The

STRONGEST
STRONG'S

EXHAUSTIVE
CONCORDANCE
OF THE BIBLE

About the Authors

Dr. James Strong (LL.D., S.T.D.) devoted 35 years of his life to the creation of his concordance. *Strong's Exhaustive Concordance of the Bible* was first published in the 1890s and has been acclaimed an indispensable reference work of Bible students and scholars ever since. Dr. Strong was professor of exegetical theology at Drew Theological Seminary from 1868 to 1893.

John R. Kohlenberger III is a specialist in the application of computers to Bible-related reference projects. He has taught at Multnomah School of Bible and Western Seminary in Portland and has produced *The NIV Interlinear Hebrew-English Old Testament*, the *Zondervan NIV Exhaustive Concordance*, and *The NRSV Concordance, Unabridged*.

James A. Swanson, associate editor, is a specialist in applying database management to biblical studies and has degrees in theology and ministry. He has taught at Multnomah Bible College and is coeditor with John R. Kohlenberger III on several Old and New Testament language concordances. He is also author of the ground-breaking *Dictionary of Biblical Languages With Semantic Domains: Hebrew and Aramaic*.

The STRONGEST STRONG'S

EXHAUSTIVE CONCORDANCE OF THE BIBLE

JAMES STRONG, LL.D., S.T.D.

FULLY REVISED AND CORRECTED BY

John R. Kohlenberger III *and* James A. Swanson

ZONDERVAN.com/
AUTHORTRACKER
follow your favorite authors

We want to hear from you. Please send your comments about this book to us in care of zreview@zondervan.com. Thank you.

ZONDERVAN

The Strongest Strongs's Exhaustive Concordance of the Bible
Copyright © 2001 by Zondervan

Requests for information should be addressed to:
Zondervan, Grand Rapids, Michigan 49530

Library of Congress Cataloging-in-Publication Data

Strong, James, 1822 – 1894
 The strongest Strong's exhaustive concordance of the Bible / James Strong. —21st century ed., fully rev. and corrected / by John R. Kohlenberger III and James A. Swanson
 p. cm.
 ISBN 978-0-310-23343-5 (hardcover)
 1. Bible – Dictionaries – English. 2. Hebrew language – Dictionaries – English. 3. Greek language, Biblical – Dictionaries – English. I. Kohlenberger, John R. II. Swanson, James A., 1952 - . III. Strong, James, 1822 – 1894. Exhaustive concordance of the Bible. IV. Title.
 BS425 .S8 2001
 220.5'2033 – dc21

2001017679

Printed in China

14 15 16 17 18 19 20 /CTC/ 34 33 32 31 30 29 28 27 26 25 24 23 22 21 20 19 18 17 16 15

CONTENTS

DEDICATION

This concordance is dedicated to the memory of

Dr. James Strong

1822–1894

PREFACE

A BRIEF HISTORY OF THE STRONGEST STRONG'S EXHAUSTIVE CONCORDANCE PROJECT

The King James Version was published in 1611. Its first multilingual concordance, Robert Young's *Analytical Concordance to the Bible*, appeared 268 years later. It took forty years of manual labor. In 1894, James Strong's *Exhaustive Concordance to the Bible* joined Young's. It too involved nearly three decades of labor. The Revised Standard Version was completed in 1952, and its first multilingual concordance was issued in 1988: *Eerdmans' Analytical Concordance to the Revised Standard Version*, edited by Richard E. Whitaker. The New American Standard was published in 1971. *The New American Standard Exhaustive Concordance of the Bible* (Holman) appeared in 1981, a project that involved more than ten years and seventy contributors under the general editorship of Robert L. Thomas. Between 1979 and 1999, a team of scholars and computer analysts produced ten concordances to the New International Version. The data developed over a twenty-year period for The NIV Concordance Project form the foundation for *The Strongest Strong's Exhaustive Concordance*.

Within two years of its inception in October of 1979, and just three years after the release of the New International Version itself, The NIV Concordance Project created *The NIV Complete Concordance* (Zondervan, 1981, retitled *The New International Bible Concordance* in 1999). The following year, 1982, saw the release of *The NIV Handy Concordance*, which is also printed in millions of NIV Bibles as the NIV "Mini" or "Standard" Concordance. (Anglicized Editions of these two *Concordances* were prepared and published by Hodder and Stoughton in 1983 and 1985, respectively.) A further abridgment, known in-house as the NIV "Micro" Concordance, was also made in 1982 and is published only in NIV Bibles.

Work on *The NIV Exhaustive Concordance* began in 1983, pairing editors Edward W. Goodrick and John R. Kohlenberger III with computer analysts Dennis B. Thomas and Barbara Perz. Proofreaders James Swanson and Donald Potts put in so many hours on the project that they were named associate editors. The analysts developed software that would assist the editors to manually interrelate or "match up" the NIV to the Hebrew, Aramaic, and Greek originals. The primary focus of this "match-up" process was on the identification of the lexical or root form of each Hebrew, Aramaic, and Greek word and on the description of the interrelation of each word of the original with each word of the NIV. The "match-up" process and its several levels of proofreading took six years—from 1983 through 1989.

The database that resulted from this process contains nearly 900,000 lines, each of which has five fields of data. Thus, the database contains nearly 4,500,000 items of information that required at least ten million editorial decisions. This database, dubbed the "Portland Index" after its place of origin, can be read in either the order of the NIV or the order of the original languages. Since its completion in 1990, it has been featured in all of Zondervan's Bible software. Following Ed Goodrick's untimely passing in 1992, Kohlenberger and Swanson continued refining the Portland Index and used it to produce several other multilingual concordances, including *The Exhaustive Concordance to the Greek New Testament* (Zondervan, 1995), *The Greek-English Concordance to the New Testament* (Zondervan, 1997), *The Hebrew-English Concordance to the Old Testament* (Zondervan, 1998), and the second edition of *The NIV Exhaustive Concordance*, with expanded and enhanced dictionary-indexes (Zondervan, 1999).

Work on *The Strongest Strong's Exhaustive Concordance* began in 1998. Working from a public-domain database of the 1894 edition of Strong's Concordance provided by Scott Musser, computer analyst Ed van der Maas developed a program to compare and merge the contents of the Portland Index with Strong's analysis. Jim Swanson spent a year working through the resulting files verse-by-verse to resolve conflicts between the two analyses of the Bible. Meanwhile, working with June Gunden and her colleagues at Peachtree Editorial and Proofreading, John Kohlenberger developed the first electronic edition of the Cambridge Paragraph Bible of 1873, the best modern edition of the King James Version. John applied this KJV database to Jim's analyzed files and spent a year enhancing and correcting the Strong's edition of the Portland Index and converting the enhanced dictionary-indexes of *The NIV Exhaustive Concordance* into the order of Strong's numbering system.

As a result, *The Strongest Strong's Exhaustive Concordance* is the most thoroughly analyzed and most accurate concordance ever produced for the King James Version.

ACKNOWLEDGMENTS

The Strongest Strong's Exhaustive Concordance was conceived of and championed by Jack Kuhatschek, Executive Editor, Zondervan Publishing House. It truly would not have been done without his involvement. Stan Gundry, Vice President and Editor-in-Chief, Zondervan Publishing House, was always there to make decisions and to provide encouragement and support. Senior Editor Verlyn D. Verbrugge worked through all the proofs with his insightful attention to detail.

Scott Musser provided the original public-domain database that served as the starting point of the project. Ed van der Maas developed the programming to merge the NIV data of the Portland Index with the KJV data from Strong. Tim Hare of Telios Systems wrote the programming that created the main concordance and the KJV indexes for the dictionaries. Brent Knopf

wrote the programming to convert the related words indexes from G/K numbers to Strong numbers.

June Gunden and her colleagues at Peachtree Editorial and Proofreading did an excellent job of reading the Cambridge Paragraph Bible of 1873 against the KJV text used to produce *The Strongest Strong's Exhaustive Concordance.* Special thanks to Dr. Donald Brake of Multnomah Biblical Seminary for loaning us his personal copy of this rare Bible.

As always, we must thank our families for their patience, encouragement, and support. John Kohlenberger thanks his wife, Carolyn, and children, Sarah and Joshua. Jim Swanson thanks his wife, Sandi, and children, Jonathan, David, and Natanya.

INTRODUCTION

Dr. James Strong (1822–1894) was professor of exegetical theology at Drew Theological Seminary from 1868 to 1893. During his quarter century at Drew, his most important publication was considered to be the massive 10-volume *Cyclopaedia of Biblical, Theological, and Ecclesiastical Literature* (1867–1881), coedited with John McClintock. But today few would doubt his most important publication to be *The Exhaustive Concordance to the Bible*, still a best-seller more than a century after its initial publication in 1894.

The Exhaustive Concordance remains a monument to Strong's brilliant design and excellent editing, especially considering that all of its hundreds of thousands of contexts and thousands of dictionary entries were researched, collated, and typeset by hand without the benefit of computers! But with advances in biblical scholarship and the assistance of computer technology, even Strong's *Concordance* can be significantly improved. This introduction will first explain the nature of Bible concordances, then list the unique features of Strong's *Concordance*, and then detail the new and improved features of *The Strongest Strong's Exhaustive Concordance*.

Bible Concordances in General

A concordance is an index to a book. It is usually arranged in alphabetical order and shows the location of each word in the book. In addition, it often supplies several words of the context in which each word is found.

There are two kinds of Bible concordances for the nonspecialist: those that deal only with the English text of the Bible version on which they are based, and those that also deal with the Hebrew, Aramaic, and Greek texts from which the Bible version was translated.

Examples of English-only concordances are *Cruden's Complete Concordance* for the King James Version and the *NIV Complete Concordance*. The best-known examples of multilingual concordances are Young's *Analytical Concordance* and Strong's *Exhaustive Concordance*, both based on the King James Version (KJV).

An *analytical* concordance is organized in English alphabetical order and shows a complete index of all the different words of a given

translation (with the exception of the most common articles, conjunctions, prepositions, and pronouns, such as *a, and, to,* and *he*). Each entry is subdivided according to the Hebrew, Aramaic, or Greek words that underlie the English. Each reference in these subdivisions is listed with a brief context. The analytical concordance also contains index-lexicons of biblical language vocabulary, showing the various English words that translate them.

An *exhaustive* concordance by definition should contain every reference to every word of the Bible version on which it is based. An exhaustive concordance is organized in English alphabetical order, indexes every word of the Bible, and lists every single biblical reference in which that word appears. For all but the most common words (which are indexed by reference only), a context is also given with each reference.

Strong's *Exhaustive Concordance* in Particular

Strong's *Concordance* went beyond the mere listing of words and references to give "exhaustive" a whole new meaning in biblical reference books.

In Strong's *Concordance* the relationship of the English to the original languages is indicated by a numbering system that was originally devised for his *Concordance*. Strong made a list of the Hebrew and "Chaldee" (Aramaic) words used in the Old Testament and of the Greek words used in the New. To each word he assigned a number, indicating its alphabetical order. This number appears at the end of most context lines to indicate the word the English translates. By consulting the dictionaries in the back of Strong's *Concordance*, the user can match numbers in order to identify the biblical word, to see its "root" definition, and to find its range of translation in the KJV.

Improvements in *The Strongest Strong's*

An exhaustive word index to the KJV and a simple guide to the relation of the English Bible to the original languages, Strong's *Concordance* has remained unsurpassed for more than a century. However, advances in biblical scholarship and computer technology, as well as shortcomings in Strong's methodology, have made a new edition desirable and even necessary. Earlier "new" or "expanded"

editions of Strong did little other than minor corrections or resetting the original in new type or adding features not intrinsic to the concordance. The *Strongest Strong's Exhaustive Concordance* rebuilt the original from the ground up. Using a gentle pun based on his name, we seek to honor and improve on the strengths of Strong's innovative excellence.

First, we started with the best modern edition of KJV: the Cambridge Paragraph Bible of 1873, edited by F. H. A. Scrivener. Dr. Scrivener was commissioned by Cambridge University Press to create a standardized edition of the KJV to eliminate all of the errors and inconsistencies that had crept into the text in two and a half centuries of printing. Dr. Scrivener spent seven years comparing at least fifteen early editions and all the important editions of the eighteenth and nineteenth centuries in order to conform all matters of italicizing, punctuation and spelling to the exacting standards of the late nineteenth century, while following closely the principles evident in the first editions of 1611. To this standard *The Strongest Strong's* conforms meticulously.

Second, our contexts reflect the KJV text more accurately. As just mentioned, they follow the spelling and punctuation of the 1873 edition with computer-verified accuracy. But beyond that, we also include all the italics of the 1873 edition. The KJV translators used italic type to show English words that were supplied in translation, but did not directly translate a word in the original Hebrew, Aramaic, or Greek. Because Strong's *Concordance* shows the relationship between the original languages and the English, it is extremely significant to show these italicized words and phrases. In the 1873 edition of the KJV, 34,712 words are italicized, but only *The Strongest Strong's* shows italics in the contexts.

Third, our contexts reflect the relationship of the original languages and the English far more exhaustively than the original edition. Since most of Strong's contexts index a single word with a single number, the user gets the wrong impression that the KJV is a word-for-word, one-to-one translation. But the translators often translated single words with phrases, phrases with single words, and phrases with idiomatic phrases. *The Strongest Strong's* uses bold type and multiple Strong numbers to indicate tens of thousands of multi-word translation not indexed in any other edition.

Fourth, Strong's dictionaries are flawed by a methodology of the nineteenth century that has come to be called the "root fallacy." He assumed that biblical words could be defined by the sum of their parts. But just as we do not think that a *pineapple* is an apple that grows on a pine tree or that a *butterfly* is a fly that likes butter, so we should not use this methodology to define biblical words as was so common in the nineteenth and even the twentieth centuries. Our dictionaries are based on the latest dictionaries, lexicons, and word study books, reflecting great advances in biblical scholarship.

Fifth, the indexes in Strong's dictionaries do not list KJV words by their exact spelling, often making it more difficult to find the exact concordance entries. Our indexes are generated from the same database that generated the concordance, so the indexed words are spelled exactly as in the KJV. And, as an added feature, each word has a statistic indicating the number of times it translates any Hebrew, Aramaic, or Greek word in the KJV. No other edition of Strong's has these features.

Sixth, as one would expect with such an enormous work done over so many years and involving so many people, there are errors in Strong's concordance and dictionaries. For example, under the heading RED, the references in Acts 7:36 and Hebrews 11:29 have the number *2281* at the end of the context lines; however, this is the number for the Greek word for "sea," not "red." Even the "new" and "corrected" editions repeat this error. *The Strongest Strong's* goes farther than any other edition in correcting the generally excellent work of the original editor.

Seventh, as a bonus feature, *The Strongest Strong's* contains an updated edition of the other most significant KJV reference book: *Nave's Topical Bible*. Our edition, called *Nave's Topical Bible Reference System*, has all the features and references of the original, but does not print out the text of the KJV for selected references. No other edition of Strong's or Nave's has half of the information combined in *The Strongest Strong's*.

FEATURES OF THE STRONGEST STRONG'S EXHAUSTIVE CONCORDANCE

The Strongest Strong's is divided into four major sections: (1) the Main Concordance, (2) the Index of Articles, Conjunctions, Particles, Prepositions, and Pronouns, (3) the Biblical Language Dictionary-Indexes, and (4) the Nave's Topical Bible Reference System.

THE MAIN CONCORDANCE

Below is a typical entry from the Main Concordance:

AARON (319) [AARON'S, AARONITES]
Ex 4:14 and he said, Is not **A** the Levite thy brother? 175
 4:27 the Lᴏʀᴅ said to **A**, "Go into the wilderness 175

The heading consists of:
 (1) the indexed word (AARON);
 (2) the frequency count in parentheses (319);
 (3) the list of related words (AARON'S, AARONITES).

The context lines consist of:
 (1) the book-chapter-verse reference;
 (2) the context for the indexed word;
 (3) the number key to the Dictionary-Index.

HEADINGS

There are three kinds of headings: (1) KJV word headings, (2) KJV Index references, and (3) "See" references.

KJV Word Headings
The 1873 Edition of the KJV contains 790,915 total words (in the 66 canonical books), with a unique vocabulary of 12,858. *The Strongest Strong's* is an exhaustive alphabetic index to every word of the KJV.

The simplest heading is composed of the KJV word and its frequency count, for example:

ABBA (3)

The frequency count lists the total number of times the word appears in the KJV, which is also the number of contexts listed in the concordance. *The Strongest Strong's* is the first exhaustive KJV concordance to provide this information.

The headings show the indexed words exactly as they are spelled in the KJV. In a few instances a word occurs both as a compound word and as a hyphenated word, as in the case of "Beth-lehem," the OT spelling, and "Bethlehem," the NT spelling. For these words, both forms appear in the heading and the contexts are all organized under that heading:

BETHLEHEM, BETH-LEHEM (39)

If the English word occurs in other forms or spellings, these words appear in square brackets following the frequency count:

ABASE (4) [ABASED, ABASING]

ABASED (4) [ABASING]

ABASING (1) [ABASED]

Rather than listing all related words after each indexed word, the editors chose one indexed word to act as the "group heading." All related words are listed after the group heading, and each of the related word headings points back to the group heading. In the example above, ABASE serves as the group heading for ABASED and ABASING.

The headings also group together words that share common elements. For example:

HEART (830) [BROKEN-HEARTED, FAINTHEARTED, HARDHEARTED, HEART'S, HEARTED, HEARTS, MERRYHEARTED, STOUTHEARTED, TENDERHEARTED]

In addition to studying related words, these lists also allow *The Strongest Strong's* to be used with any edition of the KJV. Most of the differences among the countless settings and printings of the KJV are found in italics, punctuation, and spelling. Italics and punctuation do not affect a concordance, but spelling certainly does. Use the related words lists to find all forms and spelling variations of any word. For example, the past tense of "fetch" is not only spelled "fetched," but also "fet" and "fetcht." In the 1873 edition of the KJV (as in the 1611 edition), "more" is also spelled "moe" and "mo."

KJV Index References

Forty-seven words occur a total of 383,541 times—nearly half the bulk of the KJV! These words are exhaustively indexed in their own section: the Index of Articles, Conjunctions, Particles, Prepositions, and Pronouns (see page xiii). These words are also represented by headings in the Main Concordance, with a message referring to this special index:

A (8718) [AN] See Index of Articles, Etc.

"See" References

The King James or Authorized Version has been the dominant English Bible translation from the early seventeenth century to the latter half of the twentieth century. Because of this, the KJV has had profound impact on the language of the Church. Similarly in the last half of the twentieth century, new Bible translations and biblical reference books began to impact the language of the Church. *The Strongest Strong's* includes nearly 1,100 "see" references to 1,500 proper names and key words that are spelled differently in modern versions from the KJV:

CAESAR; CAESAR'S See CESAR; CESAR'S

HOLY SPIRIT See also HOLY GHOST

SINFUL NATURE See CARNAL; FLESH

CONTEXT LINES

Concordances are word indexes. At the very least, they index the book, chapter, and verse in which these words are located. Most concordances also show each word within a brief phrase or clause: a context. This gives the user a better idea of the use of the word and helps to locate a specific verse that contains that word.

The purpose of context lines in a concordance is merely to help the reader recognize or find a specific verse in the Bible. For word study—or any kind of Bible study—the context offered by a concordance is rarely enough to go on. Nevertheless, sometimes a short sentence or a whole verse fits on one line, as in the case of John 11:35: "Jesus wept." Under the heading PRAISE, *The Strongest Strong's* was able to present almost the entirety of Psalm 150 on thirteen consecutive lines!

Taken by themselves, context lines can and do misrepresent the teaching of Scripture by omitting key words. "There is no God" is a context taken straight from Psalm 14:1. Of course the Bible does not teach this; it is what "the fool hath said in his heart"! Similarly, a context for Leviticus 24:16 might read "the LORD, shall be put to death" while the text actually says "he that is born in the land, when he blasphemeth the name of the LORD, shall be put to death."

Great care has been taken by the editors, programmers, and proofreaders of *The Strongest Strong's* to create contexts that are informative and accurate. But the reader should always check word contexts by looking them up in the KJV itself. "The Wicked Bible," a KJV edition of 1631, accidentally omitted the word "not" from the seventh commandment, for which the printers were fined 300 pounds sterling! Though there are no such fines for misleading contexts, the editors are still deeply concerned that *The Strongest Strong's* be used discerningly.

Bible Translating and Concordance Making

Traduttore traditore, "the translator is a traitor," is an ancient proverb oft quoted in books about Bible translations. To a degree this proverb is true, for no translation can perfectly bring over all the meaning and nuances of one language into another. Because no two languages share identical grammar and an identical range

of word meanings, not even the best-intentioned word-for-word translation can claim to perfectly represent the original.

If the translator is a traitor, the concordance maker must be a partner in crime. For no multilingual concordance can perfectly represent both the English and biblical language texts it indexes. It can perfectly represent the vocabulary of the English text, for it needs only to list the location of each of its words. In this respect a concordance is either absolutely right or absolutely wrong. But when a concordance attempts to display the relationship between the English text and the biblical languages, it falls heir to the same difficulties that face the Bible translator.

Much of Bible translation involves one-to-one relationships. More often than not, אֱלֹהִים (Strong number 430) is translated "God," Ἰησοῦς (2424) is "Jesus," and ἀγαπάω (25) is "love." This part of translating and concordance making is easy.

Often, however, more than one word is needed in English to render a word in the originals. For example, the Greek word τεκνίον (5040) is "little child" or "little children" twelve times in the KJV. Conversely, one English word can translate several words from the originals. The simple preposition "before" translates two Hebrew words (3807.1+6440) 958 times.

Sometimes, because of differences in idiom, it takes several English words to translate two or more words from the original languages. This is called "dynamic equivalence" or "functional equivalence." For example, the famous KJV expletive "God forbid!" translates one word in Hebrew and two words in Greek—neither of which has either "God" or "forbid" as part of its "literal" meaning! Nevertheless, "God forbid!" is the *functional* equivalent of the Greek and Hebrew phrases.

Multilingual concordances of the past, following the lead of the original Strong's *Concordance*, have tended to display the relationship between English and the original languages as if it were almost always one-to-one. Scan a few columns of Strong's *Concordance*, and you see context after context presenting one indexed word followed by one number. Over the years, this has lent support to the misconception that the KJV is an absolutely "literal," word-for-word translation. However, the original preface to the KJV stated, "We have not tied our selves to an uniformity of phrasing, or to an identity of words, as some peradventure would wish that we had done."

The Strongest Strong's, by means of two different typefaces in the context line and a greatly enhanced use of Strong's numbering system, shows more fully than any previous KJV concordance the interrelation of the English text and the biblical languages.

Context Lines: Word-for-Word Translation

The simplest context line presents four items of information. First, the location of the indexed word by book, chapter, and verse. Second, the context line. Third, within the context line, the indexed word is abbreviated by its first letter and is *usually* in bold type. Fourth, a number at the right margin indicates the Hebrew, Aramaic, or Greek word the indexed word translates. For example, under the heading AARON on page 1:

Ex	4:14 and he said, Is not **A** the Levite thy brother?	175
	4:27 the LORD said to **A**, "Go into the wilderness	175

Note that the book abbreviation is not repeated in the second reference. Book abbreviations are repeated at the top of new columns (see

columns 2 and 3, page 1). A complete list of KJV book abbreviations appears at the beginning of the Main Concordance.

The numbering system indicates which biblical language is translated. Hebrew and Aramaic words are represented by numbers in normal "roman" type, from 1 through 8674. Greek word numbers are in italics, from *1* through *5624.*

After compiling his original word list, Strong added two Hebrew words and two Greek words. To keep them in order he added an apostrophe or prime symbol to the preceding number. So when you see 1699' and 6211' at the end of OT contexts, be sure to match the number *and* the symbol in the Hebrew-Aramaic dictionary-index. Though added to the Greek numbering system, Strong did not use words *2312'* and *2526'* in the concordance.

Strong also did not include the Hebrew and Aramaic articles, conjunctions, prepositions, and pronouns that attach to words as prefixes and suffixes, though he regularly refers to these terms in his dictionaries. Because of the far more exhaustive analysis of *The Strongest Strong's*, we added these fifty forms to Strong's list. But since we did not want to change his numbering system, we added decimals to his numbers. The first two additions involve the first letter of the Hebrew and Aramaic alphabet, so the first entries in the Hebrew-Aramaic dictionary-index are now 0.1 and 0.2.

Because *The Strongest Strong's* shows the italics of the KJV in its contexts, if an indexed word is italicized in the KJV, it is bold and italic in the context. For example, in Mark 5:24 *Jesus* is italicized: the KJV translators supplied the name for clarity, though it was not in the Greek. Appropriately, the context in *The Strongest Strong's* is:

	5:24 And *J* went with him; and much people	NIG

Note the abbreviation "NIG" instead of a number at the end of the context line. This indicates the word Jesus is "Not in Greek." The abbreviation "NIH" (Not in Hebrew [Aramaic]) is used in the OT.

Context Lines: Multiple-Word Translation

One English Word—Multiple Original Words. When the indexed word translates more than one word from the original, this is indicated by an appropriate number of Strong numbers at the end of the line. This is especially true of numbers. "Twelve," for example, always translates a combination of two Hebrew or Aramaic words in the OT, though it is one-to-one in the NT:

Nu	1:44 the princes of Israel, being **t** men:	6240+8147
Mk	3:14 And he ordained **t**, that they should be with	*1427*

The original Strong's usually shows multiple numbers for such numerals (though some "new" editions do not), but rarely shows multiple numbers for the more than 14,000 times that KJV translators used this multi-word translation technique.

Multiple-word Translation. As mentioned above, the Greek word τεκνίον (*5040*) is translated "little child" or "little children" twelve times in the KJV. If you were to look up the word "little" in any edition of Strong's and look at the context for 1 John 2:1, you would find the word abbreviated by its first letter with the number *5040* at the end of the line. However, if you looked up the word "children" you would find the same thing:

1Jo 2: 1 My *l* children, these things write 5040

1Jo 2: 1 My little *c*, these things write I 5040

In these examples, it would appear that the Greek word number *5040* meant only "little" or "children," depending on which entry you looked up first. Nothing in the context line would inform you that Greek word *5040* actually means "little children."

The Strongest Strong's has solved the problem of indicating such multiple-word translations by putting *all* the words in bold type. Here is the same example of 1 John 2:1, under the headings "little" and "children":

1Jn 2: 1 My **l children**, these *things* write I unto 5040

1Jn 2: 1 My **little c**, these *things* write I unto you, 5040

If more than one English word is used to render several words from the original, the typefaces and the Strong numbers show all the words involved in this multiple-word translation. Such is the case of "with child" in Matthew 1:18, as indexed under CHILD:

Mt 1:18 **with c** of the Holy Ghost. *1064+1722+2192*

The use of multiple Strong numbers and bold type, first introduced in *The NIV Exhaustive Concordance*, show at a glance all the words involved in more than 44,000 instances of multiple-word translation in English and in more than 14,000 instances of multiple-word translation of the original languages. For these conventions alone, *The Strongest Strong's* is truly the most exhaustive concordance to the KJV.

Context Lines: "Substitution" Translation
Bible translators often substitute nouns for pronouns and pronouns for nouns for clarity. For example, Matthew 9:10 reads "as Jesus sat at meat in the house, behold, . . ." "Jesus" here translates Greek word *846*, which is not the proper name Ἰησοῦς (*2424*), but the pronoun αὐτός, "he." Such "substitutionary" translations are common and acceptable in Bible translations, but other concordances treat them as if they were one-to-one translations.

The Strongest Strong's indicates substitutionary translation by attaching a raised "S" to the bolded letter:

Mt 9:10 as **J**[S] sat at meat in the house, behold, *846*

The KJV is not unique in using substitutionary translation. *The Strongest Strong's* is unique in displaying it.

Context Lines: "Not in Hebrew" and "Not in Greek"
Because modern English and ancient Hebrew, Aramaic, and Greek do not have identical rules of grammar and style, translators must often add words for the sake of clarity. For example, Mark 16:9 begins, "Now when Jesus was risen early. . . ." Other editions of Strong have no number at the end of this context line under the entry JESUS because there is no Greek word for "Jesus" in this verse; it was supplied by the translators to give a subject to the verb.

The Strongest Strong's indicates KJV words that are not in

the originals by using the code NIH, "Not In Hebrew," for both the Hebrew and Aramaic of the Old Testament and NIG, "Not In Greek," for the New. Under the heading ABRAHAM, we find, for example:

Ge 21:33 **A** planted a grove in Beer-sheba, and NIH

Ac 7: 8 and so **A** begat Isaac, and circumcised him NIG

As in the case of Mark 16:9, these proper names were supplied for clarity, for the benefit of the reader.

Context Lines: Red-Letter Text
Because most editions of the KJV produced today have the words of Jesus in red letter, all contexts that contain words of Jesus are similarly printed in red.

THE INDEX OF ARTICLES, CONJUNCTIONS, PARTICLES, PREPOSITIONS, AND PRONOUNS

The Main Concordance indexes 407,296 references to 12,811 KJV words. The Index of Articles, Conjunctions, Particles, Prepositions, and Pronouns indexes 383,541 references to 47 KJV words.

The format of the Index of Articles, Etc. is very simple. Each of the 47 words has its own heading, followed by a frequency count. For example:

A (8718)

The 47 words of this section are indexed without contexts, since providing contexts would be of little benefit to the reader and would double the size of *The Strongest Strong's*! Book, chapter, and verse references appear in biblical order. Each book starts a new paragraph and is set in bold print for easy location.

THE BIBLICAL LANGUAGE DICTIONARY-INDEXES

At the end of each context line in the Main Concordance is a code or a Strong number, describing the relationship of the KJV to the original languages. Two Biblical Language Dictionary-Indexes list all of the words that are found in the Hebrew, Aramaic, and Greek texts from which the KJV was translated. These lists are in the alphabetical order of each of the languages, which is also the order of the Strong numbering system.

Note that in keeping with some reference works of the nineteenth century, Strong merged Hebrew and Aramaic (or "Chaldee") into one list. All major reference works of the twentieth century treat these as two separate languages. Further, he also alphabetized the letters שׂ and שׁ as though they were the same character, though again all major reference works since have

treated them as distinct. In order to preserve Strong's numbering system, *The Strongest Strong's* retained his sorting conventions.

The Dictionary-Indexes to *The Strongest Strong's* have three features not found in the indexes or dictionaries of any other KJV concordance. First, for all but sixteen highly frequent words, *The Strongest Strong's* lists all the KJV words and phrases that translate each word of the original, showing multiple-word translation and substitution translation. Second, *The Strongest Strong's* sorts the KJV word indexes according to their frequency and provides the exact number of times these words and phrases are used in the KJV. Third, the KJV words and phrases indexed are in their exact textual spelling, so the user can locate its heading in the Main Concordance without any further cross-referencing.

The entry for Greek word *26* can serve as an example for most features of both Dictionary-Indexes:

> **26** ἀγάπη, *agapē*, n. GK: *27* [→ *25*]. love, in the NT usually the active love of God for his Son and his people, and the active love his people are to have for God, each other, and even enemies; love feast, the common meal shared by Christians in connection with church meetings:– love [85], charity [27], charitably (+*2596*) [1], dear [1], feasts of charity [1], love's [1]

The entry begins with the Strong number, in bold type for easy location. Next is the lexical form or dictionary form of the Greek word, followed by its transliteration (in bold italics), the part of speech (abbreviated), the Goodrick/Kohlenberger number, and related words (listed by Strong number in square brackets, see below for more on related words).

The transliteration follows the system used in Zondervan's *New International Dictionary of New Testament Theology* and *New International Dictionary of Old Testament Theology and Exegesis*. A complete transliteration and pronunciation guide, as well as a list of abbreviations, appears before each index.

The Goodrick/Kohlenberger or G/K numbering system was developed for *The NIV Exhaustive Concordance*. Since it takes into account thousands of words and word forms not in Strong's system, the G/K numbering system is widely used in modern reference books. For those who wish to consult these more up-to-date and thorough resources, the G/K number (or numbers) is included for every entry in both Dictionary-Indexes.

The six heading elements are concluded by a period. Following the period is an essential definition for the word as it is used in the NT. These definitions can be as brief as one or two words. In the case of hundreds of theologically and culturally significant words, like ἀγάπη, the definition functions as a concise expository dictionary. In the case of a proper name, like "Bethlehem," the definition will include the possible meaning of the name in the originals: "*house of bread;* poss. *temple [house] of Lakhmu.*"

The definition ends with a colon and a dash (:–). Following this symbol is a list of all the ways in which the word is translated in the KJV, in descending order of frequency. If two words (or phrases) have the same frequency, they are listed in alphabetical order. Following the KJV word is its frequency count, in square brackets. Word *3588* (the article ὁ), which occurs almost 20,000 times in the NT, and fifteen highly-frequent Hebrew words are not indexed exhaustively, but their most frequent KJV equivalents are listed. These sixteen entries end with an asterisk (*).

One-to-one translations are indicated by one KJV word, as in the case of the first and last KJV words in the example above. Multiple-word translations are indicated in two ways: by multiple KJV words and/or multiple Strong numbers. The next-to-the-last word, "feasts of charity [1]," indicates a multiple-word KJV translation. If you look up "charity" and "feasts" in the Main Concordance, you will find the following contexts under Jude 1:12:

Jude 1:12 These are spots in your **feasts of c** when they 26

Jude 1:12 These are spots in your **f of charity** when 26

Under both headings, the phrase "feasts of charity" is shown to be the definition of Greek word *26*. (Multiple-word translation is described above on pages xii-xiii.)

When a KJV word or phrase translates more than one word of the original, the Strong number of the additional word (or words) precedes the frequency count in parentheses. This is seen in entry *26* in "charitably (+*2596*) [1]."

"Substitution" translation (see above, page xiii) is noted with a raised "s," as in the Main Concordance. The example on page xiii cited a substitute translation of word *846* by the word "Jesus" in Mt 9:10. The corresponding index in the entry for word *846* is "Jesus^s [1]."

Related Words

One popular element of Strong's original dictionaries has been intentionally omitted in *The Strongest Strong's*. Following the majority of nineteenth century scholarship, Strong attempted to explain the meaning of each word by referring to its alleged "root" meaning. Though popularized in many other dated reference books like Vine's *Expository Dictionary of New Testament Words*, this practice has been largely abandoned by modern scholars, who often label it the "root fallacy."

In his original entry on Hebrew word 3563, Strong explains:

> *koce . . .* [is] from an unused root mean. to *hold* together; a *cup* (as a container), often fig. a *lot* (as if a potion); also some unclean bird, prob. an *owl* (perh.from the cup-like cavity of its eye)

In his attempt to relate the "unused root meaning" to both "cup" and "owl," he stretches for an explanation that would apply to almost any animal with an eyeball, since all eyeballs are set in cup-like cavities!

Modern scholars understand that word 3563 is actually two completely different words, one meaning "cup" and the other "owl." Though spelled identically in Hebrew, in other related ancient languages they have different spellings. This is seen in the KJV word "cleave," which means both "stick together" (Ge 2:24) and "cut apart" (Zec 14:4). Though spelled the same in the KJV, in Old English the two meanings had separate spellings: *clifan* and *cleofan* respectively. One should not attempt to relate the meanings of these separate words, just as Strong should not have in thousands of cases.

Instead of attempting such speculative analysis and perpetuating the root fallacy, the Dictionary-Indexes of *The Strongest Strong's* list all biblical words that are related by common elements. The arrow symbol (→) points to a word or a list of words

that share common elements with the word in the entry. These related words lists are provided to allow the user to do more thorough word studies. These studies, however, should be done carefully with more attention paid to contextual definitions than fanciful etymologies.

Dictionary Definition versus KJV Translation

The original dictionaries in Strong's *Concordance* often give a single "root" definition for each word. This is often misunderstood as the *only* definition or the "literal" meaning of the word and can be misused to criticize other valid translations of the word—even in the KJV itself! The entry for ποιέω (*4160*) lists 76 different KJV words and phrases that translate this common word, yet Strong's original dictionary simply defines this word as "to *make* or *do*." Either the KJV translators were wrong in 96% of their definitions or there is more to the meaning of ποιέω than "to *make* or *do*"!

The KJV translations that follow the definition are listed in order from most used to least used. They represent careful choices the KJV translators made to render each word accurately and understandably in its context. But they also represent the translators' express principle not to tie themselves to "a uniformity of phrasing or identity of words." The KJV translations list is a good indicator of the range of a word's meaning in seventeenth-century English, as the dictionary definition is a good summary of meaning in modern English. Use these resources together, not in opposition.

For further and more detailed word studies, there are a wide variety of resources available that are keyed to Strong's numbering system.

On a basic level, there is the popular but dated *Expository Dictionary of Biblical Words* (Nelson), indexed to Strong numbers. More up-to-date and superior in methodology and OT word studies is Zondervan's *New International Encyclopedia of Bible Words*, edited by Larry Richards and indexed to G/K numbers.

On an intermediate level, there is *The NIV Theological Dictionary of New Testament Words* (Zondervan), edited by Verlyn D. Verbrugge from the four-volume *New International Dictionary of New Testament Theology* (Zondervan), edited by Colin Brown. This excellent tool gives important information for the most theologically significant words of the NT. It is keyed to G/K numbers, but also has indexes to convert G/K to Strong and Strong to G/K. For the OT, *The Theological Wordbook of the Old Testament* (Moody) uses its own numbering system, but does have a key to Strong numbers.

On an advanced level the four-volume *New International Dictionary of New Testament Theology* (Zondervan), edited by Colin Brown, and the five-volume *New International Dictionary of Old Testament Theology and Exegesis*, edited by Willem VanGemeren, are outstanding resources for deeper research. Both have English indexes and indexes to Greek and Hebrew words spelled in the same transliteration system used in *The Strongest Strong's*. The *NIDOTTE* is also keyed to G/K numbers and has an index to Strong's numbers.

Less conservative, but excellent in scholarship, are the three-volume *Theological Lexicon of the New Testament* (Hendrickson) by Ceslas Spicq and the *Theological Lexicon of the Old Testament* (Hendrickson) edited by Jenni and Westermann. Both of these sets are keyed to Strong's numbers and to a variety of more advanced resources for students of biblical languages.

NAVE'S TOPICAL BIBLE REFERENCE SYSTEM

Just as Strong's *Exhaustive Concordance* is the best and most popular concordance to the KJV, so *Nave's Topical Bible* is the best and most popular conceptual index to the KJV—and *The Strongest Strong's Exhaustive Concordance* is the best edition of both of these indispensable resources!

The original edition of *Nave's Topical Bible* fills 1464 pages, but most of that space is used by the KJV verse text, which is printed in full for many of the biblical references. Without this Bible text, and with 500 new headings and many other enhancements, all of the other content of *Nave's Topical Bible* fits in just 162 pages in *The Strongest Strong's*! Because it does not include the Bible text of the original, we have titled this section *Nave's Topical Bible Reference System*.

What is a Topical Bible?

A Topical Bible combines the most useful features of a Bible Handbook, a Bible Dictionary, and a Bible Concordance. Like a Bible Handbook, this Topical Bible introduces the reader to each book of the Bible and surveys its contents. Like a Bible Dictionary, this Topical Bible is an alphabetically organized presentation of biblical and extrabiblical information on Bible people, places, events, and objects. Like a Concordance, this Topical Bible indexes the Scriptures with thousands of biblical references and biblical text samplings.

Nave's Topical Bible Reference System is also much more than these other general reference works. A Bible Handbook offers only selected comments on the biblical text; *Nave's Topical Bible Reference System* offers a thorough survey of most biblical topics, people, places, and events. A Bible Dictionary cites a handful of biblical texts to document its articles; *Nave's Topical Bible Reference System* cites more than 100,000 verses. A Bible Concordance is limited to the vocabulary of the Bible it indexes; *Nave's Topical Bible Reference System* is based on the vocabulary of the NIV and the KJV, the two best-selling English translations today.

How to Use *Nave's Topical Bible Reference System*

Nave's Topical Bible Reference System offers quick and easy access to more than 7,000 biblical topics. Simply look up any subject, person, place, or book of the Bible in alphabetical order. There you will find a concise summary of biblical insights, well documented with Scripture references.

Entry Headings

The following shows the two types of headings used in *Nave's Topical Bible Reference System*:

ABIJAH (*[my] father is Yahweh*).

ABI See Abijah, 7.

ABIA, ABIAH See Abijah, 1 & 3.

Proper and place names are indexed according to NIV spell-

ing. When KJV spelling differs, as in the case of "Abi," "Abia," and "Abijah," those spellings are listed in "See" references that specify both the entry word and the subdivision of the entry. The definition of the name follows in parentheses and italics. When sources disagree on the definitions, these differences are listed and documented:

ASA (possibly *healer* BDB; *myrtle* KB).

The abbreviations are explained on the example page 1548.

Sometimes an entry heading contains only a cross reference to another article. This is often the case of KJV terms, such as:

WINEBIBBER *See Drunkard; Drunkenness; Wine.*

The Entry Proper

An entry can be as simple as:

JAGUR. A town of Judah (Jos 15:21).

or as complex as JESUS THE CHRIST, which fills 12 columns with 454 paragraphs of information including 84 primary subdivisions, 20 secondary subdivisions, 43 cross references to 68 topics, and more than 4,100 biblical references.

Subdivisions. Short articles appear as single paragraphs. Longer articles are usually subdivided to one or two levels.

Proper names that refer to more than one person or place are subdivided by numbered paragraphs. For example, there are three listings for Abel; thirty-one for Zechariah. More than 3,000 proper name subdivisions are identified.

Primary subdivisions are set flush left in bold print. Secondary subdivisions are indented, italicized, and followed by a dash:

JESUS THE CHRIST
Death of:
Purpose of His Death—

Biblical References. More than 100,000 biblical references are indexed in the entries, but no biblical text is printed out. This is the main difference between the full sized and compact editions of the NIV Nave's Topical Bibles.

The ampersand symbol (&) and "w" (with) are used to indicate closely related texts, often New Testament citations of the Old and parallel passages, as in this example from JESUS THE CHRIST; Head of the Church:

(Ps 118:22-23, w Mt 21:42-43, & Mk 12:10; Isa 28:16, w Eph 2:2-22, & 1Pe 2:6; Lk 20:17-18, w 1Pe 2:7; Jn 15:1-8; 1Co 3:11; Eph 1:22-23; 4:15; 5:23-32; Col 1:18; 2:10, 19; 3:11; Rev 2:2-28; 3:1, 7; 22:16).

The biblical citations index and illustrate the information of the entries. *Nave's Topical Bible Reference System* is an index to the Bible, not a substitute for the Bible. Always look up each reference in the Bible itself. Read the whole context in order to see how the text functions in the KJV or in any other translation. The easiest way to misinterpret the Bible is to study its texts out of their contexts. The editors have taken great care to select only relevant texts, but we strongly encourage users not only to double check our work, but to double check your own insights.

Cross References. More than 3,700 cross references to 6,100 entries are set in italics:

See Jesus the Christ, Second Coming; Millennium.

Entry headings are separated by semicolons; entry subdivisions follow commas.

How to Use *Nave's Topical Bible Reference System* With *The Strongest Strong's*

Nave's Topical Bible Reference System and *The Strongest Strong's* are made for each other. The *Concordance* provides an exhaustive index of every word in the KJV, listed in alphabetical order, and an exhaustive index of the relationship of the KJV to the original biblical languages. *Nave's Topical Bible Reference System* provides a biblical index that is organized by subjects, is not limited to KJV vocabulary, and is arranged by thematic development rather than by biblical order. Together these works provide endless access to the riches of God's Word.

Exhaustive KJV Word Studies

The Strongest Strong's indexes every reference to every KJV word. *Nave's Topical Bible Reference System*, while not exhaustive in its treatment of KJV vocabulary, does list every person and place in the KJV, subdivided by individual people and locations.

When you want to study any KJV word in full, begin with *The Strongest Strong's*. Look up the word exactly as it is spelled in the KJV. *The Strongest Strong's* also gives you complete listings of related KJV words you can work through. Then check the same words in *Nave's Topical Bible Reference System* for insights from its analysis and cross references.

Thorough Synonym Studies

While working through any entry in *Nave's Topical Bible Reference System*, you will notice that the verses cited regularly contain key words that are synonymns of the entry heading. This is one major advantage of the Topical Bible over the Concordance. For example, the entry on Truth contains the synonymns "faithful," "faithfulness," "just," "love," and "right." The Strongest Strong's indexes 235 verses on "truth" and another 127 on its related words. When you add the five synonymns identified in *Nave's Topical Bible Reference System*, you get another 864 references—and that does not even count their related words!

IN CONCLUSION

To Ralph Waldo Emerson, "A foolish consistency is the hobgoblin of little minds." To the editors of the *The Strongest Strong's Exhaustive Concordance*, there is no such thing as a foolish consistency in a biblical reference book. Every effort has been made by the editors, programmers, and proofreaders to make the *The Strongest Strong's* consistent and error-free. Strong's and Young's *Concordances* have each been through more than two dozen revisions, and we realize that our work has not been perfect either.

If you find anything that appears to be an error, write to The KJV Concordance Project, c/o Zondervan, 5300 Patterson Avenue, S.E., Grand Rapids, MI 49530.

THE STRONGEST STRONG'S EXHAUSTIVE CONCORDANCE

FEATURES OF THE MAIN CONCORDANCE

KJV WORD HEADING	FREQUENCY COUNT	RELATED WORD LIST
The indexed word as spelled in the KJV (see the introduction, pages x, xi).	Total number of occurrences in the KJV (see the introduction, page xi).	Other spellings and related words in the KJV (see the introduction, page xi).

ACCEPT (25) [ACCEPTABLE, ACCEPTABLY, ACCEPTANCE, ACCEPTATION, ACCEPTED]

Ex 22:11 the owner of it shall **a** *thereof*, and he shall 3947

ITALIC TYPEFACE	STRONG NUMBER
Indicates words that are italicized in the KJV (see the introduction, pages x, xii).	Refers to the biblical-language dictionary-indexes; one-to four-digit normal "roman" type is Hebrew or Aramaic; *italic* is Greek (see the introduction, pages xii–xiv).

BIBLICAL REFERENCE	INDEXED WORD
See the abbreviations table below.	Abbreviated by its first letter, usually in **bold** type.

Ge 32:20 peradventure he will **a** of me. 5375+6440

ADDITIONAL STRONG NUMBER(S)
Indicates more than one Hebrew, Aramaic, or Greek word is represented by the KJV translation (see the introduction, pages xii, xiii).

BOLD TYPEFACE
In addition to the indexed word, indicates multiple-word translation (introduction, pages xii, xiii).

Eph 1: 6 wherein he hath **made** us **a** in the beloved: *5487*

Ge 41:25 God hath shewed Pharaoh what he is **a** to NIH

NIG OR NIH
"Not in Greek" and "Not in Hebrew/ Aramaic" indicates the indexed word was supplied for clarity in translation (see the introduction, pages xii, xiii).

Lk 4:24 No prophet is **a** in his own country. *1884*

RED-LETTER TEXT
Contexts containing the words of Jesus, printed in red letter in most editions of the KJV, are printed in red in the contexts (see the introduction, page xiii).

A (8718) [AN] See Index of Articles, Etc.

KJV INDEX REFERENCES
Refers to an index of highly frequent words (see the introduction, page xi).

ABYSS See BOTTOMLESS

ACHBOR See ACBOR

"SEE" REFERENCES
Cross-references key words from various editions of the KJV and from modern translations and reference books to KJV vocabulary (see the introduction, page xi).

ABBREVIATIONS FOR THE BOOKS OF THE BIBLE

Ge Genesis	1Ch 1 Chronicles	La Lamentations	Hag Haggai	Eph Ephesians	2Pe 2 Peter
Ex. Exodus	2Ch 2 Chronicles	Eze Ezekiel	Zec Zechariah	Php Philippians	1Jn 1 John
Lev Leviticus	Ezr Ezra	Da Daniel	Mal Malachi	Col Colossians	2Jn 2 John
Nu Numbers	Ne. Nehemiah	Hos Hosea	Mt. Matthew	1Th . . . 1 Thessalonians	3Jn 3 John
Dt. Deuteronomy	Est Esther	Joel Joel	Mk Mark	2Th . . . 2 Thessalonians	Jude Jude
Jos Joshua	Job Job	Am Amos	Lk Luke	1Ti. 1 Timothy	Rev. Revelation
Jdg Judges	Ps Psalms	Ob. Obadiah	Jn. John	2Ti. 2 Timothy	
Ru Ruth	Pr Proverbs	Jnh Jonah	Ac Acts	Tit Titus	
1Sa 1 Samuel	Ecc Ecclesiastes	Mic Micah	Ro Romans	Phm Philemon	
2Sa 2 Samuel	SS . . . Song of Solomon	Na. Nahum	1Co 1 Corinthians	Heb Hebrews	Other Abbreviations
1Ki 1 Kings	Isa Isaiah	Hab Habakkuk	2Co 2 Corinthians	Jas James	S. Epistle subscript
2Ki 2 Kings	Jer Jeremiah	Zep Zephaniah	Gal Galatians	1Pe 1 Peter	T Psalm title

THE
STRONGEST STRONG'S
EXHAUSTIVE
CONCORDANCE

A

A (8718) [AN] See Index of Articles, Etc.

AARON (319) [AARON'S, AARONITES]

Ex 4:14 and he said, Is not **A** the Levite thy brother? 175
4:27 the Lord said to **A**, Go into the wilderness 175
4:28 Moses told **A** all the words of the Lord 175
4:29 Moses and **A** went and gathered together all 175
4:30 **A** spake all the words which the Lord had 175
5: 1 afterward Moses and **A** went in, 175
5: 4 Wherefore do ye, Moses and **A**, let 175
5:20 they met Moses and **A**, who stood in 175
6:13 the Lord spake unto Moses and unto **A**, 175
6:20 to wife; and she bare him **A** and Moses: 175
6:23 **A** took him Elisheba, daughter of 175
6:26 *These are* that **A** and Moses, to whom 175
6:27 from Egypt: *these are* that Moses and **A**. 175
7: 1 and **A** thy brother shall be thy prophet. 175
7: 2 and **A** thy brother shall speak unto Pharaoh, 175
7: 6 and **A** did as the Lord commanded them, 175
7: 7 **A** fourscore and three years old, when they 175
7: 8 the Lord spake unto Moses and unto **A**, 175
7: 9 then thou shalt say unto **A**, Take thy rod, 175
7:10 And Moses and **A** went in unto Pharaoh, 175
7:10 and **A** cast down his rod before Pharaoh, 175
7:19 Say unto **A**, Take thy rod, and stretch out 175
7:20 Moses and **A** did so, as the Lord 175
8: 5 The Lord spake unto Moses, Say unto **A**, 175
8: 6 **A** stretched out his hand over the waters of 175
8: 8 Pharaoh called for Moses and **A**, and said, 175
8:12 Moses and **A** went out from Pharaoh: 175
8:16 Say unto **A**, Stretch out thy rod, 175
8:17 for **A** stretched out his hand with his rod, 175
8:25 Pharaoh called for Moses and for **A**, 175
9: 8 the Lord said unto Moses and unto **A**, 175
9:27 called for Moses and **A**, and said unto them, 175
10: 3 Moses and **A** came in unto Pharaoh, 175
10: 8 and **A** were brought again unto Pharaoh: 175
10:16 Pharaoh called for Moses and **A** in haste; 175
11:10 and **A** did all these wonders before Pharaoh: 175
12: 1 unto Moses and **A** in the land of Egypt, 175
12:28 the Lord had commanded Moses and **A**, 175
12:31 And he called for Moses and **A** by night, 175
12:43 the Lord said unto Moses and **A**, This *is* 175
12:50 as the Lord commanded Moses and **A**, so 175
15:20 the sister of **A**, took a timbrel in her hand; 175
16: 2 against Moses and **A** in the wilderness: 175
16: 6 and **A** said unto all the children of Israel, 175
16: 9 Moses spake unto **A**, Say unto all 175
16:10 as **A** spake unto the whole congregation of 175
16:33 Moses said unto **A**, Take a pot, and put an 175
16:34 so **A** laid it up before the Testimony, to be 175
17:10 **A**, and Hur went up *to* the top of the hill. 175
17:12 **A** and Hur stayed up his hands, the one on 175
18:12 **A** came, and all the elders of Israel, to eat 175
19:24 thou shalt come up, thou, and **A** with thee: 175
24: 1 thou, and **A**, Nadab, and Abihu, 175
24: 9 **A**, Nadab, and Abihu, and seventy of 175
24:14 behold, and Hur *are* with you: if any man 175
27:21 **A** and his sons shall order it from evening to 175
28: 1 take thou unto thee **A** thy brother, and his 175
28: 1 *even* **A**, Nadab and Abihu, Eleazar 175
28: 2 thou shalt make holy garments for **A** thy 175
28: 4 they shall make holy garments for **A** thy 175
28:12 **A** shall bear their names before the Lord 175

Ex 28:29 **A** shall bear the names of the children of 175
28:30 **A** shall bear the judgment of the children of 175
28:35 it shall be upon **A** to minister: and his sound 175
28:38 that **A** may bear the iniquity of the holy 175
28:41 thou shalt put them upon **A** thy brother, 175
28:43 they shall be upon **A**, and upon his sons, 175
29: 4 and his sons thou shalt bring unto the 175
29: 5 put upon **A** the coat, and the robe of 175
29: 9 **A** and his sons, and put the bonnets on 175
29: 9 and thou shalt consecrate **A** and his sons. 175
29:10 and his sons shall put their hands upon 175
29:15 and his sons shall put their hands upon 175
29:19 and his sons shall put their hands upon 175
29:20 put *it* upon the tip of the *right* ear of **A**, 175
29:21 sprinkle *it* upon **A**, and upon his garments, 175
29:24 And thou shalt put all in the hands of **A**, 175
29:27 *even of that* which *is* for **A**, and of *that* 175
29:29 the holy garments of **A** shall be his sons' 175
29:32 **A** and his sons shall eat the flesh of the ram, 175
29:35 thus shalt thou do unto **A**, and to his sons, 175
29:44 I will sanctify also both **A** and his sons, 175
30: 7 **A** shall burn thereon sweet incense every 175
30: 8 when **A** lighteth the lamps at even, he shall 175
30:10 **A** shall make an atonement upon the horns 175
30:19 For **A** and his sons shall wash their hands 175
30:30 thou shalt anoint **A** and his sons, 175
31:10 the holy garments for **A** the priest, and 175
32: 1 gathered themselves together unto **A**, 175
32: 2 **A** said unto them, Break off the golden 175
32: 3 in their ears, and brought *them* unto **A**. 175
32: 5 when **A** saw *it*, he built an altar before it; 175
32: 5 **A** made proclamation, and said, To morrow 175
32:21 Moses said unto **A**, What did this people 175
32:22 **A** said, Let not the anger of my lord wax 175
32:25 (for **A** had made them naked unto *their* 175
32:35 because they made the calf, which **A** made. 175
34:30 when **A** and all the children of Israel saw 175
34:31 **A** and all the rulers of the congregation 175
35:19 *place*, the holy garments for **A** the priest, 175
38:21 by the hand of Ithamar, son to **A** the priest. 175
39: 1 and made the holy garments for **A**; 175
39:27 coats *of* fine linen *of* woven work for **A**, 175
39:41 and the holy garments for **A** the priest, 175
40:12 shalt bring **A** and his sons unto the door 175
40:13 thou shalt put upon **A** the holy garments, 175
40:31 Moses and **A** and his sons washed their 175
Lev 1: 7 the sons of **A** the priest shall put fire upon 175
3:13 the sons of **A** shall sprinkle the blood 175
6: 9 Command **A** and his sons, saying, This *is* 175
6:14 the sons of **A** shall offer it before 175
6:16 the remainder thereof shall **A** and his sons 175
6:18 All the males among the children of **A** shall 175
6:20 This *is* the offering of **A** and of his sons, 175
6:25 Speak unto **A** and to his sons, saying, This 175
7:10 and dry, shall all the sons of **A** have, 175
7:33 He among the sons of **A**, that offereth 175
7:34 have given them unto **A** the priest 175
7:35 This *is the portion* of the anointing of **A**, 175
8: 2 Take **A** and his sons with him, and 175
8: 6 Moses brought **A** and his sons, 175
8:14 **A** and his sons laid their hands upon 175
8:18 **A** and his sons laid their hands upon 175
8:22 **A** and his sons laid their hands upon 175
8:30 sprinkled *it* upon **A**, *and* upon his garments, 175
8:30 sanctified **A**, *and* his garments, and his sons, 175
8:31 Moses said unto **A** and to his sons, Boil 175
8:31 **A** and his sons shall eat it. 175
8:36 So **A** and his sons did all things which 175
9: 1 *that* Moses called **A** and his sons, and 175
9: 2 he said unto **A**, Take thee a young calf for a 175
9: 7 Moses said unto **A**, Go unto the altar, 175
9: 8 **A** therefore went unto the altar, and slew 175
9: 9 the sons of **A** brought the blood unto him: 175
9:21 the right shoulder **A** waved *for* a wave 175

Lev 9:22 **A** lift up his hand towards the people, 175
9:23 **A** went into the tabernacle of 175
10: 1 Nadab and Abihu, the sons of **A**, took either 175
10: 3 Moses said unto **A**, This *is it* that 175
10: 3 I will be glorified. And **A** held his peace. 175
10: 4 the sons of Uzziel the uncle of **A**, 175
10: 6 Moses said unto **A**, and unto Eleazar 175
10: 8 And the Lord spake unto **A**, saying, 175
10:12 Moses spake unto **A**, and unto Eleazar 175
10:16 Ithamar the sons of **A** which were left *alive*, 175
10:19 **A** said unto Moses, Behold, *this* day have 175
11: 1 And the Lord spake unto Moses and to **A**, 175
13: 1 the Lord spake unto Moses and **A**, 175
13: 2 then he shall be brought unto **A** the priest, 175
14:33 the Lord spake unto Moses and unto **A**, 175
15: 1 And the Lord spake unto Moses and to **A**, 175
16: 1 Moses after the death of the two sons of **A**, 175
16: 2 said unto Moses, Speak unto **A** thy brother, 175
16: 3 Thus shall **A** come into the holy *place:* with 175
16: 6 **A** shall offer *his* bullock of the sin offering, 175
16: 8 **A** shall cast lots upon the two goats; one lot 175
16: 9 **A** shall bring the goat upon which 175
16:11 **A** shall bring the bullock of the sin offering, 175
16:21 **A** shall lay both his hands upon the head of 175
16:23 **A** shall come into the tabernacle of 175
17: 2 Speak unto **A**, and unto his sons, and unto 175
21: 1 Speak unto the priests the sons of **A**, 175
21:17 Speak unto **A**, saying, Whosoever *he be* of 175
21:21 hath a blemish, of the seed of **A** the priest, 175
21:24 Moses told *it* unto **A**, and to his sons, 175
22: 2 Speak unto **A** and to his sons, that they 175
22: 4 What man soever of the seed of **A** *is* a leper, 175
22:18 Speak unto **A**, and to his sons, and unto all 175
24: 3 shall **A** order it from the evening unto 175
Nu 1: 3 and **A** shall number them by their armies. 175
1:17 **A** took these men which are expressed by 175
1:44 which Moses and **A** numbered, 175
2: 1 the Lord spake unto Moses and unto **A**, 175
3: 1 These also *are* the generations of **A** 175
3: 2 these *are* the names of the sons of **A**; 175
3: 3 These *are* the names of the sons of **A**, 175
3: 4 priest's office in the sight of **A** their father. 175
3: 6 and present them before **A** the priest, 175
3: 9 thou shalt give the Levites unto **A** and to 175
3:10 thou shalt appoint **A** and his sons, 175
3:32 Eleazar the son of **A** the priest *shall be* chief 175
3:38 *shall be* Moses, and **A** and his sons, 175
3:39 numbered at the commandment of 175
3:48 *is to be* redeemed, unto **A** and to his sons. 175
3:51 money of them that were redeemed unto **A** 175
4: 1 the Lord spake unto Moses and unto **A**, 175
4: 5 **A** shall come, and his sons, and they shall 175
4:15 when **A** and his sons have made an end of 175
4:16 *to* the office of Eleazar the son of **A** 175
4:17 the Lord spake unto Moses and unto **A**, 175
4:19 they approach unto the most holy *things:* **A** 175
4:27 At the appointment of **A** and his sons shall 175
4:28 the hand of Ithamar the son of **A** the priest. 175
4:33 under the hand of Ithamar the son of **A** 175
4:34 Moses and **A** and the chief of 175
4:37 **A** did number according to 175
4:41 **A** did number according to 175
4:45 **A** numbered according to the word of 175
4:46 whom Moses and **A** and the chief of Israel 175
6:23 Speak unto **A** and unto his sons, saying, 175
7: 8 under the hand of Ithamar the son of **A** 175
8: 2 Speak unto **A**, and say unto him, When 175
8: 3 **A** did so; he lighted the lamps thereof over 175
8:11 **A** shall offer the Levites before the Lord 175
8:13 And thou shalt set the Levites before **A**, 175
8:19 I have given the Levites *as* a gift to **A** 175
8:20 **A**, and all the congregation of the children 175
8:21 **A** offered them *as* an offering before 175
8:21 **A** made an atonement for them to cleanse 175

A

Nu 8:22 the tabernacle of the congregation before **A**, 175
 9: 6 before Moses and before **A** on that day: 175
 10: 8 the sons of **A**, the priests, shall blow with 175
 12: 1 and **A** spake against Moses because 175
 12: 4 unto Moses, and unto **A**, and unto Miriam, 175
 12: 5 of the tabernacle, and called **A** and Miriam: 175
 12:10 **A** looked upon Miriam, and behold, *she* 175
 12:11 **A** said unto Moses, Alas, my lord, I beseech 175
 13:26 to **A**, and to all the congregation of 175
 14: 2 murmured against Moses and against **A**: 175
 14: 5 **A** fell on their faces before all the assembly 175
 14:26 the Lord spake unto Moses and unto **A**, 175
 15:33 sticks brought him unto Moses and to **A**, 175
 16: 3 together against Moses and against **A**, 175
 16:11 and what *is* **A**, that ye murmur against him? 175
 16:16 thou, and they, and **A**, to morrow: 175
 16:17 thou also, and **A**, each *of you* his censer. 175
 16:18 of the congregation with Moses and **A**, 175
 16:20 the Lord spake unto Moses and unto **A**, 175
 16:37 Speak unto Eleazar the son of **A** the priest, 175
 16:40 no stranger, which *is* not of the seed of **A**, 175
 16:41 murmured against Moses and against **A**, 175
 16:42 was gathered against Moses and against **A**, 175
 16:43 **A** came before the tabernacle of 175
 16:46 Moses said unto **A**, Take a censer, 175
 16:47 **A** took as Moses commanded, and ran into 175
 16:50 **A** returned unto Moses unto the door of 175
 17: 6 and the rod of **A** *was* among their rods. 175
 17: 8 the rod of **A** for the house of Levi was 175
 18: 1 the Lord said unto **A**, Thou and thy sons 175
 18: 8 the Lord spake unto **A**, Behold, I also 175
 18:20 the Lord spake unto **A**, Thou shalt have 175
 18:28 the Lord's heave offering to **A** the priest. 175
 19: 1 the Lord spake unto Moses and unto **A**, 175
 20: 2 together against Moses and against **A**. 175
 20: 6 **A** went from the presence of the assembly 175
 20: 8 **A** thy brother, and speak ye unto the rock 175
 20:10 **A** gathered the congregation together before 175
 20:12 the Lord spake unto Moses and **A**, 175
 20:23 spake unto Moses and **A** in mount Hor, 175
 20:24 **A** shall be gathered unto his people: for he 175
 20:25 Take **A** and Eleazar his son, and bring them 175
 20:26 strip **A** of his garments, and put them upon 175
 20:26 and **A** shall be gathered *unto his people,* 175
 20:28 Moses stripped **A** of his garments, 175
 20:28 and **A** died there in the top of the mount: 175
 20:29 when all the congregation saw that **A** was 175
 20:29 they mourned for **A** thirty days, *even* all 175
 25: 7 the son of Eleazar, the son of **A** the priest, 175
 25:11 the son of Eleazar, the son of **A** the priest, 175
 26: 1 and unto Eleazar the son of **A** the priest, 175
 26: 9 and against **A** in the company of Korah, 175
 26:59 and she bare unto Amram **A** and Moses, 175
 26:60 unto **A** was born Nadab, and Abihu, 175
 26:64 whom Moses and **A** the priest numbered, 175
 27:13 thy people, as **A** thy brother was gathered. 175
 33: 1 armies under the hand of Moses and **A**. 175
 33:38 **A** the priest went up into mount Hor at 175
 33:39 **A** *was* an hundred and twenty 175
Dt 9:20 the Lord was very angry with **A** to have 175
 9:20 and I prayed for **A** also the same time. 175
 10: 6 there **A** died, and there he was buried: 175
 32:50 as **A** thy brother died in mount Hor, 175
Jos 21: 4 the children of **A** the priest, *which were* of 175
 21:10 Which the children of **A**, *being* of 175
 21:13 Thus they gave to the children of **A** 175
 21:19 All the cities of the children of **A**, 175
 24: 5 I sent Moses also and **A**, and I plagued 175
 24:33 Eleazar the son of **A** died; and they buried 175
Jdg 20:28 the son of Eleazar, the son of **A**, 175
1Sa 12: 6 *It is* the Lord that advanced Moses and **A**, 175
 12: 8 then the Lord sent Moses and **A**, 175
1Ch 6: 3 of Amram; **A**, and Moses, and Miriam. 175
 6: 3 The sons also of **A**; Nadab, and Abihu, 175
 6:49 **A** and his sons offered upon the altar of 175
 6:50 these *are* the sons of **A**; Eleazar his son, 175
 6:54 of the sons of **A**, of the families of 175
 6:57 to the sons of **A** they gave the cities of 175
 15: 4 And David assembled the children of **A**, 175
 23:13 The sons of Amram; **A** and Moses: 175
 23:13 **A** was separated, that he should sanctify 175
 23:28 **A** for the service of the house of 175
 23:32 the charge of the sons of **A** their brethren, 175
 24: 1 *these are* the divisions of the sons of **A**. 175
 24: 1 The sons of **A**; Nadab, and Abihu, Eleazar, 175
 24:19 to their manner, under **A** their father, 175
 24:31 sons of **A** in the presence of David the king, 175
2Ch 13: 9 the sons of **A**, and the Levites, 175
 13:10 *are* the sons of **A**, and the Levites *wait* upon 175
 26:18 the Lord, but to the priests the sons of **A** 175
 29:21 he commanded the priests the sons of **A** to 175
 31:19 Also of the sons of **A** the priests, *which* 175
 35:14 the priests the sons of **A** *were* busied in 175
 35:14 and for the priests the sons of **A**. 175
Ezr 7: 5 son of Eleazar, the son of **A** the chief priest: 175
Ne 10:38 the priest the son of **A** shall be with 175
 12:47 sanctified *them* unto the children of **A**. 175
Ps 77:20 like a flock by the hand of Moses and **A**. 175
 99: 6 Moses and **A** among his priests, 175
 105:26 his servant; *and* **A** whom he had chosen. 175
 106:16 in the camp, *and* **A** the saint of the Lord. 175
 115:10 O house of **A**, trust in the Lord: he *is* their 175
 115:12 house of Israel; he will bless the house of **A**. 175
 118: 3 Let the house of **A** now say, that his mercy 175
 135:19 of Israel: bless the Lord, O house of **A**: 175

Mic 6: 4 I sent before thee Moses, **A**, and Miriam. 175
Lk 1: 5 and his wife *was* of the daughters of **A**, 2
Ac 7:40 unto **A**, Make us gods to go before us: 2
Heb 5: 4 but he that is called of God, as *was* **A**. 2
 7:11 and not be called after the order of **A**? 2

AARON'S (31) [AARON]
Ex 6:25 Eleazar **A** son took him *one* of the daughters 175
 7:12 but **A** rod swallowed up their rods. 175
 28: 1 and Abihu, Eleazar and Ithamar, **A** sons. 175
 28: 3 that they may make **A** garments to 175
 28:30 they shall be upon **A** heart, when he goeth 175
 28:38 it shall be upon **A** forehead, that Aaron may 175
 28:40 for **A** sons thou shalt make coats, 175
 29:26 thou shalt take the breast of the ram of **A** 175
 29:28 it shall be **A** and his sons' by a 175+3807.1
Lev 1: 5 the priests, **A** sons, shall bring the blood, 175
 1: 8 the priests, **A** sons, shall lay the parts, 175
 1:11 the priests, **A** sons, shall sprinkle his blood 175
 2: 2 he shall bring it to **A** sons the priests: 175
 2: 3 of the meat offering *shall be* **A** 175+3807.1
 2:10 left of the meat offering *shall be* **A** 175+3807.1
 3: 2 **A** sons the priests shall sprinkle the blood 175
 3: 5 **A** sons shall burn it on the altar upon 175
 3: 8 **A** sons shall sprinkle the blood thereof 175
 7:31 but the breast shall be **A** and his sons'. 175
 8:12 he poured of the anointing oil upon **A** head, 175
 8:13 Moses brought **A** sons, and put coats upon 175
 8:23 put *it* upon the tip of **A** right ear, 175
 8:24 he brought **A** sons, and Moses put of 175
 8:27 he put all upon **A** hands, and upon his sons' 175
 9:12 **A** sons presented unto him the blood, 175
 9:18 **A** sons presented unto him the blood, 175
 24: 9 it shall be **A** and his sons': 175+3807.1
Nu 17: 3 thou shalt write **A** name upon the rod of 175
 17:10 Bring **A** rod again before the Testimony, 175
Ps 133: 2 ran down upon the beard, *even* **A** beard: 175
Heb 9: 4 and **A** rod that budded, and the tables of 2

AARONITES (2) [AARON]
1Ch 12:27 Jehoiada *was* the leader of the **A**, 175
 27:17 the son of Kemuel: of the **A**, Zadok: 175

ABADDON (1)
Rev 9:11 pit, whose name in the Hebrew tongue *is* **A**, 3

ABAGTHA (1)
Est 1:10 Harbona, Bigtha, and **A**, Zethar, and Carcas, 5

ABANA (1)
2Ki 5:12 *Are* not **A** and Pharpar, rivers of Damascus, 71

ABARIM (4) [IJE-ABARIM]
Nu 27:12 Get thee up into this mount **A**, and see 5682
 33:47 pitched in the mountains of **A**, before 5682
 33:48 they departed from the mountains of **A**, 5682
Dt 32:49 Get thee up into this mountain **A**, 5682

ABASE (4) [ABASED, ABASING]
Job 40:11 every one *that is* proud, and **a** him. 8213
Isa 31: 4 nor **a** himself for the noise of them: 6031
Eze 21:26 *him that is* low, and **a** *him that is* high. 8213
Da 4:37 those that walk in pride he *is* able to **a**. 8214

ABASED (4) [ABASING]
Mt 23:12 whosoever shall exalt himself shall be **a**; 5013
Lk 14:11 For whosoever exalteth himself shall be **a**; 5013
 18:14 every one that exalteth himself shall be **a**; 5013
Php 4:12 I know both *how* to be **a**, and I know *how* 5013

ABASING (1) [ABASED]
2Co 11: 7 Have I committed an offence in **a** myself 5013

ABATED (6)
Ge 8: 3 and fifty days the waters were **a**. 2637
 8: 8 see if the waters were **a** from off the face 7043
 8:11 Noah knew that the waters were **a** from 7043
Lev 27:18 and it shall be **a** from thy estimation. 1639
Dt 34: 7 eye was not dim, nor his natural force **a**. 5127
Jdg 8: 3 their anger was **a** toward him, when he 7503

ABBA (3)
Mk 14:36 And he said, **A**, Father, all *things are* possible 5
Ro 8:15 Spirit of adoption, whereby we cry, **A**, Father. 5
Gal 4: 6 into your Son into your hearts, crying, **A**, Father. 5

ABDA (2)
1Ki 4: 6 Adoniram the son of **A** *was* over 5653
Ne 11:17 **A** the son of Shammua, the son of Galal, 5653

ABDEEL (1)
Jer 36:26 Shelemiah the son of **A**, to take Baruch 5655

ABDI (3)
1Ch 6:44 of Kishi, the son of **A**, the son of Malluch, 5660
2Ch 29:12 Kish the son of **A**, and Azariah the son of 5660
Ezr 10:26 Jehiel, and **A**, and Jeremoth, and Eliah. 5660

ABDIEL (1)
1Ch 5:15 Ahi the son of **A**, the son of Guni, chief of 5661

ABDON (8)
Jos 21:30 with her suburbs, **A** with her suburbs, 5658
Jdg 12:13 after him **A** the son of Hillel, a Pirathonite, 5658
 12:15 **A** the son of Hillel the Pirathonite died, 5658
1Ch 6:74 with her suburbs, **A** with her suburbs, 5658

1Ch 8:23 And **A**, and Zichri, and Hanan, 5658
 8:30 his firstborn son **A**, and Zur, and Kish, 5658
 9:36 his firstborn son **A**, then Zur, and Kish, 5658
2Ch 34:20 **A** the son of Micah, and Shaphan 5658

ABED-NEGO (15) [AZARIAH]
Da 1: 7 of Meshach; and to Azariah, of **A**. 5664
 2:49 and he set Shadrach, Meshach, and **A**, 5665
 3:12 of Babylon, Shadrach, Meshach, and **A**; 5665
 3:13 to bring Shadrach, Meshach, and **A**. 5665
 3:14 *Is it* true, O Shadrach, Meshach, and **A**, 5665
 3:16 and **A**, answered and said to the king, 5665
 3:19 against Shadrach, Meshach, and **A**: 5665
 3:20 **A**, *and* to cast *them* into the burning fiery 5665
 3:22 that took up Shadrach, Meshach, and **A**. 5665
 3:23 three men, Shadrach, Meshach, and **A**, 5665
 3:26 and said, Shadrach, Meshach, and **A**, 5665
 3:26 *hither.* Then Shadrach, Meshach, and **A**, 5665
 3:28 Meshach, and **A**, who hath sent his angel, 5665
 3:29 Meshach, and **A**, shall be cut in pieces, 5665
 3:30 Meshach, and **A**, in the province of 5665

ABEL (16) [ABEL-BETH-MAACHAH]
Ge 4: 2 she again bare his brother **A**. And Abel 1893
 4: 2 **A** was a keeper of sheep, but Cain was a 1893
 4: 4 **A**, he also brought of the firstlings of his 1893
 4: 4 the Lord had respect unto **A** and to his 1893
 4: 8 Cain talked with **A** his brother: and it 1893
 4: 8 that Cain rose up against **A** his brother, 1893
 4: 9 said unto Cain, Where *is* **A** thy brother? 1893
 4:25 appointed me another seed instead of **A**, 1893
1Sa 6:18 even unto the great *stone* of **A**, 59
2Sa 20:14 went through all the tribes of Israel unto **A**, 59
 20:15 and besieged him in **A** of Beth-maachah, 59
 20:18 They shall surely ask *counsel* at **A**: 59
Mt 23:35 from the blood of righteous **A** unto the blood 6
Lk 11:51 From the blood of **A** unto the blood of 6
Heb 11: 4 By faith **A** offered unto God a more excellent 6
 12:24 that speaketh better *things* than *that* of **A**. 6

ABEL-BETH-MAACHAH (2) [BETH-MAACHAH]
1Ki 15:20 and Dan, and **A**, and all Cinneroth, 59
2Ki 15:29 **A**, and Janoah, and Kedesh, and Hazor, 59

ABEL-MAIM (1)
2Ch 16: 4 and **A**, and all the store cities of Naphtali. 66

ABEL-MEHOLAH (3)
Jdg 7:22 *and* to the border of **A**, unto Tabbath. 65
1Ki 4:12 beneath Jezreel, from Beth-shean to **A**, 65
 19:16 Elisha the son of Shaphat of **A** shalt thou 65

ABEL-MIZRAIM (1) [MIZRAIM]
Ge 50:11 wherefore the name of it was called **A**, 67

ABEL-SHITTIM (1) [SHITTIM]
Nu 33:49 from Beth-jesimoth *even* unto **A** in the plains 63

ABEZ (1)
Jos 19:20 And Rabbith, and Kishion, and **A**, 77

ABHOR (19) [ABHORRED, ABHORREST,
ABHORRETH, ABHORRING]
Lev 26:11 amongst you: and my soul shall not **a** you. 1602
 26:15 or if your soul **a** my judgments, so that *ye* 1602
 26:30 of your idols, and my soul shall **a** you. 1602
 26:44 neither will I **a** them, to destroy them 1602
Dt 7:26 detest it, and thou shalt **utterly a** it; 8581+8581
 23: 7 Thou shalt not **a** an Edomite; for he *is* thy 8581
 23: 7 thou shalt not **a** an Egyptian; because 8581
1Sa 27:12 **made** his people Israel **utterly to a** 887+887
Job 9:31 and mine own clothes shall **a** me. 8581
 30:10 They **a** me, they flee far from me, 8581
 42: 6 Wherefore I **a** *myself*, and repent in dust 3988
Ps 5: 6 the Lord will **a** the bloody 8581
 119:163 I hate and **a** lying: *but* thy law do I love. 8581
Pr 24:24 shall the people curse, nations shall **a** him: 2194
Jer 14:21 Do not **a** *us*, for thy name's sake, do not 5006
Am 5:10 and they **a** him that speaketh uprightly. 8581
 6: 8 I **a** the excellency of Jacob, and hate his 8374
Mic 3: 9 that a judgment, and pervert all equity. 8581
Ro 12: 9 **A** *that which is* evil; cleave to *that which is* 655

ABHORRED (16) [ABHOR]
Ex 5:21 you have **made** our savour **to be a** in 887
Lev 20:23 all these *things*, and therefore I **a** them. 6973
 26:43 and because their soul **a** my statutes. 1602
Dt 32:19 when the Lord saw *it*, he **a** *them*, 5006
1Sa 2:17 for men **a** the offering of the Lord. 5006
2Sa 16:21 all Israel shall hear that thou art **a** of thy 887
1Ki 11:25 mischief that Hadad *did*: and he **a** Israel, 6973
Job 19:19 All my inward friends **a** me: 8581
Ps 22:24 he hath not despised nor **a** the affliction 8262
 78:59 *this*, he was wroth, and greatly **a** Israel: 3988
 89:38 thou hast cast off and **a**, thou hast been 3988
 106:40 insomuch that he **a** his own inheritance. 8581
Pr 22:14 he that is **a** of the Lord shall fall therein. 2194
La 2: 7 cast off his altar, he hath **a** his sanctuary, 5010
Eze 16:25 hast **made** thy beauty **to be a**, 8581
Zec 11: 8 soul lothed them, and their soul also **a** me. 973

ABHORREST (2) [ABHOR]
Isa 7:16 the land that thou **a** shall be forsaken of 6973
Ro 2:22 thou that **a** idols, dost thou commit 948

ABHORRETH (5) [ABHOR]

Job	33:20	So that his life **a** bread, and his soul dainty	2092
Ps	10: 3	blesseth the covetous, *whom* the Lord **a**.	5006
	36: 4	in a way *that is* not good; he **a** not evil.	3988
	107:18	Their soul **a** all *manner of* meat;	8581
Isa	49: 7	to him whom the nation **a**, to a servant of	8581

ABHORRING (1) [ABHOR]

Isa	66:24	and they shall be an **a** unto all flesh.	1860

ABI (1)

2Ki	18: 2	His mother's name also *was* **A**, the daughter	21

ABIA (4)

1Ch	3:10	**A** his son, Asa his son, Jehoshaphat his son,	29
Mt	1: 7	and Roboam begat **A**; and Abia begat Asa;	7
	1: 7	and Roboam begat Abia; and **A** begat Asa;	7
Lk	1: 5	priest named Zacharias, of the course of **A**:	7

ABIAH (4)

1Sa	8: 2	was Joel; and the name of his second, **A**:	29
1Ch	2:24	**A** Hezron's wife bare him Ashur the father	29
	6:28	sons of Samuel; the firstborn Vashni, and **A**.	29
	7: 8	Jerimoth, and **A**, and Anathoth, and Alameth.	29

ABIALBON (1)

2Sa	23:31	**A** the Arbathite, Azmaveth the Barhumite,	45

ABIASAPH (1)

Ex	6:24	sons of Korah; Assir, and Elkanah, and **A**:	23

ABIATHAR (30) [ABIATHAR'S]

1Sa	22:20	named **A**, escaped, and fled after David.	54
	22:21	**A** shewed David that Saul had slain	54
	22:22	David said unto **A**, I knew *it* that day,	54
	23: 6	when **A** the son of Ahimelech fled to David	54
	23: 9	said to **A** the priest, Bring hither the ephod.	54
	30: 7	David said to **A** the priest, Ahimelech's son,	54
	30: 7	And **A** brought thither the ephod to David.	54
2Sa	8:17	Ahimelech the son of **A**, were the priests;	54
	15:24	went up, until all the people had done	54
	15:27	Ahimaaz thy son, and Jonathan the son of **A**.	54
	15:29	**A** carried the ark of God again *to* Jerusalem;	54
	15:35	not there with thee Zadok and **A** the priests?	54
	15:35	thou shalt tell *it* to Zadok and **A** the priests.	54
	17:15	said Hushai unto Zadok and to **A** the priests,	54
	19:11	David sent to Zadok and to **A** the priests,	54
	20:25	scribe: and Zadok and **A** *were* the priests:	54
1Ki	1: 7	the son of Zeruiah, and with **A** the priest:	54
	1:19	the priest, and Joab the captain of the host:	54
	1:25	and the captains of the host, and **A** the priest;	54
	1:42	Jonathan the son of **A** the priest came:	54
	2:22	for **A** the priest, and for Joab the son of	54
	2:26	unto **A** the priest said the king, Get thee *to*	54
	2:27	So Solomon thrust out **A** from being priest	54
	2:35	the priest did the king put in the room of **A**.	54
	4: 4	the host: and Zadok and **A** *were* the priests:	54
1Ch	15:11	David called for Zadok and **A** the priests,	54
	18:16	Abimelech the son of **A**, were the priests;	54
	24: 6	Ahimelech the son of **A**, and *before* the chief	54
	27:34	was Jehoiada the son of Benaiah, and **A**:	54
Mk	2:26	house of God in the days of **A** the high priest,	8

ABIATHAR'S (1) [ABIATHAR]

2Sa	15:36	Zadok's *son*, and Jonathan **A** son;	54+3807.1

ABIB (6)

Ex	13: 4	*This* day came ye out in the month **A**.	24
	23:15	in the time appointed of the month **A**;	24
	34:18	thee, in the time of the month **A**:	24
	34:18	for in the month **A** thou camest out from	24
Dt	16: 1	Observe the month of **A**, and keep	24
	16: 1	for in the month of **A** the Lord thy God	24

ABIDA (1) [ABIDAH]

1Ch	1:33	and Epher, and Henoch, and **A**, and Eldaah.	28

ABIDAH (1) [ABIDA]

Ge	25: 4	and Epher, and Hanoch, and **A**, and Eldaah.	28

ABIDAN (5)

Nu	1:11	Of Benjamin; **A** the son of Gideoni.	27
	2:22	captain of the sons of Benjamin *shall be* **A**	27
	7:60	On the ninth day **A** the son of Gideoni,	27
	7:65	this *was* the offering of **A** the son of Gideoni.	27
	10:24	of Benjamin *was* **A** the son of Gideoni.	27

ABIDE (81) [ABIDETH, ABIDING, ABODE, ABODEST]

Ge	19: 2	Nay; but we will **a** in the street **all night**.	3885
	22: 5	his young men, **A** you here with the ass;	3427
	24:55	Let the damsel **a** with us *a few* days, at	3427
	29:19	give her to another man: **a** with me.	3427
	44:33	let thy servant **a** instead of the lad a	3427
Ex	16:29	**a** ye every man in his place, let no man go	3427
Lev	8:35	Therefore shall ye **a** *at* the door of	3427
	19:13	not **a** with thee **all night** until the	3885
Nu	22: 5	of the earth, and they **a** over against me:	3427
	31:19	do ye **a** without the camp seven days:	2583
	31:23	Every thing that may **a** the fire,	935+871.1
	35:25	he shall **a** in it unto the death of the high	3427
Dt	3:19	shall **a** in your cities which I have given	3427
Jos	18: 5	Judah shall **a** in their coast on the south,	5975
	18: 5	the house of Joseph shall **a** in their coasts	5975
Ru	2: 8	hence, but **a** here **fast** by my maidens;	1692
1Sa	1:22	before the Lord, and there **a** for ever.	3427

1Sa	5: 7	The ark of the God of Israel shall not **a**	3427
	19: 2	and **a** in a secret place, and hide thyself:	3427
	22: 5	Gad said unto David, **A** in not the hold;	3427
	22:23	**A** thou with me, fear not: for he that	3427
	30:21	they had **made** also to **a** at the brook	3427
2Sa	11:11	The ark, and Israel, and Judah, **a** in tents;	3427
	15:19	return to thy place, and **a** with the king:	3427
	16:18	his will I be, and with him will I **a**.	3427
1Ki	8:13	a settled place for thee to **a** in for ever.	3427
2Ch	25:19	**a** now at home; why shouldest thou	3427
	32:10	that ye **a** in the siege in Jerusalem?	3427
Job	24:13	ways thereof, nor **a** in the paths thereof.	3427
	38:40	and **a** in the covert to lie in wait?	3427
	39: 9	be willing to serve thee, or **a** by thy crib?	3885
Ps	15: 1	Lord, who shall **a** in thy tabernacle?	1481
	61: 4	I will **a** in thy tabernacle for ever: I will	1481
	61: 7	He shall **a** before God for ever: O prepare	3427
	91: 1	shall **a** under the shadow of the Almighty.	3885
Pr	7:11	and stubborn; her feet **a** not in her house:	7931
	19:23	*he that hath it* shall **a** satisfied; he shall	3885
Ecc	8:15	for that shall **a** with him of his labour	3867
Jer	10:10	the nations shall not be **able to a** his	3557
	42:10	If ye will still **a** in this land, then will I	3427
	49:18	saith the Lord, no man shall **a** there,	3427
	49:33	there shall no man **a** there, nor *any* son of	3427
	50:40	*so* shall no man **a** there, neither shall any	3427
Hos	3: 3	unto her, Thou shalt **a** for me many days;	3427
	3: 4	the children of Israel shall **a** many days	3427
	11: 6	the sword shall **a** on his cities,	2342
Joel	2:11	great and very terrible; and who can **a** it?	3557
Mic	5: 4	of the Lord his God; and they shall **a**:	3427
Na	1: 6	who can **a** in the fierceness of his anger?	6965
Mal	3: 2	who *may* **a** the day of his coming?	3557
Mt	10:11	is worthy; and there **a** till ye go thence.	3306
Mk	6:10	there **a** till ye depart from that place.	3306
Lk	9: 4	ye enter into, there **a**, and thence depart.	3306
	19: 5	for to day I must **a** at thy house.	3306
	24:29	they constrained him, saying, **A** with us:	3306
Jn	12:46	believeth on me should not **a** in darkness.	3306
	14:16	that he may **a** with you for ever;	3306
	15: 4	in me, and I in you. As the branch	3306
	15: 4	bear fruit of itself, except it **a** in the vine;	3306
	15: 4	no more can ye, except ye **a** in me.	3306
	15: 6	If a man **a** not in me, he is cast forth as a	3306
	15: 7	If ye **a** in me, and my words abide in you,	3306
	15: 7	If ye **a** in me, and my words **a** in you,	3306
	15:10	my commandments, ye shall **a** in my love;	3306
	15:10	Father's commandments, and **a** in his love.	3306
Ac	15:34	Notwithstanding it pleased Silas to **a** there	1961
	16:15	and **a** *there*. And she constrained us.	3306
	20:23	saying that bonds and afflictions **a** me.	3306
	27:31	to the soldiers, Except these **a** in the ship,	3306
1Co	3:14	If any *man's* work **a** which he hath built	3306
	7: 8	It is good for them if they **a** even as I.	3306
	7:20	Let every man **a** in the same calling	3306
	7:24	wherein he is called, therein **a** with God.	3306
	7:40	But she is happier if she so **a**, after my	3306
	16: 6	And it may be that I will **a**, yea,	3887
Php	1:24	Nevertheless to **a** in the flesh *is* more	1961
	1:25	know that I shall **a** and continue with you	3306
1Ti	1: 3	As I besought thee to **a** *still* at Ephesus,	4357
1Jn	2:24	Let *that* therefore **a** in you, which ye have	3306
	2:27	as it hath taught you, ye shall **a** in him.	3306
	2:28	And now, little children, **a** in him; that,	3306

ABIDETH (30) [ABIDE]

Nu	31:23	all that **a** not the fire ye shall make	935+871.1
2Sa	16: 3	unto the king, Behold, he **a** at Jerusalem:	3427
Job	39:28	She dwelleth and **a** on the rock, upon	3885
Ps	49:12	Nevertheless man *being* in honour **a** not:	3885
	55:19	and afflict them, even he that **a** of old.	3427
	119:90	thou hast established the earth, and it **a**.	5975
	125: 1	*which* cannot be removed, *but* **a** for ever.	3427
Pr	15:31	The ear that heareth the reproof of life **a**	3885
Ecc	1: 4	cometh: but the earth **a** for ever.	5975
Jer	21: 9	that at this city shall die by the sword,	3427
Jn	3:36	see life; but the wrath of God **a** on him.	3306
	8:35	the servant **a** not in the house for ever:	3306
	8:35	in the house for ever: *but* the son **a** ever.	3306
	12:24	fall into the ground and die, it **a** alone:	3306
	12:34	We have heard out of the law that Christ **a**	3306
	15: 5	He that **a** in me, and I in him, the same	3306
1Co	13:13	now **a** faith, hope, charity, these three;	3306
2Ti	2:13	If we believe not, *yet* he **a** faithful:	3306
Heb	7: 3	unto the Son of God; **a** a priest continually.	3306
1Pe	1:23	word of God, which liveth and **a** for ever.	3306
1Jn	2: 6	He that saith he **a** in him ought himself	3306
	2:10	He that loveth his brother **a** in the light,	3306
	2:14	the word of God **a** in you, and ye have	3306
	2:17	he that doeth the will of God **a** for ever.	3306
	2:27	which ye have received of him **a** in you,	3306
	3: 6	Whosoever **a** in him sinneth not:	3306
	3:14	He that loveth not *his* brother **a** in death.	3306
	3:24	And hereby we know that he **a** in us, by	3306
2Jn	1: 9	and **a** not in the doctrine of Christ, hath	3306
	1: 9	He that **a** in the doctrine of Christ, he hath	3306

ABIDING (9) [ABIDE]

Nu	24: 2	he saw Israel **a** *in his tents* according to	7931
Jdg	16: 9	lying in wait, **a** with her in the chamber.	3427
	16:12	*there were* liers in wait in the chamber.	3427
1Sa	26:19	they have driven me out *this* day from **a**	5596
1Ch	29:15	*are* as a shadow, and *there is* none **a**.	4723
Lk	2: 8	in the same **country** shepherds **a** in the	63
Jn	5:38	And ye have not his word **a** in you:	3306

Ac	16:12	and we were in that city **a** certain days.	1304
1Jn	3:15	that no murderer hath eternal life **a** in him.	3306

ABIEL (3)

1Sa	9: 1	the son of **A**, the son of Zeror, the son of	22
	14:51	Ner the father of Abner *was* the son of **A**.	22
1Ch	11:32	of the brooks of Gaash, **A** the Arbathite,	22

ABIEZER, ABI-EZER (7) [ABI-EZRITE, ABI-EZRITES]

Jos	17: 2	for the children of **A**, for the children of	44
Jdg	6:34	a trumpet; and **A** was gathered after him.	44
	8: 2	of Ephraim better than the vintage of **A**?	44
2Sa	23:27	the Anethothite, Mebunnai the Hushathite,	44
1Ch	7:18	bare Ishod, and **A**, and Mahalah.	44
	11:28	son of Ikkesh the Tekoite, **A** the Antothite,	44
	27:12	ninth *captain* for the ninth month *was* **A**	44

ABI-EZRITE (1) [ABI-EZER]

Jdg	6:11	in Ophrah, that *pertained* unto Joash the **A**:	33

ABI-EZRITES (2) [ABI-EZER]

Jdg	6:24	unto this day it *is* yet in Ophrah of the **A**:	33
	8:32	of Joash his father, in Ophrah of the **A**.	33

ABIGAIL (17)

1Sa	25: 3	man *was* Nabal; and the name of his wife **A**:	26
	25:14	one of the young men told **A**, Nabal's wife,	26
	25:18	**A** made haste, and took two hundred loaves,	26
	25:23	when **A** saw David, she hasted,	26
	25:32	David said to **A**, Blessed *be* the Lord God	26
	25:36	**A** came to Nabal; and, behold, he held a feast	26
	25:39	David sent and communed with **A**, to take	26
	25:40	when the servants of David were come to **A**	26
	25:42	**A** hasted, and rose, and rode upon an ass,	26
	27: 3	and **A** the Carmelitess, Nabal's wife.	26
	30: 5	and **A** the wife of Nabal the Carmelite.	26
2Sa	2: 2	and **A** Nabal's wife the Carmelite.	26
	3: 3	of **A** the wife of Nabal the Carmelite;	26
	17:25	that went in to **A** the daughter of Nahash,	26
1Ch	2:16	Whose sisters *were* Zeruiah, and **A**.	26
	2:17	**A** bare Amasa: and the father of Amasa *was*	26
	3: 1	the second Daniel, of **A** the Carmelitess:	26

ABIHAIL (6)

Nu	3:35	families of Merari *was* Zuriel the son of **A**:	32
1Ch	2:29	And the name of the wife of Abishur *was* **A**,	32
	5:14	These *are* the children of **A** the son of Huri,	32
2Ch	11:18	*and* **A** the daughter of Eliab the son of Jesse;	32
Est	2:15	the daughter of **A** the uncle of Mordecai,	32
	9:29	the daughter of **A**, and Mordecai the Jew,	32

ABIHU (12)

Ex	6:23	Nadab, and **A**, Eleazar, and Ithamar.	30
	24: 1	and **A**, and seventy of the elders of Israel;	30
	24: 9	and **A**, and seventy of the elders of Israel:	30
	28: 1	Nadab and **A**, Eleazar and Ithamar.	30
Lev	10: 1	Nadab and **A**, the sons of Aaron, took either	30
Nu	3: 2	the firstborn, and **A**, Eleazar, and Ithamar.	30
	3: 4	Nadab and **A** died before the Lord,	30
	26:60	born Nadab, and **A**, Eleazar, and Ithamar.	30
	26:61	Nadab and **A** died, when they offered	30
1Ch	6: 3	Nadab, and **A**, Eleazar, and Ithamar.	30
	24: 1	Nadab, and **A**, Eleazar, and Ithamar.	30
	24: 2	But Nadab and **A** died before their father,	30

ABIHUD (1)

1Ch	8: 3	sons of Bela were, Addar, and Gera, and **A**,	31

ABIJAH (20) [ABIJAM]

1Ki	14: 1	At that time **A** the son of Jeroboam fell sick.	29
1Ch	24:10	The seventh to Hakkoz, the eighth to **A**,	29
2Ch	11:20	which bare him **A**, and Attai, and Ziza,	29
	11:22	Rehoboam made **A** the son of Maachah	29
	12:16	of David: and **A** his son reigned in his stead.	29
	13: 1	king Jeroboam *began* **A** to reign over Judah.	29
	13: 2	there was war between **A** and Jeroboam.	29
	13: 3	**A** set the battle in array with an army of	29
	13: 4	**A** stood up upon mount Zemaraim, which	29
	13:15	and all Israel before **A** and Judah.	29
	13:17	And his people slew them *with* a great	29
	13:19	**A** pursued after Jeroboam, and took cities	29
	13:20	recover strength again in the days of **A**:	29
	13:21	**A** waxed mighty, and married fourteen	29
	13:22	the rest of the acts of **A**, and his ways,	29
	14: 1	So **A** slept with his fathers, and they buried	29
	29: 1	his mother's name *was* **A**, the daughter of	29
Ne	10: 7	Meshullam, **A**, Mijamin,	29
	12: 4	Iddo, Ginnetho, **A**,	29
	12:17	Of **A**, Zichri; of Miniamin, of Moadiah,	29

ABIJAM (5) [ABIJAH]

1Ki	14:31	And **A** his son reigned in his stead.	38
	15: 1	the son of Nebat reigned **A** over Judah.	38
	15: 7	Now the rest of the acts of **A**, and all that he	38
	15: 7	there was war between **A** and Jeroboam.	38
	15: 8	slept with his fathers; and they buried him	38

ABILENE (1)

Lk	3: 1	of Trachonitis, and Lysanias the tetrarch of **A**,	9

ABILITY (7) [ABLE]

Lev	27: 8	according to his **a** that vowed shall	3027+5381
Ezr	2:69	They gave after their **a** unto the treasure	3581
Ne	5: 8	after our **a** have redeemed our brethren	1767
Da	1: 4	as *had* **a** in them to stand in the king's	3581
Mt	25:15	to every man according to his several **a**;	1411

A

Ac 11:29 disciples, every man according to his **a**, 2141
1Pe 4:11 *let him do it* as of the **a** which God giveth: 2479

ABIMAEL (2)

Ge 10:28 And Obal, and **A**, and Sheba, 39
1Ch 1:22 And Ebal, and **A**, and Sheba, 39

ABIMELECH (65) [ABIMELECH'S]

Ge 20: 2 and **A** king of Gerar sent, and took Sarah. 40
20: 3 But God came to **A** in a dream by night, 40
20: 4 had not come near her: and he said, Lord, 40
20: 8 Therefore **A** rose early in the morning, 40
20: 9 Then **A** called Abraham, and said unto him, 40
20:10 **A** said unto Abraham, What sawest thou, 40
20:14 **A** took sheep, and oxen, and menservants, 40
20:15 And **A** said, Behold, my land *is* before thee: 40
20:17 God healed **A**, and his wife, 40
20:18 closed up all the wombs of the house of **A**, 40
21:22 that **A** and Phichol the chief captain of his 40
21:25 Abraham reproved **A** because of a well of 40
21:26 **A** said, I wot not who hath done this thing: 40
21:27 took sheep and oxen, and gave *them* unto **A**; 40
21:29 **A** said unto Abraham, What *mean* these 40
21:32 **A** rose up, and Phichol the chief captain of 40
26: 1 Isaac went unto **A** king of the Philistims unto 40
26: 8 that **A** king of the Philistims looked out at a 40
26: 9 **A** called Isaac, and said, Behold, of a surety 40
26:10 **A** said, What *is* this thou hast done unto us? 40
26:11 **A** charged all *his* people, saying, He that 40
26:16 **A** said unto Isaac, Go from us; for thou art 40
26:26 **A** went to him from Gerar, and Ahuzzath 40
Jdg 8:31 bare him a son, whose name he called **A**. 40
9: 1 **A** the son of Jerubbaal went to Shechem 40
9: 3 hearts inclined to follow **A**; for they said, 40
9: 4 wherewith **A** hired vain and light persons, 40
9: 6 house of Millo, and went, and made **A** king, 40
9:16 in that ye have made **A** king, and if ye have 40
9:18 upon one stone, and have made **A**, 40
9:19 *then* rejoice ye in **A**, and let him also rejoice 40
9:20 let fire come out from **A**, and devour the 40
9:20 and from the house of Millo, and devour **A**. 40
9:21 and dwelt there, for fear of **A** his brother. 40
9:22 When **A** had reigned three years over Israel, 40
9:23 God sent an evil spirit between **A** and the 40
9:23 men of Shechem dealt treacherously with **A**: 40
9:24 and their blood be laid upon **A** their brother, 40
9:25 along *that* way by them: and it was told **A**. 40
9:27 god, and did eat and drink, and cursed **A**. 40
9:28 Who *is* **A**, and who *is* Shechem, that we 40
9:29 under my hand; then would I remove **A**. 40
9:29 he said to **A**, Increase thine army, 40
9:31 he sent messengers unto **A** privily, saying, 40
9:34 **A** rose up, and all the people that *were* with 40
9:35 **A** rose up, and the people that *were* with 40
9:38 mouth, wherewith thou saidst, Who *is* **A**, 40
9:39 the men of Shechem, and fought with **A**. 40
9:40 **A** chased him, and he fled before him, 40
9:41 **A** dwelt at Arumah: and Zebul thrust out 40
9:42 went out *into* the field; and they told **A**. 40
9:44 And **A**, and the company that *was* with him, 40
9:45 And **A** fought against the city all that day; 40
9:47 it was told **A**, that all the men of the tower 40
9:48 And **A** gat him up *to* mount Zalmon, he 40
9:48 **A** took an axe in his hand, and cut down a 40
9:49 and followed **A**, and put *them* to the hold, 40
9:50 went **A** to Thebez, and encamped against 40
9:52 **A** came unto the tower, and fought against 40
9:55 when the men of Israel saw that **A** was dead, 40
9:56 Thus God rendered the wickedness of **A**, 40
10: 1 after **A** there arose to defend Israel Tola 40
2Sa 11:21 Who smote **A** the son of Jerubbesheth? did 40
1Ch 18:16 and **A** the son of Abiathar, *were* the priests; 40
Ps 34: T when he changed his behaviour before **A**; 40

ABIMELECH'S (2) [ABIMELECH]

Ge 21:25 which **A** servants had violently taken away. 40
Jdg 9:53 cast a piece of a millstone upon **A** head, 40

ABINADAB (13)

1Sa 7: 1 and brought it into the house of **A** in the hill, 41
16: 8 Jesse called **A**, and made him pass before 41
17:13 next unto him, and the third Shammah. 41
31: 2 and **A**, and Malchishua, Saul's sons. 41
2Sa 6: 3 brought it out of the house of **A** that *was* in 41
6: 3 Uzzah and Ahio, the sons of **A**, drave the 41
6: 4 they brought it out of the house of **A** which 41
1Ki 4:11 The son of **A**, *in* all the region of Dor; 41
1Ch 2:13 And **A** the second, and Shimma the third, 41
8:33 and Malchishua, and **A**, and Eshbaal. 41
9:39 and Malchishua, and **A**, and Eshbaal. 41
10: 2 and **A**, and Malchishua, the sons of Saul. 41
13: 7 of God in a new cart out of the house of **A**: 41

ABINOAM (4)

Jdg 4: 6 called Barak the son of **A** out of 42
4:12 they shewed Sisera that Barak the son of **A** 42
5: 1 and Barak the son of **A** on that day, 42
5:12 and lead thy captivity captive, thou son of **A**. 42

ABIRAM (11)

Nu 16: 1 the son of Levi, and Dathan and **A**, the sons 48
16:12 Moses sent to call Dathan and **A**, the sons of 48
16:24 the tabernacle of Korah, Dathan, and **A**. 48
16:25 Moses rose up and went unto Dathan and **A**; 48
16:27 of Korah, Dathan, and **A**, on every side: 48

Nu 16:27 Dathan and **A** came out, and stood *in* the 48
26: 9 sons of Eliab; Nemuel, and Dathan, and **A**. 48
26: 9 *that* Dathan and **A**, *which were* famous 48
Dt 11: 6 what he did unto Dathan and **A**, the sons of 48
1Ki 16:34 he laid the foundation thereof in **A** his 48
Ps 106:17 up Dathan, and covered the company of **A**. 48

ABISHAG (5)

1Ki 1: 3 found **a** a Shunammite, and brought her to 49
1:15 **A** the Shunammite ministered unto the king. 49
2:17 he give me **A** the Shunammite to wife. 49
2:21 Let **A** the Shunammite be given to Adonijah 49
2:22 why dost thou ask **A** the Shunammite for 49

ABISHAI (25)

1Sa 26: 6 and to **A** the son of Zeruiah, brother to Joab, 52
26: 6 And **A** said, I will go down with thee. 52
26: 7 So David and **A** came to the people by night: 52
26: 8 said **A** to David, God hath delivered thine 52
26: 9 David said to **A**, Destroy him not: for who 52
2Sa 2:18 of Zeruiah there, Joab, and **A**, and Asahel: 52
2:24 Joab also and **A** pursued after Abner. 52
3:30 So Joab and **A** his brother slew Abner, 52
10:10 he delivered into the hand of **A** his brother, 52
10:14 *then* fled they *also* before **A**, and entered 52
16: 9 said **A** the son of Zeruiah unto the king, 52
16:11 And David said to **A**, and to all his servants, 52
18: 2 a third part under the hand of **A** the son of 52
18: 5 the king commanded Joab and **A** and Ittai, 52
18:12 the king charged thee and **A** and Ittai, 52
19:21 But **A** the son of Zeruiah answered and said, 52
20: 6 David said to **A**, Now shall Sheba the son of 52
20:10 **A** his brother pursued after Sheba the son of 52
21:17 But **A** the son of Zeruiah succoured him, 52
23:18 **A**, the brother of Joab, the son of Zeruiah, 52
1Ch 2:16 of Zeruiah; **A**, and Joab, and Asahel, three. 52
11:20 **A** the brother of Joab, he was chief of 52
18:12 Moreover **A** the son of Zeruiah slew of 52
19:11 he delivered into the hand of **A** his brother, 52
19:15 they likewise fled before **A** his brother, 52

ABISHALOM (2)

1Ki 15: 2 name *was* Maachah, the daughter of **A**. 53
15:10 name *was* Maachah, the daughter of **A**. 53

ABISHUA (5)

1Ch 6: 4 Eleazar begat Phinehas, Phinehas begat **A**, 50
6: 5 And **A** begat Bukki, and Bukki begat Uzzi, 50
6:50 Eleazar his son, Phinehas his son, **A** his son, 50
8: 4 And **A**, and Naaman, and Ahoah, 50
Ezr 7: 5 The son of **A**, the son of Phinehas, the son of 50

ABISHUR (2)

1Ch 2:28 And the sons of Shammai; Nadab, and **A**. 51
2:29 And the name of the wife of **A** *was* Abihail, 51

ABITAL (2)

2Sa 3: 4 and the fifth, Shephatiah the son of **A**; 37
1Ch 3: 3 The fifth, Shephatiah of **A**: the sixth, 37

ABITUB (1)

1Ch 8:11 And of Hushim he begat **A**, and Elpaal. 36

ABIUD (2)

Mt 1:13 And Zorobabel begat **A**; and Abiud begat 10
1:13 and **A** begat Eliakim; and Eliakim begat Azor; 10

ABJECTS (1)

Ps 35:15 *yea,* the **a** gathered themselves together 5222

ABLE (160) [ABILITY]

Ge 13: 6 the land was not **a to bear** them, that 5375
15: 5 tell the stars, if thou be **a** to number them: 3201
33:14 and the children be **a to endure**, 7272+3807.1
Ex 10: 5 that *one* cannot be **a** to see the earth: 3201
18:18 thou art not **a** to perform it thyself alone. 3201
18:21 shalt provide out of all the people **a** men, 2428
18:23 *so,* then thou shalt be **a** to endure, 3201
18:25 Moses chose **a** men out of all Israel, 2428
40:35 Moses was not **a** to enter into the tent of 3201
Lev 5: 7 if he be not **a** to bring a lamb, then he 1767
5:11 if he be not **a to bring** two 3027+5381
12: 8 if she be not **a to bring** a 1767+3027+4672
14:22 such as he is **a to get**; 3027+5381
14:31 *Even* such as he is **a to get**, the one 3027+5381
14:32 whose **hand is** not **a** to get *that* 3027+5381
25:26 be **a** to redeem it; 1767+3027+5381+3509.1
25:28 if he be not **a** to restore *it* to 1767+3027+4672
25:49 if he be **a**, he may redeem himself. 3027+5381
Nu 1: 3 all that *are* **a** to go forth *to* war in Israel: NIH
1:20 upward, all that *were* **a** to go forth *to* war; NIH
1:22 upward, all that *were* **a** to go forth *to* war; NIH
1:24 upward, all that *were* **a** to go forth *to* war; NIH
1:26 upward, all that *were* **a** to go forth *to* war; NIH
1:28 upward, all that *were* **a** to go forth *to* war; NIH
1:30 upward, all that *were* **a** to go forth *to* war; NIH
1:32 upward, all that *were* **a** to go forth *to* war; NIH
1:34 upward, all that *were* **a** to go forth *to* war; NIH
1:36 upward, all that *were* **a** to go forth *to* war; NIH
1:38 upward, all that *were* **a** to go forth *to* war; NIH
1:40 upward, all that *were* **a** to go forth *to* war; NIH
1:42 upward, all that *were* **a** to go forth *to* war; NIH
1:45 all that *were* **a** to go forth *to* war in Israel; NIH
11:14 I am not **a** to bear all this people alone, 3201
13:30 for we are **well a to overcome** it. 3201+3201
13:31 We be not **a** to go up against the people; 3201

Nu 14:16 Because the Lᴏʀᴅ was not **a** to bring this 3201
22:11 peradventure I shall be **a** to overcome 3201
22:37 am I not **a** indeed to promote thee to NIH
26: 2 all that *are* **a** to go *to* war in Israel. NIH
Dt 1: 9 I am not **a** to bear you myself alone: 3201
7:24 shall no man be **a** to stand before thee, NIH
9:28 Because the Lᴏʀᴅ was not **a** to bring them 3201
11:25 There shall no man *be* **a** to stand before NIH
14:24 for thee, so that thou art not **a** to carry it; 3201
16:17 Every man *shall give* as he is **a**, 3027+4979
Jos 1: 5 shall not any man *be* **a** to stand before NIH
14:12 I shall *be* **a** to drive them out, as the Lᴏʀᴅ NIH
23: 9 no man hath *been* **a** to stand before you NIH
Jdg 8: 3 what was I **a** to do in comparison of you? 3201
1Sa 6:20 Who is **a** to stand before this holy Lᴏʀᴅ 3201
17: 9 If he be **a** to fight with me, and *to* kill me, 3201
17:33 Thou art not **a** to go against this Philistine 3201
1Ki 3: 9 for who is **a** to judge this thy *so* great a 3201
9:21 the children of Israel also were not **a** 3201
2Ki 3:21 they gathered all that *were* **a** to put on NIH
18:23 if thou be **a** on thy part to set riders upon 3201
18:29 for he shall not be **a** to deliver you out of 3201
1Ch 5:18 men **a** *to* bear buckler and sword, NIH
9:13 **very a** men *for* the work of the service of 2428
26: 8 **a** men for strength for the service, 2428
29:14 that we should be **a** to offer *so* NIH
2Ch 2: 6 who is **a** to build him a house, 3581+6113
7: 7 was not **a** to receive the burnt offerings, 3201
20: 6 that none is **a to withstand** thee? 3320+5973
20:37 that they were not **a** to go to Tarshish. 6113
25: 5 thousand choice *men,* **a** *to* go forth *to* war, NIH
25: 9 The Lᴏʀᴅ **is a** to give thee much more 3426
32:13 **any ways a** to deliver their lands 3201+3201
32:14 that your God should be **a** to deliver you 3201
32:15 kingdom was **a** to deliver his people out of 3201
Ezr 10:13 and *we are* not **a** to stand without, 3581
Ne 4:10 so that we are not **a** to build the wall. 3581
Job 41:10 him up: who then is **a** to stand before me? NIH
Ps 18:38 I have wounded them that they were not **a** 3201
21:11 *which* they are not **a** *to* perform. 3201
36:12 are cast down, and shall not be **a** to rise. 3201
40:12 that I am not **a** to look *up*; they are moe 3201
Pr 27: 4 but who is **a to stand** before envy? 5975
Ecc 8:17 to know *it*, yet shall he not be **a** to find *it*. NIH
Isa 36: 8 if thou be **a** on thy part to set riders upon 3201
36:14 for he shall not be **a** to deliver you. 3201
47:11 upon thee; thou shalt not be **a** to put it off: 3201
47:12 if so be thou shalt be **a** to profit, if so 3201
Jer 10:10 the nations shall not be **a to abide** his 3557
11:11 which they shall not be **a** to escape; 3201
49:10 and he shall not be **a** to hide himself: 3201
La 1:14 *from whom* I am not **a** to rise up. 3201
Eze 7:19 their gold shall not be **a** to deliver them in 3201
33:12 neither shall the righteous be **a** to live for 3201
46: 5 for the lambs **as** he shall be **a** to give, 3027
46:11 to the lambs **as** he is **a** to give, and a hin 3027
Da 2:26 Art thou **a** to make known unto me 3546
3:17 our God whom we serve *is* **a** to deliver us 3202
4:18 **a** to make known unto me 3202
4:18 thou *art* **a**; for the spirit of the holy gods *is* 3546
4:37 those that walk in pride his *is* **a** to abase. 3202
6:20 **a** to deliver thee from the lions? 3202
Am 7:10 the land is not **a** to bear all his words. 3201
Zep 1:18 their silver nor their gold shall be **a** 3201
Mt 3: 9 God is **a** of these stones to raise up 1410
9:28 Believe ye that I am **a** to do this? 1410
10:28 kill the body, but are not **a** to kill the soul: 1410
10:28 rather fear him which is **a** to destroy both 1410
19:12 He that is **a** to receive *it,* let him receive *it*. 1410
20:22 Are ye **a** to drink *of* the cup that I shall 1410
20:22 They say unto him, We are **a**. 1410
22:46 And no *man* was **a** to answer him a word, 1410
26:61 I am **a** to destroy the temple of God, 1410
Mk 4:33 word unto them, as they were **a** to hear *it*. 1410
Lk 1:20 thou shalt be dumb, and not **a** to speak, 1410
3: 8 That God is **a** of these stones to raise up 1410
12:26 be not **a** *to do that thing which is* least, 1410
13:24 will seek to enter in, and shall not be **a**. 2480
14:29 is not **a** to finish *it,* all that behold *it* begin 2480
14:30 began to build, and was not **a** to finish. 2480
14:31 consulteth whether he be **a** with ten 1415
21:15 which all your adversaries shall not be **a** to 1410
Jn 10:29 no *man* is **a** to pluck *them* out of my 1410
21: 6 now they were not **a** to draw it for 2480
Ac 6:10 And they were not **a** to resist the wisdom 2480
15:10 which neither our fathers nor we were **a** to 2480
20:32 which is **a** to build *you* up, and to give you 1410
25: 5 said he, which among you are **a**, go down 1415
Ro 4:21 he had promised, he was **a** also to perform. 1415
8:39 shall be **a** to separate us from the love of 1410
11:23 for God is **a** to graff them in again. 1415
14: 4 holden up: for God is **a** to make him stand. 1415
15:14 **a** also to admonish one another. 1410
1Co 3: 2 for hitherto ye were not **a** *to bear it,* 1410
3: 2 **able** *to bear it,* neither yet now are ye **a**. 1410
6: 5 not one that shall be **a** to judge between 1410
10:13 you to be tempted above that you are **a**; 1410
10:13 way to escape, that ye may be **a** to bear it. 1410
2Co 1: 4 that we may be **a** to comfort them which 1410
3: 6 Who also hath **made** us **a** ministers of 2427
9: 8 And God *is* **a** to make all grace abound 1415
Eph 3:18 May be **a** to comprehend with all saints 1840
3:20 Now unto him that is **a** to do exceeding 1410
6:11 that ye may be **a** to stand against the wiles 1410
6:13 that ye may be **a** to withstand in the evil 1410

Eph 6:16 wherewith ye shall be **a** to quench all *1410*
Php 3:21 according to the working whereby he is **a** *1410*
2Ti 1:12 I am persuaded that he is **a** to keep that *1415*
 2: 2 who shall be **a** to teach others also. *2425*
 3: 7 never **a** to come to the knowledge of *1410*
 3:15 which are **a** to make thee wise unto *1410*
Tit 1: 9 that he may be **a** by sound doctrine both *1415*
Heb 2:18 he is **a** to succour them that are tempted. *1410*
 5: 7 tears unto him that was **a** to save him from *1410*
 7:25 Wherefore he is **a** also to save them to *1410*
 11:19 Accounting that God was **a** to raise *him* *1415*
Jas 1:21 which is **a** to save your souls. *1410*
 3: 2 *and* **a** also to bridle the whole body. *1415*
 4:12 who is **a** to save and to destroy: *1410*
2Pe 1:15 **a** after my decease to have these *things* *4160*
Jude 1:24 Now unto him that is **a** to keep you from *1410*
Rev 5: 3 under the earth, was **a** to open the book, *1410*
 6:17 is come; and who shall be **a** to stand? *1410*
 13: 4 beast: who is **a** to make war with him? *1410*
 15: 8 no *man* was **a** to enter into the temple, *1410*

ABNER (62) [ABNER'S]

1Sa 14:50 the name of the captain of his host *was* **A**, 74
 14:51 and Ner the father of **A** *was* the son of Abiel. 74
 17:55 said unto **A**, the captain of the host, Abner, 74
 17:55 said unto Abner, the captain of the host, **A**, 74
 17:55 **A** said, *As* thy soul liveth, O king, I cannot 74
 17:57 **A** took him, and brought him before Saul 74
 20:25 **A** sat by Saul's side, and David's place was 74
 26: 5 and **A** the son of Ner, the captain of his host: 74
 26: 7 but **A** and the people lay round about him. 74
 26:14 to **A** the son of Ner, saying, Answerest thou 74
 26:14 son of Ner, saying, Answerest thou not, **A**? 74
 26:14 answered and said, Who *art* thou *that* 74
 26:15 David said to **A**, *Art* not thou a *valiant* man? 74
2Sa 2: 8 But **A** the son of Ner, captain of Saul's host, 74
 2:12 the son of Ner, and the servants of 74
 2:14 **A** said to Joab, Let the young men now arise, 74
 2:17 **A** was beaten, and the men of Israel, before 74
 2:19 Asahel pursued after **A**; and in going he 74
 2:19 right hand nor to the left from following **A**. 74
 2:20 **A** looked behind him, and said, *Art* thou 74
 2:21 **A** said to him, Turn thee aside to thy right 74
 2:22 **A** said again to Asahel, Turn thee aside from 74
 2:23 wherefore **A** with the hinder end of the spear 74
 2:24 Joab also and Abishai pursued after **A**: 74
 2:25 gathered themselves together after **A**, 74
 2:26 **A** called to Joab, and said, Shall the sword 74
 2:29 **A** and his men walked all that night through 74
 2:30 Joab returned from following **A**: and when 74
 3: 6 that **A** made himself strong for the house of 74
 3: 7 *Ish-bosheth* said to **A**, Wherefore hast thou 74
 3: 8 was **A** very wroth for the words of 74
 3: 9 So do God to **A**, and more also, except, as 74
 3:11 he could not answer **A** a word again, 74
 3:12 **A** sent messengers to David on his behalf, 74
 3:16 said **A** unto him, Go, return. And he 74
 3:17 **A** had communication with the elders of 74
 3:19 **A** also spake in the ears of Benjamin: 74
 3:19 **A** went also to speak in the ears of David in 74
 3:20 So **A** came to David *to* Hebron, 74
 3:20 David made **A** and the men that *were* with 74
 3:21 **A** said unto David, I will arise and go, 74
 3:21 David sent **A** away; and he went in peace. 74
 3:22 **A** *was* not with David in Hebron; for he had 74
 3:23 **A** the son of Ner came to the king, 74
 3:24 **A** came unto thee; why *is* it *that* thou 74
 3:25 Thou knowest **A** the son of Ner, that he 74
 3:26 out from David, he sent messengers after **A**, 74
 3:27 when **A** was returned *to* Hebron, Joab took 74
 3:28 for ever from the blood of **A** the son of Ner: 74
 3:30 So Joab and Abishai his brother slew **A**, 74
 3:31 you with sackcloth, and mourn before **A**. 74
 3:32 they buried **A** in Hebron: and the king lift up 74
 3:32 lift up his voice, and wept at the grave of **A**; 74
 3:33 the king lamented over **A**, and said, Died 74
 3:33 over Abner, and said, Died **A** as a fool dieth? 74
 3:37 was not of the king to slay **A** the son of Ner. 74
 4: 1 when Saul's son heard that **A** was dead in 74
 4:12 buried *it* in the sepulchre of **A** in Hebron. 74
1Ki 2: 5 unto **A** the son of Ner, and unto Amasa 74
 2:32 knowing *thereof, to wit,* **A** the son of Ner, 74
1Ch 26:28 **A** the son of Ner, and Joab the son of 74
 27:21 of Benjamin, Jaasiel the son of **A**: 74

ABNER'S (1) [ABNER]

2Sa 2:31 of **A** men, *so that* three hundred 74

ABOARD (1)

Ac 21: 2 unto Phenicia, we **went a**, and set forth. *1910*

ABODE (69) [ABIDE]

Ge 29:14 And he **a** with him the space of a month. 3427
 49:24 his bow **a** in strength, and the arms of his 3427
Ex 24:16 the glory of the LORD **a** upon mount 7931
 40:35 because the cloud **a** thereon, and the glory 7931
Nu 9:17 in the place where the cloud **a**, there 7931
 9:18 as long as the cloud **a** upon the tabernacle 7931
 9:20 of the LORD they **a** in their *tents*, 2583
 9:21 when the cloud **a** from even unto 1961
 9:22 the children of Israel **a** in their *tents*, 2583
 11:35 *unto* Hazeroth; and **a** at Hazeroth. 1961
 20: 1 the people **a** in Kadesh; and Miriam died 3427
 22: 8 and the princes of Moab **a** with Balaam. 3427
 25: 1 Israel **a** in Shittim, and the people begun 3427

Dt 1:46 So ye **a** in Kadesh many days, 3427
 1:46 according unto the days that ye **a** *there*. 3427
 3:29 So we **a** in the valley over against 3427
 9: 9 I **a** in the mount forty days and forty 3427
Jos 2:22 unto the mountain, and **a** there three days, 3427
 5: 8 that they **a** in their places in the camp, 3427
 8: 9 between Beth-el and Ai, on the west 3427
Jdg 5:17 Gilead **a** beyond Jordan: and why did Dan 7931
 5:17 on the sea shore, and **a** in his breaches. 7931
 11:17 would not consent: and Israel **a** in Kadesh. 3427
 19: 4 and he **a** with him three days: 3427
 20:47 and **a** in the rock Rimmon four months. 3427
 21: 2 **a** there till even before God, and lift up 3427
1Sa 1:23 So the woman **a**, and gave her son suck 3427
 7: 2 to pass, while the ark **a** in Kirjath-jearim, 3427
 13:16 with them, **a** in Gibeah of Benjamin: 3427
 22: 6 now Saul **a** in Gibeah under a tree in 3427
 23:14 David **a** in the wilderness in strong holds, 3427
 23:18 David **a** in the wood, and Jonathan went 3427
 23:25 a rock, and **a** in the wilderness of Maon. 3427
 25:13 and two hundred **a** by the stuff. 3427
 26: 3 David **a** in the wilderness, and he saw that 3427
 30:10 for two hundred **a** *behind*, which were so 5975
2Sa 1: 1 and David had **a** two days in Ziklag; 3427
 11:12 So Uriah **a** in Jerusalem that day, and 3427
 15: 8 For thy servant vowed a vow while I **a** at 3427
1Ki 17:19 **a**, and laid him upon his own bed. 3427
2Ki 19:27 I know thy **a**, and thy going out, 3427
Ezr 8:15 and there **a** we in *tents* three days: 2583
 8:32 came *to* Jerusalem, and **a** there three days. 3427
Isa 37:28 I know thy **a**, and thy going out, and thy 3427
Jer 38:28 So Jeremiah **a** in the court of the prison 3427
Mt 17:22 while they **a** in Galilee, Jesus said unto *390*
Lk 1:56 And Mary **a** with her about three months, *3306*
 8:27 neither **a** in *any* house, but in the tombs. *3306*
 21:37 **a** in the mount that is called *the mount* of *835*
Jn 1:32 heaven like a dove, and it **a** upon him. *3306*
 1:39 where he dwelt, and **a** with him that day: *3306*
 4:40 tarry with them: and he **a** there two days. *3306*
 7: 9 *words* unto them, he **a** *still* in Galilee. *3306*
 8:44 and **a** not in the truth, because there is no *2476*
 10:40 John at first baptized; and there he **a**. *3306*
 11: 6 he **a** two days *still* in the *same* place *3306*
 14:23 come unto him, and make our **a** with him. *3438*
Ac 1:13 where **a** both Peter, and James, and John, *2650*
 12:19 down from Judea to Cesarea, and *there* **a**. *1304*
 14: 3 a they speaking boldly in the Lord, *1304*
 14:28 And there they **a** long time with *1304*
 17:14 but Silas and Timotheus **a** there *still*. *5278*
 18: 3 same craft, he **a** with them, and wrought: *3306*
 20: 3 And *there* **a** three months: and when *4160*
 20: 6 Troas in five days; where we **a** seven days. *1304*
 21: 7 the brethren, and **a** with them one day. *3306*
 21: 8 was *one* of the seven; and **a** with him. *3306*
Gal 1:18 to see Peter, and **a** with him fifteen days. *1961*
2Ti 4:20 Erastus **a** at Corinth: but Trophimus have *3306*

ABODEST (1) [ABIDE]

Jdg 5:16 Why **a** thou among the sheepfolds, to hear 3427

ABOLISH (1) [ABOLISHED]

Isa 2:18 And the idols he shall utterly **a**. 2498

ABOLISHED (5) [ABOLISH]

Isa 51: 6 and my righteousness shall not be **a**. 2865
Eze 6: 6 be cut down, and your works may be **a**. 4229
2Co 3:13 look to the end of that which is **a**: *2673*
Eph 2:15 Having **a** in his flesh the enmity, *even* *2673*
2Ti 1:10 who hath **a** death, and hath brought life *2673*

ABOMINABLE (23) [ABOMINATION]

Lev 7:21 any **a** unclean *thing*, and eat of the flesh 8263
 11:43 Ye shall not **make** yourselves **a** with any 8262
 18:30 that *ye* commit not *any one* of these **a** 8441
 19: 7 if it be eaten at all on the third day, it *is* **a**; 6292
 20:25 ye shall not **make** your souls **a** by beast, 8262
Dt 14: 3 Thou shalt not eat any **a** *thing*. 8441
1Ch 21: 6 for the king's word was **a** to Joab. 8581
2Ch 15: 8 put away the **a idols** out of all the land of 8251
Job 15:16 How much more **a** and filthy *is* man, 8581
Ps 14: 1 are corrupt, they have **done a** works, 8581
 53: 1 are they, and have **done a** iniquity: 8581
Isa 14:19 thou art cast out of thy grave like an **a** 8581
 65: 4 and broth of **a** *things is in* their vessels; 6292
Jer 16:18 carcases of their detestable and **a things**. 8441
 44: 4 Oh, do not this **a** thing that I hate. 8441
Eze 4:14 neither came there **a** flesh into my mouth. 6292
 8:10 **a** beasts, and all the idols of the house of 8263
 16:52 thou hast committed more **a** than they: 8581
Mic 6:10 wicked, and the scant measure *that is* **a**? 2194
Na 3: 6 I will cast **a filth** upon thee, and make 8251
Tit 1:16 but in works they deny *him*, being **a**, *947*
1Pe 4: 3 revellings, banquetings, and **a** idolatries: *111*
Rev 21: 8 and the **a**, and murderers, *948*

ABOMINABLY (1) [ABOMINABLE]

1Ki 21:26 he did very **a** in following idols, 8581

ABOMINATION (76) [ABOMINABLE, ABOMINABLY, ABOMINATIONS]

Ge 43:32 for that *is* an **a** unto the Egyptians. 8441
 46:34 for every shepherd *is* an **a** unto 8441
Ex 8:26 we shall sacrifice the **a** of the Egyptians 8441
 8:26 shall we sacrifice the **a** of the Egyptians 8441
Lev 7:18 it shall be an **a**, and the soul that eateth 6292

Lev 11:10 in the waters, they *shall be* an **a** unto you: 8263
 11:11 They shall be even an **a** unto you: ye shall 8263
 11:11 but you shall have their carcases in **a**. 8262
 11:12 in the waters, that *shall be* an **a** unto you. 8263
 11:13 these *are they which* ye shall have in **a**: 8262
 11:13 they shall not be eaten, they *are* an **a**: 8263
 11:20 upon *all* four, *shall be* an **a** unto you. 8263
 11:23 have four feet, *shall be* an **a** unto you. 8263
 11:41 creepeth upon the earth *shall be* an **a**; 8263
 11:42 them ye shall not eat; for they *are* an **a**. 8263
 18:22 mankind, as with womankind: it *is* **a**. 8441
 20:13 both of them have committed an **a**: 8441
Dt 7:25 for it *is* an **a** to the LORD thy God. 8441
 7:26 Neither shalt thou bring an **a** into thine 8441
 12:31 for every **a** to the LORD, which he hateth, 8441
 13:14 *that* such a **a** is wrought among you; 8441
 17: 1 for that *is* an **a** unto the LORD thy God. 8441
 17: 4 *that* such a **a** is wrought in Israel: 8441
 18:12 For all that do these *things are* an **a** unto 8441
 22: 5 that do so *are* an **a** unto the LORD thy God. 8441
 23:18 for even both these *are* an **a** unto the LORD 8441
 24: 4 is defiled; for that *is* an **a** before the LORD: 8441
 25:16 *are* an **a** unto the LORD thy God. 8441
 27:15 or molten image, an **a** unto the LORD, 8441
1Sa 13: 4 *that* Israel also was **had in a** with 887
1Ki 11: 5 and after Milcom the **a** of the Ammonites. 8251
 11: 7 the **a** of Moab, in the hill that *is* before 8251
 11: 7 the **a** of the children of Ammon. 8251
2Ki 23:13 for Ashtoreth the **a** of the Zidonians, 8251
 23:13 and for Chemosh the **a** of the Moabites, 8251
 23:13 for Milcom the **a** of the children of 8441
Ps 88: 8 thou hast made me an **a** unto them: 8441
Pr 3:32 For the froward *is* **a** to the LORD: 8441
 6:16 LORD hate: yea, seven *are* an **a** unto him: 8441
 8: 7 and wickedness *is* an **a** to my lips. 8441
 11: 1 A false balance *is* **a** to the LORD: 8441
 11:20 *They that* are of a froward heart *are* **a** 8441
 12:22 Lying lips *are* **a** to the LORD: 8441
 13:19 but *it* is **a** to fools to depart from evil. 8441
 15: 8 The sacrifice of the wicked *is* an **a** to 8441
 15: 9 The way of the wicked *is* an **a** unto 8441
 15:26 The thoughts of the wicked *are* an **a** to 8441
 16: 5 Every one *that* is proud in heart *is* an **a** to 8441
 16:12 *It is* an **a** to kings to commit wickedness: 8441
 17:15 even they both *are* **a** to the LORD. 8441
 20:10 both of them *are* alike **a** to the LORD. 8441
 20:23 Divers weights *are* an **a** unto the LORD; 8441
 21:27 The sacrifice of the wicked *is* **a**: how 8441
 24: 9 *is* sin: and the scorner *is* an **a** to men. 8441
 28: 9 the law, even his prayer *shall be* **a**. 8441
 29:27 An unjust man is an **a** to the just: 8441
 29:27 *he that is* upright in the way *is* **a** to 8441
Isa 1:13 incense *is* an **a** unto me; the new moons 8441
 41:24 of nought: an **a** *is he that* chooseth you. 8441
 44:19 and shall I make the residue thereof an **a**? 8441
 66:17 swine's flesh, and the **a**, and the mouse, 8263
Jer 2: 7 my land, and made mine heritage an **a**. 8441
 6:15 ashamed when they had committed **a**? 8441
 8:12 ashamed when they had committed **a**? 8441
 32:35 that *they* should do this **a**, to cause Judah 8441
Eze 16:50 haughty, and committed **a** before me: 8441
 18:12 his eyes to the idols, hath committed **a**, 8441
 22:11 hath committed **a** with his neighbour's 8441
 33:26 ye work **a**, and ye defile every one his 8441
Da 11:31 shall place the **a** that maketh desolate. 8251
 12:11 the **a** that maketh desolate set up, 8251
Mal 2:11 an **a** is committed in Israel 8441
Mt 24:15 therefore shall see the **a** of desolation, *946*
Mk 13:14 But when ye shall see the **a** of desolation, *946*
Lk 16:15 amongst men is **a** in the sight of God. *946*
Rev 21:27 neither *whatsoever* worketh **a**, or *maketh* a *946*

ABOMINATIONS (76) [ABOMINATION]

Lev 18:26 and shall not commit any of these **a**; 8441
 18:27 (For all these **a** have the men of the land 8441
 18:29 whosoever shall commit any of these **a**, 8441
Dt 18: 9 thou shalt not learn to do after the **a** of 8441
 18:12 of these the LORD thy God doth drive 8441
 20:18 they teach you not to do after all their **a**, 8251
 29:17 ye have seen their **a**, and their idols, wood 8251
 32:16 *gods*, with **a** provoked they him to anger. 8441
1Ki 14:24 they did according to all the **a** of 8441
2Ki 16: 3 the fire, according to the **a** of the heathen, 8441
 21: 2 after the **a** of the heathen, whom 8441
 21:11 king of Judah hath done these **a**, 8441
 23:24 all the **a** that were spied in the land of 8441
2Ch 28: 3 burnt his children in the fire after the **a** 8441
 33: 2 the LORD, like unto the **a** of the heathen, 8441
 34:33 Josiah took away all the **a** out of all 8441
 36: 8 his **a** which he did, and that which was 8441
 36:14 transgressed very much after all the **a** of 8441
Ezr 9: 1 *doing* according to their **a**, *even* of 8441
 9:11 of the people of the lands, with their **a**, 8441
 9:14 join in affinity with the people of these **a**? 8441
Pr 26:25 him not: for *there are* seven **a** in his heart. 8441
Isa 66: 3 and their soul delighteth in their **a**. 8251
Jer 4: 1 if thou wilt put away thine **a** out of my 8251
 7:10 say, We are delivered to do all these **a**? 8441
 7:30 they have set their **a** in the house which 8251
 13:27 *and* thine **a** on the hills in the fields. 8251
 32:34 they set their **a** in the house, which is 8251
 44:22 of the **a** which ye have committed; 8441
Eze 5: 9 any more the like, because of all thine **a**. 8441
 5:11 with all thine **a**, therefore will I also 8441
 6: 9 which they have committed in all their **a**. 8441

A

Eze	6:11 for all the evil **a** of the house of Israel:	8441
	7: 3 will recompense upon thee all thine **a**.	8441
	7: 4 and thine **a** shall be in the midst of thee:	8441
	7: 8 and will recompense thee for all thine **a**.	8441
	7: 9 and thine **a** *that* are in the midst of thee;	8441
	7:20 they made the images of their **a** *and* of	8441
	8: 6 even the great **a** that the house of Israel	8441
	8: 6 yet again, *and* thou shalt see great **a**.	8441
	8: 9 behold the wicked **a** that they do here.	8441
	8:13 *and* thou shalt see great **a** that they do.	8441
	8:15 *and* thou shalt see greater **a** than these.	8441
	8:17 commit the **a** which they commit here?	8441
	9: 4 that cry for all the **a** that be done in	8441
	11:18 and all the **a** thereof from thence.	8441
	11:21 heart of their detestable things and their **a**,	8441
	12:16 that they may declare all their **a** among	8441
	14: 6 and turn away your faces from all your **a**.	8441
	16: 2 of man, cause Jerusalem to know her **a**,	8441
	16:22 in all thine **a** and thy whoredoms thou	8441
	16:36 with all the idols of thy **a**, and by the	8441
	16:43 commit *this* lewdness above all thine **a**.	8441
	16:47 after their ways, nor done after their **a**:	8441
	16:51 thou hast multiplied thine **a** more than	8441
	16:51 justified thy sisters in all thine **a** which	8441
	16:58 Thou hast borne thy lewdness and thine **a**,	8441
	18:13 hath done all these **a**; he shall surely die;	8441
	18:24 according to all the **a** that the wicked	8441
	20: 4 cause them to know the **a** of their fathers:	8441
	20: 7 Cast ye away every man the **a** of his eyes,	8251
	20: 8 they did not every man cast away the **a** of	8251
	20:30 and commit ye whoredom after their **a**?	8251
	22: 2 yea, thou shalt shew her all her **a**.	8441
	23:36 yea, declare unto them their **a**;	8441
	33:29 of all their **a** which they have committed.	8441
	36:31 sight for your iniquities and for your **a**.	8441
	43: 8 name by their **a** that they have committed:	8441
	44: 6 of Israel, let it suffice you of all your **a**,	8441
	44: 7 broken my covenant because of all your **a**.	8441
	44:13 and their **a** which they have committed.	8441
Da	9:27 for the overspreading of **a** he *shall* make *it*	8251
Hos	9:10 and *their* **a** were according as they loved.	8251
Zec	9: 7 and his **a** from between his teeth:	8251
Rev	17: 4 having a golden cup in her hand full of **a**	946
	17: 5 THE MOTHER OF HARLOTS AND **A** OF	946

ABOUND (19) [ABOUNDED, ABOUNDETH, ABOUNDING, ABUNDANCE, ABUNDANT, ABUNDANTLY]

Pr	28:20 A faithful man shall **a** with blessings:	7227
Mt	24:12 And because iniquity shall **a**, the love of	4129
Ro	5:20 the law entered, that the offence might **a**.	4121
	5:20 sin abounded, grace did **much more a**:	5248
	6: 1 Shall we continue in sin, that grace may **a**?	4121
	15:13 peace in believing, that ye may **a** in hope,	4052
2Co	1: 5 For as the sufferings of Christ **a** in us, so	4052
	8: 7 as ye **a** in every *thing*, in faith,	4052
	8: 7 to us, *see* that ye **a** in this grace also.	4052
	9: 8 And God *is* able to make all grace **a**	4052
	9: 8 in all *things*, may **a** to every good work:	4052
Php	1: 9 that your love may **a** yet more and more	4052
	4:12 *how* to be abased, and I know *how* to **a**:	4052
	4:12 to be hungry, both to **a** and to suffer need.	4052
	4:17 I desire fruit that *may* **a** to your account.	4121
	4:18 But I have all, and **a**: I am full,	4052
1Th	3:12 and **a** in love one toward another,	4052
	4: 1 *so* ye would **a** more *and more*.	4052
2Pe	1: 8 For if these *things* be in you, and **a**,	4121

ABOUNDED (5) [ABOUND]

Ro	3: 7 if the truth of God hath *more* **a** through	4052
	5:15 one man, Jesus Christ, hath **a** unto many.	4052
	5:20 But where sin **a**, grace did much more	4121
2Co	8: 2 their deep poverty **a** unto the riches of	4052
Eph	1: 8 he hath **a** toward us in all wisdom	4052

ABOUNDETH (3) [ABOUND]

Pr	29:22 and a furious man **a** in transgression.	7227
2Co	1: 5 in us, so our consolation also **a** by Christ.	4052
2Th	1: 3 every one of you all towards each other **a**;	4121

ABOUNDING (3) [ABOUND]

Pr	8:24 there were no fountains **a** with water.	3513
1Co	15:58 always **a** in the work of the Lord,	4052
Col	2: 7 been taught, **a** therein with thanksgiving.	4052

ABOUT (632)

Ge	23:17 that *were* in all the borders **round a**,	5439
	35: 5 upon the cities that *were* **round a** them,	5439
	37: 7 your sheaves **stood round a**,	5437
	38:24 it came to pass **a** three months after,	3509.1
	39:11 it came to pass **a** this time, that *Joseph*	3509.1
	41:25 God hath shewed Pharaoh what he *is* **a** to	NIH
	41:28 What God *is* **a** to do he sheweth unto	NIH
	41:42 fine linen, and put a gold chain **a** his neck;	5921
	41:48 of the field, which *was* **round a** every city,	5439
	42:24 he **turned a** from them, and wept;	5437
	46:34 servants' **trade** hath been **a** cattle	376+4735
Ex	7:24 all the Egyptians digged **round a** the river	5439
	9:18 to morrow **a** *this* time I will cause it to	3509.1
	11: 4 **A** midnight will I go out into the midst	3509.1
	12:37 a six hundred thousand on foot *that*	3509.1
	13:18 God **led** the people **a**, *through* the way of	5437
	16:13 in the morning the dew lay **round a**	5439
	19:12 shalt set bounds unto the people **round a**,	5439
	19:23 **Set bounds a** the mount, and sanctify it.	1379

Ex	25:11 make upon it a crown *of* gold **round a**.	5439
	25:24 make thereto a crown *of* gold **round a**.	5439
	25:25 unto it a border of a handbreadth **round a**,	5439
	25:25 crown to the border thereof **round a**.	5439
	27:17 All the pillars **round a** the court shall *be*	5439
	28:32 of woven work **round a** the hole of it,	5439
	28:33 and of scarlet, **round a** the hem thereof;	5439
	28:33 and bells of gold between them **round a**;	5439
	28:34 upon the hem of the robe **round a**.	5439
	29:16 and sprinkle *it* **round a** upon the altar.	5439
	29:20 sprinkle the blood upon the altar **round a**	5439
	30: 3 the sides thereof **round a**, and the horns	5439
	30: 3 make unto it a crown *of* gold **round a**.	5439
	32:28 there fell of the people that day **a** three	3509.1
	37: 2 and made a crown *of* gold to it **round a**.	5439
	37:11 made thereunto a crown *of* gold **round a**	5439
	37:12 a border of a handbreadth **round a**;	5439
	37:12 of gold for the border thereof **round a**.	5439
	37:26 the sides thereof **round a**, and the horns	5439
	37:26 he made unto it a crown *of* gold **round a**	5439
	38:16 All the hangings of the court **round a**	5439
	38:20 and of the court **round a**, *were* of brass.	5439
	38:31 the sockets of the court **round a**,	5439
	38:31 and all the pins of the court **round a**.	5439
	39:23 *with* a band **round a** the hole, *that* it	5439
	39:25 **round a** between the pomegranates;	5439
	39:26 **round a** the hem of the robe to minister	5439
	40: 8 thou shalt set up the court **round a**,	5439
	40:33 he reared up the court **round a**	5439
Lev	1: 5 sprinkle the blood **round a** upon the altar	5439
	1:11 shall sprinkle his blood **round a** upon	5439
	3: 2 sprinkle the blood upon the altar **round a**	5439
	3: 8 the blood thereof **round a** upon the altar.	5439
	3:13 the blood thereof upon the altar **round a**.	5439
	6: 5 Or all *that* which he hath sworn falsely;	NIH
	7: 2 blood thereof shall he sprinkle **round a**	5439
	8:15 put *it* upon the horns of the altar **round a**	5439
	8:19 the blood upon the altar **round a**.	5439
	8:24 the blood upon the altar **round a**.	5439
	9:12 he sprinkled **round a** upon the altar.	5439
	9:18 he sprinkled upon the altar **round a**,	5439
	14:41 the house to be scraped within **round a**,	5439
	16:18 put *it* upon the horns of the altar **round a**	5439
	25:31 **round a** them shall be counted as the	5439
	25:44 shall *be* of the heathen that *are* **round a**	5439
Nu	1:50 and shall encamp **round a** the tabernacle.	5439
	1:53 the Levites shall pitch **round a**	5439
	2: 2 far off **a** the tabernacle of the congregation	5439
	3:26 by the altar **round a**, and the cords of it	5439
	3:37 the pillars of the court **round a**,	5439
	4: 4 the congregation, **a** the most holy *things*:	NIH
	4:14 wherewith they minister **a** it, *even*	5921
	4:26 the tabernacle and by the altar **round a**,	5439
	4:32 the pillars of the court **round a**,	5439
	11: 8 *And* the people **went a**, and gathered *it*,	7751
	11:24 and set them **round a** the tabernacle.	5439
	11:31 **round a** the camp, as it were two	5439
	11:32 abroad for themselves **round a** the camp.	5439
	16:24 Get you up from **a** the tabernacle of Korah,	5439
	16:34 all Israel that *were* **round a** them fled at	5439
	16:49 beside them that died **a** the matter of	5921
	22: 4 company lick up all *that* are **round a** us,	5439
	32:33 *even* the cities of the country **round a**.	5439
	34:12 your land with the coasts thereof **round a**.	5439
	35: 2 suburbs for the cities **round a** them.	5439
	35: 4 and outward a thousand cubits **round a**.	5439
Dt	6:14 gods of the people which *are* **round a** you;	5439
	12:10 rest from all your enemies **round a**,	4480+5439
	13: 7 gods of the people which *are* **round a** you,	5439
	17:14 like as all the nations that *are* **a** me;	5439
	21: 2 cities which *are* **round a** him that is slain:	5439
	25:19 from all thine enemies **round a**,	4480+5439
	31:21 I know their imagination which they **go a**,	6213
	32:10 he **led** him **a**, he instructed, he kept	5437
Jos	2: 5 it came to pass **a** the *time* of shutting of	NIH
	3: 4 a two thousand cubits by measure:	3509.1
	4:13 **A** forty thousand prepared for war	3509.1
	6: 3 men of war, *and* **go round a** the city once.	5362
	6:11 compassed the city, **going a** it once:	5362
	6:15 that they rose early **a** the dawning of	3509.1
	7: 3 let a two or three thousand men **go up**	3509.1
	7: 4 So there went up thither of the people **a**	3509.1
	7: 5 the men of Ai smote of them **a** thirty	3509.1
	8:12 he took **a** five thousand men,	3509.1
	10:13 hasted not to **go down a** a whole day.	3509.1
	11: 6 for to morrow **a** this time I will deliver	3509.1
	15:12 Judah **round a** according to their families.	5439
	16: 6 the border **went a** eastward *unto*	5437
	18:20 by their coasts thereof **round a**, according	5439
	19: 8 all the villages that *were* **round a** these	5439
	21:11 with the suburbs thereof **round a** it.	5439
	21:42 one with their suburbs **round a** them:	5439
	21:44 the LORD gave them rest **round a**,	5439
	23: 1 from all their enemies **round a**,	4480+5439
Jdg	2:12 the gods of the people that *were* **round a**,	5439
	2:14 the hands of their enemies **round a**,	4480+5439
	3:29 they slew of Moab at that time **a** ten	3509.1
	7:21 they stood every man in his place **round a**	5439
	8:10 a fifteen thousand *men*, all that were left	3509.1
	8:26 the chains that *were* **a** their camels'	871.1
	9:49 died also, **a** a thousand men and women.	3509.1
	16:27 *were* upon the roof **a** three thousand	3509.1
	17: 2 **a** which thou cursedst, and spakest of also	NIH
	19:22 **beset** the house **round a**, *and* beat at	5437
	20: 5 **beset** the house **round a** upon me by	5437

Jdg	20:29 Israel set liers in wait **round a** Gibeah.	5439
	20:31 in the field, **a** thirty men of Israel.	3509.1
	20:39 kill of the men of Israel **a** thirty persons:	3509.1
	20:43 they **inclosed** the Benjamites **round a**,	3803
Ru	1: 4 and they dwelled there **a** ten years.	3509.1
	1:19 that all the city was moved **a** them,	5921
	2:17 and it was **a** an ephah of barley.	3509.1
1Sa	1:20 when the time was **come a** after	8622+3509.1
	4: 2 they slew of the army in the field **a** four	3509.1
	4:20 **a** the time of her death the *women* that	3509.1
	5: 8 the God of Israel be **carried a** unto Gath.	5437
	5: 8 they **carried** the ark of the God of Israel **a**	5437
	5: 9 it was so, that after they had **carried** it **a**,	5437
	5:10 They have **brought a** the ark of the God	5437
	9:13 you up; for **a** *this* time ye shall find him.	3509.1
	9:16 To morrow **a** *this* time I will send thee **a**	3509.1
	9:22 bidden, *which* were **a** thirty persons.	3509.1
	9:26 it came to pass **a** the spring of the day,	3509.1
	13:15 present with him, **a** six hundred men.	3509.1
	14: 2 people that *were* with him *were* **a** six	3509.1
	14:14 armourbearer made, was **a** twenty men,	3509.1
	14:21 into the camp *from the country* **round a**,	5439
	15:12 is **gone a**, and passed on, and gone down	5437
	15:27 as Samuel **turned a** to go away, he laid	5437
	17:42 when the Philistine **looked a**,	5027
	20:12 when I have sounded my father **a** to	3509.1
	21: 5 *been* kept from us **a** these three days,	3509.1
	22: 2 were with him **a** four hundred men.	3509.1
	22: 6 and all his servants *were* standing **a** him;)	5921
	22: 7 said unto his servants that stood **a** him,	5921
	22:17 king said unto the footmen that stood **a**	5921
	23:13 *which* were **a** six hundred, arose	3509.1
	23:26 **compassed** David and his men **round a**	5849
	25:13 went up after David **a** four hundred	3509.1
	25:38 it came to pass **a** ten days *after*, that	3509.1
	26: 5 and the people pitched **round a** him.	5439
	26: 7 Abner and the people lay **round a** him,	5439
	31: 9 into the land of the Philistines **round a**,	5439
2Sa	3:12 with thee, to **bring a** all Israel unto thee.	5437
	4: 5 came **a** the heat of the day to the house	3509.1
	5: 9 David built **round a** from Millo	5437
	7: 1 rest **round a** from all his enemies;	4480+5439
	14:20 To **fetch a** *this* form of speech hath thy	5437
	18:15 that bare Joab's armour **compassed a**	5437
	20:26 Ira also the Jairite was a chief ruler **a**	3807.1
	22: 6 The sorrows of hell **compassed** me **a**;	5437
	22:12 he made darkness pavilions **round a** him,	5439
	24: 6 they came to Dan-jaan, and **a** to Zidon,	5437
1Ki	2: 5 war upon his girdle that *was* **a** his loins,	871.1
	2:15 howbeit the kingdom is **turned a**,	5437
	3: 1 and the wall of Jerusalem **round a**.	5439
	4:24 had peace on all sides **round a** him.	4480+5439
	4:31 and his fame was in all nations **round a**.	5439
	5: 3 wars which *were* **a** him on **every side**,	5437
	6: 5 of the house he built chambers **round a**,	5439
	6: 5 *against* the walls of the house **round a**,	5439
	6: 5 oracle: and he made chambers **round a**:	5439
	6: 6 house he made narrowed rests **round a**,	5439
	6:29 carved all the walls of the house **round a**	4524
	7:12 the great court **round a** *was* with three	5439
	7:15 cubits did **compass** either of them **a**.	5437
	7:18 two rows **round a** upon the one network,	5439
	7:20 in rows **round a** upon the other chapter.	5439
	7:23 *it was* round **all a**, and his height *was* five	5439
	7:23 cubits did **compass** it **round a**.	5437+5439
	7:24 **round a** there were knops **compassing**	5437+5439
	7:24 ten in a cubit, compassing the sea **round a**:	5439
	7:36 of every one, and additions **round a**.	5439
	8:14 the king **turned** his face **a**, and blessed all	5437
	18:32 he made a trench **a** the altar, as great as	5439
	18:35 the water ran **round a** the altar;	5439
	19: 2 of them **by** to morrow **a** *this* time.	3509.1
	20: 6 unto thee to morrow **a** *this* time,	3509.1
	22: 6 a four hundred men, and said unto	3509.1
	22:36 the host **a** the going down of the sun,	3509.1
2Ki	1: 8 girt *with* a girdle of leather **a** his loins.	871.1
	3:25 the slingers **went a** *it*, and smote it.	5437
	4:16 he said, **A** this season, according to	3807.1
	6:14 came by night, and **compassed** the city **a**.	5362
	6:17 and chariots of fire **round a** Elisha.	5439
	7: 1 To morrow **a** *this* time *shall* a measure	3509.1
	7:18 be to morrow **a** this time in the gate	3509.1
	8:21 the Edomites which **compassed** him **a**,	5437
	11: 7 watch of the house of the LORD **a** the king.	413
	11: 8 ye shall compass the king **round a**,	5439
	11:11 weapons in his hand, **round a** the king,	5439
	17:15 went after the heathen that *were* **round a**	5439
	23: 5 and in the **places round a** Jerusalem;	4524
	25: 1 and they built forts against it **round a**.	5439
	25: 4 Chaldees *were* against the city **round a**:)	5439
	25:10 down the walls of Jerusalem **round a**,	5439
	25:17 pomegranates upon the chapiter **round a**,	5439
1Ch	4:33 all their villages that *were* **round a**	5439
	6:55 and the suburbs thereof **round a** it.	5439
	9:27 they lodged **round a** the house of God,	5439
	10: 9 into the land of the Philistines **round a**,	5439
	11: 8 he built the city **round a**, even from Millo	5439
	11: 8 round about, even from Millo **round a**:	5439
	15:22 he instructed the song, because he *was*	871.1
	18:17 of David *were* chief **a** the king.	3027+3807.1
	22: 9 rest from all his enemies **round a**:	4480+5439
	28:12 of all the chambers **round a**, of	5439
2Ch	2: 9 for the house which I am **a** to build *shall*	NIH
	4: 2 of thirty cubits did compass it **round a**.	5439

A

2Ch	4: 3	which did compass it **round a:**	5439+5439
	4: 3	in a cubit, compassing the sea **round a.**	5439
	13:13	**caused** an ambushment to come a	5437
	14: 7	**make** a *them* walls, and towers, gates,	5437
	14:14	they smote all the cities **round a** Gerar;	5437
	15:15	the Lord gave them rest **round a.**	4480+5439
	17: 9	**went** a throughout all the cities of Judah,	5437
	17:10	of the lands that *were* **round a** Judah,	5439
	18:31	Therefore they compassed a him to fight:	5921
	18:34	a the time of the sun going down he	3807.1
	20:30	for his God gave him rest **round a.**	4480+5439
	23: 2	they **went** a in Judah, and gathered	5437
	23: 7	Levites shall compass the king **round a,**	5439
	23:10	and the temple, by the king **round a.**	5439
	26: 6	built cities a Ashdod, and among	871.1
	33:14	compassed a Ophel, and raised it up a	3807.1
	34: 6	Naphtali, with their mattocks **round a.**	5439
Ezr	1: 6	all *they* that *were* a them strengthened	5439
	10:15	of Tikvah were employed a this *matter:*	5921
Ne	5:17	us from among the heathen that *are* a us.	5439
	6:16	all the heathen that *were* a us saw *these*	5439
	12:28	both out of the plain country **round a**	5439
	12:29	builded them villages **round a** Jerusalem.	5439
	13:21	said unto them, Why lodge ye a the wall?	5048
Job	1: 5	the days of *their* feasting were **gone a,**	5362
	1:10	Hast not thou made a hedge a him,	1157
	1:10	a his house, and about all that he hath on	1157
	1:10	and a all that he hath on every side?	1157
	8:17	His roots are wrapped a the heap, *and*	5921
	10: 8	and fashioned me together **round a;**	5439
	11:18	thou shalt dig a *thee, and* thou shalt take	NIH
	16:13	His archers **compass** me **round a,** he	5437
	19:12	and encamp **round a** my tabernacle.	5439
	20:23	*When* he is **a** to fill his belly, *God* shall	3807.1
	22:10	Therefore snares *are* **round a** thee,	5439
	29: 5	with me, *when* my children *were* a me;	5439
	30:18	it **bindeth** me a as the collar of my coat.	247
	37:12	it is turned **round a** by his counsels:	4524
	40:22	the willows of the brook **compass** him **a.**	5437
	41:14	of his face? his teeth *are* terrible **round a.**	5439
Ps	3: 6	have set *themselves* against me **round a.**	5439
	7: 7	of the people **compass** thee **a:**	5437
	17: 9	my deadly enemies, *who* **compass** me **a.**	5362
	18: 5	The sorrows of hell **compassed** me **a:**	5437
	18:11	pavilion **round** a him *were* dark waters	5439
	27: 6	lifted up above mine enemies **round a** me:	5439
	32: 7	thou shalt **compass** me **a** *with* songs of	5437
	32:10	in the Lord, mercy shall **compass** him **a.**	5437
	34: 7	encampeth **round a** them that fear him,	5439
	40:12	innumerable evils have **compassed** me **a:**	661
	44:13	a derision to them that are **round a** us.	5439
	48:12	**Walk** a Zion, and go round about her:	5437
	48:12	Walk about Zion, and **go round a** her:	5362
	49: 5	iniquity of my heels shall **compass** me **a?**	5437
	50: 3	it shall be very tempestuous **round a** him.	5439
	55:10	night they **go a** it upon the walls thereof:	5437
	59: 6	noise like a dog, and **go round a** the city.	5437
	59:14	noise like a dog, and **go round a** the city.	5437
	73: 6	pride **compasseth** them **a as a chain;**	6059
	76:11	let all that be **round a** him bring presents	5439
	78:28	of their camp, **round a** their habitations.	5439
	79: 3	they shed like water **round a** Jerusalem;	5439
	79: 4	and derision to them that are **round a** us.	5439
	88:17	They **came round a** me daily like water;	5437
	88:17	water; they **compassed** me a together.	5362
	89: 7	be had in reverence of all them that are **a**	5439
	89: 8	or *to* thy faithfulness **round a** thee?	5439
	97: 2	Clouds and darkness *are* **round a** him:	5439
	97: 3	and burneth up his enemies **round a.**	5439
	109: 3	They **compassed** me **a** also *with* words	5437
	118:10	All nations **compassed** me **a:** but in	5437
	118:11	They **compassed** me **a;** yea,	5437
	118:11	me about; yea, they **compassed** me **a.**	5437
	118:12	They **compassed** me **a** like bees; they are	5437
	125: 2	*As* the mountains *are* **round a** Jerusalem,	5439
	125: 2	the Lord *is* **round a** his people from	5439
	128: 3	thy children like olive plants **round a** thy	5439
	139:11	even the night *shall be* light a me.	1157
	140: 9	*for* the head of those that **compass** me **a,**	4524
	142: 7	The righteous shall **compass** me **a;** for	3803
Pr	1: 9	unto thy head, and chains a thy neck.	3807.1
	3: 3	bind them a thy neck; write them upon	5921
	6:21	upon thine heart, *and* tie them a thy neck.	5921
	20:19	He that **goeth a** *as* a talebearer revealeth	1980
Ecc	1: 6	to the south, and **turneth a** unto the north;	5437
	1: 6	it **whirleth a** continually,	1980+5437+5437
	2:20	Therefore I **went a** to cause my heart to	5437
	12: 5	and the mourners **go a** the streets:	5437
SS	3: 2	**go a** the city in the streets and in the broad	5437
	3: 3	watchmen that **go a** the city found me:	5437
	3: 7	threescore valiant *men are* **a** it, of	5439
	5: 7	The watchmen that **went a** the city found	5437
	7: 2	thy belly *is like* a heap of wheat **set a** with	5473
Isa	3:18	of *their* tinkling ornaments **a** *their feet,*	NIH
	15: 8	For the cry is **gone round a** the borders	5362
	23:16	Take a harp, **go a** the city, thou harlot that	5437
	26:20	thy chambers, and shut thy doors a thee:	1157
	28:27	a cart wheel **turned a** upon the cummin;	5437
	29: 3	against thee **round a,**	1754+1886.1+3509.1
	42:25	it hath set him on fire **round a,**	4480+5439
	49:18	Lift up thine eyes **round a,** and behold:	5439
	50:11	that **compass** *yourselves* **a** with sparks:	247
	60: 4	Lift up thine eyes **round a,** and see:	5439
Jer	1:15	against all the walls thereof **round a,**	5439
	2:36	Why **gaddest** thou a *so* much to change	235

Jer	4:17	field, are they against her **round a;**	4480+5439
	6: 3	shall pitch *their* tents against her **round a;**	5439
	12: 9	the birds **round a** *are* against her;	5439
	14:18	the priest **go a** into a land that they know	5503
	17:26	from the places a Jerusalem, and from	5439
	21:14	and it shall devour all things **round a** it.	5439
	25: 9	against all these nations **round a,**	5439
	31:22	How long wilt thou **go a,** O thou	2559
	31:39	hill Gareb, and shall **compass** a to Goath.	5437
	32:44	in the places a Jerusalem, and in the cities	5439
	33:13	in the places a Jerusalem, and in the cities	5439
	41:14	carried away captive from Mizpah **cast a**	5437
	46: 5	fear *was* **round a,** saith the Lord.	4480+5439
	46:14	for the sword shall devour **round a** thee.	5439
	48:17	All ye that are a him, bemoan him;	5439
	48:39	and a dismaying to all them a him.	5439
	49: 5	of hosts, from all those that be a thee;	5439
	50:14	in array against Babylon **round a:**	5439
	50:15	Shout against her **round a:** she hath given	5439
	50:29	bend the bow, camp against it **round a;**	5439
	50:32	and it shall devour all **round a** him.	5439
	51: 2	they shall be against her **round a.**	4480+5439
	52: 4	and built forts against it **round a.**	5439
	52: 7	the Chaldeans *were* by the city **round a:)**	5439
	52:14	down all the walls of Jerusalem **round a.**	5439
	52:22	pomegranates upon the chapiters **round a,**	5439
	52:23	the network *were* an hundred **round a.**	5439
La	1:17	his adversaries *should be* **round a** him:	5439
	2: 3	a flaming fire, *which* devoureth **round a.**	5439
	2:22	a solemn day my terrors **round a,**	4480+5439
	3: 7	hath hedged me a, that I cannot get out:	1157
Eze	1: 4	a brightness *was* a it, and out of the midst	5439
	1:18	their rings were full *of* eyes **round a** them	5439
	1:27	the appearance of fire **round a** within it,	5439
	1:27	of fire, and it had brightness **round a.**	5439
	1:28	the appearance of the brightness **round a.**	5439
	4: 2	and set *battering* rams against it **round a.**	5439
	5: 2	a third *part, and* smite a it with a knife:	5439
	5: 5	and countries *that are* **round a** her.	5439
	5: 6	than the countries that *are* **round a** her:	5439
	5: 7	than the nations that *are* **round a** you,	5439
	5: 7	of the nations that *are* **round a** you;	5439
	5:12	third *part* shall fall by the sword **round a**	5439
	5:14	among the nations that *are* **round a** thee,	5439
	5:15	unto the nations that *are* **round a** thee,	5439
	6: 5	I will scatter your bones **round a** your	5439
	6:13	be among their idols **round a** their altars,	5439
	8:10	pourtrayed upon the wall **round a.**	5439+5439
	8:16	the altar, *were* a five and twenty men,	3509.1
	10:12	and the wheels, *were* full *of* eyes **round a,**	5439
	11:12	of the heathen that *are* **round a** you.	5439
	12:14	every wind all that *are* **a** him to help him,	5439
	16:10	and I **girded** thee **a** with fine linen,	2280
	16:37	I will gather them **round a**	4480+5439
	16:57	all *that* are **round a** her, the daughters of	5439
	16:57	which despise thee **round a.**	4480+5439
	23:24	and shield and helmet **round a,**	5439
	27:11	thine army *were* upon thy walls **round a,**	5439
	27:11	their shields upon thy walls **round a;**	5439
	28:24	thorn of all *that are* **round a** them,	5439
	28:26	that despise them **round a** them;	4480+5439
	31: 4	with her rivers running **round a** his plants,	5439
	32:22	his graves *are* a him: all of them slain,	5439
	32:23	and her company is **round a** her grave:	5439
	32:24	and all her multitude **round a** her grave,	5439
	32:25	her graves *are* **round a** him: all of them	5439
	32:26	her graves *are* **round a** him: all of them	5439
	34:26	and the **places round a** my hill a blessing;	5439
	36: 4	of the heathen that *are* **round a,**	4480+5439
	36: 7	Surely the heathen that *are* a you,	5439
	36:36	the heathen that are left **round a** you shall	5439
	37: 2	me to pass by them **round a:**	5439+5439
	40: 5	the outside of the house **round a,**	5439+5439
	40:14	post of the court **round a** the gate.	5439+5439
	40:16	their posts within the gate **round a,**	5439+5439
	40:16	windows *were* **round a** inward:	5439+5439
	40:17	made for the court **round a:**	5439+5439
	40:25	and in the arches thereof **round a,**	5439+5439
	40:29	and in the arches thereof **round a:**	5439+5439
	40:30	the arches **round a** *were* five	5439+5439
	40:33	in the arches thereof **round a.**	5439+5439
	40:36	and the windows to it **round a:**	5439+5439
	40:43	a hand broad, fastened **round a:**	5439+5439
	41: 5	**round a** the house on every side.	5439+5439
	41: 6	for the side chambers **round a,**	5439+5439
	41: 7	a **winding** still upward to the side	5437
	41: 7	for the **winding a** of the house *went* still	5437
	41: 7	still upward **round a** the house:	5439+5439
	41: 8	the height of the house **round a:**	5439+5439
	41:10	cubits **round a** the house on every side.	5439
	41:11	was left *was* five cubits **round a.**	5439+5439
	41:12	*was* five cubits thick **round a,**	5439+5439
	41:16	galleries **round a** on their three *stories,*	5439
	41:16	cieled with wood **round a,**	5439+5439
	41:17	by all the wall **round a** within	5439+5439
	41:19	through all the house **round a.**	5439
	42:15	the east, and measured it a **round a.**	5439+5439
	42:16	with the measuring reed **round a.**	5439
	42:17	with the measuring reed **round a.**	5439
	42:19	He **turned a** to the west side, *and*	5437
	42:20	it had a wall **round a,** a five hundred	5439+5439
	43:12	thereof **round a** *shall be* most holy.	5439+5439
	43:13	the edge thereof **round a** *shall be* a span:	5439
	43:17	the border **a** it *shall be* half a cubit;	5439
	43:17	the bottom thereof *shall be* a cubit **a;**	5439

Eze	43:20	the settle, and upon the border **round a:**	5439
	45: 1	*be* holy in all the borders thereof **round a.**	5439
	45: 2	five hundred *in breadth,* square **round a;**	5439
	45: 2	fifty cubits **round a** *for* the suburbs	5439
	46:23	there was a row *of building* **round a** in	5439
	46:23	**round a** them four, and *it was* made *with*	5439
	46:23	boiling places under the rows **round a.**	5439
	47: 2	**led** me a the way without unto the utter	5437
	48:35	*It was* **round a** eighteen thousand	5439
Da	5: 7	*have* a chain of gold a his neck,	5922
	5:16	*have* a chain of gold a thy neck,	5922
	5:29	*put* a chain of gold a his neck, and made a	5922
	5:31	*being* a threescore and two year old.	3509.4
	9:16	*are* become a reproach to all *that are* a us.	5439
	9:21	touched me a the time of the evening	3509.1
Hos	7: 2	now their own doings have **beset** them **a;**	5437
	11:12	Ephraim **compasseth** me a with lies,	5437
Joel	3:11	gather yourselves together **round a:**	4480+5439
	3:12	sit to judge all the heathen **round a.**	4480+5439
Am	3:11	An adversary *there* shall be even **round a**	5439
Jnh	2: 3	the seas; and the floods **compassed** me **a:**	5437
	2: 5	The waters **compassed** me a, *even* to	661
	2: 5	the depth **closed** me **round a,** the weeds	5437
	2: 5	the weeds *were* **wrapt a** my head.	2280
	2: 6	the earth *with* her bars *was* a me for ever:	1157
Na	3: 8	*that had* the waters **round a** it,	5439
Hab	1: 4	for the wicked doth **compass a**	3803
Zec	2: 5	will be unto her a wall of fire **round a,**	5439
	7: 7	and the cities thereof **round a** her,	5439
	9: 8	I will **encamp a** mine house because of	2583
	12: 2	of trembling unto all the people **round a,**	5439
	12: 6	they shall devour all the people **round a,**	5439
	14:14	wealth of all the heathen **round a** shall	5439
Mt	1:11	**a** the time they were carried away to	1909
	3: 4	and a leathern girdle a his loins;	4012
	3: 5	and all the **region round a** Jordan;	4066
	4:23	And Jesus **went a** all Galilee, teaching in	4013
	8:18	Now when Jesus saw great multitudes **a**	4012
	9:22	But Jesus **turned** him **a,** and when he saw	1994
	9:35	Jesus **went a** all the cities and villages,	4013
	14:21	And they that had eaten were a five	5616
	14:35	sent out into all that **country round a,**	4066
	18: 6	that a millstone were hanged a his neck,	1909
	20: 3	And he went out a the third hour,	4012
	20: 5	Again he went out a the sixth	4012
	20: 6	And a the eleventh hour he went out,	4012
	20: 9	And when they came that were *hired* a	4012
	21:33	and hedged it **round a,** and digged a	4060
	27:46	And the ninth hour Jesus cried with a	4012
Mk	1: 6	and with a girdle of a skin a his loins;	4012
	1:28	throughout all the **region round a** Galilee.	4066
	2: 2	*them,* no, not so much as a the door:	4314
	3: 5	when he had **looked round a** on them	4017
	3: 8	and they a Tyre and Sidon, a great	4012
	3:32	And *the* multitude sat a him, and they said	4012
	3:34	he looked **round a** on them which sat	2945
	3:34	round about on them which sat a him,	4012
	4:10	that were a him with the twelve asked	4012
	5:13	into the sea, (they were a two thousand,)	5613
	5:30	**turned** him a in the press, and said,	1994
	5:32	he **looked round a** to see her that had	4017
	6: 6	And he went **round a** the villages,	2945
	6:36	they may go into the country **round a,**	2945
	6:44	And they that did eat *of* the loaves were a	5616
	6:48	a the fourth watch of the night he cometh	4012
	6:55	ran through that whole **region round a,**	4066
	6:55	began to **carry a** in beds those that were	4064
	8: 9	And they that had eaten were a four	5613
	8:33	But when he had **turned a** and looked on	1994
	9: 8	when they had **looked round a,** they	4017
	9:14	he saw a great multitude a them,	4012
	9:42	that a millstone were hanged a his neck,	4012
	10:23	And Jesus **looked round a,** and saith unto	4017
	11:11	when he had **looked round a** upon all	4017
	12: 1	and **set** a hedge **a** it, and digged *a place*	4060
	14:51	having a linen cloth cast a *his* naked *body;*	1909
	15:17	a crown of thorns, and **put** it **a** his *head,*	4060
Lk	1:56	And Mary abode with her a three months,	5616
	1:65	And fear came on all that **dwelt round a**	4039
	2: 9	glory of the Lord **shone round a** them:	4034
	2:37	And she *was* a widow of a fourscore	5613
	2:49	wist ye not that I must be a my Father's	1722
	3: 3	he came into all the **country a** Jordan,	4066
	3:23	And Jesus himself began to *be* a thirty	5616
	4:14	of him through all the **region round a.**	4066
	4:37	into every place of the **country round a.**	4066
	6:10	And **looking round a** upon them all,	4017
	7: 9	and turned him **a,** and said unto the people	NIG
	7:17	and throughout all the **region round a.**	4066
	8:37	**country** of the Gadarenes **round a**	4066
	8:42	a twelve years of age, and she lay a dying.	5613
	9:12	go into the towns and country **round a,**	2945
	9:14	For they were **a** five thousand men.	5616
	9:28	And it came to pass a an eight days after	5616
	10:40	Martha was cumbered a much serving,	4012
	10:41	art careful and troubled a many *things:*	4012
	12:35	Let your loins be **girded a,** and *your* lights	4024
	13: 8	year also, till I shall dig a it, and dung *it:*	4012
	17: 2	that a millstone were hanged a his neck,	4029
	19:43	that thine enemies shall cast a trench a	4016
	22:41	And he was withdrawn from them a a	5616
	22:49	When they which were a him saw what	4012
	22:59	And a the space of one hour after another	5616
	23:44	And it was a the sixth hour, and there	5616
	24:13	which was from Jerusalem *a* threescore	NIG

A

Jn	1:39	him that day: for it was **a** the tenth hour.	5613
	3:25	John's disciples and the Jews **a** purifying.	4012
	4: 6	on the well: *and* it was **a** the sixth hour.	5616
	6:10	men sat down, *in* number **a** five thousand.	5616
	6:19	So when they had rowed **a** five and twenty	5613
	7:14	**Now a** the midst of the feast Jesus	1161+2235
	7:19	keepeth the law? Why go ye **a** to kill me?	2212
	7:20	hast a devil: who **goeth a** to kill thee?	2212
	10:24	Then **came** the Jews round **a** him,	2944
	11:18	nigh unto Jerusalem, a fifteen furlongs off:	5613
	11:44	and his face was **bound a** with a napkin.	4019
	19:14	of the passover, and **a** the sixth hour:	5616
	19:39	and aloes, **a** an hundred pound *weight*.	5616
	20: 7	And the napkin, that was **a** his head,	1909
	21:20	Then Peter, **turning a**, seeth the disciple	1994
Ac	1:15	(the number of names together were **a** an	5613
	2:10	and in the parts of Libya **a** Cyrene,	2596
	2:41	same day there were added *unto them* **a**	5616
	3: 3	and John **a to** go into the temple,	3195
	4: 4	number of the men was **a** five thousand.	5616
	5: 7	And it was **a** the space of three hours after,	5613
	5:16	*out* of the cities round **a** unto Jerusalem,	4038
	5:36	of men, **a** four hundred, joined themselves:	5616
	9: 3	there **shined** round **a** him a light	4015
	9:29	the Grecians: but they **went a** to slay him.	2021
	10: 3	**a** the ninth hour of the day,	5616
	10: 9	Peter went up upon the house to pray **a**	4012
	10:38	who **went a** doing good, and healing all	1330
	11:19	arose **a** Stephen travelled as far as Phenice,	1909
	12: 1	Now **a** that time Herod the king stretched	2596
	12: 8	**Cast** thy garment **a** thee, and follow me.	4016
	13:11	he **went a** seeking *some* to lead him by	4013
	13:18	And **a** the time of forty years suffered he	5613
	13:20	And after that he gave *unto them* judges **a**	4012
	14: 6	and *unto* the **region that lieth round a**:	4066
	14:20	as the disciples **stood** round **a** him,	2944
	15: 2	the apostles and elders **a** this question.	4012
	18:14	And when Paul was *now* **a to** open *his*	3195
	19: 7	And all the men were **a** twelve.	5616
	19:23	time there arose no small stir **a** *that* way.	4012
	19:34	all with one voice **a** the space of two hours	5613
	20: 3	wait for him, as he was **a** to sail into Syria,	3195
	21:31	And as *they* **went a** to kill him,	2212
	22: 6	was come nigh unto Damascus **a** noon,	4012
	22: 6	from heaven a great light **round a** me.	4012
	24: 6	Who also hath **gone a** to profane	3985
	25: 7	down from Jerusalem **stood** round **a**,	4026
	25:15	**A** whom, when I was at Jerusalem,	4012
	25:24	ye see this *man*, **a** whom all the multitude	4012
	26:13	**shining** round **a** me and them which	4034
	26:21	me in the temple, and **went a** to kill *me*.	3987
	27:27	**a** midnight the shipmen deemed that they	2596
	27:30	And as the shipmen were **a** to flee out of	2212
Ro	4:19	when he was **a** an hundred year old,	4225
	10: 3	*going* **a** to establish their own	2212
	15:19	and **round a** unto Illyricum,	2945
1Co	9: 5	Have we not power to **lead a** a sister,	4013
	9:13	Do ye not know that they which minister **a**	NIG
2Co	4:10	Always **bearing a** in the body the dying of	4064
Eph	4:14	and **carried a** with every wind of doctrine,	4064
	6:14	having your loins **girt a** with truth,	4024
1Ti	5:13	idle, **wandering a** from house to house;	4022
	6: 4	but doting **a** questions and strifes of words,	4012
2Ti	2:14	that *they* **strive** not **a words** to no profit,	3054
Tit	3: 9	and contentions, and strivings **a** the **law**;	3544
Heb	8: 5	when he was **a** to make the tabernacle:	3195
	9: 4	the ark of the covenant overlaid **round a**	3840
	11:30	after they were **compassed a** seven days.	2944
	11:37	they **wandered a** in sheepskins	4022
	12: 1	seeing we also are **compassed a**	4029
	13: 9	Be not **carried a** with divers	4064
Jas	3: 3	obey us; and we **turn a** their whole body.	3329
	3: 4	*yet* are they **turned a** with a very small	3329
1Pe	5: 8	the devil, as a roaring lion, **walketh a**,	4043
Jude	1: 7	and Gomorrha, and the cities **a** them,	4012
	1: 9	the devil he disputed **a** the body of Moses,	4012
	1:12	*are* without water, **carried a** of winds;	4064
Rev	1:13	and girt **a** the paps with a golden girdle.	4314
	4: 3	*there was* a rainbow **round a** the throne,	2943
	4: 4	And **round a** the throne *were* four	2943
	4: 6	of the throne, and **round a** the throne,	2943
	4: 8	beasts had each of them six wings **a** *him*;	2943
	5:11	I heard the voice of many angels **round a**	2943
	7:11	And all the angels stood **round a**	2945
	7:11	and *a* the elders and the four beasts,	NIG
	8: 1	there was silence in heaven **a** the space of	5613
	10: 4	had uttered their voices, I was **a to** write:	3195
	16:21	*every* stone **a** the weight of a talent:	5613
	20: 9	and **compassed a** the camp of the saints **a**,	2944

ABOVE (223)

Ge	1: 7	which *were* **a** the firmament:	4480+5921
	1:20	fowl *that* may fly **a** the earth in the open	5921
	3:14	thou *art* cursed **a** all cattle, and above	4480
	3:14	all cattle, and **a** every beast of the field;	4480
	6:16	thou finish it **a**; 4480+4605+1886.5+3807.1	
	7:17	ark, and it was lift up **a** the earth.	4480+5921
	27:39	earth, and of the dew of heaven from **a**;	5920
	28:13	the LORD stood **a** it, and said,	5921
	48:22	given to thee one portion **a** thy brethren,	5921
	49:25	thee *with* blessings of heaven **a**,	4480+5920
	49:26	blessings of thy father have prevailed **a**	5921
Ex	18:11	wherein they dealt proudly *he was* **a** them.	4480
	19: 5	shall be a peculiar treasure unto me **a** all	4480
	20: 4	*of any thing* that *is* in heaven **a**,	4480+4605

Ex	25:21	**a** upon the ark; 4480+4605+1886.5+3807.1	
	25:22	I will commune with thee from **a** the	5921
	26:14	of badgers' skins. 4480+4605+1886.5+3807.1	
	26:24	they shall be coupled together **a** the head	5921
	28:27	the *other* coupling thereof, **a**	4480+4605
	28:28	that *it* may be the curious girdle of	5921
	29:13	the caul *that is* **a** the liver, and the two	5921
	29:22	the caul **a** the liver, and the two kidneys,	NIH
	30:14	from twenty years old and **a**,	4605+1886.5
	36:19	skins **a** that. 4480+4605+1886.5+3807.1	
	39:20	the *other* coupling thereof, **a**	4480+4605
	39:21	that *it* might be the curious girdle of	5921
	40:19	the tent up it; 4480+4605+1886.5+3807.1	
	40:20	**a** upon the ark: 4480+4605+1886.5+3807.1	
Lev	3: 4	the caul **a** the liver, with the kidneys,	5921
	3:10	the caul **a** the liver, with the kidneys,	5921
	3:15	the caul **a** the liver, with the kidneys,	5921
	4: 9	the caul **a** the liver, with the kidneys,	5921
	7: 4	caul *that is* **a** the liver, with the kidneys,	5921
	8:16	the caul **a** the liver, and the two kidneys,	NIH
	8:25	the caul **a** the liver, and the two kidneys,	NIH
	9:10	and the caul **a** the liver of the sin offering,	4480
	9:19	and the kidneys, and the caul **a** the liver:	NIH
	11:21	have legs **a** their feet, 4480+4605+3807.1	
	27: 7	*if it be* from sixty years old and **a**; 4605+1886.5	
Nu	3:49	of them that were **over and a**	5736+5921
	4:25	that *is* **a** upon it, 4480+4605+1886.5+3807.1	
	12: 3	**a** all the men which *were* upon the face of	4480
	16: 3	lift you up yourselves **a** the congregation	5921
Dt	4:39	the LORD he *is* God in heaven **a**,	4480+4605
	5: 8	*of any thing* that *is* in heaven **a**,	4480+4605
	7: 6	**a** all people that *are* upon the face of	4480
	7:14	Thou shalt be blessed **a** all people:	4480
	10:15	*even* you **a** all people, as *it is* this day.	4480
	14: 2	**a** all the nations that *are* upon the earth.	4480
	17:20	That his heart be not lifted up **a** his	4480
	25: 3	beat him **a** these with many stripes,	5921
	26:19	to make thee high **a** all nations which he	5921
	28: 1	set thee on high **a** all nations of the earth:	5921
	28:13	thou shalt be **a** only, 4605+1886.5+3807.1	
	28:43	within thee shall get up **a** thee very high;	5921
	30: 5	thee good, and multiply thee **a** thy fathers.	4480
Jos	2:11	he *is* God in heaven **a**, and in earth	4480+4605
	3:13	that come down from **a**; 4605+1886.5+3807.1	
	3:16	came down from **a** stood 4605+1886.5+3807.1	
Jdg	5:24	Blessed **a** women shall Jael the wife of	4480
	5:24	blessed shall she be **a** women in the tent.	4480
1Sa	2:29	honourest thy sons **a** me, to make	4480
2Sa	22:17	He sent from **a**, he took me; he drew me	4791
	22:49	thou also hast lifted me up on high **a** them	4480
1Ki	7: 3	*it was* covered with cedar **a** upon	4480+4605
	7:11	**a** *were* costly stones,	
		4480+4605+1886.5+3807.1	
	7:20	pillars *had* pomegranates also **a**,	4480+4605
	7:25	the sea *was set* **a** 4480+4605+1886.5+3807.1	
	7:29	upon the ledges *there was* a base **a**: 4480+4605	
	7:31	the chapiter and *a* *was* a cubit:	4605+1886.5
	8: 7	staves thereof **a**. 4480+4605+1886.5+3807.1	
	8:23	in heaven **a**, or on earth beneath,	4480+4605
	14: 9	hast done evil **a** all that were before thee:	4480
	14:22	**a** all that their fathers had done.	4480
	16:30	of the LORD **a** all that *were* before him.	4480
2Ki	21:11	hath done wickedly **a** all that the Amorites	4480
	25:28	set his throne **a** the throne of	4480
1Ch	5: 2	For Judah prevailed **a** his brethren, and of	871.1
	16:25	he also *is* to be feared **a** all gods.	5921
	23:27	twenty years old and **a**: 4605+1886.5+3807.1	
	27: 6	mighty among the thirty, and **a** the thirty:	5921
	29: 3	God, **over and a** 4480+4605+1886.5+3807.1	
	29:11	and *thou* art **exalted** as head **a** all.	5375
2Ch	2: 5	*is* great: for great *is* our God **a** all gods.	4480
	4: 4	the sea *was set* **a** 4480+4605+1886.5+3807.1	
	5: 8	staves thereof **a**. 4480+4605+1886.5+3807.1	
	11:21	the daughter of Absalom **a** all his wives	4480+5921
	24:20	which stood **a** the people,	4480+5921
	25: 5	from twenty years old and **a**, 4605+1886.5	
	34: 4	the images, that *were* on high **a**	4480+5921
Ne	3:28	From **a** the horse gate repaired the priests,	5921
	7: 2	a faithful man, and feared God **a** many.	4480
	8: 5	(for he was **a** all the people;)	4480+5921
	9: 5	which *is* **exalted a** all blessing and praise.	5921
	12:37	at the going up of the wall, **a**	4480+5921
	12:39	from **a** the gate of Ephraim, and above	5921
	12:39	the old gate, and above the fish gate,	5921
	12:39	**a** the fish gate, and the tower of Hananeel,	5921
Est	2:17	the king loved Esther **a** all the women,	4480
	3: 1	set his seat **a** all the princes that	4480+5921
	5:11	how he had advanced him **a** the princes	5921
Job	3: 4	let not God regard it from **a**, neither let	4605
	18:16	**a** shall his branch be cut off.	4480+4605
	28:18	for the price of wisdom *is* **a** rubies.	4480
	31: 2	portion of God *is there* **from a**?	4480+4605
	31:28	have denied the God that *is* **a**.	4480+4605
Ps	8: 1	who hast set thy glory **a** the heavens.	5921
	10: 5	thy judgments *are* **far a** out of his sight:	4791
	18:16	He sent from **a**, he took me, he drew me	4791
	18:48	thou liftest me up **a** those that rise up	4480
	27: 6	now shall mine head be lifted up **a** mine	5921
	45: 7	thee *with* the oil of gladness **a** thy fellows.	4480
	50: 4	He shall call to the heavens from **a**,	5920
	57: 5	Be thou exalted, O God, **a** the heavens;	5921
	57: 5	heavens; *let* thy glory *be* **a** all the earth.	5921
	57:11	Be thou exalted, O God, **a** the heavens:	5921
	57:11	heavens: *let* thy glory *be* **a** all the earth.	5921
	78:23	he had commanded the clouds from **a**,	4605

Ps	95: 3	*is* a great God, and a great King **a** all gods.	5921
	96: 4	to be praised: he *is* to be feared **a** all gods.	5921
	97: 9	For thou, LORD, *art* High **a** all the earth:	5921
	97: 9	all the earth: thou art exalted far **a** all gods.	5921
	99: 2	in Zion; and he *is* high **a** all the people.	5921
	103:11	For as the heaven is high **a** the earth, *so*	5921
	104: 6	the waters stood **a** the mountains.	5921
	108: 4	thy mercy *is* great **a** the heavens:	4480+5921
	108: 5	Be thou exalted, O God, **a** the heavens:	5921
	108: 5	the heavens: and thy glory **a** all the earth.	5921
	113: 4	The LORD *is* high **a** all nations, *and*	5921
	113: 4	all nations, *and* his glory **a** the heavens.	5921
	119:127	Therefore I love thy commandments **a**	4480
	119:127	above gold; yea, **a** fine gold.	4480
	135: 5	*is* great, and *that* our Lord *is* **a** all gods.	4480
	136: 6	To him that stretched out the earth **a**	5921
	137: 6	if I prefer not Jerusalem **a** my chief joy.	5921
	138: 2	for thou hast magnified thy word **a** all thy	5921
	144: 7	Send thine hand from **a**; rid me,	4791
	148: 4	ye waters that *be* **a** the heavens.	4480+5921
	148:13	his glory *is* **a** the earth and heaven.	5921
Pr	8:28	When he established the clouds **a**: 4480+4605	
	15:24	The way of life *is* **a** to 4480+1886.5+3807.1	
	31:10	for her price *is* far **a** rubies.	4480
Ecc	2: 7	small cattle **a** all that were in Jerusalem	4480
	3:19	that a man hath no preeminence **a** a beast:	4480
Isa	2: 2	and *shall be* exalted **a** the hills;	4480
	6: 2	**A** it stood the seraphims: each one	4480+4605
	7:11	or in the height **a**. 4605+1886.5+3807.1	
	14:13	exalt my throne **a** the stars of God: 4480+4605	
	14:14	I will ascend **a** the heights of the clouds;	5921
	45: 8	from **a**, and let the skies pour down	4605
Jer	4:28	and the heavens **a** be black:	4480+4605
	15: 8	Their widows are increased to me **a**	4480
	17: 9	The heart is deceitful **a** all *things*,	4480
	31:37	If heaven **a** can be 4480+4605+1886.5+3807.1	
	35: 4	which *was* **a** the chamber of	4480+4605
	52:32	set his throne **a** the throne of	4480+4605
La	1:13	From **a** hath he sent fire into my bones,	4791
Eze	1:22	over their heads **a**. 4480+4605+1886.5+3807.1	
	1:26	**a** the firmament that *was* over their 4480+4605	
	1:26	of a man **a** upon it. 4480+4605+1886.5+3807.1	
	10: 1	in the firmament that *was* **a** the head of	5921
	10:19	*was* over them **a**. 4480+4605+1886.5+3807.1	
	11:22	*was* over them **a**. 4480+4605+1886.5+3807.1	
	16:43	thou shalt not commit *this* lewdness **a** all	5921
	29:15	neither shall it exalt itself any more **a**	5921
	31: 5	Therefore his height was exalted **a** all	4480
	37: 8	covered them **a**: 4480+4605+1886.5+3807.1	
	41:17	To *that* **a** the door, even unto	4480+5921
	41:20	From the ground unto **a** the door	4480+5921
Da	6: 3	this Daniel was preferred **a** the presidents	5922
	11: 5	he shall be strong **a** him,	5921
	11:36	magnify himself **a** every god,	5921
	11:37	any god: for he shall magnify himself **a** all.	5921
Am	2: 9	yet I destroyed his fruit from **a**,	4605
Mic	4: 1	and *it shall be* exalted **a** the hills;	4480
Na	3:16	Thou hast multiplied thy merchants **a**	4480
Mt	10:24	The disciple is not **a** *his* master, nor	5228
	10:24	*his* master, nor the servant **a** his lord.	5228
Lk	3:20	Added yet this **a** all, that he shut up John	1909
	6:40	The disciple is not **a** *his* master:	5228
	13: 2	Galileans were sinners **a** all the Galileans,	3844
	13: 4	think ye that they were sinners **a** all men	3844
Jn	3:31	He that cometh **from a** is above all: he that	509
	3:31	He that cometh from above is **a** all: he that	1883
	3:31	he that cometh from heaven is **a** all.	1883
	6:13	which **remained over and a** unto them	4052
	8:23	ye are from beneath; I am **from a**:	507
	19:11	except it were given thee **from a**:	509
Ac	2:19	And I will shew wonders in heaven **a**,	507
	4:22	For the man was **a** forty years old,	4183
	26:13	**a** the brightness of the sun, shining round	5228
Ro	10: 6	(that is, to bring Christ down *from* **a**:)	NIG
	14: 5	One man esteemeth one day **a** another:	3844
1Co	4: 6	to think of *men* **a** *that* which is written,	5228
	10:13	will not suffer you to be tempted **a** that	5228
	15: 6	he was seen of **a** five hundred brethren at	1883
2Co	1: 8	were pressed out of measure, **a** strength,	5228
	11:23	in stripes **a measure**, in prisons more	5234
	12: 2	I knew a man in Christ **a** fourteen years	4253
	12: 6	lest any *man* should think of me **a** that	5228
	12: 7	And lest I should be **exalted a measure**	5229
	12: 7	lest I should be **exalted a measure**.	5229
Gal	1:14	And profited in the Jews' religion **a** many	5228
	4:26	But Jerusalem which is **a** free, which is	507
Eph	1:21	**Far a** all principality, and power,	5231
	3:20	do exceeding abundantly **a** all that we ask	5228
	4: 6	who *is* **a** all, and through all, and in you all.	1909
	4:10	also that ascended up **far a** all heavens,	5231
	6:16	**A** all, taking the shield of faith,	1909
Php	2: 9	given him a name which is **a** every name:	5228
Col	3: 1	with Christ, seek those *things* which are **a**,	507
	3: 2	Set your affection on *things* **a**, not on *things*	507
	3:14	And **a** all these *things* put on charity,	1909
2Th	2: 4	exalteth himself **a** all that is called God,	1909
Phm	1:16	but **a** a servant, a brother beloved,	5228
Heb	1: 9	anointed thee **a** with the oil of gladness **a**	3844
	10: 8	**A** when he said, Sacrifice and offering	511
Jas	1:17	good gift and every perfect gift is **from a**,	509
	3:15	This wisdom descendeth not **from a**,	509
	3:17	But the wisdom that is **from a** is first pure,	509
	5:12	But **a** all *things*, my brethren, swear not,	4253
1Pe	4: 8	And **a** all *things* have fervent charity	4253
3Jn	1: 2	wish **a** all *things* that thou mayest prosper	4012

ABRAHAM (231) [ABRAHAM'S, ABRAM, ABRAM'S]

Ge	17: 5 be called Abram, but thy name shall be **A**;	85
	17: 9 God said unto **A**, Thou shalt keep my	85
	17:15 And God said unto **A**, *As for* Sarai thy wife,	85
	17:17 then fell upon his face, and laughed,	85
	17:18 **A** said unto God, O that Ishmael might live	85
	17:22 talking with him, and God went up from **A**.	85
	17:23 **A** took Ishmael his son, and all that were	85
	17:24 **A** *was* ninety years old and nine, when he	85
	17:26 In the selfsame day was **A** circumcised,	85
	18: 6 And **A** hastened into the tent unto Sarah,	85
	18: 7 **A** ran unto the herd, and fetcht a calf tender	85
	18:11 Now **A** and Sarah *were* old *and* well stricken	85
	18:13 the Lord said unto **A**, Wherefore did Sarah	85
	18:16 **A** went with them to bring them on the way.	85
	18:17 Shall I hide from **A** *that thing* which I do;	85
	18:18 Seeing that **A** shall surely become a great	85
	18:19 that the Lord may bring upon **A** that which	85
	18:22 but **A** stood yet before the Lord.	85
	18:23 drew near, and said, Wilt thou also destroy	85
	18:27 **A** answered and said, Behold now, I have	85
	18:33 as soon as he had left communing with **A**:	85
	18:33 Abraham: and **A** returned unto his place.	85
	19:27 **A** gat up early in the morning to the place	85
	19:29 that God remembered **A**, and sent Lot out of	85
	20: 1 **A** journeyed from thence toward the south	85
	20: 2 **A** said of Sarah his wife, She *is* my sister:	85
	20: 9 Abimelech called **A**, and said unto him,	85
	20:10 Abimelech said unto **A**, What sawest thou,	85
	20:11 **A** said, Because I thought, Surely the fear of	85
	20:14 gave *them* unto **A**, and restored him Sarah	85
	20:17 So **A** prayed unto God: and God healed	85
	21: 2 and bare **A** a son in his old age,	85
	21: 3 **A** called the name of his son that was born	85
	21: 4 circumcised his son Isaac being eight days	85
	21: 5 *was* an hundred years old, when his son	85
	21: 7 And she said, Who would have said unto **A**,	85
	21: 8 **A** made a great feast the *same* day that Isaac	85
	21: 9 which she had born unto **A**, mocking.	85
	21:10 Wherefore she said unto **A**, Cast out this	85
	21:12 God said unto **A**, Let it not be grievous in thy	85
	21:14 **A** rose up early in the morning,	85
	21:22 the chief captain of his host spake unto **A**,	85
	21:24 And **A** said, I will swear.	85
	21:25 **A** reproved Abimelech because of a well of	85
	21:27 **A** took sheep and oxen, and gave *them* unto	85
	21:28 **A** set seven ewe lambs of the flock by	85
	21:29 Abimelech said unto **A**, What *mean* these	85
	21:33 *A* planted a grove in Beer-sheba,	NIH
	21:34 **A** sojourned in the Philistines' land many	85
	22: 1 that God did tempt **A**, and said unto him,	85
	22: 1 did tempt Abraham, and said unto him, **A**:	85
	22: 3 **A** rose up early in the morning,	85
	22: 4 Then on the third day **A** lift up his eyes,	85
	22: 5 **A** said unto his young men, Abide you here	85
	22: 6 **A** took the wood of the burnt offering,	85
	22: 7 And Isaac spake unto **A** his father, and said,	85
	22: 8 **A** said, My son, God will provide himself a	85
	22: 9 **A** built an altar there, and laid the wood in	85
	22:10 **A** stretched forth his hand, and took the	85
	22:11 him out of heaven, and said, **A**, Abraham:	85
	22:11 him out of heaven, and said, Abraham, **A**:	85
	22:13 **A** lifted up his eyes, and looked,	85
	22:13 **A** went and took the ram, and offered him	85
	22:14 **A** called the name of that place Jehovah-jireh:	85
	22:15 the angel of the Lord called unto **A** out of	85
	22:19 So **A** returned unto his young men,	85
	22:19 to Beer-sheba; and **A** dwelt at Beer-sheba.	85
	22:20 that it was told **A**, saying, Behold, Milcah,	85
	23: 2 **A** came to mourn for Sarah, and to weep for	85
	23: 3 **A** stood up from before his dead,	85
	23: 5 the children of Heth answered **A**, saying unto	85
	23: 7 **A** stood up, and bowed himself to the people	85
	23:10 the Hittite answered **A** in the audience	85
	23:12 **A** bowed down himself before the people of	85
	23:14 And Ephron answered **A**, saying unto him,	85
	23:16 **A** hearkened unto Ephron;	85
	23:16 **A** weighed to Ephron the silver, which he	85
	23:18 Unto **A** for a possession in the presence of	85
	23:19 **A** buried Sarah his wife in the cave of	85
	23:20 were made sure unto **A** for a possession of a	85
	24: 1 And **A** was old, *and* well stricken in age:	85
	24: 1 and the Lord had blessed **A** in all things.	85
	24: 2 **A** said unto his eldest servant in all his house	85
	24: 6 **A** said unto him, Beware thou that thou	85
	24: 9 servant put his hand under the thigh of **A**	85
	24:12 O Lord God of my master **A**, I pray thee,	85
	24:12 and shew kindness unto my master **A**.	85
	24:27 Blessed *be* the Lord God of my master **A**,	85
	24:42 and said, O Lord God of my master **A**,	85
	24:48 and blessed the Lord God of my master **A**,	85
	25: 1 again **A** took a wife, and her name *was*	85
	25: 5 And **A** gave all that he had unto Isaac.	85
	25: 6 which **A** had, Abraham gave gifts,	85
	25: 6 **A** gave gifts, and sent them away from Isaac	85
	25: 8 **A** gave up the ghost, and died in a good old	85
	25:10 The field which **A** purchased of the sons of	85
	25:10 there was **A** buried, and Sarah his wife.	85
	25:11 it came to pass after the death of **A**, that God	85
	25:12 the Egyptian, Sarah's handmaid, bare unto **A**:	85
	25:19 of Isaac, Abraham's son: **A** begat Isaac:	85
	26: 1 the first famine that was in the days of **A**.	85
	26: 3 I will perform the oath which I sware unto **A**	85

Ge	26: 5 Because that **A** obeyed my voice, and kept	85
	26:15 had digged in the days of **A** his father,	85
	26:18 which they had digged in the days of **A** his	85
	26:18 had stopped them after the death of **A**:	85
	26:24 and said, I *am* the God of **A** thy father:	85
	28: 4 And give thee the blessing of **A**, to thee,	85
	28: 4 thou art a stranger, which God gave unto **A**.	85
	28:13 I *am* the Lord God of **A** thy father,	85
	31:42 the God of **A**, and the fear of Isaac, had been	85
	31:53 The God of **A**, and the God of Nahor,	85
	32: 9 O God of my father **A**, and God of my father	85
	35:12 the land which I gave **A** and Isaac, to thee I	85
	35:27 *is* Hebron, where **A** and Isaac sojourned.	85
	48:15 before whom my fathers **A** and Isaac did	85
	48:16 and the name of my fathers **A** and Isaac;	85
	49:30 which **A** bought with the field of Ephron	85
	49:31 There they buried **A** and Sarah his wife;	85
	50:13 which **A** bought with the field for a	85
	50:24 this land unto the land which he sware to **A**,	85
Ex	2:24 God remembered his covenant with **A**,	85
	3: 6 the God of **A**, the God of Isaac, and the God	85
	3:15 the God of **A**, the God of Isaac, and the God	85
	3:16 the God of **A**, of Isaac, and of Jacob,	85
	4: 5 the God of **A**, the God of Isaac, and the God	85
	6: 3 appeared unto **A**, unto Isaac, and unto Jacob,	85
	6: 8 the which I did swear to give it to **A**,	85
	32:13 Remember **A**, Isaac, and Israel, thy servants,	85
	33: 1 unto the land which I sware unto **A**, to Isaac,	85
Lev	26:42 also my covenant with **A** will I remember;	85
Nu	32:11 shall see the land which I sware unto **A**,	85
Dt	1: 8 **A**, Isaac, and Jacob, to give unto them	85
	6:10 to **A**, to Isaac, and to Jacob, to give thee great	85
	9: 5 sware unto thy fathers, **A**, Isaac, and Jacob,	85
	9:27 Remember thy servants, **A**, Isaac, and Jacob;	85
	29:13 unto thy fathers, to **A**, to Isaac, and to Jacob.	85
	30:20 to **A**, to Isaac, and to Jacob, to give them.	85
	34: 4 This *is* the land which I sware unto **A**,	85
Jos	18:36 said, Lord God of **A**, Isaac, and of Israel,	85
	24: 3 I took your father **A** from the *other* side of	85
1Ki	18:36 said, Lord God of **A**, Isaac, and of Israel,	85
2Ki	13:23 because of his covenant with **A**, Isaac,	85
1Ch	1:27 Abram; the same *is* **A**.	85
	1:28 The sons of **A**; Isaac, and Ishmael.	85
	1:34 begat Isaac. The sons of Isaac; Esau	85
	16:16 *of the covenant* which he made with **A**,	85
	29:18 O Lord God of **A**, Isaac, and of Israel,	85
2Ch	20: 7 gavest it to the seed of **A** thy friend for ever?	85
	30: 6 turn again unto the Lord God of **A**, Isaac,	85
Ne	9: 7 the Chaldees, and gavest him the name of **A**;	85
Ps	47: 9 even the people of the God of **A**:	85
	105: 6 O ye seed of **A** his servant, ye children of	85
	105: 9 *covenant* he made with **A**, and his oath	85
	105:42 his holy promise, *and* **A** his servant.	85
Isa	29:22 who redeemed **A**, concerning the house of	85
	41: 8 I have chosen, the seed of **A** my friend.	85
	51: 2 Look unto **A** your father, and unto Sarah	85
	63:16 though **A** be ignorant of us,	85
Jer	33:26 of his seed *to be* rulers over the seed of **A**,	85
Eze	33:24 saying, **A** was one, and he inherited the land:	85
Mic	7:20 the truth to Jacob, *and* the mercy to **A**,	85
Mt	1: 1 Jesus Christ, the son of David, the son of **A**.	11
	1: 2 **A** begat Isaac; and Isaac begat Jacob;	11
	1:17 So all the generations from **A** to David *are*	11
	3: 9 within yourselves, We have **A** to *our* father:	11
	3: 9 of these stones to raise up children unto **A**.	11
	8:11 and shall sit down with **A**, and Isaac,	11
	22:32 I am the God of **A**, and the God of Isaac,	11
Mk	12:26 I am the God of **A**, and the God of Isaac,	11
Lk	1:55 to our fathers), to **A**, and to his seed for ever.	11
	1:73 The oath which he sware to our father **A**,	11
	3: 8 within yourselves, We have **A** to *our* father:	11
	3: 8 of these stones to raise up children unto **A**.	11
	3:34 *the son* of Isaac, which was *the son* of **A**,	11
	13:16 ought not this *woman*, being a daughter of **A**,	11
	13:28 when ye shall see **A**, and Isaac, and Jacob,	11
	16:23 and seeth **A** afar off, and Lazarus in his	11
	16:24 And he cried and said, Father **A**, have mercy	11
	16:25 But **A** said, Son, remember that thou in thy	11
	16:29 **A** saith unto him, They have Moses	11
	16:30 he said, Nay, Father **A**: but if one went	11
	19: 9 this house, forsomuch as he also is a son of **A**.	11
	20:37 when he calleth the Lord the God of **A**,	11
Jn	8:39 and said unto him, **A** is our father.	11
	8:39 ye would do the works of **A**.	11
	8:40 which I have heard of God: this did not **A**.	11
	8:52 **A** is dead, and the prophets; and thou sayest,	11
	8:53 Art thou greater than our father **A**, which is	11
	8:56 Your father **A** rejoiced to see my day:	11
	8:57 not yet fifty years old, and hast thou seen **A**?	11
	8:58 verily, I say unto you, Before **A** was, I am.	11
Ac	3:13 The God of **A**, and of Isaac, and of Jacob,	11
	3:25 God made with our fathers, saying unto **A**,	11
	7: 2 The God of glory appeared unto our father **A**,	11
	7: 8 and so **A** begat Isaac, and circumcised him	NIG
	7:16 laid in the sepulchre that **A** bought for a sum	11
	7:17 which God had sworn to **A**, the people grew	11
	7:32 The God of **A**, and the God of Isaac,	11
	13:26 children of the stock of **A**,	11
Ro	4: 1 What shall we say then that **A** our father,	11
	4: 2 For if **A** were justified by works, he hath	11
	4: 3 **A** believed God, and it was counted unto him	11
	4: 9 for we say that faith was reckoned to **A** for	11
	4:12 walk in the steps of *that* faith of our father **A**,	11
	4:13 *was* not to **A**, or to his seed, through the law,	11
	4:16 but to that also which is of the faith of **A**;	11

Ro	9: 7 Neither, because they are the seed of **A**,	11
	11: 1 of the seed of **A**, *of* the tribe of Benjamin.	11
2Co	11:22 so am I. Are they the seed of **A**? so am I.	11
Gal	3: 6 as **A** believed God, and it was accounted	11
	3: 7 are of faith, the same are the children of **A**.	11
	3: 8 preached before the gospel unto **A**, *saying,*	11
	3: 9 which be of faith are blessed with faithful **A**.	11
	3:14 That the blessing of **A** might come on	11
	3:16 Now to **A** and his seed were the promises	11
	3:18 of promise: but God gave *it* to **A** by promise.	11
	4:22 it is written, that **A** had two sons, the one	11
Heb	2:16 *of* angels; but he took on *him* the seed of **A**.	11
	6:13 For when God made promise to **A**, because	11
	7: 1 who met **A** returning from the slaughter of	11
	7: 2 To whom also **A** gave a tenth *part* of all;	11
	7: 4 the patriarch **A** gave the tenth of the spoils.	11
	7: 5 though they come out of the loins of **A**:	11
	7: 6 not counted from them received tithes of **A**,	11
	7: 9 who receiveth tithes, payed tithes in **A**.	11
	11: 8 By faith **A**, when he was called to go out into	11
	11:17 By faith **A**, when he was tried, offered up	11
Jas	2:21 Was not **A** our father justified by works,	11
	2:23 **A** believed God, and it was imputed unto him	11
1Pe	3: 6 *Even* as Sara obeyed **A**, calling him lord:	11

ABRAHAM'S (19) [ABRAHAM]

Ge	17:23 every male among the men of **A** house;	85
	20:18 of Abimelech, because of Sarah **A** wife.	85
	21:11 the thing was very grievous in **A** sight	85
	22:23 eight Milcah did bear to Nahor, **A** brother.	85
	24:15 son of Milcah, the wife of Nahor, **A** brother,	85
	24:34 And he said, I *am* **A** servant.	85
	24:52 that, when **A** servant heard their words,	85
	24:59 and her nurse, and **A** servant, and his men.	85
	25: 7 *these are* the days of the years of **A** life	85
	25:12 **A** son, whom Hagar the Egyptian,	85
	25:19 these *are* the generations of Isaac, **A** son:	85
	26:24 and multiply thy seed for my servant **A** sake.	85
	28: 9 had Mahalath the daughter of Ishmael **A** son,	85
1Ch	1:32 Now the sons of Keturah, **A** concubine:	85
Lk	16:22 and was carried by the angels into **A** bosom:	11
Jn	8:33 We be **A** seed, and were never in bondage to	11
	8:37 I know that ye are **A** seed; but ye seek to kill	11
	8:39 Jesus saith unto them, If ye were **A** children,	11
Gal	3:29 then are ye **A** seed, and heirs according to	11

ABRAM (54) [ABRAHAM]

Ge	11:26 and begat **A**, Nahor, and Haran.	87
	11:27 Terah begat **A**, Nahor, and Haran;	87
	11:29 And **A** and Nahor took them wives: the name	87
	11:31 Terah took **A** his son, and Lot the son of	87
	12: 1 Now the Lord had said unto **A**, Get thee	87
	12: 4 So **A** departed, as the Lord had spoken	87
	12: 4 *A was* seventy and five years old when he	87
	12: 5 **A** took Sarai his wife, and Lot his brother's	87
	12: 6 **A** passed through the land unto the place of	87
	12: 7 And the Lord appeared unto **A**, and said,	87
	12: 9 **A** journeyed, going on still toward the south.	87
	12:10 **A** went down into Egypt to sojourn there;	87
	12:14 to pass, that, when **A** was come into Egypt,	87
	12:16 he entreated **A** well for her sake: and he had	87
	12:18 Pharaoh called **A**, and said, What *is* this *that*	87
	13: 1 **A** went up out of Egypt, he, and his wife,	87
	13: 2 *A was* very rich in cattle, in silver,	87
	13: 4 there **A** called on the name of the Lord.	87
	13: 5 which went with **A**, had flocks, and herds,	87
	13: 8 **A** said unto Lot, Let there be no strife, I pray	87
	13:12 **A** dwelled in the land of Canaan,	87
	13:14 the Lord said unto **A**, after that Lot was	87
	13:18 **A** removed his tent, and came and dwelt in	87
	14:13 that had escaped, and told **A** the Hebrew;	87
	14:13 of Aner: and these *were* confederate with **A**.	87
	14:14 when **A** heard that his brother was taken	87
	14:19 and said, Blessed *be* **A** of the most high God,	87
	14:21 the king of Sodom said unto **A**, Give me	87
	14:22 **A** said to the king of Sodom, I have lift up	87
	14:23 lest thou shouldest say, I have made **A** rich:	87
	15: 1 word of the Lord came unto **A** in a vision,	87
	15: 1 unto Abram in a vision, saying, Fear not, **A**:	87
	15: 2 **A** said, Lord God, what wilt thou give me,	87
	15: 3 **A** said, Behold, to me thou hast given no	87
	15:11 down upon the carcases, **A** drove them away.	87
	15:12 was going down, a deep sleep fell upon **A**;	87
	15:13 said unto **A**, Know of a surety that thy seed	87
	15:18 day the Lord made a covenant with **A**,	87
	16: 2 Sarai said unto **A**, Behold now, the Lord	87
	16: 2 And **A** hearkened to the voice of Sarai.	87
	16: 3 after **A** had dwelt ten years in the land of	87
	16: 3 gave her to her husband **A** to be his wife.	87
	16: 5 Sarai said unto **A**, My wrong *be* upon thee:	87
	16: 6 **A** said unto Sarai, Behold, thy maid *is* in thy	87
	16:15 Hagar bare **A** a son: and Abram called his	87
	16:15 **A** called his son's name, which Hagar bare,	87
	16:16 **A** *was* fourscore and six years old,	87
	16:16 six years old, when Hagar bare Ishmael to **A**.	87
	17: 1 when **A** was ninety years old and nine,	87
	17: 1 the Lord appeared to **A**, and said unto him,	87
	17: 3 **A** fell on his face: and God talked with him,	87
	17: 5 Neither shall thy name any more be called **A**,	87
1Ch	1:27 **A**; the same *is* Abraham.	87
Ne	9: 7 didst choose **A**, and broughtest him forth	87

ABRAM'S (7) [ABRAHAM]

Ge	11:29 the name of **A** wife *was* Sarai; and the name	87
	11:31 and Sarai his daughter in law, his son **A** wife;	87

A

Ge	12:17 with great plagues because of Sarai **A** wife.	87
	13: 7 there was a strife between the herdmen of **A**	87
	14:12 they took Lot, **A** brother's son, who dwelt in	87
	16: 1 Now Sarai **A** wife bare him no *children:*	87
	16: 3 Sarai **A** wife took Hagar her maid	87

ABROAD (80)

Ge	10:18 the families of the Canaanites **spread a.**	6327
	11: 4 lest we be **scattered a** upon the face of	6327
	11: 8 So the Lord **scattered** them a from	6327
	11: 9 from thence did the Lord **scatter** them a	6327
	15: 5 he brought him forth a, and said,	2351+1886.5
	19:17 they had brought them forth a,	2351+1886.5
	28:14 thou shalt **spread a** to the west, and to	6555
Ex	5:12 the people were **scattered a** throughout	6327
	9:29 I will **spread a** my hands unto the Lord;	6566
	9:33 **spread a** his hands unto the Lord:	6566
	12:46 of the flesh a out of the house;	2351+1886.5
	21:19 walk a upon his staff,	2351+871.1+1886.1
	40:19 he **spread a** the tent over the tabernacle,	6566
Lev	13: 7 if the scab **spread much a** in	6581+6581
	13:12 if a leprosy **break out a** in the skin,	6524+6524
	13:22 if it **spread much a** in the skin,	6581+6581
	13:27 *and* if it be **spread much a** in	6581+6581
	14: 8 shall **tarry a** out of his tent seven days.	3427
	18: 9 *whether she be* born at home, or born a,	2351
Nu	11:32 they **spread them all a** for	7849+7849
Dt	23:10 shall he go a out of the camp,	2351+4480
	23:12 the camp, whither thou shalt go forth a:	2351
	23:13 it shall be, when thou wilt ease thyself a,	2351
	24:11 Thou shalt stand a, and the man to whom	2351
	24:11 bring out the pledge a unto thee.	2351+1886.5
	32:11 **spreadeth a** her wings, taketh them,	6566
Jdg	12: 9 he sent a, and took in thirty	2351+1886.5
	12: 9 thirty daughters from a for his sons.	2351
1Sa	9:26 both of them, he and Samuel, **a.**	2351+1886.5
	30:16 behold *they were* **spread a** upon all	5203
2Sa	22:43 mire of the street, *and* did **spread** them a.	7554
1Ki	2: 8 walkest a any whither, that thou shalt	NIH
2Ki	3: 3 of all thy neighbours,	2351+4480+1886.1
1Ch	13: 2 us send a unto our brethren **every where**,	6555
	14:13 again **spread** themselves a in the valley.	6584
2Ch	26: 8 his name **spread** a even to the entering in	1980
	26:15 name spread **far a**,	4480+5704+7350+3807.1
	29:16 Levites took *it*, to carry *it* out a	2351+1886.5
	31: 5 as soon as the commandment **came a,**	6555
Ne	1: 8 I will **scatter** you a among the nations:	6327
Est	1:17 For *this* deed of the queen shall **come a**	3318
	3: 8 There is a certain people **scattered a**	6340
Job	4:11 the stout lion's whelps are **scattered a.**	6504
	15:23 He **wandereth a** for bread, *saying,* Where	5074
	40:11 **Cast a** the rage of thy wrath:	6327
Ps	41: 6 he goeth a, he telleth *it.*	2351+1886.1+3807.1
	77:17 out a sound: thine arrows also **went a**.	1980
Pr	5:16 Let thy fountains be dispersed a,	2351+1886.5
Isa	24: 1 and **scattereth a** the inhabitants thereof.	6327
	28:25 doth he not **cast a** the fitches,	6327
	44:24 that **spreadeth a** the earth by myself;	7554
Jer	6:11 I *will* pour it upon the children a,	2351
La	1:20 a the sword bereaveth, at home	2351+4480
Eze	34:21 **scattered** them a;	413+2351+1886.1+1886.1
Zec	1:17 through prosperity shall yet be **spread a**;	6327
	2: 6 for I have **spread** you a as the four winds	6566
Mt	9:26 And the fame hereof **went a** into all that	1831
	9:31 **spread a** his fame in all that country.	1310
	9:36 they fainted, and were **scattered a,**	4496
	12:30 that gathereth not with me **scattereth a.**	4650
	26:31 the sheep of the flock shall be **scattered a.**	1287
Mk	1:28 And immediately his fame **spread a**	1831
	1:45 publish *it* much, and to **blaze** the matter,	1310
	4:22 secret, but that it should **come a.**	1519+5318
	6:14 heard *of him;* (for his name was **spread a:)**	5318
Lk	1:65 all these sayings were **noised a** throughout	1255
	2:17 **made known** the saying which was told	1232
	5:15 the more **went** there a fame a of him:	1330
	8:17 shall not be known and **come a.**	1519+5318
Jn	11:52 the children of God that were **scattered a.**	1287
	21:23 Then **went** this saying a among	1831
Ac	2: 6 when this **was noised a,**	1096+3588+5456
	8: 1 they were all **scattered a** throughout	1289
	8: 4 Therefore they that were **scattered a** went	1289
	11:19 Now they which were **scattered a** upon	1289
Ro	5: 5 the love of God is **shed a** in our hearts by	1632
	16:19 your obedience is **come a** unto all *men.* I	864
2Co	9: 9 (As it is written, He hath **dispersed a**;	4650
1Th	1: 8 place your faith to God-ward is **spread a**;	1831
Jas	1: 1 tribes which are **scattered a**,	1290+1722+3588

ABRONAH See EBRONAH

ABSALOM (104) [ABSALOM'S]

2Sa	3: 3 **A** the son of Maacah the daughter of Talmai	53
	13: 1 that **A** the son of David had a fair sister,	53
	13:20 **A** her brother said unto her, Hath Amnon thy	53
	13:22 **A** spake unto his brother Amnon neither	53
	13:22 for **A** hated Amnon, because he had forced	53
	13:23 that **A** had sheepshearers in Baal-hazor,	53
	13:23 and **A** invited all the king's sons.	53
	13:24 **A** came to the king, and said, Behold now,	53
	13:25 the king said to **A**, Nay, my son, let us not all	53
	13:26 said **A**, If not, I pray thee, let my brother	53
	13:27 **A** pressed him, that he let Amnon and all	53
	13:28 Now had commanded his servants, saying,	53
	13:29 servants of **A** did unto Amnon as Absalom	53
	13:29 servants of Absalom did unto Amnon as **A**	53

2Sa	13:30 **A** hath slain all the king's sons, and there is	53
	13:32 for by the appointment of **A** *this* hath been	53
	13:34 **A** fled. And the young man that kept	53
	13:37 **A** fled, and went to Talmai, the son of	53
	13:38 So **A** fled, and went to Geshur, and was	53
	13:39 soul of king David longed to go forth unto **A:**	53
	14: 1 perceived that the king's heart *was* toward **A.**	53
	14:21 go therefore, bring the young man **A** again.	53
	14:23 went to Geshur, and brought **A** *to* Jerusalem.	53
	14:24 So **A** returned to his own house, and saw not	53
	14:25 to be so much praised as for his beauty:	53
	14:27 unto **A** there were born three sons,	53
	14:28 So **A** dwelt two full years in Jerusalem,	53
	14:29 Therefore **A** sent for Joab, to have sent him	53
	14:31 came to **A** unto *his* house, and said unto him,	53
	14:32 **A** answered Joab, Behold, I sent unto thee,	53
	14:33 when he had called for **A**, he came to	53
	14:33 before the king: and the king kissed **A.**	53
	15: 1 that **A** prepared him chariots and horses,	53
	15: 2 **A** rose up early, and stood beside the way of	53
	15: 2 **A** called unto him, and said, Of what city *art*	53
	15: 3 said unto him, See, thy matters *are* good	53
	15: 4 said moreover, Oh that I were made judge	53
	15: 6 on this manner did **A** to all Israel that came	53
	15: 6 so **A** stole the hearts of the men of Israel.	53
	15: 7 that **A** said unto the king, I pray thee, let me	53
	15:10 **A** sent spies throughout all the tribes of	53
	15:10 then ye shall say, **A** reigneth in Hebron.	53
	15:11 with **A** went two hundred men out of	53
	15:12 **A** sent *for* Ahithophel the Gilonite,	53
	15:12 for the people increased continually with **A.**	53
	15:13 The hearts of the men of Israel are after **A.**	53
	15:14 us flee; for we shall not *else* escape from **A:**	53
	15:31 Ahithophel *is* among the conspirators with **A.**	53
	15:34 and say unto **A**, I will be thy servant, O king;	53
	15:37 *into* the city, and **A** came *into* Jerusalem.	53
	16: 8 the kingdom into the hand of **A** thy son:	53
	16:15 And **A**, and all the people the men of Israel,	53
	16:16 Archite, David's friend, was come unto **A**,	53
	16:16 that Hushai said unto **A**, God save the king,	53
	16:17 **A** said to Hushai, *Is* this thy kindness to thy	53
	16:18 Hushai said unto **A**, Nay; but whom	53
	16:20 said **A** to Ahithophel, Give counsel among	53
	16:21 Ahithophel said unto **A**, Go in unto thy	53
	16:22 So they spread **A** a tent upon the top of	53
	16:22 **A** went in unto his father's concubines in	53
	16:23 of Ahithophel both with David and with **A.**	53
	17: 1 Moreover Ahithophel said unto **A**, Let me	53
	17: 4 the saying pleased **A** well, and all the elders	53
	17: 5 said **A**, Call now Hushai the Archite also,	53
	17: 6 when Hushai was come to **A**, Absalom spake	53
	17: 6 come to Absalom, **A** spake unto him, saying,	53
	17: 7 Hushai said unto **A**, The counsel that	53
	17: 9 a slaughter among the people that follow **A.**	53
	17:14 **A** and all the men of Israel said, The counsel	53
	17:14 that the Lord might bring evil upon **A.**	53
	17:15 Thus and thus did Ahithophel counsel **A.**	53
	17:18 Nevertheless a lad saw them, and told **A:**	53
	17:24 **A** passed over Jordan, he and all the men of	53
	17:25 **A** made Amasa captain of the host instead of	53
	17:26 So Israel and **A** pitched *in* the land of Gilead.	53
	18: 5 my sake with the young man, *even* with **A.**	53
	18: 5 gave all the captains charge concerning **A.**	53
	18: 9 **A** met the servants of David. And Absalom	53
	18: 9 **A** rode upon a mule, and the mule went	53
	18: 9 and said, Behold, I saw **A** hanged in an oak.	53
	18:12 Beware *that* none *touch* the young man **A,**	53
	18:14 and thrust them through the heart of **A,**	53
	18:15 Joab's armour compassed about and smote **A,**	53
	18:17 they took **A**, and cast him into a great pit in	53
	18:18 **A** in his lifetime had taken and reared up	53
	18:29 And the king said, *Is* the young man **A** safe?	53
	18:32 said unto Cushi, *Is* the young man **A** safe?	53
	18:33 he went, thus he said, O my son **A**, my son,	53
	18:33 O my son Absalom, my son, my son **A:**	53
	18:33 I had died for thee, O **A**, my son, my son.	53
	19: 1 the king weepeth and mourneth for **A.**	53
	19: 4 O my son **A**, O Absalom, my son, my son.	53
	19: 4 O my son Absalom, O **A**, my son, my son.	53
	19: 6 that if **A** had lived, and all we had died *this*	53
	19: 9 and now he is fled out of the land for **A.**	53
	19:10 **A**, whom we anointed over us, is dead in	53
	20: 6 son of Bichri do us more harm than *did* **A:**	53
1Ki	1: 6 goodly *man;* and *his* mother bare him after **A.**	53
	2: 7 to me when I fled because of **A** thy brother.	53
	2:28 after Adonijah, though he turned not after **A.**	53
1Ch	3: 2 **A** the son of Maachah the daughter of Talmai	53
2Ch	11:20 after her he took Maachah the daughter of **A;**	53
	11:21 Rehoboam loved Maachah the daughter of **A**,	53
Ps	3: T Psalm of David, when he fled from **A** his son.	53

ABSALOM'S (5) [ABSALOM]

2Sa	13: 4 unto him, I love Tamar, my brother **A** sister.	53
	13:20 So Tamar remained desolate *in* her brother **A**	53
	14:30 lit on fire. And **A** servants set the field on fire.	53
	17:20 when **A** servants came to the woman to	53
	18:18 and it is called unto this day, **A** place.	53

ABSENCE (2) [ABSENT]

| Lk | 22: 6 him unto them **in the a** of the multitude. | 817 |
| Php | 2:12 presence only, but now much more in my **a**, | 666 |

ABSENT (11) [ABSENCE]

| Ge | 31:49 thee, when we are **a** one from another. | 5641 |
| 1Co | 5: 3 I verily, as **a** in body, but present in spirit, | 548 |

2Co	5: 6 home in the body, we are **a** from the Lord:	1553
	5: 8 and willing rather to be **a** from the body,	1553
	5: 9 we labour, that, whether present or **a**,	1553
	10: 1 you, but being **a** am bold toward you:	548
	10:11 as we are in word by letters when we are **a**,	548
	13: 2 being **a** now I write to them which	548
	13:10 Therefore I write these *things* being **a**,	548
Php	1:27 whether I come and see you, or *else* be **a**,	548
Col	2: 5 For though I be **a** in the flesh, yet am I with	548

ABSTAIN (6) [ABSTINENCE]

Ac	15:20 that *they* **a** from pollutions of idols,	568
	15:29 That *ye* **a from** meats offered to idols,	568
1Th	4: 3 that ye should **a** from fornication:	568
	5:22 **A** from all appearance of evil.	568
1Ti	4: 3 marry, *and commanding* to **a** from meats,	568
1Pe	2:11 and pilgrims, **a** from fleshly lusts,	568

ABSTINENCE (1) [ABSTAIN]

| Ac | 27:21 after long **a** Paul stood *forth* in the midst | 776 |

ABUNDANCE (68) [ABOUND]

Dt	28:47 gladness of heart, for the **a** of all *things;*	7230
	33:19 for they shall suck *of* the **a** of the seas,	8228
1Sa	1:16 for out of the **a** of my complaint	7230
2Sa	12:30 forth the spoil of the city in great **a.**	7235
1Ki	1:19 slain oxen and fat cattle and sheep in **a,**	7230
	1:25 slain oxen and fat cattle and sheep in **a,**	7230
	10:10 there came no more such **a** of	7230+3807.1
	10:27 sycomore trees *that are in* the vale, for **a.**	7230
	18:41 and drink; for *there is* a sound of **a**, of rain.	1995
1Ch	22: 3 David prepared iron in **a** for the nails for	7230
	22: 3 joinings; and brass in **a** without weight;	7230
	22: 4 Also cedar trees in **a:** for	369+4557
	22:14 and iron without weight; for it is in **a:**	7230
	22:15 there are workmen with thee in **a,**	7230
	29: 2 *of* precious stones, and marble stones in **a.**	7230
	29:21 and sacrifices in **a** for all Israel:	7230
2Ch	1:15 sycomore trees that *are* in the vale for **a.**	7230
	2: 9 Even to prepare me timber in **a:** for	7230
	4:18 Solomon made all these vessels in great **a:**	7230
	9: 1 and gold in **a**, and precious stones:	7230
	9: 9 spices great **a**, and precious	7230+3807.1
	9:27 trees that *are* in the low plains in **a.**	7230
	11:23 he gave them victual in **a.** And he desired	7230
	14:15 carried away sheep and camels in **a,**	7230
	15: 9 for they fell to him out of Israel in **a,**	7230
	17: 5 and he had riches and honour in **a.**	7230
	18: 1 Jehoshaphat had riches and honour in **a.**	7230
	18: 2 Ahab killed sheep and oxen for him in **a,**	7230
	20:25 they found among them in **a** both riches	7230
	24:11 did day by day, and gathered money in **a.**	7230
	29:35 also the burnt offerings *were* in **a**, with	7230
	31: 5 the children of Israel **brought in a**	7235
	32: 5 of David, and made darts and shields in **a.**	7230
	32:29 and possessions of flocks and herds in **a:**	7230
Ne	9:25 oliveyards, and fruit trees in **a:**	7230+3807.1
Est	1: 7 royal wine **in a**, according to the state of	7227
Job	22:11 canst not see; and **a** of waters cover thee.	8229
	36:31 judgeth he the people; he giveth meat in **a.**	4342
	38:34 clouds, that **a** of waters may cover thee?	8229
Ps	37:11 shall delight themselves in the **a** of peace.	7230
	52: 7 trusted in the **a** of his riches, *and*	7230
	72: 7 **a** of peace so long as the moon endureth.	7230
	105:30 Their land **brought forth** frogs in **a**, in	8317
Ecc	5:10 nor he that loveth **a** *with* increase:	1995
	5:12 the **a** of the rich will not suffer him to	7647
Isa	7:22 for the **a** of milk *that they* shall give he	7230
	15: 7 Therefore the **a** they have gotten,	3502
	47: 9 for the great **a** of thine enchantments.	6109
	60: 5 the **a** of the sea shall be converted unto	1995
	66:11 and be delighted with the **a** of her glory.	2123
Jer	33: 6 will reveal unto them the **a** of peace	6283
Eze	16:49 **a** of idleness was in her and in her	7962
	26:10 By reason of the **a** of his horses their dust	8229
Zec	14:14 gold, and silver, and apparel, in great **a.**	7230
Mt	12:34 speak good *things?* for out of the **a** of	4051
	13:12 shall be given, and he shall **have** *more* **a:**	4052
	25:29 hath shall be given, and he shall **have a:**	4052
Mk	12:44 For all *they* did cast in of their **a;**	4051
Lk	6:45 of the **a** of the heart his mouth speaketh.	4051
	12:15 for a man's life consisteth not in the **a** of	4052
	21: 4 For all these have of their **a** cast in unto	4052
Ro	5:17 much more they which receive **a** of grace	4050
2Co	8: 2 How that in a great trial of affliction the **a**	4050
	8:14 *that* now at *this* time your **a** *may be* a	4051
	8:14 that their **a** also may be *a supply* for your	4051
	8:20 no *man* should blame us in this **a** which	100
	12: 7 measure through the **a** of the revelations,	5236
Rev	18: 3 waxed rich through the **a** of her delicacies.	1411

ABUNDANT (13) [ABOUND]

Ex	34: 6 longsuffering, and **a** in goodness and truth,	7227
Isa	56:12 shall be as this day, *and* much more **a.**	3499
Jer	51:13 **a** in treasures, thine end is come, *and*	7227
1Co	12:23 upon these we bestow **more a** honour;	4055
	12:23 our uncomely *parts* have **more a.**	4055
	12:24 having given **more a** honour to that *part*	4055
2Co	4:15 that the grace might through	4121
	7:15 And his inward affection is **more a** toward	4056
	9:12 is **a** also by many thanksgivings unto God;	4052
	11:23 in labours **more a**, in stripes above	4056
Php	1:26 That your rejoicing may be *more* **a** in Jesus	4052
1Ti	1:14 the grace of our Lord was **exceeding a**	5250
1Pe	1: 3 which according to his **a** mercy hath	4183

ABUNDANTLY (32) [ABOUND]
Ge 1:20 Let the waters **bring forth** a 8317+8318
1:21 which the waters **brought forth** a, 8317
8:17 that they may **breed** a in the earth, 8317
9: 7 **bring forth** a in the earth, 8317
Ex 1: 7 **increased** a, and multiplied, 8317
8: 3 the river shall **bring forth** frogs a, 8317
Nu 20:11 water came out a, and the congregation 7227
1Ch 12:40 and oil, and oxen, and sheep a: 7230+3807.1
22: 5 David prepared a before his death. 7230+3807.1
22: 8 Thou hast shed blood a, 7230+3807.1
2Ch 31: 5 the tithe of all *things* brought they in a. 7230
Job 12: 6 into whose hand God bringeth a. NIH
36:28 the clouds do drop *and* distil upon man a. 7227
Ps 36: 8 They shall be a **satisfied** with the fatness 7301
65:10 *Thou* **waterest** the ridges thereof a: 7301
132:15 I will a **bless** her provision: I will 1288+1288
145: 7 They shall a **utter** the memory of thy great 5042
SS 5: 1 O friends; drink, yea, **drink** a, O beloved. 7937
Isa 15: 3 every one shall howl, weeping a. 3381
35: 2 It shall **blossom** a and rejoice even 6524+6524
55: 7 and to our God, for he will a pardon. 7235
Jn 10:10 and that they might have it *more* a. 4053
1Co 15:10 but I laboured **more** a than they all: 4054
2Co 1:12 in the world, and **more** a to you-wards. 4056
2: 4 the love which I have **more** a unto you. 4056
10:15 by you according to our rule a, 1519+4050
12:15 though the **more** a I love you, the less I be 4056
Eph 3:20 do exceeding a above all that we ask 1537+4053
1Th 2:17 endeavoured the **more** a to see your face 4056
Tit 3: 6 he shed on us a through Jesus Christ 4146
Heb 6:17 willing **more** a to shew unto the heirs of 4054
2Pe 1:11 an entrance shall be ministered unto you a 4146

ABUSE (3) [ABUSED, ABUSERS, ABUSING]
1Sa 31: 4 and thrust me through, and a me. 5953
1Ch 10: 4 lest these uncircumcised come and a me. 5953
1Co 9:18 that I a not my power in the gospel. 2710

ABUSED (1) [ABUSE]
Jdg 19:25 and a her all the night until the morning: 5953

ABUSERS (1) [ABUSE]
1Co 6: 9 nor a of themselves **with mankind,** 733

ABUSING (1) [ABUSE]
1Co 7:31 as not a *it*: for the fashion of this world 2710

ABYSS See BOTTOMLESS

ACBOR See ACHBOR

ACCAD (1)
Ge 10:10 Erech, and **A**, and Calneh, in the land of 390

ACCEPT (25) [ACCEPTABLE, ACCEPTABLY,
 ACCEPTANCE, ACCEPTATION, ACCEPTED,
 ACCEPTEST, ACCEPTETH, ACCEPTING]
Ge 32:20 peradventure he will a of me. 5375+6440
Ex 22:11 the owner of it shall a *thereof*, and he shall 3947
Lev 26:41 then a of the punishment of their iniquity: 7521
26:43 they shall a of the punishment of their 7521
Dt 33:11 his substance, and a the work of his hands: 7521
1Sa 26:19 thee up against me, let him a an offering: 7306
2Sa 24:23 unto the king, The Lord thy God a thee. 7521
Job 13: 8 Will ye a his person? will ye contend for 5375
13:10 reprove you, if ye do secretly a persons. 5375
32:21 me not, I pray you, a *any* man's person, 5375
42: 8 for him will I a: lest I deal with you 5375+6440
Ps 20: 3 all thy offerings, and a thy burnt sacrifice. 1878
82: 2 and a the persons of the wicked? 5375
119:108 **A**, I beseech thee, the freewill offerings of 7521
Pr 18: 5 not good to a the person of the wicked, 5375
Jer 14:10 therefore the Lord doth not a them; 7521
14:12 and an oblation, I will not a them: 7521
Eze 20:40 there will I a them, and there will I 7521
20:41 I will a you with *your* sweet savour, 7521
43:27 and I will a you, saith the Lord God. 7521
Am 5:22 I will not a *them*: neither will I regard 7521
Mal 1: 8 he be pleased with thee, or a thy person? 5375
1:10 neither will I a an offering at your hand. 7521
1:13 should I a this of your hand? saith 7521
Ac 24: 3 We a *it* always, and in all places, most 588

ACCEPTABLE (23) [ACCEPT]
Lev 22:20 ye not offer: for it shall be a for you. 7522
Dt 33:24 let him be a to his brethren, and let him 7521
Ps 19:14 be a in thy sight, O Lord, 7522+3807.1
69:13 *is* unto thee, O Lord, *in* an a time: 7522
Pr 10:32 The lips of the righteous know what is a: 7522
21: 3 judgment *is* more a to the Lord than 977
Ecc 12:10 The Preacher sought to find out a words: 2656
Isa 49: 8 In an a time have I heard thee, and in a 7522
58: 5 call this a fast, and an a day to the Lord? 7522
61: 2 To proclaim the a year of the Lord, 7522
Jer 6:20 your burnt offerings *are* not a, nor your 7522
Da 4:27 let my counsel be a unto thee, and break 8232
Lk 4:19 To preach the a year of the Lord. 1184
Ro 12: 1 holy, a unto God, *which is* your reasonable 2101
12: 2 *that* good, and a, and perfect, will of God. 2101
14:18 in these *things* serveth Christ *is* a to God, 2101
15:16 the offering up of the Gentiles might be a, 2144
Eph 5:10 Proving what is a unto the Lord. 2101
Php 4:18 a sacrifice, wellpleasing to God. 1184
1Ti 2: 3 and a in the sight of God our Saviour; 587
5: 4 for that is good and a before God. 587

1Pe 2: 5 a to God by Jesus Christ. 2144
2:20 *it*, ye take it patiently, this *is* a with God. 5485

ACCEPTABLY (1) [ACCEPT]
Heb 12:28 whereby we may serve God a with 2102

ACCEPTANCE (1) [ACCEPT]
Isa 60: 7 they shall come up with a on mine altar, 7522

ACCEPTATION (2) [ACCEPT]
1Ti 1:15 *This is* a faithful saying, and worthy of all a, 594
4: 9 *This is* a faithful saying, and worthy of all a, 594

ACCEPTED (29) [ACCEPT]
Ge 4: 7 If thou doest well, *shalt thou* not be a? 7613
19:21 I have a thee concerning this thing, 5375+6440
Ex 28:38 that they may be a before the Lord. 7522
Lev 1: 4 it shall be a for him to make atonement for 7521
7:18 it shall not be a, neither shall it be imputed 7521
10:19 should it have been a in the sight of 3190
19: 7 day, it *is* abominable; it shall not be a. 7521
22:21 or sheep, it shall be perfect to be a; 7522
22:23 but for a vow it shall not be a. 7521
22:25 *be in* them: they shall not be a for you. 7521
22:27 thenceforth it shall be a for an offering 7521
23:11 sheaf before the Lord, to be a for you: 7522
1Sa 18: 5 he was a in the sight of all the people, 3190
25:35 to thy voice, and have a thy person. 5375
Est 10: 3 and a of the multitude of his brethren, 7521
Job 42: 9 the Lord also a Job. 5375+6440
Isa 56: 7 their sacrifices *shall be* a upon mine altar; 7522
Jer 37:20 I pray thee, be a before thee, 5307
42: 2 our supplication be a before thee, 5307
Lk 4:24 No prophet is a in his own country. 1184
Ac 10:35 and worketh righteousness, is a with him. 1184
Ro 15:31 have for Jerusalem may be a of the saints; 2144
2Co 5: 9 or absent, we may be a of him. 2101
6: 2 I have heard thee in a time a, and in the 1184
6: 2 behold, now *is* the a time; behold, now *is* 2144
8:12 *it is* a according to that a man hath, *and* 2144
8:17 For indeed he a the exhortation; 1209
11: 4 or another gospel, which ye have not a, 1209
Eph 1: 6 he hath **made** us a in the beloved: 5487

ACCEPTEST (1) [ACCEPT]
Lk 20:21 neither a thou the person of *any,* 2983

ACCEPTETH (4) [ACCEPT]
Job 34:19 *How* much less *to him* that a not 5375
Ecc 9: 7 a merry heart; for God now a thy works. 7521
Hos 8:13 and eat *it; but* the Lord a them not; 7521
Gal 2: 6 God a no man's person:) for they who 2983

ACCEPTING (1) [ACCEPT]
Heb 11:35 others were tortured, not a deliverance; 4327

ACCESS (3)
Ro 5: 2 By whom also we have a by faith into this 4318
Eph 2:18 For through him we both have a by one 4318
3:12 and a with confidence by the faith of him. 4318

ACCESSORIES See FURNITURE

ACCHO (1)
Jdg 1:31 did Asher drive out the inhabitants of **A**, 5910

ACCIDENTALLY See UNAWARES

ACCO See ACCHO

ACCOMPANIED (4) [ACCOMPANY]
Ac 10:23 and certain brethren from Joppa a him. 4905
11:12 Moreover these six brethren a me, 2064+4862
20: 4 And there a him into Asia Sopater of 4902
20:38 no more. And they a him unto the ship. 4311

ACCOMPANY (1) [ACCOMPANIED,
 ACCOMPANYING]
Heb 6: 9 and *things* that a salvation, though we 2192

ACCOMPANYING (1) [ACCOMPANY]
2Sa 6: 4 which *was* at Gibeah, a the ark of God: 5973

ACCOMPLISH (13) [ACCOMPLISHED,
 ACCOMPLISHING, ACCOMPLISHMENT]
Lev 22:21 offerings unto the Lord to a *his* vow, 6381
1Ki 5: 9 receive *them:* and thou shalt a my desire, 6213
Job 14: 6 till he shall a, as a hireling, his day. 7521
Ps 64: 6 out iniquities; they a diligent search: 8552
Isa 55:11 it shall a that which I please, and it shall 6213
Jer 44:25 ye will **surely** a your vows, 6965+6965
Eze 6:12 thus will I a my fury upon them. 3615
7: 8 upon thee, and a mine anger upon thee: 3615
13:15 Thus will I a my wrath upon the wall, 3615
20: 8 to a my anger against them in the midst of 3615
20:21 to a my anger against them in 3615
Da 9: 2 that *he* would a seventy years in 4390
Lk 9:31 spake of his decease which he should a at 4137

ACCOMPLISHED (26) [ACCOMPLISH]
2Ch 36:22 by the mouth of Jeremiah might be a, 3615
Est 2:12 so were the days of their purifications a, 4390
Job 15:32 shall be a before his time, and his branch 4390
Pr 13:19 The desire is sweet to the soul: but *it is* 1961
Isa 40: 2 cry unto her, that her warfare is a, 4390
Jer 25:12 come to pass, when seventy years are a, 4390
25:34 and of your dispersions are a.

Jer 29:10 That after seventy years be a at Babylon I 4390
39:16 and they shall be a in that day before thee. NIH
La 4:11 The Lord hath a his fury; he hath poured 3615
4:22 The punishment of thine iniquity is a, 8552
Eze 4: 6 when thou hast a them, lie again on thy 3615
5:13 Thus shall mine anger be a, and I will 3615
5:13 my zeal, when I have a my fury in them. 3615
Da 11:36 and shall prosper till the indignation be a: 3615
12: 7 when *he* shall have a to scatter the power 3615
Lk 1:23 as the days of his ministration were a, 4130
2: 6 the days were a that she should be 4130
2:21 And when eight days were a for 4130
2:22 according to the law of Moses were a, 4130
2:50 and how am I straitened till it be a! 5055
18:31 concerning the Son of man shall be a. 5055
22:37 this that is written must yet be a in me, 5055
Jn 19:28 Jesus knowing that all *things* were now a, 5055
Ac 21: 5 And when we had a *those* days, 1822
1Pe 5: 9 knowing that the same afflictions are a in 2005

ACCOMPLISHING (1) [ACCOMPLISH]
Heb 9: 6 the first tabernacle, a the service *of* God. 2005

ACCOMPLISHMENT (1) [ACCOMPLISH]
Ac 21:26 to signify the a of the days of purification, 1604

ACCORD (16) [ACCORDING, ACCORDINGLY]
Lev 25: 5 **That which groweth** of it own a of thy 5599
Jos 9: 2 with Joshua and with Israel, *with* one a. 6310
Ac 1:14 These all continued **with one a** in prayer 3661
2: 1 they were all **with one a** in one place. 3661
2:46 continuing daily **with one a** in the temple, 3661
4:24 they lift up their voice to God **with one a,** 3661
5:12 they were all **with one a** in Solomon's 3661
7:57 their ears, and ran upon him **with one a,** 3661
8: 6 And the people **with one a** gave heed unto 3661
12:10 which opened to them **of** his own a. 844
12:20 but they came **with one a** to him, and, 3661
15:25 good unto us, being assembled **with one a,** 3661
18:12 the Jews made insurrection **with one a** 3661
19:29 they rushed **with one a** into the theatre. 3661
2Co 8:17 of his **own** a he went unto you. 830
Php 2: 2 same love, *being* of **one** a, of one mind. 4861

ACCORDING (793) [ACCORD]
Ge 6:22 a **to** all that God commanded him, so 3509.1
7: 5 Noah did a **unto** all that the Lord 3509.1
18:10 I will certainly return unto thee a **to** 3509.1
18:14 to the time of life, and Sarah shall 3509.1
18:21 have done altogether a **to** the cry of it, 3509.1
21:23 a **to** the kindness that I have done unto 3509.1
25:13 by their names, a **to** their generations: 3807.1
25:16 twelve princes a **to** their nations. 3807.1
27: 8 obey my voice a **to** *that* which I 3509.1
27:19 I have done a as thou badest me: 3509.1
30:34 I would it might be a **to** thy word. 3509.1
33:14 a as the cattle that goeth before me 3807.1
34:12 will give a as ye shall say unto me: 834+3509.1
36:40 a **to** their families, after their places, 3807.1
36:43 a **to** their habitations in the land of their 3807.1
39:17 she spake unto him a **to** these words, 3509.1
40: 5 each man a **to** the interpretation of his 3509.1
41:11 we dreamed each man a **to** a 3509.1
41:12 man a **to** his dream he did interpret. 3509.1
41:40 a **unto** thy word shall all my people be 5921
41:54 to come, a as Joseph had said: 834+3509.1
43: 7 we told him a **to** the tenor of these words: 5921
43:33 the firstborn a **to** his birthright, 3509.1
43:33 and the youngest a **to** his youth: 3509.1
44: 2 he did a **to** the word that Joseph had 3509.1
44: 7 thy servants should do a **to** this thing: 3509.1
44:10 Now also *let it* be a **unto** your words: 5921
45:21 a **to** the commandment of Pharaoh, 5921
47:12 with bread, a **to** *their* families. 6310+3807.1
49:28 every one a **to** his blessing he blessed 3509.1
50: 6 father, a as he made thee swear. 834+3509.1
50:12 sons did unto him a as he commanded 3651
Ex 6:16 the sons of Levi a **to** their generations; 3807.1
6:17 Libni, and Shimi, a **to** their families. 3807.1
6:19 these *are* the families of Levi a **to** their 3807.1
6:25 fathers of the Levites a **to** their families. 3807.1
6:26 from the land of Egypt a **to** their armies. 5921
8:10 he said, Be *it* a **to** thy word: that thou 3509.1
8:13 the Lord did a **to** the word of Moses; 3509.1
8:31 the Lord did a **to** the word of Moses; 3509.1
12: 3 to the house of *their* fathers, a lamb 3807.1
12: 4 take *it* a **to** the number of the souls; 871.1
12: 4 every man a **to** his eating shall 6310+3807.1
12:21 and take you a lamb a **to** your families, 3807.1
12:25 a as he hath promised, that ye 834+3509.1
12:35 the children of Israel did a **to** the word 3509.1
16:16 Gather of it every man a **to** his 6310+3807.1
16:16 man, a **to** the number of your persons; NIH
16:18 every man a **to** his eating. 6310+3807.1
16:21 every man a **to** his eating: 6310+3509.1
17: 1 a **to** the commandment of the Lord, 5921
21:22 a as the woman's husband will lay 834+3509.1
21:31 a **to** this judgment shall it be done unto 3509.1
22:17 he shall pay money a **to** the dowry of 3509.1
24: 4 to the twelve tribes of Israel. 3807.1
25: 9 A **to** all that I shew thee, *after the* 3509.1
25:35 to the six branches that proceed out of 3807.1
26:30 thou shalt rear up the tabernacle a **to** 3509.1

A

Ex 28: 8 be of the same, **a to** the work thereof; 3509.1
28:10 rest on the other stone, **a to** their birth. 3509.1
28:21 twelve, **a to** their names, *like* 5921
28:21 one with his name shall they be **a to** 3807.1
29:35 **a to** all *things* which I have commanded 3509.1
29:41 **a to** the meat offering of 3509.1
29:41 **a to** the drink offering thereof, for a 3509.1
30:37 you shall not make to yourselves **a to** 871.1
31:11 sweet incense for the holy *place:* **a to** all 3509.1
32:28 the children of Levi did **a to** the word of 3509.1
36: 1 **a to** all that the Lord had commanded. 3807.1
37:21 **a to** the six branches going out of it. 3807.1
37:29 **a** *to* the work of the apothecary. NIH
38:21 **a to** the commandment of Moses, 5921
39: 5 *was* of the same, **a to** the work thereof; 3509.1
39:14 twelve, **a to** their names, *like* 5921
39:14 the stones *were* **a to** the names of 5921
39:14 with his name, **a to** the twelve tribes. 3807.1
39:32 the children of Israel did **a to** all that 3509.1
39:42 **A to** all that the Lord commanded 3509.1
40:16 **a to** all that the Lord commanded him, 3509.1
Lev 4: 3 If the priest that is anointed do sin **a to** 3807.1
4:35 **a to** the offerings made by fire unto 5921
5:10 *for* a burnt offering, **a to** the manner: 3509.1
5:12 **a to** the offerings made by fire unto 5921
9:16 and offered it **a to** the manner. 3509.1
10: 7 And they did **a to** the word of Moses. 3509.1
12: 2 **a to** the days of the separation for her 3509.1
25:15 **A to** the number of years after the jubile 871.1
25:15 **a unto** the number of years of the fruits 871.1
25:16 **A to** the multitude of years thou 6310+3807.1
25:16 **a to** the fewness of years thou 6310+3807.1
25:16 **a** *to* the number *of the years* of the fruits NIH
25:50 the price of his sale shall be **a unto** 871.1
25:50 **a to** the year of a hired servant shall it 3509.1
25:51 **a unto** them he shall give again 6310+3807.1
25:52 **a unto** his years shall he give *him* 6310+3509.1
26:21 moe plagues upon you **a to** your sins. 3509.1
27: 8 **a to** his ability that vowed 834+5921+6310
27:16 thy estimation shall be **a to** 6310+3807.1
27:17 **a to** thy estimation it shall stand. 3509.1
27:18 money **a to** the years that remain, 5921+6310
27:25 all thy estimations shall be **a to** the shekel 871.1
27:27 he shall redeem *it* **a to** thine estimation, 871.1
27:27 then it shall be sold **a to** thy estimation. 871.1
Nu 1:18 **a to** the number of the names, from 871.1
1:20 **a to** the number of the names, by their 871.1
1:22 **a to** the number of the names, by their 871.1
1:24 **a to** the number of the names, from 871.1
1:26 **a to** the number of the names, from 871.1
1:28 **a to** the number of the names, from 871.1
1:30 **a to** the number of the names, from 871.1
1:32 **a to** the number of the names, from 871.1
1:34 **a to** the number of the names, from 871.1
1:36 **a to** the number of the names, from 871.1
1:38 **a to** the number of the names, from 871.1
1:40 **a to** the number of the names, from 871.1
1:42 **a to** the number of the names, from 871.1
1:54 the children of Israel did **a to** all that 3509.1
2:10 of the camp of Reuben **a to** their armies: 3807.1
2:18 the camp of Ephraim **a to** their armies: 3807.1
2:34 the children of Israel did **a to** all that 3509.1
2:34 **a to** the house of their fathers. 5921
3:16 Moses numbered them **a to** the word of 5921
3:20 These *are* the families of the Levites **a to** 3807.1
3:22 **a to** the number of all the males, from a 871.1
3:34 **a to** the number of all the males, from a 871.1
3:51 to his sons, **a to** the word of the Lord, 5921
4:31 **a to** all their service in the tabernacle of 3807.1
4:33 **a to** all their service, in the tabernacle of 3807.1
4:37 Aaron did number **a to** the commandment 5921
4:41 Aaron did number **a to** the commandment 5921
4:45 Aaron numbered **a to** the word of 5921
4:49 **A to** the commandment of the Lord they 5921
4:49 every one **a to** his service, and according 5921
4:49 to his service, and **a to** his burden: 5921
6:21 **a to** the vow which he vowed, 6310+3509.1
7: 5 to every man **a to** his service. 6310+3509.1
7: 7 of Gershon, **a to** their service: 6310+3509.1
7: 8 of Merari, **a unto** their service, 6310+3509.1
8: 4 **a unto** the pattern which the Lord had 3509.1
8:20 did to the Levites **a unto** all that 3509.1
9: 3 **a to** all the rites of it, and according to 3509.1
9: 3 **a to** all the ceremonies thereof, shall ye 3509.1
9: 5 **a to** all that the Lord commanded 3509.1
9:12 **a to** all the ordinances of the passover 3509.1
9:14 **a to** the ordinance of the passover, 3509.1
9:14 **a to** the manner thereof, so shall he do: 3509.1
9:20 **a to** the commandment of the Lord they 5921
9:20 **a to** the commandment of the Lord they 5921
10:13 they first took their journey **a to** 5921
10:14 the children of Judah **a to** their armies: 3807.1
10:18 of Reuben set forward **a to** their armies: 3807.1
10:22 of Ephraim set forward **a to** their armies: 3807.1
10:28 of the children of Israel **a to** their armies, 3807.1
14:17 **a as** thou hast spoken, saying, 834+3509.1
14:19 the iniquity of this people **a unto** 3509.1
14:20 I have pardoned **a to** thy word: 3509.1
14:29 **a to** your whole number, from twenty 3807.1
15:12 **A to** the number that ye shall prepare, 3509.1
15:12 ye do to *every* one **a to** their number. 5921
15:24 **a to** the manner, and one kid of the 3509.1
17: 2 take of every one of them a rod **a to** 3807.1
17: 2 all their princes **a to** the house of their 3807.1
17: 6 **a to** their fathers' houses, *even* twelve 3807.1

Nu 18:16 **a to** thine estimation, *for* the money of 871.1
23:23 **a to** *this* time it shall be said of Jacob 3509.1
24: 2 he saw Israel abiding *in his tents* **a to** 3807.1
26:18 **a to** those that were numbered of them, 3807.1
26:22 These *are* the families of Judah **a to** 3807.1
26:25 These *are* the families of Issachar **a to** 3807.1
26:27 **a to** those that were numbered of them, 3807.1
26:37 **a to** those that were numbered of them, 3807.1
26:43 **a to** those that were numbered of them, 3807.1
26:47 **a to** those that were numbered of them; 3807.1
26:50 These *are* the families of Naphtali **a to** 3807.1
26:53 an inheritance **a to** the number of names. 871.1
26:54 **a to** those that were numbered of 6310+3807.1
26:55 **a to** the names of the tribes of their 3807.1
26:56 **A to** the lot shall the possession 5921+6310
29: 6 **a unto** their manner, for a sweet savour, 3509.1
29:18 for the lambs, *shall be* **a to** their number, 871.1
29:21 for the lambs, *shall be* **a to** their number, 871.1
29:24 for the lambs, *shall be* **a to** their number, 871.1
29:27 for the lambs, *shall be* **a to** their number, 871.1
29:30 for the lambs, *shall be* **a to** their number, 871.1
29:33 for the lambs, *shall be* **a to** their number, 871.1
29:37 for the lambs, *shall be* **a to** their number, 871.1
29:40 Moses told the children of Israel **a to** all 3509.1
30: 2 he shall do **a to** all that proceedeth out 3509.1
33: 2 Moses wrote their goings out **a to** their 3807.1
33: 2 these *are* their journeys **a to** their goings 3807.1
33:54 **a to** the tribes of your fathers ye shall 3807.1
34:14 Reuben **a to** the house of their fathers, 3807.1
34:14 the tribe of the children of Gad **a to** 3807.1
35: 8 **a to** his inheritance which he 6310+3509.1
35:24 revenger of blood **a to** these judgments: 5921
36: 5 of Israel **a to** the word of the Lord, 5921
Dt 1: 3 **a unto** all that the Lord had given him 3509.1
1:30 **a to** all that he did for you in Egypt 3509.1
1:41 **a to** all that the Lord our God 3509.1
1:46 **a unto** the days that ye abode *there.* 3509.1
3:24 that can do **a to** thy works, 3509.1
3:24 to thy works, and **a to** thy might? 3509.1
4:34 **a to** all that the Lord your God did for 3509.1
9:10 on them *was written* **a to** all the words, 3509.1
10: 4 **a to** the first writing, the ten 3509.1
10: 9 **a as** the Lord thy God promised 834+3509.1
10:10 **a to** the first time, forty days 3509.1
12:15 **a to** the blessing of the Lord thy God 3509.1
16:10 **a as** the Lord thy God hath 834+3509.1
16:17 **a to** the blessing of the Lord thy God 3509.1
17:10 thou shalt do **a to** the sentence, 5921+6310
17:10 thou shalt observe to do **a to** all that 3509.1
17:11 **A to** the sentence of the law which 5921+6310
17:11 **a to** the judgment which they shall tell 5921
18:16 **A to** all that thou desiredst of the Lord 3509.1
23:23 **a as** thou hast vowed unto 834+3509.1
24: 8 do **a to** all that the priests 834+3509.1
25: 2 before his face, **a to** his fault, 1767+3509.1
26:13 **a to** all thy commandments which thou 3509.1
26:14 have done **a to** all that thou hast 3509.1
29:21 **a to** all the curses of the covenant that 3509.1
30: 2 shalt obey his voice **a to** all that I 3509.1
31: 5 that ye may do unto them **a unto** all 3509.1
32: 8 he set the bounds of the people **a to** 3807.1
34: 5 land of Moab, **a to** the word of the Lord. 5921
Jos 1: 7 that *thou* mayest observe to do **a to** all 3509.1
1: 8 that thou mayest observe to do **a to** all 3509.1
1:17 **A as** we hearkened unto Moses in all 3509.1
2:21 she said, **A unto** your words, so *be* it. 3509.1
4: 5 **a unto** the number of the tribes of 3807.1
4: 8 **a to** the number of the tribes of 3807.1
4:10 to all that Moses commanded Joshua: 3509.1
7:14 ye shall be brought **a to** your tribes: 3807.1
7:14 shall come **a to** the families *thereof;* 3807.1
8: 8 **a to** the commandment of the Lord 3509.1
8:27 **a unto** the word of the Lord which he 3509.1
8:34 **a to** all that is written in the book of 3509.1
10:32 **a to** all that he had done to Libnah. 3509.1
10:35 **a to** all that he had done to Lachish. 3509.1
10:37 **a to** all that he had done to Eglon; 3509.1
11:23 **a to** all that the Lord said unto Moses; 3509.1
11:23 Israel **a to** their divisions by their tribes. 3509.1
12: 7 *for* a possession **a to** their divisions; 3509.1
13:15 of Reuben *inheritance* **a to** their families. 3807.1
13:24 *even* unto the children of Gad **a to** their 3807.1
15:12 of Judah round about **a to** their families. 3807.1
15:13 **a to** the commandment of the Lord to 413
15:20 the children of Judah **a to** their families. 3807.1
16: 5 border of the children of Ephraim **a to** 3807.1
17: 4 Therefore **a to** the commandment of 413
18: 4 it **a to** the inheritance of them; 6310+3807.1
18:10 the children of Israel **a to** their divisions. 3509.1
18:11 of Benjamin came up **a to** their families: 3807.1
18:20 thereof round about, **a to** their families. 3807.1
18:21 **a to** their families were Jericho, 3807.1
18:28 children of Benjamin **a to** their families. 3807.1
19: 1 children of Simeon **a to** their families: 3807.1
19: 8 children of Simeon **a to** their families. 3807.1
19:10 children of Zebulun **a to** their families: 3807.1
19:16 children of Zebulun **a to** their families, 3807.1
19:17 for the children of Issachar **a to** their 3807.1
19:23 children of Issachar **a to** their families, 3807.1
19:24 the children of Asher **a to** their families. 3807.1
19:31 the children of Asher **a to** their families, 3807.1
19:32 *even* for the children of Naphtali **a to** 3807.1
19:39 children of Naphtali **a to** their families, 3807.1
19:40 the children of Dan **a to** their families. 3807.1
19:48 the children of Dan **a to** their families, 3807.1

Jos 19:50 **A to** the word of the Lord they gave him 5921
21:33 the cities of the Gershonites **a to** their 3807.1
21:44 **a to** all that he sware unto their fathers: 3509.1
22: 9 **a to** the word of the Lord by the hand of 5921
24: 5 **a to** *that* which I did amongst them: 3509.1
Jdg 8:35 **a to** all the goodness which he had 3509.1
9:16 have done unto him **a to** the deserving 3509.1
11:10 if we do not so **a to** thy words. 3509.1
11:36 to me **a to** that which hath proceeded 3509.1
11:39 who did with her **a to** his vow which NIH
20:10 **a to** all the folly that they have wrought 3509.1
21:23 took *them* wives, **a to** their number, 3807.1
Ru 3: 6 **a to** all that her mother in law bade her. 3509.1
1Sa 2:35 *that* shall do **a to** *that* which *is* in my 3509.1
6: 4 **a** *to* the number of the lords of NIH
6:18 **a** *to* the number of all the cities of NIH
8: 8 **A to** all the works which they have 3509.1
13: 8 **a to** the set time that Samuel *had* 3807.1
14: 7 behold, I *am* with thee **a to** thy heart. 3509.1
17:23 and spake **a to** the same words: 3509.1
23:20 down **a to** all the desire of thy soul 3807.1
25: 9 they spake to Nabal **a to** all those words 3509.1
25:30 **a to** all the good that he hath spoken 3509.1
2Sa 3:39 the doer of evil **a to** his wickedness. 3509.1
7:17 **A to** all these words, and according to 3509.1
7:17 **a to** all this vision, so did Nathan speak 3509.1
7:21 word's sake, and **a to** thine own heart, 3509.1
7:22 **a to** all that we have heard with our ears. 871.1
9:11 **A to** all that my lord the king hath 3509.1
14:20 **a to** the wisdom of an angel of God, 3509.1
22:21 The Lord rewarded me **a to** my 3509.1
22:21 **a to** the cleanness of my hands hath he 3509.1
22:25 recompensed me **a to** my righteousness; 3509.1
22:25 **a to** my cleanness in his eye sight. 3509.1
24:19 David, **a to** the saying of Gad, went up 3509.1
1Ki 2: 6 Do therefore **a to** thy wisdom, and let 3509.1
3: 6 **a** as he walked before thee in truth, 834+3509.1
3:12 Behold, I have done **a to** thy word: lo, 3509.1
4:28 *officers* were, every man **a to** his charge. 3509.1
5: 6 servants **a to** all that thou shalt appoint: 3509.1
5:10 cedar trees and fir trees **a** *to* all his desire. NIH
6: 3 **a to** the breadth of the house; 5921+6440
6:38 and **a to** all the fashion of it. 3807.1
7: 9 **a to** the measures of hewed stones, 3509.1
7:36 **a to** the proportion of every one, 3509.1
8:32 to give him **a to** his righteousness. 3509.1
8:39 do, and give to every man **a to** his ways, 3509.1
8:43 do **a to** all that the stranger calleth to 3509.1
8:56 people Israel, **a to** all that he promised: 3509.1
9: 4 to do **a to** all that I have commanded 3509.1
9:11 and with gold, **a to** all his desire,) 3807.1
11:37 thou shalt reign **a to** all that thy soul 871.1
12:24 to depart, **a to** the word of the Lord. 3509.1
13: 5 **a to** the sign which the man of God had 3509.1
13:26 slain him, **a to** the word of the Lord, 3509.1
14:18 for him, **a to** the word of the Lord, 3509.1
14:24 they did **a to** all the abominations of 3509.1
15:29 **a unto** the saying of the Lord, 3509.1
16:12 of Baasha, **a to** the word of the Lord, 3509.1
16:34 **a to** the word of the Lord, which he 3509.1
17: 1 these years, but **a to** my word. 6310+3807.1
17: 5 and did **a unto** the saying of Elijah: 3509.1
17:15 and did **a to** the saying of Elijah: 3509.1
17:16 **a to** the word of the Lord, which he 3509.1
18:31 **a to** the number of the tribes of the sons 3509.1
20: 4 said, My lord, O king, **a to** thy saying, 3509.1
21:26 **a to** all *things* as did the Amorites, 3509.1
22:38 **a unto** the word of the Lord which he 3509.1
22:53 **a unto** all that his father had done. 3509.1
2Ki 1:17 So he died **a to** the word of the Lord 3509.1
2:22 **a to** the saying of Elisha which he spake. 3509.1
4:16 About this season, **a to** the time of life, 3509.1
4:17 had said unto her, **a to** the time of life. 3509.1
4:44 left *thereof,* **a to** the word of the Lord. 3509.1
5:14 **a to** the word of the man of God: 3509.1
6:18 he smote them with blindness **a to** 3509.1
7:16 for a shekel, **a to** the word of the Lord, 3509.1
9:26 cast him into the plat *of ground,* **a to** 3509.1
10:17 **a to** the saying of the Lord, which he 3509.1
10:30 done unto the house of Ahab **a to** all 3509.1
11: 9 captains over the hundreds did **a to** all 3509.1
14: 3 he did **a to** all *things* as Joash his father 3509.1
14: 6 **a unto** that which is written in the book 3509.1
14:25 **a to** the word of the Lord God of 3509.1
15: 3 **a to** all that his father Amaziah had 3509.1
15:34 he did **a to** all that his father Uzziah had 3509.1
16: 3 **a to** the abominations of the heathen, 3509.1
16:10 of it, **a to** the workmanship thereof. 3807.1
16:11 Urijah the priest built an altar **a to** all 3509.1
16:16 **a to** all that king Ahaz commanded. 3509.1
17:13 **a to** all the law which I commanded 3509.1
18: 3 **a to** all that David his father did. 3509.1
21: 8 only if they will observe to do **a to** all 3509.1
21: 8 **a to** all the law that my servant Moses 3807.1
22:13 to do **a unto** all that which is written 3509.1
23:16 **a to** the word of the Lord which 3509.1
23:19 did to them **a to** all the acts that he had 3509.1
23:25 all his might, **a to** all the law of Moses; 3509.1
23:32 **a to** all that his fathers had done. 3509.1
23:35 he taxed the land to give the money **a to** 5921
23:35 of every one **a to** his taxation, to give *it* 3509.1
23:37 **a to** all that his fathers had done. 3509.1
24: 2 destroy it, **a to** the word of the Lord, 3509.1
24: 3 sins of Manasseh, **a to** all that he did; 3509.1
24: 9 **a to** all that his father had done. 3509.1

A

2Ki 24:19 **a** to all that Jehoiakim had done. 3509.1
1Ch 6:19 these *are* the families of the Levites **a** to 3807.1
 6:32 waited on their office **a** to their order. 3509.1
 6:49 **a** to all that Moses the servant of God 3509.1
 9: 9 **a** to their generations, nine hundred 3807.1
 11: 3 **a** to the word of the LORD by Samuel. 3509.1
 11:10 to the word of the LORD concerning 3509.1
 12:23 Saul to him, **a** to the word of the LORD. 3509.1
 15:15 as Moses commanded **a** to the word of 3509.1
 16:40 to do **a** to all that is written in the law 3807.1
 17:15 **A** to all these words, and according to 3509.1
 17:15 **a** to this vision, so did Nathan speak 3509.1
 17:17 regarded me **a** to the estate of a man 3509.1
 17:19 servant's sake, and **a** to thine own heart, 3509.1
 17:20 **a** to all that we have heard with our ears. 871.1
 23:11 one reckoning, **a** to *their* father's house. 3807.1
 23:31 **a** to the order commanded unto them, 3509.1
 24: 3 **a** to their offices in their service. 3807.1
 24: 4 eight among the sons of Ithamar **a** to 3807.1
 24:19 **a** to their manner, under Aaron their 3509.1
 25: 1 the number of the workmen **a** to their 3807.1
 25: 2 prophesied **a** to the order of the king. 5921
 25: 6 **a** to the king's order *to* Asaph, Jeduthun, 5921
 26:13 to the house of their fathers, for every 3807.1
 26:31 **a** to the generations of his fathers. 3807.1
 28:15 **a** to the use of every candlestick. 3509.1
2Ch 3: 4 was **a** to the breadth of the house, 5921+6440
 3: 8 the length whereof *was* **a** to 5921+6440
 4: 7 he made ten candlesticks of gold **a** to 3509.1
 6:23 by giving him **a** to his righteousness. 3509.1
 6:30 unto every man **a** unto all his ways, 3509.1
 6:33 do **a** to all that the stranger calleth to 3509.1
 7:17 do **a** to all that I have commanded thee, 3509.1
 7:18 **a** as I have covenanted with David 834+3509.1
 8:13 offering at the commandment of 3509.1
 8:14 **a** to the order of David his father, 3509.1
 17:14 these *are* the numbers of them **a** to 3807.1
 23: 8 all Judah did **a** to all *things* that Jehoiada 3509.1
 24: 6 **a** to *the commandment* of Moses NIH
 25: 5 to the houses of *their* fathers, 3807.1
 26: 4 **a** to all that his father Amaziah did. 3509.1
 26:11 **a** to the number of their account by 871.1
 27: 2 **a** to all that his father Uzziah did: 3509.1
 29: 2 **a** to all that David his father had done. 3509.1
 29:15 **a** to the commandment of the king, 3509.1
 29:25 **a** to the commandment of David, 871.1
 30: 6 and **a** to the commandment of the king, 3509.1
 30:16 to the law of Moses the man of God: 3509.1
 30:19 though *he be* not *cleansed* **a** to 3509.1
 31: 2 every man **a** to his service, 6310+3509.1
 31:16 in their charges **a** to their courses; 3509.1
 32:25 Hezekiah rendered not again **a** to 3509.1
 33: 8 **a** to the whole law and the statutes 3807.1
 34:32 Jerusalem did **a** to the covenant of God, 3509.1
 35: 4 **a** to the writing of David king of Israel, 871.1
 35: 4 and **a** to the writing of Solomon his son. 871.1
 35: 5 stand in the holy *place* **a** to the divisions 3807.1
 35: 6 that *they* may do **a** to the word of 3509.1
 35:10 **a** to the king's commandment. 3509.1
 35:12 that they might give **a** to the divisions 3807.1
 35:13 they roasted the passover with fire **a** to 3509.1
 35:15 **a** to the commandment of David, 3509.1
 35:16 **a** to the commandment of king Josiah. 3509.1
 35:26 **a** to that which was written in the law 3509.1
Ezr 3: 4 **a** to **the custom**, as the duty of every 3509.1
 3: 7 **a** to the grant that they had of Cyrus 3509.1
 6: 9 **a** to the appointment of the priests 3509.4
 6:13 their companions, **a** to that which 6903+3807.2
 6:14 finished *it*, **a** to the commandment of 4481
 6:14 at the commandment of Cyrus, 4481
 6:17 **a** to the number of the tribes of Israel. 3807.2
 7: 6 **a** to the hand of the LORD his God 3509.1
 7: 9 **a** to the good hand of his God upon 3509.1
 7:14 **a** to the law of thy God which *is* in thine 871.2
 9: 1 *doing* **a** to their abominations, *even of* 3509.1
 10: 3 **a** to the counsel of my lord, and of those 871.1
 10: 3 our God; and let it be done **a** to the law. 3509.1
 10: 5 that *they* should do **a** to this word. 3509.1
 10: 8 **a** to the counsel of the princes 3509.1
Ne 2: 8 **a** to the good hand of my God upon me. 3509.1
 5:12 that *they* should do **a** to this promise. 3509.1
 5:13 And the people did **a** to this promise. 3509.1
 5:19 **a** to all that I have done for this people. NIH
 6: 6 mayest be their king, **a** to these words. 3509.1
 6: 7 now shalt it be reported to the king **a** to 3509.1
 6:14 and Sanballat **a** to these works, 3509.1
 8:18 a solemn assembly, **a** unto the manner. 3509.1
 9:27 **a** to thy manifold mercies thou gavest 3509.1
 9:28 many times didst thou deliver them **a** to 3509.1
 12:24 at the commandment of David 871.1
 12:45 **a** to the commandment of David, *and* 3509.1
 13:22 spare me **a** to the greatness of thy mercy. 3509.1
 13:24 but **a** to the language of each people. 3509.1
Est 1: 7 in abundance, **a** to the state of the king. 3509.1
 1: 8 the drinking *was* **a** to the law; none did 3509.1
 1: 8 that *they* should do **a** to every man's 3509.1
 1:15 we do unto the queen Vashti **a** to law, 3509.1
 1:21 the king did **a** to the word of Memucan: 3509.1
 1:22 into every province **a** to the writing 3509.1
 1:22 that it should be published **a** to 3509.1
 2:12 **a** to the manner of the women, (for so 3509.1
 2:18 and gave gifts, **a** to the state of the king. 3509.1
 3:12 was written **a** to all that Haman had 3509.1
 3:12 every province **a** to the writing thereof, 3509.1
 4:16 unto the king, which *is* not **a** to the law: 3509.1

Est 4:17 did **a** to all that Esther had commanded 3509.1
 8: 9 it was written **a** to all that Mordecai 3509.1
 8: 9 *unto* every province **a** to the writing 3509.1
 8: 9 to the Jews **a** to their writing, 3509.1
 8: 9 to their writing, and **a** to their language. 3509.1
 9:13 to morrow also **a** unto *this* day's decree, 3509.1
 9:27 they would keep these two days **a** to 3509.1
 9:27 **a** to their *appointed* time every year; 3509.1
 9:31 *appointed*, **a** as Mordecai the Jew 834+3509.1
Job 1: 5 offered burnt offerings **a** to the number of NIH
 20:18 **a** to *his* substance *shall* the restitution 3509.1
 33: 6 Behold, I *am* **a** to thy wish in God's 3509.1
 34:11 cause every man to find **a** to *his* ways. 3509.1
 34:33 *Should it be* **a** to thy **mind**? he will 4480+5973
 36:27 they pour down rain **a** to the vapour 3807.1
 42: 9 **a** **as** the LORD commanded them: 834+3509.1
Ps 7: 8 **a** to my righteousness, and according to 3509.1
 7: 8 and **a** to mine integrity *that is* in me. 3509.1
 7:17 I will praise the LORD **a** to his 3509.1
 18:20 The LORD rewarded me **a** to my 3509.1
 18:20 **a** to the cleanness of my hands hath he 3509.1
 18:24 recompensed me **a** to my righteousness, 3509.1
 18:24 **a** to the cleanness of my hands in his 3509.1
 20: 4 Grant thee **a** to thine own heart, 3509.1
 25: 7 **a** to thy mercy remember thou me for 3509.1
 28: 4 Give them **a** to their deeds, 3509.1
 28: 4 to the wickedness of their endeavours: 3509.1
 33:22 be upon us, **a** **as** we hope in thee. 834+3509.1
 35:24 LORD my God, **a** to thy righteousness; 3509.1
 48:10 **A** to thy name, O God, so *is* thy praise 3509.1
 51: 1 O God, **a** to thy lovingkindness, 3509.1
 51: 1 **a** unto the multitude of thy tender 3509.1
 62:12 for thou renderest to *every* man **a** to his 3509.1
 69:16 turn unto me **a** to the multitude of thy 3509.1
 74: 5 *A man* was famous **a as** he had lifted up 3509.1
 78:72 So he fed them **a** to the integrity of his 3509.1
 79:11 to the greatness of thy power; 3509.1
 90:11 even **a** to thy fear, *so is* thy wrath. 3509.1
 90:15 Make us glad **a** to the days *wherein* 3509.1
 103:10 nor rewarded us **a** to our iniquities. 3509.1
 106:45 **a** to the multitude of his mercies. 3509.1
 109:26 my God: O save me **a** to thy mercy: 3509.1
 119: 9 by taking heed *thereto* **a** to thy word. 3509.1
 119:25 quicken thou me **a** to thy word. 3509.1
 119:28 strengthen thou me **a** unto thy word. 3509.1
 119:41 *even* thy salvation, **a** to thy word. 3509.1
 119:58 be merciful unto me **a** to thy word. 3509.1
 119:65 thy servant, O LORD, **a** unto thy word. 3509.1
 119:76 **a** to thy word unto thy servant. 3509.1
 119:91 They continue *this* day **a** to thine 3807.1
 119:107 quicken me, O LORD, **a** unto thy word. 3509.1
 119:116 Uphold me **a** unto thy word, that I may 3509.1
 119:124 Deal with thy servant **a** unto thy mercy, 3509.1
 119:149 Hear my voice **a** unto thy 3509.1
 119:149 quicken me **a** to thy judgment. 3509.1
 119:154 deliver me: quicken me **a** to thy word. 3807.1
 119:156 quicken me **a** to thy judgments. 3509.1
 119:159 O LORD, **a** to thy lovingkindness. 3509.1
 119:169 give me understanding **a** to thy word. 3509.1
 119:170 before thee: deliver me **a** to thy word. 3509.1
 150: 2 praise him **a** to his excellent greatness. 3509.1
Pr 12: 8 A man shall be commended **a** to 6310+3807.1
 24:12 shall *not* he render to *every* man **a** to his 3509.1
 24:29 I will render to the man **a** to his work. 3509.1
 26: 4 Answer not a fool **a** to his folly, lest 3509.1
 26: 5 Answer a fool **a** to his folly, lest he be 3509.1
Ecc 1: 6 the wind returneth *again* **a** to his circuits. 5921
 8:14 happeneth **a** to the work of the wicked; 3509.1
 8:14 **a** to the work of the righteous: 3509.1
Isa 8:20 if they speak not **a** to this word, *it is* 3509.1
 9: 3 they joy before thee **a** to the joy in 3509.1
 10:26 **a** to the slaughter of Midian at the rock 3509.1
 21:16 **a** to the years of a hireling, and all 3509.1
 23:15 seventy years, **a** to the days of one king: 3509.1
 27: 7 is he slain **a** to the slaughter of them 3509.1
 44:13 of a man, **a** to the beauty of a man; 3509.1
 59:18 **A** to *their* deeds, accordingly he 5921+3509.1
 63: 7 **a** to all that the LORD hath 5921+3509.1
 63: 7 he hath bestowed on them **a** to his 3509.1
 63: 7 **a** to the multitude of his 3509.1
Jer 2:28 for **a** to the number of thy cities are thy NIH
 3:15 I will give you pastors **a** to mine heart, 3509.1
 11: 4 do them, **a** to all which I command you: 3509.1
 11:13 For **a** to the number of thy cities were thy NIH
 11:13 **a** to the number of the streets of Jerusalem NIH
 13: 2 **a** to the word of the LORD, and put *it* 3509.1
 17:10 to give every man **a** to his ways, *and* 3509.1
 17:10 his ways, *and* **a** to the fruit of his doings. 3509.1
 21: 2 be that the LORD will deal with us **a** to 3509.1
 21:14 I will punish you **a** to the fruit of your 3509.1
 25:14 I will recompense them **a** to their deeds, 3509.1
 25:14 and **a** to the works of their own hands. 3509.1
 26:20 against this land **a** to all the words of 3509.1
 27:12 king of Judah **a** to all these words, 3509.1
 31:32 Not **a** to the covenant that I made with 3509.1
 32: 8 the prison **a** to the word of the LORD, 3509.1
 32:11 *both* that which was sealed **a** to the law NIH
 32:19 to give every one **a** to his ways, 3509.1
 32:19 his ways, and **a** to the fruit of his doings: 3509.1
 35:10 done **a** to all that Jonadab our father 3509.1
 35:18 **a** unto all that he hath commanded 3509.1
 36: 8 Baruch the son of Neriah did **a** to 3509.1
 38:27 he told them **a** to all these words that 3509.1
 40: 3 and done **a** as he hath said: 834+3509.1
 42: 4 the LORD your God **a** to your words; 3509.1

Jer 42: 5 if we do not even **a** to all things *for* 3509.1
 42:20 unto all that the LORD our God shall 3509.1
 50:21 do **a** to all that I have commanded thee. 3509.1
 50:29 recompense her **a** to her work; 3509.1
 50:29 **a** to all that she hath done, do unto her: 3509.1
 52: 2 **a** to all that Jehoiakim had done. 3509.1
La 3:32 yet will he have compassion **a** to 3509.1
 3:64 O LORD, **a** to the work of their hands. 3509.1
Eze 4: 4 **a** to the number of the days that thou NIH
 4: 5 **a** to the number of the days, 3807.1
 4: 9 **a** to the number of the days that thou NIH
 5: 7 neither have done **a** to the judgments 3509.1
 7: 3 will judge thee **a** to thy ways, 3509.1
 7: 8 I will judge thee **a** to thy ways, 3509.1
 7: 9 I will recompense thee **a** to thy ways 3509.1
 7:27 and **a** to their deserts will I judge them; 871.1
 8: 4 the vision that I saw in the plain. 871.1
 14: 4 cometh **a** to the multitude of his idols; 871.1
 18:24 doeth **a** to all the abominations that 3509.1
 18:30 O house of Israel, every one **a** to his 3509.1
 20:44 not **a** to your wicked ways, nor 3509.1
 20:44 nor **a** to your corrupt doings, O ye 3509.1
 23:24 shall judge thee **a** to their judgments. 871.1
 24:14 to thy ways, and according to thy 3509.1
 24:14 **a** to thy doings, shall they judge thee, 3509.1
 24:24 to all that he hath done shall ye do: 3509.1
 25:14 shall do in Edom **a** to mine anger 3509.1
 25:14 to mine anger and **a** to my fury; 3509.1
 35:11 I will even do **a** to thine anger, 3509.1
 35:11 **a** to thine envy which thou hast used 3509.1
 36:19 **a** to their way and according to their 3509.1
 36:19 and **a** to their doings I judged them. 3509.1
 39:24 **A** to their uncleanness and according to 3509.1
 39:24 **a** to their transgressions have I done 3509.1
 40:24 the arches thereof **a** to these measures; 3509.1
 40:28 he measured the south gate **a** to these 3509.1
 40:29 the arches thereof, **a** to these measures; 3509.1
 40:32 measured the gate **a** to these measures. 3509.1
 40:33 thereof, *were* **a** to these measures: 3509.1
 40:35 and measured *it* **a** to these measures; 3509.1
 42:11 all their goings out *were* both **a** to their 3509.1
 42:11 to their fashions, and **a** to their doors. 3509.1
 42:12 **a** to the doors of the chambers that 3509.1
 43: 3 *it was* **a** to the appearance of the vision 3509.1
 43: 3 *even* **a** to the vision that I saw when I 3509.1
 44:24 they shall judge it **a** to my judgments: 871.1
 45: 8 to the house of Israel **a** to their tribes. 3807.1
 45:25 **a** to the sin offering, according to 3509.1
 45:25 **a** to the burnt offering, and according to 3509.1
 45:25 **a** to the meat offering, and according to 3509.1
 45:25 to the meat offering, and **a** to the oil. 3509.1
 46: 7 for the lambs **a as** his hand shall 834+3509.1
 47:10 their fish shall be **a** to their kinds, as 3807.1
 47:12 it shall bring forth new fruit **a** to his 3807.1
 47:13 whereby ye shall inherit the land **a** to 3807.1
 47:21 So shall ye divide this land unto you **a** to 3807.1
Da 4: 8 **a** to the name of my god, and in whom 3509.4
 4:35 he doeth **a** to his will in the army of 3509.4
 6: 8 to the law of the Medes and Persians, 3509.4
 6:12 **a** to the law of the Medes and Persians, 3509.4
 8: 4 he did **a** to his will, and became great. 3509.1
 9:16 O Lord, **a** to all thy righteousness, 3509.1
 11: 3 great dominion, and do **a** to his will. 3509.1
 11: 4 nor **a** to his dominion which he ruled: 3509.1
 11:16 he that cometh against him shall do **a** to 3509.1
 11:36 the king shall do **a** to his will; 3509.1
Hos 3: 1 **a** to the love of the LORD toward 3509.1
 9:10 abominations were **a** **as** they loved. 3509.1
 10: 1 **a** to the multitude of his fruit he hath 3509.1
 10: 1 **a** to the goodness of his land they have 3509.1
 12: 2 and *will* punish Jacob **a** to his ways; 3509.1
 12: 2 **a** to his doings will he recompense him. 3509.1
 13: 2 *and* idols **a** to their own understanding, 3509.1
 13: 6 **A** to their pasture, so were they filled; 3509.1
Jnh 3: 3 **a** to the word of the LORD. 3509.1
Mic 7:15 **A** to the days of thy coming out of 3509.1
Hab 3: 9 **a** to the oaths of the tribes, *even thy* word. NIH
Hag 2: 5 **A** *to* the word that I covenanted with you NIH
Zec 1: 6 **a** to our ways, and according to our 3509.1
 1: 6 to our doings, so hath he dealt with 3509.1
 5: 3 shall be cut off *as* on this *side* **a** to it; 3644
 5: 3 shall be cut off *as* on that *side* **a** to it. 3644
Mal 2: 9 **a** **as** ye have not kept my 834+6310+3509.1
Mt 2:16 **a** to the time which he had diligently 2596
 9:29 saying, **A** to your faith be it unto you. 2596
 16:27 he shall reward every man **a** to his works. 2596
 25:15 to every man **a** to his several ability; 2596
Mk 7: 5 Why walk not thy disciples **a** to 2596
Lk 1: 9 **A** to the custom of the priest's office, 2596
 1:38 of the Lord; be it unto me **a** to thy word. 2596
 2:22 And when the days of her purification **a** to 2596
 2:24 And to offer a sacrifice **a** to that which is 2596
 2:29 thy servant depart in peace, **a** to thy word: 2596
 2:39 all *things* **a** to the law of the Lord, 2596
 5:14 for thy cleansing, **a** **as** Moses commanded, 2531
 12:47 prepared not *himself*, neither did **a** to his 4314
 23:56 rested the sabbath day **a** to 2596
Jn 7:24 Judge not **a** to the appearance, 2596
 18:31 Take ye him, and judge him **a** to your law. 2596
Ac 2:30 that of the fruit of his loins, **a** to the flesh, 2596
 4:35 was made unto every man **a** as 2530
 7:44 that *he* should make it **a** to the fashion 2596
 11:29 the disciples, every man **a** to his ability, 2531
 13:23 Of this *man's* seed hath God **a** to *his* 2596
 22: 3 taught **a** to the perfect manner of the law 2596

A

Ac	22:12	one Ananias, a devout man **a to** the law,	2596
	24:	6 and would have judged **a to** our law.	2596
Ro	1:	3 which was made of the seed of David **a to**	2596
	1:	4 **a to** the Spirit of holiness, by	2596
	2:	2 **a to** truth against them which commit	2596
	2:	6 Who will render to every man **a to** his	2596
	2:16	of men by Jesus Christ **a to** my gospel.	2596
	4:18	**a to** that which was spoken, So shall thy	2596
	8:27	he maketh intercession for the saints **a to**	2596
	8:28	them who are the called **a to** his purpose.	2596
	9:	3 my brethren, my kinsmen **a to** the flesh:	2596
	9:11	the purpose of God **a to** election might	2596
	10:	2 a zeal of God, but not **a to** knowledge.	2596
	11:	5 this present time also there is a remnant **a**	2596
	11:	8 (**A as** it is written, God hath given them	2531
	12:	3 a **as** God hath dealt to every man	5613
	12:	6 gifts differing **a to** the grace that is given to	2596
	12:	6 prophesy **a to** the proportion of faith;	2596
	15:	5 one towards another **a to** Christ Jesus:	2596
	16:25	is of power to stablish you **a to** my gospel,	2596
	16:25	**a to** the revelation of the mystery,	2596
	16:26	**a to** the commandment of the everlasting	2596
1Co	1:31	That, **a as** it is written, He that glorieth,	2531
	3:	8 man shall receive his own reward **a to**	2596
	3:10	**A to** the grace of God which is given unto	2596
	15:	3 how that Christ died for our sins **a to**	2596
	15:	4 that he rose again the third day **a to**	2596
2Co	1:17	that I purpose, do I purpose **a to** the flesh,	2596
	4:13	a **as** it is written, I believed, and therefore	2531
	5:10	**a to** that he hath done, whether it be good	4314
	8:12	it is accepted **a to** that a man hath,	1437+2526
	8:12	a man hath, and not **a to** that he hath not.	2526
	9:	7 Every man **a as** he purposeth in his heart,	2531
	10:	2 which think of us as if we walked **a to**	2596
	10:13	**a to** the measure of the rule which God	2596
	10:15	that we shall be enlarged by you **a to** our	2596
	11:15	whose end shall be **a to** their works.	2596
	13:10	**a to** the power which the Lord hath given	2596
Gal	1:	4 **a to** the will of God and our Father:	2596
	2:14	not uprightly **a to** the truth of the gospel,	4314
	3:29	and heirs **a to** the promise.	2596
	6:16	And as many as walk **a to** this rule, peace	NIG
Eph	1:	4 **A as** he hath chosen us in him before	2531
	1:	5 **a to** the good pleasure of his will,	2596
	1:	7 of sins, **a to** the riches of his grace;	2596
	1:	9 **a to** his good pleasure which he had	2596
	1:11	predestinated **a to** the purpose of him	2596
	1:19	**a to** the working of his mighty power,	2596
	2:	2 Wherein in time past ye walked **a to**	2596
	2:	2 **a to** the prince of the power of the air,	2596
	3:	7 **a to** the gift of the grace of God given unto	2596
	3:11	**A to** the eternal purpose which he	2596
	3:16	grant you, **a to** the riches of his glory,	2596
	3:20	**a to** the power that worketh in us,	2596
	4:	7 unto every one of us is given grace **a to**	2596
	4:16	**a to** the effectual working in the measure	2596
	4:22	which is corrupt **a to** the deceitful lusts;	2596
	6:	5 them that are your masters **a to** the flesh,	2596
Php	1:20	**A to** my earnest expectation and my hope,	2596
	3:21	**a to** the working whereby he is able	2596
	4:19	But my God shall supply all your need **a to**	2596
Col	1:11	**a to** his glorious power, unto all patience	2596
	1:25	**a to** the dispensation of God which is	2596
	1:29	I also labour, striving **a to** his working,	2596
	3:22	obey in all things your masters **a to**	2596
2Th	1:12	**a to** the grace of our God and the Lord	2596
1Ti	1:11	**A to** the glorious gospel of the blessed	2596
	1:18	**a to** the prophecies which went before on	2596
	6:	3 and to the doctrine which is **a to** godliness;	2596
2Ti	1:	1 **a to** the promise of life which is in Christ	2596
	1:	8 of the gospel **a to** the power of God;	2596
	1:	9 not **a to** our works, but according to his	2596
	1:	9 but **a to** his own purpose and grace,	2596
	2:	8 was raised from the dead **a to** my gospel:	2596
	4:14	the Lord reward him **a to** his works:	2596
Tit	1:	1 **a to** the faith of God's elect,	2596
	1:	3 which is committed unto me **a to**	2596
	3:	5 but **a to** his mercy he saved us, by	2596
	3:	7 we should be made heirs **a to** the hope of	2596
Heb	2:	4 gifts of the Holy Ghost, **a to** his own will?	2596
	7:	5 to take tithes of the people **a to** the law,	2596
	8:	4 are priests that offer gifts **a to** the law:	2596
	8:	5 saith he, that thou make all things **a to**	2596
	8:	9 Not **a to** the covenant that I made with	2596
	9:19	precept to all the people **a to** the law,	2596
Jas	2:	8 If ye fulfil the royal law **a to** the scripture,	2596
1Pe	1:	2 Elect **a to** the foreknowledge of God	2596
	1:	3 which **a to** his abundant mercy hath	2596
	1:14	not **fashioning** yourselves **a to** the former	4964
	1:17	without respect of persons judgeth **a to**	2596
	3:	7 dwell with them **a to** knowledge,	2596
	4:	6 that they might be judged **a to** men in	2596
	4:	6 in the flesh, but live **a to** God in the spirit.	2596
	4:19	let them that suffer **a to** the will	2596
2Pe	1:	3 **A as** his divine power hath given unto us	5613
	2:22	But it is happened unto them **a to** the true	NIG
	3:13	Nevertheless we, **a to** his promise, look for	2596
	3:15	even as our beloved brother Paul also **a to**	2596
1Jn	5:14	that, if we ask any thing **a to** his will,	2596
Rev	2:23	I will give unto every one of you **a to** your	2596
	18:	6 double unto her double **a to** her works:	2596
	20:12	written in the books, **a to** their works.	2596
	20:13	they were judged every man **a to** their	2596
	21:17	a to the measure of a man, that is,	NIG
	22:12	to give every man **a as** his work shall be.	5613

ACCORDINGLY (1) [ACCORD]

Isa	59:18	**a** he will repay, fury to his	5921+3509.1

ACCOUNT (17) [ACCOUNTED, ACCOUNTING, ACCOUNTS]

2Ki	12:	4 the **a**, the money that every man is set at,	NIH
1Ch	27:24	neither was the number put in the **a** of	4557
2Ch	26:11	according to the number of their **a** by	6486
Job	33:13	for he **giveth** not **a** of any of his matters.	6030
Ps	144:	3 son of man, that thou **makest a** of him?	2803
Ecc	7:27	counting one by one, to find out the **a**:	2808
Mt	12:36	they shall give **a** thereof in the day of	3056
	18:23	which would take **a** of his servants.	3056
Lk	16:	2 give an **a** of thy stewardship; for thou	3056
Ac	19:40	we may give an **a** of this concourse.	3056
Ro	14:12	every one of us shall give **a** of himself to	3056
1Co	4:	1 Let a man so **a** of us, as of the ministers of	3049
Php	4:17	I desire fruit that may abound to your **a**.	3056
Phm	1:18	or oweth thee ought, **put** that **on** mine **a**;	1677
Heb	13:17	as they that must give **a**, that they may do	3056
1Pe	4:	5 Who shall give **a** to him that is ready to	3056
2Pe	3:15	And a that the longsuffering of our Lord is	2233

ACCOUNTED (12) [ACCOUNT]

Dt	2:11	Which also were **a** giants, as the Anakims;	2803
	2:20	(That also was **a a** land of giants:	2803
1Ki	10:21	it was nothing **a** of in the days of Solomon.	2803
2Ch	9:20	it was not any thing **a** of in the days of	2803
Ps	22:30	it shall be **a** to the Lord for a generation.	5608
Isa	2:22	in his nostrils: for wherein is he to be **a** of?	2803
Mk	10:42	Ye know that they which are **a** to rule over	1380
Lk	20:35	they which shall be **a worthy** to obtain	2661
	21:36	ye may be **a worthy** to escape all these	2661
	22:24	which of them should be the **a** the greatest.	1380
Ro	8:36	we are **a** as sheep for the slaughter.	3049
Gal	3:	6 and it was **a** to him for righteousness.	3049

ACCOUNTING (1) [ACCOUNT]

Heb	11:19	**A** that God was able to raise him up,	3049

ACCOUNTS (1) [ACCOUNT]

Da	6:	2 that the princes might give **a** unto them,	2942

ACCURSED (20) [CURSE]

Dt	21:23	(for he that is hanged is **a** of God;) that thy	7045
Jos	6:17	the city shall be **a**, even it, and all that are	2764
	6:18	keep yourselves from the **a thing**,	2764
	6:18	lest ye **make** yourselves **a**, when ye take	2763
	6:18	when ye take of the **a thing**, and make	2764
	7:	1 Israel committed a trespass in the **a thing**:	2764
	7:	1 of the tribe of Judah, took of the **a thing**:	2764
	7:11	for they have even taken of the **a thing**,	2764
	7:12	before their enemies, because they were **a**:	2764
	7:12	except ye destroy the **a** from amongst you.	2764
	7:13	There is an **a thing** in the midst of thee,	2764
	7:13	until ye take away the **a thing** from	2764
	7:15	that he that is taken with the **a thing** shall	2764
	22:20	of Zerah commit a trespass in the **a thing**,	2764
1Ch	2:	7 of Israel, who transgressed in the **thing a**.	2764
Isa	65:20	being an hundred years old shall be **a**.	7043
Ro	9:	3 For I could wish that myself were **a** from	331
1Co	12:	3 by the Spirit of God calleth Jesus **a**:	331
Gal	1:	8 we have preached unto you, let him be **a**.	331
	1:	9 than that ye have received, let him be **a**.	331

ACCUSATION (10) [ACCUSE]

Ezr	4:	6 wrote they unto him an **a** against	7855
Mt	27:37	And set up over his head his **a** written,	156
Mk	15:26	And the superscription of his **a** was written	156
Lk	6:	7 that they might find an **a against** him.	2724
	19:	8 taken any thing from any man by **false a**,	4811
Jn	18:29	said, What **a** bring you against this man?	2724
Ac	25:18	none **a** of such things as I supposed:	156
1Ti	5:19	Against an elder receive not an **a**,	2724
2Pe	2:11	bring not railing **a** against them before	2920
Jude	1:	9 durst not bring against him a railing **a**,	2920

ACCUSE (16) [ACCUSATION, ACCUSED, ACCUSER, ACCUSERS, ACCUSETH, ACCUSING]

Pr	30:10	**A** not a servant unto his master, lest he	3960
Mt	12:10	the sabbath days? that they might **a** him.	2723
Mk	3:	2 on the sabbath day; that they might **a** him.	2723
Lk	3:14	violence to no man, neither **a** any **falsely**;	4811
	11:54	out of his mouth, that they might **a** him.	2723
	23:	2 they began to **a** him, saying, We found	2723
	23:14	touching those things whereof ye **a** him:	2723
Jn	5:45	not think that I will **a** you to the Father:	2723
	8:	6 that they might have to **a** him.	2723
Ac	24:	2 forth, Tertullus began to **a** him, saying,	2723
	24:	8 of all these things, whereof we **a** him.	2723
	24:13	prove the things whereof they now **a** me.	2723
	25:	5 able, go down with me, and **a** this man,	2723
	25:11	none of these things whereof they **a** me,	2723
	28:19	not that I had ought to **a** my nation of.	2723
1Pe	3:16	they may be ashamed that **falsely a** your	1908

ACCUSED (14) [ACCUSE]

Da	3:	8 came near, and **a** the Jews.	399+7170
	6:24	brought those men which had **a**	399+7170
Mt	27:12	And when he was **a** of the chief priests	2723
Mk	15:	3 the chief priests **a** him of many things:	2723
Lk	16:	1 same was **a** unto him that he had wasted	1225
	23:10	and scribes stood and vehemently **a** him.	2723
Ac	22:30	certainty wherefore he was **a** of the Jews,	2723
	23:28	known the cause whereby they **a** him,	1458

Ac	23:29	Whom I perceived to be **a** of questions of	1458
	25:16	before that he which is **a** have the accusers	2723
	26:	2 all the things whereof I am **a** of the Jews.	1458
	26:	7 king Agrippa, I am **a** of the Jews.	1458
Tit	1:	6 having faithful children not **a** of riot	1722+2724
Rev	12:10	which **a** them before our God day	2723

ACCUSER (1) [ACCUSE]

Rev	12:10	for the **a** of our brethren is cast down,	2725

ACCUSERS (8) [ACCUSE]

Jn	8:10	her, Woman, where are those thine **a**?	2725
Ac	23:30	gave commandment to his **a** also to say	2725
	23:35	said he, when thine **a** are also come.	2725
	24:	8 Commanding his **a** to come unto thee:	2725
	25:16	that he which is accused have the **a**	2725
	25:18	Against whom when the **a** stood up, they	2725
2Ti	3:	3 trucebreakers, **false a**, incontinent, fierce,	1228
Tit	2:	3 not **false a**, not given to much wine,	1228

ACCUSETH (1) [ACCUSE]

Jn	5:45	there is one that **a** you, even Moses,	2723

ACCUSING (1) [ACCUSE]

Ro	2:15	and their thoughts the mean while **a** or	2723

ACCUSTOMED (1) [CUSTOM]

Jer	13:23	may ye also do good, that are **a** to do evil.	3928

ACELDAMA (1)

Ac	1:19	**A**, that is to say, The field of blood.	184

ACHAIA (11)

Ac	18:12	And when Gallio was the deputy of **A**,	882
	18:27	And when he was disposed to pass into **A**,	882
	19:21	he had passed through Macedonia and **A**,	882
Ro	15:26	To make a certain contribution for the	882
	16:	5 who is the firstfruits of **A** unto Christ.	882
1Co	16:15	that it is the firstfruits of **A**, and that they	882
2Co	1:	1 with all the saints which are in all **A**:	882
	9:	2 of Macedonia, that **A** was ready a year ago;	882
	11:10	stop me of this boasting in the regions of **A**.	882
1Th	1:	7 to all that believe in Macedonia and **A**.	882
	1:	8 of the Lord not only in Macedonia and **A**,	882

ACHAICUS (2)

1Co	16:17	coming of Stephanas and Fortunatus and **A**:	883
	16:	S and Fortunatus, and **A**, and Timotheus.	883

ACHAN (6) [ACHAR]

Jos	7:	1 for **A**, the son of Carmi, the son of Zabdi,	5912
	7:18	**A**, the son of Carmi, the son of Zabdi,	5912
	7:19	Joshua said unto **A**, My son, give, I pray	5912
	7:20	**A** answered Joshua, and said, Indeed I	5912
	7:24	took **A** the son of Zerah, and the silver,	5912
	22:20	Did not **A** the son of Zerah commit a	5912

ACHAR (1) [ACHAN]

1Ch	2:	7 **A**, the troubler of Israel, who transgressed	5917

ACHAZ (2) [AHAZ]

Mt	1:	9 and Joatham begat **A**; and Achaz begat	881
	1:	9 Joatham begat Achaz; and **A** begat Ezekias;	881

ACHBOR (7)

Ge	36:38	Baal-hanan the son of **A** reigned in his	5907
	36:39	Baal-hanan the son of **A** died,	5907
2Ki	22:12	**A** the son of Michaiah, and Shaphan,	5907
	22:14	and **A**, and Shaphan, and Asahiah,	5907
1Ch	1:49	Baal-hanan the son of **A** reigned in his	5907
Jer	26:22	namely, Elnathan the son of **A**,	5907
	36:12	Elnathan the son of **A**, and Gemariah	5907

ACHIM (2)

Mt	1:14	and Sadoc begat **A**; and Achim begat Eliud;	885
	1:14	and Sadoc begat Achim; and **A** begat Eliud;	885

ACHISH (21)

1Sa	21:10	fear of Saul, and went to **A** the king of Gath.	397
	21:11	The servants of **A** said unto him, Is not this	397
	21:12	and was sore afraid of **A** the king of Gath.	397
	21:14	said **A** unto his servants, Lo, ye see	397
	27:	2 hundred men that were with him unto **A**,	397
	27:	3 David dwelt with **A** at Gath, he and his	397
	27:	5 David said unto **A**, If I have now found	397
	27:	6 **A** gave him Ziklag that day: wherefore	397
	27:	9 the apparel, and returned, and came to **A**.	397
	27:10	**A** said, Whither have ye made a road	397
	27:12	**A** believed David, saying, He hath made his	397
	28:	1 **A** said unto David, Know thou assuredly,	397
	28:	2 David said to **A**, Surely thou shalt know	397
	28:	2 a said to David, Therefore will I make thee	397
	29:	2 his men passed on in the rereward with **A**.	397
	29:	3 What do these Hebrews here? And **A** said	397
	29:	6 **A** called David, and said unto him, Surely,	397
	29:	8 David said unto **A**, But what have I done?	397
	29:	9 **A** answered and said to David, I know that	397
1Ki	2:39	away unto **A** son of Maachah king of Gath.	397
	2:40	and went to Gath to **A** to seek his servants:	397

ACHMETHA (1)

Ezr	6:	2 there was found at **A**, in the palace that	307

ACHOR (5)

Jos	7:24	they brought them unto the valley of **A**.	5911
	7:26	was called, The valley of **A**, unto this day.	5911

Jos 15: 7 up toward Debir from the valley of **A**, 5911
Isa 65:10 the valley of **A** a place for the herds to lie 5911
Hos 2:15 and the valley of **A** for a door of hope: 5911

ACHSAH (5)

Jos 15:16 to him will I give **A** my daughter to wife. 5915
15:17 and he gave **A** his daughter to wife. 5915
Jdg 1:12 to him will I give **A** my daughter to wife. 5915
1:13 and he gave **A** his daughter to wife. 5915
1Ch 2:49 Gibea: and the daughter of Caleb *was* **A**. 5915

ACHSHAPH (3)

Jos 11: 1 the king of Shimron, and to the king of **A**, 407
12:20 of Shimron-meron, one; the king of **A**, one; 407
19:25 was Helkath, and Hali, and Beten, and **A**, 407

ACHZIB (4)

Jos 15:44 Keilah, and **A**, and Mareshah; nine cities 392
19:29 thereof are at the sea from the coast to **A**: 392
Jdg 1:31 nor of Ahlab, nor of **A**, nor of Helbah, nor 392
Mic 1:14 the houses of **A** *shall be* a lie to the kings 392

ACKNOWLEDGE (16) [ACKNOWLEDGED, ACKNOWLEDGEMENT, ACKNOWLEDGETH, ACKNOWLEDGING]

Dt 21:17 he shall **a** the son of the hated *for* 5234
33: 9 neither did he **a** his brethren, nor knew 5234
Ps 51: 3 For I **a** my transgressions: and my sin *is* 3045
Pr 3: 6 In all thy ways **a** him, and he shall direct 3045
Isa 33:13 and ye *that are* near, **a** my might. 3045
61: 9 all that see them shall **a** them, that they 5234
63:16 be ignorant of us, and Israel **a** us not: 5234
Jer 3:13 Only **a** thine iniquity, that thou hast 3045
14:20 We **a**, O Lord, our wickedness, *and* 3045
24: 5 will I **a** them that are carried away captive 5234
Da 11:39 whom he shall **a** *and* increase *with* glory: 5234
Hos 5:15 till they **a** their **offence**, and seek my face: 816
1Co 14:37 let him **a** that *the* things that I write unto 1921
16:18 therefore **a** ye *them that are* such. 1921
2Co 1:13 *things* unto you, than what you read or **a**; 1921
1:13 and I trust you shall **a** even to the end; 1921

ACKNOWLEDGED (3) [ACKNOWLEDGE]

Ge 38:26 Judah **a** them, and said, She hath been 5234
Ps 32: 5 I **a** my sin unto thee, and mine iniquity 3045
2Co 1:14 As also you have **a** us in part, that we are 1921

ACKNOWLEDGEMENT (1) [ACKNOWLEDGE]

Col 2: 2 to the **a** of the mystery of God and of 1922

ACKNOWLEDGETH (1) [ACKNOWLEDGE]

1Jn 2:23 *but he that* **a** *the Son hath the* [Father also.] NIG

ACKNOWLEDGING (3) [ACKNOWLEDGE]

2Ti 2:25 give them repentance to the **a** of the truth; 1922
Tit 1: 1 the **a** of the truth which is after godliness, 1922
Phm 1: 6 **a** of every good *thing* which is in you in 1922

ACQUAINT (1) [ACQUAINTANCE, ACQUAINTED, ACQUAINTING]

Job 22:21 **A** now thyself with him, and be at peace: 5532

ACQUAINTANCE (11) [ACQUAINT]

2Ki 12: 5 priests take *it* to them, every man of his **a**: 4378
12: 7 receive no *more* money of your **a**, 4378
Job 19:13 and mine **a** are verily estranged from me. 3045
42:11 all *they that had been of* his **a** before, 3045
Ps 31:11 my neighbours, and a fear to mine **a**: 3045
55:13 a man mine equal, my guide, and mine **a**. 3045
88: 8 Thou hast put away mine **a** far from me; 3045
88:18 put far from me, *and* mine **a** *into* darkness. 3045
Lk 2:44 sought him among *their* kinsfolk and **a**. 1110
23:49 all his **a**, and the women that followed 1110
Ac 24:23 that *he* should forbid none of his **a** to 2398

ACQUAINTED (2) [ACQUAINT]

Ps 139: 3 lying down, and art **a** *with* all my ways. 5532
Isa 53: 3 a man of sorrows, and **a** with grief: 3045

ACQUAINTING (1) [ACQUAINT]

Ecc 2: 3 wine, (yet a mine heart with wisdom) 5090

ACQUIT (2)

Job 10:14 thou wilt not **a** me from mine iniquity. 5352
Na 1: 3 will not **at all a** *the wicked*: 5352+5352

ACRE (1) [ACRES]

1Sa 14:14 within as it were a half **a** of land, 4618

ACRES (1) [ACRE]

Isa 5:10 ten **a** of vineyard shall yield one bath, 6776

ACSAH See ACHSA; ACHSAH

ACSHAPH See ACHSHAPH

ACT (4) [ACTIONS, ACTIVITY, ACTS]

Isa 28:21 and bring to pass his **a**, his strange act. 5656
28:21 and bring to pass his act, his strange **a**. 5656
59: 6 and the **a** of violence *is* in their hands. 6467
Jn 8: 4 was taken in adultery, **in the very a**. 1888

ACTIONS (1) [ACT]

1Sa 2: 3 of knowledge, and by him **a** are weighed. 5949

ACTIVITY (1) [ACT]

Ge 47: 6 if thou knowest *any* man of **a** amongst 2428

ACTS (66) [ACT]

Dt 11: 3 his miracles, and his **a**, which he did in 4639
11: 7 your eyes have seen all the great **a** of 4639
Jdg 5:11 rehearse the **righteous a** of the Lord, 6666
5:11 *even* the **righteous a** *towards* 6666
1Sa 12: 7 of all the **righteous a** of the Lord, 6666
2Sa 23:20 of Kabzeel, who had **done** many **a**, 6467
1Ki 10: 6 that I heard in mine own land of thy **a** 1697
11:41 the rest of the **a** of Solomon, and all that 1697
11:41 they not written in the book of the **a** of 1697
14:19 the rest of the **a** of Jeroboam, how he 1697
14:29 Now the rest of the **a** of Rehoboam, 1697
15: 7 Now the rest of the **a** of Abijam, 1697
15:23 The rest of all the **a** of Asa, and all his 1697
15:31 Now the rest of the **a** of Nadab, and all 1697
16: 5 Now the rest of the **a** of Baasha, 1697
16:14 Now the rest of the **a** of Elah, and all that 1697
16:20 Now the rest of the **a** of Zimri, 1697
16:27 Now the rest of the **a** of Omri which he 1697
22:39 Now the rest of the **a** of Ahab, and all that 1697
22:45 Now the rest of the **a** of Jehoshaphat, 1697
2Ki 1:18 Now the rest of the **a** of Ahaziah which he 1697
8:23 the rest of the **a** of Joram, and all that he 1697
10:34 Now the rest of the **a** of Jehu, and all the 1697
12:19 the rest of the **a** of Joash, and all that he 1697
13: 8 Now the rest of the **a** of Jehoahaz, 1697
13:12 the rest of the **a** of Joash, and all that he 1697
14:15 the rest of the **a** of Jehoash which he 1697
14:18 the rest of the **a** of Amaziah, *are* they not 1697
14:28 Now the rest of the **a** of Jeroboam, 1697
15: 6 Now the rest of the **a** of Azariah, and all that he 1697
15:11 the rest of the **a** of Zachariah, behold, 1697
15:15 the rest of the **a** of Shallum, 1697
15:21 the rest of the **a** of Menahem, and all that 1697
15:26 the rest of the **a** of Pekahiah, and all that 1697
15:31 the rest of the **a** of Pekah, and all that he 1697
15:36 the rest of the **a** of Jotham, and all 1697
16:19 Now the rest of the **a** of Ahaz which he 1697
20:20 the rest of the **a** of Hezekiah, and all his 1697
21:17 Now the rest of the **a** of Manasseh, 1697
21:25 Now the rest of the **a** of Amon which he 1697
23:19 did to them according to all the **a** that he 4639
23:28 Now the rest of the **a** of Josiah, and all 1697
24: 5 Now the rest of the **a** of Jehoiakim, 1697
1Ch 11:22 man of Kabzeel, who had **done** many **a**; 6467
29:29 Now the **a** of David the king, first and last, 1697
2Ch 9: 5 I heard in mine own land of thine **a**, 1697
9:29 Now the rest of the **a** of Solomon, first 1697
12:15 Now the rest of the **a** of Rehoboam, first and last, 1697
13:22 the rest of the **a** of Abijah, and his ways, 1697
16:11 behold, the **a** of Asa, first and last, lo, 1697
20:34 Now the rest of the **a** of Jehoshaphat, first 1697
25:26 Now the rest of the **a** of Amaziah, first 1697
26:22 Now the rest of the **a** of Uzziah, first 1697
27: 7 Now the rest of the **a** of Jotham, and all 1697
28:26 Now the rest of his **a** and of all his ways, 1697
32:32 Now the rest of the **a** of Hezekiah, 1697
33:18 Now the rest of the **a** of Manasseh, 1697
35:26 Now the rest of the **a** of Josiah, 1697
36: 8 Now the rest of the **a** of Jehoiakim, 1697
Est 10: 2 all the **a** of his power and of his might, 4639
Ps 103: 7 his **a** unto the children of Israel. 5949
106: 2 Who can utter the **mighty a** of 1369
145: 4 another, and shall declare thy **mighty a**. 1369
145: 6 shall speak of the might of thy **terrible a**: 3372
145:12 known to the sons of men his **mighty a**, 1369
150: 2 Praise him for his **mighty a**: praise him 1369

ACTS OF RIGHTEOUSNESS See ALMS

ACZIB See ACHZIB

ADADAH (1)

Jos 15:22 And Kinah, and Dimonah, and **A**, 5735

ADAH (8)

Ge 4:19 the name of the one *was* **A**, and the name 5711
4:20 **A** bare Jabal: he was the father of such as 5711
4:23 his wives, **A** and Zillah, Hear my voice; 5711
36: 2 **A** the daughter of Elon the Hittite, 5711
36: 4 **A** bare to Esau Eliphaz; 5711
36:10 Eliphaz the son of **A** the wife of Esau, 5711
36:12 these *were* the sons of **A** Esau's wife. 5711
36:16 land of Edom; these *were* the sons of **A**. 5711

ADAIAH (9)

2Ki 22: 1 *was* Jedidah, the daughter of **A** of Boscath. 5718
1Ch 6:41 of Ethni, the son of Zerah, the son of **A**, 5718
8:21 **A**, and Beraiah, and Shimrath, the sons of 5718
9:12 **A** the son of Jeroham, the son of Pashur, 5718
Ezr 10:29 and **A**, Jashub, and Sheal, and Ramoth. 5718
10:39 And Shelemiah, and Nathan, and **A**, 5718
Ne 11: 5 Hazaiah, the son of **A**, the son of Joiarib, 5718
11:12 **A** the son of Jeroham, the son of Pelaliah, 5718

ADALIA (1)

Est 9: 8 And Poratha, and **A**, and Aridatha, 118

ADAM (30) [ADAM'S]

Ge 2:19 brought *them* unto **A** to see what he would 120
2:19 whatsoever **A** called every living creature, 120
2:20 **A** gave names to all cattle, and to the fowl 120
2:20 for **A** there was not found a help meet for 120
2:21 God caused a deep sleep to fall upon **A**, 120

Ge 2:23 **A** said, This *is* now bone of my bones, 120
3: 8 **A** and his wife hid themselves from 120
3: 9 the Lord God called unto **A**, 120
3:17 unto he said, Because thou hast 120
3:20 **A** called his wife's name Eve; because 120
3:21 Unto **A** also and to his wife did the Lord 120
4: 1 knew Eve his wife; and she conceived, 120
4:25 knew his wife again; and she bare a son, 120
5: 1 *This is* the book of the generations of **A**. 120
5: 2 blessed them, and called their name **A**, in 120
5: 3 And **A** lived an hundred and thirty years, 120
5: 4 the days of **A** after he had begotten Seth 120
5: 5 all the days **A** lived were nine hundred 120
Dt 32: 8 when he separated the sons of **A**, 120
Jos 3:16 from the city **A**, that *is* beside Zaretan: 121
1Ch 1: 1 **A**, Sheth, Enosh, 121
Job 31:33 If I covered my transgressions as **A**, by 120
Lk 3:38 which was *the son* of **A**, which was 76
Ro 5:14 Nevertheless death reigned from **A** to Moses, 76
1Co 15:22 For as in **A** all die, even so in Christ shall all 76
15:45 The first man **A** was made a living soul; 76
15:45 the last **A** *was made* a quickening spirit. 76
1Ti 2:13 For **A** was first formed, then Eve. 76
2:14 And **A** was not deceived, but the woman 76
Jude 1:14 And Enoch also, the seventh from **A**, 76

ADAM'S (1) [ADAM]

Ro 5:14 sinned after the similitude of **A** transgression, 76

ADAMAH (1)

Jos 19:36 And **A**, and Ramah, and Hazor, 128

ADAMANT (2)

Eze 3: 9 As an **a** harder than flint have I made thy 8068
Zec 7:12 Yea, they made their hearts *as an* **a** **stone**, 8068

ADAMI (1)

Jos 19:33 and **A**, Nekeb, and Jabneel, unto Lakum; 129

ADAR (10)

Jos 15: 3 went up to **A**, and fetched a compass to 146
Ezr 6:15 finished on the third day of the month **A**, 144
Est 3: 7 *to* the twelfth *month*, that *is*, the month **A**. 143
3:13 which *is* the month **A**, and *to take* the spoil 143
8:12 the twelfth month, which *is* the month **A**. 143
9: 1 in the twelfth month, that *is*, the month **A**, 143
9:15 on the fourteenth day also of the month **A**, 143
9:17 On the thirteenth day of the month **A**; 143
9:19 made the fourteenth day of the month **A** *a* 143
9:21 keep the fourteenth day of the month **A**, 143

ADBEEL (2)

Ge 25:13 Nebajoth; and Kedar, and **A**, and Mibsam, 110
1Ch 1:29 Nebajoth; then Kedar, and **A**, and Mibsam, 110

ADD (33) [ADDED, ADDETH, ADDITION, ADDITIONS]

Ge 30:24 The Lord shall **a** to me another son. 3254
Lev 5:16 holy *thing*, and shall **a** the fifth *part* 3254
6: 5 shall **a** the fifth *part* more thereto, *and* 3254
27:13 he shall **a** a fifth *part* thereof unto thy 3254
27:15 he shall **a** the fifth *part* of the money of 3254
27:19 he shall **a** the fifth *part* of the money of 3254
27:27 and shall **a** a fifth *part* of it thereto: 3254
27:31 he shall **a** thereto the fifth *part* thereof. 3254
Nu 5: 7 and he shall **a** the fifth *part* thereof, and give *it* 3254
35: 6 to them ye shall **a** forty and two cities. 5414
Dt 4: 2 Ye shall not **a** unto the word which I 3254
12:32 shalt not **a** thereto, nor diminish 3254
19: 9 shalt thou **a** three cities moe for thee, 3254
29:19 of mine heart, to **a** drunkenness *to* thirst: 5595
2Sa 24: 3 Now the Lord thy God **a** unto 3254
1Ki 12:11 with a heavy yoke, I will **a** to your yoke: 3254
12:14 your yoke heavy, and I will **a** to your yoke: 3254
2Ki 20: 6 I will **a** unto thy days fifteen years; 3254
1Ch 22:14 I prepared; and thou mayest **a** thereto. 3254
2Ch 10:14 your yoke heavy, but I will **a** thereto: 3254
28:13 *already*, ye intend to **a** *more* to our sins 3254
Ps 69:27 **A** iniquity unto their iniquity: and let them 5414
Pr 3: 2 long life, and peace, shall they **a** to thee. 3254
30: 6 **A** thou not unto his words, lest he reprove 3254
Isa 29: 1 **a** ye year to year; let them kill sacrifices. 5595
30: 1 not of my Spirit, that *they* may **a** sin to sin: 5595
38: 5 behold, I will **a** unto thy days fifteen years. 3254
Mt 6:27 Which of you by taking thought can **a** one 4369
Lk 12:25 which of you with taking thought can **a** 4369
Php 1:16 supposing to **a** affliction to my bonds: 2018
2Pe 1: 5 giving all diligence, **a** to your faith virtue; 2023
Rev 22:18 If any *man* shall **a** unto these things, God 2007
22:18 unto him the plagues that are written in 2007

ADDAN (1)

Ezr 2:59 Tel-harsa, Cherub, **A**, *and* Immer: 135

ADDAR (1) [HAZAR-ADDAR]

1Ch 8: 3 of Bela were, **A**, and Gera, and Abihud, 146

ADDED (16) [ADD]

Dt 5:22 he **a** no more. And he wrote them in two 3254
1Sa 12:19 for we have **a** unto all our sins *this* evil, 3254
Jer 36:32 there were **a** besides unto them many like 3254
45: 3 for the Lord hath **a** grief to my sorrow; 3254
Da 4:36 and excellent majesty was **a** unto me. 3255
Mt 6:33 and all these *things* shall be **a** unto you. 4369
Lk 3:20 **A** yet this above all, that he shut up John 4369
12:31 and all these *things* shall be **a** unto you. 4369

A

Lk 19:11 And as they heard these *things,* he a 4369
Ac 2:41 same day there were a *unto them* about 4369
2:47 the Lord a to the church daily such as 4369
5:14 believers were the more a to the Lord, 4369
11:24 and much people was a unto the Lord. 4369
Gal 2: 6 in conference a nothing to me: 4323
3:15 no *man* disannulleth, or a thereto. 1928
3:19 It was a because of transgressions, till 4369

ADDER (4) [ADDER'S]
Ge 49:17 an a in the path, that biteth the horse 8207
Ps 58: 4 *they are* like the deaf a *that* stoppeth her 6620
91:13 Thou shalt tread upon the lion and a: 6620
Pr 23:32 like a serpent, and stingeth like an a. 6848

ADDER'S (1) [ADDER]
Ps 140: 3 like a serpent; a poison *is* under their lips. 5919

ADDETH (3) [ADD]
Job 34:37 he a rebellion unto his sin, he clappeth 3254
Pr 10:22 it maketh rich, and he a no sorrow with it. 3254
16:23 his mouth, and a learning to his lips. 3254

ADDI (1)
Lk 3:28 which was *the son* of A, which was *the son* 78

ADDICTED (1)
1Co 16:15 they have a themselves to the ministry 5021

ADDITION (1) [ADD]
1Ki 7:30 undersetters molten, at the side of every a. 3914

ADDITIONS (2) [ADD]
1Ki 7:29 oxen *were certain* a made of thin work. 3914
7:36 of every one, and a round about. 3914

ADDON (1)
Ne 7:61 Tel-haresha, Cherub, A, and Immer: 114

ADER (1)
1Ch 8:15 And Zebadiah, and Arad, and A, 5738

ADIEL (3)
1Ch 4:36 Asaiah, and A, and Jesimiel, and Benaiah, 5717
9:12 Maasiai the son of A, the son of Jahzerah, 5717
27:25 treasures *was* Azmaveth the son of A: 5717

ADIN (4)
Ezr 2:15 The children of A, four hundred fifty 5720
8: 6 Of the sons also of A; Ebed the son of 5720
Ne 7:20 The children of A, six hundred fifty 5720
10:16 Adonijah, Bigvai, A, 5720

ADINA (1)
1Ch 11:42 A the son of Shiza the Reubenite, 5721

ADINO (1)
2Sa 23: 8 the captains; the same *was* A the Eznite: 5722

ADITHAIM (1)
Jos 15:36 and A, and Gederah, and Gederothaim; 5723

ADJURE (5) [ADJURED]
1Ki 22:16 How many times shall I a thee that thou 7650
2Ch 18:15 How many times shall I a thee that thou 7650
Mt 26:63 said unto him, I a thee by the living God, 1844
Mk 5: 7 I a thee by God, that thou torment me not. 3726
Ac 19:13 We a you by Jesus whom Paul preacheth. 3726

ADJURED (2) [ADJURE]
Jos 6:26 Joshua a *them* at that time, saying, 7650
1Sa 14:24 Saul had a the people, saying, Cursed *be* 422

ADLAI (1)
1Ch 27:29 in the valleys *was* Shaphat the son of A: 5724

ADMAH (5)
Ge 10:19 Gomorrah, and A, and Zeboim, even unto 126
14: 2 Shinab king of A, and Shemeber king of 126
14: 8 the king of A, and the king of Zeboiim, 126
Dt 29:23 of Sodom, and Gomorrah, A, and Zeboim, 126
Hos 11: 8 how shall I make thee as A? *how* shall I set 126

ADMATHA (1)
Est 1:14 Shethar, A, Tarshish, Meres, Marsena, *and* 133

ADMINISTERED (2) [ADMINISTRATION]
2Co 8:19 which is a by us to the glory of the same 1247
8:20 us in this abundance which is a by us: 1247

ADMINISTRATION (1) [ADMINISTERED, ADMINISTRATIONS]
2Co 9:12 For the a of this service not only supplieth 1248

ADMINISTRATIONS (1) [ADMINISTRATION]
1Co 12: 5 there are differences of a, but the same 1248

ADMIRATION (2) [ADMIRED]
Jude 1:16 words, having men's persons in a 2296+4383
Rev 17: 6 when I saw her, I wondered *with* great a. 2295

ADMIRED (1) [ADMIRATION]
2Th 1:10 and to be a in all them that believe 2296

ADMONISH (3) [ADMONISHED, ADMONISHING, ADMONITION]
Ro 15:14 all knowledge, able also to a one another. 3560

1Th 5:12 and are over you in the Lord, and a you; 3560
2Th 3:15 not as an enemy, but a *him* as a brother. 3560

ADMONISHED (5) [ADMONISH]
Ecc 4:13 and foolish king, who will no more be a. 2094
12:12 further, by these, my son, be a: of making 2094
Jer 42:19 know certainly that I have a you *this* day. 5749
Ac 27: 9 fast was now already past, Paul a *them,* 3867
Heb 8: 5 a of God when he was about to make 5537

ADMONISHING (1) [ADMONISH]
Col 3:16 and a one another in psalms and hymns 3560

ADMONITION (3) [ADMONISH]
1Co 10:11 they are written for our a, upon whom 3559
Eph 6: 4 them up in the nurture and a of the Lord. 3559
Tit 3:10 *is* a heretick after the first and second a, 3559

ADNA (2)
Ezr 10:30 A, and Chelal, Benaiah, Maaseiah, 5733
Ne 12:15 Of Harim, A; of Meraioth, Helkai; 5733

ADNAH (2)
1Ch 12:20 A, and Jozabad, and Jediael, and Michael, 5734
2Ch 17:14 A the chief, and with him mighty *men* of 5734

ADO (1)
Mk 5:39 them, Why make ye this a, and weep? 2350

ADONI-BEZEK (3)
Jdg 1: 5 they found A in Bezek: and they fought 137
1: 6 A fled; and they pursued after him, 137
1: 7 A said, Threescore and ten kings, 137

ADONIJAH (26)
2Sa 3: 4 the fourth, A the son of Haggith; 138
1Ki 1: 5 A the son of Haggith exalted himself, 138
1: 7 priest: and they following A helped *him.* 138
1: 8 *belonged* to David, were not with A. 138
1: 9 A slew sheep and oxen and fat cattle by 138
1:11 Hast thou not heard that A the son of 138
1:13 upon my throne? why then doth A reign? 138
1:18 now behold, A reigneth; and now, my lord 138
1:24 A shall reign after me, and he shall sit upon 138
1:25 before him, and say, God save king A. 138
1:41 A and all the guests that *were* with him 138
1:42 A said *unto him,* Come in; for thou *art* a 138
1:43 Jonathan answered and said to A, Verily 138
1:49 all the guests that *were* with A were afraid, 138
1:50 A feared because of Solomon, and arose, 138
1:51 Behold, A feareth king Solomon: 138
2:13 A the son of Haggith came to Bath-sheba 138
2:19 king Solomon, to speak unto him for A. 138
2:21 Let Abishag the Shunammite be given to 138
2:22 thou ask Abishag the Shunammite for A? 138
2:23 if I have not spoken this word against his 138
2:24 promised, A shall be put to death *this* day. 138
2:28 Joab had turned after A, though he turned 138
1Ch 3: 2 of Geshur: the fourth, A the son of Haggith: 138
2Ch 17: 8 A, and Tobijah, and Tob-adonijah, Levites; 138
Ne 10:16 A, Bigvai, Adin, 138

ADONIKAM (3)
Ezr 2:13 children of A, six hundred sixty and six. 140
8:13 the last sons of A, whose names *are* these, 140
Ne 7:18 The children of A, six hundred threescore 140

ADONIRAM (2)
1Ki 4: 6 and A the son of Abda *was* over the tribute. 141
5:14 months at home: and A *was* over the levy. 141

ADONI-ZEDEK (2)
Jos 10: 1 when A king of Jerusalem had heard how 139
10: 3 Wherefore A king of Jerusalem sent unto 139

ADOPTION (5)
Ro 8:15 but ye have received the Spirit of a, 5206
8:23 waiting for the a, *to wit,* the redemption 5206
9: 4 to whom pertaineth the a, and the glory, 5206
Gal 4: 5 that we might receive the a of sons. 5206
Eph 1: 5 a of children by Jesus Christ to himself, 5206

ADORAIM (1)
2Ch 11: 9 And A, and Lachish, and Azekah, 115

ADORAM (2)
2Sa 20:24 A *was* over the tribute: and Jehoshaphat 151
1Ki 12:18 king Rehoboam sent A, who *was* over 151

ADORN (2) [ADORNED, ADORNETH, ADORNING]
1Ti 2: 9 that women a themselves in modest 2885
Tit 2:10 that they may a the doctrine of God our 2885

ADORNED (4) [ADORN]
Jer 31: 4 thou shalt again be a *with* thy tabrets, 5710
Lk 21: 5 how it was a with goodly stones and gifts, 2885
1Pe 3: 5 who trusted in God, a themselves, being 2885
Rev 21: 2 prepared as a bride a for her husband. 2885

ADORNETH (1) [ADORN]
Isa 61:10 and as a bride a *herself* with her jewels. 5710

ADORNING (2) [ADORN]
1Pe 3: 3 Whose a let it not be that outward 2889
3: 3 adorning let it not be that outward a NIG

ADRAMMELECH (3)
2Ki 17:31 Sepharvites burnt their children in fire to A 152
19:37 that A and Sharezer *his sons* smote him 152
Isa 37:38 that A and Sharezer his sons smote him 152

ADRAMYTTIUM (1)
Ac 27: 2 And entering into a ship of A, we launched, 98

ADRIA (1)
Ac 27:27 as we were driven up and down in A, 99

ADRIATIC See ADRIA

ADRIEL (2)
1Sa 18:19 that she was given unto A the Meholathite 5741
2Sa 21: 8 whom she brought up for A the son of 5741

ADULLAM (8) [ADULLAMITE]
Jos 12:15 king of Libnah, one; the king of A, one; 5725
15:35 Jarmuth, and A, Socoh, and Azekah, 5725
1Sa 22: 1 thence, and escaped to the cave of A: 5725
2Sa 23:13 in the harvest time unto the cave of A: 5725
1Ch 11:15 to the rock to David, into the cave of A; 5725
2Ch 11: 7 And Beth-zur, and Shoco, and A, 5725
Ne 11:30 A, and *in* their villages, *at* Lachish, 5725
Mic 1:15 he shall come unto A the glory of Israel. 5725

ADULLAMITE (3) [ADULLAM]
Ge 38: 1 turned in to a certain A, whose name *was* 5726
38:12 Timnath, and his friend Hirah the A. 5726
38:20 the kid by the hand of his friend the A, 5726

ADULTERER (3) [ADULTERY]
Lev 20:10 the a and the adulteress shall surely put 5003
Job 24:15 The eye also of the a waiteth for 5003
Isa 57: 3 the seed of the a and the whore. 5003

ADULTERERS (9) [ADULTERY]
Ps 50:18 with him, and hast been partaker with a. 5003
Jer 9: 2 for they *be* all a, an assembly of 5003
23:10 For the land is full of a; for because 5003
Hos 7: 4 They *are* all a, as an oven heated by 5003
Mal 3: 5 against the a, and against false swearers, 5003
Lk 18:11 unjust, a, or even as this publican. 3432
1Co 6: 9 nor idolaters, nor a, nor effeminate, 3432
Heb 13: 4 but whoremongers and a God will judge. 3432
Jas 4: 4 Ye a and adulteresses, know ye not that 3432

ADULTERESS (5) [ADULTERY]
Lev 20:10 and the a shall surely be put to death. 5003
Pr 6:26 a will hunt for the precious life. 376+802
Hos 3: 1 a woman beloved of *her* friend, yet an a, 5003
Ro 7: 3 to another man, she shall be called an a: 3428
7: 3 so that she is no a, though she be married 3428

ADULTERESSES (3) [ADULTERY]
Eze 23:45 shall judge them after the manner of a, 5003
23:45 because they *are* a, and blood *is* in their 5003
Jas 4: 4 Ye adulterers and a, know ye not that 3428

ADULTERIES (5) [ADULTERY]
Jer 13:27 I have seen thine a, and thy neighings, 5004
Eze 23:43 said I unto *her that was* old *in* a, Will 5004
Hos 2: 2 and her a from between her breasts; 5005
Mt 15:19 murders, a, fornications, thefts, 3430
Mk 7:21 evil thoughts, a, fornications, murders, 3430

ADULTEROUS (4) [ADULTERY]
Pr 30:20 Such *is* the way of an a woman; she 5003
Mt 12:39 and a generation seeketh after a sign; 3428
16: 4 and a generation seeketh after a sign; 3428
Mk 8:38 and of my words in this a 3428

ADULTERY (40) [ADULTERER, ADULTERERS, ADULTERESS, ADULTERESSES, ADULTERIES, ADULTEROUS]
Ex 20:14 Thou shalt not commit a. 5003
Lev 20:10 man that committeth a with *another* 5003
20:10 *even* he that committeth a with his 5003
Dt 5:18 Neither shalt thou commit a. 5003
Pr 6:32 *But* whoso committeth a with a woman 5003
Jer 3: 8 Israel committed a I had put her away, 5003
3: 9 committed a with stones and with stocks. 5003
5: 7 they then committed a, 5003
7: 9 commit a, and swear falsely, 5003
23:14 *they* commit a, and walk in lies: 5003
29:23 have committed a with their neighbours' 5003
Eze 16:32 *But as* a wife that committeth a, 5003
23:37 That they have committed a, and blood 5003
23:37 with their idols have they committed a, 5003
Hos 4: 2 killing, and stealing, and committing a, 5003
4:13 and your spouses shall commit a. 5003
4:14 nor your spouses when they commit a: 5003
Mt 5:27 of old time, Thou shalt not commit a: 3431
5:28 committed a with her already in his heart. 3431
5:32 of fornication, causeth her to commit a: 3429
5:32 marry her that is divorced committeth a. 3429
19: 9 and shall marry another, committeth a. 3429
19: 9 her which is put away doth commit a. 3429
19:18 Thou shalt not commit a, Thou shalt not 3431
Mk 10:11 marry another, committeth a against her. 3429
10:12 be married to another, she committeth a. 3429
10:19 Do not commit a, Do not kill, Do not 3431
Lk 16:18 and marrieth another, committeth a: 3431
16:18 away from *her* husband committeth a. 3431
18:20 not commit a, Do not kill, Do not steal, 3431

A

Jn 8: 3 brought unto him a woman taken in a; 3430
 8: 4 Master, this woman was taken in **a**, in 3431
Ro 2:22 that sayest a man should not **commit a**, 3431
 2:22 not commit adultery, dost thou **commit a**? 3431
 13: 9 For this, Thou shalt not **commit a**, 3431
Gal 5:19 which are these; **A**, fornication, 3430
Jas 2:11 Do not **commit a**, said also, Do not kill. 3431
 2:11 Now if thou **commit** no a, yet if thou kill, 3431
2Pe 2:14 Having eyes full of **a** and that cannot cease 3428
Rev 2:22 them that **commit a** with her into great 3431

ADUMMIM (2)
Jos 15: 7 that is before the going up to **A**, 131
 18:17 which is over against the going up of **A**, 131

ADVANCED (4)
1Sa 12: 6 It is the LORD that a Moses and Aaron, 6213
Est 3: 1 a him, and set his seat above all the 5375
 5:11 how he had a him above the princes 5375
 10: 2 of Mordecai, whereunto the king a him, 1431

ADVANTAGE (4) [ADVANTAGED, ADVANTAGETH]
Job 35: 3 thou saidst, What a will it be unto thee? 5532
Ro 3: 1 What a then hath the Jew? or what profit 4053
2Co 2:11 Lest Satan should **get an** a of us: for we 4122
Jude 1:16 men's persons in admiration because of a. 5622

ADVANTAGED (1) [ADVANTAGE]
Lk 9:25 For what is a man a, if he gain the whole 5623

ADVANTAGETH (1) [ADVANTAGE]
1Co 15:32 what a it me, if the dead rise not? 3786

ADVENTURE (2) [ADVENTURED]
Dt 28:56 which would not a to set the sole of her 5254
Ac 19:31 desiring him that he would not a himself 1325

ADVENTURED (1) [ADVENTURE]
Jdg 9:17 a his life far, and delivered you out of 7993

ADVERSARIES (36) [ADVERSARY]
Ex 23:22 and an adversary unto thine a. 6887
Dt 32:27 lest their a should behave themselves 6862
 32:43 will render vengeance to his a, and will 6862
Jos 5:13 unto him, Art thou for us, or for our a? 6862
1Sa 2:10 The a of the LORD shall be broken to 7378
2Sa 19:22 that ye should this day be a unto me? 7854
Ezr 4: 1 Now when the a of Judah 6862
Ne 4:11 our a said, They shall not know, 6862
Ps 38:20 also that render evil for good are mine a; 7853
 69:19 my dishonour: mine a are all before thee. 6887
 71:13 and consumed that are a to my soul; 7853
 81:14 and turned my hand against their a. 6862
 89:42 Thou hast set up the right hand of his a; 6862
 109: 4 For my love they are my a: but I give 7853
 109:20 Let this be the reward of mine a from 7853
 109:29 Let mine a be clothed with shame, 7853
Isa 1:24 will ease me of mine a, and avenge me 6862
 9:11 Therefore the LORD shall set up the a of 6862
 11:13 and the a of Judah shall be cut off: 6887
 59:18 accordingly he will repay, fury to his a, 6862
 63:18 our a have trodden down thy sanctuary. 6862
 64: 2 boil, to make thy name known to thine a, 6862
Jer 30:16 all thine a, every one of them, shall go 6862
 46:10 that he may avenge him of his a: 6862
 50: 7 their a said, We offend not, because they 6862
La 1: 5 Her a are the chief, her enemies prosper; 6862
 1: 7 the a saw her, and did mock at her 6862
 1:17 that his a should be round about him: 6862
 2:17 he hath set up the horn of thine a. 6862
Mic 5: 9 Thine hand shall be lift up upon thine a, 6862
Na 1: 2 the LORD will take vengeance on his a, 6862
Lk 13:17 that had seen those things, all his a 480
 21:15 which all your a shall not be able to gainsay 480
1Co 16: 9 is opened unto me, and there are many a. 480
Php 1:28 And in nothing terrified by your a: which is 480
Heb 10:27 indignation, which shall devour the a. 5227

ADVERSARY (22) [ADVERSARIES]
Ex 23:22 and an a unto thine adversaries. 6696
Nu 22:22 stood in the way for an a against him. 7854
1Sa 1: 6 her a also provoked her sore, for to make 6869
 29: 4 battle, lest in the battle he be an a to us: 7854
1Ki 5: 4 that there is neither a nor evil occurrent. 7854
 11:14 the LORD stirred up an a unto Solomon, 7854
 11:23 God stirred him up another a, Rezon 7854
 11:25 he was an a to Israel all the days of 7854
Est 7: 6 a and enemy is this wicked Haman. 376+6862
Job 31:35 and that mine a had written a book. 376+7379
Ps 74:10 O God, how long shall the a reproach? 6862
Isa 50: 8 is mine a? let him come near to me. 1167+4941
La 1:10 The a hath spread out his hand upon all 6862
 2: 4 he stood with his right hand as an a, 6862
 4:12 would not have believed that the a 6862
Am 3:11 An a there shall be even round about 6862
Mt 5:25 Agree with thine a quickly, whiles thou art 476
 5:25 lest at any time the a deliver thee to 476
Lk 12:58 When thou goest with thine a to 476
 18: 3 unto him, saying, Avenge me of mine a. 476
1Ti 5:14 give none occasion to the a to speak 480
1Pe 5: 8 because your a the devil, as a roaring lion, 476

ADVERSITIES (2) [ADVERSITY]
1Sa 10:19 who himself saved you out of all your a 7451
Ps 31: 7 trouble; thou hast known my soul in a; 6869

ADVERSITY (10) [ADVERSITIES]
2Sa 4: 9 who hath redeemed my soul out of all a, 6869
2Ch 15: 6 of city: for God did vex them with all a. 6869
Ps 10: 6 not be moved: for I shall never be in a. 7451
 35:15 in mine a they rejoiced, 6761
 94:13 mayest give him rest from the days of a, 7451
Pr 17:17 at all times, and a brother is born for a. 6869
 24:10 If thou faint in the day of a, thy strength 6869
Ecc 7:14 be joyful, but in the day of a consider: 7451
Isa 30:20 though the Lord give you the bread of a, 6862
Heb 13: 3 with them; and them which suffer a, 2558

ADVERTISE (2)
Nu 24:14 I will a thee what this people shall do 3289
Ru 4: 4 I thought to a thee, saying, Buy it 241+1540

ADVICE (9) [ADVISE]
Jdg 19:30 of it, **take a**, and speak your minds. 5779
 20: 7 of Israel; give here your a and counsel. 1697
1Sa 25:33 blessed be thy a, and blessed be thou, 2940
2Sa 19:43 that our a should not be first had in 1697
2Ch 10: 9 What a **give** ye that we may return 3289
 10:14 answered them after the a of the young 6098
 25:17 Amaziah king of Judah **took a**, and sent to 3289
Pr 20:18 by counsel: and with **good a** make war. 8458
2Co 8:10 And herein I give my a: for this is 1106

ADVISE (3) [ADVICE, ADVISED, ADVISEMENT]
2Sa 24:13 now a, and see what answer I shall return 3045
1Ki 12: 6 How do you a that I may answer this 3289
1Ch 21:12 a thyself what word I shall bring again to 7200

ADVISED (2) [ADVISE]
Pr 13:10 but with the **well a** is wisdom. 3289
Ac 27:12 the more part a to depart thence 1012+5087

ADVISEMENT (1) [ADVISE]
1Ch 12:19 for the lords of the Philistines upon a sent 6098

ADVOCATE (1)
1Jn 2: 1 man sin, we have an a with the Father, 3875

AENEAS (2)
Ac 9:33 And there he found a certain man named **A**, 132
 9:34 And Peter said unto him, **A**, Jesus Christ 132

AENON (1)
Jn 3:23 And John also was baptizing in **A** near to 137

AFAR (51) [FAR]
Ge 22: 4 his eyes, and saw the place **a off**. 4480+7350
 37:18 when they saw him **a off**, even 4480+7350
Ex 2: 4 his sister stood **a off**, to wit what 4480+7350
 20:18 it, they removed, and stood **a off**. 4480+7350
 20:21 the people stood **a off**, 4480+7350
 24: 1 of Israel; and worship ye **a off**. 4480+7350
 33: 7 a off from the camp, and called it 7368
Nu 9:10 or be in a journey **a off**, yet he shall keep 7350
1Sa 26:13 and stood on the top of a hill **a off**; 4480+7350
2Ki 2: 7 and stood to view **a off**: 4480+7350
 4:25 the man of God saw her **a off**, 4480+5048
Ezr 3:13 was heard **a off**. 4480+5704+7350+3807.1
Ne 12:43 of Jerusalem was heard **even a off**. 4480+7350
Job 2:12 when they lift up their eyes **a off**, 4480+7350
 36: 3 my knowledge from **a**, 7350
 36:25 see it; man may behold it **a off**. 4480+7350
 39:25 he smelleth the battle **a off**, 4480+7350
 39:29 prey, and her eyes behold **a off**. 4480+7350
Ps 10: 1 Why standest thou **a off**, O LORD? 7350+871.1
 38:11 and my kinsmen stand **a off**. 4480+7350
 65: 5 and of them that are **a off** upon the sea: 7350
 138: 6 but the proud he knoweth **a off**. 4480+4801
 139: 2 understandest my thought **a off**. 4480+7350
Pr 31:14 she bringeth her food from **a**. 4801
Isa 23: 7 own feet shall carry her **a off** to 4480+7350
 49: 1 unto me; and hearken, ye people, from **a**; 7350
 59:14 and justice standeth **a off**: 4480+7350
 66:19 to Tubal, and Javan, to the isles **a off**, 7350
Jer 23:23 the LORD, and not a God **a off**? 4480+7350
 30:10 I will save thee from **a**, and thy seed 7350
 31:10 declare it in the isles **a off**, and say, 4480+4801
 46:27 I will save thee from **a off**, and thy seed 7350
 51:50 remember the LORD **a off**, 4480+7350
Mic 4: 3 and rebuke strong nations **a off**; 5704+7350
Mt 26:58 But Peter followed him **a off** unto the high 3113
 27:55 And many women were there beholding **a** 3113
Mk 5: 6 But when he saw Jesus **a off**, he ran 3113
 11:13 And seeing a fig tree **a off** having leaves, 3113
 14:54 And Peter followed him **a off**, even into 3113
 15:40 There were also women looking on **a off**: 3113
Lk 16:23 and seeth Abraham **a off**, 575+3113
 17:12 men that were lepers, which stood **a off**: 4207
 18:13 standing **a off**, would not lift up so much 3113
 22:54 priest's house. And Peter followed **a off**. 3113
 23:49 stood **a off**, beholding these things. 3113
Ac 2:39 and to all that are **a off**, 1519+3112
Eph 2:17 preached peace to you which were **a off**, 3112
Heb 11:13 but having seen them **a off**, 4207
Rev 18:10 Standing **a off** for the fear of her 575+3113
 18:15 shall stand **a off** for the fear of her 575+3113
 18:17 as many as trade by sea, stood **a off**, 575+3113

AFFAIRS (8)
1Ch 26:32 pertaining to God, and a of the king. 1697
Ps 112: 5 he will guide his a with discretion. 1697

Da 2:49 over the a of the province of Babylon: 5673
 3:12 set over the a of the province of Babylon, 5673
Eph 6:21 But that ye also know my a, 2596+3588
 6:22 that ye might know our a, and that 3588+4012
Php 1:27 or else be absent, I may hear of your a, 4012
2Ti 2: 4 entangleth himself with the a of this life; 4230

AFFECT (2) [AFFECTED, AFFECTETH]
Gal 4:17 They **zealously a** you, but not well; yea, 2206
 4:17 exclude you, that you might a them. 2206

AFFECTED (2) [AFFECT]
Ac 14: 2 made their minds **evil a** against 2559
Gal 4:18 But it is good to be **zealously a** always in 2206

AFFECTETH (1) [AFFECT]
La 3:51 Mine eye a mine heart because of all 5953

AFFECTION (6) [AFFECTIONATELY, AFFECTIONED, AFFECTIONS]
1Ch 29: 3 I have **set** my a to the house of my God, 7521
Ro 1:31 **without natural a**, implacable, unmerciful: 794
2Co 7:15 his **inward a** is more abundant toward 4698
Col 3: 2 **Set** your a on things above, not on things 5426
 3: 5 fornication, uncleanness, **inordinate a**, 3806
2Ti 3: 3 **Without natural a**, trucebreakers, 794

AFFECTIONATELY (1) [AFFECTION]
1Th 2: 8 So being a **desirous** of you, we were 2442

AFFECTIONED (1) [AFFECTION]
Ro 12:10 Be kindly a one to another with brotherly 5387

AFFECTIONS (2) [AFFECTION]
Ro 1:26 this cause God gave them up unto vile a: 3806
Gal 5:24 Christ's have crucified the flesh with the a 3804

AFFINITY (3)
1Ki 3: 1 Solomon **made a** with Pharaoh king of 2859
2Ch 18: 1 in abundance, and **joined a** with Ahab. 2859
Ezr 9:14 **join in a** with the people of these 2859

AFFIRM (3) [AFFIRMED]
Ro 3: 8 and as some a that we say,) 5346
1Ti 1: 7 neither what they say, nor whereof they a. 1226
Tit 3: 8 these things I will that thou a **constantly**, 1226

AFFIRMED (3) [AFFIRM]
Lk 22:59 of one hour after another **confidently a**, 1340
Ac 12:15 But she **constantly a** that it was even so. 1340
 25:19 which was dead, whom Paul a to be alive. 5335

AFFLICT (36) [AFFLICTED, AFFLICTEST, AFFLICTION, AFFLICTIONS]
Ge 15:13 and they shall a them four hundred years; 6031
 31:50 If thou shalt a my daughters, or if thou 6031
Ex 1:11 taskmasters to a them with their burdens. 6031
 22:22 Ye shall not a any widow, or 6031
 22:23 If thou a them **in any wise**, 6031+6031
Lev 16:29 shall a your souls, and do no work at all, 6031
 16:31 ye shall a your souls, by a statute for ever. 6031
 23:27 ye shall a your souls, and offer an offering 6031
 23:32 a sabbath of rest, and ye shall a your souls: 6031
Nu 24:24 shall a Asshur, and shall afflict Eber, 6031
 24:24 shall a Eber, and he also shall perish for 6031
 29: 7 and ye shall a your souls: 6031
 30:13 and every binding oath to a the soul, 6031
Jdg 16: 5 that we may bind him to a him: 6031
 16: 6 wherewith thou mightest be bound to a 6031
 16:19 she began to a him, and his strength went 6031
2Sa 7:10 neither shall the children of wickedness a 6031
1Ki 11:39 I will for this a the seed of David, 6031
2Ch 6:26 from their sin, when thou dost a them; 6031
Ezr 8:21 that we might a ourselves before our God, 6031
Job 37:23 and in plenty of justice: he will not a. 6031
Ps 44: 2 how thou didst a the people, and cast 7489
 55:19 God shall hear, and a them, even he that 6031
 89:22 him; nor the son of wickedness a him. 6031
 94: 5 thy people, O LORD, and a thine heritage. 6031
 143:12 and destroy all them that a my soul: 6887
Isa 51:23 did **more grievously a** her by 3513
 51:23 I will put it into the hand of them that a 3013
 58: 5 a day for a man to a his soul? is it to bow 6031
 64:12 thou hold thy peace, and a us very sore? 6031
Jer 31:28 to throw down, and to destroy, and to a; 7489
La 3:33 For he doth not a willingly nor grieve 6031
Am 5:12 they a the just, they take a bribe, 6887
 6:14 they shall a you from the entering in of 3905
Na 1:12 I have afflicted thee, I will a thee no more. 6031
Zep 3:19 at that time I will undo all that a thee: 6031

AFFLICTED (55) [AFFLICT]
Ex 1:12 the more they a them, the more they 6031
Lev 23:29 whatsoever soul it be that shall not be a 6031
Nu 11:11 Wherefore hast thou a thy servant? 7489
Dt 26: 6 and a us, and laid upon us hard bondage: 6031
Ru 1:21 against me, and the Almighty hath a me? 7489
2Sa 22:28 the a people thou wilt save: but thine eyes 6041
1Ki 2:26 thou hast been a in all where in my father 6031
 2:26 afflicted in all where in my father was a. 6031
2Ki 17:20 a them, and delivered them into the hand 6031
Job 6:14 To him that is a pity should be shewed 4523
 30:11 he hath loosed my cord, and a me, 6031
 34:28 unto him, and he heareth the cry of the a. 6031
Ps 18:27 For thou wilt save the a people; 6041
 22:24 nor abhorred the affliction of the a; 6041

A

Ps	25:16 mercy upon me; for I *am* desolate and a. 6041
	82: 3 fatherless: do justice to the a. and needy. 6041
	88: 7 and thou hast a *me* with all thy waves. 6031
	88:15 I *am* a and ready to die from *my* youth *up*: 6041
	90:15 to the days *wherein* thou hast a us, 6031
	102: T A Prayer of the a, when he is 6041
	107:17 because of their iniquities, are a. 6031
	116:10 therefore have I spoken: I was greatly a: 6031
	119:67 Before I was a I went astray: but now 6031
	119:71 *It is* good for me that I have been a; that I 6031
	119:75 and *that* thou *in* faithfulness hast a me. 6031
	119:107 I am a very much: quicken me, O LORD, 6031
	129: 1 Many a time have they a me from my 6887
	129: 2 Many a time have they a me from my 6887
	140:12 LORD will maintain the cause of the a, 6041
Pr	15:15 All the days of the a *are* evil: but 6041
	22:22 poor: neither oppress the a in the gate: 6041
	26:28 lying tongue hateth *those that are* a by it; 1790
	31: 5 the judgment of any of the a. 1121+6040
Isa	9: 1 when at the first he lightly a the land of 7043
	49:13 people, and will have mercy upon his a. 6041
	51:21 thou a, and drunken, but not with wine: 6041
	53: 4 him stricken, smitten of God, and a. 6031
	53: 7 He was oppressed, and he was a, yet he 6031
	54:11 O thou a, tossed with tempest, *and* 6041
	58: 3 *wherefore* have we a our soul, 6031
	58:10 soul to the hungry, and satisfy the a soul; 6031
	60:14 The sons also of them that a thee shall 6031
	63: 9 In all their affliction he was a, 6862
La	1: 4 her virgins *are* a, and she *is* in bitterness. 3013
	1: 5 for the LORD hath a her for the multitude 3013
	1:12 wherewith the LORD hath a me in the day 3013
Mic	4: 6 that is driven out, and *her* that I have a; 7489
Na	1:12 Though I have a thee, I will afflict thee no 6031
Zep	3:12 I will also leave in the midst of thee an a 6041
Mt	24: 9 Then shall they deliver you up to be a, 2347
2Co	6: 4 And whether we be a, it is for your 2346
1Ti	5:10 the saints' feet, if she have relieved the a, 2346
Heb	11:37 being destitute, a, tormented; 2346
Jas	4: 9 Be a, and mourn, and weep: let your 5003
	5:13 Is any among you a? let him pray. Is any 2553

AFFLICTEST (1) [AFFLICT]

1Ki	8:35 turn from their sin, when thou a them: 6031

AFFLICTION (75) [AFFLICT]

Ge	16:11 because the LORD hath heard thy a. 6040
	29:32 Surely the LORD hath looked upon my a; 6040
	31:42 God hath seen mine a and the labour of 6040
	41:52 me to be fruitful in the land of my a. 6040
Ex	3: 7 I have surely seen the a of my people 6040
	3:17 I will bring you up out of the a of Egypt 6040
	4:31 that he had looked upon their a, 6040
Dt	16: 3 bread therewith, *even* the bread of a; 6040
	26: 7 looked on our a, and our labour, 6040
1Sa	1:11 if thou wilt indeed look on the a of thine 6040
2Sa	16:12 be that the LORD will look on mine a, 5771
1Ki	22:27 feed him with bread of a and with water 3906
	22:27 bread of affliction and with water of a, 3906
2Ki	14:26 For the LORD saw the a of Israel, *that it* 6040
2Ch	18:26 feed him with bread of a and with water 3906
	18:26 bread of affliction and with water of a, 3906
	20: 9 cry unto thee in our a, then thou wilt hear 6869
	33:12 when he was in a, he besought the LORD 6887
Ne	1: 3 there in the province *are* in great a 7451
	9: 9 didst see the a of our fathers in Egypt, 6040
Job	5: 6 Although a cometh not forth of the dust, 205
	10:15 of confusion; therefore see thou mine a; 6040
	30:16 the days of a have taken hold upon me. 6040
	30:27 rested not: the days of a prevented me. 6040
	36: 8 in fetters, *and* be holden in cords of a; 6040
	36:15 He delivereth the poor in his a, 6040
	36:21 for this hast thou chosen rather than a. 6040
Ps	22:24 he hath not despised nor abhorred the a 6039
	25:18 Look upon mine a and my pain; 6040
	44:24 and forgettest our a and our oppression? 6040
	66:11 into the net; thou laidst a upon our loins. 4157
	88: 9 Mine eye mourneth by reason of a: 6040
	106:44 Nevertheless he regarded their a, when he 6862
	107:10 of death, *being* bound in a and iron; 6040
	107:39 low through oppression, a, and sorrow. 7451
	107:41 Yet setteth he the poor on high from a, 6040
	119:50 This *is* my comfort in my a: for thy word 6040
	119:92 I should then have perished in mine a. 6040
	119:153 Consider mine a, and deliver me: for I do 6040
Isa	30:20 the bread of adversity, and the water of a, 3906
	48:10 I have chosen thee in the furnace of a. 6040
	63: 9 In all their a he was afflicted, and the 6869
Jer	4:15 and publisheth a from mount Ephraim. 205
	15:11 in the time of evil, and in the time of a. 6869
	16:19 my fortress, and my refuge in the day of a, 6869
	30:15 Why criest thou for thine a? thy sorrow *is* 7667
	48:16 *is* near to come, and his a hasteth fast. 7451
La	1: 3 Judah is gone into captivity because of a, 6040
	1: 7 Jerusalem remembered in the days of her a 6040
	1: 9 O LORD, behold my a: for the enemy 6040
	3: 1 I *am* the man *that* hath seen a by the rod 6040
	3:19 Remembering mine a and my misery, 6040
Hos	5:15 my face: in their a they will seek me early. 6862
Am	6: 6 they are not grieved for the a of Joseph. 7667
Ob	1:13 shouldest not have looked on their a in 7451
Jnh	2: 1 I cried by reason of mine a unto 6869
Na	1: 9 a shall not rise up the second time. 6869
Hab	3: 7 I saw the tents of Cushan in a: *and* 205
Zec	1:15 and they helped forward the a. 7451

Zec	8:10 that went out or came in because of the a: 6862
	10:11 he shall pass through the sea with a, 6869
Mk	4:17 when a or persecution ariseth for 2347
	13:19 For *in* those days shall be a, such as was 2347
Ac	7:11 the land of Egypt and Canaan, and great a: 2347
	7:34 I have seen the a of my people which is in 2561
2Co	2: 4 For out of much a and anguish of heart I 2347
	4:17 For our light a, which is but for a moment, 2347
	8: 2 that in a great trial of a the abundance 2347
Php	1:16 supposing to add a to my bonds: 2347
	4:14 that ye did communicate with my a. 2347
1Th	1: 6 having received the word in much a, 2347
	3: 7 we were comforted over you in all our a 2347
Heb	11:25 rather to suffer a with the people 4778
Jas	1:27 visit the fatherless and widows in their a, 2347
	5:10 for an example of suffering a, 2552

AFFLICTIONS (13) [AFFLICT]

Ps	34:19 Many *are* the a of the righteous: 7451
	132: 1 LORD, remember David, *and* all his a: 6031
Ac	7:10 And delivered him out of all his a, 2347
	20:23 saying that bonds and a abide me. 2347
2Co	6: 4 in a, in necessities, in distresses, 2347
Col	1:24 fill up that which is behind of the a of 2347
1Th	3: 3 That no *man* should be moved by these a: 2347
2Ti	1: 8 be thou partaker of the a of the gospel 4777
	3:11 Persecutions, a, which came unto me at 3804
	4: 5 But watch thou in all *things*, endure a, 2553
Heb	10:32 ye endured a great fight of a; 3804
	10:33 a gazingstock both by reproaches and a; 2347
1Pe	5: 9 knowing that the same a are accomplished 3804

AFFORDING (1)

Ps	144:13 garners *may be* full, a all manner of store: 6329

AFFRIGHT (1) [AFFRIGHTED]

2Ch	32:18 the wall, to a them, and to trouble them; 3372

AFFRIGHTED (9) [AFFRIGHT]

Dt	7:21 Thou shalt not be a at them: for the LORD 6206
Job	18:20 as they that went before were a. 270+8178
	39:22 He mocketh at fear, and is not a; 2865
Isa	21: 4 My heart panted, fearfulness a me: 1204
Jer	51:32 burnt with fire, and the men of war are a. 926
Mk	16: 5 in a long white garment; and they were a. 1568
	16: 6 he saith unto them, Be not a: Ye seek 1568
Lk	24:37 But they were terrified and a, 1719
Rev	11:13 and the remnant were a, and gave glory to 1719

AFOOT (2) [FOOT]

Mk	6:33 and ran a thither out of all cities, 3979
Ac	20:13 he appointed, minding himself to go a. 3978

AFORE (7) [AFOREHAND, AFORETIME]

2Ki	20: 4 a Isaiah was gone out *into* the middle 3808
Ps	129: 6 which withereth a it groweth up: 6927
Isa	18: 5 For a the harvest, when the bud 6440+3807.1
Eze	33:22 was upon me in the evening, a 6440+3807.1
Ro	2: 2 he had promised a by his prophets 4279
	9:23 which he had a prepared unto glory, 4282
Eph	3: 3 the mystery; (as I wrote a in few *words*, 4270

AFOREHAND (1) [AFORE]

Mk	14: 8 she is come a to anoint my body to 4301

AFORETIME (7) [AFORE]

Ne	13: 5 where a they had a. 6440+3807.1
Job	17: 6 people; and a I was *as* a tabret. 6440+3807.1
Isa	52: 4 My people went down a 7223+871.1+1886.1
Jer	30:20 Their children also shall be as a, 6924
Da	6:10 before his God, as he did a. 1836+4481+6928
Jn	9:13 They brought to the Pharisees him that a 4218
Ro	15: 4 whatsoever *things* were written a were 4270

AFRAID (193) [FEAR]

Ge	3:10 and I was a, because I *was* naked; 3372
	18:15 saying, I laughed not; for she was a. 3372
	20: 8 in their ears: and the men were sore a. 3372
	28:17 he was a, and said, How dreadful *is* this 3372
	31:31 and said to Laban, Because I was a: 3372
	32: 7 Jacob was greatly a and distressed: 3372
	42:28 their heart failed *them*, and they were a, 2729
	42:35 saw the bundles of money, they were a. 3372
	43:18 the men were a, because they were 3372
Ex	3: 6 his face; for he was a to look upon God. 3372
	14:10 marched after them; and they were sore a: 3372
	15:14 The people shall hear, *and be* a: 7264
	34:30 and they were a to come nigh him. 3372
Lev	26: 6 lie down, and none shall make *you* a: 2729
Nu	12: 8 were ye not a to speak against my servant 3372
	22: 3 Moab was sore a of the people, because 1481
Dt	1:17 you shall not be a of the face of man; 1481
	1:29 you, Dread not, neither be a of them. 3372
	2: 4 dwell in Seir; and they shall be a of you: 3372
	5: 5 for ye were a by reason of the fire, 3372
	7:18 Thou shalt not be a of them: *but* shalt 3372
	7:19 unto all the people of whom thou art a. 3373
	9:19 For I was a of the anger 3025
	18:22 thou shalt not be a of him. 1481
	20: 1 people more than thou, be not a of them: 3372
	28:10 of the LORD; and they shall be a of thee. 3372
	28:60 diseases of Egypt, which thou wast a of; 3025
	31: 6 good courage, fear not, nor be a of them: 6206
Jos	1: 9 be not a, neither be thou dismayed: 6206
	9:24 were sore a of our lives because of you, 3372
	11: 6 unto Joshua, Be not a because of them: 3372

Jdg	7: 3 saying, Whosoever *is* fearful and a, let him 2730
Ru	3: 8 that the man was a, and turned himself: 2729
1Sa	4: 7 The Philistines were a, for they said, God 3372
	7: 7 heard *it*, they were a of the Philistines. 3372
	17:11 they were dismayed, and greatly a. 3372
	17:24 the man, fled from him, and were sore a. 3372
	18:12 Saul was a of David, because the LORD 3372
	18:15 himself very wisely, he was a of him. 1481
	18:29 Saul was yet the more a of David; 3372
	21: 1 Ahimelech was a at the meeting of David, 2729
	21:12 and was sore a of Achish the king of Gath. 3372
	23: 3 unto him, Behold, we *be* a here in Judah: 3373
	28: 5 he was a, and his heart greatly trembled. 3372
	28:13 the king said unto her, Be not a: for what 3372
	28:20 was sore a, because of the words of 3372
	31: 4 would not; for he was sore a: 3372
2Sa	1:14 How wast thou not a to stretch forth thine 3372
	6: 9 David was a of the LORD that day, 3372
	14:15 *it is* because the people have made me a: 3372
	17: 2 and weak handed, and will make him a: 2729
	22: 5 the floods of ungodly men made me a; 1204
	22:46 they shall be a out of their close places. 2296
1Ki	1:49 guests that *were* with Adonijah were a, 2729
2Ki	1:15 be not a of him. And he arose, 3372
	10: 4 they were exceedingly a, and said, Behold, 3372
	19: 6 Be not a of the words which thou hast 3372
	25:26 to Egypt: for they were a of the Chaldees. 3372
1Ch	10: 4 would not; for he was sore a. 3372
	13:12 David was a of God that day, saying, 3372
	21:30 for he was a because of the sword of 1204
2Ch	20:15 Be not a nor dismayed by reason of this 3372
	32: 7 be not a nor dismayed for the king of 3372
Ne	2: 2 sorrow of heart. Then I was very sore a, 3372
	4:14 the rest of the people, Be not ye a of them: 3372
	6: 9 they all made us a, saying, Their hands 7503
	6:13 that I should be a, and do so, and sin, 3372
Est	7: 6 Haman was a before the king 1204
Job	3:25 *that* which I was a of is come unto me, 3025
	5:21 neither shalt thou be a of destruction 3372
	5:22 neither shalt thou be a of the beasts of 3372
	6:21 ye see *my* casting down, and are a. 3372
	9:28 I am a of all my sorrows, I know that thou 3025
	11:19 lie down, and none shall make *thee* a; 2729
	13:11 Shall not his excellency make you a? 1204
	13:21 and let not thy dread make me a. 1204
	15:24 Trouble and anguish shall make him a; 1204
	18:11 Terrors shall make him a on every side, 1204
	19:29 Be ye a of the sword: for wrath bringeth 1481
	21: 6 Even when I remember I am a, 926
	23:15 when I consider, I am a of him. 6342
	32: 6 wherefore I was a, and durst not shew 2119
	33: 7 Behold, my terror shall not make thee a, 1204
	39:20 Canst thou make him a as a grasshopper? 7493
	41:25 he raiseth up *himself*, the mighty are a. 1481
Ps	3: 6 I will not be a of ten thousands of people, 3372
	18: 4 the floods of ungodly men made me a. 1204
	18:45 and be a out of their close places. 2727
	27: 1 strength of my life; of whom shall I be a? 6342
	49:16 Be not thou a when one is made rich, 3372
	56: 3 *What* time I am a, I will trust in thee. 3372
	56:11 I will not be a what man can do unto me. 3372
	65: 8 in the uttermost parts are a at thy tokens: 3372
	77:16 O God, the waters saw thee; they were a: 2342
	83:15 and make them a with thy storm. 926
	91: 5 Thou shalt not be a for the terror by night; 3372
	112: 7 He shall not be a of evil tidings: his heart 3372
	112: 8 His heart *is* established, he shall not be a, 3372
	119:120 fear of thee; and I am a of thy judgments. 3372
Pr	3:24 thou liest down, thou shalt not be a: 6342
	3:25 Be not a of sudden fear, neither of 3372
	31:21 She is not a of the snow for her household: 3372
Ecc	12: 5 Also *when* they shall be a of *that which is* 3372
	12: 5 neither fear ye their fear, nor be a. 6206
Isa	8:12 dwellest in Zion, be not a of the Assyrian: 3372
	10:24 Ramah is a; Gibeah of Saul is fled. 2729
	10:29 thy salvation; I will trust, and not be a: 6342
	12: 2 they shall be a: pangs and sorrows shall 926
	13: 8 lie down, and none shall make *them* a. 2729
	17: 2 it shall be a and fear because of the 2729
	19:16 mention thereof shall be a in himself, 6342
	19:17 They shall be a and ashamed of Ethiopia 2865
	20: 5 he will not be a of their voice, nor abase 2865
	31: 4 his princes shall be a of the ensign, 2865
	31: 9 the sinners in Zion are a; fearfulness hath 6342
	33:14 Be not a of the words that thou hast heard, 3372
	37: 6 lift *it* up, be not a; say unto the cities of 3372
	40: 9 the ends of the earth were a, drew near, 2729
	41: 5 Fear ye not, neither be a: have not I told 7297
	44: 8 of men, neither be ye a of their revilings. 2865
	51: 7 thou shouldest be a of a man *that* shall 3372
	57:11 of whom hast thou been a or feared, 1672
Jer	1: 8 Be not a of their faces: for I *am* with thee 3372
	2:12 O ye heavens, at this, and be horribly a, 8175
	10: 5 be a of them; for they cannot do evil, 3372
	26:21 when Urijah heard *it*, he was a, and fled, 3372
	30:10 be quiet, and none shall make *him* a. 2729
	36:16 they were a both one and other, 6342
	36:24 Yet they were not a, nor rent their 6342
	38:19 I am a of the Jews that are fallen to 1672
	39:17 the hand of the men of whom thou *art* a. 3016
	41:18 for they were a of them, because 3372
	42:11 Be not a of the king of Babylon, of whom 3372
	42:11 of the king of Babylon, of whom ye *are* a; 3373
	42:11 be not a of him, saith the LORD: 3372
	42:16 the famine, whereof ye were a, shall 1672

A

Jer	46:27 and at ease, and none shall **make** *him* a.	2729
Eze	2: 6 thou, son of man, be not a of them,	3372
	2: 6 neither be a of their words, though briers	3372
	2: 6 be not a of their words, nor be dismayed	3372
	27:35 their kings shall be **sore** a, they	8175+8178
	30: 9 ships to **make** the careless Ethiopians a,	2729
	32:10 and their kings shall be horribly a for thee,	8175
	34:28 dwell safely, and none shall **make** *them* a.	2729
	39:26 in their land, and none **made** *them* a.	2729
Da	4: 5 I saw a dream which **made** me a,	1763
	8:17 he came, I was a, and fell upon my face:	1204
Joel	2:22 Be not a, ye beasts of the field: for	3372
Am	3: 6 blown in the city, and the people not be a?	2729
Jnh	1: 5 the mariners were a, and cried every man	3372
	1:10 the men **exceedingly** a,	1419+3372+3374
Mic	4: 4 his fig tree; and none shall **make** *them* a:	2729
	7:17 they shall be a of the LORD our God,	6342
Na	2:11 the lion's whelp, and none **made** *them* a?	2729
Hab	2:17 **which made** them a, because of men's	2865
	3: 2 I have heard thy speech, *and* was a:	3372
Zep	3:13 lie down, and none shall **make** *them* a.	2729
Mal	2: 5 he feared me, and was a before my name.	2865
Mt	2:22 of his father Herod, he was a to go thither:	5399
	14:27 saying, Be of good cheer; it is I, be not a.	5399
	14:30 he saw the wind boysterous, he was a;	5399
	17: 6 *it*, they fell on their face, and were sore a.	5399
	17: 7 them, and said, Arise, and be not a.	5399
	25:25 I was a, and went and hid thy talent in	5399
	28:10 said Jesus unto them, Be not a: go tell	5399
Mk	5:15 and in his right mind: and they were a.	5399
	5:36 of the synagogue, Be not a, only believe.	5399
	6:50 Be of good cheer: it is I; be not a.	5399
	9: 6 wist not what to say; for they were **sore** a.	1630
	9:32 not *that* saying, and were a to ask him.	5399
	10:32 and as they followed, they were a.	5399
	16: 8 any *thing* to any *man;* for they were a.	5399
Lk	2: 9 about them: and they were sore a.	5399+5401
	8:25 And they being a wondered, saying one to	5399
	8:35 and in his right mind: and they were a.	5399
	12: 4 Be not a of them that kill the body,	5399
	24: 5 as they were a, and bowed down *their*	1719
Jn	6:19 nigh unto the ship: and they were a.	5399
	6:20 But he saith unto them, It is I; be not a.	5399
	14:27 your heart be troubled, neither let it be a.	1168
	19: 8 heard that saying, he was the more a;	5399
Ac	9:26 they were all a of him, and believed not	5399
	10: 4 he was a, and said, What is it, Lord?	1719
	18: 9 Be not a, but speak, and hold not thy	5399
	22: 9 with me saw indeed the light, and were a;	1719
	22:29 and the chief captain also was a, after he	5399
Ro	13: 3 Wilt thou then not be a of the power?	5399
	13: 4 But if thou do *that which is* evil, be a;	5399
Gal	4:11 I am a of you, lest I have bestowed upon	5399
Heb	11:23 they were not a of the king's	5399
1Pe	3: 6 and are not a *with* any amazement.	5399
	3:14 happy *are ye:* and be not a of their terror,	5399
2Pe	2:10 they are not a to speak evil of dignities.	5141

AFRESH (1) [FRESH]

| Heb | 6: 6 **crucify** to themselves the Son of God a, | 388 |

AFTER (1180) [AFTERWARD, AFTERWARDS, HEREAFTER]

Ge	1:11 the fruit tree yielding fruit a his kind,	3807.1
	1:12 *and* herb yielding seed a his kind,	3807.1
	1:12 whose seed *was* in itself, a his kind:	3807.1
	1:21 a their kind, and every winged fowl	3807.1
	1:21 and every winged fowl a his kind:	3807.1
	1:24 bring forth the living creature a his kind,	3807.1
	1:24 and beast of the earth a his kind:	3807.1
	1:25 God made the beast of the earth a his	3807.1
	1:25 cattle a their kind, and every thing that	3807.1
	1:25 thing that creepeth upon the earth a	3807.1
	1:26 make man in our image, a our likeness:	3509.1
	4:17 of the city, a the name of his son, Enoch.	3509.1
	5: 3 *a son* in his own likeness, a his image;	3509.1
	5: 4 the days of Adam a he had begotten Seth	310
	5: 7 Seth lived a he begat Enos eight hundred	310
	5:10 Enos lived a he begat Cainan eight hundred	310
	5:13 Cainan lived a he begat Mahalaleel eight	310
	5:16 Mahalaleel lived a he begat Jared eight	310
	5:19 Jared lived a he begat Enoch eight hundred	310
	5:22 Enoch walked with God a he begat	310
	5:26 Methuselah lived a he begat Lamech seven	310
	5:30 Lamech lived a he begat Noah five hundred	310
	6: 4 also a that, when the sons of God came in	310
	6:20 Of fowls a their kind, and of cattle after	3807.1
	6:20 their kind, and of cattle a their kind,	3807.1
	6:20 every creeping thing of the earth a his	3807.1
	7:10 it came to pass a seven days, that	3807.1
	7:14 every beast a his kind, and all the cattle	3807.1
	7:14 all the cattle a their kind,	3807.1
	7:14 that creepeth upon the earth a his kind,	3807.1
	7:14 every fowl a his kind, every bird of	3807.1
	8: 3 the end of the hundred and fifty days	4480
	8:19 a their kinds, went forth out of the ark.	3807.1
	9: 9 with you and with your seed a you;	310
	9:28 Noah lived a the flood three hundred	310
	10: 1 and unto them were sons born a the flood.	310
	10: 5 every one a his tongue, after their	3807.1
	10: 5 a their families, in their nations.	3807.1
	10:20 a their families, after their tongues,	3807.1
	10:20 a their tongues, in their countries, *and*	3807.1
	10:31 a their families, after their tongues,	3807.1
	10:31 a their tongues, in their lands, after their	3807.1

Ge	10:31 in their lands, a their nations.	3807.1
	10:32 a their generations, in their nations:	3807.1
	10:32 the nations divided in the earth a the flood.	310
	11:10 and begat Arphaxad two years a the flood:	310
	11:11 Shem lived a he begat Arphaxad five	310
	11:13 Arphaxad lived a he begat Salah four	310
	11:15 Salah lived a he begat Eber four hundred	310
	11:17 Eber lived a he begat Peleg four hundred	310
	11:19 Peleg lived a he begat Reu two hundred	310
	11:21 Reu lived a he begat Serug two hundred	310
	11:23 Serug lived a he begat Nahor two hundred	310
	11:25 Nahor lived a he begat Terah an hundred	310
	13:14 a that Lot was separated from him, Lift up	310
	14:17 the king of Sodom went out to meet him a	310
	15: 1 A these things the word of the LORD came	310
	16: 3 a Abram had dwelt ten years in	4480+7093
	16:13 I also here looked a him that seeth me?	310
	17: 7 thy seed a thee in their generations for an	310
	17: 7 be a God unto thee, and to thy seed a thee.	310
	17: 8 I will give unto thee, and to thy seed a thee,	310
	17: 9 and thy seed a thee in their generations.	310
	17:10 between me and you and thy seed a thee;	310
	17:19 *and* with his seed a him.	310
	18: 5 ye your hearts; *a that* you shall pass on:	310
	18:11 ceased to be with Sarah a the manner of	3509.1
	18:12 A I am waxed old shall I have pleasure,	310
	18:19 his children and his household a him,	310
	18:25 be far from thee to do a this manner,	3509.1
	19: 6 door unto them, and shut the door a him,	310
	19:31 in unto us a the manner of all the earth:	3509.1
	22: 1 it came to pass a these things, that God did	310
	22:20 it came to pass a these things, that it was	310
	23:19 a this, Abraham buried Sarah his wife in	310
	24:55 days; a the least ten; a *that* she shall go.	310
	24:67 Isaac was comforted a his mother's *death.*	310
	25:11 And it came to pass a the death of Abraham,	310
	25:26 a that came his brother out, and his hand	310
	26:18 for the Philistins had stopped them a	310
	26:18 he called their names a the names by	3509.1
	31:23 and pursued a him seven days' journey;	310
	31:30 thou sore longedst a thy father's house,	3807.1
	31:36 that thou hast *so* hotly pursued a me?	310
	32:29 Wherefore *is it that* thou dost ask a my	3807.1
	33: 2 and Leah and her children a, and Rachel	314
	33: 7 a came Joseph near and Rachel,	310
	35: 5 and they did not pursue a the sons of Jacob.	310
	35:12 and to thy seed a thee will I give the land.	310
	36:40 a their places, by their names;	3807.1
	37:17 Joseph went a his brethren, and found them	310
	38:24 it came to pass about three months a, that	4480
	39: 7 it came to pass a these things, that his	310
	39:19 A this manner did thy servant to me;	3509.1
	40: 1 it came to pass a these things, that the	310
	40:13 a the former manner when thou wast	3509.1
	41: 3 seven other kine came up a them out of	310
	41: 6 with the east wind sprang up a them.	310
	41:19 seven other kine came up a them, poor	310
	41:23 with the east wind, sprung up a them:	310
	41:27 ill favoured kine that came up a them *are*	310
	41:30 there shall arise a them seven years of	310
	44: 4 unto his steward, Up, follow a the men;	310
	45:15 and a that his brethren talked with him.	310
	45:23 to his father he sent a this manner;	3509.1
	48: 1 it came to pass a these things, that *one* told	310
	48: 4 will give this land to thy seed a thee *for* an	310
	48: 6 which thou begettest a them, shall be thine,	310
	48: 6 shall be called a the name of their brethren	5921
	50:14 bury his father, a he had buried his father.	310
Ex	3:20 midst thereof: and a that he will let you go.	310
	5:19 they *were* in evil *case,* it was said,	3807.1
	7:25 a *that* the LORD had smitten the river.	310
	10:14 as they, neither a them shall be such.	310
	11: 8 a that I will go out. And he went out from	310
	14: 4 heart, that he shall follow a them;	310
	14: 8 and he pursued a the children of Israel:	310
	14: 9 Egyptians pursued a them (all the horses	310
	14:10 and behold, the Egyptians marched a them;	310
	14:23 went in a them to the midst of the sea,	310
	14:28 of Pharaoh that came into the sea a them;	310
	15:20 the women went out a her with timbrels	310
	16: 1 a their departing out of the land of Egypt.	3807.1
	17: 1 a their journeys, according to	3807.1
	18: 2 Moses' wife, a he had sent her *back,*	310
	21: 9 he shall deal with her a the manner of	3509.1
	23: 2 cause to decline a many to wrest *judgment:*	310
	23:24 nor serve them, nor do a their works:	3509.1
	25: 9 a the pattern of the tabernacle, and	NIH
	25:40 look that thou make *them* a their pattern,	871.1
	28:15 a the work of the ephod thou shalt make	3509.1
	28:43 for ever unto him and his seed a him.	310
	29:29 garments of Aaron shall be his sons' a him,	310
	30:12 of the children of Israel a their number,	3807.1
	30:13 a shekel a the shekel of the sanctuary:	871.1
	30:24 cassia five hundred *shekels,* a the shekel	871.1
	30:25 an ointment compound a the art of	NIH
	30:32 *any other* like it, a the composition of it:	871.1
	30:35 a confection a the art of the apothecary,	NIH
	32: 4 a he had made it a molten calf:	2050.1
	33: 8 man a *the* tent door, and looked a Moses,	310
	34:15 they go a whoring a their gods,	310
	34:16 their daughters go a whoring a their gods,	310
	34:16 make thy sons go a whoring a their gods.	310
	34:27 for a the tenor of these words I have made	5921
	37:19 **made** a the fashion of almonds in one	8246
	38:24 a the shekel of the sanctuary.	871.1

Ex	38:25 a the shekel of the sanctuary:	871.1
	38:26 a shekel, a the shekel of the sanctuary,	871.1
Lev	5:15 a the shekel of the sanctuary, for a	871.1
	11:14 And the vulture, and the kite a his kind;	3807.1
	11:15 Every raven a his kind;	3807.1
	11:16 the cuckow, and the hawk a his kind,	3807.1
	11:19 the heron a her kind, and the lapwing,	3807.1
	11:22 the locust a his kind, and the bald locust	3807.1
	11:22 the bald locust a his kind, and the beetle	3807.1
	11:22 the beetle a his kind, and the	3807.1
	11:22 his kind, and the grasshopper a his kind.	3807.1
	11:29 the mouse, and the tortoise a his kind,	3807.1
	13: 7 a that he hath been seen of the priest for	310
	13:35 if the scall spread much in the skin a his	310
	13:55 shall look on the plague, a *that* it is washed:	310
	13:56 plague *be* somewhat dark a the washing	310
	14: 8 a *that* he shall come into the camp,	310
	14:43 a *that* he hath taken away the stones,	310
	14:43 a he hath scraped the house, and after it is	310
	14:43 scraped the house, and a it is plaistered;	310
	14:48 in the house, a the house was plaistered:	310
	15:28 seven days, and a *that* she shall be clean.	310
	16: 1 the LORD spake unto Moses a the death of	310
	17: 7 a whom they have gone a whoring.	310
	18: 3 A the doings of the land of Egypt,	3509.1
	18: 3 a the doings of the land of Canaan,	3509.1
	19:31 neither seek a wizards, to be defiled by	413
	20: 5 cut him off, and all that go a whoring a him,	310
	20: 6 the soul that turneth a such as have familiar	413
	20: 6 wizards, to go a whoring after them, I will	413
	20: 6 after wizards, to go a whoring a them, I will	310
	23:11 on the morrow a the sabbath the priest	NIH
	23:15 ye shall count unto you from the morrow a	NIH
	23:16 Even unto the morrow a the seventh	NIH
	25:15 According to the number of years a	310
	25:29 may redeem it within a whole year a it is	5704
	25:46 as an inheritance for your children a you,	310
	25:48 A *that* he is sold he may be redeemed	310
	26:33 and will draw out a sword a you:	310
	27: 3 of silver, a the shekel of the sanctuary.	871.1
	27:18 if he sanctify his field a the jubile,	310
Nu	1: 1 in the second year a they were come	3807.1
	1: 2 a their families, by the house of their	3807.1
	1:18 they declared their pedigrees a their	5921
	1:20 *by* their generations, a their families,	3807.1
	1:22 *by* their generations, a their families,	3807.1
	1:24 *by* their generations, a their families,	3807.1
	1:26 *by* their generations, a their families,	3807.1
	1:28 *by* their generations, a their families,	3807.1
	1:30 *by* their generations, a their families,	3807.1
	1:32 *by* their generations, a their families,	3807.1
	1:34 *by* their generations, a their families,	3807.1
	1:36 *by* their generations, a their families,	3807.1
	1:38 *by* their generations, a their families,	3807.1
	1:40 *by* their generations, a their families,	3807.1
	1:42 a their families, by the house of their	3807.1
	1:47 the Levites a the tribe of their fathers	3807.1
	2:34 set forward, every one a their families,	3807.1
	3:15 Number the children of Levi a the house	3807.1
	3:47 a the shekel of the sanctuary shalt thou	871.1
	3:50 *shekels,* a the shekel of the sanctuary:	871.1
	4: 2 a their families, by the house of their	3807.1
	4:15 a that, the sons of Kohath	310+3651+2050.1
	4:29 thou shalt number them a their families,	3807.1
	4:34 sons of the Kohathites a their families,	3807.1
	4:34 and of the house of their fathers,	3807.1
	4:44 those that were numbered of them a	3807.1
	4:46 a their families, and after the house of	3807.1
	4:46 and a the house of their fathers,	3807.1
	6:19 a *the hair of* his separation is shaven:	310
	6:20 and a *that* the Nazarite may drink wine.	310
	6:21 so he must do a the law of his separation.	5921
	7:13 a the shekel of the sanctuary;	871.1
	7:19 a the shekel of the sanctuary;	871.1
	7:25 a the shekel of the sanctuary;	871.1
	7:31 a the shekel of the sanctuary;	871.1
	7:37 a the shekel of the sanctuary;	871.1
	7:43 a the shekel of the sanctuary;	871.1
	7:49 a the shekel of the sanctuary;	871.1
	7:55 a the shekel of the sanctuary;	871.1
	7:61 a the shekel of the sanctuary;	871.1
	7:67 a the shekel of the sanctuary;	871.1
	7:73 a the shekel of the sanctuary;	871.1
	7:79 a the shekel of the sanctuary;	871.1
	7:85 four hundred *shekels,* a the shekel of	871.1
	7:86 a the shekel of the sanctuary:	871.1
	7:88 of the altar, a *that* it was anointed.	310
	8:15 a that shall the Levites go in to do	310+3651
	8:22 a that went the Levites in to do their	310
	9: 1 in the first month of the second year a	3807.1
	9:17 then a that the children of Israel journeyed:	310
	12:14 and a *that* let her be received in *again.*	310
	13:25 searching of the land a forty days.	4480+7093
	14:34 A the number of the days *in* which ye	871.1
	15:13 shall do these *things* a **this manner,**	3602
	15:39 that ye seek not a your own heart	310
	15:39 own eyes, a which ye use to go a whoring:	310
	16:29 if they be visited a the visitation of all men;	NIH
	18:16 a the shekel of the sanctuary, which *is*	871.1
	25: 8 he went a the man of Israel into the tent,	310
	25:13 he shall have it, and his seed a him, *even*	310
	26: 1 it came to pass a the plague, that the LORD	310
	26:12 The sons of Simeon a their families:	3807.1
	26:15 The children of Gad a their families:	3807.1
	26:20 the sons of Judah a their families were,	3807.1

A

Nu	26:23 *Of* the sons of Issachar **a** their families: 3807.1
	26:26 *Of* the sons of Zebulun **a** their 3807.1
	26:28 The sons of Joseph **a** their families *were* 3807.1
	26:35 These *are* the sons of Ephraim **a** their 3807.1
	26:37 These *are* the sons of Joseph **a** their 3807.1
	26:38 The sons of Benjamin **a** their families: 3807.1
	26:41 These *are* the sons of Benjamin **a** their 3807.1
	26:42 These *are* the sons of Dan **a** their 3807.1
	26:42 These *are* the families of Dan **a** their 3807.1
	26:44 *Of* the children of Asher **a** their families: 3807.1
	26:48 *Of* the sons of Naphtali **a** their families: 3807.1
	26:57 numbered of the Levites **a** their families: 3807.1
	27:21 who shall ask *counsel* for him **a** 871.1
	28:24 **A** this **manner** ye shall offer daily, 3509.1
	28:26 **a** your weeks *be out,* ye shall have a holy 871.1
	29:18 to your number, **a** the manner: 3509.1
	29:21 to their number, **a** the manner: 3509.1
	29:24 to your number, **a** the manner: 3509.1
	29:27 to their number, **a** the manner: 3509.1
	29:30 to their number, **a** the manner: 3509.1
	29:33 to their number, **a** the manner: 3509.1
	29:37 to their number, **a** the manner: 3509.1
	30:15 if he shall any ways make them void **a** *that* 310
	32:15 For if ye turn away from **a** him, he will yet 310
	32:42 and called it Nobah, **a** his own name. 871.1
	33: 3 on the morrow **a** the passover the children NIH
	33:38 the fortieth year **a** the children of Israel 3807.1
	35:28 **a** the death of the high priest the slayer 310
Dt	1: 4 **A** he had slain Sihon the king of 310
	1: 8 to give unto them and to their seed **a** them. 310
	3:11 the breadth of it, **a** the cubit of a man. 871.1
	3:14 called them **a** his own name, 5921
	4:37 therefore he chose their seed **a** them, 310
	4:40 with thy children **a** thee, and that thou 310
	4:45 of Israel, **a** they came forth out of Egypt, 310
	4:46 **a** they were come forth out of Egypt: 871.1
	6:14 Ye shall not go **a** other gods, of the gods of 310
	8:19 walk **a** other gods, and serve them, 310
	9: 4 **a** that the LORD thy God hath cast them 871.1
	10:15 he chose their seed **a** them, *even* you 310
	11: 4 to overflow them as they pursued **a** you, 310
	11:28 to go **a** other gods, which ye have not 310
	12: 8 Ye shall not do **a** all *the things* that we 3509.1
	12:15 all thy gates, whatsoever thy soul **lusteth a,** 185
	12:20 eat flesh, whatsoever thy soul **lusteth a.** 185
	12:21 in thy gates whatsoever thy soul **lusteth a.** 185
	12:25 with thee, and with thy children **a** thee, 310
	12:28 and with thy children **a** thee for ever, 310
	12:30 **a** that they be destroyed from before thee; 310
	12:30 thou inquire not **a** their gods, saying, 3807.1
	13: 2 saying, Let us go **a** other gods, which thou 310
	13: 4 Ye shall walk **a** the LORD your God, 310
	14:13 and the kite, and the vulture **a** his kind, 3807.1
	14:14 And every raven **a** his kind, 3807.1
	14:15 the cuckow, and the hawk **a** his kind, 3807.1
	14:18 the heron **a** her kind, and the lapwing, 3807.1
	14:26 money for whatsoever thy soul **lusteth a,** 183
	16:13 **a** that thou hast gathered in thy corn 871.1
	18: 9 thou shalt not learn to do **a** 3509.1
	20:18 That they teach you not to do **a** all their 3509.1
	21:13 **a** that thou shalt go in unto her, 310+3651
	22: 2 shall be with thee until thy brother **seek a** 1875
	24: 4 again to be his wife, that she is defiled; 310
	24: 9 **a** that ye were come forth out of Egypt. 871.1
	28:14 *to* the left, to go **a** other gods to serve them. 310
	29:22 your children that shall rise up **a** you, 310+4480
	31:16 go a whoring **a** the gods of the strangers of 310
	31:27 and how much more **a** my death? 310
	31:29 For I know that **a** my death ye will utterly 310
Jos	1: 1 Now **a** the death of Moses the servant of 310
	2: 5 Pursue **a** them quickly; for ye shall overtake 310
	2: 7 the men pursued **a** them the way to Jordan 310
	2: 7 as soon as they which pursued **a** them were 310
	3: 2 it came to pass **a** three days, that 4480+7097
	3: 3 shall remove from your place, and go **a** it. 310
	5: 4 by the way, **a** they came out of Egypt. 871.1
	5:11 of the land on the **morrow a** the passover, 4283
	5:12 the manna ceased on the **morrow a** they 4283
	6: 9 the rereward came **a** the ark, *the priests* 310
	6:13 the rereward came **a** the ark of the LORD, 310
	6:15 compassed the city **a** the same manner 3509.1
	7:25 a they had stoned them with stones. 2050.1
	8: 6 (For they will come out **a** us) till we have 310
	8:16 Ai were called *together* to pursue **a** them: 310
	8:16 they pursued **a** Joshua, and were drawn 310
	8:17 in Ai or Beth-el, that went not out **a** Israel: 310
	8:17 they left the city open, and pursued **a** Israel. 310
	9:16 it came to pass at the end of three days **a** 310
	10:14 there was no day like that before it or **a** it, 310
	10:19 *but* pursue **a** your enemies, and smite 310
	13:23 the children of Reuben **a** their families, 3807.1
	13:28 the children of Gad **a** their families, 3807.1
	19:47 Dan, **a** the name of Dan their father. 3509.1
	20: 5 if the avenger of blood pursue **a** him, 310
	22:27 and you, and our generations **a** us, 310
	23: 1 it came to pass a long time **a** that 310
	24: 6 the Egyptians pursued **a** your fathers with 310
	24:20 you, **a** that he hath done you good. 310
	24:29 it came to pass **a** these things, that Joshua 310
Jdg	1: 1 Now **a** the death of Joshua it came to pass, 310
	1: 6 and they pursued **a** him, and caught him, 310
	2:10 there arose another generation **a** them, 310
	2:17 they went a whoring **a** other gods, 310
	3:22 the haft also went in **a** the blade; and the 310
	3:28 he said unto them, Follow **a** me: for 310

Jdg	3:28 they went down **a** him, and took the fords 310
	3:31 **a** him was Shamgar the son of Anath, 310
	4:14 mount Tabor, and ten thousand men **a** him. 310
	4:16 Barak pursued **a** the chariots, and after 310
	4:16 **a** him, unto Harosheth of the Gentiles: 310
	5:14 **a** thee, Benjamin, among thy people; out of 310
	6:34 a trumpet; and Abi-ezer was gathered **a** him. 310
	6:35 all Manasseh; who also was gathered **a** him: 310
	7:23 all Manasseh, and pursued **a** the Midianites. 310
	8: 5 I am pursuing **a** Zebah and Zalmunna, 310
	8:12 he pursued **a** them, and took the two kings 310
	8:27 all Israel went thither a whoring **a** it: 310
	8:33 went a whoring **a** Baalim, 310
	10: 1 **a** Abimelech there arose to defend Israel 310
	10: 3 **a** him arose Jair, a Gileadite, 310
	12: 8 **a** him Ibzan of Beth-lehem judged Israel. 310
	12:11 And **a** him Elon, a Zebulonite, judged Israel; 310
	12:13 **a** him Abdon the son of Hillel, a Pirathonite, 310
	13:11 went **a** his wife, and came to the man, 310
	13:18 Why askest thou thus **a** my name, 3807.1
	14: 8 **a** a time he returned to take her, 4480
	15: 1 it came to pass **within a while a,** 3117+4480
	15: 7 I be avenged of you, and **a** *that* I will cease. 310
	16:22 to grow *again* **a** he was shaven. 834+3509.1
	18: 7 **a** the manner of the Zidonians, quiet 3509.1
	18:29 **a** the name of Dan their father, who was 871.1
	19: 3 her husband arose, and went **a** her, to speak 310
	20:45 pursued hard **a** them unto Gidom, 310
Ru	1:15 her gods: return thou **a** thy sister in law. 310
	1:16 *or* to return from *following* **a** thee: 310
	2: 2 glean ears of corn **a** *him* in whose sight I 310
	2: 3 came, and gleaned in the field **a** the reapers: 310
	2: 7 gather **a** the reapers amongst the sheaves: 310
	2: 9 field that they do reap, and go thou **a** them: 310
	2:18 to her that she had reserved **a** she was 4480
	4: 4 to redeem *it* besides thee; and I *am* **a** thee. 310
1Sa	1: 9 So Hannah rose up **a** *they* had eaten in 310
	1: 9 had eaten in Shiloh, and **a** *they* had drunk. 310
	1:20 the time was come about **a** Hannah 2050.1
	5: 9 it was so, that **a** they had carried it about, 310
	6:12 the lords of the Philistines went **a** them unto 310
	7: 2 all the house of Israel lamented **a** 310
	8: 3 but turned aside **a** lucre, and took bribes, 310
	10: 5 **A** that thou shalt come to the hill of God, 310
	11: 5 Saul came **a** the herd out of the field; 310
	11: 7 Whosoever cometh not forth **a** Saul 310
	11: 7 cometh not forth after Saul and **a** Samuel, 310
	12:21 *should ye go* **a** vain *things,* which cannot 310
	13: 4 the people were called together **a** Saul *to* 310
	13:14 the LORD hath sought him a man **a** his 3509.1
	14:12 said unto his armourbearer, Come up **a** me: 310
	14:13 upon his feet, and his armourbearer **a** him: 310
	14:13 and his armourbearer slew **a** him. 310
	14:22 even they also followed hard **a** them in 310
	14:36 Let us go down **a** the Philistines by night, 310
	14:37 of God, Shall I go down **a** the Philistines? 310
	15:31 So Samuel turned again **a** Saul; 310
	17:27 the people answered him **a** this manner, 3509.1
	17:30 and spake **a** the same manner: 3509.1
	17:30 the people answered him again **a** 3509.1
	17:35 I went out **a** him, and smote him, 310
	17:53 returned from chasing **a** the Philistines, 310
	18:30 it came to pass, **a** they went forth, 1767+4480
	20:37 Jonathan cried **a** the lad, and said, *Is* not 310
	20:38 Jonathan cried **a** the lad, Make speed, haste, 310
	22:20 named Abiathar, escaped, and fled **a** David. 310
	23:25 when Saul heard *that,* he pursued **a** David 310
	23:28 Wherefore Saul returned from pursuing **a** 310
	24: 8 and cried **a** Saul, saying, My lord the king. 310
	24:14 **A** whom is the king of Israel come out? 310
	24:14 **a** whom dost thou pursue? after a dead dog, 310
	24:14 dost thou pursue? **a** a dead dog, after a flea. 310
	24:14 dost thou pursue? after a dead dog, **a** a flea. 310
	24:21 that thou wilt not cut off my seed **a** me, 310
	25:13 there went up **a** David about four hundred 310
	25:19 Go on before me; behold, I come **a** you. 310
	25:38 it came to pass about ten days **a,** that NIH
	25:42 damsels of hers that went **a** her; 7272+3807.1
	25:42 and she went **a** the messengers of David, 310
	26: 3 he saw that Saul came **a** him into 310
	26:18 Wherefore doth my lord thus pursue **a** his 310
	30: 8 saying, Shall I pursue **a** this troop? 310
2Sa	1: 1 Now it came to pass **a** the death of Saul, 310
	1: 6 and horsemen **followed hard a** him. 1692
	1:10 I was sure that he could not live **a** *that* he 310
	2: 1 it came to pass **a** this, that David inquired 310
	2:19 Asahel pursued **a** Abner; and in going he 310
	2:24 Joab also and Abishai pursued **a** Abner: 310
	2:25 gathered themselves together **a** Abner, 310
	2:28 stood still, and pursued **a** Israel no more, 310
	3:26 from David, he sent messengers **a** Abner, 310
	5:13 of Jerusalem, **a** he was come from Hebron: 310
	7:12 thy fathers, I will set up thy seed **a** thee, 310
	8: 1 **a** this it came to pass, that David smote 310
	10: 1 it came to pass **a** this, that the king of 310
	11: 1 it came to pass, the year was expired, 3807.1
	11: 3 David sent and inquired the woman. 3807.1
	12:28 I take the city, and it be called **a** my name. 5921
	13: 1 it came to pass **a** this, that Absalom the son 310
	13:17 out from me, and bolt the door **a** her. 310
	13:18 brought her out, and bolted the door **a** her. 310
	13:23 it came to pass **a** two full years, 3807.1
	14:26 two hundred shekels **a** the king's weight. 871.1
	15: 1 it came to pass **a** this, that Absalom 310+4480
	15: 7 it came to pass **a** forty years, 4480+7093

2Sa	15:13 The hearts of the men of Israel are **a** 310
	15:16 and all his household **a** him. 7272+871.1
	15:17 all the people **a** him, and tarried 7272+871.1
	15:18 hundred men which came **a** him 7272+871.1
	17: 1 I will arise and pursue **a** David *this* night: 310
	17: 6 Ahithophel hath spoken **a** this manner: 3509.1
	17: 6 shall we do **a** his saying? if not; speak thou. NIH
	17:21 it came to pass, **a** they were departed, 310
	18:16 the people returned from pursuing **a** Israel: 310
	18:18 he called the pillar **a** his own name: 5921
	18:22 let me, I pray thee, also run **a** Cushi. 310
	20: 2 So every man of Israel went up from **a** 310
	20: 6 pursue **a** him, lest he get him fenced cities, 310
	20: 7 there went out **a** him Joab's men, 310
	20: 7 to pursue **a** Sheba the son of Bichri. 310
	20:10 Abishai his brother pursued **a** Sheba the son 310
	20:11 and he that *is* for David, *let him go* **a** Joab. 310
	20:13 all the people went on **a** Joab, to pursue 310
	20:13 to pursue **a** Sheba the son of Bichri. 310
	20:14 gathered together, and went also **a** him. 310
	21: 1 in the days of David three years, year **a** year; 310
	21:14 And **a** that God was intreated for the land. 310
	21:18 it came to pass **a** this, that there was again 310
	23: 4 out of the earth by clear shining **a** rain. 4480
	23: 9 **a** him *was* Eleazar the son of Dodo 310
	23:10 the people returned **a** him only to spoil. 310
	23:11 **a** him *was* Shammah the son of Agee 310
	24:10 David's heart smote him **a** that he had 310
1Ki	1: 6 and *his* mother bare him **a** Absalom. 310
	1:13 Solomon thy son shall reign **a** me, 310
	1:14 I also will come in **a** thee, and confirm thy 310
	1:17 Solomon thy son shall reign **a** me, 310
	1:20 sit on the throne of my lord the king **a** him. 310
	1:24 Adonijah shall reign **a** me, and he shall sit 310
	1:27 sit on the throne of my lord the king **a** him? 310
	1:30 Solomon thy son shall reign **a** me, 310
	1:35 ye shall come up **a** him, that he may come 310
	1:40 all the people came up **a** him, and the 310
	2:28 for Joab had turned **a** Adonijah, though he 310
	2:28 though he turned not **a** Absalom. 310
	3:12 neither shall there any arise like unto thee. 310
	3:18 came to pass the third day **a** *that* I was 3807.1
	6: 1 eightieth year **a** the children of Israel 3807.1
	7:11 **a** the measures of hewed stones, 3509.1
	7:31 the mouth thereof *was* round **a** the work NIH
	7:37 **A** this *manner* he made the ten bases: 3509.1
	9:21 Their children that were left **a** them in 310
	11: 2 *for* surely they will turn away your heart **a** 310
	11: 4 *that* his wives turned away his heart **a** other 310
	11: 5 For Solomon went **a** Ashtoreth the goddess 310
	11: 5 **a** Milcom the abomination of 310
	11: 6 went not fully **a** the LORD, as *did* David 310
	11:10 that *he* should not go **a** other gods: 310
	11:15 he had smitten every male in Edom; 2050.1
	12:14 spake to them **a** the counsel of the 3509.1
	13:14 went **a** the man of God, and found him 310
	13:23 **a** he had eaten bread, and after he had 310
	13:23 he had eaten bread, and **a** he had drunk, 310
	13:31 it came to pass, **a** he had buried him, that 310
	13:33 **A** this thing Jeroboam returned not from his 310
	15: 4 to set up his son **a** him, and to establish 310
	16:24 **a** the name of Shemer, owner of the hill, 5921
	17: 7 it came to pass **a** a while, that 4480+7093
	17:13 make for thee and for thy 314+871.1+1886.1
	17:17 it came to pass **a** these things, *that* the son 310
	18: 1 it came to pass **a** many days, that the word NIH
	18:28 cut themselves **a** their manner with 3509.1
	19:11 the wind an earthquake; *but* the LORD 310
	19:12 the earthquake a fire; *but* the LORD *was* 310
	19:12 in the fire: and **a** the fire a still small voice. 310
	19:20 ran **a** Elijah, and said, Let me, I pray thee, 310
	19:21 went **a** Elijah, and ministered unto him. 310
	20:15 **a** them he numbered all the people, *even* 310
	21: 1 it came to pass **a** these things, *that* Naboth 310
2Ki	1: 1 Moab rebelled against Israel **a** the death of 310
	5:20 I will run **a** him, and take somewhat of 310
	5:21 So Gehazi followed **a** Naaman. And 310
	5:21 when Naaman saw *him* running **a** him, 310
	6:24 it came to pass **a** this, that Ben-hadad king 310
	7:14 the king sent **a** the host of the Syrians, 310
	7:15 they went **a** them unto Jordan: and lo, all 310
	8: 2 and did **a** the saying of the man of God: 3509.1
	9:25 thou rode together **a** Ahab his father, 310
	9:27 Jehu followed **a** him, and said, Smite him 310
	10:29 to sin, Jehu departed not from **a** them, 310
	14:17 the death of Jehoash son of Jehoahaz king 310
	14:19 they sent **a** him to Lachish, and slew him 310
	14:22 that the king slept with his fathers. 310
	17:15 *went* **a** the heathen that *were* round about 310
	17:33 the manner of the nations whom they 3509.1
	17:34 Unto this day they do **a** the former 3509.1
	17:34 neither do they **a** their statutes, or 3509.1
	17:34 **a** their ordinances, or after the law 3509.1
	17:34 or **a** the law and commandment which 3509.1
	17:40 but they did **a** their former manner. 3509.1
	18: 5 that **a** him was none like him among all 310
	21: 2 **a** the abominations of the heathen, 3509.1
	23: 3 to walk **a** the LORD, and to keep his 310
	23:25 neither **a** him arose there *any* like him. 310
	25: 5 army of the Chaldees pursued **a** the 310
1Ch	2:24 **a** that Hezron was dead in Caleb-ephratah, 310
	5: 1 the genealogy is not to be reckoned **a** 3807.1
	5:25 went a whoring **a** the gods of the people of 310
	6:31 of the LORD, **a** that the ark had rest. 4480
	7: 4 **a** the house of their fathers, 3807.1

A

1Ch 7: 9 the **number** of them, a their **genealogy** 3187
8: 8 of Moab, a he had sent them away; 4480
9:25 *were* to come a seven days from time to 3807.1
10: 2 the Philistines followed hard a Saul, 310
10: 2 followed hard after Saul, and a his sons; 310
11:12 him *was* Eleazar the son of Dodo, 310
14:14 God said unto him, Go not up a them; 310
15:13 that we sought him not a the due order. 3509.1
17:11 that I will raise up thy seed a thee, David 310
18: 1 Now a this it came to pass, that David 310
19: 1 Now it came to pass a this, that Nahash 310
20: 1 that a the year was expired, 6256+3807.1
20: 4 it came to pass a this, that there arose war 310
23:24 These *were* the sons of Levi a the house 3807.1
24:30 These *were* the sons of the Levites a 3807.1
27: 1 Now the children of Israel a their 3807.1
27: 7 of Joab, and Zebadiah his son a him: 310
27:34 Ahithophel *was* Jehoiada the son of 310
28: 8 for an inheritance for your children a 310
29:14 willingly a this *sort?* for all *things* come 3509.1
29:21 on the **morrow** a that day, *even* a 4283

2Ch 1:12 neither shall there any a thee have the like. 310
2:17 a the numbering where*with* David his 310
3: 3 The length *by* cubits a the first measure 871.1
4:20 they should burn a the manner before 3509.1
8: 8 who were left a them in the land, 310
8:13 Even a a certain rate every day, offering 871.1
10: 5 Come again unto me a three days. 5750
10:14 answered them a the advice of the 3509.1
11:16 a them out of all the tribes of Israel such as 310
11:20 a her he took Maachah the daughter of 310
13: 9 have made you priests **the manner of** 3509.1
13:19 Abijah pursued a Jeroboam, and took cities 310
17: 4 and not a the doings of Israel. 3509.1
18: 2 a *certain* years he went down to Ahab to 7093
18:19 one spake saying **a this manner,** 3602
18:19 and another saying **a that manner.** 3602
20: 1 It came to pass a this also, *that* the children 310
20:35 a this did Jehoshaphat king of Judah join 310
21:18 a all this the LORD smote him in his 310
21:19 a the end of two years, 3318+3509.1+6256
22: 4 for they were his counsellers a the death of 310
22: 5 He walked also a their counsel, 871.1
23:21 a that they had slain Athaliah with 2050.1
24: 4 it came to pass a this, *that* Joash was 310
24:17 Now a the death of Jehoiada came 310
25:14 a that Amaziah was come from the 310
25:15 Why hast thou **sought** a the gods of 1875
25:20 because they **sought** a the gods of Edom. 1875
25:25 a the death of Joash son of Jehoahaz king of 310
25:27 Now a the time that Amaziah did turn 4480
25:27 they sent to Lachish a him, and slew him 310
26: 2 a that the king slept with his fathers. 310
26:17 Azariah the priest went in a him, 310
28: 3 burnt his children in the fire a 3509.1
30:16 they stood in their place a their manner, 3509.1
31: 2 the priests and the Levites a their courses, 5921
32: 1 A these things, and the establishment 310
32: 9 A this did Sennacherib king of Assyria send 310
33:14 Now a this he built a wall without the city 310
34: 3 he began to seek a the God of David his 3807.1
34:21 to do a all that is written in this book. 3509.1
34:31 to walk a the LORD, and to keep his 310
35: 4 a your courses, according to the writing 3509.1
35: 5 a the division of the families of the Levites. NIH
35:20 A all this, when Josiah had prepared 310
36:14 transgressed very much a all 3509.1

Ezr 2:61 the Gileadite, and was called a their name: 5921
2:69 gave a their ability unto the treasure 3509.1
3:10 a the ordinance of David king of Israel. 5921
5: 4 said we unto them **a this manner,** What 3660
5:12 a that our fathers had provoked the God 4481
7: 1 Now a these things, in the reign of 310
7:18 and gold, *that* do a the will of your God. 3509.4
7:25 thou, Ezra, a the wisdom of thy God, 3509.4
9:10 O our God, what shall we say a this? 310
9:13 a all that is come upon us for our evil deeds, 310
10:16 a the house of their fathers, and all of 3807.1

Ne 3:16 A him repaired Nehemiah the son of Azbuk, 310
3:17 A him repaired the Levites, Rehum the son 310
3:18 A him repaired their brethren, Bavai the 310
3:20 A him repaired Baruch the son of Zabbai earnestly 310
3:21 A him repaired Meremoth the son of Urijah 310
3:22 a him repaired the priests, the men of 310
3:23 A him repaired Benjamin and Hashub over 310
3:23 A him repaired Azariah the son of Maaseiah 310
3:24 A him repaired Binnui the son of Henadad 310
3:25 A him Pedaiah the son of Parosh. 310
3:27 A them the Tekoites repaired another piece, 310
3:29 A them repaired Zadok the son of Immer 310
3:29 A him repaired also Shemaiah the son of 310
3:30 A him repaired Hananiah the son of 310
3:30 A him repaired Meshullam the son of 310
3:31 A him repaired Malchiah the goldsmith's 310
4:13 I even set the people a *their* families 3807.1
5: 8 We a our ability have redeemed our 3509.1
6: 4 Yet they sent unto me four times a this 3509.1
6: 4 I answered them a the same manner. 3509.1
7:63 *to* wife, and was called a their name. 5921
9:28 a they had rest, they did evil again 3509.1
10:34 the houses of our fathers, at times 3807.1
11: 8 a him Gabbai, Sallai, nine hundred twenty 310
12:32 a them went Hoshaiah, and half of 310
12:38 went over against *them,* and I a them, 310
13: 6 a certain days obtained I *leave* of 7093+3807.1

Ne 13:19 that they should not be opened till a 310
Est 1:22 to every people a their language, 3509.1
2: 1 A these things, when the wrath of king 310
2:12 a that she had been twelve 1961+4480+7093
3: 1 A these things did king Ahasuerus promote 310
3:12 and *to* every people a their language; 3509.1
8: 9 unto every people a their language, 3509.1
9:26 Wherefore they called these days Purim a 5921
Job 3: 1 A this opened Job his mouth, and cursed his 310
10: 6 That thou enquirest a mine iniquity, 3807.1
10: 6 mine iniquity, and searchest a my sin? 3807.1
18:20 They that **come** a *him* shall be astonied at 314
19:26 *though* a my skin *worms* destroy this *body,* 310
21: 3 and a that I have spoken, mock on. 310
21:21 For what pleasure hath he in his house a 310
21:33 every man shall draw a him, as *there are* 310
29:22 A my words they spake not again; 310
30: 5 (they cried a them as *after* a thief;) 5921
30: 5 (they cried after them as *a* a thief;) NIH
31: 7 mine heart walked a mine eyes, and *if any* 310
37: 4 A it a voice roareth: he thundereth with 310
39: 8 and he searcheth a every green thing. 310
39:10 or will he harrow the valleys a thee? 310
41:32 He maketh a path to shine a him; 310
42: 7 that a the LORD had spoken these words 310
42: 8 lest *I* deal with you a your folly, in that ye NIH
42:16 A this lived Job an hundred and forty years, 310
Ps 4: 2 will ye love vanity, *and* **seek** a leasing? 1245
10: 4 will not seek a *God:* God *is* not in all his NIH
16: 4 a another *god:* their drink offerings of blood NIH
27: 4 I desired of the LORD, that will I **seek** a; 1245
28: 4 give them a the work of their hands; 3509.1
35: 4 and put to shame that **seek** a my soul: 1245
38:12 They also that **seek** a my life lay snares 1245
40:14 confounded together that **seek** a my soul 1245
42: 1 As the hart panteth a the water brooks, so 5921
42: 1 so panteth my soul a thee, O God. 413
49:11 they call *their* lands a their own names. 5921
49:17 his glory shall not descend a him. 310
51: T a he had gone in to Bath-sheba. 834+3509.1
54: 3 me, and oppressors **seek** a my soul: 1245
63: 8 My soul followeth hard a thee: thy right 310
68:25 the players on instruments *followed* a; 310
70: 2 and confounded that **seek** a my soul: 1245
78:34 they returned and **inquired early** a God. 7836
86:14 of violent *men* have **sought** a my soul; 1245
103:10 He hath not dealt with us a our sins; 3509.1
104:21 The young lions roar a *their* prey, 3807.1
110: 4 Thou *art* a priest for ever a the order of 5921
119:40 Behold, I have longed a thy precepts; 3807.1
119:85 pits for me, which *are* not a thy law. 3509.1
119:88 Quicken me a thy lovingkindness; so 3509.1
119:150 They draw nigh that **follow** a mischief: 7291
143: 6 soul *thirsteth* a thee, as a thirsty land. 3807.1
144:12 polished *a* the similitude of a palace: NIH
Pr 2: 3 if thou criest a knowledge, *and* liftest up 3807.1
6:25 **Lust** not a her beauty in thine heart; 2530
7:22 He goeth a her straightway, as an ox goeth 310
15: 9 he loveth him that **followeth** a 7291
20: 7 his integrity: his children *are* blessed a him. 310
20:25 which *is* holy, and a vows to make inquiry. 310
21:21 He that **followeth** a righteousness 7291
28:19 he that **followeth** a vain *persons* shall 7291
Ecc 1:11 are to come with *those* that shall come a. 314
2:12 for what *can* the man *do* that cometh a 310
2:18 should leave it unto the man that shall be a 310
3:22 shall bring him to see what shall be a him? 310
4:16 they also that **come** a shall not rejoice in 314
6:12 for who can tell a man what shall be a him 310
7:14 to the end that man should find nothing a 310
9: 3 they live, and a that *they go* to the dead. 310
10:14 what shall be a him, who can tell 310+4480
11: 1 for thou shalt find it a many days. 871.1
12: 2 nor the clouds return a the rain: 310
SS 1: 4 Draw me, we will run a thee: the king hath 310
Isa 1:23 one loveth gifts, and **followeth** a rewards: 7291
5:17 shall the lambs feed a their manner, 3509.1
10:24 staff against thee, a the manner of Egypt. 871.1
10:26 shall he lift it up a the manner of Egypt. 871.1
11: 3 he shall not judge a the sight of his eyes, 3807.1
11: 3 neither reprove a the hearing of his ears: 3807.1
23:15 a the end of seventy years shall Tyre sing 4480
23:17 it shall come to pass a the end of seventy 4480
24:22 and a many days shall they be visited. 4480
43:10 no God formed, neither shall there be a me. 310
44:13 maketh a the figure of a man, 3509.1
45:14 they shall come a thee, in chains they shall 310
49:20 a thou hast lost the other, shall say again in NIH
51: 1 to me, ye that **follow** a righteousness, 7291
65: 2 *that was* not good, a their own thoughts; 310
Jer 2: 2 when thou wentest a me in the wilderness, 310
2: 5 have walked a vanity, and are become vain? 310
2: 8 and walked a *things that* do not profit. 310
2:23 am not polluted, I have not gone a Baalim? 310
2:25 I have loved strangers, and a them will I go. 310
3: 7 I said a she had done all these *things,* Turn 310
3:17 neither shall they walk any more a 310
5: 8 every one neighed a his neighbour's wife. 413
7: 6 neither walk a other gods to your hurt: 310
7: 9 and walk a other gods whom ye know not; 310
8: 2 a whom they have walked, and whom they 310
9:14 have walked a the imagination of their own 310
9:14 a Baalim, which their fathers taught them: 310
9:16 I will send a sword a them, till I have 310
9:22 as the handful a the harvestman, 310+4480

Jer 11:10 and they went a other gods to serve them: 310
12: 6 yea, they have called a multitude a thee: 310
12:15 a that I have plucked them out, I will 310
13: 6 it came to pass a many days, that 4480+7093
13: 9 A this manner will I mar the pride of 3602
13:10 walk a other gods, to serve them, 310
16:11 have walked a other gods, and have served 310
16:12 ye walk every one a the imagination of his 310
16:16 a will I send for many hunters, 310
18:12 we will walk a our own devices, and we 310
23:17 they say *unto* every one that walketh a 871.1
24: 1 a that Nebuchadrezzar king of Babylon had 310
25: 6 go not a other gods to serve them, 310
25:26 the king of Sheshach shall drink a them. 310
28:12 a that Hananiah the prophet had broken 310
29: 2 (A that Jeconiah the king, and the queen, 310
29:10 That a seventy years be 6310+3807.1
30:17 This *is* Zion, whom no man **seeketh** a. 1875
30:18 the palace shall remain a the manner 5921
31:19 Surely a that I was turned, I repented; 310
31:19 a that I was instructed, I smote upon *my* 310
31:33 A those days, saith the LORD, I will put 310
32:18 into the bosom of their children a them: 310
32:39 good of them, and of their children a them: 310
34: 8 a that the king Zedekiah had made a 310
35:15 go not a other gods to serve them, 310
36:27 a that the king had burnt the roll, and 310
39: 5 the Chaldeans' army pursued a them, 310
40: 1 a that Nebuzar-adan the captain of the 310
41: 4 it came to pass the second day a *he* had 3807.1
41:16 a *that* he had slain Gedaliah the son of 310
42: 7 it came to pass a ten days, that 4480+7093
42:16 shall follow close a you there *in* Egypt; 310
49:37 I will send the sword a them, till I have 310
50:21 waste and utterly destroy a them, saith 310
51:46 a that in *another* year *shall come* a rumour, 310
52: 8 the army of the Chaldeans pursued a 310
Eze 5: 2 and I will draw out a sword a them. 310
5:12 and I will draw out a sword a them. 310
6: 9 eyes, which go a whoring a their idols: 310
7:27 I will do unto them a their way, 4480
9: 5 Go ye a him through the city, and smite: 310
11:12 have done a the manners of the heathen 3509.1
11:21 *them* whose heart walketh a the heart 413
12:14 and I will draw out the sword a them. 310
16:23 it came to pass a all thy wickedness, (woe, 310
16:47 Yet hast thou not walked a their ways, 871.1
16:47 ways, nor done a their abominations: 871.1
20:16 for their heart went a their idols. 310
20:24 and their eyes were a their fathers' idols. 310
20:30 Are ye polluted a the manner of your 871.1
20:30 ye whoredom a their abominations? 310
23:15 a the manner of the Babylonians of NIH
23:30 thou hast gone a whoring a the heathen, 310
23:45 they shall judge them a the manner of 4941
23:45 a the manner of *women* that shed blood; 4941
23:48 all women may be taught not to do a 3509.1
29:16 when they shall look a them: 310
33:20 I will judge you every one a his ways. 3509.1
33:31 *but* their heart goeth a their covetousness. 310
34: 6 and none did search or seek a *them.* NIH
36:11 I will settle you a your old estates, 3509.1
38: 8 A many days thou shalt be visited: in 4480
39:14 a the end of seven months shall they 4480
39:26 A that they have borne their shame, 2050.1
40: 1 in the fourteenth year a that the city was 310
40:21 the arches thereof were a the measure 3509.1
40:22 *were* a the measure of the gate that 3509.1
40:24 A that he brought me toward the south, 2050.1
41: 5 A he measured the wall of the house, 2050.1
43:13 these *are* the measures of the altar a 871.1
44:10 which went astray away from me a their 310
44:26 a he is cleansed, they shall reckon unto him 310
45:11 the measure thereof shall be a the homer. 413
46:12 a his going forth *one* shall shut the gate. 310
46:17 of liberty; a, it shall return to the prince: 2050.1
46:19 A, he brought me through the entry, 310
48:31 the gates of the city *shall be* a the names 5921
Da 2:39 a thee shall arise another kingdom inferior 870
3:29 other God that can deliver a this *sort.* 3509.4
4:26 a that thou shalt have known that 4481
7: 6 A this I beheld, and lo another, like a 870
7: 7 A this I saw in the night visions, and 870
7:24 another shall rise a them; and he shall be 311
8: 1 a that which appeared unto me at the first. 310
9:26 a threescore and two weeks shall Messiah 310
11:13 shall certainly come a certain years with a 7093
11:18 A this shall he turn his face unto the 2050.1
11:23 the league *made* with him he shall work 4480
Hos 2: 5 for she said, I will go a my lovers, that give 310
2: 7 she shall **follow** a her lovers, but she shall 7291
2:13 and she went a her lovers, and forgat me, 310
5: 8 cry aloud *at* Beth-aven, a thee, O Benjamin. 310
5:11 he willingly walked a the commandment. 310
6: 2 A two days will he revive us: in the third 4480
7: 4 ceaseth from raising a *he* hath kneaded 4480
11:10 They shall walk a the LORD: he shall roar 310
12: 1 on wind, and **followeth** a the east wind: 7291
Joel 2: 2 ever the like, neither shall be any more a it, 310
Am 2: 4 err, a the which their fathers have walked: 310
2: 7 That pant a the dust of the earth on 5921
4: 4 *and* your sins a three years: 3807.1
4:10 I have sent among you the pestilence a 871.1
7: 1 *it was* the latter growth a the king's 310
Zec 2: 8 A the glory hath he sent me unto the 310

A

| Zec | 6: 6 the white go forth **a** them; | 310+413 |

Mt
1:12 And **a** they were brought to Babylon, 3326
3:11 but he that cometh **a** me is mightier than I, 3694
5: 6 do hunger and thirst **a** righteousness: NIG
5:28 lust **a** her hath committed adultery with 1937
6: 9 **A** this manner therefore pray ye: 3779
6:32 **a** all these *things* do the Gentiles **seek**): 1934
10:38 and followeth **a** me, is not worthy of me. 3694
12:39 adulterous generation **seeketh a** a sign; 1934
15:12 were offended, **a** they heard *this* saying? NIG
15:23 saying, Send her away; for she crieth **a** us. 3693
16: 4 adulterous generation **seeketh a** a sign; 1934
16:24 If any **man** will come **a** me, let him deny 3694
17: 1 And **a** six days Jesus taketh Peter, James, 3326
18:32 Then his lord, **a** that he had called him, NIG
23: 3 and do; but do not ye **a** their works: 2596
24:29 Immediately **a** the tribulation of those days 3326
25:19 **A** a long time the lord of those servants 3326
26: 2 Ye know that **a** two days is *the feast of* 3326
26:32 But **a** I am risen *again*, I will go 3326+3588
26:73 And **a** a while came unto *him* they that 3326
27:31 And **a** that they had mocked him, they 3753
27:53 And came out of the graves **a** his 3326
27:63 yet alive, **A** three days I will rise *again*. 3326

Mk
1: 7 There cometh one mightier than I **a** me, 3694
1:14 Now **a** that John was put in prison, 3326+3588
1:17 Come ye **a** me, and I will make you to 3694
1:20 with the hired servants, and went **a** him. 3694
1:36 they that were with him **followed a** him. 2614
2: 1 And again he entered into Capernaum **a** 1223
4:28 then the ear, **a** that the full corn in the ear. 1534
8:12 Why doth this generation **seek a** a sign? 1934
8:25 **A** that he put *his* hands again upon his 1534
8:31 and be killed, and **a** three days rise again. 3326
8:34 unto them, Whosoever will come **a** me, 3694
9: 2 a six days Jesus taketh with *him* Peter, 3326
9:31 **a** that he is killed, he shall rise the third NIG
12:34 And no *man* **a** that durst ask him *any* 3765
13:24 in those days, **a** that tribulation, the sun 3326
14: 1 **A** two days was *the feast of* the passover, 3326
14:28 But **a** that I am risen, I will go 3326+3588
14:70 And a little **a**, they that stood by said again 3326
16:12 **A** that he appeared in another form unto 3326
16:14 them which had seen him **a** he was risen. 3326
16:19 So then **a** the Lord had spoken unto 3326+3588

Lk
1:24 And **a** those days his wife Elisabeth 3326
1:59 him Zacharias, **a** the name of his father. 1909
2:27 to do for him **a** the custom of the law, 2596
2:42 they went up to Jerusalem **a** the custom of 2596
2:46 *that* **a** three days they found him in 3326
5:27 And **a** these *things* he went forth, and saw 3326
6: 1 to pass on the **second** sabbath **a** the first, 1207
7:11 it came to pass the *day* **a**, 1722+1836+3588
9:23 If any *man* will come **a** me, let him deny 3694
9:28 And it came to pass about an eight days **a** 3326
10: 1 **A** these *things* the Lord appointed other 3326
12: 4 and **a** that have no more that *they* can do. 3326
12: 5 which **a** he hath killed hath power 3326+3588
12:30 *things* do the nations of the world **seek a**: 1934
13: 9 **a** that thou shalt cut it down. 1519+3195+3588
14:27 and come **a** me, cannot be my disciple. 3694
14:29 **a** he hath laid the foundation, and is not 2443
15: 4 and go **a** that which is lost, until he find it? 1909
15:13 And not many days **a** the younger son 3326
17:23 see there: **go** not **a** *them*, nor follow *them*. 565
19:14 and sent a message **a** him, saying, 3694
20:40 And **a** that they durst not ask him any 3765
21: 8 draweth near: **go** ye not therefore **a** them. 3694
21:26 for **looking a** those *things* which are 4329
22:20 Likewise also the cup **a** supper, saying, 3326
22:58 And **a** a little while another saw him, 3326
22:59 about the **space** of one hour **a** another 1339
23:26 laid the cross, that *he* might bear *it* **a** Jesus. 3693
23:55 **followed a**, and beheld the sepulchre, 2628

Jn
1:15 He that cometh **a** me is preferred before 3694
1:27 who coming **a** me is preferred before me, 3694
1:30 **A** me cometh a man which is preferred 3694
1:35 Again the next day **a** John stood, and two NIG
2: 6 **a** the manner of the purifying of the Jews, 2596
2:12 **A** this he went down to Capernaum, he 3326
3:22 **A** these *things* came Jesus and his disciples 3326
4:43 Now **a** two days he departed thence, 3326
5: 1 **A** this there was a feast of the Jews; 3326
5: 4 first **a** the troubling of the water stepped 3326
6: 1 **A** these *things* Jesus went over the sea of 3326
6:23 bread, **a** that the Lord had given thanks:) NIG
7: 1 **A** these *things* Jesus walked in Galilee: 3326
8:15 Ye judge **a** the flesh; I judge no *man*. 2596
11: 7 Then **a** that saith he to *his* disciples, Let us 3326
11:11 and **a** that he saith unto them, Our friend 3326
12:19 behold, the world is gone **a** him. 3694
13: 5 **A** that, he poureth water into a bason, 1534
13:12 So **a** he had washed their feet, 3753
13:27 And **a** the sop Satan entered into him. 3326
19:28 **A** this, Jesus knowing that all *things* were 3326
19:38 And **a** this Joseph of Arimathea, being a 3326
20:26 And **a** eight days again his disciples were 3326
21: 1 **A** these *things* Jesus shewed himself again 3326
21:14 **a** that he was risen from the dead. NIG

Ac
1: 2 **a** that he through the Holy Ghost had given NIG
1: 3 **a** his passion by many infallible 3326+3588
1: 8 **a** that the Holy Ghost is come upon you: NIG
3:24 from Samuel and those that **follow a**, 2517
5: 4 and **a** it was sold, was it not in thine own NIG

Ac
5: 7 it was about the **space** of three hours **a**, 1292
5:37 **A** this *man* rose up Judas of Galilee in 3326
5:37 and drew away much people **a** him: 3694
7: 5 and to his seed **a** him, when *as yet* he had 3326
7: 7 and **a** that shall they come forth, 3326
7:36 **a** that he had shewed wonders and signs in NIG
7:45 also our fathers that **came a** brought 1237
9:23 And **a** that many days were fulfilled, 5613
10:24 And the morrow **a** they entered into NIG
10:37 **a** the baptism which John preached; 3326
10:41 with him **a** he rose from the dead. 3326+3588
12: 4 intending **a** Easter to bring him forth to 3326
13:15 And **a** the reading of the law 3326
13:20 And **a** that he gave *unto them* judges 3326
13:22 a man **a** mine own heart, which shall fulfil 2596
13:25 But behold, there cometh *one* **a** me, 3326
13:36 he had served his own generation by NIG
14:24 And **a** they had passed throughout Pisidia, NIG
15: 1 *said*, Except ye be circumcised **a** NIG
15:13 And **a** they had held their peace, 3326+3588
15:16 **A** this I will return, and will build again 3326
15:17 That the residue of men might **seek a** 1567
15:23 they wrote *letters* by them **a** this manner; 3592
15:33 And **a** they had tarried *there* a space, NIG
15:36 And some days **a** Paul said unto Barnabas, 3326
16: 7 **A** they were come to Mysia, they assayed NIG
16:10 And **a** he had seen the vision, 5613
16:17 if haply they might **feel a** him, 5584
18: 1 **A** these *things* Paul departed from Athens, 3326
18:18 And Paul **a** this tarried *there* yet a good NIG
18:23 And **a** he had spent some time there, he NIG
19: 4 believe on him which should come **a** him, 3326
19:21 **A** these *things* were ended, Paul purposed 5613
19:21 saying, **A** I have been there, 3326+3588
20: 1 And **a** the uproar was ceased, Paul 3326+3588
20: 6 And we sailed away from Philippi **a** 3326
20:18 **a** what manner I have been with you at 4459
20:29 that **a** my departing shall grievous wolves 3326
20:30 *things*, to draw away disciples **a** them. 3694
21: 1 that **a** we were gotten from them, NIG
21:15 And **a** those days we took up our carriages, 3326
21:21 neither to walk **a** the customs. NIG
21:36 For the multitude of the people followed **a**, NIG
22:29 **a** he knew that he was a Roman, NIG
23: 3 for sittest thou to judge me **a** the law, 2596
23:25 And he wrote a letter **a** this manner: 4023
24: 1 And **a** five days Ananias the high priest 3326
24:10 **a** that the governor had beckoned unto NIG
24:14 that **a** the way which they call heresy, so 2596
24:17 Now **a** many years I came to bring alms to 1223
24:24 And **a** a certain days, when Felix came with 3326
24:27 But **a** two years Porcius Festus came into 4137
25: 1 **a** three days he ascended from Cesarea to 3326
25:13 And **a** a certain days king Agrippa 1230
25:26 O king Agrippa, that, **a** examination had, NIG
26: 5 that **a** the most straitest sect of our religion 2596
27:14 But not long **a** there arose against it a 3326
27:21 But **a** long abstinence Paul stood 5119+5225
28: 6 but **a** they had looked a great while, NIG
28:11 And **a** three months we departed in a ship 3326
28:13 And **a** one day the south wind blew, 3326
28:17 that **a** three days Paul called the chief of 3326
28:25 **a** that Paul had spoken one word, NIG

Ro
2: 5 But **a** thy hardness and impenitent heart 2596
3:11 there is none that seeketh **a** God. 1567
5:14 even over them that had not sinned **a** 1909
6:19 I speak **a** the manner of men because of 442
7:22 I delight in the law of God **a** the inward 2596
8: 1 in Christ Jesus who walk not **a** the flesh, 2596
8: 1 walk not after the flesh, but **a** the Spirit. 2596
8: 4 who walk not **a** the flesh, but after 2596
8: 4 walk not after the flesh, but **a** the Spirit. 2596
8: 5 For they that are **a** the flesh do mind 2596
8: 5 they *that* are **a** the Spirit the *things* of 2596
8:12 not to the flesh, to live **a** the flesh. 2596
8:13 For if ye live **a** the flesh, ye shall die: 2596
9:30 which followed not **a** righteousness, NIG
9:31 which followed **a** the law of righteousness, NIG
10:20 manifest unto them that **asked** not **a** me, 1905
14:19 follow **a** the *things* which make for peace, NIG

1Co
1:21 For **a** that in the wisdom of God the world 1804
1:22 a sign, and the Greeks **seek a** wisdom: 2212
1:26 how that not many wise *men* **a** the flesh, 2596
7: 7 his proper gift of God, one **a** this manner, 3779
7: 7 one after this manner, and another **a** that. 3779
7:40 is happier if she so abide, **a** my judgment: 2596
10: 6 to the intent we should not **lust a** evil 1938
10:18 Behold Israel **a** the flesh: are not they 2596
11:25 **A** the same manner also *he* took the cup, 5615
12:28 **a** that miracles, then gifts of healings, 1899
14: 1 **Follow** a charity, and desire spiritual *gifts*, 1377
15: 6 **A** that, he was seen of above five hundred 1899
15: 7 **A** that, he was seen of James; then of all 1899
15:32 If **a** the manner of men I have fought 2596

2Co
5:16 Wherefore henceforth know we no man **a** 2596
5:16 though we have known Christ **a** the flesh, 2596
7: 9 for ye were made sorry **a** a godly **manner**, 2596
7:11 *thing*, that ye sorrowed **a** a godly **sort**, 2596
9:14 which **long a** you for the exceeding grace 1971
10: 3 in the flesh, we do not war **a** the flesh: 2596
10: 7 Do ye look on *things* **a** the outward 2596
11:17 I speak *it* not **a** the Lord, but as *it were* 2596
11:18 Seeing that many glory **a** the flesh, I will 2596

Gal
1:11 which was preached of me is not **a** man. 2596
1:18 Then **a** three years I went up to Jerusalem 3326

Gal
2: 1 Then fourteen years **a** I went up again to 1223
2:14 livest **a** the manner of Gentiles, and not 1483
3:15 Brethren, I speak **a** the manner of men; 2596
3:17 was four hundred and thirty years **a**, 3326
3:25 But **a** that faith is come, we are no longer NIG
4: 9 **a** that ye have known God, or rather are NIG
4:23 of the bondwoman was born **a** the flesh; 2596
4:29 that was born **a** the flesh persecuted him 2596
4:29 persecuted him that was *born* **a** the Spirit, 2596

Eph
1:11 all *things* **a** the counsel of his own will: 2596
1:13 In whom ye also **trusted, a** that ye heard NIG
1:13 in whom also **a** that ye believed, ye were NIG
1:15 **a** I heard of your faith in the Lord Jesus, NIG
4:24 which **a** God is created in righteousness 2596

Php
1: 8 how *greatly* I **long a** you all in the bowels 1971
2:26 For he **longed a** you all, and *was* full of 1971
3:12 I follow **a**, if that I may apprehend *that* for NIG

Col
2: 8 and vain deceit, **a** the tradition of men, 2596
2: 8 **a** the rudiments of the world, and not after 2596
2: 8 rudiments of the world, and not **a** Christ. 2596
2:22 **a** the commandments and doctrines of 2596
3:10 **a** the image of him that created him: 2596

1Th
2: 2 But even **a** that we had suffered before, NIG

2Th
2: 9 *Even him*, whose coming is **a** the working 2596
3: 6 not **a** the tradition which he received of 2596

1Ti
5:15 For some are already turned aside **a** Satan. 3694
5:24 judgment; and some *men* they **follow a**. 1872
6:10 which while some **coveted a**, they have 3713
6:11 these *things;* and follow **a** righteousness, NIG

2Ti
4: 3 **a** their own lusts shall they heap to 2596

Tit
1: 1 the acknowledging of the truth which is **a** 2596
1: 4 *mine* own son **a** the common faith: 2596
3: 4 But **a** that the kindness and love of God 3753
3:10 A man *that is* a heretick **a** the first 3326

Heb
3: 5 those *things* which were to be spoken **a**; NIG
4: 7 saying in David, To day, **a** so long a time; 3326
4:11 lest any *man* fall **a** the same example of 1722
5: 6 priest for ever **a** the order of Melchisedec. 2596
5:10 Called of God a high priest **a** the order of 2596
6:15 And so, **a** he had patiently endured, NIG
6:20 made a high priest for ever **a** the order of 2596
7: 2 and **a** that also King of Salem, which is, 1899
7:11 should rise **a** the order of Melchisedec, 2596
7:11 and not be called **a** the order of Aaron? 2596
7:15 for that **a** the similitude of Melchisedec 2596
7:16 not **a** the law of a carnal commandment, 2596
7:16 but **a** the power of an endless life. 2596
7:17 Thou *art* a priest for ever **a** the order of 2596
7:21 Thou *art* a priest for ever **a** the order of 2596
8:10 make with the house of Israel **a** those days, 3326
9: 3 And **a** the second vail, the tabernacle 3326
9:17 For a testament *is* of force **a** men are dead: 1909
9:27 men once to die, but **a** this the judgment: 3326
10:12 But this *man*, **a** he had offered one sacrifice NIG
10:15 to us: for **a** that *he* had said before, 3326+3588
10:16 that I will make with them **a** those days, 3326
10:26 For if we sin wilfully **a** that *we* have 3326+3588
10:32 which, **a** ye were illuminated, ye endured NIG
10:36 that, **a** ye have done the will of God, NIG
11: 8 he should a receive for an inheritance, 3195
11:30 **a** they were compassed about seven days. NIG
12:10 days chastened *us* **a** their own pleasure; 2596

Jas
3: 9 which are made **a** the similitude of God. 2596

1Pe
3: 5 For **a** this manner in the old time the 3779
5:10 **a** that ye have suffered a while, make you NIG

2Pe
1:15 **a** my decease to have these *things* always 3326
2: 6 *them* an ensample unto those that **a** 3195
2:10 But chiefly them that walk **a** the flesh in 3694
2:20 For if **a** they have escaped the pollutions of NIG
2:21 **a** they have known *it*, to turn from the holy NIG
3: 3 days scoffers, walking **a** their own lusts, 2596

2Jn
: 6 love, that we walk **a** his commandments. 2596

3Jn
: 6 forward on their journey **a** a godly **sort**, 516

Jude
: 7 and going a strange flesh, are set forth for 3694
:11 **ran greedily a** the error of Balaam for 1632
:16 complainers, walking **a** their own lusts; 2596
:18 should walk **a** their own ungodly lusts. 2596

Rev
4: 1 **A** this I looked, and behold, a door *was* 3326
7: 1 And **a** these *things* I saw four angels 3326
7: 9 **A** this I beheld, and, lo, a great multitude, 3326
11:11 And **a** three days and a half the spirit of life 3326
12:15 his mouth water as a flood **a** the woman, 3694
13: 3 and all the world wondered **a** the beast. 3694
15: 5 And **a** that I looked, and behold, the 3326
18: 1 And **a** these *things* I saw another angel 3326
18:14 And the fruits that thy soul **lusted a** are 1939
19: 1 And **a** these *things* I heard a great voice of 3326
20: 3 **a** that he must be loosed a little season. 3326

AFTERNOON (1)

| Jdg | 19: 8 they tarried until **a**, | 3117+5186+1886.1 |

AFTERWARD (64) [AFTER]

Ge
10:18 were the families of the Canaanites spread 310
15:14 **a** shall they come out with great 310+3651
32:20 before me, and **a** I will see his face; 310+3651
38:30 **a** came out his brother, that had the scarlet 310

Ex
5: 1 **a** Moses and Aaron went in, 310
34:32 **a** all the children of Israel came nigh: 310+3651

Lev
14:19 and **a** he shall kill the burnt offering: 310
14:36 the priest shall go in to see 310+3651
16:26 in water, and **a** come into the camp. 310+3651
16:28 and **a** he shall come into the camp. 310+3651
22: 7 shall **a** eat of the holy *things*; because it *is* 310

Nu
5:26 **a** shall cause the woman to drink the water. 310

Nu	12:16 **a** the people removed from Hazeroth,	310
	19: 7 **a** he shall come into the camp, and the	310
	31: 2 **a** shalt thou be gathered unto thy people.	310
	31:24 clean, and a ye shall come into the camp.	310
	32:22 **a** ye shall return, and be guiltless before	310
Dt	17: 7 **a** the hands of all the	314+871.1+1886.1
	24:21 of thy vineyard, thou shalt not glean *it* **a**:	310
Jos	2:16 be returned: and **a** may ye go your way.	310
	8:34 **a** he read all the words of the law,	310+3651
	10:26 **a** Joshua smote them, and slew	310+3651
	24: 5 amongst them: and **a** I brought you out.	310
Jdg	1: 9 **a** the children of Judah went down to fight	310
	7:11 **a** shall thine hands be strengthened to go	310
	16: 4 it came to pass **a**, that he loved a woman	310
	19: 5 *with* a morsel of bread, and **a** go your way.	310
1Sa	24: 5 it came to pass **a**, that David's heart	310+3651
	24: 8 David also rose **a**, and went out of	310+3651
2Sa	3:28 **a** when David heard *it*,	310+3651+4480
1Ch	2:21 Hezron went in to the daughter of Machir	310
2Ch	35:14 **a** they made ready for themselves,	310
Ezr	3: 5 **a** *offered* the continual burnt	310+3651
Ne	6:10 **A** I came *unto* the house of Shemaiah	2050.1
Ps	73:24 thy counsel, and **a** receive me *to* glory.	310
Isa	1:26 **a** thou shalt be called, The city of	310+3651
	9: 1 **a** did more grievously afflict *her by* the way	314
Jer	21: 7 **a**, saith the LORD, I will deliver	310+3651
	49: 6 **a** I will bring again the captivity of	310+3651
Eze	41: 1 **A** he brought me to the temple,	2050.1
	43: 1 **A** he brought me to the gate, *even*	2050.1
	47: 1 **A** he brought me again unto the door of	2050.1
	47: 5 **A** he measured a thousand; *and it was*	2050.1
Da	8:27 **a** I rose up, and did the king's business;	2050.1
Hos	3: 5 **A** shall the children of Israel return,	310
Joel	2:28 shall come to pass **a**, that I will pour	310+3651
Mt	4: 2 and forty nights, he was **a** hungered.	5306
	21:29 I will not: but **a** he repented, and went.	5306
	21:32 ye, when ye had seen *it*, repented not **a**,	5306
	25:11 **A** came also the other virgins, saying,	5306
Mk	4:17 **a**, when affliction or persecution ariseth	1534
	16:14 **A** he appeared unto the eleven as they sat	5306
Lk	4: 2 when they were ended, he **a** hungered.	5306
	8: 1 And it came to pass **a**, that	1722+2517+3588
	17: 8 and **a** thou shalt eat and drink?	3326+3778
	18: 4 but **a** he said within himself,	3326+3778
Jn	5:14 **a** Jesus findeth him in the temple,	3326+3778
Ac	13:21 **And a** they desired a king: and God gave	2547
1Co	15:23 **a** they that are Christ's at his coming.	1899
	15:46 *is* natural; and **a** *that which is* spiritual.	1899
Heb	4: 8 not **a** have spoken of another day.	3326+3778
	12:11 nevertheless **a** it yieldeth the peaceable	5306
	12:17 For ye know how that **a**, when he would	3347
Jude	1: 5 **a** destroyed them that believed not.	1208

AFTERWARDS (15) [AFTER]

Ge	30:21 **a** she bare a daughter, and called her name	310
Ex	11: 1 **a** he will let you go hence:	310+3651
Dt	13: 9 to death, and **a** the hand of all the people.	314
1Sa	9:13 *and* **a** they eat that be bidden.	310+3651
Job	18: 2 end of words? mark, and **a** we will speak.	310
Pr	20:17 but **a** his mouth shall be filled *with* gravel.	310
	24:27 thyself in the field; and **a** build thine house.	310
	28:23 **a** shall find more favour than he that	310
	29:11 mind: but a wise *man* keepeth it in *till* **a**.	268
Jer	34:11 **a** they turned, and caused the	310+3651
	46:26 **a** it shall be inhabited, as *in* the days	310+3651
Eze	11:24 **A** the spirit took me up, and brought me	2050.1
Jn	13:36 me now; but thou shalt follow me **a**.	5306
Gal	1:21 **A** I came into the regions of Syria	1899
	3:23 shut up unto the faith which should **a** be	3195

AGABUS (2)

Ac	11:28 And there stood up one of them named **A**,	13
	21:10 from Judea a certain prophet, named **A**.	13

AGAG (8) [AGAGITE]

Nu	24: 7 his king shall be higher than **A**,	90
1Sa	15: 8 he took **A** the king of the Amalekites alive,	90
	15: 9 Saul and the people spared **A**, and the best	90
	15:20 and have brought **A** the king of Amalek,	90
	15:32 Bring you hither to me **A** the king of	90
	15:32 **A** came unto him delicately. And Agag said,	90
	15:32 **A** said, Surely the bitterness of death is past.	90
	15:33 Samuel hewed **A** in pieces before the LORD	90

AGAGITE (5) [AGAG]

Est	3: 1 Haman the son of Hammedatha the **A**,	91
	3:10 unto Haman the son of Hammedatha the **A**,	91
	8: 3 to put away the mischief of Haman the **A**,	91
	8: 5 by Haman the son of Hammedatha the **A**,	91
	9:24 the **A**, the enemy of all the Jews,	91

AGAIN (672)

Ge	4: 2 she bare his brother Abel. And Abel was	3254
	4:25 Adam knew his wife **a**; and she bare a son,	5750
	8:10 **a** he sent forth the dove out of the ark;	3254
	8:12 which returned not **a** unto him any more.	3254
	8:21 I will not **a** curse the ground any more for	3254
	8:21 neither will I **a** smite any more every *thing*	3254
	14:16 also **brought a** his brother Lot,	7725
	15:16 generation they shall **come** hither **a**:	7725
	18:29 he spake unto him **yet a**, and said,	3254+5750
	19: 9 they said **a**, This one *fellow* came in to	NIH
	22: 5 yonder and worship, and **come a** to you.	7725
	24: 5 **must** I **needs bring** thy son **a** unto	7725+7725
	24: 6 thou that thou **bring** not my son thither **a**.	7725

Ge	24: 8 my oath: only **bring** not my son thither **a**.	7725
	24:20 ran **a** unto the well to draw *water*,	5750
	25: 1 **a** Abraham took a wife, and her name *was*	3254
	26:18 Isaac digged **a** the wells of water,	7725
	28:15 and will **bring** thee **a** into this land;	7725
	28:21 So that I **come a** to my father's house in	7725
	29: 3 **put** the stone **a** upon the well's mouth in	7725
	29:33 she conceived **a**, and bare a son; and said,	5750
	29:34 she conceived **a**, and bare a son; and said,	5750
	29:35 she conceived **a**, and bare a son:	5750
	30: 7 Bilhah Rachel's maid conceived **a**,	5750
	30:19 Leah conceived **a**, and bare Jacob the sixth	5750
	30:31 for me, I will **a** feed *and* keep thy flock:	7725
	35: 9 God appeared unto Jacob **a**, when he came	5750
	37:14 with the flocks; and **bring** me word **a**.	7725
	37:22 their hands, to deliver him to his father **a**.	7725
	38: 4 she conceived **a**, and bare a son;	7725
	38: 5 **yet a** conceived, and bare a son;	3254+5750
	38: 9 son. And he knew her **a** no more.	3254
	40:21 **restored** the chief butler unto his	
	butlership **a**	7725
	42:24 returned to them **a**, and communed with	NIH
	42:37 my hand, and I will **bring** him to thee **a**.	7725
	43: 2 said unto them, **Go a**, buy us a little food.	7725
	43:12 money that was **brought a** in the mouth	7725
	43:12 of your sacks, **carry** *it* in your hand;	7725
	43:13 brother, and arise, **go a** unto the man:	7725
	43:21 we have **brought** it **a** in our hand.	7725
	44: 8 we **brought a** unto thee out of the land of	7725
	44:25 father said, **Go a**, *and* buy us a little food.	7725
	46: 4 I will also surely bring thee up **a**:	NIH
	48:21 **bring** you **a** unto the land of your fathers.	7725
	50: 5 and bury my father, and I will **come a**.	7725
Ex	4: 7 he said, **Put** thine hand into thy bosom **a**.	7725
	4: 7 he **put** his hand into his bosom **a**;	7725
	4: 7 behold, it was **turned a** as his *other* flesh.	7725
	8: 8 and Aaron were **brought a** unto Pharaoh:	7725
	10:29 spoken well, I will see thy face **a** no more.	3254
	14:13 ye shall see them **a** no more for ever.	3254
	14:26 that the waters may **come a** upon	7725
	15:19 the LORD **brought a** the waters of the sea	7725
	21:19 If he **rise a**, and walk abroad upon his	6965
	23: 4 shalt **surely bring** it **back** to him **a**.	7725+7725
	24:14 ye here for us, until we **come a** unto you:	7725
	33:11 he **turned a** into the camp: but his servant	7725
	34:35 Moses **put** the vail upon his face **a**, until	7725
Lev	13: 6 the priest shall look on him **a** the seventh	8145
	13: 7 he shall see **a** of the priest **a**:	8145
	13:16 Or if the raw flesh **turn a**, and be changed	7725
	13:39 the priest shall **come a** the seventh day,	7725
	14:43 if the plague **come a**, and break out in	7725
	20: 2 **A**, thou shalt say to the children of	2050.1
	24:20 in a man, so shall it be done to him **a**.	NIH
	25:48 After *that* he is sold he may be redeemed **a**;	NIH
	25:51 **give** a the price of his redemption out of	7725
	25:52 unto his years shall he **give** *him* **a**	7725
	26:26 they shall **deliver** *you* your bread **a** by	7725
Nu	11: 4 children of Israel also wept **a**, and said,	7725
	12:14 and after *that* let her be received in **a**.	NIH
	12:15 journeyed not till Miriam was brought in **a**.	NIH
	17:10 **Bring** Aaron's rod **a** before the Testimony,	7725
	22: 8 *this* night, and I will **bring** you word **a**,	7725
	22:15 Balak sent yet **a** princes, more,	3254
	22:25 foot against the wall: and he smote her **a**.	3254
	22:34 if it displease thee, I will **get** me **back a**.	7725
	23:16 and said, **Go a** unto Balak, and say thus.	7725
	32:15 he will yet **a** leave them in the wilderness;	3254
	33: 7 **turned a** unto Pi-hahiroth, which *is* before	7725
	35:32 he should **come a** to dwell in the land,	7725
Dt	1:22 **bring** us word **a** by what way we must go	7725
	1:25 unto us, and **brought** us word **a**, and said,	7725
	5:30 Go say to them, **Get** you into your tents **a**.	7725
	13:16 be a heap for ever; it shall not be built **a**.	5750
	15: 3 Of a foreigner thou mayest exact *it* **a**:	NIH
	18:16 Let me not hear **a** the voice of the LORD	3254
	22: 1 shalt **in any case bring** them **a**	7725+7725
	22: 2 after it, and thou shalt **restore** it to him **a**.	7725
	22: 4 **surely** help him to **lift** *them* **up a**.	6965+6965
	23:11 is down, he shall **come** into the camp **a**.	NIH
	24: 4 away, may not take her **a** to be his wife,	7725
	24:13 **In any case** thou shalt **deliver** him	
	the pledge **a**	7725+7725
	24:19 in the field, thou shalt not **go a** to fetch it:	7725
	24:20 thou shalt not go over the boughs **a**:	310
	28:68 the LORD shall **bring** thee *into* Egypt **a**	7725
	28:68 unto thee, Thou shalt see it no more **a**:	7725
	30: 9 for the LORD will **a** rejoice over thee for	7725
	33:11 them that hate him, that they rise **not a**.	4480
Jos	5: 2 circumcise **a** the children of Israel	7725
	8:21 they **turned a**, and slew the men of Ai.	7725
	14: 7 I **brought** him word **a** as *it was* in mine	7725
	18: 4 of them; and they shall come **a** to me.	NIH
	18: 8 land, and describe it, and **come a** to me,	7725
	18: 9 and came **a** to Joshua to the host *at* Shiloh.	NIH
	22:28 that we may say **a**, Behold the pattern of	NIH
	22:32 of Israel, and **brought** them word **a**.	7725
Jdg	3:12 the children of Israel did evil **a** in the sight	3254
	3:19 he himself **turned a** from the quarries that	7725
	4: 1 the children of Israel **a** did evil in the sight	3254
	4:20 **A** he said unto her, Stand in the door of	2050.1
	6:18 he said, I will tarry until thou **come a**.	7725
	8: 9 saying, When I **come a** in peace, I will	7725
	8:33 that the children of Israel **turned a**,	7725
	9:37 Gaal spake **a** and said, See there	3254+5750
	10: 6 the children of Israel did evil **a** in the sight	3254

Jdg	11: 8 Therefore we **turn a** to thee now, that	7725
	11: 9 If ye **bring** me **home a** to fight against	7725
	11:13 therefore **restore** those *lands* peaceably.	7725
	11:14 Jephthah sent messengers **a** unto	3254+5750
	13: 1 the children of Israel did evil **a** in the sight	3254
	13: 8 God which thou didst send come **a** unto	5750
	13: 9 the angel of God came **a** unto the woman	5750
	15:19 his spirit **came a**, and he revived:	7725
	16:22 head began to grow **a** after he was shaven.	NIH
	19: 3 friendly unto her, *and* to **bring** her **a**,	7725
	19: 7 urged him: therefore he lodged there **a**.	7725
	20:22 set *their* **battle** in array in the place	3254
	20:23 Shall I go *up* **a** to battle against the	3254
	20:25 of Israel **a** eighteen thousand men;	5750
	20:28 Shall I **yet a** go out to battle against	3254+5750
	20:41 when the men of Israel turned **a**, the men	NIH
	20:48 the men of Israel **turned a** upon	7725
	21:14 Benjamin **came a** at that time;	7725
Ru	1:11 Naomi said, **Turn a**, my daughters: why	7725
	1:12 **Turn a**, my daughters, go *your way*; for I	7725
	1:14 they lift up their voice, and wept **a**:	5750
	1:21 the LORD hath **brought** me *home* **a**	7725
	4: 3 that is **come a** out of the country of Moab,	7725
1Sa	3: 5 he said, I called not; lie down **a**. And he	7725
	3: 6 the LORD called yet **a**, Samuel.	3254
	3: 6 I called not, my son; lie down **a**.	7725
	3: 8 the LORD called Samuel **a** the third time.	3254
	3:21 the LORD appeared **a** in Shiloh: for	3254
	4: 5 a great shout, so that the earth **rang a**.	1949
	5: 3 took Dagon, and **set** him in his place **a**.	7725
	5:11 let it **go a** to his own place, that it slay us	7725
	6:21 The Philistines have **brought a** the ark of	7725
	9: 8 the servant answered Saul **a**, and said,	3254
	15:25 pardon my sin, and **turn a** with me,	7725
	15:30 and before Israel, and **turn a** with me,	7725
	15:31 So Samuel **turned a** after Saul;	7725
	16:10 **A**, Jesse made seven of his sons to pass	2050.1
	17:30 people answered him **a** after the former	7725
	19: 8 there was war **a**: and David went out,	3254
	19:15 Saul sent the messengers **a** to see David,	NIH
	19:21 Saul sent messengers **a** the third time,	3254
	20:17 Jonathan **caused** David to swear **a**,	3254
	23: 4 David inquired of the LORD yet **a**.	3254
	23:23 and **come** ye **a** to me with the certainty,	7725
	25:12 **went a**, and came and told him all those	7725
	27: 4 *to* Gath: and he sought no more **a** for him.	3254
	29: 4 return, that he may **go a** to his place,	7725
	30:12 he had eaten, his spirit **came a** to him:	7725
2Sa	1: 9 He said unto me, Stand, I pray thee,	2050.1
	2:22 Abner said **a** to Asahel, Turn thee	3254+5750
	3:11 he could not answer Abner a word **a**,	5750
	3:26 which **brought** him **a** from the well of	7725
	3:34 And all the people wept **a** over him.	3254
	5:22 the Philistines came up yet **a**,	3254
	6: 1 **A**, David gathered together all	5750+2050.1
	12:23 can I bring him back **a**? I shall go to him,	5750
	14:13 in that the king doth not **fetch** *home* **a** his	7725
	14:14 which cannot be gathered up **a**; neither	NIH
	14:21 **bring** the young man Absalom **a**.	7725
	14:29 when he sent **a** the second time, he would	7725
	15: 8 **bring** me **a indeed** *to* Jerusalem,	7725+7725
	15:25 he will **bring** me **a**, and shew me *both* it,	7725
	15:29 Abiathar **carried** the ark of God **a** to	7725
	16:19 **a**, whom should I serve? *should I* not	8145
	18:22 said Ahimaaz the son of Zadok **yet a**	3254+5750
	19:24 departed until the day he came **a** in peace.	NIH
	19:30 forasmuch as my lord the king is come **a** in	NIH
	19:37 Let thy servant, I pray thee, **turn back a**	7725
	20:10 to the ground, and strake him not **a**;	8138
	21:15 the Philistines had **yet a** war with	5750
	21:18 there was **a** a battle with the Philistines	5750
	21:19 there was **a** a battle in Gob with	5750
	22:38 **turned** not **a** until I had consumed them.	7725
	24: 1 **a** the anger of the LORD was kindled	3254
1Ki	1:45 thence rejoicing, so that the city **rang a**.	1949
	2:30 Benaiah **brought** the king word **a**, saying,	7725
	2:41 from Jerusalem *to* Gath, and was **come a**.	7725
	8:33 shall **turn a** to thee, and confess thy name,	7725
	8:34 **bring** them **a** unto the land which thou	7725
	12: 5 yet *for* three days, then **come a** to me.	7725
	12:12 saying, **Come** to me **a** the third day.	7725
	12:20 Israel heard that Jeroboam was **come a**,	7725
	12:21 to **bring** the kingdom **a** to Rehoboam	7725
	12:27 shall the heart of this people **turn a** unto	7725
	12:27 and **go a** to Rehoboam king of Judah.	7725
	13: 4 so that he could not **pull** it **a** to him.	7725
	13: 6 that my hand may be **restored** me **a**.	7725
	13: 6 the king's hand was **restored** him **a**,	7725
	13: 9 nor **turn a** by the *same* way that thou	7725
	13:17 nor **turn a** to go by the way that thou	7725
	13:33 made **a** of the lowest of the people priests	7725
	17:21 let this child's soul **come** into him **a**.	7725
	17:22 the soul of the child **came** into him **a**,	7725
	18:37 *that* thou hast turned their heart back **a**.	322
	18:43 *is* nothing. And he said, **Go a** seven times.	7725
	19: 6 he did eat and drink, and laid him down **a**.	7725
	19: 7 the angel of the LORD **came a** the second	7725
	19:20 he said unto him, **Go back a**: for what	7725
	20: 5 the messengers **came a**, and said,	7725
	20: 9 and **brought** him word **a**.	7725
2Ki	1: 6 **turn a** unto the king that sent you,	7725
	1:11 **A** also he sent unto him another captain of	7725
	1:13 he sent **a** a captain of the third fifty with	7725
	2:18 when they **came a** to him, (for he tarried	7725
	4:22 I may run to the man of God, and **come a**.	7725

A

2Ki	4:29	answer him not **a**: and lay my staff upon	NIH
	4:31	Wherefore he **went a** to meet him,	7725
	4:38	Elisha **came a** to Gilgal: and *there was a*	7725
	4:43	He said **a**, Give the people, that they	2050.1
	5:10	thy flesh shall **come a** to thee,	7725
	5:14	his flesh **came a** like unto the flesh of a	7725
	5:26	turned **a** from his chariot to meet thee?	NIH
	7: 8	went and hid *it;* and **came a**,	7725
	9:18	came to them, but he **cometh** not **a**.	7725
	9:20	came even unto them, and **cometh** not **a**:	7725
	9:36	Wherefore they **came a**, and told him.	7725
	13:25	Jehoash the son of Jehoahaz took **a** out of	7725
	19: 9	he sent messengers **a** unto Hezekiah,	7725
	19:30	of Judah shall *yet* **a** take root downward,	3254
	20: 5	**Turn a**, and tell Hezekiah the captain of	7725
	21: 3	For he built *up* **a** the high places which	7725
	22: 9	and **brought** the king word **a**, and said,	7725
	22:20	And they **brought** the king word **a**.	7725
	24: 7	the king of Egypt came not **a** any more out	3254
1Ch	13: 3	let us **bring a** the ark of our God to us:	5437
	14:13	the Philistines yet **a** spread	3254+5750
	14:14	Therefore David inquired **a** of God;	5750
	20: 5	there was war **a** with the Philistines,	5750
	20: 6	yet **a** there was war at Gath, where was a	5750
	21:12	advise thyself what word I shall **bring a** to	7725
	21:27	he **put up** his sword **a** into the sheath	7725
2Ch	6:25	**bring** them **a** unto the land which thou	7725
	10: 5	**Come a** unto me after three days.	7725
	10:12	saying, **Come a** to me on the third day.	7725
	11: 1	that *he might* **bring** the kingdom **a** to	7725
	12:11	**brought** them **a** into the guard chamber.	7725
	13:20	Neither did Jeroboam recover strength **a**	5750
	18:18	**A** he said, Therefore hear the word of	2050.1
	18:32	they turned back **a** from pursuing him.	NIH
	19: 4	he went out **a** through the people from	7725
	20:27	of them, to **go a** to Jerusalem with joy;	7725
	24:11	and took it, and **carried** it **a** to his place **a**.	7725
	24:19	to them, to **bring** them **a** unto the LORD;	7725
	25:10	to go home **a**: wherefore their anger was	NIH
	28:11	me therefore, and **deliver** the captives **a**,	7725
	28:17	For **a** the Edomites had come	5750
	30: 6	**turn a** unto the LORD God of Abraham,	7725
	30: 9	For if ye **turn a** unto the LORD,	7725
	30: 9	so that *they shall* **come a** into this land:	7725
	32:25	Hezekiah **rendered** not **a** according to	7725
	33: 3	For he built **a** the high places which	7725
	33:13	**brought** him **a** *to* Jerusalem into his	7725
	34:16	brought the king word back **a**, saying,	5750
	34:28	So they **brought** the king word **a**.	7725
Ezr	2: 1	**came a** unto Jerusalem and Judah,	7725
	4:13	the walls set up **a**, *then* will they not pay	NIH
	4:16	if this city be builded **a**, and the walls	NIH
	6: 5	brought **a** unto the temple which *is* at	NIH
	6:21	which were **come a** out of captivity,	7725
	9:14	Should we **a** break thy commandments,	7725
Ne	7: 6	**came a** to Jerusalem and to Judah,	7725
	8:17	**come a** out of the captivity made booths,	7725
	9:28	they had rest, they did evil **a** before thee:	7725
	9:29	that *thou* mightest **bring** them **a** unto thy	7725
	13: 9	**brought** I **a** the vessels of the house	7725
	13:21	if ye **do** *so* **a**, I will lay hands on you.	8138
Est	4:10	**a** Esther spake unto Hatach,	2050.1
	6:12	Mordecai **came a** to the king's gate.	7725
	7: 2	the king said **a** unto Esther on the second	1571
	8: 3	And Esther spake yet **a** before the king,	3254
Job	2: 1	**A** there was a day when the sons of God	2050.1
	6:29	yea, return **a**, my righteousness *is* in it.	7725
	10: 9	and wilt thou **bring** me into dust **a**?	7725
	10:16	a thou shewest thyself marvellous upon	NIH
	12:14	it cannot be built **a**: he shutteth up a man,	NIH
	12:23	the nations, and straiteneth them **a**.	NIH
	14: 7	that it will sprout **a**, and that the tender	5750
	14:14	shall he live **a**? all the days of my appointed	NIH
	20:15	riches, and he shall vomit them up **a**:	NIH
	29:22	After my words they spake not **a**;	8138
	34:15	and man shall **turn a** unto dust.	7725
Ps	18:37	neither did I **turn a** till they were	7725
	37:21	The wicked borroweth, and **payeth** not **a**:	7999
	60: 1	been displeased; O **turn** thyself to us **a**.	7725
	68:22	The Lord said, I will **bring a** from Bashan,	7725
	68:22	I will **bring** *my people* **a** from the depths	7725
	71:20	shalt quicken me **a**, and shalt bring me up	7725
	71:20	shalt bring me up **a** from the depths of	7725
	78:39	that passeth away, and **cometh** not **a**.	7725
	80: 3	**Turn** us **a**, O God, and cause thy face to	7725
	80: 7	**Turn** us **a**, O God *of* hosts, and cause thy	7725
	80:19	**Turn** us **a**, O LORD God *of* hosts,	7725
	85: 6	Wilt thou not revive us **a**: that thy people	NIH
	85: 8	his saints: but let them not turn **a** to folly.	7725
	104: 9	*that* they **turn** not **a** to cover the earth.	7725
	107:26	the heaven, they go down **a** *to* the depths:	NIH
	107:39	**A**, they are minished and brought low	2050.1
	126: 1	When the LORD **turned a** the captivity of	7725
	126: 4	**Turn a** our captivity, O LORD, as	7725
	126: 6	**doubtless come a** with rejoicing,	935+935
	140:10	into deep pits, *that* they **rise** not **up a**.	6965
Pr	2:19	None that go *unto* her return **a**, neither	NIH
	3:28	and **come a**, and to morrow I will give;	7725
	19:17	which he hath given will he **pay** him **a**.	7999
	19:19	deliver *him*, yet thou must **do** *it* **a**.	3254+5750
	19:24	not so much as **bring** it to his mouth **a**.	7725
	23:35	shall I awake? I will seek it **yet a**.	3254+5750
	24:16	*man* falleth seven *times*, and riseth up **a**:	NIH
	26:15	it grieveth him to **bring** it **a** to his mouth.	7725
Ecc	1: 6	the wind returneth **a** according to his	NIH

Ecc	1: 7	rivers come, thither they **return a**.	1980+7725
	3:20	all are of the dust, and all **turn** to dust **a**.	7725
	4: 4	**A**, I considered all travail, and every	2050.1
	4:11	**A**, if two lie together, then they have heat:	1571
	8:14	a, there be wicked **men**, to whom it	2050.1
Isa	7:10	Moreover the LORD spake **a** unto Ahaz,	3254
	8: 5	The LORD spake also unto me **a**,	3254+5750
	10:20	shall no more **a** stay upon him that smote	5750
	11:11	the Lord shall **set** his hand **a** the second	3254
	24:20	upon it; and it shall fall, and not rise **a**.	3254
	37:31	house of Judah shall **a** take root	3254
	38: 8	I will **bring a** the shadow of the degrees,	7725
	46: 8	**bring** it **a** to mind, O ye transgressors.	7725
	49: 5	to **bring** Jacob **a** to him, Though Israel be	7725
	49:20	lost the other, shall say **a** in thine ears,	5750
	51:22	of my fury; thou shalt no more drink it **a**:	5750
	52: 8	when the LORD shall **bring a** Zion.	7725
Jer	3: 1	another man's, shall he return unto her **a**?	5750
	3: 1	yet **return a** to me, saith the LORD.	7725
	12:15	will **bring** them **a**, every man to his	7725
	15:19	will **bring** thee **a**, *and* thou shalt stand	7725
	16:15	I will **bring** them **a** into their land that I	7725
	18: 4	so he made it **a** another vessel, as seemed	7725
	19:11	that cannot be made whole **a**:	5750
	23: 3	and will **bring** them **a** to their folds;	7725
	24: 4	**A** the word of the LORD came unto me,	2050.1
	24: 6	and I will **bring** them **a** to this land:	7725
	25: 5	**Turn** ye **a** now every one from his evil	7725
	27:16	now shortly be **brought a** from Babylon:	7725
	28: 3	Within two full years *will* I **bring a** into	7725
	28: 4	I will **bring a** to this place Jeconiah the	7725
	28: 6	to **bring a** the vessels of the LORD's	7725
	29:14	I will **bring** you **a** into the place whence I	7725
	30: 3	that I will **bring a** the captivity of my	7725
	30:18	I *will* **bring a** the captivity of Jacob's tents,	7725
	31: 4	I will build thee, and thou shalt be built,	5750
	31: 4	thou shalt **a** be adorned *with* thy tabrets,	5750
	31:16	they shall **come a** from the land of	7725
	31:17	*thy* children shall **come a** to their own	7725
	31:21	**turn a**, O virgin of Israel, turn again to	7725
	31:21	virgin of Israel, **turn a** to these thy cities,	7725
	31:23	when I shall **bring a** their captivity;	7725
	32:15	vineyards shall be possessed **a** in this land.	5750
	32:37	I will **bring** them **a** unto this place,	7725
	33:10	**A** there shall be heard in this place, which	5750
	33:12	**A** in this place, *which is* desolate without	5750
	33:13	shall the flocks pass **a** under the hands of	5750
	36:28	Take thee **a** another roll, and write in it all	7725
	37: 8	the Chaldeans shall **come a**,	7725
	41:16	whom he had **brought a** from Gibeon:	7725
	46:16	let us **go a** to our own people, and to	7725
	48:47	Yet will I **bring a** the captivity of Moab in	7725
	49: 6	afterward I will **bring a** the captivity of	7725
	49:39	*that* I will **bring a** the captivity of Elam,	7725
	50:19	I will **bring** Israel **a** to his habitation,	7725
La	3:40	try our ways, and **turn a** to the LORD.	7725
Eze	3:20	**A**, When a righteous **man** doth turn	2050.1
	4: 6	lie **a** on thy right side, and thou shalt bear	8145
	5: 4	take of them **a**, and cast them into the	5750
	7: 7	and not the **sounding a** of the mountains.	1906
	8: 6	**turn** thee yet **a**, *and* thou shalt see great*er*	7725
	8:13	**Turn** thee yet **a**, *and* thou shalt see	7725
	8:15	**turn** thee yet **a**, *and* thou shalt see great*er*	7725
	11:14	**A** the word of the LORD came unto me,	2050.1
	12:26	**A** the word of the LORD came to me,	2050.1
	14:12	The word of the LORD came **a** to me,	2050.1
	16: 1	**A** the word of the LORD came unto me,	2050.1
	16:53	When I shall **bring a** their captivity,	7725
	16:53	*will I bring* **a** the captivity of thy captives	NIH
	18: 1	the word of the LORD came unto me **a**,	2050.1
	18:27	**A**, when the wicked *man* turneth away	2050.1
	21: 8	**A** the word of the LORD came unto me,	2050.1
	21:18	The word of the LORD came unto me **a**,	2050.1
	23: 1	The word of the LORD came **a** unto me,	2050.1
	24: 1	**A** in the ninth year, in the tenth month,	2050.1
	25: 1	The word of the LORD came **a** unto me,	2050.1
	26:21	yet shalt thou never be found **a**, saith	5750
	27: 1	The word of the LORD came **a** unto me,	2050.1
	28: 1	The word of the LORD came **a** unto me,	2050.1
	28:20	**A** the word of the LORD came unto me,	2050.1
	29:14	I will **bring a** the captivity of Egypt,	7725
	30: 1	The word of the LORD came **a** unto me,	2050.1
	33: 1	**A** the word of the LORD came unto me,	2050.1
	33:14	**A**, when I say unto the wicked,	2050.1
	33:15	**give a** that he had robbed, walk in	7999
	34: 4	neither have ye **brought a** that which was	7725
	34:16	**bring a** that which was driven away,	7725
	37: 4	**A** he said unto me, Prophesy upon these	2050.1
	37:15	The word of the LORD came **a** unto me,	2050.1
	39:25	Now will I **bring a** the captivity of Jacob,	7725
	39:27	When I have **brought** them **a** from	7725
	47: 1	Afterward he **brought** me **a** unto the door	7725
	47: 4	**A** he measured a thousand,	2050.1
	47: 4	**A** he measured a thousand,	2050.1
Da	2: 7	They answered **a** and said, Let the king	8579
	9:25	the street shall be built **a**, and the wall,	7725
	10:18	there **came a** and touched me one like	3254
Hos	1: 6	she conceived **a**, and bare a daughter.	5750
Joel	3: 1	when I shall **bring a** the captivity of Judah	7725
Am	7: 8	I will not **a** pass by them any more:	3254
	7:13	prophesy not **a** any more *at* Beth-el: for it	3254
	8: 2	I will not **a** pass by them any more.	3254
	8:14	they shall fall, and **never** rise up **a**.	3808+5750
	9:14	I will **bring a** the captivity of my people	7725
Jnh	2: 4	yet I will look **a** toward thy holy temple.	3254

Mic	7:19	He will **turn a**, he will have compassion	7725
Zep	3:20	At that time will I bring you **a**, even in	NIH
Hag	2:20	**a** the word of the LORD came unto	8145
Zec	2: 1	I lift up mine eyes **a**, and looked,	2050.1
	2:12	holy land, and shall choose Jerusalem **a**.	5750
	4: 1	the angel that talked with me **came a**,	7725
	4:12	I answered **a**, and said unto him, What	8145
	8: 1	**A** the word of the LORD of hosts came	2050.1
	8:15	So **a** have I thought in these days to do	7725
	10: 6	and I will bring them **a** to place them;	NIH
	10: 9	shall live with their children, and **turn a**.	7725
	10:10	I will **bring** them **a** also out of the land of	7725
	12: 6	Jerusalem shall be inhabited **a** in her own	5750
Mal	2:13	this have ye done **a**, covering the altar of	8145
Mt	2: 8	ye have found *him*, **bring** me word **a**,	518
	4: 7	Jesus said unto him, It is written **a**,	3825
	4: 8	**A**, the devil taketh him *up* into an	3825
	5:33	**A**, ye have heard that it hath been said by	3825
	7: 2	ye mete, it shall be **measured** to you **a**.	488
	7: 6	under their feet, and turn **a** and rent you.	NIG
	11: 4	**shew** John **a** *those things* which ye do	518
	13:44	**A**, the kingdom of heaven is like unto	3825
	13:45	**A**, the kingdom of heaven is like unto a	3825
	13:47	**A**, the kingdom of heaven is like unto a	3825
	16:21	be killed, and be raised **a** the third day.	NIG
	17: 9	the Son of man be **risen a** from the dead.	450
	17:23	the third day he shall be raised **a**.	NIG
	18:19	**A** I say unto you, That if two of you shall	3825
	19:24	And **a** I say unto you, It is easier for a	3825
	20: 5	**A** he went out about the sixth	3825
	20:19	and the third day he shall **rise a**.	450
	21:36	**A**, he sent other servants moe than the	3825
	22: 1	and spake unto them **a** by parables,	3825
	22: 4	**A**, he sent forth other servants, saying,	3825
	26:32	But after I am **risen a**, I will go before you	NIG
	26:42	He went away **a** the second time,	3825
	26:43	And he came and found them asleep **a**:	3825
	26:44	went away **a**, and prayed the third time,	3825
	26:52	him, **Put up a** thy sword into his place:	654
	26:72	And **a** he denied with an oath, I do not	3825
	27: 3	**brought a** the thirty pieces of silver to	654
	27:50	when he had cried **a** with a loud voice,	3825
	27:63	was yet alive, After three days I will **rise a**.	NIG
Mk	2: 1	And he entered **a** into Capernaum after	3825
	2:13	And he went forth **a** by the sea side;	3825
	3: 1	And he entered **a** into the synagogue;	3825
	3:20	And *the* multitude cometh together **a**, so	3825
	4: 1	And he began **a** to teach by the sea side:	3825
	5:21	And when Jesus was passed over **a** by ship	3825
	7:31	And **a**, departing from the coasts of Tyre	3825
	8:13	entering into the ship **a** departed to	3825
	8:25	that he put *his* hands **a** upon his eyes,	3825
	8:31	be killed, and after three days **rise a**.	450
	10: 1	and the people resort unto him **a**; and,	3825
	10: 1	and, as he was wont, he taught them **a**,	3825
	10:10	And in the house his disciples asked him **a**	3825
	10:24	Jesus answereth **a**, and saith unto them,	3825
	10:32	he took the twelve, and began to tell	3825
	10:34	kill him: and the third day he shall **rise a**.	450
	11:27	And they come **a** to Jerusalem: and as he	3825
	12: 4	And **a** he sent unto them another servant;	3825
	12: 5	**a** he sent another; and him they killed,	3825
	13:16	**a** for to take up his garment.	1519+3588+3694
	14:39	And **a** he went away, and prayed,	3825
	14:40	he returned, he found them asleep **a**,	3825
	14:61	**A** the high priest asked him, and said unto	3825
	14:69	And a maid saw him **a**, and began to say	3825
	14:70	And he denied *it* **a**. And a little after,	3825
	14:70	they that stood by said **a** to Peter,	3825
	15: 4	And Pilate asked him **a**, saying,	3825
	15:12	Pilate answered and said **a** unto them,	3825
	15:13	And they cried out **a**, Crucify him.	3825
Lk	2:34	for the fall and **rising a** of many in Israel;	386
	2:45	they **turned back a** to Jerusalem,	5290
	4:20	he **gave** *it* **a** to the minister,	591
	6:30	that taketh away thy *goods* **ask** *them* not **a**.	523
	6:34	also lend to sinners, to **receive** as much **a**.	618
	6:35	do good, and lend, **hoping for** nothing **a**;	560
	6:38	mete withal it shall be **measured** to you **a**.	488
	8:37	*up* into the ship, and returned *back* **a**.	NIG
	8:55	And her spirit **came a**, and she arose	1994
	9: 8	that one of the old prophets was **risen a**.	450
	9:19	*say*, that one of the old prophets is **risen a**.	450
	9:39	and it teareth him that he foameth **a**,	2532
	9:42	child, and **delivered** him **a** to his father.	591
	10: 6	rest upon it: if not, it shall **turn** to you **a**.	344
	10:17	the seventy returned **a** with joy, saying,	NIG
	10:35	when I **come a**, I will repay thee.	1880
	13:20	And **a** he said, Whereunto shall I liken	3825
	14: 6	And they could not **answer** him **a** to these	470
	14:12	lest they also **bid** thee **a**, and a recompence	479
	15:24	For this my son was dead, and is **alive a**;	326
	15:32	this thy brother was dead, and is **alive a**,	326
	17: 4	and seven times in a day **turn a** to thee,	1994
	18:33	to death: and the third day he shall **rise a**.	450
	20:11	And **a** he sent another servant:	4369
	20:12	And **a** he sent a third: and they wounded	4369
	23:11	a gorgeous robe, and **sent** him **a** to Pilate.	375
	23:20	willing to release Jesus, spake **a** to *them*.	3825
	24: 7	and be crucified, and the third day **rise a**.	450
Jn	1:35	The next day *after* John stood, and two	3825
	3: 3	I say unto thee, Except a man be born **a**,	509
	3: 7	that I said unto thee, Ye must be born **a**.	509
	4: 3	He left Judea, and departed **a** into Galilee.	3825
	4:13	drinketh of this water shall thirst **a**:	3825

Jn
4:46 So Jesus came **a** into Cana of Galilee, — 3825
4:54 This *is* a the second miracle *that* Jesus did, — 3825
6:15 he departed **a** into a mountain himself — 3825
6:39 but should raise it up *a* at the last day. — NIG
8: 2 And early in the morning he came **a** into — 3825
8: 8 And he stooped down, and wrote on — 3825
8:12 Then spake Jesus **a** unto them, saying, — 3825
8:21 Then said Jesus **a** unto them, I go my way, — 3825
9:15 Then **a** the Pharisees also asked him how — 3825
9:17 They say unto the blind man **a**, What — 3825
9:24 Then **a** called they the man that — 1208+1537
9:26 Then said they to him **a**, What did he to — 3825
9:27 wherefore would you hear it **a**? will ye — 3825
10: 7 Then said Jesus unto them **a**, Verily, verily, — 3825
10:17 I lay down my life, that I might take it **a**. — 3825
10:18 lay it down, and I have power to take it **a**. — 3825
10:19 **a** among the Jews for these sayings. — 3825
10:31 Then the Jews took up stones **a** to stone — 3825
10:39 Therefore they sought **a** to take him: — 3825
10:40 And went away **a** beyond Jordan into — 3825
11: 7 he to *his* disciples, Let us go into Judea **a**. — 3825
11: 8 to stone thee; and goest thou thither **a**? — 3825
11:23 saith unto her, Thy brother shall **rise a**. — 450
11:24 that he shall **rise a** in the resurrection — 450
11:38 **a** groaning in himself cometh to the grave. — 3825
12:22 and **a** Andrew and Philip tell Jesus. — 3825
12:28 I have both glorified *it*, and will glorify *it* **a**. — 3825
12:39 not believe, because that Esaias said **a**, — 3825
13:12 and was set down **a**, he said unto them, — 3825
14: 3 will come **a**, and receive you unto myself; — 3825
14:28 unto you, I go away, and come *a* unto you. — NIG
16:16 **a** little while, and ye shall see me, — 3825
16:17 and **a**, a little while, and ye shall see me: — 3825
16:19 and **a**, a little while, and ye shall see me? — 3825
16:22 but I will see you **a**, and your heart shall — 3825
16:28 **a**, I leave the world, and go to the Father. — 3825
18: 7 Then asked he them **a**, Whom seek ye? — 3825
18:27 Peter then denied **a**: and immediately — 3825
18:33 Pilate entered into the judgment hall **a**, — 3825
18:38 he went out **a** unto the Jews, and saith — 3825
18:40 cried they all **a**, saying, Not this *man*, — 3825
19: 4 Pilate therefore went forth **a**, — 3825
19: 9 And went **a** into the judgment hall, — 3825
19:37 And **a** another scripture saith, They shall — 3825
20: 9 that he must **rise a** from the dead. — 450
20:10 Then the disciples went away **a** unto their — 3825
20:21 Then said Jesus to them **a**, Peace *be* unto — 3825
20:26 And after eight days **a** his disciples were — 3825
21: 1 After these *things* Jesus shewed himself **a** — 3825
21:16 He saith to him **a** the second time, Simon, — 3825

Ac
1: 6 thou at this time **restore a** the kingdom — 600
7:26 and would have set them at one **a**, saying, — NIG
7:39 in their hearts turned *back a* into Egypt, — NIG
10:15 the voice *spake* unto him **a** the second — 3825
10:16 the vessel was received up **a** into heaven. — 3825
11: 9 But the voice answered me **a** from — 1208+1537
11:10 and all were drawn up **a** into heaven. — 3825
13:33 in that he hath **raised up** Jesus **a**; — 450
13:37 whom God raised **a**, saw no corruption. — NIG
14:21 they returned *a* to Lystra, and *to* Iconium, — NIG
15:16 and will **build a** the tabernacle of David, — 456
15:16 and I will **build a** the ruins thereof, — 456
15:36 Let us **go a** and visit our brethren in every — 1994
17: 3 have suffered, and **risen a** from the dead; — 3825
17:32 We will hear thee **a** of this *matter*. — 3825
18:21 but I will return **a** unto you, if God will. — 3825
20:11 When he therefore was come up **a**, — NIG
21: 6 we took ship; and they returned home **a**. — NIG
22:17 that, when I was **come a** to Jerusalem, — 5290
27:28 they sounded **a**, and found *it* fifteen — 3825

Ro
4:25 and was raised **a** for our justification. — NIG
8:15 not received the spirit of bondage to fear; — 3825
8:34 is risen **a**, who is even at the right hand — NIG
10: 7 to **bring up** Christ **a** from the dead.) — 321
11:23 for God is able to graff them in **a**. — NIG
11:35 and it shall be recompensed unto him **a**? — NIG
15:10 And **a** *he* saith, Rejoice, *ye* Gentiles, — 3825
15:11 And **a**, Praise the Lord, all ye Gentiles; — 3825
15:12 And **a** Esaias saith, There shall be a root of — 3825

1Co
3:20 And **a**, The Lord knoweth the thoughts of — 3825
7: 5 fasting and prayer, and come together **a**, — 3825
12:21 nor **a** the head to the feet, I have no need — 3825
15: 4 that he rose **a** the third day according to — NIG

2Co
1:16 and to come **a** out of Macedonia unto you, — 3825
2: 1 that I would not come **a** to you in — 3825
3: 1 Do we begin **a** to commend ourselves? or — 3825
5:12 we commend not ourselves **a** unto you, — 3825
5:15 unto him which died for them, and rose **a**. — NIG
10: 7 let him of himself think this **a**, that, as he — 3825
11:16 I say **a**, Let no *man* think me a fool; — 3825
12:19 **A**, think you that we excuse ourselves — 3825
12:21 *And* lest, when I come **a**, my God will — 3825
13: 2 and to all other, that, if I come **a**, I will not — 3825

Gal
1: 9 As we said before, so say I now **a**, If any — 3825
1:17 Arabia, and returned **a** unto Damascus. — 3825
2: 1 Then fourteen years after I went up **a** to — 3825
2:18 For if I build **a** the *things* which I — 3825
4: 9 how turn ye **a** to the weak — 3825
4: 9 whereunto ye **a** desire to be in bondage? — 509
4:19 of whom I travail in birth **a** until Christ be — 3825
5: 1 be not entangled **a** with the yoke of — 3825
5: 3 For I testify **a** to every man that is — 3825

Php
1:26 Jesus Christ for me by my coming to you **a**. — 3825
2:28 that, when ye see him **a**, ye may rejoice, — 3825
4: 4 in the Lord alway: *and* **a** I say, Rejoice. — 3825

Php
4:10 the last your care of me hath **flourished a**; — 330
4:16 ye sent once and **a** unto my necessity. — 1364

1Th
2:18 come unto you, even I Paul, once and **a**; — 1364
3: 9 For what thanks can we **render** to God **a** — 467
4:14 For if we believe that Jesus died and **rose a**, — 450

Tit
2: 9 *them* well in all *things;* not **answering a**; — 483

Phm
1:12 Whom I have **sent a**: thou therefore — 375

Heb
1: 5 And **a**, I will be to him a Father, — 3825
1: 6 And **a**, when he bringeth in — 3825
2:13 And **a**, I will put my trust in him. — 3825
2:13 And **a**, Behold, I, and the children which — 3825
4: 5 And in this *place* **a**, If they shall enter into — 3825
4: 7 **A** he limiteth a certain day, saying in — 3825
5:12 ye have need that one teach you **a** which — 3825
6: 1 not laying **a** the foundation of repentance — 3825
6: 6 away, to renew *them* **a** unto repentance; — 3825
10: 3 a remembrance **a** *made* of sins every year. — NIG
10:30 And **a**, The Lord shall judge his people. — 3825
11:35 received their dead **raised to** life **a**: — 386+1537
13:20 that **brought a** from the dead our Lord — 321

Jas
5:18 he prayed **a**, and the heaven gave rain, — 3825

1Pe
1: 3 **begotten** us **a** unto a lively hope by — 313
1:23 Being **born a**, not of corruptible seed, — 313
2:23 Who, when he was reviled, **reviled** not **a**; — 486

2Pe
2:20 are **a** entangled therein, and overcome, — 3825
2:22 The dog *is* **turned** to his own vomit **a**; — 1994

1Jn
2: 8 **A**, a new commandment I write unto you, — 3825

Rev
10: 8 I heard from heaven spake unto me **a**, — 3825
10:11 Thou must prophesy **a** before many — 3825
19: 3 And **a** they said, Alleluia. And her smoke — 1208
20: 5 But the rest of the dead **lived** not **a** until — 326

AGAINST (1667)

Ge
4: 8 that Cain rose up **a** Abel his brother, — 413
14:15 he divided himself **a** them, he — 5921
15:10 and laid each piece one **a** another: — 7125
16:12 his hand will be **a** every man, — 871.1
16:12 every man, and every man's hand **a** him; — 871.1
20: 6 also withheld thee from sinning **a** me; — 3807.1
21: 6 sat her down over **a** *him* a good way off, — 5048
21:16 she sat over **a** *him*, and lift up her voice, — 5048
30: 2 Jacob's anger was kindled **a** Rachel. — 871.1
32:25 he saw that he prevailed not **a** him, — 3807.1
34:30 shall gather themselves together **a** me, — 5921
37:18 they **conspired a** him to slay him. — 5230
39: 9 this great wickedness, and sin **a** God? — 3807.1
40: 2 Pharaoh was wroth **a** two *of* his officers, — 5921
40: 2 **a** the chief of the butlers, and against — 5921
40: 2 the butlers, and **a** the chief of the bakers. — 5921
41:36 *that* food shall be for store to the land **a** — 3807.1
42:22 unto you, saying, Do not sin **a** the child; — 3807.1
42:36 Benjamin *away:* all these things are **a** me. — 5921
43:18 that he may seek occasion **a** us, and fall — 5921
43:25 they made ready the present **a** Joseph — 5704
44:18 let not thine anger burn **a** thy servant: — 871.1
50:20 as for you, ye thought evil **a** me; *but* — 5921

Ex
1:10 fight **a** us, and *so* get them up out of — 871.1
4:14 the anger of the Lord was kindled **a** — 871.1
7:15 thou shalt stand by the river's brink **a** the — 5921
8:12 of the frogs which he had brought **a** — 3807.1
9:17 As yet exaltest thou thyself **a** my people, — 871.1
10:16 I have sinned **a** the Lord your God, — 3807.1
10:16 against the Lord your God, and **a** you. — 3807.1
11: 7 **a** any of the children of Israel shall not **a** — 3807.1
11: 7 a dog move his tongue, **a** man or beast: — 3807.1
12:12 **a** all the gods of Egypt I will execute — 871.1
14: 2 and the sea, over **a** Baal-zephon: — 6440
14: 5 of his servants was turned **a** the people, — 413
14:25 for the Lord fighteth for them **a** — 871.1
14:27 the Egyptians fled **a** it; and the Lord — 7125
15: 7 overthrown them that **rose up a** thee: — 6965
15:24 the people murmured **a** Moses, saying, — 5921
16: 2 the children of Israel murmured **a** Moses — 5921
16: 7 for that he heareth your murmurings **a** — 5921
16: 7 and what *are* we, that ye murmur **a** us? — 5921
16: 8 murmurings which ye murmur **a** him: — 5921
16: 8 your murmurings *are* not **a** us, — 5921
16: 8 *are* not against us, but **a** the Lord. — 5921
17: 3 the people murmured **a** Moses, and said, — 5921
19:11 ready the third day: for the third day — 3807.1
19:15 the people, Be ready the third day: — 3807.1
20:16 Thou shalt not bear false witness **a** thy — 871.1
23:29 and the beast of the field multiply **a** thee. — 5921
23:33 thy land, lest they make thee sin **a** me: — 3807.1
25:27 Over **a** the border shall the rings be for — 5980
25:37 that they may give light over **a** it. — 5676+6440
26:17 *be* in one board, set in order one **a** another: — 413
26:35 candlestick **over a** the table on the side — 5227
28:27 the forepart thereof, **over a** — 5980+3807.1
32:10 that my wrath may wax hot **a** them, — 871.1
32:11 doth thy wrath wax hot **a** thy people, — 871.1
32:12 and repent of *this* evil **a** thy people. — 3807.1
32:33 Whosoever hath sinned **a** me, him will — 3807.1
37:14 **Over a** the border were the rings, — 5980+3807.1
39:20 of it, over **a** the *other* coupling thereof, — 5980
40:24 **over a** the table, on the side of — 5227

Lev
4: 2 If a soul shall sin through ignorance **a** any — 4480
4: 2 to be done), and shall do **a** any of them: — 4480
4:13 they have done somewhat **a** any of — 4480
4:14 which they have sinned **a** it, is known, — 4480
4:22 done somewhat through ignorance **a** any — 4480
4:27 while he doeth somewhat **a** *any of* — 4480
5:19 hath certainly trespassed **a** the Lord. — 3807.1
6: 2 commit a trespass **a** the Lord, — 871.1
17:10 I will even set my face **a** *that* soul — 871.1

Lev
19:16 neither shalt thou stand **a** the blood of thy — 5921
19:18 nor **bear any grudge a** the children of — 5201
20: 3 I will set my face **a** that man, and will cut — 871.1
20: 5 I will set my face **a** that man, — 871.1
20: 5 **a** his family, and will cut him off, and all — 871.1
20: 6 I will even set my face **a** that soul, — 871.1
26:17 I will set my face **a** you, and ye shall be — 871.1
26:40 their trespass which they trespassed **a** — 871.1

Nu
5: 6 to do a trespass **a** the Lord, — 871.1
5: 7 give *it* unto *him* **a** whom he hath — 3807.1
5:12 go aside, and commit a trespass **a** him, — 871.1
5:13 defiled, and *there be* no witness **a** her, — 871.1
5:27 and have done trespass **a** her husband, — 871.1
8: 2 light **over a** the candlestick. — 413+4136+6440
8: 3 thereof **over a** the candlestick, — 413+4136+6440
10: 9 if ye go *to* war in your land **a** the enemy — 5921
10:21 the *other* did set up the tabernacle **a** they — 5704
11:18 Sanctify yourselves **a** to morrow, — 3807.1
11:33 the wrath of the Lord was kindled **a** — 871.1
12: 1 and Aaron spake **a** Moses because — 871.1
12: 8 were ye not afraid to speak **a** my servant — 871.1
12: 9 the anger of the Lord was kindled **a** — 871.1
13:31 We be not able to go up **a** the people; — 413
14: 2 the children of Israel murmured **a** Moses — 5921
14: 2 murmured against Moses and **a** Aaron, — 5921
14: 9 Only rebel not ye **a** the Lord, — 871.1
14:27 evil congregation, which murmur **a** me? — 5921
14:27 of Israel, which they murmur **a** me. — 5921
14:29 and upward, which have murmured **a** me, — 5921
14:35 that are gathered together **a** me: — 5921
14:36 made all the congregation to murmur **a** — 5921
16: 3 gathered themselves together **a** Moses — 5921
16: 3 together against Moses and **a** Aaron, — 5921
16:11 all thy company *are* gathered together **a** — 5921
16:11 what *is* Aaron, that ye murmur **a** him? — 5921
16:19 Korah gathered all the congregation **a** — 5921
16:38 The censers of these sinners **a** their own — 871.1
16:41 the children of Israel murmured **a** Moses — 5921
16:41 murmured against Moses and **a** Aaron, — 5921
16:42 when the congregation was gathered **a** — 5921
16:42 was gathered against Moses and **a** Aaron, — 5921
17: 5 of Israel, whereby they murmur **a** you. — 5921
17:10 to be kept for a token **a** the rebels; — 3807.1
20: 2 gathered themselves together **a** Moses — 5921
20: 2 together against Moses and **a** Aaron. — 5921
20:18 lest I come out **a** thee with the sword. — 7125
20:20 Edom came out **a** him with much people, — 7125
20:24 ye rebelled **a** my word at the water of — 854
21: 1 he fought **a** Israel, and took *some* of them — 871.1
21: 5 the people spake **a** God, — 871.1
21: 5 people spake against God, and **a** Moses, — 871.1
21: 7 for we have spoken **a** the Lord, — 871.1
21: 7 spoken against the Lord, and **a** thee; — 871.1
21:23 and went out **a** Israel into the wilderness; — 7125
21:23 and he came *to* Jahaz, and fought **a** Israel. — 871.1
21:26 who had fought **a** the former king of — 871.1
21:33 Og the king of Bashan went out **a** them, — 7125
22: 5 earth, and they abide **over a** me: — 4136+4480
22:22 stood in the way for an adversary **a** him. — 3807.1
22:25 and crusht Balaam's foot **a** the wall: — 413
22:34 not that thou stoodest in the way **a** me: — 7125
23:23 Surely *there is* no enchantment **a** Jacob, — 871.1
23:23 neither *is there* any divination **a** Israel: — 871.1
24:10 Balak's anger was kindled **a** Balaam, — 413
25: 3 the anger of the Lord was kindled **a** — 871.1
25: 4 hang them up before the Lord **a** the sun, — 5048
26: 9 who strove **a** Moses and against Aaron in — 5921
26: 9 and Aaron in the company of Korah, — 5921
26: 9 of Korah, when they strove **a** the Lord: — 5921
27: 3 **a** the Lord in the company of Korah; — 5921
27:14 For ye **rebelled a** my commandment in — 4784
30: 9 have bound their souls, shall stand **a** her. — 5921
31: 3 let them go **a** the Midianites, and avenge — 5921
31: 7 they warred **a** the Midianites, as — 5921
31:16 to commit trespass **a** the Lord, — 871.1
32:13 the Lord's anger was kindled **a** Israel, — 871.1
32:23 behold, ye have sinned **a** the Lord: — 3807.1
35:30 one witness shall not testify **a** *any* person — 871.1

Dt
1: 1 in the plain **over a** the Red *sea*, between — 4136
1:26 rebelled **a** the commandment of the Lord — 854
1:41 unto me, We have sinned **a** the Lord, — 3807.1
1:43 rebelled **a** the commandment of the Lord — 854
1:44 came out **a** you, and chased you, as bees — 7125
2:15 For indeed the hand of the Lord was **a** — 871.1
2:19 thou comest nigh **over a** the children — 4136
2:32 Sihon came out **a** us, he and all his people, — 7125
3: 1 Og the king of Bashan came out **a** us, he — 7125
3:29 So we abode in the valley **over a** — 4136
4:26 and earth to witness **a** you *this* day, — 871.1
4:46 Jordan, in the valley **over a** Beth-peor, — 4136
5:20 shalt thou bear false witness **a** thy — 871.1
6:15 of the Lord thy God be kindled **a** thee, — 871.1
7: 4 will the anger of the Lord be kindled **a** — 871.1
8:19 I testify **a** you *this* day that ye shall surely — 871.1
9: 7 ye have been rebellious **a** the Lord, — 5973
9:16 ye had sinned **a** the Lord your God, — 3807.1
9:19 wherewith the Lord was wroth **a** you to — 5921
9:23 you rebelled **a** the commandment of — 854
9:24 You have been rebellious **a** the Lord — 5973
11:17 *then* the Lord's wrath be kindled **a** you, — 871.1
11:30 which dwell in the champaign **over a** — 4136
15: 9 thine eye be evil **a** thy poor brother, — 5973
15: 9 he cry unto the Lord **a** thee, and it be sin — 5921
19:11 rise up **a** him, and smite him mortally that — 5921
19:15 One witness shall not rise up **a** a man for — 871.1

Dt	19:16 If a false witness rise up **a** any man to	871.1
	19:16 man to testify a him *that which* is wrong;	871.1
	19:18 *and* hath testified falsely **a** his brother;	871.1
	20: 1 When thou goest out to battle **a** thine	5921
	20: 3 you approach *this* day unto battle **a** your	5921
	20: 4 to fight for you **a** your enemies, to save	5973
	20:10 thou comest nigh unto a city to fight **a** it,	5921
	20:12 will make war **a** thee, then thou shalt	5973
	20:18 so should ye sin **a** the LORD your God.	3807.1
	20:19 a long time, in making war **a** it to take it,	5921
	20:19 the trees thereof by forcing an axe **a** them:	4480
	20:20 thou shalt build bulwarks **a** the city that	5921
	21:10 When thou goest forth to war **a** thine	5921
	22:14 give occasions of speech **a** her,	3807.1
	22:17 he hath given occasions of speech **a** her,	NIH
	22:26 for as when a man riseth **a** his neighbour,	5921
	23: 4 they hired **a** thee Balaam the son of Beor	5921
	23: 9 the host goeth forth **a** thine enemies,	5921
	24:15 lest he cry **a** thee unto the LORD,	5921
	28: 7 rise up **a** thee *to be* smitten before thy	5921
	28: 7 they shall come out **a** thee one way,	413
	28:25 thou shalt go out one way **a** them,	413
	28:48 which the LORD shall send **a** thee,	871.1
	28:49 The LORD shall bring a nation **a** thee	5921
	29: 7 came out **a** us unto battle, and we smote	7125
	29:20 and his jealousy shall smoke **a** that man,	871.1
	29:27 the anger of the LORD was kindled **a** this	871.1
	30:19 and earth to record *this* day **a** you,	871.1
	31:17 my anger shall be kindled **a** them in that	871.1
	31:19 that this song may be a witness for me **a**	871.1
	31:21 that this song shall testify **a** them 6440+3807.1	
	31:26 that it may be there for a witness **a** thee.	871.1
	31:27 ye have been rebellious **a** the LORD;	5973
	31:28 call heaven and earth to record **a** them.	871.1
	32:49 of Moab, that *is* **over a** Jericho, 5921+6440	
	32:51 Because ye trespassed **a** me among	871.1
	33:11 smite through the loins of them that rise **a**	NIH
	34: 1 top of Pisgah, that *is* **over a** Jericho. 5921+6440	
	34: 6 in the land of Moab, **over a** Beth-peor:	4136
Jos	1:18 Whosoever *he be* that doth rebel **a** thy	854
	3:16 and the people passed over **right a** Jericho.	5048
	5:13 there stood a man **over a** him 5048+3807.1	
	7: 1 the anger of the LORD was kindled **a**	871.1
	7:13 say, Sanctify yourselves **a** to morrow:	3807.1
	7:20 Indeed I have sinned **a** the LORD God	3807.1
	8: 3 and all the people of war, to go up **a** Ai:	NIH
	8: 4 Behold, ye shall **lie in wait a** the city,	693
	8: 5 when they come out **a** us, as at the first,	7125
	8:14 the men of the city went out **a** Israel to	7125
	8:14 liers in ambush **a** him behind the city.	3807.1
	8:22 the other issued out of the city **a** them;	7125
	8:33 half of them **over a** mount Gerizim, 413+4136	
	8:33 and half of them **over a** mount Ebal;	4136
	9: 1 in all the coasts of the great sea **over a**	4136
	9:18 all the congregation murmured **a**	5921
	10: 5 before Gibeon, and made war **a** it.	5921
	10: 6 the mountains are gathered together **a** us.	413
	10:21 none moved his tongue **a** any of	3807.1
	10:25 do to all your enemies **a** whom ye fight.	854
	10:29 *unto* Libnah, and fought **a** Libnah:	5973
	10:31 and encamped **a** it, and fought against it:	5921
	10:31 and encamped against it, and fought **a** it:	871.1
	10:34 they encamped **a** it, and fought against it:	5921
	10:34 they encamped against it, and fought **a** it:	5921
	10:36 unto Hebron; and they fought **a** it:	5921
	10:38 Israel with him, to Debir; and fought **a** it:	5921
	11: 5 at the waters of Merom, to fight **a** Israel.	5973
	11: 7 **a** them by the waters of Merom suddenly;	5921
	11:20 that *they* should **come a** Israel *in* battle,	7125
	18:17 *is* **over a** the going up of Adummim,	5227
	18:18 along toward the side **over a** Arabah	4136
	19:47 the children of Dan went up to fight **a**	5973
	22:11 built an altar **over a** the land of Canaan,	4136
	22:12 together *at* Shiloh, to go up to war **a** them.	5921
	22:16 ye have committed **a** the God of Israel,	871.1
	22:16 that ye might rebel *this* day **a** the LORD?	871.1
	22:18 *seeing* ye rebel to day **a** the LORD,	871.1
	22:19 rebel **a** the LORD, nor rebel against	871.1
	22:19 rebel not against the LORD, nor rebel **a** us,	854
	22:22 or if in transgression **a** the LORD,	871.1
	22:29 God forbid that we should rebel **a**	871.1
	22:31 ye have not committed this trespass **a**	871.1
	22:33 did not intend to go up **a** them in battle,	5921
	23:16 shall the anger of the LORD be kindled **a**	871.1
Jdg	24: 9 arose and warred **a** Israel, and sent	871.1
	24:11 the men of Jericho fought **a** you,	871.1
	24:22 Ye *are* witnesses **a** yourselves that ye have	871.1
Jdg	1: 1 Who shall go up for us **a** the Canaanites	413
	1: 1 the Canaanites first, to fight **a** them?	871.1
	1: 3 lot, that we may fight **a** the Canaanites;	871.1
	1: 5 they fought **a** him, and they slew	871.1
	1: 8 Now the children of Judah had fought **a**	871.1
	1: 9 went down to fight **a** the Canaanites,	871.1
	1:10 Judah went **a** the Canaanites that dwelt in	413
	1:11 from thence he went **a** the inhabitants of	413
	1:22 of Joseph, they also went up **a** Beth-el:	NIH
	2:14 the anger of the LORD was hot **a** Israel,	871.1
	2:14 the hand of the LORD was **a** them for	871.1
	2:20 the anger of the LORD was hot **a** Israel;	871.1
	3: 8 the anger of the LORD was hot **a** Israel:	871.1
	3:10 his hand prevailed **a** Chushan-rishathaim.	5921
	3:12 Eglon the king of Moab **a** Israel,	5921
	4:24 prevailed **a** Jabin the king of Canaan,	5921
	5:14 of Ephraim *was there* a root of them **a**	871.1
	5:20 the stars in their courses fought **a** Sisera.	5973

Jdg	5:23 to the help of the LORD **a** the mighty.	871.1
	6: 2 the hand of Midian prevailed **a** Israel: *and*	5921
	6: 3 of the east, even they came up **a** them;	5921
	6: 4 they encamped **a** them, and destroyed	5921
	6:31 Joash said unto all that stood **a** him, Will	5921
	6:32 saying, Let Baal plead **a** him, because	871.1
	6:39 Let not thine anger be hot **a** me, and I	871.1
	7: 2 lest Israel vaunt themselves **a** me, saying,	5921
	7:22 the LORD set every man's sword **a** his	871.1
	7:24 Come down **a** the Midianites,	7125
	9:18 ye are risen up **a** my father's house this	5921
	9:31 and behold, they fortify the city **a** thee.	5921
	9:33 people that *is* with him come out **a** thee,	413
	9:34 they laid wait **a** Shechem *in* four	5921
	9:43 and he rose up **a** them, and smote them.	5921
	9:45 Abimelech fought **a** the city all that day;	871.1
	9:50 and encamped **a** Thebez, and took it.	871.1
	9:52 fought **a** it, and went hard unto the door	871.1
	10: 7 the anger of the LORD was hot **a** Israel,	871.1
	10: 9 passed over Jordan to fight also **a** Judah,	871.1
	10: 9 **a** Benjamin, and against the house of	871.1
	10: 9 **a** and the house of Ephraim;	871.1
	10:10 We have sinned **a** thee, both because	3807.1
	10:18 What man *is he* that will begin to fight **a**	871.1
	11: 4 that the children of Ammon made war **a**	5973
	11: 5 the children of Ammon made war **a** Israel,	5973
	11: 8 fight **a** the children of Ammon, and be	871.1
	11: 9 If ye bring me *home* again to fight **a**	871.1
	11:12 thou art come **a** me to fight in my land?	413
	11:20 and pitched in Jahaz, and fought **a** Israel.	5973
	11:25 did he ever strive **a** Israel, or did he ever	5973
	11:25 against Israel, or did he ever fight **a** them,	5973
	11:27 Wherefore I have not sinned **a** thee,	3807.1
	11:27 but thou doest me wrong to war **a** me:	871.1
	11:32 the children of Ammon to fight **a** them;	871.1
	12: 1 Wherefore passedst thou over to fight **a**	871.1
	12: 3 passed over **a** the children of Ammon,	413
	12: 3 come up unto me this day, to fight **a** me?	871.1
	14: 4 he sought an occasion **a** the Philistines:	4480
	14: 5 behold, a young lion roared **a** him.	7125
	15:10 of Judah said, Why are ye come up **a** us?	5921
	15:14 unto Lehi, the Philistines shouted **a** him:	7125
	16: 5 by what *means* we may prevail **a** him,	3807.1
	18: 9 said, Arise, that we may go up **a** them:	5921
	19: 2 his concubine played the whore **a** him,	5921
	19:10 and departed, and came over **a** Jebus,	5227
	20: 5 the men of Gibeah rose **a** me, and beset	5921
	20: 9 do to Gibeah; *we will go up* by lot **a** it;	5921
	20:11 So all the men of Israel were gathered **a**	413
	20:14 to go out to battle **a** the children of Israel.	5973
	20:18 Which of us shall go up first to the battle **a**	5973
	20:19 in the morning, and encamped **a** Gibeah.	5921
	20:20 the men of Israel went out to battle **a**	5973
	20:20 in array to fight **a** them at Gibeah.	854
	20:23 Shall I go *up* again to battle **a** the children	5973
	20:23 And the LORD said, Go up **a** him.)	413
	20:24 the children of Israel came near **a**	413
	20:25 Benjamin went forth **a** them out of Gibeah	7125
	20:28 Shall I yet again go out to battle **a**	5973
	20:30 children of Israel went up **a** the children	413
	20:30 put *themselves* in array **a** Gibeah, as at	413
	20:31 the children of Benjamin went out **a**	7125
	20:34 there came a Gibeah ten thousand 4480+5048	
	20:43 trode them down with ease **over a** Gibeah	5227
Ru	1:13 the hand of the LORD is gone out **a** me.	871.1
	1:21 seeing the LORD hath testified **a** me,	871.1
1Sa	2:25 If one man sin **a** another, the judge shall	3807.1
	2:25 if a man sin **a** the LORD, who shall	3807.1
	3:12 In that day I will perform **a** Eli all *things*	413
	4: 1 Now Israel went out **a** the Philistines to	7125
	4: 2 the Philistines put *themselves* in array **a**	7125
	5: 9 the hand of the LORD was **a** the city *with*	871.1
	7: 6 said there, We have sinned **a** the LORD.	3807.1
	7: 7 lords of the Philistines went up **a** Israel.	413
	7:10 the Philistines drew near to battle **a** Israel:	871.1
	7:13 the hand of the LORD was **a**	871.1
	9:14 Samuel came out **a** them, for to go	7125
	11: 1 came up, and encamped **a** Jabesh-gilead:	5921
	12: 3 here I *am*: witness **a** me before	871.1
	12: 5 The LORD *is* witness **a** you,	871.1
	12: 9 king of Moab, and they fought **a** them.	871.1
	12:12 of the children of Ammon came **a** you,	5921
	12:14 not rebel **a** the commandment of	854
	12:15 rebel **a** the commandment of the LORD,	854
	12:15 shall the hand of the LORD be **a** you,	871.1
	12:15 be against you, as *it was* **a** your fathers.	871.1
	12:23 God forbid that I should sin **a** the LORD	3807.1
	14: 5 situate northward **over a** Michmash,	4136
	14: 5 and the other southward **over a** Gibeah.	4136
	14:20 every man's sword was **a** his fellow, *and*	871.1
	14:33 Behold, the people sin **a** the LORD,	3807.1
	14:34 sin not **a** the LORD in eating with	3807.1
	14:47 fought **a** all his enemies on every side,	871.1
	14:47 **a** Moab, and against the children of	871.1
	14:47 **a** the children of Ammon,	871.1
	14:47 **a** Edom, and against the kings of Zobah,	871.1
	14:47 **a** the kings of Zobah, and against	871.1
	14:47 the kings of Zobah, and the Philistines:	871.1
	14:52 there was sore war **a** the Philistines all	5921
	15: 7 *to* Shur, that *is* **over a** Egypt. 5921+6440	
	15:18 and fight **a** them until they be consumed.	871.1
	17: 2 set the battle in array **a** the Philistines.	7125
	17: 9 if I prevail **a** him, and kill him,	3807.1
	17:21 had put *the battle* in array, army **a** army.	7125
	17:28 Eliab's anger was kindled **a** David,	871.1

1Sa	17:33 Thou art not able to go **a** this Philistine to	413
	17:35 when he arose **a** me, I caught *him* by his	5921
	17:55 when Saul saw David go forth **a**	7125
	18:21 that the hand of the Philistines may be **a**	871.1
	19: 4 Let not the king sin **a** his servant,	871.1
	19: 4 the king sin against his servant, **a** David,	871.1
	19: 4 because he hath not sinned **a** thee,	3807.1
	19: 5 then wilt thou sin **a** innocent blood,	871.1
	20:30 Saul's anger was kindled **a** Jonathan,	871.1
	22: 8 That all of you have conspired **a** me,	5921
	22: 8 my son hath stirred up my servant **a** me,	5921
	22:13 Why have ye conspired **a** me, thou	5921
	22:13 that *he* should rise **a** me, to lie in wait, as	413
	23: 1 Philistines fight **a** Keilah, and they rob	871.1
	23: 3 if we come *to* Keilah **a** the armies of	413
	23: 9 Saul secretly practised mischief **a** him;	5921
	23:28 after David, and went **a** the Philistines:	7125
	24: 6 to stretch forth mine hand **a** him,	871.1
	24: 7 and suffered them not to rise **a** Saul.	413
	24:10 I will not put forth mine hand **a** my lord;	871.1
	24:11 hand, and I have not sinned **a** thee;	3807.1
	25:17 for evil is determined **a** our master,	413
	25:17 our master, and **a** all his household:	5921
	25:20 David and his men came down **a** her;	7125
	25:22 morning light *any that* pisseth **a** the wall.	871.1
	25:34 morning light *any that* pisseth **a** the wall.	871.1
	26: 9 for who can stretch forth his hand **a**	871.1
	26:11 forth mine hand **a** the LORD's anointed;	871.1
	26:19 If the LORD have stirred thee up **a** me,	871.1
	26:23 I would not stretch forth mine hand **a**	871.1
	27:10 **A** the south of Judah, and against the	5921
	27:10 **a** the south of the Jerahmeelites,	5921
	27:10 and **a** the south of the Kenites.	413
	28:15 for the Philistines make war **a** me,	871.1
	29: 8 that I may not go fight **a** the enemies	871.1
	30:23 delivered the company that came **a** us	5921
	31: 1 Now the Philistines fought **a** Israel:	871.1
	31: 3 battle went sore **a** Saul, and the archers	413
2Sa	1:16 thy mouth hath testified **a** thee, saying,	871.1
	3: 8 which **a** Judah do shew kindness	3807.1
	5:23 them **over a** the mulberry trees. 4136+4480	
	6: 7 the anger of the LORD was kindled **a**	871.1
	8:10 because he had fought **a** Hadadezer,	871.1
	10: 9 that the front of the battle was **a** him	413
	10: 9 and put *them* in array **a** the Syrians:	7125
	10:10 that he might put *them* in array **a**	7125
	10:13 with him, unto the battle **a** the Syrians:	871.1
	10:17 Syrians set *themselves* in array **a** David,	7125
	11:23 Surely the men prevailed **a** us,	5921
	11:25 make thy battle *more* strong **a** the city,	413
	12: 5 David's anger was greatly kindled **a**	871.1
	12:11 I will raise up evil **a** thee out of thine own	5921
	12:13 unto Nathan, I have sinned **a** the LORD.	3807.1
	12:26 Joab fought **a** Rabbah of the children of	871.1
	12:27 I have fought **a** Rabbah, and have taken	871.1
	12:28 and encamp **a** the city, and take it:	5921
	12:29 to Rabbah, and fought **a** it, and took it.	871.1
	14: 7 whole family is risen **a** thine handmaid,	5921
	14:13 thou thought such a thing **a** the people	5921
	16:13 Shimei went along on the hill's side **over a**	5980
	17:21 for thus hath Ahithophel counselled **a** you.	5921
	18: 6 So the people went out *into* the field **a**	7125
	18:12 *yet* would I not put forth mine hand **a**	413
	18:13 have wrought falsehood **a** mine own life:	871.1
	18:13 wouldest have set thyself **a** me. 4480+5048	
	18:28 that lift up their hand **a** my lord the king.	871.1
	18:31 *this* day of all them that rose up **a** thee.	5921
	18:32 all that rise **a** thee to do *thee* hurt, be as	5921
	20:15 they cast up a bank **a** the city, and it stood	413
	20:21 hath lift up his hand **a** the king,	871.1
	20:21 his hand against the king, *even* **a** David:	871.1
	21: 5 that devised **a** us *that* we should be	3807.1
	21:15 with him, and **fought a** the Philistines:	3898
	22:40 them that rose up **a** me hast thou subdued	NIH
	22:49 up on high above them that rose up **a** me:	NIH
	23: 8 *he lift up his spear* a eight hundred,	5921
	23:18 he lift up his spear **a** three hundred,	5921
	24: 1 anger of the LORD was kindled **a** Israel,	871.1
	24: 1 he moved David **a** them to say, Go,	871.1
	24: 4 the king's word prevailed **a** Joab,	413
	24: 4 Joab, and **a** the captains of the host.	5921
	24:17 be **a** me, and against my father's house.	871.1
	24:17 be against me, and **a** my father's house.	871.1
1Ki	2:23 if Adonijah have not spoken this word **a**	871.1
	6: 5 the wall of the house he built chambers	5921
	6: 5 **a** the walls of the house round about,	NIH
	6:10 *then* he built chambers **a** all the house,	5921
	7: 4 and light *was* **a** light *in* three ranks.	413
	7: 5 and light *was* a light *in* three ranks. 413+4136	
	7:20 **a** the belly which *was* by 5980+3807.1	
	7:39 of the house eastward **over a** the south.	4136
	8:31 If any man trespass **a** his neighbour,	NIH
	8:33 because they have sinned **a** thee,	3807.1
	8:35 rain, because they have sinned **a** thee;	3807.1
	8:44 thy people go out to battle **a** their enemy,	5921
	8:46 If they sin **a** thee, (for *there is* no man	3807.1
	8:50 forgive thy people that have sinned **a**	3807.1
	8:50 wherein they have transgressed **a** thee,	871.1
	11:26 even he lift up *his* hand **a** the king.	5921
	11:27 *was* the cause that he lift up *his* hand **a**	5921
	12:19 So Israel rebelled **a** the house of David	871.1
	12:21 warriors, to fight **a** the house of Israel,	5973
	12:24 nor fight **a** your brethren the children of	5973
	13: 2 he cried **a** the altar in the word of	5921
	13: 4 which had cried **a** the altar in Beth-el,	5921

A

1Ki 13: 4	which he put forth **a** him, dried up, so	5921
13:32	word of the LORD **a** the altar in Beth-el,	5921
13:32	**a** all the houses of the high places which	5921
14:10	Jeroboam *him that* pisseth **a** the wall,	871.1
14:25	*that* Shishak king of Egypt came up **a**	5921
15:17	Baasha king of Israel went up **a** Judah,	5921
15:20	hosts which he had **a** the cities of Israel,	5921
15:27	of the house of Issachar, conspired **a** him;	5921
16: 1	came to Jehu the son of Hanani **a** Baasha,	5921
16: 7	came the word of the LORD **a** Baasha,	413
16: 7	**a** his house, even for all the evil that he did	413
16: 9	conspired **a** him, as he *was* in Tirzah,	5921
16:11	he left him not *one that* pisseth **a** wall,	871.1
16:12	which he spake **a** Baasha by Jehu	413
16:15	the people *were* encamped **a** Gibbethon,	5921
16:22	the people that followed Omri prevailed **a**	854
20: 1	and besieged Samaria, and warred **a** it.	871.1
20:12	they set *themselves in array* **a** the city.	5921
20:22	year the king of Syria will come up **a** thee.	5921
20:23	let us fight **a** them in the plain, and surely	854
20:25	we will fight **a** them in the plain, *and*	854
20:26	and went up to Aphek, to fight **a** Israel.	5973
20:27	and were all present, and went **a** them:	7125
20:29	they pitched one **over a** the other seven	5227
21:10	him, to **bear witness a** him, saying,	5749
21:13	the men of Belial **witnessed a** him,	5749
21:13	*even* a Naboth, in the presence of	NIH
21:21	will cut off from Ahab *him that* pisseth **a**	871.1
22: 6	Shall I go up **a** Ramoth-gilead to battle, or	5921
22:15	shall we go **a** Ramoth-gilead to battle, or	413
22:32	they turned aside to fight **a** him:	5921
22:35	the king was stayed up in *his* chariot **a**	5227
2Ki 1: 1	Moab rebelled **a** Israel after the death of	871.1
3: 5	that the king of Moab rebelled **a** the king	871.1
3: 7	The king of Moab hath rebelled **a** me:	871.1
3: 7	wilt thou go with me **a** Moab to battle?	413
3:21	the kings were come up to fight **a** them,	871.1
3:27	there was great indignation **a** Israel:	5921
5: 7	and see how he seeketh a quarrel **a** me.	3807.1
6: 8	the king of Syria warred **a** Israel,	871.1
7: 6	the king of Israel hath hired **a** us the kings	5921
8:28	**a** Hazael king of Syria in Ramoth-gilead;	5973
8:29	when he fought **a** Hazael king of Syria.	854
9: 8	will cut off from Ahab *him that* pisseth **a**	871.1
9:14	the son of Nimshi conspired **a** Joram.	413
9:21	they went out **a** Jehu, and met him in	7125
10: 9	I conspired **a** my master, and slew him:	5921
12:17	went up, and fought **a** Gath, and took it:	5921
13: 3	the anger of the LORD was kindled **a**	871.1
13:12	his might where*with* he fought **a** Amaziah	5973
14:19	Now they made a conspiracy **a** him in	5921
15:10	Shallum the son of Jabesh conspired **a** him,	5921
15:19	*And* Pul the king of Assyria came **a**	5921
15:25	conspired **a** him, and smote him in	5921
15:30	a conspiracy **a** Pekah the son of Remaliah,	5921
15:37	In those days the LORD began to send **a**	871.1
16: 7	of the king of Israel, which rise up **a** me.	5921
16: 9	the king of Assyria went up **a** Damascus,	413
16:11	Urijah the priest made *it* **a** king Ahaz came	5704
17: 3	**A** him came up Shalmaneser king of	5921
17: 7	that the children of Israel had sinned **a**	3807.1
17: 9	that were not right **a** the LORD their God,	5921
17:13	Yet the LORD testified **a** Israel,	871.1
17:13	**a** Judah, by all the prophets, *and by* all	871.1
17:15	his testimonies which he testified **a** them;	871.1
18: 7	he rebelled **a** the king of Assyria,	5921
18: 9	king of Assyria came up **a** Samaria,	5921
18:13	come up **a** all the fenced cities of Judah,	5921
18:17	Hezekiah with a great host **a** Jerusalem.	NIH
18:20	dost thou trust, that thou rebellest **a** me?	871.1
18:25	Am I now come up without the LORD **a**	5921
18:25	to me, Go up **a** this land, and destroy it.	5921
19: 8	found the king of Assyria warring **a**	5921
19: 9	Behold, he is come out to fight **a** thee:	854
19:20	*That* which thou hast prayed to me **a**	413
19:22	**a** whom hast thou exalted *thy* voice,	5921
19:22	on high? *even* **a** the Holy One of Israel.	5921
19:27	and thy coming in, and thy rage **a** me.	413
19:28	Because thy rage **a** me and thy tumult is	413
19:32	before it *with* shield, nor cast a bank **a** it.	5921
21:23	the servants of Amon conspired **a** him,	5921
21:24	all them that had conspired **a** king Amon;	5921
22:13	wrath of the LORD that is kindled **a** us,	871.1
22:17	my wrath shall be kindled **a** this place,	871.1
22:19	when thou heardest what I spake **a** this	5921
22:19	**a** the inhabitants thereof, that *they* should	5921
23:17	that thou hast done **a** the altar of Beth-el.	5921
23:26	where*with* his anger was kindled **a** Judah,	871.1
23:29	**a** the king of Assyria to the river	5921
23:29	king Josiah went **a** him; and he slew him	7125
24: 1	then he turned and rebelled **a** him.	871.1
24: 2	the LORD sent **a** him bands of	871.1
24: 2	and sent them **a** Judah to destroy it,	871.1
24:10	king of Babylon came up **a** Jerusalem,	NIH
24:11	Nebuchadnezzar king of Babylon came **a**	5921
24:20	that Zedekiah rebelled **a** the king of	871.1
25: 1	**a** Jerusalem, and pitched against it;	5921
25: 1	against Jerusalem, and pitched **a** it;	5921
25: 1	and they built forts **a** it round about.	5921
25: 4	(now the Chaldees *were* **a** the city round	5921
1Ch 5:11	the children of Gad dwelt over **a** them,	5048
5:20	were helped **a** them, and the Hagarites	5921
5:25	they transgressed **a** the God of their	871.1
8:32	their brethren in Jerusalem, **over a** them.	5048
9:38	at Jerusalem, over **a** their brethren.	5973

1Ch 10: 1	Now the Philistines fought **a** Israel;	871.1
10: 3	battle went sore **a** Saul, and the archers	5921
10:13	which he committed **a** the LORD,	871.1
10:13	*even* **a** the word of the LORD, which he	5921
11:11	he lift up his spear **a** three hundred slain	5921
11:20	for lifting up his spear **a** three hundred,	5921
12:19	when he came with the Philistines **a** Saul	5921
12:21	helped David **a** the band *of the* rovers:	5921
13:10	the anger of the LORD was kindled **a**	5921
14: 8	heard *of it,* and went out **a** them.	6440+3807.1
14:10	saying, Shall I go up **a** the Philistines?	5921
14:14	them **over a** the mulberry trees.	4136+4480
18:10	because he had fought **a** Hadarezer,	871.1
19:10	when Joab saw that the battle was set **a**	413
19:10	and put *them* in array **a** the Syrians.	7125
19:11	they set *themselves* in array **a** the children	7125
19:17	them, and set *the battle* in array **a** them.	413
19:17	when David had put the battle in array **a**	7125
21: 1	Satan stood up **a** Israel,	5921
21: 4	Nevertheless the king's word prevailed **a**	5921
24:31	These likewise cast lots over **a** their	5980
24:31	*even* the principal fathers over **a** their	5980
25: 8	a *ward,* as well the small as	5980+3807.1
26:12	*having* wards one **a** another,	5980+3807.1
26:16	of the going up, ward **a** ward.	5980+3807.1
27:24	because there fell wrath for it **a** Israel;	5921
2Ch 4:10	side of the east end, over **a** the south.	4136
6:22	If a man sin **a** his neighbour, and an	3807.1
6:24	because they have sinned **a** thee;	3807.1
6:26	rain, because they have sinned **a** thee;	3807.1
6:34	thy people go out to war **a** their enemies	5921
6:36	If they sin **a** thee, (for *there is* no man	3807.1
6:39	forgive thy people which have sinned **a**	3807.1
8: 3	went *to* Hamath-zobah, and prevailed **a** it.	5921
9:29	in the visions of Iddo the seer **a** Jeroboam	5921
10:19	Israel rebelled **a** the house of David unto	871.1
11: 1	to fight **a** Israel, that *he* might bring	5973
11: 4	shall not go up, nor fight **a** your brethren:	5973
11: 4	and returned from going **a** Jeroboam.	413
12: 2	king of Egypt came up **a** Jerusalem,	5921
12: 2	they had transgressed **a** the LORD,	871.1
12: 9	So Shishak king of Egypt came up **a**	5921
13: 3	Jeroboam also set the battle in array **a** him	5973
13: 6	is risen up, and hath rebelled **a** his lord.	5921
13: 7	strengthened themselves **a** Rehoboam	5921
13:12	sounding trumpets to cry alarm **a** you.	5921
13:12	fight ye not **a** the LORD God of your	5973
14: 9	came out **a** them Zerah the Ethiopian	413
14:10	Asa went out **a** him, and they set	6440+3807.1
14:11	and in thy name we go **a** this multitude.	5921
14:11	*art* our God; let not man prevail **a** thee.	5973
16: 1	Asa Baasha king of Israel came up **a** Judah,	5921
16: 4	sent the captains of his armies **a** the cities	413
17: 1	stead, and strengthened himself **a** Israel.	5921
17:10	so that they made no war **a** Jehoshaphat.	5973
18:22	the LORD hath spoken evil **a** thee.	5921
18:34	in *his* chariot **a** the Syrians until the even:	5227
19:10	them that they trespass not **a** the LORD,	3807.1
20: 1	came **a** Jehoshaphat to battle.	5921
20: 2	There cometh a great multitude **a** thee	5921
20:12	for we have no might **a** this great	6440+3807.1
20:12	this great company that cometh **a** us;	5921
20:16	To morrow go ye down **a** them: behold,	5921
20:17	to morrow go out **a** them:	6440+3807.1
20:22	the LORD set ambushments **a** the children	5921
20:22	mount Seir, which were come **a** Judah;	3807.1
20:23	Moab stood up **a** the inhabitants of mount	5921
20:29	the LORD fought **a** the enemies of Israel.	5973
20:37	of Mareshah prophesied **a** Jehoshaphat,	5921
21:16	Moreover the LORD stirred up **a** Jehoram	5921
22: 5	**a** Hazael king of Syria at Ramoth-gilead:	5921
22: 7	he went out with Jehoram **a** Jehu the son	413
24:19	the LORD; and they testified **a** them:	871.1
24:21	they conspired **a** him, and stoned him	5921
24:23	*that* the host of Syria came up **a** him:	5921
24:24	So they executed judgment **a** Joash.	NIH
24:25	his own servants conspired **a** him for	5921
24:26	these *are* they that conspired **a** him;	5921
25:10	their anger was greatly kindled **a** Judah,	871.1
25:15	of the LORD was kindled **a** Amaziah,	871.1
25:27	made a conspiracy **a** him in Jerusalem;	5921
26: 6	went forth and warred **a** the Philistines,	871.1
26: 7	God helped him **a** the Philistines,	5921
26: 7	the Arabians that dwelt in Gur-baal,	5921
26:13	to help the king **a** the enemy.	5921
26:16	for he transgressed **a** the LORD his God,	871.1
27: 5	of the Ammonites, and prevailed **a** them.	5921
28:10	with you, sins **a** the LORD your God?	3807.1
28:12	stood up **a** them that came from the war,	5921
28:13	for whereas we have offended **a**	5921
28:13	is great, and *there is* fierce wrath **a** Israel.	5921
28:19	and transgressed sore **a** the LORD.	871.1
28:22	did he trespass yet more **a** the LORD:	871.1
30: 7	which trespassed **a** the LORD God of	871.1
32: 1	encamped **a** the fenced cities,	5921
32: 2	that he was purposed to fight **a** Jerusalem,	5921
32: 9	(but he *himself laid siege* **a** Lachish,	5921
32:16	his servants spake yet *more* **a** the LORD	5921
32:16	LORD God, and **a** his servant Hezekiah.	5921
32:17	God of Israel, and to speak **a** him, saying,	5921
32:19	they spake **a** the God of Jerusalem,	413
32:19	as **a** the gods of the people of the earth,	5921
33:24	servants conspired **a** him, and slew him	5921
33:25	all them that had conspired **a** king Amon;	5921
34:27	when thou heardest his words **a** this place,	5921

2Ch 34:27	**a** the inhabitants thereof,	5921
35:20	Necho king of Egypt came up to fight **a**	871.1
35:20	by Euphrates: and Josiah went out **a** him.	7125
35:21	*I come* not **a** thee *this* day, but against	5921
35:21	but **a** the house wherewith I have war:	413
36: 6	**A** him came up Nebuchadnezzar king of	5921
36:13	he also rebelled **a** king Nebuchadnezzar,	871.1
36:16	until the wrath of the LORD arose **a** his	871.1
Ezr 4: 5	hired counsellers **a** them, to frustrate their	5921
4: 6	wrote they *unto him* an accusation **a**	5921
4: 8	Shimshai the scribe wrote a letter **a**	5922
4:19	old time *hath* made insurrection **a** kings,	5922
7:23	for why should there be wrath **a** the realm	5922
8:22	horsemen to help us **a** the enemy in	4480
8:22	his wrath *is* **a** all them that forsake him.	5921
10: 2	We have trespassed **a** our God,	871.1
Ne 1: 6	of Israel, which we have sinned **a** thee:	3807.1
1: 7	We have dealt very corruptly **a** thee,	3807.1
2:19	thing that ye do? will ye rebel **a** the king?	5921
3:10	son of Harumaph, even **over a** his house.	5048
3:16	unto *the place* **over a** the sepulchres of	5048
3:19	another piece **over a** the going up	4480+5048
3:23	and Hashub **over a** their house.	5048
3:25	Palal the son of Uzai, **over a**	4480+5048
3:26	unto *the place* **over a** the water gate	5048
3:27	**over a** the great tower that lieth	4480+5048
3:28	every one **over a** his house.	5048+3807.1
3:29	Zadok the son of Immer **over a** his house.	5048
3:30	the son of Berechiah **over a** his chamber.	5048
3:31	**over a** the gate Miphkad, and to the going	5048
4: 8	together to come **and** to fight **a** Jerusalem,	871.1
4: 9	set a watch **a** them day and night, because	5921
5: 1	of their wives **a** their brethren the Jews.	413
5: 7	And I set a great assembly **a** them.	5921
6:12	*that* he pronounced this prophecy **a** me:	5921
7: 3	and every one *to be* **a** his house.	5048
9:10	thou knewest that they dealt proudly **a**	5921
9:26	rebelled **a** thee, and cast thy law behind	871.1
9:26	slew thy prophets which testified **a** them	871.1
9:29	testifiedst **a** them, that *thou* mightest	871.1
9:29	sinned **a** thy judgments, (which if a man	871.1
9:30	testifiedst **a** them by thy spirit in thy	871.1
9:34	where*with* thou didst testify **a** them.	871.1
12: 9	brethren, *were* **over a** them in	5048+3807.1
12:24	with their brethren **over a** them,	5048+3807.1
12:24	man of God, ward **over a** ward,	5980+3807.1
12:37	the fountain gate, which *was* **over a** them,	5048
12:38	*them that gave* thanks went **over a** *them,*	4136
13: 2	and with water, but hired Balaam **a** them,	5921
13:15	I testified **a** *them* in the day wherein they	NIH
13:21	I testified **a** them, and said unto them,	871.1
13:27	to transgress **a** our God in marrying	871.1
Est 2: 1	I had done, and what was decreed **a** her.	5921
3:14	that *they* should be ready **a** that day.	3807.1
5: 1	the king's house, **over a** the king's house:	5227
5: 1	royal house, **over a** the gate of the house.	5227
5: 9	he was full *of* indignation **a** Mordecai.	5921
6:13	thou shalt not prevail **a** him,	3807.1
7: 7	he saw that there was evil determined **a**	413
8: 3	his device that he had devised **a** the Jews.	5921
8:13	that the Jews should be ready **a** that day	3807.1
9:24	had devised **a** the Jews to destroy them,	5921
9:25	he devised **a** the Jews, should return	5921
Job 2: 3	although thou movedst me **a** him,	871.1
6: 4	of God do set *themselves* in array **a** me.	NIH
7:20	why hast thou set me as a mark **a** thee,	3807.1
8: 4	If thy children have sinned **a** him,	3807.1
9: 4	who hath hardened *himself* **a** him,	413
10:17	Thou renewest thy witnesses **a** me,	5048
10:17	upon me; changes and war *are* **a** me.	5973
11: 5	God would speak, and open his lips **a** thee;	5973
13:26	For thou writest bitter *things* **a** me,	5921
14:20	Thou **prevailest** for ever **a** him,	8630
15: 6	not I; yea, thine own lips testify **a** thee.	871.1
15:13	That thou turnest thy spirit **a** God,	413
15:24	*they* shall **prevail a** him, as a king ready	8630
15:25	For he stretcheth out his hand **a** God,	413
15:25	and strengtheneth himself **a** the Almighty.	413
16: 4	I could heap up words **a** you,	5921
16: 8	*which* is a witness **a** *me:* and my leanness	NIH
16:10	they have gathered themselves together **a**	5921
17: 8	the innocent shall stir up himself **a**	5921
18: 9	heel, *and* the robber shall prevail **a** him.	5921
19: 5	If indeed ye will magnify *yourselves* **a** me	5921
19: 5	against me, and plead **a** me my reproach:	5921
19:11	He hath also kindled his wrath **a** me,	5921
19:12	raise up their way **a** me, and encamp	5921
19:18	I arose, and they spake **a** me.	871.1
19:19	and they whom I loved are turned **a** me.	871.1
20:27	and the earth shall rise up **a** him.	3807.1
21:27	devices *which* ye wrongfully imagine **a**	5921
23: 6	Will he plead **a** me with *his* great power?	5978
24:13	They are of those that **rebel a** the light;	4775
27: 7	he that riseth up **a** me as the unrighteous.	NIH
30:12	they raise up **a** me the ways of their	5921
30:21	thy strong hand thou opposest thyself **a**	NIH
31:21	If I have lift up my hand **a** the fatherless,	5921
31:38	If my land cry **a** me, or that the furrows	5921
32: 2	**a** Job was his wrath kindled, because	871.1
32: 3	Also **a** his three friends was his wrath	871.1
32:14	Now he hath not directed *his* words **a** me:	413
33:10	Behold, he findeth occasions **a** me,	5921
33:13	Why dost thou strive **a** him? for he giveth	413
34: 6	Should I lie **a** my right? my wound *is*	5921
34:29	whether *it be done* **a** a nation, or against a	5921

Job
34:29 *it be done* against a nation, or **a** a man 5921
34:37 and multiplieth his words **a** God. 3807.1
35: 6 If thou sinnest, what doest thou **a** him? 871.1
38:23 Which I have reserved **a** the time of 3807.1
38:23 of trouble, the day of battle and war? 3807.1
39:16 She is **hardened a** her young ones, 7188
39:23 The quiver rattleth **a** him, the glittering 5921
42: 7 My wrath is kindled **a** thee, and against 871.1
42: 7 against thee, and **a** thy two friends: 871.1

Ps
2: 2 **a** the Lord, and against his anointed, 5921
2: 2 the Lord, and **a** his anointed, *saying,* 5921
3: 1 many *are they that* rise up **a** me. 5921
3: 6 have set *themselves* **a** me round about. 5921
5:10 for they have rebelled **a** thee. 871.1
7:13 ordaineth his arrows **a** the persecutors. 3807.1
10: 8 his eyes are privily set **a** the poor. 3807.1
13: 4 mine enemy say, I have **prevailed a** him, 3201
15: 3 nor taketh up a reproach **a** his neighbour. 5921
15: 5 to usury, nor taketh reward **a** the innocent. 5921
17: 7 *in thee* from those that rise up **a** *them.* NIH
18:39 under me those that **rose up a** me. 6965
18:48 liftest me up above those that rise up **a** NIH
21:11 For they intended evil **a** thee: 5921
21:12 *arrows* upon thy strings **a** the face of them. 5921
27: 3 Though a host should encamp **a** me, 5921
27: 3 though war should rise **a** me, in this *will* I 5921
27:12 For false witnesses are risen up **a** me, 871.1
31:13 while they took counsel together **a** me, 5921
31:18 and contemptuously **a** the righteous. 5921
34:16 The face of the Lord *is* **a** them that do 871.1
35: 1 fight **a** them that fight against me. 854
35: 1 fight against them that fight **a** me. NIH
35: 3 stop *the way* **a** them that persecute me: 7125
35:15 abjects gathered themselves together **a** me, 5921
35:20 they devise deceitful matters **a** *them that* 5921
35:21 they opened their mouth wide **a** me, *and* 5921
35:26 dishonour that magnify *themselves* **a** me. 5921
36:11 Let not the foot of pride come **a** me, NIH
37: 1 neither be thou envious **a** the workers of 871.1
37:12 The wicked plotteth **a** the just, 3807.1
38:16 they magnify *themselves* **a** me. 5921
41: 4 heal my soul; for I have sinned **a** thee. 3807.1
41: 7 All that hate me whisper together **a** me: 5921
41: 7 against me: **a** me do they devise my hurt. 5921
41: 9 eat *of* my bread, hath lift up *his* heel **a** me. 5921
43: 1 and plead my cause **a** an ungodly nation: 4480
44: 5 will we tread them under that rise up **a** us. NIH
50: 7 O Israel, and I will testify **a** thee: 871.1
50:20 Thou sittest and speakest **a** thy brother; 871.1
51: 4 **A** thee, thee only, have I sinned, 3807.1
53: 5 the bones of him that encampeth **a** thee: NIH
54: 3 For strangers are risen up **a** me, 5921
55:12 hated me *that* did magnify *himself* **a** me; 5921
55:18 in peace from the battle *that was* **a** me: 3807.1
55:20 He hath put forth his hands **a** such as be 871.1
56: 2 for *they* be many that fight **a** me, 3807.1
56: 5 all their thoughts *are* **a** me for evil. 5921
59: 1 defend me from them that rise up **a** me. NIH
59: 3 the mighty are gathered **a** me; not *for my* 5921
62: 3 How long will ye imagine mischief **a** us 5921
65: 3 Iniquities prevail **a** me: *as for our* 4480
69:12 They that sit in the gate speak **a** me; 871.1
71:10 For mine enemies speak **a** me; 3807.1
73: 9 They set their mouth **a** the heavens, 871.1
73:15 I should offend **a** the generation of thy NIH
74: 1 *why* doth thine anger smoke **a** the sheep 871.1
74:23 the tumult of those that rise up **a** thee NIH
78:17 sinned yet more **a** him by provoking 3807.1
78:19 they spake **a** God; they said, Can God 871.1
78:21 so a fire was kindled **a** Jacob, 871.1
78:21 and anger also came up **a** Israel; 871.1
79: 8 O remember not **a** us former iniquities: 3807.1
80: 4 how long wilt thou be angry **a** the prayer 871.1
81:14 and turned my hand **a** their adversaries. 5921
83: 3 They have taken crafty counsel **a** thy 5921
83: 3 and consulted **a** thy hidden ones. 5921
83: 5 *one* consent: they are confederate **a** thee: 5921
86:14 the proud are risen **a** me, 5921
91:12 lest thou dash thy foot **a** a stone. 871.1
92:11 *my desire* of the wicked that rise up **a** me. 5921
94:16 Who will rise up for me **a** the evildoers? 5973
94:16 who will stand up for me **a** the workers of 5973
94:21 They gather themselves together **a** the soul 5921
102: 8 they that are mad **a** me are sworn against NIH
102: 8 they that are mad against me are sworn **a** 871.1
105:28 it dark; and they rebelled not **a** his word. 854
106:26 Therefore he lifted up his hand **a** them, 3807.1
106:40 wrath of the Lord kindled **a** his people, 871.1
107:11 Because they rebelled **a** the words of God, NIH
109: 2 mouth of the deceitful are opened **a** me: 5921
109: 2 they have spoken **a** me *with* a lying tongue. 854
109: 3 hatred; and fought **a** me without a cause. NIH
109:20 and of them that speak evil **a** my soul. 5921
119:11 mine heart, that I might not sin **a** thee. 3807.1
119:23 Princes also did sit *and* speak **a** me: *but* 871.1
119:69 The proud have forged a lie **a** me: *but* I 5921
124: 2 was on our side, when men rose up **a** us: 5921
124: 3 when their wrath was kindled **a** us: 871.1
129: 2 yet they have not prevailed **a** me. 3807.1
137: 9 and dasheth thy little ones **a** the stones. 413
138: 7 thou shalt stretch forth thine hand **a** 5921
139:20 For they speak **a** thee wickedly, *and* NIH
139:21 am not I grieved with those that rise up **a** NIH

Pr
3:29 Devise not evil **a** thy neighbour, seeing he 5921
8:36 that sinneth **a** me wrongeth his own soul: NIH

Pr
14:35 but his wrath is **a** him that causeth shame. NIH
17:11 a cruel messenger shall be sent **a** him. 871.1
19: 3 and his heart fretteth **a** the Lord. 5921
20: 2 provoketh him to anger sinneth **a** his NIH
21:30 nor counsel **a** the Lord. 5048+3807.1
21:31 horse *is* prepared **a** the day of battle: 3807.1
24: 1 Be not thou envious **a** evil men, 871.1
24:15 O wicked *man,* **a** the dwelling of 3807.1
24:28 Be not a witness **a** thy neighbour 871.1
25:18 A man that beareth false witness **a** his 871.1
30:31 and a king, **a** whom *there is* no rising up. 5973

Ecc
4:12 if one **prevail a** him, two shall withstand 8630
7:14 God also hath set the one **over a** 5980+3807.1
8:11 Because sentence **a** an evil work is not NIH
9:14 there came a great king **a** it, and besieged 413
9:14 besieged it, and built great bulwarks **a** it: 5921
10: 4 If the spirit of the ruler rise up **a** thee, 5921

Isa
1: 2 up children, and they have rebelled **a** me. 871.1
2: 4 nation shall not lift up sword **a** nation, 413
3: 5 the child shall behave himself proudly **a** 871.1
3: 5 ancient, and the base **a** the honourable. 871.1
3: 8 and their doings *are* **a** the Lord, 413
3: 9 their countenance doth witness **a** them; 871.1
5:25 anger of the Lord kindled **a** his people, 871.1
5:25 he hath stretched forth his hand **a** them, 5921
5:30 in that day they shall roar **a** them like 5921
7: 1 went up *towards* Jerusalem to war **a** it, 5921
7: 1 war against it, but could not prevail **a** it. 5921
7: 5 have taken evil counsel **a** thee, saying, 5921
7: 6 Let us go up **a** Judah, and vex it, and let 871.1
9:11 shall set up the adversaries of Rezin **a** him, 5921
9:21 *and* they together *shall be* **a** Judah. For all 5921
10: 6 I will send him **a** a hypocritical nation, 871.1
10: 6 **a** the people of my wrath will I give him **a** 5921
10:15 Shall the axe boast itself **a** him that 5921
10:15 shall the saw magnify itself **a** him that 5921
10:15 as if the rod should shake *itself* **a** them NIH
10:24 shall lift up his staff **a** thee, after 5921
10:32 he shall shake his hand **a** the mount of NIH
13:17 Behold, I will stir up the Medes **a** them, 5921
14: 4 That thou shalt take up this proverb **a** 5921
14: 8 art laid down, no feller is come up **a** us. 5921
14:22 For I will rise up **a** them, saith the Lord 5921
19: 2 I will set the Egyptians **a** the Egyptians: 871.1
19: 2 they shall fight every one **a** his brother, 871.1
19: 2 brother, and every one **a** his neighbour; 871.1
19: 2 city **a** city, *and* kingdom against kingdom. 871.1
19: 2 city against city, *and* kingdom **a** kingdom. 871.1
19:17 of hosts, which he hath determined **a** it. 5921
20: 1 and fought **a** Ashdod, and took it; 871.1
23: 8 Who hath taken this counsel **a** Tyre, 5921
23:11 the Lord hath given a commandment **a** 413
25: 4 of the terrible ones *is* as a storm **a** the wall. NIH
27: 4 set the briers *and* thorns **a** me in battle? NIH
29: 3 I will camp **a** thee round about, and will 5921
29: 3 will lay siege **a** thee with a mount, 5921
29: 3 *with* a mount, and I will raise forts **a** thee. 5921
29: 7 the multitude of all the nations that fight **a** 5921
29: 7 even all that fight **a** her and her munition, NIH
29: 8 all the nations be, that fight **a** mount Zion. 5921
31: 2 will arise **a** the house of the evildoers, 5921
31: 2 and **a** the help of them that work iniquity. 5921
31: 4 of shepherds is called forth **a** him, 5921
32: 6 and to utter error **a** the Lord, 413
36: 1 Sennacherib king of Assyria came up **a** 5921
36: 5 dost thou trust, that thou rebellest **a** me? 871.1
36:10 am I now come up without the Lord **a** 5921
36:10 unto me, Go up **a** this land, and destroy it. 413
37: 8 found the king of Assyria warring **a** 5921
37:21 Whereas thou hast prayed to me **a** 413
37:23 **a** whom hast thou exalted *thy* voice, 5921
37:23 on high? *even* **a** the Holy One of Israel. 413
37:28 and thy coming in, and thy rage **a** me. 413
37:29 Because thy rage **a** me, and thy tumult, 413
37:33 before it *with* shields, nor cast a bank **a** it. 5921
41:11 all they that were incensed **a** thee shall 871.1
41:12 they that war **a** thee shall be as nothing, NIH
42:13 yea, roar; he shall prevail **a** his enemies. 5921
42:24 the Lord, he **a** whom we have sinned? 3807.1
43:27 and thy teachers have transgressed **a** me. 871.1
45:24 all that are incensed **a** him shall be 871.1
54:15 whosoever shall gather together **a** thee 854
54:17 No weapon *that* is formed **a** thee shall 5921
54:17 every tongue *that* shall rise **a** thee in 854
57: 4 **A** whom do ye sport yourselves? 5921
57: 4 **a** whom make ye a wide mouth, *and* 5921
59:12 before thee, and our sins testify **a** us: 5921
59:13 In transgressing and lying **a** the Lord, 871.1
59:19 the Lord shall lift up a standard **a** him. 5921
63:10 to be their enemy, *and* he fought **a** them. 871.1
66:24 of the men that have transgressed **a** me: 871.1

Jer
1:15 **a** all the walls thereof round about, 5921
1:15 round about, and **a** all the cities of Judah. 5921
1:16 I will utter my judgments **a** them NIH
1:18 and brasen walls **a** the whole land, 5921
1:18 **a** the kings of Judah, against the princes 3807.1
1:18 the princes thereof, against the priests 3807.1
1:18 the priests thereof, and against 3807.1
1:18 and **a** the people of the land. 3807.1
1:19 they shall fight **a** thee; but they shall not 413
1:19 they shall not prevail **a** thee; for I *am* 413
2: 8 the pastors also transgressed **a** me, 871.1
2:29 ye all have transgressed **a** me, saith 871.1
3:13 that thou hast transgressed **a** the Lord 871.1
3:25 for we have sinned **a** the Lord our 3807.1

Jer
4:12 now also will I give sentence **a** them. 854
4:16 behold, publish **a** Jerusalem, *that* watchers 5921
4:16 give out their voice **a** the cities of Judah. 5921
4:17 of a field, are they **a** her round about; 5921
4:17 because she hath been rebellious **a** me, 854
5:11 Judah have dealt very treacherously **a** me, 871.1
6: 3 they shall pitch *their* tents **a** her round 5921
6: 4 Prepare ye war **a** her; arise, and let us go 5921
6: 6 down trees, and cast a mount **a** Jerusalem: 5921
6:23 set in array as men for war **a** thee, 5921
8:14 because we have sinned **a** the Lord. 3807.1
8:18 *When* I would comfort myself **a** sorrow, 5921
11:17 planted thee, hath pronounced evil **a** thee, 5921
11:17 which they have done **a** themselves to 3807.1
11:19 knew not that they had devised a device **a** 5921
12: 8 as a lion in the forest; it crieth out **a** me: 5921
12: 9 the birds round about *are* **a** her; 5921
12:14 Thus saith the Lord **a** all mine evil 5921
13:14 I will dash them **a** one another, even 413
14: 7 though our iniquities testify **a** us, 5921
14: 7 are many; we have sinned **a** thee. 3807.1
14:20 our fathers: for we have sinned **a** thee. 3807.1
15: 6 will I stretch out my hand **a** thee, 5921
15: 8 I have brought upon them **a** the mother 5921
15:20 they shall fight **a** thee, but they shall not 413
15:20 but they shall not prevail **a** thee: 3807.1
16:10 Lord pronounced all this great evil **a** us? 5921
16:10 our sin that we have committed **a** the Lord? 3807.1
18: 8 If that nation, **a** whom I have pronounced, 5921
18:11 I frame evil **a** you, and devise a device 5921
18:11 against you, and devise a device **a** you: 5921
18:18 and let us devise devices **a** Jeremiah; 5921
18:23 knowest all their counsel **a** me to slay 5921
19:15 all the evil that I have pronounced **a** it, 5921
20:10 we shall prevail **a** him, and we shall take 3807.1
21: 2 king of Babylon maketh war **a** us; 5921
21: 4 wherewith ye fight **a** the king of Babylon, NIH
21: 4 **a** the Chaldeans, which besiege you NIH
21: 5 I myself will fight **a** you with an 854
21:10 For I have set my face **a** this city for evil, 871.1
21:13 Behold, I *am* **a** thee, O inhabitant of 413
21:13 which say, Who shall come down **a** us? 413
22: 7 I will prepare destroyers **a** thee, every one 5921
23: 2 Israel **a** the pastors that feed my people; 5921
23:30 I *am* **a** the prophets, saith the Lord, 5921
23:31 Behold, I *am* **a** the prophets, saith 5921
23:32 I *am* **a** them that prophesy false dreams, 5921
25: 9 will bring them **a** this land, and against 5921
25: 9 **a** the inhabitants thereof, and against all 5921
25: 9 **a** all these nations round about, 5921
25:13 my words which I have pronounced **a** it, 5921
25:13 which Jeremiah hath prophesied **a** all 5921
25:30 Therefore prophesy thou **a** them all these 413
25:30 as they that tread the grapes, **a** all 413
26: 9 all the people were gathered **a** Jeremiah in 413
26:11 for he hath prophesied **a** this city, as ye 413
26:12 The Lord sent me to prophesy **a** this 413
26:12 **a** this city all the words that ye have heard. 413
26:13 of the evil that he hath pronounced **a** you. 5921
26:19 evil which he had pronounced **a** them? 5921
26:19 Thus *might* we procure great evil **a** our 5921
26:20 who prophesied **a** this city and against 5921
26:20 **a** this land according to all the words of 5921
27:13 as the Lord hath spoken **a** the nation that 413
28: 8 before thee of old prophesied both **a** many 413
28: 8 **a** great kingdoms, of war, and of evil, 5921
28:16 thou hast taught rebellion **a** the Lord. 413
29:32 he hath taught rebellion **a** the Lord. 5921
31:20 for since I spake **a** him, I do earnestly 871.1
31:39 measuring line shall yet go forth **over a** 5048
32:24 that fight **a** it, because of the sword, 5921
32:29 that fight **a** this city, shall come and set 5921
33: 8 whereby they have sinned **a** me, 3807.1
33: 8 whereby they have transgressed **a** me. 871.1
34: 1 fought **a** Jerusalem, and against all 5921
34: 1 and **a** all the cities thereof, saying, 5921
34: 7 When the king of Babylon's army fought **a** 5921
34: 7 **a** all the cities of Judah that were left, 5921
34: 7 were left, **a** Lachish, and against Azekah: 413
34: 7 were left, against Lachish, and **a** Azekah: 413
34:22 they shall fight **a** it, and take it, and burn 5921
35:17 all the evil that I have pronounced **a** them: 5921
36: 2 that I have spoken unto thee **a** Israel, 5921
36: 2 **a** Judah, and against all the nations, 5921
36: 2 against Judah, and **a** all the nations, 5921
36: 7 for the fury that the Lord hath pronounced **a** 413
36:31 all the evil that I have pronounced **a** them; 413
37: 8 fight **a** this city, and take it, and burn it 5921
37:10 army of the Chaldeans that fight **a** you, 854
37:18 What have I offended **a** thee, or 3807.1
37:18 or **a** thy servants, or against this people, 3807.1
37:18 or against thy servants, or **a** this people, 3807.1
37:19 The king of Babylon shall not come **a** you, 5921
37:19 not come against you, nor **a** this land? 5921
38: 5 the king is not *he that* can do *any* thing **a** 854
38:22 set thee on, and have prevailed **a** thee: 3807.1
39: 1 of Babylon and all his army **a** Jerusalem, 413
40: 3 because ye have sinned **a** the Lord, 3807.1
43: 3 the son of Neriah setteth thee on **a** 871.1
44: 7 Wherefore commit ye *this* great evil **a** your 413
44:11 we will not face **a** you for evil, NIH
44:23 because ye have sinned **a** the Lord, 3807.1
44:29 my words shall surely stand **a** you for evil: 5921
46: 1 to Jeremiah the prophet **a** the Gentiles; NIH
46: 2 **A** Egypt, against the army of 3807.1

Jer 46: 2 **a** the army of Pharaoh-necho king of 5921
46:12 for the mighty *man* hath stumbled **a** 871.1
46:22 come **a** her with axes, as hewers of 3807.1
47: 1 to Jeremiah the prophet **a** the Philistines, 413
47: 7 seeing the LORD hath given it a charge **a** 413
47: 7 against Ashkelon, and **a** the sea shore? 413
48: 1 **A** Moab thus saith the LORD of hosts, 3807.1
48: 2 in Heshbon they have devised evil **a** it; 5921
48:26 for he magnified *himself* **a** the LORD: 5921
48:42 he hath magnified *himself* **a** the LORD. 5921
49:14 and come **a** her, and rise up to the battle. 5921
49:19 of Jordan **a** the habitation of the strong: 413
49:20 come **a** her, that he hath taken **a** Edom; 413
49:20 that he hath purposed **a** the inhabitants of 413
49:30 king of Babylon hath taken counsel **a** you, 5921
49:30 and hath conceived a purpose **a** you. 5921
49:34 **a** Elam in the beginning of the reign of 5921
50: 1 The word that the LORD spake **a** Babylon 413
50: 1 the land of the Chaldeans by Jeremiah 413
50: 3 the north there cometh up a nation **a** her, 5921
50: 7 because they have sinned **a** the LORD, 3807.1
50: 9 cause to come up **a** Babylon an assembly 5921
50: 9 they shall set *themselves* in array **a** her; 3807.1
50:14 Put *yourselves* in array **a** Babylon round 5921
50:14 for she hath sinned **a** the LORD. 3807.1
50:15 Shout **a** her round about: she hath given 5921
50:21 Go up **a** the land of Merethaim, 5921
50:21 *even* **a** it, and against the inhabitants of 5921
50:21 against it, and **a** the inhabitants of Pekod: 413
50:24 because thou hast striven **a** the LORD. 871.1
50:26 Come **a** her from the utmost border, 3807.1
50:29 Call together the archers **a** Babylon: all ye 413
50:29 that bend the bow, camp **a** it round about; 5921
50:29 for she hath been proud **a** the LORD, 413
50:29 the LORD, **a** the Holy One of Israel. 413
50:31 Behold, I *am* **a** thee, O thou most proud, 413
50:42 in array, like a man to the battle, **a** thee, 5921
50:45 of the LORD, that he hath taken **a** Babylon, 413
50:45 that he hath purposed **a** the land of 413
51: 1 I *will* raise up **a** Babylon, and against them 5921
51: 1 **a** them that dwell in the midst of them that 413
51: 1 in the midst of them that rise up **a** me, NIH
51: 2 in the day of trouble they shall be **a** her 5921
51: 3 **A** *him that* bendeth let the archer bend his 413
51: 3 a *him that* lifteth himself up in his 413
51: 5 though their land was filled *with* a sin a 4480
51:11 for his device *is* **a** Babylon, to destroy it; 5921
51:12 done that which he spake **a** the inhabitants 413
51:14 and they shall lift up a shout **a** thee. 5921
51:25 I *am* **a** thee, O destroying mountain, 413
51:27 the nations, prepare the nations **a** her, 5921
51:27 call together **a** her the kingdoms of Ararat, 5921
51:27 and Aschenaz; appoint a captain **a** her; 5921
51:28 Prepare **a** her the nations with the kings 5921
51:29 the LORD shall be performed **a** Babylon, 5921
51:46 and violence in the land, ruler **a** ruler. 5921
51:60 *even* all these words that are written **a** 413
51:62 O LORD, thou hast spoken **a** this place, 413
52: 3 that Zedekiah rebelled **a** the king of 871.1
52: 4 **a** Jerusalem, and pitched against it, 5921
52: 4 pitched **a** it, and built forts against it 5921
52: 4 against it, and built forts **a** it round about. 5921
La 1:13 into my bones, and it prevaileth **a** them: 871.1
1:15 he hath called an assembly **a** me to crush 5921
1:18 for I have rebelled **a** his commandment: NIH
2: 3 he burned **a** Jacob like a flaming fire, 871.1
2:16 enemies have opened their mouth **a** thee: 5921
3: 3 Surely **a** me is he turned; he turneth his 871.1
3: 3 he turneth his hand **a** me all the day. NIH
3: 5 He hath builded **a** me, and compassed *me* 5921
3:46 enemies have opened their mouths **a** us. 5921
3:60 *and* all their imaginations **a** me. 3807.1
3:61 O LORD, *and* all their imaginations **a** me; NIH
3:62 The lips of those that rose up **a** me, NIH
3:62 and their device **a** me all the day. 5921
5:22 rejected us; thou art very wroth **a** us. 5921
Eze 1:20 were lifted up **over a** them: 5980+3807.1
1:21 were lifted up **over a** them: 5980+3807.1
2: 3 to a rebellious nation that hath rebelled **a** 871.1
2: 3 and their fathers have transgressed **a** me, 871.1
3: 8 I have made thy face strong **a** 5980+3807.1
3: 8 forehead strong **a** their foreheads. 5980+3807.1
3:13 the noise of the wheels **over a** 5980+3807.1
4: 2 lay siege **a** it, and build a fort against it, 5921
4: 2 build a fort **a** it, and cast a mount against 5921
4: 2 a fort against it, and cast a mount **a** it; 5921
4: 2 set the camp also **a** it, and set *battering* 5921
4: 2 and set *battering* rams **a** it round about. 5921
4: 3 set thy face **a** it, and it shall be besieged, 413
4: 3 be besieged, and thou shalt lay siege **a** it. 5921
4: 7 uncovered, and thou shalt prophesy **a** it. 5921
5: 8 *am* **a** thee, and will execute judgments in 5921
6: 2 mountains of Israel, and prophesy **a** them, 413
11: 4 Therefore prophesy **a** them, prophesy, 5921
13: 2 prophesy **a** the prophets of Israel that 413
13: 8 seen lies, therefore behold, I *am* **a** you, 413
13:17 set thy face **a** the daughters of thy people, 413
13:17 own heart; and prophesy thou **a** them, 5921
13:20 Behold, I *am* **a** your pillows, where*with* 413
14: 8 I will set my face **a** that man, 871.1
14:13 when the land sinneth **a** me by 3807.1
15: 7 I will set my face **a** them; they shall go 871.1
15: 7 the LORD, when I set my face **a** them. 871.1
16:37 will even gather them round about **a** thee, 5921
16:40 They shall also bring up a company **a** thee, 5921

Eze 16:44 proverbs shall use *this* proverb **a** thee, 5921
17:15 he rebelled **a** him in sending his 871.1
17:20 his trespass that he hath trespassed **a** me. 871.1
19: 8 the nations set **a** him on every side from 5921
20: 8 they rebelled **a** me, and would not 871.1
20: 8 to accomplish my anger **a** them in 871.1
20:13 the house of Israel rebelled **a** me in 871.1
20:21 Notwithstanding the children rebelled **a** 871.1
20:21 to accomplish my anger **a** them in 871.1
20:27 in that they have committed a trespass **a** 871.1
20:38 the rebels, and them that transgress **a** me: 871.1
20:46 and prophesy **a** the forest of the south field; 413
21: 2 and prophesy **a** the land of Israel, 413
21: 3 I *am* **a** thee, and will draw forth my sword 413
21: 4 shall my sword go forth out of his sheath **a** 413
21:15 I have set the point of the sword **a** all their 5921
21:22 to appoint *battering* rams **a** the gates, 5921
21:31 I will blow **a** thee in the fire of my wrath, 5921
22: 3 maketh idols **a** herself to defile *herself.* 5921
23:22 Behold, I will raise up thy lovers **a** thee, 5921
23:22 and I will bring them **a** thee on every side; 5921
23:24 they shall come **a** thee *with* chariots, 5921
23:24 *which* shall set **a** thee buckler and shield 5921
23:25 I will set my jealousy **a** thee, and they 871.1
24: 2 the king of Babylon set himself **a** Jerusalem 413
25: 2 set thy face **a** the Ammonites, 413
25: 2 the Ammonites, and prophesy **a** them; 5921
25: 3 Because thou saidst, Aha, **a** my sanctuary, 413
25: 3 **a** the land of Israel, when it was desolate; 413
25: 3 **a** the house of Judah, when they went into 413
25: 6 rejoiced in heart with all thy despite **a** 413
25:12 that Edom hath dealt **a** the house 3807.1
26: 2 because that Tyrus hath said **a** Jerusalem, 5921
26: 3 Behold, I *am* **a** thee, O Tyrus, 5921
26: 3 cause many nations to come up **a** thee, 5921
26: 8 he shall make a fort **a** thee, and cast a 5921
26: 8 cast a mount **a** thee, and lift up the 5921
26: 8 thee, and lift up the buckler **a** thee. 5921
26: 9 he shall set engines of war **a** thy walls, 871.1
27:30 shall cause their voice to be heard **a** thee, 5921
28: 7 they shall draw their swords **a** the beauty 5921
28:21 set thy face **a** Zidon, and prophesy against 413
28:21 thy face against Zidon, and prophesy **a** it, 5921
28:22 Behold, I *am* **a** thee, O Zidon; and I will 5921
29: 2 set thy face **a** Pharaoh king of Egypt, 5921
29: 2 and prophesy **a** him, and against all Egypt: 5921
29: 2 and prophesy against him, and **a** all Egypt: 5921
29: 3 Behold, I *am* **a** thee, Pharaoh king of 5921
29:10 I *am* **a** thee, and against thy rivers, and I 413
29:10 **a** thy rivers, and I will make the land of 413
29:18 his army to serve a great service **a** Tyrus: 413
29:18 for the service that he had served **a** it: 5921
29:20 *for* his labour wherewith he served **a** it, 871.1
30:11 they shall draw their swords **a** Egypt, 5921
30:22 I *am* **a** Pharaoh king of Egypt, and will 413
33:30 children of thy people still are talking **a** 871.1
34: 2 prophesy **a** the shepherds of Israel, 5921
34:10 Behold, I *am* **a** the shepherds; and I will 413
35: 2 set thy face **a** mount Seir, 5921
35: 2 face against mount Seir, and prophesy **a** it, 5921
35: 3 I *am* **a** thee, and I will stretch out mine 413
35: 3 I will stretch out mine hand **a** thee, 5921
35:11 thou hast used out of thy hatred **a** them; 871.1
35:12 hast spoken **a** the mountains of Israel, 5921
35:13 Thus with your mouth ye have boasted **a** 5921
35:13 and have multiplied your words **a** me: 5921
36: 2 Because the enemy hath said **a** you, Aha, 5921
36: 5 I spoken **a** the residue of the heathen, 5921
36: 5 residue of the heathen, and **a** all Idumea, 5921
38: 2 Son of man, set thy face **a** Gog, the land 413
38: 2 and Tubal, and prophesy **a** him, 5921
38: 3 I *am* **a** thee, O Gog, the chief prince 413
38: 8 **a** the mountains of Israel, which have 5921
38:16 thou shalt come up **a** my people of Israel, 5921
38:16 latter days, and I will bring thee **a** my land, 5921
38:17 that *I* would bring **a** them? 5921
38:18 when Gog shall come **a** the land of Israel, 5921
38:21 I will call *for* a sword **a** him throughout all 5921
38:21 every man's sword shall be **a** his brother. 871.1
38:22 I will plead **a** him with pestilence 854
39: 1 son of man, prophesy **a** Gog, and say, 5921
39: 1 I *am* **a** thee, O Gog, the chief prince 413
39:23 because they trespassed **a** me, therefore 871.1
39:26 whereby they have trespassed **a** me, 871.1
40:13 *was* five and twenty cubits, door **a** door. 5048
40:18 **over a** the length of the gates 5980+3807.1
40:23 the gate of the inner court *was* **over a** 5048
41:15 **over a** the separate place which *was* 413+6440
41:16 on their three *stories,* **over a** the door, 5048
42: 1 that *was* **over a** the separate place, 5048
42: 3 **Over a** the twenty *cubits* which *were* for 5048
42: 3 **over a** the pavement which *was* for 5048
42: 3 *was* gallery **a** gallery in three *stories.* 413+6440
42: 7 the wall that *was* without **over a** 5980+3807.1
42:10 **over a** the separate place, and *over* 413+6440
42:10 and **over a** the building. 413+6440
44:12 therefore have I lift up mine hand **a** them, 5921
45: 6 **over a** the oblation of the holy 5980+3807.1
45: 7 the length *shall be* **over a** one of 5980+3807.1
46: 9 he came in, but go forth **over a** it. 5226
47:20 border, till *a man* come **over a** Hamath. 5227
48:13 **over a** the border of the priests, 5980+3807.1
48:15 that are left in the breadth **over a** 5921+6440
48:18 the residue in length **over a** 5980+3807.1
48:18 it shall be **over a** the oblation of 5980+3807.1

Eze 48:21 **over a** the five and twenty thousand 413+6440
48:21 westward **over a** the five 5921+6440
48:21 **over a** the portions for the prince: 5980+3807.1
Da 3:19 the form of his visage was changed **a** 5922
3:29 which speak any thing amiss **a** the God of 5922
5: 5 wrote **over a** the candlestick upon 6903
5: 6 and his knees smote one **a** another. 3807.2
5:23 hast lifted up thyself **a** the Lord of heaven; 5922
6: 4 princes sought to find occasion **a** Daniel 5922
6: 5 We shall not find any occasion **a** this 3807.2
6: 5 we find *it* **a** him concerning the law 5922
7:21 with the saints, and prevailed **a** them; 5922
7:25 he shall speak *great* words **a** 6655+3807.2
8: 7 he was moved with choler **a** him, 413
8:12 a host was given *him* **a** the daily *sacrifice* 5921
8:25 he shall also stand up **a** the Prince of 5921
9: 7 their trespass that they have trespassed **a** 871.1
9: 8 because we have sinned **a** thee. 3807.1
9: 9 though we have rebelled **a** him; 871.1
9:11 of God, because we have sinned **a** him. 3807.1
9:12 he spake **a** us, and against our judges 5921
9:12 us, and **a** our judges that judged us, 5921
11: 2 he shall stir up all **a** the realm of Grecia. 854
11: 7 and shall deal **a** them, and shall prevail: 871.1
11:14 in those times there shall many stand up **a** 5921
11:16 he that cometh **a** him shall do according to 413
11:24 he shall **forecast** his devices **a** the strong 2803
11:25 his courage **a** the king of the south with a 5921
11:25 for they shall forecast devices **a** him. 5921
11:28 his heart *shall be* **a** the holy covenant; 5921
11:30 *the* ships of Chittim shall come **a** him: 871.1
11:30 and have indignation **a** the holy covenant: 5921
11:32 such as do wickedly **a** the covenant shall NIH
11:36 shall speak marvellous *things* **a** the God of 5921
11:40 the king of the north shall come **a** him like 5921
Hos 4: 7 were increased, so they sinned **a** me: 3807.1
5: 7 They have dealt treacherously **a** 871.1
6: 7 there have they dealt treacherously **a** me. 871.1
7:13 because they have transgressed **a** me: 871.1
7:13 yet they have spoken lies **a** me. 5921
7:14 for corn and wine, *and* they rebel **a** me. 871.1
7:15 yet do they imagine mischief **a** me. 413
8: 1 *He shall come* as an eagle **a** the house of 5921
8: 1 my covenant, and trespassed **a** my law. 5921
8: 5 *thee* off; mine anger is kindled **a** them: 871.1
10: 9 the battle in Gibeah **a** the children of 5921
10:10 *the* people shall be gathered **a** them, 5921
13:16 for she hath rebelled **a** her God: 871.1
Joel 3:19 for the violence **a** the children of Judah, NIH
Am 1: 8 and I will turn mine hand **a** Ekron: 5921
3: 1 word that the LORD hath spoken **a** you, 5921
3: 1 **a** the whole family which I brought up 5921
5: 1 Hear ye this word which I take up **a** you, 5921
5: 9 strengtheneth the spoiled **a** the strong, 5921
5: 9 that the spoiled shall come **a** the fortress. 5921
6:14 behold, I *will* raise up **a** you a nation, 5921
7: 9 I will rise **a** the house of Jeroboam 5921
7:10 Amos hath conspired **a** thee in the midst 7130
7:16 Prophesy not **a** Israel, and drop not *thy* 5921
7:16 drop not *thy word* **a** the house of Isaac. 5921
Ob 1: 1 Arise ye, and let us rise up **a** her in battle. 5921
1: 7 deceived thee, *and* prevailed **a** thee; 3807.1
1:10 For *thy* violence **a** thy brother Jacob shame NIH
Jnh 1: 2 go to Nineveh, *that* great city, and cry **a** it; 5921
1:13 wrought, and was tempestuous **a** them. 5921
Mic 1: 2 let the Lord GOD be witness **a** you, 871.1
2: 3 Behold, **a** this family do I devise an evil, 5921
2: 4 In that day shall *one* take up a parable **a** 5921
3: 5 mouths, they even prepare war **a** him. 5921
4: 3 nation shall not lift up a sword **a** nation, 413
4:11 also many nations are gathered **a** thee, 5921
5: 1 he hath laid siege **a** us: they shall smite 5921
5: 5 shall we raise **a** him seven shepherds, 5921
6: 3 have I wearied thee? testify **a** me. 871.1
6: 6 the daughter riseth up **a** her mother, 871.1
7: 6 the daughter in law **a** her mother in law; 871.1
7: 8 Rejoice not **a** me, O mine enemy: 3807.1
7: 9 because I have sinned **a** him, until he 3807.1
Na 1: 9 What do ye imagine **a** the LORD? he *will* 413
1:11 that imagineth evil **a** the LORD, a wicked 5921
2: 4 they shall **justle** one **a** another in the 8264
2:13 Behold, I *am* **a** thee, saith the LORD of 413
3: 5 Behold, I *am* **a** thee, saith the LORD of 413
Hab 2: 6 Shall not all these take up a parable **a** him, 5921
2: 6 and a taunting proverb **a** him, and say, 3807.1
2:10 many people, and *hast* sinned **a** thy soul. NIH
3: 8 Was the LORD displeased **a** the rivers? 871.1
3: 8 *was* thine anger **a** the rivers? *was* thy 871.1
3: 8 *was* thy wrath **a** the sea, that thou didst 871.1
Zep 1:16 the trumpet and alarm **a** the fenced cities, 5921
1:16 the fenced cities, and **a** the high towers. 5921
1:17 because they have sinned **a** the LORD: 3807.1
2: 5 the word of the LORD *is* **a** you; 5921
2: 8 and magnified *themselves* **a** their border. 5921
2:10 magnified *themselves* **a** the people of 5921
2:13 he will stretch out his hand **a** the north, 5921
3:11 wherein thou hast transgressed **a** me: 871.1
Zec 1:12 **a** which thou hast had indignation these NIH
7:10 let none of you imagine evil **a** his brother NIH
8:10 let all men every one **a** his neighbour. 871.1
8:17 none of you imagine evil in your hearts **a** NIH
9:13 O Zion, **a** thy sons, O Greece, 5921
10: 3 Mine anger was kindled **a** the shepherds, 5921
12: 2 when they shall be in the siege both **a** 5921
12: 2 siege both against Judah *and* **a** Jerusalem. 5921

Zec 12: 3 of the earth be gathered together **a** it. 5921
12: 7 do not magnify *themselves* **a** Judah. 5921
12: 9 all the nations that come **a** Jerusalem. 5921
13: 7 **a** my shepherd, and against the man 5921
13: 7 and **a** the man *that is* my fellow, 5921
14: 2 For I will gather all nations **a** Jerusalem to 413
14: 3 LORD go forth, and fight **a** those nations, 871.1
14:12 the people that have fought **a** Jerusalem, 5921
14:13 his hand shall rise up **a** the hand of his 5921
14:16 **a** Jerusalem shall even go up from year to 5921
Mal 1: 4 The people **a** whom the LORD hath NIH
2:10 do we deal treacherously every man **a** 871.1
2:14 **a** whom thou hast dealt treacherously: 871.1
2:15 let none deal treacherously **a** the wife of 871.1
3: 5 I will be a swift witness **a** the sorcerers, 871.1
3: 5 the adulterers, and against false 871.1
3: 5 a false swearers, and against those that 871.1
3: 5 **a** those that oppress the hireling in *his* 871.1
3:13 Your words have been stout **a** me, saith 5921
3:13 What have we spoken so much **a** thee? 5921
Mt 4: 6 lest at any time thou dash thy foot **a** 4314
5:11 shall say all manner of evil **a** you falsely, 2596
5:23 that thy brother hath ought **a** thee; 2596
10: 1 he gave them power **a** unclean spirits, NIG
10:18 for a testimony **a** them and the Gentiles. NIG
10:21 children shall **rise up a** *their* parents, 1881
10:35 For I am come to set a man at variance **a** 2596
10:35 and the daughter **a** her mother, 2596
10:35 the daughter in law **a** her mother in law. 2596
12:14 went out, and held a council **a** him, 2596
12:25 Every kingdom divided **a** itself is brought 2596
12:25 or house divided **a** itself shall not stand: 2596
12:26 cast out Satan, he is divided **a** himself; 1909
12:30 He that is not with me is **a** me; and he 2596
12:31 the blasphemy **a** the *Holy* Ghost shall not NIG
12:32 whosoever speaketh a word **a** the Son 2596
12:32 but whosoever speaketh **a** the Holy Ghost, 2596
16:18 and the gates of hell shall not **prevail a** it. 2729
18:15 Moreover if thy brother shall trespass **a** 1519
18:21 how oft shall my brother sin **a** me, and I 1519
20:11 murmured **a** the goodman of the house, 2596
20:24 with indignation **a** the two brethren. 4012
21: 2 Go into the village **over a** you, 561
23:13 for ye shut up the kingdom of heaven **a** 1715
24: 7 For nation shall rise **a** nation, 1909
24: 7 against nation, and kingdom **a** kingdom: 1909
26:55 Are ye come out as **a** a thief with swords 1909
26:59 the council, sought false witness **a** Jesus, 2596
26:62 what *is it which* these **witness a** thee? 2649
27: 1 elders of the people took counsel **a** Jesus 2596
27:13 how many *things* they **witness a** thee? 2649
27:61 other Mary, sitting **over a** the sepulchre. 561
Mk 3: 6 took counsel with the Herodians **a** him, 2596
3:24 And if a kingdom be divided **a** itself, 1909
3:25 And if a house be divided **a** itself, 1909
3:26 And if Satan rise up **a** himself, 1909
3:29 But he that shall blaspheme **a** the Holy 1519
6:11 under your feet for a testimony **a** NIG
6:19 Therefore Herodias **had a quarrel a** him, 1758
9:40 For he that is not **a** us is on our part. 2596
10:11 marry another, committeth adultery **a** her. 1909
11: 2 Go your way into the village **over a** you: 2713
11:25 forgive, if ye have ought **a** any: 2596
12:12 that he had spoken the parable **a** them: 4314
12:41 And Jesus sat **over a** the treasury, 2713
13: 3 the mount of Olives **over a** the temple, 2713
13: 8 For nation shall rise **a** nation, 1909
13: 8 against nation, and kingdom **a** kingdom: 1909
13: 9 kings for my sake, for a testimony **a** them. NIG
13:12 and children shall rise up **a** *their* parents, 1909
14: 5 to the poor. And they **murmured a** her. 1690
14:48 as **a** a thief, with swords and *with* staves 1909
14:55 all the council sought for witness **a** Jesus 2596
14:56 For many bare false witness **a** him, 2596
14:57 and bare false witness **a** him, saying, 2596
14:60 what *is it which* these **witness a** thee? 2649
15: 4 behold how many *things* they **witness a** 2649
15:39 which stood **over a** him, saw that 1537+1727
Lk 2:34 and for a sign which shall be **spoken a**; 483
4:11 lest at any time thou dash thy foot **a** a 4314
5:30 and Pharisees murmured **a** his disciples, 4314
6: 7 that they might find an **accusation a** him. 2724
6:49 **a** which the stream did **beat vehemently**, 4366
7:30 lawyers rejected the counsel of God **a** 1519
8:26 of the Gadarenes, which is **over a** Galilee. 495
9: 5 dust from your feet for a testimony **a** them. 1909
9:50 him not: for he that is not **a** us is for us. 2596
10:11 cleaveth on us, we do **wipe off a** you: 631
11:17 Every kingdom divided **a** itself is brought 1909
11:17 and a house *divided* **a** a house falleth. 1909
11:18 If Satan also be divided **a** himself, 1909
11:23 He that is not with me is **a** me: and he 2596
12:10 And whosoever shall speak a word **a** 1519
12:10 unto him that blasphemeth **a** the Holy 1519
12:52 three **a** two, and two against three. 1909
12:52 three against two, and two **a** three. 1909
12:53 The father shall be divided **a** the son, 1909
12:53 against the son, and the son **a** the father; 1909
12:53 the mother **a** the daughter, and the 1909
12:53 and the daughter **a** the mother; 1909
12:53 the mother in law **a** her daughter in law, 1909
12:53 the daughter in law **a** her mother in law. 1909
14:31 to **make war a** another king, 1519+4171+4820
14:31 that cometh **a** him with twenty thousand? 1909
15:18 I have sinned **a** heaven, and before thee, 1519

Lk 15:21 I have sinned **a** heaven, and in thy sight, 1519
17: 3 If thy brother trespass **a** thee, rebuke him; 1519
17: 4 And if he trespass **a** thee seven times in a 1519
19:30 Go ye into the village **over a** *you;* in 2713
20:19 that he had spoken this parable **a** them. 4314
21:10 Nation shall rise **a** nation, 1909
21:10 against nation, and kingdom **a** kingdom: 1909
22:52 as **a** a thief, with swords and staves? 1909
22:53 ye stretched forth no hands **a** me: 1909
22:65 *things* blasphemously spake they **a** him. 1519
Jn 12: 7 the day of my burying hath she kept *this.* 1519
13:18 bread with me hath lift up his heel **a** me. 1909
13:29 Buy *those things* that we have need of **a** 1519
18:29 What accusation bring you **a** this man? 2596
19:11 Thou couldest have no power **a** all **a** me, 2596
19:12 maketh himself a king **speaketh a** 483
Ac 4:14 with them, they could **say** nothing **a** *it.* 471
4:26 the rulers were gathered together **a** 2596
4:26 together against the Lord, and **a** his Christ. 2596
4:27 For of a truth **a** thy holy child Jesus, 1909
5:39 lest haply ye be found even to **fight a God.** 2314
6: 1 there arose a murmuring of the Grecians **a** 4314
6:11 him speak blasphemous words **a** Moses, 1519
6:11 words against Moses, and **a** God. NIG
6:13 blasphemous words **a** this holy place, 2596
8: 1 **a** the church which was at Jerusalem; 1909
9: 1 and slaughter **a** the disciples of the Lord, 1519
9: 5 *it is* hard for thee to kick **a** the pricks. 4314
9:29 Lord Jesus, and disputed **a** the Grecians: 4314
13:45 **spake a** those *things* which were spoken 483
13:50 and raised persecution **a** Paul 1909
13:51 But they shook off the dust of their feet **a** 1909
14: 2 made their minds evil affected **a** 2596
16:22 the multitude rose up together **a** them: 2596
18:12 **made insurrection** with one accord **a** 2721
19:16 prevailed **a** them, so that they fled 2596
19:36 that these *things* **cannot be spoken a**, 368
19:38 have a matter **a** any *man,* the law is open, 4314
20:15 and came the next *day* **over a** Chios; 481
21:28 that teacheth all *men* every where **a** 2596
22:24 he might know wherefore they **cried** so **a** 2019
23: 9 spoken to him, let us not **fight a God.** 2313
23:30 to say before thee what *they had* **a** him. 4314
24: 1 who informed the governor **a** Paul. 2596
24:19 and object, if they had ought **a** me. 4314
25: 2 the chief of the Jews informed him **a** Paul, 2596
25: 3 And desired favour **a** him, that he would 2596
25: 7 laid many and grievous complaints **a** Paul, 2596
25: 8 Neither **a** the law of the Jews, 1519
25: 8 neither **a** the temple, nor *yet* against Cesar, 1519
25: 8 neither against the temple, nor *yet* **a** Cesar, 1519
25:15 me, desiring to have judgment **a** him. 2596
25:16 himself concerning the crime laid **a** him. NIG
25:18 A whom when the accusers stood *up,* 4012
25:19 But had certain questions **a** him of their 4314
25:27 not withal to signify the crimes *laid* **a** him. 2596
26:10 put to death, I gave my **voice a** them. 5586
26:11 and being exceedingly **mad a** them, 1693
26:14 *it is* hard for thee to kick **a** the pricks. 4314
27: 7 and scarce were come **over a** Cnidus, 2596
27: 7 we sailed under Crete, **over a** Salmone, 2596
27:14 But not long after there arose **a** it a 2596
28:17 though I have committed nothing **a** 1727
28:19 But when the Jews **spake a** *it,* I was 483
28:22 we know that every where it is **spoken a**. 483
Ro 1:18 is revealed from heaven **a** all ungodliness 1909
1:26 the natural use into that which is **a** nature: 3844
2: 2 to truth **a** them which commit such *things.* 1909
2: 5 up unto thyself wrath **a** the day of wrath 1722
4:18 Who **a** hope believed in hope, that he 3844
7:23 **warring a** the law of my mind, 497
8: 7 Because the carnal mind *is* enmity **a** God: 1519
8:31 *things?* If God *be* for us, who can *be* **a** us? 2596
9:20 O man, who art thou that **repliest a** God? 470
11: 2 how he maketh intercession to God **a** 2596
11:18 **Boast** not **a** the branches: but if thou 2620
1Co 4: 6 that no one of you be puffed up for one **a** 2596
6: 1 any of you, having a matter **a** another, 4314
6:18 that committeth fornication sinneth **a** his 1519
8:12 But when ye sin so **a** the brethren, 1519
8:12 their weak conscience, ye sin **a** Christ. 1519
7:17 if **a** my **will**, a dispensation *of the gospel* 210
2Co 10: 2 wherewith I think to be bold **a** some, 1909
10: 5 every high thing that exalteth itself **a** 2596
13: 8 For we can do nothing **a** the truth, 2596
Gal 3:21 *Is* the law then **a** the promises of God? 2596
5:17 For the flesh lusteth **a** the Spirit, 2596
5:17 the Spirit, and the Spirit **a** the flesh: 2596
5:23 **a** such there is no law. 2596
Eph 6:11 that ye may be able to stand **a** the wiles of 4314
6:12 For we wrestle not **a** flesh and blood, 4314
6:12 flesh and blood, but **a** principalities, 4314
6:12 blood, but against principalities, **a** powers, 4314
6:12 **a** the rulers of the darkness of this world, 4314
6:12 **a** spiritual wickedness in high *places.* 4314
Col 2:14 handwriting of ordinances that was **a** us, 2596
3:13 if any *man* have a quarrel **a** any: 4314
3:19 love *your* wives, and be not bitter **a** them. 4314
1Ti 5:11 when they have *begun to* **wax wanton a** 2691
5:19 **A** an elder receive not an accusation, 2596
6:19 a good foundation **a** the time to come, 1519
2Ti 1:12 I have committed unto *him* **a** that day. 1519
Heb 12: 3 such contradiction of sinners **a** himself, 1519
12: 4 not yet resisted unto blood, striving **a** sin. 4314
Jas 2:13 mercy; and mercy **rejoiceth a** judgment. 2620

Jas 3:14 glory not, and lie *not* **a** the truth. 2596
5: 3 the rust of them shall be a witness **a** you, 1519
5: 9 Grudge not one **a** another, brethren, lest 2596
1Pe 2:11 from fleshly lusts, which war **a** the soul; 2596
2:12 whereas they **speak a** you as evildoers, 2635
3:12 the face of the Lord *is* **a** them that do evil. 1909
2Pe 2:11 bring not railing accusation **a** them before 2596
3: 7 reserved unto fire **a** the day of judgment 1519
3Jn 1:10 **prating a** us with malicious words: 5396
Jude 1: 9 durst not **bring a** him a railing accusation, 2018
1:15 which ungodly sinners have spoken **a** him. 2596
Rev 2: 4 Nevertheless I have **somewhat a** thee, 2596
2:14 But I have a few *things* **a** thee, because 2596
2:16 will fight **a** them with the sword of my 3326
2:20 I have a few *things* **a** thee, 2596
11: 7 the bottomless *pit* shall make war **a** them, 3326
12: 7 and his angels fought **a** the dragon; 2596
13: 6 And he opened his mouth in blasphemy **a** 4314
19:19 gathered together to make war **a** him that 3326
19:19 him that sat on the horse, and **a** his army. 3326

AGAR (2) [HAGAR]

Gal 4:24 which gendereth to bondage, which is **A**. 28
4:25 For *this* **A** is mount Sinai in Arabia, 28

AGATE (3) [AGATES]

Ex 28:19 third row a ligure, an **a**, and an amethyst. 7618
39:12 third row, a ligure, an **a**, and an amethyst. 7618
Eze 27:16 and fine linen, and coral, and **a**. 3539

AGATES (1) [AGATE]

Isa 54:12 I will make thy windows *of* **a**, and thy 3539

AGE (42) [AGED, AGES]

Ge 15:15 thou shalt be buried in a good old **a**. 7872
18:11 Sarah were old *and* well stricken in **a**; 3117
21: 2 and bare Abraham a son in his old **a**, 2208
21: 7 for I have born *him* a son in his old **a**. 2208
24: 1 Abraham was old, *and* well stricken in **a**: 3117
25: 8 died in a good old **a**, an old man, 7872
37: 3 because he *was* the son of his old **a**: 2208
44:20 and a child of *his* old **a**, a little one; 2208
47:28 *whole a* of Jacob was an 2416+3117+8141
48:10 Now the eyes of Israel were dim for **a**, 2207
Nu 8:25 from the **a** of fifty years they shall cease 1121
Jos 3: 1 that Joshua waxed old *and* stricken in **a**, 3117
23: 2 unto them, I am old *and* stricken in **a**: 3117
Jdg 8:32 the son of Joash died in a good old **a**, 7872
Ru 4:15 of *thy* life, and a nourisher of thine old **a**. 7872
1Sa 2:33 house shall die **in the flower of** their **a**. 376
1Ki 14: 4 for his eyes were set by reason of his **a**. 7869
15:23 Nevertheless in the time of his old **a** he 2209
1Ch 23: 3 the Levites were numbered from the **a** 1121
23:24 from the **a** of twenty years and upward. 1121
29:28 he died in a good old **a**, full of days, 7872
2Ch 36:17 old man, or **him** that **stooped for a**: 3486
Job 5:26 Thou shalt come to *thy* grave in a **full a**, 3624
8: 8 of the former **a**, and prepare *thyself* to 1755
11:17 *thine* **a** shall be clearer than the noonday; 2465
30: 2 profit me, in whom old **a** was perished? 3624
Ps 39: 5 and mine **a** *is as* nothing before thee: 2465
71: 9 Cast me not off in the time of old **a**; 2209
92:14 They shall still bring forth fruit in old **a**; 7872
Isa 38:12 Mine **a** is departed, and is removed from 1755
46: 4 *even* to *your* old **a** I *am* he; and *even* to 2209
Zec 8: 4 man with his staff in his hand for very **a**. 3117
Mk 5:42 for she was *of the* **a** of twelve years. NIG
Lk 1:36 she hath also conceived a son in her old **a**: 1094
2:36 of Aser: she was of a great **a**, 1722+2250+4260
3:23 began to be about thirty **years of a**, 2094
8:42 about twelve **years of a**, and she lay **a** 2094
Jn 9:21 he is of **a**; ask him: he shall speak for 2244
9:23 Therefore said his parents, He is of **a**; 2244
1Co 7:36 if she **pass the flower of** her **a**, 1510+5230
Heb 5:14 meat belongeth to *them that are* of **full a**, 5046
11:11 of a child when *she* was past **a**, 2244+2540

AGED (9) [AGE]

2Sa 19:32 Now Barzillai was a very **a** man, 2204
Job 12:20 taketh *away* the understanding of the **a**. 2205
15:10 both the grayheaded and **very a** men, 3453
29: 8 and the **a** arose, *and* stood up. 3453
32: 9 neither do the **a** understand judgment. 2205
Jer 6:11 taken, the **a** with *him that is* full of days. 2205
Tit 2: 2 the **a men** be sober, grave, temperate, 4246
2: 3 The **a women** likewise, that they *be* in 4247
Phm 1: 9 *thee,* being such a one as Paul the **a**, 4246

AGEE (1)

2Sa 23:11 after him *was* Shammah the son of **A** 89

AGES (4) [AGE]

Eph 2: 7 That in the **a** to come he might shew 165
3: 5 Which in other **a** was not made known 1074
3:21 church by Christ Jesus throughout all **a**, 1074
Col 1:26 the mystery which hath been hid from **a** 165

AGO (13)

1Sa 9:20 thine asses that were lost three days **a**, 3117
2Ki 19:25 thou not heard **long a** 4480+7350+3807.1
Ezr 5:11 was builded these many years **a**, 4481+6928
Isa 22:11 unto him that fashioned it **long a**. 4480+7350
37:26 thou not heard **long a**, 4480+7350+3807.1
Mt 11:21 Sidon they would have repented **long a** 3819
Mk 9:21 How **long** is it is since this came unto him? 5550
Lk 10:13 they had a **great while a** repented, 3819

Ac	10:30	Four days a I was fasting until this hour;	575
	15: 7	how that **a good while a**	575+744+2250
2Co	8:10	but also to be forward **a year a**.	575+4070
	9: 2	that Achaia was ready **a year a;**	575+4070
	12: 2	a man in Christ above fourteen years a,	NIG

AGONE (1)
1Sa	30:13	left me, because three days **a** I fell sick.	NIH

AGONY (1)
Lk	22:44	And being in an **a** he prayed more earnestly:	74

AGREE (7) [AGREED, AGREEMENT, AGREETH]
Mt	5:25	**A with** thine adversary quickly,	2132
	18:19	That if two of you shall **a** on earth as	4856
	20:13	didst not thou **a with** me for a penny?	4856
Mk	14:59	so did their witness **a together**.	1510+2470
Ac	15:15	And to this **a** the words of the prophets;	4856
1Jn	5: 8	and the blood: and *these* three **a** in one.	1510
Rev	17:17	to fulfil his will, and to **a**,	1106+1520+4160

AGREED (8) [AGREE]
Am	3: 3	Can two walk together, except they be **a**?	3259
Mt	20: 2	when he had **a** with the labourers for a	4856
Mk	14:56	but *their* witness **a** not **together**.	4856
Jn	9:22	for the Jews had **a** already, that if any *man*	4934
Ac	5: 9	How *is it* that ye have **a together** to tempt	4856
	5:40	And to him they **a**: and when they had	3982
	23:20	The Jews have **a** to desire thee that thou	4934
	28:25	And when they **a** not among	800+1510

AGREEMENT (6) [AGREE]
2Ki	18:31	Make an **a** with me *by* a present,	NIH
Isa	28:15	with death, and with hell are we at **a;**	2374
	28:18	and your **a** with hell shall not stand;	2380
	36:16	Make an **a** with me *by* a present,	NIH
Da	11: 6	to the king of the north to make an **a:**	4339
2Co	6:16	And what **a** hath the temple of God with	4783

AGREETH (2) [AGREE]
Mk	14:70	art a Galilean, and thy speech **a** *thereto*.	3662
Lk	5:36	the piece that was *taken* out of the new **a**	4856

AGRIPPA (12)
Ac	25:13	And after certain days king **A**	67
	25:22	Then **A** said unto Festus, I would also hear	67
	25:23	when **A** was come, and Bernice, with great	67
	25:24	King **A**, and all men which are here present	67
	25:26	and specially before thee, O king **A**, that,	67
	26: 1	Then **A** said unto Paul, Thou art permitted	67
	26: 2	king **A**, because I shall answer for myself	67
	26: 7	For which hope's sake, king **A**, I am accused	67
	26:19	Whereupon, O king **A**, I was not disobedient	67
	26:27	King **A**, believest thou the prophets?	67
	26:28	Then **A** said unto Paul, Almost thou	67
	26:32	Then said **A** unto Festus, This man might	67

AGROUND (1) [GROUND]
Ac	27:41	where two seas met, they **ran** the ship **a;**	2027

AGUE (1)
Lev	26:16	consumption, and the **burning a**, that	6920

AGUR (1)
Pr	30: 1	The words of **A** the son of Jakeh, *even*	94

AH (18) [AHA]
Ps	35:25	say in their hearts, **A**, so would we have	1889
Isa	1: 4	A sinful nation, a people laden with	1945
	1:24	of hosts, the mighty One of Israel, **A**,	1945
Jer	1: 6	said I, **A**, Lord GOD, behold, I cannot	162
	4:10	(Then said I, **A**, Lord GOD! surely thou	162
	14:13	said I, **A** Lord GOD! behold, the prophets	162
	22:18	not lament for him, *saying*, **A** my brother!	1945
	22:18	or, **A** sister! they shall not lament for him,	1945
	22:18	shall not lament for him, *saying*, **A** lord!	1945
	22:18	for him, *saying*, Ah lord! or, **A** his glory.	1945
	32:17	**A** Lord GOD! behold, thou hast made	162
	34: 5	and they will lament thee, *saying*, **A** lord!	1945
Eze	4:14	said I, **A** Lord GOD, behold, my soul *hath*	162
	9: 8	my face, and cried, and said, **A** Lord GOD,	162
	11:13	*with* a loud voice, and said, **A** Lord GOD,	162
	20:49	said I, **A** Lord GOD, they say of me, Doth	162
	21:15	**a**, *it is* made bright, *it is* wrapt up for	253
Mk	15:29	wagging their heads, and saying, **A**,	3758

AHA (10) [AH, HA]
Ps	35:21	*and* said, **A**, aha, our eye hath seen *it*.	1889
	35:21	*and* said, Aha, **a**, our eye hath seen *it*.	1889
	40:15	of their shame that say unto me, **A**, aha!	1889
	40:15	of their shame that say unto me, Aha, **a**!	1889
	70: 3	a reward of their shame that say, **A**, aha.	1889
	70: 3	a reward of their shame that say, Aha, **a**.	1889
Isa	44:16	saith, **A**, I am warm, I have seen the fire:	1889
Eze	25: 3	Because thou saidst, **A**, against my	1889
	26: 2	Tyrus hath said against Jerusalem, **A**,	1889
	36: 2	the enemy hath said against you, **A**,	1889

AHAB (92) [AHAB'S]
1Ki	16:28	and **A** his son reigned in his stead.	256
	16:29	eighth year of Asa king of Judah *began* **A**	256
	16:29	**A** the son of Omri reigned over Israel in	256
	16:30	**A** the son of Omri did evil in the sight of	256
	16:33	**A** made a grove; and Ahab did more to	256
	16:33	**A** did more to provoke the LORD God of	256
	17: 1	said unto **A**, *As* the LORD God of Israel	256

1Ki	18: 1	third year, saying, Go, shew thyself unto **A**;	256
	18: 2	Elijah went to shew himself unto **A**.	256
	18: 3	A called Obadiah, which *was* the governor	256
	18: 5	said unto Obadiah, Go into the land,	256
	18: 6	A went one way by himself,	256
	18: 9	deliver thy servant into the hand of **A**,	256
	18:12	*so* when I come and tell **A**, and he cannot	256
	18:16	So Obadiah went to meet **A**, and told him:	256
	18:16	and told him: and **A** went to meet Elijah.	256
	18:17	it came to pass, when **A** saw Elijah,	256
	18:17	Ahab saw Elijah, that **A** said unto him,	256
	18:20	So **A** sent unto all the children of Israel,	256
	18:41	And Elijah said unto **A**, Get thee up, eat	256
	18:42	So **A** went up to eat and to drink.	256
	18:44	he said, Go up, say unto **A**, Prepare thy	256
	18:45	great rain. And **A** rode, and went to Jezreel.	256
	18:46	and ran before **A** to the entrance of Jezreel.	256
	19: 1	A told Jezebel all that Elijah had done,	256
	20: 2	he sent messengers to **A** king of Israel into	256
	20:13	there came a prophet unto **A** king of Israel,	256
	20:14	A said, By whom? And he said, Thus saith	NIH
	20:34	said **A**, I will send thee away with *this*	NIH
	21: 1	hard by the palace of **A** king of Samaria.	256
	21: 2	A spake unto Naboth, saying, Give me thy	256
	21: 3	Naboth said to **A**, The LORD forbid it me,	256
	21: 4	A came into his house heavy and displeased	256
	21:15	was dead, that Jezebel said to **A**, Arise,	256
	21:16	when **A** heard that Naboth was dead,	256
	21:16	that **A** rose up to go down to the vineyard	256
	21:18	Arise, go down to meet **A** king of Israel,	256
	21:20	A said to Elijah, Hast thou found me,	256
	21:21	will cut off from **A** him that pisseth against	256
	21:24	Him that dieth of **A** in the city the dogs	256
	21:25	(But there was none like unto **A**, which did	256
	21:27	it came to pass, when **A** heard those words,	256
	21:29	Seest thou how **A** humbleth himself before	256
	22:20	Who shall persuade **A**, that he may go up	256
	22:39	Now the rest of the acts of **A**, and all that	256
	22:40	So **A** slept with his fathers; and Ahaziah his	256
	22:41	Judah in the fourth year of **A** king of Israel.	256
	22:49	Ahaziah the son of **A** unto Jehoshaphat,	256
	22:51	Ahaziah the son of **A** *began* to reign over	256
2Ki	1: 1	rebelled against Israel after the death of **A**.	256
	3: 1	Now Jehoram the son of **A** *began* to reign	256
	3: 5	it came to pass, when **A** was dead, that	256
	8:16	in the fifth year of Joram the son of **A** king	256
	8:18	of the kings of Israel, as did the house of **A:**	256
	8:18	for the daughter of **A** was his wife:	256
	8:25	In the twelfth year of Joram the son of **A**	256
	8:27	he walked in the way of the house of **A**,	256
	8:27	sight of the LORD, as *did* the house of **A:**	256
	8:27	for he *was* the son in law of the house of **A**.	256
	8:28	went with Joram the son of **A** to the war	256
	8:29	down to see Joram the son of **A** in Jezreel,	256
	9: 7	thou shalt smite the house of **A** thy master,	256
	9: 8	For the whole house of **A** shall perish:	256
	9: 9	I will cut off from **A** him that pisseth	256
	9: 9	I will make the house of **A** like the house	256
	9:25	and thou rode together after **A** his father,	256
	9:29	in the eleventh year of Joram the son of **A**	256
	10: 1	had seventy sons in Samaria. And Jehu	256
	10:10	LORD spake concerning the house of **A:**	256
	10:11	that remained of the house of **A** in Jezreel,	256
	10:17	slew all that remained unto **A** in Samaria,	256
	10:18	and said unto them, **A** served Baal a little;	256
	10:30	hast done unto the house of **A** according to	256
	21:13	and the plummet of the house of **A**.	256
2Ch	18: 1	in abundance, and joined affinity with **A**.	256
	18: 2	after *certain* years he went down to **A** to	256
	18: 2	A killed sheep and oxen for him in	256
	18: 3	king of Israel said unto Jehoshaphat king	256
	18:19	Who shall entice **A** king of Israel, that he	256
	21: 6	kings of Israel, as did the house of **A:**	256
	21: 6	for he had the daughter of **A** to wife:	256
	21:13	like to the whoredoms of the house of **A**,	256
	22: 3	also walked in the ways of the house of **A:**	256
	22: 4	the sight of the LORD, like the house of **A:**	256
	22: 5	went with Jehoram the son of **A** king of	256
	22: 6	to see Jehoram the son of **A** at Jezreel,	256
	22: 7	had anointed to cut off the house of **A**.	256
	22: 8	executing judgment upon the house of **A**,	256
Jer	29:21	of **A** the son of Kolaiah, and of Zedekiah,	256
	29:22	LORD make thee like Zedekiah and like **A**,	256
Mic	6:16	the works of the house of **A**, and ye walk	256

AHAB'S (2) [AHAB]
1Ki	21: 8	So she wrote letters in **A** name,	256
2Ki	10: 1	them that brought up **A** *children*, saying,	256

AHARAH (1)
1Ch	8: 1	Ashbel the second, and **A** the third,	315

AHARHEL (1)
1Ch	4: 8	and the families of **A** the son of Harum.	316

AHASAI (1)
Ne	11:13	the son of **A**, the son of Meshillemoth,	273

AHASBAI (1)
2Sa	23:34	Eliphelet the son of **A**, the son of	308

AHASUERUS (30) [AHASUERUS']
Ezr	4: 6	in the reign of **A**, in the beginning of his	325
Est	1: 1	Now it came to pass in the days of **A**,	325

Est	1: 1	(this *is* **A** which reigned, from India even	325
	1: 2	when the king **A** sat on the throne of his	325
	1: 9	the royal house which *belonged* to king **A**.	325
	1:10	that served in the presence of **A** the king,	325
	1:15	of the king **A** by the chamberlains?	325
	1:16	that *are* in all the provinces of the king **A**.	325
	1:17	The king **A** commanded Vashti the queen	325
	1:19	That Vashti come no *more* before king **A;**	325
	2: 1	when the wrath of king **A** was appeased,	325
	2:12	maid's turn was come to go in to king **A**,	325
	2:16	So Esther was taken unto king **A** into his	325
	2:21	and sought to lay hand on the king **A**.	325
	3: 1	After these things did king **A** promote	325
	3: 6	*were* throughout the whole kingdom of **A**,	325
	3: 7	in the twelfth year of king **A**, they cast Pur,	325
	3: 8	Haman said unto **A**, There is a certain	325
	3:12	in the name of king **A** was it written,	325
	6: 2	who sought to lay hand on the king **A**.	325
	7: 5	the king **A** answered and said unto Esther	325
	8: 1	On that day did the king **A** give the house	325
	8: 7	the king **A** said unto Esther the queen	325
	8:12	one day in all the provinces of king **A**,	325
	9: 2	throughout all the provinces of the king **A**,	325
	9:20	that *were* in all the provinces of the king **A**,	325
	9:30	and seven provinces of the kingdom of **A**,	325
	10: 1	the king **A** laid a tribute upon the land,	325
	10: 3	Mordecai the Jew *was* next unto king **A**,	325
Da	9: 1	In the first year of Darius the son of **A**,	325

AHASUERUS' (1) [AHASUERUS]
Est	8:10	he wrote in the king **A** name, and sealed *it*	325

AHAVA (3)
Ezr	8:15	together to the river that runneth to **A;**	163
	8:21	I proclaimed a fast there, at the river **A**,	163
	8:31	we departed from the river of **A** on	163

AHAZ (42) [ACHAZ]
2Ki	15:38	father: and **A** his son reigned in his stead.	271
	16: 1	A the son of Jotham king of Judah *began* to	271
	16: 2	Twenty years old *was* **A** when he *began* to	271
	16: 5	they besieged, but could not overcome	271
	16: 7	So **A** sent messengers to Tiglath-pileser	271
	16: 8	A took the silver and gold that was found	271
	16:10	king **A** went *to* Damascus to meet	271
	16:10	king **A** sent to Urijah the priest the fashion	271
	16:11	to all that king **A** had sent from Damascus:	271
	16:11	Urijah the priest made *it* against king **A**	271
	16:15	king **A** commanded Urijah the priest,	271
	16:16	according to all that king **A** commanded.	271
	16:17	And king **A** cut off the borders of the bases,	271
	16:19	Now the rest of the acts of **A** which he did,	271
	16:20	And **A** slept with his fathers, and was buried	271
	17: 1	In the twelfth year of **A** king of Judah	271
	18: 1	*that* Hezekiah the son of **A** king of Judah	271
	20:11	which it had gone down in the dial of **A**.	271
	23:12	on the top of the upper chamber of **A**,	271
1Ch	3:13	his son, Hezekiah his son, Manasseh his	271
	8:35	Pithon, and Melech, and Tarea, and **A**.	271
	8:36	A begat Jehoadah; and Jehoadah begat	271
	9:41	and Melech, and Tahrea, and **A**.	NIH
	9:42	A begat Jarah; and Jarah begat Alemeth,	271
2Ch	27: 9	David: and **A** his son reigned in his stead.	271
	28: 1	A *was* twenty years old when he *began* to	271
	28:16	At that time did king **A** send unto the kings	271
	28:19	Judah low because of **A** king of Israel;	271
	28:21	For **A** took away a portion *out* of the house	271
	28:22	more against the LORD: this *is that* king **A**.	271
	28:24	gathered together the vessels of the	271
	28:27	A slept with his fathers, and they buried	271
	29:19	which king **A** in his reign did cast away in	271
Isa	1: 1	Jotham, **A**, *and* Hezekiah, kings of Judah.	271
	7: 1	it came to pass in the days of **A** the son of	271
	7: 3	Go forth now to meet **A**, thou,	271
	7:10	Moreover the LORD spake again unto **A**,	271
	7:12	A said, I will not ask, neither will I tempt	271
	14:28	the year that king **A** died was this burden.	271
	38: 8	which is gone down in the sun dial of **A**.	271
Hos	1: 1	Jotham, **A**, *and* Hezekiah, kings of Judah,	271
Mic	1: 1	A, *and* Hezekiah, kings of Judah, which he	271

AHAZIAH (37)
1Ki	22:40	and **A** his son reigned in his stead.	274
	22:49	said **A** the son of Ahab unto Jehoshaphat,	274
	22:51	A the son of Ahab *began* to reign over	274
2Ki	1: 2	A fell down through a lattice in his upper	274
	1:18	Now the rest of the acts of **A** which he did,	274
	8:24	David: and **A** his son reigned in his stead.	274
	8:25	A the son of Jehoram king of Judah *begin*	274
	8:26	twenty years old *was* **A** when he *began* to	274
	8:29	A the son of Jehoram king of Judah went	274
	9:16	A king of Judah was come down to see	274
	9:21	of Israel and **A** king of Judah went out,	274
	9:23	fled, and said to **A**, *There is* treachery,	274
	9:23	said to Ahaziah, *There is* treachery, O **A**.	274
	9:27	when **A** the king of Judah saw *this*, he fled	274
	9:29	son of Ahab *began* **A** to reign over Judah.	274
	10:13	Jehu met with the brethren of **A** king of	274
	10:13	they answered, We *are* the brethren of **A;**	274
	11: 1	when Athaliah the mother of **A** saw that	274
	11: 2	the daughter of king Joram, sister of **A**,	274
	11: 2	took Joash the son of **A**, and stale him from	274
	12:18	Jehoram, and **A**, his fathers, kings of Judah,	274
	13: 1	twentieth year of Joash the son of **A** king	274
	14:13	the son of Jehoash the son of **A**,	274

A

1Ch 3:11 Joram his son, **A** his son, Joash his son, 274
2Ch 20:35 of Judah join himself with **A** king of Israel, 274
 20:37 Because thou hast joined thyself with **A**, 274
 22: 1 the inhabitants of Jerusalem made **A** his 274
 22: 1 So **A** the son of Jehoram king of Judah 274
 22: 2 years old was **A** when he began to reign, 274
 22: 7 the destruction of **A** was of God by coming 274
 22: 8 sons of the brethren of **A**, that ministered 274
 22: 8 that ministered to **A**, he slew them. 274
 22: 9 he sought **A**: and they caught him, (for he 274
 22: 9 the house of **A** had no power to keep still 274
 22:10 when Athaliah the mother of **A** saw that 274
 22:11 took Joash the son of **A**, and stole him from 274
 22:11 the priest, (for she was the sister of **A**,) 274

AHBAN (1)
1Ch 2:29 Abihail, and she bare him **A**, and Molid. 257

AHER (1)
1Ch 7:12 children of Ir, and Hushim, the sons of **A**. 313

AHI (2)
1Ch 5:15 **A** the son of Abdiel, the son of Guni, 277
 7:34 **A**, and Rohgah, Jehubbah, and Aram. 277

AHIAH (4)
1Sa 14: 3 **A**, the son of Ahitub, Ichabod's brother, 281
 14:18 Saul said unto **A**, Bring hither the ark of 281
1Ki 4: 3 Elihoreph and **A**, the sons of Shisha, 281
1Ch 8: 7 and **A**, and Gera, he removed them, 281

AHIAM (2)
2Sa 23:33 **A** the son of Sharar the Hararite, 279
1Ch 11:35 **A** the son of Sacar the Hararite, Eliphal 279

AHIAN (1)
1Ch 7:19 **A**, and Shechem, and Likhi, and Aniam. 291

AHIEZER (6)
Nu 1:12 Of Dan; **A** the son of Ammishaddai. 295
 2:25 captain of the children of Dan shall be **A** 295
 7:66 the tenth day **A** the son of Ammishaddai, 295
 7:71 this was the offering of **A** the son of 295
 10:25 over his host was **A** the son of 295
1Ch 12: 3 The chief was **A**, then Joash, the sons of 295

AHIHUD (2)
Nu 34:27 children of Asher, **A** the son of Shelomi. 282
1Ch 8: 7 he removed them, and begat Uzza, and **A**. 284

AHIJAH (20)
1Ki 11:29 that the prophet **A** the Shilonite found him 281
 11:30 **A** caught the new garment that was on 281
 12:15 which the LORD spake by **A** the Shilonite 281
 14: 2 behold, there is **A** the prophet, which told 281
 14: 4 to Shiloh, and came to the house of **A**. 281
 14: 4 **A** could not see; for his eyes were set by 281
 14: 5 the LORD said unto **A**, Behold, the wife of 281
 14: 6 so, when he heard the sound of her feet, 281
 14:18 he spake by the hand of his servant **A** 281
 15:27 Baasha the son of **A**, of the house of 281
 15:29 which he spake by his servant **A** 281
 15:33 son of **A** to reign over all Israel in Tirzah, 281
 21:22 like the house of Baasha the son of **A**, for 281
2Ki 9: 9 and like the house of Baasha the son of **A**: 281
1Ch 2:25 and Bunah, and Oren, and Ozem, and **A**. 281
 11:36 Hepher the Mecherathite, **A** the Pelonite, 281
 26:20 **A** was over the treasures of the house of 281
2Ch 9:29 in the prophecy of **A** the Shilonite, and in 281
 10:15 which he spake by the hand of **A** 281
Ne 10:26 And **A**, Hanan, Anan, 281

AHIKAM (20)
2Ki 22:12 **A** the son of Shaphan, and Achbor the son 296
 22:14 **A**, and Achbor, and Shaphan, and Asahiah, 296
 25:22 over them he made Gedaliah the son of **A**, 296
2Ch 34:20 **A** the son of Shaphan, and Abdon the son 296
Jer 26:24 Nevertheless the hand of **A** the son of 296
 39:14 committed him unto Gedaliah the son of **A** 296
 40: 5 Gedaliah the son of **A** the son of Shaphan, 296
 40: 6 went Jeremiah unto Gedaliah the son of **A** 296
 40: 7 Gedaliah the son of **A** governor in the land, 296
 40: 9 Gedaliah the son of **A** the son of Shaphan 296
 40:11 Gedaliah the son of **A** the son of Shaphan, 296
 40:14 Gedaliah the son of **A** believed them not. 296
 40:16 Gedaliah the son of **A** said unto Johanan 296
 41: 1 unto Gedaliah the son of **A** to Mizpah; 296
 41: 2 smote Gedaliah the son of **A** the son of 296
 41: 6 them, Come to Gedaliah the son of **A**. 296
 41:10 had committed to Gedaliah the son of **A**: 296
 41:16 that he had slain Gedaliah the son of **A**, 296
 41:18 Nethaniah had slain Gedaliah the son of **A**, 296
 43: 6 Gedaliah the son of **A** the son of Shaphan, 296

AHILUD (5)
2Sa 8:16 Jehoshaphat the son of **A** was recorder; 286
 20:24 Jehoshaphat the son of **A** was recorder. 286
1Ki 4: 3 Jehoshaphat the son of **A**, the recorder. 286
 4:12 Baana the son of **A**; to him pertained 286
1Ch 18:15 and Jehoshaphat the son of **A**, recorder. 286

AHIMAAZ (15)
1Sa 14:50 wife was Ahinoam, the daughter of **A**: 290
2Sa 15:27 **A** thy son, and Jonathan the son of 290
 15:36 **A** Zadok's son, and Jonathan Abiathar's 290
 17:17 Now Jonathan and **A** stayed by En-rogel; 290

2Sa 17:20 they said, Where is **A** and Jonathan? 290
 18:19 said **A** the son of Zadok, Let me now run, 290
 18:22 said **A** the son of Zadok yet again to Joab, 290
 18:23 **A** ran by the way of the plain, 290
 18:27 is like the running of **A** the son of Zadok. 290
 18:28 called, and said unto the king, All is well. 290
 18:29 answered, When Joab sent the king's 290
1Ki 4:15 **A** was in Naphtali; he also took Basmath 290
1Ch 6: 8 Ahitub begat Zadok, and Zadok begat **A**, 290
 6: 9 begat Azariah, and Azariah begat 290
 6:53 Zadok his son, **A** his son. 290

AHIMAN (4)
Nu 13:22 where **A**, Sheshai, and Talmai, the children 289
Jos 15:14 Sheshai, and **A**, and Talmai, the children of 289
Jdg 1:10 and they slew Sheshai, and **A**, and Talmai. 289
1Ch 9:17 and Talmon, and **A**, and their brethren: 289

AHIMELECH (16) [AHIMELECH'S]
1Sa 21: 1 Then came David to Nob to **A** the priest: 288
 21: 1 **A** was afraid at the meeting of David, 288
 21: 2 David said unto **A** the priest, The king hath 288
 21: 8 David said unto **A**, And is there not here 288
 22: 9 coming to Nob, to **A** the son of Ahitub: 288
 22:11 the king sent to call **A** the priest, the son of 288
 22:14 **A** answered the king, and said, And who is 288
 22:16 **A**, thou, and all thy father's house. 288
 22:20 And one of the sons of **A** the son of Ahitub, 288
 23: 6 when Abiathar the son of **A** fled to David 288
 26: 6 answered David and said to **A** the Hittite, 288
2Sa 8:17 **A** the son of Abiathar, were the priests; 288
1Ch 24: 3 of Eleazar, and **A** of the sons of Ithamar, 288
 24: 6 of Abiathar, and before the chief 288
 24:31 **A**, and the chief of the fathers of the priests 288
Ps 52: T unto him, David is come to the house of **A**. 288

AHIMELECH'S (1) [AHIMELECH]
1Sa 30: 7 son, I pray thee, bring me hither 288

AHIMOTH (1)
1Ch 6:25 And the sons of Elkanah; Amasai, and **A**. 287

AHINADAB (1)
1Ki 4:14 **A** the son of Iddo had Mahanaim: 292

AHINOAM (7)
1Sa 14:50 name of Saul's wife was **A**, the daughter 293
 25:43 David also took **A** of Jezreel; and they were 293
 27: 3 the Jezreelitess, and Abigail 293
 30: 5 **A** the Jezreelitess, and Abigail the wife of 293
2Sa 2: 2 **A** the Jezreelitess, and Abigail Nabal's wife 293
 3: 2 firstborn was Amnon, of **A** the Jezreelitess; 293
1Ch 3: 1 the firstborn Amnon, of **A** the Jezreelitess; 293

AHIO (6)
2Sa 6: 3 Uzzah and **A**, the sons of Abinadab, 283
 6: 4 the ark of God: and **A** went before the ark. 283
1Ch 8:14 And **A**, Shashak, and Jeremoth, 283
 8:31 And Gedor, and **A**, and Zacher. 283
 9:37 and **A**, and Zechariah, and Mikloth. 283
 13: 7 Abinadab: and Uzza and **A** drave the cart. 283

AHIRA (5)
Nu 1:15 Of Naphtali; **A** the son of Enan. 299
 2:29 of Naphtali shall be **A** the son of Enan. 299
 7:78 On the twelfth day **A** the son of Enan, 299
 7:83 this was the offering of **A** the son of Enan. 299
 10:27 of Naphtali was **A** the son of Enan. 299

AHIRAM (1) [AHIRAMITES]
Nu 26:38 of **A**, the family of the Ahiramites: 297

AHIRAMITES (1) [AHIRAM]
Nu 26:38 of Ahiram, the family of the **A**: 298

AHISAMACH (3)
Ex 31: 6 the son of **A**, of the tribe of Dan: 294
 35:34 both he, and Aholiab, the son of **A**, of 294
 38:23 son of **A**, of the tribe of Dan, an engraver, 294

AHISHAHAR (1)
1Ch 7:10 and Zethan, and Tharshish, and **A**. 300

AHISHAR (1)
1Ki 4: 6 **A** was over the household: 301

AHITHOPHEL (20)
2Sa 15:12 Absalom sent for **A** the Gilonite, 302
 15:31 is among the conspirators with Absalom. 302
 15:31 turn the counsel of **A** into foolishness. 302
 15:34 thou for me defeat the counsel of **A**. 302
 16:15 came to Jerusalem, and **A** with him. 302
 16:20 said Absalom to **A**, Give counsel among 302
 16:21 **A** said unto Absalom, Go in unto thy 302
 16:23 the counsel of **A**, which he counselled in 302
 16:23 so was all the counsel of **A** both with David 302
 17: 1 Moreover **A** said unto Absalom, Let me 302
 17: 6 hath spoken after this manner: 302
 17: 7 The counsel that **A** hath given is not good 302
 17:14 the Archite is better than the counsel of **A**, 302
 17:14 appointed to defeat the good counsel of **A**, 302
 17:15 Thus and thus did **A** counsel Absalom 302
 17:21 for thus hath **A** counselled against you. 302
 17:23 when **A** saw that his counsel was not 302
 23:34 Eliam the son of **A** the Gilonite, 302
1Ch 27:33 **A** was the king's counsellor: and Hushai 302

1Ch 27:34 after **A** was Jehoiada the son of Benaiah, 302

AHITUB (15)
1Sa 14: 3 Ahiah, the son of **A**, Ichabod's brother, 285
 22: 9 coming to Nob, to Ahimelech the son of **A**: 285
 22:11 the son of **A**, and all his father's house, 285
 22:12 Saul said, Hear now, thou son of **A**. 285
 22:20 one of the sons of Ahimelech the son of **A**, 285
2Sa 8:17 Zadok the son of **A**, and Ahimelech the son 285
1Ch 6: 7 begat Amariah, and Amariah begat **A**, 285
 6: 8 **A** begat Zadok, and Zadok begat Ahimaaz, 285
 6:11 begat Amariah, and Amariah begat **A**, 285
 6:12 begat Amariah, and Amariah begat Shallum, 285
 6:52 his son, Amariah his son, **A** his son, 285
 9:11 Zadok, the son of Meraioth, the son of **A**, 285
 18:16 Zadok the son of **A**, and Abimelech the son 285
Ezr 7: 2 of Shallum, the son of Zadok, the son of **A**, 285
Ne 11:11 Zadok, the son of Meraioth, the son of **A**, 285

AHLAB (1)
Jdg 1:31 nor of **A**, nor of Achzib, nor of Helbah, 303

AHLAI (2)
1Ch 2:31 Sheshan. And the children of Sheshan; **A**. 304
 11:41 Uriah the Hittite, Zabad the son of **A**, 304

AHOAH (1)
1Ch 8: 4 And Abishua, and Naaman, and **A**, 265

AHOHITE (5)
2Sa 23: 9 was Eleazar the son of Dodo the **A**, 266+1121
 23:28 Zalmon the **A**, Maharai the Netophathite, 266
1Ch 11:12 the **A**, who was one of the three mighties. 266
 11:29 Sibbecai the Hushathite, Ilai the **A**, 266
 27: 4 of the second month was Dodai an **A**, 266

AHOLAH (5)
Eze 23: 4 the names of them were **A** the elder, 170
 23: 4 Samaria is **A**, and Jerusalem Aholibah. 170
 23: 5 **A** played the harlot when she was mine; 170
 23:36 of man, wilt thou judge **A** and Aholibah? 170
 23:44 so went they in unto **A** and unto Aholibah, 170

AHOLIAB (5)
Ex 31: 6 behold, I have given with him **A**, the son 171
 35:34 both he, and **A**, the son of Ahisamach, of 171
 36: 1 wrought Bezaleel and **A**, and every wise 171
 36: 2 Moses called Bezaleel and **A**, and every 171
 38:23 with him was **A**, son of Ahisamach, of 171

AHOLIBAH (6)
Eze 23: 4 were Aholah the elder, and **A** her sister: 172
 23: 4 Samaria is Aholah, and Jerusalem **A**. 172
 23:11 when her sister **A** saw this, she was more 172
 23:22 Therefore, O **A**, thus saith the Lord GOD; 172
 23:36 Son of man, wilt thou judge Aholah and **A**? 172
 23:44 so went they in unto Aholah and unto **A**, 172

AHOLIBAMAH (8)
Ge 36: 2 **A** the daughter of Anah the daughter of 173
 36: 5 bare Jeush, and Jaalam, and Korah: 173
 36:14 these were the sons of **A**, the daughter of 173
 36:18 these are the sons of **A** Esau's wife; 173
 36:18 these were the dukes that came of **A** 173
 36:25 Dishon, and **A** the daughter of Anah. 173
 36:41 Duke **A**, duke Elah, duke Pinon, 173
1Ch 1:52 Duke **A**, duke Elah, duke Pinon, 173

AHUMAI (1)
1Ch 4: 2 Jahath; and Jahath begat **A**, and Lahad. 267

AHUZAM (1)
1Ch 4: 6 Naarah bare him **A**, and Hepher, 275

AHUZZAM See AHUZAM

AHUZZATH (1)
Ge 26:26 **A** one of his friends, and Phichol the chief 276

AHZAI See AHASAI

AI (36) [HAI]
Jos 7: 2 Joshua sent men from Jericho to **A**, 5857
 7: 2 And the men went up and viewed **A**. 5857
 7: 3 three thousand men go up and smite **A**; 5857
 7: 4 and they fled before the men of **A**. 5857
 7: 5 the men of **A** smote of them about thirty 5857
 8: 1 of war with thee, and arise, go up to **A**: 5857
 8: 1 I have given into thy hand the king of **A**, 5857
 8: 2 thou shalt do to **A** and her king as thou 5857
 8: 3 all the people of war, to go up against **A**: 5857
 8: 9 abode between Beth-el and **A**, on the 5857
 8: 9 and Ai, on the west side of **A**: 5857
 8:10 the elders of Israel, before the people to **A**. 5857
 8:11 city, and pitched on the north side of **A**: 5857
 8:11 there was a valley between them and **A**. 5857
 8:12 to lie in ambush between Beth-el and **A**, 5857
 8:14 the king of **A** saw it, that they hasted 5857
 8:16 all the people that were in **A** were called 5857
 8:17 there was not a man left in **A** or Beth-el, 5857
 8:18 the spear that is in thy hand toward **A**: 5857
 8:20 when the men of **A** looked behind them, 5857
 8:21 turned again, and slew the men of **A**. 5857
 8:23 the king of **A** they took alive, 5857
 8:24 slaying all the inhabitants of **A** in the field, 5857
 8:24 that all the Israelites returned unto **A**, 5857
 8:25 twelve thousand, even all the men of **A**. 5857

Jos 8:26 utterly destroyed all the inhabitants of **A**. 5857
 8:28 Joshua burnt **A**, and made it a heap for 5857
 8:29 the king of **A** he hanged on a tree until 5857
 9: 3 Joshua had done unto Jericho and to **A**, 5857
 10: 1 had heard how Joshua had taken **A**, 5857
 10: 1 king, so he had done to **A** and her king; 5857
 10: 2 because it *was* greater than **A**, and all 5857
 12: 9 the king of **A**, which *is* beside Beth-el, 5857
Ezr 2:28 The men of Beth-el and **A**, two hundred 5857
Ne 7:32 The men of Beth-el and **A**, an hundred 5857
Jer 49: 3 Howl, O Heshbon, for **A** is spoiled: cry, 5857

AIAH (6)
Ge 36:24 the children of Zibeon; both **A**, and Anah: 345
2Sa 3: 7 name *was* Rizpah, the daughter of **A**: 345
 21: 8 the two sons of Rizpah the daughter of **A**, 345
 21:10 Rizpah the daughter of **A** took sackcloth, 345
 21:11 told David what Rizpah the daughter of **A**, 345
1Ch 1:40 And the sons of Zibeon; **A**, and Anah. 345

AIATH (1)
Isa 10:28 He is come to **A**, he is passed to Migron; 5857

AIDED (1)
Jdg 9:24 **A** him in the killing of his 853+2388+3027

AIJA (1)
Ne 11:31 and **A**, and Beth-el, and *in* their villages, 5857

AIJALON (8)
Jos 19:42 And Shaalabbin, and **A**, and Jethlah, 357
 21:24 **A** with her suburbs, Gath-rimmon with 357
Jdg 1:35 would dwell in mount Heres in **A**, 357
 12:12 was buried in **A** in the country of Zebulun. 357
1Sa 14:31 Philistines that day from Michmash to **A**: 357
1Ch 6:69 **A** with her suburbs, and Gath-rimmon 357
 8:13 of the fathers of the inhabitants of **A**, 357
2Ch 11:10 Zorah, and **A**, and Hebron, which *are* in 357

AIJELETH (1)
Ps 22: T To the chief Musician upon **A** Shahar, 365

AILED (1) [AILETH]
Ps 114: 5 What **a** thee, O thou sea, that thou 3807.1

AILETH (7) [AILED]
Ge 21:17 unto her, **What a** thee, Hagar? 4100+3807.1
Jdg 18:23 and said unto Micah, What **a** thee, 3807.1
 18:24 this *that* ye say unto me, What **a** thee? 3807.1
1Sa 11: 5 What **a** the people that they weep? 3807.1
2Sa 14: 5 the king said unto her, What **a** thee? 3807.1
2Ki 6:28 the king said unto her, What **a** thee? 3807.1
Isa 22: 1 What **a** thee now, that thou art wholly 3807.1

AIN (5)
Nu 34:11 Shepham *to* Riblah, on the east side of **A**; 5871
Jos 15:32 and Shilhim, and **A**, and Rimmon: 5871
 19: 7 **A**, Remmon, and Ether, and Ashan; 5871
 21:16 **A** with her suburbs, and Juttah with her 5871
1Ch 4:32 **A**, Rimmon, and Tochen, and Ashan, 5871

AIR (39)
Ge 1:26 over the fowl of the **a**, and over the cattle, 8064
 1:28 over the fowl of the **a**, and over every 8064
 1:30 to every fowl of the **a**, and to every *thing* 8064
 2:19 beast of the field, and every fowl of the **a**; 8064
 2:20 to the fowl of the **a**, and to every beast of 8064
 6: 7 the creeping thing, and the fowls of the **a**; 8064
 7: 3 Of fowls also of the **a** by sevens, the male 8064
 9: 2 upon every fowl of the **a**, upon all that 8064
Dt 4:17 of any winged fowl that flieth in the **a**, 8064
 28:26 shall be meat unto all fowls of the **a**, 8064
1Sa 17:44 will give thy flesh unto the fowls of the **a**, 8064
 17:46 Philistines this day unto the fowls of the **a**, 8064
2Sa 21:10 suffered neither the birds of the **a** to rest 8064
1Ki 14:11 in the field that the fowls of the **a** eat: 8064
 16: 4 in the fields shall the fowls of the **a** eat. 8064
 21:24 in the field that the fowls of the **a** eat. 8064
Job 12: 7 the fowls of the **a**, and they shall tell thee: 8064
 28:21 and kept close from the fowls of the **a**. 8064
 41:16 that no **a** can come between them. 7307
Ps 8: 8 The fowl of the **a**, and the fish of the sea, 8064
Pr 30:19 The way of an eagle in the **a**; the way of 8064
Ecc 10:20 for a bird of the **a** shall carry the voice, 8064
Mt 6:26 the fowls of the **a**: for they sow not, 3772
 8:20 and the birds of the **a** *have* nests; 3772
 13:32 so that the birds of the **a** come and lodge 3772
Mk 4: 4 the fowls of the **a** came and devoured it 3772
 4:32 that the fowls of the **a** may lodge under 3772
Lk 8: 5 and the fowls of the **a** devoured it. 3772
 9:58 have holes, and birds of the **a** *have* nests; 3772
 13:19 the fowls of the **a** lodged in the branches 3772
Ac 10:12 and creeping things, and fowls of the **a**, 3772
 11: 6 and creeping things, and fowls of the **a**. 3772
 22:23 *their* clothes, and threw dust into the **a**, 109
1Co 9:26 So fight I, not as one that beateth the **a**: 109
 14: 9 is spoken? for ye shall speak into the **a**. 109
Eph 2: 2 to the prince of the power of the **a**, 109
1Th 4:17 in the clouds, to meet the Lord in the **a**: 109
Rev 9: 2 were darkened by reason of the smoke 109
 16:17 angel poured out his vial into the **a**; 109

AJALON (2)
Jos 10:12 and thou, Moon, in the valley of **A**. 357
2Ch 28:18 **A**, and Gederoth, and Shocho with 357

AKAN (1)
Ge 36:27 *are* these; Bilhan, and Zaavan, and **A**. 6130

AKELDAMA See ACELDAMA

AKIM See ACHIM

AKKAD See ACCAD

AKKUB (8)
1Ch 3:24 **A**, and Johanan, and Dalaiah, and Anani, 6126
 9:17 **A**, and Talmon, and Ahiman, 6126
Ezr 2:42 the children of **A**, the children of Hatita, 6126
 2:45 children of Hagabah, the children of **A**, 6126
Ne 7:45 the children of **A**, the children of Hatita, 6126
 8: 7 and Sherebiah, Jamin, **A**, Shabbethai, 6126
 11:19 **A**, Talmon, and their brethren that kept 6126
 12:25 Obadiah, Meshullam, Talmon, **A**, 6126

AKRABBIM (2)
Nu 34: 4 turn from the south to the ascent of **A**, 6137
Jdg 1:36 the Amorites *was* from the going up to **A**, 6137

ALABASTER (3)
Mt 26: 7 having an **a box** of very precious ointment, *211*
Mk 14: 3 there came a woman having an **a box** of *211*
Lk 7:37 brought an **a box** of ointment, *211*

ALAMETH (1)
1Ch 7: 8 and Abiah, and Anathoth, and **A**. 5964

ALAMMELECH (1)
Jos 19:26 **A**, and Amad, and Misheal; and reacheth 487

ALAMOTH (2)
1Ch 15:20 and Benaiah, with psalteries on **A**; 5961
Ps 46: T for the sons of Korah, A Song upon **A**. 5961

ALARM (10)
Nu 10: 5 When ye blow an **a**, then the camps that 8643
 10: 6 When you blow an **a** the second time, 8643
 10: 6 they shall blow an **a** for their journeys. 8643
 10: 7 shall blow, but you shall not **sound an a**. 7321
 10: 9 ye shall **blow an a** with the trumpets; 7321
2Ch 13:12 priests with sounding trumpets to **cry a** 7321
Jer 4:19 the sound of the trumpet, the **a** of war. 8643
 49: 2 that I will cause an **a** of war to be heard 8643
Joel 2: 1 and **sound an a** in my holy mountain: 7321
Zep 1:16 trumpet and **a** against the fenced cities, 8643

ALAS (20)
Nu 12:11 **A**, my lord, I beseech thee, lay not the sin 994
 24:23 he took up his parable, and said, **A**, 188
Jos 7: 7 Joshua said, **A**, O Lord GOD, 162
Jdg 6:22 the LORD, Gideon said, **A**, O Lord GOD! 162
 11:35 rent his clothes, and said, **A**, my daughter, 162
1Ki 13:30 mourned over him, *saying*, **A**, my brother. 1945
2Ki 3:10 the king of Israel said, **A**, that the LORD 162
 6: 5 he cried, and said, **A**, master, for it *was* 162
 6:15 unto him, **A**, my master, how shall we do? 162
Jer 30: 7 **A**! for that day *is* great, so that none *is* 1945
Eze 6:11 **A** for all the evil abominations of the house 253
Joel 1:15 **A** for the day! for the day of the LORD *is* 162
Am 5:16 and they shall say in all the highways, **A**! 1930
 5:16 **a**! and they shall call the husbandman to 1930
Rev 18:10 saying, **A**, alas, *that* great city Babylon, 3759
 18:10 saying, Alas, **a**, *that* great city Babylon, 3759
 18:16 And saying, **A**, alas, *that* great city, 3759
 18:16 And saying, Alas, **a**, *that* great city, 3759
 18:19 weeping and wailing, saying, **A**, alas, 3759
 18:19 weeping and wailing, saying, Alas, **a**, 3759

ALBEIT (2)
Eze 13: 7 The LORD saith *it*; **a** I have not spoken? 2050.1
Phm 1:19 I will repay *it*: **a** I do not say to thee how *2443*

ALEMETH (3)
1Ch 6:60 **A** with her suburbs, and Anathoth with 5964
 8:36 Jehoadah begat **A**, and Azmaveth, 5964
 9:42 Jarah begat **A**, and Azmaveth, and Zimri, 5964

ALEXANDER (6)
Mk 15:21 the father of **A** and Rufus, to bear his cross. 223
Ac 4: 6 and **A**, and as many as were of the kindred 223
 19:33 And they drew **A** out of the multitude, 223
 19:33 And **A** beckoned with the hand, 223
1Ti 1:20 Of whom is Hymeneus and **A**; whom I 223
2Ti 4:14 **A** the coppersmith did me much evil: 223

ALEXANDRIA (3) [ALEXANDRIANS]
Ac 18:24 born **at A**, an eloquent man, *and* mighty 221
 27: 6 And there the centurion found a ship of **A** 222
 28:11 three months we departed in a ship of **A**, 222

ALEXANDRIANS (1) [ALEXANDRIA]
Ac 6: 9 and **A**, and of them of Cilicia and of Asia, 221

ALGUM (3) [ALMUG]
2Ch 2: 8 fir trees, and **a trees**, out of Lebanon; 418
 9:10 brought **a trees** and precious stones. 418
 9:11 the king made *of* the **a trees** terraces to 418

ALIAH (1)
1Ch 1:51 duke Timnah, duke **A**, duke Jetheth, 5933

ALIAN (1)
1Ch 1:40 **A**, and Manahath, and Ebal, Shephi, 5935

ALIEN (5) [ALIENATE, ALIENATED, ALIENS]
Ex 18: 3 said, I have been an **a** in a strange land: 1616
Dt 14:21 eat it; or thou mayest sell *it* unto an **a**: 5237
Job 19:15 me for a stranger: I am an **a** in their sight. 5237
Ps 69: 8 and an **a** unto my mother's children. 5237
Isa 61: 5 the sons of the **a** *shall be* your plowmen 5236

ALIENATE (1) [ALIEN]
Eze 48:14 nor **a** the firstfruits of the land: 5674

ALIENATED (7) [ALIEN]
Eze 23:17 them, and her mind was **a** from them. 3363
 23:18 my mind was **a** from her, like as my mind 3363
 23:18 like as my mind was **a** from her sister. 5361
 23:22 from whom thy mind is **a**, and I will bring 5361
 23:28 hand *of them* from whom thy mind is **a**: 5361
Eph 4:18 being **a** from the life of God through *526*
Col 1:21 were sometime **a** and enemies in *your* *526*

ALIENS (3) [ALIEN]
La 5: 2 is turned to strangers, our houses to **a**. 5237
Eph 2:12 being **a** from the commonwealth of Israel, *526*
Heb 11:34 fight, turned to flight the armies of the **a**. *245*

ALIKE (11) [LIKE]
Dt 12:22 and the clean shall eat of them **a**. 3162
 15:22 and the clean *person shall eat it* **a**, 3162
1Sa 30:24 that tarrieth by the stuff: they shall part **a**. 3162
Job 21:26 They shall lie down **a** in the dust, 3162
Ps 33:15 He fashioneth their hearts **a**; he 3162
 139:12 and the light *are* both **a** to thee. 3509.1
Pr 20:10 both of them *are* **a** abomination to 1571
 27:15 day and a contentious woman are **a**. 7737
Ecc 9: 2 All *things come* **a** to all: *there is* 834+3509.1
 11: 6 whether they both **a** be good. 259+3509.1
Ro 14: 5 another esteemeth every day **a**. Let every NIG

ALIVE (88) [LIVE]
Ge 6:19 into the ark, to **keep** *them* **a** with thee; 2421
 6:20 shall come unto thee, to **keep** *them* **a**. 2421
 7: 3 to **keep** seed **a** upon the face of all 2421
 7:23 Noah only remained **a**, and *they* that NIH
 12:12 will kill me, but they will **save** thee **a**. 2421
 43: 7 our kindred, saying, *Is* your father yet **a**? 2416
 43:27 old man of whom ye spake? *Is* he yet **a**? 2416
 43:28 our father *is* yet **a**, and he *is* in good 2416
 45:26 Joseph *is* yet **a**, and he *is* governor over all 2416
 45:28 *It is* enough; Joseph my son *is* yet **a**: 2416
 46:30 have seen thy face, because thou *art* yet **a**. 2416
 50:20 as *it is* this day, to **save** much people **a**. 2421
Ex 1:17 but **saved** the men children **a**. 2421
 1:18 and have **saved** the men children **a**? 2421
 1:22 and every daughter ye shall **save a**. 2421
 4:18 in Egypt, and see whether they be yet **a**. 2416
 22: 4 the theft be certainly found in his hand **a**, 2416
Lev 10:16 sons of Aaron which were left **a**, saying, NIH
 14: 4 for him that is to be cleansed two birds **a** 2416
 16:10 shall be presented **a** before the LORD, 2416
 26:36 them that are left **a** of you I will send a NIH
Nu 16:33 went down **a** into the pit, and the earth 2416
 21:35 people, until there was none left him **a**: 8300
 22:33 also I had slain thee, and **saved** her **a**. 2421
 31:15 then, Have ye **saved** all the women **a**? 2421
 31:18 by lying with him, **keep a** for yourselves. 2421
Dt 4: 4 your God *are* **a** every one of you this day. 2416
 5: 3 *even* us, who *are* all of us here **a** this day. 2416
 6:24 he might **preserve** us **a**, as *it is* at this 2421
 20:16 thou shalt **save a** nothing that breatheth: 2421
 31:27 while I am yet **a** with you *this* day, 2416
 32:39 I kill, and I **make a**; I wound, and I heal: 2421
Jos 2:13 that will **save a** my father, 2421
 6:25 Joshua **saved** Rahab the harlot **a**, and her 2421
 8:23 king of Ai they took **a**, and brought him 2416
 14:10 the LORD hath **kept** me **a**, as he said, 2421
Jdg 8:19 if ye had **saved** them **a**, I would not slay 2421
 21:14 **saved a** of the women of Jabesh-gilead: 2421
1Sa 2: 6 The LORD killeth, and **maketh a**: 2421
 15: 8 he took Agag the king of the Amalekites **a**, 2416
 27: 9 **left** neither man nor woman **a**, 2421
 27:11 David **saved** neither man nor woman **a**, 2421
2Sa 8: 2 to death, and *with* one full line to **keep a**. 2421
 12:18 Behold, while the child was yet **a**, 2416
 12:21 and weep for the child, *while it was* **a**; 2416
 12:22 While the child *was* yet **a**, I fasted 2416
 18:14 while he *was* yet **a** in the midst of the oak. 2416
1Ki 18: 5 find grass to **save** the horses and mules **a**, 2421
 20:18 they be come out for peace, take them **a**; 2416
 20:18 they be come out for war, take them **a**. 2416
 20:32 And he said, *Is* he yet **a**? he *is* my brother. 2416
 21:15 for money: for Naboth is not **a**, but dead. 2416
2Ki 5: 7 said, *Am* I God, to kill and to **make a**, 2421
 7: 4 if they **save** us **a**, we shall live; and if they 2416
 7:12 shall catch them **a**, and get into the city. 2416
 10:14 he said, Take them **a**. And they took them 2416
 10:14 took them **a**, and slew them at the pit 2416
2Ch 25:12 ten thousand *left* **a** did the children of 2416
Ps 22:29 and none can **keep a** his own soul. 2421
 30: 3 thou hast **kept** me **a**, that I should not go 2421
 33:19 death, and to **keep** them **a** in famine. 2421
 41: 2 LORD will preserve him, and **keep** him **a**; 2421
Pr 1:12 Let us swallow them up **a** as the grave; 2416
Ecc 4: 2 dead more than the living which are yet **a**. 2416
Jer 49:11 children, I will **preserve** *them* **a**; 2421
Eze 7:13 although they were yet **a**: 2416+871.1+1886.1
 13:18 will ye **save** the souls **a** *that* come unto 2421

Eze 13:19 to **save** the souls **a** that should not live, 2421
 18:27 lawful and right, he shall **save** his soul **a**. 2421
Da 5:19 whom he would he **kept a**; and whom he 2418
Mt 27:63 while he was yet **a**, After three days I will 2198
Mk 16:11 when they had heard that he was **a**, 2198
Lk 15:24 For this my son was dead, and is **a again**; 326
 15:32 this thy brother was dead, and is **a again**; 326
 24:23 vision of angels, which said that he was **a**. 2198
Ac 1: 3 To whom also he shewed himself **a** after 2198
 9:41 the saints and widows, presented her **a**. 2198
 20:12 And they brought the young man **a**, 2198
 25:19 was dead, whom Paul affirmed to be **a**. 2198
Ro 6:11 **a** unto God through Jesus Christ our Lord. 2198
 6:13 as *those that are* **a** from the dead, 2198
 7: 9 For I was **a** without the law once: 2198
1Co 15:22 even so in Christ shall all be **made a**. 2227
1Th 4:15 that we which are **a** *and* remain unto 2198
 4:17 Then we which are **a** *and* remain shall be 2198
Rev 1:18 and behold, I am **a** for evermore, Amen; 2198
 2: 8 the last, which was dead, and is **a**; 2198
 19:20 *These* both were cast **a** into a lake of fire 2198

ALL (5621)

Ge 1:26 over **a** the earth, and over every creeping 3605
 1:29 which *is* upon the face of **a** the earth, 3605
 2: 1 were finished, and **a** the host of them. 3605
 2: 2 he rested on the seventh day from **a** his 3605
 2: 3 that in it he had rested from **a** his work 3605
 2:20 Adam gave names to **a** cattle, and to 3605
 3:14 thou *art* cursed above **a** cattle, 3605
 3:14 dust shalt thou eat **a** the days of thy life: 3605
 3:17 in sorrow shalt thou eat *of it* **a** the days of 3605
 3:20 because she was the mother of **a** living. 3605
 4:21 he was the father of **a** such as handle 3605
 5: 5 the days that Adam lived were nine 3605
 5: 8 the days of Seth were nine hundred 3605
 5:11 **a** the days of Enos were nine hundred 3605
 5:14 the days of Cainan were nine hundred 3605
 5:17 **a** the days of Mahalaleel were eight 3605
 5:20 the days of Jared were nine hundred 3605
 5:23 the days of Enoch were three hundred 3605
 5:27 the days of Methuselah were nine 3605
 5:31 **a** the days of Lamech were seven hundred 3605
 6: 2 they took them wives of **a** which they 3605
 6:12 for **a** flesh had corrupted his way upon 3605
 6:13 The end of **a** flesh is come before me; 3605
 6:17 to destroy **a** flesh, wherein *is* the breath of 3605
 6:19 of every living *thing* of **a** flesh, two of 3605
 6:21 take thou unto thee of **a** food that is eaten, 3605
 6:22 according to **a** that God commanded him, 3605
 7: 1 Come thou and **a** thy house into the ark; 3605
 7: 3 to keep seed alive upon the face of **a** 3605
 7: 5 Noah did according unto **a** that the Lᴏʀᴅ 3605
 7:11 the same day were **a** the fountains of 3605
 7:14 the cattle after their kind, 3605
 7:15 two and two of **a** flesh, wherein *is* 3605
 7:16 went in male and female of **a** flesh, 3605
 7:19 the high hills, that *were* under the 3605
 7:21 **a** flesh died that moved upon the earth, 3605
 7:22 **A** in whose nostrils *was* the breath of **a** 3605
 7:22 of life, of **a** that *was* in the dry *land*, died. 3605
 8: 1 **a** the cattle that *was* with him in the ark: 3605
 8:17 of **a** flesh, *both* of fowl, and of cattle, 3605
 9: 2 upon **a** that moveth *upon* the earth, 3605
 9: 2 the earth, and upon **a** the fishes of the sea; 3605
 9: 3 *even* as the green herb have I given you **a** 3605
 9:10 from **a** that go out of the ark, to every 3605
 9:11 neither shall **a** flesh be cut off any more by 3605
 9:15 and every living creature of **a** flesh; 3605
 9:15 no more become a flood to destroy **a** flesh. 3605
 9:16 every living creature of **a** flesh that *is* upon 3605
 9:17 and **a** flesh that *is* upon the earth. 3605
 9:29 the days of Noah were nine hundred 3605
 10:21 the father of **a** the children of Eber, 3605
 10:29 Jobab: **a** these *were* the sons of Joktan. 3605
 11: 6 *is* one, and they have **a** one language; 3605
 11: 8 from thence upon the face of **a** the earth: 3605
 11: 9 confound the language of **a** the earth: 3605
 11: 9 them abroad upon the face of **a** the earth. 3605
 12: 3 in thee shall **a** families of the earth be 3605
 12: 5 their substance that they had gathered, 3605
 12:20 him away, and his wife, and **a** that he had. 3605
 13: 1 and **a** that he had, and Lot with him, 3605
 13:10 his eyes, and beheld **a** the plain of Jordan, 3605
 13:11 Lot chose him **a** the plain of Jordan; 3605
 13:15 For **a** the land which thou seest, to thee 3605
 14: 3 **A** these were joined together in the vale 3605
 14: 7 smote **a** the country of the Amalekites, 3605
 14:11 they took **a** the goods of Sodom 3605
 14:11 and **a** their victuals, and went their way. 3605
 14:16 he brought back **a** the goods, 3605
 14:20 into thy hand. And he gave him tithes of **a**. 3605
 15:10 took unto him **a** these, and divided them 3605
 16:12 he shall dwell in the presence of **a** his 3605
 17: 8 **a** the land of Canaan, for an everlasting 3605
 17:23 **a** that were born in his house, and all that 3605
 17:23 and **a** that were bought with his money, 3605
 17:27 **a** the men of his house, born in the house, 3605
 18:18 **a** the nations of the earth shall be blessed 3605
 18:25 Shall not the Judge of **a** the earth do right? 3605
 18:26 then I will spare **a** the place for their sakes. 3605
 18:28 wilt thou destroy **a** the city for *lack of* five? 3605
 19: 2 **tarry a night**, and wash your feet, 3885
 19: 2 but we will **abide** in the street **a night**. 3885
 19: 4 young, **a** the people from every quarter: 3605

Ge 19:17 thee, neither stay thou in **a** the plain; 3605
 19:25 **a** the plain, and all the inhabitants of 3605
 19:25 **a** the inhabitants of the cities, 3605
 19:28 toward **a** the land of the plain, and beheld, 3605
 19:31 in unto us after the manner of **a** the earth: 3605
 20: 7 shalt surely die, thou, and **a** that *are* thine. 3605
 20: 8 called **a** his servants, and told all these 3605
 20: 8 and told **a** these things in their ears: 3605
 20:16 unto a that *are* with thee, and with all 3605
 20:16 and with **a** *other*: thus she was reproved. 3605
 20:18 For the Lᴏʀᴅ had fast closed up **a** 3605
 21: 6 *so that* **a** that hear will laugh with me. 3605
 21:12 in **a** that Sarah hath said unto thee, 3605
 21:22 God *is* with thee in **a** that thou doest: 3605
 22:18 in thy seed shall **a** the nations of the earth 3605
 23:10 of **a** that went in *at* the gate of his city, 3605
 23:17 **a** the trees that *were* in the field, 3605
 23:17 that *were* in the borders round about, 3605
 23:18 before **a** that went in *at* the gate of his city. 3605
 24: 1 Lᴏʀᴅ had blessed Abraham in **a** things. 3605
 24: 2 of his house that ruled over **a** that he had, 3605
 24:10 for **a** the goods of his master *were* in his 3605
 24:20 to draw *water*, and drew for **a** his camels. 3605
 24:36 unto him hath he given **a** that he hath. 3605
 24:54 that *were* with him, and **tarried a night**, 3885
 24:66 the servant told Isaac **a** things that he had 3605
 25: 4 **A** these *were* the children of Keturah. 3605
 25: 5 Abraham gave **a** that he had unto Isaac. 3605
 25:18 he died in the presence of **a** his brethren. 3605
 25:25 came out red, **a over** like a hairy garment; 3605
 26: 3 I will give **a** these countries, and I will 3605
 26: 4 will give unto thy seed **a** these countries; 3605
 26: 4 **a** in thy seed shall **a** the nations of the earth 3605
 26:11 Abimelech charged **a** *his* people, saying, 3605
 26:15 For **a** the wells which his father's servants 3605
 27:33 I have eaten of **a** before thou camest, 3605
 27:37 **a** his brethren have I given to him for 3605
 28:11 **tarried** there **a night**, because the sun 3885
 28:14 in thy seed shall **a** the families of the earth 3605
 28:15 will keep thee in **a** *places* whither thou 3605
 28:22 of **a** that thou shalt give me I will surely 3605
 29: 3 thither were **a** the flocks gathered: 3605
 29: 8 until **a** the flocks be gathered together, 3605
 29:13 And he told Laban **a** these things. 3605
 29:22 Laban gathered together **a** the men of 3605
 30:32 I will pass through **a** thy flock to day, 3605
 30:32 removing from thence **a** the speckled 3605
 30:32 the brown cattle among the sheep, 3605
 30:35 **a** the she goats that were speckled 3605
 30:35 the brown amongst the sheep, 3605
 30:40 and **a** the brown in the flock of Laban; 3605
 31: 1 Jacob hath taken away **a** that *was* our 3605
 31: 1 of our father's hath he gotten **a** this glory. 3605
 31: 6 ye know that with **a** my power I have 3605
 31: 8 thy wages; then **a** the cattle bare speckled: 3605
 31: 8 thy hire; then bare **a** the cattle ringstraked. 3605
 31:12 the rams which leap upon the cattle *are* 3605
 31:12 for I have seen **a** that Laban doeth unto 3605
 31:16 For **a** the riches which God hath taken 3605
 31:18 he carried away **a** his cattle, and all his 3605
 31:18 his goods which he had gotten, **a** his 3605
 31:21 So he fled with **a** that he had; and he rose 3605
 31:34 Laban searched **a** the tent, but found 3605
 31:37 Whereas thou hast searched **a** my stuff, 3605
 31:37 what hast thou found of **a** thy household 3605
 31:43 my cattle, and **a** that thou seest *is* mine: 3605
 31:54 and **tarried a night** in the mount. 3885
 32:10 I am not worthy of the least of **a** 3605
 32:10 of **a** the truth, which thou hast shewed 3605
 32:19 and **a** that followed the droves, saying, 3605
 33: 8 What meanest thou by **a** this drove 3605
 33:13 them one day, **a** the flock will die. 3605
 34:19 he *was* more honourable than **a** the house 3605
 34:24 unto Shechem his son hearkened **a** that 3605
 34:24 that went out of the gate of his city. 3605
 34:25 upon the city boldly, and slew **a** the males. 3605
 34:29 **a** their wealth, and all their little ones, 3605
 34:29 **a** their little ones, and their wives took 3605
 34:29 and spoiled even **a** that *was* in the house. 3605
 35: 2 household, and to **a** that *were* with him, 3605
 35: 4 they gave unto Jacob **a** the strange gods 3605
 35: 4 **a** their earrings which *were* in their ears; NIH
 35: 6 he and **a** the people that *were* with him, 3605
 36: 6 **a** the persons of his house, and his cattle, 3605
 36: 6 and **a** his beasts, and all his substance, 3605
 36: 6 and all his beasts, and **a** his substance, 3605
 37: 3 Now Israel loved Joseph more than **a** his 3605
 37: 4 father loved him more than **a** his brethren, 3605
 37:35 **a** his sons and all his daughters rose up to 3605
 37:35 **a** his daughters rose up to comfort him; 3605
 39: 3 *that* the Lᴏʀᴅ made **a** that he did to 3605
 39: 4 and **a** *that* he had he put into his hand. 3605
 39: 5 over **a** that he had, that the Lᴏʀᴅ blessed 3605
 39: 5 the blessing of the Lᴏʀᴅ was upon **a** that 3605
 39: 6 he left **a** that he had in Joseph's hand; 3605
 39: 8 he hath committed **a** that he hath to my 3605
 39:22 **a** the prisoners that *were* in the prison; 3605
 40:17 in the uppermost basket *there was of* **a** 3605
 40:20 that he made a feast unto **a** his servants: 3605
 41: 8 and called for **a** the magicians of Egypt, 3605
 41: 8 of Egypt, and **a** the wise men thereof: 3605
 41:19 such as I never saw in **a** the land of Egypt 3605
 41:29 plenty throughout **a** the land of Egypt: 3605
 41:30 **a** the plenty shall be forgotten in the land 3605
 41:35 let them gather **a** the food of those good 3605

Ge 41:37 and in the eyes of **a** his servants. 3605
 41:39 as God hath shewed thee **a** this, 3605
 41:40 unto thy word shall **a** my people 3605
 41:41 I have set thee over **a** the land of Egypt. 3605
 41:43 made him *ruler* over **a** the land of Egypt. 3605
 41:44 up his hand or foot in **a** the land of Egypt. 3605
 41:45 Joseph went out over **a** the land of Egypt. NIH
 41:46 and went throughout **a** the land of Egypt. 3605
 41:48 he gathered up **a** the food of the seven 3605
 41:51 *said* he, hath made me forget **a** my toil, 3605
 41:51 forget all my toil, and **a** my father's house. 3605
 41:54 dearth was in **a** lands; but in all the land 3605
 41:54 but in **a** the land of Egypt there was bread. 3605
 41:55 when **a** the land of Egypt was famished, 3605
 41:55 Pharaoh said unto **a** the Egyptians, Go 3605
 41:56 famine was over **a** the face of the earth: 3605
 41:56 Joseph opened **a** the storehouses, 3605
 41:57 **a** countries came into Egypt to Joseph for 3605
 41:57 that the famine was *so* sore in **a** lands. 3605
 42: 6 he *it was* that sold to **a** the people of 3605
 42:11 We *are* **a** one man's sons; we *are* true 3605
 42:17 he **put** them **a together** into ward three 622
 42:29 and told him **a** that befell unto them; 3605
 42:36 ye will take Benjamin *away*: **a** these things 3605
 45: 1 Joseph could not refrain himself before **a** 3605
 45: 8 lord of **a** his house, and a ruler throughout 3605
 45: 8 and a ruler throughout **a** the land of Egypt. 3605
 45: 9 God hath made me lord of **a** Egypt: 3605
 45:10 my herds, and **a** that thou hast: 3605
 45:11 and thy household, and **a** that thou hast, 3605
 45:13 you shall tell my father of **a** my glory in 3605
 45:13 in Egypt, and of **a** that you have seen; 3605
 45:15 Moreover he kissed **a** his brethren, 3605
 45:20 the good of **a** the land of Egypt *is* yours. 3605
 45:22 To **a** of them he gave each man changes 3605
 45:26 he *is* governor over **a** the land of Egypt. 3605
 45:27 they told him **a** the words of Joseph, 3605
 46: 1 Israel took his journey with **a** that he had, 3605
 46: 6 into Egypt, Jacob, and **a** his seed with him: 3605
 46: 7 **a** his seed brought he with him into Egypt. 3605
 46:15 **a** the souls of his sons and his daughters 3605
 46:22 born to Jacob: **a** the souls *were* fourteen. 3605
 46:25 these unto Jacob: **a** the souls *were* seven. 3605
 46:26 **A** the souls that came with Jacob into 3605
 46:26 **a** the souls *were* threescore and six; 3605
 46:27 **a** the souls of the house of Jacob, 3605
 46:32 and their herds, and **a** that they have. 3605
 47: 1 and their herds, and **a** that they have, 3605
 47:12 and **a** his father's household, *with* bread, 3605
 47:13 *there was* no bread in **a** the land; for 3605
 47:13 **a** the land of Canaan fainted by reason of NIH
 47:14 Joseph gathered up **a** the money that was 3605
 47:15 the Egyptians came unto Joseph, 3605
 47:17 he fed them with bread for **a** their cattle 3605
 47:20 Joseph bought **a** the land of Egypt for 3605
 48:15 God which fed me **a** my **life long** 4480+5750
 48:16 Angel which redeemed me from **a** evil, 3605
 49:28 **A** these *are* the twelve tribes of Israel: 3605
 50: 7 with him went up **a** the servants of 3605
 50: 7 and **a** the elders of the land of Egypt, 3605
 50: 8 the house of Joseph, and his brethren, 3605
 50:14 **a** that went up with him to bury his father, 3605
 50:15 will certainly require us **a** the evil which 3605

Ex 1: 5 the souls that came *out of* the loins of 3605
 1: 6 and **a** his brethren, and all that generation. 3605
 1: 6 and all his brethren, and **a** that generation. 3605
 1:14 and in **a manner** of service in the field: 3605
 1:14 their service, wherein they made them 3605
 1:22 Pharaoh charged **a** his people, saying, 3605
 3:15 my memorial unto **a generations**. 1755+1755
 3:20 smite Egypt with **a** my wonders which I 3605
 4:19 for **a** the men are dead which sought thy 3605
 4:21 see that thou do **a** *those* wonders before 3605
 4:28 Moses told Aaron **a** the words of 3605
 4:28 **a** the signs which he had commanded 3605
 4:29 gathered together **a** the elders of 3605
 4:30 Aaron spake **a** the words which the Lᴏʀᴅ 3605
 5:12 **a** the land of Egypt to gather stubble 3605
 5:23 thou **delivered** thy people **at a**. 5337+5337
 6:29 speak thou unto Pharaoh king of Egypt **a** 3605
 7: 2 Thou shalt speak **a** that I command thee: 3605
 7:19 and upon **a** their pools of water, 3605
 7:19 *that* there may be blood throughout **a** 3605
 7:20 the waters that *were* in the river were 3605
 7:21 there was blood throughout **a** the land of 3605
 7:24 the Egyptians digged round about 3605
 8: 2 I will smite **a** thy borders with frogs: 3605
 8: 6 upon thy people, and upon **a** thy servants. 3605
 8:16 that it may become lice throughout **a** 3605
 8:17 the dust of the land became lice 3605
 8:17 lice throughout **a** the land of Egypt. 3605
 8:24 and into **a** the land of Egypt: 3605
 9: 4 there shall nothing die of **a** *that is* 3605
 9: 6 morrow, and **a** the cattle of Egypt died: 3605
 9: 9 it shall become small dust in **a** the land of 3605
 9: 9 beast, throughout **a** the land of Egypt. 3605
 9:11 the magicians, and upon **a** the Egyptians. 3605
 9:14 For I will at this time send **a** my plagues 3605
 9:14 that *there is* none like me in **a** the earth. 3605
 9:16 may be declared throughout **a** the earth. 3605
 9:19 cattle, and **a** that thou hast in the field; 834
 9:22 that there may be hail in **a** the land of 3605
 9:24 as there was none like it in **a** the land 3605
 9:25 the hail smote throughout **a** the land of 3605
 9:25 the land of Egypt **a** that *was* in the field, 3605

A

Ex	10: 6 houses of **a** thy servants, and the houses	3605
	10: 6 and the houses of **a** the Egyptians;	3605
	10:12 of the land, *even* **a** that the hail hath left.	3605
	10:13 an east wind upon the land **a** that day,	3605
	10:13 the land all that day, and **a** that night;	3605
	10:14 the locusts went up over **a** the land of	3605
	10:14 and rested in **a** the coasts of Egypt:	3605
	10:15 **a** the fruit of the trees which the hail had	3605
	10:15 of the field, through **a** the land of Egypt.	3605
	10:19 there remained not one locust in **a**	3605
	10:22 there was a thick darkness in **a** the land	3605
	10:23 the children of Israel had light in their	3605
	11: 5 the firstborn in the land of Egypt shall	3605
	11: 5 the mill; and **a** the firstborn of beasts.	3605
	11: 6 there shall be a great cry throughout **a**	3605
	11: 8 these thy servants shall come down	3605
	11: 8 out, and **a** the people that follow thee:	3605
	11:10 did **a** these wonders before Pharaoh:	3605
	12: 3 Speak ye unto **a** the congregation of Israel,	3605
	12: 9 nor **sodden at a** with water, but	1310+1311
	12:12 will smite the firstborn in the land of	3605
	12:12 against **a** the gods of Egypt I will execute	3605
	12:20 in **a** your habitations shall ye eat	3605
	12:21 Moses called for **a** the elders of Israel,	3605
	12:29 that at midnight the Lord smote **a**	3605
	12:29 the dungeon; and **a** the firstborn of cattle.	3605
	12:30 he, and **a** his servants, and all	3605
	12:30 and all his servants, and **a** the Egyptians;	3605
	12:33 in haste; for they said, We *be* **a** dead *men.*	3605
	12:41 *that* **a** the hosts of the Lord went out	3605
	12:42 **a** the children of Israel in their generations.	3605
	12:47 **A** the congregation of Israel shall keep it.	3605
	12:48 let **a** his males be circumcised, and	3605
	12:50 Thus did **a** the children of Israel; as	3605
	13: 2 Sanctify unto me **a** the firstborn,	3605
	13: 7 be leaven seen with thee in **a** thy quarters.	3605
	13:12 That thou shalt set apart unto the Lord **a**	3605
	13:13 **a** the firstborn of man amongst thy	3605
	13:15 that the Lord slew **a** the firstborn in	3605
	13:15 I sacrifice to the Lord **a** that openeth	3605
	13:15 **a** the firstborn of my children I redeem.	3605
	14: 4 upon Pharaoh, and upon **a** his host;	3605
	14: 7 **a** the chariots of Egypt, and captains over	3605
	14: 9 the Egyptians pursued after them (**a**	3605
	14:17 upon **a** his host, upon his chariots,	3605
	14:20 that the one came not near the other **a**	3605
	14:21 go *back* by a strong east wind **a** *that* night,	3605
	14:23 *even* **a** Pharaoh's horses, his chariots,	3605
	14:28 the host of Pharaoh that came into the	3605
	15:15 **a** the inhabitants of Canaan shall melt	3605
	15:20 the women went out after her with	3605
	15:26 commandments, and keep **a** his statutes,	3605
	16: 1 **a** the congregation of the children of Israel	3605
	16: 6 Aaron said unto **a** the children of Israel,	3605
	16: 9 Say unto **a** the congregation of the	3605
	16:22 the rulers of the congregation came	3605
	17: 1 **a** the congregation of the children of Israel	3605
	18: 1 heard of **a** that God had done for Moses,	3605
	18: 8 Moses told his father in law **a** that	3605
	18: 8 the travail that had come upon them by	3605
	18: 9 Jethro rejoiced for **a** the goodness which	3605
	18:11 that the Lord *is* greater than **a** gods:	3605
	18:12 Aaron came, and **a** the elders of Israel,	3605
	18:14 when Moses' father in law saw **a** that he	3605
	18:14 **a** the people stand by thee from morning	3605
	18:21 Moreover thou shalt provide out of **a**	3605
	18:22 let them judge the people at **a** seasons:	3605
	18:23 **a** this people shall also go to their place in	3605
	18:24 father in law, and did **a** that he had said.	3605
	18:25 Moses chose able men out of **a** Israel,	3605
	18:26 they judged the people at **a** seasons:	3605
	19: 5 peculiar treasure unto me above **a** people:	3605
	19: 5 above **a** people: for **a** the earth *is* mine:	3605
	19: 7 laid before their faces **a** these words	3605
	19: 8 the people answered together, and said,	3605
	19: 8 **A** that the Lord hath spoken we will do.	3605
	19:11 sight of **a** the people upon mount Sinai.	3605
	19:16 that **a** the people that *was* in the camp	3605
	20: 1 And God spake **a** these words, saying,	3605
	20: 9 days shalt thou labour, and do **a** thy work:	3605
	20:11 **a** that in them *is,* and rested the seventh	3605
	20:18 **a** the people saw the thunderings, and	3605
	20:24 in **a** places where I record my name I will	3605
	22: 9 For **a** manner of trespass, *whether it be* for	3605
	22:23 they **cry at a** unto me, I will surely	6817+6817
	22:26 **at a take** thy neighbour's raiment	
	to pledge,	2254+2254
	23:13 in **a** *things* that I have said unto you be	3605
	23:17 Three times in the year **a** thy males shall	3605
	23:22 obey his voice, and do **a** that I speak;	3605
	23:27 will destroy **a** the people to whom thou	3605
	23:27 make **a** thine enemies turn their backs	3605
	24: 3 told the people **a** the words of the Lord,	3605
	24: 3 words of the Lord, and **a** the judgments:	3605
	24: 3 the people answered *with* one voice,	3605
	24: 3 **A** the words which the Lord hath said	3605
	24: 4 Moses wrote **a** the words of the Lord,	3605
	24: 7 **A** that the Lord hath said will we do,	3605
	24: 8 made with you concerning **a** these words.	3605
	25: 9 According to **a** that I shew thee, *after*	3605
	25: 9 the pattern of **a** the instruments thereof,	3605
	25:22 of **a** *things* which I will give thee in	3605
	25:36 **a** it *shall be* one beaten work *of* pure gold.	3605
	25:39 gold shall he make it, with **a** these vessels.	3605
	26: 8 the eleven curtains *shall be* **a** of one	NIH

Ex	26:17 thus shalt thou make for **a** the boards of	3605
	27: 3 **a** the vessels thereof thou shalt make *of*	3605
	27:17 **A** the pillars round about the court	3605
	27:19 **A** the vessels of the tabernacle in all	3605
	27:19 All the vessels of the tabernacle in **a**	3605
	27:19 the pins thereof, and all the pins of	3605
	27:19 **a** the pins of the court, *shall be of* brass.	3605
	28: 3 thou shalt speak unto **a** *that are* wise	3605
	28:31 shalt make the robe of the ephod **a** of	3632
	28:38 of Israel shall hallow in **a** their holy gifts;	3605
	29:12 pour **a** the blood beside the bottom of	3605
	29:13 thou shalt take **a** the fat that covereth	3605
	29:24 thou shalt put **a** in the hands of Aaron,	3605
	29:35 according to **a** *things* which I have	3605
	30:27 the table and **a** his vessels, and	3605
	30:28 the altar of burnt offering with **a** his	3605
	31: 3 and in **a** *manner of* workmanship,	3605
	31: 5 to work in **a** *manner of* workmanship.	3605
	31: 6 in the hearts of **a** that are wise hearted I	3605
	31: 6 that they may make **a** that I have	3605
	31: 7 **a** the furniture of the tabernacle,	3605
	31: 8 the pure candlestick with **a** his furniture,	3605
	31: 9 the altar of burnt offering with **a** his	3605
	31:11 **a** that I have commanded thee shall they	3605
	32: 3 **a** the people brake off the golden earrings	3605
	32:13 **a** this land that I have spoken of will I give	3605
	32:26 **a** the sons of Levi gathered themselves	3605
	33: 8 *that* **a** the people rose up, and stood every	3605
	33:10 **a** the people saw the cloudy pillar stand *at*	3605
	33:10 **a** the people rose up and worshipped,	3605
	33:16 from **a** the people that *are* upon the face	3605
	33:19 I will make **a** my goodness pass before	3605
	34: 3 neither let any man be seen throughout **a**	3605
	34:10 before **a** thy people I will do marvels,	3605
	34:10 such as have not been done in **a** the earth,	3605
	34:10 **a** the people among which thou *art* shall	3605
	34:19 **A** that openeth the matrix *is* mine;	3605
	34:20 **A** the firstborn of thy sons thou shalt	3605
	34:23 Thrice in the year shall **a** your men	3605
	34:30 and **a** the children of Israel saw Moses,	3605
	34:31 **a** the rulers of the congregation returned	3605
	34:32 afterward **a** the children of Israel came	3605
	34:32 he gave them in commandment **a** that	3605
	35: 1 Moses gathered **a** the congregation of	3605
	35: 4 Moses spake unto **a** the congregation of	3605
	35:10 make **a** that the Lord hath commanded;	3605
	35:13 and **a** his vessels, and the shewbread,	3605
	35:16 and **a** his vessels, the laver and his foot,	3605
	35:20 **a** the congregation of the children of Israel	3605
	35:21 **a** his service, and for the holy garments.	3605
	35:22 and rings, and tablets, **a** jewels of gold:	3605
	35:25 the women that were wise hearted did	3605
	35:26 **a** the women whose heart stirred them up	3605
	35:29 willing to bring for **a** *manner of* work,	3605
	35:31 and in **a** *manner of* workmanship;	3605
	35:35 work **a** *manner of* work, of the engraver,	3605
	36: 1 understanding to know how to work **a**	3605
	36: 1 according to **a** that the Lord had	3605
	36: 3 they received of Moses **a** the offering,	3605
	36: 4 **a** the wise *men,* that wrought all the work	3605
	36: 4 all the wise *men,* that wrought **a** the work	3605
	36: 7 For the stuff *they had* was sufficient for **a**	3605
	36: 9 cubits: the curtains *were* **a** of one size.	3605
	36:22 thus did he make for **a** the boards of	3605
	37:22 **a** of it *was* one beaten work *of* pure gold.	3605
	37:24 gold made he it, and **a** the vessels thereof.	3605
	38: 3 made **a** the vessels of the altar, the pots,	3605
	38: 3 the vessels thereof made he *of* brass.	3605
	38:16 **A** the hangings of the court round about	3605
	38:17 **a** the pillars of the court *were* filleted *with*	3605
	38:20 **a** the pins of the tabernacle, and of	3605
	38:22 made **a** that the Lord commanded	3605
	38:24 **A** the gold that was occupied for the work	3605
	38:24 **a** the work of the holy *place,* even the	3605
	38:30 grate for it, and **a** the vessels of the altar,	3605
	38:31 **a** the pins of the tabernacle, and all the	3605
	38:31 and **a** the pins of the court round about.	3605
	39:22 of the ephod *of* woven work, **a** of blue.	3632
	39:32 Thus was **a** the work of the tabernacle of	3605
	39:32 children of Israel did according to **a** that	3605
	39:33 the tent, and **a** his furniture, his taches,	3605
	39:36 *and* **a** the vessels thereof, and	3605
	39:37 the vessels thereof, and the oil for light,	3605
	39:39 and **a** his vessels, the laver and his foot,	3605
	39:40 the vessels of the service of	3605
	39:42 According to **a** that the Lord	3605
	39:42 so the children of Israel made **a** the work.	3605
	39:43 Moses did look upon **a** the work,	3605
	40: 9 **a** that *is* therein, and shalt hallow it,	3605
	40: 9 shalt hallow it, and **a** the vessels thereof:	3605
	40:10 and **a** his vessels, and sanctify the altar:	3605
	40:16 according to **a** that the Lord commanded	3605
	40:36 the children of Israel went onward in **a**	3605
	40:38 in the sight of **a** the house of Israel,	3605
	40:38 throughout **a** their journeys.	3605
Lev	1: 9 the priest shall burn **a** on the altar, *to be* a	3605
	1:13 the priest shall bring *it* **a,** and burn *it* upon	3605
	2: 2 thereof, with **a** the frankincense thereof;	3605
	2:13 with **a** thine offerings thou shalt offer salt.	3605
	2:16 thereof, with **a** the frankincense thereof:	3605
	3: 3 and **a** the fat that *is* upon the inwards,	3605
	3: 9 and **a** the fat that *is* upon the inwards,	3605
	3:14 and **a** the fat that *is* upon the inwards,	3605
	3:16 a sweet savour: **a** the fat *is* the Lord's.	3605
	3:17 generations throughout **a** your dwellings,	

Lev	4: 7 shall pour **a** the blood of the bullock at	3605
	4: 8 he shall take off from it **a** the fat of	3605
	4: 8 and **a** the fat that *is* upon the inwards,	3605
	4:11 **a** his flesh, with his head, and with his	3605
	4:18 shall pour out **a** the blood at the bottom	3605
	4:19 shall take **a** his fat from him, and burn *it*	3605
	4:26 he shall burn **a** his fat upon the altar, as	3605
	4:30 shall pour out **a** the blood thereof at	3605
	4:31 he shall take away **a** the fat thereof, as	3605
	4:34 shall pour out **a** the blood thereof at	3605
	4:35 he shall take away **a** the fat thereof, as	3605
	6: 3 any of **a** *these* that a man doeth, sinning	3605
	6: 5 Or **a** *that* about which he hath sworn	3605
	6: 7 it shall be forgiven him for any *thing* of **a**	3605
	6: 9 of the burning upon the altar **a** night unto	3605
	6:15 the frankincense which *is* upon the meat	3605
	6:18 **A** the males among the children of Aaron	3605
	6:29 **A** the males among the priests shall eat	3605
	7: 3 he shall offer of it **a** the fat thereof;	3605
	7: 9 the meat offering that is baken in	3605
	7: 9 **a** *that* is dressed in the fryingpan, and in	3605
	7:10 and dry, shall **a** the sons of Aaron have,	3605
	7:18 be **eaten at a** on the third day,	398+398
	7:19 the flesh, **a** that be clean shall eat thereof.	3605
	8: 3 gather thou **a** the congregation together	3605
	8:10 the tabernacle and **a** that *was* therein,	3605
	8:11 anointed the altar and **a** his vessels,	3605
	8:16 took **a** the fat that *was* upon the inwards,	3605
	8:25 the fat that *was* upon the inwards,	3605
	8:27 he put **a** upon Aaron's hands, and upon	3605
	8:36 his sons did **a** things which the Lord	3605
	9: 5 **a** the congregation drew near	3605
	9:23 the glory of the Lord appeared unto **a**	3605
	9:24 *which* when **a** the people saw, they	3605
	10: 3 and before **a** the people I will be glorified.	3605
	10: 6 and lest wrath come upon **a** the people:	3605
	10:11 that *ye* may teach the children of Israel **a**	3605
	11: 2 among **a** the beasts that *are* on the earth.	3605
	11: 9 These shall ye eat of **a** that *are* in	3605
	11:10 **a** that have not fins nor scales in the seas,	3605
	11:10 of **a** that move in the waters, and of any	3605
	11:20 **A** fowls that creep, going upon *all* four,	3605
	11:20 All fowls that creep, going upon **a** four,	NIH
	11:21 creeping thing that goeth upon **a** four,	NIH
	11:23 **a** *other* flying creeping things, which have	3605
	11:27 among **a** *manner of* beasts that go on *all*	3605
	11:27 among all *manner of* beasts that go on **a**	NIH
	11:31 These *are* unclean to you among **a** that	3605
	11:34 Of a meat which may be eaten, *that* on	3605
	11:34 a drink that may be drunk in every *such*	3605
	11:42 whatsoever goeth upon **a** four, or	NIH
	11:42 whatsoever hath more feet among **a**	3605
	13:12 the leprosy cover **a** the skin of *him that*	3605
	13:13 *if* the leprosy have covered **a** his flesh,	3605
	13:13 plague: it is **a** turned white: he *is* clean.	3605
	13:46 **A** the days wherein the plague *shall be* in	3605
	14: 8 shave off **a** his hair, and wash *himself* in	3605
	14: 9 *that* he shall shave **a** his hair off his head	3605
	14: 9 even **a** his hair he shall shave off:	3605
	14:36 that **a** that *is* in the house be not *made*	3605
	14:45 and **a** the morter of the house;	3605
	14:46 Moreover he that goeth into the house **a**	3605
	14:54 This *is* the law for **a** *manner of* plague of	3605
	15:16 he shall wash **a** his flesh in water,	3605
	15:24 if any man **lie with** her at **a,**	854+7901+7901
	15:24 **a** the bed whereon he lieth shall be	3605
	15:25 the days of the issue of her uncleanness	3605
	15:26 Every bed whereon she lieth **a** the days of	3605
	16: 2 that he come not at **a** times into the holy	3605
	16:16 of their transgressions in **a** their sins:	3605
	16:17 and for **a** the congregation of Israel.	3605
	16:21 confess over him **a** the iniquities of	3605
	16:21 **a** their transgressions in all their sins,	3605
	16:21 all their transgressions in **a** their sins,	3605
	16:22 the goat shall bear upon him **a** their	3605
	16:29 do no work at **a,** *whether it be* one of	NIH
	16:30 *that* ye may be clean from **a** your sins	3605
	16:33 and for **a** the people of the congregation.	3605
	16:34 of Israel for **a** their sins once a year.	3605
	17: 2 unto **a** the children of Israel, and say unto	3605
	17:14 For *it is* the life of **a** flesh; the blood of it	3605
	17:14 for the life of **a** flesh *is* the blood thereof:	3605
	18:24 **a** these nations are defiled which I cast	3605
	18:27 (For **a** these abominations have the men	3605
	19: 2 Speak unto **a** the congregation of	3605
	19: 7 if it be **eaten at a** on the third day, it	398+398
	19:13 **abide** with thee **a night** until the	3885
	19:20 not **at a redeemed,** nor freedom	6299+6299
	19:23 shall have planted **a** *manner of* trees for	3605
	19:24 in the fourth year **a** the fruit thereof shall	3605
	19:37 Therefore shall ye observe **a** my statutes,	3605
	19:37 and **a** my judgments, and do them:	3605
	20: 5 off, and **a** that go a whoring after him,	3605
	20:22 Ye shall therefore keep **a** my statutes,	3605
	20:22 and **a** my judgments, and do them:	3605
	20:23 for they committed **a** these *things,*	3605
	21:24 his sons, and unto **a** the children of Israel.	3605
	22: 3 Whosoever *he be* of **a** your seed among	3605
	22:18 unto **a** the children of Israel, and say unto	3605
	22:18 that will offer his oblation for **a** his vows,	3605
	22:18 his vows, and for **a** his freewill offerings,	3605
	23: 3 sabbath of the Lord in **a** your dwellings.	3605
	23:14 your generations in **a** your dwellings.	3605
	23:21 **a** your dwellings throughout your	3605
	23:31 your generations in **a** your dwellings.	3605

A

Reference	Text	Number
Lev 23:38	beside **a** your vows, and beside all your	3605
23:38	and beside **a** your freewill offerings,	3605
23:42	that are Israelites born shall dwell in	3605
24:14	**a** that heard *him* lay their hands upon his	3605
24:14	and let **a** the congregation stone him.	3605
24:16	**a** the congregation shall certainly stone	3605
25: 7	shall **a** the increase thereof be meat.	3605
25: 9	trumpet sound throughout **a** your land.	3605
25:10	proclaim liberty throughout *a* the land	NIH
25:10	*all* the land unto **a** the inhabitants thereof:	3605
25:24	in **a** the land of your possession ye shall	3605
26:14	and will not do **a** these commandments;	3605
26:15	that *ye* will not do **a** my commandments,	3605
26:18	ye will not yet for *a* this hearken unto me,	NIH
26:27	if ye will not for **a** this hearken unto me,	NIH
26:44	yet for **a** that, when they be in the land of	NIH
27: 9	**a** that *any man* giveth of such unto	3605
27:10	if he shall **at a change** beast for	4171+4171
27:13	if he will **at a redeem** it,	1350+1350
27:25	**a** thy estimations shall be according to	3605
27:28	devote unto the LORD of **a** that he hath,	3605
27:30	**a** the tithe of the land, *whether* of the seed	3605
27:31	if a man will **at a redeem** *ought* of	1350+1350
27:33	if he **change** it **at a**, then both it	4171+4171
Nu 1: 2	Take ye the sum of **a** the congregation of	3605
1: 3	**a** that *are able to go* forth *to* war in Israel:	3605
1:18	they assembled **a** the congregation together	3605
1:20	**a** that *were able to go* forth *to* war;	3605
1:22	**a** that *were able to go* forth *to* war;	3605
1:24	**a** that *were able to go* forth *to* war;	3605
1:26	**a** that *were able to go* forth *to* war;	3605
1:28	**a** that *were able to go* forth *to* war;	3605
1:30	**a** that *were able to go* forth *to* war;	3605
1:32	**a** that *were able to go* forth *to* war;	3605
1:34	**a** that *were able to go* forth *to* war;	3605
1:36	**a** that *were able to go* forth *to* war;	3605
1:38	**a** that *were able to go* forth *to* war;	3605
1:40	**a** that *were able to go* forth *to* war;	3605
1:42	**a** that *were able to go* forth *to* war;	3605
1:45	So were **a** those that were numbered of	3605
1:45	**a** that *were able to go* forth *to* war in	3605
1:46	Even **a** they that were numbered were six	3605
1:50	over **a** the vessels thereof, and over all	3605
1:50	and over **a** *things* that *belong* to it:	3605
1:50	the tabernacle, and **a** the vessels thereof;	3605
1:54	children of Israel did according to **a** that	3605
2: 9	**A** that were numbered in the camp of	3605
2:16	**A** that were numbered in the camp of	3605
2:24	**A** that were numbered of the camp of	3605
2:31	**A** they that were numbered in the camp	3605
2:32	**a** those that were numbered of the camps	3605
2:34	children of Israel did according to **a** that	3605
3: 8	they shall keep **a** the instruments of	3605
3:12	**a** the firstborn that openeth the matrix	3605
3:13	Because **a** the firstborn *are* mine; *for* on	3605
3:13	on the day that I smote **a** the firstborn in	3605
3:13	hallowed unto me **a** the firstborn in Israel,	3605
3:22	according to the number of **a** the males,	3605
3:26	the cords of it for **a** the service thereof.	3605
3:28	the number of **a** the males, from a month	3605
3:31	the hanging, and **a** the service thereof.	3605
3:34	according to the number of **a** the males,	3605
3:36	the vessels thereof, and all that serveth	3605
3:36	vessels thereof, and **a** that serveth thereto,	3605
3:39	**A** that were numbered of the Levites,	3605
3:39	the males from a month old and upward	3605
3:40	Number **a** the firstborn of the males of	3605
3:41	instead of **a** the firstborn among	3605
3:41	the cattle of the Levites instead of **a**	3605
3:42	the firstborn among the children of Israel	3605
3:43	the firstborn males by the number of	3605
3:45	Take the Levites instead of **a** the firstborn	3605
4: 3	fifty years old, **a** that enter into the host,	3605
4: 9	and **a** the oil vessels thereof,	3605
4:10	the vessels thereof within a covering of	3605
4:12	they shall take **a** the instruments of	3605
4:14	they shall put upon it **a** the vessels thereof,	3605
4:14	and the basons, **a** the vessels of the altar;	3605
4:15	and the vessels of the sanctuary, as the camp	3605
4:16	*and* the oversight of **a** the tabernacle,	3605
4:16	of **a** that therein *is*, in the sanctuary,	3605
4:23	**a** that enter in to perform the service,	3605
4:26	**a** the instruments of their service, and all	3605
4:26	their service, and **a** that is made for them:	3605
4:27	his sons shall be **a** the service of the sons	3605
4:27	in **a** their burdens, and in all their service:	3605
4:27	in all their burdens, and in **a** their service:	3605
4:27	shall appoint unto them in charge **a** their	3605
4:31	according to **a** their service in	3605
4:32	with **a** their instruments, and with all	3605
4:32	instruments, and with **a** their service:	3605
4:33	according to **a** their service, in	3605
4:37	**a** that *might* do service in the tabernacle	3605
4:41	**a** that *might* do service in the tabernacle	3605
4:46	**A** those that were numbered of the	3605
5: 9	every offering of **a** the holy *things* of	3605
5:30	priest shall execute upon her **a** this law.	3605
6: 4	**A** the days of his separation shall he eat	3605
6: 5	**A** the days of the vow of his separation	3605
6: 6	**A** the days that he separateth *himself* unto	3605
6: 8	**A** the days of his separation he *is* holy	3605
7: 1	sanctified it, and **a** the instruments	3605
7: 1	both the altar and **a** the vessels thereof,	3605
7:85	**a** the silver vessels *weighed* two thousand	3605
7:86	**a** the gold of the spoons *was* an hundred	3605

Reference	Text	Number
Nu 7:87	**A** the oxen for the burnt offering *were*	3605
7:88	**a** the oxen for the sacrifice of the peace	3605
8: 7	let them shave **a** their flesh, and let them	3605
8:16	*even instead of* the firstborn of **a**	3605
8:17	For **a** the firstborn of the children of Israel	3605
8:18	I have taken the Levites for **a** the firstborn	3605
8:20	**a** the congregation of the children of Israel	3605
8:20	did to the Levites according unto **a** that	3605
9: 3	according to **a** the rites of it,	3605
9: 3	according to **a** the ceremonies thereof,	3605
9: 5	according to **a** that the LORD commanded	3605
9:12	according to **a** the ordinances of	3605
10: 3	**a** the assembly shall assemble themselves	3605
10:25	*which was* the rereward of **a** the camps	3605
11: 6	*there is* nothing at **a**, beside **a** this manna,	3605
11:11	*thou* layest the burden of **a** this people	3605
11:12	Have I conceived **a** this people? have I	3605
11:13	Whence should I have flesh to give unto **a**	3605
11:14	I am not able to bear **a** this people alone,	3605
11:22	shall **a** the fish of the sea be gathered	3605
11:29	would God that **a** the LORD's people	3605
11:32	the people stood up **a** that day, and all	3605
11:32	*a* that night, and all the next day,	3605
11:32	the next day, and they gathered	3605
11:32	they **spread** *them* **a abroad** for	7849+7849
12: 3	above **a** the men which *were* upon the	3605
12: 7	*is* not so, who *is* faithful in **a** mine house.	3605
13: 3	**a** those men *were* heads of the children of	3605
13:26	**a** the congregation of the children of	3605
13:26	unto **a** the congregation, and shewed	3605
13:32	**a** the people that we saw in it *are* men of	3605
14: 1	**a** the congregation lifted up their voice,	3605
14: 2	**a** the children of Israel murmured against	3605
14: 5	Aaron fell on their faces before **a**	3605
14: 7	they spake unto **a** the company of	3605
14:10	**a** the congregation bade stone them with	3605
14:10	before **a** the children of Israel.	3605
14:11	for **a** the signs which I have shewed	3605
14:15	Now *if* thou shalt kill **a** this people as one	NIH
14:21	**a** the earth shall be filled *with* the glory of	3605
14:22	Because **a** *those* men which have seen my	3605
14:29	**a** that were numbered of you, according to	3605
14:35	I will surely do it unto **a** this evil	3605
14:36	made **a** the congregation to murmur	3605
14:39	Moses told these sayings unto **a**	3605
15:13	**A** that are born of the country shall do	3605
15:22	and not observed **a** these commandments,	3605
15:23	*Even* **a** that the LORD hath commanded	3605
15:24	that **a** the congregation shall offer one	3605
15:25	the priest shall make an atonement for **a**	3605
15:26	it shall be forgiven **a** the congregation of	3605
15:26	seeing **a** the people were in ignorance.	3605
15:33	and Aaron, and unto **a** the congregation.	3605
15:35	**a** the congregation shall stone him with	3605
15:36	**a** the congregation brought him without	3605
15:39	remember **a** the commandments of	3605
15:40	do **a** my commandments, and be holy	3605
16: 3	seeing **a** the congregation *are* holy,	3605
16: 5	spake unto Korah and unto **a** his company	3605
16: 6	you censers, Korah, and **a** his company;	3605
16:10	**a** thy brethren the sons of Levi with thee:	3605
16:11	**a** thy company *are* gathered together	3605
16:16	and **a** thy company before the LORD,	3605
16:19	Korah gathered **a** the congregation against	3605
16:19	the glory of the LORD appeared unto **a**	3605
16:22	O God, the God of the spirits of **a** flesh,	3605
16:22	thou be wroth with **a** the congregation?	3605
16:26	lest ye be consumed in **a** their sins.	3605
16:28	LORD hath sent me to do **a** these works;	3605
16:29	If these *men* die the common death of **a**	3605
16:29	if they be visited after the visitation of **a**	3605
16:30	with **a** that *appertain* unto them,	3605
16:31	he had made an end of speaking **a** these	3605
16:32	the men that *appertained* unto Korah,	3605
16:32	unto Korah, and **a** *their* goods.	3605
16:33	They, and **a** that *appertained* to them,	3605
16:34	**a** Israel that *were* round about them fled	3605
16:41	on the morrow **a** the congregation of	3605
17: 2	of **a** their princes according to the house	3605
17: 9	Moses brought out **a** the rods from before	3605
17: 9	the LORD unto **a** the children of Israel:	3605
17:12	Behold, we die, we perish, we **a** perish.	3605
18: 3	and the charge of **a** the tabernacle:	3605
18: 4	for **a** the service of the tabernacle:	3605
18: 8	**a** the hallowed *things* of the children of	3605
18:11	with **a** the wave offerings of the children	3605
18:12	**A** the best of the oil, and all the best of	3605
18:12	**a** the best of the wine, and of the wheat,	3605
18:15	Every thing that openeth the matrix in **a**	3605
18:19	**A** the heave offerings of the holy *things*,	3605
18:21	have given the children of Levi **a** the tenth	3605
18:28	offering unto the LORD of **a** your tithes,	3605
18:29	Out of **a** your gifts ye shall offer every	3605
18:29	of **a** the best thereof, *even* the hallowed	3605
19:14	**a** that come into the tent, and all that *is* in	3605
19:14	into the tent, and **a** that *is* in the tent,	3605
19:18	upon **a** the vessels, and upon the persons	3605
20:14	Thou knowest **a** the travail that hath	3605
20:27	Hor in the sight of **a** the congregation.	3605
20:29	when **a** the congregation saw that Aaron	3605
20:29	thirty days, *even* **a** the house of Israel.	3605
21:23	Sihon gathered **a** his people together,	3605
21:25	Israel took **a** these cities: and Israel dwelt	3605
21:25	Israel dwelt in **a** the cities of the Amorites,	3605
21:25	in Heshbon, and in **a** the villages thereof.	3605

Reference	Text	Number
Nu 21:26	taken **a** his land out of his hand,	3605
21:33	he, and **a** his people, to the battle *at* Edrei.	3605
21:34	thy hand, and **a** his people, and his land;	3605
21:35	smote him, and his sons, and **a** his people,	3605
22: 2	Balak the son of Zippor saw **a** that Israel	3605
22: 4	Now shall *this* company lick up **a** *that are*	3605
22:38	have I now **any power at a** to say	3201+3201
23: 6	he, and **a** the princes of Moab.	3605
23:13	part of them, and shalt not see them **a**:	3605
23:25	Neither **curse** them **at a**, nor bless	5344+5344
23:25	them at all, nor **bless** them **at a**.	1288+1288
23:26	saying, **A** that the LORD speaketh, that I	3605
24:17	and destroy **a** the children of Sheth.	3605
25: 4	Take **a** the heads of the people,	3605
25: 6	in the sight of **a** the congregation of	3605
26: 2	Take the sum of **a** the congregation of	3605
26: 2	**a** that *are able to go* to war in Israel.	3605
26:43	**A** the families of the Shuhamites,	3605
26:62	**a** males from a month old and upward:	3605
27: 2	before the princes and **a** the congregation,	3605
27:16	the God of the spirits of **a** flesh,	3605
27:19	the priest, and before **a** the congregation;	3605
27:20	that **a** the congregation of the children of	3605
27:21	and **a** the children of Israel with him,	3605
27:21	Israel with him, even **a** the congregation:	3605
27:22	the priest, and before **a** the congregation:	3605
29:40	to **a** that the LORD commanded Moses.	3605
30: 2	he shall **a** according to **a** that proceedeth	3605
30: 4	her vows shall stand, and every bond	3605
30: 6	if she **had at a** a husband,	1961+1961+3807.1
30:11	**a** her vows shall stand, and every bond	3605
30:14	establisheth **a** her vows, or all her bonds,	3605
30:14	or **a** her bonds, which *are* upon her:	3605
31: 4	throughout **a** the tribes of Israel, shall ye	3605
31: 7	and they slew **a** the males.	3605
31: 9	the children of Israel took **a** the women of	NIH
31: 9	took the spoil of **a** their cattle, and all their	3605
31: 9	and **a** their flocks, and all their goods.	3605
31: 9	and all their flocks, and **a** their goods.	3605
31:10	burnt **a** their cities wherein they dwelt,	3605
31:10	and **a** their goodly castles, with fire.	3605
31:11	they took **a** the spoil, and all the prey,	3605
31:11	and the prey, *both* of men and of beasts.	3605
31:13	and **a** the princes of the congregation,	3605
31:15	Have ye saved **a** the women alive?	3605
31:18	**a** the women children, that have not	3605
31:20	purify **a** *your* raiment, and all that is made	3605
31:20	**a** that is made of skins, and all work of	3605
31:20	**a** work of goats' *hair*, and all things made	3605
31:20	of goats' *hair*, and **a** things made of wood.	3605
31:23	that abideth not the fire ye shall make	3605
31:27	to battle, and between **a** the congregation:	3605
31:30	of a *manner of* beasts, and give them unto	3605
31:35	thirty and two thousand persons in **a**,	3605
31:51	the gold of them, *even* **a** wrought jewels.	3605
31:52	**a** the gold of the offering that they offered	3605
32:13	until **a** the generation, that had done evil	3605
32:15	and ye shall destroy **a** this people.	3605
32:21	will go **a** of you armed over Jordan before	3605
32:26	our wives, our flocks, and **a** our cattle,	3605
33: 3	high hand in the sight of **a** the Egyptians.	3605
33: 4	For the Egyptians buried **a** *their* firstborn,	3605
33:52	ye shall drive out **a** the inhabitants of	3605
33:52	destroy **a** their pictures, and destroy all	3605
33:52	destroy **a** their molten images, and quite	3605
33:52	and quite pluck down **a** their high places:	3605
35: 3	and for their goods, and for **a** their beasts.	3605
35: 7	*So* **a** the cities which ye shall give to	3605
35:29	your generations in **a** your dwellings.	3605
Dt 1: 1	**a** Israel on *this* side Jordan in	3605
1: 3	according unto **a** that the LORD had given	3605
1: 7	unto **a** *the places* nigh thereunto, in	3605
1:18	commanded you at that time **a** the things	3605
1:19	we went *through* **a** that great and terrible	3605
1:30	according to **a** that he did for you in Egypt	3605
1:31	bear his son, in **a** the way that ye went,	3605
1:41	according to **a** that the LORD our God	3605
2: 7	blessed thee in **a** the works of thy hand:	3605
2:14	until **a** the generation of the men of war	3605
2:16	when **a** the men of war were consumed	3605
2:32	he and **a** his people, to fight *at* Jahaz.	3605
2:33	smote him, and his sons, and **a** his people.	3605
2:34	we took **a** his cities at that time,	3605
2:36	the LORD our God delivered **a** unto us:	3605
3: 1	he and **a** his people, to battle *at* Edrei.	3605
3: 2	**a** his people, and his land, into thy hand;	3605
3: 3	the king of Bashan, and **a** his people:	3605
3: 4	we took **a** his cities at that time, there was	3605
3: 4	threescore cities, **a** the region of Argob,	3605
3: 5	**A** these cities *were* fenced *with* high walls,	3605
3: 7	the cattle, and the spoil of the cities,	3605
3:10	**A** the cities of the plain, and all Gilead,	3605
3:10	**a** Gilead, and all Bashan, unto Salchah	3605
3:10	all Gilead, and **a** Bashan, unto Salchah	3605
3:13	the rest of Gilead, and **a** Bashan, *being*	3605
3:13	**a** the region of Argob, with all Bashan,	3605
3:13	all the region of Argob, with **a** Bashan,	3605
3:14	the son of Manasseh took **a** the country	3605
3:18	of Israel, **a** *that are* meet for the war.	3605
3:21	Thine eyes have seen **a** that the LORD	3605
3:21	shall the LORD do unto **a** the kingdoms	3605
4: 3	for **a** the men that followed Baal-peor,	3605
4: 6	which shall hear **a** these statutes, and say,	3605
4: 7	as the LORD our God *is* in **a** *things that*	3605
4: 8	and judgments *so* righteous as **a** this law,	3605

A

Dt 4: 9 lest they depart from thy heart **a** the days 3605
4:10 that they may learn to fear me **a** the days 3605
4:19 and the stars, *even* **a** the host of heaven, 3605
4:19 unto **a** nations under the whole heaven. 3605
4:29 shalt find *him*, if thou seek him with **a** 3605
4:29 him with all thy heart and with **a** thy soul. 3605
4:30 **a** these things are come upon thee, 3605
4:34 according to **a** that the LORD your God 3605
4:49 the plain on *this* side Jordan eastward, 3605
5: 1 Moses called **a** Israel, and said unto them, 3605
5: 3 us, who *are* **a** of us here alive *this* day. 3605
5:13 thou shalt labour, and do **a** thy work: 3605
5:22 These words the LORD spake unto **a** your 3605
5:23 *even* **a** the heads of your tribes, 3605
5:26 who *is there of* **a** flesh, that hath heard 3605
5:27 hear **a** that the LORD our God shall say: 3605
5:27 speak thou unto us **a** that the LORD our 3605
5:28 they have well *said* **a** that they have 3605
5:29 and keep **a** my commandments always, 3605
5:31 I will speak unto thee **a** 3605
5:33 You shall walk in **a** the ways which 3605
6: 2 to keep **a** his statutes 3605
6: 2 and thy son's son, **a** the days of thy life; 3605
6: 5 thou shalt love the LORD thy God with **a** 3605
6: 5 with **a** thy soul, and with all thy might. 3605
6: 5 with all thy soul, and with **a** thy might. 3605
6:11 houses full *of* **a** good *things*, which thou 3605
6:19 To cast out **a** thine enemies from before 3605
6:22 upon Pharaoh, and upon **a** his household, 3605
6:24 the LORD commanded us to do **a** these 3605
6:25 we observe to do **a** these commandments 3605
7: 6 above **a** people that *are* upon the face of 3605
7: 7 for ye *were* the fewest of **a** people: 3605
7:14 Thou shalt be blessed above **a** people: 3605
7:15 the LORD will take away from thee **a** 3605
7:15 will lay them upon **a** *them* that hate thee. 3605
7:16 thou shalt consume **a** the people which 3605
7:18 God did unto Pharaoh, and unto **a** Egypt; 3605
7:19 shall the LORD thy God do unto **a** 3605
8: 1 **A** the commandments which I command 3605
8: 2 thou shalt remember **a** the way which 3605
8:13 and **a** that thou hast is multiplied; 3605
8:19 if thou **do a forget** the LORD 7911+7911
9:10 on them *was written* according to **a** 3605
9:18 because of **a** your sins which ye sinned, 3605
10:12 to walk in **a** his ways, and to love him, 3605
10:12 to serve the LORD thy God with **a** thy 3605
10:12 God with all thy heart and with **a** thy soul, 3605
10:14 the earth *also*, with **a** that therein *is*. 3605
10:15 *even* you above **a** people, as *it is* this day. 3605
11: 3 the king of Egypt, and unto **a** his land; 3605
11: 6 **a** the substance that *was* in their 3605
11: 6 their possession, in the midst of **a** Israel: 3605
11: 7 your eyes have seen **a** the great acts of 3605
11: 8 Therefore shall ye keep **a** 3605
11:13 serve him with **a** your heart and with all 3605
11:13 with all your heart and with **a** your soul, 3605
11:22 For if ye shall diligently keep **a** these 3605
11:22 to walk in **a** his ways, and to cleave unto 3605
11:23 will the LORD drive out **a** these nations 3605
11:25 the dread of you upon **a** the land that ye 3605
11:32 ye shall observe to do **a** the statutes 3605
12: 1 **a** the days that ye live upon the earth. 3605
12: 2 Ye shall utterly destroy **a** the places, 3605
12: 5 out of **a** your tribes to put his name there, 3605
12: 7 shall rejoice in **a** that you put your hand 3605
12: 8 shall not do after **a** *the things* that we do 3605
12:10 *when* he giveth you rest from **a** your 3605
12:11 thither shall ye bring **a** that I command 3605
12:11 **a** your choice vows which ye vow unto 3605
12:14 thou shalt do **a** that I command thee. 3605
12:15 mayest kill and eat flesh in **a** thy gates, 3605
12:18 God in **a** that thou puttest thine hands 3605
12:28 hear **a** these words which I command 3605
13: 3 the LORD your God with **a** your heart 3605
13: 3 with all your heart and with **a** your soul. 3605
13: 9 and afterwards the hand of **a** the people. 3605
13:11 And Israel shall hear, and fear, and shall do 3605
13:15 **a** that *is* therein, and the cattle thereof, 3605
13:16 thou shalt gather **a** the spoil of it into 3605
13:16 **a** the spoil thereof every whit, for 3605
13:18 to keep **a** his commandments which I 3605
14: 2 above **a** the nations that *are* upon the 3605
14: 9 These ye shall eat of **a** that *are* in 3605
14: 9 **a** that have fins and scales shall ye eat: 3605
14:11 *Of* **a** clean birds ye shall eat. 3605
14:20 *But* of **a** clean fowls ye may eat. 3605
14:22 Thou shalt truly tithe **a** the increase of thy 3605
14:28 the tithe of thine increase the same year, 3605
14:29 **a** the work of thine hand which thou 3605
15: 5 to observe to do **a** these commandments 3605
15:10 thy God shall bless thee in **a** thy works, 3605
15:10 in **a** that thou puttest thine hand unto. 3605
15:18 the LORD thy God shall bless thee in **a** 3605
15:19 **A** the firstling males that come of thy herd 3605
16: 3 of the land of Egypt **a** the days of thy life. 3605
16: 4 seen with thee in **a** thy coast seven days; 3605
16: 4 even, **remain a night** until the morning. 3885
16:15 the LORD thy God shall bless thee in **a** 3605
16:15 in **a** the works of thine hands, therefore 3605
16:16 Three times in a year shall **a** thy males 3605
16:18 shalt thou make thee in **a** thy gates, 3605
17: 7 and afterward the hands of **a** the people. 3605
17:10 shalt observe to do according to **a** that 3605
17:13 **a** the people shall hear, and fear, and do 3605

Dt 17:14 like as **a** the nations that *are* about me; 3605
17:19 he shall read therein **a** the days of his life: 3605
17:19 to keep **a** the words of this law 3605
18: 1 priests the Levites, *and* **a** the tribe of Levi, 3605
18: 5 God hath chosen him out of **a** thy tribes, 3605
18: 6 come from any of thy gates out of **a** Israel, 3605
18: 6 come with **a** the desire of his mind unto 3605
18: 7 as **a** his brethren the Levites *do*, which 3605
18:12 For **a** that do these *things are* an 3605
18:16 According to **a** that thou desiredst of 3605
18:18 he shall speak unto them **a** that I shall 3605
19: 8 give thee **a** the land which he promised 3605
19: 9 If thou shalt keep **a** these commandments 3605
20:11 *that* **a** the people that is found therein 3605
20:14 and the cattle, and **a** that is in the city, 3605
20:14 that is in the city, *even* **a** the spoil thereof, 3605
20:15 Thus shalt thou do unto **a** the cities *which* 3605
20:18 That they teach you not to do after **a** their 3605
21: 6 **a** the elders of that city, *that are* next unto 3605
21:14 thou shalt not **sell** her at **a** for 4376+4376
21:17 by giving him a double portion of **a** that he 3605
21:21 **a** the men of his city shall stone him with 3605
21:21 and **a** Israel shall hear, and fear. 3605
21:23 His body shall not **remain a night** upon 3885
22: 3 with a lost *thing* of thy brother's, which 3605
22: 5 for **a** that do so *are* abomination unto 3605
22:19 he may not put her away **a** his days. 3605
22:29 he may not put her away **a** his days. 3605
23: 6 nor their prosperity **a** thy days for ever. 3605
23:20 the LORD thy God may bless thee in **a** 3605
24: 8 do according to **a** that the priests 3605
24:19 bless thee in **a** the work of thine hands. 3605
25:16 For **a** that do such *things, and* all that do 3605
25:16 such *things, and* **a** that do unrighteously, 3605
25:18 *even* **a** that were feeble behind thee, 3605
25:19 rest from **a** thine enemies round about, 3605
26: 2 That thou shalt take of the first of **a** 3605
26:12 When thou hast made an end of tithing **a** 3605
26:13 according to **a** thy commandments which 3605
26:14 have done according to **a** that thou hast 3605
26:16 keep and do them with **a** thine heart, 3605
26:16 with all thine heart, and with **a** thy soul. 3605
26:18 that *thou* shouldest keep **a** his 3605
26:19 to make thee high above **a** nations which 3605
27: 1 Keep **a** the commandments which I 3605
27: 3 thou shalt write upon them **a** the words 3605
27: 8 thou shalt write upon the stones **a** 3605
27: 9 the priests the Levites spake unto **a** Israel, 3605
27:14 say unto **a** the men of Israel *with* **a** loud 3605
27:15 putteth *it* in *a* secret *place*. And **a** 3605
27:16 And **a** the people shall say, Amen. 3605
27:17 And **a** the people shall say, Amen. 3605
27:18 And **a** the people shall say, Amen. 3605
27:19 And **a** the people shall say, Amen. 3605
27:20 And **a** the people shall say, Amen. 3605
27:21 And **a** the people shall say, Amen. 3605
27:22 And **a** the people shall say, Amen. 3605
27:23 And **a** the people shall say, Amen. 3605
27:24 And **a** the people shall say, Amen. 3605
27:25 And **a** the people shall say, Amen. 3605
27:26 Cursed *be* he that confirmeth not **a** NIH
27:26 And **a** the people shall say, Amen. 3605
28: 1 to do **a** his commandments which I 3605
28: 1 thee on high above **a** nations of the earth: 3605
28: 2 **a** these blessings shall come on thee, 3605
28: 8 and in **a** that thou settest thine hand unto; 3605
28:10 **a** people of the earth shall see that thou 3605
28:12 and to bless **a** the work of thine hand: 3605
28:15 to observe to do **a** his commandments 3605
28:15 that **a** these curses shall come upon thee, 3605
28:20 in **a** that thou settest thine hand unto for 3605
28:25 shalt be removed into **a** the kingdoms of 3605
28:26 thy carcase shall be meat unto **a** fowls of 3605
28:32 fail *with longing* for them **a** the day long: 3605
28:33 The fruit of thy land, and **a** thy labours, 3605
28:37 among **a** nations whither the LORD shall 3605
28:40 Thou shalt have olive trees throughout **a** 3605
28:42 **A** thy trees and fruit of thy land shall 3605
28:45 Moreover **a** these curses shall come upon 3605
28:47 of heart, for the abundance of **a** *things;* 3605
28:48 want of **a** *things:* and he shall put a yoke 3605
28:52 he shall besiege thee in **a** thy gates, 3605
28:52 thou trustedst, throughout **a** thy land: 3605
28:52 he shall besiege thee in **a** thy gates 3605
28:52 in all thy gates throughout **a** thy land, 3605
28:55 enemies shall distress thee in **a** thy gates. 3605
28:57 for she shall eat them for want of **a** *things* 3605
28:58 If thou wilt not observe to do **a** the words 3605
28:60 Moreover he will bring upon thee **a** 3605
28:64 the LORD shall scatter thee among **a** 3605
29: 2 Moses called unto **a** Israel, and said unto 3605
29: 2 Ye have seen **a** that the LORD did before 3605
29: 2 unto **a** his servants, and unto all his land; 3605
29: 2 unto all his servants, and unto **a** his land; 3605
29: 9 that ye may prosper *in* **a** that ye do. 3605
29:10 Ye stand *this* day **a** of you before 3605
29:10 and your officers, *with* **a** the men of Israel, 3605
29:20 **a** the curses that are written in this book 3605
29:21 him unto evil out of **a** the tribes of Israel, 3605
29:21 according to **a** the curses of the covenant 3605
29:24 Even **a** nations shall say, Wherefore hath 3605
29:27 bring upon it **a** the curses that are written 3605
29:29 that *we* may do **a** the words of this law. 3605
30: 1 when **a** these things are come upon thee, 3605
30: 1 thou shalt call *them* to mind among **a** 3605

Dt 30: 2 shalt obey his voice according to **a** that I 3605
30: 2 with **a** thine heart, and with all thy soul; 3605
30: 2 with all thine heart, and with **a** thy soul; 3605
30: 3 and gather thee from **a** the nations, 3605
30: 6 to love the LORD thy God with **a** thine 3605
30: 6 and with **a** thy soul, that thou mayest live. 3605
30: 7 the LORD thy God will put **a** these curses 3605
30: 8 do **a** his commandments which I 3605
30:10 the LORD thy God with **a** thine heart, 3605
30:10 with all thine heart, and with **a** thy soul. 3605
31: 1 and spake these words unto **a** Israel. 3605
31: 5 ye may do unto them according unto **a** 3605
31: 7 said unto him in the sight of **a** Israel, 3605
31: 9 the LORD, and unto **a** the elders of Israel. 3605
31:11 When **a** Israel is come to appear before 3605
31:11 thou shalt read this law before **a** Israel in 3605
31:12 and observe to do **a** the words of this law: 3605
31:18 I will surely hide my face in that day for **a** 3605
31:28 Gather unto me **a** the elders of your tribes 3605
31:30 Moses spake in the ears of **a** 3605
32: 4 his ways *are* judgment: a God of truth 3605
32:27 and the LORD hath not done **a** this. 3605
32:44 spake **a** the words of this song in the ears 3605
32:45 Moses made an end of speaking **a** these 3605
32:45 end of speaking all these words to **a** Israel: 3605
32:46 Set your hearts unto **a** the words which I 3605
32:46 to observe to do, **a** the words of this law. 3605
33: 3 the people; **a** his saints *are* in thy hand: 3605
33:12 *the* LORD shall cover him **a** the day long, 3605
34: 1 the LORD shewed him **a** the land of 3605
34: 2 **a** Naphtali, and the land of Ephraim, 3605
34: 2 Manasseh, and **a** the land of Judah, unto 3605
34:11 In **a** the signs and the wonders, which 3605
34:11 and to **a** his servants, and to all his land, 3605
34:11 and to all his servants, and to **a** his land, 3605
34:12 in *that* mighty hand, and in all the great 3605
34:12 in **a** the great terror which Moses shewed 3605
34:12 Moses shewed in the sight of **a** Israel. 3605

Jos 1: 2 over this Jordan, thou, and **a** this people, 3605
1: 4 **a** the land of the Hittites, and unto the 3605
1: 5 *to* stand before thee **a** the days of thy life: 3605
1: 7 observe to do according to **a** the law, 3605
1: 8 do according to **a** that is written therein: 3605
1:14 the mighty *men* of valour, and help 3605
1:16 **A** that thou commandest us we will do, 3605
1:17 as we hearkened unto Moses in **a** 3605
1:18 will not hearken unto thy words in **a** that 3605
2: 3 for they be come to search out **a** 3605
2: 9 that **a** the inhabitants of the land faint 3605
2:13 that they have, and deliver our lives 3605
2:18 thy brethren, and **a** thy father's household, 3605
2:22 the pursuers sought *them* throughout **a** 3605
2:23 and told him **a** *things* that befell them: 3605
2:24 hath delivered into our hands **a** the land; 3605
2:24 even **a** the inhabitants of the country do 3605
3: 1 he and **a** the children of Israel, 3605
3: 7 to magnify thee in the sight of **a** Israel, 3605
3:11 *even* the Lord of **a** the earth passeth over 3605
3:13 the Lord of **a** the earth, shall rest in 3605
3:15 (for Jordan overfloweth **a** his banks all 3605
3:15 (for Jordan overfloweth all his banks 3605
3:17 **a** the Israelites passed over on dry *ground,* 3605
3:17 **a** the people were passed clean over 3605
4: 1 when **a** the people were clean passed over 3605
4:10 according to **a** that Moses commanded 3605
4:11 when **a** the people were clean passed over 3605
4:14 magnified Joshua in the sight of **a** Israel; 3605
4:14 as they feared Moses, **a** the days of his life. 3605
4:18 flowed over **a** his banks, as *they did* 3605
4:24 That **a** the people of the earth might know 3605
5: 1 to pass, when **a** the kings of the Amorites, 3605
5: 1 **a** the kings of the Canaanites, which *were* 3605
5: 4 **A** the people that came out of Egypt, 3605
5: 4 *that were* males, *even* **a** the men of war, 3605
5: 5 Now **a** the people that came out were 3605
5: 5 **a** the people *that were* born in 3605
5: 6 till **a** the people *that were* men of war, 3605
5: 8 when they had done circumcising **a** 3605
6: 3 **a** *ye* men of war, *and* go round about 3605
6: 5 **a** the people shall shout *with* a great shout 3605
6:17 *even* it, and **a** that *are* therein, to 3605
6:17 she and **a** that *are* with her in the house, 3605
6:19 the silver, and gold, and vessels of brass 3605
6:21 utterly destroyed **a** that *was* in the city, 3605
6:22 and **a** that she hath, as ye sware unto her. 3605
6:23 and her brethren, and **a** that she had; 3605
6:23 they brought out **a** her kindred, 3605
6:24 the city with fire, and **a** that *was* therein: 3605
6:25 father's household, and **a** that she had; 3605
6:27 his fame was *noised* throughout **a** 3605
7: 3 said unto him, Let not **a** the people go up; 3605
7: 3 make not **a** the people to labour thither; 3605
7: 7 **at a brought** this people **over** 5674+5674
7: 9 **a** the inhabitants of the land shall hear 3605
7:15 be burnt with fire, he and **a** that he hath: 3605
7:23 unto the children of Israel, and laid them 3605
7:24 Joshua, and **a** Israel with him, took Achan 3605
7:24 his sheep, and his tent, and **a** that he had: 3605
7:25 **a** Israel stoned him *with* stones, 3605
8: 1 take **a** the people of war with thee, 3605
8: 3 So Joshua arose, and **a** the people of war, 3605
8: 4 very far from the city, but be ye **a** ready: 3605
8: 5 I, and **a** the people that *are* with me, 3605
8:11 the people, *even the people* of war that 3605
8:13 *even* **a** the host that *was* on the north of 3605

A

Jos	8:14 he and **a** his people, at a time appointed,	3605
	8:15 **a** Israel *made as if they* were beaten	3605
	8:16 **a** the people that *were* in Ai were called	3605
	8:21 **a** Israel saw that the ambush had taken	3605
	8:24 when Israel had made an end of slaying **a**	3605
	8:24 *when* they were **a** fallen on the edge of	3605
	8:24 that **a** the Israelites returned *unto* Ai,	3605
	8:25 *so* it was, *that* **a** that fell that day, both of	3605
	8:25 twelve thousand, *even* **a** the men of Ai.	3605
	8:26 until *he* had utterly destroyed **a**	3605
	8:33 **a** Israel, and their elders, and officers,	3605
	8:34 afterward he read **a** the words of the law,	3605
	8:34 according to **a** that is written in the book	3605
	8:35 There was not a word of **a** that Moses	3605
	8:35 which Joshua read not before **a**	3605
	9: 1 when **a** the kings which *were* on *this* side	3605
	9: 1 in **a** the coasts of the great sea over against	3605
	9: 5 **a** the bread of their provision was dry *and*	3605
	9: 9 fame of him, and **a** that he did in Egypt,	3605
	9:10 **a** that he did to the two kings of	3605
	9:11 **a** the inhabitants of our country spake to	3605
	9:18 **a** the congregation murmured against	3605
	9:19 **a** the princes said unto all the	3605
	9:19 the princes said unto **a** the congregation,	3605
	9:21 drawers of water unto **a** the congregation;	3605
	9:24 his servant Moses to give you **a** the land,	3605
	9:24 destroy **a** the inhabitants of the land from	3605
	10: 2 and **a** the men thereof *were* mighty.	3605
	10: 5 they and **a** their hosts,	3605
	10: 6 for **a** the kings of the Amorites that dwell	3605
	10: 7 he, and **a** the people of war with him,	3605
	10: 7 with him, and **a** the mighty *men* of valour.	3605
	10: 9 *and* went up from Gilgal **a** night.	3605
	10:15 Joshua returned, and **a** Israel with him,	3605
	10:21 **a** the people returned to the camp to	3605
	10:24 that Joshua called for **a** the men of Israel,	3605
	10:25 for thus shall the Lᴏʀᴅ do to **a** your	3605
	10:28 them, and **a** the souls that *were* therein;	3605
	10:29 **a** Israel with him, *unto* Libnah,	3605
	10:30 and **a** the souls that *were* therein;	3605
	10:31 **a** Israel with him, unto Lachish,	3605
	10:32 and **a** the souls that *were* therein,	3605
	10:32 according to **a** that he had done to Libnah.	3605
	10:34 passed unto Eglon, and **a** Israel with him;	3605
	10:35 **a** the souls that *were* therein he utterly	3605
	10:35 to **a** that he had done to Lachish.	3605
	10:36 and **a** Israel with him, unto Hebron;	3605
	10:36 the cities thereof, and all the souls that	3605
	10:37 and **a** the souls that *were* therein;	3605
	10:37 according to **a** that he had done to Eglon;	3605
	10:37 utterly, and **a** the souls that *were* therein.	3605
	10:38 and **a** Israel with him, to Debir;	3605
	10:39 the king thereof, and **a** the cities thereof;	3605
	10:39 utterly destroyed **a** the souls that *were*	3605
	10:40 So Joshua smote **a** the country of the hills,	3605
	10:40 and of the springs, and **a** their kings:	3605
	10:40 but utterly destroyed **a** that breathed,	3605
	10:41 **a** the country of Goshen, even unto	3605
	10:42 **a** these kings and their land did Joshua	3605
	10:43 Joshua returned, and **a** Israel with him,	3605
	11: 4 they and **a** their hosts with them,	3605
	11: 5 when **a** these kings were met together,	3605
	11: 6 will I deliver them up **a** slain before Israel:	3605
	11: 7 and **a** the people of war with him,	3605
	11:10 for Hazor beforetime *was* the head of **a**	3605
	11:11 they smote **a** the souls that *were* therein	3605
	11:12 **a** the cities of those kings, and all the	3605
	11:12 **a** the kings of them, did Joshua take,	3605
	11:14 the spoil of these cities, and the cattle,	3605
	11:15 he left nothing undone of **a** that the Lᴏʀᴅ	3605
	11:16 So Joshua took **a** that land, the hills,	3605
	11:16 **a** the south *country,* and all the land of	3605
	11:16 south *country,* and **a** the land of Goshen,	3605
	11:17 their kings he took, and smote them,	3605
	11:18 Joshua made war a long time with **a** those	3605
	11:19 of Gibeon: **a** *other* they took in battle.	3605
	11:21 from **a** the mountains of Judah,	3605
	11:21 and from **a** the mountains of Israel:	3605
	11:23 according to **a** that the Lᴏʀᴅ said unto	3605
	12: 1 Hermon, and **a** the plain on the east:	3605
	12: 5 and in Salcah, and in **a** Bashan,	3605
	12:24 of Tirzah, one: **a** the kings thirty and one.	3605
	13: 2 **a** the borders of the Philistines,	3605
	13: 2 borders of the Philistines, and **a** Geshuri,	3605
	13: 4 the land of the Canaanites,	3605
	13: 5 and **a** Lebanon, *toward* the sunrising,	3605
	13: 6 **A** the inhabitants of the hill country from	3605
	13: 6 *and* **a** the Sidonians, them will I drive out	3605
	13: 9 and **a** the plain of Medeba unto Dibon;	3605
	13:10 **a** the cities of Sihon king of the Amorites,	3605
	13:11 **a** mount Hermon, and all Bashan unto	3605
	13:11 Hermon, and **a** Bashan unto Salcah;	3605
	13:12 **A** the kingdom of Og in Bashan,	3605
	13:16 of the river, and **a** the plain by Medeba;	3605
	13:17 and **a** her cities that *are* in the plain;	3605
	13:21 **a** the cities of the plain, and all	3605
	13:21 **a** the kingdom of Sihon king of	3605
	13:25 **a** the cities of Gilead, and half the land of	3605
	13:30 coast was from Mahanaim, **a** Bashan,	3605
	13:30 **a** the kingdom of Og king of Bashan,	3605
	13:30 **a** the towns of Jair, which *are* in Bashan,	3605
	15:32 the cities *are* twenty and nine, with	3605
	15:46 **a** that *lay* near Ashdod, with their villages:	3605
	16: 9 **a** the cities with their villages.	3605
	17:16 **a** the Canaanites that dwell in the land of	3605

Jos	19: 8 **a** the villages that *were* round about these	3605
	20: 9 These were the cities appointed for **a**	3605
	21:19 **a** the cities of the children of Aaron,	3605
	21:26 **A** the cities *were* ten with their suburbs	3605
	21:33 **A** the cities of the Gershonites according	3605
	21:39 Jazer with her suburbs; four cities in **a.**	3605
	21:40 So **a** the cities for the children of Merari	3605
	21:41 **A** the cities of the Levites within	3605
	21:42 about them: thus *were* **a** these cities.	3605
	21:43 The Lᴏʀᴅ gave unto Israel **a** the land	3605
	21:44 according to **a** that he sware unto their	3605
	21:44 there stood not a man of **a** their enemies	3605
	21:44 the Lᴏʀᴅ delivered **a** their enemies into	3605
	21:45 unto the house of Israel; **a** came to pass.	3605
	22: 2 Ye have kept **a** that Moses the servant of	3605
	22: 2 have obeyed my voice in **a** that I	3605
	22: 5 to walk in **a** his ways, and to keep his	3605
	22: 5 serve him with **a** your heart and with all	3605
	22: 5 with all your heart and with **a** your soul.	3605
	22:14 of each chief house **a** prince throughout **a**	3605
	22:20 wrath fell on **a** the congregation of Israel?	3605
	23: 1 Israel from **a** their enemies round about,	3605
	23: 2 Joshua called for **a** Israel, *and* for their	3605
	23: 3 ye have seen **a** that the Lᴏʀᴅ your God	3605
	23: 3 your God hath done unto **a** these nations	3605
	23: 4 with **a** the nations that I have cut off,	3605
	23: 6 do **a** that is written in the book of the law	3605
	23:14 *this* day I am going the way of **a** the earth:	3605
	23:14 ye know in **a** your hearts and in all your	3605
	23:14 in all your hearts and in **a** your souls,	3605
	23:14 not one thing hath failed of **a** the good	3605
	23:14 are come to pass unto you, *and* **a** not one	3605
	23:15 *that* as **a** good things are come upon you,	3605
	23:15 shall the Lᴏʀᴅ bring upon you **a** evil	3605
	24: 1 Joshua gathered **a** the tribes of Israel to	3605
	24: 2 Joshua said unto the people, Thus saith	3605
	24: 3 led him throughout **a** the land of Canaan,	3605
	24:17 preserved us in **a** the way wherein we	3605
	24:17 among **a** the people through whom we	3605
	24:18 the Lᴏʀᴅ drave out from before us **a**	3605
	24:27 Joshua said unto the people, Behold,	3605
	24:27 for it hath heard **a** the words of the Lᴏʀᴅ	3605
	24:31 Israel served the Lᴏʀᴅ **a** the days of	3605
	24:31 **a** the days of the elders that overlived	3605
	24:31 which had known **a** the works of	3605
Jdg	1:25 but they let go the man and **a** his family.	3605
	2: 4 these words unto **a** the children of Israel,	3605
	2: 7 The people served the Lᴏʀᴅ **a** the days of	3605
	2: 7 **a** the days of the elders that outlived	3605
	2: 7 who had seen the great works of	3605
	2:10 also **a** that generation were gathered unto	3605
	2:18 of their enemies **a** the days of the judge:	3605
	3: 1 as many *of Israel* as had not known **a**	3605
	3: 3 **a** the Canaanites, and the Sidonians,	3605
	3:19 **a** that stood by him went out from him.	3605
	3:29 **a** lusty, and all men of valour;	3605
	3:29 all lusty, and **a** men of valour;	3605
	4:13 Sisera gathered together **a** his chariots,	3605
	4:13 and **a** the people that *were* with him,	3605
	4:15 and **a** *his* chariots, and all *his* host,	3605
	4:15 and all *his* chariots, and **a** *his* host,	3605
	4:16 the host of Sisera fell upon the edge of	3605
	5:31 So let **a** thine enemies perish, O Lᴏʀᴅ:	3605
	6: 9 out of the hand of **a** that oppressed you,	3605
	6:13 be with us, why then is **a** this befallen us?	3605
	6:13 where *be* **a** his miracles which our fathers	3605
	6:31 Joash said unto **a** that stood against him,	3605
	6:33 the Midianites and the Amalekites	3605
	6:35 sent messengers throughout **a** Manasseh;	3605
	6:37 *it be* dry upon **a** the earth *beside,*	3605
	6:39 upon **a** the ground let there be dew.	3605
	6:40 and there was dew on **a** the ground.	3605
	7: 1 **a** the people that *were* with him, rose up	3605
	7: 6 the rest of the people bowed down upon	3605
	7: 7 let **a** the *other* people go every man unto	3605
	7: 8 he sent **a** the *rest of* Israel every man	376+3605
	7:12 the children of the east lay along in	3605
	7:14 God delivered Midian, and **a** the host.	3605
	7:18 I and **a** the host with me, then blow ye	3605
	7:18 trumpets also on every side of **a** the camp,	3605
	7:21 and **a** the host ran, and cried, and fled.	3605
	7:22 his fellow, even throughout **a** the host:	3605
	7:23 out of **a** Manasseh, and pursued after	3605
	7:24 Gideon sent messengers throughout **a**	3605
	7:24 the men of Ephraim gathered themselves	3605
	8:10 fifteen thousand *men,* **a** that were left	3605
	8:10 of **a** the hosts of the children of the east:	3605
	8:12 and Zalmunna, and discomfited **a** the host.	3605
	8:27 **a** Israel went thither a whoring after it:	3605
	8:34 the hands of **a** their enemies on every side:	3605
	8:35 according to **a** the goodness which he had	3605
	9: 1 with **a** the family of the house of his	3605
	9: 2 in the ears of **a** the men of Shechem,	3605
	9: 2 either that **a** the sons of Jerubbaal,	3605
	9: 3 of **a** the men of Shechem all these words:	3605
	9: 3 of all the men of Shechem **a** these words:	3605
	9: 6 **a** the men of Shechem gathered together,	3605
	9: 6 **a** the house of Millo, and went,	3605
	9:14 said **a** the trees unto the bramble,	3605
	9:25 they robbed **a** that came along *that* way	3605
	9:34 **a** the people that *were* with him, by night,	3605
	9:44 the two *other* companies ran upon **a**	3605
	9:45 Abimelech fought against the city **a** that	3605
	9:46 when **a** the men of the tower of Shechem	3605
	9:47 that **a** the men of the tower of Shechem	3605

Jdg	9:48 he and **a** the people that *were* with him;	3605
	9:49 **a** the people likewise cut down every man	3605
	9:49 that **a** the men of the tower of Shechem	3605
	9:51 thither fled **a** the men and women,	3605
	9:51 **a** they of the city, and shut *it* to them,	3605
	9:53 and **a to brake** his skull.	7533
	9:57 **a** the evil of the men of Shechem did God	3605
	10: 8 **a** the children of Israel that *were* on	3605
	10:18 he shall be head over **a** the inhabitants of	3605
	11: 8 be our head over **a** the inhabitants of	3605
	11:11 Jephthah uttered **a** his words before	3605
	11:20 Sihon gathered **a** his people together,	3605
	11:21 and **a** his people into the hand of Israel,	3605
	11:21 Israel possessed **a** the land of the Amorites	3605
	11:22 they possessed **a** the coasts of	3605
	11:26 in **a** the cities that *be* along by the coasts	3605
	12: 4 Jephthah gathered together **a** the men of	3605
	13:13 Of **a** that I said unto the woman let her	3605
	13:14 nor eat any unclean *thing:* **a** that I	3605
	13:23 neither would he have shewed us **a** these	3605
	14: 3 of thy brethren, or among **a** my people,	3605
	16: 2 laid wait for him **a** night in the gate of	3605
	16: 2 were quiet **a** the night, saying, In	3605
	16: 3 and **a,** and put *them* upon his shoulders,	NIH
	16:17 That he told her **a** his heart, and said unto	3605
	16:18 Delilah saw that he had told her **a** his	3605
	16:18 for he hath shewed me **a** his heart.	3605
	16:27 **a** the lords of the Philistines *were* there;	3605
	16:30 he bowed *himself* with **a** his might;	NIH
	16:30 and upon **a** the people that *were* therein.	3605
	16:31 and **a** the house of his father came down,	3605
	18: 1 **a** *their* inheritance had not fallen unto	NIH
	18:31 **a** the time that the house of God was in	3605
	19: 6 **tarry a night**, and let thine heart be merry	3885
	19: 9 towards evening, I pray you **tarry a night**:	3885
	19:13 to one of *these* places to **lodge a night**,	3885
	19:20 howsoever *let* **a** thy wants *lie* upon me;	3605
	19:25 abused her **a** the night until the morning:	3605
	19:29 and sent her into **a** the coasts of Israel.	3605
	19:30 was so, that **a** that saw it said, There was	3605
	20: 1 the children of Israel went out,	3605
	20: 2 the chief of **a** the people, *even* of all	3605
	20: 2 the people, *even* of **a** the tribes of Israel,	3605
	20: 6 sent her throughout **a** the country of	3605
	20: 7 Behold, ye *are* **a** children of Israel;	3605
	20: 8 **a** the people arose as one man, saying,	3605
	20:10 hundred throughout **a** the tribes of Israel,	3605
	20:10 according to **a** the folly that they have	3605
	20:11 So **a** the men of Israel were gathered	3605
	20:12 the tribes of Israel sent men through **a**	3605
	20:16 Among **a** this people *there* were seven	3605
	20:17 drew sword: **a** these *were* men of war.	3605
	20:25 thousand men; **a** these drew the sword.	3605
	20:26 **a** the children of Israel, and all the people,	3605
	20:26 **a** the people, went up, and came *unto*	3605
	20:33 **a** the men of Israel rose up out of their	3605
	20:34 ten thousand chosen men out of **a** Israel,	3605
	20:35 an hundred men: **a** these drew the sword.	3605
	20:37 smote **a** the city with the edge of the	3605
	20:44 men; **a** these *were* men of valour.	3605
	20:46 So that **a** which fell that day of Benjamin	3605
	20:46 the sword; **a** these *were* men of valour.	3605
	20:48 as the beast, and **a** that came to hand:	3605
	20:48 also they set on fire **a** the cities that they	3605
	21: 5 Who *is there* among **a** the tribes of Israel	3605
Ru	1:19 that **a** the city was moved about them,	3605
	2:11 a that thou hast done unto thy mother in	3605
	2:21 until they have ended **a** my harvest.	3605
	3: 5 **A** that thou sayest unto me I will do.	3605
	3: 6 did according to **a** that her mother in law	3605
	3:11 I will do to thee **a** that thou requirest:	3605
	3:11 for **a** the city of my people doth know that	3605
	3:16 told her **a** that the man had done to her.	3605
	4: 7 for to confirm **a** things;	3605
	4: 9 *unto* **a** the people, Ye *are* witnesses *this*	3605
	4: 9 that I have bought **a** that *was* Elimelech's,	3605
	4: 9 **a** that *was* Chilion's and Mahlon's, of	3605
	4:11 **a** the people that *were* in the gate,	3605
1Sa	1: 4 to **a** her sons and her daughters, portions:	3605
	1:11 I will give him unto the Lᴏʀᴅ **a** the days	3605
	1:21 man Elkanah, and **a** his house, went up	3605
	2:14 that the fleshhook brought up the priest	3605
	2:14 So they did in Shiloh unto **a** the Israelites	3605
	2:22 heard **a** that his sons did unto all Israel;	3605
	2:22 heard all that his sons did unto **a** Israel;	3605
	2:23 for I hear of your evil dealings by **a** this	3605
	2:28 I choose him out of **a** the tribes of Israel	3605
	2:28 did I give unto the house of thy father **a**	3605
	2:29 make yourselves fat with the chiefest of **a**	3605
	2:32 **a** *the* wealth which *God* shall give Israel:	3605
	2:33 the increase of thine house shall die in **a**	3605
	3:12 In that day I will perform against Eli **a**	3605
	3:17 if thou hide *any* thing from me of **a**	3605
	3:20 **a** Israel from Dan even to Beer-sheba	3605
	4: 1 the word of Samuel came to **a** Israel.	3605
	4: 5 **a** Israel shouted *with* a great shout, so	3605
	4: 8 with **a** the plagues in the wilderness.	3605
	4:13 the city, and told *it,* **a** the city cried out.	3605
	5: 8 gathered **a** the lords of the Philistines unto	3605
	5:11 gathered together **a** the lords of	3605
	5:11 deadly destruction throughout **a** the city;	3605
	6: 4 for one plague *was* on you **a,** and on your	3605
	6:18 *according to* the number of **a** the cities of	3605
	7: 2 the house of Israel lamented after	3605
	7: 3 Samuel spake unto **a** the house of Israel,	3605

1Sa
7: 3 If ye do return unto the Lord with **a** your 3605
7: 5 Gather **a** Israel to Mizpeh, and I will pray 3605
7:13 the Philistines **a** the days of Samuel. 3605
7:15 Samuel judged Israel **a** the days of his life. 3605
7:16 and judged Israel **a** in those places. 3605
8: 4 **a** the elders of Israel gathered themselves 3605
8: 5 now make us a king to judge us like **a** 3605
8: 7 Hearken unto the voice of the people in **a** 3605
8: 8 According to **a** the works which they have 3605
8:10 Samuel told **a** the words of the Lord 3605
8:20 That we also may be like **a** the nations; 3605
8:21 Samuel heard **a** the words of the people, 3605
9: 6 **a** that he saith cometh surely to pass: 3605
9:19 and will tell thee **a** that *is* in thine heart. 3605
9:20 on whom *is* **a** the desire of Israel? *Is it* not 3605
9:20 not on thee, and on **a** thy father's house? 3605
9:21 my family the least of **a** the families of 3605
10: 9 and **a** those signs came to pass that day. 3605
10:11 when **a** that knew him beforetime saw 3605
10:18 of the hand of **a** kingdoms, *and* of them 3605
10:19 who himself saved you out of **a** your 3605
10:20 when Samuel had caused **a** the tribes of 3605
10:24 Samuel said to **a** the people, See ye him 3605
10:24 that *there is* none like him among **a** 3605
10:24 **a** the people shouted, and said, God save 3605
10:25 Samuel sent **a** the people away, every 3605
11: 1 **a** the men of Jabesh said unto Nahash, 3605
11: 2 that *I* may thrust out **a** your right eyes, 3605
11: 2 and lay it for a reproach upon **a** Israel. 3605
11: 3 that we may send messengers unto **a** 3605
11: 4 **a** the people lift up their voices, and wept. 3605
11: 7 *them* throughout the coasts of Israel 3605
11:10 ye shall do with us **a** that seemeth good 3605
11:15 the people went *to* Gilgal; and there 3605
11:15 and **a** the men of Israel rejoiced greatly. 3605
12: 1 Samuel said unto **a** Israel, Behold, I have 3605
12: 1 I have hearkened unto your voice in **a** that 3605
12: 7 of **a** the righteous acts of the Lord, 3605
12:18 **a** the people greatly feared the Lord 3605
12:19 **a** the people said unto Samuel, Pray for 3605
12:19 we have added unto **a** our sins *this* evil, 3605
12:20 ye have done **a** this wickedness: yet turn 3605
12:20 but serve the Lord with **a** your heart; 3605
12:24 and serve him in truth with **a** your heart: 3605
13: 3 blew the trumpet throughout **a** the land, 3605
13: 4 **a** Israel heard say *that* Saul had smitten **a** 3605
13: 7 and **a** the people followed him trembling. 3605
13:19 found throughout **a** the land of Israel: 3605
13:20 **a** the Israelites went down *to* 3605
14: 7 said unto him, Do **a** that *is* in thine heart: 3605
14:15 in the field, and among **a** the people: 3605
14:20 **a** the people that *were* with him 3605
14:22 the men of Israel which had hid 3605
14:25 And **a** *they of* the land came to a wood; 3605
14:34 **a** the people brought every man his ox 3605
14:38 ye near hither, **a** the chief of the people. 3605
14:39 *there was* not *a man* among **a** the people 3605
14:40 said he unto **a** Israel, Be ye on one side, 3605
14:47 fought against **a** his enemies on every side, 3605
14:52 was sore war against the Philistines **a** 3605
15: 3 utterly destroy **a** that they have, 3605
15: 6 ye shewed kindness to **a** the children of 3605
15: 8 destroyed **a** the people with the edge 3605
15: 9 **a** *that was* good, and would not utterly 3605
15:11 and he cried unto the Lord **a** night. 3605
16:11 said unto Jesse, Are here **a** *thy* children? 8552
17:11 **a** Israel heard those words of the Philistine 3605
17:19 and they, and **a** the men of Israel, 3605
17:24 the men of Israel, when they saw 3605
17:46 that **a** the earth may know that there is a 3605
17:47 **a** this assembly shall know that the Lord 3605
18: 5 he was accepted in the sight of **a** 3605
18: 6 that the women came out of **a** cities of 3605
18:14 David behaved himself wisely in **a** his 3605
18:16 **a** Israel and Judah loved David, because 3605
18:22 in thee, and **a** his servants love thee: 3605
18:30 more wisely than **a** the servants of Saul; 3605
19: 1 to **a** his servants, that they should kill 3605
19: 5 the Lord wrought a great salvation for **a** 3605
19: 7 and Jonathan shewed him **a** those things. 3605
19:18 and told him **a** that Saul had done to him. 3605
19:24 lay down naked all that day and all *that* 3605
19:24 down naked all that day and a *that* night. 3605
20: 6 If thy father **at a miss** me, then say, 6485+6485
20: 6 for *there is* a yearly sacrifice there for **a** 3605
22: 1 **a** his father's house heard *it*, they went 3605
22: 4 dwelt with him **a** the while that David 3605
22: 6 **a** his servants *were* standing about him;) 3605
22: 7 *and* make you **a** captains of thousands, 3605
22: 8 That **a** of you have conspired against me, 3605
22:11 son of Ahitub, and **a** his father's house, 3605
22:11 and they came **a** of them to the king. 3605
22:14 *so* faithful among **a** thy servants as David, 3605
22:15 servant, *nor* to **a** the house of my father: 3605
22:15 for thy servant knew nothing of **a** this, 3605
22:16 thou, and **a** thy father's house. 3605
22:22 I have occasioned *the death* of **a** 3605
23: 8 Saul called **a** the people together to war, 3605
23:20 come down according to **a** the desire of 3605
23:23 take knowledge of **a** the lurking places 3605
23:23 that I will search him out throughout **a** 3605
24: 2 three thousand chosen men out of **a** Israel 3605
25: 1 **a** the Israelites were gathered together, 3605
25: 6 and peace *be* unto **a** that thou hast. 3605
25: 7 **a** the while they were in Carmel. 3605

1Sa
25: 9 they spake to Nabal according to **a** those 3605
25:12 and came and told him **a** those sayings. 3605
25:16 **a** the while we were with them keeping 3605
25:17 our master, and against **a** his household: 3605
25:21 in vain have I kept **a** that this *fellow* 3605
25:21 nothing was missed of **a** that *pertained* 3605
25:22 if I leave of **a** that *pertain* to him by 3605
25:28 evil hath not been found in thee **a** thy days. NIH
25:30 **a** the good that he hath spoken 3605
26:12 for they *were* **a** asleep; because a deep 3605
26:24 let him deliver me out of **a** tribulation. 3605
27:11 his manner **a** the while he dwelleth 3605
28: 3 **a** Israel had lamented him, and buried him 3605
28: 4 Saul gathered **a** Israel together, 3605
28:20 Saul fell straightway **a along** on 4393+6967
28:20 he had eaten no bread **a** the day, nor all 3605
28:20 eaten no bread all the day, nor **a** the night. 3605
29: 1 Now the Philistines gathered together **a** 3605
30: 6 the soul of **a** the people was grieved, 3605
30: 8 overtake *them,* and without fail recover **a.** NIH
30:16 behold *they were* spread abroad upon **a** 3605
30:16 of **a** the great spoil that they had taken out 3605
30:18 David recovered **a** that the Amalekites had 3605
30:19 had taken to them: David recovered **a.** 3605
30:20 David took **a** the flocks and the herds, 3605
30:22 answered **a** the wicked men and *men* of 3605
30:31 to **a** the places where David himself 3605
31: 6 and his armourbearer, and **a** his men, 3605
31:12 **A** the valiant men arose, and went all 3605
31:12 went **a** night, and took the body of Saul 3605
2Sa 1:11 likewise **a** the men that *were* with him: 3605
2: 9 and over Benjamin, and over **a** Israel. 3605
2:28 **a** the people stood still, and pursued after 3605
2:29 his men walked **a** that night through 3605
2:29 went *through* **a** Bithron, and they came 3605
2:30 when he had gathered **a** the people 3605
2:32 Joab and his men went **a** night, and they 3605
3:12 thee, to bring about **a** Israel unto thee. 3605
3:18 and out of the hand of **a** their enemies. 3605
3:19 in Hebron **a** that seemed good to Israel, 3605
3:21 will gather **a** Israel unto my lord the king, 3605
3:21 that thou mayest reign over **a** that thine 3605
3:23 **a** the host that *was* with him were come, 3605
3:25 coming in, and to know **a** that thou doest. 3605
3:29 head of Joab, and on **a** his father's house; 3605
3:31 to **a** the people that *were* with him, 3605
3:32 the grave of Abner; and **a** the people wept. 3605
3:34 And **a** the people wept again over him. 3605
3:35 when **a** the people came to cause David to 3605
3:36 **a** the people took notice of *it,* and it 3605
3:36 the king said, pleased **a** the people. 3605
3:37 For **a** the people and all Israel understood 3605
3:37 **a** Israel understood that day that it was 3605
4: 1 and **a** the Israelites were troubled. 3605
4: 7 gat them away through the plain **a** night. 3605
4: 9 who hath redeemed my soul out of **a** 3605
5: 1 came **a** the tribes of Israel to David unto 3605
5: 3 So **a** the elders of Israel came to the king 3605
5: 5 and three years over **a** Israel and Judah. 3605
5:17 **a** the Philistines came up to seek David; 3605
6: 1 David gathered together **a** the chosen *men* 3605
6: 2 with **a** the people that *were* with him 3605
6: 5 **a** the house of Israel played before 3605
6: 5 **a** *manner of instruments made of* fir 3605
6:11 blessed Obed-edom, and **a** his household. 3605
6:12 **a** that *pertaineth* unto him, because of 3605
6:14 David danced before the Lord with **a** *his* 3605
6:15 the house of Israel brought up the ark of 3605
6:19 he dealt among **a** the people, *even* among 3605
6:19 a flagon *of wine.* So **a** the people departed 3605
6:21 before thy father, and before **a** his house, 3605
7: 1 him rest round about from **a** his enemies; 3605
7: 3 to the king, Go, do **a** that *is* in thine heart; 3605
7: 7 In **a** *the places* wherein I have walked 3605
7: 7 **a** the children of Israel spake I a word 3605
7: 9 have cut off **a** thine enemies out of thy 3605
7:11 have caused thee to rest from **a** thine 3605
7:17 According to **a** these words, 3605
7:17 according to **a** this vision, so did Nathan 3605
7:21 hast thou done **a** these great things, 3605
7:22 according to **a** that we have heard with 3605
8: 4 David houghed **a** the chariot *horses,* 3605
8: 9 had smitten **a** the host of Hadadezer, 3605
8:11 gold that he had dedicated of **a** nations 3605
8:14 throughout **a** Edom put he garrisons, 3605
8:14 **a** they of Edom became David's servants. 3605
8:15 David reigned over **a** Israel; and David 3605
8:15 and justice unto **a** his people. 3605
9: 7 will restore thee **a** the land of Saul thy 3605
9: 9 I have given unto thy master's son **a** that 3605
9: 9 that pertained to Saul and to **a** his house. 3605
9:11 According to **a** that my lord the king hath 3605
9:12 **a** that dwelt in the house of Ziba *were* 3605
10: 7 and **a** the host *of* the mighty *men.* 3605
10: 9 he chose of **a** the choice *men* of Israel, 3605
10:17 he gathered **a** Israel together, 3605
10:19 when **a** the kings *that were* servants to 3605
11: 1 his servants with him, and **a** Israel; 3605
11: 9 house with **a** the servants of his lord, 3605
11:18 David **a** the things concerning the war; 3605
11:22 shewed David **a** that Joab had sent him 3605
12:12 I will do this thing before **a** Israel, 3605
12:16 went in, and lay **a** **night** upon the earth. 3885
12:29 David gathered **a** the people together, 3605
12:31 did he unto **a** the cities of the children 3605

2Sa
12:31 **a** the people returned *unto* Jerusalem. 3605
13: 9 Amnon said, Have out **a** men from me. 3605
13:21 when king David heard of **a** these things, 3605
13:23 and Absalom invited **a** the king's sons. 3605
13:25 Nay, my son, let us not **a** now go, 3605
13:27 and **a** the king's sons go with him. 3605
13:29 the king's sons arose, and every man gat 3605
13:30 Absalom hath slain **a** the king's sons, 3605
13:31 his servants stood *by* with their clothes 3605
13:32 slain **a** the young men the king's sons; 3605
13:33 to think *that* **a** the king's sons are dead: 3605
13:36 also and **a** his servants wept very sore. 3605
14:19 *not* the hand of Joab with thee in **a** this? 3605
14:19 he put **a** these words in the mouth of 3605
14:20 to know **a** *things* that *are* in the earth. 3605
14:25 in **a** Israel there was none to be so 3605
15: 6 on this manner did Absalom to **a** Israel 3605
15:10 Absalom sent spies throughout **a** the tribes 3605
15:14 David said unto **a** his servants that *were* 3605
15:16 went forth, and **a** his household after him. 3605
15:17 **a** the people after him, and tarried *in* a 3605
15:18 **a** his servants passed on beside him; 3605
15:18 **a** the Cherethites, and all the Pelethites, 3605
15:18 and the Pelethites, and all the Gittites, 3605
15:18 and all the Pelethites, and **a** the Gittites, 3605
15:22 **a** his men, and all the little ones that *were* 3605
15:22 and **a** the little ones that *were* with him. 3605
15:23 **a** the country wept *with* a loud voice, 3605
15:23 loud voice, and **a** the people passed over: 3605
15:23 **a** the people passed over, toward the way 3605
15:24 and **a** the Levites *were* with him, 3605
15:24 until **a** the people had done passing out of 3605
15:30 **a** the people that *was* with him covered 3605
16: 4 thine *are* **a** that *pertained* unto 3605
16: 6 and at **a** the servants of king David: 3605
16: 6 **a** the people and all the mighty *men were* 3605
16: 6 **a** the mighty *men were* on his right hand 3605
16: 8 The Lord hath returned upon thee **a** 3605
16:11 and to **a** his servants, Behold, my son, 3605
16:14 **a** the people that *were* with him, 3605
16:15 and **a** the people the men of Israel, 3605
16:18 people, and **a** the men of Israel, choose, 3605
16:21 **a** Israel shall hear that thou art abhorred 3605
16:21 shall the hands of **a** that *are* with thee be 3605
16:22 father's concubines in the sight of **a** Israel. 3605
16:23 *was* **a** the counsel of Ahithophel both 3605
17: 2 **a** the people that *are* with him shall flee; 3605
17: 3 I will bring back **a** the people unto thee: 3605
17: 3 the man whom thou seekest *is* as if **a** 3605
17: 3 *so* **a** the people shall be *in* peace. 3605
17: 4 Absalom well, and **a** the elders of Israel. 3605
17:10 for **a** Israel knoweth that thy father *is* a 3605
17:11 Therefore I counsel *that* **a** Israel be 3605
17:12 of **a** the men that *are* with him there shall 3605
17:13 shall **a** Israel bring ropes to that city, 3605
17:14 Absalom and **a** the men of Israel said, 3605
17:16 and **a** the people that *are* with him, 3605
17:22 **a** the people that *were* with him, 3605
17:24 he and **a** the men of Israel with him. 3605
18: 4 the people came out by hundreds 3605
18: 5 **a** the people heard when the king gave all 3605
18: 5 all the people heard when the king gave **a** 3605
18: 8 scattered over the face of **a** the country: 3605
18:17 and **a** Israel fled every one to his tent. 3605
18:28 and said unto the king, **A is well.** 7965
18:31 day of **a** them that rose up against thee. 3605
18:32 **a** that rise against thee to do *thee* hurt, 3605
19: 2 *turned* into mourning unto **a** the people: 3605
19: 5 Thou hast shamed *this* day the faces of **a** 3605
19: 6 **a** we had died *this* day, then it had 3605
19: 7 *will be* worse unto thee than **a** the evil 3605
19: 8 they told unto **a** the people, saying, 3605
19: 8 **a** the people came before the king: 3605
19: 9 **a** the people were at strife throughout all 3605
19: 9 all the people were at strife throughout **a** 3605
19:11 seeing the speech of **a** Israel is come to 3605
19:14 he bowed the heart of **a** the men of Judah, 3605
19:14 the king, Return thou, and **a** thy servants. 3605
19:20 I am come the first *this* day of **a** the house 3605
19:28 For **a** *of* my father's house were but dead 3605
19:30 said unto the king, Yea, let him take **a,** 3605
19:39 **a** the people went over Jordan. And 3605
19:40 the people of Judah conducted the king, 3605
19:41 **a** the men of Israel came to the king, 3605
19:41 and **a** David's men with him, over Jordan? 3605
19:42 the men of Judah answered the men of 3605
19:42 have we **eaten at a** of the king's *cost?* 398+398
20: 7 the mighty *men:* and they went out of 3605
20:12 the man saw that **a** the people stood 3605
20:13 the people went on after Joab, to pursue 3605
20:14 he went through **a** the tribes of Israel 3605
20:14 and *to* Beth-maachah, and **a** the Berites: 3605
20:15 **a** the people that *were* with Joab battered 3605
20:22 the woman went unto **a** the people in her 3605
20:23 Now Joab *was* over **a** the host of Israel: 3605
21: 9 they fell **a** seven together, and were put to NIH
21:14 performed **a** that the king commanded. 3605
22: 1 him out of the hand of **a** his enemies, 3605
22:23 For **a** his judgments *were* before me: 3605
22:31 he *is* a buckler to **a** them that trust in him. 3605
23: 5 ordered in **a** *things,* and sure: 3605
23: 5 *this is* **a** my salvation, and all *my* desire, 3605
23: 5 *this is* all my salvation, and **a** *my* desire, 3605
23: 6 *the sons of* Belial *shall be* **a** of them as 3605
23:39 Uriah the Hittite: thirty and seven *in* **a.** 3605

A

2Sa 24: 2	Go now through **a** the tribes of Israel,	3605

2Sa 24: 2 Go now through **a** the tribes of Israel, 3605
24: 7 *to* **a** the cities of the Hivites, and of 3605
24: 8 when they had gone through **a** the land, 3605
24:23 **A** these things did Araunah, *as* a king, 3605
1Ki 1: 3 damsel throughout **a** the coasts of Israel, 3605
1: 9 called **a** his brethren the king's sons, 3605
1: 9 **a** the men of Judah the king's servants. 3605
1:19 hath called **a** the sons of the king, 3605
1:20 O king, the eyes of **a** Israel *are* upon thee, 3605
1:25 hath called the king's sons, and 3605
1:29 that hath redeemed my soul out of **a** 3605
1:39 **a** the people said, God save king Solomon. 3605
1:40 **a** the people came up after him, 3605
1:41 **a** the guests that *were* with him heard *it* 3605
1:49 **a** the guests that *were* with Adonijah were 3605
2: 2 I go the way of **a** the earth: be thou strong 3605
2: 3 that thou mayest prosper *in* **a** that thou 3605
2: 4 walk before me in truth with **a** their heart 3605
2: 4 with all their heart and with **a** their soul, 3605
2:15 *that* **a** Israel set their faces on me, that *I* 3605
2:26 thou hast been afflicted in **a** where*in* my 3605
2:44 Thou knowest **a** the wickedness which 3605
3:13 among the kings like unto thee **a** thy days. 3605
3:15 and made a feast to **a** his servants. 3605
3:28 **a** Israel heard of the judgment which 3605
4: 1 So king Solomon was king over **a** Israel. 3605
4: 7 Solomon had twelve officers over **a** Israel, 3605
4:10 and **a** the land of Hepher. 3605
4:11 son of Abinadab, *in* **a** the region of Dor; 3605
4:12 and Megiddo, and **a** Beth-shean, 3605
4:21 Solomon reigned over **a** kingdoms from 3605
4:21 and served Solomon **a** the days of his life. 3605
4:24 he had dominion over **a** *the region* on 3605
4:24 over **a** the kings on *this* side the river: 3605
4:24 he had peace on **a** sides round about him. 3605
4:25 to Beer-sheba, **a** the days of Solomon. 3605
4:27 for **a** that came unto king Solomon's table, 3605
4:30 of **a** the children of the east country, 3605
4:30 east country, and **a** the wisdom of Egypt. 3605
4:31 For he was wiser than **a** men; than Ethan 3605
4:31 his fame was in **a** nations round about. 3605
4:34 came of **a** people to hear the wisdom 3605
4:34 **a** kings of the earth, which had heard 3605
5: 6 according to **a** that thou shalt appoint: 3605
5: 8 I will do **a** thy desire concerning timber 3605
5:10 and fir trees *according to* **a** his desire. 3605
5:13 king Solomon raised a levy out of **a** Israel; 3605
6:10 he built chambers against **a** the house, 3605
6:12 keep **a** my commandments to walk in 3605
6:18 *a* was cedar; there was no stone seen. 3605
6:22 gold, until *he* had finished **a** the house: 3605
6:29 he carved **a** the walls of the house round 3605
6:38 was the house finished throughout **a** 3605
6:38 and according to **a** the fashion of it. 3605
7: 1 thirteen years, and he finished **a** his house. 3605
7: 5 **a** the doors and posts *were* square, *with* 3605
7: 9 **A** these *were* of costly stones, according 3605
7:14 and cunning to work **a** works in brass. 3605
7:14 king Solomon, and wrought **a** his work. 3605
7:23 *it was* round **a** about, and his height *was* 5439
7:25 and **a** their hinder parts *were* inward. 3605
7:33 and their spokes, *were* **a** molten. 3605
7:37 **a** of them had one casting, one measure, 3605
7:40 Hiram made an end of doing **a** the work 3605
7:45 **a** these vessels, which Hiram made to 3605
7:47 Solomon left **a** the vessels *unweighed,* 3605
7:48 Solomon made **a** the vessels that 3605
7:51 So was ended **a** the work that king 3605
8: 1 of Israel, and **a** the heads of the tribes, 3605
8: 2 **a** the men of Israel assembled themselves 3605
8: 3 **a** the elders of Israel came, and the priests 3605
8: 4 **a** the holy vessels that *were* in 3605
8: 5 and **a** the congregation of Israel, 3605
8:14 and blessed **a** the congregation of Israel: 3605
8:14 (and **a** the congregation of Israel stood;) 3605
8:16 I chose no city out of **a** the tribes of Israel 3605
8:22 presence of **a** the congregation of Israel, 3605
8:23 that walk before thee with **a** their heart: 3605
8:38 by any man, *or* by **a** thy people Israel, 3605
8:39 knowest the hearts of **a** the children of 3605
8:40 That they may fear thee **a** the days that 3605
8:43 do according to **a** that the stranger calleth 3605
8:43 that **a** people of the earth may know thy 3605
8:48 *so* return unto thee with **a** their heart, 3605
8:48 with **a** their soul, in the land of their 3605
8:50 **a** their transgressions wherein they have 3605
8:52 hearken unto them in **a** that they call for 3605
8:53 thou didst separate them from among **a** 3605
8:54 had made an end of praying **a** this prayer 3605
8:55 blessed the congregation of Israel *with* **a** 3605
8:56 according to **a** that he promised: 3605
8:56 hath not failed one word of **a** his good 3605
8:58 to walk in **a** his ways, and to keep his 3605
8:59 his people Israel **at a times,** 3117+3117+871.1
8:60 That **a** the people of the earth may know 3605
8:62 the king, and **a** Israel with him, 3605
8:63 **a** the children of Israel dedicated the 3605
8:65 **a** Israel with him, a great congregation, 3605
8:66 glad of heart for **a** the goodness that 3605
9: 1 **a** Solomon's desire which he was pleased 3605
9: 4 to do according to **a** that I have 3605
9: 6 *But* if you shall **at a** turn from 7725+7725
9: 7 a proverb and a byword among **a** people: 3605
9: 9 hath the LORD brought upon them **a** this 3605
9:11 and with gold, according to **a** his desire,) 3605

1Ki 9:19 **a** the cities of store that Solomon had, 3605
9:19 and in **a** the land of his dominion. 3605
9:20 *And* **a** the people that were left of 3605
10: 2 she communed with him of **a** that was in 3605
10: 3 Solomon told her **a** her questions: there 3605
10: 4 when the queen of Sheba had seen **a** 3605
10:13 gave unto the queen of Sheba **a** her desire, 3605
10:15 of **a** the kings of Arabia, and of 3605
10:21 a king Solomon's drinking vessels *were of* 3605
10:21 **a** the vessels of the house of the forest of 3605
10:23 So king Solomon exceeded **a** the kings of 3605
10:24 the earth sought to Solomon, to hear his 3605
10:29 so for **a** the kings of the Hittites, and for 3605
11: 8 likewise did he for **a** his strange wives, 3605
11:13 Howbeit I will not rend away **a** 3605
11:16 did Joab remain there with **a** Israel, 3605
11:25 he was an adversary to Israel **a** the days of 3605
11:28 he made him ruler over **a** the charge of 3605
11:32 the city which I have chosen out of **a** 3605
11:34 will make him prince **a** the days of his life 3605
11:37 shalt reign according to **a** that thy soul 3605
11:38 thou wilt hearken unto **a** that I command 3605
11:41 and **a** that he did, and his wisdom, 3605
11:42 in Jerusalem over **a** Israel *was* forty years. 3605
12: 1 for **a** Israel were come *to* Shechem to 3605
12: 3 and **a** the congregation of Israel came, 3605
12:12 **a** the people came to Rehoboam the third 3605
12:16 So when **a** Israel saw that the king 3605
12:18 **a** Israel stoned him with stones, that he 3605
12:20 when **a** Israel heard that Jeroboam was 3605
12:20 and made him king over **a** Israel: 3605
12:21 he assembled **a** the house of Judah, with 3605
12:23 unto **a** the house of Judah and Benjamin, 3605
13:11 told him **a** the works that the man of God 3605
13:32 against **a** the houses of the high places 3605
14: 8 and who followed me with **a** his heart, 3605
14: 9 hast done evil above **a** that were before 3605
14:10 *a man* taketh away dung, till it be **a** gone. 8552
14:13 **a** Israel shall mourn for him, and bury him 3605
14:18 **a** Israel mourned for him, according to 3605
14:21 did choose out of **a** the tribes of Israel, 3605
14:22 above **a** that their fathers had done. 3605
14:24 they did according to **a** the abominations 3605
14:26 of the king's house; he even took away **a:** 3605
14:26 he took away **a** the shields of gold which 3605
14:29 the acts of Rehoboam, and **a** that he did, 3605
14:30 and Jeroboam *their* days. 3605
15: 3 he walked in **a** the sins of his father, 3605
15: 5 he commanded him **a** the days of his life, 3605
15: 6 **a** the days of his life. 3605
15: 7 of the acts of Abijam, and **a** that he did, 3605
15:12 removed **a** the idols that his fathers had 3605
15:14 was perfect with the LORD **a** his days. 3605
15:16 and Baasha king of Israel **a** their days. 3605
15:18 Asa took **a** the silver and the gold that 3605
15:20 and Abel-beth-maachah, and **a** Cinneroth, 3605
15:20 all Cinneroth, with **a** the land of Naphtali. 3605
15:22 made a proclamation **throughout** **a** Judah; 3605
15:23 The rest of **a** the acts of Asa, and all his 3605
15:23 **a** his might, and all that he did, 3605
15:23 **a** that he did, and the cities which he built 3605
15:27 and **a** Israel laid siege to Gibbethon. 3605
15:29 *that* he smote **a** the house of Jeroboam; 3605
15:31 of the acts of Nadab, and **a** that he did, 3605
15:32 and Baasha king of Israel **a** their days. 3605
15:33 of Ahijah to reign over **a** Israel in Tirzah, 3605
16: 7 for **a** the evil that he did in the sight of 3605
16:11 *that* he slew **a** the house of Baasha. 3605
16:12 Thus did Zimri destroy **a** the house of 3605
16:13 For **a** the sins of Baasha, and the sins of 3605
16:14 rest of the acts of Elah, and **a** that he did, 3605
16:16 wherefore **a** Israel made Omri, the captain 3605
16:17 **a** Israel with him, and they besieged 3605
16:25 did worse than **a** that *were* before him. 3605
16:26 For he walked in **a** the way of Jeroboam 3605
16:30 the LORD above **a** that *were* before him. 3605
16:33 **a** the kings of Israel that were before him. 3605
18: 5 unto **a** fountains of water, and unto all 3605
18: 5 all fountains of water, and unto **a** brooks: 3605
18: 5 alive, that we leese not **a** the beasts. 4480
18:19 gather to me **a** Israel unto mount Carmel, 3605
18:20 So Ahab sent unto **a** the children of Israel, 3605
18:21 Elijah came unto **a** the people, and said, 3605
18:24 the people answered and said, It is well 3605
18:30 Elijah said unto **a** the people, Come near 3605
18:30 **a** the people came near unto him. And he 3605
18:36 I have done **a** these things at thy word. 3605
18:39 when **a** the people saw *it,* they fell on 3605
19: 1 Ahab told Jezebel **a** that Elijah had done, 3605
19: 1 how he had slain **a** the prophets with 3605
19:18 the knees which have not bowed unto 3605
20: 1 Ben-hadad the king of Syria gathered **a** his 3605
20: 4 thy saying, I *am* thine, and **a** that I have. 3605
20: 7 the king of Israel called **a** the elders of 3605
20: 8 the elders and all the people said unto 3605
20: 8 the elders and **a** the people said unto him, 3605
20: 9 **A** that thou didst send for to thy servant at 3605
20:10 handfuls for **a** the people that follow me. 3605
20:13 Hast thou seen **a** this great multitude? 3605
20:15 after them he numbered **a** the people, 3605
20:15 *even* **a** the children of Israel, *being* seven 3605
20:27 were **a** present, and went against them: NIH
20:28 will I deliver **a** this great multitude into 3605
21:26 according to **a** *things* as did the Amorites, 3605
22:10 the prophets prophesied before them. 3605

1Ki 22:12 **a** the prophets prophesied so, saying, Go 3605
22:17 I saw **a** Israel scattered upon the hills, 3605
22:19 the host of heaven standing by him on 3605
22:22 I will be a lying spirit in the mouth of **a** his 3605
22:23 spirit in the mouth of **a** these thy prophets, 3605
22:28 If thou **return at a** in peace, 7725+7725
22:39 and that he did, and the ivory house which 3605
22:39 he made, and **a** the cities that he built, 3605
22:43 he walked in **a** the ways of Asa his father; 3605
22:53 according unto **a** that his father had done. 3605
2Ki 3: 6 the same time, and numbered **a** Israel. 3605
3:19 stop **a** wells of water, and mar every good 3605
3:21 when **a** the Moabites heard that the kings 3605
3:21 they gathered **a** that *were* able to put on 3605
3:25 they stopped **a** the wells of water, 3605
3:25 wells of water, and felled **a** the good trees: 3605
4: 3 borrow thee vessels abroad of **a** thy 3605
4: 4 shalt pour out into **a** those vessels, 3605
4:13 thou hast been careful for us with **a** this 3605
5:12 better than **a** the waters of Israel? 3605
5:15 he and **a** his company, and came, 3605
5:15 now I know that *there is* no God in **a** 3605
5:21 chariot to meet him, and said, *Is* **a** well? NIH
5:22 said, *A is* well. My master hath sent me, NIH
6:24 Ben-hadad king of Syria gathered **a** his 3605
7:13 they *are* as **a** the multitude of Israel that 3605
7:13 *I say,* they *are even* as **a** the multitude of 3605
7:15 **a** the way *was* full *of* garments and vessels 3605
8: 4 **a** the great *things* that Elisha hath done. 3605
8: 6 Restore **a** that *was* hers, and all the fruits 3605
8: 6 **a** the fruits of the field since the day that 3605
8:21 over to Zair, and **a** the chariots with him: 3605
8:23 of the acts of Joram, and **a** that he did, 3605
9: 5 Jehu said, Unto which of us? And he 3605
9: 7 the blood of **a** the servants of the LORD, 3605
9:11 *one* said unto him, *Is* **a** well? NIH
9:14 he and **a** Israel, because of Hazael king of 3605
10: 5 and will do **a** that thou shalt bid us; 3605
10: 9 stood, and said to the people, Ye *be* 3605
10: 9 and slew him: but who slew **a** these? 3605
10:11 So Jehu slew **a** that remained of the house 3605
10:11 **a** his great *men,* and his kinsfolks, 3605
10:17 he slew **a** that remained unto Ahab in 3605
10:18 Jehu gathered **a** the people together, 3605
10:19 call unto me **a** the prophets of Baal, 3605
10:19 of Baal, **a** his servants, and **a** his priests; 3605
10:19 of Baal, all his servants, and all his priests; 3605
10:21 Jehu sent through **a** Israel: and all 3605
10:21 **a** the worshippers of Baal came, so 3605
10:22 forth vestments for **a** the worshippers 3605
10:30 according to **a** that *was* in mine heart, 3605
10:31 the LORD God of Israel with **a** his heart: 3605
10:32 smote them in **a** the coasts of Israel; 3605
10:33 the land of Gilead, the Gadites, 3605
10:34 Jehu, and **a** that he did, and all his might, 3605
10:34 Jehu, and all that he did, and **a** his might, 3605
11: 1 she arose and destroyed **a** the seed royal. 3605
11: 7 two parts of **a** you that go forth on 3605
11: 9 **a** *things* that Jehoiada the priest 3605
11:14 the people of the land rejoiced, 3605
11:18 **a** the people of the land went *into* the 3605
11:19 the guard, and **a** the people of the land; 3605
11:20 **a** the people of the land rejoiced, 3605
12: 2 **a** his days where*in* Jehoiada the priest 3605
12: 4 **A** the money of the dedicated *things* that 3605
12: 4 **A** the money that cometh into any man's 3605
12: 9 the priests that kept the door put therein **a** 3605
12:12 for **a** that was laid out for the house to 3605
12:18 Jehoash king of Judah took **a** the hallowed 3605
12:18 and the gold that was found in the treasures 3605
12:19 rest of the acts of Joash, and **a** that he did, 3605
13: 3 Ben-hadad the son of Hazael, **a** *their* days. 3605
13: 8 and **a** that he did, and his might, 3605
13:11 he departed not from **a** the sins of 3605
13:12 **a** that he did, and his might where*with* he 3605
13:22 Hazael king of Syria oppressed Israel **a** 3605
14: 3 he did according to **a** *things* as Joash his 3605
14:14 he took **a** the gold and silver, and all 3605
14:14 the vessels that were found *in* the house 3605
14:21 **a** the people of Judah took Azariah, which 3605
14:24 he departed not from **a** the sins of 3605
14:28 **a** that he did, and his might, how he 3605
15: 3 according to **a** that his father Amaziah had 3605
15: 6 of the acts of Azariah, and **a** that he did, 3605
15:16 **a** that *were* therein, and the coasts thereof 3605
15:16 **a** the women therein that were with child 3605
15:18 he departed not **a** his days from the sins of 3605
15:20 *even* of **a** the mighty *men* of wealth, 3605
15:21 of the acts of Menahem, and **a** that he did, 3605
15:26 acts of Pekahiah, and **a** that he did, 3605
15:29 the land of Naphtali, and carried them 3605
15:31 the acts of Pekah, and **a** that he did, 3605
15:34 did according to **a** that his father Uzziah 3605
15:36 of the acts of Jotham, and **a** that he did, 3605
16:10 according to **a** the workmanship thereof. 3605
16:11 the priest built an altar according to **a** 3605
16:15 with the burnt offering of **a** the people of 3605
16:15 sprinkle upon it **a** the blood of the burnt 3605
16:15 and **a** the blood of the sacrifice. 3605
16:16 to **a** that king Ahaz commanded. 3605
17: 5 the king of Assyria came up throughout **a** 3605
17: 9 built them high places in **a** their cities, 3605
17:11 there they burnt incense in **a** the high 3605
17:13 by **a** the prophets, *and by* all the seers, 3605
17:13 all the prophets, *and by* **a** the seers, 3605

A

2Ki 17:13	to **a** the law which I commanded	3605
17:16	they left **a** the commandments of	3605
17:16	worshipped **a** the host of heaven,	3605
17:20	the LORD rejected **a** the seed of Israel,	3605
17:22	For the children of Israel walked in **a**	3605
17:23	as he had said by **a** his servants	3605
17:39	he shall deliver you out of the hand of **a**	3605
18: 3	according to **a** that David his father did.	3605
18: 5	after him was none like him among **a**	3605
18:12	that Moses the servant of the LORD	3605
18:13	up against **a** the fenced cities of Judah,	3605
18:15	Hezekiah gave *him* **a** the silver that was	3605
18:21	*is* Pharaoh king of Egypt unto **a** that trust	3605
18:33	**delivered at a** his land out of	5337+5337
18:35	Who *are they* among **a** the gods of	3605
19: 4	It may be the LORD thy God will hear **a**	3605
19:11	the kings of Assyria have done to **a** lands,	3605
19:15	alone, of **a** the kingdoms of the earth;	3605
19:19	**a** the kingdoms of the earth may know	3605
19:24	with the sole of my feet have I dried up **a**	3605
19:35	behold, they *were* **a** dead corpses.	3605
20:13	shewed them **a** the house of his precious	3605
20:13	**a** house of his armour, and all that	3605
20:13	and **a** that was found in his treasures:	3605
20:13	in his house, nor in **a** his dominion,	3605
20:15	**A** *the things that are* in mine house have	3605
20:17	that **a** that *is* in thine house, and *that*	3605
20:20	**a** his might, and how he made a pool,	3605
21: 3	worshipped **a** the host of heaven,	3605
21: 5	he built altars for **a** the host of heaven in	3605
21: 7	which I have chosen out of **a** tribes of	3605
21: 8	to **a** that I have commanded them,	3605
21: 8	according to **a** the law that my servant	3605
21:11	hath done wickedly above **a** that	3605
21:14	a prey and a spoil to **a** their enemies;	3605
21:17	**a** that he did, and his sin that he sinned,	3605
21:21	he walked in **a** the way that his father	3605
21:24	the people of the land slew **a** them that	3605
22: 2	walked in **a** the way of David his father,	3605
22:13	me, and for the people, and for **a** Judah,	3605
22:13	do according unto **a** that which is written	3605
22:16	*even* **a** the words of the book which	3605
22:17	they might provoke me to anger with **a**	3605
22:20	thine eyes shall not see **a** the evil which I	3605
23: 1	they gathered unto him **a** the elders of	3605
23: 2	**a** the men of Judah and all the inhabitants	3605
23: 2	**a** the inhabitants of Jerusalem with him,	3605
23: 2	and **a** the people, both small and great:	3605
23: 2	he read in their ears **a** the words of	3605
23: 3	statutes with **a** *their* heart and all *their*	3605
23: 3	with all *their* heart and **a** *their* soul,	3605
23: 3	And **a** the people stood to the covenant.	3605
23: 4	**a** the vessels that were made for Baal,	3605
23: 4	the grove, and for **a** the host of heaven:	3605
23: 5	the planets, and to **a** the host of heaven.	3605
23: 8	he brought **a** the priests out of the cities	3605
23:19	the houses also of the high places that	3605
23:19	did to them according to **a** the acts that	3605
23:20	he slew **a** the priests of the high places	3605
23:21	the king commanded **a** the people, saying,	3605
23:22	nor *in* **a** the days of the kings of Israel,	3605
23:24	the abominations that were spied in	3605
23:25	that turned to the LORD with **a** his heart,	3605
23:25	with **a** his soul, and with all his might,	3605
23:25	with all his soul, and with **a** his might,	3605
23:25	might, according to **a** the law of Moses;	3605
23:26	of **a** the provocations that Manasseh had	3605
23:28	of the acts of Josiah, and **a** that he did,	3605
23:32	according to **a** that his fathers had done.	3605
23:37	according to **a** that his fathers had done.	3605
24: 3	of Manasseh, according to **a** that he did;	3605
24: 5	the acts of Jehoiakim, and **a** that he did,	3605
24: 7	that pertained to the king of Egypt.	3605
24: 9	according to **a** that his father had done.	3605
24:13	he carried out thence **a** the treasures of	3605
24:13	cut in pieces **a** the vessels of gold which	3605
24:14	he carried away **a** Jerusalem, and all	3605
24:14	the princes, and all the mighty *men* of	3605
24:14	and **a** the mighty *men* of valour,	3605
24:14	and **a** the craftsmen and smiths:	3605
24:16	the men of might, *even* seven thousand,	3605
24:16	**a** *that were* strong *and* apt for war,	3605
24:19	according to **a** that Jehoiakim had done.	3605
25: 1	he, and **a** his host, against Jerusalem,	3605
25: 4	**a** the men of war *fled* by night *by* the way	3605
25: 5	and **a** his army were scattered from him.	3605
25: 9	the houses of Jerusalem, and every great	3605
25:10	the army of the Chaldees, that *were*	3605
25:14	the vessels of brass wherewith they	3605
25:16	the brass of **a** these vessels was without	3605
25:17	upon the chapiter round about, **a** of brass:	3605
25:23	And when **a** the captains of the armies,	3605
25:26	**a** the people, both small and great,	3605
25:29	he did eat bread continually before him **a**	3605
25:30	rate for every day, **a** the days of his life.	3605
1Ch 1:23	Jobab. **A** these *were* the sons of Joktan.	3605
1:33	Eldaah. **A** these *are* the sons of Keturah.	3605
2: 4	and Zerah. **A** the sons of Judah *were* five.	3605
2: 6	and Calcol, and Dara: five of them in **a**.	3605
2:23	**A** these *belonged to* the sons of Machir	3605
3: 9	*These were* **a** the sons of David, beside	3605
4:27	neither did **a** their family multiply, like to	3605
4:33	**a** their villages that *were* round about	3605
5:10	they dwelt in their tents throughout **a**	3605
5:16	her towns, and in **a** the suburbs of Sharon,	3605

1Ch 5:17	**A** these were reckoned by genealogies in	3605
5:20	their hand, and **a** that *were* with them:	3605
6:48	a *manner of* service of the tabernacle of	3605
6:49	appointed for **a** the work of the *place*	3605
6:49	according to **a** that Moses the servant of	3605
6:60	**A** their cities throughout their families	3605
7: 3	Joel, Ishiah, five: **a** of them chief *men*.	3605
7: 5	their brethren among **a** the families of	3605
7: 5	reckoned in **a** by their genealogies	3605
7: 8	Alameth. **A** these *are* the sons of Becher.	3605
7:11	**A** these the sons of Jediael, by the heads	3605
7:40	**A** these *were* the children of Asher,	3605
8:38	Hanan. **A** these *were* the sons of Azel.	3605
8:40	fifty. **A** these *are* of the sons of Benjamin.	3605
9: 1	So **a** Israel were reckoned by genealogies;	3605
9: 9	**A** these men *were* chief of the fathers in	3605
9:22	**A** these which were chosen to be porters	3605
9:29	**a** the instruments of the sanctuary, and	3605
10: 6	three sons, and **a** his house died together.	3605
10: 7	when **a** the men of Israel that *were* in	3605
10:11	when **a** Jabesh-gilead heard all that	3605
10:11	when all Jabesh-gilead heard **a** that	3605
10:12	**a** the valiant men, and took away the	3605
11: 1	**a** Israel gathered themselves to David	3605
11: 3	Therefore came **a** the elders of Israel to	3605
11: 4	David and **a** Israel went *to* Jerusalem,	3605
11:10	*and* with **a** Israel, to make him king,	3605
12:15	when it had overflown **a** his banks;	3605
12:15	they put to flight **a** *them* of the valleys,	3605
12:21	for they *were* **a** mighty men of valour,	3605
12:32	**a** their brethren *were* at their	3605
12:33	expert in war, with **a** instruments of war,	3605
12:37	with **a** *manner of* instruments of war for	3605
12:38	**A** these men of war, that could keep rank,	3605
12:38	to make David king over **a** Israel:	3605
12:38	the rest also of Israel *were* **a** of one heart	3605
13: 2	David said unto **a** the congregation of	3605
13: 2	that are left in **a** the land of Israel,	3605
13: 4	**a** the congregation said that *they* would	3605
13: 4	for the thing was right in the eyes of **a**	3605
13: 5	So David gathered **a** Israel together,	3605
13: 6	David went up, and **a** Israel, to Baalah,	3605
13: 8	**a** Israel played before God with all *their*	3605
13: 8	all Israel played before God with **a** *their*	3605
13:14	house of Obed-edom, and **a** that he had.	3605
14: 8	David was anointed king over **a** Israel,	3605
14: 8	**a** the Philistines went up to seek David.	3605
14:17	the fame of David went out into **a** lands;	3605
14:17	the LORD brought the fear of him upon **a**	3605
15: 3	David gathered **a** Israel together to	3605
15:27	**a** the Levites that bare the ark,	3605
15:28	Thus **a** Israel brought up the ark of	3605
16: 9	talk you of **a** his wondrous works.	3605
16:14	our God; his judgments *are* in **a** the earth.	3605
16:23	Sing unto the LORD, **a** the earth;	3605
16:24	his marvellous works among **a** nations.	3605
16:25	he also *is* to be feared above **a** gods.	3605
16:26	For **a** the gods of the people *are* idols:	3605
16:30	Fear before him, **a** the earth: the world	3605
16:32	let the fields rejoice, and **a** that *is* therein.	3605
16:36	**a** the people said, Amen, and praised	3605
16:40	*to do* according to **a** that is written in	3605
16:43	**a** the people departed every man to his	3605
17: 2	unto David, Do **a** that *is* in thine heart;	3605
17: 6	Wheresoever I have walked with **a** Israel,	3605
17: 8	have cut off **a** thine enemies from before	3605
17:10	Moreover I will subdue **a** thine enemies.	3605
17:15	According to **a** these words,	3605
17:15	according to **a** this vision, so did Nathan	3605
17:19	heart, hast thou done **a** this greatness,	3605
17:19	in making known **a** *these* great things.	3605
17:20	according to **a** that we have heard with	3605
18: 4	David also houghed **a** the chariot *horses*,	3605
18: 9	the host of Hadarezer king of Zobah;	3605
18:10	*with him* a *manner of* vessels of gold	3605
18:11	the gold that he brought from **a** *these*	3605
18:13	**a** the Edomites became David's servants.	3605
18:14	So David reigned over **a** Israel,	3605
18:14	and justice among **a** his people.	3605
19: 8	and **a** the host *of* the mighty *men*.	3605
19:10	he chose out of **a** the choice of Israel,	3605
19:17	he gathered **a** Israel, and passed over	3605
20: 3	David with **a** the cities of the children	3605
20: 3	and **a** the people returned *to* Jerusalem.	3605
21: 3	king, *are* they not **a** my lord's servants?	3605
21: 4	went throughout **a** Israel, and came to	3605
21: 5	*they of* Israel were a thousand thousand	3605
21:12	throughout **a** the coasts of Israel.	3605
21:23	wheat for the meat offering; I give *it* **a**.	3605
22: 5	and of glory throughout **a** countries:	3605
22: 9	I will give him rest from **a** his enemies	3605
22:15	*a manner of* cunning *men* for every	3605
22:17	David also commanded **a** the princes of	3605
23: 2	gathered together **a** the princes of Israel,	3605
23:28	in the purifying of **a** holy *things*,	3605
23:29	and for **a** *manner of* measure and size;	3605
23:31	to offer **a** burnt sacrifices unto the LORD	3605
25: 5	**A** these *were* the sons of Heman	3605
25: 6	**A** these *were* under the hands of their	3605
25: 7	*even* **a** that were cunning, was two	3605
26: 8	**A** these of the sons of Obed-edom: they	3605
26:11	**a** the sons and brethren of Hosah *were*	3605
26:26	his brethren *were* over **a** the treasures of	3605
26:28	**a** that Samuel the seer, and Saul the son	3605
26:30	westward in **a** the business of the LORD,	3605

1Ch 27: 1	went out month by month throughout **a**	3605
27: 3	the children of Perez *was* the chief of **a**	3605
27:31	**A** these *were* the rulers of the substance	3605
28: 1	David assembled **a** the princes of Israel,	3605
28: 1	the stewards over **a** the substance	3605
28: 1	mighty *men*, and with **a** the valiant men,	3605
28: 4	**a** the house of my father to be king over	3605
28: 4	liked me to make *me* king over **a** Israel:	3605
28: 5	of **a** my sons, (for the LORD hath given	3605
28: 8	in the sight of **a** Israel the congregation of	3605
28: 8	seek for **a** the commandments of	3605
28: 9	for the LORD searcheth **a** hearts,	3605
28: 9	understandeth **a** the imaginations of	3605
28:12	the pattern of **a** that he had by the spirit,	3605
28:12	of **a** the chambers round about, of	3605
28:13	for **a** the work of the service of the house	3605
28:13	for **a** the vessels of service in the house of	3605
28:14	for **a** instruments of all manner of service;	3605
28:14	of **a** **manner of service;**	5656+5656+2050.1
28:14	*silver also* for **a** instruments of silver by	3605
28:14	for **a** instruments of every kind of service:	3605
28:19	**A** *this, said David,* the LORD made me	3605
28:19	me, *even* **a** the works of *this* pattern.	3605
28:20	until *thou* hast finished **a** the work for	3605
28:21	*even* they shall be with thee for **a**	3605
28:21	there shall be with thee for a *manner of*	3605
28:21	the people *will be* wholly at thy	3605
29: 1	Furthermore David the king said unto **a**	3605
29: 2	Now I have prepared with **a** my might for	3605
29: 2	a *manner of* precious stones,	3605
29: 3	above **a** *that* I have prepared for the holy	3605
29: 5	for a *manner of* work *to be made* by	3605
29:10	the LORD before **a** the congregation:	3605
29:11	for **a** *that is* in the heaven and in the earth	3605
29:11	and *thou* art exalted as head above **a**.	3605
29:12	*come* of thee, and thou reignest over **a**;	3605
29:12	to make great, and to give strength unto **a**.	3605
29:14	willingly after this *sort?* for **a** *things come*	3605
29:15	and sojourners, as *were* **a** our fathers:	3605
29:16	**a** this store that we have prepared to build	3605
29:16	*cometh* of thine hand, and *is* **a** thine own.	3605
29:17	I have willingly offered **a** these *things*:	3605
29:19	do **a** *these things*, and to build the palace,	3605
29:20	David said to **a** the congregation,	3605
29:20	**a** the congregation blessed the LORD God	3605
29:21	and sacrifices in abundance for **a** Israel:	3605
29:23	and prospered; and **a** Israel obeyed him.	3605
29:24	And **a** the princes, and the mighty *men*,	3605
29:24	and **a** the sons likewise of king David,	3605
29:25	exceedingly in the sight of **a** Israel,	3605
29:26	David the son of Jesse reigned over **a**	3605
29:30	With **a** his reign and his might,	3605
29:30	and over **a** the kingdoms of the countries.	3605
2Ch 1: 2	Solomon spake unto **a** Israel, to	3605
1: 2	and to every governor in **a** Israel,	3605
1: 3	and **a** the congregation with him,	3605
1:17	brought they out *horses* for **a** the kings of	3605
2: 5	*is* great: for great *is* our God above **a** gods.	3605
2:17	Solomon numbered **a** the strangers that	3605
4: 4	and **a** their hinder parts *were* inward.	3605
4:16	the fleshhooks, and **a** their instruments,	3605
4:18	Thus Solomon made **a** these vessels in	3605
4:19	Solomon made **a** the vessels that *were for*	3605
5: 1	Thus **a** the work that Solomon made for	3605
5: 1	Solomon brought in **a** *the things* that	NIH
5: 1	and the gold, and **a** the instruments,	3605
5: 2	of Israel, and **a** the heads of the tribes,	3605
5: 3	Wherefore **a** the men of Israel assembled	3605
5: 4	the elders of Israel came; and the Levites	3605
5: 5	**a** the holy vessels that *were*	3605
5: 6	**a** the congregation of Israel that were	3605
5:11	**a** the priests that were present were	3605
5:12	of them of Asaph, of Heman,	3605
6: 3	and **a** the congregation of Israel stood.	3605
6: 5	the tribes of Israel to build a house *in*,	3605
6:12	presence of **a** the congregation of Israel,	3605
6:13	kneeled *down* upon his knees before **a**	3605
6:14	that walk before thee with **a** their hearts:	3605
6:29	or of **a** thy people Israel, when every one	3605
6:30	unto every man according unto **a** his	3605
6:33	do according to **a** that the stranger calleth	3605
6:33	that **a** people of the earth may know thy	3605
6:38	If they return to thee with **a** their heart	3605
6:38	with **a** their soul in the land of their	3605
7: 3	when **a** the children of Israel saw how	3605
7: 4	the people offered sacrifices before	3605
7: 5	**a** the people dedicated the house of God.	3605
7: 6	trumpets before them, and **a** Israel stood.	3605
7: 8	**a** Israel with him, a very great	3605
7:11	that came into Solomon's heart to make	3605
7:17	do according to **a** that I have commanded	3605
7:20	a proverb and a byword among **a** nations.	3605
7:22	hath he brought **a** this evil upon them.	3605
8: 4	the store cities, which he built in	3605
8: 6	the store cities that Solomon had,	3605
8: 6	**a** the chariot cities, and the cities of	3605
8: 6	**a** that Solomon desired to build in	3605
8: 6	throughout **a** the land of his dominion.	3605
8: 7	*As for* **a** the people that were left of	3605
8:16	Now **a** the work of Solomon was prepared	3605
9: 1	she communed with him of **a** that was in	3605
9: 2	Solomon told her **a** her questions:	3605
9:12	Solomon gave to the queen of Sheba **a**	3605
9:14	the kings of Arabia and governors of	3605
9:20	**a** the drinking vessels of king Solomon	3605

A

2Ch 9:20 a the vessels of the house of the forest of 3605
9:22 king Solomon passed a the kings of 3605
9:23 the kings of the earth sought a the 3605
9:26 he reigned over a the kings from the river 3605
9:28 horses out of Egypt, and out of a lands. 3605
9:30 Solomon reigned in Jerusalem over a Israel 3605
10: 1 to Shechem were a Israel come to make 3605
10: 3 So Jeroboam and a Israel came 3605
10:12 the people came to Rehoboam on 3605
10:16 when a Israel saw that the king would not 3605
10:16 own house. So a Israel went to their tents. 3605
11: 3 to a Israel in Judah and Benjamin, saying, 3605
11:13 the Levites that were in a Israel resorted 3605
11:13 Israel resorted to him out of a their coasts. 3605
11:16 after them out of a the tribes of Israel such 3605
11:21 daughter of Absalom above a his wives 3605
11:23 dispersed of a his children throughout all 3605
11:23 dispersed of all his children throughout a 3605
12: 1 law of the Lord, and a Israel with him. 3605
12: 9 treasures of the king's house; he took a: 3605
12:13 had chosen out of a the tribes of Israel, 3605
13: 4 Hear me, thou Jeroboam, and a Israel; 3605
13:15 and a Israel before Abijah and Judah. 3605
14: 5 Also he took away out of a the cities of 3605
14: 8 a these were mighty men of valour. 3605
14:14 they smote a the cities round about Gerar; 3605
14:14 they spoiled a the cities; for there was 3605
15: 2 ye me, Asa, and a Judah and Benjamin; 3605
15: 5 vexations were upon a the inhabitants 3605
15: 6 for God did vex them with a adversity. 3605
15: 8 put away the abominable idols out of a 3605
15: 9 he gathered a Judah and Benjamin, 3605
15:12 God of their fathers with a their heart 3605
15:12 with all their heart and with a their soul; 3605
15:15 a Judah rejoiced at the oath: for they had 3605
15:15 for they had sworn with a their heart, 3605
15:17 the heart of Asa was perfect a 3605
16: 4 and a the store cities of Naphtali. 3605
16: 6 Asa the king took a Judah; and they 3605
17: 2 he placed forces in a the fenced cities of 3605
17: 5 a Judah brought to Jehoshaphat presents; 3605
17: 9 about throughout a the cities of Judah, 3605
17:10 the fear of the Lord fell upon a 3605
17:19 the fenced cities throughout a Judah. 3605
18: 9 a the prophets prophesied before them. 3605
18:11 a the prophets prophesied so, saying, Go 3605
18:16 I did see a Israel scattered upon 3605
18:18 a the host of heaven standing on his right 3605
18:21 be a lying spirit in the mouth of a his 3605
18:27 by me. And he said, Hearken, a ye people. 3605
19: 5 he set judges in the land throughout a 3605
19:11 Amariah the chief priest is over you in a 3605
19:11 house of Judah, for a the king's matters: 3605
20: 3 and proclaimed a fast throughout a Judah. 3605
20: 4 out of a the cities of Judah they came 3605
20: 6 rulest not thou over a the kingdoms of 3605
20:13 a Judah stood before the Lord, 3605
20:15 a Judah, and ye inhabitants of Jerusalem, 3605
20:18 a Judah and the inhabitants of Jerusalem 3605
20:29 the fear of God was on a the kingdoms of 3605
21: 2 a these were the sons of Jehoshaphat king 3605
21: 4 slew a his brethren with the sword, 3605
21: 9 his princes, and a his chariots with him: 3605
21:14 and thy wives, and a thy goods: 3605
21:17 carried away a the substance that was 3605
21:18 after a this the Lord smote him in his 3605
22: 1 to the camp had slain a the eldest. 3605
22: 9 who sought the Lord with a his heart. 3605
22:10 destroyed the seed royal of the house of 3605
23: 2 gathered the Levites out of a the cities of 3605
23: 3 a the congregation made a covenant with 3605
23: 5 a the people shall be in the courts of 3605
23: 6 a the people shall keep the watch of 3605
23: 8 a Judah did according to all things that 3605
23: 8 all Judah did according to a things that 3605
23:10 he set a the people, every man having his 3605
23:13 a the people of the land rejoiced, 3605
23:16 between a the people, and between 3605
23:17 a the people went to the house of Baal, 3605
23:20 a the people of the land, and brought 3605
23:21 a the people of the land rejoiced: 3605
24: 2 Lord a the days of Jehoiada the priest. 3605
24: 5 of a Israel money to repair the house 3605
24: 7 also the dedicate things of the house of 3605
24:10 the princes and all the people rejoiced, 3605
24:10 all the princes and a the people rejoiced, 3605
24:14 Lord continually a the days of Jehoiada. 3605
24:23 destroyed a the princes of the people from 3605
24:23 sent a the spoil of them unto the king of 3605
25: 5 throughout a Judah and Benjamin: 3605
25: 7 to wit, with a the children of Ephraim. 3605
25:12 rock, that they a were broken in pieces. 3605
25:24 he took a the gold and the silver, and all 3605
25:24 a the vessels that were found in the house 3605
26: 1 a the people of Judah took Uzziah, who 3605
26: 4 according to a that his father Amaziah did. 3605
26:14 Uzziah prepared for them throughout a 3605
26:20 the priests, looked upon a, and 3605
27: 2 according to a that his father Uzziah did: 3605
27: 7 of Jotham, and a his wars, and his ways, 3605
28: 6 in one day, which were a valiant men; 3605
28:14 before the princes and a the congregation. 3605
28:15 with the spoil clothed a that were naked 3605
28:15 carried a the feeble of them upon asses, 3605
28:23 they were the ruin of him, and of a Israel. 3605

2Ch 28:26 Now the rest of his acts and of a his ways, 3605
29: 2 according to a that David his father had 3605
29:16 brought out a the uncleanness that they 3605
29:18 We have cleansed a the house of 3605
29:18 with a the vessels thereof, and 3605
29:18 table, with a the vessels thereof. 3605
29:19 Moreover a the vessels, which king Ahaz 3605
29:24 altar, to make an atonement for a Israel: 3605
29:24 sin offering should be made for a Israel. 3605
29:28 a the congregation worshipped, 3605
29:28 a this continued until the burnt offering 3605
29:29 a that were present with him bowed 3605
29:32 a these were for a burnt offering to 3605
29:34 that they could not flay a the burnt 3605
29:36 Hezekiah rejoiced, and a the people, that 3605
30: 1 Hezekiah sent to a Israel and Judah, 3605
30: 2 and a the congregation in Jerusalem, 3605
30: 4 pleased the king and a the congregation. 3605
30: 5 to make proclamation throughout a Israel, 3605
30: 6 his princes throughout a Israel and Judah, 3605
30:14 a the altars for incense took they away, 3605
30:22 Hezekiah spake comfortably unto a 3605
30:25 a the congregation of Judah, with 3605
30:25 a the congregation that came out of Judah, 3605
31: 1 Now when a this was finished, all Israel 3605
31: 1 a Israel that were present went out to 3605
31: 1 the altars out of a Judah and Benjamin, 3605
31: 1 until they had utterly destroyed them a. NIH
31: 1 all. Then a the children of Israel returned, 3605
31: 5 honey, and of a the increase of the field; 3605
31: 5 the tithe of a things brought they in 3605
31:18 to the genealogy of a their little ones, 3605
31:18 daughters, through a the congregation: 3605
31:19 to give portions to a the males among 3605
31:19 a that were reckoned by genealogies 3605
31:20 thus did Hezekiah throughout a Judah, 3605
31:21 he did a with a his heart, and prospered. 3605
32: 4 who stopt a the fountains, and the brook 3605
32: 5 and built up a the wall that was broken, 3605
32: 7 nor a the multitude that is with him: 3605
32: 9 Lachish, and a his power with him,) 3605
32: 9 unto a Judah that were at Jerusalem, 3605
32:13 my fathers have done unto a the people of 3605
32:14 Who was there among a the gods of those 3605
32:21 which cut off a the mighty men of valour, 3605
32:22 from the hand of a other, and guided 3605
32:23 that he was magnified in the sight of a 3605
32:27 and for a manner of pleasant jewels; 3605
32:28 stalls for a manner of beasts, and cotes for 3605
32:30 And Hezekiah prospered in a his works. 3605
32:31 he might know a that was in his heart. 3605
32:33 a Judah and the inhabitants of Jerusalem 3605
33: 3 worshipped a the host of heaven, 3605
33: 5 he built altars for a the host of heaven in 3605
33: 7 which I have chosen before a the tribes of 3605
33: 8 that they will take heed to do a that I have 3605
33:14 put captains of war in a the fenced cities 3605
33:15 a the altars that he had built in the mount 3605
33:19 a his sin, and his trespass, and the places 3605
33:22 for Amon sacrificed unto a the carved 3605
33:25 the people of the land slew a them that 3605
34: 7 cut down a the idols throughout all the 3605
34: 7 down all the idols throughout a the land 3605
34: 9 of a the remnant of Israel, and of all Judah 3605
34: 9 of Israel, and of a Judah and Benjamin; 3605
34:12 a that could skill of instruments of musick. 3605
34:13 overseers of a that wrought the work 3605
34:16 A that was committed to thy servants, 3605
34:21 to do after a that is written in this book. 3605
34:24 even a the curses that are written in 3605
34:25 they might provoke me to anger with a 3605
34:28 neither shall thine eyes see a the evil that 3605
34:29 gathered together a the elders of Judah 3605
34:30 the men of Judah, and the inhabitants 3605
34:30 and a the people, great and small: 3605
34:31 he read in their ears a the words of 3605
34:31 with a his heart, and with all his soul, 3605
34:31 with all his heart, and with a his soul, 3605
34:32 caused a that were present in Jerusalem 3605
34:33 Josiah took away a the abominations out 3605
34:33 a the countries that pertained to 3605
34:33 made a that were present in Israel to serve 3605
34:33 And a his days they departed not from 3605
35: 3 said unto the Levites that taught a Israel, 3605
35: 7 a for the passover offerings, for all that 3605
35: 7 all for the passover offerings, for a that 3605
35:13 divided them speedily among a the people 3605
35:16 So a the service of the Lord was 3605
35:18 neither did a the kings of Israel keep such 3605
35:18 a Judah and Israel that were present, 3605
35:20 After a this, when Josiah had prepared 3605
35:24 a Judah and Jerusalem mourned for Josiah. 3605
35:25 the singing men and the singing women 3605
36:14 Moreover a the chief of the priests, 3605
36:14 transgressed very much after a 3605
36:17 for age: he gave them a into his hand. 3605
36:18 a the vessels of the house of God, great 3605
36:18 princes; a these he brought to Babylon. 3605
36:19 burnt a the palaces thereof with fire, 3605
36:19 destroyed a the goodly vessels thereof. 3605
36:22 he made a proclamation throughout a 3605
36:23 A the kingdoms of the earth hath 3605
36:23 Who is there among you of a his people? 3605
Ezr 1: 1 that he made a proclamation throughout a 3605
1: 2 given me a the kingdoms of the earth; 3605

Ezr 1: 3 Who is there among you of a his people? 3605
1: 5 with a them whose spirit God had raised, 3605
1: 6 a they that were about them strengthened 3605
1: 6 beside a that was willingly offered. 3605
1:11 A the vessels of gold and of silver were 3605
1:11 A these did Sheshbazzar bring up with 3605
2:42 Shobai, in a an hundred thirty and nine. 3605
2:58 A the Nethinims, and the children of 3605
2:70 in their cities, and a Israel in their cities. 3605
3: 5 of a the set feasts of the Lord that were 3605
3: 8 a they that were come out of the captivity 3605
3:11 a the people shouted with a great shout, 3605
4: 5 a the days of Cyrus king of Persia, 3605
4:20 which have ruled over a countries beyond 3606
5: 7 thus: Unto Darius the king, a peace. 3606
6:12 his name to dwell there destroy a kings 3606
6:17 for a sin offering for Israel, twelve he 3606
6:20 of them were pure, and killed 3605
6:20 killed the passover for a the children of 3605
6:21 such as had separated themselves unto 3605
7: 6 the king granted him a his request, 3605
7:13 that a they of the people of Israel, 3606
7:16 a the silver and gold that thou canst find 3606
7:16 gold that thou canst find in a the province 3606
7:21 make a decree to a the treasurers which 3606
7:25 which may judge a the people that are 3606
7:25 a such as know the laws of thy God; 3606
7:28 and before a the king's mighty princes. 3606
8:20 a of them were expressed by name. 3605
8:21 for our little ones, and for a our substance. 3605
8:22 The hand of our God is upon a them for 3605
8:22 his wrath is against a them that forsake 3605
8:25 his lords, and a Israel there present, had 3605
8:34 and a the weight was written at that time. 3605
8:35 twelve bullocks for a Israel, ninety 3605
8:35 a this was a burnt offering unto 3605
9:13 after a that is come upon us for our evil 3605
10: 3 with our God to put away a the wives, 3605
10: 5 the chief priests, the Levites, and a Israel, 3605
10: 7 Jerusalem unto a the children of 3605
10: 8 a his substance should be forfeited, 3605
10: 9 a the men of Judah and Benjamin gathered 3605
10: 9 a the people sat in the street of the house 3605
10:12 a the congregation answered and said 3605
10:14 Let now our rulers of a the congregation 3605
10:14 let a them which have taken strange wives 3605
10:16 a of them by their names, were separated, 3605
10:17 they made an end with a the men that 3605
10:44 A these had taken strange wives: 3605
Ne 4: 6 the wall was joined together unto the 3605
4: 8 conspired a of them together to come 3605
4:12 From a places whence ye shall return 3605
4:15 that we returned a of us to the wall, 3605
4:16 the rulers were behind a the house of 3605
5:13 a the congregation said, Amen, 3605
5:16 a my servants were gathered thither unto 3605
5:18 once in ten days store of a sorts of wine: 3605
5:18 yet for a this required not I the bread of NIH
5:19 according to a that I have done for this 3605
6: 9 For they a made us afraid, saying, 3605
6:16 that when a our enemies heard thereof, 3605
6:16 a the heathen that were about us saw 3605
7:60 A the Nethinims, and the children of 3605
7:73 people, and the Nethinims, and a Israel, 3605
8: 1 a the people gathered themselves together 3605
8: 2 and a that could hear with understanding, 3605
8: 3 ears of a the people were attentive unto 3605
8: 5 Ezra opened the book in the sight of a 3605
8: 5 (for he was above a the people;) 3605
8: 5 when he opened it, a the people stood up: 3605
8: 6 a the people answered, Amen, Amen, 3605
8: 9 taught the people, said unto a the people, 3605
8: 9 For a the people wept, when they heard 3605
8:11 So the Levites stilled a the people, saying, 3605
8:12 a the people went their way to eat, 3605
8:13 the chief of the fathers of a the people, 3605
8:15 and proclaim in a their cities, 3605
8:17 a the congregation of them that were 3605
9: 2 separated themselves from a strangers, 3605
9: 5 which is exalted above a blessing 3605
9: 6 with a their host, the earth, and all things 3605
9: 6 a things that are therein, the seas, 3605
9: 6 a that is therein, and thou preservest them 3605
9: 6 is therein, and thou preservest them a; 3605
9:10 on a his servants, and on all the people of 3605
9:10 and on a the people of his land: 3605
9:25 and possessed houses full of a goods, 3605
9:32 not a the trouble seem little before thee, 3605
9:32 and on our fathers, and on a thy people, 3605
9:33 Howbeit thou art just in a that is brought 3605
9:38 of a this we make a sure covenant, 3605
10:28 a they that had separated themselves from 3605
10:29 do a the commandments of the Lord our 3605
10:33 for a the work of the house of our God. 3605
10:35 the firstfruits of a fruit of all trees, year by 3605
10:35 the firstfruits of all fruit of a trees, year by 3605
10:37 the fruit of a manner of trees, of wine 3605
10:37 have the tithes in a the cities of our tillage. 3605
11: 2 people blessed a the men, that willingly 3605
11: 6 A the sons of Perez that dwelt at 3605
11:18 A the Levites in the holy city were two 3605
11:20 the Levites, were in a the cities of Judah, 3605
11:24 a at the king's hand in a matters 3605
12:27 sought the Levites out of a their places, 3605
12:47 a Israel in the days of Zerubbabel, 3605

A

Ne	13: 3 they separated from Israel **a** the mixed	3605
	13: 6 in **a** this *time* was not I at Jerusalem:	3605
	13: 8 I cast forth **a** the household stuff of Tobiah	3605
	13:12 brought **a** Judah the tithe of the corn	3605
	13:15 and figs, and **a** *manner of* burdens,	3605
	13:16 **a** *manner of* ware, and sold on the	3605
	13:18 *did not* our God bring **a** this evil upon us,	3605
	13:20 sellers of **a** *kind of* ware lodged without	3605
	13:26 and God made him king over **a** Israel:	3605
	13:27 hearken unto you to do **a** this great evil,	3605
	13:30 Thus cleansed I them from **a** strangers,	3605
Est	1: 3 he made a feast unto **a** his princes	3605
	1: 5 the king made a feast unto **a** the people	3605
	1: 8 the king had appointed to **a** the officers of	3605
	1:13 the king's manner towards **a** that knew	3605
	1:16 *also* to **a** the princes, and to all the people	3605
	1:16 **a** the people that *are* in all the provinces	3605
	1:16 all the people that *are* in **a** the provinces	3605
	1:17 queen shall come abroad unto **a** women,	3605
	1:18 Media say this day unto **a** the king's	3605
	1:20 be published throughout **a** his empire,	3605
	1:20 **a** the wives shall give to their husbands	3605
	1:22 For he sent letters into **a** the king's	3605
	2: 3 let the king appoint officers in **a**	3605
	2: 3 that they may gather together **a** the fair	3605
	2:15 Esther obtained favour in the sight of **a**	3605
	2:17 the king loved Esther above **a** the women,	3605
	2:17 favour in his sight more than **a** the virgins;	3605
	2:18 the king made a great feast unto **a** his	3605
	3: 1 set his seat above **a** the princes that *were*	3605
	3: 2 **a** the king's servants, that *were* in	3605
	3: 6 wherefore Haman sought to destroy **a**	3605
	3: 8 dispersed among the people in **a**	3605
	3: 8 their laws *are* diverse from **a** people;	3605
	3:12 there was written according to **a** that	3605
	3:13 the letters were sent by posts into **a**	3605
	3:13 **a** Jews, both young and old, little children	3605
	3:14 province *was* published unto **a** people,	3605
	4: 1 Mordecai perceived **a** that was done,	3605
	4: 7 Mordecai told him of **a** that had happened	3605
	4:11 **A** the king's servants, and the people of	3605
	4:13 in the king's house, more than **a** the Jews.	3605
	4:16 gather together **a** the Jews that are present	3605
	4:17 did according to **a** that Esther had	3605
	5:11 **a** the *things* where*in* the king had	3605
	5:13 Yet **a** this availeth me nothing, so long as I	3605
	5:14 Zeresh his wife and **a** his friends unto	3605
	6:10 let nothing fail of **a** that thou hast spoken.	3605
	6:13 **a** his friends every *thing* that had befallen	3605
	8: 5 Jews which *are* in **a** the king's provinces:	3605
	8: 9 was written according to **a** that Mordecai	3605
	8:11 **a** the power of the people and province	3605
	8:12 Upon one day in **a** the provinces of king	3605
	8:13 province *was* published unto **a** people,	3605
	9: 2 **a** the provinces of the king Ahasuerus	3605
	9: 2 for the fear of them fell upon **a** people.	3605
	9: 3 **a** the rulers of the provinces,	3605
	9: 4 his fame went out throughout **a**	3605
	9: 5 Thus the Jews smote **a** their enemies *with*	3605
	9:20 letters unto **a** the Jews that *were* in all	3605
	9:20 letters unto all the Jews that *were* in **a**	3605
	9:24 the Agagite, the enemy of **a** the Jews,	3605
	9:26 Therefore for **a** the words of this letter,	3605
	9:27 upon **a** such as joined themselves unto	3605
	9:29 Mordecai the Jew, wrote with **a** authority,	3605
	9:30 he sent the letters unto **a** the Jews, to	3605
	10: 2 the acts of his power and of his might,	3605
	10: 3 and speaking peace to **a** his seed.	3605
Job	1: 3 this man was the greatest of **a** the men	3605
	1: 5 *according to* the number of them **a:**	3605
	1:10 and about **a** that he hath on every side?	3605
	1:11 touch **a** that he hath, and he will curse	3605
	1:12 Behold, **a** that he hath *is* in thy power;	3605
	1:22 In **a** this Job sinned not, nor charged God	3605
	2: 4 **a** that a man hath will he give for his life.	3605
	2:10 In **a** this did not Job sin with his lips.	3605
	2:11 Now when Job's three friends heard of **a**	3605
	4:14 which made **a** my bones to shake.	7230
	8:13 So *are* the paths of **a** that forget God;	3605
	9:28 I am afraid of **a** my sorrows, I know that	3605
	12: 9 Who knoweth not in **a** these that the	3605
	12:10 living *thing*, and the breath of **a** mankind.	3605
	13: 1 mine eye hath seen **a** *this*, mine ear hath	3605
	13: 4 of lies, ye *are* **a** physicians of no value.	3605
	13:27 and lookest narrowly unto **a** my paths;	3605
	14:14 shall he live *again?* **a** the days of my	3605
	15:20 The wicked *man* travaileth with pain **a** his	3605
	16: 2 *things:* miserable comforters *are* ye **a.**	3605
	16: 7 thou hast made desolate **a** my company.	3605
	17: 7 and **a** my members *are* as a shadow.	3605
	17:10 *as for* you **a**, do you return, and come	3605
	19:19 **A** my inward friends abhorred me:	3605
	20:26 **A** darkness *shall* be hid in his secret	3605
	24:24 they are taken out of the way as **a** *other,*	3605
	27: 3 **A** the while my breath *is* in me,	3605
	27:12 **a** ye yourselves have seen *it;* why	3605
	28: 3 searcheth out **a** perfection, the stones of	3605
	28:21 Seeing it is hid from the eyes of **a** a living,	3605
	29:19 the dew **lay a night** upon my branch.	3885
	30:23 and *to* the house appointed for **a** living,	3605
	31: 4 he see my ways, and count **a** my steps?	3605
	31:12 and would root out **a** mine increase.	3605
	33: 1 my speeches, and hearken to **a** my words.	3605
	33:11 feet in the stocks, he marketh **a** my paths.	3605
	33:29 **a** these *things* worketh God oftentimes	3605

Job	34:15 **A** flesh shall perish together, and man	3605
	34:19 for they **a** *are* the work of his hands.	3605
	34:21 ways of man, and he seeth **a** his goings.	3605
	36:19 *no,* not gold, nor **a** the forces of strength.	3605
	37: 7 man; that **a** men may know his work.	3605
	38: 7 when the sons of God shouted for joy?	3605
	38:18 of the earth? declare if thou knowest it **a**.	3605
	40:20 where **a** the beasts of the field play.	3605
	41:34 He beholdeth a high *things:* he *is* a king	3605
	41:34 he *is* a king over **a** the children of pride.	3605
	42:11 came there unto him **a** his brethren,	3605
	42:11 **a** his sisters, and all *they that had been of*	3605
	42:11 **a** *they that had been of* his acquaintance	3605
	42:11 comforted him over **a** the evil that	3605
	42:15 in **a** the land were no women found *so*	3605
Ps	2:12 blessed *are* **a** they that put their trust in	3605
	3: 7 thou hast smitten **a** mine enemies *upon*	3605
	5: 5 sight: thou hatest **a** workers of iniquity.	3605
	5:11 let **a** those that put their trust in thee	3605
	6: 6 **a** the night make I my bed to swim;	3605
	6: 7 it waxeth old because of **a** mine enemies.	3605
	6: 8 Depart from me, **a** ye workers of iniquity;	3605
	6:10 Let **a** mine enemies be ashamed	3605
	7: 1 save me from **a** them that persecute me,	3605
	8: 1 how excellent *is* thy name in **a** the earth!	3605
	8: 6 thou hast put **a** *things* under his feet:	3605
	8: 7 **A** sheep and oxen, yea, and the beasts of	3605
	8: 9 how excellent *is* thy name in **a** the earth!	3605
	9: 1 I will shew forth **a** thy marvellous works.	3605
	9:14 That I may shew forth **a** thy praise in	3605
	9:17 hell, *and* **a** the nations that forget God.	3605
	10: 4 not seek *after God:* God *is* not in **a** his	3605
	10: 5 *as for* **a** his enemies, he puffeth at them.	3605
	12: 3 The LORD shall cut off **a** flattering lips,	3605
	14: 3 They are **a** gone aside, they are *all* together	3605
	14: 3 they are **a** *together* become filthy:	NIH
	14: 4 Have **a** the workers of iniquity no	3605
	16: 3 *to* the excellent, in whom *is* **a** my delight.	3605
	18: 1 him from the hand of **a** his enemies,	3605
	18:22 For **a** his judgments *were* before me,	3605
	18:30 he *is* a buckler to **a** those that trust in him.	3605
	19: 4 Their line is gone out through **a** the earth,	3605
	20: 3 Remember **a** thy offerings, and accept thy	3605
	20: 4 thine own heart, and fulfil **a** thy counsel.	3605
	20: 5 the LORD fulfil **a** thy petitions.	3605
	21: 8 Thine hand shall find out **a** thine enemies:	3605
	22: 7 **A** they that see me laugh me to scorn:	3605
	22:14 water, and **a** my bones are out of joint:	3605
	22:17 I may tell **a** my bones: they look *and*	3605
	22:23 **a** ye the seed of Jacob, glorify him;	3605
	22:23 and fear him, **a** ye the seed of Israel.	3605
	22:27 **A** the ends of the world shall remember	3605
	22:27 **a** the kindreds of the nations shall worship	3605
	22:29 **A** *they that be* fat upon earth shall eat	3605
	22:29 **a** they that go down to the dust shall bow	3605
	23: 6 mercy shall follow me **a** the days of my	3605
	25:10 **A** the paths of the LORD *are* mercy	3605
	25:18 and my pain; and forgive **a** my sins.	3605
	25:22 O God, out of **a** his troubles.	3605
	26: 7 and tell of **a** thy wondrous works.	3605
	27: 4 house of the LORD **a** the days of my life,	3605
	31:11 I was a reproach among **a** mine enemies,	3605
	31:23 O love the LORD, **a** ye his saints: *for*	3605
	31:24 your heart, **a** ye that hope in the LORD.	3605
	32: 3 bones waxed old through my roaring **a**	3605
	32:11 for joy, **a** ye that are upright in heart.	3605
	33: 4 right; and **a** his works *are done* in truth.	3605
	33: 6 the host of them by the breath of his	3605
	33: 8 Let **a** the earth fear the LORD: let all	3605
	33: 8 let **a** the inhabitants of the world stand in	3605
	33:11 his heart to **a** generations. 1755+1755+2050.1	
	33:13 he beholdeth **a** the sons of men.	3605
	33:14 upon **a** the inhabitants of the earth.	3605
	33:15 hearts alike; he considereth **a** their works.	3605
	34: 1 I will bless the LORD at **a** times:	3605
	34: 4 and delivered me from **a** my fears.	3605
	34: 6 and saved him out of **a** his troubles.	3605
	34:17 delivereth them out of **a** their troubles.	3605
	34:19 the LORD delivereth him out of **a** them.	3605
	34:20 He keepeth **a** his bones: not one of them	3605
	35:10 **A** my bones shall say, LORD, who *is* like	3605
	35:28 and of thy praise **a** the day long.	3605
	38: 6 I go mourning **a** the day long.	3605
	38: 9 Lord, **a** my desire *is* before thee;	3605
	38:12 and imagine deceits **a** the day long.	3605
	39: 8 Deliver me from **a** my transgressions:	3605
	39:12 and a sojourner, as **a** my fathers *were.*	3605
	40:16 Let **a** those that seek thee rejoice	3605
	41: 3 thou wilt make **a** his bed in his sickness.	3605
	41: 7 **A** that hate me whisper together against	3605
	42: 7 **a** thy waves and thy billows are gone over	3605
	44: 8 In God we boast **a** the day long,	3605
	44:17 **A** this is come upon us; yet have we not	3605
	44:22 for thy sake are we killed **a** the day long;	3605
	45: 8 **A** thy garments *smell of* myrrh, and aloes,	3605
	45:13 The king's daughter *is* **a** glorious within:	3605
	45:16 whom thou mayest make princes in **a**	3605
	45:17 in **a** generations: 1755+1755+3605+2050.1	
	47: 1 O clap *your* hands, **a** ye people; shout unto	3605
	47: 2 he *is* a great King over **a** the earth.	3605
	47: 7 For God *is* the King of **a** the earth: sing ye	3605
	49: 1 Hear this, **a** ye people; give ear, all ye	3605
	49: 1 give ear, **a** ye inhabitants of the world:	3605
	49:11 places to **a** generations; 1755+1755+2050.1	

Ps	50:11 I know **a** the fowls of the mountains:	3605
	51: 9 my sins, and blot out **a** mine iniquities.	3605
	52: 4 Thou lovest **a** devouring words, O thou	3605
	54: 7 For he hath delivered me out of **a** trouble:	3605
	56: 5 **a** their thoughts *are* against me for evil.	3605
	57: 2 unto God that performeth **a** *things* for me.	NIH
	57: 5 let thy glory *be* above **a** the earth.	3605
	57:11 let thy glory *be* above **a** the earth.	3605
	59: 5 of Israel, awake to visit **a** the heathen:	3605
	59: 8 thou shalt have **a** the heathen in derision.	3605
	62: 3 ye shall be slain **a** of you: as a bowing wall	3605
	62: 8 Trust in him at **a** times; ye people, pour	3605
	64: 8 **a** that see them shall flee away.	3605
	64: 9 **a** men shall fear, and shall declare the	3605
	64:10 and **a** the upright in heart shall glory.	3605
	65: 2 prayer, unto thee shall **a** flesh come.	3605
	65: 5 *who* art the confidence of **a** the ends of	3605
	66: 1 Make a joyful noise unto God, **a** ye lands:	3605
	66: 4 **A** the earth shall worship thee,	3605
	66:16 **a** ye that fear God, and I will declare what	3605
	67: 2 thy saving health among **a** nations.	3605
	67: 3 O God; let **a** the people praise thee.	3605
	67: 5 O God; let **a** the people praise thee.	3605
	67: 7 and **a** the ends of the earth shall fear him.	3605
	69:19 mine adversaries *are* **a** before thee.	3605
	70: 4 Let **a** those that seek thee rejoice	3605
	71: 8 thy praise *and* with thy honour **a** the day.	3605
	71:15 *and* thy salvation **a** the day;	3605
	71:24 talk of thy righteousness **a** the day long:	3605
	72: 5 throughout **a** generations. 1755+1755	
	72:11 Yea, **a** kings shall fall down before him:	3605
	72:11 before him: **a** nations shall serve him.	3605
	72:17 in him: **a** nations shall call him blessed.	3605
	73:14 For **a** the day long have I been plagued,	3605
	73:27 thou hast destroyed **a** them that go a	3605
	73:28 that *I* may declare **a** thy works.	3605
	74: 3 *even* **a** *that* the enemy hath done	3605
	74: 8 they have burnt up **a** the synagogues of	3605
	74:17 Thou hast set **a** the borders of the earth:	3605
	75: 3 **a** the inhabitants thereof *are* dissolved:	3605
	75: 8 **a** the wicked of the earth shall wring them	3605
	75:10 **A** the horns of the wicked also will I cut	3605
	76: 9 to save **a** the meek of the earth.	3605
	76:11 **a** that be round about him bring presents	3605
	77:12 I will meditate also of **a** thy work,	3605
	78:14 a cloud, and **a** the night with a light of fire.	3605
	78:32 For **a** this they sinned still, and believed	3605
	78:38 away, and did not stir up **a** his wrath.	3605
	78:51 smote the firstborn in Egypt; the chief	3605
	79:13 praise to **a** generations. 1755+1755+2050.1	
	80:12 that **a** they which pass by the way do	3605
	82: 5 the foundations of the earth are out of	3605
	82: 6 **a** of you *are* children of the most High.	3605
	82: 8 the earth: for thou shalt inherit **a** nations.	3605
	83:11 **a** their princes as Zebah, and as Zalmunna:	3605
	83:18 *art* the most High over **a** the earth.	3605
	85: 2 thy people, thou hast covered **a** their sin.	3605
	85: 3 Thou hast taken away **a** thy wrath:	3605
	85: 3 anger to **a** generations? 1755+1755+2050.1	
	86: 5 plenteous in mercy unto **a** them that call	3605
	86: 9 **A** nations whom thou hast made shall	3605
	86:12 O Lord my God, with **a** my heart:	3605
	87: 2 Zion more than **a** the dwellings of Jacob.	3605
	87: 7 *shall be there:* **a** my springs *are* in thee.	3605
	88: 7 thou hast afflicted *me with* **a** thy waves.	3605
	89: 1 to **a** generations. 1755+1755+2050.1	
	89: 4 throne to **a** generations. 1755+1755+2050.1	
	89: 7 to be had in reverence of **a** them that are	3605
	89:16 In thy name shall they rejoice **a** the day:	3605
	89:40 Thou hast broken down **a** his hedges;	3605
	89:41 **A** that pass by the way spoil him: he is **a**	3605
	89:42 thou hast made **a** his enemies to rejoice.	3605
	89:47 wherefore hast thou made **a** men in vain?	3605
	89:50 *the reproach of* **a** the mighty people;	3605
	90: 1 place in **a** generations. 1755+1755+2050.1	
	90: 9 For **a** our days are passed away in thy	3605
	90:14 we may rejoice and be glad **a** our days.	3605
	91:11 over thee, to keep thee in **a** thy ways.	3605
	92: 7 **a** the workers of iniquity do flourish;	3605
	92: 9 **a** the workers of iniquity shall be scattered	3605
	94: 4 **a** the workers of iniquity boast themselves	3605
	94:15 and **a** the upright in heart shall follow it.	3605
	95: 3 great God, and a great King above **a** gods.	3605
	96: 1 sing unto the LORD, **a** the earth.	3605
	96: 3 heathen, his wonders among **a** people.	3605
	96: 4 praised: he *is* to be feared above **a** gods.	3605
	96: 5 For **a** the gods of the nations *are* idols:	3605
	96: 9 of holiness: fear before him, **a** the earth.	3605
	96:12 the field be joyful, and **a** that *is* therein:	3605
	96:12 shall **a** the trees of the wood rejoice	3605
	97: 6 and **a** the people see his glory.	3605
	97: 7 Confounded be **a** they that serve graven	3605
	97: 7 of idols: worship him, **a** ye gods.	3605
	97: 9 LORD, *art* High above **a** the earth:	3605
	97: 9 earth: thou art exalted far above **a** gods.	3605
	98: 3 **a** the ends of the earth have seen	3605
	98: 4 a joyful noise unto the LORD, **a** the earth:	3605
	99: 2 in Zion; and he *is* high above **a** the people.	3605
	100: 1 a joyful noise unto the LORD, **a** ye lands.	3605
	100: 5 to **a** generations. 1755+1755+2050.1	
	101: 8 I will early destroy **a** the wicked of	3605
	101: 8 that *I* may cut off **a** wicked doers from	3605
	102: 8 Mine enemies reproach me **a** the day;	3605
	102:12 unto **a** generations. 1755+1755+2050.1	
	102:15 and **a** the kings of the earth thy glory.	3605

A

Ps 102:24	*are* throughout **a generations**. 1755+1755
102:26	a of them shall wax old like a garment; 3605
103: 1	a that is within me, *bless* his holy name. 3605
103: 2	O my soul, and forget not **a** his benefits: 3605
103: 3	Who forgiveth **a** thine iniquities; 3605
103: 3	iniquities; who healeth **a** thy diseases; 3605
103: 6	and judgment for **a** that are oppressed. 3605
103:19	heavens; and his kingdom ruleth over **a**. 3605
103:21	Bless ye the Lᴏʀᴅ, **a** ye his hosts. 3605
103:22	a his works in all places of his dominion: 3605
103:22	all his works in a places of his dominion: 3605
104:20	wherein **a** the beasts of the forest do creep 3605
104:24	in wisdom hast thou made them **a**: 3605
104:27	These wait **a** upon thee; that *thou* mayest 3605
105: 2	him: talk ye of **a** his wondrous works. 3605
105: 7	God: his judgments *are* in **a** the earth. 3605
105:21	of his house, and ruler of **a** his substance: 3605
105:31	sorts *of flies, and* lice in **a** their coasts. 3605
105:35	And did eat up **a** the herbs in their land, 3605
105:36	He smote also **a** the firstborn in their land, 3605
105:36	in their land, the chief of **a** their strength. 3605
106: 2	*who* can shew forth **a** his praise? 3605
106: 3	he that doeth righteousness at **a** times. 3605
106:31	**a generations** for 1755+1755+2050.1
106:46	He made them also to be pitied of **a** those 3605
106:48	let **a** the people say, Amen. Praise ye 3605
107:18	Their soul abhorreth **a** *manner of* meat; 3605
107:42	and **a** iniquity shall stop her mouth. 3605
108: 5	and thy glory above **a** the earth. 3605
109:11	Let the extortioner catch **a** that he hath; 3605
111: 2	sought out of **a** them that have pleasure 3605
111: 7	judgment; **a** his commandments *are* sure. 3605
111:10	a good understanding have **a** they that do 3605
113: 4	The Lᴏʀᴅ *is* high above **a** nations, *and* 3605
116:11	I said in my haste, **A** men *are* liars. 3605
116:12	What shall I render unto the Lᴏʀᴅ *for* **a** 3605
116:14	now in the presence of **a** his people, 3605
116:18	now in the presence of **a** his people, 3605
117: 1	O praise the Lᴏʀᴅ, **a** ye nations: 3605
117: 1	all ye nations: praise him, **a** ye people. 3605
118:10	**A** nations compassed me about: but in 3605
119: 6	when I have respect unto **a** thy 3605
119:13	With my lips have I declared **a** 3605
119:14	of thy testimonies, as *much as* in **a** riches. 3605
119:20	*that it hath* unto thy judgments at **a** times. 3605
119:63	a companion of **a** *them* that fear thee, 3605
119:86	**A** thy commandments *are* faithful: 3605
119:90	*is* unto **a generations**. 1755+1755+2050.1
119:91	to thine ordinances: for **a** *are* thy servants. 3605
119:96	I have seen an end of **a** perfection: *but* 3605
119:97	I thy law! it *is* my meditation **a** the day. 3605
119:99	I have more understanding than **a** my 3605
119:118	Thou hast trodden down **a** them that err 3605
119:119	puttest away **a** the wicked of the earth 3605
119:128	Therefore I esteem **a** *thy* precepts 3605
119:128	precepts concerning **a** *things* to be right; 3605
119:151	and **a** thy commandments *are* truth. 3605
119:168	for **a** my ways *are* before thee. 3605
119:172	**a** thy commandments *are* righteousness. 3605
121: 7	The Lᴏʀᴅ shall preserve thee from **a** 3605
128: 5	thou shalt see the good of Jerusalem **a** 3605
129: 5	Let them **a** be confounded and turned 3605
130: 8	shall redeem Israel from **a** his iniquities. 3605
132: 1	remember David, *and* **a** his afflictions: 3605
134: 1	the Lᴏʀᴅ, **a** ye servants of the Lᴏʀᴅ, 3605
135: 5	great, and *that* our Lord *is* above **a** gods. 3605
135: 6	in earth, in the seas, and **a** deep places. 3605
135: 9	upon Pharaoh, and upon **a** his servants. 3605
135:11	Bashan, and **a** the kingdoms of Canaan: 3605
135:13	throughout **a generations**. 1755+1755+2050.1
136:25	Who giveth food to **a** flesh: for his mercy 3605
138: 2	for thou hast magnified thy word above **a** 3605
138: 4	**A** the kings of the earth shall praise thee, 3605
139: 3	and art acquainted *with* **a** my ways. 3605
139:16	in thy book **a** *my members* were written, 3605
143: 5	the days of old; I meditate on **a** thy works; 3605
143:12	and destroy **a** them that afflict my soul: 3605
144:13	**a manner of store**: 413+2177+2177+4480
145: 9	The Lᴏʀᴅ *is* good to **a**: and his tender 3605
145: 9	his tender mercies *are* over **a** his works. 3605
145:10	**A** thy works shall praise thee, O Lᴏʀᴅ; 3605
145:13	thy dominion *endureth* throughout **a** 3605
145:14	The Lᴏʀᴅ upholdeth **a** that fall, 3605
145:14	raiseth up **a** those that be bowed down. 3605
145:15	The eyes of **a** wait upon thee; 3605
145:17	The Lᴏʀᴅ *is* righteous in **a** his ways, 3605
145:17	in all his ways, and holy in **a** his works. 3605
145:18	The Lᴏʀᴅ *is* nigh unto **a** them that call 3605
145:18	him, to **a** that call upon him in truth. 3605
145:20	The Lᴏʀᴅ preserveth **a** them that love 3605
145:20	him: but **a** the wicked will he destroy. 3605
145:21	let **a** flesh bless his holy name for ever 3605
146: 6	and earth, the sea, and **a** that therein is: 3605
146:10	Zion, unto **a generations**. 1755+1755+2050.1
147: 4	stars; he calleth them **a** *by their* names. 3605
148: 2	Praise ye him, **a** his angels: praise ye him, 3605
148: 2	all his angels: praise ye him, **a** his hosts. 3605
148: 3	and moon: praise him, **a** ye stars of light. 3605
148: 7	from the earth, ye dragons, and **a** deeps: 3605
148: 9	Mountains, and **a** hills; fruitful trees, 3605
148: 9	all hills; fruitful trees, and **a** cedars: 3605
148:10	Beasts, and **a** cattle; creeping things, 3605
148:11	Kings of the earth, and **a** people; princes, 3605
148:11	princes, and **a** judges of the earth: 3605
148:14	of his people, the praise of **a** his saints; 3605

Ps 149: 9	this honour have **a** his saints. Praise ye 3605
Pr 1:13	We shall find **a** precious substance, 3605
1:14	thy lot among us; let us **a** have one purse: 3605
1:25	ye have set at nought **a** my counsel, 3605
1:30	of my counsel: they despised **a** my reproof. 3605
3: 5	Trust in the Lᴏʀᴅ with **a** thine heart; 3605
3: 6	In **a** thy ways acknowledge him, 3605
3: 9	and with the firstfruits of **a** thine increase: 3605
3:15	**a** the things thou canst desire are not to be 3605
3:17	of pleasantness, and **a** her paths *are* peace. 3605
4: 7	and with **a** thy getting get understanding. 3605
4:22	that find them, and health to **a** their flesh. 3605
4:23	Keep thy heart with **a** diligence; for out of 3605
4:26	thy feet, and let **a** thy ways be established. 3605
5:14	I was almost in **a** evil in the midst of 3605
5:19	let her breasts satisfy thee at **a** times; 3605
5:21	the Lᴏʀᴅ, and he pondereth **a** his goings. 3605
6:31	he shall give **a** the substance of his house. 3605
8: 8	**A** the words of my mouth *are* in 3605
8: 9	*are* **a** plain to him that understandeth, 3605
8:11	**a** the things that may be desired are not 3605
8:16	nobles, *even* **a** the judges of the earth. 3605
8:36	own soul: **a** they that hate me love death. 3605
10:12	strifes: but love covereth **a** sins. 3605
14:23	In **a** labour there is profit: but the talk of 3605
15:15	**A** the days of the afflicted *are* evil: 3605
16: 2	**A** the ways of a man *are* clean in his own 3605
16: 4	The Lᴏʀᴅ hath made **a** *things* for 3605
16:11	**a** the weights of the bag *are* his work. 3605
17:17	A friend loveth at **a** times, and a brother 3605
18: 1	*and* intermeddleth with **a** wisdom. 3605
19: 7	**A** the brethren of the poor do hate him: 3605
20: 8	scattereth *away* **a** evil with his eyes. 3605
20:27	searching **a** the inward parts of the belly. 3605
21:26	He coveteth greedily **a** the day long: 3605
22: 2	the Lᴏʀᴅ *is* the Maker of them **a**. 3605
23:17	*be thou* in the fear of the Lᴏʀᴅ **a** the day 3605
24: 4	the chambers be filled *with* **a** precious 3605
24:31	it was **a** grown over *with* thorns, *and* 3605
26:10	The great *God* that formed **a** *things* both 3605
28: 5	they that seek the Lᴏʀᴅ understand **a** 3605
29:11	A fool uttereth **a** his mind: but a wise 3605
29:12	hearken to lies, **a** his servants *are* wicked. 3605
30: 4	who hath established **a** the ends of 3605
30:27	yet go they forth **a** of them by bands; 3605
31: 8	of **a** such as are appointed to destruction. 3605
31:12	good and not evil **a** the days of her life. 3605
31:21	for **a** her household *are* clothed with 3605
31:29	virtuously, but thou excellest them **a**. 3605
Ecc 1: 2	Preacher, vanity of vanities; **a** *is* vanity. 3605
1: 3	What profit hath a man of **a** his labour 3605
1: 7	**A** the rivers run into the sea; yet the sea 3605
1: 8	**A** things *are* full of labour; man cannot 3605
1:13	search out by wisdom concerning **a** *things* 3605
1:14	I have seen **a** the works that are done 3605
1:14	behold, **a** *is* vanity and vexation of spirit. 3605
1:16	have gotten more wisdom than **a** *they* that 3605
2: 3	which they should do under the heaven **a** 4557
2: 5	I planted trees in them of **a** *kind of* fruits: 3605
2: 7	small cattle above **a** that were in Jerusalem 3605
2: 8	**musical instruments**, and that
	of **a** sorts. 7705+7705
2: 9	increased more than **a** that were before 3605
2:10	for my heart rejoiced in **a** my labour: 3605
2:10	and this was my portion of **a** my labour. 3605
2:11	I looked on **a** the works that my hands 3605
2:11	**a** *was* vanity and vexation of spirit, 3605
2:14	also that one event happeneth to them **a**. 3605
2:16	*in* the days to come shall **a** be forgotten. 3605
2:17	for **a** *is* vanity and vexation of spirit. 3605
2:18	I hated **a** my labour which I *had* taken 3605
2:19	yet shall he have rule over **a** my labour 3605
2:20	**a** the labour which I took under the sun. 3605
2:22	For what hath man of **a** his labour, 3605
2:23	For **a** his days *are* sorrows, and his travail 3605
3:13	drink, and enjoy the good of **a** his labour, 3605
3:19	yea, they have **a** one breath; so that a man 3605
3:19	preeminence above a beast: for **a** *is* vanity. 3605
3:20	**A** go unto one place; all are of the dust, 3605
3:20	a are of the dust, and all turn to dust 3605
3:20	are of the dust, and **a** turn to dust again. 3605
4: 1	considered **a** the oppressions that *are* done 3605
4: 4	considered a travail, and every right work, 3605
4: 8	yet *is there* no end of **a** his labour; 3605
4:15	I considered **a** the living which walk 3605
4:16	*There is* no end of **a** the people, *even* of 3605
4:16	*even* of **a** that have been before them: 3605
5: 9	Moreover the profit of the earth *is* for **a**: 3605
5:16	*that* in **a** points as he came, so shall he go: 3605
5:17	**A** his days also he eateth in darkness, 3605
5:18	to enjoy the good of **a** his labour that he 3605
5:18	taketh under the sun **a** the days of his life, 4557
6: 2	that he wanteth nothing for his soul of **a** 3605
6: 6	seen no good: do not **a** go to one place? 3605
6: 7	**A** the labour of man *is* for his mouth, 3605
6:12	the days of his vain life which he 4557
7: 2	that *is* the end of **a** men; and the living 3605
7:15	**A** *things* have I seen in the days of my 3605
7:18	feareth God shall come forth of them **a**. 3605
7:21	Also take no heed unto **a** words that are 3605
7:23	**A** this have I proved by wisdom: I said, 3605
7:28	a woman among **a** those have I not found. 3605
8: 9	**A** this have I seen, and applied my heart 3605
8:17	I beheld **a** the work of God, that a man 3605
9: 1	For **a** this I considered in my heart even 3605

Ecc 9: 1	in my heart even to declare **a** this, 3605
9: 1	or hatred *by* **a** *that is* before them. 3605
9: 2	**A** *things* come alike to all: there is one 3605
9: 2	All *things* come alike to **a**: there is one 3605
9: 3	This *is* an evil among **a** *things* that are 3605
9: 3	the sun, that *there* is one event unto **a**. 3605
9: 4	For him that is joined to **a** the living 3605
9: 9	lovest **a** the days of the life of thy vanity, 3605
9: 9	under the sun, **a** the days of thy vanity: 3605
9:11	time and chance happeneth to them **a**. 3605
10:19	but money answereth **a** *things*. 3605
11: 5	not the works of God who maketh **a**. 3605
11: 8	live many years, *and* rejoice in them **a**. 3605
11: 8	shall be many. **A** that cometh *is* vanity. 3605
11: 9	that for *these things* God will bring thee 3605
12: 4	the daughters of musick shall be brought 3605
12: 8	of vanities, saith the Preacher; **a** *is* vanity. 3605
SS 1:13	he shall **lie a night** betwixt my breasts. 3885
3: 6	with **a** powders of the merchant? 3605
3: 8	They **a** hold swords, *being* expert in war: 3605
4: 4	a shields of mighty *men*. 3605
4: 7	Thou *art* **a** fair, my love; *there is* no spot 3605
4:10	the smell of thine ointments than **a** spices! 3605
4:14	cinnamon, with **a** trees of frankincense; 3605
4:14	myrrh and aloes, with **a** the chief spices: 3605
7:13	our gates *are* **a** *manner of* pleasant *fruits*, 3605
8: 7	if a man would give **a** the substance of his 3605
Isa 1:25	away thy dross, and take away **a** thy tin: 3605
2:13	the hills; and **a** nations shall flow unto it. 3605
2:13	upon **a** the cedars of Lebanon, that are 3605
2:13	lifted up, and upon **a** the oaks of Bashan, 3605
2:14	upon **a** the high mountains, and upon all 3605
2:14	upon **a** the hills that are lifted up, 3605
2:16	upon **a** the ships of Tarshish, and upon all 3605
2:16	of Tarshish, and upon **a** pleasant pictures. 3605
4: 5	for upon **a** the glory *shall be* a defence. 3605
5:25	For **a** this his anger is not turned away, 3605
5:28	arrows *are* sharp, and **a** their bows bent, 3605
7:19	shall rest **a** of them in the desolate valleys, 3605
7:19	and upon **a** thorns, and upon all bushes. 3605
7:19	and upon all thorns, and upon **a** bushes. 3605
7:24	**a** the land shall become briers and thorns. 3605
7:25	on **a** hills that shall be digged with 3605
8: 7	*even* the king of Assyria, and **a** his glory: 3605
8: 7	he shall come up over **a** his channels, 3605
8: 7	**a** his channels, and go over **a** his banks: 3605
8: 9	and give ear, **a** ye of far countries: 3605
8:12	to **a** *them* to whom this people shall say, 3605
9: 9	the people shall know, *even* Ephraim 3605
9:12	For **a** this his anger is not turned away, 3605
9:17	For **a** this his anger is not turned away, 3605
9:21	For **a** this his anger is not turned away, 3605
10: 4	For **a** this his anger is not turned away, 3605
10:14	*that are* left, have I gathered **a** the earth; 3605
10:23	*in* the midst of **a** *the land*. 3605
11: 9	They shall not hurt nor destroy in **a** my 3605
12: 5	this *is* known in **a** the earth. 3605
13: 7	Therefore shall **a** hands be faint, 3605
14: 9	thee, *even* **a** the chief ones of the earth; 3605
14: 9	it hath raised up from their thrones **a** 3605
14:10	**A** they shall speak and say unto thee, 3605
14:18	**A** the kings of the nations, *even* all of 3605
14:18	of the nations, *even* **a** of them, lie in glory, 3605
14:26	*is* the hand that is stretched out upon **a** 3605
15: 2	on **a** their heads *shall be* baldness, *and* 3605
16:14	contemned, with **a** *that* great multitude; 3605
18: 3	**A** ye inhabitants of the world, 3605
18: 6	to the beasts of the earth shall winter upon 3605
19: 8	**a** they that cast angle into the brooks shall 3605
19:10	a that make sluces *and* ponds for fish. 3605
21: 2	the sighing thereof have I made to cease. 3605
21: 9	**a** the graven images of her gods he hath 3605
21:16	and **a** the glory of Kedar shall fail: 3605
22: 3	**A** thy rulers are fled together, they are 3605
22: 3	**a** that are found in thee are bound 3605
22:24	they shall hang upon him **a** the glory of 3605
22:24	and the issue, **a** vessels of small quantity, 3605
22:24	of cups, even to **a** the vessels of flagons. 3605
23: 9	to stain the pride of **a** glory, to bring 3605
23: 9	to bring into contempt **a** the honourable 3605
23:17	shall commit fornication with **a** 3605
24: 7	**a** the merryhearted do sigh. 3605
24:11	a joy is darkened, the mirth of the land is 3605
25: 6	make unto **a** people a feast of fat things, 3605
25: 7	face of the covering cast over **a** people, 3605
25: 7	and the vail that is spread over **a** nations. 3605
25: 8	will wipe away tears from off **a** faces; 3605
25: 8	shall he take away from off **a** the earth: 3605
26:12	for thou also hast wrought **a** our works in 3605
26:14	and made **a** their memory to perish. 3605
26:15	hadst removed *it* far unto **a** the ends of 3605
27: 9	and this *is* **a** the fruit to take away his sin; 3605
27: 9	when he maketh **a** the stones of the altar 3605
28: 8	For **a** tables are full *of* vomit *and* filthiness, 3605
28:24	Doth the plowman plow **a** day to sow? 3605
29: 7	the multitude of **a** the nations that fight 3605
29: 7	even **a** that fight against her 3605
29: 8	so shall the multitude of **a** the nations be, 3605
29:11	the vision of **a** is become unto you as 3605
29:20	and **a** that watch for iniquity are cut off: 3605
30: 5	They were **a** ashamed of a people *that* 3605
30:18	blessed *are* **a** they that wait for him. 3605
31: 3	fall down, and they **a** shall fail together. 3605
32:13	upon the houses of joy *in* the joyous city: 3605
32:20	Blessed *are* ye that sow beside **a** waters, 3605

Isa		
34: 1	let the earth hear, and **a** that is therein;	4393
34: 1	and **a things** that come forth of it.	3605
34: 2	the indignation of the LORD *is* upon **a**	3605
34: 2	and *his* fury upon **a** their armies:	3605
34: 4	the host of heaven shall be dissolved,	3605
34: 4	**a** their host shall fall down, as the leaf	3605
34:12	there, and **a** her princes shall be nothing.	3605
36: 1	up against **a** the defenced cities of Judah,	3605
36: 6	*is* Pharaoh king of Egypt to **a** that trust in	3605
36:20	Who *are they* amongst **a** the gods of these	3605
37:11	to **a** lands by destroying them utterly;	3605
37:16	alone, of **a** the kingdoms of the earth:	3605
37:17	hear **a** the words of Sennacherib,	3605
37:18	the kings of Assyria have laid waste **a**	3605
37:20	**a** the kingdoms of the earth may know	3605
37:25	with the sole of my feet have I dried up **a**	3605
37:36	behold, they *were* **a** dead corpses.	3605
38:13	as a lion, so will he break **a** my bones:	3605
38:15	himself hath done *it:* I shall go softly **a** my	3605
38:16	in **a** these *things* is the life of my spirit:	3605
38:17	for thou hast cast **a** my sins behind thy	3605
38:20	the days of our life in the house of	3605
39: 2	**a** the house of his armour, and all that	3605
39: 2	and **a** that was found in his treasures:	3605
39: 2	in his house, nor in **a** his dominion.	3605
39: 4	**A** that *is in* mine house have they seen:	3605
39: 6	that **a** that *is* in thine house, and *that*	3605
40: 2	of the LORD's hand double for **a** her sins.	3605
40: 5	and **a** flesh shall see *it* together:	3605
40: 6	**A** flesh *is* grass, and all the goodliness	3605
40: 6	**a** the goodliness thereof *is* as the flower	3605
40:17	**A** nations before him *are* as nothing;	3605
40:26	he calleth them **a** by names by	3605
41:11	**a** they that were incensed against thee	3605
41:29	Behold, they *are* **a** vanity; their works *are*	3605
42:10	down to the sea, and **a** that is therein;	4393
42:15	and hills, and dry up **a** their herbs;	3605
42:22	they *are* **a** of them snared in holes,	3605
43: 9	Let **a** the nations be gathered together,	3605
43:14	have brought down **a** their nobles,	3605
44: 9	They that make a graven image *are* **a** of	3605
44:11	Behold, **a** his fellows shall be ashamed:	3605
44:11	let them **a** be gathered together, let them	3605
44:24	*am* the LORD that maketh **a** *things;* that	3605
44:28	and shall perform **a** my pleasure:	3605
45: 7	create evil: I the LORD do **a** these *things.*	3605
45:12	and **a** their host have I commanded.	3605
45:13	and I will direct **a** his ways:	3605
45:16	and also confounded, **a** of them:	3605
45:22	and be ye saved, **a** the ends of the earth:	3605
45:24	**a** that are incensed against him shall be	3605
45:25	In the LORD shall **a** the seed of Israel be	3605
46: 3	and **a** the remnant of the house of Israel,	3605
46:10	shall stand, and I will do **a** my pleasure:	3605
48: 6	Thou hast heard, see **a** this; and will not	3605
48:14	**A** ye, assemble yourselves, and hear;	3605
49: 9	their pastures *shall be* in **a** high places.	3605
49:11	I will make **a** my mountains a way,	3605
49:18	**a** these gather themselves together, *and*	3605
49:18	thou shalt surely clothe thee with them **a,**	3605
49:26	**a** flesh shall know that I the LORD *am* thy	3605
50: 2	Is mine hand **shortened at a,** that *it*	7114+7114
50: 9	lo, they **a** shall wax old as a garment;	3605
50:11	Behold, **a** ye that kindle a fire,	3605
51: 3	he will comfort **a** her waste places;	3605
51:18	*There is* none to guide her among **a**	3605
51:18	hand of **a** the sons *that* she hath brought	3605
51:20	they lie at the head of **a** the streets, as a	3605
52:10	his holy arm in the eyes of **a** the nations;	3605
52:10	**a** the ends of the earth shall see	3605
53: 6	**A** we like sheep have gone astray; we	3605
53: 6	hath laid on him the iniquity of us **a.**	3605
54:12	**a** thy borders of pleasant stones.	3605
54:13	thy children *shall be* taught of	3605
55:12	**a** the trees of the field shall clap *their*	3605
56: 7	be called a house of prayer for **a** people.	3605
56: 9	**A** ye beasts of the field, come to devour,	3605
56: 9	to devour, *yea,* **a** ye beasts in the forest.	3605
56:10	are **a** ignorant, they *are* all dumb dogs,	3605
56:10	they *are* **a** dumb dogs, they cannot bark;	3605
56:11	they **a** look to their own way, every one	3605
57:13	the wind shall carry them **a** away;	3605
58: 3	find pleasure, and exact **a** your labours.	3605
59:11	We roar **a** like bears, and mourn sore like	3605
60: 4	**a** they gather themselves together,	3605
60: 6	and Ephah; **a** they from Sheba shall come:	3605
60: 7	**A** the flocks of Kedar shall be gathered	3605
60:14	**a** they that despised thee shall bow	3605
60:21	Thy people also *shall be* **a** righteous:	3605
61: 2	of our God; to comfort **a** that mourn;	3605
61: 9	**a** that see them shall acknowledge them,	3605
61:11	praise to spring forth before **a** the nations.	3605
62: 2	thy righteousness, and **a** kings thy glory:	3605
63: 3	garments, and I will stain **a** my raiment.	3605
63: 7	according to **a** that the LORD hath	3605
63: 9	In **a** their affliction he was afflicted,	3605
63: 9	and carried them **a** the days of old.	3605
64: 6	we are **a** as an unclean *thing,* and all our	3605
64: 6	**a** our righteousnesses *are* as filthy rags;	3605
64: 6	we **a** do fade as a leaf; and our iniquities,	3605
64: 8	and we **a** *are* the work of thine hand.	3605
64: 9	we beseech thee, we *are* **a** thy people.	3605
64:11	and **a** our pleasant things are laid waste.	3605
65: 2	I have spread out mine hands **a** the day	3605
65: 5	in my nose, a fire that burneth **a** the day.	3605

Isa		
65: 8	that *I* may not destroy them **a.**	3605
65:12	and ye shall **a** bow down to the slaughter:	3605
65:25	They shall not hurt nor destroy in **a** my	3605
66: 2	For **a** those *things* hath mine hand made,	3605
66: 2	**a** those *things* have been, saith the LORD:	3605
66:10	and be glad with her, **a** ye that love her:	3605
66:10	for joy with her, **a** ye that mourn for her:	3605
66:16	by his sword will the LORD plead with **a**	3605
66:18	that *I* will gather **a** nations and tongues;	3605
66:20	they shall bring **a** your brethren *for* an	3605
66:20	the LORD out of **a** nations upon horses,	3605
66:23	shall **a** flesh come to worship before me,	3605
66:24	they shall be an abhorring unto **a** flesh.	3605

Jer		
1: 7	for thou shalt go to **a** that I shall send thee,	3605
1:14	forth upon **a** the inhabitants of the land.	3605
1:15	I will call **a** the families of the kingdoms of	3605
1:15	against **a** the walls thereof round about,	3605
1:15	and against **a** the cities of Judah.	3605
1:16	against them touching **a** their wickedness,	3605
1:17	speak unto them **a** that I command thee:	3605
2: 3	**a** that devour him shall offend; evil shall	3605
2: 4	and **a** the families of the house of Israel:	3605
2:24	**a** they that seek her will not weary	3605
2:29	ye **a** have transgressed against me, saith	3605
2:34	it by secret search, but upon **a** these.	3605
3: 7	I said after she had done **a** these *things,*	3605
3: 8	for **a** the causes whereby backsliding	3605
3:10	yet for **a** this her treacherous sister Judah	3605
3:17	**a** the nations shall be gathered unto it,	3605
4:24	and **a** the hills moved lightly.	3605
4:25	and **a** the birds of the heavens were fled.	3605
4:26	**a** the cities thereof were broken down at	3605
5:16	open sepulchre, they *are* **a** mighty *men.*	3605
5:19	Wherefore doth the LORD our God **a**	3605
6:15	nay, they were not **at a ashamed,**	954+954
6:28	They *are* **a** grievous revolters, walking	3605
6:28	*are* brass and iron; they *are* **a** corrupters.	3605
7: 2	the word of the LORD, **a** *ye of* Judah,	3605
7:10	We are delivered to do **a** these	3605
7:13	because ye have done **a** these works,	3605
7:15	as I have cast out **a** your brethren, *even*	3605
7:23	walk ye in **a** the ways that I have	3605
7:25	I have even sent unto you **a** my servants	3605
7:27	Therefore thou shalt speak **a** these words	3605
8: 2	the moon, and **a** the host of heaven,	3605
8: 3	death shall be chosen rather than life by **a**	3605
8: 3	which remain in **a** the places whither I	3605
8:12	nay, they were not **at a ashamed,**	954+954
8:16	devoured the land, and **a that is in** it;	4393
9: 2	for they **be a** adulterers, an assembly of	3605
9:25	that I will punish **a** *them which are*	3605
9:26	and **a** *that are* in the utmost corners,	3605
9:26	for **a** *these* nations *are* uncircumcised,	3605
9:26	**a** the house of Israel *are* uncircumcised in	3605
10: 7	forasmuch as among **a** the wise *men* of	3605
10: 7	in **a** their kingdoms, *there is* none like	3605
10: 9	they *are* **a** the work of cunning *men.*	3605
10:16	for he *is* the former of **a** *things;*	3605
10:20	is spoiled, and **a** my cords are broken:	3605
10:21	and **a** their flocks shall be scattered.	3605
11: 4	according to **a** which I command you:	3605
11: 6	Proclaim **a** these words in the cities of	3605
11: 8	I will bring upon them **a** the words of this	3605
11:12	they shall not **save** them **at a** in	3467+3467
12: 1	*wherefore* are **a** they happy that deal very	3605
12: 9	ye, assemble **a** the beasts of the field,	3605
12:12	The spoilers are come upon **a** high places	3605
12:14	Thus saith the LORD against **a** mine evil	3605
13:13	I *will* fill **a** the inhabitants of this land,	3605
13:13	and **a** the inhabitants of Jerusalem,	3605
13:19	Judah shall be carried away captive **a** of it,	3605
14:22	for thou hast made **a** these *things.*	3605
15: 4	I will cause them to be removed into **a**	3605
15:13	*that* for **a** thy sins, even in all thy borders.	3605
15:13	*that* for all thy sins, even in **a** thy borders.	3605
16:10	when thou shalt shew this people **a** these	3605
16:10	Wherefore hath the LORD pronounced **a**	3605
16:15	from **a** the lands whither he had driven	3605
16:17	For mine eyes *are* upon **a** their ways:	3605
17: 3	*and* **a** thy treasures to the spoil,	3605
17: 3	places for sin, throughout **a** thy borders.	3605
17: 9	The heart *is* deceitful above **a** *things,*	3605
17:13	**a** that forsake thee shall be ashamed,	3605
17:19	go out, and in **a** the gates of Jerusalem;	3605
17:20	**a** Judah, and all the inhabitants of	3605
17:20	and **a** the inhabitants of Jerusalem,	3605
18:23	thou knowest **a** their counsel against me	3605
19: 8	and hiss because of **a** the plagues thereof.	3605
19:13	of the houses upon whose roofs they	3605
19:13	burnt incense unto **a** the host of heaven,	3605
19:14	LORD's house; and said to **a** the people,	3605
19:15	upon **a** her towns all the evil that I have	3605
19:15	upon all her towns **a** the evil that I have	3605
20: 4	a terror to thyself, and to **a** thy friends:	3605
20: 4	and I will give **a** Judah into the hand of	3605
20: 5	Moreover I will deliver **a** the strength of	3605
20: 5	the labours thereof, and all the precious	3605
20: 5	the precious things thereof, and all	3605
20: 5	the treasures of the kings of Judah will I	3605
20: 6	a that dwell in thine house shall go into	3605
20: 6	be buried there, thou, and **a** thy friends,	3605
20:10	**A** my familiars watched for my halting,	3605
21: 2	us according to **a** his wondrous works,	3605
21:14	it shall devour **a things** round about it.	3605
22:20	passages: for **a** thy lovers are destroyed.	3605

Jer		
22:22	The wind shall eat up **a** thy pastors,	3605
22:22	and confounded for **a** thy wickedness.	3605
23: 3	gather the remnant of my flock out of **a**	3605
23: 8	from **a** countries whither I had driven	3605
23: 9	of the prophets; **a** my bones shake;	3605
23:14	they are **a** of them unto me as Sodom,	3605
23:15	is profaneness gone forth into **a** the land.	3605
23:32	shall not **profit** this people **at a,**	3276+3276
24: 9	I will deliver them to be removed into **a**	3605
24: 9	in **a** places whither I shall drive them.	3605
25: 1	**a** the people of Judah in the fourth year of	3605
25: 2	prophet spake unto **a** the people of Judah,	3605
25: 2	to **a** the inhabitants of Jerusalem, saying,	3605
25: 4	the LORD hath sent unto you **a** his	3605
25: 9	and take **a** the families of the north,	3605
25: 9	against **a** these nations round about,	3605
25:13	I will bring upon that land **a** my words	3605
25:13	*even* **a** that is written in this book, which	3605
25:13	which Jeremiah hath prophesied against **a**	3605
25:15	cause **a** the nations, to whom I send thee,	3605
25:17	made **a** the nations to drink, unto whom	3605
25:19	and his princes, and **a** his people;	3605
25:20	**a** the mingled people, and all the kings of	3605
25:20	**a** the kings of the land of Uz, and all	3605
25:20	**a** the kings of the land of the Philistines,	3605
25:22	**a** the kings of Tyrus, and all the kings of	3605
25:22	**a** the kings of Zidon, and the kings of	3605
25:23	and **a** *that are* in the utmost corners,	3605
25:24	**a** the kings of Arabia, and all the kings of	3605
25:24	**a** the kings of the mingled people that	3605
25:25	**a** the kings of Zimri, and all the kings of	3605
25:25	**a** the kings of Elam, and all the kings of	3605
25:25	of Elam, and **a** the kings of the Medes,	3605
25:26	**a** the kings of the north, far and near,	3605
25:26	and **a** the kingdoms of the world,	3605
25:29	for I *will* call for a sword upon **a**	3605
25:30	Therefore prophesy thou against them **a**	3605
25:30	as they that tread *the grapes,* against **a**	3605
25:31	the nations, he *will* plead with **a** flesh;	3605
26: 2	and speak unto **a** the cities of Judah,	3605
26: 2	**a** the words that I command thee to speak	3605
26: 6	will make this city a curse to **a** the nations	3605
26: 7	**a** the people heard Jeremiah speaking	3605
26: 8	**a** that the LORD had commanded *him* to	3605
26: 8	*him* to speak unto **a** the people,	3605
26: 8	the prophets and **a** the people took him,	3605
26: 9	**a** the people were gathered against	3605
26:11	unto the princes and to **a** the people,	3605
26:12	Then spake Jeremiah unto **a** the princes	3605
26:12	unto all the princes and to **a** the people,	3605
26:12	against this city **a** the words that ye have	3605
26:15	you to speak **a** these words in your ears.	3605
26:16	**a** the people unto the priests and to	3605
26:17	spake to **a** the assembly of the people,	3605
26:18	spake to **a** the people of Judah, saying,	3605
26:19	and **a** Judah put him at all to death?	3605
26:19	all Judah **put** him **at a to death?**	4191+4191
26:20	against this land according to **a** the words	3605
26:21	**a** his mighty *men,* and all the princes,	3605
26:21	all his mighty *men,* and **a** the princes,	3605
27: 6	now have I given **a** these lands into	3605
27: 7	**a** nations shall serve him, and his son,	3605
27:12	king of Judah according to **a** these words,	3605
27:16	I spake to the priests and to **a** this people,	3605
27:20	and **a** the nobles of Judah and Jerusalem;	3605
28: 1	presence of the priests and of **a** the people,	3605
28: 3	place **a** the vessels of the LORD's house,	3605
28: 4	with **a** the captives of Judah, that went	3605
28: 5	in the presence of **a** the people that stood	3605
28: 6	**a** that is carried away captive,	3605
28: 7	thine ears, and in the ears of **a** the people.	3605
28:11	Hananiah spake in the presence of **a**	3605
28:11	**a** nations within the space of two full	3605
28:14	have put a yoke of iron upon the neck of **a**	3605
29: 1	to **a** the people whom Nebuchadnezzar	3605
29: 4	unto **a** that are carried away captives,	3605
29:13	when ye shall search for me with **a**	3605
29:14	I will gather you from **a** the nations,	3605
29:14	from **a** the places whither I have driven	3605
29:16	of **a** the people that dwelleth in this city,	3605
29:18	will deliver them to be removed to **a**	3605
29:18	**a** the nations whither I have driven	3605
29:20	word of the LORD, **a** *ye of* the captivity,	3605
29:22	of them shall be taken up a curse by **a**	3605
29:25	unto **a** the people that *are* at Jerusalem,	3605
29:25	the priest, and to **a** the priests, saying,	3605
29:31	Send to **a** them of the captivity, saying,	3605
30: 2	Write thee **a** the words that I have spoken	3605
30: 6	and **a** faces are turned into paleness?	3605
30:11	though I make a full end of **a** nations	3605
30:14	**A** thy lovers have forgotten thee; they	3605
30:16	Therefore **a** they that devour thee shall be	3605
30:16	thine adversaries, every one of them,	3605
30:16	**a** that prey upon thee will I give for a prey	3605
30:20	and I will punish **a** that oppress them.	3605
31: 1	I be the God of **a** the families of Israel,	3605
31:12	shall not sorrow **any more at a.**	3254+5750
31:24	in **a** the cities thereof together,	3605
31:34	for they shall **a** know me, from the least	3605
31:37	I will also cast off **a** the seed of Israel for	3605
31:37	seed of Israel for **a** that they have done,	3605
31:40	the fields unto the brook of Kidron,	3605
32:12	before **a** the Jews that sat in the court of	3605
32:19	for thine eyes *are* open upon **a** the ways	3605
32:23	they have done nothing of **a** that thou	3605

A

Jer	32:23 thou hast caused **a** this evil to come upon 3605
	32:27 I **am** the Lord, the God of **a** flesh: 3605
	32:32 Because of **a** the evil of the children of 3605
	32:37 I **will** gather them out of **a** countries, 3605
	32:42 Like as I have brought **a** this great evil 3605
	32:42 will I bring upon them **a** the good that I 3605
	33: 5 a whose wickedness I have hid my face 3605
	33: 8 I will cleanse them from **a** their iniquity, 3605
	33: 8 I will pardon **a** their iniquities, 3605
	33: 9 honour before **a** the nations of the earth, 3605
	33: 9 which shall hear **a** the good that I do unto 3605
	33: 9 and tremble for **a** the goodness 3605
	33: 9 for a the prosperity that I procure unto it. 3605
	33:12 without beast, and in **a** the cities thereof, 3605
	34: 1 a his army, and all the kingdoms of 3605
	34: 1 a the kingdoms of the earth of his 3605
	34: 1 a the people, fought against Jerusalem, 3605
	34: 1 and against **a** the cities thereof, saying, 3605
	34: 6 Jeremiah the prophet spake **a** these words 3605
	34: 7 against **a** the cities of Judah that were left, 3605
	34: 8 a the people which *were* at Jerusalem, 3605
	34:10 when **a** the princes, and all the people, 3605
	34:10 when all the princes, and **a** the people, 3605
	34:17 I will make you to be removed into **a** 3605
	34:19 the priests, and **a** the people of the land, 3605
	35: 3 a his sons, and the whole house of 3605
	35: 7 but **a** your days ye shall dwell in tents; 3605
	35: 8 our father in **a** that he hath charged us, 3605
	35: 8 drink no wine **a** our days, we, our wives, 3605
	35:10 according to **a** that Jonadab our father 3605
	35:15 I have sent also unto you **a** my servants 3605
	35:17 upon **a** the inhabitants of Jerusalem all 3605
	35:17 upon all the inhabitants of Jerusalem **a** 3605
	35:18 kept **a** his precepts, and done according 3605
	35:18 done according unto **a** that he hath 3605
	36: 2 therein **a** the words that I have spoken 3605
	36: 2 against Judah, and against **a** the nations, 3605
	36: 3 a the evil which I purpose to do unto 3605
	36: 4 wrote from the mouth of Jeremiah **a** 3605
	36: 6 also thou shalt read them in the ears of **a** 3605
	36: 8 the son of Neriah did according to **a** 3605
	36: 9 the Lord *to* **a** the people in Jerusalem, 3605
	36: 9 *to* **a** the people that came from the cities 3605
	36:10 in the ears of **a** the people. 3605
	36:11 had heard out of the book **a** the words of 3605
	36:12 lo, the princes sat there, *even* Elishama 3605
	36:12 the son of Hananiah, and **a** the princes. 3605
	36:13 Michaiah declared unto them **a** the words 3605
	36:14 Therefore **a** the princes sent Jehudi the 3605
	36:16 it came to pass when they had heard **a** 3605
	36:16 We will surely tell the king of **a** these 3605
	36:17 How didst thou write **a** these words at his 3605
	36:18 He pronounced **a** these words unto me 3605
	36:20 told the words in the ears of the king. 3605
	36:21 in the ears of **a** the princes which stood 3605
	36:23 until a the roll was consumed in the fire 3605
	36:24 nor any of his servants that heard **a** these 3605
	36:28 write in it **a** the former words that were 3605
	36:31 a the evil that I have pronounced against 3605
	36:32 a the words of the book which Jehoiakim 3605
	37:21 until **a** the bread in the city were spent. 3605
	38: 1 Jeremiah had spoken unto **a** the people, 3605
	38: 4 the hands of **a** the people, in speaking 3605
	38: 9 these men have done evil in **a** that they 3605
	38:22 a the women that are left in the king of 3605
	38:23 So they *shall* bring out **a** thy wives and 3605
	38:27 came **a** the princes unto Jeremiah, 3605
	38:27 he told them according to **a** these words 3605
	39: 1 and **a** his army against Jerusalem, 3605
	39: 3 the princes of the king of Babylon came 3605
	39: 3 with **a** the residue of the princes of the 3605
	39: 4 a the men of war, then they fled, 3605
	39: 6 also the king of Babylon slew **a** the nobles 3605
	39:13 and **a** the king of Babylon's princes; 3605
	40: 1 a that were carried away captive of 3605
	40: 4 a the land *is* before thee: whither it 3605
	40: 7 *Now* when **a** the captains of the forces 3605
	40:11 Likewise when **a** the Jews, that *were* in 3605
	40:11 in Edom, and that *were* in **a** the countries, 3605
	40:12 Even **a** the Jews returned out of all places 3605
	40:12 Even all the Jews returned out of **a** places 3605
	40:13 a the captains of the forces that *were* in 3605
	40:15 that **a** the Jews which are gathered unto 3605
	41: 3 Ishmael also slew **a** the Jews that were 3605
	41: 6 weeping **a** along as he went: 1980+1980
	41: 9 Now the pit wherein Ishmael had cast **a** 3605
	41:10 Ishmael carried away captive **a** the residue 3605
	41:10 and **a** the people that remained in Mizpah, 3605
	41:11 a the captains of the forces that *were* with 3605
	41:11 heard of **a** the evil that Ishmael the son of 3605
	41:12 they took **a** the men, and went to fight 3605
	41:13 *that* when **a** the people which *were* with 3605
	41:13 a the captains of the forces that *were* with 3605
	41:14 So **a** the people that Ishmael had carried 3605
	41:16 a the captains of the forces that *were* with 3605
	41:16 a the remnant of the people whom he had 3605
	42: 1 a the captains of the forces, 3605
	42: 1 a the people from the least even unto 3605
	42: 2 Lord thy God, *even* for **a** this remnant; 3605
	42: 5 if we do not even according to **a** things 3605
	42: 8 a the captains of the forces which *were* 3605
	42: 8 a the people from the least even to 3605
	42:17 So shall it be with **a** the men that set their 3605
	42:20 according unto **a** that the Lord our God 3605
	43: 1 a the people all the words of the Lord 3605

Jer	43: 1 a the words of the Lord their God, 3605
	43: 1 sent him to them, *even* **a** these words; 3605
	43: 2 the proud men, saying unto Jeremiah, 3605
	43: 4 a the captains of the forces, and all 3605
	43: 4 captains of the forces, and **a** the people, 3605
	43: 5 a the captains of the forces, took all 3605
	43: 5 the forces, took **a** the remnant of Judah, 3605
	43: 5 that were returned from **a** nations, 3605
	44: 1 a the Jews which dwell in the land of 3605
	44: 2 Ye have seen **a** the evil that I have 3605
	44: 2 and upon **a** the cities of Judah; 3605
	44: 8 Howbeit I sent unto you **a** my servants 3605
	44: 8 a reproach among **a** the nations of 3605
	44:11 against you for evil, and to cut off **a** Judah. 3605
	44:12 they shall **a** be consumed, *and* fall in 3605
	44:15 a the men which knew that their wives 3605
	44:15 a the women that stood *by,* a great 3605
	44:15 even **a** the people that dwelt in the land 3605
	44:18 we have wanted **a** *things,* and have been 3605
	44:20 Jeremiah said unto **a** the people, to 3605
	44:20 to **a** the people which had given him *that* 3605
	44:24 Jeremiah said unto **a** the people, 3605
	44:24 to **a** the women, Hear the word of 3605
	44:24 a Judah that *are* in the land of Egypt: 3605
	44:26 a Judah that dwell in the land of Egypt; 3605
	44:26 any man of Judah in **a** the land of Egypt, 3605
	44:27 a the men of Judah that *are* in the land of 3605
	44:28 a the remnant of Judah, that are gone into 3605
	45: 5 for behold, I *will* bring evil upon **a** flesh, 3605
	45: 5 thy life will I give unto thee for a prey in **a** 3605
	46:25 Pharaoh, and **a** them that trust in him: NIH
	46:28 for I will make a full end of **a** the nations 3605
	47: 2 overflow the land, and **a** that is therein; 4393
	47: 2 a the inhabitants of the land shall howl. 3605
	47: 4 Because of the day that cometh to spoil **a** 3605
	48:17 A ye that are about him, bemoan him; 3605
	48:17 a ye that know his name, say, How is 3605
	48:24 upon **a** the cities of the land of Moab, far 3605
	48:31 for Moab, and I will cry out for **a** Moab; 3605
	48:37 upon **a** the hands *shall be* cuttings, 3605
	48:38 generally upon **a** the housetops of Moab, 3605
	48:39 and a dismaying to **a** them about him. 3605
	49: 5 of hosts, from **a** those that be about thee; 3605
	49:13 the cities thereof shall be perpetual 3605
	49:17 and shall hiss at **a** the plagues thereof. 3605
	49:26 the men of war shall be cut off in that 3605
	49:29 and **a** their vessels, and their camels; 3605
	49:32 I will scatter into **a** winds them *that are* 3605
	49:32 I will bring their calamity from **a** sides 3605
	49:36 will scatter them towards **a** those winds; 3605
	50: 7 A that found them have devoured them: 3605
	50:10 a that spoil her shall be satisfied, saith 3605
	50:13 be astonished, and hiss at **a** her plagues. 3605
	50:14 a ye that bend the bow, shoot at her, 3605
	50:21 do according to **a** that I have commanded 3605
	50:27 Slay **a** her bullocks; let them go down to 3605
	50:29 a ye that bend the bow, camp against it 3605
	50:29 according to **a** that she hath done, do unto 3605
	50:30 her men of war shall be cut off in that 3605
	50:32 and it shall devour **a** round about him. 3605
	50:33 a that took them captives held them fast; 3605
	50:37 upon **a** the mingled people that *are* in 3605
	51: 3 young men; destroy ye utterly **a** her host. 3605
	51: 7 that made **a** the earth drunken: 3605
	51:19 for he *is* the former of **a** *things:* 3605
	51:24 to **a** the inhabitants of Chaldea all their 3605
	51:24 all the inhabitants of Chaldea **a** their evil 3605
	51:25 the Lord, which destroyest **a** the earth: 3605
	51:28 the rulers thereof, and all the land of his 3605
	51:28 and **a** the land of his dominion. 3605
	51:47 her slain shall fall in the midst of her. 3605
	51:48 and the earth, and **a** that *is* therein, 3605
	51:49 Babylon shall fall the slain of **a** the earth. 3605
	51:52 through **a** her land the wounded shall 3605
	51:60 So Jeremiah wrote in a book **a** the evil 3605
	51:60 *even* **a** these words that are written 3605
	51:61 shalt see, and shalt read **a** these words; 3605
	52: 2 according to **a** that Jehoiakim had done. 3605
	52: 4 he and **a** his army, against Jerusalem, 3605
	52: 7 the men of war fled, and went forth 3605
	52: 8 and **a** his army was scattered from him. 3605
	52:10 he slew also **a** the princes of Judah in 3605
	52:13 the houses of Jerusalem, and all 3605
	52:13 the houses of the great *men,* burnt he 3605
	52:14 the army of the Chaldeans, that *were* 3605
	52:14 brake down **a** the walls of Jerusalem round 3605
	52:17 and carried **a** the brass of them to Babylon. 3605
	52:18 the vessels of brass wherewith they 3605
	52:20 the brass of **a** these vessels was without 3605
	52:22 the chapiters round about, **a** of brass. 3605
	52:23 the pomegranates upon the network 3605
	52:30 the persons *were* four thousand 3605
	52:33 he did continually eat bread before him **a** 3605
	52:34 the day of his death, **a** the days of his life. 3605
La	1: 2 among **a** her lovers she hath none to 3605
	1: 2 a her friends have dealt treacherously 3605
	1: 3 a her persecutors overtook her between 3605
	1: 4 a her gates are desolate: her priests sigh: 3605
	1: 6 from the daughter of Zion **a** her beauty is 3605
	1: 7 of her miseries **a** her pleasant things that 3605
	1: 8 a that honoured her despise her, because 3605
	1:10 out his hand upon **a** her pleasant things: 3605
	1:11 A her people sigh, they seek bread; 3605
	1:12 *Is it* nothing to you, **a** ye that pass by? 3605
	1:13 made me desolate *and* faint **a** the day. 3605

La	1:15 The Lord hath trodden under foot **a** my 3605
	1:18 you, **a** people, and behold my sorrow: 3605
	1:21 a mine enemies have heard of my trouble; 3605
	1:22 Let **a** their wickedness come before thee; 3605
	1:22 as thou hast done unto me for **a** my 3605
	2: 2 The Lord hath swallowed up **a** 3605
	2: 3 He hath cut off in *his* fierce anger **a** 3605
	2: 4 slew **a** *that were* pleasant to the eye, in 3605
	2: 5 he hath swallowed up **a** her palaces: 3605
	2:15 A that pass by clap *their* hands at thee; 3605
	2:16 A thine enemies have opened their mouth 3605
	3: 3 he turneth his hand *against me* **a** the day. 3605
	3:14 I was a derision to **a** my people; *and* 3605
	3:14 to all my people; *and* their song **a** the day. 3605
	3:34 To crush under his feet **a** the prisoners of 3605
	3:46 A our enemies have opened their mouths 3605
	3:51 because of **a** the daughters of my city. 3605
	3:60 Thou hast seen **a** their vengeance *and* 3605
	3:60 *and* **a** their imaginations against me. 3605
	3:61 *and a* their imaginations against me; 3605
	3:62 and their device against me **a** the day. 3605
	4:12 and **a** the inhabitants of the world, 3605
Eze	3: 7 for **a** the house of Israel *are* impudent 3605
	3:10 a my words that I shall speak unto thee 3605
	5: 4 *for* thereof shall a fire come forth into **a** 3605
	5: 9 the like, because of **a** thine abominations. 3605
	5:10 of thee will I scatter into **a** the winds. 3605
	5:11 thou hast defiled my sanctuary with **a** thy 3605
	5:11 with **a** thine abominations, therefore will 3605
	5:12 I will scatter a third *part* into **a** the winds, 3605
	5:14 about thee, in the sight of **a** that pass by. 3605
	6: 6 In **a** your dwelling places the cities shall 3605
	6: 9 have committed in **a** their abominations. 3605
	6:11 Alas for **a** the evil abominations of 3605
	6:13 in **a** the tops of the mountains, 3605
	6:13 did offer sweet savour to **a** their idols. 3605
	6:14 toward Diblath, in **a** their habitations: 3605
	7: 3 will recompense upon thee **a** thine 3605
	7: 8 will recompense thee for **a** thine 3605
	7:12 for wrath *is* upon **a** the multitude thereof. 3605
	7:14 blown the trumpet, even to make **a** ready; 3605
	7:14 for my wrath *is* upon **a** the multitude 3605
	7:16 a of them mourning, every one for his 3605
	7:17 A hands shall be feeble, and all knees 3605
	7:17 and **a** knees shall be weak *as* water. 3605
	7:18 shame *shall* be upon **a** faces, 3605
	7:18 all faces, and baldness upon **a** their heads. 3605
	8:10 and **a** the idols of the house of Israel, 3605
	9: 4 cry for **a** the abominations that be done 3605
	9: 8 *wilt* thou destroy **a** the residue of Israel in 3605
	11:15 and **a** the house of Israel wholly, 3605
	11:18 shall take away **a** the detestable things 3605
	11:18 a the abominations thereof from thence. 3605
	11:25 I spake unto them of the captivity **a** 3605
	12:10 a the house of Israel that *are* among them. 3605
	12:14 I will scatter toward every wind **a** that *are* 3605
	12:14 about him to help him, and **a** his bands; 3605
	12:16 they may declare **a** their abominations. 3605
	12:19 may be desolate from **a** that is therein, 4393
	12:19 the violence of **a** them that dwell therein. 3605
	13:18 Woe to *the women* that sew pillows to **a** 3605
	14: 3 I be **inquired of at a** by them? 1875+1875
	14: 5 they are estranged from me through 3605
	14: 6 turn away your faces from **a** your 3605
	14:11 neither be polluted any more with **a** their 3605
	14:22 concerning **a** that I have brought upon 3605
	14:23 without cause **a** that I have done in it, 3605
	16: 4 *thee;* thou wast not **salted at a,** 4414+4414
	16: 4 salted at all, nor **swaddled at a.** 2853+2853
	16:22 a thine abominations and thy whoredoms 3605
	16:23 it came to pass after **a** thy wickedness, 3605
	16:30 seeing thou doest **a** these *things,* the work 3605
	16:33 They give gifts to **a** whores: but thou 3605
	16:33 thou givest thy gifts to **a** thy lovers, 3605
	16:36 with **a** the idols of thy abominations, 3605
	16:37 therefore, I will gather **a** thy lovers, 3605
	16:37 a *them* that thou hast loved, with all 3605
	16:37 with **a** *them* that thou hast hated; 3605
	16:37 that they may see **a** thy nakedness. 3605
	16:43 hast fretted me in **a** these *things;* behold 3605
	16:43 *this* lewdness above **a** thine abominations. 3605
	16:47 corrupted more than they in **a** thy ways. 3605
	16:51 hast justified thy sisters in **a** thine 3605
	16:54 mayest be confounded in **a** that thou hast 3605
	16:57 a *that are* round about her, the daughters 3605
	16:63 when I am pacified toward thee for **a** that 3605
	17: 9 shall wither *in* **a** the leaves of her spring, 3605
	17:18 hath done **a** these *things,* he shall not 3605
	17:21 a his fugitives with all his bands shall fall 3605
	17:21 all his fugitives with **a** his bands shall fall 3605
	17:21 remain shall be scattered towards **a** winds: 3605
	17:23 under it shall dwell a fowl of every wing; 3605
	17:24 a the trees of the field shall know that I 3605
	18: 4 Behold, **a** souls *are* mine; as the soul of 3605
	18:13 he hath done **a** these abominations; 3605
	18:14 that seeth **a** his father's sins which he 3605
	18:19 hath kept **a** my statutes, and hath done 3605
	18:21 if the wicked will turn from **a** his sins that 3605
	18:21 keep **a** my statutes, and do that which is 3605
	18:22 A his transgressions that he hath 3605
	18:23 Have I **any pleasure at a** that 2654+2654
	18:24 doeth according to **a** the abominations 3605
	18:24 a his righteousness that he hath done 3605
	18:28 turneth away from **a** his transgressions 3605
	18:30 *yourselves* from **a** your transgressions; 3605

A

Eze 18:31 Cast away from you **a** your transgressions, 3605
20: 6 and honey, which *is* the glory of **a** lands: 3605
20:15 and honey, which *is* the glory of **a** lands; 3605
20:26 through *the fire* a that openeth the womb, 3605
20:28 **a** the thick trees, and they offered there 3605
20:31 ye pollute yourselves with **a** your idols, 3605
20:32 into your mind shall not **be at a,** 1961+1961
20:40 there shall **a** the house of Israel, 3605
20:40 of Israel, **a** of them in the land, serve me: 3605
20:40 of your oblations, with **a** your holy *things.* 3605
20:43 **a** your doings, wherein ye have been 3605
20:43 for **a** your evils that ye have committed. 3605
20:47 **a** faces from the south to the north shall 3605
20:48 **a** flesh shall see that I the LORD have 3605
21: 4 against **a** flesh from the south *to* the north: 3605
21: 5 That **a** flesh may know that I the LORD 3605
21: 7 **a** hands shall be feeble, and every spirit 3605
21: 7 and **a** knees shall be weak *as* water: 3605
21:12 it *shall be* upon **a** the princes of Israel: 3605
21:15 I have set the point of the sword against **a** 3605
21:24 that in **a** your doings your sins do appear; 3605
22: 2 thou shalt shew her **a** her abominations. 3605
22: 4 the heathen, and a mocking to **a** countries. 3605
22:18 **a** they *are* brass, and tin, and iron, 3605
22:19 Because ye are **a** become dross, 3605
23: 6 rulers, **a** of them desirable young men, 3605
23: 7 *with* **a** them *that were* the chosen men of 3605
23: 7 Assyria, and with **a** *on* whom she doted: 3605
23: 7 with **a** their idols she defiled herself. 3605
23:12 **a** of them desirable young men. 3605
23:15 their heads, **a** of them princes to look to, 3605
23:23 **a** the Chaldeans, Pekod, and Shoa, 3605
23:23 and Koa, **a** the Assyrians with them: 3605
23:23 **a** of them desirable young men, captains 3605
23:23 renowned, **a** of them riding upon horses. 3605
23:29 shall take *away* **a** thy labour, 3605
23:48 that **a** women may be taught not to do 3605
24:24 according to **a** that he hath done shall ye 3605
25: 6 rejoiced in heart with **a** thy despite against 3605
25: 8 the house of Judah *is* like unto **a** 3605
26:11 horses shall he tread down **a** thy streets: 3605
26:16 the princes of the sea shall come down 3605
26:17 which cause their terror *to be* on **a** that 3605
27: 5 They have made **a** thy *ship* boards of fir 3605
27: 9 **a** the ships of the sea with their mariners 3605
27:12 reason of the multitude of **a** *kind of* riches; 3605
27:18 thy making, for the multitude of **a** riches; 3605
27:21 Arabia, and the princes of Kedar, 3605
27:22 they occupied in thy fairs with chief of **a** 3605
27:22 and with **a** precious stones, and gold. 3605
27:24 *were* thy merchants in **a sorts of things,** 4360
27:27 **a** thy men of war, that *are* in thee, 3605
27:27 in **a** thy company which *is* in the midst of 3605
27:29 And **a** that handle the oar, the mariners, 3605
27:29 the mariners, *and* **a** the pilots of the sea, 3605
27:34 **a** thy company in the midst of thee shall 3605
27:35 **A** the inhabitants of the isles shall be 3605
28:18 in the sight of **a** them that behold thee. 3605
28:19 **A** they that know thee among the people 3605
28:24 nor *any* grieving thorn of **a** *that are* round 3605
28:26 when I have executed judgments upon **a** 3605
29: 2 prophesy against him, and against **a** Egypt: 3605
29: 4 **a** the fish of thy rivers shall stick unto thy 3605
29: 5 thee and **a** the fish of thy rivers: 3605
29: 6 **a** the inhabitants of Egypt shall know that 3605
29: 7 didst break, and rent **a** their shoulder: 3605
29: 7 and madest **a** their loins to be at a stand. 3605
30: 5 **a** the mingled people, and Chub, 3605
30: 8 and *when* **a** her helpers shall be destroyed. 3605
30:12 **a that is therein,** by the hand of strangers: 4393
31: 4 sent out her little rivers unto **a** the trees of 3605
31: 5 Therefore his height was exalted above **a** 3605
31: 6 **A** the fowls of heaven made their nests in 3605
31: 6 under his branches did **a** the beasts of 3605
31: 6 under his shadow dwelt **a** great nations. 3605
31: 9 so that **a** the trees of Eden, that *were* in 3605
31:12 in **a** the valleys his branches are fallen, 3605
31:12 his boughs are broken by **a** the rivers of 3605
31:12 **a** the people of the earth are gone down 3605
31:13 Upon his ruin shall **a** the fowls of 3605
31:13 **a** the beasts of the field shall be upon his 3605
31:14 To the end that none of **a** the trees by 3605
31:14 up in their height, **a** that drink water: 3605
31:14 for they are **a** delivered unto death, to 3605
31:15 and **a** the trees of the field fainted for him. 3605
31:16 **a** the trees of Eden, the choice and best of 3605
31:16 and best of Lebanon, **a** that drink water, 3605
31:18 This *is* Pharaoh and **a** his multitude, 3605
32: 4 will cause the fowls of the heaven to 3605
32: 8 **A** the bright lights of heaven will I make 3605
32:12 fall, the terrible of the nations, **a** of them: 3605
32:12 **a** the multitude thereof shall be destroyed. 3605
32:13 I will destroy also **a** the beasts thereof 3605
32:15 when I shall smite **a** them that dwell 3605
32:16 *even* for Egypt, and for **a** her multitude, 3605
32:20 the sword: draw **a** her multitudes. 3605
32:22 Asshur *is* there and **a** her company: 3605
32:22 **a** of them slain, fallen by the sword, 3605
32:23 **a** of them slain, fallen by the sword, 3605
32:24 **a** her multitude round about her grave, 3605
32:24 **a** of them slain, fallen by the sword, 3605
32:25 midst of the slain with **a** her multitude: 3605
32:25 **a** of them uncircumcised, slain by 3605
32:26 *is* Meshech, Tubal, and **a** her multitude: 3605
32:26 **a** of them uncircumcised, slain by 3605

Eze 32:29 *is* Edom, her kings, and **a** her princes, 3605
32:30 north, **a** of them, and all the Zidonians, 3605
32:30 north, all of them, and **a** the Zidonians, 3605
32:31 shall be comforted over **a** his multitude, 3605
32:31 and **a** his army slain by the sword, 3605
32:32 *even* Pharaoh and **a** his multitude, saith 3605
33:13 **a** his righteousnesses shall not be 3605
33:29 of **a** their abominations which they have 3605
34: 5 they became meat to **a** the beasts of 3605
34: 6 My sheep wandered through **a** 3605
34: 6 my flock was scattered upon **a** the face of 3605
34:12 will deliver them out of **a** places where 3605
34:13 in the inhabited places of the country. 3605
34:21 and pusht **a** the diseased with your horns, 3605
35: 8 in thy valleys, and in **a** thy rivers, 3605
35:12 *that* I have heard **a** thy blasphemies which 3605
35:15 O mount Seir, and **a** Idumea, *even* all of it: 3605
35:15 O mount Seir, and all Idumea, *even* **a** of it: 3605
36: 5 of the heathen, and against **a** Idumea, 3605
36: 5 possession with the joy of **a** *their* heart, 3605
36:10 **a** the house of Israel, *even* all of it: 3605
36:10 all the house of Israel, *even* **a** of it: 3605
36:24 gather you out of **a** countries, 3605
36:25 from **a** your filthiness, and from all your 3605
36:25 and from **a** your idols, will I cleanse you. 3605
36:29 I will also save you from **a** your 3605
36:33 have cleansed you from **a** your iniquities, 3605
36:34 it lay desolate in the sight of **a** that 3605
37:16 *for* **a** the house of Israel his companions: 3605
37:22 and one king shall be king to them **a:** 3605
37:22 into two kingdoms **any more at a:** 5750+5750
37:23 I will save them out of **a** their dwelling 3605
37:24 and they **a** shall have one shepherd: 3605
38: 4 and **a** thine army, horses and horsemen, 3605
38: 4 of them clothed with all sorts of *armour,* 3605
38: 4 of them clothed with **a sorts** of *armour,* 4358
38: 4 and shields, **a** of them handling swords: 3605
38: 5 **a** of them *with* shield and helmet: 3605
38: 6 Gomer, and **a** his bands; the house of 3605
38: 6 *of* the north quarters, and **a** his bands: 3605
38: 7 **a** thy company that are assembled unto 3605
38: 8 and they shall dwell safely of **a** of them. 3605
38: 9 **a** thy bands, and many people with thee. 3605
38:11 **a** of them dwelling without walls, 3605
38:13 with **a** the young lions thereof, shall say 3605
38:15 **a** of them riding upon horses, a great 3605
38:20 a creeping things that creep upon the 3605
38:20 and the men that *are* upon the face of 3605
38:21 against him throughout **a** my mountains, 3605
39: 4 **a** thy bands, and the people that *is* with 3605
39:11 shall they bury Gog and **a** his multitude: 3605
39:13 the people of the land shall bury *them;* 3605
39:18 of bullocks, **a** of them fatlings of Bashan. 3605
39:20 with mighty *men,* and *with* **a** men of war, 3605
39:21 **a** the heathen shall see my judgment that 3605
39:23 their enemies: so fell they **a** by the sword. 3605
39:26 **a** their trespasses whereby they have 3605
40: 4 thine heart upon **a** that I shall shew thee; 3605
40: 4 declare **a** that thou seest to the house of 3605
41:17 by **a** the wall round about within 3605
41:19 *it was* made through **a** the house round 3605
42:11 their goings out *were* both according to 3605
43:11 if they be ashamed of **a** that they have 3605
43:11 **a** the forms thereof, and all the ordinances 3605
43:11 **a** the ordinances thereof, and all the forms 3605
43:11 **a** the forms thereof, and all the laws 3605
43:11 the forms thereof, and **a** the laws thereof: 3605
43:11 **a** the ordinances thereof, and do them. 3605
44: 5 hear with thine ears **a** that I say unto thee 3605
44: 5 **a** the ordinances of the house of 3605
44: 5 of the LORD, and **a** the laws thereof; 3605
44: 6 let it suffice you of **a** your abominations, 3605
44: 7 because of **a** your abominations. 3605
44:14 for the service thereof, and for all that 3605
44:14 and for **a** that shall be done therein. 3605
44:24 and my statutes in **a** mine assemblies; 3605
44:30 the first of **a** the firstfruits of all *things,* 3605
44:30 the first of all the firstfruits of **a** *things,* 3605
44:30 of all *things,* and every oblation of **a,** 3605
45: 1 This *shall be* holy in **a** the borders thereof 3605
45:16 **A** the people of the land shall give this 3605
45:17 in the sabbaths in **a** solemnities of 3605
45:22 for **a** the people of the land a bullock *for* **a** 3605
47:12 on that side, shall grow **a** trees for meat, 3605
48:13 **a** the length *shall be* five 3605
48:19 **a** shall serve it out of **a** the tribes of Israel. 3605
48:20 **A** the oblation *shall be* five 3605

Da 1: 4 skilful in **a** wisdom, and cunning in 3605
1:15 fatter in flesh than **a** the children which 3605
1:17 and skill in **a** learning and wisdom: 3605
1:17 Daniel had understanding in **a** visions 3605
1:19 them **a** was found none like Daniel, 3605
1:20 in **a** matters of wisdom *and* understanding 3605
1:20 he found them ten times better than **a** 3605
1:20 *and* astrologers that *were* in **a** his realm. 3605
2:12 commanded to destroy **a** the wise *men* of 3606
2:38 and hath made thee ruler over them **a.** 3606
2:39 which shall bear rule over **a** the earth. 3606
2:40 subdueth **a** *things:* and as iron that 3606
2:40 and as iron that breaketh **a** these, 3606
2:44 in pieces and consume **a** these kingdoms, 3606
2:48 chief of the governors over **a** the wise 3606
3: 2 and **a** the rulers of the provinces, 3606
3: 3 and **a** the rulers of the provinces, 3606
3: 5 psaltery, dulcimer, and **a** kinds of musick, 3606

Da 3: 7 when **a** the people heard the sound of 3606
3: 7 sackbut, psaltery, and **a** kinds of musick, 3606
3: 7 **a** the people, the nations, 3606
3:10 and dulcimer, and **a** kinds of musick, 3606
3:15 and dulcimer, and **a** kinds of musick, 3606
4: 1 unto **a** people, nations, and languages, 3606
4: 1 languages, that dwell in **a** the earth; 3606
4: 6 Therefore made I **a** decree to bring in **a** 3606
4:11 the sight thereof to the end of **a** the earth: 3606
4:12 thereof much, and in it *was* meat for **a:** 3606
4:12 boughs thereof, and **a** flesh was fed of it. 3606
4:18 forasmuch as **a** the wise *men* of my 3606
4:20 and the sight thereof to **a** the earth: 3606
4:21 thereof much, and in it *was* meat for **a;** 3606
4:28 **A** this came upon the king 3606
4:35 **a** the inhabitants of the earth *are* reputed 3606
4:37 **a** whose works *are* truth, and his ways 3606
5: 8 came in **a** the king's wise *men:* 3606
5:19 **a** people, nations, and languages, trembled 3606
5:22 thine heart, though thou knewest **a** this; 3606
5:23 thy breath *is,* and whose *are* **a** thy ways, 3606
6: 7 **A** the presidents of the kingdom, 3606
6:24 brake **a** their bones in pieces or ever they 3606
6:25 king Darius wrote unto **a** people, nations, 3606
6:25 languages, that dwell in **a** the earth; 3606
7: 7 it *was* diverse from **a** the beasts that *were* 3606
7:14 that **a** people, nations, and languages, 3606
7:16 and asked him the truth of **a** this. 3606
7:19 which was diverse from **a** the others, 3606
7:23 which shall be diverse from **a** kingdoms, 3606
7:27 **a** dominions shall serve and obey him. 3606
9: 6 fathers, and to **a** the people of the land. 3605
9: 7 unto **a** Israel, *that are* near, and *that are* 3605
9: 7 through **a** the countries whither thou hast 3605
9:11 Yea, **a** Israel have transgressed thy law, 3605
9:13 law of Moses, **a** this evil is come upon us: 3605
9:14 for the LORD our God *is* righteous in **a** 3605
9:16 O Lord, according to **a** thy righteousness, 3605
9:16 thy people *are become* a reproach to **a** 3605
10: 3 neither did I **anoint** myself at **a,** 5480+5480
11: 2 the fourth shall be far richer than *they* **a:** 3605
11: 2 shall stir up **a** against the realm of Grecia. 3605
11:37 for he shall magnify himself above **a.** 3605
11:43 and over **a** the precious *things* of Egypt: 3605
12: 7 **a** these *things* shall be finished. 3605

Hos 2:11 I will also cause **a** her mirth to cease, 3605
2:11 and her sabbaths, and **a** her solemn feasts. 3605
5: 2 though I *have been* a rebuker of them **a.** 3605
7: 2 hearts *that* I remember **a** their wickedness: 3605
7: 4 They *are* **a** adulterers, as an oven heated 3605
7: 6 their baker sleepeth **a** the night; *in* 3605
7: 7 They are **a** hot as an oven, 3605
7: 7 their judges; **a** their kings are fallen: 3605
7:10 LORD their God, nor seek him for **a** this. 3605
9: 4 **a** that eat thereof shall be polluted: 3605
9: 8 the prophet *is* a snare of a fowler in **a** his 3605
9:15 **A** their wickedness *is* in Gilgal, for there I 3605
9:15 no more: **a** their princes *are* revolters. 3605
10:14 and **a** thy fortresses shall be spoiled, 3605
11: 7 most High, none **a** at would exalt *him.* 3162
12: 8 *in* **a** my labours they shall find none 3605
13: 2 **a** of it the work of the craftsmen: 3605
13:10 where *is any other* that may save thee in **a** 3605
13:15 he shall spoil the treasure of a pleasant 3605
14: 2 Take away **a** iniquity, and receive *us* 3605

Joel 1: 2 and give ear, **a** ye inhabitants of the land. 3605
1: 5 howl, **a** ye drinkers of wine, because of 3605
1:12 *even* **a** the trees of the field, are withered: 3605
1:13 lie **a night** in sackcloth, ye ministers 3885
1:14 **a** the inhabitants of the land *into* the 3605
1:19 flame hath burnt **a** the trees of the field. 3605
2: 1 let **a** the inhabitants of the land tremble: 3605
2: 6 **a** faces shall gather blackness. 3605
2:12 turn ye *even* to me with **a** your heart, 3605
2:28 that I will pour out my spirit upon **a** flesh; 3605
3: 2 I will also gather **a** nations, and will bring 3605
3: 4 and Zidon, and **a** the coasts of Palestine? 3605
3: 9 wake up the mighty *men,* let **a** the men 3605
3:11 **a** ye heathen, and gather yourselves 3605
3:12 for there will I sit to judge **a** the heathen 3605
3:18 the rivers of Judah shall flow *with* 3605

Am 1:11 did cast off **a** pity, and his anger did tear NIH
2: 3 will slay **a** the princes thereof with him, 3605
3: 2 You only have I known of **a** the families 3605
3: 2 I will punish you for **a** your iniquities. 3605
3: 5 and have **taken** nothing at **a?** 3920+3920
4: 6 you cleanness of teeth in **a** your cities, 3605
4: 6 and want of bread in **a** your places: 3605
5:16 Wailing *shall be* in **a** streets; and they 3605
5:16 and they shall say in **a** the highways, Alas! 3605
5:17 in **a** vineyards *shall be* wailing: for I will 3605
6: 8 deliver up the city with **a that is therein.** 4393
7:10 the land is not able to bear **a** his words. 3605
8:10 and **a** your songs into lamentation, 3605
8:10 I will bring up sackcloth upon **a** loins, 3605
9: 1 cut them in the head, **a** of them; and I 3605
9: 5 and **a** that dwell therein shall mourn: 3605
9: 9 I will sift the house of Israel among **a** 3605
9:10 **A** the sinners of my people shall die by 3605
9:12 of **a** the heathen, which are called by my 3605
9:13 sweet wine, and **a** the hills shall melt. 3605

Ob 1: 7 **A** the men of thy confederacy have 3605
1:15 For the day of the LORD *is* near upon **a** 3605
1:16 *so* shall the heathen drink continually, 3605

Jnh 2: 3 **a** thy billows and thy waves passed over 3605

A

Mic
1: 2 Hear, a ye people; hearken, O earth, 3605
1: 2 hearken, O earth, and **a that therein is:** 4393
1: 5 For the transgression of Jacob *is* a this, 3605
1: 7 a the graven images thereof shall be 3605
1: 7 a the hires thereof shall be burnt with 3605
1: 7 and a the idols thereof will I lay desolate: 3605
1:10 ye *it* not at Gath, **weep** ye not at a: 1058+1058
2:12 I will surely assemble, O Jacob, **a** of thee; 3605
3: 7 yea, they shall a cover their lips; for *there* 3605
3: 9 that abhor judgment, and pervert a equity. 3605
4: 5 For a people will walk every one in 3605
5: 9 and a thine enemies shall be cut off. 3605
5:11 and throw down a thy strong holds: 3605
6:16 the works of the house of Ahab, 3605
7: 2 they a lie in wait for blood; they hunt 3605
7:16 and be confounded at a their might: 3605
7:19 thou wilt cast a their sins into the depths 3605

Na
1: 3 will not at a acquit *the wicked:* 5352+5352
1: 4 maketh it dry, and drieth up a the rivers: 3605
1: 5 yea, the world, and a that dwell therein. 3605
2: 9 *and* glory out of a the pleasant furniture. 3605
2:10 much pain *is* in a loins, and the faces of 3605
2:10 the faces of them a gather blackness. 3605
3: 1 it *is* a full *of* lies *and* robbery; the prey 4392
3: 7 that a they that look upon thee shall flee 3605
3:10 dashed in pieces at the top of a the streets: 3605
3:10 a her great *men* were bound in chains. 3605
3:12 **A** thy strong holds *shall be like* fig trees 3605
3:19 a that hear the bruit of thee shall clap 3605

Hab
1: 9 They shall come a for violence: their faces 3605
1:15 They take up a of them with the angle, 3605
2: 5 gathereth unto him a nations, 3605
2: 5 nations, and heapeth unto him a people: 3605
2: 6 Shall not a these take up a parable against 3605
2: 8 a the remnant of the people shall spoil 3605
2: 8 *of* the city, and *of* a that dwell therein. 3605
2:17 *of* the city, and *of* a that dwell therein. 3605
2:19 *there is* no breath at a in the midst of it. 3605
2:20 let a the earth keep silence before him. 3605

Zep
1: 2 I will utterly consume a *things* from off 3605
1: 4 and upon a the inhabitants of Jerusalem; 3605
1: 8 a such as are clothed with strange apparel. 3605
1: 9 In the same day also will I punish a those 3605
1:11 for a the merchant people are cut down; 3605
1:11 down; a they that bear silver are cut off. 3605
1:18 riddance of a them that dwell in the land. 3605
2: 3 ye the LORD, a ye meek of the earth, 3605
2:11 for he will famish the gods of the earth; 3605
2:11 his place, *even* a the isles of the heathen. 3605
2:14 midst of her, a the beasts of the nations: 3605
3: 7 rose early, *and* corrupted a their doings. 3605
3: 8 mine indignation, *even* a my fierce anger: 3605
3: 8 for a the earth shall be devoured with 3605
3: 9 that they may a call upon the name of 3605
3:11 that day shalt thou not be ashamed for a 3605
3:14 be glad and rejoice with a the heart, 3605
3:19 at that time I *will* undo a that afflict thee; 3605
3:20 and a praise among a people of the earth, 3605

Hag
1:11 and upon a the labour of the hands. 3605
1:12 with a the remnant of the people, 3605
1:14 the spirit of a the remnant of the people; 3605
2: 4 be strong, a ye people of the land, saith 3605
2: 7 I will shake a nations, and the desire of all 3605
2: 7 and the desire of a nations shall come: 3605
2:17 with hail *in* a the labours of your hands; 3605

Zec
1:11 a the earth sitteth still, and is at rest. 3605
2:13 Be silent, O a flesh, before the LORD: 3605
4: 2 and behold, a candlestick a of gold, 3605
5: 6 This *is* their resemblance through a 3605
6: 5 standing before the Lord of a the earth. 3605
7: 5 Speak unto a the people of the land, 3605
7: 5 did ye **at a fast** *unto* me, 6684+6684
7:14 scattered them with a whirlwind among a 3605
8:10 for I set a men every one against his 3605
8:12 of this people to possess a these *things.* 3605
8:17 for a these *are things* that I hate, saith 3605
8:23 hold out of a languages of the nations, 3605
9: 1 the eyes of man, as of a the tribes of Israel, 3605
10:11 and a the deeps of the river shall dry up: 3605
11:10 which I had made with a the people. 3605
12: 2 trembling unto a the people round about, 3605
12: 3 a burdensome stone for a people: 3605
12: 3 a that burden themselves with it shall be 3605
12: 3 though a the people of the earth be 3605
12: 6 shall devour a the people round about, 3605
12: 9 I will seek to destroy a the nations that 3605
12:14 **A** the families that remain, every family 3605
13: 8 to pass, *that* in a the land, saith the LORD, 3605
14: 2 For I will gather a nations against 3605
14: 5 God shall come, *and* a the saints with 3605
14: 9 the LORD shall be king over a the earth: 3605
14:10 **A** the land shall be turned as a plain from 3605
14:12 the people that fought against 3605
14:14 the wealth of a the heathen round about 3605
14:15 of a the beasts that shall be in these tents, 3605
14:16 *that* every one that is left of a the nations 3605
14:17 *that* whoso will not come up of a NIH
14:19 the punishment of a nations that come 3605
14:21 a they that sacrifice shall come and take 3605

Mal
2: 9 and base before a the people, 3605
2:10 Have we not a one father? hath not one 3605
3:10 Bring ye a the tithes into the storehouse, 3605
3:12 a nations shall call you blessed: for ye shall 3605
4: 1 a the proud, yea, and all that do wickedly, 3605
4: 1 all the proud, yea, and a that do wickedly, 3605

Mal
4: 4 unto him in Horeb for a Israel, 3605

Mt
1:17 So a the generations from Abraham to 3956
1:22 Now a this was done, that it might be 3650
2: 3 was troubled, and a Jerusalem with him. 3956
2: 4 And when he had gathered a the chief 3956
2:16 the children that were in Bethlehem, 3956
2:16 and in a the coasts thereof, from two years 3956
3: 5 a Judea, and all the region round about 3956
3: 5 and a the region round about Jordan, 3956
3:15 for thus it becometh us to fulfil a 3956
4: 8 sheweth him a the kingdoms of the world, 3956
4: 9 unto him, **A** these *things* will I give thee, 3956
4:23 And Jesus went about a Galilee, 1722+3650
4:23 and healing a manner *of* sickness 3956
4:23 a manner *of* disease among the people. 3956
4:24 And his fame went throughout a Syria: 3956
4:24 they brought unto him a sick people that 3956
5:11 shall say a **manner** of evil against you 3956
5:15 it giveth light unto a that are in the house. 3956
5:18 wise pass from the law, till a be fulfilled. 3956
5:34 But I say unto you, Swear not **at a;** 3654
6:29 That even Solomon in a his glory was not 3956
6:32 (For after a these *things* do the Gentiles 3956
6:32 that ye have need of a these *things.* 537
6:33 a these *things* shall be added unto you. 3956
7:12 Therefore **A** *things* whatsoever ye would 3956
8:16 his word, and healed a that were sick: 3956
9:26 And the fame hereof went abroad into a 3650
9:31 spread abroad his fame in a that country. 3650
9:35 And Jesus went about a the cities 3956
10: 1 and to heal a manner *of* sickness 3956
10: 1 *of* sickness and a manner *of* disease. 3956
10:22 And ye shall be hated of a men for my 3956
10:30 But the very hairs of your head are a 3956
11:13 For a the prophets and the law prophesied 3956
11:27 **A** *things* are delivered unto me of my 3956
11:28 a ye that labour and are heavy laden, and 3956
12:15 followed him, and he healed them a, 3956
12:23 And a the people were amazed, and said, 3956
12:31 a manner *of* sin and blasphemy shall be 3956
13:32 Which indeed is the least of a seeds: 3956
13:34 **A** these *things* spake Jesus unto 3956
13:41 they shall gather out of his kingdom a 3956
13:44 thereof goeth and selleth a that he hath, 3956
13:46 and sold a that he had, and bought it. 3956
13:51 Have ye understood a these *things?* 3956
13:56 And his sisters, are they not a with us? 3956
13:56 then hath this *man* a these *things?* 3956
14:20 And they did a eat, and were filled: 3956
14:35 they sent out into a that country round 3650
14:35 brought unto him a that were diseased; 3956
15:37 And they did a eat, and were filled: 3956
17:11 truly shall first come, and restore a *things.* 3956
18:25 a that he had, and payment to be made. 3956
18:26 patience with me, and I will pay thee a. 3956
18:29 patience with me, and I will pay thee a. 3956
18:31 and told unto their lord a that was done. 3956
18:32 I forgave thee a that debt, because 3956
18:34 he should pay a that was due unto him. 3956
19:11 a men cannot receive this saying, 3956
19:20 **A** these *things* have I kept from my youth 3956
19:26 but with God a *things* are possible. 3956
19:27 we have forsaken a, and followed thee; 3956
20: 6 Why stand ye here a the day idle? 3650
21: 4 **A** this was done, that it might be fulfilled 3650
21:10 a the city was moved, saying, Who is this? 3956
21:12 cast out a them that sold and bought in 3956
21:22 And a *things,* whatsoever ye shall ask in 3956
21:26 the people; for a hold John as a prophet. 3956
21:37 But last of a he sent unto them his son, NIG
22: 4 fatlings *are* killed, and a *things are* ready: 3956
22:10 gathered together a as many as they found, 3956
22:27 And last of a the woman died also. 3956
22:28 she be of the seven? for they a had her. 3956
22:37 Thou shalt love the Lord thy God with a 3650
22:37 and with a thy soul, and with all thy mind. 3650
22:37 and with all thy soul, and with a thy mind. 3650
22:40 On these two commandments hang a 3650
23: 3 **A** therefore whatsoever they bid you 3956
23: 5 But a their works they do for to be seen of 3956
23: 8 *even* Christ; and a ye are brethren. 3956
23:20 sweareth by it, and by a *things* thereon. 3956
23:27 dead *men's* bones, and of a uncleanness. 3956
23:35 That upon you may come a the righteous 3956
23:36 **A** these *things* shall come upon this 3956
24: 2 See ye not a these *things?* verily I say 3956
24: 6 for a *these things* must come to pass, 3956
24: 8 **A** these *are* the beginning of sorrows. 3956
24: 9 ye shall be hated of a nations for my 3956
24:14 a the world for a witness unto all nations; 3650
24:14 all the world for a witness unto a nations; 3956
24:30 then shall a the tribes of the earth mourn, 3956
24:33 when ye shall see a these *things,* know 3956
24:34 not pass, till a these *things* be fulfilled. 3956
24:39 the flood came, and took *them* a away; 537
24:47 That he shall make him ruler over a his 3956
25: 5 they a slumbered and slept. 3956
25: 7 Then a those virgins arose, 3956
25:31 and a the holy angels with him, 3956
25:32 before him shall be gathered a nations: 3956
26: 1 when Jesus had finished a these sayings, 3956
26:27 gave *it* to them, saying, Drink ye a of it; 3956
26:31 **A** ye shall be offended because of me this 3956
26:33 Though a *men* shall be offended because 3956
26:35 Likewise also said a the disciples. 3956

Mt
26:52 for a they that take the sword shall perish 3956
26:56 But a this was done, that the scriptures of 3956
26:56 Then a the disciples forsook him, and fled. 3956
26:59 priests, and elders, and a the council, 3650
26:70 But he denied before *them* a, saying, 3956
27: 1 a the chief priests and elders of the people 3956
27:22 *They* a say unto him, Let him be crucified. 3956
27:25 Then answered a the people, and said, 3956
27:45 over a the land unto the ninth hour. 3956
28: 9 behold, Jesus met them, saying, **A** hail. NIG
28:11 shewed unto the chief priests a the things 537
28:18 **A** power is given unto me in heaven 3956
28:19 Go ye therefore, and teach a nations, 3956
28:20 Teaching them to observe a *things* 3956

Mk
1: 5 And there went out unto him a the land 3956
1: 5 were a baptized of him in the river of 3956
1:27 And they were a amazed, insomuch that 3956
1:28 a the region round about Galilee. 3650
1:32 brought unto him a that were diseased, 3956
1:33 And a the city was gathered together at 3650
1:37 they said unto him, **A** men seek for thee. 3956
1:39 in their synagogues throughout a Galilee, 3650
2:12 up the bed, and went forth before *them* a; 3956
2:12 insomuch that they were a amazed, 3956
2:13 and a the multitude resorted unto him, 3956
3:28 **A** sins shall be forgiven unto the sons of 3956
4:11 a these *things* are done in parables: 3956
4:13 and how then will ye know a parables? 3956
4:31 less than a the seeds that be in the earth: 3956
4:32 and becometh greater than a herbs, 3956
4:34 he expounded a *things* to his disciples. 3956
5:12 And a the devils besought him, saying, 3956
5:20 had done for him: and a men did marvel. 3956
5:26 and had spent a that she had, 3956
5:33 before him, and told him a the truth. 3956
5:40 when he had put *them* a out, he taketh 537
6:30 him a *things,* both what they had done, 3956
6:33 and ran afoot thither out of a cities, 3956
6:39 And he commanded them to make a sit 3956
6:41 the two fishes divided he among *them* a. 3956
6:42 And they did a eat, and were filled. 3956
6:50 For they a saw him, and were troubled. 3956
7: 3 For the Pharisees, and a the Jews, 3956
7:14 And when he had called a the people unto 3956
7:19 out into the draught, purging a meats? 3956
7:23 **A** these evil *things* come from within, 3956
7:37 saying, He hath done a *things* well: 3956
9:12 restoreth a *things;* and how it is written 3956
9:15 And straightway a the people, when they 3956
9:23 *They* a *things are* possible to him that believeth. 3956
9:35 *the same* shall be last of a, and servant of 3956
9:35 same shall be last of all, and servant of a. 3956
10:20 a these have I observed from my youth. 3956
10:27 for with God a *things* are possible. 3956
10:28 we have left a, and have followed thee. 3956
10:44 will be the chiefest, shall be servant of a. 3956
11:11 when he had looked round about upon a 3956
11:17 My house shall be called of a nations 3956
11:18 a the people was astonished at his 3956
11:32 for a *men* counted John, that he was a 537
12:22 left no seed: last of a the woman died also. 3956
12:28 Which is the first commandment of a? 3956
12:29 The first of a the commandments *is,* Hear, 3956
12:30 thou shalt love the Lord thy God with a 3650
12:30 with a thy soul, and with all thy mind, 3650
12:30 and with a thy mind, and with all thy 3650
12:30 with all thy mind, and with a thy strength: 3650
12:33 And to love him with a the heart, 3650
12:33 with a the understanding, and with all 3650
12:33 and with a the soul, and with all 3650
12:33 and with a the strength, and to love *his* 3650
12:33 is more than a whole burnt offerings 3956
12:43 than a they which have cast into 3956
12:44 For a *they* did cast in of their abundance; 3956
12:44 she of her want did cast in a that she had, 3650
12:44 cast in all that she had, *even* a her living. 3650
13: 4 shall be the sign when a these *things* 3956
13:10 must first be published among a nations. 3956
13:13 And ye shall be hated of a *men* for my 3956
13:23 behold, I have foretold you a *things.* 3956
13:30 shall not pass, till a these *things* be done. 3956
13:37 And what I say unto a, I say unto a. 3956
14:23 he gave *it* to them: and they a drank of it. 3956
14:27 **A** ye shall be offended because of me this 3956
14:29 Although a shall be offended, yet *will* not 3956
14:31 in any wise. Likewise also said they a. 3956
14:36 a *things are* possible unto thee; 3956
14:50 And they a forsook him, and fled. 3956
14:53 him were assembled a the chief priests 3956
14:55 a the council sought for witness against 3650
14:64 And they a condemned him to be guilty 3956
16:15 Go ye into a the world, and preach 537

Lk
1: 3 having had perfect understanding of a 3956
1: 6 walking in a the commandments 3956
1:48 henceforth a generations shall call me 3956
1:63 His name is John. And they marvelled a. 3956
1:65 fear came on a that dwelt round about 3956
1:65 a these sayings were noised abroad 3956
1:65 throughout a the hill country of Judea. 3650
1:66 And a they that heard *them* laid *them* up 3956
1:71 and from the hand of a that hate us; 3956
1:75 before him, a the days of our life. 3956
2: 1 that a the world should be taxed. 3956
2: 3 And a went to be taxed, every one into 3956
2:10 of great joy, which shall be to a people. 3956

A

Lk	2:18	And **a** they that heard *it* wondered at	3956
	2:19	But Mary kept **a** these things,	3956
	2:20	praising God for **a** *the* things that they had	3956
	2:31	hast prepared before the face of **a** people;	3956
	2:38	spake of him to **a** them that looked for	3956
	2:39	And when they had performed **a** *things*	537
	2:47	And a that heard him were astonished at	3956
	2:51	mother kept **a** these sayings in her heart.	3956
	3: 3	And he came into **a** the country about	3956
	3: 6	And a flesh shall see the salvation of God.	3956
	3:15	and **a** men mused in their hearts of John,	3956
	3:16	John answered, saying unto them **a**,	537
	3:19	and for **a** the evils which Herod had done,	3956
	3:20	Added yet this above **a**, that he shut up	3956
	3:21	Now when **a** the people were baptized,	537
	4: 5	shewed unto him **a** the kingdoms of	3956
	4: 6	**A** this power will I give thee, and the glory	537
	4: 7	wilt worship me, **a** shall be thine.	3956
	4:13	And when the devil had ended **a**	3956
	4:14	there went out a fame of him through **a**	3650
	4:15	in their synagogues, being glorified of **a**.	3956
	4:20	And the eyes of **a** *them that were* in	3956
	4:22	And **a** bare him witness, and wondered at	3956
	4:25	when great famine was throughout **a**	3956
	4:28	And **a** *they* in the synagogue, when they	3956
	4:36	And they were **a** amazed, and spake	3956
	4:40	they that had *any* sick with divers	3956
	5: 5	we have toiled **a** the night, and have taken	3650
	5: 9	was astonished, and **a** that were with him,	3956
	5:11	brought *their* ships to land, they forsook **a**,	537
	5:26	And they were **a** amazed,	537
	5:28	And he left **a**, rose up, and followed him.	537
	6:10	And looking round about upon them **a**,	3956
	6:12	and continued **a night** in prayer to God.	1273
	6:17	a great multitude of people out of **a** Judea,	3956
	6:19	virtue out of him, and healed *them* **a**.	3956
	6:26	when **a** men shall speak well of you:	3956
	7: 1	Now when he had ended **a** his sayings in	3956
	7:16	And there came a fear on **a**:	537
	7:17	of him went forth throughout **a** Judea,	3650
	7:17	and throughout **a** the region round about.	3956
	7:18	And the disciples of John shewed him of **a**	3956
	7:29	And **a** the people that heard *him*,	3956
	7:35	But wisdom is justified of **a** her children.	3956
	8:40	for they were **a** waiting for him.	3956
	8:43	which had spent **a** *her* living upon	3650
	8:45	When a denied, Peter and they that were	3956
	8:47	she declared unto him before **a** the people	3956
	8:52	**a** wept, and bewailed her: but he said,	3956
	8:54	And he put *them* **a** out, and took her by	3956
	9: 1	them power and authority over **a** devils,	3956
	9: 7	Herod the tetrarch heard of **a** that was	3956
	9:10	told him **a that** they had done.	3745
	9:13	should go and buy meat for **a** this people.	3956
	9:15	they did so, and made *them* **a** sit down.	537
	9:17	And they did eat, and were **a** filled:	3956
	9:23	And he said to *them* **a**, If any *man* will	3956
	9:43	And they were **a** amazed at the mighty	3956
	9:43	But while they wondered every one at **a**	3956
	9:48	for he that is least among you **a**, the same	3956
	10:19	and over **a** the power of the enemy:	3956
	10:22	**A** *things* are delivered to me of my Father:	3956
	10:27	Thou shalt love the Lord thy God with **a**	3650
	10:27	and with **a** thy soul, and with all thy	3650
	10:27	and with **a** thy strength, and with all thy	3650
	10:27	with all thy strength, and with **a** thy mind;	3650
	11:22	he taketh *from him* **a** his **armour** wherein	3833
	11:41	and behold, **a** *things* are clean unto you.	3956
	11:42	tithe the mint and rue and **a** *manner of* herbs,	3956
	11:50	That the blood of **a** the prophets, which	3956
	12: 1	he began to say unto his disciples first of **a**,	NIG
	12: 7	But even the *very* hairs of your head are **a**	3956
	12:18	and there will I bestow **a** my fruits	3956
	12:27	Solomon in **a** his glory was not arrayed	3956
	12:30	For **a** these *things* do the nations of	3956
	12:31	**a** these *things* shall be added unto you.	3956
	12:41	thou this parable unto us, or even to **a**?	3956
	12:44	that he will make him ruler over **a** that he	3956
	13: 2	were sinners above **a** the Galileans,	3956
	13: 3	ye repent, ye shall **a** likewise perish.	3956
	13: 4	think ye that they were sinners above **a**	3956
	13: 5	ye repent, ye shall **a** likewise perish.	3956
	13:17	And when he had said these *things*, **a** his	3956
	13:17	**a** the people rejoiced for all the glorious	3956
	13:17	all the people rejoiced for **a** the glorious	3956
	13:27	depart from me, **a** *ye* workers of iniquity.	3956
	13:28	and Isaac, and Jacob, and **a** the prophets,	3956
	14:17	Come; for **a** *things* are now ready.	3956
	14:18	they **a** with one *consent* began to make	3956
	14:29	not able to finish *it*, **a** that behold *it* begin	3956
	14:33	*he be* of you that forsaketh not **a**	3956
	15: 1	Then drew near unto him **a** the publicans	3956
	15:13	after the younger son gathered **a** together,	537
	15:14	And when he had spent **a**, there arose a	3956
	15:31	ever with me, and **a** that I have is thine.	3956
	16:14	heard **a** these *things:* and they derided	3956
	16:26	And besides **a** this, between us	3956
	17:10	when ye shall have done **a** those *things*	3956
	17:27	the flood came, and destroyed *them* **a**.	537
	17:29	from heaven, and destroyed *them* **a**.	537
	18:12	the week, I give tithes of **a** that I possess.	3956
	18:21	**A** these have I kept from my youth up.	3956
	18:22	Yet lackest thou one *thing:* sell **a** that thou	3956
	18:28	Then Peter said, Lo, we have left **a**,	3956
	18:31	**a** *things* that are written by the prophets	3956

Lk	18:43	and **a** the people, when they saw *it,* gave	3956
	19: 7	And when they saw *it,* they **a** murmured,	537
	19:37	praise God with a loud voice for **a**	3956
	19:48	for **a** the people were very attentive to	537
	20: 6	say, Of men; **a** the people will stone us:	3956
	20:32	Last of **a** the woman died also.	3956
	20:38	but of the living: for **a** live unto him.	3956
	20:40	they durst not ask him any *question at* **a**.	NIG
	20:45	Then in the audience of **a** the people he	3956
	21: 3	widow hath cast in more than *they* **a**:	3956
	21: 4	For **a** these have of their abundance cast	537
	21: 4	she of her penury hath cast in **a** the living	537
	21:12	before **a** these, they shall lay their hands	537
	21:15	which **a** your adversaries shall not be able	3956
	21:17	And ye shall be hated of **a** *men* for my	3956
	21:22	that **a** *things* which are written may be	3956
	21:24	shall be led away captive into **a** nations:	3956
	21:29	Behold the fig tree, and **a** the trees;	3956
	21:32	shall not pass away, till **a** be fulfilled.	3956
	21:35	For as a snare shall it come on **a** them	3956
	21:36	**a** these *things* that shall come to pass,	3956
	21:38	And **a** the people came early in	3956
	22:70	Then said they **a**, Art thou then the Son of	3956
	23: 5	the people, teaching throughout **a** Jewry,	3650
	23:18	And they cried out **a** at once, saying,	3826
	23:44	there was a darkness over **a** the earth until	3650
	23:48	And **a** the people that came together to	3956
	23:49	And **a** his acquaintance, and the women	3956
	24: 9	told **a** these *things* unto the eleven,	3956
	24: 9	*things* unto the eleven, and *to* **a** the rest.	3956
	24:14	And they talked together of **a** these *things*	3956
	24:19	and word before God and **a** the people:	3956
	24:21	And beside **a** this, to day is the third day	3956
	24:25	of heart to believe **a** that the prophets	3956
	24:27	beginning at Moses and **a** the prophets,	3956
	24:27	expounded unto them in **a** the scriptures	3956
	24:44	with you, that **a** *things* must be fulfilled,	3956
	24:47	preached in his name among **a** nations,	3956
Jn	1: 3	**A** *things* were made by him;	3956
	1: 7	that **a** *men* through him might believe.	3956
	1:16	And of his fulness have **a** we received,	3956
	2:15	he drove *them* **a** out of the temple,	3956
	2:24	unto them, because he knew **a** *men,*	3956
	3:26	same baptizeth, and **a** *men* come to him.	3956
	3:31	He that cometh from above is above **a**:	3956
	3:31	he that cometh from heaven is above **a**.	3956
	3:35	and hath given **a** *things* into his hand.	3956
	4:25	when he is come, he will tell us **a** *things.*	3956
	4:29	which told me **a** *things* that ever I did:	3956
	4:39	He told me **a** that ever I did.	3956
	4:45	having seen **a** *the things* that he did at	3956
	5:20	sheweth him **a** *things* that himself doeth:	3956
	5:22	hath committed **a** judgment unto the Son:	3956
	5:23	That **a** *men* should honour the Son, even	3956
	5:28	in the which **a** that are in the graves shall	3956
	6:37	**A** that the Father giveth me shall come to	3956
	6:39	that of **a** which he hath given me I should	3956
	6:45	And they shall be **a** taught of God.	3956
	7:21	I have done one work, and ye **a** marvel.	3956
	8: 2	and **a** the people came unto him;	3956
	10: 8	**A** that ever came before me are thieves	3956
	10:29	which gave them **a**, is greater than **a**;	3956
	10:41	**a** *things* that John spake of this *man* were	3956
	11:48	thus alone, **a** *men* will believe on him.	3956
	11:49	unto them, Ye know **nothing at a**,	3756+3762
	12:32	from the earth, will draw **a** *men* unto me.	3956
	13: 3	Jesus knowing that the Father had given **a**	3956
	13:10	every whit: and ye are clean, but not **a**.	3956
	13:11	therefore said he, Ye are not **a** clean.	3956
	13:18	I speak not of you **a**: I know whom I have	3956
	13:35	By this shall **a** *men* know that ye are my	3956
	14:26	he shall teach you **a** *things,* and bring all	3956
	14:26	and bring **a** *things* to your remembrance,	3956
	15:15	for **a** *things* that I have heard of my Father	3956
	15:21	But **a** these *things* will they do unto you	3956
	16:13	is come, he will guide you into **a** truth:	3956
	16:15	**A** *things* that the Father hath are mine:	3956
	16:30	Now are we sure that thou knowest **a**	3956
	17: 2	thou hast given him power over **a** flesh,	3956
	17: 7	Now they have known that **a** *things*	3956
	17:10	And **a** mine are thine, and thine are mine;	3956
	17:21	That they **a** may be one; as thou, Father,	3956
	18: 4	knowing **a** *things* that should come upon	3956
	18:38	saith unto them, I find in him no fault *at* **a**.	NIG
	18:40	Then cried they **a** again, saying, Not this	3956
	19:11	Thou couldest have no power *at* **a** against	NIG
	19:28	Jesus knowing that **a** *things* were now	3956
	21:11	for **a** there were **so many**, *yet* was not	5118
	21:17	thou knowest **a** *things;* thou knowest that	3956
Ac	1: 1	of **a** that Jesus began both to do and teach,	3956
	1: 8	and in **a** Judea, and in Samaria,	3956
	1:14	These **a** continued with one accord in	3956
	1:18	in the midst, and **a** his bowels gushed out.	3956
	1:19	And it was known unto **a** the dwellers at	3956
	1:21	us **a** the time that the Lord Jesus went in	3956
	1:24	which knowest the hearts of **a** *men,* shew	3956
	2: 1	they were **a** with one accord in one place.	537
	2: 2	filled **a** the house where they were sitting.	3650
	2: 4	they were **a** filled with the Holy Ghost,	537
	2: 7	And they were **a** amazed and marvelled,	3956
	2: 7	are not **a** these which speak Galileans?	3956
	2:12	And they were **a** amazed, and were in	3956
	2:14	of Judea, and **a** *ye* that dwell at Jerusalem,	537
	2:17	I will pour out of my Spirit upon **a** flesh:	3956
	2:32	raised up, whereof we **a** are witnesses.	3956

Ac	2:36	Therefore let **a** the house of Israel know	3956
	2:39	to your children, and to **a** that are afar off,	3956
	2:44	And **a** that believed were together,	3956
	2:44	were together, and had *things* common;	537
	2:45	parted them to **a** *men,* as every *man* had	3956
	2:47	and having favour with **a** the people.	3650
	3: 9	And **a** the people saw him walking	3956
	3:11	**a** the people ran together unto them in	3956
	3:16	perfect soundness in the presence of you **a**.	3956
	3:18	shewed by the mouth of **a** his prophets,	3956
	3:21	**a** *things,* which God hath spoken by	3956
	3:21	a his holy prophets since the world began.	3956
	3:22	shall ye hear in **a** *things* whatsoever he	3956
	3:24	and **a** the prophets from Samuel	3956
	3:25	And in thy seed shall **a** the kindreds of	3956
	4:10	Be it known unto you **a**, and to all	3956
	4:10	unto you all, and to **a** the people of Israel,	3956
	4:16	manifest to **a** them that dwell in Jerusalem;	3956
	4:18	commanded them not to speak **at a** nor	2527
	4:21	for **a** *men* glorified God for that which	3956
	4:23	and reported **a** that the chief priests	3745
	4:24	earth, and the sea, and **a** that in them is:	3956
	4:29	that with a boldness *they* may speak thy	3956
	4:31	and they were **a** filled with the Holy Ghost,	537
	4:32	his own; but they had **a** *things* common.	537
	4:33	and great grace was upon them **a**.	3956
	5: 5	great fear came on **a** them that heard these	3956
	5:11	And great fear came upon **a** the church,	3650
	5:12	they were **a** with one accord in Solomon's	537
	5:17	rose up, and **a** they that were with him,	3956
	5:20	speak in the temple to the people **a**	3956
	5:21	and **a** the senate of the children of Israel,	3956
	5:23	The prison truly found we shut with **a**	3956
	5:34	had in reputation among **a** the people,	3956
	5:36	and **a**, as many as obeyed him,	3956
	5:37	and **a**, *even* as many as obeyed him,	3956
	6:15	And **a** that sat in the council,	537
	7:10	And delivered him out of **a** his afflictions,	3956
	7:10	him governor over Egypt and **a** his house.	3650
	7:11	Now there came a dearth over **a** the land	3650
	7:14	his father Jacob to *him,* and **a** his kindred,	3956
	7:22	And Moses was learned in **a** the wisdom	3956
	7:50	Hath not my hand made **a** these *things?*	3956
	8: 1	they were **a** scattered abroad throughout	3956
	8:10	To whom they **a** gave heed, from the least	3956
	8:27	who had the charge of **a** her treasure,	3956
	8:37	If thou believest with **a** *thine* heart,	3650
	8:40	through he preached in **a** the cities,	3956
	9:14	priests to bind **a** that call on thy name.	3956
	9:21	But **a** that heard *him* were amazed,	3956
	9:26	but they were **a** afraid of him,	3956
	9:31	Then had the churches rest throughout **a**	3956
	9:32	as Peter passed throughout **a** *quarters,* he	3956
	9:35	And **a** that dwelt at Lydda and Saron saw	3956
	9:39	and **a** the widows stood by him weeping,	3956
	9:40	But Peter put *them* **a** forth,	3956
	9:42	And it was known throughout **a** Joppa;	3650
	10: 2	and one that feared God with **a** his house,	3956
	10: 8	And when he had declared **a** these *things*	537
	10:12	Wherein were **a** *manner of* fourfooted	3956
	10:22	of good report among **a** the nation of	3650
	10:33	are we **a** here present before God,	3956
	10:33	to hear **a** *things* that are commanded thee	3956
	10:36	peace by Jesus Christ: (he is Lord of **a**:)	3956
	10:37	which was published throughout **a** Judea,	3650
	10:38	healing **a** that were oppressed of the devil;	3956
	10:39	And we are witnesses of **a** *things* which	3956
	10:41	Not to **a** the people, but unto witnesses	3956
	10:43	To him give **a** the prophets witness,	3956
	10:44	the Holy Ghost fell on **a** them which heard	3956
	11:10	and **a** were drawn up again into heaven.	537
	11:14	and **a** thy house shall be saved.	3956
	11:23	of God, was glad, and exhorted *them* **a**,	3956
	11:28	be great dearth throughout **a** the world:	3650
	12:11	*from* **a** the expectation of the people of	3956
	13:10	O full of **a** subtilty and all mischief,	3956
	13:10	O full of all subtilty and **a** mischief,	3956
	13:10	the devil, *thou* enemy of **a** righteousness,	3956
	13:22	own heart, which shall fulfil **a** my will.	3956
	13:24	of repentance to **a** the people of Israel.	3956
	13:29	And when they had fulfilled **a** that was	537
	13:39	And by him **a** that believe are justified	3956
	13:39	**a** *things, from* which ye could not be	3956
	13:49	was published throughout **a** the region.	3650
	14:15	and the sea, and **a** *things* that are therein:	3956
	14:16	Who in times past suffered **a** nations to	3956
	14:27	they rehearsed **a** that God had done with	3745
	15: 3	they caused great joy unto **a** the brethren.	3956
	15: 4	they declared **a** *things* that God had done	3745
	15:12	Then **a** the multitude kept silence,	3956
	15:17	and **a** the Gentiles, upon whom my name	3956
	15:17	saith the Lord, who doeth **a** these *things.*	3956
	15:18	Known unto God are **a** his works from	3956
	16: 3	for they knew **a** that his father was a Greek.	537
	16:26	and immediately the doors were opened,	3956
	16:28	Do thyself no harm: for we are **a** here.	3956
	16:32	the Lord, and to **a** that were in his house.	3956
	16:33	was baptized, he and **a** his, straightway.	3956
	16:34	believing in God with **a** his **house**.	3832
	17: 5	and set the city on an uproar,	NIG
	17: 7	do contrary to the decrees of Cesar,	3956
	17:11	in that they received the word with **a**	3956
	17:15	for to come to him **with a speed**,	5030+5613
	17:21	(For **a** the Athenians and strangers which	3956
	17:22	I perceive that in **a** *things* ye are too	3956

A

Ac 17:24 that made the world and *a things* therein,	3956
17:25 any *thing,* seeing he giveth to *a* life,	3956
17:25 giveth to all life, and breath, and *a things;*	3956
17:26 And hath made of one blood *a* nations of	3956
17:26 for to dwell on *a* the face of the earth,	3956
17:30 now commandeth *a* men every where to	3956
17:31 *whereof* he hath given assurance unto *a*	3956
18: 2 that Claudius had commanded *a* Jews to	3956
18: 8 believed on the Lord with *a* his house;	3650
18:17 Then *a* the Greeks took Sosthenes,	3956
18:21 I must *by a means* keep *this* feast that	3843
18:23 and went over *a* the country of Galatia	NIG
18:23 in order, strengthening *a* the disciples.	
19: 7 And *a* the men were about twelve.	3956
19:10 that *a* they which dwelt in Asia heard	3956
19:17 And this was known to *a* the Jews	3956
19:17 and fear fell on them *a,* and the name of	3956
19:19 and burned *them* before *a men:*	3956
19:26 but almost throughout *a* Asia, this Paul	3956
19:27 whom *a* Asia and the world worshippeth.	3650
19:34 *a* with one voice about the space of two	3956
20:18 manner I have been with you at *a* seasons,	3956
20:19 Serving the Lord with *a* humility of mind,	3956
20:25 And now behold, I know that ye *a,*	3956
20:26 that I *am* pure from the blood of *a men.*	3956
20:27 to declare unto you *a* the counsel of God.	3956
20:28 unto yourselves, and to *a* the flock,	3956
20:32 to give you an inheritance among *a* them	3956
20:35 I have shewed you *a things,* how that so	3956
20:36 kneeled down, and prayed with them *a.*	3956
20:37 And *they a* wept sore, and fell on Paul's	3956
20:38 Sorrowing most *of a* for the words which	NIG
21: 5 and *they a* brought us on our way,	3956
21:18 unto James; and *a* the elders were present.	3956
21:20 and they are *a* zealous of the law:	3956
21:21 that thou teachest *a* the Jews which are	3956
21:24 *a* may know that *those things,* whereof	3956
21:27 stirred up *a* the people, and laid hands on	3956
21:28 that teacheth *a* men every where against	3956
21:30 And *a* the city was moved, and the people	3650
21:31 band, that *a* Jerusalem was in an uproar.	3650
22: 3 zealous towards God, as ye *a* are this day.	3956
22: 5 me witness, and *a* the estate of the elders:	3956
22:10 there it shall be told thee of *a things*	3956
22:12 having a good report of *a* the Jews which	3956
22:15 For thou shalt be his witness unto *a* men	3956
22:30 chief priests and *a* their council to appear,	3650
23: 1 I have lived in *a* good conscience before	3956
24: 3 and *in a places,* most noble Felix,	3837
24: 3 most noble Felix, with *a* thankfulness.	3956
24: 5 a mover of sedition among *a* the Jews	3956
24: 8 of *a* these *things,* whereof we accuse him.	3956
24:14 believing *a things* which are written in	3956
25: 8 have I offended any *thing* at *a.*	NIG
25:24 *a* men which are here present with us,	3956
25:24 ye see this *man,* about whom *a*	3956
26: 2 *a the things* whereof I am accused of	3956
26: 3 *I know* thee to be expert in *a* customs	3956
26: 4 nation at Jerusalem, know *a* the Jews;	3956
26:14 And when we were *a* fallen to the earth,	3956
26:20 and throughout *a* the coasts of Judea,	3956
26:29 also *a* that hear me this day, were both	3956
27:20 no small tempest lay on *us, a* hope that	3956
27:24 God hath given thee *a* them that sail with	3956
27:33 Paul besought *them a* to take meat, saying,	537
27:35 gave thanks to God in presence of *them a:*	3956
27:36 Then were they *a* of good cheer,	3956
27:37 we were in *a* in the ship two hundred	3956
27:44 to pass, that *they* escaped *a* safe to land.	3956
28:30 and received *a* that came in unto him,	3956
28:31 with *a* confidence, no man forbidding him.	3956
Ro 1: 5 obedience to the faith among *a* nations,	3956
1: 7 To *a* that be in Rome, beloved of God,	3956
1: 8 my God through Jesus Christ for you *a,*	3956
1:18 from heaven against *a* ungodliness	3956
1:29 Being filled with *a* unrighteousness,	3956
3: 9 and Gentiles, that *they* are *a* under sin;	3956
3:12 They are *a* gone out of the way, they are	3956
3:19 *a* the world may become guilty before God	3956
3:22 *which* is by faith of Jesus Christ unto *a*	3956
3:22 unto all and upon *a* them that believe:	3956
3:23 For *a* have sinned, and come short of	3956
4:11 that he might be the father of *a* them that	3956
4:16 to the end the promise might be sure to *a*	3956
4:16 of Abraham; who is the father of us *a,*	3956
5:12 so death passed upon *a* men, for that all	3956
5:12 upon all men, for that *a* have sinned:	3956
5:18 *came* upon *a* men to condemnation;	3956
5:18 *came* upon all men unto justification of life.	3956
7: 8 in me *a manner of* concupiscence.	3956
8:28 And we know that *a things* work together	3956
8:32 own Son, but delivered him up for us *a,*	3956
8:32 not with him also freely give us *a things?*	3956
8:36 For thy sake we are killed *a* the day long;	3650
8:37 in *a* these *things* we are more than	3956
9: 5 the flesh Christ *came,* who is over *a,*	3956
9: 6 For they *are* not *a* Israel, which are of	3956
9: 7 the seed of Abraham, *are they a* children:	3956
9:17 might be declared throughout *a* the earth.	3956
10:12 for the same Lord over *a* is rich unto all	3956
10:12 for the same Lord over all *is* rich unto *a*	3956
10:16 But they have not *a* obeyed the gospel.	3956
10:18 their sound went into *a* the earth,	3956
10:21 **A** day *long* have I stretched forth my	3650
11:26 And so *a* Israel shall be saved: as it is	3956

Ro 11:32 God hath concluded *them* **a** in unbelief,	3956
11:32 that he might have mercy upon *a.*	3956
11:36 *are a things:* to whom *be* glory for ever.	3956
12: 4 and *a* members have not the same office:	3956
12:17 *things* honest in the sight of *a* men.	3956
12:18 as lieth in you, live peaceably with *a* men.	3956
13: 7 Render therefore to *a their* dues: tribute to	3956
14: 2 one believeth that *he* may eat *a things:*	3956
14:10 for we shall *a* stand before the judgment	3956
14:20 *A things* indeed *are* pure; but *it is* evil for	3956
15:11 And again, Praise the Lord, *a* ye Gentiles;	3956
15:11 all ye Gentiles; and laud him, *a* ye people.	3956
15:13 Now the God of hope fill you with *a* joy	3956
15:14 full of goodness, filled with *a* knowledge,	3956
15:33 Now the God of peace *be* with you *a.*	3956
16: 4 but also *a* the churches of the Gentiles.	3956
16:15 and *a* the saints which are with them.	3956
16:19 For your obedience is come abroad unto *a*	3956
16:24 of our Lord Jesus Christ *be* with you *a.*	3956
16:26 known to *a* nations for the obedience	3956
1Co 1: 2 with *a* that in every place call upon	3956
1: 5 in *a* utterance, and *in* all knowledge;	3956
1: 5 in all utterance, and *in a* knowledge;	3956
1:10 that ye *a* speak the same *thing,*	3956
2:10 for the Spirit searcheth *a things,* yea,	3956
2:15 But he that is spiritual judgeth *a things,*	3956
3:21 *man* glory in men. For *a things* are yours;	3956
3:22 or *things* to come; *a* are yours;	3956
4:13 *are* the offscouring of *a things* unto this	3956
6:12 *A things* are lawful unto me, but all *things*	3956
6:12 unto me, but *a things* are not expedient:	3956
6:12 *a things* are lawful for me, but I will not	3956
7: 7 For I would that *a* men were even as I	3956
7:17 him walk. And so ordain I in *a* churches.	3956
8: 1 we know that we *a* have knowledge.	3956
8: 6 of whom *are a things,* and we in him;	3956
8: 6 by whom *are a things,* and we by him.	3956
9:12 suffer *a things,* lest we should hinder	3956
9:19 For though I be free from *a men,* yet have I	3956
9:19 yet have I made myself servant unto *a,*	3956
9:22 I am made *a things* to all *men,* that I	3956
9:22 I am made all *things* to *a men,* that I	3956
9:22 *men,* that I might *by a means* save some.	3843
9:24 ye not that they which run in a race run *a,*	3956
9:25 *a things.* Now they *do* it to obtain a	3956
10: 1 how that *a* our fathers were under	3956
10: 1 the cloud, and *a* passed through the sea;	3956
10: 2 And were *a* baptized unto Moses in	3956
10: 3 And did *a* eat the same spiritual meat;	3956
10: 4 And did *a* drink the same spiritual drink:	3956
10:11 Now *a* these things happened unto them	3956
10:17 for we are *a* partakers of *that* one bread.	3956
10:23 *A things* are lawful for me, but all *things*	3956
10:23 for me, but *a things* are not expedient:	3956
10:23 *a things* are lawful for me, but all *things*	3956
10:23 are lawful for me, but *a things* edify not.	3956
10:31 ye do, do *a* to the glory of God.	3956
10:33 Even as I please *a* men in all *things,* not	3956
10:33 Even as I please all *men* in *a things,* not	3956
11: 2 that you remember me in *a things,*	3956
11: 5 **even a one as if** she 846+1520+2532+3588	
11:12 also by the woman; but *a things* of God.	3956
11:18 For **first** of *a,* when ye come together in	4412
12: 6 it is the same God which worketh *a* in all.	3956
12: 6 it is the same God which worketh all in *a.*	3956
12:11 But *a* these worketh *that* one	3956
12:12 and *a* the members of *that* one body,	3956
12:13 by one Spirit are we *a* baptized into one	3956
12:13 have been *a* made to drink into one Spirit.	3956
12:19 And if they were *a* one member,	3956
12:26 the members suffer with *it;* or	3956
12:26 the members rejoice with *it.*	3956
12:29 *Are a* apostles? *are* all prophets? *are* all	3956
12:29 *are* prophets? *are* all teachers? *are* all	3956
12:29 *are* teachers? *are* all workers of miracles?	3956
12:29 *are* all teachers? *are* a workers of miracles?	3956
12:30 Have *a* the gifts of healing? do all speak	3956
12:30 do *a* speak with tongues? do all interpret?	3956
12:30 do all speak with tongues? do *a* interpret?	3956
13: 2 and understand *a* mysteries,	3956
13: 2 all mysteries, and *a* knowledge;	3956
13: 2 and though I have *a* faith, so that *I* could	3956
13: 3 And though I bestow *a* my goods to feed	3956
13: 7 Beareth *a things,* believeth all *things,*	3956
13: 7 Beareth all *things,* believeth *a things,*	3956
13: 7 hopeth *a things,* endureth all *things.*	3956
13: 7 hopeth all *things,* endureth *a things.*	3956
14: 5 I would that ye *a* spake with tongues,	3956
14:18 I speak with tongues more than you *a:*	3956
14:21 and yet **for a** that will they not hear me,	3779
14:23 and *a* speak with tongues, and there come	3956
14:24 But if *a* prophesy, and there come in one	3956
14:24 or *one* unlearned, he is convinced of *a,*	3956
14:24 he is convinced of all, he is judged of *a:*	3956
14:26 Let *a things* be done unto edifying.	3956
14:31 For ye may *a* prophesy one by one, that all	3956
14:31 a may learn, and all may be comforted.	3956
14:31 all may learn, and *a* may be comforted.	3956
14:33 of peace, as in *a* churches of the saints.	3956
14:40 Let *a things* be done decently and in order	3956
15: 3 For I delivered unto you first *of a* that	NIG
15: 7 was seen of James; then *of a* the apostles.	3956
15: 8 And last of *a* he was seen of me also, as of	3956
15:10 I laboured more abundantly than they *a:*	3956
15:19 In Christ, we are of *a* men most miserable.	3956

1Co 15:22 For as in Adam *a* die, even so in Christ	3956
15:22 even so in Christ shall *a* be made alive.	3956
15:24 when he shall have put down *a* rule	3956
15:24 down all rule and *a* authority and power.	3956
15:25 till he hath put *a* enemies under his feet.	3956
15:27 For he hath put *a things* under his feet.	3956
15:27 *a things* are put under *him, it is* manifest	3956
15:27 which did put *a things* under him.	3956
15:28 And when *a things* shall be subdued unto	3956
15:28 unto him that put *a things* under him,	3956
15:28 under him, that God may be *a* in all.	3956
15:28 under him, that God may be all in *a.*	3956
15:29 for the dead, if the dead rise not at *a?*	3654
15:39 **A** flesh *is* not the same flesh: but *there is*	3956
15:51 We shall not *a* sleep, but we shall *a* be	3956
15:51 not all sleep, but we shall *a* be changed,	3956
16:12 *his* will was not at *a* to come at this time;	3843
16:14 Let *a* your *things* be done with charity.	3956
16:20 *A* the brethren greet you. Greet ye one	3956
16:24 My love *be* with you *a* in Christ Jesus.	3956
2Co 1: 1 with *a* the saints which are in all Achaia:	3956
1: 1 with all the saints which are in *a* Achaia:	3650
1: 3 of mercies, and the God of *a* comfort;	3956
1: 4 Who comforteth us in *a* our tribulation,	3956
1:20 For the promises of God in him *are* yea,	3745
2: 3 having confidence in you *a,* that my joy is	3956
2: 3 in you all, that my joy is *the joy* of you *a.*	3956
2: 5 in part: that I may not overcharge you *a.*	3956
2: 9 of you, whether ye be obedient in *a things.*	3956
3: 2 in our hearts, known and read of *a* men:	3956
3:18 But we *a,* with open face beholding as in a	3956
4:15 For *a things are* for your sakes, that	3956
5:10 For we must *a* appear before the judgment	3956
5:14 that if one died for *a,* then were all dead:	3956
5:14 that if one died for all, then were *a* dead:	3956
5:15 *that* he died for *a,* that they which live	3956
5:17 behold, *a things* are become new.	3956
5:18 And *a things are* of God, who hath	3956
6: 4 But in *a things* approving ourselves as	3956
6:10 and *yet* possessing *a things.*	3956
7: 1 let us cleanse ourselves from *a* filthiness	3956
7: 4 I am exceeding joyful in *a* our tribulation.	3956
7:11 In *a things* ye have approved yourselves to	3956
7:13 because his spirit was refreshed by you *a.*	3956
7:14 but as we spake *a things* to you in truth,	3956
7:15 he remembereth the obedience of you *a,*	3956
7:16 that I have confidence in you in *a things.*	3956
8: 7 and *in a* diligence, and *in* your love to us,	3956
8:18 whose praise *is* in the gospel throughout *a*	3956
9: 8 And God *is* able to make *a* grace abound	3956
9: 8 always having *a* sufficiency in all *things,*	3956
9: 8 always having all sufficiency in *a things,*	3956
9:11 Being enriched in every *thing* to *a*	3956
9:13 distribution unto them, and unto *a* men;	3956
10: 6 And having in *a* readiness to revenge *a*	3956
11: 6 made manifest among you in *a things.*	3956
11: 9 in *a things* I have kept myself from being	3956
11:28 upon me daily, the care of *a* the churches.	3956
12:12 were wrought among you in *a* patience,	3956
12:19 but *we* do *a things,* dearly beloved, for	3956
13: 2 and to *a* other, that, if I come again, I will	3956
13:13 **A** the saints salute you.	3956
13:14 of the Holy Ghost, *be* with you *a.*	3956
Gal 1: 2 And *a* the brethren which are with me,	3956
2:14 I said unto Peter before *them a,* If thou,	3956
3: 8 *saying,* In thee shall *a* nations be blessed.	3956
3:10 *is* every one that continueth not in *a*	3956
3:22 But the scripture hath concluded *a* under	3956
3:26 For ye are *a* the children of God by faith in	3956
3:28 female: for ye are *a* one in Christ Jesus.	3956
4: 1 from a servant, though he be lord of *a;*	3956
4:12 *am* as ye *are:* ye have **not** injured me *at a.*	3762
4:26 above is free, which is the mother of us *a.*	3956
5:14 For the law is fulfilled in one word,	3956
6: 6 unto him that teacheth in *a* good *things.*	3956
6:10 let us do good unto *a* men, especially unto	3956
Eph 1: 3 who hath blessed us with *a* spiritual	3956
1: 8 Wherein he hath abounded toward us in *a*	3956
1:10 gather together in one *a things* in Christ,	3956
1:11 *a things* after the counsel of his own will:	3956
1:15 the Lord Jesus, and love unto *a* the saints,	3956
1:21 Far above *a* principality, and power,	3956
1:22 And hath put *a things* under his feet,	3956
1:22 gave him *to be* the head over *a things* to	3956
1:23 the fulness of him that filleth *a* in all.	3956
1:23 the fulness of him that filleth all in *a.*	3956
2: 3 Among whom also we *a* had our	3956
2:21 In whom *a* the building fitly framed	3956
3: 8 *who am* less than the least of *a* saints,	3956
3: 9 And to make *a* men see what *is*	3956
3: 9 who created *a things* by Jesus Christ:	3956
3:18 May be able to comprehend with *a* saints	3956
3:19 that ye might be filled with *a* the fulness	3956
3:20 exceeding abundantly above *a* that we ask	3956
3:21 church by Christ Jesus throughout *a* ages,	3956
4: 2 With *a* lowliness and meekness, with	3956
4: 6 One God and Father of *a,* who *is* above all,	3956
4: 6 who *is* above *a,* and through all, and in	3956
4: 6 is above all, and through *a,* and in you all.	3956
4: 6 *is* above all, and through all, and in you *a.*	3956
4:10 that ascended up far above *a* heavens,	3956
4:10 all heavens, that he might fill *a things.)*	3956
4:13 Till we *a* come in the unity of the faith,	3956
4:15 may grow *up* into him in *a things,* which	3956
4:19 to work *a* uncleanness with greediness.	3956

Eph	4:31 Let **a** bitterness, and wrath, and anger,	3956
	4:31 be put away from you, with **a** malice:	3956
	5: 3 and **a** uncleanness, or covetousness,	3956
	5: 9 (For the fruit of the Spirit *is* in **a** goodness	3956
	5:13 But **a** things that are reproved are made	3956
	5:20 thanks always for **a** things unto God	3956
	6:13 the evil day, and having done **a**, to stand.	537
	6:16 Above **a**, taking the shield of faith,	3956
	6:16 wherewith ye shall be able to quench **a**	3956
	6:18 Praying always with **a** prayer	3956
	6:18 watching thereunto with **a** perseverance	3956
	6:18 and supplication for **a** saints;	3956
	6:21 shall make known to you **a** things:	3956
	6:24 Grace *be* with **a** them that love our Lord	3956
Php	1: 1 to **a** the saints in Christ Jesus which are at	3956
	1: 4 Always in every prayer of mine for you **a**	3956
	1: 7 as it is meet for me to think this of you **a**,	3956
	1: 7 the gospel, ye **a** are partakers of my grace.	3956
	1: 8 *greatly* I long after you **a** in the bowels	3956
	1: 9 more in knowledge and *in* **a** judgment;	3956
	1:13 in Christ are manifest in **a** the palace,	3650
	1:13 in all the palace, and *in* **a** other *places;*	3956
	1:20 but *that* with **a** boldness, as always, *so*	3956
	1:25 continue with you **a** for your furtherance	3956
	2:14 Do **a** things without murmurings	3956
	2:17 of your faith, I joy, and rejoice with you **a**.	3956
	2:21 For **a** seek their own, not the *things which*	3956
	2:26 For he longed after you **a**, and *was* full of	3956
	2:29 therefore in the Lord with **a** gladness;	3956
	3: 8 and I count **a** things *but* loss for	3956
	3: 8 for whom I have suffered the loss of **a**	3956
	3:21 able even to subdue **a** things unto himself.	3956
	4: 5 your moderation be known unto **a** men.	3956
	4: 7 which passeth **a** understanding, shall keep	3956
	4:12 in **a** things I am instructed both to be full	3956
	4:13 I can do **a** things through Christ which	3956
	4:18 But I have **a**, and abound: I am full,	3956
	4:19 But my God shall supply **a** your need	3956
	4:22 **A** the saints salute you, chiefly they that	3956
	4:23 of our Lord Jesus Christ *be* with you **a**.	3956
Col	1: 4 of the love which *ye have* to **a** the saints,	3956
	1: 6 is come unto you, as *it is* in **a** the world;	3956
	1: 9 the knowledge of his will in **a** wisdom	3956
	1:10 walk worthy of the Lord unto **a** pleasing,	3956
	1:11 Strengthened with **a** might, according to	3956
	1:11 unto **a** patience and longsuffering with	3956
	1:16 For by him were **a** things created, that are	3956
	1:16 **a** things were created by him, and for him:	3956
	1:17 And he is before **a** things, and by him **a**	3956
	1:17 all *things*, and by him **a** things consist.	3956
	1:18 that in **a** things he might have	3956
	1:19 *Father* that in him should **a** fulness dwell;	3956
	1:20 by him to reconcile **a** things unto himself;	3956
	1:28 and teaching every man in **a** wisdom;	3956
	2: 2 unto **a** riches of the full assurance of	3956
	2: 3 whom are hid **a** the treasures of wisdom	3956
	2: 9 For in him dwelleth **a** the fulness of	3956
	2:10 which is the head of **a** principality	3956
	2:13 him, having forgiven you **a** trespasses;	3956
	2:19 from which **a** the body by joints	3956
	2:22 Which **a** are to perish with the using;)	3956
	3: 8 But now you also put off **a** *these;* anger,	3956
	3:11 bond *nor* free: but Christ *is* **a**, and in all.	3956
	3:11 bond *nor* free: but Christ *is* all, and in **a**.	3956
	3:14 And above **a** these *things* put on charity,	3956
	3:16 of Christ dwell in you richly in **a** wisdom;	3956
	3:17 deed, *do* **a** in the name of the Lord Jesus,	3956
	3:20 obey *your* parents in **a** *things:* for this is	3956
	3:22 obey in **a** *things your* masters according to	3956
	4: 7 **A** my state shall Tychicus declare unto	3956
	4: 9 They shall make known unto you **a** *things*	3956
	4:12 and complete in **a** the will of God.	3956
1Th	1: 2 We give thanks to God always for you **a**,	3956
	1: 7 So that ye were ensamples to **a** that believe	3956
	2:15 please not God, and are contrary to **a** men:	3956
	3: 7 we were comforted over you in **a** our	3956
	3: 9 for **a** the joy wherewith we joy for your	3956
	3:12 towards **a** *men*, even as we **a** do towards	3956
	3:13 of our Lord Jesus Christ with **a** his saints.	3956
	4: 6 that the Lord *is* the avenger of **a** such,	3956
	4:10 indeed ye do it towards **a** the brethren	3956
	4:10 all the brethren which are in **a** Macedonia:	3650
	5: 5 Ye are **a** the children of light,	3956
	5:14 the weak, be patient toward **a** men.	3956
	5:15 both among yourselves, and to **a** men.	3956
	5:21 Prove **a** *things;* hold fast *that which is*	3956
	5:22 Abstain from **a** appearance of evil.	3956
	5:26 Greet **a** the brethren with **a** holy kiss.	3956
	5:27 epistle be read unto **a** the holy brethren.	3956
2Th	1: 3 the charity of every one of you **a** towards	3956
	1: 4 and faith in **a** your persecutions	3956
	1:10 and to be admired in **a** them that believe	3956
	1:11 fulfil **a** the good pleasure of *his* goodness,	3956
	2: 4 exalteth himself above **a** that is called God,	3956
	2: 9 is after the working of Satan with **a** power	3956
	2:10 And with **a** deceivableness of	3956
	2:12 That they **a** might be damned who	3956
	3: 2 wicked men: for **a** men have not faith.	3956
	3:11 working not **a** at **a**, but are busybodies.	3367
	3:16 himself give you peace always by **a** means.	3956
	3:16 by all means. The Lord *be* with you **a**.	3956
	3:18 of our Lord Jesus Christ *be* with you **a**.	3956
1Ti	1:15 and worthy of **a** acceptation,	3956
	1:16 Christ might shew forth **a** longsuffering,	3956
	2: 1 I exhort therefore that, first of **a**,	3956

1Ti	2: 1 *and* giving of thanks, be made for **a** men;	3956
	2: 2 For kings, and *for* **a** that are in authority;	3956
	2: 2 and peaceable life in **a** godliness	3956
	2: 4 Who will have **a** men to be saved,	3956
	2: 6 Who gave himself a ransom for **a**, to be	3956
	2:11 Let the woman learn in silence with **a**	3956
	3: 4 having *his* children in subjection with **a**	3956
	3:11 not slanderers, sober, faithful in **a** *things*.	3956
	4: 8 godliness is profitable unto **a** *things,*	3956
	4: 9 faithful saying and worthy of **a** acceptation.	3956
	4:10 living God, who is the Saviour of **a** men,	3956
	4:15 them; that thy profiting may appear to **a**.	3956
	5: 2 the younger as sisters, with **a** purity.	3956
	5:20 Them that sin rebuke before **a**, that others	3956
	6: 1 their own masters worthy of **a** honour,	3956
	6:10 For the love of money is the root of **a** evil:	3956
	6:13 quickeneth **a** *things,* and *before* Christ	3956
	6:17 who giveth us richly **a** *things* to enjoy;	3956
2Ti	1:15 that **a** they which are in Asia be turned	3956
	2: 7 the Lord give thee understanding in **a**	3956
	2:10 Therefore I endure **a** *things* for the elects'	3956
	2:24 but be gentle unto **a** men, apt to teach,	3956
	3: 9 their folly shall be manifest unto **a** men,	3956
	3:11 but out of *them* **a** the Lord delivered me.	3956
	3:12 **a** that will live godly in Christ Jesus shall	3956
	3:16 **A** scripture *is* given by inspiration of God,	3956
	3:17 throughly furnished unto **a** good works.	3956
	4: 2 exhort with **a** longsuffering and doctrine.	3956
	4: 5 But watch thou in **a** things, endure	3956
	4: 8 unto **a** them also that love his appearing.	3956
	4:16 stood with me, but **a** *men* forsook me:	3956
	4:17 and *that* **a** the Gentiles might hear:	3956
	4:21 Linus, and Claudia, and **a** the brethren.	3956
Tit	1:15 Unto the pure *a* things *are* pure:	3956
	2: 7 In **a** *things* shewing thyself a pattern of	3956
	2: 9 to please *them* well in **a** *things;* not	3956
	2:10 but shewing **a** good fidelity;	3956
	2:10 doctrine of God our Saviour in **a** *things.*	3956
	2:11 salvation hath appeared to **a** men,	3956
	2:14 that he might redeem us from **a** iniquity,	3956
	2:15 and exhort, and rebuke with **a** authority.	3956
	3: 2 gentle, shewing **a** meekness unto all men.	3956
	3: 2 gentle, shewing all meekness unto **a** men.	3956
	3:15 **A** that are with me salute thee. Greet them	3956
	3:15 in the faith. Grace *be* with you **a**. Amen.	3956
Phm	1: 5 the Lord Jesus, and toward **a** saints;	3956
Heb	1: 2 whom he hath appointed heir of **a** *things,*	3956
	1: 3 upholding **a** *things* by the word of his	3956
	1: 6 And let **a** the angels of God worship him.	3956
	1:11 they **a** shall wax old as *doth* **a** garment;	3956
	1:14 Are they not **a** ministering spirits, sent	3956
	2: 8 Thou hast put **a** *things* in subjection under	3956
	2: 8 For in that *he* put **a** in subjection under	3956
	2: 8 But now we see not yet **a** *things* put under	3956
	2:10 for whom *are* **a** *things,* and by whom *are*	3956
	2:10 by whom *are* **a** *things,* in bringing many	3956
	2:11 and they who are sanctified *are* **a** of one:	3956
	2:15 were **a** their lifetime subject to bondage.	3956
	2:17 Wherefore in **a** *things* it behoved him to	3956
	3: 2 as also Moses *was faithful* in **a** his house.	3650
	3: 4 man; but he that built **a** *things* is God.	3956
	3: 5 And Moses verily *was* faithful in **a** his	3650
	3:16 howbeit not **a** that came out of Egypt by	3956
	4: 4 And God did rest the seventh day from **a**	3956
	4:13 but **a** *things are* naked and opened unto	3956
	4:15 was in **a** points tempted like as *we are,*	3956
	5: 9 salvation unto **a** them that obey him;	3956
	6:16 confirmation *is* to them an end of **a** strife.	3956
	7: 2 also Abraham gave a tenth *part* of **a**;	3956
	7: 7 And without **a** contradiction the less is	3956
	8: 5 *he,* that thou make **a** *things* according	3956
	8:11 for **a** shall know me, from the least to	3956
	9: 3 which is called the *holiest of* **a**;	40+40
	9: 8 the way into the holiest *of* **a** was not yet	NIG
	9:17 otherwise it is of **no** strength **at a** whilst	3379
	9:19 to **a** the people according to the law,	3956
	9:19 sprinkled both the book, and **a** the people,	3956
	9:21 and **a** the vessels of the ministry.	3956
	9:22 And almost **a** *things* are by the law purged	3956
	10:10 of the body of Jesus Christ **once for a**.	2178
	11:13 These **a** died in faith, not having received	3956
	11:39 And these **a**, having obtained a good report	3956
	12: 8 whereof **a** are partakers, then are ye	3956
	12:14 Follow peace with **a** *men,* and holiness,	3956
	12:23 to God the Judge of **a**, and to the spirits	3956
	13: 4 Marriage *is* honourable in **a**, and the bed	3956
	13:18 in **a** *things* willing to live honestly.	3956
	13:24 Salute **a** them that have the rule over you,	3956
	13:24 have the rule over you, and **a** the saints.	3956
	13:25 Grace *be* with you **a**. Amen.	3956
Jas	1: 2 count *it* **a** joy when ye fall into divers	3956
	1: 5 that giveth to **a** men liberally,	3956
	1: 8 A double minded man *is* unstable in **a** his	3956
	1:21 Wherefore lay apart **a** filthiness	3956
	2:10 *yet* offend in one *point*, he is guilty of **a**.	3956
	3: 2 For *in* many *things* we offend **a**. If any	537
	4:16 in your boastings: **a** such rejoicing is evil.	3956
	5:12 above **a** *things*, my brethren, swear not,	3956
1Pe	1:15 so be ye holy in **a** *manner of* conversation;	3956
	1:24 For **a** flesh *is* as grass, and all the glory of	3956
	1:24 **a** the glory of man as the flower of grass.	3956
	2: 1 Wherefore laying aside **a** malice,	3956
	2: 1 and **a** guile, and hypocrisies, and envies,	3956
	2: 1 and envies, and **a** evil speakings,	3956
	2:17 Honour **a** *men.* Love the brotherhood.	3956

1Pe	2:18 be subject to *your* masters with **a** fear;	3956
	3: 8 Finally, *be ye* **a** of one mind,	3956
	4: 7 But the end of **a** *things* is at hand: be ye	3956
	4: 8 And above *a things* have fervent charity	3956
	4:11 that God in **a** *things* may be glorified	3956
	5: 5 **a** *of you* be subject one to another,	3956
	5: 7 Casting **a** your care upon him; for he	3956
	5:10 the God of **a** grace, who hath called us	3956
	5:14 Peace *be* with you **a** that are in Christ	3956
2Pe	1: 3 unto us **a** *things* that *pertain* unto life	3956
	1: 5 And beside this, giving **a** diligence, add to	3956
	3: 4 *a things* continue as *they were* from	3956
	3: 9 but that **a** should come to repentance.	3956
	3:11 then that **a** these *things* shall be dissolved,	3956
	3:11 manner *of persons* ought ye to be in **a**	NIG
	3:16 As also in **a** *his* epistles, speaking in them	3956
1Jn	1: 5 is light, and in him is no darkness at **a**.	3762
	1: 7 Christ his Son cleanseth us from **a** sin.	3956
	1: 9 and to cleanse us from **a** unrighteousness.	3956
	2:16 For **a** that is in the world, the lust of	3956
	2:19 made manifest that they were not **a** of us.	3956
	2:20 from the Holy One, and ye know **a** *things.*	3956
	2:27 as the same anointing teacheth you of **a**	3956
	3:20 than our heart, and knoweth **a** *things.*	3956
	5:17 **A** unrighteousness is sin: and there is a sin	3956
2Jn	1: 1 but also **a** they that have known the truth;	3956
3Jn	1: 2 I wish above **a** *things* that thou mayest	3956
	1:12 Demetrius hath good report of **a** *men,*	3956
Jude	1: 3 when I gave **a** diligence to write unto you	3956
	1:15 To execute judgment upon **a**,	3956
	1:15 convince **a** *that are* ungodly among them	3956
	1:15 their ungodly deeds which they have	3956
	1:15 of **a** *their* hard *speeches* which ungodly	3956
Rev	1: 2 Jesus Christ, and of **a** *things* that he saw.	3745
	1: 7 and **a** kindreds of the earth shall wail	3956
	2:23 **a** the churches shall know that I am he	3956
	3:10 which shall come upon **a** the world, to try	3650
	4:11 for thou hast created **a** *things,* and for thy	3956
	5: 6 spirits of God sent forth into **a** the earth.	3956
	5:13 and **a** that are in them, heard I saying,	3956
	7: 4 thousand of **a** the tribes of the children	3956
	7: 9 of **a** nations, and kindreds, and people,	3956
	7:11 And **a** the angels stood round about	3956
	7:17 God shall wipe away **a** tears from their	3956
	8: 3 he should offer *it* with the prayers of **a**	3956
	8: 7 burnt up, and **a** green grass was burnt up.	3956
	11: 6 and to smite the earth with **a** plagues,	3956
	12: 5 who was to rule **a** nations with a rod of	3956
	13: 3 and **a** the world wondered after the beast.	3650
	13: 7 and power was given him over **a** kindreds,	3956
	13: 8 And **a** that dwell upon the earth shall	3956
	13:12 And he exerciseth **a** the power of the first	3956
	13:16 And he causeth **a**, *both* small and great,	3956
	14: 8 she made **a** nations drink of the wine of	3956
	15: 4 for **a** nations shall come and worship	3956
	18: 3 For **a** nations have drunk of the wine of	3956
	18:12 and **a** thyine wood, and all *manner* vessels	3956
	18:12 and **a** *manner* vessels of ivory,	3956
	18:12 **a** *manner* vessels of most precious wood,	3956
	18:14 **a** *things* which were dainty and goodly	3956
	18:14 find them **no more at a**.	3361+3756+3765
	18:17 and **a** the company in ships,	3956
	18:19 wherein were made rich **a** that had ships	3956
	18:21 and shall be found **no more at a**.	3364
	18:22 shall be heard **no more at a** in thee;	3364
	18:22 shall be heard **no more at a** in thee;	3364
	18:23 a candle shall shine **no more at a** in thee;	3364
	18:23 of the bride shall be heard **no more at a** in	3364
	18:23 for by thy sorceries were **a** nations	3956
	18:24 and of **a** that were slain upon the earth.	3956
	19: 5 a ye his servants, and ye that fear him,	3956
	19:17 saying to **a** the fowls that fly in the midst	3956
	19:18 the flesh of **a** *men,* both free and bond,	3956
	19:21 the fowls were filled with their flesh.	3956
	21: 4 And God shall wipe away **a** tears from	3956
	21: 5 throne said, Behold, I make **a** *things* new.	3956
	21: 7 He that overcometh shall inherit **a** *things;*	3956
	21: 8 and sorcerers, and idolaters, and **a** liars,	3956
	21:19 with **a** *manner of* precious stones.	3956
	21:25 And the gates of it shall **not** be shut at **a**	3364
	22:21 of our Lord Jesus Christ *be* with you **a**.	3956

ALLAMMELECH See ALAMMELECH

ALLEGING (1)

Ac 17: 3 Opening and **a**, that Christ must needs 3908

ALLEGORY (1)

Gal 4:24 Which *things* are an **a**: for these are the two 238

ALLELUIA (4)

Rev	19: 1 voice of much people in heaven, saying, **A**;	239
	19: 3 And again they said, **A**. And her smoke rose	239
	19: 4 that sat on the throne, saying, Amen; **A**.	239
	19: 6 the voice of mighty thunderings, saying, **A**:	239

ALLIED (1)

Ne 13: 4 the house of our God, *was* **a** unto Tobiah: 7138

ALLON (2)

Jos	19:33 from **A** to Zaanannim, and Adami, Nekeb,	438
1Ch	4:37 the son of **A**, the son of Jedaiah, the son of	438

ALLON BACUTH See ALLON-BACHUTH

A

ALLON-BACHUTH (1)

Ge 35: 8 an oak: and the name of it was called **A.** 439

ALLOW (3) [ALLOWANCE, ALLOWED, ALLOWETH]

Lk 11:48 Truly ye bear witness that ye **a** the deeds 4909
Ac 24:15 which they themselves also **a,** 4327
Ro 7:15 For *that* which I do I **a** not: for what I 1097

ALLOWANCE (2) [ALLOW]

2Ki 25:30 his **a** was a continual allowance given him 737
 25:30 his allowance was a continual **a** given him 737

ALLOWED (1) [ALLOW]

1Th 2: 4 But as we were **a** of God to be put in trust 1381

ALLOWETH (1) [ALLOW]

Ro 14:22 not himself in *that thing* which he **a.** 1381

ALLURE (2)

Hos 2:14 I *will* **a** her, and bring her *into* 6601
2Pe 2:18 they **a** through the lusts of the flesh, 1185

ALMIGHTY (57) [MIGHT]

Ge 17: 1 and said unto him, I *am* the **A** God; 7706
 28: 3 God **A** bless thee, and make thee fruitful, 7706
 35:11 said unto me, I *am* God **A:** be fruitful 7706
 43:14 God **A** give you mercy before the man, 7706
 48: 3 God **A** appeared unto me at Luz in the 7706
 49:25 *by* the **A,** who shall bless thee *with* 7706
Ex 6: 3 by *the name of* God **A,** but *by* my name 7706
Nu 24: 4 which saw the vision of the **A,** falling 7706
 24:16 *which* saw the vision of the **A,** falling 7706
Ru 1:20 for the **A** hath dealt very bitterly with me. 7706
 1:21 against me, and the **A** hath afflicted me? 7706
Job 5:17 despise not thou the chastening of the **A:** 7706
 6: 4 For the arrows of the **A** *are* within me, 7706
 6:14 but he forsaketh the fear of the **A.** 7706
 8: 3 or doth the **A** pervert justice? 7706
 8: 5 and make thy supplication to the **A;** 7706
 11: 7 canst thou find out the **A** unto perfection? 7706
 13: 3 Surely I would speak to the **A,** and I 7706
 15:25 and strengtheneth himself against the **A.** 7706
 21:15 What *is* the **A,** that we should serve him? 7706
 21:20 and he shall drink of the wrath of the **A.** 7706
 22: 3 *Is it any* pleasure to the **A,** that thou art 7706
 22:17 from us: and what can the **A** do for them? 7706
 22:23 If thou return to the **A,** thou shalt be built 7706
 22:25 the **A** shall be thy defence, and thou shalt 7706
 22:26 then shalt thou have thy delight in the **A,** 7706
 23:16 my heart soft, and the **A** troubleth me: 7706
 24: 1 seeing times are not hidden from the **A,** 7706
 27: 2 and the **A,** *who* hath vexed my soul; 7706
 27:10 Will he delight himself in the **A**? will he 7706
 27:11 which *is* with the **A** will I not conceal. 7706
 27:13 *which* they shall receive of the **A.** 7706
 29: 5 When the **A** *was* yet with me, *when* my 7706
 31: 2 *what* inheritance of the **A** from on high? 7706
 31:35 my desire *is, that* the **A** would answer me, 7706
 32: 8 the inspiration of the **A** giveth them 7706
 33: 4 and the breath of the **A** hath given me life. 7706
 34:10 the **A,** *that he should commit* iniquity. 7706
 34:12 neither will the **A** pervert judgment. 7706
 35:13 hear vanity, neither will the **A** regard it. 7706
 37:23 *Touching* the **A,** we cannot find him out: 7706
 40: 2 he that contendeth with the **A** instruct 7706
Ps 68:14 When the **A** scattered kings in it, it was 7706
 91: 1 shall abide under the shadow of the **A.** 7706
Isa 13: 6 it shall come as a destruction from the **A.** 7706
Eze 1:24 as the voice of the **A,** the voice of speech, 7706
 10: 5 as the voice of the **A** God when he 7706
Joel 1:15 as a destruction from the **A** shall it come. 7706
2Co 6:18 my sons and daughters, saith the Lord **A.** 3841
Rev 1: 8 which was, and which is to come, the **A.** 3841
 4: 8 saying, Holy, holy, holy, Lord God **A,** 3841
 11:17 O Lord God **A,** which art, and wast, 3841
 15: 3 marvellous *are* thy works, Lord God **A;** 3841
 16: 7 Lord God **A,** true and righteous *are* thy 3841
 16:14 to the battle of that great day of God **A.** 3841
 19:15 of the fierceness and wrath of **A** God. 3841
 21:22 for the Lord God **A** and the Lamb are 3841

ALMODAD (2)

Ge 10:26 Joktan begat **A,** and Sheleph, 486
1Ch 1:20 Joktan begat **A,** and Sheleph, 486

ALMON (1)

Jos 21:18 with her suburbs, and **A** with her suburbs; 5960

ALMOND (2) [ALMONDS]

Ecc 12: 5 the **a** tree shall flourish, 8247
Jer 1:11 And I said, I see a rod of an **a** tree. 8247

ALMON-DIBLATHAIM (2)

Nu 33:46 from Dibon-gad, and encamped in **A.** 5963
 33:47 they removed from **A,** and pitched in 5963

ALMONDS (8) [ALMOND]

Ge 43:11 honey, spices, and myrrh, nuts, and **a:** 8247
Ex 25:33 bowls **made like unto a,** *with* a knop 8246
 25:33 three bowls **made like a** in the other 8246
 25:34 *shall be* four bowls **made like unto a,** 8246
 37:19 Three bowls **made after the fashion of a** 8246
 37:19 bowls **made like a** in another branch, 8246
 37:20 candlestick *were* four bowls **made like a,** 8246
Nu 17: 8 and bloomed blossoms, and yielded **a.** 8247

ALMOST (11)

Ex 17: 4 I do unto this people? they be **a** 4592+5750
Ps 73: 2 *as for* me, my feet were **a** gone; 4592+3509.1
 94:17 my soul had **a** dwelt *in* silence. 4592+3509.1
 119:87 They had **a** consumed me upon 4592+3509.1
Pr 5:14 I was **a** in all evil in the midst of 4592+3509.1
Ac 13:44 the next sabbath day came **a** the whole 4975
 19:26 but **a** throughout all Asia, this Paul hath 4975
 21:27 when the seven days were **a** ended, 3195
 26:28 **A** thou persuadest me to be a 1722+3641
 26:29 that hear me this day, were both **a,** 1722+3641
Heb 9:22 And **a** all *things* are by the law purged 4975

ALMS (13) [ALMSDEEDS]

Mt 6: 1 Take heed that *ye* do not your **a** before 1654
 6: 2 Therefore when thou doest *thine* **a,** do not 1654
 6: 3 when thou doest **a,** let not thy left hand 1654
 6: 4 That thine **a** may be in secret: 1654
Lk 11:41 But rather give **a** of such *things* as *you* 1654
 12:33 Sell that ye have, and give **a;** 1654
Ac 3: 2 to ask **a** of them that entered into 1654
 3: 3 about to go into the temple, asked an **a.** 1654
 3:10 sat for **a** at the Beautiful gate of the temple 1654
 10: 2 which gave much **a** to the people, 1654
 10: 4 thine **a** are come up for a memorial before 1654
 10:31 thine **a** are had in remembrance in the 1654
 24:17 Now after many years I came to bring **a** to 1654

ALMSDEEDS (1) [ALMS]

Ac 9:36 full of good works and **a** which she did. 1654

ALMUG (3) [ALGUM]

1Ki 10:11 brought in from Ophir great plenty of **a** 484
 10:12 the king made *of* the **a** trees pillars for 484
 10:12 there came no such **a** trees, nor were seen 484

ALOES (5)

Nu 24: 6 as the **trees of lign a** *which* the LORD hath 174
Ps 45: 8 and cassia, out of the ivory palaces, 174
Pr 7:17 my bed *with* myrrh, **a,** and cinnamon. 174
SS 4:14 myrrh and **a,** with all the chief spices: 174
Jn 19:39 and brought a mixture of myrrh and **a,** 250

ALONE (108)

Ge 2:18 not good that the man should be **a** 905+3807.1
 32:24 Jacob was left **a;** and there 905+3807.1
 42:38 brother is dead, and he is left **a:** 905+3807.1
 44:20 he is left of his mother, 905+3807.1
Ex 14:12 saying, Let us **a,** that we may serve 2308+4480
 18:14 why sittest thou thyself **a,** and all 905+3807.1
 18:18 art not able to perform it thyself **a.** 905+3807.1
 24: 2 Moses **a** shall come near 905+3807.1
 32:10 Now therefore **let** me **a,** that my wrath 3240
Lev 13:46 he shall dwell **a;** without the camp 910
Nu 11:14 not able to bear all this people **a,** 905+3807.1
 11:17 that thou bear *it* not thyself **a.** 905+3807.1
 23: 9 lo, the people shall dwell **a,** 910+3807.1
Dt 1: 9 I am not able to bear you myself **a:** 905+3807.1
 1:12 How can I myself **a** bear your 905+3807.1
 9:14 **Let** me **a,** that I may destroy them, 7503
 32:12 *So* the LORD **a** did lead him, and *there was* 910
 33:28 Israel then shall dwell *in* safety **a:** 910
Jos 22:20 that man perished not **a** in his iniquity. 259
Jdg 3:20 he had for himself **a.** 905+2050.2+3807.1
 11:37 **let** me **a** two months, that I may go up 7503
1Sa 21: 1 *art* thou **a,** and no man with thee? 905+3807.1
2Sa 16:11 *may this* Benjamite *do it?* **let** him **a,** 3240
 18:24 and behold a man running **a.** 905+3807.1
 18:25 the king said, If he *be* **a,** *there is* 905+3807.1
 18:26 Behold *another* man running **a.** 905+3807.1
1Ki 11:29 and they two *were* **a** in the field: 905+3807.1
2Ki 4: 27 man of God said, **Let** her **a;** for her soul 7503
 19:15 thou *art* the God, *even* thou **a,** 905+3807.1
 23:18 he said, **Let** him **a;** let no man move his 3240
 23:18 So they **let** his bones **a,** with the bones of 4422
1Ch 29: 1 whom **a** God hath chosen, *is yet* young 259
Ezr 5: 2 Let the work of this house of God **a;** 7662
Ne 9: 6 Thou, *even* thou, *art* LORD **a;** thou 905+3807.1
Est 3: 6 scorn to lay hands on Mordecai **a;** 905+3807.1
Job 1:15 I only am escaped **a** to tell thee. 905+3807.1
 1:16 I only am escaped **a** to tell thee. 905+3807.1
 1:17 I only am escaped **a** to tell thee. 905+3807.1
 1:19 I only am escaped **a** to tell thee. 905+3807.1
 7:16 let me **a;** for my days *are* vanity. 2308
 7:19 **let** me **a** till I swallow down my spittle? 7503
 9: 8 a spreadeth out the heavens, 905+3807.1
 10:20 then, and let me **a,** that I may 4480+7896
 13:13 **let** me **a,** that I may speak, and let come 4480
 15:19 Unto whom **a** the earth was given, 905+3807.1
 31:17 Or have eaten my morsel myself **a,** 3807.1
Ps 83:18 whose name *is* JEHOVAH, 905+3807.1
 86:10 wondrous *things:* thou *art* God **a.** 905+3807.1
 102: 7 and am as a sparrow upon the housetop. 909
 136: 4 him who **a** doeth great wonders: 905+3807.1
 148:13 his name *is* excellent; his glory **a** 905+3807.1
Pr 9:12 thou scornest, thou **a** shalt bear *it.* 905+3807.1
Ecc 4: 8 There is one **a,** and *there is* not a second; NIH
 4:10 woe to him *that is* **a** when he falleth; 259
 4:11 have heat: but how can one be warm **a**? NIH
Isa 2:11 **a** shall be exalted in that day. 905+3807.1
 2:17 **a** shall be exalted in that day. 905+3807.1
 5: 8 that they may be placed **a** in 905+3807.1
 14:31 and none *shall be* **a** in his appointed times. 909
 37:16 thou *art* the God, *even* thou **a,** 905+3807.1
 44:24 stretcheth forth the heavens **a;** 905+3807.1

Isa 49:21 Behold, I was left **a;** these, 905+3807.1
 51: 2 for I called him **a,** and blessed him, 259
 63: 3 I have trodden the winepress **a;** 905+3807.1
Jer 15:17 nor rejoiced; I sat **a** because of thy hand: 910
 49:31 have neither gates nor bars, *which* dwell **a.** 910
La 3:28 He sitteth **a** and keepeth silence, because 910
Da 10: 7 I Daniel **a** saw the vision: for 905+3807.1
 10: 8 Therefore I was left **a,** and saw this 905+3807.1
Hos 4:17 Ephraim *is* joined to idols: **let** him **a.** 3240
 8: 9 gone up *to* Assyria, a wild ass **a** by himself: 909
Mt 4: 4 Man shall not live by bread **a,** but by every 3441
 14:23 the evening was come, he was there **a.** 3441
 15:14 **Let** them **a:** they be blind leaders of 863
 18:15 tell him his fault between thee and him **a:** 3441
Mk 1:24 Saying, **Let** *us* **a;** what have we to do with 1436
 4:10 And when he was **a,** they that were about 2651
 4:34 *when they were* **a,** he expounded 2398+2596
 6:47 the midst of the sea, and he **a** on the land. 3441
 14: 6 And Jesus said, **Let** her **a;** why trouble you 863
 15:36 reed, and gave him to drink, saying, **Let a;** 863
Lk 4: 4 That man shall not live by bread **a,** 3441
 4:34 Saying, **Let** *us* **a;** what have we to do with 1436
 5:21 Who can forgive sins, but God **a?** 3441
 6: 4 it is not lawful to eat but for the priests **a?** 3441
 9:18 And it came to pass, as he was **a** 2596+3441
 9:36 the voice was past, Jesus was found **a.** 3441
 10:40 care that my sister hath left me to serve **a?** 3441
 13: 8 Lord, **let** it **a** this year also, till I shall dig 863
Jn 6:15 departed again into a mountain himself **a.** 3441
 6:22 but *that* his disciples were gone away **a;** 3441
 8: 9 and Jesus was left **a,** and the woman 3441
 8:16 for I am not **a,** but I and the Father that 3441
 8:29 the Father hath not left me **a;** for I do 3441
 11:48 If we **let** him thus **a,** all *men* will believe 863
 12: 7 Then said Jesus, **Let** her **a:** against the day 863
 12:24 fall into the ground and die, it abideth **a:** 3441
 16:32 man to his own, and shall leave me **a:** 3441
 16:32 and *yet* I am not **a,** because the Father is 3441
 17:20 Neither pray I for these **a,** but for them 3440
Ac 5:38 Refrain from these men, and **let** them **a:** 1439
 19:26 that not **a** at Ephesus, 3440
Ro 4:23 Now it was not written for his sake **a,** 3440
 11: 3 and I am left **a,** and they seek my life. 3441
Gal 6: 4 then shall he have rejoicing in himself **a,** 3441
1Th 3: 1 we thought it good to be left at Athens **a;** 3441
Heb 9: 7 But into the second *went* the high priest **a** 3441
Jas 2:17 it hath not works, is dead, *being* **a.** 1438+2596

ALONG (30)

Ex 2: 5 her maidens walked **a** by the river's side; 5921
 9:23 hail, and the fire **ran a** upon the ground; 1980
Nu 21:22 *but* we will **go a** by the king's *high* way, 1980
 34: 3 wilderness of Zin **a** *by* the coast of Edom, 5921
Dt 2:27 I will **go a** by the high way, I will neither 1980
Jos 10:10 chased them **a** the way that goeth up to NIH
 15: 3 **passed a** to Zin, and ascended up on 5674
 15: 3 **passed a** *to* Hezron, and went up to Adar, 5674
 15: 6 and **passed a** by the north of Beth-arabah; 5674
 15:10 **passed a** unto the side of mount Jearim, 5674
 15:11 **passed a** *to* mount Baalah, and went out 5674
 16: 2 **passeth a** unto the borders of Archi *to* 5674
 17: 7 the border went **a** on the right hand unto NIH
 18:18 **passed a** toward the side over against 5674
 18:19 the border **passed a** to the side of 5674
 19:13 from thence **passeth on a** on the east to 5674
Jdg 7:12 all the children of the east **lay a** in 5307
 7:13 fell, and overturned it, that the tent **lay a.** 5307
 9:25 they robbed all that **came a** *that* way by 5674
 9:37 another company come **a** by 1870+4480
 11:18 they **went a** through the wilderness, 1980
 11:26 in all the cities that *be* **a** by the coasts of 5921
 20:37 the liers in wait **drew** *themselves* **a,** 4900
1Sa 6:12 *and* **went a** the highway, lowing as they 1980
 28:20 Saul fell straightway **all a** on 4393+6967
2Sa 15:30 husband went with her **a** weeping 1980
 16:13 Shimei **went a** on the hill's side over 1980
2Ki 11:11 the temple, **a** by the altar and the temple. NIH
2Ch 23:10 **a** by the altar and the temple, by the king NIH
Jer 41: 6 weeping **all a** as he **went:** 1980+1980

ALOOF (1)

Ps 38:11 my friends stand **a** from my sore; 4480+5048

ALOTH (1)

1Ki 4:16 the son of Hushai *was* in Asher and in **A:** 1175

ALOUD (19) [LOUD]

Ge 45: 2 he **wept a:** 1065+5414+6963+871.1
1Ki 18:27 and said, Cry **a:** 1419+6963+871.1
Ezr 3:12 **shouted a** 6963+7311+8643+871.1+3807.1
Job 19: 7 heard: I **cry a,** but *there is* no judgment. 7768
Ps 51:14 my tongue shall **sing a** of thy 7442
 55:17 and at noon, will I pray, and **cry a:** 1993
 59:16 I will **sing a** of thy mercy in the morning: 7442
 81: 1 **Sing a** unto God our strength: make a 7442
 132:16 and her saints shall **shout a for joy.** 7442+7444
 149: 5 in glory: let them **sing a** upon their beds. 7442
Isa 24:14 the LORD, they shall **cry a** from the sea. 6670
 54: 1 break forth *into* singing, and **cry a,** 6670
 58: 1 Cry **a,** spare not, lift up thy voice 1627+871.1
Da 3: 4 a herald cried **a,** To you it is 2429+871.2
 4:14 He cried **a,** and said thus, Hew 2429+871.2
 4:14 the king cried **a** to bring in 2429+871.2
Hos 5: 8 **cry a** at Beth-aven, after thee, 7321
Mic 4: 9 Now why dost thou **cry out a?** 7321+7452

Mk 15: 8 the multitude **crying a** began to desire *310*

ALPHA (4)
Rev 1: 8 I am **A** and Omega, the beginning *1*
1:11 Saying, I am **A** and Omega, the first *1*
21: 6 am **A** and Omega, the beginning and the end. *1*
22:13 am **A** and Omega, the beginning and the end, *1*

ALPHEUS (5)
Mt 10: 3 James the *son* of **A**, and Lebbeus, *256*
Mk 2:14 he saw Levi the *son* of **A** sitting at *256*
3:18 and James the *son* of **A**, and Thaddeus, *256*
Lk 6:15 James the *son* of **A**, and Simon called *256*
Ac 1:13 James the *son* of **A**, and Simon Zelotes, *256*

ALREADY (31) [READY]
Ex 1: 5 seventy souls: for Joseph was in Egypt **a**. NIH
2Ch 28:13 LORD **a**, ye intend to add *more* to our sins NIH
Ne 5: **a**: neither *is it* in our power to redeem NIH
Ecc 1:10 it hath been **a** of old time, which was 3528
2:12 *even* that which hath been a done. 3528
3:15 *that* which *is* to be hath **a** been; and God 3528
4: 2 Wherefore I praised the dead which are **a** 3528
6:10 That which hath been is named **a**, and 3528
Mal 2: 2 yea, I have cursed them **a**, because ye do NIH
Mt 5:28 committed adultery with her **a** in his heart 2235
17:12 That Elias is come **a**, and they knew him 2235
Mk 15:44 And Pilate marvelled if he were **a** dead: 2235
Lk earth; and what will I, if it be **a** kindled? 2235
Jn 3:18 but he that believeth is condemned **a**, 2235
4:35 the fields; for they are white **a** to harvest. 2235
9:22 for the Jews had agreed **a**, that if any *man* 2235
9:27 I have told you **a**, and ye did not hear: 2235
11:17 that he had *lien* in the grave four days **a**. 2235
19:33 saw that he was dead **a**, they brake not 2235
Ac 11:11 **immediately** there were three men **a** 1824
27: 9 because the fast was **now a** past, Paul 2235
1Co 5: 3 but present in spirit, have judged **a**, 2235
2Co 12:21 I shall bewail many which have **sinned a**, 4258
Php 3:12 Not as though I had **a** attained, either 2235
3:12 already attained, either were **a** perfect: 2235
3:16 whereto we have **a** attained, NIG
2Th 2: 7 For the mystery of iniquity doth **a** work: 2235
1Ti 5:15 For some are **a** turned aside after Satan. 2235
2Ti 2:18 saying that the resurrection is past **a**; 2235
1Jn 4: 3 and *even* now **a** is it in the world. 2235
Rev 2:25 But *that* which ye have **a** hold fast till I NIG

ALSO (1768)
Ge 1:16 to rule the night: *he* made the stars **a**. 2050.1
2: 9 tree of life **a** in the midst of the garden, NIH
3: 6 and gave **a** unto her husband with her; 1571
3:18 Thorns **a** and thistles shall it bring forth 2050.1
3:21 Unto Adam **a** and to his wife did 2050.1
3:22 take **a** of the tree of life, and eat, 1571
4: 4 he **a** brought of the firstlings of his flock 1571
4:22 Zillah, she **a** bare Tubal-cain, an instructor 1571
4:26 to Seth, *to* him **a** there was born a son; 1571
6: 3 strive with man, for that he **a** *is* flesh; 1571
6: 4 **a** after that, when the sons of God came 1571
6:11 The earth **a** was corrupt before God, 2050.1
7: 3 Of fowls **a** of the air by sevens, the male 1571
8: 2 The fountains **a** of the deep 2050.1
8: 8 **A** he sent forth a dove from him, to see 2050.1
10:21 Unto Shem **a**, the father of all 2050.1
12:15 The princes **a** of Pharaoh saw her, 2050.1
13: 5 Lot **a**, which went with Abram, had flocks 1571
13:16 *then* shall thy seed **a** be numbered. 1571
14: 7 **a** the Amorites, that dwelt in 1571
14:16 **a** brought again his brother Lot, 1571
14:16 and the women **a**, and the people. 1571
15:14 **a** that nation, whom they shall serve, will 1571
16:13 Have I **a** here looked after him that seeth 1571
17:16 bless her, and give thee a son **a** of her: 1571
18:12 I have pleasure, my lord being old **a**? 2050.1
18:23 Wilt thou **a** destroy the righteous with 637
18:24 wilt thou **a** destroy and not spare the place 637
19:34 let us make him drink wine this night **a**; 1571
19:35 made their father drink wine that night **a**: 1571
19:38 she **a** bare a son, and called his name 1571
20: 4 Lord, wilt thou slay **a** a righteous nation? 1571
20: 6 for I **a** withheld thee from sinning against 1571
21:13 **a** of the son of the bondwoman will I 1571
22:20 she hath **a** born children unto thy brother 1571
22:24 she bare **a** Tebah, and Gaham, 1571
24:14 Drink, and I will give thy camels drink **a**: 1571
24:19 said, I will draw *water* for thy camels **a**, 1571
24:44 and I will **a** draw for thy camels: 1571
24:46 Drink, and I will give thy camels drink **a**: 1571
24:46 I drank, and she made the camels drink **a**. 1571
24:53 he gave **a** to her brother and to her 2050.1
26:21 digged another well, and strove for that **a**: 1571
27:31 he **a** had made savoury meat, and brought 1571
27:34 Bless me, *even* me **a**, O my father. 1571
27:38 Bless me, *even* me **a**, O my father. 1571
27:45 why should I be deprived **a** of you both *in* 1571
29:27 we will give thee this **a** for the service 1571
29:28 he gave him Rachel his daughter to wife **a**. NIH
29:30 he went in **a** unto Rachel, and he loved 1571
29:30 he loved **a** Rachel more than Leah, 1571
29:33 he hath therefore given me this *son* **a**: 1571
30: 3 that I may **a** have children by her. 1571
30: 6 hath **a** heard my voice, and hath given me 1571
30:15 thou take away my son's mandrakes **a**? 2050.1
30:30 shall I provide for mine own house **a**? 1571

Ge 31:15 and hath quite devoured **a** our money. 1571
32: 6 **a** he cometh to meet thee, and four 1571
32:18 lord Esau: and behold, he *is* behind us. 1571
33: 7 Leah **a** with her children came near, 1571
35:17 Fear not; thou shalt have this son **a**. 1571
37: 7 lo, my sheaf arose, and **a** stood upright; 1571
38:10 the LORD: wherefore he slew him **a**. 1571
38:11 for he said, Lest peradventure he die **a**, 1571
38:22 **a** the men of the place said, *that* there was 1571
38:24 **a**, behold, she *is* with child by whoredom. 1571
40:15 here a have I done nothing that they 1571
40:16 I **a** *was* in my dream, and behold, 637
42:22 therefore, behold, a his blood is required. 1571
43: 8 both we, and thou, *and* **a** our little ones. 1571
43:13 Take **a** your brother, and arise, go again 2050.1
44: 9 we **a** will be my lord's bondmen. 1571
44:10 **a** *let it be* according unto your words: 1571
44:16 and he **a** with whom the cup is found. 1571
44:29 if ye take this **a** from me, 1571
45:20 **A** regard not your stuff; for the good of 2050.1
46: 4 I will **a** surely bring thee up *again*: 1571
46:34 until now, both we, *and* **a** our fathers. 1571
47: 3 *are* shepherds, both we, *and* **a** our fathers. 1571
47:18 my lord **a** had our herds of cattle; 2050.1
48:11 and lo, God hath shewed me **a** thy seed. 1571
48:19 I know *it*: he **a** shall become a people, 1571
48:19 become a people, and he **a** shall be great: 1571
50:18 his brethren **a** went and fell down before 1571
50:23 **a** of Machir the son of Manasseh were 1571
Ex 1:10 they join **a** unto our enemies, 1571
2:19 **a** drew water enough for us, 1571
3: 9 I have **a** seen the oppression wherewith 1571
4: 9 if they will not believe **a** these two signs, 1571
4:14 **a**, behold, he cometh forth to meet thee: 1571
6: 4 I have **a** established my covenant with 1571
6: 5 I have **a** heard the groaning of the children 1571
7:11 Pharaoh **a** called the wise men and 1571
7:11 they **a** did in like manner with their 1571
7:23 neither did he set his heart to this **a**. 1571
8:21 and **a** the ground whereon they *are*. 1571
8:32 Pharaoh hardened his heart at this time **a**, 1571
10:24 stayed: let your little ones **a** go with you. 1571
10:25 Thou must give us **a** sacrifices 1571
10:26 Our cattle **a** shall go with us; there shall 1571
12:32 **A** take your flocks and your herds, as ye 1571
12:32 ye have said, and be gone; and bless me **a**. 1571
12:38 a mixed multitude went up **a** with them; 1571
15: 4 his chosen captains **a** are drowned in 2050.1
18:23 all this people shall **a** go to their place in 1571
19:22 let the priests **a**, which come near to 2050.1
21: 6 he shall **a** bring him to the door, or 2050.1
21:29 and his owner **a** shall be put to death. 1571
21:35 of it; and the dead *ox* **a** they shall divide. 1571
23: 9 **A** thou shalt not oppress a stranger: for 2050.1
24:11 **a** they saw God, and did eat and drink. 2050.1
25:23 Thou shalt **a** make a table *of* shittim 2050.1
29:15 Thou shalt **a** take one ram; and Aaron 2050.1
29:22 **A** thou shalt take of the ram the fat 2050.1
29:44 I will sanctify **a** both Aaron and his sons 2050.1
30:18 Thou shalt **a** make a laver *of* brass, 2050.1
30:18 his foot **a** *of* brass, to wash *withal*: NIH
30:23 Take thou **a** unto thee principal spices, 2050.1
31:13 Speak thou **a** unto the children of Israel, 2050.1
33:12 and thou hast **a** found grace in my sight. 1571
33:17 will do this thing **a** that thou hast spoken: 1571
35:14 The candlestick **a** for the light, and his 2050.1
37:12 **A** he made thereunto a border of a 2050.1
37:26 **a** he made unto it a crown *of* gold round 2050.1
Lev 5: 2 he **a** shall be unclean, and guilty. 2050.1
7:16 on the morrow **a** the remainder of it 2050.1
8: 8 he **a** put in the breastplate the Urim 2050.1
8: 9 **a** upon the mitre, *even* upon his 2050.1
9: 4 **a** a bullock and a ram for peace 2050.1
9:18 He slew **a** the bullock and the ram *for* a 2050.1
11:29 These **a** *shall be* unclean unto you 2050.1
11:40 he **a** that beareth the carcase of it shall 2050.1
13:18 The flesh **a**, in which, *even* in the skin 2050.1
13:38 If a man **a** or a woman have in the skin 2050.1
13:47 The garment **a** that the plague of leprosy 2050.1
14: 9 he **a** shall wash his flesh in water, 2050.1
15:18 The woman **a** with whom man shall lie 2050.1
15:20 every *thing* **a** that she sitteth upon shall 2050.1
18:19 **A** thou shalt not approach unto a 2050.1
18:28 That the land spue not you out **a**, when 1571
20:13 **If** a man **a** lie with mankind, as he lieth 2050.1
20:27 A man **a** or woman that hath a familiar 2050.1
22:12 If the priest's daughter **a** be *married* 2050.1
23:27 **A** on the tenth *day* of this seventh month 389
23:39 **A** in the fifteenth *day* of the seventh month 389
26:16 I **a** will do this unto you; I will even 637
26:22 I will **a** send wild beasts among you, 2050.1
26:24 will I **a** walk contrary unto you, 637
26:28 **Then** I will walk contrary unto you **a** in 2050.1
26:39 **a** in the iniquities of their fathers shall they 637
26:40 that **a** they have walked contrary unto me; 637
26:41 *And that* I have walked contrary unto 637
26:42 **a** my covenant with Isaac, and also my 637
26:42 **a** my covenant with Abraham will I 637
26:43 The land **a** shall be left of them, 2050.1
Nu 3: 1 These **a** *are* the generations of Aaron 2050.1
4:22 Take **a** the sum of the sons of Gershon, 1571
6:17 the priest **a** offer **a** his meat offering, 2050.1
9: 2 Let the children of Israel **a** keep 2050.1
10:10 **A** in the day of your gladness, and in 2050.1
11: 4 children of Israel **a** wept again, 1571+2050.1

Nu 11:10 kindled greatly; Moses **a** was displeased. 2050.1
12: 2 hath he not spoken **a** by us? 1571
15:15 **and a** for the stranger that sojourneth 2050.1
16:10 with thee: and seek ye the priesthood **a**? 1571
16:17 **a**, and Aaron, each *of you* his censer. 2050.1
16:34 they said, Lest the earth swallow us up **a**. NIH
18: 2 brethren **a** *of* the tribe of Levi, the tribe 1571
18: 3 altar, that neither they, nor you **a**, die. 1571
18: 8 I have given thee the charge of mine 2050.1
18:28 Thus you **a** shall offer a heave offering 1571
20:11 the congregation drank, and their beasts **a**. NIH
22:19 I pray you, tarry ye **a** here *this* night, 1571
22:33 surely now **a** I had slain thee, and saved 1571
24:12 Spake I not **a** to thy messengers which 1571
24:18 Seir **a** shall be a possession for his 2050.1
24:24 afflict Eber, and he **a** shall perish for ever. 1571
24:25 to his place: and Balak **a** went his way. 1571
27:13 thou **a** shalt be gathered unto thy people 2050.1
28:26 **A** in the day of the firstfruits, when ye 2050.1
30: 3 If a woman **a** vow a vow unto 2050.1
31: 8 Balaam **a** the son of Beor they slew with 2050.1
33: 4 upon their gods **a** the LORD executed 2050.1
35: 2 ye shall give **a** unto the Levites suburbs for NIH
Dt 1:37 **A** the LORD was angry with me for your 1571
1:37 Thou **a** shalt not go in thither. 1571
2: 6 ye shall **a** buy water of them for money, 1571
2:11 Which **a** were accounted giants, as 637
2:12 The Horims **a** dwelt in Seir beforetime; 2050.1
2:20 (That **a** was accounted a land of giants: 637
3: 3 our God delivered into our hands Og **a**, 1571
3:17 The plain **a**, and Jordan, and the coast 2050.1
3:20 *until* they **a** possess the land which 1571
7:13 he will **a** bless the fruit of thy womb, 2050.1
8: 5 Thou shalt **a** consider in thine heart, 2050.1
9: 8 **A** in Horeb ye provoked the LORD to 2050.1
9:19 LORD hearkened unto me at that time **a**. 1571
9:20 and I prayed for Aaron the same time. 1571
10:10 LORD hearkened unto me at that time **a**, 1571
10:14 God, the earth **a**, with all that therein *is*. NIH
15:17 **a** unto thy maidservant thou shalt do 637
18: 4 The firstfruit **a** of thy corn, of thy wine, NIH
20: 6 let him **a** go and return unto his house, NIH
23:12 Thou shalt have a place **a** without 2050.1
26:13 a have given them unto the Levite, 1571
28:51 which **a** shall not leave thee *either* corn, NIH
28:61 **A** every sickness, and every plague, 1571
29:15 **and a** with *him* that *is* not here with us 2050.1
31: 2 **a** the LORD hath said unto me, 2050.1
32:24 I will **a** send the teeth of beasts upon 2050.1
32:25 The suckling **a** with the man of gray hairs. NIH
33:28 wine; **a** his heavens shall drop down dew. 637
Jos 1:15 they **a** have possessed the land which 1571
2:12 that ye will **a** shew kindness unto my 1571
7:11 they have **a** transgressed my covenant 1571
7:11 have **a** stolen, and dissembled also, 1571
7:11 dissembled **a**, and they have put *it* even 1571
10:30 the LORD delivered it **a**, and the king 1571
10:39 as he had done **a** to Libnah, and to her 2050.1
13: 3 and the Ekronites; **a** the Avites: 2050.1
13:22 Balaam **a** the son of Beor, the soothsayer 2050.1
15:19 a south land; give me **a** springs of water. 2050.1
17: 1 There was **a** a lot for the tribe of 2050.1
17: 2 There was **a** *a lot* for the rest of 2050.1
17: 9 coast of Manasseh **a** *was* on the north 2050.1
19:30 Ummah **a**, and Aphek, and Rehob: 2050.1
20: 1 The LORD **a** spake unto Joshua, saying, 2050.1
22: 7 when Joshua sent them away **a** unto 1571
24: 5 I sent Moses **a** and Aaron, and I plagued 2050.1
24:18 *therefore* will we **a** serve the LORD; 1571
Jdg 1:15 a south land; give me **a** springs of water. 2050.1
1:18 **A** Judah took Gaza with the coast 2050.1
1:22 of Joseph, they **a** went up *against* Beth-el: 1571
2: 3 Wherefore I **a** said, I will not drive them 1571
2:10 **a** all that generation were gathered unto 1571
2:21 I **a** will not henceforth drive out any from 1571
3:22 the haft **a** went in after the blade; 1571
3:31 with an ox goad: and he **a** delivered Israel. 1571
5: 4 the clouds **a** dropped water. 1571
5:15 with Deborah; even Issachar, *and* **a** Barak: 3651
6:35 who **a** was gathered after him: NIH
7:18 blow ye the trumpets **a** on every side of all 1571
8: 9 he spake **a** unto the men of Penuel, 1571
8:22 and thy son, **and** thy son's son **a**: 1571
8:31 she **a** bare him a son, whose name he 1571
9: 2 remember that I *am* your bone NIH
9:19 in Abimelech, and let him **a** rejoice in you: 1571
9:49 the men of the tower of Shechem died **a**, 1571
10: 9 over Jordan to fight **a** against Judah, 1571
10:10 forsaken our God, and **a** served Baalim. NIH
10:12 The Zidonians **a**, and the Amalekites, 2050.1
15: 5 **a** the standing corn, with the vineyards 5704
17: 2 spakest of **a** in mine ears, behold, the 1571
19:10 his concubine **a** *was* with him. 2050.1
19:16 at even, which *was* **a** of mount Ephraim; 376
19:19 there is bread **and** wine **a** for me, 2050.1
20:48 **a** they set on fire all the cities that they 1571
Ru 1: 5 Mahlon and Chilion died **a** both of them; 1571
1:12 *if* I should have a husband **a** to night, 1571
1:12 also to night, and should **a** bear sons; 1571
1:17 The LORD do so to me, and more **a**, 3541
2:16 let fall **a** *some* of the handfuls of purpose 1571
2:21 the Moabitess, said, He said unto me **a**, 1571
3:15 **A** he said, Bring the vail that *thou hast* 2050.1
4: 5 thou must buy *it* **a** of Ruth the Moabitess, 854
1Sa 1: 6 her adversary **a** provoked her sore, for to 1571

A

1Sa	1:28	Therefore **a** I have lent him to the Lord;	1571

1Sa 1:28 Therefore **a** I have lent him to the Lord; 1571
2:15 **A** before they burnt the fat, the priest's 1571
2:26 both with the Lord, and with men. 1571
3:12 when I begin, I will **a** make an end. 2050.1
3:17 God do so to thee, and more **a**, if thou 3541
4:17 there hath been **a** a great slaughter among 1571
4:17 thy two sons **a**, Hophni and Phinehas, 1571
8: 8 served other gods, so do they **a** unto thee. 1571
8:20 That we **a** may be like all the nations; 1571
10:11 son of Kish? *Is* Saul **a** among the prophets? 1571
10:12 a proverb, *Is* Saul among the prophets? 1571
10:26 Saul **a** went home to Gibeah; 1571
12:14 **a** the king that reigneth over you continue 1571
13: 4 *that* Israel **a** was had in abomination with 1571
14:15 they **a** trembled, and the earth quaked: 1571
14:21 they **a** turned to be with the Israelites 1571
14:22 even they **a** followed hard after them in 1571
14:44 Saul answered, God do so and more **a**: 2050.1
15: 1 Samuel **a** said unto Saul, The Lord 2050.1
15:23 he hath **a** rejected thee from *being* king. 2050.1
15:29 the Strength of Israel will not lie nor 1571
17:38 he armed him with a coat of *mail.* 2050.1
18: 5 and **a** in the sight of Saul's servants. 1571
19:11 Saul **a** sent messengers unto David's 2050.1
19:20 of Saul, and they **a** prophesied. 1571
19:21 the third time, and they prophesied **a**. 1571
19:22 went he **a** to Ramah, and came to a great 1571
19:23 the spirit of God was upon him **a**, 1571
19:24 he stript off his clothes **a**, 1571
19:24 they say, *Is* Saul **a** among the prophets? 1571
20:15 **a** thou shalt not cut off thy kindness from NIH
22:17 because their hand **a** *is* with David, 1571
23:17 and that **a** Saul my father knoweth. 1571
23:25 Saul **a** and his men went to seek *him.* 2050.1
24: 8 David **a** rose afterward, and went out 2050.1
25:13 and David **a** girded on his sword: 1571
25:22 more **a** do God unto the enemies of David 3541
25:43 David **a** took Ahinoam of Jezreel; 2050.1
25:43 and they were **a** both of them his wives. 1571
26:25 do great things, and **a** shalt still prevail. 1571
28:19 Moreover the Lord will **a** deliver Israel 1571
28:19 the Lord **a** shall deliver the host of Israel 1571
28:22 hearken thou **a** unto the voice of thine 1571
30:21 whom they had made **a** to abide at. 2050.1

2Sa 1: 4 many of the people **a** are fallen and dead; 1571
1: 4 and Saul and Jonathan his son are dead **a**. 1571
1:18 (A he bade *them* teach the children of 1571
2: 2 his two wives **a**, Ahinoam the Jezreelitess, 1571
2: 6 I **a** will requite you this kindness, because 1571
2: 7 **a** the house of Judah have anointed me 1571
2:24 Joab **a** and Abishai pursued after Abner: 2050.1
3: 9 So do God to Abner, and more **a**, except, 3541
3:12 saying **a**, Make thy league with me, NIH
3:19 Abner **a** spake in the ears of Benjamin: 1571
3:19 Abner went **a** to speak in the ears of David 1571
3:35 and more **a**, if I taste bread, or ought else, 3588
4: 2 (for Beeroth **a** was reckoned to Benjamin: 1571
5: 2 **A** in time past, when Saul was king over 1571
5:15 Ibhar **a**, and Elishua, and Nepheg, 2050.1
5:18 The Philistines **a** came 2050.1
7:11 **A** the Lord telleth thee that he will 2050.1
7:19 thou hast spoken **a** of thy servant's house 1571
8: 3 David smote **a** Hadadezer, the son of 2050.1
8:11 Which **a** king David did dedicate unto 1571
10:14 *then* fled they **a** before Abishai, NIH
11:12 Tarry here to day **a**, and to morrow I will 1571
11:17 of David; and Uriah the Hittite died **a**. 1571
11:21 Thy servant Uriah the Hittite is dead **a**. 1571
11:24 thy servant Uriah the Hittite is dead **a**. 1571
12:13 The Lord **a** hath put away thy sin; 1571
12:14 the child **a** that is born unto thee shall 1571
13:36 the king **a** and all his servants wept very 1571
14: 7 he slew; and we will destroy the heir **a**: 1571
15:19 Gittite, Wherefore goest thou **a** with us? 1571
15:19 for thou *art* a stranger, and **a** an exile. 1571
15:21 or life, even there **a** will thy servant be. NIH
15:23 the king *himself* passed over the brook 2050.1
15:24 lo Zadok **a**, and all the Levites *were* with 1571
15:27 The king said **a** unto Zadok the priest, 2050.1
15:34 so *will* I now **a** be thy servant: 2050.1
17: 5 Call now Hushai the Archite **a**, and let us 1571
17:10 he **a** *that is* valiant, whose heart *is* as 1571
18: 2 I will surely go forth with you myself **a**. 1571
18:22 let me, I pray thee, **a** run after Cushi. 1571
18:26 And the king said, He **a** bringeth tidings. 1571
19:13 God do so to me, and **more a**, if 3254+3541
19:40 the king, and **a** half the people of Israel. 1571
19:43 and we have **a** more *right* in David than ye: 1571
20:14 gathered together, and went **a** after him. 637
20:26 Ira **a** the Jairite was a chief ruler about 1571
21:20 *in* number; and he **a** was born to the giant. 1571
22:10 He bowed the heavens **a**, and came 2050.1
22:20 He brought me forth **a** into a large place: 2050.1
22:24 I was **a** upright before him, and have 2050.1
22:36 Thou hast **a** given me the shield of thy 2050.1
22:41 Thou hast **a** given me the necks of mine 2050.1
22:44 Thou **a** hast delivered me from 2050.1
22:49 Thou **a** hast lifted me up on high above 2050.1
23:20 he went down **a** and slew a lion in 2050.1

1Ki 1: 6 he **a** *was* a very goodly *man;* 2050.1
1:14 I **a** will come in after thee, 2050.1
1:22 the king, Nathan the prophet **a** came in. 2050.1
1:33 The king **a** said unto them, Take with 2050.1
1:46 **a** Solomon sitteth on the throne of 1571
1:48 **a** thus said the king, Blessed *be* the Lord 1571

1Ki 2: 5 Moreover thou knowest **a** what Joab 1571
2:22 ask for him the kingdom **a**; for he *is* 2050.1
2:23 God do so to me, and **more a**, 3254
3:13 I have **a** given thee *that* which thou hast 2050.1
3:18 that this woman was delivered **a**: 1571
4:13 to him **a** *pertained* the region of Argob, NIH
4:15 he **a** took Basmath the daughter of 1571
4:28 Barley **a** and straw for the horses 2050.1
4:33 he spake **a** of beasts, and of fowl, 2050.1
6:22 the whole altar *that was* by the oracle 2050.1
6:32 The two doors **a** *were* of olive tree; 2050.1
6:33 So **a** made he for the door of the temple 2050.1
7: 2 He built **a** the house of the forest of 2050.1
7: 8 Solomon made **a** a house for Pharaoh's 2050.1
7:20 two pillars *had* pomegranates **a** above, 1571
7:31 **a** upon the mouth of it *were* gravings 1571
8:24 thou spakest **a** with thy mouth, 2050.1
9:21 whom the children of Israel **a** were not 1571
10:11 the navy **a** of Hiram, that brought gold 1571
10:12 harps **a** and psalteries for singers: 2050.1
12:14 my father **a** chastised you with whips, NIH
13: 5 The altar **a** *was* rent, and the ashes 2050.1
13:11 king, them they told **a** to their father. 2050.1
13:18 I *am* a prophet **a** as thou *art;* and an angel 1571
13:24 by it, the lion **a** stood by the carcase. 2050.1
14:23 For they **a** built them high places, 1571
14:24 there were **a** sodomites in the land: 1571
15:13 **a** Maachah his mother, even her he 1571
16: 7 **a** by the hand of the prophet Jehu the son 1571
16:16 hath conspired, and hath **a** slain the king: 1571
17:20 hast thou **a** brought evil upon the widow 1571
18:35 and he filled the trench **a** with water. 1571
19: 2 So let the gods do *to me*, and more **a**, 3541
20: 3 thy wives **a** and thy children, *even* 2050.1
20:10 The gods do so unto me, and more **a**, 3541
21:19 Hast thou killed, and **a** taken possession? 1571
21:23 And of Jezebel **a** spake the Lord, saying, 1571
22:22 Thou shalt persuade *him*, and prevail **a**: 1571

2Ki 1:11 he sent unto him another captain 2050.1
2:13 took up **a** the mantle of Elijah that fell 2050.1
2:14 when he **a** had smitten the waters, they 2050.1
3:18 he will deliver the Moabites **a** into your 2050.1
5: 1 he was **a** a mighty *man* in valour, *but* 2050.1
6:31 he said, God do so and more **a** to me, 3541
7: 4 if we sit still here, we die **a**. Now 2050.1
7: 8 and carried thence **a**, and went and hid *it.* NIH
8: 1 it shall **a** come upon the land seven years. 1571
9:27 and said, Smite him **a** in the chariot. 1571
10: 2 and horses, a fenced city **a**, and armour; 2050.1
10: 5 the elders **a**, and the bringers up of 2050.1
11:17 between the king **a** and the people. 2050.1
13: 6 there remained the grove **a** in Samaria.) 1571
16:14 he brought **a** the brasen altar, which 2050.1
17:19 **A** Judah kept not the commandments of 1571
18: 2 His mother's name *was* Abi, 2050.1
21:11 hath made Judah **a** to sin with his idols: 1571
22:19 I have heard *thee*, saith the Lord. 1571
23: 5 them **a** that burnt incense unto Baal, 2050.1
23:19 all the houses **a** of the high places that 1571
23:27 I will remove Judah **a** out of my sight, 1571
24: 4 **a** *for* the innocent blood that he shed: 1571

1Ch 1:14 The Jebusite **a**, and the Amorite, and 2050.1
1:21 Hadoram **a**, and Uzal, and Diklah, 2050.1
1:51 Hadad died **a**. And the dukes of Edom 2050.1
2: 9 The sons **a** of Hezron, that were born 2050.1
2:26 Jerahmeel had **a** another wife, 2050.1
2:49 She bare **a** Shaaph the father of 2050.1
3: 6 Ibhar **a**, and Elishama, and Eliphelet, 2050.1
3:18 Malchiram **a**, and Pedaiah, 2050.1
6: 3 The sons **a** of Aaron; Nadab, and Abihu, 2050.1
6:48 Their brethren **a** the Levites *were* 2050.1
6:67 *they gave* **a** Gezer with her suburbs, 2050.1
6:79 Kedemoth **a** with her suburbs, 2050.1
7:10 The sons **a** of Jediael; Bilhan: 2050.1
7:12 Shuppim **a**, and Huppim, the children 1571
7:25 **a** Resheph, and Telah his son, 2050.1
7:28 Shechem **a** and the towns thereof, 2050.1
8:13 Beriah **a**, and Shema, who *were* heads 2050.1
8:18 Ishmerai **a**, and Jezliah, and Jobab, 2050.1
8:32 these **a** dwelt with their brethren in 637
9:29 *Some* of them **a** were appointed to 2050.1
9:38 they **a** dwelt with their brethren at 2050.1
10:13 a for asking *counsel* of one that had **a** 1571
11:10 These **a** *are* the chief of the mighty *men* 2050.1
11:22 **a** he went down and slew a lion in a pit 2050.1
11:26 **A** the valiant *men* of the armies *were*, 2050.1
12:38 all the rest **a** of Israel *were* of one heart to 1571
13: 2 with them **a** to the priests and Levites NIH
15:27 David **a** *had* upon him an ephod of 2050.1
16: 6 Benaiah **a** and Jahaziel the priests with 2050.1
16:25 he **a** *is* to be feared above all gods. 1571
16:30 the world **a** shall be stable, that it be not 637
16:38 Obed-edom **a** the son of Jeduthun 2050.1
17: 9 **A** I will ordain a place for my people 2050.1
17:17 for thou hast **a** spoken of thy servant's NIH
18: 4 David **a** houghed all the chariot *horses*, 2050.1
18:11 Them **a** king David dedicated unto 1571
20: 2 and he brought **a** exceeding much spoil 2050.1
20: 6 *foot*: and he **a** was the son of the giant. 1571
21:23 I give *thee* the oxen **a** for burnt offerings, NIH
22: 4 **A** cedar trees in abundance: for 2050.1
22:14 timber **a** and stone have I prepared; 2050.1
22:17 David **a** commanded all the princes of 2050.1
23:26 **a** unto the Levites; *they* shall no *more* 1571
24:30 The sons **a** of Mushi; Mahli, and Eder, 2050.1

1Ch 26: 6 **a** unto Shemaiah his son were sons 2050.1
26:10 **A** Hosah, of the children of Merari, 2050.1
27: 4 *of* his course *was* Mikloth **a** the ruler: 2050.1
27:30 Over the camels **a** *was* Obil 2050.1
27:32 **A** Jonathan David's uncle *was* a 2050.1
28:13 **A** for the courses of the priests 2050.1
28:14 silver **a** for all instruments of silver by NIH
28:15 candlestick, and **a** *for* the lamps thereof, NIH
28:17 **a** pure gold *for* the fleshhooks, 2050.1
28:21 **a** the princes and all the people will **a** be 2050.1
29: 9 David the king **a** rejoiced *with* great joy. 1571
29:17 I know **a**, my God, that thou triest 2050.1

2Ch 2: 8 Send me **a** cedar trees, fir trees, 2050.1
2:14 **a** to grave any *manner of* graving, 2050.1
3: 7 He overlaid **a** the house, the beams, 2050.1
3:12 the other wing *was* five cubits **a**, joining NIH
3:15 **A** he made before the house two pillars 2050.1
4: 2 **A** he made a molten sea of ten cubits 2050.1
4: 6 He made **a** ten lavers, and put five on 2050.1
4: 8 He made **a** ten tables, and placed *them* 2050.1
4:14 He made **a** bases and lavers made he 2050.1
4:16 The pots **a**, and the shovels, and 2050.1
4:19 the golden altar **a**, and the tables 2050.1
5: 6 **A** king Solomon, and all the 2050.1
5:12 **A** the Levites *which were* the singers, 2050.1
7: 6 Levites **a** with instruments of musick 2050.1
7: 8 **A** at the same time Solomon kept 2050.1
8: 5 **A** he built Beth-horon the upper, 2050.1
8:14 the porters **a** by their courses at every 2050.1
9: 4 his cupbearers **a**, and their apparel; 2050.1
9:10 servants **a** of Huram, and the servants 1571
12: 5 have I left you in the hand of Shishak. 637
12: 9 he carried away **a** the shields of gold 2050.1
12:12 and **a** in Judah things went well. 1571
13: 2 His mother's name **a** *was* Michaiah 2050.1
13: 3 Jeroboam **a** set the battle in array 2050.1
13:11 the *shewbread* **a** *set they* in order upon 2050.1
14: 5 **A** he took away out of all the cities of 2050.1
14:15 They smote **a** the tents of cattle, 1571+2050.1
15:16 **a** *concerning* Maachah the mother of Asa 2050.1
17: 7 **A** in the third year of his reign he sent 2050.1
17:11 **A** *some* of the Philistines brought 2050.1
18:21 shalt entice *him*, and thou shalt **a** prevail: 1571
19:11 **a** the Levites *shall be* officers before you 2050.1
20: 1 It came to pass after this **a**, *that* 2050.1
21: 4 and *divers* **a** of the princes of Israel. 1571
21:10 The same time **a** did Libnah revolt from 227
21:13 **a** hast slain thy brethren of thy father's 1571
21:17 house, and his sons **a**, and his wives; 1571
22: 2 His mother's name *was* Athaliah 2050.1
22: 3 He **a** walked in the ways of the house of 1571
22: 5 He walked **a** after their counsel, 1571
23:13 the singers **a** with instruments of 2050.1
23:18 **A** Jehoiada appointed the offices of 2050.1
24: 1 His mother's name *was* Zibiah of 2050.1
24: 7 **a** all the dedicate *things* of the house of 1571
24:12 **a** such as wrought iron and brass to mend 1571
24:20 the Lord, he hath **a** forsaken you. 2050.1
25: 6 He hired **a** an hundred thousand mighty 2050.1
25:24 the hostages **a**, and returned *to* Samaria. 2050.1
26: 3 His mother's name **a** *was* Jecoliah of 2050.1
26:10 **A** he built towers in the desert, 2050.1
26:10 husbandmen **a**, and vinedressers in NIH
26:20 yea, himself hasted **a** to go out, because 2050.1
27: 1 His mother's name **a** *was* Jerushah, 2050.1
27: 5 He fought **a** with the king of 2050.1
28: 2 and made **a** molten images for Baalim. 1571
28: 4 He sacrificed **a** and burnt incense in 2050.1
28: 5 was **a** delivered into the hand of the king 1571
28: 8 took **a** away much spoil from them, 1571
28:18 The Philistines **a** had invaded the cities 2050.1
28:18 Gimzo **a** and the villages thereof: 2050.1
29: 7 **A** they have shut up the doors of the 1571
29:22 they killed **a** the lambs, 2050.1
29:27 the song of the Lord began **a** with NIH
29:35 the burnt offerings *were* in abundance, 1571
30: 1 wrote letters **a** to Ephraim and Manasseh, 1571
30:12 **A** in Judah the hand of God was to give 1571
31: 1 Benjamin **a**, in Ephraim and Manasseh, 2050.1
31: 3 *He appointed* **a** the king's portion of his 2050.1
31: 6 they **a** brought in the tithe of oxen 1571
31:19 **A** of the sons of Aaron the priests, 2050.1
32: 5 **A** he strengthened himself, and built up 2050.1
32:17 He wrote **a** letters to rail on the Lord 2050.1
32:28 Storehouses **a** for the increase of corn, 2050.1
32:30 This same Hezekiah **a** stopped the upper 2050.1
33: 4 He **a** built altars in the house of 2050.1
33: 6 **a** he observed times, 2050.1
33:19 His prayer **a**, and *how God* was 2050.1
34:13 **A** *they were* over the bearers of burdens 2050.1
34:27 I have even heard *thee* **a**, saith the Lord. 1571
35: 9 Conaniah **a**, and Shemaiah 2050.1
36: 7 Nebuchadnezzar **a** carried of the vessels 2050.1
36:13 he **a** rebelled against king 1571
36:22 kingdom, and *put it* **a** in writing, saying, 1571

Ezr 1: 1 kingdom, and *put it* **a** in writing, saying, 1571
1: 7 **A** Cyrus the king brought forth 2050.1
3: 4 They kept **a** the feast of tabernacles, as 2050.1
3: 7 They gave money **a** unto the masons, 2050.1
4:20 There have been mighty kings **a** over 2050.3
5:10 We asked their names **a**, to certify 638+2050.3
5:14 the vessels **a** of gold and silver of the house 638
6: 5 a let the golden and silver vessels of 638
6:11 **A** I have made a decree, that whosoever 2050.3
7:19 The vessels **a** that *are* given thee for 2050.3

Ezr	7:24	**A** we certify you, that *touching* any of	2050.3
	8: 6	Of the sons **a** of Adin; Ebed the son of	2050.1
	8:14	Of the sons **a** of Bigvai; Uthai,	2050.1
	8:16	**a** for Joiarib, and for Elnathan,	2050.1
	8:20	**A** of the Nethinims, whom David	2050.1
	8:27	**A** twenty basons of gold, of a thousand	2050.1
	8:28	the vessels *are* holy **a**; and the silver	2050.1
	8:35	**A** the children of those that had been	NIH
	10: 4	we **a** *will be* with thee: be of good	2050.1
	10:23	**A** of the Levites; Jozabad, and Shimei,	2050.1
	10:24	Of the singers **a**; Eliashib: and of	2050.1
	10:28	Of the sons **a** of Bebai; Jehohanan,	2050.1
Ne	1: 3	the wall of Jerusalem **a** *is* broken down,	2050.1
	2: 6	unto me, (the queen **a** sitting by him,)	2050.1
	2:18	as **a** the king's words that he had spoken	637
	3: 3	who **a** laid the beams thereof, and set up	NIH
	3: 8	Next unto him **a** repaired Hananiah	2050.1
	3:29	After him repaired **a** Shemaiah the son	2050.1
	5: 3	*Some* **a** there were that said, We have	2050.1
	5: 4	There were **a** that said, We have	2050.1
	5: 9	**A** I said, It *is* not good that ye do: ought	2050.1
	5:11	the hundredth *part* of the money,	2050.1
	5:13	**A** I shook my lap, and said, So God shake	1571
	5:16	Yea **a** I continued in the work of this	2050.1
	5:18	a fowls were prepared for me,	2050.1
	6: 7	thou hast **a** appointed prophets to preach	1571
	6:19	**A** they reported his good deeds before me,	1571
	7:61	these *were* they which went up **a** from	NIH
	8: 7	**A** Jeshua, and Bani, and Sherebiah,	2050.1
	8:18	**A** day by day, from the first day unto	2050.1
	9:13	Thou camest down **a** upon mount Sinai,	2050.1
	9:20	Thou gavest **a** thy good spirit to instruct	2050.1
	9:23	Their children **a** multipliedst thou as	2050.1
	9:37	**a** they have dominion over our bodies,	2050.1
	10:32	**A** we made ordinances for us, to charge	2050.1
	10:36	**A** the firstborn of our sons, and of our	2050.1
	11: 1	rest of the people **a** cast lots, to bring	2050.1
	11:15	**A** of the Levites: Shemaiah the son of	2050.1
	11:22	The overseer **a** of the Levites at	2050.1
	11:31	The children **a** of Benjamin from Geba	2050.1
	12: 9	**A** Bakbukiah and Unni, their brethren,	2050.1
	12:10	Joiakim **a** begat Eliashib,	2050.1
	12:22	**a** the priests, to the reign of Darius	2050.1
	12:29	**A** from the house of Gilgal, and out of	2050.1
	12:43	that day they offered great sacrifices,	2050.1
	12:43	the wives **a** and the children rejoiced: so	1571
	13:15	as **a** wine, grapes, and figs, and all *manner*	637
	13:16	There dwelt men of Tyre **a** therein,	2050.1
	13:22	*concerning* this **a**, and spare me according	1571
	13:23	those days **a** saw I Jews *that* had married	1571
Est	1: 9	**A** Vashti the queen made a feast for	1571
	1:16	**a** to all the princes, and to all the people	NIH
	2: 8	that Esther was brought **a** unto the king's	NIH
	3:11	The silver *is* given to thee, the people **a**,	2050.1
	4: 8	**A** he gave him the copy of the writing	2050.1
	4:16	I **a** and my maidens will fast likewise;	1571
	5:12	to morrow *am* I invited unto her **a** with	1571
	7: 8	Will he force the queen **a** before me in	1571
	7: 9	said before the king, Behold **a**,	1571
	8: 8	Write ye **a** for the Jews, as it liketh you,	2050.1
	9:13	**a** according unto *this* day's decree,	1571
	9:15	the fourteenth day **a** of the month Adar,	1571
Job	1: 3	His substance **a** was seven thousand	2050.1
	1: 6	and Satan came **a** among them.	1571
	1:16	there came **a** another, and said,	2050.1
	1:17	there came **a** another, and said,	2050.1
	1:18	there came **a** another, and said, Thy	2050.1
	2: 1	Satan came **a** among them to present	1571
	5:25	Thou shalt know **a** that thy seed *shall*	2050.1
	7: 1	*are not* his days **a** like the days of a	2050.1
	9:11	he passeth on **a**, but I perceive him not.	2050.1
	9:20	perfect, it shall **a** prove me perverse.	2050.1
	11:11	seeth wickedness **a**; will he not	2050.1
	11:19	**A** thou shalt lie down, and none shall	2050.1
	12:15	**a** he sendeth them out, and they	2050.1
	13: 2	What ye know, *the same* do I know **a**.	1571
	13:16	He **a** *shall be* my salvation: for a hypocrite	1571
	13:27	Thou puttest my feet **a** in the stocks,	2050.1
	14: 2	he fleeth **a** as a shadow,	2050.1
	16: 4	I **a** could speak as ye *do:* if your soul	1571
	16:12	he hath **a** taken *me* by my neck,	2050.1
	16:17	in mine hands: **a** my prayer is pure.	2050.1
	16:19	Now, behold my witness *is* in heaven,	1571
	17: 6	He hath made me **a** a byword of	2050.1
	17: 7	Mine eye **a** is dim by reason of sorrow,	2050.1
	17: 9	The righteous **a** shall hold on his way,	2050.1
	19:11	He **a** hath kindled his wrath against me,	2050.1
	20: 9	The eye **a** *which* saw him shall *see him*	2050.1
	22:28	Thou shalt **a** decree a thing, and it shall	2050.1
	24:15	The eye **a** of the adulterer waiteth for	2050.1
	24:22	draweth **a** the mighty with his power:	2050.1
	30:11	have **a** let loose the bridle before me.	2050.1
	30:31	My harp **a** is *turned* to mourning,	2050.1
	31:28	This **a** *were* an iniquity *to be punished*	1571
	32: 3	**A** against his three friends was his wrath	2050.1
	32:10	Hearken to me; I **a** will shew mine	637
	32:17	*I said,* I will answer **a** my part, I also will	637
	32:17	also my part, I **a** will shew mine opinion.	637
	33: 6	stead: I **a** am formed out of the clay.	1571
	33:19	is chastened **a** with pain upon his bed,	2050.1
	36: 1	Elihu **a** proceeded, and said,	2050.1
	36:10	He openeth **a** their ear to discipline,	2050.1
	36:29	**A** can *any* understand the spreadings	518+637
	36:33	the cattle **a** concerning the vapour.	637
	37: 1	At this **a** my heart trembleth, and is	637

Job	37:11	**A** by watering he wearieth the thick cloud	637
	39:30	Her young ones **a** suck up blood:	2050.1
	40: 8	Wilt thou **a** disannul my judgment?	637
	40:14	will I **a** confess unto thee that thine own	1571
	42: 9	the LORD **a** accepted Job.	2050.1
	42:10	**a** the LORD gave Job twice as much as	2050.1
	42:11	every man **a** gave him a piece of money,	2050.1
	42:13	had **a** seven sons and three daughters.	2050.1
Ps	1: 3	his leaf **a** shall not wither;	2050.1
	5:11	let them **a** that love thy name be joyful	2050.1
	6: 3	My soul **a** is sore vexed: but thou,	2050.1
	7:13	He hath **a** prepared for him	2050.1
	9: 9	The LORD **a** will be a refuge for	2050.1
	16: 7	my reins **a** instruct me *in* the night	637
	16: 9	rejoiceth: my flesh **a** shall rest in hope.	637
	18: 7	the foundations **a** of the hills moved	2050.1
	18: 9	He bowed the heavens **a**, and came	2050.1
	18:13	The LORD **a** thundered in the heavens,	2050.1
	18:19	He brought me forth **a** into a large place	2050.1
	18:23	I was **a** upright before him, and I kept	2050.1
	18:35	Thou hast **a** given me the shield of thy	2050.1
	18:40	Thou hast **a** given me the necks of mine	2050.1
	19:10	sweeter **a** than honey and the	2050.1
	19:13	Keep back thy servant **a** from	1571
	26: 1	I have trusted **a** in the LORD; *therefore*	2050.1
	27: 7	have mercy **a** upon me, and answer me.	2050.1
	28: 9	feed them **a**, and lift them up for ever.	2050.1
	29: 6	He maketh them **a** to skip like a calf;	2050.1
	35: 3	Draw out **a** the spear, and stop *the way*	2050.1
	37: 4	Delight thyself **a** in the LORD;	2050.1
	37: 5	**a** in him; and he shall bring *it* to pass.	2050.1
	38:10	light of mine eyes, it **a** is gone from me.	1571
	38:12	They **a** that seek after my life lay snares	2050.1
	38:20	They **a** that render evil for good are	2050.1
	40: 2	brought me up **a** out of a horrible pit,	2050.1
	45:10	forget **a** thine own people,	2050.1
	52: 6	The righteous **a** shall see, and fear,	2050.1
	55:10	mischief **a** and sorrow *are* in the midst	2050.1
	60: 7	Ephraim **a** *is* the strength of mine head;	2050.1
	62:12	**A** unto thee, O Lord, *belongeth* mercy:	2050.1
	65: 8	They **a** that dwell in the uttermost parts	2050.1
	65:13	the valleys **a** are covered over with corn;	2050.1
	65:13	with corn; they shout for joy, they **a** sing.	637
	68: 1	let them **a** that hate him flee before him.	2050.1
	68: 8	the heavens **a** dropped at the presence of	637
	68:18	yea, *for* the rebellious **a**, that the LORD	2050.1
	69:11	I made sackcloth **a** my garment;	2050.1
	69:21	They gave me **a** gall for my meat;	2050.1
	69:31	This **a** shall please the LORD better	2050.1
	69:36	The seed **a** of his servants shall inherit it:	2050.1
	71:18	Now **a** when I am old and grayheaded,	1571
	71:19	righteousness **a**, O God, *is* very high,	2050.1
	71:22	I will **a** praise thee with the psaltery,	1571
	71:24	tongue **a** shall talk of thy righteousness	1571
	72: 8	shall have dominion **a** from sea to sea,	2050.1
	72:12	the poor **a**, and *him* that hath no helper.	2050.1
	72:15	prayer **a** shall be made for him	2050.1
	74:16	The day *is* thine, the night **a** *is* thine:	637
	75:10	All the horns of the wicked **a** will I cut	2050.1
	76: 2	In Salem **a** is his tabernacle,	2050.1
	77:12	I will meditate **a** of all thy work,	2050.1
	77:16	were afraid: the depths **a** were troubled.	637
	77:17	out **a** a sound: thine arrows **a** went abroad.	637
	78:14	In the daytime he led them with **a**	2050.1
	78:16	He brought streams **a** out of the rock,	2050.1
	78:20	streams overflowed; can he give bread **a**?	1571
	78:21	and anger **a** came up against Israel;	1571
	78:27	He rained flesh **a** upon them as dust,	2050.1
	78:46	He gave **a** their increase unto	2050.1
	78:48	He gave up **a** their cattle **a** to the hail,	2050.1
	78:55	He cast out the heathen **a** before them,	2050.1
	78:62	He gave his people over **a** unto	2050.1
	78:70	He chose David **a** his servant,	2050.1
	81:16	should have fed them **a** with the finest	2050.1
	83: 8	Assur **a** is joined with them: they have	1571
	84: 6	make it a well; the rain **a** filleth the pools.	1571
	89: 5	thy faithfulness **a** in the congregation of	637
	89:11	The heavens *are* thine, the earth **a** *is* thine:	637
	89:21	mine arm **a** shall strengthen him.	637
	89:25	I will set his hand **a** in the sea,	2050.1
	89:27	**A** I will make him *my* firstborn, higher	637
	89:29	seed **a** will I make *to endure* for ever,	2050.1
	89:43	Thou hast **a** turned the edge of his sword,	637
	92:11	Mine eye **a** shall see *my desire* on mine	2050.1
	93: 1	the world is **a** stablished, *that* it cannot	637
	95: 4	earth: the strength of the hills *is* his **a**.	2050.1
	96:10	the world **a** shall be established *that* it	637
	99: 4	The king's strength **a** loveth judgment;	2050.1
	105:23	Israel **a** came *into* Egypt;	2050.1
	105:33	smote their vines **a** and their fig trees;	2050.1
	105:36	smote **a** all the firstborn in their land,	2050.1
	105:37	He brought them forth **a** with silver	2050.1
	106: 9	He rebuked the Red sea **a**, and it was	2050.1
	106:16	They envied Moses **a** in the camp, *and*	2050.1
	106:27	To overthrow their seed **a** among	2050.1
	106:28	joined themselves **a** unto Baal-peor,	2050.1
	106:32	They angered *him* **a** at the waters of	2050.1
	106:42	Their enemies **a** oppressed them,	2050.1
	106:46	He made them **a** to be pitied of all those	2050.1
	107:32	them exalt him **a** in the congregation	2050.1
	107:38	He blesseth them **a**, so that they are	2050.1
	108: 8	Ephraim **a** *is* the strength of mine head;	2050.1
	109: 3	They compassed me about **a** *with* words	2050.1
	109:10	let them seek *their bread* **a** out of their	2050.1
	109:25	I became **a** a reproach unto them:	2050.1

Ps	119: 3	They **a** do no iniquity: they walk in his	637
	119:23	Princes **a** did sit and speak against me:	1571
	119:24	Thy testimonies **a** *are* my delight *and*	1571
	119:41	Let thy mercies come **a** unto me,	2050.1
	119:46	I will speak of thy testimonies **a** before	2050.1
	119:48	My hands **a** will I lift up unto thy	2050.1
	132:12	their children **a** shall sit upon thy throne	1571
	132:16	I will **a** clothe her priests with salvation:	2050.1
	139:17	precious **a** are thy thoughts unto me,	2050.1
	141: 5	for yet my prayer **a** *shall be* in their	2050.1
	145:19	he will hear their cry, and will save them.	2050.1
	148: 6	He hath **a** stablished them for ever	2050.1
	148:14	He **a** exalteth the horn of his people,	2050.1
Pr	1:26	I **a** will laugh at your calamity; I will	1571
	4: 4	He taught me **a**, and said unto me,	2050.1
	9: 2	her wine; she hath **a** furnished her table.	637
	11:25	that watereth shall be watered **a** himself.	1571
	17:26	**A** to punish the just *is* not good, *nor* to	1571
	18: 3	*then* cometh **a** contempt,	1571
	18: 9	He **a** that is slothful in his work *is* brother	1571
	19: 2	**A**, *that* the soul *be* without knowledge,	1571
	21:13	he **a** shall cry himself, but shall not be	1571
	23:23	**a** wisdom, and instruction,	NIH
	23:28	She **a** lieth in wait as *for* a prey,	637
	24:23	These *things* **a** *belong* to the wise.	1571
	25: 1	These *are* **a** proverbs of Solomon,	1571
	26: 4	to his folly, lest thou **a** be like unto him.	1571
	28:16	understanding *is* **a** a great oppressor:	2050.1
	30:31	a he goat **a**; and a king, against whom	176
	31:15	She riseth **a** while *it* is yet night,	2050.1
	31:28	her husband **a**, and he praiseth her.	NIH
Ecc	1: 5	The sun **a** ariseth, and the sun goeth	2050.1
	1:17	I perceived that this **a** is vexation of spirit.	1571
	2: 1	pleasure: and behold, this **a** is vanity.	1571
	2: 7	I **a** had great possessions of great	1571
	2: 8	I gathered me **a** silver and gold,	1571
	2: 9	**a** my wisdom remained with me.	637
	2:14	I myself perceived **a** that one event	1571
	2:15	I said in my heart, that this **a** *is* vanity.	1571
	2:19	wise under the sun. This *is* **a** vanity.	1571
	2:21	This **a** *is* vanity and a great evil.	1571
	2:23	not rest in the night. This *is* **a** vanity.	1571
	2:24	This **a** I saw, that it *was* from the hand of	1571
	2:26	This **a** *is* vanity and vexation of spirit.	1571
	3:11	**a** he hath set the world in their heart, so	1571
	3:13	**a** that every man should eat and drink,	1571
	4: 4	This **a** *is* vanity and vexation of spirit.	1571
	4: 8	This **a** *is* vanity, yea, it *is* a sore travail.	1571
	4:14	whereas **a** *he* that *is* born in his kingdom	1571
	4:16	they **a** that come after shall not rejoice in	1571
	4:16	Surely this **a** *is* vanity and vexation of	1571
	5: 7	many words *there are* **a** *divers* vanities:	2050.1
	5:10	abundance *with* increase: this **a** *is* vanity.	1571
	5:16	this **a** *is* a sore evil, *that* in all points as he	1571
	5:17	All his days **a** he eateth in darkness,	1571
	5:19	Every man **a** to whom God hath given	1571
	6: 3	with good, and **a** *that* he have no burial;	1571
	6: 9	this *is* **a** vanity and vexation of spirit.	1571
	7: 6	of the fool: this **a** *is* vanity.	1571+2050.1
	7:14	God **a** hath set the one over against	1571
	7:18	yea, **a** from this withdraw not thine hand:	1571
	7:21	**A** take no heed unto all words that are	1571
	7:22	For oftentimes **a** thine own heart knoweth	1571
	8:10	where they had so done: this *is* **a** vanity.	1571
	8:14	of the righteous: I said that this **a** *is* vanity.	1571
	8:16	(for **a** *there is that* neither day nor night	1571
	9: 3	**a** the heart of the sons of men is full *of* evil	1571
	9: 6	**A** their love, and their hatred,	1571
	9:12	For man **a** knoweth not his time: as	1571
	9:13	This wisdom have I seen **a** under the sun,	1571
	10: 3	Yea **a**, when he that is a fool walketh by	1571
	10:14	A fool **a** is full of words: a man cannot	2050.1
	11: 2	Give a portion to seven, and **a** to eight;	1571
	12: 5	**A** *when* they shall be afraid of *that which*	1571
SS	1:16	yea, pleasant: **a** our bed *is* green.	637
	7: 8	**a** now **a** thy breasts shall be as clusters of	2050.1
Isa	2: 7	Their land **a** is full *of* silver and gold,	2050.1
	2: 7	their land **a** is full *of* horses, neither *is*	2050.1
	2: 8	Their land **a** is full *of* idols; they worship	2050.1
	5: 2	of it, and **a** made a winepress therein:	1571
	5: 6	I will **a** command the clouds that they	2050.1
	6: 1	the year that king Uzziah died I saw **a**	2050.1
	6: 8	**A** I heard the voice of the Lord, saying,	2050.1
	7:13	weary men, but will ye weary my God **a**?	1571
	7:20	the feet: and it shall **a** consume the beard.	1571
	8: 5	The LORD spake **a** unto me again,	2050.1
	11: 6	The wolf **a** shall dwell with the lamb,	2050.1
	11:13	The envy **a** of Ephraim shall depart,	2050.1
	12: 2	*my* song; he **a** is become my salvation.	2050.1
	13: 3	I have **a** called my mighty ones for mine	1571
	13:16	children **a** shall be dashed to pieces	2050.1
	13:18	bows **a** shall dash the young men to	2050.1
	14:10	thee, Art thou **a** become weak as we?	1571
	14:13	I will sit **a** upon the mount of	2050.1
	14:23	I will **a** make it a possession for	2050.1
	17: 3	The fortress **a** shall cease from Ephraim,	2050.1
	19: 8	The fishers **a** shall mourn, and all they	2050.1
	19:13	they have **a** seduced Egypt,	NIH
	21:12	The morning cometh, and **a** the night:	1571
	22: 9	Ye have seen **a** the breaches of the city	2050.1
	22:11	made **a** a ditch between the two walls	2050.1
	23:12	Chittim; there **a** shalt thou have no rest.	1571
	24: 5	The earth **a** is defiled under	2050.1
	26:12	thou **a** hast wrought all our works in us.	1571
	26:21	the earth **a** shall disclose her blood,	2050.1

A

Isa 28: 7 they **a** have erred through wine, 1571
28:17 Judgment **a** will I lay to the line, 2050.1
28:29 This **a** cometh forth from the LORD of 1571
29:19 The meek **a** shall increase *their* joy in 2050.1
29:24 They **a** that erred in spirit shall come to 2050.1
30: 5 nor profit, but a shame, and a **a** reproach. 1571
30:22 Ye shall defile **a** the covering of thy 2050.1
31: 2 Yet he **a** *is* wise, and will bring evil, 1571
31: 5 defending **a** he will deliver *it*; 2050.1
32: 4 The heart **a** of the rash shall understand 2050.1
32: 7 The instruments **a** of the churl *are* evil: 2050.1
33: 2 our salvation **a** in the time of trouble. 637
34: 3 Their slain **a** shall be cast out, 2050.1
34:11 the owl **a** and the raven shall dwell in it: 2050.1
34:14 wild beasts of the desert shall **a** meet 2050.1
34:14 the shrich owl **a** shall rest there, and find 389
34:15 there shall the vultures **a** be gathered, 389
38:22 Hezekiah **a** had said, What *is* the sign 1571
40:24 he shall **a** blow upon them, and they shall 1571
44:19 a I have baked bread upon the coals 2050.1
45:16 ashamed, and **a** confounded, all of them: 1571
46:11 I have spoken *it*, I will **a** bring it to pass; 637
46:11 it to pass; I have purposed *it*, I will **a** do it. 637
48:12 I *am* he; I *am* the first, I **a** *am* the last. 637
48:13 Mine hand **a** hath laid the foundation of 637
48:19 Thy seed **a** had been as the sand, 2050.1
48:21 he clave the rock **a**, and the waters 2050.1
49: 6 I will **a** give thee for a light to 2050.1
49: 7 and arise, princes **a** shall worship, 2050.1
56: 6 **A** the sons of the stranger, that join 2050.1
57: 8 Behind the doors **a** and the posts hast 2050.1
57:15 *place*, with him **a** *that is* of a contrite 2050.1
57:18 I will lead him **a**, and restore comforts 2050.1
60:14 The sons **a** of them that afflicted thee 2050.1
60:16 Thou shalt **a** suck the milk of 2050.1
60:17 I will **a** make thy officers peace, 2050.1
60:21 Thy people **a** *shall be* all righteous: 2050.1
62: 3 Thou shalt **a** be a crown of glory in 2050.1
66: 4 I **a** will choose their delusions, 1571
66:21 I will **a** take of them for priests *and* 1571
Jer 1: 3 It came **a** in the days of Jehoiakim 2050.1
2: 8 the pastors **a** transgressed against me, 1571
2:16 **A** the children of Noph 1571
2:33 hast thou **a** taught the wicked ones thy 1571
2:34 **A** in thy skirts is found the blood of 1571
2:36 thou **a** shalt be ashamed of Egypt, as thou 1571
3: 6 The LORD said **a** unto me in the days of 2050.1
3: 8 but went and played the harlot **a**. 1571
4:12 now **a** will I give sentence against them. 1571
6:14 They have healed **a** the hurt of 2050.1
6:17 **A** I set watchmen over you, 1571
7:27 thou shalt **a** call unto them; but they 2050.1
9:16 I will scatter them **a** among the heathen, 2050.1
10: 5 do evil, neither **a** *is it* in them to do good. 1571
13:23 *then* may ye **a** do good, that are 1571
14: 5 the hind **a** calved in the field, 1571
16: 1 The word of the LORD came **a** unto me, 2050.1
16: 8 Thou shalt not **a** go *into* the house of 2050.1
19: 5 They have built **a** the high places of Baal, 2050.1
20: 1 who was a chief governor in the house 2050.1
23:14 have seen **a** in the prophets of Jerusalem 2050.1
23:14 they strengthen **a** the hands of evildoers, 2050.1
25:14 kings shall serve themselves of them **a**: 1571
26:20 there was **a** a man that prophesied in 1571
27: 6 beasts of the field have I given him **a** to 1571
27:12 I spake **a** to Zedekiah king of Judah 2050.1
27:16 **A** I spake to the priests and to all this 1571
28:14 I have given him the beasts of the field **a**. 1571
29:24 *Thus* shalt thou **a** speak to Shemaiah 1571
30:19 I will **a** glorify them, and they shall not 2050.1
30:20 Their children **a** shall be as aforetime, 2050.1
31:36 the seed of Israel **a** shall cease from being 1571
31:37 I will **a** cast off all the seed of Israel for all 1571
33:21 *Then* may **a** my covenant be broken with 1571
35:15 I have sent **a** unto you all my servants 1571
36: 6 **a** thou shalt read them in the ears of all 1571
38:25 to death; **a** what the king said unto thee: 2050.1
39: 6 **a** the king of Babylon slew all the nobles 2050.1
40: 5 *he said*, Go back **a** to Gedaliah the son 1571
41: 3 Ishmael **a** slew all the Jews that were 1571
43:13 He shall break **a** the images of 2050.1
46:21 **A** her hired men *are* in the midst of her 1571
46:21 for they **a** are turned back, *and* are fled 1571
48: 2 **A** thou shalt be cut down, O Madmen; 1571
48: 7 and in thy treasures, thou shalt **a** be taken: 1571
48: 8 the valley **a** shall perish, and the plain 2050.1
48:26 Moab **a** shall wallow in his vomit, 2050.1
48:26 in his vomit, and he **a** shall be in derision. 1571
48:34 for the waters **a** of Nimrim shall be 1571
49:17 **A** Edom shall be a desolation: every one 2050.1
50:24 thou art **a** taken, O Babylon, and thou 1571
50:24 a caught, because thou hast striven against 1571
51:22 With thee **a** will I break in pieces man 1571
51:23 I will **a** break in pieces with thee 2050.1
52:10 he slew **a** all the princes of Judah 1571+2050.1
52:17 **A** the pillars of brass that *were* in 2050.1
52:18 The caldrons **a**, and the shovels, and 2050.1
52:22 second pillar **a** and the pomegranates 2050.1
52:25 He took **a** out of the city an eunuch, 2050.1
La 2: 9 the law *is* no *more*; her prophets **a** find no 1571
3: 8 **A** when I cry and shout, he shutteth out 1571
3:16 He hath **a** broken my teeth with gravel 2050.1
4:21 the cup **a** shall pass through unto thee: 1571
Eze 1: 5 **A** out of the midst thereof *came* 2050.1
1:10 they four **a** had the face of an eagle, 2050.1

Eze 3:13 *I heard* **a** the noise of the wings of 2050.1
3:21 warned; **a** thou hast delivered thy soul. 2050.1
4: 1 Thou **a**, son of man, take thee a tile, 2050.1
4: 2 set the camp **a** against it, and set 2050.1
4: 4 Lie thou **a** upon thy left side, and lay 2050.1
4: 9 Take thou **a** unto thee wheat, and 2050.1
4:11 Thou shalt drink **a** water by measure, 2050.1
5: 3 Thou shalt **a** take thereof a few in 2050.1
5:11 will I **a** diminish *thee*; neither shall mine 1571
7: 2 **A**, thou son of man, thus saith the Lord 2050.1
7:18 They shall **a** gird *themselves* with 2050.1
7:22 My face will I turn **a** from them, 2050.1
7:24 I will **a** make the pomp of the strong to 2050.1
8:13 He said **a** unto me, Turn thee yet again, 2050.1
8:18 Therefore will I **a** deal in fury: mine eye 2050.1
9: 1 I cried **a** in mine ears *with* a loud voice, 2050.1
9:10 *as for* me **a**, mine eye shall not spare, 1571
10:16 the same wheels **a** turned not from beside 1571
10:17 *these* lift up themselves **a**: for the spirit NIH
10:19 the wheels *were* **a** besides them, 2050.1
12: 1 The word of the LORD **a** came unto me, 2050.1
12:13 My net **a** will I spread upon him, 2050.1
13:21 Your kerchiefs **a** will I tear, 2050.1
16:10 I clothed thee **a** with broidered work, 2050.1
16:11 I decked thee **a** *with* ornaments, and I 2050.1
16:17 Thou hast **a** taken thy fair jewels of my 2050.1
16:19 My meat **a** which I gave thee, fine flour, 2050.1
16:24 *That* thou hast **a** built unto thee an 2050.1
16:26 Thou hast **a** committed fornication with 2050.1
16:28 Thou hast played the whore **a** with, 2050.1
16:39 **And** I will **a** give thee into their hand, 2050.1
16:39 they shall strip thee **a** of thy clothes, 2050.1
16:40 They shall **a** bring up a company against 2050.1
16:41 and thou **a** shalt give no hire any more. 1571
16:43 I **a** will recompense thy way upon *thine* 1571
16:52 Thou **a**, which hast judged thy sisters, 1571
16:52 thou confounded **a**, and bear thy shame, 1571
17: 5 He took **a** of the seed of the land, 2050.1
17: 7 There was **a** another great eagle with 2050.1
17:13 he hath **a** taken the mighty of the land: 2050.1
17:22 I will **a** take of the highest branch of 2050.1
18: 4 so **a** the soul of the son *is* mine: 2050.1
19: 4 The nations **a** heard of him; he was 2050.1
20:12 Moreover **a** I gave them my sabbaths, 1571
20:15 Yet **a** I lifted up my hand unto them in 1571
20:23 I lifted up mine hand unto them **a** in 1571
20:25 I gave them **a** statutes *that were* 1571
20:28 there **a** they made their sweet savour, 2050.1
20:39 **a**, if ye will not hearken unto me: NIH
21: 9 a sword is sharpened, and **a** furbished: 1571
21:17 will **a** smite mine hands together, 1571+2050.1
21:19 **A**, thou son of man, appoint thee two 1571
23:26 They shall **a** strip thee out of thy clothes, 2050.1
23:35 therefore bear thou **a** thy lewdness and 1571
23:37 have **a** caused their sons, whom they bare 1571
24: 3 a pot, set *it* on, and **a** pour water into it: 1571
24: 5 burn **a** the bones under it, *and* make it 1571
24:15 **A** the word of the LORD came unto me, 2050.1
24:25 **A**, thou son of man, *shall it* not *be* in 1571
25:13 I will **a** stretch out mine hand upon 2050.1
26: 4 I will **a** scrape her dust from her, 2050.1
27:19 Dan **a** and Javan going to 2050.1
30: 6 They **a** that uphold Egypt shall fall; 2050.1
30:10 I will **a** make the multitude of Egypt to 2050.1
30:13 I will **a** destroy the idols, and I will 2050.1
30:18 At Tehaphnehes **a** the day shall be 2050.1
31:17 They **a** went down into hell with him 1571
32: 6 I will **a** water with thy blood the land 2050.1
32: 9 I will **a** vex the hearts of many people, 2050.1
32:13 I will **a** destroy **a** all the beasts thereof 2050.1
32:17 It came to pass **a** in the twelfth year, 2050.1
33:30 **A**, thou son of man, the children of thy 1571
36: 1 **A**, thou son of man, prophesy unto 2050.1
36:26 A new heart **a** will I give you, and a 2050.1
36:29 I will **a** save you from all your 2050.1
36:33 I will **a** cause *you* to dwell in the cities, 2050.1
37:24 they shall **a** walk in my judgments, 2050.1
37:27 My tabernacle **a** shall be with them: 2050.1
38:10 It shall **a** come to pass, *that* at the same 2050.1
39:16 **a** the name of the city *shall be* Hamonah. 1571
40: 8 He measured **a** the porch of the gate 2050.1
40:12 The space **a** before the little chambers 2050.1
40:14 He made **a** posts *of* threescore cubits, 2050.1
40:42 whereupon **a** they laid the instruments 2050.1
41: 8 I saw **a** the height of the house round 2050.1
41:14 the breadth **a** of the face of the house, 2050.1
43:21 Thou shalt take the bullock **a** of the sin 2050.1
43:25 they shall **a** prepare a young bullock, 2050.1
44:30 ye shall **a** give unto the priest the first of 2050.1
45: 5 shall **a** the Levites, the ministers of 2050.1
47:20 The west side *a shall be* the great sea 2050.1
Da 6:22 a before thee, O king, have I done no 638
7: 6 the beast had **a** four heads; 2050.1
8:25 through his policy **a** he shall cause craft 2050.1
8:25 he shall **a** stand up against the Prince of 2050.1
10: 6 His body **a** *was* like the beryl, 2050.1
11: 1 **A** I in the first year of Darius the Mede, 2050.1
11: 8 a carry captives *into* Egypt their gods, 1571
11:14 the robbers of thy people shall exalt 2050.1
11:17 He shall **a** set his face to enter with 2050.1
11:22 yea **a**, the prince of the covenant. 1571
11:41 He shall **a** enter **a** into the glorious land, 2050.1
11:42 He shall stretch forth his hand **a** upon 2050.1
Hos 2:11 I will **a** cause all her mirth to cease, 2050.1
3: 3 be for *another* man: so *will* I **a** *be* for thee. 1571

Hos 4: 3 the fishes of the sea **a** shall be taken away. 1571
4: 5 the prophet **a** shall fall with thee *in* 1571
4: 6 rejected knowledge, I will **a** reject thee, 2050.1
4: 6 law of thy God, I will **a** forget thy children. 1571
5: 5 their iniquity; Judah **a** shall fall with them. 1571
6:11 **A**, O Judah, he hath set a harvest for thee, 1571
7:11 Ephraim **a** is like a silly dove, 2050.1
8: 6 for from Israel *was* it **a**: the workman 1571
9:12 woe **a** to them when I depart from them! 1571
10: 6 It shall be **a** carried unto Assyria *for* a 1571
10: 8 The high places **a** of Aven, the sin of 2050.1
11: 3 I taught Ephraim **a** to go, taking them by 2050.1
12: 2 The LORD hath **a** controversy with 2050.1
12:10 I have **a** spoken by the prophets, 2050.1
Joel 1:12 the palm tree **a**, and the apple tree, NIH
1:20 The beasts of the field cry **a** unto thee: 1571
2:12 Therefore **a** now, saith the LORD, turn ye 1571
2:29 **a** upon the servants and upon 1571
3: 2 I will **a** gather all nations, and will bring 2050.1
3: 6 The children **a** of Judah and the children 2050.1
3:16 The LORD **a** shall roar out of Zion, 2050.1
Am 1: 5 I will break **a** the bar of Damascus, 2050.1
2:10 **A** I brought you up from the land of 2050.1
3:14 him I will **a** visit the altars of Beth-el: 2050.1
4: 6 I **a** have given you cleanness of teeth in all 1571
4: 7 a I have withholden the rain from you, 1571
7: 6 This **a** shall not be, saith the Lord GOD. 1571
7:12 **A** Amaziah said unto Amos, O thou seer 2050.1
9:14 they shall **a** make gardens, and eat 2050.1
Jnh 4:11 and their left hand; and **a** much cattle? NIH
Mic 3: 3 Who **a** eat the flesh of my people, 2050.1
4:11 Now **a** many nations are gathered 2050.1
5:13 Thy graven images **a** will I cut off, 2050.1
6:13 Therefore **a** will I make *thee* sick in 1571
7:12 *In* that day **a** he shall come even to thee NIH
Na 3:10 young children **a** were dashed in pieces 1571
3:11 Thou shalt **a** be drunken: thou shalt be 1571
3:11 thou **a** shalt seek strength because of 1571
Hab 1: 8 Their horses **a** are swifter than 2050.1
2: 5 Yea **a**, because he transgresseth by wine, 637
2:15 bottle to *him*, and makest *him* drunken **a**, 637
2:16 drink thou **a**, and let thy foreskin be 1571
Zep 1: 4 I will **a** stretch out mine hand upon 2050.1
1: 9 In the same day **a** will I punish all those 2050.1
1:13 they shall **a** build houses, but not inhabit 2050.1
2:12 Ye Ethiopians **a**, ye *shall be* slain by my 1571
3:12 I will **a** leave in the midst of thee an 2050.1
Zec 3: 7 thou shalt **a** judge my house, and shalt 1571
3: 7 shalt **a** keep my courts, and I will give 1571
4: 9 his hands shall **a** finish *it*; and thou shalt 2050.1
8: 6 should it **a** be marvellous in my eyes? 1571
8:21 to seek the LORD of hosts: I will go **a**. 1571
9: 2 Hamath **a** shall border thereby; Tyrus, 1571
9: 5 Gaza *shall see it*, and be very 2050.1
9:11 thee **a**, by the blood of thy covenant 1571
10:10 I will bring them again **a** out of the land 2050.1
11: 8 shepherds **a** I cut off in one month; 2050.1
11: 8 them, and their soul **a** abhorred me. 1571
12: 7 The LORD **a** shall save the tents of 2050.1
13: 2 **a** I will cause the prophets and the 1571
14:14 Judah **a** shall fight at Jerusalem; 1571
Mal 1:13 Ye said **a**, Behold, what a weariness 2050.1
2: 9 Therefore have I **a** made you contemptible 1571
Mt 2: 8 that I may come and worship him **a**. 2504
3:10 And now **a** the axe is laid unto the root of 2532
5:39 thy right cheek, turn to him the other **a**. 2532
5:40 *away* thy coat, let him have *thy* cloke **a**. 2532
6:14 your heavenly Father will **a** forgive you: 2532
6:21 treasure is, there will your heart be **a**. 2532
10: 4 and Judas Iscariot, who **a** betrayed him. 2532
10:32 him will I confess **a** before my Father 2504
10:33 him will I **a** deny before my Father which 2504
12:45 shall it be **a** unto this wicked generation. 2532
13:22 He **a** that received seed among the thorns 1161
13:23 understandeth *it;* which **a** beareth fruit, 1211
13:26 forth fruit, then appeared the tares **a**. 2532
13:29 tares, ye root up **a** the wheat with them. NIG
15: 3 Why do you **a** transgress 2532
15:16 Are ye **a** yet without understanding? 2532
16: 1 The Pharisees with the Sadducees came, 2532
16:18 And I say **a** unto thee, That thou art Peter, 2504
17:12 Likewise shall **a** the Son of man suffer of 2532
18:33 Shouldest not thou **a** have had compassion 2532
18:35 So likewise shall my heavenly Father do **a** NIG
19: 3 The Pharisees **a** came unto him, 2532
19:28 ye **a** shall sit upon twelve thrones, 2532
20: 4 Go ye **a** into the vineyard, 2532
20: 7 unto them, Go ye **a** into the vineyard; 2532
21:21 but **a** if ye shall say unto this mountain, 2579
21:24 unto them, I **a** will ask you one thing, 2504
22:26 Likewise the second **a**, and the third, 2532
22:27 And last of all the woman died **a**. 2532
23:26 that the outside of them may be clean **a**. 2532
23:28 ye **a** outwardly appear righteous unto men 2532
24:27 shall **a** the coming of the Son of man be. 2532
24:37 shall **a** the coming of the Son of man be. 2532
24:39 shall **a** the coming of the Son of man be. 2532
24:44 Therefore be ye **a** ready: for in such an 2532
25:11 Afterward came **a** the other virgins, 2532
25:17 *had received* two, he **a** gained other two. 2532
25:22 He **a** that had received two talents came 2532
25:41 Then shall he say **a** unto them on the left 2532
25:44 Then shall they **a** answer him, saying, 2532
26:13 *there* shall **a** *this*, that this *woman* hath 2532
26:35 deny thee. Likewise **a** said all the disciples. 2532

Mt	26:69 saying, Thou **a** wast with Jesus of Galilee.	2532
	26:71 This *fellow* was **a** with Jesus of Nazareth.	2532
	26:73 to Peter, Surely thou **a** art *one* of them;	2532
	27:41 Likewise **a** the chief priests mocking *him,*	2532
	27:44 The thieves **a,** which were crucified with	2532
	27:57 who **a** himself was Jesus' disciple:	2532
Mk	1:19 **a** *were* in the ship mending *their* nets.	2532
	1:38 next towns, that I may preach **there a:**	2532
	2:15 and sinners **sat a together with** Jesus	4873
	2:21 No **man** a seweth a piece of new cloth on	2532
	2:26 and gave **a** to them which were with him?	2532
	2:28 Therefore the Son of man is Lord **a** of	2532
	3:19 And Judas Iscariot, which **a** betrayed him.	2532
	4:36 And there were **a** with him other little	2532
	5:16 the devil, and **a** concerning the swine.	NIG
	7:18 Are ye so without understanding **a?**	2532
	8: 7 commanded to set them **a** before *them.*	2532
	8:34 the people unto *him* **with** his disciples **a,**	4862
	8:38 of him **a** shall the Son of man be ashamed,	2532
	11:25 that your Father **a,** which is in heaven may	2532
	11:29 I will **a** ask of you one question,	2504
	12: 6 he sent them **a** last unto them, saying,	2532
	12:22 left no seed: last of all the woman died **a.**	2532
	14: 9 *this* **a** that she hath done shall be spoken	2532
	14:31 thee in any wise. Likewise **a** said they all.	2532
	14:67 *And* thou **a** wast with Jesus of Nazareth.	2532
	15:31 Likewise **a** the chief priests mocking said	2532
	15:40 There were **a** women looking on afar off:	2532
	15:41 (Who **a,** when he was in Galilee,	2532
	15:43 which **a** waited for the kingdom of God,	2532
Lk	1: 3 It seemed good to **me a,** having had	2504
	1:35 **a** *that* holy thing which shall be born of	2532
	1:36 she hath **a** conceived a son in her old age:	2532
	2: 4 And Joseph **a** went up from Galilee, out of	2532
	2:35 shall pierce through thy own soul **a,)**	2532
	3: 9 And now **a** the axe is laid unto the root of	2532
	3:12 Then came **a** publicans to be baptized,	2532
	3:21 *that* Jesus **a** being baptized, and praying,	2532
	4:23 in Capernaum, do **a** here in thy country.	2532
	4:41 devils **a** came out of many, crying out,	2532
	4:43 the kingdom of God to other cities **a:**	2532
	5:10 so *was* **a** James, and John, the sons of	2532
	5:36 And he spake **a** a parable unto them;	2532
	5:39 No *man* **a** having drunk old *wine*	2532
	6: 4 and gave **a** to them that were with him;	2532
	6: 5 That the Son of man is Lord **a** of	2532
	6: 6 And it came to pass **a** on another sabbath,	2532
	6:13 chose twelve, whom **a** he named apostles;	2532
	6:14 Simon, (whom he **a** named Peter,)	2532
	6:16 and Judas Iscariot, which **a** was the traitor.	2532
	6:29 thee on the *one* cheek offer **a** the other;	2532
	6:29 thy cloke forbid not *to take* thy coat **a.**	2532
	6:31 do to you, do ye **a** to them likewise.	2532
	6:32 for sinners **a** love those that love them.	2532
	6:33 have ye? for sinners **a** do *even* the same.	2532
	6:34 for sinners **a** lend to sinners, to receive as	2532
	6:36 merciful, as your Father **a** is merciful.	2532
	7: 8 For I **a** am a man set under authority,	2532
	7:49 Who is this that forgiveth sins **a?**	2532
	8:36 They **a** which saw *it* told them by what	2532
	9:61 And another **a** said, Lord, I will follow	2532
	10: 1 the Lord appointed other seventy **a,**	2532
	10:39 which **a** sat at Jesus' feet, and heard his	2532
	11: 1 us to pray, as John **a** taught his disciples.	2532
	11: 4 for we **a** forgive every one *that* is indebted	2532
	11:18 If Satan **a** be divided against himself,	2532
	11:30 shall **a** the Son of man be to this	2532
	11:34 is single, thy whole body **a** is full of light;	2532
	11:34 *eye* is evil, thy body **a** is full of darkness.	2532
	11:40 *is* without make that *which is* within **a?**	2532
	11:45 Master, thus saying thou reproachest us **a.**	2532
	11:46 And he said, Woe unto you **a,** *ye* lawyers!	2532
	11:49 Therefore **a** said the wisdom of God,	2532
	12: 8 **A** I say unto you, Whosoever shall confess	1161
	12: 8 him shall the Son of man **a** confess before	2532
	12:34 treasure is, there will your heart be **a.**	2532
	12:40 ye therefore ready **a:** for the Son of man	2532
	12:54 he said **a** to the people, When ye see a	2532
	13: 6 spake **a** this parable; A certain *man* had	1161
	13: 8 Lord, let it alone this year **a,** till I shall dig	2532
	14:12 Then said he **a** to him that bade him,	2532
	14:12 lest they **a** bid thee again,	2532
	14:26 and sisters, yea, and his own life **a,**	2532
	16: 1 he said **a** unto his disciples, There was	2532
	16:10 in *that which is* least is faithful **a** in much:	2532
	16:10 he that is unjust in the least is unjust **a** in	2532
	16:14 And the Pharisees **a,** who were covetous,	2532
	16:22 the rich *man* **a** died, and was buried;	2532
	16:28 they **a** come into this place of torment.	2532
	17:24 so shall **a** the Son of man be in his day.	2532
	17:26 shall it be **a** in the days of the Son of man.	2532
	17:28 Likewise **a** as it was in the days of Lot;	2532
	18:15 And they brought unto him **a** infants,	2532
	19: 9 forsomuch as he **a** is a son of Abraham.	2532
	19:19 likewise to him, Be thou **a** over five cities.	2532
	20: 3 said unto them, I will **a** ask you one thing;	2504
	20:11 and they beat **him a,** and entreated *him*	2548
	20:12 they wounded him **a,** and cast *him* out.	2532
	20:31 took her; and in like manner the seven **a:**	2532
	20:32 Last of all the woman died **a.**	2532
	21: 2 he saw **a** a certain poor widow casting	2532
	22:20 Likewise **a** the cup after supper, saying,	2532
	22:24 And there was **a** a strife among them,	2532
	22:39 of Olives; and his disciples **a** followed him.	2532
	22:56 and said, This *man* **a** was with him.	2532

Lk	22:58 saw him, and said, Thou art **a** of them.	2532
	22:59 Of a truth this *fellow* **a** was with him:	2532
	22:68 if I **a** ask you, you will not answer me,	2532
	23: 7 who himself **a** was at Jerusalem at that	2532
	23:27 which **a** bewailed and lamented him.	2532
	23:32 And there were **a** two other, malefactors,	2532
	23:35 And the rulers **a** with them derided *him,*	2532
	23:36 And the soldiers **a** mocked him, coming	2532
	23:38 And a superscription **a** was written over	2532
	23:51 who **a** himself waited for the kingdom of	2532
	23:55 And the women **a,** which came with him	2532
	24:22 certain women **a** of our company made us	NIG
	24:23 that *they* had **a** seen a vision of angels,	2532
Jn	3:23 And John **a** was baptizing in Aenon near	2532
	4:45 the feast: for they **a** went unto the feast.	2532
	5:18 but said **a** that God was his Father,	2532
	5:19 he doeth, these **a** doeth the Son likewise.	2532
	5:27 him authority to execute judgment **a,**	2532
	6:24 neither his disciples, they **a** took shipping,	2532
	6:36 That ye **a** have seen me, and believe not.	2532
	6:67 Jesus unto the twelve, Will ye **a** go away?	2532
	7: 3 that thy disciples **a** may see the works that	2532
	7:10 then went he **a** up unto the feast,	2532
	7:47 them the Pharisees, Are ye **a** deceived?	2532
	7:52 and said unto him, Art thou **a** of Galilee?	2532
	8:17 It is **a** written in your law, that	2532
	8:19 ye should have known my Father **a.**	2532
	9:15 Then again the Pharisees **a** asked him	2532
	9:27 hear *it* again? will ye **a** be his disciples?	2532
	9:40 and said unto him, Are we blind **a?**	2532
	10:16 **them a** I must bring, and they shall hear	2548
	11:16 unto *his* fellow-disciples, Let us **a** go,	2532
	11:33 **and** the Jews **a** weeping which came	2532
	11:52 that **a** he should gather together in one	2532
	12: 9 but that they might see Lazarus **a,**	2532
	12:10 that they might put Lazarus **a** to death;	2532
	12:18 For this cause the people **a** met him,	2532
	12:26 where I am, there shall **a** my servant be:	2532
	12:42 Nevertheless among the *chief* rulers **a**	2532
	13: 9 feet only, but **a** my hands and *my* head.	2532
	13:14 ye **a** ought to wash one another's feet.	2532
	13:32 him, God **a** glorify him in himself,	2532
	13:34 loved you, that ye **a** love one another.	2532
	14: 1 ye believe in God, believe **a** in me.	2532
	14: 3 that where I am, *there* ye may be **a.**	2532
	14: 7 ye should have known my Father **a:**	2532
	14:12 on me, the works that I do shall **he** do **a;**	2548
	14:19 ye see me: because I live, ye shall live **a.**	2532
	15:20 persecuted me, they will **a** persecute you;	2532
	15:20 kept my saying, they will keep yours **a.**	2532
	15:23 He that hateth me hateth my Father **a.**	2532
	15:27 And ye **a** shall bear witness, because	2532
	17: 1 thy Son, that thy Son **a** may glorify thee:	2532
	17:18 **even** *so* have I **a** sent them into the world	2504
	17:19 that they **a** might be sanctified through	2532
	17:20 for them **a** which shall believe on me	2532
	17:21 I in thee, that they **a** may be one in us:	2532
	17:24 Father, I will that **they a,** whom thou hast	2548
	18: 2 And Judas **a,** which betrayed him, knew	2532
	18: 5 I am *he.* And Judas **a,** which betrayed him	2532
	18:17 Art not thou **a** one of this man's disciples?	2532
	18:25 Art not thou **a** one of his disciples?	2532
	19:23 to every soldier a part; and **a** *his* coat:	NIG
	19:39 And there came **a** Nicodemus, which at	2532
	20: 8 Then went in **a** *that* other disciple,	2532
	21: 3 They say unto him, We **a** go with thee.	2532
	21:20 which **a** leaned on his breast at supper,	2532
	21:25 And there are **a** many other *things* which	2532
Ac	1: 3 To whom **a** he shewed himself alive after	2532
	1:11 Which **a** said, Ye men of Galilee,	2532
	2:22 the midst of you, as ye yourselves **a** know:	2532
	2:26 moreover **a** my flesh shall rest in hope:	2532
	3:17 ignorance ye did *it,* as *did* **a** your rulers.	2532
	5: 2 his wife **a** being privy *to it,* and brought a	2532
	5:16 There came **a** a multitude *out of* the cities	2532
	5:32 *so* is **a** the Holy Ghost, whom God hath	1161
	5:37 **he a** perished; and all, *even* as many as	2548
	7:45 Which **a** our fathers that came after	2532
	8:13 Then Simon himself believed **a:**	2532
	8:19 Saying, Give **me a** this power, that on	2504
	9:32 **a** to the saints which dwelt at Lydda.	2532
	10:26 saying, Stand up; I myself **a** am a man.	2504
	10:45 that on the Gentiles **a** was poured out	2532
	11: 1 Gentiles had **a** received the word of God.	2532
	11:18 Then hath God **a** to the Gentiles granted	2532
	11:30 Which they did, and sent it to the elders	2532
	12: 3 he proceeded further to take Peter **a.**	2532
	13: 5 and they had **a** John to *their* minister.	2532
	13: 9 Then Saul, (who **a** *is called* Paul,)	2532
	13:22 to whom **a** he gave testimony, and said,	2532
	13:33 as it is **a** written in the second psalm,	2532
	13:35 Wherefore he saith **a** in another *psalm,*	2532
	14: 1 of the Jews and **a** of the Greeks believed.	NIG
	14: 5 and **a** of the Jews with their rulers, to use	NIG
	14:15 why do ye these *things?* We **a** are men of	2532
	15:27 who shall **a** tell *you* the same *things* by	2532
	15:32 and Silas, being prophets **a** themselves,	2532
	15:35 Paul **a** and Barnabas continued in Antioch,	1161
	15:35 the word of the Lord, with many others **a.**	2532
	17: 6 the world upside down are come hither **a;**	2532
	17:12 **a** of honourable women which were	2532
	17:13 they came **thither a,** and stirred up	2546
	17:28 as certain **a** of your own poets have said,	2532
	17:28 poets have said, For we are **a** his offspring.	2532
	19:17 Jews and Greeks **a** dwelling at Ephesus;	5037

Ac	19:19 Many **a** of them which used curious arts	1161
	19:21 I have been there, I must **a** see Rome.	2532
	19:27 **a** that the temple of the great goddess	2532
	20:21 and **a** to the Greeks, repentance toward	NIG
	20:30 **A** of your own selves shall men arise,	2532
	21:13 **a** to die at Jerusalem for the name of	2532
	21:16 There went with us **a** *certain* of	2532
	21:24 but *that* thou thyself **a** walkest orderly,	2532
	21:28 further brought Greeks **a** into the temple,	2532
	22: 5 As the high priest doth bear me witness,	2532
	22: 5 from whom **a** I received letters unto	2532
	22:20 I was standing by, and consenting unto	2532
	22:29 and the chief captain **a** was afraid, after he	1161
	23:11 so must thou bear witness **a** at Rome.	2532
	23:30 commandment to *his* accusers **a** to say	2532
	23:33 governor, presented Paul **a** before him.	2532
	23:35 said he, when thine accusers are **a** come.	2532
	24: 6 Who **a** hath gone about to profane	2532
	24: 9 And the Jews **a** assented, saying that these	2532
	24:15 which they themselves **a** allow,	2532
	24:26 He hoped **a** that money should have	260+2532
	25:22 Festus, I would **a** hear the man myself.	2532
	25:24 at Jerusalem, and **a** here, crying that he	NIG
	26:10 Which *thing* I **a** did in Jerusalem:	2532
	26:26 these *things,* before whom **a** I speak freely:	2532
	26:29 but **a** all that hear me this day, were both	2532
	27:10 of the lading and ship, but **a** of our lives.	2532
	27:12 the more part advised to depart **thence a,**	2547
	27:36 of good cheer, and they **a** took *some* meat.	2532
	28: 9 when this was done, others **a,** which had	2532
	28:10 Who **a** honoured us with many honours;	2532
Ro	1: 6 Among whom are ye **a** *the* called of Jesus	2532
	1:13 That I might have some fruit among you **a,**	2532
	1:15 the gospel to you that are at Rome **a.**	2532
	1:16 to the Jew first, and **a** to the Greek.	NIG
	1:24 Wherefore God **a** gave them up to	2532
	1:27 likewise **a** the men, leaving the natural	2532
	2: 9 of the Jew first, and **a** of the Gentile;	NIG
	2:10 to the Jew first, and **a** to the Gentile:	NIG
	2:12 without law shall **a** perish without law:	2532
	2:15 their conscience **a bearing witness,**	4828
	3: 7 why yet am **I a** judged as a sinner?	2504
	3:29 *is he* not **a** of the Gentiles? Yes, of	2532
	3:29 of the Gentiles? Yes, of the Gentiles **a:**	2532
	4: 6 as David **a** describeth the blessedness	2532
	4: 9 or upon the uncircumcision **a?**	2532
	4:11 might be imputed unto them **a:**	2532
	4:12 who **a** walk in the steps of *that* faith of our	2532
	4:16 to that **a** which is of the faith of Abraham;	2532
	4:21 had promised, he was able **a** to perform.	2532
	4:24 But for us **a,** to whom it shall be imputed,	2532
	5: 2 By whom **a** we have access by faith into	2532
	5: 3 not only *so,* but we glory in tribulations **a:**	2532
	5:11 we **a** joy in God through our Lord Jesus	2532
	5:15 But not as the offence, so **a** *is* the free gift.	2532
	6: 4 so we **a** should walk in newness of life.	2532
	6: 5 we **a** shall be **a** *in the likeness of his*	235+2532
	6: 8 we believe that we shall **a** live with him:	2532
	6:11 Likewise reckon ye **a** yourselves to be dead	2532
	7: 4 ye **a** are become dead to the law by	2532
	8:11 **a** quicken your mortal bodies by his Spirit	2532
	8:17 *him,* that we may be **a** glorified together.	2532
	8:21 Because the creature itself **a** shall be	2532
	8:23 And not only *they,* but ourselves **a,**	2532
	8:26 Likewise the Spirit **a** helpeth our	2532
	8:29 he **a** did predestinate *to be* conformed to	2532
	8:30 he did predestinate, them he **a** called:	2532
	8:30 and whom he called, them he **a** justified:	2532
	8:30 whom he justified, them he **a** glorified.	2532
	8:32 how shall he not with him **a** freely give us	2532
	8:34 of God, who **a** maketh intercession for us.	2532
	9: 1 my conscience **a bearing** me **witness** in	4828
	9:10 when Rebecca **a** had conceived by one,	2532
	9:24 of the Jews only, but **a** of the Gentiles?	2532
	9:25 As he saith **a** in Osee, I will call *them* my	2532
	9:27 Esaias **a** crieth concerning Israel,	1161
	11: 1 For I **a** am an Israelite, of the seed of	2532
	11: 5 at *this* present time **a** there is a remnant	2532
	11:16 the lump *is* **a** *holy:* and if the root *be* holy,	2532
	11:21 take heed lest he **a** spare **not** thee.	3761
	11:22 otherwise thou **a** shalt be cut off.	2532
	11:23 they **a,** if they bide not still in unbelief,	2532
	11:31 *Even* so have these **a** now not believed,	2532
	11:31 through your mercy they **a** may obtain	2532
	13: 5 only for wrath, but **a** for conscience sake.	2532
	13: 6 For for this cause pay you tribute **a:**	2532
	15: 7 Christ **a** received us, to the glory of God.	2532
	15:14 And I myself **a** am persuaded of you,	2532
	15:14 brethren, that ye **a** are full of goodness,	2532
	15:14 able **a** to admonish one another.	2532
	15:22 For which cause **a** I have been much	2532
	16: 2 been a succourer of many, and of myself **a.**	NIG
	16: 4 but **a** all the churches of the Gentiles.	2532
	16: 7 who **a** were in Christ before me.	2532
1Co	1: 8 Who shall **a** confirm you unto the end,	2532
	1:16 And I baptized **a** the household of	2532
	2:13 Which *things* **a** we speak, not in the	2532
	4: 8 did reign, that we **a** might reign with you.	2532
	5:12 For what have I to do to judge them **a** that	2532
	6:14 and will **a** raise up us by his own power.	NIG
	7: 3 and likewise **a** the wife unto the husband.	2532
	7: 4 likewise **a** the husband hath not power of	2532
	7:22 likewise **a** he that is called, *being* free,	2532
	7:34 There is difference **a** between a wife and a	NIG

A

1Co 7:40 and I think a that *I* have the Spirit of God. 2504
9: 8 as a man? or saith not the law the same a? 2532
10: 6 not lust after evil *things,* as **they** a lusted. 2548
10: 9 as some of them a tempted, 2532
10:10 as some of them a murmured, 2532
10:13 will with the temptation a make a way to 2532
11: 1 followers of me, even as I **a** *am* of Christ. 2504
11: 6 woman be not covered, let her a be shorn: 2532
11:12 *even* so *is* the man a by the woman; 2532
11:19 For there must be a heresies among you, 2532
11:23 Lord *that* which a I delivered unto you, 2532
11:25 After the same manner a *he took* the cup, 2532
12:12 being many, are one body: so a is Christ. 2532
13:12 then shall I know even as a I am known. 2532
14:15 and will pray with the understanding **a:** 2532
14:15 and I will sing with the understanding a. 2532
14:19 that *by my voice* I might teach others **a,** 2532
14:34 to be under obedience, as a saith the law. 2532
15: 1 which **a** you have received, and wherein 2532
15: 2 By which a ye are saved, if ye keep in 2532
15: 3 you first *of all* that which I a received, 2532
15: 8 And last of all he was seen of **me a,** as of 2504
15:14 preaching vain, and your faith *is* a vain. 2532
15:18 Then they a which are fallen asleep in 2532
15:21 man *came* a the resurrection of the dead. 2532
15:28 the Son a himself be subject unto him 2532
15:40 *There are* a celestial bodies, 2532
15:42 So a *is* the resurrection of the dead. It is 2532
15:48 the earthy, such *are* they a that *are* earthy: 2532
15:48 such *are* they a that *are* heavenly. 2532
15:49 we shall a bear the image of the heavenly. 2532
16: 4 And if it be meet that I go a, they shall go 2504
16:10 worketh the work of the Lord, as I **a** *do.* 2504
2Co 1: 5 so our consolation a aboundeth by Christ. 2532
1: 6 of the same sufferings which we a suffer: 2532
1: 7 so *shall ye be* a of the consolation. 2532
1:11 You a helping together by prayer for us, 2532
1:14 As **a** you have acknowledged us in part, 2532
1:14 as ye **a** *are* ours in the day of the Lord 2532
1:22 hath a sealed us, and given the earnest 2532
2: 9 For to this end a did I write, that I might 2532
2:10 To whom ye forgive any *thing,* I *forgive* **a:** 2532
3: 6 Who a hath made us able ministers of 2532
4:10 that the life a of Jesus might be made 2532
4:11 that the life a of Jesus might be made 2532
4:13 we a believe, and therefore speak; 2532
4:14 the Lord Jesus shall raise up us a by Jesus, 2532
5: 5 Who a hath given unto us the earnest of 2532
5:11 I trust a are made manifest in your 2532
6: 1 workers together *with him,* beseech *you* a 2532
6:13 as unto *my* children,) be ye a enlarged. 2532
8: 6 he would a finish in you the same grace 2532
8: 6 would also finish in you the same grace a. 2532
8: 7 to us, *see* that ye abound in this grace a. 2532
8:10 only to do, but a to be forward a year ago. 2532
8:11 *there may be* a performance a out of that 2532
8:14 that their abundance a may be a *supply* for 2532
8:19 was a chosen of the churches to travel 2532
8:21 of the Lord, but a in the sight of men. 2532
9: 6 soweth sparingly shall reap a sparingly; 2532
9: 6 he which soweth bountifully shall reap a 2532
9:12 is abundant a by many thanksgivings unto 2532
10:11 such *will we be* a in deed when we are 2532
10:14 for we are come as far as to you a in 2532
11:15 *if* his ministers a be transformed as 1499
11:18 many glory after the flesh, I will glory a. 2504
11:21 is bold, (I speak foolishly,) I am bold a. 2504
13: 4 we a are weak in him, but we shall live 2532
13: 9 and this a we wish, *even* your perfection. 2532
Gal 2: 1 with Barnabas, and took Titus with *me* **a.** 2532
2:10 the same which I a was forward to do. 2532
2:13 that Barnabas a was carried away 2532
2:17 we ourselves a are found sinners, *is* 2532
5:21 as I have a told *you* in time past, 2532
5:25 in the Spirit, let us a walk in the Spirit. 2532
6: 1 thyself, lest thou a be tempted. 2532
6: 7 a man soweth, that shall he a reap. 2532
Eph 1:11 In whom a we have obtained an 2532
1:13 In whom ye a *trusted,* after that ye heard 2532
1:13 In whom a after that ye believed, ye were 2532
1:15 Wherefore I **a,** after I heard of your faith 2504
1:21 this world, but a in that which is to come: 2532
2: 3 Among whom a we all had our 2532
2:22 In whom you a are builded together for a 2532
4: 9 that he a descended first into the lower 2532
4:10 He that descended is the same a that 2532
5: 2 as Christ a hath loved us, and hath given 2532
5:25 even as Christ a loved the church, 2532
6: 9 knowing that your Master a is in heaven; 2532
6:21 But that ye a may know my affairs, *and* 2532
Php 1:15 envy and strife; and some a of good will: 2532
1:20 now a Christ shall be magnified in my 2532
1:29 believe on him, but a to suffer for his sake; 2532
2: 4 but every man a on the *things* of others. 2532
2: 5 be in you, which *was* a in Christ Jesus: 2532
2: 9 Wherefore God a hath highly exalted him, 2532
2:18 For the same *cause* a do ye joy, 2504
2:19 that I a may be of good comfort, when I 2504
2:24 But I trust in the Lord that I a myself shall 2532
2:27 and not on him only, but on me a, lest I 2532
3: 4 Though I *might* a have confidence in 2532
3:12 which a I am apprehended of Christ Jesus. 2532
3:20 from whence a we look for the Saviour, 2532
4: 3 **And** I intreat thee a, true yokefellow, 2532
4: 3 with Clement a, and *with* other my 2532

Php 4:10 wherein ye were a careful, but ye lacked 2532
4:15 Now ye Philippians know a, that in 2532
Col 1: 6 and bringeth forth fruit, as *it doth* a in you, 2532
1: 7 As ye a learned of Epaphras our dear 2532
1: 9 For this cause we a, since the day we 2532
1:29 Whereunto I a labour, striving according 2532
2:11 In whom a ye are circumcised with 2532
2:12 wherein a you are risen with *him* through 2532
3: 4 then shall ye a appear with him in glory. 2532
3: 7 In the which ye a walked sometime, 2532
3: 8 But now you a put off all *these;* anger, 2532
3:13 even as Christ a forgave you, so a *do* ye. 2532
3:15 to the which a ye are called in one body; 2532
4: 1 that ye a have a Master in heaven. 2532
4: 3 Withal praying a for us, that God would 2532
4: 3 of Christ, for which I am a in bonds: 2532
4:16 cause that it be read a in the church of 2532
1Th 1: 5 but a in power, and in the Holy Ghost, 2532
1: 8 in every place your faith to God-ward is 2532
2: 8 but a our own souls, because ye were dear 2532
2:10 and God a, how holily and justly NIG
2:13 For this cause a thank we God without 2532
2:13 which effectually worketh a in you that 2532
2:14 for ye a have suffered like *things* of your 2532
3: 6 greatly to see us, as we a *to see* you: 2532
4: 6 we a have forewarned you and testified. 2532
4: 8 who hath a given unto us his holy Spirit. 2532
4:14 them a which sleep in Jesus will God 2532
5:11 and edify one another, even as a ye do. 2532
5:24 *is* he that calleth you, who a will do *it.* 2532
2Th 1: 5 the kingdom of God, for which ye a suffer: 2532
1:11 Wherefore a we pray always for you, 2532
1Ti 2: 9 In like manner a, that women adorn 2532
3:10 And let these a first be proved; 2532
5:13 only idle, but tattlers a and busybodies, 2532
5:20 rebuke before all, that others a may fear. 2532
5:25 Likewise a the good works *of some* are 2532
6:12 whereunto thou art a called, 2532
2Ti 1: 5 and I am persuaded that in thee a. 2532
1:12 the which cause I a suffer these *things:* 2532
2: 2 who shall be able to teach others a. 2532
2: 5 And if a man a strive for masteries, *yet* is 2532
2:10 that they may a obtain the salvation which 2532
2:11 For if we be dead with *him,* we shall a live 2532
2:12 we shall a reign with *him:* if we deny *him,* 2532
2:12 *him:* if we deny *him,* **he** a will deny us: 2548
2:20 and of silver, but a of wood and of earth; 2532
2:22 Flee a youthful lusts: 1161
3: 1 This know a, that in the last days perilous 1161
3: 8 so do these a resist the truth: 2532
3: 9 be manifest unto all *men,* as theirs a was. 2532
4: 8 unto all them a that love his appearing. 2532
4:15 Of whom be thou ware a; for he hath 2532
Tit 3: 3 we ourselves a were sometimes foolish, 2532
3:14 And let ours a learn to maintain good 2532
Phm 1: 9 and now a a prisoner of Jesus Christ. 2532
1:21 knowing that thou wilt a do more than I 2532
1:22 But withal prepare me a a lodging: for I 2532
Heb 1: 2 *things,* by whom a he made the worlds; 2532
2: 4 God a bearing them **witness,** both with 4901
2:14 a himself likewise took part of the same; 2532
3: 2 as a Moses *was* faithful in all his house. 2532
4:10 he a hath ceased from his own works, 2532
5: 2 for that he himself a is compassed with 2532
5: 3 so a for himself, to offer for sins. 2532
5: 5 So a Christ glorified not himself to be 2532
6: 6 As he saith in another *place,* Thou *art* a 2532
7: 2 To whom a Abraham gave a tenth *part* of 2532
7: 2 and after that a King of Salem, which is, 2532
7: 9 And as *I* may so say, Levi, who receiveth 2532
7:12 there is made of necessity a change a of 2532
7:25 Wherefore he is able a to save them to 2532
8: 3 that this *man* have somewhat a to offer. 2532
8: 6 by how much a he is the mediator of a 2532
9: 1 Then verily the first *covenant* had a 2532
9:16 For where a testament *is,* there must a a NIG
10:15 *Whereof* the Holy Ghost is a witness to 2532
11:11 Through faith a Sara herself received 2532
11:19 whence a he received him in a figure. 2532
11:32 *of* David a, and Samuel, and *of* 5037
12: 1 Wherefore seeing we a are compassed 2532
12:26 I shake not the earth only, but a heaven. 2532
13: 3 as being yourselves a in the body. 2532
13:12 Wherefore Jesus a, that he might sanctify 2532
Jas 1:11 a shall the rich *man* fade away in his ways. 2532
2: 2 come in a a poor *man* in vile raiment; 2532
2:11 not commit adultery, said a, Do not kill. 2532
2:19 the devils a believe, and tremble. 2532
2:25 Likewise a was not Rahab the harlot 2532
2:26 is dead, so faith without works is dead a. 2532
3: 2 *and* able to a bridle the whole body. 2532
3: 4 Behold a the ships, which though they be 2532
5: 8 Be ye a patient; stablish your hearts: for 2532
1Pe 2: 5 Ye a, as lively stones, are built *up* a 2532
2: 6 a it is contained in the scripture, 2532
2: 8 whereunto a they were appointed. 2532
2:18 the good and gentle, but a to the froward. 2532
2:21 because Christ a suffered for us, leaving 2532
3: 1 they a may without the word be won by 2532
3: 5 manner in the old time the holy women a, 2532
3:18 For Christ a hath once suffered for sins, 2532
3:19 By which a he went and preached unto 2532
3:21 a now save us (not the putting away of 2532
4: 6 gospel preached a to *them that are* dead, 2532

1Pe 4:13 ye may be glad a with exceeding joy. 2532
5: 1 who am **a an elder,** and a witness of 4850
5: 1 **and** a a partaker of the glory that shall be 2532
2Pe 1:19 We have a more sure word of prophecy; 2532
2: 1 But there were prophets a among 2532
3:10 the earth a and the works that are therein 2532
3:15 even as our beloved brother Paul a 2532
3:16 As a in all *his* epistles, speaking in them of 2532
3:16 as *they do* a the other scriptures, 2532
3:17 *these things* before, beware lest ye **a,** NIG
1Jn 1: 3 that ye a may have fellowship with us: 2532
1: 2 but a for *the sins of* the whole world. 2532
2: 6 saith *he* abideth in him ought himself a 2532
2:23 *acknowledgeth the Son hath the Father* **a.** NIG
2:24 ye a shall continue in the Son, and in 2532
3: 4 Whosoever committeth sin transgresseth a 2532
4:11 loved us, we ought a to love one another. 2532
4:21 he who loveth God love his brother **a.** 2532
5: 1 begat loveth him a that is begotten of him. 2532
2Jn 1: 1 but a all they that have known the truth; 2532
3Jn 1:12 and we a bear record; and ye know that NIG
Jude 1: 8 Likewise a these *filthy* dreamers defile 2532
1:14 And Enoch a, the seventh from Adam, 2532
Rev 1: 7 see him, and they a which pierced him: NIG
1: 9 who a am your brother, and companion 2532
2: 6 deeds of the Nicolaitans, which I **a** hate. 2504
2:15 hast thou a them that hold the doctrine 2532
3:10 I **a** will keep thee from the hour of 2504
3:21 *even* as I **a** overcame, and am set down 2504
6:11 until their fellowservants a and their 2532
11: 8 Egypt, where a our Lord was crucified. 2532
14:17 is in heaven, he a having a sharp sickle. 2532

ALTAR (378) [ALTARS]

Ge 8:20 Noah builded an a unto the LORD; 4196
8:20 and offered burnt offerings on the **a.** 4196
12: 7 there builded he an a unto the LORD, 4196
12: 8 there he builded an a unto the LORD, 4196
13: 4 Unto the place of the a, which he had 4196
13:18 and built there an a unto the LORD. 4196
22: 9 Abraham built an a there, and laid 4196
22: 9 and laid him on the a upon the wood. 4196
26:25 he builded an a there, and called upon 4196
33:20 he erected there an a, and called it 4196
35: 1 make there an a unto God, that appeared 4196
35: 3 I will make there an a unto God, 4196
35: 7 he built there an a, and called the place 4196
Ex 17:15 Moses built an a, and called the name of 4196
20:24 An a of earth thou shalt make unto me, 4196
20:25 if thou wilt make me an a of stone, 4196
20:26 shalt thou go up by steps unto mine a, 4196
21:14 thou shalt take him from mine a, that he 4196
24: 4 builded an a under the hill, 4196
24: 6 half of the blood he sprinkled on the **a.** 4196
27: 1 thou shalt make an a *of* shittim wood, 4196
27: 1 five cubits broad; the a shall be foursquare 4196
27: 5 shalt put it under the compass of the a, 4196
27: 5 the net may be even to the midst of the **a.** 4196
27: 6 thou shalt make staves for the a, staves of 4196
27: 7 shall be upon the two sides of the a, 4196
28:43 they come near unto the a to minister 4196
29:12 put *it* upon the horns of the a with thy 4196
29:12 shalt pour all the blood beside the bottom of the **a.** 4196
29:13 *is* upon them, and burn *them* upon the **a.** 4196
29:16 and sprinkle *it* round about upon the **a.** 4196
29:18 shalt burn the whole ram upon the **a.** 4196
29:20 the blood upon the a round about. 4196
29:21 shalt take of the blood that *is* upon the a, 4196
29:25 burn *them* upon the a for a burnt offering, 4196
29:36 thou shalt cleanse the a, when thou hast 4196
29:37 thou shalt make an atonement for the a, 4196
29:37 sanctify it; and it shall be an a most holy: 4196
29:37 whatsoever toucheth the a shall be holy. 4196
29:38 *is that* which thou shalt offer upon the a; 4196
29:44 tabernacle of the congregation, and the **a:** 4196
30: 1 shalt make an a to burn incense upon: 4196
30:18 tabernacle of the congregation and the a, 4196
30:20 when they come near to the a to minister, 4196
30:27 and his vessels, and the a of incense, 4196
30:28 the a of burnt offering with all his vessels, 4196
31: 8 with all his furniture, and the a of incense, 4196
31: 9 a of burnt offering with all his furniture, 4196
32: 5 when Aaron saw *it,* he built an a before it; 4196
35:15 the incense a and his staves, and 4196
35:16 The a of burnt offering with his brasen 4196
37:25 he made the incense a *of* shittim wood: 4196
38: 1 he made the a of burnt offering *of* shittim 4196
38: 3 he made all the vessels of the a, the pots, 4196
38: 4 made for the a a brasen grate of network 4196
38: 7 staves into the rings on the sides of the a, 4196
38: 7 withal; he made the a hollow with boards. NIH
38:30 the brasen a, and the brasen grate for it, 4196
38:30 grate for it, and all the vessels of the a, 4196
39:38 the golden a, and the anointing oil, 4196
39:39 The brasen a, and his grate of brass, his 4196
40: 5 thou shalt set the a of gold for the incense 4196
40: 6 thou shalt set the a of the burnt offering 4196
40: 6 the tent of the congregation and the a, 4196
40:10 shalt anoint the a of the burnt offering, 4196
40:10 and all his vessels, and sanctify the **a.** 4196
40:10 the altar: and it shall be an a most holy. 4196
40:26 he put the golden a in the tent of 4196
40:29 he put the a of burnt offering *by* the door 4196
40:30 the tent of the congregation and the a, 4196
40:32 when they came near unto the a, 4196

Ex 40:33 round about the tabernacle and the a, 4196
Lev 1: 5 sprinkle the blood round about upon the a 4196
1: 7 Aaron the priest shall put fire upon the a, 4196
1: 8 that *is* on the fire which *is* upon the a: 4196
1: 9 the priest shall burn all on the a, *to be* a 4196
1:11 he shall kill it on the side of the a 4196
1:11 sprinkle his blood round about upon the a. 4196
1:12 that *is* on the fire which *is* upon the a: 4196
1:13 shall bring *it* all, and burn *it* upon the a. 4196
1:15 the priest shall bring it unto the a, 4196
1:15 wring off his head, and burn *it* on the a; 4196
1:15 shall be wrung out at the side of the a 4196
1:16 cast it beside the a on the east part, by 4196
1:17 the priest shall burn it upon the a, upon 4196
2: 2 shall burn the memorial of it upon the a, 4196
2: 8 the priest, he shall bring it unto the a. 4196
2: 9 and shall burn *it* upon the a: 4196
2:12 they shall not be burnt on the a for 4196
3: 2 sprinkle the blood upon the a round about 4196
3: 5 Aaron's sons shall burn it on the a upon 4196
3: 8 the blood thereof round about upon the a. 4196
3:11 the priest shall burn it upon the a: *it is* 4196
3:13 the blood thereof upon the a round about. 4196
3:16 the priest shall burn them upon the a: *it is* 4196
4: 7 the a of sweet incense before the LORD, 4196
4: 7 the bottom of the a of the burnt offering, 4196
4:10 the priest shall burn them upon the a of 4196
4:18 horns of the a which *is* before the LORD, 4196
4:18 the bottom of the a of the burnt offering, 4196
4:19 his fat from him, and burn *it* upon the a. 4196
4:25 put *it* upon the horns of the a of burnt 4196
4:25 at the bottom of the a of burnt offering. 4196
4:26 he shall burn all his fat upon the a, as 4196
4:30 put *it* upon the horns of the a of burnt 4196
4:30 the blood thereof at the bottom of the a. 4196
4:31 the priest shall burn *it* upon the a for a 4196
4:34 put *it* upon the horns of the a of burnt 4196
4:34 the blood thereof at the bottom of the a; 4196
4:35 the priest shall burn them upon the a, 4196
5: 9 of the sin offering upon the side of the a; 4196
5: 9 shall be wrung out at the bottom of the a 4196
5:12 a memorial thereof, and burn *it* on the a, 4196
6: 9 of the burning upon the a all night unto 4196
6: 9 and the fire of the a shall be burning in it. 4196
6:10 with the burnt offering on the a, 4196
6:10 and he shall put them besides the a. 4196
6:12 the fire upon the a shall be burning in it; 4196
6:13 The fire shall ever be burning upon the a; 4196
6:14 offer it before the LORD, before the a. 4196
6:15 burn *it* upon the a *for* a sweet savour, 4196
7: 2 shall he sprinkle round about upon the a. 4196
7: 5 the priest shall burn them upon the a *for* 4196
7:31 the priest shall burn the fat upon the a. 4196
8:11 he sprinkled thereof upon the a seven 4196
8:11 anointed the a and all his vessels, both 4196
8:15 put *it* upon the horns of the a round about 4196
8:15 purified the a, and poured the blood at 4196
8:15 poured the blood at the bottom of the a, 4196
8:16 their fat, and Moses burned *it* upon the a. 4196
8:19 Moses sprinkled the blood upon the a 4196
8:21 Moses burnt the whole ram upon the a: 4196
8:24 Moses sprinkled the blood upon the a 4196
8:28 burnt *them* on the a upon the burnt 4196
8:30 of the blood which *was* upon the a, 4196
9: 7 Go unto the a, and offer thy sin offering, 4196
9: 8 Aaron therefore went unto the a, 4196
9: 9 put *it* upon the horns of the a, and poured 4196
9: 9 out the blood at the bottom of the a: 4196
9:10 of the sin offering, he burnt upon the a; 4196
9:12 he sprinkled round about upon the a. 4196
9:13 the head: and he burnt *them* upon the a. 4196
9:14 *them* upon the burnt offering on the a. 4196
9:17 a handful thereof, and burnt *it* upon the a, 4196
9:18 he sprinkled upon the a round about, 4196
9:20 breasts, and he burnt the fat upon the a. 4196
9:24 consumed upon the a the burnt offering 4196
10:12 and eat it without leaven beside the a: 4196
14:20 and the meat offering upon the a: 4196
16:12 of fire from off the a before the LORD, 4196
16:18 he shall go out unto the a that *is* before 4196
16:18 *it* upon the horns of the a round about. 4196
16:20 and the a, he shall bring the live goat: 4196
16:25 the sin offering shall he burn upon the a. 4196
16:33 for the a, and he shall make an atonement 4196
17: 6 a of the LORD *at* the door of 4196
17:11 I have given it to you upon the a to make 4196
21:23 come nigh unto the a, because he hath a 4196
22:22 fire of them upon the a unto the LORD. 4196
Nu 3:26 by the a round about, and the cords of it 4196
4:11 the golden a they shall spread a cloth 4196
4:13 they shall take away the ashes from the a, 4196
4:14 and the basons, all the vessels of the a, 4196
4:26 the tabernacle and by the a round about, 4196
5:25 before the LORD, and offer it upon the a: 4196
5:26 burn *it* upon the a, and afterward shall 4196
7: 1 both the a and all the vessels thereof, 4196
7:10 the princes offered *for* dedicating of the a 4196
7:10 princes offered their offering before the a. 4196
7:11 on *his* day, for the dedicating of the a. 4196
7:84 This *was* the dedication of the a, in the 4196
7:88 This *was* the dedication of the a, after 4196
16:38 them broad plates *for* a covering of the a: 4196
16:39 made broad *plates for* a covering of the a: 4196
16:46 put fire therein from off the a, and put on 4196
18: 3 the vessels of the sanctuary and the a, 4196

Nu 18: 5 of the sanctuary, and the charge of the a: 4196
18: 7 your priest's office for every thing of the a, 4196
18:17 thou shalt sprinkle their blood upon the a, 4196
23: 2 Balaam offered on *every* a a bullock 4196
23: 4 I have offered upon *every* a a bullock 4196
23:14 offered a bullock and a ram on *every* a. 4196
23:30 offered a bullock and a ram on *every* a. 4196
Dt 12:27 upon the a of the LORD thy God: 4196
12:27 out upon the a of the LORD thy God, 4196
16:21 near unto the a of the LORD thy God, 4196
26: 4 set it down before the a of the LORD thy 4196
27: 5 there shalt thou build an a unto the LORD 4196
27: 5 unto the LORD thy God, an a of stones: 4196
27: 6 Thou shalt build the a of the LORD thy 4196
33:10 and whole *burnt sacrifice* upon thine a. 4196
Jos 8:30 Joshua built an a unto the LORD God of 4196
8:31 an a of whole stones, over which no *man* 4196
9:27 for the a of the LORD, *even* unto this day, 4196
22:10 the half tribe of Manasseh built there an a 4196
22:10 an altar by Jordan, a great a to see to. 4196
22:11 the half tribe of Manasseh have built an a 4196
22:16 in that ye have builded you an a, that ye 4196
22:19 in building you an a beside the altar of 4196
22:19 in building you an altar beside the a of 4196
22:23 That we have built us an a to turn from 4196
22:26 Let us now prepare to build us an a, 4196
22:28 Behold the pattern of the a of the LORD, 4196
22:29 to build an a for burnt offerings, for meat 4196
22:29 besides the a of the LORD our God that *is* 4196
22:34 the children of Gad called the a *Ed:* for it 4196
Jdg 6:24 Gideon built an a there unto the LORD, 4196
6:25 throw down the a of Baal that thy father 4196
6:26 build an a unto the LORD thy God upon 4196
6:28 the a of Baal was cast down, and the 4196
6:28 the second bullock was offered upon the a 4196
6:30 because he hath cast down the a of Baal, 4196
6:31 because *one* hath cast down his a. 4196
6:32 because he hath thrown down his a. 4196
13:20 went up toward heaven from off the a, 4196
13:20 the LORD ascended in the flame of the a. 4196
21: 4 built there an a, and offered burnt 4196
1Sa 2:28 to offer upon mine a, to burn incense, 4196
2:33 *whom* I shall not cut off from mine a, 4196
7:17 and there he built an a unto the LORD. 4196
14:35 Saul built an a unto the LORD: the same 4196
14:35 the same was the first a that he built unto 4196
2Sa 24:18 rear an a unto the LORD in 4196
24:21 of thee, to build an a unto the LORD, 4196
24:25 David built there an a unto the LORD, 4196
1Ki 1:50 and caught hold on the horns of the a. 4196
1:51 he hath caught hold on the horns of the a, 4196
1:53 and they brought him down from the a. 4196
2:28 and caught hold on the horns of the a. 4196
2:29 of the LORD; and behold, *he is* by the a. 4196
3: 4 offerings did Solomon offer up on that a. 4196
6:20 and *so* covered the a *which was of* cedar. 4196
6:22 also the whole a that *was* by the oracle he 4196
7:48 the a of gold, and the table *of* gold, 4196
8:22 Solomon stood before the a of the LORD 4196
8:31 oath come before thine a in this house: 4196
8:54 he arose from before the a of the LORD, 4196
8:64 the brasen a that *was* before the LORD 4196
9:25 peace offerings upon the a which he built 4196
9:25 he burnt incense upon **the a**[5] that *was* 2050.2
12:32 offered upon the a (so did he in Beth-el,) 4196
12:33 So he offered upon the a which he had 4196
12:33 he offered upon the a, and burnt incense. 4196
13: 1 Jeroboam stood by the a to burn incense. 4196
13: 2 he cried against the a in the word of 4196
13: 2 and said, O a, altar, thus saith the LORD; 4196
13: 2 and said, O altar, thus saith the LORD; 4196
13: 3 the a *shall be* rent, and the ashes that *are* 4196
13: 4 which had cried against the a in Beth-el, 4196
13: 4 that he put forth his hand from the a, 4196
13: 5 The a also *was* rent, and the ashes poured 4196
13: 5 and the ashes poured out from the a, 4196
13:32 of the LORD against the a in Beth-el, 4196
16:32 he reared up an a for Baal *in* the house of 4196
18:26 they leapt upon the a which was made. 4196
18:30 he repaired the a of the LORD that was 4196
18:32 *with* the stones he built an a in the name 4196
18:32 he made a trench about the a, as great as 4196
18:35 the water ran round about the a; 4196
2Ki 11:11 the temple, *along* by the a and the temple. 4196
12: 9 hole in the lid of it, and set it beside the a, 4196
16:10 and saw an a that *was* at Damascus: 4196
16:10 to Urijah the priest the fashion of the a, 4196
16:11 Urijah the priest built an a according to all 4196
16:12 come from Damascus, the king saw the a: 4196
16:12 the king approached to the a, 4196
16:13 blood of his peace offerings, upon the a. 4196
16:14 he brought also the brasen a, which *was* 4196
16:14 from between the a and the house of 4196
16:14 and put it on the north side of the a. 4196
16:15 Upon the great a burn the morning burnt 4196
16:15 the brasen a shall be for me to inquire *by.* 4196
18:22 Ye shall worship before this a in 4196
23: 9 not up to the a of the LORD in Jerusalem, 4196
23:15 Moreover the a that *was* at Beth-el, *and* 4196
23:15 both that a and the high place he brake 4196
23:16 burnt *them* upon the a, and polluted it, 4196
23:17 thou hast done against the a of Beth-el. 4196
1Ch 6:49 his sons offered upon the a of the burnt 4196
6:49 on the a of incense, *and were appointed* 4196
16:40 a of the burnt offering continually morning 4196

1Ch 21:18 set up an a unto the LORD in 4196
21:22 that I may build an a therein unto 4196
21:26 David built there an a unto the LORD, 4196
21:26 by fire upon the a of burnt offering. 4196
21:29 and the a of the burnt offering, 4196
22: 1 this *is* the a of the burnt offering for Israel. 4196
28:18 for the a of incense refined gold by weight; 4196
2Ch 1: 5 Moreover the brasen a, that Bezaleel 4196
1: 6 Solomon went up thither to the brasen a 4196
4: 1 Moreover he made an a of brass, 4196
4:19 the golden a also, and the tables whereon 4196
5:12 stood *at* the east *end* of the a, 4196
6:12 he stood before the a of the LORD in 4196
6:22 oath come before thine a in this house; 4196
7: 7 the brasen a which Solomon had made 4196
7: 9 for they kept the dedication of the a seven 4196
8:12 unto the LORD on the a of the LORD, 4196
15: 8 renewed the a of the LORD, that *was* 4196
23:10 by the a and the temple, by the king 4196
26:16 to burn incense upon the a of incense. 4196
26:19 of the LORD, from beside the incense a. 4196
29:18 the a of burnt offering, with all the vessels 4196
29:19 they *are* before the a of the LORD. 4196
29:21 to offer *them* on the a of the LORD. 4196
29:22 the blood, and sprinkled *it* on the a: 4196
29:22 they sprinkled the blood upon the a: 4196
29:22 and they sprinkled the blood upon the a. 4196
29:24 reconciliation with their blood upon the a, 4196
29:27 to offer the burnt offering upon the a. 4196
32:12 Ye shall worship before one a, 4196
33:16 he repaired the a of the LORD, 4196
35:16 to offer burnt offerings upon the a of 4196
Ezr 3: 2 and builded the a of the God of Israel, 4196
3: 3 they set the a upon his bases; for fear *was* 4196
7:17 offer them upon the a of the house of your 4056
Ne 10:34 to burn upon the a of the LORD our God, 4196
Ps 26: 6 so will I compass thine a, O LORD: 4196
43: 4 will I go unto the a of God, unto God my 4196
51:19 then shall they offer bullocks upon thine a. 4196
118:27 with cords, *even* unto the horns of the a. 4196
Isa 6: 6 he had taken with the tongs from off the a: 4196
19:19 In that day shall there be an a to 4196
27: 9 when he maketh all the stones of the a as 4196
36: 7 Ye shall worship before this a? 4196
56: 7 sacrifices *shall be* accepted upon mine a; 4196
60: 7 shall come up with acceptance on mine a, 4196
La 2: 7 The Lord hath cast off his a, he hath 4196
Eze 8: 5 northward at the gate of the a this image 4196
8:16 between the porch and the a, *were* about 4196
9: 2 went in, and stood beside the brasen a. 4196
40:46 the keepers of the charge of the a: 4196
40:47 and the a *that was* before the house. 4196
41:22 The a *of* wood was three cubits high, 4196
43:13 these *are* the measures of the a after 4196
43:13 and this *shall be* the higher place of the a. 4196
43:15 So the a *shall be* four cubits; and from 2025
43:15 from the a and upward *shall be* four horns. 741
43:16 the a *shall be* twelve *cubits* long, twelve 741
43:18 *are* the ordinances of the a in the day 4196
43:22 shall cleanse the a, as they did cleanse 4196
43:26 Seven days shall they purge the a 4196
43:27 make your burnt offerings upon the a, 4196
45:19 the four corners of the settle of the a, 4196
47: 1 of the house, at the south *side* of the a. 4196
Joel 1:13 howl, ye ministers of the a: come, lie all 4196
2:17 weep between the porch and the a, 4196
Am 2: 8 upon clothes laid to pledge by every a, 4196
3:14 the horns of the a shall be cut off, 4196
9: 1 I saw the Lord standing upon the a: 4196
Zec 9:15 like bowls, *and* as the corners of the a. 4196
14:20 house shall be like the bowls before the a. 4196
Mal 1: 7 *Ye* offer polluted bread upon mine a; 4196
1:10 do ye kindle *fire on* mine a for nought. 4196
2:13 covering the a of the LORD *with* tears, 4196
Mt 5:23 Therefore if thou bring thy gift to the a, 2379
5:24 Leave there thy gift before the a, 2379
23:18 Whosoever shall swear by the a, it is 2379
23:19 the gift, or the a that sanctifieth the gift? 2379
23:20 Whoso therefore shall swear by the a, 2379
23:35 ye slew between the temple and the a. 2379
Lk 1:11 on the right side of the a of incense. 2379
11:51 which perished between the a 2379
Ac 17:23 I found an a with this inscription, 1041
1Co 9:13 they which wait at the a are partakers 2379
9:13 wait at the altar are partakers with the a? 2379
10:18 eat *of* the sacrifices partakers of the a? 2379
Heb 7:13 which no *man* gave attendance at the a. 2379
13:10 We have an a, whereof they have no right 2379
Jas 2:21 he had offered Isaac his son upon the a? 2379
Rev 6: 9 I saw under the a the souls of them that 2379
8: 3 another angel came and stood at the a, 2379
8: 3 the golden a which was before the throne. 2379
8: 5 and filled it with fire of the a, and cast *it* 2379
9:13 of the golden a which is before God, 2379
11: 1 and the a, and them that worship therein. 2379
14:18 And another angel came out from the a, 2379
16: 7 And I heard another out of the a say, 2379

ALTARS (55) [ALTAR]

Ex 34:13 shall destroy their a, break their images, 4196
Nu 3:31 the a, and the vessels of the sanctuary 4196
23: 1 Build me here seven a, and prepare me 4196
23: 4 have prepared seven a, and I have offered 4196
23:14 and built seven a, and offered a bullock 4196
23:29 Build me here seven a, and prepare me 4196

A

Dt	7: 5 ye shall destroy their **a**, and break down	4196
	12: 3 you shall overthrow their **a**, and break	4196
Jdg	2: 2 of this land; you shall throw down their **a**:	4196
1Ki	19:10 thrown down thine **a**, and slain thy	4196
	19:14 thrown down thine **a**, and slain thy	4196
2Ki	11:18 his **a** and his images brake they in pieces	4196
	11:18 Mattan the priest of Baal before the **a**.	4196
	18:22 and whose **a** Hezekiah hath taken away,	4196
	21: 3 reared up a for Baal, and made a grove,	4196
	21: 4 he built **a** in the house of the LORD,	4196
	21: 5 he built **a** for all the host of heaven in	4196
	23:12 the **a** that *were* on the top of the upper	4196
	23:12 the **a** which Manasseh had made in the	4196
	23:20 high places that *were* there upon the **a**,	4196
2Ch	14: 3 he took away the **a** of the strange *gods*,	4196
	23:17 brake his **a** and his images in pieces,	4196
	23:17 Mattan the priest of Baal before the **a**.	4196
	28:24 he made him **a** in every corner of	4196
	30:14 took away the **a** that *were* in Jerusalem,	4196
	30:14 all the **a for incense** took they away,	6999
	31: 1 and the **a** out of all Judah and Benjamin,	4196
	32:12 taken away his high places and his **a**,	4196
	33: 3 he reared up **a** for Baalim,	4196
	33: 4 Also he built **a** in the house of the LORD,	4196
	33: 5 he built **a** for all the host of heaven in	4196
	33:15 all the **a** that he had built in the mount of	4196
	34: 4 they brake down the **a** of Baalim in his	4196
	34: 5 the bones of the priests upon their **a**,	4196
	34: 7 when he had broken down the **a** and	4196
Ps	84: 3 *even* thine **a**, O LORD of hosts, my King,	4196
Isa	17: 8 he shall not look to the **a**, the work of his	4196
	36: 7 and whose **a** Hezekiah hath taken away,	4196
	65: 3 and burneth incense upon **a of brick**;	3843
Jer	11:13 have ye set up **a** to *that* shameful thing,	4196
	11:13 *even* **a** to burn incense unto Baal.	4196
	17: 1 their heart, and upon the horns of your **a**;	4196
	17: 2 Whilst their children remember their **a**	4196
Eze	6: 4 your **a** shall be desolate, and your images	4196
	6: 5 scatter your bones round about your **a**.	4196
	6: 6 that your **a** may be laid waste	4196
	6:13 be among their idols round about their **a**,	4196
Hos	8:11 Ephraim hath made many **a** to sin,	4196
	8:11 altars to sin, **a** shall be unto him to sin.	4196
	10: 1 of his fruit he hath increased the **a**;	4196
	10: 2 he shall break down their **a**, he shall spoil	4196
	10: 8 and the thistle shall come up on their **a**;	4196
	12:11 their **a** *are* as heaps in the furrows of	4196
Am	3:14 upon him I will also visit the **a** of Beth-el:	4196
Ro	11: 3 thy prophets, and digged down thine **a**;	2379

AL-TASCHITH (4)

Ps	57: T the chief Musician, **A**, Michtam of David.	516
	58: T the chief Musician, **A**, Michtam of David.	516
	59: T the chief Musician, **A**, Michtam of David;	516
	75: T **A**, A Psalm *or* Song of Asaph.	516

ALTER (4) [ALTERED, ALTERETH]

Lev	27:10 He shall not **a** it, nor change it, a good for	2498
Ezr	6:11 decree, that whosoever shall **a** this word,	8133
	6:12 that shall put to their hand to **a** and	8133
Ps	89:34 nor **a** the thing that is gone out of my lips.	8138

ALTERED (2) [ALTER]

Est	1:19 Persians and the Medes, that it be not **a**,	5674
Lk	9:29 the fashion of his countenance was **a**,	2087

ALTERETH (2) [ALTER]

Da	6: 8 of the Medes and Persians, which **a** not.	5709
	6:12 of the Medes and Persians, which **a** not.	5709

ALTHOUGH (16) [THOUGH]

Ex	13:17 the land of the Philistines, **a** that *was* near;	3588
Jos	22:17 **a** there was a plague in the congregation	2050.1
2Sa	23: 5 **A** my house *be* not so with God; yet he	3588
	23: 5 all *my* desire, **a** he make *it* not to grow.	3588
1Ki	20: 5 **A** I have sent unto thee, saying,	3588
Est	7: 4 **a** the enemy could not countervail	3588
Job	2: 3 **a** thou movedst me against him,	2050.1
	5: 6 **A** affliction cometh not forth of the dust,	3588
	35:14 **A** thou sayest thou shalt not see him,	637+3588
Jer	31:32 **a** I was a husband unto them, saith	2050.1
Eze	7:13 that which is sold, **a** they were yet alive:	2050.1
	11:16 **A** I have cast them far off among	3588
	11:16 **a** I have scattered them among	3588
Hab	3:17 **A** the fig tree shall not blossom,	3588
Mk	14:29 **A** all shall be offended, yet *will* not	1487+2532
Heb	4: 3 **a** the works were finished from	2543

ALTOGETHER (29) [TOGETHER]

Ge	18:21 see whether they have done **a** according	3617
Ex	11: 1 he shall surely thrust you out hence **a**.	3617
	19:18 mount Sinai was **a** on a smoke, because	3605
Nu	16:13 thou **make** thyself **a a prince**	8323+8323
	23:11 behold, thou hast **blessed** *them* **a**.	1288+1288
	24:10 **a blessed** *them* these three times.	1288+1288
	30:14 if her husband **a hold** his **peace** at	2790+2790
Dt	16:20 That which is **a just** shalt thou	6664+6664
2Ch	12:12 him, that *he* would not destroy *him* **a**.	3617
Est	4:14 For if thou **a holdest** thy **peace** at	2790+2790
Job	13: 5 that you would **a hold** your **peace**,	2790+2790
	27:12 why then are ye thus **a vain**?	1891+1892
Ps	19: 9 of the LORD *are* true *and* righteous **a**.	3162
	39: 5 verily every man at his best state *is* **a**	3605
	50:21 thou thoughtest that I **was a** *such a*	1961+1961
	53: 3 is gone back, they are **a** become filthy;	3162

Ps	62: 9 the balance, they *are* **a** *lighter* than vanity.	3162
	139: 4 *but* lo, O LORD, thou knowest it **a**.	3605
SS	5:16 yea, he *is* **a** lovely. This *is* my beloved,	3605
Isa	10: 8 For he saith, *Are* not my princes **a** kings?	3162
Jer	5: 5 these have **a** broken the yoke, *and* burst	3162
	10: 8 they are **a** brutish and foolish:	259+871.1
	15:18 wilt thou **be a** unto me as a liar,	1961+1961
	30:11 will not **leave** thee **a unpunished**.	5352+5352
	49:12 he *that* shall **a go unpunished**?	5352+5352
Jn	9:34 Thou wast **a** born in sins, and dost thou	3650
Ac	26:29 were both almost, and **a** such as I	1722+4183
1Co	5:10 Yet not **a** with the fornicators of this world,	3843
	9:10 Or saith he **a** for our sakes? For our	3843

ALUSH (2)

Nu	33:13 from Dophkah, and encamped in **A**.	442
	33:14 they removed from **A**, and encamped at	442

ALVAH (1)

Ge	36:40 duke Timnah, duke **A**, duke Jetheth,	5933

ALVAN (1)

Ge	36:23 **A**, and Manahath, and Ebal, Shepho,	5935

ALWAY (23) [ALWAYS]

Ex	25:30 set upon the table shewbread before me **a**.	8548
Nu	9:16 So it was **a**: the cloud covered it *by day*,	8548
Dt	11: 1 and his commandments **a**,	3117+3605+1886.1
	28:33 and crushed **a**:	3117+3605+1886.1
2Sa	9:10 master's son shall eat bread **a** at my table.	8548
1Ki	11:36 **a** before me in Jerusalem,	3117+3605+1886.1
2Ki	8:19 him to give to him **a**	3117+3605+1886.1
Job	7:16 I loathe *it*; I would not live **a**:	5769+3807.1
Ps	9:18 For the needy shall not **a** be	5331+3807.1
	119:112 heart to perform thy statutes **a**,	5769+3807.1
Pr	28:14 Happy *is* the man that feareth **a**: but he	8548
Mt	28:20 and lo, I am with you **a**,	2250+3588+3956
Jn	7: 6 is not your time: but your time is **a** ready.	3842
Ac	10: 2 alms to the people, and prayed to God **a**.	1275
Ro	11:10 may not see, and bow down their back **a**.	1275
2Co	4:11 we which live are **a** delivered unto death	104
	6:10 As sorrowful, yet **a** rejoicing; as poor,	104
Php	4: 4 Rejoice in the Lord **a**: *and* again I say,	3842
Col	4: 6 Let your speech *be* **a** with grace,	3842
1Th	2:16 they might be saved, to fill up their sins **a**:	3842
2Th	2:13 But we are bound to give thanks **a** to God	3842
Tit	1:12 said, The Cretians *are* **a** liars, evil beasts,	104
Heb	3:10 and said, They do **a** err in *their* heart;	104

ALWAYS (62) [ALWAY]

Ge	6: 3 spirit shall not **a** strive with man,	5769+3807.1
Ex	27:20 for the light, to cause the lamp to burn **a**.	8548
	28:38 it shall be **a** upon his forehead, that they	8548
Dt	5:29 all my commandments **a**,	3117+3605+1886.1
	6:24 our God, for our good **a**,	3117+3605+1886.1
	11:12 the eyes of the LORD thy God *are* **a** upon	8548
	14:23 fear the LORD thy God **a**.	3117+3605+1886.1
1Ch	16:15 Be ye mindful **a** of his covenant;	5769+3807.1
2Ch	18: 7 good unto me, but **a** evil:	3117+3605
Job	27:10 will he **a** call upon God?	3605+6256+871.1
	32: 9 Great men are not **a** wise: neither do	NIH
Ps	10: 5 His ways are **a** grievous;	3605+871.1
	16: 8 I have set the LORD **a** before me: because	8548
	103: 9 He will not **a** chide: neither will	5331+3807.1
Pr	5:19 be thou ravisht **a** with her love.	8548
	8:30 rejoicing **a** before him;	3605+6256+871.1
Ecc	9: 8 Let thy garments be **a** white;	3605+6256+871.1
Isa	57:16 for ever, neither will I be **a** wroth:	5331+3807.1
Jer	20:17 and her womb *to be* **a** great *with me*.	5769
Eze	38: 8 of Israel, which have been **a** waste:	8548
Mt	18:10 That in heaven their angels do **a**	1223+3956
	26:11 For ye have the poor **a** with you; but me	3842
	26:11 **always** with you; but me ye have not **a**.	3842
Mk	5: 5 And **a**, night and day, he was in	1275
	14: 7 For ye have the poor with you **a**,	3842
	14: 7 may do them good: but me ye have not **a**.	3842
Lk	18: 1 *to this end*, that *men* ought **a** to pray,	3842
	21:36 ye therefore, and pray **a**,	1722+2540+3956
Jn	8:29 for I do **a** those *things* that please him.	3842
	11:42 And I knew that thou hearest me **a**:	3842
	12: 8 For the poor **a** ye have with you; but me	3842
	12: 8 ye have with you; but me ye have not **a**.	3842
	18:20 in the temple, whither the Jews **a** resort;	3842
Ac	2:25 I foresaw the Lord **a** before my face,	1223+3956
	7:51 and ears, ye do **a** resist the Holy Ghost:	104
	24: 3 We accept *it* **a**, and in all places,	3839
	24:16 to have **a** a conscience void of offence	1275
Ro	1: 9 I make mention of you **a** in my prayers,	3842
1Co	1: 4 I thank my God **a** on your behalf, for	3842
	15:58 **a** abounding in the work of the Lord,	3842
2Co	2:14 which **a** causeth us to triumph in Christ,	3842
	4:10 **A** bearing about in the body the dying of	3842
	5: 6 Therefore we are **a** confident, knowing	3842
	9: 8 **a** having all sufficiency in all *things*, may	3842
Gal	4:18 But *it is* good to be zealously affected **a** in	3842
Eph	5:20 Giving thanks for all *things* unto God	3842
	6:18 Praying **a** with all prayer	1722+2540+3956
Php	1: 4 **A** in every prayer of mine for you all	3842
	1:20 as **a**, *so* now also Christ shall be magnified	3842
	2:12 my beloved, as ye have **a** obeyed,	3842
Col	1: 3 of our Lord Jesus Christ, praying **a** for you,	3842
	4:12 **a** labouring fervently for you in prayers,	3842
1Th	1: 2 We give thanks to God **a** for you all,	3842
	3: 6 that ye have good remembrance of us **a**,	3842
2Th	1: 3 We are bound to thank God **a** for you,	3842

2Th	1:11 Wherefore also we pray **a** for you, that our	3842
	3:16 give you peace **a** by all means.	1223+3956
Phm	1: 4 making mention of thee **a** in my prayers,	3842
Heb	9: 6 the priests went **a** into the first tabernacle,	1275
1Pe	3:15 *be* ready **a** to *give* an answer to every *man*	104
2Pe	1:12 **a** in remembrance of these *things*, though	104
	1:15 to have these *things* **a** in remembrance.	1539

AM (874) [BE]

Ge	4: 9 I know not: **A** I my brother's keeper?	NIH
	15: 1 I **a** thy shield, *and* thy exceeding great	NIH
	15: 7 I **a** the LORD that brought thee out of Ur	NIH
	17: 1 and said unto him, I **a** the Almighty God;	NIH
	18:12 After I **a** waxed old shall I have pleasure,	NIH
	18:13 I of a surety bear *a child*, which **a** old?	NIH
	18:27 unto the Lord, which **a** *but* dust and ashes:	NIH
	22: 1 Abraham: and he said, Behold, *here* I **a**.	NIH
	22: 7 he said, Here **a** I, my son. And he said,	NIH
	22:11 Abraham, Abraham: and he said, Here **a** I.	NIH
	23: 4 I **a** a stranger and a sojourner with you:	NIH
	24:24 I **a** the daughter of Bethuel the son of	NIH
	24:34 And he said, I **a** Abraham's servant.	NIH
	25:22 and said, If *it be* so, why **a** I thus?	NIH
	25:30 with that same red *pottage*; for I **a** faint:	NIH
	25:32 Esau said, Behold, I **a** at the point to die:	NIH
	26:24 said, I **a** the God of Abraham thy father:	NIH
	26:24 for I **a** with thee, and will bless thee,	NIH
	27: 1 and he said unto him, Behold, *here* **a** I.	NIH
	27: 2 he said, Behold now, I **a** old, I know not	NIH
	27:11 *is* a hairy man, and I **a** a smooth man:	NIH
	27:18 he said, Here **a** I; who *art* thou, my son?	NIH
	27:19 said unto his father, I **a** Esau thy firstborn;	NIH
	27:24 thou my very son Esau? And he said, I **a**.	NIH
	27:32 And he said, I **a** thy son, thy firstborn Esau.	NIH
	27:46 I **a** weary of my life because of	NIH
	28:13 I *am* the LORD God of Abraham thy father,	NIH
	28:15 I **a** with thee, and will keep thee in all	NIH
	30: 2 he said, **A** I in God's stead, who hath	NIH
	30:13 Leah said, Happy **a** I, for the daughters will	NIH
	31:11 dream, *saying*, Jacob: And I said, Here **a** I.	NIH
	31:13 I **a** the God of Beth-el, where thou	NIH
	32:10 I **a** not worthy of the least of all the mercies	NIH
	32:10 Jordan; and now I **a** become two bands.	NIH
	35:11 God said unto him, I **a** God Almighty:	NIH
	37:13 unto them. And he said to him, Here **a** I.	NIH
	38:25 the man, whose these *are*, **a** I with child:	NIH
	41:44 I **a** Pharaoh, and without thee shall no	NIH
	43:14 I be bereaved of my children, I **a** bereaved.	NIH
	45: 3 Joseph said unto his brethren, I **a** Joseph;	NIH
	45: 4 he said, I **a** Joseph your brother, whom ye	NIH
	46: 2 said, Jacob, Jacob. And he said, Here **a** I.	NIH
	46: 3 he said, I **a** God, the God of thy father:	NIH
	49:29 I **a** to be gathered unto my people:	NIH
	50:19 Fear not: for **a** I in the place of God?	NIH
Ex	3: 4 said, Moses, Moses. And he said, Here **a** I.	NIH
	3: 6 he said, I **a** the God of thy father,	NIH
	3: 8 I **a** come down to deliver them out of	NIH
	3:11 Moses said unto God, Who **a** I, that I	NIH
	3:14 God said unto Moses, I **A** THAT I AM:	1961
	3:14 God said unto Moses, I AM THAT I **A**:	1961
	3:14 of Israel, I **A** hath sent me unto you.	1961
	3:19 I **a** sure that the king of Egypt will not let	NIH
	4:10 O my Lord, I **a** not eloquent, neither	NIH
	4:10 I **a** slow of speech, and of a slow tongue.	NIH
	6: 2 and said unto him, I **a** the LORD:	NIH
	6: 6 I **a** the LORD, and I will bring you out	NIH
	6: 7 ye shall know that I **a** the LORD your	NIH
	6: 8 give it you *for* an heritage: I **a** the LORD.	NIH
	6:12 hear me, who **a** of uncircumcised lips?	NIH
	6:29 spake unto Moses, saying, I **a** the LORD:	NIH
	6:30 I **a** of uncircumcised lips, and how shall	NIH
	7: 5 the Egyptians shall know that I **a**	NIH
	7:17 In this thou shalt know that I **a** the LORD:	NIH
	8:22 to the end thou mayest know that I **a**	NIH
	9:29 As soon as I **a** gone out of the city,	NIH
	10: 2 that ye may know how that I **a** the LORD.	NIH
	12:12 I will execute judgment: I **a** the LORD.	NIH
	14: 4 that the Egyptians may know that I **a**	NIH
	14:18 the Egyptians shall know that I **a**	NIH
	15:26 for I **a** the LORD that healeth thee.	NIH
	16:12 ye shall know that I **a** the LORD your	NIH
	18: 6 I thy father in law Jethro **a** come unto thee,	NIH
	20: 2 I **a** the LORD thy God, which have	NIH
	20: 5 for I the LORD thy God **a a** jealous God,	NIH
	22:27 unto me, that I will hear; for I **a** gracious.	NIH
	29:46 they shall know that I **a** the LORD their	NIH
	29:46 amongst them: I **a** the LORD their God.	NIH
	31:13 that *ye* may know that I **a** the LORD that	NIH
Lev	8:35 that ye die not: for so I **a** commanded.	NIH
	10:13 made by fire: for so I **a** commanded.	NIH
	11:44 For I **a** the LORD your God: ye shall	NIH
	11:44 and ye shall be holy; for I **a** holy:	NIH
	11:45 For I **a** the LORD that bringeth you up out	NIH
	11:45 ye shall therefore be holy, for I **a** holy.	NIH
	18: 2 say unto them, I **a** the LORD your God.	NIH
	18: 4 to walk therein: I **a** the LORD your God.	NIH
	18: 5 he shall live in them: I **a** the LORD.	NIH
	18: 6 to uncover *their* nakedness: I **a** the LORD.	NIH
	18:21 the name of thy God: I **a** the LORD.	NIH
	18:30 I **a** the LORD your God.	NIH
	19: 2 be holy: for I the LORD your God **a** holy.	NIH
	19: 3 my sabbaths: I **a** the LORD your God.	NIH
	19: 4 molten gods: I **a** the LORD your God.	NIH
	19:10 and stranger: I **a** the LORD your God.	NIH
	19:12 the name of thy God: I **a** the LORD.	NIH

A

Lev 19:14 but shalt fear thy God: I *a* the LORD. NIH
19:16 the blood of thy neighbour: I *a* the LORD. NIH
19:18 thy neighbour as thyself: I *a* the LORD. NIH
19:25 increase thereof: I *a* the LORD your God. NIH
19:28 print any marks upon you: I *a* the LORD. NIH
19:30 reverence my sanctuary: I *a* the LORD. NIH
19:31 defiled by them: I *a* the LORD your God. NIH
19:32 old man, and fear thy God: I *a* the LORD. NIH
19:34 the land of Egypt: I *a* the LORD your God. NIH
19:36 I *a* the LORD your God, which brought NIH
19:37 and do them: I *a* the LORD. NIH
20: 7 be ye holy: for I *a* the LORD your God. NIH
20: 8 I *a* the LORD which sanctify you. NIH
20:24 I *a* the LORD your God, which have NIH
20:26 for I the LORD *a* holy, and have severed NIH
21: 8 I the LORD, which sanctify you, *a* holy. NIH
21:12 oil of his God *is* upon him: I *a* the LORD. NIH
22: 2 which they hallow unto me: I *a* the LORD. NIH
22: 3 cut off from my presence: I *a* the LORD. NIH
22: 8 to defile *himself* therewith: I *a* the LORD. NIH
22:30 none of it until the morrow: I *a* the LORD. NIH
22:31 and do them: I *a* the LORD. NIH
22:32 of Israel: I *a* the LORD which hallow you, NIH
22:33 of Egypt, to be your God: I *a* the LORD. NIH
23:22 to the stranger: I *a* the LORD your God. NIH
23:43 the land of Egypt: I *a* the LORD your God. NIH
24:22 own country: for I *a* the LORD your God. NIH
25:17 fear your God: for I *a* the LORD your God. NIH
25:38 I *a* the LORD your God, which brought NIH
25:55 the land of Egypt: I *a* the LORD your God. NIH
26: 1 down unto it: for I *a* the LORD your God. NIH
26: 2 reverence my sanctuary: I *a* the LORD. NIH
26:13 I *a* the LORD your God, which brought NIH
26:44 with them: for I *a* the LORD their God. NIH
26:45 that *I* might be their God: I *a* the LORD. NIH
Nu 3:13 beast: mine they shall be: I *a* the LORD. NIH
3:41 thou shalt take the Levites for me (I *a* NIH
3:45 the Levites shall be mine: I *a* the LORD. NIH
10:10 before your God: I *a* the LORD your God. NIH
11:14 I *a* not able to bear all this people alone, NIH
11:21 amongst whom I *a, are* six hundred NIH
15:41 I *a* the LORD your God, which brought NIH
15:41 to be your God: I *a* the LORD your God. NIH
18:20 I *a* thy part and thine inheritance among NIH
22:30 the ass said unto Balaam, *A* not I thine ass, NIH
22:37 *a* I not able indeed to promote thee to NIH
22:38 said unto Balak, Lo, I *a* come unto thee: NIH
Dt 1: 9 I *a* not able to bear you myself alone: NIH
1:42 neither fight; for I *a* not among you; NIH
5: 6 I *a* the LORD thy God, which brought thee NIH
5: 9 for I the LORD thy God *a a* jealous God, NIH
26: 3 that I *a* come unto the country which NIH
29: 6 that ye might know that I *a* the LORD NIH
31: 2 I *a* an hundred and twenty years old *this* NIH
31:27 while I *a* yet alive with you *this* day, NIH
32:39 even I, *a* he, and *there is* no god with me: NIH
Jos 5:14 as captain of the host of the LORD *a* I now NIH
14:10 I *a* this day fourscore and five years old. NIH
14:11 As yet I *a as* strong *this* day as *I was* in NIH
17:14 portion to inherit, seeing I *a a* great people, NIH
23: 2 said unto them, I *a* old and stricken in age; NIH
23:14 *this* day I *a* going the way of all the earth: NIH
Jdg 4:19 a little water to drink; for I *a* thirsty. NIH
6:10 I said unto you, I *a* the LORD your God; NIH
6:15 *a* the least in my father's house. NIH
8: 5 I *a* pursuing after Zebah and Zalmunna, NIH
9: 2 remember also that I *a* your bone NIH
13:11 spakest unto the woman? And he said, I *a.* NIH
17: 9 I *a a* Levite of Beth-lehem-judah, and I go NIH
18: 4 and hath hired me, and I *a* his priest. 1961
19:18 side of mount Ephraim; from thence *a* I: NIH
19:18 I *a* now going *to* the house of the LORD; NIH
Ru 1:12 go *your way;* for I *a* too old to have a NIH
2:10 knowledge of me, seeing I *a a* stranger? NIH
3: 9 she answered, I *a* Ruth thine handmaid: NIH
3:12 now it is true that I *a* thy near kinsman: NIH
4: 4 redeem *it* besides thee; and I *a* after thee. NIH
1Sa 1: 8 *a* not I better to thee than ten sons? NIH
1:15 my lord, I *a a* woman of a sorrowful spirit: NIH
1:26 I *a* the woman that stood by thee here, NIH
3: 4 called Samuel: and he answered, Here *a* I. NIH
3: 5 he ran unto Eli, and said, Here *a* I; for NIH
3: 6 and went to Eli, and said, Here *a* I; NIH
3: 8 arose and went to Eli, and said, Here *a* I; NIH
3:16 my son. And he answered, Here *a* I. NIH
4:16 I *a* he that came out of the army, and I fled NIH
9:19 answered Saul, and said, I *a* the seer: NIH
9:21 and said, *A* not I a Benjamite, NIH
12: 2 I *a* old and grayheaded; and behold, NIH
12: 3 here I *a:* witness against me before NIH
14: 7 I *a* with thee according to thy heart. NIH
16: 2 say, I *a* come to sacrifice to the LORD. NIH
16: 5 I *a* come to sacrifice unto the LORD: NIH
17: 8 *a* not I a Philistine, and you servants to NIH
17:43 the Philistine said unto David, *A* I a dog, NIH
17:58 I *a* the son of thy servant Jesse NIH
18:18 David said unto Saul, Who *a* I? and what NIH
18:23 seeing that I *a a* poor man, NIH
22:12 And he answered, Here *a* I, my lord. NIH
28:15 Saul answered, I *a* sore distressed; for NIH
30:13 he said unto him, I *a a* young man of Egypt, NIH
2Sa 1: 3 Out of the camp of Israel *a* I escaped. NIH
1: 7 called unto me. And I answered, Here *a* I. NIH
1: 8 And I answered him, I *a a*n Amalekite. NIH
1:13 I *a* the son of a stranger, an Amalekite. NIH

2Sa 1:26 I *a* distressed for thee, my brother NIH
2:20 *Art* thou Asahel? And he answered, I *a.* NIH
3: 8 of Ish-bosheth, and said, *A* I a dog's head, NIH
3:39 I *a this* day weak, though anointed king; NIH
7:18 and he said, Who *a* I, O LORD GOD? NIH
9: 8 look upon such a dead dog as I *a?* NIH
11: 5 and told David, and said, I *a* with child. NIH
14: 5 I *a* indeed a widow woman, NIH
14:15 that I *a* come to speak of this thing unto NIH
14:32 to say, Wherefore *a* I come from Geshur? NIH
15:26 behold, *here a* I, let him do to me as NIH
19:20 I *a* come the first *this* day of all the house NIH
19:22 do not I know that I *a this* day king over NIH
19:35 I *a this* day fourscore years old: *and* can I NIH
20:17 I *a* he. Then she said unto him, NIH
20:19 I *a* one of them that are peaceable and NIH
24:14 David said unto Gad, I *a* in a great strait: NIH
1Ki 3: 7 I *a* but a little child: I know not *how* to go NIH
8:20 I *a* risen up in the room of David my father NIH
13:14 that camest from Judah? And he said, I *a.* NIH
13:18 I *a* a prophet also as thou *art;* and an angel NIH
13:31 When I *a* dead, then bury me in NIH
14: 6 for I *a* sent to thee *with* heavy *tidings.* NIH
17:12 behold, I *a* gathering two sticks, that I may NIH
18: 8 I *a:* go, tell thy lord, Behold, Elijah *is* here. NIH
18:12 to pass, *as soon as* I *a* gone from thee, NIH
18:36 I *a* thy servant, and *that* I have done all NIH
19: 4 my life; for I *a* not better than my fathers. NIH
19:10 I, *even* I only, *a* left; and they seek my life, NIH
19:14 I, *even* I only, *a* left; and they seek my life, NIH
20: 4 to thy saying, I *a* thine, and all that I have. NIH
20:13 and thou shalt know that I *a* the LORD. NIH
20:28 and ye shall know that I *a* the LORD. NIH
22: 4 I *a* as thou *art*, my people as thy people, NIH
22:34 carry me out of the host; for I *a* wounded. NIH
2Ki 2:10 if thou see me *when I a* taken NIH
3: 7 I *a* as thou *art*, my people as thy people, NIH
5: 7 said, *A* I God, to kill and to make alive, NIH
16: 7 saying, I *a* thy servant and thy son: NIH
18:25 *A* I now come up without the LORD NIH
19:23 the multitude of my chariots I *a* come NIH
21:12 I *a* bringing *such* evil upon Jerusalem NIH
1Ch 17:16 said, Who *a* I, O LORD God, and what *is* NIH
21:13 David said unto Gad, I *a* in a great strait: NIH
29:14 who *a* I, and what *is* my people, that we NIH
2Ch 2: 6 who *a* I then, that I should build him a NIH
2: 9 for the house which I *a* about to build NIH
6:10 for I *a* risen up in the room of David my NIH
6:10 a set on the throne of Israel, as the LORD NIH
18: 3 I *a* as thou *art*, and my people as thy NIH
18:33 carry me out of the host; for I *a* wounded. NIH
35:23 Have me away; for I *a* sore wounded. NIH
Ezr 9: 6 I *a* ashamed and blush to lift up my face to NIH
Ne 6: 3 I *a* doing a great work, so that I cannot NIH
6:11 being as I *a,* would go into the temple to NIH
Est 5:12 to morrow *a* I invited unto her also with NIH
Job 1:15 and I only *a* escaped alone to tell thee. NIH
1:16 and I only *a* escaped alone to tell thee. NIH
1:17 and I only *a* escaped alone to tell thee. NIH
1:19 and I only *a* escaped alone to tell thee. NIH
7: 3 So I *a* made to possess months of vanity, NIH
7: 4 I *a* full *of* tossings to and fro unto NIH
7: 8 *more:* thine eyes *are* upon me, and I *a* not. NIH
7:12 *A* I a sea, or a whale, that thou settest a NIH
7:20 thee, so that I *a a* burden to myself? 1961
9:20 *if I say,* I *a* perfect, it shall also prove me NIH
9:28 I *a* afraid of all my sorrows, I know that NIH
9:32 as I *a, that* I should answer him, *and* NIH
10: 7 Thou knowest that I *a* not wicked; NIH
10:15 I *a* full of confusion; therefore see thou NIH
11: 4 is pure, and I *a* clean in thine eyes. 1961
12: 3 as well as you; I *a* not inferior to you: NIH
12: 4 I *a as* one mocked of his neighbour, 1961
13: 2 do I know also. I *a* not inferior unto you. NIH
16: 6 and *though* I forbear, what *a* I eased? NIH
19: 7 I cry out *of* wrong, but I *a* not heard: NIH
19:10 destroyed me on every side, and I *a* gone: NIH
19:15 for a stranger: I *a* an alien in their sight. 1961
19:20 and I *a* escaped with the skin of my teeth. NIH
21: 6 Even when I remember I *a* afraid, NIH
23:15 Therefore *a* I troubled at his presence: NIH
23:15 when I consider, I *a* afraid of him. NIH
30: 9 now *a* I their song, yea, I am their byword. 1961
30: 9 now am I their song, yea, I *a* their byword. 1961
30:19 and I *a* become like dust and ashes. NIH
30:29 I *a a* brother to dragons, and a companion 1961
32: 6 and said, I *a* young, and ye *are* very old; NIH
32:18 For I *a* full *of* matter, the spirit within me NIH
33: 6 I *a* according to thy wish in God's stead: NIH
33: 6 God's stead: I also *a* formed out of the clay. NIH
33: 9 I *a* clean without transgression, I *am* NIH
33: 9 clean without transgression, I *a* innocent; NIH
34: 5 For Job hath said, I *a* righteous: NIH
40: 4 Behold, I *a* vile; what shall I answer thee? NIH
Ps 6: 2 mercy upon me, O LORD; for I *a* weak: NIH
6: 6 I *a* weary with my groaning; all the night NIH
13: 4 those that trouble me rejoice when I *a* NIH
17: 3 I *a* purposed *that* my mouth shall not NIH
22: 2 and in the night season, and *a* not silent. NIH
22: 6 I *a a* worm, and no man; a reproach of NIH
22:14 I *a* poured out like water, and all my NIH
25:16 upon me; for I *a* desolate and afflicted. NIH
28: 7 my heart trusted in him, and I *a* helped: NIH
31: 9 upon me, O LORD, for I *a* in trouble: NIH
31:12 I *a* forgotten as a dead man out of mind: NIH

Ps 31:12 man out of mind: I *a* like a broken vessel. 1961
31:22 I *a* cut off from before thine eyes: NIH
35: 3 say unto my soul, I *a* thy salvation. NIH
37:25 I have been young, and *now a* old; NIH
38: 6 I *a* troubled; I am bowed down greatly; NIH
38: 6 I am troubled; I *a* bowed down greatly; NIH
38: 8 I *a* feeble and sore broken: I have roared NIH
38:17 For I *a* ready to halt, and my sorrow *is* NIH
39: 4 what it *is; that* I may know how frail I *a.* NIH
39:10 I *a* consumed by the blow of thine hand. NIH
39:12 I *a* a stranger with thee, *and a* sojourner, NIH
40:12 that I *a* not able to look *up;* they are moe NIH
40:17 I *a* poor and needy; *yet* the Lord thinketh NIH
46:10 Be still, and know that I *a* God: I will be NIH
50: 7 testify against thee: I *a* God, *even* thy God. NIH
52: 8 I *a* like a green olive tree in the house of NIH
56: 3 *What* time I *a* afraid, I will trust in thee. NIH
69: 2 I *a* come into deep waters, where the NIH
69: 3 I *a* weary of my crying: my throat is dried: NIH
69: 8 I *a* become a stranger unto my brethren, NIH
69:17 thy face from thy servant; for I *a* in trouble: NIH
69:20 broken my heart; and I *a* full of heaviness. NIH
69:29 I *a* poor and sorrowful: let thy salvation, NIH
70: 5 I *a* poor and needy: make haste unto me, NIH
71: 7 I *a* as a wonder unto many; but thou *art* 1961
71:18 Now also when I *a* old and grayheaded, NIH
73:23 Nevertheless I *a* continually with thee: NIH
77: 4 I *a so* troubled that I cannot speak. NIH
81:10 I *a* the LORD thy God, which brought thee NIH
86: 1 O LORD, hear me: for I *a* poor and needy. NIH
86: 2 Preserve my soul; for I *a* holy: O thou my NIH
88: 4 I *a* counted with them that go down into NIH
88: 4 the pit: I *a* as a man *that hath* no strength: 1961
88: 5 *I a* shut up, and I cannot come forth. NIH
88:15 I *a* afflicted and ready to die from *my* youth NIH
88:15 *up: while* I suffer thy terrors I *a* distracted. NIH
102: 2 from me in the day *when* I *a* in trouble; NIH
102: 6 I *a* like a pelican of the wilderness: I am NIH
102: 6 wilderness: I *a* like an owl of the desert. 1961
102: 7 *a* as a sparrow alone upon the housetop. 1961
102:11 that declineth; and I *a* withered like grass. NIH
109:22 For I *a* poor and needy, and my heart is NIH
109:23 I *a* gone like the shadow when it declineth: NIH
109:23 I *a* tossed up and down as the locust. NIH
116:16 Oh LORD, truly I *a* thy servant; I *am* thy NIH
116:16 I *a* thy servant, *and* the son of thy NIH
119:19 I *a a* stranger in the earth: hide not thy NIH
119:63 I *a a* companion of all *them* that fear thee, NIH
119:83 For I *a* become like a bottle in the smoke; NIH
119:94 I *a* thine, save me; for I have sought thy NIH
119:107 I *a* afflicted very much: quicken me, NIH
119:120 of thee; and I *a* afraid of thy judgments, NIH
119:125 I *a* thy servant; give me understanding, NIH
119:141 I *a* small and despised: *yet* do not I forget NIH
120: 7 I *a for* peace: but when I speak, they *are* NIH
139:14 for I a fearfully and wonderfully made: NIH
139:18 the sand: when I awake, I *a* still with thee. NIH
139:21 am not I grieved with those that rise up NIH
142: 6 unto my cry; for I *a* brought very low: NIH
143:12 that afflict my soul: for I *a* thy servant. NIH
Pr 8:14 I *a* understanding; I have strength. NIH
20: 9 my heart clean, I *a* pure from my sin? NIH
26:19 his neighbour, and saith, *A* not I in sport? NIH
30: 2 Surely I *a* more brutish than *any* man, NIH
Ecc 1:16 I *a* come to great estate, and have gotten NIH
SS 1: 5 I *a* black, but comely, O ye daughters of NIH
1: 6 because I *a* black, because the sun hath NIH
2: 1 I *a* the rose of Sharon, *and* the lily of NIH
2: 5 comfort me with apples: for I *a* sick of love. NIH
2:16 My beloved *is* mine, and I *a* his: NIH
5: 1 I *a* come into my garden, my sister, NIH
5: 8 that ye tell him, that I *a* sick of love. NIH
6: 3 I *a* my beloved's, and my beloved is mine: NIH
7:10 I *a* my beloved's, and his desire *is* towards NIH
8:10 I *a a* wall, and my breasts like towers: NIH
Isa 1:11 I *a* full *of* the burnt offerings of rams, NIH
1:14 a trouble unto me; I *a* weary to bear *them.* NIH
6: 5 for I *a* undone; because I *am* a man of NIH
6: 5 because I *a a* man of unclean lips, NIH
6: 8 go for us? Then I said, Here *a* I; send me. NIH
10:13 and by my wisdom; for I *a* prudent: NIH
19:11 I *a* the son of the wise, the son of ancient NIH
21: 8 and *a* set in my ward whole nights: NIH
29:12 I pray thee: and he saith, I *a* not learned. NIH
33:24 the inhabitant shall not say, I *a* sick: NIH
36:10 I *a* now come up without the LORD NIH
37:24 By the multitude of my chariots I *a* come NIH
38:10 I *a* deprived of the residue of my years. NIH
38:14 O LORD, I *a* oppressed; undertake for me. NIH
41: 4 the first, and with the last; I *a* he. NIH
41:10 Fear thou not; for I *a* with thee: be not NIH
41:10 be not dismayed; for I *a* thy God: I will NIH
42: 8 I *a* the LORD: that *is* my name: NIH
43: 3 For I *a* the LORD thy God, the Holy One NIH
43: 5 for I *a* with thee: I will bring thy seed from NIH
43:10 believe me, and understand that I *a* he: NIH
43:11 I, *even* I, *a* the LORD; and beside me *there* NIH
43:12 saith the LORD, that I *a* God. NIH
43:13 before the day was I *a* he; and *there is* NIH
43:15 I *a* the LORD, your Holy One, the creator NIH
43:25 *a* he that blotteth out thy transgressions for NIH
44: 5 One shall say, I *a* the LORD's; NIH
44: 6 I *a* the first, and I *am* the last; and besides NIH
44: 6 I *am* the first, and I *a* the last; and besides NIH
44:16 saith, Aha, I *a* warm, I have seen the fire: NIH

A

Isa 44:24 I *a* the LORD that maketh all *things;* that NIH
45: 3 call *thee* by thy name, the God of Israel. NIH
45: 5 I *a* the LORD, and *there is* none else, NIH
45: 6 I *a* the LORD, and *there is* none else. NIH
45:18 I *a* the LORD; and *there is* none else. NIH
45:22 for I *a* God, and *there is* none else. NIH
46: 4 *even* to *your* old age I *a* he; and *even* to NIH
46: 9 I *a* God, and *there is* none else; *I am* NIH
46: 9 I *a* God, and *there is* none like me, NIH
47: 8 thine heart, I, *a*, and none else besides me; NIH
47:10 thine heart, I, *a*, and none else besides me. NIH
48:12 I *a* he; I *am* the first, I also *am* the last. NIH
48:12 I *am* he; I *a* the first, I also *am* the last. NIH
48:12 I *am* he; I *am* the first, I also *a* the last. NIH
48:16 from the time that it was, there *a* I: NIH
48:17 I *a* the LORD thy God which teacheth thee NIH
49:21 *a* desolate, a captive, and removing to NIH
49:23 and thou shalt know that I *a* the LORD: NIH
49:26 all flesh shall know that I the LORD *a* thy NIH
51:12 I, *even* I, *a* he that comforteth you: NIH
51:15 I *a* the LORD thy God, that divided NIH
52: 6 *they shall know* in that day that I *a* he that NIH
56: 3 let the eunuch say, Behold, I *a* a dry tree. NIH
58: 9 Here I *a*. If thou take away from the midst NIH
60:16 thou shalt know that I the LORD *a* thy NIH
65: 1 I *a* sought of *them* that asked not *for me:* I NIH
65: 1 *me:* I *a* found of *them* that sought me not: NIH
65: 5 not near to me; for I *a* holier than thou. NIH
Jer 1: 6 behold, I cannot speak: for I *a* a child. NIH
1: 7 LORD said unto me, Say not, I *a* a child: NIH
1: 8 for I *a* with thee to deliver thee, saith NIH
1:19 for I *a* with thee, saith the LORD, NIH
2:23 How canst thou say, I *a* not polluted, NIH
2:35 Yet thou sayest, Because I *a* innocent, NIH
3:12 for I *a* merciful, saith the LORD, *and* I will NIH
3:14 saith the LORD; for I *a* married unto you: NIH
4:19 I *a* pained *at* my very heart; my heart NIH
6:11 Therefore I *a* full *of* the fury of the LORD; NIH
6:11 of the LORD; I *a* weary with holding in: NIH
8:21 For the hurt of the daughter of my people *a* NIH
8:21 I *a* black; astonishment hath taken hold on NIH
9:24 that I the LORD which exercise NIH
15: 6 and destroy thee; I *a* weary with repenting. NIH
15:16 for I *a* called by thy name, O LORD God NIH
15:20 for I *a* with thee to save thee and to deliver NIH
20: 7 I *a* in derision daily, every one mocketh 1961
21:13 Behold, I *a* against thee, O inhabitant of NIH
23: 9 I *a* like a drunken man, and like a man 1961
23:23 *A* I *a* God at hand, saith the LORD, NIH
23:30 I *a* against the prophets, saith the LORD, NIH
23:31 Behold, I *a* against the prophets, saith NIH
23:32 I *a* against them that prophesy false dreams NIH
24: 7 a heart to know me, that I *a* the LORD: NIH
26:14 for me, behold, I *a* in your hand: do with NIH
29:23 even I know, and *a* a witness, saith NIH
30:11 For I *a* with thee, saith the LORD, to save 1961
31: 9 I *a* a father to Israel, and Ephraim *is* my 1961
32:27 Behold, I *a* the LORD, the God of all NIH
36: 5 commanded Baruch, saying, I *a* shut up; NIH
38:19 I *a* afraid of the Jews that are fallen to NIH
42:11 for I *a* with you to save you, and to deliver NIH
46:28 for I *a* with thee; for I will make a full end NIH
50:31 I *a* against thee, O thou most proud, NIH
51:25 Behold, I *a* against thee, O destroying NIH
La 1:11 and consider; for I *a* become vile. NIH
1:14 *from whom* I *a* not able to rise up. NIH
1:20 Behold, O LORD; for I *a* in distress: my NIH
3: 1 I *a* the man that hath seen affliction by NIH
3:54 over mine head; *then* I said, I *a* cut off. NIH
3:63 and their rising up; I *a* their musick. NIH
Eze 5: 8 *a* against thee, and will execute judgments NIH
6: 7 and ye shall know that I *a* the LORD. NIH
6: 9 I *a* broken with their whorish heart, NIH
6:10 they shall know that I *a* the LORD, *and* NIH
6:13 shall ye know that I *a* the LORD, NIH
6:14 and they shall know that I *a* the LORD. NIH
7: 4 and ye shall know that I *a* the LORD. NIH
7: 9 ye shall know that I *a* the LORD that NIH
7:27 and they shall know that I *a* the LORD. NIH
11:10 and ye shall know that I *a* the LORD. NIH
11:12 ye shall know that I *a* the LORD: for ye NIH
12:11 Say, I *a* your sign: like as I have done, so NIH
12:15 they shall know that I *a* the LORD, when I NIH
12:16 and they shall know that I *a* the LORD. NIH
12:20 and ye shall know that I *a* the LORD. NIH
12:25 For I *a* the LORD: I will speak, NIH
13: 8 lies, therefore behold, I *a* against you, NIH
13: 9 and ye shall know that I *a* the Lord GOD. NIH
13:14 and ye shall know that I *a* the LORD. NIH
13:20 Behold, I *a* against your pillows, NIH
13:21 and ye shall know that I *a* the LORD. NIH
13:23 and ye shall know that I *a* the LORD. NIH
14: 8 and ye shall know that I *a* the LORD. NIH
15: 7 ye shall know that I *a* the LORD, when I NIH
16:62 and thou shalt know that I *a* the LORD: NIH
16:63 when I *a* pacified toward thee for all that NIH
20: 5 saying, I *a* the LORD your God; NIH
20: 7 idols of Egypt: I *a* the LORD your God. NIH
20:12 that *they* might know that I *a* the LORD NIH
20:19 I *a* the LORD your God; walk in my NIH
20:20 that *ye* may know that I *a* the LORD your NIH
20:26 to the end that they might know that I *a* NIH
20:38 and ye shall know that I *a* the LORD. NIH
20:42 ye shall know that I *a* the LORD, when I NIH
20:44 ye shall know that I *a* the LORD, when I NIH

Eze 21: 3 I *a* against thee, and will draw forth my NIH
22:16 and thou shalt know that I *a* the LORD. NIH
22:26 sabbaths, and I *a* profaned among them, NIH
23:49 and ye shall know that I *a* the Lord GOD. NIH
24:24 ye shall know that I *a* the Lord GOD. NIH
24:27 and they shall know that I *a* the LORD. NIH
25: 5 and ye shall know that I *a* the LORD. NIH
25: 7 and thou shalt know that I *a* the LORD. NIH
25:11 and they shall know that I *a* the LORD. NIH
25:17 they shall know that I *a* the LORD, when I NIH
26: 3 Behold, I *a* against thee, O Tyrus, NIH
26: 6 and they shall know that I *a* the LORD. NIH
27: 3 thou hast said, I *a* of perfect beauty. NIH
28: 2 thou hast said, I *a* a God, I sit *in* the seat of NIH
28: 9 say before him that slayeth thee, I *a* God? NIH
28:22 Behold, I *a* against thee, O Zidon; and I NIH
28:22 they shall know that I *a* the LORD, when I NIH
28:23 and they shall know that I *a* the LORD. NIH
28:24 they shall know that I *a* the Lord GOD. NIH
28:26 they shall know that I *a* the LORD their NIH
29: 3 Behold, I *a* against thee, Pharaoh king of NIH
29: 6 of Egypt shall know that I *a* the LORD, NIH
29: 9 and they shall know that I *a* the LORD: NIH
29:10 I *a* against thee, and against thy rivers, NIH
29:16 but they shall know that I *a* the Lord GOD. NIH
29:21 and they shall know that I *a* the LORD. NIH
30: 8 they shall know that I *a* the LORD, when I NIH
30:19 and they shall know that I *a* the LORD. NIH
30:22 I *a* against Pharaoh king of Egypt, NIH
30:25 they shall know that I *a* the LORD, when I NIH
30:26 and they shall know that I *a* the LORD. NIH
32:15 shall they know that I *a* the LORD. NIH
33:29 shall they know that I *a* the LORD, when I NIH
34:10 Behold, I *a* against the shepherds; and I NIH
34:27 and shall know that I *a* the LORD, NIH
34:30 that I the LORD their God *a* with them, NIH
34:31 *are* men, *and* I *a* your God, saith the Lord NIH
35: 3 I *a* against thee, and I will stretch out mine NIH
35: 4 and thou shalt know that I *a* the LORD. NIH
35: 9 and ye shall know that I *a* the LORD. NIH
35:12 thou shalt know that I *a* the LORD, *and* NIH
35:15 and they shall know that I *a* the LORD. NIH
36: 9 I *a* for you, and I will turn unto you, NIH
36:11 and ye shall know that I *a* the LORD. NIH
36:23 the heathen shall know that I *a* the LORD, NIH
36:38 and they shall know that I *a* the LORD. NIH
37: 6 and ye shall know that I *a* the LORD. NIH
37:13 ye shall know that I *a* the LORD, when I NIH
38: 3 Behold, I *a* against thee, O Gog, the chief NIH
38:23 and they shall know that I *a* the LORD. NIH
39: 1 Behold, I *a* against thee, O Gog, the chief NIH
39: 6 and they shall know that I *a* the LORD. NIH
39: 7 the heathen shall know that I *a* the LORD, NIH
39:22 So the house of Israel shall know that I *a* NIH
39:27 a sanctified in them in the sight of many NIH
39:28 shall they know that I *a* the LORD their NIH
44:28 I *a* their inheritance: and ye shall give them NIH
44:28 no possession in Israel: I *a* their possession. NIH
Da 9:22 I *a* now come forth to give thee skill NIH
9:23 I *a* come to shew *thee;* for thou *art* greatly NIH
10:11 for unto thee *a* I now sent. And when he NIH
10:12 were heard, and I *a* come for thy words. NIH
10:14 Now I *a* come to make thee understand NIH
10:20 I *a* gone forth, lo, the prince of Grecia NIH
Hos 2: 2 *is* not my wife, neither *a* I her husband: NIH
11: 9 for I *a* God, and not man; the Holy One in NIH
12: 8 Ephraim said, Yet I *a* become rich, I have NIH
12: 9 I *that a* the LORD thy God from the land NIH
13: 4 Yet I *a* the LORD thy God from the land NIH
14: 8 I *a* like a green fir tree. From me is thy fruit NIH
Joel 2:27 shall know that I *a* in the midst of Israel, NIH
2:27 *that* I *a* the LORD your God, NIH
3:10 into spears: let the weak say, I *a* strong. NIH
3:17 So shall ye know that I *a* the LORD your NIH
Am 2:13 Behold, I *a* pressed under you, as a cart is NIH
Jnh 1: 9 he said unto them, I *a* a Hebrew; and I NIH
2: 4 I said, I *a* cast out of thy sight; yet I will NIH
Mic 3: 8 truly I *a* full *of* power by the spirit of NIH
7: 1 for I *a* as when they have gathered 1961
Na 2:13 Behold, I *a* against thee, saith the LORD NIH
3: 5 Behold, I *a* against thee, saith the LORD NIH
Hab 2: 1 what I shall answer when I *a* reproved. NIH
Zep 2:15 heart, I, *a*, and *there is* none beside me: NIH
Hag 1:13 I *a* with you, saith the LORD. NIH
2: 4 for I *a* with you, saith the LORD of hosts: NIH
Zec 1:14 I *a* jealous for Jerusalem and for Zion *with* NIH
1:15 I *a* very sore displeased with the heathen NIH
1:16 I *a* returned to Jerusalem with mercies: NIH
8: 3 I *a* returned unto Zion, and will dwell in NIH
10: 6 for I *a* the LORD their God, and will hear NIH
11: 5 Blessed *be* the LORD; for I *a* rich: NIH
13: 5 he said, I *a* no prophet, I *a* a NIH
13: 5 I *am* no prophet, I *a* a husbandman; NIH
Mal 1:14 Lord a corrupt *thing:* for I *a* a great King, NIH
3: 6 For I *a* the LORD, I change not; therefore NIH
Mt 3:11 whose shoes I *a* not worthy to bear: 1510
3:17 my beloved Son, in whom I *a*. well pleased. NIG
5:17 Think not that I *a* come to destroy the law, NIG
5:17 I *a* not come to destroy, but to fulfil. NIG
8: 8 I *a* not worthy that thou shouldest come 1510
8: 9 For I *a* a man under authority, 1510
9:13 For I *a* not come to call *the* righteous, NIG
9:28 Believe ye that I *a* able to do this? NIG
10:34 Think not that I *a* come to send peace on NIG
10:35 For I *a* come to set a man at variance NIG

Mt 11:29 of me; for I *a* meek and lowly in heart: 1510
15:24 I *a* not sent but unto the lost sheep of NIG
16:13 do men say that I the Son of man *a*? 1510
16:15 saith unto them, But whom say ye that I *a*? 1510
17: 5 my beloved Son, in whom I *a* well pleased; NIG
18:20 my name, there *a* I in the midst of them. 1510
20:15 Is thine eye evil, because I *a* good? 1510
20:22 to be baptized *with* the baptism that I *a* NIG
20:23 be baptized *with* the baptism that I *a* NIG
22:32 I *a* the God of Abraham, and the God of 1510
24: 5 shall come in my name, saying, I *a* Christ; 1510
26:32 But after I *a* risen *again,* I will go before NIG
26:61 I *a* able to destroy the temple of God, NIG
27:24 I *a* innocent of the blood of this just 1510
27:43 have him: for he said, I *a* the Son of God. 1510
28:20 and lo, I *a* with you alway, *even* unto 1510
Mk 1: 7 the latchet of whose shoes I *a* not worthy 1510
1:11 beloved Son, in whom I *a* well pleased. NIG
8:27 unto them, Whom do men say that I *a*? 1510
8:29 unto them, But whom say ye that I *a*? 1510
10:38 be baptized *with* the baptism that I *a* NIG
10:39 *with* the baptism that I *a* baptized *withal.* NIG
12:26 I *a* the God of Abraham, and the God of NIG
13: 6 saying, I *a* Christ; and shall deceive many. 1510
14:28 after that I *a* risen, I will go before you NIG
14:62 And Jesus said, I *a*: and ye shall see 1510
Lk 1:18 for I *a* an old man, and my wife well 1510
1:19 I *a* Gabriel, that stand in the presence of 1510
1:19 *a* sent to speak unto thee, and to shew 1510
3:16 latchet of whose shoes I *a* not worthy to 1510
3:22 my beloved Son; in thee I *a* well pleased. NIG
4:43 to other cities also: for therefore *a* I sent. NIG
5: 8 from me; for I *a* a sinful man, O Lord. 1510
7: 6 I *a* not worthy that thou shouldest enter 1510
7: 8 For I also *a* a man set under authority, 1510
9:18 saying, Whom say the people that I *a*? 1510
9:20 unto them, But whom say ye that I *a*? 1510
12:49 I *a* come to send fire on the earth; NIG
12:50 how *a* I straitened till it be accomplished! NIG
12:51 Suppose ye that I *a* come to give peace on NIG
15:19 And *a* no more worthy to be called thy 1510
15:21 *a* no more worthy to be called thy son. 1510
16: 3 I cannot dig; to beg I *a* ashamed. NIG
16: 4 I *a* resolved what to do, that, when I am NIG
16: 4 that, when I *a* put out of the stewardship, NIG
16:24 my tongue; for I *a* tormented in this flame. NIG
18:11 I *a* not as other men *are,* extortioners, 1510
21: 8 I *a* Christ; and the time draweth near: 1510
22:27 but I *a* among you as he that serveth. 1510
22:33 Lord, I *a* ready to go with thee, both into 1510
22:58 of them. And Peter said, Man, I *a* not. 1510
22:70 And he said unto them, Ye say that I *a*. 1510
Jn 1:20 but confessed, I *a* not the Christ. 1510
1:21 he saith, I *a* not. Art thou *that* prophet? 1510
1:23 I *a* the voice of one crying in NIG
1:27 whose shoe's latchet I *a* not worthy to 1510
1:31 therefore I *a* come baptizing with water. NIG
3:28 I *a* not the Christ, but that I am sent 1510
3:28 not the Christ, but that I *a* sent before 1510
4: 9 of me, which *a* a woman of Samaria? 1510
4:26 unto her, I *that* speak unto thee *a* he. 1510
5: 7 but while I *a* coming, another steppeth NIG
5:43 I *a* come in my Father's name, 1510
6:35 Jesus said unto them, I *a* the bread of life: 1510
6:41 I *a* the bread which came down from 1510
6:48 I *a* *that* bread of life. 1510
6:51 I *a* the living bread which came down 1510
7:28 both know me, and ye know whence I *a*: 1510
7:28 I *a* not come of myself, but he that sent NIG
7:29 for I *a* from him, and he hath sent me. 1510
7:33 Yet a little while *a* I with you, and *then* I 1510
7:34 and shall not find *me:* and where I *a*, 1510
7:36 and shall not find *me:* and where I *a*, 1510
8:12 saying, I *a* the light of the world: 1510
8:16 for I *a* not alone, but I and the Father that 1510
8:18 I *a* *a* one that bear witness of myself, 1510
8:23 Ye are from beneath; I *a* from above: 1510
8:23 ye are of this world; I *a* not of this world. 1510
8:24 if ye believe not that I *a* he, ye shall die 1510
8:28 shall ye know that I *a* he, and *that* I do 1510
8:58 I say unto you, Before Abraham was, I *a*. 1510
9: 5 As long as I *a* in the world, I am the light 1510
9: 5 in the world, I *a* the light of the world. 1510
9: 9 *said,* He is like him: *but* he said, I *a* he. 1510
9:39 For judgment I *a* come into this world, NIG
10: 7 I say unto you, I *a* the door of the sheep. 1510
10: 9 I *a* the door: by me if any *man* enter in, 1510
10:10 I *a* come that they might have life, 1510
10:11 I *a* the good shepherd: the good shepherd 1510
10:14 I *a* the good shepherd, and know my 1510
10:14 know my *sheep,* and a known of mine. NIG
10:36 because I said, I *a* the Son of God? 1510
11:15 And I *a* glad for your sakes that I was not 1510
11:25 unto her, I *a* the resurrection, and the life: 1510
12:26 and where I *a*, there shall also my servant 1510
12:46 I *a* come a light into the world, NIG
13:13 and Lord: and ye say well; for *so* I *a*. 1510
13:19 come to pass, ye may believe that I *a* he. 1510
13:33 yet a little while *a* I with you. 1510
14: 3 that where I *a*, *there* ye may be also. 1510
14: 6 I *a* the way, the truth, and the life: 1510
14:10 Believest thou not that I *a* in the Father, 1510
14:11 Believe me that I *a* in the Father, NIG
14:20 At that day ye shall know that I *a* in my NIG
15: 1 I *a* the true vine, and my Father is 1510

A

Jn	15: 5 I *a* the vine, ye *are* the branches; He that	1510
	16:28 the Father, and *a* come into the world:	NIG
	16:32 *yet* I *a* not alone, because the Father is	1510
	17:10 thine are mine; and I *a* glorified in them.	NIG
	17:11 And *now* I *a* no more in the world,	1510
	17:14 of the world, even as I *a* not of the world.	1510
	17:16 of the world, even as I *a* not of the world.	1510
	17:24 hast given me, be with me where I *a*;	NIG
	18: 5 I *a he*. And Judas also, which betrayed	1510
	18: 6 unto them, I *a he*, they went backward,	1510
	18: 8 I have told you that I *a he*: if therefore	1510
	18:17 of this man's disciples? He saith, I *a* not.	1510
	18:25 He denied *it*, and said, I *a* not.	1510
	18:35 Pilate answered, A I a Jew? Thine own	1510
	18:37 answered, Thou sayest that I *a* a king.	1510
	19:21 but that he said, I *a* King of the Jews.	NIG
	20:17 for I *a* not yet ascended to my Father:	NIG
Ac	7:32 I *a* the God of thy fathers, the God	NIG
	7:34 and *a* come down to deliver them.	NIG
	9: 5 said, I *a* Jesus whom thou persecutest:	NIG
	9:10 And he said, Behold, I *a* here, Lord.	NIG
	10:21 and said, Behold, I *a* he whom ye seek:	1510
	10:26 saying, Stand up; I myself also *a* a man.	1510
	13:25 course, he said, Whom think ye that I *a*?	1510
	13:25 I *a* not *he*. But behold, there cometh *one*	1510
	13:25 whose shoes of *his* feet I *a* not worthy to	1510
	18: 6 blood *be* upon your own heads; I *a* clean:	NIG
	18:10 For I *a* with thee, and no *man* shall set	1510
	20:26 that I *a* pure from the blood of all *men*.	NIG
	21:13 for I *a* ready not to be bound only,	2192
	21:39 I *a* a man *which am* a Jew of Tarsus,	1510
	21:39 I *a* a man *which am* a Jew of Tarsus,	NIG
	22: 3 I *a* verily a man *which am* a Jew, born in	1510
	22: 3 I *a* verily a man *which am* a Jew, born in	NIG
	22: 8 he said unto me, I *a* Jesus of Nazareth,	1510
	23: 6 Men *and* brethren, I *a* a Pharisee, the son	1510
	23: 6 resurrection of the dead I *a* called in	NIG
	24:21 Touching the resurrection of the dead I *a*	NIG
	26: 2 *things* whereof I *a* accused of the Jews:	NIG
	26: 6 *a* judged for the hope of the promise made	NIG
	26: 7 king Agrippa, I *a* accused of the Jews.	NIG
	26:15 he said, I *a* Jesus whom thou persecutest.	1510
	26:25 he said, I *a* not mad, most noble Festus;	NIG
	26:26 for I *a* persuaded that none of these *things*	NIG
	26:29 both almost, and altogether such as I *a*,	1510
	27:23 of God, whose I *a*, and whom I serve,	1510
	28:20 that for the hope of Israel I *a* bound with	NIG
Ro	1:14 I *a* debtor both to the Greeks, and to	1510
	1:15 I *a* ready to preach the gospel to you that	NIG
	1:16 I *a* not ashamed of the gospel of Christ:	NIG
	3: 7 why yet *a* I also judged as a sinner?	NIG
	7:14 is spiritual: but I *a* carnal, sold under sin.	1510
	7:24 wretched man that I *a*! who shall deliver	NIG
	8:38 For I *a* persuaded, that neither death,	NIG
	11: 1 For I also *a* an Israelite, of the seed of	1510
	11: 3 and I *a* left alone, and they seek my life.	NIG
	11:13 as I *a* the apostle of the Gentiles,	1510
	14:14 know, and *a* persuaded by the Lord Jesus,	NIG
	15:14 And I myself also *a* persuaded of you,	NIG
	15:29 And I *a* sure that, when I come unto you,	NIG
	16:19 is come abroad unto all *men*. I *a* glad	NIG
1Co	1:12 that every one of you saith, I *a* of Paul;	1510
	3: 4 For while one saith, I *a* of Paul;	1510
	3: 4 I am of Paul; and another, I *a* of Apollos;	NIG
	4: 4 by myself; yet *a* I not hereby justified:	NIG
	9: 1 I *a* not an apostle? am I not free? have I	1510
	9: 1 *a* I not free? have I not seen Jesus Christ	NIG
	9: 2 unto others, yet doubtless I *a* to you:	NIG
	9:22 I *a* made all *things* to all *men*, that I might	NIG
	10:30 why I evil spoken of for *that for* which I	NIG
	11: 1 followers of me, even as I also *a* of Christ.	NIG
	12:15 foot shall say, Because I *a* not the hand,	1510
	12:15 I am not the hand, I *a* not of the body;	1510
	12:16 Because I *a* not the eye, I am not of	1510
	12:16 I am not the eye, I *a* not of the body;	1510
	13: 1 I *a* become *as* sounding brass, or a tinkling	NIG
	13: 2 and have no charity, I *a* nothing.	1510
	13:12 then shall I know even as also I *a* known.	NIG
	15: 9 I *a* the least of the apostles, that am not	1510
	15: 9 that *a* not meet to be called an apostle,	1510
	15:10 But by the grace of God I *a* what I am:	1510
	15:10 But by the grace of God I am what I *a*:	1510
2Co	7: 4 I *a* glad of the coming of Stephanas	NIG
	7: 4 I *a* filled with comfort, I am exceeding	NIG
	7: 4 I *a* exceeding joyful in all our tribulation.	NIG
	7:14 any *thing* to him of you, I *a* not ashamed;	NIG
	10: 1 who in presence *a* base among you,	NIG
	10: 1 but being absent *a* bold toward you:	NIG
	10: 2 when I *a* present with *that* confidence,	NIG
	11: 2 For I *a* jealous over you with godly	NIG
	11:21 is bold, (I speak foolishly,) I *a* bold also.	NIG
	11:22 so *a* I. Are they Israelites? so *am* I.	NIG
	11:22 so *a* I. Are they the seed of Abraham? so *a* I.	NIG
	11:22 Are they the seed of Abraham? so *a* I.	NIG
	11:23 (I speak as a fool) I *a* more; in labours	NIG
	11:29 Who is weak, and I *a* not weak? who is	NIG
	12:10 for when I *a* weak, then am I strong.	NIG
	12:10 for when I am weak, then *a* I strong.	1510
	12:11 I *a* become a fool in glorying; ye have	NIG
	12:11 for *in* nothing *a* I behind the very chiefest	NIG
	12:14 the third *time* I *a* ready to come to you;	2192
	13: 1 This *is* the third *time* I *a* coming to you.	NIG
Gal	2:19 For I through the law *a* dead to the law,	NIG
	2:20 I *a* crucified with Christ: nevertheless I live	NIG
	4:11 I *a* afraid of you, lest I have bestowed	NIG

Gal	4:12 be as I *a*; for I *am* as ye *are*: ye have not	NIG
	4:12 be as I *am*; for I *am* as ye *are*: ye have not	NIG
	4:16 *a* I therefore become your enemy, because	NIG
	4:18 and not only when I *a* present with you.	NIG
Eph	3: 8 who *a* less than the least of all saints,	NIG
	6:20 For which I *a* an ambassador in bonds:	NIG
Php	1:17 knowing that I *a* set for the defence of	NIG
	1:23 For I *a* in a strait betwixt two, having a	NIG
	3:12 also I *a* apprehended of Christ Jesus.	NIG
	4:11 I have learned, in whatsoever *state* I *a*,	1510
	4:12 in all *things* I *a* instructed both to be full	NIG
	4:18 I *a* full, having received of Epaphroditus	NIG
Col	1:23 whereof I Paul *a* made a minister;	NIG
	1:25 Whereof I *a* made a minister, according to	NIG
	2: 5 yet *a* I with you in the spirit, joying	1510
	4: 3 of Christ, for which I *a* also in bonds:	NIG
1Ti	1:15 world to save sinners; of whom I *a* chief.	1510
	2: 7 Whereunto I *a* ordained a preacher,	NIG
	2: 7 and *a* persuaded that in thee also.	NIG
2Ti	1: 5 and I *a* persuaded that in thee also.	NIG
	1:11 Whereunto I *a* appointed a preacher,	NIG
	1:12 *things*: nevertheless I *a* not ashamed:	NIG
	1:12 I *a* persuaded that he is able to keep that	NIG
	4: 6 For I *a* now ready to be offered,	NIG
Jas	1:13 when he is tempted, I *a* tempted of God:	NIG
1Pe	1:16 it is written, Be ye holy; for I *a* holy.	1510
	5: 1 who *a* also an elder, and a witness of	NIG
2Pe	1:13 it meet, as long as I *a* in this tabernacle,	1510
	1:17 beloved Son, in whom I *a* well pleased.	NIG
Rev	1: 8 I *a* Alpha and Omega, the beginning	1510
	1: 9 who also *a* your brother, and companion	NIG
	1:11 Saying, I *a* Alpha and Omega, the first	1510
	1:17 Fear not; I *a* the first and the last:	1510
	1:18 I *a* he that liveth, and was dead;	NIG
	1:18 and behold, I *a* alive for evermore, Amen;	1510
	2:23 all the churches shall know that I *a he*.	1510
	3:17 I *a* rich, and increased with goods,	1510
	3:21 *a* set down with my Father in his throne.	NIG
	18: 7 and *a* no widow, and shall see no sorrow.	1510
	19:10 I *a* thy fellowservant, and of thy brethren	1510
	21: 6 I *a* Alpha and Omega, the beginning	1510
	22: 9 for I *a* thy fellowservant, and of thy	1510
	22:13 I *a* Alpha and Omega, the beginning	1510
	22:16 I *a* the root and the offspring of David,	1510

AMAD (1)

Jos	19:26 Alammelech, and *A*, and Misheal;	6008

AMAL (1)

1Ch	7:35 Zophah, and Imna, and Shelesh, and *A*.	6000

AMALEK (24) [AMALEKITE, AMALEKITES]

Ge	36:12 Esau's son; and she bare to Eliphaz *A*:	6002
	36:16 Duke Korah, duke Gatam, *and* duke *A*:	6002
Ex	17: 8 came *A*, and fought with Israel in	6002
	17: 9 us out men, and go out, fight with *A*:	6002
	17:10 had said to him, and fought with *A*:	6002
	17:11 when he let down his hand, *A* prevailed.	6002
	17:13 Joshua discomfited *A* and his people with	6002
	17:14 remembrance of *A* from under heaven.	6002
	17:16 war with *A* from generation *to* generation	6002
Nu	24:20 when he looked on *A*, he took up his	6002
	24:20 and said, *A was* the first of the nations;	6002
Dt	25:17 Remember what *A* did unto thee by	6002
	25:19 remembrance of *A* from under heaven;	6002
Jdg	3:13 unto him the children of Ammon and *A*,	6002
	5:14 *was* there a root of them against *A*;	6002
1Sa	15: 2 I remember *that* which *A* did to Israel,	6002
	15: 3 go and smite *A*, and utterly destroy all	6002
	15: 5 Saul came to a city of *A*, and laid wait in	6002
	15:20 have brought Agag the king of *A*,	6002
	28:18 nor executedst his fierce wrath upon *A*,	6002
2Sa	8:12 of *A*, and of the spoil of Hadadezer, son	6002
1Ch	1:36 and Gatam, Kenaz, and Timna, and *A*.	6002
	18:11 and from the Philistines, and from *A*.	6002
Ps	83: 7 Gebal, and Ammon, and *A*; the Philistines	6002

AMALEKITE (3) [AMALEK]

1Sa	30:13 man of Egypt, servant to an *A*;	376+6003
2Sa	1: 8 And I answered him, I *am* an *A*.	6003
	1:13 I *am* the son of a stranger, an *A*.	6003

AMALEKITES (24) [AMALEK]

Ge	14: 7 smote all the country of the *A*, and also	6003
Nu	13:29 The *A* dwell in the land of the south:	6002
	14:25 (Now the *A* and the Canaanites dwelt in	6003
	14:43 For the *A* and the Canaanites *are* there	6003
	14:45 Then the *A* came down, and the Canaanites	6003
Jdg	6: 3 the *A*, and the children of the east,	6002
	6:33 all the Midianites and the *A*	6002
	7:12 the Midianites and the *A* and all	6002
	10:12 the *A*, and the Maonites, did oppress you;	6002
	12:15 land of Ephraim, in the mount of the *A*.	6003
1Sa	14:48 smote the *A*, and delivered Israel out of	6002
	15: 6 depart, get you down from among the *A*,	6003
	15: 6 the Kenites departed from among the *A*.	6002
	15: 7 Saul smote the *A* from Havilah *until* thou	6002
	15: 8 he took Agag the king of the *A* alive,	6002
	15:15 They have brought them from the *A*:	6003
	15:18 Go and utterly destroy the sinners the *A*,	6002
	15:20 and have utterly destroyed the *A*.	6002
	15:32 you hither to me Agag the king of the *A*.	6002
	27: 8 Geshurites, and the Gezrites, and the *A*:	6003
	30: 1 that the *A* had invaded the south,	6002
	30:18 David recovered all that the *A* had carried	6002
2Sa	1: 1 was returned from the slaughter of the *A*,	6002

1Ch	4:43 they smote the rest of the *A* that were	6002

AMAM (1)

Jos	15:26 *A*, and Shema, and Moladah,	538

AMANA (1)

SS	4: 8 look from the top of *A*, from the top of	549

AMARIAH (16)

1Ch	6: 7 Meraioth begat *A*, and Amariah begat	568
	6: 7 begat Amariah, and *A* begat Ahitub,	568
	6:11 begat *A*, and Amariah begat Ahitub,	568
	6:11 begat Amariah, and *A* begat Ahitub,	568
	6:52 Meraioth his son, *A* his son, Ahitub his son,	568
	23:19 Jeriah the first, *A* the second, Jahaziel	568
	24:23 the sons of *Hebron; Jeriah the first, A*	568
2Ch	19:11 *A* the chief priest *is* over you in all matters	568
	31:15 Jeshua, and Shemaiah, *A*, and Shecaniah,	568
Ezr	7: 3 The son of *A*, the son of Azariah, the son	568
	10:42 Shallum, *A, and* Joseph.	568
Ne	10: 3 Pashur, *A*, Malchijah,	568
	11: 4 the son of Zechariah, the son of *A*, the son	568
	12: 2 *A*, Malluch, Hattush,	568
	12:13 Of Ezra, Meshullam; of *A*, Jehohanan;	568
Zep	1: 1 The son of *A*, the son of Hizkiah,	568

AMASA (16)

2Sa	17:25 Absalom made *A* captain of the host	6021
	17:25 which *A was* a man's son, whose name	6021
	19:13 say ye to *A*, *Art* thou not *of* my bone,	6021
	20: 4 said the king to *A*, Assemble me the men	6021
	20: 5 So *A* went to assemble *the men of* Judah:	6021
	20: 8 which *is* in Gibeon, *A* went before them.	6021
	20: 9 Joab said to *A*, *Art* thou in health,	6021
	20: 9 Joab took *A* by the beard with the right	6021
	20:10 *A* took no heed to the sword that *was* in	6021
	20:12 *A* wallowed in blood in the midst of	6021
	20:12 he removed *A* out of the highway into	6021
1Ki	2: 5 unto *A* the son of Jether, whom he slew,	6021
	2:32 the host of Israel, and *A* the son of Jether,	6021
1Ch	2:17 Abigail bare *A*: and the father of Amasa	6021
	2:17 the father of *A was* Jether the Ishmeelite.	6021
2Ch	28:12 son of Shallum, and *A* the son of Hadlai,	6021

AMASAI (5)

1Ch	6:25 And the sons of Elkanah; *A*, and Ahimoth.	6022
	6:35 the son of Mahath, the son of *A*,	6022
	12:18 the spirit came upon *A*, *who was* chief of	6022
	15:24 and Zechariah, and Benaiah,	6022
2Ch	29:12 Mahath the son of *A*, and Joel the son of	6022

AMASHAI (1)

Ne	11:13 *A* the son of Azareel, the son of Ahasai,	6023

AMASHSAI See AMASHAI

AMASIAH (1)

2Ch	17:16 next him *was A* the son of Zichri,	6007

AMAZED (21) [AMAZEMENT]

Ex	15:15 the dukes of Edom shall be *a*; the mighty	926
Jdg	20:41 turned *again*, the men of Benjamin were *a*:	926
Job	32:15 They were *a*, they answered no more:	2865
Isa	13: 8 they shall be *a* one at another; their faces	8539
Eze	32:10 I will **make** many people *a* at thee,	8074
Mt	12:23 And all the people were *a*, and said, Is this	1839
	19:25 disciples heard *it*, they were exceedingly *a*,	1605
Mk	1:27 And they were all *a*, insomuch that *they*	2284
	2:12 insomuch that *they* were all *a*,	1839
	6:51 they were sore *a* in themselves beyond	1839
	9:15 were **greatly** *a*, and running to *him*	1568
	10:32 and they were *a*; and as they followed,	2284
	14:33 and began to be sore *a*, and to be very	1568
	16: 8 for they trembled and were *a*:	1611
Lk	2:48 And when they saw him, they were *a*:	1605
	4:36 And they were all *a*, and spake among	2285
	5:26 And they were all *a*,	1611+2983
	9:43 And they were all *a* at the mighty power	1605
Ac	2: 7 And they were all *a* and marvelled,	1839
	2:12 And they were all *a*, and were in doubt,	1839
	9:21 But all that heard *him* were *a*, and said;	1839

AMAZEMENT (2) [AMAZED]

Ac	3:10 *a* at that which had happened unto him.	1611
1Pe	3: 6 ye do well, and are not afraid *with* any *a*.	4423

AMAZIAH (40) [OZIAS]

2Ki	12:21 David: and *A* his son reigned in his stead.	558
	13:12 his might wherewith he fought against *A*	558
	14: 1 reigned *A* the son of Joash king of Judah.	558
	14: 8 *A* sent messengers to Jehoash, the son of	558
	14: 9 Jehoash the king of Israel sent to *A* king of	558
	14:11 *A* would not hear. Therefore Jehoash king	558
	14:11 *A* king of Judah looked one another in	558
	14:13 Jehoash king of Israel took *A* king of Judah,	558
	14:15 and how he fought with *A* king of Judah,	558
	14:17 *A* the son of Joash king of Judah lived after	558
	14:18 rest of the acts of *A*, *are* they not written	558
	14:21 and made him king instead of his father *A*.	558
	14:23 In the fifteenth year of *A* the son of Joash	558
	15: 1 Azariah son of *A* king of Judah to reign.	558
	15: 3 according to all that his father *A* had done;	558
1Ch	3:12 *A* his son, Azariah his son, Jotham his son,	558
	4:34 and Jamlech, and Joshah the son of *A*,	558
	6:45 the son of *A*, the son of Hilkiah,	558
2Ch	24:27 And *A* his son reigned in his stead.	558

A

2Ch 25: 1 **A** *was* twenty and five years old *when* he 558
25: 5 Moreover **A** gathered Judah together, 558
25: 9 **A** said to the man of God, But what 558
25:10 **A** separated them, to wit, the army that 558
25:11 **A** strengthened himself, and led forth his 558
25:13 the soldiers of the army which **A** sent back, 558
25:14 after that **A** was come from the slaughter 558
25:15 anger of the LORD was kindled against **A**, 558
25:17 **A** king of Judah took advice, and sent to 558
25:18 Joash king of Israel sent to **A** king of Judah, 558
25:20 **A** would not hear; for it *came* of God, 558
25:21 *both* he and **A** king of Judah, 558
25:23 Joash the king of Israel took **A** king of 558
25:25 **A** the son of Joash king of Judah lived after 558
25:26 Now the rest of the acts of **A**, first and last, 558
25:27 Now after the time that **A** did turn away 558
26: 1 made him king in the room of his father **A**. 558
26: 4 according to all that his father **A** did. 558
Am 7:10 **A** *the* priest of Beth-el sent to Jeroboam 558
7:12 Also **A** said unto Amos, O thou seer, go, 558
7:14 and said to **A**, I *was* no prophet, 558

AMBASSADOR (4) [AMBASSADORS, AMBASSAGE]
Pr 13:17 into mischief: but a faithful **a** *is* health. 6735
Jer 49:14 an **a** *is* sent unto the heathen, 6735
Ob 1: 1 an **a** is sent among the heathen, Arise ye, 6735
Eph 6:20 For which I am an **a** in bonds: that therein 4243

AMBASSADORS (8) [AMBASSADOR]
Jos 9: 4 went and **made as if** they had been **a**, 6737
2Ch 32:31 Howbeit in *the business of* the **a** of 3887
35:21 he sent **a** to him, saying, What have I to 4397
Isa 18: 2 That sendeth **a** by the sea, even in vessels 6735
30: 4 were at Zoan, and his **a** came to Hanes. 4397
33: 7 the **a** of peace shall weep bitterly. 4397
Eze 17:15 he rebelled against him in sending his **a** 4397
2Co 5:20 *Now* then we are **a** for Christ, as though 4243

AMBASSAGE (1) [AMBASSADOR]
Lk 14:32 he sendeth an **a**, and desireth conditions 4242

AMBER (3)
Eze 1: 4 out of the midst thereof as the colour of **a**, 2830
1:27 I saw as the colour of **a**, as the appearance 2830
8: 2 of brightness, as the colour of **a**. 2830

AMBUSH (7) [AMBUSHES, AMBUSHMENT, AMBUSHMENTS]
Jos 8: 2 lay thee an **a** for the city behind it. 693
8: 7 ye shall rise up from the **a**, and seize upon 693
8: 9 they went to **lie in a**, and abode between 3993
8:12 them to **lie in a** between Beth-el and Ai, 693
8:14 wist not that *there were* **liers in a** against 693
8:19 the **a** arose quickly out of their place, 693
8:21 all Israel saw that the **a** had taken the city, 693

AMBUSHES (1) [AMBUSH]
Jer 51:12 set up the watchmen, prepare the **a**: 693

AMBUSHMENT (2) [AMBUSH]
2Ch 13:13 Jeroboam caused an **a** to come about 3993
13:13 before Judah, and the **a** *was* behind them. 3993

AMBUSHMENTS (1) [AMBUSH]
2Ch 20:22 the LORD set **a** against the children of 693

AMEN (78)
Nu 5:22 to rot: And the woman shall say, **A**, amen. 543
5:22 to rot: And the woman shall say, Amen, **a**. 543
Dt 27:15 And all the people shall answer and say, **A**. 543
27:16 his mother. And all the people shall say, **A**. 543
27:17 And all the people shall say, **A**. 543
27:18 of the way. And all the people shall say, **A**. 543
27:19 and widow. And all the people shall say, **A**. 543
27:20 And all the people shall say, **A**. 543
27:21 *of* beast. And all the people shall say, **A**. 543
27:22 his mother. And all the people shall say, **A**. 543
27:23 in law. And all the people shall say, **A**. 543
27:24 And all the people shall say, **A**. 543
27:25 And all the people shall say, **A**. 543
27:26 to do them. And all the people shall say, **A**. 543
1Ki 1:36 of Jehoiada answered the king, and said, **A**: 543
1Ch 16:36 the people said, **A**, and praised the LORD. 543
Ne 5:13 **A**, and praised the LORD. 543
8: 6 **A**, Amen, with lifting up their hands: 543
8: 6 Amen, **A**, with lifting up their hands: 543
Ps 41:13 and to everlasting. **A**, and Amen. 543
41:13 and to everlasting. Amen, and **A**. 543
72:19 earth be filled *with* his glory; **A**, and Amen. 543
72:19 earth be filled *with* his glory; Amen, and **A**. 543
89:52 *be* the LORD for evermore. **A**, and Amen. 543
89:52 *be* the LORD for evermore. Amen, and **A**. 543
106:48 let all the people say, **A**. Praise ye 543
Jer 28: 6 Even the prophet Jeremiah said, **A**: 543
Mt 6:13 and the power, and the glory, for ever. **A**. 281
28:20 *even* unto the end of the world. **A**. 281
Mk 16:20 the word with signs following. **A**. 281
Lk 24:53 the temple, praising and blessing God. **A**. 281
Jn 21:25 the books that should be written. **A**. 281
Ro 1:25 the Creator, who is blessed for ever. **A**. 281
9: 5 who is over all, God blessed for ever. **A**. 281
11:36 all *things:* to whom *be* glory for ever. **A**. 281
15:33 Now the God of peace *be* with you all. **A**. 281
16:20 of our Lord Jesus Christ *be* with you. **A**. 281
16:24 of our Lord Jesus Christ *be* with you all. **A**. 281

Ro 16:27 *be* glory through Jesus Christ for ever. **A**. 281
1Co 14:16 the unlearned say **A** at thy giving of thanks, 281
16:24 My love *be* with you all in Christ Jesus. **A**. 281
2Co 1:20 and in him **A**, unto the glory of God by us. 281
13:14 of the Holy Ghost, *be* with you all. **A**. 281
Gal 1: 5 To whom *be* glory for ever and ever. **A**. 281
6:18 Lord Jesus Christ *be* with your spirit. **A**. 281
Eph 3:21 throughout all ages, world without end. **A**. 281
6:24 love our Lord Jesus Christ in sincerity. **A**. 281
Php 4:20 our Father *be* glory for ever and ever. **A**. 281
4:23 of our Lord Jesus Christ *be* with you all. **A**. 281
Col 4:18 my bonds. Grace *be* with you. **A**. 281
1Th 5:28 of our Lord Jesus Christ *be* with you. **A**. 281
2Th 3:18 of our Lord Jesus Christ *be* with you all. **A**. 281
1Ti 1:17 *be* honour and glory for ever and ever. **A**. 281
6:16 *be* honour and power everlasting. **A**. 281
6:21 the faith. Grace *be* with thee. **A**. 281
2Ti 4:18 to whom *be* glory for ever and ever. **A**. 281
4:22 *be* with thy spirit. Grace *be* with you. **A**. 281
Tit 3:15 in the faith. Grace *be* with you all. **A**. 281
Phm 1:25 Lord Jesus Christ *be* with your spirit. **A**. 281
Heb 13:21 to whom *be* glory for ever and ever. **A**. 281
13:25 Grace *be* with you all. **A**. 281
1Pe 4:11 praise and dominion for ever and ever. **A**. 281
5:11 glory and dominion for ever and ever. **A**. 281
5:14 *be* with you all that are in Christ Jesus. **A**. 281
2Pe 3:18 To him *be* glory both now and for ever. **A**. 281
1Jn 5:21 keep yourselves from idols. **A**. 281
2Jn 1:13 children of thy elect sister greet thee. **A**. 281
Jude 1:25 and power, both now and ever. **A**. 281
Rev 1: 6 glory and dominion for ever and ever. **A**. 281
1: 7 shall wail because of him. Even so, **A**. 281
1:18 and behold, I am alive for evermore, **A**; 281
3:14 These *things* saith the **A**, the faithful 281
5:14 And the four beasts said, **A**. And the four 281
7:12 Saying, **A**: Blessing, and glory, and wisdom, 281
7:12 *be* unto our God for ever and ever. **A**. 281
19: 4 God that sat on the throne, saying, **A**; 281
22:20 **A**. Even so, come, Lord Jesus. 281
22:21 our Lord Jesus Christ *be* with you all. **A**. 281

AMEND (5) [AMENDS]
Jer 7: 3 **A** your ways and your doings, and I will 3190
7: 5 For if you **throughly** **a** your ways 3190+3190
26:13 Therefore now **a** your ways 3190
35:15 **a** your doings, and go not after other gods 3190
Jn 4:52 the hour when he **began to a**. 2192+2866

AMENDS (1) [AMEND]
Lev 5:16 he shall **make a** for the harm that he hath 7999

AMERCE (1)
Dt 22:19 they shall **a** him in an hundred *shekels* of 6064

AMETHYST (3)
Ex 28:19 the third row a ligure, an agate, and an **a**. 306
39:12 the third row, a ligure, an agate, and an **a**. 306
Rev 21:20 the eleventh, a jacinth; the twelfth, an **a**. 271

AMI (1)
Ezr 2:57 of Pochereth of Zebaim, the children of **A**. 532

AMIABLE (1)
Ps 84: 1 How **a** *are* thy tabernacles, O LORD of 3039

AMINADAB (3)
Mt 1: 4 And Aram begat **A**; and Aminadab begat 284
1: 4 and **A** begat Naasson; and Naasson begat 284
Lk 3:33 Which was *the son* of **A**, which was 284

AMISS (4) [MISS]
2Ch 6:37 have **done**, and have dealt wickedly; 5753
Da 3:29 which speak **any thing a** against the God 7960
Lk 23:41 deeds: but this *man* hath done nothing **a**. 824
Jas 4: 3 Ye ask, and receive not, because ye ask **a**, 2560

AMITTAI (2)
2Ki 14:25 the son of **A**, the prophet, which *was* 573
Jnh 1: 1 the LORD came unto Jonah the son of **A**, 573

AMMAH (1) [METHEG-AMMAH]
2Sa 2:24 when they were come to the hill of **A**, 522

AMMI (1) [LO-AMMI]
Hos 2: 1 Say ye unto your brethren, **A**; 5971+2967.1

AMMIEL (4)
Nu 13:12 Of the tribe of Dan, **A** the son of Gemalli. 5988
2Sa 9: 4 of Machir, the son of **A**, in Lo-debar. 5988
9: 5 of Machir, the son of **A**, from Lo-debar. 5988
17:27 Machir the son of **A** of Lo-debar, 5988
1Ch 3: 5 four, of Bath-shua the daughter of **A**: 5988
26: 5 **A** the sixth, Issachar the seventh, 5988

AMMIHUD (10)
Nu 1:10 of Ephraim; Elishama the son of **A**: 5989
2:18 Ephraim *shall be* Elishama the son of **A**. 5989
7:48 the seventh day Elishama the son of **A**, 5989
7:53 *was* the offering of Elishama the son of **A**. 5989
10:22 over his host *was* Elishama the son of **A**. 5989
34:20 children of Simeon, Shemuel the son of **A**. 5989
34:28 children of Naphtali, Pedahel the son of **A**. 5989
2Sa 13:37 to Talmai, the son of **A**, king of Geshur. 5989
1Ch 7:26 Laadan his son, **A** his son, Elishama his 5989
9: 4 Uthai the son of **A**, the son of Omri, 5989

AMMINADAB (13)
Ex 6:23 daughter of **A**, sister of Naashon, to wife; 5992
Nu 1: 7 Of Judah; Nahshon the son of **A**. 5992
2: 3 Nahshon the son of **A** *shall be* captain of 5992
7:12 the first day was Nahshon the son of **A**, 5992
7:17 *was* the offering of Nahshon the son of **A**. 5992
10:14 over his host *was* Nahshon the son of **A**. 5992
Ru 4:19 Hezron begat Ram, and Ram begat **A**, 5992
4:20 **A** begat Nahshon, and Nahshon begat 5992
1Ch 2:10 Ram begat **A**; and Amminadab begat 5992
2:10 **A** begat Nahshon, prince of the children 5992
6:22 **A** his son, Korah his son, Assir his son, 5992
15:10 **A** the chief, and his brethren an hundred 5992
15:11 and Joel, Shemaiah, and Eliel, and **A**, 5992

AMMI-NADIB (1)
SS 6:12 my soul made me *like* the chariots of **A**. 5993

AMMISHADDAI (5)
Nu 1:12 Of Dan; Ahiezer the son of **A**. 5996
2:25 of Dan *shall be* Ahiezer the son of **A**. 5996
7:66 On the tenth day Ahiezer the son of **A**, 5996
7:71 *was* the offering of Ahiezer the son of **A**. 5996
10:25 over his host *was* Ahiezer the son of **A**. 5996

AMMIZABAD (1)
1Ch 27: 6 thirty: and *in* his course *was* **A** his son. 5990

AMMON (91) [AMMONITE, AMMONITES, AMMONITESS]
Ge 19:38 the same *is* the father of the children of **A** 5983
Nu 21:24 unto Jabbok, *even* unto the children of **A**: 5983
21:24 for the border of the children of **A** *was* 5983
Dt 2:19 nigh over against the children of **A**, 5983
2:19 land of the children of **A** *any* possession; 5983
2:37 Only unto the land of the children of **A** 5983
3:11 *is* it not in Rabbath of the children of **A**? 5983
3:16 *which is* the border of the children of **A**; 5983
Jos 12: 2 *which is* the border of the children of **A**; 5983
13:10 unto the border of the children of **A**; 5983
13:25 and half the land of the children of **A**, 5983
Jdg 3:13 he gathered unto him the children of **A** 5983
10: 6 gods of the children of **A**, and the gods 5983
10: 7 and into the hands of the children of **A**, 5983
10: 9 Moreover the children of **A** passed over 5983
10:11 from the children of **A**, and from 5983
10:17 the children of **A** were gathered together, 5983
10:18 begin to fight against the children of **A**? 5983
11: 4 that the children of **A** made war against 5983
11: 5 that when the children of **A** made war 5983
11: 6 that we may fight with the children of **A**. 5983
11: 8 fight against the children of **A**, and be our 5983
11: 9 again to fight against the children of **A**, 5983
11:12 unto the king of the children of **A**, 5983
11:13 king of the children of **A** answered unto 5983
11:14 again unto the king of the children of **A**: 5983
11:15 Moab, nor the land of the children of **A**: 5983
11:27 children of Israel and the children of **A**: 5983
11:28 Howbeit the king of the children of **A** 5983
11:29 he passed over *unto* the children of **A**. 5983
11:30 deliver the children of **A** into mine hands, 5983
11:31 I return in peace from the children of **A**, 5983
11:32 the children of **A** to fight against them; 5983
11:33 Thus the children of **A** were subdued 5983
11:36 thine enemies, *even* of the children of **A**. 5983
12: 1 over to fight against the children of **A**, 5983
12: 2 at great strife with the children of **A**; 5983
12: 3 passed over against the children of **A**, 5983
1Sa 12:12 king of the children of **A** came against you 5983
14:47 against the children of **A**, 5983
2Sa 8:12 of the children of **A**, and of the Philistines, 5983
10: 1 that the king of the children of **A** died, 5983
10: 2 came *into* the land of the children of **A**. 5983
10: 3 the princes of the children of **A** said unto 5983
10: 6 the children of **A** saw that they stank 5983
10: 6 children of **A** sent and hired the Syrians 5983
10: 8 the children of **A** came out, and put 5983
10:10 *them* in array against the children of **A**. 5983
10:11 if the children of **A** be too strong for thee, 5983
10:14 the children of **A** saw that the Syrians 5983
10:14 So Joab returned from the children of **A**, 5983
10:19 feared to help the children of **A** any more. 5983
11: 1 they destroyed the children of **A**, 5983
12: 9 him with the sword of the children of **A**. 5983
12:26 against Rabbah of the children of **A**, 5983
12:31 he unto all the cities of the children of **A**. 5983
17:27 of Nahash of Rabbah of the children of **A**, 5983
1Ki 11: 7 the abomination of the children of **A**. 5983
11:33 Milcom the god of the children of **A**, 5983
2Ki 23:13 the abomination of the children of **A**, 5983
24: 2 bands of the children of **A**, and sent them 5983
1Ch 18:11 from the children of **A**, and from 5983
19: 1 Nahash the king of the children of **A** 5983
19: 2 the land of the children of **A** to Hanun, 5983
19: 3 the princes of the children of **A** said to 5983
19: 6 when the children of **A** saw that they had 5983
19: 6 the children of **A** sent a thousand talents 5983
19: 7 the children of **A** gathered themselves 5983
19: 9 the children of **A** came out, and put 5983
19:11 in array against the children of **A**. 5983
19:12 if the children of **A** be too strong for thee, 5983
19:15 the children of **A** saw that the Syrians 5983
19:19 Syrians help the children of **A** any more. 5983
20: 1 wasted the country of the children of **A**, 5983
20: 3 with all the cities of the children of **A**. 5983

A

2Ch	20: 1 the children of **A**, and with them *other*	5983
	20:10 the children of **A** and Moab	5983
	20:22 ambushments against the children of **A**,	5983
	20:23 For the children of **A** and Moab stood up	5983
	27: 5 the children of **A** gave him the same year	5983
	27: 5 So much did the children of **A** pay unto	5983
Ne	13:23 wives of Ashdod, **of A**, *and* of Moab:	5984
Ps	83: 7 Gebal, and **A**, and Amalek; the Philistines	5983
Isa	11:14 and the children of **A** shall obey them.	5983
Jer	9:26 the children of **A**, and Moab, and all *that*	5983
	25:21 Edom, and Moab, and the children of **A**,	5983
	49: 6 again the captivity of the children of **A**,	5983
Da	11:41 Moab, and the chief of the children of **A**.	5983
Am	1:13 three transgressions of the children of **A**,	5983
Zep	2: 8 and the revilings of the children of **A**,	5983
	2: 9 the children of **A** as Gomorrah, *even*	5983

AMMONITE (9) [AMMON]

Dt	23: 3 An **A** or Moabite shall not enter into	5984
1Sa	11: 1 Nahash the **A** came up,	5984
	11: 2 Nahash the **A** answered them, On this	5984
2Sa	23:37 Zelek the **A**, Naharai the Beerothite,	5984
1Ch	11:39 Zelek the **A**, Naharai the Berothite,	5984
Ne	2:10 and Tobiah the servant, the **A**,	5984
	2:19 the **A**, and Geshem the Arabian,	5984
	4: 3 Tobiah the **A** *was* by him, and he said,	5984
	13: 1 the **A** and the Moabite should not come	5984

AMMONITES (23) [AMMON]

Dt	2:20 and the **A** call them Zamzummims;	5984
1Sa	11:11 and slew the **A** until the heat of the day:	5983
1Ki	11: 1 **A**, Edomites, Zidonians, *and* Hittites;	5984
	11: 5 after Milcom the abomination of the **A**.	5984
2Ch	20: 1 and with them *other* beside the **A**,	5984
	26: 8 the **A** gave gifts to Uzziah: and his name	5984
	27: 5 fought also with the king of the **A**,	1121+5984
Ezr	9: 1 the Jebusites, the **A**, the Moabites,	5984
Ne	4: 7 and the **A**, and the Ashdodites,	5984
Jer	27: 3 the king of the **A**, and to the king	1121+5983
	40:11 among the **A**, and in Edom,	1121+5983
	40:14 hath sent Ishmael the son of	1121+5983
	41:10 and departed to go over to the **A**.	1121+5983
	41:15 with eight men, and went to the **A**.	1121+5983
	49: 1 Concerning the **A**, thus saith	1121+5983
	49: 2 war to be heard in Rabbah of the **A**;	1121+5983
Eze	21:20 may come to Rabbath of the **A**,	1121+5983
	21:28 the Lord GOD concerning the **A**,	1121+5983
	25: 2 set thy face against the **A**,	1121+5983
	25: 3 say unto the **A**, Hear the word of	1121+5983
	25: 5 the **A** a couching place for flocks:	1121+5983
	25:10 the men of the east with the **A**,	1121+5983
	25:10 **A** may not be remembered	1121+5983

AMMONITESS (4) [AMMON]

1Ki	14:21 his mother's name *was* Naamah an **A**.	5984
	14:31 his mother's name *was* Naamah an **A**.	5984
2Ch	12:13 his mother's name *was* Naamah an **A**.	5984
	24:26 Zabad the son of Shimeath an **A**,	5984

AMNON (25) [AMNON'S]

2Sa	3: 2 his firstborn was **A**, of Ahinoam	550
	13: 1 and **A** the son of David loved her.	550
	13: 2 **A** was *so* vexed, that he fell sick for his	550
	13: 2 A thought it hard for him to do any thing	550
	13: 3 **A** had a friend, whose name *was* Jonadab,	550
	13: 4 **A** said unto him, I love Tamar, my brother	550
	13: 6 So **A** lay down, and made himself sick:	550
	13: 6 **A** said unto the king, I pray thee, let Tamar	550
	13: 9 **A** said, Have out all men from me.	550
	13:10 **A** said unto Tamar, Bring the meat *into*	550
	13:10 brought *them* into the chamber to **A** her	550
	13:15 **A** hated her exceedingly; so that the hatred	550
	13:15 And **A** said unto her, Arise, be gone.	550
	13:20 her, Hath **A** thy brother been with thee?	550
	13:22 Absalom spake unto his brother **A** neither	550
	13:22 Absalom hated **A**, because he had forced	550
	13:26 I pray thee, let my brother **A** go with us.	550
	13:27 that he let **A** and all the king's sons go	550
	13:28 and when I say unto you, Smite **A**;	550
	13:29 the servants of Absalom did unto **A** as	550
	13:32 men the king's sons; for **A** only is dead:	550
	13:33 the king's sons are dead: for **A** only is dead.	550
	13:39 for he was comforted concerning **A**,	550
1Ch	3: 1 firstborn **A**, of Ahinoam the Jezreelitess;	550
	4:20 the sons of Shimon *were*, **A**, and Rinnah,	550

AMNON'S (3) [AMNON]

2Sa	13: 7 Go now to thy brother **A** house,	550
	13: 8 So Tamar went *to* her brother **A** house;	550
	13:28 Mark ye now when **A** heart is merry with	550

AMOK (2)

Ne	12: 7 Sallu, **A**, Hilkiah, Jedaiah. These *were*	5987
	12:20 Of Sallai, Kallai; of **A**, Eber;	5987

AMON (19)

1Ki	22:26 carry him back unto **A** the governor of	526
2Ki	21:18 of Uzza: and **A** his son reigned in his stead.	526
	21:19 **A** *was* twenty and two years old when he	526
	21:23 the servants of **A** conspired against him,	526
	21:24 all them that had conspired against king **A**;	526
	21:25 Now the rest of the acts of **A** which he did,	526
1Ch	3:14 **A** his son, Josiah his son.	526
2Ch	18:25 him back to **A** the governor of the city,	526
	33:20 and **A** his son reigned in his stead.	526

2Ch	33:21 **A** *was* two and twenty years old when he	526
	33:22 for **A** sacrificed unto all the carved images	526
	33:23 but **A** trespassed more and more.	526
	33:25 all them that had conspired against king **A**;	526
Ne	7:59 of Pochereth Zebaim, the children of **A**.	526
Jer	1: 2 days of Josiah the son of **A** king of Judah,	526
	25: 3 year of Josiah the son of **A** king of Judah,	526
Zep	1: 1 in the days of Josiah the son of **A**, king of	526
Mt	1:10 and Manasses begat **A**; and Amon begat	300
	1:10 Manasses begat Amon; and **A** begat Josias;	300

AMONG (859) [AMONGST]

Ge	17:10 Every man *child* a you shall be	3807.1
	17:12 days old shall be circumcised a you,	3807.1
	17:23 male a the men of Abraham's house;	871.1
	23: 6 thou *art* a mighty prince **a** us: in	8432+871.1
	30:32 all the brown cattle a the sheep,	871.1
	30:32 and the spotted and speckled **a** the goats:	871.1
	30:41 that they might conceive **a** the rods.	871.1
	34:22 if every male **a** us be circumcised,	3807.1
	34:30 have troubled me to make me to stink **a**	871.1
	35: 2 away the strange gods that *are* **a**	8432+871.1
	36:30 Hori, **a** their dukes in the land of Seir.	3807.1
	40:20 of the chief baker **a** his servants.	8432+871.1
	42: 5 sons of Israel came to buy *corn* **a**	8432+871.1
Ex	2: 5 when she saw the ark **a** the flags,	8432+871.1
	7: 5 bring out the children of Israel from **a**	8432
	12:49 the stranger that sojourneth **a** you.	8432+871.1
	13: 2 whatsoever openeth the womb **a**	871.1
	15:11 *is* like unto thee, O LORD, **a** the gods?	871.1
	28: 1 with him, from **a** the children of Israel,	8432
	30:13 every one that passeth **a** them that are	5921
	30:14 Every one that passeth **a** them that are	5921
	34:10 all the people **a** which thou *art*	7130+871.1
	35:10 every wise hearted **a** you shall come,	871.1
	36: 8 every wise hearted *man* **a** them that	871.1
Lev	6:18 All the males **a** the children of Aaron	871.1
	6:29 All the males **a** the priests shall eat	871.1
	7: 6 Every male **a** the priests shall eat thereof:	871.1
	7:33 He **a** the sons of Aaron, that offereth	4480
	7:34 unto his sons by a statute for ever from **a**	854
	11: 2 the beasts which ye shall eat **a** all	4480
	11: 3 cheweth cud, **a** the beasts,	871.1
	11:13 ye shall have in abomination **a** the fowls;	4480
	11:27 **a** all *manner of* beasts that go on *all* four,	871.1
	11:29 These also *shall* be unclean unto you **a**	871.1
	11:31 These *are* unclean to you **a** all that creep:	871.1
	11:42 hath more feet **a** all creeping	871.1
	15:31 defile my tabernacle that *is* **a** them.	8432+871.1
	16:16 remaineth **a** them in the midst of their	854
	16:29 a stranger that sojourneth **a** you:	8432+871.1
	17: 4 man shall be cut off from **a** his people:	7130
	17: 8 of the strangers which sojourn **a**	8432+871.1
	17: 9 even that man shall be cut off **from a** his	4480
	17:10 or of the strangers that sojourn **a**	8432+871.1
	17:10 and will cut him off from **a** his people.	7130
	17:12 that sojourneth **a** you eat blood.	8432+871.1
	17:13 or of the strangers that sojourn **a**	8432+871.1
	18:26 any stranger that sojourneth **a** you:	8432+871.1
	18:29 *them* shall be cut off **a** their people.	7130
	19: 8 soul shall be cut off **from a** his people.	4480
	19:16 and down *as* a talebearer **a** thy people:	871.1
	20: 3 and will cut him off from **a** his people	7130
	20: 5 with Molech, from **a** their people.	7130
	20: 6 and will cut him off from **a** his people.	7130
	20:14 that there be no wickedness **a** you.	8432+871.1
	20:18 both of them shall be cut off from **a** their	7130
	21: 1 There shall none be defiled for the dead **a**	871.1
	21: 4 *being* a chief man **a** his people, to profane	871.1
	21:10 he that *is* the high priest **a** his brethren,	4480
	21:15 Neither shall he profane his seed **a** his	871.1
	22: 3 Whosoever *he be* of all your seed **a** your	3807.1
	22:32 hallowed **a** the children of Israel:	8432+871.1
	23:29 he shall be cut off **from a** his people.	4480
	23:30 the same soul will I destroy from **a** his	7130
	24:10 went out **a** the children of Israel:	8432+871.1
	25:33 possession **a** the children of Israel.	8432+871.1
	25:45 of the strangers that do sojourn **a** you,	5973
	26:12 I will walk **a** you, and will be your	8432+871.1
	26:22 I will also send wild beasts **a** you, which	871.1
	26:25 I will send the pestilence **a** you;	8432+871.1
	26:33 I will scatter you **a** the heathen,	871.1
	26:38 shall perish **a** the heathen, and the land	871.1
Nu	1:47 were not numbered **a** them.	8432+871.1
	1:49 neither take the sum of them **a**	8432+871.1
	2:33 the Levites were not numbered **a**	8432+871.1
	3:12 have taken the Levites from **a** the children	8432
	3:12 the matrix **a** the children of Israel:	4480
	3:41 instead of all the firstborn **a** the children	871.1
	3:41 **a** the cattle of the children of Israel.	871.1
	3:42 all the firstborn **a** the children of Israel.	871.1
	3:45 of all the firstborn **a** the children of Israel,	871.1
	4: 2 the sum of the sons of Kohath from **a**	8432
	4:18 of the Kohathites from **a** the Levites:	8432
	5:21 a curse and an oath **a** thy people,	8432+871.1
	5:27 shall be a curse **a** her people.	7130+871.1
	8: 6 Take the Levites from **a** the children of	8432
	8:14 shalt thou separate the Levites from **a**	8432
	8:16 they *are* wholly given unto me from **a**	8432
	8:19 to his sons from **a** the children of Israel,	8432
	8:19 that there be no plague **a** the children of	871.1
	9: 7 season **a** the children of Israel?	8432+871.1
	9:13 even the same soul shall be cut off **from a**	4480
	9:14 if a stranger shall sojourn **a** you,	854
	11: 1 the fire of the LORD burnt **a** them,	871.1

Nu	11: 3 the fire of the LORD burnt **a** them.	871.1
	11: 4 mixt multitude that *was* **a** them	7130+871.1
	11:20 despised the LORD which *is* **a** you,	7130+871.1
	12: 6 If there be a prophet **a** you, *I* the LORD	NIH
	13: 2 ye send a man, every one a ruler **a** them.	871.1
	14:11 signs which I have shewed **a** them?	7130+871.1
	14:13 this people in thy might from **a** them;)	7130
	14:14 that thou LORD *art* **a** this people,	7130+871.1
	14:42 Go not up, for the LORD *is* not **a**	7130+871.1
	15:14 or whosoever *be* **a** you in your	8432+871.1
	15:23 and henceforward **a** your generations;	3807.1
	15:26 stranger that sojourneth **a** them;	8432+871.1
	15:29 stranger that sojourneth **a** them.	8432+871.1
	15:30 that soul shall be cut off from **a** his people.	7130
	16: 3 of them, and the LORD *is* **a** them:	8432+871.1
	16:21 Separate yourselves from **a** this	8432
	16:33 they perished from **a** the congregation.	8432
	16:45 Get you up from **a** this congregation,	8432
	16:47 the plague was begun **a** the people:	871.1
	17: 6 the rod of Aaron *was* **a** their rods.	8432+871.1
	18: 6 the Levites from **a** the children of Israel:	8432
	18:20 shalt thou have any part **a** them:	8432+871.1
	18:20 inheritance **a** the children of Israel.	8432+871.1
	18:23 that **a** the children of Israel they	8432+871.1
	18:24 **A** the children of Israel they shall	8432+871.1
	19:10 stranger that sojourneth **a** them,	8432+871.1
	19:20 that soul shall be cut off from **a**	8432
	21: 6 the LORD sent fiery serpents **a**	871.1
	23: 9 and shall not be reckoned **a** the nations.	871.1
	23:21 and the shout of a king *is* **a** them.	871.1
	25:11 was zealous for my sake **a** them,	8432+871.1
	25:14 prince of a chief house **a** the Simeonites.	3807.1
	26:62 for they were not numbered **a**	8432+871.1
	26:62 given them **a** the children of Israel.	8432+871.1
	26:64 a these there was not a man of them	871.1
	27: 4 our father be done away from **a** his family,	8432
	27: 4 **a** the brethren of our father.	8432+871.1
	27: 7 a their father's brethren;	8432+871.1
	31:16 there was a plague **a** the congregation of	871.1
	31:17 therefore kill every male **a** the little ones,	871.1
	32:30 they shall have possessions **a** you	8432+871.1
	33: 4 which the LORD had smitten **a** them:	871.1
	33:54 **divide** the land by lot for	
	an inheritance a	5157
	35: 6 **a** the cities which ye shall give unto	NIH
	35:15 and for the sojourner **a** them:	8432+871.1
	35:34 for I the LORD dwell **a**	8432+871.1
Dt	1:13 known **a** your tribes, and I will make	3807.1
	1:15 over tens, and officers **a** your tribes.	3807.1
	1:42 neither fight; for I *am* not **a** you;	7130+871.1
	2:14 of war were wasted out from **a** the host,	7130
	2:15 to destroy them from **a** the host, until	7130
	2:16 and dead from **a** the people,	7130
	4: 3 thy God hath destroyed them from **a** you.	7130
	4:27 the LORD shall scatter you **a** the nations,	871.1
	4:27 ye shall be left few in number **a**	871.1
	6:15 thy God *is* a jealous God **a** you)	7130+871.1
	7:14 shall not be male or female barren **a** you,	871.1
	7:14 barren among you, or **a** your cattle.	871.1
	7:20 thy God will send the hornet **a** them,	871.1
	7:21 for the LORD thy God *is* **a** you,	7130+871.1
	13: 1 If there arise **a** you a prophet, or	7130+871.1
	13:11 such wickedness as this is **a** you.	7130+871.1
	13:13 are gone out from **a** you,	7130
	13:14 abomination is wrought **a** you;	7130+871.1
	15: 4 Save when there shall be no poor **a** you;	871.1
	15: 7 If there be **a** you a poor man of one of	871.1
	16:11 and the widow, that *are* **a** you,	7130+871.1
	17: 2 If there be found **a** you, within any	7130+871.1
	17: 7 thou shalt put the evil away from **a** you.	7130
	17:15 from a thy brethren shalt thou set king	7130
	18: 2 no inheritance **a** their brethren:	7130+871.1
	18:10 There shall not be found **a** you *any one*	871.1
	18:18 will raise them up a Prophet from **a** their	7130
	19:19 shalt thou put the evil away from **a** you.	7130
	19:20 no more any such evil **a** you.	7130+871.1
	21: 9 the *guilt of* innocent blood from **a** you,	7130
	21:11 seest a the captives a beautiful woman,	871.1
	21:21 so shalt thou put evil away from **a** you;	7130
	22:21 so shalt thou put evil away from **a** you.	7130
	22:24 so thou shalt put away evil from **a** you.	7130
	23:10 there be **a** you any man, that is not clean	871.1
	23:16 He shall dwell with thee, *even* **a**	7130+871.1
	24: 7 and thou shalt put evil away from **a** you.	7130
	26:11 and the stranger that *is* **a** you.	7130+871.1
	28:37 **a** all nations whither the LORD shall lead	871.1
	28:54 *So that* the man *that is* tender **a** you,	871.1
	28:56 The tender and delicate woman **a** you,	871.1
	28:64 the LORD shall scatter thee **a** all people,	871.1
	28:65 **a** these nations shalt thou find no ease,	871.1
	29:17 silver and gold, which *were* **a** them;)	5973
	29:18 Lest there should be **a** you a man,	871.1
	29:18 lest there should be **a** you a root that	871.1
	30: 1 thou shalt call *them* to mind **a** all	871.1
	32:26 of them to cease **from a** men:	4480
	32:34 with me, *and* sealed up **a** my treasures?	871.1
	32:46 the words which I testify **a** you *this* day,	871.1
	32:51 ye trespassed against me **a**	8432+871.1
Jos	3: 5 the LORD will do wonders **a** you.	7130+871.1
	3:10 know that the living God *is* **a** you,	7130+871.1
	4: 6 That this may be a sign **a** you,	7130+871.1
	7:13 take away the accursed thing from **a** you.	7130
	7:21 When I saw **a** the spoils a goodly	871.1
	8: 9 lodged that night **a** the people.	8432+871.1
	8:33 the stranger, as he that was **born a** them;	249

A

Jos 8:35 that were conversant *a* them. 7130+871.1
9: 7 Peradventure ye dwell a us; 7130+871.1
9:16 and *that* they dwelt a them. 7130+871.1
9:22 far from you; when ye dwell a us? 7130+871.1
10: 1 with Israel, and were a them; 7130+871.1
13:13 the Maachathites dwell a 7130+871.1
13:22 the sword a them that were slain by them. 413
14: 3 he gave none inheritance a them. 8432+871.1
14:15 which *Arba was* a great man a 871.1
15:13 a part a the children of Judah, 8432+871.1
16: 9 a the inheritance of the children 8432+871.1
16:10 the Canaanites dwell a 7130+871.1
17: 4 us an inheritance a our brethren. 8432+871.1
17: 4 a the brethren of their father. 8432+871.1
17: 6 had an inheritance a his sons: 8432+871.1
17: 9 these cities of Ephraim *are* a 8432+871.1
18: 2 there remained a the children of Israel 871.1
18: 4 Give out *from* a you three men for 3807.1
18: 7 the Levites have no part a you; 7130+871.1
19:49 to Joshua the son of Nun a them: 8432+871.1
20: 4 him a place, that he may dwell a them. 5973
20: 9 stranger that sojourneth a them, 8432+871.1
22: 7 unto the *other* half thereof gave Joshua a 5973
22:14 of their fathers a the thousands of Israel. 3807.1
22:19 and take possession a us: 8432+871.1
22:31 we perceive that the Lord *is* a us, 8432+871.1
23: 7 That *ye* come not a these nations, these 871.1
23:12 *even* these that remain a you, and shall 854
24:17 a all the people through whom we 871.1
24:23 the strange gods which *are* a 7130+871.1

Jdg 1:16 and they went and dwelt a the people. 854
1:29 Canaanites dwelt in Gezer a them. 7130+871.1
1:30 the Canaanites dwelt a them, 7130+871.1
1:32 the Asherites dwelt a 7130+871.1
1:33 he dwelt a the Canaanites, 7130+871.1
3: 5 the children of Israel dwelt a 7130+871.1
5: 8 or spear seen a forty thousand in Israel? 871.1
5: 9 that offered themselves willingly a 871.1
5:13 dominion over the nobles *a* the people: NIH
5:14 after thee, Benjamin, a thy people; out of 871.1
5:16 Why abodest thou a the sheepfolds, 996
10:16 they put away the strange gods from a 7130
12: 4 Ye Gileadites *are* fugitives of Ephraim a 8432
12: 4 and a the Manassites. 8432+871.1
14: 3 *Is there* never a woman a the daughters 871.1
14: 3 of thy brethren, or a all my people, 871.1
18: 1 unto them a the tribes of Israel. 8432+871.1
18:25 Let not thy voice be heard a us, lest angry 5973
20:12 wickedness *is* this that is done a you? 871.1
20:16 A all this people *there were* seven 4480
21: 5 Who *is there* a all the tribes of Israel that 4480
21:12 they found a the inhabitants of 4480

Ru 2:15 Let her glean even a the sheaves, 996
4:10 dead be not cut off *from* a his brethren, 5973

1Sa 2: 8 to set *them* a princes, and to make them 5973
4: 3 that when it cometh a us, it may 7130+871.1
4:17 there hath been also a great slaughter a 871.1
6: 6 he had wrought wonderfully a them, 871.1
7: 3 strange gods and Ashtaroth from a you, 8432
9: 2 *there was* not a the children of Israel a 4480
9:22 them sit a the chiefest place a them 871.1
10:10 and he prophesied a them. 8432+871.1
10:11 he prophesied a the prophets, 5973
10:11 son of Kish? *Is* Saul also a the prophets? 871.1
10:12 a proverb, *Is* Saul also a the prophets? 871.1
10:22 Behold, he hath hid himself a the stuff. 413
10:23 when he stood a the people, he 8432+871.1
10:24 *there is* none like him a all the people? 871.1
14:15 host, in the field, and a all the people: 871.1
14:30 much greater slaughter a the Philistines? 871.1
14:34 Disperse yourselves a the people, 871.1
14:39 *there was* not *a* a man a all the people *that* 4480
15: 6 get you down *from* a the Amalekites, 8432
15: 6 So the Kenites departed from a 8432
15:33 so shall thy mother be childless a women. 4480
16: 1 for I have provided me a king a his sons. 871.1
17:12 the man went a men *for* an old man in 871.1
19:24 they say, *Is* Saul also a the prophets? 871.1
22:14 *so* faithful a all thy servants as David, 871.1
31: 9 the house of their idols, and a the people. 854

2Sa 6:19 he dealt a all the people, *even* among 3807.1
6:19 *even* a the whole multitude of Israel, 3807.1
15:31 Ahithophel *is* a the conspirators with 871.1
16:20 Give counsel a you what we shall do. 3807.1
17: 9 There is a slaughter a the people that 871.1
19:28 yet didst thou set thy servant a them that 871.1
22:50 a the heathen, and I will sing praises unto 871.1
23: 8 that sat in the seat, chief a the captains; NIH
23:18 the son of Zeruiah, *was* chief a three. NIH
23:18 slew them, and had the name a three. NIH
23:22 and had the name a three mighty *men.* 871.1

1Ki 3:13 that there shall not be any a the kings 871.1
5: 6 thou knowest that *there is* not a us any 871.1
6:13 I will dwell a the children of Israel, 8432+871.1
7:51 did he put a the treasures of the house of 871.1
8:53 For thou didst separate them *from* a all 4480
9: 7 be a proverb and a byword a all people: 871.1
11:20 household a the sons of Pharaoh. 8432+871.1
14: 7 Forasmuch as I exalted thee *from* a 8432
21: 9 fast, and set Naboth on high a the people: NIH
21:12 fast, and set Naboth on high a the people. NIH

2Ki 4:13 I dwell a mine own people. 8432+871.1
9: 2 make him arise up *from* a his brethren, 8432
11: 2 stale him *from* a the king's sons which 8432
17:25 therefore the Lord sent lions a them, 871.1

2Ki 17:26 therefore he hath sent lions a them, 871.1
18: 5 that after him was none like him a all 871.1
18:35 Who *are they* a all the gods of 871.1
20:15 there is nothing a my treasures that I 871.1
23: 9 unleavened bread a their brethren. 8432+871.1

1Ch 7: 5 their brethren a all the families of 3807.1
11:20 slew *them,* and had a name a the three. 871.1
11:24 and had the name a the three mighties. 871.1
11:25 he was honourable a the thirty, 4480
12: 1 they *were* a the mighty *men,* helpers of 871.1
12: 4 a mighty *man* a the thirty, and over 871.1
16: 8 make known his deeds a the people. 871.1
16:24 Declare his glory a the heathen; 871.1
16:24 his marvellous works a all nations. 871.1
16:31 let *men* say a the nations, The Lord 871.1
18:14 and justice a all his people. 871.1
21: 6 Benjamin counted he not a them: 8432+871.1
23: 6 David divided them *into* courses a 3807.1
24: 4 A the sons of Eleazar *there were* sixteen 3807.1
24: 4 eight a the sons of Ithamar according to 3807.1
26:12 A these *were* the divisions of the 3807.1
26:12 *even* the chief men, *having* wards one 3807.1
26:19 These *are* the divisions of the porters a 3807.1
26:19 sons of Kore, and a the sons of Merari. 3807.1
26:30 officers a them of Israel on *this* side 5921
26:31 A the Hebronites *was* Jerijah the chief, 3807.1
26:31 *even* the Hebronites, according to 3807.1
26:31 there were found a them mighty *men* of 871.1
27: 6 *who was* mighty a the thirty, and above NIH
28: 4 a the sons of my father he liked me to 871.1

2Ch 5: 1 he a the treasures of the house of God. 871.1
6: 5 a all the tribes of Israel to build a house 4480
7:13 or if I send pestilence a my people; 871.1
7:20 a proverb and a byword a all nations. 871.1
11:22 the chief, to be ruler a his brethren: 871.1
20:25 they found a them in abundance both 871.1
22:11 stole him *from* a the king's sons that were 8432
24:16 they buried him in the city of David a 5973
24:23 princes of the people *from* a the people, 4480
26: 6 cities about Ashdod, and a the Philistines. 871.1
28:15 the spoil clothed all *that* were naked a NIH
31:19 to give portions to all the males a 871.1
31:19 all that were reckoned by genealogies a 871.1
32:14 Who *was there* a all the gods of those 871.1
33:11 which took Manasseh a the thorns, 871.1
33:19 they *are* written a the sayings of the seers. 5921
35:13 divided them speedily a all the people. 3807.1
36:23 Who *is there* a you of all his people? 871.1

Ezr 1: 3 Who *is there* a you of all his people? 871.1
2:62 These sought their register a those that NIH
2:65 *there were* a them two hundred singing 3807.1
10:18 a the sons of the priests there were found 4480

Ne 1: 8 I will scatter you abroad a the nations: 871.1
4:11 till we come in the midst a them, 8432
5:17 besides those that came unto us *from* a 4480
6: 6 It *is* reported a the heathen, 871.1
7:64 These sought their register a those that NIH
9:17 of thy wonders that thou didst a them; 5973
10:34 we cast the lots a the priests, the Levites, NIH
11:17 Bakbukiah the second a his brethren, 4480
13:26 a many nations was there no king like 871.1

Est 1:19 let it be written a the laws of the Persians 871.1
3: 8 dispersed a the people in all the provinces 996
3: 9 *there was* great mourning a the Jews, 3807.1
9:21 To stablish *this* a them, that they should 5921
9:28 of Purim should not fail from a the Jews, 8432
10: 3 great a the Jews, and accepted of 3807.1

Job 1: 6 and Satan came also a them. 8432+871.1
2: 1 Satan came also a them to present 8432+871.1
2: 8 and he sat down a the ashes. 8432+871.1
15:19 and no stranger passed a them. 8432+871.1
17:10 for I cannot find *one* wise *man* a you. 871.1
18:19 shall neither have son nor nephew a his 871.1
28:10 He cutteth out rivers a the rocks; 871.1
30: 5 They were driven forth from a men, 1460
30: 7 A the bushes they brayed; under the 996
33:23 an interpreter, one a a thousand, 4480
34: 4 let us know a ourselves what *is* good. 996
36:14 in youth, and their life *is* a the unclean. 871.1
39:25 He saith a the trumpets, Ha, ha; 1767+871.1
41: 6 shall they part him a the merchants? 996
42:15 father gave them inheritance a 8432+871.1

Ps 9:11 in Zion: declare a the people his doings. 871.1
12: 1 for the faithful fail *from* a the children of 4480
18:49 a the heathen, and sing *praises* unto thy 871.1
21:10 their seed *from* a the children of men. 4480
22:18 They part my garments a them, 3807.1
22:28 and *he is* the governor a the nations. 871.1
31:11 I was a reproach a all mine enemies, 4480
31:11 especially a my neighbours, and a fear 3807.1
35:18 I will praise thee a much people. 871.1
44:11 and hast scattered us a the heathen. 871.1
44:14 Thou makest us a byword a the heathen, 871.1
44:14 a shaking of the head a the people. 871.1
45: 9 Kings' daughters *were* a thy honourable 871.1
45:12 *even* the rich a the people shall intreat thy NIH
46:10 I will be exalted a the heathen, I will be 871.1
55:15 *is* in their dwellings, *and* a them. 7130+871.1
57: 4 My soul *is* a lions: *and* I lie *even* 8432+871.1
57: 4 *and* I lie *even* a them that are set on fire, NIH
57: 9 I will praise thee, O Lord, a the people: 871.1
57: 9 I will sing unto thee a the nations. 871.1
67: 2 earth, thy saving health a all nations. 871.1
68:13 Though ye have lien a the pots, 996
68:17 Lord *is* a them, *as in* Sinai, in the holy 871.1

Ps 68:18 that the Lord God might dwell *a* them. NIH
68:25 a *them* were the damsels playing with 8432
74: 9 neither *is there* a us any that knoweth 854
77:14 thou hast declared thy strength a 871.1
78:45 He sent divers sorts of *flies* a them, 871.1
78:49 trouble, *by* sending evil angels *a* them. NIH
78:60 Shiloh, the tent *which* he placed a men; 871.1
79:10 let him be known a the heathen in our 871.1
80: 6 and our enemies laugh a themselves. 3807.1
82: 1 the mighty; he judgeth a the gods. 7130+871.1
86: 8 A the gods *there is* none like unto thee, 871.1
88: 5 Free a the dead, like the slain that lie in 871.1
89: 6 *who* a the sons of the mighty can be 871.1
94: 8 Understand, ye brutish a the people: 871.1
96: 3 Declare his glory a the heathen, 871.1
96: 3 the heathen, his wonders a all people. 871.1
96:10 Say a the heathen that the Lord 871.1
99: 6 Moses and Aaron a his priests, 871.1
99: 6 Samuel a them that call upon his name; 871.1
104:10 into the valleys, *which* run a the hills. 996
104:12 *which* sing a the branches. 996+4480
105: 1 make known his deeds a the people. 871.1
105:27 They shewed his signs a them, 871.1
105:37 *there was* not *one* feeble *person* a their 871.1
106:27 overthrow their seed also a the nations, 871.1
106:35 were mingled a the heathen, 871.1
106:47 God, and gather us *from* a the heathen, 4480
108: 3 I will praise thee, O Lord, a the people: 871.1
108: 3 will sing *praises* unto thee a the nations. 871.1
109:30 I will praise him a the multitude. 8432+871.1
110: 6 He shall judge a the heathen, he shall fill 871.1
126: 2 said they a the heathen, The Lord hath 871.1
136:11 brought out Israel from a them: for his 8432

Pr 1:14 Cast in thy lot a us; let us all have 8432+871.1
6:19 and he that soweth discord a brethren. 996
7: 7 beheld a the simple ones, I discerned 871.1
7: 7 the simple ones, I discerned a the youths, 871.1
14: 9 at sin: but a the righteous *there is* favour. 996
15:31 reproof of life abideth a the wise. 7130+871.1
17: 2 shall have part of the inheritance a 8432+871.1
23:28 and increaseth the transgressors a men. 871.1
27:22 in a mortar a wheat with a pestle, 8432+871.1
30:14 off the earth, and the needy from a men. NIH
30:30 A lion *which is* strongest a beasts, 871.1
31:23 when he sitteth a the elders of the land. 5973

Ecc 6: 1 under the sun, and it *is* common a men: 5921
7:28 one man a a thousand have I found; 4480
7:28 a woman a all those have I not found. 871.1
9: 3 This *is* an evil a all *things* that are done 871.1
9:17 more than the cry of him that ruleth a 871.1

SS 1: 8 thou know not, O thou fairest a women, 871.1
2: 2 As the lily a thorns, so *is* my love among 996
2: 2 thorns, so *is* my love a the daughters. 996
2: 3 As the apple tree a the trees of the wood, 871.1
2: 3 of the wood, so *is* my beloved a the sons. 996
2:16 and I *am* his: he feedeth a the lilies. 871.1
4: 2 twins, and none *is* barren a them. 871.1
4: 5 *that are* twins, which feed a the lilies. 871.1
5: 9 beloved, O thou fairest a women? 871.1
5:10 and ruddy, the chiefest a ten thousand. 4480
6: 1 beloved gone, O thou fairest a women? 871.1
6: 3 beloved *is* mine: he feedeth a the lilies. 871.1
6: 6 and *there is* not one barren a them. 871.1

Isa 4: 4 he shall judge a the nations, and shall 996
4: 3 every one that is written a the living 3807.1
8:15 many a them shall stumble, and fall, 871.1
8:16 testimony, seal the law a my disciples. 871.1
10:16 of hosts, send a his fat ones leanness; 871.1
12: 4 name, declare his doings a the people, 871.1
24:13 midst of the land a the people, 8432+871.1
29:19 poor a men shall rejoice in the Holy One NIH
33:14 Who a us shall dwell *with* the 3807.1
39: 4 there is nothing a my treasures that I 871.1
42:23 Who a you will give ear to this? *who* will 871.1
43: 9 who a them can declare this, and shew 871.1
43:12 when *there was* no strange god a you: 871.1
44: 4 they shall spring up *as* a the grass, 996+871.1
44:14 which he strengtheneth for himself a 871.1
48:14 which a them hath declared these 871.1
50:10 Who *is* a you that feareth the Lord, 871.1
51:18 *There is* none to guide her a all the sons 4480
57: 6 A the smooth *stones* of the stream *is* thy 871.1
61: 9 their seed shall be known a the Gentiles, 871.1
61: 9 and their offspring a the people: 8432+871.1
65: 4 Which remain a the graves, and lodge in 871.1
66:19 I will set a sign a them, and I will send 871.1
66:19 they shall declare my glory a the Gentiles. 871.1

Jer 3:19 How shall I put thee a the children, 871.1
4: 3 your fallow ground, and sow not a thorns. 413
5:26 For a my people are found wicked *men:* 871.1
6:15 therefore they shall fall a them that fall: 871.1
6:18 know, O congregation, what *is* a them. 871.1
6:27 *for* a tower *and* a fortress a my people, 871.1
8:12 therefore shall they fall a them that fall: 871.1
8:17 I will send serpents, cockatrices, a you, 871.1
9:16 I will scatter them also a the heathen, 871.1
10: 7 forasmuch as a all the wise *men* of 871.1
11: 9 conspiracy is found a the men of Judah, 871.1
11: 9 and a the inhabitants of Jerusalem. 871.1
12:14 pluck out the house of Judah a them. 8432
14:22 there *any* a the vanities of the Gentiles 871.1
18:13 Ask ye now a the heathen, who hath 871.1
24:10 the famine, and the pestilence, a them, 871.1
25:16 of the sword that I will send a them. 996
25:27 of the sword which I will send a you. 996

Jer	29:18 **a** all the nations whither I have driven	871.1
	29:32 he shall not have a man to dwell **a**	8432+871.1
	31: 7 and shout **a** the chief of the nations:	871.1
	37: 4 came in and went out **a** the people:	8432+871.1
	37:10 remained *but* wounded men **a** them,	871.1
	39:14 home: so he dwelt **a** the people.	8432+871.1
	40: 1 **a** all that were carried away	8432+871.1
	40: 5 and dwell with him **a** the people:	8432+871.1
	40: 6 dwelt with him **a** the people that	8432+871.1
	40:11 the Ammonites, and in Edom,	871.1
	41: 8 ten men were found **a** them that said	871.1
	41: 8 slew them not **a** their brethren.	871.1
	44: 8 a reproach **a** all the nations of the earth?	871.1
	46:18 Surely as Tabor *is* **a** the mountains,	871.1
	48:27 was he found **a** thieves? for since thou	871.1
	49:15 I will make thee small **a** the heathen,	871.1
	49:15 among the heathen, *and* despised **a** men.	871.1
	50: 2 Declare ye **a** the nations, and publish,	871.1
	50:23 how is Babylon become a desolation **a**	871.1
	50:46 and the cry is heard **a** the nations.	871.1
	51:27 blow the trumpet **a** the nations, prepare	871.1
	51:41 is Babylon become an astonishment **a**	871.1
La	1: 1 she *that was* great **a** the nations, *and*	871.1
	1: 1 *and* princess **a** the provinces, *how is* she	871.1
	1: 2 **a** all her lovers she hath none to comfort	4480
	1: 3 she dwelleth **a** the heathen, she findeth	871.1
	1:17 is as a menstruous *woman* **a** them.	996
	2: 9 king and her princes *are* **a** the Gentiles:	871.1
	4:15 they said **a** the heathen, They shall no	871.1
	4:20 Under his shadow we shall live **a**	871.1
Eze	1: 1 as I *was* **a** the captives by the river	8432+871.1
	1:13 it went up and down **a** the living creatures;	996
	2: 5 there hath been a prophet **a** them.	8432+871.1
	2: 6 thee, and thou dost dwell **a** scorpions:	413
	3:15 remained there astonished **a** them	8432+871.1
	3:25 and thou shalt not go out **a** them:	8432+871.1
	4:13 eat their defiled bread **a** the Gentiles,	871.1
	5:14 a reproach **a** the nations that *are* round	871.1
	6: 8 that shall escape the sword **a** the nations,	871.1
	6: 9 a the nations whither they shall be carried	871.1
	6:13 their slain *men* shall be **a** their	8432+871.1
	9: 2 a them *was* clothed *with* linen,	8432+871.1
	11: 1 **a** whom I saw Jaazaniah the son	8432+871.1
	11: 9 and will execute judgments **a** you.	871.1
	11:16 Although I have cast them far off **a**	871.1
	11:16 although I have scattered them **a**	871.1
	12:10 the house of Israel that *are* **a** them.	871.1
	12:12 the prince that *is* **a** them shall bear	8432+871.1
	12:15 when I shall scatter them **a** the nations,	871.1
	12:16 **a** the heathen whither they come;	871.1
	13:19 ye pollute me **a** my people for handfuls	413
	15: 2 *than* a branch which is **a** the trees of	871.1
	15: 6 As the vine tree **a** the trees of the forest,	871.1
	16:14 thy renown went forth **a** the heathen for	871.1
	18:18 did *that* which *is* not good **a** his	8432+871.1
	19: 2 she lay down **a** lions, she nourished her	996
	19: 2 her whelps **a** young lions.	8432+871.1
	19: 6 he went up and down **a** the lions,	8432+871.1
	19:11 her stature was exalted **a** the thick	996+5921
	20: 9 **a** whom they *were*, in whose sight	871.1
	20:23 that *I* would scatter them **a** the heathen,	871.1
	20:38 I will purge out **from a** you the rebels,	4480
	22:15 I will scatter thee **a** the heathen,	871.1
	22:26 and I am profaned **a** them.	8432+871.1
	22:30 I sought for a man **a** them, that *should*	4480
	23:10 she became famous **a** women; for they	3807.1
	25:10 may not be remembered **a** the nations.	871.1
	27:24 and made of cedar, **a** thy merchandise.	871.1
	27:36 The merchants **a** the people shall hiss **a**	871.1
	28:19 All they that know thee **a** the people shall	871.1
	28:25 the people **a** whom they are scattered,	871.1
	29:12 her cities **a** the cities that *are* laid	8432+871.1
	29:12 I will scatter the Egyptians **a** the nations,	871.1
	30:23 I will scatter the Egyptians **a** the nations,	871.1
	30:26 I will scatter the Egyptians **a** the nations,	871.1
	30:26 and disperse them **a** the countries;	871.1
	31: 3 and his top was **a** the thick boughs.	996
	31:10 shot up his top **a** the thick boughs,	413+996
	31:14 neither shoot up their top **a** the thick	413+996
	31:18 and in greatness **a** the trees of Eden?	871.1
	32: 9 when I shall bring thy destruction **a**	871.1
	32:21 strong **a** the mighty shall speak to him	NIH
	33: 6 and take *any* person **from a** them,	4480
	33:33 that a prophet hath been **a** them.	8432+871.1
	34:12 he is **a** his sheep *that are* scattered;	8432+871.1
	34:24 my servant David a prince **a** them;	8432+871.1
	36:19 I scattered them **a** the heathen,	871.1
	36:21 which the house of Israel had profaned **a**	871.1
	36:22 which ye have profaned **a** the heathen,	871.1
	36:23 which was profaned **a** the heathen,	871.1
	36:24 For I will take you **from a** the heathen,	4480
	36:30 more reproach of famine **a** the heathen.	871.1
	37:21 I *will* take the children of Israel **from a**	996
	39: 6 a them that dwell carelessly in the isles:	871.1
	39:21 I will set my glory **a** the heathen,	871.1
	39:28 caused them to be led into captivity **a**	413
	40:46 these *are* the sons of Zadok **a** the sons of	4480
	44: 9 any stranger that *is* **a** the children	8432+871.1
	47:22 to the strangers that sojourn **a** you:	8432+871.1
	47:22 which shall beget children **a** you:	8432+871.1
	47:22 in the country **a** the children of Israel;	871.1
	47:22 with you **a** the tribes of Israel.	8432+871.1
Da	1: 6 **a** these were of the children of Judah,	871.1
	1:19 **a** them all was found none like Daniel,	4480
	4:35 heaven, and *a* the inhabitants of the earth:	NIH

Da	7: 8 there came up **a** them another little horn,	997
	11:24 he shall scatter **a** them the prey,	3807.1
	11:33 they that understand **a** the people shall	3807.1
Hos	5: 9 **a** the tribes of Israel have I made known	871.1
	7: 7 none **a** them that calleth unto me.	871.1
	7: 8 he hath mixed himself **a** the people;	871.1
	8: 8 shall they be **a** the Gentiles as a vessel	871.1
	8:10 though they have hired **a** the nations,	871.1
	9:17 they shall be wanderers **a** the nations.	871.1
	10:14 shall a tumult arise **a** thy people,	871.1
	13:15 Though he be fruitful **a** *his* brethren,	996
Joel	2:17 wherefore should they say **a** the people,	871.1
	2:19 I will no more make you a reproach **a**	871.1
	2:25 my great army which I sent **a** you.	871.1
	3: 2 whom they have scattered **a** the nations,	871.1
	3: 9 Proclaim ye this **a** the Gentiles;	871.1
Am	1: 1 who was **a** the herdmen of Tekoa,	871.1
	2:16 he *that is* courageous **a** the mighty shall	871.1
	4:10 I have sent **a** you the pestilence after	871.1
	9: 9 I will sift the house of Israel **a** all nations,	871.1
Ob	1: 1 an ambassador is sent **a** the heathen,	871.1
	1: 2 I have made thee small **a** the heathen:	871.1
	1: 4 though *thou* set thy nest **a** the stars,	996
Mic	3:11 and say, *Is* not the LORD **a** us?	7130+871.1
	4: 3 he shall judge **a** many people,	996
	5: 2 *though thou* be little **a** the thousands of	871.1
	5: 8 the remnant of Jacob shall be **a**	871.1
	5: 8 people as a lion **a** the beasts of the forest,	871.1
	5: 8 as a young lion **a** the flocks of sheep:	871.1
	7: 2 *there is* none upright **a** men: they all lie	871.1
Na	3: 8 No, that was situate **a** the rivers,	996
Hab	1: 5 Behold ye **a** the heathen, and regard,	871.1
Zep	3:20 and a praise **a** all people of the earth,	871.1
Hag	2: 3 Who *is* left **a** you that saw this house in	871.1
	2: 5 so my spirit remaineth **a** you:	8432+871.1
Zec	1: 8 he stood **a** the myrtle trees that *were* in	996
	1:10 the man that stood **a** the myrtle trees	996
	1:11 of the LORD that stood **a** the myrtle trees,	996
	3: 7 I will give thee places to walk **a** these that	996
	7:14 I scattered them with a whirlwind **a** all	5921
	8:13 *that* as ye were a curse **a** the heathen,	871.1
	10: 9 I will sow them **a** the people: and they	871.1
	12: 6 of Judah like a hearth of fire **a** the wood,	871.1
	12: 8 he that is feeble **a** them at that day shall	871.1
	14:13 tumult from the LORD shall be **a** them;	871.1
Mal	1:10 Who *is there* even **a** you that would shut	871.1
	1:11 my name shall be great **a** the Gentiles;	871.1
	1:11 my name *shall be* great **a** the heathen,	871.1
	1:14 and my name *is* dreadful **a** the heathen.	871.1
Mt	2: 6 art not the least **a** the princes of Juda:	1722
	4:23 and all *manner of* disease **a** the people.	1722
	9:35 and every disease **a** the people.	1722
	11:11 **A** them that are born of women there	1722
	12:11 them, What man shall there be **a** you,	1537
	13: 7 And some fell **a** thorns; and the thorns	1909
	13:22 He also that received seed **a** the thorns	1519
	13:25 and sowed tares **a** the wheat,	303+3319
	13:32 it is the greatest **a** herbs, and becometh a	NIG
	13:49 and sever the wicked from **a** the just,	3319
	16: 7 And they reasoned **a** themselves, saying,	1722
	16: 8 why reason ye **a** yourselves, because	1722
	20:26 But it shall not be so **a** you:	1722
	20:26 but whosoever will be great **a** you, let him	1722
	20:27 whosoever will be chief **a** you, let him	1722
	21:38 they said **a** themselves, This is the heir;	1722
	23:11 But he that is greatest **a** you shall be your	NIG
	26: 5 *day*, lest there be an uproar **a** the people.	1722
	27:35 They parted my garments **a** them,	NIG
	27:56 **A** which was Mary Magdalene,	1722
	28:15 this saying is commonly reported **a**	3844
Mk	1:27 insomuch that *they* questioned **a**	4314
	4: 7 some fell **a** thorns, and the thorns grew	1519
	4:18 And these are they which are sown **a**	1519
	5: 3 Who had *his* dwelling **a** the tombs;	1722
	6: 4 **a** his own kin, and in his own house.	1722
	6:41 and the two fishes divided he **a** *them* all.	1722
	8:16 And they reasoned **a** themselves, saying,	4314
	8:19 When I brake the five loaves **a** five	1519
	8:20 And when the seven **a** four thousand,	1519
	9:33 What *was* it that ye disputed **a** yourselves	4314
	9:34 for by the way they had disputed **a**	4314
	10:26 saying **a** themselves, Who then can be	4314
	10:43 But so shall it not be **a** you:	1722
	10:43 whosoever will be great **a** you, shall be	1722
	13:10 the gospel must first be published **a** all	1519
	15:31 said **a** themselves with the scribes,	4314
	15:40 **a** whom was Mary Magdalene,	1722
	16: 3 they said **a** themselves, Who shall roll	4314
Lk	1: 1 which are most surely believed **a** us,	1722
	1:25 on *me*, to take away my reproach **a** men.	1722
	1:28 *is* with thee: blessed *art* thou **a** women.	1722
	1:42 Blessed *art* thou **a** women, and blessed *is*	1722
	2:44 and they sought him **a** *their* kinsfolk	1722
	4:36 and spake **a** themselves, saying, What **a**	4314
	7:16 That a great prophet is risen up **a** us;	1722
	7:28 **A** *those that are* born of women there is	1722
	8: 7 And some fell **a** thorns;	1722+3319
	8:14 And that which fell **a** thorns are they,	1519
	9:46 Then there arose a reasoning **a** them,	1722
	9:48 for he that is least **a** you all, the same shall	1722
	10: 3 I send you forth as lambs **a** wolves.	1722+3319
	10:30 and **fell a** thieves, which stripped him of	4045
	10:36 was neighbour unto him that fell **a**	1519
	19: 2 which was *the* **chief a** the **publicans**,	754
	19:39 And some of the Pharisees **from a**	575

Lk	20:14 they reasoned **a** themselves, saying, This	4314
	22:17 said, Take this, and divide *it* **a** yourselves:	1519
	22:23 And they began to inquire **a** themselves,	4314
	22:24 And there was also a strife **a** them, which	1722
	22:26 but he that is greatest **a** you, let him be as	1722
	22:27 but I am **a** you as he that serveth.	1722+3319
	22:37 And he was reckoned **a** the transgressors:	3326
	22:55 Peter sat down **a** them.	1722+3319
	24: 5 Why seek ye the living **a** the dead?	3326
	24:47 be preached in his name **a** all nations,	1519
Jn	1:14 and dwelt **a** us, (and we beheld his glory,	1722
	1:26 but there standeth one **a** you, whom ye	3319
	6: 9 fishes: but what are they **a** so many?	1519
	6:43 unto them, Murmur not **a** yourselves.	3326
	7:12 And there was much murmuring **a**	1722
	7:35 Then said the Jews **a** themselves,	4314
	7:35 will he go unto the **dispersed a**	1290
	7:43 So there was a division **a** the people	1722
	8: 7 unto them, He that is without sin **a** you,	NIG
	9:16 And there was a division **a** them.	1722
	10:19 again the Jews for these sayings.	1722
	11:54 walked no more openly **a** the Jews;	1722
	11:56 and spake **a** themselves, as they stood in	3326
	12:19 The Pharisees therefore said **a** themselves,	4314
	12:20 there were certain Greeks **a** them that	1537
	12:42 Nevertheless **a** the *chief* rulers also many	1537
	15:24 If I had not done **a** them the works which	1722
	16:17 Then said *some* of his disciples **a**	4314
	16:19 Do ye inquire **a** yourselves of that I said,	3326
	19:24 They said therefore **a** themselves, Let us	4314
	19:24 They **parted** my raiment **a** them,	1266
	21:23 then went this saying abroad **a**	1519
Ac	1:21 that the Lord Jesus went in and out **a** us,	1909
	2:22 a man approved of God **a** you by miracles	1519
	3:23 shall be destroyed **from a** the people.	1537
	4:12 other name under heaven given **a** men,	1722
	4:15 the council, they conferred **a** themselves,	4314
	4:17 But that it spread no further **a** the people,	1519
	4:34 Neither was there any **a** them that lacked:	1722
	5:12 and wonders wrought **a** the people;	1722
	5:34 had in reputation **a** all the people,	NIG
	6: 3 look ye out **a** you seven men of honest	1537
	6: 8 great wonders and miracles **a** the people.	1722
	10:22 of good report **a** all the nation of the Jews,	5259
	12:18 there was no small stir **a** the soldiers,	1722
	13:26 and whosoever **a** you feareth God,	1722
	14:14 and ran in **a** the people, crying out,	1519
	15: 7 a good while ago God made choice **a** us,	1722
	15:12 wonders God had wrought **a** the Gentiles	1722
	15:19 which **from a** the Gentiles are turned to	575
	15:22 and Silas, chief *men* **a** the brethren:	1722
	17:33 So Paul departed **from a** them.	3319
	17:34 **a** the which *was* Dionysius the Areopagite,	1722
	18:11 teaching the word of God **a** them.	1722
	20:25 **a** whom I have gone preaching	1722
	20:29 shall grievous wolves enter **in a** you,	1519
	20:32 to give you an inheritance **a** all them	1722
	21:19 wrought **a** the Gentiles by his ministry.	1722
	21:21 thou teachest all the Jews which are **a**	2596
	21:34 one *thing*, some another, **a** the multitude:	1722
	23:10 and to take him by force **from a** them,	3319
	24: 5 a mover of sedition **a** all the Jews	NIG
	24:21 one voice, that I cried standing **a** them,	1722
	25: 5 said he, which **a** you are able, go down	1722
	25: 6 when he had tarried **a** them more than	1722
	26: 3 and questions which are **a** the Jews:	2596
	26: 4 was at the first **a** mine own nation at	1722
	26:18 inheritance **a** them which are sanctified	1722
	27:22 shall be no loss of *any man's* life **a** you,	1537
	28: 4 they said **a** themselves, No doubt this	4314
	28:25 And when they agreed not **a** themselves,	4314
	28:29 and had great reasoning **a** themselves.	1722
Ro	1: 5 for obedience to the faith **a** all nations,	1722
	1: 6 **A** whom are ye also *the* called of Jesus	1722
	1:13 That I might have some fruit **a** you also,	1722
	1:13 among you also, even as **a** other Gentiles.	1722
	2:24 For the name of God is blasphemed **a**	1722
	12: 3 given unto me, to every *man* that is **a** you	1722
	15: 9 For this cause I will confess to thee **a**	1722
	16: 7 who are of note **a** the apostles,	1722
1Co	1:10 and *that* there be no divisions **a** you;	1722
	1:11 Chloe, that there are contentions **a** you.	1722
	2: 2 For I determined not to know any *thing* **a**	1722
	2: 6 we speak wisdom **a** them that are	1722
	3: 3 for whereas *there is* **a** you envying,	1722
	5: 1 If any *man* **a** you seemeth to be wise in	1722
	5: 1 commonly *that there is* fornication **a** you,	1722
	5: 2 this deed might be taken away from **a** you.	3319
	5:13 Therefore put away **from a** yourselves	1537
	6: 7 therefore there is utterly a fault **a** you,	1722
	11:18 I hear that there be divisions **a** you;	1722
	11:19 For there must be also heresies **a** you,	1722
	11:19 approved may be made manifest **a** you.	1722
	11:30 cause many *are* weak and sickly **a** you,	1722
	15:12 how say some **a** you that there is no	1722
2Co	1:19 who was preached **a** you by us,	1722
	6:17 Wherefore come out **from a** them,	3319
	10: 1 who in presence *am* base **a** you,	1722
	11: 6 we *have been* throughly made manifest **a**	1519
	11:26 perils in the sea, *in* perils **a** false brethren;	1722
	12:12 were wrought **a** you in all patience,	1722
	12:21 my God will humble *me* **a** you, and *that*	4314
Gal	1:16 that I might preach him **a** the heathen;	1722
	2: 2 *that* gospel which I preach **a** the Gentiles,	1722
	3: 1 been evidently set forth, crucified **a** you?	1722

A

Gal 3: 5 the Spirit, and worketh miracles **a** you, 1722
Eph 2: 3 **A** whom also we all had our conversation 1722
3: 8 that *I* should preach to the Gentiles 1722
Php 2:15 a whom ye shine as lights in the world; 1722
Col 1:27 of the glory of this mystery **a** the Gentiles; 1722
1Th 1: 5 ye know what manner of *men* we were **a** 1722
2: 7 But we were gentle **a** you, *even as* 1722+3319
2:10 unblameably we behaved ourselves **a** you NIG
5:12 to know them which labour **a** you, 1722
5:13 work's sake. *And* be at peace **a** yourselves. 1722
5:15 *is* good, both **a** yourselves, and to all *men*. 1519
2Th 1:10 our testimony **a** you was believed) 1909
3: 7 for we behaved not ourselves disorderly **a** 1722
3:11 among you which walk **a** you disorderly, 1722
2Ti 2: 2 *the things* that thou hast heard of me **a** 1223
Heb 5: 1 For every high priest taken **from a** men is 1537
Jas 1:26 If any *man* **a** you seem to be religious, 1722
4: 1 whence *come* wars and fightings **a** you? 1722
5:13 Is any **a** you afflicted? let him pray. Is any 1722
5:14 any sick **a** you? let him call for the elders 1722
1Pe 2:12 Having your conversation honest **a** 1722
4: 8 above all *things* have fervent charity **a** 1519
5: 1 The elders which are **a** you I exhort, 1722
5: 2 Feed the flock of God which is **a** you, 1722
2Pe 2: 1 But there were false prophets also **a** 1722
2: 1 even as there shall be false teachers **a** you, 1722
2: 8 (For *that* righteous *man* dwelling **a** them, 1722
3Jn 1: 9 who **loveth to have** the preeminence **a** 5383
Jude 1:15 to convince all *that are* ungodly **a** them of 4012
Rev 2:13 was slain **a** you, where Satan dwelleth. 3844
7:15 he that sitteth on the throne shall dwell **a** 1909
14: 4 These were redeemed **from a** men, *being* 575

AMONGST (59) [AMONG]

Ge 3: 8 God **a** the trees of the garden. 8432+871.1
23: 9 possession of a buryingplace **a** you. 8432+871.1
23:10 Ephron dwelt **a** the children of 8432+871.1
24: 3 of the Canaanites, **a** whom I dwell: 7130+871.1
30:33 *is* not speckled and spotted **a** the goats, 871.1
30:33 the goats, and brown **a** the sheep, 871.1
30:35 all the brown **a** the sheep, and gave 871.1
34:30 **a** the Canaanites and the Perizzites: 871.1
47: 6 knowest *any* man of activity **a** them, 871.1
Ex 9:20 He that feared the word of the LORD **a** 4480
10: 2 and my signs which I have done **a** them; 871.1
12:31 *and* get you forth from **a** my people, 8432
13:13 all the firstborn of man **a** thy children 871.1
17: 7 Is the LORD **a** us, or not? 7130+871.1
25: 8 that I may dwell **a** them, 8432+871.1
29:45 I will dwell **a** the children of Israel, 8432+871.1
29:46 of Egypt, that I may dwell **a** them: 8432+871.1
30:12 that there be no plague **a** them, when 871.1
31:14 soul shall be cut off from **a** his people. 7130
32:25 naked unto *their* shame a their enemies:) 871.1
34: 9 let my Lord, I pray thee, go **a** us; 7130+871.1
34:19 every firstling **a** thy cattle, *whether* ox or NIH
35: 5 Take ye from **a** you an offering unto 854
Lev 19:34 you shall be unto you as **one born a** you, 249
26:11 I will set my tabernacle **a** you: 8432+871.1
Nu 11:21 **a** whom I *am*, *are* six hundred 7130+871.1
15:29 him that is born **a** the children of 871.1
25: 7 he rose up from **a** the congregation, 8432
Dt 14: 6 *and* cheweth the cud **a** the beasts: 871.1
31:16 whither they go *to be* **a** them, 7130+871.1
31:17 because our God *is* not **a** us? 7130+871.1
Jos 7:11 they have put *it* even **a** their own stuff. 871.1
7:12 ye destroy the accursed from **a** you. 7130
23: 7 these nations, these that remain **a** you; 854
24: 5 to *that* which I did **a** them: 7130+871.1
Ru 2: 7 gather after the reapers **a** the sheaves: 871.1
1Ch 4:23 those that **dwelt a** plants and hedges: 3427
Job 34:37 he clappeth *his* hands **a** us, 996
Pr 23:20 Be not a winebibbers; amongst riotous 871.1
23:20 a riotous eaters of flesh: 871.1
Isa 5:27 *shall be* weary nor stumble **a** them; 871.1
29:14 I will proceed to do a marvellous work **a** NIH
33:14 who **a** us shall dwell *with* everlasting 3807.1
36:20 *are they* **a** all the gods of these lands, 871.1
41:28 **a** them, and *there was* no counseller. 4480
Jer 32:20 this day, and in Israel, and **a** *other* men; 871.1
Eze 35:11 I will make myself known **a** them, when 871.1
Mk 12: 7 But those husbandmen said **a** themselves, 4314
Lk 16:15 for that which is highly esteemed **a** men 1722
Jn 6:52 The Jews therefore strove **a** themselves, 4314
Ro 8:29 that he might be the firstborn **a** many 1722
11:17 wert graffed in **a** them, and with *them* 1722
1Co 5: 1 as is not so much as named **a** the Gentiles, 1722
6: 5 it so, that there is not a wise *man* **a** you? 1722
2Co 10:12 and **comparing** themselves **a** themselves, 4793
Eph 5: 3 let it not be once named **a** you, 1722
Col 4:16 And when *this* epistle is read **a** you, 3844
Jas 3: 6 so is the tongue **a** our members, that it 1722
3:13 and endued with knowledge **a** you? 1722

AMORITE (14) [AMORITES]

Ge 10:16 the Jebusite, and the **A**, and the Girgashite, 567
14:13 for he dwelt in the plain of Mamre the **A**, 567
48:22 which I took out of the hand of the **A** with 567
Ex 33: 2 the **A**, and the Hittite, and the Perizzite, 567
34:11 I drive out before thee the **A**, 567
Nu 32:39 and dispossessed the **A** which *was* in it. 567
Dt 2:24 I have given into thy hand Sihon the **A**, 567
Jos 9: 1 the Hittite, and the **A**, the Canaanite, 567
11: 3 *to* the **A**, and the Hittite, and the Perizzite, 567
1Ch 1:14 also, and the **A**, and the Girgashite, 567

Eze 16: 3 thy father *was* an **A**, and thy mother a 567
16:45 mother *was* a Hittite, and your father an **A**. 567
Am 2: 9 Yet destroyed I the **A** before them, 567
2:10 wilderness, to possess the land of the **A**. 567

AMORITES (73) [AMORITE]

Ge 14: 7 also the **A**, that dwelt in Hazezon-tamar. 567
15:16 for the iniquity of the **A** *is* not yet full. 567
15:21 the **A**, and the Canaanites, and 567
Ex 3: 8 the **A**, and the Perizzites, and the Hivites, 567
3:17 the **A**, and the Perizzites, and the Hivites, 567
13: 5 the **A**, and the Hivites, and the Jebusites, 567
23:23 bring thee in unto the **A**, and the Hittites, 567
Nu 13:29 the Hittites, and the Jebusites, and the **A**: 567
21:13 that cometh out of the coasts of the **A**: 567
21:13 border of Moab, between Moab and the **A**. 567
21:21 sent messengers unto Sihon king of the **A**, 567
21:25 Israel dwelt in all the cities of the **A**, 567
21:26 *was* the city of Sihon the king of the **A**, 567
21:29 into captivity unto Sihon king of the **A**. 567
21:31 Thus Israel dwelt in the land of the **A**. 567
21:32 and drove out the **A** that *were* there. 567
21:34 as thou didst unto Sihon king of the **A**, 567
22: 2 saw all that Israel had done to the **A**. 567
32:33 the kingdom of Sihon king of the **A**, and 567
Dt 1: 4 After he had slain Sihon the king of the **A**, 567
1: 7 go *to* the mount of the **A**, and unto all 567
1:19 saw *by* the way of the mountain of the **A**, 567
1:20 Ye are come unto the mountain of the **A**, 567
1:27 to deliver us into the hand of the **A**, 567
1:44 the **A**, which dwelt in that mountain, came 567
3: 2 him as thou didst unto Sihon king of the **A**, 567
3: 8 the **A** the land that *was* on *this* side Jordan, 567
3: 9 call Sirion; and the **A** call it Shenir;) 567
4:46 in the land of Sihon king of the **A**, 567
4:47 of Og king of Bashan, two kings of the **A**, 567
7: 1 the **A**, and the Canaanites, and the Perizzites, 567
20:17 the **A**, the Canaanites, and the Perizzites, 567
31: 4 kings of the **A**, and unto the land of them, 567
Jos 2:10 what you did unto the two kings of the **A**, 567
3:10 Girgashites, and the **A**, and the Jebusites. 567
5: 1 came to pass, when all the kings of the **A**, 567
7: 7 to deliver us into the hand of the **A**, 567
9:10 all that he did to the two kings of the **A**, 567
10: 5 Therefore the five kings of the **A**, the king 567
10: 6 for all the kings of the **A** that dwell in 567
10:12 up the **A** before the children of Israel, 567
12: 2 Sihon king of the **A**, who dwelt in 567
12: 8 the **A**, and the Canaanites, the Perizzites, 567
13: 4 unto Aphek, to the borders of the **A**: 567
13:10 all the cities of Sihon king of the **A**, 567
13:21 all the kingdom of Sihon king of the **A**, 567
24: 8 I brought you into the land of the **A**, 567
24:11 **A**, and the Perizzites, and the Canaanites, 567
24:12 before you, *even* the two kings of the **A**; 567
24:15 the gods of the **A**, in whose land ye dwell: 567
24:18 even the **A** which dwelt in the land: 567
Jdg 1:34 the **A** forced the children of Dan into 567
1:35 the **A** would dwell in mount Heres in 567
1:36 the coast of the **A** *was* from the going up 567
3: 5 **A**, and Perizzites, and Hivites, 567
6:10 fear not the gods of the **A**, in whose land 567
10: 8 the *other* side Jordan in the land of the **A**, 567
10:11 from the **A**, from the children of Ammon, 567
11:19 sent messengers unto Sihon king of the **A**, 567
11:21 so Israel possessed all the land of the **A**, 567
11:22 they possessed all the coasts of the **A**, 567
11:23 the **A** from before his people Israel, 567
1Sa 7:14 there was peace between Israel and the **A**. 567
2Sa 21: 2 of Israel, but of the remnant of the **A**; 567
1Ki 4:19 *in* the country of Sihon king of the **A**, 567
9:20 *And* all the people that were left of the **A**, 567
21:26 according to all *things* as did the **A**, 567
2Ki 21:11 done wickedly above all that the **A** did, 567
2Ch 8: 7 the **A**, and the Perizzites, and the Hivites, 567
Ezr 9: 1 the Moabites, the Egyptians, and the **A**. 567
Ne 9: 8 the **A**, and the Perizzites, and the Jebusites, 567
Ps 135:11 Sihon king of the **A**, and Og king of Bashan 567
136:19 Sihon king of the **A**: for his mercy 567

AMOS (8)

Am 1: 1 The words of **A**, who was among 5986
7: 8 LORD said unto me, **A**, what seest thou? 5986
7:10 **A** hath conspired against thee in the midst 5986
7:11 For thus **A** saith, Jeroboam shall die by 5986
7:12 Amaziah said unto **A**, O thou seer, go, 5986
7:14 answered **A**, and said to Amaziah, I *was* 5986
7: 8 he said, **A**, what seest thou? And I said, 5986
Lk 3:25 was *the son* of **A**, which was *the son* 301

AMOUNTING (1)

2Ch 3: 8 it with fine gold, *a* to six hundred talents. NIH

AMOZ (13)

2Ki 19: 2 to Esai the prophet the son of **A**. 531
19:20 the son of **A** sent to Hezekiah, 531
20: 1 prophet Isaiah the son of **A** came to him, 531
2Ch 26:22 did Isaiah the prophet, the son of **A**, write. 531
32:20 the prophet Isaiah the son of **A** prayed 531
32:32 son of **A**, *and* in the book of the kings of 531
Isa 1: 1 The vision of Isaiah the son of **A**, which he 531
1: 1 The word that Isaiah the son of **A** saw 531
13: 1 which Isaiah the son of **A** did see. 531
20: 2 spake the LORD by Isaiah the son of **A**, 531
37: 2 unto Isaiah the prophet the son of **A**. 531

Isa 37:21 Isaiah the son of **A** sent unto Hezekiah, 531
38: 1 Isaiah the prophet the son of **A** came unto 531

AMPHIPOLIS (1)

Ac 17: 1 Now when they had passed through **A** 295

AMPLIAS (1)

Ro 16: 8 Greet **A** my beloved in the Lord. 291

AMPLIATUS See AMPLIAS

AMRAM (14) [AMRAM'S, AMRAMITES]

Ex 6:18 **A**, and Izhar, and Hebron, and Uzziel: 6019
6:20 took him Jochebed his father's sister to 6019
6:20 years of the life of **A** *were* an hundred 6019
Nu 3:19 **A**, and Izehar, Hebron, and Uzziel. 6019
26:58 of the Korahites. And Kohath begat **A**. 6019
26:59 she bare unto **A** Aaron and Moses, 6019
1Ch 1:41 **A**, and Eshban, and Ithran, and Cheran. 2566
6: 2 **A**, Izhar, and Hebron, and Uzziel. 6019
6: 3 the children of **A**; Aaron, and Moses, 6019
6:18 the sons of Kohath *were*, **A**, and Izhar, 6019
23:12 **A**, Izhar, Hebron, and Uzziel, four. 6019
23:13 The sons of **A**; Aaron and Moses: 6019
24:20 sons of Levi *were these:* Of the sons of **A**; 6019
Ezr 10:34 Of the sons of Bani; Maadai, **A**, and Uel, 6019

AMRAM'S (1) [AMRAM]

Nu 26:59 the name of **A** wife *was* Jochebed, 6019

AMRAMITES (2) [AMRAM]

Nu 3:27 of Kohath *was* the family of the **A**, 6020
1Ch 26:23 the **A**, *and* the Izharites, the Hebronites, 6020

AMRAPHEL (2)

Ge 14: 1 it came to pass in the days of **A** king of 569
14: 9 **A** king of Shinar, and Arioch king of 569

AMZI (2)

1Ch 6:46 The son of **A**, the son of Bani, the son of 557
Ne 11:12 the son of Pelaliah, the son of **A**, the son 557

AN (1267) [A] See Index of Articles, Etc.

ANAB (2)

Jos 11:21 from **A**, and from all the mountains of 6024
15:50 And **A**, and Eshtemoh, and Anim, 6024

ANAH (12)

Ge 36: 2 Aholibamah the daughter of **A** the 6034
36:14 the daughter of **A**, daughter of Zibeon, 6034
36:18 *came* of Aholibamah the daughter of **A**, 6034
36:20 Lotan, and Shobal, and Zibeon, and **A**, 6034
36:24 the children of Zibeon; both Aiah, and **A**: 6034
36:24 this *was that* **A** that found the mules in 6034
36:25 the children of **A** *were* these; Dishon, 6034
36:25 and Aholibamah the daughter of **A**. 6034
36:29 duke Shobal, duke Zibeon, duke **A**, 6034
1Ch 1:38 **A**, and Dishon, and Ezer, and Dishan. 6034
1:40 And the sons of Zibeon; Aiah, and **A**. 6034
1:41 The sons of **A**; Dishon. And the sons of 6034

ANAHARATH (1)

Jos 19:19 And Hapharaim, and Shion, and **A**, 588

ANAIAH (2)

Ne 8: 4 **A**, and Urijah, and Hilkiah, and Maaseiah, 6043
10:22 Pelatiah, Hanan, **A**, 6043

ANAK (9) [ANAKIMS]

Nu 13:22 Sheshai, and Talmai, the children of **A**, 6061
13:28 moreover we saw the children of **A** there. 6061
13:33 the sons of **A**, *which come* of the giants: 6061
Dt 9: 2 Who can stand before the children of **A**! 6061
Jos 15:13 *even* the city of Arba the father of **A**, 6061
15:14 Caleb drove thence the three sons of **A**, 6061
15:14 Ahiman, and Talmai, the children of **A**, 6061
21:11 them the city of Arbah the father of **A**, 6061
Jdg 1:20 he expelled thence the three sons of **A**. 6061

ANAKIMS (9) [ANAK]

Dt 1:28 moreover we have seen the sons of the **A** 6062
2:10 people great, and many, and tall, as the **A**; 6062
2:11 also were accounted giants, as the **A**; 6062
2:21 great, and many, and tall, as the **A**; 6062
9: 2 great and tall, the children of the **A**, 6062
Jos 11:21 cut off the **A** from the mountains, 6062
11:22 There was none of the **A** left in the land 6062
14:12 for thou heardest in that day how the **A** 6062
14:15 *Arba was* a great man among the **A**. 6062

ANAKITE See ANAKIMS

ANAMIM (2)

Ge 10:13 and **A**, and Lehabim, and Naphtuhim, 6047
1Ch 1:11 and **A**, and Lehabim, and Naphtuhim, 6047

ANAMITES See ANAMIM

ANAMMELECH (1)

2Ki 17:31 children in fire to Adrammelech and **A**, 6048

ANAN (1)

Ne 10:26 And Ahijah, Hanan, **A**, 6052

ANANI (1)

1Ch 3:24 and Johanan, and Dalaiah, and **A**, seven. 6054

A

ANANIAH (2)
Ne	3:23	of Maaseiah the son of **A** by his house.	6055
	11:32	*And at* Anathoth, Nob, **A**,	6055

ANANIAS (11)
Ac	5: 1	But a certain man named **A**, with Sapphira	367
	5: 3	But Peter said, **A**, why hath Satan filled	367
	5: 5	And **A** hearing these words fell down,	367
	9:10	a certain disciple at Damascus, named **A**;	367
	9:10	and to him said the Lord in a vision, A.	367
	9:12	And hath seen in a vision a man named **A**	367
	9:13	Then **A** answered, Lord, I have heard by	367
	9:17	And **A** went his way, and entered into	367
	22:12	And one **A**, a devout man according to	367
	23: 2	and the high priest **A** commanded them	367
	24: 1	And after five days **A** the high priest	367

ANATH (2) [BETH-ANATH]
Jdg	3:31	after him was Shamgar the son of **A**,	6067
	5: 6	In the days of Shamgar the son of **A**, in	6067

ANATHEMA (1)
1Co	16:22	Lord Jesus Christ, let him be **a**, Maran-atha.	331

ANATHOTH (16)
Jos	21:18	**A** with her suburbs, and Almon with her	6068
1Ki	2:26	Get thee *to* **A**, unto thine own fields;	6068
1Ch	6:60	her suburbs, and **A** with her suburbs.	6068
	7: 8	and Abiah, and **A**, and Alameth.	6068
Ezr	2:23	The men of **A**, an hundred twenty	6068
Ne	7:27	The men of **A**, an hundred twenty	6068
	10:19	Hariph, **A**, Nebai,	6068
	11:32	*And at* **A**, Nob, Ananiah,	6068
Isa	10:30	*it* to be heard unto Laish, O poor **A**.	6068
Jer	1: 1	the priests that *were* in **A** in the land of	6068
	11:21	thus saith the Lord of the men of **A**,	6068
	11:23	for I will bring evil upon the men of **A**,	6068
	29:27	hast thou not reproved Jeremiah of **A**,	6069
	32: 7	saying, Buy thee my field that *is* in **A**:	6068
	32: 8	Buy my field, I pray thee, that *is* in **A**.	6068
	32: 9	*was* in **A**, and weighed him the money,	6068

ANATHOTHITE See ANETHOTHITE; ANETOTHITE

ANCESTORS (1)
Lev	26:45	sakes remember the covenant of their **a**,	7223

ANCHOR (1) [ANCHORS]
Heb	6:19	Which *hope* we have as an **a** of the soul,	45

ANCHORS (3) [ANCHOR]
Ac	27:29	they cast four **a** out of the stern,	45
	27:30	they would have cast **a** out of the foreship,	45
	27:40	And when they had taken up the **a**,	45

ANCIENT (26) [ANCIENTS]
Dt	33:15	for the chief things of the **a** mountains,	6924
Jdg		them away, *that* a river, the river Kishon.	6917
2Ki	19:25	*and of* a times that I have formed it?	6924
1Ch	4:22	Jashubi-lehem. And *these are* **a** things.	6267
Ezr		*who were* **a** *men* that had seen the first	2205
Job	12:12	With the **a** *is* wisdom; and *in* length of	3453
Ps	77: 5	the days of old, the years of **a times**.	5769
Pr	22:28	Remove not the **a** landmark, which thy	5769
Isa	3: 2	the prophet, and the prudent, and the **a**,	2205
	3: 5	behave himself proudly against the **a**,	2205
	9:15	The **a** and honourable, he *is* the head;	2205
	19:11	the son of the wise, the son of **a** kings?	6924
	23: 7	joyous *city,* whose antiquity *is* of **a** days?	6924
	37:26	*and of* a times, that I have formed it?	6924
	44: 7	for me, since I appointed the **a** people?	5769
	45:21	who hath declared this from **a** time?	6924
	46:10	from **a times** *the things* that are not *yet*	6924
	47: 6	upon the **a** hast thou very heavily laid thy	2205
	51: 9	as *in* the days, *in* the generations	6924
Jer	5:15	*is* a mighty nation, it *is* an **a**,	4480+5769
	18:15	to stumble in their ways *from* the **a** paths,	5769
Eze	9: 6	they began at the **a** men which *were*	2205
	36: 2	even the **a** high places are ours *in*	5769
Da	7: 9	were cast *down,* and the **A** of days did sit,	6268
	7:13	came to the **A** of days, and they brought	6268
	7:22	Until the **A** of days came,	6268

ANCIENTS (10) [ANCIENT]
1Sa	24:13	As saith the proverb of the **a**,	6931
Ps	119:100	I understand more than the **a**, because	2205
Isa	3:14	into judgment with the **a** of his people,	2205
	24:23	in Jerusalem, and before his **a** gloriously.	2205
Jer	19: 1	*take* of the **a** of the people, and of	2205
	19: 1	of the people, and of the **a** of the priests;	2205
Eze	7:26	from the priest, and counsel from the **a**.	2205
	8:11	men of the **a** of the house of Israel,	2205
	8:12	hast thou seen what the **a** of the house of	2205
	27: 9	The **a** of Gebal and the wise *men* thereof	2205

AND (51713) See Index of Articles, Etc.

ANDREW (13)
Mt	4:18	Simon called Peter, and **A** his brother,	406
	10: 2	who is called Peter, and **A** his brother;	406
Mk	1:16	**A** his brother casting a net into the sea:	406
	1:29	entered into the house of Simon and **A**,	406
	3:18	And **A**, and Philip, and Bartholomew,	406
	13: 3	James and John and **A** asked him privately,	406
Lk	6:14	and **A** his brother, James and John, Philip	406
Jn	1:40	and followed him, was **A**, Simon Peter's	406

Jn	1:44	was of Bethsaida, the city of **A** and Peter.	406
	6: 8	One of his disciples, **A**, Simon Peter's	406
	12:22	Philip cometh and telleth **A**:	406
	12:22	and again **A** and Philip tell Jesus.	406
Ac	1:13	and John, and **A**, Philip, and Thomas,	406

ANDRONICUS (1)
Ro	16: 7	Salute **A** and Junia, my kinsmen,	408

ANEM (1)
1Ch	6:73	her suburbs, and **A** with her suburbs:	6046

ANER (3)
Ge	14:13	brother of Eshcol, and brother of **A**:	6063
	14:24	went with me, **A**, Eshcol, and Mamre;	6063
1Ch	6:70	**A** with her suburbs, and Bileam with her	6063

ANETHOTHITE (1) [ANETOTHITE]
2Sa	23:27	Abiezer the **A**, Mebunnai the Hushathite,	6069

ANETOTHITE (1) [ANETHOTHITE]
1Ch	27:12	for the ninth month *was* Abiezer the **A**,	6069

ANGEL (201) [ANGEL'S, ANGELS, ANGELS', ARCHANGEL]
Ge	16: 7	the **a** of the Lord found her by a	4397
	16: 9	the **a** of the Lord said unto her,	4397
	16:10	the **a** of the Lord said unto her, I will	4397
	16:11	the **a** of the Lord said unto her, Behold,	4397
	21:17	**a** of God called to Hagar out of heaven,	4397
	22:11	the **a** of the Lord called unto him out of	4397
	22:15	the **a** of the Lord called unto Abraham	4397
	24: 7	he shall send his **a** before thee,	4397
	24:40	will send his **a** with thee, and prosper thy	4397
	31:11	the **a** of God spake unto me in a dream,	4397
	48:16	The **A** which redeemed me from all evil,	4397
Ex	3: 2	the **a** of the Lord appeared unto him in a	4397
	14:19	of God, which went before the camp	4397
	23:20	Behold, I send an **A** before thee, to keep	4397
	23:23	For mine **A** shall go before thee,	4397
	32:34	behold, mine **A** shall go before thee:	4397
	33: 2	I will send an **a** before thee; and I will	4397
Nu	20:16	an **a**, and hath brought us forth out of	4397
	22:22	the **a** of the Lord stood in the way for an	4397
	22:23	the ass saw the **a** of the Lord standing in	4397
	22:24	the **a** of the Lord stood in a path of	4397
	22:25	when the ass saw the **a** of the Lord, she	4397
	22:26	the **a** of the Lord went further,	4397
	22:27	when the ass saw the **a** of the Lord, she	4397
	22:31	he saw the **a** of the Lord standing in	4397
	22:32	the **a** of the Lord said unto him,	4397
	22:34	Balaam said unto the **a** of the Lord,	4397
	22:35	the **a** of the Lord said unto Balaam,	4397
Jdg	2: 1	an **a** of the Lord came up from Gilgal to	4397
	2: 4	when the **a** of the Lord spake these	4397
	5:23	Curse ye Meroz, said the **a** of the Lord,	4397
	6:11	there came an **a** of the Lord,	4397
	6:12	the **a** of the Lord appeared unto him,	4397
	6:20	the **a** of God said unto him, Take the flesh	4397
	6:21	the **a** of the Lord put forth the end of	4397
	6:21	the unleavened *cakes.* Then the **a** of	4397
	6:22	Gideon perceived that he *was* an **a** of	4397
	6:22	I have seen an **a** of the Lord face to face.	4397
	13: 3	the **a** of the Lord appeared unto	4397
	13: 6	*was* like the countenance of an **a** of God,	4397
	13: 9	the **a** of God came again unto the woman	4397
	13:13	the **a** of the Lord said unto Manoah,	4397
	13:15	Manoah said unto the **a** of the Lord,	4397
	13:16	the **a** of the Lord said unto Manoah,	4397
	13:16	Manoah knew not that he *was* an **a** of	4397
	13:17	Manoah said unto the **a** of the Lord,	4397
	13:18	the **a** of the Lord said unto him, Why	4397
	13:19	*the* **a** did wondrously; and Manoah	NIH
	13:20	that the **a** of the Lord ascended in	4397
	13:21	the **a** of the Lord did no more appear to	4397
	13:21	Manoah knew that he *was* an **a** of	4397
1Sa	29: 9	thou *art* good in my sight, as an **a** of God:	4397
2Sa	14:17	as an **a** of God, so *is* my lord the king to	4397
	14:20	according to the wisdom of an **a** of God,	4397
	19:27	but my lord the king *is* as an **a** of God:	4397
	24:16	when the **a** stretched out his hand *upon*	4397
	24:16	said to the **a** that destroyed the people,	4397
	24:16	the **a** of the Lord was by	4397
	24:17	when he saw the **a** that smote the people,	4397
1Ki	13:18	An **a** spake unto me by the word of	4397
	19: 5	an **a** touched him, and said unto him,	4397
	19: 7	the **a** of the Lord came again the second	4397
2Ki	1: 3	the **a** of the Lord said to Elijah	4397
	1:15	the **a** of the Lord said unto Elijah,	4397
	19:35	that the **a** of the Lord went out,	4397
1Ch	21:12	the **a** of the Lord destroying throughout	4397
	21:15	God sent an **a** unto Jerusalem to destroy	4397
	21:15	said to the **a** that destroyed, *It is* enough,	4397
	21:15	the **a** of the Lord stood by	4397
	21:16	saw the **a** of the Lord stand between	4397
	21:18	the **a** of the Lord commanded Gad to	4397
	21:20	Ornan turned back, and saw the **a**;	4397
	21:27	the Lord commanded the **a**; and he put	4397
	21:30	of the sword of the **a** of the Lord.	4397
2Ch	32:21	the Lord sent an **a**, which cut off all	4397
Ps	34: 7	The **a** of the Lord encampeth round	4397
	35: 5	and let the **a** of the Lord chase *them.*	4397
	35: 6	and let the **a** of the Lord persecute them.	4397
Ecc	5: 6	neither say thou before the **a**, that it *was*	
Isa	37:36	the **a** of the Lord went forth,	4397

Isa	63: 9	and the **a** of his presence saved them:	4397
Da	3:28	who hath sent his **a**, and delivered his	4398
	6:22	My God hath sent his **a**, and hath shut	4398
Hos	12: 4	he had power over *the* **a**, and prevailed:	4397
Zec	1: 9	the **a** that talked with me said unto me,	4397
	1:11	they answered the **a** of the Lord that	4397
	1:12	the **a** of the Lord answered and said,	4397
	1:13	the Lord answered the **a** that talked with	4397
	1:14	the **a** that communed with me said	4397
	1:19	I said unto the **a** that talked with me,	4397
	2: 3	the **a** that talked with me went forth,	4397
	2: 3	and another **a** went out to meet him,	4397
	3: 1	priest standing before the **a** of the Lord,	4397
	3: 3	filthy garments, and stood before the **a**.	4397
	3: 5	And the **a** of the Lord stood *by.*	4397
	3: 6	the **a** of the Lord protested unto Joshua,	4397
	4: 1	the **a** that talked with me came again,	4397
	4: 4	and spake to the **a** that talked with me,	4397
	4: 5	the **a** that talked with me answered	4397
	5: 5	the **a** that talked with me went forth,	4397
	5:10	said I to the **a** that talked with me,	4397
	6: 4	and said unto the **a** that talked with me,	4397
	6: 5	the **a** answered and said unto me, These	4397
	12: 8	as the **a** of the Lord before them.	4397
Mt	1:20	*the* **a** of the Lord appeared unto him in a	32
	1:24	did as the **a** of the Lord had bidden him,	32
	2:13	*the* **a** of the Lord appeareth to Joseph in a	32
	2:19	an **a** of the Lord appeareth in a dream to	32
	28: 2	*the* **a** of the Lord descended from heaven,	32
	28: 5	the **a** answered and said unto the women,	32
Lk	1:11	there appeared unto him an **a** of the Lord	32
	1:13	the **a** said unto him, Fear not, Zacharias:	32
	1:18	Zacharias said unto the **a**, Whereby shall	32
	1:19	And the **a** answering said unto him, I am	32
	1:26	in the sixth month the **a** Gabriel was sent	32
	1:28	And the **a** came in unto her, and said, Hail,	32
	1:30	And the **a** said unto her, Fear not, Mary:	32
	1:34	said Mary unto the **a**, How shall this be,	32
	1:35	And the **a** answered and said unto her,	32
	1:38	to thy word. And the **a** departed from her.	32
	2: 9	*the* **a** of the Lord came upon them,	32
	2:10	And the **a** said unto them, Fear not:	32
	2:13	And suddenly there was with the **a** a	32
	2:21	named of the **a** before he was conceived in	32
	22:43	And there appeared an **a** unto him from	32
Jn	5: 4	For an **a** went down at a *certain* season into	32
	12:29	it thundered: others said, An **a** spake to him.	32
Ac	5:19	But the **a** of the Lord by night opened	32
	6:15	saw his face as it had been the face of an **a**.	32
	7:30	an **a** of the Lord in a flame of fire in a bush.	32
	7:35	a deliverer by the hand of the **a** which	32
	7:38	the **a** which spake to him in the mount Sina,	32
	8:26	And *the* **a** of the Lord spake unto Philip,	32
	10: 3	an **a** of God coming in to him,	32
	10: 7	when the **a** which spake unto Cornelius	32
	10:22	warned from God by a holy **a** to send for	32
	11:13	he shewed us how he had seen an **a** in his	32
	12: 7	*the* **a** of the Lord came upon *him,* and	32
	12: 8	And the **a** said unto him, Gird thyself,	32
	12: 9	that it was true which was done by the **a**;	32
	12:10	and forthwith the **a** departed from him.	32
	12:11	that the Lord hath sent his **a**,	32
	12:15	it was *even* so. Then said they, It is his **a**.	32
	12:23	And immediately *the* **a** of the Lord smote	32
	23: 8	there is no resurrection, neither **a** nor spirit:	32
	23: 9	but if a spirit or an **a** hath spoken to him,	32
	27:23	there stood by me this night *the* **a** of God,	32
2Co	11:14	for Satan himself is transformed into an **a** of	32
Gal	1: 8	But though we, or an **a** from heaven,	32
	4:14	but received me as an **a** of God, *even* as	32
Rev	1: 1	signified it by his **a** unto his servant John:	32
	2: 1	Unto the **a** of the church of Ephesus write;	32
	2: 8	unto the **a** of the church in Smyrna write;	32
	2:12	to the **a** of the church in Pergamos write;	32
	2:18	And unto the **a** of the church in Thyatira	32
	3: 1	unto the **a** of the church in Sardis write;	32
	3: 7	And to the **a** of the church in Philadelphia	32
	3:14	And unto the **a** of the church of	32
	5: 2	I saw a strong **a** proclaiming with a loud	32
	7: 2	I saw another **a** ascending from the east,	32
	8: 3	And another **a** came and stood at the altar,	32
	8: 5	And the **a** took the censer, and filled it with	32
	8: 7	first **a** sounded, and there followed hail	NIG
	8: 8	And the second **a** sounded, and as *it were* a	32
	8:10	the third **a** sounded, and there fell a great	32
	8:12	the fourth **a** sounded, and the third *part*	32
	8:13	an **a** flying through the midst of heaven,	32
	9: 1	And the fifth **a** sounded, and I saw a star fall	32
	9:11	*which is* the **a** of the bottomless *pit,* whose	32
	9:13	And the sixth **a** sounded, and I heard a voice	32
	9:14	Saying to the sixth **a** which had the trumpet,	32
	10: 1	I saw another mighty **a** come down from	32
	10: 5	And the **a** which I saw stand upon the sea	32
	10: 7	in the days of the voice of the seventh **a**,	32
	10: 8	hand of the **a** which standeth upon the sea	32
	10: 9	And I went unto the **a**, and said unto him,	32
	11: 1	and the **a** stood, saying, Rise, and measure	32
	11:15	And the seventh **a** sounded; and there were	32
	14: 6	And I saw another **a** fly in the midst of	32
	14: 8	And there followed another **a**, saying,	32
	14: 9	And *the* third **a** followed them, saying with	32
	14:15	And another **a** came out of the temple,	32
	14:17	And another **a** came out of the temple,	32
	14:18	And another **a** came out from the altar,	32
	14:19	And the **a** thrust in his sickle into the earth,	32

A

| Rev | 16: | 3 And the second **a** poured out his vial upon | 32 |

Rev 16: 3 And the second **a** poured out his vial upon 32
16: 4 And the third **a** poured out his vial upon 32
16: 5 I heard the **a** of the waters say, Thou art 32
16: 8 And the fourth **a** poured out his vial upon 32
16:10 And the fifth **a** poured out his vial upon 32
16:12 And the sixth **a** poured out his vial upon 32
16:17 And the seventh **a** poured out his vial into 32
17: 7 the **a** said unto me, Wherefore didst thou 32
18: 1 And after these *things* I saw another **a** come 32
18:21 And a mighty **a** took up a stone like a great 32
19:17 And I saw an **a** standing in the sun; 32
20: 1 And I saw an **a** come down from heaven, 32
21:17 *to* the measure of a man, that is, of the **a**. 32
22: 6 the Lord God of the holy prophets sent his **a** 32
22: 8 fell down to worship before the feet of the **a** 32
22:16 I Jesus have sent mine **a** to testify unto you 32

ANGEL'S (2) [ANGEL]

Rev 8: 4 ascended up before God out of the **a** hand. 32
10:10 And I took the little book out of the **a** hand, 32

ANGELS (93) [ANGEL]

Ge 19: 1 there came two **a** to Sodom at even; 4397
19:15 the **a** hastened Lot, saying, Arise, take thy 4397
28:12 behold the **a** of God ascending 4397
32: 1 on his way, and the **a** of God met him. 4397
Job 4:18 and his **a** he charged with folly: 4397
Ps 8: 5 hast made him a little lower than the **a**, 430
68:17 twenty thousand, *even* thousands of **a**: 8136
78:49 trouble, *by* sending evil **a** *among them*. 4397
91:11 For he shall give his **a** charge over thee, 4397
103:20 Bless the Lord, ye his **a**, that excel in 4397
104: 4 Who maketh his **a** spirits; his ministers a 4397
148: 2 Praise ye him, all his **a**: praise ye him, 4397
Mt 4: 6 He shall give his **a** charge concerning thee: 32
4:11 behold, **a** came and ministered unto him. 32
13:39 end of the world; and the reapers are *the* **a**. 32
13:41 The Son of man shall send forth his **a**, 32
13:49 the **a** shall come forth, and sever the wicked 32
16:27 come in the glory of his Father with his **a** 32
18:10 That in heaven their **a** do always behold 32
22:30 but are as *the* **a** of God in heaven. 32
24:31 And he shall send his **a** with a great sound 32
24:36 not *the* **a** of heaven, but my Father only. 32
25:31 all the holy **a** with him, then shall he sit 32
25:41 prepared for the devil and his **a**: 32
26:53 give me more than twelve legions of **a**? 32
Mk 1:13 wild beasts; and the **a** ministered unto him. 32
8:38 in the glory of his Father with the holy **a**. 32
12:25 but are as *the* **a** which are in heaven. 32
13:27 then shall he send his **a**, and shall gather 32
13:32 the **a** which are in heaven, neither the Son, 32
Lk 2:15 as the **a** were gone away from them into 32
4:10 He shall give his **a** charge over thee, to keep 32
9:26 and *in his* Father's, and of the holy **a**. 32
12: 8 Son of man also confess before the **a** of God: 32
12: 9 men shall be denied before the **a** of God. 32
15:10 there is joy in the presence of the **a** of God 32
16:22 was carried by the **a** into Abraham's bosom: 32
20:36 for they are **equal unto** the **a**; and are 2465
24:23 saying, that *they* had also seen a vision of **a**, 32
Jn 1:51 and the **a** of God ascending 32
Ac 20:12 And seeth two **a** in white sitting, the one at 32
7:53 have received the law by the disposition of **a**, 32
Ro 8:38 nor life, nor **a**, nor principalities, nor powers, 32
1Co 4: 9 unto the world, and to **a**, and to men. 32
6: 3 Know ye not that we shall judge **a**? 32
11:10 to have power on *her* head because of the **a**. 32
13: 1 I speak with the tongues of men and of **a**, 32
Gal 3:19 *it was* ordained by **a** in the hand of a 32
Col 2:18 in a voluntary humility and worshipping of **a**, 32
2Th 1: 7 be revealed from heaven with his mighty **a**, 32
1Ti 3:16 justified in the Spirit, seen of **a**, preached 32
5:21 and the Lord Jesus Christ, and the elect **a**, 32
Heb 1: 4 Being made so much better than the **a**, as he 32
1: 5 For unto which of the **a** said he at any time, 32
1: 6 And let all the **a** of God worship him 32
1: 7 of the **a** he saith, Who maketh his angels 32
1: 7 Who maketh his **a** spirits, and his ministers 32
1:13 But to which of the **a** said he at any time, 32
2: 2 For if the word spoken by **a** was stedfast, 32
2: 5 For unto *the* **a** hath he not put in subjection 32
2: 7 Thou madest him a little lower than the **a**; 32
2: 9 who was made a little lower than the **a**, 32
2:16 verily he took not on *him the nature of* **a**; 32
12:22 and to an innumerable company of **a**, 32
13: 2 for thereby some have entertained **a** 32
1Pe 1:12 which *things the* **a** desire to look into. 32
3:22 **a** and authorities and powers being made 32
2Pe 2: 4 For if God spared not the **a** that sinned, 32
2:11 Whereas **a**, which are greater in power 32
Jude 1: 6 And the **a** which kept not their first estate, 32
Rev 1:20 The seven stars are the **a** of the seven 32
3: 5 his name before my Father, and before his **a**. 32
5:11 I heard the voice of many **a** round about 32
7: 1 And after these *things* I saw four **a** standing 32
7: 2 and he cried with a loud voice to the four **a**, 32
7:11 And all the **a** stood round about the throne, 32
8: 2 And I saw the seven **a** which stood before 32
8: 6 And the seven **a** which had the seven 32
8:13 other voices of the trumpet of the three **a**, 32
9:14 Loose the four **a** which are bound in the 32
9:15 And the four **a** were loosed, which were 32
12: 7 Michael and his **a** fought against the dragon; 32
12: 7 the dragon; and the dragon fought and his **a**, 32

Rev 12: 9 the earth, and his **a** were cast *out* with him. 32
14:10 and brimstone in the presence of the holy **a**, 32
15: 1 seven **a** having the seven last plagues; 32
15: 6 And the seven **a** came out of the temple, 32
15: 7 a seven golden vials full of the wrath of God, 32
15: 8 till the seven plagues of the seven **a** were 32
16: 1 out of the temple saying to the seven **a**, 32
17: 1 And there came one of the seven **a** which 32
21: 9 And there came unto me one of the seven **a** 32
21:12 at the gates twelve **a**, and names written 32

ANGELS' (1) [ANGEL]

Ps 78:25 Man did eat **a** food: he sent them meat to 47

ANGER (234) [ANGERED, ANGRY]

Ge 27:45 Until thy brother's **a** turn away from thee, 639
30: 2 Jacob's **a** was kindled against Rachel: 639
44:18 let not thine **a** burn against thy servant: 639
49: 6 for in their **a** they slew a man, and in their 639
49: 7 Cursed *be* their **a**, for *it was* fierce; 639
Ex 4:14 he went out from Pharaoh in a great **a**. 639
11: 8 he went out from Pharaoh in a great **a**. 639
32:19 Moses' **a** waxed hot, and he cast the tables 639
32:22 Let not the **a** of my lord wax hot: 639
Nu 11: 1 the Lord heard *it;* and his **a** was kindled; 639
11:10 and the **a** of the Lord was kindled greatly; 639
12: 9 the **a** of the Lord was kindled against 639
22:22 God's **a** was kindled because he went: 639
22:27 Balaam's **a** was kindled, and he smote 639
24: 10 Balak's **a** was kindled against Balaam, 639
25: 3 the **a** of the Lord was kindled against Israel, 639
25: 4 that the fierce **a** of the Lord may be 639
32:10 the Lord's **a** was kindled the same time, 639
32:13 the Lord's **a** was kindled against Israel, 639
32:14 to augment yet the fierce **a** of the Lord 639
Dt 4:25 the Lord thy God, to **provoke** him to **a**: 3707
6:15 lest the **a** of the Lord thy God be kindled 639
7: 4 will the **a** of the Lord be kindled against 639
9:18 sight of the Lord, to **provoke** him to **a**. 3707
9:19 I was afraid of the **a** and hot displeasure, 639
13:17 may turn from the fierceness of his **a**, 639
29:20 then the **a** of the Lord and his jealousy 639
29:23 which the Lord overthrew in his **a**, 639
29:24 what *meaneth* the heat of this great **a**? 639
29:27 the **a** of the Lord was kindled against this 639
29:28 Lord rooted them out of their land in **a**, 639
31:17 my **a** shall be kindled against them in that 639
31:29 to **provoke** him to **a** through the work of 3707
32:16 abominations **provoked** they him to **a**. 3707
32:21 they have **provoked** me to **a** with their 3707
32:21 I will **provoke** them to **a** with a foolish 3707
32:22 a fire is kindled in my **a**, and shall burn 639
Jos 7: 1 the **a** of the Lord was kindled against 639
7:26 Lord turned from the fierceness of his **a**. 639
23:16 shall the **a** of the Lord be kindled against 639
Jdg 2:12 unto them, and **provoked** the Lord to **a**. 3707
2:14 the **a** of the Lord was hot against Israel, 639
2:20 the **a** of the Lord was hot against Israel; 639
3: 8 Therefore the **a** of the Lord was hot 639
6:39 Let not thine **a** be hot against me, and I 639
8: 3 their **a** was abated toward him, when he 7307
9:30 of Gaal the son of Ebed, his **a** was kindled. 639
10: 7 the **a** of the Lord was hot against Israel, 639
14:19 his **a** was kindled, and he went up *to* his 639
1Sa 11: 6 tidings, and his **a** was kindled greatly. 639
17:28 and Eliab's **a** was kindled against David, 639
20:30 Saul's **a** was kindled against Jonathan, 639
20:34 Jonathan arose from the table in fierce **a**, 639
2Sa 6: 7 the **a** of the Lord was kindled against 639
12: 5 David's **a** was greatly kindled against 639
24: 1 again the **a** of the Lord was kindled 639
1Ki 14: 9 to **provoke** me to **a**, and hast cast me 3707
14:15 their groves, **provoking** the Lord to **a**. 3707
15:30 **provoked** the Lord God of Israel to **a**. 3707
16: 2 to sin, to **provoke** me to **a** with their sins; 3707
16: 7 in **provoking** him to **a** with the work of 3707
16:13 **provoking** the Lord God of Israel to **a** 3707
16:26 to **provoke** the Lord God of Israel **to a** 3707
16:33 **provoke** the Lord God of Israel to **a** 3707
21:22 wherewith thou hast **provoked** *me* to **a**, 3707
22:53 **provoked** to **a** the Lord God of Israel, 3707
2Ki 13: 3 the **a** of the Lord was kindled against 639
17:11 wicked things to **provoke** the Lord to **a**: 3707
17:17 sight of the Lord, to **provoke** him to **a**. 3707
21: 6 sight of the Lord, to **provoke** *him* to **a**. 3707
21:15 have **provoked** me to **a**, since the day 3707
22:17 that they might **provoke** me to **a** with all 3707
23:19 had made to **provoke** the Lord to **a**, 3707
23:26 his **a** was kindled against Judah, 639
24:20 For through the **a** of the Lord it came to 639
1Ch 13:10 the **a** of the Lord was kindled against 639
2Ch 25:10 to go home *again:* wherefore their **a** was 639
25:10 and they returned home in great **a**. 639
25:15 Wherefore the **a** of the Lord was kindled 639
28:25 **provoked** to **a** the Lord God of his 3707
33: 6 sight of the Lord, to **provoke** him to **a**. 3707
34:25 that *they* might **provoke** me to **a** with all 3707
Ne 4: 5 for they have **provoked** *thee* to **a** before 3707
9:17 slow to **a**, and of great kindness, 639
Est 1:12 king very wroth, and his **a** burned in him. 2534
Job 9: 5 which overturneth them in his **a**. 639
9:13 *If* God will not withdraw his **a**, the proud 639
18: 4 He teareth himself in his **a**: shall the earth 639
21:17 *God* distributeth sorrows in his **a**. 639
35:15 *it is* not *so,* he hath visited *in* his **a**; 639

Ps 6: 1 O Lord, rebuke me not in thine **a**, 639
7: 6 Arise, O Lord, in thine **a**, lift up thyself 639
21: 9 as a fiery oven in the time of thine **a**: 6440
27: 9 from me; put not thy servant away in **a**: 639
30: 5 For his **a** *endureth but* a moment; in his 639
37: 8 Cease from **a**, and forsake wrath: fret not 639
38: 3 soundness in my flesh because of thine **a**; 2195
56: 7 in *thine* **a** cast down the people, O God. 639
69:24 and let thy wrathful **a** take hold of them. 639
74: 1 *why* doth thine **a** smoke against the sheep 639
77: 9 hath he in **a** shut up his tender mercies? 639
78:21 and **a** also came up against Israel; 639
78:38 many a time turned he his **a** away, 639
78:49 He cast upon them the fierceness of his **a**, 639
78:50 He made a way to his **a**; he spared not 639
78:58 they **provoked** him to **a** with their high 3707
85: 3 *thyself* from the fierceness of thine **a**. 639
85: 4 and cause thine **a** towards us to cease. 3708
85: 5 thou draw out thine **a** to all generations? 639
90: 7 For we are consumed by thine **a**, and by 639
90:11 Who knoweth the power of thine **a**? 639
103: 8 slow to **a**, and plenteous in mercy. 639
103: 9 neither will he keep *his* **a** for ever. NIH
106:29 Thus they **provoked** *him* to **a** with their 3707
145: 8 slow to **a**, and of great mercy. 639
Pr 15: 1 away wrath: but grievous words stir up **a**. 639
15:18 but *he that is* slow to **a** appeaseth strife. 639
16:32 *that is* slow to **a** is better than the mighty; 639
19:11 The discretion of a man deferreth his **a**; 639
20: 2 *whoso* **provoketh** him to **a** sinneth 5674
21:14 A gift in secret pacifieth **a**: and a reward 639
21:24 reap vanity: and the rod of his **a** shall fail. 5678
27: 4 Wrath *is* cruel, and **a** *is* outrageous; 639
Ecc 7: 9 for **a** resteth in the bosom of fools. 3708
Isa 1: 4 **provoked** the Holy One of Israel **unto a**, 5006
5:25 Therefore is the **a** of the Lord kindled 639
5:25 For all this his **a** is not turned away, 639
7: 4 for the fierce **a** of Rezin with Syria, 639
9:12 For all this his **a** is not turned away, 639
9:17 For all this his **a** is not turned away, 639
9:21 For all this his **a** is not turned away, 639
10: 4 For all this his **a** is not turned away, 639
10: 5 rod of mine **a**, and the staff in their hand 639
10:25 shall cease, and mine **a** in their destruction. 639
12: 1 thine **a** is turned away, and thou 639
13: 3 also called my mighty ones for mine **a**, 639
13: 9 cruel both *with* wrath and fierce **a**, to lay 639
13:13 of hosts, and in the day of his fierce **a**. 639
14: 6 that ruled the nations in **a**, *is* persecuted, 639
30:27 burning *with* his **a**, and the burden 639
30:30 with the indignation *of his* **a**, and *with* 639
42:25 he hath poured upon him the fury of his **a**, 639
48: 9 For my name's sake will I defer mine **a**, 639
63: 3 for I will tread them in mine **a**, 639
63: 6 I will tread down the people in mine **a**, 639
65: 3 A people that **provoketh** me to **a** 3707
66:15 to render his **a** with fury, and his rebuke 639
Jer 2:35 innocent, surely his **a** shall turn from me. NIH
3: 5 Will he reserve his **a** for ever? will he keep NIH
3:12 I will not cause mine **a** to fall upon you: 6440
3:12 the Lord, *and* I will not keep **a** for ever. NIH
4: 8 for the fierce **a** of the Lord is not turned 639
4:26 presence of the Lord, *and* by his fierce **a**. 639
7:18 gods, that *they* may **provoke** me to **a**. 3707
7:19 Do they **provoke** me to **a**? saith 3707
7:20 mine **a** and my fury *shall be* poured out 639
8:19 Why have they **provoked** me to **a** with a 3707
10:24 in thine **a**, lest thou bring me to nothing. 639
11:17 **provoke** me to **a** in offering incense unto 3707
12:13 because of the fierce **a** of the Lord. 639
15:14 for a fire is kindled in mine **a**, *which* shall 639
17: 4 for ye have kindled a fire in mine **a**, 639
18:23 deal *thus* with them in the time of thine **a**. 639
21: 5 even in **a**, and in fury, and in great wrath. 639
23:20 The **a** of the Lord shall not return, 639
25: 6 **provoke** me not to **a** with the works of 3707
25: 7 that *ye* might **provoke** me to **a** with 3707
25:37 because of the fierce **a** of the Lord. 639
25:38 the oppressor, and because of his fierce **a**. 639
30:24 The fierce **a** of the Lord shall not return, 639
32:29 unto other gods, to **provoke** me to **a**. 3707
32:30 **provoked** me to **a** with the work of their 3707
32:31 been to me *as a* **provocation** of mine **a** 639
32:32 they have done to **provoke** me to **a**, 3707
32:37 whither I have driven them in mine **a**, 639
33: 5 I have slain in mine **a** and in my fury, 639
36: 7 for great *is* the **a** and the fury that 639
42:18 As mine **a** and my fury hath been poured 639
44: 3 they have committed to **provoke** me to **a**, 3707
44: 6 my fury and mine **a** was poured forth, 639
49:37 *even* my fierce **a**, saith the Lord; 639
51:45 his soul from the fierce **a** of the Lord. 639
52: 3 For through the **a** of the Lord it came to 639
La 1:12 hath afflicted *me* in the day of his fierce **a**. 639
2: 1 the daughter of Zion with a cloud in his **a**, 639
2: 1 not his footstool in the day of his **a**! 639
2: 3 He hath cut off in *his* fierce **a** all the horn 639
2: 6 hath despised in the indignation of his **a** 639
2:21 thou hast slain *them* in the day of thine **a**; 639
2:22 that in the day of the Lord's **a** none 639
3:43 hast covered with **a**, and persecuted us: 639
3:66 destroy them in **a** from under the heavens 639
4:11 he hath poured out his fierce **a**, 639
4:16 The **a** of the Lord hath divided them; 6440
Eze 5:13 Thus shall mine **a** be accomplished, 639

Eze	5:15 I shall execute judgments in thee in a	639
	7: 3 will send mine a upon thee, and will judge	639
	7: 8 and accomplish mine a upon thee:	639
	8:17 and have returned to **provoke** me a:	3707
	13:13 shall be an overflowing shower in mine a,	639
	16:26 thy whoredoms, to **provoke** me to a	3707
	20: 8 to accomplish my a against them in	639
	20:21 to accomplish my a against them in	639
	22:20 to melt it; so will I gather you in mine a	639
	25:14 they shall do in Edom according to mine a	639
	35:11 I will even do according to thine a,	639
	43: 8 I have consumed them in mine a.	639
Da	9:16 let thine a and thy fury be turned away	639
	11:20 be destroyed, neither in a, nor in battle.	639
Hos	8: 5 thee off; mine a is kindled against them:	639
	11: 9 I will not execute the fierceness of mine a,	639
	12:14 Ephraim **provoked** him to a most bitterly	3707
	13:11 I gave thee a king in mine a, and took him	639
	14: 4 for mine a is turned away from him.	639
Joel	2:13 slow to a, and of great kindness,	639
Am	1:11 his a did tear perpetually, and he kept his	639
Jnh	3: 9 repent, and turn away from his fierce a,	639
	4: 2 slow to a, and of great kindness,	639
Mic	5:15 I will execute vengeance in a and fury	639
	7:18 he retaineth not his a for ever, because	639
Na	1: 3 The Lord is slow to a, and great in power,	639
	1: 6 who can abide in the fierceness of his a?	639
Hab	3: 8 thine a against the rivers? was thy wrath	639
	3:12 thou didst thresh the heathen in a.	639
Zep	2: 2 before the fierce a of the Lord come upon	639
	2: 2 before the day of the Lord's a come upon	639
	2: 3 ye shall be hid in the day of the Lord's a.	639
	3: 8 mine indignation, even all my fierce a:	639
Zec	10: 3 Mine a was kindled against the shepherds,	639
Mk	3: 5 had looked round about on them with a,	3709
Ro	10:19 and by a foolish nation I will a you.	3949
Eph	4:31 and a, and clamour, and evil speaking,	3709
Col	3: 8 now you also put off all these; a, wrath,	3709
	3:21 provoke not your children to a, lest they	NIG

ANGERED (1) [ANGER]

Ps	106:32 They a him also at the waters of strife, so	7107

ANGLE (2)

Isa	19: 8 all they that cast a into the brooks shall	2443
Hab	1:15 They take up all of them with the a,	2443

ANGRY (44) [ANGER]

Ge	18:30 said unto him, Oh let not the Lord be a,	2734
	18:32 Oh let not the Lord be a, and I will speak	2734
	45: 5 be not grieved, nor a with yourselves,	2734
Lev	10:16 he was a with Eleazar and Ithamar the	7107
Dt	1:37 Also the Lord was a with me for your	599
	4:21 Furthermore the Lord was a with me for	599
	9: 8 that the Lord was a with you to have	599
	9:20 the Lord was very a with Aaron to have	599
Jdg	18:25 lest a fellows run upon thee,	4751+5315
2Sa	19:42 wherefore then be ye a for this matter?	2734
1Ki	8:46 thou be a with them, and deliver them to	599
	11: 9 the Lord was a with Solomon, because	599
2Ki	17:18 Therefore the Lord was very a with	599
2Ch	6:36 thou be a with them, and deliver them	599
Ezr	9:14 wouldest thou not be a with us till thou	599
Ne	5: 6 I was very a when I heard their cry	2734
Ps	2:12 lest he be a, and ye perish from the way,	599
	7:11 and God is a with the wicked every day.	2194
	76: 7 stand in thy sight when once thou art a?	639
	79: 5 wilt thou be a, for ever? shall thy jealousy	599
	80: 4 how long wilt thou be a against the prayer	6225
	85: 5 Wilt thou be a with us for ever? wilt thou	599
Pr	14:17 He that is soon a dealeth foolishly:	639
	21:19 than with a contentious and an a woman.	3708
	22:24 Make no friendship with an a man;	639
	25:23 an a countenance a backbiting tongue.	2194
	29:22 An a man stirreth up strife, and a furious	639
Ecc	5: 6 wherefore should God be a at thy voice,	7107
	7: 9 Be not hasty in thy spirit to be a: for anger	3707
SS	1: 6 my mother's children were a with me;	2787
Isa	12: 1 though thou wast a with me, thine anger	599
Eze	16:42 and I will be quiet, and will be no more a.	3707
Da	2:12 For this cause the king was a	1149
Jnh	4: 1 Jonah exceedingly, and he was **very a**.	2734
	4: 4 said the Lord, Doest thou well to be a?	2734
	4: 9 Doest thou well to be a for the gourd?	2734
	4: 9 said, I do well to be a, even unto death.	2734
Mt	5:22 That whosoever is a with his brother	3710
Lk	14:21 of the house being a said to his servant,	3710
	15:28 And he was a, and would not go in:	3710
Jn	7:23 ye a at me, because I have made a man	5520
Eph	4:26 Be ye a, and sin not: let not the sun go	3710
Tit	1: 7 not selfwilled, not **soon** a, not given to	3711
Rev	11:18 And the nations were a, and thy wrath is	3710

ANGUISH (17)

Ge	42:21 in that we saw the a of his soul, when he	6869
Ex	6: 9 they hearkened not unto Moses for a of	7115
Dt	2:25 shall tremble, and be in a because of thee.	2342
2Sa	1: 9 for a is come upon me, because my life is	7661
Job	7:11 I will speak in the a of my spirit;	6862
	15:24 Trouble and a shall make him afraid;	4691
Ps	119:143 Trouble and a have taken hold on me:	4689
Pr	1:27 when distress and a cometh upon you:	6695
Isa	8:22 trouble and darkness, dimness of a;	6695
	30: 6 the land of trouble and a, from whence	6695
Jer	4:31 the a as of her that bringeth forth her first	6869

Jer	6:24 a hath taken hold of us, and pain, as of a	6869
	49:24 fear hath seized on her: a and sorrows	6869
	50:43 a took hold of him, and pangs as of a	6869
Jn	16:21 child, she remembereth no more the a,	2347
Ro	2: 9 Tribulation and a, upon every soul of man	4730
2Co	2: 4 a of heart I wrote unto you with many	4928

ANIAM (1)

1Ch	7:19 Ahian, and Shechem, and Likhi, and A.	593

ANIM (1)

Jos	15:50 And Anab, and Eshtemoh, and A,	6044

ANISE (1)

Mt	23:23 ye pay tithe of mint and a and cummin,	432

ANKLE (1) [ANKLES]

Ac	3: 7 his feet and a bones received strength,	4974

ANKLES (1) [ANKLE]

Eze	47: 3 the waters; the waters were to the a.	657

ANNA (1)

Lk	2:36 And there was one A, a prophetess,	451

ANNAS (4)

Lk	3: 2 A and Caiaphas being the high priests,	452
Jn	18:13 And led him away to A first; for he was	452
	18:24 had sent him bound unto Caiaphas	452
Ac	4: 6 And A the high priest, and Caiaphas,	452

ANOINT (35) [ANOINTED, ANOINTEDST, ANOINTEST, ANOINTING]

Ex	28:41 shalt a them, and consecrate them,	4886
	29: 7 and pour it upon his head, and a him.	4886
	29:36 for it, and thou shalt a it, to sanctify it.	4886
	30:26 thou shalt a the tabernacle of	4886
	30:30 thou shalt a Aaron and his sons,	4886
	40: 9 a the tabernacle, and all that is therein,	4886
	40:10 shalt a the altar of the burnt offering,	4886
	40:11 thou shalt a the laver and his foot,	4886
	40:13 a him, and sanctify him;	4886
	40:15 thou shalt a them, as thou didst anoint	4886
	40:15 anoint them, as thou didst a their father,	4886
Lev	16:32 whom he shall a, and whom he shall	4886
Dt	28:40 but thou shalt not a thyself with the oil;	5480
Jdg	9: 8 The trees went forth on a time to a a king	4886
	9:15 If in truth ye a me king over you, then	4886
Ru	3: 3 a thee, and put thy raiment upon thee,	5480
1Sa	9:16 thou shalt a him to be captain over my	4886
	15: 1 The Lord sent me to a thee to be king	4886
	16: 3 thou shalt a unto me him whom I name	4886
	16:12 the Lord said, Arise, a him: for this is	4886
2Sa	14: 2 a not thyself with oil, but be as a woman	5480
1Ki	1:34 Nathan the prophet a him there king over	4886
	19:15 Hazael to be king over Syria:	4886
	19:16 Jehu the son of Nimshi shalt thou a to be	4886
	19:16 shalt thou a to be prophet in thy room.	4886
Isa	21: 5 drink: arise, ye princes, and a the shield.	4886
Da	9:24 and prophecy, and to a the most Holy.	4886
	10: 3 neither did I a myself at all, till	5480+5480
Am	6: 6 a themselves with the chief ointments:	4886
Mic	6:15 but thou shalt not a thee with oil;	5480
Mt	6:17 fastest, a thine head, and wash thy face;	218
Mk	14: 8 she is come aforehand to a my body to	3462
	16: 1 that they might come and a him.	218
Lk	7:46 Mine head with oil thou didst not a:	218
Rev	3:18 and a thine eyes with eyesalve, that thou	1472

ANOINTED (98) [ANOINT]

Ex	29: 2 oil, and wafers unleavened a with oil:	4886
	29:29 to be a therein, and to be consecrated in	4888
Lev	2: 4 with oil, or unleavened wafers a with oil.	4886
	4: 3 If the priest that is a do sin according to	4899
	4: 5 the priest that is a shall take of	4899
	4:16 the priest that is a shall bring of	4899
	6:20 unto the Lord in the day when he is a;	4886
	6:22 the priest of his sons that is a in his stead	4899
	7:12 unleavened wafers a with oil,	4886
	7:36 in the day that he a them, by a statute for	4886
	8:10 a the tabernacle and all that was therein,	4886
	8:11 a the altar and all his vessels, both the	4886
	8:12 Aaron's head, and a him, to sanctify him.	4886
Nu	3: 3 sons of Aaron, the priests which were a,	4886
	6:15 wafers of unleavened bread a with oil,	4886
	7: 1 had a it, and sanctified it, and all	4886
	7: 1 and had a them, and sanctified them;	4886
	7:10 of the altar in the day that it was a,	4886
	7:84 in the day when it was a, by the princes	4886
	7:88 dedication of the altar, after that it was a.	4886
	35:25 high priest, which was a with the holy oil.	4886
1Sa	2:10 unto his king, and exalt the horn of his a.	4899
	2:35 and he shall walk before mine a for ever.	4886
	10: 1 the Lord hath a thee to be captain over	4886
	12: 3 me before the Lord, and before his a:	4899
	12: 5 against you, and his a is witness this day,	4899
	15:17 and the Lord a thee king over Israel?	4886
	16: 6 said, Surely the Lord's a is before him.	4899
	16:13 and a him in the midst of his brethren:	4886
	24: 6 the Lord's a, to stretch forth mine hand	4899
	24: 6 seeing he is the a of the Lord.	4899
	24:10 against my lord; for he is the Lord's a.	4899
	26: 9 forth his hand against the Lord's a,	4899
	26:11 forth mine hand against the Lord's a:	4899
	26:16 have not kept your master, the Lord's a.	4899
	26:23 forth mine hand against the Lord's a.	4899

2Sa	1:14 thine hand to destroy the Lord's a?	4899
	1:16 saying, I have slain the Lord's a.	4899
	1:21 as though he had not been a with oil.	4899
	2: 4 there they a David king over the house of	4886
	2: 7 also the house of Judah have a me king	4886
	3:39 And I am this day weak, though a king;	4886
	5: 3 and they a David king over Israel.	4886
	5:17 when the Philistines heard that they had a	4886
	12: 7 I a thee king over Israel, and I delivered	4886
	12:20 and a himself, and changed his apparel,	5480
	19:10 Absalom, whom we a over us, is dead in	4886
	19:21 because he cursed the Lord's a?	4899
	22:51 sheweth mercy to his a, unto David,	4899
	23: 1 the a of the God of Jacob, and the sweet	4899
1Ki	1:39 oil out of the tabernacle, and a Solomon.	4886
	1:45 Nathan the prophet have a him king in	4886
	5: 1 for he had heard that they had a him king	4886
2Ki	9: 3 the Lord, I have a thee king over Israel.	4886
	9: 6 I have a thee king over the people of	4886
	9:12 the Lord, I have a thee king over Israel.	4886
	11:12 they made him king, and a him;	4886
	23:30 a him, and made him king in his father's	4886
1Ch	11: 3 they a David king over Israel, according to	4886
	14: 8 the Philistines heard that David was a	4886
	16:22 Saying, Touch not mine a, and do my	4899
	29:22 a him unto the Lord to be the chief	4886
2Ch	6:42 turn not away the face of thine a:	4899
	22: 7 whom the Lord had a to cut off	4886
	23:11 Jehoiada and his sons a him, and said,	4886
	28:15 a them, and carried all the feeble of them	5480
Ps	2: 2 the Lord, and against his a, saying,	4899
	18:50 sheweth mercy to his a, to David, and to	4899
	20: 6 Now know I that the Lord saveth his a;	4899
	28: 8 and he is the saving strength of his a.	4899
	45: 7 hath a thee with the oil of gladness above	4886
	84: 9 and look upon the face of thine a.	4899
	89:20 servant; with my holy oil have I a him:	4886
	89:38 thou hast been wroth with thine a.	4899
	89:51 have reproached the footsteps of thine a.	4899
	92:10 of an unicorn: I shall be a with fresh oil.	1101
	105:15 Saying, Touch not mine a, and do my	4899
	132:10 sake turn not away the face of thine a.	4899
	132:17 bud: I have ordained a lamp for mine a.	4899
Isa	45: 1 Thus saith the Lord to his a, to Cyrus,	4899
	61: 1 the Lord hath a me to preach good	4886
La	4:20 the a of the Lord, was taken in their pits,	4899
Eze	16: 9 thy blood from thee, and I a thee with oil.	5480
	28:14 Thou art the a cherub that covereth;	4473
Hab	3:13 people, even for salvation with thine a;	4899
Zec	4:14 These are the two a ones, that stand	3323
Mk	6:13 a with oil many that were sick,	218
Lk	4:18 he hath a me to preach the gospel to	5548
	7:38 his feet, and a them with the ointment.	218
	7:46 this woman hath a my feet with ointment.	218
Jn	9: 6 he the eyes of the blind man with	2025
	9:11 and a mine eyes, and said unto me, Go to	2025
	11: 2 (It was that Mary which a the Lord with	218
	12: 3 and a the feet of Jesus, and wiped his feet	218
Ac	4:27 whom thou hast a, both Herod,	5548
	10:38 How God a Jesus of Nazareth with	5548
2Co	1:21 with you in Christ, and hath a us, is God;	5548
Heb	1: 9 hath a thee with the oil of gladness above	5548

ANOINTEDST (1) [ANOINT]

Ge	31:13 where thou a the pillar, and where thou	4886

ANOINTEST (1) [ANOINT]

Ps	23: 5 thou a my head with oil; my cup runneth	1878

ANOINTING (28) [ANOINT]

Ex	25: 6 spices for a oil, and for sweet incense,	4888
	29: 7 shalt thou take the a oil, and pour it upon	4888
	29:21 of the a oil, and sprinkle it upon Aaron,	4888
	30:25 of the apothecary: it shall be a holy a oil.	4888
	30:31 This shall be a holy a oil unto me	4888
	31:11 the a oil, and sweet incense for the holy	4888
	35: 8 spices for a oil, and for the sweet incense,	4888
	35:15 the a oil, and the sweet incense, and	4888
	35:28 for the a oil, and for the sweet incense.	4888
	37:29 he made the holy a oil, and the pure	4888
	39:38 the a oil, and the sweet incense, and	4888
	40: 9 thou shalt take the a oil, and anoint	4888
	40:15 for their a shall surely be an everlasting	4888
Lev	7:35 This is the portion of the a of Aaron,	4888
	7:35 of Aaron, and of the a of his sons,	4888
	8: 2 a oil, and a bullock for the sin offering,	4888
	8:10 Moses took the a oil, and anointed	4888
	8:12 he poured on the a oil upon Aaron's head,	4888
	8:30 Moses took of the a oil, and of the blood	4888
	10: 7 for the a oil of the Lord is upon you.	4888
	21:10 upon whose head the a oil was poured,	4888
	21:12 for the crown of the a oil of his God is	4888
Nu	4:16 the a oil, and the oversight of all	4888
	18: 8 have I given them by reason of the a,	4888
Isa	10:27 yoke shall be destroyed because of the a.	8081
Jas	5:14 a him with oil in the name of the Lord:	218
1Jn	2:27 But the a which ye have received of him	5545
	2:27 as the same a teacheth you of all things,	5545

ANON (2)

Mt	13:20 the word, and a with joy receiveth it;	2112
Mk	1:30 sick of a fever, and a they tell him of her.	2112

ANOTHER (448) [ANOTHER'S]

Ge	4:25 hath appointed me a seed instead of	312

A

Ge 11: 3 they said one to a^s, Go to, let us make 7453

Ge 11: 3 they said one to aˢ, Go to, let us make 7453
15:10 and laid each piece one against aˢ: 7453
26:21 digged a well, and strove for that also: 312
26:22 removed from thence, and digged a well; 312
26:31 in the morning, and sware one to a: 251
29:19 than that I should give her to a man: 312
30:24 and said, The LORD shall add to me a son. 312
31:49 thee, when we are absent one from aˢ. 7453
37: 9 he dreamed yet a dream, and told it his 312
37:19 they said one to aˢ, Behold, this dreamer 251
42: 1 his sons, Why do ye look one upon a? NIH
42:21 they said one to aˢ, We are verily guilty 251
42:28 and they were afraid, saying one to aˢ, 251
43: 7 have ye a brother? and we told him NIH
43:33 youth: and the men marvelled one at aˢ. 7453
Ex 10:23 They saw not one aˢ, neither rose any 251
16:15 of Israel saw it, they said one to aˢ, 251
18:16 I judge between one and aˢ, and I do 7453
21:10 If he take him a wife; her food, her 312
21:18 one smite aˢ with a stone, or with his fist, 7453
22: 5 his beast, and shall feed in a man's field; 312
22: 9 for any manner of lost thing, which a NIH
25:20 and their faces shall look one to aˢ; 251
26: 3 shall be coupled together one to aˢ: 269
26: 3 five curtains shall be coupled one to aˢ. 269
26: 4 make in the uttermost edge of a curtain, NIH
26: 5 that the loops may take hold one of aˢ. 269
26:17 in one board, set in order one against aˢ: 269
26:19 two sockets under a board for his two 259
26:21 one board, and two sockets under a board. 259
26:25 one board, and two sockets under a board. 259
36:10 he coupled the five curtains one unto a: 259
36:10 other five curtains he coupled one unto a. 259
36:11 he made in the uttermost side of a NIH
36:12 the second: the loops held one curtain to a. 259
36:13 coupled the curtains one unto a with 259
36:22 had two tenons, equally distant one from a: 259
36:24 two sockets under a board for his two 259
36:26 one board, and two sockets under a board. 259
37: 8 a cherub on the other end on that side: 259
37: 9 the mercy seat, with their faces one to a: 251
37:19 bowls made like almonds in a branch, 259
Lev 7:10 sons of Aaron have, one as much as aˢ. 251
9:11 neither deal falsely, neither lie one to aˢ. 5997
20:10 the man that committeth adultery with a NIH
25:14 ye shall not oppress one aˢ: 251
25:17 Ye shall not therefore oppress one aˢ; 5997
25:46 ye shall not rule one over aˢ with rigour. 251
26:37 they shall fall one upon aˢ, as it were before 251
27:20 or if he have sold the field to a man, it shall 312
Nu 5:19 uncleanness with a instead of thy husband, NIH
5:20 if thou hast gone aside to a instead of thy NIH
5:29 when a wife goeth aside to a instead of her NIH
8: 8 a young bullock shalt thou take for a sin 8145
14: 4 they said one to aˢ, Let us make a captain, 251
14:24 because he had a spirit with him, 312
23:13 Come, I pray thee, with me unto a place, 312
23:27 I pray thee, I will bring thee unto a place; 312
36: 9 remove from one tribe to a tribe; 312
Dt 4:34 take him a nation from the midst of a NIH
20: 5 he die in the battle, and a man dedicate it. 312
20: 6 he die in the battle, and a man eat of it. 312
20: 7 he die in the battle, and a man take her. 312
21:15 a hated, and they have born him children, 259
24: 2 house, she may go and be a man's wife. 312
25:11 When men strive together one with aˢ, 251
28:30 a wife, and a man shall lie with her: 312
28:32 daughters shall be given unto a people, 312
29:28 and cast them into a land, as it is this day. 312
Jdg 2:10 there arose a generation after them, 312
6:29 they said one to aˢ, Who hath done this 7453
9:37 a company come along by the plain of 259
10:18 and princes of Gilead said one to aˢ, 7453
16: 7 then shall I be weak, and be as a man. 259
16:11 shall I be weak, and be as a man. 259
Ru 2: 8 Go not to glean in a field, neither go from 312
3:14 she rose up before one could know aˢ. 7453
1Sa 2:25 If one man sin against aˢ, the judge shall 376
10: 3 a carrying three loaves of bread, 259
10: 3 of bread, and a carrying a bottle of wine: 259
10: 6 with them, and shalt be turned into a man. 312
10: 9 to go from Samuel, God gave him a heart: 312
10:11 prophets, then the people said one to aˢ, 7453
13:18 a company turned the way to Beth-horon: 259
13:18 a company turned to the way of the border 259
14:16 and they went on beating down one a. NIH
17:30 he turned from him towards a, 312
18: 7 women answered one a as they played, NIH
20:41 they kissed one aˢ, and wept one with 7453
20:41 wept one with aˢ, until David exceeded. 7453
21:11 they not sing one to a of him in dances, NIH
29: 5 of whom they sang one to a in dances, NIH
2Sa 11:25 for the sword devoureth one as well as a: 2088
18:20 this day, but thou shalt bear tidings a day: 312
18:26 the watchman saw a man running: 312
18:26 and said, Behold a man running alone. NIH
1Ki 6:27 their wings touched one a in 413+3671+3671
7: 8 house where he dwelt had a court within 312
11:23 God stirred him up a adversary, Rezon NIH
13:10 So he went a way, and returned not by 312
14: 5 she shall feign herself to be a woman. 5234
14: 6 why feignest thou thyself to be a? 5234
18: 6 Obadiah went a way by himself. 259
20:37 he found a man, and said, Smite me, 312
21: 6 I will give thee a vineyard for it: NIH

1Ki 22:20 this manner, and a said on that manner. 2088
2Ki 1:11 Again also he sent unto him a captain of 312
3:23 surely slain, and they have smitten one aˢ: 7453
7: 3 they said one to aˢ, Why sit we here until 7453
7: 6 they said one to aˢ, Lo, the king of Israel 251
7: 8 entered into a tent, and carried thence 312
7: 9 they said one to aˢ, We do not well: this 7453
10:21 house of Baal was full from one end to aˢ. 6310
14: 8 Come, let us look one a in the face. NIH
14:11 Amaziah king of Judah looked one a in NIH
21:16 had filled Jerusalem from one end to aˢ. 6310
1Ch 2:26 Jerahmeel had also a wife, whose name 312
16:20 and from one kingdom to a people; 312
17: 5 tent to tent, and from one tabernacle to a. NIH
24: 5 were they divided by lot, one sort with a; 428
26:12 chief men, having wards one against aˢ, 251
2Ch 18:19 and a saying after that manner. 2088
20:23 of Seir, every one helped to destroy aˢ. 7453
25:17 Come, let us see one a in the face. NIH
25:21 they saw one a in the face, both he NIH
32: 5 a wall without, and repaired Millo in the 312
Ezr 4:21 until a commandment shall be given from NIH
9:11 have filled it from one end to aˢ with 6310
Ne 3:19 a piece over against the going up to 8145
3:21 the son of Urijah the son of Koz a piece, 8145
3:24 Binnui the son of Henadad a piece, 8145
3:27 After them the Tekoites repaired a piece, 8145
3:30 Hanun the sixth son of Zalaph, a piece. 8145
4:19 separated upon the wall, one far from aˢ. 251
9: 3 a fourth part they confessed, NIH
Est 1: 7 (the vessels being diverse one from aˢ,) 3627
1:19 let the king give her royal estate unto aˢ 7468
4:14 deliverance arise to the Jews from a place; 312
9:19 and of sending portions one to aˢ. 7453
9:22 of sending portions one to aˢ, and gifts to 7453
Job 1:16 yet speaking, there came also a, and said, 2088
1:17 yet speaking, there came also a, and said, 2088
1:18 there came also a, and said, Thy sons 2088
13: 9 or as one man mocketh aˢ, do ye so 582
19:27 and mine eyes shall behold, and not a; 2114
21: 8 dieth in the bitterness of his soul, 2088
31: 8 Then let me sow, and let a eat; yea, let 312
31:10 Then let my wife grind unto a, and let 312
41:16 One is so near to a, that no air can come 259
41:17 They are joined one to aˢ, they stick 251
Ps 16: 4 a god: their drink offerings of blood will I 312
75: 7 he putteth down one, and setteth up a. 2088
105:13 When they went from one nation to a, 1471
105:13 to another, from one kingdom to a people; 312
109: 8 his days be few; and let a take his office. 312
145: 4 generation shall praise thy works to aˢ, 1755
Pr 25: 9 and discover not a secret to a: 312
27: 2 Let a man praise thee, and not thine own 2114
Ecc 1: 4 passeth away, and a generation cometh: NIH
4:10 falleth; for he hath not a to help him up. 8145
8: 9 one man ruleth over a to his own hurt. 120
SS 5: 9 What is thy beloved more than a beloved, NIH
5: 9 what is thy beloved more than a beloved, NIH
Isa 3: 5 every one by a, and every one by his 376
6: 3 one cried unto a, and said, Holy, holy, 2088
13: 8 they shall be amazed one at aˢ; their faces 7453
28:11 and a tongue will he speak to this people. 312
42: 8 my glory will I not give to a, neither my 312
44: 5 a shall call himself by the name of Jacob; 2088
44: 5 a shall subscribe with his hand unto 2088
48:11 and I will not give my glory unto a. 312
57: 8 for thou hast discovered thyself to a than NIH
65:15 slay thee, and call his servants by a name: 312
65:22 They shall not build, and a inhabit; 312
65:22 they shall not plant, and a eat: 312
66:23 that from one new moon to a, 2320
66:23 to another, and from one sabbath to aˢ, 7676
Jer 3: 1 she go from him, and become a man's, 312
13:14 I will dash them one against aˢ, even 251
18: 4 so he made it again a vessel, as seemed 312
18:14 that come from a place be forsaken? 2114
22:26 into a country, where ye were not born; 312
25:26 one with aˢ, and all the kingdoms of 251
36:28 Take thee again a roll, and write in it all 312
36:32 took Jeremiah a roll, and gave it to Baruch 312
46:16 made many to fall, yea, one fell upon aˢ: 7453
51:31 One post shall run to meet a, 7323
51:31 and one messenger to meet aˢ, 5046
51:46 after that in a year shall come a rumour, NIH
Eze 1: 9 Their wings were joined one to aˢ; they 269
1:11 wings of every one were joined one to aˢ, 376
3:13 of the living creatures that touched one aˢ, 269
4: 8 shalt not turn thee from one side to aˢ, 6654
4:17 astonied one with aˢ, and consume away 251
10: 9 cherub, and a wheel by another cherub: 259
10: 9 cherub, and another wheel by a cherub: 259
12: 3 shalt remove from thy place to a place 312
15: 7 one fire, and a fire shall devour them; NIH
17: 7 There was also a great eagle with great 259
19: 5 she took a of her whelps, and made him a 259
22:11 aˢ hath lewdly defiled his daughter in law; 376
22:11 aˢ in their hath humbled his sister, 376
24:23 your iniquities, and mourn one towards aˢ. 251
33:30 speak one to a, every one to his brother, 259
37:16 take a stick, and write upon it, For Joseph, 259
37:17 join them one to a into one stick; 259
40:13 of one little chamber to the roof of aˢ: 2050.2
40:26 one on this side, and a on that side, 259
40:49 one on this side, and a on that side. 259
41: 6 three, one over aˢ, and thirty in order; 6763

Eze 41:11 the north, and a door toward the south: 259
47:14 ye shall inherit it, one as well as aˢ: 251
Da 2:39 after thee shall arise a kingdom inferior to 317
2:39 a third kingdom of brass, which shall bear 317
2:43 they shall not cleave one to a, even as iron 1836
5: 6 and his knees smote one against a. 1668
5:17 be to thyself, and give thy rewards to a; 321
7: 3 came up from the sea, diverse one from a. 1668
7: 5 behold, a beast, a second, like to a bear, 317
7: 6 After this I beheld, and lo a, like a leopard, 317
7: 8 there came up among them a little horn, 317
7:24 a shall rise after them; and he shall be 321
8:13 a saint said unto that certain saint which 259
Hos 3: 3 harlot, and thou shalt not be for a man: NIH
4: 4 Yet let no man strive, nor reprove aˢ: 376
Joel 1: 3 and their children a generation. 312
2: 8 Neither shall one thrust aˢ; they shall walk 251
Am 4: 7 and caused it not to rain upon a city: 259
Na 2: 4 they shall justle one against a in the broad NIH
Zec 2: 3 and a angel went out to meet him, 312
8:21 the inhabitants of one city shall go to a, 259
11: 9 let the rest eat every one the flesh of aˢ. 7468
Mal 3:16 feared the LORD spake often one to aˢ: 7453
Mt 2:12 departed into their own country a way. 243
8: 9 to a, Come, and he cometh; and to my 243
8:21 And a of his disciples said unto him, Lord, 2087
10:23 persecute you in this city, flee ye into a: 243
11: 3 he that should come, or do we look for a? 2087
13:24 A parable put he forth unto them, saying, 243
13:31 A parable put he forth unto them, saying, 243
13:33 A parable spake he unto them; 243
19: 9 and shall marry a, committeth adultery: 243
21:33 Hear a parable: There was a certain 243
21:35 one, and killed a, and stoned another. 3739
21:35 one, and killed another, and stoned a. 3739
22: 5 one to his farm, a to his merchandise: 3739
24: 2 shall not be left here one stone upon aˢ, 3037
24:10 and shall betray one a, and shall hate one 240
24:10 betray one another, and shall hate one a. 240
25:15 five talents, to a two, and to another one; 3739
25:15 five talents, to another two, and to a one; 3739
25:32 and he shall separate them one from a, 243
26:71 a maid saw him, and said unto them that 243
27:38 one on the right hand, and a on the left. 1520
Mk 4:41 and said one to a, What manner of man is 240
9:10 questioning one with a what the thing NIG
9:50 in yourselves, and have peace one with a. 240
10:11 and marry a, committeth adultery against 243
10:12 and be married to a, she committeth 243
12: 4 And again he sent unto them a servant; 243
12: 5 And again he sent a; and him they killed, 243
13: 2 there shall not be left one stone upon aˢ, 3037
14:19 him one by one, Is it I? and a said, Is it I? 243
14:58 three days I will build a made without 243
16:12 After that he appeared in a form unto two 2087
Lk 2:15 shepherds said one to a, Let us now go 240
6: 6 it came to pass also on a sabbath, 2087
6:11 communed one with a what they might do 240
7: 8 and to a, Come, and he cometh; and to my 243
7:19 he that should come? or look we for a? 243
7:20 he that should come? or look we for a? 243
7:32 and calling one to a, and saying, We have 240
8:25 saying one to a, What manner of man is 240
9:56 to save them. And they went to a village. 2087
9:59 And he said unto a, Follow me. But he 2087
9:61 And a also said, Lord, I will follow thee; 2087
12: 1 insomuch that they trode one upon a, 240
14:19 And a said, I have bought five yoke of 2087
14:20 And a said, I have married a wife, 2087
14:31 going to make war against a king, 2087
16: 7 Then said he to a, And how much owest 2087
16:12 a man's, who shall give you that which is 245
16:18 and marrieth a, committeth adultery: 2087
19:20 And a came, saying, Lord, behold, here is 2087
19:44 shall not leave in thee one stone upon aˢ; 3037
20:11 And again he sent a servant: and they beat 2087
21: 6 there shall not be left one stone upon aˢ, 3037
22:58 after a little while a saw him, and said, 2087
22:59 hour after a confidently affirmed, 243+5100
24:17 are these that ye have one to a, 240
24:32 And they said one to a, Did not our heart 240
Jn 4:33 Therefore said the disciples one to a, 240
4:37 saying true, One soweth, and a reapeth. 243
5: 7 I am coming, a steppeth down before me. 243
5:32 There is a that beareth witness of me; 243
5:43 if a shall come in his own name, him ye 243
5:44 receive honour one of a, and seek not 243
13:22 Then the disciples looked one on a, 240
13:34 I give unto you, That ye love one a; 240
13:34 I have loved you, that ye also love one a. 240
13:35 are my disciples, if ye have love one to a. 240
14:16 and he shall give you a Comforter, 243
15:12 That ye love one a, as I have loved you. 240
15:17 things I command you, that ye love one a. 240
18:15 Peter followed Jesus, and so did a disciple: 243
19:37 again a scripture saith, They shall look 2087
21:18 a shall gird thee, and carry thee whither 2087
Ac 1:20 therein: and his bishoprick let a take. 2087
2: 7 and marvelled, saying one to a, Behold, 243
2:12 and were in doubt, saying one to a, 243
7:18 Till a king arose, which knew not Joseph. 2087
7:26 are brethren; why do ye wrong one to a? 240
10:28 or come unto one of a nation; 246
12:17 And he departed, and went into a place. 2087
13:35 Wherefore he saith also in a psalm, 2087

A

Ac	17: 7 saying that there is a king, *one* Jesus.	2087
	19:32 therefore cried one *thing*, and some **a**:	243
	19:38 are deputies: let them implead **one a**.	240
	21: 6 when we had taken our leave **one** of **a**,	240
	21:34 And some cried one *thing*, some **a**,	243
Ro	1:27 burned in their lust **one** towards **a**;	240
	2: 1 for wherein thou judgest **a**,	2087
	2:15 while accusing or else excusing **one a**;)	240
	2:21 Thou therefore which teachest **a**,	2087
	7: 3 husband liveth, she be married to **a** man,	2087
	7: 3 though she be married to **a** man.	2087
	7: 4 ye should be married to **a**, *even* to him	2087
	7:23 But I see **a** law in my members,	2087
	9:21 honour, and **a** unto dishonour?	3303+3739
	12: 5 in Christ, and every one members **one** of **a**.	240
	12:10 *Be* kindly affectioned **one** to **a** with	240
	12:10 brotherly love; in honour preferring **one a**;	240
	12:16 *Be* of the same mind **one** towards **a**.	240
	13: 8 Owe no *man* any *thing*, but to love **one a**:	240
	13: 8 for he that loveth **a** hath fulfilled the law.	2087
	14: 2 one believeth that *he* may eat all *things:*	3588
	14: 4 Who art thou that judgest **a** *man's* servant?	245
	14: 5 One man esteemeth one day above **a**^s:	2250
	14: 5 a esteemeth every day *alike*. Let every	3739
	14:13 Let us not therefore judge **one a** any more:	240
	14:19 and *things* wherewith **one** may edify **a**.	240
	15: 5 **one** towards **a** according to Christ Jesus:	240
	15: 7 Wherefore receive ye **one a**, as Christ also	240
	15:14 knowledge, able also to admonish **one a**.	240
	15:20 I should build upon **a** *man's* foundation:	245
	16:16 Salute **one a** with a holy kiss.	240
1Co	3: 4 I am of Paul; and **a**, *I am* of Apollos;	2087
	3:10 the foundation, and **a** buildeth thereon.	243
	4: 6 one of you be puffed up for one against **a**.	2087
	4: 7 For who maketh thee to differ *from* **a**?	NIG
	6: 1 any of you, having a matter against **a**,	2087
	6: 7 because ye go to law **one** with **a**.	1438
	7: 7 one after this manner, and **a** after that.	3739
	10:29 for why is my liberty judged of **a** *man's*	243
	11:21 and one is hungry, and **a** is drunken.	3739
	11:33 ye come together to eat, tarry **one** for **a**.	240
	12: 8 to **a** the word of knowledge by the same	243
	12: 9 To **a** faith by the same Spirit; to another	2087
	12: 9 the gifts of healing by the same Spirit;	243
	12:10 To **a** the working of miracles; to another	243
	12:10 to **a** prophecy; to another discerning of	243
	12:10 another prophecy; to **a** discerning of spirits;	243
	12:10 of spirits; to **a** *divers* kinds of tongues;	2087
	12:10 tongues; to **a** the interpretation of tongues:	243
	12:25 should have the same care **one** for **a**.	240
	14:30 If *any thing* be revealed to **a** that sitteth *by*,	243
	15:39 **a** flesh of beasts, another of fishes, *and*	243
	15:39 of beasts, **a** of fishes, *and* another of birds.	243
	15:39 beasts, another of fishes, *and* **a** of birds.	243
	15:40 *is* one, and the *glory* of the terrestrial *is* **a**.	2087
	15:41 and a glory of the moon, and another glory	243
	15:41 glory of the moon, and **a** glory of the stars:	243
	15:41 for *one* star differeth from **a** star in glory.	NIG
	16:20 greet you. Greet ye **one a** with a holy kiss.	240
2Co	10:16 not to boast in **a** *man's* line of *things* made	245
	11: 4 For if he that cometh preacheth **a** Jesus,	243
	11: 4 or *if* ye receive a spirit, which ye have not	2087
	11: 4 which ye have not received, or **a** gospel,	2087
	13:12 Greet **one** a with a holy kiss.	240
Gal	1: 6 you into the grace of Christ unto **a** gospel:	2087
	1: 7 Which is not **a**; but there be some that	243
	5:13 to the flesh, but by love serve **one a**.	240
	5:15 But if ye bite and devour **one a**, take heed	240
	5:15 take heed ye be not consumed **one** of **a**.	240
	5:26 provoking **one a**, envying one another.	240
	5:26 provoking one another, envying **one a**.	240
	6: 4 rejoicing in himself alone, and not in **a**.	2087
Eph	4: 2 longsuffering, forbearing **one a** in love;	240
	4:25 neighbour: for we are members **one** of **a**.	240
	4:32 And be ye kind **one** to **a**, tenderhearted,	240
	4:32 another, tenderhearted, forgiving **one a**,	1438
	5:21 Submitting yourselves **one** to **a** in the fear	240
Col	3: 9 Lie not **one** to **a**, seeing that ye have put	240
	3:13 Forbearing **one a**, and forgiving one	240
	3:13 one another, and forgiving **one a**,	1438
	3:16 and admonishing **one a** in psalms	1438
1Th	3:12 and abound in love **one** towards **a**,	240
	4: 9 are taught of God to love **one a**.	240
	4:18 comfort **one a** with these words.	240
	5:11 one **a**, even as also ye do.	1520+1520+3588
1Ti	5:21 *one* before **a**, doing nothing by partiality.	NIG
Tit	3: 3 and envy, hateful, *and* hating **one a**.	240
Heb	3:13 But exhort **one a** daily, while it is called	1438
	4: 8 would he not afterward have spoken of **a**	243
	5: 6 he saith also in **a** *place*, Thou *art* a priest	2087
	7:11 what further need *was there* that **a** priest	2087
	7:13 *things* are spoken pertaineth to **a** tribe,	2087
	7:15 of Melchisedec there ariseth **a** priest,	2087
	10:24 And let us consider **one a** to provoke unto	240
	10:25 exhorting *one* **a**: and so much the more,	NIG
Jas	2:25 and had sent *them* out **a** way?	2087
	4:11 Speak not evil **one** of **a**, brethren. He that	240
	4:12 to destroy: who art thou that judgest **a**?	2087
	5: 9 Grudge not **one** against **a**, brethren, lest	240
	5:16 Confess *your* faults **one** to **a**, and pray one	240
	5:16 and pray **one** for **a**, that ye may be healed.	240
1Pe	1:22 *see that* ye love **one a** with a pure heart	240
	3: 8 having **compassion** one of **a**, love as	4835
	4: 9 Use hospitality **one** to **a** without grudging.	240
	4:10 gift, *even so* minister the same **one** to **a**,	1438

1Pe	5: 5 all *of you* be subject **one** to **a**, and be	240
	5:14 Greet ye **one a** with a kiss of charity.	240
1Jn	1: 7 we have fellowship **one** with **a**,	240
	3:11 the beginning, that we should love **one a**.	240
	3:23 and love **one a**, as he gave us	240
	4: 7 Beloved, let us love **one a**: for love is of	240
	4:11 so loved us, we ought also to love **one a**.	240
	4:12 If we love **one a**, God dwelleth in us,	240
2Jn	1: 5 from the beginning, that we love **one a**.	240
Rev	6: 4 And there went out a horse *that was* red:	240
	6: 4 the earth, and that they should kill **one a**:	240
	7: 2 And I saw **a** angel ascending from the east,	243
	8: 3 And **a** angel came and stood at the altar,	243
	10: 1 And I saw a mighty angel come down from	243
	11:10 make merry, and shall send gifts **one** to **a**;	240
	12: 3 And there appeared **a** wonder in heaven;	243
	13:11 And I beheld **a** beast coming up out of	243
	14: 6 I saw **a** angel fly in the midst of heaven,	243
	14: 8 And there followed **a** angel, saying,	243
	14:15 And **a** angel came out of the temple,	243
	14:17 And **a** angel came out of the temple	243
	14:18 And **a** angel came out from the altar,	243
	15: 1 And I saw **a** sign in heaven, great	243
	16: 7 And I heard **a** out of the altar say, Even so,	243
	18: 1 And after these *things* I saw **a** angel come	243
	18: 4 And I heard **a** voice from heaven, saying,	243
	20:12 and a book was opened, which is the *book*	243

ANOTHER'S (5) [ANOTHER]

Ge	11: 7 that they may not understand one **a**^s	7453
Ex	21:35 if one man's ox hurt **a**^s, that he die;	7453+7794
Jn	13:14 feet; ye also ought to wash **one a** feet.	240
1Co	10:24 seek his own, but every man **a** *wealth*.	2087
Gal	6: 2 Bear ye **one a** burdens, and so fulfil the	240

ANSWER (131) [ANSWERABLE, ANSWERED, ANSWEREDST, ANSWEREST, ANSWERETH, ANSWERING, ANSWERS]

Ge	30:33 So shall my righteousness **a** for me in time	6030
	41:16 God shall **give** Pharaoh **an a** of peace.	6030
	45: 3 his brethren could not **a** him; for they	6030
Dt	20:11 if it **make** thee **a** of peace, and open unto	6030
	21: 7 they shall **a** and say, Our hands have not	6030
	25: 9 and spit in his face, and shall **a** and say,	6030
	27:15 *a* secret *place*. And all the people shall **a**	6030
Jos	4: 7 ye shall **a** them, That the waters of Jordan	559
Jdg	5:29 *her*, yea, she returned **a** to herself,	561
1Sa	2:16 he would **a** him, *Nay*; but thou shalt give	559
	20:10 or what *if* thy father **a** thee roughly?	6030
2Sa	3:11 he could not **a** Abner a word again,	7725
	24:13 see what **a** I shall return *to* him that sent	1697
1Ki	9: 9 they shall **a**, Because they forsook	559
	12: 6 How do you advise that *I* may **a** this	1697
	12: 7 **a** them, and speak good words to them,	6030
	12: 9 What counsel give ye that we may **a** this	1697
	18:29 nor any to **a**, nor any that regarded.	6030
2Ki	4:29 **a** him not *again:* and lay my staff upon	6030
	18:36 commandment was, saying, **A** him not.	6030
2Ch	10: 6 What counsel give ye *me* to return **a** to	1697
	10: 9 What advice give ye that we may return **a**	1697
	10:10 Thus shalt thou **a** the people that spake	559
Ezr	4:17 *Then* sent the king an **a** unto Rehum	6600
	5: 5 they **returned a** by letter concerning this	8421
	5:11 thus they returned us **a**, saying, We are	6600
Ne	2:20 Then I answered them, and found nothing to **a**.	NIH
Est	4:13 Mordecai commanded to **a** Esther,	7725
	4:15 Esther bade *them* return Mordecai this **a**:	NIH
Job	5: 1 Call now, if there be *any* that will **a** thee;	6030
	9: 3 he cannot **a** him one of a thousand.	6030
	9:14 How much less shall I **a** him, *and*	6030
	9:15 *yet* would I not **a**, *but* I would make	6030
	9:32 *that* I should **a** him, *and* we should	6030
	13:22 call thou, and I will **a**: or let me speak,	6030
	13:22 or let me speak, and **a** thou me.	7725
	14:15 Thou shalt call, and I will **a** thee: thou	6030
	19:16 I called my servant, and he **gave** *me* no **a**;	6030
	20: 2 Therefore do my thoughts **cause** me to **a**,	7725
	20: 3 of my understanding causeth me to **a**.	6030
	23: 5 would know the words *which* he would **a**	6030
	31:14 and when he visiteth, what shall I **a** him?	7725
	31:35 my desire *is, that* the Almighty would **a**	6030
	32: 1 So these three men ceased to **a** Job,	6030
	32: 3 because they had found no **a**, and *yet* had	4617
	32: 5 When Elihu saw that *there was* no **a** in	4617
	32:14 neither will I **a** him with your speeches.	7725
	32:17 I will **a** also my part, I also will shew	6030
	32:20 be refreshed: I will open my lips and **a**.	6030
	33: 5 If thou canst, **a** me, set *thy words* in order	7725
	33:12 will **a** thee, that God is greater than man.	6030
	33:32 If *thou* hast any thing to say, **a** me: speak,	7725
	35: 4 I will **a** thee, and thy companions	4405+7725
	35:12 none **giveth a**, because of the pride of evil	6030
	38: 3 for I will demand of thee, and **a** thou.	3045
	40: 2 *him*? he that reproveth God, let him **a** it.	6030
	40: 4 Behold, I am vile; what shall I **a** thee?	7725
	40: 5 Once have I spoken; but I will not **a**: yea,	6030
Ps	27: 7 have mercy also upon me, and **a** me.	6030
	65: 5 *things* in righteousness wilt thou **a** us,	6030
	86: 7 I will call upon thee: for thou wilt **a** me.	6030
	91:15 He shall call upon me, and I will **a** him:	6030
	102: 2 in the day *when* I call **a** me speedily.	6030
	108: 6 save *with* thy right hand, and **a** me.	6030
	119:42 So shall I have wherewith to **a** him that	6030
	143: 1 in thy faithfulness **a** me, *and* in thy	6030
Pr	1:28 shall they call upon me, but I will not **a**;	6030

Pr	15: 1 A soft **a** turneth away wrath:	4617
	15:23 A man hath joy by the **a** of his mouth:	4617
	15:28 The heart of the righteous studieth to **a**:	6030
	16: 1 the **a** of the tongue, *is* from the Lᴏʀᴅ.	4617
	22:21 that *thou* mightest **a** the words *of* truth to	7725
	24:26 *man* shall kiss *his* lips that giveth a right **a**.	1697
	26: 4 **A** not a fool according to his folly, lest	6030
	26: 5 **A** a fool according to his folly, lest he be	6030
	27:11 I may **a** him that reproacheth me.	1697+7725
	29:19 for though he understand he will not **a**.	4617
SS	5: 6 I called him, but he **gave** me no **a**.	6030
Isa	14:32 then **a** the messengers of the nation?	6030
	30:19 when *he* shall hear it, he will **a** thee.	6030
	36:21 commandment was, saying, **A** him not.	6030
	41:28 when I asked of them, could **a** a word.	7725
	46: 7 *one* shall cry unto him, yet can he not **a**,	6030
	50: 2 when I called, *was there* none to **a**? Is my	6030
	58: 9 shalt thou call, and the Lᴏʀᴅ shall **a**;	6030
	65:12 because when I called, ye did not **a**;	6030
	65:24 to pass, that before they call, I will **a**;	6030
	66: 4 because when I called, none did **a**; when	6030
Jer	5:19 thou **a** them, Like as ye have forsaken	559
	7:27 call unto them; but they will not **a** thee.	6030
	22: 9 they shall **a**, Because they have forsaken	559
	33: 3 I will **a** thee, and shew thee great	6030
	42: 4 *that* whatsoever thing the Lᴏʀᴅ shall **a**	6030
	44:20 the people which had **given** him *that* **a**,	6030
Eze	14: 4 I the Lᴏʀᴅ will **a** him that cometh	6030
	14: 7 I the Lᴏʀᴅ will **a** him by myself:	6030
	21: 7 that thou shalt **a**, For the tidings; because	559
Da	3:16 we *are* not careful to **a** thee in this matter.	8421
Joel	2:19 the Lᴏʀᴅ will **a** and say unto his people,	6030
Mic	3: 7 cover their lips; for *there is* no **a** of God.	4617
Hab	2: 1 and what I shall **a** when I am reproved.	7725
	2:11 and the beam out of the timber shall **a** it.	6030
Zec	13: 6 he shall **a**, *Those with* which I was	559
Mt	22:46 And no *man* was able to **a** him a word,	611
	25:37 shall the righteous **a** him, saying, Lord,	611
	25:40 And the King shall **a** and say unto them,	611
	25:44 Then shall they also **a** him, saying, Lord,	611
	25:45 Then shall he **a** them, saying, Verily I say	611
Mk	11:29 and **a** me, and I will tell you by what	611
	11:30 was *it* from heaven, or of men? **a** me.	611
	14:40 neither wist they what to **a** him.	611
Lk	11: 7 And he from within shall **a** and say,	611
	12:11 no thought how or what *thing* ye shall **a**,	626
	13:25 he shall **a** and say unto you, I know you	611
	14: 6 And they could not **a** him **again** to these	470
	20: 3 I will also ask you one thing; and **a** me:	3004
	20:26 and they marvelled at his **a**, and held their	612
	21:14 not to meditate before *what ye* shall **a**:	626
	22:68 And if I also ask *you,* you will not **a** me,	611
Jn	1:22 that we may give an **a** to them that sent us.	612
	19: 9 Whence art thou? But Jesus gave him no **a**.	612
Ac	24:10 I do the more cheerfully **a** for myself:	626
	25:16 have licence to **a** **for** himself concerning	627
	26: 2 I shall **a** **for** myself this day before thee	626
Ro	11: 4 But what saith the **a** of **God** unto him?	5538
1Co	9: 3 Mine **a** to them that do examine me is	627
2Co	5:12 that you may have *somewhat* to **a** them	NIG
Col	4: 6 *you* may know how ye ought to **a** every	611
2Ti	4:16 At my first **a** no *man* stood with me,	627
1Pe	3:15 be ready always to **give** an **a** to every *man*	627
	3:21 the **a** of a good conscience toward God,)	1906

ANSWERABLE (1) [ANSWER]

Ex	38:18 in the breadth *was* five cubits, **a**	5980+3807.1

ANSWERED (492) [ANSWER]

Ge	18:27 Abraham **a** and said, Behold now, I have	6030
	23: 5 the children of Heth **a** Abraham, saying	6030
	23:10 Ephron the Hittite **a** Abraham in	6030
	23:14 And Ephron **a** Abraham, saying unto him,	6030
	24:50 Laban and Bethuel **a** and said, The thing	6030
	27:37 Isaac **a** and said unto Esau, Behold, I have	6030
	27:39 Isaac his father **a** and said unto him,	6030
	31:14 Rachel and Leah **a** and said unto him,	6030
	31:31 Jacob **a** and said to Laban, Because I was	6030
	31:36 Jacob **a** and said to Laban, What *is* my	6030
	31:43 Laban **a** and said unto Jacob, These	6030
	34:13 the sons of Jacob **a** Shechem and Hamor	6030
	35: 3 who **a** me in the day of my distress,	6030
	40:18 Joseph **a** and said, This *is* the	6030
	41:16 Joseph **a** Pharaoh, saying, *It is* not in me:	6030
	42:22 Reuben **a** them, saying, Spake I not unto	6030
	43:28 they **a**, Thy servant our father *is* in good	559
Ex	4: 1 Moses **a** and said, But behold, they will	6030
	15:21 Miriam **a** them, Sing ye to the Lᴏʀᴅ,	6030
	19: 8 all the people **a** together, and said, All that	6030
	19:19 Moses spake, and God **a** him by a voice.	6030
	24: 3 all the people **a** *with* one voice, and said,	6030
Nu	11:28 **a** and said, My lord Moses, forbid them.	6030
	22:18 Balaam **a** and said unto the servants of	6030
	23:12 he **a** and said, Must I not take heed to	6030
	23:26 Balaam **a** and said unto Balak, Told not I	6030
	32:31 Of Gad and the children of Reuben **a**,	6030
Dt	1:14 ye **a** me, and said, The thing which thou	6030
	1:41 ye **a** and said unto me, We have sinned	6030
Jos	1:16 they **a** Joshua, saying, All that thou	6030
	2:14 men **a** her, Our life for yours, if ye utter	559
	7:20 Achan **a** Joshua, and said, Indeed I have	6030
	9:24 they **a** Joshua, and said, Because it was	6030
	15:19 Who **a**, Give me a blessing; for thou hast	559
	17:15 Joshua **a** them, If thou *be* a great people,	559
	22:21 of Gad and the half tribe of Manasseh **a**,	6030

A

Jos	24:16 the people **a** and said, God forbid that we	6030
Jdg	5:29 Her wise ladies **a** *her*, yea, she returned	6030
	7:14 his fellow **a** and said, This *is* nothing else	6030
	8: 8 the men of Penuel **a** him as the men of	6030
	8: 8 him as the men of Succoth had **a** *him*.	6030
	8:18 they **a**, As thou *art*, so *were* they; *each one*	559
	8:25 they **a**, We will willingly give *them*.	559
	11:13 the king of the children of Ammon **a** unto	6030
	15: 6 they **a**, Samson, the son in law of	559
	15:10 they **a**, To bind Samson are we come up,	559
	18:14 **a** the five men that went to spy out	6030
	19:28 none **a**. Then the man took her *up* upon	6030
	20: 4 of the woman that was slain, **a** and said,	6030
Ru	2: 4 And they **a** him, The Lord bless thee.	559
	2: 6 servant that was set over the reapers **a**	6030
	2:11 Boaz **a** and said unto her, It hath fully	6030
	3: 9 she **a**, I *am* Ruth thine handmaid: spread	559
1Sa	1:15 Hannah **a** and said, No, my lord, I *am* **a**	6030
	1:17 Eli **a** and said, Go in peace: and the God	6030
	3: 4 Lord called Samuel: and he **a**, Here am I.	559
	3: 6 he **a**, I called not, my son; lie down again.	559
	3:10 Samuel **a**, Speak; for thy servant heareth.	559
	3:16 Samuel, my son. And he **a**, Here *am* I.	559
	4:17 the messenger **a** and said, Israel is fled	6030
	4:20 But she **a** not, neither did she regard *it*.	6030
	5: 8 they **a**, Let the ark of the God of Israel be	559
	6: 4 They **a**, Five golden emerods,	559
	9: 8 the servant **a** Saul again, and said, Behold,	6030
	9:12 they **a** them, and said, He is; behold, *he is*	6030
	9:19 Samuel **a** Saul, and said, I *am* the seer:	559
	9:21 Saul **a** and said, *Am* not I **a** Benjamite,	6030
	10:12 one of the same place **a** and said, But who	6030
	10:22 the Lord **a**, Behold, he hath hid himself	559
	11: 2 Nahash the Ammonite **a** them, On this	559
	12: 5 in my hand. And they **a**, *He is* witness.	559
	14:12 And the men of the garrison **a** Jonathan	6030
	14:28 one of the people, and said, Thy father	6030
	14:37 hand of Israel? But he **a** him not that day.	6030
	14:39 a *man* among all the people that **a** him.	6030
	14:44 Saul **a**, God do so and more also: for thou	6030
	16:18 **a** one of the servants, and said, Behold,	6030
	17:27 people **a** him after this manner, saying,	559
	17:30 the people **a** him again after the former	1697
	17:58 David **a**, I *am* the son of thy servant Jesse	559
	18: 7 the women **a** *one another* as they played,	559
	19:17 Michal **a** Saul, He said unto me, Let me	559
	20:28 Jonathan **a** Saul, David earnestly asked	6030
	20:32 Jonathan **a** Saul his father, and said unto	6030
	21: 4 the priest **a** David, and said, *There is* no	6030
	21: 5 David **a** the priest, and said unto him,	6030
	22: 9 **a** Doeg the Edomite, which *was* set over	6030
	22:12 of Ahitub. And he **a**, Here I *am*, my lord.	559
	22:14 Ahimelech **a** the king, and said, And who	6030
	23: 4 the Lord **a** him and said, Arise, go down	6030
	25:10 Nabal **a** David's servants, and said, Who	6030
	26: 6 **a** David and said to Ahimelech the Hittite,	6030
	26:14 Abner **a** and said, Who *art* thou *that* criest	6030
	26:22 David **a** and said, Behold, the king's spear;	6030
	28: 6 the Lord **a** him not, neither by dreams,	6030
	28:15 Saul **a**, I am sore distressed; for	559
	29: 9 Achish **a** and said to David, I know that	6030
	30: 8 he **a** him, Pursue: for thou shalt surely	559
	30:22 **a** all the wicked men and *men* of Belial,	6030
2Sa	1: 4 he **a**, That the people are fled from the	559
	1: 7 and called unto me. And I **a**, Here *am* I.	559
	1: 8 *art* thou? And I **a** him, I *am* an Amalekite.	559
	1:13 he **a**, I *am* the son of a stranger, an	559
	2:20 and said, *Art* thou Asahel? And he **a**, I *am*.	559
	4: 9 David **a** Rechab and Baanah his brother,	6030
	9: 6 And he **a**, Behold thy servant.	559
	13:12 she **a** him, Nay, my brother, do not force	559
	13:32 of Shimeah David's brother, **a** and said,	6030
	14: 5 And she **a**, I *am* indeed a widow woman,	559
	14:18 the king **a** and said unto the woman,	6030
	14:19 the woman **a** and said, *As* thy soul liveth,	6030
	14:32 Absalom **a** Joab, Behold, I sent unto thee,	559
	15:21 Ittai **a** the king, and said, *As* the Lord	6030
	18: 3 the people **a**, Thou shalt not go forth: for	559
	18:29 Ahimaaz **a**, When Joab sent the king's	559
	18:32 Cushi **a**, The enemies of my lord the king,	559
	19:21 Abishai the son of Zeruiah **a** and said,	6030
	19:26 he **a**, My lord, O king, my servant deceived	559
	19:38 king **a**, Chimham shall go over with me,	559
	19:42 all the men of Judah **a** the men of Israel,	6030
	19:43 the men of Israel **a** the men of Judah,	6030
	20:17 he **a**, I *am* he. Then she said unto him,	559
	20:17 of thine handmaid. And he **a**, I do hear.	559
	20:20 Joab **a** and said, Far be it, far be it from	6030
	21: 1 the Lord **a**, *It is* for Saul, and for *his*	559
	21: 5 they **a** the king, The man that consumed	559
	22:42 *even* unto the Lord, but he **a** them not.	6030
1Ki	1:28 king David **a** and said, Call me Bath-sheba	6030
	1:36 Benaiah the son of Jehoiada **a** the king,	6030
	1:43 Jonathan **a** and said to Adonijah, Verily	6030
	2:22 king Solomon **a** and said unto his mother,	6030
	2:30 Thus said Joab, and thus he **a** me.	6030
	3:27 the king **a** and said, Give her the living	6030
	11:22 he **a**, Nothing: howbeit let me go in any	559
	12:13 the king **a** the people roughly,	6030
	12:16 the people **a** the king, saying,	1697+7725
	13: 6 the king **a** and said unto the man of God,	6030
	18: 8 he **a** him, I *am:* go, tell thy lord, Behold,	559
	18:18 he **a**, I have not troubled Israel; but thou,	559
	18:21 And the people **a** him not a word.	6030
	18:24 all the people **a**, It is well spoken.	6030

1Ki	18:26 *there was* no voice, nor any that **a**.	6030
	20: 4 the king of Israel **a** and said, My lord,	6030
	20:11 the king of Israel **a** and said, Tell *him*,	6030
	20:14 shall order the battle? And he **a**, Thou.	559
	21: 6 and he **a**, I will not give thee my vineyard.	559
	21:20 he **a**, I have found *thee:* because thou hast	559
	22:15 he **a** him, Go, and prosper: for the Lord	559
2Ki	1: 8 they **a** him, *He was* a hairy man,	559
	1:10 Elijah **a** and said to the captain of fifty,	6030
	1:11 he **a** and said unto him, O man of God,	6030
	1:12 Elijah **a** and said unto them, If I *be* a man	6030
	2: 5 he **a**, Yea, I know *it;* hold you your peace.	559
	3: 8 he **a**, The way through the wilderness of	559
	3:11 one of the king of Israel's servants **a**	6030
	4:13 she **a**, I dwell among mine own people.	559
	4:14 And Gehazi **a**, Verily she hath no child,	559
	4:26 well with the child? And she **a**, *It is* well.	559
	6: 2 where we may dwell. And he **a**, Go ye.	559
	6: 3 go with thy servants. And he **a**, I will go.	559
	6:16 he **a**, Fear not: for *they* that *be* with us *are*	559
	6:22 he **a**, Thou shalt not smite *them:* wouldest	559
	6:28 she **a**, This woman said unto me, Give thy	559
	7: 2 a lord on whose hand the king leaned **a**	6030
	7:13 one of his servants **a** and said, Let *some*	6030
	7:19 *that* lord **a** the man of God, and said,	6030
	8:12 he **a**, Because I know the evil that thou	559
	8:13 Elisha **a**, The Lord hath shewed me *that*	559
	8:14 he **a**, He told me *that* thou shouldest surely	559
	9:19 Jehu **a**, What hast thou to do with peace?	559
	9:22 he **a**, What peace, so long as the	559
	10:13 they **a**, We *are* the brethren of Ahaziah;	559
	10:15 Jehonadab **a**, It is. If it be, give *me* thine	559
	18:36 held their peace, and **a** him not a word:	6030
	20:10 Hezekiah **a**, It is a light thing for the	559
	20:15 Hezekiah **a**, All *the things* that *are* in	559
1Ch	12:17 to meet them, and **a** and said unto them,	6030
	21: 3 Joab **a**, The Lord make his people an	559
	21:26 he **a** him from heaven by fire upon the	6030
	21:28 **a** him in the threshingfloor of Ornan	6030
2Ch	2:11 Huram the king of Tyre **a** in writing,	559
	7:22 it shall be **a**, Because they forsook	559
	10:13 the king **a** them roughly; and king	6030
	10:14 **a** them after the advice of the young men,	1696
	10:16 people **a** the king, saying, What portion	7725
	18: 3 he **a** him, I am as thou *art*, and my people	559
	25: 9 the man of God, The Lord is able to	559
	29:31 Hezekiah **a** and said, Now ye have	6030
	31:10 chief priest of the house of Zadok **a** him,	559
	34:15 Hilkiah **a** and said to Shaphan the scribe,	6030
	34:23 she **a** them, Thus saith the Lord God of	559
Ezr	10: 2 of the sons of Elam, **a** and said unto Ezra,	6030
	10:12 all the congregation **a** and said *with* a loud	6030
Ne	2:20 I **a** them, and said unto them,	1697+7725
	6: 4 and I **a** them after the same manner.	7725
	8: 6 all the people **a**, Amen, Amen, with lifting	559
Est	1:16 Memucan **a** before the king and the	559
	5: 4 Esther **a**, If *it seem* good unto the king,	559
	5: 7 **a** Esther, and said, My petition	6030
	6: 7 Haman **a** the king, *For* the man whom	559
	7: 3 Esther the queen **a** and said, If I have	6030
	7: 5 the king Ahasuerus **a** and said unto Esther	559
Job	1: 7 Satan **a** the Lord, and said, From going	6030
	1: 9 Satan **a** the Lord, and said, Doth Job	6030
	2: 2 Satan **a** the Lord, and said, From going	6030
	2: 4 Satan **a** the Lord, and said, Skin for	6030
	4: 1 Then Eliphaz the Temanite **a** and said,	6030
	6: 1 But Job **a** and said,	6030
	8: 1 Then **a** Bildad the Shuhite, and said,	6030
	9: 1 Then Job **a** and said,	6030
	9:16 If I had called, and he had **a** me;	6030
	11: 1 Then **a** Zophar the Naamathite, and said,	6030
	11: 2 Should not the multitude of words be **a**?	6030
	12: 1 And Job **a** and said,	6030
	15: 1 Then **a** Eliphaz the Temanite, and said,	6030
	16: 1 Then Job **a** and said,	6030
	18: 1 Then **a** Bildad the Shuhite, and said,	6030
	19: 1 Then Job **a** and said,	6030
	20: 1 Then **a** Zophar the Naamathite, and said,	6030
	21: 1 But Job **a** and said,	6030
	22: 1 Then Eliphaz the Temanite **a** and said,	6030
	23: 1 Then Job **a** and said,	6030
	25: 1 Then **a** Bildad the Shuhite, and said,	6030
	32: 6 Elihu the son of Barachel the Buzite **a**	6030
	32:12 that convinced Job, *or* that **a** his words:	6030
	32:15 They were amazed, they **a** no more:	6030
	32:16 spake not, but stood still, *and* **a** no more:)	6030
	34: 1 Furthermore Elihu **a** and said,	6030
	38: 1 the Lord **a** Job out of the whirlwind,	6030
	40: 1 Moreover the Lord **a** Job, and said,	6030
	40: 3 Then Job **a** the Lord, and said,	6030
	40: 6 **a** the Lord unto Job out of	6030
	42: 1 Then Job **a** the Lord, and said,	6030
Ps	18:41 *even* unto the Lord, but he **a** them not.	6030
	81: 7 I **a** thee in the secret place of thunder:	6030
	99: 6 called upon the Lord, and he **a** them.	6030
	118: 5 the Lord **a** me, *and set me* in a large	6030
Isa	6:11 he **a**, Until the cities be wasted without	559
	21: 9 he **a** and said, Babylon is fallen, is fallen;	6030
	36:21 held their peace, and **a** him not a word:	559
	39: 4 Hezekiah **a**, All *that is* in mine house	559
Jer	7:13 heard not; and I called you, but ye **a** not;	6030
	11: 5 Then **a** I, and said, So be it, O Lord.	559
	23:35 to his brother, What hath the Lord **a**?	6030
	23:37 the prophet, What hath the Lord **a** thee?	6030

Jer	35:17 called unto them, but they have not **a**.	6030
	36:18 Baruch **a** them, He pronounced all these	559
	44:15 of Egypt, in Pathros, **a** Jeremiah, saying,	6030
Eze	24:20 I **a** them, The word of the Lord came	559
	37: 3 And I **a**, O Lord God, thou knowest.	559
Da	2: 5 The king **a** and said to the Chaldeans,	6032
	2: 7 They **a** again and said, Let the king tell his	6032
	2: 8 The king **a** and said, I know of certainty	6032
	2:10 The Chaldeans **a** before the king, and said,	6032
	2:14 Daniel **a** with counsel and wisdom to	8421
	2:15 He **a** and said to Arioch the king's captain,	6032
	2:20 Daniel **a** and said, Blessed be the name of	6032
	2:26 The king **a** and said to Daniel, whose	6032
	2:27 Daniel **a** in the presence of the king,	6032
	2:47 The king **a** unto Daniel, and said, Of a	6032
	3:16 and Abed-nego, **a** and said to the king,	6032
	3:24 They **a** and said unto the king, True,	6032
	3:25 He **a** and said, Lo, I see four men loose,	6032
	4:19 Belteshazzar **a** and said, My lord,	6032
	5:17 Daniel **a** and said before the king, Let thy	6032
	6:12 The king **a** and said, The thing *is* true,	6032
	6:13 **a** they and said before the king,	6032
Am	7:14 **a** Amos, and said to Amaziah, I *was* no	6030
Mic	6: 5 and what Balaam the son of Beor **a** him;	6030
Hab	2: 2 the Lord **a** me, and said, Write	6030
Hag	2:12 it be holy? And the priests **a** and said, No.	6030
	2:13 the priests **a** and said, It shall be unclean.	6030
	2:14 **a** Haggai, and said, So *is* this people,	6030
Zec	1:10 man that stood among the myrtle trees **a**	6030
	1:11 they **a** the angel of the Lord that stood	6030
	1:12 the angel of the Lord **a** and said,	6030
	1:13 the Lord **a** the angel that talked with me	559
	1:19 he **a** me, These *are* the horns which have	559
	3: 4 he **a** and spake unto those that stood	6030
	4: 4 So I **a** and spake to the angel that talked	6030
	4: 5 the angel that talked with me **a**	6030
	4: 6 he **a** and spake unto me, saying, This *is*	6030
	4:11 **a** I, and said unto him, What *are* these	6030
	4:12 I **a** again, and said unto him, What *be*	6030
	4:13 he **a** me and said, Knowest thou not what	559
	5: 2 I **a**, I see a flying roll; the length thereof *is*	559
	6: 4 I **a** and said unto the angel that talked	6030
	6: 5 the angel **a** and said unto me, These *are*	6030
Mt	4: 4 he **a** and said, It is written, Man shall not	611
	8: 8 The centurion **a** and said, Lord, I am not	611
	11: 4 Jesus **a** and said unto them, Go	611
	11:25 At that time Jesus **a** and said, I thank thee,	611
	12:38 of the scribes and of the Pharisees **a**,	611
	12:39 But he **a** and said to them, An evil	611
	12:48 But he **a** and said unto him that told him,	611
	13:11 He **a** and said unto them, Because it is	611
	13:37 He **a** and said unto them, He that soweth	611
	14:28 Peter **a** him and said, Lord, if it be thou,	611
	15: 3 he **a** and said unto them, Why do you	611
	15:13 But he **a** and said, Every plant, which my	611
	15:15 Then **a** Peter and said unto him,	611
	15:23 But he **a** her not a word. And his disciples	611
	15:24 But he **a** and said, I am not sent but unto	611
	15:26 But he **a** and said, It is not meet to take	611
	15:28 Then Jesus **a** and said unto her, O woman,	611
	16: 2 He **a** and said unto them, When it is	611
	16:16 And Simon Peter **a** and said, Thou art	611
	16:17 And Jesus **a** and said unto him, Blessed art	611
	17: 4 Then **a** Peter, and said unto Jesus, Lord,	611
	17:11 Jesus **a** and said unto them, Elias truly	611
	17:17 Then Jesus **a** and said, O faithless	611
	19: 4 And he **a** and said unto them, Have ye not	611
	19:27 Then **a** Peter and said unto him, Behold,	611
	20:13 he **a** one of them, and said, Friend, I do	611
	20:22 But Jesus **a** and said, Ye know not what ye	611
	21:21 Jesus **a** and said unto them, Verily I say	611
	21:24 And Jesus **a** and said unto them, I also will	611
	21:27 And they **a** Jesus, and said, We cannot tell.	611
	21:29 He **a** and said, I will not: but afterward he	611
	21:30 And he **a** and said, I go, sir: and went not.	611
	22: 1 And Jesus **a** and spake unto them again by	611
	22:29 Jesus **a** and said unto them, Ye do err,	611
	24: 4 Jesus **a** and said unto them, Take heed	611
	25: 9 the wise **a**, saying, *Not so;* lest there be	611
	25:12 But he **a** and said, Verily I say unto you,	611
	25:26 His lord **a** and said unto him, *Thou* wicked	611
	26:23 he **a** and said, He that dippeth *his* hand	611
	26:25 betrayed him, **a** and said, Master, is it I?	611
	26:33 Peter **a** and said unto him, Though all *men*	611
	26:63 And the high priest **a** and said unto him,	611
	26:66 They **a** and said, He is guilty of death.	611
	27:12 the chief priests and elders, he **a** nothing.	611
	27:14 And he **a** him to never a word;	611
	27:21 The governor **a** and said unto them,	611
	27:25 Then **a** all the people, and said, His blood	611
	28: 5 And the angel **a** and said unto the women,	611
Mk	3:33 he **a** them, saying, Who is my mother,	611
	5: 9 he **a**, saying, My name *is* Legion:	611
	6:37 He **a** and said unto them, Give ye them to	611
	7: 6 He **a** and said unto them, Well hath Esaias	611
	7:28 And she **a** and said unto him, Yes, Lord:	611
	8: 4 And his disciples **a** him, From whence can	611
	8:28 And they **a**, John the Baptist: but some *say*,	611
	9: 5 And Peter **a** and said to Jesus, Master, it is	611
	9:12 he **a** and told them, Elias verily cometh	611
	9:17 one of the multitude **a** and said, Master,	611
	9:38 John **a** him, saying, Master, we saw one	611
	10: 3 And he **a** and said unto them, What did	611
	10: 5 And Jesus **a** and said unto them, For	611
	10:20 And he **a** and said unto him, Master,	611

A

Mk 10:29 Jesus **a** and said, Verily I say unto you, 611
10:51 And Jesus **a** and said unto him, What wilt 611
11:14 And Jesus **a** and said unto it, No man eat 611
11:29 And Jesus **a** and said unto them, I will also 611
11:33 they **a** and said unto Jesus, We cannot 611
12:28 and perceiving that he had **a** them well, 611
12:29 And Jesus **a** him, The first of all 611
12:34 And when Jesus saw that he **a** discreetly, 611
12:35 And Jesus **a**, while he taught in 611
14:20 And he **a** and said unto them, *It is* one of 611
14:48 And Jesus **a** and said unto them, Are ye 611
14:61 But he held his peace, and **a** nothing. 611
15: 3 him of many *things:* but he **a** nothing. 611
15: 5 But Jesus yet **a** nothing; so that Pilate 611
15: 9 But Pilate **a** them, saying, Will ye that I 611
15:12 And Pilate **a** and said again unto them, 611
Lk 1:35 the angel **a** and said unto her, The Holy 611
1:60 And his mother **a** and said, Not so; 611
3:16 John **a**, saying unto *them* all, I indeed 611
4: 4 And Jesus **a** him, saying, It is written, 611
4: 8 And Jesus **a** and said unto him, Get thee 611
7:43 Simon **a** and said, I suppose that *he,* to 611
8:21 he **a** and said unto them, My mother 611
8:50 when Jesus heard *it,* he **a** him, saying, 611
9:49 And John **a** and said, Master, we saw one 611
10:28 And he said unto him, Thou hast **a** right: 611
10:41 And Jesus **a** and said unto her, Martha, 611
11:45 Then **a** one of the lawyers, and said unto 611
13:14 And the ruler of the synagogue **a** with 611
13:15 The Lord then **a** him, and said, 611
14: 5 And **a** them, saying, Which of you shall 611
17:20 of God should come, he **a** them and said, 611
17:37 they **a** and said unto him, Where, Lord? 611
19:40 he **a** and said unto them, I tell you that, 611
20: 3 he **a** and said unto them, I will also ask 611
20: 7 they **a**, that *they* could not tell whence 611
20:24 They **a** and said, Cesar's. 611
22:51 And Jesus **a** and said, Suffer ye thus far. 611
23: 3 And he **a** him and said, Thou sayest *it.* 611
23: 9 in many words; but he **a** him nothing. 611
Jn 1:21 Art thou *that* prophet? And he **a**, No. 611
1:26 John **a** them, saying, I baptize with water: 611
1:48 Jesus **a** and said unto him, Before that 611
1:49 Nathanael **a** and saith unto him, Rabbi, 611
1:50 Jesus **a** and said unto him, Because I said 611
2:18 Then **a** the Jews and said unto him, 611
2:19 Jesus **a** and said unto them, Destroy this 611
3: 3 Jesus **a** and said unto him, Verily, verily, 611
3: 5 Jesus **a**, Verily, verily, I say unto thee, 611
3: 9 Nicodemus **a** and said unto him, How can 611
3:10 Jesus **a** and said unto him, Art thou a 611
3:27 John **a** and said, A man can receive 611
4:10 Jesus **a** and said unto her, If thou knewest 611
4:13 Jesus **a** and said unto her, 611
4:17 The woman **a** and said, I have no husband. 611
5: 7 impotent *man* **a** him, Sir, I have no man, 611
5:11 He **a** them, He that made me whole, 611
5:17 But Jesus **a** them, My Father worketh 611
5:19 Then **a** Jesus and said unto them, Verily, 611
6: 7 Philip **a** him, Two hundred pennyworth of 611
6:26 Jesus **a** them and said, Verily, verily, I say 611
6:29 Jesus **a** and said unto them, This is the 611
6:43 Jesus therefore **a** and said unto them, 611
6:68 Then Simon Peter **a** him, Lord, to whom 611
6:70 Jesus **a** them, Have not I chosen you 611
7:16 Jesus **a** them, and said, My doctrine is not 611
7:20 The people **a** and said, Thou hast a devil: 611
7:21 Jesus **a** and said unto them, I have done 611
7:46 The officers **a**, Never man spake like this 611
7:47 Then **a** them the Pharisees, Are ye also 611
7:52 They **a** and said unto him, Art thou also of 611
8:14 Jesus **a** and said unto them, Though I bear 611
8:19 Jesus **a**, Ye neither know me, nor my 611
8:33 They **a** him, We be Abraham's seed, 611
8:34 Jesus **a** them, Verily, verily, I say unto you, 611
8:39 They **a** and said unto him, Abraham is our 611
8:48 Then **a** the Jews, and said unto him, Say 611
8:49 Jesus **a**, I have not a devil; but I honour 611
8:54 Jesus **a**, If I honour myself, my honour is 611
9: 3 Jesus **a**, Neither hath this *man* sinned, 611
9:11 He **a** and said, A man *that is* called Jesus 611
9:20 His parents **a** them and said, We know 611
9:25 He **a** and said, Whether he be a sinner *or* 611
9:27 He **a** them, I have told you already, 611
9:30 The man **a** and said unto them, Why 611
9:34 They **a** and said unto him, Thou wast 611
9:36 He **a** and said, Who is he, Lord, that I 611
10:25 Jesus **a** them, I told you, and ye believe not 611
10:32 Jesus **a** them, Many good works have I 611
10:33 The Jews **a** him, saying, For a good work 611
10:34 Jesus **a** them, Is it not written in your law, 611
11: 9 Jesus **a**, Are there not twelve hours in 611
12:23 Jesus **a** them, saying, The hour is come, 611
12:30 Jesus **a** and said, This voice came not 611
12:34 The people **a** him, We have heard out of 611
13: 7 Jesus **a** and said unto him, What I do thou 611
13: 8 Jesus **a** him, If I wash thee not, thou hast 611
13:26 Jesus **a**, He it is, to whom I shall give a sop 611
13:36 Jesus **a**, Whither I go, thou canst not 611
13:38 Jesus **a** him, Wilt thou lay down thy life 611
14:23 Jesus **a** and said unto him, If a man love 611
16:31 Jesus **a** them, Do ye now believe? 611
18: 5 They **a** him, Jesus of Nazareth. Jesus saith 611
18: 8 Jesus **a**, I have told you that I am *he:* 611
18:20 Jesus **a** him, I spake openly to the world; 611

Jn 18:23 Jesus **a** him, If I have spoken evil, 611
18:30 They **a** and said unto him, If he were not a 611
18:34 Jesus **a** him, Sayest thou this *thing* of 611
18:35 Pilate **a**, Am I a Jew? Thine own nation 611
18:36 Jesus **a**, My kingdom is not of this world: 611
18:37 Jesus **a**, Thou sayest that I am a king. 611
19: 7 The Jews **a** him, We have a law, and by 611
19:11 Jesus **a**, Thou couldest have no power 611
19:15 The chief priests **a**, We have no king 611
19:22 Pilate **a**, What I have written I have 611
20:28 Thomas **a** and said unto him, My Lord 611
21: 5 have ye any meat? They **a** him, No. 611
Ac 3:12 when Peter saw *it,* he **a** unto the people, 611
4:19 But Peter and John **a** and said unto them, 611
5: 8 And Peter **a** unto her, Tell me whether ye 611
5:29 Peter and the *other* apostles **a** and said, 611
8:24 Then **a** Simon, and said, Pray ye to the 611
8:34 And the eunuch **a** Philip, and said, I pray 611
8:37 he **a** and said, I believe that Jesus Christ 611
9:13 Ananias **a**, Lord, I have heard by many 611
10:46 and magnify God. Then **a** Peter, 611
11: 9 But *the* voice **a** me again from heaven, 611
15:13 James **a**, saying, Men *and* brethren, 611
19:15 the evil spirit **a** and said, Jesus I know, 611
21:13 Then Paul **a**, What mean ye to weep 611
22: 8 And I **a**, Who art thou, Lord? And he said 611
22:28 And the chief captain **a**, With a great sum 611
24:10 had beckoned unto him to speak, **a**, 611
24:25 judgment to come, Felix trembled, and **a**, 611
25: 4 But Festus **a**, that Paul should be kept at 611
25: 8 While he **a** for himself, Neither against 626
25: 9 **a** Paul, and said, Wilt thou go up to 611
25:12 **a**, Hast thou appealed unto Cesar? 611
25:16 To whom I **a**, It is not the manner of 611
26: 1 stretched forth the hand, and **a** for himself: 626
Rev 7:13 And one of the elders **a**, saying unto me, 611

ANSWEREDST (2) [ANSWER]
Ps 99: 8 Thou **a** them, O LORD our God: 6030
138: 3 In the day when I cried thou **a** me, *and* 6030

ANSWEREST (6) [ANSWER]
1Sa 26:14 son of Ner, saying, **A** thou not, Abner? 6030
Job 16: 3 or what emboldeneth thee that thou **a**? 6030
Mt 26:62 and said unto him, **A** thou nothing? 6030
Mk 14:60 and asked Jesus, saying, **A** thou nothing? 611
15: 4 asked him again, saying, **A** thou nothing? 611
Jn 18:22 hand, saying, **A** thou the high priest so? 611

ANSWERETH (13) [ANSWER]
1Sa 28:15 **a** me no more, neither by prophets, nor 6030
1Ki 18:24 the God that **a** by fire, let him be God. 6030
Job 12: 4 who calleth upon God, and he **a** him: 6030
Pr 18:13 He that **a** a matter before he heareth *it,* 7725
18:23 useth intreaties; but the rich **a** roughly. 6030
27:19 As *in* water face **a** to face, so the heart of NIH
Ecc 5:20 because God **a** *him* in the joy of his heart. 6031
10:19 maketh merry: but money **a** all *things.* 6030
Mk 8:29 And Peter **a** and saith unto him, Thou art 611
9:19 He **a** him, and saith, O faithless generation, 611
10:24 But Jesus **a** again, and saith unto them, 611
Lk 3:11 He **a** and saith unto them, He that hath 611
Gal 4:25 and **a** to Jerusalem which now is, and is 4960

ANSWERING (31) [ANSWER]
Mt 3:15 Jesus **a** said unto him, Suffer *it* to be so 611
Mk 11:22 Jesus **a** saith unto them, Have faith in 611
11:33 And Jesus **a** saith unto them, Neither do I 611
12:17 Jesus **a** said unto them, Render to Cesar 611
12:24 And Jesus **a** said unto them, Do ye not 611
13: 2 Jesus **a** said unto them, Seest thou these 611
13: 5 And Jesus **a** them began to say, Take heed 611
15: 2 And he **a** said unto him, Thou sayest *it.* 611
Lk 1:19 the angel **a** said unto him, I am Gabriel, 611
4:12 And Jesus **a** said unto him, It is said, 611
5: 5 And Simon **a** said unto him, Master, 611
5:22 he **a** said unto them, What reason ye in 611
5:31 And Jesus **a** said unto them, They that are 611
6: 3 And Jesus **a** them said, Have ye not read so 611
7:22 Then Jesus **a** said unto them, Go *your way,* 611
7:40 And Jesus **a** said unto him, Simon, I have 611
9:19 They **a** said, John the Baptist; but some *say,* 611
9:20 that I am? Peter **a** said, The Christ of God. 611
9:41 And Jesus **a** said, O faithless 611
10:27 And he **a** said, Thou shalt love the Lord 611
10:30 Jesus **a** said, A certain man went down 5274
13: 2 Jesus **a** said, Suppose ye that 611
13: 8 And he **a** said unto him, Lord, let it alone 611
14: 3 Jesus **a** spake unto the lawyers 611
15:29 And he **a** said to *his* father, Lo, these many 611
17:17 And Jesus **a** said, Were there not ten 611
20:34 Jesus **a** said unto them, The children of 611
20:39 Then certain of the scribes said, Master, 611
23:40 But the other **a** rebuked him, saying, Dost 611
24:18 **a** said unto him, Art thou only a stranger 611
Tit 2: 9 please *them* well in all *things;* not **a** *again;* 483

ANSWERS (3) [ANSWER]
Job 21:34 *in* your **a** there remaineth falsehood? 8666
34:36 the end because of his **a** for wicked men. 8666
Lk 2:47 astonished at his understanding and **a**. 612

ANT (1) [ANTS]
Pr 6: 6 Go to the **a**, thou sluggard; consider her 5244

ANTHOTHIJAH See ANTOTHIJAH

ANTICHRIST (4) [CHRIST]
1Jn 2:18 and as ye have heard that **a** shall come, 500
2:22 He is **a**, that denieth the Father and the Son 500
4: 3 this is *that spirit* of **a**, whereof you have 500
2Jn 1: 7 in the flesh. This is a deceiver and an **a**. 500

ANTICHRISTS (1) [CHRIST]
1Jn 2:18 shall come, even now are there many **a**; 500

ANTIOCH (19)
Ac 6: 5 Parmenas, and Nicolas a proselyte of **A**: 491
11:19 and Cyprus, and **A**, preaching the word to 490
11:20 which, when they were come to **A**, 490
11:22 Barnabas, that *he* should go as far as **A**. 490
11:26 had found him, he brought him unto **A**. 490
11:26 disciples were called Christians first in **A**. 490
11:27 came prophets from Jerusalem unto **A**. 490
13: 1 there were in the church that was at **A** 490
13:14 they came to **A** in Pisidia, and went into 490
14:19 there came thither *certain* Jews from **A** 490
14:21 *again* to Lystra, and to Iconium, and **A**, 490
14:26 And thence sailed to **A**, from whence they 490
15:22 men of their own company to **A** with Paul 490
15:23 brethren which are of the Gentiles in **A**. 490
15:30 they were dismissed, they came to **A**: 490
15:35 Paul also and Barnabas continued in **A**, 490
18:22 saluted the church, he went down to **A**. 490
Gal 2:11 when Peter was come to **A**, I withstood 490
2Ti 3:11 afflictions, which came unto me at **A**, 490

ANTIPAS (1)
Rev 2:13 even in *those* days wherein **A** *was* my 493

ANTIPATRIS (1)
Ac 23:31 took Paul, and brought *him* by night to **A**. 494

ANTIQUITY (1)
Isa 23: 7 *Is* this your joyous *city,* whose **a** *is* of 6927

ANTOTHIJAH (1)
1Ch 8:24 And Hananiah, and Elam, and **A**, 6070

ANTOTHITE (2)
1Ch 11:28 son of Ikkesh the Tekoite, Abi-ezer the **A**, 6069
12: 3 and Berachah, and Jehu the **A**, 6069

ANTS (1) [ANT]
Pr 30:25 The **a** *are* a people not strong, yet they 5244

ANUB (1)
1Ch 4: 8 Coz begat **A**, and Zobebah, and the 6036

ANVIL (1)
Isa 41: 7 *with* the hammer him that smote the **a**, 6471

ANY (916) [ANYTHING]
Ge 3: 1 Now the serpent was more subtil than **a** 3605
4:15 lest **a** finding him should kill him. 3605
8:12 returned not again unto him **a** more. 5750
8:21 I will not again curse the ground **a** more 5750
9:11 neither will I again smite **a** more every 5750
9:11 neither shall all flesh be cut off **a** more by 5750
9:11 neither shall there **a** more be a flood to 5750
14:23 that I will not take **a** thing that *is* thine, 3605
17: 5 Neither shall thy name **a** more be called 5750
17:12 or bought with money of **a** stranger, 3605
18:14 Is **a** thing too hard for the LORD? At 1697
19:12 said unto Lot, Hast thou here **a** besides? 4310
19:22 for I cannot do **a** thing till thou be come 1697
22:12 the lad, neither do thou **a** thing unto him: 3972
24:16 a virgin, neither had **a** *man* known her: 376
30:31 said, Thou shalt not give me **a** thing: 3972
31:14 *Is there* yet **a** portion or inheritance for us NIH
35:10 name shall not be called **a** more Jacob, 5750
36:31 before there reigned **a** king over NIH
39: 9 hath he kept back **a** thing from me 3972
39:23 to **a** thing *that was* under his hand; 3605+3972
42:16 proved, whether *there be* **a** truth in you: NIH
43:34 was five times so much as **a** of theirs. 3605
47: 6 if thou knowest **a** *man* of activity amongst NIH
Ex 1:10 to pass, that, when there falleth out **a** war, NIH
8:29 let not Pharaoh deal deceitfully **a** more in 3254
9:29 neither shall there be **a** more hail; 5750
10:15 there remained not **a** green thing in 3605
10:23 neither rose **a** from his place for three days: 376
11: 6 none like it, nor shall be like it **a** more. 3254
11: 7 against **a** of the children of Israel shall not 3605
12:39 neither had they prepared for themselves **a** NIH
16:24 stink, neither was there **a** worm therein. NIH
20: 4 Thou shalt not make unto thee **a** graven NIH
20: 4 a likeness *of any thing* that *is* in heaven 3605
20: 4 any likeness *of a thing* that *is* in heaven NIH
20:10 in it thou shalt not do **a** work, thou, nor 3605
20:17 nor **a** thing that *is* thy neighbour's. 3605
21:23 if **a** mischief follow, then thou shalt give NIH
22: 9 for **a** *manner* of lost *thing,* which 3605
22:10 or an ox, or a sheep, or a beast, to keep; 3605
22:20 He that sacrificeth unto **a** god, save unto 3605
22:22 Ye shall not afflict **a** widow, or NIH
22:23 If thou **afflict** *them* in **a** wise, 6031+6031
22:25 If thou lend money to **a** of my people NIH
22:31 neither shall ye eat **a** flesh that is torn of NIH
24:14 if **a** man have any matters to do, let him 4310
24:14 if any man have **a** matters to do, let him NIH
30:32 neither shall ye make **a** *other* like it, NIH
30:33 Whosoever compoundeth **a** like it, or NIH

A

Ex	30:33 whosoever putteth *a* of it upon a stranger, — NIH
	31:14 for whosoever doeth *a* work therein, that — NIH
	31:15 doeth *a* work in the sabbath day, — NIH
	32:24 Whosoever hath *a* gold, let them break *it* — NIH
	34: 3 neither let a **man** be seen throughout all — 376
	34:10 done in all the earth, nor in a nation: — 3605
	34:24 neither shall a **man** desire thy land, — 376
	35:24 with whom was found shittim wood for a — 3605
	35:33 to make a *manner of* cunning work. — 3605
	35:35 *even* of them that do a work, and of those — 3605
	36: 6 Let neither man nor woman make a **more** — 5750
Lev	1: 2 If *a* man of you bring an offering unto — NIH
	2: 1 when a will offer a meat offering unto — 5315
	2:11 for ye shall burn no leaven, nor *a* honey, — 3605
	2:11 *in* a offering of the Lord made by fire. — NIH
	4: 2 a of the commandments of the Lord — 3605
	4: 2 be done), and shall do against a of them: — 259
	4:13 they have done somewhat against *a* of — 3605
	4:22 a of the commandments of the Lord his — 3605
	4:27 if a one of the common people sin through — 259
	4:27 while he doeth somewhat against *a of* — NIH
	5: 2 Or if a soul touch a unclean thing, — 3605
	5:11 neither shall he put a frankincense — NIH
	5:17 commit a *of these things* which are — 259+3605
	6: 3 in a of all *these* that a man doeth, sinning — 259
	6: 7 it shall be forgiven him for a *thing* of all — 259
	6:27 of the blood thereof upon *a* garment, — NIH
	6:30 whereof *a* of the blood is brought into — NIH
	7: 8 the priest that offereth a man's burnt — NIH
	7:15 he shall not leave *a* of it until the morning. — NIH
	7:18 if *a* of the flesh of the sacrifice of his peace — NIH
	7:19 the flesh that toucheth a unclean *thing* — 3605
	7:21 Moreover the soul that shall touch a — 3605
	7:21 or *a* unclean beast, or any abominable — NIH
	7:21 or a abominable unclean *thing*, and eat of — 3605
	7:24 *with beasts*, may be used in a *other* use: — 3605
	7:26 of fowl or of beast, in a of your dwellings. — 3605
	7:27 soul *it be* that eateth a manner — 3605
	11:10 of a living thing which *is* in the waters, — 3605
	11:32 upon whatsoever *a* of them, when they — NIH
	11:32 *it be* a vessel of wood, or raiment, — NIH
	11:32 whatsoever vessel *it be*, wherein *a* work — NIH
	11:33 vessel, whereinto *a* of them falleth, — NIH
	11:35 every *thing* whereupon *a* part of their — NIH
	11:37 if *a* part of their carcase fall upon any — NIH
	11:37 if *any part* of their carcase fall upon a — 3605
	11:38 if *a* water be put upon the seed, and — NIH
	11:38 a *part* of their carcase fall thereon, it *shall* — NIH
	11:39 if a beast, of which ye may eat, die; — 4480
	11:43 with a creeping thing that creepeth, — 3605
	11:44 neither shall ye defile yourselves with a — 3605
	13:24 Or if there be *a* flesh, in the skin whereof — NIH
	13:48 in a skin, or in a **thing** made of skin; — 3605
	13:49 in the woof, or in a thing of skin; — 3605
	13:51 a skin, *or* in a work that is made of skin; — 3605
	13:52 in woollen or in linen, or a thing of skin, — 3605
	13:53 or in the woof, or in a thing of skin; — 3605
	13:57 or in the woof, or in a thing of skin; — 3605
	13:59 *in* the warp, or woof, or a thing of skins, — 3605
	15: 2 When a **man** hath a running issue out — 376+376
	15: 6 he that sitteth on *a* thing whereon he sat — NIH
	15:10 whosoever toucheth a *thing* that was — 3605
	15:10 that beareth *a of* those *things* shall wash — NIH
	15:16 if a **man's** seed of copulation go out from — 376
	15:22 whosoever toucheth a thing that she sat — 3605
	15:23 or on *a* thing whereon she sitteth, when — NIH
	15:24 if a **man** lie with her at all, and her flowers — 376
	17:10 that eateth a *manner of* blood; — 3605
	17:12 neither shall a^s stranger that sojourneth — 1886.1
	17:13 which hunteth and catcheth *a* beast or — NIH
	18: 6 None of you shall approach to a that is — 3605
	18:21 thou shalt not let *a* of thy seed pass — NIH
	18:23 Neither shalt thou lie with a beast to — NIH
	18:23 neither shall a woman stand before a beast — NIH
	18:24 Defile not you yourselves in a of these — 3605
	18:26 shall not commit a of these abominations; — 3605
	18:26 *neither* a of your own nation, nor any — NIH
	18:26 nor a stranger that sojourneth among you: — NIH
	18:29 For whosoever shall commit a of these — 3605
	18:30 that *ye* commit not *a* one of *these* — NIH
	19:17 thou shalt **in a wise rebuke** thy — 3198+3198
	19:18 nor **bear a grudge against** the children — 5201
	19:26 Ye shall not eat *a thing* with the blood: — NIH
	19:28 Ye shall not make a cuttings in your flesh — NIH
	19:28 for the dead, nor print a marks upon you: — 3793
	20: 2 that giveth *a* of his seed unto Molech; — NIH
	20: 4 a **ways hide** their eyes from the — 5956+5956
	20:16 if a woman approach unto a beast, — 3605
	20:25 by a *manner of living thing* that creepeth — 3605
	21: 5 nor **make a cuttings** in their flesh. — 8295+8296
	21: 9 the daughter of a priest, if she profane — 376
	21:11 Neither shall he go in to a dead body, — NIH
	21:17 in their generations that hath *a* blemish, — NIH
	21:18 hath a flat nose, or a thing superfluous, — NIH
	22: 4 whoso toucheth a *thing that is* unclean — 3605
	22: 5 Or whosoever toucheth a creeping thing, — 3605
	22: 6 The soul that hath touched a such shall — NIH
	22:11 if the priest buy a soul with his money, — NIH
	22:23 a lamb that **hath a thing superfluous** or — 8311
	22:24 neither shall you make a offering *thereof* — NIH
	22:25 offer the bread of your God of a of these; — 3605
	23:22 neither shalt thou gather a gleaning of thy — NIH
	23:30 whatsoever soul *it be* that doeth a work — 3605
	24:17 he that killeth a man shall surely be put to — 3605
	25: 25 if *a* of his kin come to redeem it, — NIH

Lev	25:32 may the Levites redeem at **a time.** — 5769
	25:49 *a* that is nigh of kin unto him of his family — NIH
	26: 1 neither shall ye set up *a* image of stone in — NIH
	27: 9 all that *a man* giveth of such unto — NIH
	27:11 if *it be* a unclean beast, of which they do — 3605
	27:19 the field will **in a wise redeem** it, — 1350+1350
	27:20 it shall not be redeemed a **more.** — 5750
Nu	4:15 they shall not touch *a holy thing*, lest they — NIH
	5: 6 woman shall commit a sin that men — 3605
	5:10 whatsoever *a man* giveth the priest, it shall — 376
	5:12 If a man's wife go aside, and commit a — 376
	6: 3 neither shall he drink a liquor of grapes, — 3605
	6: 9 And if a man die very suddenly by him, — NIH
	9:10 If a man of you or of your posterity shall — 376
	9:12 unto the morning, nor break a bone of it: — NIH
	14:23 neither shall a of them that provoked me — 3605
	15:27 if a soul sin through ignorance, then he — 259
	17:13 Whosoever cometh **a thing** near unto — 3605
	18: 5 that there be no wrath a **more** upon — 5750
	18:20 shalt thou have a part among them: — NIH
	19:11 He that toucheth the dead *body* of a man — 3605
	19:13 Whosoever toucheth the dead *body* of a — NIH
	20: 5 neither *is there* a water to drink. — NIH
	20:19 without *doing* a thing *else*, go through on — NIH
	21: 5 there *is* no bread, neither *is there* a water; — NIH
	21: 9 to pass, that if a serpent had bitten a man, — NIH
	22:38 I now a **power at all** to say any — 3201+3201
	22:38 I now any power at all to say a **thing**? — 3972
	23:23 neither *is there* a divination against Israel: — NIH
	29: 7 your souls: ye shall not do a work *therein:* — 3605
	30: 5 not a of her vows, or of her bonds — 3605
	30:15 if he shall a **ways make** them **void** — 6565+6565
	31:19 whosoever hath killed *a* person, — NIH
	31:19 whosoever hath touched a slain, purify — NIH
	35:11 which killeth *a* person at unawares. — NIH
	35:15 that every one that killeth **a** person — NIH
	35:22 cast upon him a thing without laying — NIH
	35:23 with a stone, wherewith *a* man may die, — 3605
	35:26 if the slayer shall **at a time come** — 3318+3318
	35:30 Whoso killeth a person, the murderer shall — NIH
	35:30 one witness shall not testify against *a* — NIH
	36: 3 *if* they be married to a of the sons of — 259
	36: 8 that possesseth an inheritance in a tribe of — NIH
Dt	2:19 of the children of Ammon a possession; — NIH
	2:37 nor unto a place of the river Jabbok, — NIH
	4:16 the similitude of a figure, the likeness of — 3605
	4:17 likeness of a beast that *is* on the earth, — 3605
	4:17 the likeness of a winged fowl that flieth — 3605
	4:18 The likeness of *a thing* that creepeth on — 3605
	4:18 the likeness of **a** fish that *is* in the waters — 3605
	4:23 the likeness of a *thing*, which the Lord — 3605
	4:25 the likeness of a *thing*, and shall do evil — 3605
	4:32 there hath been *a* such thing as this — NIH
	5: 8 Thou shalt not make thee **a** graven image, — NIH
	5: 8 a likeness *of any thing* that *is* in heaven — 3605
	5: 8 any likeness *of a thing* that *is* in heaven — NIH
	5:14 thou shalt not do a work, thou, nor thy — 3605
	5:14 thine ox, nor thine ass, nor a of thy cattle, — 3605
	5:21 his ass, or a *thing* that *is* thy neighbour's. — 3605
	5:25 of the Lord our God a **more,** — 3254+5750
	7: 7 ye were moe in number than a people; — 3605
	8: 9 thou shalt not lack a *thing* in it; — 3605
	12:17 nor a of thy vows which thou vowest, — 3605
	13:11 shall do no more a such wickedness as — 3509.1
	14: 1 nor make *a* baldness between your eyes — NIH
	14: 3 Thou shalt not eat a abominable *thing*. — 3605
	14:21 Ye shall not eat of a **thing** that dieth of — 3605
	15: 7 a of thy gates in thy land which the Lord — 259
	15:21 if there be *a* blemish therein, *as if it be* — NIH
	15:21 lame, or blind, *or have* a ill blemish, — 3605
	16: 4 neither shall there *a thing* of the flesh, — NIH
	16: 5 sacrifice the passover within a of thy gates, — 259
	16:21 shalt not plant thee a grove *of* a trees — 3605
	16:22 Neither shalt thou set thee up a image; — NIH
	17: 1 unto the Lord thy God a bullock, — NIH
	17: 1 is blemish, *or* any evil favouredness: — 3605
	17: 2 within a of thy gates which the Lord thy — 259
	17: 3 or moon, or a of the host of heaven, — 3605
	17:15 Thou shalt **in a wise set** *him* king — 7760+7760
	18: 6 if a Levite come from a of thy gates out of — 259
	18:10 There shall not be found among you *a one* — NIH
	18:16 neither let me see this great fire a **more,** — 5750
	19:11 a **man** hate his neighbour, and lie in wait — 376
	19:15 not rise up against a man for a iniquity, — 3605
	19:15 or for a sin, in any sin that he sinneth: — 3605
	19:15 or for any sin, in a sin that he sinneth: — 3605
	19:16 If a false witness rise up against a **man** to — 376
	19:20 shall henceforth commit no more a^s such — 1697
	21:23 shalt **in a wise bury** him that day; — 6912+6912
	22: 1 **in a case bring** them **again** unto — 7725+7725
	22: 6 to be before thee in the way in a tree, — 3605
	22: 7 shalt **in a wise let** the dam **go,** — 7971+7971
	22: 8 thine house, if a man fall from thence. — NIH
	22:13 If a **man** take a wife, and go in unto her, — 376
	23:10 If there be among you a **man,** that is not — 376
	23:18 *into* the house of the Lord thy God for a — 3605
	23:19 usury of a thing that is lent upon usury: — NIH
	23:24 but thou shalt not put *a* in thy vessel. — NIH
	24: 5 shall he be charged with a business: — NIH
	24: 7 a man be found stealing a of his brethren — 5315
	24:10 When thou dost lend thy brother **a thing,** — 3972
	24:13 **In a case** thou shalt **deliver** him the pledge **again** — 7725+7725
	26:14 have I taken away *ought* thereof for a — NIH
	27: 5 shalt not lift up *a* iron *tool* upon them. — NIH

Dt	27:15 Cursed *be* the man that maketh *a* graven — NIH
	27:21 Cursed *be* he that lieth with a *manner of* — 3605
	28:14 shalt not go aside from **a** of the words — 3605
	28:55 So that *he* will not give to a of them of — 259
	29:23 nor beareth, nor a grass groweth therein, — 3605
	30: 4 If *a* of thine be driven out unto the — NIH
	31:13 which have not known *a thing*, may hear, — NIH
	32:28 neither *is there* a understanding in them. — NIH
	32:39 neither *is there* a that can deliver out of — NIH
Jos	1: 5 There shall not a **man** *be able to* stand — 376
	2:11 neither did there remain a **more** courage — 5750
	2:11 there remain any more courage in a **man,** — 376
	2:19 on our head, if a hand be upon him. — NIH
	5: 1 neither was there spirit in them a **more,** — 5750
	5:12 had the children of Israel manna a **more;** — 5750
	6:10 nor make a noise with your voice, — NIH
	6:10 neither shall *a* word proceed out of your — NIH
	6:18 **in a wise** keep *yourselves* from — 7535
	7:12 neither will I be with you a **more,** — 3254
	8:31 over which no *man* hath lift up *a* iron: — NIH
	10:21 none moved his tongue against a of — NIH
	11:11 destroying *them:* there was not a left — 3605
	11:14 neither left they a to breathe. — 3605
	13:33 unto the tribe of Levi Moses gave not *a* — NIH
	20: 3 That the slayer that killeth *a* person — NIH
	20: 9 whosoever killeth a person at unawares — NIH
	21:45 There failed not ought of a good thing — 3605
	23:12 Else if ye do **in a wise go back,** — 7725+7725
	23:13 out *a of* these nations from before you; — NIH
Jdg	2:14 that they could not **a longer** stand before — 5750
	2:21 I also will not henceforth drive out a from — 376
	4:20 when a man doth come and inquire of — NIH
	4:20 of thee, and say, Is there a man here? — NIH
	11:25 now *art* thou a **thing better** than — 2896+2896
	13: 4 strong drink, and eat not a unclean *thing:* — 3605
	13: 7 neither eat a unclean *thing:* for the child — 3605
	13:14 She may not eat of a *thing* that cometh of — 3605
	13:14 nor eat a unclean *thing:* all that I — 3605
	16:17 become weak, and be like a *other* man. — 3605
	18: 7 that might put *them* to shame in a thing; — NIH
	18: 7 and had no business with a man. — NIH
	18:10 a place where *there is* no want of a thing — 3605
	18:28 and they had no business with a man; — NIH
	19:19 thy servants: there *is* no want of a thing. — 3605
	20: 8 We will not a *of us* go to his tent, — 376
	20: 8 neither will we a *of us* turn into his house. — 376
	21: 1 There shall not a of us give his daughter — 376
	21:12 that had known no man by lying with a — NIH
Ru	1:11 *are there* yet a **moe** sons in my womb, — NIH
	2:22 that they meet thee not in a other field. — NIH
1Sa	2: 2 **neither** *is there* a rock like our — 369+2050.1
	2:13 *was, that* when a man offered sacrifice, — 3605
	2:16 *if* a man said unto him, Let them not fail — NIH
	3:17 if thou hide a thing from me of all — NIH
	5: 5 nor a that come *into* Dagon's house, — 3605
	6: 3 **in a wise return** him a trespass — 7725+7725
	9: 2 *he was* higher than a of the people. — 3605
	10:23 he was higher than a of the people from — 3605
	12: 3 of whose hand have I received *a* bribe to — NIH
	12: 4 neither hast thou taken ought of a **man's** — 376
	13:22 of a of the people that *were* with Saul — 3605
	14:24 Cursed *be* the man that eateth *a* food until — NIH
	14:24 So none of the people tasted *a* food. — NIH
	14:28 Cursed *be* the man that eateth *a* food this — NIH
	14:52 Saul saw a strong man, or any valiant — 3605
	14:52 or a valiant man, he took him unto him. — 3605
	18:25 The king desireth not a dowry, but an — NIH
	20:12 my father about to morrow a time, — NIH
	20:26 Nevertheless Saul spake not **a thing** that — 3972
	20:39 the lad knew not a **thing:** only Jonathan — 3972
	21: 2 Let no man know a **thing** of the business — 3972
	22:15 let not the king impute a thing unto his — NIH
	22:15 were not hurt, neither missed we a **thing,** — 3972
	25:22 light *a that* pisseth against the wall. — NIH
	25:34 light *a that* pisseth against the wall. — NIH
	27: 1 to seek me a **more** in any coast of Israel: — 5750
	27: 1 to seek me any more in a coast of Israel: — 3605
	30: 2 they slew not a, either great or small, — 376
	30:12 nor drunk a water, three days — NIH
	30:19 nor a *thing* that they had taken to them: — 3605
2Sa	2: 1 shall I go up into a of the cities of Judah? — 259
	2:28 no more, neither fought they a **more.** — 5750
	7: 6 I have not dwelt in a house since — NIH
	7: 7 a word with a of the tribes of Israel, — 259
	7:10 of wickedness afflict them a **more,** — 3254
	7:22 thee, neither *is there* a God beside thee, — NIH
	9: 1 Is there yet a that is left of the house of — NIH
	9: 3 *Is there* not yet a of the house of Saul, — 376
	10:19 to help the children of Ammon a **more.** — 5750
	13: 2 it hard for him to do a **thing** to her. — 3972
	14:10 he shall not touch thee a **more.** — 3254+5750
	14:11 the revengers of blood to destroy a **more,** — 7235
	14:14 neither doth God respect *a* person: — NIH
	14:32 if there *be* a iniquity in me, let him kill me. — NIH
	15: 2 *that when* a man that had a controversy — 3605
	15: 4 that every man which hath *a* suit or — NIH
	15: 5 that when a **man** came nigh *to him* to do — 376
	15:11 simplicity, and they knew not a **thing.** — 3605
	19:22 shall there a **man** be put to death *this* day — NIH
	19:28 have I yet to cry a **more** unto the king? — 5750
	19:29 speakest thou a **more** of thy matters? — 5750
	19:35 I hear a **more** the voice of singing *men* — 5750
	19:42 the king's *cost?* or hath he given us a gift? — NIH
	21: 4 for us *shalt thou* kill a **man** in Israel. — 376
	21: 5 from remaining in a of the coasts of Israel, — 3605

1Ki	1: 6 father had not displeased him at **a time**	3117
	2:36 **a whither**. 575+575+1886.5+1886.5+2050.1	
	2:42 **a whither**, 575+575+1886.5+1886.5+2050.1	
	3:12 after thee shall **a** arise like unto thee.	NIH
	3:13 there shall not be **a** among the kings like **a**	376
	5: 6 thou knowest that *there is* not among us **a**	376
	6: 7 axe *nor* **a** tool of iron heard in the house,	3605
	8:31 If **a man** trespass against his neighbour,	376
	8:38 supplication soever be *made* by **a man**,	3605
	10: 3 there was not **a** thing hid from the king,	NIH
	10:20 there was not the like made in a kingdom.	3605
	11:22 howbeit **let me go in a wise**.	7971+7971
	15: 5 turned not aside from **a** *thing* that he	3605
	15:17 that *he* might not suffer **a** to go out or	NIH
	15:29 he left not to Jeroboam **a** that breathed,	3605
	18:26 *there was* no voice, nor **a** that answered.	369
	18:29 **nor a** to answer, nor any that	369+2050.1
	18:29 to answer, **nor a** that regarded.	369+2050.1
	20:33 whether **a** *thing would come* from him,	NIH
	20:39 if **by a means** be **missing**,	6485+6485
2Ki	2:21 shall not be from thence **a more** death	5750
	4: 2 Thine handmaid hath not **a** thing in	3605
	4:29 go *thy way:* if thou meet **a man**, salute him	376
	4:29 if **a** salute thee, answer him not *again:*	376
	6:33 should I wait for the Lord **a longer**?	5750
	10: 5 thou shalt bid us; we will not make a king:	376
	10:14 and forty men; neither left he **a** of them.	376
	10:24 *If* **a** of the men whom I *have* brought into	376
	12: 4 the money that cometh into **a man's** heart	376
	12: 5 **wheresoever** a breach shall	834+3605+8033
	12:13 **a** vessels of gold, or vessels of silver,	3605
	14:26 for *there was* **not a** shut up, nor any left,	657
	14:26 *there was* not any shut up, **nor a**	657+2050.1
	14:26 nor any left, **nor a** helper for Israel.	369+2050.1
	18: 5 kings of Judah, nor **a** that were before him.	NIH
	18:33 Hath **a** of the gods of the nations delivered	376
	21: 8 **a more** out of the land which I gave their	3254
	23:25 neither after him arose there **a** like him.	NIH
	24: 7 the king of Egypt came not again **a more**	5750
1Ch	1:43 **a** king reigned over the children of Israel,	NIH
	17: 6 spake I **a** word to **a** of the judges of Israel,	259
	17: 9 of wickedness waste them **a more**,	3254
	17:20 neither *is there* **a** God besides thee,	NIH
	19:19 help the children of Ammon **a more**.	5750
	23:26 nor **a** vessels of it for the service thereof.	3605
	27: 1 their officers that served the king in **a**	3605
	28:21 skilful *man*, for **a** *manner of* service:	3605
	29:25 not been on **a** king before him in Israel.	3605
2Ch	1:12 **neither** shall there **a** after thee	3808+2050.1
	2:14 also to grave **a** *manner of* graving,	3605
	6: 5 neither chose I **a man** to be a ruler over	376
	6:29 supplication soever shall be *made* of **a**	3605
	8:15 priests and Levites concerning **a** matter,	3605
	9: 9 **neither** was there **a** such spice	3808+2050.1
	9:19 was not the like made in **a** kingdom.	NIH
	9:20 was *not* **a thing** accounted in the days	3972
	23:19 that none *which* was unclean in **a** thing	3605
	32:13 **a ways able** to deliver their lands	3201+3201
	32:15 no god of **a** nation or kingdom was able	3605
	33: 8 Neither will I **a more** remove the foot of	3254
	34:13 in **a manner of service**:	5656+5656+2050.1
Ezr	1: 4 **a** whosoever remaineth in **a** place where he	3605
	7:24 that *touching* **a** of the priests and Levites,	3606
Ne	2:12 neither told I **a** man what my God had put	NIH
	2:12 neither was there **a** beast with me, save	NIH
	5:16 of this wall, neither bought we **a** land:	NIH
	10:31 or **a** victuals on the sabbath day to sell,	3605
Job	4:20 they perish for ever without **a** regarding *it.*	NIH
	5: 1 now, if there be **a** that will answer thee;	NIH
	5: 4 **neither** *is there* **a** to deliver *them.*	369+2050.1
	6: 6 or is there **a** taste in the white of an egg?	NIH
	7:10 neither shall his place know him **a more**.	5750
	8:12 down, it withereth before **a** *other* herb.	3605
	9:33 Neither is there **a** daysman betwixt us,	NIH
	10:22 **without a** order, and *where*	3808+2050.1
	15:11 is there **a** secret thing with thee?	NIH
	16:17 Not for **a** injustice in mine hands: also my	NIH
	18:19 people, nor **a** remaining in his dwellings.	NIH
	20: 9 neither shall his place **a more** behold him.	5750
	21:22 shall **a** teach God knowledge? seeing he	NIH
	22: 3 *Is it* **a** pleasure to the Almighty, that thou	NIH
	25: 3 Is there **a** number of his armies?	NIH
	31: 7 and *if* **a** blot hath cleaved to my hands;	NIH
	31:19 If I have seen **a** perish for want of clothing,	NIH
	31:19 of clothing, or **a** poor without covering;	NIH
	32:21 me not, I pray you, accept **a** man's person,	NIH
	33:13 for he giveth not account of **a** of his	3605
	33:27 if **a** say, I have sinned, and perverted *that*	NIH
	33:32 If *thou* hast **a thing to say**, answer me:	4405
	34:27 and would not consider **a** of his ways:	3605
	34:31 *chastisement,* I will not offend **a more:**	NIH
	36: 5 despiseth not **a**: *he is* mighty in strength	NIH
	36:29 Also can **a** understand the spreadings of	NIH
	37:24 he respecteth not **a** *that are* wise of heart.	3605
Ps	4: 6 many that say, Who will shew us **a** good?	NIH
	14: 2 to see if there were **a** that did understand,	NIH
	33:17 neither shall he deliver **a** by his great	NIH
	34:10 they that seek the Lord shall not want **a**	NIH
	37: 8 fret not thyself **in a wise** to do evil.	389
	38: 3 neither *is there* **a** rest in my bones because	NIH
	49: 7 **by a means** redeem *his* brother,	6299+6299
	53: 2 to see if there were **a** that did understand,	NIH
	59: 5 be not merciful to **a** wicked transgressors,	3605
	74: 9 *there is* no more **a** prophet: neither	NIH
	74: 9 neither *is there* among us that knoweth	NIH

Ps	81: 9 neither shall thou worship **a** strange god.	NIH
	86: 8 neither *are there* **a** works like unto thy	NIH
	91:10 neither shall **a** plague come nigh thy	NIH
	109:12 let there be **a** to favour his fatherless	NIH
	115:17 neither **a** that go down into silence.	3605
	119:133 let not **a** iniquity have dominion over me.	3605
	135:17 neither is there **a** breath in their mouths.	NIH
	139:24 And see if *there be* **a** wicked way in me,	NIH
	141: 4 Incline not my heart to **a** evil thing,	NIH
	146: 2 unto my God while I have **a** being.	NIH
	147:20 He hath not dealt so with **a** nation:	3605
Pr	1:17 vain the net *is* spread in the sight of **a** bird.	3605
	6:35 He will not regard **a** ransom; neither will	3605
	14:34 a nation: but sin *is* a reproach to **a** people.	NIH
	28:17 man that doeth violence to the blood of **a**	NIH
	30: 2 Surely I *am* more brutish than **a** man,	NIH
	30:30 among beasts, and turneth not away for **a;**	3605
	31: 5 pervert the judgment of **a** of the afflicted.	3605
Ecc	1:10 Is there **a** thing whereof it may be said,	NIH
	1:11 **a** remembrance of *things* that are to come	NIH
	2:10 I withheld not my heart from **a** joy;	3605
	3:14 to it, **nor a thing** taken from it:	369+2050.1
	5: 2 not thine heart be hasty to utter **a** thing	NIH
	6: 5 nor known **a** *thing:* this hath more rest	NIH
	9: 5 the dead know not **a** thing, neither have	3972
	9: 5 neither have they **a more** a reward;	5750
	9: 6 neither have they **a more** a portion for	5750
	9: 6 ever in **a** thing that is done under the sun.	3605
Isa	1: 5 Why should ye be stricken **a more**?	5750
	2: 4 neither shall they learn war **a more**.	5750
	2: 7 neither *is there* **a** end of their treasures;	NIH
	2: 7 neither *is there* **a** end of their chariots;	NIH
	19:15 Neither shall there be **a** work for Egypt,	NIH
	26:18 we have not wrought **a** deliverance *in*	NIH
	27: 3 lest **a** hurt it, I will keep it night and day.	NIH
	30:20 be removed into a corner **a more**,	5750
	33:20 neither shall **a** of the cords thereof be	3605
	35: 9 nor **a** ravenous beast shall go up thereon,	3605
	36:18 Hath **a** of the gods of the nations delivered	376
	44: 8 yea, *there is* no God; I know not **a.**	NIH
	51:18 *is there* **a** that taketh her by the hand	NIH
	52:14 visage *was* so marred more than **a** man,	NIH
	53: 9 neither *was* **a** deceit in his mouth.	NIH
	54: 4 the reproach of thy widowhood **a more**.	5750
	56: 2 and keepeth his hand from doing **a** evil.	3605
	59: 2 justice, **nor a** pleadeth for truth:	369+2050.1
	62: 4 neither shall thy land **a more** be termed	5750
Jer	3:16 visit *it;* neither shall *that* be done **a more**.	5750
	3:17 neither shall they walk **a more** after	5750
	5: 1 if there be **a** that executeth judgment,	NIH
	9: 4 neighbour, and trust ye not in **a** brother:	3605
	10:20 *is* none to stretch forth my tent **a more**,	5750
	14:22 Are there **a** among the vanities of	NIH
	17:22 neither do ye **a** work, but hallow ye	3605
	18:18 and let us not give heed to **a** of his words.	3605
	20: 9 of him, nor speak **a more** in his name.	5750
	22:11 He shall not return thither **a more:**	5750
	22:30 of David, and ruling **a more** in Judah.	5750
	23:24 Can **a** hide himself in secret places that I	376
	31:12 they shall not sorrow **a more at all**.	3254+5750
	31:40 nor thrown down **a more** for ever.	5750
	32:27 all flesh: is there **a** thing too hard for me?	3605
	33:26 *I* will not take **a** of his seed *to be* rulers	NIH
	34:10 should serve themselves of them **a more**,	5750
	35: 7 nor have **a**: but all your days ye shall dwell	NIH
	36:24 nor **a** of his servants that heard all these	3605
	37:17 and said, Is there **a** word from the Lord?	NIH
	38: 5 for the king *is* not *he* that can do **a** thing	NIH
	42:21 nor **a** *thing* for the which he hath sent me	3605
	44:26 of **a** man of Judah in all the land of Egypt,	3605
	48: 9 be desolate, without **a** to dwell therein.	NIH
	49:33 abide there, nor **a** son of man dwell in it.	NIH
	50:40 **neither** shall a son of man dwell	3808+2050.1
	51:43 neither doth **a** son of man pass thereby.	NIH
	51:44 the nations shall not flow together **a more**	5750
La	1:12 see if there be **a** sorrow like unto my	NIH
	3:49 ceaseth not, **without a** intermission,	369+4480
Eze	5: 9 whereunto I will not do **a more** the like,	5750
	5:11 mine eye spare, neither will I have **a** pity.	1571
	7:11 nor of their multitude, nor of **a** of theirs:	4480
	7:13 neither shall **a** strengthen himself in	376
	9: 6 come not near **a** man upon whom *is*	3605
	12:24 there shall be no more **a** vain vision nor	NIH
	12:28 none of my words be prolonged **a more**,	5750
	14:11 neither be polluted **a more** with all their	5750
	15: 2 What is the vine tree more than **a** tree, *or*	3605
	15: 3 Shall wood be taken thereof to do **a** work?	NIH
	15: 3 will *men* take a pin of it to hang **a** vessel	3605
	15: 4 midst of it is burnt. Is it meet for **a** work?	NIH
	15: 5 how much less shall it be meet yet for **a**	NIH
	16: 5 eye pitied thee, to do **a** of these unto thee,	259
	16:41 and thou also shalt give no hire **a more**.	5750
	16:63 never open thy mouth **a more**, because	5750
	18: 3 ye shall not have *occasion* **a more** to use	5750
	18: 7 hath not oppressed **a**, *but* hath restored to	376
	18: 8 upon usury, neither hath taken **a** increase,	NIH
	18:10 *that* doeth the like to **a** one of these *things,*	NIH
	18:11 that doeth not **a** of those *duties,*	3605
	18:16 Neither hath oppressed **a**, hath not	376
	18:23 Have I **a pleasure at all** that	2654+2654
	21: 5 of his sheath: it shall not return **a more**.	5750
	23:27 unto them, nor remember Egypt **a more**.	5750
	24:13 not be purged from thy filthiness **a more**,	5750
	27:36 terror, and never *shalt be* **a more**.	5704+5769
	28:19 and never *shalt* be **a more**.	5704+5769

Eze	28:24 nor **a** grieving thorn of all *that are* round	NIH
	29:15 neither shall it exalt itself **a more** above	5750
	31: 8 nor a tree in the garden of God was like	3605
	32:13 the foot of man trouble them **a more**,	5750
	33: 6 and take **a** person from among them,	NIH
	34:10 the shepherds feed themselves **a more;**	5750
	34:29 bear the shame of the heathen **a more**.	5750
	36:14 neither bereave thy nations **a more**,	5750
	36:15 in thee the shame of the heathen **a more**,	5750
	36:15 bear the reproach of the people **a more**,	5750
	36:15 thou cause thy nations to fall **a more**,	5750
	37:22 into two kingdoms **a more at all**:	5750+5750
	37:23 shall they defile themselves **a more**	5750
	37:23 nor with **a** of their transgressions:	3605
	39: 7 let *them* pollute my holy name **a more**	5750
	39:10 neither cut down **a** out of the forests;	NIH
	39:15 when **a** seeth a man's bone, then shall he	NIH
	39:28 and have left none of them **a more** there.	5750
	39:29 Neither will I hide my face **a more** from	5750
Da	2:10 *that* asked such things at a magician, or	3606
	2:30 this secret *is* not revealed to me for **a**	NIH
	2:30 wisdom that I have more than **a** living,	3606
	3:28 that they might not serve nor worship **a**	3606
	3:29 speak **a thing amiss** against the God	7960
	6: 4 neither was there **a** error or fault found in	3606
	6: 5 We shall not find **a** occasion against this	3606
	6: 7 that whosoever shall ask **a** petition of **a**	3606
	6:12 every man that shall ask **a** *petition* of **a**	3606
	8: 4 neither *was there* **a** that could deliver out	NIH
	11:15 neither *shall there be* **a** to strength to	NIH
	11:37 the desire of women, nor regard **a** god:	3605
Hos	13: 4 where *is* **a** *other* that may save thee in all	NIH
	14: 3 neither will we say **a more** to the work of	5750
	14: 8 say, What have I to do **a more** with idols?	5750
Joel	2: 2 the like, neither shall be **a** more after it,	5704
	3:17 no strangers pass through her **a more**.	5750
Am	6:10 of the house, *Is there* yet **a** with thee?	NIH
	7: 8 I will not again pass by them **a more:**	5750
	7:13 prophesy not again **a more** at Beth-el:	5750
	8: 2 I will not again pass by them **a more**.	5750
	8: 7 Surely I will never forget **a** of their works.	3605
Ob	1:18 shall not be **a** remaining of the house	NIH
Jnh	3: 7 nor beast, herd nor flock, taste **a** thing:	3972
Mic	4: 3 neither shall they learn war **a more**.	5750
Zep	3:15 of thee: thou shalt not see evil **a more**.	5750
Hag	2:12 or pottage, or wine, or oil, or **a** meat,	3605
	2:13 unclean *by* a dead body touch **a** of these,	3605
Zec	8:10 hire for man, **nor a** hire for beast;	369+2050.1
	8:10 neither *was there* **a** peace to him that	NIH
	9: 8 oppressor shall pass through them **a more:**	5750
	13: 3 *that* when **a** shall yet prophesy,	376
Mal	2:13 that he regardeth not the offering **a more**,	5750
Mt	4: 6 **lest at a time** thou dash thy foot against a	3379
	5:25 **lest at a time** the adversary deliver thee	3379
	5:40 And if **a** man will sue thee at the law,	3588
	10: 5 into **a** city of the Samaritans enter ye not:	NIG
	11:27 neither knoweth **a** man the Father, save	5100
	12:19 neither shall **a** *man* hear his voice in	5100
	13:15 **lest at a time** they should see with *their*	3379
	13:19 When **a** one heareth the word of	3956
	16:24 If **a** *man* will come after me, let him deny	1536
	18:19 as touching **a** thing that they shall ask,	3956
	21: 3 And if **a** *man* say ought unto you, ye shall	5100
	22:16 neither carest thou for **a** *man:* for thou	3762
	22:46 neither durst **a** *man* from that day forth	5100
	22:46 that day forth ask him **a moe** *questions.*	3765
	24:17 down to take **a** *thing* out of his house:	5100
	24:23 Then if **a** *man* shall say unto you, Lo,	5100
Mk	1:44 See thou say nothing to **a** *man:* but go thy	3367
	4:12 **lest at a time** they should be converted,	3379
	4:22 neither was **a** *thing* kept secret, but that it	NIG
	4:23 If **a** *man* have ears to hear, let him hear.	1536
	5: 4 in pieces: neither could **a** *man* tame him.	3762
	5:35 why troublest thou the Master **a further**?	2089
	7:16 If **a** *man* have ears to hear, let him hear.	1536
	8:26 into the town, nor tell *it* to **a** in the town.	5100
	9: 8 they saw no *man* **a** more, save Jesus only	3765
	9:22 if thou canst do **a** *thing,* have compassion	5100
	9:30 he would not that **a** *man* should know *it.*	5100
	9:35 unto them, If **a** *man* desire to be first,	1536
	11: 3 And if **a** *man* say unto you, Why do ye	5100
	11:13 if haply he might find **a** thing thereon:	5100
	11:16 And would not suffer that **a** *man* should	5100
	11:16 should carry **a** vessel through the temple.	NIG
	11:25 forgive, if ye have ought against **a:**	5100
	12:21 took her, and died, neither left he **a** seed:	NIG
	12:34 And no *man* after that durst ask him **a**	NIG
	13: 5 to say, Take heed lest **a** *man* deceive you:	5100
	13:15 neither enter *therein*, to take **a** *thing* out	5100
	13:21 And then if **a** *man* shall say to you, Lo,	5100
	14:31 with thee, I will **not** deny thee **in a wise**.	3364
	14:63 saith, What need we **a further** witnesses?	2089
	15:44 asked him whether he had been **a while**	3819
	16: 8 **neither** said they **a** thing to any	2532+3762
	16: 8 neither said they any *thing* to **a** *man;*	3762
	16:18 they drink **a** deadly *thing*, it shall not hurt	5100
Lk	3:14 to no man, neither accuse **a** falsely;	NIG
	4:11 **lest at a time** thou dash thy foot agains	3379
	4:40 all they that had **a** sick with divers diseases	NIG

A

Lk	8:17	neither *a thing* hid, that shall not be	NIG
	8:27	neither abode in *a* house, but in the tombs.	NIG
	8:43	**neither** could be healed of *a*,	3756+3762
	9:23	If *a man* will come after me, let him deny	5100
	9:36	no *man* in those days *a* of *those things*	3762
	10:19	and nothing shall **by a means** hurt you.	3364
	11:11	*If a* son shall ask bread of *a* of you that is	5101
	14: 8	When thou art bidden of *a man* to *a*	5100
	14:26	**If** *a man* come to me, and hate not his	1536
	15:29	**neither** transgressed I **at a time**	2532+3763
Jn	19: 8	if I have taken *a thing* from any *man* by	5100
	19: 8	if I have taken any *thing* from *a man* by	5100
	19:31	And if *a man* ask you, Why do ye loose	5100
	20:21	neither acceptest thou the person *of a*,	NIG
	20:27	which deny that there is *a* resurrection;	3361
	20:28	If *a man's* brother die, having a wife,	5100
	20:36	Neither can they die **a more**: for they are	2089
	20:40	And after that they durst not ask him *a*	3762
	21:34	**lest at a time** your hearts be overcharged	3379
	22:16	unto you, I will not **a more** eat thereof,	3765
	22:35	shoes, lacked ye *a thing*? And they said,	5100
	22:71	What need we **a further** witness?	2089
	24:41	he said unto them, Have ye here a meat?	5100
Jn	1: 3	without him was not *a thing* made that	1520
	1:18	No *man* hath seen God **at a time**;	4455
	1:46	Can there a good *thing* come out of	5100
	2:25	And needed not that *a* should testify of	5100
	4:33	Hath a *man* brought him *ought* to eat?	3385
	5:37	Ye have neither heard his voice **at a time**,	4455
	6:46	Not that *a man* hath seen the Father,	5100
	6:51	if *a man* eat of this bread, he shall live for	5100
	7: 4	For *there is* no *man that* doeth *a thing* in	5100
	7:17	If *a man* will do his will, he shall know of	5100
	7:37	and cried, saying, If *a man* thirst,	5100
	7:48	Have *a* of the rulers or of the Pharisees	3385
	7:51	Doth our law judge *a* man, before it hear	3588
	8:33	were never in bondage to *a* **man:** how	3762
	9:22	if *a man* did confess that he *was* Christ,	5100
	9:31	but if *a man* be a worshipper of God,	5100
	9:32	*a man* opened the eyes of one that was	5100
	10: 9	by me if *a man* enter in, he shall be saved,	5100
	10:28	neither shall *a man* pluck them out of my	5100
	11: 9	If *a man* walk in the day, he stumbleth not	5100
	11:57	that, if *a man* knew where he were,	5100
	12:26	If *a man* serve me, let him follow me;	5100
	12:26	if *a man* serve me, him will *my* Father	5100
	12:47	And if *a man* hear my words,	5100
	14:14	If ye shall ask *a thing* in my name, I will	5100
	16:30	needest not that *a man* should ask thee:	5100
	18:31	not lawful for us to put *a man* to death:	3762
	21: 5	unto them, Children, have ye *a* meat?	3385
Ac	4:12	Neither is there salvation in *a* **other:**	3762
	4:32	neither said *a* of *them* that ought of	1520
	4:34	Neither was there *a* among them that	5100
	9: 2	if he found *a* of *this* way, whether they	5100
	10:14	for I have never eaten *a thing that is*	3956
	10:28	me that *I* should not call *a* man common	3367
	10:47	Can *a* man forbid water, that these should	5100
	11: 8	**nothing** common or unclean hath	3763+3956
		at a time	
	13:15	if ye have *a* word of exhortation for	NIG
	17:25	as though he needed *a thing*, seeing he	5100
	19: 2	much as heard whether there be *a* Holy	NIG
	19:38	have a matter against *a man*, the law is	5100
	19:39	But if ye inquire *a thing* concerning other	5100
	24:12	with *a man*, neither raising up the people,	5100
	24:20	**if** they have found *a* evil doing in me,	1536
	25: 5	this man, **if** there be *a* **wickedness** in him.	1536
	25: 8	have I offended *a thing* at all.	5100
	25:11	have committed *a thing* worthy of death,	5100
	25:16	of the Romans to deliver a man to die,	5100
	25:17	they were come hither, **without** a delay,	3367
	25:24	crying that he ought not to live **a longer.**	3371
	27:12	**if by a means** they might attain to	1513
	27:22	for there shall be no loss of *a man's* life	NIG
	27:34	**not** a hair fall from the head of *a* of you.	3762
	27:42	lest *a* of *them* should swim out,	5100
	28:21	neither *a* of the brethren that came	5100
	28:21	came shewed or spake a harm of thee.	5100
Ro	1:10	**if by a means** now at length I might have	1513
	6: 2	that are dead to sin, live **a longer** therein?	2089
	8: 9	Now **if** *a man* have not the Spirit of Christ,	1536
	8:33	Who shall lay a thing to the charge of	NIG
	8:39	height, nor depth, nor *a* other creature,	5100
	9:11	neither having done a good or evil,	5100
	11:14	**If by a means** I may provoke to	1513
	13: 8	Owe no man *a* thing, but to love one	3367
	13: 9	and **if** *there be a* other commandment,	1536
	14:13	**not** therefore judge one another **a more:**	3371
	14:14	him that esteemeth *a thing* to be unclean,	5100
	14:21	*a* thing whereby thy brother stumbleth,	NIG
	15:18	For I will not dare to speak of *a* of *those*	5100
1Co	1:15	Lest a should say that I **at a time**	5100
	1:16	I know not **whether** I baptized a other.	1536
	2: 2	For I determined not to know *a thing*	NIG
	3: 7	neither is he that planteth *a thing*, neither	5100
	3:12	Now **if** *a man* build upon this foundation	1536
	3:14	**If** *a man's* work abide which he hath built	1536
	3:15	If *a man's* work shall be burnt, he shall	1536
	3:17	**If** *a man* defile the temple of God,	1536
	3:18	**If** *a man* among you seemeth to be wise	1536
	5:11	if *a man that is* called a brother be *a*	5100
	6: 1	Dare *a* of you, having a matter against	5100
	6:12	will not be brought under the power of *a*.	5100
	7:12	**If** a brother hath a wife that believeth not,	1536

1Co	7:18	Is *a man* called being circumcised? let him	5100
	7:18	Is *a* called in uncircumcision? let him not	5100
	7:36	if *a man* think that *he* behaveth himself	5100
	8: 2	And if *a man* think that *he* knoweth any	5100
	8: 2	And if any *man* think that he knoweth a	5100
	8: 3	But if *a man* love God, the same is known	5100
	8: 9	But take heed **lest by a means** this liberty	3381
	8:10	For if *a man* see thee which hast	5100
	9: 7	Who goeth a warfare **a time** at his own	4218
	9:15	than that *a man* should make my glorying	5100
	9:27	**lest that by a means**, when I have	3381
	10:19	that the idol is *a thing*, or that which is	5100
	10:19	is offered in sacrifice to idols is *a thing*?	5100
	10:27	of them that believe not bid you *to a*	5100
	10:28	But if *a man* say unto you, This is offered	5100
	11:16	But if *a man* seem to be contentious,	5100
	11:34	And if *a man* hunger, let him eat at home;	5100
	14:27	If *a man* speak in an *unknown* tongue,	5100
	14:30	If *a thing* be revealed to another that	NIG
	14:35	And if they will learn *a thing*, let them ask	5100
	14:37	If *a man* think himself to be a prophet, or	1536
	14:38	But if *a man* be ignorant, let him be	1536
	16:22	If *a man* love not the Lord Jesus Christ,	1536
2Co	1: 4	to comfort them which are in a trouble,	3956
	2: 5	But if *a* have caused grief, he hath not	5100
	2:10	To whom ye forgive *a thing*, *I forgive* also:	5100
	2:10	for **if** I forgave *a thing*, to whom I forgave	1536
	3: 5	ourselves to think *a thing* as of ourselves;	5100
	5:17	if *a man* be in Christ, he *is* a new	1536
	6: 3	Giving no offence in *a thing*, that	3367
	7:14	For **if** I have boasted *a thing* to him of you	1536
	8:23	Whether *a* do inquire of Titus, he is my	NIG
	10: 7	If *a man* trust to himself that *he is* Christ's	1536
	11: 3	But I fear, **lest by a means**, as the serpent	3381
	11:21	Howbeit whereinsoever *a* is bold, (I speak	5100
	12: 6	lest *a man* should think of me above *that*	5100
	12:17	Did I make a gain of you by *a* of them	5100
Gal	1: 8	preach *a* other gospel unto you **than** *that*	3844
	1: 9	**If** *a man* preach any other gospel unto you	1536
	1: 9	*a* other gospel unto you **than** *that* ye have	3844
	2: 2	**lest by a means** I should run, or had run,	3381
	5: 6	availeth a *thing*, nor uncircumcision;	5100
	6:15	availeth *a thing*, nor uncircumcision,	5100
Eph	2: 9	Not of works, lest *a man* should boast.	5100
	5: 5	*a* inheritance in the kingdom of Christ	NIG
	5:27	or a such *thing*; but that it should be holy	5100
	6: 8	that whatsoever good *thing* **a** man doeth,	1538
Php	2: 1	**If** *there be* therefore a consolation in	1536
	2: 1	consolation in Christ, **if** a comfort of love,	1536
	2: 1	**if** a fellowship of the Spirit, if any bowels	1536
	2: 1	of the Spirit, **if a** bowels and mercies,	1536
	3: 4	**If a** other *man* thinketh that *he hath*	1536
	3:11	**If by a means** I might attain unto	1513
	3:15	and **if** in *a thing* ye be otherwise minded,	1536
	4: 8	**if** *there be* a virtue, and *if there be* any	1536
	4: 8	any virtue, and **if** *there be* a praise,	1536
Col	2: 4	lest *a man* should beguile you with	5100
	2: 8	Beware lest *a man* spoil you through	5100
	2:23	not in a honour to the satisfying of	5100
	3:13	if *a man* have a quarrel against any:	5100
	3:13	if any *man* have a quarrel against *a*:	5100
1Th	1: 8	so that we need not to speak *a thing*.	5100
	2: 5	For neither **at a time** used we flattering	4218
	2: 9	would not be chargeable unto *a* of you,	5100
	4: 6	and defraud his brother in *a* matter:	NIG
	5:15	See that none render evil for evil unto *a*	5100
2Th	2: 3	Let no *man* deceive you by a means:	3367
	3: 8	Neither did we eat *a man's* bread for	5100
	3: 8	that *we* might not be chargeable to *a* of	5100
	3:10	that if *a* would not work, neither should	1536
	3:14	And if *a man* obey not our word by *this*	1536
1Ti	1:10	**if** *there be* **a** other *thing that* is contrary to	1536
	5: 4	But if *a* widow have children or nephews,	5100
	5: 8	But if *a* provide not for his own,	5100
	5:16	If *a* man or woman that believeth have	5100
	6: 3	**If** *a man* teach otherwise, and consent not	1536
Tit	1: 6	If *a* be blameless, the husband of one wife,	5100
Heb	1: 5	which of the angels said he **at a time**,	4218
	1:13	to which of the angels said he **at a time**,	4218
	2: 1	**at a time** we should let *them* slip.	3379
	3:12	lest there be in *a* of you an evil heart of	5100
	3:13	lest *a* of you be hardened through	5100
	4: 1	**a** of you should seem to come short *of it*.	5100
	4:11	lest *a man* fall after the same example of	5100
	4:12	and sharper than a twoedged sword,	3956
	4:13	Neither is there a creature *that is* not	NIG
	10:38	if *a man* draw back, my soul shall have	NIG
	12:15	Looking diligently lest *a man* fail of	5100
	12:15	lest a root of bitterness springing up	5100
	12:16	Lest there be *a* fornicator, or	5100
	12:19	should not be spoken to them **a more:**	4369
Jas	1: 5	If *a* of you lack wisdom, let him ask of	5100
	1: 7	that he shall receive *a thing* of the Lord.	5100
	1:13	**neither** tempteth he a man:	1161+3762
	1:23	For **if** a be a hearer of the word, and not a	1536
	1:26	**If** *a man* among you seem to be religious,	1536
	3: 2	**If** *a man* offend not in word, the same *is* a	1536
	5:12	by the earth, neither by a other oath:	5100
	5:13	Is *a* among you afflicted? let him pray.	5100
	5:13	Is *a* merry? let him sing psalms.	5100
	5:14	Is a sick among you? let him call for	5100
	5:19	if *a* of you do err from the truth,	5100
1Pe	3: 1	that, if *a* obey not the word, they also may	5100
	3: 6	and are **not** afraid **with** *a* amazement.	3367
	4:11	If *a man* speak, *let him speak* as the	1536

1Pe	4:11	**if** *a man* minister, *let him do it* as of	1536
	4:16	Yet if *a man* suffer as a Christian, let him	NIG
2Pe	1:20	that no prophecy of the scripture is of *a*	NIG
	3: 9	not willing that *a* should perish, but that	5100
1Jn	2: 1	And if *a man* sin, we have an advocate	5100
	2:15	If *a man* love the world, the love of	5100
	2:27	and ye need not that *a man* teach you:	5100
	4:12	No *man* hath seen God **at a time**. If we	4455
	5:14	if we ask *a thing* according to his will,	5100
	5:16	If *a* man see his brother sin *a* which *is*	5100
2Jn	1:10	If there come *a* unto you, and bring not	5100
Rev	3:20	if *a man* hear my voice, and open the door	5100
	7: 1	on the earth, nor on the sea, nor on a tree.	3956
	7:16	hunger no more, neither thirst **a more;**	2089
	7:16	shall the sun light on them, nor a heat.	3956
	9: 4	neither *a* green *thing*, neither any tree;	3956
	9: 4	neither any green *thing*, neither *a* tree;	3956
	11: 5	And if *a man* will hurt them,	1536
	11: 5	and if *a man* will hurt them, he must in	1536
	12: 8	neither was their place found *a* **more** in	2089
	13: 9	If *a man* have an ear, let him hear.	1536
	14: 9	If *a man* worship the beast and his image,	1536
	18:11	no *man* buyeth their merchandise **a more:**	3765
	18:22	craft he be, shall be found **a more** in thee;	2089
	21: 4	neither shall there be **a more** pain:	2089
	21:27	And there shall in no wise enter into it *a*	3956
	22:18	If *a man* shall add unto these *things*, God	5100
	22:19	And if *a man* shall take away from	5100

ANYTHING (1) [ANY]

1Ch	26:28	whosoever had dedicated *a*, *it was* under	NIH

APACE (3)

2Sa	18:25	And he **came a**, and drew near.	1980+1980
Ps	68:12	Kings of armies did **flee a:**	5074+5074
Jer	46: 5	and are **fled a**, and look not back:	4498+5127

APART (24) [PART]

Ex	13:12	That thou shalt **set a** unto the LORD all	5674
Lev	15:19	if she be blood, she shall be **put a** seven days:	5079
	18:19	as long as she is **put a** for her uncleanness.	5079
Ps	4: 3	know that the LORD hath **set a** *him that is*	6395
Eze	22:10	humbled her **that was set a** for pollution.	5079
Zec	12:12	land shall mourn, every family **a;**	905+3807.1
	12:12	the family of the house of David **a**,	905+3807.1
	12:12	of David apart, and their wives **a;**	905+3807.1
	12:12	family of the house of Nathan **a**,	905+3807.1
	12:12	of Nathan apart, and their wives **a;**	905+3807.1
	12:13	The family of the house of Levi **a**,	905+3807.1
	12:13	of Levi apart, and their wives **a;**	905+3807.1
	12:13	the family of Shimei **a**,	905+3807.1
	12:13	of Shimei apart, and their wives **a;**	905+3807.1
	12:14	family apart, and their wives **a.**	905+3807.1
	12:14	family apart, and their wives **a.**	905+3807.1
Mt	14:13	thence by ship into a desert place **a:**	2398+2596
	14:23	went up into a mountain **a** to pray:	2398+2596
	17: 1	them up into a high mountain **a**,	2398+2596
	17:19	Then came the disciples to Jesus **a**,	2398+2596
	20:17	the twelve disciples **a** in the way,	2398+2596
Mk	6:31	Come ye yourselves **a** into a desert	2398+2596
	9: 2	a high mountain **a** by themselves:	2398+2596
Jas	1:21	Wherefore **lay a** all filthiness	659

APELLES (1)

Ro	16:10	Salute **A** approved in Christ. Salute them	559

APES (2)

1Ki	10:22	and silver, ivory, and **a**, and peacocks.	6971
2Ch	9:21	and silver, ivory, and **a**, and peacocks.	6971

APHARSACHITES (2)

Ezr	5: 6	Shethar-boznai, and his companions the **A**,	671
	6: 6	Shethar-boznai, and your companions the **A**,	671

APHARSATHCHITES (1)

Ezr	4: 9	the Dinaites, the **A**, the Tarpelites,	671

APHARSITES (1)

Ezr	4: 9	the Tarpelites, the **A**, the Archevites,	670

APHEK (8)

Jos	12:18	The king of **A**, one; the king of Lasharon,	663
	13: 4	unto **A**, to the borders of the Amorites:	663
	19:30	Ummah also, and **A**, and Rehob: twenty	663
1Sa	4: 1	and the Philistines pitched in **A**.	663
	29: 1	gathered together all their armies to **A:**	663
1Ki	20:26	and went up to **A**, to fight against Israel.	663
	20:30	the rest fled to **A**, into the city; and *there* a	663
2Ki	13:17	for thou shalt smite the Syrians in **A**,	663

APHEKAH (1)

Jos	15:53	And Janum, and Beth-tappuah, and **A**,	664

APHIAH (1)

1Sa	9: 1	of Bechorath, the son of **A**, a Benjamite,	647

APHIK (1)

Jdg	1:31	nor of Helbah, nor of **A**, nor of Rehob:	663

APHRAH See HOUSE OF APHRAH

APHSES (1)

1Ch	24:15	seventeenth to Hezir, the eighteenth to **A**,	6483

APIECE (8)

Nu	3:47	Thou shalt even take **five** shekels **a**	2568+2568

A

Nu 7:86 incense, *weighing ten shekels* a, 3709+1886.1
17: 6 every one of their princes gave him a rod a, 259
1Ki 7:15 of brass, of eighteen cubits high a's: 259+5982
Eze 10:21 Every one had **four** faces a, and every 702+702
41:24 the doors had two leaves a, two turning NIH
Lk 9: 3 neither money; neither have two coats a. 303
Jn 2: 6 the Jews, containing two or three firkins a. 303

APOLLONIA (1)
Ac 17: 1 they had passed through Amphipolis and **A**, 624

APOLLOS (10)
Ac 18:24 And a certain Jew named **A**, born at 625
19: 1 came to pass that, while **A** was at Corinth, 625
1Co 1:12 and I of **A**; and I of Cephas; and I of Christ. 625
3: 4 I am of Paul; and another, I *am* of **A**; 625
3: 5 and who *is* **A**, but ministers by whom ye 625
3: 6 I have planted, **A** watered; but God gave 625
3:22 or **A**, or Cephas, or the world, or life, or 625
4: 6 to myself and to **A** for your sakes; 625
16:12 As touching *our* brother **A**, I greatly desired 625
Tit 3:13 lawyer and **A** on their journey diligently, 625

APOLLYON (1)
Rev 9:11 but in the Greek *tongue* hath *his* name **A**. 623

APOSTLE (19) [APOSTLES, APOSTLES', APOSTLESHIP]
Ro 1: 1 a servant of Jesus Christ, called *to be* an a, 652
11:13 inasmuch as I am the a of the Gentiles, 652
1Co 1: 1 called *to be* an a of Jesus Christ through 652
9: 1 Am I not an a? am I not free? have I not 652
9: 2 If I be not an a unto others, yet doubtless I 652
15: 9 that am not meet to be called an a, because 652
2Co 1: 1 an a of Jesus Christ by the will of God, 652
12:12 Truly the signs of an a were wrought 652
Gal 1: 1 Paul, an a, (not of men, neither by man, 652
Eph 1: 1 Paul, an a of Jesus Christ by the will of God 652
Col 1: 1 Paul, an a of Jesus Christ by the will of God, 652
1Ti 1: 1 an a of Jesus Christ by the commandment 652
2: 7 and an a, (I speak the truth in Christ, *and* 652
2Ti 1: 1 Paul, an a of Jesus Christ by the will of God 652
1:11 and an a, and a teacher of the Gentiles. 652
Tit 1: 1 a servant of God, and an a of Jesus Christ, 652
Heb 3: 1 consider the **A** and High Priest of our 652
1Pe 1: 1 Peter, an a of Jesus Christ, to the strangers 652
2Pe 1: 1 a servant and an a of Jesus Christ, 652

APOSTLES (55) [APOSTLE]
Mt 10: 2 Now the names of the twelve a are these; 652
Mk 6:30 the a gathered themselves together unto 652
Lk 6:13 he chose twelve, whom also he named a; 652
9:10 And the a, when they were returned, 652
11:49 I will send them prophets and a, and 652
17: 5 And the a said unto the Lord, Increase our 652
22:14 he sat down, and the twelve a with him. 652
24:10 which told these *things* unto the a. 652
Ac 1: 2 unto the **A** whom he had chosen: 652
1:26 and he was numbered with the eleven a. 652
2:37 and said unto Peter and *to* the rest of the a, 652
2:43 wonders and signs were done by the a. 652
4:33 with great power gave the a witness of 652
4:36 who by the a was surnamed Barnabas, 652
5:12 And by the hands of the a were many signs 652
5:18 laid their hands on the a, and put them 652
5:29 and the *other* a answered and said, 652
5:34 commanded to put the a forth a little space; 652
5:40 and when they had called the a, 652
6: 6 Whom they set before the a: and when 652
8: 1 regions of Judea and Samaria, except the a. 652
8:14 Now when the a which were at Jerusalem 652
9:27 brought *him* to the a, and declared unto 652
11: 1 And the a and brethren that were in Judea 652
14: 4 held with the Jews, and part with the a. 652
14:14 *Which* when the a, Barnabas and Paul, 652
15: 2 should go up to Jerusalem unto the a 652
15: 4 *of* the a and elders, and they declared all 652
15: 6 And the a and elders came together for to 652
15:22 Then pleased it the a and elders, with 652
15:23 The a and elders and brethren *send* 652
15:33 go in peace from the brethren unto the a. 652
16: 4 that were ordained of the a and elders 652
Ro 16: 7 who are of note among the a, 652
1Co 4: 9 For I think that God hath set forth us the a 652
9: 5 as well as other a, and *as* the brethren of 652
12:28 first a, secondarily prophets, 652
12:29 *Are* all a? *are* all prophets? *are* all teachers? 652
15: 7 he was seen of James; then of all the a. 652
15: 9 I am the least of the a, that am not meet 652
2Co 11: 5 was not a whit behind the very chiefest a, 652
11:13 For such *are* false a, deceitful workers, 5570
11:13 themselves into the a of Christ. 652
12:11 *in* nothing am I behind the very chiefest a, 652
Gal 1:17 Jerusalem to them which were a before 652
1:19 But other of the a saw I none, save James 652
Eph 2:20 And are built upon the foundation of the a 652
3: 5 as it is now revealed unto his holy a 652
4:11 And he gave some, a; and some, prophets; 652
1Th 2: 6 have been burdensome, as *the* a of Christ. 652
2Pe 3: 2 the commandment of us the a of the Lord 652
Jude 1:17 before of the a of our Lord Jesus Christ; 652
Rev 2: 2 thou hast tried them which say *they* are a, 652
18:20 *thou* heaven, and ye holy a and prophets; 652
21:14 in them the names of the twelve a of 652

APOSTLES' (5) [APOSTLE]
Ac 2:42 And they continued stedfastly in the a 652
4:35 And laid *them down* at the a feet: 652
4:37 brought the money, and laid *it* at the a feet. 652
5: 2 a certain part, and laid *it* at the a feet. 652
8:18 of the a hands the Holy Ghost was given, 652

APOSTLESHIP (4) [APOSTLE]
Ac 1:25 *he* may take part of this ministry and a, 651
Ro 1: 5 By whom we have received grace and a, 651
1Co 9: 2 for the seal of mine a are ye in the Lord. 651
Gal 2: 8 in Peter to the a of the circumcision, 651

APOTHECARIES (1) [APOTHECARY]
Ne 3: 8 repaired Hananiah the son of *one of* the a, 7546

APOTHECARIES' (1) [APOTHECARY]
2Ch 16:14 kinds *of spices* prepared by the a art: 4842

APOTHECARY (4) [APOTHECARIES, APOTHECARIES']
Ex 30:25 ointment compound *after* the art of the a: 7543
30:35 a confection *after* the art of the a, 7543
37:29 *according to* the work of the a. 7543
Ecc 10: 1 Dead flies cause the ointment of the a to 7543

APPAIM (2)
1Ch 2:30 the sons of Nadab; Seled, and **A**: 649
2:31 the sons of **A**; Ishi. And the sons of Ishi; 649

APPAREL (28) [APPARELLED]
Jdg 17:10 by the year, and a suit of a, and thy victuals. 899
1Sa 27: 9 the a, and returned, and came to Achish. 899
2Sa 1:24 put on ornaments of gold upon your a. 3830
12:20 anointed *himself*, and changed his a, 8071
14: 2 put on now mourning a, and anoint not 899
1Ki 10: 5 their a, and his cupbearers, and his ascent 4403
2Ch 9: 4 attendance of his ministers, and their a; 4403
9: 4 his cupbearers also, and their a; 4403
Ezr 3:10 set the priests in their a with trumpets, 3847
Est 5: 1 that Esther put on *her* royal a, and stood NIH
6: 8 Let the royal a be brought which the king 3830
6: 9 let *this* a and horse be delivered to the 3830
6:10 Make haste, *and* take the a and the horse, 3830
6:11 took Haman the a and the horse, 3830
8:15 the presence of the king in royal a *of* blue 3830
Isa 3:22 The **changeable suits** of a, 4254
4: 1 eat our own bread, and wear our own a: 8071
63: 1 this *that is* glorious in his a, travelling in 3830
63: 2 Wherefore *art thou* red in thine a, 3830
Eze 27:24 broidered work, and in chests of **rich** a, 1264
Zep 1: 8 and all such as are clothed with strange a. 4403
Zec 14:14 and silver, and a, in great abundance. 899
Ac 1:10 two men stood by them in white a; 2066
12:21 arrayed in royal a, sat upon his throne, 2066
20:33 coveted no *man's* silver, or gold, or a. 2441
1Ti 2: 9 women adorn themselves in modest a, 2689
Jas 2: 2 in goodly a, and there come in also a poor 2066
1Pe 3: 3 of wearing of gold, or of putting on of a; 2440

APPARELLED (2) [APPAREL]
2Sa 13:18 the king's daughters *that were* virgins a. 3847
Lk 7:25 they which are gorgeously a, 2441

APPARENTLY (1)
Nu 12: 8 mouth, even a, and not in dark speeches; 4758

APPEAL (2) [APPEALED]
Ac 25:11 deliver me unto them. I a unto Cesar. 1941
28:19 *it*, I was constrained to a unto Cesar; 1941

APPEALED (4) [APPEAL]
Ac 25:12 answered, Hast thou a unto Cesar? 1941
25:21 But when Paul had a to be reserved unto 1941
25:25 and *that* he himself hath a to Augustus, 1941
26:32 set at liberty, if he had not a unto Cesar. 1941

APPEAR (54) [APPEARANCE, APPEARANCES, APPEARED, APPEARETH, APPEARING]
Ge 1: 9 unto one place, and let the dry *land* a: 7200
30:37 **made** the white a which *was* in the rods. 4286
Ex 23:15 and none shall a before me empty: 7200
23:17 times in the year all thy males shall a 7200
34:20 and none shall a before me empty. 7200
34:23 men children a before the Lord God, 7200
34:24 when thou shalt go up to a before 7200
Lev 9: 4 for to day the Lord will a unto you. 7200
9: 6 the glory of the Lord shall a unto you. 7200
13:57 if it a still in the garment, either in 7200
16: 2 for I will a in the cloud upon the mercy 7200
Dt 16:16 Three times in a year shall all thy males a 7200
16:16 they shall not a before the Lord empty: 7200
31:11 When all Israel is come to a before 7200
Jdg 13:21 the angel of the Lord did no more a to 7200
1Sa 1:22 that he may a before the Lord, 7200
2:27 Did I **plainly** a unto the house of 1540+1540
2Ch 1: 7 In that night did God a unto Solomon, 7200
Ps 42: 2 when shall I come and a before God? 7200
90:16 Let thy work a unto thy servants, 7200
102:16 shall build up Zion, he shall a in his glory. 7200
SS 2:12 The flowers a on the earth; the time of 7200
4: 1 a flock of goats, that a from mount Gilead. 1570
6: 5 thy hair *is* as a flock of goats that a from 1570
7:12 *whether* the tender grape a, *and* 6605
Isa 1:12 When ye come to a before me, who hath 7200

Isa 66: 5 he *shall* a to your joy, and they shall be 7200
Jer 13:26 upon thy face, that thy shame may a. 7200
Eze 21:24 so that in all your doings your sins do a; 7200
Mt 6:16 that they may a unto men to fast. 5316
6:18 That thou a not unto men to fast, 5316
23:27 which indeed a beautiful outward, 5316
23:28 ye also outwardly a righteous unto men, 5316
24:30 shall a the sign of the Son of man in 5316
Lk 11:44 ye are as graves which a **not**, and the men 82
19:11 the kingdom of God should immediately a. 398
Ac 22:30 the chief priests and all their council to a, 2064
26:16 of those things in the which I will a unto 3700
Ro 7:13 But sin, that it might a sin, working death 5316
2Co 5:10 we must all a before the judgment seat 5319
7:12 you in the sight of God might a unto you. 5319
13: 7 not that we should a approved, but that 5316
Col 3: 4 shall a, then shall ye also appear with him 5319
3: 4 then shall ye also a with him in glory. 5319
1Ti 4:15 to them; that thy profiting may a to all. 5318
Heb 9:24 now to a in the presence of God for us: 1718
9:28 unto them that look for him shall he a 3700
11: 3 seen were not made of *things* which do a. 5316
1Pe 4:18 where shall the ungodly and the sinner a? 5316
5: 4 And when the chief Shepherd shall a, 5319
1Jn 2:28 that, when he shall a, we may have 5319
3: 2 and it doth not yet a what we shall be: 5319
3: 2 we know that, when he shall a, we shall 5319
Rev 3:18 *that* the shame of thy nakedness do not a; 5319

APPEARANCE (38) [APPEAR]
Nu 9:15 the tabernacle as it were the a of fire, 4758
9:16 it *by day*, and the a of fire by night. 4758
1Sa 16: 7 for man looketh on the **outward** a, 5869
Eze 1: 5 this *was* their a; they had the likeness of 4758
1:13 their a *was* like burning coals of fire, *and* 4758
1:13 coals of fire, *and* like the a of lamps: 4758
1:14 returned as the a of a flash of lightning. 4758
1:16 The a of the wheels and their work *was* 4758
1:16 their a and their work *was* as it were a 4758
1:26 of a throne, as the a of a sapphire stone: 4758
1:26 likeness as the a of a man above upon it. 4758
1:27 as the a of fire round about within it, 4758
1:27 from the a of his loins even upward, 4758
1:27 from the a of his loins even downward, 4758
1:27 I saw as it were the a of fire, and it had 4758
1:28 As the a of the bow that is in the cloud in 4758
1:28 the a of the brightness round about. 4758
1:28 This *was* the a of the likeness of the glory 4758
8: 2 I beheld, and lo, a likeness as the a of fire: 4758
8: 2 from the a of his loins even downward, 4758
8: 2 as the a of brightness, as the colour of 4758
10: 1 as the a of the likeness of a throne. 4758
10: 9 the a of the wheels *was* as the colour of a 4758
40: 3 whose a *was* like the appearance of brass, 4758
40: 3 whose appearance *was* like the a of brass, 4758
41:21 the a *of the one* as the appearance of 4758
41:21 the appearance *of the one was* like the a of 4758
42:11 the way before them *was* like the a of 4758
43: 3 *it was* according to the a of the vision 4758
Da 8:15 there stood before me as the a of a man. 4758
10: 6 his face as the a of lightning, and his eyes 4758
10:18 and touched me *one* like the a of a man, 4758
Joel 2: 4 The a of them *is* as the appearance of 4758
2: 4 The appearance of them *is* as the a of 4758
Jn 7:24 Judge not according to the a, 3799
2Co 5:12 to *answer* them which glory in a, 4383
10: 7 Do ye look on *things* after the **outward** a? 4383
1Th 5:22 Abstain from all a of evil. 1491

APPEARANCES (2) [APPEAR]
Eze 10:10 *as for* their a, they four had one likeness, 4758
10:22 river of Chebar, their a and themselves: 4758

APPEARED (70) [APPEAR]
Ge 12: 7 the Lord a unto Abram, and said, 7200
12: 7 an altar unto the Lord, who a unto him. 7200
17: 1 the Lord a to Abram, and said unto him, 7200
18: 1 the Lord a unto him in the plains of 7200
26: 2 the Lord a unto him, and said, Go not 7200
26:24 And the Lord a unto him the same night, 7200
35: 1 that a unto thee when thou fleddest from 7200
35: 7 because there God a unto him, when he 1540
35: 9 God a unto Jacob again, when he came 7200
48: 3 God Almighty a unto me at Luz in the 7200
Ex 3: 2 the angel of the Lord a unto him in a 7200
3:16 of Isaac, and of Jacob, a unto me, saying, 7200
4: 1 will say, The Lord hath not a unto thee. 7200
4: 5 and the God of Jacob, hath a unto thee. 7200
6: 3 I unto Abraham, unto Isaac, 7200
14:27 strength **when** the morning a; 6437+3807.1
16:10 the glory of the Lord a in the cloud. 7200
Lev 9:23 the glory of the Lord a unto all 7200
Nu 14:10 the glory of the Lord a in the tabernacle 7200
16:19 the glory of the Lord a unto all 7200
16:42 covered it, and the glory of the Lord a. 7200
20: 6 and the glory of the Lord a unto them. 7200
Dt 31:15 the Lord a in the tabernacle in a pillar of 7200
Jdg 6:12 the angel of the Lord a unto him, 7200
13: 3 the angel of the Lord a unto the woman, 7200
13:10 him, Behold, the man hath a unto me, 7200
1Sa 3:21 the Lord a again in Shiloh: for 7200
2Sa 22:16 the channels of the sea a, the foundations 7200
1Ki 3: 5 In Gibeon the Lord a to Solomon in a 7200
9: 2 That the Lord a to Solomon the second 7200
9: 2 as he had a unto him at Gibeon. 7200

A

1Ki	11: 9 God of Israel, which had **a** unto him twice	7200
2Ki	2:11 *there* **a** a chariot of fire, and horses of fire,	NIH
2Ch	3: 1 where *the* LORD **a** unto David his father,	7200
	7:12 the LORD **a** to Solomon by night,	7200
Ne	4:21 the rising of the morning till the stars **a**.	3318
Jer	31: 3 The LORD hath **a** of old unto me,	7200
Eze	10: 1 **a** over them as it were a sapphire stone,	7200
	10: 8 there **a** in the cherubims the form of a	7200
	19:11 she **a** in her height with the multitude of	7200
Da	1:15 the end of ten days their countenances **a**	7200
	8: 1 of king Belshazzar a vision **a** unto me,	7200
	8: 1 after that which **a** unto me at the first.	7200
Mt	1:20 *the* angel of the Lord **a** unto him in a	5316
	2: 7 of them diligently what time the star **a**.	5316
	13:26 brought forth fruit, then **a** the tares also.	5316
	17: 3 there **a** unto them Moses and Elias talking	3700
	27:53 went into the holy city, and **a** unto many.	1718
Mk	9: 4 And there **a** unto them Elias with Moses:	3700
	16: 9 he **a** first to Mary Magdalene, out of	5316
	16:12 After that he **a** in another form unto two	5319
	16:14 Afterward he **a** unto the eleven as they sat	5319
Lk	1:11 And there **a** unto him an angel of the Lord	3700
	9: 8 And of some, that Elias had **a**;	5316
	9:31 Who **a** in glory, and spake of his decease	3700
	22:43 And there **a** an angel unto him from	3700
	24:34 Lord is risen indeed, and hath **a** to Simon.	3700
Ac	2: 3 And there **a** unto them cloven tongues like	3700
	7: 2 The God of glory **a** unto our father	3700
	7:30 there **a** to him in the wilderness of mount	3700
	7:35 deliverer by the hand of the angel which **a**	3700
	9:17 **a** unto thee in the way as thou camest,	3700
	16: 9 And a vision **a** to Paul in the night;	3700
	26:16 for I have **a** unto thee for this *purpose, to*	3700
	27:20 neither sun nor stars in many days **a**,	2014
Tit	2:11 that bringeth salvation hath **a** to all men,	2014
	3: 4 love of God our Saviour toward man **a**,	2014
Heb	9:26 once in the end of the world hath he **a**	5319
Rev	12: 1 And there **a** a great wonder in heaven;	3700
	12: 3 And there **a** another wonder in heaven;	3700

APPEARETH (10) [APPEAR]

Lev	13:14 when raw flesh **a** in him, he shall be	7200
	13:43 as the leprosy **a** in the skin of the flesh;	4758
Dt	2:30 deliver him into thy hand, as **a** this day.	NIH
Ps	84: 7 *every one of them* in Zion **a** before God.	7200
Pr	27:25 The hay **a**, and the tender grass sheweth	1540
Jer	6: 1 for evil **a** out of the north,	8259
Mal	3: 2 who *shall* stand when he **a**? for he *is* like	7200
Mt	2:13 *the* angel of the Lord **a** to Joseph in a	5316
	2:19 angel of the Lord **a** in a dream to Joseph	5316
Jas	4:14 that **a** for a little *time*, and	5316

APPEARING (6) [APPEAR]

1Ti	6:14 until the **a** of our Lord Jesus Christ:	2015
2Ti	1:10 But is now made manifest by the **a** of our	2015
	4: 1 and the dead at his **a** and his kingdom;	2015
	4: 8 but unto all them also that love his **a**.	2015
Tit	2:13 and the glorious **a** of the great God	2015
1Pe	1: 7 honour and glory at the **a** of Jesus Christ:	602

APPEASE (1) [APPEASED, APPEASETH]

Ge	32:20 I will **a** him with the present that	3722+6440

APPEASED (2) [APPEASE]

Est	2: 1 when the wrath of king Ahasuerus was **a**,	7918
Ac	19:35 when the townclerk had **a** the people,	2687

APPEASETH (1) [APPEASE]

Pr	15:18 but *he that is* slow to anger **a** strife.	8252

APPERTAIN (2) [APPERTAINED, APPERTAINETH]

Nu	16:30 with all that *a* unto them, and they go	NIH
Jer	10: 7 for to thee doth it **a**: forasmuch as among	2969

APPERTAINED (3) [APPERTAIN]

Nu	16:32 all the men that *a* unto Korah, and all	NIH
	16:33 They, and all that *a* to them, went down	NIH
Ne	2: 8 gates of the palace which *a* to the house,	NIH

APPERTAINETH (1) [APPERTAIN]

Lev	6: 5 *and* give it unto him to whom it **a**, in	NIH

APPETITE (4)

Job	38:39 the lion? or fill the **a** of the young lions,	2416
Pr	23: 2 to thy throat, if thou *be* a man *given* to **a**.	5315
Ecc	6: 7 *is* for his mouth, and yet the **a** is not filled.	5315
Isa	29: 8 behold, *he is* faint, and his soul hath **a**:	8264

APPHIA (1)

Phm	1: 2 And to *our* beloved **A**,	682

APPII (1)

Ac	28:15 they came to meet us as far as **A** forum,	675

APPIUS See APPII

APPLE (8) [APPLES]

Dt	32:10 he kept him as the **a** of his eye.	380
Ps	17: 8 Keep me as the **a** of the eye, hide me	380+1323
Pr	7: 2 and live; and my law as the **a** of thine eye.	380
SS	2: 3 the **a tree** among the trees of the wood,	8598
	8: 5 I raised thee up under the **a** tree: there	8598
La	2:18 no rest; let not the **a** of thine eye cease.	1323
Joel	1:12 the palm tree also, and the **a tree**,	8598
Zec	2: 8 he that toucheth you toucheth the **a** of his	892

APPLES (3) [APPLE]

Pr	25:11 A word fitly spoken *is like* **a** of gold in	8598
SS	2: 5 Stay me with flagons, comfort me with **a**:	8598
	7: 8 the vine, and the smell of thy nose like **a**;	8598

APPLIED (3) [APPLY]

Ecc	7:25 I **a** mine heart to know, and to search,	5437
	8: 9 my heart unto every work that is done	5414
	8:16 When I **a** mine heart to know wisdom,	5414

APPLY (4) [APPLIED]

Ps	90:12 that we may **a** *our* hearts *unto* wisdom.	935
Pr	2: 2 and **a** thine heart to understanding;	5186
	22:17 and **a** thine heart unto my knowledge.	7896
	23:12 **A** thine heart unto instruction, and thine	935

APPOINT (41) [APPOINTED, APPOINTETH, APPOINTMENT]

Ge	30:28 he said, **A** me thy wages, and I will give *it*.	5344
	41:34 and let him **a** officers over the land,	6485
Ex	21:13 I will **a** thee a place whither he shall flee.	7760
	30:16 shalt **a** it for the service of the tabernacle	5414
Lev	26:16 will even **a** over you terror, consumption,	6485
Nu	1:50 shalt **a** the Levites over the tabernacle	6485
	3:10 thou shalt **a** Aaron and his sons,	6485
	4:19 when every one to his service and to his	7760
	4:27 ye shall **a** unto them in charge all their	6485
	35: 6 which ye shall **a** for the manslayer, he	5414
	35:11 ye shall **a** you cities to be cities of refuge	7136
Jos	20: 2 **A** out for you cities of refuge,	5414
1Sa	8:11 and **a** *them* for himself, for his chariots,	7760
	8:12 he will **a** him captains over thousands,	7760
2Sa	6:21 to **a** me ruler over the people of	6680
	7:10 Moreover I will **a** a place for my people	7760
	15:15 *to do* whatsoever my lord the king shall **a**.	977
1Ki	5: 6 servants according to all that thou shalt **a**:	559
	5: 9 unto the place that thou shalt **a** me,	7971
1Ch	15:16 spake to the chief of the Levites to **a**	5975
Ne	7: 3 **a** watches of the inhabitants of Jerusalem,	5975
Est	2: 3 let the king **a** officers in all the provinces	6485
Job	14:13 that thou wouldest **a** me a set time,	7896
Isa	26: 1 salvation will God **a** *for* walls	7896
	61: 3 To **a** unto them that mourn in Zion,	7760
Jer	15: 3 I will **a** over them four kinds, saith	6485
	49:19 who *is* a chosen *man, that* I may **a** over	6485
	49:19 who will **a** me *the* **time**? and who *is* that	3259
	50:44 who *is* a chosen *man, that* I may **a** over	6485
	50:44 who will **a** me *the* **time**? and who *is* that	3259
	51:27 and Ashchenaz; **a** a captain against her;	6485
Eze	21:19 Also, thou son of man, **a** thee two ways,	7760
	21:20 **A** a way, that the sword may come to	7760
	21:22 to **a** captains, to open the mouth in	7760
	21:22 to **a** *battering* rams against the gates,	7760
	45: 6 ye shall **a** the possession of the city five	5414
Hos	1:11 **a** themselves one head, and they shall	7760
Mt	24:51 and **a** *him* his portion with the hypocrites:	5087
Lk	12:46 **a** *him* his portion with the unbelievers.	5087
	22:29 And I **a** unto you a kingdom, as my Father	1303
Ac	6: 3 whom we may **a** over this business.	2525

APPOINTED (126) [APPOINT]

Ge	4:25 hath **a** me another seed instead of	7896
	18:14 At the **time** I will return unto thee,	4150
	24:14 *let the same* be she *that* thou hast **a** for	3198
	24:44 the LORD hath **a** out for my master's son.	3198
Ex	9: 5 the LORD **a** a set time, saying,	7760
	23:15 in the **time** of the month Abib;	4150
Nu	9: 2 also keep the passover at his **a season**.	4150
	9: 3 at even, ye shall keep it in his **a season**:	4150
	9: 7 his **a season** among the children of Israel?	4150
	9:13 the offering of the LORD in his **a season**,	4150
Jos	8:14 he and all his people, at a **time a**, before	4150
	20: 7 they **a** Kedesh in Galilee in mount	6942
	20: 9 These were the cities **a** for all the children	4152
Jdg	18:11 six hundred men *with* weapons of war.	2296
	18:16 six hundred men **a** with their weapons	2296
	18:17 men that were **a** with weapons of war.	2296
	20:38 there was an **a sign** between the men	4150
1Sa	13: 8 to the set time that Samuel had **a**:	NIH
	13:11 *that* thou camest not within the days **a**,	4150
	19:20 Samuel standing *as* **a** over them, the spirit	5324
	20:35 *into* the field at the **time a** with David,	4150
	21: 2 I have **a** *my* servants to such and such a	3045
	25:30 and shall have **a** thee ruler over Israel;	6680
	29: 4 thou hast **a** him, and let him not go	6485
2Sa	17:14 For the LORD had **a** to defeat the good	6680
	20: 5 than the set time which he had **a** him.	3259
	24:15 from the morning even to the time **a**:	4150
1Ki	1:35 I have **a** him to be ruler over Israel	6680
	11:18 and **a** him victuals, and gave him land.	559
	12:12 as the king had **a**, saying, Come to me	1696
	20:42 a man whom I **a** to **utter destruction**,	2764
2Ki	7:17 the king **a** the lord on whose hand he	6485
	8: 6 So the king **a** unto her a certain officer,	5414
	10:24 Jehu **a** fourscore men without, and said,	7760
	11:18 the priest **a** officers over the house of	7760
	18:14 the king of Assyria **a** unto Hezekiah king	7760
1Ch	6:48 brethren also the Levites *were* **a** unto	5414
	6:49 *were* **a** for all the work of the *place* most	NIH
	9:29 *Some* of them also *were* **a** to oversee	4487
	15:17 So the Levites **a** Heman the son of Joel;	5975
	15:19 *were* **a** to sound with cymbals of brass;	NIH
	16: 4 he **a** *certain* of the Levites to minister	5414
2Ch	8:14 he **a**, according to the order of David his	5975
	20:21 he **a** singers unto the LORD,	5975

2Ch	23:18 Also Jehoiada **a** the offices of the house of	7760
	31: 2 Hezekiah **a** the courses of the priests	5975
	31: 3 *He* **a** also the king's portion of his	NIH
	33: 8 the land which I have **a** for your fathers;	5975
	34:22 *they* that the king had **a**, went to Huldah	NIH
Ezr	3: 8 **a** the Levites from twenty years old	5975
	8:20 the princes had **a** for the service of	5414
	10:14 wives in our cities come at **a** times,	2163
Ne	5:14 Moreover from the time that I was **a** to	6680
	6: 7 thou hast also **a** prophets to preach of thee	5975
	7: 1 and the singers and the Levites were **a**,	6485
	9:17 in their rebellion **a** a captain to return to	5414
	10:34 of our fathers, at times a year by year,	2163
	12:31 a two great *companies of them that* gave	5975
	12:44 that time were some **a** over the chambers	6485
	13:30 **a** the wards of the priests and the Levites,	5975
	13:31 at times **a**, and for the firstfruits.	2163
Est	1: 8 the king had **a** to all the officers of his	3245
	2:15 the keeper of the women, **a**.	559
	4: 5 whom he had **a** to attend upon her,	5975
	9:27 and according to their **a** time every year;	NIH
	9:31 times **a**, according as Mordecai the Jew	NIH
Job	7: 1 *Is there* not an **a time** to man upon earth?	6635
	7: 3 and wearisome nights are **a** to me.	4487
	14: 5 hast **a** his bounds that he cannot pass;	6213
	14:14 all the days of my **a time** will I wait,	6635
	20:29 and the heritage **a** unto him by God.	561
	23:14 For he performeth the **thing** that is **a** for	2706
	30:23 *to* death, and *to* the house **a** for all living.	4150
Ps	44:11 Thou hast given us like sheep **a** for meat;	NIH
	78: 5 a law in Israel, which he commanded	7760
	79:11 thou those that are **a to die**;	1121+8546
	81: 3 in the **time a**, on our solemn feast day.	3677
	102:20 to loose those that are **a to death**;	1121+8546
	104:19 He made the moon for seasons: the sun	6213
Pr	7:20 him, *and* will come home at the day **a**.	3677
	8:29 when he **a** the foundations of the earth:	2710
	31: 8 of all such as are **a** to **destruction**.	1121+2475
Isa	1:14 and your **a feasts** my soul hateth:	4150
	14:31 and none *shall be* alone in his **a** times.	4151
	28:25 the barley and the rye in their **a** place?	5567
	44: 7 order for me, since I **a** the ancient people?	7760
Jer	5:24 he reserveth unto us the weeks of	2708
	8: 7 stork in the heaven knoweth her **a** times;	4150
	33:25 *if* I have not **a** the ordinances of heaven	7760
	46:17 *but* a noise; he hath passed the **time a**.	4150
	47: 7 against the sea shore? there hath he **a** it.	3259
Eze	4: 6 I have **a** thee each day for a year.	5414
	36: 5 have **a** my land into their possession	5414
	43:21 shall burn it in the **a place** of the house,	4662
Da	1: 5 the king **a** them a daily provision of	4487
	1:10 who hath **a** your meat and your drink:	4487
	8:19 for at the **time a** the end *shall be*.	4150
	10: 1 thing *was* true, but the **time a** *was* long:	6635
	11:27 for yet the end *shall be* at the **time a**.	4150
	11:29 At the **time a** he shall return,	4150
	11:35 of the end: because *it is* yet for a **time a**.	4150
Mic	6: 9 hear ye the rod, and who hath **a** it.	3259
Hab	2: 3 For the vision *is* yet for an **a time**,	4150
Mt	26:19 And the disciples did as Jesus had **a** them;	4929
	27:10 for the potter's field, as the Lord **a** me.	4929
	28:16 into a mountain where Jesus had **a** them.	5021
Lk	3:13 Exact no more than that which is **a** you.	1299
	10: 1 After these *things* the Lord **a** other seventy	322
	22:29 a kingdom, as my Father hath **a** unto me;	1303
Ac	1:23 And they **a** two, Joseph called Barsabas,	2476
	7:44 as he had **a**, speaking unto Moses,	1299
	17:26 and hath determined the times **before a**,	4384
	17:31 Because he hath **a** a day, in the which he	2476
	20:13 for so had he **a**, minding himself to go	1299
	22:10 of all *things* which are **a** for thee to do.	5021
	28:23 And when they had **a** him a day,	5021
1Co	4: 9 us the apostles last, as *it were* **a to death**:	1935
Gal	4: 2 governors until the **time a** of the father.	4287
1Th	3: 3 for yourselves know that we are **a**	2749
	5: 9 For God hath not **a** us to wrath,	5087
2Ti	1:11 Whereunto I am **a** a preacher,	5087
Tit	1: 5 ordain elders in every city, as I had **a** thee:	1299
Heb	1: 2 whom he hath **a** heir of all *things*,	5087
	3: 2 Who was faithful to him that **a** him,	4160
	9:27 And as it is **a** unto men once to die,	606
1Pe	2: 8 whereunto also they were **a**.	5087

APPOINTETH (1) [APPOINT]

Da	5:21 and *that* he **a** over it whomsoever he will.	6966

APPOINTMENT (4) [APPOINT]

Nu	4:27 At the **a** of Aaron and his sons shall be all	6310
2Sa	13:32 by the **a** of Absalom *this* hath been	6310
Ezr	6: 9 according to the **a** of the priests which *are*	3983
Job	2:11 they had **made an a** together to come to	3259

APPREHEND (2) [APPREHENDED]

2Co	11:32 *with a garrison*, desirous to **a** me:	4084
Php	3:12 follow *after*, if that I may **a** *that* for which	2638

APPREHENDED (3) [APPREHEND]

Ac	12: 4 And when he had **a** him, he put *him* in	4084
Php	3:12 *that* for which also I am **a** of Christ Jesus.	2638
	3:13 Brethren, I count not myself to have **a**:	2638

APPROACH (19) [APPROACHED, APPROACHETH, APPROACHING]

Lev	18: 6 None of you shall **a** to any that is near of	7126
	18:14 thou shalt not **a** to his wife:	7126

A

Lev 18:19 Also thou shalt not **a** unto a woman to 7126
 20:16 if a woman **a** unto any beast, and lie down 7126
 21:17 let him not **a** to offer the bread of his God; 7126
 21:18 *he be* that hath a blemish, he shall not **a**: 7126
Nu 4:19 when they **a** unto the most holy *things:* 5066
Dt 20: 2 that the priest shall **a** and speak unto 5066
 20: 3 you **a** *this* day unto battle against your 7131
 31:14 Behold, thy days **a** that *thou* must die: 7126
Jos 8: 5 that *are* with me, will **a** unto the city: 7126
Job 40:19 that made him can **make** his sword **to a** 5066
Ps 65: 4 **causest** to **a** *unto* thee, *that* he may dwell 7126
Jer 30:21 him to draw near, and he shall **a** unto me: 5066
 30:21 for who *is* this that engaged his heart to **a** 5066
Eze 42:13 where the priests that **a** unto the LORD 7138
 42:14 shall **a** to *those* things which *are* for 7126
 43:19 which **a** unto me, to minister unto me, 7138
1Ti 6:16 in the light **which no** *man* **can a** unto; 676

APPROACHED (2) [APPROACH]
2Sa 11:20 Wherefore **a** ye **so nigh** unto the city 5066
2Ki 16:12 king **a** to the altar, and offered thereon. 7126

APPROACHETH (1) [APPROACH]
Lk 12:33 where no thief **a**, neither moth corrupteth. 1448

APPROACHING (2) [APPROACH]
Isa 58: 2 of justice; they take delight in **a to** God. 7132
Heb 10:25 so much the more, as ye see the day **a.** 1448

APPROVE (3) [APPROVED, APPROVEST, APPROVETH, APPROVING]
Ps 49:13 yet their posterity **a** their sayings. Selah. 7521
1Co 16: 3 whomsoever you shall **a** by *your* letters, 1381
Php 1:10 That ye may **a** *things* that are excellent; 1381

APPROVED (8) [APPROVE]
Ac 2:22 a man **a** of God among you by miracles 584
Ro 14:18 Christ *is* acceptable to God, and **a** of men. 1384
 16:10 Salute Apelles **a** in Christ. Salute them 1384
1Co 11:19 that they *which are* **a** may be made 1384
2Co 7:11 In all *things* ye have **a** yourselves to be 4921
 10:18 For not he that commendeth himself is **a,** 1384
 13: 7 not that we should appear **a**, but that ye 1384
2Ti 2:15 Study to shew thyself **a** unto God, 1384

APPROVEST (1) [APPROVE]
Ro 2:18 and **a** the *things* that are more excellent, 1381

APPROVETH (1) [APPROVE]
La 3:36 subvert a man in his cause, the Lord **a** not. 7200

APPROVING (1) [APPROVE]
2Co 6: 4 But in all *things* **a** ourselves as 4921

APRONS (2)
Ge 3: 7 leaves together, and made themselves **a.** 2290
Ac 19:12 brought unto the sick handkerchiefs or **a,** 4612

APT (4)
2Ki 24:16 all *that* were strong, *and* **a** for war, 6213
1Ch 7:40 genealogy of them *that were* **a** to the war NIH
1Ti 3: 2 given to hospitality, **a to teach;** 1317
2Ti 2:24 but be gentle unto all *men*, **a to teach,** 1317

AQUEDUCT See CONDUIT

AQUILA (6)
Ac 18: 2 And found a certain Jew named **A**, born in 207
 18:18 into Syria, and with him Priscilla and **A:** 207
 18:26 whom when **A** and Priscilla had heard, 207
Ro 16: 3 and **A** my helpers in Christ Jesus: 207
1Co 16:19 **A** and Priscilla salute you much in the Lord, 207
2Ti 4:19 Salute Prisca and **A**, and the household of 207

AR (6)
Nu 21:15 that goeth down to the dwelling of **A,** 6144
 21:28 hath consumed **A** of Moab, *and* the lords 6144
Dt 2: 9 I have given **A** unto the children of Lot 6144
 2:18 Thou art to pass over *through* **A,** the coast 6144
 2:29 the Moabites which dwell in **A**, did unto 6144
Isa 15: 1 Because in the night **A** of Moab is laid 6144

ARA (1)
1Ch 7:38 of Jether; Jephunneh, and Pispah, and **A.** 690

ARAB (1) [ARABIA, ARABIAN, ARABIANS]
Jos 15:52 **A**, and Dumah, and Eshean, 694

ARABAH (2) [BETH-ARABAH]
Jos 18:18 along toward the side over against **A** 6160
 18:18 northward, and went down unto **A:** 6160

ARABIA (8) [ARAB]
1Ki 10:15 *of* all the kings of **A**, and *of* the governors 6153
2Ch 9:14 all the kings of **A** and governors of 6152
Isa 21:13 burden upon **A**. In the forest in Arabia 6152
 21:13 In the forest in **A** shall ye lodge, O ye 6152
Jer 25:24 all the kings of **A**, and all the kings of 6152
Eze 27:21 **A**, and all the princes of Kedar, 6152
Gal 1:17 I went into **A**, and returned again unto 688
 4:25 For *this* Agar is mount Sinai in **A,** 688

ARABIAN (4) [ARAB]
Ne 2:19 the Ammonite, and Geshem the **A,** 6163
 6: 1 Geshem the **A**, and the rest of our 6163
Isa 13:20 neither shall the **A** pitch tent there; 6163
Jer 3: 2 sat for them, as the **A** in the wilderness; 6163

ARABIANS (6) [ARAB]
2Ch 17:11 the **A** brought him flocks, seven thousand 6163
 21:16 of the **A**, that *were* near the Ethiopians: 6163
 22: 1 the band *of men* that came with the **A** to 6163
 26: 7 against the **A** that dwelt in Gur-baal, 6163
Ne 4: 7 the **A**, and the Ammonites, 6163
Ac 2:11 Cretes and **A**, we do hear them speak in 690

ARAD (3)
Nu 21: 1 king **A** the Canaanite, which dwelt *in* 6166
 33:40 king **A** the Canaanite, which dwelt in 6166
Jos 12:14 king of Hormah, one; the king of **A**, one; 6166
Jdg 1:16 of Judah, which *lieth* in the south of **A;** 6166
1Ch 8:15 And Zebadiah, and **A**, and Ader, 6166

ARAH (4)
1Ch 7:39 the sons of Ulla; **A**, and Haniel, and Rezia. 733
Ezr 2: 5 The children of **A**, seven hundred seventy 733
Ne 6:18 the son in law of Shechaniah the son of **A;** 733
 7:10 The children of **A**, six hundred fifty and 733

ARAM (10) [ARAM-NAHARAIM, ARAM-ZOBAH, ARAMITESS, BETH-ARAM, PADAN-ARAM]
Ge 10:22 Asshur, and Arphaxad, and Lud, and **A.** 758
 10:23 the children of **A**; Uz, and Hul, and Gether, 758
 22:21 his brother, and Kemuel the father of **A,** 758
Nu 23: 7 the king of Moab hath brought me from **A,** 758
1Ch 1:17 **A**, and Uz, and Hul, and Gether, 758
 2:23 he took Geshur, and **A**, with the towns of 758
 7:34 Ahi, and Rohgah, Jehubbah, and **A.** 758
Mt 1: 3 Phares begat Esrom; and Esrom begat **A;** 689
 1: 4 And **A** begat Aminadab; 689
Lk 3:33 which was *the son* of **A**, which was 689

ARAM MAACAH See SYRIA-MAACHAH

ARAMAIC See SYRIACK

ARAMEAN See ARAMITESS

ARAMEANS See SYRIANS

ARAMITESS (1) [ARAM]
1Ch 7:14 his concubine the **A** bare Machir the father 761

ARAM-NAHARAIM (1) [ARAM]
Ps 60: T when he strove with **A** 763

ARAM-ZOBAH (1) [ARAM, ZOBAH]
Ps 60: T he strove with Aram-naharaim and with **A,** 760

ARAN (2)
Ge 36:28 children of Dishan *are* these; Uz, and **A.** 765
1Ch 1:42 *and* Jakan. The sons of Dishan; Uz, and **A.** 765

ARARAT (2)
Ge 8: 4 of the month, upon the mountains of **A.** 780
Jer 51:27 call together against her the kingdoms of **A,** 780

ARAUNAH (9) [ORNAN]
2Sa 24:16 was by the threshingplace of **A** the Jebusite. 728
 24:18 in the threshingfloor of **A** the Jebusite. 728
 24:20 **A** looked, and saw the king and his servants 728
 24:20 **A** went out, and bowed himself before 728
 24:21 **A** said, Wherefore is my lord the king come 728
 24:22 **A** said unto David, Let my lord the king 728
 24:23 All *these things* did **A**, *as* a king, give unto 728
 24:23 **A** said unto the king, The LORD thy God 728
 24:24 the king said unto **A**, Nay; but I will surely 728

ARBA (2) [ARBAH, KIRJATH-ARBA]
Jos 14:15 which *A was* a great man among NIH
 15:13 *even* the city of **A** the father of Anak, 704

ARBAH (2) [ARBA]
Ge 35:27 unto the city of **A**, which *is* Hebron, 704
Jos 21:11 they gave them the city of **A** the father of 704

ARBATHITE (2)
2Sa 23:31 Abialbon the **A**, Azmaveth the Barhumite, 6164
1Ch 11:32 Hurai of the brooks of Gaash, Abiel the **A,** 6164

ARBITE (1)
2Sa 23:35 Hezrai the Carmelite, Paarai the **A,** 701

ARCHANGEL (2) [ANGEL]
1Th 4:16 with the voice of the **a**, and with the trump 743
Jude 1: 9 Yet Michael the **a**, when contending with 743

ARCHELAUS (1)
Mt 2:22 when he heard that **A** did reign in Judea 745

ARCHER (2) [ARCHERS]
Ge 21:20 in the wilderness, and became an **a.** 7199+7235
Jer 51: 3 Against *him that* bendeth let the **a** bend 1869

ARCHERS (12) [ARCHER]
Ge 49:23 have a sorely grieved him, 1167+2671
Jdg 5:11 *that are* delivered from the noise of **a** 2686
1Sa 31: 3 the **a** hit him; 376+3384+7198+871.1+1886.1
 31: 3 and he was sore wounded of the **a.** 3384
1Ch 8:40 **a**, and had many sons, 1869+7198
 10: 3 the **a** hit him, 4175+7198+871.1+1886.1
 10: 3 hit him, and he was wounded of the **a.** 3384
2Ch 35:23 the **a** shot at king Josiah; and the king said 3384
Job 16:13 His **a** compass me round about, 7228
Isa 21:17 the residue of the number of **a**, the mighty 7198

ARABIANS (6) [ARAB]
Isa 22: 3 are fled together, they are bound by the **a:** 7198
Jer 50:29 Call together the **a** against Babylon: all ye 7228

ARCHES (15)
Eze 40:16 gate round about, and likewise to the **a:** 361
 40:21 the **a** thereof were after the measure of 361
 40:22 and their **a**, and their palm trees, 361
 40:22 and the **a** thereof *were* before them. 361
 40:24 the **a** thereof according to these measures. 361
 40:25 in it and in the **a** thereof round about, 361
 40:26 and the **a** thereof *were* before them: 361
 40:29 the posts thereof, and the **a** thereof, 361
 40:29 in it and in the **a** thereof round about: 361
 40:30 the **a** round about *were* five 361
 40:31 the **a** thereof *were* toward the utter court; 361
 40:33 and the posts thereof, and the **a** thereof, 361
 40:33 and in the **a** thereof round about: 361
 40:34 the **a** thereof *were* toward the outward 361
 40:36 the **a** thereof, and the windows to it round 361

ARCHEVITES (1)
Ezr 4: 9 the Tarpelites, the Apharsites, the **A,** 756

ARCHI (1)
Jos 16: 2 passeth along unto the borders of **A** to 757

ARCHIPPUS (2)
Col 4:17 And say to **A**, Take heed to the ministry 751
Phm 1: 2 and **A** our fellowsoldier, and to the church 751

ARCHITE (5)
2Sa 15:32 Hushai the **A** came to meet him with his 757
 16:16 to pass, when Hushai the **A**, David's friend, 757
 17: 5 Call now Hushai the **A** also, and let us hear 757
 17:14 The counsel of Hushai the **A** *is* better than 757
1Ch 27:33 Hushai the **A** *was* the king's companion: 757

ARCTURUS (2)
Job 9: 9 Which maketh **A**, Orion, and Pleiades, 5906
 38:32 or canst thou guide **A** with his sons? 5906

ARD (3) [ARDITES]
Ge 46:21 and Rosh, Muppim, and Huppim, and **A.** 714
Nu 26:40 the sons of Bela were **A** and Naaman: 714
 26:40 *of* **A**, the family of the Ardites: *and* NIH

ARDITES (1) [ARD]
Nu 26:40 of Ard, the family of the **A**: *and* of Naaman, 716

ARDON (1)
1Ch 2:18 sons *are* these; Jesher, and Shobab, and **A.** 715

ARE (2946) [BE] See Index of Articles, Etc.

ARELI (2) [ARELITES]
Ge 46:16 Shuni, and Ezbon, Eri, and Arodi, and **A.** 692
Nu 26:17 Arodites: of **A**, the family of the Arelites. 692

ARELITES (1) [ARELI]
Nu 26:17 of the Arodites: of Areli, the family of the **A.** 692

AREOPAGITE (1) [AREOPAGUS]
Ac 17:34 among the which *was* Dionysius the **A,** 698

AREOPAGUS (1) [AREOPAGITE, MARS' HILL]
Ac 17:19 took him, and brought him unto **A**, saying, 697

ARETAS (1)
2Co 11:32 Damascus the governor under **A** the king 702

ARGOB (5)
Dt 3: 4 threescore cities, all the region of **A,** 709
 3:13 all the region of **A**, with all Bashan, which 709
 3:14 the country of **A** unto the coasts of Geshuri 709
1Ki 4:13 to him *also pertained* the region of **A,** 709
2Ki 15:25 of the king's house, with **A** and Arieh; 709

ARGUING (1) [ARGUMENTS]
Job 6:25 but what doth your **a** reprove? 3198

ARGUMENTS (1) [ARGUING]
Job 23: 4 before him, and fill my mouth *with* **a.** 8433

ARIDAI (1)
Est 9: 9 and Arisai, and **A**, and Vajezatha, 742

ARIDATHA (1)
Est 9: 8 And Poratha, and Adalia, and **A,** 743

ARIEH (1)
2Ki 15:25 of the king's house, with Argob and **A;** 745

ARIEL (6)
Ezr 8:16 for **A**, for Shemaiah, and for Elnathan, 740
Isa 29: 1 Woe to **A**, to Ariel, the city *where* David 740
 29: 1 Woe to Ariel, to **A**, the city *where* David 740
 29: 2 Yet I will distress **A**, and there shall be 740
 29: 2 and sorrow: and it shall be unto me as **A.** 740
 29: 7 of all the nations that fight against **A,** 740

ARIGHT (5) [RIGHT]
Ps 50:23 him that ordereth *his* conversation **a** will NIH
 78: 8 a generation *that* set not their heart **a,** 3559
Pr 15: 2 tongue of the wise **useth** knowledge **a:** 3190
 23:31 in the cup, *when* it moveth itself **a.** 4339+871.1
Jer 8: 6 and heard, *but* they spake not **a:** 3651

A

ARIMATHEA (4)

Mt	27:57 there came a rich man of **A**, named Joseph,	*707*
Mk	15:43 Joseph of **A**, an honourable counseller,	*707*
Lk	23:51 of them;) he *was* of **A**, a city of the Jews:	*707*
Jn	19:38 And after this Joseph of **A**, being a disciple	*707*

ARIOCH (7)

Ge	14: 1 **A** king of Ellasar, Chedorlaomer king of	746
	14: 9 king of Shinar, and **A** king of Ellasar;	746
Da	2:14 to **A** the captain of the king's guard,	746
	2:15 and said to **A** the king's captain,	746
	2:15 Then **A** made the thing known to Daniel.	746
	2:24 Therefore Daniel went in unto **A**, whom	746
	2:25 **A** brought in Daniel before the king in	746

ARISAI (1)

Est	9: 9 and **A**, and Aridai, and Vajezatha,	747

ARISE (149) [RISE]

Ge	13:17 **A**, walk through the land in the length of	6965
	19:15 saying, **A**, take thy wife, and thy two	6965
	21:18 **A**, lift up the lad, and hold him in thine	6965
	27:19 a, I pray thee, sit and eat of my venison,	6965
	27:31 Let my father **a**, and eat of his son's	6965
	27:43 a, flee thou to Laban my brother to Haran;	6965
	28: 2 **A**, go to Padan-aram, to the house of	6965
	31:13 now **a**, get thee out from this land,	6965
	35: 1 **A**, go up to Beth-el, and dwell there:	6965
	35: 3 let us **a**, and go up to Beth-el; and I will	6965
	41:30 there shall **a** after them seven years of	6965
	43: 8 the lad with me, and we will **a** and go;	6965
	43:13 brother, and **a**, go again unto the man:	6965
Dt	9:12 said unto me, **A**, get thee down	6965
	10:11 the LORD said unto me, **A**, take thy	6965
	13: 1 If there **a** among you a prophet, or	6965
	17: 8 If there **a** a matter too hard for thee in	NIH
	17: 8 shalt thou **a**, and get thee up into the place	6965
Jos	1: 2 now therefore **a**, go over this Jordan, thou,	6965
	8: 1 of war with thee, and **a**, go up *to* Ai:	6965
Jdg	5:12 **a**, Barak, and lead thy captivity captive,	6965
	7: 9 unto him, **A**, get thee down unto the host;	6965
	7:15 into the host of Israel, and said, **A**;	6965
	18: 9 they said, **A**, that we may go up against	6965
	20:40 when the flame began to **a** up out of	5927
1Sa	9: 3 with thee, and **a**, go seek the asses.	6965
	16:12 the LORD said, **A**, anoint him: for this *is*	6965
	23: 4 And the LORD answered him and said, **A**,	6965
2Sa	2:14 Let the young men now **a**, and play before	6965
	2:14 play before us. And Joab said, Let them **a**.	6965
	3:21 I will **a** and go, and will gather all Israel	6965
	11:20 if so be that the king's wrath **a**, and he say	5927
	13:15 And Amnon said unto her, **A**, be gone.	6965
	15:14 with him at Jerusalem, **A**, and let us flee;	6965
	17: 1 I will **a** and pursue after David this night:	6965
	17:21 **A**, and pass quickly over the water:	6965
	19: 7 Now therefore **a**, go forth,	6965
	22:39 and wounded them, that they could not **a**:	6965
1Ki	3:12 after thee shall any **a** like unto thee.	6965
	14: 2 **A**, I pray thee, and disguise thyself,	6965
	14:12 **A** thou therefore, get thee to thine own	6965
	17: 9 **A**, get thee to Zarephath, which	6965
	19: 5 and said unto him, **A** *and* eat.	6965
	19: 7 and touched him, and said, **A** *and* eat;	6965
	21: 7 **a**, *and* eat bread, and let thine heart be	6965
	21:15 was dead, that Jezebel said to Ahab, **A**,	6965
	21:18 **A**, go down to meet Ahab king of Israel,	6965
2Ki	1: 3 **A**, go up to meet the messengers of	6965
	8: 1 **A**, and go thou and thine household,	6965
	9: 2 **make** him **a** up from among his brethren,	6965
1Ch	22:16 **A** *therefore*, and be doing, and the LORD	6965
	22:19 **a** therefore, and build ye the sanctuary of	6965
2Ch	6:41 Now therefore **a**, O LORD God, into thy	6965
Ezr	10: 4 **A**; for *this* matter *belongeth* unto thee:	6965
Ne	2:20 therefore we his servants will **a** and build:	6965
Est	1:18 Thus *shall there* **a** too much contempt	NIH
	4:14 deliverance **a** to the Jews from another	5975
Job	7: 4 When shall I **a**, and the night be gone?	6965
	25: 3 and upon whom doth not his light **a**?	6965
Ps	3: 7 **A**, O LORD; save me, O my God:	6965
	7: 6 **A**, O LORD, in thine anger, lift up thyself	6965
	9:19 **A**, O LORD; let not man prevail: let	6965
	10:12 **A**, O LORD; O God, lift up thine hand:	6965
	12: 5 the needy, now will I **a**, saith the LORD;	6965
	17:13 **A**, O LORD, disappoint him, cast him	6965
	44:23 O Lord? **a**, cast *us* not off for ever.	6974
	44:26 **A** for our help, and redeem us for thy	6965
	68: 1 Let God **a**, let his enemies be scattered:	6965
	74:22 **A**, O God, plead thine own cause:	6965
	78: 6 *who* should **a** and declare *them* to their	6965
	82: 8 **A**, O God, judge the earth: for thou shalt	6965
	88:10 shall the dead **a** *and* praise thee? Selah.	6965
	89: 9 when the waves thereof **a**, thou stillest	5375
	102:13 Thou shalt **a**, *and* have mercy upon Zion:	6965
	109:28 when they **a**, let them be ashamed:	6965
	132: 8 **A**, O LORD, into thy rest; thou,	6965
Pr	6: 9 when wilt thou **a** out of thy sleep?	6965
	31:28 Her children **a** up, and call her blessed;	6965
SS	2:13 **A**, my love, my fair one, and come away.	6965
Isa	21: 5 drink: **a**, ye princes, *and* anoint the shield.	6965
	23:12 a, pass over *to* Chittim; there also shalt	6965
	26:19 *together with* my dead body shall they **a**.	6965
	31: 2 will **a** against the house of the evildoers,	6965
	49: 7 a servant of rulers, Kings shall see and **a**,	6965
	52: 2 the dust; **a**, *and* sit down, O Jerusalem:	6965
	60: 1 **A**, shine; for thy light is come,	6965

Isa	60: 2 the LORD shall **a** upon thee, and his glory	2224
Jer	1:17 **a**, and speak unto them all that I	6965
	2:27 their trouble they will say, **A**, and save us.	6965
	2:28 them **a**, if they can save thee in the time	6965
	6: 4 against her; **a**, and let us go up at noon.	6965
	6: 5 **A**, and let us go by night, and let us	6965
	8: 4 the LORD; Shall they fall, and not **a**?	6965
	13: 4 **a**, go to Euphrates, and hide it there in a	6965
	13: 6 **A**, go to Euphrates, and take the girdle	6965
	18: 2 **A**, and go down *to* the potter's house,	6965
	31: 6 **A** ye, and let us go up *to* Zion unto	6965
	46:16 a, and let us go again to our own people,	6965
	49:28 **A** ye, go up to Kedar, and spoil the men	6965
	49:31 **A**, get you up unto the wealthy nation,	6965
La	2:19 **A**, cry out in the night: in the beginning	6965
Eze	3:22 said unto me, **A**, go forth into the plain,	6965
Da	2:39 after thee shall **a** another kingdom inferior	6966
	7: 5 said thus unto it, **A**, devour much flesh.	6966
	7:17 four kings, *which* shall **a** out of the earth.	6966
	7:24 of this kingdom *are* ten kings *that* shall **a**:	6966
Hos	10:14 Therefore shall **a** tumult among thy	6965
Am	7: 2 *by* whom shall Jacob **a**? for he *is* small.	6965
	7: 5 *by* whom shall Jacob **a**? for he *is* small.	6965
Ob	1: 1 **A** ye, and let us rise up against her in	6965
Jnh	1: 2 **A**, go to Nineveh, *that* great city,	6965
	1: 6 a, call upon thy God, if so be that God	6965
	3: 2 **A**, go unto Nineveh, *that* great city,	6965
	4: 8 it came to pass, when the sun did **a**,	2224
Mic	2:10 **A** ye, and depart; for this *is* not *your* rest:	6965
	4:13 **A** and thresh, O daughter of Zion: for I	6965
	6: 1 **A**, contend thou before the mountains,	6965
	7: 8 I fall, I shall **a**; when I sit in darkness,	6965
Hab	2:19 to the dumb stone, **A**, it shall teach!	5782
Mal	4: 2 righteousness **a** with healing in his wings;	2224
Mt	2:13 **A**, and take the young child and his	1453
	2:20 **A**, and take the young child and his	1453
	9: 5 be forgiven thee; or to say, **A**, and walk?	1453
	9: 6 **A**, take up thy bed, and go unto thine	1453
	17: 7 and said, **A**, and be not afraid.	1453
	24:24 For there shall **a** false Christs,	1453
Mk	2: 9 to say, **A**, and take up thy bed, and walk?	1453
	2:11 **A**, and take up thy bed, and go thy way	1453
	5:41 Damsel (I say unto thee) **a**.	1453
Lk	5:24 **A**, and take up thy couch, and go into	1453
	7:14 he said, Young man, I say unto thee, **A**.	1453
	8:54 by the hand, and called, saying, Maid, **a**.	1453
	15:18 I will **a** and go to my father, and will say	450
	17:19 And he said unto him, **A**, *go thy way: thy*	450
	24:38 and why do thoughts **a** in your hearts?	305
Jn	14:31 *even* so I do. **A**, let us go hence.	1453
Ac	8:26 **A**, and go toward the south unto the way	450
	9: 6 **A**, and go into the city, and it shall be told	450
	9:11 **A**, and go into the street which is called	450
	9:34 **a**, and make thy bed. And he arose	450
	9:40 turning *him* to the body said, Tabitha, **a**.	450
	10:20 **A** therefore, and get *thee* down, and go	450
	11: 7 I heard a voice saying unto me, **A**, Peter;	450
	12: 7 and raised him up, saying, **A** up quickly.	450
	20:30 Also of your own selves shall men **a**,	450
	22:10 said unto me, **A**, and go into Damascus;	450
	22:16 **a**, and be baptized, and wash away thy sins	450
Eph	5:14 and **a** from the dead, and Christ shall give	450
2Pe	1:19 dawn, and the day star **a** in your hearts:	393

ARISETH (11) [RISE]

1Ki	18:44 there **a** a little cloud out of the sea,	5927
Ps	104:22 sun **a**, they gather themselves together,	2224
	112: 4 Unto the upright there **a** light in	2224
Ecc	1: 5 The sun also **a**, and the sun goeth down,	2224
Isa	2:19 when he **a** to shake terribly the earth.	6965
	2:21 when he **a** to shake terribly the earth.	6965
Na	3:17 *but* when the sun **a** they flee away,	2224
Mt	13:21 or persecution **a** because of the word,	1096
Mk	4:17 or persecution **a** for the word's sake,	1096
Jn	7:52 and look: for out of Galilee **a** no prophet.	1453
Heb	7:15 of Melchisedec there **a** another priest,	450

ARISING (1) [RISE]

Est	7: 7 the king **a** from the banquet of wine in his	6965

ARISTARCHUS (5)

Ac	19:29 and having caught Gaius and **A**, men of	708
	20: 4 and of the Thessalonians, **A** and Secundus;	708
	27: 2 one **A**, a Macedonian of Thessalonica,	708
Col	4:10 **A** my fellowprisoner saluteth you,	708
Phm	1:24 Marcus, **A**, Demas, Lucas,	708

ARISTOBULUS' (1)

Ro	16:10 Salute them which are of **A** household.	711

ARK (230)

Ge	6:14 Make thee an **a** of gopher wood;	8392
	6:14 rooms shalt thou make in the **a**,	8392
	6:15 of the **a** *shall be* three hundred cubits,	8392
	6:16 A window shalt thou make to the **a**,	8392
	6:16 the door of the **a** shalt thou set in the side	8392
	6:18 thou shalt come into the **a**, thou,	8392
	6:19 of every *sort* shalt thou bring into the **a**,	8392
	7: 1 Come thou and all thy house into the **a**;	8392
	7: 7 into the **a**, because of the waters of	8392
	7: 9 in two and two unto Noah into the **a**,	8392
	7:13 wives of his sons with them, into the **a**;	8392
	7:15 they went in unto Noah into the **a**, two	8392
	7:17 bare up the **a**, and it was lift up above	8392
	7:18 the **a** went upon the face of the waters.	8392

Ge	7:23 and *they* that *were* with him in the **a**.	8392
	8: 1 all the cattle that *was* with him in the **a**:	8392
	8: 4 the **a** rested in the seventh month, on	8392
	8: 6 that Noah opened the window of the **a**	8392
	8: 9 she returned unto him into the **a**, for	8392
	8: 9 and pulled her in unto him into the **a**.	8392
	8:10 again he sent forth the dove out of the **a**;	8392
	8:13 Noah removed the covering of the **a**,	8392
	8:16 Go forth of the **a**, thou, and thy wife,	8392
	8:19 after their kinds, went forth out of the **a**.	8392
	9:10 all that go out of the **a**, to every beast	8392
	9:18 that went forth of the **a**, were Shem,	8392
Ex	2: 3 she took for him an **a** of bulrushes,	8392
	2: 5 when she saw the **a** among the flags, she	8392
	25:10 they shall make an **a** of shittim wood:	727
	25:14 staves into the rings by the sides of the **a**,	727
	25:14 ark, that the **a** may be borne with them.	727
	25:15 The staves shall be in the rings of the **a**:	727
	25:16 thou shalt put into the **a** the Testimony	727
	25:21 shalt put the mercy seat above upon the **a**;	727
	25:21 in the **a** thou shalt put the Testimony that	727
	25:22 which *are* upon the **a** of the Testimony,	727
	26:33 within the vail the **a** of the Testimony:	727
	26:34 thou shalt put the mercy seat upon the **a** of	727
	30: 6 the vail that *is* by the **a** of the Testimony,	727
	30:26 and the **a** of the Testimony,	727
	31: 7 the **a** of the Testimony, and the mercy seat	727
	35:12 The **a**, and the staves thereof, *with* the	727
	37: 1 Bezaleel made the **a** *of* shittim wood:	727
	37: 5 staves into the rings by the sides of the **a**,	727
	37: 5 rings by the sides of the ark, to bear the **a**.	727
	39:35 The **a** of the Testimony, and the staves	727
	40: 3 shalt put therein the **a** of the Testimony,	727
	40: 3 Testimony, and cover the **a** with the vail.	727
	40: 5 the incense before the **a** of the Testimony,	727
	40:20 he took and put the Testimony into the **a**,	727
	40:20 set the staves on the **a**, and put the mercy	727
	40:20 and put the mercy seat above upon the **a**:	727
	40:21 And he brought the **a** into the tabernacle,	727
	40:21 and covered the **a** of the Testimony;	727
Lev	16: 2 before the mercy seat, which *is* upon the **a**;	727
Nu	3:31 their charge *shall be* the **a**, and the table,	727
	4: 5 and cover the **a** of Testimony with it:	727
	7:89 seat that *was* upon the **a** of Testimony,	727
	10:33 the **a** of the covenant of the LORD went	727
	10:35 when the **a** set forward, that Moses said,	727
	14:44 nevertheless the **a** of the covenant of	727
Dt	10: 1 the mount, and make thee an **a** of wood.	727
	10: 2 and thou shalt put them in the **a**.	727
	10: 3 I made an **a** of shittim wood, and hewed	727
	10: 5 put the tables in the **a** which I had made;	727
	31: 9 which bare the **a** of the covenant of	727
	31:25 which bare the **a** of the covenant of	727
	31:26 put it in the side of the **a** of the covenant	727
Jos	3: 3 When ye see the **a** of the covenant of	727
	3: 6 Take up the **a** of the covenant, and pass	727
	3: 6 And they took up the **a** of the covenant,	727
	3: 8 the priests that bear the **a** of the covenant,	727
	3:11 the **a** of the covenant, *even* the Lord	727
	3:13 of the priests that bear the **a** of the LORD,	727
	3:14 the priests bearing the **a** *of* the covenant	727
	3:15 as they that bare the **a** were come unto	727
	3:15 the feet of the priests that bare the **a** were	727
	3:17 the priests that bare the **a** of the covenant	727
	4: 5 Pass over before the **a** of the LORD your	727
	4: 7 before the **a** of the covenant of the LORD;	727
	4: 9 which bare the **a** of the covenant stood in	727
	4:10 For the priests which bare the **a** stood in	727
	4:11 that the **a** of the LORD passed over,	727
	4:16 Command the priests that bear the **a** of	727
	4:18 when the priests that bare the **a** of	727
	6: 4 seven priests shall bear before the **a** seven	727
	6: 6 Take up the **a** of the covenant, and let	727
	6: 6 of rams' horns before the **a** of the LORD.	727
	6: 7 him that is armed pass on before the **a** of	727
	6: 8 the **a** of the covenant of the Lord	727
	6: 9 the rereward came after the **a**, *the priests*	727
	6:11 So the **a** of the LORD compassed the city,	727
	6:12 and the priests took up the **a** of the LORD.	727
	6:13 the **a** of the LORD went on continually,	727
	6:13 the rereward came after the **a** of the LORD,	727
	7: 6 to the earth upon his face before the **a** of	727
	8:33 stood on this side the **a** and on that side	727
	8:33 which bare the **a** of the covenant of	727
Jdg	20:27 (for the **a** of the covenant of God *was* there	727
1Sa	3: 3 where the **a** of God *was*, and Samuel was	727
	4: 3 Let us fetch the **a** of the covenant of	727
	4: 4 that they might bring from thence the **a** of	727
	4: 4 *were* there with the **a** of the covenant of	727
	4: 5 when the **a** of the covenant of the LORD	727
	4: 6 they understood that the **a** of the LORD	727
	4:11 the **a** of God was taken; and the two sons	727
	4:13 for his heart trembled for the **a** of God.	727
	4:17 are dead, and the **a** of God is taken.	727
	4:18 when he made mention of the **a** of God,	727
	4:19 she heard the tidings that the **a** of God	727
	4:21 because the **a** of God was taken, and	727
	4:22 from Israel: for the **a** of God is taken.	727
	5: 1 the Philistines took the **a** of God,	727
	5: 2 When the Philistines took the **a** of God,	727
	5: 3 face to the earth before the **a** of the LORD.	727
	5: 4 to the ground before the **a** of the LORD:	727
	5: 7 The **a** of the God of Israel shall not abide	727
	5: 8 What shall we do with the **a** of the God of	727

1Sa	5: 8 Let the **a** of the God of Israel be carried	727
	5: 8 they carried the **a** of the God of Israel about	727
	5:10 Therefore they sent the **a** of God to Ekron.	727
	5:10 to pass, as the **a** of God came *to* Ekron,	727
	5:10 They have brought about the **a** of the God	727
	5:11 Send away the **a** of the God of Israel,	727
	6: 1 the **a** of the LORD was in the country of	727
	6: 2 What shall we do to the **a** of the LORD?	727
	6: 3 If ye send away the **a** of the God of Israel,	727
	6: 8 take the **a** of the LORD, and lay it upon	727
	6:11 they laid the **a** of the LORD upon the cart,	727
	6:13 and saw the **a**, and rejoiced to see *it*.	727
	6:15 the Levites took down the **a** of the LORD,	727
	6:18 whereon they set down the **a** of the LORD:	727
	6:19 they had looked into the **a** of the LORD,	727
	6:21 The Philistines have brought again the **a** of	727
	7: 1 fetched up the **a** of the LORD,	727
	7: 1 sanctified Eleazar his son to keep the **a** of	727
	7: 2 to pass, while the **a** abode in Kirjath-jearim,	727
	14:18 said unto Ahiah, Bring hither the **a** of God.	727
	14:18 For the **a** of God was at that time with	727
2Sa	6: 2 to bring up from thence the **a** of God,	727
	6: 3 they set the **a** of God upon a new cart,	727
	6: 4 *was* at Gibeah, accompanying the **a** of God:	727
	6: 4 ark of God: and Ahio went before the **a**.	727
	6: 6 Uzzah put forth *his hand* to the **a** of God,	727
	6: 7 error; and there he died by the **a** of God.	727
	6: 9 How shall the **a** of the LORD come to me?	727
	6:10 So David would not remove the **a** of	727
	6:11 the **a** of the LORD continued *in* the house	727
	6:12 unto him, because of the **a** of God.	727
	6:12 brought up the **a** of God from the house of	727
	6:13 that when they that bare the **a** of the LORD	727
	6:15 all the house of Israel brought up the **a** of	727
	6:16 as the **a** of the LORD came *into* the city of	727
	6:17 they brought in the **a** of the LORD,	727
	7: 2 but the **a** of God dwelleth within curtains.	727
	11:11 The **a**, and Israel, and Judah, abide in tents;	727
	15:24 bearing the **a** of the covenant of God:	727
	15:24 they set down the **a** of God;	727
	15:25 Carry back the **a** of God *into* the city:	727
	15:29 Abiathar carried the **a** of God again *to*	727
1Ki	2:26 thou barest the **a** of the Lord GOD before	727
	3:15 stood before the **a** of the covenant of	727
	6:19 to set there the **a** of the covenant of	727
	8: 1 that *they* might bring up the **a** of	727
	8: 3 Israel came, and the priests took up the **a**.	727
	8: 4 they brought up the **a** of the LORD,	727
	8: 5 with him before the **a**, sacrificing sheep	727
	8: 6 the priests brought in the **a** of the covenant	727
	8: 7 *their* two wings over the place of the **a**,	727
	8: 7 the cherubims covered the **a** and the staves	727
	8: 9 *There was* nothing in the **a** save the two	727
	8:21 I have set there a place for the **a**, wherein	727
1Ch	6:31 of the LORD, after that the **a** had rest.	727
	13: 3 let us bring again the **a** of our God to us:	727
	13: 5 to bring the **a** of God from Kirjath-jearim.	727
	13: 6 to bring up thence the **a** of God the LORD,	727
	13: 7 they carried the **a** of God in a new cart out	727
	13: 9 Uzza put forth his hand to hold the **a**;	727
	13:10 him, because he put his hand to the **a**:	727
	13:12 shall I bring the **a** of God *home* to me?	727
	13:13 David brought not the **a** *home* to himself	727
	13:14 the **a** of God remained with the family of	727
	15: 1 prepared a place for the **a** of God,	727
	15: 2 None ought to carry the **a** of God but	727
	15: 2 the LORD chosen to carry the **a** of God,	727
	15: 3 to bring up the **a** of the LORD unto his	727
	15:12 that you may bring up the **a** of the LORD	727
	15:14 bring up the **a** of the LORD God of Israel.	727
	15:15 children of the Levites bare the **a** of God	727
	15:23 and Elkanah *were* doorkeepers for the **a**.	727
	15:24 did blow with the trumpets before the **a** of	727
	15:24 and Jehiah *were* doorkeepers for the **a**.	727
	15:25 went to bring up the **a** of the covenant of	727
	15:26 God helped the Levites that bare the **a**	727
	15:27 all the Levites that bare the **a**,	727
	15:28 Thus all Israel brought up the **a** of	727
	15:29 *as* the **a** of the covenant of the LORD came	727
	16: 1 So they brought the **a** of God, and set it in	727
	16: 4 to minister before the **a** of the LORD,	727
	16: 6 before the **a** of the covenant of God.	727
	16:37 he left there before the **a** of the covenant	727
	16:37 to minister before the **a** continually,	727
	17: 1 the **a** of the covenant of the LORD	727
	22:19 to bring the **a** of the covenant of the LORD,	727
	28: 2 rest for the **a** of the covenant of the LORD,	727
	28:18 covered the **a** of the covenant of the LORD.	727
2Ch	1: 4 the **a** of God had David brought up from	727
	5: 2 to bring up the **a** of the covenant of	727
	5: 4 Israel came; and the Levites took up the **a**.	727
	5: 5 they brought up the **a**, and the tabernacle	727
	5: 6 that were assembled unto him before the **a**,	727
	5: 7 the priests brought in the **a** of the covenant	727
	5: 8 forth *their* wings over the place of the **a**,	727
	5: 8 the cherubims covered the **a** and the staves	727
	5: 9 they drew out the staves *of the* **a**, that	NIH
	5:10 *There was* nothing in the **a** save the two	727
	6:11 it have I put the **a**, wherein *is* the covenant	727
	6:41 place, thou, and the **a** of thy strength:	727
	8:11 whereunto the **a** of the LORD hath come.	727
	35: 3 Put the holy **a** in the house which Solomon	727
Ps	132: 8 thy rest; thou, and the **a** of thy strength.	727
Jer	3:16 The **a** of the covenant of the LORD:	727

Mt	24:38 until the day that Noe entered into the **a**,	2787
Lk	17:27 until the day that Noe entered into the **a**,	2787
Heb	9: 4 the **a** of the covenant overlaid round about	2787
	11: 7 prepared an **a** to the saving of his house;	2787
1Pe	3:20 while the **a** was a preparing, wherein few,	2787
Rev	11:19 there was seen in his temple the **a** of his	2787

ARKITE (2)

Ge	10:17 And the Hivite, and the **A**, and the Sinite,	6208
1Ch	1:15 And the Hivite, and the **A**, and the Sinite,	6208

ARKITES See ARCHI; ARCHITE

ARM (67) [ARMED, ARMHOLES, ARMIES, ARMOUR, ARMOURBEARER, ARMOURY, ARMS, ARMY]

Ex	6: 6 I will redeem you with a stretched out **a**,	2220
	15:16 by the greatness of thine **a** they shall be *as*	2220
Nu	31: 3 **A** some of yourselves unto the war,	2502
Dt	4:34 by a stretched out **a**, and by great terrors,	2220
	5:15 a mighty hand and by a stretched out **a**,	2220
	7:19 the mighty hand, and the stretched out **a**,	2220
	9:29 mighty power and by thy stretched out **a**,	2220
	11: 2 his mighty hand, and his stretched out **a**,	2220
	26: 8 with an outstretched **a**, and with great	2220
	33:20 teareth the **a** with the crown of the head.	2220
1Sa	2:31 that I will cut off thine **a**, and the arm of	2220
	2:31 thine arm, and the **a** of thy father's house,	2220
2Sa	1:10 the bracelet that *was* on his **a**,	2220
1Ki	8:42 strong hand, and of thy stretched out **a**;)	2220
2Ki	17:36 with great power and a stretched out **a**,	2220
2Ch	6:32 thy mighty hand, and thy stretched out **a**;	2220
	32: 8 With him *is* an **a** of flesh; but with us *is*	2220
Job	26: 2 savest thou the **a** *that hath* no strength?	2220
	31:22 *Then* let mine **a** fall from *my* shoulder	3802
	31:22 and mine **a** be broken from the bone.	248
	35: 9 they cry out by reason of the **a** of	2220
	38:15 and the high **a** shall be broken.	2220
	40: 9 Hast thou an **a** like God? or, canst thou	2220
Ps	10:15 Break thou the **a** of the wicked and the	2220
	44: 3 neither did their own **a** save them:	2220
	44: 3 thine **a**, and the light of thy countenance,	2220
	77:15 Thou hast with *thine* **a** redeemed thy	2220
	89:10 scattered thine enemies with thy strong **a**.	2220
	89:13 Thou hast a mighty **a**: strong is thy hand,	2220
	89:21 mine **a** also shall strengthen him.	2220
	98: 1 his holy **a**, hath gotten him the victory.	2220
	136:12 a strong hand, and with a stretched out **a**:	2220
SS	8: 6 upon thine heart, as a seal upon thine **a**:	2220
Isa	9:20 shall eat every man the flesh of his own **a**:	2220
	17: 5 the corn, and reapeth the ears *with* his **a**;	2220
	30:30 shall shew the lighting down of his **a**,	2220
	33: 2 be thou their **a** every morning,	2220
	40:10 strong *hand*, and his **a** *shall* rule for him:	2220
	40:11 he shall gather the lambs with his **a**,	2220
	48:14 and his **a** *shall be* on the Chaldeans.	2220
	51: 5 upon me, and on mine **a** shall they trust.	2220
	51: 9 awake, put on strength, O **a** of the LORD;	2220
	52:10 The LORD hath made bare his holy **a** in	2220
	53: 1 to whom is the **a** of the LORD revealed?	2220
	59:16 his **a** brought salvation unto him;	2220
	62: 8 right hand, and by the **a** of his strength,	2220
	63: 5 mine own **a** brought salvation unto me;	2220
	63:12 right hand of Moses *with* his glorious **a**,	2220
Jer	17: 5 maketh flesh his **a**, and whose heart	2220
	21: 5 an outstretched hand and with a strong **a**,	2220
	27: 5 my great power and by my outstretched **a**,	2220
	32:17 by thy great power and thy stretched out **a**,	2220
	32:21 a stretched out **a**, and with great terror;	248
	48: 25 and his **a** is broken, saith the LORD.	2220
Eze	4: 7 thine **a** *shall be* uncovered, and thou shalt	2220
	20:33 a stretched out **a**, and with fury poured	2220
	20:34 a stretched out **a**, and with fury poured	2220
	30:21 I have broken the **a** of Pharaoh king of	2220
	31: 17 *they that were* his **a**, *that* dwelt under his	2220
Da	11: 6 she shall not retain the power of the **a**;	2220
	11: 6 the arm; neither shall he stand, nor his **a**:	2220
Zec	11:17 the sword *shall be* upon his **a**, and upon	2220
	11:17 his **a** shall be clean dried up, and his right	2220
Lk	1:51 He hath shewed strength with his **a**;	1023
Jn	12:38 to whom hath the **a** of the Lord been	1023
Ac	13:17 with a high **a** brought he them out of it.	1023
1Pe	4: 1 **a** yourselves likewise with the same mind:	3695

ARMAGEDDON (1)

Rev	16:16 into a place called in the Hebrew tongue **A**.	717

ARMED (30) [ARM]

Ge	14:14 he **a** his trained *servants*, born in his own	7324
Nu	31: 5 of *every* tribe, twelve thousand **a** for war.	2502
	32:17 we ourselves will **go** ready **a** before	2502
	32:20 if ye will **go a** before the LORD to war,	2502
	32:21 will go all of you **a** over Jordan before	2502
	32:27 every man **a** for war, before the LORD to	2502
	32:29 every man **a** to battle, before the LORD,	2502
	32:30 if they will not pass over with you **a**,	2502
	32:32 We will pass over **a** before the LORD *into*	2502
Dt	3:18 ye shall pass over **a** before your brethren	2502
Jos	1:14 ye shall pass before your brethren **a**, all	2571
	4:12 passed over **a** before the children of Israel,	2571
	6: 7 let him that is **a** pass on before the ark of	2502
	6: 9 the **a** men went before the priests that	2502
	6:13 the **a** men went before them;	2502
Jdg	7:11 outside of the **a** *men that were* in the host.	2571
1Sa	17: 5 head, and he *was* **a** with a coat of mail;	3847

1Sa	17:38 Saul **a** David with his armour, and he put	3847
	17:38 head; also he **a** him with a coat *of mail*.	3847
1Ch	12: 2 *They were* **a** with bows, and could use	5401
	12:23 the bands that were **ready a** to the war,	2502
	12:24 and eight hundred, **ready a** to the war.	2502
2Ch	17:17 with him **a** men with bow and shield two	5401
	28:14 the **a** men left the captives and the spoil	2502
Job	39:21 He goeth on to meet the **a** men.	5402
Ps	78: 9 of Ephraim, *being* **a**, *and* carrying bows,	5401
Pr	6:11 that travelleth, and thy want as an **a** man.	4043
	24:34 that travelleth; and thy want as an **a** man.	4043
Isa	15: 4 the **a soldiers** of Moab shall cry out;	2502
Lk	11:21 When a strong *man* **a** keepeth his palace,	2528

ARMENIA (2)

2Ki	19:37 they escaped *into* the land of **A**.	780
Isa	37:38 and they escaped *into* the land of **A**:	780

ARMHOLES (2) [ARM, HOLE]

Jer	38:12 rags under thine **a** under the cords.	679+3027
Eze	13:18 *the women* that sew pillows to all **a**,	679+3027

ARMIES (43) [ARM]

Ex	6:26 the land of Egypt according to their **a**.	6635
	7: 4 bring forth mine **a**, *and my* people	6635
	12:17 I brought your **a** out of the land of Egypt:	6635
	12:51 Israel out of the land of Egypt by their **a**.	6635
Nu	1: 3 and Aaron shall number them by their **a**.	6635
	2: 3 camp of Judah pitch throughout their **a**:	6635
	2: 9 and four hundred, throughout their **a**.	6635
	2:10 the camp of Reuben according to their **a**:	6635
	2:16 hundred and fifty, throughout their **a**.	6635
	2:18 the camp of Ephraim according to their **a**:	6635
	2:24 and an hundred, throughout their **a**.	6635
	2:25 Dan *shall be* on the north side by their **a**:	6635
	10:14 the children of Judah according to their **a**:	6635
	10:18 Reuben set forward according to their **a**:	6635
	10:22 Ephraim set forward according to their **a**:	6635
	10:28 the children of Israel according to their **a**,	6635
	33: 1 with their **a** under the hand of Moses	6635
Dt	20: 9 that they shall make captains of the **a** to	6635
1Sa	17: 1 gathered together their **a** to battle,	4264
	17: 8 he stood and cried unto the **a** of Israel,	4634
	17:10 I defy the **a** of Israel this day;	4634
	17:23 out of the **a** of the Philistines,	4634
	17:26 he should defy the **a** of the living God?	4634
	17:36 seeing he hath defied the **a** of the living	4634
	17:45 the God of the **a** of Israel, whom thou hast	4634
	23: 3 if we come *to* Keilah against the **a** of	4634
	28: 1 the Philistines gathered their **a** together	4264
	29: 1 gathered together all their **a** to Aphek:	4264
2Ki	25:23 when all the captains of the **a**, they	2428
	25:26 and great, and the captains of the **a**,	2428
1Ch	11:26 Also the valiant *men* of the **a** were, Asahel	2428
2Ch	16: 4 sent the captains of his **a** against the cities	2428
Job	25: 3 Is there *any* number of his **a**?	1416
Ps	44: 9 to shame; and goest not forth with our **a**.	6635
	60:10 God, *which* didst not go out with our **a**?	6635
	68:12 Kings of **a** did flee apace: and she that	6635
SS	6:13 As it were the company of **two a**.	4264
Isa	34: 2 all nations, and *his* fury upon all their **a**:	6635
Mt	7 he sent forth his **a**, and destroyed those	4753
Lk	21:20 ye shall see Jerusalem compassed with **a**,	4760
Heb	11:34 in fight, turned to flight the **a** of the aliens.	3925
Rev	19:14 And the **a** which were in heaven followed	4753
	19:19 and the kings of the earth, and their **a**,	4753

ARMONI (1)

2Sa	21: 8 she bare unto Saul, **A** and Mephibosheth;	764

ARMOUR (24) [ARM]

1Sa	14: 1 said unto the young man that bare his **a**,	3627
	14: 6 said to the young man that bare his **a**,	3627
	17:38 Saul armed David with his **a**, and he put a	4055
	17:39 David girded his sword upon his **a**,	4055
	17:54 it *to* Jerusalem; but he put his **a** in his tent.	3627
	31: 9 stripped off his **a**, and sent into the land of	3627
	31:10 they put his **a** *in* the house of Ashtaroth:	3627
2Sa	2:21 of the young men, and take thee his **a**.	2488
	18:15 ten young men that bare Joab's **a**	3627
1Ki	10:25 a **a**, and spices, horses, and mules,	5402
	22:38 up his blood; and they washed his **a**	2185
2Ki	3:21 all that *were able to* **put on a**,	2290+2296
	10: 2 and horses, a fenced city also, and **a**;	5402
	20:13 all the house of his **a**, and all that was	3627
1Ch	10: 9 his **a**, and sent into the land of	3627
	10:10 they put his **a** *in* the house of their gods,	3627
Isa	22: 8 thou didst look in that day to the **a** of	5402
	39: 2 all the house of his **a**, and all that was	3627
Eze	38: 4 all of them clothed with all sorts of **a**,	NIH
Lk	11:22 he taketh *from him* **all** his **a** wherein he	3833
Ro	13:12 darkness, and let us put on the **a** of light.	3696
2Co	6: 7 the **a** of righteousness on the right hand	3696
Eph	6:11 Put on the **whole a** of God, that ye may	3833
	6:13 Wherefore take unto *you* the **whole a** of	3833

ARMOURBEARER (18) [ARM, BEAR]

Jdg	9:54 hastily unto the young man his **a**,	3627+5375
1Sa	14: 7 his **a** said unto him, Do all that *is* in	3627+5375
	14:12 answered Jonathan and his **a**,	3627+5375
	14:12 Jonathan said unto his **a**, Come up	3627+5375
	14:13 upon his feet, and his **a** after him:	3627+5375
	14:13 and his **a** slew after him.	3627+5375
	14:14 which Jonathan and his **a** made,	3627+5375
	14:17 and his **a** *were* not *there*.	3627+5375

A

1Sa 16:21	him greatly; and he became his **a**. 3627+5375
31: 4	said Saul unto his **a**, Draw thy 3627+5375
31: 4	his **a** would not; for he was sore 3627+5375
31: 5	when his **a** saw that Saul was dead, 3627+5375
31: 6	sons, and his **a**, and all his men, 3627+5375
2Sa 23:37	**a** to Joab the son of Zeruiah, 3627+5375
1Ch 10: 4	said Saul to his **a**, Draw thy sword, 3627+5375
10: 4	his **a** would not; for he was sore 3627+5375
10: 5	when his **a** saw that Saul was dead, 3627+5375
11:39	the **a** of Joab the son of Zeruiah, 3627+5375

ARMOURY (3) [ARM]
Ne	3:19 up to the **a** at the turning of the wall.	5402
SS	4: 4 like the tower of David builded for an **a**,	8530
Jer	50:25 The Lord hath opened his **a**,	214

ARMS (29) [ARM]
Ge	49:24 the **a** of his hands were made strong by	2220
Dt	33:27 and underneath are the everlasting **a**:	2220
Jdg	15:14 the cords that were upon his **a** became as	2220
	16:12 he brake them from off his **a** like a thread.	2220
2Sa	22:35 so that a bow of steel is broken by mine **a**.	2220
2Ki	9:24 smote Jehoram between his **a**,	2220
Job	22: 9 the **a** of the fatherless have been broken.	2220
Ps	18:34 so that a bow of steel is broken by mine **a**.	2220
	37:17 For the **a** of the wicked shall be broken:	2220
Pr	31:17 with strength, and strengtheneth her **a**.	2220
Isa	44:12 and worketh it with the strength of his **a**:	2220
	49:22 they shall bring thy sons in their **a**,	2684
	51: 5 and mine **a** shall judge the people;	2220
Eze	13:20 I will tear them from your **a**, and will let	2220
	30:22 will break his **a**, the strong, and that	2220
	30:24 I will strengthen the **a** of the king of	2220
	30:24 I will break Pharaoh's **a**, and he shall	2220
	30:25 I will strengthen the **a** of the king of	2220
	30:25 and the **a** of Pharaoh shall fall down;	2220
Da	2:32 his breast and his **a** of silver, his belly	1872
	10: 6 his **a** and his feet like in colour to polished	2220
	11:15 the **a** of the south shall not withstand,	2220
	11:22 with the **a** of a flood shall they be	2220
	11:31 **a** shall stand on his part, and they shall	2220
Hos	7:15 I have bound and strengthened their **a**,	2220
	11: 3 Ephraim also to go, taking them by their **a**;	2220
Mk	9:36 and when he had **taken** him in his **a**,	1723
	10:16 And he **took** them **up** in his **a**, put his	1723
Lk	2:28 Then took he him up in his **a**,	43

ARMY (82) [ARM]
Ge	26:26 and Phichol the chief captain of his **a**.	6635
Ex	14: 9 of Pharaoh, and his horsemen, and his **a**)	2428
Dt	11: 4 what he did unto the **a** of Egypt, unto	2428
Jdg	4: 7 the captain of Jabin's **a**, with his chariots	6635
	8: 6 that we should give bread unto thine **a**?	6635
	9:29 Increase thine **a**, and come out.	6635
1Sa	4: 2 they slew of the **a** in the field about four	4634
	4:12 there ran a man of Benjamin out of the **a**,	4634
	4:16 I am he that came out of the **a**, and I fled	4634
	4:16 of the army, and I fled to day out of the **a**.	4634
	17:21 had put the battle in array, **a** against army.	4634
	17:21 had put the battle in array, army against **a**.	4634
	17:22 ran into the **a**, and came and saluted his	4634
	17:48 ran toward the **a** to meet the Philistine.	4634
1Ki	20:19 the city, and the **a** which followed them.	2428
	20:25 number thee an **a**, like the army that thou	2428
	20:25 like the **a** that thou hast lost, horse for	2428
2Ki	25: 5 the **a** of the Chaldees pursued after	2428
	25: 5 and all his **a** were scattered from him.	2428
	25:10 all the **a** of the Chaldees, that were with	2428
1Ch	20: 1 Joab led forth the power of the **a**,	6635
	27:34 and the general of the king's **a** was Joab.	6635
2Ch	13: 3 Abijah set the battle in array with an **a** of	2428
	14: 8 Asa had an **a** of men that bare targets	2428
	20:21 as they went out before the **a**, and to say,	2502
	24:24 For the **a** of the Syrians came with a small	2428
	25: 7 O king, let not the **a** of Israel go with thee;	6635
	25: 9 which I have given to the **a** of Israel?	6635
	25:10 **a** that was come to him out of Ephraim,	1416
	25:13 the soldiers of the **a** which Amaziah sent	1416
	26:13 under their hand was an **a**, three 2428+6635	
Ne	2: 9 Now the king had sent captains of the **a**	2428
	4: 2 before his brethren and the **a** of Samaria,	2428
Job	29:25 and sat chief, and dwelt as a king in the **a**,	1416
SS	6: 4 as Jerusalem, terrible as an **a** with banners.	NIH
	6:10 the sun, and terrible as an **a** with banners?	NIH
Isa	36: 2 unto king Hezekiah with a great **a**.	2426
	43:17 chariot and horse, the **a** and the power;	2428
Jer	32: 2 the king of Babylon's **a** besieged	2428
	34: 1 all his **a**, and all the kingdoms of the earth	2428
	34: 7 When the king of Babylon's **a** fought	2428
	34:21 into the hand of the king of Babylon's **a**,	2428
	35:11 let us go to Jerusalem for fear of the **a** of	2428
	35:11 and for fear of the **a** of the Syrians:	2428
	37: 5 Pharaoh's **a** was come forth out of Egypt:	2428
	37: 7 Behold, Pharaoh's **a**, which is come forth	2428
	37:10 For though ye had smitten the whole **a** of	2428
	37:11 that when the **a** of the Chaldeans was	2428
	37:11 up from Jerusalem for fear of Pharaoh's **a**,	2428
	38: 3 into the hand of the king of Babylon's **a**,	2428
	39: 1 of Babylon and all his **a** against Jerusalem,	2428
	39: 5 the Chaldeans' **a** pursued after them,	2428
	46: 2 against the **a** of Pharaoh-necho king of	2428
	46:22 for they shall march with an **a**,	2428
	52: 4 he and all his **a**, against Jerusalem,	2428
	52: 8 the **a** of the Chaldeans pursued after	2428
	52: 8 and all his **a** was scattered from him.	2428

Jer	52:14 all the **a** of the Chaldeans, that were with	2428
Eze	17:17 Neither shall Pharaoh with his mighty **a**	2428
	27:10 and of Lud and of Phut were in thine **a**,	2428
	27:11 The men of Arvad with thine **a** were upon	2428
	29:18 his **a** to serve a great service against Tyrus:	2428
	29:18 yet had he no wages, nor his **a**, for Tyrus,	2428
	29:19 prey; and it shall be the wages for his **a**.	2428
	32:31 and all his **a** slain by the sword,	2428
	37:10 up upon their feet, an exceeding great **a**.	2428
	38: 4 and all thine **a**, horses and horsemen,	2428
	38:15 a great company, and a mighty **a**:	2428
Da	3:20 men that were in his **a** to bind Shadrach,	2429
	4:35 he doeth according to his will in the **a** of	2429
	11: 7 shall come with an **a**, and shall enter	2428
	11:13 come after certain years with a great **a**	2428
	11:25 the king of the south with a great **a**;	2428
	11:25 to battle with a very great and mighty **a**;	2428
	11:26 destroy him, and his **a** shall overflow:	2428
Joel	2:11 Lord shall utter his voice before his **a**:	2428
	2:20 remove far off from you the northern **a**,	NIH
	2:25 my great **a** which I sent among you.	2428
Zec	9: 8 about mine house because of the **a**,	4675
Ac	23:27 then came I with an **a**, and rescued him,	4753
Rev	9:16 And the number of the **a** of the horsemen	4753
	19:19 that sat on the horse, and against his **a**.	4753

ARNAN (1)
1Ch	3:21 the sons of **A**, the sons of Obadiah,	770

ARNON (25)
Nu	21:13 and pitched on the other side of **A**,	769
	21:13 for **A** is the border of Moab, between Moab	769
	21:14 did in the Red sea, and in the brooks of **A**,	769
	21:24 and possessed his land from **A** unto Jabbok,	769
	21:26 all his land out of his hand, even unto **A**.	769
	21:28 and the lords of the high places of **A**.	769
	22:36 which is in the border of **A**, which is in	769
Dt	2:24 your journey, and pass over the river **A**:	769
	2:36 which is by the brink of the river **A**,	769
	3: 8 from the river of **A** unto mount Hermon;	769
	3:12 which is by the river **A**, and half mount	769
	3:16 I gave from Gilead even unto the river **A**,	769
	4:48 which is by the bank of the river **A**,	769
Jos	12: 1 from the river **A** unto mount Hermon,	769
	12: 2 which is upon the bank of the river of **A**,	769
	13: 9 that is upon the bank of the river of **A**,	769
	13:16 that is on the bank of the river **A**,	769
Jdg	11:13 from **A** even unto Jabbok, and unto Jordan:	769
	11:18 pitched on the other side of **A**, but came	769
	11:18 of Moab: for **A** was the border of Moab.	769
	11:22 from **A** even unto Jabbok, and from	769
	11:26 the cities that be along by the coasts of **A**,	769
2Ki	10:33 from Aroer, which is by the river **A**,	769
Isa	16: 2 of Moab shall be at the fords of **A**.	769
Jer	48:20 cry; tell ye it in **A**, that Moab is spoiled,	769

AROD (1)
Nu	26:17 Of **A**, the family of the Arodites: of Areli,	720

ARODI (1) [ARODITES]
Ge	46:16 Shuni, and Ezbon, Eri, and **A**, and Areli.	722

ARODITES (1) [ARODI]
Nu	26:17 Of Arod, the family of the **A**: of Areli,	722

AROER (16) [AROERITE]
Nu	32:34 of Gad built Dibon, and Ataroth, and **A**,	6177
Dt	2:36 From **A**, which is by the brink of the river	6177
	3:12 from **A**, which is by the river Arnon,	6177
	4:48 From **A**, which is by the bank of the river	6177
Jos	12: 2 who dwelt in Heshbon, and ruled from **A**,	6177
	13: 9 From **A**, that is upon the bank of the river	6177
	13:16 their coast was from **A**, that is on the bank	6177
	13:25 of Ammon, unto **A** that is before Rabbah;	6177
Jdg	11:26 in **A** and her towns, and in all the cities	6177
	11:33 he smote them from **A**, even till thou	6177
1Sa	30:28 to them which were in **A**, and to them	6177
2Sa	24: 5 they passed over Jordan, and pitched in **A**,	6177
2Ki	10:33 and the Manassites, from **A**,	6177
1Ch	5: 8 the son of Joel, who dwelt in **A**, even unto	6177
Isa	17: 2 The cities of **A** are forsaken: they shall be	6177
Jer	48:19 O inhabitant of **A**, stand by the way	6177

AROERITE (1) [AROER]
1Ch	11:44 and Jehiel the sons of Hothan the **A**,	6200

AROMA See ODOUR; SAVOUR

AROSE (168) [RISE]
Ge	19:15 when the morning **a**, then the angels	5927
	19:33 not when she lay down, nor when she **a**.	6965
	19:35 The younger **a**, and lay with him;	6965
	19:35 not when she lay down, nor when she **a**.	6965
	24:10 he **a**, and went to Mesopotamia,	6965
	24:61 Rebekah **a**, and her damsels, and they	6965
	37: 7 and lo, my sheaf **a**, and also stood upright;	6965
	38:19 she **a**, and went away, and laid by her vail	6965
Ex	1: 8 Now there **a** up a new king over Egypt,	6965
Dt	34:10 there **a** not a prophet since in Israel like	6965
Jos	8: 3 So Joshua **a**, and all the people of war,	6965
	8:19 the ambush **a** quickly out of their place,	6965
	18: 8 the men **a**, and went away:	6965
	24: 9 **a** and warred against Israel, and sent	6965
Jdg	2:10 there **a** another generation after them,	6965
	3:20 God unto thee. And he **a** out of his seat.	6965
	4: 9 Deborah **a**, and went with Barak to	6965

Jdg	5: 7 ceased in Israel, until that I Deborah **a**,	6965
	5: 7 Deborah arose, that I **a** mother in Israel.	6965
	6:28 when the men of the city **a** early in	7925
	8:21 Gideon **a**, and slew Zebah and Zalmunna,	6965
	10: 1 after Abimelech there **a** to defend Israel	6965
	10: 3 after him a Jair, a Gileadite,	6965
	13:11 Manoah **a**, and went after his wife,	6965
	16: 3 a at midnight, and took the doors of	6965
	19: 3 her husband **a**, and went after her,	6965
	19: 5 when they **a** early in the morning, that he	7925
	19: 8 he **a** early in the morning on the fifth day	7925
	20: 8 all the people **a** as one man, saying,	6965
	20:18 the children of Israel **a**, and went up to	6965
Ru	1: 6 she **a** with her daughters in law, that she	6965
1Sa	3: 6 Samuel **a** and went to Eli, and said,	6965
	3: 8 he **a** and went to Eli, and said, Here am I;	6965
	5: 3 when they of Ashdod **a** early on	7925
	5: 4 when they **a** early on the morrow morning,	7925
	9:26 they **a** early: and it came to pass about	7925
	9:26 Saul **a**, and they went out both of them,	6965
	15:12 Samuel **a**, and gat him up from Gilgal	6965
	17:35 when he **a** against me, I caught him by his	6965
	17:48 when the Philistine **a**, and came	6965
	17:52 the men of Israel and of Judah **a**,	6965
	18:27 Wherefore David **a** and went, he	6965
	20:25 Jonathan **a**, and Abner sat by Saul's side,	6965
	20:34 So Jonathan **a** from the table in fierce	6965
	20:41 David **a** out of a place toward the south,	6965
	20:42 he **a** and departed: and Jonathan went	6965
	21:10 David **a**, and fled that day for fear of Saul,	6965
	23:13 David **a** and departed out of Keilah,	6965
	23:16 Jonathan Saul's son **a**, and went to David	6965
	23:24 they **a**, and went to Ziph before Saul:	6965
	24: 4 David **a**, and cut off the skirt of Saul's robe	6965
	25: 1 David **a**, and went down to the wilderness	6965
	25:41 she **a**, and bowed herself on her face to	6965
	26: 2 Saul **a**, and went down to the wilderness	6965
	26: 5 David **a**, and came to the place where Saul	6965
	27: 2 David **a**, and he passed over with the six	6965
	28:23 So he **a** from the earth, and sat upon	6965
	28:25 they **a** up, and went away that night.	6965
	31:12 All the valiant men **a**, and went all night,	6965
2Sa	2:15 there **a** and went over by number twelve	6965
	6: 2 David **a**, and went with all the people that	6965
	11: 2 that David **a** from off his bed,	6965
	12:17 the elders of his house **a**, and went to him	6965
	12:20 David **a** from the earth, and washed,	6965
	13:29 all the king's sons **a**, and every man gat	6965
	13:31 the king **a**, and tare his garments,	6965
	14:23 So Joab **a** and went to Geshur,	6965
	14:31 Joab **a**, and came to Absalom unto his	6965
	15: 9 Go in peace. So he **a**, and went to Hebron.	6965
	17:22 David **a**, and all the people that were with	6965
	17:23 **a**, and gat him home to his house, to his	6965
	23:10 He **a**, and smote the Philistines until his	6965
1Ki	1:50 **a**, and went, and caught hold on the horns	6965
	2:40 Shimei **a**, and saddled his ass, and went to	6965
	8:54 he **a** from before the altar of the Lord,	6965
	11:18 they **a** out of Midian, and came to Paran:	6965
	11:40 Jeroboam **a**, and fled into Egypt,	6965
	14: 4 **a**, and went to Shiloh, and came to	6965
	14:17 Jeroboam's wife **a**, and departed,	6965
	17:10 So he **a** and went to Zarephath. And	6965
	19: 3 when he saw that, he **a**, and went for his	6965
	19: 8 he **a**, and did eat and drink, and went in	6965
	19:21 he **a**, and went after Elijah,	6965
2Ki	1:15 he **a**, and went down with him unto	6965
	4:30 leave thee. And he **a**, and followed her.	6965
	7: 7 Wherefore they **a** and fled in the twilight,	6965
	7:12 the king **a** in the night, and said unto his	6965
	8: 2 the woman **a**, and did after the saying of	6965
	9: 6 he **a**, and went into the house;	6965
	10:12 he **a** and departed, and came to Samaria.	6965
	11: 1 she **a** and destroyed all the seed royal.	6965
	12:20 his servants **a**, and made a conspiracy,	6965
	19:35 when they **a** early in the morning,	7925
	23:25 neither after him **a** there any like him.	6965
	25:26 of the armies, **a**, and came to Egypt:	6965
1Ch	10:12 They **a**, all the valiant men, and took away	6965
	20: 4 that there **a** war at Gezer with	5975
2Ch	22:10 she **a** and destroyed all the seed royal of	6965
	29:12 the Levites **a**, Mahath the son of Amasai,	6965
	30:14 they **a** and took away the altars that	6965
	30:27 the priests the Levites **a** and blessed	6965
	36:16 until the wrath of the Lord **a** against his	5927
Ezr	9: 5 at the evening sacrifice I **a** up from my	6965
	10: 5 **a** Ezra, and made the chief priests,	6965
Ne	2:12 I **a** in the night, I and some few men with	6965
Est	8: 4 So Esther **a**, and stood before the king,	6965
Job	1:20 Job **a**, and rent his mantle, and shaved his	6965
	19:18 I **a**, and they spake against me.	6965
	29: 8 and the aged **a**, and stood up.	6965
Ps	76: 9 When God **a** to judgment, to save all	6965
Ecc	1: 5 and hasteth to his place where he **a**.	2224
Isa	37:36 when they **a** early in the morning,	7925
Jer	41: 2 a Ishmael the son of Nethaniah,	6965
Eze	3:23 I **a**, and went forth into the plain:	6965
Da	6:19 the king **a** very early in the morning,	6966
Jnh	3: 3 So Jonah **a**, and went unto Nineveh,	6965
	3: 6 he **a** from his throne, and he laid his robe	6965
Mt	2:14 When he **a**, he took the young child	1453
	2:21 And he **a**, and took the young child	1453
	8:15 and she **a**, and ministered unto them.	1453
	8:24 there **a** a great tempest in the sea,	1096
	8:26 Then he **a**, and rebuked the winds	1453

A

Mt	9: 7	And he **a**, and departed to his house.	1453
	9: 9	Follow me. And he **a**, and followed him.	450
	9:19	And Jesus **a**, and followed him, and so	1453
	9:25	and took her by the hand, and the maid **a**.	1453
	25: 7	all those virgins **a**, and trimmed their	1453
	26:62	And the high priest **a**, and said unto him,	450
	27:52	and many bodies of saints which slept **a**,	1453
Mk	2:12	And immediately he **a**, took up the bed,	1453
	2:14	Follow me. And he **a** and followed him.	450
	4:37	And there a great storm of wind, and	1096
	4:39	And he **a**, and rebuked the wind,	1326
	5:42	straightway the damsel **a**, and walked;	450
	7:24	And from thence he **a**, and went into	450
	9:27	by the hand, and lifted him up; and he **a**.	450
	14:57	And there a certain, and bare false witness	450
Lk	1:39	And Mary **a** in those days, and went into	450
	4:38	And he **a** out of the synagogue,	450
	4:39	and immediately she **a** and ministered unto	450
	6: 8	in the midst. And he **a** and stood *forth*.	450
	6:48	and when the flood **a**, the stream beat	1096
	8:55	spirit came again, and she **a** straightway:	450
	9:46	Then there **a** reasoning among them,	1525
	15:14	there **a** a mighty famine in that land;	1096
	15:20	And he **a**, and came to his father. But	450
	23: 1	And the whole multitude of them **a**,	450
	24:12	Then **a** Peter, and ran unto the sepulchre;	450
Jn	3:25	Then there **a** a question between *some* of	1096
	6:18	And the sea **a** by reason of a great wind	1326
	11:29	As soon as she heard *that*, she **a** quickly,	1453
Ac	5: 6	And the young men **a**, wound him up,	450
	6: 1	there **a** a murmuring of the Grecians	1096
	6: 9	Then there **a** certain of the synagogue,	450
	7:18	another king **a**, which knew not Joseph.	450
	8:27	And he **a** and went: and behold, a man of	450
	9: 8	And Saul **a** from the earth; and when his	1453
	9:18	sight forthwith, and **a**, and was baptized,	450
	9:34	and make thy bed. And he **a** immediately.	450
	9:39	Then Peter **a** and went with them.	450
	11:19	**a** about Stephen travelled as far as Phenice	1096
	19:23	And the same time there **a** no small stir	1096
	23: 7	there **a** a dissension between the Pharisees	1096
	23: 9	And there **a** a great cry: and the scribes	1096
	23: 9	scribes *that were* of the Pharisees' part **a**,	450
	23:10	And when there **a** a great dissension,	1096
	27:14	But not long after there **a** against it a	906
Rev	9: 2	and there **a** a smoke out of the pit, as	305

ARPAD (4) [ARPHAD]

2Ki	18:34	Where *are* the gods of Hamath, and of **A**?	774
	19:13	the king of **A**, and the king of the city of	774
Isa	10: 9	*is* not Hamath as **A**? *is* not Samaria as	774
Jer	49:23	Hamath is confounded, and **A**: for they	774

ARPHAD (2) [ARPAD]

Isa	36:19	Where *are* the gods of Hamath and **A**?	774
	37:13	the king of **A**, and the king of the city of	774

ARPHAXAD (10)

Ge	10:22	and Asshur, and **A**, and Lud, and Aram.	775
	10:24	And **A** begat Salah; and Salah begat Eber.	775
	11:10	and begat **A** two years after the flood:	775
	11:11	Shem lived after he begat **A** five hundred	775
	11:12	**A** lived five and thirty years,	775
	11:13	**A** lived after he begat Salah four hundred	775
1Ch	1:17	and **A**, and Lud, and Aram, and Uz,	775
	1:18	And **A** begat Shelah, and Shelah begat Eber.	775
	1:24	Shem, **A**, Shelah,	775
Lk	3:36	was *the son* of **A**, which was *the son*	742

ARRAY (34) [ARRAYED]

Jdg	20:20	the men of Israel **put** *themselves* **in** a to	6186
	20:22	**set** *their* battle again **in** a in the place	6186
	20:22	they **put** *themselves* **in** a in the first day.	6186
	20:30	**put** *themselves* **in** a at Gibeah, as at	6186
	20:33	and **put** *themselves* **in** a at Baal-tamar.	6186
1Sa	4: 2	Philistines **put** *themselves* **in** a against	6186
	17: 2	**set** the battle **in** a against the Philistines.	6186
	17: 8	are ye come out to **set** *your* battle **in** a?	6186
	17:21	the Philistines had **put** *the* battle **in** a,	6186
2Sa	10: 8	**put** the battle **in** a *at* the entering in of	6186
	10: 9	and **put** *them* **in** a against the Syrians:	6186
	10:10	that he might **put** *them* **in** a against	6186
	10:17	the Syrians **set** *themselves* **in** a against	6186
1Ki	20:12	**Set** *yourselves* **in** a. And they **set**	NIH
	20:12	they **set** *themselves* **in** a against the city.	NIH
1Ch	19: 9	**put** the battle **in** a before the gate of	6186
	19:10	and **put** *them* **in** a against the Syrians.	6186
	19:11	they **set** *themselves* **in** a against	6186
	19:17	and **set** the battle **in** a against them.	6186
	19:17	So when David had **put** the battle **in** a	6186
2Ch	13: 3	Abijah **set** the battle **in** a with an army of	631
	13: 3	Jeroboam also **set** the battle **in** a against	6186
	14:10	they **set** the battle **in** a in the valley of	6186
Est	6: 9	that they may **a** the man *withal* whom	3847
Job	6: 4	the terrors of God do **set** *themselves* **in** a	6186
	40:10	and **a** thyself with glory and beauty.	3847
Isa	22: 7	horsemen **set** themselves in a 7896+7896	
Jer	6:23	**set** in a as men for war against thee,	6186
	43:12	he shall **a** himself with the land of Egypt,	5844
	50: 9	they shall **set** *themselves* **in** a against her;	6186
	50:14	**Put** *yourselves* **in** a against Babylon round	6186
	50:42	*one* **put in** a, like a man to the battle,	6186
Joel	2: 5	as a strong people **set in** battle a.	6186
1Ti	2: 9	broided hair, or gold, or pearls, or costly **a**;	2441

ARRAYED (11) [ARRAY]

Ge	41:42	**a** him in vestures of fine linen, and put a	3847
2Ch	5:12	and their brethren, *being* **a** in white linen,	3847
	28:15	**a** them, and shod them, and gave them to	3847
Est	6:11	**a** Mordecai, and brought him on	3847
Mt	6:29	in all his glory was not **a** like one of these.	4016
Lk	12:27	Solomon in all his glory was not **a** like	4016
	23:11	and **a** him in a gorgeous robe,	4016
Ac	12:21	**a** in royal apparel, sat upon his throne,	1746
Rev	7:13	are these which are **a** in white robes?	4016
	17: 4	And the woman was **a** in purple	4016
	19: 8	granted that she should be **a** in fine linen,	4016

ARRIVED (2)

Lk	8:26	they **a** at the country of the Gadarenes,	2668
Ac	20:15	the next *day* we **a** at Samos, and tarried	3846

ARROGANCY (4)

1Sa	2: 3	let *not* **a** come out of your mouth:	6277
Pr	8:13	**a**, and the evil way, and the froward	1347
Isa	13:11	I will cause the **a** of the proud to cease,	1347
Jer	48:29	his **a**, and his pride, and the haughtiness	1347

ARROW (16) [ARROWS]

1Sa	20:36	as the lad ran, he shot an **a** beyond him.	2678
	20:37	the lad was come to the place of the **a**	2678
	20:37	lad, and said, *Is* not the **a** beyond thee?	2678
2Ki	9:24	**a** went out at his heart, and he sunk	2678
	13:17	The **a** of the LORD's deliverance,	2671
	13:17	and the **a** of deliverance from Syria:	2671
	19:32	nor shoot an **a** there, nor come before it	2671
Job	41:28	The **a** cannot make him flee:	1121+7198
Ps	11: 2	they make ready their **a** upon the string,	2671
	64: 7	God shall shoot at them *with* an **a**;	2671
	91: 5	by night; *nor* for the **a** that flieth by day;	2671
Pr	25:18	*is* a maul, and a sword, and a sharp **a**.	2671
Isa	37:33	nor shoot an **a** there, nor come before it	2671
Jer	9: 8	Their tongue *is as* an **a** shot out;	2671
La	3:12	his bow, and set me as a mark for the **a**.	2671
Zec	9:14	and his **a** shall go forth as the lightning:	2671

ARROWS (41) [ARROW]

Nu	24: 8	and pierce *them* through *with* his **a**.	2671
Dt	32:23	I will spend mine **a** upon them.	2671
	32:42	I will make mine **a** drunk with blood,	2671
1Sa	20:20	I will shoot three **a** on the side *thereof*, as	2671
	20:21	will send a lad, *saying*, Go, find out the **a**.	2671
	20:21	Behold, the **a** *are* on this side of thee, take	2671
	20:22	young man, Behold, the **a** *are* beyond	2671
	20:36	Run, find out now the **a** which I shoot.	2671
	20:38	Jonathan's lad gathered up the **a**,	2671
2Sa	22:15	he sent out **a**, and scattered them;	2671
2Ki	13:15	Elisha said unto him, Take bow and **a**.	2671
	13:15	arrows. And he took unto him bow and **a**.	2671
	13:18	he said, Take the **a**. And he took *them*.	2671
1Ch	12: 2	stones and *shooting* **a** out of a bow,	2671
2Ch	26:15	to shoot **a** and great stones withal.	2671
Job	6: 4	For the **a** of the Almighty *are* within me,	2671
Ps	7:13	he ordaineth his **a** against the persecutors.	2671
	18:14	Yea, he sent out his **a**, and scattered them;	2671
	21:12	*when* thou shalt make ready *thine* **a** upon	NIH
	38: 2	For thine **a** stick fast in me, and thy hand	2671
	45: 5	Thine **a** *are* sharp in the heart of the king's	2671
	57: 4	whose teeth *are* spears and **a**,	2671
	58: 7	*when* he bendeth *his bow to shoot* his **a**,	2671
	64: 3	and bend *their bows to shoot* their **a**,	2671
	76: 3	brake he the **a** of the bow, the shield,	7565
	77:17	out a sound: thine **a** also went abroad.	2687
	120: 4	Sharp **a** of the mighty, with coals of	2671
	127: 4	As **a** *are* in the hand of a mighty *man*; so	2671
	144: 6	shoot out thine **a**, and destroy them.	2671
Pr	26:18	*man* who casteth firebrands, **a**, and death,	2671
Isa	5:28	Whose **a** *are* sharp, and all their bows	2671
	7:24	With **a** and with bows shall *men* come	2671
Jer	50: 9	their **a** *shall be* as of a mighty expert *man*;	2671
	50:14	bend the bow, shoot at her, spare no **a**:	2671
	51:11	Make bright the **a**: gather the shields:	2671
La	3:13	He hath caused the **a**[s] of his quiver to	1121
Eze	5:16	When I shall send upon them the evil **a** of	2671
	21:21	he made *his* **a** bright, he consulted with	2671
	39: 3	will cause thine **a** to fall out of thy right	2671
	39: 9	the bows and the **a**, and the handstaves,	2671
Hab	3:11	at the light of thine **a** they went, *and* at	2671

ART (495) [ARTS]

Ge	3: 9	and said unto him, Where **a** thou?	NIH
	3:14	thou **a** cursed above all cattle,	NIH
	3:19	for dust thou **a**, and unto dust shalt thou	NIH
	4: 6	LORD said unto Cain, Why **a** thou wroth?	NIH
	4:11	now **a** thou cursed from the earth,	NIH
	12:11	I know that thou **a** a fair woman to look	NIH
	12:13	Say, I pray thee, thou **a** my sister: that it	NIH
	13:14	look from the place where thou **a**	NIH
	16:11	thou **a** with child, and shalt bear a son,	NIH
	17: 8	the land wherein thou **a** a stranger,	NIH
	20: 3	to him, Behold, thou **a** *but* a dead man,	NIH
	23: 6	thou **a** a mighty prince among us: in	NIH
	24:23	Whose daughter **a** thou? tell me, I pray	NIH
	24:47	and said, Whose daughter **a** thou?	NIH
	24:60	and said unto her, Thou **a** our sister,	NIH
	26:16	for thou **a** much mightier than we.	NIH
	26:29	thou **a** now the blessed of the LORD.	NIH
	27:18	he said, Here *am* I; who **a** thou, my son?	NIH
	27:24	he said, **A** thou my very son Esau? And he	NIH
	27:32	Isaac his father said unto him, Who **a** thou?	NIH

Ge	28: 4	inherit the land wherein thou **a** a stranger,	NIH
	29:14	Surely thou **a** my bone and my flesh.	NIH
	29:15	Because thou **a** my brother, shouldest thou	NIH
	32:17	and asketh thee, saying, Whose **a** thou?	NIH
	32:17	'Whose **a** thou?	NIH
	39: 9	from me but thee, because thou **a** his wife:	NIH
	41:39	*is* none so discreet and wise as thou **a**:	NIH
	44:18	thy servant: for thou **a** even as Pharaoh.	NIH
	45:19	Now thou **a** commanded, this do ye;	NIH
	46:30	seen thy face, because thou **a** yet alive.	NIH
	47: 8	Pharaoh said unto Jacob, How old **a** thou?	NIH
	49: 3	Reuben, thou **a** my firstborn, my might,	NIH
	49: 8	thou **a** *he* whom thy brethren shall praise:	NIH
	49: 9	from the prey, my son, thou **a** gone up:	NIH
Ex	4:25	Surely a bloody husband **a** thou to me.	NIH
	4:26	A bloody husband *thou* **a**, because of	NIH
	18:18	thou **a** not able to perform it thyself alone.	NIH
	30:25	an ointment compound *after* the **a** of	4639
	30:35	a confection *after* the **a** of the apothecary,	4639
	33: 3	of thee; for thou **a** a stiffnecked people:	NIH
	34:10	the people among which thou **a** shall see	NIH
Lev	27:12	valuest it, *who* **a** the priest, so shall it be.	NIH
Nu	14:14	For they have heard that thou LORD **a**	NIH
	14:14	that thou LORD **a** seen face to face,	NIH
	21:29	thou **a** undone, O people of Chemosh:	NIH
Dt	2:18	Thou **a** to pass over *through* Ar, the coast	NIH
	4:30	When thou **a** in tribulation, and all these	NIH
	4:38	and mightier than thou **a**, to bring thee in,	NIH
	7: 6	For thou **a** a holy people unto the LORD	NIH
	7:19	unto all the people of whom thou **a** afraid.	NIH
	8:10	When thou hast eaten and a full,	NIH
	8:12	Lest *when* thou hast eaten and **a** full,	NIH
	9: 1	Thou **a** to pass over Jordan *this* day, to go	NIH
	9: 6	for thou **a** a stiffnecked people.	NIH
	14: 2	For thou **a** a holy people unto the LORD	NIH
	14:21	for thou **a** a holy people unto the LORD	NIH
	14:24	for thee, so that thou **a** not able to carry it;	NIH
	17:14	When thou **a** come unto the land which	NIH
	18: 9	When thou **a** come into the land which	NIH
	26: 1	when thou **a** come in unto the land which	NIH
	27: 3	of this law, when thou **a** passed over,	NIH
	27: 9	this day thou **a** become the people of	NIH
	28:10	all people of the earth shall see that thou **a**	NIH
	32:15	thou **a** waxed fat, thou art grown thick,	NIH
	32:15	thou **a** waxed fat, thou **a** grown thick,	NIH
	32:15	thou **a** covered *with fatness;* then he	NIH
	32:18	Of the Rock *that* begat thee thou **a**	NIH
	33:29	Happy **a** thou, O Israel: who *is* like unto	NIH
Jos	5:13	**A** thou for us, or for our adversaries?	NIH
	13: 1	Thou **a** old *and* stricken in years,	NIH
	17:17	Thou **a** a great people, and hast great	NIH
Jdg	8:18	they answered, As thou **a**, so *were* they;	NIH
	11: 2	for thou **a** the son of a strange woman.	NIH
	11:12	that thou **a** come against me to fight in my	NIH
	11:25	now **a** thou any thing better than Balak	NIH
	11:35	thou **a** one of them that trouble me:	1961
	12: 5	said unto him, **A** thou an Ephraimite?	NIH
	13: 3	now, thou **a** barren, and bearest not:	NIH
	13:11	**A** thou the man that spakest unto	NIH
Ru	2: 9	when thou **a** athirst, go unto the vessels,	NIH
	2:11	**a** come unto a people which thou knewest	NIH
	2:12	under whose wings thou **a** come to trust.	NIH
	3: 9	he said, Who **a** thou? And she answered,	NIH
	3: 9	handmaid; for thou **a** a near kinsman.	NIH
	3:11	doth know that thou **a** a virtuous woman.	NIH
	3:16	she said, Who **a** thou, my daughter?	NIH
1Sa	8: 5	thou **a** old, and thy sons walk not in thy	NIH
	10: 2	When thou **a** departed from me to day,	NIH
	10: 5	when thou **a** come thither *to* the city,	NIH
	17:28	for thou **a** come down that *thou* mightest	NIH
	17:33	Thou **a** not able to go against this Philistine	NIH
	17:33	thou **a** *but* a youth, and he a man of war	NIH
	17:58	him, Whose son **a** thou, *thou* young man?	NIH
	19: 3	beside my father in the field where thou **a**,	NIH
	21: 1	Why **a** thou alone, and no man with thee?	NIH
	24:17	to David, Thou **a** more righteous than I:	NIH
	26:14	said, Who **a** thou *that* criest to the king?	NIH
	26:15	said to Abner, **A** not thou a *valiant* man?	NIH
	28:12	hast thou deceived me? for thou **a** Saul.	NIH
	29: 9	I know that thou **a** good in my sight,	NIH
	30:13	whence **a** thou? And he said, I *am* a young	NIH
2Sa	1: 8	he said unto me, Who **a** thou? And I	NIH
	1:13	young man that told him, Whence **a** thou?	NIH
	2:20	behind him, and said, **A** thou Asahel?	NIH
	7:22	Wherefore thou **a** great, O LORD God:	NIH
	7:24	and thou, LORD, **a** become their God.	NIH
	7:28	thou **a** that God, and thy words be true,	NIH
	9: 2	the king said unto him, **A** thou Ziba?	NIH
	12: 7	Nathan said to David, Thou **a** the man.	NIH
	13: 4	Why **a** thou, *being* the king's son, lean	NIH
	15: 2	unto him, and said, Of what city **a** thou?	NIH
	15:19	for thou **a** a stranger, and also an exile.	NIH
	15:27	unto Zadok the priest, **A** *not* thou a seer?	NIH
	16: 8	and, behold, thou **a** *taken* to thy mischief;	NIH
	16: 8	mischief, because thou **a** a bloody man.	NIH
	16:21	all Israel shall hear that thou **a** abhorred	NIH
	18: 3	now thou **a** worth ten thousand of us:	NIH
	19:13	**A** thou not *of* my bone, and *of* my flesh?	NIH
	20: 9	to Amasa, **A** thou in health, my brother?	NIH
	20:17	unto her, the woman said, **A** thou Joab?	NIH
	22:29	For thou **a** my lamp, O LORD:	NIH
1Ki	1:42	thou **a** a valiant man, and bringest good	NIH
	2: 9	for thou **a** a wise man, and knowest what	NIH
	2:26	own fields; for thou **a** worthy of death:	NIH
	6:12	*Concerning* this house which thou **a** in	NIH
	13:14	**A** thou the man of God that camest from	NIH

A

1Ki 13:18 I *am* a prophet also as thou *a*; and an angel NIH
17:18 a thou come unto me to call my sin to NIH
17:24 Now *by* this I know that thou *a* a man of NIH
18: 7 and said, **A** thou that my lord Elijah? NIH
18:17 unto him, **A** thou he that troubleth Israel? NIH
18:36 let it be known *this* day that thou *a* God NIH
18:37 that this people may know that thou *a* NIH
20:36 as soon as thou *a* departed from me, NIH
22: 4 I *am* as thou *a*, my people as thy people, NIH

2Ki 1: 4 from *that* bed on which thou *a* gone up, NIH
1: 6 from *that* bed on which thou *a* gone up, NIH
1:16 off *that* bed on which thou *a* gone up, NIH
3: 7 I *am* as thou *a*, my people as thy people, NIH
4: 4 when thou *a* come in, thou shalt shut NIH
19:15 thou *a* the God, *even* thou alone, of all NIH
19:19 may know that thou *a* the Lord God, NIH

1Ch 17:26 thou *a* God, and hast promised this NIH
29:11 and *thou a* exalted as head above all. NIH

2Ch 1: 9 O Lord God; let not man NIH
16:14 *of spices* prepared by the apothecaries' a: 4639
18: 3 I *am* as thou *a*, and my people as thy NIH
20: 6 of our fathers, *a* not thou God in heaven? NIH
20: 7 **A** not thou our God, who didst drive out NIH
25:16 **A** thou made of the king's counsel? NIH

Ezr 7:14 Forasmuch as *thou a* sent of the king, NIH
9:15 O Lord God of Israel, thou *a* righteous. NIH

Ne 2: 2 countenance sad, seeing thou *a* not sick? NIH
9: 6 Thou, *even* thou, *a* Lord alone; thou hast NIH
9: 7 Thou *a* the Lord the God, who didst NIH
9: 8 performed thy words; for thou *a* righteous: NIH
9:17 thou *a* God ready to pardon, gracious NIH
9:31 for thou *a* a gracious and merciful God, NIH
9:33 Howbeit thou *a* just in all that is brought NIH

Est 4:14 who knoweth whether thou *a* come to NIH

Job 4: 5 it toucheth thee, and thou *a* troubled. NIH
15: 7 **A** thou the first man *that* was born? or NIH
17:14 have said to corruption, Thou *a* my father: NIH
17:14 Thou *a* my mother, and my sister. NIH
22: 3 to the Almighty, that thou *a* righteous? NIH
30:21 Thou *a* become cruel to me: with thy NIH
31:24 to the fine gold, Thou *a* my confidence; NIH
33:12 *in* this thou *a* not just: I will answer NIH
34:18 *Is it fit* to say to a king, *Thou a* wicked? NIH
35: 8 Thy wickedness *may hurt* a man as thou *a*; NIH

Ps 2: 7 Lord hath said unto me, Thou *a* my Son; NIH
3: 3 thou, O Lord, *a* a shield for me; NIH
5: 4 For thou *a* not a God that hath pleasure in NIH
8: 4 What *is* man, that thou *a* mindful of him? NIH
10:14 the helper of the fatherless. 1961
16: 2 hast said unto the Lord, Thou *a* my Lord: NIH
22: 1 *why a thou so* far from helping me, *and* NIH
22: 3 thou *a* holy, O thou that inhabitest NIH
22: 9 thou *a* he that took me out of the womb: NIH
22:10 thou *a* my God from my mother's belly. NIH
23: 4 for thou *a* with me; thy rod and thy staff NIH
25: 5 thou *a* the God of my salvation; on thee NIH
31: 3 For thou *a* my rock and my fortress; NIH
31: 4 laid privily for me: for thou *a* my strength. NIH
31:14 in thee, O Lord: I said, Thou *a* my God. NIH
32: 7 Thou *a* my hiding place; thou shalt NIH
40:17 thou *a* my help and my deliverer; make NIH
42: 5 Why *a* thou cast down, O my soul? NIH
42: 5 *thou a* thou disquieted in me? hope thou NIH
42:11 Why *a* thou cast down, O my soul? NIH
42:11 why *a* thou disquieted within me? hope NIH
43: 2 For thou *a* the God of my strength: why NIH
43: 5 Why *a* thou cast down, O my soul? NIH
43: 5 why *a* thou disquieted within me? hope NIH
44: 4 Thou *a* my King, O God: NIH
45: 2 Thou *a* fairer than the children of men: NIH
63: 1 O God, thou *a* my God; early will I seek NIH
65: 5 *who a* the confidence of all the ends of NIH
66: 3 God, How terrible *a thou* in thy works! NIH
68:35 *thou a* terrible out of thy holy places: NIH
70: 5 thou *a* my help and my deliverer; NIH
71: 3 for thou *a* my rock and my fortress. NIH
71: 5 For thou *a* my hope, O Lord God: NIH
71: 5 *thou a* my trust from my youth. NIH
71: 6 thou *a* he that took me out of my mother's NIH
71: 7 unto many; but thou *a* my strong refuge. NIH
76: 4 Thou *a* more glorious *and* excellent than NIH
76: 7 Thou, *even* thou, *a* to be feared: NIH
76: 7 stand in thy sight when once thou *a* angry? NIH
77:14 Thou *a* the God that doest wonders: NIH
83:18 *a* the most High over all the earth. NIH
86: 5 Lord, *a* good, and ready to forgive; NIH
86:10 For thou *a* great, and doest wondrous NIH
86:10 doest wondrous *things*: thou *a* God alone. NIH
86:15 *a* a God full of compassion, and gracious, NIH
89:17 For thou *a* the glory of their strength: NIH
89:26 Thou *a* my Father, my God, and the rock NIH
90: 2 from everlasting to everlasting, thou *a* God. NIH
92: 8 Lord, *a* most high for evermore. NIH
93: 2 established of old: thou *a* from everlasting. NIH
97: 9 Lord, *a* High above all the earth: NIH
97: 9 the earth: thou *a* exalted far above all gods. NIH
102:27 thou *a* the same, and thy years shall have NIH
104: 1 O Lord my God, thou *a* very great; NIH
104: 1 thou *a* clothed with honour and majesty. NIH
110: 4 Thou *a* a priest for ever after the order of NIH
118:21 hast heard me, and *a* become my salvation. NIH
118:28 Thou *a* my God, and I will praise thee: NIH
118:28 *thou a* my God, I will exalt thee. NIH
119:12 Blessed *a* thou, O Lord: teach me thy NIH
119:57 *Thou a* my portion, O Lord: I have said NIH

Ps 119:68 Thou *a* good, and doest good; teach me NIH
119:114 Thou *a* my hiding place and my shield; NIH
119:137 Righteous *a* thou, O Lord, NIH
119:151 Thou *a* near, O Lord; and all thy NIH
137: 8 of Babylon, who *a* to be* destroyed; NIH
139: 3 and a acquainted *with* all my ways. NIH
139: 8 If I ascend up *into* heaven, thou *a* there: NIH
139: 8 make my bed in hell, behold, thou *a there*. NIH
140: 6 I said unto the Lord, Thou *a* my God: NIH
142: 5 Thou *a* my refuge and my portion in NIH
143:10 to do thy will; for thou *a* my God: NIH

Pr 6: 2 Thou *a* snared with the words of thy NIH
6: 2 thou *a* taken with the words of thy mouth, NIH
6: 3 when thou *a* come into the hand of thy NIH
7: 4 Say unto wisdom, Thou *a* my sister; NIH
24:24 saith unto the wicked, Thou *a* righteous; NIH

Ecc 10:17 Blessed *a* thou, O land, when thy king *is* NIH

SS 1:15 Behold, thou *a* fair, my love; behold; NIH
1:15 thou *art* fair, my love; behold, thou *a* fair; NIH
1:16 Behold, thou *a* fair, my beloved, yea, NIH
2:14 O my dove, *that a* in the clefts of the rock, NIH
4: 1 Behold, thou *a* fair, my love; behold, NIH
4: 1 thou *art* fair, my love; behold, thou *a* fair; NIH
4: 7 Thou *a* all fair, my love; *there* is no spot in NIH
6: 4 Thou *a* beautiful, O my love, as Tirzah, NIH
7: 6 How fair and how pleasant *a* thou, O love, NIH

Isa 14: 8 Lebanon, *saying*, Since thou *a* laid down, NIH
14:10 thee, **A** thou also become weak as we? NIH
14:10 weak as we? *a* thou become like unto us? NIH
14:12 How *a* thou fallen from heaven, O Lucifer, NIH
14:12 *how a* thou cut down to the ground, NIH
14:19 thou *a* cast out of thy grave like an NIH
14:31 O city; thou, whole Palestina, *a* dissolved: NIH
22: 1 that thou *a* wholly gone up to NIH
22: 2 Thou *that a* full *of* stirs, a tumultuous city, NIH
25: 1 O Lord, thou *a* my God; I will exalt thee, NIH
26:15 thou *a* glorified: thou hadst removed *it* far NIH
37:16 thou *a* the God, *even* thou alone, of all NIH
37:20 the earth may know that thou *a* the Lord, NIH
41: 8 thou, Israel, *a* my servant, Jacob whom I NIH
41: 9 and said unto thee, Thou *a* my servant; NIH
43: 1 have called *thee* by thy name; thou *a* mine. NIH
44:17 and saith, Deliver me; for thou *a* my god. NIH
44:21 O Jacob and Israel; for thou *a* my servant: NIH
44:21 I have formed thee; thou *a* my servant: NIH
45:15 Verily thou *a* a God that hidest thyself, NIH
47: 8 *thou that a* given to pleasures, NIH
47:13 Thou *a* wearied in the multitude of thy NIH
48: 4 Because I knew that thou *a* obstinate, NIH
49: 3 said unto me, Thou *a* my servant, O Israel, NIH
51: 9 **A** thou not it that hath cut Rahab, *and* NIH
51:10 **A** thou not it which hath dried the sea, NIH
51:12 who *a* thou, that thou shouldest be afraid NIH
51:16 and say unto Zion, Thou *a* my people. NIH
57: 8 *thyself to another* than me, and *a* gone up; NIH
57:10 Thou *a* wearied in the greatness of thy way NIH
63: 2 Wherefore *a thou* red in thine apparel, NIH
63:16 Doubtless thou *a* our father, NIH
63:16 thou, O Lord, *a* our father, our redeemer; NIH
64: 5 behold, thou *a* wroth; for we have sinned: NIH
64: 8 now, O Lord, thou *a* our father; we *are* NIH

Jer 2:21 a thou turned *into* the degenerate plant of NIH
2:23 thou *a* a swift dromedary traversing her NIH
2:27 Saying to a stock, Thou *a* my father; NIH
3: 4 my Father, thou *a* the guide of my youth? NIH
3:22 unto thee; for thou *a* the Lord our God. NIH
4:30 when thou *a* spoiled, what wilt thou do? NIH
10: 6 thou *a* great, and thy name *is* great in NIH
12: 1 Righteous *a* thou, O Lord, when I plead NIH
12: 2 thou *a* near in their mouth, and far from NIH
14: 9 *a* in the midst of us, and we are called by NIH
14:22 *a* not thou he, O Lord our God? therefore NIH
15: 6 saith the Lord, thou *a* gone backward: NIH
17:14 and I shall be saved: for thou *a* my praise. NIH
17:17 thou *a* my hope in the day of evil. NIH
20: 7 thou *a* stronger than I, and hast prevailed: NIH
22: 6 Thou *a* Gilead unto me, *and* the head of NIH
31:18 be turned; for thou *a* the Lord my God. NIH
39:17 hand of the men of whom thou *a* afraid. NIH
49:12 *a* thou he *that* shall altogether go NIH
50:24 thou *a* also taken, O Babylon, and thou NIH
50:24 thou *a* found, and also caught, because NIH
51:20 Thou *a* my battle axe *and* weapons of war: NIH

La 5:22 rejected us; thou *a* very wroth against us. NIH

Eze 3: 5 For thou *a* not sent to a people of a strange NIH
16: 7 and thou *a* come to excellent ornaments: NIH
16:34 given unto thee, therefore thou *a* contrary. 1961
16:45 Thou *a* thy mother's daughter, that lotheth NIH
16:45 thou *a* the sister of thy sisters, NIH
16:54 in that thou *a* a comfort unto them. NIH
22: 4 Thou *a* become guilty in thy blood that NIH
22: 4 and *a* come *even* unto thy years: NIH
22: 5 *which a* infamous *and* much vexed. NIH
22:24 Thou *a* the land that is not cleansed, NIH
23:30 because thou *a* polluted with their idols. NIH
26:17 to thee, How *a* thou destroyed, *that wast* NIH
27: 3 thou that *a* situate at the entry of the sea, NIH
27: 3 *which a* a merchant of the people for many NIH
28: 2 yet thou *a* a man, and not God, though NIH
28: 3 Behold, thou *a* wiser than Daniel; *there is* NIH
28:14 Thou *a* the anointed cherub that covereth; NIH
31: 2 Whom *a* thou like in thy greatness? NIH
31:18 To whom *a* thou thus like in glory NIH
32: 2 Thou *a* like a young lion of the nations, NIH
32: 2 and thou *a* as a whale in the seas: NIH

Eze 33:32 thou *a* unto them as a very lovely song *of* NIH
38:13 say unto thee, **A** thou come to take a spoil? NIH
38:17 **A** thou he of whom I have spoken in old NIH
40: 4 shew *them* unto thee *a* thou brought NIH

Da 2:26 **A** thou able to make known unto me 383
2:37 O king, *a* a king of kings: for the God NIH
2:38 over them all. Thou *a* this head of gold. NIH
4:18 thou *a* able; for the spirit of the holy gods NIH
4:22 O king, that *a* grown and become strong: NIH
5:13 and said unto Daniel, **A** thou that Daniel, NIH
5:13 which *a* of the children of the captivity of NIH
5:27 Thou *a* weighed in the balances, NIH
5:27 in the balances, and *a* found wanting. NIH
9:23 am come to shew *thee*; for thou *a* greatly NIH

Hos 2:23 *were* not my people, Thou *a* my people; NIH
2:23 and they shall say, *Thou a* my God. NIH

Ob 1: 2 the heathen: thou *a* greatly despised. NIH
1: 5 if robbers by night, (how *a* thou cut off!) NIH

Jnh 1: 8 *is* thy country? and of what people *a* thou? NIH
4: 2 for I knew that thou *a* a gracious God, NIH

Mic 2: 7 O *thou that a* named the house of Jacob, NIH

Na 1:14 I will make thy grave; for thou *a* vile. NIH
3: 8 **A** thou better than populous No, that was NIH

Hab 1:12 **A** thou not from everlasting, O Lord my NIH
1:13 *Thou a* of purer eyes than to behold evil, NIH
2:16 Thou *a* filled *with* shame for glory: NIH

Zec 4: 7 Who *a* thou, O great mountain? NIH

Mt 2: 6 a not the least among the princes of Juda: 1510
5:25 *whiles* thou *a* in the way with him; 1510
6: 9 Our Father which *a* in heaven, Hallowed NIG
8:29 a thou come hither to torment us before 1510
11: 3 **A** thou he that should come, or do we look 1510
11:23 Capernaum, which *a* exalted unto heaven, NIG
14:33 saying, Of a truth thou *a* the Son of God. 1510
16:14 Some *say* that thou *a* John the Baptist: NIG
16:16 answered and said, Thou *a* the Christ, 1510
16:17 and said unto him, Blessed *a* thou, 1510
16:18 That thou *a* Peter, and upon this rock 1510
16:23 thou *a* an offence unto me: for thou 1510
22:16 we know that thou *a* true, and teachest 1510
25:24 Lord, I knew thee that thou *a* a hard man, 1510
26:50 unto him, Friend, wherefore *a* thou come? NIG
26:73 to Peter, Surely thou also *a* one of them; 1510
27:11 saying, **A** thou the King of the Jews? 1510

Mk 1:11 Thou *a* my beloved Son, in whom I 1510
1:24 a thou come to destroy us? I know thee 1510
1:24 I know thee who thou *a*, the Holy One of 1510
3:11 and cried, saying, Thou *a* the Son of God. 1510
8:29 and saith unto him, Thou *a* the Christ. 1510
12:14 we know that thou *a* true, and carest for 1510
12:34 Thou *a* not far from the kingdom of God. 1510
14:61 and said unto him, **A** thou the Christ, 1510
14:70 again to Peter, Surely thou *a* one of them: 1510
14:70 for thou *a* a Galilean, and thy speech 1510
15: 2 asked him, **A** thou the King of the Jews? 1510

Lk 1:28 and say, Hail, *thou that a* highly favoured, NIG
1:28 with thee: blessed *a* thou among women. NIG
1:42 Blessed *a* thou among women, NIG
3:22 which said, Thou *a* my beloved Son; 1510
4:34 a thou come to destroy us? I know thee NIG
4:34 I know thee who thou *a*, the Holy One of 1510
4:41 and saying, Thou *a* Christ the Son of God. 1510
7:19 saying, **A** thou he that should come? 1510
7:20 saying, **A** thou he that should come? 1510
10:15 Capernaum, which *a* exalted to heaven, NIG
10:41 thou *a* careful and troubled about many NIG
11: 2 pray, say, Our Father which *a* in heaven, NIG
12:58 *as thou a* in the way, give diligence that NIG
13:12 Woman, thou *a* loosed from thy infirmity. NIG
14: 8 When thou *a* bidden of any *man* to a NIG
14:10 But when thou *a* bidden, go and sit down NIG
15:31 thou *a* ever with me, and all that I have is 1510
16:25 he is comforted, and thou *a* tormented. NIG
19:21 thee, because thou *a* an austere man: 1510
22:32 when thou *a* converted, strengthen thy 1510
22:58 saw him, and said, Thou *a* also of them. 1510
22:67 **A** thou the Christ? tell us. And he said 1510
22:70 said they all, **A** thou then the Son of God? 1510
23: 3 saying, **A** thou the King of the Jews? 1510
23:40 seeing thou *a* in the same condemnation? 1510
24:18 **A** thou only a stranger in Jerusalem, NIG

Jn 1:19 from Jerusalem to ask him, Who *a* thou? 1510
1:21 **A** thou Elias? And he saith, I am not. 1510
1:21 **A** thou *that* prophet? And he answered, 1510
1:22 Then said they unto him, Who *a* thou? 1510
1:42 he said, Thou *a* Simon the son of Jona: 1510
1:49 unto him, Rabbi, thou *a* the Son of God; 1510
1:49 the Son of God; thou *a* the King of Israel. 1510
3: 2 we know that thou *a* a teacher come from NIG
3:10 **A** thou a master of Israel, and knowest not 1510
4:12 thou *a* greater than our father Jacob, 1510
4:19 Sir, I perceive that thou *a* a prophet. 1510
5:14 unto him, Behold, thou *a* made whole: NIG
6:69 and are sure that thou *a* that* Christ, 1510
7:52 and said unto him, **A** thou also of Galilee? 1510
8:25 Then said they unto him, Who *a* thou? 1510
8:48 Say we not well that thou *a* a Samaritan, 1510
8:53 **A** thou greater than our father Abraham, 1510
8:57 Thou *a* not yet fifty years old, and hast 2192
9:28 reviled him, and said, Thou *a* his disciple; 1510
11:27 I believe that thou *a* the Christ, the Son of 1510
17:21 as thou, Father, *a* in me, and I in thee, 1510
18:17 **A** not thou also *one* of this man's disciples? 1510
18:25 **A** not thou also *one* of his disciples? 1510
18:33 unto him, **A** thou the King of the Jews? 1510

A

Jn 18:37 said unto him, **A** thou a king then? — *1510*
19: 9 and saith unto Jesus, Whence a thou? — *1510*
19:12 let this *man* go, thou a not Cesar's friend: — *1510*
21:12 of the disciples durst ask him, Who a thou? — *1510*
Ac 4:24 and said, Lord, thou a God, which hast — NIG
8:23 For I perceive that thou a in the gall of — *1510*
9: 5 And he said, Who a thou, Lord? — *1510*
10:33 And thou hast well done that thou **a** come. — NIG
12:15 And they said unto her, Thou a mad. — NIG
13:33 Thou a my Son, this day have I begotten — *1510*
17:29 or stone, graven by a and man's device. — *5078*
21:22 for they will hear that thou a come. — NIG
21:38 **A** not thou *that* Egyptian, which before — *1510*
22: 8 And I answered, Who a thou, Lord? — *1510*
22:27 said unto him, Tell me, a thou a Roman? — *1510*
26: 1 Thou a permitted to speak for thyself. — NIG
26:15 I said, Who a thou, Lord? And he said, — *1510*
26:24 a loud voice, Paul, thou a beside thyself; — NIG
Ro 2: 1 Therefore thou a inexcusable, O man, — *1510*
2: 1 O man, whosoever thou a that judgest: — NIG
2:17 thou a called a Jew, and restest in the law, — NIG
2:19 And a confident that thou thyself art a — NIG
2:19 art confident that thou thyself a a guide — *1510*
3: 4 mightest overcome when thou a judged. — NIG
9:20 who a thou that repliest against God? — *1510*
14: 4 Who a thou that judgest another *man's* — *1510*
1Co 7:21 **A** thou called *being* a servant? care not for — NIG
7:27 **A** thou bound unto a wife? seek not to be — NIG
7:27 **A** thou loosed from a wife? seek not a — NIG
Gal 4: 7 Wherefore thou a no more a servant, — *1510*
1Ti 6:12 whereunto thou a also called, — NIG
Heb 1: 5 Thou a my Son, this day have I begotten — *1510*
1:12 thou a the same, and thy years shall not — *1510*
2: 6 What is man, that thou a mindful of him? — NIG
5: 5 but he that said unto him, Thou a my Son, — *1510*
5: 6 As he saith also in another *place*, Thou a — NIG
7:17 Thou a a priest for ever after the order of — NIG
7:21 Thou a a priest for ever after the order of — NIG
12: 5 nor faint when thou a rebuked of him: — NIG
Jas 2:11 thou a become a transgressor of the law. — NIG
4:11 thou a not a doer of the law, but a judge. — *1510*
4:12 destroy: who a thou that judgest another? — *1510*
Rev 2: 5 therefore from whence thou a fallen, — NIG
2: 9 tribulation, and poverty, (but thou a rich) — *1510*
3: 1 hast a name that thou livest, and a dead. — *1510*
3:15 works, that thou a neither cold nor hot: — *1510*
3:16 So then because thou a lukewarm, — *1510*
3:17 and knowest not that thou a wretched, — *1510*
4:11 Thou a worthy, O Lord, to receive glory — *1510*
5: 9 Thou a worthy to take the book, — *1510*
11:17 which a, and wast, and art to come; — *1510*
11:17 which art, and wast, and a to come; — NIG
15: 4 for *thou* only a holy: for all nations shall — NIG
16: 5 Thou a righteous, O Lord, which art, — *1510*
16: 5 O Lord, which a, and wast, and shalt be, — *1510*

ARTAXERXES (14) [ARTAXERXES']
Ezr 4: 7 in the days of **A** wrote Bishlam, Mithredath, — *783*
4: 7 of their companions, unto **A** king of Persia; — *783*
4: 8 against Jerusalem to **A** the king in this sort: — *783*
4:11 they sent unto him, *even* unto **A** the king: — *783*
6:14 of Cyrus, and Darius, and **A** king of Persia. — *783*
7: 1 things, in the reign of **A** king of Persia, — *783*
7: 7 in the seventh year of **A** the king. — *783*
7:11 that the king **A** gave unto Ezra the priest, — *783*
7:12 **A**, king of kings, unto Ezra the priest, — *783*
7:21 *even* I **A** the king, do make a decree to all — *783*
8: 1 me from Babylon, in the reign of **A** the king. — *783*
Ne 2: 1 *in* the twentieth year of **A** the king, — *783*
5:14 the two and thirtieth year of **A** the king, — *783*
13: 6 thirtieth year of **A** king of Babylon came I — *783*

ARTAXERXES' (1) [ARTAXERXES]
Ezr 4:23 Now when the copy of king **A** letter *was* — *783*

ARTEMAS (1)
Tit 3:12 When I shall send **A** unto thee, — *734*

ARTEMIS See DIANA

ARTIFICER (2) [ARTIFICERS]
Ge 4:22 an instructor of every a in brass and iron: — *2794*
Isa 3: 3 the cunning a, and the eloquent orator. — *2791*

ARTIFICERS (2) [ARTIFICER]
1Ch 29: 5 *of* work *to be made* by the hands of **a**. — *2796*
2Ch 34:11 Even to the a and builders gave they *it*, — *2796*

ARTILLERY (1)
1Sa 20:40 Jonathan gave his a unto his lad, — *3627*

ARTS (1) [ART]
Ac 19:19 Many also of them which used **curious a** — *4021*

ARUBBOTH See ARUBOTH

ARUBOTH (1)
1Ki 4:10 The son of Hesed, in **A**; to him *pertained* — *700*

ARUMAH (1)
Jdg 9:41 Abimelech dwelt at **A**: and Zebul thrust — *725*

ARVAD (2) [ARVADITE]
Eze 27: 8 of Zidon and **A** were thy mariners: — *719*
27:11 The men of **A** with thine army *were* upon — *719*

ARVADITE (2) [ARVAD]
Ge 10:18 **A**, and the Zemarite, and the Hamathite: — *721*
1Ch 1:16 **A**, and the Zemarite, and the Hamathite. — *721*

ARZA (1)
1Ki 16: 9 drinking *himself* drunk *in* the house of **A** — *777*

AS (3520) [FORASMUCH, INASMUCH] See Index of Articles, Etc.

ASA (59) [ASA'S]
1Ki 15: 8 David: and **A** his son reigned in his stead. — *609*
15: 9 king of Israel reigned **A** over Judah. — *609*
15:11 **A** did *that* which *was* right in the eyes of — *609*
15:13 **A** destroyed her idol, and burnt *it* by — *609*
15:16 there was war between **A** and Baasha king — *609*
15:17 to go out or come in to **A** king of Judah. — *609*
15:18 **A** took all the silver and the gold that were — *609*
15:18 king **A** sent them to Ben-hadad, the son of — *609*
15:20 So Ben-hadad hearkened unto king **A**, — *609*
15:22 king **A** made a proclamation throughout all — *609*
15:22 king **A** built with them Geba of Benjamin, — *609*
15:23 The rest of all the acts of **A**, and all his — *609*
15:24 **A** slept with his fathers, and was buried — *609*
15:25 Israel in the second year of **A** king of Judah, — *609*
15:28 in the third year of **A** king of Judah did — *609*
15:32 there was war between **A** and Baasha king — *609*
15:33 In the third year of **A** king of Judah *began* — *609*
16: 8 sixth year of **A** king of Judah *began* Elah — *609*
16:10 and seventh year of **A** king of Judah, — *609*
16:15 seventh year of **A** king of Judah did Zimri — *609*
16:23 first year of **A** king of Judah *began* Omri to — *609*
16:29 eighth year of **A** king of Judah *began* Ahab — *609*
22:41 Jehoshaphat the son of **A** *began* to reign — *609*
22:43 he walked in all the ways of **A** his father; — *609*
22:46 remained in the days of his father **A**, — *609*
1Ch 3:10 his son, **A** his son, Jehoshaphat his son, — *609*
9:16 Berechiah the son of **A**, the son of Elkanah, — *609*
2Ch 14: 1 **A** his son reigned in his stead. In his days — *609*
14: 2 **A** did *that* which *was* good and right in — *609*
14: 8 **A** had an army *of men* that bare targets — *609*
14:10 **A** went out against him, and they set — *609*
14:11 **A** cried unto the LORD his God, and said, — *609*
14:12 the LORD smote the Ethiopians before **A**, — *609*
14:13 **A** and the people that *were* with him — *609*
15: 2 he went out to meet **A**, and said unto him, — *609*
15: 2 Hear ye me, **A**, and all Judah and Benjamin — *609*
15: 8 **A** heard these words, and the prophecy — *609*
15:10 in the fifteenth year of the reign of **A**. — *609*
15:16 also *concerning* Maachah the mother of **A** — *609*
15:16 and **A** cut down her idol, and stamped *it*, — *609*
15:17 nevertheless the heart of **A** was perfect all — *609*
15:19 the five and thirtieth year of the reign of **A**. — *609*
16: 1 thirtieth year of the reign of **A** Baasha king — *609*
16: 1 none go out or come in to **A** king of Judah. — *609*
16: 2 **A** brought out silver and gold out of — *609*
16: 4 And Ben-hadad hearkened unto king **A**, — *609*
16: 6 **A** the king took all Judah; and they carried — *609*
16: 7 that time Hanani the seer came to **A** king — *609*
16:10 **A** was wroth with the seer, and put him — *609*
16:10 of this *thing*. And **A** oppressed *some* of — *609*
16:11 behold, the acts of **A**, first and last, lo, — *609*
16:12 in the thirty and ninth year of his reign — *609*
16:13 **A** slept with his fathers, and died in the — *609*
17: 2 of Ephraim, which **A** his father had taken. — *609*
20:32 he walked in the way of **A** his father, — *609*
21:12 nor in the ways of **A** king of Judah, — *609*
Jer 41: 9 which **A** the king had made for fear of — *609*
Mt 1: 7 and Roboam begat Abia; and Abia begat **A**; — *760*
1: 8 And **A** begat Josaphat; and Josaphat begat — *760*

ASA'S (1) [ASA]
1Ki 15:14 nevertheless **A** heart was perfect with — *609*

ASAHEL (18)
2Sa 2:18 Zeruiah there, Joab, and Abishai, and **A**: — *6214*
2:18 and **A** *was* as light of foot as a wild roe. — *6214*
2:19 **A** pursued after Abner; and in going he — *6214*
2:20 looked behind him, and said, *Art* thou **A**? — *6214*
2:21 **A** would not turn aside from following of — *6214*
2:22 Abner said again to **A**, Turn thee aside — *6214*
2:23 as many as came to the place where **A** — *6214*
2:30 of David's servants nineteen men and **A**. — *6214*
2:32 they took up **A**, and buried him in — *6214*
3:27 he died, for the blood of **A** his brother. — *6214*
3:30 he had slain their brother **A** at Gibeon in — *6214*
23:24 **A** the brother of Joab *was* one of the thirty — *6214*
1Ch 2:16 Zeruiah; Abishai, and Joab, and **A**, three. — *6214*
11:26 the valiant *men* of the armies were, **A** — *6214*
27: 7 fourth month *was* **A** the brother of Joab, — *6214*
2Ch 17: 8 and Shemiramoth, and Jehonathan, — *6214*
31:13 **A**, and Jerimoth, and Jozabad, and Eliel, — *6214*
Ezr 10:15 Only Jonathan the son of **A** — *6214*

ASAHIAH (2)
2Ki 22:12 and **A** a servant of the king's, saying, — *6222*
22:14 and Achbor, and Shaphan, and **A**, — *6222*

ASAIAH (6)
1Ch 4:36 **A**, and Adiel, and Jesimiel, and Benaiah, — *6222*
6:30 his son; Haggiah his son, **A** his son. — *6222*
9: 5 Shilonites; **A** the firstborn, and his sons. — *6222*
15: 6 **A** the chief, and his brethren two hundred — *6222*
15:11 for Uriel, **A**, and Joel, Shemaiah, and Eliel, — *6222*
2Ch 34:20 and **A** a servant of the king's, saying, — *6222*

ASAPH (45) [ASAPH'S]
2Ki 18:18 and Joah the son of **A** the recorder. — *623*
18:37 and Joah the son of **A** the recorder, — *623*
1Ch 6:39 his brother **A**, who stood on his right hand, — *623*
6:39 *even* **A** the son of Berachiah, the son of — *623*
9:15 of Micah, the son of Zichri, the son of **A**, — *623*
15:17 and of his brethren **A** the son of Berechiah; — *623*
15:19 So the singers, Heman, **A**, and Ethan, — *623*
16: 5 **A** the chief, and next to him Zechariah, — *623*
16: 5 but **A** made a sound with cymbals; — *623*
16: 7 to thank the LORD into the hand of **A** — *623*
16:37 the ark of the covenant of the LORD **A** — *623*
25: 1 separated to the service of the sons of **A**, — *623*
25: 2 Of the sons of **A**; Zaccur, and Joseph, — *623*
25: 2 the sons of **A** under the hands of Asaph, — *623*
25: 2 the sons of Asaph under the hands of **A**, — *623*
25: 6 according to the king's order *to* **A**, — *623*
25: 9 the first lot came forth for **A** to Joseph: — *623*
26: 1 the son of Kore, of the sons of **A**. — *623*
2Ch 5:12 all of them of **A**, of Heman, of Jeduthun, — *623*
20:14 son of Mattaniah, a Levite of the sons of **A**, — *623*
29:13 of the sons of **A**; Zechariah, and Mattaniah: — *623*
29:30 with the words of David, and of **A** the seer. — *623*
35:15 singers the sons of **A** *were* in their place, — *623*
35:15 **A**, and Heman, and Jeduthun the king's — *623*
Ezr 2:41 the children of **A**, an hundred twenty — *623*
3:10 the Levites the sons of **A** with cymbals, — *623*
Ne 2: 8 a letter unto **A** the keeper of the king's — *623*
7:44 the children of **A**, an hundred forty — *623*
11:17 of Micha, the son of Zabdi, the son of **A**, — *623*
11:22 Of the sons of **A**, the singers *were* over — *623*
12:35 Michaiah, the son of Zaccur, the son of **A**: — *623*
12:46 **A** of old *there were* chief of the singers, — *623*
Ps 50: T A Psalm of **A**. — *623*
73: T A Psalm of **A**. — *623*
74: T Maschil of **A**. — *623*
75: T Al-taschith, A Psalm *or* Song of **A**. — *623*
76: T on Neginoth, A Psalm *or* Song of **A**. — *623*
77: T Musician, to Jeduthun, A Psalm of **A**. — *623*
78: T Maschil of **A**. — *623*
79: T A Psalm of **A**. — *623*
80: T upon Shoshannim-Eduth, A Psalm of **A**. — *623*
81: T chief Musician upon Gittith, *A Psalm* of **A**. — *623*
82: T A Psalm of **A**. — *623*
83: T A Song *or* Psalm of **A**. — *623*
Isa 36:22 and Joah, the son of **A**, the recorder, — *623*

ASAPH'S (1) [ASAPH]
Isa 36: 3 the scribe, and Joah, **A** son, the recorder. — *623*

ASAREEL (1)
1Ch 4:16 Jehaleleel; Ziph, and Ziphah, Tiria, and **A**. — *840*

ASAREL See ASAREEL

ASARELAH (1)
1Ch 25: 2 Zaccur, and Joseph, and Nethaniah, and **A**, — *841*

ASCEND (13) [ASCENDED, ASCENDETH, ASCENDING, ASCENT]
Jos 6: 5 the people shall a **up** every man straight — *5927*
Ps 24: 3 Who shall a **into** the hill of the LORD? — *5927*
135: 7 he **causeth** the vapours to a from the — *5927*
139: 8 If I a **into** heaven, thou *art* there: if I — *5266*
Isa 14:13 said in thine heart, I will a **into** heaven, — *5927*
14:14 I will a above the heights of the clouds; — *5927*
Jer 10:13 he **causeth** the vapours to a from the — *5927*
51:16 he **causeth** the vapours to a from the — *5927*
Eze 38: 9 Thou shalt a and come like a storm, — *5927*
Jn 6:62 if ye shall see the Son of man a **up** where — *305*
20:17 I a unto my Father, and *your* Father; — *305*
Ro 10: 6 in thine heart, Who shall a **into** heaven? — *305*
Rev 17: 8 and shall a out of the bottomless *pit*, — *305*

ASCENDED (19) [ASCEND]
Ex 19:18 the smoke thereof a as the smoke of a — *5927*
Nu 13:22 they a by the south, and came unto — *5927*
Jos 8:20 the smoke of the city a **up** to heaven, — *5927*
8:21 that the smoke of the city **a**, — *5927*
10: 7 So Joshua a from Gilgal, he, and all — *5927*
15: 3 a **up** on the south side unto — *5927*
Jdg 13:20 that the angel of the LORD a in the flame — *5927*
20:40 the flame of the city a **up** to heaven. — *5927*
Ps 68:18 hast a on high, thou hast led captivity — *5927*
Pr 30: 4 hath a **up** *into* heaven, or descended? — *5927*
Jn 3:13 no *man* hath a **up** to heaven, but he that — *305*
20:17 me not; for I am not yet a to my Father: — *305*
Ac 2:34 For David is not a into the heavens: — *305*
25: 1 after three days he a from Cesarea to — *305*
Eph 4: 8 *he* saith, When he a **up** on high, — *305*
4: 9 (Now that he **a**, what is it but that he also — *305*
4:10 that descended is the same also that a **up** — *305*
Rev 8: 4 before God out of the angel's hand. — *305*
11:12 And they a **up** to heaven in a cloud; — *305*

ASCENDETH (2) [ASCEND]
Rev 11: 7 the beast that a out of the bottomless *pit* — *305*
14:11 the smoke of their torment a **up** for ever — *305*

ASCENDING (5) [ASCEND]
Ge 28:12 behold the angels of God a — *5927*
1Sa 28:13 unto Saul, I saw gods a out of the earth. — *5927*
Lk 19:28 he went before, a **up** to Jerusalem. — *305*
Jn 1:51 and the angels of God a — *305*
Rev 7: 2 And I saw another angel a from the east, — *305*

A

ASCENT (4) [ASCEND]

Nu	34: 4 turn from the south to the **a** of Akrabbim,	4608
2Sa	15:30 David went up by the **a** of *mount* Olivet,	4608
1Ki	10: 5 his **a** *by* which he went up *unto* the house	5930
2Ch	9: 4 his **a** *by* which he went up *into* the house	5944

ASCRIBE (3) [ASCRIBED]

Dt	32: 3 the LORD: **a** ye greatness unto our God.	3051
Job	36: 3 and will **a** righteousness to my Maker.	5414
Ps	68:34 **A** ye strength unto God: his excellency *is*	5414

ASCRIBED (2) [ASCRIBE]

1Sa	18: 8 They have **a** unto David ten thousands,	5414
	18: 8 and to me they have **a** *but* thousands:	5414

ASENATH (3)

Ge	41:45 he gave him to wife **A** the daughter of	621
	41:50 which **A** the daughter of Poti-pherah priest	621
	46:20 which **A** the daughter of Poti-pherah priest	621

ASER (2) [ASHER]

Lk	2:36 the daughter of Phanuel, of the tribe of **A**:	768
Rev	7: 6 Of the tribe of **A** *were* sealed twelve	768

ASH (1)

Isa	44:14 he planteth an **a**, and the rain doth nourish	766

ASHAMED (122) [SHAME]

Ge	2:25 the man and his wife, and were not **a**.	954
Nu	12:14 her face, should she not be **a** seven days?	3637
Jdg	3:25 they tarried till *they* were **a**: and behold,	954
2Sa	10: 5 them, because the men were greatly **a**:	3637
	19: 3 people being a steal away when they flee	3637
2Ki	2:17 they urged him till *he* was **a**, he said,	954
	8:11 his countenance stedfastly, until *he* was **a**:	954
1Ch	19: 5 for the men were greatly **a**. And the king	3637
2Ch	30:15 the priests and the Levites were **a**,	3637
Ezr	8:22 For I was **a** to require of the king a band	954
	9: 6 I am **a** and blush to lift up my face to thee,	954
Job	6:20 hoped; they came thither, and were **a**.	2659
	11: 3 mockest, shall no man **make** *thee* **a**?	3637
	19: 3 you are not **a** *that* you make yourselves	954
Ps	6:10 Let all mine enemies be **a** and sore vexed:	954
	6:10 let them return *and* be **a** suddenly.	954
	25: 2 let me not be **a**, let not mine enemies	954
	25: 3 let none that wait on thee be **a**: let them	954
	25: 3 let them be **a** which transgress without	954
	25:20 let me not be **a**; for I put my trust in thee.	954
	31: 1 do I put my trust; let me never be **a**:	954
	31:17 Let me not be **a**, O LORD; for I have called	954
	31:17 let the wicked be **a**, *and* let them be silent	954
	34: 5 lightened: and their faces were not **a**.	2659
	35:26 Let them be **a** and brought to confusion	954
	37:19 They shall not be **a** in the evil time:	954
	40:14 Let them be **a** and confounded together	954
	69: 6 O Lord GOD of hosts, let me **a** for my sake:	954
	70: 2 Let them be **a** and confounded that seek	954
	74:21 O let not the oppressed return **a**: let	3637
	86:17 they which hate me may see *it*, and be **a**:	954
	109:28 when they arise, let them be **a**; but let thy	954
	119: 6 I not be **a**, when I have respect unto all	954
	119:46 also before kings, and will not be **a**.	954
	119:78 the proud be **a**; for they dealt perversely	954
	119:80 be sound in thy statutes; that I be not **a**.	954
	119:116 I may live: and let me not be **a** of my hope.	954
	127: 5 they shall not be **a**, but they shall speak	954
Pr	12: 4 she that **maketh a** *is* as rottenness in his	954
Isa	1:29 For they shall be **a** of the oaks which ye	954
	20: 5 afraid and **a** of Ethiopia their expectation,	954
	23: 4 thou **a**, O Zidon: for the sea hath spoken,	954
	24:23 moon shall be confounded, and the sun **a**,	954
	26:11 and be **a** for *their* envy at the people;	954
	29:22 house of Jacob, neither shall now his face **a**,	954
	30: 5 They were all **a** of a people *that* could not	954
	33: 9 Lebanon is **a** *and* hewn down: Sharon is	2659
	41:11 that were incensed against thee shall be **a**	954
	42:17 turned back, they shall be **greatly a**,	954+1322
	44: 9 see not, nor know; that they may be **a**.	954
	44:11 Behold, all his fellows shall be **a**:	954
	44:11 shall fear, *and* they shall be **a** together.	954
	45:16 They shall be **a**, and also confounded, all	954
	45:17 ye shall not be **a** nor confounded world	954
	45:24 that are incensed against him shall be **a**.	954
	49:23 for they shall not be **a** that wait for me.	954
	50: 7 a flint, and I know that I shall not be **a**.	954
	54: 4 Fear not; for thou shalt not be **a**: neither	954
	65:13 my servants shall rejoice, but ye shall be **a**:	954
	66: 5 appear to your joy, and they shall be **a**.	954
Jer	2:26 As the thief is **a** when he is found, so is	1322
	2:26 he is found, so is the house of Israel **a**;	954
	2:36 thou also shalt be **a** of Egypt, as thou wast	954
	2:36 of Egypt, as thou wast **a** of Assyria.	954
	3: 3 whore's forehead, thou refusedst to be **a**.	3637
	6:15 Were they **a** when they had committed	954
	6:15 nay, they were not **at all a**, neither	954+954
	8: 9 The wise *men* are **a**, they are dismayed	954
	8:12 Were they **a** when they had committed	954
	8:12 nay, they were not **at all a**, neither	954+954
	12:13 they shall be **a** of your revenues because	954
	14: 3 they were **a** and confounded,	954
	14: 4 the plowmen were **a**, they covered their	954
	15: 9 she hath been **a** and confounded:	954
	17:13 all that forsake thee shall be **a**, and they	954
	20:11 they shall be greatly **a**: for they shall not	954
	22:22 surely then shalt thou be **a**	954

Jer	31:19 I was **a**, yea, even confounded, because I	954
	48:13 Moab shall be **a** of Chemosh, as the house	954
	48:13 as the house of Israel was **a** of Beth-el	954
	50:12 she that bare you shall be **a**:	2659
Eze	16:27 which are **a** of thy lewd way.	3637
	16:61 be **a**, when thou shalt receive thy sisters,	3637
	32:30 with their terror *they* are **a** of their might;	954
	36:32 be **a** and confounded for your own ways,	954
	43:10 that they may be **a** of their iniquities:	3637
	43:11 if they be **a** of all that they have done,	3637
Hos	4:19 they shall be **a** because of their sacrifices.	954
	10: 6 and Israel shall be **a** of his own counsel.	954
Joel	1:11 Be ye **a**, O ye husbandmen; howl, O ye	954
	2:26 with you: and my people shall never be **a**.	954
	2:27 none else: and my people shall never be **a**.	954
Mic	3: 7 shall the seers be **a**, and the diviners	954
Zep	3:11 In that day shalt thou not be **a** for all thy	954
Zec	9: 5 her expectation shall be **a**; and the king	3001
	13: 4 *that* the prophets shall be **a** every one of	954
Mk	8:38 Whosoever therefore shall be **a** of me	1870
	8:38 of him also shall the Son of man be **a**,	1870
Lk	9:26 For whosoever shall be **a** of me and of my	1870
	9:26 of him shall the Son of man be **a**,	1870
	13:17 these *things*, and all his adversaries were **a**:	1870
	16: 3 stewardship: I cannot dig; to beg I am **a**.	153
Ro	1:16 For I am not **a** of the gospel of Christ:	1870
	5: 5 And hope **maketh** not **a**; because the love	2617
	6:21 *in* those *things* whereof ye are now **a**?	1870
	9:33 believeth on him shall not be **a**.	2617
	10:11 believeth on him shall not be **a**.	2617
2Co	7:14 any *thing* to him of you, I am not **a**;	2617
	9: 4 be **a** in this same confident boasting.	2617
	10: 8 for your destruction, I should not be **a**:	153
Php	1:20 in nothing I shall be **a**, but *that* with all	153
2Th	3:14 no company with him, that he may be **a**.	1788
2Ti	1: 8 therefore **a** of the testimony of our Lord,	1870
	1:12 these *things*: nevertheless I am not **a**:	1870
	1:16 refreshed me, and was not **a** of my chain:	1870
	2:15 a workman that **needeth not to be a**,	422
Tit	2: 8 he that is of the contrary *part* may be **a**,	1788
Heb	2:11 for which cause he is not **a** to call them	1870
	11:16 wherefore God is not **a** to be called their	1870
1Pe	3:16 may be **a** that falsely accuse your good	2617
	4:16 *suffer* as a Christian, let him not be **a**;	153
1Jn	2:28 and not be **a** before him at his coming.	153

ASHAN (4)

Jos	15:42 Libnah, and Ether, and **A**,	6228
	19: 7 Ain, Remmon, and Ether, and **A**; four	6228
1Ch	4:32 Ain, Rimmon, and Tochen, and **A**,	6228
	6:59 **A** with her suburbs, and Beth-shemesh	6228

ASHBEA (1)

1Ch	4:21 that wrought fine linen, of the house of **A**,	791

ASHBEL (3) [ASHBELITES]

Ge	46:21 and **A**, and Gera, and Naaman, Ehi, and Rosh,	788
Nu	26:38 of **A**, the family of the Ashbelites:	788
1Ch	8: 1 **A** the second, and Aharah the third,	788

ASHBELITES (1) [ASHBEL]

Nu	26:38 of Ashbel, the family of the **A**: of Ahiram,	789

ASHCHENAZ (2)

1Ch	1: 6 of Gomer; **A**, and Riphath, and Togarmah.	813
Jer	51:27 her the kingdoms of Ararat, Minni, and **A**;	813

ASHDOD (21) [ASHDODITES]

Jos	11:22 only in Gaza, in Gath, and in **A**,	795
	15:46 all that *lay* near **A**, with their villages:	795
	15:47 **A** *with* her towns and her villages, Gaza	795
1Sa	5: 1 and brought it from Eben-ezer unto **A**.	795
	5: 3 when **they** of **A** arose early on the morrow	796
	5: 5 tread on the threshold of Dagon in **A** unto	795
	5: 6 of the LORD was heavy upon **them** of **A**,	796
	5: 6 emerods, *even* **A** and the coasts thereof.	795
	5: 7 when the men of **A** saw that *it* was so,	795
	6:17 for **A** one, for Gaza one, for Askelon one,	795
2Ch	26: 6 wall of **A**, and built cities about Ashdod,	795
	26: 6 built cities about **A**, and among	795
Ne	13:23 saw I Jews *that* had married wives of **A**,	796
	13:24 children spake half **in the speech of A**,	797
Isa	20: 1 In the year that Tartan came unto **A**,	795
	20: 1 and fought against **A**, and took it;	795
Jer	25:20 and Ekron, and the remnant of **A**:	795
Am	1: 8 And I will cut off the inhabitant from **A**,	795
	3: 9 Publish in the palaces at **A**, and in	795
Zep	2: 4 they shall drive out **A** at the noon day,	795
Zec	9: 6 a bastard shall dwell in **A**, and I will cut off	795

ASHDODITES (1) [ASHDOD]

Ne	4: 7 Arabians, and the Ammonites, and the **A**,	796

ASHDOTHITES (1)

Jos	13: 3 Gazathites, and the **A**, the Eshkalonites,	796

ASHDOTH-PISGAH (3)

Dt	3:17 *even* the salt sea, under **A** eastward.	798
Jos	12: 3 and from the south, under **A**:	798
	13:20 And Beth-peor, and **A**, and Beth-jeshimoth,	798

ASHER (43) [ASER, ASHERITES]

Ge	30:13 call me blessed: and she called his name **A**.	836
	35:26 of Zilpah, Leah's handmaid; Gad, and **A**:	836
	46:17 And the sons of **A**; Jimnah, and Ishuah,	836
	49:20 Out of **A** his bread *shall be* fat, and he	836

Ex	1: 4 Dan, and Naphtali, Gad, and **A**.	836
Nu	1:13 Of **A**; Pagiel the son of Ocran.	836
	1:40 Of the children of **A**, *by* their generations,	836
	1:41 *even* of the tribe of **A**, *were* forty	836
	2:27 that encamp by him *shall be* the tribe of **A**:	836
	2:27 the captain of the children of **A** *shall be*	836
	7:72 prince of the children of **A**, offered:	836
	10:26 the host of the tribe of the children of **A**	836
	13:13 the tribe of **A**, Sethur the son of Michael.	836
	26:44 *Of* the children of **A** after their families:	836
	26:46 the name of the daughter of **A** *was* Sarah.	836
	26:47 These *are* the families of the sons of **A**	836
	34:27 the prince of the tribe of the children of **A**,	836
Dt	27:13 and **A**, and Zebulun, Dan, and Naphtali.	836
	33:24 Of **A** he said, *Let* Asher *be* blessed with	836
	33:24 he said, *Let* **A** *be* blessed with children;	836
Jos	17: 7 the coast of Manasseh was from **A** *to*	836
	17:10 and they met together in **A** on the north,	836
	17:11 and in **A** Beth-shean and her towns,	836
	19:24 children of **A** according to their families.	836
	19:31 children of **A** according to their families.	836
	19:34 reacheth to **A** on the west side,	836
	21: 6 out of the tribe of **A**, and out of the tribe	836
	21:30 out of the tribe of **A**, Mishal with her	836
Jdg	1:31 Neither did **A** drive out the inhabitants of	836
	5:17 **A** continued on the sea shore, and abode	836
	6:35 he sent messengers unto **A**,	836
	7:23 out of **A**, and out of all Manasseh,	836
1Ki	4:16 Baanah the son of Hushai *was* in **A**	836
1Ch	2: 2 and Benjamin, Naphtali, Gad, and **A**.	836
	6:62 out of the tribe of **A**, and out of the tribe	836
	6:74 out of the tribe of **A**; Mashal with her	836
	7:30 The sons of **A**; Imnah, and Isuah,	836
	7:40 All these *were* the children of **A**, heads of	836
	12:36 of **A**, such as went forth to battle, expert	836
2Ch	30:11 Nevertheless divers of **A** and Manasseh	836
Eze	48: 2 side unto the west side, a *portion for* **A**.	836
	48: 3 by the border of **A**, from the east side	836
	48:34 one gate of Gad, one gate of **A**, one gate	836

ASHERITES (1) [ASHER]

Jdg	1:32 the **A** dwelt among the Canaanites,	843

ASHES (43)

Ge	18:27 unto the Lord, which *am but* dust and **a**:	665
Ex	9: 8 Take to you handfuls of **a** of the furnace,	6368
	9:10 they took **a** of the furnace, and stood	6368
	27: 3 thou shalt make his pans to **receive** his **a**,	1878
Lev	1:16 altar on the east part, by the place of the **a**:	1880
	4:12 where the **a** are poured out, and burn him	1880
	4:12 where the **a** are poured out shall he be	1880
	6:10 the **a** which the fire hath consumed	1880
	6:11 carry forth the **a** without the camp unto a	1880
Nu	4:13 they shall **take away** the **a** from the altar,	1878
	19: 9 man *that is* clean shall gather up the **a** of	665
	19:10 he that gathereth up the **a** of the heifer shall	665
	19:17 **a** of the burnt *heifer* of purification for sin,	6083
2Sa	13:19 Tamar put **a** on her head, and rent her	665
1Ki	13: 3 the **a** that *are* upon it shall be poured out.	1880
	13: 5 and the **a** poured out from the altar,	1880
	20:38 and disguised himself with **a** upon his face.	666
	20:41 and took the **a** away from his face;	666
2Ki	23: 4 and carried the **a** of them *unto* Beth-el.	6083
Est	4: 1 put on sackcloth with **a**, and went out into	665
	4: 3 wailing; *and* many lay in sackcloth and **a**.	665
Job	2: 8 and he sat down among the **a**.	665
	13:12 Your remembrances *are* like unto **a**,	665
	30:19 the mire, and I am become like dust and **a**.	665
	42: 6 I abhor *myself*, and repent in dust and **a**.	665
Ps	102: 9 For I have eaten **a** like bread,	665
	147:16 hoar wool: he scattereth the hoarfrost like **a**.	665
Isa	44:20 He feedeth on **a**: a deceived heart hath	665
	58: 5 and a *under him?* wilt thou call this a fast,	665
	61: 3 give unto them beauty for **a**, the oil of joy	665
Jer	6:26 with sackcloth, and wallow thyself in **a**:	665
	25:34 wallow yourselves *in the* **a**, ye principal of	NIH
	31:40 of the **a**, and all the fields unto the brook	1880
La	3:16 gravel stones, he hath covered me with **a**.	665
Eze	27:30 they shall wallow themselves in the **a**:	665
	28:18 I will bring thee to **a** upon the earth in	665
Da	9: 3 with fasting, and sackcloth, and **a**:	665
Jnh	3: 6 covered *him* with sackcloth, and sat in **a**.	665
Mal	4: 3 for they shall be **a** under the soles of your	665
Mt	11:21 repented long ago in sackcloth and **a**.	4700
Lk	10:13 ago repented, sitting in sackcloth and **a**.	4700
Heb	9:13 the **a** of a heifer sprinkling the unclean,	4700
2Pe	2: 6 **turning** the cities of Sodom and Gomorrha **into a**	5077

ASHHUR See ASHUR

ASHIMA (1)

2Ki	17:30 and the men of Hamath made **A**,	807

ASHKELON (9) [ASKELON, ESHKALONITES]

Jdg	14:19 he went down *to* **A**, and slew thirty men	831
Jer	25:20 **A**, and Azzah, and Ekron, and the remnant	831
	47: 5 **A** is cut off *with* the remnant of their valley	831
	47: 7 the LORD hath given it a charge against **A**,	831
Am	1: 8 and him that holdeth the sceptre from **A**,	831
Zep	2: 4 Gaza shall be forsaken, and **A** a desolation:	831
	2: 7 in the houses of **A** shall they lie down in	831
Zec	9: 5 **A** shall see *it*, and fear; Gaza also *shall see*	831
	9: 5 from Gaza, and **A** shall not be inhabited.	831

A

ASHKENAZ (1)
Ge 10: 3 of Gomer; **A**, and Riphath, and Togarmah. 813

ASHNAH (2)
Jos 15:33 in the valley, Eshtaol, and Zoreah, and **A**, 823
 15:43 And Jiphtah, and **A**, and Nezib, 823

ASHPENAZ (1)
Da 1: 3 the king spake unto **A** the master of his 828

ASHRIEL (1)
1Ch 7:14 The sons of Manasseh; **A**, whom she bare: 844

ASHTAROTH (11) [ASHTORETH]
Jos 9:10 to Og king of Bashan, which was at **A**. 6252
 12: 4 of the giants, that dwelt at **A** and at Edrei, 6252
 13:12 Bashan, which reigned in **A** and in Edrei, 6252
 13:31 half Gilead, and **A**, and Edrei, cities of 6252
Jdg 2:13 the Lord, and served Baal and **A**, 6252
 10: 6 **A**, and the gods of Syria, and the gods of 6252
1Sa 7: 3 the strange gods and **A** from among you, 6252
 7: 4 of Israel did put away Baalim and **A**, 6252
 12:10 and have served Baalim and **A**: 6252
 31:10 they put his armour in the house of **A**: 6253
1Ch 6:71 her suburbs, and **A** with her suburbs: 6252

ASHTERATHITE (1)
1Ch 11:44 Uzzia the **A**, Shama and Jehiel the sons of 6254

ASHTEROTH KARNAIM (1)
Ge 14: 5 and smote the Rephaims in **A**, 6255

ASHTORETH (3) [ASHTAROTH]
1Ki 11: 5 For Solomon went after **A** the goddess of 6253
 11:33 have worshipped **A** the goddess of 6253
2Ki 23:13 for **A** the abomination of the Zidonians, 6253

ASHUR (2) [ASHURITES]
1Ch 2:24 Abiah Hezron's wife bare him **A** the father 806
 4: 5 **A** the father of Tekoa had two wives, 806

ASHURBANIPAL See ASNAPPER

ASHURI See ASHURITES

ASHURITES (2) [ASHUR]
2Sa 2: 9 over the **A**, and over Jezreel, 805
Eze 27: 6 the company of the **A** have made thy 839

ASHVATH (1)
1Ch 7:33 of Japhlet; Pasach, and Bimhal, and **A**. 6220

ASIA (21)
Ac 2: 9 Judea, and Cappadocia, in Pontus, and **A**, 773
 6: 9 and of them of Cilicia and of **A**, 773
 16: 6 the Holy Ghost to preach the word in **A**, 773
 19:10 that all they which dwelt in **A** heard 773
 19:22 but he himself stayed in **A** for a season. 773
 19:26 but almost throughout all **A**, this Paul 773
 19:27 whom all **A** and the world worshippeth. 773
 19:31 And certain of the chief of **A**, which were 775
 20: 4 there accompanied him into **A** Sopater 773
 20: 4 and of **A**, Tychicus and Trophimus. 774
 20:16 he would not spend the time in **A**: 773
 20:18 from the first day that I came into **A**, 773
 21:27 Jews which were of **A**, when they saw 773
 24:18 Whereupon certain Jews from **A** found me 773
 27: 2 meaning to sail by the coasts of **A**; 773
1Co 16:19 The churches of **A** salute you. Aquila 773
2Co 1: 8 of our trouble which came to us in **A**, 773
2Ti 1:15 all they which are in **A** be turned away 773
1Pe 1: 1 Galatia, Cappadocia, **A**, and Bithynia, 773
Rev 1: 4 John to the seven churches which are in **A**: 773
 1:11 it unto the seven churches which are in **A**; 773

ASIDE (72) [SIDE]
Ex 3: 3 I will now turn **a**, and see this great sight, 5493
 3: 4 when the Lord saw that he turned **a** to 5493
 32: 8 have turned **a** quickly out of the way 5493
Nu 5:12 If any man's wife go **a**, and commit a 7847
 5:19 if thou hast not gone **a** to uncleanness 7847
 5:20 if thou hast gone **a** to another instead 7847
 5:29 when a wife goeth **a** to another instead 7847
 22:23 the ass turned **a** out of the way, 5186
Dt 5:32 ye shall not turn **a** to the right hand or 5493
 9:12 turned **a** out of the way which I 5493
 9:16 ye had turned **a** quickly out of the way 5493
 11:16 ye turn **a**, and serve other gods, 5493
 11:28 turn **a** out of the way which I command 5493
 17:20 he turn not **a** from the commandment, 5493
 28:14 thou shalt not go **a** from any of the words 5493
 31:29 turn **a** from the way which I have 5493
Jos 23: 6 that ye turn not **a** therefrom to the right 5493
Jdg 14: 8 he turned **a** to see the carcase of the lion: 5493
 19:12 We will not turn **a** hither into the city of 5493
 19:15 they turned **a** thither, to go in and to 5493
Ru 4: 1 Ho, such a one, turn **a**, sit down here. 5493
 4: 1 And he turned **a**, and sat down. 5493
1Sa 6:12 turned not **a** to the right hand or to 5493
 8: 3 turned **a** after lucre, and took bribes, 5186
 12:20 yet turn not **a** from following the Lord, 5493
 12:21 turn ye not **a**: for then should ye go after 5493
2Sa 2:21 Turn thee **a** to thy right hand or to thy 5186
 2:21 Asahel would not turn **a** from following 5493
 2:22 Asahel, Turn thee **a** from following me: 5493
 2:23 Howbeit he refused to turn **a**: 5493

2Sa 3:27 Joab took him **a** in the gate to speak with 5186
 6:10 David carried it **a** into the house of 5186
 18:30 the king said unto him, Turn **a**, and 5437
 18:30 And he turned **a**, and stood still. 5437
1Ki 15: 5 turned not **a** from any thing that he 5493
 20:39 a man turned **a**, and brought a man unto 5493
 22:32 they turned **a** to fight against him: 5493
 22:43 he turned **a** not from it, doing that which 5493
2Ki 4: 4 and thou shalt set **a** that which is full. 5265
 22: 2 turned not **a** to the right hand or to the 5493
1Ch 13:13 carried it **a** into the house of Obed-edom 5186
Job 6:18 The paths of their way are turned **a**; 3943
Ps 14: 3 They are all gone **a**, they are all together 5493
 40: 4 not the proud, nor such as turn **a** to lies. 7750
 78:57 they were turned **a** like a deceitful bow. 2015
 101: 3 I hate the work of them that turn **a**; 7750
 125: 5 As for such as turn **a** unto their crooked 5186
SS 1: 7 for why should I be as one that turneth **a** 5844
 6: 1 whither is thy beloved turned **a**? that we 6437
Isa 10: 2 To turn **a** the needy from judgment, 5186
 29:21 and turn **a** the just for a thing of nought. 5186
 30:11 ye out of the way, turn **a** out of the path, 5186
 44:20 a deceived heart hath turned him **a**, 5186
Jer 14: 8 a wayfaring man that turneth **a** to tarry 5186
 15: 5 or who shall go **a** to ask how thou doest? 5493
La 3:11 He hath turned **a** my ways, and pulled 5493
 3:35 To turn **a** the right of a man before the 5186
Am 2: 7 the poor, and turn **a** the way of the meek: 5186
 5:12 they turn **a** the poor in the gate from 5186
Mal 3: 5 that turn **a** the stranger from his right, 5186
Mt 2:22 he turned **a** into the parts of Galilee, 402
Mk 7: 8 For laying **a** the commandment of God, 863
 7:33 And he took him **a** 2398+2596
Lk 9:10 went **a** privately into a desert place 5298
Jn 13: 4 from supper, and laid **a** his garments; 5087
Ac 4:15 when they had commanded them to go **a** 565
 23:19 the hand, and went with him **a** privately, 402
 26:31 And when they were gone **a**, they talked 402
1Ti 1: 6 swerved have turned **a** unto vain jangling; 1624
 5:15 For some are already turned **a** after Satan. 1624
Heb 12: 1 let us lay **a** every weight, and the sin 659
1Pe 2: 1 Wherefore laying **a** all malice, and all guile, 659

ASIEL (1)
1Ch 4:35 the son of Seraiah, the son of **A**, 6221

ASK (109) [ASKED, ASKEST, ASKETH, ASKING]
Ge 32:29 Wherefore is it that thou dost **a** after my 7592
 34:12 **A** me never so much dowry and 3966+7235
Nu 27:21 who shall **a** counsel for him after 7592
Dt 4:32 For a now of the days that are past, 7592
 4:32 **a** from the one side of heaven unto NIH
 13:14 and make search, and **a** diligently; 7592
 32: 7 **a** thy father, and he will shew thee; 7592
Jos 4: 6 that when your children **a** their fathers in 7592
 4:21 When your children shall **a** their fathers 7592
 15:18 she moved him to **a** of her father a field: 7592
Jdg 1:14 she moved him to **a** of her father a field: 7592
 18: 5 him, **A**, counsel, we pray thee, of God, 7592
1Sa 12:19 unto all our sins this evil, to **a** us a king. 7592
 25: 8 **A** thy young men, and they will shew 7592
 28:16 Wherefore then dost thou **a** of me, 7592
2Sa 14:18 I pray thee, the thing that I shall **a** thee. 7592
 20:18 shall surely **a** counsel at Abel: 7592+7592
1Ki 2:16 now I **a** one petition of thee, 7592+7596
 2:20 the king said unto her, **A**, on, my mother: 7592
 2:22 why dost thou **a** Abishag the Shunammite 7592
 2:22 **a** for him the kingdom also; for he is mine 7592
 3: 5 and God said, **A** what I shall give thee. 7592
 14: 5 the wife of Jeroboam cometh to **a** a thing 1875
2Ki 2: 9 unto Elisha, **A** what I shall do for thee, 7592
2Ch 1: 7 said unto him, **A** what I shall give thee. 7592
 20: 4 to **a** help of the Lord: 1245
Job 12: 7 a now the beasts, and they shall teach 7592
Ps 2: 8 **A** of me, and I shall give thee the heathen 7592
Isa 7:11 **A** thee a sign of the Lord thy God; ask it 7592
 7:11 a it either in the depth, or in the height 7592
 7:12 Ahaz said, I will not **a**, neither will I tempt 7592
 45:11 **A** me of things to come concerning my 7592
 58: 2 they **a** of me the ordinances of justice; 7592
Jer 6:16 the ways, and see, and **a** for the old paths, 7592
 15: 5 who shall go aside to **a** how thou doest? 7592
 18:13 **A** ye now among the heathen, who hath 7592
 23:33 the prophet, or a priest, shall **a** thee, 7592
 30: 6 **A** ye now, and see whether a man doth 7592
 38:14 said unto Jeremiah, I will **a** thee a thing; 7592
 48:19 **a** him that fleeth, and her that escapeth, 7592
 50: 5 They shall **a** the way to Zion with their 7592
La 4: 4 the young children **a** bread, and no man 7592
Da 6: 7 that whosoever shall **a** a petition of any 1156
 6:12 every man that shall **a** a petition of any 1156
Hos 4:12 My people **a** counsel at their stocks, 7592
Hag 2:11 **A** now the priests concerning the law, 7592
Zec 10: 1 **A** ye of the Lord rain in the time of 7592
Mt 6: 8 things ye have need of, before ye **a** him. 154
 7: 7 **A**, and it shall be given you; seek, 154
 7: 9 whom if his son **a** bread, will he give him 154
 7:10 if he **a** a fish, will he give him a serpent? 154
 7:11 give good things to them that **a** him? 154
 14: 7 oath to give her whatsoever she would **a**. 154
 18:19 as touching any thing that they shall **a**, 154
 20:22 and said, Ye know not what ye **a**. 154
 21:22 And all things, whatsoever ye shall **a** in 154
 21:24 unto them, I also will **a** you one thing, 2065
 22:46 durst any man from that day forth **a** 1905

Mt 27:20 the multitude that they should **a** Barabbas, 154
Mk 6:22 **A** of me whatsoever thou wilt, and I will 154
 6:23 Whatsoever thou shalt **a** of me, I will give 154
 6:24 and said unto her mother, What shall I **a**? 154
 9:32 not that saying, and were afraid to **a** him. 1905
 10:38 said unto them, Ye know not what ye **a**: 154
 11:29 I will also **a** of you one question, 1905
 12:34 And no man after that durst **a** him any 1905
Lk 6: 9 I will **a** you one thing; Is it lawful on 1905
 6:30 taketh away thy goods **a** them not again. 523
 9:45 and they feared to **a** him of that saying. 2065
 11: 9 I say unto you, **A**, and it shall be given you; 154
 11:11 If a son shall **a** bread of any of you that is a 154
 11:11 if he **a** a fish, will he for a fish give him a NIG
 11:12 Or if he shall **a** an egg, will he offer him a 154
 11:13 give the Holy Spirit to them that **a** him? 154
 12:48 of him they will **a** the more. 154
 19:31 And if any man **a** you, Why do ye loose 2065
 20: 3 unto them, I will also **a** you one thing; 2065
 20:40 And after that they durst not **a** him any 1905
 22:68 And if I also **a** you, you will not answer 2065
Jn 1:19 and Levites from Jerusalem to **a** him, 2065
 9:21 he is of age; **a** him: he shall speak for 2065
 9:23 said his parents, He is of age; **a** him. 2065
 11:22 even now, whatsoever thou wilt **a** of God, 154
 13:24 that he should **a** who it should be of 4441
 14:13 And whatsoever ye shall **a** in my name, 154
 14:14 If ye shall **a** any thing in my name, I will do 154
 15: 7 ye shall **a** what ye will, and it shall be done 154
 15:16 that whatsoever ye shall **a** of the Father in 154
 16:19 knew that they were desirous to **a** him, 2065
 16:23 And in that day ye shall **a** me nothing. 2065
 16:23 Whatsoever ye shall **a** the Father in my 154
 16:24 **a**, and ye shall receive, that your joy may 154
 16:26 At that day ye shall **a** in my name: and I 154
 16:30 needest not that any man should **a** thee: 2065
 18:21 **a** them which heard me, what I have said 1905
 21:12 And none of the disciples durst **a** him, 1833
Ac 3: 2 to **a** alms of them that entered into 154
 10:29 I therefore for what intent ye have sent 4441
1Co 14:35 And if they will learn any thing, let them **a** 1905
Eph 3:20 exceeding abundantly above all that we **a** 154
Jas 1: 5 any of you lack wisdom, let him **a** of God, 154
 1: 6 But let him **a** in faith, nothing wavering: 154
 4: 2 and war, yet ye have not, because ye **a** not. 154
 4: 3 Ye **a**, and receive not, because ye ask amiss, 154
 4: 3 Ye ask, and receive not, because ye **a** amiss, 154
1Jn 3:22 And whatsoever we **a**, we receive of him, 154
 5:14 that, if we **a** any thing according to his will, 154
 5:15 we know that he hear us, whatsoever we **a**, 154
 5:16 he shall **a**, and he shall give him life for 154

ASKED (119) [ASK]
Ge 24:47 I **a** her, and said, Whose daughter art 7592
 26: 7 the men of the place **a** him of his wife; 7592
 32:29 Jacob a him, and said, Tell me, I pray 7592
 37:15 man a him, saying, What seekest thou? 7592
 38:21 he a the men of that place, saying, Where 7592
 40: 7 he a Pharaoh's officers that were with him 7592
 43: 7 The man a us straitly of our state, 7592+7592
 43:27 he a them of their welfare, and said, 7592
 44:19 My lord a his servants, saying, Have ye a 7592
Ex 18: 7 they a each other of their welfare, 7592
Jos 9:14 a not counsel at the mouth of the Lord. 7592
 19:50 Lord they gave him the city which he **a**, 7592
Jdg 1: 1 that the children of Israel a the Lord, 7592
 5:25 He a water, and she gave him milk; 1245
 6:29 when they inquired and **a**, they said, 1245
 13: 6 I a him not whence he was, neither told 7592
 20:18 of God, and a counsel of God, and said, 7592
 20:23 and a counsel of the Lord, saying, 7592
1Sa 1:17 thee thy petition that thou hast **a** of him. 7592
 1:20 saying, Because I have a him of 7592
 1:27 given me my petition which I a of him: 7592
 8:10 unto the people that a of him a king. 7592
 14:37 Saul a counsel of God, Shall I go down 7592
 19:22 he a and said, Where are Samuel 7592
 20: 6 David earnestly a leave of me that 7592+7592
 20:28 David earnestly a leave of me 7592+7592
1Ki 3:10 the Lord, that Solomon had a this thing. 7592
 3:11 Because thou hast a this thing, and hast 7592
 3:11 and hast not a for thyself long life; 7592
 3:11 neither hast a riches for thyself, nor hast 7592
 3:11 nor hast a the life of thine enemies; 7592
 3:11 hast a for thyself understanding to discern 7592
 3:13 given thee that which thou hast not a, 7592
 10:13 whatsoever she a, besides that which 7592
2Ki 2:10 he said, Thou hast a a hard thing: 7592
 8: 6 the king a the woman, she told him. 7592
2Ch 1:11 thou hast not a riches, wealth, or honour, 7592
 1:11 thine enemies, neither yet hast a long life; 7592
 1:11 hast a wisdom and knowledge for thyself, 7592
 9:12 whatsoever she a, besides that which she 7592
Ezr 5: 9 a we those elders, and said unto them 7593
 5:10 We a their names also, to certify thee, 7593
Ne 1: 2 a them concerning the Jews that had 7592
Job 21:29 Have ye not a them that go by the way? 7592
Ps 21: 4 He a life of thee, and thou gavest it him, 7592
 105:40 The people a, and he brought quails, 7592
Isa 30: 2 a into Egypt, and have not a at my mouth; 7592
 41:28 that, when I a of them, could answer a 7592
 65: 1 I am sought of them that a not for me: 7592
Jer 36:17 they a Baruch, saying, Tell us now, 7592
 37:17 and the king a him secretly in his house, 7592
 38:27 all the princes unto Jeremiah, and a him: 7592

Da	2:10 *that* **a** such things at any magician, or	7593
	7:16 stood *by*, and **a** him the truth of all this.	1156
Mt	12:10 And they **a** him, saying, Is it lawful to heal	1905
	16:13 he **a** his disciples, saying, Whom do men	2065
	17:10 And his disciples **a** him, saying, Why	1905
	22:23 that there is no resurrection, and **a** him,	1905
	22:35 **a** *him a question*, tempting him,	1905
	22:41 were gathered together, Jesus **a** them,	1905
	27:11 and the governor **a** him, saying, Art thou	1905
Mk	4:10 that were about him when they **a** him	2065
	5: 9 And he **a** him, What *is* thy name? And he	1905
	6:25 and **a**, saying, I will that thou give me by	154
	7: 5 Then the Pharisees and scribes **a** him,	1905
	7:17 his disciples **a** him concerning the parable.	1905
	8: 5 he **a** them, How many loaves have ye?	1905
	8:23 upon him, he **a** him if he saw ought.	1905
	8:27 and by the way he **a** his disciples,	1905
	9:11 And they **a** him, saying, Why say	1905
	9:16 And he **a** the scribes, What question ye	1905
	9:21 And he **a** his father, How long is it ago	1905
	9:28 his disciples **a** him privately, Why could	1905
	9:33 and being in the house he **a** them,	1905
	10: 2 The Pharisees came to *him*, and **a** him,	1905
	10:10 And in the house his disciples **a** him again	1905
	10:17 kneeled to him, and **a** him, Good Master,	1905
	12:18 is no resurrection; and they **a** him, saying,	1905
	12:28 **a** him, Which is the first commandment	1905
	13: 3 and John and Andrew **a** him privately,	1905
	14:60 and **a** Jesus, saying, Answerest thou	1905
	14:61 Again the high priest **a** him, and said unto	1905
	15: 2 And Pilate **a** him, Art thou the King of	1905
	15: 4 And Pilate **a** him again, saying,	1905
	15:44 he **a** him whether he had been any while	1905
Lk	1:63 And he **a** for a writing table, and wrote,	154
	3:10 And the people **a** him, saying, What shall	1905
	8: 9 And his disciples **a** him, saying,	1905
	8:30 And Jesus **a** him, saying, What is thy	1905
	9:18 and he **a** them, saying, Whom say	1905
	15:26 servants, and **a** what these *things* meant.	4441
	18:18 And a certain ruler **a** him, saying,	1905
	18:36 the multitude pass by, he **a** what it meant.	4441
	18:40 and when he was come near, he **a** him,	1905
	20:21 And they **a** him, saying, Master, we know	1905
	20:27 there is any resurrection; and they **a** him,	1905
	21: 7 And they **a** him, saying, Master,	1905
	22:64 a him, saying, Prophesy, who is it that	1905
	23: 3 Pilate **a** him, saying, Art thou the King	1905
	23: 6 he **a** whether the man were a Galilean.	1905
Jn	1:21 And they **a** him, What then? Art thou	2065
	1:25 And they **a** him, and said unto him,	2065
	4:10 thou wouldest have **a** of him, and he	154
	5:12 Then they **a** him, What man is that which	2065
	9: 2 And his disciples **a** him, saying, Master,	2065
	9:15 again the Pharisees also **a** him how he	2065
	9:19 And they **a** them, saying, Is this your son,	2065
	16:24 Hitherto have ye **a** nothing in my name:	154
	18: 7 Then **a** he them again, Whom seek ye?	1905
	18:19 high priest then **a** Jesus of his disciples,	2065
Ac	1: 6 together, they **a** of him, saying, Lord,	1905
	3: about to go into the temple, **a** an alms.	2065
	4: 7 they **a**, By what power, or by what name,	4441
	5:27 the council: and the high priest **a** them,	1905
	10:18 And called, and **a** whether Simon,	4441
	23:19 **a** *him*, What is that thou hast to tell me?	4441
	23:34 *the letter*, he **a** of what province he was:	1905
	25:20 I **a** *him* whether he would go to Jerusalem,	3004
Ro	10:20 manifest unto them that **a** not *after* me.	1905

ASKELON (3) [ASHKELON]

Jdg	1:18 **A** with the coast thereof, and Ekron with	831
1Sa	6:17 for Gaza one, for **A** one, for Gath one,	831
2Sa	1:20 in Gath, publish *it* not in the streets of **A**;	831

ASKEST (3) [ASK]

Jdg	13:18 Why **a** thou thus after my name, seeing it	7592
Jn	4: 9 *is it that* thou, being a Jew, **a** drink of me,	154
	18:21 Why **a** thou me? ask them which heard	1905

ASKETH (11) [ASK]

Ge	32:17 and **a** thee, saying, Whose *art* thou?	7592
Ex	13:14 it shall be when thy son **a** thee in time to	7592
Dt	6:20 *And* when thy son **a** thee in time to come,	7592
Mic	7: 3 the prince **a**, and the judge *asketh* for a	7592
	7: 3 asketh, and the judge **a** for a reward;	NIH
Mt	5:42 Give to him that **a** thee, and from him that	154
	7: 8 For every one that **a** receiveth; and he that	154
Lk	6:30 Give to every man that **a** of thee; and	154
	11:10 For every one that **a** receiveth; and he that	154
Jn	16: 5 none of you **a** me, Whither goest thou?	2065
1Pe	3:15 **a** you a reason of the hope that is in you	154

ASKING (7) [ASK]

1Sa	12:17 in the sight of the LORD, in **a** you a king.	7592
1Ch	10:13 for a *counsel* of *one that had* a familiar	7592
Ps	78:18 they tempted God in their heart by **a** meat	7592
Lk	2:46 both hearing them, and **a** them *questions*.	1905
Jn	8: 7 So when they continued **a** him, he lift up	2065
1Co	10:25 eat, **a** no *question* for conscience sake:	350
	10:27 eat, **a** no **question** for conscience sake.	350

ASLEEP (16) [SLEEP]

Jdg	4:21 for he was **fast a** and weary. So he died.	7290
1Sa	26:12 for they *were* all **a**; because a deep sleep	3463
SS	7: 9 the lips of *those that are* **a** to speak.	3463
Jnh	1: 5 of the ship; and he lay, and was **fast a**.	7290

Mt	8:24 covered with the waves: but he was **a**.	2518
	26:40 and findeth them **a**, and saith unto Peter,	2518
	26:43 And he came and found them **a** again:	2518
Mk	4:38 the hinder part of the ship, **a** on a pillow:	2518
	14:40 when he returned, he found them **a** again,	2518
Lk	8:23 But as they sailed he **fell a**: and there	879
Ac	7:60 And when he had said this, he **fell a**.	2837
1Co	15: 6 unto this present, but some are **fallen a**.	2837
	15:18 they also which are **fallen a** in Christ	2837
1Th	4:13 brethren, concerning them which are **a**.	2837
	4:15 Lord shall not prevent them which are **a**.	2837
2Pe	3: 4 for since the fathers **fell a**, all *things*	2837

ASNAH (1)

Ezr	2:50 children of **A**, the children of Mehunim,	619

ASNAPPAR (1)

Ezr	4:10 whom the great and noble **A** brought over,	620

ASP (1) [ASPS]

Isa	11: 8 child shall play on the hole of the **a**,	6620

ASPATHA (1)

Est	9: 7 And Parshandatha, and Dalphon, and **A**,	630

ASPS (4) [ASP]

Dt	32:33 of dragons, and the cruel venom of **a**.	6620
Job	20:14 is turned, *it is* the gall of **a** within him.	6620
	20:16 He shall suck the poison of **a**: the viper's	6620
Ro	3:13 the poison of **a** *is* under their lips:	785

ASRIEL (2) [ASRIELITES]

Nu	26:31 *of* **A**, the family of the Asrielites:	844
Jos	17: 2 for the children of **A**, and for the children	844

ASRIELITES (1) [ASRIEL]

Nu	26:31 *of* Asriel, the family of the **A**:	845

ASS (86) [ASS'S, ASSES]

Ge	22: 3 saddled his **a**, and took two of his young	2543
	22: 5 young men, Abide you here with the **a**;	2543
	42:27 his sack to give his **a** provender in the inn,	2543
	44:13 laded every man his **a**, and returned to	2543
	49:14 Issachar *is* a strong **a** couching down	2543
Ex	4:20 set them upon an **a**, and he returned to	2543
	13:13 every firstling of an **a** thou shalt redeem	2543
	20:17 nor his maidservant, nor his ox, nor his **a**,	2543
	21:33 cover it, and an ox or an **a** fall therein;	2543
	22: 4 alive, whether it be ox, or **a**, or sheep;	2543
	22: 9 for **a**, for sheep, for raiment, *or* for any	2543
	22:10 If a man deliver unto his neighbour an **a**,	2543
	23: 4 thine enemy's ox or his **a** going astray,	2543
	23: 5 If thou see the **a** of him that hateth thee	2543
	23:12 that thine ox and thine **a** may rest,	2543
	34:20 the firstling of an **a** thou shalt redeem	2543
Nu	16:15 I have not taken one **a** from them,	2543
	22:21 saddled his **a**, and went with the princes	860
	22:22 Now he was riding upon his **a**, and his two	860
	22:23 the **a** saw the angel of the LORD standing	860
	22:23 the **a** turned aside out of the way,	860
	22:23 Balaam smote the **a**, to turn her *into* the	860
	22:25 when the **a** saw the angel of the LORD,	860
	22:27 when the **a** saw the angel of the LORD,	860
	22:27 kindled, and he smote the **a** with a staff.	860
	22:28 And the LORD opened the mouth of the **a**,	860
	22:29 Balaam said unto the **a**, Because thou hast	860
	22:30 the **a** said unto Balaam, *Am* not I thine ass,	860
	22:30 the ass said unto Balaam, *Am* not I thine **a**,	860
	22:32 Wherefore hast thou smitten thine **a** these	860
	22:33 the **a** saw me, and turned from me these	860
Dt	5:14 maidservant, nor thine ox, nor thine **a**,	2543
	5:21 or his **a**, or any *thing* that *is* thy	2543
	22: 3 In like manner shalt thou do with his **a**;	2543
	22: 4 shalt not see thy brother's **a** or his ox	2543
	22:10 not plow with an ox and an **a** together.	2543
	28:31 thine **a** *shall be* violently taken away from	2543
Jos	6:21 and old, and ox, and sheep, and **a**,	2543
	15:18 she lighted off *her* **a**; and Caleb said unto	2543
Jdg	1:14 she lighted from off *her* **a**; and Caleb said	2543
	6: 4 for Israel, neither sheep, nor ox, nor **a**.	2543
	10: 4 had thirty sons that rode on thirty **a colts**,	5895
	12:14 that rode on threescore and ten **a colts**,	5895
	15:15 he found a new jawbone of an **a**,	2543
	15:16 Samson said, With the jawbone of an **a**,	2543
	15:16 the jaw of an **a** have I slain a thousand	2543
	19:28 the man took her *up* upon an **a**,	2543
1Sa	12: 3 or whose **a** have I taken? or whom have	2543
	15: 3 and suckling, ox and sheep, camel and **a**.	2543
	16:20 Jesse took an *laden* with bread,	2543
	25:20 it was *so*, *as* she rode on the **a**, that she	2543
	25:23 lighted off the **a**, and fell before David on	2543
	25:42 and rose, and rode upon an **a**,	2543
2Sa	17:23 he saddled *his* **a**, and arose, and gat him	2543
	19:26 for thy servant said, I will saddle me an **a**,	2543
1Ki	2:40 saddled his **a**, and went to Gath to Achish	2543
	13:13 and said unto his sons, Saddle me the **a**.	2543
	13:13 So they saddled him the **a**: and he rode	2543
	13:23 had drunk, that he saddled for him the **a**,	2543
	13:24 was cast in the way, and the **a** stood by it,	2543
	13:27 spake to his sons, saying, Saddle me the **a**.	2543
	13:28 the **a** and the lion standing by the carcase:	2543
	13:28 had not eaten the carcase, nor torn the **a**.	2543
	13:29 laid it upon the **a**, and brought it back:	2543
2Ki	4:24 she saddled an **a**, and said to her servant,	860
Job	6: 5 Doth the **wild a** bray when he hath grass?	6501
	24: 3 They drive away the **a** of the fatherless,	2543

Job	39: 5 Who hath sent out the **wild a** free? or	6501
	39: 5 who hath loosed the bands of the **wild a**?	6171
Pr	26: 3 a bridle for the **a**, and a rod for the fools'	2543
Isa	1: 3 his owner, and the **a** his master's crib:	2543
	32:20 forth *thither* the feet of the ox and the **a**.	2543
Jer	2:24 a **wild a** used to the wilderness,	6501
	22:19 He shall be buried *with* the burial of an **a**,	2543
Hos	8: 9 up *to* Assyria, a **wild a** alone by himself:	6501
Zec	9: 9 riding upon an **a**, and upon a colt the foal	2543
	9: 9 an ass, and upon a colt the foal of an **a**.	860
	14:15 of the **a**, and of all the beasts that shall be	2543
Mt	21: 2 and straightway ye shall find an **a** tied,	3688
	21: 5 and sitting upon an **a**, and a colt the foal	3688
	21: 5 upon an ass, and a colt the foal of an **a**.	5268
Lk	13:15 sabbath loose his ox or *his* **a** from the stall,	3688
	14: 5 Which of you shall have an **a** or an ox	3688
Jn	12:14 And Jesus, when he had found a **young a**,	3678
2Pe	2:16 the dumb **a** speaking with man's voice	5268

ASS'S (4) [ASS]

Ge	49:11 vine, and his **a** colt unto the choice vine;	860
2Ki	6:25 until an **a** head was *sold* for fourscore	2543
Job	11:12 though man be born *like* a **wild a** colt.	6501
Jn	12:15 thy King cometh, sitting on an **a** colt.	3688

ASSAULT (2) [ASSAULTED]

Est	8:11 people and province that would **a** them,	6696
Ac	14: 5 And when there was an **a** made both of	3730

ASSAULTED (1) [ASSAULT]

Ac	17: 5 and a the house of Jason, and sought to	2186

ASSAY (1) [ASSAYED, ASSAYING]

Job	4: 2 *If we* **a** to commune with thee, wilt thou	5254

ASSAYED (4) [ASSAY]

Dt	4:34 hath God **a** to go *and* take him a nation	5254
1Sa	17:39 sword upon his armour, and he **a** to go;	2974
Ac	9:26 he **a** to join himself to the disciples:	3987
	16: 7 come to Mysia, they **a** to go into Bithynia:	3985

ASSAYING (1) [ASSAY]

Heb	11:29 the Egyptians **a** to do were drowned.	3984

ASSEMBLE (20) [ASSEMBLED, ASSEMBLIES, ASSEMBLING, ASSEMBLY]

Nu	10: 3 all the assembly shall **a** themselves to thee	3259
2Sa	20: 4 **A** me the men of Judah *within* three days,	2199
	20: 5 So Amasa went to **a** *the men of* Judah:	2199
Isa	11:12 shall **a** the outcasts of Israel,	622
	45:20 **A** yourselves and come; draw near	6908
	48:14 All ye, **a** yourselves, and hear;	6908
Jer	4: 5 **A** yourselves, and let us go into the	622
	8:14 **a** yourselves, and let us enter into	622
	12: 9 come ye, **a** all the beasts of the field,	622
	21: 4 I will **a** them into the midst of this city.	622
Eze	11:17 **a** you out of the countries where ye have	622
	39:17 of the field, **A** yourselves, and come;	6908
Da	11:10 and shall **a** a multitude of great forces:	622
Hos	7:14 they **a** themselves for corn and wine,	1481
Joel	2:16 **a** the elders, gather the children,	6908
	3:11 **A** yourselves, and come, all ye heathen,	5789
Am	3: 9 **A** yourselves upon the mountains of	622
Mic	2:12 I will **surely a**, O Jacob, all of thee;	622+622
	4: 6 will I **a** her that halteth, and I will gather	622
Zep	3: 8 that I may **a** the kingdoms, to pour upon	6908

ASSEMBLED (37) [ASSEMBLE]

Ex	38: 8 which **a** *at* the door of the tabernacle of	6633
Nu	1:18 they **a** the congregation **together** on	6950
Jos	18: 1 the children of Israel **a together** at Shiloh,	6950
Jdg	10:17 children of Israel **a** themselves **together**,	622
1Sa	2:22 how they lay with the women that **a** *at*	6633
	14:20 all the people that *were* with him **a**	2199
1Ki	8: 1 Solomon **a** the elders of Israel, and all	6950
	8: 2 the men of Israel **a** themselves unto king	6950
	8: 5 of Israel, that were **a** unto him,	3259
	12:21 he **a** all the house of Judah, with the tribe	6950
1Ch	15: 4 David **a** the children of Aaron, and	622
	1 David **a** all the princes of Israel,	6950
2Ch	5: 2 Solomon **a** the elders of Israel, and all	6950
	5: 3 Wherefore all the men of Israel **a**	6950
	5: 6 all the congregation of Israel that were **a**	3259
	20:26 on the fourth day they **a** themselves in	6950
	30:13 there **a** *at* Jerusalem much people to keep	622
Ezr	9: 4 were **a** unto me every one that trembled	622
	10: 1 there **a** unto him out of Israel a very great	6908
Ne	9: 1 the children of Israel were **a** with fasting,	622
Est	9:18 the Jews that *were* at Shushan **a together**	6950
Ps	48: 4 For lo, the kings were **a**, they passed by	3259
Isa	43: 9 gathered together, and let the people be **a**:	622
Jer	5: 7 **a** themselves **by troops** *in* the harlots'	1413
Eze	38: 7 all thy company that are **a** unto thee,	6950
Da	6: 6 princes **a** *together* to the king,	7284
	6:11 these men **a**, and found Daniel praying	7284
	6:15 these men **a** unto the king, and said unto	7284
Mt	26: 3 Then **a together** the chief priests,	4863
	26:57 where the scribes and the elders were **a**.	4863
	28:12 And when they were **a** with the elders,	4863
Mk	14:53 with him were **a** all the chief priests	4905
Jn	20:19 the disciples were **a** for fear of the Jews,	4863
Ac	1: 4 And, being **a together with** them,	4871
	4:31 shaken where they were **a together**;	4863
	11:26 that a whole year they **a** themselves with	4863
	15:25 good unto us, being **a** with one accord,	1096

ASSEMBLIES (6) [ASSEMBLE]

Ps	86:14 the **a** of violent *men* have sought after my	5712
Ecc	12:11 and as nails fastened *by* the masters of **a,**	627
Isa	1:13 new moons and sabbaths, the calling of **a,**	4744
	4: 5 upon her **a,** a cloud and smoke by day,	4744
Eze	44:24 my laws and my statutes in all mine **a;**	4150
Am	5:21 and I will not smell in your **solemn a.**	6116

ASSEMBLING (2) [ASSEMBLE]

Ex	38: 8 of the looking-glasses of *the women* **a,**	6633
Heb	10:25 Not forsaking the **a** of ourselves **together,**	*1997*

ASSEMBLY (49) [ASSEMBLE]

Ge	49: 6 unto their **a,** mine honour, be not thou	6951
Ex	12: 6 the whole **a** of the congregation of Israel	6951
	16: 3 to kill this whole **a** with hunger.	6951
Lev	4:13 the thing be hid from the eyes of the **a,**	6951
	8: 4 the **a** was gathered together unto the door	5712
	23:36 it *is* a **solemn a**; *and* ye shall do no servile	6116
Nu	8: 9 thou shalt gather the whole **a** of	5712
	10: 2 mayest use them for the calling of the **a,**	5712
	10: 3 all the **a** shall assemble themselves to thee	5712
	14: 5 Aaron fell on their faces before all the **a** of	6951
	16: 2 two hundred and fifty princes of the **a,**	5712
	20: 6 Aaron went from the presence of the **a**	6951
	20: 8 gather thou the **a** together, thou,	5712
	29:35 the eighth day ye shall have a **solemn a;**	6116
Dt	5:22 **a** in the mount out of the midst of the fire,	6951
	9:10 of the midst of the fire in the day of the **a,**	6951
	10: 4 of the midst of the fire in the day of the **a:**	6951
	16: 8 the seventh day *shall be* a **solemn a** to	6116
	18:16 thy God in Horeb in the day of the **a,**	6951
Jdg	20: 2 themselves in the **a** of the people	6951
	21: 8 to the camp from Jabesh-gilead to the **a.**	6951
1Sa	17:47 all this **a** shall know that the Lᴏʀᴅ saveth	6951
2Ki	10:20 Jehu said, Proclaim a **solemn a** for Baal.	6116
2Ch	7: 9 in the eighth day they made a **solemn a:**	6116
	30:23 the whole counsel to keep other	6951
Ne	5: 7 And I set a great **a** against them.	6952
	8:18 on the eighth day *was* a **solemn a,**	6116
Ps	22:16 the **a** of the wicked have inclosed me:	5712
	89: 7 God *is* greatly to be feared in the **a** of	5475
	107:32 and praise him in the **a** of the elders.	4186
	111: 1 in the **a** of the upright, and *in*	5475
Pr	5:14 in the midst of the congregation and **a.**	5712
Jer	6:11 and upon the **a** of young men together:	5475
	9: 2 all adulterers, an **a** of treacherous *men.*	6116
	15:17 I sat not in the **a** of the mockers,	5475
	26:17 spake to all the **a** of the people, saying,	6951
	50: 9 cause to come up against Babylon an **a** of	6951
La	1:15 he hath called an **a** against me to crush	4150
	2: 6 he hath destroyed his **places of** the **a:**	4150
Eze	13: 9 they shall not be in the **a** of my people,	5475
	23:24 and wheels, and with an **a** of people,	6951
Joel	1:14 call a **solemn a,** gather the elders *and*	6116
	2:15 in Zion, sanctify a fast, call a **solemn a:**	6116
Zep	3:18 *them that are* sorrowful for the **solemn a,**	4150
Ac	19:32 for the **a** was confused; and the more part	*1577*
	19:39 it shall be determined in a lawful **a.**	*1577*
	19:41 he had thus spoken, he dismissed the **a.**	*1577*
Heb	12:23 To the **general a,** and church of	*3831*
Jas	2: 2 For if there come unto your **a** a man with	*4864*

ASSENT (1) [ASSENTED]

2Ch	18:12 *declare* good to the king **with** one **a;**	6310

ASSENTED (1) [ASSENT]

Ac	24: 9 And the Jews also **a,** saying that these	*4934*

ASSES (64) [ASS]

Ge	12:16 **he a,** and menservants, and maidservants,	2543
	12:16 and maidservants, and **she a,** and camels.	860
	24:35 and maidservants, and camels, and **a.**	2543
	30:43 and menservants, and camels, and **a.**	2543
	32: 5 **a,** flocks, and menservants,	2543
	32:15 ten bulls, twenty **she a,** and ten foals.	860
	34:28 their **a,** and that which *was* in the city,	2543
	36:24 as he fed the **a** of Zibeon his father.	2543
	42:26 they laded their **a** with the corn,	2543
	43:18 and take us for bondmen, and our **a.**	2543
	43:24 their feet; and he gave their **a** provender.	2543
	44: 3 the men were sent away, they and their **a.**	2543
	45:23 ten **a** laden with the good things of Egypt,	2543
	45:23 and ten **she a** laden with corn and bread	860
	47:17 for the cattle of the herds, and for the **a:**	2543
Ex	9: 3 upon the horses, upon the **a,** upon	2543
Nu	31:28 the beeves, and of the **a,** and of the sheep:	2543
	31:30 of the beeves, of the **a,** and of the flocks,	2543
	31:34 And threescore and one thousand **a,**	2543
	31:39 the **a** *were* thirty thousand	2543
	31:45 And thirty thousand **a** and five hundred,	2543
Jos	7:24 his **a,** and his sheep, and his tent, and all	2543
	9: 4 took old sacks upon their **a,**	2543
Jdg	5:10 Speak, ye that ride on white **a,** ye that sit	860
	19: 3 his servant with him, and a couple of **a:**	2543
	19:10 *there were* with him two **a** saddled,	2543
	19:19 is both straw and provender for our **a;**	2543
	19:21 house, and gave provender unto the **a:**	2543
1Sa	8:16 and your **a,** and put *them* to his work.	2543
	9: 3 the **a** of Kish Saul's father were lost.	860
	9: 3 with thee, and arise, go seek the **a.**	860
	9: 5 lest my father lose *caring* for the **a,**	860
	9:20 for thine **a** that were lost three days ago,	860
	10: 2 The **a** which thou wentest to seek are	860
	10: 2 lo, thy father hath left the care of the **a,**	860

1Sa	10:14 said, To seek the **a:** and when we saw that	860
	10:16 He told us plainly that the **a** were found.	860
	22:19 sucklings, and oxen, and **a,** and sheep,	2543
	25:18 cakes *of figs,* and laid *them* on **a.**	2543
	27: 9 the **a,** and the camels, and the apparel,	2543
2Sa	16: 1 with a couple of **a** saddled, and upon	2543
	16: 2 The **a** *be* for the king's household to ride	2543
2Ki	4:22 one of the young men, and one of the **a,**	860
	7: 7 their tents, and their horses, and their **a,**	2543
	7:10 and **a** tied, and the tents as they *were.*	2543
1Ch	5:21 of **a** two thousand, and *of* men an	2543
	12:40 brought bread on **a,** and on camels,	2543
	27:30 over the **a** *was* Jehdeiah the Meronothite:	860
2Ch	28:15 carried all the feeble of them upon **a,**	2543
Ezr	2:67 their **a,** six thousand seven hundred	2543
Ne	7:69 six thousand seven hundred and twenty **a.**	2543
	13:15 and bringing in sheaves, and lading **a;**	2543
Job	1: 3 five hundred **she a,** and a very great	860
	1:14 and the **a** feeding beside them:	860
	24: 5 Behold, *as* **wild a** in the desert, go they	6501
	42:12 yoke of oxen, and a thousand **she a.**	860
Ps	104:11 the field: the **wild a** quench their thirst.	6501
Isa	21: 7 a chariot of **a,** *and* a chariot of camels;	2543
	30: 6 riches upon the shoulders of **young a,**	5895
	30:24 the **young a** that ear the ground shall eat	5895
	32:14 a joy of **wild a,** a pasture of flocks;	6501
Jer	14: 6 the **wild a** did stand in the high places,	6501
Eze	23:20 whose flesh *is as* the flesh of **a,**	2543
Da	5:21 and his dwelling *was* with the **wild a:**	6167

ASSHUR (8) [ASSHURIM]

Ge	10:11 Out of that land went forth **A,**	804
	10:22 and **A,** and Arphaxad, and Lud, and Aram.	804
Nu	24:22 until **A** shall carry thee away captive.	804
	24:24 and shall afflict **A,** and shall afflict Eber,	804
1Ch	1:17 **A,** and Arphaxad, and Lud, and Aram,	804
Eze	27:23 **A,** *and* Chilmad, *were* thy merchants.	804
	32:22 **A** *is* there and all her company: his graves	804
Hos	14: 3 **A** shall not save us: we will not ride upon	804

ASSHURIM (1) [ASSHUR]

Ge	25: 3 the sons of Dedan were **A,** and Letushim,	805

ASSHURITES See ASSHURIM

ASSIGNED (3)

Ge	47:22 for the priests had a portion **a** them of	3807.1
Jos	20: 8 they **a** Bezer in the wilderness upon	5414
2Sa	11:16 that he **a** Uriah unto a place where he	5414

ASSIR (5)

Ex	6:24 of Korah; **A,** and Elkanah, and Abiasaph;	617
1Ch	3:17 the sons of Jeconiah; **A,** Salathiel his son,	617
	6:22 his son, Korah his son, **A** his son,	617
	6:23 son, and Ebiasaph his son, and **A** his son,	617
	6:37 The son of Tahath, the son of **A,** the son of	617

ASSIST (1)

Ro	16: 2 *that* ye **a** her in whatsoever business she	*3936*

ASSOCIATE (1)

Isa	8: 9 **A** yourselves, O ye people, and ye shall be	7489

ASSOS (2)

Ac	20:13 we went before to ship, and sailed unto **A,**	*789*
	20:14 when he met with us at **A,** we took him	*789*

ASSUR (2)

Ezr	4: 2 since the days of Esar-haddon king of **A,**	804
Ps	83: 8 **A** also is joined with them: they have	804

ASSURANCE (7) [ASSURE]

Dt	28:66 night, and shalt have none **a** of thy life:	539
Isa	32:17 of righteousness quietness and **a** for ever.	983
Ac	17:31 *whereof* he hath given **a** unto all *men,* in	*4102*
Col	2: 2 unto all riches of the **full a** of	*4136*
1Th	1: 5 and in the Holy Ghost, and in much **a;**	*4136*
Heb	6:11 to the **full a** of hope unto the end:	*4136*
	10:22 draw near with a true heart in **full a**	*4136*

ASSURE (1) [ASSURANCE, ASSURED, ASSUREDLY]

1Jn	3:19 truth, and shall **a** our hearts before him.	*3982*

ASSURED (3) [ASSURE]

Lev	27:19 estimation unto it, and it shall be **a** to him.	6965
Jer	14:13 but I will give you **a** peace in this place.	571
2Ti	3:14 thou hast learned and hast been **a** of,	*4104*

ASSUREDLY (9) [ASSURE]

1Sa	28: 1 said unto David, **Know** thou **a,**	3045+3045
1Ki	1:13 **A** Solomon thy son shall reign after me,	3588
	1:17 **A** Solomon thy son shall reign after	3588
	1:30 **A** Solomon thy son shall reign after me,	3588
Jer	32:41 I will plant them in this land **a** with	571+871.1
	38:17 thou wilt **a go forth** unto the king	3318+3318
	49:12 drink of the cup have **a drunken;**	8354+8354
Ac	2:36 let all the house of Israel know **a,**	*806*
	16:10 a **gathering** that the Lord had called us	*4822*

ASSWAGE (1) [ASSWAGED]

Job	16: 5 the moving of my lips should **a** *your grief.*	2820

ASSWAGED (2) [ASSWAGE]

Ge	8: 1 to pass over the earth, and the waters **a;**	7918
Job	16: 6 Though I speak, my grief is not **a:**	2820

ASSYRIA (118) [ASSYRIAN, ASSYRIANS]

Ge	2:14 that *is it* which goeth toward the east of **A.**	804
	25:18 *is* before Egypt, as thou goest towards **A:**	804
2Ki	15:19 Pul the king of **A** came against the land:	804
	15:20 shekels *of* silver, to give to the king of **A.**	804
	15:20 of the king of **A** turned back, and stayed not	804
	15:29 of Israel came Tiglath-pileser king of **A,**	804
	15:29 of Naphtali, and carried them captive to **A.**	804
	16: 7 messengers to Tiglath-pileser king of **A,**	804
	16: 8 and sent it *for* a present to the king of **A.**	804
	16: 9 the king of **A** hearkened unto him: for	804
	16: 9 the king of **A** went up against Damascus,	804
	16:10 to meet Tiglath-pileser king of **A,**	804
	16:18 the house of the Lᴏʀᴅ for the king of **A.**	804
	17: 3 him came up Shalmaneser king of **A;**	804
	17: 4 the king of **A** found conspiracy in Hoshea:	804
	17: 4 brought no present to the king of **A,** as *he*	804
	17: 4 therefore the king of **A** shut him up,	804
	17: 5 the king of **A** came up throughout all	804
	17: 6 the king of **A** took Samaria,	804
	17: 6 Israel away into **A,** and placed them	804
	17:23 out of their own land to **A** unto this day.	804
	17:24 the king of **A** brought *men* from Babylon,	804
	17:26 Wherefore they spake to the king of **A,**	804
	17:27 the king of **A** commanded, saying,	804
	18: 7 he rebelled against the king of **A,**	804
	18: 9 Shalmaneser king of **A** came up against	804
	18:11 the king of **A** did carry away Israel unto	804
	18:11 of Assyria did carry away Israel unto **A,**	804
	18:13 came up against all the fenced cities of	804
	18:14 king of Judah sent to the king of **A**	804
	18:14 king of **A** appointed unto Hezekiah king	804
	18:16 had overlaid, and gave it to the king of **A.**	804
	18:17 the king of **A** sent Tartan and Rabsaris	804
	18:19 Thus saith the great king, the king of **A,**	804
	18:23 give pledges to my lord the king of **A,**	804
	18:28 the word of the great king, the king of **A:**	804
	18:30 delivered into the hand of the king of **A.**	804
	18:31 for thus saith the king of **A,** Make *an*	804
	18:33 his land out of the hand of the king of **A?**	804
	19: 4 whom the king of **A** his master hath sent	804
	19: 6 *with* which the servants of the king of **A**	804
	19: 8 found the king of **A** warring against Libnah:	804
	19:10 be delivered into the hand of the king of **A.**	804
	19:11 thou hast heard what the kings of **A** have	804
	19:17 the kings of **A** have destroyed the nations	804
	19:20 against Sennacherib king of **A** I have heard.	804
	19:32 saith the Lᴏʀᴅ concerning the king of **A,**	804
	19:36 So Sennacherib king of **A** departed,	804
	20: 6 this city out of the hand of the king of **A;**	804
	23:29 against the king of **A** to the river Euphrates:	804
1Ch	5: 6 whom Tilgath-pilneser king of **A** carried	804
	5:26 Israel stirred up the spirit of Pul king of **A,**	804
	5:26 the spirit of Tilgath-pilneser king of **A,**	804
2Ch	28:16 Ahaz send unto the kings of **A** to help him.	804
	28:20 Tilgath-pilneser king of **A** came unto him,	804
	28:21 the princes, and gave *it* unto the king of **A:**	804
	30: 6 escaped out of the hand of the kings of **A.**	804
	32: 1 *thereof,* Sennacherib king of **A** came,	804
	32: 4 Why should the kings of **A** come,	804
	32: 7 not afraid nor dismayed for the king of **A,**	804
	32: 9 After this did Sennacherib king of **A** send	804
	32:10 Thus saith Sennacherib king of **A,**	804
	32:11 deliver us out of the hand of the king of **A?**	804
	32:21 and captains in the camp of the king of **A.**	804
	32:22 the hand of Sennacherib the king of **A,**	804
	33:11 the captains of the host of the king of **A,**	804
Ezr	6:22 turned the heart of the king of **A** unto them	804
Ne	9:32 since the time of the kings of **A** unto this	804
Isa	7:17 departed from Judah; *even* the king of **A.**	804
	7:18 and for the bee that *is* in the land of **A.**	804
	7:20 by the king of **A,** the head, and the hair of	804
	8: 4 shall be taken away before the king of **A.**	804
	8: 7 *even* the king of **A,** and all his glory:	804
	10:12 the fruit of the stout heart of the king of **A,**	804
	11:11 which shall be left from **A,** and from Egypt,	804
	11:16 of his people, which shall be left from **A;**	804
	19:23 shall there be a highway out of Egypt to **A,**	804
	19:23 the Egyptian into **A,** and the Egyptians shall	804
	19:24 Israel be the third with Egypt and with **A,**	804
	19:25 **A** the work of my hands, and Israel mine	804
	20: 1 (when Sargon the king of **A** sent him,)	804
	20: 4 So shall the king of **A** lead away	804
	20: 6 for help to be delivered from the king of **A:**	804
	27:13 were ready to perish in the land of **A,**	804
	36: 1 Sennacherib king of **A** came up against	804
	36: 2 the king of **A** sent Rabshakeh from Lachish	804
	36: 4 Thus saith the great king, the king of **A,**	804
	36: 8 to my master the king of **A,** and I will give	804
	36:13 the words of the great king, the king of **A.**	804
	36:15 delivered into the hand of the king of **A.**	804
	36:16 for thus saith the king of **A,** Make *an*	804
	36:18 his land out of the hand of the king of **A?**	804
	37: 4 whom the king of **A** his master hath sent	804
	37: 6 *wherewith* the servants of the king of **A**	804
	37: 8 found the king of **A** warring against Libnah:	804
	37:10 not be given into the hand of the king of **A.**	804
	37:11 thou hast heard what the kings of **A** have	804
	37:18 the kings of **A** have laid waste all	804
	37:21 to me against Sennacherib king of **A:**	804
	37:33 saith the Lᴏʀᴅ concerning the king of **A,**	804
	37:37 So Sennacherib king of **A** departed,	804
	38: 6 this city out of the hand of the king of **A:**	804
Jer	2:18 or what hast thou to do in the way of **A,**	804

A

Jer	2:36 of Egypt, as thou wast ashamed of **A**.	804
	50:17 first the king of A hath devoured him;	804
	50:18 his land, as I have punished the king of A	804
Eze	23: 7 all them *that were* the chosen men of **A**,	804
Hos	7:11 they call to Egypt, they go to **A**.	804
	8: 9 For they are gone up to **A**, a wild ass alone	804
	9: 3 and they shall eat unclean *things* in **A**.	804
	10: 6 It shall be also carried unto **A** *for* a present	804
	11:11 Egypt, and as a dove out of the land of **A**:	804
Mic	5: 6 they shall waste the north, and destroy **A**;	804
	7:12 *also* he shall come even to thee from **A**,	804
Na	3:18 Thy shepherds slumber, O king of **A**:	804
Zep	2:13 his hand against the north, and destroy **A**;	804
Zec	10:10 land of Egypt, and gather them out of **A**;	804
	10:11 the pride of **A** shall be brought down,	804

ASSYRIAN (13) [ASSYRIA]

Isa	10: 5 **A**, the rod of mine anger, and the staff in	804
	10:24 dwellest in Zion, be not afraid of the **A**:	804
	14:25 That *I* will break the **A** in my land,	804
	19:23 the **A** shall come into Egypt,	804
	23:13 *till* the **A** founded it for them that dwell in	804
	30:31 of the LORD shall the **A** be beaten down,	804
	31: 8 shall the **A** fall with the sword, not of a	804
	52: 4 and the **A** oppressed them without cause.	804
Eze	31: 3 the **A** *was* a cedar in Lebanon with fair	804
Hos	5:13 went Ephraim to the **A**, and sent to king	804
	11: 5 shall be his king, because they refused	804
Mic	5: 5 when the **A** shall come into our land:	804
	5: 6 thus shall he deliver *us* from the **A**, when	804

ASSYRIANS (10) [ASSYRIA]

2Ki	19:35 smote in the camp of the **A** an hundred	804
Isa	19:23 and the Egyptians shall serve *with* the **A**.	804
	37:36 smote in the camp of the **A** an hundred	804
La	5: 6 and to the **A**, to be satisfied *with* bread.	804
Eze	16:28 played the whore also with the **A**,	804+1121
	23: 5 on her lovers, on the **A** her neighbours,	804
	23: 9 into the hand of the **A**, upon whom	804+1121
	23:12 doted upon the **A** *her* neighbours,	804+1121
	23:23 Shoa, and Koa, all the **A** with them:	804+1121
Hos	12: 1 and they do make a covenant with the **A**,	804

ASTAROTH (1)

Dt	1: 4 king of Bashan, which dwelt at **A** in Edrei:	6252

ASTONIED (10) [ASTONISHMENT]

Ezr	9: 3 head and of my beard, and sat down **a**.	8074
	9: 4 and I sat **a** until the evening sacrifice.	8074
Job	17: 8 Upright *men* shall be **a** at this,	8074
	18:20 They that come after *him* shall be **a** at his	8074
Isa	52:14 As many were **a** at thee; his visage *was* so	8074
Jer	14: 9 Why shouldest thou be as a man **a**, as a	1724
Eze	4:17 be **a** one with another, and consume	8074
Da	3:24 Nebuchadnezzar the king was **a**,	8429
	4:19 was **a** for one hour, and his thoughts	8075
	5: 9 *was* changed in him, and his lords *were* **a**.	7672

ASTONISHED (34) [ASTONISHMENT]

Lev	26:32 which dwell therein shall be **a** at it.	8074
1Ki	9: 8 every one that passeth by it shall be **a**,	8074
Job	21: 5 be **a**, and lay *your* hand upon *your* mouth.	8074
	26:11 of heaven tremble and are **a** at his reproof.	8539
Jer	2:12 Be **a**, O ye heavens, at this, and be	8074
	4: 9 priests shall be **a**, and the prophets shall	8074
	18:16 every one that passeth thereby shall be **a**,	8074
	19: 8 every one that passeth thereby shall be **a**,	8074
	49:17 every one that goeth by it shall be **a**,	8074
	50:13 one that goeth by Babylon shall be **a**,	8074
Eze	3:15 remained there **a** among them seven days.	8074
	26:16 at every moment, and be **a** at thee.	8074
	27:35 All the inhabitants of the isles shall be **a**	8074
	28:19 thee among the people shall be **a** at thee:	8074
Da	8:27 I was **a** at the vision, but none understood	8074
Mt	7:28 the people were **a** at his doctrine:	1605
	13:54 insomuch that they were **a**, and said,	1605
	22:33 heard *this*, they were **a** at his doctrine.	1605
Mk	1:22 And they were **a** at his doctrine: for he	1605
	5:42 they were **a** with a great astonishment.	1839
	6: 2 and many hearing *him* were **a**, saying,	1605
	7:37 And were beyond measure **a**, saying,	1605
	10:24 And the disciples were **a** at his words.	2284
	10:26 And they were **a** out of measure,	1605
	11:18 all the people was **a** at his doctrine.	1605
Lk	2:47 And all that heard him were **a** at his	1839
	4:32 And they were **a** at his doctrine: for his	1605
	5: 9 For he was **a**,	2285+4023
	8:56 And her parents were **a**: but he charged	1839
	24:22 women *also* of our company **made** us **a**,	1839
Ac	9: 6 And he trembling and **a** said, Lord,	2284
	10:45 of the circumcision which believed were **a**,	1839
	12:16 *the* door, and saw him, they were **a**.	1839
	13:12 being **a** at the doctrine of the Lord.	1605

ASTONISHMENT (21) [ASTONIED, ASTONISHED]

Dt	28:28 and blindness, and **a** of heart:	8541
	28:37 thou shalt become an **a**, a proverb, and a	8047
2Ch	7:21 be an **a** every one that passeth by it;	8074
	29: 8 to **a**, and to hissing, as ye see with your	8047
Ps	60: 3 thou hast made us to drink the wine of **a**.	8653
Jer	8:21 I am black; **a** hath taken hold on me.	8047
	25: 9 make them an **a**, and a hissing,	8047
	25:11 land shall be a desolation, *and* an **a**;	8047
	25:18 a desolation, an **a**, a hissing, and a curse;	8047
	29:18 and an **a**, and a hissing, and a reproach,	8047

Jer	42:18 and an **a**, and a curse, and a reproach;	8047
	44:12 an **a**, and a curse, and a reproach.	8047
	44:22 an **a**, and a curse, without an inhabitant,	8047
	51:37 an **a**, and a hissing, without an inhabitant,	8047
	51:41 how is Babylon become an **a** among	8047
Eze	4:16 shall drink water by measure, and with **a**:	8078
	5:15 an **a** unto the nations that *are* round	4923
	12:19 and drink their water with **a**,	8078
	23:33 sorrow, *with* the cup of **a** and desolation,	8047
Zec	12: 4 I will smite every horse with **a**,	8541
Mk	5:42 And they were astonished with a great **a**.	1611

ASTRAY (22)

Ex	23: 4 meet thine enemy's ox or his ass *going* **a**,	8582
Dt	22: 1 not see thy brother's ox or his sheep go **a**,	5080
Ps	58: 3 they go **a** as soon as they be born,	8582
	119:67 Before I was afflicted I *went* **a**:	7683
	119:176 I have **gone a** like a lost sheep; seek thy	8582
Pr	5:23 in the greatness of his folly he shall go **a**.	7686
	7:25 decline to her ways, **go** not **a** in her paths.	8582
	28:10 Whoso **causeth** the righteous to **go a** in	7686
Isa	53: 6 All we like sheep have **gone a**; we have	8582
Jer	50: 6 shepherds have **caused** them to **go a**,	8582
Eze	14:11 the house of Israel may **go** no more **a**	8582
	44:10 away far from me, when Israel **went a**,	8582
	44:10 which **went a** away from me after their	8582
	44:15 the children of Israel **went a** from me,	8582
	48:11 which **went** not **a** when the children of	8582
	48:11 astray when the children of Israel **went a**,	8582
	48:11 Israel went astray, as the Levites **went a**.	8582
Mt	18:12 and one of them be **gone a**, doth he not	4105
	18:12 and seeketh that which is **gone a**?	4105
	18:13 of the ninety and nine which **went** not **a**.	4105
1Pe	2:25 ye were as sheep **going a**; but are now	4105
2Pe	2:15 forsaken the right way, and are **gone a**,	4105

ASTROLOGER (1) [ASTROLOGERS, ASTROLOGIANS]

Da	2:10 things at any magician, or **a**, or Chaldean.	826

ASTROLOGERS (7) [ASTROLOGER]

Isa	47:13 Let now the **a**, the stargazers,	1895+8064
Da	1:20 *and* **a** that *were* in all his realm.	825
	2: 2 the **a**, and the sorcerers, and the Chaldeans	825
	4: 7 the **a**, the Chaldeans, and the soothsayers:	826
	5: 7 The king cried aloud to bring in the **a**,	826
	5:11 **a**, Chaldeans, *and* soothsayers;	826
	5:15 the wise *men*, the **a**, have been brought	826

ASTROLOGIANS (1) [ASTROLOGER]

Da	2:27 demanded cannot the wise *men*, the **a**,	826

ASUNDER (21)

Lev	1:17 the wings thereof, *but* shall not **divide** *it* **a**:	914
	5: 8 from his neck, but shall not **divide** *it* **a**;	914
Nu	16:31 that the ground **clave a** that *was* under	1234
2Ki	2:11 and horses of fire, and parted them both **a**;	996
Job	16:12 I was at ease, but he hath **broken** me **a**:	6565
	16:13 he **cleaveth** my reins **a**, and doth not	6398
Ps	2: 3 Let us **break** their bands **a**, and cast away	5423
	129: 4 he hath **cut a** the cords of the wicked.	7112
Jer	50:23 is the hammer of the whole earth **cut a**	1438
Eze	30:16 No shall be **rent a**, and Noph *shall* have	1234
Hab	3: 6 he beheld, and **drove** the nations;	5425
Zec	11:10 I took my staff, *even* Beauty, and **cut** it **a**,	1438
	11:14 I **cut a** mine other staff, *even* Bands, that	1438
Mt	19: 6 hath joined together, let not man **put a**.	5563
	24:51 And shall **cut** him **a**, and appoint *him* his	1371
Mk	5: 4 the chains had been **plucked a** by him,	1288
	10: 9 hath joined together, let not man **put a**.	5563
Ac	1:18 he **burst a** in the midst, and all his bowels	2997
	15:39 *between them*, that they **departed a**;	673
Heb	4:12 piercing even to the **dividing a** of soul	3311
	11:37 they were **sawn a**, were tempted,	4249

ASUPPIM (2)

1Ch	26:15 and to his sons the house of **A**.	624
	26:17 four a day, and toward **A** two *and* two.	624

ASWAN See SYENE

ASYNCRITUS (1)

Ro	16:14 Salute **A**, Phlegon, Hermas, Patrobas,	799

AT (1571)

Ge	3:24 he placed **a** the east of the garden of Eden	4480
	4: 7 thou doest not well, sin lieth **a** the door.	3807.1
	6: 6 the earth, and it grieved him **a** his heart.	413
	8: 6 it came to pass **a** the end of forty days,	4480
	9: 5 the hand of every beast will I require it,	4480
	9: 5 will I require it, and **a** the hand of man;	4480
	9: 5 **a** the hand of every man's brother will I	4480
	13: 3 unto the place where his tent had been **a**	871.1
	13: 4 which he had made there **a** the first:	871.1
	14:17 the valley of Shaveh, which *is* the king's	413
	17:21 which Sarah shall bear unto thee **a** this set	NIH
	18:14 **A** the time appointed I will return unto	3807.1
	19: 1 there came two angels to Sodom **a** even;	871.1
	19: 6 Lot went out **a** the door unto them,	1886.5
	19:11 they smote the men that *were* **a** the door	NIH
	20:13 **a** every place whither we shall come,	413
	21: 2 **a** the set time of which God had spoken	3807.1
	21:22 came to pass **a** that time, that Abimelech	871.1
	21:32 Thus they made a covenant **a** Beer-sheba:	871.1
	22:19 and Abraham dwelt **a** Beer-sheba.	871.1
	23:10 *even* of all that went in **a** the gate of his	NIH

Ge	23:18 all that went in **a** the gate of his city.	NIH
	24:11 well of water **a** the time of the evening,	3807.1
	24:21 man wondering **a** her held his peace,	3807.1
	24:30 behold, he stood by the camels **a** the well.	5921
	24:55 abide with us *a few* days, **a** the least ten;	176
	24:57 call the damsel, and inquire **a** her mouth.	NIH
	24:63 Isaac went out to meditate in the field **a**	3807.1
	25:32 Behold, I *am* **a the point** to die:	1980
	26: 8 of the Philistims looked out **a** a window,	1157
	27:41 of mourning for my father are **a hand**;	7126
	28:19 the name of *that* city *was* called Luz **a**	3807.1
	31:10 it came to pass **a** the time that the cattle	871.1
	33:10 then receive my present **a** my hand:	4480
	33:19 **a** the hand of the children of Hamor,	4480
	38: 1 it came to pass **a** that time, that Judah	871.1
	38: 5 he was **a** Chezib, when she bare him.	871.1
	38:11 Remain a widow **a** thy father's house,	NIH
	41: 1 came to pass **a** the end of two full years,	4480
	41:21 *were still* ill favoured, as **a** the beginning.	871.1
	43:16 for *these* men shall dine with me **a** noon.	871.1
	43:18 sacks **a** the first time *are* we brought in;	871.1
	43:19 they communed with him **a** the door of	NIH
	43:20 we came indeed down **a** the first time to	871.1
	43:25 the present against Joseph came **a** noon:	871.1
	43:33 and the men marvelled one **a** another.	413
	44:12 *and* began **a** the eldest, and left at	871.1
	44:12 at the eldest, and left **a** the youngest:	871.1
	45: 3 for they were troubled **a** his presence.	4480
	48: 3 God Almighty appeared unto me **a** Luz	871.1
	49:13 Zebulun shall dwell **a** the haven of	3807.1
	49:19 but he shall overcome **a** the last.	NIH
	49:23 him, and shot **a** *him*, and hated him:	NIH
	49:27 and **a** night he shall divide the spoil.	3807.1
Ex	2: 5 came down to wash *herself* **a** the river;	5921
	4:25 her son, and cast *it* **a** his feet, and said,	3807.1
	5:23 thou **delivered** thy people **a** all.	5337+5337
	8:32 Pharaoh hardened his heart **a** this time	871.1
	9:14 For I will **a** this time send all my plagues	871.1
	12: 9 nor **sodden a** all with water,	1310+1311
	12:18 the fourteenth day of the month **a** even,	871.1
	12:18 and twentieth day of the month **a** even.	871.1
	12:22 none of you shall go out **a** the door of his	4480
	12:29 that **a** midnight the LORD smote all	871.1
	12:41 it came to pass **a** the end of the four	4480
	16: 6 **A** even, then ye shall know that the LORD	NIH
	16:12 **A even** ye shall eat flesh,	996+6153+1886.1
	16:13 that **a** even the quails came up,	871.1
	18: 5 where he encamped **a** the mount of God:	NIH
	18:22 let them judge the people **a** all seasons:	871.1
	18:26 they judged the people **a** all seasons:	871.1
	19:15 the third day: come not **a** *your* wives.	413
	19:17 they stood **a** the nether part of the mount.	871.1
	22:23 they **cry a** all unto me, I will surely	6817+6817
	22:26 **a** all take thy neighbour's raiment to **pledge**,	2254+2254
	28: 7 *thereof* joined **a** the two edges thereof;	413
	28:14 two chains *of* pure gold **a** the ends;	NIH
	28:22 **a** the ends *of* wreathen work *of* pure gold.	NIH
	29:39 thou shalt offer **a** even;	996+6153+1886.1
	29:41 thou shalt offer **a even**,	996+6153+1886.1
	29:42 **a** the door of the tabernacle of	NIH
	30: 8 lighteth the lamps **a** even,	996+6153+1886.1
	32: 4 he received *them* **a** their hand,	4480
	33: 8 stood every man **a** his tent door,	NIH
	33: 9 stood **a** the door of the tabernacle,	NIH
	33:10 the people saw the cloudy pillar stand **a**	NIH
	34:22 the feast of ingathering **a** the year's end.	NIH
	35:15 hanging for the door **a** the entering in	3807.1
	36:29 coupled together **a** the head thereof,	413
	38: 8 which assembled **a** the door of	NIH
	39:15 upon the breastplate chains **a the ends**,	1383
	40: 8 and hang up the hanging **a** the court gate.	NIH
	40:28 he set up the hanging **a** the door of	NIH
Lev	1: 3 he shall offer it of his own voluntary will **a**	413
	1:15 the blood thereof shall be wrung out **a**	5921
	3: 2 kill it **a** the door of the tabernacle of	NIH
	4: 7 shall pour all the blood of the bullock **a**	413
	4: 7 which *is* **a** the door of the tabernacle of	NIH
	4:18 shall pour out all the blood **a** the bottom	413
	4:18 which *is* **a** the door of the tabernacle of	NIH
	4:25 shall pour out his blood **a** the bottom of	413
	4:30 shall pour out all the blood thereof **a**	413
	4:34 shall pour out all the blood thereof **a**	413
	5: 9 the rest of the blood shall be wrung out **a**	413
	6:20 in the morning, and half thereof **a** night.	871.1
	7:18 be **eaten a** all on the third day,	398+398
	8:15 poured the blood **a** the bottom of the altar,	413
	8:31 Boil the flesh **a** the door of the tabernacle	NIH
	8:33 days of your consecration be **a an end**:	4390
	8:35 Therefore shall ye abide **a** the door of	NIH
	9: 9 poured out the blood **a** the bottom of	413
	13: 5 *if* the plague in his sight be **a a stay**, *and*	5975
	13:37 if the scall be in his sight **a a stay**,	5975
	14:11 **a** the door of the tabernacle of	NIH
	15:24 if any man **lie with** her **a all**,	854+7901+7901
	16: 2 that he come not **a** all times into the holy	871.1
	16: 7 present them before the LORD **a** the door	NIH
	16:29 do no work **a** all, *whether it be* one of	NIH
	17: 6 **a** the door of the tabernacle of	NIH
	18: 9 *whether she be* born **a** home, or	NIH
	19: 5 ye shall offer it **a** your own will.	3807.1
	19: 7 if it be **eaten a all** on the third day,	398+398
	19:20 not **a all redeemed**, nor freedom	6299+6299
	22:19 *Ye shall offer* **a** your own will a male	3807.1
	22:29 unto the LORD, offer *it* **a** your own will.	3807.1

A

Lev 23: 5 In the fourteenth *day* of the first month a 996
23:32 in the ninth *day* of the month a even, 871.1
25:32 may the Levites redeem a any time. NIH
26:32 dwell therein shall be astonished a it. 5921
27:10 if he shall **a all change** beast for 4171+4171
27:13 if he will **a all redeem** it, 1350+1350
27:16 a homer of barley seed *shall be valued* a 871.1
27:31 if a man will **a all redeem** ought of 1350+1350
27:33 if he **change** it **a all,** then both it 4171+4171
Nu 3:39 Aaron numbered a the commandment of 5921
4:27 At the appointment of Aaron and his sons 5921
6: 6 the LORD he shall come a no dead body. 5921
6:18 a the door of the tabernacle of NIH
9: 2 keep the passover a his appointed season. 871.1
9: 3 the fourteenth day of this month, a even, 996
9: 5 month a even in the wilderness of Sinai: 996
9:11 The fourteenth day of the second month a 996
9:15 a even there was upon the tabernacle as 871.1
9:18 A the commandment of the LORD 5921
9:18 a the commandment of the LORD they 5921
9:23 A the commandment of the LORD they 5921
9:23 a the commandment of the LORD they 5921
9:23 a the commandment of the LORD by 5921
10: 3 a the door of the tabernacle of 413
11: 6 *there is* nothing a all, beside *this* manna, NIH
11:20 until it come out a your nostrils, and it be 4480
11:35 *unto* Hazeroth; and abode a Hazeroth. 871.1
13:30 Let us **go up a land,** and possess 5927+5927
16:34 round about them fled a the cry of them: 3807.1
19:19 in water, and shall be clean a even. NIH
20:24 ye rebelled against my word a the water 3807.1
21:11 from Oboth, and pitched a Ije-abarim, 871.1
21:15 a the stream of the brooks that goeth NIH
21:30 We have shot a them; Heshbon is perished NIH
21:33 he, and all his people, to the battle a Edrei. 871.1
21:34 of the Amorites, which dwelt a Heshbon. 871.1
22: 4 *was* king of the Moabites a that time. 871.1
22:20 God came unto Balaam a night, NIH
22:38 have I now **any power a all** to say 3201+3201
23:25 Neither **curse** them a all, nor bless 5344+5344
23:25 them at all, nor **bless** them a all. 1288+1288
24: 1 went not, as **a other times,** 6471+6471+871.1
27:14 to sanctify me a the water before their 871.1
27:21 a his word shall they go out, and at his 5921
27:21 a his word they shall come in, *both* he, 5921
28: 4 shalt thou offer **a even:** 996+6153+1886.1
28: 8 shalt thou offer **a even:** 996+6153+1886.1
30: 4 and her father shall hold his peace a her: 3807.1
30: 6 if she **had a all** a husband, 1961+1961+3807.1
30: 7 held his peace a her in the day that he 3807.1
30:11 heard *it,* and held his peace a her, 3807.1
30:14 her husband altogether hold his peace a 3807.1
30:14 held his peace a her in the day that he 3807.1
31:12 unto the camp a the plains of Moab, 413
33:14 from Alush, and encamped a Rephidim, 871.1
33:16 of Sinai, and pitched a Kibroth-hattaavah. 871.1
33:17 and encamped a Hazeroth. 871.1
33:19 and pitched a Rimmon-parez. 871.1
33:21 from Libnah, and pitched a Rissah. 871.1
33:26 Makheloth, and encamped a Tahath. 871.1
33:27 from Tahath, and pitched a Tarah. 871.1
33:30 and encamped a Moseroth. 871.1
33:32 and encamped a Hor-hagidgad. 871.1
33:34 Jotbathah, and encamped a Ebronah. 871.1
33:35 and encamped a Ezion-gaber. 871.1
33:38 the priest went up into mount Hor a 5921
34: 5 the goings out of it shall be a the sea. 1886.5
34: 9 the goings out of it shall be a Hazar-enan: NIH
34:12 the goings out of it shall be a the salt sea: NIH
35:11 which killeth *any* person a unawares. 871.1
35:20 hurl a him by laying of wait, that he die; 5921
35:26 if the slayer shall **a any time come** 3318+3318
Dt 1: 4 which dwelt a Astaroth in Edrei. 871.1
1: 9 I spake unto you a that time, saying, I am 871.1
1:16 I charged your judges a that time, saying, 871.1
1:18 I commanded you a that time all the 871.1
2:32 he and all his people, to fight a Jahaz. NIH
2:34 we took all his cities a that time, 871.1
3: 1 he and all his people, to battle a Edrei. NIH
3: 2 of the Amorites, which dwelt a Heshbon. 871.1
3: 4 we took all his cities a that time, there 871.1
3: 8 we took a that time out of the hand of 871.1
3:12 *which* we possessed a that time, from 871.1
3:18 I commanded you a that time, saying, 871.1
3:21 I commanded Joshua a that time, saying, 871.1
3:23 I besought the LORD a that time, saying, 871.1
4:14 The LORD commanded me a that time to 871.1
4:46 who dwelt a Heshbon, whom Moses 871.1
5: 5 between the LORD and you a that time, 871.1
6:24 might preserve us alive, as *it is* a this day. NIH
7:21 Thou shalt not be affrighted a them: 4480+6440
7:22 thou mayest not consume them **a once,** 4118
8:16 to do thee good a thy latter end; 871.1
8:19 if thou **do a all forget** the LORD 7911+7911
9:11 it came to pass a the end of forty days 4480
9:18 as a the first, forty days and forty nights: NIH
9:19 the LORD hearkened unto me a that time 871.1
9:22 a Taberah, and at Massah, 871.1
9:22 and a Massah, and at Kibroth-hattaavah, 871.1
9:22 and at Massah, and a Kibroth-hattaavah, 871.1
9:25 as I fell down a *the first;* because NIH
10: 1 a that time the LORD said unto me, 871.1
10: 8 A that time the LORD separated the tribe 871.1
10:10 the LORD hearkened unto me a that time 871.1
14:28 A the end of three years thou shalt bring 4480

Dt 15: 1 A the end of *every* seven years thou shalt 4480
15: 9 year, the year of release, is **a hand;** 7126
16: 4 which thou sacrificedst the first day a 871.1
16: 6 a the place which the LORD thy God shall 413
16: 6 thou shalt sacrifice the passover a even, 871.1
16: 6 a the going down of the sun, *at* the 3509.1
16: 6 a the season that thou camest forth out NIH
17: 6 A the mouth of two witnesses, or 5921
17: 6 a the mouth of one witness he shall not 5921
19:15 a the mouth of two witnesses, or at 5921
19:15 or a the mouth of three witnesses, shall 5921
21:14 thou shalt not **sell** her **a all** for 4376+4376
23:24 thou mayest eat grapes thy fill a thine 3509.1
24: 5 *but* he shall be free a home one year, 3807.1
24:15 A his day thou shalt give *him* his hire, 871.1
28:29 thou shalt grope a noondays, as the blind 871.1
28:67 a even thou shalt say, Would God it 871.1
31:10 A the end of *every* seven years, 4480
32:35 for the day of their calamity *is* **a hand,** 7138
32:51 of Israel a the waters of Meribah-Kadesh, 871.1
33: 3 they sat down a thy feet; *every one* shall 3807.1
33: 8 whom thou didst prove a Massah, *and* 871.1
33: 8 *with* whom thou didst strive a the waters 5921
Jos 5: 2 A that time the LORD said unto Joshua, 871.1
5: 3 circumcised the children of Israel a the hill 413
5:10 the month a even in the plains of Jericho. 871.1
6:16 it came to pass a the seventh time, 871.1
6:26 Joshua adjured *them* a that time, saying, 871.1
7: 7 **a all brought** this people **over** 5674+5674
8: 5 as the first, that we will flee before 871.1
8: 6 say, *They* flee before us, as a the first: 871.1
8:14 and all his people, a a time appointed, 3807.1
8:29 cast it a the entering of the gate of the city, 413
9: 6 went to Joshua unto the camp a Gilgal, NIH
9:10 king of Bashan, which *was* a Ashtaroth. 871.1
9:14 asked not *counsel* a the mouth of NIH
9:16 came to pass a the end of three days after 4480
10:10 them *with* a great slaughter a Gibeon, 871.1
10:16 hid themselves in a cave a Makkedah. 871.1
10:17 The five kings are found hid in a cave a 871.1
10:21 the camp to Joshua a Makkedah in peace: NIH
10:27 it came to pass a the time of the going 3807.1
10:42 and their land did Joshua take a one time, NIH
11: 5 pitched together a the waters of Merom, 413
11:10 Joshua a that time turned back, 871.1
11:21 a that time came Joshua, and cut off 871.1
12: 4 that dwelt a Ashtaroth and at Edrei, 871.1
12: 4 that dwelt at Ashtaroth and a Edrei, 871.1
15: 4 goings out of that coast were a the sea: 1886.5
15: 5 of the sea the uttermost part of Jordan: 1886.5
15: 7 and the goings out thereof were a En-rogel: 413
15: 8 which *is* a the end of the valley of 871.1
15:11 goings out of the border were a the sea. 1886.5
15:63 of Judah a Jerusalem unto this day. 871.1
16: 3 and the goings out thereof are a the sea. 1886.5
16: 7 came to Jericho, and went out a Jordan. NIH
16: 8 the goings out thereof were a the sea. 1886.5
17: 9 and the outgoings of it were a the sea: 1886.5
18: 1 of Israel assembled together a Shiloh, NIH
18: 9 came *again* to Joshua to the host a Shiloh. NIH
18:12 the goings out thereof were a 1886.5
18:14 the goings out thereof were a Kirjath-baal, 413
18:19 the outgoings of the border were a 1886.5
18:19 of the salt sea the south end of Jordan: 1886.5
19:22 outgoings of their border were a Jordan: NIH
19:29 the outgoings thereof are a the sea from 1886.5
19:33 and the outgoings thereof were a Jordan: NIH
19:51 a the door of the tabernacle of NIH
20: 4 stand a the entering of the gate of the city, NIH
20: 9 that whosoever killeth *any* person a 871.1
21: 2 spake unto them a Shiloh in the land 871.1
21: 3 a the commandment of the LORD, these 413
22:11 a the passage of the children of Israel. 413
22:12 gathered themselves together a Shiloh, NIH
Jdg 3: 2 a the least such as before knew nothing 7535
3:29 they slew *of* Moab a that time about ten 871.1
4: 4 of Lapidoth, she judged Israel a that time. 871.1
4:10 he went up with ten thousand men a his 871.1
5:27 A her feet he bowed, he fell, he lay down: 996
5:27 a her feet he bowed, he fell: where he 996
5:28 The mother of Sisera looked out a a 1157
7:25 Zeeb they slew a the winepress of Zeeb, 871.1
8:18 of men *were they* whom ye slew a Tabor? 871.1
9: 5 went unto his father's house a Ophrah, 1886.5
9:41 Abimelech dwelt a Arumah: 871.1
11:39 it came to pass a the end of two months, 4480
12: 2 my people were a great strife with NIH
12: 6 and slew him a the passages of Jordan: 413
12: 6 there fell a that time of the Ephraimites 871.1
12:10 died Ibzan, and was buried a Beth-lehem. 871.1
13:23 and a meat offering a our hands, 4480
13:23 *a this* time have told us *such things* as 871.1
13:25 to **move** him a times in the camp of Dan, 6470
14: 4 for a that time the Philistines had 871.1
16: 3 arose a midnight, and took the doors of 871.1
16:20 go out as **a other times** 6471+6471+871.1
16:28 that I may be a **once** avenged of 259
16:30 So the dead which he slew a his death 871.1
18:27 a people *that were* a quiet and secure: NIH
18:29 the name of the city *was* Laish a 3807.1
19:16 from his work out of the field a even, 871.1
19:22 beat a the door, and spake to the master 5921
19:26 fell down a the door of the man's house 871.1
19:27 woman his concubine *was* fallen down a NIH
20:15 children of Benjamin were numbered a 871.1

Jdg 20:16 one could sling stones a a hair *breadth,* 413
20:20 in array to fight against them a Gibeah. 413
20:30 as **a other times.** 6471+6471+871.1
20:31 **a other times,** in 6471+6471+871.1
20:32 *are* smitten down before us, as a the first. 871.1
20:33 and put *themselves* in array a Baal-tamar. 871.1
21:14 Benjamin came again a that time; 871.1
21:22 ye did not give unto them a *this* time, 3509.1
21:24 the children of Israel departed thence a 871.1
Ru 2:14 A mealtime come thou hither, and eat 3807.1
3: 7 went to lie down a the end of the heap 871.1
3: 8 it came to pass a midnight, that the man 871.1
3: 8 and behold, a woman a his feet. NIH
3:10 in the latter end than a the beginning, NIH
3:14 she lay a his feet until the morning: NIH
1Sa 2:22 a the door of the tabernacle of NIH
2:29 Wherefore kick ye a my sacrifice 871.1
2:29 ye at my sacrifice and a mine offering, 871.1
3: 2 it came to pass a that time, when Eli *was* 871.1
3:10 and called as **a other times,** 6471+6471+871.1
3:11 which both the ears of every one that NIH
6:10 the cart, and shut up their calves a home: 871.1
9: 8 I have here a hand the fourth part of a 871.1
10: 2 in the border of Benjamin a Zelzah; 871.1
13:11 themselves together a Michmash; NIH
14:18 For the ark of God was a that time with 871.1
16: 4 the elders of the town trembled a his 3807.1
17: 1 were gathered together a Shochoh, NIH
17:15 to feed his father's sheep a Beth-lehem. NIH
18:10 his hand, as **a other times:** 3117+3117+871.1
18:19 it came to pass a the time when Merab 871.1
19:19 Behold, David *is* a Naioth in Ramah. 871.1
19:22 Behold, *they* be a Naioth in Ramah. 871.1
20: 5 not fail to sit with the king a meat: 3807.1
20: 5 in the fields unto the third *day* a even. NIH
20: 6 If thy father **a all miss** me, then 6485+6485
20:16 *saying,* Let the LORD even require *it* a 4480
20:20 side *thereof,* as *though* I shot a a mark. 3807.1
20:25 as **a other times,** *even* 6471+6471+871.1
20:33 Saul cast a javelin a him to smite him: 5921
20:35 that Jonathan went out *into* the field a 3807.1
21: 1 Ahimelech was afraid a the meeting of 3807.1
21: 4 kept themselves **a least** from women. 389
22: 8 against me, to lie in wait, as a this day? NIH
22:13 against me, to lie in wait, as a this day? NIH
22:14 goeth a thy bidding, and *is* honourable in 413
23:29 and dwelt in strong holds a En-gedi. NIH
25: 1 and buried him in his house a Ramah. 871.1
25:24 fell a his feet, and said, Upon me, my lord, 5921
26: 7 his spear stuck in the ground a his bolster: NIH
26: 8 the spear even to the earth a **once,** 259+6471
26:11 thou now the spear that *is* a his bolster, NIH
26:16 the cruse of water that *was* a his bolster. NIH
27: 3 David dwelt with Achish a Gath, he 871.1
28: 7 that hath a familiar spirit a En-dor. 871.1
30: 8 David inquired a the LORD, saying, 871.1
30:21 whom they had made also to abide a 871.1
31:13 buried *them* under a tree a Jabesh, 871.1
2Sa 2:32 and they came to Hebron a **break of day.** 215
3:30 had slain their brother Asahel a Gibeon 871.1
3:32 his voice, and wept a the grave of Abner; 413
4: 5 of Ish-bosheth, who lay on a bed a noon. NIH
6: 4 house of Abinadab which *was* a Gibeah, 871.1
8: 3 he went to recover his border a the river 871.1
9: 7 shalt eat bread a my table continually. 5921
9:10 son shall eat bread alway a my table. 5921
9:11 *said the king,* he shall eat a my table, 5921
9:13 he did eat continually a the king's table; 5921
10: 5 Tarry a Jericho until your beards be 871.1
10: 8 put the battle in array a the entering in NIH
11: 1 a the time when kings go forth *to* battle, 3807.1
11: 1 But David tarried *still* a Jerusalem. 871.1
11: 9 Uriah slept a the door of the king's house NIH
11:13 a even he went out to lie on his bed with 4480
13: 5 that I may see *it,* and eat *it* a her hand. 4480
13: 6 in my sight, that I may eat a her hand. 4480
14:26 it was a every year's end that he polled 4480
14:26 he weighed the hair of his head a two NIH
15: 8 a vow while I abode a Geshur in Syria, 871.1
15:14 servants that *were* with him a Jerusalem, 871.1
16: 3 the king, Behold, he abideth a Jerusalem: 871.1
16: 6 he cast stones a David, and at all NIH
16: 6 and a all the servants of king David: NIH
16:13 threw stones a him, and cast dust 5980+3807.1
16:23 *was* as if a man had inquired a the oracle NIH
17: 7 hath given *is* not good a this time. 871.1
17: 9 when *some* of them be overthrown a 871.1
19: 9 all the people were a **strife** throughout 1777
19:28 them that did eat a thine own table. NIH
19:32 of sustenance while he lay a Mahanaim; 871.1
19:42 we **eaten a all** of the king's *cost?* 398+398
20: 3 David came to his house a Jerusalem; NIH
20: 8 When they *were* a the great stone which 5973
20:18 They shall surely ask *counsel* a Abel: 871.1
21:18 again a battle with the Philistines a Gob: 871.1
22:16 a the rebuking of the LORD, at the blast 871.1
22:16 a the blast of the breath of his nostrils. 4480
23: 8 eight hundred, whom he slew a one time. 871.1
24: 8 they came *to* Jerusalem a the end of nine 4480
24:24 but I will surely buy *it* of thee a a price: 871.1
1Ki 1: 6 his father had not displeased him a any 4480
2: 7 let them be of *those* that eat a thy table: NIH
2: 8 but he came down to meet me a Jordan, NIH
2:26 I will not a this time put thee to death, 871.1
2:39 it came to pass a the end of three years, 4480

A

1Ki
3:20 she rose a midnight, and took my son — 871.1
5:14 in Lebanon, and two months a home: — 871.1
7:30 a the side of every addition. — 4480
8: 2 Solomon a the feast in the month — 871.1
8: 9 stone, which Moses put there a Horeb, — 871.1
8:59 his people Israel a all times, — 3117+3117+871.1
8:61 to keep his commandments, as a this day. — NIH
8:65 a that time Solomon held a feast, — 871.1
9: 2 as he had appeared unto him a Gibeon. — 871.1
9: 6 But if you shall a all turn from — 7725+7725
9: 8 a this house, which is high, every one that — NIH
9:10 it came to pass a the end of twenty years, — 4480
10:22 the king had a sea a navy of Tharshish — 871.1
10:26 chariots, and with the king a Jerusalem. — 871.1
10:28 received the linen yarn a a price. — 871.1
11:29 came to pass a that time when Jeroboam — 871.1
12:27 in the house of the LORD a Jerusalem, — 871.1
13:20 it came to pass, as they sat a the table, — 413
14: 1 A that time Abijah the son of Jeroboam — 871.1
14: 6 as she came in a the door, that he said, — 871.1
15:18 of Syria, that dwelt a Damascus, saying, — 871.1
15:27 Baasha smote him a Gibbethon, — 871.1
18:19 four hundred, which eat a Jezebel's table. — NIH
18:27 came to pass a noon, that Elijah mocked — 871.1
18:36 came to pass a the time of the offering of — 871.1
18:36 that I have done all these things a thy — 871.1
18:44 came to pass a the seventh time, that he — 871.1
19: 6 coals, and a cruse of water a his head. — NIH
20: 9 that thou didst send for to thy servant a — 871.1
20:16 they went out a noon. But Ben-hadad — 871.1
20:22 for a the return of the year the king of — 3807.1
20:26 it came to pass a the return of the year, — 3807.1
22: 5 a the word of the LORD to day. — 3509.1
22:20 he may go up and fall a Ramoth-gilead? — 871.1
22:28 If thou return a all in peace, — 7725+7725
22:34 a certain man drew a bow a a venture, — 3807.1
22:35 against the Syrians, and died a even: — 871.1
22:48 for the ships were broken a Ezion-geber. — 871.1

2Ki
2: 3 sons of the prophets that were a Beth-el — NIH
2: 5 sons of the prophets that were a Jericho — 871.1
2:15 which were to view a Jericho saw him, — 871.1
2:18 again to him, (for he tarried a Jericho,) — 871.1
4:17 bare a son that season that Elisha had — 3807.1
4:37 fell a his feet, and bowed herself to — 5921
5: 9 stood a the door of the house of Elisha. — 871.1
5:20 in not receiving a his hands that which he — 4480
6:32 the door, and hold him fast a the door: — 871.1
7: 3 were four leprous men a the entering — NIH
8: 3 it came to pass a the seven years' end, — 4480
8:22 Then Libnah revolted a the same time. — 871.1
8:29 the Syrians had given him a Ramah, — 871.1
9: 7 of the LORD, a the hand of Jezebel. — 4480
9:24 the arrow went out a his heart, — 4480
9:27 And they did so a the going up to Gur, — 871.1
9:30 her head, and looked out a a window. — 1157
9:31 as Jehu entered in a a gate, she said, — 871.1
10: 8 Lay ye them in two heaps a the entering — NIH
10:12 And as he was a the shearing house in — NIH
10:14 slew them a the pit of the shearing house, — 413
11: 6 a third part shall be a the gate of Sur; — 871.1
11: 6 a third part a the gate behind the guard: — 871.1
12: 4 the money that every man is set a, — 6187
13:20 the land a the coming in of the year. — NIH
14:10 glory of this, and tarry a home: for why — 871.1
14:11 one another in the face a Beth-shemesh, — 871.1
14:13 a Beth-shemesh, and came to Jerusalem, — 871.1
14:20 was buried a Jerusalem with his fathers — 871.1
16: 6 A that time Rezin king of Syria recovered — 871.1
16:10 and saw an altar that was a Damascus: — 871.1
17:25 it was a the beginning of their dwelling — 871.1
18:10 a the end of three years they took it: — 4480
18:16 A that time did Hezekiah cut off the gold — 871.1
18:33 delivered a all his land out of — 5337+5337
19:21 of Jerusalem hath shaken her head a thee. — 310
19:36 went and returned, and dwelt a Nineveh. — 871.1
20:12 A that time Berodach-baladan, the son of — 871.1
23: 6 burnt it a the brook Kidron, and stampt — 871.1
23: 8 were on a man's left hand a the gate — 871.1
23:11 a the entering in of the house of — 4480
23:15 Moreover the altar that was a Beth-el, — 871.1
23:29 he slew him a Megiddo, when he had — 871.1
23:33 put him in bands a Riblah — 871.1
24: 3 Surely a the commandment of the LORD — 5921
24:10 A that time the servants of — 871.1
25:21 them a Riblah in the land of Hamath. — 871.1
25:25 Chaldees that were with him a Mizpah. — 871.1

1Ch
2:55 the families of the scribes which dwelt a — 3427
4:28 they dwelt a Beer-sheba, and Moladah, — 871.1
4:29 And a Bilhah, and at Ezem, and at Tolad, — 871.1
4:29 And at Bilhah, and at Ezem, and at Tolad, — 871.1
4:29 And at Bilhah, and at Ezem, and at Tolad, — 871.1
4:30 a Bethuel, and at Hormah, and at Ziklag, — 871.1
4:30 at Bethuel, and at Hormah, and at Ziklag, — 871.1
4:30 at Bethuel, and at Hormah, and at Ziklag, — 871.1
4:31 a Beth-marcaboth, and Hazar-susim, — 871.1
4:31 and a Beth-birei, and at Shaaraim. — 871.1
4:31 and at Beth-birei, and at Shaaraim. — 871.1
8:29 a Gibeon dwelt the father of Gibeon; — 871.1
9:34 generations; these dwelt a Jerusalem. — 871.1
9:38 they also dwelt with their brethren a — 871.1
11:11 three hundred slain by him a one time. — 871.1
11:13 He was with David a Pas-dammim, — 871.1
11:16 garrison was then a Beth-lehem. — 871.1
11:17 the well of Beth-lehem, that is a the gate. — 871.1
12:22 For a that time day by day there came to — 3807.1

1Ch 12:32 all their brethren were a their — 5921
13: 3 we inquired not a it in the days of Saul. — NIH
14: 3 David took moe wives a Jerusalem: — 871.1
15:13 For because ye did it not a the first, — 871.1
15:29 out a a window saw king David dancing — 1157
16:33 out a the presence of the LORD, — 4480+3807.1
16:39 in the high place that was a Gibeon, — 871.1
17: 9 waste them any more, as a the beginning, — 871.1
19: 5 Tarry a Jericho until your beards be — 871.1
20: 1 a the time that kings go out to battle, — 3807.1
20: 1 David tarried a Jerusalem. And Joab — 871.1
20: 4 that there arose war a Gezer with — 871.1
20: 4 which time Sibbechai the Hushathite — 227
20: 6 yet again there was war a Gath, where — 871.1
21:19 David went up a the saying of Gad, — 871.1
21:28 A that time when David saw that — 871.1
21:29 were a that season in the high place at — 871.1
21:29 were a that season in the high place a a — 871.1
23:30 praise the LORD, and likewise a even; — 3807.1
26:18 A Parbar westward, four at the — 3807.1
26:18 four a the causeway, and two at Parbar. — 3807.1
26:18 four at the causeway, and two a Parbar. — 871.1
26:31 mighty men of valour a Jazer of Gilead. — 871.1
28: 7 and my judgments, as a this day. — NIH
28:21 all the people will be wholly a thy — 3807.1

2Ch 1: 3 to the high place that was a Gibeon; — 871.1
1: 4 he had pitched a tent for it a Jerusalem. — 871.1
1: 6 which was a the tabernacle of — 3807.1
1:13 place that was a Gibeon to Jerusalem, — 871.1
1:14 and with the king a Jerusalem. — 871.1
1:15 gold a Jerusalem as plenteous as stones, — 871.1
1:16 received the linen yarn a a price. — 871.1
3: 1 the LORD a Jerusalem in mount Moriah, — 871.1
5:10 tables which Moses put therein a Horeb, — 871.1
5:12 stood a the east end of the altar, — NIH
7: 8 Also a the same time Solomon kept — 871.1
8: 1 it came to pass a the end of twenty years, — 4480
8:14 the porters also by their courses a every — 3807.1
8:17 Eloth, a the sea side in the land of Edom. — 5921
9: 1 with hard questions a Jerusalem, — 871.1
9:25 and with the king a Jerusalem. — 871.1
13:18 Israel were brought under a that time, — 871.1
14:10 in the valley of Zephathah a Mareshah. — 3807.1
15:10 So they gathered themselves together a — NIH
15:15 all Judah rejoiced a the oath: for they — 5921
15:16 and burnt it a the brook Kidron. — 871.1
16: 2 of Syria, that dwelt a Damascus, saying, — 871.1
16: 7 a that time Hanani the seer came to Asa — 871.1
18: 4 a the word of the LORD to day. — 3509.1
18:19 he may go up and fall a Ramoth-gilead? — 871.1
18:33 a certain man drew a bow a a venture, — 3807.1
19: 4 Jehoshaphat dwelt a Jerusalem: — 871.1
20:16 ye shall find them a the end of the brook, — 871.1
22: 5 Hazael king of Syria a Ramoth-gilead: — 871.1
22: 6 of the wounds which were given him a — 871.1
22: 6 to see Jehoram the son of Ahab a Jezreel, — 871.1
23: 3 a third part shall be a the king's house; — 871.1
23: 5 a third part a the gate of the foundation: — 871.1
23:13 the king stood a his pillar at the entering — 5921
23:13 the king stood at his pillar a the entering — 871.1
23:19 he set the porters a the gates of the house — 5921
24: 8 a the king's commandment they made a — NIH
24: 8 set it without a the gate of the house of — 871.1
24:11 that a what time the chest was brought — 871.1
24:21 stoned him with stones a — 871.1
24:23 it came to pass a the end of the year, — 3807.1
25:19 abide now a home; why shouldest thou — 871.1
25:21 Amaziah king of Judah, a Beth-shemesh, — 871.1
25:23 a Beth-shemesh, and brought him to — 871.1
26: 9 towers in Jerusalem a the corner gate, — 5921
26: 9 a the valley gate, and at the turning of — 5921
26: 9 a the turning of the wall, — 5921
28:16 A that time did king Ahaz send unto — 871.1
30: 1 to the house of the LORD a Jerusalem, — 871.1
30: 3 For they could not keep it a that time, — 871.1
30: 5 the LORD God of Israel a Jerusalem: — 871.1
30:13 there assembled a Jerusalem much people — NIH
30:21 the children of Israel that were present a — 871.1
31:13 a the commandment of Hezekiah — 871.1
32: 9 unto all Judah that were a Jerusalem, — 871.1
32:33 of Jerusalem did him honour a his death. — 871.1
33:14 even to the entering in a the fish gate, — 871.1
35:15 and the porters waited a every gate; — 3807.1
35:17 present kept the passover a that time, — 871.1
35:23 the archers shot a king Josiah; — 3807.1
36: 3 the king of Egypt put him down a — 871.1
36: 7 and put them in his temple a Babylon. — 871.1

Ezr 1: 2 hath charged me to build him a house a — 871.1
2:68 house of the LORD which is a Jerusalem, — 871.1
3: 8 unto the house of God a Jerusalem, — 3807.1
4:10 side the river, and a such a time. — NIH
4:11 on this side the river, and a such a time. — 3706
4:17 the river: Peace, and a such a time. — 3706
4:24 house of the God which is a Jerusalem. — 871.2
5: 2 to build the house of God which is a — 871.2
5: 3 A the same time came to them Tatnai, — 871.2
5:17 is there a Babylon, whether it be so, — 871.2
5:17 to build this house of God a Jerusalem, — 871.2
6: 2 was found a Achmetha, in the palace — 871.2
6: 3 the house of God a Jerusalem, — 871.2
6: 5 out of the temple which is a Jerusalem, — 871.2
6: 5 again unto the temple which is a — 871.2
6: 9 of the priests which are a Jerusalem, — 871.2
6:12 to destroy this house of God which is a — 871.2

Ezr 6:17 offered a the dedication of this house of — 3807.2
6:18 the service of God, which is a Jerusalem; — 871.2
7:12 perfect peace, and a such a time. — 3706
8:17 unto Iddo the chief a the place Casiphia, — 871.1
8:17 the Nethinims, a the place Casiphia, — 871.1
8:21 proclaimed a fast there, a the river Ahava, — 5921
8:29 chief of the fathers of Israel, a Jerusalem, — 871.1
8:34 all the weight was written a that time. — 871.1
9: 4 trembled a the words of the God of Israel, — 871.1
9: 5 a the evening sacrifice I arose up from — 871.1
10: 3 those that tremble a the commandment — 871.1
10:14 in our cities come a appointed times, — 3807.1

Ne 2:12 had put in my heart to do a Jerusalem: — 3807.1
3:19 to the armoury a the turning of the wall. — NIH
4:22 Likewise at the same time said I unto — 871.1
5:17 there were a my table an hundred — NIH
6: 1 (though a that time I had not set up — 5704
7: 7 prophets to preach of thee a Jerusalem, — 871.1
7: 5 of them which came up a the first, — 871.1
9:37 a their pleasure, and we are in great — 3509.1
10:34 a times appointed year by year, — 3807.1
11: 1 rulers of the people dwelt a Jerusalem: — 871.1
11: 2 offered themselves to dwell a Jerusalem. — 871.1
11: 4 a Jerusalem dwelt certain of the children — 871.1
11: 6 All the sons of Perez that dwelt a — 871.1
11:22 The overseer also of the Levites a — 871.1
11:24 was a the king's hand in all matters — 3807.1
11:25 some of the children of Judah dwelt a — 871.1
11:25 a Dibon, and in the villages thereof, — 871.1
11:25 a Jekabzeel, and in the villages thereof, — 871.1
11:26 a Jeshua, and at Moladah, — 871.1
11:26 and a Moladah, and at Beth-phelet, — 871.1
11:26 and at Moladah, and a Beth-phelet, — 871.1
11:27 a Hazar-shual, and at Beer-sheba, — 871.1
11:27 a Beer-sheba, and in the villages thereof, — 871.1
11:28 a Ziklag, and at Mekonah, and in — 871.1
11:28 a Mekonah, and in the villages thereof, — 871.1
11:29 a En-rimmon, and at Zareah, — 871.1
11:29 and a Zareah, and at Jarmuth, — 871.1
11:29 and at Zareah, and a Jarmuth, — 871.1
11:30 a Lachish, and the fields thereof, — NIH
11:30 a Azekah, and in the villages thereof. — NIH
11:31 Benjamin from Geba dwelt a Michmash, — NIH
11:32 And a Anathoth, Nob, Ananiah, — NIH
12:25 were porters keeping the ward a — 871.1
12:27 a the dedication of the wall of Jerusalem — 871.1
12:37 a the fountain gate, which was over — 5921
12:37 a the going up of the wall, above the — 871.1
12:44 a that time were some appointed over — 871.1
13: 6 in all this time was not I a Jerusalem: — 871.1
13:19 some of my servants set I a the gates, — 5921
13:31 a times appointed, and for the firstfruits. — 871.1

Est 1:12 the queen Vashti refused to come a — 871.1
4: 8 was given a Shushan to destroy them, — 871.1
4:14 For if thou altogether holdest thy peace a — 871.1
5: 6 the king said unto Esther a the banquet — 871.1
5:13 long as I see Mordecai the Jew sitting a — 871.1
6:10 the Jew, that sitteth a the king's gate: — 871.1
7: 2 on the second day a the banquet of wine, — 871.1
7: 3 let my life be given me a my petition, — 871.1
7: 3 my petition, and my people a my request: — 871.1
8: 3 fell down a his feet, and besought — 6440+3807.1
8: 9 were the king's scribes called a that time — 871.1
8:14 decree was given a Shushan the palace. — 871.1
9:14 decree was given a Shushan; and they — 871.1
9:15 and slew three hundred men a Shushan; — 871.1
9:18 the Jews that were a Shushan assembled — 871.1

Job 2:10 shall we receive good a the hand of — 854+4480
3:13 should have slept: then had I been a rest, — 5117
3:17 and there the weary be a rest. — 5117
5:22 A destruction and famine thou shalt — 3807.1
5:23 beasts of the field shall be a peace with — 7999
9:23 he will laugh a the trial of the innocent. — 3807.1
12: 5 in the thought of him that is a ease. — 7600
15:12 and what do thine eyes wink a, — NIH
15:23 the day of darkness is ready a his hand. — 871.1
16: 4 against you, and shake mine head a you. — 5921
16:12 I was a ease, but he hath broken me — 7961
17: 8 Upright men shall be astonied a this, — 5921
18:12 destruction shall be ready a his side. — 3807.1
18:20 after him shall be astonied a his day, — 5921
19:25 that he shall stand a the latter day upon — NIH
21:12 and rejoice a the sound of the organ. — 3807.1
21:23 strength, being wholly a ease and quiet. — 7946
22:21 now thyself with him, and be a peace: — 7999
23:15 Therefore am I troubled a his presence: — 4480
26:11 and are astonished a his reproof. — 4480
27:23 Men shall clap their hands a him, — 5921
29:21 waited, and kept silence a my counsel. — 3926
31: 9 if I have laid wait a my neighbour's door; — 5921
31:29 If I rejoiced a the destruction of him that — 871.1
34:20 shall be troubled a midnight, — 2676+3915
37: 1 A this also my heart trembleth, — 3807.1
39:22 He mocketh a fear, and is not affrighted; — 3807.1
39:27 Doth the eagle mount up a thy command, — 5921
41: 9 not one be cast down even a the sight — 413
41:26 The sword of him that layeth a him — NIH
41:29 he laugheth a the shaking of a spear. — 3807.1

Ps 7: 4 evil unto him that was a peace with me; — 7999
9: 3 they shall fall and perish a thy presence. — 4480
10: 5 as for all his enemies, he puffeth a them. — 871.1
11: 2 that they may privily shoot a the upright — 3807.1
12: 5 in safety from him that puffeth a him. — 3807.1
16: 8 because he is a my right hand, I shall not — 4480
16:11 a thy right hand there are pleasures for — 871.1

Ref	Text	Strong's
Ps 18:12	A the brightness *that was* before him his	4480
18:15	the world were discovered at thy rebuke,	4480
18:15	the blast of the breath of thy nostrils.	4480
25:13	His soul shall dwell a ease; and his seed	871.1
30: T	Song A the dedication of the house of	NIH
30: 4	give thanks a the remembrance of his	3807.1
34: 1	I will bless the LORD a all times:	871.1
35: 8	destruction come upon him a unawares;	NIH
35:26	to confusion together that rejoice a	NIH
37:13	The Lord shall laugh a him: for he seeth	3807.1
39: 5	verily every man a his **best state** *is*	5324
39:12	my cry; hold not thy peace a my tears:	NIH
42: 7	Deep calleth unto deep a the noise of	3807.1
52: 6	shall see, and fear, and shall laugh a him:	5921
55: 6	*for then* would I fly away, and be a **rest**.	7931
55:17	Evening, and morning, and a noon, will I	NIH
55:20	hands against such as be a peace with him:	NIH
59: 6	return a evening: they make a noise	3807.1
59: 8	thou, O LORD, shalt laugh a them;	3807.1
59:14	a evening let them return; *and* let them	3807.1
62: 8	Trust in him a all times; ye people,	871.1
64: 4	*they* may shoot in secret a the perfect:	NIH
64: 4	do they shoot a him, and fear not.	NIH
64: 7	God shall shoot a them *with* an arrow;	NIH
65: 8	the uttermost parts are afraid a thy tokens:	4480
68: 2	the wicked perish a the presence of God.	4480
68: 8	the heavens also dropped a the presence	4480
68: 8	Sinai itself *was moved* a the presence	4480
68:12	she that tarried a home divided the spoil.	NIH
68:29	Because of thy temple a Jerusalem shall	5921
73: 3	For I was envious a the foolish, *when* I	871.1
74: 6	carved work thereof a **once** with axes	3162
76: 6	A thy rebuke, O God of Jacob, both	4480
80:16	they perish a the rebuke of thy	4480
81: 7	I proved thee a the waters of Meribah.	5921
83: 9	Sisera, as *to* Jabin, a the brook of Kison:	871.1
83:10	*Which* perished a En-dor: they became	871.1
91: 6	*nor* for the destruction *that* wasteth a	NIH
91: 7	A thousand shall fall a thy side,	4480
91: 7	side, and ten thousand a thy right hand;	4480
97: 5	The hills melted like wax a	4480+3807.1
97: 5	at the presence of the LORD, a	4480+3807.1
97:12	give thanks a the remembrance of his	3807.1
99: 5	our God, and worship a his footstool;	3807.1
99: 9	our God, and worship a his holy hill;	3807.1
104: 7	A thy rebuke they fled; at the voice of thy	4480
104: 7	a the voice of thy thunder they hasted	4480
105:22	To bind his princes a his pleasure;	871.1
106: 3	he that doeth righteousness a all times.	871.1
106: 7	provoked *him* a the sea, even at the Red	5921
106: 7	*him* at the sea, even a the Red sea.	871.1
106:32	They angered *him* also a the waters of	5921
107:27	and are a their **wit's end**.	1104+2451+3605
109: 6	and let Satan stand a his right hand.	5921
109:31	For he shall stand a the right hand of	3807.1
110: 1	unto my Lord, Sit thou a my right hand,	3807.1
110: 5	The Lord a thy right hand shall strike	5921
114: 7	a the presence of the Lord,	4480+3807.1
114: 7	a the presence of the God of Jacob;	4480
118:13	hast thrust sore a me that *I* might fall:	NIH
119:20	unto thy judgments a all times.	871.1
119:45	I will walk a liberty: for I seek thy	871.1
119:62	A **midnight** I will rise to give	2676+3915
119:162	I rejoice a thy word, as one that findeth	5921
123: 4	*with* the scorning of those that are a **ease**,	7600
132: 6	we heard *of* it a Ephratah: we found it	871.1
132: 7	we will worship a his footstool.	3807.1
135:21	out of Zion, which dwelleth a Jerusalem.	NIH
141: 7	Our bones are scattered a the grave's	3807.1
Pr 1:23	Turn you a my reproof: behold, I will	3807.1
1:25	ye have set a **nought** all my counsel,	6544
1:26	I also will laugh a your calamity; I will	871.1
4:19	they know not a what they stumble.	871.1
5:11	thou mourn a the last, when thy flesh	871.1
5:19	let her breasts satisfy thee a all times;	871.1
7: 6	For a the window of my house I looked	871.1
7:12	streets, and lieth in wait a every corner.)	681
7:19	the goodman *is* not a home, he is gone	871.1
7:20	will come home a the day appointed.	3807.1
8: 3	She crieth a the gates, at the entry	3027+3807.1
8: 3	at the gates, a the entry of the city,	3807.1
8: 3	of the city, *a* the coming in at the doors.	NIH
8: 3	of the city, *at* the coming in a the doors.	NIH
8:34	watching daily a my gates, waiting at	5921
8:34	my gates, waiting a the posts of my doors.	NIH
9:14	For she sitteth a the door of her house,	3807.1
14: 9	Fools **make a mock** a sin: but among	3887
14:19	the wicked a the gates of the righteous.	5921
16: 7	**maketh** even his enemies **to be a peace**	7999
17: 5	he that is glad a calamities shall not be	3807.1
17:17	A friend loveth a all times, and a brother	871.1
20:21	An inheritance *may be* gotten hastily a	871.1
21:13	Whoso stoppeth his ears a the cry of	4480
23:30	They that tarry long a the wine; they that	5921
23:32	A the last it biteth like a serpent,	NIH
24:19	of evil *men*, neither be thou envious a	871.1
28:18	*that is* perverse in *his* ways shall fall a	871.1
29:21	have him become *his* son a the length.	NIH
30:17	The eye *that* mocketh a *his* father,	3807.1
Ecc 5: 6	wherefore should God be angry a thy	5921
5: 8	in a province, marvel not a the matter:	5921
10: 2	A wise *man's* heart *is* a his right hand;	3807.1
10: 2	right hand; but a fool's heart a his left.	3807.1
12: 4	he shall rise up a the voice of the bird,	3807.1
12: 6	or the pitcher be broken a the fountain,	5921
Ecc 12: 6	or the wheel broken a the cistern.	413
SS 1: 7	thou makest *thy flock* to rest a noon:	871.1
1:12	While the king *sitteth* a his table,	871.1
2: 9	our wall, he looketh forth a the windows,	NIH
7:13	a our gates *are* all *manner of* pleasant	5921
8:11	Solomon had a vineyard a Baal-hamon;	871.1
Isa 1:12	hath required this a your hand, to tread	4480
1:26	I will restore thy judges as a the first,	871.1
1:26	and thy counsellers as a the beginning:	871.1
6: 4	the posts of the door moved a the voice	4480
7: 3	a the end of the conduit of the upper pool	413
7:23	where there were a thousand vines a a	871.1
9: 1	when a the first he lightly afflicted	3509.1
10:26	the slaughter of Midian a the rock Oreb:	NIH
10:28	a Michmash he hath laid up his	3807.1
10:29	they have taken up their lodging a Geba;	NIH
10:32	As yet shall *he* remain a Nob *that day:*	871.1
13: 6	for the day of the LORD *is* a **hand;**	7138
13: 8	they shall be amazed one a another; their	413
14: 7	The whole earth is a **rest**, *and* is quiet;	5117
14: 8	fir trees rejoice a thee, *and* the cedars	3807.1
14: 9	moved for thee to meet *thee* a thy coming:	NIH
16: 2	the daughters of Moab shall be *a* the fords	NIH
16: 4	for the extortioner is **a an end**, the spoiler	656
17: 7	A that day shall a man look to his Maker,	4480
17:14	behold a eveningtide trouble; *and*	3807.1
19: 1	the idols of Egypt shall be moved a his	4480
19:19	a pillar at the border thereof to the LORD.	681
20: 2	A the same time spake the LORD by	871.1
21: 3	I was bowed down a the hearing *of it;*	4480
21: 3	*of it;* I was dismayed a the seeing *of it.*	4480
22: 7	shall set themselves in array a the gate.	1886.5
23: 5	As *a* the report concerning Egypt, so	NIH
23: 5	shall they be sorely pained *a* the report of	NIH
26:11	be ashamed for *their* envy a the people;	NIH
27:13	the LORD in the holy mount a Jerusalem.	871.1
28:15	and with hell are we a agreement;	6213
29: 5	yea, it shall be a an instant suddenly.	3807.1
30: 2	Egypt, and have not asked a my mouth;	NIH
30: 4	For his princes were a Zoan,	871.1
30:13	whose breaking cometh suddenly a an	3807.1
30:17	thousand *shall flee* a the rebuke	4480+6440
30:17	a the rebuke of five shall ye flee:	4480+6440
30:19	For the people shall dwell in Zion a	871.1
30:19	he will be very gracious unto thee a	3807.1
32: 9	Rise up, ye women that are a **ease**,	7600
32:11	Tremble, ye *women* that are a **ease;**	7600
33: 3	A the noise of the tumult the people fled;	4480
33: 3	a the lifting up of thyself the nations were	4480
37:22	of Jerusalem hath shaken her head a thee.	310
37:37	and returned, and dwelt a Nineveh.	871.1
39: 1	A that time Merodach-baladan, the son	871.1
42:14	I will destroy and devour a **once**.	3162
47:14	*shall* not be a coal to warm a, *nor* fire	3162
50: 2	Is my hand **shortened a all**, that	7114+7114
50: 2	behold, a my rebuke I dry up the sea,	871.1
51:17	which hast drunk a the hand of the LORD	4480
51:20	they lie a the head of all the streets, as a	871.1
52:14	As many were astonied a thee; his visage	5921
52:15	the kings shall shut their mouths a him:	5921
59:10	we stumble a noonday as *in* the night;	871.1
60: 4	thy daughters shall be nursed a *thy* side.	5921
60:14	themselves down a the soles of thy feet;	5921
64: 1	the mountains might flow down a thy	4480
64: 2	*that* the nations may tremble a thy	4480
64: 3	mountains flowed down a thy presence.	4480
66: 2	contrite spirit, and trembleth a my word.	5921
66: 5	to the LORD, ye that tremble a his word;	413
66: 8	*or* shall a nation be born a **once**? for	259+6471
Jer 1:15	they shall set every one his throne *a*	NIH
1:17	be not dismayed a their faces, lest I	4480
2:12	ye heavens, a this, and be horribly afraid,	5921
2:24	*that* snuffeth up the wind a her pleasure;	871.1
3:17	A that time they shall call Jerusalem	871.1
4: 9	it shall come to pass a that day, saith	871.1
4:11	A that time shall it be said to this people	871.1
4:19	I am pained a my very heart; my heart	NIH
4:26	all the cities thereof were broken down a	4480
5:22	will ye not tremble a my presence,	4480
6: 4	her; arise, and let us go up a noon.	871.1
6:15	nay, they were not a **all ashamed**,	954+954
6:15	a the time *that* I visit them they shall be	871.1
7: 2	that enter in a these gates to worship	871.1
7:12	where I set my name a the first,	871.1
8: 1	A that time, saith the LORD, they shall	871.1
8:12	nay, they were not a **all ashamed**,	954+954
8:16	the whole land trembled a the sound of	4480
10: 2	be not dismayed a the signs of heaven;	4480
10: 2	for the heathen are dismayed a them.	4480
10:10	a his wrath the earth shall tremble,	4480
10:18	sling out the inhabitants of the land a	871.1
11:12	they shall not **save** them a **all** in	3467+3467
15: 8	of the young men a spoiler a noonday:	871.1
17:11	of his days, and a his end shall be a fool.	871.1
17:27	even entering in a the gates of Jerusalem	871.1
18: 7	A *what* instant I shall speak concerning	NIH
18: 9	*a what* instant I shall speak concerning a	NIH
20:16	morning, and the shouting a noontide;	871.1
23:23	*Am* I a God a hand, saith the LORD,	4480
23:32	shall not **profit** this people a **all**,	3276+3276
25:15	the wine cup of this fury a mine hand,	4480
25:17	took I the cup a the LORD's hand,	4480
25:28	if they refuse to take the cup a thine hand	4480
25:33	the slain of the LORD shall be a that day	871.1
26:19	all Judah **put** him a **all to death**?	4191+4191
Jer 27:18	and a Jerusalem, go not to Babylon.	871.1
29:10	accomplished a Babylon I will visit you,	3807.1
29:25	unto all the people that *are* a Jerusalem,	871.1
31: 1	A the same time, saith the LORD, will I	871.1
31:12	shall not sorrow **any more a all**.	3254+5750
32:20	hast made thee a name, as a this day;	NIH
33: 7	and will build them, as a the first.	871.1
33:11	the captivity of the land as a the first,	871.1
33:15	In those days, and a that time, will I	871.1
34: 8	all the people which *were* a Jerusalem,	NIH
34:14	A the end of seven years let ye go every	4480
34:16	ye had set a liberty at their pleasure,	NIH
34:16	whom ye had set a liberty to their	3807.1
35:11	of the Syrians: so we dwell a Jerusalem.	871.1
36:10	in the higher court a the entry of the new	NIH
36:17	How didst thou write all these words a his	4480
36:27	words which Baruch wrote a the mouth	4480
39:10	vineyards and fields a the same time.	871.1
40:10	I *will* dwell a Mizpah to serve	871.1
41: 3	*even* with Gedaliah a Mizpah, and	871.1
43: 9	which *is* a the entry of Pharaoh's house	871.1
44: 1	which dwell a Migdol, and at Tahpanhes,	871.1
44: 1	a Tahpanhes, and at Noph, and in	871.1
44: 1	a Noph, and in the country of Pathros,	871.1
44: 6	are wasted *and* desolate, as a this day.	NIH
44:22	curse, without an inhabitant, as a this day.	NIH
44:23	evil is happened unto you, as *a* this day.	NIH
45: 1	words in a book a the mouth of Jeremiah,	4480
46:27	in rest and a **ease**, and none shall make	7599
47: 3	A the noise of the stamping of the hoofs	4480
47: 3	*horses,* a the rushing of his chariots,	4480
47: 3	*and a* the rumbling of his wheels,	4480
48:11	Moab hath been a **ease** from his youth,	7599
48:41	the mighty *men's* hearts in Moab a that	871.1
49:17	and shall hiss a all the plagues thereof.	5921
49:21	earth is moved a the noise of their fall,	4480
49:21	a the cry, the noise thereof was heard in	4480
49:22	a that day shall the heart of the mighty	871.1
50:11	ye are grown fat as the heifer a grass,	NIH
50:13	be astonished, and hiss a all her plagues.	5921
50:14	the bow, shoot a her, spare no arrows:	413
50:46	A the noise of the taking of Babylon	4480
51:31	Babylon that his city is taken a *one* end,	4480
51:49	a Babylon shall fall the slain of all.	3807.1
La 1: 7	saw her, *and* did mock a her sabbaths.	5921
1:20	bereaveth, a home *there is* as death.	871.1
2:15	All that pass by clap *their* hands a thee;	5921
2:15	their head a the daughter of Jerusalem,	5921
3:56	hide not thine ear a my breathing,	3807.1
3:56	not thine ear at my breathing, a my cry.	3807.1
Eze 2: 6	words, nor be dismayed a their looks,	4480
3: 9	not, neither be dismayed a their looks,	4480
3:15	I came to them of the captivity *a* Tel-abib,	NIH
3:16	it came to pass a the end of seven days,	4480
3:17	therefore hear the word a my mouth,	4480
3:18	but his blood will I require a thine hand.	4480
3:20	but his blood will I require a thine hand.	4480
8: 5	northward a the gate of the altar this	3807.1
8:16	*a* the door of the temple of the LORD,	NIH
9: 6	*is* the mark; and begin a my sanctuary.	4480
9: 6	they began a the ancient men which	871.1
10:19	*one* stood *a* the door of the east gate	NIH
11: 1	behold a the door of the gate five	871.1
12: 4	thou shalt go forth a even in their sight,	5921
12:23	The days are a **hand**, and the effect of	7126
14: 3	I be **inquired of a all** by them?	1875+1875
16: 4	thee; thou wast not **salted a all**,	4414+4414
16: 4	salted at all, nor **swaddled a all**.	2853+2853
16:25	Thou hast built thy high place a every	413
16:46	her daughters that dwell a thy left hand:	5921
16:46	that dwelleth a thy right hand, *is* Sodom	4480
16:57	as *a* the time of *thy* reproach of	NIH
18:23	Have I **any pleasure a all** that	2654+2654
20:32	into your mind shall not **be a all**,	1961+1961
21:19	a the head of the way to the city.	871.1
21:21	the king of Babylon stood a the parting	413
21:21	a the head of the two ways, to use	871.1
21:22	A his right hand was the divination for	871.1
22:13	I have smitten mine hand a thy dishonest	413
22:13	a thy blood which hath been in the midst	5921
23:42	a voice of a multitude being a **ease** *was*	7961
24:18	a even my wife died; and I did in	871.1
26:10	thy walls shall shake a the noise of	4480
26:15	Shall not the isles shake a the sound of	4480
26:16	shall tremble a every moment,	3807.1
26:16	every moment, and be astonished a thee.	5921
26:18	the sea shall be troubled a thy departure.	4480
27: 3	thou that art situate a the entry of the sea,	5921
27:28	The suburbs shall shake a the sound of	3807.1
27:35	of the isles shall be astonished a thee,	5921
27:36	among the people shall hiss a thee;	5921
28:19	the people shall be astonished a thee:	5921
29: 7	**madest** all their loins to be a a **stand**.	5976
29:13	A the end of forty years will I gather	4480
30:18	A Tehaphnehes also the day shall be	871.1
31:16	I made the nations to shake a the sound of	4480
32:10	I will make many people amazed a thee,	5921
32:10	they shall tremble a every moment,	3807.1
33: 6	his blood will I require a the watchman's	4480
33: 7	thou shalt hear the word a my mouth,	4480
33: 8	but his blood will I require a thine hand.	4480
34:10	I will require my flock a their hand,	4480
35:15	As thou didst rejoice a the inheritance	3807.1
36: 8	of Israel; for they are a **hand** to come.	7126
36:11	will do better *unto you* than a your	NIH

A

Eze	37:22	into two kingdoms **any more a all:**	5750+5750
	38:10	*that* **a** the same time shall things come	871.1
	38:11	will go to them that are **a rest,** that dwell	8252
	38:18	it shall come to pass **a** the same time	871.1
	38:20	shall shake **a** my presence,	4480
	39:20	Thus ye shall be filled **a** my table *with*	5921
	40:40	**a** the side without, as one goeth up to	413
	40:40	which *was* **a** the porch of the gate,	3807.1
	40:44	which *was* **a** the side of the north gate;	413
	40:44	one **a** the side of the east gate *having*	413
	41:12	**a** the end toward the west *was* seventy	NIH
	44:11	*having* charge **a** the gates of the house,	413
	44:17	*that* when they enter in **a** the gates of	413
	44:25	they shall come **a** no dead person to defile	413
	46: 2	shall worship **a** the threshold of the gate:	5921
	46: 3	**a** the door of this gate before the LORD in	NIH
	46:19	entry, which *was* **a** the side of the gate,	5921
	47: 1	of the house, **a** the south side of the altar.	4480
	47: 7	the bank of the river *were* very many	413
	48:28	border of Gad, **a** the south side southward,	413
	48:32	the east side four thousand	413
	48:33	**a** the south side four thousand	NIH
	48:34	**A** the west side four thousand	NIH
Da	1: 5	that **a** the end thereof they might stand	4480
	1:15	**a** the end of ten days their countenances	4480
	1:18	Now **a** the end of the days that the king	3807.1
	2:10	*that* asked such things **a** any magician,	3807.2
	3: 5	**a what time** ye hear	0.2+1768+5732+871.2
	3: 7	Therefore **a** that time, when all the	871.2
	3: 8	Wherefore **a** that time certain Chaldeans	871.2
	3:15	Now if ye be ready that **a** what time ye	871.2
	4: 4	I Nebuchadnezzar was **a** rest in mine	871.2
	4: 8	**a** the last Daniel came in before me,	5705
	4:29	**A** the end of twelve months he walked	3807.2
	4:34	**a** the end of the days I Nebuchadnezzar	3807.2
	4:36	**a** the same time my reason returned	871.2
	5: 3	house of God which *was* **a** Jerusalem;	871.2
	6:24	ever they came **a** the bottom of the den.	3807.2
	8: 1	after that which appeared unto me **a**	871.1
	8: 2	that I *was* **a** Shushan *in* the palace,	871.1
	8:17	**a** the time of the end *shall be* the vision.	3807.1
	8:19	**a** the time appointed the end *shall be*.	3807.1
	8:27	I was astonished **a** the vision,	5921
	9: 7	unto us confusion of faces, as, **a** this day;	NIH
	9:15	hast gotten thee renown, as **a** this day;	NIH
	9:21	whom I had seen in the vision **a**	871.1
	9:23	**A** the beginning of thy supplications	871.1
	10: 3	neither did I **anoint** myself **a all,**	5480+5480
	11:27	and they shall speak lies **a** one table;	5921
	11:27	for yet the end *shall be* **a** the time	3807.1
	11:29	**A** the time appointed he shall return,	3807.1
	11:40	**a** the time of the end shall the king of	871.1
	11:40	shall the king of the south push **a** him:	5973
	11:43	and the Ethiopians *shall be* **a** his steps.	871.1
	12: 1	**a** that time shall Michael stand up,	871.1
	12: 1	**a** that time thy people shall be delivered,	871.1
	12:13	stand in thy lot **a** the end of the days.	3807.1
Hos	1: 5	it shall come to pass **a** that day, that I	871.1
	2:16	it shall be **a** that day, saith the LORD,	871.1
	4:12	My people ask *counsel* **a** their stocks,	871.1
	5: 8	cry aloud **a** Beth-aven, after thee,	NIH
	9:10	firstripe in the fig tree **a** her first time:	871.1
	11: 7	most High, none **a all** would exalt *him.*	3162
Joel	1:15	for the day of the LORD *is* **a hand,**	7138
	2: 1	the LORD cometh, for *it is* **nigh a hand;**	7138
	2: 9	they shall enter in **a** the windows like a	1157
Am	1:13	they have ript up the women with child **a**	NIH
	3: 5	and have **taken** nothing **a all?**	3920+3920
	3: 9	Publish in the palaces **a** Ashdod, and in	871.1
	4: 3	ye shall go out **a** the breaches, every *cow*	NIH
	4: 3	every *cow* **a** that which *is* before her;	NIH
	4: 4	**a** Gilgal multiply transgression;	NIH
	6: 1	Woe to them that are **a ease** in Zion,	7600
	7:13	prophesy not again any more **a** Beth-el:	NIH
	8: 9	that I will cause the sun to go down **a**	871.1
Ob	1: 7	The men that were **a** peace with thee	NIH
Mic	1:10	Declare ye *it* not **a** Gath, weep ye not **a**t	871.1
	1:10	*it* not **a**t Gath, **weep** ye not **a all:**	1058+1058
	3: 4	will even hide his face from them **a** that	871.1
	7:16	and be confounded **a** all their might:	4480
Na	1: 3	will not **a all acquit** the wicked:	5352+5352
	1: 5	The mountains quake **a** him, and the hills	4480
	1: 5	the earth is burnt **a** his presence, yea,	4480
	3:10	in pieces **a** the top of all the streets:	871.1
Hab	1:10	they shall scoff **a** the kings, and the	871.1
	2: 3	but **a** the end it shall speak, and not lie:	3807.1
	2: 5	a proud man, neither **keepeth a home,**	5115
	2:19	*there is* no breath **a** all in the midst of it.	NIH
	3: 5	and burning coals went forth **a** his feet.	3807.1
	3:11	**a** the light of thine arrows they went,	3807.1
	3:11	*and* **a** the shining of thy glittering spear.	3807.1
	3:16	my lips quivered **a** the voice:	3807.1
Zep	1: 7	Hold thy peace **a** the presence of the Lord	4480
	1: 7	for the day of the LORD *is* **a hand:**	7138
	1:12	it shall come to pass **a** that time, *that* I	871.1
	2: 4	they shall drive out Ashdod **a** the noon	871.1
	3:19	**a** that time I *will* undo all that afflict thee:	871.1
	3:20	**A** that time will I bring you *again,* even	8252
Zec	1:11	all the earth sitteth still, and is **a rest.**	8252
	1:15	with the heathen *that are* **a ease:**	7600
	3: 1	Satan standing **a** his right hand to resist	5921
	3: 8	for they *are* men **wondered a:** for behold,	4159
	7: 5	ye **a all** fast *unto* me, *even* to me?	6684+6684
	11:13	a goodly price that I was prised **a** of them.	NIH
	12: 8	he that is feeble among them **a** that day	871.1

Zec	14: 7	*that* **a** evening time it shall be light.	3807.1
	14:14	Judah also shall fight **a** Jerusalem;	871.1
Mal	1:10	neither will I accept an offering **a** your	4480
	1:13	a weariness *is it!* and ye have snuffed **a** it,	NIH
	2: 7	and they should seek the law **a** his mouth:	4480
	2: 8	have caused many to stumble **a** the law;	871.1
	2:13	or receiveth *it with* good will **a** your hand.	4480
Mt	3: 2	for the kingdom of heaven is **a hand.**	1448
	4: 6	lest **a** any time thou dash thy foot against	3379
	4:17	for the kingdom of heaven is **a hand.**	1448
	5:25	lest **a** any time the adversary deliver thee	3379
	5:34	But I say unto you, Swear not **a all;**	3654
	5:40	And if any man will sue thee **a the law,**	2919
	7:13	Enter ye in **a** the strait gate: for wide *is*	1223
	7:28	the people were astonished **a** his doctrine:	1909
	8: 6	my servant lieth **a** home sick of the palsy,	1722
	9: 9	sitting **a** the receipt of custom:	1909
	9:10	as Jesus **sat a meat** in the house, behold,	345
	10: 7	saying, The kingdom of heaven is **a hand.**	1448
	10:35	For I am come to **set a** man **a variance**	1369
	11:22	for Tyre and Sidon **a** the day of judgment,	1722
	11:25	**A** that time Jesus answered and said,	1722
	12: 1	**A** that time Jesus went on the sabbath day	1722
	12:41	they repented **a** the preaching of Jonas;	1519
	13:15	lest **a** any time they should see with	3379
	13:49	So shall it be **a** the end of the world:	1722
	14: 1	**A** that time Herod the tetrarch heard of	1722
	14: 9	and them which **sat with** him **a meat,**	4873
	15:17	that whatsoever entereth in **a** the mouth	NIH
	15:30	and cast them *down* **a** Jesus' feet;	3844
	18: 1	**A** the same time came the disciples unto	1722
	18:29	And his fellowservant fell down **a** his feet,	1519
	19: 4	that he which made *them* **a** the beginning	575
	22:33	*this,* they were astonished **a** his doctrine.	1909
	23: 6	And love the uppermost rooms **a** feasts,	1722
	24:33	know that it is near, *even* **a** the doors.	1909
	24:41	Two *women shall be* grinding **a** the mill;	1722
	25: 6	And **a midnight** there was a cry	3319+3571
	25:27	**a** my coming I should have received mine	NIH
	26: 7	poured *it* on his head, as he **sat a meat.**	345
	26:18	The Master saith, My time is **a hand;**	1451
	26:18	I will keep the passover **a** thy house with	4314
	26:45	the hour is **a hand,** and the Son of man is	1448
	26:46	behold, he is **a hand** that doth betray me.	1448
	26:60	**A** the last came two false witnesses,	5306
	27:15	Now **a** *that* feast the governor was wont	2596
Mk	1:15	and the kingdom of God is **a hand:**	1448
	1:22	And they were astonished **a** his doctrine:	1909
	1:32	And **a** even, when the sun did set,	1096+3798
	1:33	And all the city was gathered together **a**	4314
	2:14	he saw Levi the *son* of Alpheus sitting **a**	1909
	2:15	that as *Jesus* **sat a meat** in his house,	2621
	4:12	lest **a** any time they should be converted,	3379
	5:22	and when he saw him, he fell **a** his feet,	4314
	5:23	**lieth a the point of death:**	2079+2192
	6: 3	with us? And they were offended **a** him.	1722
	7:25	heard of him, and came and fell **a** his feet:	4314
	9:12	suffer many *things,* and be **set a nought.**	1847
	10:22	And he was sad **a** *that* saying,	1909
	10:24	And the disciples were astonished **a** his	1909
	11: 1	and Bethany, **a** the mount of Olives,	4314
	11:18	all the people was astonished **a** his	1909
	12: 2	**a** the season he sent to the husbandmen	NIH
	12: 4	and **a** him they cast stones,	NIH
	12:17	that are God's. And they marvelled **a** him.	1909
	12:39	and the uppermost rooms **a** feasts:	1722
	13:29	know that it is nigh, *even* **a** the doors.	1909
	13:35	**a** even, or at midnight, or at	3796
	13:35	or **a** midnight, or at the cockcrowing, or	3317
	13:35	or **a** the cockcrowing, or in the morning:	NIH
	14: 3	of Simon the leper, as he **sat a meat,**	2621
	14:42	us go; lo, he that betrayeth me is **a hand.**	1448
	14:54	servants, and warmed himself **a** the fire.	4314
	15: 6	Now **a** *that* feast he released unto them	2596
	15:34	And **a** the ninth hour Jesus cried with	NIG
	16: 2	they came unto the sepulchre **a** the rising	NIG
	16:14	unto the eleven as they **sat a meat,**	345
Lk	1:10	praying without **a** the time of incense.	NIG
	1:14	and many shall rejoice **a** his birth.	1909
	1:29	when she saw *him,* she was troubled **a**	1909
	2:18	all they that heard *it* wondered **a** those	4012
	2:33	his mother marvelled **a** those *things*	1909
	2:41	every year **a** the feast of the passover.	NIG
	2:47	And all that heard him were astonished **a**	1909
	4:11	lest **a** any time thou dash thy foot against	3379
	4:18	to **set a** liberty *them that are* bruised,	1722
	4:22	wondered **a** the gracious words which	1909
	4:32	And they were astonished **a** his doctrine:	1909
	5: 5	nevertheless **a** thy word I will let down	1909
	5: 8	When Simon Peter saw *it,* he **fell down a**	4363
	5: 9	**a** the draught of the fishes which they had	1909
	5:27	Levi, sitting **a** the receipt of custom:	1909
	7: 9	heard these *things,* he marvelled **a** him,	NIG
	7:37	when she knew that *Jesus* **sat a meat** in	345
	7:38	And stood **a** his feet behind *him* weeping,	3844
	7:49	And they that **sat a meat with** *him* began	4873
	8:19	and could not **come a** him for the press.	4940
	8:26	And they arrived **a** the country of	1519
	8:35	sitting **a** the feet of Jesus, clothed,	3844
	8:41	and he fell down **a** Jesus' feet,	3844
	9:31	which he should accomplish **a** Jerusalem.	1722
	9:43	And they were all amazed **a** the mighty	1909
	9:43	But while they wondered every one **a** all	1909
	9:61	which are **a** *home* in my house.	NIG
	10:14	for Tyre and Sidon **a** the judgment,	1722

Lk	10:32	when he was **a** the place, came	2596
	10:39	which also sat **a** Jesus' feet, and heard his	3844
	11: 5	and shall go unto him **a** midnight,	NIG
	11:32	for they repented **a** the preaching of Jonas;	1519
	12:40	for the Son of man cometh **a** an hour	NIG
	12:46	and **a** an hour when he is not ware,	1722
	13: 1	There were present **a** that season some	1722
	13:24	Strive to enter in **a** the strait gate:	1223
	13:25	to knock **a** the door, saying, Lord, Lord,	NIG
	14:10	for then that **sit a meat with** thee.	4873
	14:14	for thou shalt be recompensed **a**	1722
	14:15	**sat a meat with** him heard these *things,*	4873
	14:17	And sent his servant **a** supper time to say	5610
	15:29	**neither** transgressed I **a** any time	2532+3763
	16:20	which was laid **a** his gate, full of sores,	4314
	17:16	And fell down on *his* face **a** his feet,	3844
	19: 5	for to day I must abide **a** thy house.	1722
	19:23	that **a** my coming I might have required	NIG
	19:29	**a** the mount called *the mount of* Olives,	4314
	19:30	**a** your entering ye shall find a colt tied,	NIG
	19:37	*even* now **a** the descent of the mount of	4314
	19:42	even thou, **a** least in this thy day,	1065+2532
	20:10	And **a** the season he sent a servant to	1722
	20:26	and they marvelled **a** his answer,	1909
	20:37	raised, even Moses shewed **a** the bush,	1909
	20:40	they durst not ask him any *question* **a** all.	NIG
	20:46	and the chief rooms **a** feasts;	1722
	21:30	selves that summer is now **nigh a hand.**	1451
	21:31	that the kingdom of God is **nigh a hand.**	1451
	21:34	lest **a** any time your hearts be	3379
	21:37	and **a** night he went out, and abode in	NIG
	22:27	he that **sitteth a meat,** or he that serveth?	345
	22:27	*is* not he that **sitteth a meat?** but I am	345
	22:30	and drink **a** my table in my kingdom,	1909
	22:40	And when he was **a** the place, he said	1909
	23: 7	who himself also was **a** Jerusalem at that	1722
	23: 7	who himself also was at Jerusalem **a** that	1722
	23:11	with his men of war **set** him **a nought,**	1848
	23:12	for before they were **a** enmity between	1722
	23:17	must release one unto them **a** the feast.)	2596
	23:18	And they cried out **all a** once, saying,	3826
	24:12	wondering in himself **a** that which was	NIG
	24:22	which were early **a** the sepulchre;	1909
	24:27	beginning **a** Moses and all the prophets,	575
	24:30	he **sat a meat** with them, he took bread,	2625
	24:47	among all nations, beginning **a** Jerusalem.	575
Jn	1:18	No *man* hath seen God **a** any time;	4455
	2:10	Every man **a the beginning** doth set forth	4412
	2:13	And the Jews' passover was **a hand,**	1451
	2:23	Now when he was in Jerusalem **a**	1722
	4:21	nor *yet* **a** Jerusalem, worship the Father.	1722
	4:45	having seen all the *things* that he did **a**	1722
	4:45	*things* that he did at Jerusalem **a** the feast:	1722
	4:46	whose son was sick **a** Capernaum.	1722
	4:47	his son: for he was **a the point** of death.	3195
	4:52	Yesterday **a** the seventh hour the fever left	NIG
	4:53	So the father knew that *it was* **a** the same	1722
	5: 2	Now there is **a** Jerusalem by the sheep	1722
	5: 4	an angel went down **a a** *certain* season	2596
	5:28	Marvel not **a** this: for the hour is coming,	NIG
	5:37	have neither heard his voice **a** any time,	4455
	6:21	immediately the ship was **a** the land	1909
	6:39	but should raise it up **a**gain **a** the last day.	1722
	6:40	and I will raise him up **a** the last day.	NIG
	6:41	The Jews then murmured **a** him, because	4012
	6:44	and I will raise him up **a** the last day.	NIG
	6:54	and I will raise him up **a** the last day.	NIG
	6:61	himself that his disciples murmured **a** it,	4012
	7: 2	the Jews' feast of tabernacles was **a hand.**	1451
	7:11	Then the Jews sought him **a** the feast,	1722
	7:23	are ye angry **a** me, because I have made **a**	1909
	8: 7	among you, let him first cast a stone **a** her.	1909
	8: 9	beginning **a** the eldest, *even* unto the last:	575
	8:59	Then took they up stones to cast **a** him:	1909
	10:22	And it was **a** Jerusalem *the feast of*	1722
	10:40	into the place where John **a first** baptized;	4412
	11:24	rise again in the resurrection **a** the last day.	1722
	11:32	and saw him, she fell down **a** his feet,	1519
	11:49	unto them, Ye know **nothing a all,**	3756+3762
	11:55	And the Jews' passover was **nigh a hand:**	1451
	12: 2	them that **sat a the table with** him.	4873
	12:16	understood not his disciples **a the first:**	4412
	12:20	them that came up to worship **a** the feast:	NIG
	13:28	Now no *man* **a** the table knew for what	NIG
	14:20	**A** that day ye shall know that I *am* in my	1722
	16: 4	And these *things* I said not unto you **a**	1537
	16:26	**A** that day ye shall ask in my name:	1722
	18:16	But Peter stood **a** the door without.	4314
	18:38	unto them, I find in him no fault **a** all.	NIG
	18:39	that I should release unto you one **a**	1722
	19:11	Thou couldest have no power **a** all against	NIG
	19:39	which **a** the first came to Jesus by night,	NIG
	19:42	*day;* for the sepulchre was **nigh a hand.**	1451
	20:11	But Mary stood without **a** the sepulchre	4314
	20:12	one **a** the head, and the other at the feet,	4314
	20:12	one at the head, and the other **a** the feet,	4314
	20:19	the same day **a** evening, being the first	NIG
	21: 1	again to the disciples **a** the sea of Tiberias;	1909
	21:20	which also leaned on his breast **a** supper,	1909
Ac	1: 6	wilt thou **a** this time restore again	1722
	1:19	And it was known unto all the dwellers **a**	1722
	2: 5	And there were dwelling **a** Jerusalem Jews,	1722
	2:14	of Judea, and all *ye* that dwell **a** Jerusalem,	NIG
	3: 1	John went up together into the temple **a**	1909
	3: 2	whom they laid daily **a** the gate of	4314

A

Ac 3:10 for alms **a** the Beautiful gate of the temple: *1909*
3:10 amazement **a** that which had happened *1909*
3:12 Ye men of Israel, why marvel ye **a** this? *1909*
4: 6 were gathered together **a** Jerusalem. *1519*
4:11 This is the stone which was **set a nought** *1848*
4:18 commanded them not to speak **a** all nor *2527*
4:35 And laid *them down* **a** the apostles' feet. *3844*
4:37 the money, and laid *it* **a** the apostles' feet. *3844*
5: 2 certain part, and laid *it* **a** the apostles' feet. *3844*
5: 9 have buried thy husband *are* **a** the door, *1909*
5:10 Then fell she down straightway at his feet, *3844*
5:15 **a the least** the shadow of Peter passing *2579*
7:13 And **a** the second time Joseph was made *1722*
7:26 **set** them **a one** *again,* *1515+1519+4900*
7:29 Then fled Moses **a** this saying, and was a *1722*
7:31 When Moses saw *it,* he wondered **a** NIG
7:58 the witnesses laid down their clothes **a** *3844*
8: 1 And **a** that time there was a great *1722*
8: 1 against the church which was **a** Jerusalem; *1722*
8:14 Now when the apostles which were **a** *1722*
8:35 and began **a** the same scripture, *575*
8:40 But Philip was found **a** Azotus: *1519*
9:10 And there was a certain disciple **a** *1722*
9:13 much evil he hath done to thy saints **a** *1722*
9:19 the disciples which were **a** Damascus. *1722*
9:22 confounded the Jews which dwelt **a** *1722*
9:27 how he had preached boldly **a** Damascus *1722*
9:28 coming in and going out **a** Jerusalem. *1519*
9:32 also to the saints which dwelt **a** Lydda. NIG
9:35 And all that dwelt **a** Lydda and Saron saw NIG
9:36 Now there was **a** Joppa a certain disciple *1722*
10:11 as *it had been* a great sheet knit **a** the four NIG
10:25 and fell down **a** *his* feet, *1909*
10:30 **a** the ninth hour I prayed in my house, *3360*
11: 8 **nothing** common or unclean hath
 a any time *3763+3956*
11:15 fell on them, as on us **a** the beginning. *1722*
12:13 as Peter knocked **a** the door of the gate, NIG
13: 1 Now there were in the church that was **a** *1722*
13: 5 And when they were **a** Salamis, *1722*
13:12 astonished **a** the doctrine of the Lord. *1909*
13:27 For they that dwell **a** Jerusalem, *1722*
14: 8 And there sat a certain man **a** Lystra, *1722*
15:14 Simeon hath declared how God **a** the first NIG
16: 2 of by the brethren that were **a** Lystra *1722*
16: 4 and elders which were **a** Jerusalem. *1722*
16:25 And **a** midnight Paul and Silas prayed, *2596*
17:13 of God was preached of Paul **a** Berea, *1722*
17:16 while Paul waited for them **a** Athens, *1722*
17:30 times of *this* ignorance God **winked a**; *5237*
18:22 And when he had landed **a** Cesarea, *1519*
18:24 born **a** **Alexandria**, an eloquent man, *221*
19: 1 to pass that, while Apollos was **a** Corinth, *1722*
19:17 and Greeks also **dwelling a** Ephesus; *2730*
19:26 that not alone **a** Ephesus, NIG
19:27 our craft is in danger to be **set a** nought; *1519*
20: 5 These going before tarried for us **a** Troas. *1722*
20:14 when he met with us **a** Assos, we took *1519*
20:15 and the next *day* we arrived **a** Samos, *1519*
20:15 at Samos, and tarried **a** Trogyllium; *1722*
20:16 to be **a** Jerusalem the day of Pentecost. *1519*
20:18 after what manner I have been with you **a** NIG
21: 3 and sailed into Syria, and landed **a** Tyre: *1519*
21:11 shall the Jews **a** Jerusalem bind the man *1722*
21:13 also to die **a** Jerusalem for the name of *1519*
21:24 with them, and be **a** charges with them, *1722*
22: 3 yet brought up in this city **a** the feet of *3844*
23:11 so must thou bear witness also **a** Rome. *1519*
23:23 hundred, **a** the third hour of the night; *575*
25: 4 that Paul should be kept **a** Cesarea, *1722*
25: 8 have I offended any *thing* **a** all. NIG
25:10 said Paul, I stand **a** Cesar's judgment seat, *1909*
25:15 About whom, when I was **a** Jerusalem, *1519*
25:23 a Festus' commandment Paul was brought NIG
25:24 both **a** Jerusalem, and *also* here, *1722*
26: 4 which was **a** the first among mine own *575*
26: 4 first among mine own nation **a** Jerusalem, *1722*
26:13 **A** midday, O king, I saw in the *2250+3319*
26:20 and **a** Jerusalem, and throughout all NIG
26:32 This man might have been **set a liberty**, *630*
27: 3 And the next *day* we touched **a** Sidon. *1519*
28:12 And landing **a** Syracuse, we tarried *there* *1519*

Ro 1:10 if by any means now **a length** I might *4218*
1:15 the gospel to you that are **a** Rome also. *1722*
3:26 *I say,* **a** this time his righteousness: *1722*
4:20 He staggered not **a** the promise of God *1519*
8:34 that is risen *again,* who is even **a** the right *1722*
9: 9 **A** this time will I come, and Sara shall *2596*
9:32 For they stumbled **a** *that* stumblingstone; NIG
11: 5 **a** *this* present time also there is a remnant *1722*
13:12 The night is far spent, the day is **a** hand: *1448*
14:10 why dost thou **set a nought** thy brother? *1848*
15:26 for the poor saints which are **a** Jerusalem. *1722*
16: 1 is a servant of the church which is **a** *1722*
16: S *sent* by Phebe servant of the church **a** *1722*
1Co 1: 2 the church of God which is **a** Corinth, *1722*
7:39 she is **a** liberty to be married to whom she NIG
8:10 knowledge **sit a meat** in the idol's temple *2621*
9: 7 Who goeth a warfare any time **a** his own NIG
9:13 they which **wait a** the altar are partakers *4332*
11:34 if any *man* hunger, let him eat **a** home; *1722*
14:16 say Amen **a** thy giving of thanks, *1909*
14:27 or **a** the most *by* three, and *that* by course; NIG
14:35 *thing,* let them ask their husbands **a** home: *1722*
15: 6 of above five hundred brethren **a** once, *2178*

1Co 15:23 afterward they that are Christ's **a** his *1722*
15:29 for the dead, if the dead rise not **a all**? *3654*
15:32 men I have fought with beasts **a** Ephesus, *1722*
15:52 the twinkling of an eye, **a** the last trump: *1722*
16: 8 But I will tarry **a** Ephesus until Pentecost. *1722*
16:12 *his* will was not **a all** to come at this time; *3843*
16:12 will was not at all to come **a this time**; *3568*
2Co 1: 1 the church of God which is **a** Corinth, *1722*
1:18 While we **look** not **a** the **things** which *4648*
4:18 but **a** the *things* which are not seen: NIG
5: 6 whilst we are **a home** in the body, *1736*
8:14 *that* now **a** *this* time your abundance *may* *1722*
Gal 4:12 as ye *are:* ye have **not** injured me **a all**. *3762*
4:13 I preached the gospel unto you **a** the **first**. *4387*
Eph 1: 1 to the saints which are **a** Ephesus, *1722*
1:20 set *him* **a** his own right hand in *1722*
2:12 That **a** that time ye were without Christ, *1722*
3:13 Wherefore I desire that *ye* faint not **a** my *1722*
Php 1: 1 all the saints in Christ Jesus which are **a** *1722*
2:10 That **a** the name of Jesus every knee *1722*
4: 5 known unto all men. The Lord *is* **a** hand. *1451*
4:10 that now **a** the **last** your care of me hath *4218*
Col 1: 2 faithful brethren in Christ which are **a** *1722*
2: 1 and *for* them **a** Laodicea, and *for* as many *1722*
1Th 2: 2 as ye know, **a** Philippi, *1722*
2: 5 For neither **a any time** used we flattering *1722*
2:19 our Lord Jesus Christ **a** his coming? *1722+3588*
3: 1 we thought it good to be left **a** Athens *1722*
3:13 **a** the coming of our Lord Jesus Christ with *1722*
5:13 *And* be **a** peace among yourselves. NIG
2Th 2: 2 us, as that the day of Christ is **a** hand. *1764*
2:17 working **not a all**, but are busybodies. *3367*
1Ti 1: 3 As I besought thee to abide *still* **a** Ephesus, *1722*
5: 4 let them learn first to shew piety **a** home, NIG
2Ti 1:18 *things* he ministered *unto* me **a** Ephesus, *1722*
2:26 *who are* taken captive by him **a** his will. *1519*
3:11 which came unto me **a** Antioch, *1722*
3:11 unto me at Antioch, **a** Iconium, at Lystra; *1722*
3:11 unto me at Antioch, at Iconium, **a** Lystra; *1722*
4: 1 and the dead **a** his appearing and his *2596*
4: 6 and the time of my departure is **a** hand. *2186*
4: 8 righteous judge, shall give me **a** that day: *1722*
4:13 The cloke that I left **a** Troas with Carpus, *1722*
4:16 **A** my first answer no *man* stood with me, *1722*
4:20 Erastus abode **a** Corinth: *1722*
4:20 but Trophimus have I left **a** Miletum sick. *1722*
Tit 2: 5 discreet, chaste, **keepers a home**, good, *3626*
Heb 1: 1 God, who **a** **sundry** times and in divers *3588*
1: 5 which of the angels said he **a any time**, *4218*
1:13 to which of the angels said he **a any time**, *4218*
2: 1 lest **a any time** we should let *them* slip. *3379*
2: 3 which **a** the first began to be spoken by NIG
7:13 of which no *man* **gave attendance a** *4337*
9:17 otherwise it is of **no** strength **a all** whilst *3379*
12: 2 set down **a** the right hand of the throne of *1722*
12:23 that *our* brother Timothy is **set a liberty**; *630*
Jas 3:11 a fountain send forth **a** the same place *1537*
1Pe 1: 7 and glory **a** the appearing of Jesus Christ: *1722*
1:13 unto you **a** the revelation of Jesus Christ; *1722*
2: 8 *even to them* which stumble **a** the word, NIG
4: 7 But the end of all *things* is **a** hand: *1448*
4:17 judgment must begin **a** the house of God: *575*
4:17 if *it* first **begin a** us, what *shall* the end *575*
5:13 The *church that is* **a** Babylon, *1722*
1Jn 1: 5 is light, and in him is no darkness **a** all. NIG
2:28 not be ashamed before him **a** his coming. *1722*
4:12 No *man* hath seen God **a any time**. *4455*
Rev 1: 3 written therein: for the time *is* **a** hand. *1451*
1:17 when I saw him, I fell **a** his feet as dead. *4314*
3:20 Behold, I stand **a** the door, and knock: *1909*
8: 3 another angel came and stood **a** the altar, *1909*
18:14 find them **no more a all**. *3361+3756+3765*
18:21 and shall be found **no** more **a all**. *3364*
18:22 shall be heard **no** more **a all** in thee; *3364*
18:22 shall be heard **no** more **a all** in thee; *3364*
18:23 a candle shall shine **no** more **a all** in thee; *3364*
18:23 the bride shall be heard **no** more **a all** in *3364*
19: 2 hath avenged the blood of his servants **a** *1537*
19:10 And I fell **a** his feet to worship him. *1715*
21:12 and **a** the gates twelve angels, *1909*
21:25 the gates of it shall **not** be shut **a all** by *3364*
22:10 the **a** of this book: for the time is **a** hand. *1451*

ATAD (2)

Ge 50:10 they came to the threshingfloor of **A**, *329*
50:11 saw the mourning in the floor of **A**, they *329*

ATARAH (1)

1Ch 2:26 also another wife, whose name *was* **A**; *5851*

ATAROTH (5)

Nu 32: 3 **A**, and Dibon, and Jazer, and Nimrah, *5852*
32:34 of Gad built Dibon, and **A**, and Aroer, *5852*
Jos 16: 2 along unto the borders of Archi *to* **A**, *5852*
16: 7 it went down from Janohah *to* **A**, *5852*
1Ch 2:54 **A**, the house of Joab, and half of *5852*

ATAROTH-ADAR (1) [ATAROTH-ADDAR]

Jos 18:13 the border descended *to* **A**, near the hill *5853*

ATAROTH-ADDAR (1) [ATAROTH-ADAR]

Jos 16: 5 of their inheritance on the east side was **A**, *5853*

ATE (3) [EAT]

Ps 106:28 and the sacrifices of the dead. *398*

Da 10: 3 I **a** no pleasant bread, neither came flesh *398*
Rev 10:10 book out of the angel's hand, and **a** it **up**; *2719*

ATER (5)

Ezr 2:16 The children of **A** of Hezekiah, ninety *333*
2:42 the children of **A**, the children of Talmon, *333*
Ne 7:21 The children of **A** of Hezekiah, ninety *333*
7:45 the children of **A**, the children of Talmon, *333*
10:17 **A**, Hizkijah, Azzur, *333*

ATHACH (1)

1Sa 30:30 and to *them* which *were* in **A**, *6269*

ATHAIAH (1)

Ne 11: 4 **A** the son of Uzziah, the son of Zechariah, *6265*

ATHALIAH (17)

2Ki 8:26 his mother's name *was* **A**, the daughter of *6271*
11: 1 When **A** the mother of Ahaziah saw that *6271*
11: 2 in the bedchamber from **A**, so that he was *6271*
11: 3 six years. And **A** *did* reign over the land. *6271*
11:13 when **A** heard the noise of the guard *and* *6271*
11:14 **A** rent her clothes, and cried, Treason, *6271*
11:20 they slew **A** with the sword *beside* *6271*
1Ch 8:26 And Shamsherai, and Shehariah, and **A**, *6271*
2Ch 22: 2 his mother's name also *was* **A** *6271*
22:10 when **A** the mother of Ahaziah saw that *6271*
22:11 hid him from **A**, so that she slew him not. *6271*
22:12 six years: and **A** *reigned* over the land. *6271*
23:12 when **A** heard the noise of the people *6271*
23:13 **A** rent her clothes, and said, Treason, *6271*
23:21 that they had slain **A** with the sword. *6271*
24: 7 For the sons of **A**, *that* wicked woman, *6271*
Ezr 8: 7 Jeshaiah the son of **A**, and with him *6271*

ATHENIANS (1) [ATHENS]

Ac 17:21 (For all the **A** and strangers which were *117*

ATHENS (7) [ATHENIANS]

Ac 17:15 that conducted Paul brought him unto **A**: *116*
17:16 Now while Paul waited for them **a**, his *116*
17:22 midst of Mars' hill, and said, Ye men of **A**, *117*
18: 1 After these *things* Paul departed from **A**, *116*
1Th 3: 1 we thought it good to be left **a A** alone; *116*
5: S the Thessalonians was written from **A**. *116*
2Th 3: S to the Thessalonians was written from **A**. *116*

ATHIRST (5) [THIRST]

Jdg 15:18 he was sore **a**, and called on the LORD, *6770*
Ru 2: 9 when thou art **a**, go unto the vessels, *6770*
Mt 25:44 or **a**, or a stranger, or naked, or sick, or *1372*
Rev 21: 6 will give unto him that is **a** of the fountain *1372*
22:17 And let him that is **a** come. *1372*

ATHLAI (1)

Ezr 10:28 Jehohanan, Hananiah, Zabbai, *and* **A**. *6270*

ATONEMENT (81) [ATONEMENTS]

Ex 29:33 those *things* wherewith the **a** was **made**, *3722*
29:36 every day a bullock *for* a sin offering for **a**: *3725*
29:36 when thou hast **made** an **a** for it, *3722*
29:37 Seven days thou shalt **make** an **a** for *3722*
30:10 Aaron shall **make** an **a** upon the horns of *3722*
30:10 once in the year shall he **make** an **a** upon it *3722*
30:15 the LORD, to **make** an **a** for your souls. *3722*
30:16 shalt take the money of the children *3725*
30:16 the LORD, to **make** an **a** for your souls. *3722*
32:30 peradventure I shall **make** an **a** for your *3722*
Lev 1: 4 shall be accepted for him to **make** an **a** for *3722*
4:20 the priest shall **make** an **a** for them, *3722*
4:26 the priest shall **make** an **a** for him as *3722*
4:31 the priest shall **make** an **a** for him, *3722*
4:35 the priest shall **make** an **a** for his sin that *3722*
5: 6 the priest shall **make** an **a** for him *3722*
5:10 the priest shall **make** an **a** for him for his *3722*
5:13 the priest shall **make** an **a** for him as *3722*
5:16 the priest shall **make** an **a** for him with *3722*
5:18 the priest shall **make** an **a** for him *3722*
6: 7 the priest shall **make** an **a** for him before *3722*
7: 7 the priest that **maketh** a therewith shall *3722*
8:34 commanded to do, to **make** an **a** for you. *3722*
9: 7 **make** an **a** for thyself, and for the people: *3722*
9: 7 of the people, and **make** an **a** for them; *3722*
10:17 to **make** a for them before the LORD? *3722*
12: 7 before the LORD, and **make** an **a** for her; *3722*
12: 8 the priest shall **make** an **a** for her, *3722*
14:18 the priest shall **make** an **a** for him before *3722*
14:19 **make** an **a** for him that is to be cleansed *3722*
14:20 the priest shall **make** an **a** for him, *3722*
14:21 to **make** an **a** for him, and one tenth deal *3722*
14:29 to **make** an **a** for him before the LORD. *3722*
14:31 the priest shall **make** an **a** for him that *3722*
14:53 open fields, and **make** an **a** for the house: *3722*
15:15 the priest shall **make** an **a** for him before *3722*
15:30 the priest shall **make** an **a** for her before *3722*
16: 6 **make** an **a** for himself, and for his house. *3722*
16:10 to **make** an **a** with him, *and* to let him go *3722*
16:11 shall **make** an **a** for himself, and for his *3722*
16:16 he shall **make** an **a** for the holy *place*, *3722*
16:17 **make** an **a** in the holy *place*, until he *3722*
16:17 have **made** an **a** for himself, and for his *3722*
16:18 *is* before the LORD, and **make** an **a** for it; *3722*
16:24 **make** an **a** for himself, and for the people *3722*
16:27 blood was brought in to **make** a in *3722*
16:30 on that day shall *the priest* **make** an **a** *3722*
16:32 **make** the **a**, and shall put on the linen *3722*

A

Lev 16:33 shall **make an a** for the holy sanctuary, 3722
16:33 he shall **make an a** for the tabernacle of 3722
16:33 he shall **make an a** for the priests, 3722
16:34 to **make an a** for the children of Israel for 3722
17:11 the altar to **make an a** for your souls: 3722
17:11 for it *is* the blood *that* **maketh an a** for 3722
19:22 the priest shall **make an a** for him with 3722
23:27 seventh month *there shall be* a day of **a:** 3725
23:28 for it *is* a day of **a**, to make an atonement 3725
23:28 to **make an a** for you before the Lord 3722
25: 9 in the day of **a** shall ye make the trumpet 3725
Nu 5: 8 beside the ram of the **a**, whereby an 3725
5: 8 whereby an **a** shall be **made** for him. 3722
6:11 a burnt offering, and **make an a** for him, 3722
8:12 the Lord, to **make an a** for the Levites. 3722
8:19 to **make an a** for the children of Israel: 3722
8:21 Aaron **made an a** for them to cleanse 3722
15:25 the priest shall **make an a** for all 3722
15:28 the priest shall **make an a** for the soul 3722
15:28 before the Lord, to **make an a** for him; 3722
16:46 congregation, and **make an a** for the people. 3722
16:47 incense, and **made an a** for the people. 3722
25:13 and **made an a** for the children of Israel. 3722
28:22 for a sin offering, to **make an a** for you. 3722
28:30 kid of the goats, to **make an a** for you. 3722
29: 5 for a sin offering, to **make an a** for you; 3722
29:11 beside the sin offering of **a,** 3725
31:50 to **make an a** for our souls before 3722
2Sa 21: 3 wherewith shall I **make an a**, that ye 3722
1Ch 6:49 most holy, and to **make an a** for Israel, 3722
2Ch 29:24 upon the altar, to **make an a** for all Israel: 3722
Ne 10:33 for the sin offerings to **make an a** for a 3722
Ro 5:11 by whom we have now received the **a.** 2643

ATONEMENTS (1) [ATONEMENT]
Ex 30:10 with the blood of the sin offering of **a:** 3725

ATROTH SHOPHAN (1)
Nu 32:35 **A**, and Jaazer, and Jogbehah, 5855

ATTAI (4)
1Ch 2:35 his servant to wife; and she bare him **A**. 6262
2:36 **A** begat Nathan, and Nathan begat Zabad, 6262
12:11 **A** the sixth, Eliel the seventh, 6262
2Ch 11:20 and **A**, and Ziza, and Shelomith. 6262

ATTAIN (6) [ATTAINED]
Ps 139: 6 for me; it is high, I cannot **a** unto it. 3807.1
Pr 1: 5 a man of understanding shall **a** unto wise 7069
Eze 46: 7 lambs according as his hand shall **a** unto, 5381
Hos 8: 5 long *will it be* ere they **a** to innocency? 3201
Ac 27:12 if by any means they might **a** to Phenice, 2658
Php 3:11 If by any means I might **a** unto 2658

ATTAINED (10) [ATTAIN]
Ge 47: 9 have not **a** unto the days of the years of 5381
2Sa 23:19 howbeit he **a** not unto the *first* three. 935
23:23 the thirty, but he **a** not to the *first* three. 935
1Ch 11:21 howbeit he **a** not to the *first* three. 935
11:25 the thirty, but **a** not to the *first* three: 935
Ro 9:30 have **a** to righteousness, 2638
9:31 hath not **a** to the law of righteousness. 5348
Php 3:12 Not as though I had already **a**, either were 2983
3:16 Nevertheless, whereto we have *already* **a,** 5348
1Ti 4: 6 of good doctrine, whereunto thou hast **a.** 3877

ATTALIA (1)
Ac 14:25 word in Perga, they went down into **A:** 825

ATTEND (11) [ATTENDANCE, ATTENDED, ATTENDING, ATTENT, ATTENTIVE, ATTENTIVELY]
Est 4: 5 whom he had appointed to **a upon** her, 6440
Ps 17: 1 Hear the right, O Lord, **a unto** my cry, 7181
55: 2 **A** unto me, and hear me: I mourn in my 7181
61: 1 Hear my cry, O God; **a** unto my prayer. 7181
86: 6 and **a** to the voice of my supplications. 7181
142: 6 **A** unto my cry; for I am brought very low: 7181
Pr 4: 1 of a father, and **a** to know understanding. 7181
4:20 My son, **a** to my words; incline thine ear 7181
5: 1 **a** unto my wisdom, *and* bow thine ear to 7181
7:24 and **a** to the words of my mouth. 7181
1Co 7:35 that you may **a upon** the Lord without 2145

ATTENDANCE (4) [ATTEND]
1Ki 10: 5 the **a** of his ministers, and their apparel, 4612
2Ch 9: 4 the **a** of his ministers, and their apparel; 4612
1Ti 4:13 Till I come, give **a** to reading, 4337
Heb 7:13 of which no *man* **gave a at** the altar. 4337

ATTENDED (3) [ATTEND]
Job 32:12 Yea, I **a** unto you, and behold, *there was* 995
Ps 66:19 verily God hath heard *me;* he hath **a** to 7181
Ac 16:14 that *she* **a** unto the *things* which were 4337

ATTENDING (1) [ATTEND]
Ro 13: 6 **a continually** upon this very *thing.* 4342

ATTENT (2) [ATTEND]
2Ch 6:40 *let* thine ears be **a** unto the prayer *that is* 7183
7:15 mine ears **a** unto the prayer *that is made* 7183

ATTENTIVE (5) [ATTEND]
Ne 1: 6 Let thine ear now be **a**, and thine eyes 7183
1:11 let now thine ear be **a** to the prayer of thy 7183
8: 3 the ears of all the people *were* **a** unto NIH

Ps 130: 2 let thine ears be **a** to the voice of my 7183
Lk 19:48 for all the people were **very a** to hear him. 1582

ATTENTIVELY (1) [ATTEND]
Job 37: 2 **Hear a** the noise of his voice, 8085+8085

ATTIRE (3) [ATTIRED]
Pr 7:10 there met him a woman *with* the **a** of a 7897
Jer 2:32 forget her ornaments, *or* a bride her **a?** 7196
Eze 23:15 **exceeding in dyed a** upon their 2871+5628

ATTIRED (1) [ATTIRE]
Lev 16: 4 and with the linen mitre shall he be **a:** 6801

AUDIENCE (12)
Ge 23:10 Abraham in the **a** of the children of Heth, 241
23:13 spake unto Ephron in the **a** of the people 241
23:16 which he had named in the **a** of the sons 241
Ex 24: 7 covenant, and read in the **a** of the people: 241
1Sa 25:24 speak in thine **a**, and hear the words of 241
1Ch 28: 8 in the **a** of our God, keep and seek for all 241
Ne 13: 1 the book of Moses in the **a** of the people; 241
Lk 7: 1 ended all his sayings in the **a** of the people, 189
20:45 Then **in** the **a** of all the people he said unto 191
Ac 13:16 Men of Israel, and *ye* that fear God, **give a.** 191
15:12 and **gave a** to Barnabas and Paul, 191
22:22 And they **gave** him **a** unto this word, 191

AUGMENT (1)
Nu 32:14 to **a** yet the fierce anger of the Lord 5595

AUGUSTUS (3) [AUGUSTUS']
Lk 2: 1 there went out a decree from Cesar **A,** 828
Ac 25:21 to be reserved unto the hearing of **A,** 4575
25:25 and *that* he himself had appealed to **A,** 4575

AUGUSTUS' (1) [AUGUSTUS]
Ac 27: 1 *one* named Julius, a centurion of **A** band. 4575

AUL (2)
Ex 21: 6 shall bore his ear through with an **a;** 4836
Dt 15:17 thou shalt take an **a**, and thrust *it* through 4836

AUNT (1)
Lev 18:14 not approach to his wife: she *is* thine **a.** 1733

AUSTERE (2)
Lk 19:21 I feared thee, because thou art an **a** man: 840
19:22 knewest that I was an **a** man, taking up 840

AUTHOR (3)
1Co 14:33 For God is not the **a** of confusion, NIG
Heb 5: 9 became the **a** of eternal salvation unto all 159
12: 2 Looking unto Jesus the **a** and finisher of 747

AUTHORITIES (1) [AUTHORITY]
1Pe 3:22 angels and **a** and powers being made 1849

AUTHORITY (37) [AUTHORITIES]
Est 9:29 and Mordecai the Jew, wrote with all **a,** 8633
Pr 29: 2 When the righteous are **in a**, the people 7235
Mt 7:29 For he taught them as *one* having **a,** 1849
8: 9 For I am a man under **a**, having soldiers 1849
20:25 *that* **great exercise a** upon them. 2715
21:23 By what **a** doest thou these *things?* 1849
21:23 these *things?* and who gave thee this **a?** 1849
21:24 I in like wise will tell you by what **a** I do 1849
21:27 Neither tell I you by what **a** I do these 1849
Mk 1:22 for he taught them as *one* that had **a,** 1849
1:27 with a commandment he even the unclean 1849
10:42 their **great ones exercise a** upon them. 2715
11:28 By what **a** doest thou these *things?* 1849
11:28 who gave thee this **a** to do these *things?* 1849
11:29 I will tell you by what **a** I do these *things.* 1849
11:33 Neither do I tell you by what **a** I do these 1849
13:34 and gave **a** to his servants, and to every 1849
Lk 4:36 for with **a** and power he commandeth 1849
7: 8 For I also am a man set under **a,** 1849
9: 1 gave them power and over all devils, 1849
19:17 in a very little, have thou **a** over ten cities. 1849
20: 2 by what **a** doest thou these *things?* or 1849
20: 2 or who is he that gave thee this **a?** 1849
20: 8 Neither tell I you by what **a** I do these 1849
20:20 him unto the power and **a** of the governor. 1849
22:25 that **exercise a upon** them are called 1850
Jn 5:27 hath given him **a** to execute judgment 1849
Ac 8:27 eunuch **of great a** under Candace queen 1413
9:14 here he hath **a** from the chief priests 1849
26:10 having received **a** from the chief priests; 1849
26:12 Whereupon as I went to Damascus with **a** 1849
1Co 15:24 put down all rule and all **a** and power. 1849
2Co 10: 8 I should boast somewhat more of our **a,** 1849
1Ti 2: 2 For kings, and *for* all that are in **a;** that we 5247
2:12 nor to **usurp a over** the man, but to be in 831
Tit 2:15 and exhort, and rebuke with all **a.** 2003
Rev 13: 2 him his power, and his seat, and great **a.** 1849

AVA (1)
2Ki 17:24 from **A**, and from Hamath, 5755

AVAILETH (4)
Est 5:13 Yet all this **a** me nothing, so long as I see 7737
Gal 5: 6 For in Jesus Christ neither circumcision **a** 2480
6:15 For in Christ Jesus neither circumcision **a** 2480
Jas 5:16 fervent prayer of a righteous *man* **a** much. 2480

AVEN (3) [BETH-AVEN]
Eze 30:17 The young men of **A** and of Phi-beseth shall 205
Hos 10: 8 The high places also of **A**, the sin of Israel, 205
Am 1: 5 cut off the inhabitant from the plain of **A,** 206

AVENGE (17) [VENGEANCE]
Lev 19:18 Thou shalt not **a**, nor bear any grudge 5358
26:25 shall **a the quarrel** of *my* covenant: 5358+5359
Nu 31: 2 **A** the children of Israel of 5358+5360
31: 3 and **a** the Lord of Midian. 5360+5414
Dt 32:43 for he will **a** the blood of his servants, 5358
1Sa 24:12 and thee, and the Lord **a** me of thee: 5358
2Ki 9: 7 that I may **a** the blood of my servants 5358
Est 8:13 that day to **a** themselves on their enemies. 5358
Isa 1:24 and **a** me of mine enemies: 5358
Jer 46:10 that *he* may **a** him of his adversaries: 5358
Hos 1: 4 will **a** the blood of Jezreel upon the house 6485
Lk 18: 3 unto him, saying, **A** me of mine adversary. 1556
18: 5 this widow troubleth me, I will **a** her, 1556
18: 7 And shall not God **a** his own 1557+3588+4160
18: 8 I tell you that he will **a** them speedily. 1557
Ro 12:19 **a** not yourselves, but *rather* give place 1556
Rev 6:10 **a** our blood on them that dwell on 1556

AVENGED (16) [VENGEANCE]
Ge 4:24 If Cain shall be **a** sevenfold, truly Lamech 5358
Jos 10:13 until the people had **a** themselves upon 5358
Jdg 15: 7 yet will I be **a** of you, and after *that* I will 5358
16:28 that I may be **a** at once **a** of 5358+5359
1Sa 14:24 that I may be **a** on mine enemies. 5358
18:25 to be **a** of the king's enemies. 5358
25:31 or that my lord hath **a** himself: 3467
2Sa 4: 8 the Lord hath **a** my lord the king 5360+5414
18:19 how that the Lord hath **a** him of his 8199
18:31 for the Lord hath **a** thee *this* day of all 8199
Jer 5: 9 shall not my soul be **a** on such a nation as 5358
5:29 shall not my soul be **a** on such a nation as 5358
9: 9 shall not my soul be **a** on such a nation as 5358
Ac 7:24 him that was oppressed, 1557+4160
Rev 18:20 for God hath **a** you on her. 2917+2919
19: 2 **a** the blood of his servants at her hand. 1556

AVENGER (9) [VENGEANCE]
Nu 35:12 be unto you cities for refuge from the **a;** 1350
Dt 19: 6 Lest the **a** of the blood pursue the slayer, 1350
19:12 him into the hand of the **a** of blood, 1350
Jos 20: 3 they shall be your refuge from the **a** of 1350
20: 5 if the **a** of blood pursue after him, 1350
20: 9 not die by the hand of the **a** of blood, 1350
Ps 8: 2 *thou* mightest still the enemy and the **a.** 5358
44:16 by reason of the enemy and **a.** 5358
1Th 4: 6 because that the Lord *is* the **a** of all such, 1558

AVENGETH (2) [VENGEANCE]
2Sa 22:48 *It is* God that **a** me, and that 5360+5414
Ps 18:47 *It is* God that **a** me, and subdueth 5360+5414

AVENGING (3) [VENGEANCE]
Jdg 5: 2 Praise ye the Lord for the **a** of 6544+6546
1Sa 25:26 *from* **a** thyself with thine own hand, 3467
25:33 and *from* **a** myself with mine own hand. 3467

AVERSE (1)
Mic 2: 8 that pass by securely *as men* **a** from war. 7725

AVIM (1) [AVIMS]
Jos 18:23 And **A**, and Parah, and Ophrah, 5761

AVIMS (1) [AVIM]
Dt 2:23 the **A** which dwelt in Hazerim, *even* unto 5761

AVITES (2)
Jos 13: 3 the Gittites, and the Ekronites; also the **A:** 5761
2Ki 17:31 the **A** made Nibhaz and Tartak, 5761

AVITH (2)
Ge 36:35 his stead: and the name of his city *was* **A.** 5762
1Ch 1:46 his stead: and the name of his city *was* **A.** 5762

AVOID (5) [AVOIDED, AVOIDING, AVOUCHED]
Pr 4:15 **A** it, pass not by it, turn from it, 6544
Ro 16:17 which ye have learned; and **a** them. 1578
1Co 7: 2 Nevertheless, to **a** fornication, let every 1223
2Ti 2:23 But foolish and unlearned questions **a,** 3868
Tit 3: 9 But **a** foolish questions, and genealogies, 4026

AVOIDED (1) [AVOID]
1Sa 18:11 **a** it. And David **a** out of his presence twice. 5437

AVOIDING (2) [AVOID]
2Co 8:20 **A** this, that no *man* should blame us in 4724
1Ti 6:20 **a** profane *and* vain babblings, 1624

AVOUCHED (2) [AVOID]
Dt 26:17 Thou hast **a** the Lord *this* day to be thy 559
26:18 the Lord hath **a** thee *this* day to be his 559

AVVA See AVA

AVVIM See AVIM

AVVITES See AVIMS; AVITES

AWAIT (1) [WAIT]
Ac 9:24 But their **laying a** was known of Saul. 1917

A

AWAKE (42) [WAKE]

Jdg	5:12 **A**, awake, Deborah: awake, awake, utter	5782
	5:12 Awake, **a**, Deborah: awake, awake, utter	5782
	5:12 **a**, awake, utter a song: arise, Barak,	5782
	5:12 awake, **a**, utter a song: arise, Barak,	5782
Job	8: 6 surely now he would **a** for thee,	5782
	14:12 the heavens *be* no more, they shall not **a**,	6974
Ps	7: 6 **a** for me *to* the judgment *that* thou hast	5782
	17:15 be satisfied, when *I* **a**, *with* thy likeness.	6974
	35:23 Stir up thyself, and **a** to my judgment,	6974
	44:23 **A**, why sleepest thou, O Lord? arise, cast	5782
	57: 8 **A up**, my glory; awake, psaltery and harp:	5782
	57: 8 Awake up, my glory; **a**, psaltery and harp:	5782
	57: 8 and harp: I *myself* will **a** early.	5782
	59: 4 *my* fault: **a** to help me, and behold.	5782
	59: 5 God of Israel, **a** to visit all the heathen:	6974
	108: 2 **A**, psaltery and harp: I *myself* will awake	5782
	108: 2 and harp: I *myself* will **a** early.	5782
	139:18 the sand: when I **a**, I am still with thee.	6974
Pr	23:35 when shall I **a**? I will seek it yet again.	6974
SS	2: 7 stir not up, nor **a** *my* love, till he please.	5782
	3: 5 stir not up, nor **a** *my* love, till he please.	5782
	4:16 **A**, O north wind; and come thou south;	5782
	8: 4 stir not up, nor **a** *my* love, until he please.	5782
Isa	26:19 **A** and sing, ye that dwell in dust: for thy	6974
	51: 9 **A**, awake, put on strength, O arm of	5782
	51: 9 Awake, **a**, put on strength, O arm of	5782
	51: 9 **a**, as *in* the ancient days, *in*	5782
	51:17 **A**, awake, stand up, O Jerusalem,	5782
	51:17 Awake, **a**, stand up, O Jerusalem,	5782
	52: 1 **A**, awake; put on thy strength, O Zion;	5782
	52: 1 Awake, **a**; put on thy strength, O Zion;	5782
Da	12: 2 that sleep in the dust of the earth shall **a**,	6974
Joel	1: 5 **A**, ye drunkards, and weep; and howl,	6974
Hab	2: 7 **a** that *shall* vex thee, and thou shalt be	3364
	2:19 Woe unto him that saith to the wood, **A**;	6974
Zec	13: 7 **A**, O sword, against my shepherd,	2328
Mk	4:38 and they **a** him, and say unto him, Master,	*1326*
Lk	9:32 and when they were **a**, they saw his glory,	*1235*
Jn	11:11 but I go, that I may **a** him **out of sleep**.	*1852*
Ro	13:11 that now *it is* high time to **a** out of sleep:	*1453*
1Co	15:34 **A** to righteousness, and sin not: for some	*1594*
Eph	5:14 **A** thou that sleepest, and arise from	*1453*

AWAKED (8) [WAKE]

Ge	28:16 Jacob **a** out of his sleep, and he said,	3364
Jdg	16:14 he **a** out of his sleep, and went away with	3364
1Sa	26:12 and no man saw *it*, nor knew *it*, neither **a**:	6974
1Ki	18:27 peradventure he sleepeth, and must be **a**.	3364
2Ki	4:31 and told him, saying, The child is not **a**.	6974
Ps	3: 5 I laid me down and slept; I **a**;	6974
	78:65 the Lord **a** as one out of sleep, *and* like a	3364
Jer	31:26 Upon this I **a**, and beheld; and my sleep	6974

AWAKEST (2) [WAKE]

Ps	73:20 O Lord, when *thou* **a**, thou shalt despise	5782
Pr	6:22 and *when* thou **a**, it shall talk *with* thee.	6974

AWAKETH (3) [WAKE]

Ps	73:20 As a dream when *one* **a**; *so*, O Lord,	6974
Isa	29: 8 he eateth; but he **a**, and his soul *is* empty:	6974
	29: 8 he **a**, and, behold, *he is* faint, and his soul	6974

AWAKING (1) [WAKE]

Ac	16:27 of the prison **a out of** his *sleep*,	*1096+1853*

AWARE (3) [WARE]

SS	6:12 Or ever I was **a**, my soul made me *like*	3045
Jer	50:24 also taken, O Babylon, and thou wast not **a**:	3045
Lk	11:44 the men that walk over *them* are not **a** *of*	*1492*

AWAY (916) [CASTAWAY]

Ge	12:20 they **sent** him **a**, and his wife, and all that	7971
	15:11 upon the carcases, Abram **drove** them **a**.	5380
	18: 3 **pass** not **a**, I pray thee, from thy servant:	5674
	21:14 shoulder, and the child, and **sent** her **a**:	7971
	21:25 servants had **violently taken a**.	1497
	24:54 and he said, **Send** me **a** unto my master.	7971
	24:56 send me **a** that I may go to my master.	7971
	24:59 they **sent** a Rebekah their sister, and her	7971
	25: 6 **sent** them **a** from Isaac his son, while he	7971
	26:27 ye hate me, and have **sent** me **a** from you?	7971
	26:29 but good, and have **sent** thee **a** in peace:	7971
	26:31 Isaac **sent** them **a**, and they departed from	7971
	27:35 and hath **taken a** thy blessing.	3947
	27:36 he **took a** my birthright; and behold,	3947
	27:36 behold, now he hath **taken a** my blessing.	3947
	27:44 a few days, until thy brother's fury **turn a**;	7725
	27:45 Until thy brother's anger **turn a** from thee,	7725
	28: 5 Isaac **sent a** Jacob: and he went to	7971
	28: 6 **sent** him **a** to Padan-aram, to take him a	7971
	30:15 wouldest thou **take a** my son's mandrakes	3947
	30:23 and said, God hath **taken a** my reproach:	622
	30:25 that Jacob said unto Laban, **Send** me **a**,	7971
	31: 1 Jacob hath **taken a** all that *was* our	3947
	31: 9 Thus God hath **taken a** the cattle of your	5337
	31:18 he **carried a** all his cattle, and all his goods	5090
	31:20 Jacob **stale a unawares** to Laban	1589+3820
	31:26 thou hast **stolen a unawares** to	1589+3824
	31:26 **carried a** my daughters, as captives taken	5090
	31:27 Wherefore didst thou **flee a** secretly,	1272
	31:27 flee away secretly, and **steal a from** me;	1589
	31:27 that I might have **sent** thee **a** with mirth,	7971
	31:42 surely thou hadst **sent** me **a** now empty.	7971
	35: 2 **Put a** the strange gods that *are* among you,	5493

Ge	38:19 **went a**, and laid by her vail from her,	1980
	40:15 For **indeed** I was **stolen a** out of	1589+1589
	42:36 ye will take Benjamin **a**: all these things	NIH
	43:14 that he may **send a** your other brother,	7971
	44: 3 the men were **sent a**, they and their asses.	7971
	45:24 So he **sent** his brethren **a**,	7971
Ex	2: 9 **Take** this child **a**, and nurse it for me,	1980
	2:17 the shepherds came and **drove** them **a**:	1644
	8: 8 that he may **take a** the frogs from me,	5493
	8:28 only you shall not go **very far a**:	7368+7368
	10: 7 he may **take a** from me this death only.	5493
	10:19 which **took a** the locusts, and cast them	5375
	12:15 even the first day ye shall **put a** leaven out	7673
	12:28 the children of Israel **went a**, and did as	1980
	13:19 ye shall carry up my bones a hence with	4480
	13:22 He **took a** not the pillar of the cloud by	4185
	14:11 hast thou **taken us a** to die in the	3947
	15:15 all the inhabitants of Canaan shall **melt a**.	4127
	18:18 Thou wilt **surely wear a**, both	5034+5034
	19:24 **A**, get thee down, and thou shalt come up,	1980
	22:10 it die, or be hurt, or **driven a**, no man	7617
	23:25 I will **take** sickness **a** from the midst of	5493
	33:23 I will **take a** mine hand, and thou shalt	5493
Lev	1:16 he shall **pluck a** his crop with his feathers,	5493
	3: 4 with the kidneys, it shall he **take a**.	5493
	3:10 with the kidneys, it shall he **take a**.	5493
	3:15 with the kidneys, it shall he **take a**.	5493
	4: 9 with the kidneys, it shall he **take a**,	5493
	4:31 he shall **take a** all the fat thereof, as the	5493
	4:31 as the fat is **taken a** from off the sacrifice	5493
	4:35 he shall **take a** all the fat thereof, as the fat	5493
	4:35 as the fat of the lamb is **taken a** from	5493
	6: 2 or in a **thing taken a** by violence, or	1498
	6: 4 that which he **took violently a**,	1497+1500
	7: 4 with the kidneys, it shall he **take a**:	5493
	14:40 the priest shall command that they **take a**	2502
	14:43 after *that* he hath **taken a** the stones,	2502
	16:21 shall **send** *him* **a** by the hand of a fit man	7971
	21: 7 neither shall they take **a** woman **put a**	1644
	25:25 hath sold **a** *some* of his possession,	4480
	26:39 they that are left of you shall **pine a** in	4743
	26:39 their fathers shall they **pine a** with them.	4743
	26:44 I will not **cast** them **a**, neither will I abhor	3988
Nu	4:13 they shall **take a** the ashes from the altar,	1878
	11: 6 now our soul *is* **dried a**: *there is* nothing	3002
	14:43 because ye are **turned a** from the LORD,	7725
	17:10 thou shalt **quite take a** their murmurings	3615
	20:21 Israel turned **a from** him.	4480+5921
	21: 7 that he **take a** the serpents from us.	5493
	24:22 until Asshur shall **carry** thee **a captive**.	7617
	25: 4 the LORD may be **turned a** from Israel.	7725
	25:11 hath **turned** my wrath **a** from the	7725
	27: 4 father be **done a** from among his family,	1639
	32:15 For if ye **turn a** from after him, he will yet	7725
	36: 4 shall their inheritance be **taken a** from	1639
Dt	7: 4 they will **turn a** thy son from following	5493
	7:15 the LORD will **take a** from thee all	5493
	13: 5 he hath spoken to **turn** *you* **a** from	5627
	13: 5 So shalt thou **put** the evil **a** from the midst	1197
	13:10 he hath sought to **thrust** thee **a** from	5080
	15:13 thou shalt not let him go **a** empty:	7971
	15:16 say unto thee, I will not **go a** from thee;	3318
	15:18 when thou **sendest** him **a** free from thee;	7971
	17: 7 So thou shalt **put** the evil **a** from among	1197
	17:12 and thou shalt **put a** the evil from Israel.	1197
	17:17 to himself, that his heart **turn** not **a**:	5493
	19:13 shalt **put a** *the guilt of* innocent blood	1197
	19:19 shalt thou **put** the evil **a** from among you.	1197
	21: 9 So shalt thou **put a** the *guilt of* innocent	1197
	21:21 so shalt thou **put** evil **a** from among you;	1197
	22:19 his wife; he may not **put** her **a** all his days.	7971
	22:21 so shalt thou **put** evil **a** from among you.	1197
	22:22 so shalt thou **put a** evil from Israel.	1197
	22:24 so thou shalt **put a** evil from among you.	1197
	22:29 he may not **put** her **a** all his days.	7971
	23:14 thing in thee, and turn **a from** thee.	310+4480
	24: 4 Her former husband, which **sent** her **a**,	7971
	24: 7 and thou shalt **put** evil **a** from among you.	1197
	26:13 I have **brought a** the hallowed *things* out	1197
	26:14 neither have I **taken a** *ought* thereof for	1197
	28:26 the earth, and no man shall **fray** *them* **a**.	2729
	28:31 thine ass *shall be* **violently taken a** from	1497
	29:18 whose heart **turneth a** *this* day from	6437
	30:17 if thine heart **turn a**, so that thou wilt not	6437
	30:17 shalt be **drawn a**, and worship other gods,	5080
Jos	2:21 she **sent** them **a**, and they departed:	7971
	5: 9 *This* day have I **rolled a** the reproach of	1556
	7:13 until ye **take a** the accursed thing from	5493
	8: 3 *men* of valour, and **sent** them **a** by night.	7971
	8:16 and were **drawn a** from the city.	5423
	18: 8 the men arose, and **went a**:	1980
	22: 6 So Joshua blessed them, and **sent** them **a**:	7971
	22: 7 when Joshua **sent** them **a** also unto their	7971
	22:16 to **turn a** *this* day from following	7725
	22:18 ye must **turn a** *this* day from following	7725
	24:14 **put a** the gods which your fathers served	5493
	24:23 Now therefore **put a**, *said he*, the strange	5493
Jdg	3:18 he **sent a** the people that bare the present.	7971
	4:15 off *his* chariot, and **fled a** on his feet.	5127
	4:17 Sisera **fled a** on his feet to the tent	5127
	5:21 The river of Kishon **swept** them **a**,	1640
	8:21 **took a** the ornaments that *were* on their	3947
	9:21 Jotham **ran a**, and fled, and went to Beer,	5127
	10:16 they **put a** the strange gods from among	5493
	11:13 Because Israel **took a** my land, when they	3947

Jdg	11:15 Israel **took** not **a** the land of Moab,	3947
	11:38 he **sent** her **a** *for* two months: and she	7971
	15:17 that he **cast a** the jawbone out of his hand,	7993
	16: 3 **went a** with them, bar and all, and put	5265
	16:14 **went a** with the pin of the beam,	5265
	18:24 Ye have **taken a** my gods which I made,	3947
	18:24 I made, and the priest, and ye are **gone a**:	1980
	19: 2 **went a** from him unto her father's house	1980
	20:13 them to death, and **put a** evil from Israel.	1197
	20:31 *and were* **drawn a** from the city;	5423
1Sa	1:14 be drunken? **put a** thy wine from thee.	5493
	5:11 **Send a** the ark of the God of Israel,	7971
	6: 3 If ye **send a** the ark of the God of Israel,	7971
	6: 8 side thereof; and **send** it **a**, that it may go.	7971
	7: 3 *then* **put a** the strange gods and Ashtaroth	5493
	7: 4 the children of Israel did **put a** Baalim	5493
	9:26 saying, Up, that I may **send** thee **a**.	7971
	10:25 Samuel **sent** all the people **a**, every man	7971
	14:16 the multitude **melted a**, and they went	4127
	15:27 as Samuel turned about to **go a**, he laid	5437
	17:26 and **taketh a** the reproach from Israel?	5493
	19:10 he **slipt a** out of Saul's presence,	6362
	19:17 **sent a** mine enemy, that he is escaped?	7971
	20:13 I will shew it thee, and **send** thee **a**,	7971
	20:22 *thy way:* for the LORD hath **sent** thee **a**.	7971
	20:29 let me get **a**, I pray thee, and see my	4422
	21: 6 hot bread in the day when it was **taken a**.	3947
	23: 5 **brought a** their cattle, and smote them	5090
	23:26 David made haste to **get a** for fear of Saul;	1980
	24:19 will he let him go well **a**?	1870+871.1
	25:10 that **break a** every man from his master.	6555
	26:12 they **gat** them **a**, and no man saw *it*, nor	1980
	27: 9 **took a** the sheep, and the oxen,	3947
	28: 3 Saul had **put a** those that had familiar	5493
	28:25 they arose up, and **went a** that night.	1980
	30: 2 **carried** *them* **a**, and went on their way.	5090
	30:18 all that the Amalekites had **carried a**:	3947
	30:22 that they may **lead** *them* **a**, and depart.	5090
2Sa	1:21 the shield of the mighty is **vilely cast a**,	1602
	3:21 **sent** Abner **a**; and he went in peace.	7971
	3:22 he had **sent** David **a**, and he was gone in	7971
	3:23 hath **sent** him **a**, and he is gone in peace.	7971
	3:24 why *is it that* thou hast **sent** him **a**,	7971
	4: 7 and **gat** them **a** through the plain all night.	1980
	4:11 your hand, and **take** you **a** from the earth?	1197
	5: 6 thou **take a** the blind and the lame,	5493
	7:15 my mercy shall not **depart a** from him,	5493
	7:15 Saul, whom I **put a** before thee.	4480+5493
	10: 4 *even* to their buttocks, and **sent** them **a**.	7971
	12:13 The LORD also hath **put a** thy sin;	5674
	13:16 this evil in **sending** me **a** is greater than	7971
	17:18 they **went** both of them **a** quickly,	1980
	18: 3 if we **flee a**, they will not care for	5127+5127
	18: 9 and the mule that *was* under him **went a**.	5674
	19: 3 people being ashamed **steal a** when they	1589
	19:41 brethren the men of Judah **stolen** thee **a**,	1589
	22:46 Strangers shall **fade a**, and they shall be	5034
	23: 6 *shall be* all of them as thorns **thrust a**,	5074
	23: 9 and the men of Israel were **gone a**:	5927
	24:10 **take a** the iniquity of thy servant;	5674
1Ki	2:31 thou mayest **take a** the innocent blood,	5493
	2:39 that two of the servants of Shimei **ran a**	1272
	8:46 they **carry** *them* **a captives** unto	7617+7617
	8:48 which **led** them **a captive**, and pray unto	7617
	8:66 On the eighth day he **sent** the people **a**:	7971
	11: 2 *for* surely they will **turn a** your heart after	5186
	11: 3 his wives **turned a** his heart.	5186
	11: 4 his wives **turned a** his heart after other	5186
	11:13 Howbeit I will not **rend a** all the kingdom	7167
	14: 8 **rent** the kingdom **a** from the house of	7167
	14:10 will **take a** the remnant of the house of	1197
	14:10 as *a man* **taketh a** a dung, till it be all gone.	1197
	14:26 he **took a** the treasures of the house of	3947
	14:26 of the king's house; he even **took a** all:	3947
	14:26 he **took a** all the shields of gold which	3947
	15:12 he **took a** the sodomites out of the land,	5674
	15:22 they **took a** the stones of Ramah, and	5375
	16: 3 I will **take a** the posterity of Baasha,	1197
	19: 4 *is* enough; now, O LORD, **take a** my life;	3947
	19:10 left; and they seek my life, to **take** it **a**.	3947
	19:14 left; and they seek my life, to **take** it **a**.	3947
	20: 6 shall put *it* in their hand, and **take** *it* **a**.	3947
	20:24 this thing, **Take** the kings **a**, every man	5493
	20:34 *said* Ahab, I will **send** thee **a** with *this*	7971
	20:34 a covenant with him, and **sent** him **a**.	7971
	20:41 and **took** the ashes **a** from his face;	5493
	21: 4 **turned a** his face, and would eat no bread	5437
	21:21 will **take a** thy posterity, and will cut off	1197
	22:43 the high places were not **taken a**;	5493
2Ki	2: 3 Knowest thou that the LORD will **take a**	3947
	2: 5 Knowest thou that the LORD will **take a**	3947
	2: 9 for thee, before I be **taken a** from thee.	3947
	3: 2 for he **put a** the image of Baal that his	5493
	4:27 Gehazi came near to **thrust** her **a**.	1920
	5: 2 had **brought a captive** out of the land of	7617
	5:11 and **went a**, and said, Behold, I thought,	1980
	5:12 So he turned and **went a** in a rage.	1980
	6:23 he **sent** them **a**, and they went to their	7971
	6:32 murderer hath sent to **take a** mine head?	5493
	7:15 the Syrians had **cast a** in their haste.	7993
	12: 3 the high places were not **taken a**:	5493
	12:18 of Syria: and he **went a** from Jerusalem.	5927
	14: 4 the high places were not **taken a**:	5493
	17: 6 **carried** Israel **a** into Assyria,	1540
	17:11 whom the LORD **carried a** before them;	1540

2Ki	17:23 So was Israel **carried a** out of their own	1540
	17:28 of the priests whom they had **carried a**	1540
	17:33 whom they **carried a** from thence.	1540
	18:11 the king of Assyria did **carry a** Israel unto	1540
	18:22 and whose altars Hezekiah hath **taken a**,	5493
	18:24 wilt thou **turn a** the face of one captain of	7725
	18:32 **take** you **a** to a land like your own land,	3947
	20:18 they take **a**; and they shall be eunuchs	NIH
	23:11 took **a** the horses that the kings of Judah	7673
	23:19 Josiah **took a**, and did to them according	5493
	23:24 and in Jerusalem, did Josiah **put a**,	1197
	23:34 took Jehoahaz **a**: and he came *to* Egypt,	NIH
	24:14 he **carried a** all Jerusalem, and all	1540
	24:15 he **carried a** Jehoiachin to Babylon,	1540
	25:11 the fugitives that **fell a** to the king of	5307
	25:11 the captain of the guard **carry a**.	1540
	25:14 wherewith they ministered, took they **a**.	NIH
	25:15 *in* silver, the captain of the guard took **a**.	NIH
	25:21 So Judah was **carried a** out of their land.	1540
1Ch	5: 6 king of Assyria **carried a captive**:	1540
	5:21 they **took a** their cattle; *of* their camels	7617
	5:26 he **carried** them **a**, even the Reubenites,	1540
	6:15 when the LORD **carried a** Judah.	1540
	7:21 they came down to take **a** their cattle.	NIH
	8: 8 of Moab, after he had **sent** them **a**;	7971
	8:13 who **drove a** the inhabitants of Gath:	1272
	9: 1 *who* were **carried a** to Babylon for their	1540
	10:12 **took a** the body of Saul, and the bodies of	5375
	12:19 Philistines upon advisement **sent** him **a**,	7971
	14:14 **turn a** from them, and come upon them	5437
	17:13 I will not **take** my mercy **a** from him, as I	5493
	19: 4 hard by *their* buttocks, and **sent** them **a**.	7971
	21: 8 **do a** the iniquity of thy servant;	5674
2Ch	6:36 they **carry** them **a captives** unto a	7617+7617
	6:42 **turn** not **a** the face of thine anointed:	7725
	7:10 he **sent** the people **a** into their tents,	7971
	7:19 if ye **turn a**, and forsake my statutes	7725
	9:12 **went a** to her own land, she	1980
	12: 9 **took a** the treasures of the house of	3947
	12: 9 he **carried a** also the shields of gold	3947
	14: 3 he **took a** the altars of the strange *gods,*	5493
	14: 5 he **took a** out of all the cities of Judah	5493
	14:13 and they **carried a** very much spoil.	5375
	14:15 **carried a** sheep and camels in abundance,	7617
	15: 8 **put a** the abominable idols out of all	5674
	15:17 the high places were not **taken a** out of	5493
	16: 6 they **carried a** the stones of Ramah,	5375
	17: 6 moreover he **took a** the high places	5493
	19: 3 that thou hast **taken a** the groves out of	1197
	20:25 people came to **take a** the spoil of them,	962
	20:25 more than they could **carry a**:	4853
	20:33 the high places were not **taken a**:	5493
	21:17 **carried a** all the substance that was found	7617
	25:12 did the children of Judah **carry a captive**,	7617
	25:27 after the time that Amaziah did **turn a**	5493
	28: 5 **carried a** a great multitude of them **captives,**	7617+7633
	28: 8 the children of Israel **carried a captive** of	7617
	28: 8 **took** also a much spoil from them,	962
	28:17 smitten Judah, and **carried a** captives.	7617
	28:21 Ahaz **took a** a portion *out* of the house	2505
	29: 6 have **turned a** their faces from	5437
	29:10 that his fierce wrath may **turn a**	7725
	29:19 which king Ahaz in his reign did **cast a** in	2186
	30: 8 that the fierceness of his wrath may **turn a**	7725
	30: 9 and will not **turn a** *his* face from you,	5493
	30:14 **took a** the altars that *were* in Jerusalem,	5493
	30:14 all the altars for incense **took** they **a**,	5493
	32:12 Hath not the same Hezekiah **taken a** his	5493
	33:15 he **took a** the strange gods, and the idol	5493
	34:33 Josiah **took a** all the abominations out of	5493
	35:23 the king said to his servants, **Have** me **a**;	5674
	36:20 from the sword **carried** he **a** to Babylon;	1540
Ezr	2: 1 *of* those which had been **carried a**,	1473
	2: 1 of Babylon had **carried a** unto Babylon,	1540
	5:12 **carried** the people **a** into Babylon.	1541
	8:35 children of those that had been **carried a**,	1473
	9: 4 of those that had been **carried a**;	1473
	10: 3 with our God to **put a** all the wives,	3318
	10: 6 of **them** that had been **carried a**.	1473
	10: 8 of those that had been **carried a**.	1473
	10:19 gave their hands that *they* would **put a**	3318
Ne	7: 6 of those that had been **carried a**,	1473
	7: 6 the king of Babylon had **carried a**,	1540
Est	2: 6 Who had been **carried a** from Jerusalem	1540
	2: 6 **carried a** with Jeconiah king of Judah,	1540
	2: 6 the king of Babylon had **carried a**.	1540
	4: 4 and to **take a** his sackcloth from him:	5493
	8: 3 besought him with tears to **put a**	5674
Job	1:15 Sabeans fell *upon them,* and **took** them **a**;	3947
	1:17 have **carried** them **a**, yea, and slain	3947
	1:21 the LORD hath taken **a**; blessed be	NIH
	4:21 their excellency *which is* in them **go a**?	5265
	6:15 *and* as the stream of brooks they **pass a**;	5674
	7: 9 the cloud is consumed and **vanisheth a**:	1980
	7:21 and take **a** mine iniquity?	
	8: 4 have **cast** them **a** for their transgression;	7971
	8:20 God will not **cast a** a perfect man, neither	3988
	9:12 he **taketh a**, who can hinder him?	2862
	9:25 than a post: they **flee a**, they see no good.	1272
	9:26 They are **passed a** as the swift ships: as	2498
	9:34 him **take** his rod **a** from me, and let not	5493
	11:14 **put** it **far a**, and let not wickedness dwell	7368
	11:16 *and* remember *it* as waters *that* **pass a**:	5674
	12:17 He **leadeth** counsellers **a** spoiled,	1980

Job	12:19 He **leadeth** princes **a** spoiled,	1980
	12:20 He **removeth** the speech of the trusty,	5493
	12:20 taketh **a** the understanding of the aged.	NIH
	12:24 He **taketh a** the heart of the chief of	5493
	14:10 dieth, and **wasteth a**: yea, man giveth	2522
	14:19 thou **washest a** the things which grow	7857
	14:20 his countenance, and **sendest** him **a**.	7971
	15:12 Why doth thine heart **carry** thee **a**?	3947
	15:30 by the breath of his mouth shall he **go a**.	5493
	20: 8 He shall **fly a** as a dream, and shall not be	5774
	20: 8 he shall be **chased a** as a vision of	5074
	20:19 he hath **violently taken a** a house	1497
	20:28 *his* goods *shall* **flow a** in the day of his	5064
	21:18 and as chaff *that* the storm **carrieth a**.	1589
	22: 9 Thou hast **sent** widows **a** empty,	7971
	22:23 **put** a iniquity **far** from thy tabernacles.	7368
	24: 2 they **violently take a** flocks,	1497
	24: 3 They **drive a** the ass of the fatherless,	5090
	24:10 they **take a** the sheaf *from* the hungry;	5375
	27: 2 *who* hath **taken a** my judgment;	5493
	27: 8 gained, when God **taketh a** his soul?	7953
	27:20 a tempest **stealeth** him **a** in the night.	1589
	27:21 The east wind **carrieth** him **a**,	5375
	28: 4 are dried up, they are **gone a** from men.	5128
	30:12 they **push a** my feet, and they raise up	7971
	30:15 and my welfare **passeth a** as a cloud.	5674
	32:22 my Maker would soon **take** me **a**.	5375
	33:21 His flesh is **consumed a**, that it cannot	3615
	34: 5 and God hath **taken a** my judgment.	5493
	34:20 shall be troubled at midnight, and **pass a**:	5674
	34:20 the mighty shall be **taken a** without hand.	5493
	36:18 lest he **take** thee **a** with *his* stroke:	5496
Ps	1: 4 like the chaff which the wind **driveth a**.	5086
	2: 3 and **cast a** their cords from us.	7993
	18:22 and I did not **put a** his statutes from me.	5493
	18:45 The strangers shall **fade a**, and be afraid	5034
	27: 9 from me; **put** not thy servant **a** in anger:	5186
	28: 3 **Draw** me not **a** with the wicked,	4900
	31:13 me, they devised to **take a** my life.	3947
	34: 1 who **drove** him **a**, and he departed.	1644
	37:20 into smoke shall they consume **a**.	NIH
	37:36 Yet he **passed a**, and lo, he *was* not: yea,	5674
	39:10 Remove thy stroke **a** from me:	4480+5921
	39:11 thou **makest** his beauty to **consume a**	4529
	48: 5 they were troubled, *and* **hasted a**.	2648
	49:17 when he dieth he shall **carry** nothing **a**:	3947
	51:11 **Cast** me not **a** from thy presence;	7993
	52: 5 he shall **take** thee **a**, and pluck thee out	2846
	55: 6 *for then* would I **fly a**, and be at rest.	5774
	58: 7 Let them **melt a** as waters *which* run	3988
	58: 8 let *every one of them* **pass a**:	1980
	58: 9 shall **take** them **a as with a whirlwind,**	8175
	64: 8 all that see them shall **flee a**.	5074
	65: 3 thou shalt **purge** them **a**.	3722
	66:20 which hath not **turned a** my prayer,	5493
	68: 2 As smoke is **driven a**, *so* drive *them*	5086
	68: 2 smoke is driven away, *so* **drive** *them* **a**:	5086
	69: 4 then I restored *that* which I took not **a**.	1497
	78:38 many a time **turned** he his anger **a**,	7725
	78:39 a wind that **passeth a**, and cometh not	1980
	79: 9 deliver us, and **purge a** our sins, for thy	3722
	85: 3 Thou hast **taken a** all thy wrath: thou	622
	88: 8 Thou hast **put a** mine acquaintance **far**	7368
	90: 5 Thou **carriest** them **a as with a flood;**	2229
	90: 9 all our days are **passed a** in thy wrath:	6437
	90:10 for it is soon cut off, and we **fly a**.	5774
	102:24 **take** me not **a** in the midst of my days:	5927
	104: 7 the voice of thy thunder they **hasted a**.	2648
	104:29 thou **takest a** their breath, they die,	622
	106:23 to **turn a** his wrath, lest *he* should destroy	7725
	112:10 he shall gnash *with* his teeth, and **melt a**:	4549
	119:37 **Turn a** mine eyes from beholding vanity;	5674
	119:39 **Turn a** my reproach which I fear: for thy	5674
	119:119 Thou **puttest a** all the wicked of the earth	7673
	132:10 For thy servant David's sake **turn** not **a**	7725
	137: 3 For there they that **carried** us **a captive**	7617
	144: 4 his days *are* as a shadow that **passeth a**.	5674
Pr	1:19 *which* **taketh a** the life of the owners	3947
	1:32 For the **turning a** of the simple shall slay	4878
	4:15 pass not by it, turn from it, and **pass a**.	5674
	4:16 their sleep is **taken a**, unless they cause	1497
	4:24 **Put a** from thee a froward mouth,	5493
	6:33 and his reproach shall not be **wiped a**.	4229
	10: 3 he **casteth a** the substance of the wicked.	1920
	14:32 The wicked is **driven a** in his wickedness:	1760
	15: 1 A soft answer **turneth a** wrath:	7725
	19:26 *his* father, *and* **chaseth a** *his* mother,	1272
	20: 8 judgment scattereth **a** all evil with his eyes.	NIH
	20:30 blueness of a wound **cleanseth a** evil:	8562
	22:27 why should he **take a** thy bed from under	3947
	23: 5 they **fly a** as an eagle *toward* heaven.	5774
	24:18 and he **turn a** his wrath from him.	7725
	25: 4 **Take a** the dross from the silver,	1898
	25: 5 **Take a** the wicked *from* before the king,	1898
	25:10 to shame, and thine infamy **turn** not **a**.	7725
	25:20 *As* he that **taketh a** a garment in cold	5710
	25:23 The north wind **driveth a** a rain: so *doth*	2342
	28: 9 He that **turneth a** his ear from hearing	5493
	28: 2 into a snare: but wise *men* **turn a** wrath.	7725
	30:30 among beasts, and **turneth** not **a** for any;	7725
Ecc	1: 4 One generation **passeth a**,	1980
	3: 5 A time to **cast a** stones, and a time to	7993
	3: 6 a time to keep, and a time to **cast a**;	7993
	5:15 which he may **carry a** in his hand.	1980
	11:10 thy heart, and **put a** evil from thy flesh:	5674

SS	2:10 my love, my fair one, and **come a**.	1980
	2:13 Arise, my love, my fair one, and **come a**.	1980
	2:17 the shadows **flee a**, turn, my beloved,	5127
	4: 6 the day break, and the shadows **flee a**,	5127
	5: 7 the keepers of the walls **took a** my vail	5375
Isa	1: 4 unto anger, they are **gone a** backward.	2114
	1:13 of assemblies, I **cannot a with**;	3201+3808
	1:16 **put a** the evil of your doings from before	5493
	1:25 purely **purge a** thy dross, and take away	6884
	1:25 away thy dross, and **take a** all thy tin:	5493
	3: 1 doth **take a** from Jerusalem and from	5493
	3:18 that day the Lord will **take a** the bravery	5493
	4: 1 by thy name, to **take a** our reproach.	622
	4: 4 When the Lord shall have **washed a**	7364
	5: 5 I *will* **take a** the hedge thereof, and it	5493
	5:23 **take a** the righteousness of the righteous	5493
	5:24 they have **cast a** the law of the LORD of	3988
	5:25 For all this his anger is not **turned a**,	7725
	5:29 **carry** it **a** safe, and none shall deliver	6403
	6: 7 thine iniquity is **taken a**, and thy sin	5493
	6:12 the LORD have **removed** men **far a**,	7368
	8: 4 spoil of Samaria shall be **taken a** before	5375
	9:12 For all this his anger is not **turned a**,	7725
	9:17 For all this his anger is not **turned a**,	7725
	9:21 For all this his anger is not **turned a**,	7725
	10: 2 to **take a** the right *from* the poor of my	1497
	10: 4 For all this his anger is not **turned a**,	7725
	10:27 *that* his burden shall be **taken a** from off	5493
	12: 1 thine anger is **turned a**,	7725
	15: 6 the hay is **withered a**, the grass faileth,	3001
	15: 7 shall they **carry a** to the brook of	5375
	16:10 gladness is **taken a**, and joy out of	622
	17: 1 Damascus *is* **taken a** from *being* a city,	5493
	18: 5 and **take a** *and* cut down the branches.	5493
	19: 6 they shall **turn** the rivers **far a**; *and*	2186
	19: 7 wither, be **driven a**, and *be* no *more*.	5086
	20: 4 So shall the king of Assyria **lead a**	5090
	22: 4 Therefore said I, **Look a** from me; I will	8159
	22:17 the LORD will **carry** thee **a** with a mighty	2904
	24: 4 The earth mourneth *and* **fadeth a**,	5034
	24: 4 the world languisheth *and* **fadeth a**,	5034
	25: 8 the Lord GOD will **wipe a** tears from off	4229
	25: 8 the rebuke of his people shall he **take a**	5493
	27: 9 and this *is* all the fruit to **take a** his sin;	5493
	28:17 the hail shall **sweep a** the refuge of lies,	3261
	29: 5 ones *shall be* as chaff that **passeth a**:	5674
	30:22 thou shalt **cast** them **a** as a menstruous	2219
	31: 7 For in that day every man shall **cast a** his	3988
	35:10 and sorrow and sighing shall **flee a**.	5127
	36: 7 and whose altars Hezekiah hath **taken a**,	5493
	36: 9 wilt thou **turn a** the face of one captain of	7725
	36:17 **take** you **a** to a land like your own land,	3947
	39: 7 which thou shalt beget, shall they **take a**;	3947
	40:24 whirlwind shall **take** them **a** as stubble.	5375
	41: 9 I have chosen thee, and not **cast** thee **a**.	3988
	41:16 the wind shall **carry** them **a**,	5375
	49:19 that swallowed thee up shall be **far a**.	7368
	49:25 captives of the mighty shall be **taken a**,	3947
	50: 1 divorcement, whom I have **put a**?	7971
	50: 1 your transgressions *is* your mother **put a**.	7971
	50: 5 was not rebellious, neither **turned a** back.	5472
	51: 6 the heavens shall **vanish a** like smoke,	4414
	51:11 *and* sorrow and mourning shall **flee a**.	5127
	52: 5 that my people is **taken a** for nought?	3947
	57: 1 merciful men *are* **taken a**, none	622
	57: 1 righteous is **taken a** from the evil	622
	57:13 the wind shall **carry** them all **a**;	5375
	58: 9 Here I *am*. If thou **take a** from the midst	5493
	58:13 If thou **turn a** thy foot from the sabbath,	7725
	59:13 departing **a** from our God,	5253
	59:14 judgment is **turned a** backward,	5253
	64: 6 like the wind, have **taken** us **a**.	5375
Jer	1: 3 the **carrying a** of Jerusalem **captive** in	1540
	2:24 *in* her occasion who can **turn** her **a**?	7725
	3: 1 If a man **put a** his wife, and she go from	7971
	3: 8 Israel committed adultery I had **put** her **a**,	7971
	3:19 My father; and shalt not **turn a** from me.	7725
	4: 1 if thou wilt **put a** thine abominations out	5493
	4: 4 **take a** the foreskins of your heart, ye men	5493
	5:10 **take a** her battlements; for they *are* not	5493
	5:25 Your iniquities have **turned a** these	5186
	6: 4 for the day **goeth a**, for the shadows of	6437
	6:29 for the wicked are not **plucked a**.	5423
	7:29 O Jerusalem, and **cast** it **a**, and take up a	7993
	7:33 of the earth; and none shall **fray** them **a**.	2729
	8: 4 not arise? shall he **turn a**, and not return?	7725
	8:13 have given them shall **pass a** from them.	5674
	13:17 the LORD's flock is **carried a captive**.	7617
	13:19 Judah shall be **carried a captive** all of it,	1540
	13:19 of it, it shall be wholly **carried a captive**.	1540
	13:24 **passeth a** by the wind of the wilderness.	5674
	15:15 take me not **a** in thy longsuffering;	3947
	16: 5 for I have **taken a** my peace from this	622
	18:20 *and* to **turn a** thy wrath from them.	7725
	22:10 *but* weep sore for him that **goeth a**:	1980
	23: 2 **driven** them **a**, and have not visited them:	5080
	24: 1 **carried a captive** Jeconiah the son of	1540
	24: 5 them that are **carried a captive** of Judah,	1546
	27:20 when he **carried a captive** Jeconiah	1540
	28: 3 king of Babylon **took a** from this place,	3947
	28: 6 all that is **carried a captive**, from Babylon	1473
	29: 1 the elders which were **carried a captives**,	1473
	29: 1 **carried a captive** from Jerusalem to	1540
	29: 4 unto all that are **carried a captives**,	1473

Jer 29: 4 I have **caused to be carried a** from	1540
29: 7 **caused** you **to be carried a captives,**	1540
29:14 I will **turn a** your captivity, and I will	7725
29:14 I **caused** you **to be carried a captive.**	1540
32:40 but I will not **turn a** from them, to do	7725
33:26 will I **cast a** the seed of Jacob,	3988
37:13 Thou **fallest a** to the Chaldeans.	5307
37:14 *It is* false; I **fall** not a to the Chaldeans.	5307
38:22 in the mire, *and* they are **turned a** back.	5472
39: 9 **carried a captive** *into* Babylon	1540
39: 9 those that **fell a,** that fell to him, with	5307
40: 1 that were **carried a captive** of Jerusalem	1546
40: 1 which were **carried a captive** unto	1540
40: 7 *them* that were not **carried a captive** to	1540
41:10 Ishmael **carried a captive** all the residue	7617
41:10 son of Nethaniah **carried** them **a captive,**	7617
41:14 **carried a captive** from Mizpah cast about	7617
43: 3 and **carry** us **a captives** *into* Babylon.	1540
43:12 burn them, and **carry** them **a captives:**	7617
46: 5 Let not the swift **flee a,** nor the mighty	5127
46:15 Why are thy valiant *men* **swept a?**	5502
46:21 are turned back, *and* are **fled a** together;	5127
48: 9 unto Moab, that it may flee and **get a:**	3318
49:19 suddenly make him run **a from** her:	4480+5921
49:29 flocks shall they take **a:** they shall take	NIH
50: 6 have **turned** them **a** on the mountains:	7725
50:17 the lions have **driven** him **a:**	5080
50:44 them suddenly run **a from** her:	4480+5921
51:50 escaped the sword, go **a,** stand not still:	NIH
52:15 **carried a captive** *certain* of the poor of	1540
52:15 those that **fell a,** that fell to the king of	5307
52:18 wherewith they ministered, took they **a.**	NIH
52:19 *in* silver, took the captain of the guard **a.**	NIH
52:27 Thus Judah was **carried a captive** out of	1540
52:28 Nebuchadrezzar **carried a captive:**	1540
52:29 **carried a captive** from Jerusalem eight	1540
52:30 **carried a captive** *of* the Jews seven	1540
La 2: 6 he hath **violently taken a** his tabernacle,	2554
2:14 thine iniquity, to **turn a** thy captivity;	7725
4: 9 for these **pine a,** stricken through for	2100
4:15 when they **fled a** and wandered:	5132
4:22 will no more **carry** thee **a** *into captivity:*	1540
Eze 3:14 **took** me a, and I went in bitterness, in	3947
4:17 and **consume a** for their iniquity.	4743
11:18 they shall **take a** all the detestable things	5493
14: 6 **turn a** your faces from all your	7725
16: 9 I **throughly washed a** thy blood from	7857
16:50 therefore I **took** them **a** as I saw *good.*	5493
18:24 when the righteous **turneth a** from his	7725
18:26 When a righteous *man* **turneth a** from his	7725
18:27 when the wicked *man* **turneth a** from his	7725
18:28 **turneth a** from all his transgressions that	7725
18:31 **Cast a** from you all your transgressions,	7993
20: 7 **Cast** ye **a** every man the abominations of	7993
20: 8 they did not every man **cast a**	7993
23:25 they shall **take a** thy nose and thine ears;	5493
23:26 of thy clothes, and **take a** thy fair jewels.	3947
23:29 shall take **a** all thy labour, and shall leave	NIH
24:16 I **take a** from thee the desire of thine eyes	3947
24:23 ye shall **pine a** for your iniquities,	4743
26:16 **lay a** their robes, and put off their	5493
30: 4 they shall take **a** her multitude,	NIH
33: 4 if the sword come, and **take** him **a,**	3947
33: 6 among them, he is taken **a** in his iniquity;	NIH
33:10 and we **pine a** in them, how should we	4743
34: 4 brought again that which was **driven a,**	5080
34:16 bring again that which was **driven a,**	5080
36:26 I will **take a** the stony heart out of your	5493
38:13 to **carry** a silver and gold, to take *away*	5375
38:13 and gold, to take **a** cattle and goods,	NIH
43: 9 **put a** their whoredom, and the carcases of	7368
their kings, **far**	7368
44:10 the Levites that are **gone a** far from me,	7368
44:10 which went astray **a from** me after	4480+5921
44:22 their wives a widow, nor her that is **put a:**	1644
45: 9 **take a** your exactions from my people,	7311
Da 1:16 Thus Melzar **took a** the portion of their	5375
2:35 the wind **carried** them **a,** that no place	5376
4:14 let the beasts **get a** from under it,	5111
7:12 they had their dominion **taken a:**	5709
7:14 which shall not **pass a,** and his kingdom	5709
7:26 shall **take a** his dominion, to consume	5709
8:11 by him the daily *sacrifice* was **taken a,**	7311
9:16 thy fury be **turned a** from thy city	7725
11:12 *And* when he hath **taken a** the multitude,	5375
11:31 shall **take a** the daily *sacrifice,*	5493
11:44 to destroy, and **utterly** to **make a** many.	2763
12:11 *that* the daily *sacrifice* shall be **taken a,**	5493
Hos 1: 6 but I will **utterly take** them **a.**	5375+5375
2: 2 **put a** her whoredoms out of her sight,	5493
2: 9 take **a** my corn in the time thereof,	NIH
2:17 For I will **take a** the names of Baalim out	5493
4: 3 the fishes of the sea also shall be **taken a.**	622
4:11 and wine and new wine take **a** the heart.	NIH
5:14 I, *even* I, will tear and go **a;** I will take	1980
5:14 I will **take a,** and none shall rescue *him.*	5375
6: 4 and as the early dew *it* **goeth a.**	1980
9:11 their glory shall **fly a** like a bird, from	5774
9:17 My God will **cast** them **a,** because they	3988
13: 3 and as the early dew that **passeth a,**	1980
13:11 mine anger, and took *him* **a** in my wrath.	NIH
14: 2 **Take a** all iniquity, and receive *us*	5375
14: 4 for mine anger is **turned a** from him.	7725
Joel 1: 7 he hath made it clean bare, and **cast** *it* **a;**	7993
Joel 1:12 joy is **withered a** from the sons of men.	3001
Am 1: 3 I will not **turn a** *the punishment* thereof;	7725
1: 6 I will not **turn a** *the punishment* thereof;	7725
1: 6 **carried a captive** the whole captivity,	1540
1: 9 I will not **turn a** *the punishment* thereof;	7725
1:11 I will not **turn a** *the punishment* thereof;	7725
1:13 I will not **turn a** *the punishment* thereof;	7725
2: 1 I will not **turn a** *the punishment* thereof;	7725
2: 4 I will not **turn a** *the punishment* thereof;	7725
2: 6 I will not **turn a** *the punishment* thereof;	7725
2:16 the mighty shall **flee a** naked in that day,	5127
4: 2 that he will **take** you **a** with hooks,	5375
4:10 the sword, and have **taken a** your horses;	7628
5:23 **Take** thou **a** from me the noise of thy	5493
6: 3 Ye that **put far a** the evil day,	5077
7:11 Israel shall **surely** be **led a captive**	1540+1540
7:12 go, **flee** thee **a** into the land of Judah,	1272
9: 1 he that fleeth of them shall not **flee a,**	5127
Ob 1:11 the strangers **carried a captive** his forces,	7617
Jnh 3: 9 repent, and **turn a** from his fierce anger,	7725
Mic 1:11 **Pass** ye **a,** thou inhabitant of Saphir,	5674
2: 2 violence; and houses, and **take them a:**	5375
2: 4 **turning a** he hath divided our fields.	7725
2: 9 from their children have ye taken *a* my	NIH
Na 2: 2 For the LORD hath turned **a**	NIH
2: 7 Huzzab shall be **led a captive,** she shall	1540
2: 8 they *shall* **flee a.** Stand, stand, *shall they*	5127
3:10 Yet *was* she carried **a,** she went into	1473
3:16 the cankerworm spoileth, and **flieth a.**	5774
3:17 *but* when the sun ariseth they **flee a,**	5074
Zep 2: 7 shall visit them, and **turn a** their captivity.	7725
3:11 I will **take a** out of the midst of thee them	5493
3:15 The LORD hath **taken a** thy judgments,	5493
Zec 3: 4 **Take a** the filthy garments from him.	5493
7:11 pulled **a** the shoulder, and stopped their	5637
9: 7 I will **take a** his blood out of his mouth,	5493
10:11 and the sceptre of Egypt shall **depart a.**	5493
14:12 Their flesh *shall* **consume a** while they	4743
14:12 their eyes shall **consume a** in their holes,	4743
14:12 their tongue shall **consume a** in their	4743
Mal 2: 3 and *one* shall **take** you **a** with it.	5375
2: 6 and did **turn** many **a** from iniquity.	7725
2:16 of Israel, saith that he hateth **putting a:**	7971
3: 7 ye are **gone a** from mine ordinances,	5493
Mt 1:11 about the time they were **carried a** to	3350
1:17 from David until the **carrying a** into	3350
1:17 from the **carrying a** into Babylon unto	3350
1:19 was minded to **put** her **a** privily.	630
5:31 said, Whosoever shall **put a** his wife,	630
5:32 That whosoever shall **put a** his wife,	630
5:40 take **a** thy coat, let him have *thy* cloke	NIG
5:42 would borrow of thee **turn** not thou **a.**	654
8:31 suffer us to **go a** into the herd of swine.	565
13: 6 *they* had not root, they **withered a.**	3583
13:12 him shall be **taken a** even that he hath.	142
13:19 **catcheth a** that which was sown in his	726
13:36 Then Jesus **sent** the multitude **a,**	863
13:48 the good into vessels, but cast the **bad a.**	1854
14:15 **send** the multitude **a,** that they may go	630
14:22 other side, while he **sent** the multitudes **a.**	630
14:23 And when he had **sent** the multitudes **a,**	630
15:23 and besought him, saying, **Send** her **a;**	630
15:32 I will not **send** them **a** fasting, lest they	630
15:39 he **sent a** the multitude, and took ship,	630
19: 3 Is it lawful for a man to **put a** his wife for	630
19: 7 a writing of divorcement, and to **put** her **a?**	630
19: 9 hearts suffered you to **put a** your wives:	630
19: 9 unto you, Whosoever shall **put a** his wife,	630
19: 9 whoso marrieth her *which is* **put a** doth	630
19:22 heard *that* saying, he **went a** sorrowful:	565
21:19 And presently the fig tree **withered a.**	3583
21:20 How soon is the fig tree **withered a!**	3583
22:13 Bind him hand and foot, and **take** him **a,**	142
24:35 Heaven and earth shall **pass a,**	3928
24:35 **pass away,** but my words shall not **pass a.**	3928
24:39 until the flood came, and **took** *them* all **a;**	142
25:29 him that hath not shall be **taken a** even	142
25:46 And these shall **go a** into everlasting	565
26:42 He **went a** again the second time,	565
26:42 if this cup may not **pass a** from me,	3928
26:44 **went a** again, and prayed the third time,	565
26:57 Jesus **led** *him* to Caiaphas the high priest,	520
27: 2 **led** *him* **a,** and delivered him to Pontius	520
27:31 on him, and **led** him **a** to crucify *him.*	520
27:64 and steal him **a,** and say unto the people,	NIG
28:13 by night, and stole him **a** while we slept.	NIG
28:16 Then the eleven disciples went **a** into	NIG
Mk 1:43 charged him, and forthwith **sent** him **a;**	1544
2:20 the bridegroom shall be **taken a** from	522
2:21 the new piece that filled it up **taketh a**	575
4: 6 because *it* had no root, it **withered a.**	3583
4:15 **taketh a** the word that was sown in their	142
4:36 And when they had **sent a** the multitude,	863
5:10 would not **send** them **a** out of the country.	649
6:36 **Send** them **a,** that they may go into	630
6:45 unto Bethsaida, while he **sent a** the people.	630
6:46 when he had **sent** them **a,** he departed	657
8: 3 And if I **send** them **a** fasting to their own	630
8: 9 about four thousand: and he **sent** them **a.**	630
8:26 And he **sent** him **a** to his house, saying,	630
9:18 gnasheth with his teeth, and **pineth a:**	3583
10: 2 Is it lawful for a man to **put a** his wife?	630
10: 4 a bill of divorcement, and to **put** her **a.**	630
10:11 Whosoever shall **put a** his wife,	630
10:12 And if a woman shall **put a** her husband,	630
Mk 10:22 was sad at *that* saying, and **went a** grieved:	565
10:50 **casting a** his garment, rose, and came to	577
11:21 tree which thou cursedst is **withered a.**	3583
12: 3 and beat *him,* and **sent** *him* **a** empty.	649
12: 4 and **sent** *him* **a** shamefully handled.	649
13:31 Heaven and earth shall **pass a:**	3928
13:31 away: but my words shall not **pass a.**	3928
14:36 unto thee; **take a** this cup from me:	3911
14:39 And again he **went a,** and prayed,	565
14:44 is he; take him, and **lead** *him* **a** safely.	520
14:53 And they **led** Jesus **a** to the high priest:	520
15: 1 and **carried** him **a,** and delivered *him* to	667
15:16 And the soldiers **led** him **a** into the hall,	520
16: 3 Who shall **roll** us **a** the stone from the door	617
16: 4 they saw that the stone was **rolled a:**	617
Lk 1:25 on *me,* to **take a** my reproach among men.	851
1:53 and the rich he hath **sent** empty **a.**	1821
2:15 as the angels were **gone a** from them into	565
5:35 the bridegroom shall be **taken a** from	522
6:29 him that **taketh a** thy cloke forbid not *to*	142
6:30 him that **taketh a** thy *goods* ask *them* not	142
8: 6 it **withered a,** because *it* lacked moisture.	3583
8:12 and **taketh a** the word out of their hearts,	142
8:13 and in time of temptation **fall a.**	868
8:38 be with him: but Jesus **sent** him **a,** saying,	630
9:12 And *when* the day began to **wear a,**	2827
9:12 and said unto him, **Send** the multitude **a,**	630
9:25 and lose himself, or be **cast a?**	2210
10:42 which shall not be **taken a** from her.	851
11:52 for ye have **taken a** the key of knowledge:	142
13:15 from the stall, and **lead** *him* **a** to watering?	520
16: 3 for my lord **taketh a** from me	851
16:18 Whosoever **putteth a** his wife,	630
16:18 whosoever marrieth her that is **put a** from	630
17:31 let him not come down to **take** it **a:**	142
19:26 that he hath shall be **taken a** from him.	142
20:10 beat him, and **sent** *him* **a** empty.	1821
20:11 *him* shamefully, and **sent** *him* **a** empty.	1821
21:24 and shall be **led a captive** into all nations:	163
21:32 This generation shall not **pass a,** till all be	3928
21:33 Heaven and earth shall **pass a:**	3928
21:33 pass away: but my words shall not **pass a.**	3928
23:18 **A with** this *man,* and release unto us	142
23:26 And as they **led** him **a,** they laid hold upon	520
24: 2 And they found the stone **rolled a** from	617
Jn 1:29 which **taketh a** the sin of the world.	142
4: 8 his disciples were **gone a** unto the city	565
5:13 for Jesus had **conveyed** himself **a,**	1593
6:22 but *that* his disciples were **gone a** alone;	565
6:67 Jesus unto the twelve, Will ye also **go a?**	5217
10:40 And went **a** again beyond Jordan into	565
11:39 Jesus said, **Take** ye **a** the stone. Martha,	142
11:41 Then they **took a** the stone *from the place*	142
11:48 and **take a** both our place and nation.	142
12:11 reason of him many of the Jews **went a,**	5217
12:28 you, I **go a,** and come *again* unto you.	5217
15: 2 in me that beareth not fruit he **taketh a:**	142
16: 7 truth; It is expedient for you that I **go a:**	565
16: 7 if I **go** not **a,** the Comforter will not come	565
18:13 And **led** him **a** to Annas first; for he was	520
19:15 **A with** *him,* away with *him,* crucify him.	142
19:15 **Away with** *him,* **a with** *him,* crucify him.	142
19:16 and they took Jesus, and **led** him **a.**	520
19:31 be broken, and *that* they might be **taken a.**	142
19:38 besought Pilate that he might **take a**	142
20: 1 seeth the stone **taken a** from the sepulchre.	142
20: 2 They have **taken a** the Lord out of	142
20:10 Then the disciples went **a** again unto their	565
20:13 Because they have **taken a** my Lord,	142
20:15 thou hast laid him, and I will **take** him **a.**	142
Ac 3:26 in **turning a** every one of you from *his*	654
5:37 and **drew a** much people after him:	868
7:27 that did his neighbour wrong **thrust** him **a,**	683
7:43 and I will **carry** you **a** beyond Babylon.	3351
8:33 his humiliation his judgment was **taken a:**	142
8:39 the Spirit of the Lord **caught a** Philip,	726
10:23 on the morrow Peter **went a** with them,	1831
13: 3 laid *their* hands on them, they **sent** *them* **a.**	630
13: 8 seeking to turn **a** the deputy **from** the faith.	575
17:10 And the brethren immediately **sent a** Paul	1599
17:14 the brethren **sent a** Paul to go	1821
19:26 persuaded and **turned a** much people,	3179
20: 6 And we **sailed a** from Philippi after	1602
20:30 speaking perverse *things,* to **draw a**	645
21:36 people followed *after,* crying, **A with** him.	142
22:16 be baptized, and **wash a** thy sins,	628
22:22 said, **A with** such *a fellow* from the earth:	142
24: 7 with great violence **took** *him* **a** out of our	520
27:20 we should be saved was then **taken a.**	4014
Ro 11: 1 I say then, Hath God **cast a** his people?	683
11: 2 God hath not **cast a** his people which he	683
11:15 For if the **casting a** of them	580
11:26 and shall **turn a** ungodliness from Jacob:	654
11:27 unto them, when I shall **take a** their sins.	851
1Co 5: 2 deed might be **taken a** from among you.	1808
5:13 Therefore **put a** from among yourselves	1808
7:11 and let not the husband **put a** *his* wife.	863
7:12 to dwell with her, let him not **put** her **a.**	863
7:31 *it:* for the fashion of this world **passeth a.**	3855
12: 2 carried **a** unto *these* dumb idols,	520
13: 8 *there* be knowledge, it shall **vanish a.**	2673
13:10 then that which is in part shall be **done a.**	2673
13:11 I became a man, I **put a** childish *things.*	2673
2Co 3: 7 which *glory* was to be **done a:**	2673
3:11 For if that which is **done a** *was* glorious,	2673

B

2Co	3:14 **untaken a** in the reading of the old	343+3361
	3:14 which *vail* is **done a** in Christ.	2673
	3:16 turn to the Lord, the vail shall be **taken a**.	4014
	5:17 old *things* are **past a**; behold, all *things*	3928
Gal	2:13 was **carried a** with their dissimulation.	4879
Eph	4:25 Wherefore **putting a** lying, speak every	659
	4:31 and evil speaking, be **put a** from you,	142
Col	1:23 *be* not **moved a** from the hope of	3334
2Th	2: 3 except there come a **falling a** first,	646
1Ti	1:19 some having **put a**, concerning faith	683
2Ti	1:15 which are in Asia be **turned a** from me;	654
	3: 5 the power thereof: **from** such **turn a**.	665
	3: 6 laden with sins, **led a** with divers lusts,	71
	4: 4 And they shall **turn a** *their* ears from	654
Heb	6: 6 If they shall **fall a**, to renew *them* again	3895
	8:13 and waxeth old *is* ready to **vanish a**.	854
	9:26 to **put a** sin by the sacrifice of himself.	115
	10: 4 of bulls and of goats should **take a** sins.	851
	10: 9 He **taketh a** the first, that he may establish	337
	10:11 which can never **take a** sins:	4014
	10:35 **Cast** not a therefore your confidence,	577
	12:25 **turn a** from him that *speaketh* from	654
Jas	1:10 as the flower of the grass he shall **pass a**.	3928
	1:11 also raise the rich *man* **fade a** in his ways.	3133
	1:14 when he is **drawn a** of his own lust,	1828
	4:14 for a little *time*, and then **vanisheth a**.	853
1Pe	1: 4 and undefiled, and that **fadeth not a**,	263
	1:24 and the flower thereof **falleth a:**	1601
	3:21 (not the **putting a** of the filth of the flesh,	595
	5: 4 receive a crown of glory that **fadeth not a**.	262
2Pe	3:10 which the heavens shall **pass a** with a	3928
	3:17 being **led a** with the error of the wicked,	4879
1Jn	2:17 And the world **passeth a**, and the lust	3855
	3: 5 that he was manifested to **take a** our sins;	142
Rev	7:17 God shall **wipe a** all tears from their eyes.	1813
	12:15 cause her to be **carried a of the** flood.	4216
	16:20 every island fled *a*, and the mountains	NIG
	17: 3 So he **carried** me a in the spirit into	667
	20:11 face the earth and the heaven fled *a*;	NIG
	21: 1 and the first earth were **passed a**;	3928
	21: 4 And God shall **wipe a** all tears from their	1813
	21: 4 for the former *things* are **passed a**.	505
	21:10 he **carried** me a in the spirit to a great	667
	22:19 if any *man* shall **take a** from the words	851
	22:19 God shall **take a** his part out of the book	851

AWE (3)

Ps	4: 4 **Stand in a**, and sin not: commune with	7264
	33: 8 inhabitants of the world **stand in a** of him	1481
	119:161 but my heart **standeth in a** of thy word.	6342

AWOKE (8) [WAKE]

Ge	9:24 Noah a from his wine, and knew what	3364
	41: 4 well favoured and fat kine. So Pharaoh a.	3364
	41: 7 Pharaoh a, and behold, *it was* a dream.	3364
	41:21 ill favoured, as at the beginning. So I a.	3364
Jdg	16:20 And he a out of his sleep, and said,	3364
1Ki	3:15 Solomon a; and behold, *it was* a dream.	3364
Mt	8:25 And his disciples came to *him*, and a,	1453
Lk	8:24 And they came to *him*, and a him, saying,	1326

AXE (11) [AXES]

Dt	19: 5 hand fetcheth a stroke with the **a** to cut	1631
	20:19 trees thereof by forcing an **a** against them:	1631
Jdg	9:48 Abimelech took an **a** in his hand,	7134
1Sa	13:20 his coulter, and his **a**, and his mattock.	7134
1Ki	6: 7 that there was neither hammer nor **a** *nor*	1631
2Ki	6: 5 a beam, the **a head** fell into the water:	1270
Isa	10:15 Shall the **a** boast itself against him that	1631
Jer	10: 3 of the hands of the workman, with the **a**.	4621
	51:20 Thou *art* my **battle a** *and* weapons of war:	4661
Mt	3:10 And now also the **a** is laid unto the root of	513
Lk	3: 9 And now also the **a** is laid unto the root of	513

AXES (7) [AXE]

1Sa	13:21 for the **a**, and to sharpen the goads.	7134
2Sa	12:31 under a of iron, and made them pass	4037
1Ch	20: 3 and with harrows of iron, and with **a**.	4050
Ps	74: 5 as he had lifted up a upon the thick trees.	7134
	74: 6 the carved work thereof at once with **a**	3781
Jer	46:22 come against her with **a**, as hewers of	7134
Eze	26: 9 with his **a** he shall break down thy towers.	2719

AXLETREES (2)

1Ki	7:32 **a** of the wheels *were* joined to the base:	3027
	7:33 their **a**, and their naves, and their felloes,	3027

AZAL (1)

Zec	14: 5 valley of the mountains shall reach unto **A**:	682

AZALIAH (2)

2Ki	22: 3 *that* the king sent Shaphan the son of **A**,	683
2Ch	34: 8 sent Shaphan the son of **A**, and Maaseiah	683

AZANIAH (1)

Ne	10: 9 Jeshua the son of **A**, Binnui of the sons	245

AZARAEL (1)

Ne	12:36 Shemaiah, and **A**, Milalai, Gilalai, Maai,	5832

AZAREEL (5)

1Ch	12: 6 Jesiah, and **A**, and Joezer, and Joshbeam,	5832
	25:18 The eleventh to **A**, *he*, his sons,	5832
	27:22 Of Dan, **A** the son of Jeroham. These	5832
Ezr	10:41 And Shelemiah, Shemariah,	5832
Ne	11:13 Amashai the son of **A**, the son of Ahasai,	5832

AZAREL See AZARAEL; AZAREEL

AZARIAH (49) [ABED-NEGO, UZZIAH]

1Ki	4: 2 he had; **A** the son of Zadok the priest,	5838
	4: 5 **A** the son of Nathan *was* over the officers:	5838
2Ki	14:21 all the people of Judah took **A**, which *was*	5838
	15: 1 **A** son of Amaziah king of Judah to reign.	5838
	15: 6 rest of the acts of **A**, and all that he did,	5838
	15: 7 **A** slept with his fathers; and they buried	5838
	15: 8 eighth year of **A** king of Judah did	5838
	15:17 thirtieth year of **A** king of Judah *began*	5838
	15:23 In the fiftieth year of **A** king of Judah	5838
	15:27 fiftieth year of **A** king of Judah Pekah	5838
1Ch	2: 8 And the sons of Ethan; **A**.	5838
	2:38 And Obed begat Jehu, and Jehu begat **A**,	5838
	2:39 **A** begat Helez, and Helez begat Eleasah	5838
	3:12 his son, **A** his son, Jotham his son,	5838
	6: 9 Ahimaaz begat **A**, and Azariah begat	5838
	6: 9 begat Azariah, and **A** begat Johanan,	5838
	6:10 Johanan begat **A**, (he *it is* that executed	5838
	6:11 **A** begat Amariah, and Amariah begat	5838
	6:13 begat Hilkiah, and Hilkiah begat **A**,	5838
	6:14 **A** begat Seraiah, and Seraiah begat	5838
	6:36 of Elkanah, the son of Joel, the son of **A**,	5838
	9:11 the son of Hilkiah, the son of	5838
2Ch	15: 1 the spirit of God came upon **A** the son of	5838
	21: 2 **A**, and Jehiel, and Zechariah, and Azariah,	5838
	21: 2 and **A**, and Michael, and Shephatiah:	5838
	22: 6 **A** the son of Jehoram king of Judah went	5838
	23: 1 **A** the son of Jeroham, and Ishmael the son	5838
	23: 1 **A** the son of Obed, and Maaseiah the son	5838
	26:17 **A** the priest went in after him, and with	5838
	26:20 **A** the chief priest, and all the priests,	5838
	28:12 **A** the son of Johanan, Berechiah the son	5838
	29:12 the son of Amasai, and Joel the son of **A**,	5838
	29:12 son of Abdi, and **A** the son of Jehalelel:	5838
	31:10 the chief priest of the house of Zadok	5838
	31:13 and **A** the ruler of the house of God.	5838
Ezr	7: 1 Seraiah, the son of **A**, the son of Hilkiah,	5838
	7: 3 the son of **A**, the son of Meraioth,	5838
Ne	3:23 After him repaired **A** the son of Maaseiah	5838
	3:24 from the house of **A** unto the turning *of*	5838
	7: 7 **A**, Raamiah, Nahamani, Mordecai,	5838
	8: 7 Kelita, **A**, Jozabad, Hanan, Pelaiah,	5838
	10: 2 Seraiah, **A**, Jeremiah,	5838
	12:33 And **A**, Ezra, and Meshullam,	5838
Jer	43: 2 spake **A** the son of Hoshaiah,	5838
Da	1: 6 Daniel, Hananiah, Mishael, and **A**:	5838
	1: 7 of Meshach; and to **A**, of Abed-nego.	5838
	1:11 over Daniel, Hananiah, Mishael, and **A**,	5838
	1:19 like Daniel, Hananiah, Mishael, and **A**:	5838
	2:17 Mishael, and **A**, his companions:	5839

AZAZ (1)

1Ch	5: 8 Bela the son of **A**, the son of Shema,	5811

AZAZIAH (3)

1Ch	15:21 and Obed-edom, and Jeiel, and **A**,	5812
	27:20 of Ephraim, Hoshea the son of **A**,	5812
2Ch	31:13 **A**, and Nahath, and Asahel, and Jerimoth,	5812

AZBUK (1)

Ne	3:16 repaired Nehemiah the son of **A**,	5802

AZEKAH (7)

Jos	10:10 smote them to **A**, and unto Makkedah.	5825
	10:11 stones from heaven upon them unto **A**,	5825
	15:35 Jarmuth, and Adullam, Socoh, and **A**,	5825
1Sa	17: 1 pitched between Shochoh and **A**,	5825
2Ch	11: 9 And Adoraim, and Lachish, and **A**,	5825
Ne	11:30 *at* **A**, and *in* the villages thereof.	5825
Jer	34: 7 were left, against Lachish, and against **A**:	5825

AZEL (6)

1Ch	8:37 *was* his son, Eleasah his son, **A** his son:	682
	8:38 And **A** had six sons, whose names *are*	682
	8:38 and Hanan. All these *were* the sons of **A**.	682
	9:43 his son, Eleasah his son, **A** his son.	682
	9:44 And **A** had six sons, whose names *are*	682
	9:44 and Hanan: these *were* the sons of **A**.	682

AZEM (2)

Jos	15:29 Baalah, and Iim, and **A**,	6107
	19: 3 And Hazar-shual, and Balah, and **A**,	6107

AZGAD (4)

Ezr	2:12 children of **A**, a thousand two hundred	5803
	8:12 of the sons of **A**; Johanan the son of	5803
Ne	7:17 The children of **A**, two thousand three	5803
	10:15 Bunni, A, Bebai,	5803

AZIEL (1)

1Ch	15:20 **A**, and Shemiramoth, and Jehiel,	5815

AZIZA (1)

Ezr	10:27 and Jeremoth, and Zabad, and **A**.	5819

AZMAVETH (8) [BETH-AZMAVETH]

2Sa	23:31 Abialbon the Arbathite, **A** the Barhumite,	5820
1Ch	8:36 Jehoadah begat Alemeth, and **A**,	5820
	9:42 Jarah begat Alemeth, and **A**, and Zimri;	5820
	11:33 **A** the Baharumite, Eliahba the Shaalbonite	5820
	12: 3 Jeziel, and Pelet, the sons of **A**;	5820
	27:25 over the king's treasures *was* **A** the son of	5820
Ezr	2:24 The children of **A**, forty and two.	5820
Ne	12:29 and out of the fields of Geba and **A**:	5820

AZMON (3)

Nu	34: 4 go on *to* Hazar-addar, and pass on to **A**:	6111
	34: 5 the border shall fetch a compass from **A**	6111
Jos	15: 4 *From thence* it passed toward **A**,	6111

AZNOTH-TABOR (1) [TABOR]

Jos	19:34 then the coast turneth westward *to* **A**,	243

AZOR (2)

Mt	1:13 Abiud begat Eliakim; and Eliakim begat **A**;	107
	1:14 And **A** begat Sadoc; and Sadoc begat	107

AZOTUS (1)

Ac	8:40 But Philip was found at **A**.	108

AZRIEL (3)

1Ch	5:24 **A**, and Jeremiah, and Hodaviah,	5837
	27:19 of Naphtali, Jerimoth the son of **A**:	5837
Jer	36:26 Seraiah the son of **A**, and Shelemiah	5837

AZRIKAM (6)

1Ch	3:23 Elioenai, and Hezekiah, and **A**, three.	5840
	8:38 **A**, Bocheru, and Ishmael, and Sheariah,	5840
	9:14 the son of **A**, the son of Hashabiah, of	5840
	9:44 **A**, Bocheru, and Ishmael, and Sheariah,	5840
2Ch	28: 7 **A** the governor of the house, and Elkanah	5840
Ne	11:15 the son of **A**, the son of Hashabiah,	5840

AZUBAH (4)

1Ki	22:42 his mother's name *was* **A** the daughter of	5806
1Ch	2:18 of Hezron begat *children* of **A** *his* wife,	5806
	2:19 when **A** was dead, Caleb took unto him	5806
2Ch	20:31 his mother's name *was* **A** the daughter of	5806

AZUR (2)

Jer	28: 1 *that* Hananiah the son of **A** the prophet,	5809
Eze	11: 1 whom I saw Jaazaniah the son of **A**,	5809

AZZAH (3)

Dt	2:23 *even* unto **A**, the Caphtorims,	5804
1Ki	4:24 from Tiphsah even to **A**, over all the kings	5804
Jer	25:20 **A**, and Ekron, and the remnant of Ashdod	5804

AZZAN (1)

Nu	34:26 children of Issachar, Paltiel the son of **A**.	5821

AZZUR (1)

Ne	10:17 Ater, Hizkijah, **A**,	5809

B

BAAL (63) [BAAL'S, BAAL-BERITH, BAAL-GAD, BAAL-HAMON, BAAL-HANAN, BAAL-HAZOR, BAAL-HERMON, BAAL-MEON, BAAL-PEOR, BAAL-PERAZIM, BAAL-SHALISHA, BAAL-TAMAR, BAAL-ZEBUB, BAAL-ZEPHON, BAALIM, BAMOTH-BAAL, GUR-BAAL, JERUBBAAL, KIRJATH-BAAL, MERIB-BAAL]

Nu	22:41 brought him up *into* the high places of **B**,	1168
Jdg	2:13 the LORD, and served **B** and Ashtaroth.	1168
	6:25 throw down the altar of **B** that thy father	1168
	6:28 altar of **B** was cast down, and the grove	1168
	6:30 because he hath cast down the altar of **B**,	1168
	6:31 stood against him, Will ye plead for **B**?	1168
	6:32 saying, Let **B** plead against him, because	1168
1Ki	16:31 went and served **B**, and worshipped him.	1168
	16:32 he reared up an altar for **B** *in* the house of	1168
	16:32 up an altar for **B** *in* the house of	1168
	18:19 the prophets of **B** four hundred and fifty,	1168
	18:21 if **B**, *then* follow him. And the people	1168
	18:25 Elijah said unto the prophets of **B**,	1168
	18:26 called on the name of **B** from morning	1168
	18:26 even until noon, saying, O **B**, hear us.	1168
	18:40 said unto them, Take the prophets of **B**;	1168
	19:18 the knees which have not bowed unto **B**,	1168
	22:53 For he served **B**, and worshipped him,	1168
2Ki	3: 2 for he put away the image of **B** that his	1168
	10:18 said unto them, Ahab served **B** a little;	1168
	10:19 call unto me all the prophets of **B**,	1168
	10:19 for I have a great sacrifice *to do* to **B**;	1168
	10:19 *he* might destroy the worshippers of **B**.	1168
	10:20 Proclaim a solemn assembly for **B**.	1168
	10:21 all the worshippers of **B** came, so that	1168
	10:21 they came *into* the house of **B**,	1168
	10:21 the house of **B** was full from one end to	1168
	10:22 vestments for all the worshippers of **B**.	1168
	10:23 *into* the house of **B**, and said unto	1168
	10:23 said unto the worshippers of **B**, Search,	1168
	10:23 the LORD, but the worshippers of **B** only.	1168
	10:25 and went to the city of the house of **B**.	1168
	10:26 forth the images out of the house of **B**,	1168
	10:27 they brake down the image of **B**,	1168
	10:27 brake down the house of **B**, and made it a	1168
	10:28 Thus Jehu destroyed **B** out of Israel.	1168
	11:18 of the land went *into* the house of **B**,	1168

B

2Ki	11:18 slew Mattan the priest of **B** before	1168
	17:16 and the host of heaven, and served **B**,	1168
	21: 3 reared up altars for **B**, and made a grove,	1168
	23: 4 all the vessels that were made for **B**,	1168
	23: 5 them also that burnt incense unto **B**,	1168
1Ch	4:33 *were* round about the same cities, unto **B**.	1168
	5: 5 Micah his son, Reaia his son, **B** his son,	1168
	8:30 and Zur, and Kish, and **B**, and Nadab,	1168
	9:36 and Kish, and **B**, and Ner, and Nadab,	1168
2Ch	23:17 all the people went *to* the house of **B**,	1168
	23:17 slew Mattan the priest of **B** before	1168
Jer	2: 8 the prophets prophesied by **B**,	1168
	7: 9 burn incense unto **B**, and walk after other	1168
	11:13 *even* altars to burn incense unto **B**.	1168
	11:17 me to anger in offering incense unto **B**.	1168
	12:16 as they taught my people to swear by **B**;	1168
	19: 5 They have built also the high places of **B**,	1168
	19: 5 sons with fire *for* burnt offerings unto **B**,	1168
	23:13 they prophesied in **B**, and caused my	1168
	23:27 fathers have forgotten my name for **B**.	1168
	32:29 roofs they have offered incense unto **B**,	1168
	32:35 they built the high places of **B**, which *are*	1168
Hos	2: 8 and gold, *which* they prepared for **B**.	1168
	13: 1 but when he offended in **B**, he died.	1168
Zep	1: 4 I will cut off the remnant of **B** from this	1168
Ro	11: 4 not bowed the knee to *the image of* **B**.	896

BAAL'S (1) [BAAL]

1Ki	18:22 **B** prophets *are* four hundred and fifty	1168

BAALAH (5)

Jos	15: 9 the border was drawn to **B**, which *is*	1173
	15:10 the border compassed from **B** westward	1173
	15:11 passed along *to* mount **B**, and went out	1173
	15:29 **B**, and Iim, and Azem,	1173
1Ch	13: 6 David went up, and all Israel, to **B**,	1173

BAALATH (3) [BAALATH-BEER]

Jos	19:44 And Eltekeh, and Gibbethon, and **B**,	1191
1Ki	9:18 **B**, and Tadmor in the wilderness,	1191
2Ch	8: 6 **B**, and all the store cities that Solomon	1191

BAALATH-BEER (1) [BAALATH, BEER]

Jos	19: 8 that *were* round about these cities to **B**,	1192

BAAL-BERITH (2) [BAAL, BERITH]

Jdg	8:33 after Baalim, and made **B** their god.	1170
	9: 4 ten *pieces* of silver out of the house of **B**,	1170

BAALE OF JUDAH (1) [JUDAH]

2Sa	6: 2 that *were* with him from **B**, 1184	

BAAL-GAD (3) [BAAL, GAD]

Jos	11:17 unto **B** in the valley of Lebanon under	1171
	12: 7 from **B** in the valley of Lebanon even unto	1171
	13: 5 from **B** under mount Hermon unto	1171

BAAL-HAMON (1) [BAAL]

SS	8:11 Solomon had a vineyard at **B**; he let out	1174

BAAL-HANAN (5) [BAAL, HANAN]

Ge	36:38 **B** the son of Achbor reigned in his stead.	1177
	36:39 the son of Achbor died,	1177
1Ch	1:49 **B** the son of Achbor reigned in his stead.	1177
	1:50 when **B** was dead, Hadad reigned in his	1177
	27:28 in the low plains *was* **B** the Gederite:	1177

BAAL-HAZOR (1) [BAAL, HAZOR]

2Sa	13:23 that Absalom had sheepshearers in **B**,	1178

BAAL-HERMON (2) [BAAL, HERMON]

Jdg	3: 3 from mount **B** to the entering in of	1179
1Ch	5:23 they increased from Bashan unto **B** and	1179

BAALI (1)

Hos	2:16 call *me* Ishi; and shalt call me no more **B**.	1180

BAALIM (18) [BAAL]

Jdg	2:11 in the sight of the LORD, and served **B**:	1168
	3: 7 their God, and served **B** and the groves.	1168
	8:33 went a whoring after **B**,	1168
	10: 6 served **B**, and Ashtaroth, and the gods of	1168
	10:10 have forsaken our God, and *also* served **B**.	1168
1Sa	7: 4 the children of Israel did put away **B** and	1168
	12:10 and have served **B** and Ashtaroth.	1168
1Ki	18:18 of the LORD, and thou hast followed **B**.	1168
2Ch	17: 3 his father David, and sought not unto **B**;	1168
	24: 7 of the LORD did they bestow upon **B**.	1168
	28: 2 and made also molten images for **B**.	1168
	33: 3 reared up altars for **B**, and made groves,	1168
	34: 4 they brake down the altars of **B** in his	1168
Jer	2:23 am not polluted, I have not gone after **B**?	1168
	9:14 after **B**, which their fathers taught them:	1168
Hos	2:13 I will visit upon her the days of **B**,	1168
	2:17 I will take away the names of **B** out of	1168
	11: 2 sacrificed unto **B**, and burned incense	1168

BAALIS (1)

Jer	40:14 Dost thou certainly know that **B** the king	1185

BAAL-MEON (3) [BAAL, BETH-BAAL-MEON, BETH-MEON]

Nu	32:38 and **B**, (*their* names being changed,)	1186
1Ch	5: 8 dwelt in Aroer, even unto Nebo and **B**:	1186
Eze	25: 9 Beth-jeshimoth, **B**, and Kiriathaim,	1186

BAAL-PEOR (6) [BAAL, PEOR]

Nu	25: 3 Israel joined himself unto **B**: and the anger	1187
	25: 5 one his men that were joined unto **B**.	1187
Dt	4: 3 seen what the LORD did because of **B**:	1187
	4: 3 for all the men that followed **B**, the LORD	1187
Ps	106:28 They joined themselves also unto **B**,	1187
Hos	9:10 *but* they went *to* **B**,	1187

BAAL-PERAZIM (4) [BAAL, PERAZIM]

2Sa	5:20 David came to **B**, and David smote them	1188
	5:20 he called the name of that place **B**.	1188
1Ch	14:11 So they came up to **B**; and David smote	1188
	14:11 they called the name of that place **B**.	1188

BAALS See BAALIM

BAAL-SHALISHA (1) [BAAL, SHALISHA]

2Ki	4:42 there came a man from **B**, and brought	1190

BAAL-TAMAR (1) [BAAL, TAMAR]

Jdg	20:33 and put *themselves* in array at **B**:	1193

BAAL-ZEBUB (4) [BAAL]

2Ki	1: 2 inquire of **B** the god of Ekron whether I	1176
	1: 3 ye go to inquire of **B** the god of Ekron?	1176
	1: 6 thou sendest to inquire of **B** the god of	1176
	1:16 to inquire of **B** the god of Ekron,	1176

BAAL-ZEPHON (3) [BAAL, ZEPHON]

Ex	14: 2 and the sea, over against **B**:	1189
	14: 9 by the sea, beside Pi-hahiroth, before **B**.	1189
Nu	33: 7 again unto Pi-hahiroth, which *is* before **B**:	1189

BAANA (2)

1Ki	4:12 the son of Ahilud; *to* him pertained	1195
Ne	3: 4 unto them repaired Zadok the son of **B**.	1195

BAANAH (10)

2Sa	4: 2 the name of the one *was* **B**, and the name	1196
	4: 5 Rechab and **B**, went, and came about	1196
	4: 6 and Rechab and **B** his brother escaped.	1196
	4: 9 David answered Rechab and **B** his brother	1196
	23:29 Heleb the son of **B**, a Netophathite, Ittai	1196
1Ki	4:16 **B** the son of Hushai *was* in Asher and	1195
1Ch	11:30 Heled the son of **B** the Netophathite,	1196
Ezr	2: 2 Bilshan, Mizpar, Bigvai, Rehum, **B**.	1196
Ne	7: 7 Bilshan, Mispereth, Bigvai, Nehum, **B**.	1196
	10:27 Malluch, Harim, **B**,	1196

BAARA (1)

1Ch	8: 8 away; Hushim and **B** were his wives.	1199

BAASEIAH (1)

1Ch	6:40 The son of Michael, the son of **B**, the son	1202

BAASHA (28)

1Ki	15:16 and **B** king of Israel all their days.	1201
	15:17 **B** king of Israel went up against Judah,	1201
	15:19 break thy league with **B** king of Israel,	1201
	15:21 when **B** heard *thereof*, that he left off	1201
	15:22 timber thereof, wherewith **B** had builded;	1201
	15:27 the son of Ahijah, of the house of	1201
	15:27 **B** smote him at Gibbethon,	1201
	15:28 year of Asa king of Judah did **B** slay him,	1201
	15:32 and **B** king of Israel all their days.	1201
	15:33 the son of Ahijah to reign over all Israel	1201
	16: 1 came to Jehu the son of Hanani against **B**,	1201
	16: 3 I will take away the posterity of **B**,	1201
	16: 4 Him that dieth of **B** in the city shall	1201
	16: 5 Now the rest of the acts of **B**, and what he	1201
	16: 6 So **B** slept with his fathers, and was buried	1201
	16: 7 came the word of the LORD against **B**,	1201
	16: 8 the son of **B** to reign over Israel in Tirzah,	1201
	16:11 his throne, *that* he slew all the house of **B**:	1201
	16:12 Thus did Zimri destroy all the house of **B**,	1201
	16:12 which he spake against **B** by Jehu	1201
	16:13 For all the sins of **B**, and the sins of Elah	1201
	21:22 like the house of **B** the son of Ahijah,	1201
2Ki	9: 9 and like the house of **B** the son of Ahijah:	1201
2Ch	16: 1 thirtieth year of the reign of Asa **B** king of	1201
	16: 3 go, break thy league with **B** king of Israel,	1201
	16: 5 when **B** heard *it*, that he left off building	1201
	16: 6 where*with* **B** was a building;	1201
Jer	41: 9 king had made for fear of **B** king of Israel:	1201

BABBLER (2) [BABBLING]

Ecc	10:11 and a **b** is no better.	1167+3956+1886.1
Ac	17:18 And some said, What will this **b** say?	4691

BABBLING (1) [BABBLER, BABBLINGS]

Pr	23:29 who hath **b**? who hath wounds without	7879

BABBLINGS (2) [BABBLING]

1Ti	6:20 avoiding profane *and* vain **b**,	2757
2Ti	2:16 But shun profane *and* vain **b**: for they	2757

BABE (6) [BABES]

Ex	2: 6 behold, the **b** wept. And she had	5288
Lk	1:41 of Mary, the **b** leaped in her womb;	1025
	1:44 the **b** leaped in my womb for joy.	1025
	2:12 Ye shall find *the* **b** wrapped in swaddling	1025
	2:16 and Joseph, and the **b** lying in a manger.	1025
Heb	5:13 in the word of righteousness: for he is a **b**.	3516

BABEL (2) [BABYLON]

Ge	10:10 the beginning of his kingdom was **B**,	894

Ge	11: 9 Therefore is the name of it called **B**;	894

BABES (9) [BABE]

Ps	8: 2 Out of the mouth of **b** and sucklings hast	5768
	17:14 leave the rest of their *substance* to their **b**.	5768
Isa	3: 4 their princes, and **b** shall rule over them.	8586
Mt	11:25 prudent, and hast revealed them unto **b**.	3516
	21:16 Out of the mouth of **b** and sucklings thou	3516
Lk	10:21 prudent, and hast revealed them unto **b**:	3516
Ro	2:20 instructor of the foolish, a teacher of **b**,	3516
1Co	3: 1 as unto carnal, *even* as unto **b** in Christ.	3516
1Pe	2: 2 As newborn **b**, desire the sincere milk of	1025

BABOONS See PEACOCKS

BABYLON (286) [BABEL, BABYLON'S, BABYLONIANS, BABYLONISH]

2Ki	17:24 the king of Assyria brought *men* from **B**,	894
	17:30 And the men of **B** made Succoth-benoth,	894
	20:12 king of **B**, sent letters and a present unto	894
	20:14 are come from a far country, *even* from **B**.	894
	20:17 store unto this day, shall be carried unto **B**.	894
	20:18 be eunuchs in the palace of the king of **B**.	894
	24: 1 In his days Nebuchadnezzar king of **B** came	894
	24: 7 for the king of **B** had taken from the river	894
	24:10 king of **B** came up *against* Jerusalem,	894
	24:11 Nebuchadnezzar king of **B** came against	894
	24:12 the king of Judah went out to the king of **B**,	894
	24:12 the king of **B** took him in the eighth year of	894
	24:15 he carried away Jehoiachin to **B**,	894
	24:15 he *into* captivity from Jerusalem to **B**.	894
	24:16 even them the king of **B** brought captive to	894
	24:16 the king of Babylon brought captive to **B**.	894
	24:17 the king of **B** made Mattaniah his father's	894
	24:20 Zedekiah rebelled against the king of **B**.	894
	25: 1 *that* Nebuchadnezzar king of **B** came, he,	894
	25: 6 brought him up to the king of **B** to Riblah;	894
	25: 7 with fetters of brass, and carried him to **B**.	894
	25: 8 year of king Nebuchadnezzar king of **B**,	894
	25: 8 a servant of the king of **B**, *unto* Jerusalem:	894
	25:11 the fugitives that fell away to the king of **B**,	894
	25:13 *pieces*, and carried the brass of them to **B**.	894
	25:20 brought them to the king of **B** to Riblah:	894
	25:21 the king of **B** smote them, and slew them	894
	25:22 whom Nebuchadnezzar king of **B** had left,	894
	25:23 that the king of **B** had made Gedaliah	894
	25:24 dwell in the land, and serve the king of **B**;	894
	25:27 the month, *that* Evil-merodach king of **B**,	894
	25:28 of the kings that *were* with him in **B**;	894
1Ch	9: 1 *who* were carried away to **B** for their	894
2Ch	32:31 *of* the ambassadors of the princes of **B**,	894
	33:11 him with fetters, and carried him to **B**.	894
	36: 6 him came up Nebuchadnezzar king of **B**,	894
	36: 6 bound him in fetters, to carry him to **B**.	894
	36: 7 the vessels of the house of the LORD to **B**,	894
	36: 7 Babylon, and put them in his temple at **B**.	894
	36:10 sent, and brought him to **B**,	894
	36:18 of his princes; all *these* he brought *to* **B**.	894
	36:20 from the sword carried he away to **B**;	894
Ezr	1:11 were brought up from **B** unto Jerusalem.	894
	2: 1 whom Nebuchadnezzar the king of **B** had	894
	2: 1 king of Babylon had carried away unto **B**,	894
	5:12 the hand of Nebuchadnezzar the king of **B**,	895
	5:12 and carried the people away into **B**.	895
	5:13 in the first year of Cyrus the king of **B**	895
	5:14 brought them into the temple of **B**, those	895
	5:14 Cyrus the king take out of the temple of **B**,	895
	5:17 which *is* there at **B**, whether it be *so*, that	895
	6: 1 where the treasures were laid up in **B**.	895
	6: 5 brought unto **B**, be restored,	894
	7: 6 This Ezra went up from **B**; and he *was* a	894
	7: 9 the first month began he to go up from **B**,	894
	7:16 thou canst find in all the province of **B**,	895
	8: 1 of them that went up with me from **B**,	894
Ne	7: 6 whom Nebuchadnezzar the king of **B** had	894
	13: 6 thirtieth year of Artaxerxes king of **B** came	894
Est	2: 6 whom Nebuchadnezzar the king of **B** had	894
Ps	87: 4 of Rahab and **B** to them that know me:	894
	137: 1 By the rivers of **B**, there we sat down, yea,	894
	137: 8 O daughter of **B**, who art *to be* destroyed;	894
Isa	13: 1 The burden of **B**, which Isaiah the son of	894
	13:19 **B**, the glory of kingdoms, the beauty of	894
	14: 4 take up this proverb against the king of **B**,	894
	14:22 cut off from **B** the name, and remnant,	894
	21: 9 he answered and said, **B** is fallen, is fallen;	894
	39: 1 king of **B**, sent letters and a present to	894
	39: 3 from a far country unto me, *even* from **B**.	894
	39: 6 in store until this day, shall be carried *to* **B**:	894
	39: 7 be eunuchs in the palace of the king of **B**.	894
	43:14 For your sake I have sent to **B**,	894
	47: 1 and sit in the dust, O virgin daughter of **B**,	894
	48:14 he will do his pleasure on **B**, and his arm	894
	48:20 Go ye forth of **B**, flee ye from	894
Jer	20: 4 all Judah into the hand of the king of **B**,	894
	20: 4 he shall carry them captive into **B**,	894
	20: 5 and take them, and carry them to **B**.	894
	20: 6 thou shalt come to **B**, and there thou shalt	894
	21: 2 for Nebuchadrezzar king of **B** maketh war	894
	21: 4 wherewith ye fight against the king of **B**,	894
	21: 7 into the hand of Nebuchadrezzar king of **B**,	894
	21:10 be given into the hand of the king of **B**,	894
	22:25 the hand of Nebuchadrezzar king of **B**,	894
	24: 1 after that Nebuchadrezzar king of **B** had	894
	24: 1 Jerusalem, and had brought them *to* **B**.	894
	25: 1 the first year of Nebuchadrezzar king of **B**;	894

B

Jer 25: 9 Nebuchadrezzar the king of **B**, my servant, 894
25:11 these nations shall serve the king of **B** 894
25:12 *that* I will punish the king of **B**, and that 894
27: 6 the hand of Nebuchadnezzar the king of **B**, 894
27: 8 the same Nebuchadnezzar the king of **B**, 894
27: 8 their neck under the yoke of the king of **B**, 894
27: 9 saying, Ye shall not serve the king of **B**: 894
27:11 their neck under the yoke of the king of **B**, 894
27:12 your necks under the yoke of the king of **B**, 894
27:13 the nation that will not serve the king of **B**? 894
27:14 saying, Ye shall not serve the king of **B**: 894
27:16 *shall* now shortly be brought again from **B**: 894
27:17 unto them; serve the king of **B**, and live: 894
27:18 of Judah, and at Jerusalem, go not to **B**. 894
27:20 Which Nebuchadnezzar king of **B** took not, 894
27:20 king of Judah from Jerusalem to **B**, 894
27:22 They shall be carried to **B**, and there shall 894
28: 2 I have broken the yoke of the king of **B**. 894
28: 3 that Nebuchadnezzar king of **B** took away 894
28: 3 from this place, and carried them *to* **B**: 894
28: 4 of Judah, that went into **B**, saith the Lord: 894
28: 4 for I will break the yoke of the king of **B**. 894
28: 6 away captive, from **B** into this place. 894
28:11 **B** from the neck of all nations within 894
28:14 *they* may serve Nebuchadnezzar king of **B**, 894
29: 1 carried away captive from Jerusalem to **B**; 894
29: 3 Zedekiah king of Judah sent unto **B** to 894
29: 3 Babylon to Nebuchadnezzar king of **B**, 894
29: 4 to be carried away from Jerusalem unto **B**; 894
29:10 years be accomplished at **B** I will visit you, 894
29:15 The Lord hath raised us up prophets in **B**; 894
29:20 whom I have sent from Jerusalem to **B**: 894
29:21 into the hand of Nebuchadrezzar king of **B**; 894
29:22 by all the captivity of Judah which *are* in **B**, 894
29:22 whom the king of **B** roasted in the fire; 894
29:28 For therefore he sent unto us *in* **B**, saying, 894
32: 3 give this city into the hand of the king of **B**, 894
32: 4 be delivered into the hand of the king of **B**, 894
32: 5 he shall lead Zedekiah *to* **B**, and there shall 894
32:28 into the hand of Nebuchadrezzar king of **B**, 894
32:36 into the hand of the king of **B** by the sword, 894
34: 1 when Nebuchadnezzar king of **B**, and all 894
34: 2 give this city into the hand of the king of **B**, 894
34: 3 eyes shall behold the eyes of the king of **B**, 894
34: 3 mouth to mouth, and thou shalt go to **B**. 894
35:11 when Nebuchadrezzar king of **B** came up 894
36:29 The king of **B** shall certainly come 894
37: 1 Nebuchadnezzar king of **B** made king 894
37:17 be delivered into the hand of the king of **B**. 894
38: 3 The king of **B** shall not come against you, 894
38:23 shalt be taken by the hand of the king of **B**: 894
39: 1 came Nebuchadrezzar king of **B** and all his 894
39: 3 all the princes of the king of **B** came in, 894
39: 3 the residue of the princes of the king of **B**. 894
39: 5 king of **B** to Riblah in the land of Hamath, 894
39: 6 the king of **B** slew the sons of Zedekiah 894
39: 6 also the king of **B** slew all the nobles of 894
39: 7 bound him with chains to carry him to **B**. 894
39: 9 **B** the remnant of the people that remained 894
39:11 Nebuchadrezzar king of **B** gave charge 894
40: 1 which were carried away captive unto **B**. 894
40: 4 good unto thee to come with me *into* **B**, 894
40: 4 seem ill unto thee to come with me *into* **B**, 894
40: 5 whom the king of **B** hath made governor 894
40: 7 that the king of **B** had made Gedaliah 894
40: 7 that were not carried away captive to **B**; 894
40: 9 dwell in the land and serve the king of **B**, 894
40:11 heard that the king of **B** had left a remnant 894
41: 2 the king of **B** had made governor over 894
41:18 whom the king of **B** made governor in 894
42:11 Be not afraid of the king of **B**, of whom ye 894
43: 3 to death, and carry us away captives *into* **B**. 894
43:10 and take Nebuchadrezzar the king of **B**, 894
44:30 into the hand of Nebuchadrezzar king of **B**, 894
46: 2 which Nebuchadrezzar king of **B** smote in 894
46:13 Nebuchadrezzar king of **B** should come 894
46:26 into the hand of Nebuchadrezzar king of **B**, 894
49:28 Nebuchadrezzar king of **B** shall smite, 894
49:30 for Nebuchadrezzar king of **B** hath taken 894
50: 1 The word that the Lord spake against **B** 894
50: 2 say, **B** is taken, Bel is confounded, 894
50: 8 Remove out of the midst of **B**, and go forth 894
50: 9 cause to come up against **B** an assembly of 894
50:13 every one that goeth by **B** shall be 894
50:14 Put *yourselves* in array against **B** round 894
50:16 Cut off the sower from **B**, and him that 894
50:17 last this Nebuchadrezzar king of **B** hath 894
50:18 I *will* punish the king of **B** and his land, 894
50:23 how is **B** become a desolation among 894
50:24 also taken, O **B**, and thou wast not aware: 894
50:28 that flee and escape out of the land of **B**, 894
50:29 Call together the archers against **B**: all ye 894
50:34 the land, and disquiet the inhabitants of **B**. 894
50:35 upon the inhabitants of **B**, and upon her 894
50:42 the battle, against thee, O daughter of **B**. 894
50:43 king of **B** hath heard the report of them, 894
50:45 of the Lord, that he hath taken against **B**; 894
50:46 At the noise of the taking of **B** the earth is 894
51: 1 I *will* raise up against **B**, and against them 894
51: 2 will send unto **B** fanners, that shall fan her, 894
51: 6 Flee out of the midst of **B**, and deliver 894
51: 7 **B** *hath been* a golden cup in the Lord's 894
51: 8 **B** is suddenly fallen and destroyed: howl 894
51: 9 We would have healed **B**, but she is not 894
51:11 for his device *is* against **B**, to destroy it; 894

Jer 51:12 Set up the standard upon the walls of **B**, 894
51:12 he spake against the inhabitants of **B**. 894
51:24 render unto **B** and to all the inhabitants 894
51:29 of the Lord shall be performed against **B**, 894
51:29 to make the land of **B** a desolation without 894
51:30 The mighty *men* of **B** have forborn to fight, 894
51:31 shew the king of **B** that his city is taken at 894
51:33 The daughter of **B** *is* like a threshingfloor, 894
51:34 the king of **B** hath devoured 894
51:35 done to me and *to* my flesh *be* upon **B**, 894
51:37 **B** shall become heaps, a dwelling place for 894
51:41 how is **B** become an astonishment among 894
51:42 The sea is come up upon **B**: she is covered 894
51:44 I will punish Bel in **B**, and I will bring forth 894
51:44 more unto him: yea, the wall of **B** shall fall. 894
51:47 do judgment upon the graven images of **B**: 894
51:48 and all that *is* therein, shall sing for **B**: 894
51:49 As **B** *hath caused* the slain of Israel to fall, 894
51:49 so at **B** shall fall the slain of all the earth. 894
51:53 Though **B** should mount up to heaven, 894
51:54 A sound of a cry *cometh* from **B**, 894
51:55 Because the Lord *hath* spoiled **B**, 894
51:56 upon **B**, and her mighty *men* are taken, 894
51:58 broad walls of **B** shall be utterly broken, 894
51:59 Judah *into* **B** in the fourth year of his reign. 894
51:60 book all the evil that should come upon **B**, 894
51:60 all these words that are written against **B**. 894
51:61 When thou comest *to* **B**, and shalt see, 894
51:64 Thus shall **B** sink, and shall not rise from 894
52: 3 that Zedekiah rebelled against the king of **B**. 894
52: 4 *that* Nebuchadrezzar king of **B** came, 894
52: 9 carried him up unto the king of **B** to Riblah 894
52:10 the king of **B** slew the sons of Zedekiah 894
52:11 the king of **B** bound him in chains, 894
52:11 carried him to **B**, and put him in prison till 894
52:12 year of Nebuchadrezzar king of **B**, 894
52:12 *which* served the king of **B**, into Jerusalem, 894
52:15 that fell to the king of **B**, and the rest of 894
52:17 and carried all the brass of them to **B**. 894
52:26 brought them to the king of **B** to Riblah. 894
52:27 the king of **B** smote them, and put them to 894
52:31 Evil-merodach king of **B** in the *first* year 894
52:32 of the kings that *were* with him in **B**, 894
52:34 a continual diet given him of the king of **B**, 894
Eze 12:13 I will bring him to **B** *to* the land of 894
17:12 the king of **B** is come *to* Jerusalem, 894
17:12 thereof, and led them with him to **B**: 894
17:16 with him in the midst of **B** he shall die. 894
17:20 I will bring him to **B**, and will plead with 894
19: 9 chains, and brought him to the king of **B**, 894
21:19 that the sword of the king of **B** may come: 894
21:21 For the king of **B** stood at the parting of 894
24: 2 the king of **B** set himself against Jerusalem 894
26: 7 upon Tyrus Nebuchadrezzar king of **B**, 894
29:18 Nebuchadrezzar king of **B** caused his army 894
29:19 of Egypt unto Nebuchadrezzar king of **B**; 894
30:10 by the hand of Nebuchadrezzar king of **B**. 894
30:24 I will strengthen the arms of the king of **B**, 894
30:25 I will strengthen the arms of the king of **B**, 894
30:25 my sword into the hand of the king of **B**, 894
32:11 The sword of the king of **B** shall come 894
Da 1: 1 Nebuchadnezzar king of **B** *unto* Jerusalem, 894
2:12 to destroy all the wise *men* of **B**: 895
2:14 was gone forth to slay the wise *men* of **B**: 895
2:18 perish with the rest of the wise *men* of **B**: 895
2:24 had ordained to destroy the wise *men* of **B**: 895
2:24 unto him; Destroy not the wise *men* of **B**: 895
2:48 him ruler over the whole province of **B**, 895
2:48 the governors over all the wise *men* of **B**. 895
2:49 over the affairs of the province of **B**. 895
3: 1 in the plain of Dura, in the province of **B**. 895
3:12 set over the affairs of the province of **B**, 895
3:30 and Abed-nego, in the province of **B**. 895
4: 6 to bring in all the wise *men* of **B** before me, 895
4:29 walked in the palace of the kingdom of **B**. 895
4:30 king spake, and said, *Is* not this great **B**, 895
5: 7 king spake, and said to the wise *men* of **B**, 895
7: 1 In the first year of Belshazzar king of **B**. 895
Mic 4:10 in the field, and thou shalt go *even* to **B**; 894
Zec 2: 7 Zion, that dwellest *with* the daughter of **B**. 894
6:10 which are come from **B**, and come thou 894
Mt 1:11 the time they were carried away to **B**: 897
1:12 And after they were brought to **B**, 897
1:17 from David until the carrying away into **B** 897
1:17 from the carrying away into **B** unto Christ 897
Ac 7:43 and I will carry you away beyond **B**. 897
1Pe 5:13 The *church that is* at **B**, elected together 897
Rev 14: 8 saying, **B** is fallen, is fallen, *that* great city, 897
16:19 great **B** came in remembrance before God, 897
17: 5 name written, MYSTERY, **B** THE GREAT, 897
18: 2 saying, **B** the great is fallen, is fallen, 897
18:10 saying, Alas, alas, *that* great city **B**, 897
18:21 Thus with violence shall *that* great city **B** 897

BABYLON'S (8) [BABYLON]

Jer 32: 2 the king of **B** army besieged Jerusalem: 894
34: 7 When the king of **B** army fought against 894
34:21 into the hand of the king of **B** army, 894
38: 3 given into the hand of the king of **B** army, 894
38:17 go not forth to the king of **B** princes, 894
38:18 if thou wilt not go forth to the king of **B** 894
38:22 *be* brought forth to the king of **B** princes, 894
39:13 Rab-mag, and all the king of **B** princes; 894

BABYLONIA See BABYLONISH; CHALDEA; CHALDEANS

BABYLONIANS (4) [BABYLON]

Ezr 4: 9 the Apharsites, the Archevites, the **B**, 896
Eze 23:15 *after* the manner of the **B** of Chaldea, 894+1121
23:17 **B** came to her into the bed of love, 894+1121
23:23 The **B**, and all the Chaldeans, Pekod, 894+1121

BABYLONISH (1) [BABYLON]

Jos 7:21 When I saw among the spoils a goodly **B** 8152

BACA (1)

Ps 84: 6 *Who* passing through the valley of **B** make 1056

BACHRITES (1)

Nu 26:35 of Becher, the family of the **B**: of Tahan, 1076

BACK (155) [BACKBITERS, BACKBITETH, BACKBITING, BACKBITINGS, BACKS, BACKSIDE, BACKSLIDER, BACKSLIDING, BACKSLIDINGS, BACKWARD, CROOKBACKT, HORSEBACK]

Ge 14:16 he **brought** b all the goods, 7725
19: 9 they said, Stand **b**. And they said *again*, 1973
19:26 But his wife looked **b** from behind him, NIH
38:29 to pass, as he **drew** b his hand, that, 7725
39: 9 neither hath he **kept** b any thing from me 2820
Ex 14:21 the Lord caused the sea to go **b** by a NIH
18: 2 Moses' wife, after he had sent her **b**, NIH
23: 4 **surely bring** it to him again. 7725+7725
33:23 hand, and thou shalt see my **b** parts: 268
Lev 5: 3 it shall he take off hard by the **b** bone; 6096
Nu 9: 7 are we **kept** b, that *we* may not 1639
13:26 **brought** b word unto them, and unto all 7725
22:34 if it displease thee, I will **get** me b again. 7725
24:11 the Lord hath **kept** thee **b** from honour. 4513
Dt 23:13 shalt **turn** b and cover that which cometh 7725
Jos 8:20 wilderness **turned** b upon the pursuers. 2015
8:26 For Joshua **drew** not his hand **b**, 7725
11:10 Joshua at that time **turned** b, 7725
23:12 Else if ye do **in any wise go** b, 7725+7725
Jdg 11:35 mouth unto the Lord, and I cannot **go b**. 7725
18:26 he turned and **went b** unto his house. 7725
Ru 1:15 sister in law is **gone** b unto her people, 7725
2: 6 the Moabitish damsel that **came b** with 7725
1Sa 10: 9 that when he had turned his **b** to go from 7926
15:11 for he is **turned b** from following me, 7725
25:34 which hath **kept** me b from hurting thee, 4513
2Sa 1:22 the bow of Jonathan turned not **b**, 268
12:23 can I **bring** him b again? I shall go to him, 7725
15:20 return thou, and **take b** thy brethren: 7725
15:25 **Carry b** the ark of God *into* the city: 7725
17: 3 I will **bring b** all the people unto thee: 7725
18:16 after Israel: for Joab **held b** the people. 2820
19:10 ye not a word of **bringing** the king b? 7725
19:11 Why are ye the last to **bring** the king b to 7725
19:12 then are ye the last to **bring b** the king? 7725
19:37 Let thy servant, I pray thee, **turn b again**, 7725
19:43 not be first had in **bringing b** our king? 7725
1Ki 13:18 **Bring** him b with thee into thine house, 7725
13:19 he **went b** with him, and did eat bread in 7725
13:20 unto the prophet that **brought** him b: 7725
13:22 **camest b**, and hast eaten bread and 7725
13:23 for the prophet whom he had **brought b**. 7725
13:26 when the prophet that **brought** him b 7725
13:29 and laid it upon the ass, and **brought** it b: 7725
14: 9 to anger, and hast cast me behind thy b: 1458
14:28 **brought** them b into the guard chamber. 7725
18:37 *that* thou hast **turned** their heart b again. 5437
19:20 he said unto him, Go **again**: for what 7725
19:21 he **returned** b from him, and took a yoke 7725
22:26 **carry** him b unto Amon the governor of 7725
22:33 that they **turned** b from pursuing him. 7725
2Ki 1: 5 when the messengers **turned b** unto him, 7725
1: 5 unto them, Why are ye now **turned b**? 7725
2:13 **went b**, and stood by the bank of Jordan; 7725
2:24 he turned b, and looked on them, 310
8:29 king Joram **went b** to be healed in Jezreel 7725
15:20 So the king of Assyria **turned b**, 7725
19:28 I will **turn** thee b by the way by which 7725
20: 9 forward ten degrees, or **go b** ten degrees? 7725
1Ch 21:20 Ornan **turned** b, and saw the angel; 7725
2Ch 13:14 when Judah **looked b**, behold, the battle 6437
18:25 **carry** him b to Amon the governor of 7725
18:32 they **turned** b *again* from pursuing him. 7725
19: 4 **brought** them b unto the Lord God of 7725
25:13 of the army which Amaziah **sent b**, 7725
34:16 and **brought** the king word b again, 7725
Ne 8: 3 for Joram **went b** to be healed NIH
Ne 5: 3 turned b, and entered by the gate of 7725
Job 23:12 Neither have I **gone b** from 4185
26: 9 He **holdeth b** the face of *his* throne, 270
33:18 He **keepeth b** his soul from the pit, 2820
33:30 To **bring b** his soul from the pit, to be 7725
34:27 Because they **turned b** from him, 5493
39:22 neither **turneth** he b from the sword. 7725
Ps 9: 3 When mine enemies are turned **b**, they 268
14: 7 when the Lord **bringeth b** the captivity 7725
19:13 **Keep b** thy servant also from 2820
21:12 shalt thou make them turn their **b**, 7926
35: 4 let them be turned **b** and brought to 268
44:10 makest us to turn **b** from the enemy: 268
44:18 Our heart is not turned **b**, neither have 268
53: 3 Every one of them is **gone b**, they are 5472
53: 6 When God **bringeth b** the captivity of his 7725
56: 9 then shall mine enemies turn **b**: 268

B

Ps	70: 3	Let them be **turned** b for a reward of	7725
	78: 9	bows, turned *b* in the day of battle.	NIH
	78:41	they turned *b* and tempted God,	NIH
	78:57	turned *b*, and dealt unfaithfully like their	NIH
	80:18	will not we go *b* from thee: quicken us,	NIH
	85: 1	hast **brought b** the captivity of Jacob.	7725
	114: 3	sea saw *it*, and fled: Jordan was driven **b**.	268
	114: 5	thou Jordan, *that* thou wast driven **b**?	268
	129: 3	The plowers plowed upon my **b**: they	1354
	129: 5	confounded and turned **b** that hate Zion.	268
Pr	10:13	a rod *is* for the **b** of him that is void of	1460
	19:29	for scorners, and stripes for the **b** of fools.	1460
	26: 3	for the ass, and a rod for the fools' **b**.	1460
Isa	14:27	*is* stretched out, and who shall **turn** it **b**?	7725
	31: 2	bring evil, and will not **call b** his words:	5493
	37:29	I will **turn** thee **b** by the way by which	7725
	38:17	for thou hast cast all my sins behind thy **b**.	1460
	42:17	They shall be turned **b**, they shall be	268
	43: 6	Give *up*; and to the south, **Keep** not **b**:	3607
	50: 5	not rebellious, neither turned away **b**.	268
	50: 6	I gave my **b** to the smiters, and my cheeks	1460
Jer	2:27	for they have turned *their* **b** unto me,	6203
	4: 8	of the Lord is not **turned b** from us.	7725
	4:28	not repent, neither will I **turn b** from it.	7725
	6: 9	**turn b** thine hand as a grapegatherer into	7725
	8: 5	is this people of Jerusalem **slidden b** *by a*	7725
	11:10	They are **turned b** to the iniquities of	7725
	18:17	will shew them the **b**, and not the face,	6203
	21: 4	I *will* **turn b** the weapons of war that *are*	5437
	32:33	they have turned unto me the **b**, and not	6203
	38:22	in the mire, *and* they are turned away **b**.	268
	40: 5	while he was not yet **gone b**, *he said,*	7725
	40: 5	*he said*, **Go b** also to Gedaliah the son of	7725
	42: 4	unto you; I will **keep** nothing **b** from you.	4513
	46: 5	I seen them dismayed *and* turned away **b**?	268
	46: 5	and are fled apace, and **look** not **b**:	6437
	46:21	for they also are **turned b**, *and* are fled	6437
	47: 3	fathers shall not **look** to *their* children	6437
	48:10	cursed *be* he that **keepeth b** his sword	4513
	48:39	how hath Moab turned the **b** with shame!	6203
	49: 8	Flee ye, **turn b**, dwell deep, O inhabitants	6437
La	1:13	a net for my feet, he hath turned me **b**;	268
	2: 3	hath drawn his right hand from before	268
Eze	23:35	cast me behind thy **b**, therefore bear thou	1458
	24:14	I will do *it;* I will not go **b**, neither will I	6544
	38: 4	I will **turn** thee **b**, and put hooks into thy	7725
	38: 8	land *that is* **brought b** from the sword,	7725
	39: 2	I will **turn** thee **b**, and leave but the sixth	7725
	44: 1	he **brought** me **b** the way of the gate of	7725
Da	7: 6	which had upon the **b** of it four wings of	1355
Hos	4:16	For Israel **slideth b** as a backsliding heifer:	5637
Na	2: 8	*shall they cry;* but none shall **look b**.	6437
Zep	1: 6	them that are **turned b** from the Lord;	5472
	3:20	when I **turn b** your captivity before your	7725
Mt	24:18	let him which is in the field return **b**	3694
	28: 2	and **rolled b** the stone from the door,	617
Mk	13:16	And let him that is in the field not **turn b**	1994
Lk	2:45	they **turned b** again to Jerusalem,	5290
	8:37	*up* into the ship, and returned **b** *again*.	NIG
	9:62	and looking **b**, is fit for	1519+3588+3694
	17:15	**turned b**, and with a loud voice glorified	5290
	17:31	let him likewise not return **b**.	1519+3588+3694
Jn	6:66	of his disciples **went b**,	565+1519+3588+3694
	20:14	said, she **turned** herself **b**,	1519+3588+3694
Ac	5: 2	And **kept b** *part* of the price, his wife also	3557
	5: 3	to **keep b** *part* of the price of the land?	3557
	7:39	in their hearts turned **b** *again* into Egypt,	NIG
	20:20	*And* how I **kept b** nothing that was	5288
Ro	11:10	not see, and bow down their **b** alway.	3577
Heb	10:38	but if *any* man **draw b**, my soul shall have	5288
	10:39	But we are not of *them* who **draw b** unto	5289
Jas	5: 4	which is of you **kept b** by fraud, crieth.	650

BACKBITERS (1) [BACK, BITE]

| Ro | 1:30 | **B**, haters of God, despiteful, proud, | 2637 |

BACKBITETH (1) [BACK, BITE]

| Ps | 15: 3 | *He that* **b** not with his tongue, nor doeth | 7270 |

BACKBITING (1) [BACK, BITE]

| Pr | 25:23 | so *doth* an angry countenance a **b** tongue. | 5643 |

BACKBITINGS (1) [BACK, BITE]

| 2Co | 12:20 | envyings, wraths, strifes, **b**, whisperings, | 2636 |

BACKS (8) [BACK]

Ex	23:27	I will make all thine enemies **turn** their **b**	6203
Jos	7: 8	when Israel turneth *their* **b** before their	6203
	7:12	*but* turned *their* **b** before their enemies,	6203
Jdg	20:42	Therefore they turned *their* **b** before	NIH
2Ch	29: 6	of the Lord, and turned *their* **b**.	6203
Ne	9:26	cast thy law behind their **b**, and slew thy	1458
Eze	8:16	*with* their **b** toward the temple of	268
	10:12	their **b**, and their hands, and their wings,	1354

BACKSIDE (3) [BACK, SIDE]

Ex	3: 1	he led the flock to the **b** of the desert,	310
	26:12	shall hang over the **b** of the tabernacle.	268
Rev	5: 1	a book written within and **on the b**,	3693

BACKSLIDER (1) [BACK, SLIDE]

| Pr | 14:14 | The **b** in heart shall be filled with his own | 5472 |

BACKSLIDING (12) [BACK, SLIDE]

| Jer | 3: 6 | Hast thou seen *that* which **b** Israel hath | 4878 |
| | 3: 8 | when for all the causes whereby I Israel | 4878 |

Jer	3:11	The **b** Israel hath justified herself more	4878
	3:12	say, Return, thou **b** Israel, saith	4878
	3:14	Turn, O **b** children, saith the Lord; for I	7726
	3:22	ye **b** children, *and* I will heal your	7726
	8: 5	Jerusalem slidden back *by a* perpetual **b**?	4878
	31:22	wilt thou go about, O thou **b** daughter?	7728
	49: 4	thy flowing valley, O **b** daughter?	7728
Hos	4:16	For Israel slideth back as a **b** heifer:	5637
	11: 7	my people are bent to **b** from me:	4878
	14: 4	I will heal their **b**, I will love them freely:	4878

BACKSLIDINGS (4) [BACK, SLIDE]

Jer	2:19	correct thee, and thy **b** shall reprove thee:	4878
	3:22	children, *and* I will heal your **b**.	4878
	5: 6	as many; and their **b** are increased.	4878
	14: 7	for our **b** are many; we have sinned	4878

BACKWARD (18) [BACK]

Ge	9:23	went **b**, and covered the nakedness of their	322
	9:23	their faces *were* **b**, and they saw not their	322
	49:17	the horse heels, so that his rider shall fall **b**.	268
1Sa	4:18	that he fell from off the seat **b** by the side	322
2Ki	20:10	but let the shadow return **b** ten degrees.	322
	20:11	he brought the shadow ten degrees **b**,	322
Job	23: 8	*is not there;* and **b**, but I cannot perceive	268
Ps	40:14	let them be driven **b** and put to shame that	268
	70: 2	let them be turned **b**, and put to confusion,	268
Isa	1: 4	of Israel unto anger, they are gone away **b**.	268
	28:13	fall **b**, and be broken, and snared,	268
	38: 8	in the sun dial of Ahaz, ten degrees **b**.	322
	44:25	that turneth wise *men* **b**, and maketh	268
	59:14	judgment is turned away **b**,	268
Jer	7:24	and went **b**, and not forward.	268+3807.1
	15: 6	saith the Lord, thou art gone **b**:	268
La	1: 8	yea, she sigheth, and turneth **b**.	268
Jn	18: 6	I am *he*, they went **b**,	1519+3588+3694

BAD (18) [BADNESS, WORSE, WORST]

Ge	24:50	we cannot speak unto thee **b** or good.	7451
	31:24	thou speak not to Jacob either good or **b**.	7451
	31:29	thou speak not to Jacob either good or **b**.	7451
Lev	27:10	a good for a **b**, or a bad for a good:	7451
	27:10	a good for a bad, or a **b** for a good:	7451
	27:12	shall value it, whether it be good or **b**:	7451
	27:14	shall estimate it, whether it be good or **b**:	7451
	27:33	shall not search whether it be good or **b**,	7451
Nu	13:19	they dwell in, whether it *be* good or **b**;	7451
	24:13	to do *either* good or **b** of mine own mind;	7451
2Sa	13:22	his brother Amnon neither good nor **b**:	7451
	14:17	*is my* lord the king to discern good and **b**:	7451
1Ki	3: 9	that *I* may discern between good and **b**?	7451
Ezr	4:12	building the rebellious and the **b** city,	873
Jer	24: 2	which could not be eaten, they were so **b**.	7455
Mt	13:48	the good into vessels, but cast the **b** away.	4550
	22:10	as many as they found, both **b** and good:	4190
2Co	5:10	he hath done, whether *it* be good or **b**.	2556

BADE (18) [BID]

Ge	43:17	the man did as Joseph **b**; and the man	559
Ex	16:24	laid it up till the morning, as Moses **b**:	6680
Nu	14:10	all the congregation **b** stone them with	559
Jos	11: 9	Joshua did unto them as the Lord **b** him:	559
Ru	3: 6	to all that her mother in law **b** her.	6680
1Sa	24:10	*some* **b** me kill thee: but *mine* eye spared	559
2Sa	1:18	he **b** them teach the children of Judah	559
	14:19	he **b** me, and he put all these words in	6680
2Ch	10:12	as the king **b**, saying, Come again to me	1696
Est	4:15	Esther **b** *them* return Mordecai this	559
Mt	16:12	understood they how that he **b** *them*	3004
Lk	14: 9	He that **b** thee and him come and	2564
	14:10	that when he that **b** thee cometh, he may	2564
	14:12	Then said he also to him that **b** him,	2564
	14:16	man made a great supper, and **b** many:	2564
Ac	11:12	And the Spirit **b** me go with them,	3004
	18:21	But **b** them farewell, saying, I must by all	657
	22:24	that he should be examined by	3004

BADEST (1) [BID]

| Ge | 27:19 | I have done according as thou **b** me: | 1696 |

BADGERS' (14)

Ex	25: 5	dyed red, and **b** skins, and shittim wood,	8476
	26:14	dyed red, and a covering above of **b** skins.	8476
	35: 7	dyed red, and **b** skins, and shittim wood,	8476
	35:23	skins of rams, and **b** skins, brought *them*.	8476
	36:19	and a covering of **b** skins above *that.*	8476
	39:34	the covering of **b** skins, and the vail of	8476
Nu	4: 6	shall put thereon the covering of **b** skins,	8476
	4: 8	cover the same with a covering of **b** skins,	8476
	4:10	thereof within a covering of **b** skins,	8476
	4:11	cover it with a covering of **b** skins,	8476
	4:12	cover it with a covering of **b** skins,	8476
	4:14	they shall spread upon it a covering of **b**	8476
	4:25	the covering of the **b skins** that *is* above	8476
Eze	16:10	shod thee *with* **b** skin, and I girded thee	8476

BADNESS (1) [BAD]

| Ge | 41:19 | I never saw in all the land of Egypt for **b**: | 7455 |

BAG (7) [BAGS]

Dt	25:13	shalt not have in thy **b** divers weights,	3599
1Sa	17:40	put them in a shepherd's **b** which he had,	3627
	17:49	David put his hand in his **b**,	3627
Job	14:17	My transgression *is* sealed up in a **b**,	6872
Pr	7:20	He hath taken a **b** of money with him,	6872
	16:11	all the weights of the **b** *are* his work.	3599

Isa	46: 6	They lavish gold out of the **b**,	3599
Mic	6:11	and with the **b** of deceitful weights?	3599
Hag	1: 6	wages *to put it* into a **b** with holes.	6872
Jn	12: 6	and had the **b**, and bare what was put	1101
	13:29	*of them* thought, because Judas had the **b**,	1101

BAGGAGE See STUFF

BAGS (3) [BAG]

2Ki	5:23	and bound two talents of silver in two **b**,	2754
	12:10	they put up *in* **b**, and told the money that	NIH
Lk	12:33	provide yourselves **b** which wax not old,	905

BAHARUMITE (1)

| 1Ch | 11:33 | Azmaveth the **B**, Eliahba the Shaalbonite, | 978 |

BAHURIM (5)

2Sa	3:16	with her along weeping behind her to **B**.	980
	16: 5	when king David came to **B**, behold,	980
	17:18	came to a man's house in **B**, which had a	980
	19:16	which *was* of **B**, hasted and came down	980
1Ki	2: 8	Shimei the son of Gera, a Benjamite of **B**,	980

BAJITH (1)

| Isa | 15: 2 | He is gone up *to* **B**, and *to* Dibon, the high | 1006 |

BAKBAKKAR (1)

| 1Ch | 9:15 | **B**, Heresh, and Galal, and Mattaniah | 1230 |

BAKBUK (2)

| Ezr | 2:51 | children of **B**, the children of Hakupha, | 1227 |
| Ne | 7:53 | children of **B**, the children of Hakupha, | 1227 |

BAKBUKIAH (3)

Ne	11:17	**B** the second among his brethren,	1229
	12: 9	**B** and Unni, their brethren, *were* over	1229
	12:25	Mattaniah, and **B**, Obadiah, Meshullam,	1229

BAKE (9) [BAKED, BAKEMEATS, BAKEN, BAKER, BAKERS, BAKERS', BAKETH]

Ge	19: 3	did **b** unleavened bread, and they did eat.	644
Ex	16:23	*b that* which ye will **b** *to day*, and	644
	16:23	bake *that* which you will **b** *to day*, and	644
Lev	24: 5	take fine flour, and **b** twelve cakes thereof:	644
	26:26	ten women shall **b** your bread in one oven,	644
1Sa	28:24	and did **b** unleavened bread thereof:	644
2Sa	13: 8	cakes in his sight, and did **b** the cakes.	1310
Eze	4:12	thou shalt **b** it with dung that cometh out	5746
	46:20	where they shall **b** the meat offering;	644

BAKED (4) [BAKE]

Ex	12:39	they **b** unleavened cakes of the dough	644
Nu	11: 8	and **b** *it* in pans, and made cakes *of* it:	1310
1Ch	23:29	for *that which is* **b** in the pan, and for that	NIH
Nu	44:19	also I have **b** bread upon the coals thereof;	644

BAKED GOODS See BAKEMEATS

BAKEMEATS (1) [BAKE, MEAT]

| Ge | 40:17 | all *manner of* **b** for Pharaoh; | 644+3978+4639 |

BAKEN (9) [BAKE]

Lev	2: 4	oblation of a meat offering **b** in the oven,	3989
	2: 5	if thy oblation *be* a meat offering **b** in	NIH
	2: 7	if thy oblation *be* a meat offering **b** in	NIH
	6:17	It shall not be **b** with leaven. I have given	644
	6:21	*and when it is* **b**, thou shalt bring it in:	7246
	6:21	the **b** pieces of the meat offering shalt	8601
	7: 9	all the meat offering that is **b** in the oven,	644
	23:17	*of* fine flour; they shall be **b** with leaven;	644
1Ki	19: 6	*there was* a cake **b** on the coals,	7529

BAKER (8) [BAKE]

Ge	40: 1	*his* **b** had offended their lord the king of	644
	40: 5	the butler and the **b** of the king of Egypt,	644
	40:16	the chief **b** saw that the interpretation	644
	40:20	and of the chief **b** among his servants.	644
	40:22	he hanged the chief **b**: as Joseph had	644
	41:10	*both* me and the chief **b**:	644
Hos	7: 4	all adulterers, as an oven heated by the **b**,	644
	7: 6	**b** sleepeth all the night; *in* the morning	644

BAKERS (2) [BAKE]

| Ge | 40: 2 | the butlers, and against the chief of the **b**. | 644 |
| 1Sa | 8:13 | and to be cooks, and to be **b**. | 644 |

BAKERS' (1) [BAKE]

| Jer | 37:21 | daily a piece of bread out of the **b** street, | 644 |

BAKETH (1) [BAKE]

| Isa | 44:15 | yea, he kindleth *it*, and **b** bread; yea, | 644 |

BALAAM (60) [BALAAM'S]

Nu	22: 5	therefore unto **B** the son of Beor to Pethor,	1109
	22: 7	they came unto **B**, and spake unto him	1109
	22: 8	and the princes of Moab abode with **B**.	1109
	22: 9	God came unto **B**, and said, What men	1109
	22:10	**B** said unto God, Balak the son of Zippor,	1109
	22:12	God said unto **B**, Thou shalt not go with	1109
	22:13	**B** rose up in the morning, and said unto	1109
	22:14	and said, **B** refuseth to come with us.	1109
	22:16	they came to **B**, and said to him, Thus	1109
	22:18	**B** answered and said unto the servants of	1109
	22:20	God came unto **B** at night, and said unto	1109
	22:21	**B** rose up in the morning, and saddled his	1109
	22:23	**B** smote the ass, to turn her *into* the way.	1109
	22:27	of the Lord, she fell down under **B**:	1109

B

Nu 22:28 she said unto **B**, What have I done unto 1109
22:29 **B** said unto the ass, Because thou hast 1109
22:30 the ass said unto **B**, *Am* not I thine ass, 1109
22:31 Then the LORD opened the eyes of **B**, 1109
22:34 **B** said unto the angel of the LORD, I have 1109
22:35 the angel of the LORD said unto **B**, 1109
22:35 So **B** went with the princes of Balak. 1109
22:36 when Balak heard that **B** was come, 1109
22:37 Balak said unto **B**, Did I not earnestly send 1109
22:38 **B** said unto Balak, Lo, I am come unto 1109
22:39 **B** went with Balak, and they came *unto* 1109
22:40 sent to **B**, and to the princes that *were* 1109
22:41 Balak took **B**, and brought him up *into* 1109
23: 1 **B** said unto Balak, Build me here seven 1109
23: 2 Balak did as **B** had spoken; and Balak and 1109
23: 2 and **B** offered on *every* altar a bullock and 1109
23: 3 **B** said unto Balak, Stand by thy burnt 1109
23: 4 God met **B**: and he said unto him, I have 1109
23:11 Balak said unto **B**, What hast thou done 1109
23:16 the LORD met **B**, and put a word in his 1109
23:25 Balak said unto **B**, Neither curse them at 1109
23:26 **B** answered and said unto Balak, Told not 1109
23:27 Balak said unto **B**, Come, I pray thee, 1109
23:28 Balak brought **B** *unto* the top of Peor, 1109
23:29 **B** said unto Balak, Build me here seven 1109
23:30 Balak did as **B** had said, and offered a 1109
24: 1 when **B** saw that it pleased the LORD to 1109
24: 2 **B** lift up his eyes, and he saw Israel 1109
24: 3 **B** the son of Beor hath said, and the man 1109
24:10 Balak's anger was kindled against **B**, 1109
24:10 Balak said unto **B**, I called thee to curse 1109
24:12 **B** said unto Balak, Spake I not also to thy 1109
24:15 the son of Beor hath said, and the man 1109
24:25 **B** rose up, and went and returned to his 1109
31: 8 **B** also the son of Beor they slew with 1109
31:16 of Israel, through the counsel of **B**, 1109
Dt 23: 4 they hired against thee **B** the son of Beor 1109
23: 5 thy God would not hearken unto **B**; 1109
Jos 13: 2 **B** also the son of Beor, the soothsayer, 1109
24: 9 and called the son of Beor to curse you: 1109
24:10 I would not hearken unto **B**; therefore 1109
Ne 13: 2 and with water, but hired **B** against them, 1109
Mic 6: 5 what **B** the son of Beor answered him; 1109
2Pe 2:15 following the way of **B** *the son of* Bosor, 903
Jude 1:11 ran greedily after the error of **B** for reward, 903
Rev 2:14 there them that hold the doctrine of **B**, 903

BALAAM'S (3) [BALAAM]

Nu 22:25 wall, and crusht **B** foot against the wall: 1109
22:27 **B** anger was kindled, and he smote the 1109
23: 5 the LORD put a word in **B** mouth, 1109

BALAC (1) [BALAK]

Rev 2:14 who taught **B** to cast a stumblingblock 904

BALADAN (2)

2Ki 20:12 the son of **B**, king of Babylon, sent letters 1081
Isa 39: 1 the son of **B**, king of Babylon, sent letters 1081

BALAH (1)

Jos 19: 3 And Hazar-shual, and **B**, and Azem, 1088

BALAK (42) [BALAC, BALAK'S]

Nu 22: 2 **B** the son of Zippor saw all that Israel had 1111
22: 4 **B** the son of Zippor *was* king of 1111
22: 7 and spake unto him the words of **B**. 1111
22:10 **B** the son of Zippor, king of Moab, 1111
22:13 said unto the princes of **B**, Get you into 1111
22:14 they went unto **B**, and said, 1111
22:15 **B** sent yet again princes, more, 1111
22:16 to him, Thus saith **B** the son of Zippor, 1111
22:18 and said unto the servants of **B**, 1111
22:18 If **B** would give me his house full *of* silver 1111
22:35 So Balaam went with the princes of **B**. 1111
22:36 when **B** heard that Balaam was come, 1111
22:37 **B** said unto Balaam, Did I not earnestly 1111
22:38 Balaam said unto **B**, Lo, I am come unto 1111
22:39 Balaam went with **B**, and they came *unto* 1111
22:40 **B** offered oxen and sheep, and sent to 1111
22:41 that **B** took Balaam, and brought him up 1111
23: 1 Balaam said unto **B**, Build me here seven 1111
23: 2 **B** did as Balaam had spoken; and Balak 1111
23: 2 **B** and Balaam offered on *every* altar a 1111
23: 3 Balaam said unto **B**, Stand by thy burnt 1111
23: 5 Return unto **B**, and thus thou shalt speak. 1111
23: 7 **B** the king of Moab hath brought me from 1111
23:11 **B** said unto Balaam, What hast thou done 1111
23:13 **B** said unto him, Come, I pray thee, 1111
23:15 he said unto **B**, Stand here by thy burnt 1111
23:16 and said, Go again unto **B**, and say thus. 1111
23:17 **B** said unto him, What hath the LORD 1111
23:18 his parable, and said, Rise up, **B**, and hear; 1111
23:25 **B** said unto Balaam, Neither curse them at 1111
23:26 Balaam answered and said unto **B**, Told 1111
23:27 **B** said unto Balaam, Come, I pray thee, 1111
23:28 **B** brought Balaam *unto* the top of Peor, 1111
23:29 Balaam said unto **B**, Build me here seven 1111
23:30 **B** did as Balaam had said, and offered a 1111
24:10 Balak said unto Balaam, I called thee to curse 1111
24:12 Balaam said unto **B**, Spake I not also to 1111
24:13 If **B** would give me his house full *of* silver 1111
24:25 to his place: and **B** also went his way. 1111
Jos 24: 9 **B** the son of Zippor, king of Moab, arose 1111
Jdg 11:25 *art* thou any thing better than **B** the son 1111
Mic 6: 5 remember now what **B** king of Moab 1111

BALAK'S (1) [BALAK]

Nu 24:10 **B** anger was kindled against Balaam, 1111

BALANCE (8) [BALANCES, BALANCINGS]

Job 31: 6 me be weighed in an even **b**, that God 3976
Ps 62: 9 to be laid in the **b**, they *are* altogether 3976
Pr 11: 1 A false *is* abomination to the LORD: 3976
16:11 A just weight and *are* the LORD's: 3976
20:23 unto the LORD; and a false **b** *is* not good. 3976
Isa 40:12 mountains in scales, and the hills in a **b**? 3976
40:15 are counted as the small dust of the **b**. 3976
46: 6 weigh silver in the **b**, *and* hire a goldsmith 7070

BALANCES (10) [BALANCE]

Lev 19:36 Just **b**, just weights, a just ephah, 3976
Job 6: 2 my calamity laid in the **b** together! 3976
Jer 32:10 weighed *him* the money in the **b**. 3976
Eze 5: 1 take thee **b** to weigh, and divide the *hair*. 3976
45:10 Ye shall have just **b**, and a just ephah, 3976
Da 5:27 Thou art weighed in the **b**, and art found 3977
Hos 12: 7 merchant, the **b** of deceit *are* in his hand: 3976
Am 8: 5 great, and falsifying the **b** by deceit? 3976
Mic 6:11 I count *them* pure with the wicked **b**, 3976
Rev 6: 5 he that sat on him had a **pair of b** in his 2218

BALANCINGS (1) [BALANCE]

Job 37:16 Dost thou know the **b** of the clouds, 4657

BALD (16) [BALDNESS]

Lev 11:22 the **b** locust after his kind, and the beetle 5556
13:40 whose hair is fallen off his head, he *is* **b**: 7142
13:41 *head toward* his face, he *is* **forehead b**: 1371
13:42 there be in the **b head**, or bald forehead, 7146
13:42 or **b forehead**, a white reddish sore; 1372
13:42 it *is* a leprosy sprung up in his **b head**, 7146
13:42 up in his bald head, or his **b forehead**. 1372
13:43 the sore be white reddish in his **b head**, 7146
13:43 or in his **b forehead**, as the leprosy 1372
2Ki 2:23 and said unto him, Go up, thou **b head**; 7142
2:23 up, thou bald head; go up, thou **b head**. 7142
Jer 16: 6 nor **make** themselves **b** for them: 7139
48:37 every head *shall be* **b**, and every beard 7144
Eze 27:31 **make** themselves **utterly b** for 7139+7139
29:18 every head was **made b**, 7139
Mic 1:16 **Make** thee **b**, and poll thee for thy 7139

BALDNESS (9) [BALD]

Lev 21: 5 They shall not **make b** upon their 7139+7144
Dt 14: 1 nor make *any* **b** between your eyes for 7144
Isa 3:24 instead of well set hair **b**; and instead of a 7144
15: 2 on all their heads *shall be* **b**, 7144
22:12 and to **b**, and to girding with sackcloth: 7144
Jer 47: 5 **B** is come upon Gaza; Ashkelon is cut off 7144
Eze 7:18 upon all faces, and **b** upon all their heads. 7144
Am 8:10 upon all loins, and **b** upon every head; 7144
Mic 1:16 enlarge thy **b** as the eagle; 7144

BALL (1)

Isa 22:18 and toss thee like a **b** into a large country: 1754

BALM (6)

Ge 37:25 camels bearing spicery and **b** and myrrh, 6875
43:11 a little **b**, and a little honey, spices, 6875
Jer 8:22 *Is there* no **b** in Gilead; *is there* no 6875
46:11 Go up *into* Gilead, and take **b**, O virgin, 6875
51: 8 take **b** for her pain, if so be she may be 6875
Eze 27:17 and Pannag, and honey, and oil, and **b**. 6875

BAMAH (1)

Eze 20:29 the name thereof is called **B** unto this day. 1117

BAMOTH (2) [BAMOTH-BAAL]

Nu 21:19 to Nahaliel: and from Nahaliel *to* **B**: 1120
21:20 from **B** *in* the valley, that *is in* the country 1120

BAMOTH-BAAL (1) [BAMOTH, BAAL]

Jos 13:17 Dibon, and **B**, and Beth-baal-meon, 1120

BAND (20) [BANDED, BANDS, HEADBANDS]

Ex 39:23 *with a* **b** round about the hole, *that* it 8193
1Sa 10:26 there went with him a **b** of **men**, 2428
1Ki 11:24 unto him, and became captain over a **b**, 1416
2Ki 13:21 they spied a **b** *of men*; and they cast 1416
1Ch 12:18 and made them captains of the **b**. 1416
12:21 they helped David against the **b** of 1416
2Ch 22: 1 for the **b** *of men* that came with 1416
Ezr 8:22 to require of the king a **b** *of soldiers* 2428
Job 38: 9 and thick darkness a **swaddling b** for it, 2854
39:10 Canst thou bind the unicorn *with* his **b** in 5688
Da 4:15 with a **b** of iron and brass, in the tender 613
4:23 with a **b** of iron and brass, in the tender 613
Mt 27:27 unto him the whole **b** *of soldiers*. 4686
Mk 15:16 and they call together the whole **b**. 4686
Jn 18: 3 having received a **b** *of men*, and 4686
18:12 Then the **b** and the captain and officers of 4686
Ac 10: 1 centurion of the **b** called the Italian *band*, 4686
10: 1 centurion of the band called the Italian *b*, NIG
21:31 came unto the chief captain of the **b**, 4686
27: 1 named Julius, a centurion of Augustus' **b**. 4686

BANDED (1) [BAND]

Ac 23:12 certain of the Jews **b** together, 4160+4963

BANDS (46) [BAND]

Ge 32: 7 and herds, and the camels, into two **b**; 4264
32:10 this Jordan; and now I am become two **b**. 4264

Lev 26:13 I have broken the **b** of your yoke, 4133
Jdg 15:14 and his **b** loosed from off his hands. 612
2Sa 4: 2 son had two men *that were* captains of **b**: 1416
2Ki 6:23 So the **b** of Syria came no more into 1416
13:20 the **b** of the Moabites invaded the land *at* 1416
23:33 Pharaoh-nechoh **put in b** at Riblah in 631
24: 2 the LORD sent against him **b** of 1416
24: 2 **b** of the Syrians, and bands of 1416
24: 2 **b** of the Moabites, and bands of 1416
24: 2 **b** of the children of Ammon, and sent 1416
1Ch 7: 4 *were* **b** of soldiers for war, six and 1416
12:23 these *are* the numbers of the **b** that were 7218
2Ch 26:11 fighting *men*, that went out to war by **b**, 1416
Job 1:17 The Chaldeans made out three **b**, 7218
38:31 of Pleiades, or loose the **b** of Orion? 4189
39: 5 or who hath loosed the **b** of the wild ass? 4147
Ps 2: 3 Let us break their **b** asunder, and cast 4147
73: 4 For *there are* no **b** in their death: 2784
107:14 of death, and brake their **b** in sunder. 4147
119:61 The **b** of the wicked have robbed me: 2256
Pr 30:27 no king, yet go they forth all of them **by b**, 2686
Ecc 7:26 *is* snares and nets, *and* her hands *as* **b**: 612
Isa 28:22 not mockers, lest your **b** be made strong: 4147
52: 2 loose thyself from the **b** of thy neck, 4147
58: 6 to loose the **b** of wickedness, to undo 2784
Jer 2:20 I have broken thy yoke, *and* burst thy **b**, 4147
Eze 3:25 they shall put **b** upon thee, and shall bind 5688
4: 8 I will lay **b** upon thee, and thou shalt not 5688
12:14 *are* about him to help him, and all his **b**; 102
17:21 all his fugitives with all his **b** shall fall by 4133
34:27 when I have broken the **b** of their yoke, 4133
38: 6 Gomer, and all his **b**; the house of 102
38: 6 of the north quarters, and all his **b**: 102
38: 9 and all thy **b**, and many people with thee. 102
38:22 upon his **b**, and upon the many people 102
39: 4 all thy **b**, and the people that *is* with thee: 102
Hos 11: 4 them with cords of a man, with **b** of love: 5688
Zec 11: 7 I called Beauty, and the other I called **B**; 2254
11:14 I cut asunder mine other staff, *even* **B**, 2254
Lk 8:29 and he brake the **b**, and was driven of 1199
Ac 16:26 and every one's **b** were loosed. 1199
22:30 he loosed him from his **b**, 1199
27:40 and loosed the rudder **b**, and hoised up 2202
Col 2:19 and **b** having nourishment ministered, 4886

BANI (15)

2Sa 23:36 the son of Nathan of Zobah, **B** the Gadite, 1137
1Ch 6:46 The son of Amzi, the son of **B**, the son of 1137
9: 4 son of Omri, the son of Imri, the son of **B**, 1137
Ezr 2:10 The children of **B**, six hundred forty and 1137
10:29 the sons of **B**; Meshullam, Malluch, 1137
10:34 the sons of **B**; Maadai, Amram, and Uel, 1137
10:38 And **B**, and Binnui, Shimei, 1137
Ne 3:17 repaired the Levites, Rehum the son of **B**. 1137
8: 7 **B**, and Sherebiah, Jamin, Akkub, 1137
9: 4 Jeshua, and **B**, Kadmiel, Shebaniah, Bunni, 1137
9: 4 and Chenani, and cried with a loud 1137
9: 5 Jeshua and Kadmiel, **B**, Hashabniah, 1137
10:13 Hodijah, **B**, Beninu. 1137
10:14 Parosh, Pahath-moab, Elam, Zatthu, **B**, 1137
11:22 Levites at Jerusalem *was* Uzzi the son of **B** 1137

BANISHED (2) [BANISHMENT]

2Sa 14:13 the king doth not fetch home again his **b**. 5080
14:14 that *his* **b** be not expelled from him. 5080

BANISHMENT (2) [BANISHED]

Ezr 7:26 or to **b**, or to confiscation of goods, 8332
La 2:14 for thee false burdens and **causes of b**. 4065

BANK (14) [BANKS]

Ge 41:17 behold, I stood upon the **b** of the river: 8193
Dt 4:48 which *is* by the **b** of the river Arnon, 8193
Jos 12: 2 which *is* upon the **b** of the river of Arnon, 8193
13: 9 that *is* upon the **b** of the river Arnon, 8193
13:16 that *is* on the **b** of the river Arnon, 8193
2Sa 20:15 they cast up a **b** against the city, 5550
2Ki 2:13 went back, and stood by the **b** of Jordan: 8193
19:32 with shield, nor cast a **b** against it. 5550
Isa 37:33 it *with* shields, nor cast a **b** against it. 5550
Eze 47: 7 at the **b** of the river *were* very many trees 8193
47:12 by the river upon the **b** thereof, on this 8193
Da 12: 5 the one on this side of the **b** of the river, 8193
12: 5 the other on that side of the **b** of the river, 8193
Lk 19:23 gavest not thou my money into the **b**, 5132

BANKS (5) [BANK]

Jos 3:15 for Jordan overfloweth all his **b** all 1415
4:18 flowed over all his **b**, as *they did* before. 1415
1Ch 12:15 when it had overflown all his **b**; 1415
Isa 8: 7 over all his channels, and go over all his **b**: 1415
Da 8:16 heard a man's voice between the **b** of Ulai, NIH

BANNER (3) [BANNERS]

Ps 60: 4 Thou hast given a **b** to them that fear thee 5251
SS 2: 4 and his **b** over me *was* love. 1714
Isa 13: 2 Lift ye up a **b** upon the high mountain, 5251

BANNERS (3) [BANNER]

Ps 20: 5 name of our God we will **set up** our **b**: 1713
SS 6: 4 as Jerusalem, terrible as an *army* **with b**. 1713
6:10 the sun, *and* terrible as an *army* **with b**? 1713

BANQUET (14) [BANQUETING, BANQUETINGS]

Est 5: 4 Haman come *this* day unto the **b** that I 4960
5: 5 Haman came to the **b** that Esther had 4960

B

Est	5: 6	king said unto Esther at the **b** of wine,	4960
	5: 8	Haman come to the **b** that I shall prepare	4960
	5:12	the king unto the **b** that she had prepared	4960
	5:14	in merrily with the king unto the **b**.	4960
	6:14	hasted to bring Haman unto to the **b** that	4960
	7: 1	Haman came to **b** with Esther the queen.	8354
	7: 2	Esther on the second day at the **b** of wine,	4960
	7: 7	the king arising from the **b** of wine in his	4960
	7: 8	garden into the place of the **b** of wine;	4960
Job	41: 6	Shall the companions **make a b** of him?	3739
Da	5:10	and his lords, came into the **b** house:	4961
Am	6: 7	of them that stretched themselves	4797

BANQUETING (1) [BANQUET]

SS	2: 4	He brought me to the **b** house,	3196

BANQUETINGS (1) [BANQUET]

1Pe	4: 3	revellings, **b**, and abominable idolatries:	4224

BAPTISM (22) [BAPTIZE]

Mt	3: 7	Pharisees and Sadducees come to his **b**,	908
	20:22	be baptized with the **b** that I am baptized	908
	20:23	be baptized with the **b** that I am baptized	908
	21:25	The **b** of John, whence was it?	908
Mk	1: 4	the **b** of repentance for the remission	908
	10:38	be baptized with the **b** that I am baptized	908
	10:39	with the **b** that I am baptized withal shall	908
	11:30	The **b** of John, was it from heaven, or	908
Lk	3: 3	preaching the **b** of repentance for	908
	7:29	being baptized with the **b** of John.	908
	12:50	But I have a **b** to be baptized with; and	908
	20: 4	The **b** of John, was it from heaven, or	908
Ac	1:22	Beginning from the **b** of John, unto that	908
	10:37	after the **b** which John preached;	908
	13:24	**b** of repentance to all the people of Israel.	908
	18:25	of the Lord, knowing only the **b** of John.	908
	19: 3	ye baptized? And they said, Unto John's **b**.	908
	19: 4	John verily baptized with the **b** of	908
Ro	6: 4	we are buried with him by **b** into	908
Eph	4: 5	One Lord, one faith, one **b**,	908
Col	2:12	Buried with him in **b**, wherein also you	908
1Pe	3:21	The like figure whereunto even **b** doth also	908

BAPTISMS (1) [BAPTIZE]

Heb	6: 2	Of the doctrine of **b**, and of laying on of	909

BAPTIST (14) [BAPTIZE]

Mt	3: 1	In those days came John the **B**, preaching	910
	11:11	hath not risen a greater than John the **B**:	910
	11:12	from the days of John the **B** until now	910
	14: 2	said unto his servants, This is John the **B**;	910
	16:14	said, Some say that thou art John the **B**;	910
	17:13	that he spake unto them of John the **B**.	910
Mk	6:14	That John the **B** was risen from the dead,	907
	6:24	And she said, The head of John the **B**.	910
	6:25	and by in a charger the head of John the **B**.	910
	8:28	And they answered, John the **B**:	910
Lk	7:20	John **B** hath sent us unto thee, saying,	910
	7:28	is not a greater prophet than John the **B**:	910
	7:33	For John the **B** came neither eating bread	910
	9:19	They answering said, John the **B**; but	910

BAPTIST'S (1) [BAPTIZE]

Mt	14: 8	Give me here John **B** head in a charger.	910

BAPTIZE (9) [BAPTISM, BAPTISMS, BAPTIST, BAPTIST'S, BAPTIZED, BAPTIZEST, BAPTIZETH, BAPTIZING]

Mt	3:11	indeed **b** you with water unto repentance:	907
	3:11	he shall **b** you with the Holy Ghost,	907
Mk	1: 4	John did **b** in the wilderness, and preach	907
	1: 8	but he shall **b** you with the Holy Ghost.	907
Lk	3:16	unto them all, I indeed **b** you with water;	907
	3:16	he shall **b** you with the Holy Ghost and	907
Jn	1:26	answered them, saying, I **b** with water:	907
	1:33	but he that sent me to **b** with water,	907
1Co	1:17	For Christ sent me not to **b**, but to preach	907

BAPTIZED (61) [BAPTIZE]

Mt	3: 6	And were **b** of him in Jordan,	907
	3:13	Galilee to Jordan unto John, to be **b** of	907
	3:14	I have need to be **b** of thee, and comest	907
	3:16	And Jesus, when he was **b**, went up	907
	20:22	be **b** with the baptism that I am baptized	907
	20:22	be baptized with the baptism that I am **b**	907
	20:23	be **b** with the baptism that I am baptized	907
	20:23	be baptized with the baptism that I am **b**	907
Mk	1: 5	were all **b** of him in the river of Jordan,	907
	1: 8	I indeed have **b** you with water: but he	907
	1: 9	of Galilee, and was **b** of John in Jordan.	907
	10:38	be **b** with the baptism that I am baptized	907
	10:38	be baptized with the baptism that I am **b**	907
	10:39	with the baptism that I am **b** withal shall	907
	10:39	that I am baptized withal/shall ye be **b**:	907
	16:16	He that believeth and is **b** shall be saved;	907
Lk	3: 7	multitude that came forth to be **b** of him,	907
	3:12	Then came also publicans to be **b**,	907
	3:21	Now when all the people were **b**, it came	907
	3:21	pass, that Jesus also being **b**, and praying,	907
	7:29	being **b** with the baptism of John.	907
	7:30	against themselves, being not **b** of him.	907
	12:50	But I have a baptism to be **b** with; and	907
Jn	3:22	and there he tarried with them, and **b**.	907
	3:23	water there: and they came, and were **b**.	907
	4: 1	Jesus made and **b** moe disciples than John,	907
	4: 2	(Though Jesus himself **b** not, but	907

Jn	10:40	Jordan into the place where John at first **b**;	907
Ac	1: 5	John truly **b** with water; but ye shall be	907
	1: 5	shall be **b** with the Holy Ghost not many	907
	2:38	be **b** every one of you in the name of Jesus	907
	2:41	they that gladly received his word were **b**:	907
	8:12	they were **b**, both men and women.	907
	8:13	and when he was **b**, he continued with	907
	8:16	only they were **b** in the name of the Lord	907
	8:36	is water; what doth hinder me to be **b**?	907
	8:38	both Philip and the eunuch; and he **b** him.	907
	9:18	sight forthwith, and arose, and was **b**,	907
	10:47	forbid water, that these should not be **b**,	907
	10:48	And he commanded them to be **b** in	907
	16:15	And when she was **b**, and her household,	907
	16:33	and was **b**, he and all his, straightway.	907
	18: 8	Corinthians hearing believed, and were **b**.	907
	19: 3	unto them, Unto what then were ye **b**?	907
	19: 4	John verily **b** with the baptism of	907
	19: 5	When they heard this, they were **b** in	907
	22:16	arise, and be **b**, and wash away thy sins,	907
Ro	6: 3	many of us as were **b** into Jesus Christ	907
	6: 3	into Jesus Christ were **b** into his death?	907
1Co	1:13	for you? or were ye **b** in the name of Paul?	907
	1:14	I thank God that I **b** none of you, but	907
	1:15	Lest any should say that I had **b** in mine	907
	1:16	And I **b** also the household of Stephanas;	907
	1:16	besides, I know not whether I **b** any other.	907
	10: 2	were all **b** unto Moses in the cloud and	907
	12:13	by one Spirit are we all **b** into one body,	907
	15:29	Else what shall they do which are **b** for	907
	15:29	at all? why are they then **b** for the dead?	907
Gal	3:27	For as many of you as have been **b** into	907

BAPTIZEST (1) [BAPTIZE]

Jn	1:25	and said unto him, Why **b** thou then,	907

BAPTIZETH (2) [BAPTIZE]

Jn	1:33	same is he which **b** with the Holy Ghost.	907
	3:26	the same **b**, and all men come to him.	907

BAPTIZING (4) [BAPTIZE]

Mt	28:19	**b** them in the name of the Father, and of	907
Jn	1:28	beyond Jordan, where John was **b**.	907
	1:31	Israel, therefore am I come **b** with water.	907
	3:23	And John also was **b** in Aenon near to	907

BAR (7) [BARS]

Ex	26:28	the middle **b** in the midst of the boards	1280
	36:33	he made the middle **b** to shoot through	1280
Nu	4:10	badgers' skins, and shall put it upon a **b**,	4132
	4:12	badgers' skins, and shall put them on a **b**:	4132
Jdg	16: 3	**b** and all, and put them upon his	1280
Ne	7: 3	them: and appoint watches of	270
Am	1: 5	I will break also the **b** of Damascus,	1280

BARABBAS (11)

Mt	27:16	they had then a notable prisoner, called **B**.	912
	27:17	or Jesus which is called Christ?	912
	27:20	the multitude that they should ask **B**,	912
	27:21	ye that I release unto you? They said, **B**.	912
	27:26	Then released he **B** unto them:	912
Mk	15: 7	And there was one named **B**, which lay	912
	15:11	that he should rather release **B** unto them.	912
	15:15	released **B**, and delivered Jesus,	912
Lk	23:18	Away with this man, and release unto us **B**:	912
Jn	18:40	they all again, saying, Not this man, but **B**.	912
	18:40	but Barabbas. Now **B** was a robber.	912

BARACHEL (2)

Job	32: 2	kindled the wrath of Elihu the son of **B**	1292
	32: 6	Elihu the son of **B** the Buzite answered	1292

BARACHIAS (1) [BERECHIAH]

Mt	23:35	Abel unto the blood of Zacharias son of **B**,	914

BARAK (14)

Jdg	4: 6	called **B** the son of Abinoam out of	1301
	4: 8	**B** said unto her, If thou wilt go with me,	1301
	4: 9	arose, and went with **B** to Kedesh.	1301
	4:10	**B** called Zebulun and Naphtali to Kedesh;	1301
	4:12	they shewed Sisera that **B** the son of	1301
	4:14	Deborah said unto **B**, Up; for this is the	1301
	4:14	So **B** went down from mount Tabor,	1301
	4:15	with the edge of the sword before **B**;	1301
	4:16	**B** pursued after the chariots, and after	1301
	4:22	behold, as **B** pursued Sisera, Jael came out	1301
	5: 1	and **B** the son of Abinoam on that day,	1301
	5:12	arise, **B**, and lead thy captivity captive,	1301
	5:15	with Deborah; even Issachar, and also **B**:	1301
Heb	11:32	of **B**, and of Samson, and of Jephthae;	913

BARAKEL See BARACHEL

BARBARIAN (3) [BARBARIANS, BARBAROUS]

1Co	14:11	I shall be unto him that speaketh a **b**,	915
	14:11	and he that speaketh shall be a **b** unto me.	915
Col	3:11	**b**, Scythian, bond nor free:	915

BARBARIANS (2) [BARBARIAN]

Ac	28: 4	And when the **b** saw the venomous beast	915
Ro	1:14	debtor both to the Greeks, and to the **b**;	915

BARBAROUS (1) [BARBARIAN]

Ac	28: 2	And the **b people** shewed us no little	915

BARBED (1)

Job	41: 7	Canst thou fill his skin with **b** irons? or	7905

BARBER'S (1)

Eze	5: 1	I take thee a **b** rasor, and cause it to pass	1532

BARBS See PRICKS

BARE (186) [BAREFOOT, BAREST, BEAR]

Ge	4: 1	conceived, and **b** Cain, and said, I have	3205
	4: 2	she again **b** his brother Abel. And Abel	3205
	4:17	his wife; and she conceived, and **b** Enoch:	3205
	4:20	Adah **b** Jabal: he was the father of such as	3205
	4:22	Zillah, she also **b** Tubal-cain, an instructor	3205
	4:25	she **b** a son, and called his name Seth:	3205
	6: 4	they **b** children to them, the same	3205
	7:17	**b up** the ark, and it was lift up above	5375
	16: 1	Now Sarai Abram's wife **b** him no	3205
	16:15	Hagar **b** Abram a son: and Abram called	3205
	16:15	his son's name, which Hagar **b**, Ishmael.	3205
	16:16	old, when Hagar **b** Ishmael to Abram.	3205
	19:37	the firstborn **b** a son, and called his name	3205
	19:38	she also **b** a son, and called his name	3205
	20:17	his maidservants; and they **b** children.	3205
	21: 2	and Abraham a son in his old age,	3205
	21: 3	unto him, whom Sarah **b** to him, Isaac.	3205
	22:24	she also Tebah, and Gaham,	3205
	24:24	son of Milcah, which she **b** unto Nahor.	3205
	24:36	Sarah my master's wife **b** a son to my	3205
	24:47	Nahor's son, whom Milcah **b** unto him:	3205
	25: 2	she **b** him Zimran, and Jokshan,	3205
	25:12	Sarah's handmaid, **b** unto Abraham:	3205
	25:26	Isaac was threescore years old when she **b**	3205
	29:32	**b** a son, and she called his name Reuben:	3205
	29:33	she conceived again, and **b** a son;	3205
	29:34	she conceived again, and **b** a son:	3205
	29:35	she conceived again, and **b** a son:	3205
	30: 1	when Rachel saw that she **b** Jacob no	3205
	30: 5	And Bilhah conceived, and **b** Jacob a son.	3205
	30: 7	again, and **b** Jacob a second son.	3205
	30:10	And Zilpah Leah's maid **b** Jacob a son.	3205
	30:12	Zilpah Leah's maid **b** Jacob a second son.	3205
	30:17	she conceived, and **b** Jacob the fifth son.	3205
	30:19	again, and **b** Jacob the sixth son.	3205
	30:21	afterwards she **b** a daughter, and called	3205
	30:23	she conceived, and **b** a son; and said,	3205
	31: 8	thy wages; then all the cattle **b** speckled:	3205
	31: 8	thy hire; then all the cattle **b** ringstraked.	3205
	31:39	I **b** the loss of it; of my hand didst thou	2398
	34: 1	daughter of Leah, which she **b** unto Jacob,	3205
	36: 4	Adah **b** to Esau Eliphaz;	3205
	36: 4	to Esau Eliphaz; and Bashemath **b** Reuel;	3205
	36: 5	Aholibamah **b** Jeush, and Jaalam,	3205
	36:12	Esau's son; and she **b** to Eliphaz Amalek:	3205
	36:14	she **b** to Esau Jeush, and Jaalam,	3205
	38: 3	she conceived, and **b** a son; and he called	3205
	38: 4	she conceived again, and **b** a son;	3205
	38: 5	she yet again conceived, and **b** a son;	3205
	38: 5	and he was at Chezib, when she **b** him.	3205
	41:50	of Poti-pherah priest of On **b** unto him.	3205
	44:27	Ye know that my wife **b** me two sons:	3205
	46:15	which she **b** unto Jacob in Padan-aram,	3205
	46:18	she **b** unto Jacob, even sixteen souls.	3205
	46:20	of Poti-pherah priest of On **b** unto him:	3205
	46:25	his daughter, and she **b** these unto Jacob:	3205
Ex	2: 2	the woman conceived, and **b** a son:	3205
	2:22	she **b** him a son, and he called his name	3205
	6:20	to wife; and she **b** him Aaron and Moses:	3205
	6:23	she **b** him Nadab, and Abihu, Eleazar,	3205
	6:25	of Putiel to wife; and she **b** him Phinehas:	3205
	19: 4	how I **b** you on eagles' wings,	5375
Lev	13:45	his head **b**, and he shall put a covering	6544
	13:55	whether it be **b** within or without.	7146
Nu	13:23	and they **b** it between two upon a staff;	5375
	26:59	whom her mother **b** to Levi in Egypt:	3205
	26:59	she **b** unto Amram Aaron and Moses,	3205
Dt	1:31	seen how that the Lord thy God **b** thee,	5375
	31: 9	which **b** the ark of the covenant of	5375
	31:25	which **b** the ark of the covenant of	5375
Jos	3:15	as they that **b** the ark were come unto	5375
	3:15	the feet of the priests that **b** the ark were	5375
	3:17	the priests that **b** the ark of the covenant	5375
	4: 9	which **b** the ark of the covenant stood:	5375
	4:10	For the priests which **b** the ark stood in	5375
	4:18	when the priests that **b** the ark of	5375
	8:33	which **b** the ark of the covenant of	5375
Jdg	3:18	sent away the people that **b** the present.	5375
	8:31	also **b** him a son, whose name he called	3205
	11: 2	Gilead's wife **b** him sons; and his wife's	3205
	13: 2	and his wife was barren, and **b** not.	3205
	13:24	the woman **b** a son, and called his name	3205
Ru	4:12	of Pharez, whom Tamar **b** unto Judah,	3205
	4:13	gave her conception, and she **b** a son.	3205
1Sa	1:20	that she **b** a son, and called his name	3205
	2:21	and **b** three sons and two daughters.	3205
	14: 1	unto the young man that **b** his armour,	5375
	14: 6	Jonathan said to the young man that **b** his	5375
	17:41	man that **b** the shield went before him.	5375
2Sa	6:13	that when they that **b** the ark of the Lord	5375
	11:27	she became his wife, and **b** him a son.	3205
	12:15	the child that Uriah's wife **b** unto David,	3205
	12:24	she **b** a son, and he called his name	3205
	18:15	ten young men that **b** Joab's armour	5375
	21: 8	whom she **b** unto Saul, Armoni and	3205
1Ki	1: 6	and his mother **b** him after Absalom.	3205

B

1Ki	5:15 and ten thousand that **b** burdens,	5375
	9:23 which **b** rule over the people that	7287
	10: 2 *with* camels that **b** spices, and very much	5375
	11:20 sister of Tahpenes his Genubah his	3205
	14:28 *that* the guard **b** them, and brought them	5375
2Ki	4:17 **b** a son at that season that Elisha had said	3205
	5:23 his servants; and they **b** *them* before him.	5375
1Ch	1:32 she **b** Zimran, and Jokshan, and Medan,	3205
	2: 4 Tamar his daughter in law **b** him Pharez	3205
	2:17 Abigail **b** Amasa: and the father of Amasa	3205
	2:19 took unto him Ephrath, which **b** him Hur.	3205
	2:21 years old; and she **b** him Segub.	3205
	2:24 Abiah Hezron's wife **b** him Ashur	3205
	2:29 and she **b** him Ahban, and Molid.	3205
	2:35 his servant to wife; and she **b** him Attai.	3205
	2:46 **b** Haran, and Moza, and Gazez:	3205
	2:48 concubine, **b** Sheber, and Tirhanah.	3205
	2:49 She **b** also Shaaph the father of	3205
	4: 6 Naarah **b** him Ahuzam, and Hepher,	3205
	4: 9 Because I **b** him with sorrow.	3205
	4:17 she **b** Miriam, and Shammai, and Ishbah	2029
	4:18 his wife Jehudijah **b** Jered the father of	3205
	7:14 sons of Manasseh; Ashriel, whom she **b**:	3205
	7:14 his concubine the Aramitess **b** Machir	3205
	7:16 Maachah the wife of Machir **b** a son,	3205
	7:18 his sister Hammoleketh **b** Ishod,	3205
	7:23 **b** a son, and he called his name Beriah,	3205
	12:24 The children of Judah that **b** shield and	5375
	15:15 children of the Levites **b** the ark of God	5375
	15:26 God helped the Levites that **b** the ark	5375
	15:27 all the Levites that **b** the ark,	5375
2Ch	8:10 and fifty, that **b** rule over the people.	7287
	9: 1 camels that **b** spices, and gold in	5375
	11:19 Which **b** him children; Jeush,	3205
	11:20 which **b** him Abijah, and Attai, and Ziza,	3205
	14: 8 Asa had an army of *men* that **b** targets	5375
	14: 8 that **b** shields and drew bows, two	3205
Ne	4:17 that **b** burdens, *with* those that laded,	5375
	5:15 yea, even their servants **b** rule over	7980
Pr	17:25 father, and bitterness to her that **b** him.	3205
	23:25 be glad, and she that **b** thee shall rejoice.	3205
SS	6: 9 she *is* the choice one of her that **b** her.	3205
	8: 5 there she brought *thee* forth that **b** thee.	3205
Isa	8: 3 and she conceived, and **b** a son.	3205
	22: 6 Elam **b** the quiver with chariots of men	5375
	32:11 **make** ye **b**, and gird *sackcloth* upon *your*	6209
	47: 2 **make b** the leg, uncover the thigh,	2834
	51: 2 your father, and unto Sarah *that* **b** you:	2342
	52:10 The Lord hath **made b** his holy arm in	2834
	53:12 **b** the sin of many, and made intercession	5375
	63: 9 he **b** them, and carried them all the days	5190
Jer	13:22 skirts discovered, *and* thy heels **made b**.	2554
	16: 3 concerning their mothers that **b** them,	3205
	20:14 let not the day wherein my mother **b** me	3205
	22:26 thy mother that **b** thee, into another	3205
	49:10 I have **made** Esau **b**, I have uncovered	2834
	50:12 she that **b** you shall be ashamed:	3205
Eze	12: 7 *and* I **b** *it* upon *my* shoulder in their sight.	5375
	16: 7 grown, whereas thou *wast* naked and **b**.	6181
	16:22 when thou wast naked and **b**,	6181
	16:39 fair jewels, and leave thee naked and **b**.	6181
	19:11 rods for the sceptres of them that **b** rule,	4910
	23: 4 mine, and they **b** sons and daughters.	3205
	23:29 and shall leave thee naked and **b**:	6181
	23:37 caused their sons, whom they **b** unto me,	3205
Hos	1: 3 which conceived, and **b** him a son.	3205
	1: 6 she conceived again, and **b** a daughter.	3205
	1: 8 she conceived, and **b** a son.	3205
Joel	1: 7 he hath made it clean **b**, and cast *it* away;	2834
Mt	8:17 took our infirmities, and **b** our sicknesses.	941
Mk	14:56 For many **b false witness** against him,	5576
	14:57 and **b false witness** against him, saying,	5576
Lk	4:22 And all **b** him **witness**, and wondered at	3140
	7:14 they that **b** *him* stood still. And he said,	941
	8: 8 sprang up, and **b** fruit an hundredfold.	4160
	11:27 Blessed *is* the womb that **b** thee,	941
	23:29 the wombs that never **b**, and the paps	1080
Jn	1:15 John **b witness** of him, and cried, saying,	3140
	1:32 John **b** record, saying, I saw the Spirit	3140
	1:34 and **b** record that this is the Son of God.	3140
	2: 8 the governor of the feast. And they **b** *it*.	5342
	5:33 John, and he **b witness** unto the truth.	3140
	12: 6 had the bag, and **b** what was put *therein*.	941
	12:17 and raised him from the dead, **b** record.	3140
	19:35 he that saw *it* **b** record, and his record	3140
Ac	15: 8 knoweth the hearts, **b** them **witness**,	3140
1Co	15:37 but **b** grain, it may chance of wheat,	1131
1Pe	2:24 his own self **b** our sins in his own body	399
Rev	1: 2 Who **b** record of the word of God,	3140
	22: 2 which **b** twelve *manner* of fruits,	4160

BAREFOOT (4) [BARE, FOOT]

2Sa	15:30 and had his head covered, and he went **b**:	3182
Isa	20: 2 And he did so, walking naked and **b**.	3182
	20: 3 **b** three years *for* a sign and wonder upon	3182
	20: 4 young and old, naked and **b**,	3182

BAREST (3) [BARE]

1Ki	2: 6 thou **b** the ark of the Lord God before	5375
Isa	63:19 are *thine:* thou never **b** rule over them;	4910
Jn	3:26 whom thou **b witness**, behold, the same	3140

BARHUMITE (1)

2Sa	23:31 Azmaveth the **B**,	1273

BARIAH (1)

1Ch	3:22 Igeal, and **B**, and Neariah, and Shaphat, six.	1282

BAR-JESUS (1)

Ac	13: 6 a false prophet, a Jew, whose name *was* **B**:	919

BAR-JONA (1)

Mt	16:17 said unto him, Blessed art thou, Simon **B**:	920

BARK (1) [BARKED]

Isa	56:10 they *are* all dumb dogs, they cannot **b**;	5024

BARKED (1) [BARK]

Joel	1: 7 hath laid my vine waste, and **b** my fig tree:	7111

BARKOS (2)

Ezr	2:53 The children of **B**, the children of Sisera,	1302
Ne	7:55 The children of **B**, the children of Sisera,	1302

BARLEY (37)

Ex	9:31 the flax and the **b** was smitten:	8184
	9:31 for the **b** *was* in the ear, and the flax *was*	8184
Lev	27:16 a homer of **b** seed *shall be valued* at fifty	8184
Nu	5:15 the tenth *part* of an ephah of **b** meal;	8184
Dt	8: 8 **b**, and vines, and fig trees,	8184
Jdg	7:13 a cake of **b** bread tumbled into the host of	8184
Ru	1:22 Beth-lehem in the beginning of **b** harvest.	8184
	2:17 and it was about an ephah of **b**.	8184
	2:23 of Boaz to glean unto the end of **b** harvest	8184
	3: 2 he winnoweth **b** to night in	8184
	3:15 he measured six *measures* of **b**, and laid	8184
	3:17 These six *measures* of **b** gave he me;	8184
2Sa	14:30 field is near mine, and he hath **b** there;	8184
	17:28 **b**, and flour, and parched *corn*, and beans,	8184
	21: 9 in the first *days*, in the beginning of **b**	8184
1Ki	4:28 **b** also and straw for the horses and	8184
2Ki	4:42 twenty loaves of **b** bread, and full ears of corn in	8184
	7: 1 two measures of **b** for a shekel, in the gate	8184
	7:16 two measures of **b** for a shekel,	8184
	7:18 Two measures of **b** for a shekel.	8184
1Ch	11:13 where was a parcel of ground full of **b**;	8184
2Ch	2:10 twenty thousand measures of **b**,	8184
	2:15 wheat, and the **b**, the oil, and the wine,	8184
	27: 5 of wheat, and ten thousand of **b**.	8184
Job	31:40 instead of wheat, and cockle instead of **b**.	8184
Isa	28:25 appointed the rye *in their* place?	8184
Jer	41: 8 and of **b**, and of oil, and of honey.	8184
Eze	4: 9 **b**, and beans, and lentiles, and millet,	8184
	4:12 thou shalt eat it *as* **b** cakes, and thou shalt	8184
	13:19 me among my people for handfuls of **b**	8184
	45:13 the sixth part of an ephah of a homer of **b**:	8184
Hos	3: 2 for a homer of **b**, and a half homer of	8184
	3: 2 homer of **barley**, and a half homer of **b**.	8184
Joel	1:11 vinedressers, for the wheat and for the **b**;	8184
Jn	6: 9 which hath five **b** loaves, and two small	2916
	6:13 with the fragments of the five **b** loaves,	2916
Rev	6: 6 and three measures of **b** for a penny;	2915

BARN (4) [BARNFLOOR, BARNS]

Job	39:12 home thy seed, and gather *it into* thy **b**?	1637
Hag	2:19 the seed yet in the **b**? yea, as yet the vine,	4035
Mt	13:30 them: but gather the wheat into my **b**.	596
Lk	12:24 which neither have storehouse nor **b**; and	596

BARNABAS (29) [JOSES]

Ac	4:36 who by the apostles was surnamed **B**,	921
	9:27 But **B** took him, and brought *him* to	921
	11:22 and they sent forth **B**, that *he* should go as	921
	11:25 departed **B** to Tarsus, for to seek Saul:	921
	11:30 sent it to the elders by the hands of **B** and	921
	12:25 And **B** and Saul returned from Jerusalem,	921
	13: 1 as **B**, and Simeon that was called Niger,	921
	13: 2 Separate me **B** and Saul for the work	921
	13: 7 who called for **B** and Saul, and desired to	921
	13:43 religious proselytes followed Paul and **B**:	921
	13:46 Then Paul and **B** waxed bold, and said,	921
	13:50 and raised persecution against Paul and **B**,	921
	14:12 And they called **B**, Jupiter; and Paul,	921
	14:14 *Which* when the apostles, **B** and Paul,	921
	14:20 the next day he departed with **B** to Derbe.	921
	15: 2 and **B** had no small dissension and	921
	15: 2 they determined that Paul and **B**,	921
	15:12 and gave audience to **B** and Paul,	921
	15:22 own company to Antioch with Paul and **B**;	921
	15:25 chosen men unto you with our beloved **B**	921
	15:35 Paul also and **B** continued in Antioch,	921
	15:36 some days after Paul said unto **B**, Let us	921
	15:37 And **B** determined to take with *them* John,	921
	15:39 so **B** took Mark, and sailed unto Cyprus;	921
1Co	9: 6 Or I only and **B**, have not we power to	921
Gal	2: 1 after I went up again to Jerusalem with **B**,	921
	2: 9 to me and **B** the right hands of fellowship;	921
	2:13 insomuch that **B** also was carried away	921
Col	4:10 saluteth you, and Marcus, sister's son to **B**,	921

BARNFLOOR (1) [BARN, FLOOR]

2Ki	6:27 out of the **b**, or out of the winepress?	1637

BARNS (4) [BARN]

Pr	3:10 So shall thy **b** be filled *with* plenty,	618
Joel	1:17 are laid desolate, the **b** are broken down;	4460
Mt	6:26 neither do they reap, nor gather into **b**;	596
Lk	12:18 I will pull down my **b**, and build greater;	596

BARREL (3) [BARRELS]

1Ki	17:12 a handful of meal in a **b**, and a little oil in	3537
1Ki	17:14 The **b** of meal shall not waste, neither	3537
	17:16 *And* the **b** of meal wasted not, neither did	3537

BARRELS (1) [BARREL]

1Ki	18:33 Fill four **b** *with* water, and pour *it* on	3537

BARREN (23) [BARRENNESS]

Ge	11:30 But Sarai was **b**; she had no child.	6135
	25:21 Lord for his wife, because she *was* **b**:	6135
	29:31 he opened her womb: but Rachel *was* **b**.	6135
Ex	23:26 cast their young, nor be **b**, in thy land:	6135
Dt	7:14 not be male or **female b** among you,	6135
Jdg	13: 2 and his wife *was* **b**, and bare not.	6135
	13: 3 Behold now, thou *art* **b**, and bearest not:	6135
1Sa	2: 5 so that the **b** hath born seven; and she	6135
2Ki	2:19 the water *is* naught, and the ground **b**.	7921
	2:21 be from thence any more death or **b** *land*.	7921
Job	24:21 He evil entreateth the **b** *that* beareth not:	6135
	39: 6 and the **b** *land* his dwellings.	4420
Ps	113: 9 He maketh the **b** *woman* to keep house,	6135
Pr	30:16 The grave; and the **b** womb; the earth	6115
SS	4: 2 beareth twins, and none is **b** among them.	7909
	6: 6 and *there* is not one **b** among them.	7909
Isa	54: 1 Sing, O **b**, thou *that* didst not bear;	6135
Joel	2:20 will drive him into a land **b** and desolate,	6723
Lk	1: 7 because that Elisabeth was **b**, and they	4723
	1:36 sixth month with her, who was called **b**.	4723
	23:29 Blessed *are* the **b**, and the wombs that	4723
Gal	4:27 written, Rejoice, *thou* **b** that bearest not;	4723
2Pe	1: 8 make *you* that ye shall neither *be* **b** nor	692

BARRENNESS (1) [BARREN]

Ps	107:34 A fruitful land into **b**, for the wickedness	4420

BARS (38) [BAR]

Ex	26:26 thou shalt make **b** of shittim wood; five	1280
	26:27 five **b** for the boards of the other side of	1280
	26:27 five **b** for the boards of the side of	1280
	26:29 their rings of gold for places for the **b**:	1280
	26:29 and thou shalt overlay the **b** with gold.	1280
	35:11 his **b**, his pillars, and his sockets,	1280
	36:31 he made **b** of shittim wood; five for	1280
	36:32 five **b** for the boards of the one side of	1280
	36:32 five **b** for the boards of the tabernacle for	1280
	36:34 their rings of gold *to be* places for the **b**,	1280
	36:34 for the bars, and overlaid the **b** with gold.	1280
	39:33 his **b**, and his pillars, and his sockets,	1280
	40:18 put in the **b** thereof, and reared up his	1280
Nu	3:36 the **b** thereof, and the pillars thereof,	1280
	4:31 the **b** thereof, and the pillars thereof,	1280
Dt	3: 5 were fenced *with* high walls, gates, and **b**;	1280
1Sa	23: 7 into a town that hath gates and **b**.	1280
1Ki	4:13 great cities *with* walls and brasen **b**:	1280
2Ch	8: 5 fenced cities, *with* walls, gates, and **b**;	1280
	14: 7 walls, and towers, gates, and **b**,	1280
Ne	3: 3 the locks thereof, and the **b** thereof.	1280
	3: 6 and the locks thereof, and the **b** thereof.	1280
	3:13 the **b** thereof, and a thousand cubits on	1280
	3:14 the locks thereof, and the **b** thereof.	1280
	3:15 the **b** thereof, and the wall of the pool of	1280
Job	17:16 They shall go down *to* the **b** of the pit,	905
	38:10 it my decreed *place*, and set **b** and doors,	1280
	40:18 of brass; his bones *are* like **b** of iron.	4300
Ps	107:16 of brass, and cut the **b** of iron in sunder.	1280
	147:13 he hath strengthened the **b** of thy gates;	1280
Pr	18:19 *their* contentions *are* like the **b** of a castle.	1280
Isa	45: 2 of brass, and cut in sunder the **b** of iron:	1280
Jer	49:31 which have neither gates nor **b**,	1280
	51:30 her dwelling places; her **b** are broken.	1280
La	2: 9 he hath destroyed and broken her **b**:	1280
Eze	38:11 and having neither **b** nor gates,	1280
Jnh	2: 6 earth *with* her **b** *was* about me for ever:	1280
Na	3:13 thine enemies: the fire shall devour thy **b**.	1280

BARSABAS (2)

Ac	1:23 And they appointed two, Joseph called **B**,	923
	15:22 namely, Judas surnamed **B**, and Silas,	923

BARSABBAS See BARSABAS

BARTHOLOMEW (4)

Mt	10: 3 Philip, and **B**; Thomas, and Matthew	918
Mk	3:18 and **B**, and Matthew, and Thomas,	918
Lk	6:14 his brother, James and John, Philip and **B**,	918
Ac	1:13 Philip, and Thomas, and Matthew,	918

BARTIMEUS (1)

Mk	10:46 of people, blind **B**, the son of Timeus,	924

BARUCH (26)

Ne	3:20 After him **B** the son of Zabbai earnestly	1263
	10: 6 Daniel, Ginnethon, **B**,	1263
	11: 5 Maaseiah the son of **B**, the son of	1263
Jer	32:12 I gave the evidence of the purchase unto **B**	1263
	32:13 And I charged **B** before them, saying,	1263
	32:16 of the purchase unto **B** the son of Neriah,	1263
	36: 4 Jeremiah called **B** the son of Neriah:	1263
	36: 4 **B** wrote from the mouth of Jeremiah all	1263
	36: 5 Jeremiah commanded **B**, saying, I *am* shut	1263
	36: 8 **B** the son of Neriah did according to all	1263
	36:10 read **B** in the book the words of Jeremiah	1263
	36:13 when **B** read the book in the ears of	1263
	36:14 the son of Cushi, unto **B**, saying,	1263
	36:14 So **B** the son of Neriah took the roll in his	1263
	36:15 it in our ears. So **B** read *it* in their ears.	1263
	36:16 both one and other, and said unto **B**,	1263

Jer	36:17 they asked **B**, saying, Tell us now,	1263
	36:18 **B** answered them, He pronounced all	1263
	36:19 said the princes unto **B**, Go, hide thee,	1263
	36:26 to take **B** the scribe and Jeremiah	1263
	36:27 the words which **B** wrote at the mouth of	1263
	36:32 gave it to **B** the scribe, the son of Neriah;	1263
	43: 3 **B** the son of Neriah setteth thee on against	1263
	43: 6 the prophet, and **B** the son of Neriah.	1263
	45: 1 prophet spake unto **B** the son of Neriah,	1263
	45: 2 the God of Israel, unto thee, O **B**;	1263

BARZILLAI (12)

2Sa	17:27 and **B** the Gileadite of Rogelim,	1271
	19:31 **B** the Gileadite came down from Rogelim,	1271
	19:32 Now **B** was a very aged man,	1271
	19:33 the king said unto **B**, Come thou over	1271
	19:34 **B** said unto the king, How long have I to	1271
	19:39 the king kissed **B**, and blessed him;	1271
	21: 8 for Adriel the son of **B** the Meholathite:	1271
1Ki	2: 7 shew kindness unto the sons of **B**	1271
Ezr	2:61 the children of Koz, the children of **B**;	1271
	2:61 which took a wife of the daughters of **B**	1271
Ne	7:63 the children of Koz, the children of **B**,	1271
	7:63 which took *one* of the daughters of **B**	1271

BASE (18) [BASER, BASES, BASEST]

2Sa	6:22 thus, and will be **b** in mine own sight:	8217
1Ki	7:27 four cubits *was* the length of one **b**,	4350
	7:29 upon the ledges *there was* a **b** above:	3653
	7:30 every **b** had four brasen wheels,	3653
	7:31 thereof *was* round *after* the work of the **b**,	3653
	7:32 of the wheels *were* joined to the **b**:	4350
	7:34 undersetters to the four corners of one **b**:	4350
	7:34 undersetters *were* of the *very* **b** itself.	4350
	7:35 in the top of the **b** *was there* a round	4350
	7:35 on the top of the **b** the ledges thereof and	4350
Job	30: 8 of fools, yea, children of **b** men:	1097+8034
Isa	3: 5 and the **b** against the honourable.	7034
Eze	17:14 That the kingdom might be **b**, that *it*	8217
	29:14 and they shall be there a **b** kingdom.	8217
Zec	5:11 and set there upon her own **b**.	4350
Mal	2: 9 and **b** before all the people,	8217
1Co	1:28 And **b** *things* of the world, and *things*	36
2Co	10: 1 who in presence *am* **b** among you, but	5011

BASEMATH See BASHEMATH; BASMATH

BASER (1) [BASE]

Ac	17: 5 *them* certain lewd fellows of the **b** sort,	60

BASES (16) [BASE]

1Ki	7:27 he made ten **b** of brass; four cubits *was*	4350
	7:28 the work of the **b** *was on* this manner:	4350
	7:37 After this manner he made the ten **b**: all	4350
	7:38 upon every one of the ten **b** one laver.	4350
	7:39 put five **b** on the right side of the house,	4350
	7:43 the ten **b**, and ten lavers on the bases;	4350
	7:43 the ten bases, and ten lavers on the **b**;	4350
2Ki	16:17 king Ahaz cut off the borders of the **b**,	4350
	25:13 the **b**, and the brasen sea that *was* in	4350
	25:16 the **b** which Solomon had made for	4350
2Ch	4:14 He made also **b** and lavers made he upon	4350
	4:14 also bases and lavers made he upon the **b**;	4350
Ezr	3:19 they set the altar upon his **b**; for fear *was*	4350
Jer	27:19 concerning the **b**, and concerning	4350
	52:17 the **b**, and the brasen sea that *was* in	4350
	52:20 brasen bulls that *were* under the **b**,	4350

BASEST (2) [BASE]

Eze	29:15 It shall be the **b** of the kingdoms;	8217
Da	4:17 will, and setteth up over it the **b** of men.	8215

BASHAN (59) [BASHAN-HAVOTH-JAIR]

Nu	21:33 they turned and went up *by* the way of **B**:	1316
	21:33 Og the king of **B** went out against them,	1316
	32:33 the kingdom of Og king of **B**, the land,	1316
Dt	1: 4 dwelt in Heshbon, and Og the king of **B**,	1316
	3: 1 we turned, and went up the way to **B**:	1316
	3: 1 Og the king of **B** came out against us,	1316
	3: 3 Og also, the king of **B**, and all his people:	1316
	3: 4 region of Argob, the kingdom of Og in **B**.	1316
	3:10 all Gilead, and all **B**, unto Salchah and	1316
	3:10 Edrei, cities of the kingdom of Og in **B**.	1316
	3:11 For only Og king of **B** remained of	1316
	3:13 the rest of Gilead, and all **B**, *being*	1316
	3:13 all the region of Argob, with all **B**, which	1316
	4:43 and Golan in **B**, of the Manassites.	1316
	4:47 the land of Og king of **B**, two kings of	1316
	29: 7 king of Heshbon, and Og the king of **B**,	1316
	32:14 and rams of the breed of **B**, and goats,	1316
	33:22 Dan *is* a lion's whelp: he shall leap from **B**.	1316
Jos	9:10 Og king of **B**, which *was* at Ashtaroth.	1316
	12: 4 the coast of Og king of **B**, *which was* of	1316
	12: 5 Hermon, and in Salcah, and in all **B**,	1316
	13:11 all mount Hermon, and all **B** unto Salcah;	1316
	13:12 All the kingdom of Og in **B**, which	1316
	13:30 their coast was from Mahanaim, all **B**,	1316
	13:30 all the kingdom of Og king of **B**, and all	1316
	13:30 of Jair, which *are* in **B**, threescore cities:	1316
	13:31 Edrei, cities of the kingdom of Og in **B**,	1316
	17: 1 of war, therefore he had Gilead and **B**.	1316
	17: 5 beside the land of Gilead and **B**,	1316
	20: 8 Golan in **B** out of the tribe of Manasseh.	1316
	21: 6 out of the half tribe of Manasseh in **B**,	1316
	21:27 *they gave* Golan in **B** with her suburbs,	1316
	22: 7 Moses had given *possession* in **B**:	1316

1Ki	4:13 which *is* in **B**, threescore great cities *with*	1316
	4:19 king of the Amorites, and of Og king of **B**;	1316
2Ki	10:33 *is* by the river Arnon, even Gilead and **B**.	1316
1Ch	5:11 them, in the land of **B** unto Salchah:	1316
	5:12 the next, and Jaanai, and Shaphat in **B**.	1316
	5:16 dwelt in Gilead in **B**, and in her towns,	1316
	5:23 they increased from **B** unto Baal-hermon,	1316
	6:62 out of the tribe of Manasseh in **B**,	1316
	6:71 Golan in **B** with her suburbs, and	1316
Ne	9:22 of Heshbon, and the land of Og king of **B**.	1316
Ps	22:12 strong *bulls* of **B** have beset me round.	1316
	68:15 The hill of God *is as* the hill of **B**; a high	1316
	68:15 hill of Bashan; a high hill *as* the hill of **B**.	1316
	68:22 The Lord said, I will bring again from **B**,	1316
	135:11 Og king of **B**, and all the kingdoms of	1316
	136:20 Og the king of **B**: for his mercy *endureth*	1316
Isa	2:13 and lifted up, and upon all the oaks of **B**,	1316
	33: 9 and **B** and Carmel shake off *their* fruits.	1316
Jer	22:20 lift up thy voice in **B**, and cry from	1316
	50:19 shall feed on Carmel and **B**, and his soul	1316
Eze	27: 6 the oaks of **B** have they made thine oars;	1316
	39:18 of bullocks, all of them fatlings of **B**.	1316
Am	4: 1 Hear this word, ye kine of **B**, that *are* in	1316
Mic	7:14 let them feed in **B** and Gilead, as in	1316
Na	1: 4 **B** languisheth, and Carmel, and the flower	1316
Zec	11: 2 howl, O ye oaks of **B**; for the forest of	1316

BASHAN-HAVOTH-JAIR (1) [BASHAN, HAVOTH-JAIR]

Dt	3:14 his own name, **B**, unto this day.	1316+2334

BASHEMATH (6)

Ge	26:34 and **B** the daughter of Elon the Hittite:	1315
	36: 3 **B** Ishmael's daughter, sister of Nebajoth.	1315
	36: 4 bare to Esau Eliphaz; and **B** bare Reuel;	1315
	36:10 Reuel the son of **B** the wife of Esau.	1315
	36:13 these were the sons of **B** Esau's wife.	1315
	36:17 these *are* the sons of **B** Esau's wife.	1315

BASIC PRINCIPLES See RUDIMENTS

BASIN; BASINS See BASON; BASONS; LAVER

BASKET (23) [BASKETS]

Ge	40:17 in the uppermost **b** *there was* of all	5536
	40:17 the birds did eat them out of the **b** upon	5536
Ex	29: 3 thou shalt put them into one **b**,	5536
	29: 3 bring them in the **b**, with the bullock and	5536
	29:23 one wafer out of the **b** of the unleavened	5536
	29:32 of the ram, and the bread that *is* in the **b**,	5536
Lev	8: 2 two rams, and a **b** of unleavened bread;	5536
	8:26 out of the **b** of unleavened bread, that	5536
	8:31 eat it with the bread that *is* in the **b** of	5536
Nu	6:15 a **b** of unleavened bread, cakes *of* fine	5536
	6:17 with the **b** of unleavened bread:	5536
	6:19 one unleavened cake out of the **b**,	5536
Dt	26: 2 shalt put *it* in a **b**, and shalt go unto	2935
	26: 4 priest shall take the **b** out of thine hand,	2935
	28: 5 Blessed *shall* be thy **b** and thy store.	2935
	28:17 Cursed *shall* be thy **b** and thy store.	2935
Jdg	6:19 flesh he put in a **b**, and he put the broth	5536
Jer	24: 2 had very good figs, *even* like the figs	1731
	24: 2 the other **b** *had* very naughty figs,	1731
Am	8: 1 unto me: and behold, a **b** of summer fruit.	3619
	8: 2 I said, A **b** of summer fruit. Then said	3619
Ac	9:25 and let *him* down by the wall in a **b**.	4711
2Co	11:33 And through a window in a **b** was I let	4553

BASKETS (15) [BASKET]

Ge	40:16 behold, *I had* three white **b** on my head:	5536
	40:18 The three **b** *are* three days:	5536
2Ki	10: 7 put their heads in **b**, and sent them *them*	1731
Jer	6: 9 thine hand as a grapegatherer into the **b**.	5552
	24: 1 two **b** of figs *were* set before the temple of	1736
Mt	14:20 the fragments that remained twelve **b** full.	2894
	15:37 the broken *meat* that was left seven **b** full.	4711
	16: 9 thousand, and how many **b** ye took up?	2894
	16:10 and how many **b** ye took up?	4711
Mk	6:43 And they took up twelve **b** full of	2894
	8: 8 of the broken *meat* that was left seven **b**.	4711
	8:19 how many **b** full of fragments took ye up?	2894
	8:20 how many **b** full of fragments took ye up?	4711
Lk	9:17 that remained to them twelve **b**.	2894
Jn	6:13 filled twelve **b** with the fragments of	2894

BASMATH (1)

1Ki	4:15 he also took **B** the daughter of Solomon to	1315

BASON (5) [BASONS]

Ex	12:22 dip *it* in the blood that *is* in the **b**,	5592
	12:22 side posts with the blood that *is* in the **b**;	5592
1Ch	28:17 by weight for **every b**;	3713+3713+2050.1
	28:17 for **every b** of silver:	3713+3713+2050.1
Jn	13: 5 he poureth water into a **b**, and began to	3537

BASONS (18) [BASON]

Ex	24: 6 took half of the blood, and put *it* in **b**;	101
	27: 3 his **b**, and his fleshhooks, and his firepans:	4219
	38: 3 **b**, *and* the fleshhooks and the firepans:	4219
Nu	4:14 fleshhooks, and the shovels, and the **b**,	4219
2Sa	17:28 **b**, and earthen vessels, and wheat,	5592
1Ki	7:40 the lavers, and the shovels, and the **b**.	4219
	7:45 the pots, and the shovels, and the **b**:	4219
	7:50 the **b**, and the spoons, and the censers *of*	4219
2Ki	12:13 snuffers, **b**, trumpets, any vessels of gold,	4219
1Ch	28:17 for the golden **b** *he gave gold* by weight	3713

2Ch	4: 8 And he made an hundred **b** of gold.	4219
	4:11 the pots, and the shovels, and the **b**.	4219
	4:22 the **b**, and the spoons, and the censers,	4219
Ezr	1:10 Thirty **b** of gold, silver basons of a second	3713
	1:10 silver **b** of a second sort four hundred and	3713
	8:27 Also twenty **b** of gold, of a thousand	3713
Ne	7:70 fifty **b**, five hundred and thirty priests'	4219
Jer	52:19 the **b**, and the firepans, and the bowls,	5592

BASTARD (2) [BASTARDS]

Dt	23: 2 A **b** shall not enter into the congregation	4464
Zec	9: 6 a **b** shall dwell in Ashdod, and I will cut	4464

BASTARDS (1) [BASTARD]

Heb	12: 8 are partakers, then are ye **b**, and not sons.	3541

BAT (2) [BATS]

Lev	11:19 after her kind, and the lapwing, and the **b**.	5847
Dt	14:18 after her kind, and the lapwing, and the **b**.	5847

BATH (6) [BATHS]

Isa	5:10 ten acres of vineyard shall yield one **b**,	1324
Eze	45:10 balances, and a just ephah, and a just **b**.	1324
	45:11 and the **b** shall be of one measure,	1324
	45:11 that the **b** may contain the tenth part of a	1324
	45:14 the ordinance of oil, the **b** of oil,	1324
	45:14 ye shall *offer* the tenth part of a **b** out of	1324

BATHE (18) [BATHED]

Lev	15: 5 **b** *himself* in water, and be unclean until	7364
	15: 6 **b** *himself* in water, and be unclean until	7364
	15: 7 **b** *himself* in water, and be unclean until	7364
	15: 8 **b** *himself* in water, and be unclean until	7364
	15:10 **b** *himself* in water, and be unclean until	7364
	15:11 **b** *himself* in water, and be unclean until	7364
	15:13 his flesh in running water, and shall be	7364
	15:18 they shall *both* **b** *themselves* in water,	7364
	15:21 **b** *himself* in water, and be unclean until	7364
	15:22 **b** *himself* in water, and be unclean until	7364
	15:27 **b** *himself* in water, and be unclean until	7364
	16:26 his flesh in water, and afterward come	7364
	16:28 his flesh in water, and afterward he shall	7364
	17:15 **b** *himself* in water, and be unclean until	7364
	17:16 if he wash *them* not, nor **b** his flesh; then	7364
Nu	19: 7 he shall **b** his flesh in water,	7364
	19: 8 **b** his flesh in water, and shall be unclean	7364
	19:19 **b** *himself* in water, and shall be clean at	7364

BATHED (1) [BATHE]

Isa	34: 5 For my sword shall be **b** in heaven:	7301

BATH-RABBIM (1)

SS	7: 4 the *fish*pools in Heshbon, by the gate of **B**:	1337

BATHS (9) [BATH]

1Ki	7:26 of lilies: it contained two thousand **b**.	1324
	7:38 laver contained forty **b**: *and* every laver	1324
2Ch	2:10 twenty thousand **b** of wine,	1324
	2:10 of wine, and twenty thousand **b** of oil.	1324
	4: 5 it received and held three thousand **b**.	1324
Ezr	7:22 an hundred **b** of wine, and to an hundred	1325
	7:22 to an hundred **b** *of* oil, and salt without	1325
Eze	45:14 out of the cor, *which is* a homer of ten **b**;	1324
	45:14 homer of ten baths; for ten **b** *are* a homer:	1324

BATH-SHEBA (11)

2Sa	11: 3 *one* said, *Is* not this **B**, the daughter of	1339
	12:24 David comforted **B** his wife, and went in	1339
1Ki	1:11 Nathan spake unto **B** the mother	1339
	1:15 **B** went in unto the king into the chamber:	1339
	1:16 **B** bowed, and did obeisance unto the king.	1339
	1:28 king David answered and said, Call me **B**.	1339
	1:31 **B** bowed *with her* face *to* the earth,	1339
	2:13 Adonijah the son of Haggith came to **B**	1339
	2:18 **B** said, Well; I will speak for thee unto	1339
	2:19 **B** therefore went unto king Solomon,	1339
Ps	51: T came unto him, after he had gone in to **B**.	1339

BATH-SHUA (1)

1Ch	3: 5 four, of **B** the daughter of Ammiel:	1340

BATS (1) [BAT]

Isa	2:20 to worship, to the moles and to the **b**;	5847

BATTERED (1) [BATTERING]

2Sa	20:15 all the people that *were* with Joab **b**	7843

BATTERING (2) [BATTERED]

Eze	4: 2 and set *b* rams against it round about.	NIH
	21:22 to appoint *b* rams against the gates, to cast	NIH

BATTLE (170) [BATTLEMENT, BATTLEMENTS, BATTLES]

Ge	14: 8 they joined **b** with them in the vale of	4421
Nu	21:33 he, and all his people, to the **b** *at* Edrei.	4421
	31:14 which came from the **b**.	4421+6635
	31:21 unto the men of war which went to the **b**,	4421
	31:27 who went out to **b**, and between all	6635
	31:28 of the men of war which went out to **b**:	6635
	32:27 before the LORD to **b**, as my lord saith.	4421
	32:29 your man armed to **b**, before the LORD,	6635
Dt	2: 9 neither contend with them *in* **b**:	4421
	2:24 to possess *it*, and contend with him *in* **b**.	4421
	3: 1 he and all his people, to **b** *at* Edrei.	4421
	20: 1 When thou goest out to **b** against thine	4421
	20: 2 be, when ye are come nigh unto the **b**,	4421

B

Dt 20: 3 you approach *this* day unto **b** against your 4421
20: 5 lest he die in the **b**, and another man 4421
20: 6 lest he die in the **b**, and another man eat 4421
20: 7 lest he die in the **b**, and another man take 4421
29: 7 came out against us unto **b**, and we smote 4421
Jos 4:13 war passed over before the Lᴏʀᴅ unto **b**, 4421
8:14 of the city went out against Israel to **b**, 4421
11:19 of Gibeon: all *other* they took in **b**. 4421
11:20 that *they* should come against Israel *in* **b**, 4421
22:33 did not intend to go up against them in **b**, 6635
Jdg 8:13 Gideon the son of Joash returned from **b** 4421
20:14 go out to **b** against the children of Israel. 4421
20:18 Which of us shall go up first to the **b** 4421
20:20 the men of Israel went out to **b** against 4421
20:22 set *their* **b** again in array in the place 4421
20:23 Shall I go *up* again to **b** against the 4421
20:28 Shall I yet again go out to **b** against 4421
20:34 men out of all Israel, and the **b** was sore: 4421
20:39 when the men of Israel retired in the **b**, 4421
20:39 smitten down before us, as *in* the first **b**. 4421
20:42 the **b** overtook them; and them which 4421
1Sa 4: 1 Israel went out against the Philistines to **b**, 4421
4: 2 when they joined **b**, Israel was smitten 4421
7:10 Philistines drew near to **b** against Israel: 4421
13:22 So it came to pass in the day of **b**, that 4421
14:20 and they came to the **b**: 4421
14:22 also followed hard after them in the **b**. 4421
14:23 and the **b** passed over *unto* Beth-aven. 4421
17: 1 gathered together their armies to **b**, 4421
17: 2 set the **b** in array against the Philistines. 4421
17: 8 Why are ye come out to set your**b** in 4421
17:13 of Jesse went *and* followed Saul to the **b**: 4421
17:13 went to the **b** were Eliab the firstborn, 4421
17:20 forth to the fight, and shouted for the **b**. 4421
17:21 and the Philistines had put *the* **b** in array, NIH
17:28 come down that *thou* mightest see the **b**. 4421
17:47 for the **b** *is* the Lᴏʀᴅ's, and he will give 4421
26:10 or he shall descend into **b**, and perish. 4421
28: 1 that thou shalt go out with me to **b**, thou 4264
29: 4 and let him not go down with us to **b**, 4421
29: 4 lest in the **b** he be an adversary to us: 4421
29: 9 He shall not go up with us to the **b**. 4421
30:24 as his part *is* that goeth down to the **b**, 4421
31: 3 the **b** went sore against Saul, 4421
2Sa 1: 4 That the people are fled from the **b**, 4421
1:25 are the mighty fallen in the midst of the **b**! 4421
2:17 there was a very sore **b** that day; 4421
3:30 their brother Asahel at Gibeon in the **b**. 4421
10: 8 put the **b** in array *at* the entering in of 4421
10: 9 When Joab saw that the front of the **b** was 4421
10:13 with him, unto the **b** against the Syrians: 4421
11: 1 at the time when kings go forth *to* **b**, that NIH
11:15 ye Uriah in the forefront of the hottest **b**, 4421
11:25 make thy **b** *more* strong against the city, 4421
17:11 and *that* thou go to **b** in thine own person. 7128
18: 6 and the **b** was in the wood of Ephraim; 4421
18: 8 the **b** was there scattered over the face 4421
19: 3 ashamed steal away when they flee in **b**. 4421
19:10 whom we anointed over us, is dead in **b**. 4421
21:17 Thou shalt go no more out with us to **b**, 4421
21:18 there was again a **b** with the Philistines 4421
21:19 there was again a **b** in Gob with 4421
21:20 was yet a **b** in Gath, where was a man 4421
22:40 thou hast girded me with strength to **b**: 4421
23: 9 *that* were there gathered together to **b**, 4421
1Ki 8:44 If thy people go out to **b** against their 4421
20:14 he said, Who shall order the **b**? And he 4421
20:29 that in the seventh day the **b** was joined: 4421
20:39 servant went out into the midst of the **b**; 4421
22: 4 Wilt thou go with me to **b** *to* 4421
22: 6 Shall I go against Ramoth-gilead to **b**, 4421
22:15 shall we go against Ramoth-gilead to **b**, 4421
22:30 will disguise myself, and enter into the **b**; 4421
22:30 disguised himself, and went into the **b**. 4421
22:35 the **b** increased that day: and the king was 4421
2Ki 3: 7 wilt thou go with me against Moab to **b**? 4421
3:26 the king of Moab saw that the **b** was 4421
1Ch 5:20 for they cried to God in the **b**, and he was 4421
7:11 *soldiers, fit to* go out *for* war and **b**. 4421
7:40 to **b** *was* twenty and six thousand men. 4421
10: 3 the **b** went sore against Saul, 4421
11:13 Philistines were gathered together to **b**, 4421
12: 8 *and* men of war *fit* for the **b**, that could 4421
12:19 with the Philistines against Saul to **b**: 4421
12:33 Of Zebulun, such as went forth to **b**, 6635
12:36 such as went forth to **b**, expert in war, 6635
12:37 *manner of* instruments of war for the **b**, 4421
14:15 *that* then thou shalt go out to **b**: 4421
19: 7 together from their cities, and came to **b**. 4421
19: 9 put the **b** in array *before* the gate of 4421
19:10 Now when Joab saw that the **b** was set 4421
19:14 drew nigh before the Syrians unto the **b**; 4421
19:17 and set *the* **b** in array against them. NIH
19:17 So when David had put the **b** in array 4421
20: 1 at the time that kings go out *to* **b**, Joab NIH
2Ch 13: 3 Abijah set the **b** in array with an army of 4421
13: 3 Jeroboam also set the **b** in array against 4421
13:14 behold, the **b** *was* before and behind: 4421
14:10 they set the **b** in array in the valley of 4421
18: 5 Shall we go to Ramoth-gilead to **b**, 4421
18:14 shall we go to Ramoth-gilead to **b**, 4421
18:29 will disguise myself, and will go to the **b**; 4421
18:29 disguised himself; and they went to the **b**. 4421
18:34 the **b** increased that day: howbeit the king 4421
20: 1 came against Jehoshaphat to **b**. 4421

2Ch 20:15 for the **b** *is* not yours, but God's. 4421
20:17 Ye shall not need to fight in this **b**: NIH
25: 8 if thou *wilt* go, do *it*, be strong for the **b**: 4421
25:13 that *they* should not go with him to **b**, fell 4421
Job 15:24 against him, as a king ready to the **b**. 3593
38:23 of trouble, against the day of **b** and war? 7128
39:25 he smelleth the **b** afar off, the thunder of 4421
41: 8 upon him, remember the **b**, do no more. 4421
Ps 18:39 hast girded me *with* strength unto the **b**: 4421
24: 8 and mighty, the Lᴏʀᴅ mighty *in* **b**. 4421
55:18 in peace from the **b** *that was* against me: 7128
76: 3 the shield, and the sword, and the **b**. 4421
78: 9 bows, turned *back* in the day of **b**. 7128
89:43 and hast not made him to stand in the **b**. 4421
140: 7 hast covered my head in the day of **b**. 5402
Pr 21:31 The horse *is* prepared against the day of **b**: 4421
Ecc 9:11 nor the **b** to the strong, neither yet bread 4421
Isa 9: 5 For every **b** of the warrior *is* with confused 5430
13: 4 of hosts mustereth the host of the **b**. 4421
22: 2 not slain with the sword, nor dead in **b**. 4421
27: 4 set the briers *and* thorns against me in **b**? 4421
28: 6 for strength to them that turn the **b** to 4421
42:25 the fury of his anger, and the strength of **b**: 4421
Jer 8: 6 his course, as the horse rusheth into the **b**. 4421
18:21 young men *be* slain by the sword in **b**. 4421
46: 3 buckler and shield, and draw near to **b**. 4421
49:14 come against her, and rise up to the **b**. 4421
50:22 A sound of **b** *is* in the land, and of great 4421
50:42 in array, like a man to the **b**, against thee, 4421
51:20 Thou *art* my **b** *axe and* weapons of war: 4661
Eze 7:14 make all ready; but none goeth to the **b**: 4421
13: 5 to stand in the **b** in the day of the Lᴏʀᴅ. 4421
Da 11:20 be destroyed, neither in anger, nor in **b**. 4421
11:25 king of the south shall be stirred up to **b** 4421
Hos 1: 7 nor by sword, nor by **b**, by horses, nor by 4421
2:18 and the sword and the **b** out of the earth, 4421
10: 9 the **b** in Gibeah against the children of 4421
10:14 spoiled Beth-arbel in the day of **b**: 4421
Joel 2: 5 as a strong people set in **b** array. 4421
Am 1:14 with shouting in the day of **b**, 4421
Ob 1: 1 and let us rise up against her in **b**. 4421
Zec 9:10 and the **b** bow shall be cut off: 4421
10: 3 made them as his goodly horse in the **b**. 4421
10: 4 out of him the nail, out of him the **b** bow, 4421
10: 5 in the mire of the streets in the **b**: 4421
14: 2 gather all nations against Jerusalem to **b**; 4421
14: 3 as when he fought in the day of **b**. 7128
1Co 14: 8 who shall prepare himself to the **b**? 4171
Rev 9: 7 *were* like unto horses prepared unto **b**; 4171
9: 9 of chariots of many horses running to **b**. 4171
16:14 to gather them to the **b** of that great day 4171
20: 8 and Magog, to gather them together to **b**: 4171

BATTLEMENT (1) [BATTLE]
Dt 22: 8 then thou shalt make a **b** for thy roof, 4624

BATTLEMENTS (1) [BATTLE]
Jer 5:10 take away her **b**; for they *are* not 5189

BATTLES (6) [BATTLE]
1Sa 8:20 and go out before us, and fight our **b**. 4421
18:17 valiant for me, and fight the Lᴏʀᴅ's **b**. 4421
25:28 my lord fighteth the **b** of the Lᴏʀᴅ, 4421
1Ch 26:27 the spoils won in **b** did they dedicate 4421
2Ch 32: 8 our God to help us, and to fight our **b**. 4421
Isa 30:32 and in the **b** of shaking will he fight with it. 4421

BAVAI (1) [BINNUI]
Ne 3:18 their brethren, **B** the son of Henadad, 942

BAY (6)
Jos 15: 2 sea, from the **b** that looketh southward: 3956
15: 5 **b** of the sea at the uttermost part of Jordan 3956
18:19 **b** of the salt sea at the south end of Jordan 3956
Ps 37:35 and spreading himself like a green **b** tree. 249
Zec 6: 3 in the fourth chariot grisled *and* **b** horses. 554
6: 7 the **b** went forth, and sought to go that 554

BAZLITH (1) [BAZLUTH]
Ne 7:54 The children of **B**, the children of Mehida, 1213

BAZLUTH (1) [BAZLITH]
Ezr 2:52 The children of **B**, the children of Mehida, 1213

BDELLIUM (2)
Ge 2:12 land *is* good: there *is* **b** and the onyx stone. 916
Nu 11: 7 and the colour thereof as the colour of **b**. 916

BE (7012) [AM, ARE, BEEN, BEING, HOWBEIT, IS, WAS, WAST, WERE, WERT, WILL] See Index of Articles, Etc.

BE ESHTARAH See BEESHTERAH

BEACON (1)
Isa 30:17 till ye be left as a **b** upon the top of a 8650

BEALIAH (1)
1Ch 12: 5 **B**, and Shemariah, and Shephatiah 1183

BEALOTH (1)
Jos 15:24 Ziph, and Telem, and **B**, 1175

BEAM (15) [BEAMS]
Jdg 16:14 went away with the pin of the **b**, 708
1Sa 17: 7 staff of his spear *was* like a weaver's **b**; 4500

2Sa 21:19 staff of whose spear *was* like a weaver's **b**. 4500
1Ki 7: 6 and the **thick b** *were* before them. 5646
2Ki 6: 2 take thence every man a **b**, and let us 6982
6: 5 as one was felling a **b**, the axe head fell 6982
1Ch 11:23 spear *was* a spear like a weaver's **b**; 4500
20: 5 whose spear staff *was* like a weaver's **b**. 4500
Hab 2:11 the **b** out of the timber shall answer it. 3714
Mt 7: 3 considerest not the **b** that is in thine own 1385
7: 4 and behold, a **b** *is* in thine own eye? 1385
7: 5 first cast out the **b** out of thine own eye; 1385
Lk 6:41 perceivest not the **b** that is in thine own 1385
6:42 thou thyself beholdest not the **b** that 1385
6:42 cast out first the **b** out of thine own eye, 1385

BEAMS (12) [BEAM]
1Ki 6: 6 that *the* **b** should not be fastened in NIH
6: 9 covered the house with **b** and boards of 1356
6:36 of hewed stone, and a row of cedar **b**. 3773
7: 2 pillars, with cedar **b** upon the pillars. 3773
7: 3 *was* covered with cedar above upon the **b**, 6763
7:12 a row of cedar **b**, both for the inner court 3773
2Ch 3: 7 the **b**, the posts, and the walls thereof, 6982
Ne 2: 8 that he may give me timber to **make b** for 7136
3: 3 who *also* **laid** the **b** thereof, and set up 7136
3: 6 **laid** the **b** thereof, and set up the doors 7136
Ps 104: 3 Who **layeth** the **b** of his chambers in 7136
SS 1:17 The **b** of our house *are* cedar, 6982

BEANS (2)
2Sa 17:28 parched *corn*, and **b**, and lentiles, 6321
Eze 4: 9 **b**, and lentiles, and millet, and fitches, 6321

BEAR (214) [ARMOURBEARER, BARE, BEARERS, BEAREST, BEARETH, BEARING, BEARS, BIRTH, BIRTHDAY, BIRTHRIGHT, BORN, BORNE, CHILDBEARING, CUPBEARER, CUPBEARERS, FIRSTBORN, HOMEBORN, NEWBORN, STANDARD-BEARER, TALEBEARER]
Ge 4:13 My punishment *is* greater than *I* can **b**. 5375
13: 6 land was not **able** to **b** them, that they 5375
16:11 shalt **b** a son, and shalt call his name 3205
17:17 shall Sarah, that is ninety years old, **b**? 3205
17:19 Sarah thy wife shall **b** thee a son indeed; 3205
17:21 which Sarah shall **b** unto thee at this set 3205
18:13 Shall I of a surety **b** *a child*, which am old? 3205
22:23 these eight Milcah did **b** to Nahor, 3205
30: 3 she shall **b** upon my knees, that I may 3205
36: 7 they were strangers could not **b** them 5375
43: 9 then let me **b** the **blame** for ever: 2398
44:32 I shall **b** the **blame** to my father for ever. 2398
49:15 bowed his shoulder to **b**, and became a 5445
Ex 18:22 and they shall **b** *the burden* with thee. 5375
20:16 Thou shalt not **b** false witness against thy 6030
25:27 be for places of the staves to **b** the table. 5375
27: 7 be upon the two sides of the altar, to **b** it. 5375
28:12 Aaron shall **b** their names before 5375
28:29 Aaron shall **b** the names of the children 5375
28:30 Aaron shall **b** the judgment of the 5375
28:38 that Aaron may **b** the iniquity of the holy 5375
28:43 in the holy *place*; that they **b** not iniquity, 5375
30: 4 shall be for places for the staves to **b** it 5375
37: 5 rings by the sides of the ark, to **b** the ark. 5375
37:14 the places for the staves to **b** the table. 5375
37:15 overlaid them with gold, to **b** the table. 5375
37:27 to be places for the staves to **b** it withal. 5375
38: 7 on the sides of the altar, to **b** it withal; 5375
Lev 5: 1 not utter *it*, then he shall **b** his iniquity. 5375
5:17 yet is he guilty, and shall **b** his iniquity. 5375
7:18 soul that eateth of it shall **b** his iniquity. 5375
10:17 *God* hath given it you to **b** the iniquity of 5375
12: 5 if she **b** a maid child, then she shall be 3205
16:22 goat shall **b** upon him all their iniquities 5375
17:16 his flesh; then he shall **b** his iniquity. 5375
19: 8 Therefore *every* one that eateth it shall **b** 5375
19:18 nor **b** **any grudge against** the children of 5201
20:17 sister's nakedness; he shall **b** his iniquity. 5375
20:19 his near kin: they shall **b** their iniquity. 5375
20:20 they shall **b** their sin; they shall die 5375
22: 9 lest they **b** sin for it, and die therefore, 5375
22:16 **suffer** them to **b** the iniquity of trespass, 5375
24:15 Whosoever curseth his God shall **b** his sin. 5375
Nu 1:50 they shall **b** the tabernacle, and all 5375
4:15 the sons of Kohath shall come to **b** *it*: but 5375
4:25 they shall **b** the curtains of the tabernacle, 5375
5:31 and this woman shall **b** her iniquity. 5375
7: 9 *that* they should **b** upon *their* shoulders. 5375
9:13 appointed season, that man shall **b** his sin. 5375
11:14 I am not able to **b** all this people alone, 5375
11:17 they shall **b** the burden of the people with 5375
11:17 with thee, that thou **b** *it* not thyself alone. 5375
14:27 How long *shall I* **b** with this evil NIH
14:33 **b** your whoredoms, until your carcases be 5375
14:34 shall ye **b** your iniquities, *even* forty years, 5375
18: 1 thy father's house with thee shall **b** 5375
18: 1 thy sons with thee shall **b** the iniquity of 5375
18:22 the congregation, lest they **b** sin, and die. 5375
18:23 and they shall **b** their iniquity: 5375
18:32 ye shall **b** no sin by reason of it, when ye 5375
30:15 heard *them*; then he shall **b** her iniquity. 5375
Dt 1: 9 I am not able to **b** you myself alone: 5375
1:12 can I myself alone **b** your cumbrance, 5375
1:31 as a man doth **b** his son, in all the way 5375
5:20 Neither shalt thou **b** false witness against 6030
10: 8 to **b** the ark of the covenant of the Lᴏʀᴅ, 5375
28:57 towards her children which she shall **b**: 3205

Jos 3: 8 thou shalt command the priests that **b** 5375
3:13 of the priests that **b** the ark of the LORD, 5375
4:16 Command the priests that **b** the ark of 5375
6: 4 seven priests shall **b** before the ark seven 5375
6: 6 let seven priests **b** seven trumpets of rams' 5375
Jdg 13: 3 but thou shalt conceive, and **b** a son. 3205
13: 5 For lo, thou *shalt* conceive, and **b** a son; 3205
13: 7 Behold, thou *shalt* conceive, and **b** a son; 3205
Ru 1:12 also to night, and should also **b** sons; 3205
1Sa 17:34 came a lion and a **b**, and took a lamb 1677
17:36 Thy servant slew both the lion and the **b**: 1677
17:37 of the paw of the **b**, he will deliver me 1677
2Sa 17: 8 as a **b** robbed of her whelps in the field: 1677
18:19 Let me now run, and **b** the king **tidings**, 1319
18:20 Thou *shalt* not **b**⁵ tidings this day, but 376
18:20 but thou shalt **b tidings** another day: 1319
18:20 this day thou shalt **b** no **tidings**, because 1319
1Ki 3:21 it was not my son, which I did **b**. 3205
21:10 to **b witness against** him, saying, 5749
2Ki 18:14 *that* which thou puttest on me will I **b**. 5375
19:30 take root downward, and **b** fruit upward. 6213
1Ch 5:18 men *able* to **b** buckler and sword, 5375
2Ch 2: 2 and ten thousand men to **b** burdens, NIH
Est 1:22 that every man should **b** rule in his own 8323
Ps 75: 3 *are* dissolved: I **b** up the pillars of it. 8505
89:50 I do **b** in my bosom *the reproach of* all 5375
91:12 They shall **b** thee **up** in *their* hands, 5375
Pr 9:12 but *if* thou scornest, thou alone shalt **b** *it*. 5375
12:24 The hand of the diligent shall **b rule**: 4910
17:12 Let a **b** robbed of her whelps meet a man, 1677
18:14 but a wounded spirit who can **b**? 5375
28:15 *As* a roaring lion, and a ranging **b**; *so is a* 1677
30:21 and for four *which* it cannot **b**: 5375
Isa 1:14 a trouble unto me; I am weary to **b** *them*. 5375
7:14 a Son, and shall call his name Immanuel 3205
11: 7 the cow and the **b** shall feed; their young 1677
37:31 take root downward, and **b** fruit upward. 6213
46: 4 will I carry *you:* I have made, and I will **b**; 5375
46: 7 They **b** him upon the shoulder, they carry 5375
52:11 ye clean, that **b** the vessels of the LORD. 5375
53:11 justify many; for he shall **b** their iniquities 5445
54: 1 Sing, O barren, thou *that* didst not **b**; 3205
Jer 5:31 and the priests **b rule** by their means; 7287
10:19 I said, Truly this *is* a grief, and I must **b** it. 5375
17:21 **b** no burden on the sabbath day, 5375
17:27 not to **b** a burden, even entering in at 5375
29: 6 that they may **b** sons and daughters; 3205
31:19 because I did **b** the reproach of my youth. 5375
44:22 So that the LORD could no longer **b**, 5375
La 3:10 He *was* unto me *as* a **b** lying in wait, 1677
3:27 *It is* good for a man that he **b** the yoke in 5375
Eze 4: 4 shalt lie upon it thou shalt **b** their iniquity. 5375
4: 5 shalt thou **b** the iniquity of the house of 5375
4: 6 thou shalt **b** the iniquity of the house of 5375
12: 6 In their sight shalt thou **b** *it* upon *thy* 5375
12:12 prince that *is* among them shall **b** upon 5375
14:10 they shall **b** the punishment of their 5375
16:52 **b** thine own shame for thy sins that thou 5375
16:52 thou confounded also, and **b** thy shame, 5375
16:54 That thou mayest **b** thine own shame, 5375
17: 8 that *it* might **b** fruit, that *it* might be a 6213
17:23 and **b** fruit, and be a goodly cedar: 6213
18:19 doth not the son **b** the iniquity of 5375
18:20 The son shall not **b** the iniquity of 5375
18:20 neither shall the father **b** the iniquity of 5375
23:35 therefore **b** thou also thy lewdness and 5375
23:49 and ye shall **b** the sins of your idols: 5375
32:30 **b** their shame with them that go down to 5375
34:29 neither **b** the shame of the heathen any 5375
36: 7 *are* about you, they shall **b** their shame. 5375
36:15 neither shalt thou **b** the reproach of 5375
44:10 idols; they shall even **b** their iniquity. 5375
44:12 Lord GOD, and they shall **b** their iniquity. 5375
44:13 holy *place:* but they shall **b** their shame, 5375
46:20 that *they* **b** *them* not **out** into the utter 3318
Da 2:39 which shall **b rule** over all the earth. 7981
7: 5 like to a **b**, and it raised up itself on one 1678
Hos 9:16 their root is dried up, they shall **b** no fruit: 6213
13: 8 I will meet them as a **b** *that is* bereaved of 1677
Am 5:19 man did flee from a lion, and a **b** met him; 1677
7:10 the land is not able to **b** all his words. 3557
Mic 6:16 ye shall **b** the reproach of my people. 5375
7: 9 I will **b** the indignation of the LORD, 5375
Zep 1:11 cut down; all they that **b** silver are cut off. 5187
Hag 2:12 If one **b** holy flesh in the skirt of his 5375
Zec 6:13 with me, Whither do these **b** the ephah? 1980
6:13 he shall **b** the glory, and shall sit and 5375
Mt 3:11 than I, whose shoes I am not worthy to **b**: 941
4: 6 and in *their* hands they shall **b** thee **up**, 142
19:18 not steal, Thou shalt not **b false witness**, 5576
27:32 name: him they compelled to **b** his cross. 142
Mk 10:19 Do not **b false witness**, Defraud not, 5576
15:21 of Alexander and Rufus, to **b** his cross. 142
Lk 1:13 and thy wife Elisabeth shall **b** thee a son, 1080
4:11 And in *their* hands they shall **b** thee **up**, 142
11:48 ye **b witness** that ye allow the deeds 3140
13: 9 And if *it* **b** fruit, *well:* and if not, *then* 4160
14:27 And whosoever doth not **b** his cross, and 941
18: 7 unto him, though he **b long** with them? 3114
18:20 Do not steal, Do not **b false witness**, 5576
23:26 the cross, that *he* might **b** *it* after Jesus. 5342
Jn 1: 7 for a witness, to **b witness** of the Light, 3140
1: 8 but *was* sent to **b witness** of *that* Light. 3140
2: 8 and **b** unto the governor of the feast. 5342
3:28 Ye yourselves to me **witness**, that I said, 3140

Jn 5:31 If I **b witness** of myself, my witness is not 3140
5:36 same works that I do, **b witness** of me, 3140
8:14 unto them, Though I **b record** of myself, 3140
8:18 I am *one* that **b witness** of myself, and 3140
10:25 my Father's name, they **b witness** of me. 3140
15: 4 As the branch cannot **b** fruit of itself, 5342
15: 8 my Father glorified, that ye **b** much fruit; 5342
15:27 And ye also shall **b witness**, because 3140
16:12 say unto you, but ye cannot **b** *them* now. 941
18:23 have spoken evil, **b witness** of the evil: 3140
18:37 that I should **b witness** unto the truth. 3140
Ac 9:15 to **b** my name before the Gentiles, and 941
15:10 neither our fathers nor we were able to **b**? 941
18:14 reason would that I should **b with** you: 430
22: 5 also the high priest doth **b** me **witness**, 3140
23:11 so must thou **b witness** also at Rome. 3140
27:15 could not **b up into** the wind, we let *her* 503
Ro 10: 2 For I **b** them **record** that they have a zeal 3140
13: 9 not steal, Thou shalt not **b false witness**, 5576
15: 1 that are strong ought to **b** the infirmities of 941
1Co 3: 2 hitherto ye were not able to **b** *it*, neither NIG
10:13 way to escape, that ye may be able to **b** *it*. 5297
15:49 we shall also **b** the image of the heavenly. 5409
2Co 3: 1 **b record**, *yea*, and beyond *their* power 5409
11: 1 Would *to God* you could **b with** me a little 430
11: 1 a little in *my* folly: and indeed **b with** me. 430
11: 4 not accepted, ye might well **b with** *him*. 430
Gal 4:15 for I **b** you **record**, that if *it had been* 3140
5:10 he that troubleth you shall **b** *his* judgment, 941
6: 2 **B** ye one another's burdens, and so fulfil 941
6: 5 For every man shall **b** his own burden. 941
6:17 for I **b** in my body the marks of the Lord 941
Col 4:13 For I **b** him **record**, that he hath a great 3140
1Ti 5:14 marry, **b children**, guide the house, 5041
Heb 9:28 So Christ was once offered to **b** the sins 399
Jas 3:12 the fig tree, my brethren, **b** olive berries? 4160
1Jn 1: 2 and we have seen *it*, and **b witness**, 3140
5: 7 there are three that **b record** in heaven, 3140
5: 8 there are three that **b witness** in earth, 3140
3Jn 1:12 yea, and we also **b record**; and ye know 3140
Rev 2: 2 thou canst not **b** them *which are* evil: 941
13: 2 and his feet *were* as *the feet* of a **b**, 715

BEARD (16) [BEARDS]
Lev 13:29 hath a plague upon the head or the **b**; 2206
13:30 *even* a leprosy upon the head or **b**. 2206
14: 9 off his head and his **b** and his eyebrows, 2206
19:27 shalt thou mar the corners of thy **b**. 2206
21: 5 shall they shave off the corner of their **b**, 2206
1Sa 17:35 I caught *him* by his **b**, and smote him; 2206
21:13 and let his spittle fall down upon his **b**. 2206
2Sa 19:24 trimmed his **b**, nor washed his clothes, 8222
20: 9 Joab took Amasa by the **b** with the right 2206
Ezr 9: 3 off the hair of my head and of my **b**, 2206
Ps 133: 2 that ran down upon the **b**, *even* Aaron's 2206
133: 2 down upon the beard, *even* Aaron's **b**: 2206
Isa 7:20 the feet: and it shall also consume the **b**. 2206
15: 2 *shall be* baldness, *and* every **b** cut off. 2206
Jer 48:37 head *shall be* bald, and every **b** clipt: 2206
Eze 5: 1 to pass upon thine head and upon thy **b**: 2206

BEARDS (4) [BEARD]
2Sa 10: 4 shaved off the *one* half of their **b**, 2206
10: 5 Tarry at Jericho until your **b** be grown, 2206
1Ch 19: 5 Tarry at Jericho until your **b** be grown, 2206
Jer 41: 5 having their **b** shaven, and their clothes 2206

BEARERS (3) [BEAR]
2Ch 2:18 ten thousand of them *to be* **b of burdens**, 5449
34:13 Also *they were* over the **b of burdens**, 5449
Ne 4:10 The strength of the **b of burdens** is 5449

BEAREST (5) [BEAR]
Jdg 13: 3 Behold now, thou *art* barren, and **b** not: 3205
Ps 106: 4 the favour *that thou* **b** unto thy people: NIH
Jn 8:13 said unto him, Thou **b record** of thyself; 3140
Ro 11:18 thou **b** not the root, but the root thee. 941
Gal 4:27 is written, Rejoice, *thou* barren that **b** not; 5088

BEARETH (26) [BEAR]
Lev 11:25 whosoever **b** *ought* of the carcase of them 5375
11:28 he that **b** the carcase of them shall wash 5375
11:40 he also that **b** the carcase of it shall wash 5375
15:10 he that **b** *any of* those *things* shall wash 5375
Nu 11:12 as a nursing father **b** the sucking child, 5375
Dt 25: 6 the firstborn which she **b** shall succeed 3205
29:18 there should be among you a root that **b** 6509
29:23 *and* burning, *that* it is not sown, nor **b**, 6779
32:11 taketh them, **b** them on her wings: 5375
Job 16: 8 my leanness rising up in me **b** witness 6030
24:21 He evil entreateth the barren *that* **b** not: 3205
Pr 25:18 A man that **b** false witness against his 6030
29: 2 the wicked **b rule**, the people mourn. 4910
SS 4: 2 whereof every one **b twins**, and none *is* 8382
6: 6 whereof every one **b twins**, and *there is* 8382
Joel 2:22 for the tree **b** her fruit, the fig tree and 5375
Mt 13:23 and understandeth *it*; which also **b** fruit, 2592
Jn 5:32 There is another that **b witness** of me; 3140
8:18 the Father that sent me **b witness** of me. 3140
15: 2 Every branch in me that **b** not fruit he 5342
15: 2 every *branch* that **b** fruit, he purgeth it; 5342
Ro 8:16 The Spirit itself **b witness** with our spirit, 4828
13: 4 be afraid; for he **b** not the sword in vain: 5409
1Co 13: 7 **B** all *things*, believeth all *things*, hopeth 4722
Heb 6: 8 But that which **b** thorns and briers *is* 1627

1Jn 5: 6 it is the Spirit that **b witness**, because 3140

BEARING (22) [BEAR]
Ge 1:29 I have given you every herb **b** seed, 2232
16: 2 the LORD hath restrained me from **b**. 3205
29:35 she called his name Judah; and left **b**. 3205
30: 9 When Leah saw that she had left **b**, she 3205
37:25 from Gilead with their camels spicery 5375
Nu 10:17 of Merari set forward, **b** the tabernacle. 5375
10:21 Kohathites set forward, **b** the sanctuary: 5375
Jos 3: 3 the priests the Levites **b** it, then ye shall 5375
3:14 priests **b** the ark *of* the covenant before 5375
6: 8 the seven priests **b** the seven trumpets 5375
6:13 seven priests **b** seven trumpets of rams' 5375
1Sa 17: 7 iron: and one **b** a shield went before him. 5375
2Sa 15:24 him, **b** the ark of the covenant of God: 5375
Ps 126: 6 forth and weepeth, **b** precious seed, 5375
Mk 14:13 there shall meet you a man **b** a pitcher of 941
Lk 22:10 a man meet you, **b** a pitcher of water; 941
Jn 19:17 And he **b** his cross went forth into a place 941
Ro 2:15 their conscience **also b** witness, and 4828
9: 1 my conscience **also b** me **witness** in 4828
2Co 4:10 Always **b about** in the body the dying of 4064
Heb 2: 4 God **also b** *them* **witness**, both with signs 4901
13:13 him without the camp, **b** his reproach. 5342

BEARS (2) [BEAR]
2Ki 2:24 came forth two she **b** out of the wood, 1677
Isa 59:11 We roar all like **b**, and mourn like 1677

BEAST (180) [BEAST'S, BEASTS]
Ge 1:24 and **b** of the earth after his kind: 2416
1:25 God made the **b** of the earth after his kind 2416
1:30 to every **b** of the earth, and to every fowl 2416
2:19 LORD God formed every **b** of the field, 2416
2:20 fowl of the air, and to every **b** of the field; 2416
3: 1 **b** of the field which the LORD God had 2416
3:14 all cattle, and above every **b** of the field; 2416
6: 7 **b**, and the creeping thing, and the fowls 929
7: 2 Of every clean **b** thou shalt take to thee 929
7:14 every **b** after his kind, and all the cattle 2416
7:21 of **b**, and of every creeping thing that 2416
8:19 Every **b**, every creeping thing, 2416
8:20 took of every clean **b**, and of every clean 929
9: 2 the dread of you shall be upon every **b** of 2416
9: 5 at the hand of every **b** will I require it, 2416
9:10 and of every **b** of the earth with you; 2416
9:10 go out of the ark, to every **b** of the earth. 2416
34:23 and every **b** of theirs *be* ours? 929
37:20 will say, *Some* evil **b** hath devoured him: 2416
37:33 son's coat; an evil **b** hath devoured him; 2416
Ex 8:17 and it became lice in man, and in **b**; 929
8:18 so there were lice upon man, and upon **b**. 929
9: 9 upon **b**, throughout all the land of Egypt. 929
9:10 forth *with* blains upon man, and upon **b**. 929
9:19 and **b** which shall be found in the field, 929
9:22 upon **b**, and upon every herb of the field, 929
9:25 all that *was* in the field, both man and **b**; 929
11: 7 a dog move his tongue, against man or **b**: 929
12:12 in the land of Egypt, both man and **b**; 929
13: 2 the children of Israel, *both* of man and of **b**: 929
13:12 every firstling *that* cometh of a **b** which 929
13:15 the firstborn of man, and the firstborn of **b**: 929
19:13 whether *it be* **b** or man, it shall not live: 929
21:34 of them; and the dead **b** shall be his. NIH
22: 5 shall put in his **b**, and shall feed in another 1165
22:10 or an ox, or a sheep, or any **b**, to keep; 929
22:19 Whosoever lieth with a **b** shall surely be 929
Lev 5: 2 of the field multiply against thee. 2416
5: 2 whether *it be* an unclean **b**, 2416
7:21 *any* unclean **b**, or any abominable unclean 929
7:24 And the fat of the **b** that dieth of itself, 5038
7:25 For whosoever eateth the fat of the **b**, 929
7:26 *whether it be* of fowl or of **b**, in any of 929
11:26 *The carcases* of every **b** which divideth 929
11:39 if any **b**, of which ye may eat, die; he that 929
11:47 between the **b** that may be eaten and 2416
11:47 be eaten and the **b** that may not be eaten. 2416
17:13 which hunteth and catcheth *any* **b** or 2416
18:23 Neither shalt thou lie with any **b** to defile 929
18:23 neither shall any woman stand before a **b** 929
20:15 if a man lie with a **b**, he shall surely be put 929
20:15 be put to death: and ye shall slay the **b**. 929
20:16 if a woman approach unto any **b**, 929
20:16 thou shalt kill the woman and the **b**: 929
20:25 shall not make your souls abominable by **b**, 929
24:18 he that killeth a **b** shall make it good; 929
24:18 a beast shall make it good; **b** for beast. 5315
24:18 a beast shall make it good; beast for **b**. 5315
24:21 he that killeth a **b**, he shall restore it: 929
25: 7 cattle, and for the **b** that *are* in thy land, 2416
27: 9 if *it be* a **b**, whereof *men* bring an offering 929
27:10 if he shall at all change **b** for beast, then 929
27:10 if he shall at all change beast for **b**, then 929
27:11 if *it be* any unclean **b**, of which they do not 929
27:11 he shall present the **b** before the priest: 929
27:27 *it be* of an unclean **b**, then he shall redeem 929
27:28 *both* of man and **b**, and of the field of his 929
Nu 3:13 all the firstborn in Israel, *both* man and **b**: 929
8:17 of Israel *are* mine, *both* man and **b**: 929
31:26 *both* of man and of **b**, thou, and Eleazar 929
31:47 *both* of man and of **b**, and gave them unto 929
Dt 4:17 The likeness of any **b** that *is* on the earth, 929
14: 6 every **b** that parteth the hoof, 929
27:21 be he that lieth with any *manner of* **b**. 929

B

B

Jdg	20:48 as the **b**, and all that came to hand:	929
2Ki	14: 9 there passed by a wild **b** that *was* in	2416
2Ch	25:18 there passed by a wild **b** that *was* in	2416
Ne	2:12 neither *was there any* **b** with me, save	929
	2:12 beast with me, save the **b** that I rode upon.	929
	2:14 *was* no place for the **b** *that was* under	929
Job	39:15 or *that* the wild **b** may break them.	2416
Ps	36: 6 O LORD, thou preservest man and **b**.	929
	50:10 For every **b** of the forest *is* mine,	2416
	73:22 I, and ignorant: I was *as* a **b** before thee.	929
	80:13 and the **wild b** of the field doth devour it.	2123
	104:11 They give drink to every **b** of the field:	2416
	135: 8 the firstborn of Egypt, both of man and **b**.	929
	147: 9 giveth to the **b** his food, *and* to the young	929
Pr	12:10 A righteous *man* regardeth the life of his **b**:	929
Ecc	3:19 a man hath no preeminence above a **b**:	929
	3:21 the spirit of the **b** that goeth downward to	929
Isa	35: 9 nor *any* ravenous **b** shall go up thereon,	2416
	43:20 The **b** of the field shall honour me,	2416
	46: 1 *they are* a burden to the weary **b**:	NIH
	63:14 As a **b** goeth down into the valley, the	929
Jer	7:20 upon **b**, and upon the trees of the field;	929
	9:10 the fowl of the heavens and the **b** are fled;	929
	21: 6 inhabitants of this city, both man and **b**:	929
	27: 5 man and the **b** that *are* upon the ground,	929
	31:27 the seed of man, and *with* the seed of **b**.	929
	32:43 ye say, *It is* desolate without man or **b**;	929
	33:10 desolate without man and without **b**,	929
	33:10 and without inhabitant, and without **b**,	929
	33:12 *is* desolate without man and without **b**,	929
	36:29 cause to cease from thence man and **b**?	929
	50: 3 they shall depart, both man and **b**.	929
	51:62 neither man nor **b**, but that it shall be	929
Eze	14:13 upon it, and will cut off man and **b** from it:	929
	14:17 land; so that I cut off man and **b** from it:	929
	14:19 it in blood, to cut off from it man and **b**:	929
	14:21 and the noisome **b**, and the pestilence,	2416
	14:21 pestilence, to cut off from it man and **b**?	929
	25:13 and will cut off man and **b** from it;	929
	29: 8 thee, and cut off man and **b** out of thee.	929
	29:11 it, nor foot of **b** shall pass through it,	929
	34: 8 my flock became meat to every **b** of	2416
	34:28 neither shall the **b** of the land devour	2416
	36:11 I will multiply upon you man and **b**;	929
	39:17 to every **b** of the field,	2416
	44:31 of itself, or torn, whether it be fowl or **b**.	929
Da	7: 5 another **b**, a second, like to a bear,	2423
	7: 6 the **b** had also four heads;	2423
	7: 7 behold, a fourth **b**, dreadful and terrible,	2423
	7:11 I beheld *even* till the **b** *was* slain,	2423
	7:19 I would know the truth of the fourth **b**,	2423
	7:23 The fourth **b** shall be the fourth kingdom	2423
Hos	13: 8 like a lion: the wild **b** shall tear them.	2416
Jnh	3: 7 his nobles, saying, Let neither man nor **b**,	929
	3: 8 let man and **b** be covered with sackcloth,	929
Mic	1:13 Lachish, bind the chariot to the **swift b**:	7409
Zep	1: 3 I will consume man and **b**; I will consume	929
Zec	8:10 was no hire for man, nor any hire for **b**;	929
Lk	10:34 set him on his own **b**, and brought him	2934
Ac	28: 4 saw the *venomous* **b** hang on his hand,	2342
	28: 5 And he shook off the **b** into the fire,	2342
Heb	12:20 if *so much as* a **b** touch the mountain,	2342
Rev	4: 7 And the first **b** *was* like a lion,	2226
	4: 7 and the second **b** like a calf, and the third	2226
	4: 7 and the third **b** had a face as a man,	2226
	4: 7 and the fourth **b** *was* like a flying eagle.	2226
	6: 3 I heard the second **b** say, Come and see.	2226
	6: 5 I heard the third **b** say, Come and see.	2226
	6: 7 I heard the voice of the fourth **b** say,	2226
	11: 7 the **b** that ascendeth out of the bottomless	2342
	13: 1 and saw a **b** rise up out of the sea,	2342
	13: 2 And the **b** which I saw was like unto a	2342
	13: 3 and all the world wondered after the **b**.	2342
	13: 4 which gave power unto the **b**:	2342
	13: 4 they worshipped the **b**, saying, Who *is*	2342
	13: 4 the beast, saying, Who *is* like unto the **b**?	2342
	13:11 And I beheld another **b** coming up out of	2342
	13:12 all the power of the first **b** before him,	2342
	13:12 dwell therein to worship the first **b**,	2342
	13:14 he had power to do in the sight of the **b**;	2342
	13:14 that *they* should make an image to the **b**,	2342
	13:15 power to give life unto the image of the **b**,	2342
	13:15 that the image of the **b** should both speak,	2342
	13:15 the image of the **b** should be killed.	2342
	13:17 or the name of the **b**, or the number of his	2342
	13:18 understanding count the number of the **b**:	2342
	14: 9 If any *man* worship the **b** and his image,	2342
	14:11 who worship the **b** and his image,	2342
	15: 2 that had gotten the victory over the **b**,	2342
	16: 2 the men which had the mark of the **b**,	2342
	16:10 poured out his vial upon the seat of the **b**;	2342
	16:13 and out of the mouth of the **b**, and out of	2342
	17: 3 a woman sit upon a scarlet coloured **b**,	2342
	17: 7 and of the **b** that carrieth her, which hath	2342
	17: 8 The **b** that thou sawest was, and is not;	2342
	17: 8 they behold the **b** that was, and is not,	2342
	17:11 And the **b** that was, and is not, even he is	2342
	17:12 power as kings one hour with the **b**.	2342
	17:13 give their power and strength unto the **b**.	2342
	17:16 ten horns which thou sawest upon the **b**,	2342
	17:17 and give their kingdom unto the **b**,	2342
	19:19 I saw the **b**, and the kings of the earth,	2342
	19:20 And the **b** was taken, and with him	2342
	19:20 them that had received the mark of the **b**,	2342
	20: 4 and which had not worshipped the **b**,	2342

Rev	20:10 where the **b** and the false prophet *are*,	2342

BEAST'S (1) [BEAST]

Da	4:16 and let a **b** heart be given unto him;	2423

BEASTS (156) [BEAST]

Ge	7: 2 of **b** that *are* not clean by two, the male	929
	7: 8 Of clean **b**, and of beasts that *are* not clean,	929
	7: 8 and of **b** that *are* not clean, and of fowls,	929
	31:39 That which was torn of **b** I brought not	NIH
	36: 6 cattle, and all his **b**, and all his substance,	929
	45:17 lade your **b**, and go, get you unto the land	1165
Ex	11: 5 behind the mill; and all the firstborn of **b**.	929
	22:31 eat *any* flesh *that is* torn of **b** in the field;	NIH
	23:11 they leave the **b** of the field may eat.	929
Lev	7:24 the fat of that which is torn *with* **b**, may	NIH
	11: 2 These *are* the **b** which ye shall eat among	2416
	11: 2 eat among all the **b** that *are* on the earth.	929
	11: 3 cheweth cud, among the **b**,	929
	11:27 among all *manner of* **b** that go on *all* four,	929
	11:46 This *is* the law of the **b**, and of the fowl,	929
	17:15 that which was torn *with* **b**, whether it be	NIH
	20:25 difference between clean **b** and unclean,	929
	22: 8 is torn *with* **b**, he shall not eat to defile	NIH
	26: 6 I will rid evil **b** out of the land, neither	2416
	26:22 I will also send wild **b** among you, which	2416
	27:26 Only the firstling of the **b**, which should	929
Nu	18:15 *whether it be* of men or **b**, shall be thine:	929
	18:15 firstling of unclean **b** shalt thou redeem.	929
	20: 8 give the congregation and their **b** drink.	1165
	20:11 the congregation drank, and their **b** *also*.	1165
	31:11 and all the prey, *both* of men and of **b**.	929
	31:30 of all *manner of* **b**, and give them unto	929
	35: 3 and for their goods, and for all their **b**.	2416
Dt	7:22 lest the **b** of the field increase upon thee.	2416
	14: 4 These *are* the **b** which ye shall eat: the ox,	929
	14: 6 and cheweth the cud amongst the **b**:	929
	28:26 unto the **b** of the earth, and no man shall	929
	32:24 I will also send the teeth of **b** upon them,	929
1Sa	17:44 fowls of the air, and to the **b** of the field.	929
	17:46 of the air, and to the **wild b** of the earth;	2416
2Sa	21:10 by day, nor the **b** of the field by night.	2416
1Ki	4:33 he spake also of **b**, and of fowl,	929
	18: 5 mules alive, that we leese not all the **b**.	929
2Ki	3:17 *both* ye, and your cattle, and your **b**.	929
2Ch	32:28 stalls for all *manner of* **b**,	929+929+2050.1
Ezr	1: 4 and with gold, and with goods, and with **b**,	929
	1: 6 and with **b**, and with precious things,	929
Job	5:22 neither shalt thou be afraid of the **b** of	2416
	5:23 the **b** of the field shall be at peace with	2416
	12: 7 ask now the **b**, and they shall teach thee;	929
	18: 3 Wherefore are we counted as **b**,	929
	35:11 Who teacheth us more than the **b** of	929
	37: 8 the **b** go into dens, and remain in their	2416
	40:20 food, where all the **b** of the field play.	2416
Ps	8: 7 and oxen, yea, and the **b** of the field;	929
	49:12 abideth not: he is like the **b** *that* perish.	929
	49:20 understandeth not, is like the **b** *that* perish.	929
	50:11 and the **wild b** of the field *are* mine.	2123
	79: 2 the flesh of thy saints unto the **b** of	2416
	104:20 wherein all the **b** of the forest do creep	2416
	104:25 both small and great **b**.	2416
	148:10 **B**, and all cattle; creeping things,	2416
Pr	9: 2 She hath killed her **b**; she hath mingled	2874
	30:30 A lion *which is* strongest among **b**,	929
Ecc	3:18 *they* might see that they themselves are **b**.	929
	3:19 befalleth the sons of men befalleth **b**;	929
Isa	1:11 offerings of rams, and the fat of **fed b**;	4806
	13:21 **wild b of the desert** shall lie there;	6728
	13:22 the **wild b of the islands** shall cry in their	338
	18: 6 the mountains, and to the **b** of the earth:	929
	18: 6 all the **b** of the earth shall winter upon	929
	30: 6 The burden of the **b** of the south: into	929
	34:14 The **wild b of the desert** shall also meet	6728
	34:14 also meet with the **wild b of the island**,	338
	40:16 nor the **b** thereof sufficient *for* a burnt	2416
	46: 1 their idols were upon the **b**, and upon	2416
	56: 9 All ye **b** of the field, come to devour,	2416
	56: 9 to devour, *yea*, all ye **b** in the forest.	2416
	66:20 and upon mules, and upon **swift b**,	3753
Jer	7:33 of the heaven, and for the **b** of the earth;	929
	12: 4 the **b** are consumed, and the birds;	929
	12: 9 come ye, assemble all the **b** of the field,	2416
	15: 3 the **b** of the earth, to devour and destroy.	929
	16: 4 fowls of heaven, and for the **b** of the earth.	929
	19: 7 of the heaven, and for the **b** of the earth.	929
	27: 6 the **b** of the field have I given him also to	2416
	28:14 I have given him the **b** of the field also.	2416
	34:20 of the heaven, and to the **b** of the earth.	929
	50:39 Therefore the **wild b of the desert** with	6728
	50:39 the **wild b of the islands** shall dwell	338
Eze	5:17 So will I send upon you famine and evil **b**,	2416
	8:10 abominable **b**, and all the idols of the	929
	14:15 If I cause noisome **b** to pass through	2416
	14:15 man may pass through because of the **b**:	2416
	29: 5 I have given thee for meat to the **b** of	2416
	31: 6 his branches did all the **b** of the field	2416
	31:13 all the **b** of the field shall be upon his	2416
	32: 4 will fill the **b** of the whole earth with thee.	2416
	32:13 I will destroy also all the **b** thereof from	929
	32:13 more, nor the hoofs of **b** trouble them.	929
	33:27 field will I give to the **b** to be devoured,	2416
	34: 5 they became meat to all the **b** of the field,	2416
	34:25 will cause the evil **b** to cease out of	2416
	38:20 the **b** of the field, and all creeping things	2416

Eze	39: 4 and *to* the **b** of the field to be devoured.	2416
Da	2:38 the **b** of the field and the fowls of	2423
	4:12 the **b** of the field had shadow under it,	2423
	4:14 let the **b** get away from under it,	2423
	4:15 *let* his portion *be* with the **b** in the grass	2423
	4:21 under which the **b** of the field dwelt,	2423
	4:23 *let* his portion *be* with the **b** of the field,	2423
	4:25 dwelling shall be with the **b** of the field,	2423
	4:32 dwelling *shall be* with the **b** of the field:	2423
	5:21 his heart was made like the **b**,	2423
	7: 3 four great **b** came up from the sea,	2423
	7: 7 it was diverse from all the **b** that were	2423
	7:12 As concerning the rest of the **b**, they had	2423
	7:17 These great **b**, which *are* four, *are* four	2423
	8: 4 so that no **b** might stand before him,	2416
Hos	2:12 and the **b** of the field shall eat them.	2416
	2:18 covenant for them with the **b** of the field,	2416
	4: 3 with the **b** of the field, and with the fowls	2416
Joel	1:18 How do the **b** groan! the herds of cattle	929
	1:20 The **b** of the field cry also unto thee:	929
	2:22 Be not afraid, ye **b** of the field:	929
Am	5:22 I regard the peace offerings of your **fat b**.	4806
Mic	5: 8 people as a lion among the **b** of the forest,	929
Hab	2:17 the spoil of **b**, *which* made them afraid,	929
Zep	2:14 the midst of her, all the **b** of the nations:	2416
	2:15 a desolation, a place for **b** to lie down in!	2416
Zec	14:15 and of all the **b** that shall be in these tents,	929
Mk	1:13 and was with the **wild b**; and the angels	2342
Ac	7:42 have ye offered to me **slain b** and	4968
	10:12 Wherein were all *manner of* **fourfooted b**	5074
	10:12 and **wild b**, and creeping things,	2342
	11: 6 and saw **fourfooted b** of the earth,	5074
	11: 6 **wild b**, and creeping things, and fowls	2342
	23:24 provide **b**, that they may set Paul	2934
Ro	1:23 and **fourfooted b**, and creeping things.	5074
1Co	15:32 of men I have **fought with b** at Ephesus,	2341
	15:39 another flesh of **b**, another of fishes,	2934
Tit	1:12 *are* alway liars, evil **b**, slow bellies.	2342
Heb	13:11 For the bodies of those **b**, whose blood is	2226
Jas	3: 7 For every kind of **b**, and of birds,	2342
2Pe	2:12 But these, as natural brute **b**, made to be	2226
Jude	1:10 but what they know naturally, as brute **b**,	2226
Rev	4: 6 four **b** full of eyes before and behind.	2226
	4: 8 the four **b** had each of them six wings	2226
	4: 9 And when *those* **b** give glory and honour	2226
	5: 6 the midst of the throne and of the four **b**,	2226
	5: 8 the four **b** and four *and* twenty elders fell	2226
	5:11 about the throne and the **b** and the elders:	2226
	5:14 And the four **b** said, Amen. And the four	2226
	6: 1 one of the four **b** saying, Come and see.	2226
	6: 6 a voice in the midst of the four **b** say,	2226
	6: 8 with death, and with the **b** of the earth.	2342
	7:11 and *about* the elders and the four **b**,	2226
	14: 3 and before the four **b**, and the elders:	2226
	15: 7 And one of the four **b** gave unto the seven	2226
	18:13 **b**, and sheep, and horses, and chariots,	2934
	19: 4 twenty elders and the four **b** fell down	2226

BEAT (36) [BEATEN, BEATEST, BEATETH, BEATING]

Ex	30:36 thou shalt **b** *some* of it very small,	7833
	39: 3 they did **b** the gold into thin plates,	7554
Nu	11: 8 or **b** *it* in a mortar, and baked *it* in pans,	1743
Dt	25: 3 he him above these *with* many stripes,	5221
Jdg	8:17 he **b** down the tower of Penuel,	5422
	9:45 **b** down the city, and sowed it *with* salt.	5422
	19:22 and **b** at the door, and spake to the master	1849
Ru	2:17 even, and **b** out that she had gleaned:	2251
2Sa	22:43 did I **b** them *as* small as the dust of	7833
2Ki	3:25 they **b** down the cities, and *on* every	2040
	13:25 Three times did Joash **b** him,	5221
	23:12 the king he down, and brake *them* down	5422
Ps	18:42 did I **b** them *small* as the dust before	7833
	89:23 I will **b** down his foes before his face,	3807
Pr	23:14 Thou shalt **b** him with the rod,	5221
Isa	2: 4 they shall **b** their swords into plowshares,	3807
	3:15 mean ye *that* ye **b** my people to **pieces**,	1792
	27:12 *that* the LORD shall **b** off from	2251
	41:15 **b** *them* **small**, and shalt make the hills as	1854
Joel	3:10 **B** your plowshares into swords,	3807
Jnh	4: 8 the sun **b** upon the head of Jonah, that he	5221
Mic	4: 3 they shall **b** their swords into plowshares,	3807
	4:13 thou shalt **b in pieces** many people:	1854
Mt	7:25 the winds blew, and **b upon** that house;	4363
	7:27 the winds blew, and **b upon** that house;	4350
	21:35 husbandmen took his servants, and **b** one,	1194
Mk	4:37 the waves **b** into the ship, so that it was	1911
	12: 3 and **b** *him*, and sent *him* away empty.	1194
Lk	6:48 stream **b** vehemently upon that house,	4366
	6:49 **against** which the stream did **b vehemently**,	4366
	12:45 and shall begin to **b** the menservants and	5180
	20:10 but the husbandmen **b** him, and sent *him*	1194
	20:11 and they **b** him also, and entreated *him*	1194
Ac	16:22 their clothes, and commanded to **b** them.	4463
	18:17 and **b** *him* before the judgment seat.	5180
	22:19 **b** in every synagogue them that believed	1194

BEATEN (40) [BEAT]

Ex	5:14 set over them, were **b**, *and* demanded,	5221
	5:16 behold, thy servants are **b**; but the fault is	5221
	25:18 *of* **b** work shalt thou make them, in the	4749
	25:31 *of* **b** work shall the candlestick be made:	4749
	25:36 all it *shall be* one **b** work *of* pure gold.	4749
	27:20 that they bring thee pure oil olive **b** for	3795
	29:40 with the fourth part of a hin of **b** oil;	3795

B

Ex	37: 7 **b out of one piece** made he them,	4749
	37:17 *of* **b work** made he the candlestick;	4749
	37:22 all of it *was* one **b work** *of* pure gold.	4749
Lev	2:14 by the fire, *even* corn **b out** of full ears.	1643
	2:16 *part* of the **b corn** thereof, and *part* of	1643
	16:12 his hands full of sweet incense **b small**,	1851
	24: 2 they bring unto thee pure oil olive **b** for	3795
Nu	8: 4 this work of the candlestick *was of* **b** gold,	4749
	8: 4 unto the flowers thereof, *was* **b work**:	4749
	28: 5 mingled with the fourth *part* of a hin of **b**	3795
Dt	2: 2 if the wicked *man* be worthy to be **b**,	5221
	25: 2 to be **b** before his face, according to his	5221
Jos	8:15 all Israel *made as if they* were **b** before	5060
2Sa	2:17 Abner was **b**, and the men of Israel,	5062
1Ki	10:16 made two hundred targets *of* **b** gold:	7820
	10:17 *he* made three hundred shields *of* **b** gold;	7820
2Ch	2:10 twenty thousand measures of **b** wheat,	4347
	9:15 made two hundred targets *of* **b** gold:	7820
	9:15 six hundred *shekels* of **b** gold went to one	7820
	9:16 three hundred shields *made he of* **b** gold:	7820
	34: 7 had **b** the graven images into powder,	3807
Pr	23:35 not sick; they have **b** me, *and* I felt *it* not:	1986
Isa	27: 9 altar as chalkstones that are **b in sunder**,	5310
	28:27 the fitches are **b out** with a staff,	2251
	30:31 the LORD shall the Assyrian be **b down**,	2865
Jer	46: 5 mighty ones are **b down**, and are fled	3807
Mic	1: 7 images thereof shall be **b to pieces**,	3807
Mk	13: 9 and in the synagogues ye shall be **b**:	1194
Lk	12:47 to his will, shall be **b** with many *stripes.*	1194
	12:48 shall be **b** with few *stripes.* For unto	1194
Ac	5:40 **b** *them,* they commanded that *they* should	1194
	16:37 They have **b** us openly uncondemned,	1194
2Co	11:25 Thrice was I **b with rods**, once was I	4463

BEATEST (2) [BEAT]

Dt	24:20 thou **b** thine olive tree, thou shalt not	2251
Pr	23:13 *if* thou **b** him with the rod, he shall not	5221

BEATETH (1) [BEAT]

1Co	9:26 so fight I, not as one that **b** the air:	1194

BEATING (3) [BEAT]

1Sa	14:16 and they went on **b down** *one* another.	1986
Mk	12: 5 him they killed, and many others; **b** some,	1194
Ac	21:32 and the soldiers, they left **b** of Paul.	5180

BEAUTIES (1) [BEAUTY]

Ps	110: 3 in the **b** of holiness from the womb of	1926

BEAUTIFUL (23) [BEAUTY]

Ge	29:17 Rachel was **b** and well favoured.	3303+8389
Dt	21:11 among the captives a woman,	3303+8389
1Sa	16:12 *and* withal of a **b** countenance,	3303
	25: 3 and of a **b** countenance:	3303
2Sa	11: 2 and the woman *was* very **b** to look upon.	2896
Est	2: 7 and the maid *was* fair and **b**;	2896+4758
Ps	48: 2 **B** for situation, the joy of the whole earth,	3303
Ecc	3:11 He hath made every *thing* **b** in his time:	3303
SS	6: 4 Thou *art* **b**, O my love, as Tirzah,	3303
	7: 1 How are thy feet with shoes, O prince's	3302
Isa	4: 2 day shall the branch of the LORD be **b**	6643
	52: 1 put on thy **b** garments, O Jerusalem,	8597
	52: 7 How **b** upon the mountains are the feet of	4998
	64:11 Our holy and our **b** house, where our	8597
Jer	13:20 the flock *that* was given thee, thy **b** flock?	8597
	48:17 is the strong staff broken, *and* the **b** rod!	8597
Eze	16:12 ears, and a **b** crown upon thine head.	8597
	16:13 thou wast exceeding **b**, and thou didst	3302
	23:42 hands, and **b** crowns upon their heads.	8597
Mt	23:27 which indeed appear **b** outward, but	5611
Ac	3: 2 at the gate of the temple which is called **B**,	5611
	3:10 sat for alms at the **B** gate of the temple:	5611
Ro	10:15 How **b** *are* the feet of them that preach	5611

BEAUTIFY (3) [BEAUTY]

Ezr	7:27 to **b** the house of the LORD which *is* in	6286
Ps	149: 4 he will **b** the meek with salvation.	6286
Isa	60:13 to **b** the place of my sanctuary;	6286

BEAUTY (49) [BEAUTIES, BEAUTIFUL, BEAUTIFY]

Ex	28: 2 for Aaron thy brother, for glory and for **b**.	8597
	28:40 thou make for them, for glory and for **b**.	8597
2Sa	1:19 The **b** of Israel *is* slain upon thy high	6643
	14:25 be so much praised as Absalom for his **b**:	3303
1Ch	16:29 worship the LORD in the **b** of holiness.	1927
2Ch	3: 6 the house with precious stones for **b**:	8597
	20:21 that should praise the **b** of holiness, as	1927
Est	1:11 to shew the people and the princes her **b**:	3308
Job	40:10 and array thyself with glory and **b**.	1926
Ps	27: 4 to behold the **b** of the LORD,	5278
	29: 2 worship the LORD in the **b** of holiness.	1927
	39:11 thou makest his **b** to consume away like a	2530
	45:11 So shall the king greatly desire thy **b**: for	3308
	49:14 their **b** shall consume *in* the grave from	6099
	50: 2 Out of Zion, the perfection of **b**, God hath	3308
	90:17 let the **b** of the LORD our God be upon	5278
	96: 6 strength and **b** *are* in his sanctuary.	8597
	96: 9 O worship the LORD in the **b** of holiness:	1927
Pr	6:25 Lust not after her **b** in thine heart;	3308
	20:29 and the **b** of old men *is* the gray head.	1926
	31:30 Favour *is* deceitful, and **b** *is* vain: but	3308
Isa	3:24 of sackcloth; *and* burning instead of **b**.	3308
	13:19 the **b** of the Chaldees' excellency,	8597
	28: 1 whose glorious **b** *is* a fading flower,	8597
	28: 4 the glorious **b**, which *is* on the head of	8597

Isa	28: 5 for a diadem of **b**, unto the residue of his	8597
	33:17 Thine eyes shall see the king in his **b**:	3308
	44:13 of a man, according to the **b** of a man;	8597
	53: 2 *there is* no **b** that we should desire him:	4758
	61: 3 give unto them **b** for ashes, the oil of joy	6287
La	1: 6 from the daughter of Zion all her **b** is	1926
	2: 1 down from heaven *unto* the earth the **b**	8597
	2:15 the city that *men* call The perfection of **b**,	3308
Eze	7:20 As for the **b** of his ornament, he set it in	6643
	16:14 went forth among the heathen for thy **b**:	3308
	16:15 thou didst trust in thine own **b**,	3308
	16:25 hast made thy **b** to be abhorred,	3308
	27: 3 O Tyrus, thou hast said, I *am* of perfect **b**.	3308
	27: 4 seas, thy builders have perfected thy **b**.	3308
	27:11 about; they have made thy **b** perfect.	3308
	28: 7 they shall draw their swords against the **b**	3308
	28:12 the sum, full *of* wisdom, and perfect in **b**.	3308
	28:17 Thine heart was lifted up because of thy **b**,	3308
	31: 8 garden of God was like unto him in his **b**.	3308
	32:19 Whom dost thou pass in **b**? go down,	5276
Hos	14: 6 his **b** shall be as the olive tree, and his	1935
Zec	9:17 *is* his goodness, and how great *is* his **b**!	3308
	11: 7 the one I called **B**, and the other I called	5278
	11:10 I took my staff, *even* **B**, and cut it asunder,	5278

BEBAI (6)

Ezr	2:11 The children of **B**, six hundred twenty and	893
	8:11 of the sons of **B**; Zechariah the son of Bebai,	893
	8:11 Zechariah the son of **B**, and with him	893
	10:28 Of the sons also of **B**; Jehohanan, Hananiah,	893
Ne	7:16 The children of **B**, six hundred twenty and	893
	10:15 Bunni, Azgad, **B**,	893

BECAME (106) [BECOME]

Ge	2: 7 the breath of life; and man **b** a living soul.	1961
	2:10 it was parted, and **b** into four heads.	1961
	6: 4 same *b* mighty *men* which *were* of old,	NIH
	19:26 from behind him, and she **b** a pillar of salt.	1961
	20:12 of my mother; and she **b** my wife.	1961
	21:20 dwelt in the wilderness, and **b** an archer.	1961
	24:67 and took Rebekah, and she **b** his wife;	1961
	26:13 and grew until he **b** very **great**:	1431
	44:32 For thy servant **b** surety for the lad unto	6148
	47:20 over them: so the land **b** Pharaoh's.	1961
	47:26 of the priests only, *which* **b** not Pharaoh's.	1961
	49:15 to bear, and **b** a servant unto tribute.	1961
Ex	2:10 Pharaoh's daughter, and he **b** her son.	1961
	4: 3 cast it on the ground, and it **b** a serpent;	1961
	4: 4 and it **b** a rod in his hand:	1961+3807.1
	7:10 before his servants, and it **b** a serpent.	1961
	7:12 every man his rod, and they **b** serpents:	1961
	8:17 earth, and it **b** lice in man, and in beast;	1961
	8:17 all the dust of the land **b** lice throughout	1961
	9:10 it **b** a boil breaking forth *with* blains upon	1961
	9:24 in all the land of Egypt since it **b** a nation.	1961
	36:13 with the taches: so it **b** one tabernacle.	1961
Nu	12:10 Miriam *became* leprous, *white* as snow:	NIH
	26:10 and fifty men: and they **b** a sign.	1961+3807.1
Dt	26: 5 **b** there a nation, great, mighty,	1961
Jos	7: 5 of the people melted, and **b** as water.	1961
	14:14 the inheritance of Caleb the son	1961+3807.1
	24:32 **b** the inheritance of the children	1961+3807.1
Jdg	1:30 among them, and **b** tributaries.	1961
	1:33 Beth-anath **b** tributaries unto	1961+3807.1
	1:35 so that they **b** tributaries.	1961+3807.1
	8:27 which *thing* **b** a snare unto Gideon,	1961
	15:14 cords that *were* upon his arms **b** as flax	1961
	17: 5 one of his sons, who **b** his priest.	1961
	17:12 the young man **b** his priest, and was in	1961
Ru	4:16 laid it in her bosom, and **b** nurse unto it.	1961
1Sa	10:12 Therefore it **b** a proverb, *Is* Saul also	1961
	16:21 him greatly; and he **b** his armourbearer.	1961
	18:29 and Saul **b** David's enemy continually.	1961
	22: 2 unto him; and he **b** a captain over them:	1961
	25:37 died within him, and he **b** *as* a stone.	1961
	25:42 the messengers of David, and **b** his wife.	1961
2Sa	2:25 **b** one troop, and stood on the top of a hill.	1961
	4: 4 haste to flee, that he fell, and **b lame**.	6452
	8: 2 *so* the Moabites **b** David's servants,	1961
	8: 6 the Syrians **b** servants to David,	1961
	8:14 and all they of Edom **b** David's servants.	1961
	11:27 and she **b** his wife, and bare him a son.	1961
1Ki	11:24 men unto him, and **b** a captain over a band,	1961
	12:30 this thing **b** a sin: for the people went	1961
	13: 6 restored him again, and **b** as *it was* before.	1961
	13:33 he **b** *one* of the priests of the high places.	1961
	13:34 thing **b** sin unto the house of Jeroboam,	1961
2Ki	17: 3 Hoshea **b** his servant, and gave him	1961
	17:15 **b** vain, and *went* after the heathen that	NIH
	24: 1 and Jehoiakim **b** his servant three years:	NIH
1Ch	18: 2 the Moabites **b** David's servants,	1961
	18: 6 the Syrians **b** David's servants,	1961
	18:13 and all the Edomites **b** David's servants.	1961
2Ch	27: 6 Jotham **b mighty**, because he prepared	2388
Ne	9:25 **b fat**, and delighted themselves in thy	8080
Est	8:17 many of the people of the land **b** Jews;	3054
Ps	69:11 my garment; and I **b** a proverb to them.	1961
	83:10 at En-dor: they **b** *as* dung for the earth.	1961
	109:25 I **b** also a reproach unto them: *when* they	1961
Jer	3:11 their might hath failed; they **b** as women:	1961
Eze	17: 6 and a spreading vine of low stature,	1961
	17: 6 so it **b** a vine, and brought forth branches,	1961
	19: 3 it **b** a young lion, and it learned to catch	1961
	19: 6 he **b** a young lion, and learned to catch	1961

Eze	23:10 she **b** famous among women; for they had	1961
	31: 5 his branches **b** long because of	NIH
	34: 5 they **b** meat to all the beasts of the field,	1961
	34: 8 surely because my flock **b** a prey,	1961
	34: 8 my flock **b** meat to every beast of the field,	1961
	36: 4 which **b** a prey and derision to the residue	1961
Da	2:35 **b** like the chaff of the summer	1934
	2:35 the stone that smote the image **b** a great	1934
	8: 4 he did according to his will, and **b** great.	NIH
	10:15 face toward the ground, and I **b dumb**.	481
Ob	1:12 thy brother in the day that he **b** a stranger;	NIH
Mt	28: 4 the keepers did shake, and **b** as dead *men.*	1096
Mk	9: 3 his raiment **b** shining, exceeding white	1096
Ac	10:10 And he **b** very hungry, and would have	1096
Ro	1:21 but **b** vain in their imaginations,	NIH
	1:22 *themselves* to be wise, they **b** fools,	NIG
	6:18 sin, ye **b** the servants of righteousness.	NIG
1Co	9:20 unto the Jews I **b** as a Jew, that I might	1096
	9:22 To the weak **b** I as weak, that I might gain	1096
	13:11 but when I **b** a man, I put away childish	1096
2Co	8: 9 he was rich, *yet* for your sakes he **b** poor,	NIG
Php	2: 8 and **b** obedient unto death,	1096
1Th	2: 8 And ye **b** followers of us, and of the Lord,	1096
	2:14 **b** followers of the churches of God which	1096
Heb	2:17 For it **b** him, for whom *are* all *things,* and	4241
	5: 9 he **b** the author of eternal salvation unto	1096
	7:26 For such a high priest **b** us, *who is* holy,	4241
	10:33 whilst ye **b** companions of them that were	1096
	11: 7 **b** heir of the righteousness which is by	1096
Rev	6:12 and the sun **b** black as sackcloth of hair,	1096
	6:12 sackcloth of hair, and the moon **b** as blood;	1096
	8: 8 and the third *part* of the sea **b** blood;	1096
	8:11 *part* of the waters **b** wormwood;	1096+1519
	16: 3 and it **b** as the blood of a dead *man:* and	1096
	16: 4 and fountains of waters; and they **b** blood.	1096

BECAMEST (2) [BECOME]

1Ch	17:22 for ever; and thou, LORD, **b** their God.	1961
Eze	16: 8 saith the Lord GOD, and thou **b** mine.	1961

BECAUSE (1209)

Ge	2: 3 **b** that in it he had rested from all his work	3588
	2:23 **b** she was taken out of Man.	3588
	3:10 garden, and I was afraid, **b** I *was* naked;	3588
	3:14 **B** thou hast done this, thou *art* cursed	3588
	3:17 **b** thou hast hearkened unto the voice of	3588
	3:20 **b** she was the mother of all living.	3588
	5:29 **b** of the ground which the LORD hath	4480
	7: 7 ark, **b** of the waters of the flood.	4480+6440
	11: 9 the LORD did there confound	3588
	12:13 and my soul shall live **b** of thee.	1558+871.1
	12:17 with great plagues **b** of Sarai Abram's wife.	5921
	16:11 the LORD hath heard thy affliction.	3588
	18:20 **B** the cry of Sodom and Gomorrah is great,	3588
	18:20 is great, and **b** their sin is very grievous;	3588
	19:13 the cry of them is waxen great before	3588
	20:11 Abraham said, **B** I thought, Surely the fear	3588
	20:18 **b** of Sarah Abraham's wife.	1697+5921
	21:11 in Abraham's sight **b** of his son.	182+5921
	21:12 it not be grievous in thy sight **b** of the lad,	5921
	21:12 of the lad, and **b** of thy bondwoman;	5921
	21:13 will I make a nation, **b** he *is* thy seed.	3588
	21:25 **b** of a well of water,	182+5921
	21:31 **b** there they sware both of them.	3588
	22:16 **b** thou hast done this thing,	834+3282
	22:18 **b** thou hast obeyed my voice.	834+6118
	25:21 the LORD for his wife, **b** she *was* barren:	3588
	25:28 loved Esau, **b** he did eat of *his* venison:	3588
	26: 5 **B** that Abraham obeyed my voice,	6118
	26: 7 for Rebekah; **b** she *was* fair to look upon.	3588
	26: 9 said unto him, **B** I said, Lest I die for her.	3588
	26:20 of the well Esek; **b** they strove with him,	3588
	27:20 **B** the LORD thy God brought *it* to me.	3588
	27:23 discerned him not, **b** his hands were hairy	3588
	27:41 **b** of the blessing wherewith his father	5921
	27:46 my life **b** of the daughters of Heth:	4480+6440
	28:11 tarried there all night, **b** the sun was set;	3588
	29:15 **B** thou *art* my brother, shouldest thou	3588
	29:33 **B** the LORD hath heard that I *was* hated,	3588
	29:34 unto me, **b** I have born him three sons:	3588
	30:18 **b** I have given my maiden to my husband:	834
	30:20 with me, **b** I have born him six sons:	3588
	31:30 **b** thou sore longedst after thy father's	3588
	31:31 and said to Laban, **B** I was afraid:	3588
	32:32 **b** he touched the hollow of Jacob's thigh	3588
	33:11 **b** God hath dealt graciously with me,	3588
	33:11 graciously with me, and **b** I have enough.	3588
	34: 7 **b** he had wrought folly in Israel in lying	3588
	34:13 said, **b** he had defiled Dinah their sister:	834
	34:19 **b** he had delight in Jacob's daughter:	3588
	34:27 the city, **b** they had defiled their sister.	834
	35: 7 **b** there God appeared unto him, when he	3588
	36: 7 not bear them **b** of their cattle.	4480+6440
	37: 3 **b** he *was* the son of his old age:	3588
	38:15 to be a harlot; **b** she had covered her face.	3588
	38:26 **b** that I gave her not to Shelah my son.	3588
	39: 9 me but thee, **b** thou *art* his wife:	834+871.1
	39:23 **b** the LORD *was* with him,	834+871.1
	41:32 *it is* **b** the thing *is* established by God,	3588
	41:57 **b** that the famine was *so* sore in all lands.	3588
	43:18 **b** they were brought into Joseph's house;	3588
	43:18 **B** of the money that was returned	1697+5921
	43:32 **b** the Egyptians might not eat bread with	3588
	46:30 I have seen thy face, **b** thou *art* yet alive.	3588
	47:20 field, **b** the famine prevailed over them:	3588

B

Ge 49: 4 **b** thou wentest up to thy father's bed; 3588
Ex 1:12 **b of** the children of Israel. 4480+6440
 1:19 **B** the Hebrew women *are* not as 3588
 1:21 came to pass, **b** the midwives feared God, 3588
 2:10 she said, **B** I drew him out of the water. 3588
 4:26 husband *thou art,* **b of** the circumcision. 3807.1
 5:21 **b** you have made our savour to be 834
 8:12 Moses cried unto the LORD **b** of the frogs 5921
 9:11 stand before Moses **b** of the boils; 4480+6440
 12:39 **b** they were thrust out of Egypt, 3588
 13: 8 **b of** that *which* the LORD did unto 5668+871.1
 14:11 **B** *there were* no graves in Egypt, 4480
 17: 7 **b** of the chiding of the children of Israel, 5921
 17: 7 **b** they tempted the LORD, saying, 5921
 17:16 **B** the LORD hath sworn *that* the LORD 3588
 18:15 **B** the people come unto me to inquire of 3588
 19:18 **b** the LORD descended upon it in 4480+6440
 29:33 shall not eat *thereof,* **b** they *are* holy. 3588
 29:34 with fire: it shall not be eaten, **b** it *is* holy. 3588
 32:35 **b** they made the calf, which Aaron 834+5921
 40:35 **b** the cloud abode thereon, and the glory of 3588
Lev 6: 4 it shall be, **b** he hath sinned, and is guilty, 3588
 6: 9 **b** of the burning upon the altar all night 5921
 10:13 it *is* thy due, and thy sons' due, 3588
 11: 4 **b** he cheweth the cud, but divideth not 3588
 11: 5 **b** he cheweth the cud, but divideth not 3588
 11: 6 **b** he cheweth the cud, but divideth not 3588
 14:48 the house clean, **b** the plague is healed. 3588
 15: 2 of his flesh, **b** of his issue he *is* unclean. NIH
 16:16 **b** of the uncleanness of the children of 4480
 16:16 **b** of their transgressions in all their sins: 4480
 19: 8 **b** he hath profaned the hallowed *thing* of 3588
 19:20 not be put to death, **b** she was not free. 3588
 20: 3 **b** he hath given of his seed unto Molech, 3588
 21:23 nigh unto the altar, **b** he hath a blemish; 3588
 22: 7 eat of the holy *things;* **b** it *is* his food. 3588
 22:25 **b** their corruption *is* in them, 3588
 26:10 bring forth the old **b** of the new. 4480+6440
 26:35 it did not rest in your sabbaths, when ye 834
 26:43 **b,** even because they despised my 3282
 26:43 **b** they despised my judgments, 3282+871.1
 26:43 and **b** their soul abhorred my statutes. NIH
Nu 3:13 **B** all the firstborn *are* mine; *for* on the day 3588
 6: 7 **b** the consecration of his God *is* upon his 3588
 6:12 shall be lost, **b** his separation was defiled. 3588
 7: 9 **b** the service of the sanctuary belonging 3588
 9:13 **b** he brought not the offering of 3588
 11: 3 **b** the fire of the LORD burnt among them. 3588
 11:14 this people alone, **b** *it is* too heavy for me. 3588
 11:20 **b** that ye have despised the LORD which 3282
 11:34 **b** there they buried the people that lusted. 3588
 12: 1 **b of** the Ethiopian woman whom he 182+5921
 13:24 **b of** the cluster of grapes which 182+5921
 14:16 **B** the LORD was not able to bring this 4480
 14:22 **B** all *those* men which have seen my glory 3588
 14:24 **b** he had another spirit with him, 6118
 14:43 shall fall by the sword: **b** ye 3588+3651+5921
 15:31 **b** he hath despised the word of the LORD, 3588
 15:34 **b** it was not declared what should be done 3588
 19:13 **b** the water of separation was not 3588
 19:20 **b** he hath defiled the sanctuary of 3588
 20:12 and Aaron, **B** ye believed me not, 3282
 20:13 **b** the children of Israel strove with 834
 20:24 **b** ye rebelled against my word at 834+5921
 21: 4 was much discouraged **b** of the way. 871.1
 22: 3 afraid of the people, **b** they *were* many: 3588
 22: 3 **b** of the children of Israel. 4480+6440
 22:22 God's anger was kindled **b** he went: 3588
 22:29 said unto the ass, **B** thou hast mocked me: 3588
 22:32 **b** thy way is perverse before me: 3588
 25:13 **b** he was zealous for his God, 834+8478
 26:62 **b** there was no inheritance given them 3588
 27: 4 from among his family, **b** he hath no son? 3588
 30: 5 forgive her, **b** her father disallowed her. 3588
 30:14 he held his peace at her in the day that 3588
 32:11 **b** they have not wholly followed me: 3588
 32:17 shall dwell in the fenced cities **b** of 4480+6440
 32:19 **b** our inheritance is fallen to us on *this* 3588
 35:28 **b** he should have remained in the city of 3588
Dt 1:27 and said, **B** the LORD hated us, 871.1
 1:36 **b** he hath wholly followed 834+3282
 2: 5 **b** I have given mount Seir unto Esau *for a* 3588
 2: 9 **b** I have given Ar unto the children of Lot 3588
 2:19 **b** I have given it unto the children of Lot 3588
 2:25 and be in anguish **b** of thee. 4480+6440
 4: 3 seen what the LORD did **b of** Baal-peor: 871.1
 4:37 **b** he loved thy fathers, therefore 3588+8478
 7: 7 **b** ye were moe in number than any 4480
 7: 8 **b** the LORD loved you, and because 4480
 7: 8 **b** he would keep the oath which he had 4480
 8:20 **b** ye would not be obedient unto the voice 6118
 9:18 **b** of all your sins which ye sinned, 5921
 9:25 as I fell down *at the first;* **b** the LORD had 3588
 9:28 **B** the LORD was not able to bring them 4480
 9:28 **b** he hated them, he hath brought them 4480
 12:20 eat flesh, **b** thy soul longeth to eat flesh; 3588
 13: 5 **b** he hath spoken to turn *you* away from 3588
 13:10 **b** he hath sought to thrust thee away from 3588
 14: 8 the swine, **b** it divideth the hoof, 3588
 14:29 **(b** he hath no part nor inheritance with 3588
 15: 2 **b** it is called the LORD's release. 3588
 15:10 **b** that for this thing the LORD thy God 3588
 15:16 **b** he loveth thee and thine house, because 3588
 15:16 and thine house, **b** he is well with thee; 3588
 16:15 **b** the LORD thy God shall bless thee in all 3588

Dt 18:12 **b of** these abominations the LORD 1558+871.1
 19: 6 **b** the way is long, and slay him; 3588
 20: 3 neither be ye terrified **b of** them; 4480+6440
 21:14 of her, **b** thou hast humbled her. 834+8478
 22:19 **b** hath brought up an evil name upon a 3588
 22:21 **b** she hath wrought folly in Israel, to play 3588
 22:24 the damsel, **b** she cried not, 834+1697+5921
 22:24 **b** he hath humbled her, 834+1697+5921
 22:29 **b** he hath humbled her, he may not 834+8478
 23: 4 **B** they met you not with bread 834+1697+5921
 23: 4 **b** they hired against thee Balaam the son 834
 23: 5 **b** the LORD thy God loved thee. 3588
 23: 7 **b** thou wast a stranger in his land. 3588
 24: 1 he hath found some uncleanness in her: 3588
 27:20 he uncovereth his father's skirt. 3588
 28:20 **b of** the wickedness of thy doings, 4480+6440
 28:45 thou hearkenedst not unto the voice of 3588
 28:47 **b** thou servedst not the LORD thy 834+8478
 28:55 **b** he hath nothing left him in the siege, 4480
 28:62 **b** thou wouldest not obey the voice of 3588
 29:25 **B** they have forsaken the covenant of 834+5921
 31:17 **b** our God *is* not amongst us? 3588+5921
 31:29 ye will do evil in the sight of the LORD, 3588
 32: 3 **B** I will publish the name of the LORD: 3588
 32:19 **b** of the provoking of his sons, 4480
 32:47 *is* not a vain thing for you; **b** it *is* your life: 3588
 32:51 **b** ye trespassed against me among 834+5921
 32:51 **b** ye sanctified me not in the midst 834+5921
 33:21 there, *in* a portion of the lawgiver, 3588
Jos 2: 9 of the land faint **b of** you. 4480+6440
 2:11 more courage in any man, **b** of you: 4480+6440
 2:24 of the country do faint **b of** us. 4480+6440
 5: 1 more, **b** of the children of Israel. 4480+6440
 5: 6 **b** they obeyed not the voice of the LORD: 834
 5: 7 **b** they had not circumcised them by 3588
 6: 1 shut up **b of** the children of Israel: 4480+6440
 6:17 **b** she hid the messengers that we sent. 3588
 6:25 **b** she hid the messengers, which Joshua 3588
 7:12 their enemies, **b** they were accursed: 3588
 7:15 **b** he hath transgressed the covenant of 3588
 7:15 and **b** he hath wrought folly in Israel. 3588
 9: 9 **b** of the name of the LORD thy God: 3807.1
 9:18 **b** the princes of the congregation had 3588
 9:20 **b** of the oath which we sware unto them. 5921
 9:24 said, **B** it was certainly told thy servants, 3588
 9:24 sore afraid of our lives **b** of you, 4480+6440
 10: 2 feared greatly, **b** Gibeon *was* a great city, 3588
 10: 2 **b** it *was* greater than Ai, and all the men 3588
 10:42 the LORD God of Israel fought for 3588
 11: 6 said unto Joshua, Be not afraid **b of** them: 6440
 14: 9 **b** thou hast wholly followed the LORD 3588
 14:14 **b** that he wholly followed the LORD God 3282
 17: 1 **b** he was a man of war, therefore he had 3588
 17: 6 **B** the daughters of Manasseh had an 3588
 20: 5 **b** he smote his neighbour unwittingly, 3588
 22:31 **b** ye have not committed this trespass 834
 23: 3 hath done unto all these nations **b** 4480+6440
Jdg 1:19 of the valley, **b** they had chariots of iron. 3588
 2:18 for it repented the LORD **b** of their 6440
 2:20 **B** that this people hath transgressed my 3282
 3:12 **b** they had done evil in the sight of 3588+5921
 5:23 they came not to the help of the LORD, 3588
 6: 2 **b** of the Midianites the children of 4480+6440
 6: 6 **b of** the Midianites; 4480+6440
 6: 7 unto the LORD **b** of the Midianites, 182+5921
 6:22 for **b** I have seen an angel of 3651+5921
 6:27 he feared his father's household, 834+3509.1
 6:30 **b** he hath cast down the altar of Baal, 3588
 6:30 **b** he hath cut down the grove that *was* by 3588
 6:31 himself, **b** *one* hath cast down his altar. 3588
 6:32 **b** he hath thrown down his altar. 3588
 8:20 for he feared, **b** he *was* yet a youth. 3588
 8:24 golden earrings, **b** they *were* Ishmaelites.) 3588
 9:18 men of Shechem, **b** he *is* your brother;) 3588
 10:10 both **b** we have forsaken our God, 3588
 11:13 **B** Israel took away my land, when they 3588
 12: 4 men of Gilead smote Ephraim, **b** they said, 3588
 13:22 We shall surely die, **b** we have seen God. 3588
 14:17 that he told her, **b** she lay sore upon him: 3588
 15: 6 **b** he had taken his wife, and given her to 3588
 18:28 **b** it *was* far from Zidon, and they had no 3588
 20:36 **b** they trusted unto the liers in wait which 3588
 21:15 **b** that the LORD had made a breach in 3588
 21:22 **b** we reserved not to each man his wife in 3588
1Sa 1: 6 **b** the LORD had shut up her womb. 3588
 1:20 *saying,* **b** I have asked him of the LORD. 3588
 2: 1 mine enemies; **b** I rejoice in thy salvation. 3588
 2:25 their father, **b** the LORD would slay them. 3588
 3:13 **b** his sons made themselves vile, 3588
 4:21 the ark of God was taken, and because 413
 4:21 **b** of her father in law and her husband. 413
 6:19 **b** they had looked into the ark of 3588
 6:19 **b** the LORD had smitten *many* of 3588
 8:18 cry out in that day **b of** 4480+6440+3807.1
 9:13 he come, **b** he doth bless the sacrifice; 3588
 9:16 my people, **b** their cry is come unto me. 3588
 10: 1 *Is it* not **b** the LORD hath anointed thee to 3588
 12:10 **b** we have forsaken the LORD, 3588
 12:22 **b** it hath pleased the LORD to make you 3588
 13:11 **B** I saw that the people were scattered 3588
 13:14 **b** thou hast not kept *that* which the LORD 3588
 14:29 **b** I tasted a little of this honey. 3588
 15:23 **b** thou hast rejected the word of 3282
 15:24 **b** I feared the people, and obeyed their 3588
 16: 7 height of his stature; **b** I have refused him: 3588

1Sa 17:32 to Saul, Let no man's heart fail **b of** him; 5921
 18: 3 he loved him as his own soul. 871.1
 18:12 **b** the LORD was with him, 3588
 18:16 **b** he went out and came in before them. 3588
 19: 4 **b** he hath not sinned against thee, 3588
 19: 4 **b** his works *have been* to thee-ward very 3588
 20:17 David to swear again, **b** he loved him: 3588
 20:18 shalt be missed, **b** thy seat will be empty. 3588
 20:34 **b** his father had done him shame. 3588
 21: 8 the king's business required haste. 3588
 22:17 **b** their hand also *is* with David, 3588
 22:17 **b** they knew when he fled, and did not 3588
 24: 5 **b** he had cut off Saul's skirt. 834+5921
 25:28 **b** my lord fighteth the battles of 3588
 26:12 **b** a deep sleep from the LORD was fallen 3588
 26:16 to die, **b** ye have not kept your master, 834
 26:21 **b** my soul was precious in thine eyes 834+5921
 28:18 **b** thou obeyedst not the voice of 834+3509.1
 28:20 was sore afraid, **b of** the words of Samuel: 4480
 30: 6 the soul of all the people was grieved, 3588
 30:13 left me, **b** three days agone I fell sick. 3588
 30:16 **b** of all the great spoil that they had taken 871.1
 30:22 and said, **B** they went not with us, 834+3282
2Sa 1: 9 upon me, **b** my life *is* yet whole in me. 3588
 1:10 **b** I was sure that he could not live after 3588
 1:12 of Israel; **b** they were fallen by the sword. 3588
 2: 6 this kindness, **b** ye have done this thing. 834
 3:11 Abner a word again, **b** he feared him. 4480
 3:30 **b** he had slain their brother Asahel 834+5921
 6: 8 **b** the LORD had made a breach upon 5921
 6:12 all that *pertaineth* unto him, **b of** 5668+871.1
 8:10 **b** he had fought against Hadadezer, 834+5921
 10: 5 the men were greatly ashamed, 3588
 12: 6 **b** he did this thing, and because he 834+6118
 12: 6 did this thing, and **b** he had no pity. 834+5921
 12:10 **b** thou hast despised me, 3588+6118
 12:14 by this deed thou hast given great 3588
 12:25 he called his name Jedidiah, **b of** 5668+871.1
 13:22 **b** he had forced his sister 834+1697+5921
 14:15 *it is* **b** the people have made me afraid: 3588
 14:26 he polled *it:* **b** *the hair* was heavy on him, 3588
 16: 8 to thy mischief, **b** thou *art* a bloody man. 3588
 16:10 **b** the LORD hath said unto him, 3588
 18:20 the king's son is dead. 3588+3651+5921
 19:21 **b** he cursed the LORD's anointed? 3588
 19:26 go to the king, **b** thy servant *is* lame. 3588
 19:42 of Israel, **B** the king *is* near of kin to us: 3588
 21: 1 **b** he slew the Gibeonites. 834+5921
 21: 7 **b** of the LORD's oath that *was* between 5921
 22: 8 moved and shook, **b** he was wroth. 3588
 22:20 he delivered me, **b** he delighted in me. 3588
 23: 6 **b** they cannot be taken with hands: 3588
1Ki 1:50 Adonijah feared **b of** Solomon, 4480+6440
 2: 7 I fled **b of** Absalom thy brother. 4480+6440
 2:26 thou barest the ark of the Lord GOD 3588
 2:26 thou hast been afflicted in all where*in* 3588
 3: 2 **b** there was no house built unto the name 3588
 3:11 **B** thou hast asked this thing, 834+3282
 3:19 child died in the night; **b** she overlaid it. 834
 7:47 **b** they were exceeding many: 4480
 8:11 stand to minister **b of** the cloud: 4480+6440
 8:33 **b** they have sinned against thee, 834
 8:35 no rain, **b** they have sinned against thee; 3588
 8:64 the brasen altar that *was* before 3588
 9: 9 **B** they forsook the LORD their God, 834+5921
 10: 9 **b** the LORD loved Israel for ever, 871.1
 11: 9 **b** his heart was turned from the LORD 3588
 11:33 **b** they have forsaken me, 3282
 11:34 **b** he kept my commandments and 834
 14:13 **b** in him there is found *some* good thing 3282
 14:15 **b** they have made their groves, 834+3282
 14:16 he shall give Israel up **b of** the sins 1558+871.1
 15: 5 **B** David did *that* which *was* right in the 834
 15:13 she had made an idol in a grove; 834
 15:30 **B** of the sins of Jeroboam which he sinned 5921
 16: 7 of Jeroboam; and **b** he killed him. 834+5921
 17: 7 **b** there had been no rain in the land. 3588
 19: 7 eat; **b** the journey *is* too great for thee. 3588
 19:14 the children of Israel have forsaken thy 3588
 20:28 the LORD, **B** the Syrians have said, 834+3282
 20:36 **B** thou hast not obeyed the voice of 834+3282
 20:42 **B** thou hast let go out of *thy* hand a man 3282
 21: 2 of herbs, **b** it *is* near unto my house: 3588
 21: 4 **b of** the word which Naboth the Jezreelite 5921
 21: 6 **B** I spake unto Naboth the Jezreelite, 3588
 21:20 I have found *thee:* **b** thou hast sold thyself 3282
 21:29 **b** he humbleth himself before me, 3282+3588
2Ki 1: 3 *Is it* not **b** *there is* not a God in Israel, 4480
 1: 6 *Is it* not **b** *there is* not a God in Israel, 4480
 1:16 *Is it* not **b** *there is* no God in Israel to 4480
 1:17 king of Judah; he had no son. 3588
 5: 1 by him the LORD had given deliverance 3588
 8:12 **B** I know the evil that thou wilt do unto 3588
 8:29 the son of Ahab in Jezreel, **b** he was sick. 3588
 9:14 all Israel, **b of** Hazael king of Syria. 4480+6440
 10:30 thou hast done well in executing 834+3282
 13: 4 **b** the king of Syria oppressed them. 3588
 13:23 had respect unto them, **b of** his 4616+3807.1
 15:16 **b** they opened not *to him,* therefore 3588
 17:26 **b** they know not the manner of 834+3509.1
 18:12 **B** they obeyed not the voice of 834+5921
 19:28 **b** thy rage against me and thy tumult is 3282
 21:11 **B** Manasseh king of Judah hath done 834+3282
 21:15 **b** they have done *that* which *was* evil 834+3282
 22: 7 into their hand, **b** they dealt faithfully. 3588

B

2Ki	22:13 **b** our fathers have not hearkened	834+5921
	22:17 **B** they have forsaken me,	834+4480
	22:19 **B** thine heart was tender, and thou hast	3282
	23:26 **b** of all the provocations that Manasseh	5921
1Ch	1:19 **b** in his days the earth was divided:	3588
	4: 9 saying, **B** I bare *him* with sorrow.	3588
	4:41 **b** *there was* pasture there for their flocks.	3588
	5: 9 **b** their cattle were multiplied in the land	3588
	5:20 of them; **b** they put their trust in him.	3588
	5:22 down many slain, **b** the war *was* of God.	3588
	7:21 **b** they came down to take *away* their	3588
	7:23 Beriah, **b** it went evil with his house.	3588
	9:27 **b** the charge *was* upon them,	3588
	12: 1 he yet kept himself close **b** of	4480+6440
	13:10 **b** he put his hand to the ark:	834+5921
	13:11 **b** the Lord had made a breach upon	3588
	14: 2 up on high, **b** of his people Israel.	5668+871.1
	15:13 For **b** ye *did it* not at the first,	4100+3807.1
	15:22 about the song, **b** he *was* skilful.	3588
	16:33 **b** he cometh to judge the earth.	3588
	16:41 the Lord, his mercy *endureth* for ever;	3588
	18:10 **b** he had fought against Hadarezer,	834+5921
	19: 2 he hath shewed kindness to me.	3588
	21: 8 sinned greatly, **b** I have done this thing:	834
	21:30 for he was afraid **b** of the sword of	4480+6440
	22: 8 thou hast shed much blood upon the	3588
	23:28 **B** their office *was* to wait on the sons of	3588
	27:23 the Lord had said *he* would increase	3588
	27:24 there fell wrath for it against Israel;	2050.1
	28: 3 thou *hast been* a man of war,	3588
	29: 3 I have set my affection to the house of	2050.1
	29: 9 **b** with perfect heart they offered willingly	3588
2Ch	1:11 **B** this was in thine heart,	834+3282
	2:11 **B** the Lord hath loved his people,	871.1
	6:24 enemy, **b** they have sinned against thee;	3588
	6:26 no rain, **b** they have sinned against thee;	3588
	7: 2 **b** the glory of the Lord had filled	3588
	7: 6 his mercy *endureth* for ever, when	3588
	7: 7 **b** the brasen altar which Solomon had	3588
	7:22 **B** they forsook the Lord God of	834+5921
	8:11 **b** *the places are* holy, whereunto the ark	3588
	9: 8 **b** thy God loved Israel, to establish them	871.1
	12: 2 **b** they had transgressed against	3588
	12: 5 gathered together to Jerusalem **b** of	4480+6440
	12:14 **b** he prepared not his heart to seek	3588
	13:18 **b** they relied upon the Lord God of their	3588
	14: 6 **b** the Lord had given him rest.	3588
	14: 7 **b** we have sought the Lord our God,	3588
	15:16 **b** she had made an idol in a grove:	834
	16: 7 **B** thou hast relied on the king of Syria,	871.1
	16: 8 yet, **b** thou didst rely on the Lord,	871.1
	16:10 **b** of this *thing*. And Asa oppressed *some*	5921
	17: 3 **b** he walked in the first ways of his father	3588
	20:37 **B** thou hast joined thyself with Ahaziah,	3509.1
	21: 3 he to Jehoram; **b** he *was* the firstborn.	3588
	21: 7 **b** of the covenant that he had	4616+3807.1
	21:10 **b** he had forsaken the Lord God of his	3588
	21:12 **b** thou hast not walked in the ways	834+8478
	22: 6 **b** of the wounds which were given him at	3588
	22: 6 the son of Ahab at Jezreel, he was sick.	3588
	22: 9 **B**, said they, he *is* the son of Jehoshaphat,	3588
	24:16 he had done good in Israel, both	3588
	24:20 **b** ye have forsaken the Lord, he hath	3588
	24:24 **b** they had forsaken the Lord God of	3588
	25:16 **b** thou hast done this, and hast not	3588
	25:20 **b** they sought after the gods of Edom.	3588
	26:20 to go out, **b** the Lord had smitten him.	3588
	27: 6 **b** he prepared his ways before the Lord	3588
	28: 6 **b** they had forsaken the Lord God of	871.1
	28: 9 **b** the Lord God of your fathers was	871.1
	28:19 the Lord brought Judah low **b** of	5668+871.1
	28:23 **B** the gods of the kings of Syria help them,	3588
	30: 3 **b** the priests had not sanctified themselves	3588
	34:21 **b** our fathers have not kept the word	834+5921
	34:25 **B** they have forsaken me,	834+8478
	34:27 **B** thine heart was tender, and thou didst	3282
	35:14 the priests the sons of Aaron *were*	3588
	36:15 **b** he had compassion on his people,	3588
Ezr	3: 3 **b** of the people of *those* countries:	4480
	3:11 **b** *he is* good, for his mercy *endureth* for	3588
	3:11 **b** the foundation of the house of	3588
	4:14 **b** we have maintenance	1768+3606+6903
	8:22 **b** we had spoken unto the king, saying,	3588
	9: 4 **b** of the transgression of those that had	5921
	9:15 for *we* cannot stand before thee **b** of this.	5921
	10: 6 for he mourned **b** of the transgression of	5921
	10: 9 trembling **b** of *this* matter, and for the	5921
Ne	4: 9 them day and night, **b** of them.	4480+6440
	5: 3 that we might buy corn, **b** of the dearth.	871.1
	5: 9 **b** of the reproach of the heathen our	4480
	5:15 so did not I, **b** of the fear of God.	4480+6440
	5:18 **b** the bondage was heavy upon this	3588
	6:18 he *was* the son in law of Shechaniah	3588
	8:12 **b** they had understood the words that	3588
	9:37 whom thou hast set over us **b** of our sins:	871.1
	9:38 **b** of all this we make a sure covenant,	871.1
	13: 2 **B** they met not the children of Israel with	3588
	13:29 **b** they have defiled the priesthood,	5921
Est	1:15 **b** she hath not performed	834+5921
	8: 7 he laid his hand upon the Jews.	834+5921
	9: 3 **b** the fear of Mordecai fell upon them.	3588
	9:24 Haman the son of Hammedatha,	3588
Job	3:10 **B** it shut not up the doors of my *mother's*	3588
	6:20 They were confounded **b** they had hoped;	3588
	8: 9 **b** our days upon earth *are* a shadow:)	3588

Job	11:16 **B** thou shalt forget *thy* misery,	3588
	11:18 thou shalt be secure, **b** there is hope; yea,	3588
	15:27 **B** he covereth his face with his fatness,	3588
	17:12 the light *is* short, **b** of darkness.	4480+6440
	18:15 dwell in his tabernacle, **b** *it is* none of his:	4480
	20:19 **B** he hath oppressed *and* hath forsaken	3588
	20:19 *b* he hath violently taken away a house	NIH
	23:17 **B** I was not cut off before the darkness,	3588
	29:12 **B** I delivered the poor that cried,	3588
	30:11 **B** he hath loosed my cord, and afflicted	3588
	31:25 If I rejoiced **b** my wealth *was* great,	3588
	31:25 and **b** mine hand had gotten much;	3588
	32: 1 **b** he *was* righteous in his own eyes.	3588
	32: 2 **b** he justified himself rather than God.	5921
	32: 3 **b** they had found no answer,	834+5921
	32: 4 Job had spoken, **b** they *were* elder than	3588
	34:27 **B** they turned back from him,	3651+5921
	34:36 the end **b** of *his* answers for wicked men.	5921
	35:12 none giveth answer, **b** of the pride	4480+6440
	35:15 **b** *it is* not so, he hath visited *in* his anger;	3588
	36:18 **B** *there is* wrath, *beware* lest he take thee	3588
	38:21 Knowest thou *it*, **b** thou wast then born?	3588
	38:21 or **b** the number of thy days *is* great?	NIH
	39:11 thou trust him, **b** his strength *is* great?	3588
	39:17 **B** God hath deprived her of wisdom,	3588
Ps	5: 8 **b** of mine enemies;	4616+3807.1
	5:11 shout for joy, **b** thou defendest them:	2050.1
	6: 7 Mine eye is consumed **b** of grief;	4480
	6: 7 it waxeth old **b** of all mine enemies.	871.1
	7: 6 up thyself **b** of the rage of mine enemies:	871.1
	8: 2 hast thou ordained strength **b** of	4616+3807.1
	13: 6 he hath dealt bountifully with me.	3588
	14: 6 of the poor, **b** the Lord *is* his refuge.	3588
	16: 8 **b** *he is* at my right hand, I shall not be	3588
	18: 7 and were shaken, **b** he was wroth.	3588
	18:19 he delivered me, **b** he delighted in me.	3588
	27:11 a plain path, **b** of mine enemies.	4616+3807.1
	28: 5 **B** they regard not the works of the Lord,	3588
	28: 6 **b** he hath heard the voice of my	3588
	31:10 my strength faileth **b** of mine iniquity,	871.1
	33:21 him, **b** we have trusted in his holy name.	3588
	37: 1 Fret not thyself **b** of evildoers, neither be	871.1
	37: 7 **b** of him who prospereth *in* his way,	871.1
	37: 7 **b** of the man who bringeth wicked	871.1
	37:40 and save them, **b** they trust in him.	3588
	38: 3 *is* no soundness in my flesh **b** of	4480+6440
	38: 3 *is there any* rest in my bones **b** of	4480+6440
	38: 5 My wounds stink *and* are corrupt **b**	4480+6440
	38:20 **b** I follow *the thing* that good *is*.	8478
	39: 9 I opened not my mouth; **b** thou didst *it*.	3588
	41:11 **b** mine enemy doth not triumph over me.	3588
	42: 9 **b** of the oppression of the enemy?	871.1
	43: 2 **b** of the oppression of the enemy?	871.1
	44: 3 **b** thou hadst a favour unto them.	3588
	45: 4 thy majesty ride prosperously **b** of	1697+5921
	48:11 daughters of Judah be glad, **b** of	4616+3807.1
	52: 9 **b** thou hast done *it*: and I will wait on thy	3588
	53: 5 to shame, **b** God hath despised them.	3588
	55: 3 **B** of the voice of the enemy, because of	4480
	55: 3 of the voice of the enemy, **b** of	4480+6440
	55:19 **B** they have no changes, therefore they fear	834
	59: 9 **B** *of* his strength will I wait upon thee:	NIH
	60: 4 *it* may be displayed **b** of the truth.	4480+6440
	60: 8 my shoe: Philistia, triumph thou **b** of me.	5921
	63: 3 **B** thy lovingkindness *is* better than life,	3588
	63: 7 **B** thou hast been my help, therefore in	3588
	68:29 **B** of thy temple at Jerusalem shall kings	4480
	69: 7 **B** for thy sake I have borne reproach;	3588
	69:18 deliver me **b** of mine enemies.	4616+3807.1
	78:22 **B** they believed not in God, and trusted	3588
	86:17 **b** thou, Lord, hast holpen me,	3588
	91: 9 **B** thou hast made the Lord, *which is* my	3588
	91:14 **B** he hath set his love upon me, therefore	3588
	91:14 on high, **b** he hath known my name.	3588
	97: 8 daughters of Judah rejoiced, **b** of	4616+3807.1
	102:10 **B** of thine indignation and thy	4480+6440
	106:33 **B** they provoked his spirit, so that he	3588
	107:11 **B** they rebelled against the words of God,	3588
	107:17 Fools **b** of their transgression, and because	4480
	107:17 **b** of their iniquities, are afflicted.	4480
	107:26 their soul is melted **b** of trouble.	871.1
	107:30 they glad **b** they be quiet; so he bringeth	3588
	109:16 **B** that he remembered not to shew mercy,	3282
	109:21 **b** thy mercy *is* good, deliver thou me.	3588
	116: 1 **b** he hath heard my voice *and*	3588
	116: 2 **b** he hath inclined his ear unto me,	3588
	118: 1 *he is* good: **b** his mercy *endureth* for ever.	3588
	119:53 **b** of the wicked that forsake thy law.	4480
	119:56 This I had, **b** I kept thy precepts.	3588
	119:62 unto thee **b** of thy righteous judgments.	5921
	119:74 they see me; **b** I have hoped in thy word.	3588
	119:100 than the ancients, **b** I keep thy precepts.	3588
	119:136 down mine eyes, **b** they keep not thy law.	5921
	119:139 **b** mine enemies have forgotten thy words.	3588
	119:158 was grieved; **b** they kept not thy word.	834
	119:164 I praise thee **b** of thy righteous judgments.	5921
	122: 9 **B** of the house of the Lord our	4616+3807.1
Pr	1:24 **B** I have called, and ye refused; I have	3282
	21: 7 **b** they refuse to do judgment.	3588
	22:22 Rob not the poor, **b** he *is* poor:	3588
	24:13 My son, eat thou honey, **b** *it is* good;	3588
	24:19 **b** of evil *men*, neither be thou envious at	871.1
Ecc	2:17 **b** the work that is wrought under the sun	3588
	2:18 **b** I should leave it unto the man that shall	7945
	4: 9 **b** they have a good reward for their labour.	834

Ecc	5:20 **b** God answereth *him* in the joy of his	3588
	8: 6 B to every purpose there is time and	3588
	8:11 **B** sentence *against* an evil work is not	834
	8:13 as a shadow; **b** he feareth not before God.	834
	8:15 **b** a man hath no better *thing* under the sun,	834
	8:17 **b** though a man labour to seek *it*	7945+871.1
	10:15 **b** he knoweth not how to go to the city.	834
	12: 3 the grinders cease **b** they are few,	3588
	12: 5 **b** man goeth to his long home,	3588
	12: 9 **b** the Preacher was wise, he still	7945
SS	1: 3 **B** of the savour of thy good ointments	3807.1
	1: 6 I *am* black, because the sun hath looked	7945
	1: 6 black, **b** the sun hath looked upon me:	7945
	3: 8 upon his thigh **b** of fear in the night.	4480
Isa	2: 6 **b** they be replenished from the east,	3588
	3: 8 **b** their tongue and their doings *are* against	3588
	3:16 the daughters of Zion are haughty,	3282+3588
	5:13 into captivity, **b** *they have* no knowledge:	4480
	5:24 **b** they have cast away the law of	3588
	6: 5 **b** I *am* a man of unclean lips, and I dwell	3588
	7: 5 **B** Syria, Ephraim, and the son of	3282+3588
	7:24 **b** all the land shall become briers and	3588
	8:20 this word, *it is* **b** *there is* no light in them.	834
	10:27 be destroyed **b** of the anointing.	4480+6440
	14:20 **b** thou hast destroyed thy land,	3588
	14:29 the rod of him that smote thee is broken	3588
	15: 1 **B** in the night Ar of Moab is laid waste,	3588
	15: 1 **b** in the night Kir of Moab is laid waste,	3588
	17: 9 they left **b** of the children of Israel:	4480+6440
	17:10 **B** thou hast forgotten the God of thy	3588
	19:16 **b** of the shaking of the hand of	4480+6440
	19:17 **b** of the counsel of the Lord of	4480+6440
	19:20 unto the Lord **b** of the oppressors,	4480+6440
	22: 4 **b** of the spoiling of the daughter of my	5921
	24: 5 **b** they have transgressed the laws,	3588
	26: 3 *is* stayed *on thee*: **b** he trusteth in thee.	3588
	28:15 ye have said, We have made a covenant	3588
	28:28 **b** he will not ever be threshing it, nor	3588
	30:12 **b** ye despise this word, and trust in	3282
	31: 1 and trust in chariots, **b** *they are* many;	3588
	31: 1 in horsemen, **b** they are very strong; but	3588
	32:14 **B** the palaces shall be forsaken;	3588
	37:29 **B** thy rage against me, and thy tumult,	3282
	40: 7 **b** the spirit of the Lord bloweth upon it:	3588
	43:20 **b** I give waters in the wilderness,	3588
	48: 4 **B** I knew that thou *art* obstinate,	4480
	49: 7 princes also shall worship, **b** of	4616+3807.1
	50: 2 **b** *there is* no water, and dieth for thirst.	4480
	51:13 **b** of the fury of the oppressor,	4480+6440
	53: 9 **b** he had done no violence, neither *was*	5921
	53:12 **b** he hath poured out his soul unto	834+8478
	55: 5 not thee shall run unto thee **b** of	4616+3807.1
	60: 5 the abundance of the sea shall be	3588
	60: 9 Holy One of Israel, **b** he hath glorified	3588
	61: 1 **b** the Lord hath anointed me to preach	3282
	64: 7 consumed us, **b** of our iniquities.	3027+871.1
	65:12 when I called, ye did not answer;	3282
	65:16 the former troubles are forgotten,	3588
	65:16 and **b** they are hid from mine eyes.	3588
	66: 4 when I called, none did answer; when	3282
Jer	2:35 thou sayest, **B** I am innocent, surely his	3588
	2:35 thee, **b** thou sayest, I have not sinned.	5921
	4: 4 **b** of the evil of your doings.	4480+6440
	4:17 **b** she hath been rebellious against me,	3588
	4:18 **b** *it is* bitter, because it reacheth unto	3588
	4:18 *it is* bitter, **b** it reacheth unto thine heart.	3588
	4:19 my peace, **b** thou hast heard, O my soul,	3588
	4:28 **b** I have spoken *it*, I have purposed	3588+5921
	4:31 for my soul is wearied **b** of murderers.	3807.1
	5: 6 **b** their transgressions are many,	3588
	5:14 **B** ye speak this word, behold, I will make	3282
	6:19 **b** they have not hearkened unto my	3588
	6:30 call them, **b** the Lord hath rejected them.	3588
	7:13 now, **b** ye have done all these works,	3282
	8:14 **b** we have sinned against the Lord.	3588
	8:19 **b** of them that dwell in a far country:	4480
	9:10 **b** they are burnt up, so that none can pass	3588
	9:13 **B** they have forsaken my law which I set	5921
	9:19 **b** we have forsaken the land, because	3588
	9:19 the land, **b** our dwellings have cast *us* out.	3588
	10: 5 must needs be borne, **b** they cannot go.	3588
	12: 4 **b** they said, He shall not see our last end.	3588
	12:11 desolate, **b** no man layeth *it* to heart.	3588
	12:13 **b** of the fierce anger of the Lord.	4480
	13:17 **b** the Lord's flock is carried away	3588
	13:25 **b** thou hast forgotten me, and trusted in	834
	14: 4 **B** the ground is chapt, for there	5668+871.1
	14: 5 and forsook *it*, **b** there was no grass.	3588
	14: 6 their eyes did fail, **b** *there was* no grass.	3588
	14:16 **b** of the famine and the sword;	4480+6440
	15: 4 into all kingdoms of the earth, **b** of	1558+871.1
	15:17 I sat alone **b** of thy hand:	4480+6440
	16:11 **B** your fathers have forsaken me,	834+5921
	16:18 **b** they have defiled my land, they have	5921
	17:13 **b** they have forsaken the Lord,	3588
	18:15 **b** my people hath forgotten me, they have	3588
	19: 4 **B** they have forsaken me,	834+3282
	19: 4 and hiss **b** of all the plagues thereof.	5921
	19:13 **b** of all the houses upon whose roofs	3807.1
	19:15 **b** they have hardened their necks, that	3588
	20: 8 **b** the word of the Lord was made a	3588
	20:17 **B** he slew me not from the womb; or that	834
	21:12 **b** of the evil of your doings.	4480+6440
	22: 9 **B** they have forsaken the covenant of	834+5921
	22:15 reign, **b** thou closest *thyself* in cedar?	3588

B

Jer 23: 9 within me is broken **b** of the prophets; | 3807.1
23: 9 **b** of the LORD, and because of | 4480+6440
23: 9 and **b** of the words of his holiness. | 4480+6440
23:10 **b** of swearing the land mourneth; | 4480+6440
23:38 **B** ye say this word, The burden of | 3282
25: 8 **B** ye have not heard my words, | 834+3282
25:16 **b** of the sword that I will send | 4480+6440
25:27 **b** of the sword which I will send among | 6440
25:37 **b** of the fierce anger of the LORD. | 4480+6440
25:38 **b** of the fierceness of the oppressor, | 4480+6440
25:38 and **b** of his fierce anger. | 4480+6440
26: 3 **b** of the evil of their doings. | 4480+6440
28:16 **b** thou hast taught rebellion against | 3588
29:15 ye have said, The LORD hath raised us | 3588
29:19 **B** they have not hearkened to my | 834+8478
29:23 **b** they have committed villany in | 834+3282
29:25 **b** thou hast sent letters in thy name | 834+3282
29:31 **b** that Shemaiah hath prophesied unto | 3282
29:32 **b** he hath taught rebellion against | 3588
30:14 thine iniquity; **b** thy sins were increased. | NIH
30:15 **b** thy sins were increased, I have done | NIH
30:17 **b** they called thee an Outcast, *saying,* This | 3588
31:15 for her children, **b** they *were* not. | 3588
31:19 **b** I did bear the reproach of my youth. | 3588
32:24 that fight against it, **b** of the sword, | 4480+6440
32:32 **B** of all the evil of the children of Israel | 5921
35:16 **b** the sons of Jonadab the son of Rechab | 3588
35:17 **b** I have spoken unto them, but they have | 3282
35:18 **b** ye have obeyed the commandment | 834+3282
39:18 **b** thou hast put thy trust in me, saith | 3588
40: 3 **b** ye have sinned against the LORD, | 3588
41: 9 whom he had slain **b** of Gedaliah, | 3027+871.1
41:18 **B** of the Chaldeans: for they were | 4480+6440
41:18 Ishmael the son of Nethaniah had slain | 3588
44: 3 **b** of their wickedness which they | 4480+6440
44:22 **b** of the evil of your doings, | 4480+6440
44:22 *and* **b** of the abominations which | 4480+6440
44:23 **b** you have burnt incense, | 834+4480+6440
44:23 **b** ye have sinned against the LORD, | 834
46:15 stood not, **b** the LORD did drive them. | 3588
46:21 **b** the day of their calamity was come upon | 3588
46:23 **b** they are more than the grasshoppers, | 3588
47: 4 **B** of the day that cometh to spoil all | 5921
48: 7 For **b** thou hast trusted in thy works and | 3282
48:36 the riches *that* he hath gotten are | 3651+5921
48:42 **b** he hath magnified *himself* against | 3588
48:45 the shadow of Heshbon **b** of the force: | 4480
50: 7 **b** they have sinned against | 834+8478
50:11 **B** ye were glad, because ye rejoiced, O ye | 3588
50:11 Because ye were glad, because ye rejoiced, O ye | 3588
50:11 ye are grown fat as the heifer at grass, | 3588
50:13 **B** of the wrath of the LORD it shall not be | 4480
50:24 **b** thou hast striven against the LORD. | 3588
51:11 **b** it *is* the vengeance of the LORD, | 3588
51:51 confounded, **b** we have heard reproach. | 3588
51:55 **B** the LORD *hath* spoiled Babylon, | 3588
51:56 **B** the spoiler is come upon her, *even* upon | 3588
La 1: 3 Judah is gone into captivity **b** of affliction, | 4480
1: 3 of affliction, and **b** of great servitude; | 4480
1: 4 **b** none come to the solemn feasts; | 4480
1: 8 **b** they have seen her nakedness. | 3588
1:16 **b** the comforter that *should* relieve my | 3588
1:16 are desolate, **b** the enemy prevailed. | 3588
2:11 **b** the children and the sucklings swoon in | 871.1
3:22 not consumed, **b** his compassions fail not. | 3588
3:28 **b** he hath borne *it* upon him. | 3588
3:51 **b** of all the daughters of my city. | 4480
5: 9 with *the peril of* our lives **b** of | 4480+6440
5:10 skin was black like an oven **b** of | 4480+6440
5:18 **B** of the mountain of Zion, which is | 5921
Eze 3:20 **b** thou hast not given him warning, | 3588
3:21 he shall surely live, **b** he is warned; | 3588
5: 7 **B** ye multiplied more than the nations that | 3282
5: 9 more the like, **b** of all thine abominations. | 3282
5:11 **b** thou hast defiled my sanctuary with all | 3282
6: 9 **b** I am broken with their whorish heart, | 834
7:19 **b** it is the stumblingblock of their iniquity. | 3588
12:19 **b** of the violence of all them that dwell | 4480
13: 8 **B** ye have spoken vanity, and seen lies, | 3282
13:10 **B,** even because they have seduced my | 3282
13:10 even **b** have seduced my | 3282+871.1
13:22 **B** *with* lies ye have made the heart of | 3282
14: 5 **b** they are all estranged from me through | 834
14:15 may pass through **b** of the beasts: | 4480+6440
15: 8 **b** they have committed a trespass, saith | 3282
16:15 playedst the harlot **b** of thy renown, | 5921
16:28 with the Assyrians, **b** thou wast unsatiable; | 4480
16:36 **B** thy filthiness was poured out, | 3282
16:43 **b** thou hast not remembered the days | 834+3282
16:63 open thy mouth any more, **b** of | 4480+6440
18:18 *As for* his father, **b** he cruelly oppressed, | 3588
18:28 **B** he considereth, and turneth away | 2050.1
20:16 **b** they despised my judgments, and | 3282
20:24 **b** they had not executed my judgments, | 3282
21: 7 shalt answer, For the tidings; **b** it cometh: | 3588
21:13 **b** it *is* a trial, and what if *the sword* | 3588
21:24 **b** ye have made your iniquity to be | 3282
21:24 **b,** *I say,* that ye are come to remembrance | 3282
21:28 to consume **b** of the glittering: | 4616+3807.1
22:19 **B** ye are all become dross, | 3282
23:30 **b** thou hast gone a whoring after | 871.1
23:30 **b** thou art polluted with their idols. | 834+5921
23:35 **B** thou hast forgotten me, and cast me | 3282
23:45 **b** they *are* adulteresses, and blood *is* in | 3588
24:13 **b** I have purged thee, and thou wast not | 3282

Eze 25: 3 **B** thou saidst, Aha, against my sanctuary, | 3282
25: 6 **B** thou hast clapped *thine* hands, | 3282
25: 8 **B** that Moab and Seir do say, Behold, | 3282
25:12 **B** that Edom hath dealt against the house | 3282
25:15 **B** the Philistines have dealt by revenge, | 3282
26: 2 **b** that Tyrus hath said against Jerusalem, | 3282
28: 2 **B** thine heart *is* lifted up, and thou hast | 3282
28: 5 thine heart is lifted up **b** of thy riches: | 871.1
28: 6 **B** thou hast set thine heart as the heart of | 3282
28:17 Thine heart was lifted up **b** of thy beauty, | 871.1
29: 6 **b** they have been a staff of reed to | 3282
29: 9 he hath said, The river is mine, | 3282
29:20 **b** they wrought for me, saith the Lord | 834
31: 5 became long **b** of the multitude of waters, | 4480
31:10 **B** thou hast lifted up thyself in height, | 834+3282
33:29 **b** of all their abominations which they | 5921
34: 5 were scattered, **b** *there is* no shepherd: | 4480
34: 8 surely **b** my flock became a prey, | 3282
34: 8 **b** *there was* no shepherd, neither did my | 4480
34:21 **B** ye have thrust with side and | 3282
35: 5 **b** thou hast had a perpetual hatred, | 3282
35:10 **B** thou hast said, These two nations and | 3282
35:15 it was desolate, so will I do unto | 834+5921
36: 2 **B** the enemy hath said against you, Aha, | 3282
36: 3 **B** *they* have made *you* | 3282+3282+871.1
36: 6 ye have borne the shame of the heathen: | 3282
36:13 **B** they say unto you, Thou *land* devourest | 3282
39:23 **b** they trespassed against me, | 834+5921
44: 2 **b** the LORD, the God of Israel, | 3588
44: 7 my covenant **b** of all your abominations. | 413
44:12 **B** they ministered unto them before | 834+3282
47: 9 of fish, **b** these waters shall come thither: | 3588
47:12 **b** their waters they issued out of | 3588
Da 2: 8 **b** ye see the thing is gone | 1768+3606+6903
3:22 Therefore **b** the king's | 1768+4481
3:29 shall be made a dunghill: **b** | 1768+3606+6903
4: 9 **b** I know that the spirit of the holy gods *is* | 1768
6: 3 **b** an excellent spirit *was* in | 1768+3606+6903
6:23 found upon him, **b** he believed in his God. | 1768
7:11 I beheld then **b** of the voice of the great | 4481
9: 7 **b** of their trespass that they have | 871.1
9: 8 fathers, **b** we have sinned against thee. | 834
9:11 of God, **b** we have sinned against him. | 3588
9:16 **b** for our sins, and for the iniquities of our | 3588
11:35 of the end: **b** *it is* yet for a time appointed. | 3588
Hos 4: 1 **b** *there is* no truth, nor mercy, | 3588
4: 6 **b** thou hast rejected knowledge, I will also | 3588
4:10 **b** they have left off to take heed to | 3588
4:13 and elms, **b** the shadow thereof *is* good: | 3588
4:19 they shall be ashamed **b** of their sacrifices. | 4480
5: 1 ye have been a snare on Mizpah, | 3588
5:11 **b** he willingly walked after | 3588
7:13 **b** they have transgressed against me: | 3588
8: 1 **b** they have transgressed my covenant, | 3588
8:11 **b** Ephraim hath made many altars to sin, | 3588
9: 6 For lo, they are gone **b** of destruction: | 4480
9:17 **b** they did not hearken unto him: | 3588
10: 3 have no king, **b** we feared not the LORD; | 3588
10: 5 shall fear **b** of the calves of Beth-aven: | 3807.1
10: 5 the glory thereof, **b** it is departed from it. | 3588
10:13 **b** thou didst trust in thy way, | 3588
10:15 **b** of your great wickedness: | 4480+6440
11: 5 shall be his king, **b** they refused to return. | 3588
11: 6 devour *them,* **b** of their own counsels. | 4480
Joel 1: 5 drinkers of wine, **b** of the new wine, | 5921
1:11 **b** the harvest of the field is perished. | 3588
1:12 **b** joy is withered away from the sons of | 4480
1:18 are perplexed, **b** they have no pasture; | 3588
2:20 come up, **b** he hath done great things. | 3588
3: 5 **b** ye have taken my silver and my gold, | 834
3:19 **b** they have shed innocent blood in their | 834
Am 1: 3 **b** they have threshed Gilead with | 5921
1: 6 **b** they carried away captive the whole | 5921
1: 9 **b** they delivered up the whole captivity to | 5921
1:11 **b** he did pursue his brother with the | 5921
1:13 **b** they have ript up the women with child | 5921
2: 1 **b** he burnt the bones of the king of Edom | 5921
2: 4 **b** they have despised the law of | 5921
2: 6 **b** they sold the righteous for silver, | 5921
4:12 *and* **b** I will do this unto thee, | 3588+6118
Jnh 1:10 of the LORD, **b** he had told them. | 3588
Mic 2: 1 **b** it is in the power of their hand. | 3588
2:10 for this *is* not *your* rest: **b** it is | 5668+871.1
6:13 in making thee desolate **b** of thy sins. | 5921
7: 9 I have sinned against him, until he plead | 3588
7:13 be desolate **b** of them that dwell therein, | 5921
7:17 LORD our God, and shall fear **b** of thee. | 4480
7:18 anger for ever, **b** he delighteth in mercy. | 3588
Na 3: 4 **B** of the multitude of the whoredoms of | 4480
3:11 also shalt seek strength **b** of the enemy. | 4480
Hab 1:16 by them their portion *is* fat, | 3588
2: 3 **b** it will surely come, it will not tarry. | 3588
2: 5 Yea also, **b** he transgresseth *by* wine, | 3588
2: 8 **B** thou hast spoiled many nations, all | 3588
2: 8 **b** of men's blood, and *for* the violence of | 4480
2:17 **b** of men's blood, and *for* the violence of | 4480
Zep 1:17 that they shall walk like blind *men,* **b** | 3588
2:10 **b** they have reproached and | 5921
2:10 more be haughty **b** of my holy mountain. | 871.1
Hag 1: 9 **b** of mine house that *is* waste, and ye run | 3282
Zec 8:10 went out or came in **b** of the affliction: | 4480
9: 8 encamp about mine house **b** of the army, | 4480
9: 8 **b** of him that passeth by, and because | 4480
9: 8 passeth by, and **b** of him that returneth: | 4480
10: 2 were troubled, **b** *there was* no shepherd. | 3588

Zec 10: 5 **b** the LORD *is* with them, and the riders | 3588
11: 2 cedar is fallen; **b** the mighty are spoiled: | 834
Mal 2: 2 them already, **b** ye do not lay *it* to heart. | 3588
2:14 Wherefore? **B** the LORD hath been | 3588+5921
Mt 2:18 would not be comforted, **b** they are not. | 3754
5:36 **b** thou canst not make one hair white or | 3754
7:14 **B** strait *is* the gate, and narrow *is* the way, | 3754
9:36 with compassion on them, **b** they fainted, | 3754
11:20 works were done, **b** they repented not. | 3754
11:25 **b** thou hast hid these *things* from the wise | 3754
12:41 **b** they repented at the preaching of Jonas; | 3754
13: 5 **b** *they* had not deepness of earth: | 1223+3588
13: 6 and **b** *they* had not root, | 1223+3588
13:11 **B** it is given unto you to know | 3754
13:13 **b** they seeing see not; and hearing they | 3754
13:21 or persecution ariseth **b** of the word, | 1223
13:58 mighty works there, **b** of their unbelief. | 1223
14: 5 **b** they counted him as a prophet. | 3754
15:32 **b** they continue with me now three days, | 3754
16: 7 saying, *It is* **b** we have taken no bread. | 3754
16: 8 **b** ye have brought no bread? | 3754
17:20 Jesus unto them, **B** of your unbelief: | 1223
18: 7 Woe unto the world **b** of offences! for it | 575
18:32 thee all that debt, **b** thou desiredst me: | 1893
19: 8 **b** of the hardness of your hearts suffered | 4314
20: 7 say unto him, **B** no *man* hath hired us. | 3754
20:15 mine own? Is thine eye evil, **b** I am good? | 3754
20:31 **b** they should hold their peace: | 2443
21:46 **b** they took him for a prophet. | 1894
23:29 ye build the tombs of the prophets, and | 3754
24:12 **b** iniquity shall abound, the love | 1223+3588
26:31 All ye shall be offended **b** of me this night: | 1722
26:33 all *men* shall be offended **b** of thee, | 1722
27:6 into the treasury, **b** it is the price of blood. | 1893
27:19 many *things* this day in a dream **b** of him. | 1223
Mk 1:34 not the devils to speak, **b** they knew him. | 3754
3: 9 should wait on him **b** of the multitude, | 1223
3:30 **B** they said, He hath an unclean spirit. | 3754
4: 5 up, **b** *it* had no depth of earth: | 1223+3588
4: 6 **b** *it* had no root, it withered away. | 1223+3588
4:29 the sickle, **b** the harvest is come. | 3754
5: 4 **B** that he had been often bound with | 1223
6: 6 And he marvelled **b** of their unbelief. | 1223
6:34 by they were as sheep not having a | 3754
7:19 **B** it entereth not into his heart, but into | 3754
8: 2 **b** they have now been with me three days | 3754
8:16 saying, *It is* **b** we have no bread. | 3754
8:17 Why reason ye, **b** ye have no bread? | 3754
9:38 and we forbad him, **b** he followeth not us. | 3754
9:41 ye belong to Christ, verily I say unto | 3754
11:18 **b** all the people was astonished at his | 3754
12:24 err, **b** ye know not the scriptures. | NIG
14:27 All ye shall be offended **b** of me this night: | 1722
15:42 **b** it was the preparation, that is, the day | 1893
16:14 **b** they believed not them which had seen | 3754
Lk 1: 7 **b** that Elisabeth was barren, and they | 2530
1:20 thou believest not my words, | 473+3739
2: 4 (**b** he was of the house and lineage | 1223+3588
2: 7 **b** there was no room for them in the inn. | 1360
4:18 Spirit of the Lord *is* upon me, **b** | 1752+3739
5:19 might bring him in **b** of the multitude, | 1223
8: 6 away, **b** *it* lacked moisture. | 1223+3588
8:30 **b** many devils were entered into him. | 3754
9: 7 **b** that it was said of some, | 1223+3588
9:49 forbad him, **b** he followeth not with us. | 3754
9:53 **b** his face was *as though he* would go to | 3754
10:20 your names are written in heaven. | 3754
11: 8 **b** he is his friend, yet because of his | 1223+3588
11: 8 yet **b** of his importunity he will rise and | 1223
11:18 ye say that I cast out devils through | 3754
12:17 **b** I have no room where to bestow my | 3754
13: 2 Galileans, **b** they suffered such *things*? | 3754
13:14 **b** that Jesus had healed on the sabbath | 3754
15:27 **b** he hath received him *safe and* sound. | 3754
16: 8 the unjust steward, **b** he had done wisely: | 3754
17: 9 Doth he thank that servant **b** he did | 3754
18: 5 Yet **b** this widow troubleth me, | 1223+3588
19: 3 not for the press, **b** he was little of stature. | 3754
19:11 he was nigh to Jerusalem, | 1223+3588
19:11 and **b** they thought that the kingdom of God | NIG
19:17 **b** thou hast been faithful in a very little, | 3754
19:21 I feared thee, **b** thou art an austere man: | 3754
19:31 unto him, **B** the Lord hath need of him. | 3754
19:44 **b** thou knewest not the time of thy | 473+3739
23: 8 **b** he had heard many *things* of him; | 1223+3588
Jn 1:50 and said unto him, **B** I said unto thee, | 3754
2:24 unto them, **b** he knew all *men,* | 1223+3588
3:18 **b** he hath not believed in the name of | 3754
3:19 rather than light, **b** their deeds were evil. | 1063
3:23 to Salim, **b** there was much water there: | 1223
3:29 **b** of the bridegroom's voice: | 1223
4:41 many more believed **b** of his own word; | 1223
4:42 *Now* we believe, not **b** of thy saying: | 1223
5:16 **b** he had done these *things* on the sabbath | 3754
5:18 **b** he not only had broken the sabbath, but | 3754
5:27 judgment also, **b** he is the Son of man. | 3754
5:30 is just; **b** I seek not mine own will, | 3754
6: 2 **b** they saw his miracles which he did on | 3754
6:26 not **b** ye saw the miracles, but because | 3754
6:26 but **b** ye did eat of the loaves, and | 3754
6:41 Jews then murmured at him, **b** he said, | 3754
7: 1 in Jewry, **b** the Jews sought to kill him. | 3754
7: 7 but me it hateth, **b** I testify of it, that | 3754
7:22 not **b** it is of Moses, but of the fathers; | 3754
7:23 **b** I have made a man every whit whole on | 3754

Jn	7:30 on him, **b** his hour was not yet come.	3754
	7:39 *given;* **b** that Jesus was not glorified.)	3754
	7:43 a division among the people **b** of him.	1223
	8:22 **b** he saith, Whither I go, ye cannot come.	3754
	8:37 kill me, **b** my word hath no place in you.	3754
	8:43 *even* **b** ye cannot hear my word.	3754
	8:44 not in the truth, **b** there is no truth in him.	3754
	8:45 And **b** I tell *you* the truth, ye believe me	3754
	8:47 hear *them* not, **b** ye are not of God.	3754
	9:16 of God, **b** he keepeth not the sabbath day.	3754
	9:22 spake his parents, **b** they feared the Jews:	3754
	10:13 **b** he is a hireling, and careth not for	3754
	10:17 **b** I lay down my life, that I might take it	3754
	10:26 ye are not of my sheep, as I said unto	1063
	10:33 and **b** that thou, being a man,	3754
	10:36 **b** I said, I am the Son of God?	3754
	11: 9 **b** he seeth the light of this world.	3754
	11:10 he stumbleth, **b** there is no light in him.	3754
	11:42 **b** of the people which stand by I said *it,*	1223
	12: 6 but **b** he was a thief, and had the bag,	3754
	12:11 **B** that **by reason of** him many of the Jews	1223
	12:30 This voice came not **b** of me, but for your	1223
	12:39 could not believe, **b that** Esaias said again,	3754
	12:42 **b** of the Pharisees they did not confess	1223
	13:29 *of them* thought, **b** Judas had the bag,	1893
	14:12 these shall he do; **b** I go unto my Father.	3754
	14:17 It seeth him not, neither knoweth him:	3754
	14:19 but ye see me: **b** I live, ye shall live also.	3754
	14:28 If ye loved me, ye would rejoice, **b** I said,	3754
	15:19 but **b** ye are not of the world, but I have	3754
	15:21 **b** they know not him that sent me.	3754
	15:27 **b** ye have been with me from	3754
	16: 3 **b** they have not known the Father, nor	3754
	16: 4 you at the beginning, **b** I was with you.	3754
	16: 6 But **b** I have said these *things* unto you,	3754
	16: 9 Of sin, **b** they believe not on me;	3754
	16:10 **b** I go to my Father, and ye see me no	3754
	16:11 **b** the prince of this world is judged.	3754
	16:16 and ye shall see me, **b** I go to the Father.	3754
	16:17 ye shall see me: and, **B** I go to the Father?	3754
	16:21 in travail hath sorrow, **b** her hour is come:	3754
	16:27 **b** ye have loved me, and have believed	3754
	16:32 I am not alone, **b** the Father is with me.	3754
	17:14 hated them, **b** they are not of the world,	3754
	19: 7 to die, he made himself the Son of God.	3754
	19:31 Jews therefore, **b** it was the preparation,	1893
	19:42 **b** of the Jews' preparation *day;* for	1223
	20:13 **B** they have taken away my Lord,	3754
	20:29 Thomas, **b** thou hast seen me, thou hast	3754
	21:17 Peter was grieved **b** he said unto him	3754
Ac	2: 6 **b that** every man heard them speak in his	3754
	2:24 **b** it was not possible that he should be	2530
	2:27 **B** thou wilt not leave my soul in hell,	3754
	4:21 they might punish them, **b** of the people:	1223
	6: 1 their widows were neglected in the daily	3754
	8:11 **b** that of long time *he* had bewitched them	1223
	8:20 **b** thou hast thought that the gift of God	3754
	10:45 that on the Gentiles also was poured out	3754
	12: 3 And **b** he saw it pleased the Jews,	NIG
	12:20 **b** their country was nourished by	1223
	12:23 **b** he gave not God the glory:	473+3739
	13:27 and their rulers, **b** they knew him not,	NIG
	14:12 Mercurius, **b** he was the chief speaker.	1894
	16: 3 **b** of the Jews which were in those	1223
	17:18 **b** he preached unto them Jesus,	3754
	17:31 He hath appointed a day, in the which	1360
	18: 2 (**b that** Claudius had commanded	1223+3588
	18: 3 And **b** *he* was of the same craft,	1223+3588
	20:16 he would not spend the time in Asia:	3704
	22:29 was a Roman, and be had bound him.	3754
	22:30 he would have known the certainty	NIG
	24:11 **B** that thou mayest understand, that there	NIG
	25:20 And **b** I doubted of such *manner* of	NIG
	26: 2 **b** I shall answer for myself this day before	NIG
	26: 3 Especially *b* **I** *know* thee to be expert in all	NIG
	27: 4 **b** the winds were contrary.	1223+3588
	27: 9 **b** the fast was now already past,	1223+3588
	27:12 And **b** the haven was not commodious to	NIG
	28: 2 **b** of the present rain, and because of	1223
	28: 2 of the present rain, and **b** of the cold.	1223
	28:18 there was no cause of death in	1223+3588
	28:20 **b that** for the hope of Israel I am bound	1752
Ro	1:19 **b** that which may be known of God is	1360
	1:21 **B that,** when they knew God, they	1360
	3: 2 **b** that unto them were committed	1063
	4:15 **B** the law worketh wrath: for where no	1063
	5: 5 **b** the love of God is shed abroad in our	3754
	6:15 **b** we are not under the law, but	3754
	6:19 of men **b** of the infirmity of your flesh;	1223
	8: 7 **B** the carnal mind *is* enmity against God:	1360
	8:10 Christ *be* in you, the body is dead **b** of sin	1223
	8:10 but the Spirit *is* life **b** of righteousness.	1223
	8:21 **B** the creature itself also shall be delivered	3754
	8:27 **b** he maketh intercession for the saints	3754
	9: 7 Neither, **b** they are the seed of Abraham,	3754
	9:28 **b** a short work will the Lord make upon	3754
	9:32 **B** *they* sought *it* not by faith, but as	3754
	11:20 **b** of unbelief they were broken off,	NIG
	14:23 damned if he eat, **b** *he* eateth not of faith:	3754
	15:15 **b** of the grace that is given to me of God,	1223
1Co	1:25 **B** the foolishness of God is wiser than	3754
	2:14 neither can he know *them,* **b** they are	3754
	3:13 for the day shall declare *it,* **b** it shall be	3754
	6: 7 **b** ye go to law one with another.	3754
	11:10 have power on *her* head **b** of the angels.	1223

1Co	12:15 If the foot shall say, **B** I am not the hand,	3754
	12:16 **B** I am not the eye, I am not of the body;	3754
	15: 9 **b** I persecuted the church of God.	1360
	15:15 **b** we have testified of God that he raised	3754
2Co	2:13 my spirit, **b** I found not Titus my brother:	NIG
	5: 8 **b** we thus judge, that if one died for all,	NIG
	7:13 **b** his spirit was refreshed by you all.	3754
	11: 7 **b** I have preached to you the gospel of	3754
	11:11 **b** I love you not? God knoweth.	3754
Gal	2: 4 **b** of false brethren unawares brought in,	1223
	2:11 him to the face, **b** he was to *be* blamed.	3754
	3:19 It was added **b** of transgressions, till	5484
	4: 6 And **b** ye are sons, God hath sent forth	3754
	4:16 your enemy, **b** I tell you the truth?	5620
Eph	4:18 in them, **b** of the blindness of their heart:	1223
	5: 6 **b** of these *things* cometh the wrath of God	1223
	5:16 Redeeming the time, **b** the days are evil.	3754
Php	1: 7 of you all, **b** I have you in *my* heart;	1223+3588
	2:26 **b** that ye had heard that he had been sick.	1360
	2:30 **B** for the work of Christ he was nigh unto	3754
	4:17 Not **b** I desire a gift: but I desire fruit that	3754
1Th	2: 8 our own souls, **b** ye were dear unto us.	3754
	2: 9 **b** *we* would not be chargeable unto	3588+4314
	2:13 also thank we God without ceasing, **b,**	3754
	4: 6 **b that** the Lord *is* the avenger of all such,	1360
2Th	1: 3 **b that** your faith groweth exceedingly,	3754
	1:10 to be admired in all them that believe (**b**	3754
	2:10 **b** they received not the love of	473+3739
	2:13 **b** God hath from the beginning chosen	3754
	3: 9 Not **b** we have not power, but to make	3754
1Ti	1:13 **b** I did *it* ignorantly in unbelief.	3754
	4:10 **b** we trust in the living God,	3754
	5:12 **b** they have cast off *their* first faith.	3754
	6: 2 not despise *them,* **b** they are brethren;	3754
	6: 2 **b** they are faithful and beloved,	3754
Phm	1: 7 **b** the bowels of the saints are refreshed by	3754
Heb	3:19 that they could not enter in **b** of unbelief,	1223
	4: 6 first preached entered not in **b** of unbelief,	1223
	6:13 **b** he could swear by no greater, he sware	1893
	7:23 **b** *they* were not suffered to continue by	NIG
	7:24 But this *man,* **b** he continueth ever,	1223+3588
	8: 9 **b** they continued not in my covenant,	3754
	10: 2 **b** that the worshippers once purged	1223+3588
	11: 5 was not found, **b** God had translated him:	1360
	11:11 **b** she judged him faithful who had	1893
	11:23 **b** they saw *he was* a proper child;	1360
Jas	1:10 **b** as the flower of the grass he shall pass	3754
	4: 2 war, yet ye have not, **b** ye ask not.	1223+3588
	4: 3 Ye ask, and receive not, **b** ye ask amiss,	1360
1Pe	1:16 **B** it is written, Be ye holy; for I am holy.	1360
	2:21 **b** Christ also suffered for us, leaving us an	3754
	5: 8 **b** your adversary the devil, as a roaring	3754
1Jn	2: 8 **b** the darkness is past, and the true light	3754
	2:11 **b** that darkness hath blinded his eyes.	3754
	2:12 **b** *your* sins are forgiven you for his name's	3754
	2:13 **b** ye have known him that is from	3754
	2:13 **b** you have overcome the wicked one.	3754
	2:13 children, **b** ye have known the Father.	3754
	2:14 **b** ye have known him that is from	3754
	2:14 **b** ye are strong, and the word of God	3754
	2:21 written unto you **b** ye know not the truth,	3754
	2:21 but **b** ye know it, and that no lie is or	3754
	3: 1 world knoweth us not, **b** it knew him not.	3754
	3: 9 and he cannot sin, **b** he is born of God.	3754
	3:12 **B** his own works were evil, and his	3754
	3:14 death unto life, **b** we love the brethren.	3754
	3:16 love of *God,* **b** he laid down his life for us:	3754
	3:22 **b** we keep his commandments,	3754
	4: 1 **b** many false prophets are gone out into	3754
	4: 4 **b** greater is he that is in you, than he that	3754
	4: 9 **b** that God sent his only begotten Son into	3754
	4:13 he in us, **b** he hath given us of his Spirit.	3754
	4:17 in the day of judgment: **b** as he is,	3754
	4:18 **b** fear hath torment. He that feareth is not	3754
	4:19 We love him, **b** he first loved us.	3754
	5: 6 that beareth witness, **b** the Spirit is truth.	3754
	5:10 **b** he believeth not the record that God	3754
3Jn	1: 7 **B** that for his name's sake they went forth,	NIG
Jude	1:16 persons in admiration **b** of advantage.	5484
Rev	1: 7 kindreds of the earth shall wail **b** of him.	1909
	2: 4 thee, **b** thou hast left thy first love.	3754
	2:14 **b** thou hast there them that hold	3754
	2:20 **b** thou sufferest *that* woman Jezebel,	3754
	3:10 **B** thou hast kept the word of my patience,	3754
	3:16 So then **b** thou art lukewarm, and	3754
	3:17 **b** thou sayest, I am rich, and increased	3754
	5: 4 **b** no *man* was found worthy to open and	3754
	8:11 of the waters, **b** they were made bitter.	3754
	11:10 **b** these two prophets tormented them that	3754
	11:17 **b** thou hast taken *to thee* thy great power,	3754
	12:12 **b** he knoweth that he hath *but* a short	NIG
	14: 8 **b** she made all nations drink of the wine	3754
	16: 5 and shalt be, **b** thou hast judged thus.	3754
	16:11 **b** of their pains and their sores,	1537
	16:21 **b** of the plague of the hail;	1537

BECHER (5)

Ge	46:21 and **B,** and Ashbel, Gera, and Naaman,	1071
Nu	26:35 of **B,** the family of the Bachrites: of Tahan,	1071
1Ch	7: 6 Bela, and **B,** and Jediael, three.	1071
	7: 8 the sons of **B;** Zemira, and Joash,	1071
	7: 8 and Alameth. All these *are* the sons of **B.**	1071

BECHORATH (1)

1Sa	9: 1 of Abiel, the son of Zeror, the son of **B,**	1064

B.

BECKONED (6) [BECKONING]

Lk	1:22 for he **b** unto them,	1269
	5: 7 And they **b** unto *their* partners, which	2656
Jn	13:24 Simon Peter therefore **b** to him, that *he*	3506
Ac	19:33 And Alexander **b** with the hand,	2678
	21:40 and **b** with the hand unto the people.	2678
	24:10 after that the governor had **b** unto him to	3506

BECKONING (2) [BECKONED]

Ac	12:17 **b** unto them with the hand to hold their	2678
	13:16 and **b** with *his* hand said, Men of Israel,	2678

BECOME (135) [BECAME, BECAMEST, BECOMETH]

Ge	3:22 the man is **b** as one of us, to know	1961
	9:15 the waters shall no more **b** a flood to	1961
	18:18 Seeing that Abraham shall **surely b**	1961+1961
	24:35 my master greatly; and he is **b** great:	NIH
	32:10 and now I am **b** two bands.	1961+3807.1
	34:16 and we will **b** one people.	1961+3807.1
	37:20 we shall see what will **b** of his dreams.	1961
	48:19 I know *it:* he also shall **b** a people,	1961
	48:19 his seed shall **b** a multitude of nations.	1961
Ex	4: 9 the river shall **b** blood upon the dry *land.*	1961
	7: 9 *it* before Pharaoh, *and* it shall **b** a serpent.	1961
	7:19 pools of water, that they may **b** blood;	1961
	8:16 that it may **b** lice throughout all the land	1961
	9: 9 shall **b** small dust in all the land of Egypt,	1961
	15: 2 and song, and he is **b** my salvation:	1961
	15: 6 O Lord, is **b glorious** in power:	142
	23:29 lest the land **b** desolate, and the beast of	1961
	32: 1 of Egypt, we wot not what is **b** of him.	1961
	32:23 of Egypt, we wot not what is **b** of him.	1961
Lev	19:29 and the land **b full** of wickedness.	4390
Nu	5:24 the curse shall enter into her, and **b** bitter.	NIH
	5:27 and bitter, and her belly shall swell,	NIH
Dt	27: 9 this day thou art **b** the people of	1961
	28:37 thou shalt **b** an astonishment, a proverb,	1961
Jos	9:13 our shoes are **b** old by reason of the very	1086
Jdg	16: 7 I shall **b** weak, and be like any *other* man.	1961
1Sa	28:16 departed from thee, and is **b** thine enemy?	1961
2Sa	7:24 for ever; and thou, Lord, art **b** their God.	1961
1Ki	2:15 is turned about, and is **b** my brother's:	1961
	14: 3 he shall tell thee what shall **b** of the child.	1961
2Ki	21:14 they shall **b** a prey and a spoil to all their	1961
	22:19 *they* should **b** a desolation and a curse,	1961
Est	2:11 how Esther did, and what should **b** of her.	6213
Job	2:11 my skin is broken, and **b loathsome.**	3988
	15:28 which are **ready to b** heaps.	6257
	21: 7 **b** old, yea, are mighty in power?	6275
	30:19 the mire, and I am **b like** dust and ashes.	4911
	30:21 Thou art **b** cruel to me: with thy strong	2015
Ps	14: 3 gone aside, they are *all* together **b** filthy:	NIH
	28: 1 I **b like** them that go down into the pit.	4911
	53: 3 is gone back, they are altogether **b** filthy;	NIH
	62:10 in oppression, and **b** not vain in robbery:	NIH
	69: 8 I am **b** a stranger unto my brethren,	1961
	69:22 Let their table **b** a snare before them:	1961
	69:22 *have been* for *their* welfare, *let it* **b** a trap.	NIH
	79: 4 We are **b** a reproach to our neighbours,	1961
	109: 7 be condemned: and let his prayer **b** sin.	1961
	118:14 and song, and is **b** my salvation.	1961
	118:21 hast heard me, and art **b** my salvation.	1961
	118:22 The stone *which* the builders refused is **b**	1961
	119:83 For I am **b like** a bottle in the smoke;	1961
Pr	29:21 shall have him **b** *his* son at the length.	1961
Isa	1:21 How is the faithful city **b** a harlot! *it was*	1961
	1:22 Thy silver is **b** dross, thy wine mixt with	1961
	7:24 all the land shall **b** briers and thorns.	1961
	12: 2 my song; he also is **b** my salvation.	1961
	14:10 unto thee, Art thou also **b weak** as we?	2470
	14:10 weak as we? art thou **b** like unto us?	4911
	19:11 wise counsellers of Pharaoh is **b** brutish:	NIH
	19:13 The princes of Zoan are **b** fools, the	NIH
	29:11 the vision of all is **b** unto you as the words	1961
	34: 9 and the land thereof shall **b** burning pitch.	1961
	35: 7 The parched ground shall **b** a pool,	1961
	59: 6 Their webs shall not **b** garments,	1961
	60:22 A little one shall **b** a thousand, and a small	1961
Jer	2: 5 have walked after vanity, and are **b vain?**	1891
	5: 1 from him, and **b** another man's,	1961+3807.1
	5:13 the prophets shall **b** wind, and the word *is*	1961
	5:27 they are **b** great, and waxen rich.	NIH
	7:11 my name, **b** a den of robbers in your eyes?	1961
	10:21 For the pastors are **b** brutish, and have not	NIH
	22: 5 that this house shall **b** a desolation.	1961
	26:18 Jerusalem shall **b** heaps, and the mountain	1961
	49:13 Bozrah shall **b** a desolation, a reproach,	1961
	50:23 how is Babylon **b** a desolation among	1961
	50:37 midst of her; and they shall **b** as women:	1961
	51:37 Babylon shall **b** heaps, a dwelling place for	1961
	51:41 how is Babylon **b** an astonishment among	1961
La	1: 1 is she **b** as a widow! she *that was* great	1961
	1: 1 the provinces, *how* is she **b** tributary!	1961
	1: 2 with her, they are **b** her enemies.	1961
	1: 6 her princes are **b** like harts *that* find no	1961
	1:11 O Lord, and consider; for I am **b** vile.	1961
	4: 1 How is the gold **b** dim! *how* is the most	6004
	4: 3 the daughter of my people is **b** cruel,	NIH
	4: 8 it is withered, it is **b** like a stick.	1961
Eze	22: 4 Thou art **b** guilty in thy blood that thou	NIH
	22:18 man, the house of Israel is to me **b** dross:	1961
	22:19 Because ye are all **b** dross,	1961
	26: 5 and it shall **b** a spoil to the nations.	1961
	36:35 This land that was desolate is **b** like	1961
	36:35 desolate and ruined cities *are* **b** fenced,	NIH

B

Eze 37:17 and they shall **b** in thine hand. 1961
Da 4:22 thou, O king, that art grown and **b** strong: NIH
 9:16 thy people *are* **b** a reproach to all *that are* NIH
 11:23 and shall **b** strong with a small people. NIH
Hos 12: 8 Ephraim said, Yet I am **b** rich, I have 6238
 13:15 his spring shall **b** dry, and his fountain NIH
 13:16 Samaria shall be desolate; for she hath NIH
Jnh 4: 5 till he might see what would **b** of the city. 1961
Mic 3:12 Jerusalem shall **b** heaps, and the mountain 1961
Zep 1:13 Therefore their goods shall **b** a 1961+3807.1
 2:15 is she **b** a desolation, a place for beasts 1961
Zec 4: 7 before Zerubbabel *thou shalt* **b** a plain: NIH
Mt 18: 3 ye be converted, and **b** as little children, 1096
 21:42 same is **b** the head of the corner: 1096+1519
Mk 1:17 and I will make you to **b** fishers of men. 1096
 12:10 rejected is **b** the head of the corner: 1096+1519
Lk 20:17 same is **b** the head of the corner? 1096+1519
Jn 1:12 to them gave he power to **b** the sons of 1096
Ac 4:11 which is **b** the head of the corner. 1096+1519
 7:40 of Egypt, we wot not what is **b** of him. 1096
 12:18 among the soldiers, what was **b** of Peter. 1096
Ro 3:12 the way, they are together **b** unprofitable; NIG
 3:19 and all the world may **b** guilty before God. 1096
 4:18 he might **b** the father of many nations; 1096
 6:22 and **b** servants to God, ye have your fruit NIG
 7: 4 ye also are **b** dead to the law by the body NIG
 7:13 that sin by the commandment might **b** 1096
1Co 3:18 let him **b** a fool, that he may be wise. 1096
 7:18 let him not **b uncircumcised.** Is any 1986
 8: 9 **b** a stumblingblock to them that are weak. 1096
 13: 1 I am *as* sounding brass, or a tinkling 1096
 15:20 *and* **b** the firstfruits of them that slept. 1096
2Co 5:17 past away; behold, all *things* are **b** new. 1096
 12:11 I am **b** a fool in glorying; ye have 1096
Gal 4:16 I therefore **b** your enemy, because I tell 1096
 5: 4 Christ is **b of no effect** unto you, 2673
Tit 2: 1 But speak thou *the things* which **b** sound 4241
Phm 1: 6 the communication of thy faith may **b** 1096
Heb 5:12 and are **b** such as have need of milk, 1096
Jas 2: 4 and are **b** judges of evil thoughts? 1096
 2:11 thou art **b** a transgressor of the law. 1096
Rev 11:15 The kingdoms of *this* world are **b** 1096
 18: 2 is fallen, and is **b** the habitation of devils, 1096

BECOMETH (15) [BECOME]

Ps 93: 5 holiness **b** thine house, O Lord, for ever. 4998
Pr 10: 4 He **b** poor that dealeth *with* a slack hand: NIH
 17: 7 Excellent speech **b** not a fool: much less do 5000
 17:18 **b surety** in the presence of his 6148+6161
Ecc 4:14 also *he that is* born in his kingdom **b** poor. NIH
Mt 3:15 for thus it **b** us to fulfil all righteousness. 4241
 13:22 choke the word, and he **b** unfruitful. 1096
 13:32 and **b** a tree, so that the birds of the air 1096
Mk 4:19 choke the word, and it **b** unfruitful. 1096
 4:32 and **b** greater than all herbs, and 1096
Ro 16: 2 as **b** saints, and *that* ye assist her in 516
Eph 5: 3 be once named amongst you, as **b** saints; 4241
Php 1:27 Only let your conversation be as it **b** 516
1Ti 2:10 But (which **b** women professing godliness) 4241
Tit 2: 3 *that they be* in behaviour **as b holiness,** 2412

BECORATH See BECHORATH

BED (90) [BED'S, BEDCHAMBER, BEDS, BEDSTEAD]

Ge 48: 2 strengthened himself, and sat upon the **b.** 4296
 49: 4 because thou wentest up to thy father's **b;** 4904
 49:33 he gathered up his feet into the **b,** 4296
Ex 8: 3 upon thy **b,** and into the house of thy 4296
 21:18 *his* fist, and he die not, but keepeth *his* **b:** 4904
Lev 15: 4 Every **b,** whereon he lieth that hath 4904
 15: 5 whosoever toucheth his **b** shall wash his 4904
 15:21 whosoever toucheth her **b** shall wash his 4904
 15:23 if it *be* on her **b,** or on *any* thing whereon 4904
 15:24 the **b** whereon he lieth shall be unclean. 4904
 15:26 Every **b** whereon she lieth all the days of 4904
 15:26 be unto her as the **b** of her separation: 4904
1Sa 19:13 laid *it* in the **b,** and put a pillow of goats' 4296
 19:15 saying, Bring him up to me in the **b,** that 4296
 19:16 behold *there was* an image in the **b,** 4296
 28:23 arose from the earth, and sat upon the **b.** 4296
2Sa 4: 5 who **lay on a b** at noon. 4904+7901
 4: 7 he lay on his **b** in his bedchamber, 4904
 4:11 person in his own house upon his **b?** 4904
 11: 2 that David arose from off his **b,** 4904
 11:13 at even he went out to lie on his **b** with 4904
 13: 5 Lay *thee* down on thy **b,** and make thyself 4904
1Ki 1:47 And the king bowed himself upon the **b.** 4904
 17:19 he abode, and laid him upon his own **b.** 4296
 21: 4 he laid him down upon his **b,** 4296
2Ki 1: 4 Thou shalt not come down from *that* **b** on 4296
 1: 6 thou shalt not come down from *that* **b** on 4296
 1:16 thou shalt not come down off *that* **b** on 4296
 4:10 let us set for him there a **b,** and a table, 4296
 4:21 laid him on the **b** of the man of God, 4296
 4:32 the child was dead, *and* laid upon his **b.** 4296
1Ch 5: 1 but, forasmuch as he defiled his father's **b,** 3326
2Ch 16:14 laid him in the **b** which was filled *with* 4904
 24:25 and slew him on his **b,** and he died: 4296
Est 7: 8 Haman was fallen upon the **b** whereon 4296
Job 7:13 When I say, My **b** shall comfort me, 6210
 17:13 I have made my **b** in the darkness. 3326
 33:15 upon men, in slumberings upon the **b;** 4904
 33:19 He is chastened also with pain upon his **b,** 4904
Ps 4: 4 with your own heart upon your **b,** 4904
 6: 6 all the night make I my **b** to swim; 4296

Ps 36: 4 deviseth mischief upon his **b;** he setteth 4904
 41: 3 The Lord will strengthen him upon the **b** 6210
 41: 3 thou wilt make all his **b** in his sickness. 4904
 63: 6 When I remember thee upon my **b,** 3326
 132: 3 of my house, nor go up into my **b;** 3326+6210
 139: 8 if I **make** my **b** in hell, behold, thou *art* 3331
Pr 7:16 I have deckt my **b** with coverings of 6210
 7:17 I have perfumed my **b** with myrrh, aloes, 4904
 22:27 why should he take away thy **b** from 4904
 26:14 hinges, so *doth* the slothful upon his **b.** 4296
SS 1:16 yea, pleasant: also our **b** *is* green. 6210
 3: 1 By night on my **b** I sought *him* whom my 4904
 3: 7 Behold his **b,** which *is* Solomon's; 4296
 5:13 his cheeks *are* as a **b** of spices, *as* sweet 6170
Isa 28:20 For the **b** is shorter than that *a man* can 4702
 57: 7 and high mountain hast thou set thy **b:** 4904
 57: 8 hast enlarged thy **b,** and made thee *a* 4904
 57: 8 thou lovedst their **b** where thou sawest *it.* 4904
Eze 23:17 the Babylonians came to her into the **b** of 4904
 23:41 satest upon a stately **b,** and a table 4296
 32:25 They have set her a **b** in the midst of 4904
Da 2:28 the visions of thy head upon thy **b,** 4903
 2:29 thoughts came *into thy mind* upon thy **b,** 4903
 4: 5 the thoughts upon my **b** and the visions 4903
 4:10 *were* the visions of mine head in my **b;** 4903
 4:13 saw in the visions of my head upon my **b,** 4903
 7: 1 dream and visions of his head upon his **b:** 4903
Am 3:12 that dwell in Samaria in the corner of a **b,** 4296
Mt 9: 2 him a man sick of the palsy, lying on a **b:** 2825
 9: 6 take up thy **b,** and go unto thine house. 2825
Mk 2: 4 they let down the **b** wherein the sick of 2895
 2: 9 to say, Arise, and take up thy **b,** and walk? 2895
 2:11 and take up thy **b,** and go thy way into 2895
 2:12 took up the **b,** and went forth before 2895
 4:21 to be put under a bushel, or under a **b?** 2825
 7:30 out, and *her* daughter laid upon the **b.** 2825
Lk 5:18 men brought in a **b** a man which was 2825
 8:16 it with a vessel, or putteth *it* under a **b;** 2825
 11: 7 and my children are with me in **b;** 2845
 17:34 night there shall be two *men* in one **b;** 2825
Jn 5: 8 unto him, Rise, take up thy **b,** and walk. 2895
 5: 9 and took up his **b,** and walked: 2895
 5:10 it is not lawful for thee to carry *thy* **b.** 2895
 5:11 said unto me, Take up thy **b,** and walk. 2895
 5:12 said unto thee, Take up thy **b,** and walk? 2895
Ac 9:33 which had kept his **b** eight years, and 2895
 9:34 arise, and **make** thy **b.** And he arose 4766
Heb 13: 4 *is* honourable in all, and the **b** undefiled: 2845
Rev 2:22 I will cast her into a **b,** and them that 2825

BED'S (1) [BED]

Ge 47:31 Israel bowed himself upon the **b** head. 4296

BEDAD (2)

Ge 36:35 Husham died, and Hadad the son of **B,** 911
1Ch 1:46 Husham was dead, Hadad the son of **B,** 911

BEDAN (2)

1Sa 12:11 **B,** and Jephthah, and Samuel, 917
1Ch 7:17 the sons of Ulam; **B.** These *were* the sons 917

BEDCHAMBER (6) [BED, CHAMBER]

Ex 8: 3 into thy **b,** and upon thy bed, 2315+4904
2Sa 4: 7 he lay on his bed in his **b,** 2315+4904
2Ki 6:12 words that thou speakest in thy **b.** 2315+4904
 11: 2 in the **b** from Athaliah, so that he 2315+4296
2Ch 22:11 and put him and his nurse in a **b.** 2315+4296
Ecc 10:20 and curse not the rich in thy **b:** 2315+4904

BEDEIAH (1)

Ezr 10:35 Benaiah, **B,** Chelluh, 912

BEDROOM See BEDCHAMBER

BEDS (10) [BED]

2Sa 17:28 Brought **b,** and basons, and earthen 4904
Est 1: 6 the **b** *were* of gold and silver, upon a 4296
Ps 149: 5 glory: let them sing aloud upon their **b.** 4904
SS 6: 2 to the **b** of spices, to feed in the gardens, 6170
Isa 57: 2 shall rest in their **b,** *each one* walking 4904
Hos 7:14 heart, when they howled upon their **b:** 4904
Am 6: 4 That lie upon **b** of ivory, 4296
Mic 2: 1 iniquity, and work evil upon their **b!** 4904
Mk 6:55 began to carry about in **b** those that were 2895
Ac 5:15 streets, and laid *them* on **b** and couches, 2825

BEDSTEAD (2) [BED]

Dt 3:11 behold, his **b** *was* a bedstead of iron; *is* it 6210
 3:11 behold, his bedstead *was* a **b** of iron; *is* it 6210

BEE (1) [BEES]

Isa 7:18 and for the **b** that *is* in the land of Assyria. 1682

BEELIADA (1)

1Ch 14: 7 And Elishama, and **B,** and Eliphalet. 1182

BEELZEBUB (7)

Mt 10:25 they have called the master of the house **B,** 954
 12:24 out devils, but by **B** the prince of the devils. 954
 12:27 And if I by **B** cast out devils, by whom do 954
Mk 3:22 He hath **B,** and by the prince of the devils 954
Lk 11:15 He casteth out devils through **B** the chief of 954
 11:18 ye say that I cast out devils through **B.** 954
 11:19 And if I by **B** cast out devils, by whom do 954

BEEN (331) [BE]

Ge 13: 3 unto the place where his tent had **b** at 1961
 26: 8 to pass, when he had **b** there a long time, NIH
 31: 5 The God of my father hath **b** with me. NIH
 31:38 This twenty years *have* I **b** with thee; NIH
 31:41 Thus have I **b** twenty years in thy house; NIH
 31:42 and the fear of Isaac, had **b** with me, 1961
 38:26 said, She hath **b** more righteous than I; NIH
 45: 6 For these two years *hath* the famine **b** in NIH
 46:32 for their trade hath **b** to feed cattle; 1961
 46:34 Thy servants' trade hath **b** about cattle 1961
 47: 9 evil have the days of the years of my life **b,** NIH
Ex 2:22 I have **b** a stranger in a strange land. 1961
 9:18 such as hath not **b** in Egypt since NIH
 14:12 For *it had* **b** better for us to serve NIH
 18: 3 he said, I have **b** an alien in a strange land: 1961
 21:29 it hath **b** testified to his owner, and he NIH
 34:10 such as have not **b** done in all the earth, NIH
Lev 10:19 should it have **b** accepted in the sight of NIH
 13: 7 after that he hath **b** seen of the priest for NIH
Nu 19:20 water of separation hath not **b** sprinkled NIH
Dt 2: 7 years the Lord thy God *hath* **b** with thee; NIH
 4:32 there hath **b** any such thing as this 1961
 4:32 this great thing *is,* or hath **b** heard like it? NIH
 9: 7 ye have **b** rebellious against the Lord. 1961
 9:24 You have **b** rebellious against the Lord NIH
 15:18 he hath **b** worth a double hired servant NIH
 21: 3 which hath not **b** wrought with, NIH
 31:27 ye have **b** rebellious against the Lord; 1961
Jos 7: 7 would to God we had **b** content, NIH
 9: 4 and made as if they had **b** ambassadors, NIH
 10:27 them into the cave wherein they had **b** NIH
Jdg 23: 9 no man hath **b able** to stand before you NIH
 16: 8 seven green withs which had not **b** dried, NIH
 16:17 for I *have* **b** a Nazarite unto God from my NIH
Ru 2:11 her, I had, **fully b shewed** me, 5046+5046
1Sa 1:13 therefore Eli thought she had **b** drunken. NIH
 4: 7 there hath not **b** such *a thing* heretofore. NIH
 4: 9 unto the Hebrews, as they have **b** to you: 5647
 4:17 there hath **b** also a great slaughter among 1961
 9:24 for unto *this* time *hath* I **b** kept for thee NIH
 14:29 how mine eyes have **b** enlightened, NIH
 14:30 for had there not **b** now a much greater NIH
 14:38 and see wherein this sin hath **b** *this* day. 1961
 15:21 chief of the things which should have **b** NIH
 18:19 daughter should have **b** given to David, NIH
 19: 4 his works *have* **b** to thee-ward very good: NIH
 20:13 be with thee, as he hath **b** with my father. 1961
 21: 5 Of a truth women *have* **b** kept from us NIH
 25:28 evil hath not **b** found in thee *all* thy days. NIH
 25:34 surely there had not **b** left unto Nabal by NIH
 29: 3 which hath **b** with me these days, 1961
 29: 6 thou *hast* **b** upright, and thy going out and NIH
 29: 8 long as I have **b** with thee unto this day, 1961
2Sa 1:21 *as though he* had not **b** anointed with oil. NIH
 1:26 very pleasant hast thou **b** unto me: NIH
 12: 8 if *that had* **b** too little, I would moreover NIH
 13:20 Hath Amnon thy brother **b** with thee? NIH
 13:32 **b** determined from the day that he forced NIH
 14:32 *it had* **b** good for me *to have* been there NIH
 14:32 it had been good for me *to have* **b** there NIH
 15:34 as I *have* **b** thy father's servant hitherto, NIH
1Ki 1:37 As the Lord hath **b** with my lord NIH
 2:26 thou hast **b** afflicted in all where*in* my NIH
 14: 8 *yet* thou hast not **b** as my servant David, NIH
 16:31 as if it had **b** a light thing for him to walk NIH
 17: 7 because there had **b** no rain in the land. 1961
 19:10 I have **b** very jealous for the Lord God of NIH
 19:14 I have **b** very jealous for the Lord God of NIH
2Ki 2: 3 Thy hast **b** careful for us with all this care; NIH
 20:12 for he had heard that Hezekiah had **b** sick. NIH
1Ch 17: 8 I have **b** with thee whithersoever thou NIH
 28: 3 because thou *hast* **b** a man of war, 1961
 29:25 had not **b** on any king before him in Israel. 1961
2Ch 1:12 the kings have had that *have* **b** before thee, NIH
 15: 3 for a long season Israel *hath* **b** without NIH
 23: 9 and shields, that *had* **b** king David's, NIH
Ezr 2: 1 of those which had **b** carried away, NIH
 4:18 The letter which ye sent unto us *hath* **b** NIH
 4:19 search hath **b** made, and it is found that NIH
 4:19 and sedition *have* **b** made therein. NIH
 4:20 There have **b** mighty kings also over 1934
 5:16 since that time even until now *hath it* **b** in NIH
 8:35 the children of those that had **b** carried NIH
 9: 2 and rulers hath **b** chief in this trespass. 1961
 9: 4 of the transgression of those that had **b** NIH
 9: 7 Since the days of our fathers *have we* **b** in NIH
 9: 7 **b** delivered into the hand of the kings of NIH
 9: 8 now for a little space grace hath **b** *shewed* 1961
 10: 6 of the transgression of them that had **b** NIH
 10: 8 of those that had **b** carried away. NIH
Ne 2: 1 Now I had not **b** *beforetime* sad in his NIH
 5:15 the former governors that *had* **b** before me NIH
 7: 6 of those that had **b** carried away, NIH
 13:10 had not **b** given *them:* for the Levites NIH
Est 2: 6 Who had **b** carried away from Jerusalem NIH
 2: 6 **b** carried away with Jeconiah king of Judah NIH
 2:12 after that she had **b** twelve months, NIH
 4:11 have not **b** called to come in unto the king NIH
 6: 3 dignity hath **b** done to Mordecai for this? NIH
 7: 4 if we had **b** sold for bondmen and NIH
Job 3:13 now should I have lien *still* and **b** quiet, NIH
 3:13 I should have slept: then had I **b** at rest, NIH
 3:16 Or as a hidden untimely birth I had not **b;** 1961

B

Job	10:19	I should have **b** as though I had not been; NIH
	10:19	have been as though I had not **b**; 1961+1961
	10:19	I should have **b** carried from the womb to NIH
	22: 9	the arms of the fatherless have **b** broken. NIH
	31: 9	mine heart have **b** deceived by a woman, NIH
	31:27	my heart hath **b** secretly enticed, NIH
	38:17	the gates of death **b** opened unto thee? NIH
	42:11	all *they that had* **b** *of* his acquaintance NIH
Ps	25: 6	for they *have* **b** ever of old. NIH
	27: 9	thou hast **b** my help; leave me not, 1961
	35:14	I behaved myself as though *he had* **b** my NIH
	37:25	I have **b** young, and *now* am old; yet have 1961
	42: 3	My tears have **b** my meat day and night, NIH
	50: 8	*to* have **b** continually before me. NIH
	50:18	and hast **b** partaker with adulterers. NIH
	59:16	for thou hast **b** my defence and refuge in 1961
	60: 1	hast scattered us, thou hast **b** displeased; 1961
	61: 3	For thou hast **b** a shelter for me, 1961
	63: 7	Because thou hast **b** my help, therefore 1961
	69:22	*that which should have* **b** *for their* welfare, NIH
	71: 6	thee have I **b** holden up from the womb: NIH
	73:14	For all the day long have I **b** plagued, 1961
	85: 1	thou hast **b** favourable unto thy land: NIH
	89:38	thou hast **b** wroth with thine anointed. NIH
	90: 1	thou hast **b** our dwelling place in all 1961
	94:17	Unless the Lord *had* **b** my help, my soul NIH
	115:12	The Lord hath **b** mindful of us: he will NIH
	119:54	Thy statutes have **b** my songs in the house 1961
	119:71	*It is* good for me that I have **b** afflicted; NIH
	119:92	Unless thy law *had* **b** my delights, I should NIH
	124: 1	If *it had* not **b** the Lord who was on our NIH
	124: 2	If *it had* not **b** the Lord who was on our NIH
	143: 3	darkness, as those that have **b** long dead. NIH
Pr	7:26	yea, many strong *men have* **b** slain by her. NIH
Ecc	1: 9	The thing that hath **b**, *it is* that which 1961
	1:10	it hath **b** already of old time, which was 1961
	1:16	*they* that have **b** before me in Jerusalem: 1961
	2:12	*even* that which hath **b** already done. NIH
	3:15	That which hath **b**, *is* now; and *that* 1961
	3:15	which *is* to be hath already **b**; and God 1961
	4: 3	than both they, which hath not yet **b**, 1961
	4:16	*even* of all that have **b** before them: 1961
	6:10	That which hath **b** is named already, 1961
Isa	1: 6	they have not **b** closed, neither bound up, NIH
	1: 9	we should have **b** as Sodom, *and* we 1961
	1: 9	we should have **b** like unto Gomorrah. NIH
	5: 4	What could have **b** done more to my NIH
	17:10	hast not **b** mindful of the rock of thy NIH
	23:16	the city, thou harlot that hast **b** forgotten; NIH
	25: 4	For thou hast **b** a strength to the poor, 1961
	26:17	so have we **b** in thy sight, O Lord. 1961
	26:18	have **b** with child, we have **b** in pain, NIH
	26:18	have **b** with child, we have **b** in pain, NIH
	30:24	which hath **b** winnowed with the shovel NIH
	38: 9	when he had **b** sick, and was recovered of NIH
	39: 1	for he had heard that he had **b** sick, NIH
	40:21	hath it not **b** told you from the beginning? NIH
	42:14	I have **b** still, *and* refrained myself: NIH
	43: 4	thou hast **b** honourable, and I have loved NIH
	43:22	but thou hast **b** weary of me, O Israel. NIH
	48:18	had thy peace **b** as a river, 1961
	48:19	Thy seed also had **b** as the sand, 1961
	48:19	his name should not have **b** cut off nor NIH
	49:21	I was left alone; these, where *had* they **b**? NIH
	52:15	*that* which had not **b** told them shall they NIH
	57:11	of whom hast thou **b** afraid or feared, NIH
	60:15	Whereas thou hast **b** forsaken and hated, 1961
	66: 2	all those *things* have **b**, saith the Lord: 1961
Jer	2:31	Have I **b** a wilderness unto Israel? a land 1961
	3: 2	and see where thou hast not **b** lien with. NIH
	3: 3	Therefore the showers have **b** withholden, NIH
	3: 3	and there hath **b** no latter rain; 1961
	4:17	because she hath **b** rebellious against me, NIH
	15: 9	she hath **b** ashamed and confounded: NIH
	20:17	that my mother might have **b** my grave, 1961
	22:21	This *hath* **b** thy manner from thy youth, NIH
	28: 8	The prophets that have **b** before me and 1961
	32:31	For this city hath **b** to me *as* a provocation 1961
	34:14	a Hebrew, which hath **b** sold unto thee; NIH
	42:18	my fury hath **b** poured forth upon NIH
	43: 5	whither they had **b** driven, to dwell in NIH
	44:18	have **b** consumed by the sword and by NIH
	48:11	Moab hath **b** at ease from his youth, NIH
	48:11	hath not **b** emptied from vessel to vessel, NIH
	50: 6	My people hath **b** lost sheep: 1961
	50:29	for she hath **b** proud against the Lord, NIH
	51: 5	For Israel *hath* not **b** forsaken, nor Judah NIH
	51: 7	Babylon *hath* **b** a golden cup in NIH
Eze	2: 5	yet shall know that there hath **b** a prophet 1961
	4:14	behold, my soul *hath* not **b** polluted: NIH
	10:10	if a wheel had **b** in the midst of a wheel. 1961
	11:17	of the countries where ye have **b** scattered, NIH
	16:31	not **b** as a harlot, in that *thou* scornest 1961
	20:41	the countries wherein ye have **b** scattered; NIH
	20:43	all your doings, wherein ye have **b** defiled; NIH
	22:13	at thy blood which hath **b** in the midst of NIH
	28:13	Thou hast **b** in Eden the garden of God; 1961
	29: 6	they have **b** a staff of reed to the house of NIH
	33:33	shall they know that a prophet hath **b** NIH
	34:12	where they have **b** scattered in the cloudy NIH
	38: 8	of Israel, which have **b** always waste: 1961
Da	5:15	have **b** brought in before me, that they NIH
	9:12	under the whole heaven hath not **b** done NIH
	9:12	been done as hath **b** done upon Jerusalem. NIH
Hos	5: 1	because ye have **b** a snare on Mizpah, 1961

Hos	5: 2	though I *have* **b** a rebuker of them all. NIH
Joel	1: 2	Hath this **b** in your days, or even in 1961
	2: 2	there hath not **b** ever the like, neither 1961
Ob	1:16	they shall be as though they had not **b**. 1961
Mic	5: 2	whose goings forth *have* **b** from of old, NIH
Zep	3:19	fame in every land where they have **b** put NIH
Zec	1: 2	The Lord hath **b** sore displeased with NIH
Mal	1: 9	this hath **b** by your means: will he regard NIH
	2: 9	my ways, but have **b** partial in the law. 5375
	2:14	Because the Lord hath **b** witness NIH
	3:13	Your words have **b** stout against me, NIH
Mt	1: 6	of *her that had* **b** the *wife* of Urias; NIG
	5:31	It hath **b** said, Whosoever shall put away NIG
	5:33	ye have heard that it hath **b** said by them NIG
	5:38	Ye have heard that it hath **b** said, An eye NIG
	5:43	Ye have heard that it hath **b** said, Thou NIG
	11:21	had **b** done in Tyre and Sidon they would NIG
	11:23	mighty works, which have **b** done in thee, NIG
	11:23	been done in thee, had **b** done in Sodom, NIG
	13:35	I will utter *things which have* **b** kept secret NIG
	23:30	If we had **b** in the days of our fathers, 1510
	23:30	we would not have **b** partakers with them 1510
	25:21	thou hast **b** faithful over a few *things*, 1510
	25:23	thou hast **b** faithful over a few *things*, 1510
	26: 9	For this ointment might have **b** sold for NIG
	26:24	it had **b** good for that man if he had not 1510
	26:24	good for that man if he had not **b** born. NIG
Mk	5: 4	Because that he had **b** often bound with NIG
	5: 4	the chains had **b** plucked asunder by him, NIG
	5:18	he that had **b** possessed with the devil 1510
	6:49	they supposed *it had* **b** a spirit, 1510
	8: 2	they have now **b** with me three days, 4357
	14: 5	it might have **b** sold for more than three 1410
	14: 5	and have **b** given to the poor. NIG
	14:21	were it for that man if he had never **b** NIG
	15:44	he asked him whether he had **b** any while NIG
	16:10	and told them that had **b** with him, 1096
	16:11	and had **b** seen of her, believed not. NIG
Lk	1: 4	things, wherein thou hast **b** instructed. NIG
	1:70	which have **b** since the world began: NIG
	2:44	supposing him to have **b** in the company, 1510
	4:16	to Nazareth, where he had **b** brought up: 1510
	7:10	found the servant whole that had **b** sick. NIG
	8: 2	which had **b** healed of evil spirits and 1510
	10:13	if the mighty works had **b** done in Tyre NIG
	10:13	and Sidon, which have **b** done in you, NIG
	16:11	ye have not **b** faithful in the unrighteous 1096
	16:12	And if ye have not **b** faithful in that which 1096
	19:17	because thou hast **b** faithful in a very little, 1096
	24:21	But we trusted that it had **b** he which 1510
Jn	5: 6	knew that he had **b** now a long time 2192
	9:18	that he had **b** blind, and received his sight, 1510
	11:21	Lord, if thou hadst **b** here, my brother had 1510
	11:32	unto him, Lord, if thou hadst **b** here, 1510
	11:39	he stinketh: for he hath **b** *dead* four days. 1510
	12: 1	where Lazarus was which had **b** dead, NIG
	12:38	to whom hath the arm of the Lord **b** 1510
	14: 9	Have I **b** so long time with you, and 1510
	15:27	ye have **b** with me from the beginning. 1510
Ac	1:16	this scripture must needs have **b** fulfilled, NIG
	4:13	of them, that they had **b** with Jesus. 1510
	4:16	for that indeed a notable miracle hath **b** NIG
	5:26	the people, lest they should have **b** stoned. NIG
	6:15	his face as it had **b** the face of an angel. NIG
	7:52	of whom ye have **b** now the betrayers and 1096
	9:18	there fell from his eyes **as it had b** scales: 5616
	10:11	as *it had* **b** a great sheet knit at the four NIG
	11: 5	vessel descend, as *it had* **b** a great sheet, NIG
	13: 1	which had **b** brought up with Herod NIG
	13:46	of God should first have **b** spoken to you: NIG
	14:19	out of the city, supposing he had **b** dead. NIG
	14:26	from whence they had **b** recommended to 1510
	15: 7	And when there had **b** much disputing, 1096
	16:27	supposing that the prisoners had **b** fled. NIG
	19:21	to Jerusalem, saying, After I have **b** there, 1096
	20:18	after what manner I have **b** with you at all 1096
	23:10	fearing lest Paul should have **b** pulled in NIG
	23:27	Jews, and should have **b** killed of them: NIG
	24:10	Forasmuch as I know that thou hast **b** of 1510
	24:19	Who ought to have **b** here before thee, NIG
	24:26	He hoped also that money should have **b** NIG
	25:14	And when they had **b** there many days, 1304
	26:32	This man might have **b** set at liberty, NIG
Ro	6: 5	For if we have **b** planted together in 1096
	9:29	we had **b** as Sodoma, and been made like 1096
	9:29	and **b** made like unto Gomorrha. 1096
	11:34	of the Lord? or who hath **b** his counsellor? 1096
	15:22	For which cause also I have **b** much NIG
	15:27	For if the Gentiles have **b** made partakers NIG
	16: 2	for she hath **b** a succourer of many, 1096
1Co	1:11	For it hath **b** declared unto me of you, NIG
	12:13	have **b** all made to drink into one Spirit. NIG
2Co	11: 6	we have **b** throughly made manifest NIG
	11:21	as though we had **b** weak. NIG
	11:25	a night and a day I have **b** in the deep; 4160
	12:11	for I ought to have **b** commended of you: NIG
Gal	3: 1	before whose eyes Jesus Christ hath **b** NIG
	3:21	for if there had **b** a law given which could 1510
	3:21	verily righteousness should have **b** by 1510
	3:27	For as many of you as have **b** baptized into NIG
	4:15	I bear you record, that if *it had* **b** possible, NIG
	5:13	brethren, ye have **b** called unto liberty; NIG
Eph	3: 9	beginning of the world hath **b** hid in God, NIG
	4:21	have **b** taught by him, as the truth is in NIG
Php	2:26	that ye had heard that he had **b** sick. NIG

Col	1:26	*Even* the mystery which hath **b** hid from NIG
	2: 7	stablished in the faith, as ye have **b** taught, NIG
	4:11	of God, which have **b** a comfort unto me. 1096
1Th	2: 6	when we might have **b** burdensome, 1510
2Th	2:15	hold the traditions which ye have **b** taught, NIG
1Ti	5: 9	years old, having **b** the wife of one man, 1096
2Ti	3:14	thou hast learned and hast **b** assured of, NIG
Tit	1: 9	Holding fast the faithful word as *he hath* **b** NIG
Heb	8: 7	For if that first *covenant* had **b** faultless, 1510
	10:15	no place have **b** sought for NIG
	11:15	if they had **b** mindful of that *country* from NIG
	13: 9	which have not profited them that have **b** NIG
Jas	3: 7	is tamed, and hath **b** tamed of mankind: NIG
	5: 5	in pleasure on the earth, and **b** wanton; NIG
2Pe	2:21	For it had **b** better for them not to have 1510
1Jn	2:19	if they had **b** of us, they would *no doubt* 1510
Rev	5: 6	a Lamb as *it had* **b** slain, having seven NIG
	17: 2	the inhabiters of the earth have **b** made NIG

BEER (2) [BAALATH-BEER, BEER-ELIM, BEER-LAHAI-ROI, BEER-SHEBA]
Nu	21:16	thence *they* went to **B**: that *is* the well	876
Jdg	9:21	and fled, and went to **B**, and dwelt there,	876

BEERA (1)
1Ch	7:37	Shamma, and Shilshah, and Ithran, and **B**.	878

BEERAH (1)
1Ch	5: 6	**B** his son, whom Tilgath-pilneser king of	880

BEER-ELIM (1) [BEER, ELIM]
Isa	15: 8	and the howling thereof *unto* **B**.	879

BEERI (2)
Ge	26:34	wife Judith the daughter of **B** the Hittite,	882
Hos	1: 1	son of **B**, in the days of Uzziah, Jotham,	882

BEER-LAHAI-ROI (1) [BEER, LAHAI-ROI, WELL]
Ge	16:14	Wherefore the well was called **B**; behold,	883

BEEROTH (6) [BEEROTHITE, BEEROTHITES]
Dt	10: 6	from **B** of the children of Jaakan *to* Mosera:	881
Jos	9:17	and Chephirah, and **B**, and Kirjath-jearim.	881
	18:25	Gibeon, and Ramah, and **B**,	881
2Sa	4: 2	(for **B** also was reckoned to Benjamin:	881
Ezr	2:25	Chephirah, and **B**, seven hundred and	881
Ne	7:29	Chephirah, and **B**, seven hundred forty	881

BEEROTHITE (4) [BEEROTH]
2Sa	4: 2	the sons of Rimmon a **B**, of the children of	886
	4: 5	And the sons of Rimmon the **B**, Rechab	886
	4: 9	the sons of Rimmon the **B**, and said unto	886
	23:37	Zelek the Ammonite, Naharai the **B**,	886

BEEROTHITES (1) [BEEROTH]
2Sa	4: 3	the **B** fled to Gittaim, and were sojourners	886

BEER-SHEBA (34) [BEER, SHEBA, SHEBAH]
Ge	21:14	and wandered in the wilderness of **B**.	884
	21:31	Wherefore he called that place **B**; because	884
	21:32	Thus they made a covenant at **B**: then	884
	21:33	*Abraham* planted a grove in **B**,	884
	22:19	and they rose up and went together to **B**;	884
	22:19	to Beer-sheba; and Abraham dwelt at **B**.	884
	26:23	And he went up from thence to **B**.	884
	26:33	the name of the city *is* **B** unto this day.	884
	28:10	Jacob went out from **B**, and went toward	884
	46: 1	came to **B**, and offered sacrifices unto	884
	46: 5	Jacob rose up from **B**: and the sons of Israel	884
Jos	15:28	And Hazar-shual, and **B**, and Bizjothjah,	884
	19: 2	they had in their inheritance is, or Sheba,	884
Jdg	20: 1	Dan even to **B**, with the land of Gilead,	884
1Sa	3:20	all Israel from Dan even to **B** knew that	884
	8: 2	his second, Abiah: *they were* judges in **B**.	884
2Sa	3:10	and over Judah, from Dan even to **B**.	884
	17:11	from Dan even to **B**, as the sand that *is* by	884
	24: 2	from Dan even to **B**, and number ye	884
	24: 7	went out to the south of Judah, *even to* **B**.	884
	24:15	died of the people from Dan even to **B**	884
1Ki	4:25	and under his fig tree, from Dan even to **B**,	884
	19: 3	went for his life, and came to **B**,	884
2Ki	12: 1	And his mother's name *was* Zibiah of **B**.	884
	23: 8	from Geba to **B**, and brake down the high	884
1Ch	4:28	they dwelt at **B**, and Moladah,	884
	21: 2	Go, number Israel from **B** even to Dan;	884
2Ch	19: 4	went out again through the people from **B**	884
	24: 1	His mother's name also *was* Zibiah of **B**.	884
	30: 5	throughout all Israel, from **B** even to Dan,	884
Ne	11:27	and at **B**, and *in* the villages thereof,	884
	11:30	they dwelt from **B** unto the valley of	884
Am	5: 5	nor enter *into* Gilgal, and pass not *to* **B**:	884
	8:14	Dan, liveth; and, The manner of **B** liveth;	884

BEES (3) [BEE]
Dt	1:44	as **b** do, and destroyed you in Seir,	1682
Jdg	14: 8	*there was* a swarm of **b** and honey in	1682
Ps	118:12	They compassed me about like **b**; they are	1682

BEESHTERAH (1)
Jos	21:27	and **B** with her suburbs; two cities.	1203

BEETLE (1)
Lev	11:22	the **b** after his kind, and the grasshopper	2728

BEEVES (7)
Lev	22:19	of the **b**, of the sheep, or of the goats.	1241

B

Lev 22:21 or a freewill offering in **b** or sheep, it shall 1241
Nu 31:28 the **b**, and of the asses, and of the sheep: 1241
31:30 of the **b**, of the asses, and of the flocks, 1241
31:33 And threescore and twelve thousand **b**, 1241
31:38 the **b** were thirty and six thousand; 1241
31:44 And thirty and six thousand **b**, 1241

BEFALL (9) [BEFALLEN, BEFALLETH, BEFELL]

Ge 42: 4 he said, Lest peradventure mischief **b** him. 7122
42:38 if mischief **b** him by the way in the which 7122
44:29 this also from me, and mischief **b** him, 7136
49: 1 that I may tell you that which shall **b** you 7122
Dt 31:17 and many evils and troubles shall **b** them; 4672
31:29 evil will **b** you in the latter days; because 7122
Ps 91:10 There shall no evil **b** thee, neither 413+579
Da 10:14 what shall **b** thy people in the latter days: 7136
Ac 20:22 not knowing the things that shall **b** me 4876

BEFALLEN (7) [BEFALL]

Lev 10:19 the LORD; and such things have **b** me: 7122
Nu 20:14 knowest all the travail that hath **b** us: 4672
Dt 31:21 when many evils and troubles are **b** them, 4672
Jdg 6:13 be with us, why then is all this **b** us? 4672
1Sa 20:26 for he thought, **Something** hath **b** him, 4745
Est 6:13 all his friends every thing that had **b** him. 7136
Mt 8:33 **what was b to** the possessed of the devils 3588

BEFALLETH (3) [BEFALL]

Ecc 3:19 that which the sons of men befalleth 4745
3:19 that which befalleth the sons of men **b** 4745
3:19 befalleth beasts; even one thing **b** them: 4745

BEFELL (5) [BEFALL]

Ge 42:29 and told him all that **b** unto them; 7136
Jos 2:23 Nun, and told him all things that **b** them: 4672
2Sa 19: 7 **b** thee from thy youth until now. 935+5921
Mk 5:16 they that saw it told them how it **b** to 1006
Ac 20:19 which **b** me by the lying in wait of 4819

BEFORE (1799) [BEFOREHAND, BEFORETIME]

Ge 2: 5 plant of the field **b** it was in the earth, 2962
2: 5 and every herb of the field **b** it grew: 2962
6:11 The earth also was corrupt **b** God, 6440+3807.1
6:13 The end of all flesh is come **b** me; 6440+3807.1
7: 1 thee have I seen righteous **b** me 6440+3807.1
10: 9 He was a mighty hunter **b** 6440+3807.1
10: 9 the mighty hunter **b** the LORD. 6440+3807.1
11:28 Haran died **b** his father Terah in 5921+6440
12:15 saw her, and commended her **b** Pharaoh: 413
13: 9 Is not the whole land **b** thee? 6440+3807.1
13:10 was well watered every where, **b** 6440+3807.1
13:13 and sinners **b** the LORD exceedingly. 3807.1
17: 1 walk **b** me, and be thou perfect. 6440+3807.1
17:18 O that Ishmael might live **b** thee! 6440+3807.1
18: 8 he had dressed, and set it **b** them; 6440+3807.1
18:22 Abraham stood yet **b** the LORD. 6440+3807.1
19: 4 **b** they lay down, the men of the city, 2962
19:13 cry of them is waxen great **b** the face of 854
19:27 place where he stood **b** the LORD: 854+6440
20:15 Behold, my land is **b** thee: 6440+3807.1
23: 3 Abraham stood up from **b** his dead, 6440
23:12 Abraham bowed down himself **b** 6440+3807.1
23:17 which was in Mamre, the field, 6440+3807.1
23:18 **b** all that went in at the gate of his city. 871.1
23:19 of the field of Machpelah **b** Mamre: 5921+6440
24: 7 he shall send his angel **b** thee, 6440+3807.1
24:15 **b** he had done speaking, that behold, 2962
24:33 there was set meat **b** him to eat: 6440+3807.1
24:40 The LORD, **b** whom I walk, 6440+3807.1
24:45 **b** I had done speaking in mine heart, 2962
24:51 Behold, Rebekah is **b** thee, 6440+3807.1
25: 9 the Hittite, which is **b** Mamre; 5921+6440
25:18 that is **b** Egypt, as thou goest 5921+6440
27: 4 my soul may bless thee **b** I die. 2962+871.1
27: 7 **b** the LORD before my death. 6440+3807.1
27: 7 before the LORD **b** my death. 6440+3807.1
27:10 he may bless thee **b** his death. 6440+3807.1
27:33 I have eaten of all **b** thou camest, 2962+871.1
29:26 give the younger **b** the firstborn. 6440+3807.1
30:30 it was little which thou hadst **b** 6440+3807.1
30:33 it shall come for my hire **b** thy face: 3807.1
30:38 **b** the flocks in the gutters in 5227+3807.1
30:39 the flocks conceived **b** the rods, 413
30:41 that Jacob laid the rods **b** the eyes of 3807.1
31: 2 behold, it was not toward him as **b** 8032+8543
31: 5 that it is not toward me as **b**; 8032+8543
31:32 **b** our brethren discern thou what is thine 5048
31:35 lord that I cannot rise up **b** thee; 4480+6440
31:37 set it here **b** my brethren and thy brethren, 5048
32: 3 Jacob sent messengers **b** him to 6440+3807.1
32:16 Pass over **b** me, and put a space 6440+3807.1
32:17 and whose are these **b** thee? 6440+3807.1
32:20 with the present that goeth **b** me, 6440+3807.1
32:21 So went the present over **b** him: 5921+6440
33: 3 he passed over **b** them, 6440+3807.1
33:12 and let us go, and I will go **b** thee. 5048+3807.1
33:14 pray thee, pass over **b** his servant: 6440+3807.1
33:14 as the cattle that goeth **b** 6440+3807.1
33:18 and pitched his tent **b** the city. 854+6440
34:10 the land shall be **b** you; dwell and 6440+3807.1
36:31 reigned in the land of Edom, **b** 6440+3807.1
37:18 even **b** he came near unto them, 2962+871.1
40: 9 behold, a vine was **b** me; 6440+3807.1
41:43 they cried **b** him, Bow the knee. 6440+3807.1
41:46 he stood **b** Pharaoh king of Egypt. 6440+3807.1

Ge 41:50 unto Joseph were born two sons **b** 2962+871.1
42: 6 bowed down themselves **b** him with 3807.1
42:24 and bound him **b** their eyes. 3807.1
43: 9 set him **b** thee, then let me bear 6440+3807.1
43:14 God Almighty give you mercy **b** 6440+3807.1
43:15 to Egypt, and stood **b** Joseph. 6440+3807.1
43:33 they sat **b** him, the firstborn 6440+3807.1
43:34 and sent messes unto them from **b** him: 6440
44:14 and they fell **b** him on the ground. 6440+3807.1
45: 1 Joseph could not refrain himself **b** all 3807.1
45: 5 send me **b** you to preserve life. 6440+3807.1
45: 7 God sent me **b** you to preserve 6440+3807.1
45:28 I will go and see him **b** I die. 2962+871.1
46:28 he sent Judah **b** him unto Joseph, 6440+3807.1
47: 6 The land of Egypt is **b** thee; 6440+3807.1
47: 7 his father, and set him **b** Pharaoh: 6440+3807.1
47:10 and went out from **b** Pharaoh. 6440+3807.1
47:19 Wherefore shall we die **b** thine eyes, 3807.1
48: 5 of Egypt **b** I came unto thee into Egypt, 5704
48:15 God, **b** whom my fathers 6440+3807.1
48:20 and he set Ephraim **b** Manasseh. 6440+3807.1
49: 8 thy father's children shall bow down **b** 3807.1
49:30 is **b** Mamre, in the land of Canaan, 5921+6440
50:13 of Ephron the Hittite, **b** Mamre. 5921+6440
50:16 did command **b** he died, saying, 6440+3807.1
50:18 also went and fell down **b** his face; 3807.1
Ex 4: 3 a serpent; and Moses fled from **b** it. 6440
4:21 do all those wonders **b** Pharaoh, 6440+3807.1
6:12 Moses spake **b** the LORD, saying, 6440+3807.1
6:30 Moses said **b** the LORD, Behold, 6440+3807.1
7: 9 cast it **b** Pharaoh, and it shall 6440+3807.1
7:10 Aaron cast down his rod **b** 6440+3807.1
7:10 his servants, and it became a 6440+3807.1
8:20 morning, and stand **b** Pharaoh; 6440+3807.1
8:26 of the Egyptians **b** their eyes, 3807.1
9:10 the furnace, and stood **b** Pharaoh; 6440+3807.1
9:11 the magicians could not stand **b** 6440+3807.1
9:13 stand **b** Pharaoh, and say unto 6440+3807.1
10: 1 might shew these my signs **b** him: 7130+871.1
10: 3 refuse to humble thyself **b** me? 4480+6440
10:10 look to it; for evil is **b** you. 5048+6440
10:14 very grievous were they; **b** them 6440+3807.1
11:10 did all these wonders **b** Pharaoh: 6440+3807.1
12:34 the people took their dough **b** it was 2962
13:21 the LORD went **b** them by day in 6440+3807.1
13:22 the pillar of fire by night, from **b** 6440+3807.1
14: 2 that they turn and encamp **b** 6440+3807.1
14: 2 over against Baal-zephon: **b** 5226+3807.1
14: 9 beside Pi-hahiroth, **b** Baal-zephon. 6440+3807.1
14:19 which went the camp of Israel, 6440+3807.1
14:19 pillar of the cloud went from **b** their face, 6440
16: 9 of Israel, Come near **b** the LORD: 6440+3807.1
16:33 lay it up **b** the LORD, to be kept for your 6440
16:34 so Aaron laid it up **b** 6440+3807.1
17: 5 Go on **b** the people, and take with 6440+3807.1
17: 6 I will stand **b** thee there upon 6440+3807.1
18:12 with Moses' father in law **b** God. 6440+3807.1
19: 2 and there Israel camped **b** the mount. 5048
19: 7 laid **b** their faces all these words which 3807.1
20: 3 shalt have no other gods **b** me. 5921+6440
20:20 that his fear may be **b** your faces, that ye 5921
21: 1 which thou shalt set **b** them. 6440+3807.1
22: 9 the cause of both parties shall come **b** 5704
23:15 and none shall appear **b** me empty: 6440
23:17 males shall appear **b** the Lord GOD. 413+6440
23:20 Behold, I send an Angel **b** thee, 6440+3807.1
23:23 For mine Angel shall go **b** thee, 6440+3807.1
23:27 I will send my fear **b** thee, 6440+3807.1
23:28 I will send hornets **b** thee, 6440+3807.1
23:28 and the Hittite, from **b** thee. 6440+3807.1
23:29 I will not drive them out from **b** thee in 6440
23:30 little I will drive them out from **b** thee, 6440
23:31 and thou shalt drive them out **b** thee. 6440
25:30 the table shewbread **b** me alway. 6440+3807.1
27:21 which is **b** the Testimony, Aaron and 5921
27:21 evening to morning **b** the LORD: 6440+3807.1
28:12 Aaron shall bear their names **b** 6440+3807.1
28:25 of the ephod **b** it. 413+4136+6440
28:29 **b** the LORD continually. 6440+3807.1
28:30 when he goeth in **b** the LORD: 6440+3807.1
28:30 his heart **b** the LORD continually. 6440+3807.1
28:35 unto the holy place **b** the LORD, 6440+3807.1
28:38 may be accepted **b** the LORD. 6440+3807.1
29:10 **b** the tabernacle of 6440+3807.1
29:11 thou shalt kill the bullock **b** 6440+3807.1
29:23 bread that is **b** the LORD: 6440+3807.1
29:24 for a wave offering **b** the LORD. 6440+3807.1
29:25 for a sweet savour **b** the LORD: 6440+3807.1
29:26 for a wave offering **b** the LORD: 6440+3807.1
29:42 of the congregation **b** the LORD: 6440+3807.1
30: 6 thou shalt put it **b** the vail that 6440+3807.1
30: 6 is by the ark of the Testimony, **b** 6440+3807.1
30: 8 a perpetual incense **b** the LORD 6440+3807.1
30:16 children of Israel **b** the LORD, 6440+3807.1
30:36 put of it **b** the Testimony in 6440+3807.1
32: 1 gods, which shall go **b** us; 6440+3807.1
32: 5 saw it, he built an altar **b** it; 6440+3807.1
32:23 gods, which shall go **b** us: 6440+3807.1
32:34 behold, mine Angel shall go **b** 6440+3807.1
33: 2 I will send an angel **b** thee; 6440+3807.1
33:19 I will make all my goodness pass **b** 5921+6440
33:19 the name of the LORD **b** thee; 6440+3807.1
34: 3 let the flocks nor herds feed **b** 413+4136
34: 6 the LORD passed by **b** him, 5921+6440
34:10 **b** all thy people I will do marvels, such as 5048

Ex 34:11 I drive out **b** thee the Amorite, 4480+6440
34:20 and none shall appear **b** me empty. 6440
34:23 children appear **b** the Lord GOD, 854+6440
34:24 I will cast out the nations **b** thee, 4480+6440
34:24 when thou shalt go up to appear **b** 854+6440
34:34 when Moses went in **b** the LORD 6440+3807.1
39:18 of the ephod, **b** it. 413+4136+6440
40: 5 **b** the ark of the Testimony, 6440+3807.1
40: 6 **b** the door of the tabernacle of 6440+3807.1
40:23 set the bread in order upon it **b** 6440+3807.1
40:25 he lighted the lamps **b** the LORD; 6440+3807.1
40:26 of the congregation **b** the vail: 6440+3807.1
Lev 1: 3 of the congregation **b** the LORD. 6440+3807.1
1: 5 he shall kill the bullock **b** 6440+3807.1
1:11 the altar northward **b** the LORD: 6440+3807.1
3: 1 shall offer it without blemish **b** 6440+3807.1
3: 7 then shall he offer it **b** the LORD. 6440+3807.1
3: 8 **b** the tabernacle of 6440+3807.1
3:12 then he shall offer it **b** the LORD. 6440+3807.1
3:13 **b** the tabernacle of 6440+3807.1
4: 4 of the congregation **b** the LORD, 6440+3807.1
4: 4 and kill the bullock **b** the LORD. 6440+3807.1
4: 6 of the blood seven times **b** 6440+3807.1
4: 6 seven times before the LORD, **b** 854+6440
4: 7 of sweet incense **b** the LORD, 6440+3807.1
4:14 bring him **b** the tabernacle of 6440+3807.1
4:15 head of the bullock **b** the LORD: 6440+3807.1
4:15 shall be killed **b** the LORD. 6440+3807.1
4:17 sprinkle it seven times **b** 6440+3807.1
4:17 before the LORD, even **b** the vail. 854+6440
4:18 of the altar which is **b** the LORD, 6440+3807.1
4:24 the burnt offering **b** the LORD: 6440+3807.1
6: 7 atonement for him **b** the LORD: 6440+3807.1
6:14 the sons of Aaron shall offer it **b** 6440+3807.1
6:14 shall offer it before the LORD, **b** 413+6440
6:25 offering be killed **b** the LORD: 6440+3807.1
7:30 for a wave offering **b** the LORD. 6440+3807.1
8:26 that was **b** the LORD, he took one 6440+3807.1
8:27 waved them for a wave offering **b** 6440+3807.1
8:29 for a wave offering **b** the LORD, 6440+3807.1
9: 2 and offer them **b** the LORD. 6440+3807.1
9: 4 to sacrifice **b** the LORD; 6440+3807.1
9: 5 **b** the tabernacle of the congregation: 413+6440
9: 5 drew near and stood **b** the LORD. 6440+3807.1
9:21 for a wave offering **b** the LORD; 6440+3807.1
9:24 there came a fire out from **b** 6440+3807.1
10: 1 offered strange fire **b** the LORD, 6440+3807.1
10: 2 and they died **b** the LORD. 6440+3807.1
10: 3 **b** all the people I will be glorified. 5921+6440
10: 4 carry your brethren from **b** the sanctuary 6440
10:15 to wave it for a wave offering **b** 6440+3807.1
10:17 atonement for them **b** the LORD? 6440+3807.1
10:19 their burnt offering **b** the LORD, 6440+3807.1
12: 7 Who shall offer it **b** the LORD, 6440+3807.1
14:11 those things, **b** the LORD, 6440+3807.1
14:12 wave them for a wave offering **b** 6440+3807.1
14:16 finger seven times **b** the LORD. 6440+3807.1
14:18 atonement for him **b** the LORD. 6440+3807.1
14:23 tabernacle of the congregation, **b** 6440+3807.1
14:24 for a wave offering **b** the LORD: 6440+3807.1
14:27 hand seven times **b** the LORD: 6440+3807.1
14:29 to make an atonement for him **b** 6440+3807.1
14:31 is to be cleansed **b** the LORD. 6440+3807.1
14:36 that they empty the house, **b** 2962+871.1
15:14 come **b** the LORD unto the door 6440+3807.1
15:15 for him **b** the LORD for his issue. 6440+3807.1
15:30 **b** the LORD for the issue of her 6440+3807.1
16: 1 offered **b** the LORD, and died; 6440+3807.1
16: 2 within the vail **b** the mercy seat, 413+6440
16: 7 present them **b** the LORD at 6440+3807.1
16:10 shall be presented alive **b** 6440+3807.1
16:12 off the altar **b** the LORD, 4480+6440+3807.1
16:13 upon the fire **b** the LORD, 6440+3807.1
16:14 the mercy seat shall he sprinkle 6440+3807.1
16:15 mercy seat, and **b** the mercy seat: 6440+3807.1
16:18 unto the altar that is **b** the LORD, 6440+3807.1
16:30 from all your sins **b** the LORD. 6440+3807.1
17: 4 **b** the tabernacle of the LORD; 6440+3807.1
18:23 neither shall any woman stand **b** 6440+3807.1
18:24 are defiled which I cast out **b** you: 4480+6440
18:27 were **b** you, and the land is 6440+3807.1
18:28 out the nations that were **b** you. 6440+3807.1
18:30 which were committed **b** you, 6440+3807.1
19:14 nor put a stumblingblock **b** 6440+3807.1
19:22 for him for his sin which he 6440+3807.1
19:32 shalt rise up **b** the hoary head, 4480+6440
20:23 the nation, which I cast out **b** you: 4480+6440
23:11 he shall wave the sheaf **b** 6440+3807.1
23:20 for a wave offering **b** the LORD. 6440+3807.1
23:28 to make an atonement for you **b** 6440+3807.1
23:40 ye shall rejoice **b** the LORD your 6440+3807.1
24: 3 morning **b** the LORD continually: 6440+3807.1
24: 4 **b** the LORD continually. 6440+3807.1
24: 6 upon the pure table **b** the LORD. 6440+3807.1
24: 8 in order **b** the LORD continually, 6440+3807.1
26: 7 they shall fall **b** you by the sword. 6440+3807.1
26: 8 shall fall **b** you by the sword. 6440+3807.1
26:17 ye shall be slain **b** your enemies; 6440+3807.1
26:37 as a sword, when none pursueth: 4480+6440
26:37 ye shall have no power to stand **b** 6440+3807.1
27: 8 he shall present himself **b** 6440+3807.1
27:11 present the beast **b** the priest: 6440+3807.1
Nu 3: 4 Nadab and Abihu died **b** 6440+3807.1
3: 4 when they offered strange fire **b** 6440+3807.1
3: 6 present them **b** Aaron the priest, 6440+3807.1

B

Nu
3: 7 **b** the tabernacle of — 6440+3807.1
3:38 that encamp **b** the tabernacle — 6440+3807.1
3:38 toward the east, *even* **b** — 6440+3807.1
5:16 her near, and set her **b** the LORD: — 6440+3807.1
5:18 the priest shall set the woman **b** — 6440+3807.1
5:25 shall wave the offering **b** — 6440+3807.1
5:30 shall set the woman **b** the LORD, — 6440+3807.1
6:12 the days that were **b** shall be lost, because — 7223
6:16 the priest shall bring *them* **b** — 6440+3807.1
6:20 *for* a wave offering **b** the LORD: — 6440+3807.1
7: 3 they brought their offering **b** — 6440+3807.1
7: 3 brought them **b** the tabernacle. — 6440+3807.1
7:10 offered their offering **b** the altar. — 6440+3807.1
8: 9 thou shalt bring the Levites **b** — 6440+3807.1
8:10 thou shalt bring the Levites **b** — 6440+3807.1
8:11 Aaron shall offer the Levites **b** — 6440+3807.1
8:13 shalt set the Levites **b** Aaron, — 6440+3807.1
8:13 **b** his sons, and offer them *for* an — 6440+3807.1
8:21 them *as* an offering **b** the LORD; — 6440+3807.1
8:22 of the congregation **b** Aaron, — 6440+3807.1
8:22 before Aaron, and **b** his sons: — 6440+3807.1
9: 6 they came **b** Moses and before — 6440+3807.1
9: 6 and **b** Aaron on that day: — 6440+3807.1
10: 9 ye shall be remembered **b** — 6440+3807.1
10:10 you for a memorial **b** your God: — 6440+3807.1
10:33 **b** them *in* the three days' journey, — 6440+3807.1
10:35 let them that hate thee flee **b** thee. — 4480+6440
11: 6 at all, beside this manna, **b** our eyes. — NIH
11:20 have wept **b** him, saying, Why — 6440+3807.1
13:22 built seven years **b** Zoan in Egypt.) — 6440+3807.1
13:30 Caleb stilled the people **b** Moses, and said, — 413
14: 5 Aaron fell on their faces **b** all — 6440+3807.1
14:10 the congregation **b** all the children of Israel. — 413
14:14 thou goest **b** them, by day time — 6440+3807.1
14:37 died by the plague **b** the LORD. — 6440+3807.1
14:42 be not smitten **b** your enemies. — 6440+3807.1
14:43 the Canaanites *are* there **b** you, — 6440+3807.1
15:15 shall the stranger be **b** the LORD, — 6440+3807.1
15:25 their sin offering **b** the LORD, — 6440+3807.1
15:28 when he sinneth by ignorance **b** — 6440+3807.1
16: 2 they rose up **b** Moses, with — 6440+3807.1
16: 7 put incense in them **b** the LORD — 6440+3807.1
16: 9 to stand **b** the congregation to — 6440+3807.1
16:16 and all thy company **b** the LORD, — 6440+3807.1
16:17 bring ye **b** the LORD every man — 6440+3807.1
16:38 for they offered them **b** — 6440+3807.1
16:40 near to offer incense **b** the LORD; — 6440+3807.1
16:43 Aaron came **b** the tabernacle of — 413+6440
17: 4 congregation the Testimony, — 413+6440
17: 7 Moses laid up the rods **b** — 6440+3807.1
17: 9 **b** the LORD unto all the children — 6440+3807.1
17:10 rod again **b** the Testimony, — 6440+3807.1
18: 2 sons with thee *shall minister* **b** — 6440+3807.1
18:19 it *is* a covenant of salt for ever **b** — 6440+3807.1
19: 3 and *one* shall slay her **b** his face: — 3807.1
19: 4 sprinkle of her blood directly **b** — 6440
20: 3 our brethren died **b** the LORD! — 6440+3807.1
20: 9 Moses took the rod from **b** — 3807.1
20:10 congregation together **b** the rock, — 413+6440
21:11 in the wilderness which *is* **b** Moab, — 5921+6440
22:32 because *thy* way is perverse **b** me: — 5048+3807.1
25: 4 hang them up **b** the LORD against — 3807.1
25: 6 who *were* weeping **b** the door of — NIH
26:61 when they offered strange fire **b** — 6440+3807.1
27: 2 they stood **b** Moses, and before — 6440+3807.1
27: 2 **b** Eleazar the priest, and before — 6440+3807.1
27: 2 **b** the princes and all — 6440+3807.1
27: 5 Moses brought their cause **b** — 6440+3807.1
27:14 to sanctify me at the water **b** their eyes: — 3807.1
27:17 Which may go out **b** them, — 6440+3807.1
27:17 which may go in **b** them, — 6440+3807.1
27:19 set him **b** Eleazar the priest, — 6440+3807.1
27:19 and **b** all the congregation; — 6440+3807.1
27:21 shall stand **b** Eleazar the priest, — 6440+3807.1
27:21 judgment of Urim **b** the LORD: — 6440+3807.1
27:22 set him **b** Eleazar the priest, — 6440+3807.1
27:22 and **b** all the congregation: — 6440+3807.1
31:50 for our souls **b** the LORD. — 6440+3807.1
31:54 children of Israel **b** the LORD. — 6440+3807.1
32: 4 the congregation of Israel, — 6440+3807.1
32:17 armed **b** the children of Israel, — 6440+3807.1
32:20 go armed **b** the LORD to war, — 6440+3807.1
32:21 armed over Jordan **b** the LORD, — 6440+3807.1
32:21 he hath driven out his enemies from **b** — 6440
32:22 the land be subdued **b** the LORD: — 6440+3807.1
32:22 be guiltless **b** the LORD, — 4480
32:22 guiltless before the LORD, and **b** Israel; — 4480
32:22 land shall be your possession **b** — 6440+3807.1
32:27 every man armed for war, **b** — 6440+3807.1
32:29 every man armed to battle, **b** — 6440+3807.1
32:29 the land shall be subdued **b** you; — 6440+3807.1
32:32 We will pass over armed **b** — 6440+3807.1
33: 7 which *is* **b** Baal-zephon: — 5921+6440
33: 7 and they pitched **b** Migdol, — 6440+3807.1
33: 8 they departed from **b** *Pi*hahiroth, — 6440
33:47 in the mountains of Abarim, **b** — 6440+3807.1
33:52 all the inhabitants of the land **b** you, — 6440
33:55 out the inhabitants of the land from **b** — 6440
35:12 until he stand **b** the congregation — 6440+3807.1
36: 1 **b** Moses, and before the princes, — 6440+3807.1
36: 1 before Moses, and **b** the princes, — 6440+3807.1

Dt
1: 8 Behold, I have set the land **b** you: — 6440+3807.1
1:21 thy God hath set the land **b** thee: — 6440+3807.1
1:22 We will send men **b** us, — 6440+3807.1
1:30 LORD your God which goeth **b** — 6440+3807.1
1:30 that he did for you in Egypt **b** your eyes; — 3807.1
1:33 Who went in the way **b** you, — 6440+3807.1
1:38 which standeth **b** thee, he shall go in — 6440
1:42 ye be smitten **b** your enemies. — 6440+3807.1
1:45 ye returned and wept **b** — 6440+3807.1
2:12 when they had destroyed them from **b** — 6440
2:21 The LORD destroyed them **b** them; — 4480+6440
2:22 when he destroyed the Horims from **b** — 6440
2:31 to give Sihon and his land **b** thee: — 6440+3807.1
2:33 our God delivered him **b** us; — 6440+3807.1
3:18 ye shall pass over armed **b** your — 6440+3807.1
3:28 for he shall go over **b** this people, — 6440+3807.1
4: 8 which I set **b** you *this* day? — 6440+3807.1
4:10 **b** the LORD thy God in Horeb, — 6440+3807.1
4:32 that are past, which were **b** thee, — 6440+3807.1
4:34 God did for you in Egypt **b** your eyes? — 3807.1
4:38 To drive out nations from **b** thee greater — 4480
4:44 this *is* the law which Moses set **b** — 6440+3807.1
5: 7 Thou shalt have none other gods **b** — 5921+6440
6:19 To cast out all thine enemies from **b** thee, — 6440
6:22 and upon all his household, **b** our eyes: — 3807.1
6:25 **b** the LORD our God. — 6440+3807.1
7: 1 hath cast out many nations **b** thee, — 4480+6440
7: 2 thy God shall deliver them **b** thee; — 6440+3807.1
7:22 put out those nations **b** thee by — 4480+6440
7:24 shall no man *be able to* stand **b** — 6440+871.1
8:20 which the LORD destroyeth **b** your face, — 4480
9: 2 can stand **b** the children of Anak! — 6440+3807.1
9: 3 he which goeth over **b** thee; — 6440
9: 3 he which shall bring them down **b** thy face: — 3807.1
9: 4 hath cast them out from **b** thee, — 6440+3807.1
9: 4 LORD drive them out from **b** thee. — 6440
9: 5 thy God doth drive them out from **b** thee, — 6440
9:17 two hands, and brake them **b** your eyes. — 3807.1
9:18 I fell down **b** the LORD, as at — 6440+3807.1
9:25 Thus I fell down **b** the LORD — 6440+3807.1
10: 8 to stand **b** the LORD to minister — 6440+3807.1
10:11 Arise, take thy journey **b** — 6440+3807.1
11:23 out all these nations from **b** you, — 6440+3807.1
11:25 no man *be able to* stand **b** — 6440+871.1
11:26 **b** you *this* day a blessing and — 6440+3807.1
11:32 which I set **b** you *this* day. — 6440+3807.1
12: 7 there ye shall eat **b** the LORD — 6440+3807.1
12:12 ye shall rejoice **b** the LORD your — 6440+3807.1
12:18 thou must eat them **b** the LORD — 6440+3807.1
12:18 thou shalt rejoice **b** the LORD thy — 6440+3807.1
12:29 God shall cut off the nations from **b** thee, — 6440
12:30 after that they be destroyed from **b** thee; — 6440
14:23 thou shalt eat **b** the LORD thy — 6440+3807.1
14:26 thou shalt eat **b** the LORD thy — 6440+3807.1
15:20 Thou shalt eat it **b** the LORD thy — 6440+3807.1
16:11 thou shalt rejoice **b** the LORD thy — 6440+3807.1
16:16 **b** the LORD thy God in the place — 854+6440
16:16 shall not appear **b** the LORD empty: — 854+6440
17:12 to minister there **b** the LORD thy God, — NIH
17:18 *which is* **b** the priests the Levites: — 6440+3807.1
18: 7 which stand there **b** the LORD. — 6440+3807.1
18:12 thy God doth drive them out from **b** thee. — 6440
19:17 *is,* shall stand **b** the LORD, — 6440+3807.1
19:17 *is,* shall stand before the LORD, **b** — 6440+3807.1
21:16 firstborn **b** the son of the hated, — 5921+6440
22: 6 a bird's nest chance to be **b** thee — 6440+3807.1
22:17 they shall spread the cloth **b** — 6440+3807.1
23:14 to give up thine enemies **b** thee; — 6440+3807.1
24: 4 that *is* abomination **b** the LORD: — 6440+3807.1
24:13 unto thee **b** the LORD thy God. — 6440+3807.1
25: 2 to be beaten **b** his face, according to his — 3807.1
26: 4 set it down **b** the altar of — 6440+3807.1
26: 5 and say **b** the LORD thy God, — 6440+3807.1
26:10 thou shalt set it **b** the LORD thy — 6440+3807.1
26:10 worship **b** the LORD thy God: — 6440+3807.1
26:13 thou shalt say **b** the LORD thy — 6440+3807.1
27: 7 and rejoice **b** the LORD thy God. — 6440+3807.1
28: 7 up against thee *to be* smitten **b** thy face: — 3807.1
28: 7 and flee **b** thee seven ways. — 6440+3807.1
28:25 to be smitten **b** thine enemies: — 6440+3807.1
28:25 and flee seven ways **b** them: — 6440+3807.1
28:31 Thine ox *shall be* slain **b** thine eyes, — 3807.1
28:31 be violently taken away from **b** thy face, — 3807.1
28:66 thy life shall hang in doubt **b** thee; — 4480+5048
29: 2 Ye have seen all that the LORD did **b** — 3807.1
29:10 Ye stand *this* day all of you **b** — 6440+3807.1
29:15 us *this* day **b** the LORD our God, — 6440+3807.1
30: 1 which I have set **b** thee, — 6440+3807.1
30:15 I have set **b** thee *this* day life and — 6440+3807.1
30:19 I have set **b** you life and death, — 6440+3807.1
31: 3 he will go over **b** thee, *and* he — 6440+3807.1
31: 3 destroy these nations from **b** thee, — 6440+3807.1
31: 3 Joshua, he shall go over **b** thee, — 6440+3807.1
31: 5 the LORD shall give them up **b** your — 3807.1
31: 8 he *it is* that doth go **b** thee; — 6440+3807.1
31:11 When all Israel is come to appear **b** — 854+6440
31:11 thou shalt read this law **b** all Israel in — 5048
31:21 *even* now, **b** I have brought them — 2962+871.1
32:52 Yet thou shalt see the land **b** *thee;* — 4480+5048
33: 1 the children of Israel **b** his death. — 6440+3807.1
33:10 they shall put incense **b** thee, — 639+871.1
33:27 he shall thrust out the enemy from **b** thee; — 6440

Jos
1: 5 stand **b** thee all the days of thy — 6440+3807.1
1:14 ye shall pass **b** your brethren — 6440+3807.1
2: 8 **b** they were laid down, she came up unto — 2962
3: 1 and lodged **b** they passed over. — 2962
3: 6 and pass over **b** the people. — 6440+3807.1
3: 6 and went **b** the people. — 6440+3807.1
3:10 *that* he will without fail drive out from **b** — 6440
3:11 passeth over **b** you into Jordan. — 6440+3807.1
3:14 ark *of* the covenant **b** the people; — 6440+3807.1
4: 5 Pass over **b** the ark of the LORD — 6440+3807.1
4: 7 **b** the ark of the covenant of — 4480+6440
4:12 armed **b** the children of Israel, — 6440+3807.1
4:13 over **b** the LORD unto battle, — 6440+3807.1
4:18 over all his banks, as *they did* **b**. — 8032+8543
4:23 dried up the waters of Jordan from **b** you, — 6440
4:23 which he dried up from **b** us, until we — 6440
5: 1 of Jordan from **b** the children of Israel, — 6440
6: 4 seven priests shall bear **b** the ark — 6440+3807.1
6: 5 shall ascend up every man **straight b** him. — 5048
6: 6 horns **b** the ark of the LORD. — 6440+3807.1
6: 7 let him that is armed pass on **b** — 6440+3807.1
6: 8 horns passed on **b** the LORD, — 6440+3807.1
6: 9 the armed men went **b** the priests — 6440+3807.1
6:13 **b** the ark of the LORD went on — 6440+3807.1
6:13 the armed men went **b** them; but — 6440+3807.1
6:20 every man **straight b** him, and they took — 5048
6:26 saying, Cursed *be* the man **b** — 6440+3807.1
7: 4 and they fled **b** the men of Ai. — 6440+3807.1
7: 5 for they chased them *from* **b** — 6440+3807.1
7: 6 fell to the earth upon his face **b** — 6440+3807.1
7: 8 when Israel turneth *their* backs **b** — 6440+3807.1
7:12 could not stand **b** their enemies, — 6440+3807.1
7:12 *but* turned *their* backs **b** their — 6440+3807.1
7:13 thou canst not stand **b** thine — 6440+3807.1
7:23 and laid them out **b** the LORD. — 6440+3807.1
8: 5 the first, that we will flee **b** them, — 6440+3807.1
8: 6 *They* flee **b** us, as at the first: — 6440+3807.1
8: 6 therefore we will flee **b** them. — 6440+3807.1
8:10 elders of Israel, **b** the people *to* Ai. — 6440+3807.1
8:11 came the city, and pitched on the north — 5048
8:14 at a time appointed, **b** the plain; — 6440+3807.1
8:15 *as if they* were beaten **b** them, — 6440+3807.1
8:33 and on that side **b** the priests the Levites, — 5048
8:33 LORD had commanded **b**, — 7223+871.1+1886.1
8:35 the name of Joshua read not **b** — 5048
9:24 all the inhabitants of the land from **b** you, — 6440
10: 5 encamped **b** Gibeon, and made war against — 5921
10: 8 not a man of them stand **b** thee, — 6440+871.1
10:10 the LORD discomfited them **b** — 6440+3807.1
10:11 as they fled from **b** Israel, *and* were in — 6440
10:12 Amorites **b** the children of Israel, — 6440+3807.1
10:14 there was no day like that **b** it or — 6440+3807.1
11: 6 I deliver them up all slain **b** Israel: — 6440+3807.1
13: 3 From Sihor, which *is* **b** Egypt, — 5921+6440
13: 6 them will I drive out from **b** the children — 6440
13:25 unto Aroer that *is* **b** Rabbah; — 5921+6440
14:15 the name of Hebron *was* — 6440+3807.1
15: 7 that *is* **b** the going up to Adummim, — 5227
15: 8 **b** the valley of Hinnom westward, — 5921+6440
15:15 of Debir *was* Kirjath-sepher. — 6440+3807.1
17: 4 they came near **b** Eleazar — 6440+3807.1
17: 4 to Joshua the son of Nun, — 6440+3807.1
17: 4 of Nun, and the princes, saying, — 6440+3807.1
17: 7 that *lieth* **b** Shechem; — 5921+6440
18: 1 the land was subdued **b** them. — 6440+3807.1
18: 6 that I may cast lots for you here **b** — 6440+3807.1
18: 8 that I may here cast lots for you **b** — 6440+3807.1
18:10 for them in Shiloh **b** the LORD: — 6440+3807.1
18:14 from the hill that *lieth* **b** Beth-horon — 5921+6440
18:16 the valley of the son of Hinnom, — 5921+6440
19:11 to the river that *is* **b** Jokneam; — 5921+6440
19:46 and Rakkon, with the border **b** Japho. — 4136
19:51 by lot in Shiloh **b** the LORD, — 6440+3807.1
20: 6 until he stand **b** the congregation — 6440+3807.1
20: 9 until he stood **b** the congregation. — 6440+3807.1
21:44 a man of all their enemies **b** them; — 6440+871.1
22:27 **b** him with our burnt offerings, — 6440+3807.1
22:29 our God that *is* **b** his tabernacle. — 6440+3807.1
23: 5 he shall expel them from **b** you, — 6440
23: 9 For the LORD hath driven out from **b** you — 6440
23: 9 no man hath *been able to* stand **b** — 6440+871.1
23:13 *any of* these nations from **b** you; — 6440
24: 1 they presented themselves **b** God. — 6440+3807.1
24: 8 and I destroyed them from **b** you. — 6440
24:12 I sent the hornet **b** you, — 6440+3807.1
24:12 which drave them out from **b** you, — 6440
24:18 the LORD drave out from **b** us all — 6440

Jdg
1:10 (now the name of Hebron *was* — 6440+3807.1
1:11 the name of Debir **b** *was* Kirjath-sepher. — 6440
1:23 the name of the city **b** *was* Luz.) — 6440+3807.1
2: 3 I will not drive them out from **b** you; — 6440
2:14 any longer stand **b** their enemies. — 6440+3807.1
2:21 **b** them of the nations which Joshua left — 6440
3: 2 such as **b** knew nothing thereof: — 6440+3807.1
3:27 from the mount, and he **b** them; — 6440+3807.1
4:14 is not the LORD gone out **b** thee? — 6440+3807.1
4:15 the edge of the sword **b** Barak; — 6440+3807.1
4:23 of Canaan **b** the children of Israel. — 6440+3807.1
5: 5 The mountains melted from **b** the LORD, — 6440
5: 5 *even* that Sinai from **b** the LORD God of — 6440
6: 9 drave them out from **b** you, and gave you — 6440
6:18 my present, and set *it* **b** thee. — 6440+3807.1
7:24 them the waters unto Beth-barah and — 3807.1
8:13 returned from battle **b** the sun was up, — 4480
8:28 Thus was Midian subdued **b** — 6440+3807.1
9:39 Gaal went out **b** the men of — 6440+3807.1
9:40 he fled **b** him, and many were — 4480+6440
11: 9 the LORD deliver them **b** me, — 6440+3807.1
11:11 Jephthah uttered all his words **b** — 6440+3807.1
11:23 the Amorites from **b** his people Israel, — 6440
11:24 LORD our God shall drive out from **b** us, — 6440

B

Jdg 11:33	subdued **b** the children of Israel. 4480+6440
12: 5	the passages of Jordan **b** the Ephraimites: 3807.1
14:16	Samson's wife wept **b** him, and said, 5921
14:17	she wept **b** him the seven days, while 5921
14:18	seventh day **b** the sun went down, 2962+871.1
16: 3	to the top of a hill that is **b** Hebron. 5921+6440
16:20	I will go out as at other times **b**, NIH
18: 6	**b** the LORD is your way wherein ye go. 5227
18:21	cattle and the carriage **b** them. 6440+3807.1
20:23	and wept **b** the LORD until even, 6440+3807.1
20:26	sat there **b** the LORD, 6440+3807.1
20:26	and peace offerings **b** the LORD. 6440+3807.1
20:28	Aaron, stood **b** it in those days,) 6440+3807.1
20:32	smitten down **b** us, as at the first. 6440+3807.1
20:35	the LORD smote Benjamin **b** 6440+3807.1
20:39	they are smitten down **b** us, 6440+3807.1
20:42	they turned their backs **b** 6440+3807.1
21: 2	abode there till even **b** God, 6440+3807.1
Ru 3:14	she rose up **b** one could know 2962+871.1
4: 4	Buy it **b** the inhabitants, and before 5048
4: 4	and **b** the elders of my people. 5048
1Sa 1:12	continued praying **b** the LORD, 6440+3807.1
1:15	poured out my soul **b** the LORD. 6440+3807.1
1:19	worshipped **b** the LORD, 6440+3807.1
1:22	that he may appear **b** the LORD, 854+6440
2:11	unto the LORD **b** Eli the priest. 854+6440
2:15	**b** they burnt the fat, the priest's 2962+871.1
2:17	men was very great **b** the LORD: 854+6440
2:18	Samuel ministered **b** the LORD, 854+6440
2:21	And the child Samuel grew **b** the LORD. 5973
2:28	to wear an ephod **b** me? 6440+3807.1
2:30	should walk **b** me for ever: 6440+3807.1
2:35	walk **b** mine anointed for ever. 6440+3807.1
3: 1	ministered unto the LORD **b** Eli. 6440+3807.1
4: 2	was smitten **b** the Philistines: 6440+3807.1
4: 2	us to day **b** the Philistines? 6440+3807.1
4:17	Israel is fled **b** the Philistines, 6440+3807.1
5: 3	the earth **b** the ark of the LORD. 6440+3807.1
5: 4	ground **b** the ark of the LORD: 6440+3807.1
6:20	Who is able to stand **b** this holy 6440+3807.1
7: 6	poured it out **b** the LORD, 6440+3807.1
7:10	and they were smitten **b** Israel. 6440+3807.1
8:11	and some shall run **b** his chariots. 6440+3807.1
8:20	go out **b** us, and fight our battles. 6440+3807.1
9:12	said, He is; behold, he is **b** you: 6440+3807.1
9:13	shall straightway find him, **b** he 2962+871.1
9:15	in his ear a day **b** Saul came, 6440+3807.1
9:19	go up **b** me unto the high place; 6440+3807.1
9:24	was upon it, and set it **b** Saul. 6440+3807.1
9:24	is left; set it **b** thee, and eat: 6440+3807.1
9:27	Bid the servant pass on **b** us, 6440+3807.1
10: 5	and a pipe, and a harp, **b** them; 6440+3807.1
10: 8	shalt go down **b** me to Gilgal; 6440+3807.1
10:19	present yourselves **b** the LORD 6440+3807.1
10:25	and laid it up **b** the LORD. 6440+3807.1
11:15	there they made Saul king **b** 6440+3807.1
11:15	of peace offerings **b** the LORD; 6440+3807.1
12: 2	now behold, the king walketh **b** 6440+3807.1
12: 2	I have walked **b** you from my 6440+3807.1
12: 3	here I am: witness against me **b** 5048
12: 3	me before the LORD, and **b** his anointed: 5048
12: 7	that I may reason with you **b** 6440+3807.1
12:16	which the LORD will do **b** your eyes. 3807.1
14:13	they fell **b** Jonathan; 6440+3807.1
14:21	the Philistines **b that time**, 865+8032+3509.1
15:30	**b** the elders of my people, 5048
15:30	elders of my people, and **b** Israel, 5048
15:33	Samuel hewed Agag in pieces **b** 6440+3807.1
16: 6	Surely the LORD's anointed is **b** him. 5048
16: 8	and made him pass **b** Samuel. 6440+3807.1
16:10	of his sons to pass **b** Samuel. 6440+3807.1
16:16	thy servants which are **b** thee, 6440+3807.1
16:21	David came to Saul, and stood **b** him. 6440+3807.1
16:22	David, I pray thee, stand **b** me; 6440+3807.1
17: 7	one bearing a shield went **b** him. 6440+3807.1
17:31	they rehearsed them **b** Saul: 6440+3807.1
17:41	that bare the shield went **b** him. 6440+3807.1
17:57	brought him **b** Saul with the head 6440+3807.1
18:13	out and came in **b** the people. 6440+3807.1
18:16	he went out and came in **b** them. 6440+3807.1
19:24	prophesied **b** Samuel in like 6440+3807.1
20: 1	came and said **b** Jonathan, 6440+3807.1
20: 1	what is my sin **b** thy father, that 6440+3807.1
21: 6	that was taken from **b** the LORD, 6440+3807.1
21: 7	that day, detained **b** the LORD; 6440+3807.1
21:13	he changed his behaviour **b** them, 5869+871.1
22: 4	he brought them **b** the king of Moab: 854+6440
23:18	they two made a covenant **b** 6440+3807.1
23:24	they arose, and went to Ziph **b** 6440+3807.1
25:19	unto her servants, Go on **b** me; 6440+3807.1
25:23	fell **b** David on her face, 639+3807.1
26: 1	of Hachilah, which is **b** Jeshimon? 5921+6440
26: 3	which is **b** Jeshimon, by the way. 5921+6440
26:19	cursed be they **b** the LORD; 6440+3807.1
26:20	let not my blood fall to the earth **b** 4480+5048
28:22	me set a morsel of bread **b** thee; 6440+3807.1
28:25	she brought it **b** Saul, and before 6440+3807.1
28:25	it before Saul, and **b** his servants; 6440+3807.1
30:20	which they drave **b** those other 6440+3807.1
31: 1	the men of Israel fled from **b** 6440
2Sa 2:14	men now arise, and play **b** us. 6440+3807.1
2:17	of Israel, **b** the servants of David. 6440+3807.1
2:24	that lieth by Giah by the way of 5921+6440
3:28	my kingdom are guiltless **b** 4480+5973
3:31	and mourn **b** Abner. 6440+3807.1

2Sa 3:34	as a man falleth **b** wicked men, 6440+3807.1
5: 3	them in Hebron **b** the LORD: 6440+3807.1
5:20	forth upon mine enemies **b** me, 6440+3807.1
5:24	for then shall the LORD go out **b** 6440+3807.1
6: 4	of God: and Ahio went **b** the ark. 6440+3807.1
6: 5	all the house of Israel played **b** 6440+3807.1
6:14	David danced **b** the LORD with 6440+3807.1
6:16	and dancing **b** the LORD; 6440+3807.1
6:17	and peace offerings **b** the LORD. 6440+3807.1
6:21	unto Michal, It was **b** the LORD, 6440+3807.1
6:21	chose me **b** thy father, and before all 4480
6:21	me before thy father, and **b** all his house, 4480
6:21	therefore will I play **b** the LORD: 6440+3807.1
7:15	whom I put away **b** thee. 6440+3807.1
7:16	shall be stablished for ever **b** thee: 6440+3807.1
7:18	sat **b** the LORD, and he said, 6440+3807.1
7:23	terrible, for thy land, **b** thy people, 4480+6440
7:26	David be established **b** thee. 6440+3807.1
7:29	it may continue for ever **b** thee: 6440+3807.1
10: 6	of Ammon saw that they stank **b** David, 871.1
10: 9	of the battle was against him **b** 4480+6440
10:13	the Syrians: and they fled **b** him. 4480+6440
10:14	then fled they also **b** Abishai, 4480+6440
10:15	that they were smitten **b** Israel, 6440+3807.1
10:16	host of Hadarezer went **b** them. 6440+3807.1
10:18	the Syrians fled **b** Israel; 4480+6440
10:19	that they were smitten **b** Israel, 6440+3807.1
11:13	he did eat and drink **b** him; 6440+3807.1
12:11	I will take thy wives **b** thine eyes, 3807.1
12:12	I will do this thing **b** all Israel, 5048
12:12	this thing before all Israel, and **b** the sun. 5048
12:20	they set bread **b** him, and he did eat. 3807.1
13: 9	and poured them out **b** him; 6440+3807.1
14:33	his face to the ground **b** the king: 6440+3807.1
15: 1	and fifty men to run **b** him. 6440+3807.1
15:18	from Gath, passed on **b** the king. 5921+6440
18: 7	slain **b** the servants of David, 6440+3807.1
18:28	fell down to the earth upon his face **b** 3807.1
19: 8	all the people came **b** the king: 6440+3807.1
19:13	thou be not captain of the host **b** 6440+3807.1
19:17	went over Jordan **b** the king. 6440+3807.1
19:18	the son of Gera fell down **b** 6440+3807.1
19:28	but dead men **b** my lord the king: 3807.1
20: 8	in Gibeon, Amasa went **b** them. 6440+3807.1
21: 9	them in the hill **b** the LORD: 6440+3807.1
22:13	Through the brightness **b** him were coals 5048
22:23	For all his judgments were **b** me: 5048+3807.1
22:24	I was also upright **b** him, and have kept 3807.1
24:13	thou flee three months **b** thine 3807.1
24:20	bowed himself **b** the king on his face 3807.1
1Ki 1: 2	let her stand **b** the king, and let 6440+3807.1
1: 5	and fifty men to run **b** him. 6440+3807.1
1:23	when he was come in **b** the king, 6440+3807.1
1:23	bowed himself **b** the king with his face 3807.1
1:25	they eat and drink **b** him, and say, 6440+3807.1
1:28	and stood **b** the king. 6440+3807.1
1:32	And they came **b** the king. 6440+3807.1
2: 4	to walk **b** me in truth with all 6440+3807.1
2:26	the Lord GOD **b** David my father, 6440+3807.1
2:45	established **b** the LORD for ever. 6440+3807.1
3: 6	according as he walked **b** thee in 6440+3807.1
3:12	that there was none like thee **b** 6440+3807.1
3:15	stood the ark of the covenant of 6440+3807.1
3:16	unto the king, and stood **b** him. 6440+3807.1
3:22	Thus they spake **b** the king. 6440+3807.1
3:24	they brought a sword **b** the king. 6440+3807.1
6: 3	the porch **b** the temple of the house 5921+6440
6: 3	cubits was the breadth thereof **b** 5921+6440
6: 7	was built of stone made ready **b** it was NIH
6:17	the house, that is, the temple **b** it, 6440+3807.1
6:21	by the chains of gold **b** the oracle; 6440+3807.1
7: 6	the porch **b** them: and 5921+6440
7: 6	and the thick beam were **b** them. 5921+6440
7:49	five on the left, **b** the oracle, 6440+3807.1
8: 5	were with him **b** the ark, 6440+3807.1
8: 8	out in the holy place **b** the oracle, 5921+6440
8:22	Solomon stood **b** the altar of 6440+3807.1
8:23	walk **b** thee with all their heart: 6440+3807.1
8:25	that they walk **b** me as thou hast 6440+3807.1
8:25	me as thou hast walked **b** me. 6440+3807.1
8:28	thy servant prayeth **b** thee to day: 6440+3807.1
8:31	come **b** thine altar in this house: 6440+3807.1
8:33	be smitten down **b** the enemy, 6440+3807.1
8:50	give them compassion **b** them 6440+3807.1
8:54	from **b** the altar of the LORD, 6440+3807.1
8:59	made supplication **b** the LORD, 6440+3807.1
8:62	offered sacrifice **b** the LORD. 6440+3807.1
8:64	was the house of the LORD: 6440+3807.1
8:64	the brasen altar that was **b** 6440+3807.1
8:65	unto the river of Egypt, **b** 6440+3807.1
9: 3	that thou hast made **b** me: 6440+3807.1
9: 4	if thou wilt walk **b** me, as David 6440+3807.1
9: 6	statutes which I have set **b** you, 6440+3807.1
9:25	the altar that was **b** the LORD. 6440+3807.1
10: 8	which stand continually **b** thee, 6440+3807.1
11: 7	in the hill that is **b** Jerusalem, 5921+6440
11:36	a light alway **b** me in Jerusalem, 6440+3807.1
12: 6	that stood **b** Solomon his father 854+6440
12: 8	him, and which stood **b** him: 6440+3807.1
12:30	for the people went to worship **b** 6440+3807.1
13: 6	and became as it was **b**. 7223+871.1+1886.1
14: 9	done evil above all that were **b** 6440+3807.1
14:24	cast out **b** the children of Israel. 4480+6440
15: 3	which he had done **b** him: 6440+3807.1
16:25	worse than all that were **b** him. 6440+3807.1

1Ki 16:30	LORD above all that were **b** him. 6440+3807.1
16:33	kings of Israel that were **b** him. 6440+3807.1
17: 1	the LORD God of Israel liveth, **b** 6440+3807.1
17: 3	the brook Cherith, that is **b** Jordan. 5921+6440
17: 5	the brook Cherith, that is **b** Jordan. 5921+6440
18:15	As the LORD of hosts liveth, **b** 6440+3807.1
18:46	**b** Ahab to the entrance of Jezreel. 6440+3807.1
19:11	upon the mount **b** the LORD. 6440+3807.1
19:11	in pieces the rocks **b** the LORD; 6440+3807.1
19:19	with twelve yoke of oxen **b** him, 6440+3807.1
20:27	the children of Israel pitched **b** them like 5048
21:10	set two men, sons of Belial, **b** him, to bear 5048
21:13	two men, children of Belial, and sat **b** him: 5048
21:26	whom the LORD cast out **b** 4480+6440
21:29	humbleth himself **b** me? 4480+6440+3807.1
21:29	because he humbleth himself **b** me, 4480+6440
22:10	the prophets prophesied **b** them. 6440+3807.1
2Ki 1:13	came and fell on his knees **b** 5048+6440+3807.1
2: 9	Ask what I shall do for thee, **b** I be 2962+871.1
2:15	bowed themselves to the ground **b** him. 3807.1
3:14	As the LORD of hosts liveth, **b** 6440+3807.1
3:24	so that they fled **b** them: 4480+6440
4:12	had called her, she stood **b** him. 6440+3807.1
4:31	Gehazi passed on **b** them, 6440+3807.1
4:38	the prophets were sitting **b** him: 6440+3807.1
4:43	I set this **b** an hundred men? 6440+3807.1
4:44	So he set it **b** them, and they did 6440+3807.1
5:15	and came, and stood **b** him: 6440+3807.1
5:16	the LORD liveth, **b** whom I stand, 6440+3807.1
5:23	and they bare them **b** him. 6440+3807.1
5:25	he went in, and stood **b** his master. 413
6:22	set bread and water **b** them, 6440+3807.1
6:32	the king sent a man from **b** him: 4480+6440
8: 9	came and stood **b** him, and said, 6440+3807.1
10: 4	two kings stood not **b** him: 6440+3807.1
11:18	the priest of Baal **b** the altars. 6440+3807.1
14:12	Judah was put to the worse **b** 6440+3807.1
15:10	smote him **b** the people, and slew him, 6905
16: 3	whom the LORD cast out from **b** 6440
16:14	which was **b** the LORD, from 6440+3807.1
17: 2	kings of Israel that were **b** him. 6440+3807.1
17: 8	whom the LORD cast out from **b** 6440
17:11	the LORD carried away **b** them; 4480+6440
18: 5	Judah, nor any that were **b** him. 3807.1
18:22	worship **b** this altar in Jerusalem? 6440+3807.1
19:14	and spread it **b** the LORD. 6440+3807.1
19:15	Hezekiah prayed **b** the LORD, 6440+3807.1
19:26	as corn blasted **b** it be grown up. 6440+3807.1
19:32	arrow there, nor **come b** it with shield, 6923
20: 3	I have walked **b** thee in truth 6440+3807.1
21: 2	whom the LORD cast out **b** 4480+6440
21: 9	destroyed **b** the children of Israel. 4480+6440
21:11	were **b** him, and hath made 6440+3807.1
22:10	And Shaphan read it **b** the king. 6440+3807.1
22:19	hast humbled thyself **b** the LORD, 4480+6440
22:19	rent thy clothes, and wept **b** me; 6440+3807.1
23: 3	made a covenant **b** the LORD, 6440+3807.1
23:13	the high places that were **b** 5921+6440
23:25	unto him was there no king **b** 6440+3807.1
25: 7	they slew the sons of Zedekiah **b** his 3807.1
25:29	did eat bread continually **b** him 6440+3807.1
1Ch 1:43	b any king reigned over 6440+3807.1
5:25	whom God destroyed **b** them. 4480+6440
6:32	they ministered **b** the dwelling 6440+3807.1
10: 1	the men of Israel fled from **b** 6440
11: 3	them in Hebron **b** the LORD; 6440+3807.1
11:13	and the people fled from **b** the Philistines. 6440
13: 8	played **b** God with all their might, 6440+3807.1
13:10	the ark: and there he died **b** God. 6440+3807.1
14:15	for God is gone forth **b** thee to 6440+3807.1
15:24	did blow with the trumpets **b** 6440+3807.1
16: 1	and peace offerings **b** God. 6440+3807.1
16: 4	minister **b** the ark of the LORD, 6440+3807.1
16: 6	**b** the ark of the covenant of God. 6440+3807.1
16:29	an offering, and come **b** him: 6440+3807.1
16:30	Fear **b** him, all the earth: 4480+6440+3807.1
16:37	So he left there **b** the ark of 6440+3807.1
16:37	to minister **b** the ark continually, 6440+3807.1
16:39	his brethren the priests, **b** 6440+3807.1
17: 8	cut off all thine enemies from **b** thee, 6440
17:13	took it from him that was **b** thee: 6440+3807.1
17:16	king came and sat **b** the LORD, 6440+3807.1
17:21	by driving out nations from **b** thy people, 6440
17:24	thy servant be established **b** thee. 6440+3807.1
17:25	found in his heart to pray **b** thee. 6440+3807.1
17:27	that it may be thee for ever: 6440+3807.1
19: 7	who came and pitched **b** Medeba. 6440+3807.1
19: 9	the battle in array **b** the gate of the city: NIH
19:10	saw that the battle was set against him **b** 6440
19:14	nigh **b** the Syrians unto the battle; 6440+3807.1
19:14	the battle; and they fled **b** him. 4480+6440
19:15	they likewise fled **b** Abishai his 4480+6440
19:16	were put to the worse **b** Israel, 6440+3807.1
19:16	host of Hadarezer went **b** them. 6440+3807.1
19:18	the Syrians fled **b** Israel; 4480+6440+3807.1
19:19	were put to the worse **b** Israel, 6440+3807.1
21:12	three months to be destroyed **b** thy 4480+6440
21:30	David could not go **b** it to inquire 6440+3807.1
22: 5	prepared abundantly **b** his death. 6440+3807.1
22:18	the land is subdued **b** the LORD, 6440+3807.1
22:18	the LORD, and **b** his people. 6440+3807.1
23:13	to burn incense **b** the LORD, 6440+3807.1
23:31	continually **b** the LORD: 6440+3807.1
24: 2	Nadab and Abihu died **b** their 6440+3807.1

B

1Ch 24: 6 wrote them **b** the king,	6440+3807.1
24: 6 **b** the chief of the fathers of the priests	NIH
28: 4 all the house of my father to be king	4480
29:10 the LORD **b** all the congregation:	5869+3807.1
29:15 For we *are* strangers **b** thee,	6440+3807.1
29:22 drink **b** the LORD on that day	6440+3807.1
29:25 been on any king **b** him in Israel.	6440+3807.1
2Ch 1: 5 put to the tabernacle of the LORD:	6440+3807.1
1: 6 to the brasen altar **b** the LORD,	6440+3807.1
1:10 go out and come in **b** this people:	6440+3807.1
1:12 have had that *have been* **b** thee,	6440+3807.1
1:13 from **b** the tabernacle of	6440+3807.1
2: 4 *and* to burn **b** him sweet incense,	6440+3807.1
2: 6 save only to burn sacrifice **b** him?	6440+3807.1
3:15 Also he made the house two	6440+3807.1
3:17 reared up the pillars **b** the temple,	5921+6440
4:20 after the manner **b** the oracle,	6440+3807.1
5: 6 assembled unto him **b** the ark,	6440+3807.1
5: 9 seen from the ark **b** the oracle:	5921+6440
6:12 he stood **b** the altar of the LORD	6440+3807.1
6:13 kneeled *down* upon his knees **b** all	5048
6:14 walk **b** thee with all their hearts:	6440+3807.1
6:16 law, as thou hast walked **b** me.	6440+3807.1
6:19 which thy servant prayeth **b** thee:	6440+3807.1
6:22 come **b** thine altar in this house:	6440+3807.1
6:24 be put to the worse **b** the enemy,	6440+3807.1
6:24 supplication **b** thee in this house;	6440+3807.1
6:36 them *over* **b** *their* enemies,	6440+3807.1
7: 4 all the people offered sacrifices **b**	5048
7: 6 the priests sounded trumpets **b** them,	5048
7: 7 *was* **b** the house of the LORD:	6440+3807.1
7:17 *for* thee, if thou wilt walk **b** me,	6440+3807.1
7:19 which I have set **b** you,	6440+3807.1
8:12 which he had built **b** the porch,	6440+3807.1
8:14 to praise and minister **b** the priests,	5048
9: 7 which stand continually **b** thee,	6440+3807.1
9:11 there were none such seen **b** in	6440+3807.1
10: 6 **b** Solomon his father while he *yet*	6440+3807.1
10: 8 up with him, that stood **b** him.	6440+3807.1
13:13 so they were **b** Judah,	6440+3807.1
13:14 behold, the battle *was* **b** and behind:	6440
13:15 and all Israel **b** Abijah and Judah.	6440+3807.1
13:16 the children of Israel fled **b** Judah:	4480+6440
14: 5 the kingdom was quiet **b** him.	4480
14: 7 bars, *while* the land *is* yet **b** us;	6440+3807.1
14:12 smote the Ethiopians **b** Asa,	6440+3807.1
14:12 before Asa, and **b** Judah;	6440+3807.1
14:13 for they were destroyed **b**	6440+3807.1
14:13 before the LORD, and **b** his host;	6440+3807.1
15: 8 *was* **b** the porch of the LORD.	6440+3807.1
18: 9 the prophets prophesied **b** them.	6440+3807.1
18:20 stood **b** the LORD, and said,	6440+3807.1
19: 2 upon thee from **b** the LORD.	6440+3807.1
19:11 the Levites *shall be* officers **b**	6440+3807.1
20: 5 in the house of the LORD, **b**	6440+3807.1
20: 7 land **b** thy people Israel,	4480+6440+3807.1
20: 9 this house, and in thy presence,	6440+3807.1
20:13 all Judah stood **b** the LORD,	6440+3807.1
20:16 of the brook, **b** the wilderness of Jeruel.	6440
20:18 the inhabitants of Jerusalem fell **b**	6440+3807.1
20:21 as *they* went out **b** the army,	6440+3807.1
23:17 the priest of Baal **b** the altars.	6440+3807.1
24:14 the rest of the money **b** the king	6440+3807.1
25: 8 God shall make thee fall **b**	6440+3807.1
25:14 bowed down himself **b** them,	6440+3807.1
25:22 Judah was put to the worse **b**	6440+3807.1
26:19 **b** the priests in the house of	6440+3807.1
27: 6 he prepared his ways **b** the LORD	6440+3807.1
28: 3 cast out **b** the children of Israel.	4480+6440
28: 9 went out **b** the host that came to	6440+3807.1
28:14 the spoil **b** the princes and all	6440+3807.1
29:11 hath chosen you to stand **b** him,	6440+3807.1
29:19 they *are* **b** the altar of the LORD.	6440+3807.1
29:23 for the sin offering **b** the king	6440+3807.1
30: 9 **b** them that lead them captive,	6440+3807.1
31:20 and truth **b** the LORD his God.	6440+3807.1
32:12 Ye shall worship **b** one altar,	6440+3807.1
33: 2 whom the LORD had cast out **b**	4480+6440
33: 7 which I have chosen **b** all the tribes of	4480
33: 9 whom the LORD had destroyed **b**	4480+6440
33:12 humbled himself greatly **b**	4480+6440+3807.1
33:19 images, **b** he was humbled:	6440+3807.1
33:23 humbled not himself **b**	4480+6440+3807.1
34:18 And Shaphan read it **b** the king.	6440+3807.1
34:24 have read **b** the king of Judah:	6440+3807.1
34:27 humble thyself **b** God,	4480+6440+3807.1
34:27 humbledst thyself **b** me,	6440+3807.1
34:27 rend thy clothes, and weep **b** me;	6440+3807.1
34:31 made a covenant **b** the LORD,	6440+3807.1
36:12 humbled not himself **b**	4480+6440+3807.1
Ezr 3:12 of this house was laid **b** their eyes,	871.1
4:18 sent unto us *hath been* plainly read **b** me.	6925
4:23 king Artaxerxes' letter *was* read **b** Rehum,	6925
7:19 *those* deliver thou **b** the God of Jerusalem.	6925
7:28 hath extended mercy unto me **b**	6440+3807.1
7:28 and **b** all the king's mighty princes.	3807.1
8:21 might afflict ourselves **b** our God,	6440+3807.1
8:29 keep *them*, until ye weigh *them* **b**	6440+3807.1
9:15 behold, we *are* **b** thee in our	6440+3807.1
9:15 cannot stand **b** thee because of	6440+3807.1
10: 1 himself down **b** the house of God,	6440+3807.1
10: 6 Ezra rose up from **b** the house of	6440+3807.1
Ne 1: 4 and prayed **b** the God of heaven,	6440+3807.1
1: 6 which I pray **b** thee now, day and	6440+3807.1
2: 1 the king, *that* wine *was* **b** him:	6440+3807.1

Ne 2:13 even **b** the dragon well, and to	413+6440
4: 2 he spake **b** his brethren and	6440+3807.1
4: 5 sin be blotted out from **b** thee:	4480+6440
4: 5 *thee* to anger **b** the builders.	5048+3807.1
5:15 **b** me were chargeable unto	6440+3807.1
6:19 they reported his good deeds **b**	6440+3807.1
8: 1 street that *was* **b** the water gate;	6440+3807.1
8: 2 Ezra the priest brought the law **b**	6440+3807.1
8: 3 read therein **b** the street that *was*	6440+3807.1
8: 3 *was* **b** the water gate from	6440+3807.1
8: 3 **b** the men and the women, and those that	5048
9: 8 foundest his heart faithful **b** thee,	6440+3807.1
9:11 thou didst divide the sea **b** them,	6440+3807.1
9:24 thou subduedst **b** them	6440+3807.1
9:28 rest, they did evil again **b** thee:	6440+3807.1
9:32 all the trouble seem little **b** thee,	6440+3807.1
9:35 land which thou gavest **b** them,	6440+3807.1
12:36 God, and Ezra the scribe **b** them.	6440+3807.1
13: 4 **b** this, Eliashib the priest,	6440+3807.1
13:19 Jerusalem began to be dark **b** the sabbath,	6440
Est 1: 3 of the provinces, *being* **b** him:	6440+3807.1
1:11 To bring Vashti the queen **b**	6440+3807.1
1:16 Memucan answered **b** the king	6440+3807.1
1:17 the queen to be brought in **b** him,	6440+3807.1
1:19 That Vashti come no *more* **b** king	6440+3807.1
2:11 Mordecai walked every day **b**	6440+3807.1
2:23 book of the chronicles **b** the king.	6440+3807.1
3: 7 that *is,* the lot, **b** Haman from day	6440+3807.1
4: 2 came even **b** the king's gate:	6440+3807.1
4: 6 which *was* **b** the king's gate.	6440+3807.1
4: 8 **b** him for her people.	4480+6440+3807.1
6: 1 they were read **b** the king.	6440+3807.1
6: 9 of the city, and proclaim **b** him,	6440+3807.1
6:11 of the city, and proclaimed **b** him,	6440+3807.1
6:13 *be* of the seed of the Jews, **b**	6440+3807.1
6:13 but shalt surely fall **b** him.	6440+3807.1
7: 6 was afraid **b** the king	4480+6440+3807.1
7: 8 Will he force the queen also **b** me in	5973
7: 9 said **b** the king, Behold also,	6440+3807.1
8: 1 Mordecai came **b** the king;	6440+3807.1
8: 3 Esther spake yet again **b** the king,	6440+3807.1
8: 4 arose, and stood **b** the king,	6440+3807.1
8: 5 the thing seem right **b** the king,	6440+3807.1
9:11 palace was brought **b** the king.	6440+3807.1
9:25 when *Esther* came **b** the king,	6440+3807.1
Job 1: 6 came to present themselves **b** the LORD,	5921
2: 1 came to present themselves **b** the LORD,	5921
2: 1 them to present himself **b** the LORD.	5921
3:24 For my sighing cometh **b** I eat,	6440+3807.1
4:15 a spirit passed **b** my face; the hair of my	5921
4:16 an image *was* **b** mine eyes,	5048+3807.1
4:19 which are crushed **b** the moth?	6440+3807.1
8:12 it withereth **b** any *other* herb.	6440+3807.1
8:16 He *is* green **b** the sun,	6440+3807.1
10:21 **B** I go whence I shall not return,	2962+871.1
13:15 will maintain mine own ways **b** him.	413+6440
13:16 a hypocrite shall not come **b** him.	6440+3807.1
15: 4 and restrainest prayer **b** God.	6440+3807.1
15: 7 or wast thou made **b** the hills?	6440+3807.1
15:32 It shall be accomplished **b** his time,	3808+871.1
18:20 as they that went **b** were affrighted.	6931
21: 8 and their offspring **b** their eyes.	3807.1
21:18 They are as stubble **b** the wind,	6440+3807.1
21:33 as *there are* innumerable **b** him.	6440+3807.1
23: 4 I would order *my* cause **b** him,	6440+3807.1
23:17 Because I was not cut off **b**	4480+6440
26: 6 Hell *is* naked **b** him, and destruction hath	5048
30:11 have also let loose the bridle **b** me.	4480+6440
33: 5 *words* in order **b** me, stand up.	6440+3807.1
35:14 see him, *yet* judgment *is* **b** him;	6440+3807.1
41:10 who then is able to stand **b** me?	6440+3807.1
41:22 sorrow is turned into joy **b** him.	6440+3807.1
42:10 gave Job twice as much as he had **b**.	NIH
42:11 *had been* of his acquaintance **b**,	6440+3807.1
Ps 5: 8 make thy way straight **b** my face.	3807.1
18: 6 came **b** him, *even* into his ears.	6440+3807.1
18:12 At the brightness that *was* **b** him his thick	5048
18:22 For all his judgments *were* **b** me,	5048+3807.1
18:23 I was also upright **b** him, and I kept myself	5973
18:42 did I beat them small as the dust **b**	5921+6440
22:25 I will pay my vows **b** them that fear him.	5048
22:27 the nations shall worship **b** thee.	6440+3807.1
22:29 to the dust shall bow **b** him:	6440+3807.1
23: 5 Thou preparest a table **b** me in	6440+3807.1
26: 3 For thy lovingkindness *is* **b** mine	5048+3807.1
31:19 them that trust in thee **b** the sons of men!	5048
31:22 my haste, I am cut off from **b** thine eyes.	4480+6440
34: T he changed his behaviour **b**	6440+3807.1
35: 5 Let them be as chaff **b** the wind:	6440+3807.1
36: 1 *that there is* no fear of God **b** his eyes.	5048
38: 9 Lord, all my desire *is* **b** thee;	5048
38:17 halt, and my sorrow *is* continually **b** me.	5048
39: 1 bridle, while the wicked *is* **b** me.	5048+3807.1
39: 5 mine age *is* as nothing **b** thee:	5048
39:13 that I may recover strength, **b** I go	2962+871.1
41:12 and settest me **b** thy face for ever.	3807.1
42: 2 when shall I come and appear **b** God?	6440
44:15 My confusion *is* continually **b** me,	5048
50: 3 a fire shall devour **b** him,	6440+3807.1
50: 8 *to have been* continually **b** me.	5048+3807.1
50:21 and set *them* in order **b** thine eyes.	3807.1
51: 3 transgressions: and my sin *is* ever **b** me.	5048
52: 9 on thy name; for *it is* good **b** thy saints.	5048
54: 3 have not set God **b** them. Selah.	5048+3807.1

Ps 56:13 *I* may walk **b** God in the light	6440+3807.1
57: 6 they have digged a pit **b** me,	6440+3807.1
58: 9 **B** your pots can feel the thorns,	2962+871.1
61: 7 He shall abide **b** God for ever:	6440+3807.1
62: 8 pour out your heart **b** him:	6440+3807.1
68: 1 them also that hate him flee **b** him.	4480+6440
68: 2 as wax melteth **b** the fire, *so* let	4480+6440
68: 3 be glad; let them rejoice **b** God:	6440+3807.1
68: 4 his name JAH, and rejoice **b** him.	6440+3807.1
68: 7 thou wentest forth **b** thy people,	6440+3807.1
68:25 The singers *went* **b**, the players on	6923
69:19 mine adversaries *are* all **b** thee.	5048
69:22 Let their table become a snare **b**	6440+3807.1
72: 9 the wilderness shall bow **b** him;	6440+3807.1
72:11 Yea, all kings shall fall down **b** him:	3807.1
73:22 I, and ignorant: I was *as* a beast **b** thee.	5973
78:55 cast out the heathen also **b** them,	4480+6440
79:11 sighing of the prisoner come **b**	6440+3807.1
80: 2 **B** Ephraim and Benjamin and	6440+3807.1
80: 9 Thou preparedst *room* **b** it,	6440+3807.1
83:13 wheel; as the stubble **b** the wind.	6440+3807.1
84: 7 *one of them* in Zion appeareth **b** God.	413
85:13 Righteousness shall go **b** him;	6440+3807.1
86: 9 shall come and worship **b** thee,	6440+3807.1
86:14 and have not set thee **b** them.	5048+3807.1
88: 1 I have cried day *and* night **b** thee:	5048
88: 2 Let my prayer come **b** thee:	6440+3807.1
89:14 mercy and truth shall go **b** thy face.	6923
89:23 I will beat down his foes **b** his face,	4480
89:36 for ever, and his throne as the sun **b** me.	5048
90: 2 **B** the mountains were brought	2962+871.1
90: 8 hast set our iniquities **b** thee,	5048+3807.1
95: 2 Let us **come b** his presence with	6923
95: 6 us kneel **b** the LORD our Maker.	6440+3807.1
96: 6 Honour and majesty *are* **b** him:	6440+3807.1
96: 9 of holiness: fear **b** him, all the earth.	4480+6440
96:13 the LORD, for he cometh,	6440+3807.1
97: 3 A fire goeth **b** him, and burneth	6440+3807.1
98: 6 make a joyful noise **b** the LORD,	6440+3807.1
98: 9 **B** the LORD; for he cometh to	6440+3807.1
100: 2 come **b** his presence with singing.	3807.1
101: 3 I will set no wicked thing **b** mine	5048+3807.1
102: T out his complaint **b** the LORD.	6440+3807.1
102:28 seed shall be established **b** thee.	6440+3807.1
105:17 He sent a man **b** them,	6440+3807.1
106:23 had not Moses his chosen stood **b**	6440+3807.1
109:15 Let them be **b** the LORD continually;	5048
116: 9 I will walk **b** the LORD in	6440+3807.1
119:30 of truth: thy judgments have I laid **b** me.	NIH
119:46 I will speak of thy testimonies also **b** kings,	5048
119:67 **B** I was afflicted I went astray:	2962
119:168 testimonies: for all my ways *are* **b** thee.	5048
119:169 Let my cry come near **b** thee,	6440+3807.1
119:170 Let my supplication come **b** thee:	6440+3807.1
138: 1 **b** the gods will I sing *praise* unto thee.	5048
139: 5 Thou hast beset me behind and **b**,	6924
141: 2 Let my prayer be set forth **b** thee	6440+3807.1
141: 3 Set a watch, O LORD, **b** my mouth;	3807.1
142: 2 I poured out my complaint **b** him;	6440+3807.1
142: 2 I shewed **b** him my trouble.	6440+3807.1
147:17 who can stand **b** his cold?	6440+3807.1
Pr 4:25 and let thine eyelids look straight **b** thee.	5048
5:21 For the ways of man *are* **b** the eyes of	5227
8:22 beginning of his way, **b** his works of old.	6924
8:25 **B** the mountains were settled,	2962+871.1
8:25 the mountains were settled,	6440+3807.1
8:30 delight, rejoicing always **b** him;	6440+3807.1
14:19 The evil bow **b** the good;	6440+3807.1
15:11 Hell and destruction *are* **b** the LORD:	5048
15:33 and **b** honour *is* humility.	6440+3807.1
16:18 Pride *goeth* **b** destruction,	6440+3807.1
16:18 and a haughty spirit **b** a fall.	6440+3807.1
17:14 **b** it be meddled with.	6440+3807.1
17:24 Wisdom *is* **b** him that hath	854+6440
18:12 **B** destruction the heart of man is	6440+3807.1
18:12 and **b** honour *is* humility.	6440+3807.1
18:13 He that answereth a matter **b** he	2962+871.1
18:16 and bringeth him **b** great *men*.	6440+3807.1
22:29 shall stand **b** kings; he shall not	6440+3807.1
22:29 he shall not stand **b** mean *men*.	6440+3807.1
23: 1 consider diligently what *is* **b** thee:	6440+3807.1
25: 5 Take away the wicked *from* **b**	6440+3807.1
25:26 A righteous *man* falling down **b**	6440+3807.1
26:26 his wickedness shall be shewed **b**	871.1
27: 4 but who is able to stand **b** envy?	6440+3807.1
30: 7 of thee; deny me *them* not **b** I die:	2962+871.1
Ecc 1:10 old time, which was **b** us.	4480+6440+3807.1
1:16 that have been **b** me in Jerusalem:	6440+3807.1
2: 7 all that were in Jerusalem **b** me:	6440+3807.1
2: 9 more than all that were **b**	6440+3807.1
2:26 give to *him that is* good **b** God.	6440+3807.1
3:14 *men* should fear **b** him.	4480+6440+3807.1
4:16 *even* of all that have been **b** them:	6440+3807.1
5: 2 be hasty to utter *any* thing **b** God:	6440+3807.1
5: 6 neither say thou **b** the angel, that	6440+3807.1
6: 8 poor, that knoweth to walk **b** the living?	5048
7:17 why shouldest thou die **b** thy time?	3808+871.1
8:12 God, which fear **b** him:	6440+3807.1
8:13 he feareth not **b** God.	4480+6440+3807.1
9: 1 or hatred *by all that is* **b** them.	6440+3807.1
SS 8:12 My vineyard, which *is* mine, *is* **b**	6440+3807.1
Isa 1:12 When ye come to appear **b** me, who hath	6440
1:16 put away the evil of your doings from **b**	5048
7:16 **b** the child shall know to refuse	2962+871.1
8: 4 For **b** the child shall have	2962+871.1

B

Isa 8: 4 taken away **b** the king of Assyria. 6440+3807.1
9: 3 joy **b** thee according to the joy 6440+3807.1
9:12 The Syrians **b**, and the Philistines 4480+6924
13:16 shall be dashed to pieces **b** their eyes; 3807.1
17:13 of the mountains **b** the wind, 6440+3807.1
17:13 a rolling thing **b** the whirlwind. 6440+3807.1
17:14 at eveningtide trouble; *and* **b** 2962+871.1
23:18 for them that dwell **b** the LORD, 6440+3807.1
24:23 in Jerusalem, and **b** his ancients gloriously. 5048
28: 4 as the hasty fruit **b** the summer; 2962+871.1
30: 8 write it **b** them in a table, and note it in a 854
30:11 the Holy One of Israel to cease from **b** us. 6440
36: 7 Ye shall worship **b** this altar? 6440
37:14 and spread it **b** the LORD. 6440+3807.1
37:27 *as* corn blasted **b** it be grown up. 6440+3807.1
37:33 arrow there, nor **come b** it *with* shields, 6923
38: 3 I have walked **b** thee in truth 6440+3807.1
40:10 *is* with him, and his work **b** him. 6440+3807.1
40:17 All nations **b** him *are* as nothing; 5048
41: 1 Keep silence **b** me, O islands; and let 413
41: 2 gave the nations **b** him, 6440+3807.1
42: 9 new *things* do I declare: **b** they 2962+871.1
42:16 I will make darkness light **b** them, 6440+3807.1
43:10 that I *am* he: **b** me there 6440+3807.1
43:13 Yea, the day *was* I *am* he; and *there is* 4480
45: 1 to subdue nations **b** him; 6440+3807.1
45: 1 open **b** him the two leaved gates; 6440+3807.1
45: 2 I will go **b** thee, and make 6440+3807.1
47:14 *be* a coal to warm at, *nor* fire to sit **b** it. 5048
48: 5 beginning declared *it* to thee; **b** 2962+871.1
48: 7 **b** the day when thou heardest 6440+3807.1
48:19 cut off nor destroyed from **b** me. 6440+3807.1
49:16 hands; thy walls *are* continually **b** me. 5048
52:12 for the LORD will go **b** you; 6440+3807.1
53: 2 For he shall grow up **b** him as a 6440+3807.1
53: 7 as a sheep **b** her shearers is dumb, 6440+3807.1
55:12 the hills shall break forth **b** you 6440+3807.1
57:16 for the spirit should fail **b** 4480+6440+3807.1
58: 8 thy righteousness shall go **b** thee; 6440+3807.1
59:12 For our transgressions are multiplied **b** 5048
61:11 and praise to spring forth **b** all the nations. 5048
62:11 *is* with him, and his work **b** him. 6440+3807.1
63:12 dividing the water **b** them, to make 4480+6440
65: 6 Behold, *it is* written **b** me: I will 6440+3807.1
65:12 did evil **b** mine eyes, and did choose *that* 871.1
65:24 to pass, that **b** they call, I will answer; 2962
66: 4 they did evil **b** mine eyes, and chose 871.1
66: 7 **B** she travailed, she brought forth; 2962+871.1
66: 7 she brought forth; **b** her pain came, 2962+871.1
66:22 shall remain **b** me, saith 6440+3807.1
66:23 shall all flesh come to worship **b** 6440+3807.1

Jer 1: 5 **B** I formed thee in the belly I knew 2962+871.1
1: 5 **b** thou camest forth out of the 2962+871.1
1:17 lest I confound thee **b** them. 6440+3807.1
2:22 *yet* thine iniquity is marked **b** me, 6440+3807.1
6: 7 spoil is heard in her; **b** me 5921+6440
6:21 I will lay stumblingblocks **b** this people, 413
7:10 and stand **b** me in this house, 6440+3807.1
8: 2 they shall spread them **b** the sun, 3807.1
9:13 my law which I set **b** them, 6440+3807.1
13:16 glory to the LORD your God, **b** 2962+871.1
13:16 **b** your feet stumble upon the dark 2962+871.1
15: 1 and Samuel stood **b** me, 6440+3807.1
15: 9 to the sword **b** their enemies, 6440+3807.1
15:19 *and* thou shalt stand **b** me: 6440+3807.1
17:16 out of my lips was **right b** thee. 5227+6440
18:17 *with* an east wind **b** the enemy; 6440+3807.1
18:20 Remember that I stood **b** thee to 6440+3807.1
18:23 let them be overthrown **b** thee; 6440+3807.1
19: 7 fall by the sword **b** their enemies, 6440+3807.1
21: 8 I set **b** you the way of life, 6440+3807.1
24: 1 two baskets of figs *were* set **b** 6440+3807.1
26: 4 my law, which I have set **b** you, 6440+3807.1
28: 5 prophets that have been **b** me 6440+3807.1
28: 8 **b** thee of old prophesied both 6440+3807.1
29:21 and he shall slay them **b** your eyes; 3807.1
30:20 shall be established **b** me, 6440+3807.1
31:36 If those ordinances depart from **b** 6440+3807.1
31:36 being a nation **b** me for ever. 6440+3807.1
32:12 the book of the purchase, **b** 5869+3807.1
32:13 I charged Baruch **b** them, saying, 5869+3807.1
32:30 done evil **b** me from their youth: 5869+871.1
32:31 *I* should remove it **from b** my face, 4480+5921
33: 9 an honour **b** all the nations of the earth, 3807.1
33:18 **b** me to offer burnt 4480+6440+3807.1
33:24 be no more a nation **b** them. 6440+3807.1
34: 5 the former kings which were **b** 6440+3807.1
34:15 ye had made a covenant **b** me in 6440+3807.1
34:18 which they had made **b** me, 6440+3807.1
35: 5 I set **b** the sons of the house of 6440+3807.1
35:19 a man to stand **b** me for ever. 6440+3807.1
36: 7 their supplication **b** the LORD, 6440+3807.1
36: 9 *that* they proclaimed a fast **b** 6440+3807.1
36:22 *on* the hearth burning **b** him. 6440+3807.1
37:20 I pray thee, be accepted **b** thee, 6440+3807.1
38:10 the prophet out of the dungeon, **b** 2962+871.1
38:26 my supplication **b** the king, 6440+3807.1
39: 6 sons of Zedekiah in Riblah **b** his eyes: 3807.1
39:16 shall be *accomplished* in that day **b** 6440
40: 4 behold, all the land *is* **b** thee: 6440+3807.1
42: 2 our supplication be accepted **b** 6440+3807.1
42: 9 present your supplication **b** him: 6440+3807.1
44:10 set **b** you and *before* your fathers. 6440+3807.1
44:10 set before you and **b** your fathers. 6440+3807.1
47: 1 prophet against the Philistines, **b** 2962+871.1

Jer 49:19 shepherd that will stand **b** me? 6440+3807.1
49:37 to be dismayed **b** their enemies, 6440+3807.1
49:37 and **b** them that seek their life: 6440+3807.1
50: 8 be as the he goats **b** the flocks. 6440+3807.1
50:44 shepherd that will stand **b** me? 6440+3807.1
52:10 slew the sons of Zedekiah **b** his eyes: 3807.1
52:33 did continually eat bread **b** him 6440+3807.1

La 1: 5 gone *into* captivity **b** the enemy. 6440+3807.1
1: 6 they are gone without strength **b** 6440+3807.1
1:22 Let all their wickedness come **b** 6440+3807.1
2: 3 he hath drawn back his right hand from **b** 6440
2:19 pour out thine heart like water **b** the face 5227
3:35 To turn aside the right of a man **b** the face 5048

Eze 2:10 he spread it **b** me; and it *was* 6440+3807.1
3:20 I lay a stumblingblock **b** him, 6440+3807.1
4: 1 lay it **b** thee, and pourtray upon it 6440+3807.1
6: 4 I will cast down your slain *men* **b** 6440+3807.1
6: 5 the children of Israel **b** their idols; 6440+3807.1
8: 1 and the elders of Judah sat **b** me, 6440+3807.1
8:11 there stood **b** them seventy men 6440+3807.1
9: 6 men which *were* **b** the house. 6440+3807.1
14: 1 of Israel unto me, and sat **b** me. 6440+3807.1
14: 3 put the stumblingblock of their iniquity **b** 5227
14: 4 the stumblingblock of his iniquity **b** 5227
14: 7 the stumblingblock of his iniquity **b** 5227
16:18 oil and mine incense **b** them. 6440+3807.1
16:19 thou hast even set it **b** them for a 6440+3807.1
16:50 committed abomination **b** me: 6440+3807.1
16:57 **B** thy wickedness was discovered, 2962+871.1
20: 1 of the LORD, and sat **b** me. 6440+3807.1
20: 9 not be polluted **b** the heathen, 5869+3807.1
20:14 that *it* should not be polluted **b** 5869+3807.1
20:41 sanctified in you **b** the heathen. 5869+3807.1
21: 6 and with bitterness sigh **b** their eyes. 3807.1
22:30 in the gap **b** me for the land, 6440+3807.1
23:24 I will set judgment **b** them, 6440+3807.1
23:41 and a table prepared **b** it, 6440+3807.1
28: 7 Wilt thou yet say **b** him that 6440+3807.1
30:24 he shall groan **b** him *with* 6440+3807.1
32:10 I shall brandish my sword **b** them; 5921+6440
33:31 they sit **b** thee *as* my people, 6440+3807.1
36:17 their way was **b** me as 6440+3807.1
36:23 when I shall be sanctified in you **b** their 3807.1
37:20 shall be in thine hand **b** their eyes. 3807.1
38:16 sanctified in thee, O Gog, **b** their eyes. 3807.1
40:12 The space also **b** the little 6440+3807.1
40:22 the arches thereof *were* **b** them. 6440+3807.1
40:26 the arches thereof *were* **b** them: 6440+3807.1
40:47 the altar *that was* **b** the house. 6440+3807.1
41: 4 twenty cubits, **b** the temple: 413+6440
41:12 Now the building that *was* **b** 413+6440
41:22 *is* the table that *is* **b** the LORD. 6440+3807.1
42: 1 *was* **b** the building toward the north. 5048
42: 2 **B** the length of an hundred cubits 413+6440
42: 4 **b** the chambers *was* a walk of ten 6440+3807.1
42: 8 **b** the temple *were* an hundred 5921+6440
42:11 the way **b** them *was* like 6440+3807.1
42:12 *even* the way directly **b** the wall 6440+871.1
42:13 which *are* **b** the separate place, 413+6440
43:24 thou shalt offer them **b** the LORD, 6440+3807.1
44: 3 sit in it to eat bread **b** the LORD; 6440+3807.1
44: 4 way of the north gate **b** the house: 413+6440
44:11 shall stand **b** them to minister 6440+3807.1
44:12 unto them **b** their idols, 6440+3807.1
44:15 they shall stand **b** me to offer 6440+3807.1
44:22 or a widow that *had* a priest **b** 1961+4480
45: 7 **b** the oblation of the holy *portion,* 413+6440
45: 7 and **b** the possession of the city, 413+6440
46: 3 gate **b** the LORD in the sabbaths 6440+3807.1
46: 9 **b** the LORD in the solemn feasts, 6440+3807.1

Da 1: 5 they might stand **b** the king. 6440+3807.1
1:13 be looked upon **b** thee, 6440+3807.1
1:18 them in **b** Nebuchadnezzar. 6440+3807.1
1:19 therefore stood they **b** the king. 6440+3807.1
2: 2 they came and stood **b** the king. 6440+3807.1
2: 9 and corrupt words to speak **b** me, 6925
2:10 The Chaldeans answered **b** the king, 6925
2:11 there is none other that can shew it **b** 6925
2:24 bring me in **b** the king, and I will shew 6925
2:25 Arioch brought in Daniel **b** the king in 6925
2:31 *was* excellent, stood **b** thee; 6903+3807.2
2:36 we will tell the interpretation thereof **b** 6925
3: 3 they stood **b** the image that 6903+3807.2
3:13 Then they brought these men **b** the king. 6925
4: 6 bring in all the wise *men* of Babylon **b** me, 6925
4: 7 I told the dream **b** them; but they *did* not 6925
4: 8 at the last Daniel came in **b** me, 6925
4: 8 and **b** him I told the dream, *saying,* 6925
5: 1 and drank wine **b** the thousand. 6903+3807.2
5:13 was Daniel brought in **b** the king. 6925
5:15 have been brought in **b** me, that they 6925
5:17 Daniel answered and said **b** the king, 6925
5:19 trembled and feared **b** him: 4481+6925
5:23 brought the vessels of his house **b** thee, 6925
6:10 prayed, and gave thanks **b** his God, as he 6925
6:11 and making supplication **b** his God. 6925
6:13 spake **b** the king concerning the king's 6925
6:13 answered they and said **b** the king, 6925
6:18 instruments of musick brought **b** him: 6925
6:22 forasmuch as **b** him innocency was found 6925
6:22 also **b** thee, O king, have I done no hurt. 6925
6:26 and fear **b** the God of Daniel: 4481+6925
7: 7 diverse from all the beasts that *were* **b** it; 6925
7: 8 **b** whom there were three of the 4481+6925

Da 7:10 stream issued and came forth from **b** him: 6925
7:10 ten thousand times ten thousand stood **b** 6925
7:13 of days, and they brought him near **b** him. 6925
7:20 came up, and **b** whom three fell; 4481+6925
8: 3 there stood **b** the river a ram 6440+3807.1
8: 4 so that no beasts might stand **b** 6440+3807.1
8: 6 which I had seen standing **b** 6440+3807.1
8: 7 power in the ram to stand **b** him, 6440+3807.1
8:15 stood **b** me as the appearance 5048+3807.1
9:10 which he set **b** us by his servants 6440+3807.1
9:13 yet made we not our prayer **b** the LORD 6440
9:18 **b** thee for our righteousnesses, 6440+3807.1
9:20 presenting my supplication **b** 6440+3807.1
10:12 to chasten thyself **b** thy God, 6440+3807.1
10:16 said unto him that stood **b** me, 5048+3807.1
11:16 and none shall stand **b** him: 6440+3807.1
11:22 they be overflown from **b** him, 6440+3807.1

Hos 7: 2 have beset them about; they are **b** my face. 5048

Joel 1:16 Is not the meat cut off **b** our eyes, *yea,* joy 5048
2: 3 A fire devoureth **b** them; 6440+3807.1
2: 3 land *is* as the garden of Eden **b** them. 6440+3807.1
2: 6 **B** their face *the* people shall be much 4480
2:10 The earth shall quake **b** them; 6440+3807.1
2:11 the LORD shall utter his voice **b** 6440+3807.1
2:31 the moon into blood, **b** the great 6440+3807.1

Am 1: 1 two year **b** the earthquake. 6440+3807.1
2: 9 Yet destroyed I the Amorite **b** them, 4480+6440
4: 3 every *cow at that which is* **b** her; 5048
9: 4 though they go into captivity **b** 6440+3807.1

Jnh 1: 2 wickedness is come up **b** me. 6440+3807.1
4: 2 I fled **b** unto Tarshish: for I knew 6923

Mic 1: 4 as wax **b** the fire, *and* as the waters 4480+6440
2:13 The breaker is come up **b** them: 6440+3807.1
2:13 their king shall pass **b** them, 6440+3807.1
6: 1 contend thou **b** the mountains, and let NIH
6: 4 I sent **b** thee Moses, Aaron, 6440+3807.1
6: 6 Wherewith shall I **come b** the LORD, 6923
6: 6 *and* bow myself **b** the high God? 3807.1
6: 6 shall I **come b** him with burnt offerings, 6923

Na 2: 1 Who can stand **b** his indignation? 6440+3807.1
2: 1 that dasheth in pieces is come up **b** thy 5921

Hab 1: 3 spoiling and violence *are* **b** me: 5048+3807.1
2:20 let all the earth keep silence **b** him. 4480+6440
3: 5 **B** him went the pestilence, 6440+3807.1

Zep 2: 2 **B** the decree bring forth, *before* 2962+871.1
2: 2 bring forth, *b* the day pass as the chaff, NIH
2: 2 the day pass as the chaff, **b** 2962+3808+871.1
2: 2 the LORD come upon you, **b** 2962+3808+871.1
3:20 when I turn back your captivity **b** your 3807.1

Hag 1:12 the people did fear **b** the LORD. 4480+6440
2:14 and so *is* this nation **b** me, 6440+3807.1
2:15 from **b** a stone was laid upon a stone in 2962

Zec 2:13 Be silent, O all flesh, **b** the LORD: 4480+6440
3: 1 **b** the angel of the LORD, 6440+3807.1
3: 3 and stood **b** the angel. 6440+3807.1
3: 4 unto those that stood **b** him, 6440+3807.1
3: 8 and thy fellows that sit **b** thee: 6440+3807.1
3: 9 stone that I have laid **b** Joshua; 6440+3807.1
4: 7 **b** Zerubbabel *thou shalt* become 6440+3807.1
6: 5 go forth from standing **b** the Lord of 5921
7: 2 and their men, to pray **b** the LORD, 6440
8:10 **b** these days there was no hire 6440+3807.1
8:21 Let us go speedily to pray **b** the LORD, 6440
8:22 in Jerusalem, and to pray **b** the LORD. 6440
12: 8 as the angel of the LORD **b** them. 6440+3807.1
14: 4 which *is* **b** Jerusalem on the east, 5921+6440
14: 5 like as ye fled **b** the earthquake in 6440
14:20 shall be like the bowls **b** the altar. 6440+3807.1

Mal 2: 5 and was afraid **b** my name. 4480+6440
2: 9 and base **b** all the people, 3807.1
3: 1 he shall prepare the way **b** me: 6440+3807.1
3:11 vine **cast** her **fruit b the time** in the field, 7921
3:14 that we have walked mournfully **b** 4480+6440
3:16 **b** him for them that feared 6440+3807.1
4: 5 will send you Elijah the prophet **b** 6440+3807.1

Mt 1:18 **b** they came together, she was 2228+4250
2: 9 **went b** them, till it came and stood over 4254
5:12 they the prophets which were **b** 4253
5:16 Let your light so shine **b** men, that they 1715
5:24 Leave there thy gift **b** the altar, and go thy 1715
6: 1 heed that ye do not your alms **b** men, 1715
6: 2 alms, do not sound a trumpet **b** thee, 1715
6: 8 he have need of, **b** ye ask him. 3588+4253
7: 6 neither cast ye your pearls **b** swine, 1715
8:29 art thou come hither to torment us **b** 4253
10:18 And ye shall be brought **b** governors and 1909
10:32 therefore shall confess me **b** men, 1715
10:32 him will I confess also **b** my Father which 1715
10:33 But whosoever shall deny me **b** men, 1715
10:33 him will I also deny **b** my Father which is 1715
11:10 Behold, I send my messenger **b** thy face, 4253
11:10 which shall prepare thy way **b** thee. 1715
14: 6 of Herodias danced **b** 1722+3319+3588
14: 8 being **b instructed** of her mother, said, 4264
14:22 and to **go b** him unto the other side, 4254
17: 2 And was transfigured **b** them: and his face 1715
21: 9 And the multitudes that **went b**, 4254
21:31 the harlots **go** into the kingdom of God **b** 4254
24:25 Behold, I have **told** you **b**. 4302
24:38 For as in the days that were **b** the flood 4253
25:32 And **b** him shall be gathered all nations: 1715
26:32 But after I am risen *again,* I will **go b** you 4254
26:34 thee, That this night, **b** the cock crow, 4250
26:70 But he denied **b** *them* all, saying, I know 1715
26:75 which said unto him, **B** *the* cock crow, 4250

Mt 27:11 And Jesus stood **b** the governor: 1715
27:24 and washed *his* hands **b** the multitude, 561
27:29 and they bowed the knee **b** him, 1715
28: 7 and behold, he **goeth b** you into Galilee; 4254
Mk 1: 2 Behold, I send my messenger **b** thy face, 4253
1: 2 which shall prepare thy way **b** thee. 1715
1:35 up a great while **b day**, he went out, 1773
2:12 up the bed, and went forth **b** *them* all; 1726
3:11 **fell down b** him, and cried, saying, 4363
5:33 and **fell down b** him, and told him all 4363
6:41 gave *them* to his disciples to **set b** them; 3908
6:45 to **go** to the other side **b** unto Bethsaida, 4254
8: 6 and gave to his disciples to **set b** *them;* 3908
8: 6 and they did **set** *them* **b** the people. 3908
8: 7 and commanded to **set** them also **b** *them.* 3908
9: 2 and he was transfigured **b** them. 1715
10:32 up to Jerusalem; and Jesus **went b** them: 4254
11: 9 And they that **went b**, and they that 4254
13: 9 and ye shall be brought **b** rulers and 1909
14:28 I am risen, I will **go b** you into Galilee. 4254
14:30 this night, *b the* cock crow twice, 2228+4250
14:72 **B** the cock crow twice, thou shalt deny 4250
15:42 that is, the **day b the sabbath**, 4315
16: 7 Peter that he **goeth b** you into Galilee: 4254
Lk 1: 6 And they were both righteous **b** God, 1799
1: 8 while he executed the priest's office **b** 1725
1:17 And he shall go **b** him in the spirit and 1799
1:75 In holiness and righteousness **b** him, all 1799
1:76 for thou shalt go **b** the face of the Lord to 4253
2:21 named of the angel **b** he was conceived in 4253
2:26 he he had seen the Lord's Christ. 2228+4250
2:31 Which thou hast prepared **b** the face of all 2596
5:18 to bring him in, and to lay *him* **b** him. 1799
5:19 with *his* couch into the midst **b** Jesus. 1715
5:25 And immediately he rose up **b** them, 1799
7:27 Behold, I send my messenger **b** thy face, 4253
7:27 which shall prepare thy way **b** thee. 1715
8:28 **fell down b** him, and with a loud voice 4363
8:47 came trembling, and **falling down b** him, 4363
8:47 she declared unto him **b** all the people for 1799
9:16 to the disciples to **set b** the multitude. 3908
9:52 And sent messengers **b** his face: 4253
10: 1 and two **b** his face into every city and 4253
10: 8 eat such *things* as are **set b** you: 3908
11: 6 to me, and I have nothing to **set b** him: 3908
11:38 that he had not first washed **b** dinner. 4253
12: 6 and not one of them is forgotten **b** God? 1799
12: 8 Whosoever shall confess me **b** men, 1715
12: 8 him shall the Son of man also confess **b** 1715
12: 9 But he that denieth me **b** men shall be 1799
12: 9 men shall be denied **b** the angels of God. 1799
14: 2 behold, there was a certain man **b** him, 1715
15:18 I have sinned against heaven, and **b** thee, 1799
16:15 Ye are they which justify yourselves **b** 1799
18:39 And they which **went b** rebuked him, 4254
19: 4 And he **ran b**, 4390
19:27 bring hither, and slay *them* **b** me. 1715
19:28 he went **b**, ascending up to Jerusalem. 1715
20:26 not take hold of his words **b** the people: 1726
21:12 But **b** all these, they shall lay their hands 4253
21:12 being brought **b** kings and rulers for my 1909
21:14 not to **meditate b** *what ye* shall answer: 4304
21:36 to pass, and to stand **b** the Son of man. 1715
22:15 eat this passover with you **b** I suffer: 3588+4253
22:34 that thou shalt thrice deny that 2228+4250
22:47 **went b** them, and drew near unto Jesus to 4281
22:61 **B** the cock crow, thou shalt deny me 4250
23:12 for **b** they were at enmity between 4391
23:14 behold, I, having examined *him* **b** you, 1799
23:53 wherein **never** man **b** was laid. 3756+3764
24:19 deed and word **b** God and all the people: 1726
24:43 And he took *it*, and did eat **b** them. 1799
Jn 1:15 cometh after me is **preferred b** me: 1096+1715
1:15 is preferred before me: for he was **b** me. 4413
1:27 who coming after me is preferred **b** me, 1715
1:30 a man which is **preferred** me: 1096+1715
1:30 is preferred before me: for he was **b** me. 4413
1:48 unto him, **B that** Philip called thee, 3588+4253
3:28 not the Christ, but that I am sent **b** him. 1715
5: 7 am coming, another steppeth down **b** me. 4253
6:62 Son of man ascend up where he was **b**? 4387
7:51 he it hear him, and know what he doeth? 4387
8:58 I say unto you, **B** Abraham was, I am. 4250
9: 8 they which **b** had seen him that he was 4387
10: 4 **goeth b** them, and the sheep follow him: 1715
10: 8 All that ever came **b** me are thieves and 4253
11:55 country up to Jerusalem **b** the passover, 4253
12: 1 Then Jesus six days **b** the passover came 4253
12:37 he had done so many miracles **b** them, 1715
13: 1 Now **b** the feast of the passover, 4253
13:19 Now I tell you **b** it come, that, 3588+4253
14:29 now I have told you **b** it come to pass, 4250
15:18 ye know that it hated me **b** *it hated* you. 4412
17: 5 I had with thee **b** the world was. 3588+4253
17:24 for thou lovedst me **b** the foundation of 4253
Ac 1:16 of David **spake b** concerning Judas, 4302
2:20 **b** *that* great and notable day of the Lord 4250
2:25 I foresaw the Lord always **b** my **face**, 1799
2:31 He **seeing** this **b**, spake of the resurrection 4275
3:18 *those things*, which God **b** had **shewed** 4293
3:20 which **b** was **preached** unto you: 4296
4:10 *even* by him doth this *man* stand **here b** 1799
4:28 thy counsel **determined b** to be done. 4253
5:23 the keepers standing without **b** the doors: 4253
5:27 brought them, they set *them* **b** the council: 1722

Ac 5:36 For **b** these days rose up Theudas, 4253
6: 6 Whom they set **b** the apostles: 1799
7: 2 **b** he dwelt in Charran, 2228+4250
7:40 unto Aaron, Make us gods to **go b** us: 4313
7:45 whom God drave out **b** the face of our 575
7:46 Who found favour **b** God, and desired to 1799
7:52 they have slain them which **shewed b** of 4293
8:32 and like a lamb dumb **b** his shearer, 1726
9:15 bear my name **b** the Gentiles, and kings, 1799
10: 4 thine alms are come up for a memorial **b** 1799
10:17 Simon's house, and **stood b** the gate, 2186
10:30 a man stood **b** me in bright clothing, 1799
10:33 therefore are we all here present **b** God, 1799
10:41 but unto witnesses **chosen b** of God, 4401
12: 6 *the* keepers the door kept the prison. 4253
12:14 and told how Peter stood **b** the gate. 4253
13:24 When John had first preached **b** his 4253+4383
14:13 which was **b** their city, brought oxen and 4253
16:29 and **fell down b** Paul and Silas, 4363
16:34 he set **meat b** *them*, and rejoiced, 3908+5132
17:26 hath determined the times **b** **appointed**, 4384
18:17 and beat *him* **b** the judgment seat. 1715
19: 9 but spake evil of *that* way **b** the multitude, 1799
19:19 and burned *them* **b** all *men:* and 1799
20: 5 These **going b** tarried for us at Troas. 4281
20:13 And we **went b** to ship, and sailed unto 4281
21:29 (For they had **seen b** with him in the city 4308
21:38 which **b** these days madest an uproar, 4253
22:30 brought Paul down, and set *him* **b** them. 1519
23: 1 I have lived in all good conscience **b** God NIG
23:30 to say **b** thee what *they had* against him. 1909
23:33 the governor, **presented** Paul also **b** him. 3936
24:19 Who ought to have been here **b** thee, 1909
24:20 doing in me, while I stood **b** the council, 1909
25: 9 and there be judged of these *things* **b** me? 1909
25:16 **b** that he which is accused have 2228+4250
25:26 Wherefore I have brought him forth **b** you, 1909
25:26 and specially **b** thee, O king Agrippa, that, 1909
26: 2 I shall answer for myself this day **b** thee 1909
26:26 For the king knoweth of these *things*, **b** 4314
27:24 Paul; thou must be **brought b** Cesar: 3936
Ro 2:13 (For not the hearers of the law *are* just **b** 3844
3: 9 for we have **b proved** both Jews and 4256
3:18 There is no fear of God **b** their eyes. 561
3:19 all the world may become **guilty b** God. 5267
4: 2 he hath whereof to glory; but not **b** God. 4314
4:17 **b** whom he believed, *even* God, 2713
9:29 And as Esaias **said b**, Except the Lord of 4302
14:10 for we shall all **stand b** the judgment seat 3936
14:22 have *it* to thyself **b** God. Happy *is* he that 1799
16: 2 apostles, who also were in Christ **b** me. 4253
1Co 2: 7 God ordained **b** the world unto our glory: 4253
4: 5 Therefore judge nothing **b** the time, 4253
6: 1 go to law **b** the unjust, and not before 1909
6: 1 before the unjust, and not **b** the saints? 1909
6: 6 with brother, and that **b** the unbelievers. 1909
10:27 whatsoever is **set b** you, eat, asking no 3908
11:21 For in eating every one **taketh b** *other* his 4301
2Co 1:15 I was minded to come unto you **b**, 4387
5:10 we must all appear **b** the judgment seat 1715
7: 3 *this* to condemn *you:* for I have **said b**, 4302
7:14 so our boasting, which *I made* **b** Titus, 1909
8:10 who have **begun b**, not only to do, but 4278
8:24 **b** the churches, the proof of your 1519+4383
9: 5 that they would **go b** unto you, 4281
9: 5 whereof *ye* had **notice b**, that the same 4293
12:19 we speak **b** God in Christ: but *we do* all 2714
13: 2 I told *you* **b**, and foretell *you*, as if I were 4302
Gal 1: 9 As we **said b**, so say I now again, If any 4302
1:17 to them which were apostles **b** me; 4253
1:20 I write unto you, behold, **b** God, I lie not. 1799
2:12 For **b** that certain came from James, he did 4253
2:14 I said unto Peter **b** *them* all, If thou, being 1715
3: 1 **b** whose eyes Jesus Christ hath been 2596
3: 8 **preached b** the gospel unto Abraham, 4283
3:17 that was **confirmed b** of God in Christ, 4300
3:23 But **b** faith came, we were kept 3588+4253
3:23 the faith which **I tell** you **b**, as I have also told 4302
Eph 1: 4 According as he hath chosen us in him **b** 4253
1: 4 be holy and without blame **b** him in love: 2714
2:10 God hath **b ordained** that we should 4282
Php 3:13 forth unto those *things which are* **b**, 1715
Col 1: 5 ye **heard b** in the word of the truth 4257
1:17 he is **b** all *things*, and by him all *things* 4253
1Th 2: 2 But even after that we had **suffered b**, 4310
2: 2 we **told** you **b** that we should suffer 4302
3: 9 we joy for your sakes **b** our God; 1715
3:13 hearts unblameable in holiness **b** God, 1715
1Ti 1:13 was a blasphemer, and a persecutor, 4387
1:18 according to the prophecies which **went b** 4254
5: 4 for that is good and acceptable **b** God. 1799
5:19 accusation, but **b** two or three witnesses. 1909
5:20 Them that sin rebuke **b** all, that others also 1799
5:21 I charge *thee* **b** God, and the Lord Jesus 1799
5:21 one *another*, doing nothing by partiality. NIG
5:24 open beforehand, **going b** to judgment; 4254
6:12 hast professed a good profession **b** many 1799
6:13 quickeneth all *things*, and **b** Christ Jesus, NIG
6:13 who **b** Pontius Pilate witnessed a good 1909
2Ti 1: 9 which was given us in Christ Jesus **b** 4253
2:14 charging *them* **b** the Lord that *they* strive 1799
4: 1 I charge *thee* therefore **b** God, and the Lord 1799
4:21 Do thy diligence to come **b** winter. 4253
4: S Paul was **brought b** Nero the second 3936
Tit 1: 2 cannot lie, promised **b** the world began; 4253

Heb 6:18 refuge to lay hold upon the hope **set b** *us:* 4295
7:18 commandment being **b** for the weakness 4254
10:15 witness to us: for after that *he* had **said b**, 4302
11: 5 for **b** his translation he had this testimony, 4253
12: 1 run with patience the race that is **set b** us, 4295
12: 2 for the joy that was **set b** him endured 4295
Jas 1:27 Pure religion and undefiled **b** God and 3844
2: 6 and draw you **b** the judgment seats? 1519
5: 9 the judge standeth **b** the door. 4253
1Pe 1:20 Who verily was foreordained **b** 4253
2Pe 2:11 bring not railing accusation against them **b** 3844
3: 2 were **spoken b** by the holy prophets, 4302
3:17 beloved, seeing ye **know** *these things* **b**, 4267
1Jn 2:28 and not be ashamed **b** him at his coming. 575
3:19 truth, and shall assure our hearts **b** him. 1715
3Jn 1: 6 Which have borne witness of thy charity **b** 1799
Jude 1: 4 who were **b** of old **ordained** to this 4270
1:17 **spoken b** of the apostles of our Lord Jesus 4302
1:24 to present *you* faultless **b the presence** of 2714
Rev 1: 4 from the seven spirits which are **b** his 1799
2:14 a stumblingblock **b** the children of Israel, 1799
3: 2 for I have not found thy works perfect **b** 1799
3: 5 but I will confess his name **b** my Father, 1799
3: 5 name before my Father, and **b** his angels. 1799
3: 8 I have set **b** thee an open door, and no 1799
3: 9 them to come and worship **b** thy feet, 1799
4: 5 *there were* seven lamps of fire burning **b** 1799
4: 6 And **b** the throne *there was* a sea of glass 1799
4: 6 *were* four beasts full of eyes **b** and behind. 1715
4:10 twenty elders fall down **b** him that sat on 1799
4:10 and cast their crowns **b** the throne, 1799
5: 8 *and* twenty elders fell down **b** the Lamb, 1799
7: 9 stood **b** the throne, and before the Lamb, 1799
7: 9 stood before the throne, and **b** the Lamb, 1799
7:11 and fell **b** the throne on their faces, 1799
7:15 Therefore are they **b** the throne of God, 1799
8: 2 And I saw the seven angels which stood **b** 1799
8: 3 the golden altar which was **b** the throne. 1799
8: 4 ascended up **b** God out of the angel's hand 1799
9:13 horns of the golden altar which is **b** God, 1799
10:11 must prophesy again **b** many peoples, 1909
11: 4 the two candlesticks standing **b** the God 1799
11:16 which sat **b** God on their seats, 1799
12: 4 the dragon stood **b** the woman which was 1799
12:10 which accused them **b** our God day and 1799
13:12 all the power of the first beast **b** him, 1799
14: 3 And they sung as *it were* a new song **b** 1799
14: 3 and **b** the four beasts, and the elders: 1799
14: 5 for they are without fault **b** the throne of 1799
15: 4 all nations shall come and worship **b** thee; 1799
16:19 great Babylon came in remembrance **b** 1799
19:20 false prophet that wrought miracles **b** him, 1799
20:12 the dead, small and great, stand **b** God; 1799
22: 8 I fell down to worship **b** the feet of 1715

BEFOREHAND (5) [BEFORE]

Mk 13:11 take no **thought b** what ye shall speak, 4305
2Co 9: 5 and **make up b** your bounty, whereof *ye* 4294
1Ti 5:24 Some men's sins are **open b**, going before 4271
5:25 the good works *of some* are **manifest b**; 4271
1Pe 1:11 it **testified b** the sufferings of Christ, 4303

BEFORETIME (11) [BEFORE, TIME]

Dt 2:12 The Horims also dwelt in Seir **b**; 6440+3807.1
Jos 11:10 for Hazor **b** was the head of all 6440+3807.1
20: 5 hated him not **b**. 4480+8032+8543
1Sa 9: 9 (**B** in Israel, when a man went to 6440+3807.1
9: 9 for *he that is* now *called* a Prophet was **b** 6440
10:11 knew him **b** saw that behold, 865+4480+8032
2Sa 7:10 any more, as **b**, 7223+871.1+1886.1
2Ki 13: 5 of Israel dwelt in their tents, as **b**. 8032+8543
Ne 2: 1 I had not been *b* sad in his presence. NIH
Isa 41:26 **b**, that we may say, *He is* 6440+6440+3807.1
Ac 8: 9 which **b** in the *same* city used sorcery, 4391

BEG (3) [BEGGAR, BEGGARLY, BEGGED, BEGGING]

Ps 109:10 children be continually vagabonds, and **b**: 7592
Pr 20: 4 therefore shall he **b** in harvest, 7592
Lk 16: 3 I cannot dig; to **b** I am ashamed. 1871

BEGAN (178) [BEGIN]

Ge 4:26 *b men* to call upon the name of 2490
6: 1 when men **b** to multiply on the face of 2490
9:20 Noah **b** *to be* a husbandman, and he 2490
10: 8 he **b** to be a mighty *one* in the earth. 2490
41:54 the seven years of dearth **b** to come, 2490
44:12 **b** at the eldest, and left at the youngest: 2490
Dt 1: 5 **b** Moses to declare this law, saying, 2974
Jdg 13:25 the spirit of the LORD **b** to move him at 2490
16:19 she **b** to afflict him, and his strength went 2490
16:22 Howbeit the hair of his head **b** to grow 2490
19:25 when the **day b** to spring, they let her go. 7837
20:31 they **b** to smite of the people, *and* kill, 2490
20:39 Benjamin **b** to smite *and* kill of the men 2490
20:40 the flame **b** to arise up out of the city 2490
1Sa 3: 2 his eyes *b to* wax dim, *that* he could not 2490
2Sa 2:10 years old when he **b** to reign over Israel, NIH
5: 4 David *was* thirty years old when he **b** to NIH
1Ki 6: 1 that he **b** to build the house of the LORD. NIH
14:21 and one years old when he **b** to reign, NIH
15:25 Nadab the son of Jeroboam **b** to reign over NIH
15:33 In the third year of Asa king of Judah **b** NIH
16: 8 sixth year of Asa king of Judah **b** Elah NIH
16:11 it came to pass, when he **b** to reign, as NIH

B

Ref	Text	Strong's
1Ki	16:23 first year of Asa king of Judah **b** Omri to	NIH
	16:29 eighth year of Asa king of Judah **b** Ahab	NIH
	22:41 Jehoshaphat the son of Asa **b** to reign over	NIH
	22:42 and five years old when he **b** to reign;	NIH
	22:51 Ahaziah the son of Ahab **b** to reign over	NIH
2Ki	3: 1 Now Jehoram the son of Ahab **b** to reign	NIH
	8:16 of Jehoshaphat king of Judah **b** to reign,	NIH
	8:17 two years old was he when he **b** to reign;	NIH
	8:26 twenty years old was Ahaziah when he **b**	NIH
	9:29 son of Ahab **b** Ahaziah to reign over Judah.	NIH
	10:32 In those days the LORD **b** to cut Israel	2490
	11:21 Seven years old was Jehoash when he **b** to	NIH
	12: 1 In the seventh year of Jehu Jehoash **b** to	NIH
	13: 1 of Jehu **b** to reign over Israel in Samaria,	NIH
	13:10 seventh year of Joash king of Judah **b**	NIH
	14: 2 and five years old when he **b** to reign,	NIH
	14:23 Joash king of Israel **b** to reign in Samaria,	NIH
	15: 1 seventh year of Jeroboam king of Israel **b**	NIH
	15: 2 Sixteen years old was he when he **b** to	NIH
	15:13 Shallum the son of Jabesh **b** to reign in	NIH
	15:17 thirtieth year of Azariah king of Judah **b**	NIH
	15:23 Menahem **b** to reign over Israel in Samaria,	NIH
	15:27 Remaliah **b** to reign over Israel in Samaria,	NIH
	15:32 **b** Jotham the son of Uzziah king of Judah to	NIH
	15:33 years old was he when he **b** to reign,	NIH
	15:37 In those days the LORD **b** to send against	2490
	16: 1 the year of Jotham king of Judah **b** to reign.	NIH
	16: 2 Twenty years old was Ahaz when he **b** to	NIH
	17: 1 the twelfth year of Ahaz king of Judah **b**	NIH
	18: 1 the son of Ahaz king of Judah **b** to reign.	NIH
	18: 2 five years old was he when he **b** to reign;	NIH
	21: 1 Manasseh was twelve years old when he **b**	NIH
	21:19 and two years old when he **b** to reign,	NIH
	22: 1 Josiah was eight years old when he **b** to	NIH
	23:31 and three years old when he **b** to reign;	NIH
	23:36 and five and two years old when he **b** to	NIH
	24: 8 was eighteen years old when he **b** to reign,	NIH
	24:18 and one years old when he **b** to reign,	NIH
	25:27 of Babylon, in the year that he **b** to reign,	NIH
1Ch	1:10 he **b** to be mighty upon the earth.	2490
	27:24 Joab the son of Zeruiah **b** to number, but	2490
2Ch	3: 1 Solomon **b** to build the house of	2490
	3: 2 he **b** to build in the second day of	2490
	12:13 and forty years old when he **b** to reign,	NIH
	13: 1 Jeroboam **b** Abijah to reign over Judah.	NIH
	20:22 when they **b** to sing and to praise,	2490
	20:31 and five years old when he **b** to reign,	NIH
	21: 5 and two years old when he **b** to reign,	NIH
	21:20 two years old was he when he **b** to reign,	NIH
	22: 2 two years old was Ahaziah when he **b** to	NIH
	24: 1 Joash was seven years old when he **b** to	NIH
	25: 1 and five years old when he **b** to reign,	NIH
	26: 3 Sixteen years old was Uzziah when he **b**	NIH
	27: 1 and five years old when he **b** to reign,	NIH
	27: 8 and twenty years old when he **b** to reign,	NIH
	28: 1 Ahaz was twenty years old when he **b** to	NIH
	29: 1 Hezekiah **b** to reign when he was five and	NIH
	29:17 Now they **b** on the first day of the first	2490
	29:27 when the burnt offering he, the song of	2490
	29:27 the song of the LORD **b** also with	2490
	31: 7 In the third month they **b** to lay	2490
	31:10 Since the people **b** to bring the offerings	2490
	31:21 in every work that he **b** in the service of	2490
	33: 1 Manasseh was twelve years old when he **b**	NIH
	33:21 and twenty years old when he **b** to reign,	NIH
	34: 1 Josiah was eight years old when he **b** to	NIH
	34: 3 he **b** to seek after the God of David his	2490
	34: 3 in the twelfth year he **b** to purge Judah	2490
	36: 2 and three years old when he **b** to reign,	NIH
	36: 5 and five years old when he **b** to reign,	NIH
	36: 9 Jehoiachin was eight years old when he **b**	NIH
	36:11 and twenty years old when he **b** to reign,	NIH
Ezr	3: 6 From the first day of the seventh month **b**	2490
	3: 8 **b** Zerubbabel the son of Shealtiel,	2490
	5: 2 to build the house of God which is at	8271
	7: 9 For upon the first day of the first month **b**	3246
Ne	4: 7 and that the breaches **b** to be stopped,	2490
	13:19 that when the gates of Jerusalem **b** to be	NIH
Jer	52: 1 and twenty year old when he **b** to reign,	NIH
Eze	9: 6 they **b** at the ancient men which were	2490
Jnh	3: 4 Jonah **b** to enter into the city a day's	2490
Mt	4:17 From that time Jesus **b** to preach, and to	756
	11: 7 Jesus **b** to say unto the multitudes	756
	11:20 Then **b** he to upbraid the cities wherein	756
	12: 1 and **b** to pluck the ears of corn, and to eat.	756
	16:21 From that time forth **b** Jesus to shew unto	756
	16:22 and **b** to rebuke him, saying, Be it far from	756
	26:22 and **b** every one of them to say unto him,	756
	26:37 and **b** to be sorrowful and very heavy.	756
	26:74 Then **b** he to curse and to swear, saying, I	756
	28: 1 as it **b** to dawn towards the first day of	NIG
Mk	1:45 to publish it much, and to blaze abroad	756
	2:23 and his disciples **b**, as they went, to pluck	756
	4: 1 And he **b** again to teach by the sea side:	756
	5:17 they **b** to pray him to depart out of their	756
	5:20 **b** to publish in Decapolis how great things	756
	6: 2 was come, he **b** to teach in the synagogue:	756
	6: 7 and **b** to send them forth by two and two;	756
	6:34 and he **b** to teach them many things.	756
	6:55 **b** to carry about in beds those that were	756
	8:11 came forth, and **b** to question with him,	756
	8:31 he **b** to teach them, that the Son of man	756
	8:32 And Peter took him, and **b** to rebuke him.	756
	10:28 Then Peter **b** to say unto him, Lo, we have	756
	10:32 **b** to tell them what things should happen	756

Ref	Text	Strong's
Mk	10:41 when the ten heard it, they **b** to be much	756
	10:47 he **b** to cry out, and say, Jesus, thou Son of	756
	11:15 and to cast out them that sold and	756
	12: 1 And he **b** to speak unto them by parables.	756
	13: 5 And Jesus answering them **b** to say,	756
	14:19 they **b** to be sorrowful, and to say unto	756
	14:33 and he **b** to be sore amazed, and to be very	756
	14:65 some **b** to spit on him, and to cover his	756
	14:69 and **b** to say to them that stood by, This is	756
	14:71 But he **b** to curse and to swear, saying, I	756
	15: 8 And the multitude crying aloud **b** to desire	756
	15:18 And **b** to salute him, Hail, King of the Jews.	756
Lk	1:70 which have been since the world **b**:)	575
	3:23 And Jesus himself **b** to be about thirty years	756
	4:21 And he **b** to say unto them, This day is this	756
	5: 7 filled both the ships, so that they **b** to sink.	NIG
	5:21 the scribes and the Pharisees **b** to reason,	756
	7:15 he that was dead sat up, and **b** to speak.	756
	7:24 he **b** to speak unto the people concerning	756
	7:38 and to wash his feet with tears,	756
	7:49 And they that sat at meat with him **b** to say	756
	9:12 And when the day to wear away, then	756
	11:29 he **b** to say, This is an evil generation:	756
	11:53 the Pharisees **b** to urge him vehemently,	756
	12: 1 he **b** to say unto his disciples first of all,	756
	14:18 And they all with one consent **b** to make	756
	14:30 This man **b** to build, and was not able to	756
	15:14 famine in that land; and he **b** to be in want.	756
	15:24 and is found. And they **b** to be merry.	756
	19:37 the whole multitude of the disciples **b** to	756
	19:45 and **b** to cast out them that sold therein,	756
	20: 9 Then **b** he to speak to the people this	756
	22:23 And they **b** to inquire among themselves,	756
	23: 2 And they **b** to accuse him, saying, We	756
Jn	4:52 the hour when he **b to amend.**	2192+2866
	9:32 Since the world **b** was it not heard that	1537
	13: 5 to wash the disciples' feet, and to wipe	756
Ac	1: 1 of all that Jesus **b** both to do and teach,	756
	2: 4 and to speak with other tongues,	756
	3:21 of all his holy prophets **since** the world **b**.	575
	8:35 and **b** at the same scripture,	756
	10:37 and **b** from Galilee, after the baptism which	756
	11:15 And as I **b** to speak, the Holy Ghost fell on	756
	18:26 And he **b** to speak boldly in the synagogue:	756
	24: 2 when he was called forth, Tertullus **b** to	756
	27:35 and when he had broken it, he **b** to eat.	756
Ro	16:25 was kept secret **since** the **world b**,	166+5550
2Ti	1: 9 in Christ Jesus before the **world b**,	166+5550
Tit	1: 2 promised before the **world b**;	166+5550
Heb	2: 3 which at the first **b** to be spoken by	2983

BEGAT (225) [BEGET]

Ref	Text	Strong's
Ge	4:18 Irad **b** Mehujael: and Mehujael begat	3205
	4:18 Mehujael **b** Methusael:	3205
	4:18 Methusael: and Methusael **b** Lamech.	3205
	5: 3 and **b** a son in his own likeness,	3205
	5: 4 and he **b** sons and daughters:	3205
	5: 6 an hundred and five years, and **b** Enos:	3205
	5: 7 Seth lived after he **b** Enos eight hundred	3205
	5: 7 seven years, and **b** sons and daughters:	3205
	5: 9 Enos lived ninety years, and **b** Cainan:	3205
	5:10 Enos lived after he **b** Cainan eight	3205
	5:10 fifteen years, and **b** sons and daughters:	3205
	5:12 lived seventy years, and **b** Mahalaleel:	3205
	5:13 Cainan lived after he **b** Mahalaleel eight	3205
	5:13 forty years, and **b** sons and daughters:	3205
	5:15 lived sixty and five years, and **b** Jared:	3205
	5:16 Mahalaleel lived after he **b** Jared eight	3205
	5:16 thirty years, and **b** sons and daughters:	3205
	5:18 and two years, and he **b** Enoch:	3205
	5:19 Jared lived after he **b** Enoch eight hundred	3205
	5:19 hundred years, and **b** sons and daughters:	3205
	5:21 and five years, and **b** Methuselah:	3205
	5:22 Enoch walked with God after he **b**	3205
	5:22 hundred years, and **b** sons and daughters:	3205
	5:25 and seven years, and **b** Lamech:	3205
	5:26 Methuselah lived after he **b** Lamech seven	3205
	5:26 and two years, and **b** sons and daughters:	3205
	5:28 eighty and two years, and **b** a son:	3205
	5:30 Lamech lived after he **b** Noah five	3205
	5:30 and five years, and **b** sons and daughters:	3205
	5:32 and Noah **b** Shem, Ham, and Japheth.	3205
	6:10 Noah **b** three sons, Shem, Ham,	3205
	10: 8 Cush **b** Nimrod: he began to be a mighty	3205
	10:13 Mizraim **b** Ludim, and Anamim,	3205
	10:15 Canaan **b** Sidon his firstborn, and Heth,	3205
	10:24 Arphaxad **b** Salah; and Salah begat Eber.	3205
	10:24 Arphaxad begat Salah; and Salah **b** Eber.	3205
	10:26 Joktan **b** Almodad, and Sheleph,	3205
	11:10 and Arphaxad two years after the flood:	3205
	11:11 Shem lived after he **b** Arphaxad five	3205
	11:11 hundred years, and **b** sons and daughters.	3205
	11:12 lived five and thirty years, and **b** Salah:	3205
	11:13 Arphaxad lived after he **b** Salah four	3205
	11:13 three years, and **b** sons and daughters.	3205
	11:14 And Salah lived thirty years, and **b** Eber:	3205
	11:15 Salah lived after he **b** Eber four hundred	3205
	11:15 three years, and **b** sons and daughters.	3205
	11:16 lived four and thirty years, and **b** Peleg:	3205
	11:17 Eber lived after he **b** Peleg four hundred	3205
	11:17 thirty years, and **b** sons and daughters.	3205
	11:18 And Peleg lived thirty years, and **b** Reu:	3205
	11:19 Peleg lived after he **b** Reu two hundred	3205
	11:19 nine years, and **b** sons and daughters.	3205
	11:20 lived two and thirty years, and **b** Serug:	3205

Ref	Text	Strong's
Ge	11:21 Reu lived after he **b** Serug two hundred	3205
	11:21 seven years, and **b** sons and daughters.	3205
	11:22 Serug lived thirty years, and **b** Nahor:	3205
	11:23 Serug lived after he **b** Nahor two hundred	3205
	11:23 hundred years, and **b** sons and daughters.	3205
	11:24 lived nine and twenty years, and **b** Terah:	3205
	11:25 Nahor lived after he **b** Terah an hundred	3205
	11:25 nineteen years, and **b** sons and daughters.	3205
	11:26 and **b** Abram, Nahor, and Haran.	3205
	11:27 Terah **b** Abram, Nahor, and Haran;	3205
	11:27 and Haran; and Haran **b** Lot.	3205
	22:23 Bethuel **b** Rebekah: these eight Milcah did	3205
	25: 3 Jokshan **b** Sheba, and Dedan. And the	3205
	25:19 of Isaac, Abraham's son: Abraham **b** Isaac:	3205
Lev	25:45 are with you, which they **b** in your land:	3205
Nu	26:29 Machir **b** Gilead: of Gilead come	3205
	26:58 of the Korahites. And Kohath **b** Amram.	3205
Dt	32:18 the Rock that **b** thee thou art unmindful,	3205
Jdg	11: 1 the son of a harlot: and Gilead **b** Jephthah.	3205
Ru	4:18 generations of Pharez: Pharez **b** Hezron,	3205
	4:19 Hezron **b** Ram, and Ram begat	3205
	4:19 begat Ram, and Ram **b** Amminadab,	3205
	4:20 Amminadab **b** Nahshon,	3205
	4:20 begat Nahshon, and Nahshon **b** Salmon,	3205
	4:21 Salmon **b** Boaz, and Boaz begat Obed,	3205
	4:21 Salmon begat Boaz, and Boaz **b** Obed,	3205
	4:22 And Obed **b** Jesse, and Jesse begat David.	3205
	4:22 And Obed begat Jesse, and Jesse **b** David.	3205
1Ch	1:10 Cush **b** Nimrod: he began to be mighty	3205
	1:11 Mizraim **b** Ludim, and Anamim,	3205
	1:13 Canaan **b** Zidon his firstborn, and Heth,	3205
	1:18 Arphaxad **b** Shelah, and Shelah begat	3205
	1:18 begat Shelah, and Shelah **b** Eber.	3205
	1:20 Joktan **b** Almodad, and Sheleph,	3205
	1:34 Abraham **b** Isaac. The sons of Isaac; Esau	3205
	2:10 Ram **b** Amminadab; and Amminadab	3205
	2:10 Amminadab **b** Nahshon, prince of	3205
	2:11 Nahshon **b** Salma, and Salma begat Boaz,	3205
	2:11 Nahshon begat Salma, and Salma **b** Boaz,	3205
	2:12 And Boaz **b** Obed, and Obed begat Jesse,	3205
	2:12 And Boaz begat Obed, and Obed **b** Jesse,	3205
	2:13 Jesse **b** his firstborn Eliab,	3205
	2:18 Caleb the son of Hezron **b** children of	3205
	2:20 And Hur **b** Uri, and Uri begat Bezaleel.	3205
	2:20 And Hur begat Uri, and Uri **b** Bezaleel.	3205
	2:22 Segub **b** Jair, who had three and	3205
	2:36 Attai **b** Nathan, and Nathan begat Zabad,	3205
	2:36 Attai begat Nathan, and Nathan **b** Zabad,	3205
	2:37 Zabad **b** Ephlal, and Ephlal begat Obed,	3205
	2:37 Zabad begat Ephlal, and Ephlal **b** Obed,	3205
	2:38 Obed **b** Jehu, and Jehu begat Azariah,	3205
	2:38 Obed begat Jehu, and Jehu **b** Azariah,	3205
	2:39 Azariah **b** Helez, and Helez begat Eleasah,	3205
	2:39 Azariah begat Helez, and Helez **b** Eleasah,	3205
	2:40 Eleasah **b** Sisamai, and Sisamai begat	3205
	2:40 begat Sisamai, and Sisamai **b** Shallum,	3205
	2:41 Shallum **b** Jekamiah, and Jekamiah begat	3205
	2:41 begat Jekamiah, and Jekamiah **b** Elishama.	3205
	2:44 Shema **b** Raham, the father of Jorkoam:	3205
	2:44 father of Jorkoam: and Rekem **b** Shammai.	3205
	2:46 Moza, and Gazez: and Haran **b** Gazez.	3205
	4: 2 And Reaiah the son of Shobal **b** Jahath;	3205
	4: 2 and Jahath **b** Ahumai, and Lahad.	3205
	4: 8 Coz **b** Anub, and Zobebah, and the	3205
	4:11 Chelub the brother of Shuah **b** Mehir,	3205
	4:12 Eshton **b** Beth-rapha, and Paseah,	3205
	4:14 Meonothai **b** Ophrah: and Seraiah begat	3205
	4:14 Seraiah **b** Joab, the father of the valley of	3205
	6: 4 Eleazar **b** Phinehas, Phinehas begat	3205
	6: 4 begat Phinehas, Phinehas **b** Abishua,	3205
	6: 5 Abishua **b** Bukki, and Bukki begat Uzzi,	3205
	6: 5 Abishua begat Bukki, and Bukki **b** Uzzi,	3205
	6: 6 Uzzi **b** Zerahiah, and Zerahiah begat	3205
	6: 6 begat Zerahiah, and Zerahiah **b** Meraioth,	3205
	6: 7 Meraioth **b** Amariah, and Amariah begat	3205
	6: 7 begat Amariah, and Amariah **b** Ahitub,	3205
	6: 8 Ahitub **b** Zadok, and Zadok begat	3205
	6: 8 begat Zadok, and Zadok **b** Ahimaaz,	3205
	6: 9 Ahimaaz **b** Azariah, and Azariah begat	3205
	6: 9 begat Azariah, and Azariah **b** Johanan,	3205
	6:10 Johanan **b** Azariah, (he it is that executed	3205
	6:11 Azariah **b** Amariah, and Amariah begat	3205
	6:11 begat Amariah, and Amariah **b** Ahitub,	3205
	6:12 Ahitub **b** Zadok, and Zadok begat Shallum	3205
	6:12 Ahitub begat Zadok, and Zadok **b** Shallum	3205
	6:13 Shallum **b** Hilkiah, and Hilkiah begat	3205
	6:13 begat Hilkiah, and Hilkiah **b** Azariah,	3205
	6:14 Azariah **b** Seraiah, and Seraiah begat	3205
	6:14 begat Seraiah, and Seraiah **b** Jehozadak,	3205
	7:32 Heber **b** Japhlet, and Shomer,	3205
	8: 1 Now Benjamin **b** Bela his firstborn,	3205
	8: 7 removed them, and **b** Uzza, and Ahihud.	3205
	8: 8 Shaharaim **b** children in the country of	3205
	8: 9 he **b** of Hodesh his wife, Jobab, and Zibia,	3205
	8:11 And of Hushim he **b** Abitub, and Elpaal.	3205
	8:32 Mikloth **b** Shimeah. And these also dwelt	3205
	8:33 Ner **b** Kish, and Kish begat Saul,	3205
	8:33 Kish **b** Saul, and Saul begat Jonathan,	3205
	8:33 Saul **b** Jonathan, and Malchishua,	3205
	8:34 was Merib-baal; and Merib-baal **b** Micah.	3205
	8:36 Ahaz **b** Jehoadah; and Jehoadah begat	3205
	8:36 Jehoadah **b** Alemeth, and Azmaveth,	3205
	8:36 and Zimri; and Zimri **b** Moza,	3205
	8:37 Moza **b** Binea: Rapha was his son,	3205
	9:38 Mikloth **b** Shimeam. And they also dwelt	3205

B

1Ch	9:39 Ner **b** Kish; and Kish begat Saul;	3205
	9:39 Kish **b** Saul; and Saul begat Jonathan,	3205
	9:39 Saul **b** Jonathan, and Malchishua,	3205
	9:40 *was* Merib-baal: and Merib-baal **b** Micah.	3205
	9:42 Ahaz **b** Jarah; and Jarah begat Alemeth,	3205
	9:42 Jarah **b** Alemeth, and Azmaveth,	3205
	9:42 and Zimri; and Zimri **b** Moza;	3205
	9:43 Moza **b** Binea; and Rephaiah his son,	3205
	14: 3 and David **b** moe sons and daughters.	3205
2Ch	11:21 **b** twenty and eight sons,	3205
	13:21 **b** twenty and two sons,	3205
	24: 3 two wives; and he **b** sons and daughters.	3205
Ne	12:10 Jeshua **b** Joiakim, Joiakim also begat	3205
	12:10 Joiakim also **b** Eliashib, and Eliashib begat	3205
	12:10 also begat Eliashib, and Eliashib **b** Joiada,	NIH
	12:11 Joiada **b** Jonathan, and Jonathan begat	3205
	12:11 begat Jonathan, and Jonathan **b** Jaddua.	3205
Pr	23:22 Hearken unto thy father that **b** thee,	3205
Jer	16: 3 concerning their fathers that **b** them in	3205
Da	11: 6 he that **b** her, and he that strengthened	3205
Zec	13: 3 his mother that **b** him shall say unto him,	3205
	13: 3 his mother that **b** him shall thrust him	3205
Mt	1: 2 Abraham **b** Isaac; and Isaac begat Jacob;	1080
	1: 2 and Isaac **b** Jacob; and Jacob begat Judas	1080
	1: 2 and Jacob **b** Judas and his brethren;	1080
	1: 3 And Judas **b** Phares and Zara of Thamar;	1080
	1: 3 and Phares **b** Esrom; and Esrom begat Aram;	1080
	1: 3 Phares begat Esrom; and Esrom **b** Aram;	1080
	1: 4 And Aram **b** Aminadab;	1080
	1: 4 and Aminadab **b** Naasson;	1080
	1: 4 begat Naasson; and Naasson **b** Salmon;	1080
	1: 5 And Salmon **b** Booz of Rachab;	1080
	1: 5 Booz **b** Obed of Ruth; and Obed begat	1080
	1: 5 begat Obed of Ruth; and Obed **b** Jesse;	1080
	1: 6 And Jesse **b** David the king; and David .	1080
	1: 6 David the king **b** Solomon of *her that had*	1080
	1: 7 And Solomon **b** Roboam;	1080
	1: 7 And Roboam **b** Abia; and Abia begat Asa;	1080
	1: 7 and Roboam begat Abia; and Abia **b** Asa;	1080
	1: 8 And Asa **b** Josaphat; and Josaphat begat	1080
	1: 8 and Josaphat **b** Joram; and Joram begat	1080
	1: 8 Josaphat begat Joram; and Joram **b** Ozias;	1080
	1: 9 And Ozias **b** Joatham; and Joatham begat	1080
	1: 9 and Joatham **b** Achaz; and Achaz begat	1080
	1: 9 begat Achaz; and Achaz **b** Ezekias;	1080
	1:10 And Ezekias **b** Manasses;	1080
	1:10 and Manasses **b** Amon; and Amon begat	1080
	1:10 begat Amon; and Amon **b** Josias;	1080
	1:11 And Josias **b** Jechonias and his brethren,	1080
	1:12 brought to Babylon, Jechonias **b** Salathiel;	1080
	1:12 begat Salathiel; and Salathiel **b** Zorobabel;	1080
	1:13 And Zorobabel **b** Abiud; and Abiud begat	1080
	1:13 And Abiud **b** Eliakim; and Eliakim begat	1080
	1:13 Abiud begat Eliakim; and Eliakim **b** Azor;	1080
	1:14 And Azor **b** Sadoc; and Sadoc begat	1080
	1:14 and Sadoc **b** Achim; and Achim begat	1080
	1:14 Sadoc begat Achim; and Achim **b** Eliud;	1080
	1:15 And Eliud **b** Eleazar; and Eleazar begat	1080
	1:15 Eleazar **b** Matthan; and Matthan begat	1080
	1:15 begat Matthan; and Matthan **b** Jacob;	1080
	1:16 And Jacob **b** Joseph the husband of Mary,	1080
Ac	7: 8 and so *Abraham* **b** Isaac,	1080
	7: 8 and Isaac *b* Jacob; and Jacob *begat*	NIG
	7: 8 and Jacob *b* the twelve patriarchs.	NIG
	7:29 the land of Madian, where he **b** two sons.	1080
Jas	1:18 Of his own will **b** he us with the word of	616
1Jn	5: 1 one that loveth him that **b** loveth him	1080

BEGET (10) [BEGAT, BEGETTEST, BEGETTETH, BEGOTTEN, FIRSTBEGOTTEN]

Ge	17:20 twelve princes shall he **b**, and I will make	3205
Dt	4:25 When thou shalt **b** children,	3205
	28:41 Thou shalt **b** sons and daughters, but	3205
2Ki	20:18 which thou shalt **b**, shall they take *away;*	3205
Ecc	6: 3 If a man **b** an hundred *children*, and	3205
Isa	39: 7 which thou shalt **b**, shall they take away;	3205
Jer	29: 6 Take ye wives, and **b** sons and daughters;	3205
Eze	18:10 If he **b** a son *that is* a robber, a shedder of	3205
	18:14 Now lo, *if* he **b** a son, that seeth all his	3205
	47:22 which shall **b** children among you:	3205

BEGETTEST (2) [BEGET]

Ge	48: 6 which thou **b** after them, shall be thine,	3205
Isa	45:10 that saith unto *his* father, What **b** thou?	3205

BEGETTETH (3) [BEGET]

Pr	17:21 He that **b** a fool *doeth it* to his sorrow:	3205
	23:24 that **b** a wise *child* shall have joy of him.	3205
Ecc	5:14 a son, and *there is* nothing in his hand.	3205

BEGGAR (3) [BEG]

1Sa	2: 8 lifteth up the **b** from the dunghill, to set	34
Lk	16:20 And there was a certain **b** named Lazarus,	4434
	16:22 And it came to pass that the **b** died, and	4434

BEGGARLY (1) [BEG]

Gal	4: 9 turn ye again to the weak and **b** elements,	4434

BEGGED (3) [BEG]

Mt	27:58 He went to Pilate, and **b** the body of Jesus.	154
Lk	23:52 went unto Pilate, and **b** the body of Jesus?	154
Jn	9: 8 said, Is not this he that sat and **b**?	4319

BEGGING (3) [BEG]

Ps	37:25 righteous forsaken, nor his seed **b** bread.	1245

Mk	10:46 son of Timeus, sat by the *high*way side **b**.	4319
Lk	18:35 a certain blind man sat by the way side **b**:	4319

BEGIN (27) [BEGAN, BEGINNEST, BEGINNING, BEGINNINGS, BEGUN]

Ge	11: 6 all one language; and this they **b** to do:	2490
Dt	2:24 **b** to possess *it*, and contend with him *in*	2490
	2:25 This day will I **b** to put the dread of thee	2490
	2:31 **b** to possess, that *thou* mayest inherit his	2490
	16: 9 to number the seven weeks from *such*	2490
Jos	3: 7 This day will I **b** to magnify thee in	2490
Jdg	10:18 What man *is he* that will **b** to fight against	2490
	13: 5 he shall **b** to deliver Israel out of the hand	2490
1Sa	3:12 when I, I will also make an end.	2490
	22:15 Did I then **b** to inquire of God for him?	2490
2Ki	8:25 son of Jehoram king of Judah *b* to reign.	NIH
Ne	11:17 *was* the principal to **b** the thanksgiving in	2490
Jer	25:29 I **b** to bring evil on the city which is called	2490
Eze	9: 6 whom my sanctuary at my sanctuary.	2490
Mt	24:49 And shall **b** to smite *his* fellowservants,	756
Lk	3: 8 and **b** not to say within yourselves,	756
	12:45 and shall **b** to beat the menservants and	756
	13:25 and ye **b** to stand without, and to knock at	756
	13:26 Then shall ye **b** to say, We have eaten and	756
	14: 9 with shame to take the lowest room.	756
	14:29 not able to finish *it*, all that behold *it* **b** to	756
	21:28 And when these *things* **b** to come to pass,	756
	23:30 Then shall they **b** to say to the mountains,	756
2Co	3: 1 Do we **b** again to commend ourselves? or	756
1Pe	4:17 the time *is come* that judgment must **b** at	NIG
	4:17 if *it* first **b** at us, what *shall* the end *be*	NIG
Rev	10: 7 when he shall **b** to sound, the mystery of	3195

BEGINNEST (1) [BEGIN]

Dt	16: 9 *as* thou **b** to put the sickle to the corn.	2490

BEGINNING (106) [BEGIN]

Ge	1: 1 In the **b** God created the heaven and	7225
	10:10 the **b** of his kingdom was Babel,	7225
	13: 3 place where his tent had been at the **b**,	8462
	41:21 they *were still* ill favoured, as at the **b**.	8462
	49: 3 my might, and the **b** of my strength,	7225
Ex	12: 2 This month *shall be* unto you the **b** of	7218
Dt	11:12 from the **b** of the year even unto the end	7225
	21:17 for he *is* the **b** of his strength; the right of	7225
	32:42 from the **b** of revenges upon the enemy.	7218
Jdg	7:19 unto the outside of the camp *in the* **b**	7218
Ru	1:22 came to Beth-lehem in the **b** of barley	8462
	3:10 kindness in the latter end than at the **b**,	7223
2Sa	21: 9 the first *days*, in the **b** of barley harvest.	8462
	21:10 from the **b** of harvest until water dropped	8462
2Ki	17:25 *so* it was at the **b** of their dwelling there,	8462
1Ch	17: 9 waste them any more, as at the **b**,	7223
Ezr	4: 6 reign of Ahasuerus, in the **b** of his reign,	8462
Job	8: 7 Though thy **b** was small, yet thy latter	7225
	42:12 the latter end of Job more than his **b**:	7225
Ps	111:10 The fear of the Lord *is* the **b** of wisdom:	7225
	119:160 Thy word *is* true *from* the **b**: and every	7218
Pr	1: 7 The fear of the Lord *is* the **b** of	7225
	8:22 The Lord possessed me *in* the **b** of his	7225
	8:23 from the **b**, or ever the earth was.	7218
	9:10 The fear of the Lord *is* the **b** of wisdom:	8462
	17:14 The **b** of strife *is as* when one letteth out	7225
	20:21 inheritance *may be* gotten hastily at the **b**;	7223
Ecc	3:11 that God maketh from the **b** to the end.	7218
	7: 8 Better *is* the end of a thing than the **b**	7225
	10:13 The **b** of the words of his mouth *is*	8462
Isa	1:26 at the first, and thy counsellers as at the **b**:	8462
	18: 2 to a people terrible from their **b** hitherto;	4480
	18: 7 a people terrible **from** their **b** hitherto;	4480
	40:21 hath it not been told you from the **b**?	7218
	41: 4 calling the generations from the **b**?	7218
	41:26 Who hath declared from the **b**, that we	7218
	46:10 Declaring the end from the **b**,	7225
	48: 3 declared the former *things* from the **b**;	227
	48: 5 I have even from the **b** declared *it* to thee;	227
	48: 7 They are created now, and not from the **b**;	227
	48:16 I have not spoken in secret from the **b**;	7218
	64: 4 For *since the* **b** *of the world* men	4480+5769
Jer	17:12 A glorious high throne from the **b**,	7223
	26: 1 In the **b** of the reign of Jehoiakim the son	7225
	27: 1 In the **b** of the reign of Jehoiakim the son	7225
	28: 1 in the **b** of the reign of Zedekiah king of	7225
	49:34 **b** of the reign of Zedekiah king of Judah,	7225
La	2:19 in the **b** of the watches, pour out thine	7218
Eze	40: 1 in the **b** of the year, in the tenth *day* of	7218
Da	9:21 whom I had seen in the vision at the **b**,	8462
	9:23 At the **b** of thy supplications	8462
Hos	1: 2 The **b** of the word of the Lord by Hosea.	8462
Am	7: 1 he formed grasshoppers in the **b** of	8462
Mic	1:13 she *is* the **b** of the sin to the daughter of	7225
Mt	14:30 and to sink, he cried, saying, Lord,	756
	19: 4 he which made *them* at the **b** made them	746
	19: 8 your wives: but from the **b** it was not so.	746
	20: 8 *their* hire, **b** from the last unto the first.	746
	24: 8 All these *are* the **b** of sorrows.	746
	24:21 such as was not since the **b** of the world to	746
Mk	1: 1 The **b** of the gospel of Jesus Christ, the Son	746
	10: 6 But from the **b** of the creation God made	746
	13:19 such as was not from the **b** of the creation	746
Lk	1: 2 which from the **b** were eyewitnesses,	746
	23: 5 all Jewry, **b** from Galilee to this place.	746
	24:27 And **b** at Moses and all the prophets,	756
	24:47 his name among all nations, **b** at Jerusalem.	756
Jn	1: 1 In the **b** was the Word, and the Word was	746

Jn	1: 2 The same was in the **b** with God.	746
	2:10 Every man **at the b** doth set forth good	4412
	2:11 This **b** of miracles did Jesus in Cana of	746
	6:64 For Jesus knew from the **b** who they were	746
	8: 9 by one, **b** at the eldest, *even* unto the last:	746
	8:25 the same that I said unto you *from* the **b**.	746
	8:44 He was a murderer from the **b**, and	746
	15:27 because ye have been with me from the **b**.	746
	16: 4 these *things* I said not unto you at the **b**,	746
Ac	1:22 **B** from the baptism of John, unto *that* same	756
	11: 4 But Peter *rehearsed the matter* **from the b**,	756
	11:15 Holy Ghost fell on them, as on us at the **b**.	746
	15:18 are all his works **from** the **b** of the world.	575
	26: 5 Which knew me **from** the **b**, if they would	509
Eph	3: 9 from the **b** **of the world** hath been hid	165
Php	4:15 know also, that in the **b** of the gospel,	746
Col	1:18 who is the **b**, the firstborn from the dead;	746
2Th	2:13 hath from the **b** chosen you to salvation	746
Heb	1:10 the **b** hast laid the foundation of the earth;	746
	3:14 if we hold the **b** of *our* confidence stedfast	746
	7: 3 having neither **b** of days, nor end of life;	746
2Pe	2:20 latter *end* is worse with them than the **b**.	4413
1Jn	1: 1 That which was from the **b**, which we	746
	2: 7 commandment which ye had from the **b**.	746
	2: 7 the word which ye have heard from the **b**.	746
	2:13 ye have known him that is from the **b**.	746
	2:14 ye have known him that is from the **b**.	746
	2:24 in you, which ye have heard from the **b**.	746
	2:24 *that* which ye have heard from the **b** shall	746
	3: 8 the devil; for the devil sinneth from the **b**.	746
	3:11 is the message that ye heard from the **b**,	746
2Jn	1: 5 but *that* which we had from the **b**, that we	746
	1: 6 as ye have heard from the **b**, ye should	746
Rev	1: 8 Alpha and Omega, the **b** and the ending,	746
	3:14 true witness, the **b** of the creation of God;	746
	21: 6 I am Alpha and Omega, the **b** and the end.	746
	22:13 the **b** and the end, the first and the last.	746

BEGINNINGS (4) [BEGIN]

Nu	10:10 solemn days, and in the **b** of your months,	7218
	28:11 in the **b** of your months ye shall offer a	7218
Eze	36:11 will do better *unto you* than at your **b**:	7221
Mk	13: 8 and troubles: these *are* the **b** of sorrows.	746

BEGOTTEN (24) [BEGET]

Ge	5: 4 the days of Adam after he had **b** Seth	3205
Lev	18:11 **b** of thy father, she *is* thy sister, thou shalt	4138
Nu	11:12 have I **b** them, that thou shouldest say	3205
Dt	23: 8 The children that are **b** of them shall enter	3205
Jdg	8:30 had threescore and ten sons of his body **b**:	3318
Job	38:28 a father? or who hath **b** the drops of dew?	3205
Ps	2: 7 Thou *art* my Son; this day have I **b** thee.	3205
Isa	49:21 Who hath **b** me these, seeing I have lost	3205
Hos	5: 7 for they have **b** strange children: now	3205
Jn	1:14 the glory as of the **only b** of the Father,)	3439
	1:18 the **only b** Son, which is in the bosom of	3439
	3:16 the world, that he gave his **only b** Son,	3439
	3:18 in the name of the **only b** Son of God.	3439
Ac	13:33 Thou art my Son, this day have I **b** thee.	1080
1Co	4:15 for in Christ Jesus I have **b** you through	1080
Phm	1:10 whom I have **b** in my bonds:	1080
Heb	1: 5 Thou art my Son, this day have I **b** thee?	1080
	5: 5 Thou art my Son, to day have I **b** thee.	1080
	11:17 the promises offered up *his* **only b** son,	3439
1Pe	1: 3 **b** us **again** unto a lively hope by	313
1Jn	4: 9 God sent his **only b** Son into the world,	3439
	5: 1 that begat loveth him also that is **b** of him.	1080
	5:18 but he that is **b** of God keepeth himself,	1080
Rev	1: 5 and the **first b** of the dead, and the prince	4416

BEGUILE (2) [BEGUILED, BEGUILING]

Col	2: 4 lest any *man* should **b** you with enticing	3884
	2:18 Let no *man* **b** you **of** your **reward** in a	2603

BEGUILED (5) [BEGUILE]

Ge	3:13 The serpent **b** me, and I did eat.	5377
	29:25 Rachel? wherefore then hast thou **b** me?	7411
Nu	25:18 wherewith they have **b** you in the matter	5230
Jos	9:22 Wherefore have ye **b** us, saying,	7411
2Co	11: 3 as the serpent **b** Eve through his subtilty,	1818

BEGUILING (1) [BEGUILE]

2Pe	2:14 cannot cease from sin; **b** unstable souls:	1185

BEGUN (13) [BEGIN]

Nu	16:46 gone out from the Lord; the plague is **b**.	2490
	16:47 the plague was **b** among the people:	2490
	25: 1 the people **b** to commit whoredom with	2490
Dt	2:31 I have **b** to give Sihon and his land before	2490
	3:24 thou hast **b** to shew thy servant thy	2490
Est	6:13 before whom thou hast **b** to fall, thou	2490
	9:23 the Jews undertook to do as they had **b**,	2490
Mt	18:24 And when he had **b** to reckon, one was	756
2Co	8: 6 that as he had **b**, so he would also finish	4278
	8:10 who have **b** **before**, not only to do, but	4278
Gal	3: 3 having **b** in the Spirit, are ye now	1728
Php	1: 6 **b** a good work in you will perform *it* until	1728
1Ti	5:11 for when they have *b* to wax wanton	NIG

BEHALF (13) [BEHAVE, BEHAVED, BEHAVETH, BEHAVIOUR, BEHEADED]

Ex	27:21 **on the b** of the children of Israel.	854+4480
2Sa	3:12 Abner sent messengers to David **on his b**,	8478
2Ch	16: 9 to shew himself strong **in the b of** *them*	5973

B

Job	36: 2	that *I* have yet to speak **on** God's **b**.	3807.1
Da	11:18	a prince for his own **b** shall cause	NIH
Ro	16:19	all *men*. I am glad therefore **on** your **b**:	1909
1Co	1: 4	I thank my God always **on** your **b**, for	4012
2Co	1:11	thanks may be given by many **on** our **b**.	5228
	5:12	but give you occasion to glory **on** our **b**,	5228
	8:24	your love, and of our boasting **on** your **b**,	5228
	9: 3	boasting of you should be in vain in this **b**;	3313
Php	1:29	For unto you it is given **in** the **b** of Christ,	5228
1Pe	4:16	but let him glorify God on this **b**.	3313

BEHAVE (6) [BEHALF]

Dt	32:27	should **b** themselves **strangely**,	5234
1Ch	19:13	us **b** ourselves **valiantly** for our people,	2388
Ps	101: 2	I will **b** myself wisely in a perfect way.	7919
Isa	3: 5	the child shall **b** himself **proudly** against	7292
1Co	13: 5	Doth not **b** itself **unseemly**, seeketh not	807
1Ti	3:15	oughtest to **b** thyself in the house of God,	390

BEHAVED (9) [BEHALF]

1Sa	18: 5	Saul sent him, *and* **b** himself **wisely**:	7919
	18:14	David **b** himself **wisely** in all his ways;	7919
	18:15	Saul saw that he **b** himself very **wisely**,	7919
	18:30	*that* David **b** himself more **wisely** than all	7919
Ps	35:14	I **b** myself as though *he had been* my	1980
	131: 2	Surely I have **b** and quieted myself, as a	7737
Mic	3: 4	as they have **b** themselves **ill** in their	7489
1Th	2:10	unblameably we **b** ourselves among you	1096
2Th	3: 7	for we **b** not ourselves **disorderly** among	812

BEHAVETH (1) [BEHALF]

1Co	7:36	*he* **b** himself **uncomely** toward his virgin,	807

BEHAVIOUR (4) [BEHALF]

1Sa	21:13	he changed his **b** before them,	2940
Ps	34: T	when he changed his **b** before Abimelech;	2940
1Ti	3: 2	vigilant, sober, of **good b**, given to	2887
Tit	2: 3	*that they be* in **b** as becometh holiness,	2688

BEHEADED (7) [BEHALF]

Dt	21: 6	over the heifer that is **b** in the valley:	6202
2Sa	4: 7	**b** him, and took his head,	5493+7218
Mt	14:10	And he sent, and **b** John in the prison.	607
Mk	6:16	heard *thereof*, he said, It is John, whom I **b**:	607
	6:27	and he went and **b** him in the prison,	607
Lk	9: 9	And Herod said, John have I **b**: but who is	607
Rev	20: 4	*I saw* the souls of them that were **b** for	3990

BEHELD (53) [BEHOLD]

Ge	12:14	the Egyptians **b** the woman that she *was*	7200
	13:10	up his eyes, and **b** all the plain of Jordan,	7200
	19:28	all the land of the plain, and **b**, and lo,	7200
	31: 2	And Jacob **b** the countenance of Laban,	7200
	48: 8	Israel **b** Joseph's sons, and said, Who *are*	7200
Nu	21: 9	he **b** the serpent of brass, he lived.	413+5027
	23:21	He hath not **b** iniquity in Jacob,	5027
Jdg	16:27	women, that **b** while Samson made sport.	7200
1Sa	26: 5	David **b** the place where Saul lay,	7200
1Ch	21:15	the LORD **b**, and he repented him of	7200
Job	31:26	If I **b** the sun when it shined, or the moon	7200
Ps	119:158	I **b** the transgressors, and was grieved;	7200
	142: 4	but *there was* no man that would know	7200
Pr	7: 7	**b** among the simple ones, I discerned	7200
Ecc	8:17	I **b** all the work of God, that a man cannot	7200
Isa	41:28	For I **b**, and *there was* no man;	7200
Jer	4:23	I **b** the earth, and lo, *it was* without form,	7200
	4:24	I **b** the mountains, and lo, they trembled,	7200
	4:25	I **b**, and lo, *there was* no man, and all	7200
	4:26	I **b**, and lo, the fruitful place *was* a	7200
	31:26	Upon this I awaked, and **b**; and my sleep	7200
Eze	1:15	as I **b** the living creatures, behold one	7200
	8: 2	I **b**, and lo, a likeness as the appearance of	7200
	37: 8	I **b**, lo, the sinews and the flesh came	7200
Da	7: 4	I **b** till the wings thereof were pluckt,	2370
	7: 6	After this I **b**, and lo another, like a	2370
	7: 9	I **b** till the thrones were cast *down*, and	2370
	7:11	I **b** then because of the voice of the great	2370
	7:11	I *even* till the beast was slain,	2370
	7:21	I **b**, and the same horn made war with	2370
Hab	3: 6	he **b**, and drove asunder the nations;	7200
Mt	19:26	But Jesus **b** *them*, and said unto them,	1689
Mk	9:15	when they **b** him, were greatly amazed,	1492
	12:41	how the people cast money into	2334
	15:47	Mary the *mother* of Joses **b** where he was	2334
Lk	10:18	I **b** Satan as lightning fall from heaven.	2334
	19:41	come near, he **b** the city, and wept over it,	1492
	20:17	he **b** them, and said, What is this then	1689
	22:56	But a certain maid **b** him as he sat by	1492
	23:55	and **b** the sepulchre, and how his body	2300
	24:12	he **b** the linen clothes laid by themselves,	991
Jn	1:14	and dwelt among us, (and we **b** his glory,	2300
	1:42	And when Jesus **b** him, he said, Thou art	1689
Ac	1: 9	he had spoken these *things*, while they **b**,	991
	17:23	For as I passed by, and **b** your devotions,	333
Rev	5: 6	And I **b**, and lo, in the midst of the throne	1492
	5:11	And I **b**, and I heard the voice of many	1492
	6: 5	And I **b**, and lo a black horse; and he that	1492
	6:12	And I **b** when he had opened the sixth	1492
	7: 9	After this I **b**, and, lo, a great multitude,	1492
	8:13	And I **b**, and heard an angel flying through	1492
	11:12	in a cloud; and their enemies **b** them.	2334
	13:11	And I **b** another beast coming up out of	1492

BEHEMOTH (1)

Job	40:15	Behold now **b**, which I made with thee;	930

BEHIND (74)

Ge	18:10	heard *it in* the tent door, which *was* **b** him.	310
	19:17	look not **b** thee, neither stay thou in all	310
	19:26	his wife looked back from **b** him,	310
	22:13	behold **b** *him* a ram caught in a thicket by	310
	32:18	my lord Esau: and behold, also he *is* **b** us.	310
	32:20	Behold, thy servant Jacob *is* **b** us.	310
Ex	10:26	with us; there shall not a hoof be **left b**;	7604
	11: 5	of the maidservant that *is* **b** the mill;	310
	14:19	of Israel, removed and went **b** them;	310+4480
	14:19	before their face, and stood **b** them;	310+4480
Lev	25:51	If *there be* yet many years **b**, according	NIH
Nu	3:23	families of the Gershonites shall pitch **b**	310
Dt	25:18	*even* all that were feeble **b** thee, when thou	310
Jos	8: 2	lay thee an ambush for the city **b** it.	310+4480
	8: 4	wait against the city, *even* **b** the city:	310+4480
	8:14	liers in ambush against him **b** the city.	310+4480
	8:20	when the men of Ai looked **b** them, they	310
Jdg	18:12	unto this day: behold, *it is* **b** Kirjath-jearim.	310
	20:40	the Benjamites looked **b** them, and behold,	310
1Sa	21: 9	it *is here* wrapt in a cloth **b** the ephod:	310
	24: 8	when Saul looked **b** him, David stooped	310
	30: 9	where those that were **left b** stayed.	3498
	30:10	for two hundred abode **b**, which were so	NIH
2Sa	1: 7	And when he looked **b** him, he saw me,	310
	2:20	Abner looked **b** him, and said, *Art* thou	310
	2:23	*rib*, that the spear came out **b** him;	310+4480
	3:16	husband went with her along weeping **b**	310
	5:23	fetch a compass **b** them, and come upon	310
	10: 9	battle was against him before and **b**,	268+4480
	13:34	people by the way of the hill side **b** him.	310
1Ki	10:19	the top of the throne *was* round **b**:	310+4480
	14: 9	me to anger, and hast cast me **b** thy back:	310
2Ki	6:32	*is* not the sound of his master's feet **b** him?	310
	9:18	turn thee **b** me. And the watchman	310+413
	9:19	to do with peace? turn thee **b** me.	310+413
	11: 6	and a third *part* at the gate **b** the guard:	310
1Ch	19:10	battle was set against him before and **b**,	268
2Ch	13:13	ambushment to come about **b** them:	310+4480
	13:13	and the ambushment *was* **b** them.	310+4480
	13:14	behold, the battle *was* before and **b**:	268
Ne	4:13	Therefore set I in the lower places **b**	310+4480
	4:16	the rulers *were* **b** all the house of Judah.	310
	9:26	cast thy law **b** their backs, and slew thy	310
Ps	50:17	and castest my words **b** thee.	310
	139: 5	Thou hast beset me **b** and before,	268
SS	2: 9	behold, he standeth **b** our wall, he looketh	310
Isa	9:12	Syrians before, and the Philistines **b**;	268+4480
	30:21	thine ears shall hear a word **b** thee,	310+4480
	38:17	for thou hast cast all my sins **b** thy back.	310
	57: 8	**B** the doors also and the posts hast thou set	310
	66:17	purify themselves in the gardens **b** one *tree*	310
Eze	3:12	I heard **b** me a voice of a great rushing,	310
	23:35	cast me **b** thy back, therefore bear thou	310
	41:15	the separate place which *was* **b** it,	310+5921
Joel	2: 3	before them; and **b** them a flame burneth:	310
	2: 3	and **b** them a desolate wilderness;	310
	2:14	and repent, and leave a blessing **b** him;	310
Zec	1: 8	**b** him *were there* red horses, speckled,	310
Mt	9:20	came **b** *him*, and touched the hem of his	3693
	16:23	said unto Peter, Get thee **b** me, Satan:	3694
Mk	5:27	came in the press **b**, and touched his	3693
	8:33	saying, Get thee **b** me, Satan:	3694
	12:19	and leave his wife **b** *him*, and leave no	NIG
Lk	2:43	the child Jesus **tarried b** in Jerusalem;	5278
	4: 8	and said unto him, Get thee **b** me, Satan:	3694
	7:38	And stood at his feet **b** *him* weeping,	3694
	8:44	Came **b** *him*, and touched the border of	3693
1Co	1: 7	So that ye **come b** in no gift; waiting for	5302
2Co	11: 5	For I suppose *I* was not a whit **b** the very	5302
	12:11	for in nothing am I **b** the very chiefest	5302
Php	3:13	*I do*, forgetting those *things which are* **b**,	3694
Col	1:24	fill up that which is **b** of the afflictions of	5303
Rev	1:10	and heard **b** me a great voice, as of a	3694
	4: 6	*were* four beasts full of eyes before and **b**.	3693

BEHOLD (1326) [BEHELD, BEHOLDEST, BEHOLDETH, BEHOLDING]

Ge	1:29	God said, **B**, I have given you every herb	2009
	1:31	he had made, and **b**, *it was* very good.	2009
	3:22	the LORD God said, **B**, the man is	2005
	4:14	**B**, thou hast driven me out *this* day from	2009
	6:12	upon the earth, and **b**, it was corrupt;	2009
	6:13	and **b**, I will destroy them with the earth.	2009
	6:17	**B**, I, even I, do bring a flood of waters	2009
	8:13	looked, and **b**, the face of the ground was	2009
	9: 9	I establish my covenant with you and	2009
	11: 6	**B**, the people *is* one, and they have all one	2005
	12:11	that he said unto Sarai his wife, **B** now,	2009
	12:19	now therefore **b** thy wife, take *her*, and	2009
	15: 3	Abram said, **B**, to me thou hast given no	2009
	15: 4	**b**, the word of the LORD *came* unto him,	2009
	15:17	a smoking furnace, and a burning lamp	2009
	16: 2	Sarai said unto Abram, **B** now, the LORD	2009
	16: 6	said unto Sarai, **B**, thy maid *is* in thy hand;	2009
	16:11	**B**, thou *art* with child, and shalt bear a	2009
	16:14	**B**, *it is* between Kadesh and Bered.	2009
	17: 4	*As for* me, **b**, my covenant *is* with thee,	2009
	17:20	**B**, I have blessed him, and will make him	2009
	18: 9	thy wife? And he said, **B**, in the tent.	2009
	18:27	Abraham answered and said, **B** now,	2009
	18:31	he said, **B** now, I have taken upon me to	2009
	19: 2	**B** now, my lords, turn in, I pray you,	2005
	19: 8	**B** now, I have two daughters which have	2009
	19:19	**B** now, thy servant hath found grace in	2009
Ge	19:20	**B** now, this city *is* near to flee unto,	2009
	19:34	**B**, I lay yesternight with my father:	2005
	20: 3	said to him, **B**, thou *art but* a dead man,	2009
	20:15	Abimelech said, **B**, my land *is* before thee:	2009
	20:16	unto Sarah he said, **B**, I have given thy	2009
	20:16	**b**, he *is* to thee a covering of the eyes,	2009
	22: 1	Abraham: and he said, **B**, *here* I.	2009
	22: 7	he said, **B** the fire and the wood:	2009
	22:13	behold **b** *him* a ram caught in a thicket by	2009
	22:20	it was told Abraham, saying, **B**, Milcah	2009
	24:13	**B**, I stand *here* by the well of water;	2009
	24:15	**b**, Rebekah came out, who was born to	2009
	24:30	and **b**, he stood by the camels at the well.	2009
	24:43	**B**, I stand by the well of water; and it shall	2009
	24:45	I had done speaking in mine heart, **b**,	2009
	24:51	**B**, Rebekah *is* before thee, take *her*,	2009
	24:63	he lift up his eyes, and saw, and **b**,	2009
	25:24	**b**, *there were* twins in her womb.	2009
	25:32	Esau said, **B**, I *am* at the point to die:	2009
	26: 8	saw, and **b**, Isaac *was* sporting with	2009
	26: 9	and said, **B**, of a surety she *is* thy wife:	2009
	27: 1	and he said unto him, **B**, *here am* I.	2009
	27: 2	he said, **B** now, I am old, I know not	2009
	27: 6	spake unto Jacob her son, saying, **B**,	2009
	27:11	**B**, Esau my brother *is* a hairy man,	2005
	27:36	**b**, now he hath taken away my blessing.	2009
	27:37	Isaac answered and said unto Esau, **B**,	2009
	27:39	his father answered and said unto him, **B**,	2009
	27:42	said unto him, **B**, thy brother Esau,	2009
	28:12	**b** a ladder set up on the earth, and the top	2009
	28:12	**b** the angels of God ascending and	2009
	28:13	**b**, the LORD stood above it, and said,	2009
	28:15	**B**, I *am* with thee, and will keep thee in	2009
	29: 2	looked, and **b** a well in the field, and lo,	2009
	29: 6	**b**, Rachel his daughter cometh with	2009
	29:25	pass, that in the morning, **b**, it *was* Leah:	2005
	30: 3	said, **B** my maid Bilhah, go in unto her;	2009
	30:34	Laban said, **B**, I would it might be	2005
	31: 2	and **b**, it *was* not toward him as before.	2009
	31:10	up mine eyes, and saw in a dream, and **b**,	2009
	31:51	Jacob, **B** this heap, and behold *this* pillar,	2009
	31:51	Jacob, Behold this heap, and **b** *this* pillar,	2009
	32:18	my lord Esau: and **b**, also he *is* behind us.	2009
	32:20	say ye moreover, **B**, thy servant Jacob *is*	2009
	33: 1	looked, and **b**, Esau came, and with him	2009
	34:21	the land, **b**, *it is* large enough for them;	2009
	37: 7	For, **b**, we *were* binding sheaves in	2009
	37: 7	**b**, your sheaves stood round about,	2009
	37: 9	told it his brethren, and said, **B**, I have	2009
	37: 9	**b**, the sun and the moon and the eleven	2009
	37:15	a *certain* man found him, and **b**, *he was*	2009
	37:19	one to another, **B**, this dreamer cometh.	2009
	37:25	they lift up their eyes and looked, and **b**,	2009
	37:29	**b**, Joseph *was* not in the pit; and he rent	2009
	38:13	**B** thy father in law goeth up to Timnath to	2009
	38:23	**b**, I sent this kid, and thou hast not found	2009
	38:24	also, **b**, she *is* with child by whoredom.	2009
	38:27	travail, that, **b**, twins *were* in her womb.	2009
	38:29	his hand, that, **b**, his brother came out:	2009
	39: 8	and said unto his master's wife, **B**,	2005
	40: 6	looked upon them, and **b**, they *were* sad.	2009
	40: 9	said to him, In my dream, **b** a vine *was*	2009
	40:16	Joseph, I also *was* in my dream, and **b**,	2009
	41: 1	and **b**, he stood by the river.	2009
	41: 2	**b**, there came up out of the river seven	2009
	41: 3	**b**, seven other kine came up after them	2009
	41: 5	**b**, seven ears of corn came up upon one	2009
	41: 6	**b**, seven thin ears and blasted with the	2009
	41: 7	Pharaoh awoke, and **b**, it *was* a dream.	2009
	41:17	said unto Joseph, In my dream, **b**,	2009
	41:18	**b**, there came up out of the river seven	2009
	41:19	**b**, seven other kine came up after them,	2009
	41:22	saw in my dream, and **b**, seven ears came	2009
	41:23	**b**, seven ears, withered, thin,	2009
	41:29	**B**, there come seven years of great plenty	2009
	42: 2	said, **B**, I have heard that there is corn in	2009
	42:13	**b**, the youngest *is* this day with our father,	2009
	42:22	therefore, **b**, also his blood is required.	2009
	42:27	for **b**, it *was* in his sack's mouth.	2009
	42:35	**b**, every man's bundle of money *was* in	2009
	43:21	the inn, that we opened our sacks, and **b**,	2005
	44: 8	**B**, the money, which we found in our	2005
	44:16	**b**, we *are* my lord's servants, both we,	2009
	45:12	**b**, your eyes see, and the eyes of my	2009
	47: 1	and **b**, they *are* in the land of Goshen.	2009
	47:23	**B**, I have bought you *this* day and your	2005
	48: 1	that *one* told Joseph, **B**, thy father *is* sick:	2009
	48: 2	*one* told Jacob, and said, **B**, thy son Joseph	2009
	48: 4	said unto me, **B**, I will make thee fruitful,	2009
	48:21	Israel said unto Joseph, **B**, I die:	2009
	50:18	and they said, **B**, we *be* thy servants.	2009
Ex	1: 9	he said unto his people, **B**, the people of	2009
	2: 6	**b**, the babe wept. And she had	2009
	2:13	when he went out the second day, **b**,	2009
	3: 2	and **b**, the bush burned with fire,	2009
	3: 9	therefore, **b**, the cry of the children of	2009
	3:13	Moses said unto God, **B**, *when* I come	2009
	4: 1	Moses answered and said, But **b**, they will	2009
	4: 6	when he took it out, **b**, his hand *was*	2009
	4: 7	plucked it out of his bosom, and **b**, it was	2009
	4:14	also, **b**, he cometh forth to meet thee:	2009
	4:23	**b**, I will slay thy son, *even* thy firstborn.	2009
	5: 5	Pharaoh said, **B**, the people of the land	2009
	5:16	**b**, thy servants *are* beaten; but the fault	2009
	6:12	Moses spake before the LORD, saying, **B**,	2005

Ex
6:30 **B,** I *am* of uncircumcised lips, 2005
7:16 and he, hitherto thou wouldest not hear. 2009
7:17 **b,** I will smite with the rod that *is* in mine 2009
8: 2 thou refuse to let *them* go, **b,** I will smite 2009
8:21 Else, if thou wilt not let my people go, **b,** 2009
8:29 Moses said, **B,** I go out from thee, 2009
9: 3 **B,** the hand of the LORD is upon thy 2009
9: 7 Pharaoh sent, and **b,** there was not one of 2009
9:18 **B,** to morrow about *this* time I will cause 2009
10: 4 Else, if thou refuse to let my people go, **b,** 2009
14:10 and **b,** the Egyptians marched after them; 2009
14:17 I, **b,** I will harden the hearts of 2009
16: 4 said the LORD unto Moses, **B,** I will rain 2009
16:10 looked toward the wilderness, and **b,** 2009
16:14 when the dew that lay was gone up, **b,** 2009
17: 6 **B,** I will stand before thee there upon 2009
23:20 **B,** I send an Angel before thee, to keep 2009
24: 8 and said, **B** the blood of the covenant, 2009
24:14 Aaron and Hur *are* with you: if any 2009
31: 6 **b,** I have given with him Aholiab, the son 2009
32: 9 I have seen this people, and **b,** it *is* a 2009
32:34 **b,** mine Angel shall go before thee: 2009
33:21 the LORD said, **B,** *there is* a place by me, 2009
34:10 he said, **B,** I make a covenant: before all 2009
34:11 **b,** I drive out before thee the Amorite, 2009
34:30 saw Moses, **b,** the skin of his face shone; 2009
39:43 Moses did look upon all the work, and **b,** 2009

Lev
10:16 of the sin offering, and **b,** it was burnt: 2009
10:18 **B,** the blood of it was not brought in 2005
10:19 Aaron said unto Moses, **B,** *this* day have 2005
13: 5 **b,** *if* the plague in his sight be at a stay, 2009
13: 6 **b,** *if* the plague be somewhat dark, 2009
13: 8 *if* the priest see that **b,** the scab spreadeth 2009
13:10 priest shall see *him:* and **b,** *if* the rising 2009
13:13 **b,** *if* the leprosy have covered all his flesh, 2009
13:17 **b,** *if* the plague be turned into white; then 2009
13:20 if, when the priest seeth it, **b,** it *be* in sight 2009
13:21 if the priest look on it, and **b,** *there be* no 2009
13:25 if the hair in the bright spot be turned 2009
13:26 if the priest look on it, and **b,** *there be* no 2009
13:30 **b,** *if* it *be* in sight deeper than the skin; 2009
13:31 **b,** it *be* not in sight deeper than the skin, 2009
13:32 **b,** *if* the scall spread not, and there be in 2009
13:34 **b,** *if* the scall be not spread in the skin, 2009
13:36 **b,** the scall be spread in the skin of their 2009
13:39 **b,** *if* the bright spots in the skin of their 2009
13:43 **b,** *if* the rising of the sore *be* white 2009
13:53 if the priest shall look, and **b,** the plague 2009
13:55 **b,** *if* the plague have not changed his 2009
13:56 if the priest look, and **b,** the plague *be* 2009
14: 3 the priest look, and **b,** *if* the plague 2009
14:37 he shall look on the plague, and **b,** 2009
14:39 **b,** *if* the plague be spread in the walls of 2009
14:44 the priest shall come and look, and **b,** 2009
14:48 shall come in, and look *upon it,* and **b,** 2009
25:20 **b,** we shall not sow, nor gather in our 2005

Nu
3:12 I, **b,** I have taken the Levites from among 2009
12: 8 the similitude of the LORD shall he **b:** 5027
12:10 **b,** Miriam *became* leprous, *white* as snow 2009
12:10 upon Miriam, and **b,** *she was* leprous. 2009
16:42 the cloud covered it, and the glory of 2009
16:47 **b,** the plague was begun among the 2009
17: 8 **b,** the rod of Aaron for the house of Levi 2009
17:12 **B,** we die, we perish, we all perish. 2005
18: 6 **b,** I have taken your brethren the Levites 2009
18: 8 the LORD spake unto Aaron, **B,** I also 2009
18:21 **b,** I have given the children of Levi all 2009
20:16 **b,** we *are* in Kadesh, a city in the 2009
22: 5 to call him, saying, **B,** there is a people 2009
22: 5 **b,** they cover the face of the earth, 2009
22:11 **B,** *there is* a people come out of Egypt, 2009
22:32 **b,** I went out to withstand thee, because 2009
23: 9 I see him, and from the hills I **b** him: 7789
23:11 and **b,** thou hast blessed them altogether. 2009
23:17 when he came to him, **b,** he stood by his 2009
23:20 **B,** I have received *commandment* to bless 2009
23:24 **B,** the people shall rise up as a great lion, 2005
24:10 called thee to curse mine enemies, and **b,** 2009
24:14 now **b,** I go unto my people: come 2009
24:17 shall **b** him, but not nigh: there shall come 7789
25: 6 **b,** one of the children of Israel came and 2009
25:12 Wherefore say, **B,** I give unto him my 2009
31:16 **B,** these caused the children of Israel, 2005
32: 1 the land of Gilead, that the place *was* a 2009
32:14 **b,** ye are risen up in your fathers' stead, 2009
32:23 if ye will not do so, **b,** ye have sinned 2009

Dt
1: 8 **B,** I have set the land before you: go in 7200
1:10 your God hath multiplied you, and **b,** 2009
1:21 **B,** the LORD thy God hath set the land 2009
2:24 **b,** I have given into thy hand Sihon 7200
2:31 **B,** I have begun to give Sihon and his land 7200
3:11 **b,** his bedstead *was* a bedstead of iron; 2009
3:27 eastward, and **b** *it* with thine eyes: 7200
4: 5 **B,** I have taught you statutes and 2009
5:24 ye said, **B,** the LORD our God hath 2005
9:13 saying, I have seen this people, and **b,** it 2009
9:16 I looked, and **b,** ye had sinned against 2009
10:14 **B,** the heaven and the heaven of heavens 2005
11:26 **B,** I set before you *this* day a blessing and 7200
13:14 **b,** *if it be* truth, *and* the thing certain, 2009
17: 4 and **b,** *it is* true, and the thing certain, 2009
19:18 **b,** *if* the witness *be* a false witness, 2009
26:10 now, **b,** I have brought the firstfruits of 2009
31:14 the LORD said unto Moses, **B,** thy days 2005
31:16 **B,** thou shalt sleep with thy fathers; 2009

31:27 **b,** while I am yet alive with you *this* day, 2005
32:49 **b** the land of Canaan, which I give unto 7200

Jos
2: 2 it was told the king of Jericho, saying, **B,** 2009
2:18 **B,** *when* we come into the land, thou 2009
3:11 **B,** the ark of the covenant, *even* the Lord 2009
5:13 that he lift up his eyes and looked, and **b,** 2009
7:21 **b,** they *are* hid in the earth in the midst of 2009
7:22 **b,** *it was* hid in his tent, and the silver 2009
8: 4 commanded them, saying, **B,** ye shall lie 7200
8:20 they saw, and **b,** the smoke of the city 2009
9:12 but now, **b,** it is dry, and it is mouldy: 2009
9:13 we filled, *were* new; and **b,** they be rent: 2009
9:25 **b,** we *are* in thine hand: as it seemeth 2009
14:10 And now **b,** the LORD hath kept me alive, 2009
22:11 **B,** the children of Reuben and the 2009
22:28 that we may say *again,* **B** the pattern of 7200
23: 4 **B,** I have divided unto you *by lot* these 7200
23:14 **b,** *this* day I am going the way of all 2009
24:27 Joshua said unto all the people, **B,** this 2009

Jdg
1: 2 **B,** I have delivered the land into his hand. 2009
3:24 when they saw that **b,** the doors of 2009
3:25 **b,** he opened not the doors of the parlour; 2009
3:25 they took a key, and opened *them:* and **b,** 2009
4:22 **b,** as Barak pursued Sisera, Jael came out 2009
4:22 when he came into her *tent,* **b,** Sisera lay 2009
6:15 **b,** my family *is* poor in Manasseh, 2009
6:28 **b,** the altar of Baal was cast down, 2009
6:37 **B,** I will put a fleece of wool in the floor; 2009
7:13 when Gideon was come, **b,** *there was* a 2009
7:13 and said, **B,** I dreamed a dream, and lo, 2009
7:17 **b,** when I come to the outside of the 2009
8:15 said, **B** Zebah and Zalmunna, with whom 2009
9:31 saying, **B,** Gaal the son of Ebed and 2009
9:31 **b,** they fortify the city against thee. 2009
9:33 **b,** *when* he and the people that *is* with 2009
9:36 Gaal saw the people, he said to Zebul, **B,** 2009
9:43 laid wait in the field, and looked, and **b,** 2009
11:34 came *to* Mizpeh unto his house, and **b,** 2009
13: 3 said unto her, **B** now, thou *art* barren, 2009
13: 7 **B,** thou *shalt* conceive, and bear a son; 2009
13:10 her husband, and said unto him, **B,** 2009
14: 5 **b,** a young lion roared against him. 2009
14: 8 **b,** *there was* a swarm of bees and honey 2009
14:16 he said unto her, **B,** I have not told *it* my 2009
16:10 **b,** thou hast mocked me, and told me lies: 2009
17: 2 also in mine ears, the silver *is* with me; 2009
18: 9 have seen the land, and **b,** it *is* very good: 2009
18:12 this day: **b,** *it is* behind Kirjath-jearim. 2009
19: 9 damsel's father, said unto him, **B** now, 2009
19: 9 **b,** the day groweth to an end, lodge here, 2009
19:16 **b,** there came an old man from his work 2009
19:22 **b,** the men of the city, certain sons of 2009
19:24 **B,** *here is* my daughter a maiden, 2009
19:27 **B,** the woman his concubine *was* fallen 2009
20: 7 **B,** ye *are* all children of Israel; give here 2009
20:40 Benjamites looked behind them, and **b,** 2009
21: 8 **b,** there came none to the camp from 2009
21: 9 For the people were numbered, and **b,** 2009
21:19 they said, **B,** *there is* a feast of the LORD 2009
21:21 and **b,** if the daughters of Shiloh come 2009

Ru
1:15 she said, **B,** thy sister in law is gone back 2009
2: 4 **b,** Boaz came from Beth-lehem, 2009
3: 2 **b,** he winnoweth barley to night in 2009
3: 8 and **b,** a woman lay *at* his feet. 2009
4: 1 **b,** the kinsman of whom Boaz spake came 2009

1Sa
2:31 **B,** the days come, that I will cut off thine 2009
3:11 to Samuel, **B,** I will do a thing in Israel, 2009
5: 3 of Ashdod arose early on the morrow, **b,** 2009
5: 4 arose early on the morrow morning, **b,** 2009
8: 5 **B,** thou art old, and thy sons walk not in 2009
9: 6 he said unto him, **B** now, *there is* in this 2009
9: 7 **b,** *if* we go, what shall we bring the man? 2009
9: 8 servant answered Saul again, and said, **B,** 2009
9:12 and said, He is; **b,** he is before you: 2009
9:14 **b,** Samuel came out against them, 2009
9:17 **B** the man whom I spake to thee of: 2009
9:24 *Samuel* said, **B** that which is left; set *it* 2009
10: 8 **b,** I will come down unto thee, to offer 2009
10:10 hill, **b,** a company of prophets met him; 2009
10:11 all that knew him beforetime saw that **b,** 2009
10:22 the LORD answered, **B,** he hath hid 2009
11: 5 **b,** Saul came after the herd out of the field 2009
12: 1 Samuel said unto all Israel, **B,** I have 2009
12: 2 now **b,** the king walketh before you: 2009
12: 2 grayheaded; and **b,** my sons *are* with you: 2009
12: 3 **B,** here I *am:* witness against me before 2009
12:13 the king whom ye have chosen, 2009
12:13 and **b,** the LORD hath set a king over you. 2009
13:10 the burnt offering, **b,** Samuel came; 2009
14: 7 **b,** I *am* with thee according to thy heart. 2009
14: 8 said Jonathan, **B,** we will pass over unto 2009
14:11 the Philistines said, **B,** the Hebrews come 2009
14:16 **b,** the multitude melted away, 2009
14:17 **b** Jonathan and his armourbearer *were* 2009
14:20 **b,** every man's sword was against his 2009
14:26 into the wood, **b,** the honey dropped; 2009
14:33 they told Saul, saying, **B,** the people sin 2009
15:12 Saul came to Carmel, and **b,** 2009
15:22 **B,** to obey *is* better than sacrifice, 2009
16:11 youngest, and **b,** he keepeth the sheep. 2009
16:15 Saul's servants said unto him, **B** now, 2009
16:18 answered one of the servants, and said, B, 2009
17:23 as he talked with them, **b,** there 2009
18:17 said to David, **B** my elder daughter Merab, 2009
18:22 say, **B,** the king hath delight in thee, 2009

19:16 come in, **b** there was an image in the bed, 2009
19:19 it was told Saul, saying, **B,** David *is* at 2009
19:22 one said, **B,** *they* be at Naioth in Ramah. 2009
20: 2 **b,** my father will do nothing *either* great 2009
20: 5 **B,** to morrow *is* the new moon, 2009
20:12 *or* the third *day,* and **b,** *if there be* good 2009
20:21 **b,** I will send a lad, *saying,* Go, find out 2009
20:21 If I expressly say unto the lad, **B,** 2009
20:22 man, **B,** the arrows *are* beyond thee; 2009
20:23 which thou and I have spoken of, **b,** 2009
21: 9 thou slewest in the valley of Elah, **b,** 2009
23: 1 they told David, saying, **B,** the Philistines 2009
23: 3 unto him, **B,** we *be* afraid here in Judah: 2009
24: 1 that it was told him, saying, **B,** David *is* in 2009
24: 4 **B** the day of which the LORD said unto 2009
24: 4 **B,** I will deliver thine enemy into thine 2009
24: 9 saying, **B,** David seeketh thy hurt? 2009
24:10 **B,** this day thine eyes have seen how that 2009
24:20 now **b,** I know well that thou shalt surely 2009
25:14 men told Abigail, Nabal's wife, saying, **B,** 2009
25:19 Go on before me; **b,** I come after you. 2009
25:20 **b,** David and his men came down against 2009
25:36 **b,** he held a feast in his house, like the 2009
25:41 *on her* face to the earth, and said, **B,** 2009
26: 7 **b,** Saul lay sleeping within the trench, 2009
26:21 **b,** I have played the fool, and have erred 2009
26:22 David answered and said, **B,** the king's 2009
26:24 **b,** as thy life was much set by this day in 2009
28: 7 his servants said to him, **B,** *there is* a 2009
28: 9 woman said unto him, **B,** thou knowest 2009
28:21 was sore troubled, and said unto him, **B,** 2009
30: 3 to the city, and **b,** *it was* burnt with fire; 2009
30:16 **b** *they were* spread abroad upon all 2009
30:26 **B** a present for you of the spoil of 2009

2Sa
1: 2 even to pass on the third day, that **b,** 2009
1: 6 **b,** Saul leaned upon his spear; 2009
1:18 **B,** *it is* written in the book of Jasher.) 2009
3:12 **b,** my hand *shall* be with thee, to bring 2009
3:22 **b,** the servants of David and Joab came 2009
3:24 **b,** Abner came unto thee; why *is it that* 2009
4: 8 **B** the head of Ish-bosheth the son of Saul 2009
4:10 one told me, saying, **B,** Saul is dead, 2009
5: 1 spake, saying, **B,** we *are* thy bone and 2009
9: 4 **B,** he *is in* the house of Machir, the son of 2009
9: 6 And he answered, **B** thy servant. 2009
12:11 Thus saith the LORD, **B,** I will raise up 2009
12:18 for they said, **B,** while the child was *yet* 2009
13:24 said, **B** now, thy servant hath 2009
13:34 watch lift up his eyes, and looked, and **b,** 2009
13:35 unto the king, **B,** the king's sons come: 2009
13:36 that **b,** the king's sons came, and lift up 2009
14: 7 **b,** the whole family is risen against thine 2009
14:21 unto Joab, **B** now, I have done this thing: 2009
14:32 **B,** I sent unto thee, saying, Come hither, 2009
15:15 the king's servants said unto the king, **B,** 2009
15:26 **b,** here *am* I, let him do to me as seemeth 2009
15:32 **b,** Hushai the Archite *came* to meet him 2009
15:36 **B,** *they have* there with them their two 2009
16: 1 was a little past the top *of the hill,* **b,** 2009
16: 3 unto the king, **B,** he abideth at Jerusalem: 2009
16: 4 said the king to Ziba, **B,** thine *are* all that 2009
16: 5 when king David came to Bahurim, **b,** 2009
16: 8 and, **b,** thou *art taken* to thy mischief, 2009
16:11 and to all his servants, **B,** my son, 2009
17: 9 he is hid now in some pit, or in some 2009
18:10 man saw *it,* and told Joab, and said, **B,** 2009
18:11 **b,** thou sawest *him,* and why didst thou 2009
18:24 and looked, and **b** a man running alone. 2009
18:26 and said, **B** another man running alone. 2009
18:31 **b,** Cushi came; and Cushi said, Tidings, 2009
19: 1 **B,** the king weepeth and mourneth for 2009
19: 8 **B,** the king doth sit in the gate. 2009
19:20 therefore, **b,** I am come the first *this* day 2009
19:37 **b** thy servant Chimham; let him go over 2009
19:41 **b,** all the men of Israel came to the king, 2009
20:21 woman said unto Joab, **B,** his head *shall* 2009
24:22 **b,** here *be* oxen for burnt sacrifice, 7200

1Ki
1:14 **B,** while thou yet talkest there with 2009
1:18 now **b,** Adonijah reigneth; and now, 2009
1:23 the king, saying, **B** Nathan the prophet. 2009
1:25 **b,** they eat and drink before him, and say, 2009
1:42 while he yet spake, **b,** Jonathan the son of 2009
1:51 it was told Solomon, saying, **B,** 2009
2: 8 **b,** *thou hast* with thee Shimei the son of 2009
2:29 of the LORD; and **b,** *he is* by the altar. 2009
2:39 they told Shimei, saying, **B,** thy servants 2009
3:12 **B,** I have done according to thy word: 2009
3:15 Solomon awoke; and **b,** *it was* a dream. 2009
3:21 to give my child suck, it was dead: 2009
3:21 **b,** it was not my son, which I did bear. 2009
5: 5 **b,** I purpose to build a house unto the 2009
8:27 **b,** the heaven and heaven of heavens 2009
10: 7 I came, and mine eyes had seen *it:* and **b,** 2009
11:22 what *hast* thou lacked with me, that **b,** 2009
11:31 thus saith the LORD, the God of Israel, **B,** 2009
12:28 **b** thy gods, O Israel, which brought thee 2009
13: 1 **b,** there came a man of God out of Judah 2009
13: 2 **B,** a child *shall be* born unto the house of 2009
13: 3 **B,** the altar *shall be* rent, and the ashes 2009
13:25 **b,** men passed by, and saw the carcase 2009
14: 2 **b,** there *is* Ahijah the prophet, which told 2009
14: 5 the LORD said unto Ahijah, **B,** the wife of 2009
14:10 Therefore, **b,** I will bring evil upon 2009
14:19 **b** they *are* written in the book of 2009
15:19 **b,** I have sent unto thee a present of silver 2009

B

1Ki 16: 3 **B**, I will take away the posterity of Baasha, 2009
17: 9 **b**, I have commanded a widow woman 2009
17:10 when he came to the gate of the city, **b**, 2009
17:12 **b**, I am gathering two sticks, that I may 2009
18: 7 Obadiah was in the way, **b** Elijah met 2009
18: 8 I *am:* go, tell thy lord, **B**, Elijah *is here.* 2009
18:11 Go, tell thy lord, **B**, Elijah *is here.* 2009
18:14 Go, tell thy lord, **B**, Elijah *is here:* and 2009
18:44 **B**, there ariseth a little cloud out of the 2009
19: 5 **b** then, an angel touched him, 2009+2088
19: 6 he looked, and **b**, *there was* a cake baken 2009
19: 9 **b**, the word of the LORD *came* to him, 2009
19:11 **b**, the LORD passed by, and a great and 2009
19:13 **b**, *there came* a voice unto him, and said, 2009
20:13 **b**, there came a prophet unto Ahab king 2009
20:13 **b**, I will deliver it into thine hand *this* day 2009
20:31 servants said unto him, **B** now, we have 2009
20:36 **b**, **as soon as** thou art departed from me, 2009
20:39 **b**, a man turned aside, and brought a man 2009
21:18 **b**, *he is* in the vineyard of Naboth, 2009
21:21 **B**, I will bring evil upon thee, and will 2009
22:13 Micaiah spake unto him, saying, **B** now, 2009
22:23 Now therefore **b**, the LORD hath put a 2009
22:25 Micaiah said, **B**, thou shalt see in that day, 2009
2Ki 1: 9 **b**, he sat on the top of a hill. And he spake 2009
1:14 **B**, there came fire down from heaven, 2009
2:11 *as* they still went on, and talked, that **b**, 2009
2:16 they said unto him, **B** now, there be with 2009
2:19 **B**, I pray thee, the situation of *this* city *is* 2009
3:20 the meat offering was offered, that **b**, 2009
4: 9 she said unto her husband, **B** now, 2009
4:13 he said unto him, Say now unto her, **B**, 2009
4:25 servant, **B**, *yonder is* that Shunammite: 2009
4:32 **b**, the child was dead, *and* laid upon his 2009
5: 6 when this letter is come unto thee, **b**, 2009
5:11 and went away, and said, **B**, I thought, 2009
5:15 said, **B**, now I know that *there is* no God 2009
5:20 servant of Elisha the man of God, said, **B**, 2009
5:22 My master hath sent me, saying, **B**, 2009
6: 1 of the prophets said unto Elisha, **B** now, 2009
6:13 was told him, saying, **B**, *he is* in Dothan. 2009
6:15 gone forth, **b**, a host compassed the city 2009
6:17 **b**, the mountain was full of horses and 2009
6:20 and **b**, *they were* in the midst of Samaria. 2009
6:25 **b**, they besieged it, until an ass's head 2009
6:30 the wall, and the people looked, and **b**, 2009
6:33 while he yet talked with them, **b**, 2009
6:33 he said, **B**, this evil *is* of the LORD; 2009
7: 2 said, **B**, *if* the LORD would make 2009
7: 2 said, **B**, thou shalt see *it* with thine eyes, 2009
7: 5 camp of Syria, **b**, *there was* no man there. 2009
7:10 **b**, *there was* no man there, neither voice 2009
7:13 that remain, which are left in the city, (**b**, 2009
7:13 **b**, I say, they are even as all the multitude 2009
7:19 the man of God, and said, Now **b**, 2009
7:19 said, **B**, thou shalt see *it* with thine eyes, 2009
8: 5 that **b**, the woman, whose son he had 2009
9: 5 when he came, **b**, the captains of the host 2009
10: 4 said, **B**, two kings stood not before him: 2009
10: 9 **b**, I conspired against my master, 2009
11:14 when she looked, **b**, the king stood by a 2009
13:21 that **b**, they spied a band *of men;* that 2009
15:11 rest of the acts of Zachariah, **b**, they *are* 2009
15:15 and his conspiracy which he made, **b**, 2009
15:26 acts of Pekahiah, and all that he did, **b**, 2009
15:31 the acts of Pekah, and all that he did, **b**, 2009
17:26 **b**, they slay them, because they know not 2009
18:21 Now **b**, thou trustest upon the staff of this 2009
19: 7 **B**, I will send a blast upon him, and he 2009
19: 9 **B**, he is come out to fight against thee: 2009
19:11 **B**, thou hast heard what the kings of 2009
19:35 morning, **b**, they *were* all dead corpses. 2009
20: 5 **b**, I will heal thee: on the third day thou 2009
20:17 **B**, the days come, that all that *is* in thine 2009
21:12 **B**, I *am* bringing *such* evil upon Jerusalem 2009
22:16 Thus saith the LORD, **B**, I will bring evil 2009
22:20 **B** therefore, I will gather thee unto thy 2009
1Ch 9: 1 **b**, they *were* written in the book of 2009
11: 1 **B**, we *are* thy bone and thy flesh. 2009
11:25 **b**, he was honourable among the thirty, 2009
22: 9 **b**, a son *shall* be born to thee, who shall 2009
22:14 Now **b**, in my trouble I have prepared for 2009
28:21 **b**, the courses of the priests and the 2009
29:29 acts of David the king, first and last, **b**, 2009
2Ch 2: 4 **b**, I build a house to the name of 2009
2: 8 **b**, my servants *shall be* with thy servants, 2009
2:10 **b**, I will give to thy servants, the hewers 2009
2:16 **b**, heaven and the heaven of heavens 2009
9: 6 I came, and mine eyes had seen *it:* and **b**, 2009
13:12 God *himself is* with us for *our* captain, 2009
13:14 **b**, the battle *was* before and behind: 2009
16: 3 **b**, I have sent thee silver and gold; go, 2009
16:11 **b**, the acts of Asa, first and last, lo, they 2009
18:12 to call Micaiah spake to him, saying, **B**, 2009
18:22 Now therefore **b**, the LORD hath put a 2009
18:24 Micaiah said, **B**, thou shalt see on that day 2009
19:11 **b**, Amariah the chief priest *is* over you in 2009
20: 2 **b**, they *be* in Hazazon-tamar, which *is* 2009
20:10 now **b**, the children of Ammon and Moab 2009
20:11 **B**, I say, *how* they reward us, to come to 2009
20:16 **b**, they come up by the cliff of Ziz; 2009
20:24 they looked unto the multitude, and **b**, 2009
20:34 **b** they *are* written in the book of Jehu 2009
21:14 **B**, *with* a great plague will the LORD 2009
23: 3 he said unto them, **B**, the king's son shall 2009

2Ch 23:13 she looked, and **b**, the king stood at his 2009
24:27 **b** they *are* written in the story of the book 2009
25:26 of the acts of Amaziah, first and last, **b**, 2009
26:20 all the priests, looked upon him, and **b**, 2009
28: 9 **B**, because the LORD God of your fathers 2009
28:26 acts and of all his ways, first and last, **b**, 2009
29:19 have we prepared and sanctified, and **b**, 2009
32:32 the acts of Hezekiah, and his goodness, **b**, 2009
33:18 **b**, they *are written* in the book of the 2009
33:19 **b**, they *are* written among the sayings of 2009
34:24 Thus saith the LORD, **B**, I will bring evil 2009
34:28 **B**, I will gather thee to thy fathers, 2009
35:25 **b**, they *are* written in the lamentations. 2009
35:27 deeds, first and last, **b**, they *are* written 2009
36: 8 did, and that which was found in him, **b**, 2009
Ezr 9:15 **b**, we *are* before thee in our trespasses: 2009
Ne 9:36 **b**, we *are* servants *this* day, and *for* the 2009
9:36 the fruit thereof and the good thereof, **b**, 2009
Est 6: 5 him, **B**, Haman standeth in the court. 2009
7: 9 said before the king, **B** also, 2009
8: 7 the queen and to Mordecai the Jew, **B**, 2009
Job 1:12 **B**, all that he hath *is* in thy power; 2009
1:19 **b**, there came a great wind from 2009
2: 6 said unto Satan, **B**, he *is* in thine hand; 2009
4: 3 **B**, thou hast instructed many, and thou 2009
4:18 **b**, he put no trust in his servants; and his 2009
5:17 **B**, happy *is* the man whom God 2009
8:19 **B**, this *is* the joy of his way, and out of 2005
8:20 **B**, God will not cast away a perfect *man,* 2005
9:12 **B**, he taketh away, who can hinder him? 2005
12:14 **B**, he breaketh down, and it cannot be 2005
12:15 **B**, he withholdeth the waters, and they 2005
13:18 **b** now, I have ordered *my* cause; I know 2005
15:15 **B**, he putteth no trust in his saints; yea, 2005
16:19 **b** my witness *is* in heaven, and my record 2005
19: 7 **B**, I cry out *of* wrong, but I am not heard: 2005
19:27 and mine eyes shall **b**, and not another; 7200
20: 9 neither shall his place any more **b** him. 7789
21:27 **B**, I know your thoughts, and the devices 2009
22:12 **b** the height of the stars, how high they 7200
23: 8 **B**, I go forward, but he *is not there;* and 2009
23: 9 I cannot **b** *him:* he hideth *himself* on 2372
24: 5 **B**, *as* wild asses in the desert, go they 2005
25: 5 **B** even to the moon, and it shineth not; 2005
27:12 **B**, all ye yourselves have seen *it;* why then 2005
28:28 **B**, the fear of the Lord, that *is* wisdom; 2005
31:35 **b**, my desire *is, that* the Almighty would 2005
32:11 **B**, I waited for your words; I gave ear to 2005
32:12 Yea, I attended unto you, and **b**, *there* 2009
32:19 **B**, my belly *is as* wine *which* hath no vent 2009
33: 2 **B** now I have opened my mouth, my 2005
33: 6 **B**, I *am* according to thy wish in God's 2005
33: 7 **B**, my terror shall not make thee afraid, 2005
33:10 **B**, he findeth occasions against me, 2005
33:12 **B**, *in* this thou art not just: I will answer 2005
34:29 **b** hideth *his* face, who then can **b** him? 7789
35: 5 **b** the clouds *which* are higher than thou. 7789
36: 5 **B**, God *is* mighty, and despiseth not *any:* 2005
36:22 **B**, God exalteth by his power: who 2005
36:24 thou magnify his work, which men **b**. 7891
36:25 man may see it; man may **b** it afar off. 5027
36:26 **B**, God *is* great, and we know *him* not, 2005
36:30 **B**, he spreadeth his light upon it, 2005
39:29 seeketh the prey, *and* her eyes **b** afar off. 5027
40: 4 **B**, I am vile; what shall I answer thee? 2005
40:11 **b** every one *that is* proud, and abase him. 7200
40:15 **B** now behemoth, which I made with 2005
40:23 **B**, he drinketh up a river, *and* hasteth not: 2005
41: 9 **B**, the hope of him is in vain: shall *not* 2005
Ps 7:14 **B**, he travaileth with iniquity, 2009
11: 4 his eyes **b**, his eyelids try, the children of 2372
11: 7 his countenance doth **b** the upright. 2372
17: 2 let thine eyes **b** the things that are equal. 2372
17:15 for *me,* I will **b** thy face in righteousness: 2372
27: 4 to **b** the beauty of the LORD, 2372
33:18 the eye of the LORD *is* upon them that 2009
37:37 Mark the perfect *man,* and **b** the upright: 7200
39: 5 **B**, thou hast made my days *as a* 2009
46: 8 Come, **b** the works of the LORD, 2009
51: 5 **B**, I was shapen in iniquity; and in sin did 2005
51: 6 **B**, thou desirest truth in the inward parts: 2005
54: 4 **B**, God *is* mine helper: the Lord *is* with 2009
59: 4 *my* fault: awake to help me, and **b**. 7200
59: 7 **B**, they belch out with their mouth: 2009
66: 7 his power for ever; his eyes **b** the nations: 6822
73:12 **B**, these *are* the ungodly, who prosper in 2009
73:15 **b**, I should offend *against* the generation 2009
78:20 **B**, he smote the rock, that the waters 2009
80:14 from heaven, and **b**, and visit this vine; 7200
84: 9 **B**, O God our shield, and look upon 2009
87: 4 **b** Philistia, and Tyre, with Ethiopia; 2009
91: 8 Only with thine eyes shalt thou **b** and 5027
102:19 from heaven did the LORD **b** the earth; 5027
113: 6 Who humbleth *himself* to **b** *the* things 7200
118:18 that I may **b** wondrous *things* out of thy 5027
119:40 **B**, I have longed after thy precepts: 2009
121: 4 **b**, he that keepeth Israel shall neither 2009
123: 2 **B**, as the eyes of servants *look* unto 2009
128: 4 **B**, that thus shall the man be blessed that 2009
133: 1 **B**, how good and how pleasant *it is* for 2009
134: 1 **B**, bless ye the LORD, all ye servants of 2009
139: 8 if I make my bed in hell, **b**, thou *art there.* 2009
Pr 1:23 **B**, I will pour out my spirit unto you, 2009
7:10 **b**, there met him a woman *with the attire* 2009
11:31 **B**, the righteous shall be recompensed in 2005

Pr 23:33 Thine eyes shall **b** strange *women,* and 7200
24:12 If thou sayest, **B**, we knew it not; doth 2005
Ecc 1:14 and **b**, all *is* vanity and vexation of spirit. 2009
2: 1 enjoy pleasure: and **b**, this also *is* vanity. 2009
2:11 **b**, all *was* vanity and vexation of spirit, 2009
2:12 turned myself to **b** wisdom, and madness, 7200
4: 1 **b**, the tears of such as were oppressed, 2009
5:18 **B** *that* which I have seen: *it is* good and 2009
7:27 **B**, this have I found, saith the Preacher, 7200
11: 7 a pleasant *thing it is* for the eyes to **b** 7200
SS 1:15 **B**, thou *art* fair, my love; behold, thou *art* 2009
1:15 thou *art* fair, my love; **b**, thou *art* fair; 2009
1:16 **B**, thou *art* fair, my beloved, yea, pleasant: 2009
2: 8 **b**, he cometh leaping upon the mountains, 2009
2: 9 **b**, he standeth behind our wall, 2009
3: 7 **b** his bed, which *is* Solomon's; 2009
3:11 **b** king Solomon with the crown 7200
4: 1 **B**, thou *art* fair, my love; behold, thou *art* 2009
4: 1 thou *art* fair, my love; **b**, thou *art* fair; 2009
Isa 3: 1 For **b**, the Lord, the LORD of hosts, 2009
5: 7 he looked for judgment, but **b** oppression; 2009
5: 7 for righteousness, but **b** a cry. 2009
5:26 and **b**, they shall come with speed swiftly: 2009
5:30 **b** darkness *and* sorrow, and the light is 2009
7:14 **B**, a Virgin shall conceive, and bear a Son, 2009
8: 7 Now therefore **b**, the Lord bringeth up 2009
8:18 **B**, I and the children whom the LORD 2009
8:22 **b** trouble and darkness, dimness of 2009
10:33 **B**, the Lord, the LORD of hosts, shall lop 2009
12: 2 **B**, God *is my* salvation; I will trust, 2009
13: 9 **B**, the day of the LORD cometh, 2009
13: 17 **B**, I will stir up the Medes against them, 2009
17: 1 **B**, Damascus *is* taken away from *being* a 2009
17:14 **b** at eveningtide trouble; *and* before 2009
19: 1 **B**, the LORD rideth upon a swift cloud, 2009
20: 6 in that day, **B**, such *is* our expectation, 2009
21: 9 **b**, here cometh a chariot of men, *with* a 2009
22:13 **b** joy and gladness, slaying oxen, 2009
22:17 **B**, the LORD will carry thee away with a 2009
23:13 **B** the land of the Chaldeans; this people 2005
24: 1 **B**, the LORD maketh the earth empty, 2009
26:10 and will not **b** the majesty of the LORD. 7200
26:21 For **b**, the LORD cometh out of his place 2009
28: 2 **B**, the Lord hath a mighty and 2009
28:16 Therefore thus saith the Lord GOD, **B**, 2009
29: 8 hungry *man* dreameth, and **b**, he eateth; 2009
29: 8 thirsty *man* dreameth, and **b**, he drinketh; 2009
29: 8 **b**, *he is* faint, and his soul hath appetite: 2009
29:14 Therefore, **b**, I will proceed to do a 2009
30:27 **b**, the name of the LORD cometh from 2009
32: 1 **B**, a king shall reign in righteousness, 2005
33: 7 **B**, their valiant ones shall cry without: 2009
33:17 they shall **b** the land that is very far off. 7200
34: 5 **b**, it shall come down upon Idumea, 2009
35: 4 **b**, your God will come *with* vengeance, 2009
37: 7 **B**, I will send a blast upon him, and he 2009
37:11 **B**, thou hast heard what the kings of 2009
37:36 morning, **b**, they *were* all dead corpses. 2009
38: 5 **b**, I will add unto thy days fifteen years. 2009
38: 8 **B**, I will bring again the shadow of 2009
38:11 shall **b** man no more with the inhabitants 5027
38:17 **B**, for peace I had great bitterness: 2009
39: 6 **b**, the days come, that all that *is* in thine 2009
40: 9 say unto the cities of Judah, **B** your God. 2009
40:10 **B**, the Lord GOD will come with strong 2009
40:10 **b**, his reward *is* with him, and his work 2009
40:15 **B**, the nations *are* as a drop of a bucket, 2005
40:15 **b**, he taketh up the isles as a very little 2005
40:26 **b** who hath created these *things,* that 7200
41:11 **B**, all they that were incensed against thee 2005
41:15 **B**, I will make thee a new sharp threshing 2009
41:23 we may be dismayed, and **b** it together. 7200
41:24 **B**, ye *are* of nothing, and your work of 2005
41:27 first *shall say* to Zion, **B**, behold them: 2009
41:27 first *shall say* to Zion, Behold, **b** them: 2009
41:29 **B**, they *are* all vanity; their works *are* 2005
42: 1 **B** my servant, whom I uphold; mine elect, 2005
42: 9 **B**, the former *things* are come to pass, 2009
43:19 **B**, I will do a new *thing;* now it shall 2009
44:11 **B**, all his fellows shall be ashamed: 2009
47:14 **B**, they shall be as stubble; the fire shall 2009
48: 7 lest thou shouldest say, **B**, I knew them. 2009
48:10 **B**, I have refined thee, but not with silver; 2009
49:12 **B**, these shall come from far: and lo, 2009
49:16 **B**, I have graven thee upon the palms of 2005
49:18 Lift up thine eyes round about, and **b**: 7200
49:21 **B**, I was left alone; these, where *had* they 2005
49:22 Thus saith the Lord GOD, **B**, I will lift up 2009
50: 1 **B**, for your iniquities have you sold 2005
50: 2 **b**, at my rebuke I dry up the sea, I make 2005
50: 9 **B**, the Lord GOD will help me; who *is he* 2005
50:11 **B**, all ye that kindle a fire, that compass 2005
51:22 *that* pleadeth the cause of his people, **B**, 2005
52: 6 day that I *am* he that doth speak: **b**, *it is* I. 2009
52:13 **B**, my servant shall deal prudently, he 2009
54:11 with tempest, *and* not comforted, **b**, 2005
54:15 **b**, they shall surely gather together, 2009
54:16 **B**, I have created the smith that bloweth 2005
55: 4 **B**, I have given him *for* a witness to 2005
55: 5 **B**, thou shalt call a nation *that* thou 2005
56: 3 let the eunuch say, **B**, I *am* a dry tree. 2005
58: 3 In the day of your fast you find 2005
58: 4 **B**, ye fast for strife and debate, and to 2005
59: 1 **B**, the LORD's hand is not shortened, 2005
59: 9 we wait for light, but **b** obscurity; 2009

B

Isa	60: 2 For **b**, the darkness shall cover the earth,	2009
	62:11 **B**, the Lord hath proclaimed unto	2009
	62:11 daughter of Zion, **B**, thy salvation cometh;	2009
	62:11 **b**, his reward *is* with him, and his work	2009
	63:15 **b** from the habitation of thy holiness and	7200
	64: 5 **b**, thou art wroth; for we have sinned:	2005
	64: 9 **b**, see, we beseech thee, we *are* all thy	2005
	65: 1 I said, **B** me, behold me, unto a nation	2009
	65: 1 I said, Behold me, **b** unto a nation	2009
	65: 6 **B**, *it is* written before me: I will not keep	2009
	65:13 **b**, my servants shall eat, but ye shall be	2009
	65:13 **b**, my servants shall drink, but ye shall be	2009
	65:13 **b**, my servants shall rejoice, but ye shall	2009
	65:14 **B**, my servants shall sing for joy of heart,	2009
	65:17 For, **b**, I create new heavens and a new	2009
	65:18 for **b**, I create Jerusalem a rejoicing,	2009
	66:12 For thus saith the Lord, **B**, I will extend	2009
	66:15 For **b**, the Lord will come with fire,	2009
Jer	1: 6 said I, Ah, Lord God, **b**, I cannot speak:	2009
	1: 9 the Lord said unto me, **B**, I have put my	2009
	1:18 **b**, I have made thee *this* day a defenced	2009
	2:35 **B**, I *will* plead with thee, because	2009
	3: 5 **B**, thou hast spoken and done evil *things*	2009
	3:22 **B**, we come unto thee; for thou *art*	2009
	4:13 **B**, he shall come up as clouds,	2009
	4:16 **b**, publish against Jerusalem, *that*	2009
	5:14 Because ye speak this word, **b**, I will	2009
	6:10 **b**, their ear *is* uncircumcised,	2009
	6:10 **b**, the word of the Lord is unto them a	2009
	6:19 **b**, I will bring evil upon this people,	2009
	6:21 Therefore thus saith the Lord, **B**, I will	2009
	6:22 Thus saith the Lord, **B**, a people cometh	2009
	7: 8 **b**, ye trust in lying words, *that* cannot	2009
	7:11 **B**, even I have seen *it*, saith the Lord.	2009
	7:20 **B**, mine anger and my fury *shall be*	2009
	7:32 Therefore, **b**, the days come, saith	2009
	8:15 *and* for a time of health, and **b** trouble.	2009
	8:17 For **b**, I will send serpents, cockatrices,	2009
	8:19 **B** the voice of the cry of the daughter of	2009
	9: 7 hosts, **B**, I will melt them, and try them;	2009
	9:15 **B**, I *will* feed them, *even* this people,	2009
	9:25 **B**, the days come, saith the Lord, that I	2009
	10:18 For thus saith the Lord, **B**, I will sling	2009
	10:22 **B**, the noise of the bruit is come,	2009
	11:11 the Lord, **B**, I *will* bring evil upon them,	2009
	11:22 the Lord of hosts, **B**, I will punish them:	2009
	12:14 **B**, I will pluck them out of their land,	2009
	13: 7 **b**, the girdle was marred, it was profitable	2009
	13:13 say unto them, Thus saith the Lord, **B**,	2009
	13:20 and **b** them that come from the north:	7200
	14:13 **b**, the prophets say unto them, Ye shall	2009
	14:18 the field, then **b** the slain with the sword:	2009
	14:18 then **b** them that are sick with famine:	2009
	14:19 and for the time of healing, and **b** trouble.	2009
	16: 9 **B**, I will cause to cease out of this place in	2009
	16:12 for **b**, ye walk every one after	2009
	16:14 Therefore **b**, the days come, saith	2009
	16:16 **B**, I will send for many fishers, saith	2009
	16:21 Therefore **b**, I *will* this once cause them	2009
	17:15 **b**, they say unto me, Where *is* the word	2009
	18: 3 and **b**, he wrought a work on the wheels.	2009
	18: 6 **B**, as the clay *is* in the potter's hand,	2009
	18:11 **B**, I frame evil against you, and devise a	2009
	19: 3 **B**, I *will* bring evil upon this place,	2009
	19: 6 Therefore **b**, the days come, saith	2009
	19:15 **B**, I will bring upon this city and upon all	2009
	20: 4 For thus saith the Lord, **B**, I will make	2009
	20: 4 thine eyes *shall* **b** it; and I will give all	7200
	21: 4 **B**, I *will* turn back the weapons of war	2009
	21: 8 **B**, I set before you the way of life,	2009
	21:13 **B**, I *am* against thee, O inhabitant of	2009
	23: 2 **b**, I will visit upon you the evil of your	2009
	23: 5 **B**, the days come, saith the Lord, that I	2009
	23: 7 Therefore **b**, the days come, saith	2009
	23:15 **B**, I will feed them with wormwood,	2009
	23:19 **B**, a whirlwind of the Lord is gone forth	2009
	23:30 Therefore **b**, I *am* against the prophets,	2009
	23:31 **B**, I *am* against the prophets, saith	2009
	23:32 **B**, I *am* against them that prophesy false	2009
	23:39 Therefore **b**, I, even I, will utterly forget	2009
	24: 1 The Lord shewed me, and **b**,	2009
	25: 9 **B**, I will send and take all the families of	2009
	25:32 Thus saith the Lord of hosts, **B**,	2009
	26:14 As for me, **b**, I *am* in your hand: do with	2009
	27:16 that prophesy unto you, saying, **B**,	2009
	28:16 **B**, I will cast thee from off the face of	2009
	29:17 **B**, I will send upon them the sword,	2009
	29:21 **B**, I will deliver them into the hand of	2009
	29:32 **B**, I will punish Shemaiah the Nehelamite,	2009
	29:32 neither shall he **b** the good that I will do	7200
	30:18 **B**, I *will* bring again the captivity of	2009
	30:23 **B**, the whirlwind of the Lord goeth forth	2009
	31: 8 **B**, I will bring them from the north	2009
	31:27 **B**, the days come, saith the Lord, that I	2009
	31:31 **B**, the days come, saith the Lord, that I	2009
	31:38 **B**, the days come, saith the Lord,	2009
	32: 3 and say, Thus saith the Lord, **B**,	2009
	32: 4 to mouth, and his eyes shall **b** his eyes:	7200
	32: 7 **B**, Hanameel the son of Shallum thine	2009
	32:17 **b**, thou hast made the heaven and the	2009
	32:24 **B** the mounts, they are come *unto* the	2009
	32:24 is come to pass; and **b**, thou seest *it*.	2009
	32:27 **B**, I *am* the Lord, the God of all flesh:	2009
	32:28 **B**, I *will* give this city into the hand of	2009
	32:37 **B**, I *will* gather them out of all countries,	2009

Jer	33: 6 **B**, I *will* bring it health and cure, and I	2009
	33:14 **B**, the days come, saith the Lord, that I	2009
	34: 2 **B**, I *will* give this city into the hand of	2009
	34: 3 thine eyes shall **b** the eyes of the king of	7200
	34:17 **b**, I proclaim a liberty for you, saith	2009
	34:22 **B**, I *will* command, saith the Lord,	2009
	35:17 **B**, I will bring upon Judah and upon all	2009
	37: 7 **B**, Pharaoh's army, which is come forth	2009
	38: 5 the king said, **B**, he *is* in your hand:	2009
	38:22 **b**, all the women that are left in the king	2009
	39:16 **B**, I *will* bring my words upon this city for	2009
	40: 4 **b**, I loose thee *this* day from the chains	2009
	40: 4 **b**, all the land *is* before thee: whither it	7200
	40:10 As for me, **b**, I *will* dwell at Mizpah to	2009
	42: 2 *but* a few of many, as thine eyes do **b** us:)	7200
	42: 4 said unto them, I have heard *you*; **b**,	2009
	43:10 **B**, I *will* send and take Nebuchadrezzar	2009
	44: 2 **b**, this day they *are* a desolation,	2009
	44:11 **B**, I will set my face against you for evil,	2009
	44:26 **B**, I have sworn by my great name,	2009
	44:27 **B**, I *will* watch over them for evil,	2009
	44:30 **B**, I *will* give Pharaoh-hophra king of	2009
	45: 4 **B**, *that* which I have built *will* I break	2009
	45: 5 for **b**, I *will* bring evil upon all flesh,	2009
	46:25 **B**, I *will* punish the multitude of No,	2009
	46:27 for **b**, I *will* save thee from afar off,	2009
	47: 2 **B**, waters rise up out of the north,	2009
	48:12 Therefore **b**, the days come, saith	2009
	48:40 **B**, he shall fly as an eagle, and shall spread	2009
	49: 2 Therefore **b**, the days come, saith	2009
	49: 5 **B**, I will bring a fear upon thee, saith	2009
	49:12 **B**, they whose judgment *was* not to drink	2009
	49:19 **b**, he shall come up like a lion from	2009
	49:22 **B**, he shall come up and fly as the eagle,	2009
	49:35 **B**, I *will* break the bow of Elam, the chief	2009
	50:12 **b**, the hindermost of the nations *shall be*	2009
	50:18 **B**, I *will* punish the king of Babylon and	2009
	50:31 **B**, I *am* against thee, *O thou* most proud,	2009
	50:41 **B**, a people shall come from the north,	2009
	50:44 **B**, he shall come up like a lion from	2009
	51: 1 **B**, I *will* raise up against Babylon,	2009
	51:25 **B**, I *am* against thee, O destroying	2009
	51:36 **B**, I *will* plead thy cause,	2009
	51:47 Therefore **b**, the days come, that I will do	2009
	51:52 Wherefore **b**, the days come, saith	2009
La	1: 9 O Lord, **b** my affliction: for the enemy	2009
	1:12 **b**, and see if there be any sorrow like unto	5027
	1:18 I pray you, all people, and **b** my sorrow:	7200
	1:20 **B**, O Lord; for I *am* in distress:	7200
	2:20 **B**, O Lord, and consider to whom thou	7200
	3:50 the Lord look down, and **b** from heaven.	7200
	3:63 **B** their sitting down, and their rising up;	5027
	5: 1 upon us: consider, and **b** our reproach.	7200
Eze	1: 4 I looked, and **b**, a whirlwind came out of	2009
	1:15 **b** one wheel upon the earth by the living	2009
	2: 9 I looked, **b**, a hand *was* sent unto me;	2009
	3: 8 **B**, I have made thy face strong against	2009
	3:23 **b**, the glory of the Lord stood there,	2009
	3:25 O son of man, **b**, they shall put bands	2009
	4: 8 **b**, I will lay bands upon thee, and thou	2009
	4:14 said I, Ah Lord God, **b**, my soul *hath* not	2009
	4:16 Moreover he said unto me, Son of man, **b**,	2009
	5: 8 **B**, I, even I, *am* against thee,	2009
	6: 3 **B**, I, *even* I, *will* bring a sword upon you,	2009
	7: 5 An evil, an only evil, **b**, is come:	2009
	7: 6 come: it watcheth for thee; **b**, it is come.	2009
	7:10 **B** the day, behold, it is come:	2009
	7:10 Behold the day, **b**, it is come:	2009
	8: 4 **b**, the glory of the God of Israel *was* there,	2009
	8: 5 eyes the way toward the north, and **b**,	2009
	8: 7 and when I looked, **b** a hole in the wall.	2009
	8: 8 when I had digged in the wall, **b** a door.	2009
	8: 9 **b** the wicked abominations that they do	7200
	8:10 **b** every form of creeping things,	2009
	8:14 **b**, there sat women weeping for Tammuz.	2009
	8:16 **b**, *at* the door of the temple of the Lord,	2009
	9: 2 **b**, six men came from the way of the	2009
	9:11 **b**, the man clothed with linen, which	2009
	10: 1 I looked, and **b**, in the firmament that	2009
	10: 9 **b** the four wheels by the cherubims,	2009
	11: 1 **b** at the door of the gate five and	2009
	12:27 Son of man, **b**, *they of* the house of Israel	2009
	13: 8 seen lies, therefore **b**, I *am* against you,	2009
	13:20 **B**, I *am* against your pillows, where*with*	2009
	14:22 Yet **b**, therein shall be left a remnant that	2009
	14:22 **b**, they *shall* come forth unto you,	2009
	15: 4 **B**, it is cast into the fire for fuel; the fire	2009
	15: 5 **B**, when it was whole, it was meet for no	2009
	16: 8 I passed by thee, and looked upon thee, **b**,	2009
	16:27 Therefore, I have stretched out my hand	2009
	16:37 Therefore, I will gather all thy lovers,	2009
	16:43 hast fretted me in all these *things*; **b**	1887
	16:44 **B**, every one that useth proverbs shall use	2009
	16:49 **B**, this was the iniquity of thy sister	2009
	17: 7 **b**, this vine did bend her roots toward	2009
	17:10 Yea **b**, *being* planted, shall it prosper?	2009
	17:12 not what these *things mean?* tell *them*, **B**,	2009
	18: 4 **B**, all souls *are* mine; as the soul of	2005
	20:47 **B**, I *will* kindle a fire in thee, and it shall	2009
	21: 3 **B**, I *am* against thee, and will draw forth	2009
	21: 7 **b**, it cometh, and shall be brought to pass,	2009
	22: 6 **b**, the princes of Israel, every one were in	2009
	22:13 Therefore **b**, I have smitten mine hand at	2009
	22:19 ye are all become dross, **b** therefore,	2009
	23:22 **B**, I will raise up thy lovers against thee,	2009

Eze	23:28 **B**, I *will* deliver thee into the hand	2009
	24:16 Son of man, **B**, I take away from thee	2009
	24:21 **B**, I *will* profane my sanctuary,	2009
	25: 4 **B** therefore, I *will* deliver thee to the men	2009
	25: 7 **B** therefore, I will stretch out mine hand	2009
	25: 8 Because that Moab and Seir do say, **B**,	2009
	25: 9 Therefore **b**, I *will* open the side of Moab	2009
	25:16 **B**, I *will* stretch out mine hand upon	2009
	26: 3 **B**, I *am* against thee, O Tyrus,	2009
	26: 7 **B**, I *will* bring upon Tyrus	2009
	28: 3 **B**, thou *art* wiser than Daniel; there *is* no	2009
	28: 7 **B** therefore, I *will* bring strangers upon	2009
	28:17 before kings, that *they* may **b** thee.	7200
	28:18 earth in the sight of all them that **b** thee.	7200
	28:22 **B**, I *am* against thee, O Zidon; and I will	2009
	29: 3 **B**, I *am* against thee, Pharaoh king of	2009
	29: 8 **B**, I *will* bring a sword upon thee,	2009
	29:10 Therefore **b**, I *am* against thee,	2009
	29:19 **B**, I *will* give the land of Egypt unto	2009
	30:22 **B**, I *am* against Pharaoh king of Egypt,	2009
	31: 3 **B**, the Assyrian *was* a cedar in Lebanon	2009
	34:10 **B**, I *am* against the shepherds; and I will	2009
	34:11 **B**, I, *even* I, will both search my sheep,	2009
	34:17 **B**, I judge between cattle and cattle,	2009
	34:20 **B**, I, *even* I, will judge between the fat	2009
	35: 3 **B**, O mount Seir, I *am* against thee,	2009
	36: 6 **B**, I have spoken in my jealousy and in	2009
	36: 9 For **b**, I *am* for you, and I will turn unto	2009
	37: 2 **b**, *there were* very many in the open	2009
	37: 5 **B**, I *will* cause breath to enter into you,	2009
	37: 7 **b** a shaking, and the bones came together,	2009
	37:11 **b**, they say, Our bones are dried,	2009
	37:12 **B**, O my people, I *will* open your graves,	2009
	37:19 **B**, I *will* take the stick of Joseph, which *is*	2009
	37:21 **B**, I *will* take the children of Israel from	2009
	38: 3 **B**, I *am* against thee, O Gog, the chief	2009
	39: 1 **B**, I *am* against thee, O Gog, the chief	2009
	39: 8 **B**, it is come, and it is done, saith the Lord	2009
	40: 3 me thither, and **b**, *there was* a man,	2009
	40: 4 with thine eyes, and hear with thine	7200
	40: 5 **b** a wall on the outside of the house	2009
	40:24 the south, and **b** a gate toward the south:	2009
	43: 2 **b**, the glory of the God of Israel came from	2009
	43: 5 **b**, the glory of the Lord filled the house.	2009
	43:12 most holy. **B**, this *is* the law of the house.	2009
	44: 4 I looked, and **b**, the glory of the Lord	2009
	44: 5 with thine eyes, and hear with thine	7200
	46:19 **b**, *there was* a place on the two sides	2009
	46:21 **b**, in every corner of the court *there was*	2009
	47: 1 **b**, waters issued out from under	2009
	47: 2 *by* the way that looketh east*ward;* and **b**,	2009
	47: 7 when I had returned, **b**, at the bank of	2009
Da	2:31 Thou, O king, sawest, and **b** a great image.	431
	4:10 and **b**, a tree in the midst of the earth,	431
	4:13 **b**, a watcher and a holy one came down	431
	7: 2 said, I saw in my vision by night, and **b**,	718
	7: 5 **b**, another beast, a second, like to a bear,	718
	7: 7 **b** a fourth beast, dreadful and terrible,	718
	7: 8 I considered the horns, and **b**, there came	431
	7: 8 **b**, in this horn *were* eyes like the eyes of	431
	7:13 I saw in the night visions, and **b**, *one* like	718
	8: 3 I lifted up mine eyes, and saw, and **b**,	2009
	8: 5 as I was considering, **b**, a he goat came	2009
	8:15 and sought for the meaning, then **b**,	2009
	8:19 he said, **B**, I *will* make thee know what	2009
	9:18 **b** our desolations, and the city which is	7200
	10: 5 I lift up mine eyes, and looked, and **b**,	2009
	10:10 **b**, a hand touched me, which set me	2009
	10:16 **b**, *one* like the similitude of the sons of	2009
	11: 2 **B**, there *shall* stand up yet three kings in	2009
	12: 5 and **b**, there stood other two,	2009
Hos	2: 6 Therefore **b**, I will hedge up thy way with	2009
	2:14 Therefore **b**, I *will* allure her, and bring	2009
Joel	2:19 will answer and say unto his people, **B**,	2009
	3: 1 For **b**, in those days, and in that time,	2009
	3: 7 **B**, I *will* raise them out of the place	2009
Am	2:13 **B**, I am pressed under you, as a cart is	2009
	3: 9 and **b** the great tumults in the midst	7200
	6:11 For **b**, the Lord commandeth,	2009
	6:14 **b**, I *will* raise up against you a nation,	2009
	7: 1 he formed grasshoppers in the	2009
	7: 4 **b**, the Lord God called to contend by	2009
	7: 7 **b**, the Lord stood upon a wall made by a	2009
	7: 8 said the Lord, **B**, I *will* set a plumbline in	2009
	8: 1 unto me: and **b**, a basket of summer fruit.	2009
	8:11 **B**, the days come, saith the Lord God,	2009
	9: 8 **B**, the eyes of the Lord God *are* upon	2009
	9:13 **B**, the days come, saith the Lord,	2009
Ob	1: 2 **B**, I have made thee small among	2009
Mic	1: 3 For **b**, the Lord cometh forth out of his	2009
	2: 3 **B**, against this family do I devise an evil,	2009
	7: 9 the light, *and* I shall **b** his righteousness.	7200
	7:10 mine eyes shall **b** her: now shall she be	7200
Na	1:15 **B** upon the mountains the feet of him that	2009
	2:13 **B**, I *am* against thee, saith the Lord of	2009
	3: 5 **B**, I *am* against thee, saith the Lord of	2009
	3:13 **B**, thy people in the midst of thee *are*	2009
Hab	1: 3 iniquity, and **cause** *me* to **b** grievance?	5027
	1: 5 **B** ye among the heathen, and regard,	7200
	1:13 *Thou art* of purer eyes than to **b** evil,	7200
	2: 4 **B**, his soul *which* is lifted up is not upright	2009
	2:13 **B**, *is it* not of the Lord of hosts that	2009
	2:19 **B**, it *is* laid over *with* gold and silver,	2009
Zep	3:19 **B**, at that time I *will* undo all that afflict	2009
Zec	1: 8 **b** a man riding upon a red horse,	2009

B

Zec 1:11 to and fro through the earth, and **b**, 2009
1:18 mine eyes, and saw, and **b** four horns. 2009
2: 1 mine eyes again, and looked, and **b**, 2009
2: 3 **b**, the angel that talked with me went 2009
2: 9 For **b**, I *will* shake mine hand upon them, 2009
3: 4 unto him he said, **B**, I have caused thine 7200
3: 8 for **b**, I *will* bring forth my servant 2009
3: 9 For **b** the stone that I have laid before 2009
3: 9 **b**, I *will* engrave the graving thereof, 2009
4: 2 I said, I have looked, and **b**, a candlestick 2009
5: 1 eyes, and looked, and **b**, a flying roll. 2009
5: 7 **b**, there *was* lift up a talent of lead: 2009
5: 9 lift I up mine eyes, and looked, and **b**, 2009
6: 1 and lift up mine eyes, and looked, and **b**, 2009
6: 8 upon me, and spake unto me, saying, **b**, 7200
6:12 **B** the man whose name *is* The BRANCH; 2009
7: 8 **b**, I *will* save my people from the east 2009
9: 4 **B**, the Lord will cast her out, and he will 2009
9: 9 **b**, thy King cometh unto thee: he *is* just, 2009
12: 2 **B**, I *will* make Jerusalem a cup of 2009
14: 1 **B**, the day of the LORD cometh, 2009
Mal 1:13 Ye said also, **B**, what a weariness *is it!* 2009
2: 3 **B**, I *will* corrupt your seed, 2009
3: 1 **B**, I *will* send my messenger, and he shall 2009
3: 1 **b**, he *shall* come, saith the LORD of hosts. 2009
4: 1 For **b**, the day cometh, that *shall* burn as 2009
4: 5 **B**, I *will* send you Elijah the prophet 2009
Mt 1:20 But while he thought on these *things*, **b**, 2400
1:23 **B**, a virgin shall be with child, 2400
2: 1 **b**, there came wise men from the east to 2400
2:13 when they were departed, **b**, *the* angel 2400
2:19 But when Herod was dead, **b**, an angel of 2400
4:11 and **b**, angels came and ministered unto 2400
6:26 **B** the fowls of the air: for they sow not, 1689
7: 4 and **b**, a beam *is* in thine own eye? 2400
8: 2 And **b**, there came a leper and 2400
8:24 And **b**, there arose a great tempest in 2400
8:29 And **b**, they cried out, saying, What have 2400
8:32 and **b**, the whole herd of swine ran 2400
8:34 And **b**, the whole city came out to meet 2400
9: 2 And **b**, they brought to him a man sick of 2400
9: 3 And **b**, certain of the scribes said within 2400
9:10 **b**, many publicans and sinners came and 2400
9:18 **b**, there came a *certain* ruler, 2400
9:20 (And **b**, a woman, which was diseased 2400
9:32 As they went out, **b**, they brought to him 2400
10:16 **B**, I send you forth as sheep in the midst 2400
11: 8 **b**, they that wear soft *clothing* are in 2400
11:10 For this is *he*, of whom it is written, **B**, 2400
11:19 **B** a man gluttonous, and a winebibber, 2400
12: 2 Pharisees saw *it*, they said unto him, **B**, 2400
12:10 **b**, there was a man which had *his* hand 2400
12:18 **B** my servant, whom I have chosen; 2400
12:41 and **b**, a greater than Jonas *is* here. 2400
12:42 and **b**, a greater than Solomon *is* here. 2400
12:46 **b**, *his* mother and his brethren stood 2400
12:47 **B**, thy mother and thy brethren stand 2400
12:49 and said, **B** my mother and my brethren. 2400
13: 3 saying, **B**, a sower went forth to sow; 2400
15:22 And **b**, a woman of Canaan came out of 2400
17: 3 And **b**, there appeared unto them Moses 2400
17: 5 While he yet spake, **b**, a bright cloud 2400
17: 5 **b** a voice out of the cloud, which said, 2400
18:10 That in heaven their angels do always **b** 991
19:16 And **b**, one came and said unto him, 2400
19:27 answered Peter and said unto him, **B**, 2400
20:18 **B**, we go up to Jerusalem; and the Son of 2400
20:30 And **b**, two blind men sitting by the way 2400
21: 5 **b**, thy King cometh unto thee, meek, 2400
22: 4 are bidden, **B**, I have prepared my dinner: 2400
23:34 Wherefore, **b**, I send unto you prophets, 2400
23:38 **B**, your house is left unto you desolate. 2400
24:25 **B**, I have told you before. 2400
24:26 shall say unto you, **B**, he is in the desert; 2400
24:26 **b**, *he is* in the secret chambers; believe *it* 2400
25: 6 a cry made, **B**, the bridegroom cometh; 2400
25:20 **b**, I have gained besides them five talents 2396
25:22 **b**, I have gained two other talents besides 2396
26:45 **b**, the hour is at hand, and the Son of man 2400
26:46 **b**, he is at hand that doth betray me. 2400
26:51 **b**, one of them which were with Jesus 2400
26:65 **b**, now ye have heard his blasphemy. 2396
27:51 And **b**, the vail of the temple was rent in 2400
28: 2 And **b**, there was a great earthquake: 2400
28: 7 and **b**, he goeth before you into Galilee; 2400
28: 9 **b**, Jesus met them, saying, *All* hail. 2400
28:11 Now when they were going, **b**, some of 2400
Mk 1: 2 As it is written in the prophets, **B**, I send 2400
2:24 The Pharisees said unto him, **B**, why do 2396
3:32 **B**, thy mother and thy brethren without 2396
3:34 and said, **B** my mother and my brethren. 2396
4: 3 Hearken; **B**, there went out a sower to 2400
5:22 And **b**, there cometh one of the rulers of 2400
10:33 *Saying*, **B**, we go up to Jerusalem; and 2400
11:21 the fig tree which thou cursedst 2396
13:23 ye heed: **b**, I have foretold you all *things*. 2396
14:41 **b**, the Son of man is betrayed into 2400
15: 4 what *things* they witness against 2396
15:35 they heard *it*, said, **B**, he calleth Elias. 2396
16: 6 not here: **b** the place where they laid him. 2396
Lk 1:20 And **b**, thou shalt be dumb, and not able 2400
1:31 And **b**, thou shalt conceive in *thy* womb, 2400
1:36 And **b**, thy cousin Elisabeth, she hath also 2400
1:38 Mary said, **B** the handmaid of the Lord; 2400
1:48 for **b**, from henceforth all generations 2400

Lk 2:10 for **b**, I bring you good tidings of great joy, 2400
2:25 And **b**, there was a man in Jerusalem, 2400
2:34 **B**, this *child* is set for the fall and 2400
2:48 **b**, thy father and I have sought thee 2400
5:12 in a certain city, **b** a man full of leprosy: 2400
5:18 And **b**, men brought in a bed a man 2400
6:23 ye in that day, and leap *for joy*: for **b**, 2400
7:12 **b**, there was a dead man carried out, 2400
7:25 **B**, they which are gorgeously apparelled, 2400
7:27 is *he*, of whom it is written, **B**, I send 2400
7:34 **B** a gluttonous man, and a winebibber, 2400
7:37 And **b**, a woman in the city, which was a 2400
8:41 And **b**, there came a man named Jairus, 2400
9:30 And **b**, there talked with him two men, 2400
9:38 And **b**, a man of the company cried out, 2400
10: 3 **b**, I send you forth as lambs among 2400
10:19 **b**, I give unto you power to tread on 2400
10:25 And **b**, a certain lawyer stood up, 2400
11:31 and **b**, a greater than Solomon *is* here. 2400
11:32 and **b**, a greater than Jonas *is* here. 2400
11:41 and **b**, all *things* are clean unto you. 2400
13: 7 he unto the dresser of his vineyard, **B**, 2400
13:11 And **b**, there was a woman which had a 2400
13:30 And **b**, there are last which shall be first, 2400
13:32 and tell that fox, **B**, I cast out devils, 2400
13:35 **B**, your house is left unto you desolate: 2400
14: 2 **b**, there was a certain man before him, 2400
14:29 is not able to finish *it*, all that **b** *it* begin 2334
17:21 for **b**, the kingdom of God is within you. 2400
18:31 and said unto them, **B**, we go up to 2400
19: 2 And **b**, *there was* a man named Zaccheus, 2400
19: 8 **B**, Lord, the half of my goods I give to 2400
19:20 saying, Lord, **b**, *here is* thy pound, 2400
21: 6 *As for* these *things* which ye, the days 2334
21:29 a parable; **B** the fig tree, and all the trees; 1492
22:10 And he said unto them, **B**, when ye are 2400
22:21 **b**, the hand of him that betrayeth me *is* 2400
22:31 the Lord said, Simon, Simon, **b**, Satan 2400
22:38 And they said, Lord, **b**, here *are* two 2400
22:47 **b** a multitude, and he that was called 2400
23:14 **b**, I, having examined *him* before you, 2400
23:29 For **b**, the days are coming, in the which 2400
23:50 And **b**, *there was* a man named Joseph, 2400
24: 4 they were *much* perplexed thereabout, **b**, 2400
24:13 And **b**, two of them went *that* same day 2400
24:39 **B** my hands and my feet, that it is I 1492
24:49 And **b**, I send the promise of my Father 2400
Jn 1:29 saith, **B** the Lamb of God, which taketh 2396
1:36 he walked, he saith, **B** the Lamb of God. 2396
1:47 and saith of him, **B** an Israelite indeed, 2396
3:26 **b**, the same baptizeth, and all *men* come 2400
4:35 **b**, I say unto you, Lift up your eyes, and 2400
5:14 said unto him, **B**, thou art made whole: 2396
11: 3 saying, Lord, **b**, he whom thou lovest is 2396
11:36 Then said the Jews, **B**, how he loved him. 2396
12:15 **b**, thy King cometh, sitting on an ass's colt 2396
12:19 **b**, the world is gone after him. 2396
16:32 **B**, the hour cometh, yea, is now come, 2400
17:24 they may **b** my glory, which thou hast 2334
18:21 said unto them: **b**, they know what I said. 2396
19: 4 went forth again, and saith unto them, **B**, 2396
19: 5 **B**, I and *Pilate* saith unto them, **B** the man. 2396
19:14 and he saith unto the Jews, **B** your King. 2396
19:26 saith unto his mother, Woman, **b** thy son. 2400
19:27 saith he to the disciple, **B** thy mother. 2400
20:27 Reach hither thy finger, and **b** my hands; 2396
Ac 1:10 toward heaven as he went *up*, **b**, 2400
2: 7 and marvelled, saying one to another, **B**, 2400
4:29 And now, Lord, **b** their threatenings: 1896
5: 9 **b**, the feet of them which have buried thy 2400
5:25 Then came one and told them, saying, **B**, 2400
5:28 and **b**, ye have filled Jerusalem with your 2400
7:31 as he drew near to **b** *it*, the voice of 2657
7:32 Then Moses trembled, and durst not **b**. 2657
7:56 And said, **B**, I see the heavens opened, 2400
8:27 and **b**, a man of Ethiopia, an eunuch of 2400
9:10 Ananias. And he said, **B**, I *am here*, Lord. 2400
9:11 called Saul, of Tarsus: for **b**, he prayeth, 2400
10:17 **b**, the men which were sent from 2400
10:19 said unto him, **B**, three men seek thee: 2400
10:21 and said, **B**, I am whom ye seek: 2400
10:30 ninth hour I prayed in my house, and **b**, 2400
11:11 And **b**, immediately there were three men 2400
12: 7 And **b**, *the* angel of the Lord came upon 2400
13:11 And now, **b**, the hand of the Lord *is* upon 2400
13:25 am not *he*. But **b**, there cometh *one* after 2400
13:41 **B** ye despisers, and wonder, and perish: 1492
16: 1 and **b**, a certain disciple was there, 2400
20:22 And now **b**, I go bound in the spirit unto 2400
20:25 And now **b**, I know that ye all, 2400
Ro 2:17 **B**, thou art called a Jew, and restest in 2396
9:33 As it is written, **B**, I lay in Sion a 2400
11:22 **B** therefore the goodness and severity of 2396
1Co 10:18 **B** Israel after the flesh: are not they which 991
15:51 **b**, I shew you a mystery; We shall not all 2400
2Co 3: 7 **stedfastly b** the face of Moses for the glory 816
5:17 past away; **b**, all *things* are become new. 2400
6: 2 **b**, now *is* the accepted time; behold, now 2400
6: 2 **b**, now *is* the day of salvation.) 2400
6: 9 as dying, and **b**, we live; as chastened, 2400
7:11 For **b** this selfsame *thing*, that ye sorrowed 2400
12:14 **B**, the third *time* I am ready to come to 2400
Gal 1:20 I write unto you, **b**, before God, I lie not. 2400
5: 2 **B**, I Paul say unto you, that if ye **b** 2396
Heb 2:13 **B**, I, and the children which God hath 2400

Heb 8: 8 *he* saith, **B**, the days come, saith the Lord, 2400
Jas 3: 3 **B**, we put bits in the horses' mouths, 2400
3: 4 **B** also the ships, which though they be so 2400
3: 5 **B**, how great a matter a little fire kindleth. 2400
5: 4 **B**, the hire of the labourers which have 2400
5: 7 **B**, the husbandman waiteth for the 2400
5: 9 **b**, the judge standeth before the door. 2400
5:11 **B**, we count them happy which endure. 2400
1Pe 2: 6 **B**, I lay in Sion a chief corner stone, elect, 2400
2:12 by *your* good works, which *they* shall **b**, 2029
3: 2 While they **b** your chaste conversation 2029
1Jn 3: 1 **b**, what manner of love the Father hath 1492
Jude 1:14 from Adam, prophesied of these, saying, **B**, 2400
Rev 1: 7 **B**, he cometh with clouds; and every eye 2400
1:18 **b**, I am alive for evermore, Amen; and 2400
2:10 **b**, the devil shall cast *some* of you into 2400
2:22 **B**, I *will* cast her into a bed, and them 2400
3: 8 **b**, I have set before thee an open door, 2400
3: 9 **B**, I *will* make *them* of the synagogue of 2400
3: 9 **b**, I will make them to come and 2400
3:11 **B**, I come quickly: hold *that* fast which 2400
3:20 **B**, I stand at the door, and knock: if any 2400
4: 1 After this I looked, and **b**, a door *was* 2400
4: 2 and **b**, a throne was set in heaven, 2400
5: 5 **b**, the Lion of the tribe of Juda, the root of 2400
6: 2 And I saw, and **b** a white horse: and he 2400
6: 8 And I looked, and **b** a pale horse: 2400
9:12 *and* **b**, there come two woes more 2400
11:14 *and* **b**, the third woe cometh quickly. 2400
12: 3 and **b** a great red dragon, having seven 2400
14:14 and **b** a white cloud, and upon the cloud 2400
15: 5 And after that I looked, and **b**, the temple 2400
16:15 **B**, I come as a thief. Blessed *is* he that 2400
17: 8 they **b** the beast that was, and is not, 991
19:11 saw heaven opened, and **b** a white horse; 2400
21: 3 **B**, the tabernacle of God *is* with men, 2400
21: 5 the throne said, **B**, I make all *things* new. 2400
22: 7 **B**, I come quickly: blessed *is* he that 2400
22:12 And **b**, I come quickly; and my reward *is* 2400

BEHOLDEST (4) [BEHOLD]

Ps 10:14 Thou hast seen *it*; for thou **b** mischief and 5027
Mt 7: 3 And why **b** thou the mote that is in thy 991
Lk 6:41 And why **b** thou the mote that is in thy 991
6:42 thou thyself **b** not the beam that is in 991

BEHOLDETH (4) [BEHOLD]

Job 24:18 he **b** not the way of the vineyards. 6437
41:34 He **b** all high *things*: he *is* a king over all 7200
Ps 33:13 from heaven; he **b** all the sons of men. 7200
Jas 1:24 For he **b** himself, and goeth his way, 2657

BEHOLDING (15) [BEHOLD]

Ps 119:37 Turn away mine eyes from **b** vanity; 7200
Pr 15: 3 in every place, the evil and the good. 6822
Ecc 5:11 saving the **b** *of them* with their eyes? 7207
Mt 27:55 And many women were there **b** afar off, 2334
Mk 10:21 Then Jesus **b** him loved him, and said 1689
Lk 23:35 And the people stood **b**. And the rulers 2334
23:48 **b** the *things* which were done, smote 2334
23:49 from Galilee, stood afar off, **b** these *things*. 3708
Ac 4:14 And **b** the man which was healed standing 991
8:13 **b** the miracles and signs *which* were done. 2334
14: 9 who **stedfastly b** him, and perceiving 816
23: 1 **earnestly b** the council, said, Men *and* 816
2Co 3:18 with open face **b** as in a glass the glory 2734
Col 2: 5 and **b** your order, and the stedfastness 991
Jas 1:23 he is like unto a man **b** his natural face in 2657

BEHOVED (2)

Lk 24:46 and thus it **b** Christ to suffer, and to rise 1163
Heb 2:17 Wherefore in all *things* it **b** him to be made 3784

BEING (291) [BE]

Ge 18:12 shall I have pleasure, my lord **b** old also? NIH
19:16 the LORD **b** merciful unto him: NIH
21: 4 Abraham circumcised his son Isaac **b** eight NIH
24:27 I **b** in the way, the LORD led me to NIH
34:30 I **b** few in number, they shall gather NIH
35:29 unto his people, **b** old and full of days: NIH
37: 2 Joseph, **b** seventeen years old, was feeding NIH
50:26 Joseph died, **b** an hundred and ten years NIH
Ex 12:34 their kneadingtroughs **b** bound up in their NIH
13:15 all that openeth the matrix, **b** males; NIH
22:14 or die, the owner thereof **b** not with it, NIH
28:16 Foursquare it shall be **b** doubled; a span NIH
32:18 *is it* the voice of *them that* cry for **b** NIH
39: 9 and a span the breadth thereof, **b** doubled. NIH
Lev 21: 4 **b** a chief man among his people, to profane NIH
24: 8 **b** taken from the children of Israel *by* an NIH
Nu 1:44 and the princes of Israel, **b** twelve men: NIH
22:24 wall **b** on this side, and a wall on that side. NIH
30: 3 bond, **b** in her father's house in her youth; NIH
30:16 **b** yet in her youth *in* her father's house. NIH
31:32 **b** the rest of the prey which the men of NIH
32:38 and Baal-meon, (*their* names **b** changed,) NIH
Dt 3:13 and all Bashan, **b** the kingdom of Og, NIH
17: 8 **b** matters of controversy within thy gates: NIH
22:24 because she cried not, **b** in the city; NIH
32:31 even our enemies themselves **b** judges. NIH
Jos 9:23 there shall none of you be freed from **b** NIH
21:10 **b** of the families of the Kohathites, NIH
24:29 died, **b** an hundred and ten years old. NIH
Jdg 2: 8 died, **b** an hundred and ten years old. NIH
9: 5 **b** threescore and ten persons, upon one NIH

B

1Sa 2:18 *b* a child, girded *with* a linen ephod. NIH
 15:23 he hath also rejected thee from *b* king. NIH
 15:26 the LORD hath rejected thee from *b* king 1961
 26:13 afar off; a great space *b* between them: NIH
2Sa 8:13 valley of salt, *b* eighteen thousand *men.* NIH
 13: 4 Why *art* thou, *b* the king's son, lean from NIH
 13:14 but, *b* stronger than she, forced her, NIH
 19: 3 as people *b* ashamed steal away when NIH
 21:16 he *b* girded *with* a new *sword,* thought to NIH
1Ki 1:41 Wherefore *is this* noise of the city *b* in an NIH
 2:27 So Solomon thrust out Abiathar from *b* 1961
 11:17 to go into Egypt; Hadad *b yet* a little child. NIH
 15:13 her he removed from *b* queen, because NIH
 16: 7 hands, in *b* like the house of Jeroboam; 1961
 20:15 the children of Israel, *b* seven thousand. NIH
2Ki 8:16 Israel, Jehoshaphat *b* then king of Judah, NIH
 10: 6 Now the king's sons, *b* seventy persons, NIH
 12:11 gave the money, *b* told, into the hands NIH
1Ch 9:19 their fathers, *b* over the host of the LORD, NIH
 24: 6 principal household *b* taken for Eleazar, NIH
2Ch 5:12 their brethren, *b* arrayed in white linen, NIH
 13: 3 chosen men, *b* mighty *men* of valour. NIH
 15:16 he removed her from *b* queen, because NIH
 21:20 years, and departed without *b* desired. NIH
 26:21 and dwelt *in* a several house, *b* a leper; NIH
Ezr 6:11 and *b* set up, let him be hanged thereon; NIH
 10:19 *b* guilty, *they offered* a ram of the flock NIH
Ne 6:11 *b* as I *am,* would go into the temple to NIH
Est 1: 3 princes of the provinces, *b* before him: NIH
 1: 7 (the vessels *b* diverse one from another,) NIH
 3:15 hastened by the king's commandment, NIH
 8:14 *b* hastened and pressed on by the king's NIH
Job 4: 7 pray thee, who *ever* perished, *b* innocent? NIH
 21:23 full strength, *b* wholly at ease and quiet. NIH
 42:17 So Job died, *b* old and full of days. NIH
Ps 49:12 man *b* in honour abideth not: NIH
 65: 6 fast the mountains; *b* girded with power: NIH
 69: 4 mine enemies wrongfully, are mighty: NIH
 78: 9 of Ephraim, *b* armed, *and* carrying bows, NIH
 78:38 he, *b* full of compassion, forgave *their* NIH
 83: 4 and let us cut them off from *b* a nation; NIH
 104:33 to my God **while** I **have** my **b.** 5750+871.1
 107:10 of death, *b* bound in affliction and iron; NIH
 139:16 did see my **substance, yet b unperfect;** 1564
 146: 2 unto my God **while** I **have** *any* **b.** 5750+871.1
Pr 3:26 and shall keep thy foot from *b* taken. NIH
 29: 1 that *b* often reproved hardeneth *his* neck, NIH
SS 3: 8 They all hold swords, *b* expert in war: NIH
 3:10 the midst thereof *b* paved *with* love, NIH
Isa 3:26 she *b* desolate shall sit upon the ground. NIH
 17: 1 Damascus *is* taken away from *b* a city, NIH
 40:13 or *b* his counsellor hath taught him? NIH
 65:20 the sinner *b* an hundred years old shall be NIH
Jer 2:25 Withhold thy foot from *b* unshod, NIH
 12:11 *b* desolate it mourneth unto me; NIH
 17:16 I have not hastened from *b* a pastor to NIH
 31:36 the seed of Israel also shall cease from *b* a 1961
 34: 9 *b* a Hebrew or a Hebrewess, go free; NIH
 40: 1 when he had taken him *b* bound in chains NIH
 48: 2 come, and let us cut it off from *b* a nation. NIH
 48:42 Moab shall be destroyed from *b* a people, NIH
Eze 17:10 Yea behold, *b* planted, shall it prosper? NIH
 23:42 a voice of a multitude *b* at ease *was* with NIH
 47: 8 *which* **b** brought forth into the sea, NIH
 48:22 *b* in the midst *of that* which is the NIH
Da 3:27 *b* gathered together, saw these men, NIH
 5:31 *b* about threescore and two year old. NIH
 6:10 his windows *b* open in his chamber NIH
 8:22 Now that *b* broken, whereas four stood up NIH
 9:21 at the beginning, *b* caused to fly swiftly, NIH
Mt 1:19 *b* a just *man,* and not willing to make her 1510
 1:23 which *b* interpreted is, God with us. NIG
 1:24 Then Joseph *b* raised from sleep did as NIG
 2:12 And *b* warned of God in a dream that NIG
 2:22 *b* warned of God in a dream, NIG
 7:11 If ye then, *b* evil, know how to give good 1510
 12:34 O generation of vipers, how can ye, *b* evil, 1510
 14: 8 *b* before instructed of her mother, said, NIG
Mk 3: 5 *b* grieved for the hardness of their hearts, NIG
 5:41 is, *b* interpreted, Damsel (I say unto 1510
 8: 1 In those days the multitude *b* very great, 1510
 9:33 and *b* in the house he asked them, 1096
 14: 3 And *b* in Bethany in the house of Simon 1510
 15:22 is, *b* interpreted, The place of a skull. NIG
 15:34 is, *b* interpreted, My God, my God, NIG
Lk 1:74 that we *b* delivered out of the hand of our NIG
 2: 5 his espoused wife, *b* great with child. 1510
 3: 1 Pontius Pilate *b* governor of Judea, NIG
 3: 1 and Herod *b* tetrarch of Galilee, NIG
 3: 2 Annas and Caiaphas *b* the high priests, 1909
 3:19 *b* reproved by him for Herodias his brother NIG
 3:21 *that* Jesus also *b* baptized, and praying, 1510
 3:23 thirty years of age, *b* (as was supposed) 1510
 4: 1 Jesus *b* full of the Holy Ghost returned NIG
 4: 2 *b* forty days tempted of the devil. And in NIG
 4:15 in their synagogues, *b* glorified of all. NIG
 7:29 *b* baptized *with* the baptism of John. NIG
 7:30 against themselves, *b* not baptized of him. NIG
 8:25 And they *b* afraid wondered, saying one to NIG
 11:13 If ye then, *b* evil, know how to give good 5225
 13:16 ought not this *woman, b* a daughter of 1510
 14:21 of the house *b* angry said to his servant, NIG
 16:23 *b* in torments, and seeth Abraham afar off, 5225
 20:36 of God, *b* the children of the resurrection. 1510
 21:12 *b* brought before kings and rulers for my NIG

Lk 22: 3 *b* of the number of the twelve. 1510
 22:44 And *b* in an agony he prayed more 1096
Jn 1:38 (which is to say, *b* interpreted, Master,) NIG
 1:41 which is, *b* interpreted, the Christ. NIG
 4: 6 Jesus therefore, *b* wearied with *his* NIG
 4: 9 *that* thou, *b* a Jew, askest drink of me, 1510
 5:13 himself away, *b* a multitude *b* in *that* place. 1510
 6:71 should betray him, *b* one of the twelve. 1510
 7:50 came to Jesus by night, *b* one of them,) 1510
 8: 9 And they which heard *it,* **b** convicted by NIG
 10:33 and because that thou, *b* a man, 1510
 11:49 the high priest that *same* year, said unto 1510
 11:51 but *b* high priest that year, he prophesied 1510
 13: 2 supper *b* ended, the devil having now NIG
 14:25 I spoken unto you, *b* yet present with you. NIG
 18:26 *b* his kinsman whose ear Peter cut off, 1510
 19:38 *b* a disciple of Jesus, but secretly for fear 1510
 20:19 at evening, *b* the first *day* of the week, 1510
 20:26 *then* came Jesus, the doors *b* shut, NIG
Ac 1: 3 *b* seen of them forty days, and speaking of 1510
 1: 4 And, *b* assembled together with them, NIG
 2:23 *b* delivered by the determinate counsel NIG
 2:30 Therefore *b* a prophet, and knowing that 5225
 2:33 Therefore *b* by the right hand of God NIG
 3: 1 at the hour of prayer, *b* the ninth *hour.* NIG
 4: 2 *b* grieved that they taught the people, NIG
 4:23 And *b* let go, they went to their own NIG
 4:36 (which is, *b* interpreted, The son of NIG
 5: 2 his wife also *b* privy to *it,* and brought a NIG
 7:55 But he, *b* full of the Holy Ghost, looked 5225
 13: 4 So they, *b* sent forth by the Holy Ghost, NIG
 13:12 *b* astonished at the doctrine of the Lord. NIG
 14: 8 *b* a cripple from his mother's womb, 5225
 15: 3 *b* brought on their way by the church, NIG
 15:21 *b* read in the synagogues every sabbath NIG
 15:25 unto us, *b* assembled with one accord, 1510
 15:32 and Silas, *b* prophets also themselves, 1510
 15:40 recommended by the brethren unto NIG
 16:18 *b* grieved, turned and said to the spirit, NIG
 16:20 These men, *b* Jews, do exceedingly 5225
 16:21 to receive, neither to observe, *b* Romans. 1510
 16:37 *b* Romans, and have cast *us* into prison; 5225
 17:28 we live, and move, and **have** our **b;** 1510
 18:25 and *b* fervent in the spirit, he spake and NIG
 19:40 there *b* no cause whereby we may give an 5225
 20: 9 Eutychus, *b* fallen into a deep sleep: NIG
 22:11 *b* led by the hand of them that were with NIG
 26:11 and *b* exceedingly mad against them, NIG
 27: 2 a Macedonian of Thessalonica, *b* with us. 1510
 27:18 And we *b* exceedingly tossed with a NIG
Ro 1:20 *b* understood by the things that are made, NIG
 1:29 *b* filled with all unrighteousness, NIG
 2:18 excellent, *b* instructed out of the law; NIG
 3:21 *b* witnessed by the law and the prophets; NIG
 3:24 *b* justified freely by his grace through NIG
 4:11 faith which he had *yet b* uncircumcised: 1722
 4:12 which he had *yet* uncircumcised. NIG
 4:19 And *b* not weak in faith, he considered NIG
 4:21 And *b* fully persuaded that, what he had NIG
 5: 1 Therefore *b* justified by faith, we have NIG
 5: 9 more then, *b* now justified by his blood, NIG
 5:10 more, *b* reconciled, we shall be saved NIG
 6: 9 Knowing that Christ *b* raised from the NIG
 6:18 Being then made free from sin, ye became NIG
 6:22 But now *b* made free from sin, NIG
 7: 6 law, *that b* dead wherein we were held; NIG
 9:11 (For *the children* **b** not yet born, NIG
 10: 3 they *b* ignorant of God's righteousness, NIG
 11:17 and thou, *b* a wild olive tree, wert graffed 1510
 12: 5 So we, *b* many, are one body in Christ, NIG
 15:16 *b* sanctified by the Holy Ghost. NIG
1Co 4:12 reviled, we bless; being persecuted, NIG
 4:12 we bless; *b* persecuted, we suffer *it:* NIG
 4:13 *b* defamed, we intreat: we are made as NIG
 7:18 Is any *man* called *b* circumcised? let him NIG
 7:21 Art thou called *b* a servant? care not for *it:* NIG
 7:22 Lord, *b* a servant, is the Lord's freeman: NIG
 7:22 he that is called, *b* free, is Christ's servant. NIG
 8: 7 and their conscience *b* weak is defiled. 1510
 9:21 (*b* not without law to God, but under NIG
 10:17 For we *b* many are one bread, NIG
 12:12 of *that* one body, *b* many, are one body: 1510
2Co 5: 3 be that *b* clothed we shall not be found NIG
 5: 4 in *this* tabernacle do groan, *b* burdened: NIG
 8:17 but *b* more forward, of his own accord he 5225
 9:11 *b* enriched in every *thing* to all NIG
 10: 1 but *b* absent am bold toward you: NIG
 11: 9 kept myself **from b burdensome** to you, 4
 12:16 nevertheless, *b* crafty, I caught you with 5225
 13: 2 absent now I write to them which NIG
 13:10 Therefore I write these *things b* absent, NIG
 13:10 lest *b* present I should use sharpness, NIG
Gal 1:14 *b* more exceedingly zealous of 5225
 2: 3 Titus, who was with me, *b* a Greek, 1510
 2:14 Peter before *them* all, If thou, *b* a Jew, 5225
 3:13 curse of the law, *b* made a curse for us: NIG
Eph 1:11 predestinated according to the purpose NIG
 1:18 The eyes of your understanding *b* NIG
 2:11 that ye *b* in time passed Gentiles in NIG
 2:12 *b* aliens from the commonwealth of Israel, NIG
 2:20 Jesus Christ himself *b* the chief corner 1510
 3:17 that ye, *b* rooted and grounded in love, NIG
 4:18 *b* alienated from the life of God through 1510
 4:19 Who *b* past feeling have given themselves NIG
Php 1: 6 *b* confident of this very *thing,* that he NIG

Php 1:11 *b* filled with the fruits of righteousness, NIG
 2: 2 same love, *b* of one accord, of one mind. NIG
 2: 6 Who, *b* in the form of God, thought it not 5225
 2: 8 And *b* found in fashion as a man, NIG
 3:10 be made conformable unto his death; NIG
Col 1:10 *b* fruitful in every good work, NIG
 2: 2 *b* knit together in love, and unto all riches NIG
 2:13 *b* dead in *your* sins and the 1510
1Th 2: 8 So *b* affectionately desirous of you, NIG
 2:17 *b* taken from you for a short time in NIG
1Ti 2:14 the woman *b* deceived was in NIG
 3: 6 lest *b* lifted up with pride he fall into NIG
 3:10 the office of a deacon, *b found* blameless. 1510
2Ti 1: 4 to see thee, *b* mindful of thy tears, NIG
 3:13 and worse, deceiving, and *b* deceived. NIG
Tit 1:16 in works they deny *him, b* abominable, 1510
 3: 7 That *b* justified by his grace, we should NIG
 3:11 and sinneth, *b* condemned of himself. 1510
Phm 1: 9 for love's sake I rather beseech *thee, b* 1510
Heb 1: 3 Who *b* the brightness of *his* glory, 1510
 1: 4 *b* made so much better than the angels, NIG
 2:18 For in that he himself hath suffered *b* NIG
 4: 1 promise *b* left *us* of entering into his rest, NIG
 4: 2 not *b* mixed with faith in them that heard NIG
 5: 9 And *b* made perfect, he became the author NIG
 7: 2 first *b* by interpretation King of NIG
 7:12 the priesthood *b* changed, there is made NIG
 9:11 But Christ *b* come a high priest of good NIG
 11: 4 his gifts: and by it he *b* dead yet speaketh. NIG
 11: 7 *b* warned of God of *things* not seen as yet, NIG
 11:37 *b* destitute, afflicted, tormented; NIG
 13: 3 as *b* yourselves also in the body. 1510
Jas 1:25 continueth *therein,* he *b* not a forgetful 1096
 2:17 if it hath not works, is dead, *b* alone. NIG
1Pe 1: 7 *b* much more precious than of gold that NIG
 1:23 *B* born again, not of corruptible seed, but NIG
 2: 8 which stumble at the word, *b* disobedient: NIG
 2:24 that we, *b* dead to sins, should live unto NIG
 3: 5 *b* in subjection unto their own husbands: NIG
 3: 7 and as *b* heirs together of the grace of life; NIG
 3:18 *b* put to death in the flesh, but quickened NIG
 3:22 and powers *b* made subject unto him. NIG
 5: 3 Neither as *b* lords over *God's* heritage, NIG
 5: 3 but *b* ensamples to the flock. 1096
2Pe 3: 6 then was, *b* overflowed with water, NIG
 3:12 wherein the heavens *b* on fire shall be NIG
 3:17 *b* led away with the error of the wicked, NIG
Rev 1:12 And *b* turned, I saw seven golden NIG
 12: 2 And she *b* with child cried, travailing in 2192
 14: 4 *b* the firstfruits unto God and to the Lamb. NIG

BEKA See BEKAH

BEKAH (1)
Ex 38:26 A *b* for every man, *that is,* half a shekel, 1235

BEKER See BACHRITES; BECHER

BEL (3)
Isa 46: 1 *B* boweth down, Nebo stoopeth, their 1078
Jer 50: 2 say, Babylon is taken, *B* is confounded, 1078
 51:44 I will punish *B* in Babylon, and I will 1078

BELA (13) [BELAH, BELAITES]
Ge 14: 2 and the king of *B,* which *is* Zoar. 1106
 14: 8 and the king of *B* (the same *is* Zoar); 1106
 36:32 *B* the son of Beor reigned in Edom: 1106
 36:33 *B* died, and Jobab the son of Zerah of 1106
Nu 26:38 of *B,* the family of the Belaites: of Ashbel, 1106
 26:40 the sons of *B* were Ard and Naaman: 1106
1Ch 1:43 the children of Israel; *B* the son of Beor: 1106
 1:44 when *B* was dead, Jobab the son of Zerah 1106
 5: 8 *B* the son of Azaz, the son of Shema, 1106
 7: 6 *B,* and Becher, and Jediael, three. 1106
 7: 7 sons of *B;* Ezbon, and Uzzi, and Uzziel, 1106
 8: 1 Now Benjamin begat *B* his firstborn, 1106
 8: 3 the sons of *B* were, Addar, and Gera, 1106

BELAH (1) [BELA]
Ge 46:21 the sons of Benjamin *were B,* and Becher, 1106

BELAITES (1) [BELA]
Nu 26:38 of Bela, the family of the *B:* of Ashbel, 1108

BELCH (1)
Ps 59: 7 Behold, they *b* out with their mouth: 5042

BELIAL (17)
Dt 13:13 *Certain* men, the children of *B,* are gone 1100
Jdg 19:22 the men of the city, certain sons of *B,* 1100
 20:13 deliver *us* the men, the children of *B,* 1100
1Sa 1:16 not thine handmaid for a daughter of *B:* 1100
 2:12 Now the sons of Eli *were* sons of *B;* 1100
 10:27 the children of *B* said, How shall this *man* 1100
 25:17 he *is* such a son of *B,* that a *man* cannot 1100
 25:25 I pray thee, regard this man of *B,* 1100
 30:22 all the wicked men and *men* of *B,* 1100
2Sa 16: 7 thou bloody man, and thou man of *B:* 1100
 20: 1 there happened to be there a man of *B,* 1100
 23: 6 *sons of B shall* be all of them as thorns 1100
1Ki 21:10 two men, sons of *B,* before him, to bear 1100
 21:13 men, children of *B,* and sat before him: 1100
 21:13 the men of *B* witnessed against him, 1100
2Ch 13: 7 the children of *B,* and have strengthened 1100
2Co 6:15 And what concord hath Christ with *B?* 955

BELIED (1)

Jer 5:12 They have **b** the LORD, and said, *It is* not 3584

BELIEF (1) [BELIEVE]

2Th 2:13 of the Spirit and **b** of the truth: 4102

BELIEVE (144) [BELIEF, BELIEVED, BELIEVERS, BELIEVEST, BELIEVETH, BELIEVING, UNBELIEF]

Ex	4: 1 and said, But behold, they will not **b** me,	539
	4: 5 That they may **b** that the LORD God of	539
	4: 8 shall come to pass, if they will not **b** thee,	539
	4: 8 if we **b** the voice of the latter sign.	539
	4: 9 if they will not **b** also these two signs,	539
	19: 9 I speak with thee, and **b** thee for ever.	539
Nu	14:11 how long will it be ere they **b** me, for all	539
Dt	1:32 Yet in this thing ye did not **b** the LORD	539
2Ki	17:14 that did not **b** in the LORD their God.	539
2Ch	20:20 **B** in the LORD your God, so shall you be	539
	20:20 **b** his prophets, so shall ye prosper.	539
	32:15 you on this *manner,* neither yet **b** him:	539
Job	9:16 *would I* not **b** that he had hearkened unto	539
	39:12 Wilt thou **b** him, that he will bring home	539
Pr	26:25 When he speaketh fair, **b** him not: for	539
Isa	7: 9 If ye will not **b**, surely ye shall not be	539
	43:10 that ye may know and **b** me,	539
Jer	12: 6 **b** them not, though they speak fair *words*	539
Hab	1: 5 *which* ye will not **b**, though it be told *you.*	539
Mt	9:28 unto them, **B** ye that I am able to do this?	4100
	18: 6 one of these little ones which **b** in me,	4100
	21:25 say unto us, Why did ye not then **b** him?	4100
	21:32 not afterward, that *ye might* **b** him.	4100
	24:23 Lo, here *is* Christ, or there; **b** *it* not.	4100
	24:26 he *is* in the secret chambers; **b** *it* not.	4100
	27:42 down from the cross, and we will **b** him.	4100
Mk	1:15 is at hand: repent ye, and **b** the gospel.	4100
	5:36 of the synagogue, Be not afraid, only **b**.	4100
	9:23 Jesus said unto him, If thou canst **b**,	4100
	9:24 cried out, and said with tears, Lord, I **b**;	4100
	9:42 one of *these* little ones that **b** in me,	4100
	11:23 shall **b** that *those things* which he saith	4100
	11:24 **b** that ye receive *them,* and ye shall have	4100
	11:31 he will say, Why then did ye not **b** him?	4100
	13:21 *is* Christ; or lo, *he is* there; **b** *him* not:	4100
	15:32 from the cross, that we may see and **b**.	4100
	16:17 And these signs shall follow them that **b**;	4100
Lk	8:12 lest they should **b** and be saved.	4100
	8:13 which for a while **b**, and in time of	4100
	8:50 only, and she shall be made whole.	4100
	22:67 unto them, If I tell you, you will not **b**:	4100
	24:25 slow of heart to **b** all that the prophets	4100
Jn	1: 7 that all *men* through him might **b**.	4100
	1:12 of God, *even* to them that **b** on his name:	4100
	3:12 told you earthly *things,* and ye **b** not,	4100
	3:12 and ye believe not, how shall ye **b**,	4100
	4:21 her, Woman, **b** me, the hour cometh,	4100
	4:42 *Now* we **b**, not because of thy saying:	4100
	4:48 ye see signs and wonders, ye will not **b**.	4100
	5:38 for whom he hath sent, him ye **b** not.	4100
	5:44 How can ye **b**, which receive honour one	4100
	5:47 But if ye **b** not his writings, how shall ye	4100
	5:47 his writings, how shall ye **b** my words?	4100
	6:29 that ye **b** on *him* whom he hath sent.	4100
	6:30 thou then, that we may see, and **b** thee?	4100
	6:36 That ye also have seen me, and **b** not.	4100
	6:64 But there are some of you that **b** not.	4100
	6:69 And we **b** and are sure that thou art *that*	4100
	7: 5 For neither did his brethren **b** in him.	4100
	7:39 which they that **b** on him should receive:	4100
	8:24 for if ye **b** not that I am *he,* ye shall die in	4100
	8:45 because I tell *you* the truth, ye **b** me not.	4100
	8:46 if I say the truth, why do ye not **b** me?	4100
	9:18 But the Jews did not **b** concerning him,	4100
	9:35 him, Dost thou **b** on the Son of God?	4100
	9:36 Who is he, Lord, that I might **b** on him?	4100
	9:38 he said, Lord, I **b**. And he worshipped	4100
	10:25 answered them, I told you, and ye **b** not:	4100
	10:26 But ye **b** not, because ye are not of my	4100
	10:37 do not the works of my Father, **b** me not.	4100
	10:38 But if I do, though ye **b** not me, believe	4100
	10:38 though ye believe not me, **b** the works:	4100
	10:38 that ye may know, and **b**, that the Father	4100
	11:15 I was not there, to the intent ye may **b**;	4100
	11:27 I **b** that thou art the Christ, the Son of	4100
	11:40 I not unto thee, that, if thou wouldest **b**,	4100
	11:42 *it,* that they may **b** that thou hast sent me.	4100
	11:48 let him thus alone, all *men* will **b** on him:	4100
	12:36 While ye have light, **b** in the light, that ye	4100
	12:39 Therefore they could not **b**, because	4100
	12:47 my words, and **b** not, I judge him not:	4100
	13:19 it is come to pass, ye may **b** that I am *he.*	4100
	14: 1 ye **b** in God, believe also in me.	4100
	14: 1 ye believe in God, **b** also in me.	4100
	14:11 **B** me that I *am* in the Father, and the	4100
	14:11 or else **b** me for the very works' sake.	4100
	14:29 that, when it is come to pass, ye might **b**.	4100
	16: 9 Of sin, because they **b** not on me;	4100
	16:30 by this we **b** that thou camest forth from	4100
	16:31 Jesus answered them, Do ye now **b**?	4100
	17:20 them also which shall **b** on me through	4100
	17:21 the world may **b** that thou hast sent me.	4100
	19:35 that he saith true, that ye might **b**.	4100
	20:25 thrust my hand into his side, I will not **b**.	4100
	20:31 that ye might **b** that Jesus is the Christ,	4100
Ac	8:37 I **b** that Jesus Christ is the Son of God.	4100
	13:39 And by him all that **b** are justified from all	4100

Ac	13:41 a work which you shall in no wise **b**,	4100
	15: 7 hear the word of the gospel, and **b**.	4100
	15:11 we **b** that through the grace of the Lord	4100
	16:31 **B** on the Lord Jesus Christ, and thou shalt	4100
	19: 4 that they should **b** on him which should	4100
	21:20 thousands of Jews there are which **b**;	4100
	21:25 As touching the Gentiles which **b**, we	4100
	27:25 for I **b** God, that it shall be even as it was	4100
Ro	3: 3 For what if some did **not b**? shall their	569
	3:22 Christ unto all and upon all them that **b**:	4100
	4:11 he might be the father of all them that **b**,	4100
	4:24 if we **b** on him that raised up Jesus our	4100
	6: 8 we **b** that we shall also live with him:	4100
	10: 9 shalt **b** in thine heart that God hath raised	4100
	10:14 how shall they **b** *in him* of whom they	4100
	15:31 from them that do **not b** in Judea;	544
1Co	1:21 of preaching to save them that **b**.	4100
	10:27 any of them that **b not** bid you *to a feast,*	571
	11:18 be divisions among you; and I partly **b** *it.*	4100
	14:22 not to them that **b**, but to them that	4100
	14:22 that believe, but to them that **b not**:	571
	14:22 *serveth* not for them that **b not**,	571
	14:22 that believe not, but for them which **b**.	4100
2Co	4: 4 blinded the minds of them which **b not**,	571
	4:13 I spoken; we also **b**, and therefore speak;	4100
Gal	3:22 Christ might be given to them that **b**.	4100
Eph	1:19 greatness of his power to us-ward who **b**,	4100
Php	1:29 not only to **b** on him, but also to suffer for	4100
1Th	1: 7 So that ye were ensamples to all that **b** in	4100
	2:10 we behaved ourselves among you that **b**:	4100
	2:13 effectually worketh also in you that **b**.	4100
	4:14 For if we **b** that Jesus died and rose again,	4100
2Th	1:10 and to be admired in all them that **b**	4100
	2:11 strong delusion, that they should **b** a lie:	4100
1Ti	1:16 hereafter **b** on him to life everlasting.	4100
	4: 3 with thanksgiving of them which **b**	4103
	4:10 of all men, specially of those that **b**.	4103
2Ti	2:13 If we **b** not, *yet* he abideth faithful:	569
Heb	10:39 of *them* that **b** to the saving of the soul.	4102
	11: 6 he that cometh to God must **b** that he is,	4100
Jas	2:19 dost well: the devils also **b**, and tremble.	4100
1Pe	1:21 Who by him do **b** in God, that raised him	4100
	2: 7 you therefore which **b** *he is* precious;	4100
1Jn	3:23 That we should **b** on the name of his Son	4100
	4: 1 **b** not every spirit, but try the spirits	4100
	5:13 *things* have I written unto you that **b**	4100
	5:13 that ye may **b** on the name of the Son of	4100

BELIEVED (115) [BELIEVE]

Ge	15: 6 he **b** in the LORD; and he counted it to him	539
	45:26 *Jacob's* heart fainted, for he **b** them not.	539
Ex	4:31 the people **b**: and when they heard that	539
	14:31 and the LORD, and his servant Moses.	539
Nu	20:12 and Aaron, Because ye **b** me not,	539
Dt	9:23 ye **b** him not, nor hearkened to his voice.	539
1Sa	27:12 Achish **b** David, saying, He hath made his	539
1Ki	10: 7 Howbeit I **b** not the words, until I came,	539
2Ch	9: 6 Howbeit I **b** not their words, until I came,	539
Job	29:24 *If* I laughed on them, they **b** *it* not;	539
Ps	27:13 I *had fainted,* unless I had **b** to see	539
	78:22 Because they **b** not in God, and trusted not	539
	78:32 and **b** not for his wondrous works.	539
	106:12 Then **b** they his words; they sang his praise.	539
	106:24 the pleasant land, they **b** not his word:	539
	116:10 I **b**, therefore have I spoken: I was greatly	539
	119:66 for I have **b** thy commandments.	539
Isa	53: 1 Who hath **b** our report? and to whom is	539
Jer	40:14 Gedaliah the son of Ahikam **b** them not.	539
La	4:12 would not have **b** that the adversary and	539
Da	6:23 found upon him, because he **b** in his God.	540
Jnh	3: 5 So the people of Nineveh **b** God,	539
Mt	8:13 as thou hast **b**, *so* be it done unto thee.	4100
	21:32 way of righteousness, and ye **b** him not:	4100
	21:32 the publicans and the harlots **b** him:	4100
Mk	16:11 alive, and had been seen of her, **b** not.	569
	16:13 to the residue: neither **b** they them.	4100
	16:14 they **b** not them which had seen him after	4100
Lk	1: 1 which are **most surely b** among us,	4135
	1:45 And blessed *is* she that **b**: for there shall	4100
	20: 5 he will say, Why then **b** ye him not?	4100
	24:11 them as idle tales, and they **b** them not.	569
	24:41 And while they yet **b** not for joy,	569
Jn	2:11 forth his glory; and his disciples **b** on him.	4100
	2:22 and they **b** the scripture, and the word	4100
	2:23 in the feast *day,* many **b** in his name,	4100
	3:18 he hath not **b** in the name of the only	4100
	4:39 And many of the Samaritans of that city **b**	4100
	4:41 many moe **b** because of his own word;	4100
	4:50 And the man **b** the word that Jesus had	4100
	4:53 and himself **b**, and his whole house.	4100
	5:46 For had ye **b** Moses, ye would have	4100
	5:46 ye believed Moses, ye would have **b** me:	4100
	6:64 the beginning who they were that **b** not,	4100
	7:31 many of the people **b** on him, and said,	4100
	7:48 of the rulers or of the Pharisees on him?	4100
	8:30 As he spake these *words,* many **b** on him.	4100
	8:31 Then said Jesus to those Jews which **b** on	4100
	10:42 And many **b** on him there.	4100
	11:45 *the things* which Jesus did, **b** on him.	4100
	12:11 of the Jews went away, and **b** on Jesus.	4100
	12:37 before them, *yet* they **b** not on him:	4100
	12:38 he spake, Lord, who hath **b** our report?	4100
	12:42 the *chief* rulers also many **b** on him;	4100
	16:27 and have **b** that I came out from God.	4100
	17: 8 and they have **b** that thou didst send me.	4100

Jn	20: 8 first to the sepulchre, and he saw, and **b**.	4100
	20:29 because thou hast seen me, thou hast **b**:	4100
	20:29 they that have not seen, and *yet* have **b**.	4100
Ac	2:44 And all that **b** were together,	4100
	4: 4 many of them which heard the word **b**;	4100
	4:32 And the multitude of them that **b** were of	4100
	8:12 But when they **b** Philip preaching	4100
	8:13 Then Simon himself **b** also: and when he	4100
	9:26 of him, and **b** not that he was a disciple.	4100
	9:42 all Joppa; and many **b** in the Lord.	4100
	10:45 they of the circumcision which **b** were	4103
	11:17 unto us, who **b** on the Lord Jesus Christ;	4100
	11:21 and a great number **b**, and turned unto	4100
	13:12 deputy, when he saw what was done, **b**,	4100
	13:48 as many as were ordained to eternal life **b**.	4100
	14: 1 both of the Jews and *also* of the Greeks **b**.	4100
	14:23 them to the Lord, on whom they **b**.	4100
	15: 5 of the sect of the Pharisees which **b**,	4100
	16: 1 woman, *which was* a Jewess, and **b**;	4103
	17: 4 And some of them **b**, and consorted with	3982
	17: 5 the Jews which **b** not, moved with envy,	544
	17:12 Therefore many of them **b**; also of	4100
	17:34 certain men clave unto him, and **b**:	4100
	18: 8 on the Lord with all his house;	4100
	18: 8 and many of the Corinthians hearing **b**,	4100
	18:27 helped them much which had **b** through	4100
	19: 2 ye received the Holy Ghost since ye **b**?	4100
	19: 9 **b** not, but spake evil of *that* way before	544
	19:18 And many that **b** came, and confessed,	4100
	22:19 beat in every synagogue them that **b** on	4100
	27:11 Nevertheless the centurion **b** the master	3982
	28:24 some **b** the *things* which were spoken,	3982
	28:24 which were spoken, and some **b** not.	569
Ro	4: 3 Abraham **b** God, and it was counted unto	4100
	4:17 before *him* whom he **b**, *even* God,	4100
	4:18 Who against hope **b** in hope, that he	4100
	10:14 call on *him* in whom they have not **b**?	4100
	10:16 Esaias saith, Lord, who hath **b** our report?	4100
	11:30 For as ye in times past have not **b** God,	544
	11:31 *Even* so have these also now not **b**,	544
	13:11 *is* our salvation nearer than when we **b**.	4100
1Co	3: 5 *is* Apollos, but ministers by whom ye **b**,	4100
	15: 2 unto you, unless ye have **b** in vain.	4100
	15:11 I or they, so we preach, and so ye **b**.	4100
2Co	4:13 written, I **b**, *and* therefore have I spoken;	4100
Gal	2:16 even we have **b** in Jesus Christ,	4100
	3: 6 Even as Abraham **b** God, and it was	4100
Eph	1:13 in whom also after that ye **b**, ye were	4100
2Th	1:10 (because our testimony among you was **b**)	4100
	2:12 That they all might be damned who **b** not	4100
1Ti	3:16 **b** on in the world, received up into glory.	4100
2Ti	1:12 for I know whom I have **b**, and I am	4100
Tit	3: 8 that they which have **b** in God might be	4100
Heb	3:18 enter not into his rest, but to them that **b** not?	544
	4: 3 For we which have **b** do enter into rest,	4100
	11:31 Rahab perished not with them that **b** not,	544
Jas	2:23 Abraham **b** God, and it was imputed unto	4100
1Jn	4:16 and **b** the love that God hath to us.	4100
Jude	1: 5 afterward destroyed them that **b** not.	4100

BELIEVERS (2) [BELIEVE]

Ac	5:14 And **b** were the more added to the Lord,	4100
1Ti	4:12 but be thou an example of the **b**, in word,	4103

BELIEVEST (8) [BELIEVE]

Lk	1:20 because thou **b** not my words, which shall	4100
Jn	1:50 I saw thee under the fig tree, **b** thou?	4100
	11:26 in me shall never die. **B** thou this?	4100
	14:10 **B** thou not that I am in the Father, and	4100
Ac	8:37 If thou **b** with all *thine* heart, *thou* mayest.	4100
	26:27 King Agrippa, **b** thou the prophets?	4100
	26:27 thou the prophets? I know that thou **b**.	4100
Jas	2:19 Thou **b** that there is one God; thou doest	4100

BELIEVETH (45) [BELIEVE]

Job	15:22 **b** not that *he* shall return out of darkness,	539
	39:24 neither **b** he that *it is* the sound of	539
Pr	14:15 The simple **b** every word: but the prudent	539
Isa	28:16 he that **b** shall not make haste.	539
Mk	9:23 all *things are* possible to him that **b**.	4100
	16:16 He that **b** and is baptized shall be saved;	4100
	16:16 saved; but he that **b** not shall be damned.	569
Jn	3:15 whosoever **b** in him should not perish,	4100
	3:16 whosoever **b** in him should not perish,	4100
	3:18 He that **b** on him is not condemned: but	4100
	3:18 but he that **b** not is condemned already,	4100
	3:36 He that **b** on the Son hath everlasting life:	4100
	3:36 he that **b not** the Son shall not see life;	544
	5:24 **b** on him that sent me, hath everlasting	4100
	6:35 he that **b** on me shall never thirst.	4100
	6:40 and **b** on him, may have everlasting life:	4100
	6:47 He that **b** on me hath everlasting life.	4100
	7:38 that **b** on me, as the scripture hath said,	4100
	11:25 he that **b** in me, though he were dead,	4100
	11:26 and **b** in me shall never die.	4100
	12:44 Jesus cried and said, He that **b** on me,	4100
	12:44 on me, but on him that sent me.	4100
	12:46 whosoever **b** on me should not abide in	4100
	14:12 verily, I say unto you, He that **b** on me,	4100
Ac	10:43 through his name whosoever **b** in him	4100
Ro	1:16 God unto salvation to every one that **b**;	4100
	3:26 and the justifier of him which **b** in Jesus.	4102
	4: 5 but **b** on him that justifieth the ungodly,	4100
	9:33 whosoever **b** on him shall not be ashamed	4100
	10: 4 law for righteousness to every one that **b**.	4100

B

Ro	10:10 For with the heart *man* **b** unto	4100
	10:11 Whosoever **b** on him shall not be ashamed	4100
	14: 2 For one **b** that *he* may eat all *things:*	4100
1Co	7:12 If any brother hath a wife that **b** not,	571
	7:13 woman which hath a husband that **b** not,	571
	13: 7 Beareth all *things,* **b** all *things,* hopeth all	4100
	14:24 and there come in one that **b** not,	571
2Co	6:15 what part hath he that **b** with an infidel?	4103
1Ti	5:16 any man or **woman** that **b** have widows,	4103
1Pe	2: 6 he that on him shall not be confounded:	4100
1Jn	5: 1 Whosoever **b** that Jesus is the Christ is	4100
	5: 5 but he that **b** that Jesus is the Son of God?	4100
	5:10 He that **b** on the Son of God hath	4100
	5:10 he that **b** not God hath made him a liar;	4100
	5:10 he **b** not the record that God gave of his	4100

BELIEVING (8) [BELIEVE]

Mt	21:22 ye shall ask in prayer, **b**, ye shall receive.	4100
Jn	20:27 into my side: and be not faithless, but **b**.	4103
	20:31 **b** ye might have life through his name.	4100
Ac	16:34 and rejoiced, **b** in God with all his house.	4100
	24:14 **b** all *things* which are written in the law	4100
Ro	15:13 hope fill you with all joy and peace in **b**,	4100
1Ti	6: 2 they that have **b** masters, let them not	4103
1Pe	1: 8 though now ye see *him* not, yet **b**,	4100

BELL (4) [BELLS]

Ex	28:34 A golden **b** and a pomegranate, a golden	6472
	28:34 a golden **b** and a pomegranate,	6472
	39:26 A **b** and a pomegranate, a bell and	6472
	39:26 a **b** and a pomegranate,	6472

BELLIES (1) [BELLY]

Tit	1:12 *are* alway liars, evil beasts, slow **b**.	1064

BELLOW (1) [BELLOWS]

Jer	50:11 fat as the heifer at grass, and **b** as bulls;	6670

BELLOWS (1) [BELLOW]

Jer	6:29 The **b** are burnt, the lead is consumed of	4647

BELLS (4) [BELL]

Ex	28:33 and **b** of gold between them round about:	6472
	39:25 made **b** of pure gold, and put the bells	6472
	39:25 put the **b** between the pomegranates upon	6472
Zec	14:20 In that day shall there be upon the **b** of	4698

BELLY (49) [BELLIES]

Ge	3:14 upon thy **b** shalt thou go, and dust shalt	1512
Lev	11:42 Whatsoever goeth upon the **b**,	1512
Nu	5:21 make thy thigh to rot, and thy **b** to swell;	990
	5:22 make *thy* **b** to swell, and *thy* thigh to rot:	990
	5:27 her **b** shall swell, and her thigh shall rot:	990
	25: 8 of Israel, and the woman through her **b**.	6897
Jdg	3:21 his right thigh, and thrust it into his **b**:	990
	3:22 he could not draw the dagger out of his **b**;	990
1Ki	7:20 over against the **b** which *was* by	990
Job	3:11 the ghost when I came out of the **b**?	990
	15: 2 and fill his **b** *with* the east wind?	990
	15:35 forth vanity, and their **b** prepareth deceit.	990
	20:15 up again: God shall cast them out of his **b**.	990
	20:20 Surely he shall not feel quietness in his **b**,	990
	20:23 he is about to fill his **b**, *God* shall cast	990
	32:19 my **b** *is* as wine *which* hath no vent;	990
	40:16 and his force *is* in the navel of his **b**.	990
Ps	17:14 whose **b** thou fillest *with* thy hid *treasure:*	990
	22:10 thou *art* my God from my mother's **b**.	990
	31: 9 with grief, *yea,* my soul and my **b**.	990
	44:25 to the dust: our **b** cleaveth unto the earth.	990
Pr	13:25 soul: but the **b** of the wicked shall want.	990
	18: 8 go down *into* the innermost parts of the **b**.	990
	18:20 A man's **b** shall be satisfied with the fruit	990
	20:27 searching all the inward parts of the **b**.	990
	20:30 so *do* stripes the inward parts of the **b**:	990
	26:22 go down *into* the innermost parts of the **b**.	990
SS	5:14 his **b** *is* as bright ivory overlaid *with*	4578
	7: 2 thy **b** *is like* a heap of wheat set about	990
Isa	46: 3 which are borne *by me* from the **b**, which	990
Jer	1: 5 Before I formed thee in the **b** I knew thee;	990
	51:34 he hath filled his **b** with my delicates,	3770
Eze	3: 3 cause thy **b** to eat, and fill thy bowels with	990
Da	2:32 of silver, his **b** and his thighs of brass,	4577
Jnh	1:17 Jonah was in the **b** of the fish three days	4578
	2: 1 the LORD his God out of the fish's **b**,	4578
	2: 2 out of the **b** of hell cried I, *and* thou	990
Hab	3:16 When I heard, my **b** trembled; my lips	990
Mt	12:40 and three nights in the whale's **b**;	2836
	15:17 entereth in at the mouth goeth into the **b**,	2836
Mk	7:19 entereth not into his heart, but into the **b**,	2836
Lk	15:16 And he would fain have filled his **b** with	2836
Jn	7:38 out of his **b** shall flow rivers of living	2836
Ro	16:18 our Lord Jesus Christ, but their own **b**;	2836
1Co	6:13 Meats for the **b**, and the belly for meats:	2836
	6:13 Meats for the belly, and the **b** for meats:	2836
Php	3:19 whose God *is their* **b**, and *whose* glory	2836
Rev	10: 9 it shall make thy **b** bitter, but it shall	2836
	10:10 soon as I had eaten it, my **b** was bitter.	2836

BELONG (12) [BELONGED, BELONGEST, BELONGETH, BELONGING]

Ge	40: 8 them, *Do* not interpretations **b** to God?	NIH
Lev	27:24 to whom the possession of the land *did* **b**.	NIH
Nu	1:50 and *are* all *things* that **b** to it:	NIH
Dt	29:29 The secret *things* **b** unto the LORD our	NIH
	29:29 *those things* which are revealed **b** unto us	NIH
Ps	47: 9 for the shields of the earth **b** unto God:	NIH

Ps	68:20 unto GOD the Lord **b** the issues from	NIH
Pr	24:23 These *things* also **b** to the wise. *It is* not	NIH
Da	9: 9 To the Lord our God **b** mercies and	NIH
Mk	9:41 because ye **b** to Christ, verily I say unto	1510
Lk	19:42 day, the *things* which **b** unto thy peace!	4314
1Co	7:32 careth for the *things* that **b** to the Lord,	NIG

BELONGED (11) [BELONG]

Jos	17: 8 Tappuah on the border of Manasseh **b**	NIH
1Sa	21: 7 the chiefest of the herdmen that **b** to Saul.	NIH
1Ki	1: 8 and the mighty *men* which **b** to David,	NIH
	16:15 which **b** to the Philistines.	NIH
2Ki	14:28 and Hamath, *which* **b** to Judah, for Israel,	NIH
1Ch	2:23 All these **b** to the sons of Machir the father	NIH
	13: 6 *that is,* to Kirjath-jearim, which **b** to Judah,	NIH
2Ch	26:23 the field of the burial which **b** to the kings;	NIH
Est	1: 9 royal house which **b** to king Ahasuerus.	NIH
	2: 9 with *such things as* **b** to her, and seven	4490
Lk	23: 7 And as soon as he knew that he **b** unto	1510

BELONGEST (1) [BELONG]

1Sa	30:13 David said unto him, To whom **b** thou?	NIH

BELONGETH (21) [BELONG]

Nu	8:24 This *is it* that **b** unto the Levites:	NIH
Dt	32:35 To me **b** vengeance, and recompence;	NIH
Jdg	19:14 *were* by Gibeah, which **b** to Benjamin.	NIH
	20: 4 I came into Gibeah that **b** to Benjamin,	NIH
1Sa	17: 1 which **b** to Judah, and pitched between	NIH
	30:14 upon *the coast* which **b** to Judah,	NIH
1Ki	15:27 at Gibbethon, which **b** to the Philistines;	NIH
	17: 9 which **b** to Zidon, and dwell there:	NIH
	19: 3 which **b** to Judah, and left his servant	NIH
2Ki	14:11 face at Beth-shemesh, which **b** to Judah.	NIH
2Ch	25:21 at Beth-shemesh, which **b** to Judah.	NIH
Ezr	10: 4 Arise; for *this* matter **b** unto thee: we also	NIH
Ps	3: 8 Salvation **b** unto the LORD: thy blessing *is*	NIH
	62:11 have I heard this; that power **b** unto God.	NIH
	62:12 Also unto thee, O Lord, **b** mercy: for thou	NIH
	94: 1 O LORD God, to whom vengeance **b**;	NIH
	94: 1 God, to whom vengeance **b**, shew thyself.	NIH
Da	9: 7 righteousness **b** unto thee, but unto us	NIH
	9: 8 O Lord, to us **b** confusion of face, to our	NIH
Heb	5:14 But strong meat **b** to *them that are* of full	1510
	10:30 Vengeance **b** unto me, I will recompense.	NIG

BELONGING (5) [BELONG]

Nu	7: 9 the service of the sanctuary **b** unto them	5921
Ru	2: 3 hap was to light on a part of the field **b**	NIH
1Sa	6:18 cities of the Philistines **b** to the five lords,	NIH
Pr	26:17 and meddleth with strife **b** not to him,	NIH
Lk	9:10 aside privately into a desert place **b** to	NIG

BELONGINGS See STUFF

BELOVED (111) [LOVE]

Dt	21:15 one **b**, and another hated, and they have	157
	21:15 children, *both* the **b** and the hated;	157
	21:16 *that* he may not make the son of the **b**	157
	33:12 The **b** of the LORD shall dwell in safety	3039
Ne	13:26 was **b** of his God, and God made him	157
Ps	60: 5 That thy **b** may be delivered; save *with*	3039
	108: 6 That thy **b** may be delivered: save *with*	3039
	127: 2 of sorrows: *for* so he giveth his **b** sleep.	3039
Pr	4: 3 and only *b* in the sight of my mother.	NIH
SS	1:14 My **b** *is* unto me *as* a cluster of camphire	1730
	1:16 Behold, thou *art* fair, my **b**, yea, pleasant:	1730
	2: 3 of the wood, so *is* my **b** among the sons.	1730
	2: 8 The voice of my **b**! behold, he cometh	1730
	2: 9 My **b** *is* like a roe or a young hart: behold,	1730
	2:10 My **b** spake, and said unto me, Rise up,	1730
	2:16 My **b** *is* mine, and I *am* his: he feedeth	1730
	2:17 my **b**, and be thou like a roe or a young	1730
	4:16 Let my **b** come into his garden, and eat	1730
	5: 1 drink, yea, drink abundantly, O **b**.	1730
	5: 2 *it is* the voice of my **b** that knocketh	1730
	5: 4 My **b** put in his hand by the hole *of*	1730
	5: 5 I rose up to open to my **b**; and my hands	1730
	5: 6 I opened to my **b**; but my beloved had	1730
	5: 6 my **b** had withdrawn himself,	1730
	5: 8 if ye find my **b**, that ye tell him, that I *am*	1730
	5: 9 What *is* thy **b** more than *another* beloved,	1730
	5: 9 What *is* thy beloved more than *another* **b**,	1730
	5: 9 What *is* thy **b** more than *another* beloved,	1730
	5: 9 what *is* thy beloved more than *another* **b**,	1730
	5:10 My **b** *is* white and ruddy, the chiefest	1730
	5:16 This *is* my **b**, and this *is* my friend,	1730
	6: 1 Whither *is* thy **b** gone, O thou fairest	1730
	6: 1 whither *is* thy **b** turned aside? that we	1730
	6: 2 My **b** is gone down into his garden,	1730
	6: 3 I *am* my beloved's, and my **b** *is* mine:	1730
	7: 9 for my **b**, that goeth *down* sweetly,	1730
	7:11 Come, my **b**, let us go forth into the field;	1730
	7:13 *which* I have laid up for thee, O my **b**.	1730
	8: 5 from the wilderness, leaning upon her **b**?	1730
	8:14 my **b**, and be thou like to a roe or to a	1730
Isa	5: 1 a song of my **b** touching his vineyard.	1730
Jer	11:15 What hath my **b** to do in mine house,	3033
	12: 7 I have given the **dearly b** of my soul into	3033
Da	9:23 to shew *thee;* for thou *art* **greatly b**:	2532
	10:11 said unto me, O Daniel, a man **greatly b**,	2532
	10:19 said, O man **greatly b**, fear not: peace *be*	2532
Hos	3: 1 Go yet, love a woman **b** of *her* friend,	157
	9:16 yet will I slay *even* the **b** *fruit* of their	4261
Mt	3:17 This is my **b** Son, in whom I am well	27
	12:18 my **b**, in whom my soul is well pleased:	27

Mt	17: 5 said, This is my **b** Son, in whom I am	27
Mk	1:11 *saying,* Thou art my **b** Son, in whom I am	27
	9: 7 out of the cloud, saying, This is my **b** Son:	27
Lk	3:22 heaven, which said, Thou art my **b** Son;	27
	9:35 out of the cloud, saying, This is my **b** Son:	27
	20:13 I will send my **b** son: it may be they will	27
Ac	15:25 to send chosen men unto you with our **b**	27
Ro	1: 7 in Rome, **b** of God, called *to be* saints:	27
	9:25 people; and her **b**, which was not beloved.	25
	9:25 people; and her beloved, which was not **b**.	25
	11:28 election, *they are* **b** for the fathers' sakes.	27
	12:19 **Dearly b**, avenge not yourselves, but	27
	16: 8 Greet Amplias my **b** in the Lord.	27
	16: 9 our helper in Christ, and Stachys my **b**.	27
	16:12 Salute the **b** Persis, which laboured much	27
1Co	4:14 to shame you, but as my **b** sons I warn *you.*	27
	4:17 who is my **b** son, and faithful in the Lord,	27
	10:14 Wherefore, my **dearly b**, flee from idolatry.	27
	15:58 Therefore, my **b** brethren, be ye stedfast,	27
2Co	7: 1 Having therefore these promises, **dearly b**,	27
	12:19 but *we do* all *things,* **dearly b**, for your	27
Eph	1: 6 wherein he hath made us accepted in the **b**:	25
	6:21 a **b** brother and faithful minister in the Lord,	27
Php	2:12 my **b**, as ye have always obeyed,	27
	4: 1 my brethren **dearly b** and longed for,	27
	4: 1 so stand fast in the Lord, *my* **dearly b**.	27
Col	3:12 holy and **b**, bowels of mercies, kindness,	25
	4: 7 *who is* a **b** brother, and a faithful minister	27
	4: 9 With Onesimus, a faithful and **b** brother,	27
	4:14 Luke, the **b** physician, and Demas, greet	27
1Th	1: 4 Knowing, brethren **b**, your election of God.	25
2Th	2:13 brethren **b** of the Lord, because God hath	27
1Ti	6: 2 service, because they are faithful and **b**,	27
2Ti	1: 2 To Timothy, *my* **dearly b** son: Grace,	27
Phm	1: 1 unto Philemon *our* **dearly b**,	27
	1: 2 And to *our* **b** Apphia,	27
	1:16 a brother **b**, specially to me, but how much	27
Heb	6: 9 **b**, we are persuaded better *things* of you,	27
Jas	1:16 Do not err, my **b** brethren.	27
	1:19 Wherefore, my **b** brethren, let every man be	27
	2: 5 my **b** brethren, Hath not God chosen	27
1Pe	2:11 **Dearly b**, I beseech *you* as strangers and	27
	4:12 **b**, think it not strange concerning the fiery	27
2Pe	1:17 is my **b** Son, in whom I am well pleased.	27
	3: 1 second epistle, **b**, I now write unto you;	27
	3: 8 **b**, be not ignorant of this one *thing,* that	27
	3:14 Wherefore, **b**, seeing that ye look for such	27
	3:15 even as our **b** brother Paul also according to	27
	3:17 therefore, **b**, seeing ye know *these things*	27
1Jn	3: 2 **B**, now are we the sons of God, and it doth	27
	3:21 **B**, if our heart condemn us not, *then* have	27
	4: 1 **B**, believe not every spirit, but try the spirits	27
	4: 7 **B**, let us love one another: for love is of God;	27
	4:11 **B**, if God so loved us, we ought also to love	27
3Jn	1: 2 **B**, I wish above all *things* that thou mayest	27
	1: 5 **B**, thou doest faithfully whatsoever thou	27
	1:11 **B**, follow not *that which is* evil, but	27
Jude	1: 3 **B**, when I gave all diligence to write unto	27
	1:17 But, **b**, remember ye the words which were	27
	1:20 But ye, **b**, building up yourselves on your	27
Rev	20: 9 the camp of the saints about, and the **b** city:	25

BELOVED'S (2) [LOVE]

SS	6: 3 I *am* my **b**, and my beloved *is*	1730+3807.1
	7:10 I *am* my **b**, and his desire *is*	1730+3807.1

BELOW See DOWNWARD; NETHER; NETHERMOST

BELSHAZZAR (8)

Da	5: 1 **B** the king made a great feast to a	1113
	5: 2 **B**, whiles *he* tasted the wine,	1113
	5: 9 *was* king **B** greatly troubled,	1113
	5:22 his son, O **B**, hast not humbled thine	1113
	5:29 commanded **B**, and they clothed Daniel	1113
	5:30 In that night *was* **B** the king of	1113
	7: 1 In the first year of **B** king of Babylon	1113
	8: 1 In the third year of the reign of king **B** a	1112

BELTESHAZZAR (10) [DANIEL]

Da	1: 7 for he gave unto Daniel *the name of* **B**;	1095
	2:26 and said to Daniel, whose name *was* **B**,	1096
	4: 8 name *was* **B**, according to the name	1096
	4: 9 O **B**, master of the magicians, because	1096
	4:18 Now thou, O **B**, declare the interpretation	1096
	4:19 Daniel, whose name *was* **B**, was astonied	1096
	4:19 The king spake, and said, **B**, let not	1096
	4:19 answered and said, My lord, the dream	1096
	5:12 same Daniel, whom the king named **B**:	1096
	10: 1 unto Daniel, whose name was called **B**;	1095

BEMOAN (5) [BEMOANED, BEMOANING]

Jer	15: 5 or who shall **b** thee? or who shall go aside	5110
	16: 5 neither go to lament nor **b** them:	5110
	22:10 Weep ye not for the dead, neither **b** him:	5110
	48:17 All ye that are about him, **b** him; and all	5110
Na	3: 7 who will **b** her? whence shall I seek	5110

BEMOANED (1) [BEMOAN]

Job	42:11 they **b** him, and comforted him over all	5110

BEMOANING (1) [BEMOAN]

Jer	31:18 I have surely heard Ephraim **b** himself	5110

BEN (1)

1Ch	15:18 **B**, and Jaaziel, and Shemiramoth,	1122

B

BENAIAH (42)

2Sa	8:18 **B** the son of Jehoiada *was over* both	1141
	20:23 **B** the son of Jehoiada *was* over	1141
	23:20 **B** the son of Jehoiada, the son of a valiant	1141
	23:22 These *things* did **B** the son of Jehoiada,	1141
	23:30 **B** the Pirathonite, Hiddai of the brooks of	1141
1Ki	1: 8 **B** the son of Jehoiada, and Nathan	1141
	1:10 **B**, and the mighty *men*, and Solomon his	1141
	1:26 **B** the son of Jehoiada, and thy servant	1141
	1:32 the prophet, and **B** the son of Jehoiada.	1141
	1:36 **B** the son of Jehoiada answered the king,	1141
	1:38 **B** the son of Jehoiada, and the Cherethites	1141
	1:44 **B** the son of Jehoiada, and the Cherethites	1141
	2:25 Solomon sent by the hand of **B** the son	1141
	2:29 Solomon sent **B** the son of Jehoiada,	1141
	2:30 **B** came to the tabernacle of the LORD,	1141
	2:30 **B** brought the king word again, saying,	1141
	2:34 So **B** the son of Jehoiada went up,	1141
	2:35 the king put **B** the son of Jehoiada in his	1141
	2:46 So the king commanded **B** the son of	1141
	4: 4 **B** the son of Jehoiada *was* over the host:	1141
1Ch	4:36 Asaiah, and Adiel, and Jesimiel, and **B**,	1141
	11:22 **B** the son of Jehoiada, the son of a valiant	1141
	11:24 These *things* did **B** the son of Jehoiada,	1141
	11:31 children of Benjamin, **B** the Pirathonite,	1141
	15:18 **B**, and Maaseiah, and Mattithiah,	1141
	15:20 Unni, and Eliab, and Maaseiah, and **B**,	1141
	15:24 and Zechariah, and **B**, and Eliezer,	1141
	16: 5 and Eliab, and **B**, and Obed-edom:	1141
	16: 6 **B** also and Jahaziel the priests with	1141
	18:17 **B** the son of Jehoiada *was* over	1141
	27: 5 third month *was* **B** the son of Jehoiada,	1141
	27: 6 This *is that* **B**, *who was* mighty among	1141
	27:14 the eleventh month *was* **B** the Pirathonite,	1141
	27:34 Ahithophel *was* Jehoiada the son of **B**,	1141
2Ch	20:14 the son of **B**, the son of Jeiel, the son of	1141
	31:13 Eliel, and Ismachiah, and Mahath, and **B**,	1141
Ezr	10:25 and Eleazar, and Malchijah, and **B**.	1141
	10:30 and Chelal, **B**, Maaseiah, Mattaniah,	1141
	10:35 **B**, Bedeiah, Chelluh,	1141
	10:43 Zabad, Zebina, Jadau, and Joel, **B**.	1141
Eze	11: 1 Pelatiah the son of **B**, princes of the	1141
	11:13 that Pelatiah the son of **B** died.	1141

BEN-AMMI (1)

Ge	19:38 she also bare a son, and called his name **B**:	1151

BENCHES (1)

Eze	27: 6 of the Ashurites have made thy **b** *of* ivory,	7175

BEND (8) [BENDETH, BENDING, BENT]

Ps	11: 2 lo, the wicked **b** *their* bow, they make	1869
	64: 3 and **b** *their bows* to *shoot* their arrows,	1869
Jer	9: 3 **b** their tongues *like* their bow *for* lies:	1869
	46: 9 the Lydians, that handle *and* **b** the bow.	1869
	50:14 all ye that **b** the bow, shoot at her, spare	1869
	50:29 all ye that **b** the bow, camp against it	1869
	51: 3 Against *him that* bendeth let the archer **b**	1869
Eze	17: 7 this vine did **b** her roots toward him,	3719

BEN-DEKER See SON OF DEKAR

BENDETH (2) [BEND]

Ps	58: 7 *when* he **b** *his* bow to shoot his arrows,	1869
Jer	51: 3 Against *him that* **b** let the archer bend his	1869

BENDING [BEND]

Isa	60:14 that afflicted thee shall come **b** unto thee;	7817

BENEATH (28)

Ge	35: 8 was buried **b** Beth-el under an oak:	4480+8478
Ex	20: 4 or that *is* in the earth **b**, or that *is*	4480+8478
	26:24 be coupled together **b**,	4295+4480+3807.1
	27: 5 compass of the altar **b**,	4295+4480+3807.1
	28:33 **b** upon the hem of it thou shalt make	NIH
	32:19 his hands, and brake them **b** the mount.	8478
	36:29 they were coupled **b**,	4295+4480+3807.1
	38: 4 **b** unto the midst of it.	4295+4480+3807.1
Dt	4:18 that *is* in the waters **b** the earth:	4480+8478
	4:39 above, and upon the earth **b**:	4480+8478
	5: 8 or that *is* in the earth **b**, or that *is*	4480+8478
	5: 8 or that *is* in the waters **b** the earth:	4480+8478
	28:13 be above only, and thou shalt not be **b**;	4295
	33:13 dew, and for the deep that coucheth **b**,	8478
Jos	2:11 in heaven above, and in earth **b**.	4480+8478
Jdg	7: 8 of Midian was **b** him in the valley.	4480+8478
1Ki	4:12 which *is* by Zartanah **b** Jezreel,	4480+8478
	7:29 **b** the lions and oxen *were certain*	4480+8478
	8:23 in heaven above, or on earth **b**,	4480+8478
Job	18:16 His roots shall be dried up **b**,	4480+8478
Pr	15:24 the wise, that *he* may depart from hell **b**.	4295
Isa	14: 9 Hell from **b** is moved for thee to meet	8478
	51: 6 and look upon the earth **b**:	4480+8478
Jer	31:37 of the earth searched out **b**,	4295+3807.1
Am	2: 9 his fruit from above, and his roots from **b**.	8478
Mk	14:66 And as Peter was **b** in the palace,	2736
Jn	8:23 he said unto them, Ye are from **b**; I am	2736
Ac	2:19 in heaven above, and signs in the earth **b**;	2736

BENE-BERAK (1)

Jos	19:45 And Jehud, and **B**, and Gath-rimmon,	1139

BENEFACTORS (1)

Lk	22:25 exercise authority upon them are called **b**.	2110

BENEFICIAL See EXPEDIENT

BENEFIT (5) [BENEFITS]

2Ch	32:25 again according to the **b** *done* unto him;	1576
Jer	18:10 good, wherewith I said I would **b** them.	3190
2Co	1:15 before, that you might have a second **b**;	5485
1Ti	6: 2 faithful and beloved, partakers of the **b**.	2108
Phm	1:14 that thy **b** should not be as *it were* of	18

BENEFITS (3) [BENEFIT]

Ps	68:19 daily loadeth us *with* **b**, *even* the God	NIH
	103: 2 O my soul, and forget not all his **b**:	1576
	116:12 unto the LORD *for* all his **b** towards me?	8408

BENE-JAAKAN (2) [JAAKAN]

Nu	33:31 departed from Moseroth, and pitched in **B**.	1142
	33:32 they removed from **B**, and encamped at	1142

BENEVOLENCE (1)

1Co	7: 3 the husband render unto the wife due **b**:	2133

BEN-HADAD (27)

1Ki	15:18 king Asa sent them to **B**, the son of	1130
	15:20 So **B** hearkened unto king Asa, and sent	1130
	20: 1 the king of Syria gathered all his host	1130
	20: 2 the city, and said unto him, Thus saith **B**,	1130
	20: 5 said, Thus speaketh **B**, saying, Although I	1130
	20: 9 he said unto the messengers of **B**,	1130
	20:10 And **B** sent unto him, and said, The gods	1130
	20:12 when **B** heard this message, as he *was*	NIH
	20:16 **B** *was* drinking *himself* drunk in the	1130
	20:17 **B** sent out, and they told him, saying,	1130
	20:20 the king of Syria escaped on a horse	1130
	20:26 that **B** numbered the Syrians, and went	1130
	20:30 **B** fled, and came into the city, into an	1130
	20:32 said, Thy servant **B** saith, I pray thee,	1130
	20:33 catch *it*: and they said, Thy brother **B**.	1130
	20:33 **B** came forth to him; and he caused him	1130
	20:34 **B** said unto him, The cities, which my	NIH
2Ki	6:24 that **B** king of Syria gathered all his host,	1130
	8: 7 The king of Syria was sick; and it was	1130
	8: 9 Thy son **B** king of Syria hath sent me to	1130
	13: 3 into the hand of **B** the son of Hazael,	1130
	13:24 and **B** his son reigned in his stead.	1130
	13:25 the hand of **B** the son of Hazael the cities,	1130
2Ch	16: 2 king's house, and sent to **B** king of Syria,	1130
	16: 4 **B** hearkened unto king Asa, and sent	1130
Jer	49:27 and it shall consume the palaces of **B**.	1130
Am	1: 4 which shall devour the palaces of **B**.	1130

BEN-HAIL (1)

2Ch	17: 7 *even* to **B**, and to Obadiah,	1134

BEN-HANAN (1)

1Ch	4:20 *were*, Amnon, and Rinnah, **B**, and Tilon.	1135

BEN-HESED See SON OF HESED

BENINU (1)

Ne	10:13 Hodijah, Bani, **B**.	1148

BENJAMIN (162) [BEN-ONI, BENJAMIN'S, BENJAMITE, BENJAMITES]

Ge	35:18 Ben-oni: but his father called him **B**.	1144
	35:24 The sons of Rachel; Joseph, and **B**:	1144
	42: 4 **B**, Joseph's brother, Jacob sent not with	1144
	42:36 ye will take **B** *away*: all these things are	1144
	43:14 may send away your other brother, and **B**.	1144
	43:15 took double money in their hand, and **B**;	1144
	43:16 when Joseph saw **B** with them, he said to	1144
	43:29 saw his brother **B**, his mother's son,	1144
	45:12 eyes see, and the eyes of my brother **B**,	1144
	45:14 and wept; and **B** wept upon his neck.	1144
	45:22 **B** he gave three hundred *pieces* of silver,	1144
	46:19 sons of Rachel Jacob's wife; Joseph, and **B**.	1144
	46:21 the sons of **B** *were* Belah, and Becher,	1144
	49:27 **B** shall ravin *as* a wolf: in the morning he	1144
Ex	1: 3 Issachar, Zebulun, and **B**,	1144
Nu	1:11 Of **B**; Abidan the son of Gideoni.	1144
	1:36 Of the children of **B**, *by* their generations,	1144
	1:37 *even* of the tribe of **B**, *were* thirty and	1144
	2:22 the tribe of **B**: and the captain of the sons	1144
	2:22 captain of the sons of **B** *shall be* Abidan	1144
	7:60 prince of the children of **B**, *offered*,	1144
	10:24 of the tribe of **B** *was* Abidan the son of Gideoni.	1144
	13: 9 Of the tribe of **B**, Palti the son of Raphu.	1144
	26:38 The sons of **B** after their families: of Bela,	1144
	26:41 These *are* the sons of **B** after their families:	1144
	34:21 the tribe of **B**, Elidad the son of Chislon.	1144
Dt	27:12 Judah, and Issachar, and Joseph, and **B**:	1144
	33:12 *And* of **B** he said, The beloved of	1144
Jos	18:11 the lot of the tribe of the children of **B**	1144
	18:20 *was* the inheritance of the children of **B**,	1144
	18:21 **B** according to their families were Jericho,	1144
	18:28 This *is* the inheritance of the children of **B**,	1144
	21: 4 and out of the tribe of **B**, thirteen cities.	1144
	21:17 out of the tribe of **B**, Gibeon with her	1144
Jdg	1:21 the children of **B** did not drive out	1144
	1:21 the Jebusites dwell with the children of **B**	1144
	5:14 after thee, **B**, among thy people; out of	1144
	10: 9 against **B**, and against the house of	1144
	19:14 *were* by Gibeah, which *belongeth* to **B**.	1144
	20: 3 (Now the children of **B** heard	1144
	20: 4 I came into Gibeah that *belongeth* to **B**,	1144
	20:10 may do, when they come to Gibeah of **B**,	1144
	20:12 Israel sent men through all the tribe of **B**,	1144
	20:13 the children of **B** would not hearken to	1144
	20:14 the children of **B** gathered themselves	1144
	20:15 the children of **B** were numbered at that	1144
	20:17 men of Israel, beside **B**, were numbered	1144
	20:18 first to the battle against the children of **B**?	1144
	20:20 men of Israel went out to battle against **B**;	1144
	20:21 children of **B** came forth out of Gibeah,	1144
	20:23 against the children of **B** my brother?	1144
	20:24 against the children of **B** the second day.	1144
	20:25 **B** went forth against them out of Gibeah	1144
	20:28 against the children of **B** my brother,	1144
	20:30 against the children of **B** on the third day,	1144
	20:31 the children of **B** went out against	1144
	20:32 the children of **B** said, They *are* smitten	1144
	20:35 the LORD smote **B** before Israel:	1144
	20:36 So the children of **B** saw that they were	1144
	20:39 **B** began to smite *and* kill of the men of	1144
	20:41 turned *again*, the men of **B** were amazed:	1144
	20:44 there fell of **B** eighteen thousand men; all	1144
	20:46 So that all which fell that day of **B** were	1144
	20:48 Israel turned again upon the children of **B**,	1144
	21: 1 any of us give his daughter unto **B** to wife.	1144
	21: 6 the children of Israel repented them for **B**	1144
	21:13 of **B** that *were* in the rock Rimmon,	1144
	21:14 **B** came again at that time; and they gave	1144
	21:15 the people repented them for **B**, because	1144
	21:16 seeing the women are destroyed out of **B**?	1144
	21:17 inheritance for them that be escaped of **B**,	1144
	21:18 Cursed *be* he that giveth a wife to **B**.	1144
	21:20 they commanded the children of **B**,	1144
	21:21 of Shiloh, and go *to* the land of **B**.	1144
	21:23 the children of **B** did so, and took *them*	1144
1Sa	4:12 there ran a man of **B** out of the army,	1144
	9: 1 Now there was a man of **B**, whose name	1144
	9:16 will send thee a man out of the land of **B**,	1144
	9:21 least of all the families of the tribe of **B**?	1144
	10: 2 sepulchre in the border of **B** at Zelzah;	1144
	10:20 to come near, the tribe of **B** was taken.	1144
	10:21 he had caused the tribe of **B** to come	1144
	13: 2 were with Jonathan in Gibeah of **B**:	1144
	13:15 gat him up from Gilgal *unto* Gibeah of **B**.	1144
	13:16 present with them, abode in Gibeah of **B**:	1144
	14:16 the watchmen of Saul in Gibeah of **B**	1144
2Sa	2: 9 and over **B**, and over all Israel.	1144
	2:15 and went over by number twelve of **B**,	1144
	2:25 the children of **B** gathered themselves	1144
	2:31 the servants of David had smitten of **B**,	1144
	3:19 Abner also spake in the ears of **B**:	1144
	3:19 seemed *good* to the whole house of **B**.	1144
	4: 2 Rimmon a Beerothite, of the children of **B**:	1144
	4: 2 (for Beeroth also was reckoned to **B**:	1144
	19:17 *were* a thousand men of **B** with him,	1144
	21:14 buried they in the country of **B** in Zelah,	1144
	23:29 Ribai out of Gibeah of the children of **B**,	1144
1Ki	4:18 Shimei the son of Elah, in **B**:	1144
	12:21 with the tribe of **B**, an hundred and	1144
	12:23 unto all the house of Judah and **B**,	1144
	15:22 king Asa built with them Geba of **B**,	1144
1Ch	2: 2 Dan, Joseph, and **B**, Naphtali, Gad,	1144
	6:60 out of the tribe of **B**; Geba with her	1144
	6:65 out of the tribe of the children of **B**, these	1144
	7: 6 The sons of **B**; Bela, and Becher,	1144
	7:10 **B**, and Ehud, and Chenaanah, and Zethan,	1144
	8: 1 Now **B** begat Bela his firstborn, Ashbel	1144
	8:40 and fifty. All these *are* of the sons of **B**.	1144
	9: 3 of the children of **B**, and of the children of	1144
	9: 7 of the sons of **B**; Sallu the son of	1144
	11:31 that pertained to the children of **B**,	1144
	12: 2 out of a bow, *even* of Saul's brethren of **B**.	1144
	12:16 there came of the children of **B** and	1144
	12:29 of the children of **B**, the kindred of Saul,	1144
	21: 6 and **B** counted he not among them:	1144
	27:21 of **B**, Jaasiel the son of Abner:	1144
2Ch	11: 1 *of* the house of Judah and **B** an hundred	1144
	11: 3 and to all Israel in Judah and **B**, saying,	1144
	11:10 and Hebron, which *are* in Judah and in **B**,	1144
	11:12 having Judah and **B** on his side.	1144
	11:23 all the countries of Judah and **B**,	1144
	14: 8 out of **B**, that bare shields and drew bows,	1144
	15: 2 Hear ye me, Asa, and all Judah and **B**;	1144
	15: 8 idols out of all the land of Judah and **B**,	1144
	15: 9 he gathered all Judah and **B**,	1144
	17:17 of **B**; Eliada a mighty *man* of valour,	1144
	25: 5 *their* fathers, throughout all Judah and **B**:	1144
	31: 1 and the altars out of all Judah and **B**,	1144
	34: 9 remnant of Israel, and of all Judah and **B**;	1144
	34:32 **B** to stand *to it*. And the inhabitants of	1144
Ezr	1: 5 up the chief of the fathers of Judah and **B**,	1144
	4: 1 heard that the children of the captivity	1144
	10: 9 gathered themselves together *unto*	1144
	10:32 **B**, Malluch, *and* Shemariah.	1144
Ne	3:23 After him repaired **B** and Hashub over	1144
	11: 4 of Judah, and of the children of **B**	1144
	11: 7 these *are* the sons of **B**; Sallu the son of	1144
	11:31 The children also of **B** from Geba *dwelt at*	1144
	11:36 Levites *were* divisions in Judah, *and* in **B**.	1144
	12:34 Judah, and **B**, and Shemaiah, and Jeremiah,	1144
Ps	68:27 There *is* little **B** *with* their ruler, the	1144
	80: 2 Before Ephraim and **B** and Manasseh stir	1144
Jer	1: 1 that *were* in Anathoth in the land of **B**:	1144
	6: 1 O ye children of **B**, gather yourselves to	1144
	17:26 from the land of **B**, and from the plain,	1144
	20: 2 the stocks that *were* in the high gate of **B**,	1144
	32: 8 in Anathoth, which *is* in the country of **B**:	1144
	32:44 and take witnesses in the land of **B**,	1144
	33:13 in the land of **B**, and in the places about	1144

B

Jer 37:12 out of Jerusalem to go *into* the land of **B**, 1144
37:13 when he was in the gate of **B**, a captain of 1144
38: 7 the king then sitting in the gate of **B**; 1144
Eze 48:22 the border of Judah and the border of **B**, 1144
48:23 unto the west side, **B** *shall have a portion*. 1144
48:24 by the border of **B**, from the east side unto 1144
48:32 of Joseph, one gate of **B**, one gate of Dan. 1144
Hos 5: 8 cry aloud *at* Beth-aven, after thee, O **B**. 1144
Ob 1:19 of Samaria: and **B** *shall possess* Gilead. 1144
Ac 13:21 a man of the tribe of **B**, *by the space of* 958
Ro 11: 1 of the seed of Abraham, *of* the tribe of **B**. 958
Php 3: 5 of the stock of Israel, of the tribe of **B**, 958
Rev 7: 8 Of the tribe of **B** were sealed twelve 958

BENJAMIN'S (4) [BENJAMIN]
Ge 43:34 **B** mess was five times so much as any of 1144
44:12 and the cup was found in **B** sack. 1144
45:14 fell upon his brother **B** neck, and wept; 1144
Zec 14:10 from **B** gate unto the place of the first gate 1144

BENJAMITE (9) [BENJAMIN]
Jdg 3:15 the son of Gera, a **B**, a man lefthanded: 1145
1Sa 9: 1 the son of Aphiah, a **B**, 376+1121+3227
9:21 Saul answered and said, *Am* not I a **B**, 1145
2Sa 16:11 how much more now *may this* **B** *do it*? 1145
19:16 a **B**, which *was* of Bahurim, hasted and 1145
20: 1 *was* Sheba, the son of Bichri, a **B**: 376+3227
1Ki 2: 8 Shimei the son of Gera, a **B** of Bahurim, 1145
Est 2: 5 son of Shimei, the son of Kish, a **B**; 376+3227
Ps 7: T concerning the words of Cush the **B**. 1121

BENJAMITES (8) [BENJAMIN]
Jdg 19:16 Gibeah: but the men of the place were **B**. 1145
20:35 the children of Israel destroyed of the **B** 1144
20:36 for the men of Israel gave place to the **B**, 1144
20:40 the **B** looked behind them, and behold, 1144
20:43 *Thus* they inclosed the **B** round about, 1144
1Sa 9: 4 he passed through the land of the **B**, but 3228
22: 7 that stood about him, Hear now, ye **B**; 1145
1Ch 27:12 *was* Abiezer the Anetothite, of the **B**: 1145

BENO (2)
1Ch 24:26 and Mushi: the sons of Jaaziah; **B**. 1121
24:27 **B**, and Shoham, and Zaccur, and Ibri. 1121

BEN-ONI (1) [BENJAMIN]
Ge 35:18 (for she died) that she called his name **B**: 1126

BENT (8) [BEND]
Ps 7:12 he hath **b** his bow, and made it ready. 1869
37:14 have **b** their bow, to cast down the poor 1869
Isa 5:28 arrows *are* sharp, and all their bows **b**, 1869
21:15 the **b** bow, and from the grievousness 1869
La 2: 4 He hath **b** his bow like an enemy: 1869
3:12 He hath **b** his bow, and set me as a mark 1869
Hos 11: 7 my people are **b** to backsliding from me: 8511
Zec 9:13 I have **b** Judah for me, filled the bow 1869

BEN-ZOHETH (1)
1Ch 4:20 And the sons of Ishi were, Zoheth, and **B**. 1132

BEON (1)
Nu 32: 3 Elealeh, and Shebam, and Nebo, and **B**, 1194

BEOR (10) [BOSOR]
Ge 36:32 Bela the son of **B** reigned in Edom: 1160
Nu 22: 5 unto Balaam the son of **B** to Pethor, 1160
24: 3 Balaam the son of **B** hath said, and the 1160
24:15 Balaam the son of **B** hath said, and the 1160
31: 8 Balaam also the son of **B** they slew with 1160
Dt 23: 4 hired against thee Balaam the son of **B** 1160
Jos 13:22 Balaam also the son of **B**, the soothsayer, 1160
24: 9 called Balaam the son of **B** to curse you: 1160
1Ch 1:43 the children of Israel; Bela the son of **B**: 1160
Mic 6: 5 what Balaam the son of **B** answered him; 1160

BERA (1)
Ge 14: 2 *That these* made war with **B** king of 1298

BERACAH See BERACHAH

BERACHAH (3)
1Ch 12: 3 and **B**, and Jehu the Antothite, 1294
2Ch 20:26 assembled themselves in the valley of **B**; 1293
20:26 was called, The valley of **B**, unto *this* day. 1293

BERACHIAH (1)
1Ch 6:39 *even* Asaph the son of **B**, the son of 1296

BERAIAH (1)
1Ch 8:21 Adaiah, and **B**, and Shimrath, the sons of 1256

BEREA (3)
Ac 17:10 sent away Paul and Silas by night unto **B**: 960
17:13 word of God was preached of Paul at **B**, 960
20: 4 accompanied him into Asia Sopater of **B**; 961

BEREAVE (6) [BEREAVED, BEREAVETH]
Ecc 4: 8 whom do I labour, and **b** my soul of good? 2637
Jer 15: 7 I will **b** *them* of children, I will destroy 7921
Eze 5:17 and evil beasts, and they shall **b** thee; 7921
36:12 shalt no more henceforth **b** them **of men**. 7921
36:14 neither shalt **b** thy nations any more, saith 7921
Hos 9:12 bring up their children, yet will I **b** them, 7921

BEREAVED (6) [BEREAVE]
Ge 42:36 unto them, Me have ye **b** of my **children**: 7921

Ge 43:14 If I be **b** of my **children**, I am bereaved. 7921
43:14 If I be bereaved of my children, I am **b**. 7921
Jer 18:21 let their wives be **b** of their **children**, 7909
Eze 36:13 devourest up men, and hast **b** thy nations; 7921
Hos 13: 8 them as a bear *that is* **b** of her **whelps**, 7909

BEREAVETH (1) [BEREAVE]
La 1:20 abroad the sword *is*, at home *there is* as 7921

BERECHIAH (10) [BARACHIAS]
1Ch 3:20 Ohel, and **B**, and Hasadiah, Jushabhesed, 1296
9:16 and **B** the son of Asa, the son of Elkanah, 1296
15:17 of his brethren, Asaph the son of **B**, 1296
15:23 **B** and Elkanah were doorkeepers for 1296
2Ch 28:12 **B** the son of Meshillemoth, 1296
Ne 3: 4 them repaired Meshullam the son of **B**, 1296
3:30 him repaired Meshullam the son of **B** 1296
6:18 the daughter of Meshullam the son of **B**, 1296
Zec 1: 1 the son of **B**, the son of Iddo the prophet, 1296
1: 7 the son of **B**, the son of Iddo the prophet, 1296

BERED (2)
Ge 16:14 behold, *it is* between Kadesh and **B**. 1260
1Ch 7:20 **B** his son, and Tahath his son, 1260

BEREKIAH See BARACHIAS; BERECHIAH

BERI (1)
1Ch 7:36 Harnepher, and Shual, and **B**, and Imrah, 1275

BERIAH (11) [BERIITES]
Ge 46:17 and Ishui, and **B**, and Serah their sister: 1283
46:17 and the sons of **B**; Heber, and Malchiel. 1283
Nu 26:44 of **B**, the family of the Beriites. 1283
26:45 Of the sons of **B**: of Heber, the family of 1283
1Ch 7:23 he called his name **B**, because it went evil 1283
7:30 and Ishuai, and **B**, and Serah their sister. 1283
7:31 the sons of **B**; Heber, and Malchiel, who 1283
8:13 **B** also, and Shema, who *were* heads of 1283
8:16 and Ispah, and Joha, the sons of **B**; 1283
23:10 were, Jahath, Zina, and Jeush, and **B**. 1283
23:11 Jeush and **B** had not many sons; therefore 1283

BERIITES (1) [BERIAH]
Nu 26:44 the Jesuites: of Beriah, the family of the **B**. 1284

BERITES (1)
2Sa 20:14 and *to* Beth-maachah, and all the **B**: 1276

BERITH (1) [BAAL-BERITH]
Jdg 9:46 into a hold of the house of the god **B**. 1286

BERNICE (3)
Ac 25:13 and **B** came unto Cesarea to salute Festus. 959
25:23 and **B**, with great pomp, and were entered 959
26:30 and **B**, and they that sat with them: 959

BERODACH-BALADAN (1)
[MERODACH-BALADAN]
2Ki 20:12 At that time **B**, the son of Baladan, king of 1255

BEROTHAH (1)
Eze 47:16 Hamath, **B**, Sibraim, which *is* between 1268

BEROTHAI (1) [BEROTHITE]
2Sa 8: 8 from Betah, and from **B**, cities of 1268

BEROTHITE (1) [BEROTHAI]
1Ch 11:39 Zelek the Ammonite, Naharai the **B**, 1307

BERRIES (2)
Isa 17: 6 three **b** in the top of the uppermost bough, 1620
Jas 3:12 the fig tree, my brethren, bear **olive b**? 1636

BERYL (8)
Ex 28:20 the fourth row a **b**, and an onyx, 8658
39:13 fourth row, a **b**, an onyx, and a jasper: 8658
SS 5:14 hands *are* as gold rings set with the **b**: 8658
Eze 1:16 work *was* like unto the colour of a **b**: 8658
10: 9 wheels *was* as the colour of a **b** stone. 8658
28:13 the **b**, the onyx, and the jasper, 8658
Da 10: 6 His body also *was* like the **b**, and his face 8658
Rev 21:20 the eighth, **b**; the ninth, a topaz; the tenth, 969

BESAI (2)
Ezr 2:49 the children of Paseah, the children of **B**, 1153
Ne 7:52 children of **B**, the children of Meunim, 1153

BESEECH (67) [BESEECHING, BESOUGHT]
Ex 3:18 now let us go, we **b** thee, three days' 4994
33:18 And he said, I **b** thee, shew me thy glory. 4994
Nu 12:11 my lord, I **b** thee, lay not the sin upon 4994
12:13 Heal her now, O God, I **b** thee. 4994
14:17 I **b** thee, let the power of my Lord be 4994
14:19 Pardon, I **b** thee, the iniquity of this 4994
1Sa 23:11 God of Israel, I **b** thee, tell thy servant. 4994
2Sa 14:11 his servants go with I **b** 4994
16: 4 I **humbly b** thee *that* I may find grace in 7812
24:10 now, I **b** thee, O LORD, take away 4994
2Ki 1:13 O LORD our God, I **b** thee, 4994
20: 3 I **b** thee, O LORD, remember now how I 577
1Ch 21: 8 I **b** thee, do away the iniquity of thy 4994
2Ch 6:40 Now, my God, let, I **b** thee, thine eyes 4994
Ne 1: 5 said, I **b** thee, O LORD God of heaven, 577
1: 8 Remember, I **b** thee, the word that thou 4994
1:11 O Lord, I **b** thee, let now thine ear be 577
Job 10: 9 Remember, I **b** thee, that thou hast made 4994

Job 42: 4 Hear, I **b** thee, and I will speak: I will 4994
Ps 80:14 Return, we **b** thee, O God *of* hosts: 4994
116: 4 O LORD, I **b** thee, deliver my soul. 577
118:25 Save now, I **b** thee, O LORD: O LORD, 577
118:25 O LORD, I **b** thee, send now prosperity. 577
119:108 Accept, I **b** thee, the freewill offerings of 4994
Isa 38: 3 Remember now, O LORD, I **b** thee, 4994
64: 9 behold, see, we **b** thee, we *are* all thy 4994
Jer 38: 4 We **b** thee, let this man be put to death: 4994
38:20 I **b** thee, the voice of the LORD, which I 4994
42: 2 Jeremiah the prophet, Let, we **b** thee, 4994
Da 1:12 Prove thy servants, I **b** thee, ten days; 4994
9:16 I **b** thee, let thine anger and thy fury be 4994
Am 7: 2 I said, O Lord GOD, forgive, I **b** thee: 4994
7: 5 Then said I, O Lord GOD, cease, I **b** thee: 4994
Jnh 1:14 said, We **b** thee, O LORD, we beseech 577
1:14 We beseech thee, O LORD, we **b** thee, 4994
4: 3 Therefore now, O LORD, take, I **b** thee, 4994
Mal 1: 9 God that he will be gracious unto 2470+6440
Mk 7:32 and they **b** him to put *his* hand upon him. 3870
Lk 8:28 God most high? I **b** thee, torment me not. 1189
9:38 Master, I **b** thee, look upon my son: 1189
Ac 21:39 and, I **b** thee, suffer me to speak unto 1189
26: 3 wherefore I **b** thee to hear me patiently. 1189
Ro 12: 1 I **b** you therefore, brethren, by the 3870
15:30 Now I **b** you, brethren, for the Lord Jesus 3870
16:17 Now I **b** you, brethren, mark them which 3870
1Co 1:10 Now I **b** you, brethren, by the name of 3870
4:16 Wherefore I **b** you, be ye followers of me. 3870
16:15 I **b** you, brethren, (ye know the house of 3870
2Co 2: 8 Wherefore I **b** you that *you* would confirm 3870
5:20 for Christ, as though God did **b** *you* by us: 3870
6: 1 *as* workers together *with him*, **b** *you* also 3870
10: 1 Now I Paul myself **b** you by the meekness 3870
10: 2 But I **b** *you*, that I may not be bold when 1189
Gal 4:12 Brethren, I **b** you, be as I *am*; for I *am* as 1189
Eph 4: 1 I **b** you that *ye* walk worthy of the vocation 3870
Php 4: 2 I **b** Euodias, and beseech Syntyche, 3870
4: 2 I beseech Euodias, and **b** Syntyche, 3870
1Th 4: 1 Furthermore then we **b** you, brethren, 2065
4:10 but we **b** you, brethren, that *ye* increase 3870
5:12 And we **b** you, brethren, to know them 3870
2Th 2: 1 we **b** you, brethren, by the coming of 2065
Phm 1: 9 *Yet* for love's sake I rather **b** *thee,* being 3870
1:10 I **b** thee for my son Onesimus, whom I 3870
Heb 13:19 I **b** *you* the rather to do this, that I may 3870
13:22 And I **b** you, brethren, suffer the word of 3870
1Pe 2:11 I **b** *you* as strangers and pilgrims, 3870
2Jn 1: 5 And now I **b** thee, lady, not as though I 2065

BESEECHING (3) [BESEECH]
Mt 8: 5 there came unto him a centurion, **b** him, 3870
Mk 1:40 **b** him, and kneeling down to him, 3870
Lk 7: 3 **b** him that he would come and heal his 2065

BESET (6)
Jdg 19:22 **b** the house **round about**, *and* beat at 5437
20: 5 **b** the house **round about** upon me by 5437
Ps 22:12 strong **bulls** of Bashan have **b** me **round**. 3803
139: 5 Thou hast **b** me behind and before, 6696
Hos 7: 2 their own doings have **b** them **about**; 5437
Heb 12: 1 and the sin which doth so **easily b** us, 2139

BESIDE (95) [BESIDES]
Ge 31:50 if thou shalt take *other* wives **b** my 5921
Ex 12:37 on foot *that* were men, **b** 905+4480+3807.1
14: 9 the sea, **b** Pi-hahiroth, before Baal-zephon. 5921
29:12 pour all the blood **b** the bottom of the altar. 413
Lev 1:16 cast it **b** the altar on the east part, 681
9:17 burnt *it* upon the altar, **b** 905+4480+3807.1
10:12 fire, and eat it without leaven **b** the altar: 681
23:38 **B** the sabbaths of the LORD, 905+4480+3807.1
23:38 **b** your gifts, and beside all 905+4480+3807.1
23:38 **b** all your vows, and beside 905+4480+3807.1
23:38 **b** all your freewill offerings, 905+4480+3807.1
Nu 5: 8 *even* to the priest; **b** the ram 905+4480+3807.1
5:20 man hath lain with thee **b** thine 1107+4480
11: 6 at all, **b** this manna, *before* our eyes. 1115
16:49 seven hundred, **b** them that 905+4480+3807.1
24: 6 *and* as cedar trees **b** the waters. 5921
28:10 **b** the continual burnt offering, 5921
28:23 Ye shall offer these **b** 905+4480+3807.1
28:24 it shall be offered **b** the continual burnt 5921
29: 6 **B** the burnt offering of 905+4480+3807.1
29:11 goats *for* a sin offering; **b** 905+4480+3807.1
29:16 goats *for* a sin offering; **b** 905+4480+3807.1
29:19 goats *for* a sin offering; **b** 905+4480+3807.1
29:22 goat *for* a sin offering; **b** 905+4480+3807.1
29:25 goat *for* a sin offering; **b** 905+4480+3807.1
29:28 goat *for* a sin offering; **b** 905+4480+3807.1
29:31 goat *for* a sin offering; **b** 905+4480+3807.1
29:34 goat for a sin offering; **b** 905+4480+3807.1
29:38 goat for a sin offering; **b** 905+4480+3807.1
31: 8 **b** *the* rest *of* them that were slain; 5921
Dt 3: 5 unwalled towns a great many. 905+3807.1
11:30 over against Gilgal, the plains of Moreh? 681
18: 8 shall have like portions to eat, **b** 905+3807.1
19: 9 three cities moe for thee, **b** these three: 5921
29: 1 Israel in the land of Moab, **b** 905+4480+3807.1
Jos 3:16 the city Adam, that *is* **b** Zaretan: 4480+6654
7: 2 which *is* **b** Beth-aven, on the east side of 5973
12: 9 king of Ai, which *is* **b** Beth-el; one; 4480+6654
13: 4 Mearah that *is* **b** the Sidonians, 3807.1
17: 5 the land of Gilead and 905+4480+3807.1
22:19 in building you an altar **b** the altar 1107+4480

B

Jdg 6:37 *it be* dry upon all the earth *b*, then shall I NIH
7: 1 early, and pitched *b* the well of Harod: 5921
8:26 *b* ornaments, and collars, 905+4480+3807.1
8:26 *b* the chains that *were* about 905+4480+3807.1
11:34 *b* her he had neither son nor daughter. 4480
20:15 *b* the inhabitants of Gibeah, 905+3807.1
20:17 men of Israel, *b* Benjamin, 905+4480+3807.1
20:36 liers in wait which they had set *b* Gibeah. 4480+3807.1
Ru 2:14 she sat *b* the reapers: and he 4480+6654
1Sa 2: 2 *there is* none *b* thee: neither *is there* any 1115
4: 1 to battle, and pitched *b* Eben-ezer: 5921
19: 3 stand *b* my father in the field 3027+3807.1
2Sa 7:22 like thee, neither *is there any* God *b* thee, 2108
13:23 in Baal-hazor, which *is b* Ephraim: 5973
15: 2 and stood *b* the way of the gate: 3027+5921
15:18 all his servants passed on *b* him; 3027+3807.1
1Ki 3:20 at midnight, and took my son from *b* me, 681
4:23 an hundred sheep, *b* harts, 905+4480+3807.1
9:26 which *is b* Eloth, on the shore of the Red 854
10:19 of the seat, and two lions stood *b* the stays. 681
11:25 to Israel all the days of Solomon, *b* 854+2050.1
13:31 of God *is* buried; lay my bones *b* his bones: 681
2Ki 11:20 they slew Athaliah with the sword *b* NIH
12: 9 a hole in the lid of it, and set it *b* the altar, 681
21:16 from one end to another; *b* 905+4480+3807.1
1Ch 3: 9 *were* all the sons of David, *b* 905+4480+3807.1
2Ch 20: 1 and with them *other b* the Ammonites, 4480
26:19 of the LORD, from *b* the incense altar. 3807.1
31:16 *B* their genealogy of males, 905+4480+3807.1
Ezr 1: 6 *b* all *that* was willingly 905+5921+3807.1
2:65 *B* their servants and 905+4480+3807.1
Ne 5:15 and wine, *b* forty shekels of silver; 310
7:67 *B* their manservants and 905+4480+3807.1
8: 4 and *b* him stood Mattithiah, and Shema, 681
Job 1:14 and the asses feeding *b* them: 3027+5921
Ps 23: 2 he leadeth me *b* the still waters. 5921
73:25 *none upon earth that* I desire *b* thee. 5973
SS 1: 8 and feed thy kids *b* the shepherds' tents. 5921
Isa 32:20 Blessed *are* ye that sow *b* all waters, 5921
43:11 and *b* me *there is* no saviour. 1107+4480
45:21 *there is* no God *else b* me; 1107+4480+5750
45:21 God and a saviour; *there is* none *b* me. 2108
Jer 36:21 the princes which stood *b* the king. 4480+5921
Eze 9: 2 they went in, and stood *b* the brasen altar. 681
10: 6 then he went in, and stood *b* the wheels. 681
10:16 the same wheels also turned not from *b* 681
Hos 13: 4 god but me: for *there is* no saviour *b* me. 1115
Zep 2:15 her heart, I *am*, and *there is* none *b* me: 5750
Mt 14:21 thousand men, *b* women and children. 5565
15:38 thousand men, *b* women and children. 5565
Mk 3:21 on him: for they said, He is *b* **himself.** 1839
Lk 24:21 and *b* all this, to day is the third day since 4862
Ac 26:24 a loud voice, Paul, thou art *b* **thyself,** 3105
2Pe 1: 5 And *b* this, giving all diligence, add to 2532

BESIDES (45) [BESIDE]

Ge 19:12 men said unto Lot, Hast thou here any *b*? 5750
26: 1 was a famine in the land, *b* 905+4480+3807.1
46:26 came out of his loins, *b* 905+4480+3807.1
Lev 6:10 altar, and he shall put them *b* the altar. 681
7:13 *B* the cakes, he shall offer *for* his offering 5921
18:18 her nakedness, *b* the other in her life *time.* 5921
Nu 6:21 LORD for his separation, *b* 905+4480+3807.1
28:15 the continual burnt offering, 5921
28:31 Ye shall offer *them b* 905+4480+3807.1
29:39 LORD in your set feasts, *b* 905+4480+3807.1
Dt 4:35 *there is* none else *b* him. 905+4480+3807.1
Jos 22:29 *b* the altar of the LORD our 905+4480+3807.1
Ru 4: 4 for *there is* none to redeem *it b* thee; 2108
1Ki 5:16 the chief of Solomon's 905+4480+3807.1
10:13 what*soever* she asked, *b* 905+4480+3807.1
10:15 *B that he had* of the merchantmen, 905+4480+3807.1
22: 7 *Is there* not here a prophet of the LORD *b*, 5750
1Ch 17:20 thee, neither *is there any* God *b* thee, 2108
2Ch 9:12 what*soever* she asked, *b* 905+4480+3807.1
9:14 *B that which* chapmen 905+4480+3807.1
17:19 These waited on the king, *b* 905+4480+3807.1
18: 6 *Is there* not here a prophet of the LORD *b*, 5750
Ezr 1: 4 *b* the freewill offering for the house of 5973
Ne 5:17 *b* those that came unto us from among 2050.1
Isa 26:13 *other* lords *b* thee have had dominion 2108
44: 6 the last; and *b* me *there is* no 1107+4480
44: 8 there a God *b* me? yea, *there is* no 1107+4480
45: 5 *there is* none else, *there is* no God *b* me: 2108
45: 6 from the west, that *there is* none *b* me. 1107
47: 8 in thine heart, I *am*, and none else *b* me; 5750
47: 10 in thine heart, I *am*, and none else *b* me. 5750
56: 8 *b* those that are gathered unto him. 3807.1
64: 4 neither hath the eye seen, O God, *b* thee, 2108
Jer 36:32 there were added *b* unto them many like 5750
Eze 10:19 the wheels also *were b* them, 5980+3807.1
11:22 wings, and the wheels *b* them; 5980+3807.1
32:13 the beasts thereof from *b* the great waters; 5921
Da 11: 4 even for others *b* those. 3807.1
Mt 25:20 I have gained *b* them five talents moe. 1909
25:22 I have gained two other talents *b* them. 1909
Lk 16:26 And *b* all this, between us and you there 1909
1Co 1:16 *b*, I know not whether I baptized any 3062
2Co 5:13 For whether we be *b* **ourselves,** *it is* 1839
11:28 *B* those *things* that are without, and 5565
Phm 1:19 **owest** unto me even thine own self *b*. 4359

BESIEGE (11) [BESIEGED, SIEGE]

Dt 20:12 against thee, then thou shalt *b* it: 5921+6696
20:19 When thou shalt *b* a city a long time, 6696

BESIEGED (23) [BESIEGE]

2Sa 11: 1 the children of Ammon, and *b* Rabbah. 6696
20:15 and *b* him in Abel of Beth-maachah, 6696
1Ki 16:17 and all Israel with him, and they *b* Tirzah. 6696
20: 1 he went up and *b* Samaria, 6696
2Ki 6:24 all his host, and went up, and *b* Samaria. 6696
6:25 behold, they *b* it, until an ass's head was 6696
16: 5 they *b* Ahaz, but could not overcome *him.* 6696
17: 5 went up *to* Samaria, and *b* it three years. 6696
18: 9 Assyria came up against Samaria, and *b* it. 6696
19:24 have I dried up all the rivers of *b* places. 4693
24:10 and the city was *b*. 935+4692+871.1+1886.1
25: 2 the city was *b* unto 935+4692+871.1+1886.1
1Ch 20: 1 of Ammon, and came *b* Rabbah. 6696
Ecc 9:14 *b* it, and built great bulwarks against it: 6696
Isa 1: 8 in a garden of cucumbers, as a *b* city. 5341
37:25 I dried up all the rivers of *b* places. 4693
Jer 32: 2 the king of Babylon's army *b* Jerusalem: 6696
37: 5 the Chaldeans that *b* Jerusalem heard 6696
39: 1 his army against Jerusalem, and they *b* it. 6696
52: 5 the city was *b* unto 935+4692+871.1+1886.1
Eze 4: 3 it shall be *b*, and thou 4692+871.1+1886.1
6:12 and is *b* shall die by the famine: 5341
Da 1: 1 king of Babylon *unto* Jerusalem, and *b* it. 6696

BESODEIAH (1)

Ne 3: 6 of Paseah, and Meshullam the son of *B*; 1152

BESOM (1)

Isa 14:23 I will sweep it with the *b* of destruction, 4292

BESOR (3)

1Sa 30: 9 *were* with him, and came to the brook *B*, 1308
30:10 that they could not go over the brook *B*. 1308
30:21 had made also to abide at the brook *B*: 1308

BESOUGHT (44) [BESEECH]

Ge 42:21 when he *b* us, and we would not hear; 2603
Ex 32:11 Moses *b* the LORD his God, 853+2470+6440
Dt 3:23 I *b* the LORD at that time, saying, 413+2603
2Sa 12:16 David therefore *b* God for the child; 1245
1Ki 13: 6 the man of God *b* the LORD, 2470+6440
2Ki 1:13 *b* him, and said unto him, O man of God, 2603
13: 4 Jehoahaz *b* the LORD, 2470+6440
2Ch 33:12 he *b* the LORD his God, 853+2470+6440
Ezr 8:23 So we fasted and *b* our God for this: 1245
Est 8: 3 *b* him with tears to put away the mischief 2603
Jer 26:19 *b* the LORD, and the LORD 853+2470+6440
Mt 8:31 So the devils *b* him, saying, If thou cast us 3870
8:34 they *b him* that he would depart out of 3870
14:36 And *b* him that they might only touch 3870
15:23 And his disciples came and *b* him, saying, 2065
18:29 and *b* him, saying, Have patience with me, 3870
Mk 5:10 he *b* him much that he would not send 3870
5:12 And all the devils *b* him, saying, Send us 3870
5:23 And *b* him greatly, saying, My little 3870
6:56 *b* him that they might touch if it were but 3870
7:26 *b* him that he would cast forth the devil 2065
8:22 man unto him, and *b* him to touch him. 3870
Lk 4:38 with a great fever; and they *b* him for her. 2065
5:12 *b* him, saying, Lord, if thou wilt, 1189
7: 4 to Jesus, they *b* him instantly, saying, 3870
8:31 And they *b* him that he would not 3870
8:32 they *b* him that he would suffer them to 3870
8:37 round about *b* him to depart from them; 2065
8:38 *b* him that *he* might be with him: 1189
8:41 *b* him that he would come into his house: 3870
9:40 And I *b* thy disciples to cast him out; 1189
11:37 certain Pharisee *b* him to dine with him: 2065
Jn 4:40 they *b* him that *he* would tarry with them: 2065
4:47 and *b* him that he would come down, 2065
19:31 *b* Pilate that their legs might be broken, 2065
19:38 *b* Pilate that he might take away the body 2065
Ac 13:42 the Gentiles *b* that these words might be 3870
16:15 and her household, she *b us*, saying, 3870
16:39 And they came and *b* them, 3870
21:12 place, *b* him not to go up to Jerusalem. 3870
25: 2 informed him against Paul, and *b* him, 3870
27:33 Paul *b* them all to take meat, saying, 3870
2Co 12: 8 For this *thing* I *b* the Lord thrice, that it 3870
1Ti 1: 3 As I *b* thee to abide *still* at Ephesus, 3870

BEST (25) [GOOD]

Ge 43:11 take of the *b* fruits in the land in your 2173
47: 6 in the *b* of the land make thy father and 4315
47:11 the *b* of the land, in the land of Rameses, 4315
Ex 22: 5 the *b* of his own field, and of the *b* of 4315
22: 5 the *b* of his own vineyard, shall he make 4315
Nu 18:12 All the *b* of the oil, and all the best of 2459
18:12 All the *b* of the wine, and of the wheat, 2459
18:29 all the *b* thereof, *even* the hallowed *part* 2459
18:30 ye have heaved the *b* thereof from it, 2459
18:32 when ye have heaved from it the *b* of it: 2459
36: 6 to whom they **think** *b*; 2896+5869+871.1
Dt 23:16 where it **liketh** him *b*: 2896+871.1+1886.1

Dt 28:52 he shall *b* thee in all thy gates, until thy 6887
28:52 he shall *b* thee in all thy gates throughout 6887
1Sa 23: 8 down *to* Keilah, to *b* David and his men. 6696
1Ki 8:37 if their enemy *b* them in the land of their 6887
2Ki 24:11 against the city, and his servants *did b* it. 6696
2Ch 6:28 if their enemies *b* them in the cities of 6887
Isa 21: 2 *b*, O Media; all the sighing thereof have I 6696
Jer 21: 4 with *b* you without the walls, and I will 6696
21: 9 falleth to the Chaldeans that *b* you, 6696

BESIEGED (23) [BESIEGE]

2Sa 11: 1 the children of Ammon, and *b* Rabbah. 6696
20:15 and *b* him in Abel of Beth-maachah, 6696
1Ki 16:17 and all Israel with him, and they *b* Tirzah. 6696
20: 1 he went up and *b* Samaria, 6696
2Ki 6:24 all his host, and went up, and *b* Samaria. 6696
6:25 behold, they *b* it, until an ass's head was 6696
16: 5 they *b* Ahaz, but could not overcome *him.* 6696
17: 5 went up *to* Samaria, and *b* it three years. 6696
18: 9 Assyria came up against Samaria, and *b* it. 6696
19:24 have I dried up all the rivers of *b* places. 4693
24:10 and the city was *b*. 935+4692+871.1+1886.1
25: 2 the city was *b* unto 935+4692+871.1+1886.1
1Ch 20: 1 of Ammon, and came *b* Rabbah. 6696
Ecc 9:14 *b* it, and built great bulwarks against it: 6696
Isa 1: 8 in a garden of cucumbers, as a *b* city. 5341
37:25 I dried up all the rivers of *b* places. 4693
Jer 32: 2 the king of Babylon's army *b* Jerusalem: 6696
37: 5 the Chaldeans that *b* Jerusalem heard 6696
39: 1 his army against Jerusalem, and they *b* it. 6696
52: 5 the city was *b* unto 935+4692+871.1+1886.1
Eze 4: 3 it shall be *b*, and thou 4692+871.1+1886.1
6:12 and is *b* shall die by the famine: 5341
Da 1: 1 king of Babylon *unto* Jerusalem, and *b* it. 6696

1Sa 8:14 *even the b of* them, and give *them* to his 2896
15: 9 the *b* of the sheep, and of the oxen, 4315
15:15 for the people spared the *b* of the sheep 4315
2Sa 18: 4 unto them, What seemeth you *b* I will do. 3190
1Ki 10:18 of ivory, and overlaid it with the gold. 6338
2Ki 10: 3 Look even out the *b* and meetest of your 2896
Est 2: 9 her maids unto the *b place* of the house 2896
Ps 39: 5 every man at his *b state is* altogether 5324
SS 7: 9 the roof of thy mouth like the *b* wine, 2896
Eze 31:16 choice and *b* of Lebanon, all that drink 2896
Mic 7: 4 The *b* of them *is* as a brier: the *most* 2896
Lk 15:22 Bring forth the *b* robe, and put *it* on him; 4413
1Co 12:31 But covet earnestly the *b* gifts: 2909

BESTEAD (1)

Isa 8:21 pass through it, **hardly** *b* and hungry: 7185

BESTIR (1)

2Sa 5:24 *that* then thou shalt *b* thyself: 2782

BESTOW (9) [BESTOWED]

Ex 32:29 he may *b* upon you a blessing *this* day. 5414
Dt 14:26 shalt *b that* money for whatsoever thy 5414
2Ch 24: 7 of the LORD did they *b* upon Baalim. 6213
Ezr 7:20 which thou shalt have occasion to *b*, 5415
7:20 *b it* out of the king's treasure house. 5415
Lk 12:17 I have no room where to *b* my fruits? 4863
12:18 and there will I *b* all my fruits and 4863
1Co 12:23 upon these we *b* more abundant honour; 4060
13: 3 And though I *b* all my goods **to feed** 5595

BESTOWED (14) [BESTOW]

1Ki 10:26 whom he *b* in the cities for chariots, 5148
2Ki 5:24 from their hand, and *b them* in the house: 6485
12:15 delivered the money to be *b* on workmen: 5414
1Ch 29:25 *b* upon him *such* royal majesty as had not 5414
2Ch 9:25 whom he *b* in the chariot cities, 3240
Isa 63: 7 according to all that the LORD hath *b* on 1580
63: 7 which he hath *b on* them according to his 1580
Jn 4:38 you to reap *that* whereon ye *b* no labour: 2872
Ro 16: 6 Greet Mary, who *b* much **labour** on us. 2872
1Co 15:10 his grace which was *b* upon me was not NIG
2Co 1:11 that for the gift *b* upon us by the means of NIG
8: 1 we do you to wit of the grace of God *b* on 1325
Gal 4:11 lest I have *b* upon you **labour** in vain. 2872
1Jn 3: 1 manner of love the Father hath *b* upon 1325

BETAH (1)

2Sa 8: 8 from *B*, and from Berothai, cities of 984

BETEN (1)

Jos 19:25 and Hali, and *B*, and Achshaph, 991

BETH BIRI See BETH-BIREI

BETH HAKKEREM See BETH-HACCEREM

BETH HARAM See BETH-ARAM

BETH MAACAH See BETH-MAACHAH

BETH OPHRAH See HOUSE OF APHRAH

BETH PELET See BETH-PALET; BETH-PHELET

BETHABARA (1)

Jn 1:28 These *things* were done in *B* beyond Jordan, 962

BETH-ANATH (3) [ANATH]

Jos 19:38 Horem, and *B*, and Beth-shemesh; 1043
Jdg 1:33 of Beth-shemesh, nor the inhabitants of *B*; 1043
1:33 and *B* became tributaries unto them. 1043

BETH-ANOTH (1)

Jos 15:59 Maarath, and *B*, and Eltekon; six cities 1042

BETHANY (11)

Mt 21:17 left them, and went out of the city into *B*; 963
26: 6 Now when Jesus was in *B*, in the house of 963
Mk 11: 1 unto Bethphage and *B*, at the mount of 963
11:11 he went out unto *B* with the twelve. 963
11:12 when they were come from *B*, he was 963
14: 3 And being in *B* in the house of Simon 963
Lk 19:29 he was come nigh to Bethphage and *B*, 963
24:50 And he led them out as far as to *B*, 963
Jn 11: 1 *named* Lazarus, of *B*, the town of Mary 963
11:18 Now *B* was nigh unto Jerusalem, 963
12: 1 six days before the passover came to *B*, 963

BETH-ARABAH (3) [ARABAH]

Jos 15: 6 and passed along by the north of *B*; 1026
15:61 the wilderness, *B*, Middin, and Secacah, 1026
18:22 And *B*, and Zemaraim, and Beth-el, 1026

BETH-ARAM (1) [ARAM]

Jos 13:27 *B*, and Beth-nimrah, and Succoth, 1027

BETH-ARBEL (1)

Hos 10:14 as Shalman spoiled *B* in the day of battle: 1009

BETH-AVEN (7) [AVEN]

Jos 7: 2 which *is beside B*, on the east side of 1007
18:12 out thereof were at the wilderness of *B*. 1007
1Sa 13: 5 pitched in Michmash, eastward from *B*. 1007
14:23 day: and the battle passed over *unto B*. 1007
Hos 4:15 neither go ye up *to B*, nor swear, 1007
5: 8 cry aloud *at B*, after thee, O Benjamin. 1007
10: 5 shall fear because of the calves of *B*: 1007

B

BETH-AZMAVETH (1) [AZMAVETH]
Ne 7:28 The men of **B**, forty and two. 1041

BETH-BAAL-MEON (1) [BAAL-MEON]
Jos 13:17 the plain; Dibon, and Bamoth-baal, and **B**, 1010

BETH-BARAH (2)
Jdg 7:24 take before them the waters unto **B** and 1012
 7:24 and took the waters unto **B** and Jordan. 1012

BETH-BIREI (1)
1Ch 4:31 and at **B**, and at Shaaraim. 1011

BETH-CAR (1)
1Sa 7:11 and smote them, until *they came* under **B**. 1033

BETH-DAGON (2) [DAGON]
Jos 15:41 **B**, and Naamah, and Makkedah; 1016
 19:27 turneth *toward* the sunrising to **B**, 1016

BETH-DIBLATHAIM (1)
Jer 48:22 upon Dibon, and upon Nebo, and upon **B**, 1015

BETH-EL (66) [BETHELITE, EL-BETH-EL, GOD,
 HOUSE]
Ge 12: 8 thence unto a mountain on the east of **B**, 1008
 12: 8 *having* **B** on the west, and Hai on the east: 1008
 13: 3 on his journeys from the south even to **B**, 1008
 13: 3 at the beginning, between **B** and Hai; 1008
 28:19 he called the name of that place **B**: 1008
 31:13 I *am* the God of **B**, where thou anointedst 1008
 35: 1 Arise, go up to **B**, and dwell there: 1008
 35: 3 let us arise, and go up to **B**; and I will 1008
 35: 6 that *is*, **B**, he and all the people that *were* 1008
 35: 8 she was buried beneath **B** under an oak: 1008
 35:15 the place where God spake with him, **B**. 1008
 35:16 they journeyed from **B**; and there was but 1008
Jos 7: 2 the east side of **B**, and spake unto them, 1008
 8: 9 abode between **B** and Ai, on the west side 1008
 8:12 set them to lie in ambush between **B** and 1008
 8:17 there was not a man left in Ai or **B**, 1008
 12: 9 the king of Ai, which *is* beside **B**, one; 1008
 12:16 of Makkedah, one; the king of **B**, one; 1008
 16: 1 up from Jericho throughout mount **B**, 1008
 16: 2 goeth out from **B** to Luz, and passeth 1008
 18:13 to the side of Luz, which *is* **B**, southward; 1008
 18:22 And Beth-arabah, and Zemaraim, and **B**, 1008
Jdg 1:22 of Joseph, they also went up *against* **B**: 1008
 1:23 the house of Joseph sent to descry **B**. 1008
 4: 5 between Ramah and **B** in mount Ephraim: 1008
 21:19 *in a place* which *is* on the north side of **B**, 1008
 21:19 that goeth up from **B** to Shechem, 1008
1Sa 7:16 he went from year to year in circuit *to* **B**, 1008
 10: 3 thee three men going up to God *to* **B**, 1008
 13: 2 with Saul in Michmash and in mount **B**, 1008
 30:27 To *them* which *were* in **B**, and to *them* 1008
1Ki 12:29 he set the one in **B**, and the other put he 1008
 12:32 he offered upon the altar (so did he in **B**,) 1008
 12:32 placed in **B** the priests of the high places 1008
 12:33 in the fifteenth day of the eighth month, 1008
 13: 1 Judah by the word of the LORD unto **B**: 1008
 13: 4 which had cried against the altar in **B**, 1008
 13:10 not by the way that he came to **B**. 1008
 13:11 Now there dwelt an old prophet in **B**; 1008
 13:11 the man of God had done *that* day in **B**: 1008
 13:32 word of the LORD against the altar in **B**, 1008
2Ki 2: 2 for the LORD hath sent me to **B**. 1008
 2: 2 not leave thee. So they went down *to* **B**. 1008
 2: 3 the sons of the prophets that *were* at **B** 1008
 2:23 he went up from thence *unto* **B**: and as he 1008
 10:29 *to wit*, the golden calves that *were* in **B**, 1008
 17:28 away from Samaria came and dwelt in **B**, 1008
 23: 4 and carried the ashes of them *unto* **B**. 1008
 23:15 Moreover the altar that *was* at **B**, 1008
 23:17 that thou hast done against the altar of **B**, 1008
 23:19 to all the acts that he had done in **B**. 1008
1Ch 7:28 habitations *were*, **B** and the towns thereof 1008
2Ch 13:19 **B** with the towns thereof, and Jeshanah 1008
Ezr 2:28 men of **B** and Ai, two hundred twenty 1008
Ne 7:32 men of **B** and Ai, an hundred twenty 1008
 11:31 and Aija, and **B**, and *in* their villages, 1008
Jer 48:13 as the house of Israel was ashamed of **B** 1008
Hos 10:15 So shall **B** do unto you because of your 1008
 12: 4 he found him in **B**, and there he spake 1008
Am 3:14 upon him I will also visit the altars of **B**: 1008
 4: 4 Come to **B**, and transgress; at Gilgal 1008
 5: 5 seek not **B**, nor enter *into* Gilgal, 1008
 5: 5 captivity, and **B** shall come to nought. 1008
 5: 6 and *there be* none to quench *it* in **B**. 1008
 7:10 Amaziah the priest of **B** sent to Jeroboam 1008
 7:13 prophesy not again any more *at* **B**: for *it* *is* 1008

BETHELITE (1) [BETH-EL]
1Ki 16:34 In his days did Hiel the **B** build Jericho: 1017

BETH-EMEK (1)
Jos 19:27 of Jiphthah-el toward the north side *of* **B**, 1025

BETHER (1)
SS 2:17 or a young hart upon the mountains of **B**. 1335

BETHESDA (1)
Jn 5: 2 which is called in the Hebrew tongue **B**, 964

BETH-EZEL (1) [EZEL]
Mic 1:11 came not forth *in* the mourning of **B**; 1018

BETH-GADER (1)
1Ch 2:51 of Beth-lehem, Hareph the father of **B**. 1013

BETH-GAMUL (1) [GAMUL]
Jer 48:23 and upon **B**, and upon Beth-meon, 1014

BETH-HACCEREM (1)
Ne 3:14 the son of Rechab, the ruler of part of **B**; 1021
Jer 6: 1 in Tekoa, and set up a sign of fire in **B**: 1021

BETH-HARAN (1) [HARAN]
Nu 32:36 Beth-nimrah, and **B**, fenced cities: 1028

BETH-HOGLA (1) [BETH-HOGLAH]
Jos 15: 6 the border went up *to* **B**, and passed along 1031

BETH-HOGLAH (2) [BETH-HOGLA]
Jos 18:19 the border passed along to the side of **B** 1031
 18:21 and **B**, and the valley of Keziz, 1031

BETH-HORON (14)
Jos 10:10 them *along* the way that goeth up to **B**, 1032
 10:11 *and* were in the going down to **B**, 1032
 16: 3 unto the coast of **B** the nether, 1032
 16: 5 side was Ataroth-addar, unto **B** the upper; 1032
 18:13 *lieth* on the south side of the nether **B**. 1032
 18:14 the hill that *lieth* before **B** southward; 1032
 21:22 her suburbs, and **B** with her suburbs; 1032
1Sa 13:18 another company turned the way to **B**: 1032
1Ki 9:17 Solomon built Gezer, and **B** the nether, 1032
1Ch 6:68 her suburbs, and **B** with her suburbs, 1032
 7:24 who built **B** the nether, and the upper, 1032
2Ch 8: 5 Also he built **B** the upper, and Beth-horon 1032
 8: 5 **B** the nether, fenced cities, *with* walls, 1032
 25:13 from Samaria even unto **B**, and smote 1032

BETHINK (2) [THINK]
1Ki 8:47 *Yet* if they shall **b** themselves 413+3820+7725
2Ch 6:37 *Yet* if they **b** themselves in 413+3824+7725

BETH-JESHIMOTH (3) [BETH-JESIMOTH]
Jos 12: 3 *even* the salt sea on the east, the way to **B**; 1020
 13:20 and Ashdoth-pisgah, and **B**, 1020
Eze 25: 9 the country, **B**, Baal-meon, and Kiriathaim, 1020

BETH-JESIMOTH (1) [BETH-JESHIMOTH]
Nu 33:49 *even* unto Abel-shittim in the plains 1020

BETH-LEBAOTH (1)
Jos 19: 6 and Sharuhen; thirteen cities and 1034

BETHLEHEM, BETH-LEHEM (39)
 [BETH-LEHEM-JUDAH, BETH-LEHEMITE]
Ge 35:19 buried in the way to Ephrath, which *is* **B**. 1035
 48: 7 in the way of Ephrath; the same *is* **B**. 1035
Jos 19:15 Nahallal, and Shimron, and Idalah, and **B**: 1035
Jdg 12: 8 And after him Ibzan of **B** judged Israel. 1035
 12:10 Then died Ibzan, and was buried at **B**. 1035
Ru 1:19 So they two went until they came to **B**. 1035
 1:19 came to pass, when they were come to **B**, 1035
 1:22 they came *to* **B** in the beginning of barley 1035
 2: 4 Boaz came from **B**, and said unto 1035
 4:11 worthily in Ephratah, and be famous in **B**: 1035
1Sa 16: 4 when the LORD spake, and came to **B**. 1035
 17:15 from Saul to feed his father's sheep *at* **B**. 1035
 20: 6 of me that he might run *to* **B** his city: 1035
 20:28 earnestly asked *leave* of me *to go to* **B** 1035
2Sa 2:32 sepulchre of his father, which *was* in **B**. 1035
 23:14 garrison of the Philistines *was* then *in* **B**. 1035
 23:15 drink *of* the water of the well of **B**, 1035
 23:16 drew water out of the well of **B**, that 1035
 23:24 the thirty; Elhanan the son of Dodo *of* **B**, 1035
1Ch 2:51 Salma the father of **B**, Hareph the father 1035
 2:54 **B**, and the Netophathites, Ataroth, 1035
 4: 4 the firstborn of Ephratah, the father of **B**. 1035
 11:16 the Philistines' garrison *was* then at **B**. 1035
 11:17 drink *of* the water of the well of **B**, 1035
 11:18 drew water out of the well of **B**, that 1035
 11:26 of Joab, Elhanan the son of Dodo of **B**, 1035
2Ch 11: 6 He built even **B**, and Etam, and Tekoa, 1035
Ezr 2:21 The children of **B**, an hundred twenty and 1035
Ne 7:26 The men of **B** and Netophah, an hundred 1035
Jer 41:17 which *is* by **B**, to go to enter *into* Egypt, 1035
Mic 5: 2 thou, **B** Ephratah, *though thou* be little 1035
Mt 2: 1 when Jesus was born in **B** of Judea 965
 2: 5 And they said unto him, In **B** of Judea: 965
 2: 6 And thou **B**, *in* the land of Juda, art not 965
 2: 8 And he sent them to **B**, and said, Go and 965
 2:16 and slew all the children that were in **B**, 965
Lk 2: 4 unto the city of David, which is called **B**; 965
 2:15 Let us now go *even* unto **B**, and see this 965
Jn 7:42 out of the town of **B**, where David was? 965

BETH-LEHEMITE (4) [BETH-LEHEM]
1Sa 16: 1 and go, I will send thee to Jesse the **B**: 1022
 16:18 Behold, I have seen a son of Jesse the **B**, 1022
 17:58 I *am* the son of thy servant Jesse the **B**. 1022
2Sa 21:19 a **B**, slew *the brother of* Goliath the Gittite 1022

BETH-LEHEM-JUDAH (10) [BETH-LEHEM,
 JUDAH]
Jdg 17: 7 there was a young man out of **B** of 1035+3063
 17: 8 to sojourn where he could find a 1035+3063
 17: 9 I *am* a Levite of **B**, and I go to 1035+3063
 19: 1 took to him a concubine out of **B**, 1035+3063
 19: 2 him unto her father's house to **B**, 1035+3063

BETH-MAACHAH (2) [ABEL-BETH-MAACHAH]
2Sa 20:14 unto Abel, and *to* **B**, and all the Berites: 1038
 20:15 they came and besieged him in Abel of **B**, 1038

BETH-MARCABOTH (2)
Jos 19: 5 And Ziklag, and **B**, and Hazar-susah, 1024
1Ch 4:31 at **B**, and Hazar-susim, and at Beth-birei, 1024

BETH-MEON (1) [BAAL-MEON]
Jer 48:23 and upon Beth-gamul, and upon **B**, 1010

BETH-NIMRAH (2) [NIMRAH]
Nu 32:36 And **B**, and Beth-haran, fenced cities, 1039
Jos 13:27 And **B**, and Succoth, and Zaphon, 1039

BETH-PALET (1) [BETH-PHELET]
Jos 15:27 And Hazar-gaddah, and Heshmon, and **B**, 1046

BETH-PAZZEZ (1)
Jos 19:21 and En-gannim, and En-haddah, and **B**; 1048

BETH-PEOR (4) [PEOR]
Dt 3:29 So we abode in the valley over against **B**, 1047
 4:46 side Jordan, in the valley over against **B**, 1047
 34: 6 valley in the land of Moab, over against **B**: 1047
Jos 13:20 **B**, and Ashdoth-pisgah, 1047

BETHPHAGE (3)
Mt 21: 1 and were come to **B**, unto the mount of 967
Mk 11: 1 **B** and Bethany, at the mount of Olives, 967
Lk 19:29 when he was come nigh to **B** and Bethany, 967

BETH-PHELET (1) [BETH-PALET]
Ne 11:26 And at Jeshua, and at Moladah, and at **B**, 1046

BETH-RAPHA (1) [RAPHA]
1Ch 4:12 Eshton begat **B**, and Paseah, and Tehinnah 1051

BETH-REHOB (2) [REHOB]
Jdg 18:28 and it was in the valley that *lieth* by **B**. 1050
2Sa 10: 6 of Ammon sent and hired the Syrians of **B**, 1050

BETHSAIDA (7)
Mt 11:21 unto thee, Chorazin, woe unto thee, **B**: 966
Mk 6:45 go to the other side before unto **B**, 966
 8:22 And he cometh to **B**; and they bring a blind 966
Lk 9:10 desert place belonging to the city called **B**. 966
 10:13 unto thee, Chorazin, woe unto thee, **B**: 966
Jn 1:44 Now Philip was of **B**, the city of Andrew 966
 12:21 was of **B** of Galilee, and desired him, 966

BETH-SHAN (3) [BETH-SHEAN]
1Sa 31:10 they fastened his body to the wall of **B**. 1052
 31:12 the bodies of his sons from the wall of **B**, 1052
2Sa 21:12 had stolen them from the street of **B**, 1052

BETH-SHEAN (6) [BETH-SHAN]
Jos 17:11 in Issachar and in Asher **B** and her towns, 1052
 17:16 *both they* who *are* of **B** and her towns, 1052
 1:27 Manasseh drive out *the inhabitants of* **B** 1052
1Ki 4:12 Taanach and Megiddo, and all **B** 1052
 4:12 beneath Jezreel, from **B** to Abel-meholah, 1052
1Ch 7:29 **B** and her towns, Taanach and her towns, 1052

BETH-SHEMESH (21)
Jos 15:10 down *to* **B**, and passed on *to* Timnah: 1053
 19:22 to Tabor, and Shahazimah, and **B**, 1053
 19:38 Migdal-el, Horem, and Beth-anath, and **B**; 1053
 21:16 her suburbs, and **B** with her suburbs; 1053
Jdg 1:33 Naphtali drive out the inhabitants of **B** 1053
 1:33 nevertheless the inhabitants of **B** and 1053
1Sa 6: 9 up *by* the way of his own coast *to* **B**, 1053
 6:12 took the straight way to the way of **B**, 1053
 6:12 went after them unto the border of **B**. 1053
 6:13 *of* **B** were reaping *their* wheat harvest 1053
 6:15 the men of **B** offered burnt offerings and 1053
 6:19 he smote the men of **B**, because they had 1053
 6:20 the men of **B** said, Who is able to stand 1053
1Ki 4: 9 in Shaalbim, and **B**, and Elon-beth-hanan: 1053
2Ki 14:11 Judah looked one another *in* the face at **B**, 1053
 14:13 at **B**, and came to Jerusalem, 1053
 14:59 with her suburbs, and **B** with her suburbs: 1053
1Ch 6:59 with her suburbs, and **B** with her suburbs: 1053
2Ch 25:21 *both* he and Amaziah king of Judah, at **B**, 1053
 25:23 at **B**, and brought him to Jerusalem, 1053
 28:18 had taken **B**, and Ajalon, and Gederoth, 1053
Jer 43:13 He shall break also the images of **B**, that 1053

BETH-SHEMITE (2) [BETH-SHITTAH]
1Sa 6:14 a **B**, and stood there, where *there was* a 1030
 6:18 unto this day in the field of Joshua, the **B**. 1030

BETH-SHITTAH (1) [BETH-SHEMITE]
Jdg 7:22 the host fled to **B** in Zererath, *and* to 1029

BETH-TAPPUAH (1) [TAPPUAH]
Jos 15:53 And Janum, and **B**, and Aphekah, 1054

BETHUEL (10)
Ge 22:22 Hazo, and Pildash, and Jidlaph, and **B**. 1328
 22:23 **B** begat Rebekah: these eight Milcah did 1328
 24:15 was born to **B**, son of Milcah, the wife 1328

B

Ge 24:24 I *am* the daughter of **B** the son of Milcah, 1328
 24:47 she said, The daughter of **B**, Nahor's son, 1328
 24:50 Laban and **B** answered and said, 1328
 25:20 the daughter of **B** the Syrian of 1328
 28: 2 to the house of **B** thy mother's father; 1328
 28: 5 son of **B** the Syrian, the brother of 1328
1Ch 4:30 And at **B**, and at Hormah, and at Ziklag, 1328

BETHUL (1)

Jos 19: 4 And Eltolad, and **B**, and Hormah, 1329

BETH-ZUR (4) [ZUR]

Jos 15:58 Halhul, **B**, and Gedor, 1049
1Ch 2:45 *was* Maon: and Maon *was* the father of **B**. 1049
2Ch 11: 7 And **B**, and Shoco, and Adullam, 1049
Ne 3:16 of Azbuk, the ruler of the half part of **B**, 1049

BETIMES (5) [TIME]

Ge 26:31 **rose up b** in the morning, 7925
2Ch 36:15 his messengers, **rising up b**, and sending; 7925
Job 8: 5 If thou wouldest **seek** unto God **b**, 7836
 24: 5 forth to their work; **rising b** for a prey: 7836
Pr 13:24 but he that loveth him chasteneth him **b**. 7836

BETONIM (1)

Jos 13:26 Heshbon unto Ramath-mizpeh, and **B**; 993

BETRAY (18) [BETRAYED, BETRAYERS, BETRAYEST, BETRAYETH]

1Ch 12:17 if ye be come to **b** me to mine enemies, 7411
Mt 24:10 shall **b** one another, and shall hate one 3860
 26:16 that time he sought opportunity to **b** him. 3860
 26:21 I say unto you, that one of you shall **b** me. 3860
 26:23 with me in the dish, the same shall **b** me. 3860
 26:46 behold, he is at hand that doth **b** me. 3860
Mk 13:12 Now the brother shall **b** the brother to 3860
 14:10 the chief priests, to **b** him unto them. 3860
 14:11 sought how he might conveniently **b** him. 3860
 14:18 One of you which eateth with me shall **b** 3860
Lk 22: 4 captains, how he might **b** him unto them 3860
 22: 6 sought opportunity to **b** him unto them in 3860
Jn 6:64 that believed not, and who should **b** him. 3860
 6:71 for he *it was that* should **b** him, being one 3860
 12: 4 Simon's *son*, which should **b** him, 3860
 13: 2 of Judas Iscariot, Simon's *son*, to **b** him; 3860
 13:11 For he knew who should **b** him; therefore 3860
 13:21 I say unto you, that one of you shall **b** me. 3860

BETRAYED (19) [BETRAY]

Mt 10: 4 and Judas Iscariot, who also **b** him. 3860
 17:22 The Son of man shall be **b** into the hands 3860
 20:18 the Son of man shall be **b** unto the chief 3860
 26: 2 and the Son of man is **b** to be crucified. 3860
 26:24 that man by whom the Son of man is **b**: 3860
 26:25 which **b** him, answered and said, Master, 3860
 26:45 the Son of man is **b** into the hands of 3860
 26:48 Now he that **b** him gave them a sign, 3860
 27: 3 Judas, which had **b** him, when he saw 3860
 27: 4 have sinned in that I have **b** *the* innocent 3860
Mk 3:19 And Judas Iscariot, which also **b** him. 3860
 14:21 that man by whom the Son of man is **b**: 3860
 14:41 the Son of man is **b** into the hands of 3860
 14:44 he that **b** him had given them a token, 3860
Lk 21:16 And ye shall be **b** both by parents, and 3860
 22:22 but woe unto that man by whom he is **b**. 3860
Jn 18: 2 Judas also, which **b** him, knew the place: 3860
 18: 5 Judas also, which **b** him, stood with them. 3860
1Co 11:23 *same* night in which he was **b** took bread: 3860

BETRAYERS (1) [BETRAY]

Ac 7:52 of whom ye have been now the **b** and 4273

BETRAYEST (1) [BETRAY]

Lk 22:48 Judas, **b** thou the Son of man with a kiss? 3860

BETRAYETH (3) [BETRAY]

Mk 14:42 let us go; lo, he that **b** me is at hand. 3860
Lk 22:21 the hand of him that **b** me *is* with me on 3860
Jn 21:20 and said, Lord, which is he that **b** thee? 3860

BETROTH (4) [BETROTHED]

Dt 28:30 Thou shalt **b** a wife, and another man 781
Hos 2:19 I will **b** thee unto me for ever; yea, I will 781
 2:19 I will **b** thee unto me in righteousness, 781
 2:20 I will even **b** thee unto me in faithfulness: 781

BETROTHED (9) [BETROTH]

Ex 21: 8 who hath **b** her to himself, then shall he 3259
 21: 9 if he have **b** her unto his son, he shall deal 3259
 22:16 And if a man entice a maid that is not **b**, 781
Lev 19:20 **b** to a husband, and not at all redeemed, 2778
Dt 20: 7 what man *is there* that hath **b** a wife, 781
 22:23 If a damsel *that is* a virgin be **b** unto a 781
 22:25 But if a man find a **b** damsel in the field, 781
 22:27 the **b** damsel cried, and *there was* none 781
 22:28 which is not **b**, and lay hold on her, 781

BETTER (117) [GOOD]

Ge 29:19 Laban said, *It is* **b** that I give her to thee, 2896
Ex 14:12 For *it had been* **b** for us to serve 2896
Nu 14: 3 were it not **b** for us to return into Egypt? 2896
Jdg 8: 2 of Ephraim **b** than the vintage of Abi-ezer? 2896
 9: 2 Whether *is* **b** for you, either that all 2896
 11:25 *art* thou **any thing b** than Balak 2896+2896
 18:19 **b** for thee to be a priest unto the house 2896
Ru 4:15 which *is* **b** to thee than seven sons, 2896

1Sa 1: 8 *am* not I **b** to thee than ten sons? 2896
 15:22 to obey *is* **b** than sacrifice, *and* to hearken 2896
 15:28 a neighbour of thine, *that is* **b** than thou. 2896
 27: 1 *there is* nothing **b** for me than that I 2896
2Sa 17:14 counsel of Hushai the Archite *is* **b** than 2896
 18: 3 now *it is* **b** that thou succour us out of 2896
1Ki 1:47 God **make** the name of Solomon **b** than 3190
 2:32 two men more righteous and **b** than he, 2896
 19: 4 my life; for I *am* not **b** than my fathers. 2896
 21: 2 I will give thee for it a **b** vineyard than it; 2896
2Ki 5:12 **b** than all the waters of Israel? 2896
2Ch 21:13 father's house, *which were* **b** than thyself: 2896
Est 1:19 estate unto another *that is* **b** than she. 2896
Ps 37:16 little that a righteous *man* hath *is* **b** than 2896
 63: 3 Because thy lovingkindness *is* **b** than life, 2896
 69:31 *This* also shall please the LORD **b** than 4480
 84:10 a day in thy courts *is* **b** than a thousand. 2896
 118: 8 *It is* **b** to trust in the LORD than to put 2896
 118: 9 *It is* **b** to trust in the LORD than to put 2896
 119:72 The law of thy mouth *is* **b** unto me than 2896
Pr 3:14 For the merchandise of it *is* **b** than 2896
 8:11 For wisdom *is* **b** than rubies; and all 2896
 8:19 My fruit *is* **b** than gold, yea, than fine gold 2896
 12: 9 *is* **b** than he that honoureth himself, 2896
 15:16 **b** is little with the fear of the LORD than 2896
 15:17 **B** is a dinner of herbs where love is, than 2896
 16: 8 **B** is a little with righteousness than great 2896
 16:16 much **b** *is it* to get wisdom than gold! 2896
 16:19 **B** *it is* to be of an humble spirit with 2896
 16:32 *He that* is slow to anger *is* **b** than 2896
 17: 1 **B** is a dry morsel, and quietness therewith 2896
 19: 1 **B** is the poor that walketh in his integrity, 2896
 19:22 and a poor *man* is **b** than a liar. 2896
 21: 9 **b** to dwell in a corner of the housetop, 2896
 21:19 *It is* **b** to dwell in the wilderness, than 2896
 25: 7 For **b** *it is* that it be said unto thee, 2896
 25:24 **b** to dwell in a corner of the housetop, 2896
 27: 5 Open rebuke *is* **b** than secret love. 2896
 27:10 *for* **b** *is* a neighbour *that is* near than a 2896
 28: 6 **B** *is* the poor that walketh in his 2896
Ecc 2:24 *There is* nothing **b** for a man, *than that* 2896
 3:22 I perceive that *there is* nothing **b**, 2896
 4: 3 **b** *is* he than both they, which hath not 2896
 4: 6 **B** *is* a handful *with* quietness, than both 2896
 4: 9 Two *are* **b** than one; because they have a 2896
 4:13 **B** *is* a poor and a wise child than an old 2896
 5: 5 **B** *is it* that thou shouldest not vow, 2896
 6: 3 I say, *that* an untimely birth *is* **b** than he. 2896
 6: 9 **B** *is* the sight of the eyes than 2896
 6:11 that increase vanity, what *is* man the **b**? 3148
 7: 1 A *good* name *is* **b** than precious ointment; 2896
 7: 2 *It is* **b** to go to the house of mourning, 2896
 7: 3 Sorrow *is* **b** than laughter: for by 2896
 7: 3 of the countenance the heart is **made b**. 3190
 7: 5 *It is* **b** to hear the rebuke of the wise, 2896
 7: 8 **B** is the end of a thing than the beginning 2896
 7: 8 the patient in spirit *is* **b** than the proud in 2896
 7:10 that the former days were **b** than these? 2896
 8:15 a man hath no **b** *thing* under the sun, 2896
 9: 4 for a living dog *is* **b** than a dead lion. 2896
 9:16 said I, Wisdom *is* **b** than strength: 2896
 9:18 Wisdom *is* **b** than weapons of war: 2896
 10:11 enchantment; and a babbler is no **b**. 3504
SS 1: 2 of his mouth: for thy love *is* **b** than wine. 2896
 4:10 how much **b** is thy love than wine! and 2895
Isa 56: 5 a name **b** than *of* sons and *of* daughters: 2896
La 4: 9 *that* be slain with the sword are **b** than 2896
Eze 36:11 do **b** *unto* you than at your beginnings: 2895
Da 1:20 he found them ten times **b** than all 5921
Hos 2: 7 for then *was it* **b** with me than now. 2896
Am 6: 2 *be they* **b** than these kingdoms? or 2896
Jnh 4: 3 for *it is* **b** for me to die than to live. 2896
 4: 8 and said, *It is* **b** for me to die than to live. 2896
Na 3: 8 Art thou **b** than populous No, that was 3190
Mt 6:26 Are ye not much **b than** they? 1308
 12:12 How much then is a man **b than** a sheep? 1308
 18: 6 it were **b** for him that a millstone were 4851
 18: 8 it is **b** for thee to enter into life halt or 2570
 18: 9 it is **b** for thee to enter into life with one 2570
Mk 9:42 is **b** for him that a millstone were hanged 2570
 9:43 it is **b** for thee to enter into life maimed, 2570
 9:45 it is **b** for thee to enter into life halt, 2570
 9:47 it is **b** for thee to enter into the kingdom 2570
Lk 5:39 desireth new: for he saith, The old is **b**. 5543
 12:24 how much more are ye **b than** the fowls? 1308
 17: 2 It were **b** for him that a millstone were 3081
Ro 3: 9 are we **b** *than they?* No, in no wise: 4284
1Co 7: 9 for it is **b** to marry than to burn. 2909
 7:38 that giveth *her* not in marriage doeth **b**. 2908
 8: 8 neither, if we eat, are we the **b**; neither, 4052
 9:15 for *it were* **b** for me to die, than 2570+3123
 11:17 that you come together not for the **b**, but 2909
Php 1:23 and to be with Christ; which *is* far **b**: 2909
 2: 3 *let* each esteem other **b** than themselves. 5242
Heb 1: 4 Being made so much **b than** the angels, 2909
 6: 9 we are persuaded **b** *things* of you, 2909
 7: 7 contradiction the less is blessed of the **b**. 2909
 7:19 The bringing in of a **b** hope *did;* by 2909
 7:22 much was Jesus made a surety of a **b** 2909
 8: 6 how much also he is the mediator of a **b** 2909
 8: 6 which was established upon **b** promises. 2909
 9:23 the heavenly *things* themselves with **b** 2909
 10:34 in yourselves that *ye* have in heaven a **b** 2909
 11:16 But now they desire a **b** *country,* that is, 2909
 11:35 that they might obtain a **b** resurrection: 2909

Heb 11:40 God having provided some **b** *thing* for us, 2909
 12:24 that speaketh **b** *things* than *that* of Abel. 2909
1Pe 3:17 For *it is* **b**, if the will of God be so, that *ye* 2909
2Pe 2:21 For it had been **b** for them not to have 2909

BETTERED (1) [GOOD]

Mk 5:26 and was nothing **b**, but rather grew worse, 5623

BETWEEN (232)

Ge 3:15 I will put enmity **b** thee and the woman, 996
 3:15 the woman, and **b** thy seed and her seed; 996
 9:12 token of the covenant which I make **b** me 996
 9:13 it shall be for a token of a covenant **b** me 996
 9:15 which *is* **b** me and you and every living 996
 9:16 remember the everlasting covenant **b** God 996
 9:17 which I have established **b** me and all flesh 996
 10:12 Resen **b** Nineveh and Calah: the same *is* a 996
 13: 3 been at the beginning, **b** Beth-el and Hai; 996
 13: 7 was a strife **b** the herdmen of Abram's 996
 13: 8 **b** me and thee, and between my herdmen 996
 13: 8 and **b** my herdmen and thy herdmen; 996
 15:17 a burning lamp that passed **b** those pieces. 996
 16: 5 the LORD judge **b** me and thee. 996
 16:14 behold, *it is* **b** Kadesh and Bered. 996
 17: 2 I will make my covenant **b** me and thee, 996
 17: 7 I will establish my covenant **b** me and thee 996
 17:10 **b** me and you and thy seed after thee; 996
 20: 1 dwelled **b** Kadesh and Shur, 996
 31:44 and let it be **b** for a witness **b** me and thee. 996
 31:48 This heap *is* a witness **b** me and thee *this* 996
 31:49 he said, The LORD watch **b** me and thee, 996
 48:12 Joseph brought them out from **b** his knees, 5973
 49:10 nor a lawgiver from **b** his feet, until Shiloh 996
 49:14 Issachar *is* a strong ass couching down **b** 996
Ex 8:23 I will put a division **b** my people and thy 996
 9: 4 the LORD shall sever **b** the cattle of Israel 996
 11: 7 doth put a difference **b** the Egyptians 996
 13: 9 for a memorial **b** thine eyes, that 996
 13:16 thine hand, and for frontlets **b** thine eyes: 996
 14: 2 **b** Migdol and the sea, over against 996
 14:20 And it came **b** the camp of the Egyptians 996
 16: 1 of Sin, which *is* **b** Elim and Sinai, 996
 18:16 I judge **b** one and another, and I do make 996
 22:11 Then shall an oath of the LORD be **b** them 996
 25:22 from **b** the two cherubims which *are* upon 996
 26:33 the vail shall divide unto you **b** the holy 996
 28:33 bells of gold **b** them round about: 8432+871.1
 30:18 thou shalt put it **b** the tabernacle of 996
 31:13 for it *is* a sign **b** me and you throughout 996
 31:17 It *is* a sign **b** me and the children of Israel 996
 39:25 put the bells **b** the pomegranates 8432+871.1
 39:25 round about the pomegranates; 8432+871.1
 40: 7 thou shalt set the laver **b** the tent of 996
 40:30 set the laver **b** the tent of the congregation 996
Lev 10:10 that *ye* may put difference **b** holy and 996
 10:10 and unholy, and **b** unclean and clean; 996
 11:47 To make a difference **b** the unclean and 996
 11:47 **b** the beast that may be eaten and the beast 996
 20:25 put difference **b** clean beasts and unclean, 996
 20:25 unclean, and **b** unclean fowls and clean: 996
 26:46 which the LORD made **b** him and 996
Nu 7:89 of Testimony, from **b** the two cherubims: 996
 11:33 while the flesh *was* yet **b** their teeth, ere it 996
 13:23 and they bare it **b** two upon a staff; 871.1
 16:48 he stood **b** the dead and the living; 996
 21:13 border of Moab, **b** Moab and the Amorites. 996
 26:56 the possession thereof be divided **b** many 996
 30:16 a man and his wife, between the father 996
 30:16 and his wife, **b** the father and his daughter, 996
 31:27 **b** them that took the war upon them, 996
 31:27 out to battle, and **b** all the congregation: 996
 35:24 the congregation shall judge **b** the slayer 996
Dt 1: 1 in the plain over against the Red *sea,* **b** 996
 1:16 Hear *the* causes **b** your brethren, 996
 1:16 judge righteously **b** every man and his 996
 1:39 in *that* day had no knowledge **b** good NIH
 5: 5 (I stood **b** the LORD and you at that time, 996
 6: 8 and they shall be as frontlets **b** thine eyes. 996
 11:18 that they may be as frontlets **b** your eyes. 996
 14: 1 nor make *any* baldness **b** your eyes for 996
 17: 8 **b** blood and blood, between plea and plea, 996
 17: 8 **b** plea and plea, and between stroke and 996
 17: 8 and plea, and **b** stroke and stroke, 996
 19:17 **b** whom the controversy *is,* shall stand 3807.1
 25: 1 If there be a controversy **b** men, 996
 28:57 young one that cometh out from **b** her feet, 996
 33:12 long, and he shall dwell **b** his shoulders. 996
Jos 3: 4 Yet there shall be a space **b** you and it, 996
 8: 9 abode **b** Beth-el and Ai, on the west side 996
 8:11 now *there was* a valley **b** them and Ai. 996
 8:12 set them to lie in ambush **b** Beth-el and Ai, 996
 18:11 the coast of their lot came forth **b** 996
 22:25 For the LORD hath made Jordan a border **b** 996
 22:27 *that it may* be a witness **b** us, and you, 996
 22:28 But it *is* a witness **b** us and you, 996
 22:34 *be* a witness **b** us that the LORD *is* God. 996
 24: 7 he put darkness **b** you and the Egyptians, 996
Jdg 4: 5 dwelt under the palm tree of Deborah **b** 996
 4:17 for *there was* peace **b** Jabin the king of 996
 9:23 God sent an evil spirit **b** Abimelech and 996
 11:10 The LORD be witness **b** us, if we do not so 996
 11:27 the LORD the Judge be judge *this* day **b** 996
 13:25 in the camp of Dan, **b** Zorah and Eshtaol. 996
 15: 4 put a firebrand in the midst **b** two tails. 996
 16:25 them sport: and they set him **b** the pillars. 996

B

Jdg	16:31 buried him **b** Zorah and Eshtaol in	996
	20:38 Now there was an appointed sign **b**	3807.1
1Sa	4: 4 of hosts, which dwelleth **b** the cherubims:	NIH
	7:12 set it **b** Mizpeh and Shen, and called	996
	7:14 there was peace **b** Israel and the Amorites.	996
	14: 4 **b** the passages, *by* which Jonathan sought	996
	14:42 Cast *lots* **b** me and Jonathan my son.	996
	17: 1 pitched **b** Shochoh and Azekah,	996
	17: 3 other side: and *there was* a valley **b** them.	996
	17: 6 and a target of brass **b** his shoulders.	996
	20: 3 *there is* but a step **b** me and death.	996
	20:23 The LORD be **b** thee and me for ever.	996
	20:42 The LORD be **b** me and thee,	996
	20:42 and **b** my seed and thy seed for ever.	996
	24:12 The LORD judge **b** me and thee,	996
	24:15 judge **b** me and thee, and see, and plead	996
	26:13 a hill afar off; a great space *being* **b** them:	996
2Sa	3: 1 there was long war **b** the house of Saul	996
	3: 6 there was war **b** the house of Saul and	996
	6: 2 of hosts that dwelleth *b* the cherubims.	NIH
	18: 9 was taken up **b** the heaven and the earth;	996
	18:24 David sat **b** the two gates: and the	996
	19:35 *and* can I discern **b** good and evil?	996
	21: 7 of the LORD'S oath that *was* **b** them,	996
	21: 7 **b** David and Jonathan the son of Saul.	996
1Ki	3: 9 that *I* may discern **b** good and bad:	996
	5:12 there was peace **b** Hiram and Solomon;	996
	7:28 and the borders were **b** the ledges:	996
	7:29 on the borders that *were* **b** the ledges *were*	996
	7:46 in the clay ground **b** Succoth and Zarthan.	996
	14:30 there was war **b** Rehoboam and Jeroboam	996
	15: 6 there was war **b** Rehoboam and Jeroboam	996
	15: 7 there was war **b** Abijam and Jeroboam.	996
	15:16 there was war **b** Asa and Baasha king of	996
	15:19 There is a league **b** me and thee,	996
	15:19 and thee, *and* **b** my father and thy father:	996
	15:32 there was war **b** Asa and Baasha king of	996
	18: 6 So they divided the land **b** them to pass	3807.1
	18:21 said, How long halt ye **b** two opinions?	5921
	18:42 the earth, and put his face **b** his knees,	996
	22: 1 they continued three years without war **b**	996
	22:34 smote the king of Israel **b** the joints of	996
2Ki	9:24 smote Jehoram **b** his arms, and the arrow	996
	11:17 Jehoiada made a covenant **b** the LORD	996
	11:17 the king also and the people.	996
	16:14 from the altar and the house of	996
	19:15 which dwellest *b* the cherubims, thou *art*	NIH
	25: 4 night *by* the way of the gate **b** two walls,	996
1Ch	13: 6 that dwelleth *b* the cherubims, whose	NIH
	21:16 saw the angel of the LORD stand **b**	996
2Ch	4:17 in the clay ground **b** Succoth and	996
	12:15 *there* were wars **b** Rehoboam and	NIH
	13: 2 And there was war **b** Abijah and Jeroboam.	996
	16: 3 *There is* a league **b** me and thee, as	996
	16: 3 as *there was* **b** my father and thy father:	996
	18:33 smote the king of Israel **b** the joints of	996
	19:10 **b** blood and blood, between law and	996
	19:10 and blood, **b** law and commandment,	996
	23:16 Jehoiada made a covenant **b** him,	996
	23:16 **b** all the people, and between the king,	996
	23:16 between all the people, and **b** the king,	996
Ne	3:32 the going up of the corner unto the sheep	996
Job	41:16 to another, that no air can come **b** them.	996
Ps	80: 1 thou that dwellest *b* the cherubims,	NIH
	99: 1 he sitteth *b* the cherubims; let the earth be	NIH
Pr	18:18 to cease, and parteth **b** the mighty.	996
Isa	22:11 Ye made also a ditch **b** the two walls for	996
	37:16 of Israel, that dwellest *b* the cherubims,	NIH
	59: 2 But your iniquities have separated **b** you	996
Jer	7: 5 if you throughly execute judgment **b** a man	996
	34:18 calf in twain, and passed **b** the parts thereof,	996
	34:19 which passed **b** the parts of the calf;	996
	42: 5 LORD be a true and faithful witness **b** us,	871.1
	52: 7 *by* the way of the gate **b** the two walls,	996
La	1: 3 her persecutors overtook her **b** the straits.	996
Eze	4: 3 set it *for* a wall of iron **b** thee and the city:	996
	8: 3 the spirit lift me up **b** the earth and	996
	8:16 **b** the porch and the altar, *were* about five	996
	10: 2 said, Go in **b** the wheels, *even* under	996
	10: 2 fill thine hand *with* coals of fire from **b**	996
	10: 6 saying, Take fire from **b** the wheels,	996
	10: 6 between the wheels, from **b** the cherubims;	996
	10: 7 *one* cherub stretched forth his hand from **b**	996
	10: 7 unto the fire that *was* **b** the cherubims,	996
	18: 8 executed true judgment **b** man and man,	996
	20:12 my sabbaths, to be a sign **b** me and them,	996
	20:20 they shall be a sign **b** me and you, that *ye*	996
	22:26 they have put no difference **b** the holy	996
	22:26 neither have they shewed *difference* **b**	996
	34:17 Behold, I judge **b** cattle and cattle,	996
	34:17 and cattle, **b** the rams and the he goats.	3807.1
	34:20 will judge **b** the fat cattle and between	996
	34:20 between the fat cattle and the lean cattle.	996
	34:22 a prey; and I will judge **b** cattle and cattle.	996
	40: 7 **b** the little chambers *were* five cubits;	996
	41:10 the chambers *was* the wideness of twenty	996
	41:18 so that a palm tree *was* **b** a cherub and a	996
	42:20 to make a separation **b** the sanctuary and	996
	43: 8 by my posts, and the wall **b** me and them,	996
	44:23 they shall teach my people the *difference* **b**	996
	44:23 and cause them to discern **b** the unclean	996
	47:16 which *is* **b** the border of Damascus and	996
	48:22 **b** the border of Judah and the border of	996
Da	7: 5 three ribs in the mouth of it **b** the teeth	997
	8: 5 and the goat *had* a notable horn **b** his eyes.	996

Da	8:16 I heard a man's voice **b** *the banks of* Ulai,	996
	8:21 the great horn that *is* **b** his eyes *is* the first	996
	11:45 shall plant the tabernacles of his palace **b**	996
Hos	2: 2 and her adulteries from **b** her breasts;	996
Joel	2:17 weep the porch and the altar, and let	996
Jnh	4:11 that cannot discern **b** their right hand	996
Zec	5: 9 they lift up the ephah **b** the earth and	996
	6: 1 there came four chariots out from **b** two	996
	6:13 the counsel of peace shall be **b** them both.	996
	9: 7 and his abominations from **b** his teeth:	996
	11:14 I might break the brotherhood **b** Judah	996
Mal	2:14 Because the LORD hath been witness **b**	996
	3:18 discern **b** the righteous and the wicked,	996
	3:18 **b** him that serveth God and *him* that	996
Mt	18:15 go and tell him his fault **b** thee and	3342
	23:35 whom ye slew **b** the temple and the altar.	3342
Lk	11:51 which perished **b** the altar and the temple:	3342
	16:26 **b** us and you there is a great gulf fixed:	3342
	23:12 for before they were at enmity **b**	4314
Jn	3:25 Then there arose a question **b** *some* of	1537
Ac	5: 9 one night Peter was sleeping **b** two	3342
	15: 9 And put no difference **b** us and them,	3342
	15:39 sharp **b** them, that they departed asunder	NIG
	23: 7 there arose a dissension **b** the Pharisees	NIG
	26:31 they talked **b** themselves, saying,	4314
Ro	10:12 For there is no difference **b** the Jew and	5037
	14: 2 to dishonour their own bodies **b**	1722
1Co	6: 5 not one that shall be able to judge **b**	303+3319
	7:34 There is **difference** *also* **b** a wife and a	3307
Eph	2:14 down the middle wall of partition **b** *us;*	NIG
1Ti	2: 5 and one mediator **b** God and men,	NIG

BETWIXT (16)

Ge	17:11 it shall be a token of the covenant **b** me	996
	23:15 of silver; what *is* that **b** me and thee?	996
	26:28 we said, Let there be now an oath **b** us,	996
	26:28 *even* **b** us and thee, and let us make a	996
	30:36 And he set three days' journey **b** himself	996
	31:37 brethren, that they may judge **b** us both.	996
	31:50 see, God *is* witness **b** me and thee.	996
	31:51 pillar, which I have cast **b** me and thee;	996
	31:53 Nahor, the God of their father, judge **b** us.	996
	32:16 and put a space **b** drove and drove.	996
Job	9:33 Neither is there *any* daysman **b** us,	996
	36:32 *not to shine by the cloud* that **cometh b.**	6293
SS	1:13 he shall lie all night **b** my breasts.	996
Isa	5: 3 judge, I pray you, **b** me and my vineyard.	996
Jer	39: 4 king's garden, by the gate **b** the two walls:	996
Php	1:23 For I am in a strait **b** two, having a desire	1537

BEULAH (1)

Isa	62: 4 be called Hephzi-bah, and thy land **B**:	1166

BEWAIL (6) [BEWAILED, BEWAILETH]

Lev	10: 6 **b** the burning which the LORD hath	1058
Dt	21:13 **b** her father and her mother a full month:	1058
Jdg	11:37 **b** my virginity, I and my fellows.	1058+5921
Isa	16: 9 Therefore I will **b** with the weeping of	1058
2Co	12:21 *that* I shall **b** many which have sinned	3996
Rev	18: 9 with her, shall **b** her, and lament for her,	2799

BEWAILED (3) [BEWAIL]

Jdg	11:38 and **b** her virginity upon the mountains.	1058
Lk	8:52 And all wept, and **b** her: but he said,	2875
	23:27 women, which also **b** and lamented him.	2875

BEWAILETH (1) [BEWAIL]

Jer	4:31 *that* **b** herself, *that* spreadeth her hands,	3306

BEWARE (28)

Ge	24: 6 thou that thou bring not my son thither	8104
Ex	23:21 **B** of him, and obey his voice, provoke him	8104
Dt	6:12 *Then* **b** lest thou forget the LORD,	8104
	8:11 **b** that thou forget not the LORD thy God,	8104
	15: 9 **B** that there be not a thought in thy	8104
Jdg	13: 4 therefore **b**, I pray thee, and drink not	8104
	13:13 all that I said unto the woman let her **b**.	8104
2Sa	18:12 **B** *that* none *touch* the young man	8104
2Ki	6: 9 **B** that *thou* pass not such a place;	8104
Job	36:18 **b** lest he take thee away with *his* stroke:	NIH
Pr	19:25 Smite a scorner, and the simple will **b**:	6191
Isa	36:18 *B* lest Hezekiah persuade you, saying,	NIH
Mt	7:15 **B** of false prophets, which come to you in	4337
	10:17 But **b** of men: for they will deliver you up	4337
	16: 6 and **b** of the leaven of the Pharisees and	4337
	16:11 that *ye* should **b** of the leaven of the	4337
	16:12 bade *them* not **b** of the leaven of bread,	4337
Mk	8:15 **b** of the leaven of the Pharisees, and *of*	991
	12:38 **B** of the scribes, which love to go in long	991
Lk	12: 1 *of all,* **B** ye of the leaven of the Pharisees,	4337
	12:15 Take heed, and **b** of covetousness:	5442
	20:46 **B** of the scribes, which desire to walk in	4337
Ac	13:40 **B** therefore, lest that come upon you,	991
Php	3: 2 **B** of dogs, beware of evil workers, beware	991
	3: 2 Beware of dogs, **b** of evil workers,	991
	3: 2 beware of evil workers, **b** of the concision.	991
Col	2: 8 **B** lest any *man* spoil you through	991
2Pe	3:17 know *these things* before, **b** lest ye also,	5442

BEWITCHED (3)

Ac	8: 9 and **b** the people of Samaria, giving out	1839
	8:11 that of long time he had **b** them with	1839
Gal	3: 1 O foolish Galatians, who hath **b** you,	940

BEWRAY (1) [BEWRAYETH]

Isa	16: 3 the outcasts; **b** not him that wandereth.	1540

BEWRAYETH (3) [BEWRAY]

Pr	27:16 ointment of his right hand, *which* **b** itself.	7121
	29:24 own soul: he heareth cursing, and **b** *it* not.	5046
Mt	26:73 one of them; for thy speech **b** thee.	1212+4160

BEYOND (54)

Ge	35:21 spread his tent **b** the tower of Edar.	1973+4480
	50:10 which *is* **b** Jordan, and there they	5676+871.1
	50:11 which *is* **b** Jordan.	5676+871.1
Lev	15:25 or if it run **b** the time of her separation;	5921
Nu	22:18 I cannot **go b** the word of the LORD my	5674
	24:13 I cannot **go b** the commandment of	5674
Dt	3:20 God hath given them **b** Jordan:	5676+871.1
	3:25 see the good land that *is* **b** Jordan,	5676+871.1
	30:13 Neither *is* it **b** the sea, that *thou*	4480+5676
Jos	9:10 that *were* **b** Jordan, to Sihon king	5676+871.1
	13: 8 gave them, **b** Jordan eastward,	5676+871.1
	18: 7 received their inheritance **b** Jordan on	5676
Jdg	3:26 passed **b** the quarries, and escaped unto	5674
	5:17 Gilead abode **b** Jordan: and why	5676+871.1
1Sa	20:22 Behold, the arrows *are* **b** thee;	1973+4480
	20:36 as the lad ran, he shot an arrow **b** him.	5674
	20:37 *Is* not the arrow **b** thee?	1973+4480+2050.1
2Sa	10:16 brought out the Syrians that *were* **b**	4480+5676
1Ki	4:12 unto *the place that is* **b** Jokneam;	4480+5676
	14:15 shall scatter them **b** the river,	4480+5676
1Ch	19:16 drew forth the Syrians that *were* **b**	4480+5676
2Ch	20: 2 there *be* on the sea on this side Syria;	5676
Ezr	4:17 in Samaria, and *unto* the rest **b** the river:	5675
	4:20 which have ruled over all *countries* **b**	5675
	6: 6 *therefore,* Tatnai, governor **b** the river,	5675
	6: 6 which *are* **b** the river, be ye far from	5675
	6: 8 *even* of the tribute **b** the river,	5675
	7:21 to all the treasurers which *are* **b** the river,	5675
	7:25 which may judge all the people that *are* **b**	5675
Ne	2: 7 let letters be given me to the governors **b**	5676
	2: 9 I came to the governors **b** the river,	5676
	12:38 **from b** the tower of the furnaces	4480+5921
Isa	7:20 by them **b** the river, by the king of	5676
	9: 1 the sea, **b** Jordan, in Galilee of the nations.	5676
	18: 1 which *is* **b** the rivers of Ethiopia:	4480+5676
Jer	22:19 cast forth **b** the gates of Jerusalem.	1973+4480
	25:22 of the isles which *are* **b** the sea,	5676+871.1
Am	5:27 to go into captivity **b** Damascus,	1973+4480
Zep	3:10 From **b** the rivers of Ethiopia my	5676
Mt	4:15 the way of the sea, **b** Jordan, Galilee of	4008
	4:25 and *from* Judea, and *from* **b** Jordan.	4008
	19: 1 came into the coasts of Judea **b** Jordan;	4008
Mk	3: 8 and from Idumea, and *from* **b** Jordan;	4008
	6:51 they were sore amazed in themselves **b**	1537
	7:37 And were **b** measure astonished, saying,	5249
Jn	1:28 These *things* were done in Bethabara **b**	4008
	3:26 Rabbi, *he* that was with thee **b** Jordan,	4008
	10:40 And went away again **b** Jordan into	4008
Ac	7:43 and I will carry you away **b** Babylon.	1900
2Co	8: 3 **b** *their* power *they* were willing to	5228
	10:14 For we **stretch** not ourselves **b** *our*	5239
	10:16 To preach the gospel in the *regions* **b** you,	5238
Gal	1:13 how that **b** *measure* I persecuted	2596+5236
1Th	4: 6 That no *man* **go b** and defraud his brother	5233

BEZAI (3)

Ezr	2:17 The children of **B**, three hundred twenty	1209
Ne	7:23 The children of **B**, three hundred twenty	1209
	10:18 Hodijah, Hashum, **B**,	1209

BEZALEEL (9)

Ex	31: 2 I have called by name **B** the son of Uri,	1212
	35:30 the LORD hath called by name **B** the son	1212
	36: 1 wrought **B** and Aholiab, and every wise	1212
	36: 2 Moses called **B** and Aholiab, and every	1212
	37: 1 **B** made the ark *of* shittim wood: two	1212
	38:22 **B** the son of Uri, the son of Hur, of the	1212
1Ch	2:20 And Hur begat Uri, and Uri begat **B**.	1212
2Ch	1: 5 that **B** the son of Uri, the son of Hur,	1212
Ezr	10:30 Mattaniah, **B**, and Binnui, and Manasseh.	1212

BEZALEEL See BEZALEEL

BEZEK (3)

Jdg	1: 4 they slew *of* them in **B** ten thousand men.	966
	1: 5 they found Adoni-bezek in **B**:	966
1Sa	11: 8 when he numbered them in **B**, the children	966

BEZER (5)

Dt	4:43 *Namely,* **B** in the wilderness, in the plain	1221
Jos	20: 8 they assigned **B** in the wilderness upon	1221
	21:36 **B** with her suburbs, and Jahazah with her	1221
1Ch	6:78 **B** in the wilderness with her suburbs,	1221
	7:37 **B**, and Hod, and Shamma, and Shilshah,	1221

BICHRI (8)

2Sa	20: 1 *was* Sheba, the son of **B**, a Benjamite:	1075
	20: 2 and followed Sheba the son of **B**:	1075
	20: 6 Now shall Sheba the son of **B** do us more	1075
	20: 7 to pursue after Sheba the son of **B**.	1075
	20:10 brother pursued after Sheba the son of **B**.	1075
	20:13 to pursue after Sheba the son of **B**.	1075
	20:21 Sheba the son of **B** by name,	1075
	20:22 cut off the head of Sheba the son of **B**,	1075

BICRI See BICHRI

BID (17) [BADE, BADEST, BIDDEN, BIDDETH, BIDDING]

Nu	15:38 **b** them that they make them fringes in	559

Jos 6:10 of your mouth, until the day I **b** you shout; 559
1Sa 9:27 **B** the servant pass on before us, (and 559
2Sa 2:26 thou **b** the people return from following 559
2Ki 4:24 slack not *thy* riding for me, except I **b** thee. 559
 5:13 *if* the prophet had **b** thee *do some* great 1696
 10: 5 and will do all that thou shalt **b** us; 559
Jnh 3: 2 preach unto it the preaching that I **b** thee. 1696
Zep 1: 7 prepared a sacrifice, he hath **b** his guests. 6942
Mt 14:28 thou, **b** me come unto thee on the water. 2753
 22: 9 many as ye shall find, **b** to the marriage. 2564
 23: 3 therefore whatsoever they **b** you observe, 3004
Lk 9:61 but let me first go **b** them **farewell**, 657
 10:40 **b** her therefore that she help me. 3004
 14:12 lest they also **b** thee **again**, and 479
1Co 10:27 If any of them that believe not **b** you *to a* 2564
2Jn 1:10 *your* house, neither him God speed: 3004

BIDDEN (14) [BID]
1Sa 9:13 *and* afterwards they eat that be **b**. 7121
 9:22 chiefest place among them that were **b**, 7121
2Sa 16:11 let him curse; for the LORD hath **b** him. 559
Mt 1:24 did as the angel of the Lord had **b** him, 4367
 22: 3 to call them that were **b** to the wedding: 2564
 22: 4 saying, Tell them which are **b**, Behold, 2564
 22: 8 but they which were **b** were not worthy. 2564
Lk 7:39 Now when the Pharisee which had **b** him 2564
 14: 7 put forth a parable to those which were **b**, 2564
 14: 8 thou art **b** of any *man* to a wedding, 2564
 14: 8 a more honourable *man* than thou be **b** 2564
 14:10 But when thou art **b**, go and sit down in 2564
 14:17 supper time to say to them that were **b**, 2564
 14:24 none of those men which were **b** shall 2564

BIDDETH (1) [BID]
2Jn 1:11 For he that **b** him God speed is partaker of 3004

BIDDING (1) [BID]
1Sa 22:14 goeth at thy **b**, and *is* honourable in thine 4928

BIDE (1)
Ro 11:23 they also, if they **b** not **still in** unbelief, 1961

BIDKAR (1)
2Ki 9:25 said *Jehu* to **B** his captain, Take up, 920

BIER (2)
2Sa 3:31 And king David *himself* followed the **b**. 4296
Lk 7:14 And he came and touched the **b**: 4673

BIGTHA (1)
Est 1:10 **B**, and Abagtha, Zethar, and Carcas, 903

BIGTHAN (1)
Est 2:21 **B** and Teresh, of those which kept the door, 904

BIGTHANA (1)
Est 6: 2 that Mordecai had told of **B** and Teresh, 904

BIGVAI (6)
Ezr 2: 2 Bilshan, Mizpar, **B**, Rehum, Baanah. 902
 2:14 The children of **B**, two thousand fifty and 902
 8:14 Of the sons also of **B**; Uthai, and Zabbud, 902
Ne 7: 7 Bilshan, Mispereth, **B**, Nehum, Baanah. 902
 7:19 children of **B**, two thousand threescore 902
 10:16 Adonijah, **B**, Adin, 902

BILDAD (5)
Job 2:11 **B** the Shuhite, and Zophar the 1085
 8: 1 Then answered **B** the Shuhite, and said, 1085
 18: 1 Then answered **B** the Shuhite, and said, 1085
 25: 1 Then answered **B** the Shuhite, and said, 1085
 42: 9 the Temanite and **B** the Shuhite *and* 1085

BILEAM (1)
1Ch 6:70 with her suburbs, and **B** with her suburbs, 1109

BILGAH (3)
1Ch 24:14 fifteenth to **B**, the sixteenth to Immer, 1083
Ne 12: 5 Miamin, Maadiah, **B**, 1083
 12:18 **B**, Shammua; of Shemaiah, Jehonathan; 1083

BILGAI (1)
Ne 10: 8 Maaziah, **B**, Shemaiah: these *were* 1084

BILHAH (11)
Ge 29:29 Laban gave to Rachel his daughter **B** his 1090
 30: 3 she said, Behold my maid **B**, go in unto 1090
 30: 4 she gave him **B** her handmaid to wife: 1090
 30: 5 And **B** conceived, and bare Jacob a son. 1090
 30: 7 **B** Rachel's maid conceived again, 1090
 35:22 and lay with **B** his father's concubine: 1090
 35:25 the sons of **B**, Rachel's handmaid; Dan, 1090
 37: 2 the lad *was* with the sons of **B**, and with 1090
 46:25 These *are* the sons of **B**, which Laban gave 1090
1Ch 4:29 And at **B**, and at Ezem, and at Tolad, 1090
 7:13 Jezer, and Shallum, the sons of **B**. 1090

BILHAN (4)
Ge 36:27 Ezer *are* these; **B**, and Zaavan, and Akan. 1092
1Ch 1:42 The sons of Ezer; **B**, and Zavan, *and* Jakan. 1092
 7:10 The sons also of Jediael; **B**: and the sons of 1092
 7:10 the sons of **B**; Jeush, and Benjamin, 1092

BILL (7)
Dt 24: 1 let him write her a **b** of divorcement, 5612
 24: 3 write her a **b** of divorcement, and giveth 5612

Isa 50: 1 Where *is* the **b** of your mother's 5612
Jer 3: 8 put her away, and given her a **b** of divorce 5612
Mk 10: 4 Moses suffered to write a **b** of divorcement 975
Lk 16: 6 Take thy **b**, and sit down quickly, and 1121
 16: 7 unto him, Take thy **b**, and write fourscore. 1121

BILLOWS (2)
Ps 42: 7 all thy waves and thy **b** are gone over me. 1530
Jnh 2: 3 all thy **b** and thy waves passed over me. 4867

BILSHAN (2)
Ezr 2: 2 **B**, Mizpar, Bigvai, Rehum, Baanah. 1114
Ne 7: 7 Mordecai, **B**, Mispereth, Bigvai, Nehum, 1114

BIMHAL (1)
1Ch 7:33 of Japhlet; Pasach, and **B**, and Ashvath. 1118

BIND (49) [BINDETH, BINDING, BOUND]
Ex 28:28 they shall **b** the breastplate by the rings 7405
 39:21 they did **b** the breastplate by the rings 7405
Nu 30: 2 or swear an oath to **b** his soul with a bond; 631
 30: 3 **b** *herself by* a bond, *being* in her father's 631
Dt 6: 8 thou shalt **b** them for a sign upon thine 7194
 11:18 and **b** them for a sign upon your hand, 7194
 14:25 **b up** the money in thine hand, and shalt 6696
Jos 2:18 thou shalt **b** this line of scarlet thread in 7194
Jdg 15:10 To Samson are we come up, 631
 15:12 unto him, We are come down to **b** thee, 631
 15:13 we will **b** thee **fast**, and deliver thee 631+631
 16: 5 that we may **b** him to afflict him: 631
 16: 7 If they **b** me with seven green withs that 631
 16:11 If they **b** me **fast** with new ropes that 631+631
Job 31:36 my shoulder, *and* **b** it *as* a crown to me. 6029
 38:31 Canst thou **b** the sweet influences of 7194
 39:10 Canst thou **b** the unicorn with his band in 7194
 40:13 dust together; *and* **b** their faces in secret. 2280
 41: 5 or wilt thou **b** him for thy maidens? 7194
Ps 105:22 To **b** his princes at his pleasure; 631
 118:27 **b** the sacrifice with cords, *even* unto 631
 149: 8 To **b** their kings with chains, 631
Pr 3: 3 **b** them about thy neck; write them upon 7194
 6:21 **B** them continually upon thine heart, 7194
 7: 3 **B** them upon thy fingers, write them upon 7194
Isa 8:16 **B up** the testimony, seal the law among 6887
 49:18 and **b** them *on thee*, as a bride *doth*. 7194
 61: 1 hath sent me to **b up** the broken-hearted, 2280
Jer 51:63 *that* thou shalt **b** a stone to it, and cast it 7194
Eze 3:25 shall **b** thee with them, and thou shalt not 631
 5: 3 a few in number, and **b** them in thy skirts. 6696
 24:17 the tire of thine head upon thee, 2280
 30:21 to put a roller to **b** it, to make it strong to 2280
 34:16 will **b up** that which was broken, 2280
Da 3:20 men that *were* in his army to **b** Shadrach, 3729
Hos 6: 1 he hath smitten, and he will **b** us **up**. 2280
 10:10 when *they* shall **b** themselves in their two 631
Mic 1:13 Lachish, **b** the chariot to the swift beast: 7573
Mt 12:29 except he first **b** the strong *man*? and then 1210
 13:30 and **b** them in bundles to burn them: 1210
 16:19 whatsoever thou shalt **b** on earth shall be 1210
 18:18 Whatsoever ye shall **b** on earth shall be 1210
 22:13 **B** him hand and foot, and take him away, 1210
 23: 4 For they **b** heavy burdens and grievous to 1195
Mk 3:27 except he will first **b** the strong *man*; 1210
 5: 3 and no *man* could **b** him, no, not with 1210
Ac 9:14 chief priests to **b** all that call on thy name. 1210
 12: 8 Gird thyself, and **b on** thy sandals. 5265
 21:11 So shall the Jews at Jerusalem **b** the man 1210

BINDETH (9) [BIND]
Job 5:18 For he maketh sore, and **b up**: 2280
 26: 8 He **b up** the waters in his thick clouds; 6887
 28:11 He **b** the floods from overflowing; 2280
 30:18 it **b** me about as the collar of my coat. 247
 36:13 wrath: they cry not when he **b** them. 631
Ps 129: 7 nor he that **b** sheaves his bosom. 6014
 147: 3 broken in heart, and **b up** their wounds. 2280
Pr 26: 8 As *he that* **b** a stone in a sling, so *is* he 6872
Isa 30:26 in the day that the LORD **b up** the breach 2280

BINDING (5) [BIND]
Ge 37: 7 we *were* **b** sheaves in the field, and, lo, 481
 49:11 **B** his foal unto the vine, and his ass's colt 631
Ex 28:32 it shall have a **b** of woven work round 8193
Nu 30:13 and every **b** oath to afflict the soul, 632
Ac 22: 4 **b** and delivering into prisons both men 1195

BINEA (2)
1Ch 8:37 Moza begat **B**: Rapha *was* his son, 1150
 9:43 Moza begat **B**; and Rephaiah his son, 1150

BINNUI (7) [BAVAI]
Ezr 8:33 and Noadiah the son of **B**, Levites; 1131
 10:30 Bezaleel, and **B**, and Manasseh. 1131
 10:38 And Bani, and **B**, Shimei, 1131
Ne 3:24 After him repaired **B** the son of Henadad 1131
 7:15 The children of **B**, six hundred forty and 1131
 10: 9 **B** of the sons of Henadad, Kadmiel; 1131
 12: 8 Jeshua, **B**, Kadmiel, Sherebiah, Judah, 1131

BIRD (28) [BIRD'S, BIRDS, BIRDS']
Ge 7:14 fowl after his kind, every **b** of every sort. 6833
Lev 14: 6 As for the living **b**, he shall take it, 6833
 14: 6 the living **b** in the blood of the bird *that* 6833
 14: 6 the living bird in the blood of the **b** that 6833
 14: 7 shall let the living **b** loose into the open 6833
 14:51 the living **b**, and dip them in the blood of 6833

Lev 14:51 dip them in the blood of the slain **b**, 6833
 14:52 cleanse the house with the blood of the **b**, 6833
 14:52 with the living bird, and with the cedar 6833
 14:53 he shall let go the living **b** out of the city 6833
Job 41: 5 Wilt thou play with him as with a **b**? or 6833
Ps 11: 1 to my soul, Flee *as* a **b** *to* your mountain? 6833
 124: 7 Our soul is escaped as a **b** out of the snare 6833
Pr 1:17 net *is* spread in the sight of any **b**. 1167+3605
 6: 5 and as a **b** from the hand of the fowler. 6833
 7:23 as a **b** hasteth to the snare, and knoweth 6833
 26: 2 As the **b** by wandering, as the swallow by 6833
 27: 8 As a **b** that wandereth from her nest, so 6833
Ecc 10:20 for a **b** of the air shall carry the voice, 5775
 12: 4 he shall rise up at the voice of the **b**, 5775
Isa 16: 2 as a wandering **b** cast out of the nest, 5775
 46:11 Calling a **ravenous b** from the east, 5861
Jer 12: 9 Mine heritage *is* unto me *as* a speckled **b**, 5861
La 3:52 chased me sore, like a **b**, without cause. 6833
Hos 9:11 their glory shall fly away like a **b**, from 5775
 11:11 They shall tremble as a **b** out of Egypt, 6833
Am 3: 5 Can a **b** fall in a snare upon the earth, 6833
Rev 18: 2 a cage of every unclean and hateful **b**. 3732

BIRD'S (1) [BIRD]
Dt 22: 6 If a **b** nest chance to be before thee in 6833

BIRDS (24) [BIRD]
Ge 15:10 against another: but the **b** divided he not. 6833
 40:17 the **b** did eat them out of the basket upon 5775
 40:19 and the **b** shall eat thy flesh from off thee. 5775
Lev 14: 4 for him that is to be cleansed two **b** alive 6833
 14: 5 priest shall command that one of the **b** 5775
 14:49 he shall take to cleanse the house two **b**, 6833
 14:50 he shall kill the one of the **b** in an earthen 6833
Dt 14:11 *Of* all clean **b** ye shall eat. 6833
2Sa 21:10 suffered neither the **b** of the air to rest on 5775
Ps 104:17 Where the **b** make their nests: *as for* 6833
Ecc 9:12 and as the **b** that are caught in the snare; 6833
SS 2:12 the time of the singing *of* **b** is come, NIH
Isa 31: 5 As **b** flying, so will the LORD of hosts 6833
Jer 4:25 and all the **b** of the heavens were fled. 5775
 5:27 As a cage *is* full *of* **b**, so *are* their houses 5775
 12: 4 the beasts are consumed, and the **b**; 5775
 12: 9 the **b** round about *are* against her; 5861
Eze 39: 4 I will give thee unto the ravenous **b** of 6833
Mt 8:20 holes, and the **b** of the air *have* nests; 4071
 13:32 so that the **b** of the air come and lodge in 4071
Lk 9:58 have holes, and **b** of the air *have* nests; 4071
Ro 1:23 and to **b**, and fourfooted beasts, 4071
1Co 15:39 another of fishes, *and* another of **b**. 4421
Jas 3: 7 of **b**, and of serpents, and of *things* in 4071

BIRDS' (1) [BIRD]
Da 4:33 eagles' *feathers*, and his nails like **b** *claws*. 6853

BIRSHA (1)
Ge 14: 2 with **B** king of Gomorrah, Shinab king of 1306

BIRTH (15) [BEAR]
Ex 28:10 on the other stone, according to their **b**. 8435
2Ki 19: 3 for the children are come to the **b**, 4866
Job 3:16 as a hidden **untimely b** I had not been; 5309
Ps 58: 8 *like* the **untimely b** of a woman, *that* 5309
Ecc 6: 3 *that* an **untimely b** *is* better than he, 5309
 7: 1 the day of death than the day of one's **b**. 3205
Isa 37: 3 for the children are come to the **b**, 4866
 66: 9 Shall I **bring to the b**, and not cause to 7665
Eze 16: 3 Thy **b** and thy nativity *is* of the land of 4351
Hos 9:11 from the **b**, and from the womb, 3205
Mt 1:18 the **b** of Jesus Christ was on this wise: 1083
Lk 1:14 gladness; and many shall rejoice at his **b**. 1083
Jn 9: 1 he saw a man *which was* blind from *his* **b**. 1079
Gal 4:19 of whom I **travail in b** again until Christ 5605
Rev 12: 2 **travailing in b**, and pained to be 5605

BIRTHDAY (3) [BEAR, DAY]
Ge 40:20 third day, *which was* Pharaoh's **b**, 3117+3205
Mt 14: 6 when Herod's **b** was kept, the daughter 1077
Mk 6:21 that Herod on his **b** made a supper to his 1077

BIRTHRIGHT (10) [BEAR, RIGHT]
Ge 25:31 And Jacob said, Sell me *this* day thy **b**. 1062
 25:32 what profit shall this **b** do to me? 1062
 25:33 to him: and he sold his **b** unto Jacob. 1062
 25:34 went his way: thus Esau despised *his* **b**. 1062
 27:36 he took away my **b**; and behold, now he 1062
 43:33 the firstborn according to his **b**, 1062
1Ch 5: 1 his **b** was given unto the sons of Joseph 1062
 5: 1 is not to be reckoned after the **b**. 1062
 5: 2 the chief ruler; but the **b** *was* Joseph's:) 1062
Heb 12:16 who for one morsel of meat sold his **b**. 4415

BIRZAITH See BIRZAVITH

BIRZAVITH (1)
1Ch 7:31 and Malchiel, who *is* the father of **B**. 1269

BISHLAM (1)
Ezr 4: 7 in the days of Artaxerxes wrote **B**, 1312

BISHOP (6) [BISHOPRICK, BISHOPS]
1Ti 3: 1 If a man desire the **office** of a **b**, 1984
 3: 2 A **b** then must be blameless, the husband 1985
2Ti 4: S ordained the first **b** of the church of 1985
Tit 1: 7 For a **b** must be blameless, as the steward 1985
 3: S ordained the first **b** of the church of 1985

1Pe 2:25 unto the Shepherd and **B** of your souls. *1985*

BISHOPRICK (1) [BISHOP]
Ac 1:20 dwell therein: and his **b** let another take. *1984*

BISHOPS (1) [BISHOP]
Php 1: 1 are at Philippi, with the **b** and deacons: *1985*

BIT (3) [BITE, BITS]
Nu 21: 6 among the people, and they **b** the people; 5391
Ps 32: 9 whose mouth must be held in with **b** and 4964
Am 5:19 his hand on the wall, and a serpent **b** him. 5391

BITE (7) [BACKBITERS, BACKBITETH, BACKBITING, BACKBITINGS, BIT, BITETH, BITTEN, HUNGER-BITTEN]
Ecc 10: 8 breaketh a hedge, a serpent shall **b** him. 5391
10:11 Surely the serpent will **b** without 5391
Jer 8:17 and they shall **b** you, saith the LORD. 5391
Am 9: 3 the serpent, and he shall **b** them: 5391
Mic 3: 5 that **b** with their teeth, and cry, Peace; 5391
Hab 2: 7 they not rise up suddenly that *shall* **b** 5391
Gal 5:15 But if ye **b** and devour one another, 1143

BITETH (2) [BITE]
Ge 49:17 that **b** the horse heels, so that his rider 5391
Pr 23:32 At the last it **b** like a serpent, 5391

BITHIAH (1)
1Ch 4:18 these *are* the sons of **B** the daughter of 1332

BITHRON (1)
2Sa 2:29 went *through* all **B**, and they came *to* 1338

BITHYNIA (2)
Ac 16: 7 come to Mysia, they assayed to go into **B**: 978
1Pe 1: 1 Galatia, Cappadocia, Asia, and **B**, 978

BITS (1) [BIT]
Jas 3: 3 Behold, we put **b** in the horses' mouths, 5469

BITTEN (2) [BITE]
Nu 21: 8 come to pass, that every one that is **b** 5391
21: 9 to pass, that, if a serpent had **b** *any* man, 5391

BITTER (38) [BITTERLY, BITTERNESS]
Ge 27:34 he cried with a great and exceeding **b** cry, 4751
Ex 1:14 **made** their lives **b** with hard bondage, 4843
12: 8 *and* with **b** *herbs* they shall eat it. 4844
15:23 of the waters of Marah, for they *were* **b**: 4751
Nu 5:18 priest shall have in his hand the **b** water 4751
5:19 free from this **b** water that causeth 4751
5:23 he shall blot *them* out with the **b** water: 4751
5:24 he shall cause the woman to drink the **b** 4751
5:24 curse shall enter into her, and become **b**. 4751
5:27 become **b**, and her belly shall swell, 4751
9:11 eat it with unleavened bread and **b** *herbs*. 4844
Dt 32:24 burning heat, and with **b** destruction: 4815
32:32 *are* grapes of gall, their clusters *are* **b**: 4846
2Ki 14:26 the affliction of Israel, *that it was* very **b**: 4784
Est 4: 1 city, and cried *with* a loud and a **b** cry; 4751
Job 3:20 is in misery, and life unto the **b** in soul; 4751
13:26 For thou writest **b** *things* against me, 4846
23: 2 Even to day *is* my complaint **b**: my stroke 4805
Ps 64: 3 to shoot their arrows, *even* **b** words: 4751
Pr 5: 4 her end is **b** as wormwood, sharp as a 4751
27: 7 *to* the hungry soul every *thing is* sweet. 4751
Ecc 7:26 I find more **b** than death the woman, 4751
Isa 5:20 that put **b** for sweet, and sweet for bitter! 4751
5:20 that put bitter for sweet, and sweet for **b**! 4751
24: 9 drink shall be **b** to them that drink it. 4843
Jer 2:19 and see that *it is* an evil *thing* and **b**, 4751
4:18 because *it is* **b**, because it reacheth unto 4751
6:26 *as for* an only *son*, most **b** lamentation: 8563
31:15 in Ramah, lamentation, *and* **b** weeping; 8563
Eze 27:31 with bitterness of heart *and* **b** wailing. 4751
Am 8:10 only *son*, and the end thereof as a **b** day. 4751
Hab 1: 6 the Chaldeans, *that* **b** and hasty nation, 4751
Col 3:19 *your* wives, and be not **b** against them. 4087
Jas 3:11 at the same place sweet *water* and **b**? 4089
3:14 But if ye have **b** envying and strife in your 4089
Rev 8:11 of the waters, because they were **made b**. 4087
10: 9 it shall **make** thy belly **b**, but it shall be 4087
10:10 as soon as I had eaten it, my belly was **b**. 4087

BITTERLY (9) [BITTER]
Jdg 5:23 curse ye **b** the inhabitants thereof; 779
Ru 1:20 for the Almighty hath **dealt** very **b** with 4843
Isa 22: 4 I will weep **b**, labour not to comfort me, 4843
33: 7 the ambassadors of peace shall weep **b**. 4751
Eze 27:30 shall cry **b**, and shall cast up dust upon 4751
Hos 12:14 Ephraim provoked *him* to anger **most b**: 8563
Zep 1:14 the mighty *man* shall cry there **b**. 4751
Mt 26:75 me thrice. And he went out, and wept **b**. 4090
Lk 22:62 And Peter went out, and wept **b**. 4090

BITTERN (3)
Isa 14:23 I will also make it a possession for the **b**, 7090
34:11 the cormorant and the **b** shall possess it; 7090
Zep 2:14 the **b** shall lodge in the upper lintels of it; 7090

BITTERNESS (22) [BITTER]
1Sa 1:10 she *was* in **b** of soul, and prayed unto 4751
15:32 Agag said, Surely the **b** of death is past. 4751
2Sa 2:26 knowest thou not that it will be **b** in 4751
Job 7:11 I will complain in the **b** of my soul. 4751

Job 9:18 to take my breath, but filleth me *with* **b**. 4472
10: 1 I will speak in the **b** of my soul, 4751
21:25 another dieth in the **b** of his soul, 4751
Pr 14:10 The heart knoweth his own **b**; 4787
17:25 to his father, and **b** to her that bare him. 4470
Isa 38:15 go softly all my years in the **b** of my soul. 4751
38:17 Behold, for peace I had **great b**: 4751+4843
La 1: 4 her virgins *are* afflicted, and she *is* in **b**. 4843
3:15 He hath filled me with **b**, he hath made 4844
Eze 3:14 took me away, and I went in **b**, in the 4751
21: 6 loins; and with **b** sigh before their eyes. 4814
27:31 they shall weep for thee with **b** of heart 4751
Zec 12:10 for *his* only *son*, and shall be in **b** for him, 4843
12:10 him, as one that is in **b** for *his* firstborn. 4843
Ac 8:23 I perceive that thou art in the gall of **b**, 4088
Ro 3:14 Whose mouth is full of cursing and **b**: 4088
Eph 4:31 Let all **b**, and wrath, and anger, 4088
Heb 12:15 lest any root of **b** springing up trouble *you*, 4088

BIZIOTHIAH See BIZJOTHJAH

BIZJOTHJAH (1)
Jos 15:28 And Hazar-shual, and Beer-sheba, and **B**, 964

BIZTHA (1)
Est 1:10 **B**, Harbona, Bigtha, and Abagtha, Zethar, 968

BLACK (18) [BLACKER, BLACKISH, BLACKNESS]
Lev 13:31 the skin, and *that there is* no **b** hair in it; 7838
13:37 and *that* there is **b** hair grown up therein; 7838
1Ki 18:45 that the heaven was **b** *with* clouds and 6937
Est 1: 6 red, and blue, and white, and **b** marble. 5508
Job 30:30 My skin is **b** upon me, and my bones are 7835
Pr 7: 9 in the evening, in the **b** and dark night: 380
SS 1: 5 I *am* **b**, but comely, O ye daughters of 7838
1: 6 because I *am* **b**, because the sun hath 7840
5:11 his locks *are* bushy, *and* **b** as a raven. 7838
Jer 4:28 earth mourn, and the heavens above be **b**: 6937
8:21 I am **b**; astonishment hath taken hold on 6937
14: 2 they are **b** unto the ground; and the cry of 6937
La 4:10 Our skin was **b** like an oven because of 3648
Zec 6: 2 and in the second chariot **b** horses; 7838
6: 6 The **b** horses which *are* therein go forth 7838
Mt 5:36 thou canst not make one hair white or **b**. 3189
Rev 6: 5 And I beheld, and lo a **b** horse; and he 3189
6:12 and the sun became **b** as sackcloth of hair, 3189

BLACKER (1) [BLACK]
La 4: 8 Their visage is **b** than a coal; they are not 2821

BLACKISH (1) [BLACK]
Job 6:16 Which are **b** by reason of the ice, 6937

BLACKNESS (6) [BLACK]
Job 3: 5 upon it; let the **b** of the day terrify it. 3650
Isa 50: 3 I clothe the heavens with **b**, and I make 6940
Joel 2: 6 be much pained: all faces shall gather **b**. 6289
Na 2:10 loins, and the faces of them all gather **b**. 6289
Heb 12:18 with fire, nor unto **b**, and darkness, 1105
Jude 1:13 to whom is reserved the **b** of darkness for 2217

BLADE (5)
Jdg 3:22 haft also went in after the **b**; and the fat 3851
3:22 the fat closed upon the **b**, so that he could 3851
Job 31:22 let mine arm fall from *my* **shoulder b**, 7929
Mt 13:26 But when the **b** was sprung up, and 5528
Mk 4:28 first the **b**, then the ear, after that the full 5528

BLAINS (2)
Ex 9: 9 shall be a boil breaking forth *with* **b** upon 76
9:10 because a boil breaking forth *with* **b** upon 76

BLAME (4) [BLAMED, BLAMELESS, UNBLAMEABLE]
Ge 43: 9 then let me **bear** the **b** for ever: 2398
44:32 I shall **bear the b** to my father for ever. 2398
2Co 8:20 no *man* should **b** us in this abundance 3469
Eph 1: 4 be holy and **without b** before him in love: 299

BLAMED (2) [BLAME]
2Co 6: 3 in any *thing*, that the ministry be not **b**: 3469
Gal 2:11 him to the face, because he was *to be* **b**. 2607

BLAMELESS (15) [BLAME]
Ge 44:10 shall be my servant; and ye shall be **b**. 5355
Jos 2:17 We *will be* **b** of this thine oath which thou 5355
Jdg 15: 3 Now shall I be more **b** than the Philistines, 5352
Mt 12: 5 the temple profane the sabbath, and are **b**? 338
Lk 1: 6 and ordinances of the Lord **b**. 273
1Co 1: 8 *that ye may be* **b** in the day of our Lord 410
Php 2:15 That ye may be **b** and harmless, the sons 273
3: 6 the righteousness which is in the law, **b**. 273
1Th 5:23 body be preserved **b** unto the coming of 274
1Ti 3: 2 A bishop then must be **b**, the husband of 423
3:10 use the office of a deacon, being *found* **b**. 410
5: 7 *things* give in charge, that they may be **b**. 423
Tit 1: 6 If any be **b**, the husband of one wife, 410
1: 7 For a bishop must be **b**, as the steward of 410
2Pe 3:14 of him in peace, without spot, and **b**. 298

BLASPHEME (10) [BLASPHEMED, BLASPHEMER, BLASPHEMERS, BLASPHEMEST, BLASPHEMETH, BLASPHEMIES, BLASPHEMING, BLASPHEMOUS, BLASPHEMOUSLY, BLASPHEMY]
2Sa 12:14 **given great occasion** to the enemies of 5006+5006
the LORD **to b**,
1Ki 21:10 Thou didst **b** God and the king. 1288

1Ki 21:13 Naboth did **b** God and the king. 1288
Ps 74:10 shall the enemy **b** thy name for ever? 5006
Mk 3:28 blasphemies wherewith soever they shall **b**: 987
3:29 But he that shall **b** against the Holy Ghost 987
Ac 26:11 every synagogue, and compelled *them* to **b**; 987
1Ti 1:20 unto Satan, that they may learn not to **b**. 987
Jas 2: 7 Do not they **b** *that* worthy name by 987
Rev 13: 6 to his name, and his tabernacle, 987

BLASPHEMED (16) [BLASPHEME]
Lev 24:11 the Israelitish woman's son **b** the name *of* 5344
2Ki 19: 6 servants of the king of Assyria have **b** me. 1442
19:22 Whom hast thou reproached and **b**? and 1442
Ps 74:18 *that* the foolish people have **b** thy name. 5006
Isa 37: 6 servants of the king of Assyria have **b** me. 1442
37:23 Whom hast thou reproached and **b**? and 1442
52: 5 and my name continually every day *is* **b**. 5006
65: 7 the mountains, and **b** me upon the hills: 2778
Eze 20:27 Yet in this your fathers have **b** me, in that 1442
Ac 18: 6 and **b**, he shook *his* raiment, and said unto 987
Ro 2:24 the name of God is **b** among the Gentiles 987
1Ti 6: 1 the name of God and *his* doctrine be not **b**. 987
Tit 2: 5 that the word of God be not **b**. 987
Rev 16: 9 and the name of God, which hath power 987
16:11 And **b** the God of heaven because of their 987
16:21 and men **b** God because of the plague of 987

BLASPHEMER (1) [BLASPHEME]
1Ti 1:13 Who was before a **b**, and a persecutor, 989

BLASPHEMERS (2) [BLASPHEME]
Ac 19:37 of churches, nor yet **b** of your goddess. 987
2Ti 3: 2 covetous, boasters, proud, **b**, disobedient 989

BLASPHEMEST (1) [BLASPHEME]
Jn 10:36 and sent into the world, Thou **b**; 987

BLASPHEMETH (5) [BLASPHEME]
Lev 24:11 **b** the name of the LORD, he shall 5344
24:16 when he **b** the name *of the LORD*, shall 5344
Ps 44:16 the voice of him that reproacheth and **b**; 1442
Mt 9: 3 scribes said within themselves, This *man* **b**. 987
Lk 12:10 unto him that **b** against the Holy Ghost it 987

BLASPHEMIES (6) [BLASPHEME]
Eze 35:12 *that* I have heard all thy **b** which thou hast 5007
Mt 15:19 fornications, thefts, false witness, **b**: 988
Mk 2: 7 Why doth this *man* thus speak **b**? who can 988
3:28 wherewith soever they shall blaspheme: 988
Lk 5:21 saying, Who is this which speaketh **b**? 988
Rev 13: 5 him a mouth speaking great *things* and **b**; 988

BLASPHEMING (1) [BLASPHEME]
Ac 13:45 were spoken by Paul, contradicting and **b**. 987

BLASPHEMOUS (2) [BLASPHEME]
Ac 6:11 We have heard him speak **b** words against 989
6:13 This man ceaseth not to speak **b** words 989

BLASPHEMOUSLY (1) [BLASPHEME]
Lk 22:65 many other *things* **b** spake they against 987

BLASPHEMY (14) [BLASPHEME]
2Ki 19: 3 *is* a day of trouble, and of rebuke, and **b**: 5007
Isa 37: 3 a day of trouble, and of rebuke, and **b**: 5007
Mt 12:31 *of* sin and **b** shall be forgiven unto men: 988
12:31 the **b** against the *Holy* Ghost shall not be 988
26:65 rent his clothes, saying, He hath **spoken b**; 987
26:65 behold, now ye have heard his **b**. 988
Mk 7:22 an evil eye, **b**, pride, foolishness: 988
14:64 Ye have heard the **b**: what think ye? 988
Jn 10:33 but for **b**; and because that thou, being a 988
Col 3: 8 wrath, malice, **b**, filthy communication out 988
Rev 2: 9 *I know* the **b** of them which say they are 988
13: 1 and upon his heads the name of **b**. 988
13: 6 he opened his mouth in **b** against God, 988
17: 3 full of names of **b**, having seven heads and 988

BLAST (8) [BLASTED, BLASTING]
Ex 15: 8 with the **b** of thy nostrils the waters were 7307
Jos 6: 5 that when *they* **make a long b** with 4900
2Sa 22:16 at the **b** of the breath of his nostrils. 5397
2Ki 19: 7 I will send a **b** upon him, and he shall 7307
Job 4: 9 By the **b** of God they perish, and by 5397
Ps 18:15 at the **b** of the breath of thy nostrils. 5397
Isa 25: 4 the **b** of the terrible ones *is* as a storm 7307
37: 7 I will send a **b** upon him, and he shall 7307

BLASTED (5) [BLAST]
Ge 41: 6 **b** with the east wind sprang up after them 7710
41:23 withered, thin, *and* **b** with the east wind, 7710
41:27 seven empty ears **b** with the east wind 7710
2Ki 19:26 and *as* corn **b** before it be grown up. 7711
Isa 37:27 and *as* corn **b** before it be grown up. 7711

BLASTING (5) [BLAST]
Dt 28:22 the sword, and with **b**, and with mildew; 7711
1Ki 8:37 **b**, mildew, locust, *or* if there be caterpillar 7711
2Ch 6:28 if there be **b**, or mildew, locusts, 7711
Am 4: 9 I have smitten you with **b** and mildew: 7711
Hag 2:17 I smote you with **b** and with mildew and 7711

BLASTUS (1)
Ac 12:20 having made **B** the king's chamberlain 986

B

BLAZE (1)
Mk 1:45 *it* much, and to **b** abroad the matter, *1310*

BLEATING (1) [BLEATINGS]
1Sa 15:14 then this **b** of the sheep in mine ears, 6963

BLEATINGS (1) [BLEATING]
Jdg 5:16 sheepfolds, to hear the **b** of the flocks? 8292

BLEMISH (62) [BLEMISHES]
Ex	12: 5	Your lamb shall be **without b**, a male of	8549
	29: 1	young bullock, and two rams **without b**,	8549
Lev	1: 3	the herd, let him offer a male **without b:**	8549
	1:10	he shall bring it a male **without b.**	8549
	3: 1	he shall offer it **without b** before	8549
	3: 6	or female, he shall offer it **without b.**	8549
	4: 3	a young bullock **without b** unto	8549
	4:23	a kid of the goats, a male **without b;**	8549
	4:28	a kid of the goats, a female **without b,**	8549
	4:32	he shall bring it a female **without b.**	8549
	5:15	LORD a ram **without b** out of the flocks,	8549
	5:18	he shall bring a ram **without b** out of	8549
	6: 6	a ram **without b** out of the flock, with	8549
	9: 2	**without b**, and offer *them* before	8549
	9: 3	first year, **without b**, for a burnt offering;	8549
	14:10	he shall take two he lambs **without b**,	8549
	14:10	one ewe lamb of the first year **without b**,	8549
	21:17	seed in their generations that hath *any* **b**,	3971
	21:18	For whatsoever man *he be* that hath a **b**,	3971
	21:20	or that hath a **b** in his eye, or be scurvy,	8400
	21:21	No man that hath a **b**, of the seed of	3971
	21:21	hath a **b;** he shall not come nigh to offer	3971
	21:23	nigh unto the altar, because he hath a **b;**	3971
	22:19	*offer* at your own will a male **without b,**	8549
	22:20	*But* whatsoever hath a **b**, *that* shall ye not	3971
	22:21	be accepted; there shall be no **b** therein.	3971
	23:12	**without b** of the first year for a burnt	8549
	23:18	seven lambs **without b** of the first year,	8549
	24:19	if a man cause a **b** in his neighbour; as he	3971
	24:20	as he hath caused a **b** in a man, so shall it	3971
Nu	6:14	he lamb of the first year **without b** for	8549
	6:14	ewe lamb of the first year **without b** for	8549
	6:14	one ram **without b** for peace offerings,	8549
	19: 2	wherein *is* no **b**, *and* upon which never	3971
	28:19	year: they shall be unto you **without b:**	8549
	28:31	(they shall be unto you **without b)**	8549
	29: 2	seven lambs of the first year **without b:**	8549
	29: 8	year; they shall be unto you **without b:**	8549
	29:13	of the first year; they shall be **without b:**	8549
	29:20	fourteen lambs of the first year **without b;**	8549
	29:23	fourteen lambs of the first year **without b:**	8549
	29:29	fourteen lambs of the first year **without b:**	8549
	29:32	fourteen lambs of the first year **without b;**	8549
	29:36	seven lambs of the first year **without b:**	8549
Dt	15:21	if there be *any* **b** therein, *as if it be* lame,	3971
	15:21	*as if it be* lame, or blind, *or have* any ill **b**,	3971
	17: 1	wherein is **b**, *or* any evil favouredness:	3971
2Sa	14:25	crown of his head there was no **b** in him.	3971
Eze	43:22	of the goats **without b** for a sin offering;	8549
	43:23	shalt offer a young bullock **without b.**	8549
	43:23	and a ram out of the flock **without b.**	8549
	43:25	and a ram out of the flock, **without b.**	8549
	45:18	shalt take a young bullock **without b,**	8549
	45:23	seven rams **without b** daily the seven	8549
	46: 4	sabbath day *shall be* six lambs **without b**,	8549
	46: 4	without blemish, and a ram **without b.**	8549
	46: 6	*it shall be* a young bullock **without b**,	8549
	46: 6	and a ram: they shall be **without b.**	8549
	46:13	*of* a lamb of the first year **without b:**	8549
Da	1: 4	Children in whom *was* no **b**, but	3971
Eph	5:27	but that it should be holy and **without b.**	299
1Pe	1:19	as of a lamb **without b** and without spot:	299

BLEMISHES (2) [BLEMISH]
Lev	22:25	corruption *is* in them, *and* **b** *be* in them:	3971
2Pe	2:13	Spots *they are* and **b**, sporting themselves	3470

BLENDED See APOTHECARIES'

BLENDED WINE See LIQUOR

BLESS (127) [BLESSED, BLESSEDNESS, BLESSEST, BLESSETH, BLESSING, BLESSINGS]
Ge	12: 2	I will **b** thee, and make thy name great;	1288
	12: 3	will **b** them that bless thee, and curse him	1288
	12: 3	will **b** bless them that bless thee, and curse him	1288
	17:16	will **b** her, and give thee a son also of her:	1288
	17:16	I will **b** her, and she shall be a *mother* of	1288
	22:17	That in blessing I will **b** thee,	1288
	26: 3	I will be with thee, and will **b** thee;	1288
	26:24	will **b** thee, and multiply thy seed for my	1288
	27: 4	that my soul may **b** thee before I die.	1288
	27: 7	**b** thee before the LORD before my death.	1288
	27:10	that he may **b** thee before his death.	1288
	27:19	of my venison, that thy soul may **b** me.	1288
	27:25	son's venison, that my soul may **b** thee.	1288
	27:31	son's venison, that thy soul may **b** me.	1288
	27:34	**B** me, *even* me also, O my father.	1288
	27:38	**b** me, *even* me also, O my father.	1288
	28: 3	God Almighty **b** thee, and make thee	1288
	32:26	I will not let thee go, except thou **b** me.	1288
	48: 9	I pray thee, unto me, and I will **b** them.	1288
	48:16	redeemed me from all evil, **b** the lads;	1288
	48:20	saying, In thee shall Israel **b**, saying,	1288
	49:25	who shall **b** thee *with* blessings of heaven	1288

Ex	12:32	ye have said, and be gone; and **b** me also.	1288
	20:24	I will come unto thee, and I will **b** thee.	1288
	23:25	and he shall **b** thy bread, and thy water;	1288
Nu	6:23	On this wise ye shall **b** the children of	1288
	6:24	The LORD **b** thee, and keep thee:	1288
	6:27	the children of Israel; and I will **b** them.	1288
	23:20	I have received *commandment* to **b:**	1288
	23:25	curse them at all, nor **b** them **at all.**	1288+1288
	24: 1	saw that it pleased the LORD to **b** Israel,	1288
Dt	1:11	so many moe as ye *are*, and **b** you,	1288
	7:13	love thee, and **b** thee, and multiply thee:	1288
	7:13	he will also **b** the fruit of thy womb,	1288
	8:10	thou shalt **b** the LORD thy God for	1288
	10: 8	and to **b** in his name, unto this day.	1288
	14:29	that the LORD thy God may **b** thee in all	1288
	15: 4	for the LORD shall **greatly b** thee	1288+1288
	15:10	thy God shall **b** thee in all thy works,	1288
	15:18	the LORD thy God shall **b** thee in all that	1288
	16:15	the LORD thy God shall **b** thee in all thy	1288
	21: 5	and to **b** in the name of the LORD;	1288
	23:20	that the LORD thy God may **b** thee in all	1288
	24:13	may sleep in his own raiment, and **b** thee:	1288
	24:19	that the LORD thy God may **b** thee in all	1288
	26:15	b thy people Israel, and the land which	1288
	27:12	shall stand upon mount Gerizzim to **b**	1288
	28: 8	he shall **b** thee in the land which	1288
	28:12	and to **b** all the work of thine hand:	1288
	29:19	that he **b** himself in his heart, saying,	1288
	30:16	the LORD thy God shall **b** thee in the land	1288
	33:11	**B**, LORD, his substance, and accept	1288
Jos	8:33	that they should **b** the people of Israel.	1288
Jdg	5: 9	among the people. **B** ye the LORD.	1288
Ru	2: 4	they answered him, The LORD **b** thee.	1288
1Sa	9:13	is come, because he doth **b** the sacrifice;	1288
2Sa	6:20	David returned to **b** his household.	1288
	7:29	Therefore now let it please thee to **b**	1288
	8:10	to **b** him, because he had fought against	1288
	21: 3	that ye may **b** the inheritance of	1288
1Ki	1:47	the king's servants came to **b** our	1288
1Ch	4:10	that thou wouldest **b** me **indeed**,	1288+1288
	16:43	and David returned to **b** his house.	1288
	17:27	let it please thee to **b** the house of thy	1288
	23:13	unto him, and to **b** in his name for ever.	1288
	29:20	Now **b** the LORD your God.	1288
Ne	9: 5	*and* **b** the LORD your God for ever and	1288
Ps	5:12	For thou, LORD, wilt **b** the righteous;	1288
	16: 7	I will **b** the LORD, who hath given me	1288
	26:12	in the congregations will I **b** the LORD.	1288
	28: 9	Save thy people, and **b** thine inheritance:	1288
	29:11	the LORD will **b** his people with peace.	1288
	34: 1	I will **b** the LORD at all times: his praise	1288
	62: 4	they **b** with their mouth, but they curse	1288
	63: 4	Thus will I **b** thee while I live: I will lift	1288
	66: 8	O bless our God, ye people, and make	1288
	67: 1	God be merciful unto us, and **b** us;	1288
	67: 6	and God, *even* our own God, shall **b** us.	1288
	67: 7	God shall **b** us; and all the ends of the	1288
	68:26	**B** ye God in the congregations, *even*	1288
	96: 2	Sing unto the LORD, **b** his name;	1288
	100: 4	be thankful unto him, *and* **b** his name.	1288
	103: 1	**B** the LORD, O my soul: and all that is	1288
	103: 1	all that is within me, **b** his holy name.	NIH
	103: 2	**B** the LORD, O my soul, and forget not	1288
	103:20	**B** the LORD, ye his angels, that excel in	1288
	103:21	**B** ye the LORD, all ye his hosts;	1288
	103:22	**B** the LORD, all his works in all places of	1288
	103:22	of his dominion: **b** the LORD, O my soul.	1288
	104: 1	**B** the LORD, O my soul. O LORD my	1288
	104:35	**B** thou the LORD, O my soul. Praise ye	1288
	109:28	Let them curse, but **b** thou: when they	1288
	115:12	he will **b** *us;* he will bless the house of	1288
	115:12	he will bless *us;* he will **b** the house of	1288
	115:12	of Israel; he will **b** the house of Aaron.	1288
	115:13	He will **b** them that fear the LORD, *both*	1288
	115:18	we will **b** the LORD from this time forth	1288
	128: 5	The LORD shall **b** thee out of Zion:	1288
	129: 8	we **b** you in the name of the LORD.	1288
	132:15	I will **abundantly b** her provision:	1288+1288
	134: 1	Behold, **b** ye the LORD, all ye servants of	1288
	134: 2	hands *in* the sanctuary, and **b** the LORD.	1288
	134: 3	made heaven and earth **b** thee out of Zion.	1288
	135:19	**B** the LORD, O house of Israel: bless	1288
	135:19	of Israel: **b** the LORD, O house of Aaron:	1288
	135:20	**B** the LORD, O house of Levi: ye that	1288
	135:20	ye that fear the LORD, **b** the LORD.	1288
	145: 1	and I will **b** thy name for ever and ever.	1288
	145: 2	Every day will I **b** thee; and I will praise	1288
	145:10	O LORD; and thy saints shall **b** thee.	1288
	145:21	let all flesh **b** his holy name for ever and	1288
Pr	30:11	their father, and doth not **b** their mother.	1288
Isa	19:25	Whom the LORD of hosts shall **b**, saying,	1288
	65:16	earth shall **b** himself in the God of truth;	1288
	65:16	the nations shall **b** themselves in him,	1288
Jer	4: 2	the nations shall **b** themselves in him,	1288
	31:23	The LORD **b** thee, O habitation of justice,	1288
Hag	2:19	brought forth: from this day will I **b** *you.*	1288
Mt	5:44	Love your enemies, **b** them that curse you	2127
Lk	6:28	**B** them that curse you, and pray for them	2127
Ac	3:26	raised up his Son Jesus, sent him to **b** you,	2127
Ro	12:14	**B** them which persecute you: bless;	2127
	12:14	which persecute you: **b**, and curse not.	2127
1Co	4:12	being reviled, we **b**; being persecuted,	2127
	10:16	The cup of blessing which we **b**, is it not	2127
	14:16	Else when thou shalt **b** with the spirit,	2127
Heb	6:14	Surely blessing I will **b** thee,	2127
Jas	3: 9	Therewith **b** we God, even the Father;	2127

BLESSED (302) [BLESS]
Ge	1:22	God **b** them, saying, Be fruitful,	1288
	1:28	God **b** them, and God said unto them,	1288
	2: 3	God **b** the seventh day, and sanctified it:	1288
	5: 2	**b** them, and called their name Adam,	1288
	9: 1	God **b** Noah and his sons, and said unto	1288
	9:26	he said, **B** *be* the LORD God of Shem;	1288
	12: 3	in thee shall all families of the earth be **b.**	1288
	14:19	he **b** him, and said, Blessed *be* Abram of	1288
	14:19	said, **B** *be* Abram of the most high God,	1288
	14:20	**B** *be* the most high God, which hath	1288
	17:20	I have **b** him, and will make him fruitful,	1288
	18:18	all the nations of the earth shall be **b** in	1288
	22:18	seed shall all the nations of the earth be **b;**	1288
	24: 1	the LORD had **b** Abraham in all things.	1288
	24:27	**B** *be* the LORD God of my master	1288
	24:31	he said, Come in, thou **b** of the LORD;	1288
	24:35	the LORD hath **b** my master greatly;	1288
	24:48	**b** the LORD God of my master Abraham,	1288
	24:60	they **b** Rebekah, and said unto her, Thou	1288
	25:11	of Abraham, that God **b** his son Isaac;	1288
	26: 4	seed shall all the nations of the earth be **b;**	1288
	26:12	an hundredfold: and the LORD **b** him.	1288
	26:29	in peace: thou *art* now the **b** of the LORD.	1288
	27:23	as his brother Esau's hands: so he **b** him.	1288
	27:27	of his raiment, and **b** him, and said, See,	1288
	27:27	smell of a field which the LORD hath **b:**	1288
	27:29	thee, and **b** *be* he that blesseth thee.	1288
	27:33	of all before thou camest, and have **b** him?	1288
	27:33	have blessed him? yea, *and* he shall be **b.**	1288
	27:41	the blessing wherewith his father **b** him:	1288
	28: 1	**b** him, and charged him, and said unto	1288
	28: 6	When Esau saw that Isaac had **b** Jacob,	1288
	28: 6	that as he **b** him he gave him a charge,	1288
	28:14	seed shall all the families of the earth be **b.**	1288
	30:13	am I, for the daughters will **call me b:**	833
	30:27	that the LORD hath **b** me for thy sake.	1288
	30:30	the LORD hath **b** thee since my coming:	1288
	31:55	his sons and his daughters, and **b** them:	1288
	32:29	ask after my name? And he **b** him there.	1288
	35: 9	he came out of Padan-aram, and **b** him.	1288
	39: 5	that the LORD **b** the Egyptian's house for	1288
	47: 7	him before Pharaoh: and Jacob **b** Pharaoh.	1288
	47:10	Jacob **b** Pharaoh, and went out from	1288
	48: 3	at Luz in the land of Canaan, and **b** me,	1288
	48:15	he **b** Joseph, and said, God, before whom	1288
	48:20	he **b** them that day, saying, In thee shall	1288
	49:28	their father spake unto them, and **b** them;	1288
	49:28	every one according to his blessing he **b**	1288
Ex	18:10	Jethro said, **B** *be* the LORD, who hath	1288
	20:11	wherefore the LORD **b** the sabbath day,	1288
	39:43	so had they done it: and Moses **b** them.	1288
Lev	9:22	**b** them, and came down from offering of	1288
	9:23	and came out, and **b** the people:	1288
Nu	22: 6	for I wot that *he* whom thou blessest *is* **b**,	1288
	22:12	shalt not curse the people: for they *are* **b.**	1288
	23:11	thou hast **b** *them* **altogether.**	1288+1288
	23:20	and he hath **b**; and I cannot reverse it.	1288
	24: 9	**B** *is* he that blesseth thee, and cursed *is*	1288
	24:10	thou hast **altogether b** *them* these	1288+1288
Dt	2: 7	For the LORD thy God hath **b** thee in all	1288
	7:14	Thou shalt be **b** above all people:	1288
	12: 7	where *in* the LORD thy God hath **b** thee.	1288
	14:24	when the LORD thy God hath **b** thee:	1288
	15:14	God hath **b** thee thou shalt give unto him.	1288
	16:10	as the LORD thy God hath **b** thee:	1288
	28: 3	**B** *shalt* thou *be* in the city, and blessed	1288
	28: 3	the city, and **b** *shalt thou be* in the field.	1288
	28: 4	**B** *shall be* the fruit of thy body,	1288
	28: 5	**B** *shall be* thy basket and thy store.	1288
	28: 6	**B** *shalt* thou *be* when thou comest in,	1288
	28: 6	and **b** *shalt* thou *be* when thou goest out.	1288
	33: 1	wherewith Moses the man of God **b**	1288
	33:13	he said, **B** of the LORD *be* his land,	1288
	33:20	Gad he said, **B** *be* he that enlargeth Gad:	1288
	33:24	he said, *Let* Asher *be* **b** with children;	1288
Jos	14:13	Joshua **b** him, and gave unto Caleb the	1288
	17:14	forasmuch as the LORD hath **b** me	1288
	22: 6	So Joshua **b** them, and sent them away:	1288
	22: 7	also unto their tents, then he **b** them,	1288
	22:33	the children of Israel **b** God, and did not	1288
	24:10	therefore he **b** you **still:**	1288+1288
Jdg	5:24	**B** above women shall Jael the wife of	1288
	5:24	**b** shall she be above women in the tent.	1288
	13:24	and the child grew, and the LORD **b** him.	1288
	17: 2	**B** *be thou* of the LORD, my son.	1288
Ru	2:19	be he that did take knowledge of thee.	1288
	2:20	her daughter in law, **B** *be* he of the LORD,	1288
	3:10	he said, **B** *be* thou of the LORD,	1288
	4:14	women said unto Naomi, **B** *be* the LORD,	1288
1Sa	2:20	Eli **b** Elkanah and his wife, and said,	1288
	15:13	said unto him, **B** *be* thou of the LORD:	1288
	23:21	Saul said, **B** *be ye* of the LORD; for ye	1288
	25:32	to Abigail, **B** *be* the LORD God of Israel,	1288
	25:33	**B** *be* thy advice, and blessed *be* thou,	1288
	25:33	blessed *be* thy advice, and **b** *be* thou,	1288
	25:39	Nabal was dead, he said, **B** *be* the LORD,	1288
	26:25	said to David, **B** *be* thou, my son David:	1288
2Sa	2: 5	said unto them, **B** *be ye* of the LORD,	1288
	6:11	the LORD **b** Obed-edom, and all his	1288
	6:12	The LORD hath **b** the house of	1288
	6:18	he **b** the people in the name of the LORD	1288
	7:29	let the house of thy servant be **b** for ever.	1288
	13:25	howbeit he would not go, but **b** him.	1288

2Sa	18:28 and said, **B** *be* the LORD thy God,	1288
	19:39 the king kissed Barzillai, and **b** him;	1288
	22:47 **b** *be* my rock; and exalted be the God of	1288
1Ki	1:48 the king, **B** *be* the LORD God of Israel,	1288
	2:45 king Solomon *shall be* **b**, and the throne	1288
	5: 7 and said, **B** *be* the LORD *this* day,	1288
	8:14 and **b** all the congregation of Israel:	1288
	8:15 he said, **B** *be* the LORD God of Israel,	1288
	8:55 **b** all the congregation of Israel *with* a loud	1288
	8:56 **B** *be* the LORD, that hath given rest unto	1288
	8:66 they **b** the king, and went unto their tents	1288
	10: 9 **B** *be* the LORD thy God, which delighted	1288
1Ch	13:14 the LORD **b** the house of Obed-edom,	1288
	16: 2 he **b** the people in the name of the LORD.	1288
	16:36 **B** *be* the LORD God of Israel for ever and	1288
	17:27 O LORD, and *it shall be* **b** for ever.	1288
	26: 5 Peulthai the eighth: for God *is* him.	1288
	29:10 Wherefore David **b** the LORD before all	1288
	29:10 David said, **B** *be* thou, LORD God of	1288
	29:20 all the congregation **b** the LORD God of	1288
2Ch	2:12 **B** *be* the LORD God of Israel, that made	1288
	6: 3 and **b** the whole congregation of Israel:	1288
	6: 4 he said, **B** *be* the LORD God of Israel,	1288
	9: 8 **B** be the LORD thy God, which delighted	1288
	20:26 of Berachah; for there they **b** the LORD:	1288
	30:27 priests the Levites arose and **b** the people:	1288
	31: 8 they **b** the LORD, and his people Israel.	1288
	31:10 for the LORD hath **b** his people;	1288
Ezr	7:27 **B** *be* the LORD God of our fathers,	1288
Ne	8: 6 Ezra **b** the LORD, the great God. And all	1288
	9: 5 **b** be thy glorious name, which *is* exalted	1288
	11: 2 the people **b** all the men, that willingly	1288
Job	1:10 thou hast **b** the work of his hands,	1288
	1:21 The LORD hath taken *away;* **b** be	1288
	29:11 When the ear heard *me*, then it **b** me;	833
	31:20 If his loins have not **b** me, and *if* he were	1288
	42:12 So the LORD **b** the latter end of Job more	1288
Ps	1: 1 **B** *is* the man that walketh not in the	835
	2:12 **b** *are* all they that put their trust in him.	835
	18:46 **b** be my rock; and let the God of my	1288
	21: 6 For thou hast made him most **b** for ever:	1293
	28: 6 **B** *be* the LORD, because he hath heard	1288
	31:21 **B** *be* the LORD: for he hath shewed me	1288
	32: 1 **B** *is* he whose transgression *is* forgiven,	835
	32: 2 **B** *is* the man unto whom the LORD	835
	33:12 **B** *is* the nation whose God *is* the LORD;	835
	34: 8 *is* good: **b** *is* the man *that* trusteth in him.	835
	37:22 For such as be **b** of him shall inherit	1288
	37:26 and lendeth; and his seed *is* **b**.	1293
	40: 4 **B** *is that* man that maketh the LORD his	835
	41: 1 **B** *is* he that considereth the poor:	835
	41: 2 alive; *and* he shall be **b** upon the earth:	833
	41:13 **B** *be* the LORD God of Israel from	1288
	45: 2 lips: therefore God hath **b** thee for ever.	1288
	49:18 Though whiles he lived **b** his soul:	835
	65: 4 **B** *is* the man whom thou choosest,	835
	66:20 **B** *be* God, which hath not turned away	1288
	68:19 **B** *be* the Lord, *who* daily loadeth us *with*	1288
	68:35 and power unto *his* people. **B** *be* God.	1288
	72:17 shall be **b** in him: all nations shall call	1288
	72:17 in him: all nations shall **call** him **b**.	833
	72:18 **B** *be* the LORD God, the God of Israel,	1288
	72:19 **b** *be* his glorious name for ever: and let	1288
	84: 4 **B** *are* they that dwell in thy house: they	835
	84: 5 **B** *is* the man whose strength *is* in thee;	835
	84:12 of hosts, **b** *is* the man that trusteth in thee.	835
	89:15 **B** *is* the people that know the joyful sound:	835
	89:52 **B** *be* the LORD for evermore. Amen,	1288
	94:12 **B** *is* the man whom thou chastenest,	835
	106: 3 **B** *are* they that keep judgment, *and* he that	835
	106:48 **B** *be* the LORD God of Israel from	1288
	112: 1 **B** *is* the man *that* feareth the LORD,	835
	112: 2 the generation of the upright shall be **b**.	1288
	113: 2 **B** *be* the name of the LORD from this	1288
	115:15 You *are* **b** of the LORD which made	1288
	118:26 **B** *be* he that cometh in the name of	1288
	118:26 we have **b** you out of the house of	1288
	119: 1 **B** *are* the undefiled in the way, who walk	835
	119: 2 **B** *are* they that keep his testimonies,	835
	119:12 **B** *art* thou, O LORD: teach me thy	1288
	124: 6 **B** *be* the LORD, who hath not given us *as*	1288
	128: 1 **B** *is* every one that feareth the LORD;	835
	128: 4 that thus shall the man be **b** that feareth	1288
	135:21 **B** *be* the LORD out of Zion,	1288
	144: 1 **B** *be* the LORD my strength,	1288
	147:13 he hath **b** thy children within thee.	1288
Pr	5:18 Let thy fountain be **b**: and rejoice with	1288
	8:32 for **b** *are they that* keep my ways.	835
	8:34 **B** *is* the man that heareth me, watching	835
	10: 7 The memory of the just *is* **b**: but the name	1293
	20: 7 his integrity: his children *are* **b** after him.	835
	20:21 but the end thereof shall not be **b**.	1288
	22: 9 He that hath a bountiful eye shall be **b**;	1288
	31:28 Her children arise up, and **call** her **b**;	833
Ecc	10:17 **B** *art* thou, O land, when thy king *is* the	835
SS	6: 9 The daughters saw her, and **b** her; *yea,*	833
Isa	19:25 **B** *be* Egypt my people, and Assyria	1288
	30:18 judgment: **b** *are* all they that wait for him.	835
	32:20 **B** *are* ye that sow beside all waters, that	835
	51: 2 him alone, and **b** him, and increased him.	1288
	56: 2 **B** *is* the man *that* doeth this, and the son	835
	61: 9 they *are* the seed *which* the LORD hath **b**.	1288
	65:23 for they *are* the seed of the **b** of	1288
	66: 3 he that burneth incense, *as if* he **b** an idol.	1288
Jer	17: 7 **B** *is* the man that trusteth in the LORD,	1288

Jer	20:14 the day wherein my mother bare me be **b**.	1288
Eze	3:12 *saying,* **B** *be* the glory of the LORD from	1288
Da	2:19 Then Daniel **b** the God of heaven.	1289
	2:20 be the name of God for ever and ever:	1289
	3:28 said, **B** *be* the God of Shadrach, Meshach,	1289
	4:34 I **b** the most High, and I praised and	1289
	12:12 **B** *is* he that waiteth, and cometh to	835
Zec	11: 5 they that sell them say, **B** *be* the LORD;	1288
Mal	3:12 all nations shall **call** you **b**: for ye shall be	833
Mt	5: 3 **B** *are* the poor in spirit: for theirs is	*3107*
	5: 4 **B** *are* they that mourn: for they shall be	*3107*
	5: 5 **B** *are* the meek: for they shall inherit	*3107*
	5: 6 **B** *are* they which do hunger and thirst	*3107*
	5: 7 **B** *are* the merciful: for they shall obtain	*3107*
	5: 8 **B** *are* the pure in heart: for they shall see	*3107*
	5: 9 **B** *are* the peacemakers: for they shall be	*3107*
	5:10 **B** *are* they which are persecuted for	*3107*
	5:11 **B** are ye, when *men* shall revile you, and	*3107*
	11: 6 And **b** *is* he, whosoever shall not be	*3107*
	13:16 But **b** *are* your eyes, for they see: and	*3107*
	14:19 he **b**, and brake, and gave the loaves to	*2127*
	16:17 and said unto him, **B** art thou,	*3107*
	21: 9 **B** *is* he that cometh in the name of	*2127*
	23:39 **B** *is* he that cometh in the name of	*2127*
	24:46 **B** *is* that servant, whom his lord when he	*2127*
	25:34 his right hand, Come, ye **b** of my Father,	*2127*
	26:26 and **b** *it,* and brake *it,* and gave *it* to	*2127*
Mk	6:41 and **b**, and brake the loaves, and gave	*2127*
	8: 7 he **b**, and commanded to set them also	*2127*
	10:16 put *his* hands upon them, and **b** them.	*2127*
	11: 9 **B** *is* he that cometh in the name of	*2127*
	11:10 **B** *be* the kingdom of our father David,	*2127*
	14:22 and **b**, and brake *it,* and gave to them,	*2127*
	14:61 Art thou the Christ, the Son of the **B**?	*2128*
Lk	1:28 *is* with thee: **b** *art* thou among women.	*2127*
	1:42 **B** *art* thou among women, and blessed *is*	*2127*
	1:42 and **b** *is* the fruit of thy womb.	*2127*
	1:45 And **b** *is* she that believed: for there shall	*3107*
	1:48 henceforth all generations shall **call** me **b**.	*3106*
	1:68 be the Lord God of Israel; for he hath	*2128*
	2:28 *up* in his arms, and **b** God, and said,	*2127*
	2:34 And Simeon **b** them, and said unto Mary	*2127*
	6:20 on his disciples, and said, **B** *be* ye poor:	*3107*
	6:21 **B** *are* ye that hunger now: for ye shall be	*3107*
	6:21 **B** *are* ye that weep now: for ye shall laugh	*3107*
	6:22 **B** *are* ye, when men shall hate you, and	*3107*
	7:23 And **b** is **b**, whosoever shall not be	*3107*
	9:16 he **b** them, and brake, and gave to	*2127*
	10:23 **B** *are* the eyes which see *the things that*	*3107*
	11:27 **B** *is* the womb that bare thee, and the	*3107*
	11:28 **b** *are* they that hear the word of God, and	*3107*
	12:37 **B** *are* those servants, whom the lord when	*2127*
	12:38 and find *them* so, **b** *are* those servants.	*3107*
	12:43 **B** *is* that servant, whom his lord when he	*2127*
	13:35 **B** *is* he that cometh in the name of	*2127*
	14:14 And thou shalt be **b**; for they cannot	*3107*
	14:15 **B** *is* he that shall eat bread in the kingdom	*3107*
	19:38 **B** *be* the King that cometh in the name of	*2127*
	23:29 **B** *are* the barren, and the wombs that	*2127*
	24:30 and **b** *it,* and brake, and gave to them.	*2127*
	24:50 and he lift up his hands, and **b** them.	*2127*
	24:51 And it came to pass, while he **b** them,	*2127*
Jn	12:13 **B** *is* the King of Israel that cometh in	*2127*
	20:29 **b** *are* they that have not seen, and *yet*	*3107*
Ac	3:25 shall all the kindreds of the earth be **b**.	*1757*
	20:35 said, It is more **b** to give than to receive.	*3107*
Ro	1:25 more than the Creator, who is **b** for ever.	*2128*
	4: 7 *Saying,* **B** *are* they whose iniquities are	*3107*
	4: 8 **B** *is* the man to whom the Lord will not	*3107*
	9: 5 came, who is over all, God **b** for ever.	*2128*
2Co	1: 3 **B** *be* God, even the Father of our Lord	*2128*
	11:31 which is **b** for evermore, knoweth that I	*2128*
Gal	3: 8 *saying,* In thee shall all nations be **b**.	*1757*
	3: 9 they which be of faith are **b** with faithful	*2127*
Eph	1: 3 **B** *be* the God and Father of our Lord Jesus	*2128*
	1: 3 who hath **b** us with all spiritual blessings	*2127*
1Ti	1:11 According to the glorious gospel of the **b**	*3107*
	6:15 *who is* the **b** and only Potentate, the King	*3107*
Tit	2:13 Looking for *that* **b** hope, and the glorious	*3107*
Heb	7: 1 the slaughter of the kings, and **b** him;	*2127*
	7: 6 and **b** him that had the promises.	*2127*
	7: 7 without all contradiction the less is **b**	*2127*
	11:20 By faith Isaac Jacob and Esau	*2127*
	11:21 he was a dying, **b** both the sons of Joseph;	*2127*
Jas	1:12 **B** *is* the man that endureth temptation:	*3107*
	1:25 the work, this *man* shall be **b** in his deed.	*3107*
1Pe	1: 3 **B** *be* the God and Father of our Lord Jesus	*2128*
Rev	1: 3 **B** *is* he that readeth, and they that hear	*3107*
	14:13 **B** *are* the dead which die in the Lord from	*3107*
	16:15 **B** *is* he that watcheth, and keepeth his	*3107*
	19: 9 **B** *are* they which are called unto	*3107*
	20: 6 **B** and holy *is* he that hath part in the first	*3107*
	22: 7 **b** *is* he that keepeth the sayings of	*3107*
	22:14 **B** *are* they that do his commandments,	*3107*

BLESSEDNESS (3) [BLESS]

Ro	4: 6 Even as David also describeth the **b** of	*3108*
	4: 9 this **b** then upon the circumcision	*3108*
Gal	4:15 Where is then the **b** you spake of? for I	*3108*

BLESSEST (3) [BLESS]

Nu	22: 6 for I wot that *he* whom thou **b** *is* blessed,	1288
1Ch	17:27 for thou **b**, O LORD, and *it shall be*	1288
Ps	65:10 showers: thou **b** the springing thereof.	1288

BLESSETH (8) [BLESS]

Ge	27:29 thee, and blessed *be* he that **b** thee.	1288
Nu	24: 9 Blessed *is* he that **b** thee, and cursed *is* he	1288
Dt	15: 6 For the LORD thy God **b** thee, as he	1288
Ps	10: 3 **b** the covetous, *whom* the LORD	1288
	107:38 **b** them also, so that they are multiplied	1288
Pr	3:33 but he **b** the habitation of the just.	1288
	27:14 He that **b** his friend with a loud voice,	1288
Isa	65:16 That he who **b** himself in the earth shall	1288

BLESSING (67) [BLESS]

Ge	12: 2 thy name great; and thou shalt be a **b**:	1293
	22:17 That in **b** I will bless thee,	1293
	27:12 shall bring a curse upon me, and not a **b**.	1293
	27:30 as soon as Isaac had made an end of **b**	1288
	27:35 with subtilty, and hath taken away thy **b**.	1293
	27:36 behold, now he hath taken away my **b**.	1293
	27:36 said, Hast thou not reserved a **b** for me?	1293
	27:38 father, Hast thou but one **b**, my father?	1293
	27:41 of the **b** wherewith his father blessed him:	1293
	28: 4 give thee the **b** of Abraham, to thee,	1293
	33:11 I pray thee, my **b** that is brought to thee;	1293
	39: 5 the **b** of the LORD was upon all that he	1293
	49:28 every one according to his **b** he blessed	1293
Ex	32:29 he may bestow upon you a **b** *this* day.	1293
Lev	25:21 I will command my **b** upon you in the	1293
Dt	11:26 I set before you *this* day a **b** and a curse;	1293
	11:27 A **b**, if ye obey the commandments of	1293
	11:29 that thou shalt put the **b** upon mount	1293
	12:15 according to the **b** of the LORD thy God	1293
	16:17 according to the **b** of the LORD thy God	1293
	23: 5 God turned the curse into a **b** unto thee,	1293
	28: 8 The LORD shall command the **b** upon	1293
	30: 1 the **b** and the curse, which I have set	1293
	30:19 before you life and death, **b** and cursing:	1293
	33: 1 this *is* the **b**, wherewith Moses the man of	1293
	33: 7 this *is* the **b** of Judah: and he said, Hear,	NIH
	33:16 let the **b** come upon the head of Joseph,	NIH
	33:23 and full *with* the **b** of the LORD:	1293
Jos	15:19 Who answered, Give me a **b**; for thou	1293
Jdg	1:15 she said unto him, Give me a **b**: for thou	1293
1Sa	25:27 now this **b** which thine handmaid hath	1293
2Sa	7:29 with thy **b** let the house of thy servant be	1293
2Ki	5:15 I pray thee, take a **b** of thy servant.	1293
Ne	13: 2 our God turned the curse into a **b**.	1293
Job	29:13 The **b** of him that was ready to perish	1293
Ps	3: 8 thy **b** *is* upon thy people. Selah.	1293
	24: 5 He shall receive the **b** from the LORD,	1293
	109:17 as he delighted not in **b**, so let it be far	1293
	129: 8 by say, The **b** of the LORD *be* upon you:	1293
	133: 3 for there the LORD commanded the **b**,	1293
Pr	10:22 The **b** of the LORD, it maketh rich,	1293
	11:11 By the **b** of the upright the city is exalted:	1293
	11:26 **b** *shall be* upon the head of him that	1293
	24:25 and a good **b** shall come upon them.	1293
Isa	19:24 *even* a **b** in the midst of the land:	1293
	44: 3 thy seed, and my **b** upon thine offspring:	1293
	65: 8 *one* saith, Destroy it not; for a **b** is in it:	1293
Eze	34:26 and the places round about my hill a **b**;	1293
	34:26 in his season; there shall be showers of **b**.	1293
	44:30 that he may cause the **b** to rest in thine	1293
Joel	2:14 and repent, and leave a **b** behind him;	1293
Zec	8:13 so will I save you, and ye shall be a **b**:	1293
Mal	3:10 of heaven, and pour you out a **b**,	1293
Lk	24:53 in the temple, praising and **b** God.	*2127*
Ro	15:29 I shall come in the fulness of the **b** of	*2129*
1Co	10:16 The cup of **b** which we bless, is it not	*2129*
Gal	3:14 That the **b** of Abraham might come on	*2129*
Heb	6: 7 whom it is dressed, receiveth **b** from God:	*2129*
	6:14 Surely **b** I will bless thee, and multiplying	*2127*
	12:17 when he would have inherited the **b**,	*2129*
Jas	3:10 Out of the same mouth proceedeth **b** and	*2129*
1Pe	3: 9 but contrariwise **b**; knowing that ye are	*2127*
	3: 9 called, that ye should inherit a **b**.	*2129*
Rev	5:12 strength, and honour, and glory, and **b**.	*2129*
	5:13 **b**, and honour, and glory, and power,	*2129*
	7:12 **B**, and glory, and wisdom,	*2129*

BLESSINGS (12) [BLESS]

Ge	49:25 who shall bless thee *with* **b** of heaven	1293
	49:25 **b** of the deep that lieth under, blessings of	1293
	49:25 **b** of the breasts, and of the womb:	1293
	49:26 The **b** of thy father have prevailed above	1293
	49:26 **b** of my progenitors unto the utmost	1293
Dt	28: 2 all these **b** shall come on thee,	1293
Jos	8:34 the words of the law, the **b** and cursings,	1293
Ps	21: 3 For thou preventest him *with* the **b** of	1293
Pr	10: 6 **B** *are* upon the head of the just:	1293
	28:20 A faithful man shall abound with **b**:	1293
Mal	2: 2 a curse upon you, and will curse your **b**:	1293
Eph	1: 3 who hath blessed us with all spiritual **b** in	*2129*

BLEW (23) [BLOW]

Jos	6: 8 the LORD, and **b** with the trumpets:	8628
	6: 9 the priests that **b** *with* the trumpets,	8628
	6:13 on continually, and **b** with the trumpets:	8628
	6:16 when the priests **b** with the trumpets,	8628
	6:20 the people shouted when *the priests* **b**	8628
Jdg	3:27 that he **b** a trumpet in the mountain of	8628
	6:34 came upon Gideon, and he **b** a trumpet;	8628
	7:19 **b** the trumpets, and brake the pitchers	8628
	7:20 the three companies **b** the trumpets,	8628
	7:22 the three hundred **b** the trumpets,	8628
1Sa	13: 3 the Philistines heard *of it.* And Saul **b**	8628

B

2Sa	2:28 So Joab **b** a trumpet, and all the people	8628
	18:16 Joab **b** the trumpet, and the people	8628
	20: 1 he **b** a trumpet, and said, We have no part	8628
	20:22 he **b** a trumpet, and they retired from	8628
1Ki	1:39 they **b** the trumpet; and all the people	8628
2Ki	9:13 and **b** with trumpets, saying, Jehu is king.	8628
	11:14 of the land rejoiced, and **b** with trumpets:	8628
Mt	7:25 the winds **b**, and beat upon that house;	4154
	7:27 the winds **b**, and beat upon that house;	4154
Jn	6:18 arose by reason of a great wind that **b**.	4154
Ac	27:13 And when the south wind **b** softly,	5285
	28:13 and after one day the south wind **b**,	1920

BLIND (82) [BLINDED, BLINDETH,
 BLINDFOLDED, BLINDNESS]

Ex	4:11 the dumb, or deaf, or the seeing, or the **b**?	5787
Lev	19:14 nor put a stumblingblock before the **b**, but	5787
	21:18 a **b** man, or a lame, or he that hath a flat	5787
	22:22 **B**, or broken, or maimed, or having a wen	5788
Dt	15:21 *if it be* lame, or **b**, or *have* any ill blemish,	5787
	16:19 for a gift doth **b** the eyes of the wise,	5786
	27:18 Cursed *be* he that maketh the **b** to wander	5787
	28:29 as the **b** gropeth in darkness, and thou	5787
1Sa	12: 3 *any* bribe to **b** mine eyes therewith?	5956
2Sa	5: 6 thou take away the **b** and the lame,	5787
	5: 8 the Jebusites, and the lame and the **b**,	5787
	5: 8 The **b** and the lame shall not come into	5787
Job	29:15 I was eyes to the **b**, and feet *was* I to	5787
Ps	146: 8 The Lord openeth the *eyes of* the **b**:	5787
Isa	29:18 eyes of the **b** shall see out of obscurity,	5787
	35: 5 the eyes of the **b** shall be opened,	5787
	42: 7 To open the **b** eyes, to bring out	5787
	42:16 will bring the **b** by a way *that* they knew	5787
	42:18 ye deaf; and look, ye **b**, that *ye* may see.	5787
	42:19 Who *is* **b**, but my servant? or deaf, as my	5787
	42:19 who *is* **b** as he that is perfect, and blind	5787
	42:19 is perfect, and **b** as the Lord's servant?	5787
	43: 8 Bring forth the **b** people that have eyes,	5787
	56:10 His watchmen *are* **b**: they are all ignorant,	5787
	59:10 We grope for the wall like the **b**,	5787
Jer	31: 8 *and* with them the **b** and the lame,	5787
La	4:14 They have wandered *as* **b** *men* in	5787
Zep	1:17 that they shall walk like **b** *men*, because	5787
Mal	1: 8 if ye offer the **b** for sacrifice, *is it* not evil?	5787
Mt	9:27 two **b** men followed him, crying,	5185
	9:28 into the house, the **b** men came to him:	5185
	11: 5 The **b** receive their sight, and the lame	5185
	12:22 one possessed with a devil, **b**, and dumb:	5185
	12:22 insomuch that the **b** and dumb both spake	5185
	15:14 they be **b** leaders of the blind. And if	5185
	15:14 they be blind leaders of the **b**. And if	5185
	15:14 And if the **b** lead the blind, both shall fall	5185
	15:14 And if the blind lead the **b**, both shall fall	5185
	15:30 **b**, dumb, maimed, and many others,	5185
	15:31 the lame to walk, and the **b** to see:	5185
	20:30 two **b** men sitting by the way side,	5185
	21:14 And *the* **b** and *the* lame came to him in	5185
	23:16 Woe unto you, ye **b** guides, which say,	5185
	23:17 *Ye* fools and **b**: for whether is greater,	5185
	23:19 *Ye* fools and **b**: for whether *is* greater,	5185
	23:24 *Ye* **b** guides, which strain out a gnat, and	5185
	23:26 *Thou* **b** Pharisee, cleanse first that *which*	5185
Mk	8:22 and they bring a **b** man unto him,	5185
	8:23 And he took the **b** man by the hand,	5185
	10:46 of people, **b** Bartimeus, the son of Timeus,	5185
	10:49 And they call the **b** man, saying unto him,	5185
	10:51 The **b** man said unto him, Lord, that I	5185
Lk	4:18 and recovering of sight to the **b**,	5185
	6:39 unto them, Can the **b** lead the blind?	5185
	6:39 unto them, Can the blind lead the **b**?	5185
	7:21 and unto many *that were* **b** he gave sight.	5185
	7:22 how that the **b** see, the lame walk,	5185
	14:13 the poor, the maimed, the lame, the **b**:	5185
	14:21 and the maimed, and the halt, and the **b**.	5185
	18:35 a certain **b** man sat by the way side	5185
Jn	5: 3 a great multitude of impotent *folk*, of **b**,	5185
	9: 1 saw a man *which was* **b** from *his* birth.	5185
	9: 2 or his parents, that he was born **b**?	5185
	9: 6 he anointed the eyes of the **b** man with	5185
	9: 8 which before had seen him that he was **b**,	5185
	9:13 to the Pharisees him that aforetime was **b**.	5185
	9:17 They say unto the **b** man again,	5185
	9:18 that he had been **b**, and received his sight,	5185
	9:19 Is this your son, who ye say was born **b**?	5185
	9:20 this is our son, and that he was born **b**:	5185
	9:24 again called they the man that was **b**,	5185
	9:25 I know, that, whereas I was **b**, now I see.	5185
	9:32 opened the eyes of one that was born **b**.	5185
	9:39 and that they which see might be made **b**.	5185
	9:40 and said unto him, Are we **b** also?	5185
	9:41 Jesus said unto them, If ye were **b**,	5185
	10:21 a devil. Can a devil open the eyes of the **b**?	5185
	11:37 this *man*, which opened the eyes of the **b**,	5185
Ac	13:11 thou shalt be **b**, not seeing the sun for a	5185
Ro	2:19 that thyself art a guide of the **b**,	5185
2Pe	1: 9 But he that lacketh these *things* is **b**,	5185
Rev	3:17 miserable, and poor, and **b**, and naked:	5185

BLINDED (5) [BLIND]

Jn	12:40 He hath **b** their eyes, and hardened their	5186
Ro	11: 7 hath obtained *it*, and the rest were **b**,	4456
2Co	3:14 But their minds were **b**: for until this day	4456
	4: 4 In whom the god of this world hath **b**	5186
1Jn	2:11 because that darkness hath **b** his eyes.	5186

BLINDETH (1) [BLIND]

Ex	23: 8 for the gift **b** the wise, and perverteth	5786

BLINDFOLDED (1) [BLIND]

Lk	22:64 when they had **b** him, they stroke him	4028

BLINDNESS (7) [BLIND]

Ge	19:11 *were* at the door of the house with **b**,	5575
Dt	28:28 and **b**, and astonishment of heart:	5788
2Ki	6:18 Smite this people, I pray thee, with **b**.	5575
	6:18 he smote them with **b** according to	5575
Zec	12: 4 smite every horse of the people with **b**.	5788
Ro	11:25 that **b** in part is happened to Israel, until	4457
Eph	4:18 in them, because of the **b** of their heart:	4457

BLOCKED See FENCED

BLOOD (447) [BLOODGUILTINESS,
 BLOODTHIRSTY, BLOODY]

Ge	4:10 voice of thy brother's **b** crieth unto me	1818
	4:11 to receive thy brother's **b** from thy hand.	1818
	9: 4 *which is* the **b** thereof, shall you not eat.	1818
	9: 5 surely your **b** of your lives will I require;	1818
	9: 6 Whoso sheddeth man's **b**, by man shall	1818
	9: 6 man's blood, by man shall his **b** be shed:	1818
	37:22 Shed no **b**, *but* cast him into this pit that	1818
	37:26 if we slay our brother, and conceal his **b**?	1818
	37:31 of the goats, and dipped the coat in the **b**;	1818
	42:22 therefore, behold, also his **b** is required.	1818
	49:11 in wine, and his clothes in the **b** of grapes:	1818
Ex	4: 9 river shall become **b** upon the dry *land*.	1818
	7:17 in the river, and they shall be turned to **b**.	1818
	7:19 pools of water, that they may become **b**;	1818
	7:19 there may be **b** throughout all the land	1818
	7:20 that *were* in the river were turned to **b**.	1818
	7:21 there was **b** throughout all the land of	1818
	12: 7 they shall take of the **b**, and strike *it* on	1818
	12:13 the **b** shall be to you for a token upon	1818
	12:13 where you are: and when I see the **b**,	1818
	12:22 dip *it* in the **b** that *is* in the bason,	1818
	12:22 the two side posts with the **b** that *is* in	1818
	12:23 when he seeth the **b** upon the lintel,	1818
	22: 2 he die, *there shall* no **b** *be shed* for him.	1818
	22: 3 upon him, *there shall be* **b** *shed* for him;	1818
	23:18 Thou shalt not offer the **b** of my sacrifice	1818
	24: 6 Moses took half of the **b**, and put *it in*	1818
	24: 6 and half of the **b** he sprinkled on the altar.	1818
	24: 8 Moses took the **b**, and sprinkled *it* on	1818
	24: 8 and said, Behold the **b** of the covenant,	1818
	29:12 thou shalt take of the **b** of the bullock,	1818
	29:12 all the **b** beside the bottom of the altar.	1818
	29:16 shalt take his **b**, and sprinkle *it* round	1818
	29:20 take of his **b**, and put *it* upon the tip of	1818
	29:20 sprinkle the **b** upon the altar round about.	1818
	29:21 thou shalt take of the **b** that *is* upon	1818
	30:10 the **b** of the sin offering of atonements:	1818
	34:25 Thou shalt not offer the **b** of my sacrifice	1818
Lev	1: 5 shall bring the **b**, and sprinkle the blood	1818
	1: 5 sprinkle the **b** round about upon the altar	1818
	1:11 shall sprinkle his **b** round about upon	1818
	1:15 **b** thereof shall be wrung out at the side	1818
	3: 2 sons the priests shall sprinkle the **b**	1818
	3: 8 Aaron's sons shall sprinkle the **b** thereof	1818
	3:13 the sons of Aaron shall sprinkle the **b**	1818
	3:17 dwellings, *that* ye eat neither fat nor **b**.	1818
	4: 5 is anointed shall take of the bullock's **b**,	1818
	4: 6 the priest shall dip his finger in the **b**,	1818
	4: 6 sprinkle of the **b** seven times before	1818
	4: 7 the priest shall put *some* of the **b** upon	1818
	4: 7 shall pour all the **b** of the bullock at	1818
	4:16 **b** to the tabernacle of the congregation:	1818
	4:17 priest shall dip his finger *in some* of the **b**,	1818
	4:18 he shall put *some* of the **b** upon the horns	1818
	4:18 shall pour out all the **b** at the bottom of	1818
	4:25 the priest shall take of the **b** of the sin	1818
	4:25 shall pour out his **b** at the bottom of	1818
	4:30 the priest shall take of the **b** thereof with	1818
	4:30 shall pour out all the **b** thereof at	1818
	4:34 the priest shall take of the **b** of the sin	1818
	4:34 shall pour out all the **b** thereof at	1818
	5: 9 shall sprinkle of the **b** of the sin offering	1818
	5: 9 the rest of the **b** shall be wrung out at	1818
	6:27 when there is sprinkled of the **b** thereof	1818
	6:30 whereof *any* of the **b** is brought into	1818
	7: 2 **b** thereof shall he sprinkle round about	1818
	7:14 shall be the priest's that sprinkleth the **b**	1818
	7:26 Moreover ye shall eat no *manner of* **b**,	1818
	7:27 soul *it be* that eateth any *manner of* **b**,	1818
	7:33 that offereth the **b** of the peace offerings,	1818
	8:15 slew *it;* and Moses took the **b**, and put *it*	1818
	8:15 poured the **b** at the bottom of the altar,	1818
	8:19 Moses sprinkled the **b** upon the altar	1818
	8:23 he slew *it;* and Moses took of the **b** of it,	1818
	8:24 Moses put of the **b** upon the tip of their	1818
	8:24 Moses sprinkled the **b** upon the altar	1818
	8:30 of the **b** which *was* upon the altar,	1818
	9: 9 the sons of Aaron brought the **b** unto him:	1818
	9: 9 he dipt his finger in the **b**, and put *it* upon	1818
	9: 9 out the **b** at the bottom of the altar:	1818
	9:12 Aaron's sons presented unto him the **b**,	1818
	9:18 Aaron's sons presented unto him the **b**,	1818
	10:18 the **b** of it was not brought in within	1818
	12: 4 continue in the **b** of her purifying three	1818
	12: 5 she shall continue in the **b** of her purifying	1818
	12: 7 shall be cleansed from the issue of her **b**.	1818

Lev	14: 6 living bird in the **b** of the bird *that was*	1818
	14:14 the priest shall take *some* of the **b** of	1818
	14:17 upon the **b** of the trespass offering:	1818
	14:25 the priest shall take *some* of the **b** of	1818
	14:28 upon the place of the **b** of the trespass	1818
	14:51 dip them in the **b** of the slain bird,	1818
	14:52 he shall cleanse the house with the **b** of	1818
	15:19 an issue, *and* her issue in her flesh be **b**,	1818
	15:25 if a woman have an issue of her **b** many	1818
	16:14 he shall take of the **b** of the bullock,	1818
	16:14 of the **b** with his finger seven times.	1818
	16:15 bring his **b** within the vail, and do with	1818
	16:15 do with that **b** as he did with the blood of	1818
	16:15 do with that blood as he did with the **b** of	1818
	16:18 shall take of the **b** of the bullock, and of	1818
	16:18 of the **b** of the goat, and put *it* upon	1818
	16:19 he shall sprinkle of the **b** upon it with his	1818
	16:27 **b** was brought in to make atonement	1818
	17: 4 **b** shall be imputed unto that man; he hath	1818
	17: 4 he hath shed **b**; and that man shall be cut	1818
	17: 6 priest shall sprinkle the **b** upon the altar	1818
	17:10 among you, that eateth any *manner of* **b**;	1818
	17:10 set my face against *that* soul that eateth **b**,	1818
	17:11 For the life of the flesh *is* in the **b**:	1818
	17:11 it *is* the **b** that maketh an atonement for	1818
	17:12 of Israel, No soul of you shall eat **b**,	1818
	17:12 stranger that sojourneth among you eat **b**.	1818
	17:13 he shall even pour out the **b** thereof,	1818
	17:14 all flesh; the **b** of it *is* for the life thereof:	1818
	17:14 Ye shall eat the **b** of no *manner of* flesh:	1818
	17:14 for the life of all flesh *is* the **b** thereof:	1818
	19:16 neither shalt thou stand against the **b** of	1818
	19:26 Ye shall not eat *any thing* with the **b**:	1818
	20: 9 or his mother; his **b** *shall be* upon him.	1818
	20:11 put to death; their **b** *shall be* upon them.	1818
	20:12 their **b** *shall be* upon them.	1818
	20:13 put to death; their **b** *shall be* upon them.	1818
	20:16 put to death; their **b** *shall be* upon them.	1818
	20:18 she hath uncovered the fountain of her **b**:	1818
	20:27 with stones: their **b** *shall be* upon them.	1818
Nu	18:17 thou shalt sprinkle their **b** upon the altar,	1818
	19: 4 Eleazar the priest shall take of her **b** with	1818
	19: 4 sprinkle of her **b** directly before	1818
	19: 5 skin, and her flesh, and her **b**, with her	1818
	23:24 of the prey, and drink the **b** of the slain.	1818
	35:19 The revenger of **b** himself shall slay	1818
	35:21 the revenger of **b** shall slay the murderer,	1818
	35:24 the revenger of **b** according to these	1818
	35:25 out of the hand of the revenger of **b**,	1818
	35:27 the revenger of **b** find him without	1818
	35:27 and the revenger of **b** kill the slayer;	1818
	35:27 kill the slayer; he shall not be guilty of **b**:	1818
	35:33 wherein ye *are:* for **b** it defileth the land:	1818
	35:33 land cannot be cleansed of the **b** that is	1818
	35:33 but by the **b** of him that shed it.	1818
Dt	12:16 Only ye shall not eat the **b**; ye shall pour	1818
	12:23 Only be sure that thou eat not the **b**:	1818
	12:23 the **b** *is* the life; and thou mayest not eat	1818
	12:27 the flesh and the **b**, upon the altar of	1818
	12:27 the **b** of thy sacrifices shall be poured out	1818
	15:23 Only thou shalt not eat the **b** thereof;	1818
	17: 8 between **b** and blood, between plea and	1818
	17: 8 between blood and **b**, between plea and	1818
	19: 6 the avenger of the **b** pursue the slayer,	1818
	19:10 That innocent **b** be not shed in thy land,	1818
	19:10 *for* an inheritance, and *so* **b** be upon thee.	1818
	19:12 him into the hand of the avenger of **b**,	1818
	19:13 shall put away the *guilt of* innocent **b**	1818
	21: 7 and say, Our hands have not shed this **b**,	1818
	21: 8 lay not innocent **b** unto thy people of	1818
	21: 8 And the **b** shall be forgiven them.	1818
	21: 9 the *guilt of* innocent **b** from among you,	1818
	22: 8 that thou bring not **b** upon thine house,	1818
	32:14 thou didst drink the pure **b** of the grape.	1818
	32:42 I will make mine arrows drunk with **b**,	1818
	32:42 *and that* with the **b** of the slain and of	1818
	32:43 for he will avenge the **b** of his servants,	1818
Jos	2:19 his **b** *shall be* upon his head, and we	1818
	2:19 his **b** *shall be* on our head, if *any* hand be	1818
	20: 3 be your refuge from the avenger of **b**,	1818
	20: 5 if the avenger of **b** pursue after him, then	1818
	20: 9 not die by the hand of the avenger of **b**,	1818
Jdg	9:24 their **b** be laid upon Abimelech their	1818
1Sa	14:32 and the people did eat *them* with the **b**.	1818
	14:33 the Lord, in that they eat with the **b**.	1818
	14:34 not against the Lord in eating with the **b**.	1818
	19: 5 then wilt thou sin against innocent **b**,	1818
	25:26 withholden thee from coming to *shed* **b**,	1818
	25:31 either that thou hast shed **b** causeless,	1818
	25:33 kept me this day from coming to *shed* **b**,	1818
	26:20 let not my **b** fall to the earth before the	1818
2Sa	1:16 said unto him, Thy **b** *be* upon thy head;	1818
	1:22 From the **b** of the slain, from the fat of	1818
	3:27 he died, for the **b** of Asahel his brother.	1818
	3:28 ever from the **b** of Abner the son of Ner:	1818
	4:11 therefore now require his **b** of your hand,	1818
	14:11 the revengers of **b** to destroy any more,	1818
	16: 8 upon thee all the **b** of the house of Saul,	1818
	20:12 Amasa wallowed in **b** in the midst of	1818
	23:17 *is not this* the **b** of the men that went in	1818
1Ki	2: 5 shed the **b** of war in peace, and put	1818
	2: 5 put the **b** of war upon his girdle that *was*	1818
	2: 9 bring thou down *to* the grave with **b**.	1818
	2:31 thou mayest take away the innocent **b**,	1818
	2:32 the Lord shall return his **b** upon his own	1818

B

1Ki 2:33 **b** shall therefore return upon the head 1818
 2:37 thy **b** shall be upon thine own head. 1818
 18:28 till the **b** gushed out upon them. 1818
 21:19 In the place where dogs licked the **b** of 1818
 21:19 the blood of Naboth shall dogs lick thy **b**, 1818
 22:35 the **b** ran out of the wound into the midst 1818
 22:38 the dogs licked up his **b**; and they washed 1818
2Ki 3:22 the water on the other side *as* red as **b**: 1818
 3:23 they said, This *is* **b**: the kings are surely 1818
 9: 7 that I may avenge the **b** of my servants 1818
 9: 7 the **b** of all the servants of the Lᴏʀᴅ, 1818
 9:26 Surely I have seen yesterday the **b** of 1818
 9:26 and the **b** of his sons, saith the Lᴏʀᴅ; 1818
 9:33 *some* of her **b** was sprinkled on the wall, 1818
 16:13 sprinkled the **b** of his peace offerings, 1818
 16:15 sprinkle upon it all the **b** of the burnt 1818
 16:15 offering, and all the **b** of the sacrifice. 1818
 21:16 Moreover Manasseh shed innocent **b** 1818
 24: 4 also *for* the innocent **b** that he shed: for 1818
 24: 4 for he filled Jerusalem *with* innocent **b**; 1818
1Ch 11:19 *I* should do this *thing:* shall I drink the **b** 1818
 22: 8 Thou hast shed **b** abundantly, 1818
 22: 8 thou hast shed much **b** upon the earth 1818
 28: 3 *hast been* a man of war, and hast shed **b**. 1818
2Ch 19:10 between **b** and blood, between law and 1818
 19:10 between blood and **b**, between law and 1818
 24:25 for the **b** of the sons of Jehoiada the priest, 1818
 29:22 the priests received the **b**, and sprinkled 1818
 29:22 they sprinkled the **b** upon the altar. 1818
 29:22 and they sprinkled the **b** upon the altar. 1818
 29:24 made reconciliation with their **b** upon 1818
 30:16 the priests sprinkled the **b**, *which they* 1818
 35:11 priests sprinkled the **b** from their hands, NIH
Job 16:18 cover not thou my **b**, and let my cry have 1818
 39:30 Her young ones also suck up **b**: and 1818
Ps 9:12 When he maketh inquisition for **b**, 1818
 16: 4 their drink offerings of **b** will I not offer, 1818
 30: 9 What profit *is there* in my **b**, when I go 1818
 50:13 the flesh of bulls, or drink the **b** of goats? 1818
 58:10 he shall wash his feet in the **b** of 1818
 68:23 That thy foot may be dipped in the **b** of 1818
 72:14 and precious shall their **b** be in his sight. 1818
 78:44 had turned their rivers into **b**; 1818
 79: 3 Their **b** have they shed like water round 1818
 79:10 of the **b** of thy servants which is shed. 1818
 94:21 righteous, and condemn the innocent **b**. 1818
 105:29 He turned their waters into **b**, 1818
 106:38 shed innocent **b**, *even* the blood of their 1818
 106:38 *even* the **b** of their sons and of their 1818
 106:38 and the land was polluted with **b**. 1818
Pr 1:11 Come with us, let us lay wait for **b**, 1818
 1:16 feet run to evil, and make haste to shed **b**. 1818
 1:18 they lay wait for their own **b**; they lurk 1818
 6:17 and hands that shed innocent **b**, 1818
 12: 6 of the wicked *are* to lie in wait *for* **b**: 1818
 28:17 A man that doeth violence to the **b** of *any* 1818
 30:33 the wringing of the nose bringeth forth **b**: 1818
Isa 1:11 I delight not in the **b** of bullocks, 1818
 1:15 I will not hear: your hands are full *of* **b**. 1818
 4: 4 shall have purged the **b** of Jerusalem from 1818
 9: 5 confused noise, and garments rolled in **b**; 1818
 15: 9 For the waters of Dimon shall be full *of* **b**: 1818
 26:21 the earth also shall disclose her **b**, 1818
 33:15 that stoppeth his ears from hearing of **b**, 1818
 34: 3 mountains shall be melted with their **b**. 1818
 34: 6 The sword of the Lᴏʀᴅ is filled *with* **b**, 1818
 34: 6 *and* with the **b** of lambs and goats, 1818
 34: 7 their land shall be soaked with **b**, 1818
 49:26 they shall be drunken with their own **b**, 1818
 59: 3 For your hands are defiled with **b**, 1818
 59: 7 and they make haste to shed innocent **b**: 1818
 63: 3 their **b** shall be sprinkled upon my 5332
 66: 3 an oblation, *as if he offered* swine's **b**; 1818
Jer 2:34 in thy skirts is found the **b** of the souls 1818
 7: 6 and shed not innocent **b** in this place, 1818
 18:21 pour out their **b** by the force of the sword; NIH
 19: 4 have filled this place *with* the **b** of 1818
 22: 3 neither shed innocent **b** in this place. 1818
 22:17 to shed innocent **b**, and for oppression, 1818
 26:15 ye shall surely bring innocent **b** upon 1818
 46:10 be satiate and made drunk with their **b**: 1818
 48:10 he that keepeth back his sword from **b**. 1818
 51:35 my **b** upon the inhabitants of Chaldea, 1818
La 4:13 have shed the **b** of the just in the midst 1818
 4:14 they have polluted themselves with **b**, 1818
Eze 3:18 but his **b** will I require at thine hand. 1818
 3:20 but his **b** will I require at thine hand. 1818
 5:17 pestilence and **b** shall pass through thee; 1818
 9: 9 the land is full *of* **b**, and the city full *of* 1818
 14:19 pour out my fury upon it in **b**, to cut off 1818
 16: 6 and saw thee polluted in thine own **b**, 1818
 16: 6 I said unto thee *when thou wast* in thy **b**, 1818
 16: 6 I said unto thee *when thou wast* in thy **b**, 1818
 16: 9 I throughly washed away thy **b** from thee, 1818
 16:22 and bare, *and* wast polluted in thy **b**. 1818
 16:36 by the **b** of thy children, which thou didst 1818
 16:38 that break wedlock and shed **b** are judged; 1818
 16:38 and I will give thee **b** in fury and jealousy. 1818
 18:10 a shedder of **b**, and *that* doeth the like to 1818
 18:13 shall surely die; his **b** shall be upon him. 1818
 19:10 thy mother *is* like a vine in thy **b**, 1818
 21:32 thy **b** shall be in the midst of the land; 1818
 22: 3 The city sheddeth **b** in the midst of it, 1818
 22: 4 Thou art become guilty in thy **b** that thou 1818
 22: 6 were in thee to their power to shed **b**. 1818

Eze 22: 9 In thee are men that carry tales to shed **b**: 1818
 22:12 In thee have they taken gifts to shed **b**; 1818
 22:13 at thy **b** which hath been in the midst of 1818
 22:27 to shed **b**, *and* to destroy souls, to get 1818
 23:37 **b** *is* in their hands, and with their idols 1818
 23:45 after the manner of *women* that shed **b**; 1818
 23:45 *are* adulteresses, and **b** *is* in their hands. 1818
 24: 7 For her **b** is in the midst of her; she set it 1818
 24: 8 I have set her **b** upon the top of a rock, 1818
 28:23 into her pestilence, and **b** into her streets; 1818
 32: 6 I will also water with thy **b** the land 1818
 33: 4 his **b** shall be upon his own head. 1818
 33: 5 not warning; his **b** shall be upon him. 1818
 33: 6 **b** will I require at the watchman's hand. 1818
 33: 8 but his **b** will I require at thine hand. 1818
 33:25 Ye eat with the **b**, and lift up your eyes 1818
 33:25 your eyes toward your idols, and shed **b**: 1818
 35: 5 hast shed *the* **b** *of* the children of Israel NIH
 35: 6 I will prepare thee unto **b**, and blood shall 1818
 35: 6 thee unto blood, and **b** shall pursue thee: 1818
 35: 6 sith thou hast not hated **b**, even blood 1818
 35: 6 not hated blood, even **b** shall pursue thee. 1818
 36:18 the **b** that they had shed upon the land, 1818
 38:22 against him with pestilence and with **b**; 1818
 39:17 Israel, that ye may eat flesh, and drink **b**. 1818
 39:18 drink the **b** of the princes of the earth, 1818
 39:19 *ye* be full, and drink **b** till *ye* be drunken, 1818
 43:18 and to sprinkle **b** thereon. 1818
 43:20 thou shalt take of the **b** thereof, and put *it* 1818
 44: 7 the fat and the **b**, and they have broken 1818
 44:15 me to offer unto me the fat and the **b**, 1818
 45:19 the priest shall take of the **b** of the sin 1818
Hos 1: 4 I will avenge the **b** of Jezreel upon 1818
 4: 2 they break out, and **b** toucheth blood. 1818
 4: 2 they break out, and blood toucheth **b**. 1818
 6: 8 that work iniquity, *and* is polluted with **b**. 1818
 12:14 therefore shall he leave his **b** upon him, 1818
Joel 2:30 the earth, **b**, and fire, and pillars of smoke. 1818
 2:31 the moon into **b**, before the great and 1818
 3:19 they have shed innocent **b** in their land. 1818
 3:21 For I will cleanse their **b** *that* I have not 1818
Jnh 1:14 life, and lay not upon us innocent **b**: 1818
Mic 3:10 They build up Zion with **b**, 1818
 7: 2 they all lie in wait for **b**; they hunt every 1818
Hab 2: 8 because of men's **b**, and *for* the violence 1818
 2:12 Woe to him that buildeth a town with **b**, 1818
 2:17 because of men's **b**, and *for* the violence 1818
Zep 1:17 their **b** shall be poured out as dust, 1818
Zec 9: 7 I will take away his **b** out of his mouth, 1818
 9:11 by the **b** of thy covenant I have sent forth 1818
Mt 9:20 which was **diseased with an issue of b** 131
 16:17 *flesh and* **b** hath not revealed *it* unto thee, 129
 23:30 with them in the **b** of the prophets. 129
 23:35 upon you may come all the righteous **b** 129
 23:35 the **b** of righteous Abel unto the blood 129
 23:35 the blood of righteous Abel unto the **b** 129
 26:28 For this is my **b** of the new testament, 129
 27: 4 in that I have betrayed the innocent **b**. 129
 27: 6 the treasury, because it is the price of **b**. 129
 27: 8 was called, The field of **b**, unto this day. 129
 27:24 I am innocent of the **b** of this just *person:* 129
 27:25 said, His **b** *be* on us, and on our children. 129
Mk 5:25 which had an issue of **b** twelve years, 129
 5:29 And straightway the fountain of her **b** was 129
 14:24 This is my **b** of the new testament, 129
Lk 8:43 And a woman having an issue of **b** twelve 129
 8:44 and immediately her issue of **b** stanched. 129
 11:50 That the **b** of all the prophets, which was 129
 11:51 From the **b** of Abel unto the blood of 129
 11:51 From the blood of Abel unto the **b** of 129
 13: 1 whose **b** Pilate had mingled with their 129
 22:20 This cup *is* the new testament in my **b**, 129
 22:44 his sweat was as it were great drops of **b** 129
Jn 1:13 Which were born, not of **b**, nor of the will 129
 6:53 and drink his **b**, ye have no life in you. 129
 6:54 and drinketh my **b**, hath eternal life; 129
 6:55 is meat indeed, and my **b** is drink indeed. 129
 6:56 and drinketh my **b**, dwelleth in me, and I 129
 19:34 and forthwith came there out **b** and water. 129
Ac 1:19 Aceldama, that is to say, The field of **b**. 129
 2:19 **b**, and fire, and vapour of smoke: 129
 2:20 and the moon into **b**, before *that* great and 129
 5:28 and intend to bring this man's **b** upon us. 129
 15:20 and *from* things strangled, and *from* **b**. 129
 15:29 and from **b**, and from things strangled, 129
 17:26 And hath made of one **b** all nations of men 129
 18: 6 them, Your **b** *be* upon your own heads; 129
 20:26 that I *am* pure from the **b** of all *men*. 129
 20:28 which he hath purchased with his own **b**. 129
 21:25 and from **b**, and from strangled, 129
 22:20 And when the **b** of thy martyr Stephen was 129
Ro 3:15 Their feet *are* swift to shed **b**: 129
 3:25 *to be* a propitiation through faith in his **b**, 129
 5: 9 more then, being now justified by his **b**, 129
1Co 10:16 is it not the communion of the **b** of Christ? 129
 11:25 This cup is the new testament in my **b**: 129
 11:27 shall be guilty of the body and **b** of the Lord. 129
 15:50 and **b** cannot inherit the kingdom of God; 129
Gal 1:16 I conferred not with flesh and **b**: 129
Eph 1: 7 whom we have redemption through his **b**, 129
 2:13 far off are made nigh by the **b** of Christ. 129
 6:12 For we wrestle not against flesh and **b**, but 129
Col 1:14 whom we have redemption through his **b**, 129
 1:20 having made peace through the **b** of his 129
Heb 2:14 as the children are partakers of flesh and **b**, 129

Heb 9: 7 not without **b**, which he offered for himself, 129
 9:12 by the **b** of goats and calves, 129
 9:12 by his own **b** he entered in once into 129
 9:13 For if the **b** of bulls and of goats, 129
 9:14 How much more shall the **b** of Christ, 129
 9:18 first *testament* was dedicated without **b**. 129
 9:19 he took the **b** of calves and of goats, 129
 9:20 This *is* the **b** of the testament which God 129
 9:21 Moreover he sprinkled with **b** both 129
 9:22 all *things* are by the law purged with **b**; 129
 9:22 without **shedding of b** is no remission. 130
 9:25 the holy *place* every year with **b** of others; 129
 10: 4 For *it is* not possible that the **b** of bulls and 129
 10:19 boldness to enter into the holiest by the **b** 129
 10:29 and hath counted the **b** of the covenant, 129
 11:28 kept the passover, and the sprinkling of **b**, 129
 12: 4 Ye have not yet resisted unto **b**, 129
 12:24 and to the **b** of sprinkling, that speaketh 129
 13:11 whose **b** is brought into the sanctuary by 129
 13:12 might sanctify the people with his own **b**, 129
 13:20 through the **b** of the everlasting covenant, 129
1Pe 1: 2 and sprinkling of the **b** of Jesus Christ: 129
 1:19 But with the precious **b** of Christ, as of a 129
1Jn 1: 7 the **b** of Jesus Christ his Son cleanseth us 129
 5: 6 This is he that came by water and **b**, 129
 5: 6 not by water only, but by water and **b**. 129
 5: 8 earth, the Spirit, and the water, and the **b**: 129
Rev 1: 5 and washed us from our sins in his own **b**, 129
 5: 9 hast redeemed us to God by thy **b** out of 129
 6:10 avenge our **b** on them that dwell on 129
 6:12 of hair, and the moon became as **b**; 129
 7:14 made them white in the **b** of the Lamb. 129
 8: 7 followed hail and fire mingled with **b**, 129
 8: 8 and the third *part* of the sea became **b**; 129
 11: 6 have power over waters to turn them to **b**, 129
 12:11 And they overcame him by the **b** of 129
 14:20 and **b** came out of the winepress, *even* unto 129
 16: 3 and it became as the **b** of a dead *man:* and 129
 16: 4 fountains of waters; and they became **b**. 129
 16: 6 For they have shed the **b** of saints and 129
 16: 6 and thou hast given them **b** to drink; 129
 17: 6 And I saw the woman drunken with the **b** 129
 17: 6 and with the **b** of the martyrs of Jesus: 129
 18:24 And in her was found the **b** of prophets, 129
 19: 2 hath avenged the **b** of his servants at her 129
 19:13 he *was* clothed with a vesture dipt in **b**: 129

BLOOD GUILT See BLOODGUILTINESS

BLOOD RELATIVES See KINDRED; KINDREDS

BLOODGUILTINESS (1) [BLOOD, GUILT]
Ps 51:14 Deliver me from **b**, O God, thou God of 1818

BLOODTHIRSTY (1) [BLOOD, THIRST]
Pr 29:10 The **b** hate the upright: but the just 376+1818

BLOODY (16) [BLOOD]
Ex 4:25 said, Surely a **b** husband *art* thou to me. 1818
 4:26 A **b** husband *thou art*, because of 1818
2Sa 16: 7 thou **b** man, and thou man of Belial: 1818
 16: 8 to thy mischief, because thou *art* a **b** man. 1818
 21: 1 for *his* **b** house, because he slew 1818
Ps 5: 6 the Lᴏʀᴅ will abhor the **b** and 1818
 26: 9 soul with sinners, nor my life with **b** men: 1818
 55:23 **b** and deceitful men shall not live out half 1818
 59: 2 of iniquity, and save me from **b** men. 1818
 139:19 depart from me therefore, ye **b** men. 1818
Eze 7:23 the land is full *of* **b** crimes, and the city 1818
 22: 2 thou judge, wilt thou judge the **b** city? 1818
 24: 6 Woe to the **b** city, to the pot whose scum 1818
 24: 9 saith the Lord Gᴏᴅ; Woe to the **b** city! 1818
Na 3: 1 Woe to the **b** city! it *is* all full *of* lies and 1818
Ac 28: 8 Publius lay sick of a fever and of a **b** flixe: 1420

BLOOMED (1)
Nu 17: 8 and **b** blossoms, and yielded almonds. 6692

BLOSSOM (6) [BLOSSOMED, BLOSSOMS]
Nu 17: 5 man's rod, whom I shall choose, shall **b**: 6524
Isa 5:24 and their **b** shall go up as dust: 6525
 27: 6 Israel shall **b** and bud, and fill the face of 6692
 35: 1 the desert shall rejoice, and **b** as the rose. 6524
 35: 2 It shall **b abundantly** and 6524+6524
Hab 3:17 Although the fig tree shall not **b**, 6524

BLOSSOMED (1) [BLOSSOM]
Eze 7:10 the rod hath **b**, pride hath budded. 6692

BLOSSOMS (2) [BLOSSOM]
Ge 40:10 as though it budded, *and* her **b** shot forth; 5322
Nu 17: 8 and bloomed **b**, and yielded almonds. 6731

BLOT (13) [BLOTTED, BLOTTETH, BLOTTING]
Ex 32:32 if not, **b** me, I pray thee, out of thy book 4229
 32:33 against me, him will I **b** out of my book. 4229
Nu 5:23 he shall **b** *them* out with the bitter water: 4229
Dt 9:14 and **b** out their name from under heaven: 4229
 25:19 *that* thou shalt **b** out the remembrance of 4229
 29:20 the Lᴏʀᴅ shall **b** out his name from 4229
2Ki 14:27 the Lᴏʀᴅ said not that *he* would **b** out 4229
Job 31: 7 and *if any* **b** hath cleaved to my hands; 3971
Ps 51: 1 tender mercies and **b** out my transgressions. 4229
 51: 9 my sins, and **b** out all mine iniquities. 4229
Pr 9: 7 a wicked *man* getteth himself a **b**. 3971
Jer 18:23 neither **b** out their sin from thy sight, but 4229

B

Rev 3: 5 I will not **b** out his name out of the book *1813*

BLOTTED (6) [BLOT]
Ne 4: 5 not their sin be **b** out from before thee: 4229
Ps 69:28 them be **b** out of the book of the living, 4229
 109:13 following let their name be **b** out. 4229
 109:14 let not the sin of his mother be **b** out. 4229
Isa 44:22 I have **b** out, as a thick cloud, 4229
Ac 3:19 converted, that your sins may be **b** out, *1813*

BLOTTETH (1) [BLOT]
Isa 43:25 *am* he that **b** out thy transgressions for 4229

BLOTTING (1) [BLOT]
Col 2:14 **B** out the handwriting of ordinances that *1813*

BLOW (39) [BLEW, BLOWETH, BLOWING, BLOWN]
Ex 15:10 Thou didst **b** with thy wind, the sea 5398
Nu 10: 3 when they shall **b** with them, all 8628
 10: 4 if they **b** *but* with one *trumpet*, then 8628
 10: 5 When ye **b** an alarm, then the camps that 8628
 10: 6 When you **b** an alarm the second time, 8628
 10: 6 they shall **b** an alarm for their journeys. 8628
 10: 7 you shall **b**, but you shall not sound an 8628
 10: 8 the priests, shall **b** with the trumpets: 8628
 10: 9 ye shall **b** an alarm with the trumpets; 7321
 10:10 ye shall **b** with the trumpets over your 8628
 31: 6 and the trumpets to **b** in his hand. 8643
Jos 6: 4 and the priests shall **b** with the trumpets. 8628
Jdg 7:18 When I **b** with a trumpet, I and all that 8628
 7:18 **b** ye the trumpets also on every side of all 8628
 7:20 the trumpets in their right hands to **b** 8628
1Ki 1:34 **b** ye with the trumpet, and say, God save 8628
1Ch 15:24 did **b** with the trumpets before the ark of 2690
Ps 39:10 I am consumed by the **b** of thine hand. 8409
 78:26 He **caused** an east wind to **b** in the 5265
 81: 3 **B** up the trumpet in the new moon, 8628
 147:18 he **causeth** his wind to **b**, *and* the waters 5380
SS 4:16 **b** upon my garden, *that* the spices thereof 6315
Isa 40:24 he shall also **b** upon them, and they shall 5398
Jer 4: 5 and say, **B** ye the trumpet in the land: 8628
 6: 1 **b** the trumpet in Tekoa, and set up a sign 8628
 14:17 a great breach, *with* a very grievous **b**. 4347
 51:27 **b** the trumpet among the nations, 8628
Eze 21:31 will **b** against thee in the fire of my wrath, 6315
 22:20 to **b** the fire upon it, to melt *it*; so will I 5301
 22:21 **b** upon you in the fire of my wrath, 5301
 33: 3 he **b** the trumpet, and warn the people; 8628
 33: 6 **b** not the trumpet, and the people be not 8628
Hos 5: 8 **B** ye the cornet in Gibeah, *and* the 8628
Joel 2: 1 **B** ye the trumpet in Zion, and sound an 8628
 2:15 **B** the trumpet in Zion, sanctify a fast, call 8628
Hag 1: 9 when ye brought *it* home, I did **b** upon it. 5301
Zec 9:14 the Lord GOD shall **b** the trumpet, 8628
Lk 12:55 when *ye see* the south wind **b**, ye say, *4154*
Rev 7: 1 that the wind should not **b** on the earth, *4154*

BLOWETH (4) [BLOW]
Isa 18: 3 and when *he* **b** a trumpet, hear ye. 8628
 40: 7 because the spirit of the LORD **b** upon it: 5380
 54:16 I have created the smith that **b** the coals 5301
Jn 3: 8 The wind **b** where it listeth, and *4154*

BLOWING (4) [BLOW]
Lev 23:24 a memorial of **b** of trumpets, a holy 8643
Nu 29: 1 it is a day of **b** the **trumpets** unto you. 8643
Jos 6: 9 going on, and **b** with the trumpets. 8628
 6:13 going on, and **b** with the trumpets. 8628

BLOWN (4) [BLOW]
Job 20:26 a fire not **b** shall consume him; it shall go 5301
Isa 27:13 *that* the great trumpet shall be **b**, 8628
Eze 7:14 They have **b** the trumpet, even to make 8628
Am 3: 6 Shall a trumpet be **b** in the city, 8628

BLOWS See STRIPE; STRIPES

BLUE (50) [BLUENESS]
Ex 25: 4 **b**, and purple, and scarlet, and fine linen, 8504
 26: 1 linen, and **b**, and purple, and scarlet: 8504
 26: 4 shalt make loops of **b** upon the edge of 8504
 26:31 thou shalt make a vail *of* **b**, and purple, 8504
 26:36 *of* **b**, and purple, and scarlet, 8504
 27:16 *of* **b**, and purple, and scarlet, 8504
 28: 5 **b**, and purple, and scarlet, and fine linen. 8504
 28: 6 *of* **b**, and *of* purple, *of* scarlet, 8504
 28: 8 *of* **b**, and purple, and scarlet, 8504
 28:15 *of* **b**, and *of* purple, and *of* scarlet, 8504
 28:28 the rings of the ephod with a lace of **b**, 8504
 28:31 shalt make the robe of the ephod all *of* **b**. 8504
 28:33 of it thou shalt make pomegranates of **b**, 8504
 28:37 thou shalt put it on a lace, that it may 8504
 35: 6 **b**, and purple, and scarlet, and fine linen, 8504
 35:23 with whom was found **b**, and purple, 8504
 35:25 *both* of **b**, and of purple, *and* of scarlet, 8504
 35:35 in **b**, and in purple, in scarlet, and in fine 8504
 36: 8 linen, and **b**, and purple, and scarlet: 8504
 36:11 he made loops of **b** on the edge of one 8504
 36:35 made a vail *of* **b**, and purple, and scarlet, 8504
 36:37 a hanging for the tabernacle door *of* **b**, 8504
 38:18 *of* **b**, and purple, and scarlet, 8504
 38:23 an embroiderer in **b**, and in purple, 8504
 39: 1 **b**, and purple, and scarlet, they made 8504
 39: 2 **b**, and purple, and scarlet, and fine twined 8504
 39: 3 to work *it* in the **b**, and in the purple, 8504

Ex 39: 5 **b**, and purple, and scarlet, and fine twined 8504
 39: 8 **b**, and purple, and scarlet, and fine twined 8504
 39:21 the rings of the ephod with a lace of **b**, 8504
 39:22 robe of the ephod *of* woven work, all of **b**. 8504
 39:24 the hems of the robe pomegranates of **b**, 8504
 39:29 **b**, and purple, and scarlet, *of* needlework; 8504
 39:31 they tied unto it a lace of **b**, to fasten *it* on 8504
Nu 4: 6 shall spread over *it* a cloth wholly of **b**, 8504
 4: 7 shewbread they shall spread a cloth of **b**, 8504
 4: 9 they shall take a cloth of **b**, and cover 8504
 4:11 golden altar they shall spread a cloth of **b**, 8504
 4:12 put *them* in a cloth of **b**, and cover them 8504
 4:12 **b**, and can that skill to grave with 8504
 2Ch 2: 7 **b**, and in fine linen, and in crimson; 8504
 3:14 he made the vail *of* **b**, and purple, 8504
Est 1: 6 *hangings*, fastened with cords of fine 8504
 1: 6 red, and **b**, and white, and black **marble**. 8336
 8:15 presence of the king in royal apparel of **b** 8504
Jer 10: 9 **b** and purple *is* their clothing: they *are* all 8504
Eze 23: 6 *Which were* clothed with **b**, captains and 8504
 27: 7 **b** and purple from the isles of Elishah was 8504
 27:24 in **b** clothes, and broidered work, 8504

BLUENESS (1) [BLUE]
Pr 20:30 The **b** of a wound cleanseth away evil: 2250

BLUNT (1)
Ecc 10:10 If the iron be **b**, and he do not whet 6949

BLUSH (3)
Ezr 9: 6 and **b** to lift up my face to thee, 3637
Jer 6:15 not at all ashamed, neither could they **b**: 3637
 8:12 not at all ashamed, neither could they **b**: 3637

BOANERGES (1)
Mk 3:17 (and he surnamed them **B**, which is, *993*

BOAR (1)
Ps 80:13 The **b** out of the wood doth waste it, 2386

BOARD (17) [BOARDS]
Ex 26:16 Ten cubits *shall be* the length of a **b**, 7175
 26:16 and a half *shall be* the breadth of one **b**. 7175
 26:17 Two tenons *shall there be* in one **b**, set in 7175
 26:17 sockets under one **b** for his two tenons, 7175
 26:19 two sockets under another **b** for his two 7175
 26:21 two sockets under one **b**, and two sockets 7175
 26:21 and two sockets under another **b**. 7175
 26:25 two sockets under one **b**, and two sockets 7175
 26:25 and two sockets under another **b**. 7175
 36:21 The length of a **b** *was* ten cubits, 7175
 36:21 the breadth of a **b** one cubit and a half. 7175
 36:22 One **b** had two tenons, equally distant 7175
 36:24 sockets under one **b** for his two tenons, 7175
 36:24 two sockets under another **b** for his two 7175
 36:26 two sockets under one **b**, and two sockets 7175
 36:26 and two sockets under another **b**. 7175
 36:30 *of* silver, under every **b** two sockets. 7175

BOARDS (41) [BOARD]
Ex 26:15 thou shalt make **b** for the tabernacle *of* 7175
 26:17 thus shalt thou make for all the **b** of 7175
 26:18 thou shalt make the **b** for the tabernacle, 7175
 26:18 twenty **b** on the south side southward. 7175
 26:19 forty sockets of silver under the twenty **b**; 7175
 26:20 on the north side *there shall be* twenty **b**: 7175
 26:22 westward thou shalt make six **b**. 7175
 26:23 two **b** shalt thou make for the corners of 7175
 26:25 they shall be eight **b**, and their sockets *of* 7175
 26:26 five for the **b** of the one side of 7175
 26:27 five bars for the **b** of the other side of 7175
 26:27 five bars for the **b** of the side of 7175
 26:28 the middle bar in the midst of the **b** shall 7175
 26:29 thou shalt overlay the **b** with gold, 7175
 27: 8 Hollow with **b** shalt thou make it: as it 3871
 35:11 his taches, and his **b**, his bars, his pillars, 7175
 36:20 he made **b** for the tabernacle *of* shittim 7175
 36:22 thus did he make for all the **b** of 7175
 36:23 made **b** for the tabernacle; twenty boards 7175
 36:23 twenty **b** for the south side southward: 7175
 36:24 of silver he made under the twenty **b**; 7175
 36:25 the north corner, he made twenty **b**. 7175
 36:27 the tabernacle westward he made six **b**. 7175
 36:28 two **b** made he for the corners of 7175
 36:30 there were eight **b**; and their sockets 7175
 36:31 five for the **b** of the one side 7175
 36:32 five bars for the **b** of the other side of 7175
 36:32 five bars for the **b** of the tabernacle for 7175
 36:33 the **b** from the one end to the other. 7175
 36:34 overlaid the **b** with gold, and made their 7175
 38: 7 withal; he made the *altar* hollow with **b**. 3871
 39:33 his **b**, his bars, and his pillars, 7175
 40:18 set up the **b** thereof, and put in the bars 7175
Nu 3:36 of the sons of Merari *shall be* the **b** 7175
 4:31 the **b** of the tabernacle, and the bars 7175
1Ki 6: 9 the house with beams and **b** of cedar. 7713
 6:15 walls of the house within with **b** of cedar, 6763
 6:16 the floor and the walls with **b** of cedar: 6763
SS 8: 9 door, we will inclose her with **b** of cedar. 3871
Eze 27: 5 They have made all thy *ship* **b** of fir trees 3871
Ac 27:44 some on **b**, and some on broken pieces of *4548*

BOAST (20) [BOASTED, BOASTERS, BOASTEST, BOASTETH, BOASTING, BOASTINGS]
1Ki 20:11 *harness* **b** himself as he that putteth *it* off. 1984

2Ch 25:19 and thine heart lifteth thee up to **b**: 3513
Ps 34: 2 My soul shall **make** her **b** in the LORD: 1984
 44: 8 In God we **b** all the day long, and praise 1984
 49: 6 **b** themselves in the multitude of their 1984
 94: 4 all the workers of iniquity **b** themselves? 559
 97: 7 graven images, that **b** themselves of idols: 1984
Pr 27: 1 **B** not thyself of to morrow; for thou 1984
Isa 10:15 Shall the axe **b** itself against him that 6286
 61: 6 and in their glory shall you **b** yourselves. 3235
Ro 2:17 in the law, and **makest** thy **b** of God, 2744
 2:23 Thou that **makest** thy **b** of the law, 2744
 11:18 **B** not *against* the branches: but if thou 2620
 11:18 but if thou **b**, thou bearest not the root, 2620
2Co 9: 2 which I **b** of you to them of Macedonia, 2744
 10: 8 For though I should **b** somewhat more of 2744
 10:13 But we will not **b** of *things* without our 2744
 10:16 not to **b** in another *man's* line of *things* 2744
 11:16 receive me, that I may **b** myself a little. 2744
Eph 2: 9 Not of works, lest any *man* should **b**. 2744

BOASTED (2) [BOAST]
Eze 35:13 Thus with your mouth ye have **b** against 1431
2Co 7:14 For if I have **b** any *thing* to him of you, 2744

BOASTERS (2) [BOAST]
Ro 1:30 haters of God, despiteful, proud, **b**, *213*
2Ti 3: 2 covetous, **b**, proud, blasphemers, *213*

BOASTEST (1) [BOAST]
Ps 52: 1 Why **b** thou thyself in mischief, O mighty 1984

BOASTETH (4) [BOAST]
Ps 10: 3 For the wicked **b** of his heart's desire, 1984
Pr 20:14 but when he is gone his way, then he **b**. 1984
 25:14 Whoso **b** himself of a false gift *is* like 1984
Jas 3: 5 is a little member, and **b** great things. 3166

BOASTING (9) [BOAST]
Ac 5:36 up Theudas, **b** himself to be somebody; *3004*
Ro 3:27 Where *is* **b** then? It is excluded. By what 2746
2Co 7:14 even so our **b**, which *I made* before Titus, 2746
 8:24 of your love, and of our **b** on your behalf. 2746
 9: 3 lest our **b** of you should be in vain in this 2745
 9: 4 be ashamed in this *same* confident **b**. 2746
 10:15 Not **b** of *things* without our measure, 2744
 11:10 no *man* shall stop me of this **b** in 2746
 11:17 *it were* foolishly, in this confidence of **b**. 2746

BOASTINGS (1) [BOAST]
Jas 4:16 But now ye rejoice in your **b**: all such *212*

BOAT (6) [BOATS]
2Sa 18:18 there went over a **ferry** **b** to carry over 5679
Jn 6:22 saw that there was none other **b** there, *4142*
 6:22 went not with his disciples into the **b**, *4142*
Ac 27:16 we had much work to come by the **b**. *4627*
 27:30 they had let down the **b** into the sea, *4627*
 27:32 the soldiers cut off the ropes of the **b**, *4627*

BOATS (1) [BOAT]
Jn 6:23 Howbeit there came other **b** from Tiberias *4142*

BOAZ (24) [BOOZ]
Ru 2: 1 family of Elimelech; and his name *was* **B**. 1162
 2: 3 on a part of the field *belonging* unto **B**, 1162
 2: 4 **B** came from Beth-lehem, and said unto 1162
 2: 5 said **B** unto his servant that was set over 1162
 2: 8 said **B** unto Ruth, Hearest thou not, 1162
 2:11 **B** answered and said unto her, It hath 1162
 2:14 **B** said unto her, At mealtime come thou 1162
 2:15 **B** commanded his young men, saying, 1162
 2:19 name with whom I wrought to day *is* **B**. 1162
 2:23 So she kept fast by the maidens of **B** to 1162
 3: 2 now *is* not **B** of our kindred, with whose 1162
 3: 7 **B** had eaten and drunk, and his heart 1162
 4: 1 went **B** up *to* the gate, and sat him down 1162
 4: 1 the kinsman of whom **B** spake came by; 1162
 4: 5 said **B**, What day thou buyest the field *of* 1162
 4: 8 Therefore the kinsman said unto **B**, Buy 1162
 4: 9 **B** said unto the elders, and *unto* all 1162
 4:13 So **B** took Ruth, and she was his wife: 1162
 4:21 Salmon begat **B**, and Boaz begat Obed, 1162
 4:21 Salmon begat Boaz, and **B** begat Obed, 1162
1Ki 7:21 left pillar, and called the name thereof **B**. 1162
1Ch 2:11 Nahshon begat Salma, and Salma begat **B**, 1162
 2:12 And **B** begat Obed, and Obed begat Jesse, 1162
2Ch 3:17 and the name of *that on* the left **B**. 1162

BOCHERU (2)
1Ch 8:38 **B**, and Ishmael, and Sheariah, 1074
 9:44 **B**, and Ishmael, and Sheariah, 1074

BOCHIM (2)
Jdg 2: 1 of the LORD came up from Gilgal to **B**, 1066
 2: 5 they called the name of that place **B**: 1066

BODIES (33) [BODY]
Ge 47:18 sight of my lord, *there is* not *ought* left but our **b**, and our lands: 1472
1Sa 31:12 the **b** of his sons from the wall of 1472
1Ch 10:12 the **b** of his sons, and brought them to 1480
2Ch 20:24 they *were* **dead b** fallen to the earth, 6297
 20:25 abundance both riches with the **dead b** 6297
Ne 9:37 also they have dominion over our **b**, 1472
Job 13:12 like unto ashes, your **b** to bodies of clay. 1354
 13:12 like unto ashes, your bodies to **b** of clay. 1354
Ps 79: 2 The **dead b** of thy servants have they 5038

B

Ps 110: 6 he shall fill *the places with* the **dead b**; 1472
Jer 31:40 the whole valley of the **dead b**, and of 6297
 33: 5 *it is* to fill them with the **dead b** of men, 6297
 34:20 their **dead b** shall be for meat unto 5038
 41: 9 Ishmael had cast all the **dead b** of the 6297
Eze 1:11 one to another, and two covered their **b**. 1472
 1:23 which covered on that *side*, their **b**. 1472
Da 3:27 upon whose **b** the fire had no power, 1655
 3:28 the king's word, and yielded their **b**, 1655
Am 8: 3 *shall be* many **dead b** in every place; 6297
Mt 27:52 and many **b** of saints which slept arose, 4983
Jn 19:31 the **b** should not remain upon the cross 4983
Ro 1:24 to dishonour their own **b** between 4983
 8:11 mortal **b** by his Spirit that dwelleth in you. 4983
 12: 1 that *ye* present your **b** a living sacrifice, 4983
1Co 6:15 Know ye not that your **b** are the members 4983
 15:40 There are *also* celestial **b**, 4983
 15:40 *are* also celestial bodies, and **b** terrestrial: 4983
Eph 5:28 men to love their wives as their own **b**. 4983
Heb 10:22 and *our* **b** washed with pure water. 4983
 13:11 For the **b** of those beasts, whose blood is 4983
Rev 11: 8 And their **dead b** *shall lie* in the street of 4430
 11: 9 nations shall see their **dead b** three days 4430
 11: 9 shall not suffer their **dead b** to be put in 4430

BODILY (4) [BODY]

Lk 3:22 the Holy Ghost descended in a **b** shape 4984
2Co 10:10 *his* **b** presence *is* weak, and *his* speech 4983
Col 2: 9 dwelleth all the fulness of the Godhead **b**. 4985
1Ti 4: 8 For **b** exercise profiteth little: 4984

BODY (174) [BODIES, BODILY, BODY'S, BUSYBODIES, BUSYBODY]

Ex 24:10 it were the **b** of heaven in *his* clearness. 6106
Lev 21:11 Neither shall he go in to any dead **b**, 5315
Nu 6: 6 the LORD he shall come at no dead **b**. 5315
 9: 6 were defiled by the **dead b** of a man, 5315
 9: 7 We *are* defiled by the **dead b** of a man: 5315
 9:10 shall be unclean by reason of a **dead b**, 5315
 19:11 He that toucheth the dead *b* of any man NIH
 19:13 toucheth the dead *b* of *any* man NIH
 19:16 a dead *b*, or a bone of a man, or a grave, NIH
Dt 21:23 His **b** shall not remain all night upon 5038
 28: 4 Blessed *shall be* the fruit of thy **b**, 990
 28:11 in the fruit of thy **b**, and in the fruit of thy 990
 28:18 Cursed *shall be* the fruit of thy **b**, 990
 28:53 thou shalt eat the fruit of thine own **b**, 990
 30: 9 in the fruit of thy **b**, and in the fruit of thy 990
Jdg 8:30 and ten sons of his **b** begotten: 3409
1Sa 31:10 they fastened his **b** to the wall of 1472
 31:12 took the **b** of Saul and the bodies of his 1472
2Ki 8: 5 king how he had restored a dead **b** to life, NIH
1Ch 10:12 took away the **b** of Saul, and the bodies of 1480
Job 9:17 for the children's *sake* of mine own **b**. 990
 19:26 *though* after my skin *worms* destroy this *b*, NIH
 20:25 It is drawn, and cometh out of the **b**; yea, 1465
Ps 132:11 Of the fruit of thy **b** will I set upon thy 990
Pr 5:11 when thy flesh and thy **b** are consumed, 7607
Isa 10:18 and of his fruitful field, both soul and **b**: 1320
 26:19 *together with* my **dead b** shall they arise. 5038
 51:23 thou hast laid thy **b** as the ground, 1460
Jer 26:23 cast his **dead b** into the graves of 5038
 36:30 his **dead b** shall be cast out in the day to 5038
La 4: 7 they were more ruddy *in* **b** than rubies, 6106
Eze 10:12 their whole **b**, and their backs, 1320
Da 4:33 his **b** was wet with the dew of heaven; 1655
 5:21 his **b** was wet with the dew of heaven; 1655
 7:11 his **b** destroyed, and given to the burning 1655
 7:15 grieved in my spirit in the midst of *my* **b**, 5085
 10: 6 His **b** also *was* like the beryl, and his face 1472
Mic 6: 7 the fruit of my **b** *for* the sin of my soul? 990
Hag 2:13 If *one that is* unclean by a **dead b** touch 5315
Mt 5:29 not *that* thy whole **b** should be cast into 4983
 5:30 not *that* thy whole **b** should be cast into 4983
 6:22 The light of the **b** is the eye: if therefore 4983
 6:22 single, thy whole **b** shall be full of light. 4983
 6:23 thy whole **b** shall be full of darkness. 4983
 6:25 more than meat, and the **b** than raiment? 4983
 6:25 nor yet for your **b**, what ye shall put on. 4983
 10:28 And fear not them which kill the **b**, but 4983
 10:28 is able to destroy both soul and **b** in hell. 4983
 14:12 his disciples came, and took up the **b**, 4983
 26:12 she hath poured this ointment on my **b**, 4983
 26:26 and said, Take, eat; this is my **b**. 4983
 27:58 went to Pilate, and begged the **b** of Jesus. 4983
 27:58 Then Pilate commanded the **b** to be 4983
 27:59 And when Joseph had taken the **b**, 4983
Mk 5:29 she felt in *her* **b** that she was healed of 4983
 14: 8 she is come aforehand to anoint my **b** to 4983
 14:22 to them, and said, Take, eat: this is my **b**. 4983
 14:51 a linen cloth cast about *his* naked *b*; NIG
 15:43 unto Pilate, and craved the **b** of Jesus. 4983
 15:45 of the centurion, he gave the **b** to Joseph. 4983
Lk 11:34 The light of the **b** is the eye: 4983
 11:34 is single, thy whole **b** also is full of light; 4983
 11:34 *eye* is evil, thy **b** also *is* full of darkness. 4983
 11:36 If thy whole **b** therefore *be* full of light, 4983
 12: 4 Be not afraid of them that kill the **b**, and 4983
 12:22 neither for the **b**, what ye shall put on. 4983
 12:23 meat, and the **b** *is* more than raiment. 4983
 17:37 Wheresoever the **b** *is*, thither will 4983
 22:19 This is my **b** which is given for you: 4983
 23:52 unto Pilate, and begged the **b** of Jesus. 4983
 23:55 the sepulchre, and how his **b** was laid. 4983
 24: 3 and found not the **b** of the Lord Jesus. 4983

BODY'S (1) [BODY]

Col 1:24 of Christ in my flesh for his **b** sake, 4983

Lk 24:23 when they found not his **b**, they came, 4983
Jn 2:21 But he spake of the temple of his **b**. 4983
 19:38 that he might take away the **b** of Jesus: 4983
 19:38 came therefore, and took the **b** of Jesus. 4983
 19:40 took they the **b** of Jesus, and wound it 4983
 20:12 at the feet, where the **b** of Jesus had lain. 4983
Ac 9:40 and turning *him* to the **b** said, Tabitha, 4983
 19:12 So that from his **b** were brought unto 5559
Ro 4:19 he considered not his own **b** now dead, 4983
 6: 6 *him*, that the **b** of sin might be destroyed, 4983
 6:12 not sin therefore reign in your mortal **b**, 4983
 7: 4 also are become dead to the law by the **b** 4983
 7:24 who shall deliver me from the **b** of this 4983
 8:10 *be* in you, the **b** *is* dead because of sin; 4983
 8:13 the Spirit do mortify the deeds of the **b**, 4983
 8:23 *to wit*, the redemption of our **b**. 4983
 12: 4 For as we have many members in one **b**, 4983
 12: 5 one **b** in Christ, and every one members 4983
1Co 6:13 verily, as absent in **b**, but present in spirit, 4983
 6:13 Now the **b** *is* not for fornication, but for 4983
 6:13 but for the Lord; and the Lord for the **b**. 4983
 6:16 he which is joined to a harlot is one **b**? 4983
 6:18 sin that a man doeth is without the **b**; 4983
 6:18 fornication sinneth against his own **b**. 4983
 6:19 know ye not that your **b** is the temple of 4983
 6:20 therefore glorify God in your **b**, and in 4983
 7: 4 The wife hath not power of her own **b**, 4983
 7: 4 the husband hath not power of his own **b**, 4983
 7:34 she may be holy both in **b** and in spirit: 4983
 9:27 But I keep under my **b**, and bring *it* into 4983
 10:16 it not the communion of the **b** of Christ? 4983
 10:17 we being many are one bread, *and* one **b**: 4983
 11:24 this is my **b**, which is broken for you: 4983
 11:27 shall be guilty of the **b** and blood of 4983
 11:29 to himself, not discerning the Lord's **b**. 4983
 12:12 For as the **b** is one, and hath many 4983
 12:12 and all the members of *that* one **b**, 4983
 12:12 of *that* one body, being many, are one **b**: 4983
 12:13 one Spirit are we all baptized into one **b**, 4983
 12:14 For the **b** is not one member, but many. 4983
 12:15 I am not the hand, I am not of the **b**; 4983
 12:15 of the body; is it therefore not of the **b**? 4983
 12:16 I am not the eye, I am not of the **b**; 4983
 12:16 of the body; is it therefore not of the **b**? 4983
 12:17 If the whole **b** *were* an eye, where *were* 4983
 12:18 the members every one of them in the **b**, 4983
 12:19 were all one member, where *were* the **b**? 4983
 12:20 *are they* many members, yet *but* one **b**. 4983
 12:22 Nay, much more those members of the **b**, 4983
 12:23 And those *members* of the **b**, which we 4983
 12:24 but God hath tempered the **b** together, 4983
 12:25 That there should be no schism in the **b**; 4983
 12:27 Now ye are the **b** of Christ, and members 4983
 13: 3 and though I give my **b** to be burned, 4983
 15:35 and with what **b** do they come? 4983
 15:37 thou sowest not that **b** that shall be, but 4983
 15:38 But God giveth it a **b** as it hath pleased 4983
 15:38 pleased him, and to every seed his own **b**. 4983
 15:44 is sown a natural **b**; it is raised a spiritual 4983
 15:44 a natural body; it is raised a spiritual **b**. 4983
 15:44 is a natural **b**, and there is a spiritual 4983
 15:44 a natural body, and there is a spiritual **b**. 4983
2Co 4:10 Always bearing about in the **b** the dying of 4983
 4:10 of Jesus might be made manifest in our **b**. 4983
 5: 6 whilst we are at home in the **b**, 4983
 5: 8 and willing rather to be absent from the **b**, 4983
 5:10 one may receive the *things done* in *his* **b**, 4983
 12: 2 years ago, (whether in the **b**, I cannot tell; 4983
 12: 2 or whether out of the **b**, I cannot tell: 4983
 12: 3 (whether in the **b**, or out of the body, 4983
 12: 3 in the body, or out of the **b**, I cannot tell: 4983
Gal 6:17 for I bear in my **b** the marks of the Lord 4983
Eph 1:23 Which is his **b**, the fulness of him that 4983
 2:16 both unto God in one **b** by the cross, 4983
 3: 6 and of the *same* **b**, and partakers of his 4954
 4: 4 *There is* one **b**, and one Spirit, even as ye 4983
 4:12 for the edifying of the **b** of Christ: 4983
 4:16 From whom the whole **b** fitly joined 4983
 4:16 maketh increase of the **b** unto the edifying 4983
 5:23 the church: and he is the saviour of the **b**. 4983
 5:30 For we are members of his **b**, of his flesh, 4983
Php 1:20 also Christ shall be magnified in my **b**, 4983
 3:21 Who shall change our vile **b**, that it may 4983
 3:21 may be fashioned like unto his glorious **b**, 4983
Col 1:18 And he is the head of the **b**, the church: 4983
 1:22 In the **b** of his flesh through death, 4983
 2:11 in putting off the **b** of the sins of the flesh, 4983
 2:17 of *things* to come; but the **b** *is* of Christ. 4983
 2:19 from which all the **b** by joints and 4983
 2:23 and humility, and neglecting of the **b**, 4983
 3:15 to the which also ye are called in one **b**; 4983
1Th 5:23 **b** be preserved blameless unto the coming 4983
Heb 10: 5 but a **b** hast thou prepared me: 4983
 10:10 of the **b** of Jesus Christ once for all. 4983
 13: 3 as being yourselves also in the **b**. 4983
Jas 2:16 those *things which are* needful to the **b**; 4983
 2:26 For as the **b** without the spirit is dead, 4983
 3: 2 *and* able also to bridle the whole **b**. 4983
 3: 3 obey us; and we turn about their whole **b**. 4983
 3: 6 that it defileth the whole **b**, and setteth on 4983
1Pe 2:24 self bare our sins in his own **b** on the tree, 4983
Jude 1: 9 devil he disputed about the **b** of Moses, 4983

BOHAN (2)

Jos 15: 6 border went up *to* the stone of **B** the son 932
 18:17 descended *to* the stone of **B** the son of 932

BOIL (16) [BOILED, BOILING, BOILS]

Ex 9: 9 be a **b** breaking forth *with* blains upon 7822
 9:10 it became a **b** breaking forth *with* blains 7822
 9:11 for the **b** was upon the magicians, 7822
Lev 8:31 **B** the flesh *at* the door of the tabernacle of 1310
 13:18 in the skin thereof, was a **b**, and is healed, 7822
 13:19 the place of the **b** there be a white rising, 7822
 13:20 *is* a plague of leprosy broken out of the **b**. 7822
 13:23 place, *and* spread not, it *is* a burning **b**; 7822
2Ki 20: 7 they took and laid *it* on the **b**, 7822
Job 41:31 He *maketh* the deep **to b** like a pot: 7570
Isa 38:21 lay *it* for a plaister upon the **b**, and he 7822
 64: 2 the fire **causeth** the waters to **b**, 1158
Eze 24: 5 *and* make it **b** well, and let them 7570+7571
 46:20 This *is* the place where the priests shall **b** 1310
 46:24 These *are* the places of them that **b**, 1310
 46:24 where the ministers of the house shall **b** 1310

BOILED (3) [BOIL]

1Ki 19:21 their flesh with the instruments of 1310
2Ki 6:29 we **b** my son, and did eat him: and I said 1310
Job 30:27 My bowels **b**, and rested not: the days of 7570

BOILING (1) [BOIL]

Eze 46:23 *was* made *with* **b** places under the rows 4018

BOILS (1) [BOIL]

Ex 9:11 not stand before Moses because of the **b**; 7822
Job 2: 7 smote Job with sore **b** from the sole of his 7822

BOKERU See BOCHERU

BOKIM See BOCHIM

BOLD (11) [BOLDLY, BOLDNESS, EMBOLDENED, EMBOLDENETH]

Pr 28: 1 but the righteous are **b** as a lion. 982
Ac 13:46 Paul and Barnabas **waxed b**, and said, 3955
Ro 10:20 Esaias is **very b**, and saith, I was found 662
2Co 10: 1 but being absent am **b** toward you: 2292
 10: 2 But I beseech *you*, that I may not be **b** 2292
 10: 2 wherewith I think to be **b** against some, 5111
 11:21 Howbeit whereinsoever any is **b**, (I speak 5111
 11:21 any is bold, (I speak foolishly,) I am **b** also. 5111
Php 1:14 much more **b** to speak the word without 5111
1Th 2: 2 we were **b** in our God to speak unto you 3955
Phm 1: 8 though I might be much **b** in Christ to 3954

BOLDLY (13) [BOLD]

Ge 34:25 upon the city **b**, and slew all the males. 983
Mk 15:43 and went in **b** unto Pilate, and craved 5111
Jn 7:26 he speaketh **b**, and they say nothing unto 3954
Ac 9:27 how he had **preached b** at Damascus in 3955
 9:29 And he spake **b** in the name of the Lord 3955
 14: 3 abode they **speaking b** in the Lord, 3955
 18:26 he began to speak **b** in the synagogue: 3955
 19: 8 spake **b** for the space of three months, 3955
Ro 15:15 I have written the **more b** unto you in 5112
Eph 6:19 that *I* may open my mouth **b**, 1722+3955
 6:20 that therein I may **speak b**, as I ought to 3955
Heb 4:16 come **b** unto the throne of grace, 3326+3954
 13: 6 So that we may **b** say, The Lord *is* my 2292

BOLDNESS (10) [BOLD]

Ecc 8: 1 and the **b** of his face shall be changed. 5797
Ac 4:13 Now when they saw the **b** of Peter and 3954
 4:29 that with all **b** *they* may speak thy word, 3954
 4:31 and they spake the word of God with **b**. 3954
2Co 7: 4 Great *is* my **b** of speech toward you, 3954
Eph 3:12 In whom we have **b** and access with 3954
Php 1:20 but *that* with all **b**, as always, *so* now also 3954
1Ti 3:13 great **b** in the faith which is in Christ 3954
Heb 10:19 **b** to enter into the holiest by the blood of 3954
1Jn 4:17 we may have **b** in the day of judgment: 3954

BOLLED (1)

Ex 9:31 barley *was* in the ear, and the flax *was* **b**. 1392

BOLSTER (6)

1Sa 19:13 put a pillow of goats' *hair* for his **b**. 4763
 19:16 with a pillow of goats' *hair* for his **b**. 4763
 26: 7 his spear stuck in the ground *at* his **b**: 4763
 26:11 take thou now the spear that *is at* his **b**, 4763
 26:12 and the cruse of water from Saul's **b**; 4763
 26:16 and the cruse of water that *was at* his **b**. 4763

BOLT (1) [BOLTED]

2Sa 13:17 out from me, and **b** the door after her. 5274

BOLTED (1) [BOLT]

2Sa 13:18 brought her out, and **b** the door after her. 5274

BOLTS See LOCKS

BOND (19) [BONDAGE, BONDMAID, BONDMAIDS, BONDMAN, BONDMEN, BONDS, BONDSERVANT, BONDSERVICE, BONDWOMAN, BONDWOMEN]

Nu 30: 2 or swear an oath to bind his soul with a **b**; 632
 30: 3 bind *herself by* a **b**, *being* in her father's 632
 30: 4 her **b** wherewith she hath bound her soul, 632
 30: 4 every **b** wherewith she hath bound her 632

B

Nu 30:10 or bound her soul by a **b** with an oath; 632
 30:11 every **b** wherewith she bound her soul 632
 30:12 or concerning the **b** of her soul, shall not 632
Job 12:18 He looseth the **b** of kings, and girdeth 4148
Eze 20:37 will bring you into the **b** of the covenant: 4562
Lk 13:16 be loosed from this **b** on the sabbath day? 1199
Ac 8:23 gall of bitterness, and *in* the **b** of iniquity. 4886
1Co 12:13 or Gentiles, whether *we be* **b** or free; 1401
Gal 3:28 Jew nor Greek, there is neither **b** nor free, 1401
Eph 4: 3 the unity of the Spirit in the **b** of peace. 4886
 6: 8 of the Lord, whether *he be* **b** or free. 1401
Col 3:11 barbarian, Scythian, **b** *nor* free: 1401
 3:14 *on* charity, which is the **b** of perfectness. 4886
Rev 13:16 and great, rich and poor, free and **b**, 1401
 19:18 and the flesh of all *men*, both free and **b**, 1401

BONDAGE (39) [BOND]

Ex 1:14 they made their lives bitter with hard **b**, 5656
 2:23 of Israel sighed by reason of the **b**, 5656
 2:23 cry came up unto God by reason of the **b**. 5656
 6: 5 of Israel, whom the Egyptians **keep in b**; 5647
 6: 6 I will rid you out of their **b**, and I will 5656
 6: 9 for anguish of spirit, and for cruel **b**. 5656
 13: 3 out from Egypt, out of the house of **b**; 5650
 13:14 us out from Egypt, from the house of **b**. 5650
 20: 2 the land of Egypt, out of the house of **b**. 5650
Dt 5: 6 of the land of Egypt, from the house of **b**. 5650
 6:12 of the land of Egypt, from the house of **b**. 5650
 8:14 out of the land of Egypt, from the house of **b**; 5650
 13: 5 and redeemed you out of the house of **b**, 5650
 13:10 of the land of Egypt, from the house of **b**. 5650
 26: 6 and afflicted us, and laid upon us hard **b**: 5656
Jos 24:17 from the house of **b**, and which did those 5650
Jdg 6: 8 brought you forth out of the house of **b**; 5650
Ezr 9: 8 and give us a little reviving in our **b**. 5659
 9: 9 yet our God hath not forsaken us in our **b**, 5659
Ne 5: 5 we **bring into b** our sons and our 3533
 5: 5 of our daughters are **brought unto b** 3533
 5:18 the **b** was heavy upon this people. 5656
 9:17 appointed a captain to return to their **b**: 5659
Isa 14: 3 from the hard **b** wherein thou wast made 5656
Jn 8:33 were never in **b** to any *man:* how sayest 1398
Ac 7: 6 and that they should **bring** them **into b**, 1402
 7: 7 the nation to whom they shall be in **b** 1398
Ro 8:15 For ye have not received the spirit of **b** 1397
 8:21 **b** of corruption into the glorious liberty of 1397
1Co 7:15 or a sister is not **under b** in such *cases:* 1402
2Co 11:20 For ye suffer, if a man **bring** you **into b**, 2615
Gal 2: 4 that they might **bring** us **into b**: 2615
 4: 3 in **b** under the elements of the world: 1402
 4: 9 whereunto ye desire again to be in **b**? 1398
 4:24 which gendereth to **b**, which is Agar. 1397
 4:25 now is, and is in **b** with her children. 1398
 5: 1 not entangled again with the yoke of **b**. 1397
Heb 2:15 death were all their lifetime subject to **b**. 1397
2Pe 2:19 of the same is he **brought in b**. 1402

BONDMAID (2) [BOND, MAID]

Lev 19:20 lieth carnally with a woman that *is* a **b**, 8198
Gal 4:22 the one by a **b**, the other by a freewoman. 3814

BONDMAIDS (2) [BOND, MAID]

Lev 25:44 Both thy bondmen, and thy **b**, which thou 519
 25:44 of them shall ye buy bondmen and **b**. 519

BONDMAN (7) [BOND, MAN]

Ge 44:33 let thy servant abide instead of the lad a **b** 5650
Dt 15:15 thou shalt remember that thou wast a **b** in 5650
 16:12 thou shalt remember that thou wast a **b** in 5650
 24:18 thou shalt remember that thou wast a **b** in 5650
 24:22 thou shalt remember that thou wast a **b** in 5650
1Ki 9:22 children of Israel did Solomon make no **b**: 5650
Rev 6:15 and the mighty *men*, and every **b**, 1401

BONDMEN (16) [BOND, MAN]

Ge 43:18 upon us, and take us for **b**, and our asses. 5650
 44: 9 him die, and we also will be my lord's **b**. 5650
Lev 25:42 land of Egypt: they shall not be sold as **b**. 5650
 25:44 Both thy **b**, and thy bondmaids, which 5650
 25:44 of them shall ye buy **b** and bondmaids. 5650
 25:46 possession; they shall be your **b** for ever: 5647
 26:13 of Egypt, that *ye* should not be their **b**; 5650
Dt 6:21 thy son, We were Pharaoh's **b** in Egypt; 5650
 7: 8 redeemed you out of the house of **b**, 5650
 28:68 ye shall be sold unto your enemies for **b** 5650
Jos 9:23 shall none of you be freed from being **b**, 5650
2Ki 4: 1 to take unto him my two sons to be **b**. 5650
2Ch 28:10 Jerusalem for **b** and bondwomen unto 5650
Ezr 9: 9 For we *were* **b**; yet our God hath not 5650
Est 7: 4 we had been sold for **b** and bondwomen, 5650
Jer 34:13 of Egypt, out of the house of **b**, saying, 5650

BONDS (26) [BOND]

Nu 30: 5 her **b** wherewith she hath bound her soul, 632
 30: 7 her **b** wherewith her soul shall 632
 30:14 vows, or all her **b**, which *are* upon her: 632
Ps 116:16 of thy handmaid: thou hast loosed my **b**. 4147
Jer 5: 5 broken the yoke, *and* burst the **b**. 4147
 27: 2 Make thee **b** and yokes, and put them 4147
 30: 8 will burst thy **b**, and strangers shall no 4147
Na 1:13 off thee, and will burst thy **b** in sunder. 4147
Ac 20:23 saying that **b** and afflictions abide me. 1199
 23:29 laid to his charge worthy of death or of **b**. 1199
 25:14 There is a certain man left in **b** by Felix: 1198
 26:29 altogether such as I am, except these **b**. 1199

Ac 26:31 doeth nothing worthy of death or of **b**. 1199
Eph 6:20 For which I am an ambassador in **b**: 254
Php 1: 7 inasmuch as both in my **b**, and *in* 1199
 1:13 So that my **b** in Christ are manifest in all 1199
 1:14 in the Lord, waxing confident by my **b**, 1199
 1:16 supposing to add affliction to my **b**: 1199
Col 4: 3 of Christ, for which I am also in **b**: 1210
 4:18 Remember my **b**. Grace *be* with you. 1199
2Ti 2: 9 trouble, as an evil doer, *even* unto **b**; 1199
Phm 1:10 whom I have begotten in my **b**: 1199
 1:13 ministered unto me in the **b** of the gospel: 1199
Heb 10:34 For ye had compassion *of me* in my **b**, 1199
 11:36 yea, moreover of **b** and imprisonment: 1199
 13: 3 Remember *them that are* in **b**, as bound 1198

BONDSERVANT (1) [BOND, SERVE]

Lev 25:39 thou shalt not compel him to serve as a **b**: 5650

BONDSERVICE (1) [BOND, SERVE]

1Ki 9:21 those did Solomon levy a tribute of **b** 5647

BONDWOMAN (8) [BOND, WOMAN]

Ge 21:10 Abraham, Cast out this **b** and her son: 519
 21:10 for the son of this **b** shall not be heir with 519
 21:12 because of the lad, and because of thy **b**; 519
 21:13 of the son of the **b** will I make a nation, 519
Gal 4:23 But he who was of the **b** was born after 3814
 4:30 Cast out the **b** and her son: for the son of 3814
 4:30 for the son of the **b** shall not be heir with 3814
 4:31 not children of *the* **b**, but of the free. 3814

BONDWOMEN (3) [BOND, WOMAN]

Dt 28:68 unto your enemies for bondmen and **b**, 8198
2Ch 28:10 Jerusalem for bondmen and **b** unto you: 8198
Est 7: 4 if we had been sold for bondmen and **b**, 8198

BONE (20) [BONES, JAWBONE]

Ge 2:23 This *is* now **b** of my bones, and flesh of 6106
 29:14 him, Surely thou *art* my **b** and my flesh. 6106
Ex 12:46 neither shall ye break a **b** thereof. 6106
Lev 3: 9 it shall he take off hard by the **back b**; 6096
Nu 9:12 it unto the morning, nor break any **b** of it: 6106
 19:16 a dead *body*, or a **b** of a man, or a grave, 6106
 19:18 upon him that touched a **b**, or one slain, 6106
Jdg 19: 2 remember also that I *am* your **b** and 6106
2Sa 5: 1 Behold, we *are* thy **b** and thy flesh. 6106
 19:13 *Art* thou not *of* my **b**, and *of* my flesh? 6106
1Ch 11: 1 Behold, we *are* thy **b** and thy flesh. 6106
Job 2: 5 touch his **b** and his flesh, and he will 6106
 19:20 My **b** cleaveth to my skin and to my flesh, 6106
 31:22 and mine arm be broken from the **b**. 7070
Ps 3: 7 all mine enemies *upon* the **cheek b**; 3895
Pr 25:15 and a soft tongue breaketh the **b**. 1634
Eze 37: 7 the bones came together, **b** to his bone. 6106
 37: 7 the bones came together, bone to his **b**. 6106
 39:15 *any* seeth a man's **b**, then shall he set 6106
Jn 19:36 fulfilled, A **b** of him shall not be broken. 3747

BONES (99) [BONE]

Ge 2:23 This *is* now bone of my, and flesh of my 6106
 50:25 and ye shall carry up my **b** from hence. 6106
Ex 13:19 Moses took the **b** of Joseph with him: 6106
 13:19 ye shall carry up my **b** away hence with 6106
Nu 24: 8 break their **b**, and pierce *them* through 6106
Jos 24:32 **b** of Joseph, which the children of Israel 6106
Jdg 19:29 divided her, *together* with her **b**, 6106
1Sa 31:13 they took their **b**, and buried *them* under 6106
2Sa 19:12 my brethren, ye *are* my **b** and my flesh: 6106
 21:12 David went and took the **b** of Saul and 6106
 21:12 the **b** of Jonathan his son from the men of 6106
 21:13 he brought up from thence the **b** of Saul 6106
 21:13 of Saul and the **b** of Jonathan his son; 6106
 21:13 they gathered the **b** of them that were 6106
 21:14 the **b** of Saul and Jonathan his son buried 6106
1Ki 13: 2 and men's **b** shall be burnt upon thee. 6106
 13:31 God *is* buried; lay my **b** beside his bones: 6106
 13:31 God *is* buried; lay my bones beside his **b**: 6106
2Ki 13:21 touched the **b** of Elisha, he revived, 6106
 23:14 and filled their places *with* the **b** of men. 6106
 23:16 took the **b** out of the sepulchres, 6106
 23:18 Let him alone; let no man move his **b**. 6106
 23:18 So they let his **b** alone, with the bones of 6106
 23:18 with the **b** of the prophet that came out of 6106
 23:20 burnt men's **b** upon them, and returned 6106
1Ch 10:12 buried their **b** under the oak in Jabesh, 6106
2Ch 34: 5 he burnt the **b** of the priests upon their 6106
Job 4:14 trembling, which made all my **b** to shake. 6106
 10:11 and hast fenced me with **b** and sinews, 6106
 20:11 His **b** are full *of the sin of* his youth, 6106
 21:24 and his **b** are moistened with marrow. 6106
 30:17 **b** are pierced in me in the night season: 6106
 30:30 upon me, and my **b** are burnt with heat. 6106
 33:19 the multitude of his **b** *with* strong *pain:* 6106
 33:21 and his **b** *that* were not seen stick out. 6106
 40:18 His **b** *are* as strong pieces of brass; 6106
 40:18 pieces of brass; his **b** *are* like bars of iron. 1634
Ps 6: 2 O LORD, heal me; for my **b** are vexed. 6106
 22:14 like water, and all my **b** are out of joint: 6106
 22:17 I may tell all my **b**: they look *and* 6106
 31:10 of mine iniquity, and my **b** are consumed. 6106
 32: 3 my **b** waxed old through my roaring all 6106
 34:20 He keepeth all his **b**: not one of them is 6106
 35:10 All my **b** shall say, LORD, who *is* like 6106
 38: 3 neither *is there any* rest in my **b** because 6106
 42:10 *As* with a sword in my **b**, mine enemies 6106

Ps 51: 8 *that* the **b** which thou hast broken may 6106
 53: 5 for God hath scattered the **b** of him that 6106
 102: 3 smoke, and my **b** are burnt as a hearth. 6106
 102: 5 reason of the voice of my groaning my **b** 6106
 109:18 bowels like water, and like oil into his **b**. 6106
 141: 7 Our **b** are scattered at the grave's mouth, 6106
Pr 3: 8 health to thy navel, and marrow to thy **b**. 6106
 12: 4 maketh ashamed *is* as rottenness in his **b**. 6106
 14:30 the flesh: but envy the rottenness of the **b**. 6106
 15:30 *and* a good report maketh the **b** fat. 6106
 16:24 sweet to the soul, and health to the **b**. 6106
 17:22 medicine: but a broken spirit drieth the **b**. 1634
Ecc 11: 5 *nor* how the **b** *do* grow in the womb of 6106
Isa 38:13 *that*, as a lion, so will he break all my **b**: 6106
 58:11 thy soul in drought, and make fat thy **b**: 6106
 66:14 and your **b** shall flourish like an herb: 6106
Jer 8: 1 they shall bring out the **b** of the kings of 6106
 8: 1 the **b** of his princes, and the bones of 6106
 8: 1 the **b** of the priests, and the bones of 6106
 8: 1 the **b** of the prophets, and the bones of 6106
 8: 1 the **b** of the inhabitants of Jerusalem, out 6106
 20: 9 heart as a burning fire shut up in my **b**, 6106
 23: 9 because of the prophets; all my **b** shake; 6106
 50:17 king of Babylon hath **broken** his **b**. 6105
La 1:13 From above hath he sent fire into my **b**, 6106
 3: 4 hath he made old; he hath broken my **b**. 6106
 4: 8 skin cleaveth to their **b**; it is withered, 6106
Eze 6: 5 I will scatter your **b** round about your 6106
 24: 4 and the shoulder; fill *it* with the choice **b**. 6106
 24: 5 burn also the **b** under it, *and* make it boil 6106
 24: 5 and let them seethe the **b** of it therein. 6106
 24:10 and spice it well, and let the **b** be burnt. 6106
 32:27 but their iniquities shall be upon their **b**, 6106
 37: 1 midst of the valley which *was* full *of* **b**, 6106
 37: 3 unto me, Son of man, can these **b** live? 6106
 37: 4 Prophesy upon these **b**, and say unto 6106
 37: 4 bones, and say unto them, O ye dry **b**, 6106
 37: 5 Thus saith the Lord GOD unto these **b**; 6106
 37: 7 the **b** came together, bone to his bone. 6106
 37:11 these **b** are the whole house of Israel: 6106
 37:11 Our **b** are dried, and our hope is lost: 6106
Da 6:24 brake all their **b** in pieces or ever they 1635
Am 2: 1 he burnt the **b** of the king of Edom into 6106
 6:10 to bring out the **b** out of the house, 6106
Mic 3: 2 off them, and their flesh from off their **b**; 6106
 3: 3 break their **b**, and chop *them* in pieces, 6106
Hab 3:16 rottenness entered into my **b**, 6106
Zep 3: 3 they **gnaw** not the **b** till the morrow. 1633
Mt 23:27 but are within full of dead *men's* **b**, and 3747
Lk 24:39 for a spirit hath not flesh and **b**, as ye see 3747
Ac 3: 7 his feet and ankle **b** received strength, NIG
Eph 5:30 of his body, of his flesh, and of his **b**. 3747
Heb 11:22 gave commandment concerning his **b**. 3747

BONNETS (6)

Ex 28:40 **b** shalt thou make for them, for glory and 4021
 29: 9 Aaron and his sons, and put the **b** on 4021
 39:28 goodly **b** *of* fine linen, and linen breeches 4021
Lev 8:13 them *with* girdles, and put **b** upon them; 4021
Isa 3:20 The **b**, and the ornaments of the legs, 6287
Eze 44:18 They shall have linen **b** upon their heads, 6287

BOOK (188) [BOOKS]

Ge 5: 1 This *is* the **b** of the generations of Adam. 5612
Ex 17:14 Write this *for* a memorial in a **b**, 5612
 24: 7 he took the **b** of the covenant, and read in 5612
 32:32 out of thy **b** which thou hast written. 5612
 32:33 against me, him will I blot out of my **b**. 5612
Nu 5:23 the priest shall write these curses in a **b**, 5612
 21:14 Wherefore it is said in the **b** of the wars of 5612
Dt 17:18 **b** out of *that which* is before the priests 5612
 28:58 of this law that are written in this **b**, 5612
 28:61 which *is* not written in the **b** of this law, 5612
 29:20 all the curses that are written in this **b** 5612
 29:21 that are written in this **b** of the law: 5612
 29:27 all the curses that are written in this **b**: 5612
 30:10 his statutes which are written in this **b** of 5612
 31:24 of writing the words of this law in a **b**, 5612
 31:26 Take this **b** of the law, and put it in the 5612
Jos 1: 8 This **b** of the law shall not depart out of 5612
 8:31 it is written in the **b** of the law of Moses, 5612
 8:34 according to all that is written in the **b** of 5612
 10:13 *Is* not this written in the **b** of Jasher? So 5612
 18: 9 it by cities into seven parts in a **b**, 5612
 23: 6 do all that is written in the **b** of the law 5612
 24:26 Joshua wrote these words in the **b** of 5612
1Sa 10:25 wrote *it* in a **b**, and laid *it* up before 5612
2Sa 1:18 behold, *it* is written in the **b** of Jasher.) 5612
1Ki 11:41 *are* they not written in the **b** of the acts of 5612
 14:19 behold they *are* written in the **b** of 5612
 14:29 *are* they not written in the **b** of 5612
 15: 7 *are* they not written in the **b** of 5612
 15:23 *are* they not written in the **b** of 5612
 15:31 *are* they not written in the **b** of 5612
 16: 5 *are* they not written in the **b** of 5612
 16:14 *are* they not written in the **b** of 5612
 16:20 *are* they not written in the **b** of 5612
 16:27 *are* they not written in the **b** of 5612
 22:39 *are* they not written in the **b** of 5612
 22:45 *are* they not written in the **b** of 5612
2Ki 1:18 *are* they not written in the **b** of 5612
 8:23 *are* they not written in the **b** of 5612
 10:34 *are* they not written in the **b** of 5612
 12:19 *are* they not written in the **b** of 5612
 13: 8 *are* they not written in the **b** of 5612

2Ki	13:12 *are* they not written in the **b** of	5612
	14: 6 is written in the **b** of the law of Moses,	5612
	14:15 *are* they not written in the **b** of	5612
	14:18 *are* they not written in the **b** of	5612
	14:28 *are* they not written in the **b** of	5612
	15: 6 *are* they not written in the **b** of	5612
	15:11 *are* written in the **b** of the chronicles of	5612
	15:15 *are* written in the **b** of the chronicles of	5612
	15:21 *are* written in the **b** of the chronicles of	5612
	15:26 *are* written in the **b** of the chronicles of	5612
	15:31 *are* written in the **b** of the chronicles of	5612
	15:36 *are* they not written in the **b** of	5612
	16:19 *are* they not written in the **b** of	5612
	20:20 *are* they not written in the **b** of	5612
	21:17 *are* they not written in the **b** of	5612
	21:25 *are* they not written in the **b** of	5612
	22: 8 have found the **b** of the law in the house	5612
	22: 8 Hilkiah gave the **b** to Shaphan, and he	5612
	22:10 Hilkiah the priest hath delivered me a **b**.	5612
	22:11 the king had heard the words of the **b**	5612
	22:13 concerning the words of this **b** that is	5612
	22:13 not hearkened unto the words of this **b**,	5612
	22:16 all the words of the **b** which the king	5612
	23: 2 read in their ears all the words of the **b**	5612
	23: 3 this covenant that were written in this **b**.	5612
	23:21 as it is written in the **b** of this covenant.	5612
	23:24 **b** that Hilkiah the priest found *in* the	5612
	23:28 *are* they not written in the **b** of	5612
	24: 5 *are* they not written in the **b** of	5612
1Ch	9: 1 they *were* written in the **b** of the kings of	5612
	29:29 *are* written in the **b** of Samuel the seer,	1697
	29:29 in the **b** of Nathan the prophet, and in	1697
	29:29 the prophet, and in the **b** of Gad the seer,	1697
2Ch	9:29 *are* they not written in the **b** of Nathan	1697
	12:15 *are* they not written in the **b** of Shemaiah	1697
	16:11 they *are* written in the **b** of the kings of	5612
	17: 9 had the **b** of the law of the LORD with	5612
	20:34 behold they *are* written in the **b** of Jehu	1697
	20:34 who is mentioned in the **b** of the kings of	5612
	24:27 they *are* written in the story of the **b**	5612
	25: 4 *did* as it is written in the law in the **b** of	5612
	25:26 they not written in the **b** of the kings of	5612
	27: 7 they *are* written in the **b** of the kings of	5612
	28:26 they *are* written in the **b** of the kings of	5612
	32:32 *and* in the **b** of the kings of Judah and	5612
	33:18 they *are* written in the **b** of the kings of	1697
	34:14 Hilkiah the priest found a **b** of the law of	5612
	34:15 I have found the **b** of the law in the house	5612
	34:15 And Hilkiah delivered the **b** to Shaphan.	5612
	34:16 Shaphan carried the **b** to the king,	5612
	34:18 Hilkiah the priest hath given me a **b**.	5612
	34:21 the words of the **b** that is found:	5612
	34:21 to do after all that is written in this **b**.	5612
	34:24 all the curses that are written in the **b**	5612
	34:30 he read in their ears all the words of the **b**	5612
	34:31 the covenant which are written in this **b**.	5612
	35:12 as it is written in the **b** of Moses.	5612
	35:27 they *are* written in the **b** of the kings of	5612
	36: 8 they *are* written in the **b** of the kings of	5612
Ezr	4:15 That search may be made in the **b** of	5609
	4:15 so shalt thou find in the **b** of the records,	5609
	6:18 as it is written in the **b** of Moses.	5609
Ne	8: 1 scribe to bring the **b** of the law of Moses,	5612
	8: 3 *were* attentive unto the **b** of the law.	5612
	8: 5 Ezra opened the **b** in the sight of all	5612
	8: 8 So they read in the **b** in the law of God	5612
	8:18 day, he read in the **b** in the law of God.	5612
	9: 3 read in the **b** of the law of the LORD their	5612
	12:23 *were* written in the **b** of the chronicles,	5612
	13: 1 On that day they read in the **b** of Moses	5612
Est	2:23 it was written in the **b** of the chronicles	5612
	6: 1 he commanded to bring the **b** of records	5612
	9:32 of Purim; and *it was* written in the **b**.	5612
	10: 2 *are* they not written in the **b** of	5612
Job	19:23 O that they were printed in a **b**!	5612
	31:35 and *that* mine adversary had written a **b**.	5612
Ps	40: 7 in the volume of the **b** *it is* written of me,	5612
	56: 8 tears into thy bottle: *are they* not in thy **b**?	5612
	69:28 Let them be blotted out of the **b** of	5612
	139:16 in thy **b** all *my* members were written,	5612
Isa	29:11 you as the words of a **b** that is sealed,	5612
	29:12 **b** is delivered to *him* that is not learned,	5612
	29:18 day shall the deaf hear the words of the **b**,	5612
	30: 8 before them in a table, and note it in a **b**,	5612
	34:16 Seek ye out of the **b** of the LORD,	5612
Jer	25:13 *even* all that is written in this **b**, which	5612
	30: 2 that I have spoken unto thee in a **b**.	5612
	32:12 that subscribed the **b** of the purchase,	5612
	36: 2 Take thee a roll of a **b**, and write therein	5612
	36: 4 had spoken unto him, upon a roll of a **b**.	5612
	36: 8 reading in the **b** the words of the LORD *in*	5612
	36:10 Baruch in the **b** the words of Jeremiah	5612
	36:11 had heard out of the **b** all the words of	5612
	36:13 when Baruch read the **b** in the ears of	5612
	36:18 and I wrote *them* with ink in the **b**.	5612
	36:32 **b** which Jehoiakim king of Judah had	5612
	45: 1 when he had written these words in a **b**	5612
	51:60 So Jeremiah wrote in a **b** all the evil that	5612
	51:63 thou hast made an end of reading this **b**,	5612
Eze	2: 9 unto me; and lo, a roll of a **b** *was* therein;	5612
Da	12: 1 one that *shall* be found written in the **b**.	5612
	12: 4 Daniel, shut up the words, and seal the **b**,	5612
Na	1: 1 The **b** of the vision of Nahum	
Mal	3:16 **b** of remembrance was written before him	5612
Mt	1: 1 The **b** of the generation of Jesus Christ,	976

Mk	12:26 have ye not read in the **b** of Moses, how	976
Lk	3: 4 As it is written in the **b** of the words of	976
	4:17 And there was delivered unto him the **b** of	975
	4:17 And when he had opened the **b**, he found	975
	4:20 And he closed the **b**, and he gave *it* again	975
	20:42 And David himself saith in the **b** of Psalms,	976
Jn	20:30 disciples, which are not written in this **b**:	975
Ac	1:20 For it is written in the **b** of Psalms, Let his	976
	7:42 as it is written in the **b** of the prophets,	976
Gal	3:10 are written in the **b** of the law to do them.	975
Php	4: 3 whose names *are* in the **b** of life.	976
Heb	9:19 sprinkled both the **b**, and all the people,	975
	10: 7 I come (in the volume of the **b** it is written	975
Rev	1:11 write in a **b**, and send *it* unto the seven	
	3: 5 I will not blot out his name out of the **b** of	976
	5: 1 that sat on the throne a **b** written within	975
	5: 2 Who is worthy to open the **b**, and to loose	975
	5: 3 under the earth, was able to open the **b**,	975
	5: 4 found worthy to open and to read the **b**,	975
	5: 5 hath prevailed to open the **b**, and to loose	975
	5: 7 took the **b** out of the right hand of him that	975
	5: 8 when he had taken the **b**, the four beasts	975
	5: 9 Thou art worthy to take the **b**, and to open	975
	10: 2 And he had in his hand a **little b** open:	974
	10: 8 take the **little b** which is open in the hand	974
	10: 9 and said unto him, Give me the **little b**.	974
	10:10 And I took the **little b** out of the angel's	974
	13: 8 names are not written in the **b** of life	976
	17: 8 whose names were not written in the **b** of	975
	20:12 another **b** was opened, which is *the book*	975
	20:12 book was opened, which is *the* **b** of life:	NIG
	20:15 in the **b** of life was cast into the lake of fire.	976
	21:27 they which are written in the Lamb's **b** of	975
	22: 7 The sayings of the prophecy of this **b**.	
	22: 9 of them which keep the sayings of this **b**:	975
	22:10 not the sayings of the prophecy of this **b**:	975
	22:18 the words of the prophecy of this **b**,	975
	22:18 him the plagues that are written in this **b**:	975
	22:19 from the words of the **b** of this prophecy,	975
	22:19 God shall take away his part out of the **b** of	976
	22:19 *from the things* which are written in this **b**.	975

BOOKS (8) [BOOK]

Ecc	12:12 of making many **b** *there is* no end;	5612
Da	7:10 judgment was set, and the **b** were opened	5609
	9: 2 understood by **b** the number of the years,	5612
Jn	21:25 not contain the **b** that should be written.	975
Ac	19:19 used curious arts brought their **b** together,	976
2Ti	4:13 bring *with thee*, and the **b**, *but* especially	975
Rev	20:12 stand before God; and the **b** were opened:	975
	20:12 those *things* which were written in the **b**,	975

BOOTH (2) [BOOTHS]

Job	27:18 moth, and as a **b** *that* the keeper maketh.	5521
Jnh	4: 5 there made him a **b**, and sat under it in	5521

BOOTHS (9) [BOOTH]

Ge	33:17 him a house, and made **b** for his cattle:	5521
Lev	23:42 Ye shall dwell in **b** seven days; all that are	5521
	23:42 all that are Israelites born shall dwell in **b**:	5521
	23:43 I made the children of Israel to dwell in **b**,	5521
Ne	8:14 the children of Israel should dwell in **b**	5521
	8:15 of thick trees, to make **b**, as it is written.	5521
	8:16 brought *them*, and made themselves **b**,	5521
	8:17 come again out of the captivity made **b**,	5521
	8:17 made booths, and sat under the **b**:	5521

BOOTIES (1) [BOOTY]

Hab	2: 7 and thou shalt be for **b** unto them?	4933

BOOTY (3) [BOOTIES]

Nu	31:32 the **b**, *being* the rest of the prey which	4455
Jer	49:32 camels shall be a **b**, and the multitude	957
Zep	1:13 Therefore their goods shall become a **b**,	4933

BOOZ (3) [BOAZ]

Mt	1: 5 And Salmon begat **B** of Rachab;	1003
	1: 5 **B** begat Obed of Ruth; and Obed begat	1003
Lk	3:32 the son of Obed, which was the son of **B**,	1003

BOR ASHAN See CHOR-ASHAN

BORDER (158) [BORDERS]

Ge	10:19 the **b** of the Canaanites was from Sidon,	1366
	49:13 of ships; and his **b** *shall be* unto Zidon.	3411
Ex	19:12 up into the mount, or touch the **b** of it:	7097
	25:25 thou shalt make unto it a **b** of a	4526
	25:25 thou shalt make a golden crown to the **b**	4526
	25:27 Over against the **b** shall the rings be for	4526
	28:26 ends of the breastplate in the **b** thereof,	8193
	37:12 Also he made thereunto a **b** of a	4526
	37:12 made a crown of gold for the **b** thereof	4526
	37:14 Over against the **b** were the rings,	4526
	39:19 upon the **b** of it, which *was* on the side of	8193
Nu	20:16 in Kadesh, a city in the uttermost of thy **b**:	1366
	20:21 to give Israel passage through his **b**:	1366
	21:13 Arnon *is* the **b** of Moab, between Moab	1366
	21:15 of Ar, and lieth upon the **b** of Moab.	1366
	21:23 not suffer Israel to pass through his **b**:	1366
	21:24 for the **b** of the children of Ammon *was*	1366
	22:36 which *is* in the **b** of Arnon, which *is* in	1366
	33:44 pitched in Ije-abarim, in the **b** of Moab.	1366
	34: 3 your south **b** shall be the outmost coast of	1366
	34: 4 your **b** shall turn from the south to	1366
	34: 5 the **b** shall fetch a compass from Azmon	1366
	34: 6 *as for* the western **b**, you shall even have	1366

Nu	34: 6 you shall even have the great sea for a **b**:	1366
	34: 6 sea for a border: this shall be your west **b**.	1366
	34: 7 this shall be your north **b**: from the great	1366
	34: 8 mount Hor ye shall point out *your* **b**	NIH
	34: 8 the goings forth of the **b** shall be to Zedad:	1366
	34: 9 **b** shall go on to Ziphron, and the goings	1366
	34:10 ye shall point out your east **b** from	1366
	34:11 the **b** shall descend, and shall reach unto	1366
	34:12 the **b** shall go down to Jordan,	1366
	35:26 *without* the **b** of the city of his refuge,	1366
Dt	3:16 half the valley, and the **b**, even unto	1366
	3:16 which *is* the **b** of the children of Ammon;	1366
	12:20 the LORD thy God shall enlarge thy **b**,	1366
Jos	4:19 in Gilgal, in the east **b** of Jericho.	7097
	12: 2 *which is* the **b** of the Geshurites and	1366
	12: 5 unto the **b** of the Geshurites and	1366
	12: 5 the **b** of Sihon king of Heshbon.	1366
	13:10 unto the **b** of the children of Ammon;	1366
	13:11 the **b** of the Geshurites and Maachathites,	1366
	13:23 **b** of the children of Reuben was Jordan,	1366
	13:23 *thereof*. This *was* the inheritance of	1366
	13:26 and from Mahanaim unto the **b** of Debir;	1366
	13:27 Sihon king of Heshbon, Jordan and *his* **b**,	1366
	15: 1 *even* to the **b** of Edom, the wilderness of	1366
	15: 2 south **b** was from the shore of the salt	1366
	15: 5 the east **b** *was* the salt sea, *even* unto	1366
	15: 5 *their* **b** in the north quarter *was* from	1366
	15: 6 the **b** went up *to* Beth-hogla,	1366
	15: 6 the **b** went up to the stone of Bohan the	1366
	15: 7 **b** went up toward Debir from the valley	1366
	15: 7 the **b** passed towards the waters of	1366
	15: 8 the **b** went up *by* the valley of the son of	1366
	15: 8 the **b** went up to the top of the mountain	1366
	15: 9 the **b** was drawn from the top of the hill	1366
	15: 9 the **b** was drawn *to* Baalah, which *is*	1366
	15:10 the **b** compassed from Baalah westward	1366
	15:11 the **b** went out unto the side of Ekron	1366
	15:11 the **b** was drawn to Shicron,	1366
	15:11 the goings out of the **b** were at the sea.	1366
	15:12 the west **b** *was* to the great sea,	1366
	15:47 and the great sea, and the **b** *thereof*.	1366
	16: 5 the **b** of the children of Ephraim according	1366
	16: 5 of their inheritance on the east side was	1366
	16: 6 the **b** went out toward the sea *to*	1366
	16: 6 the **b** went about eastward *unto*	1366
	16: 8 The **b** went *out* from Tappuah westward	1366
	17: 7 the **b** went *along* on the right hand unto	1366
	17: 8 Tappuah on the **b** of Manasseh *belonged*	1366
	17:10 *it was* Manasseh's, and the sea is his **b**;	1366
	18:12 their **b** on the north side was from Jordan;	1366
	18:12 the **b** went up to the side of Jericho on	1366
	18:13 the **b** went over from thence toward Luz,	1366
	18:13 the **b** descended to Ataroth-adar, near	1366
	18:14 the **b** was drawn *thence*, and compassed	1366
	18:15 the **b** went out on the west, and went out	1366
	18:16 the **b** came down to the end of	1366
	18:19 the **b** passed along to the side of	1366
	18:19 outgoings of the **b** were at the north bay	1366
	18:20 Jordan was the **b** of it on the east side.	1379
	19:10 the **b** of their inheritance was unto Sarid:	1366
	19:11 their **b** went up toward the sea,	1366
	19:12 the sunrising unto the **b** of Chisloth-tabor,	1366
	19:14 the **b** compasseth it on the north side *to*	1366
	19:18 **b** was toward Jezreel, and Chesulloth,	1366
	19:22 the outgoings of their **b** were *at* Jordan:	1366
	19:25 their **b** was Helkath, and Hali, and Beten,	1366
	19:46 and Rakkon, with the **b** before Japho.	1366
	22:25 For the LORD hath made Jordan a **b**	1366
	24:30 they buried him in the **b** of his inheritance	1366
Jdg	2: 9 they buried him in the **b** of his inheritance	1366
	7:22 *and* to the **b** of Abel-meholah,	8193
	11:18 but came not within the **b** of Moab:	1366
	11:18 of Moab: for Arnon *was* the **b** of Moab.	1366
1Sa	6:12 after them unto the **b** of Beth-shemesh.	1366
	10: 2 sepulchre in the **b** of Benjamin at Zelzah;	1366
	13:18 company turned *to* the way of the **b**	1366
2Sa	8: 3 as he went to recover his **b** at the river	3027
1Ki	4:21 of the Philistines, and unto the **b** of Egypt:	1366
2Ki	3:21 armour, and upward, and stood in the **b**.	1366
2Ch	9:26 of the Philistines, and to the **b** of Egypt.	1366
Ps	78:54 he brought them to the **b** of his sanctuary,	1366
Pr	15:25 but he will establish the **b** of the widow.	1366
Isa	19:19 and a pillar at the **b** thereof to the LORD.	1366
	37:24 I will enter *into* the height of his **b**,	7093
Jer	31:17 children shall come again to their own **b**.	1366
	50:26 Come against her from the **utmost b**,	7093
Eze	11:10 I will judge you in the **b** of Israel;	1366
	11:11 *but* I will judge you in the **b** of Israel:	1366
	29:10 from the tower of Syene even unto the **b**	1366
	43:13 the **b** thereof by the edge thereof round	1366
	43:17 the **b** about it *shall be* half a cubit;	1366
	43:20 of the settle, and upon the **b** round about:	1366
	45: 7 from the west **b** unto the east border.	1366
	45: 7 from the west border unto the east **b**.	1366
	47:13 *shall be* the **b**, whereby ye shall inherit	1366
	47:15 this *shall be* the **b** of the land toward	1366
	47:16 which *is* between the **b** of Damascus and	1366
	47:16 border of Damascus and the **b** of Hamath;	1366
	47:17 the **b** from the sea shall be Hazar-enan,	1366
	47:17 of Damascus, and the north	1366
	47:17 north northward, and the **b** of Hamath.	1366
	47:18 Jordan, from the **b** unto the east sea.	1366
	47:20 side also *shall be* the great sea from the **b**,	1366
	48: 1 the **b** of Damascus northward,	1366

B

B

Eze 48: 2 by the **b** of Dan, from the east side unto 1366
48: 3 by the **b** of Asher, from the east side even 1366
48: 4 by the **b** of Naphtali, from the east side 1366
48: 5 by the **b** of Manasseh, from the east side 1366
48: 6 by the **b** of Ephraim, from the east side 1366
48: 7 by the **b** of Reuben, from the east side 1366
48: 8 by the **b** of Judah, from the east side unto 1366
48:12 *a thing* most holy by the **b** of the Levites. 1366
48:13 against the **b** of the priests, the Levites 1366
48:21 of the oblation toward the east **b**, 1366
48:21 and twenty thousand toward the west **b**, 1366
48:22 between the **b** of Judah and the border of 1366
48:22 border of Judah and the **b** of Benjamin, 1366
48:24 by the **b** of Benjamin, from the east side 1366
48:25 by the **b** of Simeon, from the east side 1366
48:26 by the **b** of Issachar, from the east side 1366
48:27 by the **b** of Zebulun, from the east side 1366
48:28 by the **b** of Gad, at the south side 1366
48:28 the **b** shall be even from Tamar *unto* 1366
Joel 3: 6 *ye* might remove them far from their **b**. 1366
Am 1:13 at Gilead, that *they* might enlarge their **b**: 1366
6: 2 their greater than your border? 1366
6: 2 or their border greater than your **b**? 1366
Ob 1: 7 have brought thee *even* to the **b**: 1366
Zep 2: 8 and magnified *themselves* against their **b**. 1366
Zec 9: 2 Hamath also shall **b** thereby; Tyrus, 1379
Mal 1: 4 shall call them, The **b** of wickedness, and, 1366
1: 5 The Lord will be magnified from the **b** 1366
Mk 6:56 touch it were but the **b** of his garment: 2899
Lk 8:44 and touched the **b** of his garment: 2899

BORDERS (43) [BORDER]
Ge 23:17 that *were* in all the **b** round about, 1366
47:21 to Egypt even to the *other* end thereof. 1366
Ex 8: 2 behold, I will smite all thy **b** with frogs: 1366
16:35 until they came unto the **b** of the land of 7097
34:24 nations before thee, and enlarge thy **b**: 1366
Nu 15:38 **b** of their garments throughout their 3671
15:38 that they put upon the fringe of the **b** a 3671
20:17 nor *to* the left, until we have passed thy **b**. 1366
21:22 king's *high* way, until we be past thy **b**. 1366
35:27 him without the **b** of the city of his refuge, 1366
Jos 11: 2 valley, and in the **b** of Dor on the west, 5299
13: 2 all the **b** of the Philistines, and all Geshuri, 1552
13: 3 even unto the **b** of Ekron northward, 1366
13: 4 unto Aphek, to the **b** of the Amorites: 1366
16: 2 passeth along unto the **b** of Archi *to* 1366
22:10 when they came unto the **b** of Jordan, 1552
22:11 in the **b** of Jordan, at the passage of 1552
1Ki 7:28 bases *was on* this *manner:* they had **b**, 4526
7:28 and the **b** were between the ledges: 4526
7:29 on the **b** that *were* between the ledges 4526
7:31 mouth of it *were* gravings with their **b**, 4526
7:32 under the **b** were four wheels; 4526
7:35 and the **b** thereof *were* of the same. 4526
7:36 on the **b** thereof, he graved cherubims, 4526
2Ki 16:17 king Ahaz cut off the **b** of the bases, 4526
18: 8 *even* unto Gaza, and the **b** thereof, 1366
19:23 I will enter *into* the lodgings of his **b**, 7093
1Ch 5:16 all the suburbs of Sharon, upon their **b**. 8444
7:29 by the **b** of the children of Manasseh, 3027
Ps 74:17 Thou hast set all the **b** of the earth: 1367
147:14 He maketh peace *in* thy **b**, *and* filleth thee 1366
SS 1:11 We will make thee **b** of gold with studs of 8447
Isa 15: 8 For the cry is gone round about the **b** of 1366
54:12 and all thy **b** of pleasant stones. 1366
60:18 wasting nor destruction within thy **b**; 1366
Jer 15:13 and *that* for all thy sins, even in all thy **b**. 1366
17: 3 high places for sin, throughout all thy **b**. 1366
Eze 27: 4 Thy **b** *are* in the midst of the seas, 1366
45: 1 *shall* be holy in all the **b** thereof round 1366
Mic 5: 6 and when he treadeth within our **b**. 1366
Mt 4:13 in the **b** of Zabulon and Nephthalim: 3725
23: 5 and enlarge the **b** of their garments, 2899
Mk 7:24 and went into the **b** of Tyre and Sidon, 3181

BORE (2) [BORED]
Ex 21: 6 his master shall **b** his ear **through** with an 7527
Job 41: 2 or **b** his jaw **through** with a thorn? 5344

BORED (1) [BORE]
2Ki 12: 9 **b** a hole in the lid of it, and set it beside 5344

BORN (154) [BEAR]
Ge 4:18 unto Enoch was **b** Irad: and Irad begat 3205
4:26 to Seth, *to* him also there was **b** a son; 3205
6: 1 earth, and daughters were **b** unto them, 3205
10: 1 unto them were sons **b** after the flood. 3205
10:21 the elder, even to him were *children* **b**. 3205
10:25 unto Eber were **b** two sons: the name of 3205
14:14 armed his trained *servants,* **b** in his own 3211
15: 3 and lo, **one b** in my house is mine heir. 1121
17:12 he **that is b** in the house, or bought with 3211
17:13 He **that is b** in thy house, and he that is 3211
17:17 Shall *a child* be **b** unto him that is an 3205
17:23 all **that were b** in his house, and all that 3211
17:27 **b** in the house, and bought with money 3211
21: 3 the name of his son that was **b** unto him, 3205
21: 5 when his son Isaac was **b** unto him. 3205
21: 7 for *I have* **b** *him* a son in his old age. 3205
21: 9 which she had **b** unto Abraham, mocking. 3205
22:20 she hath also **b** children unto thy brother 3205
24:15 who was **b** to Bethuel, son of Milcah, 3205
29:34 me, because I have **b** him three sons: 3205
30:20 with me, because I have **b** him six sons: 3205

Ge 30:25 came to pass, when Rachel had **b** Joseph, 3205
31:43 or unto their children which they have **b**? 3205
35:26 which were **b** to him in Padan-aram. 3205
36: 5 which were **b** unto him in the land of 3205
41:50 unto Joseph were **b** two sons before 3205
46:20 unto Joseph in the land of Egypt were **b** 3205
46:22 sons of Rachel, which were **b** to Jacob: 3205
46:27 which were **b** him in Egypt, *were* two 3205
48: 5 were **b** unto thee in the land of Egypt 3205
Ex 1:22 Every son that is **b** ye shall cast into 3209
12:19 whether he be a stranger, or **b** in the land. 249
12:48 he shall be as one that is **b** in the land: 249
21: 4 and she have **b** him sons or daughters; 3205
Lev 12: 2 have conceived seed, and **b** a man child: 3205
12: 7 This *is* the law for her that hath **b** a male 3205
18: 9 *she be* **b** at home, or born abroad, 4138
18: 9 *she be* born at home, or **b** abroad, 4138
19:34 shall be unto you as **one b** amongst you, 249
22:11 eat of it, and **he that is b** in his house: 3211
23:42 that are Israelites **b** shall dwell in booths: 249
24:16 the stranger, as he **that is b** in the *land,* 249
Nu 9:14 and for him **that is b** amongst the 249
15:13 All that are **b** of the country shall do 249
15:29 *for* him **that is b** amongst the children 249
15:30 *he be* **b** in the land, or a stranger, 249
26:60 unto Aaron was **b** Nadab, and Abihu, 3205
Dt 21:15 and they have **b** him children, 3205
Jos 5: 5 the people *that were* **b** in the wilderness 3209
8:33 stranger, as he that was **b** among them; 3205
Jdg 13: 8 we shall do unto the child that shall be **b**. 3205
18:29 Dan their father, who was **b** unto Israel: 3205
Ru 4:15 to thee than seven sons, hath **b** him. 3205
4:17 name, saying, There is a son **b** to Naomi; 3205
1Sa 2: 5 so that the barren hath **b** seven; and she 3205
4:20 *unto her,* Fear not; for thou hast **b** a son. 3205
2Sa 3: 2 unto David were sons **b** in Hebron: 3205
5: 3 These were **b** to David in Hebron. 3205
5:13 were yet sons and daughters **b** to David. 3205
5:14 these *be* the names of those that were **b** 3209
12:14 the child also that is **b** unto thee shall 3205
14:27 unto Absalom there were **b** three sons, 3205
21:20 number; and he also was **b** to the giant. 3205
21:22 These four were **b** to the giant in Gath, 3205
1Ki 13: 2 child *shall be* **b** unto the house of David, 3205
1Ch 1:19 unto Eber were **b** two sons: the name of 3205
2: 3 *which* three were **b** unto him of 3205
2: 9 also of Hezron, that were **b** unto him; 3205
3: 1 which were **b** unto him in Hebron, 3205
3: 4 These six were **b** unto him in Hebron; 3205
3: 5 these were **b** unto him in Jerusalem; 3205
7:21 whom the men of Gath that were **b** in 3205
20: 8 These were **b** unto the giant in Gath; 3205
22: 9 a son *shall be* **b** to thee, who shall 3205
26: 6 Also unto Shemaiah his son were sons **b**, 3205
Ezr 10: 3 such as are **b** of them, according to 3205
Job 1: 2 there were **b** unto him seven sons and 3205
3: 3 Let the day perish wherein I was **b**, 3205
5: 7 man is **b** unto trouble, as the sparks fly 3205
11:12 though man be *like* a wild ass's colt. 3205
14: 1 Man *that is* **b** of a woman *is* of few days, 3205
15: 7 *Art* thou the first man *that was* **b**? or 7209
15:14 he which is **b** of a woman, that he should 3205
25: 4 can he be clean *that is* **b** of a woman? 3205
38:21 thou *it,* because thou wast then **b**? 3205
Ps 22:31 unto a people that *shall be* **b**, 3205
58: 3 they go astray **as soon as** they be **b**, 990+4480
78: 6 *even* the children *which* should be **b**; 3205
87: 4 Tyre, with Ethiopia; this *man* was **b** there. 3205
87: 5 be said, This and that man was **b** in her: 3205
87: 6 *up* the people, *that* this *man* was **b** there. 3205
Pr 17:17 all times, and a brother is **b** for adversity. 3205
Ecc 2: 7 maidens, and had servants **b** in *my* house; 1121
3: 2 A time to be **b**, and a time to die; a time 3205
4:14 whereas also *he that is* **b** in his kingdom 3205
Isa 9: 6 For unto us a child is **b**, unto us a Son is 3205
66: 8 *or* shall a nation be **b** at once? for as soon 3205
Jer 16: 3 concerning the daughters that are **b** in 3209
20:14 Cursed *be* the day wherein I was **b**: 3205
20:15 saying, A man child is **b** unto thee; 3205
22:26 another country, where ye were not **b**; 3205
Eze 16: 4 in the day thou wast **b** thy navel was not 3205
16: 5 of thy person, in the day that thou wast **b**. 3205
47:22 shall be unto you as **b in the country** 3205
Hos 2: 3 and set her as *in* the day that she was **b**, 3205
Mt 1:16 whom was **b** Jesus, who is called Christ. 1080
2: 1 Now when Jesus was **b** in Bethlehem of 1080
2: 2 Where is he that is **b** King of the Jews? 5088
2: 4 of them where Christ should be **b**. 1080
11:11 Among *them that are* **b** of women there 1084
19:12 so *from their* mother's womb: 1080
26:24 good for that man if he had not been **b**. 1080
Mk 14:21 it for that man if he had never been **b**. 1080
Lk 1:35 *that* holy thing which shall be **b** of thee 1080
2:11 For unto you is **b** this day in the city of 5088
7:28 Among *those that are* **b** of women there 1084
Jn 1:13 were **b**, not of blood, nor of the will 1080
3: 3 I say unto thee, Except a man be **b** again, 1080
3: 4 How can a man be **b** when he is old? 1080
3: 4 time into his mother's womb, and be **b**? 1080
3: 5 Except a man be **b** of water and *of* 1080
3: 6 That which is **b** of the flesh is flesh; and 1080
3: 6 and that which is **b** of the Spirit is spirit. 1080
3: 7 that I said unto thee, Ye must be **b** again. 1080
3: 8 so is every one that is **b** of the Spirit. 1080
8:41 they to him, We be not **b** of fornication; 1080

Jn 9: 2 or his parents, that he was **b** blind? 1080
9:19 Is this your son, who ye say was **b** blind? 1080
9:20 this is our son, and that he was **b** blind: 1080
9:32 opened the eyes of one that was **b** blind. 1080
9:34 Thou wast altogether **b** in sins, 1080
16:21 for joy that a man is **b** into the world. 1080
18:37 To this end was I **b**, and for this cause 1080
Ac 2: 8 in our own tongue, wherein we were **b**? 1080
7:20 In which time Moses was **b**, 1080
18: 2 **b** in Pontus, lately come from Italy, 1085
18:24 **b** at Alexandria, an eloquent man, 1085
22: 3 *am* a Jew, in Tarsus, *a city* in Cilicia, 1080
22:28 And Paul said, But I was *free* **b**. 1080
Ro 9:11 (For *the children* being not yet **b**, 1080
1Co 15: 8 of me also, as of one **b** out of due time. 1626
Gal 4:23 he who was of the bondwoman was **b** 1080
4:29 he that was **b** after the flesh persecuted 1080
4:29 persecuted him that was **b** after the Spirit, NIG
Heb 11:23 By faith Moses, when he was **b**, was hid 1080
1Pe 1:23 Being **b** **again**, not of corruptible seed, 313
1Jn 2:29 which doeth righteousness is **b** of him. 1080
3: 9 Whosoever is **b** of God doth not commit 1080
3: 9 he cannot sin, because he is **b** of God. 1080
4: 7 and every one that loveth is **b** of God, 1080
5: 1 that Jesus is the Christ is **b** of God: 1080
5: 4 For whatsoever is **b** of God overcometh 1080
5:18 We know that whosoever is **b** of God 1080
Rev 12: 4 to devour her child as soon as it was **b**. 5088

BORN OF A FORBIDDEN MARRIAGE See
 BASTARD; BASTARDS

BORNE (31) [BEAR]
Ex 25:14 the ark, that the ark may be **b** with them. 5375
25:28 that the table may be **b** with them. 5375
Jdg 16:29 on which it was **b up**, of the one with his 5564
Job 34:31 I have **b** *chastisement,* I will not offend 5375
Ps 55:12 I could have **b** *it:* neither *was* it he that 5375
69: 7 Because for thy sake I have **b** reproach; 5375
Isa 46: 3 which are **b** *by me* from the belly, 6006
53: 4 Surely he hath **b** our griefs, and carried 5375
66:12 ye shall be **b** upon *her* sides, 5375
Jer 10: 5 they **must needs be b**, because 5375+5375
15: 9 She that hath **b** seven languisheth: she 3205
15:10 that thou hast **b** me a man of strife and 3205
La 3:28 because he hath **b** *it* upon him. 5190
5: 7 *are* not; *and* we have **b** their iniquities. 5445
Eze 16:20 whom thou hast **b** unto me, and these 3205
16:58 Thou hast **b** thy lewdness and thine 5375
32:24 yet have they **b** their shame with them 5375
32:25 yet have they **b** their shame with them 5375
36: 6 ye have **b** the shame of the heathen; 5375
39:26 After that they have **b** their shame, and all 5375
Am 5:26 ye have **b** the tabernacle of your Moloch 5375
Mt 20:12 have **b** the burden and heat of the day. 941
23: 4 bind heavy burdens and **grievous to be b**, 1419
Mk 2: 3 one sick of the palsy, *which was* **b** of four. 142
Lk 11:46 lade men *with* burdens **grievous to be b**, 1419
Jn 5:37 hath sent me, hath **b witness** of me. 3140
20:15 if thou have **b** him *hence,* tell me where 941
Ac 21:35 he was **b** of the soldiers for the violence 941
1Co 15:49 And as we have **b** the image of the earthy, 5409
3Jn 1: 6 Which have **b witness** of thy charity 3140
Rev 2: 3 And hast **b**, and hast patience, and for my 941

BORROW (8) [BORROWED, BORROWER, BORROWETH]
Ex 3:22 every woman shall **b** of her neighbour, 7592
11: 2 let every man **b** of his neighbour, 7592
22:14 if a man **b** *ought* of his neighbour, and it 7592
Dt 15: 6 unto many nations, but thou shalt not **b**; 5670
28:12 unto many nations, and thou shalt not **b**. 3867
2Ki 4: 3 **b** thee vessels abroad of all thy neighbours, 7592
4: 3 *even* empty vessels; **b** not a few. NIH
Mt 5:42 from him that would **b** of thee turn not 1155

BORROWED (3) [BORROW]
Ex 12:35 they **b** of the Egyptians jewels of silver, 7592
2Ki 6: 5 and said, Alas, master, for it *was* **b**. 7592
Ne 5: 4 We have **b** money for the king's tribute, 3867

BORROWER (2) [BORROW]
Pr 22: 7 poor, and the **b** *is* servant to the lender. 3867
Isa 24: 2 seller; as *with* the lender, so *with* the **b**; 3867

BORROWETH (1) [BORROW]
Ps 37:21 The wicked **b**, and payeth not again: 3867

BOSCATH (1)
2Ki 22: 1 *was* Jedidah, the daughter of Adaiah of **B**. 1218

BOSOM (41)
Ge 16: 5 I have given my maid into thy **b**; 2436
Ex 4: 6 unto him, Put now thine hand into thy **b**. 2436
4: 6 he put his hand into his **b**: and when he 2436
4: 7 he said, Put thine hand into thy **b** again. 2436
4: 7 he put his hand into his **b** again; 2436
4: 7 plucked it out of his **b**, and behold, it was 2436
Nu 11:12 say unto me, Carry them in thy **b**, 2436
Dt 13: 6 or the wife of thy **b**, or thy friend, 2436
28:54 toward the wife of his **b**, and towards 2436
28:56 be evil towards the husband of her **b**, 2436
Ru 4:16 laid it in her **b**, and became nurse unto it. 2436
2Sa 12: 3 lay in his **b**, and was unto him as a 2436
12: 8 thy master's wives into thy **b**, 2436
1Ki 1: 2 her cherish him, and let her lie in thy **b**, 2436

B

1Ki 3:20 laid it in her **b**, and laid her dead child in 2436
3:20 bosom, and laid her dead child in my **b**. 2436
17:19 he took him out of her **b**, and carried him 2436
Job 31:33 as Adam, by hiding mine iniquity in my **b**: 2243
Ps 74:11 even thy right hand? pluck *it* out of thy **b**. 2436
79:12 sevenfold into their **b** their reproach, 2436
89:50 *how* I do bear in my **b** *the reproach* of all 2436
129: 7 hand; nor he that bindeth sheaves his **b**. 2683
Pr 5:20 and embrace the **b** of a stranger? 2436
6:27 Can a man take fire in his **b**, and his 2436
17:23 A wicked *man* taketh a gift out of the **b** to 2436
19:24 A slothful *man* hideth his hand in *his* **b**, 6747
21:14 and a reward in the **b** strong wrath. 2436
26:15 The slothful hideth in his **b**; 6747
Ecc 7: 9 angry: for anger resteth in the **b** of fools. 2436
Isa 40:11 carry *them* in his **b**, *and* shall gently lead 2436
65: 6 even recompense into their **b**, 2436
65: 7 I measure their former work into their **b**. 2436
Jer 32:18 into the **b** of their children after them: 2436
La 2:12 was poured out into their mothers' **b**. 2436
Mic 7: 5 of thy mouth from her that lieth in thy **b**. 2436
Lk 6:38 running over, shall *men* give into your **b**. 2859
16:22 carried by the angels into Abraham's **b**: 2859
16:23 Abraham afar off, and Lazarus in his **b**. 2859
Jn 1:18 which is in the **b** of the Father, he hath 2859
13:23 Now there was leaning on Jesus' **b** one of 2859

BOSOR (1) [BEOR]
2Pe 2:15 following the way of Balaam *the son of* **B**, 1007

BOSSES (1)
Job 15:26 *his* neck, upon the thick **b** of his bucklers: 1354

BOTCH (2)
Dt 28:27 The LORD will smite thee with the **b** of 7822
28:35 with a sore **b** that cannot be healed, 7822

BOTH (361)
Ge 2:25 they were **b** naked, the man and his wife, 8147
3: 7 the eyes of them **b** were opened, 8147
6: 7 **b** man, and beast, and the creeping thing, 4480
7:21 *b* of fowl, and of cattle, and of beast, NIH
7:23 **b** man, and cattle, and the creeping things, 4480
8:17 *b* of fowl, and of cattle, and of every NIH
9:23 laid *it* upon **b** their shoulders, 8147
19: 4 the house round, **b** old and young, 4480+5704
19:11 with blindness, **b** small and great; 4480+5704
19:36 Thus were the **b** daughters of Lot with 8147
21:27 and **b** of them made a covenant. 8147
21:31 because there they sware **b** of them. 8147
22: 6 a knife; and they went **b** of them together. 8147
22: 8 so they went **b** of them together. 8147
24:25 We have **b** straw and provender enough, 1571
24:44 **B** drink thou, and I will also draw for thy 1571
27:45 why should I be deprived also of you **b** *in* 8147
31:37 that they may judge betwixt us **b**. 8147
36:24 children of Zibeon; **b** Aiah, and Anah: 2050.1
40: 5 they dreamed a dream **b** of them, each 8147
41:10 guard's house, *b* me and the chief baker: NIH
42:35 when **b** their father saw NIH
43: 8 **b** we, and thou, *and* also our little ones. 1571
44: 9 let him die, and we also will be my 2050.1
44:16 we, and *he* also with whom the cup is 1571
46:34 until now, **b** we, *and* also our fathers: 1571
47: 3 *are* shepherds, **b** we, *and* also our fathers. 1571
47:19 die before thine eyes, **b** we and our land? 1571
48:13 Joseph took them **b**, Ephraim in his right 8147
50: 9 there went up with him **b** chariots and 1571
Ex 5:14 your task in making brick **b** yesterday 1571
7:19 **b** in *vessels of* wood, and in *vessels of* 2050.1
8: 4 the frogs shall come up **b** on thee, NIH
9:25 *was* in the field, **b** man and beast; 4480+5704
12:12 the land of Egypt, **b** man and beast; 4480+5704
12:31 people, **b** you and the children of Israel; 1571
13: 2 children of Israel, *b* of man and of beast: NIH
13:15 **b** the firstborn of man, 4480+5704
18:18 **b** thou, and this people that *is* with thee: 1571
22: 9 the cause of **b** parties shall come before 8147
22:11 an oath of the LORD be between them **b**, 8147
26:24 thus shall it be for them **b**; they shall be 8147
29:44 I will sanctify also **b** Aaron and his sons, NIH
32:15 the tables *were* written on **b** their sides; 8147
35:22 they came, **b** men **and** women, as many 5921
35:25 **b** of blue, and of purple, *and* of scarlet, NIH
35:34 *b* he, and Aholiab, the son of Ahisamach, NIH
36:29 he did to **b** of them in both the corners. 8147
36:29 he did to both of them in **b** the corners. 8147
37:26 *b* the top of it, and the sides thereof round NIH
Lev 6:28 shall be scoured, and rinsed in water. NIH
8:11 all his vessels, **b** the laver and his foot, 2050.1
9: 3 a calf and a lamb, **b** of the first year, NIH
15:18 they shall *b* bathe *themselves* in water, NIH
16:21 Aaron shall lay **b** his hands upon the head 8147
17:15 he shall **b** wash his clothes, NIH
20:11 of them shall surely be put to death; 8147
20:12 **b** of them shall surely be put to death: 8147
20:13 **b** of them have committed an 8147
20:14 they shall be burnt with fire, **b** he **and** 2050.1
20:18 **b** of them shall be cut off from among 8147
21:22 God, *b* of the most holy, and of the holy. NIH
22:28 not kill it and her young **b** in one day. NIH
25:41 *b* he and his children with him, NIH
25:44 **B** thy bondmen, and thy bondmaids, 2050.1
25:54 of jubile, *b* he, and his children with him. NIH

Lev 27:28 *b* of man and beast, and of the field of his NIH
27:33 **b** it **and** the change thereof shall be 2050.1
Nu 3:13 all the firstborn in Israel, **b** man and beast: 4480
5: 3 **B** male and female shall ye put out, 4480
7: 1 **b** the altar and all the vessels thereof, 2050.1
7:13 of them *were* full *of* fine flour mingled 8147
7:19 of them full *of* fine flour mingled with 8147
7:25 of them full *of* fine flour mingled with 8147
7:31 of them full *of* fine flour mingled with 8147
7:37 of them full *of* fine flour mingled with 8147
7:43 of them full *of* fine flour mingled with 8147
7:49 of them full *of* fine flour mingled with 8147
7:55 of them full *of* fine flour mingled with 8147
7:61 of them full *of* fine flour mingled with 8147
7:67 of them full *of* fine flour mingled with 8147
7:73 of them full *of* fine flour mingled with 8147
7:79 of them full *of* fine flour mingled with 8147
8:17 of Israel *are* mine, *b* man and beast: NIH
9:14 for the stranger, and for him that was 2050.1
12: 5 and Miriam: and they **b** came forth. 8147
15:15 One ordinance *shall be* for you *of* NIH
15:29 *b* for him that is born amongst the children NIH
16:11 which cause *b* thou and all thy company NIH
25: 8 thrust **b** of them through, the man of 8147
27:21 *b* he, and all the children of Israel with NIH
31:11 and all the prey, *b* of men and of beasts. NIH
31:19 purify **b** yourselves and your captives on NIH
31:26 *b* of man and of beast, thou, and Eleazar NIH
31:28 *b* of the persons, and of the beeves, NIH
31:47 *b* of man and of beast, and gave them unto NIH
35:15 *b* for the children of Israel, and for NIH
Dt 19:17 the men, between whom the 8147
21:15 children, *b* the beloved and the hated; NIH
22:22 they shall **b** of them die, *both* the man 8147
22:22 *b* the man that lay with the woman, NIH
22:24 ye shall bring them **b** out unto the gate of 8147
23:18 for even **b** these *are* abomination unto 8147
30:19 that *b* thou and thy seed may live: NIH
32:25 shall destroy **b** the young man and 1571
Jos 6:21 **b** man and woman, young and old, 4480+5704
8:25 **b** of men and women, *were* twelve 4480+5704
14:11 for war, **b** to go out, and to come in. 2050.1
17:16 *b* they who *are* of Beth-shean and NIH
Jdg 5:30 divers colours of needlework on **b** sides, NIH
6: 5 *for* **b** they and their camels were 2050.1
8:22 **b** thou, and thy son, and thy son's son 1571
10:10 **b** because we have forsaken our God, 2050.1
15: 5 burnt up **b** the shocks, and also the 4480
19: 6 and did eat and drink **b** of them together: 8147
19: 8 afternoon, and they did eat **b** them. 8147
19:19 Yet there is **b** straw and provender for our 1571
Ru 1: 5 and Chilion died also **b** of them; 8147
1Sa 2:26 was in favour **b** with the LORD, 1571
2:34 in one day they shall die **b** of them. 8147
3:11 *at* which the ears of every one that 8147
5: 4 the palms of his hands *were* cut off 8147
5: 9 **b** small and great, and they had emerods 4480
6:18 of fenced cities, and *of* country villages, NIH
9:26 they went out **b** of them, he and Samuel, 8147
12:14 shall **b** ye and also the king that reigneth 1571
12:25 ye shall be consumed, **b** ye and your king. 1571
14:11 **b** of them discovered themselves unto 8147
15: 3 slay **b** man and woman, infant and 4480
17:36 Thy servant slew **b** the lion and the bear: 1571
20:11 they went out **b** of them *into* the field. 8147
20:42 forasmuch as we have sworn **b** of us in 8147
22:19 **b** men and women, children and 4480
25: 6 liveth *in prosperity*, Peace *be* **b** *to* thee, 2050.1
25:16 They were a wall unto us **b** by night and 1571
25:43 and they were also **b** of them his wives. 1571
26:25 thou shalt **b** do great things, and also 1571
2Sa 8:18 Benaiah the son of Jehoiada *was over* **b** 2050.1
9:13 king's table; and *was* lame on **b** his feet. 8147
15:25 and shew me *b* it, and his habitation: NIH
16:23 *was* **b** the counsel of Ahithophel **b** with 1571
17:18 they went **b** of them away quickly, 8147
1Ki 3:13 thou hast not asked, **b** riches, and honour: 1571
6: 5 *b* of the temple and of the oracle: NIH
6:15 the floor of the house, and the walls of 4480
6:16 the floor and the walls with boards of 4480
6:25 the cherubims *were* of one measure and 8147
7:12 for the inner court of the house of 2050.1
7:50 *of* gold, *b* for the doors of the inner house, NIH
2Ki 2:11 horses of fire, and parted them **b** asunder; 8147
3:17 *b* ye, and your cattle, and your beasts. NIH
6:15 a host compassed the city **b** with horses 2050.1
17:41 **b** their children, and their children's 1571
21:12 heareth of it, **b** his ears shall tingle. 8147
23: 2 all the people, **b** small and great: 4480+3807.1
23:15 **b** that altar and the high place he brake 1571
25:26 **b** small and great, and the captains of 4480
1Ch 12: 2 could use **b** the right hand and the left in NIH
12:15 *b* toward the east, and toward the west. NIH
15:12 sanctify yourselves, *b* ye and your brethren, NIH
16: 3 *b* man and woman, to every one a loaf of 4480
23:29 *b* for the shewbread, and for the fine 2050.1
24: 3 Zadok of the sons of Eleazar, 2050.1
28:15 *b* for the candlestick, and *also for* the NIH
29:12 **B** riches and honour *come* of thee, 2050.1
2Ch 20:25 found among them in abundance **b** 2050.1
24:16 towards God, and *towards* his house. 2050.1
25:21 *b* he and Amaziah king of Judah, NIH
26:10 **b** in the low country, and in the plains: 2050.1
27: 5 the second year, and the third. 2050.1
31:17 **B** *to* the genealogy of the priests by 2050.1

2Ch 32:26 *b* he and the inhabitants of Jerusalem, NIH
Ezr 3: 5 **b** of the new moons, and of all the set 2050.1
6: 9 **b** young bullocks, and rams, and lambs, 2050.3
Ne 1: 6 **b** I and my father's house have sinned. 2050.1
4:16 the *other* half of them held **b** the spears, 2050.1
8: 2 law before the congregation **b** of 4480+5704
10: 9 **b** Jeshua the son of Azaniah, Binnui of 2050.1
12:27 **b** with thanksgivings, and with singing, 2050.1
12:28 **b** out of the plain country round about 2050.1
12:45 the singers and the porters kept 2050.1
Est 1: 5 **b** unto great and small, seven days, 4480
1:20 to great and small. 4480+3807.1
2:23 therefore they were **b** hanged on a tree: 8147
3:13 all Jews, **b** young and old, little children 4480
8:11 *b* little ones and women, and *to* take NIH
9:20 of the king Ahasuerus, **b** nigh and far, NIH
Job 9:33 *that* might lay his hand upon us **b**. 8147
15:10 With us *are* **b** the grayheaded and 1571
Ps 4: 8 I will **b** lay me down in peace, and sleep: 3162
49: 2 **B** low and high, rich and poor, together. 1571
58: 9 a whirlwind, **b** living, and in *his* wrath. 3644
64: 6 the inward *thought* of every one *of* 2050.1
76: 6 **b** the chariot and horse *are* cast into a 2050.1
104:25 **b** small and great beasts. 2050.1
115:13 that fear the LORD, **b** small and great. NIH
135: 8 the firstborn of Egypt, **b** of man and beast. NIH
139:12 and the light *are* **b** alike *to thee*. NIH
148:12 **B** young men, and maidens; old men, 2050.1
Pr 17:15 even they **b** *are* abomination to 8147
20:10 **b** of them *are* alike abomination to 8147
20:12 The LORD hath made even **b** of them. 8147
24:22 and who knoweth the ruin of them **b**? 8147
26:10 The great *God* that formed all *things* 2050.1
27: 3 but a fool's wrath *is* heavier than them **b**. 8147
29:13 the LORD lighteneth **b** their eyes. 8147
Ecc 4: 3 Yea, better *is he* than **b** they, which hath 8147
4: 6 than **b** the **hands** full *with* travail and 2651
8: 5 a wise *man's* heart discerneth **b** time and 2050.1
11: 6 or whether they **b** *shall be* alike good. 8147
Isa 1:31 they shall **b** burn together, and none shall 8147
7:16 abhorrest shall be forsaken of **b** her kings. 8147
8:14 for a rock of offence to **b** the houses of 8147
10:18 and of his fruitful field, **b** soul and body: 4480
13: 9 cruel **b** *with* wrath and fierce anger, 2050.1
18: 5 he shall **b** cut off the sprigs with pruning 2050.1
31: 3 **b** he that helpeth shall fall, and he that 2050.1
38:15 he hath **b** spoken unto me, 2050.1
44:12 The smith *with* the tongs **b** worketh in 2050.1
Jer 5:24 **b** the former and the latter, in his season: NIH
9:10 the fowl of the heavens and the beast 4480
14:18 the prophet and the priest go about 1571
16: 6 **B** the great and the small shall die in 2050.1
21: 6 inhabitants of this city, **b** man and 2050.1
23:11 For **b** prophet and priest are profane; yea, 1571
26: 5 to rising up early, and sending *them*, but 2050.1
28: 8 before thee of old prophesied **b** against 2050.1
31:13 dance, **b** young men and old together: 2050.1
32:14 **b** that which was sealed *according to* NIH
32:14 **b** which is sealed, and this evidence 2050.1
36:16 they were afraid **b** one **and** other, 413
44:25 your wives have **b** spoken with your 2050.1
46:12 mighty, *and* they are fallen **b** together. 8147
50: 3 they shall depart, **b** man and beast. 4480
51:12 for the LORD hath **b** devised and 1571
51:46 a rumour shall **b** come *one* year, 2050.1
La 3:26 *It is* good that a man should **b** hope 2050.1
Eze 9: 6 **b** maids, and little children, and women 2050.1
14:22 be brought forth, *b* sons and daughters. NIH
15: 4 the fire devoureth **b** the ends of it, 8147
21:19 **b** twain shall come forth out of one land: 8147
23:13 she was defiled, *that* they took **b** one way, 8147
23:29 **b** thy lewdness and thy whoredoms. 2050.1
34:11 **b** search my sheep, and seek them out. 2050.1
39: 9 **b** the shields and the bucklers, the bows 2050.1
42:11 all their goings out *were* **b** according to 2050.1
Da 8:13 to give **b** the sanctuary and the host to 2050.1
11:27 these kings' hearts *shall be* to do 8147
Mic 5: 8 **b** treadeth down, and teareth in pieces, 2050.1
7: 3 That *they* may do evil with **b** hands NIH
Na 3: 3 The horseman lifteth up **b** the bright 2050.1
Zep 2:14 **b** the cormorant and the bittern shall 1571
Zec 6:13 of peace shall be between them **b**. 8147
12: 2 when they shall be in the siege **b** 1571+2050.1
Mt 9:17 into new bottles, and **b** are preserved. 297
10:28 rather fear him which is able to destroy **b** 2532
12:22 that the blind and dumb **b** spake and saw. 2532
13:30 Let **b** grow together until the harvest: and 297
15:14 lead the blind, **b** shall fall into the ditch. 297
22:10 all as many as they found, **b** bad and good: 5037
Mk 6:30 told him all *things*, **b** what they had done, 2532
7:37 maketh the deaf to hear, and the dumb 2532
Lk 1: 6 And they were **b** righteous before God, 297
1: 7 they **b** were *now* well stricken in years. 297
2:46 hearing them, and asking them 2532
5: 7 and filled **b** the ships, so that they began to 297
5:36 then *b* the new maketh a rent, and the 2532
5:38 put into new bottles; and **b** are preserved. 297
6:39 blind? shall *they* not **b** fall into the ditch? 297
7:42 nothing to pay, he frankly forgave them **b**. 297
21:16 And ye shall be betrayed **b** by parents, 2532
22:33 go with thee, **b** into prison, and to death. 2532
Jn 2: 2 And **b** Jesus was called, and his disciples, 2532
4:36 that he that soweth and he that reapeth 2532
7:28 Ye **b** know **me**, and ye know whence I 2504
9:37 Thou hast **b** seen him, and it is he that 2532

B

Jn	11:48 and take away **b** our place and nation.	2532
	11:57 Now **b** the chief priests and the Pharisees	2532
	12:28 *saying*, I have **b** glorified *it*, and	2532
	15:24 but now have they **b** seen and hated both	2532
	15:24 both seen and hated **b** me and my Father.	2532
	20: 4 So they ran **b** together: and the other	1417
Ac	1: 1 of all that Jesus began **b** to do and teach,	5037
	1: 8 ye shall be witnesses unto me **b** in	5037
	1:13 abode **b** Peter, and James, and John,	5037
	2:29 that he is **b** dead and buried,	5037
	2:36 ye have crucified, **b** Lord and Christ.	2532
	4:27 **b** Herod, and Pontius Pilate, with	5037
	5:14 Lord, multitudes **b** of men and women.)	5037
	8:12 they were baptized, **b** men and women.	5037
	8:38 and they went down **b** into the water,	297
	8:38 into the water, **b** Philip and the eunuch;	5037
	10:39 which he did **b** in the land of the Jews,	5037
	14: 1 they went ***b*** together into the synagogue	NIG
	14: 1 that a great multitude **b** of the Jews and	5037
	14: 5 when there was an assault made **b** of	5037
	19:10 of the Lord Jesus, **b** Jews and Greeks.	5037
	20:21 Testifying **b** to the Jews, and *also* to	5037
	21:12 And when we heard *these things*, **b** we,	5037
	22: 4 and delivering into prisons **b** men and	5037
	23: 8 nor spirit: but the Pharisees confess **b**	297
	24:15 of the dead, **b** of the just and unjust.	5037
	25:24 **b** at Jerusalem, and *also* here, crying that	5037
	26:16 a witness **b** of *these things* which thou	5037
	26:22 this day, witnessing **b** to small and great,	5037
	26:29 all that hear me this day, were **b** almost,	NIG
	28:23 **b** out of the law of Moses, and *out of*	5037
Ro	1:12 with you by the mutual faith **b** of you	5037
	1:14 I am debtor **b** to the Greeks, and to	5037
	1:14 **b** to the wise, and to the unwise.	5037
	3: 9 for we have before proved **b** Jews and	5037
	11:33 O the depth of the riches **b** of the wisdom	2532
	14: 9 For to this end Christ **b** died, and rose,	2532
	14: 9 that he might be Lord **b** of the dead and	2532
1Co	1: 2 Jesus Christ our Lord, **b** theirs and ours:	2532
	1:24 **b** Jews and Greeks, Christ the power of	5037
	4: 5 **b** will bring to light the hidden *things*	2532
	4:11 Even unto this present hour we **b** hunger,	2532
	6:13 but God shall destroy **b** it and them.	2532
	6:14 And God hath **b** raised up the Lord,	2532
	7:29 that **b** they that have wives be as though	2532
	7:34 that she may be holy **b** in body and	2532
2Co	9:10 the sower **b** minister bread for *your* food,	2532
Eph	1:10 **b** which are in heaven, and which are on	5037
	2:14 who hath made **b** one, and hath broken	297
	2:16 *that* he might reconcile **b** unto God in	297
	2:18 For through him we **b** have access by one	297
Php	1: 7 **inasmuch as b** in my bonds, and *in*	2532
	2:13 For it is God which worketh in you **b** to	2532
	4: 9 Those *things*, which ye have **b** learned,	2532
	4:12 I know *how* to be abased, and I know	2532
	4:12 in all *things* I am instructed **b** to be full	2532
	4:12 be hungry, **b** to abound and to suffer need.	2532
1Th	2:15 Who **b** killed the Lord Jesus, and their	2532
	5:15 **b** among yourselves, and to all *men.*	2532
2Th	3: 4 that ye **b** do and will do the *things* which	2532
1Ti	4:10 For therefore we **b** labour and	2532
	4:16 for in doing this thou shalt **b** save thyself,	2532
Tit	1: 9 that he may be able by sound doctrine **b**	2532
Phm	1:16 unto thee, **b** in the flesh, and in the Lord?	2532
Heb	2: 4 **b** with signs and wonders, and with divers	5037
	2:11 For **b** he that sanctifieth and they who are	5037
	5: 1 that he may offer **b** gifts and sacrifices for	5037
	5:14 their senses exercised **b** to discern **b** good	5037
	6:19 **b** sure and stedfast, and which entereth	5037
	9: 9 in which were offered **b** gifts and	5037
	9:19 and sprinkled **b** the book, and all	5037
	9:21 Moreover he sprinkled with blood **b**	5037
	10:33 whilst ye were made a gazingstock **b** by	5037
	11:21 was a dying, blessed **b** the sons of Joseph;	1538
Jas	3:12 so *can* no fountain ***b*** yield salt water and	NIG
2Pe	3: 1 in **b** which I stir up your pure minds by	NIG
	3:18 To him *be* glory **b** now and for ever.	2532
2Jn	1: 9 Christ, he hath **b** the Father and the Son.	2532
Jude	1:25 dominion and power, **b** now and ever.	2532
Rev	3:15 the image of the beast should **b** speak,	2532
	3:16 ***b*** small and great, rich and poor, free and	NIG
	19: 5 and ye that fear him, **b** small and great.	2532
	19:18 and the flesh of all *men*, **b** free and bond,	5037
	19:18 both free and bond, **b** small and great.	2532
	19:20 *These* **b** were cast alive into a lake of fire	1417

BOTTLE (15) [BOTTLES]

Ge	21:14 and a **b** of water, and gave *it* unto Hagar,	2573
	21:15 The water was spent in the **b**, and she cast	2573
	21:19 filled the **b** *with* water, and gave the lad	2573
Jdg	4:19 she opened a **b** of milk, and gave him	4997
1Sa	1:24 a **b** of wine, and brought him *unto*	5035
	10: 3 bread, and another carrying a **b** of wine:	5035
	16:20 a **b** of wine, and a kid, and sent *them* by	4997
2Sa	16: 1 of summer fruits, and a **b** of wine.	5035
Ps	56: 8 put thou my tears into thy **b**: *are they* not	4997
	119:83 For I am become like a **b** in the smoke;	4997
Jer	13:12 of Israel, Every **b** shall be filled *with* wine:	5035
	13:12 we not certainly know that every **b** shall	5035
	19: 1 and get a potter's earthen **b**, and *take of*	1228
	19:10 shalt thou break the **b** in the sight of	1228
Hab	2:15 that puttest thy **b** to *him*, and makest *him*	2573

BOTTLES (19) [BOTTLE]

Jos	9: 4 and wine bottles, old, and rent, and bound up;	4997

Jos	9:13 **b** of wine, which we filled, *were* new;	4997
1Sa	25:18 two **b** of wine, and five sheep ready	5035
Job	32:19 no vent; it is ready to burst like new **b**.	178
	38:37 or who can stay the **b** of heaven,	5035
Jer	48:12 shall empty his vessels, and break their **b**.	5035
Hos	7: 5 have made *him* sick *with* **b** of wine;	2534
Mt	9:17 Neither do *men* put new wine into old **b**:	779
	9:17 the **b** break, and the wine runneth out,	779
	9:17 the wine runneth out, and the **b** perish:	779
	9:17 but they put new wine into new **b**, and	779
Mk	2:22 And no *man* putteth new wine into old **b**:	779
	2:22 else the new wine doth burst the **b**, and	779
	2:22 wine is spilled, and the **b** will be marred:	779
	2:22 but new wine must be put into new **b**.	779
Lk	5:37 And no *man* putteth new wine into old **b**;	779
	5:37 else the new wine will burst the **b**, and	779
	5:37 and be spilled, and the **b** shall perish.	779
	5:38 But new wine must be put into new **b**;	779

BOTTOM (20) [BOTTOMLESS, BOTTOMS]

Ex	15: 5 they sank into the **b** as a stone.	4688
	29:12 all the blood beside the **b** of the altar.	3247
Lev	4: 7 at the **b** of the altar of the burnt offering,	3247
	4:18 shall pour out all the blood at the **b** of	3247
	4:25 pour out his blood at the **b** of the altar	3247
	4:30 pour out all the blood thereof at the **b**	3247
	4:34 pour out all the blood thereof at the **b**	3247
	5: 9 shall be wrung out at the **b** of the altar:	3247
	8:15 poured the blood at the **b** of the altar,	3247
	9: 9 poured out the blood at the **b** of the altar:	3247
Job	36:30 upon it, and covereth the **b** of the sea.	8328
SS	3:10 the **b** thereof *of* gold, the covering of it *of*	7507
Eze	43:13 the **b** *shall be* a cubit, and the breadth	2436
	43:14 from the **b** *upon* the ground *even* to	2436
	43:17 and the **b** thereof *shall be* a cubit about;	2436
Da	6:24 or ever they came at the **b** of the den.	773
Am	9: 3 they be hid from my sight in the **b**	7172
Zec	1: 8 the myrtle trees that *were* in the **b**;	4699
Mt	27:51 was rent in twain from the top to the **b**;	2736
Mk	15:38 was rent in twain from the top to the **b**.	2736

BOTTOMLESS (7) [BOTTOM]

Rev	9: 1 and to him was given the key of the **b** pit.	12
	9: 2 And he opened the **b** pit; and there arose a	12
	9:11 *which is* the angel of the **b** *pit*, whose name	12
	11: 7 beast that ascendeth out of the **b** *pit* shall	12
	17: 8 and shall ascend out of the **b** *pit*, and go into	12
	20: 1 having the key of the **b** *pit* and a great chain	12
	20: 3 cast him into the **b** *pit*, and shut him up,	12

BOTTOMS (1) [BOTTOM]

Jnh	2: 6 I went down to the **b** of the mountains;	7095

BOUGH (7) [BOUGHS]

Ge	49:22 Joseph *is* a **fruitful b**, *even* a	1121+6509
	49:22 *even* a **fruitful b** by a well;	1121+6509
Jdg	9:48 cut down a **b** from the trees, and took it,	7754
	9:49 likewise cut down every man his **b**,	7754
Isa	10:33 LORD of hosts, shall lop the **b** with terror:	6288
	17: 6 berries in the top of the **uppermost b**,	534
	17: 9 shall his strong cities be as a forsaken **b**,	2793

BOUGHS (18) [BOUGH]

Lev	23:40 ye shall take you on the first day the **b** of	6529
	23:40 **b** of thick trees, and willows of	6057
Dt	24:20 thou shalt not **go over the b** again:	6286
2Sa	18: 9 mule went under the **thick b** of a great	7730
Job	14: 9 it will bud, and bring forth **b** like a plant.	7105
Ps	80:10 the **b** thereof *were* like the goodly cedars.	6057
	80:11 She sent out her **b** unto the sea,	7105
SS	7: 8 tree, I will take hold of the **b** thereof:	5577
Isa	27:11 When the **b** thereof are withered, they	7105
Eze	17:23 and it shall bring forth **b**, and bear fruit,	6057
	31: 3 and his top was among the **thick b**.	5688
	31: 5 his **b** were multiplied, and his branches	5634
	31: 6 fowls of heaven made their nests in his **b**,	5589
	31: 8 the fir trees were not like his **b**,	5589
	31:10 hath shot up his top among the **thick b**,	5688
	31:12 his **b** are broken by all the rivers of	6288
	31:14 shoot up their top among the **thick b**,	5688
Da	4:12 the fowls of the heaven dwelt in the **b**	6056

BOUGHT (44) [BUY]

Ge	17:12 or **b** with money of any stranger, which	4736
	17:13 he **that is b** with thy money, must needs	4736
	17:23 and all **that were b** with his money,	4736
	17:27 and **b** with money of the stranger,	4736
	33:19 he **b** a parcel of a field, where he had	7069
	39: 1 **b** him of the hand of the Ishmeelites,	7069
	47:14 of Canaan, for the corn which they **b**:	7666
	47:20 Joseph **b** all the land of Egypt for Pharaoh;	7069
	47:22 Only the land of the priests he **b** not; for	7069
	47:23 I have **b** you this day and your land for	7069
	49:30 Abraham **b** with the field of Ephron	7069
	50:13 which Abraham **b** with the field for a	7069
Ex	12:44 every man's servant that is **b** for money,	4736
Lev	25:28 him that hath **b** it until the year of jubile:	7069
	25:30 him that **b** it throughout his generations:	7069
	25:50 he shall reckon with him that **b** him from	7069
	25:51 out of the money that he was **b** for.	4736
	27:22 unto the LORD a field which he hath **b**,	7069
	27:24 shall return unto him of whom it was **b**,	7069
Dt	32: 6 *is* not he thy father *that* hath **b** thee?	7069
Jos	24:32 in a parcel of ground which Jacob **b** of	7069
Ru	4: 9 that I have **b** all that *was* Elimelech's,	7069

2Sa	12: 3 which he had **b** and nourished up:	7069
Ne	5:16 work of this wall, neither **b** we *any* land:	7069
Isa	43:24 hast **b** me no sweet cane with money,	7069
Jer	32: 7 I **b** the field of Hanameel my uncle's son,	7069
	32:43 fields shall be **b** in this land, whereof ye	7069
Hos	3: 2 I **b** her to me for fifteen *pieces* of silver,	3739
Mt	13:46 went and sold all that he had, and **b** it.	59
	21:12 out all them that sold and **b** in the temple,	59
	27: 7 and **b** with them the potter's field, to bury	59
Mk	11:15 out them that sold and **b** in the temple,	59
	15:46 And he **b** fine linen, and took him down,	59
	16: 1 and Salome, had **b** *sweet* spices, that they	59
Lk	14:18 have **b** a piece of ground, and I must needs	59
	14:19 have **b** five yoke of oxen, and I go to prove	59
	17:28 they did eat, they drank, they **b**, they sold,	59
	19:45 them that sold therein, and *them that* **b**;	59
Ac	7:16 laid in the sepulchre that Abraham **b** for a	5608
1Co	6:20 For ye are **b** with a price: therefore	59
	7:23 Ye are **b** with a price; be not ye the servants	59
2Pe	2: 1 even denying the Lord that **b** them,	59

BOUND (104) [BIND, BOUNDS]

Ge	22: 9 Isaac his son, and laid him on the altar	6123
	38:28 and **b** upon his hand a scarlet thread,	7194
	39:20 a place where the king's prisoners *were* **b**:	631
	40: 3 the prison, the place where Joseph *was* **b**.	631
	40: 5 king of Egypt, which *were* **b** in the prison.	631
	42:19 brethren be **b** in the house of your prison:	631
	42:24 them Simeon, and **b** him before their eyes.	631
	44:30 seeing that his life *is* **b** up in *the* lad's *life*;	7194
	49:26 unto the **utmost b** of the everlasting hills:	8379
Ex	12:34 their kneadingtroughs being **b** up in their	6887
Lev	8: 7 of the ephod, and **b** *it* unto him therewith.	640
Nu	19:15 which hath no covering **b** upon it,	6616
	30: 4 her bond wherewith she hath **b** her soul,	631
	30: 4 every bond wherewith she hath **b** her soul	631
	30: 5 her bonds wherewith she hath **b** her soul,	631
	30: 6 out of her lips, wherewith she **b** her soul;	631
	30: 7 her bonds wherewith she **b** her soul shall	631
	30: 8 wherewith she **b** her soul, of none effect:	631
	30: 9 wherewith they have **b** their souls,	631
	30:10 or **b** her soul by a bond with an oath;	631
	30:11 every bond wherewith she **b** her soul shall	631
Jos	2:21 and she **b** the scarlet line in the window.	7194
	9: 4 and wine bottles, old, and rent, and **b** up;	6887
Jdg	15:13 they **b** him with two new cords,	631
	16: 6 thou mightest be **b** to afflict thee.	631
	16: 8 not been dried, and she **b** him with them.	631
	16:10 I pray thee, wherewith thou mightest be **b**.	631
	16:12 and **b** him therewith, and said unto him,	631
	16:13 tell me wherewith thou mightest be **b**.	631
	16:21 to Gaza, and **b** him with fetters of brass;	631
1Sa	25:29 soul of my lord shall be **b** in the bundle	6887
2Sa	3:34 Thy hands *were* not **b**, nor thy feet put	631
2Ki	5:23 and **b** two talents of silver in two bags,	6696
	17: 4 Assyria shut him up, and **b** him in prison.	631
	25: 7 **b** him with fetters of brass, and carried	631
2Ch	33:11 **b** him with fetters, and carried him to	631
	36: 6 **b** him in fetters, to carry him to Babylon.	631
Job	36: 8 if *they be* **b** in fetters, *and be* holden in	631
	38:20 thou shouldest take it to the **b** thereof,	1366
Ps	68: 6 he bringeth out those which are **b** with	615
	104: 9 Thou hast set a **b** *that* they may not pass	1366
	107:10 of death, *being* **b** in affliction and iron;	615
Pr	22:15 Foolishness *is* **b** in the heart of a child;	7194
	30: 4 who hath **b** the waters in a garment?	6887
Isa	1: 6 they have not been closed, neither **b** up,	2280
	22: 3 fled together, they are **b** by the archers:	631
	22: 3 all that are found in thee are **b** together,	631
	61: 1 opening of the prison to *them that are* **b**;	631
Jer	5:22 which have placed the sand *for* the **b** of	1366
	30:13 plead thy cause, that thou mayest be **b** up:	4205
	39: 7 **b** him with chains to carry him to Babylon.	631
	40: 1 when he had taken him being **b** in chains,	631
	52:11 and the king of Babylon **b** him in chains,	631
La	1:14 The yoke of my transgressions is **b** by his	8244
Eze	27:24 **b** with cords, and made of cedar,	2280
	30:21 it shall not be **b** up, to be healed, to put a	2280
	34: 4 neither have ye **b** up that which was	2280
Da	3:21 these men were **b** in their coats,	3729
	3:23 fell down **b** into the midst of the burning	3729
	3:24 Did not we cast three men **b** into the	3729
Hos	4:19 The wind hath **b** her up in her wings,	6887
	5:10 Judah were like them that remove the **b**:	1366
	7:15 Though I have **b** *and* strengthened their	3256
	13:12 The iniquity of Ephraim *is* **b** up; his sin *is*	6887
Na	3:10 and all her great *men* were **b** in chains.	7576
Mt	14: 3 and him, and *put him* in prison for	1210
	16:19 shalt bind on earth shall be **b** in heaven:	1210
	18:18 shall bind on earth shall be **b** in heaven:	1210
	27: 2 And when they had **b** him, they led *him*	1210
Mk	5: 4 Because that he had been often **b** with	1210
	6:17 and **b** him in prison for Herodias' sake,	1210
	15: 1 and **b** Jesus, and carried *him* away,	1210
	15: 7 *which lay* **b** with them that had made	1210
Lk	8:29 and he was kept **b** with chains and	1196
	10:34 And went to *him*, and **b** up his wounds,	2611
	13:16 Satan hath **b**, lo *these* eighteen years,	1210
Jn	11:44 **b** hand and foot with graveclothes:	1210
	11:44 and his face was **b** about with a napkin.	4019
	18:12 officers of the Jews took Jesus, and **b** him,	1210
	18:24 Annas had sent him **b** unto Caiaphas.	1210
Ac	9: 2 he might bring *them* **b** unto Jerusalem.	1210

B

Ac 9:21 might bring them **b** unto the chief priests? *1210*
12: 6 between two soldiers, **b** with two chains: *1210*
20:22 I go **b** in the spirit unto Jerusalem, *1210*
21:11 and **b** his *own* hands and feet, and said, *1210*
21:13 for I am ready not to be **b** only, but also to *1210*
21:33 commanded *him* to be **b** with two chains; *1210*
22: 5 unto Jerusalem, for to be punished. *1210*
22:25 And as they **b** him with thongs, Paul said *4385*
22:29 was a Roman, and because he had **b** him. *1210*
23:12 and **b** themselves **under a curse**, *332*
23:14 ourselves **under a great curse**, *331+332*
23:21 which have **b** themselves **with an oath**, *332*
24:27 to shew the Jews a pleasure, left Paul **b**. *1210*
28:20 for the hope of Israel I am **b** with this *4029*
Ro 7: 2 the woman which hath a husband is **b** *1210*
1Co 7:27 Art thou **b** unto a wife? seek not to be *1210*
7:39 The wife is **b** by the law as long as her *1210*
2Th 1: 3 We are **b** to thank God always for you, *3784*
2:13 But we are **b** to give thanks alway to God *3784*
2Ti 2: 9 unto bonds; but the word of God is not **b**. *1210*
Heb 13: 3 as **b** with *them; and* them which suffer *4887*
Rev 9:14 Loose the four angels which are **b** in *1210*
20: 2 and Satan, and **b** him a thousand years, *1210*

BOUNDARY STONE See LANDMARK

BOUNDLESS See INFINITE

BOUNDS (8) [BOUND]

Ex 19:12 thou shalt **set b** unto the people round 1379
19:23 **Set b** about the mount, and sanctify it. 1379
23:31 I will set thy **b** from the Red sea even unto 1366
Dt 32: 8 he set the **b** of the people according to 1367
Job 14: 5 thou hast appointed his **b** that he cannot 2706
26:10 He hath compassed the waters with **b**, 2706
Isa 10:13 I have removed the **b** of the people, 1367
Ac 17:26 and the **b** of their habitation; 3734

BOUNTIFUL (2) [BOUNTY]

Pr 22: 9 He that hath a **b** eye shall be blessed; 2896
Isa 32: 5 called liberal, nor the churl said *to be* **b**. 7771

BOUNTIFULLY (6) [BOUNTY]

Ps 13: 6 because he hath **dealt b** with me. 1580
116: 7 for the LORD hath **dealt b** with thee. 1580
119:17 **Deal b** with thy servant, *that* I may live, 1580
142: 7 me about; for thou shalt **deal b** with me. 1580
2Co 9: 6 he which soweth **b** shall reap also *1909+2129*
9: 6 soweth bountifully shall reap also *1909+2129*

BOUNTIFULNESS (1) [BOUNTY]

2Co 9:11 Being enriched in every *thing* to all **b**, *572*

BOUNTY (3) [BOUNTIFUL, BOUNTIFULLY, BOUNTIFULNESS]

1Ki 10:13 which Solomon gave her of his royal **b**. 3027
2Co 9: 5 and make up beforehand your **b**, *2129*
9: 5 as *a matter of* **b**, and not as *of* *2129*

BOW (99) [BOWED, BOWETH, BOWING, BOWMEN, BOWS, BOWSHOT, RAINBOW]

Ge 9:13 I do set my **b** in the cloud, and it shall be 7198
9:14 that the **b** shall be seen in the cloud: 7198
9:16 the **b** shall be in the cloud; and I will look 7198
27: 3 thy quiver and thy **b**, and go out to 7198
27:29 serve thee, and nations **b down** to thee: 7812
27:29 let thy mother's sons **b down** to thee: 7812
37:10 thy brethren indeed come to **b down** 7812
41:43 and they cried before him, **B the knee:** 86
48:22 Amorite with my sword and with my **b**. 7198
49: 8 thy father's children shall **b down** before 7812
49:24 his **b** abode in strength, and the arms of 7198
Ex 11: 8 **b down** themselves unto me, saying, 7812
20: 5 Thou shalt not **b down** thyself to them, 7812
23:24 Thou shalt not **b down** to their gods, 7812
Lev 26: 1 of stone in your land, to **b down** unto it: 7812
Dt 5: 9 Thou shalt not **b down** thyself unto them. 7812
Jos 23: 7 serve them, nor **b** yourselves unto them. 7812
24:12 *but* not with thy sword, nor with thy **b**. 7198
Jdg 2:19 to serve them, and to **b down** unto them; 7812
1Sa 18: 4 his sword, and to his **b**, and to his girdle. 7198
2Sa 1:18 the children of Judah the *use of the* **b:** 7198
1:22 the **b** of Jonathan turned not back, 7198
22:35 that a **b** of steel is broken *by* mine arms. 7198
1Ki 22:34 a *certain* man drew a **b** at a venture, 7198
2Ki 5:18 and I **b** myself *in* the house of Rimmon, 7812
5:18 when I **b down** myself *in* the house of 7812
6:22 captive with thy sword and with thy **b**? 7198
9:24 Jehu drew a **b** with his full strength, 7198
13:15 Elisha said unto him, Take **b** and arrows. 7198
13:15 And he took unto him **b** and arrows. 7198
13:16 king of Israel, Put thine hand upon the **b**. 7198
17:35 nor **b** yourselves to them, nor serve them, 7812
19:16 LORD, **b down** thine ear, and hear: open, 5186
1Ch 5:18 and to shoot with **b**, and skilful in war, 7198
12: 2 and *shooting* arrows out of a **b**, 7198
2Ch 17:17 with him armed *men* with **b** and shield 7198
18:33 a *certain* man drew a **b** at a venture, 7198
Job 20:24 the **b** of steel shall strike him through. 7198
29:20 me, and my **b** was renewed in my hand. 7198
31:10 and let others **b down** upon her. 3766
39: 3 They **b** themselves, they bring forth their 3766
Ps 7:12 he hath bent his **b**, and made it ready. 7198
11: 2 lo, the wicked bend *their* **b**, they make 7198
18:34 that a **b** of steel is broken *by* mine arms. 7198
22:29 all they that go down to the dust shall **b** 3766

Ps 31: 2 **B down** thine ear to me; deliver me 5186
37:14 have bent their **b**, to cast down the poor 7198
44: 6 For I will not trust in my **b**, neither shall 7198
46: 9 he breaketh the **b**, and cutteth the spear 7198
58: 7 he bendeth *his* **b** *to* shoot his arrows, NIH
72: 9 They that dwell in the wilderness shall **b** 3766
76: 3 There brake he the arrows of the **b**, 7198
78:57 they were turned aside like a deceitful **b**. 7198
86: 1 **B down** thine ear, O LORD, hear me: 5186
95: 6 O come, let us worship and **b down**: 3766
144: 5 **B** thy heavens, O LORD, and come down: 5186
Pr 5: 1 *and* **b** thine ear to my understanding: 5186
14:19 evil **b** before the good; and the wicked 7817
22:17 **B down** thine ear, and hear the words of 5186
Ecc 12: 3 the strong men shall **b** themselves, 5791
Isa 10: 4 Without me they shall **b down** under 3766
21:15 the bent **b**, and from the grievousness 7198
41: 2 his sword, *and* as driven stubble to his **b**. 7198
45:23 return, That unto me every knee shall **b**, 3766
46: 2 They stoop, they **b down** together; 3766
49:23 they shall **b down** to thee *with their* face 7812
51:23 thy soul, **B down**, that we may go over: 7812
58: 5 *is it* to **b down** his head as a bulrush, 3721
60:14 themselves **down** at the soles of thy 7812
65:12 and ye shall all **b down** to the slaughter: 3766
66:19 Pul, and Lud, that draw the **b**, *to* Tubal, 7198
Jer 6:23 They shall lay hold on **b** and spear; 7198
9: 3 bend their tongues *like* their **b** *for* lies: 7198
46: 9 the Lydians, that handle *and* bend the **b**. 7198
49:35 Behold, I *will* break the **b** of Elam, 7198
50:14 all ye that bend the **b**, shoot at her, 7198
50:29 all ye that bend the **b**, camp against it 7198
50:42 They shall hold the **b** and the lance: 7198
51: 3 *that* bendeth let the archer bend his **b**, 7198
La 2: 4 hath bent his **b** like an enemy: *he* stood 7198
3:12 He hath bent his **b**, and set me as a mark 7198
Eze 1:28 As the appearance of the **b** that is in 7198
39: 3 I will smite thy **b** out of thy left hand, 7198
Hos 1: 5 I will break the **b** of Israel in the valley 7198
1: 7 will not save them by **b**, nor by sword, 7198
2:18 I will break the **b** and the sword and 7198
7:16 they are like a deceitful **b:** their princes 7198
Am 2:15 he shall stand that handleth the **b**; 7198
Mic 6: 6 *and* **b** myself before the high God? 3721
Hab 3: 6 were scattered, the perpetual hills did **b:** 7817
3: 9 Thy **b** was made quite naked, *according* 7198
Zec 9:10 and the battle **b** shall be cut off: 7198
9:13 filled the **b** *with* Ephraim, and raised up 7198
10: 4 of him the nail, out of him the battle **b**, 7198
Ro 11:10 not see, and **b down** their back alway. 4781
14:11 every knee shall **b** to me, and every 2578
Eph 3:14 this cause I **b** my knees unto the Father 2578
Php 2:10 at the name of Jesus every knee should **b**, 2578
Rev 6: 2 he that sat on him had a **b**; and a crown 5115

BOWED (78) [BOW]

Ge 18: 2 door, and **b** himself toward the ground, 7812
19: 1 he **b** himself with his face toward 7812
23: 7 and **b** himself to the people of the land, 7812
23:12 Abraham **b down** himself before the 7812
24:26 the man **b down** his **head**, 6915
24:48 I **b down** my **head**, and worshipped 6915
33: 3 and **b** himself to the ground seven times, 7812
33: 6 and their children, and they **b** themselves. 7812
33: 7 children came near, and **b** themselves. 7812
33: 7 and Rachel, and they **b** themselves. 7812
42: 6 **b down** themselves before him *with* their 7812
43:26 and **b** themselves to him to the earth. 7812
43:28 they **b down** their **heads**, 6915
47:31 And Israel **b** himself upon the bed's head. 7812
48:12 he **b** himself with his face to the earth. 7812
49:15 **b** his shoulder to bear, and became a 5186
Ex 4:31 then they **b** their **heads** and worshipped. 6915
12:27 the people **b the head** and worshipped. 6915
34: 8 **b** his **head** toward the earth, 6915
Nu 22:31 he **b down** his **head**, and fell flat on his 6915
25: 2 people did eat, and **b down** to their gods. 7812
Jos 23:16 other gods, and **b** yourselves to them; 7812
Jdg 2:12 **b** themselves unto them, and provoked 7812
2:17 other gods, and **b** themselves unto them: 7812
5:27 At her feet he **b**, he fell, he lay down: 3766
5:27 At her feet he **b**, he fell: where he bowed, 3766
5:27 where he **b**, there he fell down dead. 3766
7: 6 all the rest of the people **b down** upon 3766
16:30 he **b** *himself* with *all his* might; 5186
Ru 2:10 to the ground, and said unto him 7812
1Sa 4:19 were dead, she **b** herself and travailed; 3766
20:41 to the ground, and **b** himself three times: 7812
24: 8 *with his* face to the earth, and **b** himself. 7812
25:23 on her face, and **b** herself *to* the ground, 7812
25:41 **b** herself *on her* face to the earth, 7812
28:14 *with his* face to the ground, and **b** himself. 7812
2Sa 9: 8 **b** himself, and said, What *is* thy servant, 7812
14:22 and **b** himself, and thanked the king: 7812
14:33 **b** himself on his face to the ground before 7812
18:21 And Cushi **b** himself unto Joab, and ran. 7812
19:14 he **b** the heart of all the men of Judah, 5186
22:10 He **b** the heavens also, and came down; 5186
24:20 **b** himself before the king *on* his face upon 7812
1Ki 1:16 Bath-sheba **b**, and did obeisance unto 6915
1:23 he **b** himself before the king with his face 7812
1:31 Bath-sheba **b** *with her* face *to* the earth, 6915
1:47 And the king **b** himself upon the bed. 7812
1:53 he came and **b** himself to king Solomon: 7812
2:19 **b** himself unto her, and sat down on his 7812

1Ki 19:18 all the knees which have not **b** unto Baal, 3766
2Ki 2:15 **b** themselves to the ground before him. 7812
4:37 **b** herself to the ground, and took up her 7812
1Ch 21:21 **b** himself to David *with his* face to 7812
29:20 **b down** their **heads**, and worshipped 6915
2Ch 7: 3 they **b** themselves *with their* faces to 3766
20:18 Jehoshaphat **b** his **head** *with his* face to 6915
25:14 **b down** himself before them, 7812
29:29 all that were present with him **b** 3766
29:30 and they **b** their **heads** and worshipped. 6915
Ne 8: 6 they **b** their **heads**, and worshipped 6915
Est 3: 2 the king's gate, **b**, and reverenced Haman: 3766
3: 2 Mordecai **b** not, nor did *him* reverence. 3766
3: 5 when Haman saw that Mordecai **b** not, 3766
Ps 18: 9 He **b** the heavens also, and came down: 5186
35:14 I **b down** heavily, as one that mourneth 7817
38: 6 I am troubled; I am **b down** greatly; I go 7817
44:25 For our soul is **b down** to the dust: 7743
57: 6 a net for my steps; my soul is **b down**: 3721
145:14 and raiseth up all those that be **b down**. 3721
146: 8 the LORD raiseth them that are **b down**. 3721
Isa 2:11 the haughtiness of men shall be **b down**, 7817
2:17 the loftiness of man shall be **b down**, 7817
21: 3 I was **b down** at the hearing *of it;* I was 5753
Mt 27:29 and they **b the knee** before him, 1120
Lk 13:11 was **b together**, and could in no wise 4794
24: 5 and **b down** *their* faces to the earth, 2827
Jn 19:30 and he **b** *his* head, and gave up the ghost. 2827
Ro 11: 4 who have not **b** the knee to *the image of* 2578

BOWELS (39)

Ge 15: 4 that shall come forth out of thine own **b** 4578
25:23 of people shall be separated from thy **b**; 4578
43:30 for his **b** did yern upon his brother: 7356
Nu 5:22 that causeth the curse shall go into thy **b**, 4578
2Sa 7:12 which shall proceed out of thy **b**, and I 4578
16:11 my son, which came forth of my **b**, 4578
20:10 with *rib*, and shed out his **b** to the ground, 4578
1Ki 3:26 her **b** yearned upon her son, and she said, 7356
2Ch 21:15 have great sickness by disease of thy **b**, 4578
21:15 thy **b** fall out by reason of the sickness 4578
21:18 after all this the LORD smote him in his **b** 4578
21:19 his **b** fell out by reason of his sickness: 4578
32:21 that came forth of his own **b** slew him 4578
Job 20:14 his meat in his **b** is turned, *it is* the gall 4578
30:27 My **b** boiled, and rested not: the days of 4578
Ps 22:14 wax; it is melted in the midst of my **b**. 4578
71: 6 art he that took me out of my mother's **b**: 4578
109:18 so let it come into his **b** like water, 7130
SS 5: 4 *the door*, and my **b** were moved for him. 4578
Isa 16:11 Wherefore my **b** shall sound like a harp 4578
48:19 the offspring of thy **b** like the gravel 4578
49: 1 from the **b** of my mother hath he made 4578
63:15 the sounding of thy **b** and of thy mercies 4578
Jer 4:19 My **b**, my bowels! I am pained *at* my very 4578
4:19 My bowels, my **b**! I am pained *at* my very 4578
31:20 therefore my **b** are troubled for him; I will 4578
La 1:20 my **b** are troubled; mine heart is turned 4578
2:11 eyes do fail with tears, my **b** are troubled, 4578
Eze 3: 3 fill thy **b** with this roll that I give thee. 4578
7:19 not satisfy their souls, neither fill their **b:** 4578
Ac 1:18 in the midst, and all his **b** gushed out. 4698
2Co 6:12 in us, but ye are straitened in your own **b**. 4698
Php 1: 8 how *greatly* I long after you all in the **b** of 4698
2: 1 if the *Spirit*, if any **b** and mercies, 4698
Col 3:12 holy and beloved, **b** of mercies, kindness, 4698
Phm 1: 7 the **b** of the saints are refreshed by thee, 4698
1:12 receive him, that is, mine own **b**: 4698
1:20 in the Lord: refresh my **b** in the Lord. 4698
1Jn 3:17 shutteth up his **b** *of* compassion from him 4698

BOWETH (3) [BOW]

Jdg 7: 5 likewise every one that **b down** upon his 3766
Isa 2: 9 mean man **b down**, and the great man 7817
46: 1 Bel **b down**, Nebo stoopeth, their idols 3766

BOWING (4) [BOW]

Ge 24:52 the LORD, **b** *himself* to the earth. NIH
Ps 17:11 they have set their eyes **b down** to 5186
62: 3 as a **b** wall *shall ye be, and as* a tottering 5186
Mk 15:19 and **b** *their* knees worshipped him. *5087*

BOWL (17) [BOWLS]

Nu 7:13 thirty *shekels*, one silver **b** of seventy 4219
7:19 thirty *shekels*, one silver **b** of seventy 4219
7:25 thirty *shekels*, one silver **b** of seventy 4219
7:31 thirty *shekels*, one silver **b** of seventy 4219
7:37 thirty *shekels*, one silver **b** of seventy 4219
7:43 thirty *shekels*, a silver **b** of seventy 4219
7:49 thirty *shekels*, one silver **b** of seventy 4219
7:55 thirty *shekels*, one silver **b** of seventy 4219
7:61 thirty *shekels*, one silver **b** of seventy 4219
7:67 thirty *shekels*, one silver **b** of seventy 4219
7:73 thirty *shekels*, one silver **b** of seventy 4219
7:79 thirty *shekels*, one silver **b** of seventy 4219
7:85 and thirty *shekels*, each **b** seventy: 4219
Jdg 6:38 dew out of the fleece, a **b** full *of* water. 5602
Ecc 12: 6 the golden **b** be broken, or the pitcher be 1543
Zec 4: 2 with a **b** upon the top of it, and his seven 1531
4: 3 one upon the right *side* of the **b**, 1543

BOWLS (24) [BOWL]

Ex 25:29 and covers thereof, and **b** thereof, 4518
25:31 his **b**, his knops, and his flowers, 1375
25:33 Three **b** made like unto almonds, *with a* 1375

B

Ex 25:33 three **b** made like almonds in the other 1375
 25:34 the candlestick *shall be* four **b** made like 1375
 37:16 and his **b**, and *his* covers to cover withal, 4518
 37:17 his **b**, his knops, and his flowers, 1375
 37:19 Three **b** made after the fashion of almonds 1375
 37:19 three **b** made like almonds in another 1375
 37:20 in the candlestick *were* four **b** made like 1375
Nu 4: 7 and the **b**, and covers to cover withal: 4518
 7:84 twelve silver **b**, twelve spoons of gold: 4219
1Ki 7:41 the two **b** of the chapiters *were* on 1543
 7:41 to cover the two **b** of the chapiters which 1543
 7:42 to cover the two **b** of the chapiters that 1543
 7:50 the **b**, and the snuffers, and the basons, 5592
2Ki 12:13 *for* the house of the LORD **b** of silver, 5592
 25:15 the **b**, *and such things as were* of gold, 4219
1Ch 28:17 the fleshhooks, and the **b**, and the cups: 4219
Jer 52:18 the **b**, and the spoons, and all the vessels 4219
 52:19 the **b**, and the caldrons, 4219
Am 6: 6 That drink wine in **b**, 4219
Zec 9:15 they shall be filled like **b**, *and* as 4219
 14:20 house shall be like the **b** before the altar. 4219

BOWMEN (1) [BOW, MAN]
Jer 4:29 the noise of the horsemen and **b**; 7198+7411

BOWS (14) [BOW]
1Sa 2: 4 The **b** of the mighty *men are* broken, 7198
1Ch 12: 2 *They were* armed with **b**, and could use 7198
2Ch 14: 8 bare shields and drew **b**, two hundred 7198
 26:14 and **b**, and slings to cast stones. 7198
Ne 4:13 their swords, their spears, and their **b**. 7198
 4:16 shields, and the **b**, and the habergeons; 7198
Ps 37:15 own heart, and their **b** shall be broken. 7198
 64: 3 *and* bend *their* **b** *to shoot* their arrows, NIH
 78: 9 of Ephraim, *being* armed, *and* carrying **b**, 7198
Isa 5:28 arrows *are* sharp, and all their **b** bent, 7198
 7:24 and with **b** shall *men* come thither; 7198
 13:18 *Their* **b** also shall dash the young men to 7198
Jer 51:56 are taken, *every one of* their **b** is broken: 7198
Eze 39: 9 the **b** and the arrows, and the handstaves, 7198

BOWSHOT (1) [BOW, SHOOT]
Ge 21:16 *him* a good way off, as it were a **b**: 2909+7198

BOX (8)
2Ki 9: 1 take this **b** of oil in thine hand, and go *to* 6378
 9: 3 take the **b** of oil, and pour *it* on his head, 6378
Isa 41:19 *and* the pine, and the **b tree** together: 8391
 60:13 fir tree, the pine tree, and the **b** together, 8391
Mt 26: 7 an **alabaster b** of very precious ointment, *211*
Mk 14: 3 came a woman having an **alabaster b** *211*
 14: 3 and she brake the **b**, and poured *it* on his *211*
Lk 7:37 brought an **alabaster b** of ointment, *211*

BOY (1) [BOYS]
Joel 3: 3 have given a **b** for a harlot, and sold a girl 3206

BOYS (2) [BOY]
Ge 25:27 **b** grew: and Esau was a cunning hunter, 5288
Zec 8: 5 the streets of the city shall be full of **b** and 3206

BOYSTEROUS (1)
Mt 14:30 when he saw the wind **b**, he was afraid; *2478*

BOZEZ (1)
1Sa 14: 4 the name of the one *was* **B**, and the name 949

BOZKATH (1)
Jos 15:39 Lachish, and **B**, and Eglon, 1218

BOZRAH (9)
Ge 36:33 Jobab the son of Zerah of **B** reigned in his 1224
1Ch 1:44 Jobab the son of Zerah of **B** reigned in his 1224
Isa 34: 6 for the LORD hath a sacrifice in **B**, 1224
 63: 1 from Edom, with dyed garments from **B**? 1224
Jer 48:24 upon **B**, and upon all the cities of the land 1224
 49:13 that **B** shall become a desolation, a 1224
 49:22 as the eagle, and spread his wings over **B**: 1224
Am 1:12 which shall devour the palaces of **B**. 1224
Mic 2:12 I will put them together as the sheep of **B**, 1223

BRACELET (1) [BRACELETS]
2Sa 1:10 the **b** that *was* on his arm, and have 685

BRACELETS (10) [BRACELET]
Ge 24:22 two **b** for her hands of ten *shekels* weight 6781
 24:30 the earring and **b** upon his sister's hands, 6781
 24:47 upon her face, and the **b** upon her hands. 6781
 38:18 thy **b**, and thy staff that *is* in thine hand, 6616
 38:25 *are* these, the signet, and **b**, and staff. 6616
Ex 35:22 *and* brought **b**, and earrings, and rings, 2397
Nu 31:50 chains, and **b**, rings, earrings, and tablets, 6781
Isa 3:19 The chains, and the **b**, and the mufflers, 8285
Eze 16:11 I put **b** upon thine hands, and a chain on 6781
 23:42 which put **b** upon their hands, 6781

BRAIDED See BROIDED; PLAITING

BRAIDS See LOCKS

BRAKE (73) [BREAK]
Ex 9:25 of the field, and **b** every tree of the field. 7665
 32: 3 all the people **b** off the golden earrings 6561
 32:19 hands, and **b** them beneath the mount. 7665
Dt 9:17 two hands, and **b** them before your eyes. 7665
Jdg 7:19 **b** the pitchers that *were* in their hands. 5310
 7:20 **b** the pitchers, and held the lamps in their 7665

Jdg 9:53 Abimelech's head, and **all to b** his skull. 7533
 16: 9 **b** the withs, as a thread of tow is broken 5423
 16:12 he **b** them from off his arms like a thread. 5423
1Sa 4:18 of the gate, and his neck **b**, and he died: 7665
2Sa 23:16 three mighty *men* **b** through the host of 1234
1Ki 19:11 **b** in pieces the rocks before the LORD; 7665
2Ki 10:27 they **b** down the image of Baal, 5422
 10:27 **b down** the house of Baal, and made it a 5422
 11:18 *into* the house of Baal, and **b** it **down**; 5422
 11:18 his images **b** in pieces throughly, 7665
 14:13 **b down** the wall of Jerusalem from the 6555
 18: 4 **b** the images, and cut down the groves, 5422
 18: 4 **b** in pieces the brasen serpent that Moses 3807
 23: 7 he **b down** the houses of the sodomites, 5422
 23: 8 **b down** the high places of the gates that 5422
 23:12 **b** them **down** from thence, and cast the 7323
 23:14 he **b** in pieces the images, and cut down 7665
 23:15 that altar and the high place he **b down**, 5422
 25:10 **b down** the walls of Jerusalem round 5422
1Ch 11:18 the three **b** through the host of 1234
2Ch 23: 3 **b down** the images, and cut down 7665
 21:17 **b into** it, and carried away all the 1234
 23:17 **b** it **down**, and brake his altars and his 5422
 23:17 **b** his altars and his images **in pieces**, 7665
 25:23 **b down** the wall of Jerusalem from the 6555
 26: 6 **b down** the wall of Gath, and the wall of 6555
 33: 1 **b** the images *in pieces*, and cut down 7665
 34: 4 they **b down** the altars of Baalim in his 5422
 34: 4 he **b** *in pieces*, and made dust *of them*, 7665
 36:19 **b down** the wall of Jerusalem, and burnt 5422
Job 29:17 I **b** the jaws of the wicked, and pluckt 7665
 38: 8 the sea with doors, when it **b forth**, 1518
 38:10 **b up** for it my decreed *place*, and set bars 7665
Ps 76: 3 There he **b** the arrows of the bow, 7665
 105:16 the land: he **b** the whole staff of bread. 7665
 105:33 fig trees; and **b** the trees of their coasts. 7665
 106:29 and the plague **b** in upon them. 6555
 107:14 of death, and **b** their bands **in sunder**. 5423
Jer 28:10 off the prophet Jeremiah's neck, and **b** it. 7665
 31:32 my covenant they **b**, although I was 6565
 39: 8 and **b down** the walls of Jerusalem. 5422
 52:14 with all the walls of Jerusalem round 5422
 52:17 Chaldeans **b**, and carried all the brass of 7665
Eze 17:16 he despised, and whose covenant he **b**, 6565
Da 2: 1 was troubled, and his sleep **b** from him. 1961
 2:34 of iron and clay, and **b** them **in pieces**. 1855
 2:45 *that* it **b** in pieces the iron, the brass, 1855
 6:24 **b** all their bones **in pieces** or ever they 1855
 7: 7 it devoured and **b** in pieces, 1855
 7:19 **b** in pieces, and stamped the residue 1855
 8: 7 and smote the ram, and **b** his two horns: 7665
Mt 14:19 and **b**, and gave the loaves to *his* disciples, *2806*
 15:36 he **b** *them*, and gave to his disciples *2806*
 26:26 and blessed *it*, and **b** *it*, and gave *it* to *2806*
Mk 6:41 the loaves, and gave *them* to his 2622
 8: 6 and **b**, and gave to his disciples to set *2806*
 8:19 When I **b** the five loaves among five 2806
 14: 3 and she **b** the box, and poured *it* on his 4937
 14:22 **b** *it*, and gave to them, and said, Take, *2806*
Lk 5: 6 great multitude of fishes: and their net **b**. 1284
 8:29 and he **b** the bands, and was driven of 1284
 9:16 and **b**, and gave to the disciples to set 2622
 22:19 and **b** *it*, and gave unto them, saying, *2806*
 24:30 and blessed *it*, and **b**, and gave to them. *2806*
Jn 19:32 and **b** the legs of the first, and of the other 2608
 19:33 he was dead already, they **b** not his legs: 2608
1Co 11:24 given thanks, he **b** *it*, and said, Take, eat: *2806*

BRAKEST (5) [BREAK]
Ex 34: 1 that were in the first tables, which thou **b**. 7665
Dt 10: 2 that were in the first tables which thou **b**, 7665
Ps 74:13 thou **b** the heads of the dragons in 7665
 74:14 Thou **b** the heads of leviathan **in pieces**, 7533
Eze 29: 7 thou **b**, and madest all their loins to be at 7665

BRAMBLE (4) [BRAMBLES]
Jdg 9:14 said all the trees unto the **b**, Come thou, 329
 9:15 the **b** said unto the trees, If in truth ye 329
 9:15 let fire come out of the **b**, and devour 329
Lk 6:44 nor of a **b** bush gather they grapes. *942*

BRAMBLES (1) [BRAMBLE]
Isa 34:13 nettles and **b** in the fortresses thereof: 2336

BRANCH (37) [BRANCHES]
Ex 25:33 *with* a knop and a flower in one **b**; 7070
 25:33 bowls made like almonds in the other **b**, 7070
 37:17 his shaft, and his **b**, his bowls, his knops, 7070
 37:19 after the fashion of almonds in one **b**, 7070
 37:19 bowls made like almonds in another **b**, 7070
Nu 13:23 down from thence a **b** with one cluster 2156
Job 8:16 and his **b** shooteth forth in his garden, 3127
 14: 7 that the **tender b** thereof will not cease. 3127
 15:32 his time, and his **b** shall not be green. 3712
 18:16 and above shall his **b** be cut off. 7105
 29:19 and the dew lay all night upon my **b**. 7105
Ps 80:15 the **b** *that* thou madest strong for thyself. 1121
Pr 11:28 but the righteous shall flourish as a **b**. 5929
Isa 4: 2 In that day shall the **b** of the LORD be 6780
 9:14 off Israel head and tail, **b** and rush, 3712
 11: 1 and a **B** shall grow out of his roots: 5342
 14:19 cast out of thy grave like an abominable **b**, 5342
 17: 9 an uppermost **b**, which they left because 534
 19:15 which the head or tail, **b** or rush, may do. 3712
 25: 5 the **b** of the terrible ones shall be brought 2159

Isa 60:21 the **b** of my planting, the work of my 5342
Jer 23: 5 that I will raise unto David a righteous **B**, 6780
 33:15 will I cause the **B** of righteousness to grow 6780
Eze 8:17 and lo, they put the **b** to their nose. 2156
 15: 2 *than* a **b** which is among the trees of 2156
 17: 3 and took the **highest b** of the cedar: 6788
 17:22 I will also take of the **highest b** of the 6788
Da 11: 7 out of a **b** of her roots shall *one* stand up 5342
Zec 3: 8 I *will* bring forth my servant the **B**. 6780
 6:12 Behold the man whose name *is* The **B**; 6780
Mal 4: 1 that it shall leave them neither root nor **b**. 6057
Mt 24:32 his **b** is yet tender, and putteth forth 2798
Mk 13:28 her **b** is yet tender, and putteth forth 2798
Jn 15: 2 Every **b** in me that beareth not fruit he 2814
 15: 2 every **b** that beareth fruit, he purgeth it, NIG
 15: 4 As the **b** cannot bear fruit of itself, except 2814
 15: 6 he is cast forth as a **b**, and is withered; 2814

BRANCHES (75) [BRANCH]
Ge 40:10 in the vine *were* three **b**: and it *was* as 8299
 40:12 of it: The three **b** *are* three days: 8299
 49:22 by a well; *whose* **b** run over the wall. 1323
Ex 25:31 his shaft, and his **b**, his bowls, his knops, 7070
 25:32 six **b** shall come out of the sides of it; 7070
 25:32 three **b** of the candlestick out of the one 7070
 25:32 three **b** of the candlestick out of the other 7070
 25:33 in the six **b** that come out of 7070
 25:35 *there shall be* a knop under two **b** of 7070
 25:35 a knop under two **b** of the same, and 7070
 25:35 a knop under two **b** of the same, 7070
 25:35 according to the six **b** that proceed out of 7070
 25:36 and their **b** shall be of the same: 7070
 37:18 six **b** going out of the sides thereof; 7070
 37:18 three **b** of the candlestick out of the one 7070
 37:18 three **b** of the candlestick out of the other 7070
 37:19 throughout the six **b** going out of 7070
 37:21 a knop under two **b** of the same, and 7070
 37:21 a knop under two **b** of the same, and 7070
 37:21 and a knop under two **b** of the same, 7070
 37:21 according to the six **b** going out of it. 7070
 37:22 Their knops and their **b** were of the same: 7070
Lev 23:40 **b** of palm trees, and the boughs of thick 3709
Ne 8:15 fetch olive **b**, and pine branches, 5929
 8:15 pine **b**, and myrtle branches, 6086
 8:15 myrtle **b**, and palm branches, 5929
 8:15 palm **b**, and branches of thick trees, 5929
 8:15 palm branches, and **b** of thick trees, 5929
Job 15:30 the flame shall dry up his **b**, and by 3127
Ps 80:11 unto the sea, and her **b** unto the river. 3127
 104:12 their habitation, *which* sing among the **b**. 6073
Isa 16: 8 her **b** are stretched out, they are gone over 7976
 17: 6 *or* five in the outmost fruitful **b** thereof, 5585
 18: 5 take away *and* cut down the **b**. 5189
 27:10 he lie down, and consume the **b** thereof. 5585
Jer 11:16 fire upon it, and the **b** of it are broken. 1808
Eze 17: 6 whose **b** turned toward him, and the roots 1808
 17: 6 and brought forth **b**, and shot forth sprigs. 905
 17: 7 and shot forth her **b** toward him, 1808
 17: 8 *it* might bring forth **b**, and that *it* might 6057
 17:23 in the shadow of the **b** thereof shall they 1808
 19:10 and **full of b** by reason of many waters. 6058
 19:11 stature was exalted among the **thick b**, 5688
 19:11 in her height with the multitude of her **b**. 1808
 19:14 fire is gone out of a rod of her **b**, 905
 31: 3 *was* a cedar in Lebanon with fair **b**, 6057
 31: 5 his **b** became long because of the 6288
 31: 6 under his **b** did all the beasts of the field 6288
 31: 7 fair in his greatness, in the length of his **b** 1808
 31: 8 and the chesnut trees were not like his **b**; 6288
 31: 9 made him fair by the multitude of his **b**: 1808
 31:12 and in all the valleys his **b** are fallen, 6288
 31:13 the beasts of the field shall upon his **b**: 6288
 36: 8 ye shall shoot forth your **b**, and yield your 6057
Da 4:14 Hew down the tree, and cut off his **b**, 6056
 4:14 from under it, and the fowls from his **b**: 6056
 4:21 upon whose **b** the fowls of the heaven 6056
Hos 11: 6 shall consume his **b**, and devour *them*, 905
 14: 6 His **b** shall spread, and his beauty shall be 3127
Joel 1: 7 cast *it* away; the **b** thereof are made white. 8299
Na 2: 2 them out, and marred their **vine b**. 2156
Zec 4:12 What *be* these two olive **b** which through 7641
Mt 13:32 *of* the air come and lodge in the **b** thereof. 2798
 21: 8 others cut down **b** from the trees, 2798
Mk 4:32 than all herbs, and shooteth out great **b**; 2798
 11: 8 and others cut down **b** off the trees, 4746
Lk 13:19 the fowls of the air lodged in the **b** of it. 2798
Jn 12:13 Took **b** of palm trees, and went forth to 902
 15: 5 I am the vine, ye *are* the **b**: He that 2814
Ro 11:16 and if the root *be* holy, so *are* the **b**. 2798
 11:17 And if some of the **b** be broken off, 2798
 11:18 Boast not against the **b**: but if thou boast, 2798
 11:19 wilt say then, The **b** were broken off, 2798
 11:21 For if God spared not the natural **b**, 2798
 11:24 which be the natural *b*, be graffed into NIG

BRAND (1) [BRANDS, FIREBRAND, FIREBRANDS]
Zec 3: 2 *is* not this a **b** pluckt out of the fire? 181

BRANDISH (1)
Eze 32:10 when I shall **b** my sword before them; 5774

BRANDS (1) [BRAND]
Jdg 15: 5 when he had set the **b** on fire, he let *them* 3940

B

BRASEN (29) [BRASS]

Ex	27: 4 upon the net shalt thou make four **b** rings	5178
	35:16 The altar of burnt offering with his **b** grate,	5178
	38: 4 he made for the altar a **b** grate of network	5178
	38:10 *were* twenty, and their **b** sockets twenty;	5178
	38:30 the **b** altar, and the brasen grate for it,	5178
	38:30 the **b** grate for it, and all the vessels of	5178
	39:39 The **b** altar, and his grate of brass, his	5178
Lev	6:28 if it be sodden in a **b** pot, it shall be both	5178
Nu	16:39 Eleazar the priest took the **b** censers,	5178
1Ki	4:13 great cities *with* walls and **b** bars:	5178
	7:30 every base had four **b** wheels, and plates	5178
	8:64 the **b** altar that *was* before the LORD *was*	5178
	14:27 king Rehoboam made in their stead **b**	5178
2Ki	16:14 he brought also the **b** altar, which *was*	5178
	16:15 the **b** altar shall be for me to inquire by.	5178
	16:17 took down the sea from off the **b** oxen	5178
	18: 4 brake in pieces the **b** serpent that Moses	5178
	25:13 the **b** sea that *was* in the house of	5178
1Ch	18: 8 wherewith Solomon made the **b** sea,	5178
2Ch	1: 5 Moreover the **b** altar, that Bezaleel the	5178
	1: 6 Solomon went up thither to the **b** altar	5178
	6:13 Solomon had made a **b** scaffold, of five	5178
	7: 7 the **b** altar which Solomon had made was	5178
Jer	1:18 and **b** walls against the whole land,	5178
	15:20 make thee unto this people a fenced **b**	5178
	52:17 the **b** that *was* in the house of	5178
	52:20 twelve **b** bulls that *were* under the bases,	5178
Eze	9: 2 they went in, and stood beside the **b** altar.	5178
Mk	7: 4 cups, and pots, **b vessels**, and of tables.	*5473*

BRASS (126) [BRASEN]

Ge	4:22 an instructor of every artificer in **b** and	5178
Ex	25: 3 shalt take of them; gold, and silver, and **b**,	5178
	26:11 thou shalt make fifty taches of **b**,	5178
	26:37 thou shalt cast five sockets of **b** for them.	5178
	27: 2 the same: and thou shalt overlay it with **b**.	5178
	27: 3 the vessels thereof thou shalt make *of* **b**.	5178
	27: 4 shalt make for it a grate of network *of* **b**.	5178
	27: 6 of shittim wood, and overlay them with **b**.	5178
	27:10 and their twenty sockets *shall be of* **b**;	5178
	27:11 pillars and their twenty sockets *of* **b**.	5178
	27:17 *shall be of* silver, and their sockets *of* **b**.	5178
	27:18 fine twined linen, and their sockets *of* **b**.	5178
	27:19 and all the pins of the court, *shall be of* **b**.	5178
	30:18 Thou shalt also make a laver *of* **b**,	5178
	30:18 his foot *also of* **b**, to wash *withal:* and	5178
	31: 4 to work in gold, and in silver, and in **b**,	5178
	35: 5 of the LORD; gold, and silver, and **b**,	5178
	35:24 and **b** brought the LORD's offering:	5178
	35:32 to work in gold, and in silver, and in **b**,	5178
	36:18 made fifty taches of **b** to couple the tent	5178
	36:38 with gold: but their five sockets *were of* **b**.	5178
	38: 2 of the same: and he overlaid it with **b**.	5178
	38: 3 all the vessels thereof made he *of* **b**.	5178
	38: 5 rings for the four ends of the grate of **b**,	5178
	38: 6 shittim wood, and overlaid them with **b**.	5178
	38: 8 he made the laver *of* **b**, and the foot of it	5178
	38: 8 the laver *of* brass, and the foot of it *of* **b**,	5178
	38:11 twenty, and their sockets *of* **b** twenty;	5178
	38:17 the sockets for the pillars *were of* **b**;	5178
	38:19 *were* four, and their sockets *of* **b** four;	5178
	38:20 and of the court round about, *were of* **b**.	5178
	38:29 the **b** of the offering *was* seventy talents,	5178
	39:39 his grate of **b**, his staves, and all his	5178
Lev	26:19 your heaven as iron, and your earth as **b**:	5154
Nu	21: 9 Moses made a serpent of **b**, and put it	5178
	21: 9 he beheld the serpent of **b**, he lived.	5178
	31:22 the **b**, the iron, the tin, and the lead,	5178
Dt	8: 9 and out of whose hills thou mayest dig **b**.	5178
	28:23 heaven that *is* over thy head shall be **b**,	5178
	33:25 Thy shoes *shall be* iron and **b**; and as thy	5178
Jos	6:19 and gold, and vessels of **b** and iron,	5178
	6:24 the gold, and the vessels of **b** and of iron,	5178
	22: 8 with **b**, and with iron, and with very	5178
Jdg	16:21 to Gaza, and bound him with **fetters of b**;	5178
1Sa	17: 5 *he had* a helmet of **b** upon his head,	5178
	17: 5 of the coat *was* five thousand shekels of **b**.	5178
	17: 6 *he had* greaves of **b** upon his legs,	5178
	17: 6 and a target of **b** between his shoulders.	5178
	17:38 and he put a helmet of **b** upon his head;	5178
2Sa	8: 8 king David took exceeding much **b**.	5178
	8:10 and vessels of gold, and vessels of **b**:	5178
	21:16 three hundred *shekels* of **b** *in* weight,	5178
1Ki	7:14 father *was* a man of Tyre, a worker in **b**:	5178
	7:14 and cunning to work all works in **b**.	5178
	7:15 For he cast two pillars of **b**, of eighteen	5178
	7:16 he made two chapiters of molten **b**, to set	5178
	7:27 he made ten bases of **b**; four cubits *was*	5178
	7:30 had four brasen wheels, and plates of **b**:	5178
	7:38 made he ten lavers of **b**: one laver	5178
	7:45 the house of the LORD, *were* of bright **b**.	5178
	7:47 was the weight of the **b** found out.	5178
2Ki	25: 7 bound him with **fetters of b**,	5178
	25:13 the pillars of **b** that *were in* the house of	5178
	25:13 and carried the **b** of them to Babylon.	5178
	25:14 all the vessels of **b** wherewith they	5178
	25:16 the **b** of all these vessels was without	5178
	25:17 and the chapiter upon it *was* **b**:	5178
	25:17 upon the chapiter round about, all *of* **b**:	5178
1Ch	15:19 *appointed* to sound with cymbals of **b**;	5178
	18: 8 Hadarezer, brought David very much **b**.	5178
	18: 8 and the pillars, and the vessels of **b**.	5178
	18:10 *of* vessels of gold and silver and **b**.	5178
	22: 3 and **b** in abundance without weight;	5178
1Ch	22:14 of **b** and iron without weight; for it is in	5178
	22:16 gold, the silver, and the **b**, and the iron,	5178
	29: 2 **b** for *things of* brass, the iron for *things*	5178
	29: 2 brass for *things of* **b**, the iron for *things*	5178
	29: 7 *of* **b** eighteen thousand talents,	5178
2Ch	2: 7 in **b**, and in iron, and in purple,	5178
	2:14 in **b**, in iron, in stone, and in timber,	5178
	4: 1 Moreover he made an altar of **b**,	5178
	4: 9 and overlaid the doors of them with **b**.	5178
	4:16 for the house of the LORD *of* bright **b**.	5178
	4:18 the weight of the **b** could not be found	5178
	12:10 which king Rehoboam made shields of **b**,	5178
	24:12 and **b** to mend the house of the LORD.	5178
Job	6:12 the strength of stones? or *is my* flesh of **b**?	5153
	28: 2 earth, and **b** *is* molten *out of* the stone.	5154
	40:18 His bones *are as* strong pieces of **b**;	5154
	41:27 iron as straw, *and* **b** as rotten wood.	5154
Ps	107:16 For he hath broken the gates of **b**,	5178
Isa	45: 2 I will break in pieces the gates of **b**,	5154
	48: 4 neck *is* an iron sinew, and thy brow **b**:	5154
	60:17 For **b** I will bring gold, and for iron I will	5178
	60:17 and for wood **b**, and for stones iron:	5178
Jer	6:28 *are* **b** and iron; they *are* all corrupters.	5178
	52:17 the pillars of **b** that *were* in the house	5178
	52:17 and carried all the **b** of them to Babylon.	5178
	52:18 all the vessels of **b** wherewith they	5178
	52:20 the **b** of all these vessels was without	5178
	52:22 chapiter of **b** *was* upon it; and the height	5178
	52:22 upon the chapiters round about, all *of* **b**.	5178
Eze	1: 7 sparkled like the colour of burnished **b**.	5178
	22:18 all they *are* **b**, and tin, and iron, and lead,	5178
	22:20 and **b**, and iron, and lead, and tin,	5178
	24:11 that the **b** of it may be hot, and may burn,	5178
	27:13 of men and vessels of **b** in thy market.	5178
	40: 3 appearance *was* like the appearance of **b**,	5178
Da	2:32 of silver, his belly and his thighs of **b**,	5174
	2:35 the clay, the **b**, the silver, and the gold,	5174
	2:39 another third kingdom of **b**, which shall	5174
	2:45 the **b**, the clay, the silver, and the gold;	5174
	4:15 even with a band of iron and **b**,	5174
	4:23 even with a band of iron and **b**,	5174
	5: 4 of **b**, of iron, of wood, and of stone.	5174
	5:23 of **b**, iron, wood, and stone, which see	5174
	7:19 teeth *were of* iron, and his nails of **b**;	5174
	10: 6 and his feet like in colour to polished **b**,	5178
Mic	4:13 horn iron, and I will make thy hoofs **b**:	5178
Zec	6: 1 and the mountains *were* mountains of **b**.	5178
Mt	10: 9 nor silver, nor **b** in your purses;	*5475*
1Co	13: 1 I am become *as* sounding **b**, or a tinkling	*5475*
Rev	1:15 And his feet like unto fine **b**, as if they	*5474*
	2:18 a flame of fire, and his feet *are* like fine **b**;	*5474*
	9:20 idols of gold, and silver, and **b**, and stone,	*5470*
	18:12 and of **b**, and iron, and marble,	*5475*

BRAVE See VALIANT; VALOUR

BRAVERY (1)

Isa	3:18 that day the Lord will take away the **b** of	8597

BRAWLER (1) [BRAWLERS, BRAWLING]

1Ti	3: 3 but patient, **not a b**, not covetous;	269

BRAWLERS (1) [BRAWLER]

Tit	3: 2 To speak evil of no *man,* to be **no b**,	269

BRAWLING (2) [BRAWLER]

Pr	21: 9 than with a **b** woman in a wide house.	4066
	25:24 with a **b** woman and in a wide house.	4066

BRAY (2) [BRAYED]

Job	6: 5 Doth the wild ass **b** when he hath grass?	5101
Pr	27:22 Though thou shouldest **bray** a fool in a	3806

BRAYED (1) [BRAY]

Job	30: 7 Among the bushes they **b**; under the	5101

BRAZEN See IMPUDENT

BREACH (22) [BREACHES]

Ge	38:29 *this* **b** *be* upon thee: therefore his name	6556
Lev	24:20 **B** for breach, eye for eye, tooth for tooth:	7667
	24:20 Breach for **b**, eye for eye, tooth for tooth:	7667
Nu	14:34 and ye shall know my **b** of promise.	8569
Jdg	21:15 that the LORD had made a **b** in the tribes	6556
2Sa	5:20 enemies before me, as the **b** of waters.	6556
	6: 8 LORD had **made a b** upon Uzzah:	6555+6556
2Ki	12: 5 house, wheresoever any **b** shall be found.	919
1Ch	13:11 LORD had **made a b** upon Uzza:	6555+6556
	15:13 the LORD our God **made a b** upon us,	6555
Ne	6: 1 and *that* there was no **b** left therein;	6556
Job	16:14 He breaketh me *with* **b** upon breach,	6556
	16:14 He breaketh me *with* breach upon **b**,	6556
Ps	106:23 his chosen stood before him in the **b**,	6556
Pr	15: 4 perverseness therein *is* a **b** in the spirit.	7667
Isa	7: 6 let us **make a b** therein for us, and set a	1234
	30:13 iniquity shall be to you as a **b** ready to fall,	6556
	30:26 in the day that the LORD bindeth up the **b**	7667
	58:12 thou shalt be called, The repairer of the **b**,	6556
Jer	14:17 of my people is broken *with* a great **b**,	7667
La	2:13 thy **b** *is* great like the sea: who can heal	7667
Eze	26:10 enter into a city wherein is **made a b**.	1234

BREACHES (15) [BREACH]

Jdg	5:17 on the sea shore, and abode in his **b**.	4664
1Ki	11:27 repaired the **b** of the city of David his	6556
2Ki	12: 5 let them repair the **b** of the house,	919
2Ki	12: 6 priests had not repaired the **b** of the house.	919
	12: 7 Why repair ye not the **b** of the house?	919
	12: 7 but deliver it for the **b** of the house.	919
	12: 8 neither to repair the **b** of the house.	919
	12:12 hewed stone to repair the **b** of the house	919
	22: 5 of the LORD, to repair the **b** of the house,	919
Ne	4: 7 *and that* the **b** began to be stopped, then	6555
Ps	60: 2 heal the **b** thereof; for it shaketh.	7667
Isa	22: 9 Ye have seen also the **b** of the city of	1233
Am	4: 3 ye shall go out at the **b**, every *cow at that*	6556
	6:11 he will smite the great house *with* **b**,	7447
	9:11 that is fallen, and close up the **b** thereof;	6556

BREAD (361) [SHEWBREAD]

Ge	3:19 In the sweat of thy face shalt thou eat **b**,	3899
	14:18 king of Salem brought forth **b**	3899
	18: 5 I will fetch a morsel of **b**, and comfort ye	3899
	19: 3 did bake **unleavened b**, and they did eat.	4682
	21:14 took **b**, and a bottle of water, and gave *it*	3899
	25:34 Jacob gave Esau **b** and pottage of lentiles,	3899
	27:17 she gave the savoury meat and the **b**,	3899
	28:20 will give me **b** to eat, and raiment to put	3899
	31:54 mount, and called his brethren to eat **b**:	3899
	31:54 they did eat **b**, and tarried all night in	3899
	37:25 they sat down to eat **b**: and they lift up	3899
	39: 6 he had, save the **b** which he did eat.	3899
	41:54 but in all the land of Egypt there was **b**.	3899
	41:55 the people cried to Pharaoh for **b**:	3899
	43:25 they heard that they should eat **b** there.	3899
	43:31 and refrained himself, and said, Set on **b**.	3899
	43:32 The Egyptians might not eat **b** with	3899
	45:23 ten she asses laden with corn and **b** and	3899
	47:12 and all his father's household, *with* **b**,	3899
	47:13 *there was* no **b** in all the land; for	3899
	47:15 came unto Joseph, and said, Give us **b**:	3899
	47:17 gave them **b** *in exchange* for horses,	3899
	47:17 he fed them with **b** for all their cattle for	3899
	47:19 buy us and our land for **b**, and we and	3899
	49:20 Out of Asher his **b** *shall be* fat, and he	3899
Ex	2:20 left the man? call him, that he may eat **b**.	3899
	12: 8 roast with fire, and **unleavened b**;	4682
	12:15 Seven days shall ye eat **unleavened b**;	4682
	12:15 for whosoever eateth **leavened b** from	2557
	12:17 shall observe the *feast of* **unleavened b**;	4682
	12:18 ye shall eat **unleavened b**, until the one	4682
	12:20 habitations shall ye eat **unleavened b**.	4682
	13: 3 there shall no **leavened b** be eaten.	2557
	13: 6 Seven days thou shalt eat **unleavened b**,	4682
	13: 7 **Unleavened b** shall be eaten seven days;	4682
	13: 7 there shall no **leavened b** be seen with	2557
	16: 3 *and when* we did eat **b** to the full;	3899
	16: 4 Behold, I will rain **b** from heaven for you;	3899
	16: 8 to eat, and in the morning **b** to the full;	3899
	16:12 in the morning ye shall be filled *with* **b**;	3899
	16:15 This *is* the **b** which the LORD hath given	3899
	16:22 sixth day they gathered twice as much **b**,	3899
	16:29 giveth you on the sixth day the **b** of two	3899
	16:32 That they may see the **b** wherewith I have	3899
	18:12 to eat **b** with Moses' father in law before	3899
	23:15 shalt keep the feast of **unleavened b**:	4682
	23:15 thou shalt eat **unleavened b** seven days,	4682
	23:18 blood of my sacrifice with **leavened b**;	2557
	23:25 and he shall bless thy **b**, and thy water;	3899
	29: 2 **unleavened b**, and cakes unleavened	3899
	29:23 one loaf of **b**, and one cake of oiled bread,	3899
	29:23 one cake of oiled **b**, and one wafer out of	3899
	29:23 **unleavened b** that *is* before the LORD:	4682
	29:32 of the ram, and the **b** that *is* in the basket,	3899
	29:34 of the **b**, remain unto the morning, then	3899
	34:18 feast of **unleavened b** shalt thou keep:	4682
	34:18 seven days thou shalt eat **unleavened b**,	4682
	34:28 he did neither eat **b**, nor drink water.	3899
	40:23 he set the **b** in order upon it before	3899
Lev	6:16 *with* **unleavened b** shall it be eaten in	4682
	7:13 he shall offer *for* his offering leavened **b**	3899
	8: 2 two rams, and a basket of **unleavened b**;	4682
	8:26 out of the basket of **unleavened b**,	4682
	8:26 a cake of oiled **b**, and one wafer,	3899
	8:31 there eat it with the **b** that *is in* the basket	3899
	8:32 and of the **b** shall ye burn with fire.	3899
	21: 6 *and* the **b** of their God, they do offer:	3899
	21: 8 for he offereth the **b** of thy God:	3899
	21:17 let him not approach to offer the **b** of his	3899
	21:21 he shall not come nigh to offer the **b** of his	3899
	21:22 He shall eat the **b** of his God, *both* of	3899
	22:25 ye offer the **b** of your God of any of these;	3899
	23: 6 the feast of **unleavened b** unto the LORD:	4682
	23: 6 seven days ye must eat **unleavened b**.	4682
	23:14 ye shall eat neither **b**, nor parched *corn,*	3899
	23:18 ye shall offer with the **b** seven lambs	3899
	23:20 the priest shall wave them with the **b** of	3899
	24: 7 that it may be on the **b** for a memorial,	3899
	26: 5 ye shall eat your **b** to the full, and dwell in	3899
	26:26 when I have broken the staff of your **b**,	3899
	26:26 ten women shall bake your **b** in one oven,	3899
	26:26 they shall deliver *you* your **b** again by	3899
Nu	4: 7 and the continual **b** shall be thereon:	3899
	6:15 a basket of **unleavened b**, cakes *of* fine	4682
	6:15 wafers of **unleavened b** anointed with oil	4682
	6:17 with the basket of **unleavened b**:	4682
	9:11 *and* eat it with **unleavened b** and	4682
	14: 9 people of the land; for they *are* **b** for us:	3899
	15:19 *that* when ye eat of the **b** of the land,	3899
	21: 5 *there is* no **b**, neither *is there any* water;	3899
	21: 5 and our soul loatheth this light **b**.	3899

B

Nu	28: 2 *and* my **b** for my sacrifices made by fire,	3899
	28:17 seven days shall **unleavened b** be eaten.	4682
Dt	8: 3 know that man doth not live by **b** only,	3899
	8: 9 A land wherein thou shalt eat **b** without	3899
	9: 9 I neither did eat **b** nor drink water:	3899
	9:18 I did neither eat **b**, nor drink water,	3899
	16: 3 Thou shalt eat no **leavened b** with it;	2557
	16: 3 seven days shalt thou eat **unleavened b**	4682
	16: 3 bread therewith, *even* the **b** of affliction;	3899
	16: 4 shall be no **leavened b** seen with thee	7603
	16: 8 Six days thou shalt eat **unleavened b**:	4682
	16:16 in the feast of **unleavened b**, and in	4682
	23: 4 Because they met you not with **b** and	3899
	29: 6 Ye have not eaten **b**, neither have you	3899
Jos	9: 5 all the **b** of their provision was dry *and*	3899
	9:12 This our **b** we took hot for our provision	3899
Jdg	7:13 a cake of barley **b** tumbled into the host	3899
	8: 5 loaves of **b** unto the people that follow	3899
	8: 6 that we should give **b** unto thine army?	3899
	8:15 that we should give **b** unto thy men	3899
	13:16 thou detain me, I will not eat of thy **b**:	3899
	19: 5 Comfort thine heart *with* a morsel of **b**,	3899
	19:19 there is **b** and wine also for me, and for	3899
Ru	1: 6 had visited his people in giving them **b**.	3899
	2:14 eat of the **b**, and dip thy morsel in	3899
1Sa	2: 5 *were* full have hired out themselves for **b**;	3899
	2:36 him for a piece of silver and a morsel of **b**,	3899
	2:36 priests' offices, that *I* may eat a piece of **b**.	3899
	9: 7 for the **b** is spent in our vessels, and	3899
	10: 3 another carrying three loaves of **b**,	3899
	10: 4 salute thee, and give thee two *loaves* of **b**;	3899
	16:20 Jesse took an ass *laden* with **b**, and a	3899
	21: 3 give *me* five *loaves of* **b** in mine hand,	3899
	21: 4 *There is* no common **b** under mine hand,	3899
	21: 4 under mine hand, but there is hallowed **b**;	3899
	21: 5 and *the* **b** *is in* a manner common, yea,	NIH
	21: 6 So the priest gave him hallowed **b**:	NIH
	21: 6 hallowed *bread:* for there was no **b** there	3899
	21: 6 to put hot **b** in the day when it was taken	3899
	22:13 that thou hast given him **b** and a sword,	3899
	25:11 Shall I then take my **b**, and my water,	3899
	28:20 for he had eaten no **b** all the day, nor all	3899
	28:22 and let me set a morsel of **b** before thee;	3899
	28:24 and did bake **unleavened b** thereof:	4682
	30:11 to David, and gave him **b**, and he did eat;	3899
	30:12 he had eaten no **b**, nor drunk *any* water,	3899
2Sa	3:29 falleth on the sword, or that lacketh **b**.	3899
	3:35 and more also, if I taste **b**, or ought else,	3899
	6:19 to every one a cake of **b**, and a good piece	3899
	9: 7 thou shalt eat **b** at my table continually.	3899
	9:10 Mephibosheth thy master's son shall eat **b**	3899
	12:17 not, neither did he eat **b** with them.	3899
	12:20 they set **b** before him, and he did eat.	3899
	12:21 child was dead, thou didst rise and eat **b**.	3899
	16: 1 upon them two hundred *loaves* of **b**,	3899
	16: 2 the **b** and summer fruit for the young	3899
1Ki	13: 8 neither will I eat **b** nor drink water in this	3899
	13: 9 saying, Eat no **b**, nor drink water,	3899
	13:15 him, Come home with me, and eat **b**.	3899
	13:16 neither will I eat **b** nor drink water with	3899
	13:17 Thou shalt eat no **b** nor drink water there,	3899
	13:18 that he may eat **b** and drink water.	3899
	13:19 did eat **b** in his house, and drank water.	3899
	13:22 eaten **b** and drunk water in the place,	3899
	13:22 say to thee, Eat no **b**, and drink no water;	3899
	13:23 after he had eaten **b**, and after he had	3899
	17: 6 the ravens brought him **b** and flesh in	3899
	17: 6 and **b** and flesh in the evening;	3899
	17:11 I pray thee, a morsel of **b** in thine hand.	3899
	18: 4 a cave, and fed them *with* **b** and water.)	3899
	18:13 a cave, and fed them *with* **b** and water?	3899
	21: 4 turned away his face, and would eat no **b**.	3899
	21: 5 is thy spirit so sad, that thou eatest no **b**?	3899
	21: 7 *and* eat **b**, and let thine heart be merry:	3899
	22:27 feed him with **b** of affliction and with	3899
2Ki	4: 8 and she constrained him to eat **b**.	3899
	4: 8 passed by, he turned in thither to eat **b**.	3899
	4:42 the man of God **b** of the firstfruits,	3899
	6:22 set **b** and water before them, that they	3899
	18:32 and wine, a land of **b** and vineyards,	3899
	23: 9 they did eat of the **unleavened b** among	4682
	25: 3 there was no **b** for the people of the land.	3899
	25:29 he did eat **b** continually before him all	3899
1Ch	12:40 brought **b** on asses, and on camels,	3899
	16: 3 to every one a loaf of **b**, and a good piece	3899
2Ch	8:13 *even* in the feast of **unleavened b**,	4682
	18:26 feed him with **b** of affliction and with	3899
	30:13 feast of **unleavened b** in the second	4682
	30:21 **unleavened b** seven days with great	4682
	35:17 the feast of **unleavened b** seven days.	4682
Ezr	6:22 the feast of **unleavened b** seven days	4682
	10: 6 he did eat no **b**, nor drink water:	3899
Ne	5:14 my brethren have not eaten the **b** of	3899
	5:15 taken of them **b** and wine, beside forty	3899
	5:18 yet for *all* this required not I the **b** of	3899
	9:15 gavest them **b** from heaven for their	3899
	13: 2 they met not the children of Israel with **b**	3899
Job	15:23 He wandereth abroad for **b**, *saying,*	3899
	22: 7 thou hast withholden **b** from the hungry,	3899
	27:14 his offspring shall not be satisfied *with* **b**.	3899
	28: 5 *As for* the earth, out of it cometh **b**:	3899
	33:20 So that his life abhorreth **b**, and his soul	3899
	42:11 and did eat **b** with him in his house:	3899
Ps	14: 4 who eat up my people *as* they eat **b**,	3899
	37:25 forsaken, nor his seed begging **b**.	3899

Ps	41: 9 in whom I trusted, which did eat of my **b**,	3899
	53: 4 who eat up my people *as* they eat **b**:	3899
	78:20 streams overflowed; can he give **b** also?	3899
	80: 5 Thou feedest them with the **b** of tears;	3899
	102: 4 like grass; so that I forget to eat my **b**.	3899
	102: 9 For I have eaten ashes like **b**,	3899
	104:15 and **b** *which* strengtheneth man's heart.	3899
	105:16 the land: he brake the whole staff of **b**.	3899
	105:40 and satisfied them *with* the **b** of heaven.	3899
	109:10 let them seek *their* **b** also out of their	NIH
	127: 2 to sit up late, to eat the **b** of sorrows;	3899
	132:15 provision: I will satisfy her poor *with* **b**.	3899
Pr	4:17 For they eat the **b** of wickedness,	3899
	6:26 woman *a man is brought* to a piece of **b**:	3899
	9: 5 eat of my **b**, and drink of the wine	3899
	9:17 sweet, and **b** *eaten* in secret is pleasant.	3899
	12: 9 he that honoureth himself, and lacketh **b**.	3899
	12:11 tilleth his land shall be satisfied *with* **b**.	3899
	20:13 *and* thou shalt be satisfied *with* **b**.	3899
	20:17 **B** of deceit *is* sweet to a man; but	3899
	22: 9 for he giveth of his **b** to the poor.	3899
	23: 6 Eat thou not the **b** of *him that hath* an	3899
	25:21 thine enemy *be* hungry, give him **b** to eat;	3899
	28:19 that tilleth his land shall have plenty of **b**:	3899
	28:21 for a piece of **b** *that* man will transgress.	3899
	31:27 and eateth not the **b** of idleness.	3899
Ecc	9: 7 Go *thy way,* eat thy **b** with joy,	3899
	9:11 to the strong, neither yet **b** to the wise,	3899
	11: 1 Cast thy **b** upon the waters: for thou shalt	3899
Isa	3: 1 the whole stay of **b**, and the whole stay	3899
	3: 7 for in my house *is* neither **b** nor clothing:	3899
	4: 1 We will eat our own **b**, and wear our	3899
	21:14 they prevented with their **b** him that fled.	3899
	28:28 **B** *corn* is bruised; because he will not	3899
	30:20 *though* the Lord give you the **b** of	3899
	30:23 **b** of the increase of the earth, and it shall	3899
	33:16 **b** *shall* be given him; his waters *shall* be	3899
	36:17 and wine, a land of **b** and vineyards.	3899
	44:15 yea, he kindleth *it*, and baketh **b**; yea,	3899
	44:19 I have baked **b** upon the coals thereof;	3899
	51:14 die in the pit, nor that his **b** should fail.	3899
	55: 2 ye spend money for *that which is* not **b**?	3899
	55:10 give seed to the sower, and **b** to the eater:	3899
	58: 7 *Is it* not to deal thy **b** to the hungry,	3899
Jer	5:17 thy **b**, *which* thy sons and thy daughters	3899
	37:21 *they* should give him daily a piece of **b**	3899
	37:21 until all the **b** in the city were spent.	3899
	38: 9 he is: for *there is* no more **b** in the city.	3899
	41: 1 there they did eat **b** together in Mizpah.	3899
	42:14 of the trumpet, nor have hunger of **b**;	3899
	52: 6 that there was no **b** for the people of	3899
	52:33 he did continually eat **b** before him all	3899
La	1:11 All her people sigh, they seek **b**; they have	3899
	4: 4 the young children ask **b**, *and* no man	3899
	5: 6 *to* the Assyrians, to be satisfied *with* **b**.	3899
	5: 9 We gat our **b** with *the peril of* our lives	3899
Eze	4: 9 in one vessel, and make thee **b** thereof,	3899
	4:13 eat their defiled **b** among the Gentiles,	3899
	4:15 and thou shalt prepare thy **b** therewith.	3899
	4:16 I will break the staff of **b** in Jerusalem:	3899
	4:16 they shall eat **b** by weight, and with care;	3899
	4:17 That they may want **b** and water,	3899
	5:16 upon you, and will break your staff of **b**:	3899
	12:18 eat thy **b** with quaking, and drink thy	3899
	12:19 They shall eat their **b** with carefulness,	3899
	13:19 for handfuls of barley and for pieces of **b**,	3899
	14:13 will break the staff of **b** thereof,	3899
	16:49 fulness of **b**, and abundance of idleness	3899
	18: 7 hath given his **b** to the hungry,	3899
	18:16 *but* hath given his **b** to the hungry,	3899
	24:17 not *thy* lips, and eat not the **b** of men.	3899
	24:22 not cover *your* lips, nor eat the **b** of men.	3899
	44: 3 he shall sit in it to eat **b** before the Lord;	3899
	44: 7 when ye offer my **b**, the fat and the blood,	3899
	45:21 seven days; **unleavened b** shall be eaten.	4682
Da	10: 3 I ate no pleasant **b**, neither came flesh nor	3899
Hos	2: 5 give *me* my **b** and my water, my wool	3899
	9: 4 sacrifices *shall be* unto them as the **b**	3899
	9: 4 for their **b** for their soul shall not come	3899
Am	4: 6 and want of **b** in all your places:	3899
	7:12 and there eat **b**, and prophesy there:	3899
	8:11 not a famine of **b**, nor a thirst for water,	3899
Ob	1: 7 *they that eat* thy **b** have laid a wound	3899
Hag	2:12 with his skirt do touch **b**, or pottage,	3899
Mal	1: 7 Ye offer polluted **b** upon mine altar;	3899
Mt	4: 3 command that these stones be made **b**.	740
	4: 4 Man shall not live by **b** alone, but by	740
	6:11 Give us this day our daily **b**.	740
	7: 9 whom if his son ask **b**, will he give him a	740
	15: 2 wash not their hands when they eat **b**.	740
	15:26 It is not meet to take the children's **b**, and	740
	15:33 we have so much **b** in the wilderness,	740
	16: 5 other side, they had forgotten to take **b**.	740
	16: 7 saying, *It is* because we have taken no **b**.	740
	16: 8 because ye have brought no **b**?	740
	16:11 that I spake *it* not to you concerning **b**,	740
	16:12 bade *them* not beware of the leaven of **b**,	740
	26:17 unleavened the disciples came to Jesus,	106
	26:26 Jesus took **b**, and blessed *it,* and brake *it,*	740
Mk	3:20 so that they could not so much as eat **b**.	740
	6: 8 no scrip, no **b**, no money in *their* purse:	740
	6:36 *into* the villages, and buy themselves **b**:	740
	6:37 and buy two hundred pennyworth of **b**,	740
	7: 2 saw some of his disciples eat **b** with defiled,	740
	7: 5 the elders, but eat with unwashen hands?	740

Mk	7:27 for it is not meet to take the children's **b**,	740
	8: 4 these *men* with **b** here in the wilderness?	740
	8:14 Now *the disciples* had forgotten to take **b**,	740
	8:16 saying, *It is* because we have no **b**.	740
	8:17 Why reason ye, because ye have no **b**?	740
	14: 1 *feast* of the passover, and of **unleavened b**:	106
	14:12 And the first day of **unleavened b**,	106
	14:22 Jesus took **b**, and blessed, and brake *it,*	740
Lk	4: 3 command this stone that it be made **b**.	740
	4: 4 That man shall not live by **b** alone, but	740
	7:33 For John the Baptist came neither eating **b**	740
	9: 3 neither staves, nor scrip, neither **b**,	740
	11: 3 Give us day by day our daily **b**.	740
	11:11 *If* a son shall ask **b** of any of you that is a	740
	14: 1 chief Pharisees to eat **b** on the sabbath day,	740
	14:15 Blessed *is he* that shall eat **b** in the	740
	15:17 *servants* of my father's have **b** enough	740
	22: 1 the feast of **unleavened b** drew nigh,	106
	22: 7 Then came the day of **unleavened b**,	106
	22:19 And he took **b**, and gave thanks,	740
	24:30 he took **b**, and blessed *it*, and brake,	740
	24:35 he was known of them in breaking of **b**.	740
Jn	6: 5 shall we buy **b**, that these may eat?	740
	6: 7 Two hundred pennyworth of **b** is not	740
	6:23 nigh unto the place where they did eat **b**,	740
	6:31 He gave them **b** from heaven to eat.	740
	6:32 Moses gave you not *that* **b** from heaven;	740
	6:32 my Father giveth you the true **b** from	740
	6:33 the **b** of God is he which cometh down	740
	6:34 unto him, Lord, evermore give us this **b**.	740
	6:35 Jesus said unto them, I am the **b** of life:	740
	6:41 am the **b** which came down from heaven.	740
	6:48 I am *that* **b** of life.	740
	6:50 This is the **b** which cometh down from	740
	6:51 I am the living **b** which came down from	740
	6:51 if any *man* eat of this **b**, he shall live for	740
	6:51 the **b** that I will give is my flesh, which I	740
	6:58 This is *that* **b** which came down from	740
	6:58 he that eateth *of* this **b** shall live for ever.	740
	13:18 that eateth **b** with me hath lift up his heel	740
	21: 9 of coals there, and fish laid thereon, and **b**.	740
	21:13 and taketh **b**, and giveth them,	740
Ac	2:42 and in breaking of **b**, and in prayers.	740
	2:46 breaking **b** from house to house, did eat	740
	12: 3 (Then were the days of **unleavened b**.)	106
	20: 6 Philippi after the days of **unleavened b**,	106
	20: 7 the disciples came together to break **b**,	740
	20:11 was come up *again,* and had broken **b**,	740
	27:35 he took **b**, and gave thanks to God in	740
1Co	5: 8 but with the **unleavened b** of sincerity	106
	10:16 The **b** which we break, is it not	740
	10:17 we being many are one **b**, *and* one body:	740
	10:17 for we are all partakers of *that* one **b**.	740
	11:23 night in which he was betrayed took **b**:	740
	11:26 For as often as ye eat this **b**, and drink this	740
	11:27 Wherefore whosoever shall eat this **b**,	740
	11:28 so let him eat of *that* **b**, and drink of *that*	740
2Co	9:10 to the sower both minister **b** for *your* food,	740
2Th	3: 8 did we eat any man's **b** for nought;	740
	3:12 quietness they work, and eat their own **b**.	740

BREAD OF THE PRESENCE See SHEWBREAD

BREADTH (87) [BROAD, HANDBREADTH]

Ge	6:15 the **b** of it fifty cubits, and the height of it	7341
	13:17 land in the length of it and in the **b** of it;	7341
Ex	25:10 cubit and a half the **b** thereof, and a cubit	7341
	25:17 and a cubit and a half the **b** thereof.	7341
	25:23 cubit the **b** thereof, and a cubit and a half	7341
	26: 2 and the **b** of one curtain four cubits:	7341
	26: 8 and the **b** of one curtain four cubits.	7341
	26:16 and a half *shall be* the **b** of one board.	7341
	27:12 the **b** of the court on the west side *shall*	7341
	27:13 the **b** of the court on the east side	7341
	27:18 the **b** fifty every where, and the height	7341
	28:16 and a span *shall be* the **b** thereof.	7341
	30: 2 length thereof, and a cubit the **b** thereof;	7341
	36: 9 and the **b** of one curtain four cubits:	7341
	36:15 and four cubits *was* the **b** of one curtain:	7341
	36:21 and the **b** of a board one cubit and a half.	7341
	37: 1 a cubit and a half the **b** of it, and a cubit	7341
	37: 6 and one cubit and a half the **b** thereof.	7341
	37:10 cubit the **b** thereof, and a cubit and a half	7341
	37:25 of it *was* a cubit, and the **b** of it a cubit;	7341
	38: 1 and five cubits the **b** thereof;	7341
	38:18 and the height in the **b** *was* five cubits,	7341
	39: 9 and a span the **b** thereof, *being* doubled.	7341
Dt	2: 5 of their land, no, not so much as a foot **b**;	4096
	3:11 four cubits the **b** of it, after the cubit of a	7341
Jdg	20:16 every one could sling stones at a hair **b**,	NIH
1Ki	6: 2 the **b** thereof twenty *cubits,* and the	7341
	6: 3 according to the **b** of the house;	7341
	6: 3 ten cubits *was* the **b** thereof before	7341
	6:20 twenty cubits in **b**, and twenty cubits in	7341
	7: 2 the **b** thereof fifty cubits, and the height	7341
	7: 6 fifty cubits, and the **b** thereof thirty cubits;	7341
	7:27 four cubits the **b** thereof, and three cubits	7341
2Ch	3: 3 threescore cubits, and the **b** twenty cubits.	7341
	3: 4 *of it was* according to the **b** of the house,	7341
	3: 8 length whereof *was* according to the **b**	7341
	3: 8 and the **b** thereof twenty cubits:	7341
	4: 1 cubits the **b** thereof, and ten cubits	7341
Ezr	6: 3 *and* the **b** thereof threescore cubits;	6613
Job	37:10 and the **b** of the waters is straitened.	7341
	38:18 Hast thou perceived the **b** of the earth?	7338

B

Isa 8: 8 of his wings shall fill the **b** of thy land, 7341
Eze 40: 5 cubits *long* by the cubit and a **hand b:** 2948
 40: 5 so he measured the **b** of the building, 7341
 40:11 measured the **b** of the entry of the gate, 7341
 40:13 the **b** was five and twenty cubits, 7341
 40:19 he measured the **b** from the forefront of 7341
 40:20 the length thereof, and the **b** thereof. 7341
 40:21 and the **b** five and twenty cubits. 7341
 40:25 and the **b** five and twenty cubits. 7341
 40:36 and the **b** five and twenty cubits. 7341
 40:48 the **b** of the gate *was* three cubits on this 7341
 40:49 twenty cubits, and the **b** eleven cubits; 7341
 41: 1 *which was* the **b** of the tabernacle. 7341
 41: 2 the **b** of the door *was* ten cubits; 7341
 41: 2 forty cubits: and the **b,** twenty cubits. 7341
 41: 3 and the **b** of the door, seven cubits. 7341
 41: 4 the **b,** twenty cubits, before the temple: 7341
 41: 5 the **b** of *every* side chamber, four cubits, 7341
 41: 7 the **b** of the house *was still* upward, 7341
 41:11 the **b** of the place that was left *was* five 7341
 41:14 Also the **b** of the face of the house, 7341
 42: 2 the north door, and the **b** was fifty cubits. 7341
 42: 4 *was* a walk of ten cubits **b** inward, 7341
 43:13 The cubit *is* a cubit and a **hand b;** even 2948
 43:13 the **b** a cubit, and the border thereof by 7341
 43:14 *shall be* two cubits, and the **b** one cubit; 7341
 43:14 *shall be* four cubits, and the **b** *one* cubit. 7341
 45: 1 and the **b** *shall be* ten thousand. 7341
 45: 2 five hundred *in* **b,** square round about; NIH
 45: 3 thousand, and the **b** of ten thousand: 7341
 45: 5 the ten thousand of **b,** shall also 7341
 48: 8 *of* five and twenty thousand *reeds in* **b,** 7341
 48: 9 *in* length, and *of* ten thousand *in* **b.** 7341
 48:10 and toward the west ten thousand *in* **b,** 7341
 48:10 toward the east ten thousand *in* **b,** 7341
 48:13 *in* length, and ten thousand *in* **b:** 7341
 48:13 twenty thousand, and the **b** ten thousand. 7341
 48:15 that are left in the **b** over against the five 7341
Da 3: 1 *and* the **b** thereof six cubits: 6613
Hab 1: 6 which *shall* march through the **b** of 4800
Zec 2: 2 to see what *is* the **b** thereof, and what *is* 7341
 5: 2 cubits, and the **b** thereof ten cubits. 7341
Eph 3:18 comprehend with all saints what *is* the **b,** 4114
Rev 20: 9 And they went up on the **b** of the earth, 4114
 21:16 and the length is as large as the **b:** 4114
 21:16 The length and the **b** and the height of it 4114

BREAK (140) [BRAKE, BRAKEST, BREAKER,
 BREAKEST, BREAKETH, BREAKING, BREAKINGS,
 BROKEN, BROKEN-HEARTED, BROKENFOOTED,
 BROKENHANDED, COVENANT-BREAKERS,
 TRUCEBREAKERS]

Ge 19: 9 *even* Lot, and came near to **b** the door. 7665
 27:40 that thou shalt **b** his yoke from off thy 6561
Ex 12:46 house; neither shall ye **b** a bone thereof. 7665
 13:13 not redeem *it*, then thou shalt **b** his **neck:** 6202
 19:21 lest they **b** through unto the Lᴏʀᴅ to 2040
 19:22 lest the Lᴏʀᴅ **b** forth upon them. 6555
 19:24 the people **b** through to come up unto 2040
 19:24 the Lᴏʀᴅ, lest he **b** forth upon them. 6555
 22: 6 If fire **b** out, and catch in thorns, so that 3318
 23:24 and **quite b down** their images. 7665+7665
 32: 2 said unto them, **B off** the golden earrings, 6561
 32:24 hath *any* gold, let them **b** it **off.** 6561
 34:13 **b** their images, and cut down their groves: 7665
 34:20 *him* not, then shalt thou **b** his **neck.** 6202
Lev 11:33 *is* in it shall be unclean; and ye shall **b** it. 7665
 13:12 a leprosy **b out** abroad in the skin, 6524+6524
 14:43 come again, and **b out** in the house, 6524
 14:45 shall **b down** the house, the stones of it, 5422
 26:15 *but* that ye **b** my covenant: 6565
 26:19 I will **b** the pride of your power; and I 7665
 26:44 and to **b** my covenant with them: 6565
Nu 9:12 unto the morning, nor **b** any bone of it: 7665
 24: 8 shall **b** their bones, and pierce *them* 1633
 30: 2 he shall not **b** his word, he shall do 2490
Dt 7: 5 **b down** their images, and cut down their 7665
 12: 3 **b** their pillars, and burn their groves with 7665
 31:16 **b** my covenant which I have made with 6565
 31:20 and provoke me, and **b** my covenant. 6565
Jdg 2: 1 I will never **b** my covenant with you. 6565
 8: 9 again in peace, I will **b down** this tower. 5422
1Sa 25:10 that **b away** every man from his master. 6555
2Sa 2:32 and they came to Hebron **at b of day.** 215
1Ki 15:19 thy league with Baasha king of Israel, 6565
2Ki 3:26 **b through** *even* unto the king of Edom: 1234
 25:13 did the Chaldees **b** *in pieces*, and 7665
2Ch 16: 3 thy league with Baasha king of Israel, 6565
Ezr 9:14 Should we again **b** thy commandments, 6565
Ne 4: 3 he shall even **b down** their stone wall. 6555
Job 13:25 Wilt thou **b** a leaf driven to and fro? and 6206
 19: 2 my soul, and **b** me **in pieces** with words? 1792
 34:24 He shall **b in pieces** mighty *men* without 7489
 39:15 or *that* the wild beast may **b** them. 1758
Ps 2: 3 Let us **b** their bands **asunder,** 5423
 2: 9 Thou shalt **b** them with a rod of iron; 7489
 10:15 **B** thou the arm of the wicked and the evil 7665
 58: 6 **B** their teeth, O God, in their mouth: 2040
 58: 6 **b out** the great teeth of the young lions, 5422
 72: 4 and shall **b in pieces** the oppressor. 1792
 74: 6 they **b down** the carved work thereof 1986
 89:31 If they **b** my statutes, and keep not my 2490
 89:34 My covenant will I not **b,** nor alter 2490
 94: 5 They **b in pieces** thy people, O Lᴏʀᴅ, 1792
 141: 5 excellent oil, *which* shall not **b** my head: 5106

Ecc 3: 3 time to **b** down, and a time to build *up;* 6555
SS 2:17 Until the day **b,** and the shadows flee 6315
 4: 6 Until the day **b,** and the shadows flee 6315
Isa 5: 5 *and* **b down** the wall thereof, and it shall 6555
 14: 7 *and* is quiet: they **b forth** *into* singing. 6476
 14:25 That *I* will **b** the Assyrian in my land, 7665
 28:24 he open and **b the clods** of his ground? 7702
 28:28 nor **b** *it* with the wheel of his cart, 2000
 30:14 he shall **b** it as the breaking of the potters' 7665
 35: 6 for in the wilderness shall waters **b out,** 1234
 38:13 *that,* as a lion, so will he **b** all my bones: 7665
 42: 3 A bruised reed shall he not **b,** 7665
 44:23 **b forth** *into* singing, ye mountains, 6476
 45: 2 I will **b in pieces** the gates of brass, 7665
 49:13 and **b forth** *into* singing, O mountains: 6476
 52: 9 **B forth** into joy, sing together, ye waste 6476
 54: 1 **b forth** *into* singing, and cry aloud, 6476
 54: 3 For thou shalt **b forth** *on* the right hand 6555
 55:12 the hills shall **b forth** before you *into* 6476
 58: 6 go free, and *that* ye **b** every yoke? 5423
 58: 8 shall thy light **b forth** as the morning, 1234
Jer 1:14 of the north an evil shall **b forth** upon 6605
 4: 3 **B up** your fallow ground, and sow not 5214
 14:21 remember, **b** not thy covenant with us. 6565
 15:12 iron **b** the northern iron and the steel? 7489
 19:10 shalt thou **b** the bottle in the sight of 7665
 19:11 Even so will I **b** this people and this city, 7665
 28: 4 I will **b** the yoke of the king of Babylon. 7665
 28:11 will I **b** the yoke of Nebuchadnezzar king 7665
 30: 8 *that* I will **b** his yoke from off thy neck, 7665
 31:28 to **b down,** and to throw down, 5422
 33:20 If you can **b** my covenant of the day, 6565
 43:13 He shall **b** also the images of 7665
 45: 4 *that* which I have built *will* I **b down,** 2040
 48:12 empty his vessels, and **b** their bottles. 5310
 49:35 I *will* **b** the bow of Elam, the chief 7665
 51:20 with thee will I **b in pieces** the nations, 5310
 51:21 with thee will I **b in pieces** the horse 5310
 51:21 with thee will I **b in pieces** the chariot 5310
 51:22 With thee also will I **b in pieces** man and 5310
 51:22 thee will I **b in pieces** old and young; 5310
 51:22 thee will I **b in pieces** the young man 5310
 51:23 I will also **b in pieces** with thee 5310
 51:23 thee will I **b in pieces** the husbandman 5310
 51:23 with thee will I **b in pieces** captains and 5310
Eze 4:16 I will **b** the staff of bread in Jerusalem: 7665
 5:16 upon you, and will **b** your staff of bread: 7665
 13:14 So will I **b down** the wall that ye have 2040
 14:13 will **b** the staff of the bread thereof, 7665
 16:38 *women* that **b wedlock** and shed blood 5003
 16:39 and shall **b down** thy high places: 5422
 17:15 such *things?* or shall he **b** the covenant, 6565
 23:34 thou shalt **b** the sheards thereof, 1633
 26: 4 walls of Tyrus, and **b down** her towers: 2040
 26: 9 his axes he shall **b down** thy towers. 5422
 26:12 they shall **b down** thy walls, 2040
 29: 7 thou didst **b,** and rent all their shoulder: 7533
 30:18 when I shall **b** there the yokes of Egypt: 7665
 30:22 will **b** his arms, the strong, and that 7665
 30:24 will **b** Pharaoh's arms, and he shall groan 7665
Da 2:40 all these, shall it **b in pieces** and bruise. 1855
 2:44 *but* it shall **b in pieces** and consume all 1855
 4:27 **b off** thy sins by righteousness, 6562
 7:23 shall tread it down, and **b** it **in pieces.** 1855
Hos 1: 5 that I will **b** the bow of Israel in the valley 7665
 2:18 I will **b** the bow and the sword and 7665
 4: 2 they **b out,** and blood toucheth blood. 6555
 10: 2 he shall **b down** their altars, he shall spoil 6202
 10:11 shall plow, *and* Jacob shall **b** his **clods.** 7702
 10:12 reap in mercy; **b up** your fallow ground: 5214
Joel 2: 7 his ways, and they shall not **b** their ranks: 5670
Am 1: 5 I will **b** also the bar of Damascus, 7665
 5: 6 lest he **b out** like fire *in* the house of 6743
Mic 3: 3 they **b** their bones, and chop *them* in 6476
Na 1:13 For now will I **b** his yoke from off thee, 7665
Zec 11:10 that *I* might **b** my covenant which I had 6565
 11:14 that I might **b** the brotherhood between 6565
Mt 5:19 shall **b** one of these least commandments, 3089
 6:19 and where thieves **b through** and steal: 1358
 6:20 where thieves do not **b through** nor steal: 1358
 9:17 the bottles **b,** and the wine runneth out, 4486
 12:20 A bruised reed shall he not **b,** 2608
Ac 20: 7 when the disciples came together to **b** 2806
 20:11 *even* till **b of day,** so he departed. 827
 21:13 mean ye to weep and to **b** mine heart? 4919
1Co 10:16 The bread which we **b,** is it not 2806
Gal 4:27 **b forth** and cry, thou that travailest not: 4486

BREAKER (2) [BREAK]
Mic 2:13 The **b** is come up before them: they have 6555
Ro 2:25 but if thou be a **b** of the law, 3848

BREAKEST (1) [BREAK]
Ps 48: 7 Thou **b** the ships of Tarshish with an east 7665

BREAKETH (17) [BREAK]
Ge 32:26 he said, Let me go, for the day **b.** And he 5927
Job 9:17 For he **b** me with a tempest, 7779
 12:14 he **b down,** and it cannot be built *again:* 2040
 16:14 He **b** me *with* breach upon breach, 6555
 28: 4 The flood **b out** from the inhabitant; *even* 6555
Ps 29: 5 The voice of the Lᴏʀᴅ **b** the cedars; yea, 7665
 29: 5 yea, the Lᴏʀᴅ **b** the cedars of Lebanon. 7665
 46: 9 he **b** the bow, and cutteth the spear in 7665
 119:20 My soul **b** for the longing *that it hath* unto 1638

Pr 25:15 and a soft tongue **b** the bone. 7665
Ecc 10: 8 whoso **b** a hedge, a serpent shall bite him. 6555
Isa 59: 5 that which is crushed **b out** *into* a viper. 1234
Jer 19:11 this city, as *one* **b** a potter's vessel, 7665
 23:29 like a hammer *that* **b** the rock in pieces? 6327
La 4: 4 ask bread, *and no* man **b** *it* unto them. 6566
Da 2:40 forasmuch as iron **b in pieces** and 1855
 2:40 all *things*: and as iron **b** all these, 7490

BREAKING (18) [BREAK]
Ge 32:24 wrestled a man with him until the **b** of 5927
Ex 9: 9 shall be a boil **b forth** *with* blains upon 6524
 9:10 it became a boil **b forth** *with* blains upon 6524
 22: 2 If a thief be found **b up,** and be smitten 4290
1Ch 14:11 by mine hand like the **b forth** of waters: 6556
Job 30:14 They came *upon me* as a wide **b in** *of* 6556
Ps 144:14 *that there be* no **b in,** nor going out; 6556
Isa 22: 5 **b down** the walls, and of crying to 6979
 30:13 whose **b** cometh suddenly at an instant. 7667
 30:14 he shall break it as the **b** of the potters' 7667
Eze 16:59 which hast despised the oath in **b** 6565
 17:18 Seeing he despised the oath by **b** 6565
 21: 6 thou son of man, with the **b** of *thy* loins; 7670
Hos 13:13 in *the place of* the **b forth** of children. 4866
Lk 24:35 how he was known of them in **b** of bread. 2800
Ac 2:42 and in **b** of bread, and in prayers. 2800
 2:46 and in **b** bread from house to house, did eat 2806
Ro 2:23 through **b** the law dishonourest thou God? 3847

BREAKINGS (1) [BREAK]
Job 41:25 by reason of **b** they purify themselves. 7667

BREAST (18) [BREASTPLATE, BREASTPLATES,
 BREASTS]
Ex 29:26 shalt take the **b** of the ram of Aaron's 2373
 29:27 thou shalt sanctify the **b** of the wave 2373
Lev 7:30 fire, the fat with the **b,** it shall he bring, 2373
 7:30 that the **b** may be waved *for* a wave 2373
 7:31 but the **b** shall be Aaron's and his sons'. 2373
 7:34 For the wave **b** and the heave shoulder 2373
 8:29 Moses took the **b,** and waved it *for* a 2373
 10:14 wave **b** and heave shoulder shall ye eat 2373
 10:15 the wave **b** shall they bring with 2373
Nu 6:20 with the wave **b** and heave shoulder: 2373
 18:18 as the wave **b** and as the right shoulder 2373
Job 24: 9 They pluck the fatherless from the **b,** 7699
Isa 60:16 Gentiles, and shalt suck the **b** of kings: 7699
La 4: 3 Even the sea monsters draw out the **b,** 7699
Da 2:32 his **b** and his arms of silver, his belly and 2306
Lk 18:13 heaven, but smote upon his **b,** saying, 4738
Jn 13:25 He then lying on Jesus' **b** saith unto him, 4738
 21:20 which also leaned on his **b** at supper, 4738

BREASTPLATE (28) [BREAST, PLATE]
Ex 25: 7 to be set in the ephod, and in the **b.** 2833
 28: 4 a **b,** and an ephod, and a robe, 2833
 28:15 thou shalt make the **b** of judgment *with* 2833
 28:22 thou shalt make upon the **b** chains at 2833
 28:23 thou shalt make upon the **b** two rings of 2833
 28:23 the two rings on the two ends of the **b.** 2833
 28:24 two rings *which are* on the ends of the **b.** 2833
 28:26 two ends of the **b** in the border thereof, 2833
 28:28 they shall bind the **b** by the rings thereof 2833
 28:28 that the **b** be not loosed from the ephod. 2833
 28:29 Israel in the **b** of judgment upon his heart, 2833
 28:30 thou shalt put in the **b** of judgment 2833
 29: 5 the **b,** and gird him with the curious girdle 2833
 35: 9 to be set for the ephod, and for the **b.** 2833
 35:27 be set, for the ephod, and for the **b;** 2833
 39: 8 he made the **b** of cunning work, like 2833
 39: 9 was foursquare; they made the **b** double: 2833
 39:15 they made upon the **b** chains at the ends, 2833
 39:16 the two rings in the two ends of the **b.** 2833
 39:17 gold in the two rings on the ends of the **b.** 2833
 39:19 put *them* on the two ends of the **b,** upon 2833
 39:21 they did bind the **b** by his rings unto 2833
 39:21 that the **b** might not be loosed from 2833
Lev 8: 8 he put the **b** upon him: also he put in 2833
 8: 8 also he put in the **b** the Urim and 2833
Isa 59:17 For he put on righteousness as a **b,** 8302
Eph 6:14 and having on the **b** of righteousness; 2382
1Th 5: 8 sober, putting on the **b** of faith and love; 2382

BREASTPLATES (3) [BREAST, PLATE]
Rev 9: 9 And they had **b,** as *it were* breastplates of 2382
 9: 9 they had breastplates, as *it were* **b** of iron; 2382
 9:17 having **b** of fire, and of jacinth, 2382

BREASTS (27) [BREAST]
Ge 49:25 blessings of the **b,** and of the womb: 7699
Lev 9:20 they put the fat upon the **b,** and he burnt 2373
 9:21 the **b** and the right shoulder Aaron waved 2373
Job 3:12 or why the **b** that I should suck? 7699
 21:24 His **b** are full *of* milk, and his bones are 5845
Ps 22: 9 hope *when I was* upon my mother's **b.** 7699
Pr 5:19 let her **b** satisfy thee at all times; 1717
SS 1:13 me; he shall lie all night betwixt my **b.** 7699
 4: 5 Thy two **b** *are* like two young roes *that* 7699
 7: 3 Thy two **b** are like two young roes *that* 7699
 7: 7 palm tree, and thy **b** to clusters *of grapes.* 7699
 7: 8 now also thy **b** shall be as clusters of 7699
 8: 1 that sucked the **b** of my mother! 7699
 8: 8 We have a little sister, and she hath no **b:** 7699
 8:10 I *am* a wall, and my **b** like towers: then 7699
Isa 28: 9 from the milk, *and* drawn from the **b.** 7699

B

Isa	66:11 be satisfied with the **b** of her consolations;	7699
Eze	16: 7 thy **b** are fashioned, and thine hair is	7699
	23: 3 there were their **b** pressed, and there they	7699
	23: 8 they bruised the **b** of her virginity,	1717
	23:34 thereof, and pluck off thine own **b**:	7699
Hos	2: 2 and her adulteries from between her **b**;	7699
	9:14 give them a miscarrying womb and dry **b**.	7699
Joel	2:16 the children, and those that suck the **b**:	7699
Na	2: 7 the voice of doves, tabring upon their **b**.	3824
Lk	23:48 were done, smote their **b**, and returned.	*4738*
Rev	15: 6 having their **b** girded with golden girdles.	*4738*

BREATH (42) [BREATHE]

Ge	2: 7 and breathed into his nostrils the **b** of life;	5397
	6:17 destroy all flesh, wherein *is* the **b** of life,	7307
	7:15 two of all flesh, wherein *is* the **b** of life.	7307
	7:22 All in whose nostrils *was* the **b** of	5397+7307
2Sa	22:16 at the blast of the **b** of his nostrils.	7307
1Ki	17:17 so sore, that there was no **b** left in him.	5397
Job	4: 9 the **b** of his nostrils are they consumed.	7307
	9:18 He will not suffer me to take my **b**, but	7307
	12:10 living *thing*, and the **b** of all mankind.	7307
	15:30 by the **b** of his mouth shall he go away.	7307
	17: 1 My **b** is corrupt, my days are extinct,	7307
	19:17 My **b** is strange to my wife, though I	7307
	27: 3 All the while my **b** *is* in me, and the spirit	5397
	33: 4 the **b** of the Almighty hath given me life.	5397
	34:14 he gather unto himself his spirit and his **b**;	5397
	37:10 By the **b** of God frost is given:	5397
	41:21 His **b** kindleth coals, and a flame goeth	5315
Ps	18:15 at the blast of the **b** of thy nostrils.	7307
	33: 6 the host of them by the **b** of his mouth.	7307
	104:29 thou takest away their **b**, they die,	7307
	135:17 neither is there *any* **b** in their mouths.	7307
	146: 4 His **b** goeth forth, he returneth to his	7307
	150: 6 Let every *thing that hath* **b** praise	5397
Ecc	3:19 they have all one **b**; so that a man hath	7307
Isa	2:22 ye from man, whose **b** *is* in his nostrils:	5397
	11: 4 with the **b** of his lips shall he slay	7307
	30:28 his **b**, as an overflowing stream, shall	7307
	30:33 the **b** of the Lord, like a stream of	5397
	33:11 your **b**, *as* fire, shall devour you.	7307
	42: 5 he that giveth **b** unto the people upon it,	5397
Jer	10:14 is falsehood, and *there is* no **b** in them.	7307
	51:17 is falsehood, and *there is* no **b** in them.	7307
La	4:20 The **b** of our nostrils, the anointed of	7307
Eze	37: 5 I *will* cause **b** to enter into you, and ye	7307
	37: 6 and put **b** in you, and ye shall live;	7307
	37: 8 them above: but *there was* no **b** in them.	7307
	37: 9 O **b**, and breathe upon these slain, that	7307
	37:10 the **b** came into them, and they lived,	7307
Da	5:23 the God in whose hand thy **b** *is*, and	5396
	10:17 strength in me, neither is there **b** left in	5397
Hab	2:19 and *there is* no **b** at all in the midst of it.	7307
Ac	17:25 he giveth to all life, and, **b**, and all *things*;	*4157*

BREATHE (4) [BREATH, BREATHED, BREATHETH, BREATHING]

Jos	11:11 *them:* there was not any left to **b**:	5397
	11:14 destroyed them, neither left they any to **b**.	5397
Ps	27:12 up against me, and such as **b out** cruelty.	3307
Eze	37: 9 O breath, and **b** upon these slain, that	5301

BREATHED (4) [BREATHE]

Ge	2: 7 and **b** into his nostrils the breath of life;	5301
Jos	10:40 but utterly destroyed all that **b**,	5397
1Ki	15:29 he left not to Jeroboam any that **b**, until	5397
Jn	20:22 he **b on** *them*, and saith unto them,	*1720*

BREATHETH (1) [BREATHE]

Dt	20:16 thou shalt save alive nothing that **b**:	5397

BREATHING (2) [BREATHE]

La	3:56 hide not thine ear at my **b**, at my cry.	7309
Ac	9: 1 yet **b out** threatenings and slaughter	*1709*

BRED (1) [BREED]

Ex	16:20 the morning, and it **b** worms, and stank:	7311

BREECHES (5)

Ex	28:42 thou shalt make them linen **b** to cover	4370
	39:28 linen, and linen **b** *of* fine twined linen,	4370
Lev	6:10 *his* linen **b** shall he put upon his flesh,	4370
	16: 4 he shall have the linen **b** upon his flesh,	4370
Eze	44:18 and shall have linen **b** upon their loins;	4370

BREED (2) [BRED, BREEDING]

Ge	8:17 that they may **b abundantly** in the earth,	8317
Dt	32:14 and rams of the **b** of Bashan, and goats,	1121

BREEDING (1) [BREED]

Zep	2: 9 *even* the **b** of nettles, and saltpits,	4476

BRETHREN (563) [BROTHER]

Ge	9:22 of his father, and told his two **b** without.	251
	9:25 servant of servants shall he be unto his **b**.	251
	13: 8 herdmen and thy herdmen; for we *be* **b**.	251
	16:12 he shall dwell in the presence of all his **b**.	251
	19: 7 said, I pray you, **b**, do not *so* wickedly.	251
	24:27 led me to the house of my master's **b**.	251
	25:18 *and* he died in the presence of all his **b**.	251
	27:29 lord over thy **b**, and let thy mother's sons	251
	27:37 all his **b** have I given to him for servants;	251
	29: 4 Jacob said unto them, My **b**, whence	251
	31:23 he took his **b** with him, and pursued after	251
	31:25 Laban with his **b** pitched in the mount of	251

Ge	31:32 before our **b** discern thou what *is* thine	251
	31:37 set *it* here before my **b** and thy brethren,	251
	31:37 set *it* here before my brethren and thy **b**,	251
	31:46 Jacob said unto his **b**, Gather stones;	251
	31:54 the mount, and called his **b** to eat bread:	251
	34:11 said unto her father and unto her **b**,	251
	34:25 and Levi, Dinah's **b**, took each man	251
	37: 2 years old, was feeding the flock with his **b**;	251
	37: 4 when his **b** saw that their father loved him	251
	37: 4 their father loved him more than all his **b**,	251
	37: 5 dreamed a dream, and he told *it* his **b**:	251
	37: 8 his **b** said to him, Shalt thou indeed reign	251
	37: 9 told it his **b**, and said, Behold, I have	251
	37:10 And he told *it* to his father, and to his **b**:	251
	37:10 thy **b** indeed come to bow down ourselves	251
	37:11 his **b** envied him; but his father observed	251
	37:12 his **b** went to feed their father's flock in	251
	37:13 Do not thy **b** feed *the flock* in Shechem?	251
	37:14 see whether it be well with thy **b**, and well	251
	37:16 he said, I seek my **b**: tell me, I pray thee,	251
	37:17 Joseph went after his **b**, and found them in	251
	37:23 to pass, when Joseph was come unto his **b**,	251
	37:26 Judah said unto his **b**, What profit *is it* if	251
	37:27 *and* our flesh. And his **b** were content.	251
	37:30 he returned unto his **b**, and said, The child	251
	38: 1 that Judah went down from his **b**,	251
	38:11 as his **b** *did*. And Tamar went and dwelt *in*	251
	42: 3 Joseph's ten **b** went down to buy corn in	251
	42: 4 Joseph's brother, Jacob sent not with his **b**;	251
	42: 6 Joseph's **b** came, and bowed down	251
	42: 7 Joseph saw his **b**, and he knew them, but	251
	42: 8 Joseph knew his **b**, but they knew not him.	251
	42:13 they said, Thy servants *are* twelve **b**,	251
	42:19 *be* true *men*, let one of your **b** be bound	251
	42:28 he said unto his **b**, My money is restored;	251
	42:32 We *be* twelve **b**, sons of our father; one *is*	251
	42:33 *men*; leave one of your **b** *here* with me,	251
	44:14 and his **b** came to Joseph's house;	251
	44:33 my lord; and let the lad go up with his **b**.	251
	45: 1 Joseph made himself known unto his **b**.	251
	45: 3 Joseph said unto his **b**, I *am* Joseph; doth	251
	45: 3 his **b** could not answer him; for they were	251
	45: 4 Joseph said unto his **b**, Come near to me,	251
	45:15 Moreover he kissed all his **b**, and wept	251
	45:15 and after that his **b** talked with him.	251
	45:16 saying, Joseph's **b** are come:	251
	45:17 unto Joseph, Say unto thy **b**, This do ye;	251
	45:24 So he sent his **b** away, and they departed:	251
	46:31 Joseph said unto his **b**, and unto his	251
	46:31 unto him, My **b**, and my father's house,	251
	47: 1 My father and my **b**, and their flocks,	251
	47: 2 he took some of his **b**, *even* five men,	251
	47: 3 Pharaoh said unto his **b**, What *is* your	251
	47: 5 Thy father and thy **b** are come unto thee:	251
	47: 6 of the land make thy father and **b** to dwell;	251
	47:11 Joseph placed his father and his **b**,	251
	47:12 his **b**, and all his father's household,	251
	48: 6 shall be called after the name of their **b** in	251
	48:22 given to thee one portion above thy **b**,	251
	49: 5 Simeon and Levi *are* **b**; instruments of	251
	49: 8 Judah, thou *art* he whom thy **b** shall praise:	251
	49:26 head of him *that was* separate from his **b**.	251
	50: 8 of Joseph, and his **b**, and his father's house:	251
	50:14 and his **b**, and all that went up with him	251
	50:15 when Joseph's **b** saw that their father was	251
	50:17 now, the trespass of thy **b**, and their sin;	251
	50:18 his **b** also went and fell down before his	251
	50:24 Joseph said unto his **b**, I die: and God will	251
Ex	1: 6 and all his **b**, and all that generation.	251
	2:11 he went out unto his **b**, and looked on	251
	2:11 Egyptian smiting a Hebrew, *one* of his **b**.	251
	4:18 return unto my **b** which *are* in Egypt,	251
Lev	10: 4 carry your **b** from before the sanctuary out	251
	10: 6 let your **b**, the whole house of Israel,	251
	21:10 *he that is* the high priest among his **b**,	251
	25:46 over your **b** the children of Israel, ye shall	251
	25:48 one of his **b** may redeem him:	251
Nu	16:10 minister with their **b** in the tabernacle	251
	16:10 and all thy **b** the sons of Levi with thee:	251
	18: 2 thy **b** also *of* the tribe of Levi, the tribe of	251
	18: 6 have taken your **b** the Levites from among	251
	20: 3 Would God that we had died when our **b**	251
	25: 6 brought unto his **b** a Midianitish *woman*	251
	27: 4 a possession among the **b** of our father.	251
	27: 7 of an inheritance among their father's **b**;	251
	27: 9 ye shall give his inheritance unto his **b**.	251
	27:10 if he have no **b**, then ye shall give his	251
	27:10 give his inheritance unto his father's **b**.	251
	27:11 his father have no **b**, then ye shall give his	251
	32: 6 your **b** go to war, and shall ye sit here?	251
Dt	1:16 Hear *the causes* between your **b**,	251
	1:28 our **b** have discouraged our heart, saying,	251
	2: 4 Ye are to pass through the coast of your **b**	251
	2: 8 we passed by from our **b** the children	251
	3:18 ye shall pass over armed before your **b**	251
	3:20 the Lord have given rest unto your **b**,	251
	10: 9 hath no part nor inheritance with his **b**;	251
	15: 7 within *any* of thy gates in thy land which	251
	17:15 one from among thy **b** shalt thou set king	251
	17:20 That his heart be not lifted up above his **b**,	251
	18: 2 they have no inheritance among their **b**:	251
	18: 7 as all his **b** the Levites *do*, which stand	251
	18:15 the midst of thee, of thy **b**, like unto me;	251
	18:18 them up a Prophet from among their **b**,	251
	24: 7 If a man be found stealing any of his **b** of	251

Dt	24:14 *whether he be* of thy **b**, or of thy strangers	251
	25: 5 If **b** dwell together, and one of them die,	251
	33: 9 neither did he acknowledge his **b**, nor	251
	33:16 head of him *that was* separated from his **b**.	251
	33:24 let him be acceptable to his **b**, and let him	251
Jos	1:14 ye shall pass before your **b** armed, all	251
	1:15 Until the Lord have given your **b** rest,	251
	2:13 my **b**, and my sisters, and all that they	251
	2:18 and thy **b**, and all thy father's household,	251
	6:23 mother, and her **b**, and all that she had;	251
	14: 8 Nevertheless my **b** that went up with me	251
	17: 4 to give us an inheritance among our **b**.	251
	17: 4 an inheritance among the **b** of their father.	251
	22: 3 Ye have not left your **b** these many days	251
	22: 4 your God hath given rest unto your **b**,	251
	22: 7 among their **b** on *this* side Jordan.	251
	22: 8 the spoil of your enemies with your **b**.	251
Jdg	8:19 he said, They *were* my **b**, *even* the sons of	251
	9: 1 went to Shechem unto his mother's **b**,	251
	9: 3 mother's **b** spake of him in the ears of all	251
	9: 5 slew his **b** the sons of Jerubbaal,	251
	9:24 which aided him in the killing of his **b**,	251
	9:26 Gaal the son of Ebed came with his **b**,	251
	9:31 of Ebed and his **b** be come to Shechem;	251
	9:41 Zebul thrust out Gaal and his **b**, that *they*	251
	9:56 unto his father, in slaying his seventy **b**:	251
	11: 3 Jephthah fled from his **b**, and dwelt in	251
	14: 3 a woman among the daughters of thy **b**,	251
	16:31 his **b** and all the house of his father came	251
	18: 8 came unto their **b** *to* Zorah and Eshtaol;	251
	18: 8 and their **b** said unto them, What *say* ye?	251
	18:14 said unto their **b**, Do ye know that there is	251
	19:23 unto them, Nay, my **b**, *nay*, I pray you,	251
	20:13 the voice of their **b** the children of Israel:	251
	21:22 or their **b** come unto us to complain,	251
Ru	4:10 the dead be not cut off from among his **b**,	251
1Sa	16:13 and anointed him in the midst of his **b**;	251
	17:17 Take now for thy **b** an ephah of this	251
	17:17 ten loaves, and run *to* the camp to thy **b**;	251
	17:18 look how thy **b** fare, and take their pledge.	251
	17:22 *into* the army, and came and saluted his **b**.	251
	20:29 let me get away, I pray thee, and see my **b**.	251
	22: 1 when his **b** and all his father's house heard	251
	30:23 said David, Ye shall not do so, my **b**,	251
2Sa	2:26 the people return from following their **b**?	251
	3: 8 to his **b**, and to his friends, and have not	251
	15:20 I may, return thou, and take back thy **b**:	251
	19:12 *are* my **b**, ye *are* my bones and my flesh:	251
	19:41 Why have our **b** the men of Judah stolen	251
1Ki	1: 9 called all his **b** the king's sons, and all	251
	12:24 nor fight against your **b** the children of	251
2Ki	9: 2 make him arise up from among his **b**,	251
	10:13 Jehu met with the **b** of Ahaziah king of	251
	10:13 they answered, We *are* the **b** of Ahaziah;	251
	23: 9 eat of the unleavened bread among their **b**.	251
1Ch	4: 9 Jabez was more honourable than his **b**:	251
	4:27 his **b** had not many children, neither did all	251
	5: 2 Judah prevailed above his **b**, and of him	251
	5: 7 his **b** by their families, when the genealogy	251
	5:13 their **b** of the house of their fathers *were*,	251
	6:44 their **b** the sons of Merari *stood* on the left	251
	6:48 Their **b** also the Levites *were* appointed	251
	7: 5 their **b** among all the families of Issachar	251
	7:22 many days, and his **b** came to comfort him.	251
	8:32 these also dwelt with their **b** in Jerusalem,	251
	9: 6 Jeuel, and their **b**, six hundred and ninety.	251
	9: 9 their **b**, according to their generations,	251
	9:13 their **b**, heads of the house of their fathers,	251
	9:17 and Talmon, and Ahiman, and their **b**:	251
	9:19 of Ebiasaph, the son of Korah, and his **b**,	251
	9:25 their **b**, *which were* in their villages, *were*	251
	9:32 *other* of their **b**, of the sons of	251
	9:38 they also dwelt with their **b** at Jerusalem,	251
	9:38 brethren at Jerusalem, over against their **b**.	251
	12: 2 out of a bow, *even* of Saul's **b** of Benjamin.	251
	12:32 all their **b** *were* at their commandment.	251
	12:39 drinking: for their **b** had prepared for them.	251
	13: 2 let us send abroad unto our **b** every where,	251
	15: 5 chief, and his **b** an hundred and twenty:	251
	15: 6 chief, and his **b** two hundred and twenty:	251
	15: 7 chief, and his **b** an hundred and thirty:	251
	15: 8 the chief, and his **b** two hundred:	251
	15: 9 Eliel the chief, and his **b** fourscore:	251
	15:10 chief, and his **b** an hundred and twelve.	251
	15:12 sanctify yourselves, *both* ye and your **b**,	251
	15:16 *to be* the singers with instruments of	251
	15:17 of his **b**, Asaph the son of Berechiah;	251
	15:17 the sons of Merari their **b**, Ethan the son	251
	15:18 with them their **b** of the second degree,	251
	16: 7 Lord into the hand of Asaph and his **b**.	251
	16:37 the covenant of the Lord Asaph and his **b**,	251
	16:38 Obed-edom with their **b**, threescore and	251
	16:39 Zadok the priest, and his **b** the priests,	251
	23:22 and their **b** the sons of Kish took them.	251
	23:32 the charge of the sons of Aaron their **b**,	251
	24:31 These likewise cast lots over against their **b**	251
	24:31 fathers over against their younger **b**.	251
	25: 7 their **b** *that were* instructed in the songs	251
	25: 9 who with his **b** and sons *were* twelve:	251
	25:10 *he*, his sons, and his **b**, *were* twelve:	251
	25:11 Izri, *he*, his sons, and his **b**, *were* twelve:	251
	25:12 *he*, his sons, and his **b**, *were* twelve:	251
	25:13 *he*, his sons, and his **b**, *were* twelve:	251
	25:14 *he*, his sons, and his **b**, *were* twelve:	251
	25:15 *he*, his sons, and his **b**, *were* twelve:	251

B

1Ch	25:16 *he*, his sons, and his **b**, *were* twelve:	251
	25:17 *he*, his sons, and his **b**, *were* twelve:	251
	25:18 *he*, his sons, and his **b**, *were* twelve:	251
	25:19 *he*, his sons, and his **b**, *were* twelve:	251
	25:20 *he*, his sons, and his **b**, *were* twelve:	251
	25:21 *he*, his sons, and his **b**, *were* twelve:	251
	25:22 *he*, his sons, and his **b**, *were* twelve:	251
	25:23 *he*, his sons, and his **b**, *were* twelve:	251
	25:24 *he*, his sons, and his **b**, *were* twelve:	251
	25:25 *he*, his sons, and his **b**, *were* twelve:	251
	25:26 *he*, his sons, and his **b**, *were* twelve:	251
	25:27 *he*, his sons, and his **b**, *were* twelve:	251
	25:28 *he*, his sons, and his **b**, *were* twelve:	251
	25:29 *he*, his sons, and his **b**, *were* twelve:	251
	25:30 *he*, his sons, and his **b**, *were* twelve:	251
	25:31 *he*, his sons, and his **b**, *were* twelve.	251
	26: 7 whose **b** *were* strong men, Elihu,	251
	26: 8 they and their sons and their **b**, able men	251
	26: 9 Meshelemiah had sons and **b**, strong men,	251
	26:11 all the sons and of Hosah were thirteen.	251
	26:25 And his **b** by Eliezer; Rehabiah his son,	251
	26:26 his **b** *were* over all the treasures of	251
	26:28 under the hand of Shelomith, and of his **b**.	251
	26:30 Hashabiah and his **b**, men of valour,	251
	26:32 his **b**, men of valour, *were* two thousand	251
	27:18 Of Judah, Elihu, *one* of the **b** of David:	251
	28: 2 and said, Hear me, my **b**, and my people:	251
2Ch	5:12 of Jeduthun, with their sons and their **b**,	251
	11: 4 shall not go up, nor fight against your **b**:	251
	11:22 the chief, to be ruler among his **b**:	251
	19:10 to you of your **b** that dwell in their cities,	251
	19:10 wrath come upon you, and upon your **b**:	251
	21: 2 he had **b** the sons of Jehoshaphat, Azariah,	251
	21: 4 slew all his **b** with the sword, and *divers*	251
	21:13 also hast slain thy **b** of thy father's house,	251
	22: 8 sons of the **b** of Ahaziah, that ministered	251
	28: 8 captive of their **b** two hundred thousand,	251
	28:11 which ye have taken captive of your **b**:	251
	28:15 Jericho, the city of palm trees, to their **b**:	251
	29:15 they gathered their **b**,	251
	29:34 wherefore their **b** the Levites did help	251
	30: 7 not ye like your fathers, and like your **b**,	251
	30: 9 your **b** and your children *shall find*	251
	31:15 set office, to give to their **b** by courses,	251
	35: 5 families of the fathers of your **b** the people,	251
	35: 6 sanctify yourselves, and prepare your **b**,	251
	35: 9 his **b**, and Hashabiah and Jeiel and Jozabad,	251
	35:15 for their **b** the Levites prepared for them.	251
Ezr	3: 2 his **b** the priests, and Zerubbabel the son	251
	3: 2 his **b**, and builded the altar of the God of	251
	3: 8 the remnant of their **b** the priests and	251
	3: 9 stood Jeshua *with* his sons and his **b**,	251
	3: 9 *with* their sons and their **b** the Levites.	251
	6:20 for their **b** the priests, and for themselves.	251
	7:18 to thy **b**, to do with the rest of the silver	252
	8:17 *and to* his **b** the Nethinims, at the place	251
	8:18 with his sons and his **b**, eighteen;	251
	8:19 of Merari, his **b** and their sons, twenty;	251
	8:24 Hashabiah, and ten of their **b** with them,	251
	10:18 of Jeshua the son of Jozadak, and his **b**;	251
Ne	1: 2 one of my **b**, came, he and *certain* men of	251
	3: 1 Eliashib the high priest rose up with his **b**	251
	3:18 After him repaired their **b**, Bavai the son	251
	4: 2 he spake before his **b** and the army of	251
	4:14 *is* great and terrible, and fight for your **b**,	251
	4:23 So neither I, nor my **b**, nor my servants,	251
	5: 1 and of their wives against their **b** the Jews.	251
	5: 5 Yet now our flesh *is* as the flesh of our **b**,	251
	5: 8 We after our ability have redeemed our **b**	251
	5: 8 heathen; and will you even sell your **b**?	251
	5:10 I likewise, *and* my **b**, and my servants,	251
	5:14 my **b** have not eaten the bread of	251
	10:10 their **b**, Shebaniah, Hodijah, Kelita,	251
	10:29 They clave to their **b**, their nobles,	251
	11:12 their **b** that did the work of the house	251
	11:13 his **b**, chief of the fathers, two hundred	251
	11:14 his **b**, mighty *men* of valour, an hundred	251
	11:17 and Bakbukiah the second among his **b**,	251
	11:19 Talmon, and their **b** that kept the gates,	251
	12: 7 and of their **b** in the days of Jeshua.	251
	12: 8 *was* over the thanksgiving, he and his **b**.	251
	12: 9 Bakbukiah and Unni, their **b**, *were* over	251
	12:24 with their **b** over against them, to praise	251
	12:36 his **b**, Shemaiah, and Azarael, Milalai,	251
	13:13 their office *was* to distribute unto their **b**.	251
Est	10: 3 and accepted of the multitude of his **b**,	251
Job	6:15 My **b** have dealt deceitfully as a brook,	251
	19:13 He hath put my **b** far from me,	251
	42:11 came there unto him all his **b**, and all his	251
	42:15 gave them inheritance among their **b**.	251
Ps	22:22 I will declare thy name unto my **b**:	251
	69: 8 I am become a stranger unto my **b**,	251
	122: 8 my **b** and companions' sakes, I will now	251
	133: 1 how pleasant *it is* for **b** to dwell together	251
Pr	6:19 and he that soweth discord among **b**.	251
	17: 2 have part of the inheritance among the **b**.	251
	19: 7 All the **b** of the poor do hate him: how	251
Isa	66: 5 Your **b** that hated you, that cast you out	251
	66:20 they shall bring all your **b** *for* an offering	251
Jer	7:15 I have cast out all your **b**, *even* the whole	251
	12: 6 For even thy **b**, and the house of thy father,	251
	29:16 *of* your **b** that are not gone forth with you	251
	35: 3 his **b**, and all his sons, and the whole	251
	41: 8 forbare, and slew them not among their **b**.	251
	49:10 his **b**, and his neighbours, and he *is* not.	251

Eze	11:15 Son of man, thy **b**, *even* thy brethren,	251
	11:15 Son of man, thy brethren, *even* thy **b**,	251
Hos	2: 1 Say ye unto your **b**, Ammi; and to your	251
	13:15 Though he be fruitful among his **b**, an east	251
Mic	5: 3 the remnant of his **b** shall return unto	251
Mt	1: 2 Jacob; and Jacob begat Judas and his **b**;	80
	1:11 And Josias begat Jechonias and his **b**,	80
	4:18 saw two **b**, Simon called Peter,	80
	4:21 he saw other two **b**, James the *son of*	80
	5:47 if ye salute your **b** only, what do ye more	80
	12:46 *his* mother and his **b** stood without,	80
	12:47 thy mother and thy **b** stand without,	80
	12:48 Who is my mother? and who are my **b**?	80
	12:49 and said, Behold my mother and my **b**,	80
	13:55 called Mary? and his **b**, James, and Joses,	80
	19:29 or **b**, or sisters, or father, or mother, or wife,	80
	20:24 moved with indignation against the two **b**.	80
	22:25 Now there were with us seven **b**: and the	80
	23: 8 your Master, *even* Christ; and all ye are **b**.	80
	25:40 done *it* unto one of the least of these my **b**,	80
	28:10 go tell my **b** that they go into Galilee, and	80
Mk	3:31 There came then *his* **b** and his mother, and,	80
	3:32 thy mother and thy **b** without seek for thee.	80
	3:33 saying, Who is my mother, or my **b**?	80
	3:34 and said, Behold my mother and my **b**.	80
	10:29 **b**, or sisters, or father, or mother, or wife,	80
	10:30 **b**, and sisters, and mothers, and children,	80
	12:20 Now there were seven **b**: and the first took	80
Lk	8:19 Then came to him *his* mother and his **b**,	80
	8:20 Thy mother and thy **b** stand without,	80
	8:21 my **b** are these which hear the word of God,	80
	14:12 or a supper, call not thy friends, nor thy **b**,	80
	14:26 and wife, and children, and **b**, and sisters,	80
	16:28 For I have five **b**; that he may testify unto	80
	18:29 or parents, or **b**, or wife, or children, for	80
	20:29 There were therefore seven **b**: and the first	80
	21:16 parents, and **b**, and kinsfolks, and friends;	80
	22:32 when thou art converted, strengthen thy **b**.	80
Jn	2:12 and his mother, and his **b**, and his disciples:	80
	7: 3 His **b** therefore said unto him, Depart	80
	7: 5 For neither did his **b** believe in him.	80
	7:10 But when his **b** were gone up, then went	80
	20:17 go to my **b**, and say unto them, I ascend	80
	21:23 Then went this saying abroad among the **b**,	80
Ac	1:14 Mary the mother of Jesus, and with his **b**.	80
	1:16 Men and **b**, this scripture must needs have	80
	2:29 Men and **b**, let *me* freely speak unto you of	80
	2:37 the apostles, Men and **b**, what shall we do?	80
	3:17 now, **b**, I wot that through ignorance ye	80
	3:22 Lord your God raise up unto you of your **b**,	80
	6: 3 Wherefore, **b**, look ye out among you seven	80
	7: 2 And he said, Men, **b**, and fathers, hearken;	80
	7:13 time Joseph was made known to his **b**;	80
	7:23 it came into his heart to visit his **b**	80
	7:25 he supposed his **b** would have understood	80
	7:26 set them at one *again*, saying, Sirs, ye are **b**;	80
	7:37 Lord your God raise up unto you of your **b**,	80
	9:30 Which when the **b** knew, they brought him	80
	10:23 and certain **b** from Joppa accompanied him.	80
	11: 1 **b** that were in Judea heard that the Gentiles	80
	11:12 Moreover these six **b** accompanied me,	80
	11:29 determined to send relief unto the **b** which	80
	12:17 shew these *things* unto James, and to the **b**.	80
	13:15 Ye men and **b**, if ye have *any* word of	80
	13:26 and **b**, children of the stock of Abraham,	80
	13:38 it known unto you therefore, men and **b**,	80
	14: 2 made their minds evil affected against the **b**.	80
	15: 1 which came down from Judea taught the **b**,	80
	15: 3 and they caused great joy unto all the **b**.	80
	15: 7 rose up, and said unto them, Men and **b**,	80
	15:13 James answered, saying, Men and **b**,	80
	15:22 and Silas, chief *men* among the **b**:	80
	15:23 **b** *send* greeting unto the brethren which	80
	15:23 brethren *send* greeting unto the **b** which	80
	15:32 exhorted the **b** with many words,	80
	15:33 they were let go in peace from the **b** unto	80
	15:36 visit our **b** in every city where we have	80
	15:40 being recommended by the **b** unto the grace	80
	16: 2 was well reported of by the **b** that were	80
	16:40 when they had seen the **b**, they comforted	80
	17: 6 and certain **b** unto the rulers of the city,	80
	17:10 And the **b** immediately sent away Paul and	80
	17:14 immediately the **b** sent away Paul to go as	80
	18:18 and then took his leave of the **b**,	80
	18:27 the **b** wrote, exhorting the disciples to	80
	20:32 And now, **b**, I commend you to God,	80
	21: 7 saluted the **b**, and abode with them one	80
	21:17 come to Jerusalem, the **b** received us gladly.	80
	22: 1 Men, **b**, and fathers, hear ye my defence	80
	22: 5 whom also I received letters unto the **b**,	80
	23: 1 beholding the council, said, Men and **b**,	80
	23: 5 Then said Paul, I wist not, **b**, that he was	80
	23: 6 Men and **b**, I am a Pharisee, the son of a	80
	28:14 we found **b**, and were desired to tarry	80
	28:15 And from thence, when the **b** heard of us,	80
	28:17 together, he said unto them, Men and **b**,	80
	28:21 neither any of the **b** that came shewed or	80
Ro	1:13 Now I would not have you ignorant, **b**,	80
	7: 1 Know ye not, **b**, (for I speak to them that	80
	7: 4 Wherefore, my **b**, ye also are become dead	80
	8:12 **b**, we are debtors, not to the flesh,	80
	8:29 he might be the firstborn amongst many **b**.	80
	9: 3 myself were accursed from Christ for my **b**,	80
	10: 1 **B**, my heart's desire and prayer to God for	80
	11:25 I would not, **b**, that ye should be ignorant	80

Ro	12: 1 you therefore, **b**, by the mercies of God,	80
	15:14 my **b**, that ye also are full of goodness,	80
	15:15 Nevertheless, **b**, I have written the more	80
	15:30 Now I beseech you, **b**, for the Lord Jesus	80
	16:14 Hermes, and the **b** which are with them.	80
	16:17 Now I beseech you, **b**, mark them which	80
1Co	1:10 Now I beseech you, **b**, by the name of our	80
	1:11 my **b**, by them which are of the *house* of	80
	1:26 ye see your calling, **b**, how that not many	80
	2: 1 I, **b**, when I came to you, came not with	80
	3: 1 And I, **b**, could not speak unto you as unto	80
	4: 6 And these *things*, **b**, I have in a figure	80
	6: 5 that shall be able to judge between his **b**?	80
	6: 8 do wrong, and defraud, and that *your* **b**.	80
	7:24 **B**, let every man, wherein he is called,	80
	7:29 But this I say, **b**, the time *is* short:	80
	8:12 But when ye sin so against the **b**,	80
	9: 5 and *as* the **b** of the Lord, and Cephas?	80
	10: 1 Moreover, **b**, I would not that ye should be	80
	11: 2 I praise you, **b**, that you remember me in	80
	11:33 Wherefore, my **b**, when ye come together to	80
	12: 1 Now concerning spiritual *gifts*, **b**, I would	80
	14: 6 Now, **b**, if I come unto you speaking with	80
	14:20 **B**, be not children in understanding.	80
	14:26 How is it then, **b**? when ye come together,	80
	14:39 Wherefore, **b**, covet to prophesy,	80
	15: 1 Moreover, **b**, I declare unto you the gospel	80
	15: 6 was seen of above five hundred **b** at once;	80
	15:50 **b**, that flesh and blood cannot inherit	80
	15:58 Therefore, my beloved **b**, be ye stedfast,	80
	16:11 unto me: for I look for him with the **b**.	80
	16:12 desired him to come unto you with the **b**:	80
	16:15 I beseech you, **b**, (ye know the house of	80
	16:20 All the **b** greet you. Greet ye one another	80
2Co	1: 8 For we would not, **b**, have you ignorant of	80
	8: 1 Moreover, **b**, we do you to wit of the grace	80
	8:23 **b** *be* inquired of, they are the messengers	80
	9: 3 have I sent the **b**, lest our boasting of you	80
	9: 5 I thought it necessary to exhort the **b**,	80
	11: 9 **b** which came from Macedonia supplied:	80
	11:26 perils in the sea, *in* perils among false **b**;	5569
	13:11 Finally, **b**, farewell. Be perfect, be of good	80
Gal	1: 2 And all the **b** which are with me, unto	80
	1:11 But I certify you, **b**, that the gospel which	80
	2: 4 because of false **b** unawares brought in,	5569
	3:15 **B**, I speak after the manner of men; Though	80
	4:12 **B**, I beseech you, be as I *am*; for I *am* as ye	80
	4:28 Now we, **b**, as Isaac was, are the children	80
	4:31 So then, **b**, we are not children of	80
	5:11 I, **b**, if I yet preach circumcision, why do	80
	5:13 For, **b**, ye have been called unto liberty;	80
	6: 1 **B**, if a man be overtaken in a fault, ye	80
	6:18 **B**, the grace of our Lord Jesus Christ *be*	80
Eph	6:10 Finally, my **b**, be strong in the Lord,	80
	6:23 Peace *be* to the **b**, and love with faith,	80
Php	1:12 But I would ye should understand, **b**, that	80
	1:14 And many of the **b** in the Lord,	80
	3: 1 Finally, my **b**, rejoice in the Lord. To write	80
	3:13 **B**, I count not myself to have apprehended:	80
	3:17 **B**, be followers together of me,	80
	4: 1 my **b** dearly beloved and longed for, my joy	80
	4: 8 Finally, **b**, whatsoever *things* are true,	80
	4:21 The **b** which are with me greet you.	80
Col	1: 2 faithful **b** in Christ which are at Colosse:	80
	4:15 Salute the **b** which are in Laodicea,	80
1Th	1: 4 Knowing, **b** beloved, your election of God.	80
	2: 1 For yourselves, **b**, our entrance in	80
	2: 9 For ye remember, **b**, our labour and travail:	80
	2:14 For ye, **b**, became followers of the churches	80
	2:17 But we, **b**, being taken from you for a short	80
	3: 7 Therefore, **b**, we were comforted over you	80
	4: 1 **b**, and exhort *you* by the Lord Jesus,	80
	4:10 And indeed ye do it towards all the **b** which	80
	4:10 we beseech you, **b**, that *ye* increase more	80
	4:13 **b**, concerning them which are asleep, that	80
	5: 1 But of the times and the seasons, **b**, ye have	80
	5: 4 But ye, **b**, are not in darkness, that *that* day	80
	5:12 we beseech you, **b**, to know them which	80
	5:14 we exhort you, **b**, warn *them that are*	80
	5:25 **B**, pray for us.	80
	5:26 Greet all the **b** with a holy kiss.	80
	5:27 that *this* epistle be read unto all the holy **b**.	80
2Th	1: 3 **b**, as it is meet, because that your faith	80
	2: 1 we beseech you, **b**, by the coming of our	80
	2:13 **b** beloved of the Lord, because God hath	80
	2:15 **b**, stand fast, and hold the traditions which	80
	3: 1 Finally, **b**, pray for us, that the word of	80
	3: 6 we command you, **b**, in the name of our	80
	3:13 But ye, **b**, be not weary in well doing.	80
1Ti	4: 6 If thou put the **b** in remembrance of these	80
	5: 1 *him* as a father; *and the* younger *men* as **b**;	80
	6: 2 them not despise *them*, because they are **b**;	80
2Ti	4:21 and Linus, and Claudia, and all the **b**.	80
Heb	2:11 cause he is not ashamed to call them **b**,	80
	2:12 Saying, I will declare thy name unto my **b**,	80
	2:17 it behoved him to be made like unto his **b**,	80
	3: 1 Wherefore, holy **b**, partakers of the heavenly	80
	3:12 Take heed, **b**, lest there be in any of you an	80
	5: 7 that is, of their **b**, though they come out of	80
	10:19 Having therefore, **b**, boldness to enter into	80
	13:22 And I beseech you, **b**, suffer the word of	80
Jas	1: 2 My **b**, count *it* all joy when ye fall into	80
	1:16 Do not err, my beloved **b**.	80
	1:19 Wherefore, my beloved **b**, let every man be	80
	2: 1 My **b**, have not the faith of our Lord Jesus	80

B

Jas 2: 5 my beloved **b**, Hath not God chosen 80
 2:14 What *doth* it profit, my **b**, though a man say 80
 3: 1 My **b**, be not many masters, knowing that 80
 3:10 My **b**, these *things* ought not so to be. 80
 3:12 Can the fig tree, my **b**, bear olive berries? 80
 4:11 Speak not evil one of another, **b**. He that 80
 5: 7 Be patient therefore, **b**, unto the coming of 80
 5: 9 against another, **b**, lest ye be condemned: 80
 5:10 Take, my **b**, the prophets, who have spoken 80
 5:12 But above all *things*, my **b**, swear not, 80
 5:19 **B**, if any of you do err from the truth, 80
1Pe 1:22 the Spirit unto unfeigned **love** of the **b**, 5360
 3: 8 **love as b**, *be* pitiful, *be* courteous: 5361
 5: 9 accomplished in your **b** that are in the 81
2Pe 1:10 Wherefore the rather, **b**, give diligence to 80
1Jn 2: 7 **B**, I write no new commandment unto you, 80
 3:13 Marvel not, my **b**, if the world hate you. 80
 3:14 from death unto life, because we love the **b**. 80
 3:16 we ought to lay down *our* lives for the **b**. 80
3Jn 1: 3 when *the* **b** came and testified of the truth 80
 1: 5 faithfully whatsoever thou doest to the **b**, 80
 1:10 neither doth he himself receive the **b**, 80
Rev 6:11 until their fellowservants also and their **b**, 80
 12:10 for the accuser of our **b** is cast down, 80
 19:10 of thy **b** that have the testimony of Jesus: 80
 22: 9 of thy **b** the prophets, and of them which 80

BRETHREN'S (1) [BROTHER]
Dt 20: 8 lest his **b** heart faint as well as his heart. 251

BRIBE (2) [BRIBERY, BRIBES]
1Sa 12: 3 of whose hand have I received *any* **b** to 3724
Am 5:12 they take a **b**, and they turn aside the poor 3724

BRIBERY (1) [BRIBE]
Job 15:34 fire shall consume the tabernacles of **b**. 7810

BRIBES (3) [BRIBE]
1Sa 8: 3 and took **b**, and perverted judgment. 7810
Ps 26:10 mischief, and their right hand is full *of* **b**. 7810
Isa 33:15 that shaketh his hands from holding of **b**, 7810

BRICK (7) [BRICKKILN, BRICKS]
Ge 11: 3 **make b**, and burn *them* 3835+3843
 11: 3 they had **b** for stone, and slime had they 3843
Ex 1:14 in **b**, and in all manner of service in 3843
 5: 7 give the people straw to **make b**, 3835+3843
 5:14 your task in **making b** both yesterday 3835
 5:16 thy servants, and they say to us, Make **b**: 3843
Isa 65: 3 and burneth incense upon **altars of b**; 3843

BRICKKILN (3) [BRICK]
2Sa 12:31 iron, and made them pass through the **b**: 4404
Jer 43: 9 and hide them in the clay in the **b**, 4404
Na 3:14 and tread the morter, make strong the **b**. 4404

BRICKS (4) [BRICK]
Ex 5: 8 the tale of the **b**, which they did make 3843
 5:18 you, yet shall ye deliver the tale of **b**. 3843
 5:19 Ye shall not minish *ought* from your **b** of 3843
Isa 9:10 The **b** are fallen down, but we will build 3843

BRIDE (14) [BRIDECHAMBER, BRIDEGROOM, BRIDEGROOM'S]
Isa 49:18 and him *that* on *thee*, as a **b** *doth*. 3618
 61:10 as a **b** adorneth *herself* with her jewels. 3618
 62: 5 *as* the bridegroom rejoiceth over the **b**, 3618
Jer 2:32 forget her ornaments, *or* a **b** her attire? 3618
 7:34 the bridegroom, and the voice of the **b**: 3618
 16: 9 the bridegroom, and the voice of the **b**. 3618
 25:10 the voice of the **b**, the sound of 3618
 33:11 of the bridegroom, and the voice of the **b**, 3618
Joel 2:16 his chamber, and the **b** out of her closet. 3618
Jn 3:29 He that hath the **b** is the bridegroom: 3565
Rev 18:23 of the **b** shall be heard no more at all in 3565
 21: 2 prepared as a **b** adorned for her husband. 3565
 21: 9 *Come* hither, I will shew thee the **b**, 3565
 22:17 And the Spirit and the **b** say, Come. 3565

BRIDECHAMBER (3) [BRIDE]
Mt 9:15 Can the children of the **b** mourn, 3567
Mk 2:19 unto them, Can the children of the **b** fast, 3567
Lk 5:34 Can ye make the children of the **b** fast, 3567

BRIDEGROOM (23) [BRIDE]
Ps 19: 5 *is* as a **b** coming out of his chamber, 2860
Isa 61:10 as a **b** decketh *himself* with ornaments, 2860
 62: 5 *as* the **b** rejoiceth over the bride, 2860
Jer 7:34 the voice of the **b**, and the voice of 2860
 16: 9 the voice of the **b**, and the voice of 2860
 25:10 the voice of the **b**, and the voice of 2860
 33:11 the voice of the **b**, and the voice of 2860
Joel 2:16 let the **b** go forth of his chamber, 2860
Mt 9:15 as long as the **b** is with them? 3566
 9:15 when the **b** shall be taken from them, 3566
 25: 1 their lamps, and went forth to meet the **b**. 3566
 25: 5 While the **b** tarried, they all slumbered 3566
 25: 6 was a cry made, Behold, the **b** cometh; 3566
 25:10 And while they went to buy, the **b** came; 3566
Mk 2:19 while the **b** is with them? 3566
 2:19 as long as they have the **b** with them, 3566
 2:20 the **b** shall be taken away from them, 3566
Lk 5:34 while the **b** is with them? 3566
 5:35 the **b** shall be taken away from them, 3566
Jn 2: 9 the governor of the feast called the **b**, 3566
 3:29 He that hath the bride is the **b**: 3566

Jn 3:29 the friend of the **b**, which standeth and 3566
Rev 18:23 the voice of the **b** and of the bride shall 3566

BRIDEGROOM'S (1) [BRIDE]
Jn 3:29 rejoiceth greatly because of the **b** voice: 3566

BRIDE-PRICE See DOWRY

BRIDLE (9) [BRIDLES, BRIDLETH]
2Ki 19:28 my **b** in thy lips, and I will turn thee back 4964
Job 30:11 they have also let loose the **b** before me. 7448
 41:13 who can come *to him* with his double **b**? 7448
Ps 32: 9 mouth must be held in with bit and **b**, 7448
 39: 1 I will keep my mouth with a **b**, while 4269
Pr 26: 3 a **b** for the ass, and a rod for the fools' 4964
Isa 30:28 *shall be* a **b** in the jaws of the people, 7448
 37:29 my **b** in thy lips, and I will turn thee back 4964
Jas 3: 2 *and* able also to **b** the whole body. 5468

BRIDLES (1) [BRIDLE]
Rev 14:20 *even* unto the horse **b**, by the space of a 5469

BRIDLETH (1) [BRIDLE]
Jas 1:26 and **b** not his tongue, but deceiveth his 5468

BRIEFLY (2)
Ro 13: 9 it is **b comprehended** in this saying, 346
1Pe 5:12 I have written **b**, exhorting, 1223+3641

BRIER (3) [BRIERS]
Isa 55:13 instead of the **b** shall come up the myrtle 5636
Eze 28:24 there shall be no more a pricking **b** unto 5544
Mic 7: 4 best of them *is* as a **b**: the *most* upright 2312

BRIERS (12) [BRIER]
Jdg 8: 7 the thorns of the wilderness and with **b**. 1303
 8:16 thorns of the wilderness and **b**, 1303
Isa 5: 6 but there shall come up **b** and thorns: 8068
 7:23 it shall *even* be for **b** and thorns. 8068
 7:24 all the land shall become **b** and thorns. 8068
 7:25 there shall not come thither the fear of **b** 8068
 9:18 it shall devour the **b** and thorns, 8068
 10:17 devour his thorns and his **b** in one day; 8068
 27: 4 would set the **b** *and* thorns against me 8068
 32:13 my people shall come up thorns *and* **b**; 8068
Eze 2: 6 though **b** and thorns *be* with thee, 5621
Heb 6: 8 which beareth thorns and **b** *is* rejected, 5146

BRIGANDINE (1) [BRIGANDINES]
Jer 51: 3 against *him that* lifteth himself up in his **b**: 5630

BRIGANDINES (1) [BRIGANDINE]
Jer 46: 4 furbish the spears, *and* put on the **b**. 5630

BRIGHT (29) [BRIGHTNESS]
Lev 13: 2 or **b** spot, and it be in the skin of his flesh 934
 13: 4 the **b** spot *be* white in the skin of his flesh, 934
 13:19 or a **b** spot, white, *and* somewhat reddish, 934
 13:23 if the **b** spot stay in his place, 934
 13:24 *flesh* that burneth have a white **b** spot, 934
 13:25 *if* the hair in the **b** spot be turned white, 934
 13:26 *there be* no white hair in the **b** spot, 934
 13:28 the **b** spot stay in his place, *and* spread not 934
 13:38 have in the skin of their flesh **b** spots, 934
 13:38 flesh bright spots, *even* white **b** spots; 934
 13:39 *if* the **b** spots in the skin of their flesh *be* 934
 14:56 a rising, and for a scab, and for a **b** spot: 934
1Ki 7:45 the house of the LORD, *were of* **b** brass. 4803
2Ch 4:16 for the house of the LORD *of* **b** brass. 4838
Job 37:11 thick cloud: he scattereth his **b** cloud: 216
 37:21 now *men* see not the **b** light which *is* in 925
SS 5:14 his belly *is* as **b** ivory overlaid *with* 6247
Jer 51:11 **Make b** the arrows: gather the shields: 1305
Eze 1:13 the fire was **b**, and out of the fire went 5051
 21:15 ah, *it* is made **b**, *it is* wrapt up for 1300
 21:21 he **made** *his* arrows **b**, he consulted with 7043
 27:19 **b** iron, cassia, and calamus, were in thy 6219
 32: 8 All the **b** lights of heaven will I make dark 3974
Na 3: 3 The horseman lifteth up both the **b** sword 3851
Zec 10: 1 *so* the LORD *shall* make **b** clouds, 2385
Mt 17: 5 behold, a **b** cloud overshadowed them: 5460
Lk 11:36 when the **b shining** of a candle doth give 796
Ac 10:30 a man stood before me in **b** clothing, 2986
Rev 22:16 of David, *and* the **b** and morning star. 2986

BRIGHTNESS (22) [BRIGHT]
2Sa 22:13 Through the **b** before him were coals of 5051
Job 31:26 it shined, or the moon walking *in* **b**; 3368
Ps 18:12 At the **b** *that was* before him his thick 5051
Isa 59: 9 for **b**, *but* we walk in darkness. 5054
 60: 3 thy light, and kings to the **b** of thy rising. 5051
 60:19 neither for **b** shall the moon give light 5051
 62: 1 the righteousness thereof go forth as **b**, 5051
Eze 1: 4 a **b** *was* about it, and out of the midst 5051
 1:27 of fire, and it had **b** round about. 5051
 1:28 so *was* the appearance of the **b** round 5051
 8: 2 as the appearance of **b**, as the colour of 2096
 10: 4 the court was full of the **b** of the LORD's 5051
 28: 7 thy wisdom, and they shall defile thy **b**. 3314
 28:17 corrupted thy wisdom by reason of thy **b**: 3314
Da 2:31 This great image, whose **b** *was* excellent, 2122
 4:36 mine honour and **b** returned unto me; 2122
 12: 3 they that be wise shall shine as the **b** of 2096
Am 5:20 not light? even very dark, and no **b** in it? 5051
Hab 3: 4 **b** was as the light; he had horns *coming* 5051
Ac 26:13 above the **b** of the sun, shining round 2987

2Th 2: 8 shall destroy with the **b** of his coming: 2015
Heb 1: 3 Who being the **b** of *his* glory, 541

BRIM (10) [BRIMSTONE]
Jos 3:15 the ark were dipped in the **b** of the water, 7097
1Ki 7:23 ten cubits from the one **b** to the other: 8193
 7:24 under the **b** of it round about *there were* 8193
 7:26 the **b** thereof was wrought like the brim 8193
 7:26 brim thereof was wrought like the **b** of 8193
2Ch 4: 2 a molten sea of ten cubits from **b** to brim, 8193
 4: 2 a molten sea of ten cubits from brim to **b**, 8193
 4: 5 the **b** of it like the work of the brim of a 8193
 4: 5 the brim of it like the work of the **b** of a 8193
Jn 2: 7 And they filled them up to **the b**. 507

BRIMSTONE (15) [BRIM, STONE]
Ge 19:24 upon Gomorrah **b** and fire from 1614
Dt 29:23 *And that* the whole land thereof *is* **b**, 1614
Job 18:15 **b** shall be scattered upon his habitation. 1614
Ps 11: 6 fire and **b**, and a horrible tempest: 1614
Isa 30:33 like a stream of **b**, doth kindle it. 1614
 34: 9 the dust thereof into **b**, and the land 1614
Eze 38:22 and great hailstones, fire, and **b**. 1614
Lk 17:29 of Sodom it rained fire and **b** from heaven, 2303
Rev 9:17 breastplates of fire, and of jacinth, and **b**: 2306
 9:17 their mouths issued fire and smoke and **b**. 2303
 9:18 the fire, and by the smoke, and by the **b**, 2303
 14:10 and **b** in the presence of the holy angels, 2303
 19:20 alive into a lake of fire burning with **b**. 2303
 20:10 them was cast into the lake of fire and **b**, 2303
 21: 8 the lake which burneth with fire and **b**: 2303

BRING (727) [BRINGERS, BRINGEST, BRINGETH, BRINGING, BROUGHT, BROUGHTEST]
Ge 1:11 God said, Let the earth **b forth** grass, 1876
 1:20 Let the waters **b forth** abundantly 8317+8318
 1:24 Let the earth **b forth** the living creature 3318
 3:16 in sorrow thou shalt **b forth** children; 3205
 3:18 and thistles shall it **b forth** to thee; 6779
 6:17 I, do **b** a flood of waters upon the earth, 935
 6:19 two of every *sort* shalt thou **b** into the ark, 935
 8:17 **B forth** with thee every living thing that 3318
 9: 7 **b forth** abundantly in the earth, 8317
 9:14 when I **b** a cloud over the earth, 6049+6051
 18:16 went with them to **b** them on the **way**. 7971
 18:19 that the LORD may **b** upon Abraham that 935
 19: 5 **b** them unto us, that we may know 3318
 19: 8 **b** them **out** unto you, and do ye to them 3318
 19:12 hast in the city, **b** *them* out of *this* place: 3318
 24: 5 **must I needs b** thy son **again** 7725+7725
 24: 6 that thou **b** not my son thither **again**. 7725
 24: 8 my oath: only **b** not my son thither **again**. 7725
 27: 4 as I love, and **b** *it* to me, that I may eat; 935
 27: 5 to the field to hunt for venison, *and* to **b** *it*. 935
 27: 7 **B** me venison, and make me savoury meat, 935
 27:10 shalt **b** *it* to thy father, that he may eat, 935
 27:12 **b** a curse upon me, and not a blessing. 935
 27:25 **B** *it* **near** to me, and I will eat of my son's 5066
 28:15 and will **b** thee **again** into this land; 7725
 37:14 with the flocks; and **b** me word **again**. 7725
 38:24 **B** her **forth**, and let her be burnt. 3318
 40:14 Pharaoh, and **b** me **out** of this house: 3318
 41:32 by God, and God will shortly **b** it to **pass**. 6213
 42:20 **b** your youngest brother unto me; 935
 42:34 **b** your youngest brother unto me: then 935
 42:37 Slay my two sons, if I **b** him not to thee: 935
 42:37 my hand, and I will **b** him to thee **again**. 7725
 42:38 ye shall **b down** my gray hairs with sorrow 3381
 43: 7 that he would say, **B** your brother **down**? 3381
 43: 9 if I **b** him not unto thee, and set him 935
 43:16 **B** these men home, and slay, 935
 44:21 unto thy servants, **B** him **down** unto me, 3381
 44:29 shall **b down** my gray hairs with sorrow 3381
 44:31 thy servants shall **b down** the gray hairs 3381
 44:32 If I **b** him not unto thee, then I shall bear 935
 45:13 shall haste and **b down** my father hither. 3381
 45:19 your wives, and **b** your father, and come. 5375
 46: 4 I will also **surely b** thee **up** *again*: 5927+5927
 48: 9 **B** them, I pray thee, unto me, and I will 3947
 48:21 **b** you **again** unto the land of your fathers. 7725
 50:20 it unto good, to **b** to **pass**, as *it is* this day, 6213
 50:24 **b** you out of this land unto the land which 5927
Ex 3: 8 to **b** them **up** out of that land unto a good 5927
 3:10 that thou mayest **b forth** my people 5927
 3:11 that I should **b forth** the children of Israel 3318
 3:17 I will **b** you **up** out of the affliction of 5927
 6: 6 I will **b** you **out** from under the burdens 3318
 6: 8 I will **b** you **in** unto the land, *concerning* 935
 6:13 to the children of Israel out of the land 3318
 6:26 **B out** the children of Israel from the land 3318
 6:27 to **b** out the children of Israel from Egypt: 3318
 7: 4 **b forth** mine armies, *and* my people 3318
 7: 5 **b out** the children of Israel from among 3318
 8: 3 the river shall **b forth** frogs **abundantly**, 8317
 8:18 with their enchantments to **b forth** lice, 3318
 10: 4 will I **b** the locusts into thy coast: 935
 11: 1 will I **b** one plague *more* upon Pharaoh, 935
 12:51 **b** the children of Israel **out** of the land of 3318
 13: 5 it shall be when the LORD shall **b** thee into 935
 13:11 it shall be when the LORD shall **b** thee into 935
 15:17 Thou shalt **b** them **in**, and plant them in 935
 16: 5 they shall prepare *that* which they **b** in; 935
 18:19 that thou mayest **b** the causes unto God: 935
 18:22 *that* every great matter they shall **b** unto 935
 21: 6 his master shall **b** him unto the judges; 5066

B

Ex	21: 6 he shall also **b** him to the door, or unto	5066
	22:13 *then* let him **b** it *for* witness, *and* he shall	935
	23: 4 **surely b** it **back** to him again.	7725+7725
	23:19 **b** *into* the house of the Lord thy God.	935
	23:20 to **b** thee into the place which I have	935
	23:23 **b** thee **in** unto the Amorites.	935
	25: 2 of Israel, that they **b** me an offering:	3947
	26:33 thou mayest **b** **in** thither within the vail	935
	27:20 that they **b** thee pure oil olive beaten for	3947
	29: 3 **b** them in the basket, with the bullock	7126
	29: 4 his sons thou shalt **b** unto the door of	7126
	29: 8 thou shalt **b** his sons, and put coats upon	7126
	32: 2 of your daughters, and **b** *them* unto me.	935
	32:12 For mischief did he **b** them **out**, to slay	3318
	33:12 thou sayest unto me, **B up** this people:	5927
	34:26 the house of the Lord thy God.	935
	35: 5 let him **b** it, an offering of the Lord;	935
	35:29 heart made them willing to **b** for all	935
	36: 5 The people **b** much more than enough for	935
	40: 4 thou shalt **b** **in** the table, and set in order	935
	40: 4 thou shalt **b** **in** the candlestick, and light	935
	40:12 thou shalt **b** Aaron and his sons unto	7126
	40:14 thou shalt **b** them, and clothe them	7126
Lev	1: 2 If *any* man of you **b** an offering unto	7126
	1: 2 ye shall **b** your offering of the cattle,	7126
	1: 5 shall **b** the blood, and sprinkle the blood	7126
	1:10 he shall **b** it a male without blemish.	7126
	1:13 the priest shall **b** it all, and burn *it* upon	7126
	1:14 his offering of turtledoves, or	7126
	1:15 the priest shall **b** it unto the altar,	7126
	2: 2 he shall **b** it to Aaron's sons the priests:	935
	2: 4 if thou **b** an oblation of a meat offering	7126
	2: 8 thou shalt **b** the meat offering that is made	935
	2: 8 unto the priest, he shall **b** it unto the altar.	5066
	2:11 which ye shall **b** unto the Lord,	7126
	4: 3 him **b** for his sin, which he hath sinned,	7126
	4: 4 he shall **b** the bullock unto the door of	935
	4: 5 **b** it to the tabernacle of the congregation:	935
	4:14 **b** him before the tabernacle of	935
	4:16 the priest that is anointed shall **b** of	935
	4:23 he shall **b** his offering, a kid of the goats,	935
	4:28 he shall **b** his offering, a kid of the goats,	935
	4:32 if he **b** a lamb for a sin offering, he shall	935
	4:32 he shall **b** it a female without blemish.	935
	5: 6 he shall **b** his trespass offering unto	935
	5: 7 if he be not able to **b** a lamb, then he shall	5060
	5: 7 he shall **b** for his trespass, which he hath	935
	5: 8 he shall **b** them unto the priest, who shall	935
	5:11 if he be not **able to b** two	3027+5381
	5:11 he that sinned shall **b** for his offering	935
	5:12 shall he **b** it to the priest, and the priest	935
	5:15 he shall **b** for his trespass unto the Lord a	935
	5:18 he shall **b** a ram without blemish out of	935
	6: 6 he shall **b** his trespass offering unto	935
	6:21 *and when it is* baken, thou shalt **b** it **in:**	935
	7:29 **b** his oblation unto the Lord of	935
	7:30 His own hands shall **b** the offerings of	935
	7:30 fire, the fat with the breast, it shall he **b,**	935
	10:15 the wave breast shall they **b** with	935
	12: 6 shall **b** a lamb of the first year for a burnt	935
	12: 8 she be not **able to b** a lamb,	1767+3027+4672
	12: 8 she shall **b** two turtles, or two young	3947
	14:23 he shall **b** them on the eighth day for his	935
	15:29 young pigeons, and **b** them unto the priest,	935
	16: 9 shall **b** the goat upon which	7126
	16:11 Aaron shall **b** the bullock of the sin	7126
	16:12 beaten small, and **b** *it* within the vail:	935
	16:15 his blood within the vail, and do with	935
	16:20 and the altar, he shall **b** the live goat:	7126
	17: 5 the end that the children of Israel may **b**	935
	17: 5 even that they may **b** them unto the Lord,	935
	18: 3 Canaan, whither I **b** you, ye shall not do:	935
	19:21 he shall **b** his trespass offering unto	935
	20:22 the land, whither I **b** you to dwell therein,	935
	23:10 ye shall **b** a sheaf of the firstfruits of your	935
	23:17 Ye shall **b** out of your habitations two	935
	24: 2 they **b** unto thee pure oil olive beaten	3947
	24:14 **B forth** him that hath cursed without	3318
	24:23 that they should **b forth** him that had	3318
	25:21 it shall **b forth** fruit for three years.	6213
	26:10 **b forth** the old because of the new.	3318
	26:21 I will **b** seven *times* moe plagues upon	3254
	26:25 will **b** a sword upon you, that shall avenge	935
	26:31 **b** your sanctuaries **unto desolation,**	8074
	26:32 I will **b** the land **into desolation:**	8074
	27: 9 whereof *men* **b** an offering unto	7126
Nu	3: 6 **B** the tribe of Levi **near,** and present	7126
	5: 9 which they **b** unto the priest, shall be his.	7126
	5:15 shall the man **b** his wife unto the priest,	935
	5:15 he shall **b** her offering for her, the tenth	935
	5:16 the priest shall **b** her **near,** and set her	7126
	6:10 on the eighth day he shall **b** two turtles,	935
	6:12 shall **b** a lamb of the first year for a trespass	935
	6:16 the priest shall **b** *them* before the Lord,	7126
	8: 9 thou shalt **b** the Levites before	7126
	8:10 thou shalt **b** the Levites before the Lord:	7126
	11:16 to the tabernacle of	3947
	13:20 courage, and **b** of the fruit of the land.	3947
	14: 8 he will **b** us into this land, and give it us;	935
	14:16 Because the Lord was not able to **b** this	935
	14:24 will I **b** into the land whereinto he went;	935
	14:31 them will I **b in,** and they shall know	935
	14:37 Even *those* men that did **b up** the evil	3318
	15: 4 **b** a meat offering of a tenth deal *of* flour	7126
	15: 9 shall he **b** with a bullock a meat offering	7126

Nu	15:10 thou shalt **b** for a drink offering half a hin	7126
	15:18 ye come into the land whither I **b** you,	935
	15:25 they shall **b** their offering, a sacrifice made	935
	15:27 he shall **b** a she goat of the first year for a	7126
	16: 9 to **b** you **near** to himself to do the service	7126
	16:17 **b** ye before the Lord every man his	7126
	17:10 **B** Aaron's rod again before the Testimony	7725
	18: 2 the tribe of thy father, **b** thou with thee,	7126
	18:13 which they shall **b** unto the Lord, shall be	935
	18:15 which they **b** unto the Lord, *whether it*	7126
	19: 2 that they **b** thee a red heifer without spot,	3947
	19: 3 he may **b** her **forth** without the camp,	3318
	20: 5 of Egypt, to **b** us **in** unto this evil place?	935
	20: 8 thou shalt **b forth** to them water out of	3318
	20:12 shall not **b** this congregation into the land	935
	20:25 his son, and **b** them **up** unto mount Hor:	5927
	22: 8 *this* night, and I will **b** you word again,	7725
	23:27 thee, I will **b** thee unto another place;	3947
	27:17 lead them out, and which may **b** them **in;**	935
	28:26 when ye **b** a new meat offering unto	7126
	32: 5 a possession, *and* **b** us **not over** Jordan.	5674
Dt	1:17 for you, **b** *it* unto me, and I will hear it.	7126
	1:22 **b** us word **again** by what way we must go	7725
	4:38 and mightier than thou *art*, to **b** thee **in,**	935
	6:23 us out from thence, that he might **b** us **in,**	935
	7: 1 When the Lord thy God shall **b** thee into	935
	7:26 Neither shalt thou **b** an abomination into	935
	9: 3 he shall **b** them **down** before thy face:	3665
	9:28 Because the Lord was not able to **b** them	935
	12: 6 thither ye shall **b** your burnt offerings,	935
	12:11 thither shall ye **b** all that I command you;	935
	14:28 the end of three years thou shalt **b forth**	3318
	17: 5 thou **b forth** that man or that woman,	3318
	21: 4 the elders of that city shall **b down**	3381
	21:12 thou shalt **b** her home to thine house;	935
	21:19 **b** him **out** unto the elders of his city,	3318
	22: 1 shalt in **any case b** them **again**	7725+7725
	22: 2 thou shalt **b** it unto thine own house,	622
	22: 8 that thou **b** not blood upon thine house,	7760
	22:14 **b up** an evil name upon her, and say,	3318
	22:15 **b forth** *the tokens* of the damsel's	3318
	22:21 they shall **b out** the damsel to the door of	3318
	22:24 ye shall **b** them both **out** unto the gate of	3318
	23:18 Thou shalt not **b** the hire of a whore,	935
	24:11 man to whom thou dost lend shall **b out**	3318
	26: 2 which thou shalt **b** of thy land that	935
	28:36 The Lord shall **b** thee, and thy king	1980
	28:49 The Lord shall **b** a nation against thee	5375
	28:60 Moreover he will **b** upon thee all	7725
	28:61 them will the Lord **b** upon thee,	5927
	28:63 to destroy you, and to **b** you **to nought;**	8045
	28:68 the Lord shall **b** thee *into* Egypt **again**	7725
	29:27 to **b** upon it all the curses that are written	935
	30: 5 the Lord thy God will **b** thee into the land	935
	30:12 **b** it unto us, that we may hear it, and do	3947
	30:13 **b** it unto us, that we may hear it, and do	3947
	31:23 for thou shalt **b** the children of Israel into	935
	33: 7 voice of Judah, and **b** him unto his people:	935
Jos	2: 3 **b forth** the men that are come to thee,	3318
	2:18 thou shalt **b** thy father, and thy mother,	622
	6:22 **b out** thence the woman, and all that she	3318
	6:22 **b out** those five kings unto me out of	3318
	18: 6 and **b** *the description* hither to me,	935
	23:15 shall the Lord **b** upon you all evil things,	935
Jdg	6:13 Did not the Lord **b** us **up** from Egypt?	5927
	6:18 **b forth** my present, and set *it* before thee.	3318
	6:30 Joash, **B out** thy son, that he may die:	3381
	7: 4 **b** them **down** unto the water, and I will	3381
	11: 9 If ye **b** me *home* **again** to fight against	7725
	19: 3 friendly unto her, *and* to **b** her **again,**	7725
	19:22 **B forth** the man that came into thine	3318
	19:24 them I will **b out** now, and humble ye	3318
Ru	3:15 **B** the vail that *thou hast* upon thee,	3051
1Sa	1:22 I will **b** him, that he may appear before	935
	4: 4 that they might **b** from thence the ark of	5375
	6: 7 and **b** their calves home from them:	7725
	9: 7 if we go, what shall we **b** the man?	935
	9: 7 *is* not a present to **b** to the man of God:	935
	9:23 the portion which I gave thee, of which	5414
	11:12 **b** the men, that we may put them to	5066
	13: 9 **B hither** a burnt offering to me,	5066
	14:18 said unto Ahiah, **B hither** the ark of God.	5066
	14:34 **B** me **hither** every man his ox,	5066
	15:32 **B** you **hither** to me Agag the king of	5066
	16:17 man that can play well, and **b** *him* to me.	935
	19:15 saying, **B** him **up** to me in the bed, that I	5927
	20: 8 why shouldest thou **b** me to thy father?	935
	23: 9 Abiathar the priest, **B hither** the ephod.	5066
	27:11 to **b** *tidings* to Gath, saying, Lest they	5046
	28: 8 **b** me *him up*, whom I shall name unto	5927
	28:11 woman, Whom shall I **b up** unto thee?	5927
	28:11 unto thee? And he said, **B** me **up** Samuel.	5927
	28:15 hast thou disquieted me, to **b** me **up?**	5927
	30: 7 I pray thee, **b** me **hither** the ephod.	5066
	30:15 Canst thou **b** me **down** to this company?	3381
	30:15 and I will **b** thee **down** to this company.	3381
2Sa	2: 3 men that *were* with him did David **b up,**	5927
	3:12 with thee, to **b** about all Israel unto thee.	5437
	3:13 except thou first **b** Michal Saul's daughter,	935
	6: 2 to **b up** from thence the ark of God,	5927
	9:10 thou shalt **b in** *the fruits,* that thy master's	935
	12:23 can I **b** him **back** again? I shall go to him,	7725
	13:10 **B** the meat *into* the chamber, that I may	935
	14:10 **b** him to me, and he shall not touch thee.	935
	14:21 the young man Absalom **again.**	7725

2Sa	15: 8 **b** me **again indeed** *to* Jerusalem,	7725+7725
	15:14 evil upon us, and smite the city with	5080
	15:25 he will **b** me **again,** and shew me *both* it,	7725
	17: 3 I will **b** all the people unto thee:	7725
	17:13 shall all Israel **b** ropes to that city,	5375
	17:14 to the intent that the Lord might **b** evil	935
	19:11 Why are ye the last to **b** the king **back** to	7725
	19:12 then are ye the last to **b back** the king?	7725
	22:28 *that* thou mayest **b** them **down.**	8213
1Ki	1:33 own mule, and **b** him **down** to Gihon:	3381
	2: 9 his hoar head **b** thou **down** to the grave	3381
	3:24 the king said, **B** me a sword. And they	3947
	5: 9 My servants shall **b** *them* **down** from	3381
	8: 1 that *they* might **b up** the ark of	5927
	8: 4 those did the priests and the Levites **b up.**	5927
	8:32 the wicked, to **b** his way upon his head;	5414
	8:34 **b** them **again** unto the land which thou	7725
	10:29 did they **b** them **out** by their means.	3318
	12:21 to **b** the kingdom **again** to Rehoboam	7725
	13:18 **B** him **back** with thee into thine house,	7725
	14:10 I will **b** evil upon the house of Jeroboam,	935
	17:11 said, **B** me, I pray thee, a morsel of bread	3947
	17:13 **b** *it* unto me, and after make for thee and	3318
	20:33 he said, Go ye, **b** him. Then Ben-hadad	3947
	21:21 I will **b** evil upon thee, and will take away	935
	21:29 before me, I will not **b** the evil in his days:	935
	21:29 in his son's days will I **b** the evil upon his	935
2Ki	2:20 **B** me a new cruse, and put salt therein.	3947
	3:15 now **b** me a minstrel. And it came to pass,	5059
	4: 6 she said unto her son, **B** me yet a vessel.	5066
	4:41 he said, Then **b** meal. And he cast *it* into	3947
	6:19 I will **b** you to the man whom ye seek.	1980
	10:22 **B forth** vestments for all the worshippers	3318
	12: 4 heart to **b** *into* the house of the Lord,	935
	19: 3 and *there is* not strength to **b forth.**	3205
	22:16 I will **b** evil upon this place, and upon	935
	22:20 all the evil which I will **b** upon this place.	935
	23: 4 to **b forth** out of the temple of the Lord	3318
1Ch	9:28 that they should **b** them **in** and out by tale.	935
	13: 3 let us **b again** the ark of our God to us:	5437
	13: 5 to **b** the ark of God from Kirjath-jearim.	935
	13: 6 to **b up** thence the ark of God the Lord,	5927
	13:12 shall I **b** the ark of God *home* to me?	935
	15: 3 to **b up** the ark of the Lord unto his	5927
	15:12 that you may **b up** the ark of the Lord	5927
	15:14 the Levites sanctified themselves to **b up**	5927
	15:25 went to **b up** the ark of the covenant of	5927
	16:29 **b** an offering, and come before him:	5375
	21: 2 **b** the number of them to me, that I may	935
	21:12 advise thyself what word I shall **b again** to	7725
	22:19 to **b** the ark of the covenant of the Lord,	935
2Ch	2:16 will **b** it to thee *in* flotes by sea *to* Joppa;	935
	5: 2 to **b up** the ark of the covenant of	5927
	5: 5 these did the priests *and* the Levites **b up.**	5927
	6:25 **b** them **again** unto the land which thou	7725
	11: 1 that *he* might **b** the kingdom **again** to	7725
	24: 6 required of the Levites to **b** in out of Judah	935
	24: 9 to **b in** to the Lord the collection that	935
	24:19 to them, to **b** them **again** unto the Lord;	7725
	28:13 Ye shall not **b in** the captives hither:	935
	29:31 come near and **b** sacrifices and	935
	31:10 Since *the people* began to **b** the offerings	935
	34:24 I will **b** evil upon this place, and upon	935
	34:28 see all the evil that I will **b** upon this place,	935
Ezr	1: 8 those did Cyrus king of Persia **b forth**	3318
	1:11 All *these* did Sheshbazzar **b up** with *them*	5927
	3: 7 to **b** cedar trees from Lebanon to the sea of	935
	8:17 that *they* should **b** unto us ministers for	935
	8:30 to **b** *it* to Jerusalem unto the house of	935
Ne	1: 9 **b** them unto the place that I have chosen	935
	5: 5 we **b into bondage** our sons and our	3533
	8: 1 spake unto Ezra the scribe to **b** the book	935
	9:29 that *thou* mightest **b** them **again** unto thy	7725
	10:31 *if* the people of the land **b** ware or	935
	10:34 to **b** *it* into the house of our God,	935
	10:35 to **b** the firstfruits of our ground,	935
	10:36 of our flocks, to **b** to the house of our God,	935
	10:37 we should **b** the firstfruits of our dough,	935
	10:38 Levites shall **b up** the tithe of the tithes	5927
	10:39 the children of Levi shall **b** the offering of	935
	11: 1 to **b** one of ten to dwell in Jerusalem	935
	12:27 to **b** them to Jerusalem, to keep	935
	13:18 *did not* our God **b** all this evil upon us,	935
	13:18 yet ye **b more** wrath upon Israel by	3254
Est	1:11 To **b** Vashti the queen before the king	935
	3: 9 to **b** *it* into the king's treasuries.	935
	6: 1 he commanded to **b** the book of records	935
	6: 9 **b** him on horseback through the street of	7392
	6:14 hasted to **b** Haman unto the banquet that	935
Job	6:22 Did I say, **B** unto me? or, Give a reward	3051
	10: 9 and wilt thou **b** me into dust **again?**	7725
	14: 4 can **b** a clean *thing* out of an unclean?	5414
	14: 9 will bud, and **b forth** boughs like a plant.	6213
	15:35 **b forth** vanity, and their belly prepareth	3205
	18:14 and it shall **b** him to the king of terrors.	6805
	30:23 For I know *that* thou wilt **b** me *to* death,	7725
	33:30 To **b back** his soul from the pit, to be	7725
	38:32 Canst thou **b forth** Mazzaroth in his	3318
	39: 1 when the wild goats of the rock **b forth?**	3205
	39: 2 thou the time when they **b forth?**	3205
	39: 3 they **b forth** their young ones,	6398
	39:12 that he will **b home** thy seed, and gather	7725
	40:12 every one *that is* proud, *and* **b** him **low;**	3665
	40:20 Surely the mountains **b** him **forth** food,	5375
Ps	18:27 but wilt **b down** high looks.	8213

B

Ps
25:17 O **b** thou me **out** of my distresses. — 3318
37: 5 trust also in him; and he shall **b** *it* **to pass.** — 6213
37: 6 he shall **b forth** thy righteousness as — 3318
38: T A Psalm of David, to **b to remembrance.** — 2142
43: 3 let them **b** me unto thy holy hill, and to — 935
55:23 shalt **b** them **down** into the pit of — 3381
59:11 and **b** them **down,** O Lord our shield. — 3381
60: 9 Who will **b** me *into* the strong city? — 2986
68:22 The Lord said, I will **b again** from Bashan — 7725
68:22 I will **b** *my people* **again** from the depths — 7725
68:29 Jerusalem shall kings **b** presents unto thee — 2986
70: T *A Psalm* of David, to **b to remembrance.** — 2142
71:20 shalt **b** me **up** again from the depths of — 5927
72: 3 mountains shall **b** peace to the people, — 5375
72:10 Tarshish and of the isles shall **b** presents — 7725
76:11 let all that be round about him **b** presents — 2986
81: 2 Take a psalm, and **b** hither the timbrel, — 5414
92:14 They shall still **b forth** fruit in old age; — 5107
94:23 he shall **b** upon them their own iniquity, — 7725
96: 8 an offering, and come into his courts. — 5375
104:14 that *he* may **b forth** food out of the earth; — 3318
108:10 Who will **b** me into the strong city? — 2986
142: 7 **B** my soul **out** of prison, that *I* may praise — 3318
143:11 for thy righteousness' sake **b** my soul **out** — 3318
144:13 our sheep may **b forth** thousands and — 503

Pr
4: 8 she shall **b** thee **to honour,** when thou — 3513
19:24 not so much as **b** it to his mouth again. — 7725
26:15 it grieveth him to **b** it **again** to his mouth. — 7725
27: 1 knowest not what a day may **b forth.** — 3205
29: 8 Scornful men **b** a city **into a snare;** — 6315
29:23 A man's pride shall **b** him **low:** — 8213

Ecc
3:22 who shall **b** him to see what shall be after — 935
11: 9 for all these *things* God will **b** thee into — 935
12:14 For God shall **b** every work into judgment, — 935

SS
8: 2 *and* **b** thee into my mother's house, — 935
8:11 every one for the fruit thereof was to **b** a — 935

Isa
1:13 **B** no more vain oblations; incense *is* an — 935
5: 2 he looked that *it* should **b forth** grapes, — 6213
5: 4 I looked that *it* should **b forth grapes,** — 6213
7:17 The Lord shall **b** upon thee, and upon thy — 935
14: 2 shall take them, and **b** them to their place: — 935
15: 9 for I will **b** more upon Dimon, lions upon — 7896
23: 4 I travail not, nor **b forth children,** — 3205
23: 4 nourish up young men, nor **b up** virgins. — 7311
23: 9 to **b into contempt** all the honourable of — 7043
25: 5 Thou shalt **b down** the noise of strangers, — 3665
25:11 he shall **b down** their pride together with — 8213
25:12 high fort of thy walls shall he **b down,** — 7817
25:12 lay low, *and* **b** to the ground, *even* to — 5060
28:21 and **b to pass** his act, his strange act. — 5647
31: 2 **b** evil, and will not call back his words: — 935
33:11 conceive chaff, ye shall **b forth** stubble: — 3205
37: 3 and *there is* not strength to **b forth.** — 3205
38: 8 I will **b again** the shadow of the degrees, — 7725
41:21 **b forth** your strong *reasons,* saith the — 5066
41:22 Let them **b** them **forth,** and shew us what — 5066
42: 1 he shall **b forth** judgment to the Gentiles. — 3318
42: 3 he shall **b forth** judgment unto truth. — 3318
42: 7 to **b out** the prisoners from the prison, — 3318
42:16 I will **b** the blind by a way *that* they knew — 1980
43: 5 I will **b** thy seed from the east, — 935
43: 6 **b** my sons from far, and my daughters — 935
43: 8 **B forth** the blind people that have eyes, — 3318
43: 9 shew us former *things?* let them **b forth** — 5414
45: 8 let them **b forth** salvation, — 6509
45:21 Tell ye, and **b** them **near;** yea, let them — 5066
46: 8 **b** *it* **again** to mind, O ye transgressors. — 7725
46:11 I have spoken *it,* I will also **b** it **to pass;** — 935
46:13 I **b near** my righteousness; it shall not be — 7126
49: 5 to **b** Jacob **again** to him, Though Israel be — 7725
49:22 they shall **b** thy sons in *their* arms, — 935
52: 8 when the Lord shall **b again** Zion. — 7725
55:10 the earth, and **maketh** it **b forth** and bud, — 3205
56: 7 Even them will I **b** to my holy mountain, — 935
58: 7 thou **b** the poor that are cast out *to thy* — 935
59: 4 conceive mischief, and **b forth** iniquity. — 3205
60: 6 they shall **b** gold and incense; — 5375
60: 9 to **b** thy sons from far, their silver and — 935
60:11 that *men* may **b** unto thee the forces of — 935
60:17 For brass I will **b** gold, and for iron I will — 935
60:17 for iron I will **b** silver, and for wood brass, — 935
63: 6 I will **b down** their strength to the earth. — 3381
65: 9 I will **b forth** a seed out of Jacob, — 3318
65:23 not labour in vain, nor **b forth** for trouble; — 3205
66: 4 and will **b** their fears upon them; — 935
66: 8 the earth be **made** to **b forth** in one day? — 2342
66: 9 Shall I **b to the birth,** and not cause to — 7665
66: 9 to the birth, and not **cause** to **b forth?** — 3205
66: 9 shall I **cause** to **b forth,** and shut — 3205
66:20 shall **b** all your brethren for an offering — 935
66:20 as the children of Israel **b** an offering in a — 935

Jer
3:14 two of a family, and I will **b** you *to* Zion: — 935
4: 6 for I will **b** evil from the north, and a great — 935
5:15 Lo, I will **b** a nation upon you from far, — 935
6:19 behold, I will **b** evil upon this people, — 935
8: 1 they shall **b out** the bones of the kings of — 3318
10:24 in thine anger, lest thou **b** me **to nothing.** — 4591
11: 8 I will **b** upon them all the words of this — 935
11:11 the Lord, Behold, I *will* **b** evil upon them, — 935
11:23 for I will **b** evil upon the men of Anathoth, — 935
12: 2 they grow, yea, they **b forth** fruit: thou — 6213
12:15 will **b** them **again,** every man to his — 7725
15:19 will I **b** thee **again,** *and* thou shalt stand — 7725
16:15 I will **b** them **again** into their land that I — 7725
17:18 **b** upon them the day of evil, — 935

Jer
17:21 nor **b** *it* **in** by the gates of Jerusalem; — 935
17:24 to **b in** no burden through the gates of this — 935
18:22 when thou shalt **b** a troop suddenly upon — 935
19: 3 Behold, I *will* **b** evil upon this place, — 935
19:15 **b** upon this city and upon all her towns — 935
23: 3 and will **b** them **again** to their folds; — 7725
23:12 for I will **b** evil upon them, *even* the year — 935
23:40 I will **b** an everlasting reproach upon you, — 5414
24: 6 and I will **b** them **again** to this land: — 7725
25: 9 will **b** them against this land, and against — 935
25:13 I will **b** upon that land all my words — 935
25:29 begin to **b** evil on the city which is called — 7489
26:15 ye shall surely **b** innocent blood upon — 5414
27:11 nations that **b** their neck under the yoke — 935
27:12 **B** your necks under the yoke of the king — 935
27:22 will I **b** them **up,** and restore them to this — 5927
28: 3 Within two full years *will* I **b again** into — 7725
28: 4 I will **b again** to this place Jeconiah the — 7725
28: 6 to **b again** the vessels of the Lord's — 7725
29:14 I will **b** you **again** into the place whence — 7725
30: 3 that I will **b again** the captivity of my — 7725
30:18 I *will* **b again** the captivity of Jacob's tents — 7725
31: 8 I will **b** them from the north country, — 935
31:23 when I shall **b again** their captivity; — 7725
31:32 to **b** them **out** of the land of Egypt; — 3318
32:37 and I will **b** them **again** unto this place, — 7725
32:42 will I **b** upon them all the good that I — 935
33: 6 I *will* **b** it health and cure, and I will cure — 5927
33:11 of them that shall **b** the sacrifice of praise — 935
35: 2 and **b** them *into* the house of the Lord, — 935
35:17 I will **b** upon Judah and upon all — 935
36:31 I will **b** upon them, and upon the — 935
38:23 So they *shall* **b out** all thy wives and thy — 3318
39:16 I *will* **b** my words upon this city for evil, — 935
41: 5 to **b** *them* to the house of the Lord. — 935
42:17 from the evil that I *will* **b** upon them. — 935
45: 5 for behold, I **will** b evil upon all flesh, — 935
48:44 for I will **b** upon it, *even* upon Moab, — 935
48:47 Yet will I **b again** the captivity of Moab — 7725
49: 5 Behold, I will **b** a fear upon thee, saith — 935
49: 6 afterward I will **b again** the captivity of — 7725
49: 8 the calamity of Esau upon him, — 935
49:16 I will **b** thee **down** from thence, saith — 3381
49:32 will **b** their calamity from all sides — 935
49:36 upon Elam will I **b** the four winds from — 935
49:37 I will **b** evil upon them, *even* my fierce — 935
49:39 *that* I will **b again** the captivity of Elam, — 7725
50:19 I will **b** Israel **again** to his habitation, — 7725
51:40 I will **b** them **down** like lambs to — 3381
51:44 I will **b forth** out of his mouth that which — 3318
51:64 not rise from the evil that I *will* **b** upon — 935

La
1:21 thou wilt **b** the day *that* thou hast called, — 935

Eze
5:17 and I will **b** the sword upon thee. — 935
6: 3 *will* **b** a sword upon you, and I will destroy — 935
7:24 I will **b** the worst of the heathen, — 935
11: 7 I will **b** you **forth** out of the midst of it. — 935
11: 8 I *will* **b** a sword upon you, saith the Lord — 935
11: 9 I will **b** you **out** of the midst thereof, — 935
12: 4 shalt thou **b forth** thy stuff by day in their — 3318
12:13 I will **b** him to Babylon *to* the land of — 935
13:14 and **b** it **down** to the ground, — 5060
14:17 Or if I **b** a sword upon that land, and say, — 935
16:40 They shall also **b up** a company against — 5927
16:53 When I shall **b again** their captivity, — 7725
16:53 *will* I **b again** the captivity of thy captives — NIH
17: 8 that *it* might **b forth** branches, and that *it* — 6213
17:20 I will **b** him to Babylon, and will plead — 935
17:23 it shall **b forth** boughs, and bear fruit, — 5375
20: 6 to **b** them **forth** of the land of Egypt into — 3318
20:15 that *I* would not **b** them into the land — 935
20:34 I will **b** you **out** from the people, — 3318
20:35 I will **b** you into the wilderness of — 935
20:37 I will **b** you into the bond of the covenant: — 935
20:38 I will **b** them **forth** out of the country — 3318
20:41 when I **b** you **out** from the people, — 3318
20:42 when I shall **b** you into the land of Israel, — 935
21:29 to **b** thee upon the necks of *them that are* — 5414
23:22 I will **b** them against thee on every side; — 935
23:46 I *will* **b up** a company against them, — 5927
24: 6 **b** it **out** piece by piece; let no lot fall upon — 3318
26: 7 I will **b** upon Tyrus Nebuchadrezzar king — 935
26:19 when I shall **b up** the deep upon thee, — 5927
26:20 When I shall **b** thee **down** with them that — 3381
28: 7 I will **b** strangers upon thee, — 935
28: 8 They shall **b** thee **down** to the pit, — 3381
28:18 I **b forth** a fire from the midst of thee, — 3318
28:18 I will **b** thee to ashes upon the earth in — 5414
29: 4 I will **b** thee **up** out of the midst of thy — 935
29: 8 *will* **b** a sword upon thee, and cut off man — 935
29:14 I will **b again** the captivity of Egypt, — 7725
31: 6 beasts of the field **b forth** their **young,** — 3205
32: 3 and they shall **b** thee **up** in my net. — 5927
32: 9 when I shall **b** thy destruction among — 935
33: 2 them, When I **b** the sword upon a land, — 935
34:13 I will **b** them **out** from the people, — 3318
34:13 will **b** them to their own land, and feed — 935
34:16 **b again** that which was driven away, — 7725
36:11 beast; and they shall increase and **b fruit:** — 6509
36:24 and will **b** you into your own land. — 935
37: 6 will **b up** flesh upon you, and cover you — 5927
37:12 and **b** you into the land of Israel. — 935
37:21 side, and **b** them into their own land: — 935
38: 4 I will **b** thee **forth,** and all thine army, — 3318
38:16 days, and I will **b** thee against my land, — 935
38:17 that *I* would **b** thee against them? — 935

Eze
39: 2 will **b** thee upon the mountains of Israel: — 935
39:25 Now will I **b again** the captivity of Jacob, — 7725
47:12 it shall **b forth new fruit** according to his — 1069

Da
1: 3 that *he* should **b certain** of the children of — 935
1:18 the king had said *he* should **b** them **in,** — 935
2:24 **b** me **in** before the king, and I will shew — 5954
3:13 rage and fury commanded to **b** Shadrach, — 858
4: 6 Therefore made I a decree to **b in** all — 5954
5: 2 commanded to **b** the golden and — 858
5: 7 king cried aloud to **b in** the astrologers, — 5954
9:24 to **b in** everlasting righteousness, and to — 935

Hos
2:14 **b** her *into* the wilderness, — 1980
7:12 I will **b** them **down** as the fowls of — 3381
9:12 Though they **b up** their children, yet will — 1431
9:13 Ephraim *shall* **b forth** his children to — 3318
9:16 yea, though they **b forth,** yet will I slay — 3205

Joel
3: 1 I shall **b again** the captivity of Judah — 7725
3: 2 will **b** them **down** into the valley of — 3381

Am
3:11 he shall **b down** thy strength from thee, — 3381
4: 1 say to their masters, **B,** and let us drink. — 935
4: 4 **b** your sacrifices *every* morning, — 935
6:10 to **b out** the bones out of the house, — 3318
8:10 I will **b up** sackcloth upon all loins, — 5927
9: 2 *to* heaven, thence will I **b** them **down:** — 3381
9:14 I will **b again** the captivity of my people — 7725

Ob
1: 3 Who shall **b** me **down** *to* the ground? — 3381
1: 4 thence will I **b** thee **down,** saith — 3381

Jnh
1:13 Nevertheless the men rowed hard to **b** *it* — 7725

Mic
1:15 will I **b** an heir unto thee, O inhabitant — 935
4:10 Be in pain, and **labour** to **b forth,** — 1518
7: 9 he will **b** me **forth** to the light, *and* I shall — 3318

Zep
1:17 I will **b distress** upon men, that they — 6887
2: 2 Before the decree **b forth,** *before* the day — 3205
3: 5 every morning doth he **b** his judgment to — 5414
3:10 of my dispersed, shall **b** mine offering. — 2986
3:20 At that time will I **b** you *again,* even in — 935

Hag
1: 6 have sown much, and **b in** little; *ye* eat, — 935
1: 8 and **b** wood, and build the house; — 935

Zec
3: 8 I *will* **b forth** my servant the BRANCH. — 935
4: 7 he shall **b forth** the headstone *thereof* — 3318
5: 4 I will **b** it **forth,** saith the Lord of hosts, — 3318
8: 8 I will **b** them, and they shall dwell in — 935
10: 6 and I will **b** them *again* **to place** them; — 3427
10:10 I will **b** them **again** also out of the land of — 7725
10:10 and I will **b** them into the land of Gilead — 935
13: 9 I will **b** the third *part* through the fire, — 935

Mal
3:10 **B** ye all the tithes into the storehouse, that — 935

Mt
1:21 she shall **b forth** a son, and thou shalt — 5088
1:23 and shall **b forth** a son, and they shall call — 5088
2: 8 ye have found *him,* **b** me **word again,** — 518
2:13 and be thou there until I **b** thee **word:** — 3004
3: 8 **B forth** therefore fruits meet for — 4160
5:23 Therefore if thou **b** thy gift to the altar, — 4374
7:18 A good tree cannot **b forth** evil fruit, — 4160
7:18 neither *can* a corrupt tree **b forth** good — 4160
14:18 He said, **B** them hither to me. — 5342
17:17 shall I suffer you? **b** him hither to me. — 5342
21: 2 her: loose *them,* and **b** *them* unto me. — 71
28: 8 and did run to **b** his disciples **word.** — 518

Mk
4:20 word, and receive *it,* and **b forth fruit,** — 2592
7:32 And they **b** unto him one *that was* deaf, — 5342
8:22 and they **b** a blind man unto him, — 5342
9:19 long shall I suffer you? **b** him unto me. — 5342
11: 2 never man sat; loose him, and **b** him. — 71
12:15 ye me? **b** me a penny, that I may see *it.* — 5342
15:22 And they **b** him unto the place Golgotha, — 5342

Lk
1:31 and **b forth** a son, and shalt call his name — 5088
2:10 I **bring you good tidings** of great joy, — 2097
3: 8 **B forth** therefore fruits worthy of — 4160
5:18 and they sought *means* to **b** him **in,** — 1533
5:19 not find by what way they might **b** him in — 1533
6:43 neither doth a corrupt tree **b forth** good — 4160
8:14 of **this life,** and **b** no fruit **to perfection.** — 5052
8:15 keep *it,* and **b forth** fruit with patience. — 2592
9:41 with you, and suffer you? **B** thy son hither. — 4317
12:11 when they **b** you unto the synagogues, — 4374
14:21 and **b in** hither the poor, and the maimed, — 1521
15:22 **B forth** the best robe, and put *it* on him; — 1627
15:23 And **b hither** the fatted calf, and kill *it;* — 5342
19:27 them, **b** hither, and slay *them* before me. — 71
19:30 man sat: loose him, and **b** *him hither.* — 71

Jn
10:16 them also I must **b,** and they shall hear — 71
14:26 and **b** all *things* to your **remembrance,** — 5279
15: 2 purgeth it, that it may **b forth** more fruit. — 5342
15:16 that you should go and **b forth** fruit, and — 5342
18:29 What accusation **b** you against this man? — 5342
19: 4 unto them, Behold, I **b** him forth to you, — 71
21:10 **B** of the fish which ye have now caught. — 5342

Ac
5:28 and intend to **b** this man's blood upon us. — 1863
7: 6 that they should **b** them **into bondage,** — 1402
7:40 he might **b** *them* bound unto Jerusalem. — 71
9:21 hither for that *intent,* that he might **b** — 71
12: 4 intending after Easter to **b** him **forth** to — 321
17: 5 and sought to **b** them **out** to the people. — 71
22: 5 Damascus, to **b** them which were there, — 71
23:10 among them, and to **b** *him* into the castle. — 71
23:15 that he **b** him **down** unto you to morrow, — 2609
23:17 **B** this young man unto the chief captain: — 520
23:18 prayed *me* to **b** this young man unto thee, — 71
23:20 **b down** Paul to morrow into the council, — 2609
23:24 **b** *him* safe unto Felix the governor. — 1295
24:17 Now after many years I came to **b** alms to — 4160

Ro
7: 4 that we should **b forth fruit** unto God. — 2592
7: 5 did work in our members to **b forth fruit** — 2592
10: 6 (that is, to **b** Christ **down** *from above:*) — 2609

Ro 10: 7 to **b up** Christ **again** from the dead.) 321
10:15 and **b glad tidings** of good *things!* 2097
1Co 1:19 will **b to nothing** the understanding of 114
1:28 are not, to **b to nought** *things* that are: 2673
4: 5 both will **b to light** the hidden *things* 5461
4:17 shall **b** you **into remembrance** of my 363
9:27 under my body, and **b** *it* **into subjection:** 1396
16: 3 them will I send to **b** your liberality unto 667
16: 6 that ye may **b** me **on my journey** 4311
2Co 11:20 ye suffer, if a man **b** you **into bondage**, 2615
Gal 2: 4 that they might **b** us **into bondage:** 2615
3:24 was our schoolmaster to **b** *us* unto Christ, NIG
Eph 6: 4 but **b** them **up** in the nurture and 1625
1Th 4:14 them also which sleep in Jesus will God **b** 71
2Ti 4:11 Take Mark, and **b** *him* with thee: for he is 71
4:13 **b** *with thee,* and the books, 5342
Tit 3:13 **B** Zenas the lawyer and Apollos **on** their **journey** 4311
1Pe 3:18 for the unjust, that he might **b** us to God, 4317
2Pe 2: 1 who **privily** shall **b** in damnable heresies, 3919
2: 1 and **b upon** themselves swift destruction. 1863
2:11 **b** not railing accusation against them 5342
2Jn 1:10 any unto you, and **b** not this doctrine, 5342
3Jn 1: 6 if thou **b forward** on their **journey** 4311
Jude 1: 9 durst not **b against** *him* a railing 2018
Rev 21:24 the kings of the earth do **b** their glory and 5342
21:26 And they shall **b** the glory and honour of 5342

BRINGERS (1) [BRING]
2Ki 10: 5 the **b up** *of the children,* sent to Jehu, 539

BRINGEST (5) [BRING]
1Ki 1:42 *art* a valiant man, and **b** good **tidings**. 1319
Job 14: 3 one, and **b** me into judgment with thee? 935
Isa 40: 9 O Zion, that **b good tidings**, get thee up 1319
40: 9 O Jerusalem, that **b good tidings**, lift up 1319
Ac 17:20 For thou **b** certain strange *things* to our 1533

BRINGETH (79) [BRING]
Ex 6: 7 which **b** you out from under the burdens 3318
Lev 11:45 For I *am* the LORD that **b** you **up** out of 5927
17: 4 **b** it not unto the door of the tabernacle of 935
17: 9 **b** it not unto the door of the tabernacle of 935
Dt 8: 7 For the LORD thy God **b** thee into a good 935
14:22 seed, that the field **b forth** year by year. 935
1Sa 2: 6 he **b down** *to* the grave, and bringeth up. 3381
2: 6 he bringeth down *to* the grave, and **b** up. 5927
2: 7 and maketh rich: he **b** low, and lifteth up. 8213
2Sa 18:26 And the king said, He also **b tidings**. 1319
22:48 and that **b down** the people under me, 3381
22:49 that **b** me **forth** from mine enemies: 3318
Job 12: 6 into whose hand God **b** abundantly. 935
12:22 and **b out** to light the shadow of death. 3318
19:29 wrath *b* the punishments of the sword, NIH
28:11 the thing that is hid **b** he **forth** to light. 3318
Ps 1: 3 water, that **b forth** his fruit in his season; 5414
14: 7 when the LORD **b back** the captivity of 7725
33:10 **b** the counsel of the heathen **to nought:** 6331
37: 7 the man who **b** wicked devices **to pass.** 6213
53: 6 When God **b back** the captivity of his 7725
68: 6 he **b out** those which are bound with 3318
107:28 and he **b** them **out** of their distresses. 3318
107:30 so he **b** them unto their desired haven. 5148
135: 7 rain; he **b** the wind **out** of his treasuries. 3318
Pr 10:31 The mouth of the just **b forth** wisdom: 5107
16:30 moving his lips he **b** evil **to pass.** 3615
18:16 for him, and **b** him before great *men.* 5148
19:26 son that causeth shame, and **b reproach.** 2659
20:26 the wicked, and **b** the wheel over them. 7725
21:27 *when* he **b** it with a wicked mind? 935
29:15 left *to himself* **b** his mother to **shame.** 954
29:21 He that **delicately b** up his servant from 6445
29:25 The fear of man **b** a snare: 5414
30:33 Surely the churning of milk **b forth** butter, 3318
30:33 the wringing of the nose **b forth** blood: 3318
30:33 so the forcing of wrath **b forth** strife. 3318
31:14 merchant's ships; she **b** her food from afar. 935
Ecc 2: 6 to water therewith the wood that **b forth** 6779
Isa 8: 7 the Lord **b up** upon them the waters of 5927
26: 5 For he **b down** them that dwell on high; 7817
26: 5 to the ground; he **b** it *even* to the dust. 5060
40:23 That **b** the princes to nothing; he maketh 5414
40:26 *things,* that **b** out their host by number: 3318
41:27 to Jerusalem one that **b good tidings.** 1319
43:17 Which **b forth** the chariot and horse, 3318
52: 7 are the feet of him that **b good tidings,** 1319
52: 7 that **b good tidings** of good, that 1319
54:16 that **b forth** an instrument for his work; 3318
61:11 For as the earth **b forth** her bud, and as 3318
Jer 4:31 as of her that **b forth** her **first child,** 1069
10:13 and **b forth** the wind out of his treasures. 3318
51:16 and **b forth** the wind out of his treasures. 3318
Eze 29:16 which **b** *their* iniquity **to remembrance**, 2142
Hos 1:15 the feet of him that **b good tidings**, 1319
Na 1:15 the feet of him that **b good tidings**, 1319
Hag 1:11 upon *that* which the ground **b forth**, 3318
Mt 3:10 every tree which **b** not **forth** good fruit is 4160
7:17 so every good tree **b forth** good fruit; 4160
7:17 but a corrupt tree **b forth** evil fruit. 4160
7:19 Every tree that **b** not **forth** good fruit is 4160
12:35 *treasure of the heart* **b forth** good *things:* 1544
12:35 evil man out of the evil treasure **b forth** 1544
13:23 and **b forth,** some an hundred*fold,* some 4160
13:52 which **b forth** out of his treasure *things* 1544
17: 1 and **b** them **up** into a high mountain 399

Mk 4:28 For the earth **b forth** fruit of herself; 2592
Lk 3: 9 **b** not **forth** good fruit is hewn down, 4160
6:43 For a good tree **b** not **forth** corrupt fruit; 4160
6:45 of his heart **b forth** that which is good; 4393
6:45 of his heart **b forth** that which is evil: 4393
Jn 12:24 but if it die, it **b forth** much fruit. 5342
15: 5 and I in him, the same **b forth** much fruit: 5342
Col 1: 6 and **b forth** fruit, as *it doth* also in you, 2592
Tit 2:11 For the grace of God that **b** salvation hath NIG
Heb 1: 6 when he **b** in the firstbegotten into 1521
6: 7 **b forth** herbs meet for them by whom it is 5088
Jas 1:15 when lust hath conceived, it **b forth** sin: 5088
1:15 sin, when it is finished, **b forth** death. 616

BRINGING (24) [BRING]
Ex 12:42 for **b** them out from the land of Egypt: 3318
36: 6 So the people were restrained from **b.** 935
Nu 5:15 memorial, **b** iniquity **to remembrance**. 2142
14:36 by **b** up a slander upon the land, 935
2Sa 19:10 speak ye not a word of **b** the king **back?** 7725
19:43 not be first had in **b back** our king? 7725
1Ki 10:22 **b** gold, and silver, ivory, and apes, 5375
2Ki 21:12 am **b** such evil upon Jerusalem and Judah, 935
2Ch 9:21 once came the ships of Tarshish **b** gold, 5375
Ne 13:15 and **b** in sheaves, and lading asses; 935
Ps 126: 6 with rejoicing, **b** his sheaves *with him.* 5375
Jer 17:26 burnt offerings, and sacrifices, 935
17:26 incense, and **b** *sacrifices of* praise, 935
Eze 20: 9 in **b** them **forth** out of the land of Egypt. 3318
Da 9:12 that judged us, by **b** upon us a great evil: 935
Mt 21:43 to a nation **b forth** the fruits thereof. 4160
Mk 2: 3 **b** one sick of the palsy, *which was* borne 5342
Lk 24: 1 the spices which they had prepared, 5342
Ac 5:16 **b** sick *folks,* and *them* which *were* vexed 5342
Ro 7:23 **b** me **into captivity** to the law of sin 163
2Co 10: 5 **b** into captivity every thought to 163
Heb 2:10 by whom *are* all *things*, in **b** many sons 71
7:19 the **b in** of a better hope *did;* by the 1898
2Pe 2: 5 **b in** the flood upon the world of 1863

BRINK (6)
Ge 41: 3 stood by the *other* kine upon the **b** of 8193
Ex 2: 3 she laid *it* in the flags by the river's **b.** 8193
7:15 thou shalt stand by the river's **b** against 8193
Dt 2:36 which *is* by the **b** of the river of Arnon, 8193
Jos 3: 8 When ye are come to the **b** of the water 7097
Eze 47: 6 caused me to return to the **b** of the river. 8193

BROAD (36) [BREADTH, BROADER]
Ex 27: 1 five cubits long, and five cubits **b;** 7341
Nu 16:38 them make them **b** plates *for* a covering 7555
16:39 they were **made b** plates *for* a covering 7554
1Ki 6: 6 nethermost chamber *was* five cubits **b**, 7341
6: 6 the middle *was* six cubits **b**, and the third 7341
6: 6 and the third *was* seven cubits **b.** 7341
2Ch 6:13 and five cubits **b**, and three cubits high, 7341
Ne 3: 8 they fortified Jerusalem unto the **b** wall. 7342
12:38 of the furnaces even unto the **b** wall; 7342
Job 30:16 thou out of the strait *into* a **b** place, 7338
Ps 119:96 *but* thy commandment *is* exceeding **b.** 7342
SS 3: 2 the city in the streets and in the **b ways,** 7339
Isa 33:21 *will be* unto us a place of **b** rivers 3027+7342
Jer 5: 1 know, and seek in the **b places** thereof, 7339
51:58 The **b** walls of Babylon shall be utterly 7342
Eze 40: 6 of the gate, *which was* one reed **b;** 7341
40: 6 *the other gate, which was* one reed **b.** 7341
40: 7 *was* one reed long, and one reed **b;** 7341
40:29 cubits long, and five and twenty cubits **b.** 7341
40:30 and twenty cubits long, and five cubits **b.** 7341
40:33 cubits long, and five and twenty cubits **b.** 7341
40:42 a cubit and a half **b**, and one cubit high: 7341
40:43 a **hand b**, fastened round about: 2948
40:47 and an hundred cubits **b**, foursquare; 7341
41: 1 six cubits **b** on the one side, and six cubits 7341
41: 1 side, and six cubits **b** on the other side, 7341
41:12 toward the west *was* seventy cubits **b;** 7341
42:11 north, as long as they, *and* as **b** as they: 7341
42:20 hundred *reeds* long, and five hundred **b**, 7341
43:16 twelve **b**, square in the four squares 7341
43:17 and fourteen **b** in the four squares thereof; 7341
45: 6 the possession of the city five thousand **b**, 7341
46:22 joined *of* forty *cubits* long and thirty **b:** 7341
Na 2: 4 justle one against another in the **b ways:** 7339
Mt 7:13 for wide *is* the gate, and **b** *is* the way, 2149
23: 5 they **make b** their phylacteries, and 4115

BROADER (1) [BROAD]
Job 11: 9 longer than the earth, and **b** than the sea. 7342

BROIDED (1) [BROIDERED]
1Ti 2: 9 and sobriety; not with **b** hair, 4117

BROIDERED (8) [BROIDED]
Ex 28: 4 a robe, and a **b** coat, a mitre, and a girdle: 8665
Eze 16:10 I clothed thee also with **b work**, 7553
16:13 *was of* fine linen, and silk, and **b work;** 7553
16:18 tookest thy **b** garments, and 7553
26:16 their shame, and put off their **b** garments: 7553
27: 7 Fine linen with **b work** from Egypt was 7553
27:16 **b work**, and fine linen, and coral, 7553
27:24 and **b work**, and in chests of rich apparel, 7553

BROILED (1)
Lk 24:42 And they gave him a piece of a **b** fish, 3702

BROKEN (186) [BREAK]
Ge 7:11 all the fountains of the great deep **b up**, 1234
17:14 from his people; he hath **b** my covenant. 6565
38:29 she said, How hast thou **b forth?** 6555
Lev 6:28 vessel wherein it is sodden shall be **b:** 7665
11:35 or ranges for pots, they shall be **b down.** 5422
13:20 it *is* a plague of leprosy **b out** of the boil. 6524
13:25 it *is* a leprosy **b out** of the burning: 6524
15:12 toucheth which hath the issue, shall be **b:** 7665
21:20 scurvy, or scabbed, or hath his stones **b;** 4790
21:20 or **b**, or maimed, or having a wen, 7665
22:24 which is bruised, or crushed, or **b**, or cut; 5423
26:13 I have **b** the bands of your yoke, 7665
26:26 *And* when I have **b** the staff of your bread, 7665
Nu 15:31 hath **b** his commandment, that soul shall 6565
Jdg 5:22 were the horsehoofs **b** by the means of 1986
16: 9 as a thread of tow is **b** when it toucheth 5423
1Sa 2: 4 The bows of the mighty *men are* **b**, 2844
2:10 of the LORD shall be **b** to pieces; 2865
2Sa 22: 35 so that a bow of steel is **b** *by* mine arms. 5181
1Ki 18:30 the altar of the LORD *that* was **b down**. 2040
22:48 for the ships were **b** at Ezion-geber. 7665
2Ki 11: 6 of the house, that it be **not b down**. 4535
25: 4 the city was **b** up, and all the men of war 1234
1Ch 14:11 God hath **b** in upon mine enemies by 6555
2Ch 20:37 the LORD hath **b** thy works. 6555
20:37 the ships were **b**, that they were not able 7665
24: 7 woman, had **b up** the house of God; 6555
25:12 the rock, that they all were **b** in pieces. 1234
32: 5 built up all the wall that was **b**, and raised 6555
33: 3 which Hezekiah his father had **b down**, 5422
34: 7 when he had **b down** the altars and 5422
Ne 1: 3 the wall of Jerusalem also *is* **b down**, 6555
2:13 which were **b down**, and the gates 6555
Job 4:10 and the teeth of the young lions, are **b**. 5421
7: 5 my skin is **b**, and become loathsome. 7280
16:12 I was at ease, but he hath **b** me **asunder:** 6565
17:11 My days are past, my purposes are **b off**, 5423
22: 9 the arms of the fatherless have been **b**. 1792
24:20 and wickedness shall be **b** as a tree. 7665
31:22 and mine arm be **b** from the bone. 7665
38:15 withholden, and the high arm shall be **b**. 7665
Ps 3: 7 thou hast **b** the teeth of the ungodly. 7665
18:34 so that a bow of steel is **b** *by* mine arms. 5181
31:12 dead man out of mind: I am like a **b** vessel. 6
34:18 *is* nigh unto them that are of a **b** heart; 7665
34:20 all his bones: not one of them is **b**. 7665
37:15 own heart, and their bows shall be **b**. 7665
37:17 For the arms of the wicked shall be **b:** 7665
38: 8 I am feeble and sore **b**: I have roared by 1794
44:19 Though thou hast **sore b** us in the place 1794
51: 8 *that* the bones *which* thou hast **b** may 1794
51:17 The sacrifices of God *are* a **b** spirit: 7665
51:17 a **b** and a contrite heart, O God, thou wilt 7665
55:20 peace with him: he hath **b** his covenant. 2490
60: 2 made the earth to tremble; thou hast **b** it: 6480
69:20 Reproach hath **b** my heart; and I am full 7665
80:12 Why hast thou *then* **b down** her hedges, 6555
89:10 Thou hast **b** Rahab **in pieces**, as one that 1792
89:40 Thou hast **b down** all his hedges; thou 6555
107:16 For he hath **b** the gates of brass, and cut 7665
109:16 that *he* might even slay the **b** in heart. 3512
124: 7 the snare is **b**, and we are escaped. 7665
147: 3 He healeth the **b** in heart, and bindeth up 7665
Pr 3:20 By his knowledge the depths are **b** up, 1234
6:15 suddenly shall he be **b** without remedy. 7665
15:13 but by sorrow of the heart the spirit *is* **b**. 5218
17:22 medicine: but a **b** spirit drieth the bones. 5218
24:31 and the stone wall thereof was **b down**. 2040
25:19 *man* in time of trouble *is* like a **b** tooth, 7465
25:28 own spirit *is* like a city *that is* **b down**, 6555
Ecc 4:12 and a threefold cord is not quickly **b**. 5423
12: 6 or the golden bowl be **b**, or the pitcher be 7533
12: 6 or the pitcher be **b** at the fountain, 7665
12: 6 the fountain, or the wheel **b** at the cistern. 7533
Isa 5:27 nor the latchet of their shoes be **b:** 5423
7: 8 and five years shall Ephraim be **b**, 2865
8: 9 O ye people, and ye shall be **b in pieces**; 2865
8: 9 yourselves, and ye shall be **b in pieces**; 2865
8: 9 yourselves, and ye shall be **b in pieces**. 2865
8:15 and be **b**, and be snared, and be taken. 7665
9: 4 For thou hast **b** the yoke of his burden, 2865
14: 5 The LORD hath **b** the staff of the wicked, 7665
14:29 the rod of him that smote thee is **b:** 7665
16: 8 the lords of the heathen have **b down** 1986
19:10 they shall be **b** *in* the purposes thereof, 1792
21: 9 the graven images of her gods he hath **b** 7665
22:10 the houses have ye **b down** to fortify 5422
24: 5 the ordinance, the everlasting covenant. 6565
24:10 The city of confusion is **b down:** 7665
24:19 The earth is **utterly b down**, 7489+7489
27:11 thereof are withered, they shall be **b off:** 7665
28:13 and be **b**, and snared, and be taken. 7665
30:14 of the potters' vessel that is **b in pieces;** 3807
33: 8 he hath **b** the covenant, he hath despised 6565
33:20 neither shall any of the cords thereof be **b**. 5423
36: 6 Lo, thou trustest in the staff of this **b** reed, 7533
Jer 2:13 **b** cisterns, that can hold no water. 7665
2:16 Tahapanes have **b** the crown of thy head. 7462
2:20 For of old time I have **b** thy yoke, 7665
4:26 all the cities thereof were **b down** at 5422
5: 5 these have altogether **b** the yoke, 7665
10:20 is spoiled, and all my cords are **b:** 5423

B

Jer 11:10 the house of Judah have **b** my covenant 6565
11:16 fire upon it, and the branches of it are **b.** 7489
14:17 for the virgin daughter of my people is **b** 7665
22:28 *Is* this man Coniah a despised **b** idol? 5310
23: 9 Mine heart within me is **b** because of 7665
28: 2 I have **b** the yoke of the king of Babylon. 7665
28:12 **b** the yoke from off the neck of the 7665
28:13 Thou hast **b** the yokes of wood; but 7665
33:21 *Then* may also my covenant be **b** 6565
37:11 **b** up from Jerusalem for fear of Pharaoh's 5927
39: 2 *day* of the month, the city was **b** up. 1234
48:17 is the strong staff **b**, *and* the beautiful 7665
48:20 Moab is confounded; for it is **b** down: 2865
48:25 cut off, and his arm is **b**, saith the L ORD . 7665
48:38 for I have **b** Moab like a vessel wherein *is* 7665
48:39 they howl, *saying*, How is it **b** down! 2865
50: 2 is confounded, Merodach is **b in pieces.** 2865
50: 2 confounded, her images are **b in pieces.** 2865
50:17 king of Babylon hath **b** his bones. 6105
50:23 of the whole earth cut asunder and **b**! 7665
51:30 burnt her dwelling places; her bars are **b.** 7665
51:56 are taken, *every one* of their bows is **b:** 2865
51:58 walls of Babylon shall be **utterly b**, 6209+6209
52: 7 the city was **b** up, and all the men of war 1234
La 2: 9 he hath destroyed and **b** her bars: 7665
3: 4 hath he made old; he hath **b** my bones. 7665
3:16 hath also **b** my teeth with gravel stones, 1638
Eze 6: 4 be desolate, and your images shall be **b:** 7665
6: 6 your idols may be **b** and cease, 7665
6: 9 because I am **b** with their whorish heart, 7665
17:19 and my covenant that he hath **b**, 6331
19:12 her strong rods were **b** and withered; 6561
26: 2 she is **b** *that was* the gates of the people: 7665
27:26 the east wind hath **b** thee in the midst of 7665
27:34 the time when *thou shalt be* **b** by the seas 7665
30: 4 and her foundations shall be **b** down. 2040
30:21 have **b** the arm of Pharaoh king of Egypt; 7665
30:22 arms, the strong, and that which was **b**; 7665
31:12 his boughs are **b** by all the rivers of 7665
32:28 thou shalt be **b** in the midst of 7665
34: 4 have ye bound up that which was **b**, 7665
34:16 will bind up that which was **b**, 7665
34:27 when I have **b** the bands of their yoke, 7665
44: 7 they have **b** my covenant because of all 6565
Da 2:35 **b** to pieces together, and became like 1855
2:42 shall be partly strong, and partly **b.** 8406
8: 8 he was strong, the great horn was **b**; 7665
8:22 Now that being **b**, whereas four stood up 7665
8:25 princes; but he shall be **b** without hand. 7665
11: 4 his kingdom shall be **b**, and shall be 7665
11:22 overflown from before him, and shall be **b**; 7665
Hos 5:11 Ephraim *is* oppressed *and* **b** in judgment, 7533
8: 6 the calf of Samaria shall be **b in pieces.** 7616
Joel 1:17 are laid desolate, the barns are **b** down; 2040
Jnh 1: 4 the sea, so that the ship was like to be **b.** 7665
Mic 2:13 they have **b** up, and have passed through 6555
Zec 11:11 it was **b** in that day: and so the poor of 6565
11:16 nor heal that that is **b**, nor feed that that 7665
Mt 15:37 they took up of the **b** meat that was left 2801
21:44 shall fall on this stone shall be **b:** 4917
24:43 not have suffered his house to be **b** up. 1358
Mk 2: 4 and when they had **b** it up, they let down 1846
5: 4 by him, and the fetters **b in pieces**: 4937
8: 8 they took up of the **b** meat that was left 2801
Lk 12:39 have suffered his house to be **b through.** 1358
20:18 shall fall upon that stone shall be **b**; 4917
Jn 5:18 because he not only had **b** the sabbath, 3089
7:23 that the law of Moses should not be **b**; 3089
10:35 came, and the scripture cannot be **b**; 3089
19:31 besought Pilate that their legs might be **b**, 2608
19:36 be fulfilled, A bone of him shall not be **b.** 4937
21:11 were so many, *yet* was not the net **b.** 4977
Ac 13:43 Now when the congregation was **b** up, 3089
20:11 was come up *again*, and had **b** bread, 2806
27:35 and when he had **b** *it*, he began to eat. 2806
27:41 the hinder part was **b** with the violence of 3089
27:44 and some on **b**S **pieces** of the ship. 5100
Ro 11:17 And if some of the branches be **b** off, 1575
11:19 wilt say then, The branches were **b** off, 1575
11:20 because of unbelief they were **b** off, 1575
1Co 11:24 is my body, which is **b** for you: this do 2806
Eph 2:14 hath **b** down the middle wall of partition 3089
Rev 2:27 of a potter *shall* they be **b** to shivers: 4937

BROKENFOOTED (1) [BREAK, FOOT]

Lev 21:19 a man that is **b**, or brokenhanded, 7272+7667

BROKENHANDED (1) [BREAK, HAND]

Lev 21:19 a man that is brokenfooted, or **b**, 3027+7667

BROKEN-HEARTED (2) [BREAK, HEART]

Isa 61: 1 he hath sent me to bind up the **b**, 3820+7665
Lk 4:18 he hath sent me to heal the **b**, to preach 4937

BRONZE See BRASEN; BRASS; STEEL

BROOD (1)

Lk 13:34 a hen *doth gather* her **b** under *her* wings, 3555

BROOK (39) [BROOKS]

Ge 32:23 sent them over the **b**, and sent over that 5158
Lev 23:40 of thick trees, and willows of the **b**; 5158
Nu 13:23 came unto the **b** of Eshcol, 5158
13:24 The place was called the **b** Eshcol, 5158
Dt 2:13 *said I*, and get you over the **b** Zered. 5158
2:13 And we went over the **b** Zered. 5158

Dt 2:14 until we were come over the **b** Zered, 5158
9:21 I cast the dust thereof into the **b** that 5158
1Sa 17:40 him five smooth stones out of the **b**, 5158
30: 9 *were* with him, and came to the **b** Besor, 5158
30:10 faint that they could not go over the **b** 5158
30:21 they had made also to abide at the **b** 5158
2Sa 15:23 the **b** Kidron: and all the people 5158
17:20 They be gone over the **b** of water. 4323
1Ki 2:37 goest out, and passest over the **b** Kidron, 5158
15:13 her idol, and burnt *it* by the **b** Kidron. 5158
17: 3 and hide thyself by the **b** Cherith, 5158
17: 4 it shall be, *that* thou shalt drink of the **b;** 5158
17: 5 for he went and dwelt by the **b** Cherith, 5158
17: 6 in the evening; and he drank of the **b.** 5158
17: 7 that the **b** dried up, because there had 5158
18:40 Elijah brought them down to the **b** Kishon 5158
2Ki 23: 6 the Kidron, and burnt it at the brook 5158
23: 6 burnt it at the **b** Kidron, and stampt *it* 5158
23:12 cast the dust of them into the **b** Kidron. 5158
2Ch 15:16 stamped *it*, and burnt *it* at the **b** Kidron. 5158
20:16 ye shall find them at the end of the **b**, 5158
29:16 to carry *it* out abroad into the **b** Kidron. 5158
30:14 away, and cast *them* into the **b** Kidron. 5158
32: 4 that ran through the midst of the land, 5158
Ne 2:15 I up in the night by the **b**, and viewed 5158
Job 6:15 My brethren have dealt deceitfully as a **b**, 5158
40:22 the willows of the **b** compass him about. 5158
Ps 83: 9 as *to* Sisera, as *to* Jabin, at the **b** of Kison: 5158
110: 7 He shall drink of the **b** in the way: 5158
Pr 18: 4 the wellspring of wisdom *as a* flowing **b.** 5158
Isa 15: 7 shall they carry away to the **b** of 5158
Jer 31:40 and all the fields unto the **b** of Kidron, 5158
Jn 18: 1 forth with his disciples over the **b** Cedron, 5493

BROOKS (15) [BROOK]

Nu 21:14 did in the Red sea, and *in* the **b** of Arnon, 5158
21:15 *at* the stream of the **b** that goeth down to 5158
Dt 8: 7 a land of **b** of water, of fountains and 5158
2Sa 23:30 the Pirathonite, Hiddai of the **b** of Gaash, 5158
1Ki 18: 5 all fountains of water, and unto all **b:** 5158
1Ch 11:32 Hurai of the **b** of Gaash, Abiel 5158
Job 6:15 *and* as the stream of **b** they pass away; 5158
20:17 the floods, the **b** of honey and butter. 5158
22:24 the gold *of* Ophir as the stones of the **b.** 5158
Ps 42: 1 As the hart panteth after the water **b**, 650
Isa 19: 6 *and* the **b** of defence shall be emptied 2975
19: 7 The paper reeds by the **b**, by the mouth 2975
19: 7 by the mouth of the **b**, and every thing 2975
19: 7 every thing sown by the **b**, shall wither, 2975
19: 8 all they that cast angle into the **b** shall 2975

BROOM See BESOM

BROTH (3)

Jdg 6:19 he put the **b** in a pot, and brought *it* out 4839
6:20 *them* upon this rock, and pour out the **b.** 4839
Isa 65: 4 **b** of abominable *things is in* their vessels; 4839

BROTHER (367) [BRETHREN, BRETHREN'S, BROTHER'S, BROTHERHOOD, BROTHERLY, BROTHERS']

Ge 4: 2 she again bare his **b** Abel. And Abel was a 251
4: 8 Cain talked with Abel his **b**: and it came to 251
4: 8 that Cain rose up against Abel his **b**, 251
4: 9 said unto Cain, Where *is* Abel thy **b**? 251
9: 5 at the hand of every man's **b** will I require 251
10:21 the **b** of Japheth the elder, even to him 251
14:13 **b** of Eshcol, and brother of Aner: 251
14:13 brother of Eshcol, and **b** of Aner: 251
14:14 when Abram heard that his **b** was taken 251
14:16 brought again his **b** Lot, and his goods, 251
20: 5 she, even she herself said, He *is* my **b**, 251
20:13 we shall come, say of me, He *is* my **b**. 251
20:16 I have given thy **b** a thousand *pieces* of 251
22:20 she hath also born children unto thy **b** 251
22:21 Buz his **b**, and Kemuel the father of Aram, 251
22:23 Milcah did bear to Nahor, Abraham's **b.** 251
24:15 of Milcah, the wife of Nahor, Abraham's **b**, 251
24:29 Rebekah had a **b**, and his name *was* Laban: 251
24:53 he gave also to her **b** and to her mother 251
24:55 her **b** and her mother said, Let the damsel 251
25:26 that came his **b** out, and his hand took 251
27: 6 I heard thy father speak unto Esau thy **b**, 251
27:11 Esau my **b** *is* a hairy man, and I *am* a 251
27:23 hands were hairy, as his **b** Esau's hands: 251
27:30 that Esau his **b** came in from his hunting. 251
27:35 Thy **b** came with subtilty, and hath taken 251
27:40 shalt thou live, and shalt serve thy **b**; 251
27:41 are at hand; then will I slay my **b** Jacob. 251
27:42 said unto him, Behold, thy **b** Esau, 251
27:43 arise, flee thou to Laban my **b** to Haran; 251
28: 2 of the daughters of Laban thy mother's **b**. 251
28: 5 the **b** of Rebekah, Jacob's and 251
29:10 the daughter of Laban his mother's **b**, 251
29:10 the sheep of Laban his mother's **b**, 251
29:10 watered the flock of Laban his mother's **b**. 251
29:12 told Rachel that he *was* her father's **b**, 251
29:15 Because thou *art* my **b**, shouldest thou 251
32: 3 him to Esau his **b** unto the land of Seir, 251
32: 6 came to thy **b** Esau, and also he cometh 251
32:11 I pray thee, from the hand of my **b**, 251
32:13 came to his hand a present for Esau his **b**; 251
32:17 When Esau my **b** meeteth thee, 251
33: 3 seven times, until he came near to his **b.** 251
33: 9 Esau said, I have enough, my **b**; keep that 251

Ge 35: 1 thou fleddest from the face of Esau thy **b.** 251
35: 7 when he fled from the face of his **b.** 251
36: 6 into the country from the face of his **b** 251
37:26 What profit *is it* if we slay our **b**, 251
37:27 be upon him; for he *is* our **b** *and* our flesh. 251
38: 8 and marry her, and raise up seed to thy **b.** 251
38: 9 lest that he should give seed to his **b**, 251
38:29 his hand, that, behold, his **b** came out: 251
38:30 came out his **b**, that had the scarlet 251
42: 4 Benjamin, Joseph's **b**, Jacob sent not with 251
42:15 except your youngest **b** come hither. 251
42:16 let him fetch your **b**, and ye shall be kept 251
42:20 bring your youngest **b** unto me; so shall 251
42:21 We *are* verily guilty concerning our **b**, 251
42:34 bring your youngest **b** unto me: then shall 251
42:34 *are* true *men: so* will I deliver you your **b**, 251
42:38 for his **b** is dead, and he is left alone: 251
43: 3 see my face, except your **b** *be* with you. 251
43: 4 If thou wilt send our **b** with us, we will go 251
43: 5 see my face, except your **b** *be* with you. 251
43: 6 *as* to tell the man whether ye had yet a **b**? 251
43: 7 have ye *another* **b**? and we told him 251
43: 7 that he would say, Bring your **b** down? 251
43:13 Take also your **b**, and arise, go again unto 251
43:14 that he may send away your other **b**, 251
43:29 saw his **b** Benjamin, his mother's son, 251
43:29 and said, *Is* this your younger **b**, 251
43:30 for his bowels did yern upon his **b:** 251
44:19 saying, Have ye a father, or a **b**? 251
44:20 his **b** is dead, and he alone is left of his 251
44:23 Except your youngest **b** come down with 251
44:26 if our youngest **b** be with us, then will we 251
44:26 except our youngest **b** be with us. 251
45: 4 he said, I *am* Joseph your **b**, whom ye sold 251
45:12 eyes see, and the eyes of my **b** Benjamin, 251
45:14 And he fell upon his **b** Benjamin's neck, 251
48:19 his younger **b** shall be greater than he, 251
Ex 4:14 he said, Is not Aaron the Levite thy **b**? 251
7: 1 and Aaron thy **b** shall be thy prophet. 251
7: 2 Aaron thy **b** shall speak unto Pharaoh, 251
28: 1 take thou unto thee Aaron thy **b**, and his 251
28: 2 shalt make holy garments for Aaron thy **b** 251
28: 4 shall make holy garments for Aaron thy **b**, 251
28:41 thou shalt put them upon Aaron thy **b**, 251
32:27 slay every man his **b**, and every man his 251
32:29 every man upon his son, and upon his **b**; 251
Lev 16: 2 said unto Moses, Speak unto Aaron thy **b**, 251
18:14 uncover the nakedness of thy father's **b**, 251
19:17 Thou shalt not hate thy **b** in thine heart: 251
21: 2 his son, and for his daughter, and for his **b**, 251
25:25 If thy **b** be waxen poor, and hath sold 251
25:25 shall he redeem that which his **b** sold. 251
25:35 thy **b** be waxen poor, and fallen in decay 251
25:36 fear thy God; that thy **b** may live with thee. 251
25:39 thy **b** *that dwelleth* by thee be waxen poor, 251
25:47 thy **b** *that dwelleth* by thee wax poorer, 251
Nu 6: 7 for his **b**, or for his sister, when they die: 251
20: 8 Aaron thy **b**, and speak ye unto the rock 251
20:14 Thus saith thy **b** Israel, Thou knowest all 251
27:13 thy people, as Aaron thy **b** was gathered. 251
36: 2 of Zelophehad our **b** unto his daughters. 251
Dt 1:16 righteously between every man and his **b**, 251
13: 6 If thy **b**, the son of thy mother, or thy son, 251
15: 2 not exact *it* of his neighbour, or of his **b**; 251
15: 3 *that* which is thine with thy **b** thine hand 251
15: 7 nor shut thine hand from thy poor **b**: 251
15: 9 and thine eye be evil against thy poor **b**, 251
15:11 shalt open thine hand wide unto thy **b**, 251
15:12 *And* if thy **b**, a Hebrew man, or a Hebrew 251
17:15 a stranger over thee, which *is* not thy **b**. 251
19:18 and hath testified falsely against his **b**; 251
19:19 as he had thought to have done unto his **b**: 251
22: 1 in any case bring them again unto thy **b**. 251
22: 2 if thy **b** *be* not nigh unto thee, or *if* thou 251
22: 2 shall be with thee until thy **b** seek after it, 251
23: 7 shalt not abhor an Edomite; for he *is* thy **b**: 251
23:19 Thou shalt not lend upon usury to thy **b**; 251
23:20 unto thy **b** thou shalt not lend upon usury: 251
24:10 When thou dost lend thy **b** any thing, 7453
25: 3 then thy **b** should seem vile unto thee. 251
25: 5 **husband's b** shall go in unto her, 2993
25: 5 **perform the duty of a husband's b** unto 2992
25: 6 succeed in the name of his **b** which is dead 251
25: 7 My **husband's b** refuseth to raise up unto 2993
25: 7 to raise up unto his **b** a name in Israel, 251
25: 7 **perform the duty of my husband's b.** 2992
28:54 his eye shall be evil toward his **b**, 251
32:50 as Aaron thy **b** died in mount Hor, 251
Jos 15:17 the son of Kenaz, the **b** of Caleb, took it: 251
Jdg 1: 13 Judah said unto Simeon his **b**, Come up 251
1:13 son of Kenaz, Caleb's younger **b**, took it: 251
1:17 Judah went with Simeon his **b**, and they 251
3: 9 the son of Kenaz, Caleb's younger **b**. 251
9: 3 Abimelech; for they said, He *is* our **b**. 251
9:18 men of Shechem, because he *is* your **b**;) 251
9:21 dwelt there, for fear of Abimelech his **b**. 251
9:24 blood be laid upon Abimelech their **b**, 251
20:23 against the children of Benjamin my **b**? 251
20:28 against the children of Benjamin my **b**, 251
21: 6 Israel repented them for Benjamin their **b**, 251
Ru 4: 3 of land, which *was* our **b** Elimelech's: 251
1Sa 14: 3 Ahiah, the son of Ahitub, Ichabod's **b**, 251
17:28 Eliab his eldest **b** heard when he spake 251
20:29 my **b**, he hath commanded me *to be there*: 251
26: 6 the son of Zeruiah, **b** to Joab, saying, 251

2Sa	1:26 I am distressed for thee, my **b** Jonathan:	251
	2:22 should I hold up my face to Joab thy **b**?	251
	2:27 gone up every one from following his **b**.	251
	3:27 that he died, for the blood of Asahel his **b**.	251
	3:30 So Joab and Abishai his **b** slew Abner,	251
	3:30 he had slain their **b** Asahel at Gibeon in	251
	4: 6 and Rechab and Baanah his **b** escaped.	251
	4: 9 David answered Rechab and Baanah his **b**,	251
	10:10 delivered into the hand of Abishai his **b**,	251
	13: 3 Jonadab, the son of Shimeah David's **b**:	251
	13: 4 I love Tamar, my **b** Absalom's sister.	251
	13: 7 Go now *to* thy **b** Amnon's house,	251
	13: 8 So Tamar went *to* her **b** Amnon's house;	251
	13:10 *them* into the chamber to Amnon her **b**.	251
	13:12 answered him, Nay, my **b**, do not force me;	251
	13:20 Absalom her **b** said unto her, Hath Amnon	251
	13:20 her, Hath Amnon thy **b** been with thee?	251
	13:20 he *is* thy **b**; regard not this thing. So Tamar	251
	13:20 So Tamar remained desolate *in* her **b**	251
	13:22 Absalom spake unto his **b** Amnon neither	NIH
	13:26 I pray thee, let my **b** Amnon go with us.	251
	13:32 the son of Shimeah David's **b**, answered	251
	14: 7 they said, Deliver him that smote his **b**,	251
	14: 7 kill him, for the life of his **b** whom he slew;	251
	18: 2 Joab's **b**, and a third part under the hand	251
	20: 9 said to Amasa, *Art* thou in health, my **b**?	251
	20:10 Abishai his **b** pursued after Sheba the son	251
	21:19 slew *the* **b** of Goliath the Gittite,	NIH
	21:21 Jonathan the son of Shimea the **b** of David	251
	23:18 Abishai, the **b** of Joab, the son of Zeruiah,	251
	23:24 Asahel the **b** of Joab *was* one of the thirty;	251
1Ki	1:10 and the mighty *men*, and Solomon his **b**.	251
	2: 7 when I fled because of Absalom thy **b**.	251
	2:21 be given to Adonijah thy **b** to wife.	251
	2:22 for he *is* mine elder **b**; even for him,	251
	9:13 these which thou hast given me, my **b**?	251
	13:30 mourned over him, *saying*, Alas, my **b**.	251
	20:32 And he said, *Is* he yet alive? he *is* my **b**.	251
	20:33 catch *it:* and they said, Thy **b** Ben-hadad.	251
2Ki	24:17 Mattaniah his **father's b** king in his stead,	1730
1Ch	2:32 the sons of Jada the **b** of Shammai; Jether,	251
	2:42 Now the sons of Caleb the **b** of Jerahmeel	251
	4:11 Chelub the **b** of Shuah begat Mehir,	251
	6:39 his **b** Asaph, who stood on his right hand,	251
	7:16 name of his **b** *was* Sheresh; and his sons	251
	7:35 son of his **b** Helem; Zophah, and Imna,	251
	8:39 the sons of Eshek his **b** *were*, Ulam his	251
	11:20 Abishai the **b** of Joab, he was chief of	251
	11:26 of the armies *were*, Asahel the **b** of Joab,	251
	11:38 Joel the **b** of Nathan, Mibhar the son of	251
	11:45 son of Shimri, and Joha his **b**, the Tizite,	251
	19:11 delivered unto the hand of Abishai his **b**,	251
	19:15 they likewise fled before Abishai his **b**,	251
	20: 5 Elhanan the son of Jair slew Lahmi the **b**	251
	20: 7 Jonathan the son of Shimea David's **b** slew	251
	24:25 The **b** of Michah *was* Isshiah: of the sons	251
	26:22 Zetham, and Joel his **b**, *which were* over	251
	27: 7 the fourth month *was* Asahel the **b** of Joab,	251
2Ch	31:12 *was* ruler, and Shimei his **b** *was* the next.	251
	31:13 the hand of Cononiah and Shimei his **b**,	251
	36: 4 the king of Egypt made Eliakim his **b** king	251
	36: 4 Necho took Jehoahaz his **b**, and carried	251
	36:10 made Zedekiah his **b** king over Judah and	251
Ne	5: 7 You exact usury, every one of his **b**.	251
	7: 2 That I gave my **b** Hanani, and Hananiah	251
Job	22: 6 For thou hast taken a pledge from thy **b**	251
	30:29 I am a **b** to dragons, and a companion to	251
Ps	35:14 as though he had been my friend *or* **b**:	251
	49: 7 *of them* can by any means redeem his **b**,	251
	50:20 Thou sittest *and* speakest against thy **b**;	251
Pr	17:17 at all times, and a **b** is born for adversity.	251
	18: 9 He also that is slothful in his work *is* **b** to	251
	18:19 A **b** offended *is harder to be won* than a	251
	18:24 *is* a friend that sticketh closer than a **b**.	251
	27:10 better *is* a neighbour *that is* near than a **b**	251
Ecc	4: 8 a second; yea, he hath neither child nor **b**:	251
SS	8: 1 O that thou *wert* as my **b**, that sucked	251
Isa	3: 6 When a man shall take hold of his **b** of	251
	9:19 fuel of the fire: no man shall spare his **b**.	251
	19: 2 they shall fight every one against his **b**,	251
	41: 6 *one* said to his **b**, Be of good courage.	251
Jer	9: 4 his neighbour, and trust ye not in any **b**:	251
	9: 4 for every **b** will utterly supplant,	251
	22:18 shall not lament for him, *saying*, Ah my **b**!	251
	23:35 every one to his **b**, What hath the LORD	251
	31:34 every man his **b**, *saying*, Know the LORD:	251
	34: 9 himself of them, *to wit*, of a Jew his **b**.	251
	34:14 years let ye go every man his **b** a Hebrew,	251
	34:17 every one to his **b**, and every man to his	251
Eze	18:18 spoiled *his* **b** by violence, and did *that*	251
	33:30 every one to his **b**, saying, Come, I pray	251
	38:21 every man's sword shall be against his **b**.	251
	44:25 **b**, or for sister that hath had no husband,	251
Hos	12: 3 he took his **b** by the heel in the womb,	251
Am	1:11 he did pursue his **b** with the sword,	251
Ob	1:10 For *thy* violence against thy **b** Jacob shame	251
	1:12 by in the day that he became a stranger;	251
Mic	7: 2 they hunt every man his **b** *with* a net.	251
Hag	2:22 down, every one by the sword of his **b**.	251
Zec	7: 9 and compassions every man to his **b**	251
	7:10 let none of you imagine evil against his **b**	251
Mal	1: 2 *was* not Esau Jacob's **b**? saith the LORD:	251
	2:10 deal treacherously every man against his **b**,	251
Mt	4:18 Simon called Peter, and Andrew his **b**,	80
	4:21 James the *son* of Zebedee, and John his **b**,	80

Mt	5:22 whosoever is angry with his **b** without a	80
	5:22 and whosoever shall say to his **b**, Raca,	80
	5:23 there rememberest that thy **b** hath ought	80
	5:24 first be reconciled to thy **b**, and then come	80
	7: 4 how wilt thou say to thy **b**, Let me pull out	80
	10: 2 who is called Peter, and Andrew his **b**;	80
	10: 2 the *son* of Zebedee, and John his **b**;	80
	10:21 And the brother shall deliver up the brother to	80
	10:21 And the brother shall deliver up the **b** to	80
	12:50 the same is my **b**, and sister, and mother.	80
	14: 3 prison for Herodias' sake, his **b** Philip's wife.	80
	17: 1 and John his **b**, and bringeth them into a	80
	18:15 Moreover if thy **b** shall trespass against thee,	80
	18:15 if he shall hear thee, thou hast gained thy **b**.	80
	18:21 how oft shall my **b** sin against me, and I	80
	18:35 forgive not every one his **b** their trespasses.	80
	22:24 his **b** shall marry his wife, and raise up seed	80
	22:24 marry his wife, and raise up seed unto his **b**:	80
	22:25 having no issue, left his wife unto his **b**:	80
Mk	1:16 and Andrew his **b** casting a net into the sea:	80
	1:19 James the *son* of Zebedee, and John his **b**,	80
	3:17 *son* of Zebedee, and John the **b** of James;	80
	3:35 same is my **b**, and my sister, and mother.	80
	5:37 and James, and John the **b** of James.	80
	6: 3 the **b** of James, and Joses, and of Juda,	80
	6:17 prison for Herodias' sake, his **b** Philip's wife:	80
	12:19 If a man's **b** die, and leave his wife *behind*	80
	12:19 that his **b** should take his wife, and raise up	80
	12:19 take his wife, and raise up seed unto his **b**.	80
	13:12 Now the **b** shall betray the brother to death,	80
	13:12 Now the brother shall betray the **b** to death,	80
Lk	3: 1 his **b** Philip tetrarch of Iturea and of	80
	3:19 being reproved by him for Herodias his **b**	80
	6:14 Andrew his **b**, James and John, Philip and	80
	6:16 *And* Judas the **b** of James,	NIG
	6:42 Either how canst thou say to thy **b**, Brother,	80
	6:42 Either how canst thou say to thy brother, **B**,	80
	12:13 Master, speak to my **b**, that *he* divide	80
	15:27 And he said unto him, Thy **b** is come;	80
	15:32 for this thy **b** was dead, and is alive again;	80
	17: 3 If thy **b** trespass against thee, rebuke him;	80
	20:28 any *man's* die, having a wife, and he die	80
	20:28 that his **b** should take *his* wife, and raise up	80
	20:28 take *his* wife, and raise up seed unto his **b**.	80
Jn	1:40 him, was Andrew, Simon Peter's **b**.	80
	1:41 He first findeth his own **b** Simon,	80
	6: 8 Andrew, Simon Peter's **b**, saith unto him,	80
	11: 2 with her hair, whose **b** Lazarus was sick.)	80
	11:19 Mary, to comfort them concerning their **b**.	80
	11:21 if thou hadst been here, my **b** had not died.	80
	11:23 Jesus saith unto her, Thy **b** shall rise again.	80
	11:32 if thou hadst been here, my **b** had not died.	80
Ac	1:13 Simon Zelotes, and Judas the **b** of James.	NIG
	9:17 on him said, **B** Saul, the Lord, *even* Jesus,	80
	12: 2 And he killed James the **b** of John with	80
	21:20 the Lord, and said unto, Thou seest, **b**,	80
	22:13 me, and stood, and said unto me, **B** Saul,	80
Ro	14:10 But why dost thou judge thy **b**? or why dost	80
	14:10 or why dost thou set at nought thy **b**?	80
	14:15 But if thy **b** be grieved with *thy* meat,	80
	14:21 nor *any thing* whereby thy **b** stumbleth,	80
	16:23 of the city saluteth you, and Quartus a **b**.	80
1Co	1: 1 the will of God, and Sosthenes our **b**,	80
	5:11 if any *man that is* called a **b** be a fornicator,	80
	6: 6 But **b** goeth to law with brother,	80
	6: 6 But brother goeth to law with **b**,	80
	7:12 If any **b** hath a wife that believeth not,	80
	7:15 A **b** or a sister is not under bondage in such	80
	8:11 through thy knowledge shall the weak **b**	80
	8:13 Wherefore, if meat make my **b** to offend,	80
	8:13 world standeth, lest I make my **b** to offend.	80
	16:12 As touching our **b** Apollos, I greatly desired	80
2Co	1: 1 and Timothy our **b**, unto the church of God	80
	2:13 my spirit, because I found not Titus my **b**:	80
	8:18 And we have sent with him the **b**,	80
	8:22 And we have sent with them our **b**,	80
	12:18 I desired Titus, and with *him* I sent a **b**.	80
Gal	1:19 apostles saw I none, save James the Lord's **b**.	80
Eph	6:21 beloved **b** and faithful minister in the Lord,	80
Php	2:25 my **b**, and companion in labour,	80
Col	1: 1 by the will of God, and Timotheus our **b**,	80
	4: 7 *who is* a beloved **b**, and a faithful minister	80
	4: 9 With Onesimus, a faithful and beloved **b**,	80
1Th	2: 6 our **b**, and minister of God,	80
	4: 6 go beyond and defraud his **b** in *any* matter:	80
2Th	3: 6 ye withdraw yourselves from every **b** that	80
	3:15 not as an enemy, but admonish *him* as a **b**.	80
Phm	1: 1 prisoner of Jesus Christ, and Timothy our **b**,	80
	1: 7 of the saints are refreshed by thee, **b**.	80
	1:16 a **b** beloved, specially to me, but how much	80
	1:20 Yea, **b**, let me have joy of thee in the Lord:	80
Heb	8:11 every man his **b**, saying, Know the Lord:	80
	13:23 Know ye that our **b** Timothy is set at liberty;	80
Jas	1: 9 Let the **b** of low degree rejoice in that he is	80
	2:15 If a **b** or sister be naked, and destitute of	80
	4:11 He that speaketh evil of *his* **b**, and judgeth	80
	4:11 and judgeth his **b**, speaketh evil of the law,	80
1Pe	5:12 By Silvanus, a faithful **b** unto you, as I	80
2Pe	3:15 even as our beloved **b** Paul also according to	80
1Jn	2: 9 and hateth his **b**, is in darkness *even* until	80
	2:10 He that loveth his **b** abideth in the light,	80
	2:11 But he that hateth his **b** is in darkness,	80
	3:10 not of God, neither he that loveth not his **b**.	80
	3:12 was of *that* wicked one, and slew his **b**.	80
	3:14 He that loveth not *his* **b** abideth in death.	80

1Jn	3:15 Whosoever hateth his **b** is a murderer:	80
	3:17 seeth his **b** hath need, and shutteth up his	80
	4:20 I love God, and hateth his **b**, he is a liar:	80
	4:20 for he that loveth not his **b** whom he hath	80
	4:21 That he who loveth God love his **b** also.	80
	5:16 If any *man* see his **b** sin a sin *which is* not	80
Jude	1: 1 the servant of Jesus Christ, and **b** of James,	80
Rev	1: 9 who also am your **b**, and companion in	80

BROTHER'S (35) [BROTHER]

Ge	4: 9 he said, I know not: *Am* I my **b** keeper?	251
	4:10 the voice of thy **b** blood crieth unto me	251
	4:11 to receive thy **b** blood from thy hand.	251
	4:21 his **b** name *was* Jubal: he was the father	251
	10:25 earth divided; and his **b** name *was* Joktan.	251
	12: 5 Lot his **b** son, and all their substance that	251
	14:12 took Lot, Abram's **b** son, who dwelt in	251
	24:48 take my master's **b** daughter unto his son.	251
	27:44 a few days, until thy **b** fury turn away;	251
	27:45 Until thy **b** anger turn away from thee,	251
	38: 8 Go in unto thy **b** wife, and marry her,	251
	38: 9 to pass, when he went in unto his **b** wife,	251
Lev	18:16 not uncover the nakedness of thy **b** wife:	251
	18:16 of thy brother's wife: it *is* thy **b** nakedness.	251
	20:21 if a man shall take his **b** wife, it *is an*	251
	21:10 he hath uncovered his **b** nakedness;	251
Dt	22: 1 Thou shalt not see thy **b** ox or his sheep go	251
	22: 3 with all lost *thing* of thy **b**, which he hath	251
	22: 4 Thou shalt not see thy **b** ass or his ox fall	251
	25: 7 if the man like not to take his **b** wife,	2994
	25: 7 let his **b** wife go up to the gate unto	2994
	25: 9 shall his **b** wife come unto him in	2994
	25: 9 man that will not build up his **b** house.	251
1Ki	2:15 turned about, and is become my **b**:	251+3807.1
1Ch	1:19 was divided: and his **b** name *was* Joktan.	251
Job	1:13 and drinking wine in their eldest **b** house:	251
	1:18 and drinking wine in their eldest **b** house:	251
Pr	27:10 neither go *into* thy **b** house in the day of	251
Mt	7: 3 beholdest thou the mote that is in thy **b** eye,	80
	7: 5 clearly to cast out the mote out of thy **b** eye.	80
Mk	6:18 It is not lawful for thee to have thy **b** wife.	80
Lk	6:41 beholdest thou the mote that is in thy **b** eye,	80
	6:42 to pull out the mote that is in thy **b** eye.	80
Ro	14:13 or an occasion to fall in *his* **b** way.	80
1Jn	3:12 own works were evil, and his **b** righteous.	80

BROTHERHOOD (2) [BROTHER]

Zec	11:14 that I might break the **b** between Judah	264
1Pe	2:17 Honour all *men*. Love the **b**. Fear God.	81

BROTHERLY (6) [BROTHER]

Am	1: 9 and remembered not the **b** covenant:	251
Ro	12:10 affectioned one to another with **b** love;	5360
1Th	4: 9 But as touching **b** love ye need not that	5360
Heb	13: 1 Let **b** love continue.	5360
2Pe	1: 7 And to godliness **b** kindness;	5360
	1: 7 and to **b** kindness charity.	5360

BROTHERS See BRETHREN

BROTHERS' (1) [BROTHER]

Nu	36:11 were married unto their **father's b** sons:	1730

BROUGHT (864) [BRING]

Ge	1:12 the earth **b** forth grass, *and* herb yielding	3318
	1:21 which the waters **b** forth abundantly,	8317
	2:19 **b** them unto Adam to see what he would	935
	2:22 a woman, and **b** her unto the man.	935
	4: 3 that Cain **b** of the fruit of the ground an	935
	4: 4 he **b** also of the firstlings of his flock and	935
	14:16 he **b** back all the goods, and also brought	7725
	14:16 **b** again his brother Lot, and his goods,	7725
	14:18 Melchizedek king of Salem **b** forth bread	3318
	15: 5 he **b** him forth abroad, and said, Look	3318
	15: 7 I *am* the LORD that **b** thee *out* of Ur of	3318
	19:16 they **b** him forth, and set him without	3318
	19:17 when they had **b** them forth abroad,	3318
	20: 9 thou hast **b** on me and on my kingdom	935
	24:53 the servant **b** forth jewels of silver,	3318
	24:67 Isaac **b** her into his mother Sarah's tent,	935
	26:10 thou shouldest have **b** guiltiness upon us.	935
	27:14 and fetched, and **b** *them* to his mother:	935
	27:20 Because the LORD thy God **b** it to me.	7136
	27:25 he **b** it *near* to him, and he did eat:	5066
	27:25 did eat: and he **b** him wine, and he drank.	935
	27:31 **b** it unto his father, and said unto his father	935
	27:33 **b** it me, and I have eaten of all before thou	935
	29:13 and kissed him, and **b** him to his house.	935
	29:23 took Leah his daughter, and **b** her to him;	935
	30:14 field, and **b** them unto his mother Leah.	935
	30:39 **b** forth cattle ringstraked, speckled,	3205
	31:39 That which was torn *of beasts* I **b** not	935
	33:11 I pray thee, my blessing that is **b** to thee;	935
	37: 2 Joseph **b** unto his father their evil report.	935
	37:28 of silver: and they **b** Joseph into Egypt.	935
	37:32 many colours, and they **b** *it* to their father;	935
	38:25 When she *was* **b** forth, she sent to her	3318
	39: 1 Joseph was **b** down to Egypt;	3381
	39: 1 which had **b** him down thither.	3381
	39:14 hath **b** in a Hebrew unto us to mock us;	935
	39:17 servant, which thou hast **b** unto us,	935
	40:10 the clusters thereof **b** forth ripe grapes:	1310
	41:14 they **b** him *hastily* out of the dungeon:	7323
	41:47 years the earth **b** by handfuls.	6213
	43: 1 The corn which they had **b** out of Egypt,	935
	43:12 the money that was **b** again in the mouth	7725

B

B

Ge 43:17 the man **b** the men into Joseph's house. 935
43:18 because they were **b** into Joseph's house; 935
43:18 in our sacks at the first time *are* we **b** in; 935
43:21 and we have **b** it **again** in our hand. 7725
43:22 money have we **b** down in our hands 3381
43:23 And he **b** Simeon **out** unto them. 3318
43:24 the man **b** the men into Joseph's house, 935
43:26 they **b** him the present which *was* in their 935
44: 8 we **b** again unto thee out of the land of 7725
46: 7 and all his seed **b** he with him into Egypt. 935
46:32 they have **b** their flocks, and their herds, 935
47: 7 Joseph **b** in Jacob his father, and set him 935
47:14 Joseph the money into Pharaoh's house. 935
47:17 they their cattle unto Joseph: 935
48:10 he **b** them **near** unto him; and he kissed 5066
48:12 Joseph **b** them **out** from between his 3318
48:13 right hand, and **b** *them* **near** unto him. 5066
50:23 Manasseh were **b** up upon Joseph's knees. 3205
Ex 2:10 and she **b** him unto Pharaoh's daughter, 935
3:12 When thou hast **b** forth the people out of 3318
8: 7 and **b** up frogs upon the land of Egypt. 5927
8:12 of the frogs which he had **b** against 7760
9:19 shall not be **b** home, the hail shall come 622
10: 8 and Aaron were **b** again unto Pharaoh: 7725
10:13 the LORD **b** an east wind upon the land 5090
10:13 was morning, the east wind **b** the locusts. 5375
12:17 I **b** your armies **out** of the land of Egypt: 3318
12:39 dough which they **b** forth out of Egypt, 3318
13: 3 b you **out** from this *place*: there shall no 3318
13: 9 hand hath the LORD **b** thee **out** of Egypt. 3318
13:14 By strength of hand the LORD **b** us **out** 3318
13:16 hand the LORD **b** us **forth** out of Egypt. 3318
15:19 So the LORD **b** again the waters of the sea 7725
15:22 So Moses **b** Israel from the Red sea, 5265
15:26 which I have **b** upon the Egyptians: 7760
16: 3 ye have **b** us **forth** into this wilderness, 3318
16: 6 hath **b** you **out** from the land of Egypt: 3318
16:32 I **b** you **forth** from the land of Egypt. 3318
17: 3 Wherefore *is* this *that* thou hast **b** us **up** 5927
18: 1 that the LORD had **b** Israel **out** of Egypt; 3318
18:26 the hard causes they **b** unto Moses, 935
19: 4 on eagles' wings, and **b** you unto myself. 935
19:17 Moses **b** forth the people out of the camp 3318
20: 2 have **b** thee **out** of the land of Egypt, 3318
22: 8 the master of the house shall be **b** unto 7126
29:10 thou shalt *cause* a bullock to be **b** before 7126
29:46 that **b** them **forth** out of the land of Egypt, 3318
32: 1 the man that **b** us **up** out of the land of 5927
32: 3 in their ears, and *them* unto Aaron. 935
32: 4 which **b** thee **up** out of the land of Egypt. 5927
32: 6 burnt offerings, and **b** peace offerings; 5066
32: 8 which have **b** thee **up** out of the land of 5927
32:11 which thou hast **b** forth out of the land of 3318
32:21 thou hast **b** *so* great a sin upon them? 935
32:23 the man that **b** us **up** out of the land of 5927
33: 1 the people which thou hast **b** up out of 5927
35:21 they **b** the LORD's offering to the work of 935
35:22 *and* **b** bracelets, and earrings, and rings, 935
35:23 skins of rams, and badgers' skins, **b** *them*. 935
35:24 of silver and brass **b** the LORD's offering: 935
35:24 wood for any work of the service, **b** *it.* 935
35:25 and **b** that which they had spun, 935
35:27 rulers **b** onyx stones, and stones to be set, 935
35:29 The children of Israel **b** a willing offering 935
36: 3 which the children of Israel had **b** for 935
36: 3 to make it *withal.* And they **b** yet unto him 935
39:33 they **b** the tabernacle unto Moses, the tent, 935
40:21 he **b** the ark into the tabernacle, and set up 935
Lev 6:30 whereof *any* of the blood is **b** into 935
8: 6 Moses **b** Aaron and his sons, 7126
8:13 Moses **b** Aaron's sons, and put coats upon 7126
8:14 he **b** the bullock *for* the sin offering: 5066
8:18 he **b** the ram for the burnt offering: 7126
8:22 **b** the other ram, the ram of consecration: 7126
8:24 he **b** Aaron's sons, and Moses put of 7126
9: 5 they **b** *that* which Moses commanded 3947
9: 9 the sons of Aaron **b** the blood unto him: 7126
9:15 he **b** the people's offering, and took 7126
9:16 he **b** the burnt offering, and offered it 7126
9:17 he **b** the meat offering, and took a handful 7126
10:18 blood of it was not **b** in within the holy 935
13: 2 he shall be **b** unto Aaron the priest, 935
13: 9 a man, then he shall be **b** unto the priest; 935
14: 2 his cleansing: He shall be **b** unto the priest: 935
16:27 whose blood was **b** in to make atonement 935
19:36 which **b** you **out** of the land of Egypt. 3318
22:27 is **b** forth, then it shall be seven days 3205
22:33 That **b** you out of the land of Egypt, to be 3318
23:14 until the selfsame day that ye have **b** an 935
23:15 from the day that ye **b** the sheaf of the 935
23:43 when I **b** them **out** of the land of Egypt: 3318
24:11 they **b** him unto Moses: (and his mother's 935
25:38 **b** you out of the land of Egypt, 3318
25:42 whom I **b** forth out of the land of Egypt: 3318
26:13 **b** you **forth** out of the land of Egypt, 3318
26:41 **b** them into the land of their enemies; 935
26:45 whom I **b** forth out of the land of Egypt 3318
Nu 6:13 shall be **b** unto the door of the tabernacle 935
7: 3 And they **b** their offering before the LORD, 935
7: 3 and they **b** them before the tabernacle. 7126
9:13 he **b** not the offering of the LORD in his 7126
11:31 **b** quails from the sea, and let *them* fall by 1468
12:15 journeyed not till Miriam was **b** in *again.* 622
13:23 they **b** of the pomegranates, and of the figs. NIH

Nu 13:26 **b** back word unto them, and unto all 7725
13:32 they **b** an evil report of the land which 3318
14: 3 wherefore *hath* the LORD **b** us unto this 935
15:33 that found him gathering sticks **b** him 7126
15:36 all the congregation **b** him without 3318
15:41 which **b** you **out** of the land of Egypt, 3318
16:10 he hath **b** thee **near** to him, and all thy 7126
16:13 a small thing that thou hast **b** us **up** out 5927
16:14 Moreover thou hast not **b** us into a land 935
17: 8 **b** forth buds, and bloomed blossoms, 3318
17: 9 Moses **b** out all the rods from before 3318
20: 4 why have ye **b** up the congregation of 935
20:16 angel, and hath **b** us **forth** out of Egypt: 3318
21: 5 Wherefore have ye **b** us **up** out of Egypt 5927
22:41 and **b** him **up** *into* the high places of Baal, 5927
23: 7 Balak the king of Moab hath **b** me from 5148
23:14 he **b** him *into* the field of Zophim, 3947
23:22 God **b** them **out** of Egypt; he hath as it 3318
23:28 Balak **b** Balaam **unto** the top of Peor, 3947
24: 8 God **b** him **forth** out of Egypt; he hath as 3318
25: 6 **b** unto his brethren a Midianitish *woman* 7126
27: 5 Moses **b** their cause before the LORD. 7126
31:12 they **b** the captives, and the prey, 935
31:50 therefore **b** an oblation for the LORD, 7126
31:54 **b** it into the tabernacle of the congregation, 935
32:17 until we have **b** them unto their place: 935
Dt 1:25 **b** *it* **down** unto us, and brought us word 3381
1:25 unto us, and **b** us word **again**, and said, 7725
1:27 hath **b** us **forth** out of the land of Egypt, 3318
4:20 hath **b** you **forth** out of the iron furnace, 3318
4:37 **b** thee out in his sight with his mighty 3318
5: 6 which **b** thee **out** of the land of Egypt, 3318
5:15 *that* the LORD thy God **b** thee **out** thence 3318
6:10 when the LORD thy God shall have **b** thee 935
6:12 which **b** thee **forth** out of the land of 3318
6:21 the LORD **b** us **out** of Egypt with a 3318
6:23 he **b** us **out** from thence, that he might 3318
7: 8 hath the LORD **b** you **out** with a mighty 3318
7:19 where *by* the LORD thy God **b** thee **out:** 3318
8:14 which **b** thee **forth** out of the land of 3318
8:15 who **b** thee **forth** water out of the rock of 3318
9: 4 hath **b** me in to possess this land: 935
9:12 thy people which thou hast **b** **forth** out 3318
9:26 which thou hast **b** **forth** out of Egypt with 3318
9:28 he hath **b** them **out** to slay them in 3318
11:29 when the LORD thy God hath **b** thee in 935
13: 5 which **b** you out of the land of Egypt, 3318
13:10 which **b** thee out of the land of Egypt, 3318
16: 1 God **b** thee **forth** out of Egypt by night. 3318
20: 1 which **b** thee **up** out of the land of Egypt. 5927
22:19 he hath **b** up an evil name upon a virgin 3318
26: 8 the LORD **b** us **forth** out of Egypt with a 3318
26: 9 hath **b** us into this place, and hath given 935
26:10 behold, I have **b** the firstfruits of the land, 935
26:13 I have **b** **away** the hallowed *things* out of 1197
29:25 he **b** them **forth** out of the land of Egypt: 3318
31:20 when I shall have **b** them into the land 935
31:21 before I have **b** them into the land which 935
33:14 for the precious fruits **b** forth by the sun, NIH
Jos 2: 6 had **b** them **up** to the roof of the house, 5927
6:23 **b** out Rahab, and her father, 3318
6:23 they **b** out all her kindred, and left them 3318
7: 7 at all **b** this people **over** Jordan, 5674+5674
7:14 ye shall be **b** according to your tribes: 7126
7:16 the morning, and **b** Israel by their tribes; 7126
7:17 he **b** the family of Judah; and he took 7126
7:17 he **b** the family of the Zarhites man by 7126
7:18 he **b** his household man by man; 7126
7:23 **b** them unto Joshua, and unto all the 935
7:24 and they **b** them *unto* the valley of Achor. 5927
8:23 of Ai they took alive, and **b** him to Joshua. 7126
10:23 **b** forth those five kings unto him out of 3318
10:24 when they **b** out those kings unto Joshua, 3318
14: 7 **b** him word **again** as *it was* in mine heart. 7725
22:32 of Israel, and **b** them word **again**. 7725
24: 5 amongst them: and afterward I **b** you **out**. 3318
24: 6 I **b** your fathers **out** of Egypt: 3318
24: 7 the sea upon them, and covered them; 935
24: 8 I **b** you into the land of the Amorites, 935
24:17 he *it is* that **b** us **up** and our fathers out of 5927
24:32 which the children of Israel **b** up out of 5927
Jdg 1: 7 they **b** him *to* Jerusalem, and there he died. 935
2: 1 have **b** you unto the land which I sware 935
2:12 which **b** them **out** of the land of Egypt, 3318
3:17 he **b** the present unto Eglon king of Moab: 7126
5:25 she **b** forth butter in a lordly dish. 7126
6: 8 I **b** you **up** from Egypt, and brought you 5927
6: 8 **b** you **forth** out of the house of bondage; 3318
6:19 **b** *it* out unto him under the oak, 3318
7: 5 So he **b** down the people unto the water: 3381
7:25 **b** the heads of Oreb and Zeeb to Gideon 935
11:35 thou hast **b** me **very low**, 3766+3766
14:11 that they **b** thirty companions to be with 3947
15:13 new cords, and **b** him **up** from the rock. 5927
16: 8 the lords of the Philistines **b** up to her 5927
16:18 up unto her, and **b** money in their hand. 5927
16:21 **b** him **down** to Gaza, and bound him 3381
16:31 **b** *him* up, and buried him between Zorah 5927
18: 3 and said unto him, Who **b** thee hither? 935
19: 3 she **b** him *into* her father's house: 935
19:21 So he **b** him into his house, 935
19:25 his concubine, and **b** *her* forth unto them; 3318
21:12 they **b** them unto the camp *to* Shiloh, 935
Ru 1:21 the LORD hath **b** me **home again** empty: 7725
2:18 she **b** forth, and gave to her that she had 3318

1Sa 1:24 **b** him *unto* the house of the LORD *in* 935
1:25 they slew a bullock, and **b** the child to Eli. 935
2:14 all that the fleshhook **b** up the priest took 5927
2:19 coat, and **b** *it* to him from year to year, 5927
5: 1 and **b** it from Eben-ezer unto Ashdod. 935
5: 2 they **b** it *into* the house of Dagon, and set 935
5:10 They have **b** about the ark of the God of 5437
6:21 The Philistines have **b** again the ark of 7725
7: 1 **b** it into the house of Abinadab in the hill, 935
8: 8 **b** them **up** out of Egypt even unto this 5927
9:22 **b** them into the parlour, and made them 935
10:18 I **b** up Israel out of Egypt, 5927
10:27 they despised him, and **b** him no presents. 935
12: 6 that **b** your fathers **up** out of the land of 5927
12: 8 which **b** forth your fathers out of Egypt, 3318
14:34 the people **b** every man his ox with him 5066
15:15 They have **b** them from the Amalekites: 935
15:20 have **b** Agag the king of Amalek, 935
16:12 he sent, and **b** him in. Now he *was* ruddy, 935
17:54 of the Philistine, and **b** it *to* Jerusalem; 935
17:57 **b** him before Saul with the head of 935
18:27 David **b** their foreskins, and they gave 935
19: 7 Jonathan **b** David to Saul, and he was in 935
20: 8 for thou hast **b** thy servant into a covenant 935
21: 8 for I have neither **b** my sword nor my 3947
21:14 wherefore *then* have ye **b** him to me? 935
21:15 that ye have **b** this *fellow* to play the mad 935
22: 4 he **b** them before the king of Moab: 5148
23: 5 **b** **away** their cattle, and smote them 5090
25:27 thine handmaid hath **b** unto my lord, 935
25:35 of her hand *that* which she had **b** him, 935
28:25 she **b** *it* before Saul, and before his 5066
30: 7 Abiathar **b** **thither** the ephod to David. 5066
30:11 **b** him to David, and gave him bread, 3947
30:16 when he had **b** him **down**, behold *they* 3381
2Sa 1:10 and have **b** them hither unto my lord. 935
2: 8 of Saul, and **b** him **over** *to* Mahanaim; 5674
3:22 a troop, and **b** in a great spoil with them: 935
3:26 **b** him **again** from the well of Sirah: 7725
4: 8 they **b** the head of Ish-bosheth unto David 935
4:10 is dead, thinking to have **b** good tidings, 1319
6: 3 **b** it out of the house of Abinadab that *was* 5375
6: 4 they **b** it out of the house of Abinadab 5375
6:12 **b** up the ark of God from the house of 5927
6:15 all the house of Israel **b** up the ark of 5927
6:17 they **b** in the ark of the LORD, and set it in 935
7: 6 I **b** up the children of Israel out of Egypt, 5927
7:18 *is* my house, that thou hast **b** me hitherto? 935
8: 2 became David's servants, and **b** gifts. 5375
8: 6 became servants to David, and **b** gifts. 5375
8: 7 of Hadadezer, and **b** them *to* Jerusalem. 935
8:10 Joram **b** with him vessels of silver, 1961
10:16 **b** out the Syrians that *were* beyond 3318
12:30 he **b** forth the spoil of the city in great 3318
12:31 he **b** forth the people that *were* therein, 3318
13:10 **b** *them* into the chamber to Amnon her 935
13:11 when she had **b** *them* unto him to eat, 5066
13:18 his servant **b** her out, and bolted the door 3318
14:23 to Geshur, and **b** Absalom *to* Jerusalem. 935
17:28 **b** beds, and basons, and earthen vessels, 5066
19:41 the king, and his household, and all 5674
 David's men with him, **over**
21: 8 whom she **b** up for Adriel the son of 3205
21:13 he **b** up from thence the bones of Saul 5927
22:20 He **b** me **forth** also into a large place: 3318
23:16 by the gate, and took *it*, and **b** *it* to David: 935
1Ki 1: 3 a Shunammite, and **b** her to the king. 935
1:38 king David's mule, and **b** him to Gihon. 1980
1:53 and they **b** him **down** from the altar. 3381
2:30 Benaiah **b** the king word **again**, saying, 7725
2:40 Shimei went, and **b** his servants from Gath. 935
3: 1 and **b** her into the city of David, 935
3:24 And they **b** a sword before the king. 935
4:21 they **b** presents, and served Solomon all 5066
4:28 dromedaries **b** they unto the place where 935
5:17 they **b** great stones, costly stones, 5265
6: 7 stone made ready *before it was* **b** *thither:* 4551
7:51 Solomon **b** in the *things* which David his 935
8: 4 they **b** up the ark of the LORD, 5927
8: 6 the priests **b** in the ark of the covenant of 935
8:16 Since the day that I **b** forth my people 3318
8:21 when he **b** them **out** of the land of Egypt. 3318
9: 9 who **b** forth their fathers out of the land of 3318
9: 9 hath the LORD **b** upon them all this evil. 935
9:28 twenty talents, and **b** *it* to king Solomon. 935
10:11 also of Hiram, that **b** gold from Ophir, 5375
10:11 **b** in from Ophir great plenty of almug 935
10:25 they **b** every man his present, vessels of 935
10:28 Solomon had horses **b** out of Egypt, 4161
12:28 which **b** thee up out of the land of Egypt. 5927
13:20 came unto the prophet that **b** him **back:** 7725
13:23 for the prophet whom he had **b** back. 7725
13:26 when the prophet that **b** him **back** from 7725
13:29 and laid it upon the ass, and **b** it **back:** 7725
14:28 and **b** them **back** into the guard chamber. 7725
15:15 he **b** in *the* things which his father had 935
17: 6 the ravens **b** him bread and flesh in 935
17:20 hast thou also **b** evil upon the widow 7489
17:23 he **b** him **down** out of the chamber into 3381
18:40 Elijah **b** them **down** to the brook Kishon, 3381
20: 9 and **b** him word **again**. 7725
20:39 a man and said, Keep this man: 935
22:37 So the king died, and was **b** *to* Samaria; 935
2Ki 2:20 and put salt therein. And they **b** *it* to him. 3947
4: 5 upon her sons, who **b** the *vessels* to her; 5066

B

2Ki
4:20	**b** him to his mother, he sat on her knees	935
4:42	the man of God bread of the firstfruits,	935
5: 2	had **b away captive** out of the land of	7617
5: 6	he **b** the letter to the king of Israel, saying,	935
5:20	not receiving at his hands *that* which he **b**:	935
10: 1	to them that **b up** Ahab's *children*, saying,	539
10: 6	great *men* of the city, which **b** them **up**.	1431
10: 8	They have **b** the heads of the king's sons.	935
10:22	of Baal. And he **b** them vestments.	3318
10:24	*If* any of the men whom I *have* **b** into your	935
10:26	they **b forth** the images **out of** the house	3318
11: 4	**b** them to him *into* the house of the LORD,	935
11:12	he **b forth** the king's son, and put	3318
11:19	they **b down** the king from the house of	3381
12: 4	*things* that is **b** *into* the house of the LORD,	935
12: 9	that was **b** *into* the house of the LORD.	935
12:13	of the money that was **b** *into* the house of	935
12:16	sin money was not **b** *into* the house of	935
14:20	they **b** him on horses: and he was buried	5375
16:14	he **b** also the brasen altar, which *was*	7126
17: 4	**b** no present to the king of Assyria, as *he*	5927
17: 7	which had **b** them **up** out of the land of	5927
17:24	the king of Assyria **b** *men* from Babylon,	935
17:27	Carry thither one of the priests whom ye **b**	1540
17:36	who **b** you **up** out of the land of Egypt	5927
19:25	have I **b** it **to pass**, that thou shouldest	7725
20:11	he **b** the shadow ten degrees backward,	7725
20:20	and a conduit, and **b** water into the city,	935
22: 4	that he may sum the silver which is **b** *into*	935
22: 9	and **b** the king word **again**, and said,	7725
22:20	And they **b** the king word **again**.	7725
23: 6	he **b** out the grove from the house of	3318
23: 8	**b** all the priests out of the cities of Judah,	935
23:30	**b** him *to* Jerusalem, and buried him in his	935
24:16	even them the king of Babylon **b** captive	935
25: 6	**b** him **up** to the king of Babylon to Riblah;	5927
25:20	**b** them to the king of Babylon to Riblah:	1980

1Ch
5:26	**b** them unto Halah, and Habor, and Hara,	935
10:12	**b** them to Jabesh, and buried their bones	935
11:18	by the gate, and took *it*, and **b** *it* to David:	935
11:19	with *the jeopardy* of their lives they **b** it.	935
12:40	**b** bread on asses, and on camels,	935
13:13	So David **b** not the ark *home* to himself to	5493
14:17	the LORD **b** the fear of him upon all	5414
15:28	all Israel **b up** the ark of the covenant	5927
16: 1	So they **b** the ark of God, and set it in	935
17: 5	the day that I **b up** Israel unto this day;	5927
17:16	mine house, that thou hast **b** me hitherto?	935
18: 2	became David's servants, and **b** gifts.	5375
18: 6	became David's servants, and **b** gifts.	5375
18: 7	of Hadarezer, and **b** them *to* Jerusalem.	935
18: 8	of Hadarezer, **b** David very much brass,	3947
18:11	the gold that he **b** from all *these* nations;	5375
20: 2	he **b** also exceeding much spoil *out of*	3318
20: 3	he **b** out the people that *were* in it,	3318
22: 4	of Tyre **b** much cedar wood to David.	935

2Ch
1: 4	the ark of God had David **b up** from	5927
1:16	Solomon had horses **b out** of Egypt,	4161
1:17	**b forth** out of Egypt a chariot for six	3318
1:17	**b out** *horses* for all the kings of	3318
5: 1	Solomon **b in** *all the things* that David	935
5: 5	they **b up** the ark, and the tabernacle of	5927
5: 7	the priests **b in** the ark of the covenant of	935
6: 5	the day that I **b forth** my people out	3318
7:22	which **b** them **forth** out of the land of	3318
7:22	hath he **b** all this evil upon them.	935
8:11	Solomon **b up** the daughter of Pharaoh	5927
8:18	of gold, and **b** *them* to king Solomon.	935
9:10	which **b** gold from Ophir, brought algum	935
9:10	**b** algum trees and precious stones.	935
9:12	*that* which she had **b** unto the king.	935
9:14	*that which* chapmen and merchants **b**.	935
9:14	governors of the country **b** gold and silver	935
9:24	they **b** every man his present, vessels of	935
9:28	they **b** unto Solomon horses out of Egypt,	3318
10: 8	the young men that were **b up** with him,	1431
10:10	the young men that were **b up** with him	1431
12:11	and **b** them **again** into the guard chamber.	7725
13:18	Thus the children of Israel were **b under**	3665
15:11	the spoil *which* they had **b**, seven hundred	935
15:18	he **b** *into* the house of God *the things*	935
16: 2	Asa **b out** silver and gold out of	3318
17: 5	all Judah **b** to Jehoshaphat presents;	5414
17:11	Also *some* of the Philistines **b** Jehoshaphat	935
17:11	the Arabians **b** him flocks, seven thousand	935
19: 4	**b** them **back** unto the LORD God of their	7725
22: 9	he *was* hid in Samaria,) and **b** him to Jehu:	935
23:11	they **b out** the king's son, and put upon	3318
23:14	Jehoiada the priest **b out** the captains of	3318
23:20	**b down** the king from the house of	3381
24:10	and **b in**, and cast into the chest,	935
24:11	that at *what* time the chest was **b** unto	935
24:14	when they had finished *it*, they **b** the rest	935
25:12	**b** them unto the top of the rock,	935
25:14	that he **b** the gods of the children of Seir,	935
25:23	**b** him *to* Jerusalem, and brake down the	935
25:28	they **b** him upon horses, and buried him	5375
28: 5	of them captives, and **b** *them to* Damascus.	935
28: 8	spoil from them, and **b** the spoil to Samaria.	935
28:15	**b** them *to* Jericho, the city of palm trees,	935
28:19	For the LORD **b** Judah **low** because	3665
28:27	they **b** him not into the sepulchres of	935
29: 4	he **b** in the priests and the Levites,	935
29:16	**b out** all the uncleanness that they found	3318
29:21	they **b** seven bullocks, and seven rams,	935

2Ch
29:23	they **b forth** the he goats for the sin	5066
29:31	the congregation **b in** sacrifices and	935
29:32	which the congregation **b**, was threescore	935
30:15	**b in** the burnt offerings *into* the house of	935
31: 5	the children of Israel **b in abundance**	7235
31: 5	tithe of all *things* **b** they in abundantly.	935
31: 6	they also **b in** the tithe of oxen and sheep,	935
31:12	**b in** the offerings and the tithes and	935
32:23	many **b** gifts unto the LORD to Jerusalem,	935
32:30	**b it straight** down to the west *side* of	3474
33:11	Wherefore the LORD **b** upon them	935
33:13	**b** him **again** *to* Jerusalem into his	7725
34: 9	they delivered the money that was **b** *into*	935
34:14	when they **b out** the money that was	3318
34:14	they **b** brought out the money that was **b**	935
34:16	the king word **back** again, saying,	7725
34:28	So they **b** the king word **again**.	7725
35:24	they **b** him *to* Jerusalem, and he died,	1980
36:10	sent, and **b** him to Babylon,	935
36:17	Therefore he **b** upon them the king of	5927
36:18	of his princes; all *these* he **b** *to* Babylon.	935

Ezr
1: 7	Also Cyrus the king **b forth** the vessels of	3318
1: 7	which Nebuchadnezzar had **b forth** out	3318
1:11	were **b up** from Babylon unto Jerusalem.	5927
4: 2	king of Assur, which **b** us **up** hither.	5927
4:10	the great and noble Asnappar **b over**,	1541
5:14	**b** them into the temple of Babylon,	2987
6: 5	**b** unto Babylon, be restored,	2987
6: 5	**b** *again* unto the temple which *is* at	1946
8:18	the good hand of our God upon us they **b**	935

Ne
4:15	God had **b** their counsel to **nought**,	6565
5: 5	of our daughters are **b** unto **bondage**	3533
8: 2	Ezra the priest **b** the law before	935
8:16	and **b** *them*, and made themselves booths,	935
9:18	*is* thy God that **b** thee **up** out of Egypt,	5927
9:33	thou *art* just in all that is **b** upon us;	935
12:31	I **b up** the princes of Judah upon the wall,	5927
13: 9	thither **b** I **again** the vessels of the house	7725
13:12	**b** all Judah the tithe of the corn and the	935
13:15	they **b** *into* Jerusalem on the sabbath	935
13:16	which **b** fish, and all *manner of* ware,	935
13:19	*that* there should no burden be **b in** on	935

Est
1:17	Vashti the queen to be **b** in before him,	935
2: 7	he **b up** Hadassah, that *is*, Esther,	539
2: 8	that Esther was **b** *also* unto the king's	3947
2:20	like as when she was **b up** with him.	545
6: 8	Let the royal apparel be **b** which the king	935
6:11	**b** him **on horseback** through the street	7392
9:11	Shushan the palace was **b** before the king.	935

Job
4:12	Now a thing was **secretly b** to me,	1589
10:18	hast thou **b** me **forth** out of the womb?	3318
14:21	they are **b low**, but he perceiveth *it* not	6819
21:30	they shall be **b forth** to the day of wrath.	2986
21:32	Yet shall he be **b** to the grave,	2986
24:24	for a little while, but are gone and **b low**,	4355
31:18	(For from my youth he was **b up** *with* me,	1431
42:11	all the evil that the LORD had **b** upon him:	935

Ps
7:14	conceived mischief, and **b forth** falsehood.	3205
18:19	He **b** me **forth** also into a large place;	3318
20: 8	They are **b down** and fallen: but we are	3766
22:15	and thou hast **b** me into the dust of death.	8239
30: 3	thou hast **b up** my soul from the grave:	5927
35: 4	and **b to confusion** that devise my hurt.	2659
35:26	**b to confusion** together that rejoice at	2659
40: 2	He **b** me **up** also out of a horrible pit,	5927
45:14	She shall be **b** unto the king in raiment of	2986
45:14	that follow her *shall be* **b** unto thee.	935
45:15	gladness and rejoicing shall they be **b**:	2986
71:24	for they are **b unto shame**, that seek my	2659
73:19	How are they *b* into desolation, as *in a*	NIH
78:16	He **b** streams also **out** of the rock,	3318
78:26	and by his power he **b in** the south wind.	5090
78:54	he **b** them to the border of his sanctuary,	935
78:71	young he **b** him to feed Jacob his people,	935
79: 8	prevent us: for we are **b** very **low**.	1809
80: 8	Thou hast **b** a vine **out** of Egypt: thou	5265
81:10	which **b** thee out of the land of Egypt:	5927
85: 1	thou hast **b back** the captivity of Jacob.	7725
89:40	thou hast **b** his strong holds to ruin.	7760
90: 2	Before the mountains were **b forth**,	3205
105:30	Their land **b forth** frogs in **abundance**,	8317
105:37	He **b** them **forth** also with silver and gold	3318
105:40	he **b** quails, and satisfied them *with*	935
105:43	he **b forth** his people with joy,	935
106:42	they were **b into subjection** under their	3665
106:43	were **b low** for their iniquity.	4355
107:12	Therefore he **b down** their heart with	3665
107:14	**b** them **out** of darkness and the shadow	3318
107:39	minished and **b low** through oppression,	7817
116: 6	simple: I was **b low**, and he helped me.	1809
136:11	**b out** Israel from among them: for his	3318
142: 6	Attend unto my cry; for I am **b** very **low**:	1809

Pr
6:26	woman *a man is* **b** to a piece of bread:	NIH
8:24	*there were* no depths, I was **b forth**;	2342
8:25	settled, before the hills was I **b forth**;	2342
8:30	*as* one **b up** *with him*: and I was daily	525

Ecc
12: 4	all the daughters of musick shall be **b low**;	7817

SS
1: 4	the king hath **b** me *into* his chambers:	935
1: 4	He **b** me to the banqueting house,	935
3: 4	until I had **b** him into my mother's house,	935
8: 2	there thy mother **b** thee **forth**: there she	2254
8: 5	there she **b** *thee* **forth** *that* bare thee.	2254

Isa
1: 2	I have nourished and **b up** children,	7311
2:12	that is lifted up; and he shall be **b low**:	8213
5: 2	forth grapes, and it **b forth** wild grapes.	6213

Isa
5: 4	bring forth grapes, **b** it **forth** wild grapes?	6213
5:15	the mean man shall be **b down**,	7817
14:11	Thy pomp is **b down** *to* the grave,	3381
14:15	Yet thou shalt be **b down** to hell,	3381
15: 1	of Moab is laid waste, *and* **b to silence**;	1820
15: 1	of Moab is laid waste, *and* **b to silence**;	1820
18: 7	In that time shall the present be **b** unto	2986
21:14	inhabitants of the land of Tema **b**	857+7125
23:13	up the palaces thereof; and he **b** it to ruin.	7760
25: 5	branch of the terrible ones shall be **b low**.	6030
26:18	in pain, we have as it were **b forth** wind;	3205
29: 4	thou shalt be **b down**, *and* shalt speak	8213
29:20	For the terrible one is **b** to nought,	656
37:26	have I **b** it **to pass**, that thou shouldest	935
43:14	have **b down** all their nobles,	3381
43:23	Thou hast not **b** me the small cattle of thy	935
45:10	or to the woman, What hast thou **b forth**?	2342
48:15	I have **b** him, and he shall make his way	935
49:21	who hath **b up** these? Behold, I was left	1431
51:18	all the sons *whom* she hath **b forth**;	3205
51:18	hand of all the sons *that* she hath **b up**.	1431
53: 7	he is **b** as a lamb to the slaughter, and as	2986
59:16	therefore his arm **b salvation** unto him;	3467
60:11	Gentiles, *and that their kings may be* **b**.	5090
62: 9	they that have **b** it **together** shall drink	6908
63: 5	mine own arm **b salvation** unto me;	3467
63:11	Where *is* he that **b** them **up** out of	5927
66: 7	Before she travailed, she **b forth**; before	3205
66: 8	as Zion travailed, she **b forth** her children.	3205

Jer
2: 6	Where *is* the LORD that **b** us **up** out of	5927
2: 7	I **b** you into a plentiful country, to eat	935
2:27	and to a stone, Thou hast **b** me **forth**:	3205
7:22	day that I **b** them out of the land of Egypt,	3318
10: 9	Silver spread into plates is **b** from Tarshish,	935
11: 4	I **b** them **forth** out of the land of Egypt,	3318
11: 7	that I **b** them **up** out of the land of Egypt,	5927
11:19	a lamb *or* an ox *that* is **b** to the slaughter;	2986
15: 8	I have **b** upon them against the mother of	935
16:14	that **b up** the children of Israel out of	5927
16:15	that **b up** the children of Israel from	5927
20: 3	that Pashur **b forth** Jeremiah out of	3318
20:15	Cursed *be* the man who **b tidings** to my	1319
23: 7	which **b up** the children of Israel out of	5927
23: 8	which **b up** and which led the seed of	5927
24: 1	Jerusalem, and had **b** them *to* Babylon.	935
26:23	and **b** him unto Jehoiakim the king;	935
27:16	now shortly be **b again** from Babylon:	7725
32:21	hast **b forth** thy people Israel out of	3318
32:42	Like as I have **b** all this great evil upon	935
34:11	**b** them **into subjection** for servants and	3533
34:13	I **b** them **forth** out of the land of Egypt,	3318
34:16	and **b** them **into subjection**, to be	3533
35: 4	And I **b** them *into* the house of the LORD,	935
37:14	took Jeremiah, and **b** him to the princes.	935
38:22	**b forth** to the king of Babylon's princes,	3318
39: 5	they **b** him **up** to Nebuchadnezzar king	5927
40: 3	Now the LORD hath **b** *it*, and	935
41:16	whom he had **b again** from Gibeon:	7725
44: 2	Ye have seen all the evil that I have **b** upon	935
50:25	hath **b forth** the weapons of his	3318
51:10	The LORD hath **b forth** our	3318
52:26	**b** them to the king of Babylon to Riblah.	1980
52:31	of Judah, and **b** him **forth** out of prison;	3318

La
2: 2	he hath **b** *them* **down** to the ground:	5060
2:22	and **b up** hath mine enemy consumed.	7235
3: 2	**b** *me into* darkness, but not *into* light.	1980
4: 5	they that were **b up** in scarlet embrace	539

Eze
8: 3	**b** me in the visions of God to Jerusalem,	935
8: 7	he **b** me to the door of the court;	935
8:14	he **b** me to the door of the gate of	935
8:16	he **b** me into the inner court of the LORD's	935
11: 1	**b** me unto the east gate of the LORD's	935
11:24	**b** me in vision by the Spirit of God into	935
12: 7	I **b forth** my stuff by day, as stuff for	3318
12: 7	I **b** it **forth** in the twilight, *and* I bare *it*	3318
14:22	be left a remnant that shall be **b forth**,	3318
14:22	the evil that I have **b** upon Jerusalem,	935
14:22	*even* concerning all that I have **b** upon it.	935
17: 6	**b** forth branches, and shot forth sprigs.	6213
17:24	the LORD have **b down** the high tree,	8213
19: 3	she **b up** one of her whelps: it became a	5927
19: 4	they **b** him with chains unto the land of	935
19: 9	and **b** him to the king of Babylon:	935
19: 9	they **b** him into holds, that his voice	935
20:10	of Egypt, and **b** them into the wilderness.	935
20:14	the heathen, in whose sight I **b** them **out**.	3318
20:22	heathen, in whose sight I **b** them **forth**.	3318
20:28	*For* when I had **b** them into the land,	935
21: 7	behold, it cometh, and shall be **b to pass**,	1961
23: 8	Neither left her whoredoms *b* from	NIH
23:27	thy whoredom *b* from the land of Egypt:	NIH
23:42	with the men of the common sort *were* **b**	935
27: 6	*of* ivory, *b* out of the isles of Chittim.	NIH
27:15	**b** thee *for* a present horns of ivory	7725
27:26	Thy rowers have **b** thee into great waters:	935
29: 5	shalt not be **b together**, nor gathered:	622
30:11	the nations, *shall be* **b** to destroy the land:	935
31:18	yet shalt thou be **b down** with the trees	3381
34: 4	neither have ye **b again** that which was	7725
37:13	and **b** you **up** out of your graves,	5927
38: 8	the land *that is* **b back** from the sword,	7725
38: 8	it is **b forth** out of the nations,	3318
39:27	I have **b** them **again** from the people,	7725
40: 1	the LORD was upon me, and **b** me thither.	935
40: 2	In the visions of God **b** he me into the land	935

B

Eze 40: 3 he **b** me thither, and behold, *there was* a 935
40: 4 shew *them* unto thee art thou **b** hither: 935
40:17 Then he he me into the outward court, 935
40:24 After that he **b** me toward the south, 1980
40:28 he **b** me to the inner court by the south 935
40:32 he **b** me into the inner court toward the 935
40:35 he **b** me to the north gate, and measured 935
40:48 he **b** me to the porch of the house, 935
40:49 he *he* **b** me by the steps whereby they went NIH
41: 1 Afterward he **b** me to the temple, 935
42: 1 he **b** me **forth** into the utter court, 3318
42: 1 he **b** me into the chamber that *was* over 935
42:15 he **b** me **forth** toward the gate whose 3318
43: 1 Afterward he **b** me to the gate, *even* 1980
43: 5 took me up, and **b** me into the inner court; 935
44: 1 he **b** me **back** the way of the gate of 7725
44: 4 **b** he me the way of the north gate before 935
44: 7 In that ye have **b** *into my sanctuary* 935
46:19 After, he **b** me through the entry, which 935
46:21 Then he **b** me **forth** into the utter court, 3318
47: 1 Afterward he **b** me **again** unto the door 7725
47: 2 **b** he me **out** *of* the way of the gate 3318
47: 3 and he **b** me through the waters; 5674
47: 4 a thousand, and **b** me through the waters; 5674
47: 4 measured a thousand, and **b** me **through;** 5674
47: 6 hast thou seen *this?* Then he **b** me, 1980
47: 8 *which* being **b** forth into the sea, 3318
Da 1: 2 he **b** the vessels *into* the treasure house 935
1: 9 Now God had **b** Daniel into favour and 5414
1:18 prince of the eunuchs **b** them in before 935
2:25 **b** in Daniel before the king in haste, 5954
3:13 Then they **b** these men before the king. 858
5: 3 they **b** the golden vessels that were taken 858
5:13 was Daniel **b** in before the king. *And* 5954
5:13 whom the king my father **b** out of Jewry? 858
5:15 been **b** in before me, that they should 5954
5:23 they have **b** the vessels of his house before 858
6:16 they **b** Daniel, and cast *him* into the den 858
6:17 a stone was **b**, and laid upon the mouth of 858
6:18 neither were instruments of musick **b** 5954
6:24 **b** those men which had accused Daniel, 858
7:13 of days, and they **b** him **near** before him. 7127
9:14 watched upon the evil, and **b** it upon us: 935
9:15 hast **b** thy people **forth** out of the land 3318
11: 6 they that **b** her, and he that begat her, 935
Hos 12:13 by a prophet the Lᴏʀᴅ **b** Israel out of 5927
Am 2:10 Also I **b** you **up** from the land of Egypt, 5927
3: 1 against the whole family which I **b up** 5927
9: 7 Have not I **b up** Israel out of the land of 5927
Ob 1: 7 the men of thy confederacy have **b** thee 7971
Jnh 2: 6 hast thou **b up** my life from corruption, 5927
Mic 5: 3 *that* she which travaileth hath **b forth:** 3205
6: 4 For I **b** thee **up** out of the land of Egypt, 5927
Na 2: 7 shall be **b up**, and her maids *shall* lead 5927
Hag 1: 9 when ye **b** it home, I did blow upon it. 935
2:19 and the olive tree, hath not **b forth:** 5375
Zec 10:11 the pride of Assyria shall be **b down**, 3381
Mal 1:13 ye **b** *that which was* torn, and the lame, 935
1:13 lame, and the sick; thus ye **b** an offering: 935
Mt 1:12 And after they were **b** to Babylon, 3350
1:25 And knew her not till she had **b forth** her 5088
4:24 they **b** unto him all sick people that were 4374
8:16 **b** unto him many *that were* possessed 4374
9: 2 they **b** to him a man sick of the palsy, 4374
9:32 they **b** to him a dumb man possessed 4374
10:18 ye shall be **b** before governors and kings 71
11:23 unto heaven, shalt be **b down** to hell: 2601
12:22 Then was **b** unto him one possessed with 4374
12:25 divided against itself is **b to desolation;** 2049
13: 8 fell into good ground, and **b forth** fruit, 1325
13:26 and **b forth** fruit, then appeared the tares 4160
14:11 And his head was **b** in a charger, 5342
14:11 to the damsel: and she **b** *it* to her mother. 5342
14:35 and **b** unto him all that were diseased; 4374
16: 8 because ye have **b** no bread? 2983
17:16 And I **b** him to thy disciples, 4374
18:24 begun to reckon, one was **b** unto him, 4374
19:13 were there **b unto** him little children, 4374
21: 7 the ass, and the colt, and put on them 71
22:19 And they **b** unto him a penny. 4374
25:20 five talents came and **b** other five talents, 4374
27: 3 **b again** the thirty pieces of silver to the 654
Mk 1:32 they **b** unto him all that were diseased, 5342
4: 8 and **b forth**, some thirty, and some sixty, 5342
4:21 Is a candle **b** to be put under a bushel, or 2064
4:29 But when the fruit is **b forth**, 3860
6:27 and commanded his head to be **b**: 5342
6:28 And **b** his head in a charger, and gave it to 5342
9:17 Master, I have **b** unto thee my son, 5342
9:20 they **b** him unto him: and when he saw 5342
10:13 they **b** young children to him, that he 4374
10:13 *his* disciples rebuked those that **b** them. 4374
11: 7 they **b** the colt to Jesus, and cast their 71
12:16 And they **b** it. And he saith unto them, 5342
13: 9 and ye shall be **b** before rulers and 2476
Lk 1:57 be delivered; and she **b forth** a son. 1080
2: 7 And she **b forth** her firstborn son, 5088
2:22 they **b** him to Jerusalem, to present *him* 321
2:27 when the parents **b** in the child Jesus, 1521
3: 5 every mountain and hill shall be **b low**; 5013
4: 9 he **b** him to Jerusalem, and set him on a 71
4:16 to Nazareth, where he had been **b up**: 5142
4:40 sick with divers diseases **b** them unto him; 71
5:11 And when they had **b** *their* ships to land, 2609
5:18 men **b** in a bed a man which was taken 5342

Lk 7:37 **b** an alabaster box of ointment, 2865
10:34 **b** him to an inn, and took care of him. 71
11:17 divided against itself is **b to desolation;** 2049
12:16 of a certain rich man **b** forth plentifully: 2164
18:15 And they **b** unto him also infants, that he 4374
18:40 and commanded him to be **b** unto him: 71
19:35 And they **b** him to Jesus: and they cast 71
21:12 being **b** before kings and rulers for my 71
22:54 **b** him **into** the high priest's house. 1521
23:14 unto them, Ye have **b** this man unto me, 4374
Jn 1:42 And he **b** him to Jesus. And when Jesus 71
4:33 Hath any man **b** him *ought* to eat? 5342
7:45 said unto them, Why have ye not **b** him? 71
8: 3 Pharisees **b** unto him a woman taken in 71
9:13 They **b** to the Pharisees him that aforetime 71
18:16 her that kept the door, and **b** in Peter. 1521
19:13 he **b** Jesus forth, and sat down in 71
19:39 and **b** a mixture of myrrh and aloes, 5342
Ac 4:34 **b** the prices of *the things* that were sold, 5342
4:37 sold *it*, and **b** the money, and laid *it* at 5342
5: 2 also being privy *to it*, and **b** a certain part, 5342
5:15 Insomuch that *they* **b forth** the sick into 1627
5:19 prison doors, and **b** them **forth**, and said, 1806
5:21 and sent to the prison to have them **b**. 5342
5:26 the officers, and **b** them without violence: 71
5:27 And when they had **b** them, they set *them* 71
5:36 were scattered, and **b** to nought. 1096
6:12 and caught him, and **b** *him* to the council, 71
7:36 He **b** them **out**, after that he had shewed 1806
7:40 which **b** us **out** of the land of Egypt, 1806
7:45 also our fathers that came after **b** in 1521
9: 8 the hand, and **b** *him* **into** Damascus. 1521
9:27 and **b** *him* to the apostles, and declared 71
9:30 they **b** him **down** to Cesarea, and sent 2609
9:39 they **b** him into the upper chamber: 321
11:26 he had found him, he **b** him unto Antioch. 71
12: 6 when Herod would have **b** him **forth**, 4254
12:17 the Lord had **b** him **out** of the prison. 1806
13: 1 which had been **b up** with Herod 4939
13:17 and with a high arm **b** he them **out** of it. 1806
14:13 **b** oxen and garlands unto the gates, 5342
15: 3 And being **b** on their **way** by the church, 4311
16:16 which **b** her masters much gain by 3930
16:20 And **b** them **to** the magistrates, saying, 4317
16:30 And **b** them out, and said, Sirs, what must 4254
16:34 And when he had **b** them into his house, 321
16:39 **b** *them* **out**, and desired *them* to depart 1806
17:15 And they that conducted Paul **b** him unto 71
17:19 and **b** him unto Areopagus, saying, 71
18:12 Paul, and **b** him to the judgment seat, 71
19:12 that from his body were **b** unto the sick 2018
19:19 used curious arts **b** their books **together**, 4851
19:24 **b** no small gain unto the craftsmen; 3930
19:37 For ye have **b** *hither* these men, *which are* 71
20:12 And they **b** the young man alive, and were 71
21: 5 *our way;* and *they* all **b** us **on** our way, 4311
21:16 and **b** *with them* one Mnason of Cyprus, 71
21:28 and further **b** Greeks also into 1521
21:29 that Paul had **b into** the temple.) 1521
22: 3 yet **b up** in this city at the feet of Gamaliel, 397
22:24 The chief captain commanded him to be **b** 71
22:30 **b** Paul **down**, and set *him* before them. 2609
23:18 and **b** *him* to the chief captain, and said, 71
23:28 I **b** him **forth** into their council: 2609
23:31 took Paul, and **b** him by night to Antipatris. 71
25: 6 judgment seat, commanded Paul to be **b**. 71
25:17 and commanded the man to be **b forth**. 71
25:18 **b** none accusation of *such things* as I 2018
25:23 at Festus' commandment Paul was **b forth**. 71
25:26 Wherefore I have **b** him **forth** before you, 4254
27:24 Paul; thou must be **b** before Cesar: 3936
Ro 15:24 to be **b** on my **way** thitherward you, 4311
1Co 6:12 I will not be **b** under the **power** of any. 1850
15:54 be **b** to **pass** the saying that is written, 1096
2Co 1:16 of you to be **b** on *my* **way** toward Judea. 4311
Gal 2: 4 because of false brethren **unawares b** in, 3920
1Th 3: 6 and **b us good tidings** of your faith and 2097
1Ti 5:10 if she have **b up children**, if she have 5044
6: 7 For we **b** nothing into *this* world, *and it is* 1533
2Ti 1:10 hath **b** life and immortality to **light** 5461
4: S Paul was **b** before Nero the second 3936
Heb 13:11 whose blood is **b** into the sanctuary by 1533
13:20 **b again** from the dead our Lord Jesus, 321
Jas 5:18 gave rain, and the earth **b forth** her fruit. 985
1Pe 1:13 to the end for the grace that is *to be* **b** 5342
2Pe 2:19 of the same is he **b in bondage**. 1402
Rev 12: 5 And she **b forth** a man child, who was to 5088
12:13 he persecuted the woman which **b forth** 5088

BROUGHTEST (13) [BRING]

Ex 32: 7 which thou **b** out of the land of Egypt, 5927
Nu 14:13 the Egyptians shall hear *it*, (for thou **b up** 5927
Dt 9:28 Lest the land whence thou **b** us **out** say, 3318
9:29 which thou **b** out by thy mighty power 3318
2Sa 5: 2 wast he that leddest out and **b** in Israel: 935
1Ki 8:51 which thou **b forth** out of Egypt, 3318
8:53 when thou **b** our fathers **out** of Egypt, 3318
1Ch 11: 2 *wast* he that leddest out and **b** in Israel: 935
Ne 9: 7 **b** him **forth** out of Ur of the Chaldees, 3318
9:15 **b forth** water for them out of the rock for 3318
9:23 **b** them into the land, *concerning* which 935
Ps 66:11 Thou **b** us into the net; thou laidst affliction 935
66:12 but thou **b** us **out** into a wealthy *place*. 3318

BROW (2) [EYEBROWS]

Isa 48: 4 thy neck *is* an iron sinew, and thy **b** brass: 4696
Lk 4:29 led him unto the **b** of the hill whereon 3790

BROWN (4)

Ge 30:32 all the **b** cattle among the sheep, 2345
30:33 the goats, and **b** amongst the sheep, 2345
30:35 all the **b** amongst the sheep, and gave 2345
30:40 and all the **b** in the flock of Laban; 2345

BRUISE See STRIPE; STRIPES

BRUISE (8) [BRUISED, BRUISES, BRUISING, BRUIT]

Ge 3:15 it shall **b** thy head, and thou shalt bruise 7779
3:15 bruise thy head, and thou shalt **b** his heel. 7779
Isa 28:28 of his cart, nor **b** it *with* his horsemen. 1854
53:10 Yet it pleased the Lᴏʀᴅ to **b** him; he hath 1792
Jer 30:12 Thy **b** *is* incurable, *and* thy wound is 7667
Da 2:40 all these, shall it break in pieces and **b**. 7490
Na 3:19 *There is* no healing of thy **b**; thy wound *is* 7667
Ro 16:20 And the God of peace shall **b** Satan under 4937

BRUISED (9) [BRUISE]

Lev 22:24 not offer unto the Lᴏʀᴅ that which is **b**, 4600
2Ki 18:21 thou trustest upon the staff of this **b** reed, 7533
Isa 28:28 Bread *corn* is **b**; because he will not ever 1854
42: 3 A **b** reed shall he not break, 7533
53: 5 *he was* **b** for our iniquities: 1792
Eze 23: 3 there they **b** the teats of their virginity, 6213
23: 8 they **b** the breasts of her virginity, 6213
Mt 12:20 A **b** reed shall he not break, 4937
Lk 4:18 the blind, to set at liberty *them that are* **b**, 2352

BRUISES (1) [BRUISE]

Isa 1: 6 *but* wounds, and **b**, and putrifying sores: 2250

BRUISING (2) [BRUISE]

Eze 23:21 **b** thy teats by the Egyptians for the paps 6213
Lk 9:39 and **b** him hardly departeth from him. 4937

BRUIT (2) [BRUISE]

Jer 10:22 the noise of the **b** is come, and a great 8052
Na 3:19 all that hear the **b** of thee shall clap 8088

BRUTE (2) [BRUTISH]

2Pe 2:12 But these, as natural **b** beasts, made to be 249
Jude 1:10 but what they know naturally, as **b** beasts, 249

BRUTISH (11) [BRUTE]

Ps 49:10 likewise the fool and the **b person** perish, 1198
92: 6 A man knoweth not; neither doth a fool 1198
94: 8 Understand, ye **b** among the people: 1197
Pr 12: 1 but he that hateth reproof *is* **b**. 1198
30: 2 Surely I *am* more **b** than *any* man, 1198
Isa 19:11 wise counsellers of Pharaoh is become **b**: 1197
Jer 10: 8 they are altogether **b** and foolish: 1197
10:14 Every man is **b** in *his* knowledge: 1197
10:21 the pastors are become **b**, and have not 1197
51:17 Every man is **b** by *his* knowledge; 1197
Eze 21:31 deliver thee into the hand of **b** men, 1197

BUBASTIS See PHI-BESETH

BUCKET (1) [BUCKETS]

Isa 40:15 the nations *are* as a drop of a **b**, 1805

BUCKETS (1) [BUCKET]

Nu 24: 7 He shall pour the water out of his **b**, 1805

BUCKLER (11) [BUCKLERS]

2Sa 22:31 he *is* a **b** to all them that trust in him. 4043
1Ch 5:18 able *to* bear **b** and sword, and to shoot 4043
12: 8 the battle, that could handle shield and **b**, 7420
Ps 18: 2 my **b**, and the horn of my salvation, 4043
18:30 he *is* a **b** to all those that trust in him. 4043
35: 2 Take hold of shield and **b**, and stand up 6793
91: 4 his truth *shall be thy* shield and **b**. 5507
Pr 2: 7 he *is* a **b** to them that walk uprightly. 4043
Jer 46: 3 Order ye the **b** and shield, and draw near 4043
Eze 23:24 *which* shall set against thee **b** and shield 6793
26: 8 against thee, and lift up the **b** against thee. 6793

BUCKLERS (5) [BUCKLER]

2Ch 23: 9 **b**, and shields, that *had been* king David's 4043
Job 15:26 *his* neck, upon the thick bosses of his **b**: 4043
SS 4: 4 whereon there hang a thousand **b**, 4043
Eze 38: 4 of *armour, even* a great company *with* **b** 6793
39: 9 both the shields and the **b**, the bows and 6793

BUD (11) [BUDDED, BUDS]

Job 14: 9 *Yet* through the sent of water it will **b**, 6524
38:27 to cause the **b** of the tender herb to spring 4161
Ps 132:17 There will I **make** the horn of David to **b**: 6779
SS 7:12 *and* the pomegranates **b forth:** 5340
Isa 18: 5 when the **b** is perfect, and the sour grape 6525
27: 6 Israel shall blossom and **b**, and fill the face 6524
55:10 the earth, and maketh it bring forth and **b**, 6779
61:11 For as the earth bringeth forth her **b**, 6780
Eze 16: 7 I have caused thee to multiply as the **b** of 6780
29:21 **cause** the horn of the house of Israel
to **b forth**, 6779
Hos 8: 7 the **b** shall yield no meal: if so be it yield, 6780

BUDDED (5) [BUD]

Ge 40:10 as though it **b**, *and* her blossoms shot 6524
Nu 17: 8 rod of Aaron for the house of Levi was **b**, 6524

B

SS	6:11	vine flourished, *and* the pomegranates **b**.	5340
Eze	7:10	the rod hath blossomed, pride hath **b**.	6524
Heb	9: 4	and Aaron's rod that **b**, and the tables of	985

BUDS (1) [BUD]

Nu	17: 8	brought forth **b**, and bloomed blossoms,	6525

BUFFET (2) [BUFFETED]

Mk	14:65	and to **b** him, and to say unto him,	2852
2Co	12: 7	the messenger of Satan to **b** me, lest I	2852

BUFFETED (3) [BUFFET]

Mt	26:67	Then did they spit in his face, and **b** him;	2852
1Co	4:11	and are **b**, and have no certain dwelling	2852
1Pe	2:20	glory *is it*, if, when ye be **b** for your faults,	2852

BUILD (162) [BUILDED, BUILDEDST, BUILDER, BUILDERS, BUILDEST, BUILDETH, BUILDING, BUILDINGS, BUILT, MASTERBUILDER]

Ge	11: 4	Go to, let us **b** us a city and a tower,	1129
	11: 8	all the earth: and they left off to **b** the city.	1129
Ex	20:25	stone, thou shalt not **b** it *of* hewn stone;	1129
Nu	23: 1	**B** me here seven altars, and prepare me	1129
	23:29	**B** me here seven altars, and prepare me	1129
	32:16	We will **b** sheepfolds here for our cattle,	1129
	32:24	**B** ye cities for your little ones, and folds	1129
Dt	20:20	thou shalt **b** bulwarks against the city that	1129
	25: 9	that will not **b** up his brother's house.	1129
	27: 5	there shalt thou **b** an altar unto the LORD	1129
	27: 6	Thou shalt **b** the altar of the LORD thy	1129
	28:30	thou shalt **b** a house, and thou shalt not	1129
Jos	22:26	Let us now prepare to **b** us an altar,	1129
	22:29	to **b** an altar for burnt offerings, for meat	1129
Jdg	6:26	**b** an altar unto the LORD thy God upon	1129
Ru	4:11	which two did **b** the house of Israel:	1129
1Sa	2:35	I will **b** him a sure house; and he shall	1129
2Sa	7: 5	thou **b** me a house for me to dwell in?	1129
	7: 7	Why **b** ye not me a house of cedar?	1129
	7:13	He shall **b** a house for my name, and I	1129
	7:27	thy servant, saying, I will **b** thee a house:	1129
	24:21	of thee, to **b** an altar unto the LORD,	1129
1Ki	2:36	**B** thee a house in Jerusalem,	1129
	5: 3	**b** a house unto the name of the LORD his	1129
	5: 5	I purpose to **b** a house unto the name of	1129
	5: 5	room, he shall **b** a house unto my name.	1129
	5:18	timber and stones to **b** the house.	1129
	6: 1	that he *began* to **b** the house of the LORD.	1129
	8:16	out of all the tribes of Israel to **b** a house,	1129
	8:17	was in the heart of David my father to **b** a	1129
	8:18	it was in thine heart to **b** a house	1129
	8:19	Nevertheless thou shalt not **b** the house;	1129
	8:19	he shall **b** the house unto my name.	1129
	9:15	for to **b** the house of the LORD, and his	1129
	9:19	that which Solomon desired to **b** in	1129
	9:24	had built for her: then did he **b** Millo.	1129
	11: 7	did Solomon **b** a high place for Chemosh,	1129
	11:38	**b** thee a sure house, as I built for David,	1129
	16:34	his days did Hiel the Bethelite **b** Jericho:	1129
1Ch	14: 1	and carpenters, to **b** him a house.	1129
	17: 4	Thou shalt not **b** me a house to dwell in:	1129
	17:10	thee that the LORD will **b** thee a house.	1129
	17:12	He shall **b** me a house, and I will stablish	1129
	17:25	hast told thy servant that *thou* wilt **b** him	1129
	21:22	that I may **b** an altar therein unto	1129
	22: 2	set masons to hew wrought stones to **b**	1129
	22: 6	charged him to **b** a house for the LORD	1129
	22: 7	it was in my mind to **b** a house unto	1129
	22: 8	thou shalt not **b** a house unto my name,	1129
	22:10	He shall **b** a house for my name;	1129
	22:11	and **b** the house of the LORD thy God,	1129
	22:19	and **b** ye the sanctuary of the LORD God,	1129
	28: 2	I *had* in mine heart to **b** a house	1129
	28: 3	Thou shalt not **b** a house for my name,	1129
	28: 6	he shall **b** my house and my courts:	1129
	28:10	for the LORD hath chosen thee to **b** a	1129
	29:16	all this store that we have prepared to **b**	1129
	29:19	do all *these things*, and to **b** the palace,	1129
2Ch	2: 1	Solomon determined to **b** a house for	1129
	2: 3	didst send me cedars to **b** him a house to	1129
	2: 4	I **b** a house to the name of the LORD my	1129
	2: 5	the house which I **b** *is* great: for great *is*	1129
	2: 6	who is able to **b** him a house, seeing	1129
	2: 6	am I then, that I should **b** him a house,	1129
	2: 9	for the house which I am about to **b** *shall*	1129
	2:12	that might **b** a house for the LORD,	1129
	3: 1	Solomon began to **b** the house of	1129
	3: 2	he began to **b** in the second *day* of	1129
	6: 5	**b** a house *in*, that my name might be there	1129
	6: 7	**b** a house for the name of the LORD God	1129
	6: 8	Forasmuch as it was in thine heart to **b** a	1129
	6: 9	thou shalt not **b** the house;	1129
	6: 9	he shall **b** the house for my name.	1129
	8: 6	that Solomon desired to **b** in Jerusalem,	1129
	14: 7	Let us **b** these cities, and make about	1129
	35: 3	the son of David king of Israel did **b**;	1129
	36:23	he hath charged me to **b** him a house in	1129
Ezr	1: 2	he hath charged me to **b** him a house at	1129
	1: 3	**b** the house of the LORD God of Israel,	1129
	1: 5	to go up to **b** the house of the LORD	1129
	4: 2	and said unto them, Let us **b** with you:	1129
	4: 3	You have nothing to do with us to **b** a	1129
	4: 3	we ourselves together will **b** unto	1129
	5: 2	began to **b** the house of God which *is* at	1124
	5: 3	hath commanded you to **b** this house,	1124
	5: 9	Who commanded you to **b** this house,	1124

Ezr	5:11	**b** the house that was builded these many	1124
	5:13	made a decree to **b** this house of God.	1124
	5:17	king to **b** this house of God at Jerusalem,	1124
	6: 7	the elders of the Jews **b** this house of God	1124
Ne	2: 5	to my fathers' sepulchres, that I may **b** it.	1129
	2:17	and let us **b** up the wall of Jerusalem,	1129
	2:18	they said, Let us rise up and **b**. So they	1129
	2:20	therefore we his servants will arise and **b**:	1129
	3: 3	the fish gate did the sons of Hassenaah **b**,	1129
	4: 3	said, Even *that* which they **b**, if a fox go	1129
	4:10	so that we are not able to **b** the wall.	1129
Ps	28: 5	shall destroy them, and not **b** them **up**.	1129
	51:18	unto Zion: **b** thou the walls of Jerusalem.	1129
	69:35	save Zion, and will **b** the cities of Judah:	1129
	89: 4	and **b** up thy throne to all generations.	1129
	102:16	When the LORD shall **b** up Zion, he shall	1129
	127: 1	Except the LORD **b** the house,	1129
	127: 1	the house, they labour in vain that **b** it:	1129
	147: 2	The LORD doth **b** up Jerusalem:	1129
Pr	24:27	in the field; and afterwards **b** thine house.	1129
Ecc	3: 3	time to break down, and a time to **b** *up*;	1129
SS	8: 9	we will **b** upon her a palace of silver:	1129
Isa	9:10	but we will **b** *with* hewn stones:	1129
	45:13	he shall **b** my city, and he shall let go my	1129
	58:12	*they that shall be* of thee shall **b** the old	1129
	60:10	the sons of strangers shall **b** up thy walls,	1129
	61: 4	shall **b** the old wastes, they shall raise	1129
	65:21	they shall **b** houses, and inhabit *them;*	1129
	65:22	They shall not **b**, and another inhabit;	1129
	66: 1	where *is* the house that ye **b** unto me?	1129
Jer	1:10	and to throw down, to **b**, and to plant.	1129
	18: 9	concerning a kingdom, to **b** and to plant	1129
	22:14	I will **b** me a wide house and	1129
	24: 6	I will **b** them, and not pull *them* down;	1129
	29: 5	**B** ye houses, and dwell *in them;* and	1129
	29:28	**b** ye houses, and dwell *in them;* and	1129
	31: 4	I will **b** thee, and thou shalt be built,	1129
	31:28	to **b**, and to plant, saith the LORD.	1129
	33: 7	to return, and will **b** them, as at the first.	1129
	35: 7	Neither shall ye **b** house, nor sow seed,	1129
	35: 9	Nor to **b** houses for us to dwell in:	1129
	42:10	will I **b** you, and not pull *you* down,	1129
Eze	4: 2	**b** a fort against it, and cast a mount	1129
	11: 3	say, *It is* not near; *let us* **b** houses:	1129
	21:22	gates, to cast a mount, *and* to **b** a fort.	1129
	28:26	shall **b** houses, and plant vineyards;	1129
	36:36	know that I the LORD **b** the ruined *places,*	1129
Da	9:25	to **b** Jerusalem unto the Messiah the	1129
Am	9:11	and I will **b** it as *in* the days of old:	1129
	9:14	they shall **b** the waste cities,	1129
Mic	3:10	They **b** up Zion with blood,	1129
Zep	1:13	they shall also **b** houses, but not inhabit	1129
Hag	1: 8	and bring wood, and **b** the house;	1129
Zec	5:11	To **b** it a house in the land of Shinar:	1129
	6:12	and he shall **b** the temple of the LORD:	1129
	6:13	Even he shall **b** the temple of the LORD;	1129
	6:15	and **b** in the temple of the LORD,	1129
	9: 3	Tyrus did **b** herself a strong hold,	1129
Mal	1: 4	we will return and **b** the desolate places;	1129
	1: 4	They shall **b**, but I will throw down;	1129
Mt	16:18	and upon this rock I will **b** my church;	3618
	23:29	because ye the tombs of the prophets,	3618
	26:61	temple of God, and to **b** it in three days.	3618
Mk	14:58	within three days I will **b** another made	3618
Lk	11:47	for ye **b** the sepulchres of the prophets,	3618
	11:48	killed them, and ye **b** their sepulchres.	3618
	12:18	I will pull down my barns, and **b** greater;	3618
	14:28	For which of you, intending to **b** a tower,	3618
	14:30	This man began to **b**, and was not able to	3618
Ac	7:49	what house will ye **b** me? saith the Lord:	3618
	15:16	and will **b** again the tabernacle of David,	456
	15:16	and I will **b** again the ruins thereof,	456
	20:32	which is able to **b** *you* up, and to give	2026
Ro	15:20	lest I should **b** upon another *man's*	3618
1Co	3:12	Now if any *man* **b** upon this foundation	2026
Gal	2:18	For if I **b** again the *things* which I	3618

BUILDED (49) [BUILD]

Ge	4:17	**b** a city, and called the name of the city,	1129
	8:20	Noah **b** an altar unto the LORD;	1129
	10:11	**b** Nineveh, and the city Rehoboth,	1129
	11: 5	the tower, which the children of men **b**.	1129
	12: 7	there **b** he an altar unto the LORD,	1129
	12: 8	there he **b** an altar unto the LORD,	1129
	26:25	he **b** an altar there, and called upon	1129
Ex	24: 4	**b** an altar under the hill, and twelve	1129
Nu	32:38	other names unto the cities which they **b**.	1129
Jos	22:16	in that ye have **b** you an altar, that ye	1129
1Ki	8:27	how much less this house that I have **b**?	1129
	8:43	which I have **b**, is called by thy name.	1129
	15:22	timber thereof, wherewith Baasha had **b**;	1129
2Ki	23:13	which Solomon the king of Israel had **b**	1129
1Ch	22: 5	the house *that is* to be **b** for the LORD	1129
Ezr	3: 2	and the altar of the God of Israel,	1129
	4: 1	**b** the temple unto the LORD God of	1129
	4:13	if this city be **b**, and the walls set up	1124
	4:16	if this city be **b** *again*, and the walls thereof	1124
	4:21	*that* this city be not **b**, until *another*	1124
	5: 8	which is **b** with great stones, and timber	1124
	5:11	build the house that was **b** these many	1124
	5:11	which a great king of Israel **b** and set up.	1124
	5:15	and let the house of God be **b** in his place.	1124
	6: 3	Let the house be **b**, the place where they	1124
	6:14	elders of the Jews **b**, and they prospered	1124
	6:14	they **b**, and finished *it*, according to	1124

Ne	3: 2	next unto him **b** the men of Jericho.	1129
	3: 2	next to them **b** Zaccur the son of Imri.	1129
	4: 1	that when Sanballat heard that we **b**	1129
	4:17	They which **b** on the wall, and they that	1129
	4:18	his sword girded by his side, and *so* **b**.	1129
	6: 1	heard that I had **b** the wall, and *that* there	1129
	7: 4	few therein, and the houses *were* not **b**.	1129
	12:29	for the singers had **b** them villages round	1129
Job	20:19	taken away a house which he **b** not;	1129
Ps	122: 3	Jerusalem *is* **b** as a city that is compact	1129
Pr	9: 1	Wisdom hath **b** her house, she hath hewn	1129
	24: 3	Through wisdom is a house **b**;	1129
Ecc	2: 4	I **b** me houses; I planted me vineyards:	1129
SS	4: 4	Thy neck *is* like the tower of David **b** for	1129
Jer	30:18	the city shall be **b** upon her own heap,	1129
La	3: 5	He hath **b** against me, and compassed *me*	1129
Eze	36:10	be inhabited, and the wastes shall be **b**:	1129
	36:33	in the cities, and the wastes shall be **b**.	1129
Lk	17:28	they sold, they planted, they **b**;	3618
Eph	2:22	In whom you also are **b** together for a	4925
Heb	3: 3	inasmuch as he who hath **b** the house	2680
	3: 4	For every house is **b** by some *man;* but	2680

BUILDEDST (1) [BUILD]

Dt	6:10	and goodly cities, which thou **b** not,	1129

BUILDER (1) [BUILD]

Heb	11:10	whose **b** and maker *is* God.	5079

BUILDERS (15) [BUILD]

1Ki	5:18	Solomon's **b** and Hiram's builders did	1129
	5:18	Hiram's **b** did hew *them*, and	1129
2Ki	12:11	they laid it out to the carpenters and **b**,	1129
	22: 6	**b**, and masons, and to buy timber and	1129
2Ch	34:11	and **b** gave they *it*, to buy hewn stone,	1129
Ezr	3:10	when the **b** laid the foundation of	1129
Ne	4: 5	have provoked *thee* to anger before the **b**.	1129
	4:18	For the **b**, every one had his sword girded	1129
Ps	118:22	The stone *which* the **b** refused is become	1129
Eze	27: 4	the seas, thy **b** have perfected thy beauty.	1129
Mt	21:42	The stone which the **b** rejected,	3618
Mk	12:10	The stone which the **b** rejected is become	3618
Lk	20:17	written, The stone which the **b** rejected,	3618
Ac	4:11	stone which was set at nought of you **b**,	3618
1Pe	2: 7	the stone which the **b** disallowed,	3618

BUILDEST (5) [BUILD]

Dt	22: 8	When thou **b** a new house, then thou	1129
Ne	6: 6	for which cause thou **b** the wall, that thou	1129
Eze	16:31	In that thou **b** thine eminent place in	1129
Mt	27:40	and **b** *it* in three days, save thyself.	3618
Mk	15:29	the temple, and **b** *it* in three days,	3618

BUILDETH (9) [BUILD]

Jos	6:26	that riseth up and **b** this city Jericho:	1129
Job	27:18	He **b** his house as a moth, and as a booth	1129
Pr	14: 1	Every wise woman **b** her house:	1129
Jer	22:13	Woe unto him that **b** his house by	1129
Hos	8:14	hath forgotten his Maker, and **b** temples;	1129
Am	9: 6	*It is* he that **b** his stories in the heaven,	1129
Hab	2:12	Woe to him that **b** a town with blood,	1129
1Co	3:10	the foundation, and another **b** thereon.	2026
	3:10	man take heed how he **b** thereupon.	2026

BUILDING (37) [BUILD]

Jos	22:19	in **b** you an altar beside the altar of	1129
1Ki	3: 1	until he had made an end of **b** his own	1129
	6: 7	the house, when it was **in b**, was built *of*	1129
	6: 7	heard in the house, while it was **in b**.	1129
	6:12	this house which thou art in **b**,	1129
	6:38	So was he seven years in **b** it.	1129
	7: 1	Solomon was **b** his own house thirteen	1129
	9: 1	when Solomon had finished the **b** of	1129
	15:21	Baasha heard *thereof*, that he left off **b**	1129
1Ch	28: 2	our God, and had made ready for the **b**:	1129
2Ch	3: 3	instructed for the **b** of the house of God.	1129
	16: 5	when Baasha heard *it*, that he left off **b** of	1129
	16: 6	thereof, wherewith Baasha was a **b**;	1129
Ezr	4: 4	people of Judah, and troubled them in **b**,	1129
	4:12	the rebellious and the bad city,	1124
	5: 4	the names of the men that make this **b**?	1147
	5:16	time even until now *hath it been* in **b**,	1124
	6: 8	these Jews for the **b** of this house of God:	1124
Ecc	10:18	By much slothfulness the **b** decayeth;	4746
Eze	17:17	casting up mounts, and **b** forts, to cut off	1129
	40: 5	so he measured the breadth of the **b**,	1146
	41:12	Now the **b** that *was* before the separate	1146
	41:12	the wall of the **b** *was* five cubits thick	1146
	41:13	separate place, and the **b**, with the walls	1140
	41:15	he measured the length of the **b** over	1146
	42: 1	which *was* before the **b** toward the north.	1146
	42: 5	and than the middlemost of the **b**.	1146
	42: 6	the **b** was straitened more than the lowest	NIH
	42:10	the separate place, and over against the **b**.	NIH
	46:23	*was* a row of **b** round about in them,	NIH
Jn	2:20	Forty and six years was this temple in **b**,	3618
1Co	3: 9	ye are God's husbandry, *ye are* God's **b**.	3619
2Co	5: 1	we have a **b** of God, a house not made	3619
Eph	2:21	In whom all the **b** fitly framed together	3619
Heb	9:11	with hands, that is to say, not of this **b**,	2937
Jude	1:20	**b** up yourselves on your most holy faith,	2026
Rev	21:18	And the **b** of the wall of it was *of* jasper:	1739

BUILDINGS (3) [BUILD]

Mt	24: 1	for to shew him the **b** of the temple.	3619

B

Mk 13:	1 manner of stones and what **b** *are here.*	3619
13:	2 said unto him, Seest thou these great **b**?	3619

BUILT (171) [BUILD]

Ge 13:18	and **b** there an altar unto the LORD.	1129
22:	9 Abraham **b** an altar there, and laid	1129
33:17	**b** him a house, and made booths for his	1129
35:	7 he **b** there an altar, and called the place	1129
Ex 1:11	they **b** for Pharaoh treasure cities, Pithom	1129
17:15	Moses **b** an altar, and called the name of	1129
32:	5 Aaron saw *it,* he **b** an altar before it;	1129
Nu 13:22	were. (Now Hebron was **b** seven years	1129
21:27	let the city of Sihon be **b** and prepared:	1129
23:14	seven altars, and offered a bullock and	1129
32:34	the children of Gad **b** Dibon, and Ataroth,	1129
32:37	the children of Reuben **b** Heshbon,	1129
Dt 8:12	hast **b** goodly houses, and dwelt *therein;*	1129
13:16	be a heap for ever; it shall not be **b** again.	1129
20:	5 man *is there* that hath **b** a new house,	1129
Jos 8:30	Joshua **b** an altar unto the LORD God of	1129
19:50	and he **b** the city, and dwelt therein.	1129
22:10	the half tribe of Manasseh **b** there an altar	1129
22:11	the half tribe of Manasseh have **b** an altar	1129
22:23	That we have **b** us an altar to turn from	1129
24:13	cities which ye **b** not, and ye dwell in	1129
Jdg 1:26	**b** a city, and called the name thereof Luz:	1129
6:24	Gideon **b** an altar there unto the LORD,	1129
6:28	was offered upon the altar that was **b.**	1129
18:28	And they **b** a city, and dwelt therein,	1129
21:	4 **b** there an altar, and offered burnt	1129
1Sa 7:17	and there he **b** an altar unto the LORD.	1129
14:35	Saul **b** an altar unto the LORD: the same	1129
14:35	the same was the first altar that he **b** unto	1129
2Sa 5:	9 David **b** round about from Millo and	1129
5:11	masons: and they **b** David a house.	1129
24:25	David **b** there an altar unto the LORD,	1129
1Ki 3:	2 there was no house **b** unto the name of	1129
6:	2 the house which king Solomon **b** for	1129
6:	5 the wall of the house he **b** chambers	1129
6:	7 was **b** *of* stone made ready *before it was*	1129
6:	9 So he **b** the house, and finished it;	1129
6:10	*then* he **b** chambers against all the house,	1129
6:14	So Solomon **b** the house, and finished it.	1129
6:15	he **b** the walls of the house within with	1129
6:16	he **b** twenty cubits on the sides of	1129
6:16	he even **b** *them* for it within, *even* for	1129
6:36	he **b** the inner court *with* three rows of	1129
7:	2 He **b** also the house of the forest of	1129
8:13	have **surely b** thee a house to dwell 1129+1129	
8:20	have **b** a house for the name of the LORD	1129
8:44	*toward* the house that I have **b** for thy	1129
8:48	the house which I have **b** for thy name:	1129
9:	3 hallowed this house, which thou hast **b,**	1129
9:10	when Solomon had **b** the two houses,	1129
9:17	Solomon **b** Gezer, and Beth-horon	1129
9:24	her house which *Solomon* had **b** for her:	1129
9:25	peace offerings upon the altar which he **b**	1129
10:	4 and the house that he had **b,**	1129
11:27	Solomon **b** Millo, *and* repaired the	1129
11:38	as I **b** for David, and will give Israel unto	1129
12:25	Jeroboam **b** Shechem in mount Ephraim,	1129
12:25	went out from thence, and **b** Penuel.	1129
14:23	For they also **b** them high places,	1129
15:17	**b** Ramah, that *he* might not suffer *any* to	1129
15:22	king Asa with them Geba of Benjamin,	1129
15:23	all that he did, and the cities which he **b,**	1129
16:24	**b** *on* the hill, and called the name of	1129
16:24	called the name of the city which he **b,**	1129
16:32	house of Baal, which he had **b** in Samaria.	1129
18:32	*with* the stones he **b** an altar in the name	1129
22:39	he made, and all the cities that he **b,**	1129
2Ki 14:22	He **b** Elath, and restored it to Judah,	1129
15:35	He **b** the higher gate of the house of	1129
16:11	Urijah the priest **b** an altar according to all	1129
16:18	covert for the sabbath that they had **b** in	1129
17:	9 they **b** them high places in all their cities,	1129
21:	3 For he **b** *up* again the high places which	1129
21:	4 And he **b** altars in the house of the LORD,	1129
21:	5 he **b** altars for all the host of heaven in	1129
25:	1 and they **b** forts against it round about.	1129
1Ch 6:10	the temple that Solomon **b** in Jerusalem:)	1129
6:32	until Solomon had **b** the house of	1129
7:24	who **b** Beth-horon the nether,	1129
8:12	and Shamed, who **b** Ono, and Lod,	1129
11:	8 he **b** the city round about, even from Millo	1129
17:	6 Why have ye not **b** me a house of cedars?	1129
21:26	David **b** there an altar unto the LORD,	1129
22:19	the house that is *to be* **b** to the name of	1129
2Ch 2:	1 have **b** a house of habitation for thee,	1129
6:10	have **b** the house for the name of	1129
6:18	how much less this house which I have **b**?	1129
6:33	may know that this house which I have **b**	1129
6:34	the house which I have **b** for thy name;	1129
6:38	toward the house which I have **b** for thy	1129
8:	1 wherein Solomon had **b** the house of	1129
8:	2 Solomon **b** them, and caused the children	1129
8:	4 he **b** Tadmor in the wilderness, and all	1129
8:	4 all the store cities, which he **b** in Hamath.	1129
8:	5 Also he **b** Beth-horon the upper,	1129
8:11	unto the house that he had **b** for her:	1129
8:12	which he had **b** before the porch,	1129
9:	3 Solomon, and the house that he had **b,**	1129
11:	5 and **b** cities for defence in Judah.	1129
11:	6 He **b** even Beth-lehem, and Etam,	1129

2Ch 14:	6 he **b** fenced cities in Judah: for the land	1129
14:	7 on every side. So they **b** and prospered.	1129
16:	1 Ramah, to the intent that *he* might let	1129
16:	6 and he **b** therewith Geba and Mizpah.	1129
17:12	he **b** in Judah castles, and cities of store.	1129
20:	8 have **b** thee a sanctuary therein for thy	1129
26:	2 He **b** Eloth, and restored it to Judah,	1129
26:	6 cities about Ashdod, and among	1129
26:	9 Moreover Uzziah **b** towers in Jerusalem	1129
26:10	Also he **b** towers in the desert,	1129
27:	3 He **b** the high gate of the house of	1129
27:	3 and on the wall of Ophel he **b** much.	1129
27:	4 Moreover he **b** cities in the mountains of	1129
27:	4 and in the forests he **b** castles and towers.	1129
32:	5 **b** up all the wall that was broken,	1129
33:	3 For he **b** again the high places which	1129
33:	4 Also he **b** altars in the house of	1129
33:	5 he **b** altars for all the host of heaven in	1129
33:14	after this he **b** a wall without the city	1129
33:15	all the altars that he had **b** in the mount	1129
33:19	the places wherein he **b** high places,	1129
Ne 3:	1 the priests, and they **b** the sheep gate;	1129
3:13	they **b** it, and set up the doors thereof,	1129
3:14	he **b** it, and set up the doors thereof,	1129
3:15	he **b** it, and covered it, and set up the	1129
4:	6 So **b** we the wall; and all the wall was	1129
7:	1 when the wall was **b,** and I had set up	1129
Job 3:14	which **b** desolate places for themselves;	1129
12:14	cannot be **b** *again:* he shutteth up a man,	1129
22:23	thou shalt be **b** up, thou shalt put away	1129
Ps 78:69	he **b** his sanctuary like high *palaces,* like	1129
89:	2 I have said, Mercy shall be **b** up for ever:	1129
Ecc 9:14	and **b** great bulwarks against it:	1129
Isa 5:	2 a tower in the midst of it, and also made	1129
25:	2 strangers to be no city; it shall never be **b.**	1129
44:26	Ye shall be **b,** and I will raise up	1129
44:28	even saying to Jerusalem, Thou shalt be **b;**	1129
Jer 7:31	they have **b** the high places of Tophet,	1129
12:16	shall they be **b** in the midst of my people.	1129
19:	5 They have **b** also the high places of Baal,	1129
31:	4 and thou shalt be **b,** O virgin of Israel:	1129
31:38	that the city shall be **b** to the LORD from	1129
32:31	my fury from the day that they **b** it even	1129
32:35	they **b** the high places of Baal, which *are*	1129
45:	4 *that* which I have **b** *will* I break down,	1129
52:	4 and **b** forts against it round about.	1129
Eze 13:10	one **b** up a wall, and lo, others daubed it	1129
16:24	thou hast also **b** unto thee an eminent	1129
16:25	Thou hast **b** thy high place at every head	1129
26:14	nets upon; thou shalt be **b** no more:	1129
Da 4:30	I have **b** for the house of the kingdom	1124
9:25	the street shall be **b** again, and the wall,	1129
Am 5:11	ye have **b** houses of hewn stone, but	1129
Mic 7:11	*In* the day that thy walls are *to be* **b,**	1129
Hag 1:	2 time that the LORD's house should be **b.**	1129
Zec 1:16	my house shall be **b** in it, saith the LORD	1129
8:	9 hosts was laid, that the temple might be **b.**	1129
Mt 7:24	wise man, which **b** his house upon a rock:	3618
7:26	which **b** his house upon the sand:	3618
21:33	**b** a tower, and let it out to husbandmen,	3618
Mk 12:	1 **b** a tower, and let it out to husbandmen,	3618
Lk 4:29	brow of the hill whereon their city was **b,**	3618
6:48	He is like a man which **b** a house, and	3618
6:49	like a man that without a foundation **b** a	3618
7:	5 our nation, and he hath **b** us a synagogue.	3618
Ac 7:47	But Solomon **b** him a house.	3618
1Co 3:14	work abide which he hath **b thereupon,**	2026
Eph 2:20	And are **b** upon the foundation of	2026
Col 2:	7 Rooted and **b** up in him, and stablished in	2026
Heb 3:	4 some *man;* but he that **b** all *things is* God.	2680
1Pe 2:	5 as lively stones, are **b** *up* a spiritual house,	3618

BUKKI (5)

Nu 34:22	of the children of Dan, **B** the son of Jogli.	1231
1Ch 6:	5 Abishua begat **B,** and Bukki begat Uzzi,	1231
6:	5 Abishua begat Bukki, and **B** begat Uzzi,	1231
6:51	his son, Uzzi his son, Zerahiah his son,	1231
Ezr 7:	4 of Zerahiah, the son of Uzzi, the son of **B,**	1231

BUKKIAH (2)

1Ch 25:	4 B, Mattaniah, Uzziel, Shebuel,	1232
25:13	The sixth *to* **B,** *he,* his sons,	1232

BUL (1)

1Ki 6:38	in the eleventh year, in the month **B,**	945

BULL (2) [BULLOCK, BULLOCK'S, BULLOCKS, BULLS]

Job 21:10	Their **b** gendereth, and faileth not;	7794
Isa 51:20	of all the streets, as a **wild b** *in* a net:	8377

BULLOCK (104) [BULL]

Ex 29:	1 Take one young **b,** and two rams	1241+6499
29:	3 the basket, with the **b** and the two rams.	6499
29:10	thou shalt cause a **b** to be brought before	6499
29:10	put their hands upon the head of the **b.**	6499
29:11	thou shalt kill the **b** before the LORD,	6499
29:12	thou shalt take of the blood of the **b,**	6499
29:14	the flesh of the **b,** and his skin, and his	6499
29:36	thou shalt offer every day a **b** *for* a sin	6499
Lev 1:	5 he shall kill the **b** before the LORD:	1121+1241
4:	3 a young **b** without blemish unto	1241+6499
4:	4 he shall bring the **b** unto the door of	6499
4:	4 and kill the **b** before the LORD.	6499
4:	5 shall pour all the blood of the **b** at	6499
4:	7 priest shall put *some* of the blood	6499

Lev 4:	8 he shall take off from it all the fat of the **b**	6499
4:10	As it was taken off from the **b** of	7794
4:11	the skin of the **b,** and all his flesh, with	6499
4:12	Even the whole **b** shall he carry forth	6499
4:14	shall offer a young **b** for the sin,	1241+6499
4:15	upon the head of the **b** before the LORD:	6499
4:15	and the **b** shall be killed before the LORD.	6499
4:20	he shall do with the **b** as he did with	6499
4:20	as he did with the **b** for a sin offering,	6499
4:21	shall carry forth the **b** without the camp,	6499
4:21	and burn him as he burned the first **b:**	6499
8:	2 a **b** *for* the sin offering, and two rams,	6499
8:14	he brought the **b** for the sin offering:	6499
8:14	the head of the **b** *for* the sin offering.	6499
8:17	**b,** and his hide, his flesh, and his dung,	6499
9:	4 Also a **b** and a ram for peace offerings,	7794
9:18	He slew also the **b** and the ram *for* a	7794
9:19	the fat of the **b** and of the ram, the rump,	7794
16:	3 with a young **b** for a sin offering,	1241+6499
16:	6 Aaron shall offer *his* **b** of the sin offering,	6499
16:11	Aaron shall bring the **b** of the sin offering,	6499
16:11	shall kill the **b** of the sin offering which *is*	6499
16:14	he shall take of the blood of the **b,**	6499
16:15	blood as he did with the blood of the **b,**	6499
16:18	shall take of the blood of the **b,** and of	6499
16:27	the **b** for the sin offering, and the goat for	6499
22:23	Either a **b** or a lamb that hath any thing	7794
22:27	When a **b,** or a sheep, or a goat, is brought	7794
23:18	and one young **b,** and two rams:	1241+6499
Nu 7:15	One young **b,** one ram, one lamb	1241+6499
7:21	One young **b,** one ram, one lamb	1241+6499
7:27	One young **b,** one ram, one lamb	1241+6499
7:33	One young **b,** one ram, one lamb	1241+6499
7:39	One young **b,** one ram, one lamb	1241+6499
7:45	One young **b,** one ram, one lamb	1241+6499
7:51	One young **b,** one ram, one lamb	1241+6499
7:57	One young **b,** one ram, one lamb	1241+6499
7:63	One young **b,** one ram, one lamb	1241+6499
7:69	One young **b,** one ram, one lamb	1241+6499
7:75	One young **b,** one ram, one lamb	1241+6499
7:81	One young **b,** one ram, one lamb	1241+6499
8:	8 let them take a young **b** with his	1241+6499
8:	8 another young **b** shalt thou take	1241+6499
15:	8 when thou preparest a **b** *for* a burnt	1121+1241
15:	9 shall he bring with a **b** a meat	1121+1241
15:11	Thus shall it be done for one **b,** or for one	7794
15:24	one young **b** for a burnt offering,	6499
23:	2 and Balaam offered on *every* altar a **b** and	6499
23:	4 I have offered upon *every* altar a **b** and	6499
23:14	and offered a **b** and a ram on *every* altar.	6499
23:30	and offered a **b** and a ram on *every* altar.	6499
28:12	meat offering, mingled with oil, for one **b;**	6499
28:14	shall be half a hin of wine unto a **b,**	6499
28:20	three tenth deals shall ye offer for a **b,**	6499
28:28	three tenth deals unto one **b,** two tenth	6499
29:	2 one young **b,** one ram,	1241+6499
29:	3 three tenth deals for a **b,** *and* two tenth	6499
29:	8 one young **b,** one ram,	1241+6499
29:	9 three tenth deals to a **b,** *and* two tenth	6499
29:14	three tenth deals unto every **b** of	6499
29:36	one **b,** one ram, seven lambs of the first	6499
29:37	and their drink offerings for the **b,**	6499
Dt 15:19	do no work with the firstling of thy **b,**	7794
17:	1 sacrifice unto the LORD thy God *any* **b,**	7794
33:17	His glory *is like* the firstling of his **b,**	7794
Jdg 6:25	said unto him, Take thy father's young **b,**	7794
6:25	even the second **b** of seven years old,	6499
6:26	take the second **b,** and offer a burnt	6499
6:28	the second **b** was offered upon the altar	6499
1Sa 1:25	slew a **b,** and brought the child to Eli.	6499
1Ki 18:23	let them choose one **b** for themselves,	6499
18:23	no fire *under:* and I will dress the other **b,**	6499
18:25	Choose you one **b** for yourselves,	6499
18:26	they took the **b** which was given them,	6499
18:33	cut the **b** in pieces, and laid *him* on	6499
2Ch 13:	9 consecrate himself with a young **b**	1241+6499
Ps 50:	9 I will take no **b** out of thy house, *nor* he	6499
69:31	than an ox *or* **b** that hath horns *and* hoofs.	6499
Isa 65:25	and the lion shall eat straw like the **b:**	1241
Jer 31:18	as a **b** unaccustomed *to the yoke;* turn	5695
Eze 43:19	a young **b** for a sin offering.	1241+6499
43:21	Thou shalt take the **b** also of the sin	6499
43:22	the altar, as they did cleanse *it* with the **b.**	6499
43:23	offer a young **b** without blemish;	6499
43:25	they shall also prepare a young **b,**	1241+6499
45:18	thou shalt take a young **b** without	1241+6499
45:22	for all the people of the land a **b** *for* a sin	6499
45:24	a meat offering *of* an ephah for a **b,**	6499
46:	6 *shall be* a young **b** without blemish, 1241+6499	
46:	7 an ephah for a **b,** and an ephah for a ram,	6499
46:11	the meat offering shall be an ephah to a **b,**	6499

BULLOCK'S (3) [BULL]

Lev 4:	4 shall lay his hand upon the **b** head,	6499
4:	5 priest that is anointed shall take of the **b**	6499
4:16	**b** blood to the tabernacle of	6499

BULLOCKS (45) [BULL]

Nu 7:87	oxen for the burnt offering *were* twelve **b,**	6499
7:88	peace offerings *were* twenty and four **b,**	6499
8:12	lay their hands upon the heads of the **b:**	6499
23:29	prepare me here seven **b** and seven rams.	6499
28:11	two young **b,** and one ram,	1241+6499
28:19	two young **b,** and one ram,	1241+6499
28:27	two young **b,** one ram, seven lambs 1241+6499	

B

Nu	29:13 thirteen young **b**, two rams,	1241+6499
	29:14 deals unto every bullock of the thirteen **b**,	6499
	29:17 day ye shall offer twelve young **b**,	1241+6499
	29:18 and their drink offerings for the **b**,	6499
	29:20 on the third day eleven **b**, two rams,	6499
	29:21 and their drink offerings for the **b**,	6499
	29:23 on the fourth day ten **b**, two rams,	6499
	29:24 and their drink offerings for the **b**,	6499
	29:26 on the fifth day nine **b**, two rams,	6499
	29:27 and their drink offerings for the **b**,	6499
	29:29 And on the sixth day eight **b**, two rams,	6499
	29:30 and their drink offerings for the **b**,	6499
	29:32 on the seventh day seven **b**, two rams,	6499
	29:33 and their drink offerings for the **b**,	6499
1Sa	1:24 with three **b**, and one ephah of flour,	6499
1Ki	18:23 Let them therefore give us two **b**;	6499
1Ch	15:26 that they offered seven **b** and seven rams.	6499
	29:21 even a thousand **b**, a thousand rams,	6499
2Ch	29:21 they brought seven **b**, and seven rams.	6499
	29:22 So they killed the **b**, and the priests	1241
	29:32 threescore and ten **b**, an hundred rams,	1241
	30:24 did give to the congregation a thousand **b**	6499
	30:24 gave to the congregation a thousand **b**	6499
	35: 7 of thirty thousand, and three thousand **b**:	1241
Ezr	6: 9 both young **b**, and rams, and lambs,	8450
	6:17 of this house of God an hundred **b**,	8450
	7:17 mayest buy speedily with this money **b**,	8450
	8:35 twelve **b** for all Israel, ninety and six rams,	6499
Job	42: 8 Therefore take unto you now seven **b** and	6499
Ps	51:19 then shall they offer **b** upon thine altar.	6499
	66:15 incense of rams; I will offer **b** with goats,	1241
Isa	1:11 I delight not in the blood of **b**, or of lambs,	6499
	34: 7 with them, and the **b** with the bulls;	6499
Jer	46:21 men are in the midst of her like fatted **b**;	5695
	50:27 Slay all her **b**; let them go down to	6499
Eze	39:18 rams, of lambs, and of goats, of **b**, all of	6499
	45:23 seven **b** and seven rams without blemish	6499
Hos	12:11 they sacrifice **b** in Gilgal; yea, their altars	7794

BULLS (10) [BULL]

Ge	32:15 forty kine, and ten **b**, twenty she asses,	6499
Ps	22:12 Many **b** have compassed me: strong bulls	6499
	22:12 strong **b** of Bashan have beset me round.	NIH
	50:13 Will I eat the flesh of **b**, or drink the blood	47
	68:30 the multitude of the **b**, with the calves of	47
Isa	34: 7 with them, and the bullocks with the **b**;	47
Jer	50:11 fat as the heifer at grass, and bellow as **b**;	47
	52:20 twelve brasen **b** that were under the bases,	1241
Heb	9:13 For if the blood of **b** and of goats,	5022
	10: 4 For it is not possible that the blood of **b**	5022

BULRUSH (1) [BULRUSHES, RUSH]

Isa	58: 5 is it to bow down his head as a **b**,	100

BULRUSHES (2) [BULRUSH, RUSH]

Ex	2: 3 took for him an ark of **b**, and daubed it	1573
Isa	18: 2 even in vessels of **b** upon the waters,	1573

BULWARKS (5)

Dt	20:20 thou shalt build **b** against the city that	4692
2Ch	26:15 men, to be on the towers and upon the **b**,	6438
Ps	48:13 Mark ye well her **b**, consider her palaces;	2430
Ecc	9:14 besieged it, and built great **b** against it:	4685
Isa	26: 1 salvation will God appoint for walls and **b**.	2426

BUNAH (1)

1Ch	2:25 and **B**, and Oren, and Ozem, and Ahijah.	946

BUNCH (1) [BUNCHES]

Ex	12:22 ye shall take a **b** of hyssop, and dip it in	92

BUNCHES (3) [BUNCH]

2Sa	16: 1 an hundred **b** of raisins, and an hundred	6778
1Ch	12:40 cakes of figs, and **b** of raisins, and wine,	6778
Isa	30: 6 their treasures upon the **b** of camels, to a	1707

BUNDLE (4) [BUNDLES]

Ge	42:35 every man's **b** of money was in his sack:	6872
1Sa	25:29 soul of my lord shall be bound in the **b**	6872
SS	1:13 A **b** of myrrh is my well-beloved unto me;	6872
Ac	28: 3 And when Paul had gathered a **b** of sticks,	4128

BUNDLES (2) [BUNDLE]

Ge	42:35 and their father saw the **b** of money,	6872
Mt	13:30 tares, and bind them in **b** to burn them:	1197

BUNNI (3)

Ne	9: 4 **B**, Sherebiah, Bani, and Chenani,	1138
	10:15 **B**, Azgad, Bebai,	1138
	11:15 the son of Hashabiah, the son of **B**;	1138

BURDEN (69) [BURDENED, BURDENS, BURDENSOME]

Ex	18:22 and they shall bear the **b** with thee.	NIH
	23: 5 of him that hateth thee lying under his **b**,	4853
Nu	4:15 These things are the **b** of the sons of	4853
	4:19 every one to his service and to his **b**:	4853
	4:31 this is the charge of their **b**, according to	4853
	4:32 the instruments of the charge of their **b**:	4853
	4:47 the service of the **b** in the tabernacle of	4853
	4:49 his service, and according to his **b**:	4853
	11:11 thou layest the **b** of all this people upon	4853
	11:17 they shall bear the **b** of the people with	4853
Dt	1:12 and your **b**, and your strife?	4853
2Sa	15:33 with me, then thou shalt be a **b** unto me:	4853
	19:35 thy servant be yet a **b** unto my lord	4853

2Ki	5:17 be given to thy servant two mules' **b** of	4853
	8: 9 forty camels' **b**, and came and stood	4853
	9:25 his father, the LORD laid this **b** upon him;	4853
2Ch	35: 3 it shall not be a **b** upon your shoulders:	4853
Ne	13:19 that there should no **b** be brought in on	4853
Job	7:20 against thee, so that I am a **b** to myself?	4853
Ps	38: 4 as a heavy **b** they are too heavy for me.	4853
	55:22 Cast thy **b** upon the LORD, and he shall	3053
	81: 6 I removed his shoulder from the **b**:	5447
Ecc	12: 5 the grasshopper shall be a **b**, and desire	5445
Isa	9: 4 For thou hast broken the yoke of his **b**,	5448
	10:27 that his **b** shall be taken away from off thy	5448
	13: 1 The **b** of Babylon, which Isaiah the son of	4853
	14:25 and his **b** depart from off their shoulders.	5448
	14:28 In the year that king Ahaz died was this **b**.	4853
	15: 1 The **b** of Moab. Because in the night Ar of	4853
	17: 1 The **b** of Damascus. Behold, Damascus is	4853
	19: 1 The **b** of Egypt. Behold, the LORD rideth	4853
	21: 1 The **b** of the desert of the sea.	4853
	21:11 The **b** of Dumah. He calleth to me out of	4853
	21:13 The **b** upon Arabia. In the forest in Arabia	4853
	22: 1 The **b** of the valley of vision. What aileth	4853
	22:25 the **b** that was upon it shall be cut off:	4853
	23: 1 The **b** of Tyre. Howl, ye ships of Tarshish;	4853
	30: 6 The **b** of the beasts of the south: into	4853
	30:27 with his anger, and the **b** thereof is heavy:	4858
	46: 1 they are a **b** to the weary beast.	4853
	46: 2 they could not deliver the **b**, but	4853
Jer	17:21 bear no **b** on the sabbath day,	4853
	17:22 Neither carry forth a **b** out of your houses	4853
	17:24 to bring in no **b** through the gates of this	4853
	17:27 not to bear a **b**, even entering in at the	4853
	23:33 saying, What is the **b** of the LORD?	4853
	23:33 thou shalt then say unto them, What **b**?	4853
	23:34 that shall say, The **b** of the LORD,	4853
	23:36 the **b** of the LORD ye mention no	4853
	23:36 for every man's word shall be his **b**;	4853
	23:38 sith ye say, The **b** of the LORD; therefore	4853
	23:38 The **b** of the LORD, and I have sent unto	4853
	23:38 Ye shall not say, The **b** of the LORD;	4853
Eze	12:10 This **b** concerneth the prince in Jerusalem	4853
Hos	8:10 they shall sorrow a little for the **b** of	4853
Na	1: 1 The **b** of Nineveh. The book of the vision	4853
Hab	1: 1 The **b** which Habakkuk the prophet did	4853
Zep	3:18 to whom the reproach of it was a **b**.	4864
Zec	9: 1 The **b** of the word of the LORD in	4853
	12: 1 The **b** of the word of the LORD for Israel,	4853
	12: 3 all that **b** themselves with it shall be cut in	6006
Mal	1: 1 The **b** of the word of the LORD to Israel	4853
Mt	11:30 For my yoke is easy, and my **b** is light.	5413
	20:12 have borne the **b** and heat of the day.	922
Ac	15:28 to lay upon you no greater **b** than these	922
	21: 3 for there the ship was to unlade her **b**.	1117
2Co	12:16 But be it so, I did not **b** you: nevertheless,	2599
Gal	6: 5 For every man shall bear his own **b**.	5413
Rev	2:24 speak; I will put upon you none other **b**.	922

BURDENED (2) [BURDEN]

2Co	5: 4 are in this tabernacle do groan, being **b**:	916
	8:13 not that other men be eased, and you **b**:	2347

BURDENS (25) [BURDEN]

Ge	49:14 strong ass couching down between two **b**:	4942
Ex	1:11 taskmasters to afflict them with their **b**.	5450
	2:11 unto his brethren, and looked on their **b**:	5450
	5: 4 from their works? get you unto your **b**.	5450
	5: 5 and you make them rest from their **b**.	5450
	6: 6 I will bring you out from under the **b** of	5450
	6: 7 bringeth you out from under the **b** of	5450
Nu	4:24 of the Gershonites, to serve, and for **b**:	4853
	4:27 in all their **b**, and in all their service:	4853
	4:27 appoint them over in charge all their **b**.	4853
1Ki	5:15 and ten thousand that bare **b**,	5449
2Ch	2: 2 and ten thousand men to bear **b**,	5449
	2:18 ten thousand of them to be **bearers of b**,	5449
	24:27 the greatness of the **b** laid upon him,	4853
	34:13 Also they were over the **bearers of b**,	5449
Ne	4:10 The strength of the **bearers of b** is	5449
	4:17 they that bare **b**, with those that laded,	5447
	13:15 grapes, and figs, and all manner of **b**,	4853
Isa	58: 6 undo the heavy **b**, and to let the oppressed	92
La	2:14 have seen for thee false **b** and causes of	4864
Am	5:11 poor, and ye take from him **b** of wheat:	4864
Mt	23: 4 For they bind heavy **b** and grievous to be	5413
Lk	11:46 for ye lade men with **b** grievous to be	5413
	11:46 ye yourselves touch not the **b** with one of	5413
Gal	6: 2 Bear ye one another's **b**, and so fulfil the	922

BURDENSOME (5) [BURDEN]

Zec	12: 3 that day will I make Jerusalem a **b** stone	4614
2Co	11: 9 all things I have kept myself from being **b**	4
	12:13 it be that I myself was not **b** to you?	2655
	12:14 come to you; and I will not be **b** to you:	2655
1Th	2: 6 when we might have been **b**,	922+1722

BURIAL (6) [BURY]

2Ch	26:23 of the **b** which belonged to the kings:	6900
Ecc	6: 3 with good, and also that he have no **b**;	6900
Isa	14:20 Thou shalt not be joined with them in **b**,	6900
Jer	22:19 He shall be buried with the **b** of an ass,	6900
Mt	26:12 ointment on my body, she did it for my **b**.	1779
Ac	8: 2 And devout men carried Stephen to his **b**,	NIG

BURIED (106) [BURY]

Ge	15:15 peace; thou shalt be **b** in a good old age.	6912

Ge	23:19 Abraham **b** Sarah his wife in the cave of	6912
	25: 9 Ishmael **b** him in the cave of Machpelah,	6912
	25:10 there was Abraham **b**, and Sarah his wife.	6912
	35: 8 she was **b** beneath Beth-el under an oak:	6912
	35:19 and was **b** in the way to Ephrath,	6912
	35:29 and his sons Esau and Jacob **b** him.	6912
	48: 7 I **b** her there in the way of Ephrath;	6912
	49:31 There they **b** Abraham and Sarah his wife;	6912
	49:31 there they **b** Isaac and Rebekah his wife;	6912
	49:31 and Rebekah his wife; and there I **b** Leah.	6912
	50:13 **b** him in the cave of the field of	6912
	50:14 bury his father, after he had **b** his father.	6912
Nu	11:34 there they **b** the people that lusted.	6912
	20: 1 and Miriam died there, and was **b** there.	6912
	33: 4 For the Egyptians **b** all their firstborn,	6912
Dt	10: 6 there Aaron died, and there he was **b**;	6912
	34: 6 he **b** him in a valley in the land of Moab,	6912
Jos	24:30 **b** him in the border of his inheritance	6912
	24:32 up out of Egypt, **b** they in Shechem,	6912
	24:33 they **b** him in a hill that pertained to	6912
Jdg	2: 9 **b** him in the border of his inheritance	6912
	8:32 was **b** in the sepulchre of Joash his father,	6912
	10: 2 years, and died, and was **b** in Shamir.	6912
	10: 5 And Jair died, and was **b** in Camon.	6912
	12: 7 and was **b** in one of the cities of Gilead.	6912
	12:10 died Ibzan, and was **b** at Beth-lehem.	6912
	12:12 **b** in Aijalon in the country of Zebulun.	6912
	12:15 **b** in Pirathon in the land of Ephraim,	6912
	16:31 **b** him between Zorah and Eshtaol in	6912
Ru	1:17 diest, will I die, and there will I be **b**:	6912
1Sa	25: 1 and **b** him in his house at Ramah.	6912
	28: 3 **b** him in Ramah, even in his own city.	6912
	31:13 **b** them under a tree at Jabesh,	6912
2Sa	2: 4 of Jabesh-gilead were they that **b** Saul.	6912
	2: 5 lord, even unto Saul, and have **b** him.	6912
	2:32 and **b** him in the sepulchre of his father,	6912
	3:32 they **b** Abner in Hebron: and the king lift	6912
	4:12 **b** it in the sepulchre of Abner in Hebron.	6912
	17:23 and was **b** in the sepulchre of his father.	6912
	19:37 and be **b** by the grave of my father and	NIH
	21:14 Jonathan his son **b** they in the country of	6912
1Ki	2:10 his fathers, and was **b** in the city of David.	6912
	2:34 he was **b** in his own house in	6912
	11:43 and was **b** in the city of David his father:	6912
	13:31 it came to pass, after he had **b** him, that	6912
	13:31 sepulchre wherein the man of God is **b**;	6912
	14:18 they **b** him; and all Israel mourned for	6912
	14:31 was **b** with his fathers in the city of David.	6912
	15: 8 and they **b** him in the city of David:	6912
	15:24 was **b** with his fathers in the city of David	6912
	16: 6 slept with his fathers, and was **b** in Tirzah:	6912
	16:28 with his fathers, and was **b** in Samaria:	6912
	22:37 Samaria; and they **b** the king in Samaria.	6912
	22:50 was **b** with his fathers in the city of David	6912
2Ki	8:24 was **b** with his fathers in the city of David:	6912
	9:28 **b** him in his sepulchre with his fathers in	6912
	10:35 they **b** him in Samaria. And Jehoahaz his	6912
	12:21 they **b** him with his fathers in the city of	6912
	13: 9 his fathers; and they **b** him in Samaria:	6912
	13:13 Joash was **b** in Samaria with the kings of	6912
	13:20 Elisha died, and they **b** him.	6912
	14:16 was **b** in Samaria with the kings of Israel;	6912
	14:20 he was **b** at Jerusalem with his fathers in	6912
	15: 7 they **b** him with his fathers in the city of	6912
	15:38 was **b** with his fathers in the city of David	6912
	16:20 was **b** with his fathers in the city of David:	6912
	21:18 was **b** in the garden of his own house,	6912
	21:26 he was **b** in his sepulchre in the garden of	6912
	23:30 and **b** him in his own sepulchre.	6912
1Ch	10:12 their bones under the oak in Jabesh,	6912
2Ch	9:31 he was **b** in the city of David his father:	6912
	12:16 fathers, and was **b** in the city of David:	6912
	14: 1 and they **b** him in the city of David:	6912
	16:14 they **b** him in his own sepulchres, which	6912
	21: 1 was **b** with his fathers in the city of David,	6912
	21:20 Howbeit they **b** him in the city of David,	6912
	22: 9 when they had slain him, they **b** him:	6912
	24:16 in the city of David among	6912
	24:25 they **b** him in the city of David, but	6912
	24:25 they **b** him not in the sepulchres of	6912
	25:28 **b** him with his fathers in the city of Judah.	6912
	26:23 they **b** him with his fathers in the field of	6912
	27: 9 and they **b** him in the city of David:	6912
	28:27 they **b** him in the city, even in Jerusalem:	6912
	32:33 **b** him in the chiefest of the sepulchres	6912
	33:20 and they **b** him in his own house:	6912
	35:24 was **b** in one of the sepulchres of his	6912
Job	27:15 Those that remain of him shall be **b** in	6912
Ecc	8:10 so I saw the wicked **b**, who had come	6912
Jer	8: 2 they shall not be gathered, nor be **b**;	6912
	16: 4 neither shall they be **b**; but they shall be	6912
	16: 6 they shall not be **b**, neither shall men	6912
	20: 6 shalt be **b** there, thou, and all thy friends,	6912
	22:19 He shall be **b** with the burial of an ass,	6912
	25:33 not be lamented, neither gathered, nor **b**;	6912
Eze	39:15 till the buriers have **b** it in the valley of	6912
Mt	14:12 body, and **b** it, and went and told Jesus.	2290
Lk	16:22 the rich man also died, and was **b**;	2290
Ac	2:29 that he is both dead and **b**,	2290
	5: 6 him up, and carried him out, and **b** him.	2290
	5: 9 feet of them which have **b** thy husband	2290
	5:10 carrying her forth, **b** her by her husband.	2290
Ro	6: 4 Therefore we are **b** with him by baptism	4916
1Co	15: 4 And that he was **b**, and that he rose again	2290
Col	2:12 **B** with him in baptism, wherein also you	4916

B

BURIERS (1) [BURY]
Eze 39:15 till the **b** have buried it in the valley of 6912

BURN (138) [BURNED, BURNETH, BURNING, BURNINGS, BURNT]
Ge 11: 3 **b** them thoroughly. 8313+8316+3807.1
44:18 let not thine anger **b** against thy servant; 2734
Ex 12:10 of it until the morning ye shall **b** with fire. 8313
27:20 the light, to **cause** the lamp **to b** always. 5927
29:13 is upon them, and **b** them upon the altar. 6999
29:14 shalt thou **b** with fire without the camp: 8313
29:18 thou shalt **b** the whole ram upon the altar: 6999
29:25 **b** them upon the altar for a burnt offering, 6999
29:34 then thou shalt **b** the remainder with fire: 8313
30: 1 shalt make an altar to **b** incense upon: 4729
30: 7 Aaron shall **b** thereon sweet incense every 6999
30: 7 the lamps, he shall **b** incense upon it. 6999
30: 8 lamps at even, he shall **b** incense upon it, 6999
30:20 to **b** offering made by fire unto 6999
Lev 1: 9 the priest shall **b** all on the altar, to be a 6999
1:13 shall bring it all, and **b** it upon the altar: 6999
1:15 wring off his head, and **b** it on the altar; 6999
1:17 the priest shall **b** it upon the altar, upon 6999
2: 2 the priest shall **b** the memorial of it upon 6999
2: 9 and shall **b** it upon the altar: 6999
2:11 for ye shall **b** no leaven, nor any honey, 6999
2:16 the priest shall **b** the memorial of it, part 6999
3: 5 Aaron's sons shall **b** it on the altar upon 6999
3:11 the priest shall **b** it upon the altar: it is 6999
3:16 the priest shall **b** them upon the altar: it is 6999
4:10 the priest shall **b** them upon the altar of 6999
4:12 and **b** him on the wood with fire: 8313
4:19 his fat from him, and **b** it upon the altar. 6999
4:21 and **b** him as he burned the first bullock: 8313
4:26 he shall **b** all his fat upon the altar, 6999
4:31 the priest shall **b** it upon the altar for a 6999
4:35 the priest shall **b** them upon the altar, 6999
5:12 a memorial thereof, and **b** it on the altar, 6999
6:12 priest shall **b** wood on it every morning, 1197
6:12 he shall **b** thereon the fat of the peace 6999
6:15 **b** it upon the altar for a sweet savour, 6999
7: 5 the priest shall **b** them upon the altar for 6999
7:31 the priest shall **b** the fat upon the altar: 6999
8:32 and of the bread shall ye **b** with fire. 8313
13:52 He shall therefore **b** that garment, 8313
13:55 it is unclean; thou shalt **b** it in the fire; it 8313
13:57 it is a spreading plague: thou shalt **b** that 8313
16:25 the fat of the sin offering shall he **b** upon 6999
16:27 they shall **b** in the fire their skins, 8313
17: 6 **b** the fat for a sweet savour unto 6999
24: 2 to **cause** the lamps **to b** continually. 5927
Nu 5:26 **b** it upon the altar, and afterward shall 6999
18:17 shalt **b** their fat for an offering made by 6999
19: 5 one shall **b** the heifer in his sight; her skin 8313
19: 5 and her blood, with her dung, shall he **b**: 8313
Dt 5:23 (for the mountain did **b** with fire,) 1197
7: 5 and **b** their graven images with fire. 8313
7:25 graven images of their gods shall ye **b** 8313
12: 3 their pillars, and **b** their groves with fire; 8313
13:16 shalt **b** with fire the city, and all the spoil 8313
32:22 shall **b** unto the lowest hell, 3344
Jos 11: 6 their horses, and **b** their chariots with fire. 8313
11:13 save Hazor only; that did Joshua **b**. 8313
Jdg 9:52 hard unto the door of the tower to **b** it 8313
12: 1 we will **b** thine house upon thee with fire. 8313
14:15 lest we **b** thee and thy father's house with 8313
1Sa 2:16 Let them **not fail to b** the fat 6999+6999
2:28 to offer upon mine altar, to **b** incense, 6999
1Ki 13: 1 Jeroboam stood by the altar to **b** incense. 6999
13: 2 the high places that **b** incense upon thee, 6999
2Ki 16:15 Upon the great altar **b** the morning burnt 6999
18: 4 the children of Israel did **b** incense to it: 6999
23: 5 **b** incense in the high places in the cities 6999
1Ch 23:13 for ever, to **b** incense before the LORD, 6999
2Ch 2: 4 and to **b** before him sweet incense, 6999
2: 6 save only to **b** sacrifice before him? 6999
4:20 that they should **b** after the manner before 1197
13:11 And they **b** unto the LORD every morning 6999
13:11 the lamps thereof, to **b** every evening: 1197
26:16 to **b** incense upon the altar of incense. 6999
26:18 to **b** incense unto the LORD, but to 6999
26:18 Aaron, that are consecrated to **b** incense: 6999
26:19 had a censer in his hand to **b** incense: 6999
28:25 high places to **b** incense unto other gods, 6999
29:11 should minister unto him, and **b** incense. 6999
32:12 before one altar, and **b** incense upon it? 6999
Ne 10:34 to **b** upon the altar of the LORD our God, 1197
Ps 79: 5 for ever? shall thy jealousy **b** like fire? 1197
89:46 for ever? shall thy wrath **b** like fire? 1197
Isa 1:31 they shall both **b** together, and none shall 1197
10:17 it shall **b** and devour his thorns and 1197
27: 4 through them, I would **b** them together. 6702
40:16 Lebanon is not sufficient to **b**, nor 1197
44:15 shall it be for a man to **b**: for he will take 1197
47:14 shall be as stubble; the fire shall **b** them; 8313
Jer 4: 4 lest my fury come forth like fire, and **b** 1197
7: 9 **b** incense unto Baal, and walk after other 6999
7:20 and it shall **b**, and shall not be quenched. 1197
7:31 to **b** their sons and their daughters in 8313
11:13 even altars to **b** incense unto Baal. 6999
15:14 in mine anger, which shall **b** upon you. 3344
17: 4 fire in mine anger, which shall **b** for ever. 3344
19: 5 **b** their sons with fire for burnt offerings 8313
21:10 of Babylon, and he shall **b** it with fire. 8313
21:12 **b** that none can quench it, because of 1197

Jer 32:29 fire on this city, and **b** it with the houses, 8313
34: 2 of Babylon, and he shall **b** it with fire. 8313
34: 5 thee, so shall they odours for thee; 8313
34:22 against it, and take it, and **b** it with fire: 8313
36:25 to the king that he would not **b** the roll: 8313
37: 8 this city, and take it, and **b** it with fire. 8313
37:10 man in his tent, and **b** this city with fire. 8313
38:18 they shall **b** it with fire, and thou shalt not 8313
43:12 he shall **b** them, and carry them away 8313
43:13 gods of the Egyptians shall he **b** with fire. 8313
44: 3 that they went to **b** incense, and to serve 6999
44: 5 to **b** no incense unto other gods. 6999
44:17 to **b** incense unto the queen of heaven, 6999
44:18 we left off to **b** incense to the queen 6999
44:25 to **b** incense to the queen of heaven, 6999
Eze 5: 2 Thou shalt **b** with fire a third part in 1197
5: 4 midst of the fire, and **b** them in the fire; 8313
16:41 they shall **b** thine houses with fire, 8313
23:47 and **b up** their houses with fire. 8313
24: 5 also the bones under it, and make it boil 1752
24:11 may **b**, and that the filthiness of it may be 2787
39: 9 shall set on fire and **b** the weapons, 5400
39: 9 they shall **b** them with fire seven years: 1197
39:10 for they shall **b** the weapons with fire: 1197
43:21 he shall **b** it in the appointed place of 8313
Hos 4:13 **b** incense upon the hills, under oaks and 6999
Na 2:13 I will **b** her chariots in the smoke, 1197
Hab 1:16 their net, and **b** incense unto their drag; 6999
Mal 4: 1 the day cometh, that shall **b** as an oven; 1197
4: 1 the day that cometh shall **b** them up, saith 3857
Mt 3:12 **b up** the chaff with unquenchable fire. 2618
13:30 and bind them in bundles to **b** them: 2618
Lk 1: 9 his lot was to **b** incense when he went 2370
3:17 chaff he will **b** with fire unquenchable. 2618
24:32 another, Did not our heart **b** within us, 2545
1Co 7: 9 for it is better to marry than to **b**. 4448
2Co 11:29 not weak? who is offended, and I **b** not? 4448
Rev 17:16 shall eat her flesh, and **b** her with fire. 2618

BURNED (22) [BURN]
Ex 3: 2 bush **b** with fire, and the bush was not 1197
Lev 4:21 and burn him as he **b** the first bullock: 8313
8:16 their fat, and Moses **b** it upon the altar. 6999
Dt 9:15 the mount, and the mount **b** with fire: 1197
Jos 7:25 him with stones, and **b** them with fire, 8313
11:13 Israel **b** none of them, save Hazor only; 8313
2Ch 25:14 before them, and **b** incense unto them. 6999
34:25 and have **b** incense unto other gods, 6999
Est 1:12 king very wroth, and his anger **b** in him. 1197
Ps 39: 3 within me, while I was musing the fire **b**: 1197
39: 3 then spake I with my tongue, 1197
Isa 24: 6 the inhabitants of the earth are **b**, 2787
42:25 and it **b** him, yet he laid it not to heart. 1197
La 2: 3 he **b** against Jacob like a flaming fire, 1197
Eze 15: 5 the fire hath devoured it, and it is **b**? 2787
Hos 11: 2 and **b** incense to graven images. 6999
Jn 15: 6 cast them into the fire, and they are **b**. 2545
Ac 19:19 and **b** them before all men: and 2618
Ro 1:27 **b** in their lust one towards another; 1572
1Co 13: 3 and though I give my body to be **b**, 2545
Heb 6: 8 nigh unto cursing; whose end is to be **b**. 2740
12:18 and that **b** with fire, nor unto blackness, 2545
Rev 1:15 unto fine brass, as if they **b** in a furnace; 4448

BURNETH (18) [BURN]
Lev 13:24 the quick flesh that **b** have a white bright 4348
16:28 he that **b** them shall wash his clothes, 8313
Nu 19: 8 he that **b** her shall wash his clothes in 8313
Ps 46: 9 in sunder; he **b** the chariot in the fire. 8313
83:14 As the fire **b** a wood, and as the flame 1197
97: 3 and **b up** his enemies round about. 3857
Isa 9:18 wickedness **b** as the fire: it shall devour 1197
44:16 He **b** part thereof in the fire; with part 1197
62: 1 and the salvation thereof as a lamp that **b**. 1197
64: 2 when the melting fire **b**, the fire causeth 6919
65: 3 and **b** incense upon altars of brick; 6999
65: 5 in my nose, a fire that **b** all the day. 3344
66: 3 he that **b** incense, as if he blessed an idol. 2142
Jer 48:35 and him that **b** incense to his gods. 6999
Hos 7: 6 in the morning it **b** as a flaming fire. 1197
Joel 2: 3 before them; and behind them a flame **b**: 3857
Am 6:10 shall take him up, and he that **b** him, 5635
Rev 21: 8 shall have their part in the lake which **b** 2545

BURNING (60) [BURN]
Ge 15:17 **b** lamp that passed between those pieces. 784
Ex 21:25 **B** for burning, wound for wound, stripe 3555
21:25 Burning for **b**, wound for wound, stripe 3555
Lev 6: 9 of the **b** upon the altar all night unto 4169
6: 9 and the fire of the altar shall be **b** in it. 3344
6:12 the fire upon the altar shall be **b** in it; 3344
6:13 The fire shall ever be **b** upon the altar; 3344
10: 6 bewail the **b** which the LORD hath 8316
13:23 in his place, and spread not, it is a **b** boil; 6867
13:24 in the skin whereof there is a hot **b**, 4348
13:25 skin; it is a leprosy broken out of the **b**: 4348
13:28 it is a rising of the **b**, and the priest shall 4348
13:28 for it is an inflammation of the **b**. 4348
16:12 shall take a censer full of **b coals** of fire 1513
26:16 consumption, and the **b ague**, that shall 6920
Nu 16:37 that he take up the censers out of the **b**, 8316
16:37 scatter thou the fire yonder; for they are 8316
Dt 28:22 with an **extreme b**, and with the sword, 2746
29:23 and **b**, that it is not sown, nor beareth, 8316
32:24 devoured with **b heat**, and with bitter 7565
2Ch 16:14 they **made a** very great **b** for him. 8313+8316

2Ch 21:19 his people made no **b** for him, like 8316
21:19 burning for him, like the **b** of his fathers. 8316
Job 41:19 Out of his mouth go **b lamps**, and sparks 3940
Ps 140:10 Let **b coals** fall upon them: let them be 1513
Pr 16:27 up evil: and in his lips there is as a **b** fire. 6867
26:21 As coals are to **b coals**, and wood to fire; 1513
26:23 **B** lips and a wicked heart are like a 1814
Isa 3:24 of sackcloth; and **b** instead of beauty. 3587
4: 4 spirit of judgment, and by the spirit of **b**. 1197
9: 5 but this shall be with **b** and fuel of fire. 8316
10:16 under his glory he shall kindle a **b** like 3350
10:16 shall kindle a burning like the **b** of a fire: 3350
30:27 **b** with his anger, and the burden thereof 1197
30:33 and the land thereof shall become **b** pitch. 1197
Jer 20: 9 his word was in mine heart as a **b** fire 1197
36:22 a fire on the hearth **b** before him. 1197
44: 8 **b** incense unto other gods in the land of 6999
Eze 1:13 their appearance was like **b coals** of fire, 1197
Da 3: 6 be cast into the midst of a **b** fiery furnace. 3345
3:11 he should be cast into the midst of a **b** 3345
3:15 hour into the midst of a **b** fiery furnace, 3345
3:17 able to deliver us from the **b** fiery furnace, 3345
3:20 and to cast them into the **b** fiery furnace. 3345
3:21 were cast into the midst of the **b** fiery 3345
3:23 fell down bound into the midst of the **b** 3345
3:26 near to the mouth of the **b** fiery furnace, 3345
7: 9 the fiery flame, and his wheels as **b** fire. 1815
7:11 body destroyed, and given to the **b** flame. 3346
Am 4:11 ye were as a firebrand pluckt out of the **b**: 8316
Hab 3: 5 and **b coals** went forth at his feet. 7565
Lk 12:35 loins be girded about, and your lights **b**; 2545
Jn 5:35 He was a **b** and a shining light: and ye 2545
Jas 1:11 the sun is no sooner risen with a **b heat**, 2742
Rev 4: 5 there were seven lamps of fire **b** before 2545
8: 8 as it were a great mountain **b** with fire 2545
8:10 **b** as it were a lamp, and it fell upon 2545
18: 9 when they shall see the smoke of her **b**, 4451
18:18 cried when they saw the smoke of her **b**, 4451
19:20 alive into a lake of fire **b** with brimstone. 2545

BURNINGS (3) [BURN]
Isa 33:12 the people shall be as the **b** of lime: 4955
33:14 amongst us shall dwell with everlasting **b**? 4168
Jer 34: 5 with the **b** of thy fathers, the former kings 4955

BURNISHED (1)
Eze 1: 7 they sparkled like the colour of **b** brass. 7044

BURNT (442) [BURN]
Ge 8:20 provided and offered **b offerings** on the altar. 5930
22: 2 offer him there for a **b offering** upon one 5930
22: 3 clave the wood for the **b offering**, 5930
22: 6 Abraham took the wood of the **b offering**, 5930
22: 7 but where is the lamb for a **b offering**? 5930
22: 8 provide himself a lamb for a **b offering**: 5930
22:13 him up for a **b offering** in the stead 5930
38:24 Bring her forth, and let her be **b**. 8313
Ex 3: 3 see this great sight, why the bush is not **b**. 1197
10:25 give us also sacrifices and **b offerings**, 5930
18:12 took a **b offering** and sacrifices for God: 5930
20:24 shalt sacrifice thereon thy **b offerings**, 5930
24: 5 which offered **b offerings**, 5930
29:18 it is a **b** offering unto the LORD: it is a 5930
29:25 burn them upon the altar for a **b offering**, 5930
29:42 This shall be a continual **b offering** 5930
30: 9 nor **b** sacrifice, nor meat offering; 5930
30:28 the altar of **b offering** with all his vessels, 5930
31: 9 altar of **b offering** with all his furniture, 5930
32: 6 offered **b offerings**, and brought peace 5930
32:20 **b** it in the fire, and ground it to powder, 8313
35:16 The altar of **b offering** with his brasen 5930
38: 1 he made the altar of **b offering** of shittim 5930
40: 6 thou shalt set the altar of the **b offering** 5930
40:10 shalt anoint the altar of the **b offering**, 5930
40:27 he put the altar of **b** sweet incense thereon; as the LORD 6999
40:29 he put the altar of **b offering** by the door 5930
40:29 offered upon it the **b offering** and the 5930
Lev 1: 3 If his offering be a **b sacrifice** of the herd, 5930
1: 4 his hand upon the head of the **b offering**; 5930
1: 6 he shall flay the **b offering**, and cut it into 5930
1: 9 to be a **b sacrifice**, an offering made by 5930
1:10 sheep, or of the goats, for a **b sacrifice**; 5930
1:13 is a **b sacrifice**, an offering made by fire, 5930
1:14 if the **b sacrifice** for his offering to 5930
1:17 is a **b sacrifice**, an offering made by fire, 5930
2:12 they shall not be **b** on the altar for a sweet 5927
3: 5 burn it on the altar upon the **b sacrifice**, 5930
4: 7 the bottom of the altar of the **b offering**, 5930
4:10 them upon the altar of the **b offering**. 5930
4:12 the ashes are poured out shall he be **b**. 8313
4:18 the bottom of the altar of the **b offering**, 5930
4:24 they kill the **b offering** before the LORD: 5930
4:25 upon the horns of the altar of **b offering**, 5930
4:25 at the bottom of the altar of **b offering**. 5930
4:29 sin offering in the place of the **b offering**. 5930
4:30 upon the horns of the altar of **b offering**, 5930
4:33 the place where they kill the **b offering**. 5930
4:34 upon the horns of the altar of **b offering**, 5930
5: 7 offering, and the other for a **b offering**. 5930
5:10 shall offer the second for a **b offering**, 5930
6: 9 This is the law of the **b offering**: 5930
6: 9 It is the **b offering**, because of the 5930
6:10 with the **b offering** on the altar, 5930
6:12 lay the **b offering** in order upon it; 5930
6:22 ever unto the LORD; it shall be wholly **b**. 6999

Lev 6:23 shall be wholly *b*: it shall not be eaten. NIH
6:25 the place where the **b offering** is killed 5930
6:30 shall be eaten: it shall be **b** in the fire. 8313
7: 2 the place where they kill the **b offering** 5930
7: 8 priest that offereth *any* man's **b offering**, 5930
7: 8 of the **b offering** which he hath offered. 5930
7:17 on the third day shall be **b** with fire. 8313
7:19 shall not be eaten; it shall be **b** with fire: 8313
7:37 This *is* the law of the **b offering**, 5930
8:17 dung, he **b** with fire without the camp; 8313
8:18 he brought the ram for the **b offering**: 5930
8:20 Moses **b** the head, and the pieces, 6999
8:21 Moses **b** the whole ram upon the altar; 6999
8:21 it *was* a **b** sacrifice for a sweet savour, 6999
8:28 **b** *them* on the altar upon the burnt 6999
8:28 *them* on the altar upon the **b offering**: 5930
9: 2 a ram for a **b offering**, without blemish, 5930
9: 3 without blemish, for a **b offering**; 5930
9: 7 thy **b offering**, and make an atonement 5930
9:10 of the sin offering, he **b** upon the altar; 6999
9:11 hide he **b** with fire without the camp. 8313
9:12 he slew the **b offering**; and Aaron's sons 5930
9:13 they presented the **b offering** unto him, 5930
9:13 the head: and he **b** *them* upon the altar. 6999
9:14 **b** *them* upon the burnt offering on the 6999
9:14 *them* upon the **b offering** on the altar. 5930
9:16 he brought the **b offering**, and offered it 5930
9:17 a handful thereof, and **b** *it* upon the altar, 6999
9:17 beside the **b** sacrifice of the morning. 5930
9:20 breasts, and he **b** the fat upon the altar: 6999
9:22 and the **b offering**, and peace offerings. 5930
9:24 consumed upon the altar the **b offering** 5930
10:16 of the sin offering, and behold, it was **b**: 8313
10:19 and their **b offering** before the LORD; 5930
12: 6 a lamb of the first year for a **b offering**, 5930
12: 8 the one for the **b offering**, and the other 5930
13:52 a fretting leprosy; it shall be **b** in the fire. 8313
14:13 kill the sin offering and the **b offering**, 5930
14:19 and afterward he shall kill the **b offering**: 5930
14:20 the priest shall offer the **b offering** and 5930
14:22 a sin offering, and the other a **b offering**. 5930
14:31 the other *for* a **b offering**, with the meat 5930
15:15 offering, and the other *for* a **b offering**, 5930
15:30 offering, and the other *for* a **b offering**, 5930
16: 3 a sin offering, and a ram for a **b offering**. 5930
16: 5 sin offering, and one ram for a **b offering**. 5930
16:24 offer his **b offering**, and the burnt offering 5930
16:24 the **b offering** of the people, and make 5930
17: 8 that offereth a **b offering** or sacrifice, 5930
19: 6 until the third day, it shall be **b** in the fire. 8313
20:14 shall be **b** with fire, both he and they; 8313
21: 9 her father: she shall be **b** with fire. 8313
22:18 will offer unto the LORD for a **b offering**, 5930
23:12 first year for a **b offering** unto the LORD. 5930
23:18 they shall be *for* a **b offering** unto 5930
23:37 a **b offering**, and a meat offering, 5930
Nu 6:11 the other for a **b offering**, and make an 5930
6:14 first year without blemish for a **b offering**, 5930
6:16 offer his sin offering, and his **b offering**: 5930
7:15 lamb of the first year, for a **b offering**: 5930
7:21 lamb of the first year, for a **b offering**: 5930
7:27 lamb of the first year, for a **b offering**: 5930
7:33 lamb of the first year, for a **b offering**: 5930
7:39 lamb of the first year, for a **b offering**: 5930
7:45 lamb of the first year, for a **b offering**: 5930
7:51 lamb of the first year, for a **b offering**: 5930
7:57 lamb of the first year, for a **b offering**: 5930
7:63 lamb of the first year, for a **b offering**: 5930
7:69 lamb of the first year, for a **b offering**: 5930
7:75 lamb of the first year, for a **b offering**: 5930
7:81 lamb of the first year, for a **b offering**: 5930
7:87 the oxen for the **b offering** *were* twelve 5930
8:12 the other *for* a **b offering**, unto the LORD, 5930
10:10 with the trumpets over your **b offerings**, 5930
11: 1 the fire of the LORD **b** among them, 1197
11: 3 the fire of the LORD **b** among them. 1197
15: 3 a **b offering**, or a sacrifice in performing 5930
15: 5 shalt thou prepare with the **b offering** 5930
15: 8 thou preparest a bullock *for* a **b offering**, 5930
15:24 offer one young bullock for a **b offering**, 5930
16:39 wherewith they that were **b** had offered; 8313
19:17 ashes of the **b** *heifer* of purification for sin, 5930
23: 3 Stand by thy **b offering**, and I will go: 5930
23: 6 lo, *he* stood by his **b** sacrifice, he, 5930
23:15 unto Balak, Stand here by thy **b offering**, 5930
23:17 stood by his **b offering**, and the princes 5930
28: 3 day by day, *for* a continual **b offering**. 5930
28: 6 *It is* a continual **b offering**, which was 5930
28:10 *This is* the **b offering** of every sabbath, 5930
28:10 beside the continual **b offering**, 5930
28:11 shall offer a **b offering** unto the LORD; 5930
28:13 *for* a **b offering** *of* a sweet savour, 5930
28:14 this *is* the **b offering** of every month 5930
28:15 besides the continual **b offering**, 5930
28:19 by fire *for* a **b offering** unto the LORD; 5930
28:23 Ye shall offer these beside the **b offering** 5930
28:23 which *is* for a continual **b offering**. 5930
28:24 offered beside the continual **b offering**, 5930
28:27 ye shall offer the **b offering** for a sweet 5930
28:31 *them* besides the continual **b offering**, 5930
29: 2 ye shall offer a **b offering** for a sweet 5930
29: 6 Beside the **b offering** of the month, 5930
29: 6 daily **b offering**, and his meat offering, 5930
29: 8 ye shall offer a **b offering** unto the LORD 5930
29:11 the continual **b offering**, and the meat 5930

Nu 29:13 shall offer a **b offering**, a sacrifice made 5930
29:16 beside the continual **b offering**, his meat 5930
29:19 beside the continual **b offering**, 5930
29:22 beside the continual **b offering**, 5930
29:25 beside the continual **b offering**, his meat 5930
29:28 beside the continual **b offering**, 5930
29:31 beside the continual **b offering**, his meat 5930
29:34 beside the continual **b offering**, his meat 5930
29:36 ye shall offer a **b offering**, a sacrifice 5930
29:38 beside the continual **b offering**, 5930
29:39 for your **b offerings**, and for your meat 5930
31:10 they **b** all their cities wherein they dwelt, 8313
Dt 4:11 the mountain **b** with fire unto the midst 1197
9:21 **b** it with fire, and stamped it, *and* ground 1197
12: 6 thither ye shall bring your **b offerings**, 5930
12:11 your **b offerings**, and your sacrifices, 5930
12:13 **b offerings** in every place that thou seest: 5930
12:14 there thou shalt offer thy **b offerings**, 5930
12:27 thou shalt offer thy **b offerings**, the flesh 5930
12:31 their daughters they have **b** in the fire to 8313
27: 6 thou shalt offer **b offerings** thereon unto 5930
32:24 *They shall be* **b** with hunger, 4198
33:10 and whole *b* sacrifice upon thine altar. NIH
Jos 6:24 they **b** the city with fire, and all that *was* 8313
7:15 the accursed thing shall be **b** with fire, 8313
8:28 Joshua **b** Ai, and made it a heap for ever, 8313
8:31 they offered thereon **b offerings** unto 5930
11: 9 horses, and **b** their chariots with fire. 8313
11:11 left to breathe: and he **b** Hazor with fire. 8313
22:23 or if to offer thereon **b offering** or 5930
22:26 not for **b offering**, nor for sacrifice: 5930
22:27 LORD before him with our **b offerings**, 5930
22:28 not for **b offerings**, nor for sacrifices; 5930
22:29 to build an altar for **b offerings**, for meat 5930
Jdg 6:26 offer a **b** sacrifice with the wood of 5930
11:31 and I will offer it up *for* a **b offering**. 5930
13:16 if thou wilt offer a **b offering**, thou must 5930
13:23 he would not have received a **b offering** 5930
15: 5 **b** up both the shocks, and also the 1197
15: 6 and **b** her and her father with fire. 8313
15:14 arms became as flax that was **b** with fire, 1197
18:27 of the sword, and **b** the city with fire. 8313
20:26 offered **b offerings** and peace offerings. 5930
21: 4 offered **b offerings** and peace offerings. 5930
1Sa 2:15 Also before they **b** the fat, the priest's 6999
6:14 offered the kine a **b offering** unto 5930
6:15 men of Beth-shemesh offered **b offerings** 5930
7: 9 offered it *for* a **b offering** wholly unto 5930
7:10 as Samuel was offering up the **b offering**, 5930
10: 8 to offer **b offerings**, *and* to sacrifice 5930
13: 9 Bring hither a **b offering** to me, and 5930
13: 9 And he offered the **b offering**. 5930
13:10 made an end of offering the **b offering**, 5930
13:12 therefore, and offered a **b offering**. 5930
15:22 the LORD *as great* delight in **b offerings** 5930
30: 1 and smitten Ziklag, and **b** it with fire; 8313
30: 3 to the city, and behold, *it was* **b** with fire; 8313
30:14 south of Caleb; and we **b** Ziklag with fire. 8313
31:12 and came to Jabesh, and **b** them there. 5375
2Sa 5:21 and David and his men **b** them. 5375
6:17 David offered **b offerings** and 5930
6:18 had made an end of offering **b offerings** 5930
23: 7 they shall be **utterly b** with fire in 8313+8313
24:22 *be* oxen for a **b** sacrifice, and threshing 5930
24:24 neither will I offer **b offerings** unto 5930
24:25 offered **b offerings** and peace offerings. 5930
1Ki 3: 3 sacrificed and **b incense** in high places. 6999
3: 4 a thousand **b offerings** did Solomon offer 5930
3:15 offered up **b offerings**, and offered peace 5930
8:64 for there he offered **b offerings**, and meat 5930
8:64 *was* too little to receive the **b offerings**, 5930
9:16 **b** it with fire, and slain the Canaanites 8313
9:25 in a year did Solomon offer **b offerings** 5930
9:25 he **b incense** upon the altar that *was* 6999
11: 8 which **b incense** and sacrificed unto their 6999
12:33 he offered upon the altar, and **b incense**. 6999
13: 2 and men's bones shall be **b** upon thee. 8313
15:13 her idol, and **b** *it* by the brook Kidron. 8313
16:18 **b** the king's house over him with fire, 8313
18:33 pour *it* on the **b offering**, and on the 5930
18:38 consumed the **b** sacrifice, and the wood, 5930
22:43 and **b incense** yet in the high places. 6999
2Ki 1:14 **b up** the two captains of the former fifties 398
3:27 him *for* a **b offering** upon the wall. 5930
5:17 **b offering** nor sacrifice unto other gods, 5930
10:24 went in to offer sacrifices and **b offerings**, 5930
10:25 made an end of offering the **b offering**, 5930
10:26 out of the house of Baal, and **b** them. 8313
12: 3 and **b incense** in the high places. 6999
14: 4 and **b incense** on the high places. 6999
15: 4 and **b incense** still on the high places. 6999
15:35 and **b incense** still in the high places. 6999
16: 4 and **b incense** in the high places, 6999
16:13 he **b** his burnt offering and his meat 6999
16:13 he burnt his **b offering** and his meat 5930
16:15 great altar burn the morning **b offering** 5930
16:15 the king's **b** sacrifice, and his meat 5930
16:15 with the **b offering** of all the people of 5930
16:15 upon it all the blood of the **b offering**, 5930
17:11 they **b incense** in all the high places, 6999
17:31 the Sepharvites **b** their children in fire to 8313
22:17 and have **b incense** unto other gods, 6999
23: 4 and **b** them without Jerusalem in the fields 8313
23: 5 them also that **b incense** unto Baal, 6999
23: 6 **b** it at the brook Kidron, and stamp *it* 8313

2Ki 23: 8 places where the priests had **b incense**, 6999
23:11 and **b** the chariots of the sun with fire. 8313
23:15 and **b** the high place, *and* stampt *it* small to 8313
23:15 small to powder, and **b** the grove. 8313
23:16 **b** them upon the altar, and polluted it, 8313
23:20 **b** men's bones upon them, and returned 8313
25: 9 he **b** the house of the LORD, 8313
25: 9 every great *man's* house he **b** with fire. 8313
1Ch 6:49 offered upon the altar of the **b offering**, 5930
14:12 and they were **b** with fire. 5930
16: 1 they offered **b sacrifices** and 5930
16: 2 made an end of offering the **b offerings**, 5930
16:40 To offer **b offerings** unto the LORD upon 5930
16:40 altar of the **b offering** continually 5930
21:23 I give *thee* the oxen *also* for **b offerings**, 5930
21:24 nor offer **b offerings** without cost. 5930
21:26 offered **b offerings** and peace offerings, 5930
21:26 by fire upon the altar of **b offering**. 5930
21:29 and the altar of the **b offering**, 5930
22: 1 *is* the altar of the **b offering** for Israel. 5930
23:31 to offer all **b sacrifices** unto the LORD in 5930
29:21 offered **b offerings** unto the LORD, 5930
2Ch 1: 6 offered a thousand **b offerings** upon it. 5930
2: 4 the **b offerings** morning and evening, 5930
4: 6 for the **b offering** they washed in them; 5930
7: 1 consumed the **b offering** and the 5930
7: 7 there he offered **b offerings**, and the fat 5930
7: 7 was not able to receive the **b offerings**, 5930
8:12 Solomon offered **b offerings** unto 5930
13:11 every evening **b sacrifices** and 5930
15:16 stamped *it*, and **b** *it* at the brook Kidron. 8313
23:18 to offer the **b offerings** of the LORD, as it 5930
24:14 they offered **b offerings** in the house of 5930
28: 3 Moreover he **b incense** in the valley of 6999
28: 3 his children in the fire after 1197
28: 4 and **b incense** in the high places, 6999
29: 7 have not **b incense** nor offered 6999+7004
29: 7 **b offerings** in the holy *place* unto 5930
29:18 the altar of **b offering**, with all the vessels 5930
29:24 the king commanded *that* the **b offering** 5930
29:27 to offer the **b offering** upon the altar. 5930
29:27 when the **b offering** began, the song of 5930
29:28 *this continued* until the **b offering** was 5930
29:31 many as were of a free heart **b offerings**. 5930
29:32 the number of the **b offerings**, which 5930
29:32 all these *were* for a **b offering** to 5930
29:34 they could not flay all the **b offerings**: 5930
29:35 also the **b offerings** *were* in abundance, 5930
29:35 the drink offerings for *every* **b offering**. 5930
30:15 brought in the **b offerings** *into* the house 5930
31: 2 the priests and Levites for **b offerings** 5930
31: 3 of his substance for the **b offerings**, 5930
31: 3 for the morning and evening **b offerings**, 5930
31: 3 the **b offerings** for the sabbaths, and for 5930
34: 5 he **b** the bones of the priests upon their 8313
35:12 they removed the **b offerings**, that they 5930
35:14 *were* busied in offering of **b offerings** 5930
35:16 to offer **b offerings** upon the altar of 5930
36:19 they **b** the house of God, and brake down 8313
36:19 **b** all the palaces thereof with fire, 8313
Ezr 3: 2 to offer **b offerings** thereon, 5930
3: 3 they offered **b offerings** thereon unto 5930
3: 3 *even* **b offerings** morning and evening. 5930
3: 4 *offered* the daily **b offerings** by number, 5930
3: 5 *offered* the continual **b offering**, 5930
3: 6 they to offer **b offerings** unto the LORD. 5930
6: 9 for the **b offerings** of the God of heaven, 5928
8:35 offered **b offerings** unto the God of Israel 5930
8:35 all *this* was a **b offering** unto the LORD. 5930
Ne 1: 3 and the gates thereof are **b** with fire. 3341
2:17 and the gates thereof are **b** with fire: 3341
4: 2 of the heaps of the rubbish which are **b**? 8313
10:33 for the continual **b offering**, 5930
Job 1: 5 offered **b offerings** according to 5930
1:16 hath **b up** the sheep, and the servants, 1197
30:30 upon me, and my bones are **b** with heat. 2787
42: 8 and offer up for yourselves a **b offering**; 5930
Ps 20: 3 thy offerings, and accept thy **b sacrifice**. 5930
40: 6 **b offering** and sin offering hast thou not 5930
50: 8 thee for thy sacrifices or thy **b offerings**, 5930
51:16 I give *it*: thou delightest not in **b offering**. 5930
51:19 **b offering** and whole *burnt offering*: 5930
51:19 burnt offering and whole *b offering*: then NIH
66:13 I will go *into* thy house with **b offerings**: 5930
66:15 I will offer unto thee **b sacrifices** of 5930
74: 8 they have **b up** all the synagogues of God 8313
80:16 *is* **b** with fire, *it is* cut down: they perish 8313
102: 3 smoke, and my bones are **b** as a hearth. 2787
106:18 company; the flame **b up** the wicked. 3857
Pr 6:27 in his bosom, and his clothes not be **b**? 8313
6:28 go upon hot coals, and his feet not be **b**? 3554
Isa 1: 7 *is* desolate, your cities *are* **b** *with* fire: 8313
1:11 I am full *of* the **b offerings** of rams, 5930
33:12 thorns cut up shall they be **b** in the fire. 3341
40:16 beasts thereof sufficient *for* a **b offering**. 5930
43: 2 through the fire, thou shalt not be **b**; 3554
43:23 me the small cattle of thy **b offerings**; 5930
44:19 to say, I have **b** part of it in the fire; 8313
56: 7 their **b offerings** and their sacrifices *shall* 5930
61: 8 I hate robbery for **b offering**; 5930
64:11 our fathers praised thee, is **b up** with fire: 8316
65: 7 have **b incense** upon the mountains, 6999
Jer 1:16 have **b incense** unto other gods, 6999
2:15 his cities are **b** without inhabitant. 3341
6:20 your **b offerings** *are* not acceptable, 5930

B

Jer 6:29 The bellows are **b**, the lead is consumed 2787
7:21 Put your **b offerings** unto your sacrifices, 5930
7:22 concerning **b offerings** or sacrifices: 5930
9:10 because they are **b up**, so that none can 3341
9:12 *and* is **b up** like a wilderness, 3341
14:12 they offer **b offering** and an oblation, 5930
17:26 bringing **b offerings**, and sacrifices, 5930
18:15 they have **b incense** to vanity, 6999
19: 4 and have **b incense** in it unto other gods, 6999
19: 5 burn their sons with fire *for* **b offerings** 5930
19:13 incense unto all the host of heaven, 6999
33:18 a man before me to offer **b offerings**, 5930
36:27 after that the king had **b** the roll, 8313
36:28 Jehoiakim the king of Judah hath **b**. 8313
36:29 Thou hast **b** this roll, saying, Why hast 8313
36:32 Jehoiakim king of Judah had **b** in the fire: 8313
38:17 and this city shall not be **b** with fire; 8313
38:23 shalt **cause** this city **to be b** with fire. 8313
39: 8 the Chaldeans the king's house, 8313
44:15 wives had **b incense** unto other gods, 6999
44:19 we **b incense** to the queen of heaven, 6999
44:21 incense that ye **b** in the cities of Judah, 6999
44:23 Because you have **b incense**, and because 6999
49: 2 and her daughters shall be **b** with fire: 3341
51:25 rocks, and will make thee a **b** mountain. 8316
51:30 they have **b** her dwelling places; her bars 3341
51:32 reeds they have **b** with fire, and the men 8313
51:58 her high gates shall be **b** with fire; 3341
52:13 the house of the LORD, and the king's 8313
52:13 all the houses of the great *men*, **b** he with 8313
Eze 15: 4 the ends of it, and the midst of it is **b**. 2787
20:47 the south to the north shall be **b** therein. 6866
24:10 and spice it well, and let the bones be **b**. 2787
40:38 where they washed the **b offering** 5930
40:39 to slay thereon the **b offering** and the sin 5930
40:42 *were* of hewn stone for the **b offering**, 5930
40:42 wherewith they slew the **b offering** 5930
43:18 offer **b offering** thereon, and to sprinkle 5930
43:24 they shall offer them up *for* a **b offering** 5930
43:27 the priests shall make your **b offerings** 5930
44:11 they shall slay the **b offering** and 5930
45:15 for a **b offering**, and for peace offerings, 5930
45:17 be the prince's part *to give* **b offerings**, 5930
45:17 the **b offering**, and the peace offerings, 5930
45:23 he shall prepare a **b offering** to the LORD, 5930
45:25 according to the **b offering**, 5930
46: 2 the priests shall prepare his **b offering** 5930
46: 4 the **b offering** that the prince shall offer 5930
46:12 shall prepare a voluntary **b offering** 5930
46:12 he shall prepare his **b offering** and his 5930
46:13 Thou shalt daily prepare a **b offering** unto 5930
46:15 every morning *for* a continual **b offering**. 5930
Hos 2:13 where*in* she **b** incense to them, 6999
6: 6 knowledge of God more than **b offerings**. 5930
Joel 1:19 the flame hath **b** all the trees of the field. 3857
Am 2: 1 he **b** the bones of the king of Edom into 8313
5:22 Though ye offer me **b offerings** and 5930
Mic 1: 7 the hires thereof shall be **b** with the fire, 8313
6: 6 shall I come before him with **b offerings**, 5930
Na 1: 5 the earth is **b** at his presence, yea, 5375
Mt 13:40 the tares are gathered and **b** in the fire; 2618
22: 7 those murderers, and **b up** their city. 1714
Mk 12:33 is more than all **whole b offerings** and 3646
1Co 3:15 If any *man's* work shall be **b**, he shall 2618
Heb 10: 6 In **b offerings** and *sacrifices* for sin thou 3646
10: 8 Sacrifice and offering and **b offerings** and 3646
13:11 priest for sin, are **b** without the camp. 2618
2Pe 3:10 the works that are therein shall be **b up**. 2618
Rev 8: 7 The third *part* of trees was **b up**, and all 2618
8: 7 burnt up, and all green grass was **b up**. 2618
18: 8 and she shall be **utterly b** with fire: 2618

BURST (9) [BURSTING]
Job 32:19 no vent; it is **ready to b** like new bottles. 1234
Pr 3:10 thy presses shall **b out** with new wine. 6555
Jer 2:20 I have broken thy yoke, *and* **b** thy bands; 5423
5: 5 broken the yoke, *and* **b** the bonds. 5423
30: 8 will **b** thy bonds, and strangers shall no 5423
Na 1:13 off thee, and will **b** thy bonds **in sunder**. 5423
Mk 2:22 else the new wine doth **b** the bottles, and 4486
Lk 5:37 else the new wine will **b** the bottles, and 4486
Ac 1:18 he **b asunder** in the midst, and all his 2997

BURSTING (1) [BURST]
Isa 30:14 that there shall not be found in the **b** of it 4386

BURY (39) [BURIAL, BURIED, BURIERS, BURYING,
 BURYINGPLACE]
Ge 23: 4 that I may **b** my dead out of my sight. 6912
23: 6 the choice of our sepulchres thy dead; 6912
23: 6 but that thou mayest **b** thy dead. 6912
23: 8 If it be your mind that I should **b** my dead 6912
23:11 of my people give I it thee: **b** thy dead. 6912
23:13 take *it* of me, and I will **b** my dead there. 6912
23:15 me and thee? **b** therefore thy dead. 6912
47:29 with me; **b** me not, I pray thee, in Egypt: 6912
47:30 of Egypt, and **b** me in their buryingplace. 6912
49:29 **b** me with my fathers in the cave that *is* 6912
50: 5 land of Canaan, there shalt thou **b** me. 6912
50: 5 and **b** my father, and I will come again. 6912
50: 6 Pharaoh said, Go up, and **b** thy father, 6912
50: 7 Joseph went up to **b** his father: 6912
50:14 all that went up with him to **b** his father, 6912
Dt 21:23 but **in any wise b** him that day; 6912+6912
1Ki 2:31 hath said, and fall upon him, and **b** him; 6912

1Ki 11:15 of the host was gone up to **b** the slain, 6912
13:29 came to the city, to mourn and to **b** him. 6912
13:31 **b** me in the sepulchre wherein the man 6912
14:13 all Israel shall mourn for him, and **b** him: 6912
2Ki 9:10 *there shall be* none to **b** her. 6912
9:34 see now this cursed *woman*, and **b** her: 6912
9:35 they went to **b** her: but they found no 6912
Ps 79: 3 and *there was* none to **b** them. 6912
Jer 7:32 for they shall **b** in Tophet, till there be no 6912
14:16 they *shall* have none to **b** them, them, 6912
19:11 shall **b** *them* in Tophet, till *there be* no 6912
19:11 in Tophet, till *there be* no place to **b**. 6912
Eze 39:11 there shall they **b** Gog and all his 6912
39:13 all the people of the land shall **b** *them*; 6912
39:14 passing through the land to **b** with 6912
Hos 9: 6 gather them up, Memphis shall **b** them: 6912
Mt 8:21 suffer me first to go and **b** my father. 2290
8:22 Follow me; and let the dead **b** their dead. 2290
27: 7 them the potter's field, to **b** strangers in. 5027
Lk 9:59 suffer me first to go and **b** my father. 2290
9:60 said unto him, Let the dead **b** their dead: 2290
Jn 19:40 as the manner of the Jews is to **b**. 1779

BURYING (4) [BURY]
2Ki 13:21 as they were **b** a man, that behold, 6912
Eze 39:12 months shall the house of Israel be **b** 6912
Mk 14: 8 aforehand to anoint my body to the **b**. 1780
Jn 12: 7 against the day of my **b** hath she kept this. 1780

BURYINGPLACE (7) [BURY, PLACE]
Ge 23: 4 a **b** with you, 6913
23: 9 it me for a possession of a **b** amongst you. 6913
23:20 a possession of a **b** by the sons of Heth. 6913
47:30 me out of Egypt, and bury me in their **b**. 6900
49:30 Ephron the Hittite for a possession of a **b**. 6913
49:30 a possession of a **b** of Ephron the Hittite, 6913
Jdg 16:31 and Eshtaol in the **b** of Manoah his father. 6913

BUSH (11) [BUSHES, BUSHY]
Ex 3: 2 in a flame of fire out of the midst of a **b**: 5572
3: 2 the **b** burned with fire, and the bush was 5572
3: 2 with fire, and the **b** was not consumed. 5572
3: 3 this great sight, why the **b** is not burnt. 5572
3: 4 called unto him out of the midst of the **b**, 5572
Dt 33:16 the good will of him that dwelt in the **b**: 5572
Mk 12:26 how in the **b** God spake unto him, saying, 942
Lk 6:44 nor of a **bramble b** gather they grapes. 942
20:37 are raised, even Moses shewed at the **b**, 942
Ac 7:30 angel of the Lord in a flame of fire in a **b**. 942
7:35 the angel which appeared to him in the **b**. 942

BUSHEL (3)
Mt 5:15 put it under a **b**, but on a candlestick; 3426
Mk 4:21 Is a candle brought to be put under a **b**, 3426
Lk 11:33 neither under a **b**, but on a candlestick, 3426

BUSHES (3) [BUSH]
Job 30: 4 Who cut up mallows by the **b**, 7880
30: 7 the **b** they brayed; under the nettles 7880
Isa 7:19 and upon all thorns, and upon all **b**. 5097

BUSHY (1) [BUSH]
SS 5:11 his locks *are* **b**, *and* black as a raven. 8534

BUSIED (1) [BUSY]
2Ch 35:14 the priests the sons of Aaron *were* **b** in NIH

BUSINESS (29) [BUSY]
Ge 39:11 *Joseph* went into the house to do his **b**; 4399
Dt 24: 5 neither shall he be charged with any **b**: 1697
Jos 2:14 life for yours, if ye utter not this our **b**. 1697
2:20 if thou utter this our **b**, then we will be 1697
Jdg 18: 7 Zidonians, and had no **b** with *any* man. 1697
18:28 and they had no **b** with *any* man; 1697
1Sa 20:19 hide thyself when the **b** was *in hand*, 4639
21: 2 The king hath commanded me a **b**, 1697
21: 2 Let no man know any thing of the **b**, 1697
21: 8 because the king's **b** required haste. 1697
1Ch 26:29 sons *were* for the outward **b** over Israel, 4399
26:30 Jordan westward in all the **b** of the LORD, 4399
2Ch 13:10 Aaron, and the Levites *wait* upon *their* **b**: 4399
17:13 he had much **b** in the cities of Judah: 4399
32:31 Howbeit in *the* **b** of the ambassadors of NIH
Ne 11:16 had the oversight of the outward **b** of 4399
11:22 the singers *were* over the **b** of the house 4399
13:30 and the Levites, every one in his **b**; 4399
Est 3: 9 of those that have the charge of the **b**, 4399
Ps 107:23 the sea in ships, that do **b** in great waters; 4399
Pr 22:29 Seest thou a man diligent in his **b**? 4399
Ecc 5: 3 dream cometh through the multitude of **b**; 6045
8:16 to see the **b** that is done upon the earth: 6045
Da 8:27 afterward I rose up, and did the king's **b**. 4399
Lk 2:49 ye not that I must be about my Father's **b**? NIG
Ac 6: 3 whom we may appoint over this **b**. 5532
Ro 12:11 Not slothful in **b**; fervent in spirit; 4710
16: 2 ye assist her in whatsoever **b** she hath 4229
1Th 4:11 and to do your own **b**, and to work with NIG

BUSY (1) [BUSIED, BUSINESS, BUSYBODIES,
 BUSYBODY]
1Ki 20:40 as thy servant was **b** here and there, 6213

BUSYBODIES (2) [BUSY, BODY]
2Th 3:11 working not at all, but are **b**, 4020
1Ti 5:13 and not only idle, but tattlers also and **b**, 4021

BUSYBODY (1) [BUSY, BODY]
1Pe 4:15 or as a **b in other men's matters**. 244

BUT (3994) See Index of Articles, Etc.

BUTLER (8) [BUTLERS, BUTLERSHIP]
Ge 40: 1 *that* the **b** of the king of Egypt and *his* 8248
40: 5 the **b** and the baker of the king of Egypt, 8248
40: 9 the chief **b** told his dream to Joseph, 8248
40:13 the former manner when thou wast his **b**. 8248
40:20 he lifted up the head of the chief **b** and of 8248
40:21 he restored the chief **b** unto his butlership 8248
40:23 Yet did not the chief **b** remember Joseph, 8248
41: 9 spake the chief **b** unto Pharaoh, saying, 8248

BUTLERS (1) [BUTLER]
Ge 40: 2 against the chief of the **b**, and against 8248

BUTLERSHIP (1) [BUTLER]
Ge 40:21 he restored the chief butler unto his **b** 4945

BUTTER (11)
Ge 18: 8 he took **b**, and milk, and the calf which 2529
Dt 32:14 **B** of kine, and milk of sheep, with fat of 2529
Jdg 5:25 she brought forth **b** in a lordly dish. 2529
2Sa 17:29 **b**, and sheep, and cheese of kine, 2529
Job 20:17 the floods, the brooks of honey and **b**. 2529
29: 6 When *I* washed my steps with **b**, 2529
Ps 55:21 *of* his mouth were smoother than **b**, 4260
Pr 30:33 the churning of milk bringeth forth **b**, 2529
Isa 7:15 **B** and honey shall he eat, that he may 2529
7:22 of milk *that they* shall give he shall eat **b**: 2529
7:22 for **b** and honey shall every one eat that 2529

BUTTOCKS (3)
2Sa 10: 4 *even* to their **b**, and sent them away. 8357
1Ch 19: 4 garments in the midst hard by *their* **b**, 4667
Isa 20: 4 barefoot, even with *their* **b** uncovered, 8357

BUY (56) [BOUGHT, BUYER, BUYEST, BUYETH]
Ge 41:57 came into Egypt to Joseph for to **b** *corn*; 7666
42: 2 down thither, and **b** for us from thence; 7666
42: 3 ten brethren went down to **b** corn 7666
42: 5 the sons of Israel came to **b** *corn* among 7666
42: 7 From the land of Canaan to **b** food. 7666
42:10 but to **b** food are thy servants come. 7666
43: 2 unto them, Go again, **b** us a little food. 7666
43: 4 us, we will go down and **b** thee food: 7666
43:20 came indeed down at the first time to **b** 7666
43:22 we brought down in our hands to **b** food: 7666
44:25 said, Go again, *and* **b** us a little food. 7666
47:19 **b** us and our land for bread, and we and 7069
Ex 21: 2 If thou **b** a Hebrew servant, six years he 7069
Lev 22:11 if the priest **b** *any* soul with his 7069+7075
25:15 the jubile thou shalt **b** of thy neighbour, 7069
25:44 of them shall ye **b** bondmen and 7069
25:44 of them shall ye **b**, and of their families 7069
Dt 2: 6 Ye shall **b** meat of them for money, that 7666
2: 6 ye shall also **b** water of them for money, 3739
28:68 and bondwomen, and no man shall **b** *you*. 7069
Ru 4: 4 **B** *it* before the inhabitants, and before 7069
4: 5 thou must **b** *it* also of Ruth the Moabitess, 7069
4: 8 the kinsman said unto Boaz, **B** *it* for thee. 7069
2Sa 24:21 said, To **b** the threshingfloor of thee, 7069
24:24 I will **surely b** *it* of thee at a price: 7069+7069
2Ki 12:12 to **b** timber and hewed stone to repair 7069
12: 6 to **b** timber and hewn stone to repair 7069
1Ch 21:24 I will **verily b** *it* for the full price: 7069+7069
2Ch 34:11 builders gave they *it*, to **b** hewn stone, 7069
Ezr 7:17 That thou mayest **b** speedily with this 7066
Ne 5: 3 houses, that we might **b** corn, because 3947
10:31 *that* we would not **b** *it* of them on 3947
Pr 23:23 **B** the truth, and sell *it* not; *also* wisdom, 7069
Isa 55: 1 come ye, **b**, and eat; yea, come, buy wine 7666
55: 1 b wine and milk without money and 7666
Jer 32: 7 **B** thee my field that *is* in Anathoth: 7069
32: 7 for the right of redemption *is* thine to **b** *it*. 7069
32: 8 said unto me, **B** my field, I pray thee, 7069
32: 8 the redemption *is* thine; **b** *it* for thyself. 7069
32:25 **B** thee the field for money, 7069
32:44 *Men* shall **b** fields for money, 7069
Am 8: 6 That *we* may **b** the poor for silver, 7069
Mt 14:15 the villages, and **b** themselves victuals. 59
25: 9 to them that sell, and **b** for yourselves. 59
25:10 while they went to **b**, the bridegroom 59
Mk 6:36 *into* the villages, and **b** themselves bread: 59
6:37 and two hundred pennyworth of bread, 59
Lk 9:13 we should go and **b** meat for all this people. 59
22:36 sword, let him sell his garment, and **b** one. 59
Jn 4: 8 were gone away unto the city to **b** meat.) 59
6: 5 shall we **b** bread, that these may eat? 59
1Co 7:30 they that **b**, as though they possessed not; 59
Jas 4:13 there a year, and **b and sell**, and get gain: 1710
Rev 3:18 counsel thee to **b** of me gold tried in the fire, 59
13:17 that no *man* might **b** or sell, save he that 59

BUYER (3) [BUY]
Pr 20:14 *It is* naught, *it is* naught, saith the **b**: 7069
Isa 24: 2 as *with* the **b**, so *with* the seller; 7069
Eze 7:12 let not the **b** rejoice, nor the seller mourn: 7069

BUYEST (2) [BUY]
Lev 25:14 or **b** *ought* of thy neighbour's hand, 7069
Ru 4: 5 What day thou **b** the field of the hand of 7069

BUYETH (3) [BUY]

Pr	31:16	She considereth a field, and **b** it: with	3947
Mt	13:44	selleth all that he hath, and **b** that field.	59
Rev	18:11	no *man* **b** their merchandise any more:	59

BUZ (3)

Ge	22:21	**B** his brother, and Kemuel the father of	938
1Ch	5:14	Jeshishai, the son of Jahdo, the son of **B**;	938
Jer	25:23	**B**, and all *that are* in the utmost corners,	938

BUZI (1)

| Eze | 1: 3 | the son of **B**, in the land of the Chaldeans | 941 |

BUZITE (2)

| Job | 32: 2 | wrath of Elihu the son of Barachel the **B**, | 940 |
| | 32: 6 | Elihu the son of Barachel the **B** answered | 940 |

BY (2633) [HEREBY, THEREBY, WHEREBY] See
Index of Articles, Etc.

BYWAYS (1) [WAY]

| Jdg | 5: 6 | and the travellers walked *through* **b**. | 734+6128 |

BYWORD (6) [WORD]

Dt	28:37	an astonishment, a proverb, and a **b**:	8148
1Ki	9: 7	be a proverb and a **b** among all people:	8148
2Ch	7:20	to be a proverb and a **b** among all nations.	8148
Job	17: 6	He hath made me also a **b** of the people;	4914
	30: 9	now am I their song, yea, I am their **b**.	4405
Ps	44:14	Thou makest us a **b** among the heathen,	4912

C

CABBON (1)

| Jos | 15:40 | And **C**, and Lahmam, and Kithlish, | 3522 |

CABINS (1)

| Jer | 37:16 | into the **c**, and Jeremiah had remained | 2588 |

CABUL (2)

| Jos | 19:27 | and goeth out to **C** on the left hand, | 3521 |
| 1Ki | 9:13 | called them the land of **C** unto this day. | 3521 |

CAESAR; CAESAR'S See CESAR; CESAR'S

CAESAREA See CESAREA

CAGE (2)

| Jer | 5:27 | As a **c** *is* full *of* birds, so *are* their houses | 3619 |
| Rev | 18: 2 | and a **c** of every unclean and hateful bird. | 5438 |

CAIAPHAS (9)

Mt	26: 3	of the high priest, who was called **C**,	2533
	26:57	led *him* away to **C** the high priest,	2533
Lk	3: 2	Annas and **C** being the high priests,	2533
Jn	11:49	one of them, *named* **C**, being the high	2533
	18:13	for he was father in law to **C**, which was	2533
	18:14	Now **C** was he, which gave counsel to	2533
	18:24	Now Annas had sent him bound unto **C**	2533
	18:28	led they Jesus from **C** unto the hall of	2533
Ac	4: 6	and **C**, and John, and Alexander,	2533

CAIN (20)

Ge	4: 1	conceived, and bare **C**, and said, I have	7014
	4: 2	of sheep, but **C** was a tiller of the ground.	7014
	4: 3	that **C** brought of the fruit of the ground	7014
	4: 5	unto **C** and to his offering he had not	7014
	4: 5	**C** was very wroth, and his countenance	7014
	4: 6	the Lord said unto **C**, Why art thou	7014
	4: 8	**C** talked with Abel his brother: and it	7014
	4: 8	that **C** rose up against Abel his brother,	7014
	4: 9	the Lord said unto **C**, Where *is* Abel thy	7014
	4:13	**C** said unto the Lord, My punishment *is*	7014
	4:15	him, Therefore whosoever slayeth **C**,	7014
	4:15	the Lord set a mark upon **C**, lest any	7014
	4:16	**C** went out from the presence of	7014
	4:17	**C** knew his wife; and she conceived,	7014
	4:24	If **C** shall be avenged sevenfold,	7014
	4:25	seed instead of Abel, whom **C** slew.	7014
Jos	15:57	**C**, Gibeah, and Timnah; ten cities with	7014
Heb	11: 4	God a more excellent sacrifice than **C**,	2535
1Jn	3:12	Not as **C**, *who* was of *that* wicked one,	2535
Jude	1:11	for they have gone in the way of **C**,	2535

CAINAN (7)

Ge	5: 9	And Enos lived ninety years, and begat **C**:	7018
	5:10	Enos lived after he begat **C** eight hundred	7018
	5:12	**C** lived seventy years,	7018
	5:13	**C** lived after he begat Mahalaleel eight	7018
	5:14	all the days of **C** were nine hundred	7018
Lk	3:36	was *the son* of **C**, which was *the son* of	2536
	3:37	*son* of Maleleel, which was *the son* of **C**,	2536

CAKE (13) [CAKES]

Ex	29:23	one **c** of oiled bread, and one wafer out of	2471
Lev	8:26	he took one unleavened **c**, and a cake of	2471
	8:26	a **c** of oiled bread, and one wafer,	2471

Lev	24: 5	two tenth deals shall be *in* one **c**.	2471
Nu	6:19	one unleavened **c** out of the basket,	2471
	15:20	Ye shall offer up a **c** *of* the first of your	2471
Jdg	7:13	a **c** of barley bread tumbled into the host	6742
1Sa	30:12	they gave him a piece of a **c** *of* figs, and	1690
2Sa	6:19	every one a **c** of bread, and a good piece	2471
1Ki	17:12	I have not a **c**, but a handful of meal in a	4580
	17:13	make me thereof a little **c** first, and bring	5692
	19: 6	*there was* a **c** baken on the coals,	5692
Hos	7: 8	the people; Ephraim is a **c** not turned.	5692

CAKES (25) [CAKE]

Ge	18: 6	knead *it*, and make **c** upon the hearth.	5692
Ex	12:39	they baked unleavened **c** of the dough	5692
	29: 2	unleavened tempered with oil,	2471
Lev	2: 4	*it shall be* unleavened **c** of fine flour	2471
	7:12	unleavened **c** mingled with oil,	2471
	7:12	and **c** mingled with oil, of fine flour, fried.	2471
	7:13	the **c**, he shall offer *for* his offering	2471
	24: 5	take fine flour, and bake twelve **c** thereof:	2471
Nu	6:15	**c** *of* fine flour mingled with oil,	2471
	11: 8	and baked *it* in pans, and made **c** *of* it:	5692
Jos	5:11	unleavened **c**, and parched *corn* in	NIH
Jdg	6:19	and unleavened **c** *of* an ephah of flour:	NIH
	6:20	Take the flesh and the unleavened **c**,	NIH
	6:21	touched the flesh and the unleavened **c**;	NIH
	6:21	the unleavened **c**. Then the angel of	NIH
1Sa	25:18	two hundred **c** *of* figs, and laid *them* on	1690
2Sa	13: 6	**make** *me* a couple of **c** in my sight,	3823+3834
	13: 8	kneaded *it*, and **made c** in his sight,	3823
	13: 8	cakes in his sight, and did bake the **c**.	3834
	13:10	Tamar took the **c** which she had made,	3834
1Ch	12:40	**c** *of* figs, and bunches of raisins, and wine,	1690
	23:29	for the unleavened **c**, and for *that which*	7550
Jer	7:18	to make **c** to the queen of heaven,	3561
	44:19	did we make her **c** to worship her,	3561
Eze	4:12	thou shalt eat it *as* barley **c**, and thou shalt	5692

CALAH (2)

| Ge | 10:11 | and the city Rehoboth, and **C**, | 3625 |
| | 10:12 | Resen between Nineveh and **C**: the same | 3625 |

CALAMITIES (3) [CALAMITY]

Ps	57: 1	make my refuge, until *these* **c** be overpast.	1942
	141: 5	for yet my prayer also *shall be* in their **c**.	7451
Pr	17: 5	that is glad at **c** shall not be unpunished.	343

CALAMITY (19) [CALAMITIES]

Dt	32:35	for the day of their **c** *is* at hand,	343
2Sa	22:19	They prevented me in the day of my **c**:	343
Job	6: 2	my **c** laid in the balances together!	1942
	30:13	They mar my path, they set forward my **c**,	1942
Ps	18:18	They prevented me in the day of my **c**:	343
Pr	1:26	I also will laugh at your **c**; I will mock	343
	6:15	Therefore shall his **c** come suddenly;	343
	19:13	A foolish son *is* the **c** of his father: and	1942
	24:22	For their **c** shall rise suddenly;	343
	27:10	thy brother's house in the day of thy **c**:	343
Jer	18:17	and not the face, in the day of their **c**.	343
	46:21	the day of their **c** was come upon them,	343
	48:16	The **c** of Moab *is* near to come,	343
	49: 8	for I will bring the **c** of Esau upon him,	343
	49:32	I will bring their **c** from all sides thereof,	343
Eze	35: 5	force of the sword in the time of their **c**,	343
Ob	1:13	the gate of my people in the day of their **c**;	343
	1:13	on their affliction in the day of their **c**,	343
	1:13	on their substance in the day of their **c**;	343

CALAMUS (3)

Ex	30:23	and of sweet **c** two hundred and	7070
SS	4:14	and cinnamon, with all trees of	7070
Eze	27:19	bright iron, cassia, and **c**, were in thy	7070

CALCOL (1) [CHALCOL]

| 1Ch | 2: 6 | and Ethan, and Heman, and **C**, and Dara: | 3633 |

CALDRON (6) [CALDRONS]

1Sa	2:14	*it* into the pan, or kettle, or **c**, or pot;	7037
Job	41:20	smoke, as *out of* a seething pot or **c**.	100
Eze	11: 3	this *city* is the **c**, and we *be* the flesh.	5518
	11: 7	they *are* the flesh, and this *city* is the **c**:	5518
	11:11	This *city* shall not be your **c**, neither shall	5518
Mic	3: 3	as for the pot, and as flesh within the **c**.	7037

CALDRONS (3) [CALDRON]

2Ch	35:13	in **c**, and in pans, and divided *them*	1731
Jer	52:18	The **c** also, and the shovels,	5518
	52:19	**c**, and the candlesticks, and the spoons,	5518

CALEB (32) [CALEB'S, CALEB-EPHRATAH]

Nu	13: 6	tribe of Judah, **C** the son of Jephunneh.	3612
	13:30	**C** stilled the people before Moses,	3612
	14: 6	son of Nun, and **C** the son of Jephunneh,	3612
	14:24	servant **C**, because he had another spirit	3612
	14:30	save **C** the son of Jephunneh,	3612
	14:38	son of Nun, and **C** the son of Jephunneh,	3612
	26:65	save **C** the son of Jephunneh,	3612
	32:12	**C** the son of Jephunneh the Kenezite,	3612
	34:19	tribe of Judah, **C** the son of Jephunneh.	3612
Dt	1:36	Save **C** the son of Jephunneh; he shall see	3612
Jos	14: 6	the son of Jephunneh the Kenezite said	3612
	14:13	gave unto **C** the son of Jephunneh Hebron	3612
	14:14	became the inheritance of **C** the son of	3612
	15:13	the son of Jephunneh he gave a part	3612
	15:14	**C** drove thence the three sons of Anak,	3612
	15:16	**C** said, He that smiteth Kirjath-sepher,	3612

Jos	15:17	son of Kenaz, the brother of **C**, took it:	3612
	15:18	and **C** said unto her, What wouldest thou?	3612
	21:12	gave they to **C** the son of Jephunneh for	3612
Jdg	1:12	**C** said, He that smiteth Kirjath-sepher,	3612
	1:14	and **C** said unto her, What wilt thou?	3612
	1:15	**C** gave her the upper springs and the	3612
	1:20	they gave Hebron unto **C**, as Moses said:	3612
1Sa	25: 3	doings; and he *was* of the house of **C**.	3614
	30:14	to Judah, and upon the south of **C**;	3612
1Ch	2:18	**C** the son of Hezron begat *children* of	3612
	2:19	**C** took unto him Ephrath, which bare him	3612
	2:42	the sons of **C** the brother of Jerahmeel	3612
	2:49	and the daughter of **C** *was* Achsah.	3612
	2:50	These were the sons of **C** the son of Hur,	3612
	4:15	the sons of **C** the son of Jephunneh; Iru,	3612
	6:56	they gave to **C** the son of Jephunneh.	3612

CALEB'S (4) [CALEB]

Jdg	1:13	son of Kenaz, **C** younger brother, took it:	3612
	3: 9	the son of Kenaz, **C** younger brother.	3612
1Ch	2:46	**C** concubine, bare Haran, and Moza,	3612
	2:48	Maachah, **C** concubine, bare Sheber,	3612

CALEB-EPHRATAH (1) [CALEB, EPHRATAH]

| 1Ch | 2:24 | after that Hezron was dead in **C**, then | 3613 |

CALF (29) [CALF'S, CALVE, CALVED, CALVES, CALVETH]

Ge	18: 7	fetch a **c** tender and good,	1121+1241
	18: 8	the **c** which he had dressed,	1121+1241
Ex	32: 4	after he had made it a molten **c**:	5695
	32: 8	they have made them a molten **c**,	5695
	32:19	that he saw the **c**, and the dancing:	5695
	32:20	he took the **c** which they had made,	5695
	32:24	it into the fire, and there came out this **c**.	5695
	32:35	because they made the **c**, which Aaron	5695
Lev	9: 2	Take thee a young **c** for a sin	1241+5695
	9: 3	a **c** and a lamb, both of the first year,	5695
	9: 8	altar, and slew the **c** of the sin offering,	5695
Dt	9:16	your God, *and* had made you a molten **c**:	5695
	9:21	the **c** which ye had made, and burnt it	5695
1Sa	28:24	the woman had a fat **c** in the house;	5695
Ne	9:18	when they had made them a molten **c**,	5695
Job	21:10	their cow calveth, and **casteth** not **her c**.	7921
Ps	29: 6	He maketh them also to skip like a **c**;	5695
	106:19	They made a **c** in Horeb,	5695
Isa	11: 6	the **c** and the young lion and the fatling	5695
	27:10	shall the **c** feed, and there shall he lie	5695
Jer	34:18	when they cut the **c** in twain,	5695
	34:19	which passed between the parts of the **c**;	5695
Hos	8: 5	Thy **c**, O Samaria, hath cast *thee* off;	5695
	8: 6	the **c** of Samaria shall be broken in pieces.	5695
Lk	15:23	And bring hither the fatted **c**, and kill *it*;	3448
	15:27	and thy father killed the fatted **c**,	3448
	15:30	thou hast killed for him the fatted **c**.	3448
Ac	7:41	And they **made** a **c** in those days,	3447
Rev	4: 7	the second beast like a **c**, and the third	3448

CALF'S (1) [CALF]

| Eze | 1: 7 | sole of their feet *was* like the sole of a **c** | 5695 |

CALKERS (2)

| Eze | 27: 9 | wise *men* thereof were in thee thy **c**: | 919+2388 |
| | 27:27 | thy **c**, and the occupiers of thy | 919+2388 |

CALL (196) [CALLED, CALLEDST, CALLEST, CALLETH, CALLING]

Ge	2:19	unto Adam to see what he would **c** them:	7121
	4:26	began *men* to **c** upon the name of	7121
	16:11	bear a son, and shalt **c** his name Ishmael;	7121
	17:15	thou shalt not **c** her name Sarai,	7121
	17:19	indeed; and thou shalt **c** his name Isaac:	7121
	24:57	We will **c** the damsel, and inquire at her	7121
	30:13	for the daughters will **c** me **blessed**:	833
	46:33	when Pharaoh shall **c** you, and shall say,	7121
Ex	2: 7	to thee a nurse of the Hebrew women,	7121
	2:20	the man? **c** him, that he may eat bread.	7121
	34:15	*one* **c** thee, and thou eat of his sacrifice;	7121
Nu	16: 2	Moses sent to **c** Dathan and Abiram,	7121
	22: 5	to **c** him, saying, Behold, there is a people	7121
	22:20	If the men come to **c** thee, rise up,	7121
	22:37	I not earnestly send unto thee to **c** thee?	7121
Dt	2:11	but the Moabites **c** them Emims.	7121
	2:20	the Ammonites **c** them Zamzummims;	7121
	3: 9	(*Which* Hermon the Sidonians **c** Sirion;	7121
	3: 9	call Sirion; and the Amorites **c** it Shenir;)	7121
	4: 7	*is* in all *things that* we **c** upon him *for?*	7121
	4:26	I **c** heaven and earth **to witness** against	5749
	25: 8	the elders of his city shall **c** him,	7121
	30: 1	thou shalt **c** *them* to mind among all	7725
	30:19	I **c** heaven and earth **to record** *this* day	5749
	31:14	**c** Joshua, and present yourselves in	7121
	31:28	**c** heaven and earth **to record** against	5749
	33:19	shall **c** the people *unto* the mountain;	7121
Jdg	12: 1	and didst not **c** us to go with thee?	7121
	16:25	they said, **C** for Samson, that he may	7121
	21:13	and to **c** peaceably unto them.	7121
Ru	1:20	them, **C** me not Naomi, call me Mara:	7121
	1:20	them, Call me not Naomi, **c** me Mara:	7121
	1:21	why *then* **c** ye me Naomi, seeing	7121
1Sa	3: 6	and said, Here *am* I; for thou didst **c** me.	7121
	3: 8	and said, Here *am* I; for thou didst **c** me.	7121
	3: 9	it shall be, if he **c** thee, that thou shalt say,	7121
	12:17	I will **c** unto the Lord, and he shall send	7121
	16: 3	**c** Jesse to the sacrifice, and I will shew	7121

C

Ref	Text	Strong's
1Sa 22:11	the king sent to c Ahimelech the priest,	7121
2Sa 17: 5	C now Hushai the Archite also, and let us	7121
22: 4	I will c on the LORD, who is worthy to	7121
1Ki 1:28	and said, C me Bath-sheba.	7121
1:32	C me Zadok the priest, and Nathan	7121
8:52	hearken unto them in all that they c for	7121
17:18	unto me to c my sin to remembrance,	2142
18:24	c ye on the name of your gods, and I will	7121
18:24	and I will c on the name of the LORD:	7121
18:25	c on the name of your gods, but put no	7121
22:13	the messenger that was gone to c Micaiah	7121
2Ki 4:12	to Gehazi his servant, C this Shunammite.	7121
4:15	said, C her. And when he had called her,	7121
4:36	and said, C this Shunammite.	7121
5:11	c on the name of the LORD his God,	7121
10:19	unto me all the prophets of Baal,	7121
1Ch 16: 8	thanks unto the LORD, c upon his name,	7121
2Ch 18:12	messenger that went to c Micaiah spake	7121
Job 5: 1	C now, if there be any that will answer	7121
13:22	thou, and I will answer: or let me speak,	7121
14:15	Thou shalt c, and I will answer thee:	7121
27:10	Almighty? will he always c upon God?	7121
Ps 4: 1	Hear me when I c, O God of my	7121
4: 3	the LORD will hear when I c unto him.	7121
14: 4	they eat bread, and c not upon the LORD.	7121
18: 3	I will c upon the LORD, who is worthy to	7121
20: 9	LORD: let the king hear us when we c.	7121
49:11	they c their lands after their own names.	7121
50: 4	He shall c to the heavens from above,	7121
50:15	c upon me in the day of trouble: I will	7121
55:16	As for me, I will c upon God;	7121
72:17	in him: all nations shall c him blessed.	833
77: 6	c to remembrance my song in the night:	2142
80:18	quicken us, and we will c upon thy name.	7121
86: 5	in mercy unto all them that c upon thee.	7121
86: 7	the day of my trouble I will c upon thee:	7121
91:15	shall c upon me, and I will answer him:	7121
99: 6	among them that c upon his name;	7121
102: 2	in the day when I c answer me speedily.	7121
105: 1	thanks unto the LORD; c upon his name:	7121
116: 2	will I c upon him as long as I live.	7121
116:13	and c upon the name of the LORD.	7121
116:17	and will c upon the name of the LORD.	7121
145:18	is nigh unto all them that c upon him,	7121
145:18	upon him, to all that c upon him in truth.	7121
Pr 1:28	they c upon me, but I will not answer;	7121
7: 4	and understanding thy kinswoman.	7121
8: 4	Unto you, O men, I c; and my voice is to	7121
9:15	To c passengers who go right on their	7121
31:28	Her children arise up, and c her blessed;	833
Isa 5:20	Woe unto them that c evil good, and good	559
7:14	a Son, and shall c his name Immanuel.	7121
8: 3	me, C his name Maher-shalal-hash-baz.	7121
12: 4	Praise the LORD, c upon his name,	7121
22:12	in that day did the Lord GOD of hosts c to	7121
22:20	that I will c my servant Eliakim the son of	7121
31: 2	bring evil, and will not c back his words:	5493
34:12	They shall c the nobles thereof to	7121
41:25	from the rising of the sun shall he c upon	7121
44: 5	another shall c himself by the name of	7121
44: 7	shall c, and shall declare it, and set it in	7121
45: 3	the LORD, which c thee by thy name,	7121
48: 2	For they c themselves of the holy city,	7121
48:13	I c unto them, they stand up together.	7121
55: 5	shalt c a nation that thou knowest not,	7121
55: 6	be found, c ye upon him while he is near:	7121
58: 5	ashes under him? wilt thou c this a fast,	7121
58: 9	shalt thou c, and the LORD shall answer;	7121
58:13	c the sabbath a delight, the holy of	7121
60:14	they shall c thee, The city of the LORD,	7121
60:18	thou shalt c thy walls Salvation,	7121
61: 6	men shall c you the Ministers of our God:	559
62:12	they shall c them, The holy people,	7121
65:15	and c his servants by another name:	7121
65:24	to pass, that before they c, I will answer;	7121
Jer 1:15	I will c all the families of the kingdoms of	7121
3:17	At that time they shall c Jerusalem	7121
3:19	I said, Thou shalt c me, My father;	7121
6:30	Reprobate silver shall men c them,	7121
7:27	thou shalt also c unto them; but they will	7121
9:17	c for the mourning women, that they may	7121
10:25	upon the families that c not on thy name:	7121
25:29	For I will c for a sword upon all	7121
29:12	shall ye c upon me, and ye shall go and	7121
33: 3	C unto me, and I will answer thee,	7121
50:29	C together the archers against Babylon;	8085
51:27	together against her the kingdoms of	8085
La 2:15	saying, Is this the city that men c The	559
Eze 21:23	he will c to remembrance the iniquity,	2142
36:29	I will c for the corn, and will increase it,	7121
38:21	I will c for a sword against him	7121
39:11	they shall c it The valley of Hamon-gog.	7121
Da 2: 2	the king commanded to c the magicians,	7121
Hos 1: 4	LORD said unto him, C his name Jezreel;	7121
1: 6	said unto him, C her name Lo-ruhamah;	7121
1: 9	said God, C his name Lo-ammi: for ye are	7121
2:16	saith the LORD, that thou shalt c me Ishi;	7121
2:16	me Ishi; and shalt c me no more Baali.	7121
7:11	they c to Egypt, they go to Assyria.	7121
Joel 1:14	c a solemn assembly, gather the elders	7121
2:15	sanctify a fast, c a solemn assembly:	7121
2:32	that whosoever shall c on the name of	7121
2:32	in the remnant whom the LORD shall c.	7121
Am 5:16	they shall c the husbandman to mourning,	7121
Jnh 1: 6	c upon thy God, if so be that God will	7121

Ref	Text	Strong's
Zep 3: 9	that they may all c upon the name of	7121
Zec 3:10	shall ye c every man his neighbour, under	7121
13: 9	they shall c on my name, and I will hear	7121
Mal 1: 4	they shall c, The border of	7121
3:12	all nations shall c you blessed: for ye shall	833
3:15	now we c the proud happy; yea, they that	833
Mt 1:21	a son, and thou shalt c his name JESUS:	2564
1:23	son, and they shall c his name Emmanuel,	2564
9:13	for I am not come to c the righteous,	2564
10:25	how much more shall they c them of his	NIG
20: 8	C the labourers, and give them their hire,	2564
22: 3	And sent forth his servants to c them that	2564
22:43	then doth David in spirit c him Lord,	2564
22:45	If David then c him Lord, how is he his	2564
23: 9	And c no man your father upon the earth:	2564
Mk 2:17	I came not to c the righteous, but sinners	2564
10:49	they c the blind man, saying unto him,	5455
15:12	that I shall do unto him whom ye c	3004
15:16	and they c together the whole band.	4779
Lk 1:13	a son, and thou shalt c his name John.	2564
1:31	forth a son, and shalt c his name JESUS.	2564
1:48	all generations shall c me blessed.	3106
5:32	I came not to c the righteous, but sinners	2564
6:46	And why c ye me, Lord, Lord, and do not	2564
14:12	a dinner or a supper, c not thy friends,	5455
14:13	c the poor, the maimed, the lame, the	2564
Jn 4:16	Go, c thy husband, and come hither.	5455
13:13	Ye c me Master and Lord: and ye say well;	5455
15:15	Henceforth I c you not servants;	3004
Ac 2:21	that whosoever shall c on the name of	1941
2:39	even as many as the Lord our God shall c.	4341
9:14	chief priests to bind all that c on thy name.	1941
10: 5	and c for one Simon, whose surname is	3343
10:15	hath cleansed, that c not thou common.	2840
10:28	God hath shewed me that I should not c	3004
10:32	therefore to Joppa, and c hither Simon,	3333
11: 9	hath cleansed, that c not thou common.	2840
11:13	Send men to Joppa, and c for Simon,	3343
19:13	took upon them to c over them which had	3687
24:14	that after the way which they c heresy,	3004
24:25	a convenient season, I will c for thee.	3333
Ro 9:25	also in Osee, I will c them my people,	2564
10:12	over all is rich unto all that c upon him.	1941
10:13	For whosoever shall c upon the name of	1941
10:14	shall they c on him in whom they have	1941
1Co 1: 2	with all that in every place c upon	1941
2Co 1:23	Moreover I c God for a record upon my	1941
2Ti 1: 5	When I c to remembrance the unfeigned	2983
2:22	them that c on the Lord out of a pure	1941
Heb 2:11	for which cause he is not ashamed to c	2564
10:32	But c to remembrance the former days,	363
Jas 5:14	let him c for the elders of the church;	4341
1Pe 1:17	And if ye c on the Father, who without	1941

CALLED (623) [CALL]

Ref	Text	Strong's
Ge 1: 5	God c the light Day, and the darkness he	7121
1: 5	light Day, and the darkness he c Night.	7121
1: 8	God c the firmament Heaven.	7121
1:10	God c the dry land Earth; and the	7121
1:10	the gathering together of the waters he c	7121
2:19	whatsoever Adam c every living creature,	7121
2:23	she shall be c Woman, because she was	7121
3: 9	the LORD God c unto Adam,	7121
3:20	Adam c his wife's name Eve; because	7121
4:17	builded a city, and c the name of the city,	7121
4:25	she bare a son, and c his name Seth:	7121
4:26	c his name Enos; then began men to call	7121
5: 2	blessed them, and c their name Adam,	7121
5: 3	after his image; and c his name Seth:	7121
5:29	he c his name Noah, saying, This same	7121
11: 9	Therefore is the name of it c Babel;	7121
12: 8	and c upon the name of the LORD.	7121
12:18	Pharaoh c Abram, and said, What is this	7121
13: 4	there Abram c on the name of the LORD.	7121
16:13	she c the name of the LORD that spake	7121
16:14	Wherefore the well was c Beer-lahai-roi;	7121
16:15	Abram c his son's name, which Hagar	7121
17: 5	Neither shall thy name any more be c	7121
19: 5	they c unto Lot, and said unto him,	7121
19:22	the name of the city was c Zoar.	7121
19:37	bare a son, and c his name Moab:	7121
19:38	bare a son, and c his name Ben-ammi:	7121
20: 8	c all his servants, and told all these things	7121
20: 9	Abimelech c Abraham, and said unto him	7121
21: 3	Abraham c the name of his son that was	7121
21:12	her voice; for in Isaac shall thy seed be c.	7121
21:17	angel of God c to Hagar out of heaven,	7121
21:31	Wherefore he c that place Beer-sheba;	7121
21:33	c there on the name of the LORD,	7121
22:11	the angel of the LORD c unto him out of	7121
22:14	Abraham c the name of that place	7121
22:15	the angel of the LORD c unto Abraham	7121
24:58	they c Rebekah, and said unto her, Wilt	7121
25:25	hairy garment; and they c his name Esau.	7121
25:26	on Esau's heel; and his name was c Jacob:	7121
25:30	am faint: therefore was his name c Edom.	7121
26: 9	Abimelech c Isaac, and said, Behold, of a	7121
26:18	he c their names after the names by	7121
26:18	names by which his father had c them.	7121
26:20	he c the name of the well Esek; because	7121
26:21	that also: and he c the name of it Sitnah.	7121
26:22	he c the name of it Rehoboth; and he said,	7121
26:25	c upon the name of the LORD,	7121
26:33	he c it Shebah: therefore the name of	7121
27: 1	he c Esau his eldest son, and said unto	7121

Ref	Text	Strong's
Ge 27:42	she sent and c Jacob her younger son,	7121
28: 1	Isaac c Jacob, and blessed him,	7121
28:19	he c the name of that place Beth-el: but	7121
28:19	name of that city was c Luz at the first.	NIH
29:32	bare a son, and she c his name Reuben:	7121
29:33	this son also: and she c his name Simeon.	7121
29:34	three sons: therefore was his name c Levi.	7121
29:35	therefore she c his name Judah;	7121
30: 6	me a son: therefore c she his name Dan.	7121
30: 8	and she c his name Naphtali.	7121
30:11	A troop cometh: and she c his name Gad.	7121
30:13	me blessed: and she c his name Asher.	7121
30:18	my husband: and she c his name Issachar.	7121
30:20	him six sons: and she c his name Zebulun.	7121
30:21	bare a daughter, and c her name Dinah.	7121
30:24	she c his name Joseph; and said,	7121
31: 4	Jacob sent and c Rachel and Leah to	7121
31:47	Laban c it Jegar-sahadutha: but	7121
31:47	it Jegar-sahadutha: but Jacob c it Galeed.	7121
31:48	Therefore was the name of it c Galeed;	7121
31:54	mount, and c his brethren to eat bread:	7121
32: 2	he c the name of that place Mahanaim.	7121
32:28	Thy name shall be c no more Jacob,	559
32:30	Jacob c the name of the place Peniel: for I	7121
33:17	the name of the place is c Succoth.	7121
33:20	there an altar, and c it El-Elohe-Israel.	7121
35: 7	there an altar, and c the place El-beth-el:	7121
35: 8	and the name of it was c Allon-bachuth.	7121
35:10	thy name shall not be c any more Jacob,	7121
35:10	be thy name: and he c his name Israel.	7121
35:15	Jacob c the name of the place where God	7121
35:18	(for she died) that she c his name Ben-oni:	7121
35:18	but his father c him Benjamin.	7121
38: 3	and bare a son; and he c his name Er.	7121
38: 4	and bare a son; and she c his name Onan.	7121
38: 5	and bare a son; and she c his name Shelah:	7121
38:29	therefore his name was c Pharez.	7121
38:30	upon his hand: and his name was c Zarah.	7121
39:14	That she c unto the men of her house,	7121
41: 8	c for all the magicians of Egypt,	7121
41:14	Pharaoh sent and c Joseph,	7121
41:45	Pharaoh c Joseph's name	7121
41:51	Joseph c the name of the firstborn	7121
41:52	the name of the second c he Ephraim:	7121
47:29	he c his son Joseph, and said unto him,	7121
48: 6	shall be c after the name of their brethren	7121
49: 1	Jacob c unto his sons, and said,	7121
50:11	wherefore the name of it was c	7121
Ex 1:18	the king of Egypt c for the midwives,	7121
2: 8	the maid went and c the child's mother.	7121
2:10	she c his name Moses: and she said,	7121
2:22	him a son, and c his name Gershom:	7121
3: 4	God c unto him out of the midst of	7121
7:11	Pharaoh also c the wise men and	7121
8: 8	Pharaoh c for Moses and Aaron, and said,	7121
8:25	Pharaoh c for Moses and for Aaron,	7121
9:27	c for Moses and Aaron, and said unto	7121
10:16	Pharaoh c for Moses and Aaron in haste:	7121
10:24	Pharaoh c unto Moses, and said, Go ye,	7121
12:21	Moses c for all the elders of Israel,	7121
12:31	he c for Moses and Aaron by night,	7121
15:23	the name of it was c Marah.	7121
16:31	the house of Israel c the name thereof	7121
17: 7	he c the name of the place Massah,	7121
17:15	altar, and c the name of it Jehovah-nissi:	7121
19: 3	the LORD c unto him out of the mountain,	7121
19: 7	and c for the elders of the people,	7121
19:20	the LORD c Moses up to the top of	7121
24:16	the seventh day he c unto Moses out of	7121
31: 2	I have c by name Bezaleel the son of Uri,	7121
33: 7	c it the Tabernacle of the Congregation.	7121
34:31	Moses c unto them; and Aaron and all	7121
35:30	the LORD hath c by name Bezaleel	7121
36: 2	Moses c Bezaleel and Aholiab, and every	7121
Lev 1: 1	the LORD c unto Moses, and spake unto	7121
9: 1	that Moses c Aaron and his sons,	7121
10: 4	Moses c Mishael and Elzaphan, the sons	7121
Nu 11: 3	he c the name of the place Taberah:	7121
11:34	he c the name of that place	7121
12: 5	the tabernacle, and c Aaron and Miriam:	7121
13:16	Moses c Oshea the son of Nun, Jehoshua.	7121
13:24	The place was c the brook Eshcol, because	7121
21: 3	and he c the name of the place Hormah.	7121
24:10	I c thee to curse mine enemies, and	7121
25: 2	they c the people unto the sacrifices of	7121
32:41	towns thereof, and c them Havoth-jair.	7121
32:42	and c it Nobah, after his own name.	7121
Dt 3:13	Bashan, which was c the land of giants.	7121
3:14	c them after his own name,	7121
5: 1	Moses c all Israel, and said unto them,	7121
15: 2	because it is c the LORD's release.	7121
25:10	his name shall be c in Israel, The house of	7121
28:10	that thou art c by the name of the LORD;	7121
29: 2	Moses c unto all Israel, and said unto	7121
31: 7	Moses c unto Joshua, and said unto	7121
Jos 4: 4	Joshua c the twelve men, whom he had	7121
5: 9	the name of the place is c Gilgal.	7121
6: 6	Joshua the son of Nun c the priests,	7121
7:26	Wherefore the name of that place was c,	7121
8:16	all the people that were in Ai were c	2199
9:22	Joshua c for them, and he spake unto	7121
10:24	that Joshua c for all the men of Israel,	7121
19:47	and dwelt therein, and c Leshem, Dan,	7121
22: 1	Joshua c the Reubenites, and the Gadites,	7121
22:34	the children of Gad c the altar Ed: for it	7121

C

Jos 23: 2	Joshua **c** for all Israel, *and* for their elders,	7121
24: 1	**c** for the elders of Israel, and for their	7121
24: 9	**c** Balaam the son of Beor to curse you:	7121
Jdg 1:17	and the name of the city was **c** Hormah.	7121
1:26	built a city, and **c** the name thereof Luz:	7121
2: 5	they **c** the name of that place Bochim.	7121
4: 6	**c** Barak the son of Abinoam out of	7121
4:10	Barak **c** Zebulun and Naphtali to Kedesh;	2199
6:24	unto the LORD, and **c** it Jehovah-shalom:	7121
6:32	Therefore on that day he **c** him Jerubbaal,	7121
8:31	him a son, whose name he **c** Abimelech.	7760
9:54	he **c** hastily unto the young man his	7121
10: 4	which are **c** Havoth-jair unto this day,	7121
12: 2	when I **c** you, ye delivered me not out of	2199
13:24	bare a son, and **c** his name Samson:	7121
14:15	have ye **c** us to take that we have?	7121
15:17	of his hand, and **c** that place Ramath-lehi.	7121
15:18	sore athirst, and **c** on the LORD, and said,	7121
15:19	wherefore he **c** the name thereof	7121
16:18	and **c** for the lords of the Philistines,	7121
16:19	she **c** for a man, and she caused *him* to	7121
16:25	they **c** for Samson out of the prison house;	7121
16:28	Samson **c** unto the LORD, and said,	7121
18:12	wherefore they **c** that place Mahaneh-dan	7121
18:29	they **c** the name of the city Dan, after	7121
Ru 4:17	to Naomi; and they **c** his name Obed:	7121
1Sa 1:20	she bare a son, and **c** his name Samuel,	7121
3: 4	That the LORD **c** Samuel: and	7121
3: 5	he said, I **c** not; lie down again. And he	7121
3: 6	the LORD **c** yet again, Samuel.	7121
3: 6	he answered, I **c** not, my son; lie down	7121
3: 8	the LORD **c** Samuel again the third time.	7121
3: 8	Eli perceived that the LORD had **c**	7121
3:10	stood, and **c** as at other times, Samuel,	7121
3:16	Eli **c** Samuel, and said, Samuel, my son.	7121
6: 2	the Philistines **c** for the priests and	7121
7:12	Shen, and **c** the name of it Eben-ezer,	7121
9: 9	for *he that is* now **c** a Prophet was	NIH
9: 9	*called* a Prophet was beforetime **c** a Seer.)	7121
9:26	that Samuel **c** Saul to the top of the house,	7121
10:17	Samuel **c** the people **together** unto	6817
12:18	So Samuel **c** unto the LORD;	7121
13: 4	the people were **c together** after Saul *to*	6817
16: 5	and his sons, and **c** them to the sacrifice.	7121
16: 8	Jesse **c** Abinadab, and made him pass	7121
19: 7	Jonathan **c** David, and Jonathan shewed	7121
23: 8	Saul **c** all the people **together** to war,	8085
23:28	they **c** that place Sela-hammahlekoth.	7121
28:15	therefore I have **c** thee, that *thou* mayest	7121
29: 6	Achish **c** David, and said unto him,	7121
2Sa 1: 7	behind him, he saw me, and **c** unto me.	7121
1:15	David **c** one of the young men, and said,	7121
2:16	wherefore that place was **c**	7121
2:26	Abner **c** to Joab, and said, Shall the sword	7121
5: 9	in the fort, and **c** it the city of David.	7121
5:20	Therefore he **c** the name of that place	7121
6: 2	whose name is **c** *by* the name of	7121
6: 8	he **c** *the* name of the place Perez-uzzah to	7121
9: 2	they had **c** him unto David, the king	7121
9: 9	the king **c** to Ziba, Saul's servant,	7121
11:13	when David had **c** him, he did eat and	7121
12:24	bare a son, and he **c** his name Solomon:	7121
12:25	he **c** his name Jedidiah, because of	7121
12:28	I take the city, and it be **c** after my name.	7121
13:17	he his servant that ministered unto him,	7121
14:33	when he had **c** for Absalom, he came to	7121
15: 2	Absalom **c** unto him, and said, Of what	7121
15:11	men out of Jerusalem, *that were* **c**;	7121
18:18	the pillar after his own name: and it	7121
18:18	and it is **c** unto this day, Absalom's place.	7121
18:26	the watchman **c** unto the porter, and said,	7121
18:28	Ahimaaz **c**, and said unto the king, All is	7121
21: 2	the king of the Gibeonites, and said unto	7121
22: 7	In my distress I **c upon** the LORD,	7121
1Ki 1: 9	**c** all his brethren the king's sons, and all	7121
1:10	and Solomon his brother, he **c** not.	7121
1:19	hath **c** all the sons of the king,	7121
1:19	but Solomon thy servant hath he not **c**.	7121
1:25	hath **c** all the king's sons, and the captains	7121
1:26	and thy servant Solomon, hath he not **c**.	7121
2:36	the king sent and **c** for Shimei,	7121
2:42	the king sent and **c** for Shimei,	7121
7:21	pillar, and **c** the name thereof Jachin.	7121
7:21	left pillar, and **c** the name thereof Boaz.	7121
8:43	which I have builded, is **c** by thy name.	7121
9:13	**c** them the land of Cabul unto this day.	7121
12: 3	That they sent and **c** him. And Jeroboam	7121
12:20	sent and **c** him unto the congregation,	7121
16:24	and **c** the name of the city which he built,	7121
17:10	he to her, and said, Fetch me, I pray	7121
17:11	as she was going to fetch *it*, he **c** to her,	7121
18: 3	Ahab **c** Obadiah, which *was* the governor	7121
18:26	**c** on the name of Baal from morning even	7121
20: 7	the king of Israel **c** all the elders of	7121
22: 9	the king of Israel **c** an officer, and said,	7121
2Ki 3:10	that the LORD hath **c** these three kings	7121
3:13	for the LORD hath **c** these three kings	7121
4:12	when he had **c** her, she stood before him.	7121
4:15	when he had **c** her, she stood in the door.	7121
4:22	she **c** unto her husband, and said, Send	7121
4:36	he **c** Gehazi, and said, Call this	7121
4:36	So he **c** her. And when she was come in	7121
6:11	he his servants, and said unto them, Will	7121
7:10	came and **c** unto the porter of the city:	7121
7:11	he **c** the porters; and they told *it* to	7121

2Ki 8: 1	for the LORD hath **c** for a famine;	7121
9: 1	Elisha the prophet **c** one of the children of	7121
12: 7	king Jehoash **c** for Jehoiada the priest,	7121
14: 7	**c** the name of it Joktheel unto this day.	7121
18: 4	burnt incense to it: and he **c** it Nehushtan.	7121
18:18	they had **c** to the king, there came out	7121
1Ch 4: 9	his mother **c** his name Jabez, saying,	7121
4:10	Jabez **c** on the God of Israel, saying,	7121
6:65	these cities, which are **c** by *their* names.	7121
7:16	bare a son, and she **c** his name Peresh;	7121
7:23	**c** his name Beriah, because it went evil	7121
11: 7	therefore they **c** it the city of David.	7121
13: 6	the cherubims, whose name is **c** on it.	7121
13:11	wherefore that place is **c** Perez-uzza to	7121
14:11	the name of that place Baal-perazim.	7121
15:11	**c** for Zadok and Abiathar the priests,	7121
21:26	peace offerings, and **c** upon the LORD;	7121
22: 6	he **c** for Solomon his son, and charged	7121
2Ch 3:17	**c** the name of *that on* the right hand	7121
6:33	house which I have built is **c** by thy name.	7121
7:14	If my people, which are **c** by my name,	7121
10: 3	they sent and **c** him. So Jeroboam and	7121
18: 8	the king of Israel **c** for one *of his* officers,	7121
20:26	the name of the same place was **c**,	7121
24: 6	the king **c** for Jehoiada the chief,	7121
Ezr 2:61	the Gileadite, and was **c** after their name:	7121
Ne 5:12	I **c** the priests, and took an oath of them,	7121
7:63	*to* wife, and was **c** after their name.	7121
Est 2:14	in her, and *that* she were **c** by name.	7121
3:12	were the king's scribes **c** on the thirteenth	7121
4: 5	**c** Esther for Hatach, *one* of the king's	7121
4:11	who is not **c**, *there is* one law of his to	7121
4:11	have not been **c** to come in unto the king	7121
5:10	he sent and **c for** his friends, and Zeresh	935
8: 9	were the king's scribes **c** at that time in	7121
9:26	Wherefore they **c** these days Purim after	7121
Job 1: 4	sent and **c** for their three sisters to eat and	7121
9:16	If I had **c**, and he had answered me;	7121
19:16	**c** my servant, and he gave *me* no answer;	7121
42:14	And he **c** the name of the first, Jemima;	7121
Ps 17: 6	have **c upon** thee, for thou wilt hear me,	7121
18: 6	In my distress I **c upon** the LORD,	7121
31:17	O LORD; for I have **c upon** thee:	7121
50: 1	**c** the earth from the rising of the sun unto	7121
53: 4	eat bread: they have not **c upon** God.	7121
79: 6	the kingdoms that have not **c** upon thy	7121
88: 9	LORD, I have **c** daily **upon** thee, I have	7121
99: 6	they **c upon** the LORD, and he answered	7121
105:16	he **c** *for* a famine upon the land:	7121
116: 4	I **c** upon the name of the LORD;	7121
118: 5	I **c upon** the LORD in distress:	7121
Pr 1:24	Because I have **c**, and ye refused; I have	7121
16:21	The wise in heart shall be **c** prudent: and	7121
24: 8	He that deviseth to do evil shall be **c** a	7121
SS 5: 6	I **c** him, but he gave me no answer.	7121
Isa 1:26	afterward thou shalt be **c**, The city of	7121
4: 1	let us be **c** by thy name, to take away	7121
4: 3	remaineth in Jerusalem, shall be **c** holy,	559
9: 6	name shall be **c** Wonderful, Counseller,	7121
13: 3	I have also **c** my mighty ones for mine	7121
19:18	one shall be **c**, The city of destruction.	559
31: 4	when a multitude of shepherds is **c forth**	7121
32: 5	The vile person shall be no more **c** liberal,	7121
35: 8	and it shall be **c** The way of holiness;	7121
41: 2	**c** him to his foot, gave the nations before	7121
41: 9	thee from the chief men thereof,	7121
42: 6	I the LORD have **c** thee in righteousness,	7121
43: 1	thee, I have **c** *thee* by thy name;	7121
43: 7	*Even* every one that is **c** by my name:	7121
43:22	thou hast not **c upon** me, O Jacob;	7121
45: 4	elect, I have even **c** thee by thy name:	7121
47: 1	for thou shalt no more be **c** tender and	7121
47: 5	for thou shalt no more be **c**, The lady of	7121
48: 1	which are **c** by the name of Israel,	7121
48: 8	wast **c** a transgressor from the womb.	7121
48:12	unto me, O Jacob, and Israel my **c**;	7121
48:15	I, *even* I, have spoken; yea, I have **c** him:	7121
49: 1	The LORD hath **c** me from the womb;	7121
50: 2	when I **c**, *was there* none to answer?	7121
51: 2	for I **c** him alone, and blessed him,	7121
54: 5	The God of the whole earth shall he be **c**.	7121
54: 6	For the LORD hath **c** thee as a woman	7121
56: 7	mine house shall be **c** a house of prayer	7121
58:12	shalt be **c**, The repairer of the breach,	7121
61: 3	they might be **c** trees of righteousness,	7121
62: 2	thou shalt be **c** by a new name, which	7121
62: 4	thou shalt be **c** Hephzi-bah, and thy land	7121
62:12	thou shalt be **c**, Sought out, A city not	7121
63:19	over them; they were not **c** by thy name.	7121
65: 1	a nation *that* was not **c** by my name.	7121
65:12	because when I **c**, ye did not answer;	7121
66: 4	because when I **c**, none did answer;	7121
Jer 7:10	house, which is **c** by my name, and say,	7121
7:11	Is this house, which is **c** by my name,	7121
7:13	not; and I **c** you, but ye answered not;	7121
7:14	which is **c** by my name, wherein ye trust,	7121
7:30	in the house which is **c** by my name,	7121
7:32	that it shall no more be **c** Tophet,	559
11:16	The LORD **c** thy name, A green olive	7121
12: 6	yea, they have **c** a multitude after thee:	7121
14: 9	midst of us, and we are **c** by thy name;	7121
15:16	for I am **c** by thy name, O LORD God of	7121
19: 6	that this place shall no more be **c** Tophet,	7121
20: 3	The LORD hath not **c** thy name Pashur,	7121
23: 6	this *is* his name whereby he shall be **c**,	7121

Jer 25:29	I begin to bring evil on the city which is **c**	7121
30:17	because they **c** thee an Outcast,	7121
32:34	which is **c** by my name, to defile it.	7121
33:16	this *is the name* wherewith she shall be **c**,	7121
34:15	me in the house which is **c** by my name.	7121
35:17	I have **c** unto them, but they have not	7121
36: 4	Jeremiah **c** Baruch the son of Neriah: and	7121
42: 8	he Johanan the son of Kareah, and all	7121
La 1:15	he hath **c** an assembly against me to crush	7121
1:19	I **c** for my lovers, *but* they deceived me:	7121
1:21	thou wilt bring the day *that* thou hast **c**,	7121
2:22	Thou hast **c** as *in* a solemn day my terrors	7121
3:55	I **c upon** thy name, O LORD, out of	7121
3:57	drewest near in the day that I **c upon**	7121
Eze 9: 3	he **c** to the man clothed *with* linen,	7121
20:29	name thereof is **c** Bamah unto this day.	7121
Da 5:12	now let Daniel be **c**, and he will shew	7123
8:16	which **c**, and said, Gabriel, make this	7121
9:18	and the city which is **c** by thy name:	7121
9:19	city and thy people are **c** by thy name.	7121
10: 1	whose name was **c** Belteshazzar;	7121
Hos 11: 1	I loved him, and **c** my son out of Egypt.	7121
11: 2	*As* they **c** them, so they went from them:	7121
11: 7	though they **c** them to the most High,	7121
Am 7: 4	the Lord GOD **c** to contend by fire,	7121
9:12	all the heathen, which are **c** by my name,	7121
Hag 1:11	I **c** *for* a drought upon the land,	7121
Zec 8: 3	Jerusalem shall be **c** a city of truth;	7121
11: 7	the one I **c** Beauty, and the other I called	7121
11: 7	I **c** Beauty, and the other I **c** Bands;	7121
Mt 1:16	of whom was born Jesus, who is **c** Christ.	3004
1:25	firstborn son: and *he* **c** his name JESUS.	2564
2: 7	when he had privily **c** the wise men,	2564
2:15	saying, Out of Egypt have I **c** my son.	2564
2:23	he came and dwelt in a city **c** Nazareth:	3004
2:23	the prophets, He shall be **c** a Nazarene.	2564
4:18	Simon **c** Peter, and Andrew his brother,	3004
4:21	mending their nets; and he **c** them.	2564
5: 9	for they shall be **c** the children of God.	2564
5:19	he shall be **c** the least in the kingdom of	2564
5:19	teach *them*, the same shall be **c** great in	2564
10: 1	And when he had **c** unto *him* his twelve	4341
10: 2	who is **c** Peter, and Andrew his brother;	3004
10:25	If they have **c** the master of the house	2564
13:55	not his mother **c** Mary? and his brethren,	3004
15:10	he **c** the multitude, and said unto them,	4341
15:32	Then Jesus **c** his disciples **unto** *him*, and	4341
18: 2	And Jesus **c** a little child **unto** *him*, and	4341
18:32	Then his lord, after that he had **c** him,	4341
20:16	first last: for many be **c**, but few chosen.	2822
20:25	But Jesus **c** them **unto** *him*, and said,	4341
20:32	Jesus stood still, and **c** them, and said,	5455
21:13	My house shall be **c** the house of prayer;	2564
22:14	For many are **c**, but few *are* chosen.	2822
23: 7	and to be **c** of men, Rabbi, Rabbi.	2564
23: 8	But be not ye **c** Rabbi: for one is your	2564
23:10	Neither be ye **c** masters: for one is your	2564
25:14	*who* **c** his own servants, and delivered	2564
26: 3	of the high priest, who was **c** Caiaphas,	3004
26:14	Then one of the twelve, **c** Judas Iscariot,	3004
26:36	with them unto a place **c** Gethsemane,	2564
27: 8	Wherefore that field was **c**, The field of	2564
27:16	then a notable prisoner, **c** Barabbas.	3004
27:17	Barabbas, or Jesus which is **c** Christ?	3004
27:22	I do then with Jesus which is **c** Christ?	3004
27:33	when they were come unto a place **c**	3004
Mk 1:20	And straightway he **c** them: and they left	2564
3:23	And he **c** them **unto** *him*, and said	4341
7:14	And when he had **c** all the people **unto**	4341
8: 1	Jesus **c** his disciples **unto** *him*, and	4341
8:34	And when he had **c** the people **unto** *him*	4341
9:35	and the twelve, and saith unto them,	5455
10:42	But Jesus **c** them **to** *him*, and saith unto	4341
10:49	stood still, and commanded him to be **c**.	5455
11:17	house shall be **c** of all nations the house	2564
12:43	And he **c** **unto** *him* his disciples,	4341
14:72	Peter **c to mind** the word that Jesus said	363
15:16	led him away into the hall, *c* Pretorium;	3739
Lk 1:32	and shall be **c** the Son of the Highest:	2564
1:35	be born of thee shall be **c** the Son of God.	2564
1:36	sixth month with her, who was **c** barren.	2564
1:59	they **c** him Zacharias, after the name of	2564
1:60	and said, Not *so;* but he shall be **c** John.	2564
1:61	There is none of thy kindred that is **c** by	2564
1:62	to his father, how he would have him **c**.	2564
1:76	shalt be **c** the prophet of the Highest:	2564
2: 4	the city of David, which is **c** Bethlehem;	2564
2:21	his name was **c** JESUS, which was *so*	2564
2:23	the womb shall be **c** holy to the Lord;)	2564
6:13	it was day, he **c** unto *him* his disciples:	4377
6:15	the *son* of Alpheus, and Simon **c** Zelotes,	2564
7:11	*day* after, *that* he went into a city **c** Nain;	2564
8: 2	and infirmities, Mary **c** Magdalene,	2564
8:54	by the hand, and **c**, saying, Maid, arise.	5455
9: 1	Then he **c** his twelve disciples **together**,	4779
9:10	place belonging to the city **c** Bethsaida.	2564
10:39	she had a sister **c** Mary, which also sat	2564
13:12	he **c** *her* to *him*, and said unto her,	4377
15:19	And am no more worthy to be **c** thy son:	2564
15:21	and am no more worthy to be **c** thy son.	2564
15:26	And he **c** one of the servants,	4341
16: 2	he **c** him, and said unto him, How *is it*	5455
16: 5	he **c** every one of his lord's debtors **unto**	4341
18:16	But Jesus **c** them **unto** *him*, and said,	4341
19:13	And he **c** his ten servants,	2564

C

Ref	Text	Strong's
Lk 19:15	commanded these servants to be c unto	5455
19:29	at the mount c the mount of Olives,	2564
21:37	abode in the mount that is c the mount of	2564
22: 1	bread drew nigh, which is c the Passover.	3004
22:25	that exercise authority upon them are c	2564
22:47	he that was c Judas, one of the twelve,	3004
23:13	when he had c together the chief priests	4779
23:33	which is c Calvary, there they crucified	2564
24:13	that same day to a village c Emmaus,	3686
Jn 1:42	thou shalt be c Cephas, which is by	2564
1:48	said unto him, Before that Philip c thee,	5455
2: 2	And both Jesus was c, and his disciples,	2564
2: 9	governor of the feast c the bridegroom,	5455
4: 5	he to a city of Samaria, which is c Sychar,	3004
4:25	that Messias cometh, which is c Christ:	3004
5: 2	is c in the Hebrew tongue Bethesda,	1951
9:11	A man that is c Jesus made clay,	3004
9:18	until they c the parents of him that had	5455
9:24	Then again c they the man that was blind,	5455
10:35	If he c them gods, unto whom the word	3004
11:16	Then said Thomas, which is c Didymus,	3004
11:28	and c Mary her sister secretly, saying,	5455
11:54	a city c Ephraim, and there continued	3004
12:17	was with him when he c Lazarus out of	5455
15:15	I have c you friends; for all things that I	3004
18:33	and c Jesus, and said unto him, Art thou	5455
19:13	seat in a place that is c the Pavement,	3004
19:17	forth into a place c the place of a skull,	3004
19:17	skull, which is c in the Hebrew Golgotha:	3004
20:24	Thomas, one of the twelve, c Didymus,	3004
21: 2	Thomas c Didymus, and Nathanael of	3004
Ac 1:12	unto Jerusalem from the mount c Olivet,	2564
1:19	insomuch as that field is c in their proper	2564
1:23	they appointed two, Joseph c Barsabas,	2564
3: 2	gate of the temple which is c Beautiful,	2564
3:11	them in the porch that is c Solomon's,	2564
4:18	they c them, and commanded them not	2564
5:21	and the council together, and all	4779
5:40	and when they had c the apostles,	4341
6: 2	c the multitude of the disciples unto	4341
6: 9	is c the synagogue of the Libertines,	3004
7:14	and c his father Jacob to him, and all his	3333
8: 9	But there was a certain man, c Simon,	3686
9:11	and go into the street which is c Straight,	2564
9:11	in the house of Judas for one c Saul,	3686
9:21	this he that destroyed them which c on	1941
9:36	which by interpretation is c Dorcas:	3004
9:41	when he had c the saints and widows,	5455
10: 1	There was a certain man in Cesarea c	3686
10: 1	centurion of the band c the Italian band,	2564
10: 7	he c two of his household servants,	5455
10:18	And c, and asked whether Simon,	5455
10:23	Then c he them in, and lodged them.	1528
10:24	and had c together his kinsmen and near	4779
11:26	the disciples were c Christians first in	5537
13: 1	Simeon that was c Niger, and Lucius of	2564
13: 2	for the work whereunto I have c them.	4341
13: 7	who c for Barnabas and Saul,	4341
13: 9	Saul, (who also is c Paul,) filled with	NIG
14:12	And they c Barnabas, Jupiter; and Paul,	2564
15:17	upon whom my name is c, saith the Lord,	1941
16:10	assuredly gathering that the Lord had c us	4341
16:29	Then he c for a light, and sprang in,	154
19:25	Whom he c together with the workmen	4867
19:40	we are in danger to be c in question for	1458
20: 1	Paul c unto him the disciples,	4341
20:17	Ephesus, and c the elders of the church.	3333
23: 6	of the dead I am c in question.	2919
23:17	Then Paul c one of the centurions unto	4341
23:18	Paul the prisoner c me unto him, and	4341
23:23	he c unto him two centurions, saying,	4341
24: 2	And when he was c forth, Tertullus began	2564
24:21	that I am c in question by you this day.	2919
27: 8	came unto a place which is c The fair	2564
27:14	it a tempestuous wind, c Euroclydon.	2564
27:16	under a certain island which is c Clauda,	2564
28: 1	they knew that the island was c Melita.	2564
28:17	Paul c the chief of the Jews together:	4779
28:20	For this cause therefore have I c for you,	3870
Ro 1: 1	servant of Jesus Christ, c to be an apostle,	2822
1: 6	Among whom are ye also the c of Jesus	2822
1: 7	in Rome, beloved of God, c to be saints:	2822
2:17	thou art c a Jew, and restest in the law,	2028
7: 3	another man, she shall be c an adulteress:	5537
8:28	to them who are the c according to his	2822
8:30	he did predestinate, them he also c:	2564
8:30	and whom he c, them he also justified:	2564
9: 7	but, In Isaac shall thy seed be c.	2564
9:24	Even us, whom he hath c, not of the Jews	2564
9:26	there shall they be c the children of	2564
1Co 1: 1	c to be an apostle of Jesus Christ through	2822
1: 2	sanctified in Christ Jesus, c to be saints,	2822
1: 9	by whom ye were c unto the fellowship	2564
1:24	unto them which are c, both Jews and	2822
1:26	not many mighty, not many noble, are c:	NIG
5:11	if any man that is c a brother be a	3687
7:15	such cases: but God hath c us to peace.	2564
7:17	as the Lord hath c every one, so let him	2564
7:18	Is any man c being circumcised? let him	2564
7:18	Is any c in uncircumcision? let him not be	2564
7:20	in the same calling wherein he was c.	2564
7:21	Art thou c being a servant? care not for it:	2564
7:22	he that is c in the Lord, being a servant,	2564
7:22	likewise also he that is c, being free,	2564
7:24	Brethren, let every man, wherein he is c,	2564
1Co 8: 5	For though there be that are c gods,	3004
15: 9	that am not meet to be c an apostle,	2564
Gal 1: 6	soon removed from him that c you into	2564
1:15	mother's womb, and c me by his grace,	2564
5:13	brethren, ye have been c unto liberty,	2564
Eph 2:11	who are c Uncircumcision by that which	3004
2:11	c the Circumcision in the flesh made by	3004
4: 1	of the vocation wherewith ye are c,	2564
4: 4	even as ye are c in one hope of your	2564
Col 3:15	to the which also ye are c in one body;	2564
4:11	And Jesus, which is c Justus, who are of	3004
1Th 2:12	who hath c you into his kingdom and	2564
4: 7	For God hath not c us unto uncleanness,	2564
2Th 2: 4	exalteth himself above all that is c God,	3004
2:14	Whereunto he c you by our gospel,	2564
1Ti 6:12	whereunto thou art also c,	2564
6:20	and oppositions of science falsely so c:	5581
2Ti 1: 9	saved us, and c us with a holy calling,	2564
Heb 3:13	one another daily, while it is c To day;	2564
5: 4	but he that is c of God, as was Aaron.	2564
5:10	C of God a high priest after the order of	4316
7:11	and not be c after the order of Aaron?	3004
9: 2	the shewbread; which is c the sanctuary.	3004
9: 3	the tabernacle which is c the holiest of all;	3004
9:15	which are c might receive the promise	2564
11: 8	when he was c to go out into a place	2564
11:16	God is not ashamed to be c their	1941
11:18	said, That in Isaac shall thy seed be c:	2564
11:24	refused to be c the son of Pharaoh's	3004
Jas 2: 7	that worthy name by the which ye are c?	1941
2:23	and he was c the Friend of God.	2564
1Pe 1:15	as he which hath c you is holy, so be ye	2564
2: 9	c you out of darkness into his marvellous	2564
2:21	For even hereunto were ye c: because	2564
3: 9	knowing that ye are thereunto c, that ye	2564
5:10	who hath c us into his eternal glory by	2564
2Pe 1: 3	through the knowledge of him that hath c	2564
1Jn 3: 1	that we should be the sons of God:	2564
Jude 1: 1	and preserved in Jesus Christ, and c:	2822
Rev 1: 9	was in the isle that is c Patmos,	2564
8:11	And the name of the star is c Wormwood:	3004
11: 8	which spiritually is c Sodom and Egypt,	2564
12: 9	c the devil, and Satan, which deceiveth	2564
16:16	in the Hebrew tongue Armageddon.	2564
17:14	and they that are with him are c,	2822
19: 9	Blessed are they which are c unto	2564
19:11	he that sat upon him was c Faithful and	2564
19:13	and his name is c The Word of God.	2564

CALLEDST (4) [CALL]

Ref	Text	Strong's
Jdg 8: 1	thou served us thus, that thou c us not,	7121
1Sa 3: 5	and said, Here am I; for thou c me.	7121
Ps 81: 7	Thou c in trouble, and I delivered thee;	7121
Eze 23:21	thou c to remembrance the lewdness	6485

CALLEST (3) [CALL]

Ref	Text	Strong's
Mt 19:17	he said unto him, Why c thou me good?	3004
Mk 10:18	said unto him, Why c thou me good?	3004
Lk 18:19	said unto him, Why c thou me good?	3004

CALLETH (31) [CALL]

Ref	Text	Strong's
1Ki 8:43	do according to all that the stranger c to	7121
2Ch 6:33	do according to all that the stranger c to	7121
Job 12: 4	who c upon God, and he answereth him:	7121
Ps 42: 7	Deep c unto deep at the noise of thy	7121
147: 4	of the stars; he c them all by their names.	7121
Pr 18: 6	and his mouth c for strokes.	7121
Isa 21:11	He c to me out of Seir, Watchman, what	7121
40:26	he c them all by names by the greatness	7121
59: 4	None c for justice, nor any pleadeth for	7121
64: 7	there is none that c upon thy name,	7121
Hos 7: 7	none among them that c unto me.	7121
Am 5: 8	that c for the waters of the sea,	7121
9: 6	he that c for the waters of the sea,	7121
Mt 27:47	they heard that, said, This man c for Elias.	5455
Mk 3:13	and c unto him whom he would:	4341
6: 7	And he c unto him the twelve,	4341
10:49	Be of good comfort, rise; he c thee.	5455
12:37	David therefore himself c him Lord;	3004
15:35	they heard it, said, Behold, he c Elias.	5455
Lk 15: 6	he c together his friends and neighbours,	4779
15: 9	c her friends and her neighbours together,	4779
20:37	when he c the Lord the God of Abraham,	3004
20:44	David therefore c him Lord, how is he	2564
Jn 10: 3	and he c his own sheep by name,	2564
11:28	The Master is come, and c for thee.	5455
Ro 4:17	c those things which be not as though	2564
9:11	not of works, but of him that c;)	2564
1Co 12: 3	no man speaking by the Spirit of God c	3004
Gal 5: 8	This persuasion cometh not of him that c	2564
1Th 5:24	Faithful is he that c you, who also will do	2564
Rev 2:20	which c herself a prophetess, to teach	3004

CALLING (24) [CALL]

Ref	Text	Strong's
Nu 10: 2	that thou mayest use them for the c of	4744
Isa 1:13	and sabbaths, the c of assemblies,	7121
41: 4	done it, c the generations from	7121
46:11	C a ravenous bird from the east, the man	7121
Eze 23:19	in c to remembrance the days of her	2142
Mt 11:16	in the markets, and c unto their fellows,	4377
Mk 5:14	standing without, sent unto him, c him.	5455
11:21	And Peter c to remembrance saith unto	363
15:44	and c unto him the centurion, he asked	4341
Lk 7:19	And John c unto him two of his disciples	4341
7:32	c one to another, and saying, We have	4377

Ref	Text	Strong's
Ac 7:59	c upon God, and saying, Lord Jesus,	1941
22:16	away thy sins, c on the name of the Lord.	1941
Ro 11:29	and c of God are without repentance.	2821
1Co 1:26	For ye see your c, brethren, how that not	2821
7:20	every man abide in the same c wherein	2821
Eph 1:18	ye may know what is the hope of his c,	2821
4: 4	as ye are called in one hope of your c;	2821
Php 3:14	prize of the high c of God in Christ Jesus.	2821
2Th 1:11	God would count you worthy of this c,	2821
2Ti 1: 9	saved us, and called us with a holy c,	2821
1Pe 3: 6	Even as Sara obeyed Abraham, c him lord:	2564
2Pe 1:10	give diligence to make your c and	2821

CALLOUS See FAT; FATNESS

CALLOUSED See GROSS

CALM (6)

Ref	Text	Strong's
Ps 107:29	maketh the storm a c, so that the waves	1827
Jnh 1:11	unto thee, that the sea may be c unto us?	8367
1:12	the sea; so shall the sea be c unto you:	8367
Mt 8:26	and the sea; and there was a great c.	1055
Mk 4:39	the wind ceased, and there was a great c.	1055
Lk 8:24	and they ceased, and there was a c.	1055

CALNEH (2)

Ref	Text	Strong's
Ge 10:10	Erech, and Accad, and C, in the land of	3641
Am 6: 2	Pass ye unto C, and see; and from thence	3641

CALNO (1)

Ref	Text	Strong's
Isa 10: 9	Is not C as Carchemish? is not Hamath as	3641

CALVARY (1) [GOLGOTHA]

Ref	Text	Strong's
Lk 23:33	is called C, there they crucified him,	2898

CALVE (2) [CALF]

Ref	Text	Strong's
Job 39: 1	or canst thou mark when the hinds do c?	2342
Ps 29: 9	voice of the LORD maketh the hinds to c,	2342

CALVED (1) [CALF]

Ref	Text	Strong's
Jer 14: 5	the hind also c in the field, and forsook it,	3205

CALVES (18) [CALF]

Ref	Text	Strong's
1Sa 6: 7	cart, and bring their c home from them:	1121
6:10	to the cart, and shut up their c at home:	1121
14:32	c, and slew them on the ground:	1121+1241
1Ki 12:28	made two c of gold, and said unto them,	5695
12:32	sacrificing unto the c that he had made:	5695
2Ki 10:29	to wit, the golden c that were in Beth-el,	5695
17:16	even two c, and made a grove,	5695
2Ch 11:15	and for the c which he had made.	5695
13: 8	and there are with you golden c,	5695
Ps 68:30	of the bulls, with the c of the people,	5695
Hos 10: 5	shall fear because of the c of Beth-aven:	5697
13: 2	Let the men that sacrifice kiss the c.	5695
14: 2	so will we render the c of our lips.	6499
Am 6: 4	and the c out of the midst of the stall;	5695
Mic 6: 6	with burnt offerings, with c of a year old?	5695
Mal 4: 2	go forth, and grow up as c of the stall.	5695
Heb 9:12	Neither by the blood of goats and c,	3448
9:19	he took the blood of c and of goats,	3448

CALVETH (1) [CALF]

Ref	Text	Strong's
Job 21:10	their cow c, and casteth not her calf.	6403

CAME (2096) [COME]

Ref	Text	Strong's
Ge 4: 3	in process of time it c to pass, that Cain	1961
4: 8	it c to pass, when they were in the field,	1961
6: 1	it c to pass, when men began to multiply	1961
6: 4	when the sons of God c in unto	935
7:10	c to pass after seven days, that the waters	1961
8: 6	it c to pass at the end of forty days,	1961
8:11	And the dove c in to him in the evening;	935
8:13	it c to pass in the six hundredth and	1961
10:14	and Casluhim, (out of whom c Philistim)	3318
11: 2	it c to pass, as they journeyed from	1961
11: 5	the LORD c down to see the city and	3381
11:31	and they c unto Haran, and dwelt there.	935
12: 5	and into the land of Canaan they c.	935
12:11	it c to pass, when he was come near to	1961
12:14	it c to pass, that, when Abram was come	1961
13:18	c and dwelt in the plain of Mamre, which	935
14: 1	it c to pass in the days of Amraphel king	1961
14: 5	in the fourteenth year c Chedorlaomer,	935
14: 7	c to En-mishpat, which is Kadesh,	935
14:13	there c one that had escaped, and told	935
15: 1	of the LORD c unto Abram in a vision,	1961
15: 4	the word of the LORD c unto him, saying,	NIH
15:11	the fowls c down upon the carcases,	3381
15:17	it c to pass, that, when the sun went	1961
19: 1	there c two angels to Sodom at even;	935
19: 5	Where are the men which c in to thee	935
19: 8	c they under the shadow of my roof.	935
19: 9	they said again, This one fellow c in	935
19: 9	even Lot, and c near to break the door.	5066
19:17	it c to pass, when they had brought them	1961
19:29	it c to pass, when God destroyed the	1961
19:34	it c to pass on the morrow, that	1961
20: 3	God c to Abimelech in a dream by night,	935
20:13	it c to pass, when God caused me to	935
21:22	it c to pass at that time, that Abimelech	1961
22: 1	it c to pass after these things, that God	1961
22: 9	they c to the place which God had told	935
22:20	it c to pass after these things, that it was	1961
23: 2	Abraham c to mourn for Sarah, and to	935

Ge 24:15 it **c to pass**, before he had done speaking,	1961
24:15 behold, Rebekah **c out**, who was born	3318
24:16 the well, and filled her pitcher, and **c up**.	5927
24:22 it **c to pass**, as the camels had done	1961
24:30 it **c to pass**, when he saw the earring and	1961
24:30 he **c** unto the man; and behold, he stood	935
24:32 man **c** into the house: and he ungirded	935
24:42 I **c** this day unto the well, and said,	935
24:45 Rebekah **c forth** with her pitcher on her	3318
24:52 it **c to pass**, that, when Abraham's	1961
24:62 Isaac **c** from the way of the well Lahai-roi;	935
25:11 it **c to pass** after the death of Abraham,	1961
25:25 the first **c out** red, all over like a hairy	3318
25:26 after that **c** his brother **out**, and his hand	3318
25:29 Esau **c** from the field, and he *was* faint:	935
26: 8 it **c to pass**, when he had been there a	1961
26:32 it **c to pass** the same day, that Isaac's	1961
26:32 that Isaac's servants **c**, and told him	935
27: 1 it **c to pass**, that when Isaac was old,	1961
27:18 he **c** unto his father, and said, My father:	935
27:27 he **c near**, and kissed him: and he smelled	5066
27:30 it **c to pass**, as soon as Isaac had made an	1961
27:30 Esau his brother **c** from his hunting.	935
27:35 Thy brother **c** with subtilty, and hath	935
29: 1 **c** into the land of the people of the east.	1980
29: 9 them, Rachel **c** with her father's sheep:	935
29:10 it **c to pass**, when Jacob saw Rachel	1961
29:13 **c to pass**, when Laban heard the tidings	1961
29:23 it **c to pass** in the evening, that he took	1961
29:25 it **c to pass**, that in the morning, behold,	1961
30:16 Jacob **c out** of the field in the evening,	935
30:25 **c to pass**, when Rachel had born Joseph,	1961
30:30 *it was* little which thou hadst before I **c**,	935
30:38 troughs when the flocks **c** to drink,	935
30:38 that they should conceive when they **c** to	935
30:41 it **c to pass**, whensoever the stronger	1961
31:10 it **c to pass** at the time that the cattle	1961
31:24 God **c** to Laban the Syrian in a dream by	935
32: 6 We **c** to thy brother Esau, and also he	935
32:13 took of that which **c** to his hand a present	935
33: 1 Esau **c**, and with him four hundred men.	935
33: 3 times, until he **c near** to his brother.	5066
33: 6 the handmaidens **c near**, they and	5066
33: 7 Leah also with her children **c near**,	5066
33: 7 after **c** Joseph **near** and Rachel,	5066
33:18 Jacob **c** to Shalem, a city of Shechem,	935
33:18 of Canaan, when he **c** from Padan-aram;	935
34: 7 the sons of Jacob **c out** of the field when	935
34:20 his son **c** unto the gate of their city,	935
34:25 it **c to pass** on the third day, when they	1961
34:25 **c** upon the city boldly, and slew all	935
34:27 The sons of Jacob **c** upon the slain,	935
35: 6 So Jacob **c** to Luz, which *is* in the land of	935
35: 9 when he **c** out of Padan-aram,	935
35:17 it **c to pass**, when she was in hard labour,	1961
35:18 it **c to pass**, as her soul was in departing	1961
35:22 **c to pass**, when Israel dwelt in that land,	1961
35:27 Jacob **c** unto Isaac his father unto Mamre,	935
36:16 these *are* the dukes *that* **c** of Eliphaz in	NIH
36:17 these *are* the dukes *that* **c** of Reuel in	NIH
36:18 *were* the dukes *that* **c** of Aholibamah	NIH
36:29 These *are* the dukes *that* **c** of the Horites;	NIH
36:30 these *are* the dukes *that* **c** of Hori,	NIH
36:40 these *are* the names of the dukes *that* **c** of	NIH
37:14 the vale of Hebron, and he **c** to Shechem.	935
37:18 afar off, even before he **c near** unto them,	7126
37:23 it **c to pass**, when Joseph was come unto	1961
37:25 a company of Ishmeelites **c** from Gilead	935
38: 1 it **c to pass** at that time, that Judah went	1961
38: 9 it **c to pass**, when he went in unto his	1961
38:18 and **c in** unto her, and she conceived by	935
38:24 it **c to pass** about three months after,	1961
38:27 it **c to pass** in the time of her travail, that,	1961
38:28 it **c to pass**, when she travailed, that	1961
38:28 a scarlet thread, saying, This **c out** first.	3318
38:29 it **c to pass**, as he drew back his hand,	1961
38:29 his hand, that, behold, his brother **c out**:	3318
38:30 afterward **c out** his brother, that had	3318
39: 5 it **c to pass** from the time *that* he had	1961
39: 7 it **c to pass** after these things, that his	1961
39:10 it **c to pass**, as she spake to Joseph day	1961
39:11 it **c to pass** about this time, that *Joseph*	1961
39:13 it **c to pass**, when she saw that he had left	1961
39:14 **c in** unto me to lie with me, and I cried	935
39:15 it **c to pass**, when he heard that I lifted	1961
39:16 his garment by her, until his lord **c** home.	935
39:17 unto us, **c in** unto me to mock me:	935
39:18 it **c to pass**, as I lift up my voice and	1961
39:19 it **c to pass**, when his master heard	1961
40: 1 it **c to pass** after these things, *that* the	1961
40: 6 Joseph **c in** unto them in the morning,	935
40:20 it **c to pass** the third day, *which was*	1961
41: 1 it **c to pass** at the end of two full years,	1961
41: 2 there **c up** out of the river seven well	5927
41: 3 seven other kine **c up** after them out of	5927
41: 5 seven ears of corn **c up** upon one stalk,	5927
41: 8 it **c to pass** in the morning that his spirit	1961
41:13 it **c to pass**, as he interpreted to us,	1961
41:14 his raiment, and **c in** unto Pharaoh.	935
41:18 there **c up** out of the river seven kine,	5927
41:19 seven other kine **c up** after them, poor	5927
41:22 seven ears **c up** in one stalk, full and	5927
41:27 ill favoured kine that **c up** after them *are*	5927
41:50 two sons before the years of famine **c**,	935
41:57 all countries **c** into Egypt to Joseph for to	935

Ge 42: 5 the sons of Israel **c** to buy *corn* among	935
42: 5 came to buy *corn* among those that **c**:	935
42: 6 Joseph's brethren **c**, and bowed down	935
42:29 they **c** unto Jacob their father unto the	935
42:35 it **c to pass** as they emptied their sacks,	1961
43: 2 it **c to pass**, when they had eaten up	1961
43:19 they **c near** to the steward of Joseph's	5066
43:20 we **c indeed down** at the first	3381+3381
43:21 it **c to pass**, when we came to the inn,	1961
43:21 it came to pass, when we **c** to the inn,	935
43:25 made ready the present against Joseph **c**	935
43:26 when Joseph **c** home, they brought him	935
44:14 and his brethren **c** to Joseph's house;	935
44:18 Judah **c near** unto him, and said, O my	5066
44:24 it **c to pass** when we came up unto thy	1961
44:24 it came to pass when we **c up** unto thy	5927
45: 4 they **c near**. And he said, I *am* Joseph	5066
45:25 **c** *into* the land of Canaan unto Jacob their	935
46: 1 to Beer-sheba, and offered sacrifices unto	935
46: 6 into Egypt, Jacob, and all his seed with	935
46: 8 which **c** into Egypt, Jacob and his sons:	935
46:26 All the souls that **c** with Jacob into Egypt,	935
46:26 which **c out** of his loins, besides Jacob's	3318
46:27 which **c** into Egypt, *were* threescore and	935
46:28 and they **c** into the land of Goshen.	935
47: 1 Joseph **c** and told Pharaoh, and said,	935
47:15 all the Egyptians **c** unto Joseph, and said,	935
47:18 they **c** unto him the second year,	935
48: 1 it **c to pass** after these things, that *one*	1961
48: 5 of Egypt before I **c** unto thee into Egypt,	935
48: 7 for me, when I **c** from Padan, Rachel died	935
50:10 they **c** to the threshingfloor of Atad, which	935
Ex 1: 1 the children of Israel, which **c** into Egypt;	935
1: 1 man and his household **c** with Jacob.	935
1: 5 the souls that **c** *out* of the loins of Jacob	3318
1:21 it **c to pass**, because the midwives feared	1961
2: 5 the daughter of Pharaoh **c down** to wash	3381
2:11 it **c to pass** in those days, when Moses	1961
2:16 **c** and drew water, and filled the troughs	935
2:17 the shepherds **c** and drove them away:	935
2:18 when they **c** to Reuel their father, he said,	935
2:23 it **c to pass** in process of time, that the	1961
2:23 their cry **c up** unto God by reason of	5927
3: 1 **c** to the mountain of God, *even* to Horeb.	935
4:24 it **c to pass** by the way in the inn, that	1961
5:15 the officers of the children of Israel **c** and	935
5:20 in the way, as they **c forth** from Pharaoh:	3318
5:23 For since I **c** to Pharaoh to speak in thy	935
6:28 it **c to pass** on the day *when* the LORD	1961
8: 6 the frogs **c up**, and covered the land of	5927
8:24 there **c** a grievous swarm *of flies* into	935
10: 3 Moses and Aaron **c in** unto Pharaoh,	935
12:29 it **c to pass**, that at midnight the LORD	1961
12:41 it **c to pass** at the end of the four hundred	1961
12:41 even the selfsame day it **c to pass**,	1961
12:51 it **c to pass** the selfsame day, *that*	1961
13: 3 this day, *in* which ye **c out** from Egypt,	3318
13: 4 *This* day ye **c out** in the month Abib.	3318
13: 8 did unto me when I **c forth** out of Egypt.	3318
13:15 it **c to pass**, when Pharaoh would hardly	1961
13:17 it **c to pass**, when Pharaoh had let	1961
14:20 it **c** between the camp of the Egyptians	935
14:20 that the one **c** not **near** the other all	7126
14:24 it **c to pass**, that in the morning watch	1961
14:28 all the host of Pharaoh that **c** into the sea	935
15:23 they **c** to Marah, they could not drink	935
15:27 they **c** to Elim, where *were* twelve wells of	935
16: 1 of Israel **c** unto the wilderness of Sin,	935
16:10 it **c to pass**, as Aaron spake unto the	1961
16:13 it **c to pass**, that at even the quails came	1961
16:13 that at even the quails **c up**,	5927
16:22 it **c to pass**, *that* on the sixth day they	1961
16:22 all the rulers of the congregation **c** and	935
16:27 it **c to pass**, *that* there went out *some* of	1961
16:35 forty years, until they **c** to a land inhabited;	935
16:35 until they **c** unto the borders of the land	935
17: 8 **c** Amalek, and fought with Israel in	935
17:11 it **c to pass**, when Moses held up his hand,	1961
18: 5 **c** with his sons and his wife unto Moses	935
18: 7 of *their* welfare; and they **c** into the tent.	935
18:12 Aaron **c**, and all the elders of Israel, to eat	935
18:13 it **c to pass** on the morrow, that Moses	1961
19: 1 the same day **c** they *into* the wilderness of	935
19: 7 Moses **c** and called for the elders of	935
19:16 it **c to pass** on the third day in the morning,	1961
19:20 And the LORD **c down** upon mount Sinai,	3381
21: 3 If he **c** in by himself, he shall go out by	935
22:15 good: if it *be* a hired *thing*, it **c** for his hire.	935
24: 3 Moses **c** and told the people all the words	935
32:19 it **c to pass**, as soon as he came nigh unto	1961
32:19 as soon as he **c nigh** unto the camp, that	7126
32:24 into the fire, and there **c out** this calf.	3318
32:30 it **c to pass** on the morrow, that Moses	1961
33: 7 it **c to pass**, that every one which sought	1961
33: 8 it **c to pass**, when Moses went out unto	1961
33: 9 it **c to pass**, as Moses entered into	1961
34:29 it **c to pass**, when Moses came down	1961
34:29 when Moses **c down** from mount Sinai	3381
34:29 when Moses **c down** from the mount,	3381
34:32 afterward all the children of Israel **c nigh**:	5066
34:34 he took the vail off, until he **c out**.	3318
34:34 he **c out**, and spake unto the children of	3318
35:21 they **c**, every one whose heart stirred him	935
35:22 they **c**, both men and women, as many as	935
36: 4 **c** every man from his work which they	935

Ex 40:17 it **c to pass** in the first month in the	1961
40:32 when they **c near** unto the altar,	7126
Lev 9: 1 it **c to pass** on the eighth day, *that* Moses	1961
9:22 **c down** from offering of the sin offering,	3381
9:23 and **c out**, and blessed the people:	3318
9:24 there **c** a fire **out** from before the LORD,	3318
Nu 4:47 every one that **c** to do the service of	935
7: 1 it **c to pass** on the day that Moses had	1961
9: 6 they **c** before Moses and before Aaron on	7126
10:11 it **c to pass** on the twentieth *day* of	1961
10:21 did set up the tabernacle against they **c**.	935
10:35 it **c to pass**, when the ark set forward,	1961
11:20 saying, Why **c** we **forth** out of Egypt?	3318
11:25 the LORD **c down** in a cloud,	3381
11:25 it **c to pass**, that when the spirit rested	1961
12: 4 of the congregation. And they three **c out**.	3318
12: 5 the LORD **c down** in the pillar of	3381
12: 5 and Miriam: and they both **c forth**.	3318
13:22 ascended by the south, and **c** unto Hebron;	935
13:23 they **c** unto the brook of Eshcol,	935
13:26 they went and **c** to Moses, and to Aaron,	935
13:27 We **c** unto the land whither thou sentest	935
14:45 Amalekites **c down**, and the Canaanites	3381
16:27 Dathan and Abiram **c out**, and stood *in*	3318
16:31 it **c to pass**, as he had made an end of	1961
16:35 there **c out** a fire from the LORD,	3318
16:42 it **c to pass**, when the congregation was	1961
16:43 Aaron **c** before the tabernacle of	935
17: 8 it **c to pass**, that on the morrow Moses	1961
19: 2 blemish, *and* upon which never **c** yoke:	5927
20: 1 **c** the children of Israel, *even* the whole	935
20:11 the water **c out** abundantly,	3318
20:20 Edom **c out** against him with much	3318
20:22 from Kadesh, and **c** *unto* mount Hor.	935
20:28 and Eleazar **c down** from the mount.	3381
21: 1 heard *tell* that Israel **c** *by* the way of	935
21: 7 Therefore the people **c** to Moses, and said,	935
21: 9 put it upon a pole, and it **c to pass**, that	1961
21:23 he **c** *to* Jahaz, and fought against Israel.	935
22: 7 they **c** unto Balaam, and spake unto him	935
22: 9 God **c** unto Balaam, and said, What men	935
22:16 they **c** to Balaam, and said to him, Thus	935
22:20 God **c** unto Balaam at night, and said unto	935
22:39 Balak, and they **c** *unto* Kirjath-huzoth.	935
22:41 it **c to pass** on the morrow, that Balak	1961
23:17 when he **c** to him, behold, he stood by	935
24: 2 and the spirit of God **c** upon him.	935
25: 6 one of the children of Israel **c** and	935
26: 1 it **c to pass** after the plague, that	1961
27: 1 **c** the daughters of Zelophehad, the son of	7126
31:14 over hundreds, which **c** from the battle.	935
31:48 captains of hundreds, **c near** unto Moses:	7126
32: 2 the children of Reuben **c** and spake unto	935
32:11 Surely none of the men that **c up** out of	5927
32:16 they **c near** unto him, and said, We will	5066
33: 9 removed from Marah, and **c** unto Elim:	935
36: 1 **c near**, and spake before Moses,	7126
Dt 1: 3 it **c to pass** in the fortieth year,	1961
1:19 us; and we **c** to Kadesh-barnea.	935
1:22 ye **c near** unto me every one of you,	7126
1:24 **c** unto the valley of Eshcol, and searched	935
1:31 that ye went, until ye **c** into this place.	935
1:44 **c out** against you, and chased you, as bees	3318
2:14 the space in which we **c** from	1980
2:16 So it **c to pass**, when all the men of war	1961
2:23 which **c forth** out of Caphtor,	3318
2:32 Sihon **c out** against us, he and all his	3318
3: 1 Og the king of Bashan **c out** against us,	3318
4:11 ye **c near** and stood under the mountain;	7126
4:45 of Israel, after they **c forth** out of Egypt,	3318
5:23 it **c to pass**, when ye heard the voice out	1961
5:23 that ye **c near** unto me, *even* all the	7126
9: 7 until ye **c** unto this place, ye have been	935
9:11 it **c to pass** at the end of forty days and	1961
9:15 So I turned and **c down** from the mount,	3381
10: 5 myself and **c down** from the mount,	3381
11: 5 the wilderness, until ye **c** into this place;	935
11:10 the land of Egypt, from whence ye **c out**,	3318
22:14 I took this woman, and when I **c** to her,	7126
23: 4 in the way, when ye **c forth** out of Egypt;	3318
29: 7 when ye **c** unto this place, Sihon the king	935
29: 7 **c out** against us into battle, and we smote	3318
29:16 how we **c** through the nations which ye	5674
31:24 it **c to pass**, when Moses had made an	1961
32:17 knew not, *to* new *gods that* **c** newly **up**,	935
32:44 Moses **c** and spake all the words of this	935
33: 2 The LORD **c** from Sinai, and rose up from	935
33: 2 and he **c** with ten thousands of saints:	857
33:21 he **c** *with* the heads of the people,	857
Jos 1: 1 the servant of the LORD it **c to pass**,	1961
2: 1 **c** *into* a harlot's house, named Rahab,	935
2: 2 there **c** men in hither to night of the	935
2: 4 There **c** men unto me, but I wist not	935
2: 5 it **c to pass** *about the time* of shutting of	1961
2: 8 she **c up** unto them upon the roof;	5927
2:10 sea for you, when you **c out** of Egypt;	3318
2:22 **c** unto the mountain, and abode there	935
2:23 **c** to Joshua the son of Nun, and told him	935
3: 1 to Jordan, he and all the children of	935
3: 2 it **c to pass** after three days, that	1961
3:14 it **c to pass**, when the people removed	1961
3:16 the waters which **c down** from above	3381
3:16 those that **c down** toward the sea of	3381
4: 1 it **c to pass**, when all the people were	1961
4:11 it **c to pass**, when all the people were	1961

C

C

Jos
4:18 it **c to pass**, when the priests that bare — 1961
4:19 people **c up** out of Jordan on the tenth — 5927
4:22 Israel **c over** this Jordan on dry *land.* — 5674
5: 1 it **c to pass**, when all the kings of — 1961
5: 4 All the people that **c out** of Egypt, — 3318
5: 4 by the way, after they **c out** of Egypt. — 3318
5: 5 Now all the people that **c out** were — 3318
5: 5 by the way as they **c forth** out of Egypt, — 3318
5: 6 which **c out** of Egypt, were consumed, — 3318
5: 8 it **c to pass**, when they had done — 1961
5:13 it **c to pass**, when Joshua was by Jericho, — 1961
6: 1 of Israel: none went out, and none **c in**. — 935
6: 8 it **c to pass**, when Joshua had spoken — 1961
6: 9 the rereward **c** after the ark, *the priests* — 1980
6:11 they **c** *into* the camp, and lodged in — 935
6:13 the rereward **c** after the ark of the LORD, — 1980
6:15 it **c to pass** on the seventh day, that they — 1961
6:16 it **c to pass** at the seventh time, when — 1961
6:20 it **c to pass**, when the people heard — 1961
8:11 **c** before the city, and pitched on the north — 935
8:14 it **c to pass**, when the king of Ai saw *it,* — 1961
8:24 it **c to pass**, when Israel had made an end — 1961
9: 1 it **c to pass**, when all the kings which — 1961
9:12 on the day we **c forth** to go unto you; — 3318
9:16 it **c to pass** at the end of three days after — 1961
9:17 and **c** unto their cities on the third day. — 935
10: 1 it **c to pass**, when Adoni-zedek king — 1961
10: 9 Joshua therefore **c** unto them suddenly, — 935
10:11 **c to pass**, as they fled from before Israel, — 1961
10:20 **c to pass**, when Joshua and the children — 1961
10:24 **c to pass**, when they brought out those — 1961
10:24 they **c near**, and put their feet upon — 7126
10:27 it **c to pass** at the time of the going down — 1961
10:33 king of Gezer **c up** to help Lachish; — 5927
11: 1 it **c to pass**, when Jabin king of Hazor — 1961
11: 5 they **c** and pitched at the waters — 935
11: 7 Joshua **c**, and all the people of war with — 935
11:21 at that time **c** Joshua, and cut off — 935
14: 6 the children of Judah **c** unto Joshua in — 5066
15:18 it **c to pass**, as she came *unto him,* that — 1961
15:18 she **c** *unto him,* that she moved him to ask — 935
16: 7 and **c** to Jericho, and went out at Jordan. — 6293
17: 4 they **c near** before Eleazar the priest, — 7126
17:13 it **c to pass**, when the children of Israel — 1961
18: 9 **c** *again* to Joshua to the host at Shiloh. — 935
18:11 Benjamin **c up** according to their families: — 5927
18:11 the coast of their lot **c forth** between — 3318
18:16 the border **c down** to the end of — 3381
19: 1 the second lot **c forth** to Simeon, *even* for — 3318
19:10 the third lot **c up** for the children of — 5927
19:17 *And* the fourth lot **c out** to Issachar, — 3318
19:24 the fifth lot **c out** for the tribe of — 3318
19:32 The sixth lot **c out** to the children of — 3318
19:40 *And* the seventh lot **c out** for the tribe of — 3318
21: 1 **c near** the heads of the fathers of — 5066
21: 4 the lot **c out** for the families of — 3318
21:45 unto the children of Israel; all **c to pass**. — 935
22:10 when they **c** unto the borders of Jordan, — 935
22:15 And they **c** unto the children of Reuben, — 935
23: 1 it **c to pass** a long time after that — 1961
24: 6 you **c** unto the sea; and the Egyptians — 935
24:11 ye went over Jordan, and **c** unto Jericho: — 935
24:29 it **c to pass** after these things, that Joshua — 1961

Jdg
1: 1 after the death of Joshua it **c to pass**, — 1961
1:14 it **c to pass**, when she came *to him,* that — 1961
1:14 when she **c** *to him,* that she moved him — 935
1:28 it **c to pass**, when Israel was strong, — 1961
2: 1 an angel of the LORD **c up** from Gilgal to — 5927
2: 4 it **c to pass**, when the angel of the LORD — 1961
2:19 it **c to pass**, when the judge was dead, — 1961
3:10 the spirit of the LORD **c** upon him, — 1961
3:20 Ehud **c** unto him; and he was sitting in a — 935
3:22 dagger out of his belly; and the dirt **c out**. — 3318
3:24 When he was gone out, his servants **c**; — 935
3:27 it **c to pass**, when he was come, that he — 1961
4: 5 the children of Israel **c up** to her for — 5927
4:22 Jael **c out** to meet him, and said unto him, — 3318
4:22 when he **c** into her *tent,* behold, Sisera lay — 935
5:14 out of Machir **c down** governors, and out — 3381
5:19 The kings **c** *and* fought, then fought — 935
5:23 they **c** not to the help of the LORD, — 935
6: 3 that the Midianites **c up**, — 5927
6: 3 of the east, even they **c up** against them; — 5927
6: 5 For they **c up** with their cattle and — 5927
6: 5 and they **c** as grasshoppers for multitude; — 935
6: 7 it **c to pass**, when the children of Israel — 1961
6:11 there **c** an angel of the LORD, — 935
6:25 it **c to pass** the same night, that the LORD — 1961
6:34 the spirit of the LORD **c** upon Gideon, — 3847
6:35 Naphtali; and they **c up** to meet him. — 5927
7: 9 it **c to pass** the same night, that the LORD — 1961
7:13 and **c** unto a tent, and smote it that it fell, — 935
7:19 **c** unto the outside of the camp *in* — 935
8: 4 Gideon **c** to Jordan, *and* passed over, — 935
8:15 he **c** unto the men of Succoth, and said, — 935
8:33 it **c to pass**, as soon as Gideon was dead, — 1961
9:25 they robbed all that **c along** *that* way by — 5674
9:26 Gaal the son of Ebed **c** with his brethren. — 935
9:42 it **c to pass** on the morrow, that the — 1961
9:52 Abimelech **c** unto the tower, — 935
9:57 upon them **c** the curse of Jotham the son — 935
11: 4 it **c to pass** in process of time, that — 1961
11:13 when they **c up** out of Egypt, from Arnon — 5927
11:16 when Israel **c up** from Egypt, — 5927
11:16 unto the Red sea, and **c** to Kadesh; — 935

Jdg
11:18 **c** by the east side of the land of Moab, — 935
11:18 but **c** not within the border of Moab: — 935
11:29 the spirit of the LORD **c** upon Jephthah, — 1961
11:34 Jephthah **c** *to* Mizpeh unto his house, — 935
11:34 his daughter **c** out to meet him with — 3318
11:35 it **c to pass**, when he saw her, that he — 1961
11:39 it **c to pass** at the end of two months, — 1961
13: 6 woman **c** and told her husband, saying, — 935
13: 6 A man of God **c** unto me, — 935
13: 9 the angel of God **c** again unto the woman — 935
13:10 unto me, that **c** unto me the *other* day. — 935
13:11 and **c** to the man, and said unto him, — 935
13:20 For it **c to pass**, when the flame went up — 5927
14: 2 he **c up**, and told his father and his — 5927
14: 5 and **c** to the vineyards of Timnath: — 935
14: 6 the spirit of the LORD **c** mightily upon — 6743
14: 9 **c** to his father and mother, and he gave — 1980
14:11 it **c to pass**, when they saw him, that — 1961
14:14 Out of the eater **c forth** meat, and out of — 3318
14:14 and out of the strong **c forth** sweetness. — 3318
14:15 it **c to pass** on the seventh day, that they — 1961
14:17 it **c to pass** on the seventh day, that he — 1961
14:19 the spirit of the LORD **c** upon him, — 6743
15: 1 it **c to pass** within a while after, in the — 1961
15: 6 the Philistines **c up**, and burnt her and her — 5927
15:14 *And* when he **c** unto Lehi, the Philistines — 935
15:14 the spirit of the LORD **c** mightily upon — 6743
15:17 it **c to pass**, when he had made an end of — 1961
15:19 in the jaw, and there **c** water thereout; — 3318
15:19 his spirit **c** again, and he revived: — 7725
16: 4 it **c to pass** afterward, that he loved a — 1961
16: 5 the lords of the Philistines **c up** unto her, — 5927
16:16 it **c to pass**, when she pressed him daily — 1961
16:18 the lords of the Philistines **c up** unto her, — 5927
16:25 **c to pass**, when their hearts were merry, — 1961
16:31 and all the house of his father **c down**, — 3381
17: 8 he **c** *to* mount Ephraim to the house of — 935
18: 2 who when they **c** *to* mount Ephraim, — 935
18: 7 **c** to Laish, and saw the people that *were* — 935
18: 8 they **c** unto their brethren *to* Zorah and — 935
18:13 and **c** unto the house of Micah. — 935
18:15 **c** to the house of the young man the Levite, — 935
18:17 **c in** thither, *and* took the graven image, — 935
18:27 the priest which he had, and **c** unto Laish, — 935
19: 1 it **c to pass** in those days, when *there* — 1961
19: 5 it **c to pass** on the fourth day, when they — 1961
19:10 and departed, and **c** over against Jebus, — 935
19:16 there **c** an old man from his work out of — 935
19:22 Bring forth the man that **c** into thine — 935
19:26 the woman in the dawning of the day, — 935
19:30 **c up** out of the land of Egypt unto this — 5927
20: 4 into Gibeah that *belongeth* to Benjamin, — 935
20:21 the children of Benjamin **c forth** out of — 3318
20:24 the children of Israel **c near** against — 7126
20:26 **c** *unto* the house of God, and wept, — 935
20:33 the liers in wait of Israel **c forth** out of — 1518
20:34 there **c** against Gibeah ten thousand — 935
20:42 them which **c** out of the cities they — NIH
20:48 as the beast, and all that **c to hand**; — 4672
20:48 set on fire all the cities that they **c** to. — 4672
21: 2 the people **c** to the house of God, — 935
21: 4 it **c to pass** on the morrow, that the — 1961
21: 5 **c** not **up** with the congregation unto — 5927
21: 5 *him* that **c** not up to the LORD to Mizpeh, — 5927
21: 8 that **c** not **up** to Mizpeh to the LORD? — 5927
21: 8 **c** none to the camp from Jabesh-gilead — 935
21:14 Benjamin **c** again at that time; — 7725

Ru
1: 1 Now it **c to pass** in the days when — 1961
1: 2 they **c** *into* the country of Moab, — 935
1:19 they two went until they **c** *to* Beth-lehem. — 935
1:19 it **c to pass**, when they were come *to* — 1961
1:22 they **c** *to* Beth-lehem in the beginning of — 935
2: 3 **c**, and gleaned in the field after the reapers: — 935
2: 4 Boaz **c** from Beth-lehem, and said unto — 935
2: 6 the Moabitish damsel that **c back** with — 7725
2: 7 so she **c**, and hath continued even from — 935
3: 7 end of the heap of corn: and she **c** softly, — 935
3: 8 it **c to pass** at midnight, that the man was — 1961
3:14 Let it not be known that a woman **c** into — 935
3:16 she **c** to her mother in law, she said, — 935
4: 1 the kinsman of whom Boaz spake **c by**; — 5674

1Sa
1:12 it **c to pass**, she continued praying — 1961
1:19 returned, and **c** to their house to Ramah: — 935
1:20 Wherefore it **c to pass**, when the time — 1961
2:13 the priest's servant **c**, while the flesh was — 935
2:14 Shiloh unto all the Israelites that **c** thither. — 935
2:15 the priest's servant **c**, and said to the man — 935
2:19 when she **c up** with her husband to offer — 5927
2:27 there **c** a man of God unto Eli, and said — 935
3: 2 **c** to pass at that time, when Eli *was* laid — 1961
3:10 the LORD **c**, and stood, and called as at — 935
4: 1 the word of Samuel **c** to all Israel. — 1961
4: 5 the covenant of the LORD **c** into the camp, — 935
4:12 **c** to Shiloh the same day with his clothes — 935
4:13 when he **c**, lo, Eli sat upon a seat *by* — 935
4:13 when the man **c** into the city, and told *it,* — 935
4:14 And the man **c** in hastily, and told Eli. — 935
4:16 I *am* he that **c out** of the army, and I fled — 935
4:18 it **c to pass**, when he made mention of — 1961
4:19 and travailed; for her pains **c** upon her. — 2015
5:10 it **c to pass**, as the ark of God came *to* — 1961
5:10 came to pass, as the ark of God **c** to Ekron, — 935
6:14 the cart **c** into the field of Joshua, — 935
7: 1 the men of Kirjath-jearim **c**, and fetched — 935
7: 2 it **c to pass**, while the ark abode in — 1961

1Sa
7:11 smote them, until *they* **c** under Beth-car. — NIH
7:13 they **c** no more into the coast of Israel: — 935
8: 1 it **c to pass**, when Samuel was old, that — 1961
8: 4 and **c** to Samuel unto Ramah, — 935
9:12 haste now, for he **c** to day to the city; — 935
9:14 behold, Samuel **c** out against them, for to — 3318
9:15 told Samuel in his ear a day before Saul **c**, — 935
9:26 it **c to pass** about the spring of the day, — 1961
10: 9 and all those signs **c to pass** that day. — 935
10:10 when they **c** thither to the hill, behold, — 935
10:10 the spirit of God **c** upon him, — 6743
10:11 it **c to pass**, when all that knew him — 1961
10:13 of prophesying, he **c** to the high place. — 935
10:14 *they were* no where, we **c** to Samuel. — 935
11: 1 Nahash the Ammonite **c up**, — 5927
11: 4 **c** the messengers *to* Gibeah of Saul, — 935
11: 5 Saul **c** after the herd out of the field; — 935
11: 6 the spirit of God **c** upon Saul when he — 6743
11: 7 and they **c** out with one consent. — 3318
11: 9 they said unto the messengers that **c**, — 935
11: 9 messengers **c** and shewed *it* to the men — 935
11:11 they **c** into the midst of the host in — 935
11:11 it **c to pass**, that they which remained — 1961
12:12 of the children of Ammon **c** against you, — 935
13: 5 they **c up**, and pitched in Michmash, — 5927
13: 8 *appointed:* but Samuel **c** not to Gilgal; — 935
13:10 it **c to pass**, that as soon as he had made — 1961
13:10 the burnt offering, behold, Samuel **c**; — 935
13:17 the spoilers **c out** of the camp of — 3318
13:22 So it **c to pass** in the day of battle, — 1961
14: 1 it **c to pass** upon a day, that Jonathan — 1961
14:19 it **c to pass**, while Saul talked unto — 1961
14:20 and they **c** to the battle: — 935
14:25 all *they* of the land **c** to a wood; — 935
15: 2 in the way, when he **c up** from Egypt. — 5927
15: 5 Saul **c** to a city of Amalek, and laid wait in — 935
15: 6 of Israel, when they **c up** out of Egypt. — 5927
15:10 **c** the word of the LORD unto Samuel, — 1961
15:12 Saul **c** to Carmel, and behold, — 935
15:13 Samuel **c** to Saul: and Saul said unto him, — 935
15:32 Agag **c** unto him delicately. And Agag — 1980
15:35 Samuel **c** no **more** to see Saul until the — 3254
16: 4 the LORD spake, and **c** to Beth-lehem. — 935
16: 6 it **c to pass**, when they were come, that — 1961
16:13 the spirit of the LORD **c** upon David from — 6743
16:21 David **c** to Saul, and stood before him: — 935
16:23 **c to pass**, when the *evil* spirit from God — 1961
17:20 he **c** to the trench, as the host was going — 935
17:22 the army, and **c** and saluted his brethren. — 935
17:23 behold, there **c up** the champion, — 5927
17:34 there **c** a lion and a bear, and took a lamb — 935
17:41 the Philistine **c on** and drew near — 1980+1980
17:48 it **c to pass**, when the Philistine arose, — 1961
17:48 **c** and drew nigh to meet David, that — 1980
18: 1 it **c to pass**, when he had made an end — 1961
18: 6 it **c to pass** as they came, when David — 1961
18: 6 it came to pass as they **c**, when David was — 935
18: 6 the women **c out** of all cities of Israel, — 3318
18:10 it **c to pass** on the morrow, that the evil — 1961
18:10 that the evil spirit from God **c** upon Saul, — 6743
18:13 he went out and **c in** before the people. — 935
18:16 he went out and **c in** before them. — 935
18:19 it **c to pass** at the time when Merab — 1961
18:30 it **c to pass**, after they went forth, — 1961
19:18 to Samuel to Ramah, and told him all — 935
19:22 and **c** to a great well that *is* in Sechu: — 935
19:23 prophesied, until he **c** to Naioth in Ramah. — 935
20: 1 **c** and said before Jonathan, What have I — 935
20:27 it **c to pass** on the morrow, *which was* — 1961
20:35 it **c to pass** in the morning, that Jonathan — 1961
20:38 the arrows, and **c** to his master. — 935
21: 1 **c** David to Nob to Ahimelech the priest: — 935
21: 5 since I **c** out, and the vessels of the young — 3318
22: 5 and **c** *into* the forest of Hareth. — 935
22:11 in Nob: and they **c** all of them to the king. — 935
23: 6 it **c to pass**, when Abiathar the son of — 1961
23: 6 he **c down** *with* an ephod in his hand. — 3381
23:19 **c up** the Ziphites to Saul to Gibeah, — 5927
23:25 wherefore he **c down** *into* a rock, — 3381
23:27 there **c** a messenger unto Saul, saying, — 935
24: 1 it **c to pass**, when Saul was returned from — 1961
24: 3 he **c** to the sheepcotes by the way, where — 935
24: 5 it **c to pass** afterward, that David's heart — 1961
24:16 it **c to pass**, when David had made an end — 1961
25: 9 when David's young men **c**, they spake to — 935
25:12 and **c** and told him all those sayings. — 935
25:20 that she **c down** by the covert of the hill, — 3381
25:20 David and his men **c down** against her; — 3381
25:36 Abigail **c** to Nabal; and behold, he held a — 935
25:37 **c to pass** in the morning, when the wine — 1961
25:38 it **c to pass** about ten days *after,* that — 1961
26: 1 Ziphites **c** unto Saul to Gibeah, saying, — 935
26: 3 he saw that Saul **c** after him into — 935
26: 5 **c** to the place where Saul had pitched: — 935
26: 7 and Abishai **c** to the people by night: — 935
26:15 for there **c** one of the people **in** to destroy — 935
27: 9 apparel, and returned, and **c** to Achish. — 935
28: 1 it **c to pass** in those days, that — 1961
28: 4 and **c** and pitched in Shunem: — 935
28: 8 and they **c** to the woman by night: — 935
28:21 the woman **c** unto Saul, and saw that he — 935
30: 1 it **c to pass**, when David and his men — 1961
30: 3 So David and his men **c** to the city, — 935
30: 9 *were* with him, and **c** to the brook Besor, — 935
30:12 he had eaten, his spirit **c** again to him: — 7725

C

1Sa 30:21	David **c** to the two hundred men, which	935
30:21	when David **c near** to the people,	5066
30:23	delivered the company that **c** against us	935
30:26	David **c** to Ziklag, he sent of the spoil	935
31: 7	and the Philistines **c** and dwelt in them.	935
31: 8	it **c to pass** on the morrow, when	1961
31: 8	when the Philistines **c** to strip the slain,	935
31:12	and **c** to Jabesh, and burnt them there.	935
2Sa 1: 1	Now it **c to pass** after the death of Saul,	1961
1: 2	It **c** even **to pass** on the third day, that	1961
1: 2	a man **c** out of the camp from Saul with	935
1: 2	it was, when he **c** to David, that he fell to	935
2: 1	it **c to pass** after this, that David inquired	1961
2: 4	men of Judah **c**, and there they anointed	935
2:23	fifth **rib**, that the spear **c** out behind him;	3318
2:23	it **c to pass**, that as many as came to	1961
2:23	as many as **c** to the place where Asahel	935
2:29	all Bithron, and they **c** to Mahanaim.	935
2:32	and they **c** to Hebron at break of day.	NIH
3: 6	it **c to pass**, while there was war	1961
3:20	So Abner **c** to David **to** Hebron,	935
3:22	David and Joab **c** from *pursuing* a troop,	935
3:23	Abner the son of Ner **c** to the king,	935
3:24	Joab **c** to the king, and said, What hast	935
3:24	behold, Abner **c** unto thee; why *is* it *that*	935
3:25	that he **c** to deceive thee, and to know	935
3:35	all the people **c** to cause David to eat	935
4: 4	five years old when the tidings **c** of Saul	935
4: 4	it **c to pass**, as she made haste to flee,	1961
4: 5	**c** about the heat of the day to the house	935
4: 6	they **c** thither into the midst of the house,	935
4: 7	For when they **c** *into* the house, he lay on	935
5: 1	**c** all the tribes of Israel to David unto	935
5: 3	So all the elders of Israel **c** to the king to	935
5:17	all the Philistines **c up** to seek David;	5927
5:18	Philistines also **c** and spread themselves	935
5:20	David **c** to Baal-perazim, and David smote	935
5:22	the Philistines **c up** yet again,	5927
6: 6	when they **c** to Nachon's threshingfloor,	935
6:16	as the ark of the Lord **c** *into* the city of	935
6:20	Michal the daughter of Saul **c** out to meet	3318
7: 1	it **c to pass**, when the king sat in his house,	1961
7: 4	it **c to pass** that night, that the word of	1961
7: 4	that the word of the Lord **c** unto Nathan,	1961
8: 1	after this it **c to pass**, that David smote	1961
8: 5	the Syrians of Damascus **c** to succour	935
10: 1	it **c to pass** after this, that the king of	1961
10: 2	David's servants **c** *into* the land of	935
10: 8	the children of Ammon **c out**, and put	3318
10:14	children of Ammon, and **c** to Jerusalem.	935
10:16	they **c** *to* Helam; and Shobach the captain	935
10:17	and passed over Jordan, and **c** to Helam.	935
11: 1	it **c to pass**, after the year was expired,	1961
11: 2	it **c to pass** in an eveningtide, that David	1961
11: 4	she **c in** unto him, and he lay with her;	935
11:14	it **c to pass** in the morning, that David	1961
11:16	it **c to pass**, when Joab observed the city,	1961
11:22	**c** and shewed David all that Joab had sent	935
11:23	**c out** unto us *into* the field, and we were	3318
12: 1	he **c** unto him, and said unto him,	935
12: 4	there **c** a traveller unto the rich man,	935
12:18	it **c to pass** on the seventh day, that	1961
12:20	**c** *into* the house of the Lord,	935
12:20	to his own house; and when he required,	935
13: 1	it **c to pass** after this, that Absalom the	1961
13:23	it **c to pass** after two full years,	1961
13:24	Absalom **c** to the king, and said,	935
13:30	it **c to pass**, while they *were* in the way,	1961
13:30	in the way, that tidings **c** to David, saying,	935
13:34	there **c** much people by the way of the hill	1980
13:36	**c to pass**, as soon as he had made an end	1961
13:36	the king's sons **c**, and lift up their voice	935
14:31	**c** to Absalom unto *his* house, and said	935
14:33	So Joab **c** to the king, and told him: and	935
14:33	he **c** to the king, and bowed himself on	935
15: 1	it **c to pass** after this, that Absalom	1961
15: 2	*when* any man that had a controversy **c**	935
15: 5	when any man **c nigh** *to him* to do him	7126
15: 6	all Israel that **c** to the king for judgment:	935
15: 7	it **c to pass** after forty years, that Absalom	1961
15:13	there **c** a messenger to David, saying,	935
15:18	six hundred men which **c** after him from	935
15:32	it **c to pass**, that *when* David was come	1961
15:32	Hushai the Archite **c** to meet him with	NIH
15:37	So Hushai David's friend **c** *into* the city,	935
15:37	the city, and Absalom **c** *into* Jerusalem.	935
16: 5	And when king David **c** to Bahurim,	935
16: 5	thence **c out** a man of the family of	3318
16: 5	he **c forth**, and cursed still as he came.	3318
16: 5	he came forth, and cursed still as he **c**.	3318
16:11	my son, which **c forth** of my bowels,	3318
16:14	**c** weary, and refreshed themselves there.	935
16:15	**c** *to* Jerusalem, and Ahithophel with him.	935
16:16	it **c to pass**, when Hushai the Archite,	1961
17:18	**c** to a man's house in Bahurim, which had	935
17:20	when Absalom's servants **c** to the woman	935
17:21	it **c to pass**, after they were departed,	1961
17:21	that they **c up** out of the well, and went	5927
17:24	David **c** to Mahanaim. And Absalom	935
17:27	it **c to pass**, when David was come to	1961
18: 4	all the people **c out** by hundreds and	3318
18:25	And he **c apace**, and drew near.	1980+1980
18:31	behold, Cushi **c**; and Cushi said, Tidings,	935
19: 5	Joab **c** *into* the house to the king, and said,	935
19: 8	all the people **c** before the king: for Israel	935

2Sa 19:15	So the king returned, and **c** to Jordan.	935
19:15	Judah **c** to Gilgal, to go to meet the king,	935
19:16	**c** down with the men of Judah to meet	NIH
19:24	Mephibosheth the son of Saul **c down** to	3381
19:24	departed until the day he **c** *again* in peace.	935
19:25	it **c to pass**, when he was come *to*	1961
19:31	Barzillai the Gileadite **c down** from	3381
19:41	all the men of Israel **c** to the king,	935
20: 3	David **c** to his house *at* Jerusalem;	935
20:12	when he saw that every one that **c** by him	935
20:15	they **c** and besieged him in Abel of	935
21:18	it **c to pass** after this, that there was again	1961
22:10	He bowed the heavens also, and **c down**;	3381
23:13	**c** to David in the harvest time unto the	935
24: 6	they **c** to Gilead, and to the land of	935
24: 6	they **c** to Dan-jaan, and about to Zidon,	935
24: 7	**c** *to* the strong hold of Tyre, and *to* all	935
24: 8	they **c** *to* Jerusalem at the end of nine	935
24:11	the word of the Lord **c** unto the prophet	1961
24:13	So Gad **c** to David, and told him,	935
24:18	Gad **c** that day to David, and said unto	935
1Ki 1:22	the king, Nathan the prophet also **c in**.	935
1:28	she **c** into the king's presence,	935
1:32	of Jehoiada. And they **c** before the king.	935
1:40	all the people **c up** after him,	5927
1:42	Jonathan the son of Abiathar the priest **c**:	935
1:47	moreover the king's servants **c** to bless	935
1:53	he **c** and bowed himself to king Solomon:	935
2: 7	for so they **c** to me when I fled because of	7126
2: 8	he **c down** to meet me *at* Jordan,	3381
2:13	Adonijah the son of Haggith **c** to	935
2:28	tidings **c** to Joab: for Joab had turned after	935
2:30	Benaiah **c** to the tabernacle of the Lord,	935
2:39	it **c to pass** at the end of three years,	1961
3:15	he **c** *to* Jerusalem, and stood before the ark	935
3:16	**c** there two women, *that were* harlots,	935
3:18	it **c to pass** the third day after that I was	1961
4:27	for all that **c** unto king Solomon's table,	7131
4:34	there **c** of all people to hear the wisdom of	935
5: 7	it **c to pass**, when Hiram heard the words	1961
6: 1	it **c to pass** in the four hundred and	1961
6:11	the word of the Lord **c** to Solomon,	1961
7:14	he **c** to king Solomon, and wrought all his	935
8: 3	the elders of Israel **c**, and the priests took	935
8: 9	when they **c out** of the land of Egypt.	3318
8:10	it **c to pass**, when the priests were come	1961
9: 1	it **c to pass**, when Solomon had finished	1961
9:10	it **c to pass** at the end of twenty years,	1961
9:12	Hiram **c out** from Tyre to see the cities	3318
9:24	Pharaoh's daughter **c up** out of the city of	5927
9:28	they **c** to Ophir, and fet from thence gold,	935
10: 1	she **c** to prove him with hard questions.	935
10: 2	she **c** to Jerusalem with a very great train,	935
10: 7	until I **c**, and mine eyes had seen *it:* and	935
10:10	there **c** no more such abundance of spices	935
10:12	there **c** no such almug trees, nor were seen	935
10:14	the weight of gold that **c** to Solomon in	935
10:22	in three years the navy of Tharshish,	935
10:29	chariot **c up** and went out of Egypt for six	5927
11: 4	For it **c to pass**, when Solomon was old,	1961
11:15	it **c to pass**, when David was in Edom,	1961
11:18	they arose out of Midian, and **c** *to* Paran:	935
11:18	**c** *to* Egypt, unto Pharaoh king of Egypt;	935
11:29	it **c to pass** at that time when Jeroboam	1961
12: 2	it **c to pass**, when Jeroboam the son of	1961
12: 3	and all the congregation of Israel **c**,	935
12:12	the people **c** to Rehoboam the third day,	935
12:20	it **c to pass**, when all Israel heard that	1961
12:22	the word of God **c** unto Shemaiah the	1961
13: 1	there **c** a man of God out of Judah by	935
13: 4	it **c to pass**, when king Jeroboam heard	1961
13:10	not by the way that he **c** to Beth-el.	935
13:11	his son **c** and told him all the works that	935
13:12	man of God went, which **c** from Judah.	935
13:20	it **c to pass**, as they sat at the table, that	1961
13:20	that the word of the Lord **c** unto	1961
13:21	he cried unto the man of God that **c** from	935
13:23	it **c to pass**, after he had eaten bread,	1961
13:25	they **c** and told *it* in the city where the old	935
13:29	the old prophet **c** to the city, to mourn and	935
13:31	it **c to pass**, after he had buried him,	1961
14: 4	*to* Shiloh, and **c** *to* the house of Ahijah.	935
14: 6	she **c in** at the door, that he said, Come in,	935
14:17	wife arose, and departed, and **c** to Tirzah:	935
14:17	when she **c** to the threshold of the door,	935
14:25	it **c to pass** in the fifth year of king	1961
14:25	*that* Shishak king of Egypt **c up** against	5927
15:21	it **c to pass**, when Baasha heard *thereof,*	1961
15:29	it **c to pass**, when he reigned, *that* he	1961
16: 1	the word of the Lord **c** to Jehu the son of	1961
16: 7	**c** the word of the Lord against Baasha,	1961
16:11	it **c to pass**, when he *began* to reign,	1961
16:18	it **c to pass**, when Zimri saw that the city	1961
16:31	it **c to pass**, as if it had been a light thing	1961
17: 2	the word of the Lord **c** unto him, saying,	1961
17: 7	it **c to pass** after a while, that the brook	1961
17: 8	the word of the Lord **c** unto him, saying,	1961
17:10	when he **c** to the gate of the city, behold,	935
17:17	it **c to pass** after these things, *that* the son	1961
17:22	the soul of the child **c** into him **again**,	7725
18: 1	it **c to pass** *after* many days, that the word	1961
18: 1	that the word of the Lord **c** to Elijah in	1961
18:17	it **c to pass**, when Ahab saw Elijah,	1961
18:21	Elijah **c** unto all the people, and said,	5066
18:27	it **c to pass** at noon, that Elijah mocked	1961

1Ki 18:29	it **c to pass**, when midday was past,	1961
18:30	all the people **c near** unto him. And he	5066
18:31	unto whom the word of the Lord **c**,	1961
18:36	it **c to pass** at *the time of* the offering of	1961
18:36	that Elijah the prophet **c near**, and said,	5066
18:44	it **c to pass** at the seventh *time*, that he	1961
18:45	it **c to pass** in the mean while, that	1961
19: 3	went for his life, and **c** *to* Beer-sheba,	935
19: 4	and **c** and sat down under a juniper tree:	935
19: 7	the angel of the Lord **c again** the second	7725
19: 9	he **c** thither unto a cave, and lodged there;	935
19: 9	the word of the Lord **c** to him,	NIH
19:13	*there* **c** a voice unto him, and said,	NIH
20: 5	the messengers **c again**, and said,	7725
20:12	it **c to pass**, when *Ben-hadad* heard this	1961
20:13	there **c** a prophet unto Ahab king of Israel,	5066
20:19	princes of the provinces **c out** of the city,	3318
20:22	the prophet **c** to the king of Israel,	5066
20:26	it **c to pass** at the return of the year,	1961
20:28	there **c** a man of God, and spake unto	5066
20:30	Ben-hadad fled, and **c** into the city, into	935
20:32	and **c** to the king of Israel, and said,	935
20:33	Ben-hadad **c forth** to him; and he caused	3318
20:43	and displeased, and **c** to Samaria.	935
21: 1	it **c to pass** after these things, *that* Naboth	1961
21: 4	Ahab **c** into his house heavy and	935
21: 5	Jezebel his wife **c** to him, and said unto	935
21:13	there **c in** two men, children of Belial,	935
21:15	it **c to pass**, when Jezebel heard that	1961
21:16	it **c to pass**, when Ahab heard that Naboth	1961
21:17	the word of the Lord **c** to Elijah	1961
21:27	it **c to pass**, when Ahab heard those words,	1961
21:28	the word of the Lord **c** to Elijah	1961
22: 2	it **c to pass** on the third year, that	1961
22: 2	Jehoshaphat the king of Judah **c down**	3381
22:15	he **c** to the king. And the king said unto	935
22:21	there **c forth** a spirit, and stood before	3318
22:32	it **c to pass**, when the captains of	1961
22:33	it **c to pass**, when the captains of	1961
2Ki 1: 6	There **c** a man **up** to meet us, and said	5927
1: 7	manner of man *was he* which **c up** to	5927
1:10	there **c down** fire from heaven,	3381
1:12	the fire of God **c down** from heaven,	3381
1:13	and **c** and fell on his knees before Elijah,	935
1:14	there **c** fire **down** from heaven,	3381
2: 1	it **c to pass**, when the Lord would take	1961
2: 3	that *were* at Beth-el **c forth** to Elisha,	3318
2: 4	I will not leave thee. So they **c** *to* Jericho.	935
2: 5	prophets that *were* at Jericho **c** to Elisha,	5066
2: 9	it **c to pass**, when they were gone over,	1961
2:11	it **c to pass**, *as* they still went on,	1961
2:15	they **c** to meet him, and bowed themselves	935
2:18	when they **c again** to him, (for he tarried	7725
2:23	there **c forth** little children out of the city,	3318
2:24	there **c forth** two she bears out of	3318
3: 5	it **c to pass**, when Ahab was dead, that	1961
3:15	it **c to pass**, when the minstrel played,	1961
3:15	that the hand of the Lord **c** upon him.	1961
3:20	it **c to pass** in the morning, when the	1961
3:20	there **c** water by the way of Edom,	935
3:24	when they **c** to the camp of Israel,	935
4: 6	it **c to pass**, when the vessels were full,	1961
4: 7	she **c** and told the man of God. And he	935
4:11	that he **c** thither, and he turned into	935
4:25	**c** unto the man of God to mount Carmel.	935
4:25	it **c to pass**, when the man of God saw	1961
4:27	when she **c** to the man of God to the hill,	935
4:27	Gehazi **c near** to thrust her away.	5066
4:38	Elisha **c again** to Gilgal: and *there was a*	7725
4:39	**c** and shred *them* into the pot of pottage:	935
4:40	it **c to pass**, as they were eating of	1961
4:42	there **c** a man from Baal-shalisha,	935
5: 7	it **c to pass**, when the king of Israel had	1961
5: 9	Naaman **c** with his horses and with his	935
5:13	his servants **c near**, and spake unto him,	5066
5:14	his flesh **c again** like unto the flesh of a	7725
5:15	his company, and, **c**, and stood before him:	935
5:24	he **c** to the tower, he took them from	935
6: 4	they **c** to Jordan, they cut down wood.	935
6:14	they **c** by night, and compassed the city	935
6:18	when they **c down** to him, Elisha prayed	3381
6:20	it **c to pass**, when they were come *into*	1961
6:23	the bands of Syria **c** no more into the land	935
6:24	it **c to pass** after this, that Ben-hadad king	1961
6:30	it **c to pass**, when the king heard the words	1961
6:32	ere the messenger **c** to him, he said to	935
6:33	the messenger **c down** unto him:	3381
7: 8	when these lepers **c** to the uttermost part	935
7: 8	went and hid *it;* and **c again**,	7725
7:10	So they **c** and called unto the porter of	935
7:10	We **c** to the camp of the Syrians,	935
7:17	who spake when the king **c down** to him.	3381
7:18	it **c to pass** as the man of God had spoken	1961
8: 3	it **c to pass** at the seven years' end, that	1961
8: 5	it **c to pass**, *as* he was telling the king	1961
8: 7	Elisha **c** *to* Damascus; and Ben-hadad	935
8: 9	and **c** and stood before him, and said,	935
8:14	departed from Elisha, and **c** to his master;	935
8:15	it **c to pass** on the morrow, that he took	1961
9: 5	he **c**, behold, the captains of the host	935
9:11	Jehu **c forth** to the servants of his lord:	3318
9:11	wherefore **c** this mad *fellow* to thee?	935
9:17	he spied the company of Jehu as he **c**,	935
9:18	messenger **c** to them, but he cometh not	935
9:19	which **c** to them, and said, Thus saith	935

C

2Ki 9:20 He **c** even unto them, and cometh not 935
9:22 it **c to pass**, when Joram saw Jehu, that 1961
9:36 Wherefore they **c** again, and told him. 7725
10: 7 it **c to pass**, when the letter came to 1961
10: 7 it came to pass, when the letter **c** to them, 935
10: 8 there **c** a messenger, and told him, saying, 935
10: 9 it **c to pass** in the morning, that he went 1961
10:12 he arose and departed, and **c** to Samaria. 1980
10:17 when he **c** to Samaria, he slew all that 935
10:21 all the worshippers of Baal **c**, so that there 935
10:21 so that there was not a man left that **c** not. 935
10:21 they **c** into the house of Baal; and the 935
10:25 it **c to pass**, as soon as he had made an 1961
11: 9 the sabbath, and **c** to Jehoiada the priest. 935
11:13 she **c** to the people into the temple of 935
11:16 which the horses **c** into the king's house: 3996
11:19 **c** by the way of the gate of the guard to 935
12:10 the king's scribe and the high priest **c** up, 5927
13:14 Joash the king of Israel **c down** unto him, 3381
13:21 it **c to pass**, as they were burying a man, 1961
14: 5 it **c to pass**, as soon as the kingdom was 1961
14:13 **c** to Jerusalem, and brake down the wall 935
15:12 fourth generation. And so it **c to pass**. 1961
15:14 **c** to Samaria, and smote Shallum the son 935
15:19 And Pul the king of Assyria **c** against 935
15:29 In the days of Pekah king of Israel **c** 935
16: 5 Pekah son of Remaliah king of Israel **c up** 5927
16: 6 the Syrians **c** to Elath, and dwelt there 935
16:11 the priest made it against king Ahaz **c** 935
17: 3 Against him **c up** Shalmaneser king of 5927
17: 5 the king of Assyria **c up** throughout all 5927
17:28 they had carried away from Samaria **c** 935
18: 1 it **c to pass** in the third year of Hoshea 1961
18: 9 it **c to pass** in the fourth year of king 1961
18: 9 that Shalmaneser king of Assyria **c up** 5927
18:17 they went up and **c** to Jerusalem. 935
18:17 they **c** and stood by the conduit of the 935
18:18 there **c out** to them Eliakim the son of 3318
18:37 **c** Eliakim the son of Hilkiah, which was 935
19: 1 it **c to pass**, when king Hezekiah heard it, 1961
19: 5 the servants of king Hezekiah **c** to Isaiah. 935
19:33 By the way that he **c**, by the same shall he 935
19:35 it **c to pass** that night, that the angel of 1961
19:37 it **c to pass**, as he was worshipping in 1961
20: 1 prophet Isaiah the son of Amoz **c** to him, 935
20: 4 it **c to pass**, afore Isaiah was gone out 1961
20: 4 that the word of the Lord **c** to him, 1961
20:14 Isaiah the prophet unto king Hezekiah, 935
20:14 from whence **c** they unto thee? 935
21:15 since the day their fathers **c forth** out of 3318
22: 3 it **c to pass** in the eighteenth year of king 1961
22: 9 Shaphan the scribe **c** to the king, 935
22:11 it **c to pass**, when the king had heard 1961
23: 9 **c** not up to the altar of the Lord in 5927
23:17 which **c** from Judah, and proclaimed these 935
23:18 with the bones of the prophet that **c** out 935
23:34 took Jehoahaz away; and he **c** to Egypt, 935
24: 1 Nebuchadnezzar king of Babylon **c up**, 5927
24: 3 of the Lord **c** this upon Judah, 1961
24: 7 king of Egypt **c** not again any more **out** 3318
24:10 king of Babylon **c up** against Jerusalem, 5927
24:11 Nebuchadnezzar king of Babylon **c** against 935
24:20 of the Lord it **c to pass** in Jerusalem 1961
25: 1 it **c to pass** in the ninth year of his reign, 1961
25: 1 that Nebuchadnezzar king of Babylon **c**, 935
25: 8 **c** Nebuzar-adan, captain of the guard, 935
25:23 there **c** to Gedaliah to Mizpah, even 935
25:25 it **c to pass** in the seventh month, 1961
25:25 **c**, and ten men with him, 935
25:26 of the armies, arose, and **c** to Egypt: 935
25:27 it **c to pass** in the seven and thirtieth year 1961
1Ch 1:12 Casluhim, (of whom **c** the Philistines,) 3318
2:53 of them **c** the Zareathites, 3318
2:55 These are the Kenites that **c** of Hemath, 935
4:41 these written by name **c** in the days of 935
5: 2 his brethren, and of him **c** the chief ruler; NIH
7:21 they **c down** to take away their cattle. 3381
7:22 and his brethren **c** to comfort him. 935
7:40 and the Philistines and dwelt in them. 935
10: 8 it **c to pass** on the morrow, when 1961
10: 8 when the Philistines **c** to strip the slain, 935
11: 3 Therefore **c** all the elders of Israel to the 935
12: 1 these are they that **c** to David to Ziklag, 935
12:16 And there **c** of the children of Benjamin 935
12:18 the spirit **c** upon Amasai, who was chief 3847
12:19 he **c** with the Philistines against Saul 935
12:22 at that time day by day there **c** to David 935
12:23 and **c** to David to Hebron, to turn 935
12:38 rank, with a perfect heart to Hebron, 935
13: 9 when they **c** unto the threshingfloor of 935
14: 9 the Philistines and spread themselves in 935
14:11 So they **c up** to Baal-perazim; 5927
15:26 it **c to pass**, when God helped the Levites 1961
15:29 it **c to pass**, as the ark of the covenant of 1961
15:29 as the ark of the covenant of the Lord **c** to 935
17: 1 it **c to pass**, as David sat in his house, 1961
17: 3 it **c to pass** the same night, that the word 1961
17: 3 that the word of God **c** to Nathan, saying, 935
17:16 David the king **c** and sat before the Lord, 935
18: 1 Now after this it **c to pass**, that David 1961
18: 5 when the Syrians of Damascus **c** to help 935
19: 1 Now it **c to pass** after this, that Nahash 1961
19: 2 So the servants of David **c** into the land 935
19: 7 who **c** and pitched before Medeba. 935
19: 7 together from their cities, and **c** to battle. 935

1Ch 19: 9 the children of Ammon **c out**, and put 3318
19:15 into the city. Then Joab **c** to Jerusalem. 935
19:17 **c** upon them, and set the battle in array 935
20: 1 **c to pass**, that after the year was expired, 1961
20: 1 of Ammon, and **c** and besieged Rabbah. 935
20: 4 it **c to pass** after this, that there arose war 1961
21: 4 throughout all Israel, and **c** to Jerusalem. 935
21:11 So Gad **c** to David, and said unto him, 935
21:21 And as David **c** to Ornan, Ornan looked 935
22: 8 the word of the Lord **c** to me, saying, 1961
24: 7 Now the first lot **c forth** to Jehoiarib, 3318
24:28 Of Mahli **c** Eleazar, who had no sons. NIH
25: 9 Now the first lot **c forth** for Asaph to 3318
26:14 cast lots; and his lot **c out** northward. 3318
26:16 and Hosah the lot **c forth** westward, NIH
27: 1 which **c in** and went out month by month 935
2Ch 1:13 Solomon **c** from his journey to the high 935
5: 4 the elders of Israel **c**; and the Levites took 935
5:10 of Israel, when they **c** out of Egypt. 3318
5:11 it **c to pass**, when the priests were come 1961
5:13 It **c** even **to pass**, as the trumpeters and 1961
7: 1 the fire **c down** from heaven, 3381
7: 3 of Israel saw how the fire **c down**, 3381
7:11 all that **c** into Solomon's heart to make in 935
8: 1 it **c to pass** at the end of twenty years, 1961
9: 1 **c** to prove Solomon with hard questions 935
9: 6 until I **c**, and mine eyes had seen it: and 935
9:13 the weight of gold that **c** to Solomon in 935
9:21 every three years once **c** the ships of 935
10: 2 it **c to pass**, when Jeroboam the son of 1961
10: 3 So Jeroboam and all Israel **c** and spake to 935
10:12 all the people **c** to Rehoboam on the third 935
11: 2 the word of the Lord **c** to Shemaiah 1961
11:14 and **c** to Judah and Jerusalem: 1980
11:16 the Lord God of Israel **c** to Jerusalem, 935
12: 1 it **c to pass**, when Rehoboam had 1961
12: 2 it **c to pass**, that in the fifth year of king 1961
12: 2 king of Egypt **c up** against Jerusalem, 5927
12: 3 people were without number that **c** with 935
12: 4 pertained to Judah, and **c** to Jerusalem. 935
12: 5 Shemaiah the prophet to Rehoboam, 935
12: 7 the word of the Lord **c** to Shemaiah, 1961
12: 9 So Shishak king of Egypt **c up** against 5927
12:11 the guard **c** and fet them, and brought 935
13:15 it **c to pass**, that God smote Jeroboam 1961
14: 9 there **c out** against them Zerah 3318
14: 9 hundred chariots; and **c** unto Mareshah. 935
14:14 for the fear of the Lord **c** upon them: 1961
15: 1 the spirit of God **c** upon Azariah the son 1961
15: 5 to him that **c in**, but great vexations were 935
16: 1 Baasha king of Israel **c up** against Judah, 5927
16: 5 it **c to pass**, when Baasha heard it, that he 1961
16: 7 at that time Hanani the seer **c** to Asa king 935
18:20 there **c out** a spirit, and stood before 3318
18:23 Zedekiah the son of Chenaanah **c near**, 5066
18:31 it **c to pass**, when the captains of 1961
18:32 For it **c to pass**, that when the captains of 1961
20: 1 it **c to pass** after this also, that the children 1961
20: 1 **c** against Jehoshaphat to battle. 935
20: 2 there **c** some that told Jehoshaphat, 935
20: 4 even out of all the cities of Judah they **c** to 935
20:10 when they **c** out of the land of Egypt, 935
20:14 **c** the spirit of the Lord in the midst of 1961
20:24 when Judah **c** toward the watch tower in 935
20:25 his people **c** to take away the spoil of them, 935
20:28 **c** to Jerusalem with psalteries and harps 935
21:12 there **c** a writing to him from Elijah 935
21:17 they **c up** into Judah, and brake into it, 5927
21:19 it **c to pass**, that in process of time, after 1961
22: 1 the band of men that **c** with the Arabians 935
22: 8 **c to pass**, that when Jehu was executing 1961
23: 2 fathers of Israel, and they **c** to Jerusalem. 935
23:12 she **c** to the people into the house of 935
23:20 they **c** through the high gate into the 935
24: 4 it **c to pass** after this, that Joash was 1961
24:11 it **c to pass**, that at what time the chest 1961
24:11 and the high priest's officer and 935
24:17 after the death of Jehoiada **c** the princes 935
24:18 wrath upon Judah and Jerusalem for this 935
24:20 the spirit of God **c** upon Zechariah the son 3847
24:23 it **c to pass** at the end of the year, that 1961
24:23 that the host of Syria **c up** against him: 5927
24:23 they **c** to Judah and Jerusalem, 935
24:24 For the army of the Syrians **c** with a small 935
25: 3 Now it **c to pass**, when the kingdom was 1961
25: 7 there **c** a man of God to him, saying, 935
25:14 Now it **c to pass**, after that Amaziah was 1961
25:16 it **c to pass**, as he talked with him, that 1961
25:20 for it **c** of God, that he might deliver them NIH
28: 9 he went out before the host that **c** to 935
28:12 stood up against them that **c** from the war, 935
28:20 Tilgath-pilneser king of Assyria **c** unto him, 935
29:15 and sanctified themselves, and **c**, 935
29:17 on the eighth day of the month **c** they to 935
30:11 humbled themselves, and **c** to Jerusalem. 935
30:25 all the congregation that **c** out of Israel, 935
30:25 strangers that **c** out of the land of Israel, 935
30:27 prayer **c** up to his holy dwelling place, 935
31: 5 as soon as the commandment **c abroad**, 6555
31: 8 and the princes **c** and saw the heaps, 935
32: 1 thereof, Sennacherib king of Assyria **c**, 935
32:21 they that **c forth** of his own bowels slew 3329
32:26 that the wrath of the Lord **c** not upon 935
34: 9 when they **c** to Hilkiah the high priest, 935
34:19 it **c to pass**, when the king had heard 1961

2Ch 35:20 Necho king of Egypt **c up** to fight against 5927
35:22 and **c** to fight in the valley of Megiddo. 935
36: 6 Against him **c up** Nebuchadnezzar king of 5927
Ezr 2: 1 **c again** unto Jerusalem and Judah, 7725
2: 2 Which **c** with Zerubbabel: Jeshua, 935
2:68 when they **c** to the house of the Lord 935
4: 2 they **c** to Zerubbabel, and to the chief of 5066
4:12 that the Jews which **c up** from thee to us 5559
5: 3 At the same time **c** to them Tatnai, 858
5: 5 them to cease, till the matter **c** to Darius: 1946
5:16 **c** the same Sheshbazzar, and laid 858
7: 8 he **c** to Jerusalem in the fifth month, 935
7: 9 on the first day of the fifth month **c** he to 935
8:32 we **c** to Jerusalem, and abode there three 935
10: 5 the princes **c** to me, saying, The people of 5066
10: 6 when he **c** thither, he did eat no bread, 1980
Ne 1: 1 it **c to pass** in the month Chisleu, 1961
1: 2 brethren, **c**, he and certain men of Judah; 935
1: 4 it **c to pass**, when I heard these words, 1961
2: 1 it **c to pass** in the month Nisan, 1961
2: 9 I **c** to the governors beyond the river, 935
2:11 So I **c** to Jerusalem, and was there three 935
4: 1 it **c to pass**, that when Sanballat heard 1961
4: 7 it **c to pass**, that when Sanballat, 1961
4:12 it **c to pass**, that when the Jews which 1961
4:12 when the Jews which dwelt by them **c**, 935
4:15 it **c to pass**, when our enemies heard that 1961
4:16 it **c to pass** from that time forth, that 1961
5:17 besides those that **c** unto us from among 935
6: 1 Now it **c to pass**, when Sanballat, 1961
6:10 Afterward I **c** unto the house of Shemaiah 935
6:16 it **c to pass**, that when all our enemies 1961
6:17 and the letters of Tobiah **c** unto them. 935
7: 1 it **c to pass**, when the wall was built, 1961
7: 5 genealogy of them which **c up** at the first, 5927
7: 6 **c** again to Jerusalem and to Judah, 7725
7: 7 Who **c** with Zerubbabel, Jeshua, 935
7:73 when the seventh month **c**, the children 5060
13: 3 Now it **c to pass**, when they had heard 1961
13: 6 king of Babylon **c** I unto the king, 935
13: 7 I **c** to Jerusalem, and understood of the evil 935
13:19 it **c to pass**, that when the gates of 1961
13:21 From that time forth **c** they no more on 935
Est 1: 1 it **c to pass** in the days of Ahasuerus, 1961
1:17 be brought in before him, but she **c** not. 935
2: 8 So it **c to pass**, when the king's 1961
2:13 thus **c** every maiden unto the king; 935
2:14 she **c** in unto the king no more, except 935
3: 4 Now it **c to pass**, when they spake daily 1961
4: 2 **c** even before the king's gate: for none 935
4: 3 king's commandment and his decree **c**, 5060
4: 4 and her chamberlains **c** and told it her. 935
4: 9 Hatach **c** and told Esther the words of 935
5: 1 Now it **c to pass** on the third day, 1961
5: 5 Haman **c** to the banquet that Esther had 935
5:10 he **c** home, he sent and called for his 935
6: 6 Haman **c** in. And the king said unto him, 935
6:12 Mordecai **c again** to the king's gate. 7725
6:14 the king's chamberlains **c**, and hasted to 5060
7: 1 Haman **c** to banquet with Esther the 935
8: 1 Mordecai **c** before the king; for Esther had 935
8:17 king's commandment and his decree **c**, 5060
9:25 when Esther **c** before the king, 935
Job 1: 6 there was a day when the sons of God **c** 935
1: 6 the Lord, and Satan **c** also among them. 935
1:14 there **c** a messenger unto Job, and said, 935
1:16 speaking, there **c** also another, and said, 935
1:17 speaking, there **c** also another, and said, 935
1:18 there **c** also another, and said, Thy sons 935
1:19 there **c** a great wind from the wilderness, 935
1:21 Naked **c** I out of my mother's womb, 3318
2: 1 **c** to present themselves before the Lord, 935
2: 1 Satan **c** also among them to present himself 935
2:11 they **c** every one from his own place; 935
3:11 the ghost when I **c** out of the belly? 3318
3:26 I rest, neither was I quiet; yet trouble **c**. 935
4:14 Fear **c** upon me, and trembling, 7122
6:20 hoped; they **c** thither, and were ashamed. 935
26: 4 and whose spirit **c** from thee? 3318
29:13 him that was ready to perish **c** upon me: 935
30:14 They **c** upon me as a wide breaking in of 857
30:26 evil **c** unto me: and when I waited for light, 935
30:26 when I waited for light, there **c** darkness. 935
38:29 Out of whose womb **c** the ice? and 3318
42:11 **c** there unto him all his brethren, and all 935
Ps 18: 6 my cry **c** before him, even into his ears. 935
18: 9 He bowed the heavens also, and **c down**: 3381
27: 2 my foes, **c** upon me to eat up my flesh, 7126
51: 1 T when Nathan the prophet **c** unto him, 935
52: 1 T when Doeg the Edomite **c** and told Saul, 935
54: 1 T when the Ziphims **c** and said to Saul, 935
78:21 and anger also **c up** against Israel; 5927
78:31 The wrath of God **c** upon them, 5927
88:17 They **c round about** me daily like water; 5437
105:19 Until the time that his word **c**: the word 935
105:23 Israel also **c** into Egypt; and Jacob 935
105:31 there **c** divers sorts of flies, and lice in all 935
105:34 the locusts **c**, and caterpillars, 935
Pr 7:15 therefore **c** I forth to meet thee, 3318
Ecc 5:15 As he **c forth** of his mother's womb, 3318
5:15 naked shall he return to go as he **c**, 935
5:16 that in all points as he **c**, so shall he go: 935
9:14 there **c** a great king against it, 935
SS 4: 2 shorn, which **c up** from the washing; 5927
Isa 7: 1 it **c to pass** in the days of Ahaz the son of 1961

C

Isa 11:16 day that he **c up** out of the land of Egypt.	5927
20: 1 In the year that Tartan **c** unto Ashdod,	935
30: 4 at Zoan, and his ambassadors **c** to Hanes.	5060
36: 1 Now it **c to pass** in the fourteenth year of	1961
36: 1 *that* Sennacherib king of Assyria **c up**	5927
36: 3 **c forth** unto him Eliakim, Hilkiah's son,	3318
36:22 **c** Eliakim, the son of Hilkiah, *that was* over	935
37: 1 it **c to pass**, when king Hezekiah heard *it*,	1961
37: 5 the servants of king Hezekiah **c** to Isaiah.	935
37:34 By the way that he **c**, *by the same* shall	935
37:38 it **c to pass**, as he was worshipping *in*	1961
38: 1 Isaiah the prophet the son of Amoz **c** unto	935
38: 4 **c** the word of the LORD to Isaiah, saying,	1961
39: 3 **c** Isaiah the prophet unto king Hezekiah,	935
39: 3 from whence **c** they unto thee?	935
41: 5 of the earth were afraid, drew near, and **c**.	857
48: 3 I did *them* suddenly, and they **c to pass**.	935
48: 5 before it **c to pass** I shewed *it* thee:	935
50: 2 Wherefore, when I **c**, *was there* no man?	935
66: 7 before her pain **c**, she was delivered of a	935
Jer 1: 2 To whom the word of the LORD **c** in	1961
1: 3 It also in the days of Jehoiakim the son	1961
1: 4 the word of the LORD **c** unto me, saying,	1961
1:11 the word of the LORD **c** unto me, saying,	1961
1:13 the word of the LORD **c** unto me	1961
2: 1 Moreover the word of the LORD **c** to me,	1961
3: 9 it **c to pass** through the lightness of her	1961
7: 1 The word that **c** to Jeremiah from	1961
7:25 Since the day that your fathers **c forth** out	3318
7:31 *them* not, neither **c** it into my heart.	5927
8:15 no good **c**, *and* for a time of health,	NIH
11: 1 The word that **c** to Jeremiah from	1961
13: 3 the word of the LORD **c** unto me	1961
13: 6 it **c to pass** after many days, that	1961
13: 8 the word of the LORD **c** unto me, saying,	1961
14: 1 The word of the LORD that **c** to Jeremiah	1961
14: 3 they **c** to the pits, *and* found no water;	935
16: 1 the word of the LORD **c** also unto me,	1961
17:16 **that which c out of** my lips was right	4161
18: 1 The word which **c** to Jeremiah from	1961
18: 5 the word of the LORD **c** to me, saying,	1961
19: 5 nor spake *it*, neither **c** *it* into my mind:	5927
19:14 **c** Jeremiah from Tophet, whither the LORD	935
20: 3 it **c to pass** on the morrow, that Pashur	1961
20:18 Wherefore **c** I **forth** out of the womb to	3318
21: 1 The word which **c** unto Jeremiah from	1961
24: 4 Again the word of the LORD **c** unto me,	1961
25: 1 The word that **c** to Jeremiah concerning	1961
26: 1 king of Judah **c** this word from the LORD,	1961
26: 8 it **c to pass**, when Jeremiah had made	1961
26:10 they **c up** from the king's house *unto*	5927
27: 1 **c** this word unto Jeremiah from	1961
28: 1 **c to pass** the same year, in the beginning	1961
28:12 the word of the LORD **c** unto Jeremiah	1961
29:30 **c** the word of the LORD unto Jeremiah	1961
30: 1 The word that **c** to Jeremiah from	1961
32: 1 The word that **c** to Jeremiah from	1961
32: 6 The word of the LORD **c** unto me, saying,	1961
32: 8 So Hanameel mine uncle's son **c** to me in	935
32:23 **c in**, and possessed it; but they obeyed	935
32:26 **c** the word of the LORD unto Jeremiah,	1961
32:35 them not, neither **c** it into my mind,	5927
33: 1 Moreover the word of the LORD **c** unto	1961
33:19 the word of the LORD **c** unto Jeremiah,	1961
33:23 Moreover the word of the LORD **c** to	1961
34: 1 The word which **c** unto Jeremiah from	1961
34: 8 *This is* the word that **c** unto Jeremiah	1961
34:12 Therefore the word of the LORD **c** to	1961
35: 1 The word which **c** unto Jeremiah from	1961
35:11 it **c to pass**, when Nebuchadrezzar king	1961
35:11 king of Babylon **c up** into the land,	5927
35:12 **c** the word of the LORD unto Jeremiah,	1961
36: 1 **c to pass** in the fourth year of Jehoiakim	1961
36: 1 *that* this word **c** unto Jeremiah from	1961
36: 9 it **c to pass** in the fifth year of Jehoiakim	1961
36: 9 *to* all the people that **c** from the cities of	935
36:14 took the roll in his hand, and **c** unto them.	935
36:16 Now it **c to pass** when they had heard all	1961
36:23 it **c to pass**, *that* when Jehudi had read	935
36:27 the word of the LORD **c** to Jeremiah,	1961
37: 4 Now Jeremiah **c in** and went out among	935
37: 6 **c** the word of the LORD unto the prophet	1961
37:11 it **c to pass**, *that* when the army of	1961
38:27 **c** all the princes unto Jeremiah,	935
39: 1 Nebuchadrezzar king of Babylon and	935
39: 3 all the princes of the king of Babylon **c in**,	935
39: 4 it **c to pass**, *that* when Zedekiah the king	1961
39:15 Now the word of the LORD **c** unto	1961
40: 1 The word which **c** to Jeremiah from	1961
40: 8 they **c** to Gedaliah to Mizpah, even	935
40:12 **c** *to* the land of Judah, to Gedaliah, unto	935
40:13 in the fields, **c** to Gedaliah to Mizpah,	935
41: 1 Now it **c to pass** in the seventh month,	1961
41: 1 **c** unto Gedaliah the son of Ahikam to	935
41: 4 it **c to pass** the second day after *he* had	1961
41: 5 That there **c** certain from Shechem,	935
41: 6 it **c to pass**, as he met them, he said unto	1961
41: 7 *so*, when they **c** into the midst of the city,	935
41:13 it **c to pass**, *that* when all the people	1961
42: 1 the least even unto the greatest, **c** near,	5066
42: 7 it **c to pass** after ten days, that the word	1961
42: 7 that the word of the LORD **c** unto	1961
43: 1 it **c to pass**, *that* when Jeremiah had made	1961
43: 7 So they **c** *into* the land of Egypt: for they	935
43: the LORD: thus **c** they *even* to Tahpanhes.	935

Jer 43: 8 **c** the word of the LORD unto Jeremiah in	1961
44: 1 The word that **c** to Jeremiah concerning	1961
44:21 them, and **c** it *not* into his mind?	5927
46: 1 The word of the LORD which **c** to	1961
47: 1 The word of the LORD that **c** to Jeremiah	1961
49:34 The word of the LORD that **c** to Jeremiah	1961
52: 3 the anger of the LORD **c to pass** in Jerusalem	1961
52: 4 it **c to pass** in the ninth year of his reign,	1961
52: 4 *that* Nebuchadrezzar king of Babylon **c**,	935
52:12 **c** Nebuzar-adan, captain of the guard,	935
52:31 it **c to pass** in the seven and thirtieth year	1961
La 1: 9 therefore she **c down** wonderfully:	3381
Eze 1: 1 Now it **c to pass** in the thirtieth year,	1961
1: 3 The word of the LORD **c expressly**	1961+1961
1: 4 behold, a whirlwind **c** out of the north,	935
1: 5 out of the midst thereof **c** the likeness	NIH
3:15 I **c** to them of the captivity at Tel-abib,	935
3:16 it **c to pass** at the end of seven days,	1961
3:16 that the word of the LORD **c** unto me,	1961
4:14 neither **c** there abominable flesh into my	935
6: 1 the word of the LORD **c** unto me, saying,	1961
7: 1 Moreover the word of the LORD **c** unto	1961
8: 1 it **c to pass** in the sixth year, in the sixth	1961
9: 2 six men **c** from the way of the higher gate,	935
9: 8 it **c to pass**, while they were slaying	1961
10: 6 **c to pass**, *that* when he had commanded	1961
11:13 it **c to pass**, when I prophesied,	1961
11:14 Again the word of the LORD **c** unto me,	1961
12: 1 The word of the LORD also **c** unto me,	1961
12: 8 in the morning **c** the word of the LORD	1961
12:17 Moreover the word of the LORD **c** to me,	1961
12:21 the word of the LORD **c** unto me, saying,	1961
12:26 Again the word of the LORD **c** to me,	1961
13: 1 the word of the LORD **c** unto me, saying,	1961
14: 1 **c** certain of the elders of Israel unto me,	935
14: 2 the word of the LORD **c** unto me, saying,	1961
14:12 The word of the LORD **c** again to me,	1961
15: 1 the word of the LORD **c** unto me, saying,	1961
16: 1 Again the word of the LORD **c** unto me,	1961
16:23 it **c to pass** after all thy wickedness, (woe,	1961
17: 1 the word of the LORD **c** unto me, saying,	1961
17: 3 **c** unto Lebanon, and took the highest	935
17:11 Moreover the word of the LORD **c** unto	1961
18: 1 the word of the LORD **c** unto me again,	1961
20: 1 it **c to pass** in the seventh year, in the	1961
20: 1 certain of the elders of Israel **c** to inquire	935
20: 2 **c** the word of the LORD unto me, saying,	1961
20:45 Moreover the word of the LORD **c**	1961
21: 1 the word of the LORD **c** unto me, saying,	1961
21: 8 Again the word of the LORD **c** unto me,	1961
21:18 The word of the LORD **c** unto me again,	1961
22: 1 Moreover the word of the LORD **c**	1961
22:17 the word of the LORD **c** unto me, saying,	1961
22:23 the word of the LORD **c** unto me, saying,	1961
23: 1 The word of the LORD **c** again unto me,	1961
23:17 Babylonians **c** to her into the bed of love,	935
23:39 they **c** the same day into my sanctuary to	935
23:40 a messenger *was* sent; and lo, they **c**:	935
24: 1 the word of the LORD **c** unto me, saying,	1961
24:15 Also the word of the LORD **c** unto me,	1961
24:20 The word of the LORD **c** unto me, saying,	1961
25: 1 The word of the LORD **c** again unto me,	1961
26: 1 it **c to pass** in the eleventh year, in the	1961
26: 1 *that* the word of the LORD **c** unto me,	1961
27: 1 The word of the LORD **c** again unto me,	1961
28: 1 The word of the LORD **c** again unto me,	1961
28:11 Moreover the word of the LORD **c** unto	1961
28:20 Again the word of the LORD **c** unto me,	1961
29: 1 the word of the LORD **c** unto me, saying,	1961
29:17 it **c to pass** in the seven and twentieth	1961
29:17 the word of the LORD **c** unto me, saying,	1961
30: 1 The word of the LORD **c** again unto me,	1961
30:20 it **c to pass** in the eleventh year, in the	1961
30:20 *that* the word of the LORD **c** unto me,	1961
31: 1 it **c to pass** in the eleventh year, in the	1961
31: 1 *that* the word of the LORD **c** unto me,	1961
32: 1 it **c to pass** in the twelfth year,	1961
32: 1 *that* the word of the LORD **c** unto me,	1961
32:17 It **c to pass** also in the twelfth year,	1961
32:17 *that* the word of the LORD **c** unto me,	1961
33: 1 Again the word of the LORD **c** unto me,	1961
33:21 it **c to pass** in the twelfth year of our	1961
33:21 one that had escaped out of Jerusalem **c**	935
33:22 the evening, afore he that was escaped **c**;	935
33:22 mouth, until *he* **c** to me in the morning;	935
33:23 the word of the LORD **c** unto me, saying,	1961
34: 1 the word of the LORD **c** unto me, saying,	1961
35: 1 Moreover the word of the LORD **c** unto	1961
36:16 Moreover the word of the LORD **c** unto	1961
37: 7 the bones **c together**, bone to his bone.	7126
37: 8 the sinews and the flesh **c up** upon them,	5927
37:10 the breath **c** into them, and they lived,	935
37:15 the word of the LORD **c** again unto me,	1961
38: 1 the word of the LORD **c** unto me, saying,	1961
40: 6 **c** he unto the gate which looketh toward	935
43: 2 glory of the God of Israel **c** from the way	935
43: 3 that I saw when I **c** to destroy the city:	935
43: 4 the glory of the LORD **c** into the house by	935
46: 9 *by* the way of the gate whereby he **c** in,	935
47: 1 the waters **c down** from under from	3381
Da 1: 1 Nebuchadnezzar king of Babylon *unto*	935
2: 2 So they **c** and stood before the king.	935
2:29 thoughts **c** *into thy mind* upon thy bed,	5559
3: 8 at that time certain Chaldeans **c near**,	7127
3:26 Nebuchadnezzar **c near** to the mouth of	7127

Da 3:26 **c forth** of the midst of the fire.	5312
4: 7 **c** in the magicians, the astrologers,	5954
4: 8 at the last Daniel **c in** before me,	5954
4:13 and a holy one **c down** from heaven;	5182
4:28 All this **c** upon the king Nebuchadnezzar.	4291
5: 5 In the same hour **c forth** fingers of a	5312
5: 8 **c in** all the king's wise *men*: but they	5954
5:10 and his lords, **c** into the banquet house:	5954
6:12 they **c near**, and spake before the king	7127
6:20 when he **c** to the den, he cried with a	7127
6:24 or ever they **c** at the bottom of the den.	4291
7: 3 four great beasts **c up** from the sea,	5559
7: 8 **c up** among them another little horn,	5559
7:10 issued and **c forth** from before him:	5312
7:13 *one* like the Son of man **c** with the clouds	858
7:13 **c** to the Ancient of days, and they brought	4291
7:16 I **c near** unto one of them that stood *by*,	7127
7:20 the other which **c up**, and before whom	5559
7:22 Until the Ancient of days **c**,	858
7:22 the time **c** that the saints possessed	4291
8: 2 it **c to pass**, when I saw, that I *was* at	1961
8: 3 than the other, and the higher **c up** last.	5927
8: 5 a he goat **c** from the west on the face of	935
8: 6 he **c** to the ram that had two horns, which	935
8: 8 for it **c up** four notable ones toward	5927
8: 9 out of one of them **c forth** a little horn,	3318
8:15 it **c to pass**, when I, *even* I Daniel, had	1961
8:17 So he **c near** where I stood: and when he	935
8:17 when he **c**, I was afraid, and fell upon my	935
9: 2 where *of* the word of the LORD **c** to	1961
9:23 supplications the commandment **c forth**,	3318
10: 3 neither **c** flesh nor wine in my mouth,	935
10:13 one of the chief princes, **c** to help me;	935
10:18 there **c again** and touched me *one* like	3254
Hos 1: 1 The word of the LORD that **c** unto Hosea,	1961
2:15 *in* the day when she **c up** out of the land	5927
Joel 1: 1 The word of the LORD that **c** to Joel	1961
Am 6: 1 nations, to whom the house of Israel **c**!	935
7: 2 it **c to pass**, *that* when they had made an	1961
Ob 1: 5 If thieves **c** to thee, if robbers by night,	935
1: 5 if the grape-gatherers **c** to thee, would	935
Jnh 1: 1 Now the word of the LORD **c** unto Jonah	1961
1: 6 So the shipmaster **c** to him, and said unto	7126
2: 7 my prayer **c in** unto thee, into thine holy	935
3: 1 the word of the LORD **c** unto Jonah	1961
3: 6 For word **c** unto the king of Nineveh,	5060
4: 8 it **c to pass**, when the sun did arise,	1961
4:10 which **c up** in a night, and perished in a	1961
Mic 1: 1 The word of the LORD that **c** to Micah	1961
1:11 the inhabitant of Zaanan **c** not **forth** *in*	3318
1:12 evil **c down** from the LORD unto the gate	3381
Hab 3: 3 God **c** from Teman, and the Holy One	935
3:14 they **c out as a whirlwind** to scatter me:	5590
Zep 1: 1 The word of the LORD which **c** unto	1961
Hag 1: 1 **c** the word of the LORD by Haggai	1961
1: 3 **c** the word of the LORD by Haggai	1961
1: 9 *Ye* looked for much, and lo, *it* **c** to little;	NIH
1:14 they **c** and did work in the house of	935
2: 1 the word of the LORD by the prophet	1961
2: 5 with you when ye **c out** of Egypt,	3318
2:10 **c** the word of the LORD by Haggai	1961
2:16 one **c** to a heap of twenty *measures*,	935
2:16 one **c** to the pressfat for to draw out	935
2:20 again the word of the LORD **c** unto	1961
Zec 1: 1 **c** the word of the LORD unto Zechariah,	1961
1: 7 **c** the word of the LORD unto Zechariah,	1961
4: 1 the angel that talked with me **c again**,	7725
4: 8 Moreover the word of the LORD **c** unto	1961
5: 9 there **c out** two women, and the wind	3318
6: 1 there **c** four chariots **out** from between	3318
6: 9 the word of the LORD **c** unto me, saying,	1961
7: 1 it **c to pass** in the fourth year of king	1961
7: 1 *that* the word of the LORD **c** unto	1961
7: 4 **c** the word of the LORD of hosts unto me,	1961
7: 8 the word of the LORD **c** unto Zechariah,	1961
7:12 **c** a great wrath from the LORD of hosts.	1961
8: 1 Again the word of the LORD of hosts **c** *to*	1961
8:10 went out or **c in** because of the affliction:	935
8:18 the word of the LORD of hosts **c** unto me,	1961
10: 4 Out of him **c forth** the corner, out of him	3318
14:16 **c** against Jerusalem shall even go up from	935
Mt 1:18 before they **c together**, she was found	4905
2: 1 there **c** wise men from the east to	3854
2: 9 till it **c** and stood over where the young	2064
2:21 his mother, and **c** into the land of Israel.	2064
2:23 And he **c** and dwelt in a city called	2064
3: 1 In those days **c** John the Baptist,	3854
4: 3 And when the tempter **c** to him, he said,	4334
4:11 behold, angels **c** and ministered unto him.	4334
4:13 he **c** and dwelt in Capernaum,	2064
5: 1 he was set, his disciples **c** unto him:	4334
7:25 and the floods **c**, and the winds blew,	2064
7:27 and the floods **c**, and the winds blew,	2064
7:28 it **c to pass**, when Jesus had ended	1096
8: 2 there **c** a leper and worshipped him,	2064
8: 5 there **c** unto him a centurion,	4334
8:19 And a certain scribe **c**, and said unto him,	4334
8:25 his disciples **c to** *him*, and awoke him,	4334
8:34 the whole city **c out** to meet Jesus:	1831
9: 1 and passed over, and **c** into his own city.	2064
9:10 And it **c to pass**, as Jesus sat at meat in	1096
9:10 many publicans and sinners **c** and sat	2064
9:14 Then **c** to him the disciples of John,	4334
9:18 there **c** a *certain* ruler, and worshipped	2064
9:20 **c** behind *him*, and touched the hem of his	4334

C

Mt
9:23 And when Jesus c into the ruler's house, 2064
9:28 into the house, the blind men c to him: 4334
10:34 I c not to send peace, but a sword. 2064
11: 1 And it c to pass, when Jesus had made an 1096
11:18 For John c neither eating nor drinking, 2064
11:19 The Son of man c eating and drinking, 2064
12:42 for she c from the uttermost parts of the 2064
12:44 into my house from whence I c out; 1831
13: 4 and the fowls c and devoured them up: 2064
13:10 And the disciples c, and said unto him, 4334
13:25 his enemy c and sowed tares among 2064
13:27 So the servants of the householder c and 4334
13:36 and his disciples c unto him, saying, 4334
13:53 And it c to pass, that when Jesus had 1096
14:12 And his disciples c, and took up the body, 4334
14:15 his disciples c to him, saying, This is a 4334
14:33 Then they that were in the ship c and 2064
14:34 they c into the land of Gennesaret. 2064
15: 1 Then c to Jesus scribes and Pharisees, 4334
15:12 Then c his disciples, and said unto him, 4334
15:22 a woman of Canaan c out of the same 1831
15:23 And his disciples c and besought him, 4334
15:25 Then c she and worshipped him, saying, 2064
15:29 and c nigh unto the sea of Galilee; 2064
15:30 And great multitudes c unto him, 4334
15:39 ship, and c into the coasts of Magdala. 2064
16: 1 The Pharisees also with the Sadducees c, 4334
16:13 When Jesus c into the coasts of Cesarea 2064
17: 7 And Jesus c and touched them, and said, 4334
17: 9 And as they c down from the mountain, 2597
17:14 there c to him a certain man, kneeling 4334
17:19 Then c the disciples to Jesus apart, 4334
17:24 that received tribute money c to Peter, 4334
18: 1 the same time the disciples unto Jesus, 4334
18:21 Then c Peter to him, and said, Lord, 4334
18:31 and c and told unto their lord all that 2064
19: 1 And it c to pass, that when Jesus had 1096
19: 1 c into the coasts of Judea beyond Jordan; 2064
19: 3 The Pharisees also c unto him, 4334
19:16 And behold, one c and said unto him, 4334
20: 9 And when they c that were hired about 2064
20:10 But when the first c, they supposed that 2064
20:20 Then c to him the mother of Zebedee's 4334
20:28 Even as the Son of man c not to be 2064
21:14 And the lame c to him in the temple; 4334
21:19 he c to it, and found nothing thereon, 2064
21:23 the elders of the people c unto him as he 4334
21:28 he c to the first, and said, Son, go work 4334
21:30 And he c to the second, 4334
21:32 For John c unto you in the way of 2064
22:11 And when the king c in to see the guests, 1525
22:23 The same day c to him the Sadducees, 4334
24: 1 his disciples c to him for to shew him 4334
24: 3 the disciples c unto him privately, saying, 4334
24:39 And knew not until the flood c, 2064
25:10 they went to buy, the bridegroom c; 2064
25:11 Afterward c also the other virgins, saying, 2064
25:20 so he that had received five talents c and 4334
25:22 also that had received two talents c and 4334
25:24 he which had received the one talent c 4334
25:36 I was in prison, and ye c unto me. 2064
25:39 sick, or in prison, and c unto thee? 2064
26: 1 And it c to pass, when Jesus had finished 1096
26: 7 There c unto him a woman having an 4334
26:17 unleavened bread the disciples c to Jesus, 4334
26:43 And he c and found them asleep again: 2064
26:47 c, and with him a great multitude with 2064
26:49 forthwith he c to Jesus, and said, Hail, 4334
26:50 Then c they, and laid hands on Jesus, 4334
26:60 yea, though many false witnesses c, 4334
26:60 At the last c two false witnesses, 4334
26:69 a damsel c unto him, saying, Thou also 4334
26:73 And after a while c unto him they that 4334
27:32 And as they c out, they found a man of 1831
27:53 And c out of the graves after his 1831
27:57 there c a rich man of Arimathea, 2064
27:62 and Pharisees c together unto Pilate, 4863
28: 1 c Mary Magdalene and the other Mary to 2064
28: 2 and c and rolled back the stone from 4334
28: 9 And they c and held him by the feet, 4334
28:11 some of the watch c into the city, 2064
28:13 His disciples c by night, and stole him 2064
28:18 And Jesus c and spake unto them, saying, 4334

Mk
1: 9 And it c to pass in those days, that Jesus 1096
1: 9 that Jesus c from Nazareth of Galilee, 2064
1:11 And there c a voice from heaven, 1096
1:14 John was put in prison, Jesus c into 2064
1:26 cried with a loud voice, he c out of him. 1831
1:31 And he c and took her by the hand, 4334
1:38 preach there also: for therefore I c forth. 1831
1:40 there c a leper to him, beseeching him, 2064
1:45 and they c to him from every quarter. 2064
2:15 it c to pass, that as Jesus sat at meat in 1096
2:17 I c not to call the righteous, but sinners to 2064
2:23 And it c to pass, that he went through 1096
3: 8 what great things he did, c unto him. 2064
3:13 whom he would: and they c unto him. 565
3:22 And the scribes which c down 2597
3:31 There c then his brethren and his mother, 2064
4: 4 it c to pass, as he sowed, some fell by 1096
4: 4 and the fowls of the air c and devoured it 2064
5: 1 And they c over unto the other side of 2064
5:27 c in the press behind, and touched his 2064
5:33 c and fell down before him, and told him 2064
5:35 there c from the ruler of the synagogue's 2064

Mk
6: 1 from thence, and c into his own country; 2064
6:22 the daughter of the said Herodias c in, 1525
6:25 And she c in straightway with haste unto 1525
6:29 And when his disciples heard of it, they c 2064
6:33 outwent them, and c together unto him. 4905
6:34 And Jesus, when he c out, saw much 1831
6:35 his disciples c unto him, and said, This is 4334
6:53 they c into the land of Genesaret, 2064
7: 1 Then c together unto him the Pharisees, 4863
7: 1 of the scribes, which c from Jerusalem. 2064
7:25 heard of him, and c and fell at his feet: 2064
7:31 and Sidon, he c unto the sea of Galilee, 2064
8: 3 by the way: for divers of them c from far. 2240
8:10 and c into the parts of Dalmanutha. 2064
8:11 And the Pharisees c forth, and began to 1831
9: 7 and a voice c out of the cloud, saying, 2064
9: 9 And as they c down from the mountain, 2597
9:14 And when he c to his disciples, he saw a 2064
9:21 How long is it ago since this c unto him? 1096
9:25 saw that the people c running together, 1998
9:26 c out of him: and he was as one dead; 1831
9:33 And he c to Capernaum: and being in 2064
10: 2 The Pharisees c to him, and asked him, 4334
10:17 there c one running, and kneeled to him, 4370
10:45 For even the Son of man c not to be 2064
10:46 And they c to Jericho: and as he went out 2064
10:50 away his garment, rose, and c to Jesus. 2064
11: 1 And when they c nigh to Jerusalem, 1448
11:13 he c, if haply he might find any thing 2064
11:13 when he c to it, he found nothing but 2064
12:28 one of the scribes c, and having heard 4334
12:42 And there c a certain poor widow, 2064
14: 3 there c a woman having an alabaster box 2064
14:16 c into the city, and found as he had said 2064
14:32 And they c to a place which was named 2064
15:41 many other women which c up with him 4872
15:43 c, and went in boldly unto Pilate, 2064
16: 2 they c unto the sepulchre at the rising of 2064

Lk
1: 8 And it c to pass, that while he executed 1096
1:22 And when he c out, he could not speak 1831
1:23 And it c to pass that, as soon as the days 1096
1:28 the angel c in unto her, and said, Hail, 1525
1:41 it c to pass that, when Elisabeth heard 1096
1:57 Elisabeth's full time c that she should 4130
1:59 it c to pass, that on the eighth day they 1096
1:59 on the eighth day they c to circumcise 2064
1:65 And fear c on all that dwelt round about 1096
2: 1 And it c to pass in those days, that there 1096
2: 9 the angel of the Lord c upon them, 2186
2:15 And it c to pass, as the angels were gone 1096
2:16 And they c with haste, and found Mary, 2064
2:27 And he c by the Spirit into the temple: 2064
2:46 And it c to pass, that after three days they 1096
2:51 and c to Nazareth, and was subject unto 2064
3: 2 the word of God c unto John the son of 1096
3: 3 he c into all the country about Jordan, 2064
3: 7 said he to the multitude that c forth 1607
3:12 Then c also publicans to be baptized, 2064
3:21 it c to pass, that Jesus also being baptized, 1096
3:22 and a voice c from heaven, which said, 1096
4:16 And he c to Nazareth, where he had been 2064
4:31 And c down to Capernaum, a city of 2718
4:35 he c out of him, and hurt him not. 1831
4:41 And devils also c out of many, crying out, 1831
4:42 and c unto him, and stayed him, 2064
5: 1 it c to pass that, as the people pressed 1096
5: 7 And they c, and filled both the ships, 2064
5:12 it c to pass, when he was in a certain 1096
5:15 and great multitudes c together to hear, 4905
5:17 it c to pass on a certain day, as he was 1096
5:32 I c not to call the righteous, but sinners to 2064
6: 1 it c to pass on the second sabbath after 1096
6: 6 And it c to pass also on another sabbath, 1096
6:12 it c to pass in those days, that he went 1096
6:17 And he c down with them, and stood in 2597
6:17 which c to hear him, and to be healed of 2064
7: 4 And when they c to Jesus, they besought 3854
7:11 it c to pass the day after, that he went 1096
7:12 when he c nigh to the gate of the city, 1448
7:14 And he c and touched the bier: and 4334
7:16 And there c a fear on all: 2983
7:33 John the Baptist c neither eating bread 2064
7:45 this woman since the time I c in hath not 1525
8: 1 it c to pass afterward, that he went 1096
8:19 c to him his mother and his brethren, 3854
8:22 Now it c to pass on a certain day, that he 1096
8:23 c down a storm of wind on the lake; 2597
8:24 And they c to him, and awoke him, 4334
8:35 and c to Jesus, and found the man, out of 2064
8:40 And it c to pass that, when Jesus was 1096
8:41 there c a man named Jairus, and he was a 2064
8:44 C behind him, and touched the border of 4334
8:47 she c trembling, and falling down before 2064
8:51 And when he c into the house, 1525
8:55 And her spirit c again, and she arose 1994
9:12 then c the twelve, and said unto him, 4334
9:18 And it c to pass, as he was alone praying, 1096
9:28 And it c to pass about an eight days after 1096
9:33 And it c to pass, as they departed from 1096
9:34 there c a cloud, and overshadowed them: 1096
9:35 And there c a voice out of the cloud, 1096
9:37 And it c to pass, that on the next day, 1096
9:51 it c to pass, when the time was come 1096
9:57 it c to pass, that, as they went in 1096
10:31 And by chance there c down a certain 2597

Lk
10:32 c and looked on him, and passed by on 2064
10:33 as he journeyed, c where he was: 2064
10:38 Now it c to pass, as they went, that he 1096
10:40 serving, and c to him, and said, Lord, 2186
11: 1 it c to pass that, as he was praying in a 1096
11:14 it c to pass, when the devil was gone 1096
11:24 return unto my house whence I c out. 1831
11:27 it c to pass, as he spake these things, a 1096
11:31 she c from the utmost parts of the earth 2064
13: 6 and he c and sought fruit thereon, 2064
13:31 The same day there c certain of 4334
14: 1 it c to pass, as he went into the house 1096
14:21 that servant c, and shewed his lord these 3854
15:17 And when he c to himself, he said, 2064
15:20 And he arose, and c to his father. 2064
15:25 and as he c and drew nigh to the house, 2064
15:28 therefore c his father out and intreated 1831
16:21 moreover the dogs c and licked his sores. 2064
16:22 And it c to pass that the beggar died, 1096
17:11 And it c to pass, as he went to Jerusalem, 1096
17:14 And it c to pass that, as they went, 1096
17:27 and the flood c, and destroyed them all. 2064
18: 3 she c unto him, saying, Avenge me of 2064
18:35 it c to pass, that as he was come nigh 1096
19: 5 And when Jesus c to the place, he looked 2064
19: 6 and c down, and received him joyfully. 2597
19:15 And it c to pass, that when he was 1096
19:16 Then c the first, saying, Lord, thy pound 3854
19:18 And the second c, saying, Lord, thy pound 2064
19:20 another c, saying, Lord, behold, here is 2064
19:29 it c to pass, when he was come nigh to 1096
20: 1 it c to pass, that on one of those days, 1096
20: 1 the scribes c upon him with the elders, 2186
20:27 Then c to him certain of the Sadducees, 4334
21:38 all the people c early in the morning 3719
22: 7 Then c the day of unleavened bread, 2064
22:39 And he c out, and went, as he was wont, 1831
22:66 chief priests and the scribes c together, 4863
23:48 And all the people that c together to that 4836
23:55 which c with him from Galilee, 4905
24: 1 in the morning, they c unto the sepulchre, 2064
24: 4 And it c to pass, as they were much 1096
24:15 it c to pass, that while they communed 1096
24:23 they found not his body, they c, saying, 2064
24:30 And it c to pass, as he sat at meat with 1096
24:51 And it c to pass, while he blessed them, 1096

Jn
1: 7 The same c for a witness, to bear witness 2064
1:11 He c unto his own, and his own received 2064
1:17 but grace and truth c by Jesus Christ. 1096
1:39 They c and saw where he dwelt, 2064
3: 2 The same c to Jesus by night, and said 2064
3:13 but he that c down from heaven, even 2597
3:22 After these things c Jesus and his disciples 2064
3:23 and they c, and were baptized. 3854
3:26 And they c unto John, and said unto him, 2064
4:27 And upon this c his disciples, 2064
4:30 they went out of the city, and c unto him. 2064
4:46 So Jesus c again into Cana of Galilee, 2064
6:23 (Howbeit there c other boats from Tiberias 2064
6:24 and c to Capernaum, seeking for Jesus. 2064
6:38 For I c down from heaven, not to do 2597
6:41 the bread which c down from heaven. 2597
6:42 that he saith, I c down from heaven? 2597
6:51 I am the living bread which c down from 2597
6:58 This is that bread which c down from 2597
7:45 Then c the officers to the chief priests and 2064
7:50 (he that c to Jesus by night, being one of 2064
8: 2 And early in the morning he c again into 3854
8: 2 temple, and all the people c unto him; 2064
8:14 for I know whence I c, and whither I go; 2064
8:42 for I proceeded forth and c from God; 2240
8:42 and came from God; neither c I of myself, 2064
9: 7 way therefore, and washed, and c seeing. 2064
10: 8 All that ever c before me are thieves and 2064
10:24 Then c the Jews round about him, 2944
10:35 unto whom the word of God c, 1096
11:17 Then when Jesus c, he found that he had 2064
11:19 And many of the Jews c to Martha and 2064
11:29 that, she arose quickly, and c unto him. 2064
11:33 the Jews also weeping which c with her, 4905
11:44 he that was dead c forth, bound hand 1831
11:45 Then many of the Jews which c to Mary, 2064
12: 1 Then Jesus six days before the passover c 2064
12: 9 and they c not for Jesus' sake only, 2064
12:20 them that c up to worship at the feast: 305
12:21 The same c therefore to Philip, which was 4334
12:27 but for this cause c I unto this hour. 2064
12:28 Then c there a voice from heaven, 2064
12:30 This voice c not because of me, 1096
12:47 for I c not to judge the world, but to save 2064
16:27 and have believed that I c out from God. 1831
16:28 I c forth from the Father, and am come 1831
17: 8 have known surely that I c out from thee, 1831
18:37 and for this cause c I into the world, 2064
19: 5 Then c Jesus forth, wearing the crown of 1831
19:32 the soldiers, and brake the legs of 2064
19:33 But when they c to Jesus, and saw that he 2064
19:34 forthwith c there out blood and water. 1831
19:38 He c therefore, and took the body of Jesus. 2064
19:39 And there c also Nicodemus, which at 2064
19:39 which at the first c to Jesus by night, 2064
20: 3 that other disciple, and c to the sepulchre. 2064
20: 4 outrun Peter, and c first to the sepulchre. 2064
20: 6 which c first to the sepulchre, and he saw, 2064
20:18 Mary Magdalene c and told the disciples 2064

C

Jn	20:19 c Jesus and stood in the midst, 2064
20:24 was not with them when Jesus c. 2064	
20:26 then c Jesus, the doors being shut, 2064	
21: 8 And the other disciples c in a little ship; 2064	
Ac	2: 2 suddenly there c a sound from heaven 1096
2: 6 the multitude c together, 4905	
2:43 And fear c upon every soul: and 1096	
4: 1 and the Sadducees, c upon them, 2186	
4: 5 And it c to pass on the morrow, that their 1096	
5: 5 great fear c on all them that heard these 1096	
5: 7 wife, not knowing what was done, c in. 1525	
5:10 and the young men c in, and found her 1525	
5:11 And great fear c upon all the church, 1096	
5:16 There c also a multitude out of the cities 4905	
5:21 But the high priest c, and they that were 3854	
5:22 But when the officers c, and found them 3854	
5:25 Then c one and told them, saying, 3854	
6:12 and c upon him, and caught him, 2186	
7: 4 c he out of the land of the Chaldeans, 1831	
7:11 Now there c a dearth over all the land of 2064	
7:23 c into his heart to visit his brethren 305	
7:31 the voice of the Lord c unto him, 1096	
7:45 also our fathers that c after brought 1237	
8: 7 c out of many that were possessed with 1831	
8:36 on their way, they c unto a certain water: 2064	
8:40 in all the cities, till he c to Cesarea. 2064	
9: 3 as he journeyed, he c near Damascus: 1448	
9:21 c hither for that intent, that he might 2064	
9:32 it c to pass, as Peter passed throughout 1096	
9:32 c down also to the saints which dwelt at 2718	
9:37 it c to pass in those days, that she was 1096	
9:43 it c to pass, that he tarried many days 1096	
10:13 there c a voice to him, Rise, Peter; kill, 1096	
10:29 c I unto you without gainsaying, 2064	
10:45 as many as c with Peter, because that on 4905	
11: 5 by four corners; and it c even to me: 2064	
11:22 tidings of these things c unto the ears 191	
11:23 he c, and had seen the grace of God, 3854	
11:26 And it c to pass, that a whole year they 1096	
11:27 And in these days c prophets from 2718	
11:28 which c to pass in the days of Claudius 1096	
12: 7 the angel of the Lord c upon him, and 2186	
12:10 they c unto the iron gate that leadeth unto 2064	
12:12 when he had considered the thing, he c 2064	
12:13 a damsel c to hearken, named Rhoda. 4334	
12:20 but they c with one accord to him, and, 3918	
13:13 Paphos, they c to Perga in Pamphylia: 2064	
13:14 they c to Antioch in Pisidia, and went into 3854	
13:31 c up with him from Galilee to Jerusalem, 4872	
13:44 c almost the whole city together to hear 4863	
13:51 feet against them, and c unto Iconium. 2064	
14: 1 it c to pass in Iconium, that they went 1096	
14:19 And there c thither certain Jews from 1904	
14:20 he rose up, and c into the city: 1525	
14:24 throughout Pisidia, they c to Pamphylia. 2064	
15: 1 certain men which c down from Judea 2718	
15: 6 elders c together for to consider of this 4863	
15:30 they were dismissed, they c to Antioch: 2064	
16: 1 Then c he to Derbe and Lystra: 2658	
16: 8 And they passing by Mysia c down to 2597	
16:11 we c with a straight course to 2113	
16:16 And it c to pass, as we went to prayer, 1096	
16:18 out of her. And he c out the same hour. 1831	
16:29 c trembling, and fell down before Paul 1096	
16:39 And they c and besought them, 2064	
17: 1 and Apollonia, they c to Thessalonica, 2064	
17:13 they c thither also, and stirred up 2064	
18: 1 departed from Athens, and c to Corinth; 2064	
18: 2 to depart from Rome:) and c unto them. 4334	
18:19 And he c to Ephesus, and left them there: 2658	
18:24 mighty in the scriptures, c to Ephesus. 2658	
19: 1 it c to pass that, while Apollos was at 1096	
19: 1 through the upper coasts c to Ephesus: 2064	
19: 6 upon them, the Holy Ghost c on them; 2064	
19:18 And many that believed c, and confessed, 2064	
20: 2 much exhortation, he c into Greece, 2064	
20: 6 and c unto them to Troas in five days; 2064	
20: 7 when the disciples c together to break 4863	
20:14 we took him in, and c to Mitylene. 2064	
20:15 and the next day over against Chios; 2658	
20:15 and the next day we c to Miletus. 2064	
20:18 from the first day that I c into Asia, 1910	
21: 1 it c to pass, that after we were gotten 1096	
21: 1 we c with a straight course unto Cos, 2064	
21: 7 c to Ptolemais, and saluted the brethren, 2658	
21: 8 company departed, and c unto Cesarea: 2064	
21:10 c down from Judea a certain prophet, 2718	
21:31 c unto the chief captain of the band, 305	
21:33 Then the chief captain c near, 1448	
21:35 And when he c upon the stairs, so it was, 1096	
22: 6 it c to pass that, as I made my journey, 1096	
22:11 that were with me, I c into Damascus. 2064	
22:13 C unto me, and stood, and said unto me, 2064	
22:17 And it c to pass that, when I was come 1096	
22:27 the chief captain c, and said unto him, 4334	
23:14 And they c to the chief priests and elders, 4334	
23:27 then c I with an army, and rescued him, 2186	
23:33 when they c to Cesarea, 1525	
24: 7 But the chief captain Lysias c upon us, 3928	
24:17 Now after many years I c to bring alms to 3854	
24:24 when Felix c with his wife Drusilla, 3854	
24:27 Porcius Festus came into Felix' room: 1240+2983	
25: 7 the Jews which c down from Jerusalem 2597	
25:13 Bernice c unto Cesarea to salute Festus. 2658	
27: 5 of Cilicia and Pamphylia, we c to Myra, 2718	

Ac	27: 8 c unto a place which is called The fair 2064
27:44 And so it c to pass, that they escaped all 1096	
28: 3 there c a viper out of the heat, 1831	
28: 8 it c to pass, that the father of Publius 1096	
28: 9 diseases in the island, c, and were healed: 4334	
28:13 we fet a compass, and c to Rhegium: 2658	
28:13 and we the next day to Puteoli: 2064	
28:15 they c to meet us as far as Appii forum, 1831	
28:16 And when we c to Rome, the centurion 2064	
28:17 it c to pass, that after three days Paul 1096	
28:21 neither any of the brethren that c shewed 3854	
28:23 there c many to him into his lodging; 2240	
28:30 and received all that c in unto him, 1531	
Ro	5:18 judgment c upon all men to condemnation NIG
5:18 by the righteousness of one the free gift c NIG	
7: 9 when the commandment c, sin revived, 2064	
9: 5 of whom as concerning the flesh Christ c, NIG	
1Co	2: 1 I, brethren, when I c to you, came not 2064
2: 1 c not with excellency of speech or 2064	
14:36 c the word of God out from you? 1831	
14:36 out from you? or c it unto you only? 2658	
15:21 For since by man c death, by man came NIG	
15:21 by man c also the resurrection of the dead. NIG	
2Co	1: 8 you ignorant of our trouble which c to 1096
1:23 to spare you I c not as yet unto Corinth. 2064	
2: 3 wrote this same unto you, lest, when I c, 2064	
2:12 to Troas to preach Christ's gospel, 2064	
11: 9 which c from Macedonia supplied: 2064	
Gal	1:21 Afterwards I c into the regions of Syria 2064
2: 4 who c in privily to spy out our liberty 3922	
2:12 before that certain c from James, he did 2064	
3:23 But before faith c, we were kept under 2064	
Eph	2:17 And c and preached peace to you which 2064
1Th	1: 5 our gospel c not unto you in word only, 1096
3: 4 even as it c to pass, and ye know. 1096	
3: 6 now when Timotheus c from you unto 2064	
1Ti	1:15 that Christ Jesus c into the world to save 2064
2Ti	3:11 afflictions, which c unto me at Antioch, 1096
Heb	3:16 howbeit not all that c out of Egypt by 1831
11:15 of that country from whence they c out, 1831	
2Pe	1:17 when there c such a voice to him from 5342
1:18 And this voice which c from heaven we 5342	
1:21 For the prophecy c not in old time by 5342	
1Jn	5: 6 This is he that c by water and blood, 2064
3Jn	1: 3 when the brethren c and testified of 2064
Rev	5: 7 he c and took the book out of the right 2064
7:13 in white robes? and whence c they? 2064	
14: 3 These are they which c out of great 2064	
8: 3 another angel c and stood at the altar, 2064	
8: 4 which c with the prayers of the saints, NIG	
9: 3 there c out of the smoke locusts upon 1831	
14:15 And another angel c out of the temple, 1831	
14:17 And another angel c out of the temple 1831	
14:18 And another angel c out from the altar, 1831	
15: 6 And the seven angels c out of the temple, 1831	
16:17 there c a great voice out of the temple of 1831	
16:19 great Babylon c in remembrance 3415	
17: 1 there c one of the seven angels which 2064	
19: 5 And a voice c out of the throne, saying, 1831	
20: 9 And fire c down from God out of heaven, 2597	
21: 9 And there c unto me one of the seven 2064	

CAMEL (9) [CAMEL'S, CAMELS, CAMELS']

Ge	24:64 when she saw Isaac, she lighted off the c. 1581
Lev	11: 4 as the c, because he cheweth the cud, 1581
Dt	14: 7 as the c, and the hare, and the coney: 1581
1Sa	15: 3 and suckling, ox and sheep, c and ass. 1581
Zec	14:15 the c, and of the ass, and of all the beasts 1581
Mt	19:24 It is easier for a c to go through the eye of 2574
23:24 which strain out a gnat, and swallow a c. 2574	
Mk | 10:25 It is easier for a c to go through the eye of 2574
Lk | 18:25 For it is easier for a c to go through a 2574

CAMEL'S (3) [CAMEL]

Ge | 31:34 put them in the c furniture, and sat upon 1581
Mt | 3: 4 And the same John had his raiment of c 2574
Mk | 1: 6 And John was clothed with c hair, 2574

CAMELS (47) [CAMEL]

Ge	12:16 and maidservants, and she asses, and c. 1581
24:10 the servant took ten c of the camels of his 1581	
24:10 the servant took ten camels of the c of his 1581	
24:11 he made his c to kneel down without 1581	
24:14 Drink, and I will give thy c drink also: 1581	
24:19 she said, I will draw water for thy c also, 1581	
24:20 well to draw water, and drew for all his c. 1581	
24:22 came to pass, as the c had done drinking, 1581	
24:30 and behold, he stood by the c at the well. 1581	
24:31 prepared the house, and room for the c. 1581	
24:32 he ungirded his c, and gave straw and 1581	
24:32 and gave straw and provender for the c, 1581	
24:35 and maidservants, and c, and asses. 1581	
24:44 drink thou, and I will also draw for thy c: 1581	
24:46 Drink, and I will give thy c drink also: 1581	
24:46 I drank, and she made the c drink also. 1581	
24:61 they rode upon the c, and followed 1581	
24:63 and saw, and behold, the c were coming. 1581	
30:43 and menservants, and c, and asses. 1581	
31:17 and set his sons and his wives upon c; 1581	
32: 7 the flocks, and herds, and the c, into two 1581	
32:15 Thirty milch c with their colts, forty kine, 1581	
37:25 from Gilead with their c bearing spicery 1581	
Ex | 9: 3 upon the c, upon the oxen, and upon 1581
Jdg | 6: 5 they and their c were without number: 1581

Jdg	7:12 their c were without number, as the sand 1581
1Sa	27: 9 the c, and the apparel, and returned, 1581
30:17 young men, which rode upon c, and fled. 1581	
1Ki	10: 2 with c that bare spices, and very much 1581
1Ch	5:21 of their c fifty thousand, and of sheep two 1581
12:40 on c, and on mules, and on oxen, 1581	
27:30 Over the c also was Obil the Ishmaelite: 1581	
2Ch	9: 1 c that bare spices, and gold in abundance, 1581
14:15 carried away sheep and c in abundance, 1581	
Ezr	2:67 Their c, four hundred thirty and five; 1581
Ne	7:69 Their c, four hundred thirty and five: 1581
Est	8:10 on mules, c, and young dromedaries: 327
8:14 that rode upon mules and c went out, 327	
Job	1: 3 three thousand c, and five hundred yoke 1581
1:17 fell upon the c, and have carried them 1581	
42:12 six thousand c, and a thousand yoke of 1581	
Isa	21: 7 a chariot of asses, and a chariot of c; 1581
30: 6 their treasures upon the bunches of c, to 1581	
60: 6 The multitude of c shall cover thee, 1581	
Jer	49:29 and all their vessels, and their c; 1581
49:32 their c shall be a booty, and the multitude 1581	
Eze | 25: 5 I will make Rabbah a stable for c, 1581

CAMELS' (3) [CAMEL]

Jdg	8:21 the ornaments that were on their c necks. 1581
8:26 beside the chains that were about their c 1581	
2Ki | 8: 9 forty c burden, and came and stood 1581

CAMEST (28) [COME]

Ge	16: 8 said, Hagar, Sarai's maid, whence c thou? 935
24: 5 again unto the land from whence thou c? 3318	
27:33 I have eaten of all before thou c, 935	
Ex	23:15 for in it thou c out from Egypt: 3318
34:18 for in the month Abib thou c out from 3318	
Nu	22:37 wherefore c thou not unto me? am I not 1980
Dt	2:37 of the children of Ammon thou c not, 7126
16: 3 for thou c forth out of the land of Egypt 3318	
16: 3 c forth out of the land of Egypt all the 3318	
16: 6 the season that thou c forth out of Egypt. 3318	
1Sa	13:11 thou c not within the days appointed, 935
17:28 and he said, Why c thou down hither? 3381	
2Sa	11:10 unto Uriah, C thou not from thy journey? 935
15:20 Whereas thou c but yesterday, should 935	
1Ki	13: 9 turn again by the same way that thou c. 1980
13:14 thou the man of God that c from Judah? 935	
13:17 turn again to go by the way that thou c. 1980	
13:22 c back, and hast eaten bread and 7725	
2Ki	19:28 the back by the way by which thou c. 935
Ne	9:13 Thou c down also upon mount Sinai, 3381
Isa	37:29 the back by the way by which thou c. 935
64: 3 thou c down, the mountains flowed 3381	
Jer	1: 5 before thou c forth out of the womb I 3318
Eze	32: 2 thou c forth with thy rivers, 1518
Mt	22:12 how c thou in hither not having a 1525
Jn	6:25 unto him, Rabbi, when c thou hither? 1096
16:30 by this we believe that thou c forth from 1831	
Ac | 9:17 appeared unto thee in the way as thou c, 2064

CAMON (1)

Jdg | 10: 5 And Jair died, and was buried in C. 7056

CAMP (136) [CAMPED, CAMPS, ENCAMP, ENCAMPED, ENCAMPETH, ENCAMPING]

Ex	14:19 which went before the c of Israel, 4264
14:20 it came between the c of the Egyptians 4264	
14:20 camp of the Egyptians and the c of Israel; 4264	
16:13 the quails came up, and covered the c 4264	
19:16 that all the people that was in the c 4264	
19:17 brought forth the people out of the c 4264	
29:14 shalt thou burn with fire without the c: 4264	
32:17 There is a noise of war in the c. 4264	
32:19 soon as he came nigh unto the c, that he 4264	
32:26 Moses stood in the gate of the c, and said, 4264	
32:27 out from gate to gate throughout the c, 4264	
33: 7 pitched it without the c, afar off from 4264	
33: 7 afar off from the c, and called it 4264	
33: 7 Congregation, which was without the c. 4264	
33:11 he turned again into the c: but his servant 4264	
36: 6 it to be proclaimed throughout the c, 4264	
Lev	4:12 forth without the c unto a clean place, 4264
4:21 carry forth the bullock without the c, 4264	
6:11 carry forth the ashes without the c unto a 4264	
8:17 dung, he burnt with fire without the c; 4264	
9:11 the hide he burnt with fire without the c. 4264	
10: 4 from before the sanctuary out of the c. 4264	
10: 5 carried them in their coats out of the c; 4264	
13:46 without the c shall his habitation be. 4264	
14: 3 the priest shall go forth out of the c; 4264	
14: 8 after that he shall come into the c, 4264	
16:26 in water, and afterward come into the c. 4264	
16:27 place, shall one carry forth without the c; 4264	
16:28 and afterward he shall come into the c. 4264	
17: 3 in the c, or that killeth it out of the camp, 4264	
17: 3 in the camp, or that killeth it out of the c, 4264	
24:10 forth him that hath cursed without the c; 4264	
24:14 forth him that hath cursed without the c, 4264	
24:23 forth him that had cursed out of the c, 4264	
Nu	1:52 every man by his own c, and every man 4264
2: 3 of Judah pitch throughout their armies: 4264	
2: 9 All that were numbered in the c of Judah 4264	
2:10 the c of Reuben according to their armies: 4264	
2:16 that were numbered in the c of Reuben 4264	
2:17 c of the Levites in the midst of the camp: 4264	
2:17 camp of the Levites in the midst of the c: 4264	
2:18 c of Ephraim according to their armies: 4264	

C

Nu	2:24 that were numbered of the **c** of Ephraim	4264
	2:25 The standard of the **c** of Dan *shall be* on	4264
	2:31 All they that were numbered in the **c** of	4264
	4: 5 when the **c** setteth forward, Aaron shall	4264
	4:15 the sanctuary, as the **c** is to set forward;	4264
	5: 2 that they put out of the **c** every leper,	4264
	5: 3 put out, without the **c** shall ye put them;	4264
	5: 4 did so, and put them out without the **c:**	4264
	10:14 the first *place* went the standard of the **c**	4264
	10:18 standard of the **c** of Reuben set forward	4264
	10:22 the standard of the **c** of the children of	4264
	10:25 standard of the **c** of the children of Dan	4264
	10:34 by day, when they went out of the **c.**	4264
	11: 1 *that were* in the uttermost parts of the **c.**	4264
	11: 9 the dew fell upon the **c** in the night,	4264
	11:26 there remained two *of* the men in the **c,**	4264
	11:26 and they prophesied in the **c.**	4264
	11:27 Eldad and Medad do prophesy in the **c.**	4264
	11:30 Moses gat him into the **c,** he and the	4264
	11:31 from the sea, and let *them* fall by the **c,**	4264
	11:31 about the **c,** and as it were two cubits	4264
	11:32 abroad for themselves round about the **c.**	4264
	12:14 let her be shut out from the **c** seven days,	4264
	12:15 Miriam was shut out from the **c** seven	4264
	14:44 and Moses, departed not out of the **c.**	4264
	15:35 shall stone him with stones without the **c.**	4264
	15:36 congregation brought him without the **c,**	4264
	19: 3 that he may bring her forth without the **c,**	4264
	19: 7 afterward he shall come into the **c,**	4264
	19: 9 *them* up without the **c** in a clean place,	4264
	31:12 unto the **c** at the plains of Moab, which	4264
	31:13 went forth to meet them without the **c.**	4264
	31:19 do ye abide without the **c** seven days:	4264
	31:24 and afterward ye shall come into the **c.**	4264
Dt	23:10 he go abroad out of the **c,** he shall not	4264
	23:10 the camp, he shall not come within the **c:**	4264
	23:11 is down, he shall come into the **c** *again.*	4264
	23:12 shalt have a place also without the **c,**	4264
	23:14 thy God walketh in the midst of thy **c,**	4264
	23:14 before thee; therefore shall thy **c** be holy:	4264
	29:11 wives, and thy stranger that *is* in thy **c,**	4264
Jos	5: 8 that they abode in their places in the **c,**	4264
	6:11 they came *into* the **c,** and lodged in	4264
	6:11 came *into* the camp, and lodged in the **c.**	4264
	6:14 the city once, and returned *into* the **c:**	4264
	6:18 make the **c** of Israel a curse, and trouble	4264
	6:23 and left them without the **c** of Israel.	4264
	9: 6 they went to Joshua unto the **c** *at* Gilgal,	4264
	10: 6 men of Gibeon sent unto Joshua to the **c**	4264
	10:15 all Israel with him, unto the **c** to Gilgal.	4264
	10:21 all the people returned to the **c** to Joshua	4264
	10:43 all Israel with him, unto the **c** to Gilgal.	4264
Jdg	7:17 when I come to the outside of the **c,**	4264
	7:18 trumpets also on every side of all the **c,**	4264
	7:19 came unto the outside of the **c** *in*	4264
	7:21 every man in his place round about the **c:**	4264
	13:25 to move him at times in the **c** of Dan,	4264
	21: 8 there came none to the **c** from	4264
	21:12 they brought them unto the **c** *to* Shiloh,	4264
1Sa	4: 3 when the people were come into the **c,**	4264
	4: 5 covenant of the Lord came into the **c,**	4264
	4: 6 this great shout in the **c** of the Hebrews?	4264
	4: 6 the ark of the Lord was come into the **c.**	4264
	4: 7 for they said, God is come into the **c.**	4264
	13:17 the spoilers came out of the **c** of	4264
	14:21 which went up with them into the **c** *from*	4264
	17: 4 there went out a champion out of the **c** of	4264
	17:17 loaves, and run to the **c** to thy brethren;	4264
	26: 6 will go down with me to Saul to the **c?**	4264
2Sa	1: 2 a man came out of the **c** from Saul with	4264
	1: 3 Out of the **c** of Israel am I escaped.	4264
1Ki	16:16 the host, king over Israel that day in the **c.**	4264
2Ki	3:24 when they came to the **c** of Israel,	4264
	6: 8 In such and such a place *shall be* my **c.**	8466
	7: 5 twilight, to go unto the **c** of the Syrians:	4264
	7: 5 to the uttermost part of the **c** of Syria,	4264
	7: 7 *even* the **c** as it *was,* and fled for their life.	4264
	7: 8 lepers came to the uttermost part of the **c,**	4264
	7:10 We came to the **c** of the Syrians,	4264
	7:12 are they gone out of the **c** to hide	4264
	19:35 smote in the **c** of the Assyrians an hundred	4264
2Ch	22: 1 Arabians to the **c** had slain all the eldest.	4264
	32:21 captains in the **c** of the king of Assyria.	4264
Ps	78:28 he let *it* fall in the midst of their **c,**	4264
	106:16 They envied Moses also in the **c,**	4264
Isa	29: 3 I will **c** against thee round about,	2583
	37:36 smote in the **c** of the Assyrians an hundred	2583
Jer	50:29 bend the bow, **c** against it round about;	2583
Eze	4: 2 set the **c** also against it, and set *battering*	4264
Joel	2:11 for his **c** *is* very great: for *he* is strong that	2583
Na	3:17 which **c** in the hedges in the cold day,	2583
Heb	13:11 high priest for sin, are burnt without the **c.**	*3925*
	13:13 go forth therefore unto him without the **c,**	*3925*
Rev	20: 9 and compassed the **c** of the saints about,	*3925*

CAMPED (1) [CAMP]

Ex	19: 2 and there Israel **c** before the mount.	2583

CAMPFIRES See SHEEPFOLD

CAMPHIRE (2)

SS	1:14 My beloved *is* unto me *as* a cluster of **c** in	3724
	4:13 with pleasant fruits; **c,** with spikenard,	3724

CAMPS (7) [CAMP]

Nu	2:32 all those that were numbered of the **c**	4264
	5: 3 that they defile not their **c,** in the midst	4264
	10: 2 and for the journeying of the **c.**	4264
	10: 5 the **c** that lie on the east parts shall go	4264
	10: 6 the **c** that lie on the south side shall take	4264
	10:25 *which was* the rereward of all the **c**	4264
Am	4:10 have made the stink of your **c** to come up	4264

CAN (235) [CANNOT, CANST]

Ge	4:13 My punishment *is* greater than I **c** bear.	NIH
	13:16 if a man **c** number the dust of the earth,	3201
	31:43 what I **c** do *this* day unto these my	NIH
	39: 9 how then **c** I do this great wickedness,	NIH
	41:15 and *there is* none that **c** interpret it:	NIH
	41:38 **C** we find *such a one* as this *is,* a man in	NIH
	44: 1 as much as they **c** carry, and put every	3201
	44:15 wot ye not that such a man as I **c** certainly	NIH
Ex	4:14 I know that he **c** speak well. And also,	NIH
	5:11 get you straw where you **c** find *it:* yet not	NIH
Lev	14:30 young pigeons, such as he **c** get;	3027+5381
Nu	23:10 Who **c** count the dust of Jacob,	NIH
Dt	1:12 **c** I myself alone bear your cumbrance,	NIH
	3:24 that **c** do according to thy works,	NIH
	7:17 *are* moe than I, how **c** I dispossess them?	3201
	9: 2 *whom* thou hast heard *say,* Who **c** stand	NIH
	31: 2 *this* day; I **c** no more go out and come in:	3201
	32:39 neither *is there any* that **c** deliver out of	NIH
Jdg	14:12 if you **c** certainly declare it me *within*	NIH
1Sa	9: 6 peradventure he **c** shew us our way that	NIH
	16: 2 Samuel said, How **c** I go? if Saul hear *it,*	NIH
	16:17 Provide me now a man that **c** play well,	NIH
	18: 8 *what* **c** he have more but the kingdom?	NIH
	26: 9 for who **c** stretch forth his hand against	NIH
	28: 2 Surely thou shalt know what thy servant **c**	NIH
2Sa	7:20 what **c** David say more unto thee?	NIH
	12:22 Who **c** tell *whether* God will be gracious	NIH
	12:23 **c** I bring him back again? I shall go to him,	3201
	14:19 none **c** turn to the right hand or to the left	786
	15:36 send unto me every thing that ye **c** hear.	NIH
	19:35 *and* **c** I discern between good and evil?	NIH
	19:35 **c** thy servant taste what I eat or what I	NIH
	19:35 **c** I hear any more the voice of singing *men*	NIH
1Ki	5: 6 **c** skill to hew timber like unto	3045
1Ch	17:18 What **c** David *speak* **more** to thee	3254+5750
2Ch	1:10 for who **c** judge this thy people, *that is* so	NIH
	2: 7 that **c** skill to grave with the cunning *men*	NIH
	2: 8 for I know that thy servants **c** skill to cut	NIH
Est	8: 6 how **c** I endure to see the evil that shall	NIH
	8: 6 how **c** I endure to see the destruction of	NIH
Job	3:22 are glad, when they **c** find the grave?	NIH
	4: 2 who **c** withhold himself from speaking?	3201
	6: 6 **C** that which is unsavoury be eaten	NIH
	8:11 **C** the rush grow up without mire?	NIH
	8:11 **c** the flag grow without water?	NIH
	9:12 he taketh away, who **c** hinder him?	NIH
	10: 7 *there is* none that **c** deliver out of thine	NIH
	11:10 gather together, then who **c** hinder him?	NIH
	12:14 up a man, and there **c** be no opening.	NIH
	14: 4 Who **c** bring a clean *thing* out of an	NIH
	15: 3 speeches wherewith he **c** do no good?	NIH
	22: 2 **C** a man be profitable unto God, as he that	NIH
	22:13 **c** he judge through the dark *cloud?*	NIH
	22:17 and what **c** the Almighty do for them?	NIH
	23:13 he *is* in one *mind,* and who **c** turn him?	NIH
	25: 4 How then **c** man be justified with God?	NIH
	25: 4 **c** he be clean *that is* born of a woman?	NIH
	26:14 thunder of his power who **c** understand?	NIH
	34:29 quietness, who then **c** make trouble?	NIH
	34:29 hideth *his* face, who then **c** behold him?	NIH
	36:23 or who **c** say, Thou hast wrought iniquity?	NIH
	36:26 neither **c** the number of his years be	NIH
	36:29 Also **c** *any* understand the spreadings of	NIH
	38:37 Who **c** number the clouds in wisdom?	NIH
	38:37 or who **c** stay the bottles of heaven,	NIH
	40:14 that thine own right hand **c** save thee.	NIH
	40:19 he that made him **c** make his sword to	NIH
	40:23 he trusteth that he **c** draw up Jordan into	NIH
	41:13 Who **c** discover the face of his garment?	NIH
	41:13 who **c** come *to him* with his double bridle?	NIH
	41:14 Who **c** open the doors of his face?	NIH
	41:16 that no air **c** come between them.	NIH
	42: 2 no thought **c** be withholden from thee.	NIH
Ps	11: 3 be destroyed, what **c** the righteous do?	NIH
	19:12 Who **c** understand *his* errors? cleanse thou	NIH
	22:29 and none **c** keep alive his own soul.	NIH
	40: 5 speak *of them,* they are moe than **c** be	NIH
	49: 7 None *of them* **c** by any means redeem *his*	NIH
	56: 4 I will not fear what flesh **c** do unto me.	NIH
	56:11 will not be afraid what man **c** do unto me.	NIH
	58: 9 Before your pots **c** feel the thorns, he shall	NIH
	78:19 **C** God furnish a table in the wilderness?	3201
	78:20 streams overflowed; **c** he give bread also?	3201
	78:20 **c** he provide flesh for his people?	NIH
	89: 6 for in the heaven **c** he compared	NIH
	89: 6 *who* among the sons of the mighty **c** be	NIH
	106: 2 Who **c** utter the mighty acts of the Lord?	NIH
	106: 2 *who* **c** shew forth all his praise?	NIH
	118: 6 I will not fear: what **c** man do unto me?	NIH
	147:17 like morsels: who **c** stand before his cold?	NIH
Pr	6:27 **C** a man take fire in his bosom,	NIH
	6:28 **C** one go upon hot coals, and his feet not	NIH
	18:14 but a wounded spirit who **c** bear?	NIH
	20: 6 but a faithful man who **c** find?	NIH
	20: 9 Who **c** say, I have made my heart clean,	NIH

Pr	20:24 **c** a man then understand his own way?	NIH
	26:16 than seven *men* that **c** render a reason.	NIH
	31:10 Who **c** find a virtuous woman?	NIH
Ecc	2:12 for what **c** the man *do* that cometh after	NIH
	2:25 For who **c** eat, or who else can hasten	NIH
	2:25 who else **c** hasten *hereunto,* more than I?	NIH
	3:11 that no man **c** find out the work that God	NIH
	3:14 nothing **c** be put to it, nor any thing taken	NIH
	4:11 heat: but **how c** one be warm *alone?*	349
	6:12 who **c** tell a man what shall be after him	NIH
	7:13 who **c** make *that* straight, which he hath	3201
	7:24 and exceeding deep, who **c** find it out?	NIH
	8: 7 for who **c** tell him when it shall be?	NIH
	10:14 what shall be after him, who **c** tell him?	NIH
SS	8: 7 love, neither **c** the floods drown it:	NIH
Isa	28:20 For the bed is shorter than that *a man* **c**	NIH
	28:20 covering narrower than that *he* **c** wrap	NIH
	38:18 praise thee, death **c** not celebrate thee:	NIH
	43: 9 who among them **c** declare this,	NIH
	43:13 *is* none that **c** deliver out of my hand:	NIH
	46: 7 shall cry unto him, yet **c** he not answer,	NIH
	49:15 **C** a woman forget her sucking child,	NIH
	56:11 *they are* greedy dogs *which* **c** never have	NIH
Jer	2:13 broken cisterns, that **c** hold no water.	NIH
	2:24 *in* her occasion who **c** turn her away?	NIH
	2:28 they **c** save thee in the time of thy trouble:	NIH
	2:32 **C** a maid forget her ornaments, *or* a bride	NIH
	4: 4 burn that none **c** quench *it,* because of	NIH
	5: 1 broad places thereof, if ye **c** find a man,	NIH
	5:22 toss themselves, yet **c** they not prevail;	NIH
	5:22 they roar, yet **c** they not pass over it?	NIH
	9:10 none **c** pass through *them;* neither can	NIH
	9:10 none **c** pass through *them;* neither **c**	NIH
	13:23 **C** the Ethiopian change his skin,	NIH
	14:22 vanities of the Gentiles that **c** cause rain?	NIH
	14:22 or **c** the heavens give showers?	NIH
	17: 9 and desperately wicked: who **c** know it?	NIH
	21:12 burn that none **c** quench *it,* because of	NIH
	23:24 **C** any hide himself in secret places that I	NIH
	31:37 If heaven above **c** be measured,	NIH
	33:20 If you **c** break my covenant of the day,	NIH
	38: 5 for the king *is* not *he that* **c** do *any* thing	3201
	47: 7 How **c** it be quiet, seeing the Lord hath	NIH
La	2:13 *is* great like the sea: who **c** heal thee?	NIH
Eze	22:14 **C** thine heart endure, or can thine hands	NIH
	22:14 heart endure, or **c** thine hands be strong,	NIH
	28: 3 no secret *that* they **c** hide *from* thee:	NIH
	33:32 and **c** play well on an instrument:	NIH
	37: 3 unto me, Son of man, **c** these bones live?	NIH
Da	2: 9 I shall know that ye **c** shew me	NIH
	2:10 There is not a man upon the earth that **c**	3202
	2:11 there is none other that **c** shew it before	NIH
	3:29 there is no other God that **c** deliver after	3202
	4:35 none **c** stay his hand, or say unto him,	NIH
	10:17 For how **c** the servant of this my lord talk	3201
Joel	2:11 and very terrible; and who **c** abide it?	NIH
Am	3: 3 **C** two walk together, except they be	NIH
	3: 5 **C** a bird fall in a snare upon the earth,	NIH
	3: 8 God hath spoken, who **c** but prophesy?	NIH
Jnh	3: 9 Who **c** tell *if* God will turn and repent,	NIH
Mic	3:11 among us? none evil **c** come upon us.	NIH
	5: 8 and teareth in pieces, and none **c** deliver.	NIH
Na	1: 6 Who **c** stand before his indignation? and	NIH
	1: 6 who **c** abide in the fierceness of his anger?	NIH
Mt	6:24 No man **c** serve two masters: for either he	1410
	6:27 Which of you by taking thought **c** add one	1410
	7:18 neither **c** a corrupt tree bring forth good	NIG
	9:15 **C** the children of the bridechamber mourn	1410
	12:29 else how **c** one enter into a strong *man's*	1410
	12:34 generation of vipers, how **c** ye, being evil,	1410
	16: 3 ye **c** discern the face of the sky;	1097
	16: 3 **c** ye not *discern* the signs of the times?	1410
	19:25 saying, Who then **c** be saved?	1410
	23:33 **how c** ye escape the damnation of hell?	4459
	27:65 go your way, make *it* as sure as you **c.**	1492
Mk	2: 7 who **c** forgive sins but God only?	1410
	2:19 **C** the children of the bridechamber fast,	1410
	3:23 in parables, How **c** Satan cast out Satan?	1410
	3:27 No *man* **c** enter into a strong *man's* house	1410
	7:15 a man, that entering into him **c** defile him:	1410
	8: 4 From whence **c** a man satisfy these *men*	1410
	9: 3 so as no fuller on earth **c** white *them.*	1410
	9:29 This kind **c** come forth by nothing, but by	1410
	9:39 my name, that **c** lightly speak evil of me.	1410
	10:26 among themselves, Who then **c** be saved?	1410
	10:38 **c** ye drink of the cup that I drink of? and	1410
	10:39 And they said unto him, We **c.** And Jesus	1410
Lk	5:21 Who **c** forgive sins, but God alone?	1410
	5:34 **C** ye make the children of	1410
	6:39 unto them, **C** the blind lead the blind?	1410
	12: 4 after that have no more that *they* **c** do.	NIG
	12:25 And which of you with taking thought **c**	1410
	12:56 ye **c** discern the face of the sky and of	1492
	16:13 No servant **c** serve two masters: for either	1410
	16:26 neither **c** they pass to us, that	NIG
	18:26 that heard *it* said, Who then **c** be saved?	1410
	20:36 Neither **c** they die any more: for they are	1410
Jn	1:46 **C** there any good *thing* come out of	1410
	3: 2 for no *man* **c** do these miracles that thou	1410
	3: 4 How **c** a man be born when he is old?	1410
	3: 4 **c** he enter the second time into his	1410
	3: 9 said unto him, How **c** these *things* be?	1410
	3:27 and said, A man **c** receive nothing,	1410
	5:19 The Son **c** do nothing of himself,	1410
	5:30 I **c** of mine own self do nothing: as I hear,	1410

C

Jn	5:44 How **c** ye believe, which receive honour	1410
	6:44 No *man* **c** come to me, except the Father	1410
	6:52 How **c** this *man* give us *his* flesh to eat?	1410
	6:60 This is a hard saying; who **c** hear it?	1410
	6:65 I unto you, that no *man* **c** come unto me,	1410
	9: 4 the night cometh, when no *man* **c** work.	1410
	9:16 How **c** a man *that is* a sinner do such	1410
	10:21 **C** a devil open the eyes of the blind?	1410
	14: 5 thou goest; and how **c** we know the way?	1410
	15: 4 no more **c** ye, except ye abide in me.	3779
	15: 5 fruit: for without me ye **c** do nothing.	1410
Ac	8:31 And he said, How **c** I, except some *man*	1410
	10:47 **C** any *man* forbid water, that these should	1410
	24:13 Neither **c** they prove *the things* whereof	1410
Ro	8: 7 to the law of God, neither indeed **c** be.	1410
	8:31 If God *be* for us, who **c** *be* against us?	NIG
1Co	2:14 neither **c** he know *them*, because they are	1410
	3:11 other foundation **c** no *man* lay than that	1410
	12: 3 *that* no *man* **c** say that Jesus is the Lord,	1410
2Co	13: 8 For we **c** do nothing against the truth,	1410
Php	4:13 I **c** do all *things* through Christ which	2480
1Th	3: 9 what thanks **c** we render to God again	1410
1Ti	6: 7 *and it is* certain we **c** carry nothing out.	1410
	6:16 light **which no** *man* **c approach unto**;	676
	6:16 whom no man hath seen, nor **c** see:	1410
Heb	5: 2 Who **c** have compassion on the ignorant,	1410
	10: 1 **c** never with those sacrifices which they	1410
	10:11 which **c** never take away sins:	1410
Jas	2:14 and have not works? **c** faith save him?	1410
	3: 8 But the tongue **c** no man tame; *it is* an	1410
	3:12 **C** the fig tree, my brethren, bear olive	1410
	3:12 so **c** no fountain *both* yield salt water and	NIG
1Jn	4:20 **c** he love God whom he hath not seen?	1410
Rev	3: 8 thee an open door, and no *man* **c** shut it:	1410
	9:20 which neither **c** see, nor hear, nor walk:	1410

CANA (4)

Jn	2: 1 the third day there was a marriage in **C**	2580
	2:11 This beginning of miracles did Jesus in **C**	2580
	4:46 So Jesus came again into **C** of Galilee,	2580
	21: 2 Nathanael of **C** in Galilee, and the *sons*	2580

CANAAN (93) [CANAANITE, CANAANITES, CANAANITISH, CANAANITISH]

Ge	9:18 and Japheth: and Ham *is* the father of **C**.	3667
	9:22 Ham, the father of **C**, saw the nakedness	3667
	9:25 said, Cursed *be* **C**; a servant of servants	3667
	9:26 God of Shem; and **C** shall be his servant.	3667
	9:27 tents of Shem; and **C** shall be his servant.	3667
	10: 6 Cush, and Mizraim, and Phut, and **C**.	3667
	10:15 **C** begat Sidon his firstborn, and Heth,	3667
	11:31 of the Chaldees, to go into the land of **C**;	3667
	12: 5 they went forth to go into the land of **C**;	3667
	12: 5 and into the land of **C** they came.	3667
	13:12 Abram dwelled in the land of **C**,	3667
	16: 3 had dwelt ten years in the land of **C**,	3667
	17: 8 all the land of **C**, for an everlasting	3667
	23: 2 the same *is* Hebron in the land of **C**:	3667
	23:19 the same *is* Hebron in the land of **C**.	3667
	28: 1 not take a wife of the daughters of **C**.	3667
	28: 6 not take a wife of the daughters of **C**;	3667
	28: 8 seeing that the daughters of **C** pleased	3667
	31:18 to go to Isaac his father in the land of **C**.	3667
	33:18 of Shechem, which *is* in the land of **C**,	3667
	35: 6 which *is* in the land of **C**, that *is*, Beth-el,	3667
	36: 2 Esau took his wife of the daughters of **C**;	3667
	36: 5 were born unto him in the land of **C**.	3667
	36: 6 which he had got in the land of **C**;	3667
	37: 1 his father was a stranger, in the land of **C**.	3667
	42: 5 for the famine was in the land of **C**.	3667
	42: 7 they said, From the land of **C** to buy food.	3667
	42:13 the sons of one man in the land of **C**;	3667
	42:29 Jacob their father unto the land of **C**,	3667
	42:32 *this* day with our father in the land of **C**.	3667
	44: 8 again unto thee out of the land of **C**:	3667
	45:17 and go, get you unto the land of **C**;	3667
	45:25 came *into* the land of **C** unto Jacob their	3667
	46: 6 which they had gotten in the land of **C**,	3667
	46:12 Er and Onan died in the land of **C**.	3667
	46:31 *were* in the land of **C**, are come unto	3667
	47: 1 they have, are come out of the land of **C**;	3667
	47: 4 for the famine *is* sore in the land of **C**:	3667
	47:13 *all* the land of **C** fainted by reason of	3667
	47:14 in the land of **C**, for the corn which they	3667
	47:15 in the land of **C**, all the Egyptians came	3667
	48: 3 appeared unto me at Luz in the land of **C**,	3667
	48: 7 Rachel died by me in the land of **C** in	3667
	49:30 which *is* before Mamre, in the land of **C**,	3667
	50: 5 I have digged for me in the land of **C**,	3667
	50:13 his sons carried him into the land of **C**,	3667
Ex	6: 4 give them the land of **C**, the land of their	3667
	15:15 all the inhabitants of **C** shall melt away.	3667
	16:35 came unto the borders of the land of **C**.	3667
Lev	14:34 When ye be come into the land of **C**,	3667
	18: 3 after the doings of the land of **C**, whither	3667
	25:38 to give you the land of **C**, *and* to be your	3667
Nu	13: 2 that they may search the land of **C**,	3667
	13:17 Moses sent them to spy out the land of **C**,	3667
	26:19 and Er and Onan died in the land of **C**.	3667
	32:30 possessions among you in the land of **C**.	3667
	32:32 before the LORD *into* the land of **C**,	3667
	33:40 which dwelt in the south in the land of **C**,	3667
	33:51 are passed over Jordan into the land of **C**;	3667
	34: 2 When ye come into the land of **C**;	3667
	34: 2 the land of **C** with the coasts thereof:)	3667

Nu	34:29 the children of Israel in the land of **C**.	3667
	35:10 be come over Jordan into the land of **C**;	3667
	35:14 three cities shall ye give in the land of **C**,	3667
Dt	32:49 behold the land of **C**, which I give unto	3667
Jos	5:12 did eat of the fruit of the land of **C** that	3667
	14: 1 of Israel inherited in the land of **C**,	3667
	21: 2 unto them at Shiloh in the land of **C**,	3667
	22: 9 which *is* in the land of **C**, to go unto	3667
	22:10 that *are* in the land of **C**, the children of	3667
	22:11 built an altar over against the land of **C**,	3667
	22:32 the land of **C**, to the children of Israel,	3667
	24: 3 led him throughout all the land of **C**,	3667
Jdg	3: 1 *Israel* had not known all the wars of **C**;	3667
	4: 2 sold them into the hand of Jabin king of **C**,	3667
	4:23 the king of **C** before the children of Israel.	3667
	4:24 prevailed against Jabin the king of **C**,	3667
	4:24 until they had destroyed Jabin king of **C**.	3667
	5:19 fought the kings of **C** in Taanach by	3667
	21:12 camp *to* Shiloh, which *is* in the land of **C**.	3667
1Ch	1: 8 of Ham; Cush, and Mizraim, Put, and **C**.	3667
	1:13 begat Zidon his firstborn, and Heth,	3667
	16:18 Saying, Unto thee will I give the land of **C**,	3667
Ps	105:11 Saying, Unto thee will I give the land of **C**,	3667
	106:38 whom they sacrificed unto the idols of **C**:	3667
	135:11 king of Bashan, and all the kingdoms of **C**:	3667
Isa	19:18 the land of Egypt speak the language of **C**,	3667
Eze	16: 3 and thy nativity *is* of the land of **C**;	3669
	16:29 fornication in the land of **C** unto Chaldea;	3669
Zep	2: 5 **C**, the land of the Philistines, I will even	3667
Mt	15:22 a woman of **C** came out of the same	5478
Ac	7:11 a dearth over all the land of Egypt and **C**,	5477
	13:19 destroyed seven nations in the land of **C**,	5477

CANAANITE (14) [CANAAN]

Ge	12: 6 And the **C** *was* then in the land.	3669
	13: 7 the **C** and the Perizzite dwelled then in	3669
	38: 2 Judah saw there a daughter of a certain **C**,	3669
Ex	23:28 the **C**, the Hittite, from before thee.	3669
	33: 2 I will drive out the **C**, the Amorite,	3669
	34:11 the **C**, and the Hittite, and the Perizzite,	3669
Nu	21: 1 when king Arad the **C**, which dwelt *in*	3669
	33:40 Arad the **C**, which dwelt in the south	3669
Jos	9: 1 the Hittite, and the Amorite, the **C**,	3669
	11: 3 *And to* the **C** on the east and on the west,	3669
	13: 3 *which* is counted to the **C**:	3669
Zec	14:21 that day there shall be no more the **C** in	3669
Mt	10: 4 Simon the **C**, and Judas Iscariot, who also	2581
Mk	3:18 and Thaddeus, and Simon the **C**,	2581

CANAANITES (55) [CANAAN]

Ge	10:18 were the families of the **C** spread	3669
	10:19 the border of the **C** was from Sidon,	3669
	15:21 the **C**, and the Girgashites,	3669
	24: 3 unto my son of the daughters of the **C**,	3669
	24:37 wife to my son of the daughters of the **C**,	3669
	34:30 land, amongst the **C** and the Perizzites:	3669
	50:11 when the inhabitants of the land, the **C**,	3669
Ex	3: 8 unto the place of the **C**, and the Hittites,	3669
	3:17 affliction of Egypt unto the land of the **C**,	3669
	13: 5 shall bring thee into the land of the **C**,	3669
	13:11 shall bring thee into the land of the **C**,	3669
	23:23 and the **C**, the Hivites, and the Jebusites:	3669
Nu	13:29 the **C** dwell by the sea, and by the coast	3669
	14:25 and the **C** dwelt in the valley.)	3669
	14:43 and the **C** *are* there before you,	3669
	14:45 the **C** which dwelt in that hill,	3669
	21: 3 voice of Israel, and delivered up the **C**;	3669
Dt	1: 7 *to* the land of the **C**, and *unto* Lebanon,	3669
	7: 1 the **C**, and the Perizzites, and the Hivites,	3669
	11:30 the sun goeth down, in the land of the **C**,	3669
	20:17 the **C**, and the Perizzites, the Hivites,	3669
Jos	3:10 fail drive out from before you the **C**,	3669
	5: 1 all the kings of the **C**, which *were* by	3669
	7: 9 the **C** and all the inhabitants of the land	3669
	12: 8 the Amorites, and the **C**, the Perizzites,	3669
	13: 4 all the land of the **C**, and Mearah that *is*	3669
	16:10 they drave not out the **C** that dwelt in	3669
	16:10 the **C** dwell among the Ephraimites unto	3669
	17:12 but the **C** would dwell in that land:	3669
	17:13 strong, that they put the **C** to tribute;	3669
	17:16 the **C** that dwell in the land of the valley	3669
	17:18 for thou shalt drive out the **C**, though	3669
	24:11 **C**, and the Hittites, and the Girgashites,	3669
Jdg	1: 1 Who shall go up for us against the **C** first,	3669
	1: 3 my lot, that we may fight against the **C**;	3669
	1: 4 the LORD delivered the **C** and	3669
	1: 5 and they slew the **C** and the Perizzites.	3669
	1: 9 Judah went down to fight against the **C**,	3669
	1:10 Judah went against the **C** that dwelt in	3669
	1:17 they slew the **C** that inhabited Zephath,	3669
	1:27 but the **C** would dwell in that land.	3669
	1:28 that they put the **C** to tribute, and did not	3669
	1:29 Neither did Ephraim drive out the **C** that	3669
	1:29 but the **C** dwelt in Gezer among them.	3669
	1:30 the **C** dwelt among them,	3669
	1:32 the Asherites dwelt among the **C**,	3669
	1:33 he dwelt among the **C**, the inhabitants of	3669
	3: 3 all the **C**, and the Sidonians,	3669
	3: 5 the children of Israel dwelt among the **C**,	3669
2Sa	24: 7 all the cities of the Hivites, and of the **C**:	3669
1Ki	9:16 slain the **C** that dwelt in the city,	3669
Ezr	9: 1 *even* of the **C**, the Hittites, the Perizzites,	3669
Ne	9: 8 with him to give the land of the **C**,	3669
	9:24 the **C**, and gavest them into their hands,	3669
Ob	1:20 of Israel *shall* possess *that* of the **C**,	3669

CANAANITESS (1) [CANAAN]

1Ch	2: 3 unto him of the daughter of Shua the **C**.	3669

CANAANITISH (2) [CANAAN]

Ge	46:10 Zohar, and Shaul the son of a **C** woman.	3669
Ex	6:15 Zohar, and Shaul the son of a **C** woman:	3669

CANDACE (1)

Ac	8:27 eunuch of great authority under **C** queen	2582

CANDLE (16) [CANDLES, CANDLESTICK, CANDLESTICKS]

Job	18: 6 and his **c** shall be put out with him.	5216
	21:17 How oft is the **c** of the wicked put out!	5216
	29: 3 When his **c** shined upon my head,	5216
Ps	18:28 For thou wilt light my **c**: the LORD my	5216
Pr	20:27 The spirit of man *is* the **c** of the LORD,	5216
	24:20 man; the **c** of the wicked shall be put out.	5216
	31:18 *is* good: her **c** goeth not out by night.	5216
Jer	25:10 of the millstones, and the light of the **c**.	5216
Mt	5:15 Neither do men light a **c**, and put it under	3088
Mk	4:21 Is a **c** brought to be put under a bushel,	3088
Lk	8:16 No *man*, when he hath lighted a **c**,	3088
	11:33 No *man*, when he hath lighted a **c**,	3088
	11:36 when the bright shining of a **c** doth give	3088
	15: 8 doth not light a **c**, and sweep the house,	3088
Rev	18:23 And the light of a **c** shall shine no more at	3088
	22: 5 they need no **c**, neither light of the sun;	3088

CANDLES (1) [CANDLE]

Zep	1:12 *that* I will search Jerusalem with **c**,	5216

CANDLESTICK (41) [CANDLE, STICK]

Ex	25:31 shalt make a **c** of pure gold: *of* beaten	4501
	25:31 *of* beaten work shall the **c** be made:	4501
	25:32 three branches of the **c** out of the one	4501
	25:32 three branches of the **c** out of the other	4501
	25:33 the six branches that come out of the **c**.	4501
	25:34 in the **c** *shall be* four bowls made like	4501
	25:35 six branches that proceed out of the **c**.	4501
	26:35 the **c** over against the table on the side of	4501
	30:27 the **c** and his vessels, and the altar of	4501
	31: 8 the pure **c** with all his furniture,	4501
	35:14 The **c** also for the light, and his furniture,	4501
	37:17 made the **c** *of* pure gold: *of* beaten work	4501
	37:17 *of* beaten work made he the **c**; his shaft,	4501
	37:18 three branches of the **c** out of the one	4501
	37:18 three branches of the **c** out of the other	4501
	37:19 the six branches going out of the **c**.	4501
	37:20 in the **c** *were* four bowls made like	4501
	39:37 The pure **c**, *with* the lamps thereof,	4501
	40: 4 thou shalt bring in the **c**, and light	4501
	40:24 put the **c** in the tent of the congregation,	4501
Lev	24: 4 He shall order the lamps upon the pure **c**	4501
Nu	3:31 the **c**, and the altars, and the vessels of	4501
	4: 9 cover the **c** of the light, and his lamps,	4501
	8: 2 lamps shall give light over against the **c**.	4501
	8: 3 the lamps thereof over against the **c**,	4501
	8: 4 this work of the **c** *was* of beaten gold,	4501
	8: 4 had shewed Moses, so he made the **c**.	4501
2Ki	4:10 a bed, and a table, and a stool, and a **c**:	4501
1Ch	28:15 by weight for **every c**,	4501+4501+2050.1
	28:15 *both* for the **c**, and *also for* the lamps	4501
	28:15 to the use of **every c**,	4501+4501+2050.1
2Ch	13:11 the **c** of gold with the lamps thereof,	4501
Da	5: 5 wrote over against the **c** upon the plaister	5043
Zec	4: 2 I have looked, and behold, a **c** all of gold,	4501
	4:11 olive trees upon the right *side* of the **c**	4501
Mt	5:15 and put it under a bushel, but on a **c**;	3087
Mk	4:21 or under a bed? *and* not to be set on a **c**?	3087
Lk	8:16 but setteth *it* on a **c**, that they which enter	3087
	11:33 neither under a bushel, but on a **c**,	3087
Heb	9: 2 wherein *was* the **c**, and the table,	3087
Rev	2: 5 and will remove thy **c** out of his place,	3087

CANDLESTICKS (12) [CANDLE, STICK]

1Ki	7:49 the **c** *of* pure gold, five on the right side,	4501
1Ch	28:15 Even the weight for the **c** of gold,	4501
	28:15 for the **c** of silver by weight, *both* for	4501
2Ch	4: 7 he made ten **c** of gold according to their	4501
	4:20 Moreover the **c** with their lamps, that	4501
Jer	52:19 and the **c**, and the spoons, and the cups;	4501
Rev	1:12 And being turned, I saw seven golden **c**;	3087
	1:13 And in the midst of the seven **c** one like	3087
	1:20 in my right hand, and the seven golden **c**.	3087
	1:20 the seven **c** which thou sawest are the	3087
	2: 1 in the midst of the seven golden **c**;	3087
	11: 4 the two **c** standing before the God of	3087

CANE (2)

Isa	43:24 Thou hast bought me no **sweet c** with	7070
Jer	6:20 and the sweet **c** from a far country?	7070

CANKER (1) [CANKERED]

2Ti	2:17 And their word will eat as *doth* a **c**:	1044

CANKERED (1) [CANKER]

Jas	5: 3 Your gold and silver is **c**; and the rust of	2728

CANKERWORM (6) [WORM]

Joel	1: 4 that which the locust hath left hath the **c**	3218
	1: 4 that which the **c** hath left hath	3218
	2:25 the **c**, and the caterpillar,	3218
Na	3:15 cut thee off, it shall eat thee up like the **c**:	3218
	3:15 make thyself many as the **c**, make thyself	3218

C

Na 3:16 of heaven: the **c** spoileth, and flieth away. 3218

CANNEH (1)
Eze 27:23 Haran, and **C**, and Eden, the merchants 3656

CANNOT (184) [CAN]
Ge 19:19 I **c** escape to the mountain, lest 3201+3808
19:22 I **c** do any thing till thou be come 3201+3808
24:50 we **c** speak unto thee bad or good. 3201+3808
29: 8 they said, We **c**, until all the flocks 3201+3808
31:35 Let it not displease my lord that I **c** 3201+3808
32:12 which **c** be numbered for multitude. 3808
34:14 said unto them, We **c** do this thing, 3201+3808
38:22 returned to Judah, and said, I **c** find her; 3808
43:22 we **c** tell who put our money in our sacks. 3808
44:22 my lord, The lad **c** leave his father: 3201+3808
44:26 we said, We **c** go down: if our 3201+3808
Ex 10: 5 that *one* **c** be able to see the earth: 3808
19:23 people **c** come up to mount Sinai: 3201+3808
Lev 14:21 **c** get *so much*; then he shall take one lamb 369
Nu 22:18 I **c** go beyond the word of 3808
23:20 and he hath blessed; and I **c** reverse it. 3808
24:13 I **c** go beyond the commandment 3808
35:33 the land **c** be cleansed of the blood that is 3808
Dt 28:35 with a sore botch that **c** be healed, 3201+3808
Jos 24:19 the people, Ye **c** serve the LORD: 3201+3808
Jdg 11:35 unto the LORD, and I **c** go back. 3201+3808
14:13 if ye **c** declare *it* me, then shall ye 3201+3808
Ru 4: 6 I **c** redeem *it* for myself, 3201+3808
4: 6 my right to thyself; for I **c** redeem 3201+3808
1Sa 12:21 *should* ye go after vain *things*, which **c** 3808
17:39 said unto Saul, I **c** go with these; 3201+3808
17:55 *As* thy soul liveth, O king, I **c** tell. 518
25:17 a son of Belial, that *a man* **c** speak to him. 4480
2Sa 5: 6 hither: thinking, David **c** come in hither. 3808
14:14 which **c** be gathered up *again*; neither 3808
23: 6 because they **c** be taken with hands: 3808
1Ki 3: 8 that **c** be numbered nor counted for 3808
8:27 and heaven of heavens **c** contain thee; 3808
18:12 I come and tell Ahab, and he **c** find thee, 3808
2Ch 2: 6 and heaven of heavens **c** contain him? 3808
6:18 the heaven of heavens **c** contain thee; 3808
24:20 of the LORD, that ye **c** prosper? 3808
Ezr 9:15 for *we* **c** stand before thee because of this. 369
Ne 6: 3 great work, so that I **c** come down: 3201+3808
Job 5:12 their hands **c** perform *their* enterprise. 3808
6:30 **c** my taste discern perverse things? 518+3808
9: 3 he **c** answer him one of a thousand. 3808
12:14 it **c** be built *again*: he shutteth up a man, 3808
14: 5 thou hast appointed his bounds that he **c** 3808
17:10 for I **c** find *one* wise *man* among you. 3808
19: 8 He hath fenced up my way that I **c** pass, 3808
23: 8 and backward, but I **c** perceive him: 3808
23: 9 I **c** behold *him*: he hideth *himself on* 3808
23: 9 *on* the right hand, that I **c** see *him*: 3808
28:15 It **c** be gotten for gold, neither shall silver 3808
28:16 It **c** be valued with the gold of Ophir, 3808
28:17 The gold and the crystal **c** equal it: and 3808
31:31 that we had of his flesh! we **c** be satisfied. 3808
33:21 flesh is consumed away, that it **c** be seen; 4480
36:18 then a great ransom **c** deliver thee. 408
37: 5 *things* doeth he, which we **c** comprehend. 3808
37:19 for we **c** order *our speech* by reason of 3808
37:23 the Almighty, we **c** find him out: 3808
41:17 stick together, that they **c** be sundered. 3808
41:23 are firm in themselves; they **c** be moved. 1077
41:26 sword of him that layeth at him **c** hold: 1097
41:28 The arrow **c** make him flee: slingstones 3808
Ps 40: 5 they be reckoned up in order unto thee: 369
77: 4 I am *so* troubled that I **c** speak. 3808
88: 8 *I am* shut up, and I **c** come forth. 3808
93: 1 also is stablished, *that* it **c** be moved. 1077
125: 1 *which* **c** be removed, *but* abideth for ever. 3808
139: 6 for me; it is high, I **c** attain unto it. 3201+3808
Pr 30:21 and for four *which* it **c** bear: 3201+3808
Ecc 1: 8 **c** utter *it*: the eye is not satisfied 3201+3808
1:15 *That* which is crooked **c** be made 3201+3808
1:15 which is wanting **c** be numbered. 3201+3808
8:17 a man **c** find out the work that is 3201+3808
10:14 a man **c** tell what shall be; and what shall 3808
SS 8: 7 Many waters **c** quench love, 3808+3201
Isa 1:13 of assemblies, I **c** **away with**; 3201+3808
29:11 and he saith, I **c**; for it *is* sealed: 3201+3808
38:18 For the grave **c** praise thee, death *can not* 3808
38:18 they that go down into the pit **c** hope for 3808
44:18 he hath shut their eyes, that *they* **c** see; 4480
44:18 *and* their hearts, that *they* **c** understand. 4480
44:20 that he **c** deliver his soul, nor say, *Is there* 3808
45:20 and pray unto a god *that* **c** save. 3808
50: 2 hand shortened at all, that it **c** redeem? 3808
56:10 *are* all dumb dogs, they **c** bark; 3201+3808
56:11 and they *are* shepherds that **c** understand: 3808
57:20 when it **c** rest, whose waters cast 3201+3808
59: 1 hand is not shortened, that it **c** save; 4480
59: 1 neither his ear heavy, that it **c** hear: 4480
59:14 in the street, and equity **c** enter. 3201+3808
Jer 1: 6 Ah, Lord GOD, behold, I **c** speak: 3045+3808
4:19 I **c** hold my peace, because thou hast 3808
5:22 sea *by* a perpetual decree, that it **c** pass it: 3808
6:10 and they **c** hearken: 3201+3808
7: 8 ye trust in lying words, *that* **c** profit. 1115
10: 5 must needs be borne, because they **c** go. 3808
10: 5 they **c** do evil, neither also *is it* in them 3808
14: 9 as a mighty *man* that **c** save? 3201+3808
18: 6 **c** I do with you as this potter? 3201+3808

Jer 19:11 that **c** be made whole again: 3201+3808
24: 3 very evil, that **c** be eaten, they are so evil. 3808
24: 8 figs, which **c** be eaten, they are so evil. 3808
29:17 vile figs, that **c** be eaten, they are so evil. 3808
33:22 As the host of heaven **c** be numbered, 3808
36: 5 I **c** go *into* the house of the LORD: 3201+3808
46:23 saith the LORD, though it **c** be searched; 3808
49:23 *is* sorrow on the sea; it **c** be quiet. 3808
La 3: 7 hath hedged me about, that I **c** get out: 3808
4:18 hunt our steps, that we **c** go in our streets: 4480
Da 2:27 which the king hath demanded **c** 3809+3202
Hos 1:10 which **c** be measured nor numbered; 3808
Jnh 1:13 but they **c**: for the sea wrought, and was 3201
Hab 2: 5 **c** be satisfied, but gathereth unto him all 3808
Mt 5:14 A city that is set on a hill **c** be hid. 1410+3756
6:24 Ye **c** serve God and mammon. 1410+3756
7:18 A good tree **c** bring forth evil fruit, 1410+3756
19:11 unto them, All *men* **c** receive this saying, 3756
21:27 they answered Jesus, and said, We **c** tell. 3756
26:53 Thinkest thou that I **c** now pray to 3756
27:42 He saved others; himself he **c** save. 1410+3756
Mk 2:19 bridegroom with them, they **c** fast. 1410+3756
3:24 against itself, that kingdom **c** stand. 1410+3756
3:25 against itself, that house **c** stand. 1410+3756
3:26 he **c** stand, but hath an end. 1410+3756
7:18 into the man, *it* **c** defile him; 1410+3756
11:33 and said unto Jesus, We **c** tell. 3756
15:31 He saved others; himself he **c** save. 1410+3756
Lk 11: 7 me in bed; I **c** rise and give thee? 1410+3756
13:33 for it **c** be that a prophet perish 1735+4350
14:14 for they **c** recompense thee: 2192+3756
14:20 a wife, and therefore I **c** come. 1410+3756
14:26 own life also, he **c** be my disciple. 1410+3756
14:27 come after me, **c** be my disciple. 1410+3756
14:33 that he hath, he **c** be my disciple. 1410+3756
16: 3 I **c** dig; to beg I am ashamed. 2480+3756
16:13 Ye **c** serve God and mammon. 1410+3756
16:26 would pass from hence to you **c**; 1410+3361
Jn 3: 3 he **c** see the kingdom of God. 3756
3: 5 **c** enter into the kingdom of God. 1410+3756
7: 7 The world **c** hate you; but me it 1410+3756
7:34 and where I am, *thither* ye **c** come. 1410+3756
7:36 and where I am, *thither* ye **c** come. 1410+3756
8:14 ye **c** tell whence I come, and whither I 3756
8:21 your sins: whither I go, ye **c** come. 1410+3756
8:22 he saith, Whither I go, ye **c** come. 1410+3756
8:43 *even* because ye **c** hear my word. 1410+3756
10:35 and the scripture **c** be broken; 1410+3756
13:33 the Jews, Whither I go, ye **c** come; 1410+3756
13:37 Lord, why **c** I follow thee now? 1410+3756
14:17 whom the world **c** receive, because 1410+3756
15: 4 As the branch **c** bear fruit of itself, 1410+3756
16:12 unto you, but ye **c** bear *them* now. 1410+3756
16:18 A little while? we **c** tell what he saith. 3756
Ac 4:16 in Jerusalem; and we **c** deny it. 1410+3756
4:20 we **c** but speak *the things* which 1410+3756
5:39 if it be of God, ye **c** overthrow it; 1410+3756
15: 1 manner of Moses, ye **c** be saved. 1410+3756
19:36 that these *things* **c** be spoken against, 368
27:31 abide in the ship, ye **c** be saved. 1410+3756
Ro 8: 8 that are in the flesh **c** please God. 1410+3756
8:26 with groanings which **c** be uttered. 215
1Co 7: 9 but if they **c** contain, let them marry: 3756
10:21 Ye **c** drink the cup of the Lord, 1410+3756
10:21 ye **c** be partakers of the Lord's table, 1410+3756
12:21 And the eye **c** say unto the hand, 1410+3756
15:50 blood **c** inherit the kingdom of God; 1410+3756
2Co 2: 2 years ago, (whether in the body, I **c** tell; 3756
12: 2 or whether out of the body, I **c** tell: 3756
12: 3 in the body, or out of the body, I **c** tell; 3756
Gal 3:17 hundred and thirty years after, **c** disannul, 3756
5:17 so that ye **c** do the *things* that ye would. 3361
1Ti 5:25 they that are otherwise **c** be hid. 1410+3756
2Ti 2:13 abideth faithful: he **c** deny himself. 1410+3756
Tit 1: 2 hope of eternal life, which God, that **c** lie, 893
2: 8 Sound speech that **c** be **condemned**; 176
Heb 4:15 we have not a high priest which **c** 1410+3361
9: 5 which we **c** now speak particularly. 1510+4250
12:27 that those *things* which **c** be shaken may 3361
12:28 receiving a kingdom which **c** be **moved**, 761
Jas 1:13 for God **c** be tempted with evil, 551+1510
4: 2 ye kill, and desire *to have*, and **c** 1410+3756
2Pe 1: 9 and **c** see far off, and hath forgotten that 3467
2:14 full of adultery and that **c** cease from sin; 180
1Jn 3: 9 he **c** sin, because he is born of God. 1410+3756

CANNOT SPEAK See DUMB

CANST (51) [CAN]
Ge 41:15 thou **c** understand a dream to interpret NIH
Ex 33:20 he said, Thou **c** not see my face: for there 3201
Dt 28:27 the itch, where*of* thou **c** not be healed. 3201
Jos 7:13 thou **c** not stand before thine enemies, 3201
Jdg 16:15 unto him, How **c** thou say, I love thee, NIH
1Sa 30:15 **C** thou bring me down to this company? NIH
2Ki 8: 1 and sojourn wheresoever thou **c** sojourn: NIH
Ezr 7:16 gold that thou **c** find in all the province of NIH
Job 11: 7 **C** thou by searching find out God? NIH
11: 7 **c** thou find out the Almighty unto NIH
11: 8 *It is* as high as heaven; what **c** thou do? NIH
11: 8 deeper than hell; what **c** thou know? NIH
22:11 Or darkness, *that* thou **c** not see; NIH
33: 5 thou **c**, answer me, set *thy words* in order 3201
38:31 **C** thou bind the sweet influences of NIH
38:32 **C** thou bring forth Mazzaroth in his NIH

Job 38:32 or **c** thou guide Arcturus with his sons? NIH
38:33 **c** thou set the dominion thereof in the NIH
38:34 **C** thou lift up thy voice to the clouds, NIH
38:35 **C** thou send lightnings, that they may go, NIH
39: 1 or **c** thou mark when the hinds do calve? NIH
39: 2 **c** thou number the months *that* they fulfil? NIH
39:10 **C** thou bind the unicorn *with* his band in NIH
39:20 **C** thou make him afraid as a grasshopper? NIH
40: 9 **c** thou thunder with a voice like him? 3807.1
41: 1 **C** thou draw out leviathan with a hook? NIH
41: 2 **C** thou put a hook into his nose? or bore NIH
41: 7 **C** thou fill his skin with barbed irons? NIH
Pr 3:15 all the things thou **c** desire are not to be NIH
5: 6 are moveable, *that* thou **c** not know *them*. NIH
30: 4 and what *is* his son's name, if thou **c** tell? NIH
Isa 33:19 a people of a deeper speech than *thou* **c** NIH
33:19 *that* thou **c** not understand. NIH
Jer 2:23 How **c** thou say, I am not polluted, I have NIH
12: 5 then how **c** thou contend with horses? NIH
Eze 3: 6 whose words thou **c** not understand. NIH
Da 5:16 that thou **c** make interpretations, 3202
5:16 now if thou **c** read the writing, 3202
Hab 1:13 to behold evil, and **c** not look on iniquity: 3201
Mt 5:36 thou **c** not make one hair white or black. 1410
8: 2 Lord, if thou wilt, thou **c** make me clean. 1410
Mk 1:40 If thou wilt, thou **c** make me clean. 1410
9:22 if thou **c** do any *thing*, have compassion 1410
9:23 Jesus said unto him, If thou **c** believe, 1410
Lk 5:12 Lord, if thou wilt, thou **c** make me clean. 1410
6:42 Either how **c** thou say to thy brother, 1410
Jn 3: 8 but **c** not tell whence it cometh, NIG
13:36 Whither I go, thou **c** not follow me now; 1410
Ac 21:37 Who said, **C** thou **speak** Greek? 1097
Rev 2: 2 how thou **c** not bear *them* which are evil: 1410

CAPABLE See VALOUR

CAPERNAUM (16)
Mt 4:13 Nazareth, he came and dwelt in **C**, 2584
8: 5 And when Jesus was entered into **C**, 2584
11:23 And thou, **C**, which art exalted unto 2584
17:24 when they were come to **C**, they that 2584
Mk 1:21 they went into **C**; and straightway on 2584
2: 1 And again he entered into **C** after *some* 2584
9:33 he came to **C**: and being in the house 2584
Lk 4:23 whatsoever we have heard done in **C**, 2584
4:31 And came down to **C**, a city of Galilee, 2584
7: 1 of the people, he entered into **C**. 2584
10:15 thou, **C**, which art exalted to heaven, 2584
Jn 2:12 After this he went down to **C**, he, 2584
4:46 nobleman, whose son was sick at **C**. 2584
6:17 ship, and went over the sea towards **C**. 2584
6:24 and came to **C**, seeking for Jesus. 2584
6:59 he in the synagogue, as he taught in **C**. 2584

CAPHTHORIM (1) [CAPHTOR]
1Ch 1:12 (of whom came the Philistines,) and **C**. 3732

CAPHTOR (3) [CAPHTHORIM, CAPHTORIM, CAPHTORIMS]
Dt 2:23 came forth out of **C**, destroyed them, 3731
Jer 47: 4 the remnant of the country of **C**. 3731
Am 9: 7 the Philistines from **C**, and the Syrians 3731

CAPHTORIM (1) [CAPHTOR]
Ge 10:14 (out of whom came Philistim) and **C**. 3732

CAPHTORIMS (1) [CAPHTOR]
Dt 2:23 unto Azzah, the **C**, which came forth 3732

CAPITAL; CAPITALS See CHAPTER; CHAPTERS

CAPPADOCIA (2)
Ac 2: 9 and in Judea, and **C**, in Pontus, and Asia, 2587
1Pe 1: 1 Galatia, **C**, Asia, and Bithynia, 2587

CAPTAIN (139) [CAPTAINS]
Ge 21:22 Phichol the **chief** of his host spake unto 8269
21:32 Phichol the **chief** of his host, 8269
26:26 and Phichol the **chief** of his army. 8269
37:36 officer of Pharaoh's, *and* **c** of the guard. 8269
39: 1 of Pharaoh, **c** of the guard, an Egyptian, 8269
40: 3 put them in ward *in* the house of the **c** of 8269
40: 4 the **c** of the guard charged Joseph with 8269
41:10 put me in ward *in* the **c** of the guard's 8269
41:12 a Hebrew, servant to the **c** of the guard; 8269
Nu 2: 3 Nahshon the son of Amminadab *shall be* **c** 5387
2: 5 Nethaneel the son of Zuar *shall be* **c** of 5387
2: 7 Eliab the son of Helon *shall be* **c** of 5387
2:10 the **c** of the children of Reuben *shall be* 5387
2:12 the **c** of the children of Simeon *shall be* 5387
2:14 the **c** of the sons of Gad *shall be* Eliasaph 5387
2:18 the **c** of the children of Ephraim *shall be* 5387
2:20 the **c** of the children of Manasseh *shall be* 5387
2:22 the **c** of the sons of Benjamin *shall be* 5387
2:25 the **c** of the children of Dan *shall be* 5387
2:27 the **c** of the children of Asher *shall be* 5387
2:29 the **c** of the children of Naphtali *shall be* 5387
14: 4 Let us make a **c**, and let us return into 7218
Jos 5:14 *as* **c** of the host of the LORD am I now 8269
5:15 the **c** of the LORD's host said unto 8269
Jdg 4: 2 the **c** of whose host *was* Sisera, which 8269
4: 7 the **c** of Jabin's army, with his chariots 8269
11: 6 said unto Jephthah, Come, and be our **c**, 7101
11:11 people made him head and **c** over them: 7101

C

1Sa 9:16 thou shalt anoint him to be c over my 5057
10: 1 the LORD hath anointed thee to be c over 5057
12: 9 c of the host of Hazor, and into the hand 8269
13:14 the LORD hath commanded him to be c 5057
14:50 the name of the c of his host was Abner, 8269
17:18 carry these ten cheeses unto the c of their 8269
17:55 said unto Abner, the c of the host, Abner, 8269
18:13 and made him his c over a thousand; 8269
22: 2 unto him; and he became a c over them: 8269
26: 5 Abner the son of Ner, the c of his host: 8269
2Sa 2: 8 Abner the son of Ner, c of Saul's host, 8269
5: 2 and thou shalt be a c over Israel. 5057
5: 8 he shall be chief and c. Wherefore they NIH
10:16 Shobach the c of the host of Hadarezer 8269
10:18 Shobach the c of their host, who died 8269
17:25 Absalom made Amasa c⁵ of the host 5921
19:13 if thou be not c of the host before me 8269
23:19 therefore he was their c: howbeit he 8269
24: 2 For the king said to Joab the c of the host, 8269
1Ki 1:19 the priest, and Joab the c of the host: 8269
2:32 c of the host of Israel, and Amasa the son 8269
2:32 the son of Jether, c of the host of Judah. 8269
11:15 Joab the c of the host was gone up to 8269
11:21 that Joab the c of the host was dead, 8269
11:24 unto him, and became a c over a band, 8269
16: 9 c of half his chariots, conspired against 8269
16:16 all Israel made Omri, the c of the host, 8269
2Ki 1: 9 the king sent unto him a c of fifty with 8269
1:10 Elijah answered and said to the c of fifty, 8269
1:11 Again also he sent unto him another c of 8269
1:13 he sent again a c of the third fifty with his 8269
1:13 the third c of fifty went up, and came and 8269
4:13 for to the king, or to the c of the host? 8269
5: 1 c of the host of the king of Syria, 8269
9: 5 he said, I have an errand to thee, O c. 8269
9: 5 of all us? And he said, To thee, O c. 8269
9:25 said Jehu to Bidkar his c, Take up, 7991
15:25 a c of his, conspired against him, 7991
18:24 wilt thou turn away the face of one c of 6346
20: 5 and tell Hezekiah the c of my people, 5057
25: 8 came Nebuzar-adan, c of the guard, 7227
25:10 that were with the c of the guard, 7227
25:11 Nebuzar-adan the c of the guard carry 7227
25:12 the c of the guard left of the poor of 7227
25:15 in silver, the c of the guard took away. 7227
25:18 the c of the guard took Seraiah the chief 7227
25:20 Nebuzar-adan the c of the guard took these, 7227
1Ch 11: 6 the Jebusites first shall be chief and c. 8269
11:21 than the two; for he was their c: 8269
11:42 c of the Reubenites, and thirty with him, 7218
19:16 Shophach the c of the host of Hadarezer 8269
19:18 killed Shophach the c of the host. 8269
27: 5 The third c of the host for the third 8269
27: 7 The fourth c for the fourth month was NIH
27: 8 The fifth c for the fifth month was 8269
27: 9 The sixth c for the sixth month was Ira NIH
27:10 The seventh c for the seventh month was NIH
27:11 The eighth c for the eighth month was NIH
27:12 ninth c for the ninth month was Abiezer NIH
27:13 The tenth c for the tenth month was NIH
27:14 eleventh c for the eleventh month was NIH
27:15 The twelfth c for the twelfth month was NIH
2Ch 13:12 God himself is with us for our c, 7218
17:15 next to him was Jehohanan the c, 8269
Ne 9:17 in their rebellion appointed a c to return 7218
Isa 3: 3 The c of fifty, and the honourable man, 8269
36: 9 wilt thou turn away the face of one c of 6346
Jer 37:13 a c of the ward was there, whose name 1167
39: 9 Nebuzar-adan the c of the guard carried 7227
39:10 Nebuzar-adan the c of the guard left of 7227
39:11 to Nebuzar-adan the c of the guard, 7227
39:13 So Nebuzar-adan the c of the guard sent, 7227
40: 1 after that Nebuzar-adan the c of the guard 7227
40: 2 the c of the guard took Jeremiah, 7227
40: 5 So the c of the guard gave him victuals 7227
41:10 whom Nebuzar-adan the c of the guard 7227
43: 6 every person that Nebuzar-adan the c of 7227
51:27 and Ashchenaz; appoint a c against her; 2951
52:12 came Nebuzar-adan, c of the guard, 7227
52:14 that were with the c of the guard 7227
52:15 Nebuzar-adan the c of the guard carried 7227
52:16 Nebuzar-adan the c of the guard left 7227
52:19 in silver, took the c of the guard away. 7227
52:24 the c of the guard took Seraiah the chief 7227
52:26 So Nebuzar-adan the c of the guard took 7227
52:30 c of the guard carried away captive of 7227
Da 2:14 to Arioch the c of the king's guard, 7229
2:15 and said to Arioch the king's c, 7990
Jn 18:12 Then the band and the c and officers of 5506
Ac 4: 1 the c of the temple, and the Sadducees, 4755
5:24 the high priest and the c of the temple 4755
5:26 Then went the c with the officers, 4755
21:31 tidings came unto the chief c of the band, 5506
21:32 and when they saw the chief c and 5506
21:33 the chief c came near, and took him, 5506
21:37 said unto the chief c, May I speak unto 5506
22:24 chief c commanded him to be brought 5506
22:26 heard that, he went and told the chief c, 5506
22:27 Then the chief c came, and said unto him, 5506
22:28 the chief c answered, With a great sum 5506
22:29 and the chief c also was afraid, after he 5506
23:10 there arose a great dissension, the chief c, 5506
23:15 ye with the council signify to the chief c 5506
23:17 Bring this young man unto the chief c: 5506
23:18 and brought him unto the chief c, and said, 5506

Ac 23:19 Then the chief c took him by the hand, 5506
23:22 So the chief c then let the young man 5506
24: 7 But the chief c Lysias came upon us, and 5506
24:22 Lysias the chief c shall come down, 5506
28:16 the prisoners to the c of the guard: 4759
Heb 2:10 to make the c of their salvation perfect 747

CAPTAINS (119) [CAPTAIN]
Ex 14: 7 of Egypt, and c over every one of them. 7991
15: 4 his chosen c also are drowned in the Red 7991
Nu 31:14 with the c over thousands, 8269
31:14 c over hundreds, which came from 8269
31:48 the c of thousands, and captains of 8269
31:48 c of hundreds, came near unto Moses: 8269
31:52 the c of thousands, and of the captains of 8269
31:52 of thousands, and of the c of hundreds, 8269
31:54 Eleazar the priest took the gold of the c 8269
Dt 1:15 c over thousands, and captains over 8269
1:15 c over hundreds, and captains over fifties, 8269
1:15 c over fifties, and captains over tens, 8269
1:15 c over tens, and officers among your 8269
20: 9 they shall make c of the armies to lead 7218
29:10 your c of your tribes, your elders, 7218
Jos 10:24 said unto the c of the men of war which 7101
1Sa 8:12 he will appoint him c over thousands, 8269
8:12 over thousands, and c over fifties; 8269
22: 7 and make you all c of thousands, 8269
22: 7 captains of thousands, and c of hundreds; 8269
2Sa 4: 2 Saul's son had two men that were c of 8269
18: 1 set of thousands and captains of 8269
18: 1 thousands and c of hundreds over them. 8269
18: 5 gave all the c charge concerning Absalom. 8269
23: 8 that sat in the seat, chief among the c; 7991
24: 4 against Joab, and against the c of the host. 8269
24: 4 the c of the host went out from the 8269
1Ki 1:25 the c of the host, and Abiathar the priest; 8269
2: 5 what he did to the two c of the hosts of 8269
9:22 his c, and rulers of his chariots, 7991
15:20 sent the c of the hosts which he had 8269
20:24 out of his place, and put c in their rooms: 6346
22:31 and two c that had rule over his chariots, 8269
22:32 the c of the chariots saw Jehoshaphat, 8269
22:33 the c of the chariots perceived that it 8269
2Ki 1:14 burnt up the two c of the former fifties 8269
8:21 him about, and the c of the chariots: 8269
9: 5 behold, the c of the host were sitting; 8269
10:25 that Jehu said to the guard and to the c, 7991
10:25 the guard and the c cast them out, 7991
11: 4 the c and the guard, and brought them 3746
11: 9 the c over the hundreds did according to 8269
11:10 to the c over hundreds did the priest give 8269
11:15 Jehoiada the priest commanded the c of 8269
11:19 the c, and the guard, and all the people of 3746
25:23 when all the c of the armies, they and 8269
25:26 and great, and the c of the armies, 8269
1Ch 4:42 having for their c Pelatiah, and Neariah, 7218
11:11 a Hachmonite, the chief of the c: 7991
11:15 Now three of the thirty c went down to 7218
12:14 were of the sons of Gad, c of the host: 7218
12:18 who was chief of the c, and he said, 7970
12:18 and made them c of the band. 7218
12:20 c of the thousands that were of Manasseh. 7218
12:21 men of valour, and were c in the host. 8269
12:28 of his father's house twenty and two c. 8269
12:34 of Naphtali a thousand c, and with them 8269
13: 1 David consulted with the c of thousands 8269
15:25 elders of Israel, and the c over thousands, 8269
25: 1 the c of the host separated to the service 8269
26:26 the c over thousands and hundreds, 8269
26:26 and hundreds, and the c of the host, 8269
27: 1 and c of thousands and hundreds, 8269
27: 3 of all the c of the host for the first month. 8269
28: 1 the c of the companies that ministered to 8269
28: 1 the c over the thousands, and captains 8269
28: 1 c over the hundreds, and the stewards 8269
29: 6 and the c of thousands and of hundreds, 8269
2Ch 1: 2 to the c of thousands and of hundreds, 8269
8: 9 chief of his c, and captains of his chariots 7991
8: 9 and c of his chariots and horsemen. 8269
11:11 put c in them, and store of victual, 5057
16: 4 sent the c of his armies against the cities 8269
17:14 Of Judah, the c of thousands; Adnah 8269
18:30 the c of the chariots that were with him, 8269
18:31 the c of the chariots saw Jehoshaphat, 8269
18:32 that when the c of the chariots perceived 8269
21: 9 him in, and the c of the chariots. 8269
23: 1 took the c of hundreds, Azariah the son 8269
23: 9 delivered to the c of hundreds spears, 8269
23:14 Jehoiada the priest brought out the c of 8269
23:20 took the c of hundreds, and the nobles, 8269
25: 5 made them c over thousands, 8269
25: 5 over thousands, and c over hundreds, 8269
26:11 hand of Hananiah, one of the king's c. 8269
32: 6 he set c of war over the people, 8269
32:21 and in the camp of the king of Assyria. 8269
33:11 the c of the host of the king of Assyria, 8269
33:14 put c of war in all the fenced cities of 8269
Ne 2: 9 Now the king had sent c of the army and 8269
Job 39:25 the thunder of the c, and the shouting. 8269
Jer 13:21 for thou hast taught them to be c, 441
40: 7 Now when all the c of the forces which 8269
40: 7 all the c of the forces that were in the fields, 8269
41:11 all the c of the forces that were with him, 8269
41:13 all the c of the forces that were with him, 8269
41:16 all the c of the forces that were with him, 8269

Jer 42: 1 all the c of the forces, and Johanan the 8269
42: 8 the c of the forces which were with him, 8269
43: 4 all the c of the forces, and all the people, 8269
43: 5 the c of the forces, took all the remnant 8269
51:23 thee will I break in pieces c and rulers. 6346
51:28 the c thereof, and all the rulers thereof, 6346
51:57 her wise men, her c, and her rulers, 6346
Eze 21:22 to appoint c, to open the mouth in 3733
23: 6 were clothed with blue, c and rulers, 6346
23:12 c and rulers clothed most gorgeously, 6346
23:23 c and rulers, great lords and renowned, 6346
Da 3: 2 and the c, the judges, the treasurers, 6347
3: 3 the governors and c, the judges, 6347
3:27 c, and the king's counsellors 6347
6: 7 the princes, the counsellors and the c, 6347
Na 3:17 and thy c as the great grasshoppers, 2951
Mk 6:21 high c, and chief estates of Galilee; 5506
Lk 22: 4 communed with the chief priests and c, 4755
22:52 and of the temple, and the elders, 4755
Ac 25:23 with the chief c, and principal men of 5506
Rev 6:15 and the rich men, and the chief c, 5506
19:18 and the flesh of c, and the flesh of mighty 5506

CAPTIVE (59) [CAPTIVES, CAPTIVITY]
Ge 14:14 heard that his brother was taken c, 7617
34:29 their wives took they c, and spoiled even 7617
Ex 12:29 firstborn of the c that was in the dungeon; 7628
Nu 24:22 until Ashur shall carry thee away c. 7617
Dt 21:10 and thou hast taken them c, 7617+7628
Jdg 5:12 arise, Barak, and lead thy captivity c, 7617
1Ki 8:48 led them away c, and pray unto thee 7617
8:50 before them who carried them c, 7617
2Ki 5: 2 had brought away c out of the land of 7617
6:22 whom thou hast taken c with thy sword 7617
15:29 Naphtali, and carried them c to Assyria. 1540
16: 9 carried the people of it c to Kir, and slew 1540
24:16 them the king of Babylon brought c to 1473
1Ch 5: 6 king of Assyria carried away c. 1540
2Ch 6:37 in the land whither they are carried c, 7617
25:12 did the children of Judah carry away c, 7617
28: 8 the children of Israel carried away c of 7617
28:11 which ye have taken c of your brethren: 7617
30: 9 before them that lead them c, 7617
Ps 68:18 on high, thou hast led captivity c: 7617
137: 3 For there they that carried us away c 7617
Isa 49:21 desolate, a c, and removing to and fro? 1540
49:24 the mighty, or the lawful c delivered? 7628
51:14 The c exile hasteneth that he may be 6808
52: 2 bands of thy neck, O c daughter of Zion. 7628
Jer 1: 3 the carrying away of Jerusalem c in 1540
13:17 the LORD's flock is carried away c. 7617
13:19 Judah shall be carried away c all of it, 1540
13:19 it shall be wholly carried away c. 1540
20: 4 he shall carry them c into Babylon, 1540
22:12 in the place whither they have led him c, 1540
24: 1 carried away c Jeconiah the son 1540
24: 5 them that are carried away c of Judah, 1546
27:20 he carried away c Jeconiah the son 1540
28: 6 all that is carried away c, from Babylon 1473
29: 1 carried away c from Jerusalem to 1540
29:14 I caused you to be carried away c. 1540
39: 9 carried away c into Babylon the remnant 1540
40: 1 all that were carried away c of Jerusalem 1546
40: 1 were carried away c unto Babylon. 1540
40: 7 of them that were not carried away c to 1540
41:10 Ishmael carried away c all the residue of 7617
41:10 son of Nethaniah carried them away c, 7617
41:14 carried away c from Mizpah cast about 7617
52:15 carried away c certain of the poor of 1540
52:27 Judah was carried away c out of his 1540
52:28 whom Nebuchadrezzar carried away c: 1540
52:29 carried away c from Jerusalem eight 1540
52:30 carried away c of the Jews seven 1540
Am 1: 6 they carried away c the whole captivity, 1540
6: 7 Therefore now shall they go c with the 1540
6: 7 they go captive with the first that go c, 1540
7:11 Israel shall surely be led away c 1540+1540
Ob 1:11 the day that the strangers carried away c 7617
Na 2: 7 Huzzab shall be led away c, she shall be 1540
Lk 21:24 shall be led away c into all nations: 163
Eph 4: 8 led captivity c, and gave gifts unto men. 162
2Ti 2:26 who are taken c by him at his will. 2221
3: 6 and lead c silly women laden with sins, 162

CAPTIVES (43) [CAPTIVE]
Ge 31:26 my daughters, as c taken with the sword? 7617
Nu 31: 9 of Israel took all the women of Midian c, 7617
31:12 they brought the c, and the prey, 7628
31:19 yourselves and your c on the third day, 7628
Dt 21:11 seest among the c a beautiful woman, 7633
32:42 with the blood of the slain and of the c, 7633
1Sa 30: 2 had taken the women c, that were 7617
30: 3 and their daughters, were taken c. 7617
30: 5 David's two wives were taken c. 7617
1Ki 8:46 that they carry them away c unto 7617+7617
8:47 in the land whither they were carried c, 7617
8:47 in the land of them that carried them c, 7617
2Ki 24:14 even ten thousand c, and all the craftsmen 1540
2Ch 6:36 carry them away c unto a land 7617+7617
6:38 whither they have carried them c, 7617
28: 5 carried away a great multitude
 of them c, 7617+7633
28:11 hear me therefore, and deliver the c again, 7633
28:13 Ye shall not bring in the c hither: 7633
28:14 So the armed men left the c and the spoil 7633

C

2Ch 28:15 took the **c**, and with the spoil clothed all 7633
28:17 and smitten Judah, and carried away **c**. 7628
Ps 106:46 pitied of all those that **carried** them **c**. 7617
Isa 14: 2 they shall **take** them **c**, whose captives 7617
14: 2 take them captives, whose **c** they were; 7617
20: 4 the Ethiopians **c**, young and old, naked 1546
45:13 build my city, and let he shall let go my **c**, 1546
49:25 Even the **c** of the mighty shall be taken 7628
61: 1 proclaim liberty to the **c**, and the opening 7617
Jer 28: 4 with all the **c** of Judah, that went into 1546
29: 1 of the elders which were **carried away c**, 1473
29: 4 of Israel, unto all that are **carried away c**, 1473
29: 7 I have **caused** you **to be carried away c**, 1540
43: 3 and **carry** us **away c** *into* Babylon. 1540
43:12 shall burn them, and **carry** them **away c**: 7617
48:46 for thy sons are taken **c**, and thy daughters 7628
48:46 are taken captives, and thy daughters **c**. 7633
50:33 all that **took** them **c** held them fast; 7617
Eze 1: 1 as I *was* among the **c** by the river of 1473
6: 9 nations whither they shall be **carried c**, 7617
16:53 *will I bring again* the captivity of thy **c** in 7622
Da 2:25 have found a man of the **c** of Judah, 1123+1547
11: 8 shall also carry **c** *into* Egypt their gods, 7628
Lk 4:18 to preach deliverance to the **c**, *164*

CAPTIVITY (127) [CAPTIVE]

Nu 21:29 his daughters into **c** unto Sihon king of 7622
Dt 21:13 she shall put the raiment of her **c** from off 7628
28:41 not enjoy them; for they shall go into **c**. 7628
30: 3 then the LORD thy God will turn thy **c**, 7622
Jdg 5:12 arise, Barak, and lead thy **c** captive, 7628
18:30 of Dan until the day of the **c** of the land. 1540
2Ki 24:15 *those* carried he *into* **c** from Jerusalem to 1473
25:27 thirtieth year of the **c** of Jehoiachin king 1546
1Ch 5:22 And they dwelt in their steads until the **c**. 1473
6:15 Jehozadak went *into* **c**, when the LORD NIH
2Ch 6:37 and pray unto thee in the land of their **c**, 7628
6:38 with all their soul in the land of their **c**, 7628
29: 9 and our wives *are* in **c** for this. 7628
Ezr 1:11 **c** that were brought up from Babylon unto 1473
2: 1 of the province that went up out of the **c**, 7628
3: 8 all they that were come out of the **c** *unto* 7628
4: 1 Benjamin heard that the children of the **c** 1547
6:16 and the rest of the children of the **c**, 1547
6:19 the children of the **c** kept the passover 1473
6:20 the passover for all the children of the **c**, 1473
6:21 which were come again out of **c**, 1473
8:35 which were come out of the **c**, offered 7628
9: 7 to **c**, and to a spoil, and to confusion of 7628
10: 7 Jerusalem unto all the children of the **c**, 1473
10:16 the children of the **c** did so. And Ezra 1473
Ne 1: 2 which were left of the **c**, 7628
1: 3 The remnant that are left of the **c** there in 7628
4: 4 and give them for a prey in the land of **c**: 7633
7: 6 that went up out of the **c**, *of* those that 7628
8:17 come again out of the **c** made booths, 7628
Est 2: 6 **c** which had been carried away with 1473
Job 42:10 the LORD turned the **c** of Job, when he 7622
Ps 14: 7 when the LORD bringeth back the **c** of his 7622
53: 6 When God bringeth back the **c** of his 7622
68:18 ascended on high, thou hast led **c** captive: 7628
78:61 delivered his strength into **c**, and his glory 7628
85: 1 thou hast brought back the **c** of Jacob. 7622
126: 1 When the LORD turned again the **c** of 7870
126: 4 Turn again our **c**, O LORD, as the streams 7622
Isa 5:13 Therefore my people are **gone into c**, 1540
22:17 will carry thee away with a mighty **c**, 2925
46: 2 burden, but themselves are gone into **c**. 7628
Jer 15: 2 and such as *are* for the **c**, to the captivity. 7628
15: 2 and such as *are* for the captivity, to the **c**. 7628
20: 6 that dwell in thine house shall go into **c**: 7628
22:22 thy pastors, and thy lovers shall go into **c**: 7628
29:14 I will turn away your **c**, and I will gather 7622
29:16 that are not gone forth with you into **c**; 1473
29:20 the word of the LORD, all *ye of* the **c**, 1473
29:22 all the **c** of Judah which *are* in Babylon, 1546
29:28 unto us *in* Babylon, saying, This **c** *is* long: NIH
29:31 Send to all them of the **c**, saying, Thus 1473
30: 3 that I will bring again the **c** of my people 7622
30:10 and thy seed from the land of their **c**; 7628
30:16 every one of them, shall go into **c**; 7628
30:18 I *will* bring again the **c** of Jacob's tents, 7622
31:23 when I shall bring again their **c**; 7622
32:44 for I will cause their **c** to return, saith 7622
33: 7 will cause the **c** of Judah and the captivity 7622
33: 7 of Judah and the **c** of Israel to return, 7622
33:11 For I will cause to return the **c** of the land 7622
33:26 for I will cause their **c** to return, 7622
43:11 such *as are* for **c** to captivity; and such *as* 7628
43:11 such *as are* for captivity to **c**; and such *as* 7628
46:19 in Egypt, furnish thyself to **go into c**: 1473
46:27 and thy seed from the land of their **c**; 7628
48: 7 Chemosh shall go forth into **c** *with* his 1473
48:11 to vessel, neither hath he gone into **c**: 1473
48:47 Yet will I bring again the **c** of Moab in 7622
49: 3 their king shall go into **c**, *and* his priests 1473
49: 6 afterward I will bring again the **c** of 7622
49:39 *that* I will bring again the **c** of Elam, 7622
52:31 thirtieth year of the **c** of Jehoiachin king 1546
La 1: 3 Judah is **gone into c** because of affliction, 1540
1: 5 her children are gone *into* **c** before 7628
1:18 and my young men are gone into **c**. 7628
2:14 thine iniquity, to turn away thy **c**; 7622
4:22 he will no more **carry** thee **away into c**: 1540
Eze 1: 2 *was* the fifth year of king Jehoiachin's **c**, 1546

Eze 3:11 go, get thee to them of the **c**, unto 1473
3:15 I came to them of the **c** *at* Tel-abib, 1473
11:24 of God into Chaldea, to them of the **c**. 1473
11:25 I spake unto them of the **c** all the things 1473
12: 4 in their sight, as they that go forth into **c**. 1473
12: 7 as stuff for **c**, and in the even I digged 1473
12:11 them: they shall remove *and* go into **c**. 7628
16:53 When I shall bring again their **c**, 7622
16:53 the **c** of Sodom and her daughters, 7622
16:53 the **c** of Samaria and her daughters, then 7622
16:53 *will I bring again* the **c** of thy captives in 7622
25: 3 house of Judah, when they went into **c**; 1473
29:14 I will bring again the **c** of Egypt, 7622
30:17 the sword: and these *cities* shall go into **c**. 7628
30:18 her, and her daughters shall go into **c**. 7628
33:21 came to pass in the twelfth year of our **c**, 1546
39:23 of Israel **went into c** for their iniquity: 1540
39:25 Now will I bring again the **c** of Jacob, 7622
39:28 which **caused** them **to be led into c** 1540
40: 1 In the five and twentieth year of our **c**, 1546
Da 5:13 *art* of the children of the **c** of Judah, 1547
6:13 which *is* of the children of the **c** of Judah, 1547
11:33 by flame, by **c**, and by spoil, *many* days. 7628
Hos 6:11 when I returned the **c** of my people. 7622
Joel 3: 1 when I shall bring again the **c** of Judah 7622
Am 1: 5 people of Syria shall **go into c** unto Kir, 1540
1: 6 they carried away captive the whole **c**, 1546
1: 9 they delivered up the whole **c** to Edom, 1546
1:15 king shall go into **c**, he and his princes 1473
5: 5 for Gilgal shall **surely go into c**, 1540+1540
5:27 Therefore will I **cause** you **to go into c** 1540
Ob 1:20 they go into **c** before their enemies, 7628
9:14 I will bring again the **c** of my people of 7622
1:20 the **c** of this host of the children of Israel 1546
1:20 the **c** of Jerusalem, which *is* in Sepharad, 1546
Mic 1:16 for they are **gone into c** from thee. 1540
Na 3:10 *was* she carried away, she went into **c**: 7628
Hab 1: 9 and they shall gather the **c** as the sand. 7628
Zep 2: 7 shall visit them, and turn away their **c**. 7622
3:20 when I turn back your **c** before your eyes, 7622
Zec 6:10 Take of *them of* the **c**, *even* of Heldai, 1473
14: 2 and half of the city shall go forth into **c**, 1473
Ro 7:23 **bringing** me **into c** to the law of sin *163*
2Co 10: 5 **bringing** into **c** every thought to *163*
Eph 4: 8 he led **c** captive, and gave gifts unto men. *161*
Rev 13:10 that leadeth into **c** *shall* go into captivity: *161*
13:10 that leadeth into captivity *shall* go into **c**: *161*

CAPTURE See FETCH; FETCHED

CARAWAY See FITCHES

CARBUNCLE (3) [CARBUNCLES]

Ex 28:17 row *shall be* a sardius, a topaz, and a **c**: 1304
39:10 *first* row *shall be* a sardius, a topaz, and a **c**: 1304
Eze 28:13 the emerald, and the **c**, and gold: 1304

CARBUNCLES (1) [CARBUNCLE]

Isa 54:12 thy gates of **c**, and all thy borders of 68+688

CARCAS (1)

Est 1:10 Bigtha, and Abagtha, Zethar, and **C**, 3752

CARCASE (34) [CARCASES]

Lev 5: 2 whether *it be* an unclean beast, or a 5038
5: 2 or a **c** of unclean cattle, or the carcase of 5038
5: 2 the **c** of unclean creeping things, and *if* it 5038
11: 8 ye not eat, and their **c** shall ye not touch; 5038
11:24 whosoever toucheth the **c** of them shall 5038
11:25 whosoever beareth *ought* of the **c** of them 5038
11:27 whoso toucheth their **c** shall be unclean 5038
11:28 he that beareth the **c** of them shall wash 5038
11:35 every *thing* whereupon *any part* of their **c** 5038
11:36 that which toucheth their **c** shall be 5038
11:37 if *any part* of their **c** fall upon any sowing 5038
11:38 *any part* of their **c** fall thereon, it *shall be* 5038
11:39 he that toucheth the **c** thereof shall be 5038
11:40 he that eateth of the **c** of it shall wash his 5038
11:40 he also that beareth the **c** of it shall wash 5038
Dt 14: 8 eat of their flesh, nor touch their **dead c**. 5038
28:26 **c** shall be meat unto all fowls of the air, 5038
Jos 8:29 should take his **c** down from the tree, 5038
Jdg 14: 8 he turned aside to see the **c** of the lion: 4658
14: 8 of bees and honey in the **c** of the lion. 1472
14: 9 taken the honey out of the **c** of the lion. 1472
1Ki 13:22 thy **c** shall not come unto the sepulchre 5038
13:24 **c** was cast in the way, and the ass stood 5038
13:24 stood by it, the lion also stood by the **c**. 5038
13:25 saw the **c** cast in the way, and the lion 5038
13:25 in the way, and the lion standing by the **c**: 5038
13:28 he went and found his **c** cast in the way, 5038
13:28 and the ass and the lion standing by the **c**: 5038
13:28 the lion had not eaten the **c**, nor torn 5038
13:29 the prophet took up the **c** of the man of 5038
13:30 he laid his **c** in his own grave; 5038
2Ki 9:37 of Jezebel shall be as dung upon 5038
Isa 14:19 stones of the pit; as a **c** trodden under feet. 6297
Mt 24:28 For wheresoever the **c** is, there will 4430

CARCASES (22) [CARCASE]

Ge 15:11 when the fowls came down upon the **c**, 6297
Lev 11:11 but you shall have their **c** in abomination. 5038
11:26 The **c** of every beast which divideth NIH
26:30 your **c** upon the carcases of your idols, 6297
26:30 your carcases upon the **c** of your idols, 6297

Nu 14:29 Your **c** shall fall in this wilderness; 6297
14:32 *as for* you, your **c**, they shall fall in this 6297
14:33 until your **c** be wasted in the wilderness. 6297
1Sa 17:46 I will give the **c** of the host of 6297
Isa 5:25 **c** were torn in the midst of the streets. 5038
34: 3 their stink shall come up *out of* their **c**, 6297
66:24 look upon the **c** of the men that have 6297
Jer 7:33 the **c** of this people shall be meat for 5038
9:22 Even the **c** of men shall fall as dung upon 5038
16: 4 their **c** shall be meat for the fowls of 5038
16:18 have filled mine inheritance with the **c** 5038
19: 7 their **c** will I give to be meat for the fowls 5038
Eze 6: 5 I will lay the **dead c** of the children of 6297
43: 7 nor by the **c** of their kings *in* their high 6297
43: 9 the **c** of their kings, far from me, and I 6297
Na 3: 3 of slain, and a great number of **c**; 6297
Heb 3:17 sinned, whose **c** fell in the wilderness? *2966*

CARCASS; CARCASSES See CARCASE; CARCASES

CARCHEMISH (3)

2Ch 35:20 came up to fight against **C** by Euphrates: 3751
Isa 10: 9 not Calno as **C**? *is* not Hamath as Arpad? 3751
Jer 46: 2 which was by the river Euphrates in **C**, 3751

CARE (20) [CARED, CAREFUL, CAREFULLY, CAREFULNESS, CARELESS, CARELESSLY, CARES, CAREST, CARETH, CARING]

1Sa 10: 2 lo, thy father hath left the **c** of the asses, 1697
2Sa 18: 3 for if we flee away, they will not **c** 3820+7760
18: 3 if half of us die, will they **c** for us: 3820+7760
2Ki 4:13 hast been careful for us with all this **c**; 2731
Jer 49:31 that dwelleth **without c**, saith the LORD, 983
Eze 4:16 they shall eat bread by weight, and with **c**; 1674
Mt 13:22 and the **c** of this world, 3308
Lk 10:34 brought him to an inn, and **took c** of him. 1959
10:35 host, and said unto him, **Take c** of him: 1959
10:40 dost thou not **c** that my sister hath left me 3199
1Co 7:21 thou called *being* a servant? **c** not **for** it: 3199
9: 9 out the corn. Doth God **take c** for oxen? 3199
12:25 the members should **have** the same **c** 3309
2Co 7:12 our **c** for you in the sight of God might 4710
8:16 put the same **earnest c** into the heart 4710
11:28 upon me daily, the **c** of all the churches. 3308
Php 2:20 who will naturally **c for** your state. 3309
4:10 that now at the last your **c** of me hath 5426
1Ti 3: 5 shall he **take c** of the church of God? 1959
1Pe 5: 7 Casting all your **c** upon him; for he careth 3308

CAREAH (1)

2Ki 25:23 Johanan the son of **C**, and Seraiah the son 7143

CARED (3) [CARE]

Ps 142: 4 refuge failed me; no man **c** for my soul. 1875
Jn 12: 6 This he said, not that he **c** for the poor; 3199
Ac 18:17 And Gallio **c** for none of those *things*. 3199

CAREFUL (7) [CARE]

2Ki 4:13 thou hast been **c** for us with all this care; 2729
Jer 17: 8 shall not be **c** in the year of drought, 1672
Da 3:16 *are* not **c** to answer thee in this matter. 2818
Lk 10:41 art **c** and troubled about many *things*: 3309
Php 4: 6 Be **c** for nothing; but in every *thing* by 3309
4:10 wherein ye were also **c**, but ye lacked 5426
Tit 3: 8 might be **c** to maintain good works. 5431

CAREFULLY (4) [CARE]

Dt 15: 5 Only if thou **c hearken** unto 8085+8085
Mic 1:12 the inhabitant of Maroth **waited c** for 2342
Php 2:28 I sent him therefore the **more c**, that, 4708
Heb 12:17 though he **sought** it **c** with tears. 1567

CAREFULNESS (4) [CARE]

Eze 12:18 thy water with trembling and with **c**; 1674
12:19 They shall eat their bread with **c**, 1674
1Co 7:32 But I would have you **without c**. 275
2Co 7:11 what **c** it wrought in you, yea, 4710

CARELESS (5) [CARE]

Jdg 18: 7 that *were* therein, how they dwelt **c**, 983
Isa 32: 9 ye **c** daughters, give ear unto my speech. 982
32:10 ye **c women**: for the vintage shall fail, 982
32:11 that are at ease; be troubled, ye **c** ones: 982
Eze 30: 9 in ships to make the **c** Ethiopians afraid, 983

CARELESSLY (3) [CARE]

Isa 47: 8 that dwellest **c**, that sayest in thine 983+3807.1
Eze 39: 6 them that dwell **c** in the isles: 983+3807.1
Zep 2:15 *is* the rejoicing city that dwelt **c**, 983+3807.1

CARES (3) [CARE]

Mk 4:19 And the **c** of this world, 3308
Lk 8:14 and are choked with **c** and riches and 3308
21:34 and **c** of *this* life, and *so* that day come 3308

CARESSING See SPORTING

CAREST (3) [CARE]

Mt 22:16 neither **c** thou for any *man*: for thou 3199
Mk 4:38 Master, **c** thou not that we perish? 3199
12:14 **c** for no *man*: for thou regardest not 3199

CARETH (7) [CARE]

Dt 11:12 A land which the LORD thy God **c for**: 1875
Jn 10:13 he is a hireling, and **c** not for the sheep. 3199
1Co 7:32 He *that is* unmarried **c for** the *things* that 3309

1Co 7:33 he that is married **c** for the *things* that 3309
7:34 The unmarried *woman* **c** for the *things* of 3309
7:34 she that is married **c** for the *things* of 3309
1Pe 5: 7 all your care upon him; for he **c** for you. 3199

CARING (1) [CARE]
1Sa 9: 5 lest my father leave **c** for the asses, NIH

CARMEL (26) [CARMELITE, CARMELITESS]
Jos 12:22 one; the king of Jokneam of **C**, one; 3760
15:55 Maon, **C**, and Ziph, and Juttah, 3760
19:26 reacheth to **C** westward, 3760
1Sa 15:12 Saul came to **C**, and behold, 3760
25: 2 in Maon, whose possessions *were* in **C**; 3760
25: 2 and he was shearing his sheep in **C**. 3760
25: 5 Get you up to **C**, and go to Nabal, 3760
25: 7 unto them, all the while they were in **C**. 3760
25:40 of David were come to Abigail to **C**, 3760
1Ki 18:19 *and* gather to me all Israel unto mount **C**, 3760
18:20 the prophets together unto mount **C**. 3760
18:42 Elijah went up to the top of **C**; and he cast 3760
2Ki 2:25 he went from thence to mount **C**, 3760
4:25 came unto the man of God to mount **C**. 3760
19:23 his borders, *and into* the forest of his **C**. 3760
2Ch 26:10 vinedressers in the mountains, and in **C**: 3760
SS 7: 5 head upon thee *is* like **C**, and the hair 3760
Isa 33: 9 and Bashan and **C** shake off *their fruits*. 3760
35: 2 the excellency of **C** and Sharon, they shall 3760
37:24 of his border, *and* the forest of his **C**. 3760
Jer 46:18 and as **C** by the sea, *so* shall he come. 3760
50:19 shall feed on **C** and Bashan, and his soul 3760
Am 1: 2 mourn, and the top of **C** shall wither. 3760
9: 3 they hide themselves in the top of **C**, 3760
Mic 7:14 solitarily *in* the wood, in the midst of **C**: 3760
Na 1: 4 **C**, and the flower of Lebanon languisheth. 3760

CARMELITE (5) [CARMEL]
1Sa 30: 5 and Abigail the wife of Nabal the **C**. 3761
2Sa 2: 2 and Abigail Nabal's wife the **C**. 3761
3: 3 of Abigail the wife of Nabal the **C**; 3761
23:35 Hezrai the **C**, Paarai the Arbite, 3761
1Ch 11:37 Hezro the **C**, Naarai the son of Ezbai, 3761

CARMELITESS (2) [CARMEL]
1Sa 27: 3 and Abigail the **C**, Nabal's wife. 3761
1Ch 3: 1 the second Daniel, of Abigail the **C**: 3761

CARMI (8) [CARMITES]
Ge 46: 9 Hanoch, and Phallu, and Hezron, and **C**. 3756
Ex 6:14 Hanoch, and Pallu, Hezron, and **C**: 3756
Nu 26: 6 of **C**, the family of the Carmites. 3756
Jos 7: 1 for Achan, the son of **C**, the son of Zabdi, 3756
7:18 Achan, the son of **C**, the son of Zabdi, 3756
1Ch 2: 7 sons of **C**; Achar, the troubler of Israel, 3756
4: 1 Hezron, and **C**, and Hur, and Shobal. 3756
5: 3 *were*, Hanoch, and Pallu, Hezron, and **C**. 3756

CARMITE See CARMITES

CARMITES (1) [CARMI]
Nu 26: 6 of Carmi, the family of the **C**. 3757

CARNAL (11) [CARNALLY]
Ro 7:14 law is spiritual: but I am **c**, sold under sin. 4559
8: 7 Because the **c** mind *is* enmity against God: 4561
15:27 is also to minister unto them in **c** *things*. 4559
1Co 3: 1 as unto **c**, *even* as unto babes in Christ. 4559
3: 3 ye are yet **c**: for whereas *there is* among 4559
3: 3 divisions, are ye not **c**, and walk as men? 4559
3: 4 another, I *am* of Apollos; are ye not **c**? 4559
9:11 great *thing* if we shall reap your **c** *things*? 4559
2Co 10: 4 For the weapons of our warfare *are* not **c**, 4559
Heb 7:16 not after the law of a **c** commandment, 4559
9:10 and divers washings, and **c** ordinances, 4561

CARNALLY (4) [CARNAL]
Lev 18:20 not **lie c** with thy 2233+5414+7903+3807.1
19:20 **lieth c with** a woman 854+2233+7901+7902
Nu 5:13 a *man* lie with her **c**, and it 376+2233+7902
Ro 8: 6 For to be **c** minded *is* death; 4561

CARNELIAN See SARDINE

CARPENTER (3) [CARPENTER'S, CARPENTERS]
Isa 41: 7 So the **c** encouraged the goldsmith, 2796
44:13 The **c** stretcheth out *his* rule; 2796+6086
Mk 6: 3 Is not this the **c**, the son of Mary, 5045

CARPENTER'S (1) [CARPENTER]
Mt 13:55 Is not this the **c** son? is not his mother 5045

CARPENTERS (9) [CARPENTER]
2Sa 5:11 cedar trees, and **c**, and masons: 2796+6086
2Ki 12:11 laid it out to the **c** and builders, 2796+6086
22: 6 Unto **c**, and builders, and masons, 2796
1Ch 14: 1 of cedars, with masons and **c**, 2796+6086
2Ch 24:12 and **c** to repair the house of the LORD, 2796
Ezr 3: 7 money also unto the masons, and to the **c**; 2796
Jer 24: 1 with the **c** and smiths, from Jerusalem, 2796
29: 2 and Jerusalem, and the **c**, and the smiths, 2796
Zec 1:20 And the LORD shewed me four **c**. 2796

CARPUS (1)
2Ti 4:13 The cloke that I left at Troas with **C**, 2591

CARRIAGE (3) [CARRIAGES]
Jdg 18:21 and the cattle and the **c** before them. 3520

1Sa 17:22 David left his **c** in the hand of the keeper 3627
17:22 carriage in the hand of the keeper of the **c**, 3627

CARRIAGES (3) [CARRIAGE]
Isa 10:28 at Michmash he hath laid up his **c**: 3627
46: 1 your **c** *were* heavy loaden; *they are* a 5385
Ac 21:15 And after those days we **took up** our **c**, 643

CARRIED (145) [CARRY]
Ge 31:18 he **c away** his cattle, and all his goods 5090
31:26 **c away** my daughters, as captives taken 5090
46: 5 the sons of Israel **c** Jacob their father, 5375
50:13 his sons **c** him into the land of Canaan, 5375
Lev 10: 5 and **c** them in their coats out of the camp; 5375
Jos 4: 8 **c** them **over** with them unto the place 5674
Jdg 16: 3 **c** them **up** to the top of a hill that *is* before 5927
1Sa 5: 8 Let the ark of the God of Israel be **c about** 5437
5: 8 they **c** the ark of the God of Israel **about** 5437
5: 9 it was *so*, that after they had **c** it **about**, 5437
30: 2 but **c** *them* **away**, and went on their way. 5090
30:18 all that the Amalekites had **c away**: 3947
2Sa 6:10 David **c** it **aside** *into* the house of 5186
15:29 Abiathar **c** the ark of God **again** *to* 7725
1Ki 8:47 in the land whither they were **c captives**, 7617
8:47 in the land that **c** them **captives**, 7617
8:50 before them who **c** them **captive**, 7617
17:19 **c** him **up** into a loft, where he abode, 5927
21:13 they **c** him **forth** out of the city, 3318
2Ki 7: 8 **c** thence silver, and gold, and raiment, 5375
7: 8 and **c** thence *also*, and went and hid *it*. 5375
9:28 servants **c** him *in a chariot* to Jerusalem, 7392
15:29 Naphtali, and **c** them **captive** to Assyria. 1540
16: 9 **c** *the people of* it **captive** to Kir, and slew 1540
17: 6 **c** Israel **away** into Assyria, and placed 1540
17:11 whom the LORD **c away** before them; 1540
17:23 was Israel **c away** out of their own land 1540
17:28 one of the priests whom they had **c away** 1540
17:33 nations whom they **c away** from thence. 1540
20:17 unto this day, shall be **c** unto Babylon: 5375
23: 4 and **c** the ashes of them *unto* Beth-el. 5375
23:30 his servants **c** him *in a chariot* dead from 7392
24:13 he **c out** thence all the treasures of 3318
24:14 he **c away** all Jerusalem, and all 1540
24:15 he **c away** Jehoiachin to Babylon, 1540
25: 7 those **c** him *into* captivity from Jerusalem 1980
25: 7 fetters of brass, and **c** him to Babylon. 935
25:13 and **c** the brass of them to Babylon. 5375
25:21 So Judah was **c away** out of their land. 1540
1Ch 5: 6 king of Assyria **c away captive**: 1540
5:26 he **c** them **away**, even the Reubenites, 1540
6:15 *captivity*, when the LORD **c away** Judah 1540
9: 1 *who* were **c** to Babylon for their 1540
13: 7 they **c** the ark of God in a new cart out of 7392
13:13 **c** it **aside** into the house of Obed-edom 5186
2Ch 6:37 in the land whither they are **c captive**, 7617
6:38 whither they have **c** them **captives**, 7617
12: 9 he **c away** also the shields of gold which 3947
14:13 host; and they **c away** very much spoil. 5375
14:15 **c away** sheep and camels in abundance, 7617
16: 6 they **c away** the stones of Ramah, 5375
21:17 **c away** all the substance that was found 7617
24:11 and took it, and **c** it to his place **again**. 7725
28: 5 **c away** a great multitude of
them **captives**, 7617+7633
28: 8 the children of Israel **c away captive** of 7617
28:15 **c** all the feeble them upon asses, 5095
28:17 and smitten Judah, and **c away** captives. 7617
33:11 him with fetters, and **c** him to Babylon. 1980
34:16 Shaphan **c** the book to the king, 935
36: 4 Jehoahaz his brother, and **c** him to Egypt. 935
36: 7 Nebuchadnezzar also **c** of the vessels of 935
36:20 from the sword he **c away** to Babylon; 1540
Ezr 2: 1 *of those* which had been **c away**, 1473
2: 1 king of Babylon had **c away** unto Babylon, 1540
5:12 and **c** the people **away** into Babylon. 1541
8:35 children of those that had been **c away**, 1473
9: 4 of those that had been **c away**; 1473
10: 6 of **them** that had been **c away**. 1473
10: 8 of those that had been **c away**. 1473
Ne 7: 6 *of those* that had been **c away**, 1473
7: 6 the king of Babylon had **c away**, 1540
Est 2: 6 Who had been **c away** from Jerusalem 1540
2: 6 been **c away** with Jeconiah king of Judah, 1540
2: 6 the king of Babylon had **c away**. 1540
Job 1:17 have **c** them **away**, yea, and slain 3947
5:13 the counsel of the froward is **c headlong**. 4116
10:19 I should have been **c** from the womb to 2986
Ps 46: 2 the mountains be **c** into the midst of 4131
106:46 pitied of all those that **c** them **captives**, 7617
137: 3 For they that **c** us **away captive** 7617
Isa 39: 6 store until this day, shall be **c** *to* Babylon: 5375
46: 3 the belly, which are **c** from the womb: 5375
49:22 thy daughters shall be **c** upon *their* 5375
53: 4 hath borne our griefs, and **c** our sorrows: 5445
63: 9 bare them, and **c** them all the days of old. 5375
Jer 13:17 the LORD's flock is **c away captive**. 7617
13:19 Judah shall be **c away captive** all of it, 1540
13:19 of it, it shall be wholly **c away captive**. 1540
24: 1 **c away captive** Jeconiah the son of 1540
24: 5 them that are **c away captive** of Judah, 1546
27:20 he **c away captive** Jeconiah the son 1540
27:22 They shall be **c** to Babylon, and there 935
28: 3 from this place, and **c** them *to* Babylon: 935
28: 6 all that is **c away captive**, from Babylon 1473
29: 1 the elders which were **c away captives**, 1473

Jer 29: 1 **c away captive** from Jerusalem to 1540
29: 4 Israel, unto all that are **c away captives**, 1473
29: 4 whom I have **caused to be c away** from 1540
29: 7 have **caused** you to be **c away captives**, 1540
29:14 I **caused** you **to be c away captive**. 1540
39: 9 **c away captive** *into* Babylon the remnant 1540
40: 1 all that were **c away captive** of Jerusalem 1546
40: 1 were **c away captive** unto Babylon. 1540
40: 7 of *them* that were not **c away captive** to 1540
41:10 Ishmael **c away captive** all the residue of 7617
41:10 son of Nethaniah **c** them **away captive**, 7617
41:14 **c away captive** from Mizpah cast about 7617
52: 9 **c** him **up** unto the king of Babylon to 5927
52:11 **c** him to Babylon, and put him in prison 935
52:15 **c away captive** *certain* of the poor of 1540
52:17 and **c** all the brass of them to Babylon. 5375
52:27 Thus Judah was **c away captive** out of 1540
52:28 whom Nebuchadrezzar **c away captive**: 1540
52:29 **c away captive** from Jerusalem eight 1540
52:30 **c away captive** *of* the Jews seven 1540
Eze 6: 9 nations whither they shall be **c captives**, 7617
17: 4 twigs, and **c** it into a land of traffick; 935
37: 1 **c** me **out** in the spirit of the LORD, 3318
Da 1: 2 which he *into* the land of Shinar to 935
2:35 the wind **c** them **away**, that no place was 5376
Hos 10: 6 It shall be also **c** unto Assyria *for* a present 2986
12: 1 with the Assyrians, and oil is **c** into Egypt. 2986
Joel 3: 5 have **c** into your temples my goodly 935
Am 1: 6 they **c away captive** the whole captivity, 1540
Ob 1:11 the day that the strangers **c away captive** 7617
Na 3:10 Yet *was* she **c away**, she went into 3807.1
Mt 1:11 about the time they were **c away** to 3350
Mk 15: 1 **c** *him* **away**, and delivered *him* to Pilate. 667
Lk 7:12 behold, there was a dead man **c out**, 1580
16:22 was **c** by the angels into Abraham's bosom: 667
24:51 parted from them, and **c up** into heaven. 399
Ac 3: 2 man lame from his mother's womb was **c**, 941
5: 6 him up, and **c** *him* **out**, and buried *him*. 1627
7:16 And were **c over** into Sychem, and laid in 3346
8: 2 And devout men **c** Stephen *to his burial*, 4792
21:34 he commanded him to be **c** into the castle. 71
1Co 12: 2 **c away** unto *these* dumb idols, *even* as ye 520
Gal 2:13 also was **c away with** their dissimulation. 4879
Eph 4:14 and **c about** with every wind of doctrine, 4064
Heb 13: 9 Be not **c about** with divers and 4064
2Pe 2:17 clouds that are **c** with a tempest; 1643
Jude 1:12 *they are* without water, **c about** of winds; 4064
Rev 12:15 cause her to be **c away** of the flood. 4216
17: 3 So he **c** me **away** in the spirit into 667
21:10 And he **c** me **away** in the spirit to a great 667

CARRIEST (1) [CARRY]
Ps 90: 5 Thou **c** them **away** as with a flood; 2229

CARRIETH (3) [CARRY]
Job 21:18 and as chaff that the storm **c away**. 1589
27:21 The east wind **c** him **away**, 5375
Rev 17: 7 and of the beast that **c** her, which hath 941

CARRY (90) [CARRIED, CARRIEST, CARRIETH, CARRYING]
Ge 37:25 and myrrh, going to **c** *it* **down** to Egypt. 3381
42:19 go ye, **c** corn *for* the famine of your houses: 935
43:11 **c down** the man a present, a little balm, 3381
43:12 of your sacks, **c** *it* **again** in your hand; 7725
44: 1 much as they can **c**, and put every man's 5375
45:27 wagons which Joseph had sent to **c** him, 5375
46: 5 the wagons which Pharaoh had sent to **c** 5375
47:30 thou shalt **c** me out of Egypt, and bury me 5375
50:25 and ye shall **c up** my bones from hence. 5927
Ex 12:46 thou shalt not **c forth** *ought* of the flesh 3318
13:19 ye shall **c up** my bones away hence with 5927
14:11 thus with us, to **c** us **forth** out of Egypt? 3318
33:15 thy presence go not *with me*, **c** us not **up** 5927
Lev 4:12 Even the whole bullock shall he **c forth** 3318
4:21 he shall **c forth** the bullock without 3318
6:11 **c forth** the ashes without the camp unto 3318
10: 4 **c** your brethren from before the sanctuary 5375
14:45 he shall **c** them **forth** out of the city unto 3318
16:27 place, shall one **c forth** without the camp; 3318
Nu 11:12 say unto me, **C** them in thy bosom, 5375
24:22 until Asshur shall **c** thee **away** captive. 7617
Dt 14:24 for thee, so that thou art not able to **c** it; 5375
28:38 Thou shalt **c** much seed **out** *into* the field, 3318
Jos 4: 3 ye shall **c** them **over** with you, 5674
1Sa 17:18 **c** these ten cheeses unto the captain of 935
20:40 and said unto him, Go, **c** *them* to the city. 935
2Sa 15:25 **C back** the ark of God *into* the city: 7725
19:18 there went over a ferry boat to **c over** 5674
1Ki 8:46 they **c** them **away captives** unto 7617+7617
18:12 that the spirit of the LORD shall **c** thee 5375
21:10 *then* **c** him **out**, and stone him, that he 3318
22:26 **c** him **back** unto Amon the governor of 7725
22:34 thine hand, and **c** me **out** of the host; 3318
2Ki 4:19 And he said to a lad, **C** him to his mother. 5375
9: 2 brethren, and **c** him *to* an inner chamber; 935
17:27 **C** thither one of the priests whom ye 1980
18:11 the king of Assyria did **c away** Israel unto 1540
25:11 the captain of the guard **c away**. 1540
1Ch 10: 9 to **c tidings** unto their idols, and to 1319
15: 2 None ought to **c** the ark of God but 5375
15: 2 for them hath the LORD chosen to **c** 5375
23:26 *they* shall no *more* **c** the tabernacle, nor 5375
2Ch 2:16 and thou shalt **c** it **up** to Jerusalem. 5927
6:36 they **c** them **away captives** unto a 7617+7617

C

2Ch 18:25 **c** him **back** to Amon the governor of	7725
18:33 that thou mayest **c** me **out** of the host;	3318
20:25 more than they could **c away**:	4853
25:12 did the children of Judah **c away captive**,	7617
29: 5 **c forth** the filthiness out of the holy *place*.	3318
29:16 the Levites took *it*, to **c** *it* **out** abroad into	3318
36: 6 bound him in fetters, to **c** him to Babylon.	1980
Ezr 5:15 **c** them into the temple that *is* in	5182
7:15 to **c** the silver and gold, which the king	2987
Job 15:12 Why doth thine heart **c** thee **away**? and	3947
Ps 49:17 when he dieth he shall **c** nothing **away**:	3947
Ecc 5:15 which he may **c away** in his hand.	1980
10:20 for a bird of the air shall **c** the voice,	1980
Isa 5:29 **c** *it* **away** safe, and none shall deliver	6403
15: 7 shall they **c away** to the brook of	5375
22:17 the Lord will **c** thee **away** with a mighty	2904
23: 7 own feet shall **c** her afar off to sojourn.	2986
30: 6 will **c** their riches upon the shoulders	5375
40:11 **c** *them* in his bosom, *and* shall gently lead	5375
41:16 the wind shall **c** them **away**,	5375
46: 4 *even* to hoar hairs will I **c** *you:* I have	5445
46: 4 even I will **c**, and will deliver *you.*	5445
46: 7 they **c** him, and set him in his place,	5445
57:13 the wind shall **c** them **all away**; vanity	5375
Jer 17:22 Neither **c forth** a burden **out** of your	3318
20: 4 he shall **c** them **captive** into Babylon,	1540
20: 5 and take them, and **c** them to Babylon.	935
39: 7 him with chains to **c** him to Babylon.	935
39:14 of Shaphan, that *he* should **c** him **home**:	3318
43: 3 and **c** us **away** captives *into* Babylon.	1540
43:12 burn them, and **c** them **away captives**;	7617
La 4:22 will no more **c** thee **away into captivity**.	1540
Eze 12: 5 the wall in their sight, and **c out** thereby.	3318
12: 6 shoulders, *and* **c** *it* **forth** in the twilight:	3318
12:12 they shall dig through the wall to **c out**	3318
22: 9 In thee are men that **c tales** to shed blood	7400
38:13 to **c away** silver and gold, to take *away*	5375
Da 11: 8 shall also **c** captives *into* Egypt their gods,	935
Mk 6:55 began to **c about** in beds those that were	4064
11:16 should **c** *any* vessel through the temple.	1308
Lk 10: 4 **C** neither purse, nor scrip, nor shoes:	941
Jn 5:10 it is not lawful for thee to **c** thy bed.	142
21:18 and **c** *thee* whither thou wouldest not.	5342
Ac 5: 9 *are* at the door, and shall **c** thee **out**.	1627
7:43 and I will **c** you **away** beyond Babylon.	3351
1Ti 6: 7 and *it is* certain we can **c** nothing **out**.	1627

CARRYING (8) [CARRY]

1Sa 10: 3 one **c** three kids, and another carrying	5375
10: 3 another **c** three loaves of bread,	5375
10: 3 of bread, and another **c** a bottle of wine:	5375
Ps 78: 9 of Ephraim, *being* armed, *and* **c** bows,	7411
Jer 1: 3 unto the **c away** of Jerusalem **captive** in	1540
Mt 1:17 from David until the **c away** into Babylon	3350
1:17 from the **c away** into Babylon unto Christ	3350
Ac 5:10 and found her dead, and, **c** *her* **forth**,	1627

CARSHENA (1)

Est 1:14 the next unto him *was* **C**, Shethar,	3771

CART (15)

1Sa 6: 7 therefore make a new **c**, and take two	5699
6: 7 tie the kine to the **c**, and bring their	5699
6: 8 ark of the Lord, and lay it upon the **c**;	5699
6:10 tied them to the **c**, and shut up their	5699
6:11 they laid the ark of the Lord upon the **c**,	5699
6:14 the **c** came into the field of Joshua,	5699
6:14 they clave the wood of the **c**, and offered	5699
2Sa 6: 3 they set the ark of God upon a new **c**,	5699
6: 3 the sons of Abinadab, drave the new **c**.	5699
1Ch 13: 7 they carried the ark of God in a new **c** out	5699
13: 7 and Uzza and Ahio drave the **c**.	5699
Isa 5:18 of vanity, and sin as it were with a **c** rope:	5699
28:27 a **c** wheel turned about upon the cummin;	5699
28:28 nor break *it with* the wheel of his **c**,	5699
Am 2:13 as a **c** is pressed *that is* full *of* sheaves.	5699

CARVED (13) [CARVING]

Jdg 18:18 fetched the **c image**, the ephod,	6459
1Ki 6:18 the cedar of the house within *was* **c** with	4734
6:29 he **c** all the walls of the house round	7049
6:29 about *with* **c** figures of cherubims	4734+6603
6:32 he **c** upon them carvings of cherubims	7049
6:35 he **c** *thereon* cherubims and palm trees	7049
6:35 *them* with gold fitted upon the **c work**.	2707
2Ch 33: 7 he set a **c image**, the idol which he had	6459
33:22 for Amon sacrificed unto all the **c images**	6456
34: 3 and the **c images**, and the molten images,	6456
34: 4 and the **c images**, and the molten images,	6456
Ps 74: 6 they break down the **c work** thereof at	6603
Pr 7:16 *with* **c** works, *with* fine linen of Egypt.	2405

CARVING (2) [CARVED, CARVINGS]

Ex 31: 5 of stones, to set *them*, and in **c** of timber,	2799
35:33 of stones, to set *them*, and in **c** of wood,	2799

CARVINGS (1) [CARVING]

1Ki 6:32 he carved upon them **c** of cherubims and	4734

CASE (8) [CASES]

Ex 5:19 see *that* they *were* in evil **c**, after it was	NIH
Dt 19: 4 this *is* the **c** of the slayer, which shall flee	1697
22: 1 shalt **in any c bring** them **again**	7725+7725
24:13 **In any c** thou shalt **deliver** him the pledge **again**	7725+7725

Ps 144:15 Happy *is that* people, that is **in such a c**:	3602
Mt 5:20 ye shall **in no c** enter into the kingdom of	3364
19:10 If the **c** of the man be so with *his* wife, it is	*156*
Jn 5: 6 now a long time *in that* **c**, he saith unto	NIG

CASEMENT (1)

Pr 7: 6 of my house I looked through my **c**,	822

CASES (1) [CASE]

1Co 7:15 or a sister is not under bondage in such **c**	NIG

CASIPHIA (2)

Ezr 8:17 unto Iddo the chief at the place **C**,	3703
8:17 brethren the Nethinims, at the place **C**,	3703

CASLUHIM (2)

Ge 10:14 Pathrusim, and **C**, (out of whom came	3695
1Ch 1:12 Pathrusim, and **C**, (of whom came	3695

CASLUHITES See CASLUHIM

CASSIA (3)

Ex 30:24 of **c** five hundred *shekels*, after the shekel	6916
Ps 45: 8 and aloes, *and* **c**, out of the ivory palaces,	7102
Eze 27:19 bright iron, **c**, and calamus, were in thy	6916

CAST (501) [CASTAWAY, CASTEDST, CASTEST, CASTETH, CASTING, OUTCAST, OUTCASTS]

Ge 21:10 **C out** this bondwoman and her son:	1644
21:15 she **c** the child under one of the shrubs.	7993
31:38 and thy she goats have not **c** their **young**,	7921
31:51 which I have **c** betwixt me and thee;	3384
37:20 and **c** him into some pit, and we will say,	7993
37:22 **c** him into this pit that *is* in the wilderness	7993
37:24 they took him, and **c** him into a pit: and	7993
39: 7 that his master's wife **c** her eyes upon	5375
Ex 1:22 Every son that is born ye shall **c** into	7993
4: 3 said, **C** it on the ground. And he cast it	7993
4: 3 he **c** it on the ground, and it became a	7993
4:25 of her son, and **c** *it* at his feet, and said,	5060
7: 9 **c** *it* before Pharaoh, *and* it shall become a	7993
7:10 Aaron **c down** his rod before Pharaoh,	7993
7:12 For they **c down** every man his rod,	7993
10:19 the locusts, and **c** them into the Red sea;	8628
15: 4 and his host hath he **c** into the sea:	3384
15:25 *which* when he had **c** into the waters,	7993
22:31 in the field; ye shall **c** it to the dogs.	7993
23:26 There shall nothing **c** their **young**, nor be	7921
25:12 thou shalt **c** four rings of gold for it,	3332
26:37 thou shalt **c** five sockets of brass for them.	3332
32:19 he **c** the tables out of his hands,	7993
32:24 I **c** it into the fire, and there came out this	7993
34:24 For I will **c out** the nations before thee,	3423
36:36 and he **c** for them four sockets of silver.	3332
37: 3 he **c** for it four rings of gold, *to be set* by	3332
37:13 he **c** for it four rings of gold, and put	3332
38: 5 **c** four rings for the four ends of the grate	3332
38:27 of the hundred talents of silver were **c**	3332
Lev 1:16 **c** it beside the altar on the east part,	7993
14:40 they shall **c** them into an unclean place	7993
16: 8 Aaron shall **c** lots upon the two goats;	5414
18:24 are defiled which I **c out** before you:	7971
20:23 of the nation, which I **c out** before you:	7971
26:30 your carcases upon the carcases of your	5414
26:44 not **c** them **away**, neither will I abhor	3988
Nu 19: 6 **c** *it* into the midst of the burning of	7993
35:22 have **c** upon him any thing without laying	7993
35:23 **c** *it* upon him, that he die, and *was* not	5307
Dt 6:19 To **c out** all thine enemies from before	1920
7: 1 hath **c out** many nations before thee,	5394
9: 4 God hath **c** them **out** from before thee,	1920
9:17 **c** them out of my two hands,	7993
9:21 I **c** the dust thereof into the brook that	7993
28:40 the oil; for thine olive shall **c** *his fruit*.	5394
29:28 **c** them into another land, as *it is* this day.	7993
Jos 8:29 **c** it at the entering of the gate of the city,	7993
10:11 the Lord **c down** great stones from	7993
10:27 **c** them into the cave wherein they had	7993
13:12 these did Moses smite, and **c** them **out**.	3423
18: 6 that I may **c** lots for you here before	3384
18: 8 that I may here **c** lots for you before	7993
18:10 Joshua **c** lots for them in Shiloh before	7993
Jdg 6:28 altar of Baal was **c down**, and the grove	5422
6:30 because he hath **c down** the altar of Baal,	5422
6:31 because *one* hath **c down** his altar.	5422
8:25 did **c** therein every man the earrings of his	7993
9:53 a certain woman **c** a piece of a millstone	7993
15:17 he **c away** the jawbone out of his hand,	7993
1Sa 14:42 **C** lots between me and Jonathan my son.	5307
18:11 Saul **c** the javelin; for he said, I will smite	2904
20:33 Saul **c** a javelin at him to smite him:	2904
2Sa 1:21 the shield of the mighty is **vilely c away**,	1602
11:21 did not a woman **c** a piece of a millstone	7993
16: 6 **c** stones at David, and at all the servants	5619
16:13 and threw stones at him, and **c** dust.	6080
18:17 **c** him into a great pit in the wood,	7993
20:12 *into* the field, and **c** a cloth upon him,	7993
20:15 they **c up** a bank against the city,	8210
20:22 the son of Bichri, and **c** *it* out to Joab.	7993
1Ki 7:15 For he **c** two pillars *of* brass, of eighteen	6696
7:24 the knops were **c** in two rows, when it	3332
7:24 *were* cast in two rows, when it was **c**.	3333
7:46 the plain of Jordan did the king **c** them,	3332
9: 7 for my name, will I **c out** of my sight;	7971
13:24 his carcase was **c** in the way, and the ass	7993
13:25 saw the carcase **c** in the way, and the lion	7993

1Ki 13:28 went and found his carcase **c** in the way,	7993
14: 9 to anger, and hast **c** me behind thy back:	7993
14:24 Lord **c out** before the children of Israel.	3423
18:42 he **c** himself **down** upon the earth,	1457
19:19 by him, and **c** his mantle upon him,	7993
21:26 whom the Lord **c out** before the children	3423
2Ki 2:16 **c** him upon some mountain, or into some	7993
2:21 **c** the salt **in** there, and said, Thus saith	7993
3:25 *on* every good piece of land **c** every man	7993
4:41 he **c** it into the pot; and he said, Pour out	7993
6: 6 he cut down a stick, and **c** *it* in thither;	7993
7:15 which the Syrians had **c away** in their	7993
9:25 **c** him in the portion of the field of Naboth	7993
9:26 **c** him into the plat *of ground*, according	7993
10:25 the guard and the captains **c** *them* **out**,	7993
13:21 **c** the man into the sepulchre of Elisha:	7993
13:23 neither **c** he them from his presence as	7993
16: 3 whom the Lord **c out** from before	3423
17: 8 whom the Lord **c out** from before	3423
17:20 until *he* had **c** them out of his sight.	7993
19:18 have **c** their gods into the fire: for they	5414
19:32 *with* shield, nor **c** a bank against it.	8210
21: 2 whom the Lord **c out** before the children	3423
23: 6 **c** the powder thereof upon the graves of	7993
23:12 **c** the dust of them into the brook Kidron.	7993
23:27 will **c off** this city Jerusalem which I have	3988
24:20 he had **c** them **out** from his presence,	7993
1Ch 24:31 These likewise **c** lots over against their	5307
25: 8 they **c** lots, ward against *ward*, as well	5307
26:13 they **c** lots, as well the small as the great,	5307
26:14 his son, a wise counseller, they **c** lots;	5307
28: 9 forsake him, he will **c** thee **off** for ever.	2186
2Ch 4: 3 Two rows *of* oxen *were* **c**, when it was	3332
4: 3 rows *of* oxen *were* cast, when it was **c**,	4166
4:17 In the plain of Jordan did the king **c** them,	3332
7:20 will I **c** out of my sight, and will make it	7993
11:14 his sons had **c** them **off** from executing	2186
13: 9 Have ye not **c out** the priests of	5080
20:11 to come to **c** us **out** of thy possession,	1644
24:10 and brought in, and **c** into the chest,	7993
25: 8 God hath power to help, and to **c down**.	3782
25:12 **c** them **down** from the top of the rock,	7993
26:14 and bows, and slings to **c** stones.	NIH
28: 3 had **c out** before the children of Israel.	3423
29:19 king Ahaz in his reign did **c away** in	2186
30:14 and **c** *them* into the brook Kidron.	7993
33: 2 whom the Lord had **c out** before	3423
33:15 in Jerusalem, and **c** *them* out of the city.	7993
Ne 1: 9 though there were of you **c out** unto	5080
6:16 were much **c down** in their own eyes:	5307
9:26 **c** thy law behind their backs, and slew	7993
10:34 the lots *among* the priests, the Levites,	5307
11: 1 the rest of the people also **c** lots, to bring	5307
13: 8 I **c forth** all the household stuff of Tobiah	7993
Est 3: 7 they **c** Pur, that *is*, the lot, before Haman	5307
9:24 had **c** Pur, that *is*, the lot, to consume	5307
Job 8: 4 he have **c** them **away** for their	7971
8:20 God will not **c away** a perfect *man*,	3988
15:33 and shall **c off** her flower as the olive.	7993
18: 7 and his own counsel shall **c** him **down**.	7993
18: 8 For he is **c** into a net by his own feet,	7568
20:15 again: God shall **c** them **out** of his belly.	3423
20:23 shall **c** the fury of his wrath upon him,	7971
22:29 When *men* are **c down**, then thou shalt	8213
27:22 For *God* shall **c** upon him, and not spare:	7993
29:24 light of my countenance they **c** not **down**.	5307
30:19 He hath **c** me into the mire, and I am	3384
39: 3 young ones, they **c out** their sorrows.	7971
40:11 **C abroad** the rage of thy wrath: and	6327
41: 9 shall not one be **c down** even at the sight	2904
Ps 2: 3 and **c away** their cords from us.	7993
5:10 **c** them **out** in the multitude of their	5080
17:13 O Lord, disappoint him, **c** him **down**:	3766
18:42 I did **c** them **out** as the dirt in the streets.	7324
22:10 I was **c** upon thee from the womb: thou	7993
22:18 among them, and **c** lots upon my vesture.	5307
36:12 they are **c down**, and shall not be able to	1760
37:14 **c down** the poor and needy, *and* to slay	5307
37:24 he fall, he shall not be **utterly c down**:	2904
42: 5 Why art thou **c down**, O my soul? and	7817
42: 6 my God, my soul is **c down** within me:	7817
42:11 Why art thou **c down**, O my soul? and	7817
43: 2 why dost thou **c** me **off**? why go I	2186
43: 5 Why art thou **c down**, O my soul? and	7817
43: 5 Why art thou **c down**, O my soul? and	7817
44: 2 didst afflict the people, and **c** them **out**.	7971
44: 9 thou hast **c off**, and put us to shame;	2186
44:23 O Lord? arise, **c** *us* not **off** for ever.	2186
51:11 **C** me not **away** from thy presence;	7993
55: 3 for they **c** iniquity upon me, and in wrath	4131
55:22 **C** thy burden upon the Lord,	7993
56: 7 *thine* anger **c down** the people, O God.	3381
60: 1 O God, thou hast **c** us **off**, thou hast	2186
60: 8 over Edom will I **c out** my shoe:	7993
60:10 not thou, O God, *which* hadst **c** us **off**?	2186
62: 4 They only consult to **c** him **down** from	5080
71: 9 **C** me not **off** in the time of old age;	7993
74: 1 O God, why hast thou **c** us **off** for ever?	2186
74: 7 They have **c** fire into thy sanctuary,	7971
76: 6 and horse *are* **c into** a dead sleep.	7290
77: 7 Will the Lord **c off** for ever? and will he	2186
78:49 **c** upon them the fierceness of his anger,	7971
78:55 He **c out** the heathen also before them,	1644
80: 8 hast **c out** the heathen, and planted it.	1644
89:38 thou hast **c off** and abhorred, thou hast	2186
89:44 and **c** his throne **down** to the ground.	4048

C

Ps	94:14 For the LORD will not **c off** his people,	5203
	102:10 thou hast lifted me up, and **c** me **down**.	7993
	108: 9 over Edom will I **c out** my shoe;	7993
	108:11 Wilt not thou, O God, who hast **c** us **off**?	2186
	140:10 let them be **c** into the fire; into deep pits,	5307
	144: 6 **C forth lightning**, and scatter	1299+1300
Pr	1:14 **C** in thy lot among us; let us all have one	5307
	7:26 For she hath **c down** many wounded:	5307
	16:33 The lot is **c** into the lap; but the whole	2904
	22:10 **C out** the scorner, and contention shall go	1644
Ecc	3: 5 A time to **c away** stones, and a time to	7993
	3: 6 a time to keep, and a time to **c away**;	7993
	11: 1 **C** thy bread upon the waters: for thou	7971
Isa	2:20 In that day a man shall **c** his idols of silver,	7993
	5:24 they have **c away** the law of the LORD of	3988
	6:13 when they **c** their leaves: so the holy seed	7995
	14:19 thou art **c** out of thy grave like an	7993
	16: 2 as a wandering bird **c out** of the nest,	7971
	19: 8 all they that **c** angle into the brooks shall	7993
	25: 7 the face of the covering **c** over all people,	3874
	26:19 herbs, and the earth shall **c out** the dead.	5307
	28: 2 shall **c down** to the earth with the hand.	3240
	28:25 doth he not **c abroad** the fitches,	6327
	28:25 **c** in the principal wheat and the appointed	7760
	30:22 thou shalt **c** them **away** as a menstruous	2219
	31: 7 For in that day every man shall **c away** his	3988
	34: 3 Their slain also shall be **c** out,	7993
	34:17 he hath **c** the lot for them, and his hand	5307
	37:19 have **c** their gods into the fire: for they	5414
	37:33 it with shields, nor **c** a bank against it.	8210
	38:17 thou hast **c** all my sins behind thy back.	7993
	41: 9 I have chosen thee, and not **c** thee **away**.	3988
	57:14 say, **C ye up**, cast ye up, prepare	5549
	57:14 shall say, Cast ye up, **c** ye **up**, prepare	5549
	57:20 whose waters **c up** mire and dirt.	1644
	58: 7 thou bring the poor that are **c out** to thy	4788
	62:10 **c up**, cast up the highway; gather out	5549
	62:10 cast up, **c up** the highway; gather out	5549
	66: 5 that **c** you **out** for my name's sake, said,	5077
Jer	6: 6 and **c** a mount against Jerusalem:	8210
	6:15 that I visit them they shall be **c down**,	3782
	7:15 I will **c** you out of my sight, as I have cast	7993
	7:15 as I have **c out** all your brethren, even	7993
	7:29 O Jerusalem, and **c** it **away**, and take up	7993
	8:12 of their visitation they shall be **c down**,	3782
	9:19 because our dwellings have **c** us **out**.	7993
	14:16 shall be **c** out in the streets of Jerusalem	7993
	15: 1 **c** them **out** of my sight, and let them go	7971
	16:13 Therefore will I **c** you out of this land	2904
	18:15 to walk in paths, in a way not **c up**;	5549
	22: 7 choice cedars, and **c** them into the fire.	5307
	22:19 beyond the gates of Jerusalem.	7993
	22:26 will **c** thee **out**, and thy mother that bare	2904
	22:28 are they **c out**, he and his seed,	2904
	22:28 are **c** into a land which they know not?	7993
	23:39 fathers, and **c** you out of my presence:	NIH
	26:23 **c** his dead body into the graves of	7993
	28:16 I will **c** thee from off the face of the earth:	7971
	31:37 I will also **c off** all the seed of Israel for all	3988
	33:24 hath chosen, he hath even **c** them **off**?	3988
	33:26 will I **c away** the seed of Jacob,	3988
	36:23 **c** it into the fire that was on the hearth,	7993
	36:30 his dead body shall be **c out** in the day to	7993
	38: 6 **c** him into the dungeon of Malchiah the	7993
	38: 9 whom they have **c** into the dungeon;	7993
	38:11 thence old **c clouts** and old rotten rags,	5499
	38:12 Put now these old **c clouts** and rotten	5499
	41: 7 and **c** them into the midst of the pit, he,	NIH
	41: 9 Now the pit wherein Ishmael had **c** all	7993
	41:14 away captive from Mizpah **c about**	5437
	50:26 **c** her **up** as heaps, and destroy her utterly:	5549
	51:34 belly with my delicates, he hath **c** me **out**.	1740
	51:63 to it, and **c** it into the midst of Euphrates:	7993
	52: 3 till he had **c** them **out** from his presence,	7993
La	2: 1 **c down** from heaven unto the earth	7993
	2: 7 The Lord hath **c off** his altar, he hath	2186
	2:10 they have **c up** dust upon their heads;	5927
	3:31 For the Lord will not **c off** for ever:	2186
	3:53 in the dungeon, and **c** a stone upon me.	3034
Eze	4: 2 a fort against it, and **c** a mount against it;	8210
	5: 4 **c** them into the midst of the fire,	7993
	6: 4 I will **c down** your slain men before your	5307
	7:19 They shall **c** their silver in the streets,	7993
	11:16 Although I have **c** them **far off** among	7368
	15: 4 it is **c** into the fire for fuel; the fire	5414
	16: 5 thou wast **c out** in the open field,	7993
	18:31 **C away** from you all your transgressions,	7993
	19:12 was **c down** to the ground, and the east	7993
	20: 7 **C ye away** every man the abominations	7993
	20: 8 they did not every man **c away**	7993
	21:22 gates, to **c** a mount, and to build a fort.	8210
	23:35 **c** me behind thy back, therefore bear thou	7993
	26: 8 **c** a mount against thee, and lift up	8210
	27:30 and shall **c up** dust upon their heads,	5927
	28:16 **c** thee **as profane** out of the mountain	2490
	28:17 I will **c** thee to the ground, I will lay thee	7993
	31:16 when I **c** him **down** to hell with them	3381
	32: 4 I will **c** thee **forth** upon the open field,	2904
	32:18 **c** them **down**, even her, and the	3381
	36: 5 despiteful minds, to **c** it **out** for a prey.	4054
	43:24 the priests shall **c** salt upon them,	7993
Da	3: 6 worshippeth shall the same hour be **c** into	7412
	3:11 that he should be **c** into the midst of a	7412
	3:15 ye shall be **c** the same hour into the midst	7412
	3:20 to **c** them into the burning fiery furnace.	7412

Da	3:21 were **c** into the midst of the burning fiery	7412
	3:24 Did not we **c** three men bound into	7412
	6: 7 O king, he shall be **c** into the den of lions.	7412
	6:12 O king, shall be **c** into the den of lions?	7412
	6:16 and **c** him into the den of lions.	7412
	6:24 they **c** them into the den of lions, them,	7412
	7: 9 I beheld till the thrones were **c down**,	7412
	8: 7 he **c** him **down** to the ground,	7993
	8:10 **c down** some of the host and of the stars	5307
	8:11 the place of his sanctuary was **c down**.	7993
	8:12 and it **c down** the truth to the ground;	7993
	11:12 he shall **c down** many ten thousands:	5307
	11:15 **c up** a mount, and take the most fenced	8210
Hos	8: 3 Israel hath **c off** the thing that is good:	2186
	8: 5 Thy calf, O Samaria, hath **c** thee **off**;	2186
	9:17 My God will **c** them **away**, because	3988
Joel	1: 7 hath made it clean bare, and **c** it **away**;	7993
	3: 3 they have **c** lots for my people;	3032
Am	1:11 did **c off** all pity, and his anger did tear	7843
	4: 3 ye shall **c** them into the palace, saith	7993
	8: 3 they shall **c** them **forth** with silence.	7993
	8: 8 it shall be **c** out and drowned, as by	1644
Ob	1:11 c lots upon Jerusalem, even thou wast as	3032
Jnh	1: 5 **c forth** the wares that were in the ship	2904
	1: 7 one to his fellow, Come, and let us **c** lots,	5307
	1: 7 So they **c** lots, and the lot fell upon Jonah.	5307
	1:12 Take me up, and **c** me **forth** into the sea;	2904
	1:15 up Jonah, and **c** him **forth** into the sea:	2904
	2: 3 For thou hadst **c** me into the deep,	7993
	2: 4 I said, I am **c** out of thy sight; yet I will	1644
Mic	2: 5 thou shalt have none that shall **c**	7993
	2: 9 The women of my people have ye **c out**	1644
	4: 7 her that was **c far off** a strong nation:	1972
	7:19 thou wilt **c** all their sins into the depths of	7993
Na	3: 6 I will **c** abominable filth upon thee,	7993
	3:10 they **c** lots for her honourable men, and	3032
Zep	3:15 judgments, he hath **c** out thine enemy:	6437
Zec	1:21 to **c out** the horns of the Gentiles,	3034
	5: 8 he **c** it into the midst of the ephah;	7993
	5: 8 he **c** the weight of lead upon the mouth	7993
	9: 4 the Lord will **c** her **out**, and he will smite	3423
	10: 6 shall be as though I had not **c** them **off**:	2186
	11:13 LORD said unto me, **C** it unto the potter:	7993
	11:13 **c** them to the potter in the house of	7993
Mal	3:11 **c** her **fruit before the time** in the field,	7921
Mt	3:10 fruit is hewn down, and **c** into the fire.	906
	4: 6 If thou be the Son of God, **c** thyself down:	906
	4:12 had heard that John was **c into prison**,	3860
	5:13 to be **c** out, and to be trodden under foot	906
	5:25 to the officer, and thou be **c** into prison.	906
	5:29 offend thee, pluck it out, and **c** it from	906
	5:29 not that thy whole body should be **c** into	906
	5:30 offend thee, cut it off, and **c** it from thee:	906
	5:30 not that thy whole body should be **c** into	906
	6:30 and to morrow is **c** into the oven,	906
	7: 5 first **c out** the beam out of thine own eye;	1544
	7: 5 thou see clearly to **c out** the mote out	1544
	7: 6 neither **c** ye your pearls before swine,	906
	7:19 fruit is hewn down, and **c** into the fire.	906
	7:22 and in thy name have **c out** devils?	1544
	8:12 shall be **c** into outer darkness:	1544
	8:16 and he **c out** the spirits with his word,	1544
	8:31 besought him, saying, If thou **c** us **out**,	1544
	9:33 And when the devil was **c out**, the dumb	1544
	10: 1 to **c** them **out**, and to heal all manner of	1544
	10: 8 the lepers, raise the dead, **c out** devils:	1544
	12:24 This fellow doth not **c out** devils, but by	1544
	12:26 And if Satan **c out** Satan, he is divided	1544
	12:27 And if I by Beelzebub **c out** devils,	1544
	12:27 by whom do your children **c** them **out**?	1544
	12:28 But if I **c** out devils by the Spirit of God,	1544
	13:42 And shall **c** them into a furnace of fire:	906
	13:47 that was **c** into the sea, and gathered of	906
	13:48 the good into vessels, but **c** the bad away.	906
	13:50 And shall **c** them into the furnace of fire:	906
	15:17 the belly, and is **c out** into the draught?	1544
	15:26 the children's bread, and to **c** it to dogs.	906
	15:30 and **c** them down at Jesus' feet;	4496
	17:19 and said, Why could not we **c** him **out**?	1544
	17:27 **c** a hook, and take up the fish that first	906
	18: 8 cut them off, and **c** them from thee:	906
	18: 8 or two feet to be **c** into everlasting fire.	906
	18: 9 offend thee, pluck it out, and **c** it from	906
	18: 9 than having two eyes to be **c** into hell	906
	18:30 went and **c** him into prison, till he should	906
	21:12 and **c out** all them that sold and bought in	1544
	21:21 removed, and be thou **c** into the sea;	906
	21:39 and **c** him **out** of the vineyard,	1544
	22:13 him away, and **c** him into outer darkness;	1544
	25:30 **c** ye the unprofitable servant into outer	1544
	27: 5 And he **c down** the pieces of silver in	4496
	27:35 and upon my vesture did they **c** lots.	906
	27:44 with him, **c** the same in his **teeth**.	3679
Mk	1:34 of divers diseases, and **c** out many devils;	1544
	1:39 throughout all Galilee, and **c** out devils.	1544
	3:15 to heal sicknesses, and to **c out** devils:	1544
	3:23 in parables, How can Satan **c out** Satan?	1544
	4:26 as if a man should **c** seed into the ground,	906
	6:13 And they **c** out many devils,	1544
	7:26 she besought him that he would **c forth**	1544
	7:27 children's bread, and to **c** it unto the dogs.	906
	9:18 thy disciples that they should **c** him **out**;	1544
	9:22 And ofttimes it hath **c** him into the fire,	906
	9:28 Why could not we **c** him **out**?	1544

Mk	9:42 his neck, and he were **c** into the sea.	906
	9:45 than having two feet to be **c** into hell;	906
	9:47 than having two eyes to be **c** into hell fire:	906
	11: 7 colt to Jesus, and **c** their garments **on** him;	1911
	11:15 and began to **c out** them that sold and	1544
	11:23 removed, and be thou **c** into the sea;	906
	12: 4 at him they **c stones**, and wounded him	3036
	12: 8 killed him, and **c** him **out** of the vineyard.	1544
	12:41 beheld how the people **c** money into	906
	12:41 and many that were rich **c** in much.	906
	12:43 That this poor widow hath **c** more in,	906
	12:43 all they which have **c** into the treasury:	906
	12:44 For all they did **c** in of their abundance;	906
	12:44 she of her want did **c** in all that she had,	906
	14:51 having a linen cloth **c** about his naked	4016
	16: 9 out of whom he had **c** seven devils.	1544
	16:17 In my name shall they **c out** devils;	1544
Lk	1:29 **c** in her **mind** what manner of salutation	1260
	3: 9 fruit is hewn down, and **c** into the fire.	906
	4: 9 Son of God, **c** thyself down from hence:	906
	4:29 that they might **c** him **down headlong**.	2630
	6:22 and **c out** your name as evil,	1544
	6:42 **c out** first the beam out of thine own eye,	1544
	9:25 and lose himself, or be **c away**?	2210
	9:40 And I besought thy disciples to **c** him **out**;	1544
	11:18 ye say that I **c out** devils through	1544
	11:19 And if I by Beelzebub **c out** devils,	1544
	11:19 by whom do your sons **c** them **out**?	1544
	11:20 if I with the finger of God **c out** devils,	1544
	12: 5 after he hath killed hath power to **c**	1685
	12:28 field, and to morrow is **c** into the oven;	906
	12:58 officer, and the officer **c** thee into prison.	906
	13:19 which a man took, and **c** into his garden;	906
	13:32 I **c** out devils, and I do cures to day and	1544
	14:35 nor yet for the dunghill; but men **c** it out.	906
	17: 2 and he **c** into the sea, than that he should	4496
	19:35 and they **c** their garments **upon** the colt,	1977
	19:43 that thine enemies shall **c** a trench **about**	4016
	19:45 and began to **c out** them that sold therein,	1544
	20:12 they wounded him also, and **c** him **out**.	1544
	20:15 So they **c** him **out** of the vineyard,	1544
	21: 3 that this poor widow hath **c** in more than	906
	21: 4 For all these have of their abundance **c** in	906
	21: 4 she of her penury hath **c** in all the living	906
	22:41 withdrawn from them about a stone's **c**,	1000
	23:19 city, and for murder, was **c** into prison.)	906
	23:25 for sedition and murder was **c** into prison,	906
	23:34 And they parted his raiment, and **c** lots.	906
Jn	3:24 For John was not yet **c** into prison.	906
	6:37 that cometh to me I will in no wise **c out**.	1544
	8: 7 among you, let him first **c** a stone at her.	906
	8:59 Then took they up stones to **c** at him: but	906
	9:34 dost thou teach us? And they **c** him **out**.	1544
	9:35 Jesus heard that they had **c** him **out**;	1544
	12:31 shall the prince of this world be **c out**.	1544
	15: 6 he is **c** forth as a branch, and is withered;	906
	15: 6 **c** them into the fire, and they are burned.	906
	19:24 Let us not rent it, but **c** lots for it, whose	2975
	19:24 and for my vesture they did **c** lots.	906
	21: 6 **C** the net on the right side of the ship,	906
	21: 6 They **c** therefore, and now they were not	906
	21: 7 was naked,) and did **c** himself into the sea.	906
Ac	7:19 they **c** out their young children,	1570+4160
	7:21 And when he was **c out**,	1620
	7:58 **c** him **out** of the city, and stoned him:	1544
	12: 8 **C** thy garment **about** thee, and follow me.	4016
	16:23 they **c** them into prison, charging the jailor	906
	16:37 being Romans, and have **c** us into prison;	906
	22:23 **c off** their clothes, and threw dust into	4495
	27:19 And the third day we **c** out with our own	4496
	27:26 Howbeit we must be **c** upon a certain	1601
	27:29 they **c** four anchors out of the stern,	4496
	27:30 under colour as though they would have **c**	1614
	27:38 the ship, and **c** out the wheat into the sea.	1544
	27:43 should **c** themselves first into the sea,	641
Ro	11: 1 I say then, Hath God **c away** his people?	683
	11: 2 God hath not **c away** his people which he	683
	13:12 therefore **c off** the works of darkness,	659
1Co	7:35 not that I may **c** a snare upon you,	1911
2Co	4: 9 not forsaken; **c down**, but not destroyed;	2598
	7: 6 that comforteth those that are **c down**,	5011
Gal	4:30 **C** out the bondwoman and her son: for	1544
1Ti	5:12 because they have **c off** their first faith.	114
Heb	10:35 **C** not **away** therefore your confidence,	577
2Pe	2: 4 but **c** them **down to hell**,	5020
Rev	2:10 the devil shall **c** some of you into prison,	906
	2:14 who taught Balac to **c** a stumblingblock	906
	2:22 I will **c** her into a bed, and them that	906
	4:10 **c** their crowns before the throne,	906
	8: 5 with fire of the altar, and **c** it into the earth:	906
	8: 7 blood, and they were **c** upon the earth:	906
	8: 8 burning with fire was **c** into the sea:	906
	12: 4 stars of heaven, and did **c** them to the earth	906
	12: 9 And the great dragon was **c** out, that old	906
	12: 9 he was **c out** into the earth, and his angels	906
	12: 9 and his angels were **c out** with him.	906
	12:10 for the accuser of our brethren is **c down**,	2598
	12:13 when the dragon saw that he was **c** unto	906
	12:15 the serpent **c** out of his mouth water as	906
	12:16 swallowed up the flood which the dragon **c**	906
	14:19 **c** it into the great winepress of the wrath of	906
	18:19 And they **c** dust on their heads, and cried,	906
	18:21 millstone, **c** it into the sea, saying,	906
	19:20 These both were **c** alive into a lake of fire	906
	20: 3 And **c** him into the bottomless pit, and	906

C

Rev 20:10 the devil that deceived them was **c** into *906*
20:14 and hell were **c** into the lake of fire. *906*
20:15 in the book of life was **c** into the lake of fire. *906*

CASTAWAY (1) [AWAY, CAST]

1Co 9:27 preached to others, I myself should be a **c**. *96*

CASTEDST (1) [CAST]

Ps 73:18 thou **c** them **down** into destruction. *5307*

CASTEST (3) [CAST]

Job 15: 4 thou **c off** fear, and restrainest prayer *6565*
Ps 50:17 and **c** my words behind thee. *7993*
88:14 Lord, why **c** thou **off** my soul? *2186*

CASTETH (16) [CAST]

Job 21:10 their cow calveth, and **c** not **her calf**. *7921*
Ps 147: 6 he **c** the wicked **down** to the ground. *8213*
147:17 he **c forth** his ice like morsels: who can *7993*
Pr 10: 3 he **c away** the substance of the wicked. *1920*
19:15 Slothfulness **c into** a deep sleep; *5307*
21:22 **c down** the strength of the confidence *3381*
26:18 As a mad *man* who **c** firebrands, arrows, *3384*
Isa 40:19 it over with gold, and **c** silver chains. *6884*
Jer 6: 7 As a fountain **c out** her waters, *6979*
6: 7 her waters, so she **c out** her wickedness: *6979*
Mt 9:34 He **c out** the devils through the prince of *1544*
Mk 3:22 by the prince of the devils he **c out** devils *1544*
Lk 11:15 He **c out** devils through Beelzebub *1544*
1Jn 4:18 no fear in love; but perfect love **c** out fear: *906*
3Jn 1:10 that would, and **c** *them* out of the church. *1544*
Rev 6:13 *even* as a fig tree **c** her untimely figs, *906*

CASTING (21) [CAST]

2Sa 8: 2 with a line, **c** them **down** to the ground; *7901*
1Ki 7:37 all of them had one **c**, one measure, *4165*
Ezr 10: 1 **c** himself **down** before the house of God, *5307*
Job 6:21 ye see *my* **c down**, and are afraid. *2866*
Ps 74: 7 they have defiled *by* **c** *down* the dwelling NIH
89:39 thou hast profaned his crown *by* **c** it to NIH
Eze 17:17 by **c up** mounts, and building forts, to cut *8210*
Mic 6:14 thy **c down** *shall* be in the midst of thee; *3445*
Mt 4:18 Andrew his brother, **c** a net into the sea: *906*
27:35 and parted his garments, **c** lots: *906*
Mk 1:16 Andrew his brother **c** a net into the sea: *906*
9:38 we saw one **c out** devils in thy name, *1544*
10:50 **c away** his garment, rose, and came to *577*
15:24 they parted his garments, **c** lots upon them, *906*
Lk 9:49 we saw one **c out** devils in thy name; *1544*
11:14 he was **c out** a devil, and it was dumb. *1544*
21: 1 saw the rich *men* **c** their gifts into *906*
21: 2 And he saw also a certain poor widow **c** in *906*
Ro 11:15 if the **c away** of them *be* the reconciling *580*
2Co 10: 5 **C down** imaginations, and every high *2507*
1Pe 5: 7 **C** all your care upon him; for he careth for *1977*

CASTLE (9) [CASTLES]

1Ch 11: 5 Nevertheless David took the **c** of Zion, *4686*
11: 7 David dwelt in the **c**; therefore they called *4679*
Pr 18:19 *their* contentions *are* like the bars of a **c**. *759*
Ac 21:34 commanded him to be carried into the **c**. *3925*
21:37 And as Paul was to be led into the **c**, *3925*
22:24 commanded him to be brought into the **c**, *3925*
23:10 among them, and to bring *him* into the **c**, *3925*
23:16 he went and entered into the **c**, *3925*
23:32 to go with him, and returned to the **c**: *3925*

CASTLES (6) [CASTLE]

Ge 25:16 names, by their towns, and by their **c**; *2918*
Nu 31:10 dwelt, and all their **goodly c**, with fire. *2918*
1Ch 6:54 places throughout their **c** in their coasts, *2918*
27:25 cities, and in the villages, and in the **c**, *4026*
2Ch 17:12 he built in Judah a, and cities of store. *1003*
27: 4 and in the forests he built **c** and towers. *1003*

CASTOR (1)

Ac 28:11 in the isle, *whose* sign *was* **C and Pollux**. *1359*

CATCH (15) [CATCHETH, CAUGHT]

Ex 22: 6 **c** in thorns, so that the stacks of corn, *4672*
Jdg 21:21 **c** you every man his wife of the daughters *2414*
1Ki 20:33 did hastily **c** *it*: and they said, Thy brother *2480*
2Ki 7:12 shall **c** them alive, and get into the city. *8610*
Ps 10: 9 lieth in wait to **c** the poor: he doth catch *2414*
10: 9 doth **c** the poor, when he draweth him *2414*
35: 8 and let his net that he hath hid **c** himself: *3920*
109:11 Let the extortioner **c** all that he hath; *5367*
Jer 5:26 setteth snares; they set a trap, they **c** men. *3920*
Eze 19: 3 a young lion, and it learned to **c** the prey; *2963*
19: 6 learned to **c** the prey, *and* devoured men. *2963*
Hab 1:15 they **c** them in their net, and gather them *1641*
Mk 12:13 of the Herodians, to **c** him in *his* words. *64*
Lk 5:10 from henceforth thou shalt **c** men. *2221*
11:54 seeking to **c** something out of his mouth, *2340*

CATCHETH (3) [CATCH]

Lev 17:13 which hunteth and **c** *any* beast or fowl *6718*
Mt 13:19 **c away** that which was sown in his heart. *726*
Jn 10:12 and the wolf **c** them, and scattereth *726*

CATERPILLAR (5) [CATERPILLARS]

1Ki 8:37 blasting, mildew, locust, *or* if there be **c**; *2625*
Ps 78:46 He gave also their increase unto the **c**, *2625*
Isa 33: 4 be gathered *like* the gathering of the **c**: *2625*
Joel 1: 4 cankerworm hath left hath the **c** eaten. *2625*
2:25 and the **c**, and the palmerworm, *2625*

CATERPILLARS (4) [CATERPILLAR]

2Ch 6:28 there be blasting, or mildew, locusts, or **c**; *2625*
Ps 105:34 and **c**, and that without number, *3218*
Jer 51:14 Surely I will fill thee *with* men, as *with* **c**; *3218*
51:27 the horses to come up as the rough **c**. *3218*

CATTLE (153)

Ge 1:24 **c**, and creeping thing, and beast of the *929*
1:25 **c** after their kind, and every thing that *929*
1:26 over the **c**, and over all the earth, *929*
2:20 Adam gave names to all **c**, and to the fowl *929*
3:14 thou *art* cursed above all **c**, and above *929*
4:20 as dwell in tents, and *of such as have* **c**. *4735*
6:20 after their kind, and of **c** after their kind, *929*
7:14 the **c** after their kind, and every creeping *929*
7:21 of **c**, and of beast, and of every creeping *929*
7:23 **c**, and the creeping things, and the fowl of *929*
8: 1 and all the **c** that *was* with him in the ark: *929*
8:17 of **c**, and of every creeping thing that *929*
9:10 the **c**, and of every beast of the earth with *929*
13: 2 Abram *was* very rich in **c**, in silver, *4735*
13: 7 strife between the herdmen of Abram's **c** *4735*
13: 7 cattle and the herdmen of Lot's **c**: *4735*
29: 7 neither *is it* time that the **c** should be *4735*
30:29 served thee, and how thy **c** was with me. *4735*
30:32 thence all the speckled and spotted **c**, *7716*
30:32 all the brown **c** among the sheep, *7716*
30:39 brought forth **c** ringstraked, speckled, *6629*
30:40 put them not unto Laban's **c**. *6629*
30:41 whensoever the stronger **c** did conceive, *6629*
30:41 before the eyes of the **c** in the gutters, *6629*
30:42 the **c** were feeble, he put *them* not in: *6629*
30:43 had much **c**, and maidservants, *4735*
31: 8 thy wages; then all the **c** bare speckled: *6629*
31: 8 thy hire; then bare all the **c** ringstraked. *6629*
31: 9 Thus God hath taken away the **c** of your *4735*
31:10 it came to pass at the time that the **c** *6629*
31:10 the rams which leaped upon the **c** *were* *6629*
31:12 all the rams which leap upon the **c** *are* *6629*
31:18 carried away all his **c**, and all his goods *4735*
31:18 which he had gotten, the **c** of his getting, *4735*
31:41 thy two daughters, and six years for thy **c**: *6629*
31:43 **c** *are* my cattle, and all that thou seest *6629*
31:43 cattle *are* my **c**, and all that thou seest *6629*
33:14 according as the **c** that goeth before me *4399*
33:17 him a house, and made booths for his **c**: *4735*
34: 5 now his sons were with his **c** in the field: *4735*
34:23 *Shall* not their **c** and their substance and *4735*
36: 6 his **c**, and all his beasts, and all his *4735*
36: 7 could not bear them because of their **c**. *4735*
46: 6 they took their **c**, and their goods, *4735*
46:32 for their **trade** hath been to feed **c**; *376+4735*
46:34 servants' **trade** hath been about **c** *376+4735*
47: 6 then make them rulers over my **c**. *4735*
47:16 Joseph said, Give your **c**; and I will give *4735*
47:16 I will give you for your **c**, if money fail. *4735*
47:17 they brought their **c** unto Joseph: and *4735*
47:17 for the **c** of the herds, and for the asses: *4735*
47:17 he fed them with bread for all their **c** for *4735*
47:18 is spent; my lord also had our herds of **c**; *929*
Ex 9: 3 the hand of the Lord is upon thy **c** which *4735*
9: 4 the Lord shall sever between the **c** of *4735*
9: 4 the cattle of Israel and the **c** of Egypt: *4735*
9: 6 the morrow, and all the **c** of Egypt died: *4735*
9: 6 of the **c** of the children of Israel died not *4735*
9: 7 was not one of the **c** of the Israelites *4735*
9:19 *and* gather thy **c**, and all that thou hast in *4735*
9:20 servants and his **c** flee into the houses: *4735*
9:21 left his servants and his **c** in the field. *4735*
10:26 Our **c** also shall go with us; there shall not *4735*
12:29 in the dungeon; and all the firstborn of **c**. *929*
12:38 and flocks, and herds, *even* very much **c**. *4735*
17: 3 and our children and our **c** with thirst? *4735*
20:10 nor thy maidservant, nor thy **c**, *929*
34:19 every firstling amongst thy **c**, *whether* ox *4735*
Lev 1: 2 ye shall bring your offering of the **c**, *even* *929*
5: 2 or a carcase of unclean **c**, or the carcase of *929*
19:19 shalt not let thy **c** gender with a diverse *929*
25: 7 for thy **c**, and for the beast that *are* in thy *929*
26:22 destroy your **c**, and make you few in *929*
Nu 3:41 the **c** of the Levites instead of all *929*
3:41 among the **c** of the children of Israel. *929*
3:45 the **c** of the Levites instead of their cattle; *929*
3:45 the cattle of the Levites instead of their **c**; *929*
20: 4 that we and our **c** should die there? *1165*
20:19 I and my **c** drink *of* thy water, then I will *4735*
31: 9 took the spoil of all their **c**, and all their *929*
32: 1 of Gad had a very great multitude of **c**: *4735*
32: 1 behold, the place *was* a place for **c**; *4735*
32: 4 a land for **c**, and thy servants have cattle: *4735*
32: 4 a land for cattle, and thy servants have **c**: *4735*
32:16 We will build sheepfolds here for our **c**, *4735*
32:26 our wives, our flocks, and all our **c**, *929*
35: 3 the suburbs of them shall be for their **c**, *929*
Dt 2:35 the **c** we took for a prey unto ourselves, *929*
3: 7 the **c**, and the spoil of the cities, we took *929*
3:19 wives, and your little ones, and your **c**, *4735*
3:19 (*for* I know that ye have much **c**,) *4735*
5:14 thine ox, nor thine ass, nor any of thy **c**, *929*
7:14 barren among you, or among your **c**. *929*
11:15 I will send grass in thy fields for thy **c**, *929*
13:15 and all that *is* therein, and the **c** thereof, *929*
20:14 and the **c**, and all that is in the city, *929*
28: 4 fruit of thy ground, and the fruit of thy **c**, *929*
28:11 in the fruit of thy **c**, and in the fruit of thy *929*
28:51 he shall eat the fruit of thy **c**, and the fruit *929*
30: 9 in the fruit of thy **c**, and in the fruit of thy *929*
Jos 1:14 Your wives, your little ones, and your **c**, *4735*
8: 2 only the spoil thereof, and the **c** thereof, *929*
8:27 Only the **c** and the spoil of that city Israel *929*
11:14 all the spoil of these cities, and the **c**, *929*
14: 4 to dwell *in*, with their suburbs for their **c** *4735*
21: 2 in, with the suburbs thereof for our **c**. *929*
22: 8 with very much **c**, with silver, *4735*
Jdg 6: 5 For they came up with their **c** and *4735*
18:21 the little ones and the **c** and the carriage *4735*
1Sa 23: 5 brought away their **c**, and smote them *4735*
30:20 *which* they drave before those *other* **c**, *4735*
1Ki 1: 9 oxen and **fat c** by the stone of Zoheleth, *4806*
1:19 and **fat c** and sheep in abundance, *4806*
1:25 hath slain oxen and **fat c** and sheep in *4806*
2Ki 3: 9 host, and for the **c** that followed them. *929*
3:17 *both* ye, and your **c**, and your beasts. *4735*
1Ch 5: 9 their **c** were multiplied in the land of *4735*
5:21 they took away their **c**; *of* their camels *4735*
7:21 they came down to take *away* their **c**. *4735*
2Ch 14:15 They smote also the tents of **c**, *4735*
26:10 he had much **c**, both in the low country, *4735*
35: 8 six hundred *small* **c**, and three hundred NIH
35: 9 passover *offerings* five thousand *small* **c**, NIH
Ne 9:37 over our **c**, at their pleasure, We *are in* *929*
10:36 of our **c**, as it is written in the law, *929*
Job 36:33 the **c** also concerning the vapour. *4735*
Ps 50:10 *is* mine, *and* the **c** upon a thousand hills. *929*
78:48 He gave up their **c** also to the hail, *1165*
104:14 He causeth the grass to grow for the **c**, *929*
107:38 and suffereth not their **c** to decrease. *929*
148:10 Beasts, and all **c**; creeping things, *929*
Ecc 2: 7 great possessions of **great** and small **c** *1241*
Isa 7:25 of oxen, and for the treading of **lesser c**. *7716*
30:23 in that day shall thy **c** feed *in* large *4735*
43:23 Thou hast not brought me the **small** of **c** *7716*
46: 1 were upon the beasts, and upon the **c**: *929*
Jer 9:10 neither can *men* hear the voice of the **c**; *4735*
49:32 booty, and the multitude of their **c** a spoil: *4735*
Eze 34:17 Behold, I judge between **c** and cattle, *7716*
34:17 Behold, I judge between cattle and **c**, *7716*
34:20 will judge between the fat **c** and *7716*
34:20 the fat cattle and between the lean **c**. *7716*
34:22 and I will judge between **c** and cattle. *7716*
34:22 and I will judge between cattle and **c**. *7716*
38:12 have gotten **c** and goods, that dwell *4735*
38:13 and gold, to take *away* **c** and goods, *4735*
Joel 1:18 the herds of **c** are perplexed, because *1241*
Jnh 4:11 and their left hand; and *also* much **c**? *929*
Hag 1:11 **c**, and upon all the labour of the hands. *929*
Zec 2: 4 walls for the multitude of men and **c** *929*
13: 5 man taught me *to keep* **c** from my youth. NIH
Lk 17: 7 having a servant plowing or **feeding c**, *4165*
Jn 4:12 himself, and his children, and his **c**? *2353*

CAUDA See CLAUDA

CAUGHT (37) [CATCH]

Ge 22:13 behind *him* a ram **c** in a thicket by his *270*
39:12 she **c** him by his garment, saying, Lie with *8610*
Ex 4: 4 and **c** it, and it became a rod in his hand: *2388*
Nu 31:32 of the prey which the men of war had **c**, *962*
Jdg 1: 6 **c** him, and cut off his thumbs and his *270*
8:14 **c** a young man of the men of Succoth, *3920*
15: 4 Samson went and **c** three hundred foxes, *3920*
21:23 of them that danced, whom they **c**: *1497*
1Sa 17:35 I **c** *him* by his beard, and smote him, *2388*
2Sa 2:16 they **c** every one his fellow by the head, *2388*
18: 9 his head **c hold** of the oak, and he was *2388*
1Ki 1:50 and **c hold** on the horns of the altar, *2388*
1:51 he hath **c hold** on the horns of the altar, *270*
2:28 and **c hold** on the horns of the altar, *2388*
11:30 Ahijah **c** the new garment that *was* on *8610*
2Ki 4:27 of God to the hill, she **c** him by the feet: *2388*
2Ch 22: 9 they **c** him, (for he *was* hid in Samaria,) *3920*
Pr 7:13 So she **c** him, and kissed him, and *2388*
Ecc 9:12 and as the birds that are **c** in the snare; *270*
Jer 50:24 also **c**, because thou hast striven against *8610*
Mt 14:31 and **c** him, and said unto him, O thou *of* *1949*
21:39 And they **c** him, and cast *him* out of *2983*
Mk 12: 3 And they **c** him, and beat *him*, and sent *2983*
Lk 8:29 For oftentimes it had **c** him: and he was *4884*
Jn 21: 3 and that night they **c** nothing. *4084*
21:10 Bring of the fish which ye have now **c**. *4084*
Ac 6:12 and came upon *him*, and **c** him, *4884*
8:39 the Spirit of the Lord **c away** Philip, that *726*
16:19 they **c** Paul and Silas, and drew *them* into *1949*
19:29 having **c** Gaius and Aristarchus, men of *4884*
26:21 For these causes the Jews **c** me in *4815*
27:15 And when the ship was **c**, and could not *4884*
2Co 12: 2 such a one **c up** to the third heaven. *726*
12: 4 How that he was **c up** into paradise, *726*
12:16 being crafty, I **c** you with guile. *2083*
1Th 4:17 remain shall be **c up** together with them in *726*
Rev 12: 5 her child was **c up** unto God, and *to* his *726*

CAUL (12) [CAULS]

Ex 29:13 the **c** *that is* above the liver, and the two *3508*
29:22 **c** *above* the liver, and the two kidneys, *3508*
Lev 3: 4 the **c** above the liver, with the kidneys, *3508*
3:10 the **c** above the liver, with the kidneys, *3508*
3:15 the **c** above the liver, with the kidneys, *3508*
4: 9 the **c** above the liver, with the kidneys, *3508*
7: 4 the **c** *that is* above the liver, with *3508*

Lev	8:16 **c** *above* the liver, and the two kidneys,	3508
	8:25 **c** *above* the liver, and the two kidneys,	3508
	9:10 the **c** above the liver of the sin offering,	3508
	9:19 the kidneys, and the **c** *above* the liver:	3508
Hos	13: 8 will rent the **c** of their heart, and there	5458

CAULS (1) [CAUL]

Isa	3:18 ornaments *about their feet*, and *their* **c**,	7636

CAUSE (328) [CAUSED, CAUSELESS, CAUSES, CAUSEST, CAUSETH, CAUSEWAY, CAUSING]

Ge	7: 4 will **c** it **to rain** upon the earth forty days	4305
	45: 1 he cried, **C** every man **to go out** from me.	3318
Ex	8: 5 **c** frogs **to come up** upon the land of	5927
	9:16 very deed **for** this **c** have I raised	5668+871.1
	9:18 about *this* time I will **c** it **to rain**	4305
	21:19 **c** *him* **to be thoroughly healed.**	7495+7495
	22: 5 shall **c** a field or vineyard **to be eaten**,	1197
	22: 9 the **c** of both parties shall come before	1697
	23: 2 neither shalt thou speak in a **c** to decline	7379
	23: 3 thou countenance a poor *man* in his **c**.	7379
	23: 6 wrest the judgment of thy poor in his **c**.	7379
	27:20 the light, to **c** the lamp **to burn** always.	5927
Lev	14:41 shall **c** the house **to be scraped** within	7106
	19:29 thy daughter, to **c** her **to be a whore**;	2181
	24: 2 to **c** the lamps **to burn** continually.	5927
	24:19 if a man a blemish in his neighbour;	5414
	25: 9 the trumpet of the jubile **to sound** on	5674
	26:16 consume the eyes, and **c** **sorrow** of heart:	1727
Nu	5:24 he shall **c** the woman **to drink** the bitter	8248
	5:26 afterward shall **c** the woman **to drink**	8248
	16: 5 and will **c** *him* **to come near** unto him:	7126
	16: 5 chosen will he **c** **to come near** unto him.	7126
	16:11 **For which c** *both* thou and all	3651+3807.1
	27: 5 Moses brought their **c** before the LORD.	4941
	27: 7 **c** the inheritance of their father **to pass**	5674
	27: 8 ye shall **c** his inheritance **to pass** unto his	5674
	28: 7 **c** the strong wine **to be poured** unto	5258
	35:30 testify against *any* person to **c** him to die.	NIH
Dt	1:17 the **c** that is too hard for you, bring *it* unto	1697
	1:38 for he shall **c** Israel **to inherit** it.	5157
	3:28 he shall **c** them **to inherit** the land which	5157
	12:11 shall choose to **c** his name **to dwell** there;	7931
	17:16 nor **c** the people **to return** to Egypt,	7725
	24: 4 thou shalt not **c** the land **to sin**, which	2398
	25: 2 that the judge shall **c** him **to lie down**,	5307
	28: 7 The LORD shall **c** thine enemies that rise	5414
	28:25 The LORD shall **c** thee **to be** smitten	5414
	31: 7 and thou shalt **c** them **to inherit** it.	5157
Jos	5: 4 this *is* the **c** why Joshua did circumcise:	1697
	20: 4 shall declare his **c** in the ears of the elders	1697
	23: 7 nor **c** **to swear** by them, neither serve	7650
1Sa	17:29 What have I now done? *Is there* not a **c**?	1697
	19: 5 blood, to slay David **without a c**?	2600
	24:15 plead my **c**, and deliver me out of thine	7379
	25:39 that hath pleaded the **c** of my reproach	7379
	28: 9 thou a snare for my life, to **c** me to die?	4191
2Sa	3:35 all the people came to **c** David **to eat**	1262
	13:13 I, whither shall I **c** my shame **to go**?	1980
	13:16 she said unto him, *There* is no **c**: this evil	182
	15: 4 hath *any* suit or **c** might come unto me,	4941
1Ki	1:33 **c** Solomon my son **to ride** upon mine	7392
	5: 9 will **c** them **to be discharged** there,	5310
	8:31 oath be laid upon him to **c** him **to swear**,	422
	8:45 their supplication, and maintain their **c**.	4941
	8:49 thy dwelling place, and maintain their **c**,	4941
	8:59 that he maintain the **c** of his servant,	4941
	8:59 the **c** of his people Israel at all times,	4941
	11:27 *this was* the **c** that he lift up *his* hand	1697
	12:15 for the **c** was from the LORD, that *he*	5438
2Ki	7: 7 will **c** the **c** by the sword in his	5307
1Ch	21: 3 why will he be a **c** **of trespass** to Israel?	819
2Ch	6:35 their supplication, and maintain their **c**.	4941
	6:39 maintain their **c**, and forgive thy people	4941
	10:15 for the **c** was of God, that the LORD	5252
	19:10 what **c** soever shall come to you of your	7379
	32:20 for this **c** Hezekiah the king, and the	NIH
Ezr	4:15 for which **c** was this city destroyed.	NIH
	4:21 commandment to **c** these men **to cease**,	989
	5: 5 that they could not **c** them **to cease**, till	989
Ne	4:11 and slay them, and **c** the work **to cease**.	7673
	6: 6 **for which c** thou buildest the wall,	3651+5921
	13:26 even him did outlandish women **c** **to sin**.	2398
Est	3:13 to kill, and to **c** **to perish**, all Jews,	6
	5: 5 the king said, **C** Haman **to make haste**,	4116
	8:11 to destroy, to slay, and to **c** **to perish**,	6
Job	2: 3 against him, to destroy him **without c**.	2600
	5: 8 and unto God would I commit my **c**:	1700
	6:24 **c** me **to understand** wherein I have erred.	995
	9:17 and multiplieth my wounds **without c**.	2600
	13:18 Behold now, I have ordered *my* **c**; I know	4941
	20: 2 do my thoughts **c** me **to answer**,	7725
	23: 4 I would order *my* **c** before him, and fill	4941
	24: 7 **c** the naked **to lodge** without clothing,	3885
	24:10 They **c** *him* **to go** naked without clothing,	1980
	29:16 the **c** *which* I knew not I searched out.	7379
	31:13 If I did despise the **c** of my manservant or	4941
	34:11 every man to **c** **to find** according to *his* ways	4672
	34:28 So that *they* **c** the cry of the poor **to come**	935
	38:26 **c** it **to rain** on the earth, *where* no man	4305
	38:27 **c** the bud of the tender herb **to spring forth**?	6779
Ps	7: 4 have delivered him that **without c** is mine	7387
	9: 4 thou hast maintained my right and my **c**;	1779

Ps	10:17 their heart, thou wilt **c** thine ear **to hear**:	7181
	25: 3 be ashamed which transgress **without c**.	7387
	35: 1 Plead *my* **c**, O LORD, with them that	NIH
	35: 7 For **without** **c** have they hid for me their	2600
	35: 7 *which* **without** **c** they have digged for my	2600
	35:19 *with* the eye that hate me **without a c**.	2600
	35:23 *even* unto my **c**, my God and my Lord.	7379
	35:27 and be glad, that favour my **righteous c**:	6664
	43: 1 and plead my **c** against an ungodly nation:	7379
	67: 1 *and* **c** his face **to shine** upon us; Selah.	215
	69: 4 They that hate me **without a c** are moe	2600
	71: 2 in thy righteousness, and **c** me **to escape**:	6403
	74:22 Arise, O God, plead thine own **c**:	7379
	76: 8 Thou didst **c** judgment **to be heard** from	8085
	80: 3 us again, O God, and **c** thy face **to shine**;	215
	80: 7 O God *of* hosts, and **c** thy face **to shine**;	215
	80: 9 didst **c** it **to take deep root**,	8327+8328
	80:19 O LORD God *of* hosts, **c** thy face **to shine**;	215
	85: 4 and **c** thine anger towards us **to cease**.	6565
	109: 3 and fought against me **without a c**.	2600
	119:78 dealt perversely with me **without a c**:	8267
	119:154 Plead my **c**, and deliver me: quicken me	7379
	119:161 Princes have persecuted me **without a c**:	2600
	140:12 I know that the LORD will maintain the **c**	1779
	143: 8 **C** me **to hear** thy lovingkindness in	8085
	143: 8 **c** me **to know** the way wherein I should	3045
Pr	1:11 us lurk privily for the innocent **without c**:	2600
	3:30 Strive not with a man **without c**, if he	2600
	4:16 is taken away, unless they **c** *some* **to fall**.	3782
	8:21 *I* may **c** those that love me **to inherit**	5157
	18:17 He that is first in his own **c** *seemeth* just;	7379
	22:23 For the LORD will plead their **c**,	7379
	23:11 mighty; he shall plead their **c** with thee.	7379
	23:29 who hath wounds **without c**? who hath	2600
	24:28 witness against thy neighbour **without c**;	2600
	25: 9 Debate thy **c** with thy neighbour *himself*;	7379
	29: 7 righteous considereth the **c** of the poor:	1779
	31: 8 Open thy mouth for the dumb in the **c** of	1779
	31: 9 and **plead the c** of the poor and needy.	1777
Ecc	2:20 **c** my heart **to despair** of all the labour	2976
	5: 6 Suffer not thy mouth to **c** thy flesh **to sin**;	2398
	7:10 What is *the* **c** that the former days were	NIH
	10: 1 **c** the ointment of the apothecary **to send forth**	5042
SS	8: 2 I would **c** thee **to drink** of spiced wine,	8248
	8:13 hearken to thy voice: **c** me **to hear** *it*.	8085
Isa	1:23 neither doth the **c** of the widow come	7379
	3:12 they which lead thee **c** thee **to err**,	8582
	9:16 the leaders of this people **c** *them* **to err**;	8582
	10:30 **c** *it* **to be heard** unto Laish, O poor	7181
	13:10 the moon shall not **c** her light **to shine**.	5050
	13:11 **c** the arrogancy of the proud **to cease**,	7673
	27: 6 **c** them that come of Jacob **to take root**:	8327
	28:12 *wherewith* ye may **c** the weary **to rest**;	5117
	30:11 **c** the Holy One of Israel **to cease** from	7673
	30:30 shall **c** his glorious voice **to be heard**,	8085
	32: 6 he will **c** the drink of the thirsty **to fail**.	2637
	37: 7 I will **c** him **to fall** by the sword in his	5307
	41:21 Produce your **c**, saith the LORD;	7379
	42: 2 nor **c** his voice **to be heard** in the street.	8085
	49: 8 to **c** **to inherit** the desolate heritages;	5157
	51:22 God that **pleadeth the c** of his people,	7378
	52: 4 Assyrian oppressed them **without c**.	657+871.1
	58:14 I will **c** thee **to ride** upon the high places	7392
	61:11 righteousness and praise to **c** **to spring forth**	6779
	66: 9 to the birth, and not **c** **to bring forth**?	3205
	66: 9 shall I **c** **to bring forth**, and shut	3205
Jer	3:12 I will not **c** mine anger **to fall** upon you:	5307
	5:28 they judge not the **c**, the cause of	1779
	5:28 the **c** of the fatherless, yet they prosper;	1779
	7: 3 and I will **c** you **to dwell** in this place.	7931
	7: 7 will I **c** you **to dwell** in this place,	7931
	7:34 will I **c** **to cease** from the cities of Judah,	7673
	11:20 for unto thee have I revealed my **c**.	7379
	13:16 before he **c** **darkness**, and before your	2821
	14:22 vanities of the Gentiles that can **c** **rain**?	1652
	15: 4 I will **c** them **to be** removed into all	5414
	15:11 verily I will **c** the enemy **to entreat** thee	6293
	16: 9 I will **c** **to cease** out of this place in your	7673
	16:21 I *will* this once **c** them **to know**,	3045
	16:21 I will **c** them **to know** mine hand and my	3045
	17: 4 I will **c** thee **to serve** thine enemies in	5647
	18: 2 and there I will **c** thee **to hear** my words.	8085
	19: 7 I will **c** them **to fall** by the sword before	5307
	19: 9 I will **c** them **to eat** the flesh of their sons	398
	20:12 for unto thee have I opened my **c**.	7379
	22:16 He judged the **c** of the poor and needy;	1779
	23:27 Which think to **c** my people **to forget** my	7911
	23:32 **c** my people **to err** by their lies,	8582
	25:15 **c** all the nations, to whom I send thee, **to drink**	8248
	29: 8 your dreams which ye **c** **to be dreamed**.	2492
	30: 3 I will **c** them **to return** to the land that I	7725
	30:13 *There* is none to plead thy **c**, that thou	1779
	30:21 I will **c** him **to draw near**, and he shall	7126
	31: 2 *even* Israel when *I* went to **c** him **to rest**.	7280
	31: 9 I will **c** them **to walk** by the rivers of	1980
	32:35 **c** their sons and their daughters **to pass through**	5674
	32:35 do this abomination, to **c** Judah **to sin**.	2398
	32:37 and I will **c** them **to dwell** safely;	3427
	32:44 for I will **c** their captivity **to return**,	7725
	33: 7 **c** the captivity of Judah and the captivity of Israel **to return**,	7725
	33:11 For I will **c** **to return** the captivity of	7725

Jer	33:15 **c** the Branch of righteousness **to grow up**	6779
	33:26 for I will **c** their captivity **to return**,	7725
	34:22 and **c** them **to return** to this city;	7725
	36:29 shall **c** **to cease** from thence man and	7673
	37:20 thou **c** me not **to return** *to* the house of	7725
	38:23 shalt **c** this city **to be burnt** with fire.	8313
	38:26 that *he* would not **c** me **to return** to	7725
	42:12 and **c** you **to return** to your own land.	7725
	48:12 shall **c** him **to wander**, and shall empty	6808
	48:35 Moreover will I **c** **to cease** in Moab,	7673
	49: 2 I will **c** an alarm of war **to be heard** in	8085
	49:37 For I will **c** Elam **to be dismayed** before	2865
	50: 9 **c** **to come up** against Babylon an	5927
	50:34 shall throughly plead their **c**, that he may	7379
	51:27 **c** the horses **to come up** as the rough	5927
	51:36 I *will* plead thy **c**, and take vengeance for	7379
La	3:32 though he **c** **grief**, yet will he have	3013
	3:36 To subvert a man in his **c**, the Lord	7379
	3:52 chased me sore, like a bird, **without c**.	2600
	3:59 hast seen my wrong: judge thou my **c**.	4941
Eze	3: 3 **c** thy belly **to eat**, and fill thy bowels with	398
	5: 1 **c** *it* **to pass** upon thine head and upon thy	5674
	5:13 I will **c** my fury **to rest** upon them,	5117
	9: 1 **C** them that have charge over the city **to draw near**,	7126
	14:15 If I **c** noisome beasts **to pass** through	5674
	14:23 done **without c** all that I have done in it,	2600
	16: 2 **c** Jerusalem **to know** her abominations,	3045
	16:21 them to **c** them **to pass** through	5674
	16:41 I will **c** thee **to cease** from playing	7673
	20: 4 wilt thou judge *them*? **c** them **to know**	3045
	20:37 I will **c** you **to pass** under the rod,	5674
	21:17 together, and I will **c** my fury **to rest**:	5117
	21:30 Shall I **c** *it* **to return** into his sheath?	7725
	23:48 Thus will I **c** lewdness **to cease** out of	7673
	24: 8 That *it* might **c** fury **to come up** to take	5927
	24:26 to **c** *thee* **to hear** *it* with *thine* ears?	2045
	25: 7 I will **c** thee **to perish** out of the countries:	6
	26: 3 will **c** many nations **to come up** against	5927
	26:13 I will **c** the noise of thy songs **to cease**;	7673
	26:17 which **c** their terror *to be* on all that haunt	5414
	27:30 **c** their voice **to be heard** against thee,	8085
	29: 4 I will **c** the fish of thy rivers **to stick** unto	1692
	29:14 will **c** them **to return** *into* the land of	7725
	29:21 **c** the horn of the house of Israel **to bud forth**,	6779
	30:13 will **c** *their* images **to cease** out of Noph;	7673
	30:22 I will **c** the sword **to fall** out of his hand.	5307
	32: 4 **c** all the fowls of the heaven **to remain**	7931
	32:12 the mighty will I **c** thy multitude **to fall**,	5307
	32:14 their rivers **to run** like oil, saith the Lord	1980
	34:10 **c** them **to cease** from feeding the flock;	7673
	34:15 my flock, and I will **c** them **to lie down**,	7257
	34:25 will **c** the evil beasts **to cease** out of	7673
	34:26 I will **c** the shower **to come down** in his	3381
	36:12 Yea, I will **c** men **to walk** upon you,	1980
	36:15 Neither will I **c** *men* **to hear** in thee	8085
	36:15 neither shalt thou **c** thy nations **to fall** any	3782
	36:27 **c** you to walk in my statutes, and ye shall	6213
	36:33 I will also **c** *you* **to dwell** in the cities,	3427
	37: 5 I *will* **c** breath **to enter** into you, and ye	935
	37:12 **c** you **to come up** out of your graves,	5927
	39: 2 **c** thee **to come up** from the north parts,	5927
	39: 3 will **c** thine arrows **to fall** out of thy right	5307
	44:23 will **c** them **to discern** between the unclean	3045
	44:30 that he may **c** the blessing **to rest** in thine	5117
Da	2:12 For the king was	1836+3606+6903
	8:25 he shall **c** craft **to prosper** in his hand;	6743
	9:17 **c** thy face **to shine** upon thy sanctuary	215
	9:27 **c** the sacrifice and the oblation **to cease**,	7673
	11:18 **c** the reproach offered by him **to cease**;	7673
	11:18 reproach he shall **c** *it* **to turn** upon him.	7725
	11:39 he shall **c** them **to rule over** many,	4910
Hos	1: 4 will **c** **to cease** the kingdom of the house	7673
	2:11 also **c** all her mirth **to cease**, her feast	7673
Joel	2:23 he will **c** **to come down** for you the rain,	3381
	3:11 thither **c** thy mighty ones **to come down**,	5181
Am	5:27 will I **c** you **to go into captivity**	1540
	6: 3 and **c** the seat of violence **to come near**;	5066
	8: 9 that I will **c** the sun **to go down** at noon,	935
Jnh	1: 7 we may know for whose **c** this	7945+871.1
	1: 8 for whose **c** this evil *is* upon us;	834+871.1
Mic	7: 9 until he plead my **c**, and execute	7379
Hab	1: 3 iniquity, and **c** *me* **to behold** grievance?	5027
Zec	8:12 **c** the remnant of this people **to possess** all	5157
	13: 2 **c** the prophets and the unclean spirit **to pass**	5674
Mt	5:22 **without a c** shall be in danger of	1500
	5:32 saving for the **c** of fornication, causeth her	3056
	10:21 parents, and **c** them to be put to death.	NIG
	19: 3 a man to put away his wife for every **c**?	156
	19: 5 **For this c** shall a man leave father	1752+3778
Mk	10: 7 **For this c** shall a man leave his	1752+3778
	13:12 and shall **c** them to be put to death.	NIG
Lk	8:47 people for what **c** she had touched him,	156
	21:16 of you shall they **c** to be put to death.	NIG
	23:22 I have found no **c** of death in him: I will	158
Jn	12:18 For this **c** the people also met him,	1223+3778
	12:27 **for this c** came I unto this hour.	1223+3778
	15:25 in their law, They hated me **without a c**.	1432
	18:37 **for this c** came I into the world,	1519+3778
Ac	10:21 what *is* the **c** wherefore ye are come?	156
	13:28 though they found no **c** of death in *him*,	156
	19:40 there being no **c** whereby we may give an	158
	23:28 And when I would have known the **c**	156

C

Ac	25:14 Festus declared Paul's **c** unto the king,	2596
	28:18 because there was no **c** of death in me.	156
	28:20 For this **c** therefore have I called for you,	156
Ro	1:26 For this **c** God gave them up unto	1223+3778
	13: 6 For **for this c** pay you tribute also:	1223+3778
	15: 9 **For this c** I will confess to thee	1223+3778
	15:22 For **which c** also I have been much	1352
	16:17 mark them which **c** divisions and offences	4160
1Co	4:17 **For this c** have I sent unto you	1223+3778
	11:10 **For this c** ought the woman to have	1223+3778
	11:30 **For this c** many are weak and	1223+3778
2Co	4:16 **For which c** we faint not; but though our	1352
	5:13 or whether we be sober, *it is* for your **c.**	NIG
	7:12 *I did it* not for his **c** that had done	1752
	7:12 nor **for** his **c** that suffered wrong,	1752
Eph	3: 1 **For this c** I Paul, the prisoner of Jesus	5484
	3:14 **For this c** I bow my knees unto the Father	5484
	5:31 **For this c** shall a man leave his father and	473
Php	2:18 For the same **c** also do ye joy,	NIG
Col	1: 9 **For this c** we also, since the day	1223+3778
	4:16 **c** that it be read also in the church of	4160
1Th	2:13 **For this c** also thank we God	1223+3778
	3: 5 **For this c,** when I could no longer	1223+3778
2Th	2:11 And **for this c** God shall send them	1223+3778
1Ti	1:16 Howbeit **for this c** I obtained mercy,	1223+3778
2Ti	1:12 For the **which c** I also suffer these *things:*	156
Tit	1: 5 **For this c** left I thee in Crete, that thou	5484
Heb	2:11 for which **c** he is not ashamed to call them	156
	9:15 And **for this c** he is the mediator of	1223+3778
1Pe	4: 6 For **for this c** was the gospel	1519+3778
Rev	12:15 that he might **c** her to be carried away of	4160
	13:15 **c** that as many as would not worship	4160

CAUSED (94) [CAUSE]

Ge	2: 5 for the LORD God had not **c** it to rain	4305
	2:21 the LORD God **c** a deep sleep to fall upon	5307
	20:13 when God **c** me to **wander** from my	8582
	41:52 For God hath **c** me to be fruitful in	6509
Ex	14:21 the LORD **c** the sea to go *back* by a strong	1980
	36: 6 they **c** it to be proclaimed	5674+6963
Lev	24:20 as he hath **c** a blemish in a man, so shall	5414
Nu	31:16 Behold, these **c** the children of Israel,	1961
Dt	34: 4 I have **c** thee to **see** *it* with thine eyes,	7200
Jdg	16:19 she **c** *him* to **shave off** the seven locks of	1548
1Sa	10:20 **c** all the tribes of Israel to **come near**,	7126
	10:21 **c** the tribe of Benjamin to **come near** by	7126
	20:17 Jonathan **c** David to swear **again,** because	3254
2Sa	7:11 **c** thee to **rest** from all thine enemies.	5117
1Ki	1:38 **c** Solomon to **ride** upon king David's	7392
	1:44 they have **c** him to **ride** upon the king's	7392
	2:19 **c** a seat to be set for the king's mother;	7760
	20:33 he **c** him to **come up** into the chariot.	5927
2Ki	17:17 **c** their sons and their daughters to **pass**	5674
2Ch	8: 2 and **c** the children of Israel to **dwell** there.	3427
	13:13 an ambushment to **come about**	5437
	21:11 **c** the inhabitants of Jerusalem	
	to **commit fornication**,	2181
	33: 6 he **c** his children to **pass** through the fire	5674
	34:32 **c** all that were present in Jerusalem and	
	Benjamin to **stand**	5975
Ezr	6:12 God that hath **c** his name to **dwell** there	7932
Ne	8: 7 **c** the people to **understand** the law:	995
	8: 8 and **c** *them* to **understand** the reading.	995
Est	5:14 and he **c** the gallows to be made.	6213
Job	29:13 and I **c** the widow's heart to **sing for joy.**	7442
	31:16 or have **c** the eyes of the widow to **fail;**	3615
	31:39 the owners thereof to **lose** their life:	5301
	37:15 and **c** the light of his cloud to **shine?**	3313
	38:12 *and* **c** the dayspring to **know** his place;	3045
Ps	66:12 Thou hast **c** men to **ride** over our heads;	7392
	78:13 the sea, and **c** them to **pass through;**	5674
	78:16 and **c** waters to **run down** like rivers.	3381
	78:26 He **c** an east wind to **blow** in the heaven:	5265
	119:49 upon which thou hast **c** me to **hope.**	3176
Pr	7:21 her much fair speech she **c** him to **yield,**	5186
Isa	19:14 they have **c** Egypt to **err** in every work	8582
	43:23 have not **c** thee to **serve** with an offering,	5647
	48:21 he **c** the waters to **flow** out of the rock for	5140
	63:14 the Spirit of the LORD **c** him to **rest:**	5117
Jer	12:14 I have **c** my people Israel to **inherit,**	5157
	13:11 I to **cleave** unto me the whole house	1692
	15: 8 I have **c** *him* to **fall** upon it suddenly,	5307
	18:15 have **c** them to **stumble** in their ways	3782
	23:13 in Baal, and **c** my people Israel to **err.**	8582
	23:22 had **c** my people to **hear** my words, then	8085
	29: 4 whom I have **c** to be **carried away** from	1540
	29: 7 have **c** you to be **carried away captives,**	1540
	29:14 **c** you to be **carried away captive.**	1540
	29:31 not, and he **c** you to **trust** in a lie:	982
	32:23 hast **c** all this evil to **come upon** them:	7122
	34:11 **c** the servants and the handmaids, whom	
	they had let go free, to **return,**	7725
	34:16 **c** every man his servant, . . . to **return,**	7725
	48: 4 her little ones have **c** a cry to be **heard.**	8085
	48:33 have **c** wine to **fail** from the wine presses	7673
	50: 6 their shepherds have **c** them to **go astray,**	8582
	51:49 Babylon *hath* **c** the slain of Israel to fall,	NIH
La	2: 6 **c** the solemn feasts and sabbaths	
	to be forgotten	7911
	2:17 hath **c** *thine* enemy to **rejoice** over thee,	8055
	3:13 hath **c** the arrows of his quiver to **enter**	935
Eze	3: 2 my mouth, and he **c** me to **eat** that roll.	398
	16: 7 I have **c** thee to **multiply** as the bud of	5414
	20:10 Wherefore I **c** them to **go forth** out of	3318
	20:26 in that they **c** to **pass through** *the fire* all	5674

Eze	22: 4 thou hast **c** thy days **to draw near,**	7126
	23:37 **c** their sons, whom they bare unto me,	
	to pass for them **through**	5674
	24:13 till I have **c** my fury **to rest** upon thee.	5117
	29:18 **c** his army **to serve** a great service against	5647
	31:15 went down to the grave I **c a mourning:**	56
	31:15 I **c** Lebanon **to mourn** for him, and all	6937
	32:23 which **c** terror in the land of the living.	5414
	32:24 their terror in the land of the living;	5414
	32:25 though their terror was **c** in the land of	5414
	32:26 though they **c** their terror in the land of	5414
	32:32 For I have **c** my terror in the land of	5414
	37: 2 And **c** me **to pass** by them round about:	5674
	39:28 which **c** them **to be led into captivity**	1540
	44:12 **c** the house of Israel **to fall** into iniquity;	4383
	46:21 **c** me **to pass** by the four corners of	5674
	47: 6 **c** me **to return** to the brink of the river.	7725
Da	9:21 at the beginning, being **c to fly** swiftly,	3286
Hos	4:12 spirit of whoredoms hath **c** *them* **to err,**	8582
Am	2: 4 and their lies **c** them **to err,**	8582
	4: 7 I **c** it to **rain** upon one city, and caused it	4305
	4: 7 and **c** it not to **rain** upon another city:	4305
Jnh	3: 7 he **c** it **to be proclaimed** and	2199
Zec	3: 4 I have **c** thine iniquity **to pass** from thee,	5674
Mal	2: 8 ye have **c** many to **stumble** at the law;	3782
Jn	11:37 have **c** that even this *man* should not	4160
Ac	15: 3 and they **c** great joy unto all the brethren.	4160
2Co	2: 5 if any have **c** grief, he hath not grieved	3076

CAUSELESS (2) [CAUSE]

1Sa	25:31 either that thou hast shed blood **c,**	2600
Pr	26: 2 by flying, so the curse **c** shall not come.	2600

CAUSES (7) [CAUSE]

Ex	18:19 that thou mayest bring the **c** unto God:	1697
	18:26 the hard **c** they brought unto Moses,	1697
Dt	1:16 Hear *the* **c** between your brethren,	NIH
Jer	3: 8 for all the **c** whereby backsliding Israel	182
La	2:14 thee false burdens and **c** of banishment.	4065
	3:58 Lord, thou hast pleaded the **c** of my soul;	7379
Ac	26:21 **For** these **c** the Jews caught me in	1752

CAUSEST (2) [CAUSE]

Job	30:22 thou **c** me **to ride** *upon it,* and	7392
Ps	65: 4 **c** **to approach** *unto thee,* that he may	7126

CAUSETH (32) [CAUSE]

Nu	5:18 his hand the bitter water that **c** the **curse:**	779
	5:19 from this bitter water that **c** **the curse:**	779
	5:22 this water that **c** **the curse** shall go into	779
	5:24 to drink the bitter water that **c** **the curse:**	779
	5:24 the water that **c** **the curse** shall enter into	779
	5:27 that the water that **c** **the curse** shall enter	779
Job	12:24 **c** them **to wander** in a wilderness *where*	8582
	20: 3 the spirit of my understanding **c** me to	NIH
	37:13 He **c** it **to come,** whether for correction,	4672
Ps	104:14 He **c** the grass **to grow** for the cattle,	6779
	107:40 **c** them **to wander** in the wilderness,	8582
	135: 7 **c** the vapours **to ascend** from the ends	5927
	147:18 he **c** his wind **to blow,** *and* the waters	5380
Pr	10: 5 sleepeth in harvest *is* a son that **c** shame.	954
	10:10 He that winketh with the eye **c** sorrow:	5414
	14:35 but his wrath is *against* him that **c** shame.	954
	17: 2 shall have rule over a son that **c** shame,	954
	18:18 The lot **c** contentions **to cease,**	7673
	19:26 a son that **c** shame, and bringeth reproach.	954
	19:27 to hear the instruction that **c** to **err**	NIH
	28:10 Whoso **c** the righteous **to go astray** in an	7686
Isa	61:11 **c** the things that are sown in it	
	to spring forth;	6779
	64: 2 fire burneth, the fire **c** the waters **to boil,**	1158
Jer	10:13 he **c** the vapours **to ascend** from the ends	5927
	51:16 he **c** the vapours **to ascend** from the ends	5927
Eze	26: 3 as the sea **c** his waves **to come up.**	5927
	44:18 *themselves* with any thing that **c** sweat.	871.1
Mt	5:32 of fornication, **c** her to commit adultery:	4160
2Co	2:14 which always **c** us **to triumph** in Christ,	2358
	9:11 which **c** through us thanksgiving to God.	2716
Rev	13:12 and **c** the earth and them which dwell	4160
	13:16 And he **c** all, *both* small and great, rich	4160

CAUSEWAY (2) [CAUSE]

1Ch	26:16 by the **c** of the going up, ward against	4546
	26:18 four at the **c,** *and* two at Parbar.	4546

CAUSING (4) [CAUSE]

SS	7: 9 **c** the lips of *those that are* asleep	
	to speak.	1680
Isa	30:28 in the jaws of the people, **c** *them* **to err.**	8582
Jer	29:10 in **c** you **to return** to this place.	7725
	33:12 of shepherds **c** *their* flocks **to lie down.**	7257

CAVE (33) [CAVE'S, CAVES]

Ge	19:30 he dwelt in a **c,** he and his two daughters.	4631
	23: 9 That he may give me the **c** of Machpelah,	4631
	23:11 and the **c** that *is* therein, I give it thee;	4631
	23:17 the **c** which *was* therein, and all the trees	4631
	23:19 Abraham buried Sarah his wife in the **c** of	4631
	23:20 the field, and the **c** that *is* therein, were	4631
	25: 9 buried him in the **c** of Machpelah,	4631
	49:29 bury me with my fathers in the **c** that *is*	4631
	49:30 In the **c** that *is* in the field of Machpelah,	4631
	49:32 of the **c** that *is* therein *was* from	4631
	50:13 buried him in the **c** of the field of	4631
Jos	10:16 and hid themselves in a **c** at Makkedah.	4631

Jos	10:17 The five kings are found hid in a **c** at	4631
	10:18 Roll great stones upon the mouth of the **c,**	4631
	10:22 Open the mouth of the **c,** and bring out	4631
	10:22 out those five kings unto me out of the **c.**	4631
	10:23 those five kings unto him out of the **c,**	4631
	10:27 cast them into the **c** wherein they had	4631
1Sa	22: 1 and escaped to the **c** Adullam:	4631
	24: 3 sheepcotes by the way, where *was* a **c;**	4631
	24: 3 his men remained in the sides of the **c.**	4631
	24: 7 Saul rose up out of the **c,** and went on *his*	4631
	24: 8 went out of the **c,** and cried after Saul,	4631
	24:10 thee to day into mine hand in the **c:**	4631
2Sa	23:13 in the harvest time unto the **c** of Adullam:	4631
1Ki	18: 4 hid them *by* fifty in a **c,** and fed them	4631
	18:13 of the LORD'S prophets by fifty in a **c,**	4631
	19: 9 came thither unto a **c,** and lodged there;	4631
	19:13 and stood in the entering in of the **c.**	4631
1Ch	11:15 the rock to David, into the **c** of Adullam;	4631
Ps	57: T David, when he fled from Saul in the **c.**	4631
	142: T of David; A Prayer when he was in the **c.**	4631
Jn	11:38 It was a **c,** and a stone lay upon it.	4693

CAVE'S (1) [CAVE]

Jos	10:27 laid great stones in the **c** mouth,	4631

CAVES (6) [CAVE]

Jdg	6: 2 the mountains, and **c,** and strong holds.	4631
1Sa	13: 6 the people did hide themselves in **c,**	4631
Job	30: 6 in **c** of the earth, and *in* the rocks.	2356
Isa	2:19 into the **c** of the earth, for fear of	4247
Eze	33:27 and in the **c** shall die of the pestilence.	4631
Heb	11:38 and *in* dens and **c** of the earth.	3692

CEASE (70) [CEASED, CEASETH, CEASING]

Ge	8:22 and winter, and day and night shall not **c.**	7673
Ex	9:29 the thunder shall **c,** neither shall there	2308
Nu	8:25 from the age of fifty years they shall **c**	7725
	11:25 them, they prophesied, and did not **c.**	3254
	17: 5 will **make to c** from me the murmurings	7918
Dt	15:11 For the poor shall never **c** out of the land:	2308
	32:26 **make** the remembrance of them **to c**	7673
Jos	22:25 shall your children **make** our children **c**	7673
Jdg	15: 7 avenged of you, and after *that* I will **c.**	2308
	20:28 of Benjamin my brother, or shall I **c?**	2308
1Sa	7: 8 **C** not to cry unto the LORD our God for	2790
2Ch	16: 5 off building of Ramah, and let his work **c.**	7673
Ezr	4:21 commandment to **cause** these men to **c,**	989
	4:23 and **made** them to **c** by force and power.	989
	5: 5 that they could not **cause** them to **c,** till	989
Ne	4:11 and slay them, and **cause** the work to **c.**	7673
	6: 3 why should the work **c,** whilst I leave it,	7673
Job	3:17 There the wicked **c** *from* troubling;	2308
	10:20 **c** then, and let me alone, that I may take	2308
	14: 7 that the tender branch thereof will not **c.**	2308
Ps	37: 8 **C** from anger, and forsake wrath: fret not	7503
	46: 9 He **maketh** wars to **c** unto the end of	7673
	85: 4 and **cause** thine anger towards us **to c.**	6565
	89:44 Thou hast **made** his glory **to c,** and cast	7673
Pr	18:18 The lot **causeth** contentions to **c,**	7673
	19:27 **C,** my son, to hear the instruction *that*	2308
	20: 3 *It is* an honour for a man to **c** from strife:	7674
	22:10 go out; yea, strife and reproach shall **c.**	7673
	23: 4 not to be rich: **c** from thine own wisdom.	2308
Ecc	12: 3 and the grinders **c** because they are few,	988
Isa	1:16 from before mine eyes; **c** to do evil;	2308
	2:22 **C** ye from man, whose breath *is* in his	2308
	10:25 the indignation shall **c,** and mine anger in	3615
	13:11 **cause** the arrogancy of the proud **to c,**	7673
	16:10 I have **made** *their* vintage shouting to **c.**	7673
	17: 3 The fortress also shall **c** from Ephraim,	7673
	21: 2 all the sighing thereof have I **made** to **c.**	7673
	30:11 **cause** the Holy One of Israel **to c** from	7673
	33: 1 when thou shalt **c** to spoil, thou shalt be	8552
Jer	7:34 will I **cause** to **c** from the cities of Judah,	7673
	14:17 tears night and day, and let them not **c:**	1820
	16: 9 I will **cause** to **c** out of this place in your	7673
	17: 8 neither shall **c** from yielding fruit.	4185
	31:36 the seed of Israel also shall **c** from being	7673
	36:29 shall **cause** to **c** from thence man and	7673
	48:35 Moreover I will **cause** to **c** in Moab,	7673
La	2:18 no rest; let not the apple of thine eye **c.**	1826
Eze	6: 6 your idols may be broken and **c,**	7673
	7:24 also **make** the pomp of the strong **to c;**	7673
	12:23 I will **make** this proverb **to c,**	7673
	16:41 I will **cause** thee to **c** from playing	7673
	23:27 Thus will I **make** thy lewdness **to c** from	7673
	23:48 Thus will I **cause** lewdness to **c** out of	7673
	26:13 I will **cause** the noise of thy songs to **c;**	7673
	30:10 **make** the multitude of Egypt **to c** by	7673
	30:13 will **cause** *their* images **to c** out of Noph;	7673
	30:18 the pomp of her strength shall **c** in her:	7673
	33:28 the pomp of her strength shall **c;**	7673
	34:10 **cause** them **to c** from feeding the flock,	7673
	34:25 will **cause** the evil beasts **to c** out of	7673
Da	9:27 **cause** the sacrifice and the oblation **to c,**	7673
	11:18 **cause** the reproach offered by him **to c;**	7673
Hos	1: 4 will **cause** **to c** the kingdom of the house	7673
	2:11 also **cause** all her mirth **to c,** her feast	7673
Am	7: 5 said I, O Lord GOD, **c,** I beseech thee:	2308
Ac	13:10 thou not **c** to pervert the right ways of	3973
1Co	13: 8 whether *there* be tongues, they shall **c;**	3973
Eph	1:16 **C** not to give thanks for you,	3973
Col	1: 9 the day we heard *it,* do not **c** to pray	3973
2Pe	2:14 of adultery and that **cannot c** from sin;	180

CEASED (33) [CEASE]

Ge	18:11 it **c** to be with Sarah after the manner of	2308
Ex	9:33 the thunders and hail **c**, and the rain was	2308
	9:34 and the hail and the thunders were **c**,	2308
Jos	5:12 the manna **c** on the morrow after they	7673
Jdg	2:19 they **c** not from their own doings, nor	5307
	5: 7 *The inhabitants of* the villages **c**,	2308
	5: 7 they **c** in Israel, until that I Deborah arose,	2308
1Sa	2: 5 for bread; and *they that were* hungry **c**:	2308
	25: 9 those words in the name of David, and **c**.	5117
Ezr	4:24 **c** the work of the house of the God	989
	4:24 So it **c** unto the second year of the reign of	989
Job	32: 1 So these three men **c** to answer Job,	7673
Ps	35:15 I knew *it* not; they did tear *me*, and **c** not:	1826
	77: 2 my sore ran in the night, and **c** not:	6313
Isa	14: 4 and say, How hath the oppressor **c**!	7673
	14: 4 the oppressor ceased! the golden city **c**!	7673
La	5:14 elders have **c** from the gate, the young	7673
	5:15 The joy of our heart is **c**; our dance is	7673
Jnh	1:15 the sea: and the sea **c** from her raging.	5975
Mt	14:32 they were come into the ship, the wind **c**.	2869
Mk	4:39 the wind **c**, and there was a great calm.	2869
	6:51 unto them into the ship; and the wind **c**:	2869
Lk	7:45 time I came in hath not **c** to kiss my feet.	1257
	8:24 water: and they **c**, and there was a calm.	3973
	11: 1 when he **c**, one of his disciples said unto	3973
Ac	5:42 they **c** not to teach and preach Jesus	3973
	20: 1 after the uproar was **c**, Paul called unto	3973
	20:31 that *by the space of* three years I **c** not to	3973
	21:14 **c**, saying, The will of the Lord be done.	2270
Gal	5:11 then is the offence of the cross **c**.	2673
Heb	4:10 also hath **c** from his own works, as God	2664
	10: 2 then would they not have **c** to be offered?	3973
1Pe	4: 1 he that hath suffered in the flesh hath **c**	3973

CEASETH (10) [CEASE]

Ps	12: 1 Help, Lord; for the godly *man* **c**;	1584
	49: 8 of their soul is precious, and it **c** for ever:)	1584
Pr	26:20 where *there is* no talebearer, the strife **c**.	8367
Isa	16: 4 the extortioner is at an end, the spoiler **c**,	3615
	24: 8 The mirth of tabrets **c**, the noise of them	7673
	24: 8 that rejoice endeth, the joy of the harp **c**.	7673
	33: 8 highways lie waste, the wayfaring man **c**:	7673
La	3:49 Mine eye trickleth down, and **c** not,	1820
Hos	7: 4 *who* raising after *he* hath kneaded	7673
Ac	6:13 This man **c** not to speak blasphemous	3973

CEASING (7) [CEASE]

1Sa	12:23 sin against the Lord in **c** to pray for you:	2308
Ac	12: 5 prayer was made **without c** of the church	1618
Ro	1: 9 that **without c** I make mention of you,	89
1Th	1: 3 Remembering **without c** your work of faith,	89
	2:13 this cause also thank we God **without c**,	89
	5:17 Pray **without c**.	89
2Ti	1: 3 that **without c** I have remembrance of thee	88

CEDAR (51) [CEDARS]

Lev	14: 4 and **c** wood, and scarlet, and hyssop:	730
	14: 6 **c** wood, and the scarlet, and the hyssop,	730
	14:49 **c** wood, and scarlet, and hyssop:	730
	14:51 he shall take the **c** wood, and the hyssop,	730
	14:52 with the **c** wood, and with the hyssop,	730
Nu	19: 6 the priest shall take **c** wood, and hyssop,	730
	24: 6 *and* as **c** trees beside the waters.	730
2Sa	5:11 and **c** trees, and carpenters, and masons:	730
	7: 2 I dwell in a house of **c**, but the ark of God	730
	7: 7 Why build ye not me a house of **c**?	730
1Ki	4:33 from the **c** tree that *is* in Lebanon even	730
	5: 6 command thou that they hew me **c trees**	730
	5: 8 do all thy desire concerning timber of **c**,	730
	5:10 Hiram gave Solomon **c** trees and fir trees	730
	6: 9 the house with beams and boards of **c**,	730
	6:10 they rested on the house with timber of **c**.	730
	6:15 walls of the house within with boards of **c**,	730
	6:16 the floor and the walls with boards of **c**:	730
	6:18 the **c** of the house within *was* carved with	730
	6:18 all *was* **c**; there was no stone seen.	730
	6:20 and *so* covered the altar *which was of* **c**.	730
	6:36 of hewed stone, and a row of **c** beams.	730
	7: 2 thirty cubits, upon four rows of **c** pillars,	730
	7: 2 cedar pillars, with **c** beams upon the pillars.	730
	7: 3 covered with **c** above upon the beams,	730
	7: 7 *it* was covered with **c** from one side of	730
	7:12 a row of **c** beams, both for the inner court	730
	9:11 Tyre had furnished Solomon with **c** trees	730
2Ki	19:23 will cut down the tall **c** trees thereof,	730
1Ch	22: 4 of Tyre brought much **c** wood to David.	730
2Ch	1:15 **c** trees made he as the sycomore trees that	730
	2: 8 Send me also **c** trees, fir trees,	730
	9:27 **c** trees made he as the sycomore trees that	730
	25:18 thistle that *was* in Lebanon sent to the **c**	730
Ezr	3: 7 to bring **c** trees from Lebanon to the sea of	730
Job	40:17 He moveth his tail like a **c**: the sinews of	730
Ps	92:12 tree: he shall grow like a **c** in Lebanon.	730
SS	1:17 The beams of our house *are* **c**,	730
	8: 9 door, we will inclose her with boards of **c**.	730
Isa	41:19 I will plant in the wilderness the **c**,	730
Jer	22:14 *it is* cieled with **c**, and painted with	730
	22:15 reign, because thou closest *thyself* in **c**?	730
Eze	17: 3 and took the highest branch of the **c**:	730
	17:22 take of the highest branch of the high **c**,	730
	17:23 and bear fruit, and be a goodly **c**:	730
	27:24 bound with cords, and **made of c**,	729

Eze	31: 3 the Assyrian *was* a **c** in Lebanon with fair	730
Zep	2:14 for he shall uncover the **c work**.	731
Zec	11: 2 Howl, fir tree; for the **c** is fallen; because	730

CEDARS (24) [CEDAR]

Jdg	9:15 the bramble, and devour the **c** of Lebanon.	730
1Ki	7:11 after the measures of hewed stones, and **c**.	730
	10:27 **c** made he *to be* as the sycomore trees that	730
1Ch	14: 1 timber of **c**, with masons and carpenters,	730
	17: 1 I dwell in a house of **c**, but the ark of	730
	17: 6 Why have ye not built me a house of **c**?	730
2Ch	2: 3 didst send him **c** to build him a house to	730
Ps	29: 5 The voice of the Lord breaketh the **c**; yea,	730
	29: 5 yea, the Lord breaketh the **c** of Lebanon.	730
	80:10 the boughs thereof *were like* the goodly **c**.	730
	104:16 The trees of the Lord are full of *sap*; the **c**	730
	148: 9 all hills; fruitful trees, and all **c**:	730
SS	5:15 *is* as Lebanon, excellent as the **c**.	730
Isa	2:13 upon all the **c** of Lebanon, that are high	730
	9:10 cut down, but we will change *them into* **c**.	730
	14: 8 trees rejoice at thee, *and* the **c** of Lebanon,	730
	37:24 I will cut down the tall **c** thereof,	730
	44:14 He heweth him down **c**, and taketh	730
Jer	22: 7 they shall cut down thy choice **c**,	730
	22:23 of Lebanon, that makest thy nest in the **c**,	730
Eze	27: 5 they have taken **c** from Lebanon to make	730
	31: 8 The **c** in the garden of God could not hide	730
Am	2: 9 whose height *was* like the height of the **c**,	730
Zec	11: 1 Lebanon, that the fire may devour thy **c**.	730

CEDRON (1)

Jn	18: 1 forth with his disciples over the brook **C**,	2748

CELEBRATE (3)

Lev	23:32 unto even, shall ye **c** your **sabbath**.	7673+7676
	23:41 ye shall **c** it in the seventh month.	2287
Isa	38:18 cannot praise thee, death can *not* **c** thee:	1984

CELESTIAL (2)

1Co	15:40 *There are* also **c** bodies,	2032
	15:40 the glory of the **c** *is* one, and the *glory*	2032

CELLARS (2)

1Ch	27:27 for the wine **c** *was* Zabdi the Shiphmite:	214
	27:28 Gederite: and over the **c** of oil *was* Joash:	214

CENCHREA (3)

Ac	18:18 having shorn *his* head in **C**: for he had a	2747
Ro	16: 1 is a servant of the church which is at **C**:	2747
	16: 5 *sent* by Phebe servant of the church at **C**.	2747

CENSER (12) [CENSERS]

Lev	10: 1 took either of them his **c**, and put fire	4289
	16:12 shall take a **c** full of burning coals of fire	4289
Nu	16:17 take every man his **c**, and put incense in	4289
	16:17 ye before the Lord every man his **c**,	4289
	16:17 thou also, and Aaron, each *of you* his **c**.	4289
	16:18 they took every man his **c**, and put fire in	4289
	16:46 Take a **c**, and put fire therein from off	4289
2Ch	26:19 and *had* a **c** in his hand to burn incense:	4730
Eze	8:11 with every man his **c** in his hand;	4730
Heb	9: 4 Which had the golden **c**, and the ark of	2369
Rev	8: 3 and stood at the altar, having a golden **c**;	3031
	8: 5 the angel took the **c**, and filled it with	3031

CENSERS (8) [CENSER]

Nu	4:14 the **c**, the fleshhooks, and the shovels,	4289
	16: 6 Take you **c**, Korah, and all his company;	4289
	16:17 man his censer, two hundred and fifty **c**;	4289
	16:37 that he take up the **c** out of the burning,	4289
	16:38 The **c** of these sinners against their own	4289
	16:39 Eleazar the priest took the brasen **c**,	4289
1Ki	7:50 and the spoons, and the **c** *of* pure gold;	4289
2Ch	4:22 the basons, and the spoons, and the **c**,	4289

CENSUS See NUMBER; SUM; TAXING

CENTURION (20) [CENTURION'S, CENTURIONS]

Mt	8: 5 there came unto him a **c**, beseeching him,	1543
	8: 8 The **c** answered and said, Lord, I am not	1543
	8:13 And Jesus said unto the **c**, Go thy way;	1543
	27:54 Now when the **c**, and they that were with	1543
Mk	15:39 when the **c**, which stood over against	2760
	15:44 calling unto *him* the **c**, he asked him	2760
	15:45 And when he knew *it* of the **c**, he gave	2760
Lk	7: 6 sent friends to him, saying unto him,	1543
	23:47 Now when the **c** saw what was done,	1543
Ac	10: 1 a **c** of the band called the Italian *band,*	1543
	10:22 Cornelius the **c**, a just man, and one that	1543
	22:25 Paul said unto the **c** that stood *by,* Is it	1543
	22:26 When the **c** heard *that*, he went and told	1543
	24:23 And he commanded a **c** to keep Paul,	1543
	27: 1 *one* named Julius, a **c** of Augustus' band.	1543
	27: 6 there the **c** found a ship of Alexandria	1543
	27:11 Nevertheless the **c** believed the master	1543
	27:31 Paul said to the **c** and to the soldiers,	1543
	27:43 But the **c**, willing to save Paul, kept them	1543
	28:16 the **c** delivered the prisoners to the captain	1543

CENTURION'S (1) [CENTURION]

Lk	7: 2 a certain **c** servant, who was dear unto	1543

CENTURIONS (3) [CENTURION]

Ac	21:32 Who immediately took soldiers and **c**,	1543
	23:17 Then Paul called one of the **c** unto *him*,	1543
	23:23 And he called unto *him* two **c**, saying,	1543

CEPHAS (6) [PETER]

Jn	1:42 thou shalt be called **C**, which is by	2786
1Co	1:12 I of Apollos; and I of **C**; and I of Christ.	2786
	3:22 or **C**, or the world, or life, or death,	2786
	9: 5 as the brethren of the Lord, and **C**?	2786
	15: 5 And that he was seen of **C**, then of	2786
Gal	2: 9 And when James, **C**, and John,	2786

CEREMONIES (1)

Nu	9: 3 according to all the **c** thereof, shall ye	4941

CERTAIN (196) [CERTAINLY, CERTAINTY, UNCERTAIN]

Ge	28:11 lighted upon a **c** place, and tarried there	NIH
	37:15 a **c** man found him, and, behold, *he was*	NIH
	38: 1 turned in to a **c** Adullamite, whose name	376
	38: 2 saw there a daughter of a **c** Canaanite,	376
Ex	16: 4 shall go out and gather a **c** rate every day,	1697
Nu	9: 6 there were **c** men, who were defiled by	NIH
	16: 2 with **c** of the children of Israel, two	376
Dt	13:13 **C** men, the children of Belial, are gone	NIH
	13:14 behold, *if it be* truth, *and* the thing **c**,	3559
	17: 4 and behold, *it is* true, *and* the thing **c**,	3559
	25: 2 according to his fault, by a **c** number.	NIH
Jdg	9:53 a **c** woman cast a piece of a millstone upon	259
	13: 2 there was a **c** man of Zorah, of the family	376
	19: 1 that there was a **c** Levite sojourning on	376
	19:22 the men of the city, **c** sons of Belial,	376
Ru	1: 1 a **c** man of Beth-lehem-judah went to	NIH
1Sa	1: 1 Now there was a **c** man of	259
	21: 7 Now a **c** man of the servants of Saul *was*	NIH
2Sa	18:10 a **c** man saw *it*, and told Joab, and said,	259
1Ki	2:37 shalt **know for c** that thou shalt	3045+3045
	2:42 unto thee, saying, **Know for a c**,	3045+3045
	7:29 oxen *were* **c** additions made of thin work.	NIH
	11:17 **c** Edomites of his father's servants with	376
	20:35 a **c** man of the sons of the prophets said	259
	22:34 a **c** man drew a bow at a venture,	NIH
2Ki	4: 1 Now there cried a **c** woman of the wives	259
	8: 6 So the king appointed unto her a **c** officer,	259
1Ch	9:28 **c** of them had the charge of the	NIH
	16: 4 he appointed of the Levites to minister	NIH
	19: 5 went **c**, and told David how the men	NIH
2Ch	8:13 Even after a **c** rate every day, offering	1697
	18: 2 after **c** years he went down to Ahab to	NIH
	18:33 a **c** man drew a bow at a venture,	376
	28:12 **c** of the heads of the children of Ephraim,	376
Ezr	10:16 Ezra the priest, *with* **c** chief of the fathers,	376
Ne	1: 2 brethren, came, he and **c** men of Judah;	NIH
	1: 4 mourned **c** days, and fasted,	NIH
	11: 4 at Jerusalem dwelt **c** of the children of	NIH
	11:23 that a **c portion** *should be* for the singers,	548
	12:35 **c** of the priests' sons with trumpets;	NIH
	13: 6 after **c** days obtained I *leave* of the king:	NIH
	13:25 smote **c** of them, and pluckt off their hair,	376
Est	2: 5 *Now* in Shushan the palace there was a **c**	376
	3: 8 There is a **c** people scattered abroad and	259
Jer	26:15 **know** ye **for c**, that if ye put me to	3045+3045
	26:17 Then rose up **c** of the elders of the land,	376
	26:22 Achbor, and **c** men with him into Egypt.	NIH
	41: 5 That there came **c** from Shechem,	376
	52:15 away captive **c** of the poor of the people,	NIH
	52:16 the captain of the guard left **c**	NIH
Eze	14: 1 came **c** of the elders of Israel unto me,	376
	20: 1 **c** of the elders of Israel came to inquire	376
Da	1: 3 that *he* should bring **c** of the children of	NIH
	2:45 the dream *is* **c**, and the interpretation	3330
	3: 8 Wherefore at that time **c** Chaldeans came	1400
	3:12 There are **c** Jews whom thou hast set over	1400
	8:13 another saint said unto that **c** *saint* which	6422
	8:27 I Daniel fainted, and was sick **c** days;	NIH
	10: 5 and behold, a **c** man clothed *in* linen,	259
	11:13 shall certainly come after **c** years with a	6256
Mt	8:19 And a **c** scribe came, and said unto him,	1520
	9: 3 **c** of the scribes said within themselves,	5100
	9:18 there came a **c** ruler, and worshipped him,	NIG
	12:38 Then **c** of the scribes and of the Pharisees	5100
	17:14 there came to him a **c** man, beseeching	NIG
	18:23 kingdom of heaven likened unto a **c** king,	444
	20:20 and desiring a **c** thing of him.	5100
	21:28 A **c** man had two sons; and he came to	NIG
	21:33 was a **c** householder, which planted a	5100
	22: 2 kingdom of heaven is like unto a **c** king,	444
Mk	2: 6 there were **c** of the scribes sitting there,	5100
	5:25 And a **c** woman, which had an issue of	5100
	5:35 ruler of the synagogue's *house* **c** which	NIG
	7: 1 and **c** of the scribes, which came from	5100
	7:25 For a **c** woman, whose young daughter	NIG
	11: 5 And **c** of them that stood there said unto	5100
	12: 1 A **c** man planted a vineyard, and set a	NIG
	12:13 they send unto him **c** of the Pharisees	5100
	12:42 And there came a **c** poor widow,	1520
	14:51 And there followed him a **c** young man,	5100
	14:57 And there arose **c**, and bare false witness	5100
Lk	1: 5 king of Judea, a **c** priest named Zacharias,	5100
	5:12 it came to pass, when he was in a **c** city,	1520
	5:17 that it came to pass on a **c** day, as he was	5100
	6: 2 And **c** of the Pharisees said unto them,	5100
	7: 2 And a **c** centurion's servant, who was dear	5100
	7:41 There was a **c** creditor which had two	5100
	8: 2 And **c** women, which had been healed of	5100
	8:20 And it was told him *by* **c** which said,	NIG
	8:22 Now it came to pass on a **c** day, that he	1520
	8:27 there met him out of the city a **c** man,	5100
	9:57 a **c** *man* said unto him, Lord, I will follow	5100

C

Lk	10:25 a **c** lawyer stood up, and tempted him,	5100
	10:30 A **c** man went down from Jerusalem to	5100
	10:31 by chance there came down a **c** priest	5100
	10:33 But a **c** Samaritan, as he journeyed,	5100
	10:38 went, that he entered into a **c** village:	5100
	10:38 a **c** woman named Martha received him	5100
	11: 1 pass *that*, as he was praying in a **c** place,	5100
	11:27 as he spake these *things*, a **c** woman of	5100
	11:37 a **c** Pharisee besought him to dine with	5100
	12:16 The ground of a **c** rich man brought forth	5100
	13: 6 A **c** *man* had a fig tree planted in his	5100
	13:31 The same day there came a **c** of	5100
	14: 2 behold, there was a **c** man before him,	5100
	14:16 A **c** man made a great supper,	5100
	15:11 And he said, A **c** man had two sons:	5100
	16: 1 There was a **c** rich man, which had a	5100
	16:19 There was a **c** rich man, which was	5100
	16:20 And there was a **c** beggar named Lazarus,	5100
	17:12 And as he entered into a **c** village,	5100
	18: 9 And he spake this parable unto **c** which	5100
	18:18 And a **c** ruler asked him, saying,	5100
	18:35 a **c** blind man sat by the way side begging:	5100
	19:12 A **c** nobleman went into a far country to	5100
	20: 9 A **c** man planted a vineyard, and let it	5100
	20:27 Then came to *him* **c** of the Sadducees,	5100
	20:39 Then **c** of the scribes answering said,	5100
	21: 2 he saw also a **c** poor widow casting in	5100
	22:56 But a **c** maid beheld him as he sat by	5100
	23:19 (Who for a **c** sedition made in the city,	5100
	24: 1 had prepared, and **c** *others* with them.	5100
	24:22 **c** women *also* of our company made us	5100
	24:24 And **c** of them which were with us went	5100
Jn	4:46 And there was a **c** nobleman, whose son	5100
	5: 4 For an angel went down at a **c** season into	NIG
	5: 5 And a **c** man was there, which had an	5100
	11: 1 Now a **c** *man* was sick, *named* Lazarus,	5100
	12:20 there were **c** Greeks among them that	5100
Ac	3: 2 a **c** man lame from his mother's womb	5100
	5: 1 a **c** man named Ananias, with Sapphira	5100
	5: 2 being privy to *it*, and brought a **c** part,	5100
	6: 9 Then there arose **c** of the synagogue,	5100
	8: 9 But there was a **c** man, called Simon,	5100
	8:36 on *their* way, they came unto a **c** water:	5100
	9:10 And there was a **c** disciple at Damascus,	5100
	9:19 Then was Saul **c** days with the disciples	5100
	9:33 there he found a **c** man named Aeneas,	5100
	9:36 there was at Joppa a **c** disciple named	5100
	10: 1 There was a **c** man in Cesarea called	5100
	10:11 and a **c** vessel descending unto him,	5100
	10:23 **c** brethren from Joppa accompanied him.	5100
	10:48 Then prayed they him to tarry **c** days.	5100
	11: 5 trance I saw a vision, A **c** vessel descend,	5100
	12: 1 forth *his* hands to vex **c** of the church.	5100
	13: 1 the church that was at Antioch **c** prophets	5100
	13: 6 they found a **c** sorcerer, a false prophet,	5100
	14: 8 there sat a **c** man at Lystra, impotent in	5100
	14:19 there came thither **c** Jews from Antioch	NIG
	15: 1 And **c** *men* which came down from Judea	5100
	15: 2 and Barnabas, and **c** other of them,	5100
	15: 5 But there rose up **c** of the sect of	5100
	15:24 that **c** which went out from us have	5100
	16: 1 and behold, a **c** disciple was there,	5100
	16: 1 named Timotheus, the son of a **c** woman,	5100
	16:12 and we were in that city abiding **c** days.	5100
	16:14 And a **c** woman named Lydia, a seller of	5100
	16:16 a **c** damsel possessed with a spirit of	5100
	17: 5 unto *them* **c** lewd fellows of the baser	5100
	17: 6 and **c** brethren unto the rulers of the city,	5100
	17:18 Then **c** philosophers of the Epicureans,	5100
	17:20 For thou bringest **c** strange *things* to our	5100
	17:28 as **c** also of your own poets have said,	5100
	17:34 Howbeit **c** men clave unto him,	5100
	18: 2 And found a **c** Jew named Aquila, born in	5100
	18: 7 and entered into a **c** *man's* house,	5100
	18:24 And a **c** Jew named Apollos, born at	5100
	19: 1 came to Ephesus: and finding **c** disciples,	5100
	19:13 Then **c** of the vagabond Jews, exorcists,	5100
	19:24 For a **c** *man* named Demetrius,	5100
	19:31 And **c** of the chief of Asia, which were his	5100
	20: 9 And there sat in a window a **c** young man	5100
	21:10 there came down from Judea a **c** prophet,	5100
	21:16 There went with us also **c** of the disciples	NIG
	23:12 it was day, **c** of the Jews banded together,	5100
	23:17 for he hath a **c** *thing* to tell him.	5100
	24: 1 and *with* a **c** orator *named* Tertullus,	5100
	24:18 Whereupon **c** Jews from Asia found me	5100
	24:24 And after **c** days, when Felix came with	5100
	25:13 And after **c** days king Agrippa and	5100
	25:14 There is a **c** man left in bonds by Felix:	5100
	25:19 But had **c** questions against him of their	5100
	25:26 Of whom I have no **c** *thing* to write unto	804
	27: 1 **c** other prisoners unto *one* named Julius,	5100
	27:16 And running under a **c** island *which* is	5100
	27:26 Howbeit we must be cast upon a **c** island.	5100
	27:39 they discovered a **c** creek with a shore,	5100
Ro	15:26 Achaia to make a **c** contribution for	5100
1Co	4:11 buffeted, and **have no c dwelling place;**	790
Gal	2:12 For before that **c** came from James, he did	5100
1Ti	6: 7 *and it is* **c** we can carry nothing out.	1212
Heb	2: 6 But one in a **c** place testified, saying,	4225
	4: 4 For *he* spake in a **c** place of the seventh	4225
	4: 7 Again he limiteth a **c** day, saying in David,	5100
	10:27 But a **c** fearful looking for of judgment and	5100
Jude	1: 4 For there are **c** men crept in unawares,	5100

CERTAINLY (31) [CERTAIN]

Ge	18:10 I will **c** return unto thee according	7725+7725
	26:28 **saw c** that the LORD was with	7200+7200
	43: 7 we **c** know that he would say,	3045+3045
	44:15 that such a man as I can **c** divine?	5172+5172
	50:15 will **c** requite us all the evil which	7725+7725
Ex	3:12 he said, **C** I will be with thee; and this	3588
	22: 4 If the theft be **c** found in his hand	4672+4672
Lev	5:19 hath **c** trespassed against the LORD.	816+816
	24:16 congregation shall **c** stone him:	7275+7275
Jos	9:24 Because it was **c** told thy servants,	5046+5046
Jdg	14:12 if you can **c** declare it me *within*	5046+5046
1Sa	20: 3 Thy father **c** knoweth that I have	3045+3045
	20: 9 for if I **knew c** that evil were	3045+3045
	23:10 thy servant hath **c** heard that Saul	8085+8085
	25:28 for the LORD will **c** make my lord	6213+6213
1Ki	1:30 in my stead; even so will I **c** do this day.	3651
2Ki	8:10 unto him, Thou mayest **c** recover:	2421+2421
2Ch	18:27 If thou **c** return in peace, *then*	7725+7725
Pr	23: 5 riches **c** make themselves wings;	6213+6213
Jer	8: 8 **c** in vain made he *it*; the pen of the scribes	403
	13:12 we not **c** know that every bottle	3045+3045
	25:28 LORD of hosts; Ye shall **c** drink.	8354+8354
	36:29 The king of Babylon shall **c** come	935+935
	40:14 Dost thou **c** know that Baalis	3045+3045
	42:19 **know c** that I have admonished	3045+3045
	42:22 know **c** that ye shall die by	3045+3045
	44:17 will **c** do whatsoever thing goeth	6213+6213
La	2:16 **c** this *is* the day that we looked for;	389
Da	11:10 *one* shall **c** come, and overflow,	935+935
	11:13 shall **c** come after certain years with	935+935
Lk	23:47 saying, **C** this was a righteous man.	3689

CERTAINTY (7) [CERTAIN]

Jos	23:13 **Know for a c** that the LORD your	3045+3045
1Sa	23:23 come ye again to me with the **c,**	3559
Pr	22:21 That *I* might make thee know the **c** of	7189
Da	2: 8 I know of **c** that ye would gain the time,	3330
Lk	1: 4 That thou mightest know the **c** of *those*	803
Ac	21:34 he could not know the **c** for the tumult,	804
	22:30 he would have known the **c** wherefore he	804

CERTIFIED (2) [CERTIFY]

Ezr	4:14 therefore have we sent and **c** the king:	3046
Est	2:22 Esther **c** the king *thereof* in Mordecai's	559

CERTIFY (5) [CERTIFIED]

2Sa	15:28 until there come word from you to **c** me.	5046
Ezr	4:16 We **c** the king that, if this city be builded	3046
	5:10 We asked their names also, to **c** thee,	3046
	7:24 Also *we* **c** you, that *touching* any of	3046
Gal	1:11 I **c** you, brethren, that the gospel which	1107

CESAR (21) [CESAR'S]

Mt	22:17 Is it lawful to give tribute unto **C,** or not?	2541
	22:21 unto **C** the *things* which are Cesar's;	2541
Mk	12:14 Is it lawful to give tribute to **C,** or not?	2541
	12:17 Render to **C** the *things* that are Cesar's,	2541
Lk	2: 1 *that* there went out a decree from **C**	2541
	3: 1 fifteenth year of the reign of Tiberius **C,**	2541
	20:22 Is it lawful for us to give tribute unto **C,**	2541
	20:25 unto **C** the *things* which be Cesar's,	2541
	23: 2 forbidding to give tribute to **C,** saying	2541
Jn	19:12 maketh himself a king speaketh against **C.**	2541
	19:15 priests answered, We have no king but **C.**	2541
Ac	11:28 came to pass in the days of Claudius **C.**	2541
	17: 7 these all do contrary to the decrees of **C,**	2541
	25: 8 against the temple, nor *yet* against **C,**	2541
	25:11 deliver me unto them. I appeal unto **C.**	2541
	25:12 answered, Hast thou appealed unto **C?**	2541
	25:12 unto Cesar? unto **C** shalt thou go.	2541
	25:21 him to be kept till I might send him to **C.**	2541
	26:32 at liberty, if he had not appealed unto **C.**	2541
	27:24 Paul; thou must be brought before **C:**	2541
	28:19 *it,* I was constrained to appeal unto **C;**	2541

CESAR'S (9) [CESAR]

Mt	22:21 They say unto him, **C.** Then saith he	2541
	22:21 unto Cesar the *things* which are **C;**	2541
Mk	12:16 And they said unto him, **C.**	2541
	12:17 Render to Cesar the *things* that are **C,**	2541
Lk	20:24 They answered and said, **C.**	2541
	20:25 unto Cesar the *things* which be **C,**	2541
Jn	19:12 let this *man* go, thou art not **C** friend:	2541
Ac	25:10 said Paul, I stand at **C** judgment seat,	2541
Php	4:22 chiefly they that are of **C** household.	2541

CESAREA (17)

Mt	16:13 When Jesus came into the coasts of **C**	2542
Mk	8:27 his disciples, into the towns of **C** Philippi:	2542
Ac	8:40 in all the cities, till he came to **C.**	2542
	9:30 they brought him down to **C,** and sent	2542
	10: 1 There was a certain man in **C** called	2542
	10:24 the morrow *after* they entered into **C.**	2542
	11:11 house where I was, sent from **C** unto me.	2542
	12:19 And he went down from Judea to **C,**	2542
	18:22 when he had landed at **C,** and gone up,	2542
	21: 8 company departed, and came unto **C:**	2542
	21:16 with us also *certain* of the disciples of **C,**	2542
	23:23 ready two hundred soldiers to go to **C,**	2542
	23:33 when they came to **C,** and delivered	2542
	25: 1 after three days he ascended from **C** to	2542
	25: 4 that Paul should be kept at **C,** and that	2542
	25: 6 than ten days, he went down unto **C;**	2542
	25:13 Bernice came unto **C** to salute Festus.	2542

CHAFED (1)

2Sa	17: 8 mighty *men,* and they *be* **c** in their minds,	4751

CHAFF (14)

Job	21:18 and as **c** that the storm carrieth away.	4671
Ps	1: 4 like the **c** which the wind driveth away.	4671
	35: 5 Let them be as **c** before the wind: and	4671
Isa	5:24 the flame consumeth the **c,** *so* their root	2842
	17:13 shall be chased as the **c** of the mountains	4671
	29: 5 ones *shall* be as **c** that passeth away:	4671
	33:11 Ye shall conceive **c,** ye shall bring forth	2842
	41:15 small, and shalt make the hills as **c.**	4671
Jer	23:28 What *is* the **c** to the wheat? saith	8401
Da	2:35 became like the **c** of the summer	5784
Hos	13: 3 as the **c** *that* is driven with a whirlwind	4671
Zep	2: 2 bring forth, *before* the day pass as the **c,**	4671
Mt	3:12 burn up the **c** with unquenchable fire.	892
Lk	3:17 the **c** he will burn with fire unquenchable.	892

CHAIN (13) [CHAINS]

Ge	41:42 linen, and put a gold **c** about his neck;	7242
1Ki	7:17 of checker work, *and* wreaths of **c** work,	8333
Ps	73: 6 pride **compasseth** them **about as a c;**	6059
SS	4: 9 one of thine eyes, with one **c** of thy neck.	6060
La	3: 7 cannot get out: he hath made my **c** heavy.	5178
Eze	7:23 Make a **c:** for the land is full *of* bloody	7569
	16:11 upon thine hands, and a **c** on thy neck.	7242
Da	5: 7 *have* a **c** of gold about his neck,	2002
	5:16 *have* a **c** of gold about thy neck,	2002
	5:29 *put* a **c** of gold about his neck, and made	2002
Ac	28:20 the hope of Israel I am bound with this **c.**	254
2Ti	1:16 and was not ashamed of my **c:**	254
Rev	20: 1 bottomless *pit* and a great **c** in his hand.	254

CHAINS (37) [CHAIN]

Ex	28:14 two **c** *of* pure gold at the ends;	8333
	28:14 and fasten the wreathen **c** to the ouches.	8333
	28:22 thou shalt make upon the breastplate **c** at	8331
	28:24 thou shalt put the two wreathen **c** *of* gold	NIH
	28:25 *the other* two ends of the two wreathen **c**	NIH
	39:15 they made upon the breastplate **c** at	8333
	39:17 they put the two wreathen **c** *of* gold in	NIH
	39:18 the two ends of the two wreathen **c** they	NIH
Nu	31:50 **c,** and bracelets, rings, earrings,	685
Jdg	8:26 beside the **c** that *were* about their camels'	6060
1Ki	6:21 he made a partition by the **c** of gold	7572
2Ch	3: 5 gold, and set thereon palm trees and **c.**	8333
	3:16 he made **c,** *as* in the oracle, and put *them*	8333
	3:16 and put *them* on the **c.**	8333
Ps	68: 6 out those which are bound with **c:**	3574
	149: 8 bind their kings with **c,** and their nobles	2131
Pr	1: 9 unto thy head, and **c** about thy neck.	6060
SS	1:10 rows *of* jewels, thy neck with **c** of gold.	2737
Isa	3:19 The **c,** and the bracelets, and the mufflers,	5188
	40:19 it over with gold, and casteth silver **c.**	7577
	45:14 in **c** they shall come over, and they shall	2131
Jer	39: 7 him with **c** to carry him to Babylon.	5178
	40: 1 when he had taken him being bound in **c**	246
	40: 4 I loose thee *this* day from the **c** which	246
	52:11 the king of Babylon bound him in **c,**	5178
Eze	19: 4 they brought him with **c** unto the land of	2397
	19: 9 put him in ward in **c,** and brought him	2397
Na	3:10 and all her great *men* were bound in **c.**	2131
Mk	5: 3 no *man* could bind him, no, not with **c:**	254
	5: 4 had been often bound with fetters and **c,**	254
	5: 4 the **c** had been plucked asunder by him,	254
Lk	8:29 he was kept bound with **c** and in fetters;	254
Ac	12: 6 between two soldiers, bound with two **c:**	254
	12: 7 And his **c** fell off from *his* hands.	254
	21:33 commanded *him* to be bound with two **c;**	254
2Pe	2: 4 and delivered *them* into **c** of darkness,	4577
Jude	1: 6 he hath reserved in everlasting **c** under	1199

CHALCEDONY (1)

Rev	21:19 the second, sapphire; the third, a **c;**	5472

CHALCOL (1) [CALCOL]

1Ki	4:31 Heman, and **C,** and Darda, the sons of	3633

CHALDEA (7) [CHALDEAN, CHALDEANS, CHALDEANS', CHALDEES, CHALDEES']

Jer	50:10 **C** shall be a spoil: all that spoil her shall	3778
	51:24 all the inhabitants of **C** all their evil that	3778
	51:35 my blood upon the inhabitants of **C,**	3778
Eze	11:24 me in vision by the Spirit of God into **C,**	3778
	16:29 fornication in the land of Canaan unto **C;**	3778
	23:15 *after* the manner of the Babylonians of **C,**	3778
	23:16 and sent messengers unto them into **C.**	3778

CHALDEAN (2) [CHALDEA]

Ezr	5:12 **C,** who destroyed this house,	3679
Da	2:10 at any magician, or astrologer, or **C.**	3779

CHALDEANS (66) [CHALDEA]

Job	1:17 The **C** made out three bands, and fell	3778
Isa	23:13 Behold the land of the **C;** this people was	3778
	43:14 and the **C,** whose cry *is* in the ships.	3778
	47: 1 *there is* no throne, O daughter of the **C;**	3778
	47: 5 into darkness, O daughter of the **C:**	3778
	48:14 Babylon, and his arm *shall be* on the **C.**	3778
	48:20 ye forth of Babylon, flee ye from the **C,**	3778
Jer	21: 4 against the **C,** which besiege you without	3778
	21: 9 falleth to the **C** that besiege you, he shall	3778
	22:25 of Babylon, and into the hand of the **C.**	3778
	24: 5 place *into* the land of the **C** for *their* good.	3778

C

Jer 25:12 the land of the **C**, and will make it 3778
32: 4 shall not escape out of the hand of the **C**, 3778
32: 5 though ye fight with the **C**, ye shall not 3778
32:24 the city is given into the hand of the **C**, 3778
32:25 for the city is given into the hand of the **C**. 3778
32:28 I *will* give this city into the hand of the **C**, 3778
32:29 the **C**, that fight against this city, 3778
32:43 or beast; it is given into the hand of the **C**. 3778
33: 5 They come to fight with the **C**, but *it is* to 3778
35:11 to Jerusalem for fear of the army of the **C**, 3778
37: 5 when the **C** that besieged Jerusalem heard 3778
37: 8 the **C** shall come again, and fight against 3778
37: 9 The **C** shall surely depart from us: 3778
37:10 army of the **C** that fight against you, 3778
37:11 when the army of the **C** was broken up 3778
37:13 saying, Thou fallest away to the **C**. 3778
37:14 *It is* false; I fall not away to the **C**. 3778
38: 2 he that goeth forth to the **C** shall live; 3778
38:18 this city be given into the hand of the **C**, 3778
38:19 afraid of the Jews that are fallen to the **C**, 3778
38:23 out all thy wives and thy children to the **C**: 3778
39: 8 the **C** burnt the king's house, 3778
40: 9 their men, saying, Fear not to serve the **C**: 3778
40:10 I *will* dwell at Mizpah to serve the **C**, 3778
41: 3 the **C** that were found there, *and* the men 3778
41:18 Because of the **C**: for they were afraid of 3778
43: 3 for to deliver us into the hand of the **C**, 3778
50: 1 against the land of the **C** by Jeremiah 3778
50: 8 go forth out of the land of the **C**, and be 3778
50:25 Lord G<small>OD</small> of hosts in the land of the **C**. 3778
50:35 A sword *is* upon the **C**, saith the L<small>ORD</small>, 3778
50:45 hath purposed against the land of the **C**: 3778
51: 4 the slain shall fall in the land of the **C**, 3778
51:54 great destruction from the land of the **C**: 3778
52: 7 the **C** *were* by the city round about:) 3778
52: 8 the army of the **C** pursued after the king, 3778
52:14 all the army of the **C**, that *were* with 3778
52:17 the **C** brake, and carried all the brass of 3778
Eze 1: 3 in the land of the **C** by the river Chebar; 3778
12:13 bring him to Babylon *to* the land of the **C**; 3778
23:14 the images of the **C** pourtrayed with 3778
23:23 all the, **C**, Pekod, and Shoa, and Koa, 3778
Da 1: 4 the learning and the tongue of the **C**. 3778
2: 2 and the sorcerers, and the **C**, 3778
2: 4 spake the **C** to the king in Syriack, 3778
2: 5 The king answered and said to the **C**, 3779
2:10 The **C** answered before the king, and said, 3779
3: 8 at that time certain **C** came near, 3779
4: 7 astrologers, the **C**, and the soothsayers: 3779
5: 7 astrologers, the **C**, and the soothsayers. 3779
5:11 astrologers, **C**, *and* soothsayers; 3779
5:30 *was* Belshazzar the king of the **C** slain. 3778
9: 1 was made king over the realm of the **C**; 3778
Hab 1: 6 I raise up the **C**, *that* bitter and hasty 3778
Ac 7: 4 Then came he out of the land of the **C**, 5466

CHALDEANS' (1) [CHALDEA]
Jer 39: 5 the **C** army pursued after them, 3778

CHALDEES (13) [CHALDEA]
Ge 11:28 in the land of his nativity, in Ur of the **C**. 3778
11:31 went forth with them from Ur of the **C**, 3778
15: 7 that brought thee out of Ur of the **C**, 3778
2Ki 24: 2 L<small>ORD</small> sent against him bands of the **C**, 3778
25: 4 (now the **C** *were* against the city round 3778
25: 5 the army of the **C** pursued after the king, 3778
25:10 all the army of the **C**, that *were* with 3778
25:13 did the **C** break *in pieces*, and carried 3778
25:24 Fear not to be the servants of the **C**: 3778
25:25 and the **C** that were with him at Mizpah. 3778
25:26 *to* Egypt: for they were afraid of the **C**. 3778
2Ch 36:17 he brought upon them the king of the **C**, 3778
Ne 9: 7 broughtest him forth out of Ur of the **C**, 3778

CHALDEES' (1) [CHALDEA]
Isa 13:19 the beauty of the **C** excellency, 3778

CHALKSTONES (1) [STONE]
Isa 27: 9 altar as **c** that are beaten in sunder, 68+1615

CHALLENGETH (1)
Ex 22: 9 any manner of lost *thing*, which *another* **c** 559

CHAMBER (52) [BEDCHAMBER, CHAMBERING, CHAMBERLAIN, CHAMBERLAINS, CHAMBERS, GUESTCHAMBER]
Ge 43:30 he entered into *his* **c**, and wept there. 2315
Jdg 3:24 he covereth his feet in *his* summer **c**. 2315
15: 1 he said, I will go in to my wife into the **c**. 2315
16: 9 lying in wait, abiding with her in the **c**. 2315
16:12 *there were* liers in wait abiding in the **c**. 2315
2Sa 13:10 Bring the meat *into* the **c**, that I may eat 2315
13:10 brought *them* into the **c** to Amnon her 2315
18:33 went up to the **c** over the gate, and wept: 5944
1Ki 1:15 sheba went in unto the king into the **c**: 2315
6: 6 The nethermost *was* five cubits broad, 3326
6: 6 for the middle *c was* in the right 6763
6: 8 up with winding stairs into the middle **c**, NIH
14:28 and brought them back into the guard **c**. 8372
17:23 brought him down out of the **c** into 5944
20:30 the city, into an **inner c**. 2315+2315+871.1
22:25 into an **inner c** to hide 2315+2315+871.1
2Ki 1: 2 lattice in his **upper c** that *was* in Samaria, 5944
4:10 Let us make a little **c**, I pray thee, 5944
4:11 he turned into the **c**, and lay there. 5944

2Ki 9: 2 carry him *to* an **inner c**: 2315+2315+871.1
23:11 the **c** of Nathan-melech the chamberlain, 3957
23:12 were on the top of the **upper c** of Ahaz, 5944
2Ch 12:11 and brought them again into the guard **c**. 8372
18:24 into an **inner c** to hide 2315+2315+871.1
Ezr 10: 6 went into the **c** of Johanan the son of 3957
Ne 3:30 the son of Berechiah over against his **c**. 5393
13: 4 having the oversight of the **c** of the house 3957
13: 5 he had prepared for him a great **c**, where 3957
13: 7 in preparing him a **c** in the courts of 5393
13: 8 household stuff of Tobiah out of the **c**. 3957
Ps 19: 5 *is* as a bridegroom coming out of his **c**, 2646
SS 3: 4 and into the **c** of her that conceived me. 2315
Jer 35: 4 into the **c** of the sons of Hanan, the son 3957
35: 4 which *was* by the **c** of the princes, 3957
35: 4 which *was* above the **c** of Maaseiah 3957
36:10 in the **c** of Gemariah the son of Shaphan 3957
36:12 *into* the king's house, into the scribe's **c**: 3957
36:20 they laid up the roll in the **c** of Elishama 3957
36:21 he took it out of Elishama the scribe's **c**. 3957
Eze 40: 7 *every* **little c** *was* one reed long, 8372
40:13 the gate from the roof of *one* **little c** to 8372
40:45 said unto me, This **c**, whose prospect *is* 3957
40:46 the **c** whose prospect *is* toward the north 3957
41: 5 the breadth of *every* **side c**, four cubits, 6763
41: 7 increased *from* the lowest **c** to the highest NIH
41: 9 *was* for the **side c** without, was five 6763
42: 1 he brought me into the **c** that *was* over 3957
Da 6:10 his windows being open in his **c** toward 5952
Joel 2:16 let the bridegroom go forth of his **c**, 2315
Ac 9:37 had washed, they laid *her* in an **upper c**. 5253
9:39 they brought him into the **upper c**: 5253
20: 8 there were many lights in the **upper c**, 5253

CHAMBERING (1) [CHAMBER]
Ro 13:13 not in **c** and wantonness, not in strife *and* 2845

CHAMBERLAIN (6) [CHAMBER]
2Ki 23:11 the chamber of Nathan-melech the **c**, 5631
Est 2: 3 unto the custody of Hege the king's **c**, 5631
2:14 the king's **c**, which kept the concubines: 5631
2:15 but what Hegai the king's **c**, 5631
Ac 12:20 the king's **c** their friend, 1909+2846+3588
Ro 16:23 Erastus the **c** of the city saluteth you, 3623

CHAMBERLAINS (9) [CHAMBER]
Est 1:10 the seven **c** that served in the presence of 5631
1:12 at the king's commandment by *his* **c**: 5631
1:15 of the king Ahasuerus by the **c**? 5631
2:21 two of the king's **c**, Bigthan and Teresh, 5631
4: 4 and her **c** came and told *it* her. 5631
4: 5 Esther for Hatach, *one* of the king's **c**, 5631
6: 2 and Teresh, two of the king's **c**, 5631
6:14 came the king's **c**, and hasted to bring 5631
7: 9 Harbonah, one of the **c**, said before 5631

CHAMBERS (66) [CHAMBER]
1Ki 6: 5 against the wall of the house he built **c** 3326
6: 5 of the oracle: and he made **c** round about: 6763
6:10 *then* he built **c** against all the house, 3326
1Ch 9:26 over the **c** and treasuries of the house 3957
9:33 *who remaining* in the **c** *were* free: 3957
23:28 in the **c**, and in the purifying of all holy 3957
28:11 of the **upper c** thereof, and of the inner 5944
28:12 all the **c** round about, of the treasuries of 3957
2Ch 3: 9 And he overlaid the **upper c** with gold. 5944
31:11 Hezekiah commanded to prepare **c** in 3957
Ezr 8:29 *in* the **c** of the house of the L<small>ORD</small>. 3957
Ne 10:37 priests, to the **c** of the house of our God; 3957
10:38 our God, to the, **c**, into the treasure house. 3957
10:39 of the new wine, and the oil, unto the **c**, 3957
12:44 that time were some appointed over the **c** 5393
13: 9 I commanded, and they cleansed the **c**: 3957
Job 9: 9 and Pleiades, and the **c** of the south. 2315
Ps 104: 3 Who layeth the beams of his **c** in 5944
104:13 He watereth the hills from his **c**: the earth 5944
105:30 frogs in abundance, in the **c** of their kings. 2315
Pr 7:27 way to hell, going down to the **c** of death. 2315
24: 4 by knowledge shall the **c** be filled *with* all 2315
SS 1: 4 the king hath brought me *into* his **c**: 2315
Isa 26:20 enter thou into thy **c**, and shut thy doors 2315
Jer 22:13 by unrighteousness, and his **c** by wrong; 5944
22:14 I will build me a wide house and large **c**, 5944
35: 2 into one of the **c**, and give them wine to 3957
Eze 8:12 every man in the **c** of his imagery? 2315
21:14 slain, which **entereth into** their **privy c**, 2314
40: 7 between the **little c** *were* five cubits; 8372
40:10 the **little c** of the gate eastward *were* 8372
40:12 The space also before the **little c** *was* one 8372
40:12 the **little c** *were* six cubits on this side, 8372
40:16 *were* narrow windows to the **little c**, 8372
40:17 *there were* a, and a pavement made for 3957
40:17 thirty **c** *were* upon the pavement. 3957
40:21 the **little c** thereof *were* three on this side 8372
40:29 the **little c** thereof, and the posts thereof, 8372
40:33 the **little c** thereof, and the posts thereof, 8372
40:36 The **little c** thereof, the posts thereof, 8372
40:38 the **c** and the entries thereof *were* by 3957
40:44 without the inner gate *were* the **c** of 3957
41: 6 the **side c** *were* three, one over another, 6763
41: 6 of the house for the **side c** round about, 6763
41: 7 winding about still upward to the **side c**: 6763
41: 8 the foundations of the **side c** *were* a full 6763
41: 9 the place of the **side c** that *were* within. 6763
41:10 between the **c** *was* the wideness of twenty 3957

Eze 41:11 the doors of the **side c** *were* toward 6763
41:26 *upon* the **side c** of the house, and thick 6763
42: 4 before the **c** *was* a walk of ten cubits 3957
42: 5 Now the upper **c** *were* shorter: for 3957
42: 7 wall that *was* without over against the **c**, 3957
42: 7 the utter court on the forepart of the **c**, 3957
42: 8 the length of the **c** that were in the utter 3957
42: 9 under these *was* the entry on the east 3957
42:10 The **c** *were* in the thickness of the wall of 3957
42:11 of the **c** which *were* toward the north, 3957
42:12 according to the doors of the **c** that *were* 3957
42:13 The north **c** and the south chambers, 3957
42:13 The north chambers *and* the south **c**, 3957
42:13 before the separate place, they be holy **c**, 3957
44:19 in the holy **c**, and they shall put on 3957
45: 5 for a possession *for* twenty **c**. 3957
46:19 the holy **c** of the priests, which looked 3957
Mt 24:26 he is in the **secret c**; believe *it* not. 5009

CHAMELEON (1)
Lev 11:30 the **c**, and the lizard, and the snail, 3581

CHAMOIS (1)
Dt 14: 5 the pygarg, and the wild ox, and the **c**. 2169

CHAMPAIGN (1)
Dt 11:30 which dwell in the **c** over against Gilgal, 6160

CHAMPION (3)
1Sa 17: 4 there went out a **c** out of 376+1143+1886.1
17:23 behold, there came up the **c**, 376+1143+1886.1
17:51 when the Philistines saw their **c** was dead, 1368

CHANCE (6) [CHANCETH]
Dt 22: 6 If a bird's nest **c** to be before thee in 7122
1Sa 6: 9 smote us; it *was* a **c** *that* happened to us. 4745
2Sa 1: 6 I **happened by c** upon mount 7122+7136
Ecc 9:11 but time and **c** happeneth to them all. 6294
Lk 10:31 by **c** there came down a certain priest 4795
1Co 15:37 it may **c** of wheat, or of some other 1487+5177

CHANCELLOR (3)
Ezr 4: 8 Rehum the **c** and Shimshai the 1169+2942
4: 9 *wrote* Rehum the **c**, and Shimshai 1169+2942
4:17 king an answer unto Rehum the **c**, 1169+2942

CHANCETH (1) [CHANCE]
Dt 23:10 reason of *uncleanness* that **c** him by night, 7137

CHANGE (26) [CHANGEABLE, CHANGED, CHANGERS, CHANGERS', CHANGES, CHANGEST, CHANGETH, CHANGING, UNCHANGEABLE]
Ge 35: 2 and be clean, and **c** your garments: 2498
Lev 27:10 nor **c** it, a good for a bad, or a bad for a 4171
27:10 if he shall **at all c** beast for beast, 4171+4171
27:33 it be good or bad, neither may he **c** it: 4171
27:33 if he **c** it **at all**, then both it and 4171+4171
27:33 both it and the **c** thereof shall be holy; 8545
Jdg 14:12 you thirty sheets and thirty **c** of garments: 2487
14:13 me thirty sheets and thirty **c** of garments. 2487
14:19 gave **c** *of garments* unto them which 2487
Job 14:14 appointed time will I wait, till my **c** come. 2487
17:12 They **c** the night into day: the light *is* 7760
Ps 102:26 as vesture shalt thou **c** them, 2498
Pr 24:21 not with them that are **given** to **c**: 8138
Isa 9:10 down, but we will **c** *them* into cedars. 2498
Jer 2:36 gaddest thou about *so* much to **c** thy way? 8138
13:23 Can the Ethiopian **c** his skin, 2015
Da 7:25 most High, and think to **c** times and laws: 8133
Hos 4: 7 *therefore* will I **c** their glory into shame. 4171
Hab 1:11 shall *his* mind **c**, and he shall pass over, 2498
Zec 3: 4 and *I will* clothe thee with **c** of raiment. 4254
Mal 3: 6 For I *am* the L<small>ORD</small>, I **c** not; therefore 8138
Ac 6:14 the customs which Moses delivered 236
Ro 1:26 even their women did **c** the natural use 3337
Gal 4:20 present with you now, and to **c** my voice; 236
Php 3:21 Who shall **c** our vile body, that it may be 3345
Heb 7:12 made is of necessity a **c** also of 3331

CHANGEABLE (1) [CHANGE]
Isa 3:22 The **c suits of apparel**, and the mantles, 4254

CHANGED (43) [CHANGE]
Ge 31: 7 deceived me, and **c** my wages ten times; 2498
31:41 and thou hast **c** my wages ten times. 2498
41:14 he shaved *himself*, and **c** his raiment, 2498
Lev 13:16 be **c** unto white, he shall come unto 2015
13:55 *if* the plague have not **c** his colour, 2015
Nu 32:38 and Baal-meon, (*their* names being **c**,) 5437
1Sa 21:13 he **c** his behaviour before them, 8138
2Sa 12:20 he arose, and anointed *himself*, and **c** his apparel, 2498
2Ki 24:17 in his stead, and **c** his name to Zedekiah. 5437
25:29 **c** his prison garments: and he did eat 8132
Job 30:18 great force *of my disease* is my garment **c**: 2664
Ps 34: 1 he **c** his behaviour before Abimelech, 8138
102:26 thou change them, and they shall be **c**: 2498
106:20 Thus they **c** their glory into the similitude 4171
Ecc 8: 1 and the boldness of his face shall be **c**. 8132
Isa 24: 5 transgressed the laws, **c** the ordinance, 2498
Jer 2:11 Hath a nation **c** *their* gods, which *are* yet 3235
2:11 my people have **c** their glory for *that* 4171
48:11 remained in him, and his sent is not **c**. 4171
52:33 **c** his prison garments: and he did 8138
La 4: 1 *how* is the most fine gold **c**! the stones of 8132
Eze 5: 6 she hath **c** my judgments into wickedness 4784

C

Da	2: 9 to speak before me, till the time be **c**:	8133
3:19 the form of his visage was **c** against	8133	
3:27 head singed, neither were their coats **c**,	8133	
3:28 have **c** the king's word, and yielded their	8133	
4:16 Let his heart be **c** from man's, and let a	8133	
5: 6 the king's countenance was **c**,	8133	
5: 9 countenance *was* **c** in him, and his lords	8133	
5:10 nor let thy countenance be **c**.	8133	
6: 8 and sign the writing, that *it* be not **c**,	8133	
6:15 which the king establisheth may be **c**.	8133	
6:17 the purpose might not be **c** concerning	8133	
7:28 and my countenance **c** in me:	8133	
Mic	2: 4 he hath **c** the portion of my people:	4171
Ac	28: 6 they **c** *their minds*, and said that he was	3328
Ro	1:23 And **c** the glory of the uncorruptible God	236
1:25 Who **c** the truth of God into a lie,	3337	
1Co	15:51 shall not all sleep, but we shall all be **c**,	236
15:52 be raised incorruptible, and we shall be **c**.	236	
2Co	3:18 are **c** *into* the same image from glory to	3339
Heb	1:12 thou fold them up, and they shall be **c**:	236
7:12 For the priesthood being **c**, there is made	3346	

CHANGERS (1) [CHANGE]

Jn | 2:14 and doves, and the **c of money** sitting: | 2773

CHANGERS' (1) [CHANGE]

Jn | 2:15 and poured out the **c** money, | 2855

CHANGES (7) [CHANGE]

Ge	45:22 To all of them he gave each man **c** of	2487
45:22 *pieces* of silver, and five **c** of raiment.	2487	
2Ki	5: 5 *pieces* of gold, and ten **c** of raiment.	2487
5:22 a talent of silver, and two **c** of garments.	2487	
5:23 two **c** of garments, and laid *them* upon	2487	
Job | 10:17 upon me; and **c** and war *are* against me. | 2487
Ps | 55:19 they have no **c**, therefore they fear | 2487

CHANGEST (1) [CHANGE]

Job | 14:20 thou **c** his countenance, and sendest him | 8138

CHANGETH (2) [CHANGE]

Ps | 15: 4 *that* sweareth to *his own* hurt, and **c** not. | 4171
Da | 2:21 he **c** the times and the seasons: | 8133

CHANGING (1) [CHANGE]

Ru | 4: 7 concerning redeeming and concerning **c**, | 8545

CHANNEL (1) [CHANNELS]

Isa | 27:12 *that* the Lord shall beat off from the **c** of | 7641

CHANNELS (3) [CHANNEL]

2Sa | 22:16 the **c** of the sea appeared, the foundations | 650
Ps | 18:15 the **c** of waters were seen, | 650
Isa | 8: 7 he shall come up over all his **c**, and go over | 650

CHANT (1)

Am | 6: 5 That **c** to the sound of the viol, | 6527

CHAPEL (1)

Am | 7:13 for it *is* the king's **c**, and it *is* the king's | 4720

CHAPITER (13) [CHAPITERS]

1Ki	7:16 the height of the one **c** *was* five cubits,	3805
7:16 the height of the other **c** *was* five cubits:	3805	
7:17 seven for the one **c**, and seven for the	3805	
7:17 one chapiter, and seven for the other **c**.	3805	
7:18 and so did he for the other **c**.	3805	
7:20 *in* rows round about upon the other **c**,	3805	
7:31 the mouth of it within the **c** and above	3805	
2Ki	25:17 cubits, and the **c** upon it *was* brass:	3805
25:17 the height of the three cubits;	3805	
25:17 pomegranates upon the **c** round about,	3805	
2Ch	3:15 the **c** that *was* on the top *of each* of them	6858
Jer	52:22 a **c** of brass *was* upon it; and the height of	3805
52:22 the height of one **c** *was* five cubits,	3805	

CHAPITERS (16) [CHAPITER]

Ex	36:38 he overlaid their **c** and their fillets with	7218
38:17 the overlaying of their **c** *of* silver; and all	7218	
38:19 the overlaying of their **c** and their fillets	7218	
38:28 and overlaid their **c**, and filleted them.	7218	
1Ki	7:16 he made two **c** *of* molten brass, to set	3805
7:17 for the **c** which were upon the top of	3805	
7:18 to cover the **c** that *were* upon the top,	3805	
7:19 (And the **c** that *were* upon the top of	3805	
7:20 the **c** upon the two pillars *had*	3805	
7:41 two bowls of the **c** that *were* on the top	3805	
7:41 to cover the two bowls of the **c** which	3805	
7:42 to cover the two bowls of the **c** that *were*	3805	
2Ch	4:12 the **c** which *were* on the top of the two	3805
4:12 the **c** which *were* on the top of the pillars;	3805	
4:13 to cover the two pommels of the **c** which	3805	
Jer | 52:22 pomegranates upon the **c** round about, | 3805

CHAPMEN (1) [MAN]

2Ch | 9:14 *which* **c** and merchants | 376+1886.1+8446

CHAPT (1)

Jer | 14: 4 Because the ground is **c**, for there was no | 2865

CHARASHIM (1)

1Ch | 4:14 begat Joab, the father of the valley of **C**; | 2798

CHARGE (102) [CHARGEABLE, CHARGED, CHARGEDST, CHARGES, CHARGEST, CHARGING, OVERCHARGE]

Ge	26: 5 kept my **c**, my commandments,	4931
28: 6 that as he blessed him he **gave** him a **c**,	6680	
Ex	6:13 **gave** them a **c** unto the children of Israel,	6680
19:21 said unto Moses, Go down, **c** the people,	5749	
Lev	8:35 keep the **c** of the Lord, that ye die not:	4931
Nu	1:53 the Levites shall keep the **c** of	4931
3: 7 they shall keep his **c**, and the charge of	4931	
3: 7 the **c** of the whole congregation before	4931	
3: 8 the **c** of the children of Israel, to do	4931	
3:25 the **c** of the sons of Gershon in	4931	
3:28 hundred, keeping the **c** of the sanctuary.	4931	
3:31 their **c** *shall be* the ark, and the table,	4931	
3:32 the oversight of them that keep the **c**	4931	
3:36 **c** of the sons of Merari *shall be* the boards	4931	
3:38 keeping the **c** of the sanctuary for	4931	
3:38 for the **c** of the children of Israel;	4931	
4:27 ye shall appoint unto them in **c** all their	4931	
4:28 their **c** *shall be* under the hand of Ithamar	4931	
4:31 *is* the **c** of their burden, according to all	4931	
4:32 the instruments of their **c**, and all their burden.	4931	
5:19 the priest shall **c** her **by an oath**,	7650	
5:21 **c** the woman **with an oath**	7621+7650+871.1	
8:26 to keep the **c**, and shall do no service.	4931	
8:26 thou do unto the Levites touching their **c**.	4931	
9:19 the children of Israel kept the **c** of	4931	
9:23 they kept the **c** of the Lord,	4931	
18: 3 they shall keep thy **c**, and the charge of all	4931	
18: 3 thy charge, and the **c** of all the tabernacle:	4931	
18: 4 keep the **c** of the tabernacle of	4931	
18: 5 ye shall keep the **c** of the sanctuary,	4931	
18: 5 of the sanctuary, and the **c** of the altar:	4931	
18: 8 I also have given thee the **c** of mine heave	4931	
27:19 and **give** him a **c** in their sight.	6680	
27:23 his hands upon him, and **gave** him a **c**,	6680	
31:30 which keep the **c** of the tabernacle of	4931	
31:47 which kept the **c** of the tabernacle of	4931	
31:49 the men of war which *are* under our **c**,	3027	
Dt	3:28 **c** Joshua, and encourage him,	6680
11: 1 keep his **c**, and his statutes,	4931	
21: 8 blood unto thy people of Israel's **c**.	7130	
31:14 congregation, that I may **give** him a **c**.	6680	
31:23 he **gave** Joshua the son of Nun a **c**,	6680	
Jos	22: 3 have kept the **c** of the commandment of	4931
2Sa	14: 8 and I will **give c** concerning thee.	6680
18: 5 **gave** all the captains **c** concerning	6680	
1Ki	2: 3 keep the **c** of the Lord thy God, to walk	4931
4:28 every man according to his **c**.	4941	
11:28 he made him ruler over all the **c** of	5447	
2Ki	7:17 had he leaned to **have the c** of the gate:	5921
1Ch	9:27 because the **c** *was* upon them,	4931
9:28 of them had the **c** of the ministering	5921	
22:12 and **give** them **c** concerning Israel,	6680	
23:32 that they should keep the **c** of	4931	
23:32 the **c** of the holy *place*, and the charge of	4931	
23:32 the **c** of the sons of Aaron their brethren,	4931	
2Ch	13:11 for we keep the **c** of the Lord our God;	4931
30:17 the Levites **had the c** of the killing of	5921	
Ne	7: 2 **gave** my brother Hanani, and Hananiah	6680
the ruler of the palace, **c**	6680	
10:32 to **c** ourselves yearly with the third *part*	5414	
Est	3: 9 of those that have the **c** of the business,	6213
4: 8 **c** her that *she* should go in unto the king,	6680	
Job	34:13 Who hath **given** him a **c** over the earth?	6485
Ps	35:11 they **laid to** my **c** *things* that I knew not.	7592
91:11 For he shall **give** his angels **c** over thee,	6680	
SS	2: 7 I **c** you, O ye daughters of Jerusalem,	7650
3: 5 I **c** you, O ye daughters of Jerusalem,	7650	
5: 8 I **c** you, O daughters of Jerusalem, if ye	7650	
5: 9 *another* beloved, that thou dost so **c** us?	7650	
8: 4 I **c** you, O daughters of Jerusalem, that ye	7650	
Isa	10: 6 people of my wrath will I **give** him a **c**,	6680
Jer	39:11 **gave** **c** concerning Jeremiah to	6680
47: 7 seeing the Lord hath **given** it a **c** against	6680	
52:25 which had the **c** of the men of war;	6496	
Eze	9: 1 Cause them **that have c over** the city to	6486
40:45 the keepers of the **c** of the house.	4931	
40:46 priests, the keepers of the **c** of the altar:	4931	
44: 8 have not kept the **c** of mine holy *things*:	4931	
44: 8 ye have set keepers of my **c** in my	4931	
44:11 *having* **c** at the gates of the house,	6486	
44:14 I will make them keepers of the **c** of	4931	
44:15 that kept the **c** of my sanctuary when	4931	
44:16 unto me, and they shall keep my **c**.	4931	
48:11 which have kept my **c**, which went not	4931	
Zec	3: 7 If thou wilt keep my **c**, then thou shalt	4931
Mt	4: 6 He shall **give** his angels **c** concerning thee:	1781
Mk	9:25 Thou dumb and deaf spirit, I **c** thee,	2004
Lk	4:10 shall **give** his angels **c** over thee, to keep	1781
Ac	7:60 voice, Lord, **lay** not this sin **to** their **c**.	2476
8:27 who had the **c** of all her treasure, and had	1909	
16:24 having received such a **c**, thrust them	3852	
23:29 to have nothing **laid to** his **c** worthy of	1462	
Ro	8:33 Who shall **lay** any thing **to the c** of God's	1458
1Co	9:18 may make the gospel of Christ **without c**,	77
1Th	5:27 **c** you by the Lord that *this* epistle be read	3726
1Ti	1: 3 that thou mightest **c** some *that they* teach	3853
1:18 This **c** I commit unto thee, son Timothy,	3852	
5: 7 And these *things* **give in c**, that they may	3853	
5:21 I **c** *thee* before God, and the Lord Jesus	1263	
6:13 I **give** thee **c** in the sight of God,	3853	
6:17 **C** *them that are* rich in this world, that	3853	

2Ti	4: 1 I **c** *thee* therefore before God,	1263
4:16 that it may not be **laid to** their **c**.	3049	

CHARGEABLE (5) [CHARGE]

2Sa | 13:25 not all now go, lest we be **c** unto thee. | 3513
Ne | 5:15 before me were **c** unto the people, | 3513
2Co | 11: 9 I was **c** to no *man*: for that which was | 2655
1Th | 2: 9 we would not be **c** unto any of you, | 1912
2Th | 3: 8 day, that *we* might not be **c** to any of you: | 1912

CHARGED (51) [CHARGE]

Ge	26:11 Abimelech **c** all *his* people, saying, He	6680
28: 1 blessed him, and **c** him, and said unto	6680	
40: 4 the captain of the guard **c** Joseph with	6485	
49:29 he **c** them, and said unto them, I *am* to be	6680	
Ex	1:22 Pharaoh **c** all his people, saying, Every son	6680
Dt	1:16 I **c** your judges at that time, saying,	6680
24: 5 shall he be **c** with any business:	5674+5921	
27:11 Moses **c** the people the same day, saying,	6680	
Jos	18: 8 Joshua **c** them that went to describe	6680
22: 5 which Moses the servant of the Lord **c**	6680	
Ru	2: 9 have I not **c** the young men that *they* shall	7650
1Sa	14:27 his father **c** the people **with the oath**:	7650
14:28 **straitly c** the people **with an oath**,	7650+7650	
2Sa	11:19 **c** the messenger, saying, When thou hast	6680
18:12 for in our hearing the king **c** thee and	6680	
1Ki	2: 1 and he **c** Solomon his son, saying,	6680
2:43 commandment that I have **c** thee with?	6680	
13: 9 so was it **c** me by the word of the Lord,	6680	
2Ki	17:15 *concerning* whom the Lord had **c** them,	6680
17:35 **c** them, saying, Ye shall not fear other	6680	
1Ch	22: 6 him to build a house for the Lord God	6680
22:13 judgments which the Lord **c** Moses with	6680	
2Ch	19: 9 he **c** them, saying, Thus shall ye do in	6680
36:23 he hath **c** me to build him a house in	6485	
Ezr	1: 2 he hath **c** me to build him a house at	6485
Ne	13:19 **c** that they should not be opened till after	559
Est	2:10 Mordecai had **c** her that she should not	6680
2:20 nor her mandate; as Mordecai had **c** her:	6680	
Job	1:22 Job sinned not, nor **c** God foolishly.	5414
4:18 servants; and his angels he **c** with folly:	7760	
Jer	32:13 And I **c** Baruch before them, saying,	6680
35: 8 Rechab our father in all that he hath **c** us,	6680	
Mt	9:30 and Jesus **straitly c** them, saying,	1690
12:16 And **c** them that they should not make	2008	
16:20 Then **c** he his disciples that they should	1291	
17: 9 from the mountain, Jesus **c** them, saying,	1781	
Mk	1:43 And he **straitly c** him, and forthwith sent	1690
3:12 he **straitly c** them that they should not	2008	
5:43 he **c** them straitly that no *man* should	1291	
7:36 he **c** them that they should tell no *man*:	1291	
7:36 tell no *man*: but the more he **c** them,	1291	
8:15 And he **c** them, saying, Take heed,	1291	
8:30 he **c** them that they should tell no *man*	2008	
9: 9 he **c** them that they should tell no *man*	1291	
10:48 And many **c** him that he should hold his	2008	
Lk	5:14 And he **c** him to tell no *man*: but go,	3853
8:56 he **c** them that they should tell no *man*	3853	
9:21 And he **straitly c** them,	2008	
Ac | 23:22 **c** him, *See thou* tell no *man* that thou | 3853
1Th | 2:11 and comforted and **c** every one of you, | 3143
1Ti | 5:16 relieve them, and let not the church be **c**; | 916

CHARGEDST (1) [CHARGE]

Ex | 19:23 for thou **c** us, saying, Set bounds about | 5749

CHARGER (17) [CHARGERS]

Nu	7:13 His offering *was* one silver **c**, the weight	7086
7:19 He offered *for* his offering one silver **c**	7086	
7:25 His offering *was* one silver **c**, the weight	7086	
7:31 His offering *was* one silver **c** of the weight	7086	
7:37 His offering *was* one silver **c**, the weight	7086	
7:43 His offering *was* one silver **c** of the weight	7086	
7:49 His offering *was* one silver **c**, the weight	7086	
7:55 His offering *was* one silver **c**, the weight	7086	
7:61 His offering *was* one silver **c**, the weight	7086	
7:67 His offering *was* one silver **c**, the weight	7086	
7:73 His offering *was* one silver **c**, the weight	7086	
7:79 His offering *was* one silver **c**, the weight	7086	
7:85 Each **c** of silver *weighing* an hundred and	7086	
Mt	14: 8 Give me here John Baptist's head in a **c**.	4094
14:11 And his head was brought in a **c**,	4094	
Mk	6:25 and by in a **c** the head of John the Baptist.	4094
6:28 And brought his head in a **c**, and gave it to	4094	

CHARGERS (3) [CHARGER]

Nu | 7:84 twelve **c** of silver, twelve silver bowls, | 7086
Ezr | 1: 9 thirty **c** of gold, a thousand chargers of | 105
 | 1: 9 a thousand **c** of silver, nine and | 105

CHARGES (6) [CHARGE]

2Ch | 8:14 Levites to their **c**, to praise and minister | 4931
 | 31:16 daily portion for their service in their **c** | 4931
 | 31:17 and upward, in their **c** by their courses; | 4931
 | 35: 2 he set the priests in their **c**, | 4931
Ac | 21:24 thyself with them, and be at **c** with them, | 1159
1Co | 9: 7 goeth a warfare any time at his own **c**? | 3800

CHARGEST (1) [CHARGE]

2Sa | 3: 8 that thou **c** me to day with a fault | 6485

CHARGING (2) [CHARGE]

Ac | 16:23 prison, **c** the jailor to keep them safely: | 3853
2Ti | 2:14 **c** them before the Lord that *they* strive not | 1263

C

CHARIOT (64) [CHARIOTS]
Ge	41:43 made him to ride in the second **c** which	4818
	46:29 Joseph made ready his **c**, and went up to	4818
Ex	14: 6 he made ready his **c**, and took his people	7393
	14:25 took off their **c** wheels, that they drave	4818
Jdg	4:15 so that Sisera lighted down off *his* **c**,	4818
	5:28 lattice, Why is his **c** *so* long in coming?	7393
2Sa	8: 4 David houghed all the **c** *horses*, but	7393
1Ki	7:33 wheels *was* like the work of a **c** wheel:	4818
	10:29 a came up and went out of Egypt for	4818
	12:18 made speed to get *him* up to his **c**,	4818
	18:44 Prepare *thy* **c**, and get thee down,	NIH
	20:25 lost, horse for horse, and **c** for chariot:	7393
	20:25 lost, horse for horse, and chariot for **c**:	7393
	20:33 and he caused him to come up into the **c**.	4818
	22:34 he said unto the **driver of** his **c**,	7395
	22:35 the king was stayed up in *his* **c** against	7393
	22:35 out of the wound into the midst of the **c**.	7393
	22:38 *one* washed the **c** in the pool of Samaria;	7393
2Ki	2:11 *there appeared* a **c** of fire, and horses of	7393
	2:12 the **c** of Israel, and the horsemen thereof.	7393
	5: 9 came with his horses and with his **c**,	7393
	5:21 he lighted down from the **c** to meet him,	4818
	5:26 turned *again* from his **c** to meet thee?	4818
	7:14 They took therefore two **c** horses;	7393
	9:16 So Jehu rode in a **c**, and went to Jezreel;	NIH
	9:21 his **c** was made ready. And Joram king of	7393
	9:21 each in his **c**, and they went out against	7393
	9:24 at his heart, and he sunk down in his **c**.	7393
	9:27 and said, Smite him also in the **c**.	4818
	9:28 servants carried him *in a* **c** to Jerusalem,	NIH
	10:15 and he took him up to him into the **c**.	4818
	10:16 So they made him ride in his **c**.	7393
	13:14 the **c** of Israel, and the horsemen thereof.	7393
	23:30 his servants carried him *in a* **c** dead from	NIH
1Ch	18: 4 David also houghed all the **c** *horses*, but	7393
	28:18 gold for the pattern of the **c** of	4818
2Ch	1:14 which he placed in the **c** cities, and with	4818
	1:17 brought forth out of Egypt a **c** for six	4818
	8: 6 all the **c** cities, and the cities of	7393
	9:25 whom he bestowed in the **c** cities,	7393
	10:18 made speed to get *him* up to his **c**,	4818
	18:33 therefore he said to *his* **c man**, Turn	7395
	18:34 in *his* **c** against the Syrians until the even:	4818
	35:24 therefore took him out of *that* **c**,	4818
	35:24 and put him in the second **c** that he had;	7393
Ps	46: 9 in sunder; he burneth the **c** in the fire.	5699
	76: 6 both the **c** and horse *are* cast into a dead	7393
	104: 3 who maketh the clouds his **c**: who walketh	7398
SS	3: 9 Solomon made himself a **c** of the wood	668
Isa	21: 7 he saw a **c** *with* a couple of horsemen,	7393
	21: 7 a **c** of asses, *and* a chariot of camels;	7393
	21: 7 a chariot of asses, *and* a **c** of camels;	7393
	21: 9 behold, here cometh a **c** of men, *with* a	7393
	43:17 Which bringeth forth the **c** and horse,	7393
Jer	51:21 with thee will I break in pieces the **c** and	7393
Mic	1:13 of Lachish, bind the **c** to the swift beast:	4818
Zec	6: 2 In the first **c** *were* red horses; and in	4818
	6: 2 and in the second **c** black horses;	4818
	6: 3 in the third **c** white horses; and in	4818
	6: 3 in the fourth **c** grisled *and* bay horses.	4818
	9:10 I will cut off the **c** from Ephraim,	7393
Ac	8:28 sitting in his **c** read Esaias the prophet.	716
	8:29 Go near, and join thyself to this **c**.	716
	8:38 And he commanded the **c** to stand still:	716

CHARIOTS (113) [CHARIOT]
Ge	50: 9 there went up with him both **c** and	7393
Ex	14: 7 he took six hundred chosen **c**, and all	7393
	14: 7 all the **c** of Egypt, and captains over every	7393
	14: 9 them (all the horses *and* **c** of Pharaoh,	7393
	14:17 upon his **c**, and upon his horsemen.	7393
	14:18 upon his **c**, and upon his horsemen.	7393
	14:23 Pharaoh's horses, his **c**, and his horsemen	7393
	14:26 upon their **c**, and upon their horsemen.	7393
	14:28 covered the **c**, and the horsemen, and all	7393
	15: 4 Pharaoh's **c** and his host hath he cast into	4818
	15:19 the horse of Pharaoh went in with his **c**	7393
Dt	11: 4 of Egypt, unto their horses, and to their **c**;	7393
	20: 1 and **c**, *and* a people more than thou,	7393
Jos	11: 4 multitude, with horses and **c** very many.	7393
	11: 6 their horses, and burn their **c** with fire.	4818
	11: 9 their horses, and burnt their **c** with fire.	4818
	17:16 in the land of the valley have **c** of iron,	7393
	17:18 though they have iron **c**, *and* though they	7393
	24: 6 pursued after your fathers with **c**	7393
Jdg	1:19 of the valley, because they had **c** of iron.	7393
	4: 3 for he had nine hundred **c** of iron;	7393
	4: 7 Jabin's army, with his **c** and his multitude	7393
	4:13 Sisera gathered together all his **c**,	7393
	4:13 *even* nine hundred **c** of iron, and all	7393
	4:15 and all **c**, and all *his* host,	7393
	4:16 Barak pursued after the **c**, and after	7393
	5:28 why tarry the wheels of his **c**?	4818
1Sa	8:11 for his **c**, and to be his horsemen;	4818
	8:11 and *some* shall run before his **c**.	4818
	8:12 of war, and instruments of his **c**.	7393
	13: 5 thirty thousand **c**, and six thousand	7393
2Sa	1: 6 the **c** and horsemen followed hard after	7393
	8: 4 And David took from him a thousand **c**,	NIH
	8: 4 but reserved for *an* hundred **c**.	7393
	10:18 David slew the men of seven hundred **c**	7393
	15: 1 that Absalom prepared him **c** and horses,	4818
1Ki	1: 5 he prepared him **c** and horsemen,	7393
	4:26 forty thousand stalls of horses for his **c**,	4817

1Ki	9:19 cities for his **c**, and cities for his horsemen	7393
	9:22 and rulers of his **c**, and his horsemen.	7393
	10:26 Solomon gathered together **c** and	7393
	10:26 he had a thousand and four hundred **c**,	7393
	10:26 whom he bestowed in the cities for **c**,	7393
	16: 9 captain of half *his* **c**, conspired against	7393
	20: 1 two kings with him, and horses, and **c**:	7393
	20:21 smote the horses and **c**, and slew	7393
	22:31 two captains that had rule over *his* **c**,	7393
	22:32 when the captains of the **c** saw	7393
	22:33 when the captains of the **c** perceived that	7393
2Ki	6:14 he thither horses, and **c**, and a great host:	7393
	6:15 the city both with horses and **c**.	7393
	6:17 *of* horses and **c** of fire round about Elisha.	7393
	7: 6 host of the Syrians to hear a noise of **c**,	7393
	8:21 went over to Zair, and all the **c** with him:	7393
	8:21 him about, and the captains of the **c**.	7393
	10: 2 *there are* with you **c** and horses, a fenced	7393
	13: 7 and ten **c**, and ten thousand footmen;	7393
	18:24 put thy trust on Egypt for **c** and	7393
	19:23 With the multitude of my **c** I am come up	7393
	23:11 and burnt the **c** of the sun with fire.	4818
1Ch	18: 4 David took from him a thousand **c**,	7393
	18: 4 but reserved of them *an* hundred **c**.	7393
	19: 6 thousand talents of silver to hire them **c**	7393
	19: 7 So they hired thirty and two thousand **c**,	7393
	19:18 seven thousand *men which fought in* **c**,	7393
2Ch	1:14 Solomon gathered **c** and horsemen: and	7393
	1:14 he had a thousand and four hundred **c**,	7393
	8: 9 and captains of his **c** and horsemen.	7393
	9:25 had four thousand stalls for horses and **c**,	4818
	12: 3 With twelve hundred **c**, and threescore	7393
	14: 9 thousand thousand, and three hundred **c**;	7393
	16: 8 with very many **c** and horsemen?	7393
	18:30 the captains of the **c** that *were* with him,	7393
	18:31 when the captains of the **c** saw	7393
	18:32 that when the captains of the **c** perceived	7393
	21: 9 with his princes, and all *his* **c** with him:	7393
	21: 9 him in, and the captains of the **c**.	7393
Ps	20: 7 Some *trust* in **c**, and some in horses: but	7393
	68:17 The **c** of God *are* twenty thousand,	7393
SS	1: 9 to a company of horses in Pharaoh's **c**.	7393
	6:12 my soul made me *like* the **c** of	4818
Isa	2: 7 neither *is there any* end of their **c**:	4818
	22: 6 Elam bare the quiver with **c** of men *and*	7393
	22: 7 that thy choicest valleys shall be full *of* **c**,	7393
	22:18 there the **c** of thy glory *shall be* the shame	4818
	31: 1 and trust in **c**, because *they* are many;	7393
	36: 9 put thy trust on Egypt for **c** and	7393
	37:24 By the multitude of my **c** am I come up *to*	7393
	66:15 with his **c** like a whirlwind, to render his	4818
	66:20 in **c**, and in litters, and upon mules,	7393
Jer	4:13 clouds, and his **c** *shall be* as a whirlwind:	4818
	17:25 riding in **c** and on horses, they,	7393
	22: 4 riding in **c** and on horses, he,	7393
	46: 9 rage, ye **c**; and let the mighty *men* come	7393
	47: 3 his strong *horses*, at the rushing of his **c**,	7393
	50:37 upon their **c**, and upon all the mingled	7393
Eze	23:24 they shall come against thee *with* **c**,	2021
	26: 7 **c**, and with horsemen, and companies,	7393
	26:10 of the wheels, and of the **c**, when he shall	7393
	27:20 thy merchant in precious clothes for **c**.	7396
	39:20 be filled at my table *with* horses and **c**,	7393
Da	11:40 with **c**, and with horsemen, and with	7393
Joel	2: 5 the noise of **c** on the tops of mountains	4818
Mic	5:10 the midst of thee, and I will destroy thy **c**:	4818
Na	2: 3 the **c** *shall be* with flaming torches in	7393
	2: 4 The **c** shall rage in the streets, they shall	7393
	2:13 I will burn her **c** in the smoke,	7393
	3: 2 the prancing horses, and of the jumping **c**.	4818
Hab	3: 8 upon thine horses *and* thy **c** of salvation?	4818
Hag	2:22 I will overthrow the **c**, and those that ride	4818
Zec	6: 1 there came four **c** out from between two	4818
Rev	9: 9 sound of **c** of many horses running to battle.	716
	18:13 and **c**, and slaves, and souls of men.	4480

CHARITABLY (1) [CHARITY]
Ro	14:15 *thy* meat, now walkest thou not **c**.	26+2596

CHARITY (28) [CHARITABLY]
1Co	8: 1 Knowledge puffeth up, but **c** edifieth.	26
	13: 1 of men and of angels, and have not **c**,	26
	13: 2 and have no **c**, I am nothing.	26
	13: 3 and have not **c**, it profiteth me nothing.	26
	13: 4 **C** suffereth long, *and* is kind; charity	26
	13: 4 suffereth long, *and* is kind; **c** envieth not;	26
	13: 4 vaunteth not itself, is not puffed up,	26
	13: 8 **C** never faileth:	26
	13:13 now abideth faith, hope, **c**, these three;	26
	13:13 these three; but the greatest of these *is* **c**.	26
	14: 1 Follow after **c**, and desire spiritual *gifts*,	26
	16:14 Let all your *things* be done with **c**.	26
Col	3:14 And above all these *things put on* **c**, which	26
1Th	3: 6 brought us good tidings of your faith and **c**,	26
2Th	1: 3 the **c** of every one of you all towards each	26
1Ti	1: 5 the end of the commandment is **c** out of	26
	2:15 in faith and **c** and holiness with sobriety.	26
	4:12 in **c**, in spirit, in faith, in purity.	26
2Ti	2:22 but follow righteousness, faith, **c**, peace,	26
	3:10 purpose, faith, longsuffering, **c**, patience,	26
Tit	2: 2 temperate, sound in faith, in **c**, in patience.	26
1Pe	4: 8 Above all *things* have fervent **c** among	26
	4: 8 for **c** shall cover the multitude of sins.	26
	5:14 Greet ye one another with a kiss of **c**.	26
2Pe	1: 7 and to brotherly kindness **c**.	26

3Jn	1: 6 Which have borne witness of thy **c** before	26
Jude	1:12 These are spots in your **feasts of** **c** when	26
Rev	2:19 I know thy works, and **c**, and service,	26

CHARMED (1) [CHARMER, CHARMERS, CHARMING]
Jer	8:17 *will* not be **c**, and they shall bite you,	3908

CHARMER (1) [CHARMED]
Dt	18:11 Or a **c**, or a consulter with familiar	2266+2267

CHARMERS (2) [CHARMED]
Ps	58: 5 Which will not hearken to the voice of **c**,	3907
Isa	19: 3 to the **c**, and to them that have familiar	328

CHARMING (1) [CHARMED]
Ps	58: 5 of charmers, **c** *never so* wisely.	2266+2267

CHARRAN (2) [HARAN]
Ac	7: 2 in Mesopotamia, before he dwelt in **C**,	5488
	7: 4 land of the Chaldeans, and dwelt in **C**:	5488

CHASE (6) [CHASED, CHASETH, CHASING]
Lev	26: 7 ye shall **c** your enemies, and they shall fall	7291
	26: 8 five of you shall **c** an hundred,	7291
	26:36 the sound of a shaken leaf shall **c** them;	7291
Dt	32:30 How should one **c** a thousand, and two	7291
Jos	23:10 One man of you shall **c** a thousand: for	7291
Ps	35: 5 and let the angel of the LORD **c** them.	1760

CHASED (13) [CHASE]
Dt	1:44 **c** you, as bees do, and destroyed you in	7291
Jos	7: 5 for they **c** them *from* before the gate *even*	7291
	8:24 in the wilderness wherein they **c** them,	7291
	10:10 **c** them *along* the way that goeth up to	7291
	11: 8 **c** them unto great Zidon,	7291
Jdg	9:40 Abimelech **c** him, and he fled before him,	7291
	20:43 **c** them, *and* trode them down with ease	7291
Ne	13:28 the Horonite: therefore I **c** him from me.	1272
Job	18:18 light into darkness, and **c** out of the world.	5074
	20: 8 shall be **c** away as a vision of the night.	5074
Isa	13:14 shall be as the **c** roe, and as a sheep that	5080
	17:13 shall be **c** as the chaff of the mountains	7291
La	3:52 enemies **c** me *sore*, like a bird,	6679+6679

CHASETH (1) [CHASE]
Pr	19:26 *his* father, *and* **c** away *his* mother,	1272

CHASING (1) [CHASE]
1Sa	17:53 the children of Israel returned from **c** after	1814

CHASTE (3)
2Co	11: 2 I may present *you* as a **c** virgin to Christ.	53
Tit	2: 5 *To be* discreet, **c**, keepers at home, good,	53
1Pe	3: 2 While they behold your **c** conversation	53

CHASTEN (6) [CHASTENED, CHASTENEST, CHASTENETH, CHASTENING]
2Sa	7:14 I will **c** him with the rod of men,	3198
Ps	6: 1 neither **c** me in thy hot displeasure.	3256
	38: 1 neither **c** me in thy hot displeasure.	3256
Pr	19:18 **C** thy son while there is hope, and let not	3256
Da	10:12 to **c** thyself before thy God, thy words	6031
Rev	3:19 As many as I love, I rebuke and **c**:	3811

CHASTENED (8) [CHASTEN]
Dt	21:18 mother, and *that*, when they have **c** him,	3256
Job	33:19 He is *also* with pain upon his bed,	3198
Ps	69:10 When I wept, *and* **c** my soul with fasting,	NIH
	73:14 I been plagued, and **c** every morning.	8433
	118:18 The LORD hath **c** me *sore*: but	3256+3256
1Co	11:32 when we are judged, we are **c** of the Lord,	3811
2Co	6: 9 and behold, we live; as **c**, and not killed;	3811
Heb	12:10 For they verily for a few days **c** us after	3811

CHASTENEST (1) [CHASTEN]
Ps	94:12 Blessed *is* the man whom thou **c**,	3256

CHASTENETH (5) [CHASTEN]
Dt	8: 5 as a man **c** his son, *so* the LORD thy God	3256
	8: 5 his son, *so* the LORD thy God **c** thee.	3256
Pr	13:24 but he that loveth him **c** him betimes.	4148
Heb	12: 6 For whom the Lord loveth he **c**,	3811
	12: 7 for what son is *he* whom the father **c** not?	3811

CHASTENING (6) [CHASTEN]
Job	5:17 despise not thou the **c** of the Almighty:	4148
Pr	3:11 My son, despise not the **c** of the LORD;	4148
Isa	26:16 they poured out a prayer *when* thy **c** *was*	4148
Heb	12: 5 despise not thou the **c** of the Lord,	3809
	12: 7 If ye endure **c**, God dealeth with you as	3809
	12:11 Now no **c** for the present seemeth to be	3809

CHASTISE (10) [CHASTISED, CHASTISEMENT, CHASTISETH]
Lev	26:28 I, will **c** you seven *times* for your sins.	3256
Dt	22:18 of that city shall take *that* man and **c** him;	3256
1Ki	12:11 whips, but I will **c** you with scorpions.	3256
	12:14 whips, but I will **c** you with scorpions.	3256
2Ch	10:11 whips, but I *will* **c** you with scorpions.	NIH
	10:14 whips, but I will **c** you with scorpions.	NIH
Hos	7:12 I will **c** them, as their congregation hath	3256
	10:10 *It is* in my desire that I should **c** them;	3256
Lk	23:16 I will therefore **c** him, and release *him*.	3811
	23:22 I will therefore **c** him, and let *him* go.	3811

C

CHASTISED (6) [CHASTISE]
1Ki 12:11 my father hath **c** you with whips, but I 3256
 12:14 my father *also* **c** you with whips, but I 3256
2Ch 10:11 my father **c** you with whips, but I *will* 3256
 10:14 my father **c** you with whips, but I *will* 3256
Jer 31:18 bemoaning himself *thus;* Thou hast **c** me, 3256
 31:18 I was **c**, as a bullock unaccustomed *to* 3256

CHASTISEMENT (5) [CHASTISE]
Dt 11: 2 which have not seen the **c** of the Lord 4148
Job 34:31 I have borne **c**, I will not offend *any more:* NIH
Isa 53: 5 the **c** of our peace *was* upon him; 4148
Jer 30:14 with the **c** of a cruel one, for the 4148
Heb 12: 8 But if ye be without **c**, whereof all are 3809

CHASTISETH (1) [CHASTISE]
Ps 94:10 that **c** the heathen, shall he not correct? 3256

CHATTER (1)
Isa 38:14 Like a crane *or* a swallow, so did I **c**: I did 6850

CHEBAR (8)
Eze 1: 1 *was* among the captives by the river of **C**, 3529
 1: 3 the land of the Chaldeans by the river **C**; 3529
 3:15 that dwelt by the river of **C**, and I sat 3529
 3:23 as the glory which I saw by the river of **C**: 3529
 10:15 living creature that I saw by the river of **C**. 3529
 10:20 under the God of Israel by the river of **C**; 3529
 10:22 same faces which I saw by the river of **C**, 3529
 43: 3 like the vision that I saw by the river **C**; 3529

CHECK (1)
Job 20: 3 I have heard the **c** of my reproach, 4148

CHECKER (1)
1Ki 7:17 And nets of **c** work, *and* wreaths of chain 7639

CHEDORLAOMER (5)
Ge 14: 1 **C** king of Elam, and Tidal king of nations; 3540
 14: 4 Twelve years they served **C**, and *in* 3540
 14: 5 in the fourteenth year came **C**, 3540
 14: 9 With **C** the king of Elam, and *with* Tidal 3540
 14:17 after his return from the slaughter of **C**, 3540

CHEEK (8) [CHEEK-TEETH, CHEEKS]
1Ki 22:24 and smote Micaiah on the **c**, and said, 3895
2Ch 18:23 and smote Micaiah upon the **c**, and said, 3895
Job 16:10 they have smitten me upon the **c** 3895
Ps 3: 7 all mine enemies *upon* the **c** bone; 3895
La 3:30 He giveth *his* **c** to him that smiteth him: 3895
Mic 5: 1 the judge of Israel with a rod upon the **c**. 3895
Mt 5:39 *whosoever* shall smite thee on thy right **c**, 4600
Lk 6:29 unto him that smiteth thee on the *one* **c** 4600

CHEEKS (5) [CHEEK]
Dt 18: 3 shoulder, and the **two c**, and the maw. 3895
SS 1:10 Thy **c** are comely with rows *of jewels,* thy 3895
 5:13 His **c** *are* as a bed of spices, *as* sweet 3895
Isa 50: 6 my **c** to them that plucked off the hair: 3895
La 1: 2 in the night, and her tears *are* on her **c**: 3895

CHEEK-TEETH (1) [CHEEK, TOOTH]
Joel 1: 6 of a lion, and he hath the **c** of a great lion. 4973

CHEER (10) [CHEERETH, CHEERFUL, CHEERFULLY, CHEERFULNESS]
Dt 24: 5 shall **c** up his wife which he hath taken. 8055
Ecc 11: 9 thy heart **c** thee in the days of thy youth, 2895
Mt 9: 2 *Son,* **be of good c; thy sins be forgiven** 2293
 14:27 spake unto them, saying, **Be of good c;** 2293
Mk 6:50 and saith unto them, **Be of good c:** 2293
Jn 16:33 but **be of good c; I have overcome** 2293
Ac 23:11 by him, and said, **Be of good c,** Paul: 2293
 27:22 And now I exhort you to **be of good c:** 2114
 27:25 sirs, **be of good c:** for I believe 2114
 27:36 were they all of **good c**, and they also 2115

CHEERETH (1) [CHEER]
Jdg 9:13 which **c** God and man, and go to be 8055

CHEERFUL (4) [CHEER]
Pr 15:13 A merry heart **maketh** a **c** countenance: 3190
Zec 8:19 of Judah joy and gladness, and **c** feasts; 2896
 9:17 corn shall **make** the young men **c**, 5107
2Co 9: 7 or of necessity: for God loveth a **c** giver. 2431

CHEERFULLY (1) [CHEER]
Ac 24:10 I do the **more c** answer for myself: 2115

CHEERFULNESS (1) [CHEER]
Ro 12: 8 he that sheweth mercy, with **c**. 2432

CHEESE (2) [CHEESES]
2Sa 17:29 and sheep, and **c** of kine, for David, 8194
Job 10:10 me out as milk, and cruddled me like **c**? 1385

CHEESES (1) [CHEESE]
1Sa 17:18 carry these ten **c** unto the captain 2461+2757

CHELAL (1)
Ezr 10:30 Adna, and **C**, Benaiah, Maaseiah, 3636

CHELLUH (1)
Ezr 10:35 Benaiah, Bedeiah, **C**, 3622

CHELUB (2)
1Ch 4:11 **C** the brother of Shuah begat Mehir, 3620
 27:26 of the ground *was* Ezri the son of **C**: 3620

CHELUBAI (1)
1Ch 2: 9 unto him; Jerahmeel, and Ram, and **C**. 3621

CHEMARIMS (1)
Zep 1: 4 *and* the name of the **C** with the priests; 3649

CHEMOSH (8)
Nu 21:29 thou art undone, O people of **C**: he hath 3645
 21:29 not thou possess that which **C** thy god 3645
1Ki 11: 7 did Solomon build a high place for **C**, 3645
 11:33 **C** the god of the Moabites, and Milcom 3645
2Ki 23:13 for **C** the abomination of the Moabites, 3645
Jer 48: 7 **C** shall go forth into captivity *with* his 3645
 48:13 Moab shall be ashamed of **C**, as the house 3645
 48:46 the people of **C** perisheth: for thy sons are 3645

CHENAANAH (5)
1Ki 22:11 Zedekiah the son of **C** made him horns of 3668
 22:24 Zedekiah the son of **C** went near, 3668
1Ch 7:10 **C**, and Zethan, and Tharshish, 3668
2Ch 18:10 Zedekiah the son of **C** had made him 3668
 18:23 Zedekiah the son of **C** came near, 3668

CHENANI (1)
Ne 9: 4 *and* **C**, and cried with a loud voice unto 3662

CHENANIAH (3)
1Ch 15:22 **C**, chief of the Levites, *was* for song: 3663
 15:27 **C** the master of the song *with* the singers: 3663
 26:29 **C** and his sons *were* for the outward 3663

CHEPHAR-HAAMMONAI (1)
Jos 18:24 **C**, and Ophni, and Gaba; twelve cities 3726

CHEPHIRAH (4)
Jos 9:17 and **C**, and Beeroth, and Kirjath-jearim. 3716
 18:26 And Mizpeh, and **C**, and Mozah, 3716
Ezr 2:25 **C**, and Beeroth, seven hundred and forty 3716
Ne 7:29 and Beeroth, seven hundred forty and 3716

CHERAN (2)
Ge 36:26 Hemdan, and Eshban, and Ithran, and **C**. 3763
1Ch 1:41 Amram, and Eshban, and Ithran, and **C**. 3763

CHERETHIMS (1) [CHERETHITES]
Eze 25:16 I will cut off the **C**, and destroy 3774

CHERETHITES (9) [CHERETHIMS]
1Sa 30:14 an invasion *upon* the south of the **C**, 3774
2Sa 8:18 the son of Jehoiada *was over* both the **C** 3774
 15:18 all the **C**, and all the Pelethites, and all 3774
 20: 7 the **C**, and the Pelethites, and all the mighty 3774
 20:23 the son of Jehoiada *was* over the **C** 3774
1Ki 1:38 the **C**, and the Pelethites, went down, 3774
 1:44 the **C**, and the Pelethites, and they have 3774
1Ch 18:17 the son of Jehoiada *was* over the **C** 3774
Zep 2: 5 of the sea coast, the nation of the **C**! 3774

CHERISH (1) [CHERISHED, CHERISHETH]
1Ki 1: 2 let her **c** him, and let her lie in thy 1961+5532

CHERISHED (1) [CHERISH]
1Ki 1: 4 **c** the king, and ministered to him: 1961+5532

CHERISHETH (2) [CHERISH]
Eph 5:29 but nourisheth and **c** it, even as the Lord 2282
1Th 2: 7 you, *even* as a nurse **c** her children; 2282

CHERITH (2)
1Ki 17: 3 and hide thyself by the brook **C**, 3747
 17: 5 for he went and dwelt by the brook **C**, 3747

CHERUB (30) [CHERUBIMS, CHERUBIMS']
Ex 25:19 make one **c** on the one end, and the other 3742
 25:19 end, and the other **c** on the other end: 3742
 37: 8 One **c** on the end on this side, 3742
 37: 8 another **c** on the *other* end on that side: 3742
2Sa 22:11 he rode upon a **c**, and did fly: and he was 3742
1Ki 6:24 five cubits *was* the one wing of the **c**, 3742
 6:24 and five cubits the other wing of the **c**: 3742
 6:25 the other **c** *was* ten cubits: both 3742
 6:26 The height of the one **c** *was* ten cubits, 3742
 6:26 ten cubits, and so *was it* of the other **c**. 3742
 6:27 the wing of the other **c** touched the other 3742
2Ch 3:11 *one* wing of the one **c** *was* five cubits, NIH
 3:11 reaching to the wing of the other **c**. 3742
 3:12 *one* wing of the other **c** *was* five cubits, 3742
 3:12 *also,* joining to the wing of the other **c**. 3742
Ezr 2:59 Tel-harsa, **C**, Addan, *and* Immer: 3743
Ne 7:61 Tel-haresha, **C**, Addon, and Immer: 3743
Ps 18:10 he rode upon a **c**, and did fly: yea, he did 3742
Eze 9: 3 the God of Israel was gone up from the **c**, 3742
 10: 2 *even* under the **c**, and fill thine hand *with* 3742
 10: 4 glory of the Lord went up from the **c**, 3742
 10: 7 *one* stretched forth his hand from 3742
 10: 9 one wheel by one **c**, and another wheel 3742
 10: 9 and another wheel by another **c**: 3742
 10:14 the first face *was* the face of a **c**, 3742
 28:14 Thou *art* the anointed **c** that covereth; 3742
 28:16 I will destroy thee, O covering **c**, from 3742
 41:18 so that a palm tree *was* between a **c** and 3742
 41:18 palm tree *was* between a cherub and a **c**; 3742

CHERUBIMS (64) [CHERUB]
Ge 3:24 at the east of the garden of Eden **C**, 3742
Ex 25:18 thou shalt make two **c** *of* gold, *of* beaten 3742
 25:19 of the mercy seat shall ye make the **c** 3742
 25:20 **c** shall stretch forth *their* wings on high, 3742
 25:20 the mercy seat shall the faces of the **c** be. 3742
 25:22 from between the two **c** which *are* upon 3742
 26: 1 *with* cunning work shalt thou make 3742
 26:31 *of* cunning work: *with* **c** shall it be made: 3742
 36: 8 *with* **c** *of* cunning work made he them. 3742
 36:35 *with* **c** made he it *of* cunning work. 3742
 37: 7 he made two **c** *of* gold, beaten out of one 3742
 37: 8 out of the mercy seat made he the **c** on 3742
 37: 9 the **c** spread out *their* wings on high, 3742
 37: 9 mercy seatward were the faces of the **c**. 3742
Nu 7:89 of Testimony, from between the two **c**: 3742
1Sa 4: 4 of hosts, which dwelleth *between* the **c**: 3742
2Sa 6: 2 of hosts that dwelleth *between* the **c**. 3742
1Ki 6:23 within the oracle he made two **c** *of* olive 3742
 6:25 both the **c** *were* of one measure and 3742
 6:27 And he set the **c** within the inner house: 3742
 6:27 they stretched forth the wings of the **c**, 3742
 6:28 And he overlaid the **c** with gold. 3742
 6:29 round about *with* carved figures of **c** 3742
 6:32 he carved upon them carvings of **c** and 3742
 6:32 gold upon the **c**, and upon the palm 3742
 6:35 he carved *thereon* **c** and palm trees and 3742
 7:29 the ledges *were* lions, oxen, and **c**: 3742
 7:36 he graved **c**, lions, and palm trees, 3742
 8: 6 holy *place,* even under the wings of the **c**. 3742
 8: 7 the **c** spread forth *their* two wings over 3742
 8: 7 the **c** covered the ark and the staves 3742
2Ki 19:15 which dwellest *between* the **c**, thou *art* 3742
1Ch 13: 6 that dwelleth *between* the **c**, whose name 3742
 28:18 gold for the pattern of the chariot of the **c**, 3742
2Ch 3: 7 with gold; and graved **c** on the walls. 3742
 3:10 in the most holy house he made two **c** of 3742
 3:11 wings of the **c** *were* twenty cubits long: 3742
 3:13 The wings of these **c** spread themselves 3742
 3:14 and fine linen, and wrought **c** thereon. 3742
 5: 7 holy *place,* even under the wings of the **c**: 3742
 5: 8 For the **c** spread forth *their* wings over 3742
 5: 8 the **c** covered the ark and the staves 3742
Ps 80: 1 thou that dwellest *between* the **c**, 3742
 99: 1 he sitteth *between* the **c**; let the earth be 3742
Isa 37:16 God of Israel, that dwellest *between* the **c** 3742
Eze 10: 1 **c** there appeared over them as it were a 3742
 10: 2 *with* coals of fire from between the **c**, 3742
 10: 3 Now the **c** stood on the right side of 3742
 10: 6 between the wheels, from between the **c**; 3742
 10: 7 unto the fire that *was* between 3742
 10: 8 appeared in the **c** the form of a man's 3742
 10: 9 I looked, behold the four wheels by the **c**, 3742
 10:15 the **c** were lifted up. This *is* the living 3742
 10:16 the **c** went, the wheels went by them: 3742
 10:16 the **c** lift up their wings to mount up 3742
 10:18 of the house, and stood over the **c**. 3742
 10:19 the **c** lift up their wings, and mounted up 3742
 10:20 Chebar; and I knew that they *were* the **c**. 3742
 11:22 the **c** lift up their wings, and the wheels 3742
 41:18 it *was* made *with* **c** and palm trees, so that 3742
 41:20 the ground unto above the door *were* **c** 3742
 41:25 the doors of the temple, **c** and palm trees, 3742
Heb 9: 5 And over it the **c** of glory shadowing 5502

CHERUBIMS' (1) [CHERUB]
Eze 10: 5 the sound of the **c** wings was heard *even* 3742

CHESALON (1)
Jos 15:10 which *is* **C**, on the north side, 3693

CHESED (1)
Ge 22:22 **C**, and Hazo, and Pildash, and Jidlaph, 3777

CHESIL (1)
Jos 15:30 And Eltolad, and **C**, and Hormah, 3686

CHESNUT (2)
Ge 30:37 green poplar, and of the hazel and **c** tree; 6196
Eze 31: 8 the **c** trees were not like his branches; 6196

CHEST (6) [CHESTS]
2Ki 12: 9 Jehoiada the priest took a **c**, and bored a 727
 12:10 saw that *there was* much money in the **c**, 727
2Ch 24: 8 the king's commandment they made a **c**, 727
 24:10 and brought in, and cast into the **c**, 727
 24:11 that at *what time* the **c** was brought unto 727
 24:11 priest's officer came and emptied the **c**, 727

CHESTS (1) [CHEST]
Eze 27:24 broidered work, and in **c** of rich apparel, 1595

CHESULLOTH (1)
Jos 19:18 was toward Jezreel, and **C**, and Shunem, 3694

CHEW (3) [CHEWED, CHEWETH]
Lev 11: 4 shall ye not eat of them that **c** the cud, 5927
Dt 14: 7 ye shall not eat of them that **c** the cud, 5927
 14: 7 they **c** the cud, but divide not the hoof; 5927

CHEWED (1) [CHEW]
Nu 11:33 *was* yet between their teeth, ere it was **c**, 3772

C

CHEWETH (8) [CHEW]
Lev	11: 3 *is* clovenfooted, *and* c cud, among	5927
	11: 4 because he c the cud, but divideth not	5927
	11: 5 because he c the cud, but divideth not	5927
	11: 6 because he c the cud, but divideth not	5927
	11: 7 *be* clovenfooted, yet he c not the cud;	1641
	11:26 *is* not clovenfooted, nor c the cud,	5927
Dt	14: 6 *and* c the cud amongst the beasts.	5927
	14: 8 it divideth the hoof, yet c not the cud,	NIH

CHEZIB (1)
Ge	38: 5 and he was at C, when she bare him.	3580

CHICKENS (1)
Mt	23:37 even as a hen gathereth her c under *her*	3556

CHICKS See BROOD; CHICKENS

CHIDE (4) [CHIDING]
Ex	17: 2 Wherefore the people did c with Moses,	7378
	17: 2 Moses said unto them, Why c you with	7378
Jdg	8: 1 And they did c with him sharply.	7378
Ps	103: 9 He will not always c: neither will he keep	7378

CHIDING (1) [CHIDE]
Ex	17: 7 because of the c of the children of Israel,	7379

CHIDON (1)
1Ch	13: 9 they came unto the threshingfloor of C,	3592

CHIEF (338) [CHIEFEST, CHIEFLY]
Ge	21:22 Phichol the c **captain** of his host spake	8269
	21:32 Phichol the c **captain** of his host,	8269
	26:26 and Phichol the c **captain** of his army.	8269
	40: 2 against the c of the butlers, and against	8269
	40: 2 butlers, and against the c of the bakers.	8269
	40: 9 the c butler told his dream to Joseph,	8269
	40:16 When the c baker saw that	8269
	40:20 he lifted up the head of the c butler and	8269
	40:20 and of the c baker among his servants.	8269
	40:21 restored the c butler unto his butlership	8269
	40:22 he hanged the c baker: as Joseph had	8269
	40:23 did not the c butler remember Joseph,	8269
	41: 9 spake the c butler unto Pharaoh, saying,	8269
	41:10 guard's house, *both* me and the c baker:	8269
Lev	21: 4 *being* a c **man** among his people,	1167
Nu	3:24 the c of the house of the father of	5387
	3:30 the c of the house of the father	5387
	3:32 *shall be* c **over** the chief of the Levites,	5387
	3:32 *shall be* chief over the c of the Levites,	5387
	3:35 the c of the house of the father of	5387
	4:34 the c of the congregation numbered	5387
	4:46 and Aaron and the c of Israel numbered,	5387
	25:14 prince of a c house among the Simeonites.	1
	25:15 over a people, *and* of a c house in Midian.	1
	31:26 and the c fathers of the congregation:	7218
	32:28 the c fathers of the tribes of the children	7218
	36: 1 the c fathers of the families of the children	7218
	36: 1 fathers of the children of Israel:	7218
Dt	1:15 So I took the c of your tribes, wise men,	7218
	33:15 for the c **things** of the ancient mountains,	7218
Jos	22:14 of each c house a prince throughout all	5387
Jdg	20: 2 the c of all the people, *even* of all the	6438
1Sa	14:38 ye near hither, all the c of the people:	6438
	15:21 the c of the things which should have	7225
2Sa	5: 8 *he* shall be c and captain. Wherefore they	NIH
	8:18 and David's sons were c **rulers**.	3548
	20:26 Ira also the Jairite was a c **ruler** about	3548
	23: 8 that sat in the seat, c among the captains;	7218
	23:13 three of the thirty c went down,	7218
	23:18 the son of Zeruiah, *was* c among three.	7218
1Ki	5:16 Besides the c of Solomon's officers which	8269
	8: 1 c of the fathers of the children of Israel,	5387
	9:23 These *were* the c of the officers that *were*	8269
	14:27 committed *them* unto the hands of the c	8269
2Ki	25:18 captain of the guard took Seraiah the c	7218
1Ch	5: 2 brethren, and of him came the c **ruler**;	5057
	5: 7 were the c, Jeiel, and Zechariah,	7218
	5:12 Joel the c, and Shapham the next,	7218
	5:15 of Guni, c of the house of their fathers.	7218
	7: 3 and Joel, Ishiah, five: all of them c **men.**	7218
	7:40 mighty men of valour, c of the princes.	7218
	8:28 c **men.** These dwelt in Jerusalem.	7218
	9: 9 All these men *were* c of the fathers in	7218
	9:17 and their brethren: Shallum *was* the c;	7218
	9:26 For these Levites, the four c porters,	1368
	9:33 the singers, c of the fathers of the Levites,	7218
	9:34 These c fathers of the Levites were chief	7218
	9:34 These chief fathers of the Levites *were*	7218
	11: 6 smiteth the Jebusites first shall be c	7218
	11: 6 son of Zeruiah went first up, and was c.	7218
	11:10 These also *are* the c of the mighty *men*	7218
	11:11 a Hachmonite, the c of the captains:	7218
	11:20 the brother of Joab, he was c of the three:	7218
	12: 3 The c *was* Ahiezer, then Joash, the sons	7218
	12:18 who was c of the captains, *and he said,*	7218
	15: 5 Uriel the c, and his brethren an hundred	8269
	15: 6 Asaiah the c, and his brethren two	8269
	15: 7 Joel the c, and his brethren an hundred	8269
	15: 8 Shemaiah the c, and his brethren two	8269
	15: 9 Eliel the c, and his brethren fourscore:	8269
	15:10 Amminadab the c, and his brethren an	8269
	15:12 Ye *are* the c of the fathers of the Levites:	7218
	15:16 David spake to the c of the Levites to	8269
	15:22 c of the Levites, *was* for song:	8269

1Ch	16: 5 Asaph the c, and next to him Zechariah,	7218
	18:17 the sons of David *were* c about the king.	7223
	23: 8 the c *was* Jehiel, and Zetham, and Joel,	7218
	23: 9 These *were* the c of the fathers of Laadan.	7218
	23:11 Jahath was the c, and Zizah the second:	7218
	23:16 the sons of Gershom, Shebuel *was* the c.	7218
	23:17 the sons of Eliezer *were,* Rehabiah the c.	7218
	23:18 *Of* the sons of Izhar; Shelomith the c.	7218
	23:24 *even* the c of the fathers, as they were	7218
	24: 4 were moe c men found of the sons of	7218
	24: 4 sixteen c **men** of the house of *their*	7218
	24: 6 *before* the c of the fathers of the priests	7218
	24:31 the c of the fathers of the priests and	7218
	26:10 Simri the c, (for *though* he was not	7218
	26:10 yet his father made him the c;)	7218
	26:12 *even* among the c men, *having* wards one	7218
	26:21 c fathers, *even* of Laadan the Gershonite,	7218
	26:26 the c fathers, the captains over thousands	7218
	26:31 Among the Hebronites *was* Jerijah the c,	7218
	26:32 thousand and seven hundred c fathers,	7218
	27: 1 to wit, the c fathers and captains of	7218
	27: 3 Of the children of Perez *was* the c of all	7218
	27: 5 Benaiah the son of Jehoiada, a c priest:	7218
	29: 6 c of the fathers and princes of the tribes	8269
	29:22 *him* unto the Lord to be the c **governor**,	5057
2Ch	1: 2 governor in all Israel, the c of the fathers.	7218
	5: 2 c of the fathers of the children of Israel,	5387
	8: 9 c of his captains, and captains of his	8269
	8:10 these *were* the c of king Solomon's	8269
	11:22 made Abijah the son of Maachah the c,	7218
	12:10 committed *them* to the hands of the c of	8269
	17:14 Adnah the c, and with him mighty *men*	8269
	19: 8 and of the c of the fathers of Israel,	7218
	19:11 Amariah the c priest *is* over you in all	7218
	23: 2 c of the fathers of Israel, and they came	7218
	24: 6 the king called for Jehoiada the c,	7218
	26:12 The whole number of the c of the fathers	7218
	26:20 Azariah the c priest, and all the priests,	7218
	31:10 Azariah the c priest of the house of Zadok	7218
	35: 9 and Jeiel and Jozabad, c of the Levites,	8269
	36:14 Moreover all the c of the priests,	7218
Ezr	1: 5 rose up the c of the fathers of Judah and	7218
	2:68 *some* of the c of the fathers, when they	7218
	3:12 priests and Levites and c of the fathers,	7218
	4: 2 the c of the fathers, and said unto them,	7218
	4: 3 the rest of the c of the fathers of Israel,	7218
	5:10 of the men that *were* the c of them.	7217
	7: 5 of Eleazar, the son of Aaron the c	7218
	7:28 gathered together out of Israel c **men** to go	7218
	8: 1 These *are* now the c of their fathers,	7218
	8:16 c **men;** also for Joiarib, and for Elnathan,	7218
	8:17 unto Iddo the c at the place Casiphia,	7218
	8:24 I separated twelve of the c of the priests,	8269
	8:29 until ye weigh *them* before the c	8269
	8:29 the Levites, and c of the fathers of Israel,	8269
	9: 2 and rulers hath been c in this trespass.	7223
	10: 5 made the c priests, the Levites,	8269
	10:16 Ezra the priest, *with* certain c of the	7218
Ne	7:70 some of the c of the fathers gave unto	7218
	7:71 *some* of the c of the fathers gave to	7218
	8:13 the c of the fathers of all the people,	7218
	10:14 The c of the people; Parosh, Pahath-moab,	7218
	11: 3 Now these *are* the c of the province that	7218
	11:13 brethren, c of the fathers, two hundred	7218
	11:16 and Jozabad, of the c of the Levites,	7218
	12: 7 These *were* the c of the priests and of	7218
	12:12 Joiakim were priests, the c of the fathers:	7218
	12:22 Jaddua, were recorded c of the fathers:	7218
	12:23 The sons of Levi, the c of the fathers,	7218
	12:24 the c of the Levites: Hashabiah, Sherebiah,	7218
	12:46 Asaph of old *there were* c of the singers,	7218
Job	12:24 He taketh away the heart of the c of	7218
	29:25 and sat c, and dwelt as a king in the army,	7218
	40:19 He *is* the c of the ways of God: he that	7225
Ps	4: T To the c **Musician** on Neiloth, A Psalm	5329
	5: T To the c **Musician** upon Nehiloth,	5329
	6: T To the c **Musician** upon Neginoth upon	5329
	8: T To the c **Musician** upon Gittith, A Psalm	5329
	9: T To the c **Musician** upon Muth-labben,	5329
	11: T To the c **Musician**, *A Psalm* of David.	5329
	12: T To the c **Musician** upon Sheminith,	5329
	13: T To the c **Musician**, A Psalm of David.	5329
	14: T To the c **Musician**, *A Psalm* of David.	5329
	18: T To the c **Musician**, *A Psalm* of David,	5329
	19: T To the c **Musician**, A Psalm of David.	5329
	20: T To the c **Musician**, A Psalm of David.	5329
	21: T To the c **Musician**, A Psalm of David.	5329
	22: T To the c **Musician** upon Aijeleth Shahar,	5329
	31: T To the c **Musician**, A Psalm of David.	5329
	36: T To the c **Musician**, *A Psalm* of David	5329
	39: T To the c **Musician**, *even* to Jeduthun,	5329
	40: T To the c **Musician**, A Psalm of David.	5329
	41: T To the c **Musician**, A Psalm of David.	5329
	42: T To the c **Musician**, Maschil, for the sons	5329
	44: T To the c **Musician** for the sons of Korah,	5329
	45: T To the c **Musician** upon Shoshannim,	5329
	46: T To the c **Musician** for the sons of Korah,	5329
	47: T To the c **Musician**, A Psalm for the sons	5329
	49: T To the c **Musician**, A Psalm for the sons	5329
	51: T To the c **Musician**, A Psalm of David,	5329
	52: T To the c **Musician**, Maschil, *A Psalm* of	5329
	53: T To the c **Musician** upon Mahalath,	5329
	54: T To the c **Musician** on Neginoth, Maschil,	5329
	55: T To the c **Musician** on Neginoth, Maschil,	5329
	56: T To the c **Musician** upon	5329

Ps	57: T To the c **Musician**, Al-taschith,	5329
	58: T To the c **Musician**, Al-taschith,	5329
	59: T To the c **Musician**, Al-taschith,	5329
	60: T To the c **Musician** upon Shushan-eduth,	5329
	61: T To the c **Musician** upon Neginah,	5329
	62: T To the c **Musician**, to Jeduthun, A Psalm	5329
	64: T To the c **Musician**, A Psalm of David.	5329
	65: T To the c **Musician**, A Psalm *and* Song of	5329
	66: T To the c **Musician**, A Song *or* Psalm.	5329
	67: T To the c **Musician** on Neginoth, A Psalm	5329
	68: T To the c **Musician**, A Psalm *or* Song of	5329
	69: T To the c **Musician** upon Shoshannim,	5329
	70: T To the c **Musician**, *A Psalm* of David.	5329
	75: T To the c **Musician**, Al-taschith, A Psalm	5329
	76: T To the c **Musician** on Neginoth, A Psalm	5329
	77: T To the c **Musician**, to Jeduthun, A Psalm	5329
	78:51 the c of *their* strength in the tabernacles	7225
	80: T To the c **Musician** upon	5329
	81: T To the c **Musician** upon Gittith, *A Psalm*	5329
	84: T To the c **Musician** upon Gittith, A Psalm	5329
	85: T To the c **Musician**, A Psalm for the sons	5329
	88: T To the c **Musician** upon Mahalath	5329
	105:36 in their land, the c of all their strength.	7225
	109: T To the c **Musician**, A Psalm of David.	5329
	137: 6 if I prefer not Jerusalem above my c joy.	7218
	139: T To the c **Musician**, A Psalm of David.	5329
	140: T To the c **Musician**, A Psalm of David.	5329
Pr	1:21 She crieth in the c **place** of concourse,	7218
	16:28 and a whisperer separateth c **friends.**	441
SS	4:14 myrrh and aloes, with all the c spices:	7218
Isa	14: 9 for thee, *even* all the c **ones** of the earth;	6260
	41: 9 called thee from the c **men** thereof,	678
Jer	13:21 them *to be* captains, *and* as c over thee:	7218
	20: 1 who *was* also c governor in the house of	5057
	31: 7 and shout among the c of the nations:	7218
	49:35 the bow of Elam, the c of their might.	7225
	52:24 captain of the guard took Seraiah the c	7218
La	1: 5 Her adversaries are the c, her enemies	7218
Eze	27:22 they occupied in thy fairs with c of all	7218
	38: 2 the c prince of Meshech and Tubal,	7218
	38: 3 Gog, the c prince of Meshech and Tubal:	7218
	39: 1 Gog, the c prince of Meshech and Tubal:	7218
Da	2:48 c of the governors over all the wise *men*	7229
	10:13 Michael, one of the c **princes,** came to	7223
	11:41 and the c of the children of Ammon.	7225
Am	6: 1 which *are* named c of the nations,	7225
	6: 6 anoint themselves *with* the c ointments:	7225
Hab	3:19 the c **singer** on my stringed instruments.	5329
Mt	2: 4 when he had gathered all the c **priests**	749
	16:21 of the elders and c **priests** and scribes,	749
	20:18 shall be betrayed unto the c **priests**	749
	20:27 And whosoever will be c among you,	4413
	21:15 And when the c **priests** and scribes saw	749
	21:23 the c **priests** and the elders of the people	749
	21:45 when the c **priests** and Pharisees had	749
	23: 6 feasts, and the c **seats** in the synagogues,	4410
	26: 3 Then assembled together the c **priests,**	749
	26:14 Judas Iscariot, went unto the c **priests,**	749
	26:47 from the c **priests** and elders of the people.	749
	26:59 Now the c **priests,** and elders, and all	749
	27: 1 the c **priests** and elders of the people took	749
	27: 3 the thirty pieces of silver to the c **priests**	749
	27: 6 And the c **priests** took the silver pieces,	749
	27:12 And when he was accused of the c **priests**	749
	27:20 But the c **priests** and elders persuaded	749
	27:41 Likewise also the c **priests** mocking *him,*	749
	27:62 the c **priests** and Pharisees came together	749
	28:11 shewed unto the c **priests** all the *things*	749
Mk	6:21 high captains, and c **estates** of Galilee;	4413
	8:31 elders, and *of* the c **priests,** and scribes,	749
	10:33 shall be delivered unto the c **priests,**	749
	11:18 And the scribes and c **priests** heard *it,* and	749
	11:27 there come to him the c **priests,**	749
	12:39 And the c **seats** in the synagogues,	4410
	14: 1 the c **priests** and the scribes sought how	749
	14:10 of the twelve, went unto the c **priests,**	749
	14:43 from the c **priests** and the scribes and	749
	14:53 with him were assembled all the c **priests**	749
	14:55 the c **priests** and all the council sought	749
	15: 1 straightway in the morning the c **priests**	749
	15: 3 And the c **priests** accused him of many	749
	15:10 he knew that the c **priests** had delivered	749
	15:11 the c **priests** moved the people, that he	749
	15:31 Likewise also the c **priests** mocking said	749
Lk	9:22 of the elders and c **priests** and scribes,	749
	11:15 through Beelzebub the c of the devils.	758
	14: 1 as he went into the house of one of the c	758
	14: 7 marked how they chose out the c **rooms;**	4411
	19: 2 which was *the* c **among** the publicans,	754
	19:47 But the c **priests** and the scribes and	749
	19:47 the c of the people sought to destroy him,	4413
	20: 1 the c **priests** and the scribes came upon	749
	20:19 the c **priests** and the scribes the same	749
	20:46 synagogues, and the c **rooms** at feasts;	4411
	22: 2 And the c **priests** and scribes sought how	749
	22: 4 and communed with the c **priests** and	749
	22:26 and he that is c, as he that doth serve.	2233
	22:52 Then Jesus said unto the c **priests,**	749
	22:66 the elders of the people and the c **priests**	749
	23: 4 Then said Pilate to the c **priests** and *to*	749
	23:10 And the c **priests** and scribes stood and	749
	23:13 when he had called together the c **priests**	749
	23:23 of them and of the c **priests** prevailed.	749
	24:20 And how the c **priests** and our rulers	749
Jn	7:32 and the c **priests** sent officers to take him.	749

C

Jn	7:45 came the officers to the **c** priests and	749
	11:47 Then gathered the **c** priests and	749
	11:57 Now both the **c** priests and the Pharisees	NIG
	12:10 the **c** priests consulted that they might	749
	12:42 Nevertheless among the **c** rulers also many	NIG
	18: 3 and officers from the **c** priests and	749
	18:35 the **c** priests have delivered thee unto me:	749
	19: 6 When the **c** priests therefore and officers	749
	19:15 The **c** priests answered, We have no king	749
	19:21 said the **c** priests of the Jews to Pilate,	749
Ac	4:23 reported all that the **c** priests and elders	749
	5:24 and the **c** priests heard these things,	749
	9:14 here he hath authority from the **c** priests	749
	9:21 bring them bound unto the **c** priests?	749
	13:50 and the **c** men of the city,	4413
	14:12 Mercurius, because he was the **c** speaker.	2233
	15:22 and Silas, **c** men among the brethren:	2233
	16:12 which is the **c** city of *that* part of	4413
	17: 4 and of the **c** women not a few.	4413
	18: 8 And Crispus, the **c** ruler of the synagogue,	NIG
	18:17 the **c** ruler of the synagogue, and beat *him*	NIG
	19:14 a Jew, *and* **c** of the priests, which did so.	749
	19:31 certain of the **c** of Asia, which were his	775
	21:31 tidings came unto the **c** captain of	5506
	21:32 and when they saw the **c** captain and	5506
	21:33 Then the **c** captain came near,	5506
	21:37 he said unto the **c** captain, May I speak	5506
	22:24 The **c** captain commanded him to be	5506
	22:26 he went and told the **c** captain,	5506
	22:27 Then the **c** captain came, and said unto	5506
	22:28 And the **c** captain answered, With a great	5506
	22:29 and the **c** captain also was afraid, after he	5506
	22:30 commanded the **c** priests and all their	749
	23:10 arose a great dissension, the **c** captain,	5506
	23:14 they came to the **c** priests and elders,	749
	23:15 with the council signify to the **c** captain	5506
	23:17 Bring this young man unto the **c** captain:	5506
	23:18 brought *him* to the **c** captain, and said,	5506
	23:19 Then the **c** captain took him by the hand,	5506
	23:22 So the **c** captain then let the young man	5506
	24: 7 But the **c** captain Lysias came *upon us,*	5506
	24:22 When Lysias the **c** captain shall come	5506
	25: 2 the **c** of the Jews informed him against	4413
	25:15 the **c** priests and the elders of the Jews	749
	25:23 with the **c** captains, and principal men of	5506
	26:10 received authority from the **c** priests;	749
	26:12 and commission from the **c** priests,	749
	28: 7 possessions of the **c** man of the island,	4413
	28:17 that after three days Paul called the **c** of	4413
Eph	2:20 Jesus Christ himself being the **c** corner	204
1Ti	1:15 world to save sinners; of whom I am **c.**	4413
1Pe	2: 6 I lay in Sion a **c** corner stone, elect,	204
	5: 4 And when the **c** Shepherd shall appear,	750
Rev	6:15 and the rich *men,* and the **c** captains,	5506

CHIEFEST (9) [CHIEF]

1Sa	2:29 to make yourselves fat with the **c** of all	7225
	9:22 made them sit in the **c** place among them	7218
	21: 7 **c** of the herdmen that *belonged* to Saul.	47
2Ch	32:33 they buried him in the **c** of the sepulchres	4608
SS	5:10 and ruddy, the **c** among ten thousand.	1713
Mk	10:44 And whosoever of you will be the **c,**	4413
2Co	11: 5 was not a whit behind the very **c** apostles.	3029
	12:11 for *in* nothing am I behind the very **c**	3029
1Ti	6: S which is the **c** city of Phrygia Pacatiana.	3390

CHIEFLY (3) [CHIEF]

Ro	3: 2 **c,** because that unto them were	4412
Php	4:22 **c** they that are of Cesar's household.	3122
2Pe	2:10 But **c** them that walk after the flesh in	3122

CHILD (201) [CHILD'S, CHILDBEARING, CHILDHOOD, CHILDISH, CHILDLESS, CHILDREN, CHILDREN'S]

Ge	11:30 But Sarai was barren; she had no **c.**	2056
	16:11 thou *art* **with c,** and shalt bear a son,	2030
	17:10 Every man **c** among you shall be	NIH
	17:12 every man **c** in your generations, he that	NIH
	17:14 uncircumcised man **c** whose flesh of his	NIH
	17:17 Shall a **c** be born unto him that is an	NIH
	18:13 Shall I of a surety bear a **c,** which *am* old?	NIH
	19:36 were both the daughters of Lot **with c**	2029
	21: 8 the **c** grew, and was weaned: and	3206
	21:14 shoulder, and the **c,** and sent her away:	3206
	21:15 she cast the **c** under one of the shrubs.	3206
	21:16 said, Let me not see the death of the **c.**	3206
	37:30 unto his brethren, and said, The **c** *is* not;	3206
	38:24 also, behold, she *is* **with c** by whoredom.	2030
	38:25 the man, whose these *are,* am I **with c**	2030
	42:22 you, saying, Do not sin against the **c;**	3206
	44:20 and a **c** of *his* old age, a little one;	3206
Ex	2: 2 she saw him that he *was* a goodly **c,**	NIH
	2: 3 and with pitch, and put the **c** therein;	3206
	2: 6 when she had opened *it,* she saw the **c:**	3206
	2: 7 that may nurse the **c** for thee?	3206
	2: 9 Take this *away,* and nurse it for me,	3206
	2: 9 the woman took the **c,** and nursed it.	3206
	2:10 the **c** grew, and she brought him unto	3206
	21:22 hurt a woman **with c,** so that her fruit	2030
	22:22 not afflict any widow, or **fatherless c.**	3490
Lev	12: 2 have conceived seed, and born a **man c:**	2145
	12: 5 if she bear a **maid c,** then she shall be	5347
	22:13 no **c,** and is returned unto her father's	2233
Nu	11:12 a nursing father beareth the **sucking c,**	3243
Dt	25: 5 and one of them die, and have no **c,**	1121

Jdg	11:34 she *was his* only **c;** beside her he had	3173
	13: 5 for the **c** shall be a Nazarite unto God	5288
	13: 7 eat any unclean *thing:* for the **c** shall	5288
	13: 8 teach us what we shall do unto the **c** that	5288
	13:12 How shall we order the **c,** and *how* shall	5288
	13:24 the **c** grew, and the LORD blessed him.	5288
Ru	4:16 Naomi took the **c,** and laid it in her	3206
1Sa	1:11 wilt give unto thine handmaid a man **c,**	2233
	1:22 *I will not go up* until the **c** be weaned,	5288
	1:24 the LORD *in* Shiloh: and the **c** *was* young.	5288
	1:25 slew a bullock, and brought the **c** to Eli.	5288
	1:27 For this **c** I prayed; and the LORD hath	5288
	2:11 the **c** did minister unto the LORD before	5288
	2:18 *being* a **c,** girded with a linen ephod.	5288
	2:21 And the **c** Samuel grew before the LORD.	5288
	2:26 the **c** Samuel grew on, and was in favour	5288
	3: 1 the **c** Samuel ministered unto the LORD	5288
	3: 8 perceived that the LORD had called the **c.**	5288
	4:19 Phinehas' wife, was **with c,** *near* to be	2030
	4:21 named the **c** Ichabod, saying, The glory	5288
2Sa	6:23 Saul had no **c** unto the day of her death.	2056
	11: 5 and told David, and said, I *am* **with c.**	2030
	12:14 the **c** also that is born unto thee shall	1121
	12:15 the LORD strake the **c** that Uriah's wife	5288
	12:16 David therefore besought God for the **c;**	5288
	12:18 on the seventh day, that the **c** died.	3206
	12:18 feared to tell him that the **c** was dead:	3206
	12:18 said, Behold, while the **c** was *yet* alive,	3206
	12:18 if we tell him *that* the **c** is dead?	3206
	12:19 David perceived that the **c** was dead:	3206
	12:19 said unto his servants, Is the **c** dead?	3206
	12:21 thou didst fast and weep for the **c,** *while*	3206
	12:21 when the **c** was dead, thou didst rise and	3206
	12:22 While the **c** was *yet* alive, I fasted and	3206
	12:22 be gracious to me, that the **c** may live?	3206
1Ki	3: 7 I *am but* a little **c:** I know not *how* to go	5288
	3:17 I was **delivered of a c** with her in	3205
	3:19 this woman's **c** died in the night; because	1121
	3:20 and laid her dead **c** in my bosom.	1121
	3:21 when I rose in the morning to give my **c**	1121
	3:25 Divide the living **c** in two, and give half to	3206
	3:26 give her the living **c,** and in no wise slay	1121
	3:26 give her the living **c,** and in no wise slay	3205
	3:27 Give her the living **c,** and in no wise slay	3205
	11:17 go *into* Egypt; Hadad *being yet* a little **c.**	5288
	13: 2 a **c** shall be born unto the house of David,	1121
	14: 3 shall tell thee what shall become of the **c.**	5288
	14:12 thy feet enter into the city, the **c** shall die.	3206
	14:17 to the threshold of the door, the **c** died;	5288
	17:21 stretched himself upon the **c** three times,	3206
	17:22 the soul of the **c** came into him again,	3206
	17:23 Elijah took the **c,** and brought him down	3206
2Ki	4:14 Verily she hath no **c,** and her husband *is*	1121
	4:18 when the **c** was grown, it fell on a day,	3206
	4:26 *is* it well with the **c?** And she answered,	3206
	4:29 and lay my staff upon the face of the **c.**	5288
	4:30 the mother of the **c** said, *As* the LORD	5288
	4:31 and laid the staff upon the face of the **c;**	5288
	4:31 and told him, saying, The **c** is not awaked.	5288
	4:32 the **c** was dead, *and* laid upon his bed.	5288
	4:34 lay upon the **c,** and put his mouth upon	3206
	4:34 he stretched himself upon the **c**s;	2050.2
	4:34 and the flesh of the **c** waxed warm.	3206
	4:35 the **c** neesed seven times, and the child	5288
	4:35 seven times, and the **c** opened his eyes.	5288
	5:14 came again like unto the flesh of a little **c,**	5288
	8:12 and rip up their **women with c.**	2030
	15:16 all the **women** therein that were **with c**	2030
Job	3: 3 and the night *in which* it was said, There is a **man c** conceived.	1397
Ps	131: 2 as a **c** that is **weaned** of his mother:	1580
	131: 2 mother: my soul *is even* as a **weaned c.**	1580
Pr	20:11 Even a **c** is known by his doings,	5288
	22: 6 Train up a **c** in the way he should go:	5288
	22:15 Foolishness *is* bound in the heart of a **c;**	5288
	23:13 Withhold not correction from the **c:** for *if*	5288
	23:24 he that begetteth a wise **c** shall have joy	NIH
	29:15 a **c** left to *himself* bringeth his mother to	5288
	29:21 **c** shall have him become *his* son at	5290
Ecc	4: 8 yea, he hath neither **c** nor brother:	1121
	4:13 and a wise **c** than an old and foolish king,	3206
	4:15 with the second **c** that shall stand up *in*	3206
	10:16 when thy king *is* a **c,** and thy princes eat	5288
	11: 5 **grow** in the womb of her that is **with c:**	4392
Isa	3: 5 the **c** shall behave himself proudly against	5288
	7:16 For before the **c** shall know to refuse	5288
	8: 4 For before the **c** shall have knowledge to	5288
	9: 6 For unto us a **c** is born, unto us a Son is	3206
	10:19 shall be few, that a **c** may write them.	5288
	11: 6 and a little **c** shall lead them.	5288
	11: 8 the **sucking c** shall play on the hole of	3243
	11: 8 the **weaned c** shall put his hand on	1580
	26:17 Like as a woman **with c,** *that* draweth	2030
	26:18 We have been **with c,** we have been in	2029
	49:15 Can a woman forget her **sucking c,** that	5764
	54: 1 thou *that* didst not **travail with c:**	2342
	65:20 for the **c** shall die an hundred years old;	5288
	66: 7 pain came, she was delivered of a **man c.**	2145
Jer	1: 6 behold, I cannot speak: for I *am* a **c.**	5288
	1: 7 the LORD said unto me, Say not, I *am* a **c:**	5288
	4:31 as of her that **bringeth forth** her **first c,**	1069
	20:15 saying, A **man c** is born unto thee;	1121
	30: 6 see whether a man doth **travail with c?**	3205
	31: 8 the woman **with c** and her that travaileth	2030
	31: 8 and her that **travaileth with c** together:	3205
	31:20 *is he* a pleasant **c?** for since I spake against	3206

Jer	44: 7 man and woman, **c** and suckling,	5768
La	4: 4 The tongue of the **sucking c** cleaveth to	3243
Hos	11: 1 When Israel *was* a **c,** then I loved him,	5288
	13:16 and their **women with c** shall be ript up.	2030
Am	1:13 they have ript up the **women with c** at	2030
Mt	1:18 **with c** of the Holy Ghost.	1064+1722+2192
	1:23 a virgin shall be **with c,**	1064+1722+2192
	2: 8 Go and search diligently for the **young c;**	3813
	2: 9 and stood over where the **young c** was.	3813
	2:11 they saw the **young c** with Mary his	3813
	2:13 and take the **young c** and his mother,	3813
	2:13 for Herod will seek the **young c** to destroy	3813
	2:14 he took the **young c** and his mother by	3813
	2:20 and take the **young c** and his mother,	3813
	2:21 and took the **young c** and his mother,	3813
	10:21 the **brother** to death, and the father the **c:**	5043
	17:18 and the **c** was cured from that *very* hour.	3816
	18: 2 And Jesus called a **little c** unto *him,*	3813
	18: 4 shall humble himself as this **little c,**	3813
	18: 5 whoso shall receive one such **little c** in	3813
	23:15 ye make him twofold more the **c** of hell	5207
	24:19 unto them that are **with c,**	1064+1722+2192
Mk	9:21 this came unto him? And he said, Of a **c.**	3812
	9:24 straightway the father of the **c** cried	3813
	9:36 he took a **c,** and set him in the midst of	3813
	10:15 receive the kingdom of God as a **little c,**	3813
	13:17 But woe to them that are **with c,**	1064
Lk	1: 7 they had no **c,** because that Elisabeth	5043
	1:59 eighth day they came to circumcise the **c;**	3813
	1:66 saying, What **manner** of **c** shall this be!	3813
	1:76 thou, **c,** shalt be called the prophet of	3813
	1:80 the **c** grew, and waxed strong in spirit,	3813
	2: 5 his espoused wife, being **great with c.**	1471
	2:17 which was told them concerning this **c.**	3813
	2:21 for the circumcising of the **c,**	3813
	2:27 when the parents brought in the **c** Jesus,	3813
	2:34 this **c** is set for the fall and rising again of	NIG
	2:40 the **c** grew, and waxed strong in spirit,	3813
	2:43 the **c** Jesus tarried behind in Jerusalem;	3816
	9:38 look upon my son: for he is mine **only c.**	3439
	9:42 healed the **c,** and delivered him again	3816
	9:47 their heart, took a **c,** and set him by him,	3813
	9:48 shall receive this **c** in my name	3813
	18:17 as a **little c** shall in no wise enter therein.	3813
	21:23 unto them that are **with c,**	1064+1722+2192
Jn	4:49 unto him, Sir, come down ere my **c** die.	3813
	16:21 but as soon as she is delivered of the **c,**	3813
Ac	4:27 For of a truth against thy holy **c** Jesus,	3816
	4:30 be done by the name of thy holy **c** Jesus.	3816
	7: S seed after him, when *as yet* he had no **c.**	5043
	13:10 and all mischief, *thou* **c** of the devil,	5207
1Co	13:11 When I was a **c,** I spake as a child,	3516
	13:11 When I was a **child,** I spake as a **c,**	3516
	13:11 I spake as a **child,** I understood as a **c,**	3516
	13:11 understood as a **child,** I thought as a **c:**	3516
Gal	4: 1 I say, *That* the heir, as long as he is a **c,**	3516
1Th	5: 3 upon a *woman* **with c;**	1064+1722+2192
2Ti	3:15 that from a **c** thou hast known the holy	1025
Heb	11:11 was **delivered of a c** when *she* was past	5088
	11:23 because they saw he *was* a proper **c,**	3813
Rev	12: 2 And she being **with c** cried, travailing in	1064
	12: 4 for to devour her **c** as soon as it was born.	5043
	12: 5 And she brought forth a man **c,** who was	5207
	12: 5 and her **c** was caught up unto God,	5043
	12:13 woman which brought forth the man **c.**	NIG

CHILD'S (4) [CHILD]

Ex	2: 8 the maid went and called the **c** mother.	3206
1Ki	17:21 let this **c** soul come into him again.	3206
Job	33:25 His flesh shall be fresher than a **c:** he shall	5290
Mt	2:20 they are dead which sought the **young c**	3813

CHILDBEARING (1) [BEAR, CHILD]

1Ti	2:15 Notwithstanding she shall be saved in **c,**	5042

CHILDHOOD (2) [CHILD]

1Sa	12: 2 I have walked before you from my **c** unto	5271
Ecc	11:10 from thy flesh: for **c** and youth *are* vanity.	3208

CHILDISH (1) [CHILD]

1Co	13:11 I became a man, I put away **c** *things.*	3516

CHILDLESS (7) [CHILD]

Ge	15: 2 I go **c,** and the steward of my house	6185
Lev	20:20 they shall bear their sin; they shall die **c.**	6185
	20:21 his brother's nakedness; they shall be **c.**	6185
1Sa	15:33 As thy sword hath **made** women **c,**	7921
	15:33 so shall thy mother be **c** among women.	7921
Jer	22:30 saith the LORD, Write ye this man **c,**	6185
Lk	20:30 second took her to wife, and he died **c.**	815

CHILDREN (1803) [CHILD]

Ge	3:16 in sorrow thou shalt bring forth **c;**	1121
	6: 4 they bare **c** to them, the same became	NIH
	10:21 Shem also, the father of all the **c** of Eber,	1121
	10:21 the elder, even to him were **c** born.	NIH
	10:22 The **c** of Shem; Elam, and Asshur,	1121
	10:23 the **c** of Aram; Uz, and Hul, and Gether,	1121
	11: 5 the tower, which the **c** of men builded.	1121
	16: 1 Now Sarai Abram's wife bare him no **c:**	NIH
	16: 2 it may be that I may **obtain c** by her.	1129
	18:19 that he will command his **c** and his	1121
	19:38 the same *is* the father of the **c** of Ammon	NIH
	20:17 and his maidservants; and they bare **c.**	NIH
	21: 7 that Sarah should have given **c** suck?	1121

Ge 22:20 she hath also born **c** unto thy brother 1121
23: 5 the **c** of Heth answered Abraham, saying 1121
23: 7 people of the land, *even* to the **c** of Heth. 1121
23:10 Ephron dwelt amongst the **c** of Heth: and 1121
23:10 Abraham in the audience of the **c** of Heth, 1121
23:18 in the presence of the **c** of Heth, 1121
25: 4 Eldaah. All these *were* the **c** of Keturah. 1121
25:22 the **c** struggled together within her; 1121
30: 1 Rachel saw that she bare Jacob no **c**, NIH
30: 1 said unto Jacob, Give me **c**, or else I die. 1121
30: 3 my knees, that I may also **have c** by her. 1129
30:26 Give *me* my wives and my **c**, for whom I 3206
31:43 *these* **c** *are* my children, and 1121+3807.1
31:43 *these* children *are* my **c**, and *these* 1121
31:43 or unto their **c** which they have born? 1121
32:11 and smite me, *and* the mother with the **c**. 1121
32:32 Therefore the **c** of Israel eat not *of* 1121
33: 1 he divided the **c** unto Leah, 3206
33: 2 put the handmaids and their **c** foremost, 3206
33: 2 Leah and her **c** after, and Rachel and 3206
33: 5 his eyes, and saw the women and the **c**; 3206
33: 5 The **c** which God hath graciously given 3206
33: 6 they and their **c**, and they bowed 3206
33: 7 Leah also with her **c** came near, 3206
33:13 My lord knoweth that the **c** *are* tender, 3206
33:14 before me and the **c** be able to endure, 3206
33:19 at the hand of the **c** of Hamor, 1121
36:21 the **c** of Seir in the land of Edom. 1121
36:22 the **c** of Lotan were Hori and Hemam; 1121
36:23 the **c** of Shobal *were* these; Alvan, 1121
36:24 these *are* the **c** of Zibeon; both Aiah, 1121
36:25 the **c** of Anah *were* these; Dishon, 1121
36:26 these *are* the **c** of Dishon; Hemdan, 1121
36:27 The **c** of Ezer *are* these; Bilhan, 1121
36:28 The **c** of Dishan *are* these; Uz, and Aran. 1121
36:31 before there reigned *any* king over the **c** 1121
37: 3 Israel loved Joseph more than all his **c**, 1121
42:36 them, Me have ye **bereaved of** my **c**: 7921
43:14 If I be **bereaved of** my **c**, I am bereaved. 7921
45:10 thy **c**, and thy children's children, 1121
45:10 children's **c**, and thy flocks, 1121
45:21 of Israel did so: and Joseph gave 1121
46: 8 these *are* the names of the **c** of Israel, 1121
49: 8 thy father's **c** shall bow down before thee. 1121
49:32 the cave that *is* therein *was* from the **c** of 1121
50:23 Joseph saw Ephraim's **c** of the third 1121
50:23 **c** also of Machir the son of Manasseh 1121
50:25 Joseph took an oath of the **c** of Israel, 1121
Ex 1: 1 these *are* the names of the **c** of Israel, 1121
1: 7 the **c** of Israel were fruitful, 1121
1: 9 the people of the **c** of Israel *are* moe and 1121
1:12 were grieved because of the **c** of Israel. 1121
1:13 the Egyptians made the **c** of Israel to serve 1121
1:17 but saved the **men c** alive. 3206
1:18 thing, and have saved the **men c** alive? 3206
2: 6 and said, This *is one* of the Hebrews' **c**. 3206
2:23 the **c** of Israel sighed by reason of 1121
2:25 God looked upon the **c** of Israel, 1121
3: 9 the cry of the **c** of Israel is come unto me: 1121
3:10 my people the **c** of Israel out of Egypt. 1121
3:11 that I should bring forth the **c** of Israel out 1121
3:13 *when* I come unto the **c** of Israel, 1121
3:14 Thus shalt thou say unto the **c** of Israel, 1121
3:15 Thus shalt thou say unto the **c** of Israel, 1121
4:29 gathered together all the elders of the **c** of 1121
4:31 that the LORD had visited the **c** of Israel, 1121
5:14 the officers of the **c** of Israel, 1121
5:15 the officers of the **c** of Israel came and 1121
5:19 the officers of the **c** of Israel did see *that* 1121
6: 5 I have also heard the groaning of the **c** of 1121
6: 6 Wherefore say unto the **c** of Israel, I *am* 1121
6: 9 Moses spake so unto the **c** of Israel: but 1121
6:11 he let the **c** of Israel go out of his land. 1121
6:12 the **c** of Israel have not hearkened unto 1121
6:13 gave them a charge unto the **c** of Israel, 1121
6:13 to bring the **c** of Israel out of the land of 1121
6:26 Bring out the **c** of Israel from the land of 1121
6:27 to bring out the **c** of Israel from Egypt: 1121
7: 2 that he send the **c** of Israel out of his land. 1121
7: 4 armies, *and* my people the **c** of Israel, 1121
7: 5 bring out the **c** of Israel from among them 1121
9: 6 the cattle of the **c** of Israel died not one. 1121
9:26 where the **c** of Israel *were*, was there no 1121
9:35 neither would he let the **c** of Israel go; 1121
10:20 so that he would not let the **c** of Israel go. 1121
10:23 all the **c** of Israel had light in their 1121
11: 7 any of the **c** of Israel shall not a dog 1121
11:10 he would not let the **c** of Israel go out 1121
12:26 to pass, when your **c** shall say unto you, 1121
12:27 who passed over the houses of the **c** of 1121
12:28 the **c** of Israel went away, and did as 1121
12:31 my people, both you and the **c** of Israel; 1121
12:35 the **c** of Israel did according to the word 1121
12:37 the **c** of Israel journeyed from Rameses to 1121
12:37 on foot *that were* men, beside a 2945
12:40 Now the sojourning of the **c** of Israel, 1121
12:42 of all the **c** of Israel in their generations. 1121
12:50 Thus did all the **c** of Israel; as the LORD 1121
12:51 *that* the LORD did bring the **c** of Israel out 1121
13: 2 openeth the womb among the **c** 1121
13:13 all the firstborn of man amongst thy **c** 1121
13:15 but all the firstborn of my **c** I redeem. 1121
13:18 the **c** of Israel went up harnessed out of 1121
13:19 for he had straitly sworn the **c** of Israel, 1121
14: 2 Speak unto the **c** of Israel, that they turn 1121

Ex 14: 3 For Pharaoh will say of the **c** of Israel, 1121
14: 8 and he pursued after the **c** of Israel: 1121
14: 8 the **c** of Israel went out with a high hand. 1121
14:10 the **c** of Israel lift up their eyes, 1121
14:10 the **c** of Israel cried out unto the LORD. 1121
14:15 speak unto the **c** of Israel, that they go 1121
14:16 the **c** of Israel shall go on dry *ground* 1121
14:22 the **c** of Israel went into the midst of the 1121
14:29 the **c** of Israel walked upon dry *land* in 1121
15: 1 the **c** of Israel this song unto the LORD, 1121
15:19 the **c** of Israel went on dry *land* in the 1121
16: 1 all the congregation of the **c** of Israel came 1121
16: 2 the whole congregation of the **c** of Israel 1121
16: 3 the **c** of Israel said unto them, Would to 1121
16: 6 and Aaron said unto all the **c** of Israel, 1121
16: 9 Say unto all the congregation of the **c** of 1121
16:10 the whole congregation of the **c** of Israel, 1121
16:12 I have heard the murmurings of the **c** of 1121
16:15 when the **c** of Israel saw *it*, they said one 1121
16:17 the **c** of Israel did so, and gathered, 1121
16:35 the **c** of Israel did eat manna forty years, 1121
17: 1 all the congregation of the **c** of Israel 1121
17: 3 to kill us and our **c** and our cattle with 1121
17: 7 because of the chiding of the **c** of Israel, 1121
19: 1 when the **c** of Israel were gone forth out 1121
19: 3 the house of Jacob, and tell the **c** of Israel; 1121
19: 6 thou shalt speak unto the **c** of Israel. 1121
20: 5 of the fathers upon the **c** unto the third 1121
20:22 Thus thou shalt say unto the **c** of Israel, 1121
21: 4 the wife and her **c** shall be her master's, 3206
21: 5 I love my master, my wife, and my **c**; 1121
22:24 shall be widows, and your **c** fatherless. 1121
24: 5 he sent young men of the **c** of Israel, 1121
24:11 upon the nobles of the **c** of Israel he laid 1121
24:17 of the mount in the eyes of the **c** of Israel 1121
25: 2 Speak unto the **c** of Israel, that they bring 1121
25:22 in commandment unto the **c** of Israel. 1121
27:20 thou shalt command the **c** of Israel, 1121
27:21 generations on the behalf of the **c** of Israel. 1121
28: 1 sons with him, from among the **c** of Israel, 1121
28: 9 grave on them the names of the **c** of Israel: 1121
28:11 stones with the names of the **c** of Israel: 1121
28:12 *for* stones of memorial unto the **c** of Israel: 1121
28:21 stones shall be with the names of the **c** 1121
28:29 Aaron shall bear the names of the **c** of 1121
28:30 Aaron shall bear the judgment of the **c** of 1121
28:38 of Israel shall hallow in all their holy 1121
29:28 sons' by a statute for ever from the **c** of 1121
29:28 it shall be a heave offering from the **c** of 1121
29:43 there I will meet with the **c** of Israel, 1121
29:45 I will dwell amongst the **c** of Israel, 1121
30:12 thou takest the sum of the **c** of Israel 1121
30:16 the atonement money of the **c** of Israel, 1121
30:16 that it may be a memorial unto the **c** of 1121
30:31 thou shalt speak unto the **c** of Israel, 1121
31:13 Speak thou also unto the **c** of Israel, 1121
31:16 Wherefore the **c** of Israel shall keep 1121
31:17 between me and the **c** of Israel for ever: 1121
32:20 and made the **c** of Israel drink *of it*. 1121
32:28 the **c** of Levi did according to the word of 1121
33: 5 Say unto the **c** of Israel, Ye *are* a 1121
33: 6 the **c** of Israel stript themselves of their 1121
34: 7 the iniquity of the fathers upon the **c**, 1121
34: 7 upon the children's **c**, unto the third and 1121
34:23 Thrice in the year shall all your **men c** 2138
34:30 and all the **c** of Israel saw Moses, 1121
34:32 afterward all the **c** of Israel came nigh: 1121
34:34 spake unto the **c** of Israel *that* which he 1121
34:35 the **c** of Israel saw the face of Moses, 1121
35: 1 congregation of the **c** of Israel together, 1121
35: 4 unto all the congregation of the **c** of Israel, 1121
35:20 all the congregation of the **c** of Israel 1121
35:29 The **c** of Israel brought a willing offering 1121
35:30 Moses said unto the **c** of Israel, See, 1121
36: 3 which the **c** of Israel had brought for 1121
39: 6 with the names of the **c** of Israel. 1121
39: 7 *be* stones for a memorial to the **c** of Israel; 1121
39:14 according to the names of the **c** of Israel, 1121
39:32 the **c** of Israel did according to all that 1121
39:42 so the **c** of Israel made all the work. 1121
40:36 the **c** of Israel went onward in all their 1121
Lev 1: 2 Speak unto the **c** of Israel, and say unto 1121
2: 2 Speak unto the **c** of Israel, saying, If a soul 1121
6:18 All the males among the **c** of Aaron shall 1121
7:23 Speak unto the **c** of Israel, saying, Ye shall 1121
7:29 Speak unto the **c** of Israel, saying, He that 1121
7:34 heave shoulder have I taken of the **c** of 1121
7:34 for ever from among the **c** of Israel. 1121
7:36 to be given them of the **c** of Israel, 1121
7:38 in the day that he commanded the **c** of 1121
9: 3 unto the **c** of Israel thou shalt speak, 1121
10:11 that *ye* may teach the **c** of Israel all 1121
10:14 of peace offerings of the **c** of Israel. 1121
11: 2 Speak unto the **c** of Israel, saying, 1121
12: 2 Speak unto the **c** of Israel, saying, If a 1121
15: 2 Speak unto the **c** of Israel, and say unto 1121
15:31 Thus shall ye separate the **c** of Israel from 1121
16: 5 he shall take of the congregation of the **c** 1121
16:16 of the uncleanness of the **c** of Israel, 1121
16:19 hallow it from the uncleanness of the **c** of 1121
16:21 confess over him all the iniquities of the **c** 1121
16:34 to make an atonement for the **c** of Israel 1121
17: 2 unto all the **c** of Israel, and say unto them; 1121
17: 5 To the end that the **c** of Israel may bring 1121
17:12 Therefore I said unto the **c** of Israel, 1121

Lev 17:13 whatsoever man *there be* of the **c** of Israel, 1121
17:14 therefore I said unto the **c** of Israel, 1121
18: 2 Speak unto the **c** of Israel, and say unto 1121
19: 2 Speak unto all the congregation of the **c** 1121
19:18 nor bear any grudge against the **c** of thy 1121
20: 2 Again, thou shalt say to the **c** of Israel, 1121
20: 2 Whosoever *he be* of the **c** of Israel, or of 1121
21:24 to his sons, and unto all the **c** of Israel. 1121
22: 2 from the holy *things* of the **c** of Israel, 1121
22: 3 goeth unto the holy *things* which the **c** 1121
22:15 profane the holy *things* of the **c** of Israel, 1121
22:18 of the **c** of Israel, and say unto them, 1121
22:32 I will be hallowed among the **c** of Israel: 1121
23: 2 Speak unto the **c** of Israel, and say unto 1121
23:10 Speak unto the **c** of Israel, and say unto 1121
23:24 Speak unto the **c** of Israel, saying, 1121
23:34 Speak unto the **c** of Israel, saying, 1121
23:43 I made the **c** of Israel to dwell in booths, 1121
23:44 Moses declared unto the **c** of Israel 1121
24: 2 Command the **c** of Israel, that they bring 1121
24: 8 *being taken* from the **c** of Israel *by* an 1121
24:10 went out among the **c** of Israel: 1121
24:15 thou shalt speak unto the **c** of Israel, 1121
24:23 Moses spake to the **c** of Israel, that they 1121
24:23 the **c** of Israel did as the LORD 1121
25: 2 Speak unto the **c** of Israel, and say unto 1121
25:33 *are* their possession among the **c** of Israel. 1121
25:41 he and his **c** with him, and shall return 1121
25:45 Moreover of the **c** of the strangers that do 1121
25:46 as an inheritance for your **c** after you, 1121
25:46 over your brethren the **c** of Israel, ye shall 1121
25:54 year of jubile, *both* he, and his **c** with him. 1121
25:55 For unto me the **c** of Israel *are* servants; 1121
26:22 which shall **rob** you *of* your **c**, 7921
26:46 the **c** of Israel in mount Sinai by the hand 1121
27: 2 Speak unto the **c** of Israel, and say unto 1121
27:34 Moses for the **c** of Israel in mount Sinai. 1121
Nu 1: 2 of all the congregation of the **c** of Israel, 1121
1:10 Of the **c** of Joseph: of Ephraim; 1121
1:20 the **c** of Reuben, Israel's eldest son, 1121
1:22 Of the **c** of Simeon, *by* their generations, 1121
1:24 Of the **c** of Gad, *by* their generations, 1121
1:26 Of the **c** of Judah, *by* their generations, 1121
1:28 Of the **c** of Issachar, *by* their generations, 1121
1:30 Of the **c** of Zebulun, *by* their generations, 1121
1:32 the **c** of Joseph, *namely*, of the children 1121
1:32 *namely*, of the **c** of Ephraim, *by* their 1121
1:34 the **c** of Manasseh, *by* their generations, 1121
1:36 the **c** of Benjamin, *by* their generations, 1121
1:38 Of the **c** of Dan, *by* their generations, 1121
1:40 Of the **c** of Asher, *by* their generations, 1121
1:42 *Of* the **c** of Naphtali, *throughout* their 1121
1:45 that were numbered of the **c** of Israel, 1121
1:49 neither take the sum of them among the **c** 1121
1:52 the **c** of Israel shall pitch their tents, 1121
1:53 upon the congregation of the **c** of Israel: 1121
1:54 the **c** of Israel did according to all that 1121
2: 2 Every man of the **c** of Israel shall pitch by 1121
2: 3 *shall be* captain of the **c** of Judah. 1121
2: 5 Zuar *shall be* captain of the **c** of Issachar. 1121
2: 7 Helon *shall be* captain of the **c** of Zebulun. 1121
2:10 the captain of the **c** of Reuben *shall be* 1121
2:12 the captain of the **c** of Simeon *shall be* 1121
2:20 the captain of the **c** of Manasseh *shall be* 1121
2:25 captain of the **c** of Dan *shall be* Ahiezer 1121
2:27 captain of the **c** of Asher *shall be* Pagiel 1121
2:29 the captain of the **c** of Naphtali *shall be* 1121
2:32 the **c** of Israel by the house of their fathers: 1121
2:33 Levites were not numbered among the **c** 1121
2:34 the **c** of Israel did according to all that 1121
3: 4 the wilderness of Sinai, and they had no **c**: 1121
3: 8 the charge of the **c** of Israel, to do 1121
3: 9 *are* wholly given unto him out of the **c** 1121
3:12 have taken the Levites from among the **c** 1121
3:12 openeth the matrix among the **c** of Israel: 1121
3:15 Number the **c** of Levi after the house of 1121
3:38 sanctuary for the charge of the **c** of Israel; 1121
3:40 males of the **c** of Israel from a month old 1121
3:41 instead of all the firstborn among the **c** of 1121
3:41 among the cattle of the **c** of Israel. 1121
3:42 all the firstborn among the **c** of Israel. 1121
3:45 of all the firstborn among the **c** of Israel, 1121
3:46 thirteen of the firstborn of the **c** of Israel, 1121
3:50 Of the firstborn of the **c** of Israel took he 1121
5: 2 Command the **c** of Israel, that they put 1121
5: 4 the **c** of Israel did so, and put them out 1121
5: 4 spake unto Moses, so did the **c** of Israel. 1121
5: 6 Speak unto the **c** of Israel, When a man 1121
5:12 Speak unto the **c** of Israel, and say unto 1121
6: 2 Speak unto the **c** of Israel, and say unto 1121
6:23 On this wise ye shall bless the **c** of Israel, 1121
6:27 shall put my name upon the **c** of Israel; 1121
7:24 prince of the **c** of Zebulun, *did offer*: 1121
7:30 prince of the **c** of Reuben, *did offer*: 1121
7:36 prince of the **c** of Simeon, *did offer*: 1121
7:42 of Deuel, prince of the **c** of Gad, *offered*: 1121
7:48 prince of the **c** of Ephraim, *offered*: 1121
7:54 of Pedahzur, prince of the **c** of Manasseh: 1121
7:60 prince of the **c** of Benjamin, *offered*: 1121
7:66 prince of the **c** of Dan, *offered*: 1121
7:72 Ocran, prince of the **c** of Asher, *offered*: 1121
7:78 prince of the **c** of Naphtali, *offered*: 1121
8: 6 Take the Levites from among the **c** of 1121
8: 9 whole assembly of the **c** of Israel together: 1121

C

Nu	8:10 the **c** of Israel shall put their hands upon
8:11 LORD *for* an offering of the **c** of Israel,	1121
8:14 the Levites from among the **c** of Israel:	1121
8:16 given unto me from among the **c** of Israel;	1121
8:16 *even instead of* the firstborn of all the **c** of	1121
8:17 For all the firstborn of the **c** of Israel *are*	1121
8:18 for all the firstborn of the **c** of Israel.	1121
8:19 to his sons from among the **c** of Israel,	1121
8:19 to do the service of the **c** of Israel in	1121
8:19 to make an atonement for the **c** of Israel:	1121
8:19 that there be no plague among the **c** of	1121
8:19 when the **c** of Israel come nigh unto	1121
8:20 and all the congregation of the **c** of Israel,	1121
8:20 Levites, so did the **c** of Israel unto them.	1121
9: 2 Let the **c** of Israel also keep the passover	1121
9: 4 Moses spake unto the **c** of Israel, that they	1121
9: 5 commanded Moses, so did the **c** of Israel.	1121
9: 7 appointed season among the **c** of Israel?	1121
9:10 Speak unto the **c** of Israel, saying, If any	1121
9:17 then after that the **c** of Israel journeyed:	1121
9:17 there the **c** of Israel pitched their tents.	1121
9:18 At the commandment of the LORD the **c**	1121
9:19 the **c** of Israel kept the charge of	1121
9:22 the **c** of Israel abode in their tents,	1121
10:12 the **c** of Israel took their journeys out of	1121
10:14 the **c** of Judah according to their armies:	1121
10:15 over the host of the tribe of the **c** of	1121
10:16 over the host of the tribe of the **c** of	1121
10:19 the host of the tribe of the **c** of Simeon	1121
10:20 over the host of the tribe of the **c** of Gad	1121
10:22 the standard of the camp of the **c** of	1121
10:23 over the host of the tribe of the **c** of	1121
10:24 over the host of the tribe of the **c** of	1121
10:25 the standard of the camp of the **c** of Dan	1121
10:26 over the host of the tribe of the **c** of Asher	1121
10:27 over the host of the tribe of the **c** of	1121
10:28 *were* the journeyings of the **c** of Israel	1121
11: 4 the **c** of Israel also wept again, and said,	1121
13: 2 which I give unto the **c** of Israel:	1121
13: 3 these men *were* heads of the **c** of Israel.	1121
13:22 Sheshai, and Talmai, the **c** of Anak,	3211
13:24 the cluster of grapes which the **c** of Israel	1121
13:26 to all the congregation of the **c** of Israel,	1121
13:28 moreover we saw the **c** of Anak there.	3211
13:32 they had searched unto the **c** of Israel,	1121
14: 2 the **c** of Israel murmured against Moses	1121
14: 3 our wives and our **c** should be a prey?	2945
14: 5 of the congregation of the **c** of Israel.	1121
14: 7 spake unto all the company of the **c** of	1121
14:10 the congregation before all the **c** of Israel.	1121
14:18 of the fathers upon the **c** unto the third	1121
14:27 I have heard the murmurings of the **c** of	1121
14:33 **c** shall wander in the wilderness forty	1121
14:39 Moses told these sayings unto all the **c** of	1121
15: 2 Speak unto the **c** of Israel, and say unto	1121
15:18 Speak unto the **c** of Israel, and say unto	1121
15:25 for all the congregation of the **c** of Israel,	1121
15:26 all the congregation of the **c** of Israel,	1121
15:29 *both for* him that is born amongst the **c** of	1121
15:32 the **c** of Israel were in the wilderness,	1121
15:38 Speak unto the **c** of Israel, and bid them	1121
16: 2 certain of the **c** of Israel, two hundred	1121
16:27 and their sons, and their **little c.**	2945
16:38 they shall be a sign unto the **c** of Israel.	1121
16:40 *To be* a memorial unto the **c** of Israel, that	1121
16:41 the morrow all the congregation of the **c**	1121
17: 2 Speak unto the **c** of Israel, and take of	1121
17: 5 the murmurings of the **c** of Israel,	1121
17: 6 Moses spake unto the **c** of Israel,	1121
17: 9 before the LORD unto all the **c** of Israel!	1121
17:12 the **c** of Israel spake unto Moses, saying,	1121
18: 5 there be no wrath any more upon the **c**	1121
18: 6 the Levites from among the **c** of Israel:	1121
18: 8 all the hallowed *things* of the **c** of Israel;	1121
18:11 with all the wave offerings of the **c** of	1121
18:19 which the **c** of Israel offer unto the LORD,	1121
18:20 thine inheritance among the **c** of Israel.	1121
18:21 I have given the **c** of Levi all the tenth in	1121
18:22 Neither must the **c** of Israel henceforth	1121
18:23 that among the **c** of Israel they have no	1121
18:24 tithes of the **c** of Israel, which they offer	1121
18:24 Among the **c** of Israel they shall have no	1121
18:26 When ye take of the **c** of Israel the tithes	1121
18:28 which ye receive of the **c** of Israel;	1121
18:32 pollute the holy *things* of the **c** of Israel,	1121
19: 2 Speak unto the **c** of Israel, that they	1121
19: 9 shall be kept for the congregation of the **c**	1121
19:10 it shall be unto the **c** of Israel, and unto	1121
20: 1 came the **c** of Israel, *even* the whole	1121
20:12 sanctify me in the eyes of the **c** of Israel,	1121
20:13 the **c** of Israel strove with the LORD,	1121
20:19 the **c** of Israel said unto him, We will go	1121
20:22 the **c** of Israel, *even* the whole	1121
20:24 which I have given unto the **c** of Israel,	1121
21:10 the **c** of Israel set forward, and pitched in	1121
21:24 unto Jabbok, *even* unto the **c** of Ammon:	1121
21:24 for the border of the **c** of Ammon *was*	1121
22: 1 the **c** of Israel set forward, and pitched in	1121
22: 3 was distressed because of the **c** of Israel.	1121
22: 5 *is* by the river *of* the land of the **c** of	1121
24:17 of Moab, and destroy all the **c** of Sheth.	1121
25: 6 one of the **c** of Israel came and	1121
25: 6 the sight of all the congregation of the **c**	1121
25: 8 So the plague was stayed from the **c** of	1121
25:11 hath turned my wrath away from the **c** of	1121

Nu	25:11 that I consumed not the **c** of Israel in my
25:13 made an atonement for the **c** of Israel.	1121
26: 2 of all the congregation of the **c** of Israel,	1121
26: 4 commanded Moses and the **c** of Israel,	1121
26: 5 **c** of Reuben; Hanoch, *of whom cometh*	1121
26:11 Notwithstanding the **c** of Korah died not.	1121
26:15 The **c** of Gad after their families:	1121
26:18 These *are* the families of the **c** of Gad	1121
26:44 *Of* the **c** of Asher after their families:	1121
26:51 *were* the numbered of the **c** of Israel,	1121
26:62 they were not numbered among the **c** of	1121
26:62 given them among the **c** of Israel.	1121
26:63 numbered the **c** of Israel in the plains	1121
26:64 when they numbered the **c** of Israel in	1121
27: 8 thou shalt speak unto the **c** of Israel,	1121
27:11 it shall be unto the **c** of Israel a statute of	1121
27:12 the land which I have given unto the **c**	1121
27:20 that all the congregation of the **c** of Israel	1121
27:21 *both* he, and all the **c** of Israel with him,	1121
28: 2 Command the **c** of Israel, and say unto	1121
29:40 Moses told the **c** of Israel according to all	1121
30: 1 of the tribes concerning the **c** of Israel,	1121
31: 2 Avenge the **c** of Israel of the Midianites:	1121
31: 9 the **c** of Israel took *all* the women of	1121
31:12 unto the congregation of the **c** of Israel,	1121
31:16 Behold, these caused the **c** of Israel,	1121
31:18 all the women **c**, that have not known a	2945
31:30 of the **c** of Israel's half, thou shalt take	1121
31:42 of the **c** of Israel's half, which Moses	1121
31:47 Even of the **c** of Israel's half, Moses took	1121
31:54 *for* a memorial for the **c** of Israel before	1121
32: 1 Now the **c** of Reuben and the children of	1121
32: 1 the **c** of Gad had a very great multitude of	1121
32: 2 The **c** of Gad and the children of Reuben	1121
32: 2 the **c** of Reuben came and spake unto	1121
32: 6 Moses said unto the **c** of Gad and to	1121
32: 6 children of Gad and to the **c** of Reuben,	1121
32: 7 discourage ye the heart of the **c**	1121
32: 9 discouraged the heart of the **c** of Israel,	1121
32:17 will go ready armed before the **c** of Israel,	1121
32:18 until the **c** of Israel have inherited every	1121
32:25 the **c** of Gad and the children of Reuben	1121
32:25 and the **c** of Reuben spake unto Moses,	1121
32:28 the chief fathers of the tribes of the **c** of	1121
32:29 If the **c** of Gad and the children of Reuben	1121
32:29 the **c** of Reuben will pass with you over	1121
32:31 the **c** of Gad and the children of Reuben	1121
32:31 of Gad and the **c** of Reuben answered,	1121
32:33 to the **c** of Gad, and to the children of	1121
32:33 the **c** of Reuben, and unto half the tribe	1121
32:34 the **c** of Gad built Dibon, and Ataroth,	1121
32:37 the **c** of Reuben built Heshbon,	1121
32:39 the **c** of Machir the son of Manasseh went	1121
33: 1 These *are* the journeys of the **c** of Israel,	1121
33: 3 on the morrow after the passover the **c**	1121
33: 5 the **c** of Israel removed from Rameses,	1121
33:38 in the fortieth year after the **c** of Israel	1121
33:40 heard of the coming of the **c** of Israel:	1121
33:51 Speak unto the **c** of Israel, and say unto	1121
34: 2 Command the **c** of Israel, and say unto	1121
34:13 Moses commanded the **c** of Israel, saying,	1121
34:14 For the tribe of the **c** of Reuben according	1121
34:14 the tribe of the **c** of Gad according to	1121
34:20 of the tribe of the **c** of Simeon, Shemuel	1121
34:22 the prince of the tribe of the **c** of Dan,	1121
34:23 The prince of the **c** of Joseph, for the tribe	1121
34:23 for the tribe of the **c** of Manasseh,	1121
34:24 the prince of the tribe of the **c** of Ephraim,	1121
34:25 the prince of the tribe of the **c** of Zebulun,	1121
34:26 the prince of the tribe of the **c** of Issachar,	1121
34:27 the prince of the tribe of the **c** of Asher,	1121
34:28 the prince of the tribe of the **c** of Naphtali,	1121
34:29 unto the **c** of Israel in the land of Canaan.	1121
35: 2 Command the **c** of Israel, that they give	1121
35: 8 *be* of the possession of the **c** of Israel:	1121
35:10 Speak unto the **c** of Israel, and say unto	1121
35:15 for the **c** of Israel, and for the stranger,	1121
35:34 for I the LORD dwell among the **c** of	1121
36: 1 the chief fathers of the families of the **c** of	1121
36: 1 the chief fathers of the **c** of Israel:	1121
36: 2 for an inheritance by lot to the **c** of Israel:	1121
36: 3 sons of the *other* tribes of the **c** of Israel,	1121
36: 4 when the jubile of the **c** of Israel shall be,	1121
36: 5 Moses commanded the **c** of Israel	1121
36: 7 So shall not the inheritance of the **c** of	1121
36: 7 for every one of the **c** of Israel shall keep	1121
36: 8 inheritance in any tribe of the **c** of Israel,	1121
36: 8 that the **c** of Israel may enjoy every man	1121
36: 9 every one of the tribes of the **c** of Israel	1121
36:13 in the plains of Moab by Jordan	1121
Dt	1: 3 *that* Moses spake unto the **c** of Israel,
1:36 to his **c**, because he hath wholly followed	1121
1:39 ye said should be a prey, and your **c**,	1121
2: 4 the coast of your brethren the **c** of Esau,	1121
2: 8 we passed by from our brethren the **c**	1121
2: 9 I have given Ar unto the **c** of Lot *for* a	1121
2:12 the **c** of Esau succeeded them, when they	1121
2:19 *when* thou comest nigh over against the **c**	1121
2:19 for I will not give thee of the land of the **c**	1121
2:19 I have given it unto the **c** of Lot *for* a	1121
2:22 As he did to the **c** of Esau, which dwelt in	1121
2:29 (As the **c** of Esau which dwell in Seir,	1121
2:37 Only unto the land of the **c** of Ammon	1121
3: 6 the men, women, and **c**, of every city.	2945
3:11 *is* it not in Rabbath of the **c** of Ammon?	1121

Dt	3:16 *which is* the border of the **c** of Ammon;
3:18 armed before your brethren the **c** of Israel,	1121
4:10 the earth, and *that* they may teach their **c**.	1121
4:25 When thou shalt beget **c**,	1121
4:25 children's **c**, and ye shall have remained	1121
4:40 with thy **c** after thee, and that thou mayest	1121
4:44 *is* the law which Moses set before the **c**	1121
4:45 which Moses spake unto the **c** of Israel,	1121
4:46 whom Moses and the **c** of Israel smote,	1121
5: 9 the iniquity of the fathers upon the **c**	1121
5:29 well with them, and with their **c** for ever!	1121
6: 7 shalt teach them diligently unto thy **c**,	1121
9: 2 great and tall, the **c** of the Anakims,	1121
9: 2 *say*, Who can stand before the **c** of Anak!	1121
10: 6 the **c** of Israel took their journey from	1121
10: 6 from Beeroth of the **c** of Jaakan *to* Mosera:	1121
11: 2 *I speak* not with your **c** which have not	1121
11:19 ye shall teach them your **c**, speaking of	1121
11:21 may be multiplied, and the days of your **c**,	1121
12:25 well with thee, and with thy **c** after thee,	1121
12:28 thee, and with thy **c** after thee for ever,	1121
13:13 *Certain* men, the **c** of Belial, are gone out	1121
14: 1 Ye *are* the **c** of the LORD your God:	1121
17:20 he, and his **c**, in the midst of Israel.	1121
21:15 another hated, and they have born him **c**,	1121
23: 8 The **c** that are begotten of them shall enter	1121
24: 7 any of his brethren of the **c** of Israel,	1121
24:16 fathers shall not be put to death for the **c**,	1121
24:16 neither shall the **c** be put to death for	1121
28:54 towards the remnant of his **c** which he	1121
28:55 of the flesh of his whom he shall eat:	1121
28:57 and towards her **c** which she shall bear:	1121
29: 1 with the **c** of Israel in the land of Moab,	1121
29:22 So that the generation to come of your **c**	1121
29:29 *belong* unto us and to our **c** for ever,	1121
30: 2 thou and thy **c**, with all thine heart,	1121
31:12 **c**, and thy stranger that *is* within thy	2945
31:13 *that* their **c**, which have not known *any*	1121
31:19 song for you, and teach it the **c** of Israel:	1121
31:19 be a witness for me against the **c** of Israel.	1121
31:22 the same day, and taught it the **c** of Israel.	1121
31:23 for thou shalt bring the **c** of Israel into	1121
32: 5 their spot *is* not *the spot* of his **c**:	1121
32: 8 according to the number of the **c** of Israel.	1121
32:20 froward generation, **c** in whom *is* no faith.	1121
32:46 ye shall command your **c** to observe	1121
32:49 which I give unto the **c** of Israel for a	1121
32:51 **c** of Israel at the waters of	1121
32:51 sanctified me not in the midst of the **c** of	1121
32:52 unto the land which I give the **c** of Israel.	1121
33: 1 blessed the **c** of Israel before his death.	1121
33: 9 his brethren, nor knew his own **c**:	1121
33:24 he said, *Let* Asher *be* blessed with **c**;	1121
34: 8 the **c** of Israel wept for Moses in the	1121
34: 9 the **c** of Israel hearkened unto him,	1121
Jos	1: 2 I do give to them, *even* to the **c** of Israel.
2: 2 there came men in hither to night of the **c**	1121
3: 1 he and all the **c** of Israel, and lodged there	1121
3: 9 Joshua said unto the **c** of Israel,	1121
4: 4 whom he had prepared of the **c** of Israel,	1121
4: 5 the number of the tribes of the **c** of Israel:	1121
4: 6 when your **c** ask *their fathers* in time to	1121
4: 7 a memorial unto the **c** of Israel for ever.	1121
4: 8 **c** of Israel did so as Joshua commanded,	1121
4: 8 the number of the tribes of the **c** of Israel,	1121
4:12 the **c** of Reuben, and the children of Gad,	1121
4:12 the **c** of Gad, and half the tribe of	1121
4:12 passed over armed before the **c** of Israel,	1121
4:21 he spake unto the **c** of Israel, saying,	1121
4:21 your **c** shall ask their fathers in time	1121
4:22 ye shall let your **c** know, saying,	1121
5: 1 of Jordan from before the **c** of Israel,	1121
5: 1 them any more, because of the **c** of Israel.	1121
5: 2 circumcise again the **c** of Israel the second	1121
5: 3 circumcised the **c** of Israel at the hill of	1121
5: 6 For the **c** of Israel walked forty years in	1121
5: 7 their **c**, *whom* he raised up in their stead,	1121
5:10 the **c** of Israel encamped in Gilgal,	1121
5:12 had the **c** of Israel manna any more;	1121
6: 1 straitly shut up because of the **c** of Israel:	1121
7: 1 the **c** of Israel committed a trespass in	1121
7: 1 LORD was kindled against the **c** of Israel.	1121
7:12 Therefore the **c** of Israel could not stand	1121
7:23 unto all the **c** of Israel, and laid them out	1121
8:31 of the LORD commanded the **c** of Israel,	1121
8:32 he wrote in the presence of the **c** of	1121
9:17 the **c** of Israel journeyed, and came unto	1121
9:18 And the **c** of Israel smote them not,	1121
9:26 delivered them out of the hand of the **c** of	1121
10: 4 peace with Joshua and with the **c** of Israel.	1121
10:11 whom the **c** of Israel slew with the sword.	1121
10:12 up the Amorites before the **c** of Israel,	1121
10:20 the **c** of Israel had made an end of slaying	1121
10:21 moved his tongue against any of the **c**	1121
11:14 the **c** of Israel took for a prey unto	1121
11:19 city that made peace with the **c** of Israel,	1121
11:22 Anakims left in the land of the **c** of Israel:	1121
12: 1 which the **c** of Israel smote,	1121
12: 2 *which is* the border of the **c** of Ammon;	1121
12: 6 of the LORD and the **c** of Israel smite:	1121
12: 7 the **c** of Israel smote on *this* side Jordan	1121
13: 6 them will I drive out from before the **c** of	1121
13:10 unto the border of the **c** of Ammon;	1121
13:13 (Nevertheless the **c** of Israel expelled not	1121
13:15 Moses gave unto the tribe of the **c** of	1121

Jos	13:22 did the **c** of Israel slay with the sword	1121
	13:23 the border of the **c** of Reuben was Jordan,	1121
	13:23 of the **c** of Reuben after their families,	1121
	13:24 *even* unto the **c** of Gad according to their	1121
	13:25 and half the land of the **c** of Ammon,	1121
	13:28 This *is* the inheritance of the **c** of Gad	1121
	13:29 of the **c** of Manasseh by their families.	1121
	13:31 *were* pertaining unto the **c** of Machir	1121
	13:31 *even* to the one half of the **c** of Machir by	1121
	14: 1 *are the countries* which the **c** of Israel	1121
	14: 1 heads of the fathers of the tribes of the **c**	1121
	14: 4 For the **c** of Joseph were two tribes,	1121
	14: 5 so the **c** of Israel did, and they divided	1121
	14: 6 the **c** of Judah came unto Joshua in Gilgal:	1121
	14:10 while the **c** *of* Israel wandered in	NIH
	15: 1 the lot of the tribe of the **c** of Judah by	1121
	15:12 coast *thereof*. This *is* the coast of the **c**	1121
	15:13 he gave a part among the **c** of Judah,	1121
	15:14 and Ahiman, and Talmai, the **c** of Anak.	3211
	15:20 *is* the inheritance of the tribe of the **c**	1121
	15:21 uttermost cities of the tribe of the **c** of	1121
	15:63 the **c** of Judah could not drive them out:	1121
	15:63 the Jebusites dwell with the **c** of Judah at	1121
	16: 1 the lot of the **c** of Joseph fell from Jordan	1121
	16: 4 the **c** of Joseph, Manasseh and Ephraim,	1121
	16: 5 the border of the **c** of Ephraim according	1121
	16: 8 *is* the inheritance of the tribe of the **c**	1121
	16: 9 the separate cities for the **c** of Ephraim	1121
	16: 9 the inheritance of the **c** of Manasseh,	1121
	17: 2 was also *a lot* for the rest of the **c** of	1121
	17: 2 for the **c** of Abiezer, and for the children	1121
	17: 2 for the **c** of Helek, and for the children of	1121
	17: 2 for the **c** of Asriel, and for the children of	1121
	17: 2 for the **c** of Shechem, and for the children	1121
	17: 2 for the **c** of Hepher, and for the children	1121
	17: 2 of Hepher, and for the **c** of Shemida:	1121
	17: 2 *were* the male **c** of Manasseh the son	1121
	17: 8 Manasseh *belonged* to the **c** of Ephraim;	1121
	17:12 Yet the **c** of Manasseh could not drive out	1121
	17:13 when the **c** of Israel were waxen strong,	1121
	17:14 the **c** of Joseph spake unto Joshua, saying,	1121
	17:16 the **c** of Joseph said, The hill is not	1121
	18: 1 the whole congregation of the **c** of Israel	1121
	18: 2 remained among the **c** of Israel seven	1121
	18: 3 Joshua said unto the **c** of Israel, How long	1121
	18:10 Joshua divided the land unto the **c** of	1121
	18:11 the lot of the tribe of the **c** of Benjamin	1121
	18:11 lot came forth between the **c** of Judah	1121
	18:11 the children of Judah and the **c** of Joseph.	1121
	18:14 *is* Kirjath-jearim, a city of the **c** of Judah:	1121
	18:20 This *was* the inheritance of the **c** of	1121
	18:21 Now the cities of the tribe of the **c** of	1121
	18:28 *is* the inheritance of the **c** of Benjamin	1121
	19: 1 *even* for the tribe of the **c** of Simeon	1121
	19: 1 within the inheritance of the **c** of Judah.	1121
	19: 8 *is* the inheritance of the tribe of the **c**	1121
	19: 9 Out of the portion of the **c** of Judah *was*	1121
	19: 9 *was* the inheritance of the **c** of Simeon:	1121
	19: 9 the part of the **c** of Judah was too much	1121
	19: 9 the **c** of Simeon had their inheritance	1121
	19:10 the third lot came up for the **c** of Zebulun	1121
	19:16 This *is* the inheritance of the **c** of Zebulun	1121
	19:17 for the **c** of Issachar according to how	1121
	19:23 This *is* the inheritance of the tribe of the **c**	1121
	19:24 the fifth lot came out for the tribe of the **c**	1121
	19:31 This *is* the inheritance of the tribe of the **c**	1121
	19:32 sixth lot came out to the **c** of Naphtali,	1121
	19:32 for the **c** of Naphtali according to their	1121
	19:39 This *is* the inheritance of the tribe of the **c**	1121
	19:40 of the **c** of Dan according to their families.	1121
	19:47 coast of the **c** of Dan went out *too little*	1121
	19:47 the **c** of Dan went up to fight against	1121
	19:48 *is* the inheritance of the tribe of the **c**	1121
	19:49 of Israel gave an inheritance to Joshua	1121
	19:51 heads of the fathers of the tribes of the **c**	1121
	20: 2 Speak to the **c** of Israel, saying,	1121
	20: 9 were the cities appointed for all the **c**	1121
	21: 1 the fathers of the tribes of the **c** of Israel;	1121
	21: 3 the **c** of Israel gave unto the Levites out	1121
	21: 4 the **c** of Aaron the priest, among	1121
	21: 5 the rest of the **c** of Kohath had by lot out	1121
	21: 6 the **c** of Gershon *had* by lot out of	1121
	21: 7 The **c** of Merari by their families *had* out	1121
	21: 8 the **c** of Israel gave by lot unto the Levites	1121
	21: 9 gave out of the tribe of the **c** of Judah,	1121
	21: 9 out of the tribe of the **c** of Simeon, these	1121
	21:10 the **c** of Aaron, *being* of the families	1121
	21:10 *who were* of the **c** of Levi, had:	1121
	21:13 they gave to the **c** of Aaron the priest	1121
	21:19 All the cities of the **c** of Aaron, the priests,	1121
	21:20 families of the **c** of Kohath, the Levites	1121
	21:20 the Levites which remained of the **c** of	1121
	21:26 families of the **c** of Kohath that remained.	1121
	21:27 unto the **c** of Gershon, of the families of	1121
	21:34 the families of the **c** of Merari, the rest	1121
	21:40 all the cities for the **c** of Merari by their	1121
	21:41 possession of the **c** of Israel *were* forty	1121
	22: 9 the **c** of Reuben and the children of Gad	1121
	22: 9 children of Reuben and the **c** of Gad and	1121
	22: 9 departed from the **c** of Israel out of Shiloh,	1121
	22:10 the **c** of Reuben and the children of Gad	1121
	22:10 children of Reuben and the **c** of Gad and	1121
	22:11 the **c** of Israel heard say, Behold,	1121
	22:11 the **c** of Reuben and the children of Gad	1121
	22:11 children of Reuben and the **c** of Gad and	1121

Jos	22:11 of Jordan, at the passage of the **c** of Israel.	1121
	22:12 when the **c** of Israel heard *of it*, the whole	1121
	22:12 **c** of Israel gathered themselves together *at*	1121
	22:13 the **c** of Israel sent unto the children of	1121
	22:13 the children of Israel sent unto the **c** of	1121
	22:13 to the **c** of Gad, and to the half tribe of	1121
	22:15 they came unto the **c** of Reuben, and to	1121
	22:15 to the **c** of Gad, and to the half tribe of	1121
	22:21 the **c** of Reuben and the children of Gad	1121
	22:21 children of Reuben and the **c** of Gad and	1121
	22:24 In time to come your **c** might speak unto	1121
	22:24 your children might speak unto our **c**,	1121
	22:25 ye **c** of Reuben and children of Gad;	1121
	22:25 ye children of Reuben and **c** of Gad;	1121
	22:25 shall your **c** make our children cease from	1121
	22:25 shall your children make our **c** cease from	1121
	22:27 that your **c** may not say to our children in	1121
	22:27 that your children may not say to our **c** in	1121
	22:30 heard the words that the **c** of Reuben and	1121
	22:30 **c** of Gad and the children of Manasseh	1121
	22:30 of Gad and the **c** of Manasseh spake,	1121
	22:31 the priest said unto the **c** of Reuben,	1121
	22:31 to the **c** of Gad, and to the children of	1121
	22:31 of Gad, and to the **c** of Manasseh,	1121
	22:31 ye have delivered the **c** of Israel out of	1121
	22:32 returned from the **c** of Reuben,	1121
	22:32 from the **c** of Gad, out of the land of	1121
	22:32 to the **c** of Israel, and brought them word	1121
	22:33 the thing pleased the **c** of Israel;	1121
	22:33 the **c** of Israel blessed God, and did not	1121
	22:33 destroy the land wherein the **c** of Reuben	1121
	22:34 the **c** of Reuben and the children of Gad	1121
	22:34 the **c** of Gad called the altar *Ed:* for it	1121
	24: 4 Jacob and his **c** went down *into* Egypt.	1121
	24:32 which the **c** of Israel brought up out of	1121
	24:32 became the inheritance of the **c** of Joseph.	1121
Jdg	1: 1 that the **c** of Israel asked the Lord,	1121
	1: 8 Now the **c** of Judah had fought against	1121
	1: 9 the **c** of Judah went down to fight	1121
	1:16 of the Kenite, Moses' father in law,	1121
	1:16 **c** of Judah *into* the wilderness of Judah,	1121
	1:21 the **c** of Benjamin did not drive out	1121
	1:21 Jebusites dwell with the **c** of Benjamin	1121
	1:34 the Amorites forced the **c** of Dan into	1121
	2: 4 spake these words unto all the **c** of Israel,	1121
	2: 6 the **c** of Israel went every man unto his	1121
	2:11 the **c** of Israel did evil in the sight of	1121
	3: 2 Only that the generations of the **c** of Israel	1121
	3: 5 of Israel dwelt among the Canaanites,	1121
	3: 7 the **c** of Israel did evil in the sight of	1121
	3: 8 the **c** of Israel served Chushan-rishathaim	1121
	3: 9 when the **c** of Israel cried unto the Lord,	1121
	3: 9 the Lord raised up a deliverer to the **c** of	1121
	3:12 the **c** of Israel did evil again in the sight of	1121
	3:13 he gathered unto him the **c** of Ammon	1121
	3:14 So the **c** of Israel served Eglon the king of	1121
	3:15 when the **c** of Israel cried unto the Lord,	1121
	3:15 by him the **c** of Israel sent a present unto	1121
	3:27 the **c** of Israel went down with him from	1121
	4: 1 the **c** of Israel again did evil in the sight of	1121
	4: 3 the **c** of Israel cried unto the Lord: for he	1121
	4: 3 years he mightily oppressed the **c** of	1121
	4: 5 of Israel came up to her for judgment.	1121
	4: 6 with thee ten thousand men of the **c** of	1121
	4: 6 of Naphtali and of the **c** of Zebulun?	1121
	4:11 *which was* of the **c** of Hobab the father in	1121
	4:23 the king of Canaan before the **c** of Israel.	1121
	4:24 the hand of the **c** of Israel prospered,	1121
	6: 1 the **c** of Israel did evil in the sight of	1121
	6: 2 the Midianites the **c** of Israel made them	1121
	6: 3 and the Amalekites, and the **c** of the east,	1121
	6: 6 and the **c** of Israel cried unto the Lord.	1121
	6: 7 when the **c** of Israel cried unto the Lord	1121
	6: 8 That the Lord sent a prophet unto the **c**	1121
	6:33 the **c** of the east gathered together,	1121
	7:12 all the **c** of the east lay along in the valley	1121
	8:10 left of all the hosts of the **c** of the east:	1121
	8:18 *each* one resembled the **c** of a king.	1121
	8:28 Thus was Midian subdued before the **c** of	1121
	8:33 the **c** of Israel turned again, and went a	1121
	8:34 the **c** of Israel remembered not the Lord	1121
	10: 6 the **c** of Israel did evil again in the sight of	1121
	10: 6 the gods of the **c** of Ammon, and the gods	1121
	10: 7 and into the hands of the **c** of Ammon.	1121
	10: 8 they vexed and oppressed the **c** of Israel:	1121
	10: 8 all the **c** of Israel that *were* on the *other*	1121
	10: 9 Moreover the **c** of Ammon passed over	1121
	10:10 the **c** of Israel cried unto the Lord,	1121
	10:11 the Lord said unto the **c** of Israel,	1121
	10:11 from the **c** of Ammon, and from	1121
	10:15 the **c** of Israel said unto the Lord,	1121
	10:17 the **c** of Ammon were gathered together,	1121
	10:17 the **c** of Israel assembled themselves	1121
	10:18 begin to fight against the **c** of Ammon?	1121
	11: 4 that the **c** of Ammon made war against	1121
	11: 5 that when the **c** of Ammon made war	1121
	11: 6 that we may fight with the **c** of Ammon.	1121
	11: 8 fight against the **c** of Ammon, and be our	1121
	11: 9 again to fight against the **c** of Ammon,	1121
	11:12 unto the king of the **c** of Ammon,	1121
	11:13 the king of the **c** of Ammon answered	1121
	11:14 again unto the king of the **c** of Ammon:	1121
	11:15 of Moab, nor the land of the **c** of Ammon:	1121
	11:27 be judge *this* day between the **c** of Israel	1121
	11:27 the children of Israel and the **c** of Ammon.	1121

Jdg	11:28 Howbeit the king of the **c** of Ammon	1121
	11:29 he passed over *unto* the **c** of Ammon.	1121
	11:30 If thou shalt without fail deliver the **c** of	1121
	11:31 when I return in peace from the **c** of	1121
	11:32 So Jephthah passed over unto the **c** of	1121
	11:33 Thus the **c** of Ammon were subdued	1121
	11:33 were subdued before the **c** of Israel.	1121
	11:36 thine enemies, *even* of the **c** of Ammon.	1121
	12: 1 over to fight against the **c** of Ammon,	1121
	12: 2 people were at great strife with the **c** of	1121
	12: 3 passed over against the **c** of Ammon,	1121
	13: 1 the **c** of Israel did evil again in the sight of	1121
	14:16 hast put forth a riddle unto the **c** of my	1121
	14:17 she told the riddle to the **c** of her people.	1121
	18: 2 the **c** of Dan sent of their family five men	1121
	18:16 which *were* of the **c** of Dan, stood *by*	1121
	18:22 and overtook the **c** of Dan.	1121
	18:23 they cried unto the **c** of Dan. And they	1121
	18:25 the **c** of Dan said unto him, Let not thy	1121
	18:26 the **c** of Dan went their way: and	1121
	18:30 the **c** of Dan set up the graven image: and	1121
	19:12 of a stranger, that *is* not of the **c** of Israel;	1121
	19:30 **c** of Israel came up out of the land of	1121
	20: 1 all the **c** of Israel went out,	1121
	20: 3 (Now the **c** of Benjamin heard that	1121
	20: 3 the **c** of Israel were gone up *to* Mizpeh.)	1121
	20: 3 said the **c** of Israel, Tell *us*, how was this	1121
	20: 7 Behold, ye *are* all **c** of Israel; give here	1121
	20:13 deliver *us* the men, the **c** of Belial,	1121
	20:13 of Benjamin would not hearken to	1121
	20:13 the voice of their brethren the **c** of Israel:	1121
	20:14 the **c** of Benjamin gathered themselves	1121
	20:14 to go out to battle against the **c** of Israel.	1121
	20:15 the **c** of Benjamin were numbered at that	1121
	20:18 the **c** of Israel arose, and went up *to*	1121
	20:18 to the battle against the **c** of Benjamin?	1121
	20:19 the **c** of Israel rose up in the morning,	1121
	20:21 the **c** of Benjamin came forth out of	1121
	20:23 (And the **c** of Israel went up and	1121
	20:23 I go *up* again to battle against the **c** of	1121
	20:24 the **c** of Israel came near against	1121
	20:24 children of Israel came near against the **c**	1121
	20:25 destroyed *down* to the ground of the **c** of	1121
	20:26 all the **c** of Israel, and all the people,	1121
	20:27 the **c** of Israel inquired of the Lord,	1121
	20:28 against the **c** of Benjamin my brother,	1121
	20:30 **c** of Israel went up against the children	1121
	20:30 children of Israel went up against the **c**	1121
	20:31 the **c** of Benjamin went out against	1121
	20:32 the **c** of Benjamin said, They *are* smitten	1121
	20:32 the **c** of Israel said, Let us flee,	1121
	20:35 the **c** of Israel destroyed of the Benjamites	1121
	20:36 So the **c** of Benjamin saw that they were	1121
	20:48 men of Israel turned again upon the **c** of	1121
	21: 5 the **c** of Israel said, Who *is there* among	1121
	21: 6 the **c** of Israel repented them for Benjamin	1121
	21:10 of the sword, with the women and the **c**.	2945
	21:13 **c** of Benjamin that *were* in the rock	1121
	21:18 for the **c** of Israel have sworn, saying,	1121
	21:20 Therefore they commanded the **c** of	1121
	21:23 the **c** of Benjamin did so, and took *them*	1121
	21:24 **c** of Israel departed thence at that time,	1121
1Sa	1: 2 Peninnah had **c**, but Hannah had no	3206
	1: 2 had children, but Hannah had no **c**.	3206
	2: 5 and she that hath many **c** is waxed feeble.	1121
	2:28 offerings made by fire of the **c** of Israel?	1121
	7: 4 the **c** of Israel did put away Baalim and	1121
	7: 6 Samuel judged the **c** of Israel in Mizpeh.	1121
	7: 7 when the Philistines heard that the **c** of	1121
	7: 7 when the **c** of Israel heard *it*, they were	1121
	7: 8 the **c** of Israel said to Samuel, Cease not	1121
	9: 2 *there was* not among the **c** of Israel a	1121
	10:18 said unto the **c** of Israel, Thus saith	1121
	10:27 the **c** of Belial said, How shall this *man*	1121
	11: 8 the **c** of Israel were three hundred	1121
	12:12 ye saw that Nahash the king of the **c**	1121
	14:18 was at that time with the **c** of Israel.	1121
	14:47 against the **c** of Ammon, and against	1121
	15: 6 for ye shewed kindness to all the **c** of	1121
	16:11 Samuel said unto Jesse, Are here all *thy* **c**?	5288
	17:53 the **c** of Israel returned from chasing after	1121
	22:19 **c** and sucklings, and oxen, and asses,	5768
	26:19 if *they be* the **c** of men, cursed *be* they	1121
	30:22 save *to* every man his wife and his **c**,	1121
2Sa	1:18 (Also he bade *them* teach the **c** of Judah	1121
	2:25 the **c** of Benjamin gathered themselves	1121
	4: 2 a Beerothite, of the **c** of Benjamin:	1121
	7: 6 I brought up the **c** of Israel out of Egypt,	1121
	7: 7 of Israel spake I a word with any of	1121
	7:10 neither shall the **c** of wickedness afflict	1121
	7:14 and with the stripes of the **c** of men:	1121
	8:12 of the **c** of Ammon, and of the Philistines,	1121
	10: 1 that the king of the **c** of Ammon died,	1121
	10: 2 servants came *into* the land of the **c**	1121
	10: 3 the princes of the **c** of Ammon said unto	1121
	10: 6 the **c** of Ammon saw that they stank	1121
	10: 6 **c** of Ammon sent and hired the Syrians	1121
	10: 8 the **c** of Ammon came out, and put	1121
	10:10 *them* in array against the **c** of Ammon.	1121
	10:11 if the **c** of Ammon be too strong for thee,	1121
	10:14 the **c** of Ammon saw that the Syrians	1121
	10:14 So Joab returned from the **c** of Ammon,	1121
	10:19 So the Syrians feared to help the **c** of	1121
	11: 1 they destroyed the **c** of Ammon,	1121
	12: 3 up together with him, and with his **c**;	1121

C

2Sa 12: 9 slain him with the sword of the **c** of — 1121
12:26 Joab fought against Rabbah of the **c** of — 1121
12:31 thus did he unto all the cities of the **c** of — 1121
17:27 of Nahash of Rabbah of the **c** of Ammon, — 1121
21: 2 (now the Gibeonites *were* not of the **c** of — 1121
21: 2 and the **c** of Israel had sworn unto them: — 1121
21: 2 sought to slay them in his zeal to the **c** — 1121
23:29 the son of Ribai out of Gibeah of the **c** — 1121

1Ki 2: 4 saying, If thy **c** take heed to their way, — 1121
4:30 wisdom of all the **c** of the east country, — 1121
6: 1 eightieth year after the **c** of Israel were — 1121
6:13 I will dwell among the **c** of Israel, — 1121
8: 1 the chief of the fathers of the **c** of Israel, — 1121
8: 9 made *a covenant* with the **c** of Israel, — 1121
8:25 so that thy **c** take heed to their way, — 1121
8:39 knowest the hearts of all the **c** of men;) — 1121
8:63 all the **c** of Israel dedicated the house of — 1121
9: 6 you or your **c**, and will not keep my — 1121
9:20 which *were* not of the **c** of Israel, — 1121
9:21 Their **c** that were left after them in the — 1121
9:21 whom the **c** of Israel also were not able — 1121
9:22 of the **c** of Israel did Solomon make no — 1121
11: 2 which the LORD said unto the **c** of Israel, — 1121
11: 7 the abomination of the **c** of Ammon. — 1121
11:33 Milcom the god of the **c** of Ammon, — 1121
12:17 *as for* the **c** of Israel which dwelt in — 1121
12:24 nor fight against your brethren the **c** of — 1121
12:33 and ordained a feast unto the **c** of Israel: — 1121
14:24 the LORD cast out before the **c** of Israel. — 1121
18:20 So Ahab sent unto all the **c** of Israel, — 1121
19:10 for the **c** of Israel have forsaken thy — 1121
19:14 the **c** of Israel have forsaken thy covenant, — 1121
20: 3 thy wives also and thy **c**, *even* — 1121
20: 5 and thy gold, and thy wives, and thy **c**; — 1121
20: 7 for my **c**, and for my silver, and for my — 1121
20:15 *even* all the **c** of Israel, *being* seven — 1121
20:27 the **c** of Israel were numbered, and were — 1121
20:27 the **c** of Israel pitched before them like — 1121
20:29 the **c** of Israel slew *of* the Syrians an — 1121
21:13 two men, of Belial, and sat before him: — 1121
21:26 whom the LORD cast out before the **c** of — 1121

2Ki 2:23 there came forth little **c** out of the city, — 5288
2:24 wood, and tare forty and two **c** of them. — 3206
4: 7 debt, and live thou and thy **c** of the rest. — 1121
8:12 evil that thou wilt do unto the **c** of Israel: — 1121
8:12 wilt dash their **c**, and rip up their women — 5768
8:19 to give to him alway a light, *and* to his **c**. — 1121
9: 1 Elisha the prophet called one of the **c** of — 1121
10: 1 to them that brought up Ahab's **c**, saying, — NIH
10: 5 the bringers up *of the* **c**, sent to Jehu, — NIH
10:13 we go down to salute the **c** of the king — 1121
10:13 of the king and the **c** of the queen. — 1121
10:30 thy **c** of the fourth *generation* shall sit on — 1121
13: 5 the **c** of Israel dwelt in their tents, — 1121
14: 6 the **c** of the murderers he slew not: — 1121
14: 6 fathers shall not be put to death for the **c**, — 1121
14: 6 nor the **c** be put to death for the fathers; — 1121
16: 3 LORD cast out from before the **c** of Israel. — 1121
17: 7 that the **c** of Israel had sinned against — 1121
17: 8 LORD cast out from before the **c** of Israel, — 1121
17: 9 the **c** of Israel did secretly *those* things — 1121
17:22 For the **c** of Israel walked in all the sins of — 1121
17:24 cities of Samaria instead of the **c** of Israel: — 1121
17:31 the Sepharvites burnt their **c** in fire to — 1121
17:34 the LORD commanded the **c** of Jacob, — 1121
17:41 both their **c**, and their children's children: — 1121
17:41 both their children, and their children's **c**: — 1121
18: 4 for unto those days the **c** of Israel did burn — 1121
19: 3 for the **c** are come to the birth, and *there* — 1121
19:12 the **c** of Eden which *were* in Thelasar? — 1121
21: 2 whom the LORD cast out before the **c** of — 1121
21: 9 LORD destroyed before the **c** of Israel. — 1121
23: 6 upon the graves of the **c** of the people. — 1121
23:10 which *is* in the valley of the **c** of Hinnom, — 1121
23:13 for Milcom the abomination of the **c** of — 1121
24: 2 bands of the **c** of Ammon, and sent them — 1121

1Ch 1:43 *any* king reigned over the **c** of Israel; — 1121
2:10 begat Nahshon, prince of the **c** of Judah; — 1121
2:18 the son of Hezron begat **c** of Azubah — NIH
2:30 and Appaim: but Seled died without **c**. — 1121
2:31 Sheshan. And the **c** of Sheshan; Ahlai. — 1121
2:32 and Jonathan: and Jether died without **c**. — 1121
4:27 his brethren had not many **c**, neither did — 1121
4:27 family multiply, like to the **c** of Judah. — 1121
5:11 the **c** of Gad dwelt over against them, — 1121
5:14 These *are* the **c** of Abihail the son of Huri, — 1121
5:23 the **c** of the half tribe of Manasseh dwelt — 1121
6: 3 the **c** of Amram; Aaron, and Moses, — 1121
6:33 these *are* they that waited with their **c**. — 1121
6:64 the **c** of Israel gave to the Levites *these* — 1121
6:65 gave by lot out of the tribe of the **c** of — 1121
6:65 out of the tribe of the **c** of Simeon, — 1121
6:65 out of the tribe of the **c** of Benjamin, — 1121
6:77 Unto the rest of the **c** of Merari *were* — 1121
7:12 and Huppim, the **c** of Ir, *and* Hushim, — 1121
7:29 by the borders of the **c** of Manasseh, — 1121
7:29 In these dwelt the **c** of Joseph the son of — 1121
7:33 and Ashvath. These *are* the **c** of Japhlet. — 1121
7:40 All these *were* the **c** of Asher, heads of — 1121
8: 8 Shaharaim begat **c** in the country of Moab, — NIH
9: 3 in Jerusalem dwelt of the **c** of Judah, — 1121
9: 3 of the **c** of Benjamin, and of the children — 1121
9: 3 and of the **c** of Ephraim, and Manasseh; — 1121
9: 4 Bani, of the **c** of Pharez the son of Judah. — 1121
9:18 *were* porters in the companies of the **c** — 1121

1Ch 9:23 their **c** had the oversight of the gates of — 1121
11:31 that pertained to the **c** of Benjamin, — 1121
12:16 there came of the **c** of Benjamin and — 1121
12:24 The **c** of Judah that bare shield and — 1121
12:25 Of the **c** of Simeon, mighty *men* of valour — 1121
12:26 Of the **c** of Levi four thousand and — 1121
12:29 of the **c** of Benjamin, the kindred of Saul, — 1121
12:30 of the **c** of Ephraim twenty thousand and — 1121
12:32 of the **c** of Issachar, *which were men* that — 1121
14: 4 Now these *are* the names of *his* **c** which — 3205
15: 4 David assembled the **c** of Aaron, — 1121
15:15 the **c** of the Levites bare the ark of God — 1121
16:13 servant, ye **c** of Jacob, his chosen *ones*. — 1121
17: 9 neither shall the **c** of wickedness waste — 1121
18:11 from the **c** of Ammon, and from — 1121
19: 1 that Nahash the king of the **c** of Ammon — 1121
19: 2 the land of the **c** of Ammon to Hanun, — 1121
19: 3 the princes of the **c** of Ammon said to — 1121
19: 6 when the **c** of Ammon saw that they had — 1121
19: 6 the **c** of Ammon sent a thousand talents — 1121
19: 7 the **c** of Ammon gathered themselves — 1121
19: 9 the **c** of Ammon came out, and put — 1121
19:11 set *themselves* in array against the **c** of — 1121
19:12 if the **c** of Ammon be too strong for thee, — 1121
19:15 the **c** of Ammon saw that the Syrians — 1121
19:19 neither would the Syrians help the **c** of — 1121
20: 1 wasted the country of the **c** of Ammon, — 1121
20: 3 dealt David with all the cities of the **c** of — 1121
20: 4 Sippai, *that was* of the **c** of the giant: — 3211
24: 2 died before their father, and had no **c**: — 1121
26:10 Also Hosah, of the **c** of Merari, had sons; — 1121
27: 1 Now the **c** of Israel after their number, — 1121
27: 3 Of the **c** of Perez *was* the chief of all — 1121
27:10 Helez the Pelonite, of the **c** of Ephraim: — 1121
27:14 the Pirathonite, of the **c** of Ephraim: — 1121
27:20 Of the **c** of Ephraim, Hoshea the son of — 1121
28: 8 leave *it* for an inheritance for your **c** after — 1121

2Ch 5: 2 the chief of the fathers of the **c** of Israel, — 1121
5:10 made *a covenant* with the **c** of Israel, — 1121
6:11 that he made with the **c** of Israel. — 1121
6:16 thy **c** take heed to their way to walk in — 1121
6:30 thou only knowest the hearts of the **c** of — 1121
7: 3 when all the **c** of Israel saw how the fire — 1121
8: 2 and caused the **c** of Israel to dwell there. — 1121
8: 8 of their **c**, who were left after them in — 1121
8: 8 whom the **c** of Israel consumed not, — 1121
8: 9 of the **c** of Israel did Solomon make no — 1121
10:17 the **c** of Israel that dwelt in the cities — 1121
10:18 the **c** of Israel stoned him with stones, — 1121
11:19 Which bare him; Jeush, and Shamariah, — 1121
11:23 dispersed of all his **c** throughout all — 1121
13: 7 the **c** of Belial, and have strengthened — 1121
13:12 O **c** of Israel, fight ye not against — 1121
13:16 the **c** of Israel fled before Judah: and — 1121
13:18 Thus the **c** of Israel were brought under — 1121
13:18 the **c** of Judah prevailed, because — 1121
20: 1 *that* the **c** of Moab, and the children of — 1121
20: 1 the **c** of Ammon, and with them *other* — 1121
20:10 **c** of Ammon and Moab and mount Seir, — 1121
20:13 their little ones, their wives, and their **c**. — 1121
20:19 of the **c** of the Kohathites, and of — 1121
20:19 Kohathites, and of the **c** of the Korhites, — 1121
20:22 the LORD set ambushments against the **c** — 1121
20:23 For the **c** of Ammon and Moab stood up — 1121
21:14 thy **c**, and thy wives, and all thy goods: — 1121
25: 4 slew not their **c**, but *did* as it is written in — 1121
25: 4 saying, The fathers shall not die for the **c**, — 1121
25: 4 neither shall the **c** die for the fathers, — 1121
25: 7 *to wit*, with all the **c** of Ephraim. — 1121
25:11 and smote *of* the **c** of Seir ten thousand. — 1121
25:12 *other* ten thousand *left* alive did the **c** of — 1121
25:14 that he brought the gods of the **c** of Seir, — 1121
27: 5 the **c** of Ammon gave him the same year — 1121
27: 5 So much did the **c** of Ammon pay unto — 1121
28: 3 his **c** in the fire after the abominations — 1121
28: 3 LORD had cast out before the **c** of Israel. — 1121
28: 8 the **c** of Israel carried away captive of their — 1121
28:10 now ye purpose to keep under the **c** of — 1121
28:12 certain of the heads of the **c** of Ephraim, — 1121
30: 6 of the king, saying, Ye **c** of Israel, — 1121
30: 9 your **c** *shall find* compassion before them — 1121
30:21 the **c** of Israel that were present at — 1121
31: 1 Then all the **c** of Israel returned, — 1121
31: 5 the **c** of Israel brought in abundance — 1121
31: 6 *concerning* the **c** of Israel and Judah, — 1121
33: 2 whom the LORD had cast out before the **c** — 1121
33: 6 he caused his **c** to pass through the fire in — 1121
33: 9 had destroyed before the **c** of Israel. — 1121
34:33 countries that *pertained* to the **c** of Israel, — 1121
35:17 the **c** of Israel that were present kept — 1121

Ezr 2: 1 Now these *are* the **c** of the province that — 1121
2: 3 The **c** of Parosh, two thousand an — 1121
2: 4 The **c** of Shephatiah, three hundred — 1121
2: 5 The **c** of Arah, seven hundred seventy — 1121
2: 6 The **c** of Pahath-moab, of the children of — 1121
2: 6 of the **c** of Jeshua *and* Joab, two thousand — 1121
2: 7 The **c** of Elam, a thousand two hundred — 1121
2: 8 The **c** of Zattu, nine hundred forty and — 1121
2: 9 The **c** of Zaccai, seven hundred and — 1121
2:10 The **c** of Bani, six hundred forty and two. — 1121
2:11 The **c** of Bebai, six hundred twenty and — 1121
2:12 The **c** of Azgad, a thousand two hundred — 1121
2:13 The **c** of Adonikam, six hundred sixty — 1121
2:14 The **c** of Bigvai, two thousand fifty and — 1121
2:15 The **c** of Adin, four hundred fifty and — 1121

Ezr 2:16 The **c** of Ater of Hezekiah, ninety and — 1121
2:17 The **c** of Bezai, three hundred twenty — 1121
2:18 The **c** of Jorah, an hundred and twelve. — 1121
2:19 The **c** of Hashum, two hundred twenty — 1121
2:20 The **c** of Gibbar, ninety and five. — 1121
2:21 The **c** of Beth-lehem, an hundred twenty — 1121
2:24 The **c** of Azmaveth, forty and two. — 1121
2:25 The **c** of Kirjath-arim, Chephirah, — 1121
2:26 The **c** of Ramah and Gaba, six hundred — 1121
2:29 The **c** of Nebo, fifty and two. — 1121
2:30 The **c** of Magbish, an hundred fifty and — 1121
2:31 The **c** of the other Elam, a thousand two — 1121
2:32 The **c** of Harim, three hundred and — 1121
2:33 The **c** of Lod, Hadid, and Ono, — 1121
2:34 The **c** of Jericho, three hundred forty and — 1121
2:35 The **c** of Senaah, three thousand and — 1121
2:36 the **c** of Jedaiah, of the house of Jeshua, — 1121
2:37 The **c** of Immer, a thousand fifty and two. — 1121
2:38 The **c** of Pashur, a thousand two hundred — 1121
2:39 The **c** of Harim, a thousand and — 1121
2:40 the **c** of Jeshua and Kadmiel, — 1121
2:40 of the **c** of Hodaviah, seventy and four. — 1121
2:41 The **c** of Asaph, an hundred twenty and — 1121
2:42 The **c** of the porters: the children of — 1121
2:42 the **c** of Shallum, the children of Ater, — 1121
2:42 the **c** of Ater, the children of Talmon, — 1121
2:42 children of Ater, the **c** of Talmon, — 1121
2:42 the **c** of Akkub, the children of Hatita, — 1121
2:42 children of Akkub, the **c** of Hatita, — 1121
2:42 the children of Hatita, the **c** of Shobai, — 1121
2:43 the **c** of Ziha, the children of Hasupha, — 1121
2:43 children of Ziha, the **c** of Hasupha, — 1121
2:43 children of Hasupha, the **c** of Tabbaoth, — 1121
2:44 The **c** of Keros, the children of Siaha, — 1121
2:44 the **c** of Siaha, the children of Padon, — 1121
2:44 the children of Siaha, the **c** of Padon, — 1121
2:45 **c** of Lebanah, the children of Hagabah, — 1121
2:45 the **c** of Hagabah, the children of Akkub, — 1121
2:45 the children of Hagabah, the **c** of Akkub, — 1121
2:46 The **c** of Hagab, the children of Shalmai, — 1121
2:46 the **c** of Shalmai, the children of Hanan, — 1121
2:46 the children of Shalmai, the **c** of Hanan, — 1121
2:47 The **c** of Giddel, the children of Gahar, — 1121
2:47 the **c** of Gahar, the children of Reaiah, — 1121
2:47 the children of Gahar, the **c** of Reaiah, — 1121
2:48 The **c** of Rezin, the children of Nekoda, — 1121
2:48 the **c** of Rezin, the children of Nekoda, — 1121
2:48 the children of Nekoda, the **c** of Gazzam, — 1121
2:49 The **c** of Uzza, the children of Paseah, — 1121
2:49 the **c** of Paseah, the children of Besai, — 1121
2:49 the children of Paseah, the **c** of Besai, — 1121
2:50 The **c** of Asnah, the children of Mehunim, — 1121
2:50 children of Asnah, the **c** of Mehunim, — 1121
2:50 children of Mehunim, the **c** of Nephusim, — 1121
2:51 The **c** of Bakbuk, the children of Hakupha, — 1121
2:51 the **c** of Hakupha, the children of Harhur, — 1121
2:51 the children of Hakupha, the **c** of Harhur, — 1121
2:52 The **c** of Bazluth, the children of Mehida, — 1121
2:52 the **c** of Mehida, the children of Harsha, — 1121
2:52 the children of Mehida, the **c** of Harsha, — 1121
2:53 The **c** of Barkos, the children of Sisera, — 1121
2:53 The children of Barkos, the **c** of Sisera, — 1121
2:53 The children of Sisera, the **c** of Thamah, — 1121
2:54 The **c** of Neziah, the children of Hatipha. — 1121
2:54 The children of Neziah, the **c** of Hatipha. — 1121
2:55 The **c** of Solomon's servants: the children — 1121
2:55 the **c** of Sotai, the children of Sophereth, — 1121
2:55 the children of Sotai, the **c** of Sophereth, — 1121
2:55 children of Sophereth, the **c** of Peruda, — 1121
2:56 The **c** of Jaalah, the children of Darkon, — 1121
2:56 the **c** of Darkon, the children of Giddel, — 1121
2:56 the children of Darkon, the **c** of Giddel, — 1121
2:57 **c** of Shephatiah, the children of Hattil, — 1121
2:57 children of Shephatiah, the **c** of Hattil, — 1121
2:57 of Pochereth of Zebaim, the children — 1121
2:57 of Pochereth of Zebaim, the **c** of Ami. — 1121
2:58 and the **c** of Solomon's servants, — 1121
2:60 The **c** of Delaiah, the children of Tobiah, — 1121
2:60 the **c** of Tobiah, the children of Nekoda, — 1121
2:60 **c** of Nekoda, six hundred fifty and two. — 1121
2:61 of the **c** of the priests: the children of — 1121
2:61 the **c** of Habaiah, the children of Koz, — 1121
2:61 the children of Habaiah, the **c** of Koz, — 1121
2:61 the children of Koz, the **c** of Barzillai, — 1121
3: 1 and the **c** of Israel *were* in the cities, — 1121
4: 1 Benjamin heard that the **c** of the captivity — 1121
6:16 the **c** of Israel, the priests, and the Levites, — 1123
6:16 and the rest of the **c** of the captivity, — 1123
6:19 the **c** of the captivity kept the passover — 1121
6:20 killed the passover for all the **c** of — 1121
6:21 the **c** of Israel, which were come again — 1121
7: 7 there went up *some* of the **c** of Israel, — 1121
8:35 *Also* the **c** of those that had been carried — 1121
9:12 leave *it* for an inheritance to your **c** for — 1121
10: 1 congregation *of* men and women and **c**: — 3206
10: 7 Jerusalem unto all the **c** of the captivity, — 1121
10:16 the **c** of the captivity did so. And Ezra — 1121
10:44 of them had wives by *whom* they had **c**. — 1121

Ne 1: 6 for the **c** of Israel thy servants, — 1121
1: 6 confess the sins of the **c** of Israel, which — 1121
2:10 man to seek the welfare of the **c** of Israel. — 1121
5: 5 of our brethren, our **c** as their children: — 1121
5: 5 of our brethren, our children as their **c**: — 1121
7: 6 These *are* the province, that went — 1121
7: 8 The **c** of Parosh, two thousand an — 1121

C

Ne	7: 9 The **c** of Shephatiah, three hundred	1121
	7:10 The **c** of Arah, six hundred fifty and two.	1121
	7:11 The **c** of Pahath-moab, the children of	1121
	7:11 of the **c** of Jeshua and Joab, two thousand	1121
	7:12 The **c** of Elam, a thousand two hundred	1121
	7:13 The **c** of Zattu, eight hundred forty and	1121
	7:14 The **c** of Zaccai, seven hundred and	1121
	7:15 The **c** of Binnui, six hundred forty and	1121
	7:16 The **c** of Bebai, six hundred twenty and	1121
	7:17 The **c** of Azgad, two thousand three	1121
	7:18 The **c** of Adonikam, six hundred	1121
	7:19 The **c** of Bigvai, two thousand threescore	1121
	7:20 The **c** of Adin, six hundred fifty and five.	1121
	7:21 The **c** of Ater of Hezekiah, ninety and	1121
	7:22 The **c** of Hashum, three hundred twenty	1121
	7:23 The **c** of Bezai, three hundred twenty and	1121
	7:24 The **c** of Hariph, an hundred and twelve.	1121
	7:25 The **c** of Gibeon, ninety and five.	1121
	7:34 The **c** of the other Elam, a thousand two	1121
	7:35 The **c** of Harim, three hundred and	1121
	7:36 The **c** of Jericho, three hundred forty and	1121
	7:37 The **c** of Lod, Hadid, and Ono,	1121
	7:38 The **c** of Senaah, three thousand nine	1121
	7:39 The **c** of Jedaiah, of the house of Jeshua,	1121
	7:40 The **c** of Immer, a thousand fifty and two.	1121
	7:41 The **c** of Pashur, a thousand two hundred	1121
	7:42 The **c** of Harim, a thousand *and*	1121
	7:43 The **c** of Jeshua, of Kadmiel, *and* of	1121
	7:43 of the **c** of Hodevah, seventy and four.	1121
	7:44 the **c** of Asaph, an hundred forty and	1121
	7:45 The **c** of Shallum, the children of Ater,	1121
	7:45 the **c** of Ater, the children of Talmon,	1121
	7:45 the children of Ater, the **c** of Talmon,	1121
	7:45 the **c** of Akkub, the children of Hatita,	1121
	7:45 the children of Akkub, the **c** of Hatita,	1121
	7:45 the **c** of Shobai, an hundred thirty and	1121
	7:46 the **c** of Ziha, the children of Hashupha,	1121
	7:46 the children of Ziha, the **c** of Hashupha,	1121
	7:46 children of Hashupha, the **c** of Tabbaoth,	1121
	7:47 The **c** of Keros, the children of Sia,	1121
	7:47 the **c** of Sia, the children of Padon,	1121
	7:47 the children of Sia, the **c** of Padon,	1121
	7:48 The **c** of Lebana, the children of Hagaba,	1121
	7:48 The children of Lebana, the **c** of Hagaba,	1121
	7:48 the children of Hagaba, the **c** of Shalmai,	1121
	7:49 The **c** of Hanan, the children of Giddel,	1121
	7:49 the **c** of Giddel, the children of Gahar,	1121
	7:49 the children of Giddel, the **c** of Gahar,	1121
	7:50 The **c** of Reaiah, the children of Rezin,	1121
	7:50 the **c** of Rezin, the children of Nekoda,	1121
	7:50 the children of Rezin, the **c** of Nekoda,	1121
	7:51 The **c** of Gazzam, the children of Uzza,	1121
	7:51 the **c** of Uzza, the children of Phaseah,	1121
	7:51 the children of Uzza, the **c** of Phaseah,	1121
	7:52 The **c** of Besai, the children of Meunim,	1121
	7:52 The children of Besai, the **c** of Meunim,	1121
	7:52 of Meunim, the **c** of Nephishesim,	1121
	7:53 **c** of Bakbuk, the children of Hakupha,	1121
	7:53 the **c** of Hakupha, the children of Harhur,	1121
	7:53 the children of Hakupha, the **c** of Harhur,	1121
	7:54 The **c** of Bazlith, the children of Mehida,	1121
	7:54 the **c** of Mehida, the children of Harsha,	1121
	7:54 the children of Mehida, the **c** of Harsha,	1121
	7:55 The **c** of Barkos, the children of Sisera,	1121
	7:55 the **c** of Sisera, the children of Tamah,	1121
	7:55 the children of Sisera, the **c** of Tamah,	1121
	7:56 The **c** of Neziah, the children of Hatipha.	1121
	7:56 The children of Neziah, the **c** of Hatipha.	1121
	7:57 The **c** of Solomon's servants: the children	1121
	7:57 the **c** of Sotai, the children of Sophereth,	1121
	7:57 the children of Sotai, the **c** of Sophereth,	1121
	7:57 the children of Sophereth, the **c** of Perida,	1121
	7:58 The **c** of Jaala, the children of Darkon,	1121
	7:58 The children of Jaala, the **c** of Darkon,	1121
	7:58 the children of Darkon, the **c** of Giddel,	1121
	7:59 **c** of Shephatiah, the children of Hattil,	1121
	7:59 children of Shephatiah, the **c** of Hattil,	1121
	7:59 of Hattil, the **c** of Pochereth Zebaim,	1121
	7:59 of Pochereth Zebaim, the **c** of Amon.	1121
	7:60 and the **c** of Solomon's servants,	1121
	7:62 The **c** of Delaiah, the children of Tobiah,	1121
	7:62 the **c** of Tobiah, the children of Nekoda,	1121
	7:62 **c** of Nekoda, six hundred forty and two.	1121
	7:63 the **c** of Habaiah, the children of Koz,	1121
	7:63 the children of Habaiah, the **c** of Koz,	1121
	7:63 the children of Koz, the **c** of Barzillai,	1121
	7:73 the **c** of Israel *were* in their cities.	1121
	8:14 that the **c** of Israel should dwell in booths	1121
	8:17 that day had not the **c** of Israel done so.	1121
	9: 1 fourth day of this month the **c** of Israel	1121
	9:23 Their **c** also multipliedst thou as the stars	3206
	9:24 So the **c** went in and possessed the land,	1121
	10:39 For the **c** of Israel and the children of Levi	1121
	10:39 of Levi shall bring the offering of	1121
	11: 3 and the **c** of Solomon's servants.	1121
	11: 4 Jerusalem dwelt *certain* of the **c** of Judah,	1121
	11: 4 of Judah, and of the **c** of Benjamin.	1121
	11: 4 Of the **c** of Judah; Athaiah the son of	1121
	11: 4 the son of Mahalaleel, of the **c** of Perez;	1121
	11:24 of the **c** of Zerah the son of Judah,	1121
	11:25 *some* of the **c** of Judah dwelt at	1121
	11:31 The **c** also of Benjamin from Geba *dwelt*	1121
	12:43 the wives also and the **c** rejoiced: so	3206
	12:47 the Levites sanctified *them* unto the **c** of	1121
	13: 2 Because they met not the **c** of Israel with	1121

Ne	13:16 sold on the sabbath unto the **c** of Judah,	1121
	13:24 spake half in the speech of Ashdod,	1121
Est	3:13 both young and old, **little c** and women,	2945
	5:11 the multitude of his **c**, and all *the things*	1121
Job	5: 4 His **c** are far from safety, and they are	1121
	8: 4 If thy **c** have sinned against him,	1121
	17: 5 friends, even the eyes of his **c** shall fail.	1121
	19:18 Yea, **young c** despised me; I arose,	5759
	20:10 His **c** shall *seek* to please the poor,	1121
	21:11 little ones like a flock, and their **c** dance.	3206
	21:19 God layeth up his iniquity for his **c**:	1121
	24: 5 *yieldeth* food for them *and* for *their* **c**.	5288
	27:14 If his **c** be multiplied, *it is* for the sword:	1121
	29: 5 yet with me, *when* my **c** *were* about me;	5288
	30: 8 *were* **c** of fools, yea, children of base	1121
	30: 8 *were* children of fools, yea, **c** of base men:	1121
	41:34 *things:* he *is* a king over all the **c** of pride.	1121
Ps	4: 2 sons of men, how long will ye turn my glory	1121
	11: 4 eyes behold, his eyelids try, the **c** of men.	1121
	12: 1 for the faithful fail from among the **c** of	1121
	14: 2 down from heaven upon the **c** of men,	1121
	17:14 *with* thy hid *treasure:* they are full *of* **c**,	1121
	21:10 and their seed from among the **c** of men.	1121
	34:11 Come, ye **c**, hearken unto me: I will teach	1121
	36: 7 the **c** of men put their trust under	1121
	45: 2 Thou art fairer than the **c** of men: grace is	1121
	45:16 Instead of thy fathers shall be thy **c**,	1121
	53: 2 God looked down from heaven upon the **c**	1121
	66: 5 he *is* terrible *in his* doing toward the **c** of	1121
	69: 8 and an alien unto my mother's **c**.	1121
	72: 4 he shall save the **c** of the needy,	1121
	73:15 offend *against* the generation of thy **c**.	1121
	78: 4 We will not hide *them* from their **c**,	1121
	78: 5 *they* should make them known to their **c**:	1121
	78: 6 *them, even* the **c** *which* should be born;	1121
	78: 6 should arise and declare *them* to their **c**:	1121
	78: 9 The **c** of Ephraim, *being* armed,	1121
	82: 6 and all of you *are* **c** of the most High.	1121
	83: 8 they have holpen the **c** of Lot. Selah.	1121
	89:30 If his **c** forsake my law, and walk not in	1121
	90: 3 and sayest, Return, ye **c** of men.	1121
	90:16 thy servants, and thy glory unto their **c**.	1121
	102:28 The **c** of thy servants shall continue,	1121
	103: 7 unto Moses, his acts unto the **c** of Israel.	1121
	103:13 Like as a father pitieth *his* **c**, *so* the LORD	1121
	103:17 and his righteousness unto children's **c**;	1121
	105: 6 his servant, ye **c** of Jacob, his chosen.	1121
	107: 8 for his wonderful works to the **c** of men!	1121
	107:15 for his wonderful works to the **c** of men!	1121
	107:21 for his wonderful works to the **c** of men!	1121
	107:31 for his wonderful works to the **c** of men!	1121
	109: 9 Let his **c** be fatherless, and his wife a	1121
	109:10 Let his **c** be continually vagabonds,	1121
	109:12 there be any to favour his **fatherless c**.	3490
	113: 9 to keep house, *to be* a joyful mother of **c**.	1121
	115:14 you more and more, you and your **c**.	1121
	115:16 the earth hath he given to the **c** of men.	1121
	127: 3 Lo, **c** *are* an heritage of the LORD: *and*	1121
	127: 4 of a mighty *man; so are* **c** of the youth.	1121
	128: 3 thy **c** like olive plants round about thy	1121
	128: 6 thou shalt see thy children's **c**,	1121
	132:12 If thy **c** will keep my covenant and	1121
	132:12 their **c** also shall sit upon thy throne for	1121
	137: 7 the **c** of Edom in the day of Jerusalem;	1121
	144: 7 great waters, from the hand of strange **c**;	1121
	144:11 deliver me from the hand of strange **c**,	1121
	147:13 he hath blessed thy **c** within thee.	1121
	148:12 young men, and maidens; old men, and **c**:	5288
	148:14 *even* of the **c** of Israel, a people near unto	1121
	149: 2 let the **c** of Zion be joyful in their King.	1121
Pr	4: 1 Hear, ye **c**, the instruction of a father,	1121
	5: 7 O ye **c**, and depart not from the words of	1121
	7:24 O ye **c**, and attend to the words of my	1121
	8:32 Now therefore hearken unto me, O ye **c**:	1121
	13:22 leaveth an inheritance to *his* children's **c**:	1121
	14:26 and his **c** shall have a place of refuge.	1121
	15:11 more then the hearts of the **c** of men?	1121
	17: 6 Children's **c** *are* the crown of old men;	1121
	17: 6 and the glory of **c** *are* their fathers.	1121
	20: 7 in his integrity: his **c** *are* blessed after him.	1121
	31:28 Her **c** arise up, and call her blessed;	1121
Ecc	6: 3 If a man beget an hundred **c**, and live	NIH
SS	1: 6 my mother's **c** were angry with me;	1121
Isa	1: 2 I have nourished and brought up **c**,	1121
	1: 4 a seed of evildoers, **c** that are corrupters:	3206
	2: 6 please themselves in the **c** of strangers.	3206
	3: 4 I will give **c** *to be* their princes,	5288
	3:12 **c** *are* their oppressors, and women rule	5953
	8:18 the **c** whom the LORD hath given me *are*	3206
	11:14 and the **c** of Ammon shall obey them.	1121
	13:16 Their **c** also shall be dashed to pieces	5768
	13:18 of the womb; their eye shall not spare **c**.	1121
	14:21 Prepare slaughter for his **c** for the iniquity	1121
	17: 3 they shall be as the glory of the **c** of Israel,	1121
	17: 9 which they left because of the **c** of Israel:	1121
	21:17 the mighty *men* of the **c** of Kedar, shall be	1121
	23: 4 saying, I travail not, nor **bring forth c**,	3205
	27:12 be gathered one by one, O ye **c** of Israel.	1121
	29:23 when he seeth his **c**, the work of mine	3206
	30: 1 Woe to the rebellious, saith the LORD,	1121
	30: 9 That this *is* a rebellious people, lying **c**,	1121
	30: 9 **c** *that* will not hear the law of the LORD:	1121
	31: 6 Turn ye unto *him from* whom the **c** of	1121
	37: 3 for the **c** are come to the birth, and *there*	1121
	37:12 and the **c** of Eden which *were* in Telassar?	1121
	38:19 the father to the **c** shall make known thy	1121

Isa	47: 8 neither shall I know the **loss of c**:	7908
	47: 9 one day, the **loss of c**, and widowhood:	7908
	49:17 Thy **c** shall make haste; thy destroyers and	1121
	49:20 The **c** which thou shalt have, after thou	1121
	49:21 seeing I have **lost** my **c**, and *am* desolate,	7921
	49:25 with thee, and I will save thy **c**.	1121
	54: 1 for more *are the* **c** of the desolate than	1121
	54: 1 desolate than the **c** of the married wife,	1121
	54:13 And all thy **c** *shall* be taught of the LORD;	1121
	54:13 and great *shall* be the peace of thy **c**.	1121
	57: 4 *are* ye not **c** of transgression, a seed of	3206
	57: 5 slaying the **c** in the valleys under the clifts	3206
	63: 8 they *are* my people, **c** *that* will not lie:	1121
	66: 8 as Zion travailed, she brought forth her **c**.	1121
	66:20 as the **c** of Israel bring an offering in a	1121
Jer	2: 9 and with your children's **c** will I plead.	1121
	2:16 Also the **c** of Noph and Tahapanes have	1121
	2:30 In vain have I smitten your **c**; they	1121
	3:14 Turn, O backsliding **c**, saith the LORD;	1121
	3:19 How shall I put thee among the **c**,	1121
	3:21 *and* supplications of the **c** of Israel:	1121
	3:22 ye backsliding **c**, *and* I will heal your	1121
	4:22 they *are* sottish **c**, and they have none	1121
	5: 7 thy **c** have forsaken me, and sworn by	1121
	6: 1 O ye **c** of Benjamin, gather yourselves to	1121
	6:11 I *will* pour *it* out upon the **c** abroad,	5768
	7:18 The **c** gather wood, and the fathers kindle	1121
	7:30 For the **c** of Judah have done evil in my	1121
	9:21 to cut off the **c** from without, *and* the	5768
	9:26 the **c** of Ammon, and Moab, and all	1121
	10:20 my **c** are gone forth *of* me, and they *are*	1121
	15: 7 I will **bereave** *them* of **c**, I will destroy	7921
	16:14 that brought up the **c** of Israel out of	1121
	16:15 brought up the **c** of Israel from the land	1121
	17: 2 Whilst their **c** remember their altars and	1121
	17:19 stand in the gate of the **c** of the people,	1121
	18:21 Therefore deliver up their **c** to the famine,	1121
	18:21 let their wives be **bereaved of** their **c**,	7909
	23: 7 which brought up the **c** of Israel out of	1121
	25:21 Edom, and Moab, and the **c** of Ammon,	1121
	30:20 Their **c** also shall be as aforetime,	1121
	31:15 Rahel weeping for her **c** refused to be	1121
	31:15 refused to be comforted for her **c**,	1121
	31:17 that *thy* **c** shall come again to their own	1121
	32:18 into the bosom of their **c** after them:	1121
	32:30 the **c** of Israel and the children of Judah	1121
	32:30 the **c** of Judah have only done evil before	1121
	32:30 for the **c** of Israel have only provoked me	1121
	32:32 Because of all the evil of the **c** of Israel	1121
	32:32 children of Israel and of the **c** of Judah,	1121
	32:39 good of them, and of their **c** after them:	1121
	38:23 all thy wives and thy **c** to the Chaldeans:	1121
	40: 7 and **c**, and of the poor of the land,	2945
	41:16 the women, and the **c**, and the eunuchs,	2945
	43: 6 **c**, and the king's daughters, and every	2945
	47: 3 fathers shall not look back to *their* **c** for	1121
	49: 6 again the captivity of the **c** of Ammon,	1121
	49:11 Leave thy **fatherless c**, I will preserve	3490
	50: 4 the **c** of Israel shall come, they and	1121
	50: 4 they and the **c** of Judah together, going	1121
	50:33 The **c** of Israel and the children of Judah	1121
	50:33 the **c** of Judah *were* oppressed together:	1121
La	1: 5 her **c** are gone *into* captivity before	5768
	1:16 my **c** are desolate, because the enemy	1121
	2:11 because the **c** and the sucklings swoon in	5768
	2:19 toward him for the life of thy **young c**,	5768
	2:20 women eat their fruit, *and* **c** of a span	5768
	3:33 afflict willingly nor grieve the **c** of men.	1121
	4: 4 the **young c** ask bread, *and* no man	5768
	4:10 pitiful women have sodden their own **c**:	3206
	5:13 to grind, and the **c** fell under the wood.	5288
Eze	2: 3 Son of man, I send thee to the **c** of Israel,	1121
	2: 4 For *they are* impudent **c** and stiff hearted.	1121
	3:11 unto the **c** of thy people, and speak unto	1121
	4:13 Even thus shall the **c** of Israel eat their	1121
	6: 5 I will lay the dead carcases of the **c** of	1121
	9: 6 both maids, and **little c**, and women:	2945
	16:21 That thou hast slain my **c**,	1121
	16:36 by the blood of thy **c**, which thou didst	1121
	16:45 that loatheth her husband and her **c**;	1121
	16:45 which lothed their husbands and their **c**:	1121
	20:18 I said unto their **c** in the wilderness,	1121
	20:21 Notwithstanding the **c** rebelled against	1121
	23:39 For when they had slain their **c** to their	1121
	31:14 of the earth, in the midst of the **c** of men,	1121
	33: 2 speak to the **c** of thy people, and say unto	1121
	33:12 son of man, say unto the **c** of thy people,	1121
	33:17 Yet the **c** of thy people say, The way of	1121
	33:30 the **c** of thy people still are talking against	1121
	35: 5 hast shed *the blood of* the **c** of Israel by	1121
	37:16 and for the **c** of Israel his companions:	1121
	37:18 when the **c** of thy people shall speak unto	1121
	37:21 I *will* take the **c** of Israel from among	1121
	37:25 their **c**, and their children's children for	1121
	37:25 and their children's **c** for ever:	1121
	43: 7 where I will dwell in the midst of the **c** of	1121
	44: 9 of any stranger that *is* among the **c** of	1121
	44:15 when the **c** of Israel went astray from me,	1121
	47:22 which shall beget **c** among you:	1121
	47:22 born in the country among the **c** of Israel;	1121
	48:11 went not astray when the **c** of Israel	1121
Da	1: 3 that *he* should bring *certain* of the **c** of	1121
	1: 4 **c** In whom *was* no blemish,	3206
	1: 6 Now among these were of the **c** of Judah,	1121
	1:10 liking than the **c** which *are* of your sort?	3206

Da	1:13 the countenance of the **c** that eat *of*	3206
	1:15 fatter in flesh than all the **c** which did eat	3206
	1:17 As for these four **c**, God gave them	3206
	2:38 wheresoever the **c** of men dwell,	1123
	5:13 *art* of the **c** of the captivity of Judah,	1123
	6:13 *is* of the **c** of the captivity of Judah,	1123
	6:24 of lions, them, their **c**, and their wives;	1123
	11:41 Moab, and the chief of the **c** of Ammon.	1121
	12: 1 great prince which standeth for the **c** of	1121
Hos	1: 2 wife of whoredoms and of whoredoms:	3206
	1:10 Yet the number of the **c** of Israel shall be	1121
	1:11 shall the **c** of Judah and the children of	1121
	1:11 and the **c** of Israel be gathered together,	1121
	2: 4 I will not have mercy upon her **c**; for they	1121
	2: 4 for they *be* the **c** of whoredoms.	1121
	3: 1 love of the LORD toward the **c** of Israel,	1121
	3: 4 For the **c** of Israel shall abide many days	1121
	3: 5 Afterward shall the **c** of Israel return,	1121
	4: 1 the word of the LORD, ye **c** of Israel:	1121
	4: 6 the law of thy God, I will also forget thy **c**.	1121
	5: 7 for they have begotten strange **c**: now	1121
	9:12 Though they bring up their **c**, yet will I	1121
	9:13 Ephraim *shall* bring forth his **c** to	1121
	10: 9 battle in Gibeah against the **c** of iniquity	1121
	10:14 mother was dashed in pieces upon her **c**.	1121
	11:10 then the **c** shall tremble from the west.	1121
	13:13 in *the place of* the breaking forth of **c**.	1121
Joel	1: 3 Tell ye your **c** of it, and *let* your children	1121
	1: 3 *let* your **c** *tell* their children,	1121
	1: 3 *let* your children *tell* their **c**,	1121
	1: 3 and their **c** another generation.	1121
	2:16 gather the **c**, and those that suck the	5768
	2:23 ye **c** of Zion, and rejoice in the LORD	1121
	3: 6 The **c** also of Judah and the children of	1121
	3: 6 the **c** of Jerusalem have ye sold unto	1121
	3: 8 your daughters into the hand of the **c** of	1121
	3:16 and the strength of the **c** of Israel.	1121
	3:19 for the violence against the **c** of Judah,	1121
Am	1:13 For three transgressions of the **c** of	1121
	2:11 *Is it* not even thus, O ye **c** of Israel?	1121
	3: 1 hath spoken against you, O **c** of Israel,	1121
	3:12 the **c** of Israel be taken out that dwell	1121
	4: 5 for this liketh you, O ye **c** of Israel,	1121
	9: 7 *Are* ye not as **c** of the Ethiopians unto me,	1121
	9: 7 of the Ethiopians unto me, O **c** of Israel?	1121
Ob	1:12 **c** of Judah in the day of their destruction;	1121
	1:20 the captivity of this host of the **c** of Israel	1121
Mic	1:16 thee bald, and poll thee for thy delicate **c**;	1121
	2: 9 from their **c** have ye taken *away* my glory	5768
	5: 3 brethren shall return unto the **c** of Israel.	1121
Na	3:10 her **young c** also were dashed in pieces at	5768
Zep	1: 8 the king's **c**, and all such as are clothed	1121
	2: 8 and the revilings of the **c** of Ammon,	1121
	2: 9 the **c** of Ammon as Gomorrah, *even*	1121
Zec	10: 7 yea, their **c** shall see *it*, and be glad;	1121
	10: 9 shall live with their **c**, and turn again.	1121
Mal	4: 6 shall turn the heart of the fathers to the **c**,	1121
	4: 6 the heart of the **c** to their fathers, lest I	1121
Mt	2:16 slew all the **c** that were in Bethlehem,	3816
	2:18 Rachel weeping for her **c**, and would not	5043
	3: 9 God is able of these stones to raise up **c**	5043
	5: 9 for they shall be called the **c** of God.	5207
	5:45 That ye may be the **c** of your Father	5207
	7:11 know how to give good gifts unto your **c**,	5043
	8:12 But the **c** of the kingdom shall be cast out	5207
	9:15 Can the **c** of the bridechamber mourn,	5207
	10:21 the **c** shall rise up against *their* parents,	5043
	11:16 It is like unto **c** sitting in the markets,	3808
	11:19 sinners. But wisdom is justified of her **c**.	5043
	12:27 by whom do your **c** cast *them* out?	5207
	13:38 the good seed are the **c** of the kingdom;	5207
	13:38 but the tares are the **c** of the wicked one;	5207
	14:21 five thousand men, beside women and **c**.	3813
	15:38 four thousand men, beside women and **c**.	3813
	17:25 or tribute? of their own **c**, or of strangers?	5207
	17:26 Jesus saith unto him, Then are the **c** free.	5207
	18: 3 ye be converted, and become as **little c**,	3813
	18:25 and **c**, and all that he had, and payment to	5043
	19:13 were there brought unto him **little c**,	3813
	19:14 Suffer **little c**, and forbid them not,	3813
	19:29 father, or mother, or wife, or **c**, or lands,	5043
	20:20 the mother of Zebedee's **c** with her sons,	5207
	21:15 the **c** crying in the temple, and saying,	3816
	22:24 Moses said, If a man die, having no **c**,	5043
	23:31 that ye are the **c** of them which killed	5207
	23:37 how often would I have gathered thy **c**	5043
	27: 9 whom they of the **c** of Israel did value;	5207
	27:25 said, His blood *be* on us, and on our **c**.	5207
	27:56 and Joses, and the mother of Zebedee's **c**.	5207
Mk	2:19 Can the **c** of the bridechamber fast,	5207
	7:27 said unto him, Let the **c** first be filled:	5043
	9:37 Whosoever shall receive one of such **c** in	3813
	10:13 they brought **young c** to him, that he	3813
	10:14 Suffer the **little c** to come unto me,	3813
	10:24 answereth again, and saith unto them, **C**,	5043
	10:29 father, or mother, or wife, or **c**, or lands,	5043
	10:30 sisters, and mothers, and **c**, and lands,	5043
	12:19 *his* wife behind him, and leave no **c**,	5043
	13:12 and **c** shall rise up against *their* parents,	5043
Lk	1:16 And many of the **c** of Israel shall he turn	5207
	1:17 to turn the hearts of the fathers to the **c**,	5043
	3: 8 these stones to raise up **c** unto Abraham.	5043
	5:34 Can ye make the **c** of the bridechamber	5207
	6:35 and ye shall be the **c** of the Highest:	5207
	7:32 They are like unto **c** sitting in	3813

Lk	7:35 But wisdom is justified of all her **c**.	5043
	11: 7 now shut, and my **c** are with me in bed;	3813
	11:13 know how to give good gifts unto your **c**:	5043
	13:34 how often would I have gathered thy **c**	5043
	14:26 and **c**, and brethren, and sisters, yea,	5043
	16: 8 for the **c** of this world are in their	5207
	16: 8 their generation wiser than the **c** of light.	5207
	18:16 Suffer **little c** to come unto me,	3813
	18:29 or parents, or brethren, or wife, or **c**,	5043
	19:44 with the ground, and thy **c** within thee:	5043
	20:28 having a wife, and he die **without c**,	815
	20:29 the first took a wife, and died **without c**.	815
	20:31 seven also: and they left no **c**, and died.	5043
	20:34 The **c** of this world marry, and are given	5207
	20:36 are the **c** of God, being the children of	5207
	20:36 of God, being the **c** of the resurrection.	5207
	23:28 but weep for yourselves, and for your **c**.	5043
Jn	4:12 thereof himself, and his **c**, and his cattle?	5043
	8:39 saith unto them, If ye were Abraham's **c**,	5043
	11:52 the **c** of God that were scattered abroad.	5043
	12:36 in the light, that ye may be the **c** of light.	5207
	13:33 **Little c**, yet a little while I am with you.	5040
	21: 5 saith unto them, **C**, have ye any meat?	3813
Ac	2:39 and to your **c**, and to all that are afar off,	5043
	3:25 Ye are the **c** of the prophets, and of the	5207
	5:21 and all the senate of the **c** of Israel,	5207
	7:19 so that *they* cast out their **young c**,	1025
	7:23 heart to visit his brethren the **c** of Israel.	5207
	7:37 Moses, which said unto the **c** of Israel,	5207
	9:15 Gentiles, and kings, and the **c** of Israel:	5207
	10:36 The word which *God* sent unto the **c** of	5207
	13:26 **c** of the stock of Abraham,	5207
	13:33 hath fulfilled the same unto us their **c**,	5043
	21: 5 with wives and **c**, till *we were* out of	5043
	21:21 that *they ought* not to circumcise *their* **c**,	5043
Ro	8:16 with our spirit, that we are the **c** of God:	5043
	8:17 And if **c**, then heirs; heirs of God,	5043
	8:21 into the glorious liberty of the **c** of God.	5043
	9: 7 are the seed of Abraham, *are they* all **c**:	5043
	9: 8 That is, *They which are* the **c** of the flesh,	5043
	9: 8 of the flesh, these *are* not the **c** of God:	5043
	9: 8 the **c** of the promise are counted for	5043
	9:11 (for the **c** being not yet born, neither	NIG
	9:26 shall they be called the **c** of the living	5207
	9:27 Though the number of the **c** of Israel be	5207
1Co	7:14 else were your **c** unclean; but now are	5043
	14:20 Brethren, be not **c** in understanding:	3813
	14:20 howbeit in malice be ye **c**,	3515
2Co	3: 7 that the **c** of Israel could not stedfastly	5207
	3:13 the **c** of Israel could not stedfastly look	5207
	6:13 in the same, (I speak as unto *my* **c**,)	5043
	12:14 the **c** ought not to lay up for the parents,	5043
	12:14 for the parents, but the parents for the **c**.	5043
Gal	3: 7 of faith, the same are the **c** of Abraham.	5207
	3:26 ye are all the **c** of God by faith in Christ	5207
	4: 3 Even so we, when we were **c**, were in	3516
	4:19 My **little c**, of whom I travail in birth	5040
	4:25 now is, and is in bondage with her **c**.	5043
	4:27 for the desolate hath many moe **c** than	5043
	4:28 as Isaac was, are the **c** of promise.	5043
	4:31 we are not **c** of *the* bondwoman, but of	5043
Eph	1: 5 **adoption of c** by Jesus Christ to himself,	5206
	2: 2 the spirit that now worketh in the **c** of	5207
	2: 3 were by nature the **c** of wrath, even as	5043
	4:14 we *henceforth* be no more **c**, tossed to	3516
	5: 1 ye therefore followers of God, as dear **c**;	5043
	5: 6 wrath of God upon the **c** of disobedience.	5207
	5: 8 *are ye* light in the Lord: walk as **c** of light:	5043
	6: 1 **C**, obey your parents in the Lord: for this	5043
	6: 4 ye fathers, provoke not your **c** to wrath:	5043
Col	3: 6 of God cometh on the **c** of disobedience:	5207
	3:20 **C**, obey *your* parents in all *things*: for this	5043
	3:21 provoke not your **c** *to anger*, lest they be	5043
1Th	2: 7 even as a nurse cherisheth her **c**:	5043
	2:11 every one of you, as a father *doth* his **c**,	5043
	5: 5 Ye are all the **c** of light, and the children	5207
	5: 5 the children of light, and the **c** of the day:	5207
1Ti	3: 4 having *his* **c** in subjection with all gravity;	5043
	3:12 ruling *their* **c** and their own houses well.	5043
	5: 4 But if any widow have **c** or nephews,	5043
	5:10 if she have **brought up c**, if she have	5044
	5:14 women marry, **bear c**, guide the house,	5041
Tit	1: 6 having faithful **c** not accused of riot or	5043
	2: 4 to love their husbands, to **love** their **c**,	5388
Heb	2:13 I, and the **c** which God hath given me.	3813
	2:14 then as the **c** are partakers of flesh and	3813
	11:22 made mention of the departing of the **c** of	5207
	12: 5 which speaketh unto you as unto **c**,	5043
1Pe	1:14 As obedient **c**, not fashioning yourselves	5043
2Pe	2:14 with covetous practices; cursed **c**:	5043
1Jn	2: 1 My **little c**, these *things* write I unto you,	5040
	2:12 **little c**, because *your* sins are forgiven you	5040
	2:13 **little c**, because ye have known the	3813
	2:18 **Little c**, it is the last time: and as ye have	3813
	2:28 And now, **little c**, abide in him; that,	5040
	3: 7 **Little c**, let no man deceive you: he that	5040
	3:10 In this the **c** of God are manifest,	5043
	3:10 are manifest, and the **c** of the devil:	5043
	3:18 My **little c**, let us not love in word,	5040
	4: 4 of God, **little c**, and have overcome them:	5040
	5: 2 this we know that we love the **c** of God,	5043
	5:21 **Little c**, keep yourselves from idols.	5040
2Jn	1: 1 The Elder unto the elect lady and her **c**,	5043
	1: 4 I rejoiced greatly that I found of thy **c**	5043
	1:13 The **c** of thy elect sister greet thee. Amen.	5043

3Jn	1: 4 no greater joy than to hear that my **c**	5043
Rev	2:14 a stumblingblock before the **c** of Israel,	5207
	2:23 And I will kill her **c** with death; and all	5043
	7: 4 four thousand of all the tribes of the **c** of	5207
	21:12 the twelve tribes of the **c** of Israel:	5207

CHILDREN'S (19) [CHILD]

Ge	31:16 from our father, that *is* ours, and our **c**:	1121
	45:10 thy **c** children, and thy flocks,	1121
Ex	3:22 shall nothing die of all *that is* the **c** of	1121
	34: 7 upon the **c** children, unto the third and	1121
Dt	4:25 **c** children, and ye shall have remained	1121
Jos	14: 9 thy **c** for ever, because thou hast wholly	1121
2Ki	17:41 both their children, and their **c** children:	1121
Job	17:19 though I intreated for the **c** *sake* of mine	1121
Ps	103:17 and his righteousness unto **c** children;	1121
	128: 6 thou shalt see thy **c** children, 1121+3807.1	
Pr	13:22 good *man* leaveth an inheritance to his **c**	1121
	17: 6 **C** children *are* the crown of old men;	1121
Jer	2: 9 and with your **c** children will I plead.	1121
	31:29 grape, and the **c** teeth are set on edge.	1121
Eze	18: 2 grapes, and the **c** teeth are set on edge?	1121
	37:25 children, and their **c** children for ever.	1121
Mt	15:26 It is not meet to take the **c** bread,	5043
Mk	7:27 for it is not meet to take the **c** bread,	5043
	7:28 yet the dogs under the table eat of the **c**	3813

CHILEAB (1)

2Sa	3: 3 his second, **C**, of Abigail the wife of Nabal	3609

CHILION (2) [CHILION'S]

Ru	1: 2 the name of his two sons Mahlon and **C**,	3630
	1: 5 Mahlon and **C** died also both of them;	3630

CHILION'S (1) [CHILION]

Ru	4: 9 all that *was* **C** and Mahlon's, of the hand	3630

CHILMAD (1)

Eze	27:23 Asshur, and **C**, were thy merchants.	3638

CHIMHAM (4)

2Sa	19:37 behold thy servant **C**; let him go over	3643
	19:38 **C** shall go over with me, and I will do to	3643
	19:40 on to Gilgal, and **C** went on with him:	3643
Jer	41:17 and dwelt in the habitation of **C**,	3643

CHIMNEY (1)

Hos	13: 3 of the floor, and as the smoke out of the **c**.	699

CHINNERETH (3) [CINNEROTH]

Nu	34:11 shall reach unto the side of the sea of **C**	3672
Dt	3:17 coast thereof, from **C** even unto the sea	3672
Jos	19:35 Zer, and Hammath, Rakkath, and **C**,	3672

CHIOS (1)

Ac	20:15 and came the next *day* over against **C**;	5508

CHISEL See HEW

CHISELS See PLANES

CHISLEU (2)

Ne	1: 1 it came to pass in the month **C**,	3691
Zec	7: 1 fourth *day* of the ninth month, *even* in **C**;	3691

CHISLON (1)

Nu	34:21 the tribe of Benjamin, Elidad the son of **C**.	3692

CHISLOTH-TABOR (1) [TABOR]

Jos	19:12 *toward* the sunrising unto the border of **C**,	3696

CHITTIM (6)

Nu	24:24 ships *shall come* from the coast of **C**,	3794
Isa	23: 1 from the land of **C** it is revealed to them.	3794
	23:12 arise, pass over to **C**; there also shalt	3794
Jer	2:10 For pass over the isles of **C**, and see;	3794
Eze	27: 6 of ivory, *brought* out of the isles of **C**.	3794
Da	11:30 For the ships of **C** shall come against him:	3794

CHIUN (1)

Am	5:26 of your Moloch and **C** your images,	3594

CHLOE (1)

1Co	1:11 by them which are of the *house* of **C**,	5514

CHODE (2)

Ge	31:36 Jacob was wroth, and **c** with Laban: and	7378
Nu	20: 3 the people **c** with Moses, and spake,	7378

CHOICE (21) [CHOOSE]

Ge	23: 6 in the **c** of our sepulchres bury thy dead;	4005
	49:11 vine, and his ass's colt unto the **c vine**;	8322
Dt	12:11 all your **c** vows which ye vow unto	4005
1Sa	9: 2 *was* Saul, a **c** *young man*, and a goodly:	970
2Sa	10: 9 he chose of all the **c** men of Israel,	977
2Ki	3:19 every **c** city, and shall fell every good tree,	4004
	19:23 trees thereof, *and* the **c** fir trees thereof:	4004
1Ch	7:40 **c** and mighty *men* of valour, chief of	1305
	19:10 he chose out of all the **c** of Israel,	977
2Ch	25: 5 three hundred thousand **c** *men*,	977
Ne	5:18 *for me* daily *was* one ox *and* six **c** sheep;	1305
Pr	8:10 and knowledge rather than **c** gold.	977
	8:19 fine gold; and my revenue than **c** silver.	977
	10:20 The tongue of the just *is* as **c** silver:	977
SS	6: 9 she *is* the **c** one of her that bare her.	1249
Isa	37:24 cedars thereof, *and* the **c** fir trees thereof:	4005
Jer	22: 7 they shall cut down thy **c** cedars,	4005

Eze 24: 4 and the shoulder; fill *it with* the **c** bones. 4005
 24: 5 Take the **c** of the flock, and burn also 4005
 31:16 the **c** and best of Lebanon, all that drink 4005
Ac 15: 7 a good while ago God **made c** among us, 1586

CHOICEST (2) [CHOOSE]

Isa 5: 2 planted it *with* the **c vine**, and built a 8321
 22: 7 *that* thy **c** valleys shall be full *of* chariots, 4005

CHOKE (2) [CHOKED]

Mt 13:22 **c** the word, and he becometh unfruitful. 4846
Mk 4:19 **c** the word, and it becometh unfruitful. 4846

CHOKED (6) [CHOKE]

Mt 13: 7 and the thorns sprung up, and **c** them: 638
Mk 4: 7 grew up, and **c** it, and it yielded no fruit. 4846
 5:13 two thousand,) and were **c** in the sea. 4155
Lk 8: 7 and the thorns sprang up with *it*, and **c** it. 638
 8:14 and are **c** with cares and riches and 4846
 8:33 a steep place into the lake, and were **c**. 638

CHOLER (2)

Da 8: 7 he was **moved with c** against him, 4843
 11:11 king of the south shall be **moved with c**, 4843

CHOOSE (59) [CHOICE, CHOICEST, CHOOSEST, CHOOSETH, CHOOSING, CHOSE, CHOSEN]

Ex 17: 9 **C** us **out** men, and go out, fight with 977
Nu 16: 7 be *that* the man whom the LORD doth **c**, 977
 17: 5 man's rod, whom I shall **c**, shall blossom: 977
Dt 7: 7 **c** you, because ye were moe in number 977
 12: 5 out of all your tribes to put his name 977
 12:11 God shall **c** to cause his name to dwell 977
 12:14 in the place which the LORD shall **c** in one 977
 12:18 the place which the LORD thy God shall **c**, 977
 12:26 go unto the place which the LORD shall **c**; 977
 14:23 in the place which he shall **c** to place his 977
 14:24 which the LORD thy God shall **c** to set his 977
 14:25 the place which the LORD thy God shall **c**: 977
 15:20 year in the place which the LORD shall **c**, 977
 16: 2 in the place which the LORD shall **c** to 977
 16: 6 the place which the LORD thy God shall **c**: 977
 16: 7 the place which the LORD thy God shall **c**: 977
 16:15 God in the place which the LORD shall **c**: 977
 16:16 thy God in the place which he shall **c**; 977
 17: 8 the place which the LORD thy God shall **c**; 977
 17:10 which the LORD shall **c** shall shew thee; 977
 17:15 whom the LORD thy God shall **c**: 977
 18: 6 unto the place which the LORD shall **c**; 977
 23:16 in *that* place which he shall **c** in one of 977
 26: 2 thy God shall **c** to place his name there. 977
 30:19 therefore **c** life, that *both* thou and thy seed 977
 31:11 thy God in the place which he shall **c**, 977
Jos 9:27 this day, in the place which he should **c**. 977
 24:15 **c** you *this* day whom you will serve; 977
1Sa 2:28 did I **c** him out of all the tribes of Israel 977
 17: 8 **c** you a man for you, and let him come 1262
2Sa 16:18 **c**, his will find, and with him will I abide. 977
 17: 1 Let me now **c out** twelve thousand men, 977
 21: 6 in Gibeah of Saul, whom the LORD did **c**. 972
 24:12 I offer thee three *things;* **c** thee one of 977
1Ki 14:21 the city which the LORD did **c** out of all 977
 18:23 let them **c** one bullock for themselves, 977
 18:25 **C** you one bullock for yourselves, 977
1Ch 21:10 I offer thee three *things:* **c** thee one of 977
 21:11 unto him, Thus saith the LORD, **C**hoose 6901
Ne 9: 7 who didst **c** Abram, and broughtest him 977
Job 9:14 and **c** out my words *to reason* with him? 977
 34: 4 Let us **c** to us judgment: let us know 977
 34:33 whether thou refuse, or whether thou **c**; 977
Ps 25:12 shall he teach in the way *that* he shall **c**. 977
 47: 4 He shall **c** our inheritance for us, 977
Pr 1:29 and did not **c** the fear of the LORD: 977
 3:31 not the oppressor, and **c** none of his ways. 977
Isa 7:15 know to refuse the evil, and **c** the good. 977
 7:16 know to refuse the evil, and **c** the good, 977
 14: 1 will yet **c** Israel, and set them in their own 977
 49: 7 the Holy One of Israel, and he shall **c** thee. 977
 56: 4 **c** *the things* that please me, and take hold 977
 65:12 and did **c** *that* wherein I delighted not. 977
 66: 4 I also will **c** their delusions, and will bring 977
Eze 21:19 **c** thou a place, choose *it*, at the head of 1254
 21:19 **c** *it*, at the head of the way to the city. 1254
Zec 1:17 yet comfort Zion, and shall yet **c** Jerusalem. 977
 2:12 the holy land, and shall **c** Jerusalem again. 977
Php 1:22 of my labour: yet what I shall **c** I wot not. 138

CHOOSEST (2) [CHOOSE]

Job 15: 5 and thou **c** the tongue of the crafty. 977
Ps 65: 4 Blessed *is* the man whom thou **c**, 977

CHOOSETH (3) [CHOOSE]

Job 7:15 So that my soul **c** strangling, 977
Isa 40:20 impoverished that he hath no oblation **c** a 977
 41:24 of nought: an abomination *is* he that **c** you. 977

CHOOSING (1) [CHOOSE]

Heb 11:25 **C** rather to suffer affliction with the people 138

CHOP (1)

Mic 3: 3 **c** them **in pieces**, as for the pot, and as 6566

CHOR-ASHAN (1)

1Sa 30:30 to *them* which were in **C**, and to *them* 3565

CHORAZIN (2)

Mt 11:21 unto thee, **C**, woe unto thee, Bethsaida: 5523
Lk 10:13 unto thee, **C**, woe unto thee, Bethsaida: 5523

CHOSE (29) [CHOOSE]

Ge 6: 2 they took them wives of all which they **c**. 977
 13:11 Lot **c** him all the plain of Jordan; 977
Ex 18:25 Moses **c** able men out of all Israel, 977
Dt 4:37 therefore he **c** their seed after them, 977
 10:15 he **c** their seed after them, *even* you above 977
Jos 8: 3 Joshua **c out** thirty thousand mighty *men* 977
Jdg 5: 8 **c** new gods; then *was* war in the gates: 977
1Sa 13: 2 Saul **c** him three thousand *men* of Israel; 977
 17:40 **c** him five smooth stones out of the brook, 977
2Sa 6:21 which **c** me before thy father, and before 977
 10: 9 he **c** of all the choice *men* of Israel, 977
1Ki 8:16 I **c** no city out of all the tribes of Israel to 977
 8:16 but I **c** David to be over my people Israel. 977
 11:34 whom I **c**, because he kept my 977
1Ch 19:10 he **c** out of all the choice of Israel, 977
 28: 4 Howbeit the LORD God of Israel **c** me 977
2Ch 6: 5 **c** no city among all the tribes of Israel to 977
 6: 5 neither **c** I any man to be a ruler over my 977
Job 29:25 I **c out** their way, and sat chief, and dwelt 977
Ps 78:67 of Joseph, and **c** not the tribe of Ephraim: 977
 78:68 the tribe of Judah, the mount Zion which 977
 78:70 He **c** David also his servant, and took him 977
Isa 66: 4 and **c** *that* in which I delighted not. 977
Eze 20: 5 In the day when I **c** Israel, and lifted up 977
Lk 6:13 and of them he **c** twelve, whom also he 1586
 14: 7 he marked how they **c out** the chief 1586
Ac 6: 5 they **c** Stephen, a man full of faith and 1586
 13:17 The God of this people of Israel **c** our 1586
 15:40 And Paul **c** Silas, and departed, 1951

CHOSEN (123) [CHOOSE]

Ex 14: 7 he took six hundred **c** chariots, and all 977
 15: 4 his **c** captains also are drowned in the Red 4005
Nu 16: 5 even *him* whom he hath **c** will he cause to 977
Dt 7: 6 the LORD thy God hath **c** thee to be a 977
 12:21 **c** to put his name there be too far from 977
 14: 2 the LORD hath **c** thee to be a peculiar 977
 16:11 thy God hath **c** to place his name there. 977
 18: 5 For the LORD thy God hath **c** him out of 977
 21: 5 for them the LORD thy God hath **c** to 977
Jos 24:22 yourselves that ye have **c** you the LORD, 977
Jdg 10:14 and cry unto the gods which ye have **c**; 977
 20:15 were numbered seven hundred **c** men. 977
 20:16 *were* seven hundred **c** men lefthanded; 977
 20:34 there came against Gibeah ten thousand **c** 977
1Sa 8:18 of your king which ye shall have **c** you; 977
 10:24 See ye him whom the LORD hath **c**, 977
 12:13 therefore behold the king whom ye have **c**, 977
 16: 8 And he said, Neither hath the LORD **c** this. 977
 16: 9 And he said, Neither hath the LORD **c** this. 977
 16:10 unto Jesse, The LORD hath not **c** these. 977
 20:30 **c** the son of Jesse to thine own confusion, 977
 24: 2 Saul took three thousand **c** men out of all 977
 26: 2 having three thousand **c** men of Israel with 977
2Sa 6: 1 David gathered together all the **c** *men* of 977
1Ki 3: 8 the midst of thy people which thou hast **c**, 977
 8:44 LORD toward the city which thou hast **c**, 977
 8:48 the city which thou hast **c**, and the house 977
 11:13 and for Jerusalem's sake, which I have **c**. 977
 11:32 the city which I have **c** out of all the tribes 977
 11:36 the city which I have **c** me to put my name 977
 12:21 fourscore thousand **c** *men*, which were 977
2Ki 21: 7 which I have **c** out of all tribes of Israel, 977
 23:27 cast off this city Jerusalem which I have **c**, 977
1Ch 9:22 All these which were **c** to be porters in 1305
 15: 2 for them hath the LORD **c** to carry the ark 977
 16:13 servant, ye children of Jacob, his **c** ones. 972
 16:41 and Jeduthun, and the rest that were **c**, 1305
 28: 4 for he hath **c** Judah to be the ruler; and of 977
 28: 5 he hath **c** Solomon my son to sit upon 977
 28: 6 for I have **c** him to be my son, and I will 977
 28:10 for the LORD hath **c** thee to build a house 977
 29: 1 whom alone God hath **c**, *is yet* young and 977
2Ch 6: 6 I have **c** Jerusalem, that my name might be 977
 6: 6 have **c** David to be over my people Israel. 977
 6:34 thee toward this city which thou hast **c**, 977
 6:38 *toward* the city which thou hast **c**, 977
 7:12 have **c** this place to myself for a house of 977
 7:16 For now have I **c** and sanctified this house, 977
 11: 1 fourscore thousand **c** *men*, which were 977
 12:13 the city which the LORD had **c** out of all 977
 13: 3 war, *even* four hundred thousand **c** men: 977
 13: 3 him with eight hundred thousand **c** men, 977
 13:17 slain of Israel five hundred thousand **c** men. 977
 29:11 for the LORD hath **c** you to stand before 977
 33: 7 I have **c** before all the tribes of Israel, 977
Ne 1: 9 bring them unto the place that I have **c** 977
Job 36:21 for this hast thou **c** rather than affliction. 977
Ps 33:12 the people *whom* he hath **c** for his own 977
 78:31 and smote down the **c** *men* of Israel. 970
 89: 3 I have made a covenant with my **c**, I have 977
 89:19 I have exalted *one* **c** out of the people. 977
 105: 6 his servant, ye children of Jacob, his **c**. 972
 105:26 his servant; *and* Aaron whom he had **c**. 977
 105:43 people with joy, *and* his **c** with gladness: 972
 106: 5 That *I* may see the good of thy **c**, that *I* 972
 106:23 had not Moses his **c** stood before him in 977
 119:30 I have **c** the way of truth: thy judgments 977
 119:173 hand help me; for I have **c** thy precepts. 977
 132:13 For the LORD hath **c** Zion; he hath desired 977

Ps 135: 4 For the LORD hath **c** Jacob unto himself, 977
Pr 16:16 to get understanding rather to be **c** than 977
 22: 1 A *good* name *is* rather to be **c** than great 977
Isa 1:29 confounded for the gardens that ye have **c**. 977
 41: 8 *art* my servant, whom I have **c**, 977
 41: 9 I have **c** thee, and not cast thee away. 977
 43:10 the LORD, and my servant whom I have **c**: 977
 43:20 desert, to give drink to my people, my **c**. 972
 44: 1 my servant; and Israel, whom I have **c**: 977
 44: 2 and *thou*, Jeshurun, whom I have **c**. 977
 48:10 I have **c** thee in the furnace of affliction. 977
 58: 5 Is it such a fast that I have **c**? a day for a 977
 58: 6 *Is* not this the fast that I have **c**? to loose 977
 65:15 leave your name for a curse unto my **c**: 972
 66: 3 they have **c** their own ways, and their soul 977
Jer 8: 3 death shall be **c** rather than life by all 977
 33:24 The two families which the LORD hath **c**, 977
 48:15 his **c** young men are gone down to 4005
 49:19 *is a* **c** *man, that* I may appoint over her? 977
 50:44 *is a* **c** *man, that* I may appoint over her? 977
Eze 23: 7 *with* all them *that* were the **c** men of 4005
Da 11:15 shall not withstand, neither his **c** people, 4005
Hag 2:23 for I have **c** thee, saith the LORD of hosts. 977
Zec 3: 2 even the LORD that hath **c** Jerusalem 977
Mt 12:18 Behold my servant, whom I have **c**; 140
 20:16 first last: for many be called, but few **c**. 1588
 22:14 For many are called, but few *are* **c**. 1588
Mk 13:20 but for the elect's sake, whom he hath **c**, 1586
Lk 10:42 Mary hath **c** *that* good part, which shall 1586
 23:35 save himself, if he be Christ, the **c** of God. 1588
Jn 6:70 Have not I **c** you twelve, and one of you 1586
 13:18 I know whom I have **c**: but that 1586
 15:16 Ye have not **c** me, but I have chosen you, 1586
 15:16 but I have **c** you, and ordained you, 1586
 15:19 but I have **c** you out of the world, 1586
Ac 1: 2 unto the Apostles whom he had **c**: 1586
 1:24 shew whether of these two thou hast **c**, 1586
 9:15 Go *thy way:* for he is a **c** vessel unto me, 1589
 10:41 but unto witnesses **c before** of God, 4401
 15:22 to send **c** men of their own company to 1586
 15:25 to send **c** men unto you with our beloved 1586
 22:14 said, The God of our fathers hath **c** thee, 4400
Ro 16:13 Salute Rufus **c** in the Lord, and his mother 1588
1Co 1:27 But God hath **c** the foolish *things* of 1586
 1:27 God hath **c** the weak *things* of the world 1586
 1:28 God **c**, *yea,* and *things* which are not, 1586
2Co 8:19 who was also **c** of the churches to travel 5500
Eph 1: 4 According as he hath **c** us in him before 1586
2Th 2:13 God hath from the beginning **c** you to 138
2Ti 2: 4 him who hath **c** *him* **to be a soldier**. 4758
Jas 2: 5 Hath not God **c** the poor of this world rich 1588
1Pe 2: 4 of men, but **c** of God, *and* precious, 1588
 2: 9 But ye *are a* **c** generation, a royal 1588
Rev 17:14 with him *are* called, and, **c**, and faithful. 1588

CHOZEBA (1)

1Ch 4:22 and the men of **C**, and Joash, and Saraph, 3578

CHRIST (555) [ANTICHRIST, ANTICHRISTS, CHRIST'S, CHRISTIAN, CHRISTIANS, CHRISTS]

Mt 1: 1 The book of the generation of Jesus **C**, 5547
 1:16 of whom was born Jesus, who is called **C**. 5547
 1:17 Babylon unto **C** *are* fourteen generations. 5547
 1:18 the birth of Jesus **C** was on this wise: 5547
 2: 4 he demanded of them where **C** should be 5547
 11: 2 had heard in the prison the works of **C**, 5547
 16:16 Peter answered and said, Thou art the **C**, 5547
 16:20 tell no *man* that he was Jesus the **C**. 5547
 22:42 Saying, What think ye of **C**? whose son is 5547
 23: 8 for one is your Master, *even* **C**; 5547
 23:10 for one is your Master, *even* **C**. 5547
 24: 5 shall come in my name, saying, I am **C**; 5547
 24:23 shall say unto you, Lo, here *is* **C**, or there; 5547
 26:63 that thou tell us whether thou be the **C**, 5547
 26:68 Saying, Prophesy unto us, *thou* **C**, Who is 5547
 27:17 Barabbas, or Jesus which is called **C**? 5547
 27:22 I do then with Jesus which is called **C**? 5547
Mk 1: 1 The beginning of the gospel of Jesus **C**, 5547
 8:29 and saith unto him, Thou art the **C**. 5547
 9:41 because ye belong to **C**, verily I say unto 5547
 12:35 How say the scribes that **C** is the Son of 5547
 13: 6 saying, I am **C**; and shall deceive many. NIG
 13:21 if any *man* shall say to you, Lo, here *is* **C**; 5547
 14:61 said unto him, Art thou the **C**, the Son 5547
 15:32 Let the King of Israel descend now from 5547
Lk 2:11 of David a Saviour, which is **C** the Lord. 5547
 2:26 death, before he had seen the Lord's **C**. 5547
 3:15 of John, whether he were the **C**, or not; 5547
 4:41 and saying, Thou art **C** the Son of God. 5547
 4:41 to speak: for they knew that he was **C**. 5547
 9:20 Peter answering said, The **C** of God. 5547
 20:41 How say they that **C** is David's son? 5547
 21: 8 I am **C**; and the time draweth near: NIG
 22:67 Art thou the **C**? tell us. And he said unto 5547
 23: 2 saying that he himself is **C** a King. 5547
 23:35 himself, if he be **C**, the chosen of God. 5547
 23:39 saying, If thou be **C**, save thyself and us. 5547
 24:26 Ought not **C** to have suffered these *things*, 5547
 24:46 thus it behoved **C** to suffer, and to rise 5547
Jn 1:17 *but* grace and truth came by Jesus **C**. 5547
 1:20 denied not; but confessed, I am not the **C**. 5547
 1:25 if thou be not *that* **C**, nor Elias, neither 5547
 1:41 which is, being interpreted, the **C**. 5547
 3:28 I am not the **C**, but that I am sent before 5547
 4:25 that Messias cometh, which is called **C**: 5547

C

Jn
4:29 *things* that ever I did: is not this the **C**? 5547
4:42 and know that this is indeed the **C**, 5547
6:69 believe and are sure that thou art *that* **C**, 5547
7:26 rulers know indeed that this is the very **C**? 5547
7:27 but when **C** cometh, no *man* knoweth 5547
7:31 on him, and said, When **C** cometh, 5547
7:41 Others said, This is the **C**. But some said, 5547
7:41 some said, Shall **C** come out of Galilee? 5547
7:42 That **C** cometh of the seed of David, 5547
9:22 that if any *man* did confess that he *was* **C**, 5547
10:24 to doubt? If thou be the **C**, tell us plainly. 5547
11:27 I believe that thou art the **C**, the Son of 5547
12:34 We have heard out of the law that **C** 5547
17: 3 and Jesus **C**, whom thou hast sent. 5547
20:31 that ye might believe that Jesus is the **C**, 5547

Ac
2:30 *he* would raise up **C** to sit on his throne; 5547
2:31 *this* before, spake of the resurrection of **C**, 5547
2:36 whom ye have crucified, both Lord and **C**. 5547
2:38 name of Jesus **C** for the remission of sins. 5547
3: 6 In the name of Jesus **C** of Nazareth rise up 5547
3:18 that **C** should suffer, he hath so fulfilled. 5547
3:20 And he shall send Jesus **C**, which before 5547
4:10 that by the name of Jesus **C** of Nazareth, 5547
4:26 against the Lord, and against his **C**. 5547
5:42 ceased not to teach and preach Jesus **C**. 5547
8: 5 of Samaria, and preached **C** unto them. 5547
8:12 and the name of Jesus **C**, they were 5547
8:37 I believe that Jesus is the Son of God. 5547
9:20 And straightway he preached **C** in 5547
9:22 at Damascus, proving that this is very **C**. 5547
9:34 Aeneas, Jesus **C** maketh thee whole: 5547
10:36 of Israel, preaching peace by Jesus **C** 5547
11:17 us, who believed on the Lord Jesus **C**; 5547
15:11 of the Lord Jesus **C** *we* shall be saved, 5547
15:26 lives for the name of our Lord Jesus **C**. 5547
16:18 I command thee in the name of Jesus **C** to 5547
16:31 Believe on the Lord Jesus **C**, and thou 5547
17: 3 that **C** must needs have suffered, 5547
17: 3 this Jesus, whom I preach unto you, is **C**. 5547
18: 5 and testified to the Jews *that* Jesus *was* **C**. 5547
18:28 by the scriptures that Jesus was **C**. 5547
19: 4 come after him, that is, on **C** Jesus. 5547
20:21 and faith toward our Lord Jesus **C**. 5547
24:24 and heard him concerning the faith in **C**. 5547
26:23 That **C** should suffer, *and* that he *should* 5547
28:31 *things* which concern the Lord Jesus **C**. 5547

Ro
1: 1 Paul, a servant of Jesus **C**, called *to be* an 5547
1: 3 Concerning his Son Jesus **C** our Lord, 5547
1: 6 whom are ye also *the* called of Jesus **C**: 5547
1: 7 God our Father, and the Lord Jesus **C**. 5547
1: 8 I thank my God through Jesus **C** for you 5547
1:16 For I am not ashamed of the gospel of **C**: 5547
2:16 of men by Jesus **C** according to my gospel. 5547
3:22 God *which is* by faith of Jesus **C** unto all 5547
3:24 through the redemption that is in **C** Jesus: 5547
5: 1 peace with God through our Lord Jesus **C**: 5547
5: 6 in due time **C** died for the ungodly. 5547
5: 8 while we were yet sinners, **C** died for us. 5547
5:11 also joy in God through our Lord Jesus **C**, 5547
5:15 by grace, which is by one man, Jesus **C**, 5547
5:17 shall reign in life by one, Jesus **C**. 5547
5:21 unto eternal life by Jesus **C** our Lord. 5547
6: 3 many of us as were baptized into Jesus **C** 5547
6: 4 like as **C** was raised up from the dead 5547
6: 8 if we be dead with **C**, we believe that 5547
6: 9 Knowing that **C** being raised from the 5547
6:11 alive unto God through Jesus **C** our Lord. 5547
6:23 *is* eternal life through Jesus **C** our Lord. 5547
7: 4 become dead to the law by the body of **C**; 5547
7:25 I thank God through Jesus **C** our Lord. 5547
8: 1 in **C** Jesus who walk not after the flesh, 5547
8: 2 For the law of the Spirit of life in **C** Jesus 5547
8: 9 Now if any *man* have not the Spirit of **C**, 5547
8:10 And if **C** *be* in you, the body *is* dead 5547
8:11 he that raised up **C** from the dead shall 5547
8:17 heirs of God, and joint-heirs with **C**; if so 5547
8:34 *It is* **C** that died, yea rather, that is risen 5547
8:35 Who shall separate us from the love of **C**? 5547
8:39 love of God, which is in **C** Jesus our Lord. 5547
9: 1 I say the truth in **C**, I lie not, my 5547
9: 3 were accursed from **C** for my brethren, 5547
9: 5 of whom as concerning the flesh **C** came, 5547
10: 4 For **C** *is* the end of the law for 5547
10: 6 (that is, to bring **C** down *from above:*) 5547
10: 7 to bring up **C** again from the dead.) 5547
12: 5 one body in **C**, and every one members 5547
13:14 But put ye on the Lord Jesus **C**, 5547
14: 9 For to this end **C** both died, and rose, 5547
14:10 all stand before the judgment seat of **C**. 5547
14:15 not him with thy meat, for whom **C** died. 5547
14:18 For he that in these *things* serveth **C** *is* 5547
15: 3 For even **C** pleased not himself; but, as it 5547
15: 5 one towards another according to **C** Jesus: 5547
15: 6 even the Father of our Lord Jesus **C**. 5547
15: 7 as **C** also received us, to the glory of God. 5547
15: 8 Now I say that Jesus **C** was a minister of 5547
15:16 That I should be the minister of Jesus **C** to 5547
15:17 whereof I *may* glory through Jesus **C** *in* 5547
15:18 *things* which **C** hath not wrought by me, 5547
15:19 I have fully preached the gospel of **C**. 5547
15:20 the gospel, not where **C** was named, 5547
15:29 fulness of the blessing of the gospel of **C**. 5547
16: 3 and Aquila my helpers in **C** Jesus: 5547
16: 5 who is the firstfruits of Achaia unto **C**. 5547
16: 7 apostles, who were in **C** before me. 5547

Ro
16: 9 Salute Urban our helper in **C**, 5547
16:10 Salute Apelles approved in **C**. Salute them 5547
16:16 a holy kiss. The churches of **C** salute you. 5547
16:18 *that are* such serve not our Lord Jesus **C**, 5547
16:20 grace of our Lord Jesus **C** *be* with you. 5547
16:24 grace of our Lord Jesus **C** *be* with you 5547
16:25 the preaching of Jesus **C**, according to 5547
16:27 *be* glory through Jesus **C** for ever. 5547

1Co
1: 1 called *to be* an apostle of Jesus **C** through 5547
1: 2 to them that are sanctified in **C** Jesus, 5547
1: 2 call upon the name of Jesus **C** our Lord, 5547
1: 3 our Father, and *from* the Lord Jesus **C**. 5547
1: 4 of God which is given you by Jesus **C**; 5547
1: 6 Even as the testimony of **C** was confirmed 5547
1: 7 for the coming of our Lord Jesus **C**: 5547
1: 8 blameless in the day of our Lord Jesus **C**. 5547
1: 9 the fellowship of his Son Jesus **C** our Lord. 5547
1:10 by the name of our Lord Jesus **C**, 5547
1:12 I of Apollos; and I of Cephas; and I of **C**. 5547
1:13 Is **C** divided? was Paul crucified for you? 5547
1:17 **C** sent me not to baptize, but to preach 5547
1:17 lest the cross of **C** should be made of none 5547
1:23 But we preach **C** crucified, unto the Jews 5547
1:24 the power of God, and the wisdom of 5547
1:30 But of him are ye in **C** Jesus, who of God 5547
2: 2 save Jesus **C**, and him crucified. 5547
2:16 instruct him? But we have the mind of **C**. 5547
3: 1 as unto carnal, *even* as unto babes in **C**. 5547
3:11 man lay than that is laid, which is Jesus **C**. 5547
3:23 And ye *are* Christ's; and **C** *is* God's. 5547
4: 1 as of the ministers of **C**, and stewards of 5547
4:10 for Christ's sake, but ye *are* wise in **C**; 5547
4:15 you have ten thousand instructors in **C**, 5547
4:15 for in **C** Jesus I have begotten you through 5547
4:17 remembrance of my ways which be in **C**, 5547
5: 4 In the name of our Lord Jesus **C**, when ye 5547
5: 4 with the power of our Lord Jesus **C**, 5547
5: 7 For even **C** our passover is sacrificed for 5547
6:15 that your bodies are the members of **C**? 5547
6:15 shall I then take the members of **C**, 5547
8: 6 and one Lord Jesus **C**, by whom *are* all 5547
8:11 weak brother perish, for whom **C** died? 5547
8:12 their weak conscience, ye sin against **C**. 5547
9: 1 have I not seen Jesus **C** our Lord? are not 5547
9:12 lest we should hinder the gospel of **C**. 5547
9:18 may make the gospel of **C** without charge, 5547
9:21 law to God, but under the law to **C**,) 5547
10: 4 that followed *them:* and *that* Rock was **C**. 5547
10: 9 Neither let us tempt **C**, as some of them 5547
10:16 it not the communion of the blood of **C**? 5547
10:16 it not the communion of the body of **C**? 5547
11: 1 ye followers of me, even as I also *am* of **C**. 5547
11: 3 know, that the head of every man is **C**; 5547
11: 3 *is* the man; and the head of **C** is God. 5547
12:12 being many, are one body: so also *is* **C**. 5547
12:27 Now ye are the body of **C**, and members 5547
15: 3 how that **C** died for our sins according to 5547
15:12 Now if **C** be preached that he rose from 5547
15:13 of the dead, then is **C** not risen: 5547
15:14 if **C** be not risen, then *is* our preaching 5547
15:15 have testified of God that he raised up **C**: 5547
15:16 if the dead rise not, then is not **C** raised: 5547
15:17 And if **C** be not raised, your faith *is* vain; 5547
15:18 they also which are fallen asleep in **C**. 5547
15:19 If in this life only we have hope in **C**, 5547
15:20 But now is **C** risen from the dead, 5547
15:22 die, even so in **C** shall all be made alive. 5547
15:23 the firstfruits; afterward they that are 5547
15:31 rejoicing which I have in **C** Jesus our Lord, 5547
15:57 us the victory through our Lord Jesus **C**. 5547
16:22 If any *man* love not the Lord Jesus **C**, 5547
16:23 grace of *our* Lord Jesus **C** *be* with you. 5547
16:24 My love *be* with you all in **C** Jesus. Amen. 5547

2Co
1: 1 an apostle of Jesus **C** by the will of God, 5547
1: 2 our Father, and *from* the Lord Jesus **C**. 5547
1: 3 even the Father of our Lord Jesus **C**. 5547
1: 5 For as the sufferings of **C** abound in us, 5547
1: 5 so our consolation also aboundeth by **C**. 5547
1:19 For the Son of God, Jesus **C**, who was 5547
1:21 he which stablisheth us with you in **C**, 5547
2:10 your sakes *forgave I* it in the person of **C**; 5547
2:14 which always causeth us to triumph in **C**, 5547
2:15 For we are unto God a sweet savour of **C**, 5547
2:17 of God, in the sight of God speak we in **C**. 5547
3: 3 to be the epistle of **C** ministered by us, 5547
3: 4 And such trust have we through **C** to 5547
3:14 which *vail* is done away in **C**. 5547
4: 4 lest the light of the glorious gospel of **C**, 5547
5: 5 not ourselves, but **C** Jesus the Lord; 5547
4: 6 of the glory of God in the face of Jesus **C**. 5547
5:10 all appear before the judgment seat of **C**; 5547
5:14 For the love of **C** constraineth us; because 5547
5:16 though we have known **C** after the flesh, 5547
5:17 Therefore if any *man be* in **C**, *he is* a new 5547
5:18 hath reconciled us to himself by Jesus **C**, 5547
5:19 that God was in **C** reconciling the world 5547
5:20 *Now* then we are ambassadors for **C**, 5547
8: 9 ye know the grace of our Lord Jesus **C**, 5547
6:15 what concord hath **C** with Belial? 5547
8:23 of the churches, *and* the glory of **C**. 5547
9:13 professed subjection unto the gospel of **C**, 5547
10: 1 you by the meekness and gentleness of **C**, 5547
10: 5 every thought to the obedience of **C**; 5547
10:14 to you also in *preaching* the gospel of **C**: 5547
11: 2 I may present *you as* a chaste virgin to **C**. 5547

2Co
11: 3 corrupted from the simplicity that is in **C**. 5547
11:10 *As* the truth of **C** is in me, no *man* shall 5547
11:13 themselves into the apostles of **C**. 5547
11:23 Are they ministers of **C**? (I speak as a fool) 5547
11:31 The God and Father of our Lord Jesus **C**, 5547
12: 2 I knew a man in **C** above fourteen years 5547
12: 9 that the power of **C** may rest upon me. 5547
12:19 we speak before God in **C**: but *we do* all 5547
13: 3 Since ye seek a proof of **C** speaking in me, 5547
13: 5 how that Jesus **C** is in you, except ye be 5547
13:14 grace of the Lord Jesus **C**, and the love 5547

Gal
1: 1 but by Jesus **C**, and God the Father, 5547
1: 3 the Father, and *from* our Lord Jesus **C**: 5547
1: 6 into the grace of **C** unto another gospel: 5547
1: 7 and would pervert the gospel of **C**. 5547
1:10 I should not be the servant of **C**. 5547
1:12 taught *it*, but by the revelation of Jesus **C**. 5547
1:22 the churches of Judea which were in **C**: 5547
2: 4 out our liberty which we have in **C** Jesus, 5547
2:16 but by the faith of Jesus **C**, even we have 5547
2:16 even we have believed in Jesus **C**, 5547
2:16 we might be justified by the faith of **C**, 5547
2:17 But if, while we seek to be justified by **C**, 5547
2:17 *is* therefore **C** the minister of sin? 5547
2:20 I am crucified with **C**: nevertheless I live; 5547
2:20 I live; yet not I, but **C** liveth in me: 5547
2:21 *come* by the law, then **C** is dead in vain. 5547
3: 1 before whose eyes Jesus **C** hath been 5547
3:13 **C** hath redeemed us from the curse of 5547
3:14 come on the Gentiles through Jesus **C**; 5547
3:16 as of one, And to thy seed, which is **C**. 5547
3:17 that was confirmed before of God in **C**, 5547
3:22 that the promise by faith of Jesus **C** might 5547
3:24 was our schoolmaster *to bring us* unto **C**, 5547
3:26 all the children of God by faith in **C** Jesus. 5547
3:27 been baptized into **C** have put on Christ. 5547
3:27 been baptized into Christ have put on **C**. 5547
3:28 nor female: for ye are all one in **C** Jesus. 5547
4: 7 if a son, then an heir of God through **C**. 5547
4:14 me as an angel of God, *even as* **C** Jesus. 5547
4:19 of whom I travail in birth again until **C** be 5547
5: 1 in the liberty wherewith **C** hath made us 5547
5: 2 circumcised, **C** shall profit you nothing. 5547
5: 4 **C** is become of no effect unto you, 5547
5: 6 For in Jesus **C** neither circumcision 5547
6: 2 and so fulfil the law of **C**. 5547
6:12 suffer persecution for the cross of **C**. 5547
6:14 save in the cross of our Lord Jesus **C**, 5547
6:15 For in Jesus **C** neither circumcision 5547
6:18 the grace of our Lord Jesus **C** *be* with 5547

Eph
1: 1 an apostle of Jesus **C** by the will of God, 5547
1: 1 at Ephesus, and to the faithful in **C** Jesus: 5547
1: 2 our Father, and *from* the Lord Jesus **C**. 5547
1: 3 the God and Father of our Lord Jesus **C**, 5547
1: 3 spiritual blessings in heavenly *places* in **C**: 5547
1: 5 adoption of children by Jesus **C** to himself, 5547
1:10 gather together in one all *things* in **C**, 5547
1:12 praise of his glory, who first trusted in **C**: 5547
1:17 That the God of our Lord Jesus **C**, 5547
1:20 Which he wrought in **C**, when he raised 5547
2: 5 hath quickened *us* together with **C**, 5547
2: 6 sit together in heavenly *places* in **C** Jesus: 5547
2: 7 *his* kindness towards us through **C** Jesus. 5547
2:10 created in **C** Jesus unto good works, 5547
2:12 That at that time ye were without **C**, 5547
2:13 But now in **C** Jesus ye who sometimes 5547
2:13 far off are made nigh by the blood of **C**. 5547
2:20 Jesus **C** himself being the chief corner 5547
3: 1 the prisoner of Jesus **C** for you Gentiles, 5547
3: 4 my knowledge in the mystery of **C**) 5547
3: 6 partakers of his promise in **C** by the gospel 5547
3: 8 the Gentiles the unsearchable riches of **C**; 5547
3: 9 in God, who created all *things* by Jesus **C**: 5547
3:11 which he purposed in **C** Jesus our Lord: 5547
3:14 knees unto the Father of our Lord Jesus **C**, 5547
3:17 That **C** may dwell in your hearts by faith; 5547
3:19 And to know the love of **C**, which passeth 5547
3:21 him be glory in the church by **C** Jesus 5547
4: 7 according to the measure of the gift of **C**. 5547
4:12 for the edifying of the body of **C**: 5547
4:13 measure of the stature of the fulness of **C**: 5547
4:15 in all *things*, which is the head, *even* **C**: 5547
4:20 But ye have not so learned **C**; 5547
5: 2 as **C** also hath loved us, and hath given 5547
5: 5 hath *any* inheritance in the kingdom of **C** 5547
5:14 from the dead, and **C** shall give thee light. 5547
5:20 Father in the name of our Lord Jesus **C**; 5547
5:23 even as **C** *is* the head of the church: 5547
5:24 Therefore as the church is subject unto **C**, 5547
5:25 even as **C** also loved the church, 5547
5:32 but I speak concerning **C** and the church. 5547
6: 5 in singleness of your heart, as unto **C**; 5547
6: 6 but as the servants of **C**, doing the will of 5547
6:23 God the Father and the Lord Jesus **C**. 5547
6:24 that love our Lord Jesus **C** in sincerity. 5547

Php
1: 1 and Timotheus, the servants of Jesus **C**, 5547
1: 1 to all the saints in **C** Jesus which are at 5547
1: 2 our Father, and *from* the Lord Jesus **C**. 5547
1: 6 will perform *it* until the day of Jesus **C**: 5547
1: 8 long after you all in the bowels of Jesus **C**. 5547
1:10 and without offence till the day of **C**; 5547
1:11 which are by Jesus **C** unto the glory and 5547
1:13 So that my bonds in **C** are manifest in all 5547
1:15 Some indeed preach **C** even of envy and 5547
1:16 The one preach **C** of contention, 5547

Php	1:18 in pretence, or in truth, **C** is preached;	5547
	1:19 and the supply of the Spirit of Jesus **C**,	5547
	1:20 also **C** shall be magnified in my body,	5547
	1:21 For to me to live *is* **C**, and to die *is* gain.	5547
	1:23 a desire to depart, and to be with **C**;	5547
	1:26 Jesus **C** for me by my coming to you	5547
	1:27 be as it becometh the gospel of **C**:	5547
	1:29 For unto you it is given in the behalf of **C**,	5547
	2: 1 If *there be* therefore any consolation in **C**,	5547
	2: 5 be in you, which *was* also in **C** Jesus:	5547
	2:11 should confess that Jesus **C** *is* Lord,	5547
	2:16 that I may rejoice in the day of **C**, that I	5547
	2:30 Because for the work of **C** he was nigh	5547
	3: 3 and rejoice in **C** Jesus, and have no	5547
	3: 7 gain to me, those I counted loss for **C**.	5547
	3: 8 of the knowledge of **C** Jesus my Lord:	5547
	3: 8 count *them but* dung, that I may win **C**,	5547
	3: 9 but that which is through the faith of **C**,	5547
	3:12 which also I am apprehended of **C** Jesus.	5547
	3:14 prize of the high calling of God in **C** Jesus.	5547
	3:18 *they are* the enemies of the cross of **C**:	5547
	3:20 we look for the Saviour, the Lord Jesus **C**:	5547
	4: 7 your hearts and minds through **C** Jesus.	5547
	4:13 I can do all *things* through **C** which	5547
	4:19 according to his riches in glory by **C** Jesus.	5547
	4:21 Salute every saint in **C** Jesus.	5547
	4:23 grace of our Lord Jesus **C** *be* with you	5547
Col	1: 1 an apostle of Jesus **C** by the will of God,	5547
	1: 2 brethren in **C** which are at Colosse:	5547
	1: 2 God our Father and the Lord Jesus **C**.	5547
	1: 3 God and the Father of our Lord Jesus **C**,	5547
	1: 4 Since we heard of your faith in **C** Jesus,	5547
	1: 7 who is for you a faithful minister of **C**;	5547
	1:24 of **C** in my flesh for his body's sake,	5547
	1:27 which is **C** in you, the hope of glory:	5547
	1:28 we may present every man perfect in **C**	5547
	2: 2 of God and of the Father, and of **C**;	5547
	2: 5 and the stedfastness of your faith in **C**.	5547
	2: 6 therefore received **C** Jesus the Lord,	5547
	2: 8 rudiments of the world, and not after **C**.	5547
	2:11 sins of the flesh, by the circumcision of **C**:	5547
	2:17 of *things* to come; but the body *is* of **C**.	5547
	2:20 Wherefore if ye be dead with **C** from	5547
	3: 1 If ye then be risen with **C**, seek those	5547
	3: 1 where **C** sitteth on the right hand of God.	5547
	3: 3 and your life is hid with **C** in God.	5547
	3: 4 When **C**, *who is* our life, shall appear,	5547
	3:11 bond *nor* free: but **C** is all, and in all.	5547
	3:13 even as **C** forgave you, so also *do* ye.	5547
	3:16 Let the word of **C** dwell in you richly in	5547
	3:24 of the inheritance: for ye serve the Lord **C**.	5547
	4: 3 to speak the mystery of **C**, for which I am	5547
	4:12 is *one* of you, a servant of **C**, saluteth you,	5547
1Th	1: 1 in God the Father and *in* the Lord Jesus **C**:	5547
	1: 1 God our Father, and the Lord Jesus **C**.	5547
	1: 3 and patience of hope in our Lord Jesus **C**,	5547
	2: 6 been burdensome, as *the* apostles of **C**.	5547
	2:14 of God which in Judea are in **C** Jesus:	5547
	2:19 of our Lord Jesus **C** at his coming?	5547
	3: 2 and our fellowlabourer in the gospel of **C**,	5547
	3:11 and our Father, and our Lord Jesus **C**,	5547
	3:13 at the coming of our Lord Jesus **C** with all	5547
	4:16 of God: and the dead in **C** shall rise first:	5547
	5: 9 to obtain salvation by our Lord Jesus **C**	5547
	5:18 for this *is* the will of God in **C** Jesus	5547
	5:23 unto the coming of our Lord Jesus **C**.	5547
	5:28 grace of our Lord Jesus **C** *be* with you.	5547
2Th	1: 1 our God and Father and the Lord Jesus **C**:	5547
	1: 2 God our Father and the Lord Jesus **C**.	5547
	1: 8 obey not the gospel of our Lord Jesus **C**:	5547
	1:12 That the name of our Lord Jesus **C** may	5547
	1:12 grace of our God and the Lord Jesus **C**.	5547
	2: 1 by the coming of our Lord Jesus **C**,	5547
	2: 2 as from us, as that the day of **C** is at hand.	5547
	2:14 obtaining of the glory of our Lord Jesus **C**.	5547
	2:16 Now our Lord Jesus **C** himself, and God,	5547
	3: 5 of God, and into the patient waiting for **C**.	5547
	3: 6 brethren, in the name of our Lord Jesus **C**,	5547
	3:12 and exhort by our Lord Jesus **C**,	5547
	3:18 The grace of our Lord Jesus **C** *be* with you	5547
1Ti	1: 1 apostle of Jesus **C** by the commandment	5547
	1: 1 Lord Jesus **C**, *which is* our hope;	5547
	1: 2 God our Father and Jesus **C** our Lord.	5547
	1:12 And I thank **C** Jesus our Lord, who hath	5547
	1:14 with faith and love which is in **C** Jesus.	5547
	1:15 that **C** Jesus came into the world to save	5547
	1:16 in me first Jesus **C** might shew forth all	5547
	2: 5 between God and men, the man **C** Jesus;	5547
	2: 7 (I speak the truth in **C**, *and* lie not;)	5547
	3:13 great boldness in the faith which is in **C**	5547
	4: 6 thou shalt be a good minister of Jesus **C**,	5547
	5:11 have *begun to* wax wanton against **C**,	5547
	5:21 and the Lord Jesus **C**, and the elect angels,	5547
	6: 3 *even* the *words* of our Lord Jesus **C**,	5547
	6:13 quickeneth all *things*, and *before* **C** Jesus,	5547
	6:14 until the appearing of our Lord Jesus **C**:	5547
2Ti	1: 1 an apostle of Jesus **C** by the will of God,	5547
	1: 1 to the promise of life which is in **C** Jesus,	5547
	1: 2 from God the Father and **C** Jesus our Lord.	5547
	1: 9 which was given us in **C** Jesus before	5547
	1:10 by the appearing of our Saviour Jesus **C**,	5547
	1:13 in faith and love which is in **C** Jesus.	5547
	2: 1 be strong in the grace that is in **C** Jesus.	5547
	2: 3 as a good soldier of Jesus **C**.	5547
	2: 8 Remember that Jesus **C** of the seed of	5547

2Ti	2:10 which is in **C** Jesus with eternal glory.	5547
	2:19 Let every one that nameth the name of **C**	5547
	3:12 all that will live godly in **C** Jesus shall	5547
	3:15 salvation through faith which is in **C** Jesus.	5547
	4: 1 before God, and the Lord Jesus **C**,	5547
	4:22 The Lord Jesus **C** *be* with thy spirit.	5547
Tit	1: 1 servant of God, and an apostle of Jesus **C**,	5547
	1: 4 and the Lord Jesus **C** our Saviour.	5547
	2:13 of the great God and our Saviour Jesus **C**;	5547
	3: 6 abundantly through Jesus **C** our Saviour;	5547
Phm	1: 1 a prisoner of Jesus **C**, and Timothy *our*	5547
	1: 3 God our Father and the Lord Jesus **C**.	5547
	1: 6 good *thing* which is in you in **C** Jesus.	5547
	1: 8 I might be much bold in **C** to enjoin	5547
	1: 9 and now also a prisoner of Jesus **C**.	5547
	1:23 my fellowprisoner in **C** Jesus;	5547
	1:25 The grace of our Lord Jesus **C** *be* with	5547
Heb	3: 1 High Priest of our profession, **C** Jesus;	5547
	3: 6 But **C** as a Son over his own house;	5547
	3:14 we are made partakers of **C**, if we hold	5547
	5: 5 So also **C** glorified not himself to be made	5547
	6: 1 leaving the principles of the doctrine of **C**,	5547
	9:11 But **C** being come a high priest of good	5547
	9:14 How much more shall the blood of **C**,	5547
	9:24 For **C** is not entered into the holy *places*	5547
	9:28 So **C** was once offered to bear the sins of	5547
	10:10 offering of the body of Jesus **C** once for all	5547
	11:26 Esteeming the reproach of **C** greater	5547
	13: 8 Jesus **C** the same yesterday, and to day,	5547
	13:21 well pleasing in his sight, through Jesus **C**;	5547
Jas	1: 1 a servant of God and of the Lord Jesus **C**,	5547
	2: 1 have not the faith of our Lord Jesus **C**,	5547
1Pe	1: 1 Peter, an apostle of Jesus **C**,	5547
	1: 2 and sprinkling of the blood of Jesus **C**:	5547
	1: 3 the God and Father of our Lord Jesus **C**,	5547
	1: 3 the resurrection of Jesus **C** from the dead,	5547
	1: 7 and glory at the appearing of Jesus **C**:	5547
	1:11 what manner of time the Spirit of **C** which	5547
	1:11 it testified beforehand the sufferings of **C**,	5547
	1:13 unto you at the revelation of Jesus **C**;	5547
	1:19 But with the precious blood of **C**, as of a	5547
	2: 5 acceptable to God by Jesus **C**.	5547
	2:21 because **C** also suffered for us, leaving us	5547
	3:16 accuse your good conversation in **C**.	5547
	3:18 For **C** also hath once suffered for sins,	5547
	3:21 by the resurrection of Jesus **C**:	5547
	4: 1 then as **C** hath suffered for us in the flesh,	5547
	4:11 *things* may be glorified through Jesus **C**,	5547
	4:14 If ye be reproached for the name of **C**,	5547
	5: 1 and a witness of the sufferings of **C**,	5547
	5:10 called us into his eternal glory by **C** Jesus,	5547
	5:14 Peace *be* with you all that are in **C** Jesus.	5547
2Pe	1: 1 a servant and an apostle of Jesus **C**,	5547
	1: 1 of God and our Saviour Jesus **C**:	5547
	1: 8 in the knowledge of our Lord Jesus **C**.	5547
	1:11 kingdom of our Lord and Saviour Jesus **C**.	5547
	1:14 as our Lord Jesus **C** hath shewed me.	5547
	1:16 power and coming of our Lord Jesus **C**,	5547
	2:20 of the Lord and Saviour Jesus **C**,	5547
	3:18 of our Lord and Saviour Jesus **C**.	5547
1Jn	1: 3 the Father, and with his Son Jesus **C**.	5547
	1: 7 the blood of Jesus **C** his Son cleanseth us	5547
	2: 1 with the Father, Jesus **C** the righteous:	5547
	2:22 but he that denieth that Jesus is the **C**?	5547
	3:23 believe on the name of his Son Jesus **C**,	5547
	4: 2 Every spirit that confesseth that Jesus **C** is	5547
	4: 3 Jesus **C** is come in the flesh is not of God:	5547
	5: 1 Whosoever believeth that Jesus is the **C** is	5547
	5: 6 came by water and blood, *even* Jesus **C**;	5547
	5:20 him *that* is true, *even* in his Son Jesus **C**.	5547
2Jn	1: 3 the Father, and from the Lord Jesus **C**,	5547
	1: 7 who confess not that Jesus **C** is come in	5547
	1: 9 and abideth not in the doctrine of **C**,	5547
	1: 9 He that abideth in the doctrine of **C**,	5547
Jude	1: 1 the servant of Jesus **C**, and brother of	5547
	1: 1 and preserved *in* Jesus **C**, *and* called:	5547
	1: 4 the only Lord God, and our Lord Jesus **C**.	5547
	1:17 before of the apostles of our Lord Jesus **C**;	5547
	1:21 looking for the mercy of our Lord Jesus **C**	5547
Rev	1: 1 The Revelation of Jesus **C**, which God	5547
	1: 2 and of the testimony of Jesus **C**, and of all	5547
	1: 5 And from Jesus **C**, *who is* the faithful	5547
	1: 9 in the kingdom and patience of Jesus **C**,	5547
	1: 9 of God, and for the testimony of Jesus **C**.	5547
	11:15 *the kingdoms* of our Lord, and of his **C**;	5547
	12:10 of our God, and the power of his **C**:	5547
	12:17 God, and have the testimony of Jesus **C**.	5547
	20: 4 and reigned with **C** a thousand years.	5547
	20: 6 but they shall be priests of God and of **C**,	5547
	22:21 The grace of our Lord Jesus **C** *be* with you	5547

CHRIST'S (16) [CHRIST]

Ro	15:30 for the Lord Jesus **C** sake, and for the love	5547
1Co	3:23 And ye *are* **C**; and Christ *is* God's.	5547
	4:10 We *are* fools for **C** sake, but ye *are* wise in	5547
	7:22 he that is called, *being* free, is **C** servant.	5547
	15:23 afterward they that are **C** at his coming.	5547
2Co	2:12 when I came to Troas to *preach* **C** gospel,	5547
	5:20 we pray *you* in **C** stead, be ye reconciled	5547
	10: 7 If any *man* trust to himself that *he is* **C**,	5547
	10: 7 that, as he *is* **C**, even so *are we* Christ's.	5547
	10: 7 that, as he *is* Christ's, even so *are we* **C**.	5547
	12:10 in persecutions, in distresses for **C** sake:	5547
Gal	3:29 And if ye *be* **C**, then are ye Abraham's	5547
	5:24 they that are **C** have crucified the flesh	5547

CHRISTIAN (2) [CHRIST]

Ac	26:28 Almost thou persuadest me to be a **C**.	5546
1Pe	4:16 Yet if *any man suffer* as a **C**, let him not	5546

CHRISTIANS (1) [CHRIST]

Ac	11:26 disciples were called **C** first in Antioch.	5546

CHRISTS (2) [CHRIST]

Mt	24:24 For there shall arise false **C**,	5580
Mk	13:22 For false **C** and false prophets shall rise,	5580

CHRONICLES (38)

1Ki	14:19 book of the **c** of the kings of Israel.	1697+3117
	14:29 book of the **c** of the kings of Judah?	1697+3117
	15: 7 book of the **c** of the kings of Judah?	1697+3117
	15:23 book of the **c** of the kings of Judah?	1697+3117
	15:31 book of the **c** of the kings of Israel?	1697+3117
	16: 5 book of the **c** of the kings of Israel?	1697+3117
	16:14 book of the **c** of the kings of Israel?	1697+3117
	16:20 book of the **c** of the kings of Israel?	1697+3117
	16:27 book of the **c** of the kings of Israel?	1697+3117
	22:39 book of the **c** of the kings of Israel?	1697+3117
	22:45 book of the **c** of the kings of Judah?	1697+3117
2Ki	1:18 book of the **c** of the kings of Judah?	1697+3117
	8:23 book of the **c** of the kings of Judah?	1697+3117
	10:34 book of the **c** of the kings of Judah?	1697+3117
	12:19 book of the **c** of the kings of Judah?	1697+3117
	13: 8 book of the **c** of the kings of Judah?	1697+3117
	13:12 book of the **c** of the kings of Judah?	1697+3117
	14:15 book of the **c** of the kings of Israel?	1697+3117
	14:18 book of the **c** of the kings of Israel?	1697+3117
	14:28 book of the **c** of the kings of Israel?	1697+3117
	15: 6 book of the **c** of the kings of Judah?	1697+3117
	15:11 *are* written in the book of the **c**	1697+3117
	15:15 *are* written in the book of the **c**	1697+3117
	15:21 book of the **c** of the kings of Israel?	1697+3117
	15:26 *are* written in the book of the **c**	1697+3117
	15:31 *are* written in the book of the **c**	1697+3117
	15:36 book of the **c** of the kings of Judah?	1697+3117
	16:19 book of the **c** of the kings of Judah?	1697+3117
	20:20 book of the **c** of the kings of Judah?	1697+3117
	21:17 book of the **c** of the kings of Judah?	1697+3117
	21:25 book of the **c** of the kings of Judah?	1697+3117
	23:28 book of the **c** of the kings of Judah?	1697+3117
	24: 5 book of the **c** of the kings of Judah?	1697+3117
1Ch	27:24 of the **c** of king David.	1697+3117+1886.1
Ne	12:23 in the book of the **c**,	1697+3117+1886.1
Est	2:23 of the **c** before the king.	1697+3117+1886.1
	6: 1 book of records of the **c**;	1697+3117+1886.1
	10: 2 the **c** of the kings of Media	1697+3117+1886.1

CHRYSOLITE (1)

Rev	21:20 the sixth, sardius; the seventh, **c**;	5555

CHRYSOPRASE See CHRYSOPRASUS

CHRYSOPRASUS (1)

Rev	21:20 beryl; the ninth, a topaz; the tenth, a **c**;	5556

CHUB (1)

Eze	30: 5 **C**, and the men of the land that is in	3552

CHUN (1)

1Ch	18: 8 and from **C**, cities of Hadarezer,	3560

CHURCH (80) [CHURCHES]

Mt	16:18 and upon this rock I will build my **c**;	1577
	18:17 neglect to hear them, tell *it* unto the **c**:	1577
	18:17 but if he neglect to hear the **c**, let him be	1577
Ac	2:47 And the Lord added to the **c** daily such as	1577
	5:11 And great fear came upon all the **c**,	1577
	7:38 that was in the **c** in the wilderness with	1577
	8: 1 against the **c** which was at Jerusalem;	1577
	8: 3 As for Saul, he made havock of the **c**,	1577
	11:22 the ears of the **c** which was in Jerusalem:	1577
	11:26 they assembled themselves with the **c**,	1577
	12: 1 forth *his* hands to vex certain of the **c**.	1577
	12: 5 prayer was made without ceasing of the **c**	1577
	13: 1 there were in the **c** that was at Antioch	1577
	14:23 ordained them elders **in every c**,	1577+2596
	14:27 and had gathered the **c** together,	1577
	15: 3 And being brought on their way by the **c**,	1577
	15: 4 they were received of the **c**, and *of*	1577
	15:22 the apostles and elders, with the whole **c**,	1577
	18:22 and gone up, and saluted the **c**, he went	1577
	20:17 to Ephesus, and called the elders of the **c**.	1577
	20:28 to feed the **c** of God, which he hath	1577
Ro	16: 1 which is a servant of the **c** which is at	1577
	16: 5 Likewise *greet* the **c** that is in their house.	1577
	16:23 host, and of the whole **c**, saluteth you.	1577
	16: 5 by Phebe servant of the **c** at Cenchrea.	1577
1Co	1: 2 Unto the **c** of God which is at Corinth,	1577
	4:17 Christ, as I teach every where in every **c**.	1577
	6: 4 to judge who are least esteemed in the **c**.	1577
	10:32 nor to the Gentiles, nor to the **c** of God:	1577
	11:18 of all, when ye come together in the **c**,	1577
	11:22 to drink *in?* or despise ye the **c** of God,	1577
	12:28 And God hath set some in the **c**,	1577
	14: 4 but he that prophesieth edifieth the **c**.	1577
	14: 5 that the **c** may receive edifying.	1577
	14:12 that ye may excel to the edifying of the **c**.	1577
	14:19 Yet in the **c** I had rather speak five words	1577

CHRIST'S – CHURCH

C

C

1Co 14:23 the whole **c** be come together into one — *1577*
 14:28 interpreter, let him keep silence in the **c**; — *1577*
 14:35 it is a shame for women to speak in the **c**. — *1577*
 15: 9 because I persecuted the **c** of God. — *1577*
 16:19 the Lord, with the **c** that is in their house. — *1577*
2Co 1: 1 unto the **c** of God which is at Corinth, — *1577*
Gal 1:13 that beyond measure I persecuted the **c** — *1577*
Eph 1:22 *to be* the head over all *things* to the **c**, — *1577*
 3:10 by the **c** the manifold wisdom of God, — *1577*
 3:21 Unto him *be* glory in the **c** by Christ Jesus — *1577*
 5:23 wife, even as Christ *is* the head of the **c**: — *1577*
 5:24 Therefore as the **c** is subject unto Christ, — *1577*
 5:25 even as Christ also loved the **c**, — *1577*
 5:27 he might present it to himself a glorious **c**, — *1577*
 5:29 and cherisheth it, even as the Lord the **c**: — *1577*
 5:32 but I speak concerning Christ and the **c**. — *1577*
Php 3: 6 Concerning zeal, persecuting the **c**; — *1577*
 4:15 no **c** communicated with me as — *1577*
Col 1:18 he is the head of the body, the **c**: — *1577*
 1:24 flesh for his body's sake, which is the **c**: — *1577*
 4:15 Nymphas, and the **c** which is in his house. — *1577*
 4:16 cause that it be read also in the **c** of — *1577*
1Th 1: 1 unto the **c** of the Thessalonians *which is* — *1577*
2Th 1: 1 unto the **c** of the Thessalonians in God — *1577*
1Ti 3: 5 how shall he take care of the **c** of God?) — *1577*
 3:15 which is the **c** of the living God, the pillar — *1577*
 5:16 relieve them, and let not the **c** be charged; — *1577*
2Ti 3: S ordained the first bishop of the **c** of — *1577*
Tit 3: S ordained the first bishop of the **c** of — *1577*
Phm 1: 2 fellowsoldier, and to the **c** in thy house: — *1577*
Heb 2:12 in the midst of the **c** will I sing praise unto — *1577*
 12:23 general assembly, and **c** of the firstborn, — *1577*
Jas 5:14 let him call for the elders of the **c**; — *1577*
1Pe 5:13 The **c** *that is* at Babylon, elected together — NIG
3Jn 1: 6 borne witness of thy charity before the **c**: — *1577*
 1: 9 I wrote unto the **c**: but Diotrephes, — *1577*
 1:10 that would, and casteth *them* out of the **c**. — *1577*
Rev 2: 1 Unto the angel of the **c** of Ephesus write; — *1577*
 2: 8 And unto the angel of the **c** in Smyrna — *1577*
 2:12 And to the angel of the **c** in Pergamos — *1577*
 2:18 And unto the angel of the **c** in Thyatira — *1577*
 3: 1 And unto the angel of the **c** in Sardis — *1577*
 3: 7 And to the angel of the **c** in Philadelphia — *1577*
 3:14 And unto the angel of the **c** of — *1577*

CHURCHES (37) [CHURCH]

Ac 9:31 Then had the **c** rest throughout all Judea — *1577*
 15:41 Syria and Cilicia, confirming the **c**. — *1577*
 16: 5 And so were the **c** established in the faith, — *1577*
 19:37 *which are* neither **robbers of c**, nor yet — *2417*
Ro 16: 4 but also all the **c** of the Gentiles. — *1577*
 16:16 a holy kiss. The **c** of Christ salute you. — *1577*
1Co 7:17 so let him walk. And so ordain I in all **c**. — *1577*
 11:16 no such custom, neither the **c** of God. — *1577*
 14:33 but of peace, as in all **c** of the saints. — *1577*
 14:34 Let your women keep silence in the **c**: — *1577*
 16: 1 as I have given order to the **c** of Galatia, — *1577*
 16:19 The **c** of Asia salute you. Aquila and — *1577*
2Co 8: 1 of God bestowed on the **c** of Macedonia; — *1577*
 8:18 praise is in the gospel throughout all the **c**; — *1577*
 8:19 who was also chosen of the **c** to travel — *1577*
 8:23 *of, they are* the messengers of the **c**, — *1577*
 8:24 and before the **c**, the proof of your love, — *1577*
 11: 8 I robbed other **c**, taking wages *of them,* — *1577*
 11:28 upon me daily, the care of all the **c**. — *1577*
 12:13 is it wherein ye were inferior to other **c**, — *1577*
Gal 1: 2 which are with me, unto the **c** of Galatia: — *1577*
 1:22 And was unknown by face unto the **c** of — *1577*
1Th 2:14 became followers of the **c** of God which — *1577*
2Th 1: 4 So that we ourselves glory in you in the **c** — *1577*
Rev 1: 4 John to the seven **c** which are in Asia: — *1577*
 1:11 send *it* unto the seven **c** which are in Asia; — *1577*
 1:20 seven stars are the angels of the seven **c**; — *1577*
 1:20 which thou sawest are the seven **c**. — *1577*
 2: 7 hear what the Spirit saith unto the **c**; — *1577*
 2:11 hear what the Spirit saith unto the **c**; — *1577*
 2:17 hear what the Spirit saith unto the **c**; — *1577*
 2:23 all the **c** shall know that I am he which — *1577*
 2:29 hear what the Spirit saith unto the **c**. — *1577*
 3: 6 hear what the Spirit saith unto the **c**. — *1577*
 3:13 hear what the Spirit saith unto the **c**. — *1577*
 3:22 hear what the Spirit saith unto the **c**. — *1577*
 22:16 to testify unto you these *things* in the **c**. — *1577*

CHURL (2) [CHURLISH]

Isa 32: 5 liberal, nor the **c** said *to be* bountiful. — *3596*
 32: 7 The instruments also of the **c** *are* evil. — *3596*

CHURLISH (1) [CHURL]

1Sa 25: 3 the man *was* **c** and evil *in* his doings; — *7186*

CHURNING (1)

Pr 30:33 Surely the **c** of milk bringeth forth butter, — *4330*

CHUSHAN-RISHATHAIM (4)

Jdg 3: 8 he sold them into the hand of **C** king of — *3573*
 3: 8 the children of Israel served **C** eight years. — *3573*
 3:10 the Lord delivered **C** king of — *3573*
 3:10 hand; and his hand prevailed against **C**. — *3573*

CHUZA (1)

Lk 8: 3 Joanna the wife of **C** Herod's steward, — *5529*

CIELED (4) [CIELING]

2Ch 3: 5 the greater house he **c** with fir tree, — *2645*

Jer 22:14 *it is* **c** with cedar, and painted with — *5603*
Eze 41:16 **c** with wood round about, and *from* — *7824*
Hag 1: 4 to dwell in your **c** houses, and this house — *5603*

CIELING (1) [CIELED]

1Ki 6:15 floor of the house, and the walls of the **c**: — *5604*

CILICIA (8)

Ac 6: 9 and of them of **C** and of Asia, — *2791*
 15:23 the Gentiles in Antioch and Syria and **C**: — *2791*
 15:41 And he went through Syria and **C**, — *2791*
 21:39 *a city* in **C**, a citizen of no mean city: — *2791*
 22: 3 am a Jew, born in Tarsus, *a city* in **C**, — *2791*
 23:34 when he understood that *he was* of **C**; — *2791*
 27: 5 when we had sailed over the sea of **C** — *2791*
Gal 1:21 I came into the regions of Syria and **C**; — *2791*

CINNAMON (4)

Ex 30:23 and of sweet **c** half so much, — *7076*
Pr 7:17 my bed *with* myrrh, aloes, and **c**. — *7076*
SS 4:14 calamus and **c**, with all trees of — *7076*
Rev 18:13 And **c**, and odours, and ointments, — *2792*

CINNERETH (1) [CINNEROTH]

Jos 13:27 *even* unto the edge of the sea of **C** on — *3672*

CINNEROTH (3) [CINNERETH, CHINNERETH]

Jos 11: 2 of the plains south of **C**, and in the valley, — *3672*
 12: 3 *from* the plain to the sea of **C** on the east, — *3672*
1Ki 15:20 and Abel-beth-maachah, and all **C**, — *3672*

CIRCLE (1)

Isa 40:22 he that sitteth upon the **c** of the earth, — *2329*

CIRCUIT (3) [CIRCUITS]

1Sa 7:16 he went from year to year in **c** *to* Beth-el, — *5437*
Job 22:14 and he walketh *in* the **c** of heaven. — *2329*
Ps 19: 6 the heaven, and his **c** unto the ends of it: — *8622*

CIRCUITS (1) [CIRCUIT]

Ecc 1: 6 wind returneth *again* according to his **c**. — *5439*

CIRCUMCISE (10) [CIRCUMCISED, CIRCUMCISING, CIRCUMCISION, UNCIRCUMCISED]

Ge 17:11 ye shall **c** the flesh of your foreskin; — *5243*
Dt 10:16 **C** therefore the foreskin of your heart, — *4135*
 30: 6 the Lord thy God will **c** thine heart, — *4135*
Jos 5: 2 **c** again the children of Israel the second — *4135*
 5: 4 this *is* the cause why Joshua did **c**: All — *4135*
Jer 4: 4 **C** yourselves to the Lord, and take away — *4135*
Lk 1:59 that on the eighth day they came to **c** — *4059*
Jn 7:22 and ye on the sabbath day **c** a man. — *4059*
Ac 15: 5 That it was needful to **c** them, — *4059*
 21:21 saying that they *ought* not to **c** *their* — *4059*

CIRCUMCISED (39) [CIRCUMCISE]

Ge 17:10 Every man *child* among you shall be **c**. — *4135*
 17:12 he that is eight days old shall be **c** among — *4135*
 17:13 thy money, **must needs be c**: — *4135+4135*
 17:14 *child* whose flesh of his foreskin is not **c**, — *4135*
 17:23 **c** the flesh of their foreskin in the selfsame — *4135*
 17:24 when he was **c** in the flesh of his foreskin. — *4135*
 17:25 when he was **c** in the flesh of his foreskin. — *4135*
 17:26 In the selfsame day was Abraham **c**, — *4135*
 17:27 money of the stranger, were **c** with him. — *4135*
 21: 4 Abraham **c** his son Isaac being eight days — *4135*
 34:15 be as we *be,* that every male of you be **c**; — *4135*
 34:17 if ye will not hearken unto us, to be **c**; — *4135*
 34:22 one people, if every male among us be **c**, — *4135*
 34:22 among us be circumcised, as they *are* **c**. — *4135*
 34:24 every male was **c**, all that went out of — *4135*
Ex 12:44 when thou hast **c** him, then shall he eat — *4135*
 12:48 let all his males be **c**, and then let him — *4135*
Lev 12: 3 day the flesh of his foreskin shall be **c**. — *4135*
Jos 5: 3 **c** the children of Israel at the hill of — *4135*
 5: 5 Now all the people that came out were **c**: — *4135*
 5: 5 forth out of Egypt, *them* they had not **c**. — *4135*
 5: 7 he raised up in their stead, them Joshua **c**: — *4135*
 5: 7 because they had not **c** them by the way. — *4135*
Jer 9:25 I will punish all *them* which *are* **c** with — *4135*
Ac 7: 8 begat Isaac, and **c** him the eighth day; — *4059*
 15: 1 said, Except ye be **c** after the manner of — *4059*
 15:24 saying, Ye must be **c**, and keep the law: — *4059*
 16: 3 and took and **c** him because of the Jews — *4059*
Ro 4:11 them that believe, though they be **not c**; — *203*
1Co 7:18 Is any *man* called being **c**? let him not — *4059*
 7:18 in uncircumcision? let him not be **c**. — *4059*
Gal 2: 3 being a Greek, was compelled to be **c**: — *4059*
 5: 2 I Paul say unto you, that if ye be **c**, — *4059*
 5: 3 For I testify again to every man that is **c**, — *4059*
 6:12 in the flesh, they constrain you to be **c**; — *4059*
 6:13 neither they themselves who are **c** keep — *4059*
 6:13 but desire to have you **c**, that they may — *4059*
Php 3: 5 **C** the eighth day, of the stock of Israel, — *4061*
Col 2:11 In whom also ye are **c** with — *4059*

CIRCUMCISING (2) [CIRCUMCISE]

Jos 5: 8 when they had done **c** all the people, — *4135*
Lk 2:21 were accomplished for the **c** of the child, — *4059*

CIRCUMCISION (36) [CIRCUMCISE]

Ex 4:26 bloody husband *thou art,* because of the **c**. — *4139*
Jn 7:22 Moses therefore gave unto you **c**; — *4061*
 7:23 If a man on the sabbath day receive **c**, — *4061*
Ac 7: 8 And he gave him the covenant of **c**: and — *4061*

Ac 10:45 And they of the **c** which believed were — *4061*
 11: 2 that were of the **c** contended with him, — *4061*
Ro 2:25 **c** verily profiteth, if thou keep the law: — *4061*
 2:25 of the law, thy **c** is made uncircumcision. — *4061*
 2:26 not his uncircumcision be counted for **c**? — *4061*
 2:27 by the letter and **c** dost transgress the law? — *4061*
 2:28 neither *is that* **c**, which is outward in — *4061*
 2:29 and **c** *is that* of the heart, in the spirit, — *4061*
 3: 1 hath the Jew? or what profit *is there* of **c**? — *4061*
 3:30 which shall justify the **c** by faith, — *4061*
 4: 9 this blessedness then upon the **c** *only,* or — *4061*
 4:10 when he was in **c**, or in uncircumcision? — *4061*
 4:10 Not in **c**, but in uncircumcision. — *4061*
 4:11 And he received the sign of **c**, a seal of — *4061*
 4:12 And the father of **c** to them who are not — *4061*
 4:12 to them who are not of the **c** only, — *4061*
 15: 8 a minister of the **c** for the truth of God, — *4061*
1Co 7:19 **C** is nothing, and uncircumcision is — *4061*
Gal 2: 7 as *the gospel* of the **c** was unto Peter; — *4061*
 2: 8 in Peter to the apostleship of the **c**, — *4061*
 2: 9 *go* unto the heathen, and they unto the **c**. — *4061*
 2:12 fearing them which were of the **c**. — *4061*
 5: 6 For in Jesus Christ neither **c** availeth any — *4061*
 5:11 And I, brethren, if I yet preach **c**, why do — *4061*
 6:15 For in Christ Jesus neither **c** availeth any — *4061*
Eph 2:11 is called the **C** in the flesh made by hands; — *4061*
Php 3: 3 For we are the **c**, which worship God in — *4061*
Col 2:11 whom also ye are circumcised with the **c** — *4061*
 2:11 of the sins of the flesh, by the **c** of Christ: — *4061*
 3:11 **c** nor uncircumcision, barbarian, Scythian, — *4061*
 4:11 which is called Justus, who are of the **c**, — *4061*
Tit 1:10 and deceivers, specially they of the **c**: — *4061*

CIRCUMSPECT (1) [CIRCUMSPECTLY]

Ex 23:13 all *things* that I have said unto you be **c**: — *8104*

CIRCUMSPECTLY (1) [CIRCUMSPECT]

Eph 5:15 See then that ye walk **c**, not as fools, — *199*

CIRCUMSTANCES See DEGREE; DEGREES

CIS (1)

Ac 13:21 God gave unto them Saul the son of **C**, — *2797*

CISTERN (4) [CISTERNS]

2Ki 18:31 and drink ye every one the waters of his **c**: — *953*
Pr 5:15 Drink waters out of thine own **c**, — *953*
Ecc 12: 6 the fountain, or the wheel broken at the **c**. — *953*
Isa 36:16 drink ye every one the waters of his own **c**; — *953*

CISTERNS (2) [CISTERN]

Jer 2:13 hewed them out **c**, broken cisterns, that — *953*
 2:13 broken **c**, that can hold no water. — *953*

CITIES (448) [CITY]

Ge 13:12 Lot dwelled in the **c** of the plain, — *5892*
 19:25 he overthrew those **c**, and all the plain, — *5892*
 19:25 all the inhabitants of the **c**, and that — *5892*
 19:29 when God destroyed the **c** of the plain, — *5892*
 19:29 he overthrew the **c** in the which Lot — *5892*
 35: 5 the terror of God was upon the **c** that — *5892*
 41:35 Pharaoh, and let them keep food in the **c**, — *5892*
 41:48 of Egypt, and laid up the food in the **c**: — *5892*
 47:21 he removed them to **c** from *one* end of — *5892*
Ex 1:11 they built for Pharaoh treasure **c**, Pithom — *5892*
Lev 25:32 Notwithstanding the **c** of the Levites, — *5892*
 25:32 the houses of the **c** of their possession, — *5892*
 25:33 for the houses of the **c** of the Levites *are* — *5892*
 25:34 the field of the suburbs of their **c** may not — *5892*
 26:25 ye are gathered together within your **c**, — *5892*
 26:31 I will make your **c** waste, and bring your — *5892*
 26:33 land shall be desolate, and your **c** waste. — *5892*
Nu 13:19 wear *they* be that they dwell in, — *5892*
 13:28 and the **c** *are* walled, *and* very great: — *5892*
 21: 2 hand, then I will utterly destroy their **c**. — *5892*
 21: 3 they utterly destroyed them and their **c**: — *5892*
 21:25 Israel took all these **c**: and Israel dwelt in — *5892*
 21:25 Israel dwelt in all the **c** of the Amorites, — *5892*
 31:10 they burnt all their **c** wherein they dwelt, — *5892*
 32:16 for our cattle, and **c** for our little ones: — *5892*
 32:17 our little ones shall dwell in the fenced **c** — *5892*
 32:24 Build ye **c** for your little ones, and folds — *5892*
 32:26 cattle, shall be there in the **c** of Gilead: — *5892*
 32:33 the land, with the **c** thereof in the coasts, — *5892*
 32:33 *even* the **c** of the country round about. — *5892*
 32:36 and Beth-haran, fenced **c**: — *5892*
 32:38 gave other names unto the **c** which they — *5892*
 35: 2 of their possession **c** to dwell in; — *5892*
 35: 2 suburbs for the **c** round about them. — *5892*
 35: 3 the **c** shall they have to dwell in; — *5892*
 35: 4 the suburbs of the **c**, which ye shall give — *5892*
 35: 5 this shall be to them the suburbs of the **c**. — *5892*
 35: 6 *among* the **c** which ye shall give unto — *5892*
 35: 6 the Levites *there shall be* six **c** for refuge, — *5892*
 35: 6 to them ye shall add forty and two **c**. — *5892*
 35: 7 *So* all the **c** which ye shall give to — *5892*
 35: 7 to the Levites *shall be* forty and eight **c**: — *5892*
 35: 8 the **c** which ye shall give *shall be* of — *5892*
 35: 8 every one shall give of his **c** unto — *5892*
 35:11 shall appoint you **c** to be cities of refuge — *5892*
 35:11 shall appoint you cities to be **c** of refuge — *5892*
 35:12 they shall be unto you **c** for refuge from — *5892*
 35:13 *of these* **c** which ye shall give six cities — *5892*
 35:13 *of these* cities which ye shall give six **c** — *5892*
 35:14 Ye shall give three **c** on *this* side Jordan, — *5892*
 35:14 **c** shall ye give in the land of Canaan, — *5892*

C

Nu	35:14 of Canaan, *which* shall be **c** of refuge.	5892
	35:15 These six **c** shall be a refuge, *both* for	5892
Dt	1:22 go up, and into what **c** we shall come.	5892
	1:28 the **c** *are* great and walled up to heaven;	5892
	2:34 we took all his **c** at that time,	5892
	2:35 and the spoil of the **c** which we took.	5892
	2:37 nor *unto* the **c** in the mountains,	5892
	3: 4 we took all his **c** at that time, there was	5892
	3: 4 threescore **c**, all the region of Argob,	5892
	3: 5 All these **c** *were* fenced *with* high walls,	5892
	3: 7 the cattle, and the spoil of the **c**, we took	5892
	3:10 All the **c** of the plain, and all Gilead,	5892
	3:10 Edrei, **c** of the kingdom of Og in Bashan.	5892
	3:12 half mount Gilead, and the **c** thereof, gave	5892
	3:19 shall abide in your **c** which I have given	5892
	4:41 Moses severed three **c** on *this* side Jordan	5892
	4:42 that fleeing unto one of these **c** he might	5892
	6:10 to Jacob, to give thee great and goodly **c**,	5892
	9: 1 **c** great and fenced up to heaven,	5892
	13:12 If thou shalt hear *say* in one of thy **c**,	5892
	19: 1 dwellest in their **c**, and in their houses;	5892
	19: 2 Thou shalt separate three **c** for thee in	5892
	19: 5 he shall flee unto one of those **c**, and live:	5892
	19: 7 Thou shalt separate three **c** for thee.	5892
	19: 9 shalt thou add three **c** moe for thee,	5892
	19:11 that he die, and fleeth into one of these **c**,	5892
	20:15 Thus shalt thou do unto all the **c** *which*	5892
	20:15 which *are* not of the **c** of these nations.	5892
	20:16 of the **c** of these people, which the LORD	5892
	21: 2 they shall measure unto the **c** which *are*	5892
Jos	9:17 and came unto their **c** on the third day.	5892
	9:17 their **c** *were* Gibeon, and Chephirah,	5892
	10: 2 as one of the royal **c**, and because it *was*	5892
	10:19 suffer them not to enter into their **c**:	5892
	10:20 remained of them entered into fenced **c**.	5892
	10:37 all the **c** thereof, and all the souls that	5892
	10:39 and the king thereof, and all the **c** thereof;	5892
	11:12 all the **c** of those kings, and all the kings	5892
	11:13 *for* the **c** that stood still in their strength,	5892
	11:14 the spoil of these **c**, and the cattle,	5892
	11:21 destroyed them utterly with their **c**.	5892
	13:10 all the **c** of Sihon king of the Amorites,	5892
	13:17 and all her **c** that *are* in the plain;	5892
	13:21 all the **c** of the plain, and all the kingdom	5892
	13:23 their families, the **c** and villages thereof.	5892
	13:25 all the **c** of Gilead, and half the land of	5892
	13:28 their families, the **c**, and their villages.	5892
	13:30 of Jair, which *are* in Bashan, threescore **c**:	5892
	13:31 Edrei, **c** of the kingdom of Og in Bashan,	5892
	14: 4 save **c** to dwell *in*, with their suburbs for	5892
	14:12 and *that* the **c** *were* great *and* fenced:	5892
	15: 9 and went out to the **c** of mount Ephron;	5892
	15:21 the uttermost **c** of the tribe of the children	5892
	15:32 all the **c** *are* twenty and nine, with their	5892
	15:36 fourteen **c** with their villages.	5892
	15:41 Makkedah; sixteen **c** with their villages.	5892
	15:44 and Mareshah; nine **c** with their villages.	5892
	15:51 and Giloh; eleven **c** with their villages.	5892
	15:54 and Zior; nine **c** with their villages.	5892
	15:57 and Timnah; ten **c** with their villages.	5892
	15:59 and Eltekon; six **c** with their villages.	5892
	15:60 and Rabbah; two **c** with their villages.	5892
	15:62 and En-gedi; six **c** with their villages.	5892
	16: 9 the separate **c** for the children of Ephraim	5892
	16: 9 of Manasseh, all the **c** with their villages.	5892
	17: 9 these **c** of Ephraim *are* among the cities	5892
	17: 9 cities of Ephraim *are* among the **c** of	5892
	17:12 not drive out the inhabitants *of* those **c**;	5892
	18: 9 described it by **c** into seven parts in a	5892
	18:21 Now the **c** of the tribe of the children of	5892
	18:24 and Gaba; twelve **c** with their villages.	5892
	18:28 *and* Kirjath; fourteen **c** with their villages.	5892
	19: 6 Sharuhen; thirteen **c** and their villages:	5892
	19: 7 and Ashan; four **c** and their villages:	5892
	19: 8 *were* round about these **c** to Baalath-beer,	5892
	19:15 Beth-lehem: twelve **c** with their villages.	5892
	19:16 their families, these **c** with their villages.	5892
	19:22 *at* Jordan: sixteen **c** with their villages.	5892
	19:23 to their families, the **c** and their villages.	5892
	19:30 twenty and two **c** with their villages.	5892
	19:31 their families, these **c** with their villages.	5892
	19:35 the fenced **c** *are* Ziddim, Zer,	5892
	19:38 nineteen **c** with their villages.	5892
	19:39 to their families, the **c** and their villages.	5892
	19:48 their families, these **c** with their villages.	5892
	20: 2 Appoint out for you **c** of refuge,	5892
	20: 4 he that doth flee unto one of those **c**	5892
	20: 9 These were the **c** appointed for all	5892
	21: 2 hand of Moses to give us **c** to dwell in,	5892
	21: 3 of the LORD, these **c** and their suburbs.	5892
	21: 4 out of the tribe of Benjamin, thirteen **c**.	5892
	21: 5 out of the half tribe of Manasseh, ten **c**.	5892
	21: 6 tribe of Manasseh in Bashan, thirteen **c**.	5892
	21: 7 and out of the tribe of Zebulun, twelve **c**.	5892
	21: 8 The Levites these **c** with their suburbs,	5892
	21: 9 **c** which *are* here mentioned by name,	5892
	21:16 suburbs; nine **c** out of those two tribes.	5892
	21:18 and Almon with her suburbs; four **c**.	5892
	21:19 All the **c** of the children of Aaron,	5892
	21:19 *were* thirteen **c** with their suburbs.	5892
	21:20 even they had the **c** of their lot out of	5892
	21:22 and Beth-horon with her suburbs; four **c**.	5892
	21:24 Gath-rimmon with her suburbs; four **c**.	5892
	21:25 Gath-rimmon with her suburbs; two **c**.	5892
	21:26 All the **c** *were* ten with their suburbs for	5892

Jos	21:27 and Beeshterah with her suburbs; two **c**.	5892
	21:29 En-gannim with her suburbs; four **c**.	5892
	21:31 and Rehob with her suburbs; four **c**.	5892
	21:32 and Kartan with her suburbs; three **c**.	5892
	21:33 All the **c** of the Gershonites according to	5892
	21:33 *were* thirteen **c** with their suburbs.	5892
	21:35 Nahalal with her suburbs; four **c**.	5892
	21:37 and Mephaath with her suburbs; four **c**.	5892
	21:39 Jazer with her suburbs; four **c** in all.	5892
	21:40 So all the **c** for the children of Merari by	5892
	21:40 of the Levites, were *by* their lot twelve **c**.	5892
	21:41 All the **c** of the Levites within	5892
	21:41 *were* forty and eight **c** with their suburbs.	5892
	21:42 These **c** were *every one* with their	5892+5892
	21:42 round about them: thus *were* all these **c**.	5892
	24:13 **c** which ye built not, and ye dwell in	5892
Jdg	10: 4 they had thirty **c**, which are called	5892
	11:26 in all the **c** that *be* along by the coasts of	5892
	11:33 *even* twenty **c**, and unto the plain of	5892
	12: 7 and was buried in *one of* the **c** of Gilead.	5892
	20:14 together out of the **c** unto Gibeah,	5892
	20:15 numbered at that time out of the **c** twenty	5892
	20:42 them which came out of the **c** they	5892
	20:48 they set on fire all the **c** that they came	5892
	21:23 and repaired the **c**, and dwelt in them.	5892
1Sa	6:18 *according to* the number of all the **c** of	5892
	6:18 *both* of fenced **c**, and of country villages,	5892
	7:14 the **c** which the Philistines had taken	5892
	18: 6 the women came out of all **c** of Israel,	5892
	30:29 to *them* which *were* in the **c** of	5892
	30:29 *them* which *were* in the **c** of the Kenites,	5892
	31: 7 were dead, they forsook the **c**, and fled;	5892
2Sa	2: 1 Shall I go up into any of the **c** of Judah?	5892
	2: 3 and they dwelt in the **c** of Hebron.	5892
	8: 8 and from Berothai, **c** of Hadadezer,	5892
	10:12 for our people, and for the **c** of our God:	5892
	12:31 thus did he unto all the **c** of the children	5892
	20: 6 lest he get him fenced **c**, and escape us.	5892
	24: 7 to all the **c** of the Hivites, and of	5892
1Ki	4:13 threescore great **c** with walls and	5892
	8:37 enemy besiege them in the land of their **c**;	8179
	9:11 king Solomon gave Hiram twenty **c** in	5892
	9:12 Hiram came out from Tyre to see the **c**	5892
	9:13 What *are* these which thou hast given	5892
	9:19 all the **c** of store that Solomon had,	5892
	9:19 **c** for his chariots, and cities for his	5892
	9:19 **c** for his horsemen, and that which	5892
	10:26 whom he bestowed in the **c** for chariots,	5892
	12:17 of Israel which dwelt in the **c** of Judah,	5892
	13:32 high places which *are* in the **c** of Samaria,	5892
	15:20 hosts which he had against the **c** of Israel,	5892
	15:23 all that he did, and the **c** which he built,	5892
	20:34 *Ben-hadad* said unto him, The **c**, which	5892
	22:39 he made, and all the **c** that he built,	5892
2Ki	3:25 they beat down the **c**, and *on* every good	5892
	13:25 of Ben-hadad the son of Hazael the **c**,	5892
	13:25 beat him, and recovered the **c** of Israel.	5892
	17: 6 river of Gozan, and in the **c** of the Medes.	5892
	17: 9 they built them high places in all their **c**,	5892
	17:24 placed *them* in the **c** of Samaria instead of	5892
	17:24 and dwelt in the **c** thereof.	5892
	17:26 and placed in the **c** of Samaria,	5892
	17:29 nation in their **c** wherein they dwelt.	5892
	18:11 of Gozan, and in the **c** of the Medes:	5892
	18:13 come up against all the fenced **c** of Judah,	5892
	19:25 thou shouldest be to lay waste fenced **c**	5892
	23: 5 in the high places in the **c** of Judah,	5892
	23: 8 he brought all the priests out of the **c** of	5892
	23:19 high places that *were* in the **c** of Samaria,	5892
1Ch	2:22 and twenty **c** in the land of Gilead.	5892
	2:23 the towns thereof, *even* threescore **c**.	5892
	4:31 *were* their **c** unto the reign of David.	5892
	4:32 Rimmon, and Tochen, and Ashan, five **c**:	5892
	4:33 villages that *were* round about the same **c**,	5892
	6:57 to the sons of Aaron they gave the **c** of	5892
	6:60 All their **c** throughout their families *were*	5892
	6:60 throughout their families *were* thirteen **c**.	5892
	6:61 *were* **c** given out of the half tribe,	NIH
	6:61 *of* the half *tribe* of Manasseh, by lot, ten **c**.	5892
	6:62 tribe of Manasseh in Bashan, thirteen **c**.	5892
	6:63 and out of the tribe of Zebulun, twelve **c**.	5892
	6:64 to the Levites *these* **c** with their suburbs.	5892
	6:65 these **c**, which are called by *their* names.	5892
	6:66 **c** of their coasts out of the tribe of	5892
	6:67 they gave unto them, *of* the **c** of refuge,	5892
	9: 2 possessions in their **c** *were*, the Israelites,	5892
	10: 7 then they forsook their **c**, and fled:	5892
	13: 2 Levites *which are* in their **c** *and* suburbs,	5892
	18: 8 and from Chun, **c** of Hadarezer,	5892
	19: 7 gathered themselves together from their **c**,	5892
	19:13 for our people, and for the **c** of our God:	5892
	20: 3 dealt David with all the **c** of the children	5892
	27:25 in the **c**, and in the villages, and in	5892
2Ch	1:14 which he placed in the chariot **c**,	5892
	6:28 if their enemies besiege them in the **c** of	8179
	8: 2 That the **c** which Huram had restored to	5892
	8: 4 all the store **c**, which he built in Hamath.	5892
	8: 5 fenced **c**, *with* walls, gates, and bars;	5892
	8: 6 all the store **c** that Solomon had, and all	5892
	8: 6 all the chariot **c**, and the cities of	5892
	8: 6 **c** of the horsemen, and all that Solomon	5892
	9:25 whom he bestowed in the chariot **c**,	5892
	10:17 of Israel that dwelt in the **c** of Judah,	5892
	11: 5 and built **c** for defence in Judah.	5892
	11:10 *are* in Judah and in Benjamin, fenced **c**.	5892

2Ch	12: 4 he took the fenced **c** which *pertained* to	5892
	13:19 took **c** from him, Beth-el with the towns	5892
	14: 5 he took away out of all the **c** of Judah	5892
	14: 6 he built fenced **c** in Judah: for the land	5892
	14: 7 Let us build these **c**, and make about	5892
	14:14 they smote all the **c** round about Gerar;	5892
	14:14 they spoiled all the **c**; for there was	5892
	15: 8 of the **c** which he had taken from mount	5892
	16: 4 the captains of his armies against the **c**	5892
	16: 4 and all the store of Naphtali.	5892
	17: 2 he placed forces in all the fenced **c** of	5892
	17: 2 in the **c** of Ephraim, which Asa his father	5892
	17: 7 to Michaiah, to teach in the **c** of Judah.	5892
	17: 9 went about throughout all the **c** of Judah,	5892
	17:12 he built in Judah castles, and **c** of store.	5892
	17:13 he had much business in the **c** of Judah.	5892
	17:19 put in the fenced **c** throughout all Judah.	5892
	19: 5 land throughout all the fenced **c** of Judah,	5892
	19:10 you of your brethren that dwell in their **c**,	5892
	20: 4 out of all the **c** of Judah they came to	5892
	21: 3 precious things, with fenced **c** in Judah:	5892
	23: 2 gathered the Levites out of all the **c** of	5892
	24: 5 Go out unto the **c** of Judah, and gather of	5892
	25:13 fell upon the **c** of Judah, from Samaria	5892
	26: 6 built **c** about Ashdod, and among	5892
	27: 4 Moreover he built **c** in the mountains of	5892
	28:18 The Philistines also had invaded the **c** of	5892
	31: 1 Israel that were present went out to the **c**	5892
	31: 1 man to his possession, into their own **c**.	5892
	31: 6 and Judah, that dwelt in the **c** of Judah,	5892
	31:15 and Shecaniah, in the **c** of the priests,	5892
	31:19 in the fields of the suburbs of their **c**,	5892
	32: 1 encamped against the fenced **c**,	5892
	32:29 Moreover he provided him **c**,	5892
	33:14 put captains of war in all the fenced **c** of	5892
	34: 6 so did he in the **c** of Manasseh,	5892
Ezr	2:70 in their **c**, and all Israel in their cities.	5892
	2:70 in their cities, and all Israel in their **c**.	5892
	3: 1 and the children of Israel *were* in the **c**,	5892
	4:10 set in the **c** of Samaria, and the rest *that*	7149
	10:14 wives in our **c** come at appointed times,	5892
Ne	7:73 and all Israel, dwelt in their **c**;	5892
	7:73 the children of Israel *were* in their **c**.	5892
	8:15 should publish and proclaim in all their **c**,	5892
	9:25 they took strong **c**, and a fat land,	5892
	10:37 have the tithes in all the **c** of our tillage.	5892
	11: 1 and nine parts to dwell in *other* **c**.	5892
	11: 3 in the **c** of Judah dwelt every one in his	5892
	11: 3 every one in his possession in their **c**,	5892
	11:20 *and* the Levites, *were* in all the **c** of Judah,	5892
	12:44 gather into them out of the fields of the **c**	5892
Est	9: 2 throughout all the provinces of the king	5892
Job	15:28 he dwelleth in desolate **c**, *and* in houses	5892
Ps	9: 6 thou hast destroyed; their memorial is	5892
	69:35 save Zion, and will build the **c** of Judah:	5892
Isa	1: 7 *is* desolate, your **c** *are* burnt with fire:	5892
	6:11 Until the **c** be wasted without inhabitant,	5892
	14:17 a wilderness, and destroyed the **c** thereof;	5892
	14:21 nor fill the face of the world *with* **c**.	5892
	17: 2 The **c** of Aroer *are* forsaken: they shall be	5892
	19: 2 In that day shall his strong **c** be as a	5892
	19:18 In that day shall five **c** in the land of Egypt	5892
	33: 8 he hath despised the **c**, he regardeth no	5892
	36: 1 up against all the defenced **c** of Judah,	5892
	37:26 lay waste defenced **c** *into* ruinous heaps.	5892
	40: 9 say unto the **c** of Judah, Behold your God.	5892
	42:11 the **c** thereof lift up *their* voice,	5892
	44:26 to the **c** of Judah, Ye shall be built,	5892
	54: 3 and make the desolate **c** to be inhabited.	5892
	61: 4 they shall repair the waste **c**,	5892
	64:10 Thy holy **c** are a wilderness, Zion is a	5892
Jer	1:15 about, and against all the **c** of Judah.	5892
	2:15 his **c** are burnt without inhabitant.	5892
	2:28 for *according* to the number of thy **c** are	5892
	4: 5 and let us go into the defenced **c**.	5892
	4: 7 *and* thy **c** shall be laid waste, without an	5892
	4:16 give out their voice against the **c** of Judah,	5892
	4:26 all the **c** thereof were broken down at	5892
	5: 6 a leopard shall watch over their **c**:	5892
	5:17 they shall impoverish thy fenced **c**,	5892
	7:17 Seest thou not what they do in the **c** of	5892
	7:34 will I cause to cease from the **c** of Judah,	5892
	8:14 let us enter into the defenced **c**, and let us	5892
	9:11 I will make the **c** of Judah desolate,	5892
	10:22 make the **c** of Judah desolate, *and* a den	5892
	11: 6 Proclaim all these words in the **c** of Judah	5892
	11:12 shall the **c** of Judah and inhabitants of	5892
	11:13 *according* to the number of thy **c** were	5892
	13:19 The **c** of the south shall be shut up,	5892
	17:26 they shall come from the **c** of Judah,	5892
	20:16 let that man be as the **c** which the LORD	5892
	22: 6 wilderness *and* **c** which are not inhabited.	5892
	25:18 the **c** of Judah, and the kings thereof,	5892
	26: 2 and speak unto all the **c** of Judah,	5892
	31:21 virgin of Israel, turn again to these thy **c**,	5892
	31:23 in the land of Judah and in the **c** thereof,	5892
	31:24 *in* all the **c** thereof together, husbandmen,	5892
	32:44 in the **c** of Judah, and in the cities of	5892
	32:44 in the **c** of the mountains, and in the	5892
	32:44 in the **c** of the valley, and in the cities of	5892
	32:44 of the valley, and in the **c** of the south:	5892
	33:10 *even* in the **c** of Judah, and in the streets	5892
	33:12 without beast, and in all the **c** thereof,	5892
	33:13 In the **c** of the mountains, in the cities of	5892
	33:13 in the **c** of the vale, and in the cities of	5892

C

Jer	33:13 in the **c** of the south, and in the land of	5892
	33:13 about Jerusalem, and in the **c** of Judah,	5892
	34: 1 and against all the **c** thereof, saying,	5892
	34: 7 against all the **c** of Judah that were left,	5892
	34: 7 these defenced **c** remained of the cities	5892
	34: 7 these defenced cities remained of the **c**	5892
	34:22 I will make the **c** of Judah a desolation	5892
	36: 6 ears of all Judah that come out of their **c**.	5892
	36: 9 *to* all the people that came from the **c** of	5892
	40: 5 hath made governor over the **c** of Judah,	5892
	40:10 and dwell in your **c** that ye have taken.	5892
	44: 2 and upon all the **c** of Judah;	5892
	44: 6 was kindled in the **c** of Judah and in	5892
	44:17 in the **c** of Judah, and in the streets of	5892
	44:21 incense that ye burnt in the **c** of Judah,	5892
	48: 9 for the **c** thereof shall be desolate, without	5892
	48:15 gone up *out of* her **c**, and his chosen	5892
	48:24 upon all the **c** of the land of Moab, far or	5892
	48:28 leave the **c**, and dwell in the rock,	5892
	49: 1 inherit Gad, and his people dwell in his **c**?	5892
	49:13 all the **c** thereof shall be perpetual wastes.	5892
	49:18 Gomorrah and the neighbour **c** thereof,	NIH
	50:32 I will kindle a fire in his **c**, and it shall	5892
	50:40 Gomorrah and the neighbour **c** thereof,	NIH
	51:43 Her **c** are a desolation, a dry land,	5892
La	5:11 in Zion, *and* the maids in the **c** of Judah.	5892
Eze	6: 6 In all your dwelling places the **c** shall be	5892
	12:20 **c** that are inhabited shall be laid waste,	5892
	19: 7 palaces, and he laid waste their **c**;	5892
	25: 9 I *will* open the side of Moab from the **c**,	5892
	25: 9 from his **c** *which are* in his frontiers,	5892
	26:19 like the **c** that are not inhabited;	5892
	29:12 her **c** among the cities *that are* laid waste	5892
	29:12 her cities among the **c** *that are* laid waste	5892
	30: 7 her **c** shall be in the midst of the cities	5892
	30: 7 her cities shall be in the midst of the **c**	5892
	30:17 and these **c** shall go into captivity.	NIH
	35: 4 I will lay thy **c** waste, and thou shalt be	5892
	35: 9 and thy **c** shall not return:	5892
	36: 4 to the **c** that are forsaken, which became	5892
	36:10 the **c** shall be inhabited, and the wastes	5892
	36:33 I will also cause *you* to dwell in the **c**,	5892
	36:35 and ruined **c** *are become* fenced,	5892
	36:38 shall the waste **c** be filled *with* flocks of	5892
	39: 9 they that dwell in the **c** of Israel shall go	5892
Da	11:15 up a mount, and take the most fenced **c**:	5892
Hos	8:14 and Judah hath multiplied fenced **c**:	5892
	8:14 I will send a fire upon his **c**, and it shall	5892
	11: 6 the sword shall abide on his **c**,	5892
	13:10 *any other* that may save thee in all thy **c**?	5892
Am	4: 6 given you cleanness of teeth in all your **c**,	5892
	4: 8 two *or* three **c** wandered unto one city,	5892
	9:14 they shall build the waste **c**,	5892
Ob	1:20 shall possess the **c** of the south.	5892
Mic	5:11 I will cut off the **c** of thy land,	5892
	5:14 the midst of thee: so will I destroy thy **c**.	5892
	7:12 *from* the fortified **c**, and from the fortress	5892
Zep	1:16 trumpet and alarm against the fenced **c**,	5892
	3: 6 their **c** are destroyed, so that there is no	5892
Zec	1:12 mercy on Jerusalem and on the **c** of Judah,	5892
	1:17 My **c** through prosperity shall yet be	5892
	7: 7 and the **c** thereof round about her,	5892
	8:20 and the inhabitants of many **c**:	5892
Mt	9:35 Jesus went about all the **c** and villages,	4172
	10:23 shall not have gone over the **c** of Israel,	4172
	11: 1 thence to teach and to preach in their **c**.	4172
	11:20 Then began he to upbraid the **c** wherein	4172
	14:13 they followed him on foot out of the **c**.	4172
Mk	6:33 and ran afoot thither out of all **c**,	4172
	6:56 he entered, into villages, or **c**, or country,	4172
Lk	4:43 preach the kingdom of God to other **c**	4172
	13:22 And he went through the **c** and villages,	4172
	19:17 very little, have thou authority over ten **c**	4172
	19:19 likewise to him, Be thou also over five **c**.	4172
Ac	5:16 There came also a multitude *out of* the **c**	4172
	8:40 passing through he preached in all the **c**,	4172
	14: 6 of Lycaonia, and, *unto* the region that	4172
	16: 4 And as they went through the **c**,	4172
	26:11 I persecuted *them* even unto strange **c**.	4172
2Pe	2: 6 And turning the **c** of Sodom and	4172
Jude	1: 7 and Gomorrha, and the **c** about them,	4172
Rev	16:19 three parts, and the **c** of the nations fell:	4172

CITIZEN (2) [CITIZENS, FELLOWCITIZENS]

Lk	15:15 and joined himself to a **c** of that country;	4177
Ac	21:39 a city in Cilicia, a **c** of no mean city:	4177

CITIZENS (1) [CITIZEN]

Lk	19:14 But his **c** hated him, and sent a message	4177

CITIZENSHIP See COMMONWEALTH

CITRON See THYINE

CITY (870) [CITIES]

Ge	4:17 he builded a **c**, and called the name of	5892
	4:17 a city, and called the name of the **c**,	5892
	10:11 and the **c** Rehoboth, and Calah,	5892
	10:12 and Calah: the same *is* a great **c**.	5892
	11: 4 Go to, let us build us a **c** and a tower,	5892
	11: 5 the Lord came down to see the **c** and	5892
	11: 8 the earth: and they left off to build the **c**.	5892
	18:24 there be fifty righteous within the **c**:	5892
	18:26 find in Sodom fifty righteous within the **c**,	5892
	18:28 wilt thou destroy all the **c** for *lack of* five?	5892
	19: 4 the men of the **c**, *even* the men of Sodom,	5892

Ge	19:12 and whatsoever thou hast in the **c**,	5892
	19:14 for the Lord will destroy this **c**.	5892
	19:15 thou be consumed in the iniquity of the **c**.	5892
	19:16 him forth, and set him without the **c**.	5892
	19:20 this **c** *is* near to flee unto, and it *is* a little	5892
	19:21 that I will not overthrow *this* **c**,	5892
	19:22 Therefore the name of the **c** was called	5892
	23:10 *even* of all that went in *at* the gate of his **c**,	5892
	23:18 before all that went in *at* the gate of his **c**.	5892
	24:10 to Mesopotamia, unto the **c** of Nahor.	5892
	24:11 **c** by a well of water at the time	5892
	24:13 daughters of the men of the **c** come out	5892
	26:33 the name of the **c** *is* Beer-sheba unto this	5892
	28:19 the name of that **c** was called Luz at	5892
	33:18 Jacob came to Shalem, a **c** of Shechem,	5892
	33:18 and pitched his tent before the **c**.	5892
	34:20 his son came unto the gate of their **c**,	5892
	34:20 commune with the men of their **c**,	5892
	34:24 all that went out of the gate of his **c**;	5892
	34:24 all that went out of the gate of his **c**.	5892
	34:25 came upon the **c** boldly, and slew all	5892
	34:27 spoiled the **c**, because they had defiled	5892
	34:28 that which *was* in the **c**, and that which	5892
	35:27 unto the **c** of Arbah, which *is* Hebron,	7151
	36:32 and the name of his **c** *was* Dinhabah.	5892
	36:35 stead: and the name of his **c** *was* Avith.	5892
	36:39 the name of his **c** *was* Pau; and his wife's	5892
	41:48 the field, which *was* round about every **c**,	5892
	44: 4 And when they were gone out of the **c**,	5892
	44:13 every man his ass, and returned to the **c**.	5892
Ex	9:29 As soon as I am gone out of the **c**,	5892
	9:33 Moses went out of the **c** from Pharaoh,	5892
Lev	14:40 them into an unclean place without the **c**:	5892
	14:41 off without the **c** into an unclean place:	5892
	14:45 he shall carry *them* forth out of the **c** into	5892
	14:53 he shall let go the living bird out of the **c**	5892
	25:29 a man sell a dwelling house in a walled **c**,	5892
	25:30 the house that *is* in the walled **c** shall	5892
	25:33 that was sold, and the **c** of his possession,	5892
Nu	20:16 a **c** in the uttermost of thy border:	5892
	21:26 Heshbon *was* the **c** of Sihon the king of	5892
	21:27 let the **c** of Sihon be built and prepared:	5892
	21:28 of Heshbon, a flame from the **c** of Sihon:	7151
	22:36 went out to meet him unto a **c** of Moab,	5892
	24:19 shall destroy him that remaineth of the **c**.	5892
	35: 4 shall reach from the wall of the **c** and	5892
	35: 5 ye shall measure from without the **c** on	5892
	35: 5 and the **c** *shall be* in the midst:	5892
	35:25 congregation shall restore him to the **c**	5892
	35:26 *without* the border of the **c** of his refuge,	5892
	35:27 without the borders of the **c** of his refuge,	5892
	35:28 Because he should have remained in the **c**	5892
	35:32 for him that is fled to the **c** of his refuge,	5892
Dt	2:34 women, and the little ones, of every **c**,	5892
	2:36 *from* the **c** that *is* by the river, even unto	5892
	2:36 there was not one **c** too strong for us:	7151
	3: 4 there was not a **c** which we took not from	7151
	3: 6 the men, women, and children, of every **c**.	5892
	13:13 have withdrawn the inhabitants of their **c**,	5892
	13:15 of that **c** with the edge of the sword,	5892
	13:16 burn with fire the **c**, and all the spoil	5892
	19:12 elders of his **c** shall send and fetch him	5892
	20:10 When thou comest nigh unto a **c** to fight	5892
	20:14 and the cattle, and all that is in the **c**,	5892
	20:19 When thou shalt besiege a **c** a long time,	5892
	20:20 shalt build bulwarks against the **c** that	5892
	21: 3 the **c** *which* is next unto the slain *man*,	5892
	21: 3 the elders of that **c** shall take a heifer,	5892
	21: 4 the elders of that **c** shall bring down	5892
	21: 6 all the elders of that **c**, *that are* next unto	5892
	21:19 bring him out unto the elders of his **c**,	5892
	21:20 they shall say unto the elders of his **c**,	5892
	21:21 all the men of his **c** shall stone him with	5892
	22:15 unto the elders of the **c** in the gate:	5892
	22:17 spread the cloth before the elders of the **c**.	5892
	22:18 the elders of that **c** shall take *that* man	5892
	22:21 men of her **c** shall stone her with stones	5892
	22:23 a man find her in the **c**, and lie with her;	5892
	22:24 them both out unto the gate of that **c**,	5892
	22:24 because she cried not, *being* in the **c**;	5892
	25: 8 the elders of his **c** shall call him,	5892
	28: 3 Blessed *shalt* thou *be* in the **c**,	5892
	28:16 Cursed *shalt* thou *be* in the **c**,	5892
	34: 3 of Jericho, the **c** of palm trees, unto Zoar.	5892
Jos	3:16 from the **c** Adam, that *is* beside Zaretan:	5892
	6: 3 ye shall compass the **c**, all *ye* men of war,	5892
	6: 3 of war, *and* go round about the **c** once.	5892
	6: 4 the seventh day ye shall compass the **c**	5892
	6: 5 the wall of the **c** shall fall down flat,	5892
	6: 7 compass the **c**, and let him that is armed	5892
	6:11 So the ark of the Lord compassed the **c**,	5892
	6:14 second day they compassed the **c** once,	5892
	6:15 compassed the **c** after the same manner	5892
	6:15 only on that day they compassed the **c**	5892
	6:16 Shout; for the Lord hath given you the **c**.	5892
	6:17 the **c** shall be accursed, *even* it, and all	5892
	6:20 so that the people went up into the **c**,	5892
	6:20 straight before him, and they took the **c**.	5892
	6:21 utterly destroyed all that *was* in the **c**,	5892
	6:24 they burnt the **c** with fire, and all that	5892
	6:26 that riseth up and buildeth this **c** Jericho:	5892
	8: 1 his people, and his **c**, and his land:	5892
	8: 2 lay thee an ambush for the **c** behind it.	5892
	8: 4 Behold, ye shall lie in wait against the **c**,	5892
	8: 4 wait against the city, *even* behind the **c**:	5892

Jos	8: 4 go not very far from the **c**, but be ye all	5892
	8: 5 *are* with me, will approach unto the **c**:	5892
	8: 6 till we have drawn them from the **c**;	5892
	8: 7 from the ambush, and seize upon the **c**:	5892
	8: 8 it shall be, when ye have taken the **c**,	5892
	8: 8 the city, *that* ye shall set the **c** on fire:	5892
	8:11 before the **c**, and pitched on the north	5892
	8:12 and Ai, on the west side of the **c**.	5892
	8:13 the host that *was* on the north of the **c**,	5892
	8:13 their liers in wait on the west of the **c**,	5892
	8:14 the men of the **c** went out against Israel to	5892
	8:14 liers in ambush against him behind the **c**.	5892
	8:16 and were drawn away from the **c**.	5892
	8:17 they left the **c** open, and pursued after	5892
	8:18 that *he* had in his hand toward the **c**.	5892
	8:19 they entered *into* the **c**, and took it,	5892
	8:19 took it, and hasted and set the **c** on fire.	5892
	8:20 smoke of the **c** ascended up to heaven,	5892
	8:21 saw that the ambush had taken the **c**,	5892
	8:21 that the smoke of the **c** ascended, then	5892
	8:22 other issued out of the **c** against them;	5892
	8:27 the spoil of that **c** Israel took for a prey	5892
	8:29 cast it at the entering of the gate of the **c**,	5892
	10: 2 because Gibeon *was* a great **c**,	5892
	11:19 There was not a **c** that made peace with	5892
	13: 9 the **c** that *is* in the midst of the river,	5892
	13:16 the **c** that *is* in the midst of the river,	5892
	15:13 *even* the **c** of Arba the father of Anak,	7151
	15:13 the father of Anak, which **c** is Hebron.	NIH
	15:62 and the **c** of salt, and En-gedi;	5892
	18:14 a **c** of the children of Judah:	5892
	19:29 to Ramah, and to the strong **c** Tyre;	5892
	19:50 they gave him the **c** which he asked,	5892
	19:50 and he built the **c**, and dwelt therein.	5892
	20: 4 stand *at* the entering of the gate of the **c**,	5892
	20: 4 cause in the ears of the elders of that **c**,	5892
	20: 4 they shall take him into the **c** unto them,	5892
	20: 6 he shall dwell in that **c**, until he stand	5892
	20: 6 come unto his own **c**, and unto his own	5892
	20: 6 house, unto the **c** from whence he fled.	5892
	21:11 they gave them the **c** of Arbah the father	7151
	21:11 which **c** is Hebron, in the hill *country* of	NIH
	21:12 fields of the **c**, and the villages thereof,	5892
	21:13 to be a **c** of refuge for the slayer;	5892
	21:21 to be a **c** of refuge for the slayer;	5892
	21:27 to be a **c** of refuge for the slayer;	5892
	21:32 to be a **c** of refuge for the slayer;	5892
	21:38 to be a **c** of refuge for the slayer;	5892
Jdg	1: 8 edge of the sword, and set the **c** on fire.	5892
	1:16 went up out of the **c** of palm trees with	5892
	1:17 the name of the **c** was called Hormah.	5892
	1:23 (Now the name of the **c** before *was* Luz.)	5892
	1:24 spies saw a man come forth out of the **c**,	5892
	1:24 the entrance into the **c**, and we will shew	5892
	1:25 they shewed them the entrance into the **c**,	5892
	1:25 they smote the **c** with the edge of	5892
	1:26 built a **c**, and called the name thereof Luz:	5892
	3:13 and possessed the **c** of palm trees.	5892
	6:27 the men of the **c**, that *he* could not do *it*	5892
	6:28 when the men of the **c** arose early in	5892
	6:30 the men of the **c** said unto Joash, Bring	5892
	8:16 he took the elders of the **c**, and thorns of	5892
	8:17 of Penuel, and slew the men of the **c**.	5892
	8:27 and put it in his **c**, *even* in Ophrah:	5892
	9:30 when Zebul the ruler of the **c** heard	5892
	9:31 and behold, they fortify the **c** against thee.	5892
	9:33 thou shalt rise early, and set upon the **c**:	5892
	9:35 stood in the entering of the gate of the **c**:	5892
	9:43 the people *were* come forth out of the **c**;	5892
	9:44 stood *in* the entering of the gate of the **c**:	5892
	9:45 Abimelech fought against the **c** all that	5892
	9:45 he took the **c**, and slew the people that	5892
	9:45 beat down the **c**, and sowed it *with* salt.	5892
	9:51 there was a strong tower within the **c**,	5892
	9:51 all they of the **c**, and shut *it* to them,	5892
	14:18 the men of the **c** said unto him on	5892
	16: 2 wait for him all night in the gate of the **c**,	5892
	16: 3 took the doors of the gate of the **c**,	5892
	17: 8 the man departed out of the **c** from	5892
	18:27 of the sword, and burnt the **c** with fire.	5892
	18:28 And they built a **c**, and dwelt therein,	5892
	18:29 they called the name of the **c** Dan, after	5892
	18:29 howbeit the name of the **c** was Laish at	5892
	19:11 let us turn in into this **c** of the Jebusites,	5892
	19:12 We will not turn aside hither into the **c** of	5892
	19:15 he sat him down in a street of the **c**:	5892
	19:17 a wayfaring man in the street of the **c**:	5892
	19:22 behold, the men of the **c**, certain sons of	5892
	20:11 men of Israel were gathered against the **c**,	5892
	20:31 *and* were drawn away from the **c**,	5892
	20:32 draw them from the **c** unto the highways.	5892
	20:37 smote all the **c** with the edge of the sword	5892
	20:38 flame with smoke rise up out of the **c**.	5892
	20:40 up out of the **c** *with* a pillar of smoke,	5892
	20:40 the flame of the **c** ascended up to heaven.	5892
	20:48 as well the men of *every* **c**, as the beast,	5892
Ru	1:19 that all the **c** was moved about them,	5892
	2:18 she took *it* up, and went *into* the **c**: and	5892
	3:11 for all the **c** of my people doth know that	8179
	3:15 and laid *it* on her: and he went *into* the **c**.	5892
	4: 2 he took ten men of the elders of the **c**,	5892
1Sa	1: 3 this man went up out of his **c** yearly to	5892
	4:13 the man came into the **c**, and told *it*,	5892
	4:13 the city, and told *it*, all the **c** cried out.	5892
	5: 9 the hand of the Lord was against the **c**	5892

1Sa	5: 9 he smote the men of the **c**, both small	5892
	5:11 a deadly destruction throughout all the **c**;	5892
	5:12 and the cry of the **c** went up *to* heaven.	5892
	8:22 men of Israel, Go ye every man unto his **c**.	5892
	9: 6 *there is* in this **c** a man of God, and *he is*	5892
	9:10 So they went unto the **c** where the man	5892
	9:11 *And* as they went up the hill to the **c**,	5892
	9:12 haste now, for he came to day to the **c**;	5892
	9:13 As soon as ye be come *into* the **c**, ye shall	5892
	9:14 they went up *into* the **c**: *and* when they	5892
	9:14 *and* when they were come into the **c**,	5892
	9:25 down from the high place *into* the **c**,	5892
	9:27 they were going down to the end of the **c**,	5892
	10: 5 pass, when thou art come thither *to* the **c**,	5892
	15: 5 Saul came to a **c** of Amalek, and laid wait	5892
	20: 6 me that *he* might run *to* Beth-lehem his **c**:	5892
	20:29 for our family hath a sacrifice in the **c**;	5892
	20:40 said unto him, Go, carry *them* to the **c**.	5892
	20:42 departed: and Jonathan went *into* the **c**.	5892
	22:19 Nob, the **c** of the priests, smote he with	5892
	23:10 to Keilah, to destroy the **c** for my sake.	5892
	27: 5 servant dwell in the royal **c** with thee?	5892
	28: 3 buried him in Ramah, even in his own **c**.	5892
	30: 3 So David and his men came to the **c**,	5892
2Sa	5: 7 hold of Zion: the same *is* the **c** of David.	5892
	5: 9 in the fort, and called it the **c** of David.	5892
	6:10 the LORD unto him into the **c** of David:	5892
	6:12 *into* the **c** of David with gladness.	5892
	6:16 as the ark of the LORD came into the **c** of	5892
	10: 3 to search the **c**, and to spy it out,	5892
	10:14 before Abishai, and entered *into* the **c**.	5892
	11:16 came to pass, when Joab observed the **c**,	5892
	11:17 men of the **c** went out, and fought with	5892
	11:20 so nigh unto the **c** when *ye* did fight?	5892
	11:25 thy battle *more* strong against the **c**,	5892
	12: 1 unto him, There were two men in one **c**;	5892
	12:26 children of Ammon, and took the royal **c**.	5892
	12:27 and have taken the **c** of waters.	5892
	12:28 and encamp against the **c**, and take it:	5892
	12:28 lest I take the **c**, and it be called after my	5892
	12:30 he brought forth the spoil of the **c** in great	5892
	15: 2 unto him, and said, Of what **c** *art* thou?	5892
	15:12 from his **c**, *even* from Giloh,	5892
	15:14 smite the **c** with the edge of the sword.	5892
	15:24 the people had done passing out of the **c**.	5892
	15:25 Carry back the ark of God *into* the **c**:	5892
	15:27 return *into* the **c** in peace, and your two	5892
	15:34 if thou return *to* the **c**, and say unto	5892
	15:37 So Hushai David's friend came *into* the **c**,	5892
	17:13 he be gotten into a **c**, then shall all Israel	5892
	17:13 shall all Israel bring ropes to that **c**,	5892
	17:17 might not be seen to come into the **c**:	5892
	17:23 to his **c**, and put his household in order,	5892
	18: 3 better that thou succour us out of the **c**.	5892
	19: 3 gat them by stealth that day *into* the **c**,	5892
	19:37 I may die in mine own **c**, *and be buried*	5892
	20:15 they cast up a bank against the **c**,	5892
	20:16 cried a wise woman out of the **c**, Hear,	5892
	20:19 thou seekest to destroy a **c** and a mother	5892
	20:21 him only, and I will depart from the **c**.	5892
	20:22 they retired from the **c**, every man to his	5892
	24: 5 *on* the right side of the **c** that *lieth* in	5892
1Ki	1:41 Wherefore *is this* noise of the **c** being in	7151
	1:45 thence rejoicing, so that the **c** rang again.	7151
	2:10 and was buried in the **c** of David.	5892
	3: 1 and brought her into the **c** of David,	5892
	8: 1 of the LORD out of the **c** of David,	5892
	8:16 I chose no **c** out of all the tribes of Israel	5892
	8:44 shall pray unto the LORD toward the **c**	5892
	8:48 the **c** which thou hast chosen, and the	5892
	9:16 slain the Canaanites that dwelt in the **c**,	5892
	9:24 Pharaoh's daughter came up out of the **c**	5892
	11:27 repaired the breaches of the **c** of David his	5892
	11:32 the **c** which I have chosen out of all	5892
	11:36 the **c** which I have chosen me to put my	5892
	11:43 was buried in the **c** of David his father:	5892
	13:25 in the **c** where the old prophet dwelt.	5892
	13:29 the old prophet came to the **c**, to mourn	5892
	14:11 Him that dieth of Jeroboam in the **c** shall	5892
	14:12 when thy feet enter into the **c**, the child	5892
	14:21 the **c** which the LORD did choose out of	5892
	14:31 was buried with his fathers in the **c** of	5892
	15: 8 and they buried him in the **c** of David:	5892
	15:24 was buried with his fathers in the **c** of	5892
	16: 4 Him that dieth of Baasha in the **c** shall	5892
	16:18 when Zimri saw that the **c** was taken,	5892
	16:24 called the name of the **c** which he built,	5892
	17:10 when he came to the gate of the **c**,	5892
	20: 2 to Ahab king of Israel into the **c**,	5892
	20:12 they set *themselves* in array against the **c**.	5892
	20:19 princes of the provinces came out of the **c**,	5892
	20:30 the rest fled to Aphek, into the **c**;	5892
	20:30 Ben-hadad fled, and came into the **c**,	5892
	21: 8 and to the nobles that *were* in his **c**,	5892
	21:11 the men of his **c**, *even* the elders and	5892
	21:11 nobles who *were* the inhabitants in his **c**,	5892
	21:13 they carried him forth out of the **c**,	5892
	21:24 Him that dieth of Ahab in the **c** the dogs	5892
	22:26 back unto Amon the governor of the **c**,	5892
	22:36 Every man to his **c**, and every man to his	5892
	22:50 was buried with his fathers in the **c** of	5892
2Ki	2:19 the men of the **c** said unto Elisha, Behold,	5892
	2:19 the situation of *this* **c** *is* pleasant,	5892
	2:23 came forth little children out of the **c**,	5892
	3:19 ye shall smite every fenced **c**,	5892

2Ki	3:19 every choice **c**, and shall fell every good	5892
	6:14 by night, and compassed the **c** about.	5892
	6:15 a host compassed the **c** both with horses	5892
	6:19 This *is* not the way, neither *is* this the **c**:	5892
	7: 4 We will enter *into* the **c**, then the famine	5892
	7: 4 the famine *is* in the **c**, and we shall die	5892
	7:10 and called unto the porter of the **c**:	5892
	7:12 saying, When they come out of the **c**,	5892
	7:12 shall catch them alive, and get into the **c**.	5892
	7:13 which are left in **the c**^s, (behold,	1886.3
	8:24 was buried with his fathers in the **c** of	5892
	9:15 let none go forth *nor* escape out of the **c**	5892
	9:28 with his fathers in the **c** of David.	5892
	10: 2 and horses, a fenced **c** also, and armour;	5892
	10: 5 *he* that *was* over the **c**, the elders also,	5892
	10: 6 *were* with the great *men* of the **c**,	5892
	10:25 and went to the **c** of the house of Baal.	5892
	11:20 the land rejoiced, and the **c** was in quiet:	5892
	12:21 buried him with his fathers in the **c** of	5892
	14:20 with his fathers in the **c** of David.	5892
	15: 7 buried him with his fathers in the **c** of	5892
	15:38 was buried with his fathers in the **c** of	5892
	16:20 was buried with his fathers in the **c** of	5892
	17: 9 tower of the watchmen to the fenced **c**	5892
	18: 8 tower of the watchmen to the fenced **c**.	5892
	18:30 this **c** shall not be delivered into the hand	5892
	19:13 the king of the **c** of Sepharvaim, of Hena,	5892
	19:32 He shall not come into this **c**, nor shoot	5892
	19:33 shall not come into this **c**, saith	5892
	19:34 I will defend this **c**, to save it, for mine	5892
	20: 6 this **c** out of the hand of the king of	5892
	20: 6 I will defend this **c** for mine own sake,	5892
	20:20 a conduit, and brought water into the **c**,	5892
	23: 8 the gate of Joshua the governor of the **c**,	5892
	23: 8 on a man's left hand at the gate of the **c**:	5892
	23:17 the men of the **c** told him, *It is*	5892
	23:27 will cast off this **c** Jerusalem which I have	5892
	24:10 *against* Jerusalem, and the **c** was besieged.	5892
	24:11 king of Babylon came against the **c**,	5892
	25: 2 the **c** was besieged unto the eleventh year	5892
	25: 3 month the famine prevailed in the **c**,	5892
	25: 4 the **c** was broken up, and all the men of	5892
	25: 4 the Chaldees *were* against the **c** round	5892
	25:11 rest of the people that were left in the **c**,	5892
	25:19 of the **c** he took an officer that was set	5892
	25:19 which were found in the **c**,	5892
	25:19 of the land that were found in the **c**:	5892
1Ch	1:43 and the name of his **c** *was* Dinhabah.	5892
	1:46 stead: and the name of his **c** *was* Avith.	5892
	1:50 the name of his **c** *was* Pai; and his wife's	5892
	6:56 fields of the **c**, and the villages thereof,	5892
	6:57 the **c** of refuge, and Libnah with her	NIH
	11: 5 castle of Zion, which *is* the **c** of David.	5892
	11: 7 they called it the **c** of David.	5892
	11: 8 built the **c** round about, even from Millo	5892
	11: 8 and Joab repaired the rest of the **c**.	5892
	13:13 the ark *home* to himself to the **c** of David,	5892
	15: 1 *David* made him houses in the **c** of David,	5892
	15:29 of the LORD came to the **c** of David,	5892
	19: 9 the battle in array *before* the gate of the **c**:	5892
	19:15 his brother, and entered into the **c**.	5892
	20: 2 also exceeding much spoil *out* of the **c**.	5892
2Ch	5: 2 the **c** out of the **c** of David,	5892
	6: 5 among all the tribes of Israel to build a	5892
	6:34 they pray unto thee toward this **c** which	5892
	6:38 *toward* the **c** which thou hast chosen,	5892
	8:11 **c** of David unto the house that he had	5892
	9:31 was buried in the **c** of David his father:	5892
	11:12 in every **several c** *he* put 5892+5892+2050.1	
	11:23 and Benjamin, unto every fenced **c**:	5892
	12:13 the **c** which the LORD had chosen out of	5892
	12:16 and was buried in the **c** of David:	5892
	14: 1 and they buried him in the **c** of David:	5892
	15: 6 was destroyed of nation, and **c** of city:	5892
	15: 6 was destroyed of nation, and city of **c**:	5892
	16:14 which he had made for himself in the **c** of	5892
	18:25 him back to Amon the governor of the **c**,	5892
	19: 5 all the fenced cities of Judah, **c** by city,	5892
	19: 5 all the fenced cities of Judah, city by **c**,	5892
	21: 1 was buried with his fathers in the **c** of	5892
	21:20 they buried him in the **c** of David.	5892
	23:21 the **c** was quiet, after that they had slain	5892
	24:16 they buried him in the **c** of David among	5892
	24:25 they buried him in the **c** of David,	5892
	25:28 buried him with his fathers in the **c** of	5892
	27: 9 and they buried him in the **c** of David:	5892
	28:15 the **c** of palm trees, to their brethren:	5892
	28:25 in every **several** *c* of Judah 5892+5892+2050.1	
	28:27 buried him in the **c**, *even* in Jerusalem:	5892
	29:20 gathered the rulers of the **c**, and went up	5892
	30:10 So the posts passed from **c** to city through	5892
	30:10 So the posts passed from city to **c** through	5892
	31:19 in every **several** *c* 5892+5892+2050.1	
	32: 3 the fountains which *were* without the **c**:	5892
	32: 5 repaired Millo *in* the **c** of David,	5892
	32: 6 to him in the street of the gate of the **c**,	5892
	32:18 trouble them; that they might take the **c**.	5892
	32:30 down to the west *side* of the **c** of David.	5892
	33:14 after this he built a wall without the **c**,	5892
	33:15 in Jerusalem, and cast *them* out of the **c**.	5892
	34: 8 Maaseiah the governor of the **c**, and Joah	5892
Ezr	2: 1 and Judah, every one unto his **c**,	5892
	4:12 building the rebellious and the bad **c**,	7149
	4:13 if this **c** be builded, and the walls set up	7149
	4:15 and know that this **c** *is* a rebellious city,	7149

Ezr	4:15 and know that this city *is* a rebellious **c**,	7149
	4:15 for which *cause* was this **c** destroyed.	7149
	4:16 if this **c** be builded *again*, and the walls	7149
	4:19 it is found that this **c** of old time	7149
	4:21 *that* this **c** be not builded, until *another*	7149
	10:14 the elders of **every c**, 5892+5892+2050.1	
Ne	2: 3 when the **c**, the place of my fathers'	5892
	2: 5 unto the **c** of my fathers' sepulchres,	5892
	2: 8 for the wall of the **c**, and for the house	5892
	3:15 unto the stairs that go down from the **c** of	5892
	7: 4 Now the **c** *was* large and great: but	5892
	7: 6 and to Judah, every one unto his **c**;	5892
	11: 1 of ten to dwell in Jerusalem the holy **c**,	5892
	11: 9 the son of Senuah *was* second over the **c**.	5892
	11:18 All the Levites in the holy **c** *were* two	5892
	12:37 went up by the stairs of the **c** of David,	5892
	13:18 all this evil upon us, and upon this **c**?	5892
Est	3:15 drink; but the **c** Shushan was perplexed.	5892
	4: 1 went out into the midst of the **c**,	5892
	4: 6 forth to Mordecai unto the street of the **c**,	5892
	6: 9 on horseback through the street of the **c**,	5892
	6:11 on horseback through the street of the **c**,	5892
	8:11 **every c** to gather 3605+5892+5892+2050.1	
	8:15 the **c** of Shushan rejoiced and was glad.	5892
	8:17 in **every c**, 3605+5892+5892+2050.1	
	9:28 province, and **every c**; 5892+5892+2050.1	
Job	24:12 Men groan from out of the **c**, and the soul	5892
	29: 7 I went out *to* the gate through the **c**,	7176
	39: 7 He scorneth the multitude of the **c**,	7151
Ps	31:21 me his marvellous kindness in a strong **c**.	5892
	46: 4 streams whereof shall make glad the **c**	5892
	48: 1 greatly to be praised in the **c** of our God,	5892
	48: 2 sides of the north, the **c** of the great King.	7151
	48: 8 have we seen in the **c** of the LORD of	5892
	48: 8 of the LORD of hosts, in the **c** of our God:	5892
	55: 9 I have seen violence and strife in the **c**.	5892
	59: 6 like a dog, and go round about the **c**.	5892
	59:14 like a dog, and go round about the **c**.	5892
	60: 9 Who will bring me *into* the strong **c**?	5892
	72:16 *they* of the **c** shall flourish like grass of	5892
	87: 3 *things* are spoken of thee, O **c** of God.	5892
	101: 8 all wicked doers from the **c** of the LORD.	5892
	107: 4 solitary way; they found no **c** to dwell in.	5892
	107: 7 that *they* might go to a **c** of habitation.	5892
	107:36 that they may prepare a **c** for habitation;	5892
	108:10 Who will bring me *into* the strong **c**?	5892
	122: 3 Jerusalem *is* builded as a **c** that is compact	5892
	127: 1 except the LORD keep the **c**,	5892
Pr	1:21 in the **c** she uttereth her words, *saying*,	5892
	8: 3 crieth at the gates, at the entry of the **c**,	7176
	9: 3 crieth upon the highest places of the **c**,	7176
	9:14 on a seat in the high places of the **c**,	7176
	10:15 The rich *man's* wealth *is* his strong **c**:	7151
	11:10 well with the righteous, the **c** rejoiceth:	7151
	11:11 By the blessing of the upright the **c** is	7176
	16:32 ruleth his spirit than he that taketh a **c**.	5892
	18:11 The rich *man's* wealth *is* his strong **c**,	7151
	18:19 *is harder to be won* than a strong **c**:	7151
	21:22 A wise *man* scaleth the **c** of the mighty,	5892
	25:28 own spirit *is like* a **c** *that is* broken down,	5892
	29: 8 Scornful men bring a **c** into a snare: but	7151
Ecc	7:19 than ten mighty *men* which are in the **c**.	5892
	8:10 they were forgotten in the **c** where they	5892
	9:14 There was a little **c**, and few men within	5892
	9:15 and he by his wisdom delivered the **c**;	5892
	10:15 he knoweth not how to go to the **c**.	5892
SS	3: 2 go about the **c** in the streets and in	5892
	3: 3 The watchmen that go about the **c** found	5892
	5: 7 watchmen that went about the **c** found	5892
Isa	1: 8 in a garden of cucumbers, as a besieged **c**.	5892
	1:21 How is the faithful **c** become a harlot!	7151
	1:26 The **c** of righteousness, the faithful city.	5892
	1:26 The city of righteousness, the faithful **c**.	7151
	4062 oppressor ceased! the **golden c** ceased!	4062
	14:31 cry, O **c**; thou, whole Palestina;	5892
	17: 1 Damascus is taken away from *being* a **c**,	5892
	19: 2 **c** against city, *and* kingdom against	5892
	19: 2 city against **c**, *and* kingdom against	5892
	19:18 one shall be called, The **c** of destruction.	5892
	22: 2 full *of* stirs, a tumultuous **c**, a joyous city:	5892
	22: 2 full *of* stirs, a tumultuous city, a joyous **c**:	7151
	22: 9 Ye have seen also the breaches of the **c** of	5892
	23: 7 *Is* this your joyous **c**, whose antiquity *is* of	NIH
	23: 8 the crowning **c**, whose merchants *are*	NIH
	23:11 **c**, to destroy the strong holds thereof.	NIH
	23:16 Take a harp, go about the **c**, thou harlot	5892
	24:10 The **c** of confusion is broken down:	7151
	24:12 In the **c** is left desolation, and the gate is	5892
	25: 2 For thou hast made of a **c** a heap; *of* a	5892
	25: 2 of a city a heap; *of* a defenced **c** a ruin:	7151
	25: 2 a palace of strangers to be no **c**; it shall	5892
	25: 3 the **c** of the terrible nations shall fear thee.	7151
	26: 1 We have a strong **c**; salvation will *God*	5892
	26: 5 the lofty **c**, he layeth it low; he layeth it	7151
	27:10 Yet the defenced **c** *shall be* desolate,	5892
	29: 1 Ariel, to Ariel, the **c** *where* David dwelt!	7151
	32:13 upon all the houses of joy in the joyous **c**:	7151
	32:14 multitude of the **c** shall be left; the forts	5892
	32:19 and the **c** shall be low in a low place.	5892
	33:20 Look upon Zion, the **c** of our solemnities:	7151
	36:15 this **c** shall not be delivered into the hand	5892
	37:13 the king of the **c** of Sepharvaim, Hena,	5892
	37:33 He shall not come into this **c**, nor shoot	5892
	37:34 shall not come into this **c**, saith	5892
	37:35 For I will defend this **c** to save it for mine	5892

C

Isa 38: 6 this **c** out of the hand of the king of | 5892
38: 6 king of Assyria: and I will defend this **c**. | 5892
45:13 he shall build my **c**, and he shall let go | 5892
48: 2 For they call themselves of the holy **c**, | 5892
52: 1 O Jerusalem, the holy **c**: | 5892
60:14 they shall call thee, The **c** of the LORD, | 5892
62:12 be called, Sought out, A **c** not forsaken. | 5892
66: 6 A voice of noise from the **c**, a voice from | 5892
Jer 1:18 I have made thee *this* day a defenced **c**, | 5892
3:14 I will take you one of a **c**, and two of | 5892
4:29 The whole **c** shall flee for the noise of | 5892
4:29 every **c** *shall* be forsaken, and not a man | 5892
6: 6 this is the **c** to be visited; she *is* wholly | 5892
8:16 the **c**, and those that dwell therein. | 5892
14:18 if I enter *into* the **c**, then behold them | 5892
15: 8 upon it suddenly, and terrors *upon* the **c**. | 5892
17:24 the gates of this **c** on the sabbath day, | 5892
17:25 shall there enter into the gates of this **c** | 5892
17:25 and this **c** shall remain for ever. | 5892
19: 8 I will make this **c** desolate, and a hissing; | 5892
19:11 so will I break this people and this **c**, | 5892
19:12 and *even* make this **c** as Tophet: | 5892
19:15 I will bring upon this **c** and upon all her | 5892
20: 5 I will deliver all the strength of this **c**, | 5892
21: 4 assemble them into the midst of this **c**. | 5892
21: 6 I will smite the inhabitants of this **c**, both | 5892
21: 7 as are left in this **c** from the pestilence, | 5892
21: 9 He that abideth in this **c** shall die by | 5892
21:10 For I have set my face against this **c** for | 5892
22: 8 many nations shall pass by this **c**, | 5892
22: 8 the LORD done thus unto this great **c**? | 5892
23:39 the **c** that I gave you and your fathers, | 5892
25:29 I begin to bring evil on the **c** which is | 5892
26: 6 will make this **c** a curse to all the nations | 5892
26: 9 this **c** shall be desolate without an | 5892
26:11 for he hath prophesied against this **c**, | 5892
26:12 against this **c** all the words that ye have | 5892
26:15 upon this **c**, and upon the inhabitants | 5892
26:20 who prophesied against this **c** and | 5892
27:17 wherefore should this **c** be laid waste? | 5892
27:19 of the vessels that remain in this **c**, | 5892
29: 7 seek the peace of the **c** whither I have | 5892
29:16 of all the people that dwelleth in this **c**, | 5892
30:18 the **c** shall be builded upon her own heap, | 5892
31:38 that the **c** shall be built to the LORD from | 5892
32: 3 I *will* give this **c** into the hand of the king | 5892
32:24 they are come *unto* the **c** to take it; | 5892
32:24 the **c** is given into the hand of | 5892
32:25 for the **c** is given into the hand of | 5892
32:28 I *will* give this **c** into the hand of | 5892
32:29 that fight against this **c**, shall come and | 5892
32:29 come and set fire on this **c**, and burn it | 5892
32:31 this **c** hath been to me *as* a provocation | 5892
32:36 Israel, concerning this **c**, whereof ye say, | 5892
33: 4 concerning the houses of this **c**, | 5892
33: 5 I have hid my face from this **c**. | 5892
34: 2 I *will* give this **c** into the hand of the king | 5892
34:22 and cause them to return to this **c**; | 5892
37: 8 fight against this **c**, and take it, and burn it | 5892
37:10 man in his tent, and burn this **c** with fire. | 5892
37:21 until all the bread in the **c** were spent. | 5892
38: 2 He that remaineth in this **c** shall die by | 5892
38: 3 This **c** shall surely be given into the hand | 5892
38: 4 of the men of war that remain in this **c**, | 5892
38: 9 he is: for *there is* no more bread in the **c**. | 5892
38:17 and this **c** shall not be burnt with fire; | 5892
38:18 shall this **c** be given into the hand of | 5892
38:23 shalt cause this **c** to be burnt with fire. | 5892
39: 2 *day* of the month, the **c** was broken up. | 5892
39: 4 and went forth out of the **c** by night, | 5892
39: 9 of the people that remained in the **c**, | 5892
39:16 I *will* bring my words upon this **c** for evil, | 5892
41: 7 when they came into the midst of the **c**, | 5892
46: 8 I will destroy the **c** and the inhabitants | 5892
47: 2 the **c**, and them that dwell therein: | 5892
48: 8 the spoiler shall come upon every **c**, | 5892
48: 8 upon every city, and no **c** shall escape: | 5892
49:25 How is the **c** of praise not left, the city of | 5892
49:25 the city of praise not left, the **c** of my joy! | 7151
51:31 to shew the king of Babylon that his **c** is | 5892
52: 5 So the **c** was besieged unto the eleventh | 5892
52: 6 the famine was sore in the **c**, so that there | 5892
52: 7 the **c** was broken up, and all the men of | 5892
52: 7 forth out of the **c** by night *by* the way | 5892
52: 7 (now the Chaldeans *were* by the **c** round | 5892
52:15 of the people that remained in the **c**, | 5892
52:25 He took also out of the **c** an eunuch, | 5892
52:25 king's person, which were found in the **c**; | 5892
52:25 that were found in the midst of the **c**. | 5892
La 1: 1 How doth the **c** sit solitary, *that was* full | 5892
1:19 mine elders gave up the ghost in the **c**, | 5892
2:11 sucklings swoon in the streets of the **c**. | 7151
2:12 as the wounded in the streets of the **c**, | 5892
2:15 *saying*, Is this the **c** that *men* call The | 5892
3:51 because of all the daughters of my **c**. | 5892
Eze 4: 1 pourtray upon it the **c**, *even* Jerusalem: | 5892
4: 3 *for* a wall of iron between thee and the **c**: | 5892
5: 2 with fire a third *part* in the midst of the **c**, | 5892
7:15 he that *is* in the **c**, famine and | 5892
7:23 crimes, and the **c** is full *of* violence. | 5892
9: 1 Cause them that have charge over the **c** to | 5892
9: 4 Go through the midst of the **c** through | 5892
9: 5 Go ye after him through the **c**, and smite: | 5892
9: 7 And they went forth, and slew in the **c**. | 5892
9: 9 *of* blood, and the **c** full *of* perverseness: | 5892
Eze 10: 2 cherubims, and scatter *them* over the **c**. | 5892
11: 2 and give wicked counsel in this **c**: | 5892
11: 3 this **c** *is* the caldron, and we *be* the flesh. | NIH
11: 6 Ye have multiplied your slain in this **c**, | 5892
11: 7 *are* the flesh, and this **c** *is* the caldron: | NIH
11:11 This **c** shall not be your caldron, | NIH
11:23 LORD went up from the midst of the **c**, | 5892
11:23 which *is* on the east side of the **c**. | 5892
17: 4 of traffick; he set it in a **c** of merchants. | 5892
21:19 choose *it*, at the head of the way to the **c**. | 5892
22: 2 thou judge, wilt thou judge the bloody **c**? | 5892
22: 3 The **c** sheddeth blood in the midst of it, | 5892
24: 6 Woe to the bloody **c**, to the pot whose | 5892
24: 9 saith the Lord GOD; Woe to the bloody **c**! | 5892
26:10 as men enter into a **c** wherein is made a | 5892
26:17 the renowned **c**, which wast strong in | 5892
26:19 When I shall make thee a desolate **c**, | 5892
27:32 over thee, *saying*, What *c is* like Tyrus, | NIH
33:21 came unto me, saying, The **c** is smitten. | 5892
39:16 also the name of the **c** *shall be* Hamonah. | 5892
40: 1 in the fourteenth year after that the **c** was | 5892
40: 2 by which *was* as the frame of a **c** on | 5892
43: 3 that I saw when I came to destroy the **c**: | 5892
45: 6 shall appoint the possession of the **c** five | 5892
45: 7 *portion*, and of the possession of the **c**, | 5892
45: 7 and before the possession of the **c**, | 5892
48:15 *shall be* a profane place for the **c**, | 5892
48:15 and the **c** shall be in the midst thereof. | 5892
48:17 the suburbs of the **c** shall be toward | 5892
48:18 be for food unto them that serve the **c**. | 5892
48:19 that serve the **c** shall serve it out of all | 5892
48:20 with the possession of the **c**. | 5892
48:21 of the possession of the **c**, over against | 5892
48:22 *and* from the possession of the **c**, | 5892
48:30 these *are* the goings out of the **c**: on | 5892
48:31 the gates of the **c** *shall be* after the names | 5892
48:35 the name of the **c** from *that* day *shall be*, | 5892
Da 9:16 thy fury be turned away from thy **c** | 5892
9:18 and the **c** which is called by thy name: | 5892
9:19 for thy **c** and thy people are called by thy | 5892
9:24 upon thy people and upon thy holy **c**, | 5892
9:26 prince that *shall* come shall destroy the **c** | 5892
Hos 6: 8 Gilead *is* a **c** of them that work iniquity, | 7151
11: 9 of thee: and I will not enter into the **c**. | 5892
Joel 2: 9 They shall run to and fro in the **c**; they | 5892
Am 2: 6 Shall a trumpet be blown in the **c**, | 5892
3: 6 shall there be evil in a **c**, and the LORD | 5892
4: 7 I caused it to rain upon one **c**, and caused | 5892
4: 7 and caused it not to rain upon another **c**: | 5892
4: 8 two *or* three cities wandered unto one **c**, | 5892
5: 3 The **c** that went out *by* a thousand shall | 5892
6: 8 will I deliver up the **c** with all that is | 5892
7:17 Thy wife shall be a harlot in the **c**, | 5892
Jnh 1: 2 Nineveh, *that* great **c**, and cry against it; | 5892
3: 2 *that* great **c**, and preach unto it | 5892
3: 3 Now Nineveh was an exceeding great **c** of | 5892
3: 4 Jonah began to enter into the a **c** day's | 5892
4: 5 So Jonah went out of the **c**, and sat on | 5892
4: 5 sat on the east side of the **c**, and there | 5892
4: 5 might see what would become of the **c**. | 5892
4:11 should not I spare Nineveh, *that* great **c**, | 5892
Mic 4:10 for now shalt thou go forth out of the **c**, | 7151
6: 9 The LORD's voice crieth unto the **c**, | 5892
Na 1: 1 Woe to the bloody **c**! it *is* all full *of* lies | 5892
Hab 2: 8 *of* the **c**, and *of* all that dwell therein. | 7151
2:12 blood, and stablisheth a **c** by iniquity! | 7151
2:17 *of* the **c**, and *of* all that dwell therein. | 7151
Zep 2:15 *is* the rejoicing **c** that dwelt carelessly, | 5892
3: 1 is filthy and polluted, to the oppressing **c**! | 5892
Zec 8: 3 Jerusalem shall be called a **c** of truth; | 5892
8: 5 the streets of the **c** shall be full *of* boys | 5892
8:21 inhabitants of one **c** shall go to another, | NIH
14: 2 the **c** shall be taken, and the houses rifled, | 5892
14: 2 half of the **c** shall go forth into captivity; | 5892
14: 2 the people shall not be cut off from the **c**. | 5892
Mt 2:23 he came and dwelt in a **c** called Nazareth: | 4172
4: 5 the devil taketh him *up* into the holy **c**, | 4172
5:14 A **c** that is set on a hill cannot be hid. | 4172
5:35 for it is the **c** of the great King. | 4172
8:33 and went their ways into the **c**, | 4172
8:34 the whole **c** came out to meet Jesus: | 4172
9: 1 and passed over, and came into his own **c**. | 4172
10: 5 into *any* **c** of the Samaritans enter ye not: | 4172
10:11 And into whatsoever **c** or town ye shall | 4172
10:14 when ye depart out of that house or **c**, | 4172
10:15 in the day of judgment, than for that **c**. | 4172
10:23 But when they persecute you in this **c**, | 4172
12:25 and every **c** or house divided against itself | 4172
21:10 all the **c** was moved, saying, Who is this? | 4172
21:17 and went out of the **c** into Bethany; | 4172
21:18 in the morning as he returned into the **c**, | 4172
22: 7 those murderers, and burnt up their **c**. | 4172
23:34 and persecute *them* from **c** to city: | 4172
23:34 and persecute *them* from city to **c**: | 4172
26:18 Go into the **c** to such a man, and say unto | 4172
27:53 went into the holy **c**, and appeared unto | 4172
28:11 some of the watch came into the **c**, | 4172
Mk 1:33 And all the **c** was gathered together at | 4172
1:45 could no more openly enter into the **c**, | 4172
5:14 and told *it* in the **c**, and in the country. | 4172
6:11 in the day of judgment, than for that **c**. | 4172
11:19 even was come, he went out of the **c**. | 4172
14:13 Go ye into the **c**, and there shall meet you | 4172
14:16 and came into the **c**, and found as he had | 4172
Lk 1:26 was sent from God unto a **c** of Galilee, | 4172
Lk 1:39 hill country with haste, into a **c** of Juda; | 4172
2: 3 to be taxed, every one into his own **c**. | 4172
2: 4 out of the **c** of Nazareth, into Judea, | 4172
2: 4 into Judea, unto the **c** of David, | 4172
2:11 For unto you is born this day in the **c** of | 4172
2:39 into Galilee, to their own **c** Nazareth. | 4172
4:26 save unto Sarepta, a **c** of Sidon, unto a | NIG
4:29 and thrust him out of the **c**, and led him | 4172
4:29 of the hill whereon their **c** was built, | 4172
4:31 a **c** of Galilee, and taught them on | 4172
5:12 came to pass, when he was in a certain **c**, | 4172
7:11 after, *that* he went into a **c** called Nain; | 4172
7:12 when he came nigh to the gate of the **c**, | 4172
7:12 and much people of the **c** was with her. | 4172
7:37 And behold, a woman in the **c**, which was | 4172
8: 1 that he went throughout every **c** and | 4172
8: 4 and were come to him out of every **c**, | 4172
8:27 there met him out of the **c** a certain man, | 4172
8:34 and went and told *it* in the **c** and in | 4172
8:39 published throughout the whole **c** how | 4172
9: 5 not receive you, when ye go out of that **c**, | 4172
9:10 place belonging to the **c** called Bethsaida. | 4172
10: 1 and two before his face into every **c** and | 4172
10: 8 And into whatsoever **c** ye enter, | 4172
10:10 But into whatsoever **c** ye enter, | 4172
10:11 Even the *very* dust of your **c**, | 4172
10:12 in that day for Sodom, than for that **c**. | 4172
14:21 quickly into the streets and lanes of the **c**, | 4172
18: 2 Saying, There was in a **c** a judge, | 4172
18: 3 And there was a widow in that **c**: | 4172
19:41 he beheld the **c**, and wept over it, | 4172
22:10 Behold, when ye are entered into the **c**, | 4172
23:19 (Who for a certain sedition made in the **c**, | 4172
23:51 *he was* of Arimathea, a **c** of the Jews: | 4172
24:49 tarry ye in the **c** of Jerusalem, until ye | 4172
Jn 1:44 of Bethsaida, the **c** of Andrew and Peter. | 4172
4: 5 Then cometh he to a **c** of Samaria, which | 4172
4: 8 were gone away unto the **c** to buy meat.) | 4172
4:28 and went her way into the **c**, and saith to | 4172
4:30 they went out of the **c**, and came unto | 4172
4:39 And many of the Samaritans of that **c** | 4172
11:54 into a **c** called Ephraim, and there | 4172
19:20 Jesus was crucified was nigh to the **c**: | 4172
Ac 7:58 cast *him* out of the **c**, and stoned *him*: | 4172
8: 5 Philip went down to the **c** of Samaria, | 4172
8: 8 And there was great joy in that **c**. | 4172
8: 9 which beforetime in the *same* **c** used | 4172
9: 6 and go into the **c**, and it shall be told thee | 4172
10: 9 their journey, and drew nigh unto the **c**, | 4172
11: 5 I was in the **c** of Joppa praying: and in a | 4172
12:10 the iron gate that leadeth unto the **c**; | 4172
13:44 whole **c** together to hear the word of God. | 4172
13:50 and the chief *men* of the **c**, | 4172
14: 4 But the multitude of the **c** was divided: | 4172
14:13 which was before their **c**, brought oxen | 4172
14:19 stoned Paul, drew *him* out of the **c**, | 4172
14:20 him, he rose up, and came into the **c**: | 4172
14:21 they had preached the gospel to that **c**, | 4172
15:21 Moses of old time hath in every **c** them | 4172
15:36 visit our brethren in every **c** where we | 4172
16:12 which is the chief **c** of *that* part of | 4172
16:12 we were in that **c** abiding certain days. | 4172
16:13 on the sabbath we went out of the **c** by | 4172
16:14 a seller of purple, of the **c** of Thyatira, | 4172
16:20 being Jews, do exceedingly trouble our **c**, | 4172
16:39 and desired *them* to depart out of the **c**. | 4172
17: 5 set all the **c** on an uproar, and assaulted | 4172
17: 6 certain brethren unto the **rulers of the c**, | 4172
17: 8 the people and the **rulers of the c**, | 4173
17:16 he saw the **c** wholly given to idolatry. | 4172
18:10 for I have much people in this **c**. | 4172
19:29 the whole **c** was filled with confusion: | 4172
19:35 **c** of the Ephesians is a worshipper of | 4172
20:23 that the Holy Ghost witnesseth in every **c**, | 4172
21: 5 and children, till *we were* out of the **c**: | 4172
21:29 they had seen before with him in the **c** | 4172
21:30 And all the **c** was moved, and the people | 4172
21:39 *a* **c** in Cilicia, a citizen of no mean city: | NIG
21:39 a *city* in Cilicia, a citizen of no mean **c**: | 4172
22: 3 *am* a Jew, born in Tarsus, *a* **c** in Cilicia, | NIG
22: 3 yet brought up in this **c** at the feet of | 4172
24:12 neither in the synagogues, nor in the **c**: | 4172
25:23 chief captains, and principal men of the **c**, | 4172
27: 5 Pamphylia, we came to Myra, *a* **c** of Lycia. | NIG
27: 8 nigh whereunto was the **c** *of* Lasea. | 4172
Ro 16:23 Erastus the chamberlain of the **c** saluteth | 4172
2Co 11:26 *in* perils by the heathen, *in* perils in the **c**, | 4172
11:32 **c** of the Damascenes *with a garrison*, | 4172
13: 5 *a* **c** of Macedonia, by Titus and Lucas. | NIG
1Ti 6: 5 S which is the **chiefest c** of Phrygia | 3390
Tit 1: 5 and ordain elders in every **c**, as I had | 4172
Heb 11:10 For he looked for a **c** which hath | 4172
11:16 for he hath prepared for them a **c**. | 4172
12:22 and unto the **c** of the living God, | 4172
13:14 For here have we no continuing **c**, | 4172
Jas 4:13 or to morrow we will go into such a **c**, | 4172
Rev 3:12 and the name of the **c** of my God, | 4172
11: 2 the holy **c** shall they tread under foot forty | 4172
11: 8 bodies *shall* lie in the street of the great **c**, | 4172
11:13 and the tenth *part* of the **c** fell, and in | 4172
14: 8 Babylon is fallen, is fallen, *that* great **c**, | 4172
16:19 And the great **c** was *divided* into three | 4172
17:18 woman which thou sawest *is that* great **c**, | 4172
18:10 saying, Alas, alas, *that* great **c** Babylon, | 4172

Nu	35:14 of Canaan, *which* shall be **c** of refuge.	5892
	35:15 These six **c** shall be a refuge, *both* for	5892
Dt	1:22 go up, and into what **c** we shall come.	5892
	1:28 The **c** *are* great and walled up to heaven;	5892
	2:34 we took all his **c** at that time,	5892
	2:35 and the spoil of the **c** which we took.	5892
	2:37 nor *unto* the **c** in the mountains,	5892
	3: 4 we took all his **c** at that time, there was	5892
	3: 4 threescore **c**, all the region of Argob,	5892
	3: 5 All these **c** *were* fenced *with* high walls,	5892
	3: 7 the cattle, and the spoil of the **c**, we took	5892
	3:10 All the **c** of the plain, and all Gilead,	5892
	3:10 Edrei, **c** of the kingdom of Og in Bashan.	5892
	3:12 half mount Gilead, and the **c** thereof, gave	5892
	3:19 shall abide in your **c** which I have given	5892
	4:41 Moses severed three **c** on *this* side Jordan	5892
	4:42 that fleeing unto one of these **c** he might	5892
	6:10 to Jacob, to give thee great and goodly **c**,	5892
	9: 1 **c** great and fenced up to heaven,	5892
	13:12 If thou shalt hear *say* in one of thy **c**,	5892
	19: 1 dwellest in their **c**, and in their houses;	5892
	19: 2 Thou shalt separate three **c** for thee in	5892
	19: 5 he shall flee unto one of those **c**, and live:	5892
	19: 7 Thou shalt separate three **c** for thee.	5892
	19: 9 shalt thou add three **c** moe for thee,	5892
	19:11 that he die, and fleeth into one of these **c**:	5892
	20:15 Thus shalt thou do unto all the **c** *which*	5892
	20:15 which *are* not of the **c** of these nations.	5892
	20:16 of the **c** of these people, which the Lord	5892
	21: 2 they shall measure unto the **c** which *are*	5892
Jos	9:17 and came unto their **c** on the third day.	5892
	9:17 their *were* Gibeon, and Chephirah,	5892
	10: 2 as one of the royal **c**, and because it *was*	5892
	10:19 suffer them not to enter into their **c**:	5892
	10:20 remained of them entered into fenced **c**.	5892
	10:37 all the **c** thereof, and all the souls that	5892
	10:39 and the king thereof, and all the **c** thereof;	5892
	11:12 all the **c** of those kings, and all the kings	5892
	11:13 *for* the **c** that stood still in their strength,	5892
	11:14 all the spoil of these **c**, and the cattle,	5892
	11:21 destroyed them utterly with their **c**.	5892
	13:10 all the **c** of Sihon king of the Amorites,	5892
	13:17 and all her **c** that *are* in the plain;	5892
	13:21 all the **c** of the plain, and all the kingdom	5892
	13:23 their families, the **c** and villages thereof.	5892
	13:25 all the **c** of Gilead, and half the land of	5892
	13:28 their families, the **c**, and their villages.	5892
	13:30 of Jair, which *are* in Bashan, threescore **c**:	5892
	13:31 Edrei, **c** of the kingdom of Og in Bashan,	5892
	14: 4 save **c** to dwell *in*, with their suburbs for	5892
	14:12 and *that* the **c** *were* great *and* fenced:	5892
	15: 9 and went out to the **c** of mount Ephron;	5892
	15:21 the uttermost **c** of the tribe of the children	5892
	15:32 all the **c** *are* twenty and nine, with their	5892
	15:36 fourteen **c** with their villages.	5892
	15:41 Makkedah; sixteen **c** with their villages.	5892
	15:44 and Mareshah; nine **c** with their villages.	5892
	15:51 and Giloh; eleven **c** with their villages.	5892
	15:54 and Zior; nine **c** with their villages.	5892
	15:57 and Timnah; ten **c** with their villages.	5892
	15:59 and Eltekon; six **c** with their villages.	5892
	15:60 and Rabbah; two **c** with their villages.	5892
	15:62 and En-gedi; six **c** with their villages.	5892
	16: 9 the separate **c** for the children of Ephraim	5892
	16: 9 of Manasseh, all the **c** with their villages.	5892
	17: 9 these **c** of Ephraim *are* among the cities	5892
	17: 9 cities of Ephraim *are* among the **c** of	5892
	17:12 not drive out *the inhabitants of* those **c**;	5892
	18: 9 described it by **c** into seven parts in a	5892
	18:21 Now the **c** of the tribe of the children of	5892
	18:24 and Gaba; twelve **c** with their villages.	5892
	18:28 *and* Kirjath; fourteen **c** with their villages.	5892
	19: 6 Sharuhen; thirteen **c** with their villages:	5892
	19: 7 and Ashan; four **c** and their villages:	5892
	19: 8 *were* round about these **c** to Baalath-beer,	5892
	19:15 Beth-lehem: twelve **c** with their villages.	5892
	19:16 their families, these **c** with their villages.	5892
	19:22 at Jordan: sixteen **c** with their villages.	5892
	19:23 to their families, the **c** and their villages.	5892
	19:30 twenty and two **c** with their villages.	5892
	19:31 their families, these **c** with their villages.	5892
	19:35 the fenced **c** *are* Ziddim, Zer,	5892
	19:38 nineteen **c** with their villages.	5892
	19:39 to their families, the **c** and their villages.	5892
	19:48 their families, these **c** with their villages.	5892
	20: 2 Appoint out for you **c** of refuge,	5892
	20: 4 he that doth flee unto one of those **c**	5892
	20: 9 These were the **c** appointed for all	5892
	21: 2 hand of Moses to give us **c** to dwell in,	5892
	21: 3 of the Lord, these **c** and their suburbs.	5892
	21: 4 out of the tribe of Benjamin, thirteen **c**.	5892
	21: 5 out of the half tribe of Manasseh, ten **c**.	5892
	21: 6 tribe of Manasseh in Bashan, thirteen **c**.	5892
	21: 7 and out of the tribe of Zebulun, twelve **c**.	5892
	21: 8 the Levites these **c** with their suburbs,	5892
	21: 9 **c** which are *here* mentioned by name,	5892
	21:16 suburbs; nine **c** out of those two tribes.	5892
	21:18 and Almon with her suburbs; four **c**.	5892
	21:19 All the **c** of the children of Aaron,	5892
	21:19 *were* thirteen **c** with their suburbs.	5892
	21:20 even they had the **c** of their lot out of	5892
	21:22 and Beth-horon with her suburbs; four **c**.	5892
	21:24 Gath-rimmon with her suburbs; four **c**.	5892
	21:25 Gath-rimmon with her suburbs; two **c**.	5892
	21:26 All the **c** *were* ten with their suburbs for	5892

Jos	21:27 and Beeshterah with her suburbs; two **c**.	5892
	21:29 En-gannim with her suburbs; four **c**.	5892
	21:31 and Rehob with her suburbs; four **c**.	5892
	21:32 and Kartan with her suburbs; three **c**.	5892
	21:33 All the **c** of the Gershonites according to	5892
	21:33 *were* thirteen **c** with their suburbs.	5892
	21:35 Nahalal with her suburbs; four **c**.	5892
	21:37 and Mephaath with her suburbs; four **c**.	5892
	21:39 Jazer with her suburbs; four **c** in all.	5892
	21:40 So all the **c** for the children of Merari by	5892
	21:40 of the Levites, were *by* their lot twelve **c**.	5892
	21:41 All the **c** of the Levites within	5892
	21:41 *were* forty and eight **c** with their suburbs.	5892
	21:42 These **c** were **every one** with their	5892+5892
	21:42 round about them: thus *were* all these **c**.	5892
	24:13 **c** which ye built not, and ye dwell in	5892
Jdg	10: 4 they had thirty **c**, which are called	5892
	11:26 in all the **c** that *be* along by the coasts of	5892
	11:33 *even* twenty **c**, and unto the plain of	5892
	12: 7 and was buried in *one of* the **c** of Gilead.	5892
	20:14 together out of the **c** unto Gibeah,	5892
	20:15 numbered at that time out of the **c** twenty	5892
	20:42 them which *came* out of the **c** they	5892
	20:48 they set on fire all the **c** that they came	5892
	21:23 and repaired the **c**, and dwelt in them.	5892
1Sa	6:18 *according to* the number of all the **c** of	5892
	6:18 *both* of fenced **c**, and of country villages,	5892
	7:14 the **c** which the Philistines had taken	5892
	18: 6 the women came out of all **c** of Israel,	5892
	30:29 to *them* which *were* in the **c** of	5892
	30:29 *them* which *were* in the **c** of the Kenites,	5892
	31: 7 were dead, they forsook the **c**, and fled;	5892
2Sa	2: 1 Shall I go up into any of the **c** of Judah?	5892
	2: 3 and they dwelt in the **c** of Hebron.	5892
	8: 8 and from Berothai, **c** of Hadadezer,	5892
	10:12 for our people, and for the **c** of our God:	5892
	12:31 thus did he unto all the **c** of the children	5892
	20: 6 lest he get him fenced **c**, and escape us.	5892
	24: 7 to all the **c** of the Hivites, and of	5892
1Ki	4:13 threescore great **c** *with* walls and	5892
	8:37 enemy besiege them in the land of their **c**;	8179
	9:11 king Solomon gave Hiram twenty **c** in	5892
	9:12 Hiram came out from Tyre to see the **c**	5892
	9:13 What *are* these which thou hast given	5892
	9:19 all the **c** of store that Solomon had,	5892
	9:19 for his chariots, and cities for his	5892
	9:19 for his horsemen, and that which	5892
	10:26 whom he bestowed in the **c** for chariots,	5892
	12:17 of Israel which dwelt in the **c** of Judah,	5892
	13:32 high places which *are* in the **c** of Samaria,	5892
	15:20 hosts which he had against the **c** of Israel,	5892
	15:23 all that he did, and the **c** which he built,	5892
	20:34 Ben-hadad said unto him, The **c**, which	5892
	22:39 he made, and all the **c** that he built,	5892
2Ki	3:25 they beat down the **c**, and *on* every good	5892
	13:25 of Ben-hadad the son of Hazael the **c**,	5892
	13:25 beat him, and recovered the **c** of Israel.	5892
	17: 6 river of Gozan, and in the **c** of the Medes.	5892
	17: 9 they built them high places in all their **c**,	5892
	17:24 placed *them* in the **c** of Samaria instead of	5892
	17:24 and dwelt in the **c** thereof.	5892
	17:26 and placed in the **c** of Samaria,	5892
	17:29 nation in their **c** wherein they dwelt.	5892
	18:11 of Gozan, and in the **c** of the Medes:	5892
	18:13 come up against all the fenced **c** of Judah,	5892
	19:25 thou shouldest be to lay waste fenced **c**	5892
	23: 5 in the high places in the **c** of Judah,	5892
	23: 8 he brought all the priests out of the **c** of	5892
	23:19 high places that *were* in the **c** of Samaria,	5892
1Ch	2:22 and twenty **c** in the land of Gilead.	5892
	2:23 the towns thereof, *even* threescore **c**.	5892
	4:31 *were* their **c** unto the reign of David.	5892
	4:32 Rimmon, and Tochen, and Ashan, five **c**:	5892
	4:33 villages that *were* round about the same **c**,	5892
	6:57 to the sons of Aaron they gave the **c** of	5892
	6:60 All their **c** throughout their families *were*	5892
	6:60 throughout their families *were* thirteen **c**.	5892
	6:61 *were* **c** given out of the half tribe,	NIH
	6:61 of the half *tribe* of Manasseh, by lot, ten **c**.	5892
	6:62 tribe of Manasseh in Bashan, thirteen **c**.	5892
	6:63 and out of the tribe of Zebulun, twelve **c**.	5892
	6:64 to the Levites *these* **c** with their suburbs.	5892
	6:65 these **c**, which are called by *their* names.	5892
	6:66 of their coasts out of the tribe of	5892
	6:67 they gave unto them, *of* the **c** of refuge,	5892
	9: 2 possessions in their **c** *were*, the Israelites,	5892
	10: 7 then they forsook their **c**, and fled:	5892
	13: 2 Levites *which are* in their **c** *and* suburbs,	5892
	18: 8 and from Chun, **c** of Hadarezer,	5892
	19: 7 gathered themselves together from their **c**,	5892
	19:13 for our people, and for the **c** of our God:	5892
	20: 3 dealt David with all the **c** of the children	5892
	27:25 in the **c**, and in the villages, and in	5892
2Ch	1:14 which he placed in the chariot **c**,	5892
	6:28 if their enemies besiege them in the **c** of	8179
	8: 2 That the **c** which Huram had restored to	5892
	8: 4 all the store **c**, which he built in Hamath.	5892
	8: 5 fenced **c**, *with* walls, gates, and bars;	5892
	8: 6 all the store **c** that Solomon had, and all	5892
	8: 6 all the chariot **c**, and the cities of	5892
	8: 6 of the horsemen, and all that Solomon	5892
	9:25 whom he bestowed in the chariot **c**,	5892
	10:17 of Israel that dwelt in the **c** of Judah,	5892
	11: 5 and built **c** for defence in Judah.	5892
	11:10 *are* in Judah and in Benjamin, fenced **c**.	5892

2Ch	12: 4 he took the fenced **c** which *pertained* to	5892
	13:19 took **c** from him, Beth-el with the towns	5892
	14: 5 he took away out of all the **c** of Judah	5892
	14: 6 he built fenced **c** in Judah: for the land	5892
	14: 7 Let us build these **c**, and make about	5892
	14:14 they smote all the **c** round about Gerar;	5892
	14:14 they spoiled all the **c**; for there was	5892
	15: 8 of the **c** which he had taken from mount	5892
	16: 4 the captains of his armies against the **c**	5892
	16: 4 and all the store **c** of Naphtali.	5892
	17: 2 he placed forces in all the fenced **c** of	5892
	17: 2 in the **c** of Ephraim, which Asa his father	5892
	17: 7 to Michaiah, to teach in the **c** of Judah.	5892
	17: 9 went about throughout all the **c** of Judah,	5892
	17:12 he built in Judah castles, and **c** of store.	5892
	17:13 he had much business in the **c** of Judah:	5892
	17:19 put in the fenced **c** throughout all Judah.	5892
	19: 5 land throughout all the fenced **c** of Judah,	5892
	19:10 you of your brethren that dwell in their **c**,	5892
	20: 4 out of all the **c** of Judah they came to	5892
	21: 3 precious things, with fenced **c** in Judah:	5892
	23: 2 gathered the Levites out of all the **c** of	5892
	24: 5 Go out unto the **c** of Judah, and gather of	5892
	25:13 fell upon the **c** of Judah, from Samaria	5892
	26: 6 built **c** about Ashdod, and among	5892
	27: 4 Moreover he built **c** in the mountains of	5892
	28:18 The Philistines also had invaded the **c** of	5892
	31: 1 Israel that were present went out to the **c**	5892
	31: 1 man to his possession, into their own **c**.	5892
	31: 6 and Judah, that dwelt in the **c** of Judah,	5892
	31:15 and Shecaniah, in the **c** of the priests,	5892
	31:19 in the fields of the suburbs of their **c**,	5892
	32: 1 encamped against the fenced **c**,	5892
	32:29 Moreover he provided him **c**,	5892
	33:14 put captains of war in all the fenced **c** of	5892
	34: 6 *so did he* in the **c** of Manasseh,	5892
Ezr	2:70 in their **c**, and all Israel in their cities.	5892
	2:70 in their cities, and all Israel in their **c**.	5892
	3: 1 and the children of Israel *were* in the **c**,	5892
	4:10 set in the **c** of Samaria, and the rest *that*	7149
	10:14 wives in our **c** come at appointed times,	5892
Ne	7:73 and all Israel, dwelt in their **c**;	5892
	7:73 the children of Israel *were* in their **c**.	5892
	8:15 should publish and proclaim in all their **c**,	5892
	9:25 they took strong **c**, and a fat land,	5892
	10:37 have the tithes in all the **c** of our tillage.	5892
	11: 1 and nine parts *to dwell in* other **c**.	5892
	11: 3 in the **c** of Judah dwelt every one in his	5892
	11: 3 every one in his possession in their **c**,	5892
	11:20 and the Levites, *were* in all the **c** of Judah,	5892
	12:44 gather into them out of the fields of the **c**	5892
Est	9: 2 throughout all the provinces of the king	5892
Job	15:28 he dwelleth in desolate **c**, *and* in houses	5892
Ps	9: 6 thou hast destroyed **c**; their memorial is	5892
	69:35 save Zion, and will build the **c** of Judah:	5892
Isa	1: 7 is desolate, your **c** *are* burnt *with* fire:	5892
	6:11 until the **c** be wasted without inhabitant,	5892
	14:17 a wilderness, and destroyed the **c** thereof;	5892
	14:21 nor fill the face of the world *with* **c**.	5892
	17: 2 The **c** of Aroer *are* forsaken: they shall be	5892
	17: 9 In that day shall his strong **c** be as a	5892
	19:18 In that day shall five **c** in the land of Egypt	5892
	33: 8 he hath despised the **c**, he regardeth no	5892
	36: 1 up against all the defenced **c** of Judah,	5892
	37:26 lay waste defenced **c** *into* ruinous heaps.	5892
	40: 9 say unto the **c** of Judah, Behold your God.	5892
	42:11 the **c** thereof lift up *their* voice,	5892
	44:26 to the **c** of Judah, Ye shall be built,	5892
	54: 3 and make the desolate **c** to be inhabited.	5892
	61: 4 they shall repair the waste **c**,	5892
	64:10 Thy holy **c** are a wilderness, Zion is a	5892
Jer	1:15 about, and against all the **c** of Judah.	5892
	2:15 his **c** are burnt without inhabitant.	5892
	2:28 for *according to* the number of thy **c** are	5892
	4: 5 and let us go into the defenced **c**.	5892
	4: 7 and thy **c** shall be laid waste, without an	5892
	4:16 give out their voice against the **c** of Judah.	5892
	4:26 all the **c** thereof were broken down at	5892
	5: 6 a leopard shall watch over their **c**:	5892
	5:17 they shall impoverish thy fenced **c**,	5892
	7:17 Seest thou not what they do in the **c** of	5892
	7:34 will I cause to cease from the **c** of Judah,	5892
	8:14 let us enter into the defenced **c**, and let us	5892
	9:11 I will make the **c** of Judah desolate,	5892
	10:22 make the **c** of Judah desolate, *and* a den	5892
	11: 6 Proclaim all these words in the **c** of Judah	5892
	11:12 shall the **c** of Judah and inhabitants of	5892
	11:13 *according to* the number of thy **c** *were*	5892
	13:19 The **c** of the south shall be shut up,	5892
	17:26 they shall come from the **c** of Judah,	5892
	20:16 let that man be as the **c** which the Lord	5892
	22: 6 wilderness *and* **c** *which* are not inhabited.	5892
	25:18 the **c** of Judah, and the kings thereof,	5892
	26: 2 and speak unto all the **c** of Judah,	5892
	31:21 virgin of Israel, turn again to these thy **c**,	5892
	31:23 in the land of Judah and in the **c** thereof,	5892
	31:24 in all the **c** thereof together, husbandmen,	5892
	32:44 in the **c** of Judah, and in the cities of	5892
	32:44 in the **c** of the mountains, and in the	5892
	32:44 in the **c** of the valley, and in the cities of	5892
	32:44 of the valley, and in the **c** of the south:	5892
	33:10 *even* in the **c** of Judah, and in the streets	5892
	33:12 without beast, and in all the **c** thereof,	5892
	33:13 In the **c** of the mountains, in the cities of	5892
	33:13 in the **c** of the vale, and in the cities of	5892

CITIZEN – CITY
The Strongest Strong's
218

C

Jer	33:13 in the **c** of the south, and in the land of	5892
	33:13 about Jerusalem, and in the **c** of Judah,	5892
	34: 1 and against all the **c** thereof, saying,	5892
	34: 7 against all the **c** of Judah that were left,	5892
	34: 7 these defenced **c** remained of the cities	5892
	34: 7 these defenced cities remained of the **c**	5892
	34:22 I will make the **c** of Judah a desolation	5892
	36: 6 ears of all Judah that come out of their **c**	5892
	36: 9 to all the people that came from the **c** of	5892
	40: 5 hath made governor over the **c** of Judah,	5892
	40:10 and dwell in your **c** that ye have taken.	5892
	44: 2 and upon all the **c** of Judah;	5892
	44: 6 was kindled in the **c** of Judah and in	5892
	44:17 in the **c** of Judah, and in the streets of	5892
	44:21 incense that ye burnt in the **c** of Judah,	5892
	48: 9 for the **c** thereof shall be desolate, without	5892
	48:15 gone up out of her **c**, and his chosen	5892
	48:24 upon all the **c** of the land of Moab, far or	5892
	48:28 leave the **c**, and dwell in the rock,	5892
	49: 1 inherit Gad, and his people dwell in his **c**?	5892
	49:13 all the **c** thereof shall be perpetual wastes.	5892
	49:18 Gomorrah and the neighbour **c** thereof,	NIH
	50:32 I will kindle a fire in his **c**, and it shall	5892
	50:40 Gomorrah and the neighbour **c** thereof,	NIH
	51:43 Her **c** are a desolation, a dry land,	5892
La	5:11 in Zion, and the maids in the **c** of Judah.	5892
Eze	6: 6 In all your dwelling places the **c** shall be	5892
	12:20 **c** that are inhabited shall be laid waste,	5892
	19: 7 palaces, and he laid waste their **c**;	5892
	25: 9 I will open the side of Moab from the **c**,	5892
	25: 9 from his **c** which are on his frontiers,	5892
	26:19 like the **c** that are not inhabited;	5892
	29:12 her **c** among the cities that are laid waste	5892
	29:12 her cities among the **c** that are laid waste	5892
	30: 7 her **c** shall be in the midst of the cities	5892
	30: 7 her cities shall be in the midst of the **c**	5892
	30:17 and these **c** shall go into captivity.	NIH
	35: 4 I will lay thy **c** waste, and thou shalt	5892
	35: 9 and thy **c** shall not return:	5892
	36: 4 to the **c** that are forsaken, which became	5892
	36:10 the **c** shall be inhabited, and the wastes	5892
	36:33 I will also cause you to dwell in the **c**,	5892
	36:35 and ruined **c** are become fenced,	5892
	36:38 shall the waste **c** be filled with flocks of	5892
	39: 9 they that dwell in the **c** of Israel shall go	5892
Da	11:15 up a mount, and take the most fenced **c**:	5892
Hos	8:14 and Judah hath multiplied fenced **c**:	5892
	8:14 I will send a fire upon his **c**, and it shall	5892
	11: 6 the sword shall abide on his **c**,	5892
	13:10 any other that may save thee in all thy **c**?	5892
Am	4: 6 given you cleanness of teeth in all your **c**,	5892
	4: 8 two or three **c** wandered unto one city,	5892
	9:14 they shall build the waste **c**,	5892
Ob	1:20 shall possess the **c** of the south.	5892
Mic	5:11 I will cut off the **c** of thy land,	5892
	5:14 the midst of thee: so will I destroy thy **c**.	5892
	7:12 from the fortified **c**, and from the fortress	5892
Zep	1:16 trumpet and alarm against the fenced **c**,	5892
	3: 6 their **c** are destroyed, so that there is no	5892
Zec	1:12 mercy on Jerusalem and on the **c** of Judah,	5892
	1:17 My **c** through prosperity shall yet be	5892
	7: 7 and the **c** thereof round about her,	5892
	8:20 and the inhabitants of many **c**:	5892
Mt	9:35 Jesus went about all the **c** and villages,	4172
	10:23 shall not have gone over the **c** of Israel,	4172
	11: 1 thence to teach and to preach in their **c**.	4172
	11:20 Then began he to upbraid the **c** wherein	4172
	14:13 they followed him on foot out of the **c**.	4172
Mk	6:33 and ran afoot thither out of all **c**,	4172
	6:56 he entered, into villages, or **c**, or country,	4172
Lk	4:43 preach the kingdom of God to other **c**	4172
	13:22 And he went through the **c** and villages,	4172
	19:17 very little, have thou authority over ten **c**.	4172
	19:19 likewise to him, Be thou also over five **c**.	4172
Ac	5:16 There came also a multitude out of the **c**	4172
	8:40 passing through he preached in all the **c**,	4172
	14: 6 **c** of Lycaonia, and unto the region that	4172
	16: 4 And as they went through the **c**,	4172
	26:11 I persecuted them even unto strange **c**.	4172
2Pe	2: 6 And turning the **c** of Sodom and	4172
Jude	1: 7 and Gomorrha, and the **c** about them,	4172
Rev	16:19 three parts, and the **c** of the nations fell:	4172

CITIZEN (2) [CITIZENS, FELLOWCITIZENS]

Lk	15:15 and joined himself to a **c** of that country;	4177
Ac	21:39 a city in Cilicia, a **c** of no mean city:	4177

CITIZENS (1) [CITIZEN]

Lk	19:14 But his **c** hated him, and sent a message	4177

CITIZENSHIP See COMMONWEALTH

CITRON See THYINE

CITY (870) [CITIES]

Ge	4:17 he builded a **c**, and called the name of	5892
	4:17 a city, and called the name of the **c**,	5892
	10:11 and the **c** Rehoboth, and Calah,	5892
	10:12 and Calah: the same is a great **c**.	5892
	11: 4 Go to, let us build us a **c** and a tower,	5892
	11: 5 the LORD came down to see the **c** and	5892
	11: 8 the earth: and they left off to build the **c**.	5892
	18:24 there be fifty righteous within the **c**:	5892
	18:26 find in Sodom fifty righteous within the **c**,	5892
	18:28 wilt thou destroy all the **c** for lack of five?	5892
	19: 4 the men of the **c**, even the men of Sodom,	5892

Ge	19:12 and whatsoever thou hast in the **c**,	5892
	19:14 for the LORD will destroy this **c**.	5892
	19:15 thou be consumed in the iniquity of the **c**.	5892
	19:16 him forth, and set him without the **c**.	5892
	19:20 this **c** is near to flee unto, and it is a little	5892
	19:21 that I will not overthrow this **c**,	5892
	19:22 Therefore the name of the **c** was called	5892
	23:10 even of all that went in at the gate of his **c**,	5892
	23:18 before all that went in at the gate of his **c**.	5892
	24:10 to Mesopotamia, unto the **c** of Nahor.	5892
	24:11 **c** by a well of water at the time of	5892
	24:13 daughters of the men of the **c** come out	5892
	26:33 the name of the **c** is Beer-sheba unto this	5892
	28:19 the name of that **c** was called Luz at	5892
	33:18 Jacob came to Shalem, a **c** of Shechem,	5892
	33:18 and pitched his tent before the **c**.	5892
	34:20 his son came unto the gate of their **c**,	5892
	34:20 communed with the men of their **c**,	5892
	34:24 all that went out of the gate of his **c**;	5892
	34:24 all that went out of the gate of his **c**.	5892
	34:25 came upon the **c** boldly, and slew all	5892
	34:27 spoiled the **c**, because they had defiled	5892
	34:28 that which was in the **c**, and that which	5892
	35:27 unto the **c** of Arbah, which is Hebron,	7151
	36:32 and the name of his **c** was Dinhabah.	5892
	36:35 stead: and the name of his **c** was Avith.	5892
	36:39 the name of his **c** was Pau; and his wife's	5892
	41:48 the field, which was round about every **c**,	5892
	44: 4 And when they were gone out of the **c**,	5892
	44:13 every man his ass, and returned to the **c**.	5892
Ex	9:29 As soon as I am gone out of the **c**,	5892
	9:33 Moses went out of the **c** from Pharaoh,	5892
Lev	14:40 them into an unclean place without the **c**:	5892
	14:41 off without the **c** into an unclean place:	5892
	14:45 he shall carry them forth out of the **c** into	5892
	14:53 he shall let go the living bird out of the **c**	5892
	25:29 a man sell a dwelling house in a walled **c**,	5892
	25:30 the house that is in the walled **c** shall be	5892
	25:33 that was sold, and the **c** of his possession,	5892
Nu	20:16 a **c** in the uttermost of thy border:	5892
	21:26 Heshbon was the **c** of Sihon the king of	5892
	21:27 let the **c** of Sihon be built and prepared:	5892
	21:28 of Heshbon, a flame from the **c** of Sihon:	7151
	22:36 went out to meet him unto a **c** of Moab,	5892
	24:19 shall destroy him that remaineth of the **c**.	5892
	35: 4 shall reach from the wall of the **c** and	5892
	35: 5 ye shall measure from without the **c** on	5892
	35: 5 and the **c** shall be in the midst:	5892
	35:25 congregation shall restore him to the **c**	5892
	35:26 without the border of the **c** of his refuge,	5892
	35:27 without the borders of the **c** of his refuge,	5892
	35:28 Because he should have remained in the **c**	5892
	35:32 for him that is fled to the **c** of his refuge,	5892
Dt	2:34 women, and the little ones, of every **c**,	5892
	2:36 from the **c** that is by the river, even unto	5892
	2:36 there was not one **c** too strong for us:	7151
	3: 4 there was not a **c** which we took not from	7151
	3: 6 the men, women, and children, of every **c**.	5892
	13:13 have withdrawn the inhabitants of their **c**,	5892
	13:15 of that **c** with the edge of the sword,	5892
	13:16 burn with fire the **c**, and all the spoil	5892
	19:12 elders of his **c** shall send and fetch him	5892
	20:10 When thou comest nigh unto a **c** to fight	5892
	20:14 and the cattle, and all that is in the **c**,	5892
	20:19 When thou shalt besiege a **c** a long time,	5892
	20:20 shalt build bulwarks against the **c** that	5892
	21: 3 the **c** which is next unto the slain man,	5892
	21: 3 the elders of that **c** shall take a heifer,	5892
	21: 4 the elders of that **c** shall bring down	5892
	21: 6 all the elders of that **c**, that are next unto	5892
	21:19 bring him out unto the elders of his **c**,	5892
	21:20 they shall say unto the elders of his **c**,	5892
	21:21 all the men of his **c** shall stone him with	5892
	22:15 unto the elders of the **c** in the gate:	5892
	22:17 spread the cloth before the elders of the **c**	5892
	22:18 the elders of that **c** shall take that man	5892
	22:21 men of her **c** shall stone her with stones	5892
	22:23 a man find her in the **c**, and lie with her;	5892
	22:24 them both out unto the gate of that **c**,	5892
	22:24 because she cried not, being in the **c**;	5892
	25: 8 the elders of his **c** shall call him,	5892
	28: 3 Blessed shalt thou be in the **c**,	5892
	28:16 Cursed shalt thou be in the **c**,	5892
	34: 3 of Jericho, the **c** of palm trees, unto Zoar.	5892
Jos	3:16 from the **c** Adam, that is beside Zaretan:	5892
	6: 3 ye shall compass the **c**, all ye men of war,	5892
	6: 3 of war, and go round about the **c** once.	5892
	6: 4 the seventh day ye shall compass the **c**	5892
	6: 5 the wall of the **c** shall fall down flat,	5892
	6: 7 compass the **c**, and let him that is armed	5892
	6:11 So the ark of the LORD compassed the **c**,	5892
	6:14 second day they compassed the **c** once,	5892
	6:15 compassed the **c** after the same manner	5892
	6:15 only on that day they compassed the **c**	5892
	6:16 Shout; for the LORD hath given you the **c**.	5892
	6:17 the **c** shall be accursed, even it, and all	5892
	6:20 so that the people went up into the **c**,	5892
	6:20 straight before him, and they took the **c**.	5892
	6:21 utterly destroyed all that was in the **c**,	5892
	6:24 they burnt the **c** with fire, and all that	5892
	6:26 that riseth up and buildeth this **c** Jericho:	5892
	8: 1 and his people, and his **c**, and his land:	5892
	8: 2 lay thee an ambush for the **c** behind it.	5892
	8: 4 Behold, ye shall lie in wait against the **c**,	5892
	8: 4 wait against the city, even behind the **c**:	5892

Jos	8: 4 go not very far from the **c**, but be ye all	5892
	8: 5 are with me, will approach unto the **c**:	5892
	8: 6 till we have drawn them from the **c**;	5892
	8: 7 from the ambush, and seize upon the **c**:	5892
	8: 8 it shall be, when ye have taken the **c**,	5892
	8: 8 the city, that ye shall set the **c** on fire:	5892
	8:11 before the **c**, and pitched on the north	5892
	8:12 and Ai, on the west side of the **c**.	5892
	8:13 the host that was on the north of the **c**,	5892
	8:13 their liers in wait on the west of the **c**,	5892
	8:14 the men of the **c** went out against Israel to	5892
	8:14 liers in ambush against him behind the **c**.	5892
	8:16 and were drawn away from the **c**.	5892
	8:17 they left the **c** open, and pursued after	5892
	8:18 that he had in his hand toward the **c**.	5892
	8:19 they entered into the **c**, and took it,	5892
	8:19 took it, and hasted and set the **c** on fire.	5892
	8:20 smoke of the **c** ascended up to heaven,	5892
	8:21 saw that the ambush had taken the **c**,	5892
	8:21 that the smoke of the **c** ascended, then	5892
	8:22 other issued out of the **c** against them;	5892
	8:27 The spoil of that **c** Israel took for a prey	5892
	8:29 cast it at the entering of the gate of the **c**,	5892
	10: 2 because Gibeon was a great **c**,	5892
	11:19 There was not a **c** that made peace with	5892
	13: 9 the **c** that is in the midst of the river,	5892
	13:16 the **c** that is in the midst of the river,	5892
	15:13 even the **c** of Arba the father of Anak,	7151
	15:13 the father of Anak, which **c** is Hebron.	NIH
	15:62 and the **c** of salt, and En-gedi;	5892
	18:14 a **c** of the children of Judah:	5892
	19:29 to Ramah, and to the strong **c** Tyre;	5892
	19:50 they gave him the **c** which he asked,	5892
	19:50 and he built the **c**, and dwelt therein.	5892
	20: 4 stand at the entering of the gate of the **c**,	5892
	20: 4 cause in the ears of the elders of that **c**,	5892
	20: 4 they shall take him into the **c** unto them,	5892
	20: 6 he shall dwell in that **c**, until he stand	5892
	20: 6 come unto his own **c**, and unto his own	5892
	20: 6 house, unto the **c** from whence he fled.	5892
	21:11 they gave them the **c** of Arbah the father	7151
	21:11 which **c** is Hebron, in the hill country of	NIH
	21:12 fields of the **c**, and the villages thereof,	5892
	21:13 to be a **c** of refuge for the slayer;	5892
	21:21 to be a **c** of refuge for the slayer;	5892
	21:27 to be a **c** of refuge for the slayer;	5892
	21:32 to be a **c** of refuge for the slayer;	5892
	21:38 to be a **c** of refuge for the slayer;	5892
Jdg	1: 8 edge of the sword, and set the **c** on fire.	5892
	1:16 went up out of the **c** of palm trees with	5892
	1:17 the name of the **c** was called Hormah.	5892
	1:23 (Now the name of the **c** before was Luz.)	5892
	1:24 spies saw a man come forth out of the **c**,	5892
	1:24 the entrance into the **c**, and we will shew	5892
	1:25 he shewed them the entrance into the **c**,	5892
	1:25 they smote the **c** with the edge of	5892
	1:26 built a **c**, and called the name thereof Luz:	5892
	3:13 and possessed the **c** of palm trees.	5892
	6:27 the men of the **c**, that he could not do it	5892
	6:28 when the men of the **c** arose early in	5892
	6:30 the men of the **c** said unto Joash, Bring	5892
	8:16 he took the elders of the **c**, and thorns of	5892
	8:17 of Penuel, and slew the men of the **c**.	5892
	8:27 and put it in his **c**, even in Ophrah:	5892
	9:30 when Zebul the ruler of the **c** heard	5892
	9:31 and behold, they fortify the **c** against thee.	5892
	9:33 thou shalt rise early, and set upon the **c**:	5892
	9:35 stood in the entering of the gate of the **c**:	5892
	9:43 the people were come forth out of the **c**;	5892
	9:44 stood in the entering of the gate of the **c**:	5892
	9:45 Abimelech fought against the **c** all that	5892
	9:45 he took the **c**, and slew the people that	5892
	9:45 beat down the **c**, and sowed it with salt.	5892
	9:51 there was a strong tower within the **c**,	5892
	9:51 all they of the **c**, and shut it to them,	5892
	14:18 the men of the **c** said unto him on	5892
	16: 2 wait for him all night in the gate of the **c**,	5892
	16: 3 took the doors of the gate of the **c**,	5892
	17: 8 the man departed out of the **c** from	5892
	18:27 of the sword, and burnt the **c** with fire.	5892
	18:28 And they built a **c**, and dwelt therein,	5892
	18:29 they called the name of the **c** Dan, after	5892
	18:29 howbeit the name of the **c** was Laish at	5892
	19:11 let us turn in into this **c** of the Jebusites,	5892
	19:12 We will not turn aside hither into the **c** of	5892
	19:15 he sat him down in a street of the **c**:	5892
	19:17 a wayfaring man in the street of the **c**:	5892
	19:22 behold, the men of the **c**, certain sons of	5892
	20:11 men of Israel were gathered against the **c**,	5892
	20:31 and were drawn away from the **c**,	5892
	20:32 draw them from the **c** unto the highways.	5892
	20:37 smote all the **c** with the edge of the sword	5892
	20:38 flame with smoke rise up out of the **c**.	5892
	20:40 up out of the **c** with a pillar of smoke,	5892
	20:40 the flame of the **c** ascended up to heaven.	5892
	20:48 as well the men of every **c**, as the beast,	5892
Ru	1:19 that all the **c** was moved about them,	5892
	2:18 she took it up, and went into the **c**: and	5892
	3:11 for all the **c** of my people doth know that	8179
	3:15 and laid it on her: and he went into the **c**.	5892
	4: 2 he took ten men of the elders of the **c**,	5892
1Sa	1: 3 this man went up out of his **c** yearly to	5892
	4:13 the man came into the **c**, and told it,	5892
	4:13 the city, and told it, all the **c** cried out.	5892
	5: 9 the hand of the LORD was against the **c**	5892

Rev	18:10	that great city Babylon, that mighty c!	4172
	18:16	And saying, Alas, alas, that great c,	4172
	18:18	saying, What c is like unto this great city?	NIG
	18:18	saying, What city is like unto this great c?	4172
	18:19	wailing, saying, Alas, alas, that great c,	4172
	18:21	Thus with violence shall that great c	4172
	20: 9	of the saints about, and the beloved c:	4172
	21: 2	I John saw the holy c, new Jerusalem,	4172
	21:10	mountain, and shewed me that great c,	4172
	21:14	And the wall of the c had twelve	4172
	21:15	he had a golden reed to measure the c,	4172
	21:16	And the c lieth foursquare, and the length	4172
	21:16	and he measured the c with the reed,	4172
	21:18	and the c was pure gold, like unto clear	4172
	21:19	And the foundations of the wall of the c	4172
	21:21	the street of the c was pure gold, as it	4172
	21:23	the c had no need of the sun, neither of	4172
	22:14	may enter in through the gates into the c.	4172
	22:19	out of the holy c, and from the things	4172

CITY CLERK See TOWNCLERK

CLAD (2)

1Ki	11:29	he had c himself with a new garment;	3680
Isa	59:17	clothing, and was c with zeal as a cloke.	5844

CLAMOROUS (1) [CLAMOUR]

Pr	9:13	A foolish woman is c: she is simple,	1993

CLAMOUR (1) [CLAMOROUS]

Eph	4:31	and anger, and c, and evil speaking,	2906

CLAN See KINDRED; KINDREDS

CLANGING See TINKLING

CLAP (6) [CLAPPED, CLAPPETH, CLAPT]

Job	27:23	Men shall c their hands at him,	5606
Ps	47: 1	O c your hands, all ye people; shout unto	8628
	98: 8	Let the floods c their hands: let the hills	4222
Isa	55:12	all the trees of the field shall c their hands.	4222
La	2:15	All that pass by c their hands at thee;	5606
Na	3:19	all that hear the bruit of thee shall c	8628

CLAPPED (1) [CLAP]

Eze	25: 6	Because thou hast c thine hands,	4222

CLAPPETH (1) [CLAP]

Job	34:37	he c his hands amongst us,	5606

CLAPT (1) [CLAP]

2Ki	11:12	they c their hands, and said, God save	5221

CLASP See TACHES

CLAUDA (1)

Ac	27:16	under a certain island which is called C,	2802

CLAUDIA (1)

2Ti	4:21	and Linus, and C, and all the brethren.	2803

CLAUDIUS (3)

Ac	11:28	came to pass in the days of C Cesar.	2804
	18: 2	that C had commanded all Jews to depart	2804
	23:26	C Lysias unto the most excellent governor	2804

CLAVE (14) [CLEAVE]

Ge	22: 3	c the wood for the burnt offering,	1234
	34: 3	soul c unto Dinah the daughter of Jacob,	1692
Nu	16:31	that the ground c asunder that was under	1234
Jdg	15:19	God c a hollow place that was in the jaw,	1234
Ru	1:14	her mother in law; but Ruth c unto her.	1692
1Sa	6:14	they c the wood of the cart, and offered	1234
2Sa	20: 2	the men of Judah c unto their king,	1692
	23:10	weary, and his hand c unto the sword:	1692
1Ki	11: 2	their gods: Solomon c unto these in love.	1692
2Ki	18: 6	For he c to the LORD, and departed not	1692
Ne	10:29	They c to their brethren, their nobles,	2388
Ps	78:15	He c the rocks in the wilderness,	1234
Isa	48:21	he c the rock also, and the waters gushed	1234
Ac	17:34	Howbeit certain men c unto him,	2853

CLAWS (3)

Dt	14: 6	cleaveth the cleft into two c,	6541
Da	4:33	eagles' feathers, and his nails like birds' c.	NIH
Zec	11:16	flesh of the fat, and tear their c in pieces.	6541

CLAY (33)

1Ki	7:46	in the c ground between Succoth and	4568
2Ch	4:17	in the c ground between Succoth and	5645
Job	4:19	less in them that dwell in houses of c,	2563
	10: 9	that thou hast made me as the c;	2563
	13:12	unto ashes, your bodies to bodies of c.	2563
	27:16	as the dust, and prepare raiment as the c;	2563
	33: 6	I also am formed out of the c.	2563
	38:14	It is turned as c to the seal; and they	2563
Ps	40: 2	out of the miry c, and set my feet upon a	2916
Isa	29:16	down shall be esteemed as the potter's c:	2563
	41:25	morter, and as the potter treadeth c.	2916
	45: 9	Shall the c say to him that fashioneth it,	2563
	64: 8	we are the c, and thou our potter;	2563
Jer	18: 4	the vessel that he made of c was marred	2563
	18: 6	as the c is in the potter's hand, so are ye	2563
	43: 9	and hide them in the c in the brickkiln,	4423
Da	2:33	of iron, his feet part of iron and part of c.	2635
	2:34	upon his feet that were of iron and c,	2635
	2:35	the c, the brass, the silver, and the gold,	2635

Da	2:41	toes, part of potter's c, and part of iron,	2635
	2:41	thou sawest the iron mixed with miry c.	2635
	2:42	part of c, so the kingdom shall be partly	2635
	2:43	thou sawest the iron mixt with miry c,	2635
	2:43	another, even as iron is not mixed with c.	2635
	2:45	the brass, the c, the silver, and the gold;	2635
Na	3:14	go into c, and tread the morter, make	2916
Hab	2: 6	to him that ladeth himself with thick c!	5671
Jn	9: 6	made c of the spittle, and he anointed	4081
	9: 6	the eyes of the blind man with the c,	4081
	9:11	A man that is called Jesus made c,	4081
	9:14	the sabbath day when Jesus made the c,	4081
	9:15	He put c upon mine eyes, and I washed,	4081
Ro	9:21	Hath not the potter power over the c,	4081

CLEAN (133) [CLEANNESS, CLEANSE, CLEANSED, CLEANSETH, CLEANSING, UNCLEAN]

Ge	7: 2	Of every c beast thou shalt take to thee	2889
	7: 2	of beasts that are not c by two, the male	2889
	7: 8	Of c beasts, and of beasts that are not	2889
	7: 8	of beasts that are not c, and of fowls,	2889
	8:20	took of every c beast, and of every clean	2889
	8:20	every c beast, and offered burnt offerings	2889
	35: 2	be c, and change your garments:	2891
Lev	4:12	forth without the camp unto a c place,	2889
	6:11	ashes without the camp unto a c place.	2889
	7:19	the flesh, all that be c shall eat thereof.	2889
	10:10	and unholy, and between unclean and c;	2889
	10:14	heave shoulder shall ye eat in a c place;	2889
	11:36	there is plenty of water, shall be c:	2889
	11:37	seed which is to be sown, it shall be c.	2889
	11:47	difference between the unclean and the c,	2889
	12: 8	an atonement for her, and she shall be c.	2891
	13: 6	skin, the priest shall pronounce him c:	2891
	13: 6	and he shall wash his clothes, and be c.	2891
	13:13	he shall pronounce him c that hath	2891
	13:13	the plague: it is all turned white: he is c.	2889
	13:17	the priest shall pronounce him c that	2891
	13:17	him clean that hath the plague: he is c.	2889
	13:23	and the priest shall pronounce him c.	2891
	13:28	and the priest shall pronounce him c:	2891
	13:34	then the priest shall pronounce him c:	2891
	13:34	and he shall wash his clothes, and be c.	2891
	13:37	up therein; the scall is healed, he is c:	2889
	13:37	and the priest shall pronounce him c.	2891
	13:39	spot that groweth in the skin: he is c.	2889
	13:40	fallen off his head, he is bald: yet is he c.	2889
	13:41	his face, he is forehead bald: yet is he c.	2889
	13:58	washed the second time, and shall be c.	2891
	13:59	to pronounce it c, or to pronounce it	2891
	14: 4	is to be cleansed two birds alive and c,	2889
	14: 7	shall pronounce him c, and shall let	2891
	14: 8	wash himself in water, that he may be c:	2891
	14: 9	wash his flesh in water, and he shall be c.	2891
	14:11	priest that maketh him c shall present	2891
	14:11	present the man that is to be made c,	2891
	14:20	an atonement for him, and he shall be c.	2891
	14:48	the priest shall pronounce the house c,	2891
	14:53	atonement for the house: and it shall be c.	2891
	14:57	when it is unclean, and when it is c:	2889
	15: 8	hath the issue spit upon him that is c;	2891
	15:13	his flesh in running water, and shall be c.	2891
	15:28	seven days, and after that she shall be c.	2891
	16:30	that ye may be c from all your sins before	2891
	17:15	until the even: then shall he be c.	2891
	20:25	put difference between c beasts	2889
	20:25	and between unclean fowls and c:	2889
	22: 4	not eat of the holy things, until he be c.	2891
	22: 7	he shall be c, and shall afterward eat of	2891
	23:22	thou shalt not make c riddance of	3615
Nu	5:28	if the woman be not defiled, but be c;	2889
	8: 7	their clothes, and so make themselves c.	2891
	9:13	the man that is c, and is not in a journey,	2889
	18:11	every one that is c in thy house shall eat	2889
	18:13	every one that is c in thine house shall eat	2889
	19: 9	man that is c shall gather up the ashes of	2889
	19: 9	them up without the camp in a c place,	2889
	19:12	and on the seventh day he shall be c:	2891
	19:12	then the seventh day he shall not be c.	2891
	19:18	a c person shall take hyssop, and dip it in	2889
	19:19	the c person shall sprinkle upon the	2889
	19:19	himself in water, and shall be c at even.	2891
	31:23	it go through the fire, and it shall be c:	2891
	31:24	ye shall be c, and afterward ye shall come	2891
Dt	12:15	the unclean and the c may eat thereof,	2889
	12:22	and the c shall eat of them alike.	2889
	14:11	Of all c birds ye shall eat.	2889
	14:20	But of all c fowls ye may eat.	2889
	15:22	and the c person shall eat it alike,	2889
	23:10	that is not c by reason of uncleanness that	2889
Jos	3:17	all the people were passed c over Jordan,	8552
	4: 1	when all the people were c passed over	8552
	4:11	when all the people were c passed over,	8552
1Sa	20:26	Something hath befallen him, he is not c;	2889
	20:26	he is not clean; surely he is not c.	2889
2Ki	5:10	come again to thee, and thou shalt be c.	2891
	5:12	may I not wash in them, and be c? So he	2891
	5:13	when he saith to thee, Wash, and be c?	2891
	5:14	the flesh of a little child, and he was c.	2891
2Ch	30:17	passovers for every one that was not c,	2889
Job	9:30	make my hands never so c; 1253+2141+871.1	
	11: 4	doctrine is pure, and I am c in thine eyes.	1249
	14: 4	can bring a c thing out of an unclean?	2889
	15:14	What is man, that he should be c?	2135
	15:15	yea, the heavens are not c in his sight.	2141

Job	17: 9	he that hath c hands shall be stronger	2889
	25: 4	how can he be c that is born of a woman?	2135
	33: 9	I am c without transgression, I am	2134
Ps	19: 9	The fear of the LORD is c, enduring for	2889
	24: 4	He that hath c hands, and a pure heart;	5355
	51: 7	Purge me with hyssop, and I shall be c:	2891
	51:10	Create in me a c heart, O God; and renew	2889
	73: 1	to Israel, even to such as are of a c heart.	1249
	77: 8	Is his mercy c gone for ever? doth his	656
Pr	14: 4	Where no oxen are, the crib is c: but	1249
	16: 2	All the ways of a man are c in his own	2134
	20: 9	Who can say, I have made my heart c,	2135
Ecc	9: 2	the good and to the c, and to the unclean;	2889
Isa	1:16	Wash ye, make you c; put away the evil	2135
	24:19	the earth is c dissolved, the earth 6565+6565	
	28: 8	and filthiness, so that there is no place c.	NIH
	30:24	that ear the ground shall eat c provender,	2548
	52:11	be ye c, that bear the vessels of	1305
	66:20	in a c vessel into the house of the LORD.	2889
Jer	13:27	wilt thou not be made c? when shall it	2891
Eze	22:26	difference between the unclean and the c	2889
	36:25	will I sprinkle c water upon you,	2889
	36:25	clean water upon you, and ye shall be c:	2891
	44:23	to discern between the unclean and the c.	2889
Joel	1: 7	he hath made it c bare, and cast it away;	2834
Zec	11:17	his arm shall be c dried up, 3001+3001	
Mt	8: 2	Lord, if thou wilt, thou canst make me c.	2511
	8: 3	and touched him, saying, I will; be thou c.	2511
	23:25	for ye make c the outside of the cup and	2511
	23:26	that the outside of them may be c also.	2513
	27:59	the body, he wrapped it in a c linen cloth,	2513
Mk	1:40	If thou wilt, thou canst make me c.	2511
	1:41	and saith unto him, I will; be thou c.	2511
Lk	5:12	Lord, if thou wilt, thou canst make me c.	2511
	5:13	be thou c. And immediately the leprosy	2511
	11:39	for ye Pharisees make c the outside of	2511
	11:41	and behold, all things are c unto you.	2513
Jn	13:10	save to wash his feet, but is c every whit:	2513
	13:10	clean every whit: and ye are c, but not all.	2513
	13:11	therefore said he, Ye are not all c.	2513
	15: 3	Now ye are c through the word which I	2513
Ac	18: 6	blood be upon your own heads; I am c:	2513
2Pe	2:18	those that were c escaped from them who	3689
Rev	19: 8	be arrayed in fine linen, c and white:	2513
	19:14	clothed in fine linen, white and c.	2513

CLEANNESS (5) [CLEAN]

2Sa	22:21	according to the c of my hands hath he	1252
	22:25	according to my c in his eye sight.	1252
Ps	18:20	according to the c of my hands hath he	1252
	18:24	according to the c of my hands in his	1252
Am	4: 6	I also have given you c of teeth in all your	5356

CLEANSE (33) [CLEAN]

Ex	29:36	thou shalt c the altar, when thou hast	2398
Lev	14:49	he shall take to c the house two birds,	2398
	14:52	he shall c the house with the blood of	2398
	16:19	c it, and hallow it from the uncleanness	2891
	16:30	to c you, that ye may be clean from all	2891
Nu	8: 6	among the children of Israel, and c them.	2891
	8: 7	thus shalt thou do unto them, to c them:	2891
	8:15	thou shalt c them, and offer them for an	2891
	8:21	Aaron made an atonement for them to c	2891
2Ch	29:15	the LORD, to c the house of the LORD.	2891
	29:16	c it, and brought out all the uncleanness	2891
Ne	13: 9	the Levites that they should c	2891
Ps	19:12	his errors? c thou me from secret faults.	5352
	51: 2	mine iniquity, and c me from my sin.	2891
	119: 9	shall a young man c his way?	2135
Jer	4:11	of my people, not to fan, nor to c,	1305
	33: 8	I will c them from all their iniquity,	2891
Eze	36:25	and from all your idols, will I c you.	2891
	37:23	they have sinned, and will c them:	2891
	39:12	of them, that they may c the land.	2891
	39:14	remain upon the face of the earth, to c it:	2891
	39:16	be Hamonah. Thus shall they c the land.	2891
	43:20	about: thus shalt thou c and purge it.	2398
	43:22	they shall c the altar, as they did cleanse	2891
	43:22	the altar, as they did c it with the bullock.	2398
	45:18	without blemish, and c the sanctuary:	2398
Joel	3:21	For I will c their blood that I have not	5352
Mt	10: 8	Heal the sick, c the lepers, raise the dead,	2511
	23:26	c first that which is within the cup and	2511
2Co	7: 1	let us c ourselves from all filthiness of	2511
Eph	5:26	c it with the washing of water by the	2511
Jas	4: 8	C your hands, ye sinners; and purify your	2511
1Jn	1: 9	and to c us from all unrighteousness.	2511

CLEANSED (39) [CLEAN]

Lev	11:32	be unclean until the even; so it shall be c.	2891
	12: 7	she shall be c from the issue of her blood.	2891
	14: 4	take for him that is to be c two birds alive	2891
	14: 7	he shall sprinkle upon him that is to be c	2891
	14: 8	he that is to be c shall wash his clothes,	2891
	14:14	tip of the right ear of him that is to be c,	2891
	14:17	tip of the right ear of him that is to be c,	2891
	14:18	upon the head of him that is to be c:	2891
	14:19	an atonement for him that is to be c	2891
	14:25	tip of the right ear of him that is to be c,	2891
	14:28	tip of the right ear of him that is to be c,	2891
	14:29	put upon the head of him that is to be c,	2891
	14:31	for him that is to be c before the LORD.	2891
	15:13	he that hath an issue is c of his issue;	2891
	15:28	if she be c of her issue, then she shall	2891
Nu	35:33	the land cannot be c of the blood that is	3722

C

Jos	22:17 from which we are not **c** until this day,	2891
2Ch	29:18 We have **c** all the house of the LORD,	2891
	30:18 and Zebulun, had not **c** themselves,	2891
	30:19 though *he be* not **c** according to	NIH
	34: 5 their altars, and **c** Judah and Jerusalem.	2891
Ne	13: 9 I commanded, and they **c** the chambers:	2891
	13:30 Thus **c** I them from all strangers,	2891
Job	35: 3 profit shall I have, *if I be* **c** from my sin?	NIH
Ps	73:13 Verily I have **c** my heart *in* vain,	2135
Eze	22:24 unto her, Thou *art* the land that is not **c**,	2891
	36:33 In the day that I shall have **c** you from all	2891
	44:26 after he is **c**, they shall reckon unto him	2893
Da	8:14 days; then shall the sanctuary be **c**.	6663
Joel	3:21 will cleanse their blood *that* I have not **c**:	5352
Mt	8: 3 And immediately his leprosy was **c**.	2511
	11: 5 the lepers are **c**, and the deaf hear,	2511
Mk	1:42 leprosy departed from him, and he was **c**.	2511
Lk	4:27 and none of them was **c**, saving Naaman	2511
	7:22 lame walk, the lepers are **c**, the deaf hear,	2511
	17:14 to pass *that*, as they went, they were **c**.	2511
	17:17 answering said, Were there not ten **c**?	2511
Ac	10:15 What God hath **c**, *that* call not thou	2511
	11: 9 What God hath **c**, *that* call not thou	2511

CLEANSETH (3) [CLEAN]

Job	37:21 but the wind passeth, and **c** them.	2891
Pr	20:30 The blueness of a wound **c away** evil:	8562
1Jn	1: 7 the blood of Jesus Christ his Son **c** us	2511

CLEANSING (10) [CLEAN]

Lev	13: 7 he hath been seen of the priest for his **c**,	2893
	13:35 scall spread much in the skin after his **c**;	2893
	14: 2 be the law of the leper in the day of his **c**:	2893
	14:23 on the eighth day for his **c** unto the priest,	2893
	14:32 able to get *that which pertaineth* to his **c**.	2893
	15:13 number to himself seven days for his **c**,	2893
Nu	6: 9 he shall shave his head in the day of his **c**,	2893
Eze	43:23 When thou hast made an end of **c** *it*,	2398
Mk	1:44 offer for thy **c** *those things* which Moses	2512
Lk	5:14 thyself to the priest, and offer for thy **c**,	2512

CLEAR (15) [CLEARER, CLEARING, CLEARLY, CLEARNESS]

Ge	24: 8 then thou shalt be **c** from this my oath:	5352
	24:41 shalt thou be **c** from *this* my oath,	5352
	24:41 if they give not thee *one*, thou shalt be **c**	5355
	44:16 or how shall we **c** ourselves? God hath	6663
Ex	34: 7 *that* will by no means **c** *the guilty*;	5352+5352
2Sa	23: 4 out of the earth by **c shining** after rain.	5051
Ps	51: 4 speakest, *and* be **c** when thou judgest.	2135
SS	6:10 **c** as the sun, *and* terrible as *an army* with	1249
Isa	18: 4 will consider in my dwelling place like a **c**	6703
Am	8: 9 and I will darken the earth in the **c** day:	216
Zec	14: 6 *that* the light shall not be **c**, *nor* dark:	3368
2Co	7:11 approved yourselves to be **c** in *this* matter.	53
Rev	21:11 *even* like a jasper stone, **c as crystal**;	2929
	21:18 the city *was* pure gold, like unto **c** glass.	2513
	22: 1 **c** as crystal, proceeding out of the throne	2986

CLEARER (1) [CLEAR]

Job	11:17 *thine* age shall be **c** than the noonday;	6965

CLEARING (2) [CLEAR]

Nu	14:18 by no means **c** *the guilty*, visiting	5352+5352
2Co	7:11 yea, what **c** of yourselves, yea,	627

CLEARLY (5) [CLEAR]

Job	33: 3 and my lips shall utter knowledge **c**.	1305
Mt	7: 5 shalt thou **see c** to cast out the mote out	1227
Mk	8:25 and he was restored, and saw every man **c**.	5081
Lk	6:42 shalt thou **see c** to pull out the mote that	1227
Ro	1:20 from the creation of the world are **c seen**,	2529

CLEARNESS (1) [CLEAR]

Ex	24:10 as it were the body of heaven in *his* **c**.	2892

CLEAVE (30) [CLAVE, CLEAVED, CLEAVETH, CLOVEN, CLOVENFOOTED]

Ge	2:24 and his mother, and shall **c** unto his wife:	1692
Lev	1:17 And he shall **c** it with the wings thereof,	8156
Dt	4: 4 ye that did **c** unto the LORD your God *are*	1695
	10:20 him shalt thou **c**, and swear by his name.	1692
	11:22 walk in all his ways, and to **c** unto him,	1692
	13: 4 and you shall serve him, and **c** unto him.	1692
	13:17 there shall **c** nought of the cursed thing to	1692
	28:21 The LORD shall **make** the pestilence **c**	1692
	28:60 wast afraid of; and they shall **c** unto thee.	1692
	30:20 voice, and that thou mayest **c** unto him:	1692
Jos	22: 5 to **c** unto him, and to serve him with all	1692
	23: 8 **c** unto the LORD your God, as ye have	1692
	23:12 unto the remnant of these nations,	1692
2Ki	5:27 therefore of Naaman shall **c** unto thee,	1692
Job	38:38 and the clods **c fast together**?	1692
Ps	74:15 Thou didst **c** the fountain and the flood:	1234
	101: 3 them that turn aside; *it* shall not **c** to me.	1692
	102: 5 of my groaning my bones **c** to my skin.	1692
	137: 6 let my tongue **c** to the roof of my mouth;	1692
Isa	14: 1 and they shall **c** to the house of Jacob.	5596
Jer	13:11 have I **caused** to **c** unto me the whole	1692
Eze	3:26 I will **make** thy tongue **c** to the roof of	1692
Da	2:43 shall **c** one to another, even as iron	1693
	11:34 but many shall **c** to them with flatteries.	3867
Hab	3: 9 Selah. Thou didst **c** the earth *with* rivers.	1234
Zec	14: 4 the mount of Olives shall **c** in the midst	1234
Mt	19: 5 and mother, and shall **c to** his wife:	4347
Mk	10: 7 his father and mother, and **c to** his wife;	4347

Ac	11:23 of heart *they* would **c unto** the Lord.	4357
Ro	12: 9 *which* is evil; **c** to *that* which is good.	2853

CLEAVED (3) [CLEAVE]

2Ki	3: 3 he **c** unto the sins of Jeroboam	1692
Job	29:10 their tongue **c** to the roof of their mouth.	1692
	31: 7 and *if any* blot hath **c** to my hands;	1692

CLEAVETH (13) [CLEAVE]

Dt	14: 6 **c** the cleft *into* two claws, and cheweth	8156
Job	16:13 my reins **asunder**, and doth not spare;	6398
	19:20 My bone **c** to my skin and to my flesh,	1692
Ps	22:15 my tongue **c** *to* my jaws; and thou hast	1692
	41: 8 An evil disease, *say they*, **c fast** unto him:	3332
	44:25 to the dust: our belly **c** unto the earth.	1692
	119:25 My soul **c** unto the dust: quicken thou	1692
	141: 7 One cutteth and **c wood** upon the earth.	1234
Ecc	10: 9 that **c** wood shall be endangered thereby.	1234
Jer	13:11 For as the girdle **c** to the loins of a man,	1692
La	4: 4 The tongue of the sucking child **c** to	1692
	4: 8 their skin **c** to their bones; it is withered,	6821
Lk	10:11 **c on** us, we do wipe off against you:	2853

CLEFT (2) [CLEFTS]

Dt	14: 6 cleaveth the **c** *into* two claws,	8157
Mic	1: 4 the valleys shall be **c**, as wax before	1234

CLEFTS (4) [CLEFT]

SS	2:14 O my dove, *that art* in the **c** of the rock,	2288
Jer	49:16 O thou that dwellest in the **c** of the rock,	2288
Am	6:11 *with* breaches, and the little house *with* **c**.	1233
Ob	1: 3 thou that dwellest in the **c** of the rock,	2288

CLEMENCY (1)

Ac	24: 4 wouldest hear us of thy **c** a few words.	1932

CLEMENT (1)

Php	4: 3 with **C** also, and *with* other my	2815

CLEOPAS (1)

Lk	24:18 And the one *of them*, whose name *was* **C**,	2810

CLEOPHAS (1)

Jn	19:25 Mary the *wife* of **C**, and Mary Magdalene.	2832

CLIFF (1) [CLIFT, CLIFTS]

2Ch	20:16 behold, they come up by the **c** of Ziz;	4608

CLIFT (1) [CLIFF]

Ex	33:22 that I will put thee in a **c** of the rock,	5366

CLIFTS (3) [CLIFF]

Job	30: 6 To dwell in the **c** of the valleys, *in* caves	6178
Isa	2:21 To go into the **c** of the rocks, and into	5366
	57: 5 in the valleys under the **c** of the rocks?	5585

CLIMB (4) [CLIMBED, CLIMBETH]

Jer	4:29 go into thickets, and **c up** upon the rocks:	5927
Joel	2: 7 they shall **c** the wall like men of war;	5927
	2: 9 the wall, they shall **c up** upon the houses;	5927
Am	9: 2 though they **c up** to heaven, thence will I	5927

CLIMBED (2) [CLIMB]

1Sa	14:13 Jonathan **c up** upon his hands and upon	5927
Lk	19: 4 and **c up** into a sycomore tree to see him:	305

CLIMBETH (1) [CLIMB]

Jn	10: 1 **c up** some other way, the same is a thief	305

CLING See CLEAVE; CLEAVED; CLEAVETH

CLIP OFF See MAR

CLIPT (1)

Jer	48:37 head *shall be* bald, and every beard **c**:	1639

CLOAK See CLOKE; GARMENT; RAIMENT; VESTURE

CLODS (6)

Job	7: 5 flesh is clothed with worms and **c** of dust;	1487
	21:33 The **c** of the valley shall be sweet unto	7263
	38:38 and the **c** cleave fast together?	7263
Isa	28:24 he open and **break the c** of his ground?	7702
Hos	10:11 shall plow, *and* Jacob shall **break** his **c**.	7702
Joel	1:17 The seed is rotten under their **c**,	4053

CLOKE (7)

Isa	59:17 clothing, and was clad with zeal as a **c**.	4598
Mt	5:40 **take away** thy coat, let him have thy **c**	2440
Lk	6:29 him that taketh away thy **c** forbid not *to*	2440
Jn	15:22 but now they have no **c** for their sin.	4392
1Th	2: 5 as ye know, nor a **c** of covetousness;	4392
2Ti	4:13 The **c** that I left at Troas with Carpus,	5341
1Pe	2:16 not using *your* liberty for a **c** of	1942

CLOPAS See CLEOPHAS

CLOSE (11) [CLOSED, CLOSER, CLOSEST]

Nu	5:13 be **kept c**, and she be defiled, and *there*	5641
2Sa	22:46 they shall be afraid out of their **c places**.	4526
1Ch	12: 1 he yet **kept** himself **c** because of Saul	6113
Job	28:21 and **kept c** from the fowls of the air.	5641
	41:15 pride, shut up *together* as with a **c** seal.	6862
Ps	18:45 be afraid out of their **c places**.	4526
Jer	42:16 shall **follow c** after you there *in* Egypt;	1692
Da	8: 7 I saw him **come c** unto the ram, and he	5060
Am	9:11 is fallen, and **c up** the breaches thereof;	1443

Lk	9:36 And they **kept** *it* **c**, and told no man in	4601
Ac	27:13 loosing *thence*, they sailed **c by** Crete.	788

CLOSED (11) [CLOSE]

Ge	2:21 his ribs, and **c up** the flesh instead thereof;	5462
	20:18 For the LORD had **fast c up** all	6113+6113
Nu	16:33 into the pit, and the earth **c** upon them:	3680
Jdg	3:22 the fat **c** upon the blade, so that he could	5462
Isa	1: 6 they have not been **c**, neither bound up,	2115
	29:10 spirit of deep sleep, and hath **c** your eyes:	6105
Da	12: 9 for the words *are* **c up** and sealed till	5640
Jnh	2: 5 the depth **c** me **round about**, the weeds	5437
Mt	13:15 dull of hearing, and their eyes they have **c**;	2576
Lk	4:20 And he **c** the book, and he gave *it* again to	4428
Ac	28:27 dull of hearing, and their eyes have they **c**;	2576

CLOSER (1) [CLOSE]

Pr	18:24 there is a friend *that* **sticketh c** than a	1695

CLOSEST (1) [CLOSE]

Jer	22:15 reign, because thou **c** *thyself* in cedar?	8474

CLOSET (2) [CLOSETS]

Joel	2:16 of his chamber, and the bride out of her **c**.	2646
Mt	6: 6 enter into thy **c**, and when thou hast shut	5009

CLOSETS (1) [CLOSET]

Lk	12: 3 *that* which ye have spoken in the ear in **c**	5009

CLOTH (18) [CLOTHE, SACKCLOTH, SACKCLOTHES]

Nu	4: 6 shall spread over *it* a **c** wholly of blue,	899
	4: 7 of shewbread they shall spread a **c** of blue,	899
	4: 8 they shall spread upon them a **c** of scarlet,	899
	4: 9 they shall take a **c** of blue, and cover	899
	4:11 upon the golden altar they shall spread a **c**	899
	4:12 or *them* in a **c** of blue, and cover them	899
	4:13 the altar, and spread a purple **c** thereon:	899
Dt	22:17 they shall spread the **c** before the elders of	8071
1Sa	19:13 *for* his bolster, and covered *it* with a **c**.	8071
	21: 9 it *is here* wrapt in a **c** behind the ephod:	8071
2Sa	20:12 *into* the field, and cast a **c** upon him,	899
2Ki	8:15 he took a **thick c**, and dipt *it* in water,	4346
Isa	30:22 shalt cast them away as a **menstruous c**;	1739
Mt	9:16 No *man* putteth a piece of new **c** unto an	4470
	27:59 body, he wrapped it in a clean **linen c**,	4616
Mk	2:21 No *man* also seweth a piece of new **c** on	4470
	14:51 a **linen c** cast about *his* naked *body*;	4616
	14:52 he left the **linen c**, and fled from them	4616

CLOTHE (16) [CLOTH, CLOTHED, CLOTHES, CLOTHEST, CLOTHING, GRAVECLOTHES, UNCLOTHED]

Ex	40:14 bring his sons, and **c** them with coats:	3847
Est	4: 4 she sent raiment to **c** Mordecai, and to	3847
Ps	132:16 I will also **c** her priests **with** salvation:	3847
	132:18 His enemies will I **c with** shame: but	3847
Pr	23:21 and drowsiness shall **c** *a man* **with** rags.	3847
Isa	22:21 I will **c** him with thy robe,	3847
	49:18 thou shalt surely **c** thee **with** them all,	3847
	50: 3 I **c** the heavens **with** blackness, and I	3847
Eze	26:16 they shall **c** themselves **with** trembling,	3847
	34: 3 eat the fat, and ye **c** you **with** the wool,	3847
Hag	1: 6 *ye* **c** you, but there is none warm; and he	3847
Zec	3: 4 and *I will* **c** thee **with** change of raiment.	3847
Mt	6:30 if God so **c** the grass of the field,	294
	6:30 *shall* he not much more **c** you, O ye	NIG
Lk	12:28 If then God so **c** the grass, which is to day	294
	12:28 how much more **will** he **c** you, O ye	NIG

CLOTHED (73) [CLOTHE]

Ge	3:21 God make coats of skins, and **c** them.	3847
Lev	8: 7 **c** him with the robe, and put the ephod	3847
2Sa	1:24 weep over Saul, who **c** you in scarlet,	3847
1Ch	15:27 David *was* **c** with a robe of fine linen,	3736
	21:16 the elders of *Israel*, who were **c** in	3680
2Ch	6:41 be **c** *with* salvation, and let thy saints	3847
	18: 9 **c in** *their* robes, and they sat in a void	3847
	28:15 with the spoil **c** all *that* were naked	3847
Est	4: 2 none might enter into the king's gate **c**	3830
Job	7: 5 My flesh is **c with** worms and clods of	3847
	8:22 that hate thee shall be **c with** shame;	3847
	10:11 Thou hast **c** me **with** skin and flesh,	3847
	29:14 I put on righteousness, and it **c** me:	3847
	39:19 hast thou **c** his neck **with** thunder?	3847
Ps	35:26 let them be **c with** shame and	3847
	65:13 The pastures are **c with** flocks; the valleys	3847
	93: 1 The LORD reigneth, he is **c with** majesty;	3847
	93: 1 the LORD is **c with** strength,	3847
	104: 1 thou art **c with** honour and majesty.	3847
	109:18 As he **c** himself **with** cursing like as with	3847
	109:29 Let mine adversaries be **c with** shame,	3847
	132: 9 Let thy priests be **c with** righteousness;	3847
Pr	31:21 for all her household *are* **c with** scarlet.	3847
Isa	61:10 for he hath **c** me with the garments of	3847
Eze	7:27 the prince shall be **c with** desolation,	3847
	9: 2 one man among them *was* **c with** linen,	3847
	9: 3 he called to the man *with* linen,	3847
	9:11 behold, the man **c with** linen, which *had*	3847
	10: 2 he spake unto the man **c with** linen,	3847
	10: 6 he had commanded the man **c with** linen,	3847
	10: 7 into the hands of *him that was* **c with**	3847
	16:10 I **c** thee also **with** broidered work,	3847
	23: 6 *Which were* **c with** blue, captains and	3847
	23:12 captains and rulers **c** most gorgeously,	3847

Eze 38: 4 all of them **c with** all sorts *of armour,* 3847
 44:17 they shall be **c with** linen garments; 3847
Da 5: 7 shall be **c with** scarlet, and *have* a chain 3848
 5:16 thou shalt be **c with** scarlet, and *have* a 3848
 5:29 they **c** Daniel **with** scarlet, and *put* a chain 3848
 10: 5 and behold, a certain man **c** in linen, 3847
 12: 6 one said to the man **c in** linen, which 3847
 12: 7 I heard the man **c in** linen, which *was* 3847
Zep 1: 8 and all such as are **c** with strange apparel. 3847
Zec 3: 3 Now Joshua was **c** with filthy garments; 3847
 3: 5 upon his head, and **c** him **with** garments. 3847
Mt 6:31 drink? or, Wherewithal shall we be **c?** 4016
 11: 8 A man **c** in soft raiment? behold, they 294
 25:36 Naked, and ye **c** me: I was sick, 4016
 25:38 and took *thee* in? or naked, and **c** *thee?* 4016
 25:43 naked, and ye **c** me not: sick, 4016
Mk 1: 6 And John was **c with** camel's hair, 1746
 5:15 sitting, and **c,** and in his right mind: 2439
 15:17 And they **c** him **with** purple, and platted a 1746
 16: 5 the right side, **c in** a long white garment; 4016
Lk 7:25 A man **c** in soft raiment? Behold, 294
 8:35 the feet of Jesus, and in his right mind: 2439
 16:19 which was **c in** purple and fine linen, 1737
2Co 5: 2 earnestly desiring to be **c upon** with our 1902
 5: 3 be that being **c** we shall not be found 1746
 5: 4 that we would be unclothed, but **c upon,** 1902
1Pe 5: 5 one to another, and be **c with** humility: 1463
Rev 1:13 **c with a garment** down to the foot, 1746
 3: 5 the same shall be **c** in white raiment; 4016
 3:18 thou mayest be **c,** and *that* the shame of 4016
 4: 4 twenty elders sitting, **c** in white raiment; 4016
 7: 9 **c** with white robes, and palms in their 4016
 10: 1 come down from heaven, **c with** a cloud: 4016
 11: 3 *and* threescore days, **c** in sackcloth. 4016
 12: 1 a woman **c with** the sun, and the moon 4016
 15: 6 **c** in pure and white linen, and having 1746
 18:16 that was **c** in fine linen, and purple, 4016
 19:13 he *was* **c** with a vesture dipt in blood: 4016
 19:14 **c** in fine linen, white and clean. 1746

CLOTHES (105) [CLOTHE]

Ge 37:29 was not in the pit; and he rent his **c.** 899
 37:34 Jacob rent his **c,** and put sackcloth upon 8071
 44:13 they rent their **c,** and laded every man his 8071
 49:11 in wine, and his **c** in the blood of grapes: 5497
Ex 12:34 bound up in their **c** upon their shoulders. 8071
 19:10 to morrow, and let them wash their **c,** 8071
 19:14 the people; and they washed their **c.** 8071
 31:10 the **c** of service, and the holy garments for 899
 35:19 The **c** of service, to do service in the holy 899
 39: 1 and scarlet, they made **c** of service, 899
 39:41 The **c** of service to do service in the holy 899
Lev 10: 6 not your heads, neither rend your **c;** 899
 11:25 the carcase of them shall wash his **c,** 899
 11:28 the carcase of them shall wash his **c,** 899
 11:40 eateth of the carcase of it shall wash his **c,** 899
 11:40 beareth the carcase of it shall wash his **c,** 899
 13: 6 and he shall wash his **c,** and be clean. 899
 13:34 and he shall wash his **c,** and be clean. 899
 13:45 leper in whom the plague *is,* his **c** shall 899
 14: 8 he that is to be cleansed shall wash his **c,** 899
 14: 9 he shall wash his **c,** also he shall wash his 899
 14:47 he that lieth in the house shall wash his **c;** 899
 14:47 that eateth in the house shall wash his **c.** 899
 15: 5 toucheth his bed shall wash his **c,** 899
 15: 6 he sat that hath the issue shall wash his **c,** 899
 15: 7 of him that hath the issue shall wash his **c,** 899
 15: 8 he shall wash his **c,** and bathe *himself* in 899
 15:10 *any* of those *things* shall wash his **c,** 899
 15:11 he shall wash his **c,** and bathe *himself* in 899
 15:13 wash his **c,** and bathe his flesh in running 899
 15:21 toucheth her bed shall wash his **c,** 899
 15:22 thing that she sat upon shall wash his **c,** 899
 15:27 wash his **c,** and bathe *himself* in water, 899
 16:26 the goat for the scapegoat shall wash his **c,** 899
 16:28 he that burneth them shall wash his **c,** 899
 16:32 shall put on the linen **c,** *even* the holy 899
 17:15 he shall both wash his **c,** and bathe 899
 21:10 shall not uncover his head, nor rend his **c;** 899
Nu 8: 7 let them wash their **c,** and *so* 899
 8:21 were purified, and they washed their **c;** 899
 14: 6 them that searched the land, rent their **c:** 899
 19: 7 priest shall wash his **c,** and he shall bathe 899
 19: 8 that burneth her shall wash his **c** in water, 899
 19:10 the ashes of the heifer shall wash his **c,** 899
 19:19 day he shall purify him*self,* and wash his **c,** 899
 19:21 the water of separation shall wash his **c;** 899
 31:24 ye shall wash your **c** on the seventh day, 899
Dt 29: 5 your **c** are not waxen old upon you, 8008
Jos 7: 6 Joshua rent his **c,** and fell to the earth 8071
Jdg 11:35 that he rent his **c,** and said, Alas, 899
1Sa 4:12 came to Shiloh the same day with his **c** 4055
 19:24 he stript off his **c** also, and prophesied 899
2Sa 1: 2 out of the camp from Saul with his **c** rent, 899
 1:11 David took hold on his **c,** and rent them; 899
 3:31 Rent your **c,** and gird you with sackcloth, 899
 13:31 all his servants stood *by* with their **c** rent. 899
 19:24 nor trimmed his beard, nor washed his **c,** 899
1Ki 1: 1 covered him with **c,** but he gat no heat. 899
 21:27 that he rent his **c,** and put sackcloth upon 899
2Ki 2:12 he took hold of his own **c,** and rent them 899
 5: 7 he rent his **c,** and said, *Am* I God, to kill 899
 5: 8 heard that the king of Israel had rent his **c,** 899
 5: 8 saying, Wherefore hast thou rent thy **c?** 899
 6:30 words of the woman, that he rent his **c;** 899

2Ki 11:14 Athaliah rent her **c,** and cried, Treason, 899
 18:37 to Hezekiah with *their* **c** rent, and told 899
 19: 1 king Hezekiah heard *it,* that he rent his **c** 899
 22:11 of the book of the law, that he rent his **c,** 899
 22:19 and hast rent thy **c,** and wept before me; 899
2Ch 23:13 Athaliah rent her **c,** and said, Treason, 899
 34:19 the words of the law, that he rent his **c.** 899
 34:27 and didst rend thy **c,** and weep before me; 899
Ne 4:23 followed me, none of us put off our **c,** 899
 9:21 their **c** waxed not old, and their feet 8008
Est 4: 1 Mordecai rent his **c,** and put on sackcloth 899
Job 9:31 the ditch, and mine own **c** shall abhor me. 8008
Pr 6:27 fire in his bosom, and his **c** not be burnt? 899
Isa 36:22 to Hezekiah with *their* **c** rent, and told 899
 37: 1 king Hezekiah heard *it,* that he rent his **c,** 899
Jer 41: 5 their **c** rent, and having cut themselves, 899
Eze 16:39 they shall strip thee also of thy **c,** 899
 23:26 They shall also strip thee out of thy **c,** 899
 27:20 Dedan *was* thy merchant in precious **c** for 899
 27:24 blue **c,** and broidered work, and in chests 1545
Am 2: 8 they lay *themselves* down upon **c** laid to 899
Mt 21: 7 and the colt, and put on them their **c,** 2440
 24:18 is in the field return back to take his **c.** 2440
 26:65 Then the high priest rent his **c,** saying, 2440
Mk 5:28 For she said, If I may touch but his **c,** 2440
 5:30 the press, and said, Who touched my **c?** 2440
 14:63 the high priest rent his **c,** and saith, 5509
 15:20 put his own **c** on him, and led him out 2440
Lk 2: 7 and **wrapped him** in **swaddling c,** 4683
 2:12 find the **babe wrapped in swaddling c,** 4683
 8:27 ware no **c,** neither abode in *any* house, 2440
 19:36 he went, they spread their **c** in the way. 2440
 24:12 he beheld the **linen c** laid by themselves, 3608
Jn 19:40 and wound it in **linen c** with the spices, 3608
 20: 5 and looking in, saw the **linen c** lying; 3608
 20: 6 the sepulchre, and seeth the **linen c** lie, 3608
 20: 7 not lying with the **linen c,** 3608
Ac 7:58 the witnesses laid down their **c** at a young 2440
 14:14 heard *of,* they rent their **c,** and ran in 2440
 16:22 and the magistrates rent off their **c,** 2440
 22:23 and cast *off* their **c,** and threw dust into 2440

CLOTHEST (1) [CLOTHE]

Jer 4:30 Though thou **c** thyself **with** crimson, 3847

CLOTHING (19) [CLOTHE]

Job 22: 6 nought, and stripped the naked of their **c.** 899
 24: 7 They cause the naked to lodge without **c,** 3830
 24:10 They cause *him* to go naked without **c,** 3830
 31:19 If I have seen *any* perish for want of **c,** 3830
Ps 35:13 when they were sick, my **c** *was* sackcloth: 3830
 45:13 glorious within: her **c** *is* of wrought gold. 3830
Pr 27:26 The lambs *are* for thy **c,** and the goats *are* 3830
 31:22 of tapestry; her **c** *is* silk and purple. 3830
 31:25 Strength and honour *are* her **c;** and she 3830
Isa 3: 6 *saying,* Thou hast **c,** be thou our ruler, 8071
 3: 7 for in my house *is* neither bread nor **c:** 8071
 23:18 to eat sufficiently, and for durable **c.** 4374
 59:17 **put on** the garments of vengeance
 for **c,** 3847+8516
Jer 10: 9 blue and purple *is* their **c:** they *are* all 3830
Mt 7:15 which come to you in sheep's **c,** 1742
 11: 8 they that wear soft **c** are in kings' houses. NIG
Mk 12:38 which love to go in long **c,** 4749
Ac 10:30 behold, a man stood before me in bright **c,** 2066
Jas 2: 3 respect to him that weareth the gay **c,** 2066

CLOUD (107) [CLOUDS, CLOUDY]

Ge 9:13 I do set my bow in the **c,** and it shall be 6051
 9:14 when I **bring a c** over the earth, 6049+6051
 9:14 that the bow shall be seen in the **c:** 6051
 9:16 the bow shall be in the **c;** and I will look 6051
Ex 13:21 went before them by day in a pillar of a **c,** 6051
 13:22 took not away the pillar of the **c** by day, 6051
 14:19 the pillar of the **c** went from before their 6051
 14:20 it was a **c** and darkness *to them,* but it 6051
 14:24 through the pillar of fire and of the **c,** 6051
 16:10 the glory of the LORD appeared in the **c.** 6051
 19: 9 Lo, I come unto thee in a thick **c,** 6051
 19:16 a thick **c** upon the mount, and the voice 6051
 24:15 the mount, and a **c** covered the mount. 6051
 24:16 Sinai, and the **c** covered it six days: 6051
 24:16 unto Moses out of the midst of the **c.** 6051
 24:18 Moses went into the midst of the **c,** 6051
 34: 5 The LORD descended in the **c,** 6051
 40:34 a **c** covered the tent of the congregation, 6051
 40:35 the **c** abode thereon, and the glory 6051
 40:36 when the **c** was taken up from over 6051
 40:37 if the **c** were not taken up, then 6051
 40:38 For the **c** of the LORD *was* upon 6051
Lev 16: 2 for I will appear in the **c** upon the mercy 6051
 16:13 that the **c** of the incense may cover 6051
Nu 9:15 the **c** covered the tabernacle, namely, 6051
 9:16 **c** covered it *by day,* and the appearance 6051
 9:17 when the **c** was taken up from 6051
 9:17 in the place where the **c** abode, there 6051
 9:18 as long as the **c** abode upon the tabernacle 6051
 9:19 the **c** tarried long upon the tabernacle 6051
 9:20 when the **c** was a few days upon 6051
 9:21 when the **c** abode from even unto 6051
 9:21 *that* the **c** was taken up in the morning, 6051
 9:21 day or by night that the **c** was taken up, 6051
 9:22 that the **c** tarried upon the tabernacle, 6051
 10:11 *that* the **c** was taken up from off 6051
 10:12 the **c** rested in the wilderness of Paran. 6051

Nu 10:34 the **c** of the LORD *was* upon them by day, 6051
 11:25 the LORD came down in a **c,** 6051
 12: 5 LORD came down in the pillar of the **c,** 6051
 12:10 the **c** departed from off the tabernacle; 6051
 14:14 *that* thy **c** standeth over them, and *that* 6051
 14:14 day time in a pillar of a **c,** and in a pillar 6051
 16:42 the **c** covered it, and the glory of 6051
Dt 1:33 what way ye should go, and in a **c** by day. 6051
 5:22 of the **c,** and of the thick darkness, *with* a 6051
 31:15 in the tabernacle in a pillar of a **c:** 6051
 31:15 the pillar of the **c** stood over the door of 6051
1Ki 8:10 that the **c** filled the house of the LORD, 6051
 8:11 not stand to minister because of the **c:** 6051
 18:44 there ariseth a little **c** out of the sea, 5645
2Ch 5:13 that *then* the house was filled with a **c,** 6051
 5:14 not stand to minister by reason of the **c:** 6051
Ne 9:19 the pillar of the **c** departed not from them 6051
Job 3: 5 of death stain it; let a **c** dwell upon it; 6053
 7: 9 is consumed and vanisheth away: 6051
 22:13 can he judge through the dark **c?** NIH
 26: 8 and the **c** is not rent under them. 6051
 26: 9 of *his* throne, and spreadeth his **c** upon it. 6051
 30:15 and my welfare passeth away as a **c.** 5645
 36:32 commandeth it *not to shine by the* **c** that NIH
 37:11 Also by watering he wearieth the **thick c:** 5645
 37:11 the thick cloud: he scattereth his bright **c:** 6051
 37:15 and caused the light of his **c** to shine? 6051
 38: 9 When I made the **c** the garment thereof, 6051
Ps 78:14 In the daytime also he led them with a **c,** 6051
 105:39 He spread a **c** for a covering; and fire to 6051
Pr 16:15 and his favour *is* as a **c** of the latter rain. 5645
Isa 4: 5 a **c** and smoke by day, and the shining of 6051
 18: 4 *and* like a **c** of dew in the heat of harvest. 5645
 19: 1 the LORD rideth upon a swift **c,** 5645
 25: 5 *even* the heat with the shadow of a **c:** 5645
 44:22 I have blotted out, as a **thick c,** 5645
 44:22 thy transgressions, and, as a **c,** thy sins: 6051
 60: 8 Who *are* these *that* fly as a **c,** and as 5645
La 2: 1 **covered** the daughter of Zion **with a c** in 5743
 3:44 Thou hast covered thyself with a **c,** that 6051
Eze 1: 4 a great **c,** and a fire infolding itself, 6051
 1:28 the appearance of the bow that is in the **c** 6051
 8:11 hand, and a thick **c** of incense went up. 6051
 10: 3 went in; and the **c** filled the inner court. 6051
 10: 4 the house was filled with the **c,** 6051
 30:18 shall cover her, and her daughters shall 6051
 32: 7 will cover the sun with a **c,** and the moon 6051
 38: 9 thou shalt be like a **c** to cover the land, 6051
 38:16 people of Israel, as a **c** to cover the land; 6051
Hos 6: 4 for your goodness *is* as a morning **c,** 6051
 13: 3 Therefore they shall be as the morning **c,** 6051
Mt 17: 5 behold, a **bright c** overshadowed them: 3507
 17: 5 behold a voice out of the **c,** which said, 3507
Mk 9: 7 there was a **c** that overshadowed them: 3507
 9: 7 and a voice came out of the **c,** saying, 3507
Lk 9:34 there came a **c,** and overshadowed them: 3507
 9:34 and they feared as they entered into the **c.** 3507
 9:35 there came a voice out of the **c,** saying, 3507
 12:54 When ye see a **c** rise out of the west, 3507
 21:27 they see the Son of man coming in a **c** 3507
Ac 1: 9 and a **c** received him out of their sight. 3507
1Co 10: 1 how that all our fathers were under the **c,** 3507
 10: 2 were all baptized unto Moses in the **c** 3507
Heb 12: 1 about with so great a **c** of witnesses, 3509
Rev 10: 1 down from heaven, clothed with a **c:** 3507
 11:12 And they ascended up to heaven in a **c;** 3507
 14:14 and behold a white **c,** and upon the cloud 3507
 14:14 the **c** one sat like unto the Son of man, 3507
 14:15 with a loud voice to him that sat on the **c,** 3507
 14:16 he that sat on the **c** thrust in his sickle 3507

CLOUDS (49) [CLOUD]

Dt 4:11 *with* darkness, **c,** and thick darkness. 6051
Jdg 5: 4 dropped, the **c** also dropped water. 5645
2Sa 22:12 dark waters, *and* **thick** of the skies. 5645
 23: 4 the sun riseth, *even* a morning without **c;** 5645
1Ki 18:45 the heaven was black with **c** and wind, 5645
Job 20: 6 heavens, and his head reach unto the **c;** 5645
 22:14 **Thick c** *are* a covering to him, that he 5645
 26: 8 He bindeth up the waters in his **thick c;** 5645
 35: 5 behold the **c** *which* are higher than thou. 7834
 36:28 Which the **c** do drop *and* distil upon man 7834
 36:29 *any* understand the spreadings of the **c,** 5645
 36:32 With **c** he covereth the light; 3709
 37:16 Dost thou know the balancings of the **c,** 7834
 37:21 see not the bright light which *is* in the **c:** 7834
 38:34 Canst thou lift up thy voice to the **c,** 5645
 38:37 Who can number the **c** in wisdom? or 7834
Ps 18:11 *were* dark waters *and* **thick c** of the skies. 5645
 18:12 *that was* before him his **thick c** passed, 5645
 36: 5 *and* thy faithfulness *reacheth* unto the **c.** 7834
 57:10 the heavens, and thy truth unto the **c.** 7834
 68:34 *is* over Israel, and his strength *is* in the **c.** 7834
 77:17 The **c** poured out water: the skies sent out 5645
 78:23 Though he had commanded the **c** from 7834
 97: 2 **C** and darkness *are* round about him: 6051
 104: 3 maketh the **c** his chariot: who walketh 5645
 108: 4 and thy truth *reacheth* unto the **c.** 7834
 147: 8 Who covereth the heaven with **c,** 5645
Pr 3:20 broken up, and the **c** drop down the dew. 7834
 8:28 When he established the **c** above: when 7834
 25:14 boasteth himself of a false gift *is like* **c** 5387
Ecc 11: 3 If the **c** be full *of* rain, they empty 5645
 11: 4 and he that regardeth the **c** shall not reap. 5645
 12: 2 darkened, nor the **c** return after the rain: 5645

C

Isa	5: 6 I will also command the **c** that they rain	5645
	14:14 I will ascend above the heights of the **c**;	5645
Jer	4:13 he shall come up as **c**, and his chariots	6051
Da	7:13 *one* like the Son of man came with the **c**	6050
Joel	2: 2 a day of **c** and of thick darkness,	6051
Na	1: 3 storm, and the **c** *are* the dust of his feet.	6051
Zep	1:15 gloominess, a day of **c** and thick darkness,	6051
Zec	10: 1 *so* the Lord *shall* make **bright c**,	2385
Mt	24:30 coming in the **c** of heaven with power	3507
	26:64 of power, and coming in the **c** of heaven.	3507
Mk	13:26 of man coming in the **c** with great power	3507
	14:62 of power, and coming in the **c** of heaven.	3507
1Th	4:17 be caught up together with them in the **c**,	3507
2Pe	2:17 **c** that are carried with a tempest;	3507
Jude	12 *they* are without water, carried about of	3507
Rev	1: 7 Behold, he cometh with **c**; and every eye	3507

CLOUDY (6) [CLOUD]

Ex	33: 9 the **c** pillar descended, and stood *at* the	6051
	33:10 all the people saw the **c** pillar stand *at*	6051
Ne	9:12 thou leddest them in the day by a **c** pillar;	6051
Ps	99: 7 He spake unto them in the **c** pillar:	6051
Eze	30: 3 even the day of the Lord *is* near, a **c** day;	6051
	34:12 where they have been scattered in the **c**	6051

CLOUTED (1) [CLOUTS]

Jos	9: 5 old shoes and **c** upon their feet,	2921

CLOUTS (2) [CLOUTED]

Jer	38:11 took thence old **cast c** and old rotten rags,	5499
	38:12 Put now *these* old **cast c** and rotten rags	5499

CLOVEN (2) [CLEAVE]

Dt	14: 7 the cud, or of them that divide the **c** hoof;	8156
Ac	2: 3 And there appeared unto them **c** tongues	1266

CLOVENFOOTED (3) [CLEAVE, FOOT]

Lev	11: 3 *is* **c**, *and* cheweth cud,	6541+8156+8157
	11: 7 he divide the hoof, and be **c**,	6541+8156+8157
	11:26 *is* not **c**, nor cheweth the cud,	8156+8157

CLUB See DARTS

CLUBS See STAVES

CLUNG See CLAVE; CLEAVE; CLEAVED; CLEAVETH

CLUSTER (5) [CLUSTERS]

Nu	13:23 cut down from thence a branch with one **c**	811
	13:24 of the **c of grapes** which the children of	811
SS	1:14 My beloved *is* unto me *as* a **c** of camphire	811
Isa	65: 8 As the new wine is found in the **c**,	811
Mic	7: 1 *there is* no **c** to eat: my soul desired	811

CLUSTERS (7) [CLUSTER]

Ge	40:10 the **c** thereof brought forth ripe grapes:	811
Dt	32:32 grapes *are* grapes of gall, their **c** *are* bitter:	811
1Sa	25:18 corn, and an hundred **c of raisins**,	6778
	30:12 of a cake *of* figs, and two **c of raisins**:	6778
SS	7: 7 palm tree, and thy breasts to **c** *of* grapes.	811
	7: 8 also thy breasts shall be as **c** of the vine,	811
Rev	14:18 and gather the **c** of the vine of the earth;	1009

CNIDUS (1)

Ac	27: 7 and scarce were come over against **C**,	2834

COAL (4) [COALS]

2Sa	14: 7 so they shall quench my **c** which is left,	1513
Isa	6: 6 unto me, having a **live c** in his hand,	7531
	47:14 *there shall* not *be* a **c** to warm at, *nor* fire	1513
La	4: 8 Their visage is blacker than a **c**; they are	7815

COALS (26) [COAL]

Lev	16:12 he shall take a censer full of **burning c** of	1513
2Sa	22: 9 his mouth devoured: **c** were kindled by it.	1513
	22:13 Through the brightness before him were **c**	1513
1Ki	19: 6 *there was* a cake **baken on the c**,	7529
Job	41:21 His breath kindleth **c**, and a flame goeth	1513
Ps	18: 8 his mouth devoured: **c** were kindled by it.	1513
	18:12 clouds passed, hail-*stones* and **c** of fire.	1513
	18:13 gave his voice; hail-*stones* and **c** of fire.	1513
	120: 4 arrows of the mighty, with **c** of juniper.	1513
	140:10 Let **burning c** fall upon them: let them be	1513
Pr	6:28 Can one go upon **hot c**, and his feet not	1513
	25:22 thou shalt heap **c of fire** upon his head,	1513
	26:21 *As* **c** *are* to burning coals, and wood to fire	6352
	26:21 *As* coals *are* to **burning c**, and wood to	1513
SS	8: 6 the **c** thereof *are* coals of fire, *which hath*	7565
	8: 6 the coals thereof *are* of **c**, *which hath*	7565
Isa	44:12 with the tongs both worketh in the **c**,	6352
	44:19 I have baked bread upon the **c** thereof;	6352
	54:16 have created the smith that bloweth the **c**	6352
Eze	1:13 their appearance *was* like burning **c** of fire,	1513
	10: 2 fill thine hand *with* **c** of fire from between	1513
	24:11 set it empty upon the **c** thereof, that	1513
Hab	3: 5 and **burning c** went forth at his feet.	7565
Jn	18:18 stood *there*, who had made a **fire of c**;	439
	21: 9 they saw a **fire of c** there, and fish laid	439
Ro	12:20 doing thou shalt heap **c** of fire on his head.	440

COARSE JOKING See JESTING

COAST (62) [COASTS]

Ex	10: 4 morrow will I bring the locusts into thy **c**:	1366
Nu	13:29 dwell by the sea, and by the **c** of Jordan.	3027
	20:23 by the **c** of the land of Edom, saying,	1366
	22:36 border of Arnon, which *is* in the utmost **c**.	1366

Nu	24:24 ships *shall come* from the **c** of Chittim,	3027
	34: 3 wilderness of Zin along by the **c** of Edom,	3027
	34: 3 **outmost c** of the salt sea eastward:	4480+7097
	34:11 the **c** shall go down from Shepham *to*	1366
Dt	2: 4 Ye are to pass through the **c** of your	1366
	2:18 over *through* Ar, the **c** of Moab, *this* day:	1366
	3:17 the **c** *thereof*, from Chinnereth even unto	1366
	11:24 unto the uttermost sea shall your **c** be.	1366
	16: 4 seen with thee in all thy **c** seven days;	1366
	19: 8 if the Lord thy God enlarge thy **c**, as he	1366
Jos	1: 4 going down of the sun, shall be your **c**.	1366
	12: 4 the **c** of Og king of Bashan, *which was* of	1366
	12:23 The king of Dor in the **c** of Dor, one;	5299
	13:16 their **c** was from Aroer, that *is* on the bank	1366
	13:25 their **c** was Jazer, and all the cities of	1366
	13:30 their **c** was from Mahanaim, all Bashan,	1366
	15: 1 *was* the uttermost part of the south **c**.	NIH
	15: 4 the goings out of that **c** were at the sea:	1366
	15: 4 at the sea: this shall be your south **c**.	1366
	15:12 the **c** *thereof*. This *is* the coast of	1366
	15:12 the coast *thereof*. This *is* the **c** of	1366
	15:21 the **c** of Edom southward were Kabzeel,	1366
	16: 3 goeth down westward to the **c** of Japhleti,	1366
	16: 3 unto the **c** of Beth-horon the nether,	1366
	17: 7 the **c** of Manasseh was from Asher *to*	1366
	17: 9 the **c** descended *unto* the river Kanah,	1366
	17: 9 of Manasseh also *was* on the north	1366
	18: 5 Judah shall abide in their **c** on the south,	1366
	18:11 the **c** of their lot came forth between	1366
	18:19 south end of Jordan: this *was* the south **c**.	1366
	19:22 the **c** reacheth to Tabor, and Shahazimah,	1366
	19:29 *then* the **c** turneth to Ramah, and to	1366
	19:29 the **c** turneth *to* Hosah; and the outgoings	1366
	19:29 are at the sea from the **c** to Achzib:	2256
	19:33 their **c** was from Heleph, from Allon to	1366
	19:34 the **c** turneth westward to Aznoth-tabor,	1366
	19:41 the **c** of their inheritance was Zorah,	1366
	19:47 the **c** of the children of Dan went out *too*	1366
Jdg	1:18 Also Judah took Gaza with the **c** thereof,	1366
	1:18 Askelon with the **c** thereof, and Ekron	1366
	1:18 thereof, and Ekron with the **c** thereof.	1366
	1:36 the **c** of the Amorites *was* from the going	1366
	11:20 trusted not Israel to pass through his **c**:	1366
1Sa	6: 9 it goeth up *by* the way of his own **c** *to*	1366
	7:13 they came no more into the **c** of Israel:	1366
	27: 1 to seek me any more in any **c** of Israel:	1366
	30:14 upon *the* **c** which *belongeth* to Judah,	NIH
2Ki	14:25 He restored the **c** of Israel from the	1366
1Ch	4:10 enlarge my **c**, and that thine hand might	1366
Eze	25:16 and destroy the remnant of the sea **c**.	2348
	47:16 which *is* by the **c** of Hauran.	1366
	48: 1 From the north end to the **c** of the way of	3027
	48: 1 Damascus northward, to the **c** of Hamath;	3027
Zep	2: 5 Woe unto the inhabitants of the sea **c**,	2256
	2: 6 the sea **c** shall be dwellings *and* cottages	2256
	2: 7 the **c** shall be for the remnant of the house	2256
Mt	4:13 in Capernaum, which is **upon the sea c**,	3864
Lk	6:17 and *from* the **sea c** of Tyre and Sidon,	3882

COASTS (51) [COAST]

Ex	10:14 of Egypt, and rested in all the **c** of Egypt:	1366
	10:19 remained not one locust in all the **c** of	1366
Nu	21:13 that cometh out of the **c** of the Amorites:	1366
	32:33 the land, with the cities thereof in the **c**,	1367
	34: 2 the land of Canaan with the **c** thereof:)	1367
	34:12 this shall be your land with the **c** thereof	1366
Dt	3:14 country of Argob unto the **c** of Geshuri	1366
	19: 3 thee a way, and divide the **c** of thy land,	1366
	28:40 shalt have olive trees throughout all thy **c**,	1366
Jos	9: 1 in all the **c** of the great sea over against	2348
	18: 5 house of Joseph shall abide in their **c** on	1366
	18:20 by the **c** thereof round about, according to	1367
	19:49 the land for inheritance by their **c**,	1367
Jdg	11:22 they possessed all the **c** of the Amorites,	1366
	11:26 in all the cities that *be* along by the **c** of	3027
	18: 2 sent of their family five men from their **c**,	7098
	19:29 and sent her into all the **c** of Israel.	1366
1Sa	5: 6 *even* Ashdod and the **c** thereof.	1366
	7:14 the **c** thereof did Israel deliver out of	1366
	11: 3 we may send messengers unto all the **c**	1366
	11: 7 sent *them* throughout all the **c** of Israel by	1366
2Sa	21: 5 from remaining in any of the **c** of Israel,	1366
1Ki	1: 3 fair damsel throughout all the **c** of Israel,	1366
2Ki	10:32 Hazael smote them in all the **c** of Israel;	1366
	15:16 therein, and the **c** thereof from Tirzah:	1366
1Ch	6:54 places throughout their castles in their **c**,	1366
	6:66 cities of their **c** out of the tribe of Ephraim.	1366
	21:12 destroying throughout all the **c** of Israel.	1366
2Ch	11:13 all Israel resorted to him out of all their **c**.	1366
Ps	105:31 divers sorts *of* flies, *and* lice in all their **c**.	1366
	105:33 fig trees; and brake the trees of their **c**.	1366
Jer	25:32 shall be raised up from the **c** of the earth.	3411
	31: 8 and gather them from the **c** of the earth,	3411
	50:41 many kings shall be raised up from the **c**	3411
Eze	33: 2 people of the land take a man of their **c**,	7097
Joel	3: 4 and Zidon, and all the **c** of Palestine?	1552
Mt	2:16 in all the **c** thereof, from two years old	3725
	8:34 *him* that he would depart out of their **c**.	3725
	15:21 and departed into the **c** of Tyre and Sidon.	3313
	15:22 woman of Canaan came out of the same **c**,	3725
	15:39 ship, and came into the **c** of Magdala.	3725
	16:13 When Jesus came into the **c** of Cesarea	3313
	19: 1 came into the **c** of Judea beyond Jordan;	3725
Mk	5:17 began to pray him to depart out of their **c**.	3725
	7:31 departing from the **c** of Tyre and Sidon,	3725

Mk	7:31 through the midst of the **c** of Decapolis.	3725
	10: 1 cometh into the **c** of Judea by the farther	3725
Ac	13:50 and expelled them out of their **c**.	3725
	19: 1 Paul having passed through the upper **c**	3313
	26:20 and throughout all the **c** of Judea,	5561
	27: 2 meaning to sail by the **c** of Asia;	5117

COAT (25) [COATS]

Ge	37: 3 and he made him a **c** of many colours.	3801
	37:23 that they stript Joseph out of his **c**,	3801
	37:23 *his* **c** of many colours that *was* on him;	3801
	37:31 they took Joseph's **c**, and killed a kid of	3801
	37:31 the goats, and dipped the **c** in the blood;	3801
	37:32 they sent the **c** of many colours,	3801
	37:32 now whether it *be* thy son's **c** or no.	3801
	37:33 he knew it, and said, *It is* my son's **c**;	3801
Ex	28: 4 a robe, and a broidered **c**, a mitre,	3801
	28:39 thou shalt embroider the **c** of fine linen,	3801
	29: 5 put upon Aaron the **c**, and the robe of	3801
Lev	8: 7 he put upon him the **c**, and girded him	3801
	16: 4 He shall put on the holy linen **c**,	3801
1Sa	2:19 Moreover his mother made him a little **c**,	4598
	17: 5 and he *was* armed with a **c** of mail;	8302
	17: 5 the weight of the **c** *was* five thousand	8302
	17:38 also he armed him with a **c** *of* mail.	8302
2Sa	15:32 Archite *came* to meet him with his **c** rent,	3801
Job	30:18 it bindeth me about as the collar of my **c**.	3801
SS	5: 3 I have put off my **c**; how shall I put it on?	3801
Mt	5:40 take *away* thy **c**, let him have thy **cloke**	5509
Lk	6:29 away thy cloke forbid not *to* take thy **c**	5509
Jn	19:23 to every soldier a part; and *also* his **c**:	5509
	19:23 now the **c** was without seam, woven from	5509
	21: 7 he girt *his* **fisher's c** unto him, (for he	1903

COAT OF ARMOR See HABERGEONS

COATS (14) [COAT]

Ge	3:21 to his wife did the Lord God make **c** of	3801
Ex	28:40 for Aaron's sons thou shalt make **c**,	3801
	29: 8 shalt bring his sons, and put **c** upon them.	3801
	39:27 they made **c** *of* fine linen *of* woven work	3801
	40:14 bring his sons, and clothe them with **c**:	3801
Lev	8:13 put **c** upon them, and girded them *with*	3801
	10: 5 carried them in their **c** out of the camp;	3801
Da	3:21 these men were bound in their **c**,	5622
	3:27 singed, neither were their **c** changed,	5622
Mt	10:10 two **c**, neither shoes, nor yet staves:	5509
Mk	6: 9 shod with sandals; and not put on two **c**.	5509
Lk	3:11 and saith unto them, He that hath two **c**,	5509
	9: 3 neither money; neither have two **c** apiece.	5509
Ac	9:39 and shewing the **c** and garments which	5509

COBRA See ASP; ASPS

COCK (12) [COCKCROWING]

Mt	26:34 thee, That this night, before the **c** crow,	220
	26:74 not the man. And immediately the **c** crew.	220
	26:75 which said unto him, Before the **c** crow,	220
Mk	14:30 even in this night, before the **c** crow twice,	220
	14:68 went out into the porch; and the **c** crew.	220
	14:72 And the second time the **c** crew.	220
	14:72 Before the **c** crow twice, thou shalt deny	220
Lk	22:34 thee, Peter, the **c** shall not crow this day,	220
	22:60 while he yet spake, the **c** crew.	220
	22:61 Before the **c** crow, thou shalt deny me	220
Jn	13:38 I say unto thee, The **c** shall not crow,	220
	18:27 denied again: and immediately the **c** crew.	220

COCKATRICE (1) [COCKATRICE', COCKATRICES]

Isa	14:29 of the serpent's root shall come forth a **c**,	6848

COCKATRICE' (2) [COCKATRICE]

Isa	11: 8 weaned child shall put his hand on the **c**	6848
	59: 5 They hatch **c** eggs, and weave the spider's	6848

COCKATRICES (1) [COCKATRICE]

Jer	8:17 I will send serpents, **c**, among you,	6848

COCKCROWING (1) [COCK, CROW]

Mk	13:35 at midnight, or at the **c**, or in the morning:	219

COCKLE (1)

Job	31:40 instead of wheat, and **c** instead of barley.	890

COFFER (3)

1Sa	6: 8 trespass offering, in a **c** by the side thereof;	712
	6:11 the **c** with the mice of gold and the images	712
	6:15 the **c** that *was* with it, wherein the jewels	712

COFFIN (1)

Ge	50:26 and he was put in a **c** in Egypt.	727

COGITATIONS (1)

Da	7:28 my **c** much troubled me,	7476

COINS See PENCE

COLD (18)

Ge	8:22 **c** and heat, and summer and winter,	7120
Job	24: 7 that *they* have no covering in the **c**.	7135
	37: 9 the whirlwind: and **c** out of the north.	7135
Ps	147:17 like morsels: who can stand before his **c**?	7135
Pr	20: 4 sluggard will not plow *by reason* of the **c**;	2779
	25:13 As the **c** of snow in the time of harvest,	6793
	25:20 As he that taketh away a garment in **c**	7135
	25:25 *As* **c** waters to a thirsty soul, so *is* good	7119
Jer	18:14 shall the **c** flowing waters that come from	7119

Na	3:17 which camp in the hedges in the **c** day,	7135
Mt	10:42 of **c** water only in the name of a disciple,	5593
	24:12 abound, the love of many shall **wax c**.	5594
Jn	18:18 who had made a fire of coals; for it was **c**:	5592
Ac	28: 2 of the present rain, and because of the **c**.	5592
2Co	11:27 in fastings often, in **c** and nakedness.	5592
Rev	3:15 thy works, that thou art neither **c** nor hot:	5593
	3:15 cold nor hot: I would thou wert **c** or hot.	5593
	3:16 thou art lukewarm, and neither **c** nor hot,	5593

COL-HOZEH (2)
Ne	3:15 the fountain repaired Shallun the son of **C**,	3626
	11: 5 the son of **C**, the son of Hazaiah, the son	3626

COLLAR (1) [COLLARS]
Job	30:18 it bindeth me about as the **c** of my coat.	6310

COLLARS (1) [COLLAR]
Jdg	8:26 **c**, and purple raiment that *was* on the	5188

COLLECTION (3)
2Ch	24: 6 out of Judah and out of Jerusalem the **c**,	4864
	24: 9 to bring in to the LORD the **c**ollection that Moses	4864
1Co	16: 1 Now concerning the **c** for the saints, as I	3048

COLLEGE (2)
2Ki	22:14 (now she dwelt in Jerusalem in the **c**;)	4932
2Ch	34:22 (now she dwelt in Jerusalem in the **c**:)	4932

COLLOPS (1)
Job	15:27 and maketh **c** of fat on *his* flanks.	6371

COLONY (1)
Ac	16:12 city of *that* part of Macedonia, *and* a **c**:	2862

COLORFUL See DIVERS; DIVERSE

COLOSSE (1) [COLOSSIANS]
Col	1: 2 faithful brethren in Christ which are at **C**:	2857

COLOSSIANS (1) [COLOSSE]
Col	4: S Written from Rome to the **C** by Tychicus	2858

COLOUR (14) [COLOURED, COLOURS]
Lev	13:55 *if* the plague have not changed his **c**,	5869
Nu	11: 7 the **c** thereof as the colour of bdellium.	5869
	11: 7 the colour thereof as the **c** of bdellium.	5869
Pr	23:31 when it giveth his **c** in the cup, *when* it	5869
Eze	1: 4 out of the midst thereof as the **c** of amber,	5869
	1: 7 sparkled like the **c** of burnished brass.	5869
	1:16 their work *was* like unto the **c** of a beryl:	5869
	1:22 *was* as the **c** of the terrible crystal,	5869
	1:27 saw as the **c** of amber, as the appearance	5869
	8: 2 of brightness, as the **c** of amber.	5869
	10: 9 appearance of the wheels *was* as the **c**	5869
Da	10: 6 and his feet like in **c** to polished brass,	5869
Ac	27:30 **under** as though they would have cast	4392
Rev	17: 4 was arrayed in purple and **scarlet c**,	2847

COLOURED (1) [COLOUR]
Rev	17: 3 saw a woman sit upon a **scarlet c** beast,	2847

COLOURS (12) [COLOUR]
Ge	37: 3 and he made him a coat of **many c**.	6446
	37:23 *his* coat of **many c** that *was* on him;	6446
	37:32 they sent the coat of **many c**,	6446
Jdg	5:30 Sisera a prey of **divers c**, a prey of divers	6648
	5:30 a prey of **divers c** of needlework,	6648
	5:30 of **divers c** of needlework on both sides,	6648
2Sa	13:18 *she had* a garment of **divers c** upon her:	6446
	13:19 rent her garment of **divers c** that *was* on	6446
1Ch	29: 2 of **divers c**, and all *manner of* precious	7553
Isa	54:11 I will lay thy stones with **fair c**, and lay	6320
Eze	16:16 deckedst thy high places with **divers c**,	2921
	17: 3 full *of* feathers, which had **divers c**,	7553

COLT (15) [COLTS]
Ge	49:11 and his ass's **c** unto the choice vine;	1121
Job	11:12 though man be born *like* a wild ass's **c**.	5895
Zec	9: 9 an ass, and upon a **c** the foal of an ass.	5895
Mt	21: 2 ye shall find an ass tied, and a **c** with her:	4454
	21: 5 upon an ass, and a **c** the foal of an ass.	4454
	21: 7 and the **c**, and put on them their clothes,	4454
Mk	11: 2 ye shall find a **c** tied, whereon never man	4454
	11: 4 found the **c** tied by the door without in a	4454
	11: 5 unto them, What do ye, loosing the **c**?	4454
	11: 7 And they brought the **c** to Jesus,	4454
Lk	19:30 at your entering ye shall find a **c** tied,	4454
	19:33 as they were loosing the **c**, the owners	4454
	19:33 said unto them, Why loose ye the **c**?	4454
	19:35 and they cast their garments upon the **c**,	4454
Jn	12:15 thy King cometh, sitting on an ass's **c**.	4454

COLTS (3) [COLT]
Ge	32:15 Thirty milch camels with their **c**, forty	1121
Jdg	10: 4 had thirty sons that rode on thirty **ass c**,	5895
	12:14 that rode on threescore and ten **ass c**:	5895

COME (1972) [CAME, CAMEST, COMERS, COMEST, COMETH, COMING, COMINGS]
Ge	4:14 shall **c to pass**, *that* every one that findeth	1961
	6:13 The end of all flesh is **c** before me;	935
	6:18 shalt **c** into the ark, thou, and thy sons,	935
	6:20 two of every *sort* shall **c** unto thee, to keep	935
	7: 1 **C** thou and all thy house into the ark;	935
	9:14 it shall **c to pass**, when I bring a cloud	1961
	12:11 when he was **c near** to enter into Egypt,	7126
	12:12 Therefore it shall **c to pass**, when	1961
	12:14 pass, that, when Abram was **c** into Egypt,	935
	15: 4 he that shall **c forth** out of thine own	3318
	15:14 afterward shall they **c out** with great	3318
	15:16 generation they shall **c** hither **again**:	7725
	17: 6 of thee, and kings shall **c out** of thee.	3318
	18: 5 for therefore are you **c** to your servant.	5674
	18:21 to the cry of it, which is **c** unto me;	935
	19:22 for I cannot do any thing till thou be **c**	935
	19:31 not a man in the earth to **c in** unto us	935
	19:32 let us make our father drink wine,	1980
	20: 4 Abimelech had not **c near** her: and he	7126
	20:13 every place whither we shall **c**, say of me,	7725
	22: 9 yonder and worship, and **c again** to you.	7725
	24:13 daughters of the men of the city **c out** to	3318
	24:14 let it **c to pass**, *that* the damsel to whom	1961
	24:31 he said, **C in**, thou blessed of the LORD;	935
	24:43 it shall **c to pass**, *that when* the virgin	1961
	26:27 Wherefore **c** ye to me, seeing ye hate me,	935
	27:21 **C near**, I pray thee, that I may feel thee,	5066
	27:26 **c near** now, and kiss me, my son.	5066
	27:40 it shall **c to pass** when thou shalt have	1961
	28:21 So that I **c again** to my father's house in	7725
	30:16 and said, Thou must **c in** unto me;	935
	30:33 righteousness answer for me in time **to c**,	4279
	30:33 when it shall **c** for my hire before thy face:	935
	31:44 Now therefore **c** thou, let us make a	1980
	32: 8 If Esau **c** to the one company, and smite it,	935
	32:11 lest he will **c** and smite me, *and* the mother	935
	33:14 to endure, until I **c** unto my lord unto Seir.	935
	34: 5 and Jacob held his peace until they were **c**.	935
	35:11 of thee, and kings shall **c out** of thy loins;	3318
	35:16 there was but a little way to **c** to Ephrath:	935
	37:10 thy brethren **indeed c** to bow down	935+935
	37:13 **c**, and I will send thee unto them.	1980
	37:20 **C** now therefore, and let us slay him,	1980
	37:23 when Joseph was **c** unto his brethren,	935
	37:27 **C**, and let us sell him to the Ishmeelites,	1980
	38:16 Go to, I pray thee, let me **c in** unto thee;	935
	38:16 give me, that thou mayest **c in** unto me?	935
	41:29 there **c** seven years of great plenty	935
	41:35 all the food of those good years that **c**,	935
	41:54 the seven years of dearth began to **c**,	935
	42: 7 and he said unto them, Whence **c** ye?	935
	42: 9 to see the nakedness of the land you are **c**.	935
	42:10 but to buy food are thy servants **c**.	935
	42:12 to see the nakedness of the land you are **c**.	935
	42:15 except your youngest brother **c** hither.	935
	42:21 therefore is this distress **c** upon us.	935
	44:23 Except your youngest brother **c down**	3381
	44:30 therefore when I **c** to thy servant my father,	935
	44:31 shall **c to pass**, when he seeth that the lad	1961
	44:34 I see the evil that shall **c on** my father.	4672
	45: 4 his brethren, **C near** to me, I pray you.	5066
	45: 9 of all Egypt; **c down** unto me, tarry not:	3381
	45:11 and all that thou hast, **c to poverty**.	3423
	45:16 saying, Joseph's brethren are **c**:	935
	45:18 and your households, and **c** unto me:	935
	45:19 your wives, and bring your father, and **c**.	935
	46:31 in the land of Canaan, are **c** unto me;	935
	46:33 it shall **c to pass**, when Pharaoh shall call	1961
	47: 1 they have, are **c** out of the land of Canaan;	935
	47: 4 For to sojourn in the land are we **c**;	935
	47: 5 father and thy brethren are **c** unto thee:	935
	47:24 it shall **c to pass** in the increase, that you	1961
	48: 7 *was* but a little way to **c** unto Ephrath:	935
	49: 6 O my soul, **c** not thou into their secret;	935
	49:10 from between his feet, until Shiloh **c**;	935
	50: 5 and bury my father, and I will **c again**.	7725
Ex	1:10 **C on**, let us deal wisely with them;	3051
	1:10 lest they multiply, and it **c to pass**, that,	1961
	1:19 are delivered ere the midwives **c in** unto	935
	2:18 How *is it that* you are **c** so soon to day?	935
	3: 8 I am **c down** to deliver them out of	3381
	3: 9 cry of the children of Israel is **c** unto me:	935
	3:10 **C** now therefore, and I will send thee	1980
	3:13 *when* I **c** unto the children of Israel,	935
	3:18 thou shalt **c**, thou and the elders of Israel,	935
	3:21 it shall **c to pass**, that, when ye go,	1961
	4: 8 it shall **c to pass**, if they will not believe	1961
	4: 9 it shall **c to pass**, if they will not believe	1961
	7:15 stand by the river's brink against he **c**;	7125
	8: 3 which shall go up and **c** into thine house,	935
	8: 4 the frogs shall **c up** *both* on thee,	5927
	8: 5 **cause** frogs to **c up** upon the land of	5927
	9:19 the hail shall **c down** upon them,	3381
	10:12 they may **c up** upon the land of Egypt,	5927
	10:26 must serve the LORD, until we **c** thither.	935
	11: 8 these thy servants shall **c down** unto me,	3381
	12:23 will not suffer the destroyer to **c in** unto	935
	12:25 it shall **c to pass**, when ye be come to	1961
	12:25 when ye be **c** to the land which the LORD	935
	12:26 that it shall **c to pass**, when your children	1961
	12:48 and then let him **c near** and keep it;	7126
	13:14 when thy son asketh thee **in time to c**,	4279
	14:26 that the waters may **c again** upon	7725
	16: 5 it shall **c to pass**, that on the sixth day	1961
	16: 9 of Israel, **C near** before the LORD:	7126
	17: 6 the rock, and there shall **c water out** of it,	3318
	18: 6 I thy father in law Jethro am **c** unto thee,	935
	18: 8 all the travail that had **c upon** them by	4672
	18:15 Because the people **c** unto me to inquire of	935
	18:16 When they have a matter, they **c** unto me;	935
	19: 2 **c** to the desert of Sinai, and had pitched	935

C

Ex	19: 9 Lo, I **c** unto thee in a thick cloud,	935
	19:11 for the third day the LORD will **c down** in	3381
	19:13 they shall **c up** to the mount.	5927
	19:15 against the third day: **c** not at *your* wives.	5066
	19:22 which **c near** to the LORD,	5066
	19:23 The people cannot **c up** to mount Sinai:	5927
	19:24 shalt **c up**, thou, and Aaron with thee:	5927
	19:24 the people break through to **c up** unto	5927
	20:20 for God is **c** to prove you, and that his fear	935
	20:24 all places where I record my name I will **c**	935
	21:14 if a man **c presumptuously** upon his	2102
	22: 9 the cause of both parties shall **c** before	935
	22:27 shall **c to pass**, when he crieth unto me,	1961
	23:27 all the people to whom thou shalt **c**,	935
	24: 1 **C up** unto the LORD, thou, and Aaron,	5927
	24: 2 Moses alone shall **c near** the LORD: but	5066
	24: 2 they shall not **c nigh**; neither shall	5066
	24:12 **C up** to me into the mount, and be there:	5927
	24:14 ye here for us, until we **c again** unto you:	7725
	24:14 any matters to do, let him **c** unto them.	5066
	25:32 six branches shall **c out** of the sides of it;	3318
	25:33 in the six branches that **c out** of	3318
	28:43 when they **c in** unto the tabernacle of	935
	28:43 they **c near** unto the altar to minister	5066
	30:20 when they **c near** to the altar to minister,	5066
	32: 1 Moses delayed to **c down** out of the	3381
	32:26 *let him* **c** unto me. And all the sons of	NIH
	33: 5 I will **c up** into the midst of thee in a	5927
	33:22 it shall **c to pass**, while my glory passeth	1961
	34: 2 **c up** in the morning unto mount Sinai,	5927
	34: 3 no man shall **c up** with thee, neither let	5927
	34:30 and they were afraid to **c nigh** him.	5066
	35:10 every wise hearted among you shall **c**,	935
	36: 2 stirred him up to **c** unto the work to do it:	7126
Lev	4:23 he hath sinned, **c** to his **knowledge**,	3045
	4:28 **c** to his **knowledge**, then he shall bring	3045
	10: 3 will be sanctified in them that **c nigh** me,	7138
	10: 4 of Aaron, and said unto them, **C near**,	7126
	10: 6 and lest wrath **c** upon all the people:	NIH
	12: 4 shall touch no hallowed *thing*, nor **c** into	935
	13:16 unto white, he shall **c** unto the priest;	935
	14: 8 after *that* he shall **c** into the camp,	935
	14:34 When ye be **c** into the land of Canaan,	935
	14:35 he that owneth the house shall **c** and tell	935
	14:39 the priest shall **c again** the seventh day,	7725
	14:43 if the plague **c again**, and break out in	7725
	14:44 the priest shall **c** and look, and behold,	935
	14:48 if the priest shall **c in**, and look	935+935
	15:14 **c** before the LORD unto the door of	935
	16: 2 he **c** not at all times into the holy *place*	935
	16: 3 Thus shall Aaron **c** into the holy *place*:	935
	16:17 in the holy *place*, until he **c out**,	3318
	16:23 Aaron shall **c** into the tabernacle of	935
	16:24 **c forth**, and offer his burnt offering,	3318
	16:26 in water, and afterward **c** into the camp.	935
	16:28 and afterward he shall **c** into the camp.	935
	19:19 mingled of linen and woollen **c** upon thee.	5927
	19:23 when ye shall **c** into the land, and shall	935
	21:21 shall **c nigh** to offer the offerings of	5066
	21:21 he shall not **c nigh** to offer the bread of	5066
	21:23 nor **c nigh** unto the altar, because he hath	5066
	23:10 When ye be **c** into the land which I give	935
	25: 2 When ye **c** into the land which I give you,	935
	25:22 until her fruits **c in** ye shall eat *of* the old	935
	25:25 *if any of* his kin **c** to redeem it, then shall	935
Nu	1: 1 in the second year after they were **c out**	3318
	4: 5 Aaron shall **c**, and his sons, and they shall	935
	4:15 the sons of Kohath shall **c** to bear *it*: but	935
	5:14 the spirit of jealousy **c** upon him, and he	5674
	5:14 or if the spirit of jealousy **c** upon him,	5674
	5:27 it shall **c to pass**, *that*, if she be defiled,	1961
	6: 5 there shall no razor **c** upon his head:	5674
	6: 6 unto the LORD he shall **c** at no dead body.	935
	8:19 when the children of Israel **c nigh** unto	5066
	9: 1 after they were **c out** of the land of Egypt,	3318
	10:29 **c** thou with us, and we will do thee good:	1980
	11:17 I will **c down**, and talk with thee there:	3381
	11:20 until it **c out** at your nostrils, and it be	3318
	11:23 whether my word shall **c to pass** unto	7136
	12: 4 **C out** ye three unto the tabernacle of	3318
	13:21 of Zin unto Rehob, as men **c** to Hamath.	935
	13:33 the sons of Anak, *which* **c** of the giants:	NIH
	14:30 Doubtless ye shall not **c** into the land,	935
	15: 2 When ye be **c** into the land of your	935
	15:18 When ye **c** into the land whither I bring	935
	16: 5 and will **cause** him to **c near** unto him:	7126
	16: 5 chosen will he **cause to c near** unto him.	7126
	16:12 of Eliab: which said, We will not **c up**:	5927
	16:14 the eyes of these men? we will not **c up**.	5927
	16:40 **c near** to offer incense before the LORD;	7126
	17: 5 it shall **c to pass**, *that* the man's rod,	1961
	18: 3 only they shall not **c nigh** the vessels of	7126
	18: 4 and a stranger shall not **c nigh** unto you.	7126
	18:22 **c nigh** the tabernacle of the congregation,	7126
	19: 7 afterward he shall **c** into the camp,	935
	19:14 all that **c** into the tent, and all that *is* in	935
	20:18 lest I **c out** against thee with the sword.	3318
	21: 1 it shall **c to pass**, that every one that is	1961
	21:27 **C into** Heshbon, let the city of Sihon be	935
	22: 5 there is a people **c out** from Egypt:	3318
	22: 6 **C** now therefore, I pray thee, curse me	1980
	22:11 Behold, *there is* a people **c out** of Egypt,	3318
	22:11 **c** now, curse me them; peradventure	1980
	22:14 and said, Balaam refuseth to **c** with us.	1980

C

Nu 22:17 c therefore, I pray thee, curse me this 1980
22:20 If the men c to call thee, rise up, and go 935
22:36 when Balak heard that Balaam was c, 935
22:38 said unto Balak, Lo, I am c unto thee: 935
23: 3 peradventure the LORD will c to meet 7136
23: 7 saying, C, curse me Jacob, and come, 1980
23: 7 curse me Jacob, and c, defy Israel. 1980
23:13 Balak said unto him, C, I pray thee, 1980
23:27 Balak said unto Balaam, C, I pray thee, 1980
24:14 c therefore, and I will advertise thee what 1980
24:17 there shall a Star c out of Jacob, 1869
24:19 Out of Jacob shall c he that shall have NIH
24:24 ships shall c from the coast of Chittim, NIH
26:29 of Gilead c the family of the Gileadites. NIH
27:21 at his word they shall c in, both he, 935
31:24 and afterward ye shall c into the camp. 935
33:38 of Israel were c out of the land of Egypt, 3318
33:55 c to pass, that those which ye let remain 3498
33:56 Moreover it shall c to pass, that I shall do 1961
34: 2 When ye c into the land of Canaan; 935
35:10 When ye be c over Jordan into the land of 5674
35:26 if the slayer shall at any time c 3318+3318
35:32 he should c again to dwell in the land, 7725
Dt 1:20 are c unto the mountain of the Amorites, 935
1:22 go up, and into what cities we shall c. 935
2:14 until we were c over the brook Zered, 5674
4:30 all these things are c upon thee, even in 4672
4:46 after they were c forth out of Egypt. 3318
6:20 when thy son asketh thee in time to c, 4279
7:12 Wherefore it shall c to pass, if ye hearken 1961
10: 1 c up unto me into the mount, 5927
11:13 it shall c to pass, if you shall hearken 1961
11:29 it shall c to pass, when the LORD thy 1961
12: 5 shall ye seek, and thither thou shalt c: 935
12: 9 For ye are not as yet c to the rest and to 935
13: 2 sign or the wonder c to pass, whereof he 935
14:29 shall c, and shall eat and be satisfied; 935
15:19 All the firstling males that c of thy herd 3205
17: 9 thou shalt c unto the priests the Levites, 935
17:14 When thou art c unto the land which 935
18: 6 if a Levite c from any of thy gates out of all 935
18: 6 c with all the desire of his mind unto 935
18: 9 When thou art c into the land which 935
18:19 it shall c to pass, that whosoever will not 1961
18:22 if the thing follow not, nor c to pass, 935
20: 2 when ye are c nigh unto the battle, 7126
21: 2 thy elders and thy judges shall c forth, 3318
21: 5 the priests the sons of Levi shall c near; 5066
23:10 the camp, he shall not c within the camp: 935
23:11 sun is down, he shall c into the camp 935
24: 1 it c to pass that she find no favour in his 1961
24: 9 after that ye were c forth out of Egypt. 3318
25: 1 they c unto judgment, that the judges 5066
25: 9 shall his brother's wife c unto him in 5066
25:17 when ye were c forth out of Egypt; 3318
26: 1 when thou art c in unto the land which 935
26: 3 that I am c unto the country which 935
27:12 the people, when ye are c over Jordan; 5674
28: 1 it shall c to pass, if thou shalt hearken 1961
28: 2 all these blessings shall c on thee, 935
28: 7 they shall c out against thee one way, 3318
28:15 it shall c to pass, if thou wilt not hearken 1961
28:15 that all these curses shall c upon thee, 935
28:24 from heaven shall it c down upon thee, 3381
28:43 high; and thou shalt c down very low. 3381
28:45 all these curses shall c upon thee, 935
28:52 until thy high and fenced walls c down, 3381
28:63 it shall c to pass, that as the LORD 1961
29:19 it c to pass, when he heareth the words 1961
29:22 that the generation to c of your children 314
29:22 the stranger that shall c from a far land, 935
30: 1 it shall c to pass, when all these things 1961
30: 1 when all these things are c upon thee, 935
31: 2 this day; I can no more go out and c in: 935
31:11 When all Israel is c to appear before 935
31:17 Are not these evils c upon us, because 4672
31:21 And it shall c to pass, when many evils 1961
32:35 the things that shall c upon them make 6264
33:16 let the blessing c upon the head of Joseph, 935
Jos 2: 3 Bring forth the men that are c to thee, 935
2: 3 for they be c to search out all the country. 935
2:18 when we c into the land, thou shalt 935
3: 4 c not near unto it, that ye may know 7126
3: 8 When ye are c to the brink of the water of 935
3: 9 C hither, and hear the words of the LORD 5066
3:13 it shall c to pass, as soon as the soles of 1961
3:13 from the waters that c down from above; 3381
3:15 they that bare the ark were c unto Jordan, 935
4: 6 children ask their fathers in time to c, 4279
4:16 Testimony, that they c up out of Jordan. 5927
4:17 the priests, saying, C ye up out of Jordan. 5927
4:18 were c up out of the midst of Jordan, 5927
4:21 shall ask their fathers in time to c, 4279
5:14 of the host of the LORD am I now c. 935
6: 5 it shall c to pass, that when they make a 1961
6:19 they shall c into the treasury of the LORD. 935
7:14 shall c according to the families thereof; 7126
7:14 LORD shall take shall c by households; 7126
7:14 the LORD take shall c man by man. 7126
8: 5 it shall c to pass, when they come out 1961
8: 5 when they c out against us, as at the first, 3318
8: 6 (For they will c out after us) till we have 3318
9: 6 men of Israel, We be c from a far country: 935
9: 8 Who are ye? and from whence c ye? 935
9: 9 From a very far country thy servants are c 935

Jos 10: 4 C up unto me, and help me, that we may 5927
10: 6 c up to us quickly, and save us, 5927
10:24 C near, put your feet upon the necks of 7126
11:20 that they should c against Israel in battle, 7125
14:11 for war, both to go out, and to c in. 935
18: 4 of them; and they shall c again to me. 935
18: 8 land, and describe it, and c again to me, 7725
20: 6 c unto his own city, and unto his own 935
22:24 In time to c your children might speak 4279
22:27 may not say to our children in time to c, 4279
22:28 to us or to our generations in time to c, 4279
23: 7 That ye c not among these nations, these 935
23:14 all are c to pass unto you, and not one 935
23:15 it shall c to pass, that as all good 1961
23:15 that as all good things are c upon you, 935
Jdg 1: 3 his brother, C up with me into my lot, 5927
1:24 spies saw a man c forth out of the city, 3318
1:34 they would not suffer them to c down to 3381
3:27 came to pass, when he was c, that he blew 935
4:20 when any man doth c and inquire of thee, 935
4:22 C, and I will shew thee the man whom 1980
6: 4 till thou c unto Gaza, and left them 935
6:18 until I c unto thee, and bring forth my 935
6:18 he said, I will tarry until thou c again. 7725
7:13 Gideon was c, behold, there was a man 935
7:17 when I c to the outside of the camp, 935
7:24 C down against the Midianites, 3381
8: 9 saying, When I c again in peace, I will 7725
9:10 unto the fig tree, C thou, and reign over us. 1980
9:12 unto the vine, C thou, and reign over us. 1980
9:14 the bramble, C thou, and reign over us. 1980
9:15 then c and put your trust in my shadow: 935
9:15 let fire c out of the bramble, and devour 3318
9:20 let fire c out from Abimelech, 3318
9:20 let fire c out from the men of Shechem, 3318
9:24 and ten sons of Jerubbaal might c, 935
9:29 Increase thine army, and c out. 3318
9:31 Ebed and his brethren be c to Shechem; 935
9:33 the people that is with him c out against 3318
9:36 there c people down from the top of 935
9:37 See there c people down by the middle of 3381
9:37 another company c along by the plain of 935
9:43 the people were c forth out of the city; 3318
11: 6 said unto Jephthah, C, and be our captain, 1980
11: 7 why are ye c unto me now when ye are in 935
11:12 that thou art c against me to fight in my 935
11:33 even till thou c to Minnith, even twenty 935
12: 3 are ye c up unto me this day, 5927
13: 5 a son; and no rasor shall c on his head: 5927
13: 8 the man of God which thou didst send c 935
13:12 said, Now let thy words c to pass. 935
13:17 when thy sayings c to pass we may do 935
15:10 of Judah said, Why are ye c up against us? 5927
15:10 To bind Samson are we c up, 5927
15:12 unto him, We are c down to bind thee, 3381
16: 2 the Gazites, saying, Samson is c hither. 935
16:17 There hath not c a razor upon mine head; 5927
16:18 C up this once, for he hath shewed 5927
18:10 ye shall c unto a people secure, and to a 935
19:11 C, I pray thee, and let us turn in into this 1980
19:13 C, and let us draw near to one of these 1980
19:23 seeing that this man is c into mine house, 935
19:29 when he was c into his house, he took a 935
20:10 do, when they c to Gibeah of Benjamin, 935
20:41 for they saw that evil was c upon them. 5060
21: 3 of Israel, why is this c to pass in Israel, 1961
21:21 if the daughters of Shiloh c out to dance 3318
21:21 ye c out of the vineyards, and catch you 3318
21:22 or their brethren c unto us to complain, 935
Ru 1:19 to pass, when they were c to Beth-lehem, 935
2:11 c unto a people which thou knewest not 1980
2:12 under whose wings thou art c to trust. 935
2:14 At mealtime c thou hither, and eat of 5066
4: 3 is c again out of the country of Moab, 7725
4:11 The LORD make the woman that is c into 935
1Sa 1:11 and there shall no rasor c upon his head. 5927
1:20 when the time was c about after 8622+3807.1
2: 3 let not arrogancy c out of your mouth: 3318
2:31 Behold, the days c, that I will cut off thine 935
2:34 that shall c upon thy two sons, on Hophni 935
2:36 shall c to pass, that every one that is left 1961
2:36 every one that is left in thine house shall c 935
4: 3 when the people were c into the camp, 935
4: 6 the ark of the LORD was c into the camp. 935
4: 7 for they said, God is c into the camp. 935
5: 5 Dagon, nor any that c into Dagon's house, 935
6: 7 on which there hath c no yoke, and tie 5927
6:21 ye c down, and fetch it up to you. 3381
9: 5 when they were c to the land of Zuph, 935
9: 5 that was with him, C, and let us return; 1980
9: 9 thus he spake, C, and let us go to the seer: 1980
9:10 Saul to his servant, Well said; c, let us go. 1980
9:13 As soon as ye be c into the city, ye shall 935
9:13 for the people will not eat until he c, 935
9:14 And when they were c into the city, 935
9:16 people, because their cry is c unto me. 935
9:25 when they were c down from the high 3381
10: 3 thou shalt c to the plain of Tabor, 935
10: 5 After that thou shalt c to the hill of God, 935
10: 5 it shall c to pass, when thou art come 1961
10: 5 when thou art c thither to the city, 935
10: 6 the spirit of the LORD will c upon thee, 6743
10: 7 let it be, when these signs are c unto thee, 935
10: 8 behold, I will c down unto thee, to offer 3381
10: 8 till I c to thee, and shew thee what thou 935

1Sa 10:11 What is this that is c unto the son of Kish? 1961
10:20 caused all the tribes of Israel to c near, 7126
10:21 caused the tribe of Benjamin to c near, 7126
10:22 if the man should yet c thither. 935
11: 3 no man to save us, we will c out to thee. 3318
11:10 To morrow we will c out unto you, 3318
11:14 C, and let us go to Gilgal, and renew 1980
12: 8 When Jacob was c into Egypt, 935
13:12 The Philistines will c down now upon me 3381
14: 1 C, and let us go over to the Philistines' 1980
14: 6 C, and let us go over unto the garrison of 1980
14: 9 say thus unto us, Tarry until we c to you; 5060
14:10 If they say thus, C up unto us; then we 5927
14:11 the Hebrews c forth out of the holes 3318
14:12 C up to us, and we will shew you a thing. 5927
14:12 unto his armourbearer, C up after me: 5927
14:26 when the people were c into the wood, 935
16: 2 say, I am c to sacrifice to the LORD. 935
16: 3 I am c to sacrifice unto the LORD: 935
16: 5 and c with me to the sacrifice. 935
16: 6 it came to pass, when they were c, that he 935
16:11 for we will not sit down till he c hither. 935
16:16 it shall c to pass, when the evil spirit 1961
17: 8 Why are ye c out to set your battle in 3318
17: 8 man for you, and let him c down to me. 3381
17:25 Have ye seen this man that is c up? 5927
17:25 surely to defy Israel is he c up: and it shall 5927
17:28 thou art c down that thou mightest see 3381
17:44 C to me, and I will give thy flesh unto 1980
17:45 I c to thee in the name of the LORD of 935
17:52 until thou c to the valley, and to the gates 935
19:16 when the messengers were c in, behold 935
20: 9 determined by my father to c upon thee, 935
20:11 C, and let us go out into the field. 1980
20:19 c to the place where thou didst hide thyself 935
20:21 on this side of thee, take them; then c thou: 935
20:24 the new moon was c, the king sat him 1961
20:37 the lad was c to the place of the arrow 935
21:15 shall this fellow c into my house? 935
22: 3 I pray thee, c forth, and be with you, 3318
23: 3 if we c to Keilah against the armies of 1980
23: 7 it was told Saul that David was c to Keilah. 935
23:10 heard that Saul seeketh to c to Keilah, 935
23:11 Will Saul c down, as thy servant hath 3381
23:11 And the LORD said, He will c down. 3381
23:15 David saw that Saul was c out to seek his 3318
23:20 c down according to all the desire of thy 3381
23:20 to all the desire of thy soul to c down; 3381
23:23 c ye again to me with the certainty, 7725
23:23 it shall c to pass, if he be in the land, 1961
23:27 unto Saul, saying, Haste thee, and c; 1980
24:14 After whom is the king of Israel c out? 3318
25: 8 for we c in a good day: give, I pray thee, 935
25:19 Go on before me; behold, I c after you. 935
25:30 it shall c to pass, when the LORD shall 1961
25:34 thou hadst hasted and c to meet me, 935
25:40 when the servants of David were c to 935
26: 4 understood that Saul was c in very deed. 935
26:10 his day shall c to die; or he shall descend 935
26:20 the king of Israel is c out to seek a flea, 3318
26:22 let one of the young men c over and 5674
29:10 thy master's servants that are c with thee: 935
30: 1 his men were c to Ziklag on the third day, 935
31: 4 lest these uncircumcised c and thrust me 935
2Sa 1: 9 anguish is c upon me, because my life is 270
2:24 the sun went down when they were c to 935
3:23 and all the host that was with him were c, 935
3:26 when Joab was c out from David, he sent 3318
5: 6 and the lame, thou shalt not c in hither: 935
5: 6 thinking, David cannot c in hither. 935
5: 8 and the lame shall not c into the house. 935
5:13 of Jerusalem, after he was c from Hebron; 935
5:23 c upon them over against the mulberry 935
5:25 the Philistines from Geba until thou c 935
6: 9 How shall the ark of the LORD c to me? 935
7:19 house for a great while to c. 4480+7350
9: 6 the son of Saul, was c unto David, he fell 935
10:11 for thee, then I will c and help thee. 1980
11: 7 when Uriah was c unto him, David 935
12: 4 to dress for the wayfaring man that was c 935
12: 4 dressed it for the man that was c to him. 935
13: 5 let my sister Tamar c, and give me meat, 935
13: 6 when the king was c to see him, Amnon 935
13: 6 let Tamar my sister c, and make me a 935
13:11 said unto her, C lie with me, my sister. 935
13:35 unto the king, Behold, the king's sons c: 935
14: 3 c to the king, and speak on this manner 935
14:15 that I am c to speak of this thing unto my 935
14:29 to the king; but he would not c to him: 935
14:29 again the second time, he would not c. 935
14:32 Behold, I sent unto thee, saying, C hither, 935
14:32 to say, Wherefore am I c from Geshur? 935
15: 4 hath any suit or cause might c unto me, 935
15:28 until there c word from you to certify me. 935
15:32 that when David was c to the top of 935
16: 7 C out, come out, thou bloody man, 3318
16: 7 Come out, come out, thou bloody man, 3318
16:16 David's friend, was c unto Absalom, 935
17: 2 And I will c upon him while he is weary 935
17: 6 when Hushai was c to Absalom, 935
17: 9 it will be, when some of them be c 1961
17:12 So shall we c upon him in some place 935
17:17 they might not be seen to c into the city: 935
17:27 to pass, when David was c to Mahanaim, 935
19:11 seeing the speech of all Israel is c to 935

C

2Sa	19:18 before the king, as he was **c over** Jordan;	5674
	19:20 I am **c** the first *this* day of all the house of	935
	19:25 when he was **c** *to* Jerusalem to meet	935
	19:30 forasmuch as my lord the king is **c** *again* in	935
	19:33 **c** thou **over** with me, and I will feed thee	5674
	19:39 when the king was **c over**, the king kissed	5674
	20:16 say, I pray you, unto Joab, **C near** hither,	7126
	20:17 when he was **c near** unto her, the woman	7126
	24:13 Shall seven years of famine **c** unto thee in	935
	24:21 Wherefore is my lord the king **c** to his	935
1Ki	1:12 Now therefore **c**, let me, I pray thee,	1980
	1:14 I also will **c in** after thee, and confirm thy	935
	1:21 Otherwise it shall **c to pass**, when my lord	1961
	1:23 he was **c in** before the king, he bowed	935
	1:35 ye shall **c up** after him, that he may come	5927
	1:35 that he may **c** and sit upon my throne;	935
	1:42 Adonijah said *unto him*, **C in**; for thou *art*	935
	1:45 they are **c up** from thence rejoicing,	5927
	2:30 unto him, Thus saith the king, **C forth.**	3318
	2:41 from Jerusalem *to* Gath, and was **c**	7725
	3: 7 child: I know not *how* to go out or **c in.**	935
	6: 1 of Israel were **c out** of the land of Egypt,	3318
	8:10 when the priests were **c out** of the holy	3318
	8:19 thy son that shall **c forth** out of thy loins,	3318
	8:31 the oath **c** before thine altar in this house:	935
	8:42 he shall **c** and pray towards this house;	935
	10: 2 she was **c** to Solomon, she communed	935
	11: 2 to them, neither shall they **c in** unto you:	935
	12: 1 all Israel were **c** *to* Shechem to make him	935
	12: 5 yet *for* three days, then **c again** to me.	7725
	12:12 saying, **C** to me **again** the third day.	7725
	12:20 Israel heard that Jeroboam was **c again**,	7725
	12:21 when Rehoboam was **c** *to* Jerusalem,	935
	13: 7 **C** home with me, and refresh *thyself*, and	935
	13:15 him, **C** home with me, and eat bread.	1980
	13:22 thy carcase shall not **c** unto the sepulchre	935
	13:32 of Samaria, shall **surely c to pass.**	1961+1961
	14: 6 that he said, **C in**, thou wife of Jeroboam;	935
	14:13 he only of Jeroboam shall **c** to the grave,	935
	15:17 *any* to go out or **c in** to Asa king of Judah.	935
	15:19 **c** and break thy league with Baasha king	1980
	17:18 art thou **c** unto me to call my sin to	935
	17:21 let this child's soul **c** into him **again.**	7725
	18:12 It shall **c to pass**, *as soon as* I am gone	1961
	18:12 *so* when I **c** and tell Ahab, and he cannot	935
	18:30 said unto all the people, **C near** unto me.	5066
	19:17 it shall **c to pass**, *that* him that escapeth	1961
	20:17 There are men **c** out of Samaria.	3318
	20:18 he said, Whether they be **c out** for peace,	3318
	20:18 whether they be **c out** for war, take them	5927
	20:22 the king of Syria will **c up** against thee.	935
	20:33 whether *any thing would* **c** from him,	NIH
	20:33 he **caused** him **to c up** into the chariot.	5927
	22:27 with water of affliction, until I **c** in peace.	935
2Ki	1: 4 Thou shalt not **c down** from *that* bed on	3381
	1: 6 thou shalt not **c down** from *that* bed on	3381
	1: 9 man of God, the king hath said, **C down.**	3381
	1:10 let fire **c down** from heaven,	3381
	1:11 thus hath the king said, **C down** quickly.	3381
	1:12 let fire **c down** from heaven,	3381
	1:16 thou shalt not **c down** off *that* bed on	3381
	3:21 the kings were **c up** to fight against them,	5927
	4: 1 the creditor is **c** to take unto him my two	935
	4: 4 thou art **c in**, thou shalt shut the door	935
	4:22 may run to the man of God, and **c again.**	7725
	4:32 when Elisha was **c** into the house, behold,	935
	4:36 when she was **c in** unto him, he said,	935
	5: 6 Now when this letter is **c** unto thee,	935
	5: 8 let him **c** now to me, and he shall know	935
	5:10 thy flesh shall **c again** to thee,	7725
	5:11 He will **surely c out** to me,	3318+3318
	5:22 even now there be **c** to me from mount	935
	6: 9 place; for thither the Syrians are **c down.**	5185
	6:20 when they were **c** into Samaria, that Elisha	935
	7: 4 Now therefore **c**, and let us fall unto	1980
	7: 5 when they were **c** to the uttermost part of	935
	7: 6 the kings of the Egyptians to **c** upon us.	935
	7: 9 *some* mischief will **c upon** us:	4672
	7: 9 now therefore **c**, that we may go and	1980
	7:12 saying, When they **c out** of the city,	3318
	8: 1 it shall also **c** upon the land seven years.	935
	8: 7 him, saying, The man of God is **c** hither.	935
	9:16 Ahaziah king of Judah was **c down** to see	3381
	9:30 when Jehu was **c** to Jezreel, Jezebel heard	935
	9:34 when he was **c in**, he did eat and drink,	935
	10: 6 **c** to me to Jezreel by to morrow *this* time.	935
	10:16 **C** with me, and see my zeal for	1980
	10:25 Go in, *and* slay them; let none **c forth.**	3318
	11: 9 his men that were to **c in** on the sabbath,	935
	14: 8 son of Jehu, king of Israel, saying, **C**,	1980
	16: 7 **c up**, and save me out of the hand of	5927
	16:12 when the king was **c** from Damascus,	5927
	18:13 **c up** against all the fenced cities of Judah,	5927
	18:17 when they were **c up**, they came and	5927
	18:25 Am I now **c up** without the Lord against	5927
	18:31 **c out** to me, and *then* eat ye every man of	3318
	18:32 Until I **c** and take you away to a land like	935
	19: 3 for the children are **c** to the birth,	935
	19: 9 Behold, he is **c out** to fight against thee:	3318
	19:23 I am **c up** *to* the height of the mountains,	5927
	19:28 thy tumult is **c up** into mine ears,	5927
	19:32 He shall not **c** into this city, nor shoot an	935
	19:32 arrow there, nor **c before** it *with* shield,	6923
	19:33 shall not **c** into this city, saith the Lord.	935
	20:14 They are **c** from a far country,	935

2Ki	20:17 Behold, the days **c**, that all that *is* in thine	935
1Ch	9:25 to **c** after seven days from time to time	935
	10: 4 lest these uncircumcised **c** and abuse me.	935
	11: 5 said to David, Thou shalt not **c** hither.	935
	12:17 If ye be **c** peaceably unto me to help me,	935
	12:17 *if ye be* **c** to betray me to mine enemies,	NIH
	12:31 by name, to **c** and make David king.	935
	14:14 upon them over against the mulberry	935
	16:29 bring an offering, and **c** before him:	935
	17:11 shall **c to pass**, when thy days be expired	1961
	17:17 house for a **great while to c**,	4480+7350
	17: 3 not his servants **c** unto thee for to search,	935
	19: 9 the kings that were **c** were by themselves	935
	24:19 service to **c** into the house of the Lord,	935
	29:12 Both riches and honour *c* of thee,	935
	29:14 willingly after this *sort*? for all *things* **c** of	NIH
2Ch	1:10 I may go out and **c** in before this people:	935
	5:11 when the priests were **c** *out* of the holy	3318
	6: 9 son which shall **c forth** out of thy loins,	3318
	6:22 the oath **c** before thine altar in this house;	935
	6:32 is **c** from a far country for thy great name's	935
	6:32 out arm; if they **c** and pray in this house;	935
	8:11 whereunto the ark of the Lord hath **c.**	935
	9: 1 she was **c** to Solomon, she communed	935
	10: 1 *to* Shechem were all Israel to make him	935
	10: 5 **C again** unto me after three days.	7725
	10:12 saying, **C again** to me on the third day.	7725
	11: 1 when Rehoboam was **c** *to* Jerusalem,	935
	13:13 caused an ambushment to **c** about	935
	16: 1 none go out or **c in** to Asa king of Judah.	935
	18:14 when he was **c** to the king, the king said	935
	19:10 what cause soever shall **c** to you of your	935
	19:10 *so* wrath **c** upon you, and upon your	1961
	20:11 to **c** to cast us out of thy possession,	935
	20:16 behold, they **c up** by the cliff of Ziz;	5927
	20:22 mount Seir, which were **c** against Judah;	935
	22: 7 for when he was **c**, he went out with	935
	23: 6 But let none **c** into the house of the Lord,	935
	23: 8 every man his men that were to **c in** on	935
	23:15 she was **c** to the entering of the horse	935
	25:10 the army that was **c** to him out of Ephraim,	935
	25:14 that Amaziah was **c** from the slaughter	935
	25:17 the son of Jehu, king of Israel, saying, **C**,	1980
	28:17 For again the Edomites had **c** and	935
	29:31 **c near** and bring sacrifices and	5066
	30: 1 that *they* should **c** to the house of	935
	30: 5 that *they* should **c** to keep the passover	935
	30: 9 so that *they shall* **c again** into this land:	7725
	32: 2 Hezekiah saw that Sennacherib was **c**,	935
	32: 4 Why should the kings of Assyria **c**,	935
	32:21 when he was **c** *into* the house of his god,	935
	35:21 I **c** not against thee *this* day, but against	NIH
Ezr	3: 1 when the seventh month was **c**,	5060
	3: 8 all they that were **c** out of the captivity	935
	4:12 up from thee to us are **c** unto Jerusalem,	858
	6:21 which were **c again** out of captivity,	7725
	8:35 which were **c** out of the captivity,	935
	9:13 after all that is **c** upon us for our evil deeds,	935
	10: 8 *that* whosoever would not **c** within three	935
	10:14 wives in our cities **c** at appointed times,	935
Ne	2: 7 that they may convey me over till I **c** into	935
	2:10 **c** a man to seek the welfare of the children	1980
	2:17 **c**, and let us build *up* the wall of	935
	4: 8 conspired all of them together to **c** and	935
	4:11 till we **c** in the midst among them,	935
	6: 2 and Geshem sent, saying, **C**, let us meet	1980
	6: 3 a great work, so that I cannot **c down**:	3381
	6: 3 whilst I leave it, and **c down** to you?	3381
	6: 7 **C** now therefore, and let us take counsel	1980
	6:10 they will **c** to slay thee; yea, in the night	935
	6:10 yea, in the night will they **c** to slay thee.	935
	8:17 **c again** out of the captivity made booths,	7725
	9:32 that hath **c upon** us, on our kings, on our	4672
	13: 1 the Moabite should not **c** into	935
	13:22 *that* they should **c** and keep the gates,	935
Est	1:12 the queen Vashti refused to **c** at the king's	935
	1:17 For *this* deed of the queen shall **c abroad**	3318
	1:19 That Vashti **c** no *more* before king	935
	2:12 when every maid's turn was **c** to go in	5060
	2:15 was **c** to go in unto the king, she required	5060
	4:11 shall **c** unto the king into the inner court,	935
	4:11 have not been called to **c in** unto the king	935
	4:14 who knoweth whether thou art **c** to	5060
	5: 4 Haman **c** *this* day unto the banquet that I	935
	5: 8 Haman **c** to the banquet that I shall prepare	935
	5:12 Esther the queen did let no *man* **c in** with	935
	6: 4 Haman was **c** into the outward court of	935
	6: 5 And the king said, Let him **c.**	935
	8: 6 see the evil that shall **c unto** my people?	4672
	9:26 this *matter*, and which had **c** unto them,	935
Job	2:11 heard of all this evil that was **c** upon him,	935
	2:11 together to **c** to mourn with him	935
	3: 6 let it not **c** into the number of the months.	935
	3: 7 be solitary, let no joyful voice **c** therein.	935
	3:25 thing which I greatly feared is **c** upon me,	857
	3:25 *that* which I was afraid of is **c** unto me.	935
	4: 5 now it is **c** upon thee, and thou faintest;	935
	5:26 Thou shalt **c** to *thy* grave in a full age, like	935
	7: 9 that goeth down to the grave shall **c up**	5927
	8:22 place of the wicked shall **c to nought.**	369
	9:32 *and* we should **c** together in judgment.	935
	13:13 I may speak, and let **c** on me what *will*.	5674
	13:16 For a hypocrite shall not **c** before him.	935
	14:14 time will I wait, till my change **c.**	
	14:21 His sons **c to honour**, and he knoweth *it*	3513

Job	15:21 prosperity the destroyer shall **c upon** him.	935
	16:22 When a few years are **c**, then I shall go	857
	17:10 *as for* you all, do you return, and **c** now;	935
	18:20 They that **c after** *him* shall be astonied at	314
	19:12 His troops **c** together, and raise up their	935
	20:22 hand of the wicked shall **c upon** him.	935
	22:21 at peace: thereby good shall **c** unto thee.	935
	23: 3 find him! *that* I might **c** *even* to his seat!	935
	23:10 he hath tried me, I shall **c forth** as gold.	3318
	26:10 until the day and night **c to an end.**	8503
	34:28 that *they* **cause** the cry of the poor **to c**	935
	37:13 **causeth** it **to c**, whether for correction,	4672
	38:11 Hitherto shalt thou **c**, but no further:	935
	41:13 who can **c** *to him* with his double bridle?	935
	41:16 to another, that no air can **c** between them.	935
Ps	5: 7 I will **c into** thy house in the multitude of	935
	7: 9 wickedness of the wicked **c to an end**;	1584
	7:16 his violent dealing shall **c down** upon his	3381
	9: 6 destructions are **c** to a perpetual **end:**	8552
	14: 7 that the salvation of Israel *were* **c** out of	NIH
	17: 2 my sentence **c forth** from thy presence;	3318
	22:31 They shall **c**, and shall declare his	935
	24: 7 and the King of glory shall **c in.**	935
	24: 9 and the King of glory shall **c in.**	935
	32: 6 waters they shall not **c nigh** unto him.	5060
	32: 9 and bridle, lest *they* **c near** unto thee.	7126
	34:11 **C**, ye children, hearken unto me: I will	1980
	35: 8 Let destruction **c upon** him at unawares;	935
	36:11 Let not the foot of pride **c** against me,	935
	40: 7 Lo, I **c**: in the volume of the book *it is*	935
	41: 6 if he **c** to see *me*, he speaketh vanity:	935
	42: 2 when shall I **c** and appear before God?	935
	44:17 All this is **c** upon us; yet have we not	935
	46: 8 behold the works of the Lord,	1980
	50: 3 God shall **c**, and shall not keep silence:	935
	52: T David is **c** to the house of Ahimelech.	935
	53: 6 that the salvation of Israel *were* **c** out of	NIH
	55: 5 Fearfulness and trembling are **c** upon me,	935
	65: 2 hearest prayer, unto thee shall all flesh **c.**	935
	66: 5 **C** and see the works of God: *he is* terrible	1980
	66:16 **C** *and* hear, all ye that fear God,	1980
	68:31 Princes shall **c** out of Egypt; Ethiopia shall	857
	69: 1 God; for the waters are **c in** unto *my* soul.	935
	69: 2 I am **c** into deep waters, where the floods	935
	69:27 and let them not **c** into thy righteousness.	935
	71:18 *and* thy power to every one *that is* to **c.**	935
	72: 6 He shall **c down** like rain upon the mown	3381
	78: 4 shewing to the generation to **c** the praises	314
	78: 6 the generation to **c** might know *them*,	314
	79: 1 the heathen are **c** into thine inheritance;	935
	79:11 Let the sighing of the prisoner **c** before	935
	80: 2 stir up thy strength, and **c** and save us.	1980
	83: 4 **C**, and let us cut them off from *being* a	1980
	86: 9 All nations whom thou hast made shall **c**	935
	88: 2 my prayer **c** before thee: incline thine ear	935
	88: 8 *I am* shut up, and I cannot **c forth.**	3318
	91: 7 right hand; *but* it shall not **c nigh** thee.	5066
	91:10 neither shall *any* plague **c nigh** thy	7126
	95: 1 O **c**, let us sing unto the Lord: let us	1980
	95: 2 Let us **c before** his presence with	6923
	95: 6 O **c**, let us worship and bow down: let us	935
	96: 8 bring an offering, and **c into** his courts.	935
	100: 2 **c** before his presence with singing.	935
	101: 2 O when wilt thou **c** unto me? I will walk	935
	102: 1 O Lord, and let my cry **c** unto thee.	935
	102:13 time to favour her, yea, the set time, is **c.**	935
	102:18 shall be written for the generation to **c:**	314
	109:17 As he loved cursing, so let it **c** *unto* him:	935
	109:18 so let it **c** into his bowels like water,	935
	119:41 Let thy mercies **c** also *unto* me, O Lord,	935
	119:77 Let thy tender mercies **c** *unto* me,	935
	119:169 Let my cry **c near** before thee, O Lord:	7126
	119:170 Let my supplication **c** before thee:	935
	126: 6 **doubtless c again** with rejoicing,	935+935
	132: 3 Surely I will not **c** into the tabernacle of	935
	144: 5 Bow thy heavens, O Lord, and **c down:**	3381
Pr	1:11 If they say, **C** with us, let us lay wait for	1980
	3:28 and **c again**, and to morrow I will give;	7725
	5: 8 and **c** not **nigh** the door of her house:	7126
	6: 3 thou art **c** into the hand of thy friend;	935
	6:11 shall thy poverty **c** as one that travelleth,	935
	6:15 Therefore shall his calamity **c** suddenly;	935
	7:18 **C**, let us take our fill of love until	1980
	7:20 *and* will **c** home at the day appointed.	935
	9: 5 **C**, eat of my bread, and drink of the wine	1980
	10:24 fear of the wicked, it shall **c upon** him:	935
	11:27 that seeketh mischief, it shall **c** unto him.	935
	12:13 *his* lips: but the just shall **c out** of trouble.	3318
	20:13 Love not sleep, lest thou **c to poverty**;	3423
	22:16 giveth to the rich, *shall* surely **c** to want.	NIH
	23:21 and the glutton shall **c to poverty**;	3423
	24:25 and a good blessing shall **c** upon them.	935
	24:34 shall thy poverty **c** *as* one that travelleth;	935
	25: 4 there shall **c forth** a vessel for the finer.	3318
	25: 7 *it is* that it be said unto thee, **C up** hither;	5927
	26: 2 flying, so the curse causeless shall not **c.**	935
	28:22 considereth not that poverty shall **c** upon	
	31:25 and she shall rejoice in time to **c.**	314
Ecc	1: 7 unto the place from whence the rivers **c**,	1980
	1:11 are to **c** with *those* that shall come after.	314
	1:11 are to come with *those* that shall come after.	1961
	1:16 I am **c to great estate**, and have gotten	1431
	2:16 seeing *that* which now is, *in* the days to **c**	935
	4:16 also that **c after** shall not rejoice in him.	314
	7:18 for he that feareth God shall **c forth** of	3318

C

Ecc
8:10 who had c and gone from the place of — 935
9: 2 All *things* c alike to all: *there is* one event — NIH
12: 1 while the evil days c not, nor the years — 935

SS
2:10 my love, my fair one, and c *away*. — 1980
2:12 the time of the singing of *birds* is c, — 5060
2:13 Arise, my love, my fair one, and c *away*. — 1980
4: 8 C with me from Lebanon, *my* spouse, — 935
4:16 Awake, O north wind; and c thou south; — 935
4:16 Let my beloved c into his garden, and eat — 935
5: 1 I am c into my garden, my sister, — 935
7:11 C, my beloved, let us go forth *into* — 1980

Isa
1:12 When ye c to appear before me, — 935
1:18 C now, and let us reason together, saith — 1980
1:23 doth the cause of the widow c unto — 935
2: 2 it shall c to pass in the last days, *that* — 1961
2: 3 C ye, and let us go up to the mountain of — 1980
2: 5 c ye, and let us walk in the light of — 1980
3:24 it shall c to pass, *that* instead of sweet — 1961
4: 3 shall c to pass, *that* he that is left in Zion — 1961
5: 6 but there shall c up briers and thorns: — 5927
5:19 of the Holy One of Israel draw nigh and c, — 935
5:26 behold, they shall c with speed swiftly: — 935
7: 7 shall not stand, neither shall it c to pass. — 1961
7:17 thy father's house, days that have not c, — 935
7:18 it shall c to pass in that day, *that* — 1961
7:19 they shall c, and shall rest all of them in — 935
7:21 it shall c to pass in that day, *that* a man — 1961
7:22 shall c to pass, for the abundance of milk — 1961
7:23 it shall c to pass in that day, *that* every — 1961
7:24 and with bows shall men c thither; — 935
7:25 there shall not c thither the fear of briers — 935
8: 7 he shall c up over all his channels, — 5927
8:10 counsel together, and it shall c to nought; — 6565
8:21 it shall c to pass, that when they shall be — 1961
10: 3 in the desolation *which* shall c from far? — 935
10:12 Wherefore it shall c to pass, *that* when — 1961
10:20 it shall c to pass in that day, *that* — 1961
10:27 it shall c to pass in that day, *that* his — 1961
10:28 He is c to Aiath, he is passed to Migron; — 935
11: 1 there shall c forth a rod out of the stem — 3318
11:11 it shall c to pass in that day, *that* the Lord — 1961
13: 5 They c from a far country, from the end of — 935
13: 6 shall c as a destruction from the Almighty. — 935
13:22 time *is* near to c, and her days shall not — 935
14: 3 it shall c to pass in the day that the Lord — 1961
14: 8 art laid down, no feller is c up against us. — 5927
14:24 as I have thought, so shall it c to pass; — 1961
14:29 for out of the serpent's root shall c forth — 3318
14:31 for there shall c from the north a smoke, — 935
16: 8 they are c *even* unto Jazer, they wandered — 5060
16:12 it shall c to pass, when it is seen that — 1961
16:12 that he shall c to his sanctuary to pray; — 935
17: 4 that day it shall c to pass, that the glory — 1961
19: 1 upon a swift cloud, and shall c *into* Egypt: — 935
19:23 the Assyrian shall c into Egypt, — 935
21:12 if ye will inquire, inquire ye: return, c. — 857
22: 7 it shall c to pass, *that* thy choicest valleys — 1961
22:20 shall c to pass in that day, that I will call — 1961
23:15 shall c to pass in that day, that Tyre shall — 1961
23:17 it shall c to pass after the end of seventy — 1961
24:10 house is shut up, that no *man* may c *in*. — 935
24:18 it shall c to pass, *that* he who fleeth from — 1961
24:21 it shall c to pass in that day, *that* — 1961
26:20 C, my people, enter thou into thy — 1980
27: 6 He shall cause them that c of Jacob to — 935
27:11 the women c, *and* set them on fire: for it — 935
27:12 it shall c to pass in that day, *that* — 1961
27:13 it shall c to pass in that day, *that* the — 1961
27:13 they shall c which were ready to perish in — 935
28:15 shall pass through, it shall not c *unto* us: — 935
29:24 in spirit shall c to understanding, — 998+3045
30: 6 from whence c the young and old lion, — NIH
30: 8 that it may be for the time to c for ever — 314
30:29 as when one goeth with a pipe to c into — 935
31: 4 shall the Lord of hosts c down to fight — 3381
32:10 vintage shall fail, the gathering shall not c. — 935
32:13 Upon the land of my people shall c up — 5927
34: 1 C near, ye nations, to hear; and hearken, — 7126
34: 1 the world, and all things that c forth of it. — 6631
34: 3 their stink shall c up *out of* their carcases, — 5927
34: 5 it shall c down upon Idumea, and upon — 3381
34: 7 the unicorns shall c down with them, — 3381
34:13 thorns shall c up *in* her palaces, nettles — 5927
35: 4 behold, your God will c *with* vengeance, — 935
35: 4 *with* a recompence; he will c and save you. — 935
35:10 *to* Zion with songs and everlasting joy — 935
36:10 am I now c up without the Lord against — 5927
36:16 with me *by* a present, and c *out* to me: — 3318
36:17 Until I c and take you away to a land like — 935
37: 3 for the children are c to the birth, — 935
37: 7 He is c forth to make war with thee. — 3318
37:24 By the multitude of my chariots am I c up — 5927
37:29 is c up into mine ears, therefore will I put — 5927
37:33 He shall not c into this city, nor shoot an — 935
37:33 arrow there, nor c *before* it *with* shields, — 6923
37:34 shall not c into this city, saith the Lord. — 935
39: 3 They are c from a far country unto me, — 935
39: 6 Behold, the days c, that all that *is* in thine — 935
40:10 the Lord God will c *with* strong *hand*, and — 935
41: 1 let them c near; then let them speak; — 5066
41: 1 let us c near together to judgment. — 7126
41:22 end of them; or declare us *things* for to c. — 935
41:23 Shew the *things* that are to c hereafter, — 857
41:25 up *one* from the north, and he shall c: — 857
41:25 he shall c *upon* princes as *upon* morter, — 935

Isa
42: 9 the former *things* are c to pass, — 935
42:23 will hearken and hear for the time to c? — 268
44: 7 and shall c, let them shew unto them. — 935
45:11 Ask me of *things* to c concerning my sons, — 857
45:14 shall c *over* unto thee, and they shall be — 5674
45:14 they shall c *after* thee, in chains they shall — 1980
45:14 in chains they shall c *over*, and they shall — 5674
45:20 Assemble yourselves and c; draw near — 857
45:24 *even* to him shall men c; and all that are — 935
47: 1 c *down*, and sit in the dust, O virgin — 3381
47: 9 two *things* shall c to thee *in* a moment — 935
47: 9 they shall c *upon* thee in their perfection — 935
47:11 Therefore shall evil c upon thee; thou shalt — 935
47:11 desolation shall c upon thee suddenly, — 935
47:13 from *these things* that shall c upon — 935
48: 1 and are c forth out of the waters of Judah, — 3318
48:16 C ye *near* unto me, hear ye this; I have — 7126
49:12 Behold, these shall c from far: and, lo, — 935
49:18 gather themselves together, *and* c to thee. — 935
50: 8 *is* mine adversary? let him c *near* to me. — 5066
51:11 shall return, and c with singing *unto* Zion; — 935
51:19 These two *things* are c *unto* thee; — 7122
52: 1 henceforth there shall no more c into thee — 935
54:14 from terror; for it shall not c *near* thee. — 7126
55: 1 ye to the waters, and he that hath no — 1980
55: 1 c ye, buy, and eat; yea, come, buy wine — 1980
55: 1 yea, c, buy wine and milk without money — 1980
55: 3 Incline your ear, and c unto me: hear, — 1980
55:13 Instead of the thorn shall c up the fir tree, — 5927
55:13 instead of the brier shall c up the myrtle — 5927
56: 1 for my salvation *is* near to c, — 935
56: 9 All ye beasts of the field, c to devour, — 857
56:12 C ye, *say they*, I will fetch wine, and we — 857
57: 1 righteous is taken away from the evil *to* c. — NIH
59:19 When the enemy shall c *in* like a flood, — 935
59:20 redeemer shall c to Zion, and unto them — 935
60: 1 for thy light is c, and the glory of — 935
60: 3 the Gentiles shall c to thy light, — 1980
60: 4 gather themselves together, they c to thee: — 935
60: 4 sons shall c from far, and thy daughters — 935
60: 5 forces of the Gentiles shall c unto thee. — 935
60: 6 and Ephah; all they from Sheba shall c: — 935
60: 7 they shall c up with acceptance on mine — 5927
60:13 The glory of Lebanon shall c unto thee, — 935
60:14 afflicted thee shall c bending unto thee; — 1980
63: 4 and the year of my redeemed is c. — 935
64: 1 the heavens, that thou wouldest c *down*, — 3381
65: 5 Stand by thyself, c not *near* to me; — 5066
65:17 be remembered, nor c into mind. — 5927
65:24 it shall c to pass, that before they call, — 1961
66:15 the Lord will c with fire, and with his — 935
66:18 it shall c, that *I* will gather all nations and — 935
66:18 and they shall c, and see my glory. — 935
66:23 it shall c to pass, *that* from one new moon — 1961
66:23 shall all flesh c to worship before me, — 935

Jer
1:15 they shall c, and they shall set every one — 935
2: 3 evil shall c upon them, saith the Lord. — 935
2:31 are lords; we will c no more unto thee? — 935
3:16 it shall c to pass, when ye be multiplied — 1961
3:16 neither shall it c to mind: neither shall — 5927
3:18 they shall c together out of the land of — 935
3:22 Behold, we c unto thee; for thou *art* — 857
4: 4 lest my fury c forth like fire, and burn — 3318
4: 7 The lion is c up from his thicket, — 5927
4: 9 it shall c to pass at that day, saith — 1961
4:12 *Even* a full wind from those *places* shall c — 935
4:13 he shall c up as clouds, and his chariots — 5927
4:16 *that* watchers c from a far country, — 935
5:12 *It is* not he; neither shall evil c upon us; — 935
5:19 it shall c to pass, when ye shall say, — 1961
6: 3 The shepherds with their flocks shall c — 935
6:26 for the spoiler shall suddenly c upon us. — 935
7:10 c and stand before me in this house, — 935
7:32 Therefore, behold, the days c, saith — 935
8:16 for they are c, and have devoured the land, — 935
9:17 for the mourning *women*, that they may c; — 935
9:17 send for cunning *women*, that they may c: — 935
9:21 For death is c up into our windows, — 5927
9:25 Behold, the days c, saith the Lord, that I — 935
10:22 the noise of the bruit is c, and a great — 935
12: 9 c ye, assemble all the beasts of the field, — 1980
12: 9 all the beasts of the field, c to devour. — 857
12:12 The spoilers are c upon all high places — 935
12:15 it shall c to pass, after that I have plucked — 1961
12:16 it shall c to pass, if they will diligently — 1961
13:18 for your principalities shall c *down*, — 3381
13:20 and behold them that c from the north: — 935
13:22 Wherefore c these *things* upon me? — 7122
15: 2 it shall c to pass, if they say unto thee, — 1961
16:10 it shall c to pass, when thou shalt shew — 1961
16:14 the days c, saith the Lord, — 935
16:19 Gentiles shall c unto thee from the ends — 935
17:15 *is* the word of the Lord? let it c now. — 935
17:24 whereby the kings of Judah c *in*, and by — 935
17:24 it shall c to pass, if ye diligently hearken — 1961
17:26 they shall c from the cities of Judah, — 935
18:14 shall the cold flowing waters that c from — NIH
18:18 C, and let us devise devices against — 1980
18:18 C, and let us smite him with the tongue, — 1980
19: 6 the days c, saith the Lord, — 935
20: 6 thou shalt c *to* Babylon, and there thou — 935
21:13 which say, Who shall c *down* against us? — 5181
22:23 how gracious shalt thou be when pangs c — 935
23: 5 Behold, the days c, saith the Lord, that I — 935
23: 7 the days c, saith the Lord, — 935

Jer
23:17 of his own heart, No evil shall c upon you. — 935
25: 3 the word of the Lord hath c unto me, — 1961
25:12 it shall c to pass, when seventy years are — 1961
25:31 noise shall c *even* to the ends of the earth; — 935
26: 2 which to worship *in* the Lord's house, — 935
27: 3 by the hand of the messengers which c *to* — 935
27: 7 son's son, until the very time of his land c: — 935
27: 8 it shall c to pass, *that* the nation and — 1961
28: 9 the word of the prophet shall c to pass, — 935
30: 3 For lo, the days c, saith the Lord, that I — 935
30: 8 For it shall c to pass in that day, saith — 1961
31: 9 They shall c with weeping, — 935
31:12 they shall c and sing in the height — 935
31:16 they shall c *again* from the land of — 7725
31:17 *thy* children shall c *again* to their own — 7725
31:27 Behold, the days c, saith the Lord, that I — 935
31:28 it shall c to pass, that like as I have — 1961
31:31 Behold, the days c, saith the Lord, that I — 935
31:38 Behold, the days c, saith the Lord, — 935
32: 7 of Shallum thine uncle *shall* c unto thee, — 935
32:23 thou hast **caused** all this evil to c upon — 7122
32:24 mounts, they are c *unto* the city to take it; — 935
32:24 what thou hast spoken is c to pass; — 1961
32:29 shall c and set fire on this city, and burn it — 935
33: 5 They c to fight with the Chaldeans, — 935
33:14 Behold, the days c, saith the Lord, that I — 935
35:11 C, and let us go *to* Jerusalem for fear of — 935
36: 6 ears of all Judah that c out of their cities. — 935
36:14 hast read in the ears of the people, and c. — 1980
36:29 The king of Babylon shall **certainly** c — 935+935
37: 5 Pharaoh's army was c forth out of Egypt: — 3318
37: 7 which is c forth to help you, — 3318
37: 8 the Chaldeans shall c *again*, — 7725
37:19 king of Babylon shall not c against you, — 935
38:25 and they c unto thee, and say unto thee, — 935
40: 3 voice, therefore this thing is c upon you. — 1961
40: 4 If it seem good unto thee to c with me *into* — 935
40: 4 thee to come with me *into* Babylon, c; — 935
40: 4 if it seem ill unto thee to c with me *into* — 935
40:10 serve the Chaldeans, which will c unto us: — 935
41: 6 them, C to Gedaliah the son of Ahikam. — 935
42: 4 it shall c to pass, *that* whatsoever thing — 1961
42:16 it shall c to pass, *that* the sword, which — 1961
46: 9 C up, ye horses; and rage, ye chariots; — 5927
46: 9 chariots; and let the mighty *men* c forth; — 3318
46:13 Nebuchadrezzar king of Babylon should c — 935
46:18 as and Carmel by the sea, *so* shall he c. — 935
46:21 the day of their calamity was c upon them, — 935
46:22 c against her with axes, as hewers of wood. — 935
47: 5 Baldness is c upon Gaza; Ashkelon is cut — 935
48: 2 c, and let us cut it off from *being* a nation. — 1980
48: 8 the spoiler shall c upon every city, — 935
48:12 the days c, saith the Lord, — 935
48:16 The calamity of Moab *is* near to c, — 935
48:18 c *down* from *thy* glory, and sit in thirst; — 3381
48:18 for the spoiler of Moab shall c upon thee, — 5927
48:21 judgment is c upon the plain country; — 935
48:45 a fire shall c forth out of Heshbon, — 3318
49: 2 the days c, saith the Lord, — 935
49: 4 treasures, *saying*, Who shall c unto me? — 935
49:14 and c against her, and rise up to the battle. — 935
49:19 he shall c up like a lion from the swelling — 5927
49:22 he shall c up and fly as the eagle, — 5927
49:36 whither the outcasts of Elam shall not c. — 935
49:39 it shall c to pass in the latter days, that I — 1961
50: 4 the children of Israel shall c, they and — 935
50: 5 *saying*, C, and let us join ourselves to — 935
50: 9 **cause** to c up against Babylon an — 5927
50:26 C against her from the utmost border, — 935
50:27 their day is c, the time of their visitation. — 935
50:31 thy day is c, the time *that* I will visit thee. — 935
50:41 people shall c from the north, and a great — 935
50:44 he shall c up like a lion from the swelling — 5927
51:10 c, and let us declare in Zion the work of — 935
51:13 thine end is c, *and* the measure of thy — 935
51:27 **cause** the horses to c up as the rough — 5927
51:33 and the time of her harvest shall c. — 935
51:42 The sea is c up upon Babylon: she is — 5927
51:46 a rumour shall both c *one* year, and after — 935
51:46 in *another* year *shall* c a rumour, — NIH
51:47 Therefore behold, the days c, that I will do — 935
51:48 for the spoilers shall c unto her from — 935
51:50 off, and let Jerusalem c into your mind. — 5927
51:51 for strangers are c into the sanctuaries of — 935
51:52 the days c, saith the Lord, — 935
51:53 *yet* from me shall spoilers c unto her, — 935
51:56 Because the spoiler is c upon her, — 935
51:60 all the evil that should c upon Babylon, — 935

La
1: 4 because none c to the solemn feasts: — 935
1:14 are wreathed, *and* c up upon my neck; — 5927
1:22 Let all their wickedness c before thee; — 935
3:47 Fear and a snare is c upon us, desolation — 1961
4:18 our days are fulfilled; for our end is c. — 935
5: 1 Remember, O Lord, what is c upon us: — 1961

Eze
5: 4 *for* thereof shall a fire c forth into all — 3318
7: 2 the end is c upon the four corners of — 935
7: 3 the end c upon thee, and I will send — NIH
7: 5 An evil, an only evil, behold, is c. — 935
7: 6 An end is c, the end is come: it watcheth — 935
7: 6 An end is c, the end is c: it watcheth — 935
7: 6 it watcheth for thee; behold, it is c. — 935
7: 7 The morning is c unto thee, O thou that — 935
7: 7 the time is c, the day of trouble *is* near, — 935
7:10 the day, behold, it is c: the morning — 935

Eze
7:12 The time is **c**, the day draweth near: — 935
7:26 Mischief shall **c** upon mischief, — 935
9: 6 **c** not **near** any man upon whom *is* — 5066
11: 5 for I know the **things that c into** your — 4609
11:16 in the countries where they shall **c.** — 935
11:18 they shall **c** thither, and they shall take — 935
12:16 among the heathen whither they **c**; — 935
12:25 word that I shall speak shall **c to pass**; — 6213
12:27 vision that he seeth *is* for many days to **c**, — NIH
13:18 ye save the souls alive *that* **c** unto you? — NIH
14:22 *shall* **c forth** unto you, and ye shall see — 3318
16: 7 and thou art **c** to excellent ornaments: — 935
16:16 the like things shall not **c**, neither shall it — 935
16:33 that *they* may **c** unto thee on every side — 935
17:12 the king of Babylon is **c** *to* Jerusalem, — 935
18: 6 neither hath **c near** to a menstruous — 7126
20: 3 the Lord God; Are ye **c** to inquire of me? — 935
21:19 the sword of the king of Babylon may **c**: — 935
21:19 both twain shall **c forth** out of one land: — 3318
21:20 that the sword may **c** to Rabbath of — 935
21:24 *I say*, that ye are **c to remembrance**, — 2142
21:25 wicked prince of Israel, whose day is **c**, — 935
21:27 it shall be no *more*, until he **c** whose right — 935
21:29 whose day is **c**, when *their* iniquity *shall* — 935
22: 3 that *her* time may **c**, and maketh idols — 935
22: 4 draw near, and art *even* unto thy years: — 935
23:24 they shall **c** against thee *with* chariots, — 935
23:40 that ye have sent for men to **c** from far, — 935
24: 8 That *it* might **cause** fury to **c up** to take — 5927
24:14 the Lord have spoken *it*: it shall **c to pass**, — 935
24:26 he that escapeth in that day shall **c** unto — 935
26: 3 will **cause** many nations to **c up** against — 5927
26: 3 as the sea **causeth** his waves **to c up.** — 5927
26:16 all the princes of the sea shall **c down** — 3381
27:29 of the sea, shall **c down** from their ships, — 3381
30: 4 the sword shall **c** upon Egypt, and great — 935
30: 6 and the pride of her power shall **c down**: — 3381
30: 9 great pain shall **c** upon them, as *in* the day — 1961
32:11 The sword of the king of Babylon shall **c** — 935
33: 3 when he seeth the sword **c** upon the land, — 935
33: 4 if the sword **c**, and take him away, — 935
33: 6 if the watchman see the sword **c**, — 935
33: 6 if the sword **c**, and take *any* person from — 935
33:30 saying, **C**, I pray you, and hear what *is* — 935
33:31 they **c** unto thee as the people cometh, — 935
33:33 when this cometh to pass, (lo, it will **c**) — 935
34:21 I will **cause** the shower **to c down** in — 3381
36: 8 people of Israel; for they are at hand to **c.** — 935
37: 9 **C** from the four winds, O breath, — 935
37:12 **cause** you to **c up** out of your graves, — 5927
38: 8 the latter years thou shalt **c** into the land — 935
38: 9 Thou shalt ascend and **c** like a storm, — 935
38:10 shall also **c to pass**, *that* at the same time — 1961
38:10 at the same time shall things into thy — 5927
38:13 say unto thee, Art thou **c** to take a spoil? — 935
38:15 shalt **c** from thy place out of the north — 935
38:15 shalt **c up** against my people of Israel, — 5927
38:18 it shall **c to pass** at the same time when — 1961
38:18 Gog shall **c** against the land of Israel, — 935
38:18 *that* my fury shall **c up** in my face. — 5927
39: 2 will **cause** thee to **c up** from the north — 5927
39: 8 it is **c**, and it is done, saith the Lord — 935
39:11 it shall **c to pass** in that day, *that* I will — 1961
39:17 of the field, Assemble yourselves, and **c**; — 935
40:46 which **c near** to the Lord to minister — 7131
44:13 they shall not **c near** unto me, to do — 5066
44:13 nor to **c near** to any of my holy *things*, — 5066
44:15 shall **c near** to me to minister unto me, — 7126
44:16 they shall **c near** to my table, to minister — 7126
44:17 it shall **c to pass**, *that* when they enter in — 1961
44:17 no wool shall **c** upon them, whiles they — 5927
44:25 they shall **c** at no dead person to defile — 935
45: 4 which shall **c near** to minister unto — 7131
46: 9 when the people of the land shall **c** before — 935
47: 9 it shall **c to pass**, *that* every thing that — 1961
47: 9 whithersoever the rivers shall **c**, shall live: — 935
47: 9 because these waters shall **c** thither: — 935
47:10 it shall **c to pass**, *that* the fishers shall — 1961
47:20 border, till *a man* **c** over against Hamath. — 935
47:22 it shall **c to pass**, *that* ye shall divide it *by* — 1961
47:23 it shall **c to pass**, *that* in what tribe — 1961

Da
2:29 thy bed, what should **c to pass** hereafter: — 1934
2:29 known to thee what shall **c to pass.** — 1934
2:45 to the king what shall **c to pass** hereafter: — 1934
3: 2 to **c** to the dedication of the image which — 858
3:26 **c forth**, and come *hither*. Then Shadrach, — 5312
3:26 **c hither**. Then Shadrach, Meshach, — 858
4:24 which is **c** upon my lord the king: — 4291
8: 7 I saw him **c close** unto the ram, — 5060
8:23 when the transgressors are **c to the full**, — 8552
9:13 the law of Moses, all this evil is **c** upon us: — 935
9:22 I am now **c forth** to give thee skill and — 3318
9:23 I am **c** to shew *thee*; for thou *art* greatly — 935
9:26 the people of the prince that *shall* **c** shall — 935
10:12 were heard, and I am **c** for thy words. — 935
10:14 Now I am **c** to make thee understand what — 935
10:20 Knowest thou wherefore I **c** unto thee? — 935
10:20 gone forth, lo, the prince of Grecia shall **c.** — 935
11: 6 the king's daughter of the south shall **c** to — 935
11: 7 shall **c** with an army, and shall enter — 935
11: 9 So the king of the south shall **c** into *his* — 935
11:10 *one* shall **certainly c**, and overflow, — 935+935
11:11 shall **c forth** and fight with him, — 3318
11:13 shall **certainly c** after certain years — 935+935
11:15 the king of the north shall **c**, and cast up — 935

Da
11:21 he shall **c** in peaceably, and obtain — 935
11:23 for he shall **c up**, and shall become strong — 5927
11:29 he shall return, and **c** toward the south; — 935
11:30 *the* ships of Chittim shall **c** against him: — 935
11:40 shall **c** against him **like a whirlwind**, — 8175
11:45 shall **c** to his end, and none shall help — 935

Hos
1: 5 it shall **c to pass** at that day, that I will — 1961
1:10 it shall **c to pass**, that in the place where — 1961
1:11 and they shall **c up** out of the land: — 5927
2:21 it shall **c to pass** in that day, I will hear, — 1961
4:15 **c** not ye *unto* Gilgal, neither go ye up *to* — 935
6: 1 **C** and let us return unto the Lord: for he — 1980
6: 3 he shall **c** unto us as the rain, as the latter — 935
8: 1 He shall **c** as an eagle against the house of — NIH
9: 4 for their bread for their soul shall not **c** — 935
9: 7 The days of visitation are **c**, the days of — 935
9: 7 are come, the days of recompence are **c**; — 935
10: 8 and the thistle shall **c up** on their altars; — 5927
10:12 till he **c** and rain righteousness upon you. — 935
13:13 The sorrows of a travailing *woman* shall **c** — 935
13:15 among *his* brethren, an east wind shall **c**, — 935
13:15 the wind of the Lord *shall* **c up** from — 5927

Joel
1: 6 For a nation is **c up** upon my land, strong, — 5927
1:13 **c**, lie all night in sackcloth, ye ministers of — 935
1:15 a destruction from the Almighty shall it **c.** — 935
2:20 his stink shall **c up**, and his ill savour shall — 5927
2:20 his ill savour shall **c up**, because he hath — 5927
2:23 he will **cause to c down** for you the rain, — 3381
2:28 shall **c to pass** afterward, that I will pour — 1961
2:31 and the terrible day of the Lord **c.** — 935
2:32 shall **c to pass**, *that* whosoever shall call — 1961
3: 9 the men of war draw near; let them **c up**: — 5927
3:11 **c**, all ye heathen, and gather yourselves — 935
3:11 thither **cause** thy mighty ones to **c down**, — 5181
3:12 and **c up** to the valley of Jehoshaphat: — 5927
3:13 **c**, get you down; for the press is full, — 935
3:18 it shall **c to pass** in that day, *that* — 1961
3:18 a fountain shall **c forth** of the house of — 3318

Am
4: 2 that lo, the days shall **c** upon you, that he — 935
4: 4 **C** *to* Beth-el, and transgress; at Gilgal — 935
4:10 **made** the stink of your camps **to c up** — 5927
5: 5 and Beth-el shall **c** to nought. — 1961
5: 9 that the spoiled shall **c** against the fortress. — 935
6: 3 and **cause** the seat of violence **to c near**; — 5066
6: 9 it shall **c to pass**, if there remain ten men — 1961
8: 2 The end is **c** upon my people *of* Israel; — 935
8: 9 shall **c to pass** in that day, saith the Lord — 1961
8:11 Behold, the days, saith the Lord God, — 935
9:13 Behold, the days **c**, saith the Lord, — 935

Ob
1:21 saviours shall **c up** on mount Zion to judge — 5927

Jnh
1: 2 for their wickedness is **c up** before me. — 5927
1: 7 one to his fellow, **C**, and let us cast lots, — 1980
4: 6 a gourd, and **made** *it* **to c up** over Jonah, — 5927

Mic
1: 3 **c down** and tread upon the high places — 3381
1: 9 wound *is* incurable; for it is **c** unto Judah; — 935
1: 9 he is **c** unto the gate of my people, *even to* — 5060
1:15 he shall **c** unto Adullam the glory of Israel. — 935
2:13 The breaker is **c up** before them: — 5927
3:11 Lord among us? none evil can **c** upon us. — 935
4: 1 in the last days it shall **c to pass**, *that* — 1961
4: 2 many nations shall **c**, and say, Come, — 1980
4: 2 **C**, and let us go up to the mountain of — 1980
4: 8 unto thee shall it **c**, even the first dominion — 857
4: 8 the kingdom shall **c** to the daughter of — 935
5: 2 *yet* out of thee shall he **c forth** unto me — 3318
5: 5 when the Assyrian shall **c** into our land: — 935
5:10 it shall **c to pass** in that day, saith — 1961
6: 6 Wherewith shall I **c before** the Lord, — 6923
6: 6 shall I **c before** him with burnt offerings, — 6923
7:12 *In* that day *also* he shall **c** even to thee — 935

Na
1:11 There is *one* **c out** of thee, that imagineth — 3318
2: 1 He that dasheth in pieces is **c up** before — 5927
3: 7 it shall **c to pass**, *that* all they that look — 1961

Hab
1: 8 and their horsemen shall **c** from far; — 935
1: 9 They shall **c** all for violence: their faces — 935
2: 3 it will **surely c**, it will not tarry. — 935+935

Zep
1: 8 it shall **c to pass** in the day of — 1961
1:10 it shall **c to pass** in that day, saith — 1961
1:12 it shall **c to pass** at that time, *that* I will — 1961
2: 2 before the fierce anger of the Lord **c** upon — 935
2: 2 before the day of the Lord's anger **c** upon — 935

Hag
1: 2 This people say, The time is not **c**, — 935
2: 7 and the desire of all nations shall **c**: — 935
2:22 the horses and their riders shall **c down**, — 3381

Zec
1:21 said I, What **c** these to do? And he spake, — 935
1:21 are **c** to fray them, to cast out the horns — 935
2: 6 **c** *forth*, and flee from the land of the north, — NIH
2:10 I **c**, and I will dwell in the midst of thee, — 935
6:10 which are **c** from Babylon, and come thou — 935
6:10 **c** thou the same day, and go *into* the house — 935
6:15 *they that are* far off shall **c** and build in — 935
6:15 *this* shall **c to pass**, if ye will diligently — 1961
7:13 Therefore it is **c to pass**, *that* as he cried, — 1961
8:13 it shall **c to pass**, *that* as ye were a curse — 1961
8:20 *It shall yet* **c to pass**, that there shall come — 935
8:20 *It shall* yet *come to pass*, that there shall — 935
8:22 strong nations shall **c** to seek the Lord of — 935
8:23 In those days *it shall* **c** *to pass*, that ten — NIH

11: 2 for the forest of the vintage is **c down.** — 3381
12: 9 shall **c to pass** in that day, *that* I will seek — 1961
12: 9 all the nations that **c** against Jerusalem. — 935
13: 2 it shall **c to pass** in that day, saith — 1961
13: 3 it shall **c to pass**, *that* when any shall yet — 1961
13: 4 it shall **c to pass** in that day, *that* — 1961
13: 8 it shall **c to pass**, *that* in all the land, — 1961

Zec
14: 5 the Lord my God shall **c**, *and* all — 935
14: 6 shall **c to pass** in that day, *that* the light — 1961
14: 7 it shall **c to pass**, *that* at evening time it — 1961
14:13 it shall **c to pass** in that day, *that* a great — 1961
14:16 shall **c to pass**, *that* every one that is left — 1961
14:17 whoso will not **c up** of *all* the families — 5927
14:18 if the family of Egypt go not up, and **c** not, — 935
14:18 **c** not **up** to keep the feast of tabernacles, — 5927
14:19 punishment of all nations that **c** not **up** — 5927
14:21 all they that sacrifice shall **c** and take of — 935

Mal
3: 1 ye seek, shall suddenly **c** to his temple, — 935
3: 1 behold, he *shall* **c**, saith the Lord of hosts. — 935
3: 5 I will **c near** to you to judgment; — 7126
4: 6 lest I **c** and smite the earth *with* a curse. — 935

Mt
2: 2 star in the east, and are **c** to worship him. — 2064
2: 6 for **out** of thee shall **c** a Governor, — 1831
2: 8 that I may **c** and worship him also. — 2064
2:11 And when they were **c** into the house, — 2064
3: 7 and Sadducees **c** to his baptism, — 2064
3: 7 warned you to flee from the wrath to **c**? — 3195
5:17 Think not that I am **c** to destroy the law, — 2064
5:17 I am not **c** to destroy, but to fulfil. — 2064
5:24 thy brother, and then **c** and offer thy gift. — 2064
5:26 Thou shalt by no means **c out** thence, — 1831
6:10 Thy kingdom **c**. Thy will be done in earth, — 2064
7:15 which **c** to you in sheep's clothing, — 2064
8: 1 When he was **c down** from the mountain, — 2597
8: 7 Jesus saith unto him, I will **c** and heal him. — 2064
8: 8 not worthy that thou shouldest **c** under — 1525
8: 9 and to another, **C**, and he cometh; — 2064
8:11 That many shall **c** from the east and west, — 2240
8:14 And when Jesus was **c** into Peter's house, — 2064
8:16 When the even was **c**, they brought unto — 1096
8:28 And when he was **c** to the other side into — 2064
8:29 art thou **c** hither to torment us before — 2064
8:32 when they were **c out**, they went into — 1831
9:13 for I am not **c** to call the righteous, — 2064
9:15 but the days will **c**, when the bridegroom — 2064
9:18 but **c** and lay thy hand upon her, — 2064
9:28 And when he was **c** into the house, — 2064
10:12 And when ye **c into** a house salute it. — 1525
10:13 house be worthy, let your peace **c** upon it: — 2064
10:23 cities of Israel, till the Son of man be **c.** — 2064
10:34 Think not that I am **c** to send peace on — 2064
10:35 For I am **c** to set a man at variance against — 2064
11: 3 Art thou he that should **c**, or do we look — 2064
11:14 *it*, this is Elias, which was **for to c.** — 2064+3195
11:28 **C** unto me, all *ye* that labour and are — 1205
12:28 then the kingdom of God is **c** unto you. — 5348
12:32 in this world, neither in the *world* to **c.** — 3195
12:44 and when he is **c**, he findeth *it* empty, — 2064
13:32 so that the birds of the air **c** and lodge in — 2064
13:49 the angels shall **c forth**, and sever — 1831
13:54 when he was **c** into his own country, — 2064
14:23 when the evening was **c**, he was there — 1096
14:28 thou, bid me **c** unto thee on the water. — 2064
14:29 he said, **C.** And when Peter was come — 2064
14:29 And when Peter was **c down** out of — 2597
14:32 And when they were **c** into the ship, — 1684
15:18 out of the mouth **c forth** from the heart; — 1831
16: 5 when his disciples were **c** to the other — 2064
16:24 If any *man* will **c** after me, let him deny — 2064
17:10 For the Son of man shall **c** in the glory of — 2064
17:10 then say the scribes that Elias must first **c**? — 2064
17:11 Elias truly shall first **c**, and restore all — 2064
17:12 Elias is **c** already, and they knew him — 2064
17:14 And when they were **c** to the multitude, — 2064
17:24 And when they were **c** to Capernaum, — 2064
17:25 And when he was **c into** the house, — 1525
18: 7 for it must needs be that offences **c**; — 2064
18:11 For the Son of man is **c** to save that which — 2064
19:14 and forbid them not, to **c** unto me: — 2064
19:21 treasure in heaven: and **c** and follow me. — 1204
20: 8 So when even was **c**, the lord of — 1096
21: 1 were **c** to Bethphage, unto the mount of — 2064
21:10 And when he was **c into** Jerusalem, — 1525
21:23 And when he was **c** into the temple, — 2064
21:38 **c**, let us kill him, and let us seize on his — 1205
22: 3 to the wedding: and they would not **c.** — 2064
22: 4 all *things are* ready: **c** unto the marriage. — 1205
23:35 That upon you may **c** all the righteous — 2064
23:36 All these *things* shall **c** upon this — 2240
24: 5 many shall **c** in my name, saying, I am — 2064
24: 6 for all *these things* must **c to pass**, — 1096
24:14 unto all nations; and then shall the end **c.** — 2240
24:17 **c down** to take any *thing* out of his house — 2597
24:42 ye know not what hour your Lord doth **c.** — 2064
24:43 known in what watch the thief would **c**, — 2064
24:50 The lord of that servant shall **c** in a day — 2240
25:31 When the Son of man shall **c** in his glory, — 2064
25:34 his right hand, **C**, ye blessed of my Father, — 1205
26:20 Now when the even was **c**, he sat down — 1096
26:50 unto him, Friend, wherefore art thou **c**? — 3918
26:55 ye **c out** as against a thief with swords — 1831
27: 1 When the morning was **c**, all the chief — 1096
27:33 when they were **c** unto a place called — 2064
27:40 the Son of God, **c down** from the cross. — 2597
27:42 let him now **c down** from the cross, — 2597
27:49 see whether Elias will **c** to save him. — 2064
27:57 When the even was **c**, there came a rich — 1096
27:64 lest his disciples **c** by night, and steal him — 2064
28: 6 **C**, see the place where the Lord lay. — 935
28:14 And if this **c** to the governor's **ears**, — 191+1909

Mk
1:17 **C** ye after me, and I will make you to — 1205
1:24 art thou **c** to destroy us? I know thee who — 2064

C

Mk		
1:25	saying, Hold thy peace, and **c** out of him.	1831
1:29	when they were **c** out of the synagogue,	1831
2: 3	And they **c** unto him, bringing one sick of	2064
2: 4	when they could not **c** nigh unto him	4331
2:18	and they **c** and say unto him, Why do	2064
2:20	But the days will **c**, when the bridegroom	2064
4:22	kept secret, but that it should **c** abroad.	2064
4:29	in the sickle, because the harvest is **c**.	3936
4:35	And the same day, when the even was **c**,	1096
5: 2	And when he was **c** out of the ship,	1831
5: 8	**C** out of the man, thou unclean spirit.	1831
5:15	And they **c** to Jesus, and see him that was	2064
5:18	And when he was **c** into the ship, he that	1684
5:23	I pray thee, **c** and lay thy hands on her,	2064
5:39	when he was **c** in, he saith unto them,	1525
6: 2	when the sabbath day was **c**, he began	1096
6:21	And when a convenient day was **c**,	1096
6:31	**C** ye yourselves apart into a desert place,	1205
6:47	And when even was **c**, the ship was in	1096
6:54	And when they were **c** out of the ship,	1831
7: 4	And when they **c** from the market,	NIG
7:15	but the things which **c** out of him,	1607
7:23	All these evil things **c** from within,	1607
7:30	when she was **c** to her house, she found	565
8:34	unto them, Whosoever will **c** after me,	2064
9: 1	till they have seen the kingdom of God **c**	2064
9:11	say the scribes that Elias must first **c**?	2064
9:13	Elias is indeed **c**, and they have done	2064
9:25	**c** out of him, and enter no more into him.	1831
9:28	And when he was **c** into the house,	1525
9:29	This kind can **c** forth by nothing, but by	1831
10:14	Suffer the little children to **c** unto me,	2064
10:21	and **c**, take up the cross, and follow me.	1204
10:30	and in the world to **c** eternal life.	2064
10:35	of Zebedee, **c** unto him, saying, Master,	4365
11:11	all things, and now the eventide was **c**,	1510
11:12	when they were **c** from Bethany, he was	1831
11:15	And they **c** to Jerusalem: and Jesus went	2064
11:19	And when even was **c**, he went out of	1096
11:23	things which he saith shall **c** to pass;	1096
11:27	And they **c** again to Jerusalem: and as he	2064
11:27	there **c** to him the chief priests,	2064
12: 7	**c**, let us kill him, and the inheritance shall	1205
12: 9	he will **c** and destroy the husbandmen,	2064
12:14	when they were **c**, they say unto him,	2064
12:18	Then **c** unto him the Sadducees, which	2064
13: 6	many shall **c** in my name, saying, I am	2064
13:29	when ye shall see these things **c** to pass,	1096
14: 8	she is **c** aforehand to anoint my body to	4301
14:41	enough, the hour is **c**; behold, the Son	2064
14:45	And as soon as he was **c**, he goeth	2064
14:48	and said unto them, Are ye **c** out,	1831
15:30	Save thyself, and **c** down from the cross.	2597
15:33	when the sixth hour was **c**, there was	1096
15:36	let us see whether Elias will **c** to take him	2064
15:42	And now when the even was **c**, because	1096
16: 1	that they might **c** and anoint him.	2064

Lk		
1:35	The Holy Ghost shall **c** upon thee,	1904
1:43	the mother of my Lord should **c** to me?	2064
2:15	and see this thing which is **c** to pass,	1096
3: 7	warned you to flee from the wrath to **c**?	3195
4:34	art thou **c** to destroy us? I know thee who	2064
4:35	saying, Hold thy peace, and **c** out of him.	1831
4:36	the unclean spirits, and they **c** out.	1831
5: 7	that they should **c** and help them.	2064
5:17	of the law sitting by, which were **c**	2064
5:35	the days will **c**, when the bridegroom	2064
7: 3	beseeching him that he would **c** and	2064
7: 7	thought I myself worthy to **c** unto thee:	2064
7: 8	and to another, **C**, and he cometh;	2064
7:19	Jesus, saying, Art thou he that should **c**?	2064
7:20	When then were **c** unto him,	3854
7:20	saying, Art thou he that should **c**?	2064
7:34	The Son of man is **c** eating and drinking;	2064
8: 4	and were **c** to him out of every city,	1975
8:17	that shall not be known and **c** abroad.	2064
8:19	and could not **c** at him for the press.	4940
8:29	the unclean spirit to **c** out of the man.	1831
8:41	besought him that he would **c** into	1525
9:23	If any man will **c** after me, let him deny	2064
9:26	when he shall **c** in his own glory,	2064
9:37	when they were **c** down from the hill,	2718
9:51	when the time was **c** that he should be	4845
9:54	thou that we command fire to **c** down	2597
9:56	For the Son of man is not **c** to destroy	2064
10: 1	and place, whither he himself would **c**.	2064
10: 9	The kingdom of God is **c** nigh unto you.	1448
10:11	that the kingdom of God is **c** nigh unto	1448
10:35	when I **c** again, I will repay thee.	1880
11: 2	Thy kingdom **c**. Thy will be done, as in	2064
11: 6	For a friend of mine in his journey is **c** to	3854
11:20	no doubt the kingdom of God is **c** upon	5348
11:22	when a stronger than he shall **c** upon	1904
11:33	that they which **c** in may see the light.	1531
12:37	to meat, and will **c** forth and serve them.	3928
12:38	And if he shall **c** in the second watch,	2064
12:38	or **c** in the third watch, and find them so,	2064
12:39	had known what hour the thief would **c**,	2064
12:46	The lord of that servant will **c** in a day	2240
12:49	I am **c** to send fire on the earth;	2064
12:51	Suppose ye that I am **c** to give peace on	3854
13: 7	three years I **c** seeking fruit on this fig	2064
13:14	in them therefore **c** and be healed,	2064
13:29	And they shall **c** from the east,	2240
13:35	until the time **c** when ye shall say,	2240

Lk		
14: 9	that bade thee and him **c** and say to thee,	2064
14:17	time to say to them that were bidden, **C**;	2064
14:20	married a wife, and therefore I cannot **c**.	2064
14:23	and hedges, and compel them to **c** in,	1525
14:26	any man **c** to me, and hate not his father,	2064
14:27	and **c** after me, cannot be my disciple.	2064
15:27	And he said unto him, Thy brother is **c**;	2240
15:30	But as soon as this thy son was **c**,	2064
16:26	they pass to us, that would **c** from thence.	NIG
16:28	lest they also **c** into this place of torment.	2064
17: 1	It is impossible but that offences will **c**:	2064
17: 1	but woe unto him, through whom they **c**.	2064
17: 7	when he is **c** from the field, Go and	1525
17:20	when the kingdom of God should **c**,	2064
17:22	said unto the disciples, The days will **c**,	2064
17:31	let him not **c** down to take it away:	2597
18:16	Suffer little children to **c** unto me,	2064
18:22	treasure in heaven: and **c**, follow me.	1204
18:30	and in the world to **c** life everlasting.	2064
18:35	that as he was **c** nigh unto Jericho,	1448
18:40	and when he was **c** near, he asked him,	1448
19: 5	Zaccheus, make haste, and **c** down;	2597
19: 9	This day is salvation **c** to this house,	1096
19:10	the Son of man is **c** to seek and to save	2064
19:13	and said unto them, Occupy till I **c**.	2064
19:29	when he was **c** nigh to Bethphage and	1448
19:37	And when he was **c** nigh, even now at	1448
19:41	And when he was **c** near, he beheld	1448
19:43	For the days shall **c** upon thee, that thine	2240
20:14	**c**, let us kill him, that the inheritance may	1205
20:16	He shall **c** and destroy these husbandmen,	2064
21: 6	things which ye behold, the days will **c**,	2064
21: 7	be when these things shall **c** to pass?	1096
21: 8	many shall **c** in my name, saying, I am	2064
21: 8	for these things must first **c** to pass;	1096
21:28	when these things begin to **c** to pass,	1096
21:31	when ye see these things **c** to pass,	1096
21:34	so that day **c** upon you unawares.	2186
21:35	For as a snare shall it **c** on all them	1904
21:36	all these things that shall **c** to pass,	1096
22:14	And when the hour was **c**, he sat down,	1096
22:18	vine, until the kingdom of God shall **c**.	2064
22:45	from prayer, and was **c** to his disciples,	2064
22:52	and the elders, which were **c** to him,	3854
22:52	Be ye **c** out, as against a thief, with swords	1831
23:33	when they were **c** to the place, which is	565
24:12	in himself at that which was **c** to pass.	1096
24:18	which are **c** to pass there in these days?	1096

Jn		
1:31	therefore am I **c** baptizing with water.	2064
1:39	He saith unto them, **C** and see.	2064
1:46	Can there any good thing **c** out of	1510
1:46	Philip saith unto him, **C** and see.	2064
2: 4	I to do with thee? mine hour is not yet **c**.	2240
3: 2	we know that thou art a teacher **c** from	2064
3:19	light is **c** into the world, and men loved	2064
3:26	the same baptizeth, and all men **c** to him.	2064
4:15	that I thirst not, neither **c** hither to draw.	2064
4:16	her, Go, call thy husband, and **c** hither.	2064
4:25	when he is **c**, he will tell us all things.	2064
4:29	**C**, see a man, which told me all things	1205
4:40	when the Samaritans were **c** unto him,	2064
4:45	Then when he was **c** into Galilee,	2064
4:47	When he heard that Jesus was **c** out of	2240
4:47	and besought him that he would **c** down,	2597
4:49	unto him, Sir, **c** down ere my child die.	2597
4:54	when he was **c** out of Judea into Galilee.	2064
5:14	no more, lest a worse thing **c** unto thee.	1096
5:24	and shall not **c** into condemnation;	2064
5:29	And shall **c** forth; they that have done	1607
5:40	ye will not **c** to me, that ye might have	2064
5:43	I am **c** in my Father's name, and ye	2064
5:43	if another shall **c** in his own name,	2064
6: 5	and saw a great company **c** unto him,	2064
6:14	is of a truth that prophet that should **c**	2064
6:15	therefore perceived that they would **c** and	2064
6:16	And when even was now **c**, his disciples	1096
6:17	now dark, and Jesus was not **c** to them.	2064
6:37	that the Father giveth me shall **c** to me;	2240
6:44	No man can **c** to me, except the Father	2064
6:65	I unto you, that no man can **c** unto me,	2064
7: 6	said unto them, My time is not yet **c**:	3918
7: 8	this feast; for my time is not yet full **c**.	4137
7:28	I am not **c** of myself, but he that sent	2064
7:30	on him, because his hour was not yet **c**.	2064
7:34	me: and where I am, thither ye cannot **c**.	2064
7:36	me: and where I am, thither ye cannot **c**?	2064
7:37	man thirst, let him **c** unto me, and drink.	2064
7:41	some said, Shall Christ **c** out of Galilee?	2064
8:14	ye cannot tell whence I **c**, and whither I	2064
8:20	hands on him; for his hour was not yet **c**.	2064
8:21	die in your sins: whither I go, ye cannot **c**.	2064
8:22	he saith, Whither I go, ye cannot **c**.	2064
9:39	For judgment I am **c** into this world,	2064
10:10	I am **c** that they might have life,	2064
11:27	which should **c** into the world.	2064
11:28	The Master is **c**, and calleth for thee.	3918
11:30	Now Jesus was not yet **c** into the town,	2064
11:32	Then when Mary was **c** where Jesus was,	2064
11:34	They say unto him, Lord, **c** and see.	2064
11:43	cried with a loud voice, Lazarus, **c** forth.	1204
11:48	the Romans shall **c** and take away both	2064
11:56	think ye, that he will not **c** to the feast?	2064
12:12	the next day much people that were **c** to	2064
12:23	answered them, saying, The hour is **c**,	2064
12:35	have the light, lest darkness **c** upon you:	2638

Jn		
12:46	I am **c** a light into the world,	2064
13: 1	Jesus knew that his hour was **c** that	2064
13: 3	and that he was **c** from God, and went to	1831
13:19	Now I tell you before it **c**, that, when it is	1096
13:19	that, when it is **c** to pass, ye may believe	1096
13:33	unto the Jews, Whither I go, ye cannot **c**;	2064
14: 3	will **c** again, and receive you unto myself;	2064
14:18	not leave you comfortless: I will **c** to you.	2064
14:23	and we will **c** unto him, and make our	2064
14:28	I go away, and **c** again unto you.	2064
14:29	now I have told you before it **c** to pass,	1096
14:29	when it is **c** to pass, ye might believe.	1096
15:22	If I had not **c** and spoken unto them,	2064
15:26	But when the Comforter is **c**, whom I will	2064
16: 4	I told you, that when the time shall **c**,	2064
16: 7	The Comforter will not **c** unto you;	2064
16: 8	when he is **c**, he will reprove the world	2064
16:13	Howbeit when he, the Spirit of truth, is **c**,	2064
16:13	speak: and he will shew you things to **c**.	2064
16:21	travail hath sorrow, because her hour is **c**:	2064
16:28	from the Father, and am **c** into the world:	2064
16:32	Behold, the hour cometh, yea, is now **c**,	2064
17: 1	to heaven, and said, Father, the hour is **c**;	2064
17:11	but these are in the world, and I **c** to thee.	2064
17:13	And now **c** I to thee; and these things I	2064
18: 4	all things that should **c** upon him,	2064
21: 4	But when the morning was now **c**,	1096
21: 9	As soon then as they were **c** to land,	576
21:12	Jesus saith unto them, **C** and dine.	1205
21:22	If I will that he tarry till I **c**, what is that to	2064
21:23	but, If I will that he tarry till I **c**, what is	2064

Ac		
1: 6	When they therefore were **c** together,	4905
1: 8	that the Holy Ghost is **c** upon you:	1904
1:11	**c** in like manner as ye have seen him go	2064
1:13	when they were **c** in, they went up into	1525
2: 1	when the day of Pentecost was fully **c**,	4845
2:17	And it shall **c** to pass in the last days,	1510
2:20	that great and notable day of the Lord **c**:	2064
2:21	it shall **c** to pass, that whosoever shall	1510
3:19	when the times of refreshing shall **c** from	2064
3:23	And it shall **c** to pass, that every soul,	1510
5:38	this work be of men, it will **c** to nought:	2647
7: 3	**c** into the land which I shall shew thee.	1204
7: 7	and after that shall they **c** forth,	1831
7:34	and am **c** down to deliver them.	2597
7:34	And now I, I will send thee into Egypt.	1204
8:15	when they were **c** down, prayed for	2597
8:24	which ye have spoken **c** upon me.	1904
8:27	and had to Jerusalem for to worship,	2064
8:31	he desired Philip that he would **c** up	305
8:39	when they were **c** up out of the water,	305
9:26	And when Saul was **c** to Jerusalem,	3854
9:38	desiring him that he would not delay to **c**	1330
9:39	When he was **c**, they brought him into	3854
10: 4	thine alms are **c** up for a memorial before	305
10:21	what is the cause wherefore ye are **c**?	3918
10:27	and found many that were **c** together.	4905
10:28	or **c** unto one of another nation;	4334
10:33	and thou hast well done that thou art **c**.	3854
11: 2	when Peter was **c** up to Jerusalem,	305
11:11	there were three men already **c**	2186
11:20	which, when they were **c** to Antioch,	1525
12:11	And when Peter was **c** to himself, he said,	1096
13:40	Beware therefore, lest that **c** upon you,	1904
14:11	The gods are **c** down to us in the likeness	2597
14:27	And when they were **c**, and had gathered	3854
15: 4	And when they were **c** to Jerusalem,	3854
16: 7	After they were **c** to Mysia, they assayed	2064
16: 9	**C** over into Macedonia, and help us.	1224
16:15	**c** into my house, and abide there.	1525
16:18	in the name of Jesus Christ to **c** out of her.	1831
16:37	let them **c** themselves and fetch us out.	2064
17: 6	the world upside down are **c** hither also;	3918
17:15	Timotheus for to **c** to him with all speed,	2064
18: 2	born in Pontus, lately **c** from Italy, with	2064
18: 5	and Timotheus were **c** from Macedonia,	2718
18:27	who, when he was **c**, helped them much	3854
19: 4	believe on him which should **c** after him,	2064
19:32	wherefore they were **c** together.	4905
20:11	When he therefore was **c** up again, and	305
20:18	when they were **c** to him, he said unto	3854
21:11	when he was **c** unto us, he took Paul's	2064
21:17	And when we were **c** to Jerusalem,	1096
21:22	the multitude must needs **c** together:	4905
21:22	for they will hear that thou art **c**.	2064
22: 6	was **c** nigh unto Damascus about noon,	1448
22:17	that, when I was **c** again to Jerusalem,	5290
23:15	we, or ever he **c** near, are ready to kill	1448
23:35	said he, when thine accusers are also **c**.	3854
24: 8	Commanding his accusers to **c** unto thee:	2064
24:22	Lysias the chief captain shall **c** down,	2597
24:23	acquaintance to minister or **c** unto him.	4334
24:25	temperance, and judgment to **c**, Felix	3195
25: 1	when Festus was **c** into the province,	1910
25: 7	when he was **c**, the Jews which came	3854
25:17	Therefore, when they were **c** hither,	4905
25:23	when Agrippa was **c**, and Bernice,	2064
26: 7	serving God day and night, hope to **c**.	2658
26:22	the prophets and Moses did say should **c**:	1096
27: 7	and scarce were **c** over against Cnidus,	1096
27:16	had much work to **c** by the boat:	1096+4031
27:27	But when the fourteenth night was **c**,	1096
28: 6	and saw no harm **c** to him, they changed	1096
28:17	and when they were **c** together, he said	4905

Ro		
1:10	journey by the will of God to **c** unto you.	2064

Ro 1:13 that oftentimes I purposed to **c** unto you, 2064
 3: 8 we say,) Let us do evil, that good may **c**? 5302
 3:23 and **c** *short* of the glory of God; 5302
 5:14 who is the figure of *him* that was to **c**. 3195
 8:38 nor *things* present, nor *things* to **c**, 3195
 9: 9 At this time will I **c**, and Sara shall have 2064
 9:26 And it shall **c** to **pass**, *that* in the place 1510
 11:11 through their fall salvation *is* **c** unto NIG
 11:25 until the fulness of the Gentiles be **c in**. 1525
 11:26 There shall **c** out of Sion the Deliverer, 2240
 15:23 a great desire these many years to **c** 2064
 15:24 my journey into Spain, I will **c** to you: 2064
 15:28 them this fruit, I will **c** by you into Spain. 565
 15:29 And I am sure that, when I **c** unto you, 2064
 15:29 I shall **c** in the fulness of the blessing of 2064
 15:32 That I may **c** unto you with joy by the will 2064
 16:19 For your obedience is **c** abroad unto all 864
1Co 1: 7 So that ye **c** behind in no gift; waiting for 5302
 2: 6 princes of this world, that **c** to **nought**; 2673
 3:22 or death, or *things* present, or *things* to **c**; 3195
 4: 5 nothing before the time, until the Lord **c**, 2064
 4:18 puffed up, as though I would not **c** to you. 2064
 4:19 But I will **c** to you shortly, if the Lord will, 2064
 4:21 shall I **c** unto you with a rod, or in love, 2064
 5: 5 fasting and prayer, and **c** together again, 4905
 10:11 upon whom the ends of the world are **c**. 2658
 11:17 that you **c together** not for the better, 4905
 11:18 of all, when ye **c together** in the church, 4905
 11:20 When ye **c together** therefore into one 4905
 11:26 ye do shew the Lord's death till he **c**. 2064
 11:33 my brethren, when ye **c together** to eat, 4905
 11:34 ye not **together** unto condemnation. 4905
 11:34 And the rest will I set in order when I **c**. 2064
 13:10 But when *that which* is perfect is **c**, then 2064
 14: 6 if I **c** unto you speaking with tongues, 2064
 14:23 the whole church be **c together** into one 4905
 14:23 and there **c in** *those that* are unlearned, 1525
 14:24 and there **c in** one that believeth not, 1525
 14:26 when ye **c together**, every one of you 4905
 14:35 and with what body do they **c**? 2064
 16: 2 that there be no gatherings when I **c**. 2064
 16: 3 And when I **c**, whomsoever you shall 3854
 16: 5 Now I will **c** unto you, when I shall pass 2064
 16:10 Now if Timotheus **c**, see that he may be 2064
 16:11 forth in peace, that he may **c** unto me: 2064
 16:12 I greatly desired him to **c** unto you with 2064
 16:12 *his* will was not at all to **c** at this time; 2064
 16:12 he will **c** when he shall have convenient 2064
2Co 1:15 And in this confidence I was minded to **c** 2064
 1:16 to **c** again out of Macedonia unto you, 2064
 2: 1 that *I would not* **c** again to you in 2064
 6:17 Wherefore **c out** from among them, 1831
 7: 5 For, when we were **c** into Macedonia, 2064
 9: 4 Lest haply if they of Macedonia **c** with me, 2064
 10:14 for we are **c** as far as to you also in 5348
 12: 1 I will **c** to visions and revelations of 2064
 12:14 the third *time* I am ready to **c** to you; 2064
 12:20 For I fear, lest, when I **c**, I shall not find 2064
 12:21 *And lest*, when I **c** again, my God will 2064
 13: 2 to all other, that, if I **c** again, I will not 2064
Gal 2:11 But when Peter was **c** to Antioch, 2064
 2:12 but when they were **c**, he withdrew and 2064
 2:21 for if righteousness **c** by the law, then NIG
 3:14 That the blessing of Abraham might **c** on 1096
 3:19 the seed should **c** to whom the promise 2064
 3:25 But after that faith is **c**, we are no longer 2064
 4: 4 But when the fulness of the time was **c**, 2064
Eph 1:21 this world, but also in that which is to **c**: 3195
 2: 7 That in the ages to **c** he might shew 1904
 4:13 Till we all **c** in the unity of the faith, 2658
Php 1:27 that whether I **c** and see you, or *else* be 2064
 2:24 the Lord that I also myself shall **c** shortly. 2064
Col 1: 6 Which is **c** unto you, as *it is* in all 3918
 2:17 Which are a shadow of *things* to **c**; 3195
 4:10 if he **c** unto you, receive him;) 2064
1Th 1:10 which delivered us from the wrath to **c**, 2064
 2:16 for the wrath is **c** upon them to 5348
 2:18 Wherefore we would have **c** unto you, 2064
2Th 1:10 he shall **c** to be glorified in his saints, 2064
 2: 3 *that day shall not* **c**, except there come a NIG
 2: 3 *that day shall not* **c**, except there **c** a 2064
1Ti 2: 4 and to **c** unto the knowledge of the truth. 2064
 3:14 I unto thee, hoping to **c** unto thee shortly: 2064
 4: 8 life that now is, and of that which is to **c**. 3195
 4:13 Till I **c**, give attendance to reading, 2064
 6:19 a good foundation against the **time** to **c**, 3195
2Ti 3: 1 that in the last days perilous times shall **c**. 1764
 3: 7 never able to **c** to the knowledge of 2064
 4: 3 For the time will **c** when they will not 1510
 4: 9 Do thy diligence to **c** shortly unto me: 2064
 4:21 Do thy diligence to **c** before winter. 2064
Tit 3:12 be diligent to **c** unto me to Nicopolis: 2064
Heb 2: 5 he hath not put in subjection the world to **c**, 3195
 4: 1 any of you should seem to **c** short *of it*. 5302
 4:16 boldly unto the throne of grace, 4334
 6: 5 of God, and the powers of the world to **c**, 3195
 7: 5 though they **c out** of the loins of Abraham: 1831
 7:25 to the uttermost that **c unto** God by him, 4334
 8: 8 saith, Behold, the days **c**, saith the Lord, 2064
 9:11 But Christ being a **c** high priest of good 3854
 9:11 come a high priest of good *things* to **c**, 3195
 10: 1 law having a shadow of good *things* to **c**, 3195
 10: 7 I **c** (in the volume of the book it is written 2240
 10: 9 said he, Lo, I **c** to do thy will, O God. 2240
 10:37 he that shall come will **c**, and will not 2064

Heb 10:37 he that shall come will **c**, and will not 2240
 11:20 and Esau concerning *things* **to c**. 3195
 11:24 By faith Moses, when he was **c to years**, 3173
 12:18 For ye are not **c** unto the mount that 4334
 12:22 But ye are **c** unto mount Sion, and unto 4334
 13:14 no continuing city, but we seek one to **c**. 3195
 13:23 with whom, if he **c** shortly, I will see you. 2064
Jas 2: 2 For if there **c** unto your assembly a 1525
 2: 2 there **c in** also a poor *man* in vile raiment; 1525
 4: 1 From whence **c** wars and fightings among NIG
 4: 1 *they* not hence, *even* of your lusts that NIG
 5: 1 howl for your miseries that shall **c upon** 1904
1Pe 1:10 who prophesied of the grace *that should* **c** NIG
 4:17 For the time *is* **c** that judgment must begin NIG
2Pe 3: 3 that there shall **c** in the last days scoffers, 2064
 3: 9 but that all should **c** to repentance. 5562
 3:10 But the day of the Lord will **c** as a thief in 2240
1Jn 2:18 and as ye have heard that antichrist shall **c**, 2064
 4: 2 that Jesus Christ is **c** in the flesh of God: 2064
 4: 3 Jesus Christ is **c** in the flesh is not of God: 2064
 4: 3 whereof you have heard that it should **c**; 2064
 5:20 And we know that the Son of God is **c**, 2240
2Jn 1: 7 who confess not that Jesus Christ is **c** in 2064
 1:10 If there **c** any unto you, and bring not this 2064
 1:12 I trust to **c** unto you, and speak face to 2064
3Jn 1:10 if I **c**, I will remember his deeds 2064
Rev 1: 1 *things* which must shortly **c to pass**; 1096
 1: 4 is, and which was, and which is to **c**; 2064
 1: 8 is, and which was, and which is to **c**, 2064
 2: 5 or else I *will* **c** unto thee quickly, 2064
 2:16 or else I *will* **c** unto thee quickly, 2064
 2:25 which *ye have already* hold fast till I **c**. 2240
 3: 3 I will **c** on thee as a thief, and thou shalt 2240
 3: 3 shalt not know what hour I will **c** upon 2064
 3: 9 I will make them to **c** and worship before 2240
 3:10 which shall **c** upon all the world, to try 2064
 3:11 Behold, I **c** quickly: hold *that* fast which 2064
 3:20 I will **c in** to him, and will sup with him, 1525
 4: 1 **C up** hither, and I will shew thee *things* 305
 4: 8 which was, and is, and is to **c**. 2064
 6: 1 one of the four beasts saying, **C** and see. 2064
 6: 3 I heard the second beast say, **C** and see. 2064
 6: 5 I heard the third beast say, **C** and see. 2064
 6: 7 voice of the fourth beast say, **C** and see. 2064
 6:17 For the great day of his wrath is **c**; 2064
 9:12 behold, there **c** two woes more hereafter. 2064
 10: 1 And I saw another mighty angel **c down** 2597
 11:12 saying unto them, **C** up hither. 305
 11:17 which art, and wast, and art to **c**; 2064
 11:18 thy wrath is **c**, and the time of the dead, 2064
 12:10 Now is **c** salvation, and strength, 1096
 12:12 for the devil is **c down** unto you, 2597
 13:13 he maketh fire **c down** from heaven on 2597
 14: 7 to him; for the hour of his judgment is **c**: 2064
 14:15 for the time is **c** for thee to reap; 2064
 15: 4 for all nations shall **c** and worship before 2240
 16:13 I saw three unclean spirits like frogs **c** NIG
 16:15 Behold, I **c** as a thief. Blessed *is* he that 2064
 17: 1 talked with me, saying unto me, **C** hither; NIG
 17:10 and one is, *and* the other is not yet **c**; 2064
 18: 1 I saw another angel **c down** from heaven, 2597
 18: 4 saying, **C out** of her, my people, that ye 1831
 18: 8 Therefore shall her plagues **c** in one day, 2240
 18:10 for in one hour is thy judgment **c**. 2064
 18:17 in one hour so great riches is **c to nought**. 2049
 19: 7 for the marriage of the Lamb is **c**, 2064
 19:17 **C** and gather yourselves together unto 1205
 20: 1 And I saw an angel **c down** from heaven, 2597
 21: 9 talked with me, saying, **C** hither, I will NIG
 22: 7 Behold, I **c** quickly: blessed *is* he that 2064
 22:12 behold, I **c** quickly; and my reward *is* 2064
 22:17 And the Spirit and the bride say, **C**. 2064
 22:17 And let him that heareth say, **C**. 2064
 22:17 And let him that is athirst **c**. 2064
 22:20 these *things* saith, Surely I **c** quickly. 2064
 22:20 Amen. Even so, **c**, Lord Jesus. 2064

COME O LORD See MARAN-ATHA

COMELINESS (5) [COMELY, UNCOMELY]

Isa 53: 2 he hath no form nor **c**; and when we 1926
Eze 16:14 for it *was* perfect through my **c**, which I 1926
 27:10 and helmet in thee; they set forth thy **c**. 1926
Da 10: 8 my **c** was turned in me into corruption, 1935
1Co 12:23 uncomely *parts* have more abundant **c**. 2157

COMELY (16) [COMELINESS]

1Sa 16:18 a **c** person, and the Lord *is* with him. 8389
Job 41:12 nor *his* power, nor his **c** proportion. 2433
Ps 33: 1 righteous: *for* praise is **c** for the upright. 5000
 147: 1 God; for *it is* pleasant; *and* praise is **c**. 5000
Pr 30:29 which go well, yea, four are **c** in going: 3190
Ecc 5:18 good and **c** *for one* to eat and to drink, 3303
SS 1: 5 I *am* black, but **c**, O ye daughters of 5000
 1:10 Thy cheeks are **c** with rows of *jewels*, 4998
 2:14 *is* thy voice, and thy countenance *is* **c**. 5000
 4: 3 a thread of scarlet, and thy speech *is* **c**: 5000
 6: 4 O my love, as Tirzah, *as* Jerusalem, 5000
Isa 4: 2 **c** for them that are escaped of 8597+3807.1
Jer 6: 2 I have likened the daughter of Zion *to a* **c** 5116
1Co 7:35 but for *that which is* **c**, and that you may 2158
 11:13 is it **c** that a woman pray unto God 4241
 12:24 For our **c** *parts* have no need: 2158

C

COMERS (1) [COME]

Heb 10: 1 continually make the **c** *thereunto* perfect. 4334

COMEST (29) [COME]

Ge 10:19 from Sidon, as thou **c** to Gerar, unto Gaza; 935
 13:10 like the land of Egypt, as thou **c** unto Zoar. 935
 24:41 *this* my oath, when thou **c** to my kindred; 935
Dt 2:19 thou **c nigh** over against the children 7126
 20:10 When thou **c nigh** unto a city to fight 7126
 23:24 thou **c** into thy neighbour's vineyard, 935
 23:25 When thou **c** into the standing corn of thy 935
 28: 6 Blessed *shalt* thou *be* when thou **c in**, 935
 28:19 Cursed *shalt* thou *be* when thou **c in**, 935
Jdg 17: 9 Micah said unto him, Whence **c** thou? 935
 18:23 that thou **c with** such *a company*? 2199
 19:17 Whither goest thou? and whence **c** thou? 935
1Sa 15: 7 from Havilah *until* thou **c** to Shur, 935
 16: 4 at his coming, and said, **C** thou peaceably? 935
 17:43 *Am* I a dog, that thou **c** to me with staves? 935
 17:45 Thou **c** to me with a sword, and with 935
2Sa 1: 3 David said unto him, From whence **c** thou? 935
 3:13 daughter, when thou **c** to see my face. 935
1Ki 2:13 she said, **C** thou peaceably? And he said, 935
 19:15 when thou **c**, anoint Hazael to be king 935
2Ki 5:25 said unto him, Whence **c** *thou*, Gehazi? NIH
 9: 2 when thou **c** thither, look out there Jehu 935
Job 1: 7 the Lord said unto Satan, Whence **c** thou? 935
 2: 2 said unto Satan, From whence **c** thou? 935
Jer 51:61 When thou **c** to Babylon, and shalt see, 935
Jnh 1: 8 and whence **c** thou? what *is* thy country? 935
Mt 3:14 to be baptized of thee, and **c** thou to me? 2064
Lk 23:42 remember me when thou **c** into thy 2064
2Ti 4:13 when thou **c**, bring *with thee*, and 2064

COMETH (282) [COME]

Ge 24:43 *when* the virgin **c forth** to draw *water*, 3318
 29: 6 Rachel his daughter **c** with the sheep. 935
 30:11 Leah said, A troop **c**: and she called his 935
 32: 6 also he **c** to meet thee, and four hundred 1980
 37:19 one to another, Behold, this dreamer **c**. 935
 48: 2 said, Behold, thy son Joseph **c** unto thee: 935
Ex 4:14 also, behold, he **c forth** to meet thee: 3318
 8:20 lo, he **c forth** to the water; and say unto 3318
 13:12 every firstling that **c** of a beast which thou 7698
 28:35 and when he **c out**, that he die not. 3318
 29:30 when he **c** into the tabernacle of 935
Lev 11:34 on which *such* water **c** shall be unclean: 935
Nu 1:51 the stranger that **c nigh** shall be put to 7131
 3:10 the stranger that **c nigh** shall be put to 7131
 3:38 the stranger that **c nigh** shall be put to 7131
 5:30 when the spirit of jealousy **c** upon him, 5674
 5:12 when he **c out** of his mother's womb. 3318
 17:13 Whosoever **c** any thing *near* unto 7131+7131
 18: 7 the stranger that **c nigh** shall be put to 7131
 21:13 which *is* in the wilderness that **c out** of 3318
 26: 5 *of whom* **c** the family of the Hanochites: NIH
Dt 18: 8 beside that which **c** of the **sale** of his 4465
 23:11 it shall be, when evening **c on**, he shall 6437
 23:13 and cover that which **c** from thee: 6627
 28:57 towards her young one that **c out** from 3318
Jdg 11:31 whatsoever **c forth** of the doors of my 3318
 13:14 She may not eat of any *thing* that **c** of 3318
1Sa 4: 3 when it **c** among us, it may save us out 935
 4: 6 all that he saith **c surely to pass**: 935+935
 7: 7 Whosoever **c** not forth after Saul and 3318
 20:27 Wherefore **c** not the son of Jesse to meat, 935
 20:29 Therefore he **c** not unto the king's table. 935
 25: 8 whatsoever **c** to thine hand unto thy 4672
 28:14 she said, An old man **c up**; and he *is* 5927
2Sa 3: 5 thy father **c** to see thee, say unto him, 935
 18:27 He *is* a good man, and **c** with good tidings. 935
1Ki 8:41 **c** out of a far country for thy name's sake; 935
 14: 5 wife of Jeroboam **c** to ask a thing of thee 935
 14: 5 for it shall be, when she **c in**, that she shall 935
2Ki 4:10 when he **c** to us, *that* he shall turn 935
 6:32 when the messenger **c**, shut the door, 935
 9:18 came to them, but he **c** not **again**. 7725
 9:20 came even unto them, and **c** not **again**: 7725
 10: 2 Now as soon as this letter **c** to you, 935
 11: 8 that **c** within the ranges, let him be slain: 935
 11: 8 the king as he goeth out and as he **c** in 935
 12: 4 all the money that **c** into any man's heart 5927
 12: 9 on the right side as one **c** *into* the house of 935
1Ch 16:33 before the Lord, because he **c** to judge the earth. 935
 29:16 house for thine holy name **c** of thine hand, NIH
2Ch 13: 9 whosoever **c** to consecrate himself with 935
 20: 2 There **c** a great multitude against thee from 935
 20: 9 If, *when* evil **c** upon us, *as* the sword, 935
 20:12 this great company that **c** against us; 935
 23: 7 whosoever *else* **c** into the house, he shall 935
 23: 8 be you with the king when he **c in**, 935
Job 3:21 Which long for death, but it **c** not; NIH
 3:24 For my sighing **c** before I eat, 935
 5: 6 Although affliction **c** not **forth** of the dust, 3318
 5:21 thou be afraid of destruction when it **c**. 935
 5:26 like as a shock of corn **c** in in his season. 5927
 14: 2 he **c forth** like a flower, and is cut down: 3318
 14:18 surely the mountain falling **c to nought**, 5034
 20:25 It is drawn, and **c out** of the body; yea, 3318
 20:25 yea, the glistering sword **c out** of his gall: 1980
 21:17 *how oft* is their destruction upon them! 935
 27: 9 Will God hear his cry when trouble **c** upon 935
 28: 5 *As for* the earth, out of it **c** bread: and 3318
 28:20 Whence then **c** wisdom? and where *is* 935
 36:32 *not* to shine by the cloud that **c betwixt**. 6293

C

Job 37: 9 Out of the south c the whirlwind: and | 935
37:22 Fair weather c out of the north: with God | 857
Ps 30: 5 for a night, but joy c in the morning. | NIH
62: 1 upon God: from him c my salvation. | NIH
75: 6 For promotion c neither from the east, | NIH
78:39 wind that passeth away, and c not **again**. | 7725
96:13 Before the Lord, for he c, for he cometh | 935
96:13 for he cometh, for he c to judge the earth: | 935
98: 9 the Lord; for he c to judge the earth: | 935
118:26 Blessed *be* he that c in the name of | 935
121: 1 unto the hills, from whence c my help. | NIH
121: 2 My help c from the Lord, which made | NIH
Pr 1:26 calamity; I will mock when your fear c; | 935
1:27 When your fear c as desolation, | 935
1:27 and your destruction c as a whirlwind; | 857
1:27 when distress and anguish c upon you: | 935
2: 6 out of his mouth c knowledge and | NIH
3:25 of the desolation of the wicked, when it c. | 935
11: 2 *When* pride c, then cometh shame: but | 935
11: 2 *When* pride cometh, then c shame: but | 935
11: 8 of trouble, and the wicked c in his stead. | 935
13: 5 is loathsome, and c to shame. | 2659
13:10 Only by pride c contention: but with | 5414
13:12 but *when* the desire c, *it is* a tree of life. | 935
13: 3 When the wicked c, *then* cometh also | 935
18: 3 *then* c also contempt, and with ignominy | 935
18:17 but his neighbour c and searcheth him. | 935
29:26 *every* man's judgment c from the Lord. | NIH
Ecc 1: 4 passeth away, and *another* generation c: | 935
2:12 for what *can* the man *do* that c after | 935
4:14 For out of prison he c to reign; | 3318
5: 3 For a dream c through the multitude of | 935
6: 4 For he c in with vanity, and departeth in | 935
11: 8 for they shall be many. All that c *is* vanity. | 935
SS 2: 8 behold, he c leaping upon the mountains, | 935
3: 6 Who *is* this that c out of the wilderness | 5927
8: 5 Who *is* this that c **up** from the wilderness, | 5927
Isa 13: 9 Behold, the day of the Lord c, cruel both | 935
21: 1 *so* it c from the desert, from a terrible land. | 935
21: 9 behold, here c a chariot of men, *with* a | 935
21:12 The morning c, and also the night: | 857
24:18 he that c **up** out of the midst of the pit | 5927
26:21 the Lord c **out** of his place to punish | 3318
28:29 This also c **forth** from the Lord of hosts, | 3318
30:13 whose breaking c suddenly at an instant. | 935
30:27 Behold, the name of the Lord c from far, | 935
42: 5 the earth, and **that which c out** of it; | 6631
55:10 For as the rain c **down**, and the snow | 3381
62:11 daughter of Zion, Behold, thy salvation c; | 935
63: 1 Who *is* this that c from Edom, with dyed | 935
Jer 6:20 To what purpose c there to me incense | 935
6:22 a people c from the north country, | 935
17: 6 the desert, and shall not see when good c; | 935
17: 8 not see when heat c, but her leaf shall | 935
18:14 Lebanon *which* c from the rock of the | NIH
43:11 he c, he shall smite the land of Egypt, | 935
46: 7 Who *is* this that c **up** as a flood, | 5927
46:20 a very fair heifer, *but* destruction c; | 935
46:20 destruction cometh; it c out of the north. | 935
47: 4 Because of the day that c to spoil all | 935
50: 3 For out of the north there c **up** a nation | 5927
51:54 A sound of a cry c from Babylon, | NIH
La 3:37 Who *is* he *that* saith, and it c **to pass**, | 1961
Eze 4:12 shalt bake it with dung that c **out** of | 6627
7:25 Destruction c; and they shall seek peace, | 935
14: 4 before his face, and to the prophet; | 935
14: 4 I the Lord will answer him that c | 935
14: 7 c to a prophet to inquire of him | 935
20:32 which c into your mind shall not be at | 5927
21: 7 shalt answer, For the tidings; because it c: | 935
21: 7 behold, it c, and shall be brought to pass, | 935
24:24 this c, ye shall know that I *am* the Lord | 935
30: 9 as *in* the day of Egypt: for lo, it c. | 935
33:30 hear what *is* the word that c **forth** from | 3318
33:31 they come unto thee as the people c, | 3996
33:33 when this c **to pass**, (lo, it will come) | 935
47: 9 every *thing* shall live whither the river c. | 935
Da 11:16 he that c against him shall do according to | 935
12:12 c to the thousand three hundred and five | 5060
Hos 7: 1 the thief c **in**, *and* the troop of *robbers* | 935
Joel 2: 1 for the day of the Lord c, for *it is* nigh at | 935
Mic 1: 3 the Lord c **forth** out of his place, | 3318
5: 6 when he c into our land, and when he | 935
7: 4 day of thy watchmen *and* thy visitation c; | 935
Hab 3:16 when *he* c **up** unto the people, he will | 5927
Zec 9: 9 behold, thy King c unto thee: he *is* just, | 935
14: 1 the day of the Lord c, and thy spoil shall | 935
Mal 4: 1 For behold, the day, that *shall* burn as | 935
4: 1 the day that c shall burn them up, saith | 935
Mt 3:11 but he that c after me is mightier than I, | 2064
3:13 Then c Jesus from Galilee to Jordan unto | 3854
5:37 whatsoever is more than these c of evil. | 1510
8: 9 to another, Come, and he c; and to my | 2064
13:19 c the wicked one, and catcheth away | 2064
15:11 but that which c **out** of the mouth, | 1607
17:27 hook, and take up the fish that first c **up**; | 305
18: 7 woe to that man by whom the offence c. | 2064
21: 5 thy King c unto thee, meek, | 2064
21: 9 Blessed *is* he that c in the name of | 2064
21:40 When the lord therefore of the vineyard c, | 2064
23:39 is he that c in the name of the Lord. | 2064
24:27 For as the lightning c **out** of the east, | 1831
24:44 hour as you think not the Son of man c. | 2064
24:46 whom his lord when he c shall find so | 2064
25: 6 a cry made, Behold, the bridegroom c; | 2064

Mt 25:13 nor the hour wherein the Son of man c. | 2064
25:19 a long time the lord of those servants c, | 2064
26:36 c Jesus with them unto a place called | 2064
26:40 And he c unto the disciples, | 2064
26:45 Then c he to his disciples, and saith unto | 2064
Mk 1: 7 There c one mightier than I after me, | 2064
3:20 And *the* multitude c **together** again, | 4905
4:15 Satan c immediately, and taketh away | 2064
5:22 there c one of the rulers of the synagogue, | 2064
5:38 And he c to the house of the ruler of | 2064
6:48 about the fourth watch of the night he c | 2064
7:20 he said, That which c **out** of the man, | 1607
8:22 And he c to Bethsaida; and they bring a | 2064
8:38 when he c in the glory of his Father with | 2064
9:12 Elias verily c first, and restoreth all *things;* | 2064
10: 1 c into the coasts of Judea by the farther | 2064
11: 9 Blessed *is* he that c in the name of | 2064
11:10 that c in the name of the Lord: | 2064
13:35 not when the master of the house c, | 2064
14:17 And in the evening he c with the twelve. | 2064
14:37 And he c, and findeth them sleeping, | 2064
14:41 And he c the third time, and saith unto | 2064
14:43 c Judas, one of the twelve, and with him | 3854
14:66 there c one of the maids of the high priest: | 2064
Lk 3:16 but one mightier than I c, the latchet of | 2064
6:47 Whosoever c to me, and heareth my | 2064
7: 8 to another, Come, and he c; and to my | 2064
8:12 c the devil, and taketh away the word | 2064
8:49 there c one from the ruler of | 2064
11:25 And when he c, he findeth *it* swept and | 2064
12:36 that when *he* c and knocketh, they may | 2064
12:37 whom the lord when he c shall find | 2064
12:40 for the Son of man c at an hour when ye | 2064
12:43 whom his lord when he c shall find so | 2064
12:54 straightway ye say, There c a shower; | 2064
12:55 say, There will be heat; and it c **to pass**. | 1096
13:35 Blessed *is* he that c in the name of the | 2064
14:10 when he that bade thee c, he may say | 2064
14:31 that c against him with twenty thousand? | 2064
15: 6 And when he c home, he calleth together | 2064
17:20 The kingdom of God c not with | 2064
18: 8 Nevertheless when the Son of man c, | 2064
19:38 Blessed *be* the King that c in the name of | 2064
Jn 1: 9 which lighteth every man *that* c into | 2064
1:15 He that c after me is preferred before me: | 2064
1:30 After me c a man which is preferred before | 2064
3: 8 but canst not tell whence it c, and whither | 2064
3:20 neither c to the light, lest his deeds should | 2064
3:21 But he that doeth truth c to the light, | 2064
3:31 He that c from above is above all: he that | 2064
3:31 he that c from heaven is above all. | 2064
4: 5 Then c he to a city of Samaria, which is | 2064
4: 7 c a woman of Samaria to draw water: | 2064
4:21 unto her, Woman, believe me, the hour c, | 2064
4:23 But the hour c, and now is, when the true | 2064
4:25 I know that Messias c, which is called | 2064
4:35 are yet four months, and *then* c harvest? | 2064
5:44 seek not the honour *that* c from God only? | NIG
6:33 For the bread of God is he which c **down** | 2597
6:35 he that c to me shall never hunger; | 2064
6:37 that c to me I will in no wise cast out. | 2064
6:45 hath learned of the Father, c unto me. | 2064
6:50 This is the bread which c **down** from | 2597
7:27 when Christ c, no *man* knoweth whence | 2064
7:31 believed on him, and said, When Christ c, | 2064
7:42 That Christ c of the seed of David, | 2064
9: 4 day: the night c, when no *man* can work. | 2064
10:10 The thief c not, but for to steal, and to kill, | 2064
11:38 again groaning in himself c to the grave. | 2064
12:13 Blessed *is* the King of Israel that c in | 2064
12:15 behold, thy King c, sitting on an ass's colt. | 2064
12:22 Philip c and telleth Andrew: and | 2064
13: 6 Then c he to Simon Peter: and *Peter* saith | 2064
14: 6 no *man* c unto the Father, but by me. | 2064
14:30 for the prince of this world c, | 2064
15:25 But this c to pass, that the word might be | NIG
16: 2 the time c, that whosoever killeth you | 2064
16:25 the time c, when I shall no more speak | 2064
16:32 Behold, the hour c, yea, is now come, | 2064
18: 3 thither with lanterns and torches and | 2064
20: 1 The first *day* of the week c Mary | 2064
20: 2 and c to Simon Peter, and to the other | 2064
20: 6 Then c Simon Peter following him, | 2064
21:13 Jesus then c, and taketh bread, | 2064
Ac 10:32 who, when he c, shall speak unto thee. | 3854
13:25 But behold, there c one after me, | 2064
18:21 I must by all means keep this feast that c | 2064
Ro 4: 9 *C* this blessedness then upon | NIG
10:17 So then faith c by hearing, | NIG
1Co 15:24 Then c the end, when he shall have | NIG
2Co 11: 4 For if he that c preacheth another Jesus, | 2064
11:28 which c **upon** me daily, the care of all | 1999
Gal 5: 8 *This* persuasion c not of him that calleth | NIG
Eph 5: 6 of these *things* c the wrath of God upon | 2064
Col 3: 6 which *things'* sake the wrath of God c | 2064
1Th 5: 2 day of the Lord so c as a thief in the night. | 2064
5: 3 then sudden destruction c **upon** them, | 2186
1Ti 6: 4 whereof c envy, strife, railings, | 1096
Heb 6: 7 drinketh *in* the rain that c oft upon it, | 2064
10: 5 Wherefore when he c **into** the world, | 1525
11: 6 he that c to God must believe that he is, | 4334
Jas 1:17 and c **down** from the Father of lights, | 2597
Jude 1:14 Lord c with ten thousands of his saints, | 2064
Rev 1: 7 Behold, he c with clouds; and every eye | 2064
3:12 c **down** out of heaven from my God: | 2597

Rev 11:14 *and* behold, the third woe c quickly. | 2064
17:10 and when he c, he must continue a short | 2064

COMFORT (66) [COMFORTABLE, COMFORTABLY, COMFORTED, COMFORTEDST, COMFORTER, COMFORTERS, COMFORTETH, COMFORTLESS, COMFORTS]

Ge 5:29 This *same* shall c us concerning our work | 5162
18: 5 a morsel of bread, and c ye your hearts; | 5582
27:42 as touching thee, doth c himself, | 5162
37:35 and all his daughters rose up to c him; | 5162
Jdg 19: 5 *C* thine heart *with* a morsel of bread, | 5582
19: 8 father said, *C* thine heart, I pray thee. | 5582
2Sa 10: 2 David sent to c him by the hand of his | 5162
1Ch 7:22 days, and his brethren came to c him. | 5162
19: 2 David sent messengers to c him | 5162
19: 2 children of Ammon to Hanun, to c him. | 5162
Job 2:11 to come to mourn with him and to c him. | 5162
6:10 should I yet have c; yea, I would harden | 5165
7:13 When I say, My bed shall c me, my couch | 5162
9:27 will leave off my heaviness, and c myself: | 1082
10:20 let me alone, that I may **take** c a little, | 1082
21:34 How then c ye me in vain, seeing *in* your | 5162
Ps 23: 4 with me; thy rod and thy staff they c me. | 5162
71:21 my greatness, and c me on every side. | 5162
119:50 This *is* my c in my affliction: for thy word | 5165
119:76 thy merciful kindness be for my c, | 5162
119:82 thy word, saying, When wilt thou c me? | 5162
SS 2: 5 Stay me with flagons, c me with apples: | 7502
Isa 22: 4 labour not to c me, because of the spoiling | 5162
40: 1 C ye, comfort ye my people, saith your | 5162
40: 1 Comfort ye, c my people, saith your | 5162
51: 3 For the Lord shall c Zion: he will | 5162
51: 3 he will c all her waste places; and he will | 5162
51:19 and the sword: *by* whom shall I c thee? | 5162
57: 6 offering. Should I **receive** c in these? | 5162
61: 2 of our God; to c all that mourn; | 5162
66:13 his mother comforteth, so will I c you; | 5162
Jer 8:18 *When* I would c myself against sorrow, | 4010
16: 7 in mourning, to c them for the dead; | 5162
31:13 will c them, and make them rejoice from | 5162
La 1: 2 all her lovers she hath none to c *her:* | 5162
1:17 her hands, *and* there is none to c her: | 5162
1:21 heard that I sigh; *there is* none to c me: | 5162
2:13 shall I equal to thee, that I may c thee, | 5162
Eze 14:23 they shall c you, when ye see their ways | 5162
16:54 hast done, in that thou art a c unto them. | 5162
Zec 1:17 the Lord shall yet c Zion, and shall yet | 5162
10: 2 and have told false dreams; they c in vain: | 5162
Mt 9:22 saw her, he said, Daughter, **be of good c;** | 2293
Mk 10:49 saying unto him, **Be of good c**, rise; | 2293
Lk 8:48 he said unto her, Daughter, **be of good c:** | 2293
Jn 11:19 Mary, to c them concerning their brother. | 3888
Ac 9:31 and in the c of the Holy Ghost, | 3874
Ro 15: 4 and c of the scriptures might have hope. | 3874
1Co 14: 3 to edification, and exhortation, and c. | 3889
2Co 1: 3 Father of mercies, and the God of all c; | 3874
1: 4 that we may be able to c them which are | 3870
1: 4 by the c wherewith we ourselves are | 3874
2: 7 c *him*, lest perhaps such a one should be | 3870
7: 4 I am filled with c, I am exceeding joyful | 3874
7:13 Therefore we were comforted in your c: | 3874
13:11 Be perfect, be **of good c**, be of one mind, | 3870
Eph 6:22 affairs, and *that* he might c your hearts. | 3870
Php 2: 1 any consolation in Christ, if any c of love, | 3890
2:19 I also may be **of good c**, when I know | 2174
Col 4: 8 know your estate, and c your hearts; | 3870
4:11 of God, which have been a c unto me. | 3031
1Th 3: 2 and to c you concerning your faith: | 3870
4:18 c one another with these words. | 3870
5:11 Wherefore c yourselves together, | 3870
5:14 c the feebleminded, support the weak, | 3888
2Th 2:17 C your hearts, and stablish you in every | 3870

COMFORT (2) [COMFORT]

2Sa 14:17 word of my lord the king shall now be c: | 4496
Zec 1:13 with me *with* good words *and* c words. | 5150

COMFORTABLY (5) [COMFORT]

2Sa 19: 7 and speak c unto thy servants: | 3820+5921
2Ch 30:22 Hezekiah spake c unto all the | 3820+5921
32: 6 and spake c to them, saying, | 3824+5921
Isa 40: 2 Speak ye c to Jerusalem, | 3820+5921
Hos 2:14 wilderness, and speak c unto her. | 3820+5921

COMFORTED (36) [COMFORT]

Ge 24:67 and Isaac was c after his mother's *death.* | 5162
37:35 he refused to be c; and he said, For I will | 5162
38:12 Judah was c, and went up unto his | 5162
50:21 he c them, and spake kindly unto them. | 5162
Ru 2:13 for that thou hast c me, and for that thou | 5162
2Sa 13:39 David of Bath-sheba his wife, and went unto | 5162
13:39 for he was c concerning Amnon, seeing | 5162
Job 42:11 c him over all the evil that the Lord had | 5162
Ps 77: 2 and ceased not: my soul refused to be c. | 5162
86:17 thou, Lord, hast holpen me, and c me. | 5162
119:52 of old, O Lord; and have c myself. | 5162
Isa 49:13 for the Lord hath c his people, | 5162
52: 9 for the Lord hath c his people, he hath | 5162
54:11 tossed with tempest, *and* not c, behold, | 5162
66:13 and ye shall be c in Jerusalem. | 5162
Jer 31:15 children refused to be c for her children, | 5162
Eze 5:13 fury to rest upon them, and I will be c: | 5162
14:22 ye shall be c concerning the evil that I | 5162
31:16 shall be c in the nether parts of the earth. | 5162

Eze	32:31 shall be c over all his multitude,	5162
Mt	2:18 and would not be c, because they are not.	3870
	5:4 are they that mourn: for they shall be c.	3870
Lk	16:25 Lazarus evil things: but now he is c,	3870
Jn	11:31 and c her, when they saw Mary, that she	3888
Ac	16:40 the brethren, they c them, and departed.	3870
	20:12 young man alive, and were not a little c.	3870
Ro	1:12 that I may be c together with you by	4837
1Co	14:31 one, that all may learn, and all may be c.	3870
2Co	1:4 wherewith we ourselves are c of God.	3870
	1:6 or whether we be c, it is for your	3870
	7:6 cast down, c us by the coming of Titus;	3870
	7:7 by the consolation wherewith he was c in	3870
	7:13 Therefore we were c in your comfort: yea,	3870
Col	2:2 That their hearts might be c, being knit	3870
1Th	2:11 and c and charged every one of you,	3888
	3:7 we were c over you in all our affliction	3870

COMFORTEDST (1) [COMFORT]

Isa	12:1 anger is turned away, and thou c me.	5162

COMFORTER (8) [COMFORT]

Ecc	4:1 as were oppressed, and they had no c;	5162
	4:1 there was power; but they had no c.	5162
La	1:9 she had no c. O LORD, behold my	5162
	1:16 he c that should relieve my soul is far	5162
Jn	14:16 Father, and he shall give you another C,	3875
	14:26 But the C, which is the Holy Ghost,	3875
	15:26 when the C is come, whom I will send	3875
	16:7 not away, the C will not come unto you;	3875

COMFORTERS (5) [COMFORT]

2Sa	10:3 thy father, that he hath sent c unto thee?	5162
1Ch	19:3 thy father, that he hath sent c unto thee?	5162
Job	16:2 have heard many such things: miserable c	5162
Ps	69:20 was none; and for c, but I found none.	5162
Na	3:7 whence shall I seek c for thee?	5162

COMFORTETH (5) [COMFORT]

Job	29:25 in the army, as one that c the mourners.	5162
Isa	51:12 I, even I, am he that c you: who art thou,	5162
	66:13 As one whom his mother c, so will I	5162
2Co	1:4 Who c us in all our tribulation, that we	3870
	7:6 that c those that are cast down,	3870

COMFORTLESS (1) [COMFORT]

Jn	14:18 I will not leave you c: I will come to you.	3737

COMFORTS (2) [COMFORT]

Ps	94:19 thoughts within me thy c delight my soul.	8575
Isa	57:18 restore c unto him and to his mourners.	5150

COMING (100) [COME]

Ge	24:63 and saw, and behold, the camels were c.	935
	30:30 the LORD hath blessed thee since my c:	7272
Nu	22:16 I pray thee, hinder thee from c unto me:	1980
	33:40 heard of the c of the children of Israel.	935
Jdg	5:28 the lattice, Why is his chariot so long in c?	935
1Sa	10:5 c down from the high place with	3381
	16:4 the elders of the town trembled at his c,	7125
	22:9 said, I saw the son of Jesse c to Nob,	935
	25:26 hath withholden thee from c to shed blood,	935
	25:33 which hast kept me this day from c to shed	935
	29:6 thy c in with me in the host is good in my	935
	29:6 the day of thy c unto me unto this day:	935
2Sa	3:25 to know thy going out and thy c in,	4126
	24:20 king and his servants c on toward him:	5674
2Ki	10:15 Jehonadab the son of Rechab c to meet	NIH
	13:20 invaded the land at the c in of the year.	935
	19:27 and thy c in, and thy rage against me.	935
2Ch	22:7 the destruction of Ahaziah was of God by c	935
Ezr	3:8 Now in the second year of their c unto	935
Ps	19:5 Which is as a bridegroom c out of his	935
	37:13 laugh at him: for he seeth that his day is c.	935
	121:8 going out and thy c in from this time forth,	935
Pr	8:3 entry of the city, at the c in at the doors.	3996
Isa	14:9 is moved from beneath to meet thee at thy c:	935
	32:19 When it shall hail, c down on the forest;	3381
	37:28 and thy c in, and thy rage against me.	935
	44:7 the things that are c, and shall come,	935
Jer	8:7 the swallow observe the time of their c;	935
Da	4:23 and a holy one c down from heaven,	5182
Mic	7:15 According to the days of thy c out of	3318
Hab	3:4 the light; he had horns c out of his hand:	NIH
Mal	3:2 who may abide the day of his c? and	935
	4:5 Elijah the prophet before the c of the great	935
Mt	8:28 c out of the tombs, exceeding fierce,	1831
	16:28 till they see the Son of man c in his	2064
	24:3 and what shall be the sign of thy c,	3952
	24:27 so shall also the c of the Son of man be.	3952
	24:30 they shall see the Son of man c in	2064
	24:37 so shall also the c of the Son of man be.	3952
	24:39 so shall also the c of the Son of man be.	3952
	24:48 say in his heart, My lord delayeth his c;	2064
	25:27 at my c I should have received mine own	2064
	26:64 of power, and c in the clouds of heaven.	2064
Mk	1:10 And straightway c up out of the water,	305
	6:31 for there were many c and going,	2064
	13:26 shall they see the Son of man c in	2064
	13:36 Lest c suddenly he find you sleeping.	2064
	14:62 of power, and c in the clouds of heaven.	2064
	15:21 who passed by, c out of the country,	2064
Lk	2:38 And she c in that instant gave thanks	2186
	9:42 as he was yet a c, the devil threw him	4334
	12:45 say in his heart, My lord delayeth his c;	2064

Lk	18:5 lest by her continual c she weary me.	2064
	19:23 that at my c I might have required mine	2064
	21:26 those things which are c on the earth:	1904
	21:27 shall they see the Son of man c in a cloud	2064
	23:26 c out of the country, and on him they laid	2064
	23:29 For behold, the days are c, in the which	2064
	23:36 c to him, and offering him vinegar,	4334
Jn	1:27 who c after me is preferred before me,	2064
	1:29 next day John seeth Jesus c unto him,	2064
	1:47 Jesus saw Nathanael c to him, and saith	2064
	5:7 but while I am c, another steppeth down	2064
	5:25 I say unto you, The hour is c, and now is,	2064
	5:28 for the hour is c, in the which all that	2064
	10:12 seeth the wolf c, and leaveth the sheep.	2064
	11:20 as soon as she heard that Jesus was c,	2064
	12:12 when they heard that Jesus was c to	2064
Ac	7:52 shewed before of the c of the Just One;	1660
	9:12 in a vision a man named Ananias c in,	1525
	9:28 he was with them c in and going out at	1531
	10:3 an angel of God c in to him,	1525
	10:25 And as Peter was c in, Cornelius met him,	1525
	13:24 When John had first preached before his c	1529
	17:10 who c thither went into the synagogue of	3854
	27:33 while the day was c on, Paul besought	3195
Ro	15:22 I have been much hindered from c to you.	2064
1Co	1:7 waiting for the c of our Lord Jesus Christ:	602
	15:23 afterward they that are Christ's at his c.	3952
	16:17 I am glad of the c of Stephanas and	3952
2Co	7:6 cast down, comforted us by the c of Titus;	3952
	7:7 And not by his c only, but by	3952
	13:1 This is the third time I am c to you.	2064
Php	1:26 Jesus Christ for me by my c to you again.	3952
1Th	2:19 presence of our Lord Jesus Christ at his c?	3952
	3:13 at the c of our Lord Jesus Christ with all	3952
	4:15 remain unto the c of the Lord shall not	3952
	5:23 body be preserved blameless unto the c of	3952
2Th	2:1 by the c of our Lord Jesus Christ,	3952
	2:8 shall destroy with the brightness of his c:	3952
	2:9 Even him, whose c is after the working of	3952
Jas	5:7 brethren, unto the c of the Lord.	3952
	5:8 for the c of the Lord draweth nigh.	3952
1Pe	2:4 To whom c, as unto a living stone,	4334
2Pe	1:16 the power and c of our Lord Jesus Christ,	3952
	3:4 And saying, Where is the promise of his c?	3952
	3:12 and hasting unto the c of the day of God,	3952
1Jn	2:28 and not be ashamed before him at his c.	3952
Rev	3:11 And I beheld another beast c up out of	305
	21:2 c down from God out of heaven,	2597

COMINGS (1) [COME]

Eze	43:11 the c in thereof, and all the forms thereof,	4126

COMMAND (104) [COMMANDED, COMMANDEDST, COMMANDER, COMMANDEST, COMMANDETH, COMMANDING, COMMANDMENT, COMMANDMENTS]

Ge	18:19 that he will c his children and his	6680
	27:8 obey my voice according to that which I c	6680
	50:16 Thy father did c before he died, saying,	6680
Ex	7:2 Thou shalt speak all that I c thee: and	6680
	8:27 the LORD our God, as he shall c us.	559
	18:23 God c thee so, then thou shalt be able to	6680
	27:20 thou shalt c the children of Israel, that	6680
	34:11 Observe thou that which I c thee this day:	6680
Lev	6:9 C Aaron and his sons, saying, This is	6680
	13:54 the priest shall c that they wash the thing	6680
	14:4 shall the priest c to take for him that is to	6680
	14:5 the priest shall c that one of the birds be	6680
	14:36 priest shall c that they empty the house,	6680
	14:40 the priest shall c that they take away	6680
	24:2 C the children of Israel, that they bring	6680
	25:21 I will c my blessing upon you in the sixth	6680
Nu	5:2 C the children of Israel, that they put out	6680
	9:8 I will hear what the LORD will c	6680
	28:2 C the children of Israel, and say unto	6680
	34:2 C the children of Israel, and say unto	6680
	35:2 C the children of Israel, that they give	6680
	36:6 This is the thing which the LORD doth c	6680
Dt	4:2 c thou the people, saying, Ye are to pass	6680
	4:2 Ye shall not add unto the word which I c	6680
	4:2 of the LORD your God which I c you.	6680
	4:40 commandments, which I c thee this day,	6680
	6:2 which I c thee, thou, and thy son,	6680
	6:6 these words, which I c thee this day,	6680
	7:11 which I c thee this day, to do them.	6680
	8:1 All the commandments which I c thee	6680
	8:11 and his statutes, which I c thee this day:	6680
	10:13 which I c thee this day for thy good?	6680
	11:8 commandments which I c you this day,	6680
	11:13 commandments which I c you this day,	6680
	11:22 all these commandments which I c you,	6680
	11:27 LORD your God, which I c you this day:	6680
	11:28 turn aside out of the way which I c you	6680
	12:11 thither shall ye bring all that I c you;	6680
	12:14 but there thou shalt do all that I c thee.	6680
	12:28 and hear all these words which I c thee,	6680
	12:32 What thing soever I c you, observe to do	6680
	13:18 to keep all his commandments which I c	6680
	15:5 commandments which I c thee this day.	6680
	15:11 therefore I c thee, saying, Thou shalt open	6680
	15:15 therefore I c thee this thing to day.	6680
	18:18 he shall speak unto them all that I shall c	6680
	19:7 Wherefore I c thee, saying, Thou shalt	6680
	19:9 which I c thee this day, to love the LORD	6680

Dt	24:18 therefore I c thee to do this thing.	6680
	24:22 Egypt: therefore I c thee to do this thing.	6680
	27:1 Keep all the commandments which I c	6680
	27:4 which I c you this day, in mount Ebal,	6680
	27:10 and his statutes, which I c thee this day.	6680
	28:1 to all his commandments which I c thee	6680
	28:8 The LORD shall c the blessing upon thee	6680
	28:13 which I c thee this day, to observe and	6680
	28:14 any of the words which I c thee this day,	6680
	28:15 and his statutes which I c thee this day;	6680
	30:2 obey his voice according to all that I c	6680
	30:8 do all his commandments which I c thee	6680
	30:11 For this commandment which I c thee	6680
	30:16 In that I c thee this day to love the LORD	6680
	32:46 which ye shall c your children to observe	6680
Jos	1:11 c the people, saying, Prepare you victuals;	6680
	3:8 thou shalt c the priests that bear the ark	6680
	4:3 c you, saying, Take you hence out	6680
	4:16 C the priests that bear the ark of	6680
	11:15 so did Moses c Joshua, and so did Joshua;	6680
1Sa	16:16 Let our lord now c thy servants which are	559
1Ki	5:6 c thou that they hew me cedar trees out	6680
	11:38 if thou wilt hearken unto all that I c thee,	6680
2Ch	7:13 or if I c the locusts to devour the land,	6680
Job	39:27 Doth the eagle mount up at thy c,	6310
Ps	42:8 Yet the LORD will c his lovingkindness	6680
	44:4 King, O God: c deliverances for Jacob.	6680
Isa	5:6 I will also c the clouds that they rain no	6680
	45:11 the work of my hands c ye me.	6680
Jer	1:7 and whatsoever I c thee thou shalt speak.	6680
	1:17 and speak unto them all that I c thee:	6680
	11:4 do them, according to all which I c you:	6680
	26:2 all the words that I c thee to speak unto	6680
	27:4 c them to say unto their masters, Thus	6680
	34:22 Behold, I will c, saith the LORD,	6680
La	1:10 whom thou didst c that they should not	6680
Am	9:3 will I c the serpent, and he shall bite	6680
	9:4 thence will I c the sword, and it shall slay	6680
	9:9 will I c, and I will sift the house of Israel	6680
Mt	4:3 c that these stones be made bread.	3004
	19:7 then c to give a writing of divorcement,	1781
	27:64 C therefore that the sepulchre be made	2753
Mk	10:3 said unto them, What did Moses c you?	1781
Lk	4:3 of God, c this stone that it be made bread.	3004
	8:31 they besought him that he would not c	2004
	9:54 wilt thou that we c fire to come down	3004
Jn	15:14 my friends, if ye do whatsoever I c you.	1781
	15:17 These things I c you, that ye love one	1781
Ac	5:28 Did not we straitly c you that you	3852+3853
	15:5 c to them to keep the law of Moses.	3853
	16:18 I c thee in the name of Jesus Christ to	3853
1Co	7:10 And unto the married I c, yet not I,	3853
2Th	3:4 and will do the things which we c you,	3853
	3:6 we c you, brethren, in the name of our	3853
	3:12 them that are such we c and exhort by	3853
1Ti	4:11 These things c and teach.	3853

COMMANDED (443) [COMMAND]

Ge	2:16 the LORD God c the man, saying,	6680
	3:11 whereof I c thee that thou shouldest not	6680
	3:17 eaten of the tree, of which I c thee,	6680
	6:22 according to all that God c him, so did he.	6680
	7:5 according unto all that the LORD c him.	6680
	7:9 and the female, as God had c Noah.	6680
	7:16 and female of all flesh, as God had c him:	6680
	12:20 Pharaoh c his men concerning him: and	6680
	21:4 being eight days old, as God had c him.	6680
	32:4 he c them, saying, Thus shall ye speak	6680
	32:17 he be the foremost, saying, When Esau my	6680
	32:19 so c he the second, and the third, and all	6680
	42:25 Joseph c to fill their sacks with corn,	6680
	44:1 he c the steward of his house, saying,	6680
	45:19 Now thou art c, this do ye; take you	6680
	47:11 in the land of Rameses, as Pharaoh had c.	6680
	50:2 Joseph c his servants the physicians to	6680
	50:12 his sons did unto him according as he c	6680
Ex	1:17 and did not as the king of Egypt c them,	1696
	4:28 and all the signs which he had c them.	6680
	5:6 Pharaoh c the same day the taskmasters	6680
	7:6 and Aaron did as the LORD c them,	6680
	7:10 and they did so as the LORD had c:	6680
	7:20 and Aaron did so, as the LORD c;	6680
	12:28 did as the LORD had c Moses and Aaron,	6680
	12:50 as the LORD c Moses and Aaron,	6680
	16:16 This is the thing which the LORD hath c,	6680
	16:34 As the LORD c Moses, so Aaron laid it up	6680
	19:7 all these words which the LORD c him.	6680
	23:15 as I c thee, in the time appointed of	6680
	29:35 according to all things which I have c	6680
	31:6 that they may make all that I have c thee;	6680
	31:11 to all that I have c thee shall they do.	6680
	32:8 quickly out of the way which I c them:	6680
	34:4 as the LORD had c him, and took in his	6680
	34:18 as I c thee, in the time of the month Abib:	6680
	34:34 the children of Israel that which he was c.	6680
	35:1 are the words which the LORD hath c,	6680
	35:4 This is the thing which the LORD c,	6680
	35:10 and make all that the LORD hath c;	6680
	35:29 which the LORD had c to be made by	6680
	36:1 according to all that the LORD had c.	6680
	36:5 of the work, which the LORD c to make.	6680
	38:22 made all that the LORD c Moses.	6680
	39:1 for Aaron; as the LORD c Moses.	6680
	39:5 fine twined linen; as the LORD c Moses.	6680
	39:7 children of Israel; as the LORD c Moses.	6680

C

C

Ex 39:21 from the ephod; as the Lᴏʀᴅ **c** Moses. 6680
 39:26 robe to minister *in*; as the Lᴏʀᴅ **c** Moses. 6680
 39:29 *of* needlework; as the Lᴏʀᴅ **c** Moses. 6680
 39:31 upon the mitre; as the Lᴏʀᴅ **c** Moses. 6680
 39:32 according to all that the Lᴏʀᴅ **c** Moses, 6680
 39:42 According to all that the Lᴏʀᴅ **c** Moses, 6680
 39:43 they had done it as the Lᴏʀᴅ had **c**, *even* 6680
 40:16 according to all that the Lᴏʀᴅ **c** him, 6680
 40:19 tent above upon it; as the Lᴏʀᴅ **c** Moses. 6680
 40:21 of the Testimony; as the Lᴏʀᴅ **c** Moses. 6680
 40:23 the Lᴏʀᴅ; as the Lᴏʀᴅ had **c** Moses. 6680
 40:25 the Lᴏʀᴅ; as the Lᴏʀᴅ **c** Moses. 6680
 40:27 incense thereon; as the Lᴏʀᴅ **c** Moses. 6680
 40:29 the meat offering; as the Lᴏʀᴅ **c** Moses. 6680
 40:32 they washed; as the Lᴏʀᴅ **c** Moses. 6680
Lev 7:36 Which the Lᴏʀᴅ **c** to be given them of 6680
 7:38 Which the Lᴏʀᴅ **c** Moses in mount Sinai, 6680
 7:38 in the day that he **c** the children of Israel 6680
 8: 4 Moses did as the Lᴏʀᴅ **c** him; 6680
 8: 5 This *is* the thing which the Lᴏʀᴅ **c** to be 6680
 8: 9 the holy crown; as the Lᴏʀᴅ **c** Moses. 6680
 8:13 upon them; as the Lᴏʀᴅ **c** Moses. 6680
 8:17 without the camp; as the Lᴏʀᴅ **c** Moses. 6680
 8:21 unto the Lᴏʀᴅ; as the Lᴏʀᴅ **c** Moses. 6680
 8:29 it was Moses' part; as the Lᴏʀᴅ **c** Moses. 6680
 8:31 as I **c**, saying, Aaron and his sons shall eat 6680
 8:34 done this day, as the Lᴏʀᴅ **c** to do, 6680
 8:35 the Lᴏʀᴅ, that ye die not: for so I am **c**. 6680
 8:36 his sons did all things which the Lᴏʀᴅ **c** 6680
 9: 5 they brought *that* which Moses **c** before 6680
 9: 6 This *is* the thing which the Lᴏʀᴅ **c** *that* 6680
 9: 7 an atonement for them; as the Lᴏʀᴅ **c**. 6680
 9:10 upon the altar; as the Lᴏʀᴅ **c** Moses. 6680
 9:21 offering before the Lᴏʀᴅ; as Moses **c**. 6680
 10: 1 before the Lᴏʀᴅ, which he **c** them not. 6680
 10:13 of the Lᴏʀᴅ made by fire: for so I am **c**. 6680
 10:15 by a statute for ever; as the Lᴏʀᴅ hath **c**. 6680
 10:18 have eaten it in the holy *place*, as I **c**. 6680
 16:34 a year. And he did as the Lᴏʀᴅ **c** Moses. 6680
 17: 2 This *is* the thing which the Lᴏʀᴅ hath **c**, 6680
 24:23 the children of Israel did as the Lᴏʀᴅ **c** 6680
 27:34 which the Lᴏʀᴅ **c** Moses for the children 6680
Nu 1:19 As the Lᴏʀᴅ **c** Moses, so he numbered 6680
 1:54 according to all that the Lᴏʀᴅ **c** Moses, 6680
 2:33 children of Israel; as the Lᴏʀᴅ **c** Moses, 6680
 2:34 according to all that the Lᴏʀᴅ **c** Moses: 6680
 3:16 to the word of the Lᴏʀᴅ, as he was **c**. 6680
 3:42 Moses numbered, as the Lᴏʀᴅ **c** him, 6680
 3:51 of the Lᴏʀᴅ, as the Lᴏʀᴅ **c** Moses. 6680
 4:49 numbered of him, as the Lᴏʀᴅ **c** Moses. 6680
 8: 3 the candlestick, as the Lᴏʀᴅ **c** Moses. 6680
 8:20 Lᴏʀᴅ **c** Moses concerning the Levites, 6680
 8:22 as the Lᴏʀᴅ had **c** Moses concerning 6680
 9: 5 according to all that the Lᴏʀᴅ **c** Moses, 6680
 15:23 *Even* all that the Lᴏʀᴅ hath **c** you by 6680
 15:23 from the day that the Lᴏʀᴅ **c** *Moses,* and 6680
 15:36 and he died; as the Lᴏʀᴅ **c** Moses. 6680
 16:47 Aaron took as Moses **c**, and ran into 1696
 17:11 Moses did *so*: as the Lᴏʀᴅ **c** him, 6680
 19: 2 of the law which the Lᴏʀᴅ hath **c**, 6680
 20: 9 rod from before the Lᴏʀᴅ, as he **c** him. 6680
 20:27 Moses did as the Lᴏʀᴅ **c**: and they went 6680
 26: 4 as the Lᴏʀᴅ **c** Moses and the children of 6680
 27:11 of judgment, as the Lᴏʀᴅ **c** Moses. 6680
 27:22 Moses did as the Lᴏʀᴅ **c** him: and 6680
 27:23 as the Lᴏʀᴅ **c** by the hand of Moses. 1696
 29:40 according to all that the Lᴏʀᴅ **c** Moses. 6680
 30: 1 This *is* the thing which the Lᴏʀᴅ hath **c**. 6680
 30:16 which the Lᴏʀᴅ **c** Moses, between a man 6680
 31: 7 the Midianites, as the Lᴏʀᴅ **c** Moses; 6680
 31:21 of the law which the Lᴏʀᴅ **c** Moses; 6680
 31:31 Eleazar the priest did as the Lᴏʀᴅ **c** 6680
 31:41 Eleazar the priest, as the Lᴏʀᴅ **c** Moses. 6680
 31:47 of the Lᴏʀᴅ; as the Lᴏʀᴅ **c** Moses. 6680
 32:28 So concerning them Moses **c** Eleazar 6680
 34:13 Moses **c** the children of Israel, saying, 6680
 34:13 which the Lᴏʀᴅ **c** to give unto the nine 6680
 34:29 These *are they* whom the Lᴏʀᴅ **c** to 6680
 36: 2 The Lᴏʀᴅ **c** my lord to give the land for 6680
 36: 2 my lord was **c** by the Lᴏʀᴅ to give 6680
 36: 5 Moses **c** the children of Israel according 6680
 36:10 Even as the Lᴏʀᴅ **c** Moses, so did 6680
 36:13 which the Lᴏʀᴅ **c** by the hand of Moses 6680
Dt 1:18 I **c** you at that time all the things which 6680
 1:19 the Amorites, as the Lᴏʀᴅ our God **c** us; 6680
 1:41 according to all that the Lᴏʀᴅ our God **c** 6680
 3:18 I **c** you at that time, saying, The Lᴏʀᴅ 6680
 3:21 I **c** Joshua at that time, saying, Thine eyes 6680
 4: 5 even as the Lᴏʀᴅ my God **c** me, 6680
 4:13 which he **c** you to perform, *even* ten 6680
 4:14 the Lᴏʀᴅ **c** me at that time to teach you 6680
 5:12 as the Lᴏʀᴅ thy God hath **c** thee. 6680
 5:15 the Lᴏʀᴅ thy God **c** thee to keep 6680
 5:16 as the Lᴏʀᴅ thy God hath **c** thee; 6680
 5:32 as the Lᴏʀᴅ your God hath **c** you: 6680
 5:33 which the Lᴏʀᴅ your God hath **c** you, 6680
 6: 1 which the Lᴏʀᴅ your God **c** to teach you, 6680
 6:17 and his statutes, which he hath **c** thee. 6680
 6:20 which the Lᴏʀᴅ our God hath **c** you? 6680
 6:24 the Lᴏʀᴅ **c** us to do all these statutes, 6680
 6:25 the Lᴏʀᴅ our God, as he hath **c** us. 6680
 9:12 aside out of the way which I **c** them; 6680
 9:16 of the way which the Lᴏʀᴅ had **c** you. 6680
 10: 5 and there they be, as the Lᴏʀᴅ **c** me. 6680
 12:21 as I have **c** thee, and thou shalt eat in thy 6680

Dt 13: 5 the Lᴏʀᴅ thy God **c** thee to walk in. 6680
 17: 3 the host of heaven, which I have not **c**; 6680
 18:20 which I have not **c** him to speak, 6680
 20:17 as the Lᴏʀᴅ thy God hath **c** thee: 6680
 24: 8 as I **c** them, *so* ye shall observe to do. 6680
 26:13 hy commandments which thou hast **c** me: 6680
 26:14 done according to all that thou hast **c** 6680
 27: 1 Moses with the elders of Israel, 6680
 28:45 and his statutes which he **c** thee: 6680
 29: 1 which the Lᴏʀᴅ **c** Moses to make with 6680
 31: 5 the commandments which I have **c** you. 6680
 31:10 Moses **c** them, saying, At the end of *every* 6680
 31:25 That Moses **c** the Levites, which bare 6680
 31:29 turn aside from the way which I have **c** 6680
 33: 4 Moses **c** us a law, *even* the inheritance of 6680
 34: 9 unto him, and did as the Lᴏʀᴅ **c** Moses. 6680
Jos 1: 7 the law, which Moses my servant **c** thee: 6680
 1: 9 Have not I **c** thee? Be strong and of a 6680
 1:10 Joshua **c** the officers of the people, saying, 6680
 1:13 Moses the servant of the Lᴏʀᴅ **c** you, 6680
 3: 3 they **c** the people, saying, When ye see 6680
 4: 8 the children of Israel did so as Joshua **c**, 6680
 4:10 Lᴏʀᴅ **c** Joshua to speak unto the people, 6680
 4:10 according to all that Moses **c** Joshua: 6680
 4:17 Joshua therefore **c** the priests, saying, 6680
 6:10 Joshua had **c** the people, saying, Ye shall 6680
 7:11 transgressed my covenant which I **c** them: 6680
 8: 4 he **c** them, saying, Behold, ye shall lie in 6680
 8: 8 the Lᴏʀᴅ shall ye do. See, I have **c** you. 6680
 8:27 the word of the Lᴏʀᴅ which he **c** Joshua. 6680
 8:29 Joshua **c** that they should take his carcase 6680
 8:31 As Moses the servant of the Lᴏʀᴅ **c** 6680
 8:33 as Moses the servant of the Lᴏʀᴅ had **c** 6680
 8:35 There was not a word of all that Moses **c**, 6680
 9:24 how that the Lᴏʀᴅ thy God **c** his servant 6680
 10:27 Joshua **c**, and they took them down off 6680
 10:40 as the Lᴏʀᴅ God of Israel **c**. 6680
 11:12 as Moses the servant of the Lᴏʀᴅ **c**. 6680
 11:15 As the Lᴏʀᴅ **c** Moses his servant, 6680
 11:15 undone of all that the Lᴏʀᴅ **c** Moses. 6680
 11:20 destroy them, as the Lᴏʀᴅ **c** Moses. 6680
 13: 6 for an inheritance, as I have **c** thee. 6680
 14: 2 as the Lᴏʀᴅ **c** by the hand of Moses, 6680
 14: 5 As the Lᴏʀᴅ **c** Moses, so the children of 6680
 17: 4 The Lᴏʀᴅ **c** Moses to give us an 6680
 21: 2 The Lᴏʀᴅ **c** by the hand of Moses to give 6680
 21: 8 as the Lᴏʀᴅ **c** by the hand of Moses. 6680
 22: 2 Moses the servant of the Lᴏʀᴅ **c** you, 6680
 22: 2 have obeyed my voice in all that I **c** you: 6680
 23:16 which he **c** you, and have gone and 6680
Jdg 2:20 my covenant which I **c** their fathers, 6680
 3: 4 which he **c** their fathers by the hand of 6680
 4: 6 Hath not the Lᴏʀᴅ God of Israel **c**, 6680
 13:14 nor eat any unclean *thing*: all that I **c** her 6680
 21:10 **c** them, saying, Go and smite 6680
 21:20 Therefore they **c** the children of Benjamin, 6680
Ru 2:15 to glean, Boaz **c** his young men, saying, 6680
1Sa 2:29 which I have **c** in *my* habitation; 6680
 13:13 of the Lᴏʀᴅ thy God, which he **c** thee: 6680
 13:14 the Lᴏʀᴅ hath **c** him to be captain over 6680
 13:14 thou hast not kept *that* which the Lᴏʀᴅ **c** 6680
 17:20 and took, and went, as Jesse had **c** him; 6680
 18:22 Saul's servants, *saying*, Commune 6680
 20:29 he hath **c** me *to be there:* and now, 6680
 21: 2 The king hath **c** me a business, 6680
 21: 2 I send thee, and what I have **c** thee: 6680
2Sa 4:12 David **c** *his* young men, and they slew 6680
 5:25 David did so, as the Lᴏʀᴅ had **c** him; 6680
 7: 7 whom I **c** to feed my people Israel, saying, 6680
 7:11 since the time that I **c** judges *to be* over 6680
 9:11 that my lord the king hath **c** his servant, 6680
 13:28 Now Absalom had **c** his servants, saying, 6680
 13:28 have not I **c** you? be courageous, 6680
 13:29 did unto Amnon as Absalom had **c**. 6680
 18: 5 the king **c** Joab and Abishai and Ittai, 6680
 21:14 they performed all that the king **c**. 6680
 24:19 saying of Gad, went up as the Lᴏʀᴅ **c**. 6680
1Ki 2:46 So the king **c** Benaiah the son of Jehoiada; 6680
 5:17 the king **c**, and they brought great stones, 6680
 8:58 his judgments, which he **c** our fathers. 6680
 9: 4 to do according to all that I have **c** thee, 6680
 11:10 had **c** him concerning this thing, that *he* 6680
 11:10 but he kept not *that* which the Lᴏʀᴅ **c**. 6680
 11:11 and my statutes, which I have **c** thee, 6680
 13:21 which the Lᴏʀᴅ thy God **c** thee, 6680
 15: 5 turned not aside from any *thing* that he **c** 6680
 17: 4 and I have **c** the ravens to feed thee there. 6680
 17: 9 I have **c** a widow woman there to sustain 6680
 22:31 the king of Syria **c** his thirty and 6680
2Ki 11: 5 he **c** them, saying, This *is* the thing that 6680
 11: 9 to all *things* that Jehoiada the priest **c**: 6680
 11:15 Jehoiada the priest **c** the captains of 6680
 14: 6 where *in* the Lᴏʀᴅ **c**, saying, The fathers 6680
 16:15 king Ahaz **c** Urijah the priest, saying, 6680
 16:16 priest, according to all that king Ahaz **c**. 6680
 17:13 according to all the law which I **c** your 6680
 17:27 the king of Assyria **c**, saying, Carry thither 6680
 17:34 commandment which the Lᴏʀᴅ **c** 6680
 18: 6 which the Lᴏʀᴅ **c** Moses. 6680
 18:12 all that Moses the servant of the Lᴏʀᴅ **c**, 6680
 21: 8 to do according to all that I have **c** them, 6680
 21: 8 all the law that my servant Moses **c** them. 6680
 22:12 the king **c** Hilkiah the priest, and Ahikam 6680
 23: 4 the king **c** Hilkiah the high priest, 6680

2Ki 23:21 the king **c** all the people, saying, Keep 6680
1Ch 6:49 all that Moses the servant of God had **c**. 6680
 14:16 David therefore did as God **c** him: and 6680
 15:15 as Moses **c** according to the word of 6680
 16:15 the word *which* he **c** to a thousand 6680
 16:40 in the law of the Lᴏʀᴅ, which he **c** Israel; 6680
 17: 6 whom I **c** to feed my people, saying, 6680
 17:10 since the time that I **c** judges *to be* over 6680
 21:17 not I *that* **c** the people to be numbered? 559
 21:18 the angel of the Lᴏʀᴅ **c** Gad to say to 559
 21:27 the Lᴏʀᴅ **c** the angel; and he put up his 559
 22: 2 David **c** to gather together the strangers 559
 22:17 David also **c** all the princes of Israel to help 6680
 23:31 according to the **order** **c** unto them, 4941
 24:19 as the Lᴏʀᴅ God of Israel had **c** him. 6680
2Ch 7:17 do according to all that I have **c** thee, 6680
 8:14 for so had David the man of God **c**. 4687
 14: 4 Judah to seek the Lᴏʀᴅ God of their 559
 18:30 Now the king of Syria had **c** the captains 6680
 23: 8 to all *things* that Jehoiada the priest had **c**, 6680
 25: 4 where the Lᴏʀᴅ **c**, saying, The fathers 6680
 29:21 he **c** the priests the sons of Aaron to offer 559
 29:24 for the king *that* the burnt offering and 559
 29:27 Hezekiah **c** to offer the burnt offering upon 559
 29:30 the princes **c** the Levites to *sing* praise unto 559
 31: 4 Moreover he **c** the people that dwelt in 559
 31:11 Hezekiah **c** to prepare chambers in the 559
 32:12 and **c** Judah and Jerusalem, saying, 559
 33: 8 take heed to do all that I have **c** them, 6680
 33:16 **c** Judah to serve the Lᴏʀᴅ God of Israel. 559
 34:20 the king **c** Hilkiah, and Ahikam the son of 6680
 35:21 for God **c** me to make haste: forbear thee 559
Ezr 4: 3 as king Cyrus the king of Persia hath **c** us. 6680
 4:19 I **c**, and search hath been made, 2942+7761
 5: 3 Who hath **c** you to build this house, 2942+7761
 5: 9 Who **c** you to build this house, 2942+7761
 7:23 Whatsoever *is* **c** by the God of heaven, 2941
 9:11 which thou hast **c** by thy servants 6680
Ne 8: 1 which the Lᴏʀᴅ had **c** to Israel. 6680
 8:14 the law which the Lᴏʀᴅ had **c** by Moses, 6680
 13: 5 which was **c** *to be given* to the Levites, 4687
 13: 9 I **c**, and they cleansed the chambers: and 559
 13:19 I **c** that the gates should be shut, 559
 13:22 I **c** the Levites that they should cleanse 559
Est 1:10 he **c** Mehuman, Biztha, Harbona, Bigtha, 559
 1:17 The king Ahasuerus **c** Vashti the queen 559
 3: 2 for the king had so **c** concerning him. 6680
 3:12 Haman had **c** unto the king's lieutenants, 6680
 4:13 Mordecai to answer Esther, Think not 559
 4:17 did according to all that Esther had **c** him. 6680
 6: 1 he **c** to bring the book of records of 559
 8: 9 to all that Mordecai **c** unto the Jews, 6680
 9:14 the king **c** it so to be done: and the decree 559
 9:25 he **c** by letters *that* his wicked device, 559
Job 38:12 Hast thou **c** the morning since thy days; 6680
 42: 9 and did according as the Lᴏʀᴅ **c** them: 1696
Ps 7: 6 for me *to* the judgment *that* thou hast **c**. 6680
 33: 9 and it *was* done; he **c**, and it stood fast. 6680
 68:28 Thy God hath **c** thy strength: strengthen, 6680
 78: 5 a law in Israel, which he **c** our fathers, 6680
 78:23 Though he had **c** the clouds from above, 6680
 105: 8 the word *which* he **c** to a thousand 6680
 106:34 *concerning* whom the Lᴏʀᴅ **c** them: 6680
 111: 9 he hath **c** his covenant for ever: holy and 6680
 119: 4 Thou hast **c** *us* to keep thy precepts 6680
 119:138 Thy testimonies *that* thou hast **c** *are* 6680
 133: 3 for there the Lᴏʀᴅ **c** the blessing, 6680
 148: 5 for he **c**, and they were created. 6680
Isa 13: 3 I have **c** my sanctified ones, I have also 6680
 34:16 for my mouth it hath **c**, and his spirit it 6680
 45:12 the heavens, and all their host have I **c**. 6680
 48: 5 and my molten image, hath **c** them. 6680
Jer 7:22 nor **c** them in the day that I brought them 6680
 7:23 thing **c** I them, saying, Obey my voice, 6680
 7:23 walk ye in all the ways that I have **c** you, 6680
 7:31 which I **c** *them* not, neither came it into 6680
 11: 4 Which I **c** your fathers in the day that I 6680
 11: 8 of this covenant, which I **c** *them* to do; 6680
 13: 5 hid it by Euphrates, as the Lᴏʀᴅ **c** me. 6680
 13: 6 from thence, which I **c** thee to hide there. 6680
 14:14 I **c** them not, neither have I **c** them, 6680
 17:22 ye the sabbath day, as I **c** your fathers. 6680
 19: 5 which I **c** not, nor spake *it*, neither came 6680
 23:32 yet I sent them not, nor **c** them: 6680
 26: 8 had **c** *him* to speak unto all the people, 6680
 29:23 in my name, which I have not **c** them; 6680
 32:35 which I **c** them not, neither came it into 6680
 35: 6 Jonadab the son of Rechab our father **c** 6680
 35:10 to all that Jonadab our father **c** us. 6680
 35:14 that he **c** his sons not to drink wine, 6680
 35:16 of their father, which he **c** them; 6680
 35:18 according unto all that he hath **c** you: 6680
 36: 5 Jeremiah **c** Baruch, saying, I *am* shut up; 6680
 36: 8 to all that Jeremiah the prophet **c** him, 6680
 36:26 the king **c** Jerahmeel the son of 6680
 37:21 Zedekiah the king *that* they should 6680
 38:10 the king **c** Ebed-melech the Ethiopian, 6680
 38:27 to all these words that the king had **c**. 6680
 50:21 and do according to all that I have **c** thee. 6680
 51:59 The word which Jeremiah the prophet **c** 6680
La 1:17 the Lᴏʀᴅ hath **c** concerning Jacob, 6680
 2:17 he hath fulfilled his word that he had **c** in 6680
Eze 9:11 I have done as thou hast **c** me. 6680
 10: 6 *that* when he had **c** the man clothed with 6680
 12: 7 did so as I was **c**: I brought forth my stuff 6680

C

Eze	24:18 and I did in the morning as I was **c.**	6680
	37: 7 So I prophesied as I was **c:** and as I	6680
	37:10 I prophesied as he **c** me, and the breath	6680
Da	2: 2 the king **c** to call the magicians,	559
	2:12 **c** to destroy all the wise *men* of Babylon.	560
	2:46 **c** that *they* should offer an oblation and	560
	3: 4 To you it is **c,** O people, nations,	560
	3:13 in *his* rage and fury **c** to bring Shadrach,	560
	3:19 he **c** that *they* should heat the furnace one	560
	3:20 he **c** the most mighty men that *were* in his	560
	4:26 they **c** to leave the stump of the tree	560
	5: 2 to bring the golden and silver vessels	560
	5:29 Belshazzar, and they clothed Daniel with	560
	6:16 the king **c,** and they brought Daniel,	560
	6:23 **c** that *they* should take Daniel up out of	560
	6:24 the king **c,** and they brought those men	560
Am	2:12 **c** the prophets, saying, Prophesy not.	6680
Zec	1: 6 which I **c** my servants the prophets,	6680
Mal	4: 4 which I **c** unto him in Horeb for all Israel,	6680
Mt	8: 4 offer the gift that Moses **c** for a testimony	4367
	10: 5 twelve Jesus sent forth, and **c** them,	3853
	14: 9 with him at meat, and **c** *it* to be given *her.*	2753
	14:19 And he **c** the multitude to sit down on	2753
	15: 4 For God **c,** saying, Honour thy father and	1781
	15:35 And he **c** the multitude to sit down on	2753
	18:25 his lord **c** him to be sold, and his wife,	2753
	21: 6 disciples went, and did as Jesus **c** them,	4367
	27:58 Then Pilate **c** the body to be delivered.	2753
	28:20 all *things* whatsoever I have **c** you:	1781
Mk	1:44 cleansing *those things* which Moses **c,**	4367
	5:43 **c** that *something* should be given her	3004
	6: 8 And **c** them that they should take nothing	3853
	6:27 and **c** his head to be brought:	2004
	6:39 And he **c** them to make all sit down by	2004
	8: 6 And he **c** the people to sit down on	3853
	8: 7 and **c** to set them also before *them.*	3004
	10:49 Jesus stood still, and **c** him to be called.	3004
	11: 6 they said unto them even as Jesus had **c:**	1781
	13:34 man his work, and **c** the porter to watch.	1781
Lk	5:14 for thy cleansing, according as Moses **c,**	4367
	8:29 he had **c** the unclean spirit to come out	3853
	8:55 and he **c** to give her meat.	1299
	9:21 and **c** *them* to tell no *man* that *thing;*	3853
	14:22 it is done as thou hast **c,** and yet there is	2004
	17: 9 he did the *things* that were **c** him?	1299
	17:10 done all those *things* which are **c** you,	1299
	18:40 and **c** him to be brought unto him:	2753
	19:15 he **c** these servants to be called unto him,	3004
Jn	8: 5 Now Moses in the law **c** us, that such	1781
Ac	1: 4 **c** them that *they* should not depart from	3853
	4:15 But when they had **c** them to go aside out	2753
	4:18 **c** them not to speak at all nor teach in	3853
	5:34 **c** to put the apostles forth a little space;	2753
	5:40 beaten *them,* they **c** that *they* should not	3853
	8:38 And he **c** the chariot to stand still: and	2753
	10:33 to hear all *things* that are **c** thee of God.	4367
	10:42 And he **c** us to preach unto the people,	3853
	10:48 he **c** them to be baptized in the name	4367
	12:19 and **c** that *they* should be put to death.	2753
	13:47 so hath the Lord **c** us, *saying,* I have set	1781
	16:22 rent off their clothes, and **c** to beat *them.*	2753
	18: 2 Claudius had **c** all Jews to depart from	1299
	21:33 and **c** *him* to be bound with two chains;	2753
	21:34 he **c** him to be carried into the castle.	2753
	22:24 The chief captain **c** him to be brought into	2753
	22:30 **c** the chief priests and all their council	2753
	23: 2 And the high priest Ananias **c** them that	2004
	23:10 the soldiers to go down, and to take him	2753
	23:31 as it was **c** them, took Paul,	1299
	23:35 And he **c** him to be kept in Herod's	2753
	24:23 And he **c** a centurion to keep Paul,	1299
	25: 6 the judgment seat, **c** Paul to be brought.	2753
	25:17 and **c** the man to be brought *forth.*	2753
	25:21 I **c** him to be kept till I might send him to	2753
	27:43 **c** that they which could swim should cast	2753
1Co	14:34 but *they are* **c** to be under obedience,	NIG
2Co	4: 6 who **c** the light to shine out of darkness,	3004
1Th	4:11 work with your own hands, as we **c** you;	3853
2Th	3:10 this we **c** you, that if any would not work,	3853
Heb	12:20 they could not endure that which was **c,**	1291
Rev	9: 4 it was **c** them that they should not hurt	3004

COMMANDEDST (4) [COMMAND]

Ne	1: 7 which thou **c** thy servant Moses.	6680
	1: 8 the word that thou **c** thy servant Moses,	6680
	9:14 **c** them precepts, statutes, and laws,	6680
Jer	32:23 they have done nothing of all that thou **c**	6680

COMMANDER (1) [COMMAND]

Isa	55: 4 the people, a leader and **c** to the people.	6680

COMMANDEST (3) [COMMAND]

Jos	1:16 All that thou **c** us we will do,	6680
	1:18 unto thy words in all that thou **c** him,	6680
Ac	23: 3 **c** me to be smitten contrary to the law?	2753

COMMANDETH (13) [COMMAND]

Ex	16:32 This *is* the thing which the Lord **c,**	6680
Nu	32:25 Thy servants will do as my lord **c.**	6680
Job	7: 7 Which **c** the sun, and it riseth not;	559
	36:10 and **c** that they return from iniquity.	559
	36:32 it *is* not to shine by the *cloud* that cometh	6680
	37:12 that they may do whatsoever he **c** them	6680
Ps	107:25 For he **c,** and raiseth the stormy wind,	559
La	3:37 it cometh to pass, *when* the Lord **c** *it* not?	6680

Am	6:11 the Lord **c,** and he will smite the great	6680
Mk	1:27 for with authority **c** he even the unclean	2004
Lk	4:36 and power he **c** the unclean spirits,	2004
	8:25 for he **c** even the winds and water,	2004
Ac	17:30 but now **c** all men every where to repent:	3853

COMMANDING (4) [COMMAND]

Ge	49:33 Jacob had made an end of **c** his sons,	6680
Mt	11: 1 when Jesus had made an end of **c** his	1299
Ac	24: 8 **c** his accusers to come unto thee:	2753
1Ti	4: 3 to marry, *and* **c** to abstain from meats,	NIG

COMMANDMENT (177) [COMMAND]

Ge	45:21 according to the **c** of Pharaoh,	6310
Ex	17: 1 according to the **c** of the Lord,	6310
	25:22 all *things* which I will **give** thee **in c** unto	6680
	34:32 he **gave** them **in c** all that the Lord had	6680
	36: 6 Moses **gave c,** and they caused it to be	6680
	38:21 was counted, according to the **c** of Moses,	6310
Nu	3:39 Aaron numbered at the **c** of the Lord,	6310
	4:37 Aaron did number according to the **c** of	6310
	4:41 Aaron did number according to the **c** of	6310
	4:49 According to the **c** of the Lord they	6310
	9:18 At the **c** of the Lord the children of	6310
	9:18 and at the **c** of the Lord they pitched:	6310
	9:20 according to the **c** of the Lord they	6310
	9:20 according to the **c** of the Lord they	6310
	9:23 At the **c** of the Lord they rested in	6310
	9:23 and at the **c** of the Lord they journeyed:	6310
	9:23 at the **c** of the Lord by the hand of	6310
	10:13 the **c** of the Lord by the hand of Moses.	6310
	13: 3 Moses by the **c** of the Lord sent them	6310
	14:41 Wherefore now do ye transgress the **c** of	6310
	15:31 hath broken his **c,** that soul shall utterly	4687
	23:20 Behold, I have received **c** to bless: and	NIH
	24:13 I cannot go beyond the **c** of the Lord,	6310
	27:14 For ye rebelled against my **c** in the desert	6310
	33: 2 to their journeys by the **c** of the Lord:	6310
	33:38 up into mount Hor at the **c** of the Lord,	6310
Dt	1: 3 the Lord had **given** him **in c** unto them;	6680
	1:26 rebelled against the **c** of the Lord your	6310
	1:43 rebelled against the **c** of the Lord,	6310
	9:23 you rebelled against the **c** of the Lord	6310
	17:20 that *he* turn not aside from the **c,**	4687
	30:11 this **c** which I command thee *this* day,	4687
Jos	1:18 *he be* that doth rebel against thy **c,**	6310
	8: 8 according to the **c** of the Lord shall ye	1697
	15:13 according to the **c** of the Lord to Joshua,	6310
	17: 4 Therefore according to the **c** of the Lord	6310
	21: 3 at the **c** of the Lord, these cities and	6310
	22: 3 have kept the charge of the **c** of the Lord	4687
	22: 5 diligent heed to do the **c** and the law,	6680
1Sa	12:14 not rebel against the **c** of the Lord, then	6310
	12:15 rebel against the **c** of the Lord, then	6310
	13:13 thou hast not kept the **c** of the Lord thy	4687
	15:24 for I have transgressed the **c** of the Lord,	6310
2Sa	12: 9 Wherefore hast thou despised the **c** of	1697
1Ki	2:43 and the **c** that I have charged thee with?	6310
	13:21 hast not kept the **c** which the Lord thy	4687
2Ki	17:34 **c** which the Lord commanded	4687
	17:37 the ordinances, and the law, and the **c,**	4687
	18:36 for the king's **c** was, saying, Answer him	4687
	23:35 the money according to the **c** of Pharaoh:	6310
	24: 3 Surely at the **c** of the Lord came *this*	6310
1Ch	12:32 and all their brethren *were* at their **c.**	6310
	14:12 David **gave a c,** and they were burnt with	559
	28:21 and all the people *will be* wholly at thy **c.**	1697
2Ch	8:13 offering according to the **c** of Moses,	4687
	8:15 they departed not *from* the **c** of the king	4687
	14: 4 their fathers, and to do the law and the **c.**	4687
	19:10 and blood, between law and **c,**	4687
	24: 6 *according to* the **c** of Moses the servant of	NIH
	24: 8 at the king's **c** they made a chest, and set	559
	24:21 stoned him *with* stones at the **c** of the	4687
	29:15 and came, according to the **c** of the king,	4687
	29:25 according to the **c** of David, and of Gad	4687
	29:25 *so was* the **c** of the Lord by his prophets.	4687
	30: 6 Judah, and according to the **c** of the king,	4687
	30:12 them one heart to do the **c** of the king	4687
	31: 5 as soon as the **c** came abroad, the children	1697
	31:13 at the **c** of Hezekiah the king,	4662
	35:10 in their courses, according to the king's **c.**	4687
	35:15 according to the **c** of David, and Asaph,	4687
	35:16 according to the **c** of king Josiah.	4687
Ezr	4:21 now to cause these men to cease,	2942
	4:21 until *another* shall be given from me.	2941
	6:14 finished *it,* according to the **c** of the God	2941
	6:14 according to the **c** of Cyrus, and Darius,	2942
	8:17 I **sent** them **with c** unto Iddo the chief at	6680
	10: 3 of those that tremble at the **c** of our God;	4687
Ne	11:23 For *it was* the king's **c** concerning them,	4687
	12:24 according to the **c** of David the man of	4687
	12:45 according to the **c** of David,	4687
Est	1:12 come at the king's **c** by *his* chamberlains:	1697
	1:15 she hath not performed the **c** of the king	3982
	1:19 let there go a royal **c** from him, and let it	1697
	2: 8 the king's **c** and his decree was heard,	1697
	2:20 for Esther did the **c** of Mordecai, like as	3982
	3: 3 Why transgressest thou the king's **c?**	4687
	3:14 The copy of the writing for a **c** to be given	1881
	3:15 being hastened by the king's **c,**	1697
	4: 3 whithersoever the king's **c** and his decree	1697
	4: 5 **gave** him a **c** to Mordecai, to know what	6680
	4:10 and **gave** him **c** unto Mordecai:	6680

Est	8:13 The copy of the writing for a **c** to be given	1881
	8:14 and pressed on by the king's **c,**	1697
	8:17 whithersoever the king's **c** and his decree	1697
	9: 1 the king's **c** and his decree drew near	1697
Job	23:12 Neither have I gone back from the **c** of his	4687
Ps	19: 8 the **c** of the Lord *is* pure,	4687
	71: 3 thou hast **given** to save me; for thou *art*	6680
	119:96 perfection: *but* thy **c** *is* exceeding broad.	4687
	147:15 He sendeth forth his **c** *upon* earth:	565
Pr	6:20 keep thy father's **c,** and forsake not the	4687
	6:23 For the **c** *is* a lamp; and the law *is* light;	4687
	8:29 that the waters should not pass his **c:**	6310
	13:13 he that feareth the **c** shall be rewarded.	4687
	19:16 that keepeth the **c** keepeth his own soul;	4687
Ecc	8: 2 I *counsel thee* to keep the king's **c,**	6310
	8: 5 Whoso keepeth the **c** shall feel no evil	4687
Isa	23:11 the Lord hath **given** a **c** against	6680
	36:21 for the king's **c** was, saying, Answer him	4687
Jer	35:14 they drink none, but obey their father's **c:**	4687
	35:16 have performed the **c** of their father,	4687
	35:18 Because ye have obeyed the **c** of Jonadab	4687
La	1:18 for I have rebelled against his **c:**	6310
Da	3:22 because the king's **c** *was* urgent,	4406
	9:23 the beginning of thy supplications the **c**	1697
	9:25 from the going forth of the **c** to restore	1697
Hos	5:11 because he willingly walked after the **c,**	6673
Na	1:14 the Lord hath **given** a **c** concerning thee,	6680
Mal	2: 1 And now, O ye priests, this **c** *is* for you.	4687
	2: 4 ye shall know that I have sent this **c** unto	4687
Mt	8:18 he **gave c** to depart unto the other side.	2753
	15: 3 Why do you also transgress the **c** of God	1785
	15: 6 he shall be free. Thus have ye made the **c**	1785
	22:36 Master, which *is* the great **c** in the law?	1785
	22:38 This is the first and great **c.**	1785
Mk	7: 8 For laying aside the **c** of God, ye hold	1785
	7: 9 them, Full well ye reject the **c** of God,	1785
	12:28 asked him, Which is the first **c** of all?	1785
	12:30 with all thy strength: this *is* the first **c.**	1785
	12:31 There is none other **c** greater than these.	1785
Lk	15:29 neither transgressed I at any time thy **c:**	1785
	23:56 rested the sabbath day according to the **c.**	1785
Jn	10:18 This **c** have I received of my Father.	1785
	11:57 and the Pharisees had given a **c,**	1785
	12:49 he gave me a **c,** what I should say,	1785
	12:50 And I know that his **c** is life everlasting:	1785
	13:34 A new **c** I give unto you, That ye love one	1785
	14:31 as the Father **gave** me **c,** *even* so I do.	1781
	15:12 This is my **c,** That ye love one another,	1785
Ac	15:24 the law: to whom we **gave** no such **c:**	1291
	17:15 receiving a **c** unto Silas and Timotheus	1785
	23:30 **gave c** to *his* accusers also to say before	3853
	25:23 at Festus' **c** Paul was brought *forth.*	2753
Ro	7: 8 But sin, taking occasion by the **c,**	1785
	7: 9 but when the **c** came, sin revived,	1785
	7:10 And the **c,** which *was ordained* to life,	1785
	7:11 For sin, taking occasion by the **c,**	1785
	7:12 holy, and the **c** holy, and just, and good.	1785
	7:13 that sin by the **c** might become exceeding	1785
	13: 9 and if *there be* any other **c,** it is briefly	1785
	16:26 according to the **c** of the everlasting God,	2003
1Co	7: 6 I speak this by permission, *and* not of **c.**	2003
	7:25 Now concerning virgins I have no **c** of	2003
2Co	8: 8 I speak not by **c,** but by occasion of	2003
Eph	6: 2 (which is the first **c** with promise;)	1785
1Ti	1: 1 an apostle of Jesus Christ by the **c** of God	2003
	1: 5 Now the end of the **c** is charity out of a	3852
	6:14 That thou keep *this* **c** without spot,	1785
Tit	1: 3 me according to the **c** of God our Saviour;	2003
Heb	7: 5 to take tithes of the people according to	1785
	7:16 not after the law of a carnal **c,** but after	1785
	7:18 For there is verily a disannulling of the **c**	1785
	11:22 of Israel; and **gave c** concerning his bones.	1781
	11:23 and they were not afraid of the king's **c.**	1297
2Pe	2:21 turn from the holy **c** delivered unto them.	1785
	3: 2 of the **c** of us the apostles of the Lord and	1785
1Jn	2: 7 I write no new **c** unto you, but an old	1785
	2: 7 an old **c** which ye had from the beginning.	1785
	2: 7 old **c** is the word which ye have heard	1785
	2: 8 Again, a new **c** I write unto you,	1785
	3:23 this is his **c,** That we should believe on	1785
	3:23 and love one another, as he gave us **c.**	1785
	4:21 And this **c** have we from him, That he	1785
2Jn	1: 4 as we have received a **c** from the Father.	1785
	1: 5 not as though I wrote a new **c** unto thee,	1785
	1: 6 This is the **c,** That, as ye have heard from	1785

COMMANDMENTS (171) [COMMAND]

Ge	26: 5 charge, my **c,** my statutes, and my laws.	4687
Ex	15:26 wilt give ear to his **c,** and keep all his	4687
	16:28 How long refuse ye to keep my **c** and	4687
	20: 6 of them that love me, and keep my **c.**	4687
	24:12 a law, and **c** which I have written;	4687
	34:28 the words of the covenant, the ten **c.**	1697
Lev	4: 2 **c** of the Lord (*concerning things* which	4687
	4:13 **c** of the Lord *concerning things* which	4687
	4:22 **c** of the Lord his God *concerning things*	4687
	4:27 **c** of the Lord *concerning things* which	4687
	5:17 to be done by the **c** of the Lord	4687
	22:31 Therefore shall ye keep my **c,** and do	4687
	26: 3 my statutes, and keep my **c,** and do them;	4687
	26:14 unto me, and will not do all these **c;**	4687
	26:15 so that *ye* will not do all my **c,** *but* that ye	4687
	27:34 These *are* the **c,** which the Lord	4687
Nu	15:22 have erred, and not observed all these **c,**	4687
	15:39 remember all the **c** of the Lord,	4687

C

Nu	15:40 do all my **c**, and be holy unto your God.	4687
	36:13 These *are* the **c** and the judgments,	4687
Dt	4: 2 that *ye* may keep the **c** of the LORD your	4687
	4:13 commanded you to perform, *even* ten **c**;	1697
	4:40 keep therefore his statutes, and his **c**,	4687
	5:10 of them that love me and keep my **c**.	4687
	5:29 would fear me, and keep all my **c** always,	4687
	5:31 I will speak unto thee all the **c**,	4687
	6: 1 Now these *are* the **c**, the statutes,	4687
	6: 2 to keep all his statutes and his **c**, which I	4687
	6:17 You shall diligently keep the **c** of	4687
	6:25 if we observe to do all these **c** before	4687
	7: 9 and keep his **c** to a thousand generations,	4687
	7:11 Thou shalt therefore keep the **c**,	4687
	8: 1 All the **c** which I command thee *this* day	4687
	8: 2 whether thou wouldest keep his **c**, or no.	4687
	8: 6 Therefore thou shalt keep the **c** of	4687
	8:11 in not keeping his **c**, and his judgments,	4687
	10: 4 according to the first writing, the ten **c**,	1697
	10:13 To keep the **c** of the LORD, and his	4687
	11: 1 and his judgments, and his **c** alway.	4687
	11: 8 Therefore shall ye keep all the **c** which I	4687
	11:13 if you shall hearken diligently unto my **c**	4687
	11:22 For if ye shall diligently keep all these **c**	4687
	11:27 if ye obey the **c** of the LORD your God,	4687
	11:28 if ye will not obey the **c** of the LORD	4687
	13: 4 keep his **c**, and obey his voice,	4687
	13:18 to keep all his **c** which I command thee	4687
	15: 5 to observe to do all these **c** which I	4687
	19: 9 If thou shalt keep all these **c** to do them,	4687
	26:13 according to all thy **c** which thou hast	4687
	26:13 I have not transgressed thy **c**, neither have	4687
	26:17 his **c**, and his judgments, and to hearken	4687
	26:18 and that *thou* shouldest keep all his **c**;	4687
	27: 1 Keep all the **c** which I command you *this*	4687
	27:10 do his **c** and his statutes, which I	4687
	28: 1 to do all his **c** which I command thee *this*	4687
	28: 9 if thou shalt keep the **c** of the LORD thy	4687
	28:13 if that thou hearken unto the **c** of	4687
	28:15 to observe to do all his **c** and his statutes	4687
	28:45 keep his **c** and his statutes which he	4687
	30: 8 all his **c** which I command thee *this* day.	4687
	30:10 to keep his **c** and his statutes which are	4687
	30:16 to keep his **c** and his statutes and	4687
	31: 5 all the **c** which I have commanded you.	4687
Jos	22: 5 to keep his **c**, and to cleave unto him,	4687
Jdg	2:17 walked in, obeying the **c** of the LORD;	4687
	3: 4 would hearken unto the **c** of the LORD,	4687
1Sa	15:11 and hath not performed my **c**.	1697
1Ki	2: 3 *and* his **c**, and his judgments,	4687
	3:14 keep my statutes and my **c**, as thy father	4687
	6:12 and keep all my **c** to walk in them;	4687
	8:58 to keep his **c**, and his statutes,	4687
	8:61 statutes, and to keep his **c**, as at this day.	4687
	9: 6 will not keep my **c** *and* my statutes which	4687
	11:34 he kept my **c** and my statutes:	4687
	11:38 to keep my statutes and my **c**, as David	4687
	14: 8 who kept my **c**, and who followed me	4687
	18:18 in that ye have forsaken the **c** of	4687
2Ki	17:13 evil ways, and keep my **c** *and* my statutes,	4687
	17:16 they left all the **c** of the LORD their God,	4687
	17:19 Also Judah kept not the **c** of the LORD	4687
	18: 6 not from following him, but kept his **c**,	4687
	23: 3 to keep his **c** and his testimonies and his	4687
1Ch	28: 7 if he be constant to do my **c** and	4687
	28: 8 seek for all the **c** of the LORD your God:	4687
	29:19 to keep thy **c**, thy testimonies,	4687
2Ch	7:19 and forsake my statutes and my **c**,	4687
	17: 4 walked in his **c**, and not after the doings	4687
	24:20 Why transgress ye the **c** of the LORD,	4687
	31:21 in the law, and in the **c**, to seek his God,	4687
	34:31 to keep his **c**, and his testimonies,	4687
Ezr	7:11 *even* a scribe of the words of the **c** of	4687
	9:10 say after this? for we have forsaken thy **c**,	4687
	9:14 Should we again break thy **c**, and join in	4687
Ne	1: 5 for them that love him and observe his **c**:	4687
	1: 7 have not kept the **c**, nor the statutes,	4687
	1: 9 unto me, and keep my **c**, and do them;	4687
	9:13 and true laws, good statutes and **c**:	4687
	9:16 their necks, and hearkened not to thy **c**,	4687
	9:29 hearkened not unto thy **c**,	4687
	9:34 nor hearkened unto thy **c**,	4687
	10:29 and do all the **c** of the LORD our Lord,	4687
Ps	78: 7 forget the works of God, but keep his **c**:	4687
	89:31 break my statutes, and keep not my **c**;	4687
	103:18 to those that remember his **c** to do them.	6490
	103:20 that excel in strength, that do his **c**,	1697
	111: 7 verity and judgment; all his **c** *are* sure.	6490
	111:10 that do *his* **c**: his praise endureth for ever.	NIH
	112: 1 the LORD, *that* delighteth greatly in his **c**.	4687
	119: 6 when I have respect unto all thy **c**.	4687
	119:10 O let me not wander from thy **c**.	4687
	119:19 in the earth: hide not thy **c** from me.	4687
	119:21 *that are* cursed, which do err from thy **c**.	4687
	119:32 I will run the way of thy **c**, when thou	4687
	119:35 Make me to go in the path of thy **c**;	4687
	119:47 I will delight myself in thy **c**, which I have	4687
	119:48 My hands also will I lift up unto thy **c**,	4687
	119:60 haste, and delayed not to keep thy **c**.	4687
	119:66 and knowledge: for I have believed thy **c**.	4687
	119:73 me understanding, that I may learn thy **c**.	4687
	119:86 All thy **c** *are* faithful: they persecute me	4687
	119:98 Thou through thy **c** hast made me wiser	4687
	119:115 for I will keep the **c** of my God.	4687
	119:127 Therefore I love thy **c** above gold; yea,	4687

Ps	119:131 and panted: for I longed for thy **c**.	4687
	119:143 hold on me: *yet* thy **c** *are* my delights.	4687
	119:151 *art* near, O LORD; and all thy **c** *are* truth.	4687
	119:166 hoped for thy salvation, and done thy **c**.	4687
	119:172 thy word: for all thy **c** *are* righteousness.	4687
	119:176 seek thy servant; for I do not forget thy **c**.	4687
Pr	2: 1 my words, and hide my **c** with thee;	4687
	3: 1 not my law; but let thine heart keep my **c**:	4687
	4: 4 retain my words: keep my **c**, and live.	4687
	7: 1 my words, and lay up my **c** with thee.	4687
	7: 2 Keep my **c**, and live; and my law as	4687
	7: 8 The wise in heart will receive **c**: but	4687
Ecc	12:13 Fear God, and keep his **c**: for this *is*	4687
Isa	48:18 O that thou hadst hearkened to my **c**!	4687
Da	9: 4 love him, and to them that keep his **c**;	4687
Am	2: 4 have not kept his **c**, and their lies caused	2706
Mt	5:19 therefore shall break one of these least **c**,	1785
	15: 9 teaching for doctrines the **c** of men.	1778
	19:17 but if thou wilt enter into life, keep the **c**.	1785
	22:40 On these two **c** hang all the law and	1785
Mk	7: 7 teaching for doctrines the **c** of men.	1778
	10:19 Thou knowest the **c**, Do not commit	1785
	12:29 The first of all the **c** *is*, Hear, O Israel;	1785
Lk	1: 6 walking in all the **c** and ordinances of	1785
	18:20 Thou knowest the **c**, Do not commit	1785
Jn	14: 15 If ye love me, keep my **c**.	1785
	14:21 He that hath my **c**, and keepeth them,	1785
	15:10 If ye keep my **c**, ye shall abide in my love;	1785
	15:10 even as I have kept my Father's **c**,	1785
Ac	1: 2 given unto the Apostles whom he had	1781
1Co	7:19 is nothing, but the keeping of the **c** of God.	1785
	14:37 that I write unto you are the **c** of the Lord.	1785
Eph	2:15 the law of **c** *contained* in ordinances;	1785
Col	2:22 after the **c** and doctrines of men?	1778
	4:10 (touching whom ye received **c**:	1785
1Th	4: 2 For ye know what **c** we gave you by	3852
Tit	1:14 and **c** of men, that turn from the truth.	1785
1Jn	2: 3 know that we know him, if we keep his **c**.	1785
	2: 4 keepeth not his **c**, is a liar, and the truth	1785
	3:22 we keep his **c**, and do those *things*	1785
	3:24 And he that keepeth his **c** dwelleth in him,	1785
	5: 2 when we love God, and keep his **c**.	1785
	5: 3 this is the love of God, that we keep his **c**:	1785
	5: 3 and his **c** are not grievous.	1785
2Jn	1: 6 And this is love, that we walk after his **c**.	1785
Rev	12:17 which keep the **c** of God, and have	1785
	14:12 here *are* they that keep the **c** of God,	1785
	22:14 Blessed *are* they that do his **c**, that they	1785

COMMEND (7) [COMMENDATION, COMMENDED, COMMENDETH, COMMENDING]

Lk	23:46 said, Father, into thy hands I **c** my spirit:	3908
Ac	20:32 I **c** you to God, and to the word of his	3908
Ro	3: 5 But if our unrighteousness **c**	4921
	16: 1 I **c** unto you Phebe our sister, which is a	4921
2Co	3: 1 Do we begin again to **c** ourselves?	4921
	5:12 For we **c** not ourselves again unto you,	4921
	10:12 compare ourselves with some that **c**	4921

COMMENDABLE See THANKWORTHY

COMMENDATION (2) [COMMEND]

2Co	3: 1 as some *others*, epistles of **c** to you,	4956
	3: 1 to you, or *letters* of **c** from you?	4956

COMMENDED (6) [COMMEND]

Ge	12:15 saw her, and **c** her before Pharaoh:	1984
Pr	12: 8 A man shall be **c** according to his wisdom:	1984
Ecc	8:15 I **c** mirth, because a man hath no better	7623
Lk	16: 8 And the lord **c** the unjust steward,	1867
Ac	14:23 they **c** them to the Lord, on whom they	3908
2Co	12:11 for I ought to have been **c** of you: for *in*	4921

COMMENDETH (4) [COMMEND]

Ro	5: 8 But God **c** his love toward us, in that,	4921
1Co	8: 8 But meat **c** us not to God: for neither,	3936
2Co	10:18 For not he that **c** himself is approved,	4921
	10:18 is approved, but whom the Lord **c**.	4921

COMMENDING (1) [COMMEND]

2Co	4: 2 by manifestation of the truth **c** ourselves	4921

COMMISSION (1) [COMMISSIONS]

Ac	26:12 authority and **c** from the chief priests,	2011

COMMISSIONS (1) [COMMISSION]

Ezr	8:36 they delivered the king's **c** unto the king's	1881

COMMIT (75) [COMMITTED, COMMITTEST, COMMITTETH, COMMITTING]

Ex	20:14 Thou shalt not **c** adultery.	5003
Lev	5:15 If a soul **c** a trespass,	4603+4604
	5:17 **c** any of *these things* which are forbidden	6213
	6: 2 a trespass against the LORD,	4603+4604
	18:26 and shall not **c** any of these abominations;	6213
	18:29 For whosoever shall **c** any of these	6213
	18:29 even the souls that **c** *them* shall be cut off	6213
	18:30 that *ye* **c** not *any one* of *these* abominable	6213
	20: 5 to **c** whoredom with Molech, from among	NIH
Nu	5: 6 woman shall **c** any sin that men commit,	6213
	5: 6 woman shall commit any sin that men **c**,	NIH
	5:12 and **c** a trespass against him,	4603+4604
	25: 1 the people begun to **c** whoredom with	2181
	31:16 to **c** trespass against the LORD in	4560
Dt	5:18 Neither shalt thou **c** adultery.	5003

Dt	19:20 shall henceforth **c** no more any such evil	6213
Jos	22:20 **c** a trespass in the accursed thing,	4603+4604
2Sa	7:14 If he **c** iniquity, I will chasten him with	5753
2Ch	21:11 caused the inhabitants of Jerusalem	
	to **c** fornication,	2181
Job	5: 8 and unto God would I **c** my cause:	7760
	34:10 the Almighty, *that he should* **c** iniquity.	NIH
Ps	31: 5 Into thine hand I **c** my spirit: thou hast	6485
	37: 5 **C** thy way unto the LORD; trust also in	1556
Pr	16: 3 **C** thy works unto the LORD,	1556
	16:12 *It is* an abomination to kings to **c**	6213
Isa	22:21 I will **c** thy government into his hand:	5414
	23:17 shall **c** fornication with all the kingdoms	2181
Jer	7: 9 **c** adultery, and swear falsely,	5003
	9: 5 *and* weary themselves to **c** iniquity.	5753
	23:14 they **c** adultery, and walk in lies:	5003
	37:21 **c** Jeremiah into the court of the prison,	6485
	44: 7 Wherefore **c** ye *this* great evil against your	6213
Eze	3:20 **c** iniquity, and I lay a stumblingblock	6213
	8:17 **c** the abominations which they commit	6213
	8:17 the abominations which they **c** here?	6213
	16:17 and didst **c** whoredom with them,	2181
	16:34 none followeth thee to **c** whoredoms:	2181
	16:43 thou shalt not **c** *this* lewdness above all	6213
	20:30 **c** ye whoredom after their abominations?	2181
	22: 9 in the midst of thee they **c** lewdness.	2154
	23:43 Will they now **c** whoredoms with	2181+8457
	33:13 to his own righteousness, and **c** iniquity,	6213
Hos	4:10 they shall **c** whoredom, and shall not	2181
	4:13 your daughters shall **c** whoredom,	2181
	4:13 and your spouses shall **c** adultery.	5003
	4:14 your daughters when they **c** whoredom,	2181
	4:14 nor your spouses when they **c** adultery:	5003
	6: 9 the way by consent: for they **c** lewdness.	6213
	7: 1 for they **c** falsehood; and the thief cometh	6466
Mt	5:27 of old time, Thou shalt not **c** adultery.	3431
	5:32 of fornication, causeth her to **c** adultery:	3429
	19: 9 her *which is* put away doth **c** adultery.	3429
	19:18 Thou shalt not **c** adultery, Thou shalt not	3431
Mk	10:19 Do not **c** adultery, Do not kill, Do not	3431
Lk	12:48 and did **c** *things* worthy of stripes,	4160
	16:11 who will **c** to your trust the true *riches?*	4100
	18:20 Do not **c** adultery, Do not kill, Do not	3431
Jn	2:24 But Jesus did not **c** himself unto them,	4100
Ro	1:32 they which **c** such *things* are worthy of	4238
	2: 2 to truth against them which **c** such *things*.	4238
	2:22 that sayest *a man* should not **c** adultery,	3431
	2:22 commit adultery, dost thou **c** adultery?	3431
	2:22 abhorrest idols, dost thou **c** sacrilege?	2416
	13: 9 For *this*, Thou shalt not **c** adultery,	3431
1Co	10: 8 Neither let us **c** fornication, as some of	4203
1Ti	1:18 This charge I **c** unto thee, son Timothy,	3908
2Ti	2: 2 the same **c** thou to faithful men,	3908
Jas	2: 9 ye **c** sin, and are convinced of the law as	2038
	2:11 Do not **c** adultery, said also, Do not kill.	3431
	2:11 if thou **c** no adultery, yet *if* thou kill,	3431
1Pe	4:19 **c** the keeping of their souls to *him* in	3908
1Jn	3: 9 Whosoever is born of God doth not **c** sin;	4160
Rev	2:14 sacrificed unto idols, and to **c** fornication.	4203
	2:20 to seduce my servants to **c** fornication,	4203
	2:22 them that **c** adultery with her into great	3431

COMMITTED (92) [COMMIT]

Ge	39: 8 he hath **c** all that he hath to my hand;	5414
	39:22 keeper of the prison **c** to Joseph's hand	5414
Lev	4:35 an atonement for his sin that he hath **c**,	2398
	5: 7 which he hath **c**, two turtledoves,	2398
	18:30 were **c** before you, and that ye defile	6213
	20:13 both of them have **c** an abomination:	6213
	20:23 for they **c** all these *things*, and therefore	6213
Nu	15:24 if *ought* be **c** by ignorance without	6213
Dt	17: 5 which have **c** that wicked thing,	6213
	21:22 if a man have **c** a sin worthy of death,	2399
Jos	7: 1 the children of Israel **c** a trespass	4603+4604
	22:16 trespass *is* this that ye have **c** against	4603
	22:31 ye have not **c** this trespass against	4603+4604
Jdg	20: 6 they have **c** lewdness and folly in Israel.	6213
1Ki	8:47 done perversely, we have **c** wickedness;	7561
	14:22 jealousy with their sins which they had **c**,	2398
	14:27 **c** them unto the hands of the chief of	6485
1Ch	10:13 transgression which he **c** against	4603+4604
2Ch	12:10 **c** *them* to the hands of the chief of	6485
	34:16 saying, All that was **c** to thy servants,	5414
Ps	106: 6 we have **c** iniquity, we have done	5753
Jer	2:13 For my people have **c** two evils; they have	6213
	3: 8 Israel **c** adultery I had put her away,	5003
	3: 9 **c** adultery with stones and with stocks.	5003
	5: 7 they then **c** adultery,	5003
	5:30 and horrible thing is **c** in the land;	1961
	6:15 Were they ashamed when they had **c**	6213
	8:12 Were they ashamed when they had **c**	6213
	16:10 what *is* our sin that we have **c**	2398+2403
	29:23 Because they have **c** villany in Israel,	6213
	29:23 have **c** adultery with their neighbours'	5003
	39:14 **c** him unto Gedaliah the son of Ahikam	5414
	40: 7 had **c** unto him men, and women,	6485
	41:10 had **c** to Gedaliah the son of Ahikam:	6485
	44: 3 they have **c** to provoke me to anger,	6213
	44: 9 which they have **c** in the land of Judah,	6213
	44:22 of the abominations which ye have **c**;	6213
Eze	6: 9 they have **c** in all their abominations.	6213
	15: 8 because they have **c** a trespass,	4603+4604
	16:26 Thou hast also **c** fornication with	2181
	16:50 and **c** abomination before me:	6213
	16:51 Neither hath Samaria **c** half of thy sins;	2398

Eze 16:52 **sins** that thou hast **c** more abominable	2403
18:12 his eyes to the idols, hath **c** abomination,	6213
18:21 will turn from all his sins that he hath **c,**	6213
18:22 All his transgressions that he hath **c,**	6213
18:27 away from his wickedness that he hath **c,**	6213
18:28 from all his transgressions that he hath **c,**	6213
20:27 they have **c a trespass** against me.	4603+4604
20:43 own sight for all your evils that ye have **c.**	6213
22:11 one hath **c** abomination with his	6213
23: 3 they **c whoredoms** in Egypt:	2181
23: 3 Egypt; they **c** whoredoms in their youth:	2181
23: 7 Thus she **c** her whoredoms with them,	5414
23:37 That they have **c adultery,** and blood *is*	5003
23:37 with their idols have they **c adultery,**	5003
33:13 for his iniquity that he hath **c,** he shall die	6213
33:16 None of his sins that he hath **c** shall be	2398
33:29 all their abominations which they have **c.**	6213
43: 8 by their abominations that they have **c:**	6213
44:13 their abominations which they have **c.**	6213
Da 9: 5 have **c iniquity,** and have done wickedly,	5753
Hos 1: 2 the land hath **c great whoredom,**	2181+2181
4:18 have **c whoredom continually:**	2181+2181
Mal 2:11 an abomination is **c** in Israel and	6213
Mt 5:28 **c adultery** with her already in his heart.	3431
Mk 15: 7 who had **c** murder in the insurrection.	4160
Lk 12:48 and to whom *men* have **c** much, of him	3908
Jn 5:22 but hath **c** all judgment unto the Son:	1325
Ac 8: 3 haling men and women **c** *them* to prison.	3860
25:11 or have **c** any *thing* worthy of death,	4238
25:25 But when I found that he had **c** nothing	4238
27:40 they **c** *themselves* unto the sea,	1439
28:17 I have **c** nothing against the people,	4160
Ro 3: 2 that unto them were **c** the oracles of God.	4100
1Co 9:17 a dispensation *of the gospel* is **c** unto me.	4100
10: 8 as some of them **c,** and fell in one day	4203
2Co 5:19 hath **c** unto us the word of reconciliation,	5087
11: 7 Have I **c** an offence in abasing myself that	4160
12:21 and lasciviousness which they have **c.**	4238
Gal 2: 7 of the uncircumcision was **c** unto me,	4100
1Ti 1:11 blessed God, which was **c** to my **trust.**	4100
6:20 keep that which is **c** to *thy* **trust,**	3872
2Ti 1:12 which I have **c** unto *him* against that day.	3866
1:14 *That* good thing which was **c** unto *thee*	3872
Tit 1: 3 which is **c** unto me according to	4100
Jas 5:15 if he have **c** sins, they shall be forgiven	4160
1Pe 2:23 **c** *himself* to him that judgeth righteously:	3860
Jude 1:15 deeds which they have **ungodly c,**	764
Rev 17: 2 the kings of the earth have **c fornication,**	4203
18: 3 the kings of the earth have **c fornication**	4203
18: 9 who have **c fornication** and	4203

COMMITTEST (1) [COMMIT]

Hos 5: 3 thou **c whoredom,** *and* Israel is defiled.	2181

COMMITTETH (19) [COMMIT]

Lev 20:10 man that **c adultery** with *another* man's	5003
20:10 *even* he that **c adultery** with his	5003
Ps 10:14 the poor **c** *himself* unto thee; thou art	5800
Pr 6:32 *But* whoso **c adultery** with a woman	5003
Eze 8: 6 that the house of Israel **c** here,	6213
16:32 as a wife that **c adultery,** *which* taketh	5003
18:24 **c** iniquity, *and* doeth according to all	6213
18:26 and **c** iniquity, and dieth in them;	6213
33:18 and **c** iniquity, he shall even die thereby.	6213
Mt 5:32 marry her that is divorced **c adultery:**	3429
19: 9 and shall marry another, **c adultery:**	3429
Mk 10:11 marry another, **c adultery** against her.	3429
10:12 be married to another, she **c adultery.**	3429
Lk 16:18 wife, and marrieth another, **c adultery:**	3431
16:18 put away from *her* husband **c adultery.**	3431
Jn 8:34 Whosoever **c** sin is the servant of sin.	4160
1Co 6:18 he that **c fornication** sinneth against his	4203
1Jn 3: 4 **c** sin transgresseth also the law:	4160
3: 8 He that **c** sin is of the devil; for the devil	4160

COMMITTING (2) [COMMIT]

Eze 33:15 in the statutes of life, without **c** iniquity;	6213
Hos 4: 2 and killing, and stealing, and **c adultery,**	5003

COMMODIOUS (1)

Ac 27:12 because the haven was not **c** to winter in,	428

COMMON (21) [COMMONLY]

Lev 4:27 if any one of the **c** people sin through	776
Nu 16:29 If these *men* die the **c** death of all men,	3509.1
1Sa 21: 4 *There* is no **c** bread under mine hand,	2455
21: 5 and *the* bread is in a manner **c,** yea,	2455
Ecc 6: 1 under the sun, and it *is* **c** among men:	7227
Jer 26:23 cast his dead body into the graves of the **c**	1121
31: 5 plant, and shall *eat* them **as c things.**	2490
Eze 23:42 with the men of the **c** sort *were* brought	7230
Mt 27:27 of the governor took Jesus into the **c hall,**	4232
Mk 12:37 And the **c** people heard him gladly.	4183
Ac 2:44 were together, and had all *things* **c;**	2839
4:32 was his own; but they had all *things* **c.**	2839
5:18 the apostles, and put them in the **c** prison.	1219
10:14 for I have never eaten any *thing* that is **c**	2839
10:15 God hath cleansed, *that* call not thou **c.**	2840
10:28 that *I* should not call any man **c**	2839
11: 8 for nothing **c** or unclean hath at any time	2839
11: 9 God hath cleansed, *that* call not thou **c.**	2840
1Co 10:13 taken you but such as is **c to man:**	442
Tit 1: 4 To Titus, *mine* own son after the **c** faith:	2839
Jude 1: 3 to write unto you of the **c** salvation,	2839

COMMONLY (2) [COMMON]

Mt 28:15 this saying is **c reported** among the Jews	1310
1Co 5: 1 It is reported **c** *that there* is fornication	3654

COMMONWEALTH (1)

Eph 2:12 being aliens from the **c** of Israel,	4174

COMMOTION (1) [COMMOTIONS]

Jer 10:22 and a great **c** out of the north country,	7494

COMMOTIONS (1) [COMMOTION]

Lk 21: 9 But when ye shall hear of wars and **c,**	181

COMMUNE (8) [COMMUNED, COMMUNING, COMMUNION]

Ge 34: 6 went out unto Jacob to **c** with him.	1696
Ex 25:22 I will **c** with thee from above the mercy	1696
1Sa 18:22 saying, **C** with David secretly, and say,	1696
19: 3 and I will **c** with my father of thee;	1696
Job 4: 2 If we assay to **c** with thee, wilt thou be	1697
Ps 4: 4 with your own heart upon your bed,	559
64: 5 they **c** of laying snares privily; they say,	5608
77: 6 I **c** with mine own heart: and my spirit	7878

COMMUNED (18) [COMMUNE]

Ge 23: 8 he **c** with them, saying, If it be your mind	1696
34: 6 Hamor **c** with them, saying, The soul of	1696
34:20 and **c** with the men of their city, saying,	1696
42:24 returned to them *again,* and **c** with them,	1696
43:19 they **c** with him *at* the door of the house,	1696
Jdg 9: 1 **c** with them, and with all the family of	1696
1Sa 9:25 Samuel **c** with Saul upon the top of	1696
25:39 David sent and **c** with Abigail, to take her	1696
1Ki 10: 2 she **c** with him of all that was in her heart.	1696
2Ki 22:14 in the college;) and they **c** with her.	1696
2Ch 9: 1 she **c** with him of all that was in her heart.	1696
Ecc 1:16 I **c** with mine own heart, saying, Lo, I am	1696
Da 1:19 the king **c** with them; and among them all	1696
Zec 1:14 So the angel that **c** with me said unto me,	1696
Lk 6:11 **c** one with another what they might do to	1255
22: 4 and **c** with the chief priests and captains,	4814
24:15 that while they **c** *together* and reasoned,	3656
Ac 24:26 sent for him the oftener, and **c** with him.	3656

COMMUNICATE (4) [COMMUNICATED, COMMUNICATION, COMMUNICATIONS]

Gal 6: 6 Let him that is taught in the word **c** unto	2841
Php 4:14 done, that ye did **c with** my affliction.	4790
1Ti 6:18 ready to distribute, **willing to c;**	2843
Heb 13:16 to do good and to **c** forget not: for with	2842

COMMUNICATED (2) [COMMUNICATE]

Gal 2: 2 **c** unto them *that* gospel which I preach	394
Php 4:15 no church **c with** me as concerning giving	2841

COMMUNICATION (6) [COMMUNICATE]

2Sa 3:17 Abner had **c** with the elders of Israel,	1697
2Ki 9:11 unto you, Ye know the man, and his **c.**	7879
Mt 5:37 Let your **c** be, Yea, yea; Nay, nay;	3056
Eph 4:29 no corrupt **c** proceed out of your mouth,	3056
Col 3: 8 blasphemy, **filthy c** out of your mouth.	148
Phm 1: 6 That the **c** of thy faith may become	2842

COMMUNICATIONS (2) [COMMUNICATE]

Lk 24:17 What *manner of* **c** are these that ye have	3056
1Co 15:33 deceived: evil **c** corrupt good manners.	3657

COMMUNING (2) [COMMUNE]

Ge 18:33 as soon as he had left **c** with Abraham:	1696
Ex 31:18 when he had made an end of **c** with him	1696

COMMUNION (4) [COMMUNE]

1Co 10:16 is it not the **c** of the blood of Christ?	2842
10:16 is it not the **c** of the body of Christ?	2842
2Co 6:14 and what hath light with darkness?	2842
13:14 and the **c** of the Holy Ghost, *be* with you	2842

COMPACT (1) [COMPACTED]

Ps 122: 3 Jerusalem *is* builded as a city that is **c**	2266

COMPACTED (1) [COMPACT]

Eph 4:16 and **c** by that which every joint supplieth,	4822

COMPANIED (1) [COMPANY]

Ac 1:21 of these men which have **c with**	4905

COMPANIES (17) [COMPANY]

Jdg 7:16 the three hundred men *into* three **c,**	7218
7:20 the three **c** blew the trumpets, and brake	7218
9:34 they laid wait against Shechem *in* four **c.**	7218
9:43 divided them into three **c,** and laid wait in	7218
9:44 the two *other* **c** ran upon all *the people*	7218
1Sa 11:11 that Saul put the people *in* three **c;**	7218
13:17 of the camp of the Philistines *in* three **c:**	7218
2Ki 5: 2 the Syrians had gone out *by* **c,**	1416
1Ch 9:18 they *were* porters in the **c** of the children	4264
28: 1 to that ministered to the king **by course,**	4256
Ne 12:31 appointed two great **c** of them that gave	NIH
12:40 stood the two **c** of them that gave thanks	NIH
Job 6:19 the **c** of Sheba waited for them.	1979
Isa 21:13 ye lodge, O ye **travelling c** of Dedanim.	736
57:13 When thou criest, let thy **c** deliver thee;	6899
Eze 26: 7 with horsemen, and **c,** and much people.	6951
Mk 6:39 sit down **by c** upon the green grass.	4849+4849

COMPANION (13) [COMPANIONS, COMPANIONS']

Ex 32:27 every man his **c,** and every man his	7453
Jdg 14:20 Samson's wife was *given* to his **c,**	4828
15: 2 hated her; therefore I gave her to thy **c:**	4828
15: 6 had taken his wife, and given her to his **c.**	4828
1Ch 27:33 and Hushai the Archite *was* the king's **c:**	7453
Job 30:29 I am a brother to dragons, and a **c** to owls.	7453
Ps 119:63 I *am* a **c** of all *them* that fear thee,	2270
Pr 13:20 be wise: but a **c** of fools shall be destroyed.	7462
28: 7 he that is a **c** of riotous *men* shameth his	7462
28:24 the same *is* the **c** of a destroyer.	2270
Mal 2:14 yet *is* she thy **c,** and the wife of thy	2278
Php 2:25 and **c in labour,** and fellowsoldier,	4904
Rev 1: 9 and **c in tribulation,** and in the kingdom	4791

COMPANIONS (21) [COMPANION]

Jdg 11:38 she went with her **c,** and bewailed her	7464
14:11 that they brought thirty **c** to be with her.	4828
Ezr 4: 7 Tabeel, and the rest of their **c,**	3674
4: 9 the scribe, and the rest of their **c;**	3675
4:17 *to* the rest of their **c** that dwell in Samaria,	3675
4:23 Shimshai the scribe, and their **c,** they	3675
5: 3 and their **c,** and said thus unto them,	3675
5: 6 and his **c** the Apharsachites,	3675
6: 6 and your **c** the Apharsachites,	3675
6:13 the river, Shethar-boznai, and their **c,**	3675
Job 34: 8 I will answer thee, and thy **c** with thee.	7453
41: 6 Shall the **c** make a banquet of him?	2271
Ps 45:14 the virgins her **c** that follow her *shall be*	2270
SS 1: 7 that turneth aside by the flocks of thy **c?**	2270
8:13 in the gardens, the **c** hearken to thy voice:	2270
Isa 1:23 princes *are* rebellious, and **c** of thieves:	2270
Eze 37:16 and for the children of Israel his **c:**	2270
37:16 and *for* all the house of Israel his **c:**	2270
Da 2:17 to Hananiah, Mishael, and Azariah, his **c:**	2269
Ac 19:29 men of Macedonia, Paul's **c in travel,**	4898
Heb 10:33 whilst ye became **c** of them that were so	2844

COMPANIONS' (1) [COMPANION]

Ps 122: 8 For my brethren and **c** sakes, I will now	7453

COMPANY (86) [COMPANIED, COMPANIED']

Ge 32: 8 If Esau come to the one **c,** and smite it,	4264
32: 8 then the *other* **c** which is left shall escape.	4264
32:21 and himself lodged that night in the **c.**	4264
35:11 nation and a **c** of nations shall be of thee,	6951
37:25 a **c** of Ishmeelites came from Gilead with	736
50: 9 and horsemen: and it was a very great **c.**	4264
Nu 14: 7 they spake unto all the **c** of the children	5712
16: 5 he spake unto Korah and unto all his **c,**	5712
16: 6 Take you censers, Korah, and all his **c;**	5712
16:11 all thy **c** *are* gathered together against	5712
16:16 Be thou and all thy **c** before the LORD,	5712
16:40 that he be not as Korah, and as his **c:**	5712
22: 4 shall *this* **c** lick up all *that are* round	6951
26: 9 and against Aaron in the **c** of Korah,	5712
26:10 when that **c** died, what time the fire	5712
27: 3 he was not in the **c** of them that gathered	5712
27: 3 against the LORD in the **c** of Korah;	5712
Jdg 9:37 another **c** come along by the plain of	7218
9:44 the **c** that *was* with him, rushed forward,	7218
18:23 that thou **comest with** such a **c?**	2199
1Sa 10: 5 thou shalt meet a **c** of prophets coming	2256
10:10 the hill, behold, a **c** of prophets met him;	2256
13:17 one **c** turned unto the way that leadeth to	7218
13:18 another **c** turned the way to Beth-horon:	7218
13:18 another **c** turned *to* the way of the border	7218
19:20 when they saw the **c** of the prophets	3862
30:15 Canst thou bring me down to this **c?**	1416
30:15 and I will bring thee down to this **c.**	1416
30:23 delivered the **c** that came against us into	1416
2Ki 5:15 he and all his **c,** and came, and stood	4264
9:17 he spied the **c** of Jehu as he came,	8229
9:17 of Jehu as he came, and said, I see a **c.**	8229
2Ch 9: 1 with a very great **c,** and camels that bare	2428
20:12 for we have no might against this great **c**	1995
24:24 the Syrians came with a small **c** of men,	NIH
Ne 4:22 the other **c** of them that gave thanks went	NIH
Job 16: 7 thou hast made desolate all my **c.**	5712
34: 8 Which goeth in **c** with the workers of	2274
Ps 55:14 *and* walked unto the house of God in **c.**	7285
68:11 great *was* the **c** of those that published *it.*	6635
68:30 Rebuke the **c** of spearmen, the multitude	2416
106:17 Dathan, and covered the **c** of Abiram.	5712
106:18 a fire was kindled in their **c;** the flame	5712
Pr 29: 3 he that **keepeth c** with harlots spendeth	7462
SS 1: 9 to a **c of horses** in Pharaoh's chariots.	5484
6:13 As it were the **c** of two armies.	4246
Jer 31: 8 a great **c** shall return thither.	6951
Eze 16:40 They shall also bring up a **c** against thee,	6951
17:17 and great **c** make for him in the war,	6951
23:46 bring up a **c** upon them, and *will* give	6951
23:47 the **c** shall stone them with stones,	6951
27: 6 the **c** of the Ashurites have made thy	1323
27:27 in all thy **c** which *is* in the midst of thee,	6951
27:34 and all thy **c** in the midst of thee shall fall.	6951
32: 3 spread out my net over thee with a **c** of	6951
32:22 Asshur *is* there and all her **c:** his graves	6951
32:23 pit, and her **c** is round about her grave:	6951
38: 4 *of armour, even* a great **c** *with* bucklers	6951
38: 7 all thy **c** that are assembled unto thee,	6951
38:13 hast thou gathered thy **c** to take a prey?	6951
38:15 upon horses, a great **c,** and a mighty army:	6951
Hos 6: 9 the **c** of priests murder *in* the way by	2267

C

Lk 2:44 supposing him to have been in the **c**, 4923
5:29 and there was a great **c** of publicans and 3793
6:17 and the **c** of his disciples, and a great 3793
6:22 when they shall separate you *from their* **c**, NIG
9:14 Make them sit down by fifties in a **c**. 2828
9:38 a man of the **c** cried out, saying, Master, 3793
11:27 a certain woman of the **c** lift up her voice, 3793
12:13 And one of the **c** said unto him, Master, 3793
23:27 there followed him a great **c** of people, 4128
24:22 certain women *also* **of** our **c** made us 1537
Jn 6: 5 eyes, and saw a great **c** come unto him, 3793
Ac 4:23 they went to their own **c**, and reported all NIG
6: 7 a great **c** of the priests were obedient to 3793
10:28 *thing* for a man *that is* a Jew to **keep c**, 2853
13:13 and his **c** loosed from Paphos, 3588+4012
15:22 to send chosen men of **their own c** to 846
17: 5 and **gathered** a **c**, and set all the city on 3792
21: 8 And the next day we that were of Paul's **c** 4012
Ro 15:24 if first I be somewhat filled with your **c**. NIG
1Co 5: 9 wrote unto you in an epistle not to **c with** 4874
5:11 I have written unto you not to **keep c**, 4874
2Th 3:14 note that *man*, and **have** no **c with** him, 4874
Heb 12:22 and to an **innumerable c** of angels, 3461
Rev 18:17 every shipmaster, and all the **c** in ships, 3658

COMPARABLE (1) [COMPARE]

La 4: 2 The precious sons of Zion, **c** to fine gold, 5537

COMPARE (4) [COMPARABLE, COMPARED, COMPARING, COMPARISON]

Isa 40:18 or what likeness will ye **c** unto him? 6186
46: 5 make *me* equal, and **c** me, that we may 4911
Mk 4:30 or with what comparison shall we **c** it? 3846
2Co 10:12 **c** ourselves **with** some that commend 4793

COMPARED (5) [COMPARE]

Ps 89: 6 For him in the heaven can be **c** unto 6186
Pr 3:15 thou canst desire are not to be **c** unto her. 7737
8:11 that may be desired are not to be **c** to it. 7737
SS 1: 9 I have **c** thee, O my love, to a company of 1819
Ro 8:18 **c with** the glory which shall be revealed 4314

COMPARING (2) [COMPARE]

1Co 2:13 **c** spiritual *things* with spiritual. 4793
2Co 10:12 and **c** themselves **amongst** themselves, 4793

COMPARISON (4) [COMPARE]

Jdg 8: 2 What have I done now **in c** of you? 3509.1
8: 3 what was I able to do **in c** of you? 3509.1
Hag 2: 3 *is it* not in your eyes **in c** of it as nothing? 3644
Mk 4:30 or with what **c** shall we compare it? 3850

COMPASS (39) [COMPASSED, COMPASSEST, COMPASSETH, COMPASSING]

Ex 27: 5 thou shalt put it under the **c** of the altar 3749
38: 4 the **c** thereof beneath unto the midst of it. 3749
Nu 21: 4 way of the Red sea, to **c** the land of Edom: 5437
34: 5 the border shall **fetch** a **c** from Azmon 5437
Jos 6: 3 ye shall **c** the city, all *ye* men of war, 5437
6: 4 the seventh day ye shall **c** the city seven 5437
6: 7 **c** the city, and let him that is armed pass 5437
15: 3 up to Adar, and **fetched** a **c** to Karkaa: 5437
2Sa 5:23 but **fetch** a **c** behind them, and come 5437
1Ki 7:15 twelve cubits did **c** either of them **about**. 5437
7:23 thirty cubits did **c** it **round about**. 5437+5439
7:35 in the top of the base *was* there a round **c** 5439
2Ki 3: 9 they **fetcht** a **c** of seven days' journey: 5437
11: 8 ye shall **c** the king round about, every 5362
2Ch 4: 2 round **in c**, and five cubits the height 5439
4: 2 a line of thirty cubits did **c** it round about. 5437
4: 3 of oxen, which did **c** it round about: 5437
23: 7 the Levites shall **c** the king round about, 5362
Job 16:13 archers **c** me **round about**, he cleaveth 5437
40:22 the willows of the brook **c** him **about**. 5437
Ps 5:12 **with** favour wilt thou **c** him as **with** a 5849
7: 7 congregation of the people **c** thee **about**: 5437
17: 9 my deadly enemies, *who* **c** me **about**. 5362
26: 6 so will I **c** thine altar, O **L**ORD: 5437
32: 7 thou shalt **c** me **about with** songs of 5437
32:10 in the **L**ORD, mercy shall **c** him **about**. 5437
49: 5 the iniquity of my heels shall **c** me **about**? 5437
140: 9 *As for* the head of those that **c** me **about**, 4524
142: 7 the righteous shall **c** me **about**; for thou 3803
Pr 8:27 he set a **c** upon the face of the depth: 2329
Isa 44:13 he marketh it out with the **c**, and maketh 4230
50:11 a fire, that **c** *yourselves* **about** with sparks: 247
Jer 31:22 in the earth, A woman shall **c** a man. 5437
31:39 hill Gareb, and shall **c** about to Goath. 5437
52:21 a fillet of twelve cubits did **c** it; 5437
Hab 1: 4 the wicked doth **c** **about** the righteous; 3803
Mt 23:15 for ye **c** sea and land to make one 4013
Lk 19:43 and **c** thee **round**, and keep thee in on 4033
Ac 28:13 And from thence we **fet** a **c**, 4022

COMPASSED (44) [COMPASS]

Ge 19: 4 **c** the house **round**, both old and young, 5437
Dt 2: 1 and we **c** mount Seir many days. 5437
2: 3 Ye have **c** this mountain long enough: 5437
Jos 6:11 So the ark of the **L**ORD **c** the city, 5437
6:14 the second day they **c** the city once, 5437
6:15 the city after the same manner seven 5437
6:15 on that day they **c** the city seven times. 5437
15:10 the border **c** from Baalah westward unto 5437
18:14 and the corner of the sea southward, 5437
Jdg 11:18 **c** the land of Edom, and the land of Moab, 5437

Jdg 16: 2 they **c** him **in**, and laid wait for him all 5437
1Sa 23:26 men **c** David and his men **round about** 5849
2Sa 18:15 men that bare Joab's armour **c** about 5437
22: 5 When the waves of death **c** me, the floods 661
22: 6 sorrows of hell **c** me **about**; the snares 5437
2Ki 6:14 they came by night, and **c** the city **about**. 5362
6:15 a host the city both with horses and 5437
8:21 smote the Edomites which **c** him **about**, 5437
2Ch 18:31 Therefore they **c** about him to fight: but 5437
21: 9 smote the Edomites which **c** him **in**, 5437
33:14 **c** about Ophel, and raised it up a very 5437
Job 19: 6 and hath **c** me with his net. 5362
26:10 He hath **c** the waters **with** 2328+5921+6440
Ps 17:11 They have now **c** us **in** our steps: 5437
18: 4 The sorrows of death **c** me, and the floods 661
18: 5 sorrows of hell **c** me **about**: the snares 5437
22:12 Many bulls have **c** me: strong *bulls* of 5437
22:16 For dogs have **c** me: the assembly of 5437
40:12 For innumerable evils have **c** me **about**: 661
88:17 like water; they **c** me **about** together. 5362
109: 3 They **c** me **about** also with words of 5437
116: 3 The sorrows of death **c** me, and the pains 661
118:10 All nations **c** me **about**: but in the name 5437
118:11 They **c** me **about**; yea, they compassed 5437
118:11 me **about**; yea, they **c** me **about**: 5437
118:12 They **c** me **about** like bees; they are 5437
La 3: 5 against me, and **c** *me* with gall and travail. 5362
Jnh 2: 3 of the seas; and the floods **c** me **about**: 5437
2: 5 The waters **c** me **about**, *even* to the soul: 661
Lk 21:20 And when ye shall see Jerusalem **c** with 2944
Heb 5: 2 that he himself also is **c with** infirmity. 4029
11:30 after they were **c** about seven days. 2944
12: 1 seeing we also are **c** about with 4029
Rev 20: 9 and **c** the camp of the saints **about**, 2944

COMPASSEST (1) [COMPASS]

Ps 139: 3 Thou **c** my path and my lying down, 2219

COMPASSETH (1) [COMPASS]

Ge 2:11 *is it* which **c** the whole land of Havilah, 5437
2:13 the same *is it* that **c** the whole land of 5437
Jos 19:14 the border **c** it on the north side 5437
Ps 73: 6 Therefore pride **c** them **about as a chain**; 6059
Hos 11:12 Ephraim **c** me **about** with lies, 5437

COMPASSING (3) [COMPASS]

1Ki 7:24 **round about** there were knops **c** it, 5437+5439
7:24 ten in a cubit, **c** the sea round about: 5362
2Ch 4: 3 ten in a cubit, **c** the sea round about. 5362

COMPASSION (41) [COMPASSIONS]

Ex 2: 6 she **had c** on him, and said, This *is one* 2550
Dt 13:17 and **have c** upon thee, and multiply thee, 7355
30: 3 **have c** upon thee, and will return and 7355
1Sa 23:21 *be* ye of the **L**ORD; for ye **have c** on me. 2550
1Ki 8:50 give them **c** before them who carried 7356
8:50 that they may **have c** on them: 7355
2Ki 13:23 **had c** on them, and had respect unto 2550
2Ch 30: 9 your children *shall find* **c** before them 7356
36:15 because he **had c** on his people, and on 2550
36:17 **had** no **c** upon young man or maiden, 2550
Ps 78:38 he, *being* **full of c**, forgave *their* iniquity, 7349
86:15 O Lord, *art* a God **full of c**, and gracious, 7349
111: 4 The **L**ORD *is* gracious and **full of c**. 7349
112: 4 gracious, and **full of c**, and righteous. 7349
145: 8 The **L**ORD *is* gracious, and **full of c**; 7349
Isa 49:15 *she* should not **have c** on the son of her 7355
Jer 12:15 **have c** on them, and will bring them 7355
La 3:32 yet will he **have c** according to 7355
Eze 16: 5 of these unto thee, to **have c** upon thee; 2550
Mic 7:19 will turn again, he will **have c** upon us; 7355
Mt 9:36 he was **moved with c** on them, because 4697
14:14 and was **moved with c** toward them, 4697
15:32 and said, I **have c** on the multitude, 4697
18:27 lord of that servant was **moved with c**, 4697
18:33 Shouldest not thou also have **had c** on 1653
20:34 Jesus **had c** on *them*, and touched their 4697
Mk 1:41 And Jesus, **moved with c**, put forth *his* 4697
5:19 done for thee, and hath **had c** on thee. 1653
6:34 and was **moved with c** toward them, 4697
8: 2 I **have c** on the multitude, because 4697
9:22 if thou canst do any *thing*, **have c** on us, 4697
Lk 7:13 he **had c** on her, and said unto her, 4697
10:33 and when he saw him, he **had c** on him, 4697
15:20 and **had c**, and ran, and fell on his neck, 4697
Ro 9:15 I will **have c** on whom I will have 3627
9:15 have compassion on whom I will **have c**. 3627
Heb 5: 2 Who can **have c** on the ignorant, 3356
10:34 For ye **had c** of me in my bonds, 4834
1Pe 3: 8 having **c one of another**, love as brethren 4835
1Jn 3:17 and shutteth up his bowels of **c** from him, NIG
Jude 1:22 And of some **have c**, making a difference: 1653

COMPASSIONATE See TENDERHEARTED

COMPASSIONS (2) [COMPASSION]

La 3:22 are not consumed, because his **c** fail not. 7356
Zec 7: 9 mercy and every man to his brother: 7356

COMPEL (5) [COMPELLED, COMPELLEST]

Lev 25:39 thou shalt not **c** him **to serve** as a 5647+5656
Est 1: 8 *was* according to the law; none did **c**: 597
Mt 5:41 And whosoever shall **c** thee **to go** a mile, 29
Mk 15:21 And they **c** one Simon a Cyrenian, 29
Lk 14:23 and hedges, and **c** *them* to come in, 315

COMPELLED (6) [COMPEL]

1Sa 28:23 together with the woman, **c** him; 6555
2Ch 21:11 commit fornication, and **c** Judah *thereto*. 5080
Mt 27:32 by name: him they **c** to bear his cross. 29
Ac 26:11 synagogue, and **c** *them* to blaspheme; 315
2Co 12:11 become a fool in glorying; ye have **c** me: 315
Gal 2: 3 being a Greek, was **c** to be circumcised: 315

COMPELLEST (1) [COMPEL]

Gal 2:14 why **c** thou the Gentiles to live as do 315

COMPLAIN (4) [COMPLAINED, COMPLAINERS, COMPLAINING, COMPLAINT, COMPLAINTS]

Jdg 21:22 or their brethren come unto us to **c**, 7378
Job 7:11 I will **c** in the bitterness of my soul. 7878
31:38 or that the furrows likewise thereof **c**; 1058
La 3:39 Wherefore doth a living man **c**, a man for 596

COMPLAINED (2) [COMPLAIN]

Nu 11: 1 *when* the people **c**, it displeased the **L**ORD: 596
Ps 77: 3 I **c**, and my spirit was overwhelmed. 7878

COMPLAINERS (1) [COMPLAIN]

Jude 1:16 These are murmurers, **c**, walking after 3202

COMPLAINING (1) [COMPLAIN]

Ps 144:14 that *there be* no **c** in our streets. 6682

COMPLAINT (9) [COMPLAIN]

1Sa 1:16 for out of the abundance of my **c** and 7879
Job 7:13 comfort me, my couch shall ease my **c**; 7879
9:27 If I say, I will forget my **c**, I will leave off 7879
10: 1 of my life; I will leave my **c** upon myself; 7879
21: 4 *As for* me, *is* my **c** to man? and *if it were* 7879
23: 2 Even to day *is* my **c** bitter: my stroke *is* 7879
Ps 55: 2 I mourn in my **c**, and make a noise; 7879
102: 1 T and poureth out his **c** before the **L**ORD: 7879
142: 2 I poured out my **c** before him; I shewed 7879

COMPLAINTS (1) [COMPLAIN]

Ac 25: 7 and laid many and grievous **c** against Paul, 157

COMPLETE (3)

Lev 23:15 wave offering; seven sabbaths shall be **c**: 8549
Col 2:10 And ye are **c** in him, which is the head of 4137
4:12 stand perfect and **c** in all the will of God. 4137

COMPLETELY See UTTERMOST

COMPOSITION (2)

Ex 30:32 ye make *any other* like it, after the **c** of it: 4971
30:37 to yourselves according to the **c** thereof: 4971

COMPOUND (1) [COMPOUNDETH]

Ex 30:25 an ointment **c** *after* the art of 4842

COMPOUNDETH (1) [COMPOUND]

Ex 30:33 Whosoever **c** *any* like it, 7543

COMPREHEND (2) [COMPREHENDED]

Job 37: 5 great *things* doeth he, which we cannot **c**. 3045
Eph 3:18 May be able to **c** with all saints what *is* 2638

COMPREHENDED (3) [COMPREHEND]

Isa 40:12 and **c** the dust of the earth in a measure, 3557
Jn 1: 5 and the darkness **c** it not. 2638
Ro 13: 9 it is **briefly c** in this saying, namely, 346

CONANIAH (1)

2Ch 35: 9 **C** also, and Shemaiah and Nethaneel, 3562

CONCEAL (6) [CONCEALED, CONCEALETH]

Ge 37:26 if we slay our brother, and **c** his blood? 3680
Dt 13: 8 shalt thou spare, neither shalt thou **c** him: 3680
Job 27:11 which *is* with the Almighty will I not **c**. 3582
41:12 I will not **c** his parts, nor *his* power, 2790
Pr 25: 2 *It is* the glory of God to **c** a thing: but 5641
Jer 50: 2 and set up a standard; publish, *and* **c** not: 3582

CONCEALED (2) [CONCEAL]

Job 6:10 I have not **c** the words of the Holy One. 3582
Ps 40:10 I have not **c** thy lovingkindness and 3582

CONCEALETH (2) [CONCEAL]

Pr 11:13 he that is of a faithful spirit **c** the matter. 3680
12:23 A prudent man **c** knowledge: 3680

CONCEIT (5) [CONCEITS]

Pr 18:11 city, and as a high wall in his own **c**. 4906
26: 5 to his folly, lest he be wise in his own **c**. 5869
26:12 Seest thou a man wise in his own **c**? 5869
26:16 The sluggard *is* wiser in his own **c** than 5869
28:11 The rich man *is* wise in his own **c**; 5869

CONCEITED See HIGH-MINDED

CONCEITS (3) [CONCEIT]

Ro 11:25 lest ye should be wise in your own **c**; NIG
12:16 of low estate. Be not wise in your own **c**. NIG

CONCEIVE (14) [CONCEIVED, CONCEIVING, CONCEPTION]

Ge 30:38 they should **c** when they came to drink. 3179
30:41 whensoever the stronger cattle did **c**, 3179
30:41 that they might **c** among the rods. 3179
Nu 5:28 she shall be free, and shall **c seed**. 2232+2233
Jdg 13: 3 but thou shalt **c**, and bear a son. 2029

C

Jdg 13: 5 For lo, thou *shalt* c, and bear a son; 2030
 13: 7 Behold, thou *shalt* c, and bear a son; 2030
Job 15:35 They c mischief, and bring forth vanity, 2029
Ps 51: 5 iniquity; and in sin did my mother c me. 3179
Isa 7:14 a Virgin shall c, and bear a Son, 2030
 33:11 Ye shall c chaff, ye shall bring forth 2029
 59: 4 *they* c mischief, and bring forth iniquity. 2029
Lk 1:31 thou shalt c in *thy* womb, and bring forth 4815
Heb 11:11 Sara herself received strength to c seed, 2602

CONCEIVED (46) [CONCEIVE]

Ge 4: 1 she c, and bare Cain, and said, I have 2029
 4:17 knew his wife; and she c, and bare Enoch: 2029
 16: 4 he went in unto Hagar, and she c: and 2029
 16: 4 when she saw that she had c, her mistress 2029
 16: 5 when she saw that she had c, I was 2029
 21: 2 Sarah c, and bare Abraham a son in his 2029
 25:21 intreated of him, and Rebekah his wife c. 2029
 29:32 Leah c, and bare a son, and she called his 2029
 29:33 she c again, and bare a son; and said, 2029
 29:34 she c again, and bare a son; and she said, 2029
 29:35 she c again, and bare a son: and she said, 2029
 30: 5 And Bilhah c, and bare Jacob a son. 2029
 30: 7 Bilhah Rachel's maid c again, 2029
 30:17 and she c, and bare Jacob the fifth son. 2029
 30:19 Leah c again, and bare Jacob the sixth 2029
 30:23 c, and bare a son; and said, God hath 2029
 30:39 the flocks c before the rods, 3179
 31:10 came to pass at the time that the cattle c, 3179
 38: 3 she c, and bare a son; and he called his 2029
 38: 4 she c again, and bare a son; and she 2029
 38: 5 she yet again c, and bare a son; NIH
 38:18 and came in unto her, and she c by him. 2029
Ex 2: 2 the woman c, and bare a son: and when 2029
Lev 12: 2 If a woman have c **seed**, and born a man 2232
Nu 11:12 Have I c all this people? have I begotten 2029
1Sa 1:20 time was come about after Hannah had c, 2029
 2:21 so that she c, and bare three sons and 2029
2Sa 11: 5 the woman c, and sent and told David, 2029
2Ki 4:17 woman c, and bare a son at that season 2029
1Ch 7:23 she c again, and bare a son, and he called his 2029
Job 3: 3 *it was* said, There is a man child c. 2029
Ps 7:14 hath c mischief, and brought forth 2029
SS 3: 4 and into the chamber of her that c me. 2029
Isa 8: 3 the prophetess; and she c, and bare a son. 2029
Jer 49:30 and hath c a purpose against you. 2803
Hos 1: 3 of Diblaim; which c, and bare him a son. 2029
 1: 6 she c again, and bare a daughter. 2029
 1: 8 Lo-ruhamah, she c, and bare a son. 2029
 2: 5 she that c them hath done shamefully: 2029
Mt 1:20 for that which is c in her is of the Holy 1080
Lk 1:24 And after those days his wife Elisabeth c, 4815
 1:36 she hath also c a son in her old age: 4815
 2:21 named of the angel before he was c in 4815
Ac 5: 4 why hast thou c this thing in thine heart? 5087
Ro 9:10 but when Rebecca also had c by one, 2845
Jas 1:15 when lust hath c, it bringeth forth sin: 4815

CONCEIVING (1) [CONCEIVE]

Isa 59:13 c and uttering from the heart words of 2029

CONCEPTION (3) [CONCEIVE]

Ge 3:16 will greatly multiply thy sorrow and thy c; 2032
Ru 4:13 the LORD gave her c, and she bare a son. 2032
Hos 9:11 and from the womb, and from the c. 2032

CONCERN (2) [CONCERNETH, CONCERNING]

Ac 28:31 teaching those *things* which c the Lord 4012
2Co 11:30 I will glory of the *things* which c mine NIG

CONCERNETH (2) [CONCERN]

Ps 138: 8 The LORD will perfect that which c me: 1157
Eze 12:10 This burden c the prince in Jerusalem, NIH

CONCERNING (242) [CONCERN]

Ge 5:29 This *same* shall comfort us c our work 4480
 12:20 Pharaoh commanded his men c him: and 5921
 19:21 See, I have accepted thee c this thing, 3807.1
 24: 9 master, and sware to him c that matter. 5921
 26:32 c the well which they had digged, 182+5921
 42:21 We *are* verily guilty c our brother, 5921
Ex 6: 8 c the which I did swear to give it to NIH
 24: 8 which the LORD hath made with you c all 5921
Lev 4: 2 (c *things* which ought not to be done), NIH
 4:13 LORD c *things* which should not be done, NIH
 4:22 God c *things* which should not be done, NIH
 4:26 make an atonement for him as c his sin, 4480
 4:27 c *things* which ought not to be done, NIH
 5: 6 make an atonement for him c his sin. 4480
 5:18 for him c his ignorance wherein he erred 5921
 6: 3 and lieth c it, and sweareth falsely; 871.1
 6:18 c the offerings of the LORD made by fire: 4480
 23: 2 say unto them, c The feasts of the LORD, NIH
 27:32 c the tithe of the herd, or of the flock, NIH
Nu 8:20 LORD commanded Moses c the Levites, 3807.1
 8:22 as the LORD had commanded Moses c 5921
 9: 8 what the LORD will command c you. 3807.1
 10:29 for the LORD hath spoken good c Israel. 5921
 14:30 c which I sware to make you dwell NIH
 30: 1 of the tribes c the children of Israel, 5921
 30:12 whatsoever proceeded out of her lips c 3807.1
 30:12 c the bond of her soul, shall not stand: 3807.1
 32:28 So c them Moses commanded Eleazar 3807.1
 36: 6 c the daughters of Zelophehad, 3807.1
Jos 14: 6 unto Moses the man of God c me 182+5921

Jos 23:14 which the LORD your God spake c you; 5921
Jdg 15: 3 Samson said c them, Now shall I be 3807.1
 21: 5 For *they* had made a great oath c *him* 3807.1
Ru 4: 7 in former time in Israel c redeeming 5921
 4: 7 concerning redeeming and c changing, 5921
1Sa 3:12 *things* which I have spoken c his house: 413
 25:30 to all the good that he hath spoken c thee, 5921
2Sa 3: 8 that thou chargest me to day with a fault c NIH
 7:25 the word that thou hast spoken c thy 5921
 7:25 c his house, establish *it* for ever, and do as 5921
 11:18 and told David all the **things** c the war; 1697
 13:39 for he was comforted c Amnon, seeing he 5921
 14: 8 thine house, and I will give charge c thee. 5921
 18: 5 all the captains charge c Absalom. 1697+5921
1Ki 2: 4 continue his word which he spake c me, 5921
 2:27 he spake c the house of Eli in Shiloh. 5921
 5: 8 I will do all thy desire c timber of cedar, 871.1
 5: 8 timber of cedar, and c timber of fir. 871.1
 6:12 c This house which thou art in building, NIH
 8:41 Moreover c a stranger, that *is not* of thy 413
 10: 1 of Solomon c the name of the LORD, 3807.1
 11: 2 Of the nations c which the LORD said NIH
 11:10 had commanded him c this thing, that *he* 5921
 22: 8 for he doth not prophesy good c me, 5921
 22:18 that he would prophesy no good c me, 5921
 22:23 and the LORD hath spoken evil c thee. 5921
2Ki 10:10 which the LORD spake c the house of 5921
 17:15 c whom the LORD had charged them, 5921
 19:21 word that the LORD hath spoken c him; 5921
 19:32 Therefore thus saith the LORD c the king 413
 22:13 the words of this book that is found: 5921
 22:13 unto all that which is written c us. 5921
1Ch 11:10 according to the word of the LORD c 5921
 17:23 let the thing that thou hast spoken c thy 5921
 17:23 and c thine house be established for ever, 5921
 19: 2 David sent messengers to comfort him c 5921
 22:12 and give thee charge c Israel, 5921
 22:13 the LORD charged Moses with c Israel: 5921
 23:14 Now c Moses the man of God, his sons NIH
 24:21 C Rehabiah: of the sons of Rehabiah, 3807.1
 24:29 C Kish: the son of Kish *was* Jerahmeel. 3807.1
 26: 1 C The divisions of the porters: Of 3807.1
 26:21 *As* c the sons of Laadan; the sons of NIH
2Ch 6:32 the stranger, which *is not* of thy 413
 8:15 the priests and Levites c any matter, 3807.1
 8:15 any matter, or c the treasures. 3807.1
 12:15 and of Iddo the seer c genealogies? 3807.1
 15:16 c Maachah the mother of Asa the king, NIH
 24:27 Now c his sons, and the greatness of NIH
 31: 6 c the children of Israel and Judah, NIH
 31: 9 the priests and the Levites c the heaps. 5921
 34:21 c the words of the book that is found: 5921
 34:26 Thus saith the LORD God of Israel c NIH
Ezr 5: 5 they returned answer by letter c this 5922
 5:17 let the king send his pleasure to us c this 5922
 6: 3 a decree c the house of God at Jerusalem, NIH
 7:14 to inquire c Judah and Jerusalem, 5922
 10: 2 now there is hope in Israel c this *thing.* 5921
Ne 1: 2 I asked them c the Jews that had escaped, 5921
 1: 2 were left of the captivity, and c Jerusalem. 5921
 9:23 c which thou hadst promised to their NIH
 11:23 For *it was* the king's commandment c 5921
 11:24 *was* at the king's hand in all matters c 3807.1
 13:14 c this, and wipe not out my good deeds 5921
 13:22 c this also, and spare me according to NIH
Est 3: 2 for the king had so commanded c him. 3807.1
 9:26 *of that* which they had seen c this *matter,* 5921
Job 36:33 The noise thereof sheweth c it, the cattle 5921
 36:33 concerning it, the cattle also c the vapour. 5921
Ps 7: T C the words of Cush the Benjamite. NIH
 17: 4 C the works of men, by the word of thy 3807.1
 73: 8 and speak wickedly c oppression: NIH
 90:13 and let it repent thee c thy servants. 5921
 106:34 c whom the LORD commanded them: NIH
 119:128 Therefore I esteem all *thy* precepts c all NIH
 119:152 C thy testimonies, I have known of old 4480
 135:14 and he will repent himself c his servants. 5921
Ecc 1:13 search out by wisdom c all *things* that are 5921
 3:18 I said in my heart c the estate of the sons 5921
 7:10 for thou dost not inquire wisely c this. 5921
Isa 1: 1 which he saw c Judah and Jerusalem in 5921
 2: 1 that Isaiah the son of Amoz saw c Judah 5921
 8: 1 write in it with a man's pen c 3807.1
 16:13 hath spoken c Moab since that time. 413
 23: 5 As *at* the report c Egypt, so shall they be 3807.1
 29:22 redeemed Abraham, c the house of Jacob, 413
 30: 7 therefore have I cried c this, 3807.1
 37: 9 he heard say c Tirhakah king of Ethiopia, 5921
 37:22 word which the LORD hath spoken c him; 5921
 37:33 Therefore thus saith the LORD c the king 413
 45:11 Ask me of *things* to come c my sons, 5921
 45:11 c the work of my hands command ye me. 5921
Jer 7:22 c burnt offerings or sacrifices: 1697+5921
 14: 1 that came to Jeremiah c the dearth. 1697+5921
 14:15 Therefore thus saith the LORD c the 5921
 16: 3 For thus saith the LORD c the sons and 5921
 16: 3 c the daughters that are born in this place, 5921
 16: 3 c their mothers that bare them, 5921
 16: 3 c their fathers that begat them in this land; 5921
 18: 7 *At what* instant I shall speak c a nation 5921
 18: 7 concerning a nation and c a kingdom, 5921
 18: 9 *At what* instant I shall speak c a nation, 5921
 18: 9 and c a kingdom, to build and to plant *it;* 5921
 22:18 Therefore thus saith the LORD c Jehoiakim 413
 23:15 Therefore thus saith the LORD of hosts c 5921

Jer 25: 1 The word that came to Jeremiah c all 5921
 27:19 For thus saith the LORD of hosts c 413
 27:19 c the sea, and concerning the bases, 5921
 27:19 c the bases, and concerning the residue of 5921
 27:19 c the residue of the vessels that remain in 5921
 27:21 c the vessels that remain in the house of 5921
 29:31 Thus saith the LORD c Shemaiah 413
 30: 4 these *are* the words that the LORD spake c 413
 30: 4 spake concerning Israel and c Judah. 413
 32:36 God of Israel, c this city, whereof ye say, 413
 33: 4 the houses of this city, and concerning 5921
 33: 4 and c the houses of the kings of Judah, 5921
 39:11 c Jeremiah to Nebuzar-adan the captain of 5921
 42:19 The LORD hath said c you, O ye remnant 5921
 44: 1 The word that came to Jeremiah c all 413
 49: 1 C the Ammonites, thus saith the LORD; 3807.1
 49: 7 C Edom, thus saith the LORD of hosts; 3807.1
 49:23 C Damascus. Hamath is confounded, 3807.1
 49:28 C Kedar, and concerning the kingdoms 3807.1
 49:28 and c the kingdoms of Hazor, 3807.1
 52:21 c the pillars, the height of one pillar *was* NIH
La 1:17 the LORD hath commanded c Jacob, 3807.1
Eze 13:16 of Israel which prophesy c Jerusalem, 5921
 14: 7 to a prophet to inquire of him c me; 871.1
 14:22 ye shall be comforted c the evil that 5921
 14:22 *even* c all that I have brought upon it. NIH
 18: 2 ye use this proverb c the land of Israel, 5921
 21:28 Thus saith the Lord GOD c the Ammonites, 413
 21:28 the Ammonites, and c their reproach; 413
 36: 6 Prophesy therefore c the land of Israel, 5921
 44: 5 c all the ordinances of the house of 3807.1
 45:14 C the ordinance of oil, the bath of oil, 2050.1
 47:14 c the which I lifted up mine hand to give NIH
Da 2:18 mercies of the God of heaven c this secret; 5922
 5:29 his neck, and made a proclamation c him, 5922
 6: 4 against Daniel c the kingdom; 4481+6655
 6: 5 except we find *it* against him c the law of 871.2
 6:12 spake before the king c the king's decree; 5922
 6:17 that the purpose might not be changed c 871.2
 7:12 As c the rest of the beasts, they had 2050.3
 8:13 How long *shall be* the vision c the daily NIH
Am 1: 1 he saw c Israel in the days of Uzziah 5921
Ob 1: 1 Thus saith the Lord GOD c Edom; 3807.1
Mic 1: 1 which he saw c Samaria and Jerusalem. 5921
 3: 5 Thus saith the LORD c the prophets that 5921
Na 1: T the LORD hath given a commandment c 5921
Hag 2:11 Ask now the priests c the law, saying, NIH
Mt 4: 6 He shall give his angels charge c thee: 4012
 11: 7 Jesus began to say unto the multitudes c 4012
 16:11 that I spake *it* not to you c bread, 4012
Mk 5:16 with the devil, and *also* c the swine. 4012
 7:17 his disciples asked him c the parable. 4012
Lk 2:17 saying which was told them c this child. 4012
 7:24 he began to speak unto the people c John, 4012
 18:31 *things* that are written by the prophets c NIG
 22:37 for the *things* c me have an end. 4012
 24:19 C Jesus of Nazareth, which was a prophet 4012
 24:27 in all the scriptures the *things* c himself. 4012
 24:44 in the prophets, and *in* the psalms, c me. 4012
Jn 7:12 murmuring among the people c him: 4012
 7:32 the people murmured such *things* c him; 4012
 9:18 But the Jews did not believe c him, 4012
 11:19 Mary, to comfort them c their brother. 4012
Ac 1:16 the mouth of David spake before c Judas, 4012
 2:25 For David speaketh c him, I foresaw 1519
 8:12 the *things* c the kingdom of God, 4012
 13:34 And as c that he raised him up from NIG
 19: 8 persuading the *things* c the kingdom of 4012
 19:39 If ye inquire any *thing* c other *matters,* 4012
 21:24 whereof they were informed c thee, 4012
 22:18 for they will not receive thy testimony c 4012
 23:15 inquire something more perfectly c him: 4012
 24:24 and heard him c the faith in Christ. 4012
 25:16 have licence to answer for himself c 4012
 28:21 We neither received letters out of Judea c 4012
 28:22 for as c this sect, we know that every 4012
 28:23 persuading them c Jesus, both out of 4012
Ro 1: 3 C his Son Jesus Christ our Lord, which 4012
 9: 5 of whom as c the flesh Christ *came,* 2596
 9:27 Esaias also crieth c Israel, Though 5228
 11:28 As c the gospel, *they are* enemies for your 2596
 16:19 *that which is* good, and simple c evil. 1519
1Co 3: 5 c him that hath so done this *deed,* NIG
 7: 1 Now c the *things* whereof ye wrote unto 4012
 7:25 Now c virgins I have no commandment 4012
 8: 4 As c therefore the eating of those things 4012
 12: 1 Now c spiritual *gifts,* brethren, I would 4012
 16: 1 Now c the collection for the saints, as I 4012
2Co 8:23 he *is* my partner and fellowhelper c you: 1519
 11:21 I speak as c reproach, as though we had 2596
Eph 4:22 That ye put off c the former conversation 2596
 5:32 but I speak c Christ and the church. 1519
Php 3: 6 C zeal, persecuting the church; 2596
 4:15 communicated with me as c giving 1519+3056
1Th 3: 2 and to comfort you c your faith: 4012
 4:13 c them which are asleep, that ye 4012
 5:18 for this *is* the will of God in Christ Jesus c 1519
1Ti 1:19 put away, c faith have made shipwreck: 4012
 6:21 Which some professing have erred c 4012
2Ti 2:18 Who c the truth have erred, saying that 4012
 3: 8 of corrupt minds, reprobate c the faith. 4012
Heb 7:14 of which tribe Moses spake nothing c 4012
 11:20 blessed Jacob and Esau c *things* to come. 4012
 11:22 and gave commandment c his bones. 4012
1Pe 4:12 think it not strange c the fiery trial which NIG

C

2Pe 3: 9 The Lord is not slack *c his* promise, as NIG
1Jn 2:26 These *things* have I written unto you *c* 4012

CONCISION (1)
Php 3: 2 beware of evil workers, beware of the *c.* 2699

CONCLUDE (1) [CONCLUDED, CONCLUSION]
Ro 3:28 Therefore we *c* that a man is justified by 3049

CONCLUDED (3) [CONCLUDE]
Ac 21:25 *c* that they observe no such *thing,* save 2919
Ro 11:32 For God hath *c them* all in unbelief, that 4788
Gal 3:22 But the scripture hath *c* all under sin, 4788

CONCLUSION (1) [CONCLUDE]
Ecc 12:13 Let us hear the *c* of the whole matter: 5490

CONCORD (1)
2Co 6:15 And what *c* hath Christ with Belial? or 4857

CONCOURSE (2)
Pr 1:21 She crieth in the chief place of *c,* 1993
Ac 19:40 we may give an account of this *c.* 4963

CONCUBINE (22) [CONCUBINES]
Ge 22:24 his *c,* whose name *was* Reumah, she bare 6370
 35:22 and lay with Bilhah his father's *c:* 6370
 36:12 Timna was *c* to Eliphaz Esau's son; 6370
Jdg 8:31 *c* that *was* in Shechem, she also bare 6370
 19: 1 who took to him a *c* out of 6370
 19: 2 his *c* played the whore against him, 6370
 19: 9 and his *c,* and his servant, his father in 6370
 19:10 asses saddled, his *c* also *was* with him. 6370
 19:24 *here is* my daughter a maiden, and his *c;* 6370
 19:25 the man took his *c,* and brought *her* forth 6370
 19:27 the woman his *c was* fallen down *at* 6370
 19:29 and laid hold on his *c,* and divided her, 6370
 20: 4 to Benjamin, and I and my *c,* to lodge. 6370
 20: 5 my *c* have they forced, that she is dead. 6370
 20: 6 I took my *c,* and cut her in pieces, 6370
2Sa 3: 7 Saul had a *c,* whose name *was* Rizpah, 6370
 3: 7 hast thou gone in unto my father's *c?* 6370
 21:11 daughter of Aiah, the *c* of Saul, had done. 6370
1Ch 1:32 Now the sons of Keturah, Abraham's *c:* 6370
 2:46 Caleb's *c,* bare Haran, and Moza, 6370
 2:48 Maachah, Caleb's *c,* bare Sheber, 6370
 7:14 his *c* the Aramitess bare Machir the father 6370

CONCUBINES (17) [CONCUBINE]
Ge 25: 6 the sons of the *c,* which Abraham had, 6370
2Sa 5:13 David took *him mo c* and wives out of 6370
 15:16 *which were c,* to keep the house. 6370
 16:21 unto Absalom, Go in unto thy father's *c,* 6370
 16:22 Absalom went in unto his father's *c* in 6370
 19: 5 lives of thy wives, and the lives of thy *c;* 6370
 20: 3 the king took the ten women *his c,* 6370
1Ki 11: 3 princesses, and three hundred *c:* 6370
1Ch 3: 9 beside the sons of the *c,* and Tamar their 6370
2Ch 11:21 of Absalom above all his wives and his *c:* 6370
 11:21 he took eighteen wives, and threescore *c;* 6370
Est 2:14 the king's chamberlain, which kept the *c;* 6370
SS 6: 8 fourscore *c,* and virgins without number. 6370
 6: 9 the queens and the *c,* and they praised 6370
Da 5: 2 and his princes, his wives, and his *c,* 3904
 5: 3 and his princes, his wives, and his *c,* 3904
 5:23 thou, and thy lords, thy wives, and thy *c,* 3904

CONCUPISCENCE (3)
Ro 7: 8 wrought in me all *manner of c.* 1939
Col 3: 5 evil *c,* and covetousness, which is idolatry: 1939
1Th 4: 5 Not in the lust of *c,* even as the Gentiles 1939

CONDEMN (24) [CONDEMNATION, CONDEMNED, CONDEMNEST, CONDEMNETH, CONDEMNING, UNCONDEMNED]
Ex 22: 9 whom the judges shall *c,* he shall pay 7561
Dt 25: 1 justify the righteous, and *c* the wicked. 7561
Job 9:20 myself, mine own mouth shall *c* me: 7561
 10: 2 I will say unto God, Do not *c* me; shew 7561
 34:17 and wilt thou *c* him that is most just? 7561
 40: 8 wilt thou *c* me, that thou mayest be 7561
Ps 37:33 in his hand, nor *c* him when he is judged. 7561
 94:21 the righteous, and *c* the innocent blood. 7561
 109:31 to save *him* from those that *c* his soul. 8199
Pr 12: 2 but a man of wicked devices will he *c.* 7561
Isa 50: 9 will help me; who *is he that* shall *c* me? 7561
 54:17 rise against thee in judgment thou shalt *c.* 7561
Mt 12:41 with this generation, and shall *c* it: 2632
 12:42 with this generation, and shall *c* it: 2632
 20:18 *the* scribes, and they shall *c* him to death, 2632
Mk 10:33 and they shall *c* him to death, 2632
Lk 6:37 *c* not, and ye shall not be condemned: 2613
 11:31 the men of this generation, and *c* them; 2632
 11:32 with this generation, and shall *c* it: 2632
Jn 3:17 God sent not his Son into the world to *c* 2919
 8:11 Jesus said unto her, Neither do I *c* thee: 2632
2Co 7: 3 I speak not *this* to *c* you: for I have said 2633
1Jn 3:20 For if *our* heart *c* us, God is greater than 2607
 3:21 if our heart *c* us, *then* have we 2607

CONDEMNATION (12) [CONDEMN]
Lk 23:40 fear God, seeing thou art in the same *c?* 2917
Jn 3:19 And this is the *c,* that light is come into 2920
 5:24 everlasting life, and shall not come into *c;* 2920
Ro 5:16 for the judgment *was* by one to *c,* 2631
 5:18 of one *judgment came* upon all men to *c;* 2631

Ro 8: 1 no *c* to them *which are* in Christ Jesus 2631
1Co 11:34 that ye come not together unto *c.* 2917
2Co 3: 9 For if the ministration of *c be* glory, 2633
1Ti 3: 6 with pride he fall into the *c* of the devil. 2917
Jas 3: 1 that we shall receive the greater *c.* 2917
 5:12 and *your* nay, nay; lest ye fall into *c.* 2920
Jude 1: 4 were before of old ordained to this *c,* 2917

CONDEMNED (21) [CONDEMN]
2Ch 36: 3 *c* the land in an hundred talents of silver 6064
Job 32: 3 had found no answer, and *yet* had *c* Job. 7561
Ps 109: 7 When he shall be judged, let him be *c:* 7563
Am 2: 8 they drink the wine of the *c* in the house 6064
Mt 12: 7 ye would not have *c* the guiltless, 2613
 12:37 and by thy words thou shalt be *c.* 2613
 27: 3 when he saw that he was *c,* 2632
Mk 14:64 And they all *c* him to be guilty of death. 2632
Lk 6:37 condemn not, and ye shall not be *c:* 2613
 24:20 our rulers delivered him to be *c* to death, 2917
Jn 3:18 He that believeth on him is not *c:* but 2919
 3:18 but he that believeth not is *c* already, 2919
 8:10 thine accusers? hath no *man c* thee? 2632
Ro 8: 3 sinful flesh, and for sin, *c* sin in the flesh: 2632
1Co 11:32 that we should not be *c* with the world. 2632
Tit 2: 8 Sound speech that **cannot be** *c;* that he 176
 3:11 and sinneth, being *c* of himself. 843
Heb 11: 7 by the which he *c* the world, 2632
Jas 5: 6 Ye have *c and* killed the just; *and* he doth 2613
 5: 9 one against another, brethren, lest ye be *c:* 2632
2Pe 2: 6 Gomorrha into ashes *c* them with an 2632

CONDEMNEST (1) [CONDEMN]
Ro 2: 1 thou judgest another, thou *c* thyself; 2632

CONDEMNETH (4) [CONDEMN]
Job 15: 6 Thine own mouth *c* thee, and not I; yea, 7561
Pr 17:15 the wicked, and he that *c* the just, 7561
Ro 8:34 Who *is* he that *c?* *It is* Christ that died, 2632
 14:22 Happy *is* he that *c* not himself in *that* 2919

CONDEMNING (2) [CONDEMN]
1Ki 8:32 do, and judge thy servants, *c* the wicked, 7561
Ac 13:27 they have fulfilled *them* in *c* him. 2919

CONDESCEND (1)
Ro 12:16 high *things,* but *c* to *men* of low estate. 4879

CONDITION (1)
1Sa 11: 2 On this *c* will I make *a covenant* with you, NIH

CONDITIONS (1) [CONDITION]
Lk 14:32 an ambassage, and desireth *c* of peace. 3588

CONDUCT (3) [CONDUCTED]
2Sa 19:15 meet the king, to *c* the king over Jordan. 5674
 19:31 with the king, to *c* him *over* Jordan. 7971
1Co 16:11 but *c* him *forth* in peace, that he may 4311

CONDUCTED (2) [CONDUCT]
2Sa 19:40 all the people of Judah *c* the king, 5674
Ac 17:15 And they that *c* Paul brought him unto 2525

CONDUIT (4)
2Ki 18:17 and stood by the *c* of the upper pool, 8585
 20:20 and a *c,* and brought water into the city, 8585
Isa 7: 3 at the end of the *c* of the upper pool in 8585
 36: 2 he stood by the *c* of the upper pool in 8585

CONEY (1) [CONIES, CONY]
Dt 14: 7 *as* the camel, and the hare, and the *c:* 8227

CONFECTION (1) [CONFECTIONARIES]
Ex 30:35 a *c after* the art of the apothecary, 7545

CONFECTIONARIES (1) [CONFECTION]
1Sa 8:13 he will take your daughters to be *c,* 7548

CONFEDERACY (3) [CONFEDERATE]
Isa 8:12 Say ye not, A *c,* to all *them* to whom this 7195
 8:12 *them* to whom this people shall say, A *c;* 7195
Ob 1: 7 All the men of thy *c* have brought thee 1285

CONFEDERATE (3) [CONFEDERACY]
Ge 14:13 and these *were c* with Abram. 1167+1285
Ps 83: 5 with one consent: they are *c* against thee: 1285
Isa 7: 2 of David, saying, Syria is *c* with Ephraim. 5117

CONFERENCE (1) [CONFERRED]
Gal 2: 6 be somewhat **in c** added nothing to me: 4323

CONFERRED (4) [CONFERENCE]
1Ki 1: 7 he *c* with Joab the son of Zeruiah, 1697+1961
Ac 4:15 of the council, they *c* among themselves, 4820
 25:12 he had *c* with the council, answered, 4814
Gal 1:16 immediately I *c* not with flesh and blood: 4323

CONFESS (28) [CONFESSED, CONFESSETH, CONFESSING, CONFESSION]
Lev 5: 5 shall *c* that he hath sinned in that *thing:* 3034
 16:21 *c* over him all the iniquities of the children 3034
 26:40 If they shall *c* their iniquity, 3034
Nu 5: 7 shall *c* their sin which they have done: 3034
1Ki 8:33 *c* thy name, and pray, 3034
 8:35 *c* thy name, and turn from their sin, 3034
2Ch 6:24 shall return and *c* thy name, and pray and 3034
 6:26 *c* thy name, *and* turn from their sin, 3034
Ne 1: 6 *c* the sins of the children of Israel, 3034

Job 40:14 I also *c* unto thee that thine own right 3034
Ps 32: 5 I will *c* my transgressions unto the LORD; 3034
Mt 10:32 therefore shall *c* me before men, 3670
 10:32 him will I *c* also before my Father which 3670
Lk 12: 8 Whosoever shall *c* me before men, 3670
 12: 8 him shall the Son of man also *c* before 3670
Jn 9:22 that if any *man* did *c* that he *was* Christ, 3670
 12:42 of the Pharisees they did not *c him,* lest 3670
Ac 23: 8 angel nor spirit: but the Pharisees *c* both. 3670
 24:14 But this I *c* unto thee, that after the way 3670
Ro 10: 9 if thou shalt *c* with thy mouth the Lord 3670
 14:11 to me, and every tongue shall *c* to God. 1843
 15: 9 For this cause I will *c* to thee among 1843
Php 2:11 And *that* every tongue should *c* that Jesus 1843
Jas 5:16 *C* your faults one to another, and pray one 1843
1Jn 1: 9 If we *c* our sins, he is faithful and just to 3670
 4:15 Whosoever shall *c* that Jesus is the Son of 3670
2Jn 1: 7 who *c* not that Jesus Christ is come in 3670
Rev 3: 5 but I will *c* his name before my Father, 1843

CONFESSED (7) [CONFESS]
Ezr 10: 1 when he had *c,* weeping and 3034
Ne 9: 2 and their sins, and the iniquities of 3034
 9: 3 *another* fourth *part* they *c,* 3034
Jn 1:20 And he *c,* and denied not; but confessed, 3670
 1:20 denied not; but *c,* I am not the Christ. 3670
Ac 19:18 and *c,* and shewed their deeds. 1843
Heb 11:13 and *c* that they were strangers and 3670

CONFESSETH (3) [CONFESS]
Pr 28:13 whoso *c* and forsaketh *them* shall have 3034
1Jn 4: 2 Every spirit that *c* that Jesus Christ is come 3670
 4: 3 every spirit that *c* not that Jesus Christ 3670

CONFESSING (3) [CONFESS]
Da 9:20 *c* my sin and the sin of my people Israel, 3034
Mt 3: 6 baptized of him in Jordan, *c* their sins. 1843
Mk 1: 5 of him in the river *of* Jordan, *c* their sins. 1843

CONFESSION (6) [CONFESS]
Jos 7:19 God of Israel, and make *c* unto him; 8426
2Ch 30:22 **making** *c* to the LORD God of their 3034
Ezr 10:11 make *c* unto the LORD God of your 8426
Da 9: 4 **made** my *c,* and said, O Lord, the great 3034
Ro 10:10 with the mouth *c* is **made** unto salvation. 3670
1Ti 6:13 before Pontius Pilate witnessed a good *c;* 3671

CONFIDENCE (38) [CONFIDENT]
Jdg 9:26 the men of Shechem **put** their *c* in him. 982
2Ki 18:19 What *c is* this wherein thou trustest? 986
Job 4: 6 *Is* not this thy fear, thy *c,* thy hope; 3690
 18:14 His *c* shall be rooted out of his tabernacle, 4009
 31:24 have said to the fine gold, *Thou art* my *c;* 4009
Ps 65: 5 *who art* the *c* of all the ends of the earth, 4009
 118: 8 to trust in the LORD than to **put** *c* in man. 982
 118: 9 trust in the LORD than to **put** *c* in princes. 982
Pr 3:26 For the LORD shall be thy *c,* 3689
 14:26 In the fear of the LORD *is* strong *c:* and 4009
 21:22 casteth down the strength of the *c* 4009
 25:19 *C* in an unfaithful *man* in time of trouble 4009
Isa 30:15 quietness and in *c* shall be your strength: 985
 36: 4 What *c is* this wherein thou trustest? 986
Jer 48:13 of Israel was ashamed of Beth-el their *c.* 4009
Eze 28:26 yea, they shall dwell with *c,* when I have 983
 29:16 it shall be no more the *c* of the house of 4009
Mic 7: 5 ye not in a friend, **put** ye not *c* in a guide: 982
Ac 28:31 with all *c,* no man forbidding him. 3954
2Co 1:15 And in this *c* I was minded to come unto 4006
 2: 3 having *c* in you all, that my joy is *the* joy 3982
 7:16 that I **have** *c* in you in all *things.* 2292
 8:22 upon the great *c* which *I* have in you. 4006
 10: 2 be bold when I am present with *that c,* 4006
 11:17 as *it were* foolishly, in this *c* of boasting. 5287
Gal 5:10 I have *c* in you through the Lord, that you 3982
Eph 3:12 and access with *c* by the faith of him. 4006
Php 1:25 **having** this *c,* I know that I shall abide 3982
 3: 3 Christ Jesus, and **have** no *c* in the flesh. 3982
 3: 4 Though I *might* also have *c* in the flesh. 4006
2Th 3: 4 And we have *c* in the Lord touching you, 3982
Phm 1:21 **Having** *c* in thy obedience I wrote unto 3982
Heb 3: 6 if we hold fast the *c* and the rejoicing of 3954
 3:14 if we hold the beginning of *our c* stedfast 5287
 10:35 Cast not away therefore your *c,* which 3954
1Jn 2:28 we may have *c,* and not be ashamed 3954
 3:21 us not, *then* have we *c* towards God. 3954
 5:14 this is the *c* that we have in him, that, 3954

CONFIDENCES (1) [CONFIDENCE, CONFIDENCES, CONFIDENT]
Jer 2:37 for the LORD hath rejected thy *c,* 4009

CONFIDENT (8) [CONFIDENTLY]
Ps 27: 3 should rise against me, in this *will* I *be c.* 982
Pr 14:16 from evil: but the fool rageth, and *is c.* 982
Ro 2:19 And art *c* that thou thyself art a guide of 3982
2Co 5: 6 Therefore *we are* always *c,* knowing that, 2292
 5: 8 We are *c,* I say, and willing rather to be 2292
 9: 4 be ashamed in this *same c* boasting. 5287
Php 1: 6 Being *c* of this very *thing,* that he which 3982
 1:14 in the Lord, **waxing** *c* by my bonds, 3982

CONFIDENTLY (1) [CONFIDENT]
Lk 22:59 of one hour after another *c* **affirmed,** 1340

CONFIRM (13) [CONFIRMATION, CONFIRMED, CONFIRMETH, CONFIRMING]

Ru	4: 7 concerning changing, for to c all things;	6965
1Ki	1:14 will come in after thee, and c thy words.	4390
2Ki	15:19 that his hand might be with him to c	2388
Est	9:29 to c this second letter of Purim.	6965
	9:31 To c these days of Purim in their times	6965
Ps	68: 9 whereby thou didst c thine inheritance,	3559
Isa	35: 3 the weak hands, and c the feeble knees.	553
Eze	13: 6 to hope that they would c the word.	6965
Da	9:27 he shall c the covenant with many for one	1396
	11: 1 even I, stood to c and to strengthen him.	2388
Ro	15: 8 to c the promises made unto the fathers:	950
1Co	1: 8 Who shall also c you unto the end, that ye	950
2Co	2: 8 Wherefore I beseech you that you would c	2964

CONFIRMATION (2) [CONFIRM]

Php	1: 7 and in the defence and c of the gospel,	951
Heb	6:16 an oath for c is to them an end of all strife.	951

CONFIRMED (13) [CONFIRM]

2Sa	7:24 For thou hast c to thyself thy people Israel	3559
2Ki	14: 5 as soon as the kingdom was c in his hand,	2388
1Ch	14: 2 David perceived that the LORD had c him	3559
	16:17 hath c the same to Jacob for a law,	5975
Est	9:32 the decree of Esther c these matters of	6965
Ps	105:10 c the same unto Jacob for a law,	5975
Da	9:12 he hath c his words, which he spake	6965
Ac	15:32 brethren with many words, and c them.	1991
1Co	1: 6 Even as the testimony of Christ was c in	950
Gal	3:15 it be but a man's covenant, yet if it be c,	2964
	3:17 was c before of God in Christ, the law,	4300
Heb	2: 3 was c unto us by them that heard him;	950
	6:17 of his counsel, c it by an oath:	3315

CONFIRMETH (3) [CONFIRM]

Nu	30:14 he c them, because he held his peace at	6965
Dt	27:26 Cursed be he that c not all the words of	6965
Isa	44:26 That c the word of his servant,	6965

CONFIRMING (2) [CONFIRM]

Mk	16:20 and c the word with signs following.	950
Ac	14:22 C the souls of the disciples,	1991
	15:41 through Syria and Cilicia, c the churches.	1991

CONFISCATION (1)

Ezr	7:26 or to c of goods, or to imprisonment.	6065

CONFLICT (2)

Php	1:30 Having the same c which ye saw in me,	73
Col	2: 1 I would that ye knew what great c I have	73

CONFORMABLE (1) [CONFORMED]

Php	3:10 sufferings, being made c unto his death;	4833

CONFORMED (2) [CONFORMABLE]

Ro	8:29 also did predestinate to be c to the image	4832
	12: 2 And be not c to this world: but be ye	4964

CONFOUND (5) [CONFOUNDED]

Ge	11: 7 go down, and there c their language,	1101
	11: 9 the LORD did there c the language of all	1101
Jer	1:17 at their faces, lest I c thee before them.	2865
1Co	1:27 foolish things of the world to c the wise;	2617
	1:27 world to c the things which are mighty;	2617

CONFOUNDED (50) [CONFOUND]

2Ki	19:26 of small power, they were dismayed and c;	954
Job	6:20 They were c because they had hoped;	954
Ps	22: 5 they trusted in thee, and were not c.	954
	35: 4 Let them be c and put to shame that seek	954
	40:14 c together that seek after my soul to	2659
	69: 6 let not those that seek thee be c for my	3637
	70: 2 be ashamed and c that seek after my soul:	2659
	71:13 Let them be c and consumed that are	954
	71:24 for they are c, for they are brought unto	954
	83:17 Let them be c and troubled for ever; yea,	954
	97: 7 C be all they that serve graven images,	954
	129: 5 Let them all be c and turned back that hate	954
Isa	1:29 ye shall be c for the gardens that ye have	2659
	19: 9 and they that weave networks, shall be c.	954
	24:23 moon shall be c, and the sun ashamed,	2659
	37:27 small power, they were dismayed and c:	954
	41:11 against thee shall be ashamed and c;	3637
	45:16 shall be ashamed, and also c, all of them:	3637
	45:17 ye shall not be ashamed nor c world	3637
	50: 7 will help me; therefore shall I not be c:	3637
	54: 4 neither be thou c; for thou shalt not be	3637
Jer	9:19 we are greatly c, because we have forsaken	954
	10:14 every founder is c by the graven image:	954
	14: 3 they were ashamed and c, and covered	3637
	15: 9 she hath been ashamed and c: and	2659
	17:18 Let them be c that persecute me, but let	954
	17:18 that persecute me, but let not me be c:	954
	22:22 be ashamed and c for all thy wickedness.	3637
	31:19 even c, because that I did bear the reproach	3637
	46:24 The daughter of Egypt shall be c; she shall	954
	48: 1 Kiriathaim is c and taken: Misgab is	954
	48: 1 and taken: Misgab is c and dismayed.	954
	48:20 Moab is c; for it is broken down: howl and	954
	49:23 Hamath is c, and Arpad: for they have	954
	50: 2 say, Babylon is taken, Bel is c, Merodach	954
	50: 2 her idols are c, her images are broken in	954
	50:12 Your mother shall be sore c; she that bare	954
	51:17 every founder is c by the graven image:	954

Jer	51:47 her whole land shall be c, and all her slain	954
	51:51 We are c, because we have heard reproach:	954
Eze	16:52 yea, be thou c also, and bear thy shame,	954
	16:54 mayest be c in all that thou hast done,	3637
	16:63 be c, and never open thy mouth any more,	954
	36:32 be ashamed and c for your own ways,	3637
Mic	3: 7 the seers be ashamed, and the diviners c:	2659
	7:16 shall see and be c at all their might:	954
Zec	10: 5 and the riders on horses shall be c.	3001
Ac	2: 6 were c, because that every man heard	4797
	2: 6 the Jews which dwelt at Damascus,	4797
1Pe	2: 6 he that believeth on him shall not be c.	2617

CONFUSED (2) [CONFUSION]

Isa	9: 5 battle of the warrior is with c noise,	7494
Ac	19:32 the assembly was c; and the more part	4797

CONFUSION (26) [CONFUSED]

Lev	18:23 before a beast to lie down thereto: it is c.	8397
	20:12 they have wrought c; their blood shall be	8397
1Sa	20:30 chosen the son of Jesse to thine own c,	1322
	20:30 unto the c of thy mother's nakedness?	1322
Ezr	9: 7 captivity, and to a spoil, and to c of face,	1322
Job	10:15 I am full of c; therefore see thou mine	7036
Ps	35: 4 and brought to c that desire my hurt.	2659
	35:26 brought to c together that rejoice at mine	2659
	44:15 My c is continually before me,	3639
	70: 2 and put to c, that desire my hurt.	3637
	71: 1 I put my trust: let me never be put to c.	954
	109:29 them cover themselves with their own c,	1322
Isa	24:10 The city of c is broken down: every house	8414
	30: 3 the trust in the shadow of Egypt your c.	3639
	34:11 he shall stretch out upon it the line of c,	8414
	41:29 their molten images are wind and c.	8414
	45:16 shall go to c together that are makers	3639
	61: 7 for c they shall rejoice in their portion:	3639
Jer	3:25 in our shame, and our c covereth us:	3639
	7:19 they not provoke themselves to the c of	1322
	20:11 everlasting c shall never be forgotten.	3639
Da	9: 7 but unto us c of faces, as at this day;	1322
	9: 8 O Lord, to us belongeth c of face, to our	1322
Ac	19:29 And the whole city was filled with c: and	4799
1Co	14:33 God is not the author of c, but of peace,	181
Jas	3:16 strife is, there is c and every evil work.	181

CONGEALED (1)

Ex	15: 8 the depths were c in the heart of the sea.	7087

CONGRATULATE (1)

1Ch	18:10 to c him, because he had fought against	1288

CONGREGATION (364) [CONGREGATIONS]

Ex	12: 3 Speak ye unto all the c of Israel, saying,	5712
	12: 6 the whole assembly of the c of Israel shall	5712
	12:19 that soul shall be cut off from the c of	5712
	12:47 All the c of Israel shall keep it.	5712
	16: 1 all the c of the children of Israel came	5712
	16: 2 the whole c of the children of Israel	5712
	16: 9 Say unto all the c of the children of Israel,	5712
	16:10 as Aaron spake unto the whole c of	5712
	16:22 the rulers of the c came and told Moses.	5712
	17: 1 all the c of the children of Israel journeyed	5712
	27:21 In the tabernacle of the c without the vail,	4150
	28:43 they come in unto the tabernacle of the c,	4150
	29: 4 unto the door of the tabernacle of the c,	4150
	29:10 be brought before the tabernacle of the c:	4150
	29:11 by the door of the tabernacle of the c.	4150
	29:30 of the c to minister in the holy place.	4150
	29:32 by the door of the tabernacle of the c.	4150
	29:42 the tabernacle of the c before the LORD:	4150
	29:44 I will sanctify the tabernacle of the c,	4150
	30:16 for the service of the tabernacle of the c;	4150
	30:18 put it between the tabernacle of the c	4150
	30:20 they go into the tabernacle of the c,	4150
	30:26 thou shalt anoint the tabernacle of the c	4150
	30:36 the Testimony, in the tabernacle of the c,	4150
	31: 7 The tabernacle of the c, and the ark of	4150
	33: 7 and called it the Tabernacle of the C.	4150
	33: 7 went out unto the Tabernacle of the C,	4150
	34:31 all the rulers of the c returned unto him:	5712
	35: 1 Moses gathered all the c of the children of	5712
	35: 4 Moses spake unto all the c of the children	5712
	35:20 all the c of the children of Israel departed	5712
	35:21 to the work of the tabernacle of the c,	4150
	38: 8 at the door of the tabernacle of the c.	4150
	38:25 of the c was an hundred talents,	5712
	38:30 to the door of the tabernacle of the c,	4150
	39:32 tabernacle of the tent of the c finished:	4150
	39:40 of the tabernacle, for the tent of the c,	4150
	40: 2 set up the tabernacle of the tent of the c.	4150
	40: 6 door of the tabernacle of the tent of the c.	4150
	40: 7 set the laver between the tent of the c	4150
	40:12 unto the door of the tabernacle of the c,	4150
	40:22 he put the table in the tent of the c,	4150
	40:24 he put the candlestick in the tent of the c,	4150
	40:26 he put the golden altar in the tent of the c	4150
	40:29 door of the tabernacle of the tent of the c,	4150
	40:30 he set the laver between the tent of the c	4150
	40:32 When they went into the tent of the c,	4150
	40:34 a cloud covered the tent of the c,	4150
	40:35 not able to enter into the tent of the c,	4150
Lev	1: 1 unto him out of the tabernacle of the c,	4150
	1: 3 the tabernacle of the c before the LORD.	4150
	1: 5 is by the door of the tabernacle of the c.	4150
	3: 2 at the door of the tabernacle of the c:	4150

Lev	3: 8 and kill it before the tabernacle of the c:	4150
	3:13 and kill it before the tabernacle of the c:	4150
	4: 4 the tabernacle of the c before the LORD;	4150
	4: 5 and bring it to the tabernacle of the c.	4150
	4: 7 which is in the tabernacle of the c;	4150
	4: 7 is at the door of the tabernacle of the c.	4150
	4:13 if the whole c of Israel sin through	5712
	4:14 c shall offer a young bullock for the sin,	6951
	4:14 bring him before the tabernacle of the c.	4150
	4:15 the elders of the c shall lay their hands	5712
	4:16 bullock's blood to the tabernacle of the c:	4150
	4:18 that is in the tabernacle of the c, and shall	4150
	4:18 is at the door of the tabernacle of the c.	4150
	4:21 first bullock: it is a sin offering for the c.	6951
	6:16 in the court of the tabernacle of the c they	4150
	6:26 in the court of the tabernacle of the c.	4150
	6:30 c to reconcile withal in the holy place,	4150
	8: 3 gather thou all the c together unto the	5712
	8: 3 unto the door of the tabernacle of the c.	4150
	8: 4 unto the door of the tabernacle of the c.	4150
	8: 5 Moses said unto the c, This is the thing	5712
	8:31 at the door of the tabernacle of the c:	4150
	8:33 of the tabernacle of the c in seven days,	4150
	8:35 at the door of the tabernacle of the c day	4150
	9: 5 before the tabernacle of the c:	4150
	9: 5 all the c drew near and stood before	5712
	9:23 Aaron went into the tabernacle of the c,	4150
	10: 7 from the door of the tabernacle of the c,	4150
	10: 9 when ye go into the tabernacle of the c,	4150
	10:17 given it you to bear the iniquity of the c,	5712
	12: 6 unto the door of the tabernacle of the c:	4150
	14:11 at the door of the tabernacle of the c:	4150
	14:23 unto the door of the tabernacle of the c,	4150
	15:14 unto the door of the tabernacle of the c,	4150
	15:29 to the door of the tabernacle of the c.	4150
	16: 5 he shall take of the c of the children of	5712
	16: 7 at the door of the tabernacle of the c:	4150
	16:16 so shall he do for the tabernacle of the c,	4150
	16:17 c when he goeth in to make an atonement	4150
	16:17 his household, and for all the c of Israel.	6951
	16:20 holy place, and the tabernacle of the c,	4150
	16:23 shall come into the tabernacle of the c,	4150
	16:33 an atonement for the tabernacle of the c,	4150
	16:33 the priests, and for all the people of the c.	6951
	17: 4 unto the door of the tabernacle of the c,	4150
	17: 5 unto the door of the tabernacle of the c,	4150
	17: 6 at the door of the tabernacle of the c,	4150
	17: 9 unto the door of the tabernacle of the c,	4150
	19: 2 Speak unto all the c of the children of	5712
	19:21 unto the door of the tabernacle of the c,	4150
	24: 3 the Testimony, in the tabernacle of the c,	4150
	24:14 upon his head, and let all the c stone him.	5712
	24:16 all the c shall certainly stone him:	5712
Nu	1: 1 in the tabernacle of the c, on the first day	4150
	1: 2 the sum of all the c of the children	5712
	1:16 These were the renowned of the c,	5712
	1:18 they assembled all the c together on	5712
	1:53 that there be no wrath upon the c of	5712
	2: 2 far off about the tabernacle of the c shall	4150
	2:17 the tabernacle of the c shall set forward	4150
	3: 7 the charge of the whole c before	5712
	3: 7 before the tabernacle of the c,	4150
	3: 8 the instruments of the tabernacle of the c,	4150
	3:25 tabernacle of the c shall be the tabernacle,	4150
	3:25 for the door of the tabernacle of the c,	4150
	3:38 even before the tabernacle of the c	4150
	4: 3 to do the work in the tabernacle of the c,	4150
	4: 4 sons of Kohath in the tabernacle of the c,	4150
	4:15 sons of Kohath in the tabernacle of the c,	4150
	4:23 to do the work in the tabernacle of the c,	4150
	4:25 the tabernacle of the c, his covering,	4150
	4:25 for the door of the tabernacle of the c,	4150
	4:28 sons of Gershon in the tabernacle of the c:	4150
	4:30 to do the work in the tabernacle of the c,	4150
	4:31 all their service in the tabernacle of the c;	4150
	4:33 all their service, in the tabernacle of the c,	4150
	4:34 the chief of the c numbered the sons of	5712
	4:35 for the work in the tabernacle of the c:	4150
	4:37 do service in the tabernacle of the c,	4150
	4:39 for the work in the tabernacle of the c,	4150
	4:41 do service in the tabernacle of the c,	4150
	4:43 for the work in the tabernacle of the c,	4150
	4:47 of the burden in the tabernacle of the c,	4150
	6:10 to the door of the tabernacle of the c:	4150
	6:13 unto the door of the tabernacle of the c:	4150
	6:18 at the door of the tabernacle of the c,	4150
	7: 5 do the service of the tabernacle of the c;	4150
	7:89 the tabernacle of the c to speak with him,	4150
	8: 9 the Levites before the tabernacle of the c:	4150
	8:15 do the service of the tabernacle of the c,	4150
	8:19 of Israel in the tabernacle of the c,	4150
	8:20 and all the c of the children of Israel,	5712
	8:22 in the tabernacle of the c before Aaron,	4150
	8:24 the service of the tabernacle of the c:	4150
	8:26 their brethren in the tabernacle of the c,	4150
	10: 3 at the door of the tabernacle of the c.	4150
	10: 7 when the c is to be gathered together,	6951
	11:16 bring them unto the tabernacle of the c,	4150
	12: 4 out ye three unto the tabernacle of the c.	4150
	13:26 and to all the c of the children of Israel,	5712
	13:26 unto all the c, and shewed them the fruit	5712
	14: 1 all the c lifted up their voice, and cried;	5712
	14: 2 the whole c said unto them, Would God	5712
	14: 5 assembly of the c of the children of Israel.	5712
	14:10 all the c bade stone them with stones.	5712

C

Nu	14:10 of the **c** before all the children of Israel.	4150
	14:27 How long *shall I bear* with this evil **c**,	5712
	14:35 I will surely do it unto all this evil **c**,	5712
	14:36 made all the **c** to murmur against him,	5712
	15:15 ordinance *shall be both* for you *of* the **c**,	6951
	15:24 ignorance without the knowledge of the **c**,	5712
	15:24 that all the **c** shall offer one young bullock	5712
	15:25 for all the **c** of the children of Israel,	5712
	15:26 it shall be forgiven all the **c** of the children	5712
	15:33 unto Moses and Aaron, and unto all the **c**.	5712
	15:35 all the **c** shall stone him with stones	5712
	15:36 all the **c** brought him without the camp,	5712
	16: 2 famous in the **c**, men of renown:	4150
	16: 3 all the **c** *are* holy, every one of them,	5712
	16: 3 lift you up yourselves above the **c** of	6951
	16: 9 hath separated you from the **c** of Israel,	5712
	16: 9 stand before the **c** to minister unto them?	5712
	16:18 *in* the door of the tabernacle of the **c**	4150
	16:19 Korah gathered all the **c** against him unto	5712
	16:19 unto the door of the tabernacle of the **c**	4150
	16:19 of the Lord appeared unto all the **c**.	5712
	16:21 Separate yourselves from among this **c**,	5712
	16:22 and wilt thou be wroth with all the **c**?	5712
	16:24 Speak unto the **c**, saying, Get you up from	5712
	16:26 he spake unto the **c**, saying, Depart, I pray	5712
	16:33 and they perished from among the **c**.	6951
	16:41 on the morrow all the **c** of the children of	5712
	16:42 the **c** was gathered against Moses and	5712
	16:42 looked toward the tabernacle of the **c**	4150
	16:43 Aaron came before the tabernacle of the **c**.	4150
	16:45 Get you up from among this **c**, that I may	5712
	16:46 go quickly unto the **c**, and make an	5712
	16:47 and ran into the midst of the **c**;	6951
	16:50 unto the door of the tabernacle of the **c**:	4150
	17: 4 tabernacle of the **c** before the Testimony,	4150
	18: 4 keep the charge of the tabernacle of the **c**,	4150
	18: 6 do the service of the tabernacle of the **c**.	4150
	18:21 the service of the tabernacle of the **c**,	4150
	18:22 come nigh the tabernacle of the **c**,	4150
	18:23 do the service of the tabernacle of the **c**,	4150
	18:31 for your service in the tabernacle of the **c**.	4150
	19: 4 before the tabernacle of the **c** seven times:	4150
	19: 9 it shall be kept for the **c** of the children of	5712
	19:20 soul shall be cut off from among the **c**,	6951
	20: 1 the children of Israel, *even* the whole **c**,	5712
	20: 2 there was no water for the **c**: and	5712
	20: 4 why have ye brought up the **c** of	6951
	20: 6 unto the door of the tabernacle of the **c**,	4150
	20: 8 so thou shalt give the **c** and their beasts	5712
	20:10 Aaron gathered the **c** together before	6951
	20:11 and the **c** drank, and their beasts *also*.	5712
	20:12 ye shall not bring this **c** into the land	6951
	20:22 the whole **c**, journeyed from Kadesh,	5712
	20:27 into mount Hor in the sight of all the **c**.	5712
	20:29 when all the **c** saw that Aaron was dead,	5712
	25: 6 in the sight of all the **c** of the children of	5712
	25: 6 *before* the door of the tabernacle of the **c**.	4150
	25: 7 saw *it*, he rose up from amongst the **c**,	5712
	26: 2 Take the sum of all the **c** of the children	5712
	26: 9 and Abiram, *which were* famous in the **c**,	5712
	27: 2 and before the princes and all the **c**,	5712
	27: 2 *by* the door of the tabernacle of the **c**,	4150
	27:14 in the strife of the **c**, to sanctify me at	5712
	27:16 spirits of all flesh, set a man over the **c**,	5712
	27:17 that the **c** of the Lord be not as sheep	5712
	27:19 Eleazar the priest, and before all the **c**;	5712
	27:20 that all the **c** of the children of Israel may	5712
	27:21 children of Israel with him, even all the **c**.	5712
	27:22 Eleazar the priest, and before all the **c**:	5712
	31:12 and unto the **c** of the children of Israel,	5712
	31:13 the priest, and all the princes of the **c**,	5712
	31:16 there was a plague among the **c** of	5712
	31:26 the priest, and the chief fathers of the **c**:	5712
	31:27 went out to battle, and between all the **c**:	5712
	31:43 the half that pertained unto the **c** was	5712
	31:54 brought it into the tabernacle of the **c**,	4150
	32: 2 and unto the princes of the **c**, saying,	5712
	32: 4 the Lord smote before the **c** of Israel,	5712
	35:12 until he stand before the **c** in judgment.	5712
	35:24 the **c** shall judge between the slayer and	5712
	35:25 the **c** shall deliver the slayer out of the	5712
	35:25 the **c** shall restore him to the city of his	5712
Dt	23: 1 shall not enter into the **c** of the Lord.	6951
	23: 2 A bastard shall not enter into the **c** of	6951
	23: 2 shall he not enter into the **c** of the Lord.	6951
	23: 3 Moabite shall not enter into the **c** of	6951
	23: 3 not enter into the **c** of the Lord for ever:	6951
	23: 8 **c** of the Lord *in* their third generation.	6951
	31:14 yourselves in the tabernacle of the **c**,	4150
	31:14 themselves in the tabernacle of the **c**.	4150
	31:30 spake in the ears of all the **c** of Israel	6951
	33: 4 *even* the inheritance of the **c** of Jacob.	6952
Jos	8:35 which Joshua read not before all the **c** of	6951
	9:15 and the princes of the **c** sware unto them.	5712
	9:18 the princes of the **c** had sworn unto them	5712
	9:18 all the **c** murmured against the princes.	5712
	9:19 all the princes said unto all the **c**, We	5712
	9:21 and drawers of water unto all the **c**;	5712
	9:27 of wood and drawers of water for the **c**,	5712
	18: 1 the whole **c** of the children of Israel	5712
	18: 1 and set up the tabernacle of the **c** there.	4150
	19:51 *at* the door of the tabernacle of the **c**.	4150
	20: 6 until he stand before the **c** for judgment,	5712
	20: 9 of blood, until he stood before the **c**.	5712
	22:12 **c** of the children of Israel gathered	5712

Jos	22:16 Thus saith the whole **c** of the Lord,	5712
	22:17 although there was a plague in the **c** of	5712
	22:18 will be wroth with the whole **c** of Israel.	5712
	22:20 and wrath fell on all the **c** of Israel?	5712
	22:30 the princes of the **c** and heads of	5712
Jdg	20: 1 the **c** was gathered together as one man,	5712
	21: 5 came not up with the **c** unto the Lord?	6951
	21:10 the **c** sent thither twelve thousand men of	5712
	21:13 the whole **c** sent *some* to speak to	5712
	21:16 the elders of the **c** said, How shall we do	5712
1Sa	2:22 *at* the door of the tabernacle of the **c**.	4150
1Ki	8: 4 the tabernacle of the **c**, and all the holy	4150
	8: 5 king Solomon, and all the **c** of Israel,	5712
	8:14 face about, and blessed all the **c** of Israel:	6951
	8:14 of Israel: (and all the **c** of Israel stood;)	6951
	8:22 in the presence of all the **c** of Israel,	6951
	8:55 blessed all the **c** of Israel *with* a loud	6951
	8:65 a feast, and all Israel with him, a great **c**,	6951
	12: 3 Jeroboam and all the **c** of Israel came,	6951
	12:20 that they sent and called him unto the **c**,	5712
1Ch	6:32 of the tabernacle of the **c** with singing,	4150
	9:21 of the door of the tabernacle of the **c**.	4150
	13: 2 David said unto all the **c** of Israel, If *it*	6951
	13: 4 all the **c** said that *they* would do so: for	6951
	23:32 keep the charge of the tabernacle of the **c**,	4150
	28: 8 in the sight of all Israel the **c** of	6951
	29: 1 David the king said unto all the **c**,	6951
	29:10 David blessed the Lord before all the **c**:	6951
	29:20 David said to all the **c**, Now bless	6951
	29:20 all the **c** blessed the Lord God of their	6951
2Ch	1: 3 Solomon, and all the **c** with him, went to	6951
	1: 3 for there was the tabernacle of the **c** of	4150
	1: 5 and Solomon and the **c** sought *unto* it.	6951
	1: 6 which *was* at the tabernacle of the **c**,	4150
	1:13 from before the tabernacle of the **c**,	4150
	5: 5 the tabernacle of the **c**, and all the holy	4150
	5: 6 all the **c** of Israel that were assembled	5712
	6: 3 his face, and blessed the whole **c** of Israel:	6951
	6: 3 of Israel: and all the **c** of Israel stood.	6951
	6:12 in the presence of all the **c** of Israel,	6951
	6:13 upon his knees before all the **c** of Israel,	6951
	7: 8 all Israel with him, a very great **c**, from	6951
	20: 5 Jehoshaphat stood in the **c** of Judah and	6951
	20:14 spirit of the Lord in the midst of the **c**;	6951
	23: 3 all the **c** made a covenant with the king	6951
	24: 6 of the **c** of Israel, for the tabernacle of	6951
	28:14 the spoil before the princes and all the **c**.	6951
	29:23 the sin offering before the king and the **c**;	6951
	29:28 the **c** worshipped, and the singers sang,	6951
	29:31 the **c** brought in sacrifices and	6951
	29:32 which the **c** brought, was threescore and	6951
	30: 2 his princes, and all the **c** in Jerusalem,	6951
	30: 4 the thing pleased the king and all the **c**.	6951
	30:13 in the second month, a very great **c**.	6951
	30:17 there were many in the **c** that were not	6951
	30:24 did give to the **c** a thousand bullocks	6951
	30:24 the princes gave to the **c** a thousand	6951
	30:25 all the **c** of Judah, with the priests and	6951
	30:25 all the **c** that came out of Israel,	6951
	31:18 and their daughters, through all the **c**:	6951
Ezr	2:64 The whole **c** together *was* forty *and*	6951
	10: 1 out of Israel a very great **c** *of* men	6951
	10: 8 himself separated from the **c** of those that	6951
	10:12 all the **c** answered and said *with* a loud	6951
	10:14 Let now our rulers of all the **c** stand,	6951
Ne	5:13 all the **c** said, Amen, and praised	6951
	7:66 The whole **c** together *was* forty *and*	6951
	8: 2 the priest brought the law before the **c**	6951
	8:17 all of them that were come again	6951
	13: 1 the Moabite should not come into the **c**	6951
Job	15:34 For the **c** of hypocrites *shall be* desolate,	5712
	30:28 the sun: I stood up, *and* I cried in the **c**.	6951
Ps	1: 5 nor sinners in the **c** of the righteous.	5712
	7: 7 So shall the **c** of the people compass thee	5712
	22:22 in the midst of the **c** will I praise thee.	6951
	22:25 My praise *shall be* of thee in the great **c**:	6951
	26: 5 I have hated the **c** of evildoers; and	6951
	35:18 I will give thee thanks in the great **c**: I will	6951
	40: 9 preached righteousness in the great **c**:	6951
	40:10 and thy truth from the great **c**.	6951
	58: 1 Do ye indeed speak righteousness, O **c**?	482
	68:10 Thy **c** hath dwelt therein: thou, O God,	2416
	74: 2 Remember thy **c**, *which* thou hast	5712
	74:19 forget not the **c** of thy poor for ever.	2416
	75: 2 When I shall receive the **c** I will judge	4150
	82: 1 God standeth in the **c** of the mighty;	5712
	89: 5 thy faithfulness also in the **c** of the saints.	6951
	107:32 Let them exalt him also in the **c** of	6951
	111: 1 the assembly of the upright, and *in* the **c**.	5712
	149: 1 new song, *and* his praise in the **c** of saints.	6951
Pr	5:14 was almost in all evil in the midst of the **c**	6951
	21:16 shall remain in the **c** of the dead.	6951
	26:26 shall be shewed before the *whole* **c**.	6951
Isa	14:13 I will sit also upon the mount of the **c**,	4150
Jer	6:18 hear, ye nations, and know, O **c**,	5712
	30:20 their *c* rulers shall be established before me,	5712
La	1:10 *that* they should not enter into thy **c**.	6951
Hos	7:12 I will chastise them, as their **c** hath heard.	5712
Joel	2:16 Gather the people, sanctify the **c**,	6951
Mic	2: 5 cast a cord by lot in the **c** of the Lord.	6951
Ac	13:43 Now when the **c** was broken up, many of	4864

CONGREGATIONS (3) [CONGREGATION]

Ps	26:12 even place: in the **c** will I bless the Lord.	4721
	68:26 Bless ye God in the **c**, *even* the Lord,	4721

Ps	74: 4 Thine enemies roar in the midst of thy **c**;	4150

CONIAH (3) [JEHOIACHIN]

Jer	22:24 though as the son of Jehoiakim king of	3659
	22:28 *Is* this man **C** a despised broken idol?	3659
	37: 1 reigned instead of **C** the son of Jehoiakim,	3659

CONIES (2) [CONEY]

Ps	104:18 for the wild goats; *and* the rocks for the **c**.	8227
Pr	30:26 The **c** *are but* a feeble folk, yet make they	8227

CONONIAH (2)

2Ch	31:12 over which **C** the Levite *was* ruler,	3562
	31:13 *were* overseers under the hand of **C** and	3562

CONQUER (1) [CONQUERING, CONQUERORS]

Rev	6: 2 and he went forth conquering, and to **c**.	3528

CONQUERING (1) [CONQUER]

Rev	6: 2 and he went forth **c**, and to conquer.	3528

CONQUERORS (1) [CONQUER]

Ro	8:37 in all these *things* we are **more than c**	5245

CONSCIENCE (31) [CONSCIENCES]

Jn	8: 9 heard *it*, being convicted by *their own* **c**,	4893
Ac	23: 1 I have lived in all good **c** before God until	4893
	24:16 to have always a **c** void of offence toward	4893
Ro	2:15 their **c** also bearing witness, and *their*	4893
	13: 5 not only for wrath, but also for **c** sake.	4893
1Co	8: 7 for some with **c** of the idol unto this hour,	4893
	8: 7 an idol; and their **c** being weak is defiled.	4893
	8:10 shall not the **c** of him which is weak	4893
	8:12 the brethren, and wound their weak **c**,	4893
	10:25 *that* eat, asking no question for **c** sake:	4893
	10:27 eat, asking no question for **c** sake.	4893
	10:28 and for **c** sake: for the earth *is* the Lord's,	4893
	10:29 **C**, I say, not thine own, but of the other's:	4893
	10:29 is my liberty judged of another *man's* **c**?	4893
2Co	1:12 the testimony of our **c**, that in simplicity	4893
	4: 2 to every man's **c** in the sight of God.	4893
1Ti	1: 5 and *of* a good **c**, and *of* faith unfeigned:	4893
	1:19 Holding faith, and a good **c**; which some	4893
	3: 9 the mystery of the faith in a pure **c**.	4893
	4: 2 having their **c** seared with a hot iron;	4893
2Ti	1: 3 I serve from *my* forefathers with pure **c**,	4893
Tit	1:15 but even their mind and **c** is defiled.	4893
Heb	9: 9 the service perfect, as pertaining to the **c**;	4893
	9:14 purge your **c** from dead works to serve	4893
	10: 2 purged should have had no more **c** of sins.	4893
	10:22 having *our* hearts sprinkled from an evil **c**,	4893
	13:18 we trust we have a good **c**, in all *things*	4893
1Pe	2:19 if a man for **c** toward God endure grief,	4893
	3:16 Having a good **c**; that, whereas they speak	4893
	3:21 but the answer of a good **c** toward God,)	4893

CONSCIENCES (1) [CONSCIENCE]

2Co	5:11 I trust also are made manifest in your **c**.	4893

CONSECRATE (14) [CONSECRATED, CONSECRATION, CONSECRATIONS]

Ex	28: 3 that they may make Aaron's garments to **c**	6942
	28:41 **c** them, and sanctify them,	853+3027+4390
	29: 9 thou shalt **c** Aaron and his sons.	3027+4390
	29:33 to **c** *and* to sanctify them:	853+3027+4390
	29:35 seven days shalt thou **c** them.	3027+4390
	30:30 anoint Aaron and his sons, and **c** them,	6942
	32:29 **C** yourselves to day to the Lord,	3027+4390
Lev	8:33 for seven days shall he **c** you.	853+3027+4390
	16:32 whom he shall **c** to minister	853+3027+4390
Nu	6:12 he shall **c** unto the Lord the days of his	5144
1Ch	29: 5 is willing to **c** his service this day unto	4390
2Ch	13: 9 whosoever cometh to **c** himself	3027+4390
Eze	43:26 and they shall **c** themselves.	3027+4390
Mic	4:13 and I will **c** their gain unto the Lord,	2763

CONSECRATED (14) [CONSECRATE]

Ex	29:29 and to be **c** in them.	853+3027+4390
Lev	21:10 is **c** to put on the garments,	853+3027+4390
Nu	3: 3 is **c** to minister in the priest's office.	3027+4390
Jos	6:19 of brass and iron, *are* **c** unto the Lord:	6944
Jdg	17: 5 and **c** one of his sons,	853+3027+4390
	17:12 Micah **c** the Levite;	853+3027+4390
1Ki	13:33 he **c** him, and he became *one*	853+3027+4390
2Ch	26:18 sons of Aaron, that are **c** to burn incense:	6942
	29:31 Now ye have **c** yourselves unto	3027+4390
	29:33 the **c** *things* were six hundred oxen and	6944
	31: 6 the tithe of holy *things* which were **c** unto	6942
Ezr	3: 5 all the set feasts of the Lord that were **c**,	6942
Heb	7:28 *maketh* the Son, who is **c** for evermore.	5048
	10:20 and living way, which he hath **c** for us,	1457

CONSECRATION (8) [CONSECRATE]

Ex	29:22 and the right shoulder; for it *is* a ram of **c**:	4394
	29:27 which is heaved up, of the ram of the **c**,	4394
	29:31 thou shalt take the ram of the **c**,	4394
Lev	8:22 he brought the other ram, the ram of **c**:	4394
	8:29 *for* of the ram of it was Moses' part;	4394
	8:33 until the days of your **c** be at an end:	4394
Nu	6: 7 because the **c** of his God *is* upon his head.	5145
	6: 9 and he hath defiled the head of his **c**;	5145

CONSECRATIONS (5) [CONSECRATE]

Ex	29:26 take the breast of the ram of Aaron's **c**,	4394
	29:34 if *ought* of the flesh of the **c**, or of	4394

C

Lev 7:37 of the **c**, and of the sacrifice of the peace 4394
 8:28 they *were* **c** for a sweet savour: it *is an* 4394
 8:31 it with the bread that *is* in the basket of **c**, 4394

CONSENT (15) [CONSENTED, CONSENTEDST, CONSENTING]
Ge 34:15 in this will we **c** unto you: If ye will be as 225
 34:22 Only herein will the men **c** unto us for to 225
 34:23 only let us **c** unto them, and they will dwell 225
Dt 13: 8 Thou shalt not **c** unto him, nor hearken 14
Jdg 11:17 he would not **c**: and Israel abode in Kadesh. 14
1Sa 11: 7 the people, and they came out with one **c**. 376
1Ki 20: 8 unto him, Hearken not *unto him*, nor **c**. 14
Ps 83: 5 they have consulted together *with one* **c**: 3820
Pr 1:10 My son, if sinners entice thee, **c** thou not. 14
Hos 6: 9 of priests murder *in* the way by **c**: 7926
Zep 3: 9 of the LORD, to serve him *with one* **c**. 7926
Lk 14:18 And they will with one **c** began to make NIG
Ro 7:16 would not, I **c** unto the law that *it is* good. 4852
1Co 7: 5 the other, except *it be* with **c** for a time, 4859
1Ti 6: 3 and **c** not **to** wholesome words, 4334

CONSENTED (4) [CONSENT]
2Ki 12: 8 the priests **c** to receive no *more* money of 225
Da 1:14 So he **c** to them in this matter, 8085
Lk 23:51 (The same had not **c** to the counsel and 4784
Ac 18:20 to tarry longer time with them, he **c** not; 1962

CONSENTEDST (1) [CONSENT]
Ps 50:18 thou **c** with him, and hast been partaker 7521

CONSENTING (2) [CONSENT]
Ac 8: 1 Saul was **c** unto his death. And at that 4909
 22:20 **c** unto his death, and kept the raiment 4909

CONSIDER (67) [CONSIDERED, CONSIDEREST, CONSIDERETH, CONSIDERING]
Ex 33:13 and **c** that this nation *is* thy people. 7200
Lev 13:13 priest shall **c**: and behold, *if* the leprosy 7200
Dt 4:39 therefore *this* day, and **c** *it* in thine heart, 7725
 8: 5 Thou shalt also **c** in thine heart, that, as a 3045
 32: 7 of old, **c** the years of many generations: 995
 32:29 *that* they would **c** their latter end! 995
Jdg 18:14 now therefore **c** what ye have to do. 995
 19:30 **c** of it, take advice, and speak 7760+3807.1
1Sa 12:24 **c** how great things he hath done for you. 7200
 25:17 therefore know and **c** what thou wilt do; 7200
2Ki 5: 7 wherefore **c**, I pray you, and see how he 3045
Job 11:11 wickedness also; will he not then **c** *it*? 995
 23:15 his presence: when I **c**, I am afraid of him. 995
 34:27 and would not **c** any of his ways. 7919
 37:14 and **c** the wondrous works of God. 995
Ps 5: 1 to my words, O LORD, **c** my meditation. 995
 8: 3 When I **c** thy heavens, the work of thy 7200
 9:13 **c** my trouble *which I suffer* of them that 7200
 13: 3 **C** *and* hear me, O LORD my God: 5027
 25:19 **C** mine enemies; for they are many; 7200
 37:10 thou shalt **diligently c** his place, and it 995
 45:10 O daughter, and **c**, and incline thine ear; 7200
 48:13 Mark ye well her bulwarks, **c** her palaces; 6448
 50:22 Now **c** this, ye that forget God, lest I tear 995
 64: 9 for they shall **wisely c** of his doing. 7919
 119:95 to destroy me: *but* I will **c** thy testimonies. 995
 119:153 **C** mine affliction, and deliver me: for I do 7200
 119:159 **C** how I love thy precepts: quicken me, 7200
Pr 6: 6 thou sluggard; **c** her ways, and be wise: 7200
 23: 1 ruler, **diligently** what *is* before thee: 995+995
 24:12 doth not he that pondereth the heart **c** *it*? 995
Ecc 5: 1 of fools: for they **c** not that they do evil. 3045
 7:13 the work of God: for who can make 7200
 7:14 be joyful, but in the day of adversity **c**: 7200
Isa 1: 3 doth not know, my people doth not **c**. 995
 5:12 neither **c** the operation of his hands. 7200
 14:16 narrowly look upon thee, *and* **c** thee, 995
 18: 4 I will **c** in my dwelling place like a clear 5027
 41:20 know, and **c**, and understand together, 7760
 41:22 what they *be*, that we may **c** *them*, 3820+7760
 43:18 former *things*, neither **c** the *things* of old. 995
 52:15 which they had not heard shall they **c**. 995
Jer 2:10 **c** diligently, and see if there be such a 995
 9:17 **C** ye, and call for the mourning *women*, 995
 23:20 the latter days ye shall **c** it **perfectly**. 995+998
 30:24 of his heart: in the latter days ye shall **c** it. 995
La 1:11 see, O LORD, and **c**; for I am become 5027
 2:20 and **c** to whom thou hast done this. 5027
 5: 1 upon us: **c**, and behold our reproach. 5027
Eze 12: 3 it may be they will **c**, though they *be* a 7200
Da 9:23 understand the matter, and **c** the vision. 995
Hos 7: 2 they **c** not in their hearts *that* I remember 559
Hag 1: 5 the LORD of hosts; **C** your ways. 3824+7760
 1: 7 the LORD of hosts; **C** your ways. 3824+7760
 2:15 **c** from this day and upward, 3824+7760
 2:18 **C** now from this day and upward, 3824+7760
 2:18 the LORD's temple was laid, **c** it. 3824+7760
Mt 6:28 **C** the lilies of the field, how they grow; 2648
Lk 12:24 **C** the ravens: for they neither sow nor 2657
 12:27 **C** the lilies how they grow: they toil not, 2657
Jn 11:50 Nor **c** that it is expedient for us, that one 1260
Ac 15: 6 came together for to **c** of this matter, 1492
2Ti 2: 7 **C** what I say; and the Lord give thee 3539
Heb 3: 1 **c** the Apostle and High Priest of our 2657
 7: 4 Now **c** how great this *man was*, unto 2334
 10:24 And let us **c** one another to provoke unto 2657
 12: 3 For **c** him that endured such contradiction 357

CONSIDERED (16) [CONSIDER]
1Ki 3:21 when I had **c** it in the morning, 413+995
 5: 8 I have **c** the *things* which thou sentest 8085
Job 1: 8 Hast thou **c** my servant Job, 3820+7760
 2: 3 Hast thou **c** my servant Job, 3820+7760
Ps 31: 7 thou hast **c** my trouble; thou hast known 7200
 77: 5 the days of old, the years of 2803
Pr 24:32 and **c** it well: I looked upon *it*, 3820+7896
Ecc 4: 1 **c** all the oppressions that *are* done under 7200
 4: 4 Again, I **c** all travail, and every right work, 7200
 4:15 **c** all the living which walk under the sun, 7200
 9: 1 For all this I **c** in my heart even to declare 5414
Da 7: 8 I **c** the horns, and behold, there came up 7920
Mk 6:52 For they **c** not the *miracle* of the loaves: 4920
Ac 11: 6 I **c**, and saw fourfooted beasts of the earth, 2657
 12:12 And when he had **c** *the thing*, he came to 4894
Ro 4:19 in faith, he **c** not his own body now dead, 2657

CONSIDEREST (2) [CONSIDER]
Jer 33:24 **C** thou not what this people have spoken, 7200
Mt 7: 3 **c** not the beam that is in thine own eye? 2657

CONSIDERETH (9) [CONSIDER]
Ps 33:15 their hearts alike; he **c** all their works. 995
 41: 1 Blessed *is* he that **c** the poor: the LORD 7919
Pr 21:12 The righteous *man* **wisely c** the house of 7919
 28:22 **c** not that poverty shall come *upon* him. 3045
 29: 7 The righteous **c** the cause of the poor: *but* 3045
 31:16 She **c** a field, and buyeth it: with the fruit 2161
Isa 44:19 none **c** in his heart, neither *is there* 7725
Eze 18:14 hath done, and **c**, and doeth not such like, 7200
 18:28 Because he **c**, and turneth away from all 7200

CONSIDERING (4) [CONSIDER]
Isa 57: 1 none **c** that the righteous is taken away 995
Da 8: 5 as I was **c**, behold, a he goat came from 995
Gal 6: 1 **c** thyself, lest thou also be tempted. 4648
Heb 13: 7 **c** the end of *their* conversation. 333

CONSIST (1) [CONSISTETH]
Col 1:17 before all *things*, and by him all *things* **c**. 4921

CONSISTETH (1) [CONSIST]
Lk 12:15 for a man's life **c** not in the abundance of 1510

CONSOLATION (15) [CONSOLATIONS]
Jer 16: 7 neither shall *men* give them the cup of **c** 8575
Lk 2:25 and devout, waiting for the **c** of Israel: 3874
 6:24 that are rich: for ye have received your **c**. 3874
Ac 4:36 being interpreted, The son of **c**,) 3874
 15:31 they had read, they rejoiced for the **c**. 3874
Ro 15: 5 **c** grant you to be likeminded one towards 3874
2Co 1: 5 in us, so our **c** also aboundeth by Christ. 3874
 1: 6 be afflicted, *it is* for your **c** and salvation, 3874
 1: 6 comforted, *it is* for your **c** and salvation. 3874
 1: 7 the sufferings, so *shall ye be* also of the **c**. 3874
 1: 7 by the **c** wherewith he was comforted in 3874
Php 2: 1 If *there be* therefore any **c** in Christ, if any 3874
2Th 2:16 and hath given *us* everlasting **c** and 3874
Phm 1: 7 For we have great joy and **c** in thy love, 3874
Heb 6:18 for God to lie, we might have a strong **c**, 3874

CONSOLATIONS (3) [CONSOLATION]
Job 15:11 *Are* the **c** of God small with thee? is there 8575
 21: 2 my speech, and let this be your **c**. 8575
Isa 66:11 and be satisfied with the breasts of her **c**; 8575

CONSORTED (1)
Ac 17: 4 them believed, and **c with** Paul and Silas; 4345

CONSPIRACY (10) [CONSPIRATORS, CONSPIRED]
2Sa 15:12 the **c** was strong; for the people increased 7195
2Ki 15:12 **made a c**, and slew Joash in 7194+7195
 14:19 Now they **made a c** against him in 7194+7195
 15:15 and his **c** which he made, behold, 7194+7195
 15:30 Hoshea the son of Elah **made a c** 7194+7195
 17: 4 the king of Assyria found **c** in Hoshea: 7195
2Ch 25:27 **made a c** against him in Jerusalem; 7194+7195
Jer 11: 9 A **c** is found among the men of Judah, 7195
Eze 22:25 *There is* a **c** of her prophets in the midst 7195
Ac 23:13 more *than* forty which had made this **c**. 4945

CONSPIRATORS (1) [CONSPIRACY]
2Sa 15:31 Ahithophel *is* among the **c** with Absalom. 7194

CONSPIRED (19) [CONSPIRACY]
Ge 37:18 them, they **c against** him to slay him. 5230
1Sa 22: 8 That all of you have **c** against me, 7194
 22:13 Why have ye **c** against me, thou and 7194
1Ki 15:27 of the house of Issachar, **c** against him; 7194
 16: 9 **c** against him, as he *was* in Tirzah, 7194
 16:16 Zimri hath **c**, and hath also slain the king: 7194
2Ki 9:14 the son of Nimshi **c** against Joram. 7194
 10: 9 **c** against my master, and slew him: 7194
 15:10 Shallum the son of Jabesh **c** against him, 7194
 15:25 **c** against him, and smote him in Samaria, 7194
 21:23 the servants of Amon **c** against him, 7194
 21:24 all them that had **c** against king Amon; 7194
2Ch 24:21 they **c** against him, and stoned him *with* 7194
 24:25 his own servants **c** against him for 7194
 24:26 these *are* they that **c** against him; Zabad 7194
 33:24 his servants **c** against him, and slew him 7194
 33:25 all them that had **c** against king Amon; 7194
Ne 4: 8 **c** all of them together to come *and* to fight 7194
Am 7:10 Amos hath **c** against thee in the midst of 7194

CONSTANT (1) [CONSTANTLY]
1Ch 28: 7 if he be **c** to do my commandments and 2388

CONSTANTLY (3) [CONSTANT]
Pr 21:28 the man that heareth, speaketh **c**. 5331+3807.1
Ac 12:15 But she **affirmed** that it was *even* so. 1340
Tit 3: 8 and these *things* I will that thou **affirm c**, 1226

CONSTELLATIONS (1)
Isa 13:10 and the **c** thereof shall not give their light: 3685

CONSTRAIN (1) [CONSTRAINED, CONSTRAINETH, CONSTRAINT]
Gal 6:12 in the flesh, they **c** you to be circumcised; 315

CONSTRAINED (6) [CONSTRAIN]
2Ki 4: 8 great woman; and she **c** him to eat bread. 2388
Mt 14:22 And straightway Jesus **c** his disciples to get 315
Mk 6:45 straightway he **c** his disciples to get into 315
Lk 24:29 But they **c** him, saying, Abide with us: 3849
Ac 16:15 my house, and abide *there*. And she **c** us. 3849
 28:19 when the Jews spake against *it*, I was **c** 315

CONSTRAINETH (2) [CONSTRAIN]
Job 32:18 full *of* matter, the spirit within me **c** me. 6693
2Co 5:14 the love of Christ **c** us; because we thus 4912

CONSTRAINT (1) [CONSTRAIN]
1Pe 5: 2 taking the oversight *thereof*, not **by c**, 317

CONSULT (1) [CONSULTATION, CONSULTED, CONSULTER, CONSULTETH]
Ps 62: 4 They only **c** to cast *him* down from his 3289

CONSULTATION (1) [CONSULT]
Mk 15: 1 the chief priests held a **c** with the elders 4824

CONSULTED (13) [CONSULT]
1Ki 12: 6 king Rehoboam **c with** the old men, 3289
 12: 8 **c** with the young men that were grown 3289
1Ch 13: 1 David **c** with the captains of thousands 3289
2Ch 20:21 when he had **c** with the people, 3289
Ne 5: 7 I **c** with myself, and I rebuked the nobles, 4427
Ps 83: 3 thy people, and **c** against thy hidden ones. 3289
 83: 5 they have **c** together *with one* consent: 3289
Eze 21:21 he **c** with images, he looked in the liver. 7592
Da 6: 7 **c together** to establish a royal statute, 3272
Mic 6: 5 now what Balak king of Moab **c**, 3289
Hab 2:10 Thou hast **c** shame to thy house by 3289
Mt 26: 4 And **c** that they might take Jesus by 4823
Jn 12:10 But the chief priests **c** that they might put 1011

CONSULTER (1) [CONSULT]
Dt 18:11 or a **c** with familiar spirits, or a wizard, 7592

CONSULTETH (1) [CONSULT]
Lk 14:31 **c** whether he be able with ten thousand to 1011

CONSULTS THE DEAD See NECROMANCER

CONSUME (56) [CONSUMED, CONSUMETH, CONSUMING, CONSUMPTION]
Ge 41:30 of Egypt; and the famine shall **c** the land; 3615
Ex 32:10 hot against them, and that I may **c** them: 3615
 32:12 and to **c** them from the face of the earth? 3615
 33: 3 people: lest I **c** thee in the way. 3615
 33: 5 midst of thee in a moment, and **c** thee: 3615
Lev 26:16 that shall **c** the eyes, and cause sorrow of 3615
Nu 16:21 that I may **c** them in a moment. 3615
 16:45 that I may **c** them as in a moment. 3615
Dt 5:25 for this great fire will **c** us: if we hear 398
 7:16 thou shalt **c** all the people which the LORD 398
 7:22 thou mayest not **c** them at once, lest 3615
 28:38 *but* little in; for the locust shall **c** it. 2628
 28:42 and fruit of thy land shall the locust **c**. 3423
 32:22 shall **c** the earth with her increase, and set 398
Jos 24:20 he will turn and do you hurt, and **c** you, 3615
1Sa 2:33 *be* to **c** thine eyes, and to grieve thine 3615
2Ki 1:10 from heaven, and **c** thee and thy fifty. 398
 1:12 from heaven, and **c** thee and thy fifty. 398
Ne 9:31 sake thou didst not **utterly c** them, 3617
Est 9:24 the lot, to **c** them, and to destroy them; 2000
Job 15:34 and fire shall **c** the tabernacles of bribery. 398
 20:26 a fire not blown shall **c** him; it shall go ill 398
 24:19 Drought and heat **c** the snow waters: *so* 1497
Ps 37:20 they shall **c**; into smoke shall they 3615
 37:20 into smoke shall they **c** *away*. 3615
 39:11 thou **makest** his beauty to **c** away like a 4529
 49:14 their beauty shall **c** *in* the grave from their 1086
 59:13 **C** them in wrath, consume *them*, that 3615
 59:13 **c** them, that they may not *be*: and let 3615
 78:33 Therefore their days did he **c** in vanity, 3615
Isa 7:20 of the feet: and it shall also **c** the beard. 5595
 10:18 the glory of his forest, and of his 3615
 27:10 he lie down, and **c** the branches thereof. 3615
Jer 8: 1 I will **surely c** them, saith 622+5486
 14:12 I will **c** them by the sword, and by 3615
 49:27 and it shall **c** the palaces of Ben-hadad. 398
Eze 4:17 another, and **c away** for their iniquity. 4743
 13:13 and great hailstones in *my* fury to **c** it. 3617
 20:13 upon them in the wilderness, to **c** them. 3615
 21:28 furbished, to **c** because of the glittering; 398
 22:15 and will **c** thy filthiness out of thee. 8552
 24:10 **c** the flesh, and spice it well, and let 8552
 35:12 are laid desolate, they are given us to **c**. 402
Da 2:44 break in pieces and **c** all these kingdoms, 5487

Da	7:26 to **c** and to destroy *it* unto the end.	8046
Hos	11: 6 shall **c** his branches, and devour *them,*	3615
Zep	1: 2 I will utterly **c** all *things* from off the land,	5486
	1: 3 I will **c** man and beast; I will consume	5486
	1: 3 I will **c** the fowls of the heaven,	5486
Zec	5: 4 shall **c** it with the timber thereof and	3615
	14:12 Their flesh *shall* **c** **away** while they stand	4743
	14:12 their eyes shall **c** **away** in their holes,	4743
	14:12 their tongue shall **c** **away** in their mouth.	4743
Lk	9:54 heaven, and **c** them, even as Elias did?	355
2Th	2: 8 the Lord shall **c** with the spirit of his	355
Jas	4: 3 amiss, that ye may **c** *it* upon your lusts.	1159

CONSUMED (96) [CONSUME]

Ge	19:15 lest thou be **c** in the iniquity of the city.	5595
	19:17 escape to the mountain, lest thou be **c.**	5595
	31:40 the drought **c** me, and the frost by night;	398
Ex	3: 2 burned with fire, and the bush was not **c.**	398
	15: 7 forth thy wrath, *which* **c** them as stubble.	398
	22: 6 be **c** *therewith;* he that kindled the fire	398
Lev	6:10 the ashes which the fire hath **c** with	398
	9:24 **c** upon the altar the burnt offering and	398
Nu	11: 1 **c** *them that were* in the uttermost parts of	398
	12:12 whom the flesh is half **c** when he cometh	398
	14:35 in this wilderness they shall be **c,**	8552
	16:26 of theirs, lest ye be **c** in all their sins.	5595
	16:35 the two hundred and fifty men that	398
	17:13 Lord shall die: shall we be **c** with dying?	8552
	21:28 it hath **c** Ar of Moab, *and* the lords of	398
	25:11 that I **c** not the children of Israel in my	3615
	32:13 done evil in the sight of the Lord, was **c.**	8552
Dt	2:15 from among the host, until they were **c.**	8552
	2:16 when all the men of war were **c** and	8552
	28:21 until he have **c** thee from off the land,	3615
Jos	5: 6 **c,** because they obeyed not the voice	8552
	8:24 until they were **c,** that all the Israelites	8552
	10:20 till they were **c,** that the rest *which*	8552
Jdg	6:21 **c** the flesh and the unleavened *cakes.*	398
1Sa	12:25 ye shall be **c,** both ye and your king.	5595
	15:18 and fight against them until they be **c.**	3615
2Sa	21: 5 The man that **c** us, and that devised	3615
	22:38 and turned not again until I had **c** them.	3615
	22:39 I have **c** them, and wounded them,	3615
1Ki	18:38 **c** the burnt sacrifice, and the wood,	398
	22:11 push the Syrians, until *thou* have **c** them.	3615
2Ki	1:10 fire from heaven, and **c** him and his fifty.	398
	1:12 from heaven, and **c** him and his fifty.	398
	7:13 the multitude of the Israelites that are **c:)**	8552
	13:17 Syrians in Aphek, till *thou* have **c** *them.*	3615
	13:19 thou smitten Syria till *thou* hadst **c** *it:*	3615
2Ch	7: 1 and **c** the burnt offering and the sacrifices,	398
	8: 8 land, whom the children of Israel **c** not,	3615
	8:10 thou shalt push Syria until they be **c.**	3615
Ezr	9:14 not be angry with us till *thou* hadst **c** *us,*	3615
Ne	2: 3 and the gates thereof are **c** with fire?	398
	2:13 and the gates thereof were **c** with fire.	398
Job	1:16 the sheep, and the servants, and **c** them;	398
	4: 9 by the breath of his nostrils are they **c.**	3615
	6:17 it is hot, they are **c** out of their place.	1846
	7: 9 *As* the cloud is **c** and vanisheth away: so	3615
	19:27 *though* my reins be **c** within me.	3615
	33:21 His flesh is **c** away, that it cannot be seen;	3615
Ps	6: 7 Mine eye is **c** because of grief; it waxeth	6244
	18:37 neither did I turn again till they were **c.**	3615
	31: 9 mine eye is **c** with grief, *yea,* my soul and	6244
	31:10 of mine iniquity, and my bones are **c.**	6244
	39:10 I am **c** by the blow of thine hand.	3615
	71:13 *and* **c** that are adversaries to my soul;	3615
	73:19 a moment! they are utterly **c** with terrors.	5486
	78:63 The fire **c** their young men;	398
	90: 7 For we are **c** by thine anger, and by thy	3615
	102: 3 For my days are **c** like smoke,	3615
	104:35 Let the sinners be **c** out of the earth,	8552
	119:87 They had almost **c** me upon earth;	3615
	119:139 My zeal hath **c** me, because mine enemies	6789
Pr	5:11 last, when thy flesh and thy body are **c,**	3615
Isa	1:28 and they that forsake the Lord shall be **c.**	3615
	16: 4 the oppressors are **c** out of the land.	8552
	29:20 the scorner is **c,** and all that watch for	3615
	64: 7 and hast **c** us, because of our iniquities.	4127
	66:17 and the mouse, shall be **c** together,	5486
Jer	5: 3 thou hast **c** them, *but* they have refused	3615
	6:29 bellows are burnt, the lead is **c** of the fire;	3615
	9:16 a sword after them, till I have **c** them.	3615
	10:25 **c** him, and have made his habitation	3615
	12: 4 the beasts are **c,** and the birds; because	5595
	14:15 and famine shall those prophets be **c.**	8552
	16: 4 they shall be **c** by the sword,	3615
	20:18 that my days should be **c** with shame?	3615
	24:10 till they be **c** from off the land that I gave	8552
	27: 8 until I have **c** them by his hand.	8552
	36:23 until all the roll was **c** in the fire that *was*	8552
	44:12 they shall all be **c,** *and* fall in the land of	8552
	44:12 they shall *even* be **c** by the sword,	8552
	44:18 have been **c** by the sword and by	8552
	44:27 the land of Egypt shall be **c** by the sword	8552
	49:37 the sword after them, till I have **c** them:	3615
La	2:22 and brought up hath mine enemy **c.**	3615
	3:22 *of* the Lord's mercies that we are not **c,**	8552
Eze	5:12 with famine shall they be **c** in the midst of	3615
	13:14 and ye shall be **c** in the midst thereof:	8552
	19:12 broken and withered; the fire **c** them.	398
	22:31 have **c** them with the fire of my wrath:	3615
	24:11 molten in it, *that* the scum of it may be **c.**	8552
	34:29 they shall be no more **c** with hunger in	622

Eze	43: 8 wherefore I have **c** them in mine anger.	3615
	47:12 neither shall the fruit thereof be **c:**	8552
Da	11:16 land, which by his hand shall be **c.**	3617
Mal	3: 6 therefore ye sons of Jacob are not **c.**	3615
Gal	5:15 take heed ye be not **c** one of another.	355

CONSUMETH (4) [CONSUME]

Job	13:28 as a rotten thing, **c,** as a garment that is	1086
	22:20 down, but the remnant of them the fire **c.**	398
	31:12 For it *is* a fire *that* **c** to destruction,	398
Isa	5:24 the flame **c** the chaff, *so* their root shall be	7503

CONSUMING (3) [CONSUME]

Dt	4:24 For the Lord thy God *is* a **c** fire, *even* a	398
	9: 3 *as* a **c** fire he shall destroy them, and he	398
Heb	12:29 For our God *is* a **c** fire.	2654

CONSUMMATION (1)

Da	9:27 even until the **c,** and that determined shall	3617

CONSUMPTION (5) [CONSUME]

Lev	26:16 **c,** and the burning ague, that shall	7829
Dt	28:22 The Lord shall smite thee with a **c,**	7829
Isa	10:22 the **c** decreed shall overflow *with*	3631
	10:23 for the Lord God of hosts shall make a **c,**	3617
	28:22 heard from the Lord God of hosts a **c,**	3617

CONTAIN (7) [CONTAINED, CONTAINETH, CONTAINING]

1Ki	8:27 and heaven of heavens cannot **c** thee;	3557
	18:32 as great as would **c** two measures of seed.	1004
2Ch	2: 6 and heaven of heavens cannot **c** him?	3557
	6:18 and the heaven of heavens cannot **c** thee;	3557
Eze	45:11 that the bath may **c** the tenth part of a	5375
Jn	21:25 not **c** the books that should be written.	5562
1Co	7: 9 But if they cannot **c,** let them marry: for it	1467

CONTAINED (5) [CONTAIN]

1Ki	7:26 flowers of lilies: it **c** two thousand baths.	3557
	7:38 one laver **c** forty baths: *and* every laver	3557
Ro	2:14 do by nature the *things* **c** in the law, these,	NIG
Eph	2:15 *even* the law of commandments **c** in	NIG
1Pe	2: 6 Wherefore also it is **c** in the scripture,	4023

CONTAINETH (1) [CONTAIN]

Eze	23:32 to scorn and had in derision; *it* **c** much.	3557

CONTAINING (1) [CONTAIN]

Jn	2: 6 of the Jews, **c** two or three firkins apiece.	5562

CONTEMN (2) [CONTEMNED, CONTEMNETH]

Ps	10:13 Wherefore doth the wicked **c** God?	5006
Eze	21:13 and what if *the sword* **c** even the rod?	3988

CONTEMNED (4) [CONTEMN]

Ps	15: 4 In whose eyes a vile *person* is **c;** but he	959
	107:11 God, and **c** the counsel of the most High:	5006
SS	8: 7 house for love, it would utterly be **c.**	936+936
Isa	16:14 hireling, and the glory of Moab shall be **c,**	7034

CONTEMNETH (1) [CONTEMN]

Eze	21:10 it **c** the rod of my son, *as* every tree.	3988

CONTEMPT (10) [CONTEMPTIBLE, CONTEMPTUOUSLY]

Est	1:18 *shall there arise* too much **c** and wrath.	963
Job	12:21 He poureth **c** upon princes,	937
	31:34 did the **c** of families terrify me, that I kept	937
Ps	107:40 He poureth **c** upon princes, and causeth	937
	119:22 Remove from me reproach and **c;** for I have	937
	123: 3 for we are exceedingly filled *with* **c.**	937
	123: 4 are at ease, *and with* the **c** of the proud.	937
Pr	18: 3 *then* cometh also **c,** and with ignominy	937
Isa	23: 9 to **bring into** **c** all the honourable of	7043
Da	12: 2 and some to shame *and* everlasting **c.**	1860

CONTEMPTIBLE (4) [CONTEMPT]

Mal	1: 7 In that ye say, The table of the Lord *is* **c.**	959
	1:12 the fruit thereof, *even* his meat, *is* **c.**	959
	2: 9 Therefore have I also made you **c** and	959
2Co	10:10 bodily presence *is* weak, and *his* speech **c.**	1848

CONTEMPTUOUSLY (1) [CONTEMPT]

Ps	31:18 things proudly and **c** against the righteous.	937

CONTEND (14) [CONTENDED, CONTENDEST, CONTENDETH, CONTENDING]

Dt	2: 9 Moabites, neither **c** with them *in* battle.	1624
	2:24 to possess *it,* and **c** with him *in* battle.	1624
Job	9: 3 If he will **c** with him, he cannot answer	7378
	13: 8 ye accept his person? will ye **c** for God?	7378
Pr	28: 4 but such as keep the law **c** with them.	1624
Ecc	6:10 neither may he **c** with him that *is* mightier	1777
Isa	49:25 for I will **c** **with** him that contendeth with	7378
	50: 8 that justifieth me; who will **c** with me?	7378
	57:16 For I will not **c** for ever, neither will I be	7378
Jer	12: 5 then how canst thou **c** with horses?	8474
	18:19 hearken to the voice of them that **c** **with**	3401
Am	7: 4 the Lord God called to **c** by fire,	7378
Mic	6: 1 **c** thou before the mountains, and let	7378
Jude	1: 3 exhort you that ye should **earnestly c for**	1864

CONTENDED (6) [CONTEND]

Ne	13:11 **c** I with the rulers, and said, Why is	7378
	13:17 I **c** with the nobles of Judah, and said	7378
	13:25 I **c** with them, and cursed them,	7378

Job	31:13 of my maidservant, when they **c** with me;	7379
Isa	41:12 find them, *even* them that **c with** thee:	4695
Ac	11: 2 they that were of the circumcision **c** with	1252

CONTENDEST (1) [CONTEND]

Job	10: 2 shew me wherefore thou **c** with me.	7378

CONTENDETH (3) [CONTEND]

Job	40: 2 Shall he that **c** with the Almighty instruct	7378
Pr	29: 9 If a wise man **c** with a foolish man,	8199
Isa	49:25 I will contend with him that **c with** thee,	3401

CONTENDING (1) [CONTEND]

Jude	1: 9 when **c** with the devil he disputed about	1252

CONTENT (16) [CONTENTMENT]

Ge	37:27 *and* our flesh. And his brethren were **c.**	8085
Ex	2:21 Moses was **c** to dwell with the man: and	2974
Lev	10:20 Moses heard *that,* he was **c.**	3190+5869+871.1
Jos	7: 7 would to God we had been **c,** and dwelt	2974
Jdg	17:11 the Levite was **c** to dwell with the man;	2974
	19: 6 Be **c,** I pray thee, and tarry all night,	2974
2Ki	5:23 Naaman said, Be **c,** take two talents.	2974
	6: 3 Be **c,** I pray thee, and go with thy servants	2974
Job	6:28 Now therefore be **c,** look upon me; for	2974
Pr	6:35 neither will he **rest,** though thou givest	14
Mk	15:15 And *so* Pilate, willing to **c**	2425+4160
Lk	3:14 *any* falsely; and be **c** with your wages.	714
Php	4:11 whatsoever *state* I am, *therewith* to be **c.**	842
1Ti	6: 8 and raiment let us be therewith **c.**	714
Heb	13: 5 *and be* **c** with such *things* as ye have:	714
3Jn	1:10 not **c** therewith, neither doth he himself	714

CONTENTION (9) [CONTENTIONS, CONTENTIOUS]

Pr	13:10 Only by pride cometh **c:** but with the well	4683
	17:14 therefore leave off **c,** before *it* be meddled	7379
	18: 6 A fool's lips enter into **c,** and his mouth	7379
	22:10 Cast out the scorner, and **c** shall go out;	4066
Jer	15:10 strife and a man of **c** to the whole earth!	4066
Hab	1: 3 and there are *that* raise up strife and **c.**	4066
Ac	15:39 And the **c** was so **sharp** *between them,*	3948
Php	1:16 The one preach Christ of **c,** not sincerely,	2052
1Th	2: 2 unto you the gospel of God with much **c.**	73

CONTENTIONS (6) [CONTENTION]

Pr	18:18 The lot causeth **c** to cease,	4066
	18:19 and *their* **c** *are* like the bars of a castle.	4066
	19:13 the **c** of a wife *are* a continual dropping;	4066
	23:29 who hath **c?** who hath babbling?	4066
1Co	1:11 of Chloe, that there are **c** among you.	2054
Tit	3: 9 and **c,** and strivings about the law;	2054

CONTENTIOUS (5) [CONTENTION]

Pr	21:19 than with a **c** and an angry woman.	4066
	26:21 to fire; so *is* a **c** man to kindle strife.	4066
	27:15 very rainy day and a **c** woman are alike.	4066
Ro	2: 8 unto them that are **c,**	2052
1Co	11:16 But if any *man* seem to be **c,** we have no	5380

CONTENTMENT (1) [CONTENT]

1Ti	6: 6 But godliness with **c** is great gain.	841

CONTINUAL (33) [CONTINUE]

Ex	29:42 *This shall be* a **c** burnt offering	8548
Nu	4: 7 and the **c** bread shall be thereon:	8548
	28: 3 spot day by day, *for* a **c** burnt offering.	8548
	28: 6 a **c** burnt offering, which was ordained	8548
	28:10 beside the **c** burnt offering, and his drink	8548
	28:15 besides the **c** burnt offering, and his drink	8548
	28:23 which *is* for a **c** burnt offering.	8548
	28:24 it be offered beside the **c** burnt	8548
	28:31 Ye shall offer *them* besides the **c** burnt	8548
	29:11 the **c** burnt offering, and the meat offering	8548
	29:16 beside the **c** burnt offering, his meat	8548
	29:19 beside the **c** burnt offering, and the meat	8548
	29:22 beside the **c** burnt offering, his meat	8548
	29:25 beside the **c** burnt offering, his meat	8548
	29:28 beside the **c** burnt offering, his meat	8548
	29:31 beside the **c** burnt offering, his meat	8548
	29:34 beside the **c** burnt offering, his meat	8548
	29:38 beside the **c** burnt offering, his meat	8548
2Ki	25:30 his allowance was a **c** allowance given	8548
2Ch	2: 4 for the **c** shewbread, and *for* the burnt	8548
Ezr	3: 5 afterward *offered* the **c** burnt offering,	8548
Ne	10:33 *for* the **c** meat offering, and for	8548
	10:33 for the **c** burnt offering, of the sabbaths,	8548
Pr	15:15 *he that is* of a merry heart *hath* a **c** feast.	8548
	19:13 the contentions of a wife *are* a **c** dropping.	8548
	27:15 A **c dropping** in a very rainy day	1812+2956
Isa	14: 6 the people in wrath with a **c** stroke,	1115+5627
Jer	48: 5 of Luhith **c weeping** shall go up;	1065+1065
	52:34 there was a **c** diet given him of the king	8548
Eze	39:14 shall sever out men of **c employment,**	8548
	46:15 every morning *for a* **c** burnt offering.	8548
Lk	18: 5 lest **by** her **c** coming she weary me;	1519+5056
Ro	9: 2 great heaviness and **c** sorrow in my heart.	88

CONTINUALLY (81) [CONTINUE]

Ge	6: 5 of his heart *was* only evil **c.**	3117+3605+1886.1
	8: 3 from off the earth **c:**	1980+7725+2050.1
	8: 5 the waters decreased **c** until the tenth	1980
Ex	28:29 *place,* for a memorial before the Lord **c.**	8548
	28:30 Israel upon his heart before the Lord **c.**	8548
	29:38 two lambs of the first year day by day **c.**	8548
Lev	24: 2 the light, to cause the lamps to burn **c.**	8548

Lev 24: 3 unto the morning before the LORD **c**: 8548
24: 4 the pure candlestick before the LORD **c**. 8548
24: 8 he shall set it in order before the LORD **c**, 8548
Jos 6:13 the ark of the LORD **went on c**, 1980+1980
1Sa 18:29 became David's enemy **c**. 3117+3605+1886.1
2Sa 9: 7 and thou shalt eat bread at my table **c**. 8548
9:13 for he did eat **c** at the king's table; 8548
15:12 for the people increased **c** with Absalom. 1980
19:13 me **c** in the room of Joab. 3117+3605+1886.1
1Ki 10: 8 which stand **c** before thee, *and* that hear 8548
2Ki 9: 4 holy man of God, which passeth by us **c**. 8548
25:29 he did eat bread **c** before him all the days 8548
1Ch 16: 6 Jahaziel the priests with trumpets **c** before 8548
16:11 and his strength, seek his face **c**. 8548
16:37 his brethren, to minister before the ark **c**, 8548
16:40 the altar of the burnt offering **c** morning 8548
23:31 unto them, **c** before the LORD: 8548
2Ch 9: 7 which stand **c** before thee, and hear thy 8548
12:15 and Jeroboam **c**. 3117+3605+1886.1
24:14 of the LORD **c** all the days of Jehoiada. 8548
Job 1: 5 Thus did Job **c**. 3117+3605+1886.1
Ps 34: 1 times: his praise *shall c be* in my mouth. 8548
35:27 yea, let them say **c**, Let the LORD be 8548
38:17 to halt, and my sorrow *is* **c** before me. 8548
40:11 and thy truth **c** preserve me. 8548
40:16 let such as love thy salvation say **c**, 8548
42: 3 while *they* **c** say unto me, 3117+3605+1886.1
44:15 My confusion *is* **c** before 3117+3605+1886.1
50: 8 burnt offerings, *to have been* **c** before me. 8548
52: 1 of God *endureth* **c**. 3117+3605+1886.1
58: 7 them melt away as waters *which* **run c**. 1980
69:23 see not; and make their loins **c** to shake. 8548
70: 4 let such as love thy salvation say **c**, 8548
71: 3 habitation, whereunto *I* may **c** resort: 8548
71: 6 my praise *shall be* **c** of thee. 8548
71:14 I will hope **c**, and will yet praise thee 8548
72:15 prayer also shall be made for him **c**; 8548
73:23 Nevertheless I *am* **c** with thee: thou hast 8548
74:23 that rise up against thee increaseth **c**. 8548
109:10 Let his children be **c vagabonds**, 5128+5128
109:15 Let them be before the LORD **c**, that he 8548
109:19 and for a girdle where*with* he is girded **c**. 8548
119:44 So shall I keep thy law **c** for ever and ever. 8548
119:109 soul *is* **c** in my hand: yet do I not forget 8548
119:117 I will have respect unto thy statutes **c**. 8548
140: 2 **c** are they gathered together for war. 3117+3605
Pr 6:14 he deviseth mischief **c**; 3605+6256+871.1
6:21 Bind them upon thine heart, *and* tie 8548
Ecc 1: 6 it **whirleth about c**, 1980+5437+5437
Isa 21: 8 I stand upon the watchtower in 8548
49:16 of *my* hands; thy walls *are* **c** before me. 8548
51:13 hast feared **c** every day because of the fury 8548
52: 5 and my name *is* every day *is* blasphemed. 8548
58:11 the LORD shall guide thee **c**, 8548
60:11 Therefore thy gates shall be open **c**; 8548
65: 3 A people that provoketh me to anger **c** to 8548
Jer 6: 7 in her; before me **c** *is* grief and wounds. 8548
33:18 and to do sacrifice **c**. 3117+3605+1886.1
52:33 he did **c** eat bread before him all the days 8548
Eze 46:14 a meat offering *by* a perpetual ordinance 8548
Da 6:16 God whom thou servest **c**, 0.2+8411+871.2
6:20 God, whom thou servest **c**, 0.2+8411+871.2
Hos 4:18 have **committed whoredom c**: 2181+2181
12: 6 and judgment, and wait on thy God **c**. 8548
Ob 1:16 *so* shall all the heathen drink **c**, yea, 8548
Na 3:19 whom hath not thy wickedness passed **c**? 8548
Hab 1:17 and not spare **c** to slay the nations? 8548
Lk 24:53 And were **c** in the temple, praising and 1275
Ac 6: 4 But we will **give** ourselves **c** to prayer, 4342
10: 7 soldier of them that **waited on** him **c**; 4342
Ro 13: 6 **attending c** upon this very *thing*. 4342
Heb 7: 3 of God; abideth a priest **c**. 1336+1519+3588
10: 1 **c** make the comers *thereunto* 1336+1519+3588
13:15 offer the sacrifice of praise to God **c**, 1223+3956

CONTINUANCE (5) [CONTINUE]

Dt 28:59 of **long c**, and sore sicknesses, and of long 539
28:59 and sore sicknesses, and of **long c**. 539
Ps 139:16 *which* in **c** were fashioned, when *as yet* 3117
Isa 64: 5 in those is **c**, and we shall be saved. 5769
Ro 2: 7 To them who by **patient c** in well doing 5281

CONTINUE (38) [CONTINUAL, CONTINUALLY, CONTINUANCE, CONTINUED, CONTINUETH, CONTINUING]

Ex 21:21 Notwithstanding, if he **c** a day or two, 5975
Lev 12: 4 **c** in the blood of her purifying three and 3427
12: 5 she shall **c** in the blood of her purifying 3427
1Sa 12:14 also the king that reigneth over you **c** 1961
13:14 now thy kingdom shall not **c**: the LORD 6965
2Sa 7:29 that *it* may **c** for ever before thee: 1961
1Ki 2: 4 That the LORD may **c** his word which he 6965
Job 15:29 not be rich, neither shall his substance **c**, 6965
17: 2 *doth* not mine eye **c** in their provocation? 3885
Ps 36:10 O **c** thy lovingkindness unto them that 4900
49:11 *that* their houses *shall* **c** for ever, NIH
102:28 The children of thy servants shall **c**, 7931
119:91 They **c** *this* day according to thine 5975
Isa 5:11 that **c** until night, *till* wine inflame them! 309
Jer 32:14 vessel, that they may **c** many days. 5975
Da 11: 8 he shall *more* years than the king of 5975
Mt 15:32 because they **c** with me now three days, 4357
Jn 8:31 ye **c** in my word, *then* are ye my disciples 3306
15: 9 so have I loved you: **c** ye in my love. 3306
Ac 13:43 persuaded them to **c** in the grace of God. 1961

Ac 14:22 *and* exhorting *them* to **c** in the faith, 1696
26:22 obtained help of God, I **c** unto this day, 2476
Ro 6: 1 Shall we **c** in sin, that grace may abound? 1961
11:22 goodness, if thou **c** in *his* goodness: 1961
Gal 2: 5 that the truth of the gospel might **c** with 1265
Php 1:25 and **c** **with** you all for your furtherance 4839
Col 1:23 If ye **c** in the faith grounded and settled, 1961
4: 2 **C** in prayer, and watch in the same with 4342
1Ti 2:15 if they **c** in faith and charity and 3306
4:16 and unto the doctrine; **c** in them: 1961
2Ti 3:14 But **c** thou in *the things* which thou hast 3306
Heb 7:23 *they* were not suffered to **c** by reason of 3887
13: 1 Let brotherly love **c**. 3306
Jas 4:13 there a year, and buy and sell, 4160
2Pe 3: 4 *things* **c** as *they were* from the beginning 1265
1Jn 2:24 also shall **c** in the Son, and in the Father. 3306
Rev 13: 5 power was given unto him to **c** forty *and* 4160
17:10 when he cometh, he must **c** a short *space*. 3306

CONTINUED (29) [CONTINUE]

Ge 40: 4 served them: and they **c** a season in ward. 1961
Jdg 5:17 Asher **c** on the sea shore, and abode in his 3427
Ru 1: 2 *into* the country of Moab, and **c** there. 1961
2: 7 hath **c** even from the morning until now, 5975
1Sa 1:12 as she **c** praying before the LORD, 7235
2Sa 6:17 the ark of the LORD **c** in the house of 3427
1Ki 22: 1 they **c** three years without war between 3427
2Ch 29:28 all *this* **c** until the burnt offering was NIH
Ne 5:16 Yea also I **c** in the work of this wall, 2388
Job 27: 1 Job **c** his parable, and said, 3254+5375
29: 1 Job **c** his parable, and said, 3254+5375
Ps 72:17 his name shall be **c** as long as the sun: 5125
Da 1:21 Daniel *even* unto the first year of king 1961
Lk 6:12 to pray, and **c** all night in prayer to God. 1510
22:28 Ye are they which have **c** with me in my 1265
Jn 2:12 and they **c** there not many days. 3306
8: 7 So when they **c** asking him, he lift up 1961
11:54 and there **c** with his disciples. 1304
Ac 1:14 These all **c** with one accord in prayer and 4342
2:42 And they **c stedfastly** in the apostles' 4342
8:13 he **c** with Philip, and wondered, 4342
12:16 But Peter **c** knocking: and when they had 1961
15:35 Paul also and Barnabas **c** in Antioch, 1304
18:11 And he **c** *there* a year and six months, 2523
19:10 And this **c** by the space of two years; 1096
20: 7 and *his* speech until midnight. 3905
27:33 day that ye have tarried and **c** fasting, 1300
Heb 8: 9 because they **c** not in my covenant, and I 1696
1Jn 2:19 they would *no doubt* have **c** with us: 3306

CONTINUETH (5) [CONTINUE]

Job 14: 2 he fleeth also as a shadow, and **c** not. 5975
Gal 3:10 Cursed *is* every one that **c** not in all *things* 1696
1Ti 5: 5 and **c** in supplications and prayers night 4357
Heb 7:24 But this *man*, because he **c** ever, hath an 3306
Jas 1:25 **c** *therein*, he being not a forgetful hearer, 3887

CONTINUING (4) [CONTINUE]

Jer 30:23 goeth forth *with* fury, a **c** whirlwind: 1641
Ac 2:46 And they, **c** daily with one accord in the temple, 4342
Ro 12:12 patient in tribulation; **c instant** in prayer; 4342
Heb 13:14 For here have we no **c** city, but we seek 3306

CONTRADICTING (1) [CONTRADICTION]

Ac 13:45 were spoken by Paul, **c** and blaspheming. 483

CONTRADICTION (2) [CONTRADICTING]

Heb 7: 7 And without all **c** the less is blessed of 485
12: 3 For consider him that endured such **c** of 485

CONTRARIWISE (3) [CONTRARY]

2Co 2: 7 So that **c** ye *ought* rather to forgive *him*, 5121
Gal 2: 7 But **c**, when they saw that the gospel of 5121
1Pe 3: 9 but **c** blessing; knowing that ye are 5121

CONTRARY (24) [CONTRARIWISE]

Lev 26:21 ye walk **c** unto me, and will not hearken 7147
26:23 by these *things*, but will walk **c** unto me; 7147
26:24 I also walk **c** unto you, and will punish 7147
26:27 hearken unto me, but walk **c** unto me; 7147
26:28 I will walk **c** unto you also in fury; 7147
26:40 that also they have walked **c** unto me; 7147
26:41 *And that* I also have walked **c** unto them, 7147
Est 9: 1 it was turned *to the* **c**, that the Jews NIH
Eze 16:34 the **c** is in thee *from* other women in thy 2016
16:34 is given unto thee, therefore thou art **c**. 2016
Mt 14:24 tossed with waves: for the wind was **c**. 1727
Mk 6:48 in rowing; for the wind was **c** unto them: 1727
Ac 17: 7 and these all do **c** to the decrees of Cesar, 561
18:13 men to worship God **c** to the law. 3844
23: 3 me to be smitten **c** to the **law**? 3891
26: 9 that *I* ought to do many *things* **c** to 1727
27: 4 under Cyprus, because the winds were **c**. 1727
Ro 11:24 wert graffed **c** to nature into a good olive 3844
16:17 offences **c** to the doctrine which ye have 3844
Gal 5:17 and these are **c** the one to the other: so 480
Col 2:14 which was **c** to us, and took it out of 5227
1Th 2:15 they please not God, and are **c** to all men: 1727
1Ti 1:10 *there be* any other *thing that* is **c** to sound 480
Tit 2: 8 he that is of the **c** *part* may be ashamed, 1727

CONTRIBUTION (1)

Ro 15:26 Achaia to make a certain **c** for the poor 2842

CONTRITE (5)

Ps 34:18 and saveth such as be of a **c** spirit. 1793

Ps 51:17 a broken and a **c** heart, O God, thou wilt 1794
Isa 57:15 holy *place*, with him also *that is* of a **c** 1793
57:15 and to revive the heart of the **c** ones. 1792
66: 2 *even* to him that *is* poor and of a **c** spirit, 5223

CONTROVERSIES (1) [CONTROVERSY]

2Ch 19: 8 for the judgment of the LORD, and for **c**, 7379

CONTROVERSY (13) [CONTROVERSIES]

Dt 17: 8 *being* matters of **c** within thy gates: 7379
19:17 between whom the **c** *is*, shall stand before 7379
21: 5 by their word shall every **c** and 7379
25: 1 If there be a **c** between men, and they 7379
2Sa 15: 2 *that when* any man that had a **c** came to 7379
Isa 34: 8 the year of recompences for the **c** of Zion. 7379
Jer 25:31 for the LORD hath a **c** with the nations, 7379
Eze 44:24 in **c** they shall stand in judgment; 7379
Hos 4: 1 for the LORD hath a **c** with 7379
12: 2 The LORD hath also a **c** with Judah, 7379
Mic 6: 2 the LORD's **c**, and ye strong foundations 7379
6: 2 for the LORD hath a **c** with his people, 7379
1Ti 3:16 And **without** **c** great is the mystery of 3672

CONVENIENT (9) [CONVENIENTLY]

Pr 30: 8 nor riches; feed me with food **c** for me: 2706
Jer 40: 4 and **c for** thee to go, 413+3477+1886.1
40: 5 go wheresoever it seemeth **c** unto thee to 3477
Mk 6:21 when a **c** day was come, that Herod on 2121
Ac 24:25 I have a **season**, I will call for thee. 2540
Ro 1:28 to do those *things* which are not **c**; 2520
1Co 16:12 he will come when he shall **have c time**. 2119
Eph 5: 4 talking, nor jesting, which are not **c**: 433
Phm 1: 8 in Christ to enjoin thee that which is **c**, 433

CONVENIENTLY (1) [CONVENIENT]

Mk 14:11 he sought how he might **c** betray him. 2122

CONVERSANT (2)

Jos 8:35 the strangers that were **c** among them. 1980
1Sa 25:15 long as we were **c** with them, when we 1980

CONVERSATION (20)

Ps 37:14 needy, *and* to slay such as be of upright **c**. 1870
50:23 him that ordereth *his* **c** *aright* will I shew 1870
2Co 1:12 we have **had** our **c** in the world, 390
Gal 1:13 For ye have heard of my **c** in time past in 391
Eph 2: 3 whom also we all **had** our **c** in times 390
4:22 That ye put off concerning the former **c** 391
Php 1:27 let your **c** be as it becometh the gospel 4176
3:20 For our **c** is in heaven; from whence also 4175
1Ti 4:12 in word, in **c**, in charity, in spirit, in faith, 391
Heb 13: 5 *Let* your **c** be without covetousness; 5158
13: 7 faith follow, considering the end of *their* **c**. 391
Jas 3:13 let him shew out of a good **c** his works 391
1Pe 1:15 is holy, so be ye holy in all *manner of* **c**; 391
1:18 from your vain **c** received by tradition from 391
2:12 Having your **c** honest among the Gentiles: 391
3: 1 the word be won by the **c** of the wives; 391
3: 2 While they behold your chaste **c** *coupled* 391
3:16 that falsely accuse your good **c** in Christ. 391
2Pe 2: 7 vexed with the filthy **c** of the wicked; 391
3:11 *of persons* ought ye to be in all holy **c** 391

CONVERSION (1) [CONVERT]

Ac 15: 3 Samaria, declaring the **c** of the Gentiles: 1995

CONVERT (2) [CONVERSION, CONVERTED, CONVERTETH, CONVERTING, CONVERTS]

Isa 6:10 *with* their heart, and **c**, and be healed. 7725
Jas 5:19 do err from the truth, and one **c** him; 1994

CONVERTED (9) [CONVERT]

Ps 51:13 and sinners shall be **c** unto thee. 7725
Isa 60: 5 the abundance of the sea shall be **c** unto 2015
Mt 13:15 and should be **c**, and I should heal them. 1994
18: 3 Except ye be **c**, and become as little 4762
Mk 4:12 lest at any time they should be **c**, 1994
Lk 22:32 and when thou art **c**, strengthen thy 1994
Jn 12:40 and be **c**, and I should heal them. 1994
Ac 3:19 Repent ye therefore, and be **c**, that your 1994
28:27 and should be **c**, and I should heal them. 1994

CONVERTETH (1) [CONVERT]

Jas 5:20 he which **c** the sinner from the error of 1994

CONVERTING (1) [CONVERT]

Ps 19: 7 law of the LORD *is* perfect, **c** the soul: 7725

CONVERTS (1) [CONVERT]

Isa 1:27 and her **c** with righteousness. 7725

CONVEY (2) [CONVEYED]

1Ki 5: 9 will **c** them by sea *in* flotes unto the place 7760
Ne 2: 7 that they may **c** me **over** till I come into 5674

CONVEYED (1) [CONVEY]

Jn 5:13 for Jesus had **c** himself **away**, a multitude 1593

CONVICT See REPROOF; REPROVE

CONVICTED (1)

Jn 8: 9 And they which heard *it*, being **c** by *their* 1651

CONVINCE (2) [CONVINCED, CONVINCETH]

Tit 1: 9 both to exhort and to **c** the gainsayers. 1651
Jude 1:15 to **c** all *that are* ungodly among them of all 1827

C

CONVINCED (4) [CONVINCE]

Job	32:12 *there* was none of you that c Job,	3198
Ac	18:28 For he mightily c the Jews,	1246
1Co	14:24 *one* unlearned, he is c of all, he is judged	1651
Jas	2: 9 and are c of the law as transgressors.	1651

CONVINCETH (1) [CONVINCE]

Jn	8:46 Which of you c me of sin? And if I say	1651

CONVINCING See INFALLIBLE

CONVOCATION (16) [CONVOCATIONS]

Ex	12:16 in the first day *there* shall *be* a holy c,	4744
	12:16 in the seventh day there shall be a holy c	4744
Lev	23: 3 day *is* the sabbath of rest, a holy c;	4744
	23: 7 In the first day ye shall have a holy c:	4744
	23: 8 in the seventh day *is* a holy c: ye shall do	4744
	23:21 *that* it may be a holy c unto you:	4744
	23:24 of blowing of trumpets, a holy c.	4744
	23:27 it shall be a holy c unto you; and ye shall	4744
	23:35 On the first day *shall be* a holy c: ye shall	4744
	23:36 on the eighth day shall be a holy c unto	4744
Nu	28:18 In the first day *shall be* a holy c; ye shall	4744
	28:25 on the seventh day ye shall have a holy c;	4744
	28:26 your weeks *be* out, ye shall have a holy c;	4744
	29: 1 *day* of the month, ye shall have a holy c;	4744
	29: 7 tenth *day* of this seventh month a holy c:	4744
	29:12 the seventh month ye shall have a holy c;	4744

CONVOCATIONS (3) [CONVOCATION]

Lev	23: 2 which ye shall proclaim *to be* holy c,	4744
	23: 4 *are* the feasts of the LORD, *even* holy c,	4744
	23:37 which ye shall proclaim *to be* holy c,	4744

CONVENIENTLY See TARE

CONY (1) [CONEY]

Lev	11: 5 the c, because he cheweth the cud,	8227

COOK (2) [COOKS]

1Sa	9:23 Samuel said unto the c, Bring the portion	2876
	9:24 the c took up the shoulder, and *that*	2876

COOKED See SOD; SODDEN

COOKING See SOD; SODDEN

COOKS (1) [COOK]

1Sa	8:13 and to be c, and to be bakers.	2879

COOL (2)

Ge	3: 8 walking in the garden in the c of the day:	7307
Lk	16:24 of his finger in water, and c my tongue;	2711

COPIED (1) [COPY]

Pr	25: 1 the men of Hezekiah king of Judah c out.	6275

COPING (1)

1Ki	7: 9 even from the foundation unto the c,	2947

COPPER (1) [COPPERSMITH]

Ezr	8:27 and two vessels of fine c, precious as gold.	5178

COPPERSMITH (1) [COPPER, SMITH]

2Ti	4:14 Alexander the c did me much evil;	5471

COPULATION (3)

Lev	15:16 if any man's seed of c go out from him,	7902
	15:17 and every skin, whereon is the seed of c,	7902
	15:18 with whom man shall lie *with* seed of c,	7902

COPY (9) [COPIED]

Dt	17:18 that he shall write him a c of this law in a	4932
Jos	8:32 he wrote there upon the stones a c of	4932
Ezr	4:11 This *is* the c of the letter that they sent	6573
	4:23 Now when the c of king Artaxerxes' letter	6573
	5: 6 The c of the letter that Tatnai, governor	6573
	7:11 this *is* the c of the letter that the king	6572
Est	3:14 The c of the writing for a commandment	6572
	4: 8 Also he gave him the c of the writing of	6572
	8:13 The c of the writing for a commandment	6572

COR (1)

Eze	45:14 *offer* the tenth part of a bath out of the c,	3734

CORAL (2)

Job	28:18 No mention shall be made of c,	7215
Eze	27:16 and fine linen, and c, and agate.	7215

CORBAN (1)

Mk	7:11 shall say to *his* father or mother, *It is* C,	2878

CORD (6) [CORDS]

Jos	2:15 she let them down by a c through	2256
Job	30:11 Because he hath loosed my c,	3499
	41: 1 his tongue with a c *which* thou lettest	2256
Ecc	4:12 and a threefold c is not quickly broken.	2339
	12: 6 ever the silver c be loosed, or the golden	2256
Mic	2: 5 c by lot in the congregation of the LORD.	2256

CORDS (26) [CORD]

Ex	35:18 and the pins of the court, and their c,	4340
	39:40 his c, and his pins, and all the vessels of	4340
Nu	3:26 and the c of it for all the service thereof.	4340
	3:37 their sockets, and their pins, and their c.	4340
	4:26 their c, and all the instruments of their	4340
	4:32 their sockets, and their pins, and their c,	4340

Jdg	15:13 they bound him with two new c,	5688
	15:14 the c that *were* upon his arms became as	5688
Est	1: 6 *hangings*, fastened with c of fine linen	2256
Job	36: 8 in fetters, *and* be holden in c of affliction;	2256
Ps	2: 3 and cast away their c from us.	5688
	118:27 bind the sacrifice with c, *even* unto	5688
	129: 4 he hath cut asunder the c of the wicked.	5688
	140: 5 The proud have hid a snare for me, and c;	2256
Pr	5:22 he shall be holden with the c of his sins.	2256
Isa	5:18 Woe unto them that draw iniquity with c	2256
	33:20 shall any of the c thereof be broken.	2256
	54: 2 lengthen thy c, and strengthen thy stakes;	4340
Jer	10:20 is spoiled, and all my c are broken:	4340
	38: 6 they let down Jeremiah with c. And in	2256
	38:11 let them down by c into the dungeon to	2256
	38:12 rags under thine armholes under the c.	2256
	38:13 So they drew up Jeremiah with c,	2256
Eze	27:24 bound with c, and made of cedar,	2256
Hos	11: 4 I drew them with c of a man, with bands	2256
Jn	2:15 when he had made a scourge of small c,	4979

CORE (1)

Jude	1:11 and perished in the gainsaying of C.	2879

CORIANDER (2)

Ex	16:31 *was* like c seed, white; and the taste of it	1407
Nu	11: 7 the manna *was* as c seed, and the colour	1407

CORINTH (6) [CORINTHIANS, CORINTHUS]

Ac	18: 1 departed from Athens, and came to C;	2882
	19: 1 came to pass that, while Apollos was at C,	2882
1Co	1: 2 Unto the church of God which is at C,	2882
2Co	1: 1 unto the church of God which is at C,	2882
	1:23 to spare you I came not as yet unto C.	2882
2Ti	4:20 Erastus abode at C: but Trophimus have I	2882

CORINTHIANS (4) [CORINTH]

Ac	18: 8 and many of the C hearing believed,	2881
1Co	16: S The first *epistle* to the C was written from	2881
2Co	6:11 O ye C, our mouth is open unto you,	2881
	13: S The second *epistle* to the C was written	2881

CORINTHUS (1) [CORINTH]

Ro	16: S Written to the Romans from C, *and sent*	2882

CORMORANT (4)

Lev	11:17 little owl, and the c, and the great owl,	7994
Dt	14:17 the pelican, and the gier eagle, and the c,	7994
Isa	34:11 the c and the bittern shall possess it;	6893
Zep	2:14 both the c and the bittern shall lodge in	6893

CORN (102) [CORNFLOOR]

Ge	27:28 of the earth, and plenty of c and wine:	1715
	27:37 with c and wine have I sustained him:	1715
	41: 5 seven ears of c came up upon one stalk,	7641
	41:35 lay up c under the hand of Pharaoh,	1250
	41:49 Joseph gathered c as the sand of the sea,	1250
	41:57 came into Egypt to Joseph for to buy c;	NIH
	42: 1 Now when Jacob saw that there was c in	7668
	42: 2 I have heard that there is c in Egypt:	7668
	42: 3 ten brethren went down to buy c	1250
	42: 5 the sons of Israel came to buy c among	NIH
	42:19 carry c *for* the famine of your houses:	7668
	42:25 commanded to fill their sacks *with* c,	1250
	42:26 they laded their asses with the c,	7668
	43: 2 when they had eaten up the c which they	7668
	44: 2 mouth of the youngest, and his c money.	7668
	45:23 ten she asses laden with c and bread and	1250
	47:14 of Canaan, for the c which they bought:	7668
Ex	22: 6 that the stacks of c, or the standing corn,	1430
	22: 6 or corn, or the standing c, or the field,	7054
Lev	2:14 firstfruits green ears of c dried by the fire,	24
	2:14 by the fire, *even* c beaten out of full ears.	3759
	2:16 *part* of the beaten c thereof, and *part* of	1643
	23:14 bread, nor parched c, nor green ears,	NIH
Nu	18:27 as though it were the c of	1715
Dt	7:13 land, thy c, and thy wine, and thine oil,	1715
	11:14 thou mayest gather in thy c,	1715
	12:17 not eat within thy gates the tithe of thy c,	1715
	14:23 the tithe of thy c, of thy wine, and of thine	1715
	16: 9 *thou* beginnest *to put* the sickle to the c.	7054
	16:13 after that thou hast gathered in thy c and	1637
	18: 4 The firstfruit *also* of thy c, of thy wine,	1715
	23:25 When thou comest into the standing c of	7054
	23:25 a sickle unto thy neighbour's standing c.	7054
	25: 4 the ox when he treadeth out *the* c.	NIH
	28:51 which *also* shall not leave thee *either* c,	1715
	33:28 fountain of Jacob *shall be* upon a land of c	1715
Jos	5:11 they did eat of the old c of the land on	5669
	5:11 and parched c in the selfsame day.	NIH
	5:12 they had eaten of the old c of the land;	5669
Jdg	15: 5 he *them* go into the standing c of	7054
	15: 5 also the standing c, with the vineyards	NIH
Ru	2: 2 glean ears of c after *him* in whose sight I	7641
	2:14 he reached her parched c, and she did eat,	NIH
	3: 7 to lie down at the end of the heap of c	NIH
1Sa	17:17 thy brethren an ephah of this parched c,	NIH
	25:18 five measures of parched c, and an	NIH
2Sa	17:19 and spread ground c thereon;	7383
	17:28 parched c, and beans, and lentiles,	NIH
2Ki	4:42 and full ears of c in the husk thereof.	3759
	18:32 a land of c and wine, a land of bread and	1715
	19:26 and *as c* blasted before it be grown up.	NIH
2Ch	31: 5 brought in abundance the firstfruits of c,	1715
	32:28 Storehouses also for the increase of c,	1715

Ne	5: 2 we take up c *for them*, that we may eat,	1715
	5: 3 houses, that we might buy c, because of	1715
	5:10 *might* exact of them money and c:	1715
	5:11 the c, the wine, and the oil, that ye exact	1715
	10:39 of Levi shall bring the offering of the c,	1715
	13: 5 the vessels, and the tithes of the c,	1715
	13:12 brought all Judah the tithe of the c and	1715
Job	5:26 as a shock of c cometh in in his season.	1430
	24: 6 They reap every *one* his c in the field:	1098
	24:24 and cut off as the tops of the ears of c.	7641
	39: 4 are in good liking, they grow up with c;	1250
Ps	4: 7 more than *in* the time *that* their c and	1715
	65: 9 thou preparest them c, when thou hast so	1715
	65:13 The valleys also are covered over with c;	1250
	72:16 There shall be a handful of c in the earth	1250
	78:24 and had given them of the c of heaven.	1715
Pr	11:26 He that withholdeth c, the people shall	1250
Isa	17: 5 as when the harvestman gathereth the c,	7054
	21:10 O my threshing, and the c of my floor:	1121
	28:28 Bread c is bruised; because he will not	NIH
	36:17 a land of c and wine, a land of bread and	1715
	37:27 and *as c* blasted before it be grown up.	NIH
	62: 8 I will no more give thy c *to be* meat	1715
La	2:12 to their mothers, Where *is* c and wine?	1715
Eze	36:29 I will call for the c, and will increase it,	1715
Hos	2: 8 For she did not know that I gave her c,	1715
	2: 9 and take *away* my c in the time thereof,	1715
	2:22 the earth shall hear the c, and the wine,	1715
	7:14 they assemble themselves for c and wine,	1715
	10:11 *and* loveth to tread out *the* c; but I passed	NIH
	14: 7 they shall revive *as* the c, and grow as	1715
Joel	1:10 for the c is wasted, the new wine is dried	1715
	1:17 are broken down; for the c is withered.	1715
	2:19 I *will* send you c, and wine, and oil,	1715
Am	5:11 new moon be gone, that we may sell c?	7668
	9: 9 like as c is sifted in a sieve, yet shall not	NIH
Hag	1:11 and upon the c, and upon the new wine,	1715
Zec	9:17 c shall make the young men cheerful,	1715
Mt	12: 1 went on the sabbath day through the c;	4702
	12: 1 began to pluck the ears of c, and to eat.	4719
Mk	2:23 that he went through the c fields on	4702
	2:23 as they went, to pluck the ears of c	4719
	4:28 the ear, after that the full c in the ear.	4621
Lk	6: 1 first, that he went through the c fields;	4702
	6: 1 and his disciples plucked the ears of c,	4719
Jn	12:24 Except a c of wheat fall into the ground	2848
Ac	7:12 But when Jacob heard that there was c in	4621
1Co	9: 9 mouth of the ox that treadeth out the c.	248
1Ti	5:18 not muzzle the ox that treadeth out the c.	248

CORNELIUS (10)

Ac	10: 1 was a certain man in Cesarea called C,	2883
	10: 3 coming in to him, and saying unto him, C.	2883
	10: 7 And when the angel which spake unto C	2883
	10:17 men which were sent from C had made	2883
	10:21 men which were sent unto him from C;	2883
	10:22 C the centurion, a just man, and one that	2883
	10:24 And C waited for them, and had called	2883
	10:25 C met him, and fell down at his feet,	2883
	10:30 And C said, Four days ago I was fasting	2883
	10:31 And said, C, thy prayer is heard,	2883

CORNER (37)

Ex	36:25 *which is* toward the north c, he made	6285
Lev	21: 5 neither shall they shave off the c of their	6285
Jos	18:14 compassed the c of the sea southward,	6285
2Ki	11:11 from the right c of the temple to the left	3802
	11:11 of the temple to the left c of the temple,	3802
	14:13 from the gate of Ephraim unto the c gate,	6438
2Ch	25:23 from the gate of Ephraim to the c gate,	6437
	26: 9 built towers in Jerusalem at the c gate,	6438
	28:24 made him altars in every c of Jerusalem.	6438
Ne	3:24 the turning *of the wall*, even unto the c.	6438
	3:31 Miphkad, and to the going up of the c.	6438
	3:32 between the going up of the c unto	6438
Job	38: 6 or who laid the c stone thereof;	6438
Ps	118:22 refused is become the head *stone* of the c.	6438
	144:12 *that* our daughters *may be* as c stones,	2106
Pr	7: 8 Passing through the street near her c;	6434
	7:12 in the streets, and lieth in wait at every c.)	6438
	21: 9 *It is* better to dwell in a c of the housetop,	6438
	25:24 *It is* better to dwell in a c of the housetop,	6438
Isa	28:16 a precious *stone*, a sure foundation:	6438
	30:20 teachers be removed into a c any more,	3670
Jer	31:38 tower of Hananeel unto the gate of the c.	6438
	31:40 unto the c of the horse gate towards	6438
	48:45 devour the c of Moab, and the crown	6285
	51:26 they shall not take of thee a stone for a c,	6438
Eze	46:21 every c of the court there was a	4740+4740
Am	3:12 that dwell in Samaria in the c of a bed,	6285
Zec	10: 4 Out of him came forth the c, out of him	6438
	14:10 unto the c gate, and *from* the tower of	6434
Mt	21:42 the same is become the head of the c:	1137
Mk	12:10 rejected is become the head of the c:	1137
Lk	20:17 the same is become the head of the c?	1137
Ac	4:11 which is become the head of the c.	1137
	26:26 for this *thing* was not done in a c.	1137
Eph	2:20 Christ himself being the chief *corner* *stone*;	204
1Pe	2: 6 I lay in Sion a chief c stone, elect,	204
	2: 7 the same is made the head of the c,	1137

CORNER DEFENSES See BULWARKS

CORNERS (39)

Ex	25:12 for it, and put *them* in the four c thereof;	6471

Ex	25:26	put the rings in the four **c** that *are* on	6285
	26:23	two boards shalt thou make for the **c** of	4742
	26:24	them both; they shall be for the two **c.**	4740
	27:	2 the horns of it upon the four **c** thereof:	6438
	27:	4 four brasen rings in the four **c** thereof.	7098
	30:	4 by the two **c** thereof, upon the two sides	6763
	36:28	two boards made he for the **c** of	4742
	36:29	thus he did to both of them in both the **c.**	4740
	37:	3 rings of gold, *to be set* by the four **c** of it;	6471
	37:13	put the rings upon the four **c** that *were* in	6285
	37:27	by the two **c** of it, upon the two sides	6763
	38:	2 made the horns thereof on the four **c** of	6438
Lev	19:	9 shalt not wholly reap the **c** of thy field,	6285
	19:27	Ye shall not round the **c** of your heads,	6285
	19:27	neither shalt thou mar the **c** of thy beard.	6285
	23:22	shalt not make clean riddance of the **c**	6285
Nu	24:17	shall smite the **c** of Moab, and destroy all	6285
Dt	32:26	I said, I would **scatter** them **into c,**	6284
1Ki	7:30	the four **c** thereof had undersetters: under	6471
	7:34	*were* four undersetters to the four **c** of	6438
Ne	9:22	and nations, and didst divide them into **c:**	6285
Job	1:19	smote the four **c** of the house, and it fell	6438
Isa	11:12	of Judah from the four **c** of the earth.	3671
Jer	9:26	Moab, and all *that are* in the utmost **c,**	6285
	25:23	and Buz, and all *that are* in the utmost **c,**	6285
	49:32	all winds them *that are* in the utmost **c;**	6285
Eze	7:	2 end is come upon the four **c** of the land.	3671
	41:22	the **c** thereof, and the length thereof,	4740
	43:20	on the four **c** of the settle, and upon	6438
	45:19	upon the four **c** of the settle of the altar,	6438
	46:21	caused me to pass by the four **c** of	4740
	46:22	the four **c** of the court *there were* courts	4740
	46:22	these four **c** *were* of one measure.	7106
Zec	9:15	filled like bowls, *and* as the **c** of the altar.	2106
Mt	6:	5 the synagogues and in the **c** of the streets,	*1137*
Ac	10:11	*it had been* a great sheet knit at the four **c,**	*746*
	11:	5 sheet, let down from heaven by four **c;**	*746*
Rev	7:	1 angels standing on the four **c** of the earth,	*1137*

CORNET (7)

1Ch	15:28	with sound of the **c,** and with trumpets,	7782
Ps	98:	6 sound of **c** make a joyful noise before	7782
Da	3:	5 at what time ye hear the sound of the **c,**	7162
	3:	7 all the people heard the sound of the **c,**	7162
	3:10	man that shall hear the sound of the **c,**	7162
	3:15	at what time ye hear the sound of the **c,**	7162
Hos	5:	8 Blow ye the **c** in Gibeah, *and* the trumpet	7782

CORNETS (2)

2Sa	6:	5 on timbrels, and on **c,** and on cymbals.	4517
2Ch	15:14	and with trumpets, and with **c.**	7782

CORNFLOOR (1) [CORN, FLOOR]

Hos	9:	1 hast loved a reward upon every **c.**	1637+1715

CORPSE (1) [CORPSES]

Mk	6:29	heard *of it,* they came and took up his **c,**	*4430*

CORPSES (4) [CORPSE]

2Ki	19:35	morning, behold, they *were* all dead **c.**	6297
Isa	37:36	morning, behold, they *were* all dead **c.**	6297
Na	3:	3 carcases; and *there is* none end of their **c;**	1472
	3:	3 *their* corpses; they stumble upon their **c:**	1472

CORRECT (7) [CORRECTED, CORRECTETH, CORRECTION]

Ps	39:11	When thou with rebukes dost **c** man for	3256
	94:10	chastiseth the heathen, shall not he **c?**	3198
Pr	29:17	**C** thy son, and he shall give thee rest; yea,	3256
Jer	2:19	Thine own wickedness shall **c** thee,	3256
	10:24	O Lord, **c** me, but with judgment; not in	3256
	30:11	I will **c** thee in measure, and will not leave	3256
	46:28	but **c** thee in measure;	3256

CORRECTED (2) [CORRECT]

Pr	29:19	A servant will not be **c** by words:	3256
Heb	12:	9 have had fathers of our flesh which **c** us,	*3810*

CORRECTETH (2) [CORRECT]

Job	5:17	Behold, happy *is* the man whom God **c:**	3198
Pr	3:12	For whom the Lord loveth he **c;** even as	3198

CORRECTION (12) [CORRECT]

Job	37:13	for **c,** or for his land, or for mercy.	7626
Pr	3:11	of the Lord; neither be weary of his **c:**	8433
	7:22	or as a fool to the **c** of the stocks;	4148
	15:10	**C** *is* grievous unto him that forsaketh	4148
	22:15	the rod of **c** shall drive it far from him.	4148
	23:13	Withhold not **c** from the child: for *if* thou	4148
Jer	2:30	smitten your children; they received no **c:**	4148
	5:	3 *but* they have refused to receive **c:**	4148
	7:28	the Lord their God, nor receiveth **c:**	4148
Hab	1:12	thou hast established them for **c.**	3198
Zep	3:	2 obeyed not the voice; she received not **c;**	4148
2Ti	3:16	*is* profitable for doctrine, for reproof, for **c,**	*1882*

CORRUPT (33) [CORRUPTED, CORRUPTERS, CORRUPTETH, CORRUPTIBLE, CORRUPTION, CORRUPTLY, UNCORRUPTIBLE]

Ge	6:11	The earth also was **c** before God,	7843
	6:12	upon the earth, and, behold, it was **c;**	7843
Dt	4:16	Lest ye **c** *yourselves,* and make you a	7843
	4:25	shall **c** *yourselves,* and make a graven	7843
	31:29	death ye will **utterly c** *yourselves,*	7843+7843
Job	17:	1 My breath is **c,** my days are extinct,	2254
Ps	14:	1 They are **c,** they have done abominable	7843

Ps	38:	5 My wounds stink *and* are **c** because of	4743
	53:	1 **C** are they, and have done abominable	7843
	73:	8 are **c,** and speak wickedly *concerning*	4167
Pr	25:26	*is* as a troubled fountain, and a **c** spring.	7843
Eze	20:44	nor according to your **c** doings, O ye	7843
	23:11	more **c** in her inordinate love than she,	7843
Da	2:	9 and **c** words to speak before me,	7844
	11:32	the covenant shall he **c** by flatteries:	2610
Mal	1:14	sacrificeth unto the Lord a **c** *thing:*	7843
	2:	3 I *will* **c** your seed, and spread dung upon	1605
Mt	6:19	where moth and rust doth **c,**	*853*
	6:20	where neither moth nor rust doth **c,**	*853*
	7:17	but a **c** tree bringeth forth evil fruit.	*4550*
	7:18	neither *can* a **c** tree bring forth good fruit.	*4550*
	12:33	or else make the tree **c,** and his fruit	*4550*
	12:33	make the tree corrupt, and his fruit **c.**	*4550*
Lk	6:43	For a good tree bringeth not forth **c** fruit;	*4550*
	6:43	doth a **c** tree bring forth good fruit.	*4550*
1Co	15:33	evil communications **c** good manners.	*5351*
2Co	2:17	not as many, which **c** the word of God:	*2585*
Eph	4:22	which is **c** according to the deceitful lusts;	*5351*
	4:29	Let no **c** communication proceed out of	*4550*
1Ti	6:	5 Perverse disputings of men of **c** minds,	*1311*
2Ti	3:	8 men of **c** minds, reprobate concerning	*2704*
Jude	1:10	in those *things* they **c** themselves.	*5351*
Rev	19:	2 did **c** the earth with her fornication,	*5351*

CORRUPTED (14) [CORRUPT]

Ge	6:12	for all flesh had **c** his way upon the earth.	7843
Ex	8:24	the land was **c** by reason of the swarm *of*	7843
	32:	7 of the land of Egypt, have **c** *themselves:*	7843
Dt	9:12	**c** *themselves;* they are quickly turned	7843
	32:	5 They have **c** themselves, their spot *is* not	7843
Jdg	2:19	and **c** *themselves* more than their fathers,	7843
Eze	16:47	wast **c** more than they in all thy ways.	7843
	28:17	thou hast **c** thy wisdom by reason of thy	7843
Hos	9:	9 They have deeply **c** *themselves,* as in	7843
Zep	3:	7 but they rose early, *and* **c** all their doings.	7843
Mal	2:	8 have **c** the covenant of Levi, saith	7843
2Co	7:	2 we have wronged no *man,* we have **c** no	*5351*
	11:	3 minds should be **c** from the simplicity	*5351*
Jas	5:	2 Your riches are **c,** and your garments are	*4595*

CORRUPTERS (2) [CORRUPT]

Isa	1:	4 a seed of evildoers, children that are **c:**	7843
Jer	6:28	*they are* brass and iron; they are all **c.**	7843

CORRUPTETH (1) [CORRUPT]

Lk	12:33	no thief approacheth, neither moth **c.**	*1311*

CORRUPTIBLE (7) [CORRUPT]

Ro	1:23	God into an image made like to **c** man,	*5349*
1Co	9:25	Now they *do it* to obtain a **c** crown;	*5349*
	15:53	For this **c** must put on incorruption,	*5349*
	15:54	So when this **c** shall have put on	*5349*
1Pe	1:18	not redeemed with **c** *things, as* silver	*5349*
	1:23	not of **c** seed, but *of* incorruptible,	*862*
	3:	4 *that which is* **not c,** *even the ornament* of	*862*

CORRUPTING (1) [CORRUPT]

Da	11:17	give him the daughter of women, **c** her:	7843

CORRUPTION (21) [CORRUPT]

Lev	22:25	because their **c** *is* in them, *and* blemishes	4893
2Ki	23:13	*were* on the right hand of the mount of **c,**	4889
Job	17:14	I have said to **c,** Thou *art* my father:	7845
Ps	16:10	wilt thou suffer thine Holy One to see **c.**	7845
	49:	9 he should still live for ever, *and* not see **c.**	7845
Isa	38:17	to my soul *delivered it* from the pit of **c:**	1097
Da	10:	8 my comeliness was turned in me into **c,**	4889
Jnh	2:	6 hast thou brought up my life from **c,**	7845
Ac	2:27	wilt thou suffer thine Holy One to see **c.**	*1312*
	2:31	not left in hell, neither his flesh did see **c.**	*1312*
	13:34	no more to return to **c,** he said on this	*1312*
	13:35	shalt not suffer thine Holy One to see **c.**	*1312*
	13:36	and was laid unto his fathers, and saw **c:**	*1312*
	13:37	he, whom God raised *again,* saw no **c.**	*1312*
Ro	8:21	into the glorious liberty of the children	*5356*
1Co	15:42	It is sown in **c;** it is raised in incorruption.	*5356*
	15:50	God; neither doth **c** inherit incorruption.	*5356*
Gal	6:	8 to his flesh shall of the flesh reap **c;**	*5356*
2Pe	1:	4 having escaped the **c** that is in the world	*5356*
	2:12	and shall utterly perish in their own **c;**	*5356*
	2:19	they themselves are the servants of **c:**	*5356*

CORRUPTLY (2) [CORRUPT]

2Ch	27:	2 of the Lord. And the people did yet **c.**	7843
Ne	1:	7 We have **dealt very c** against thee,	2254+2254

COS (1)

Ac	21:	1 we came with a straight course unto **C,**	*2972*

COSAM (1)

Lk	3:28	the son of Addi, which was *the son* of **C,**	*2973*

COST (4) [COSTLINESS, COSTLY]

2Sa	19:42	have we eaten at all of the king's **c?**	NIH
	24:24	God of that which doth **c** me **nothing.**	2600
1Ch	21:24	nor offer burnt offerings **without c.**	2600
Lk	14:28	sitteth not down first, and counteth the **c,**	*1160*

COSTLINESS (1) [COST]

Rev	18:19	had ships in the sea by reason of her **c?**	*5094*

COSTLY (6) [COST]

1Ki	5:17	great stones, **c** stones, *and* hewed stones,	3368

1Ki	7:	9 All these *were* of **c** stones, according to	3368
	7:10	foundation *was of* **c** stones, *even* great	3368
	7:11	above *were* **c** stones, after the measures	3368
Jn	12:	3 **very c,** and anointed the feet of Jesus,	*4186*
1Ti	2:	9 broided hair, or gold, or pearls, or **c** array;	*4185*

COTES (1)

2Ch	32:28	for all *manner of* beasts, and **c** for flocks.	220

COTTAGE (2) [COTTAGES]

Isa	1:	8 the daughter of Zion is left as a **c** in a	5521
	24:20	drunkard, and shall be removed like a **c;**	4412

COTTAGES (1) [COTTAGE]

Zep	2:	6 shall be dwellings *and* **c** for shepherds,	3741

COUCH (7) [COUCHED, COUCHES, COUCHETH, COUCHING]

Ge	49:	4 defiledst thou *it:* he went up to my **c.**	3326
Job	7:13	my **c** shall ease my complaint;	4904
	38:40	When they **c** in *their* dens, *and* abide in	7817
Ps	6:	6 bed to swim; I water my **c** with my tears.	6210
Am	3:12	corner of a bed, and in Damascus in a **c.**	6210
Lk	5:19	him down through the tiling with *his* **c**	2826
	5:24	take up thy **c,** and go into thine house.	*2826*

COUCHED (2) [COUCH]

Ge	49:	9 he **c** as a lion, and as an old lion;	7257
Nu	24:	9 He **c,** he lay down as a lion, and as a great	3766

COUCHES (2) [COUCH]

Am	6:	4 stretch themselves upon their **c,** and eat	6210
Ac	5:15	the streets, and laid *them* on beds and **c,**	*2895*

COUCHETH (1) [COUCH]

Dt	33:13	the dew, and for the deep that **c** beneath,	7257

COUCHING (1) [COUCH]

Ge	49:14	Issachar *is* a strong ass **c down** between	7257
Eze	25:	5 and the Ammonites a **c place** for flocks:	4769

COULD (166) [COLDEST]

Ge	13:	6 great, so that they **c** not dwell together.	3201
	27:	1 his eyes were dim, so that he **c** not see,	NIH
	36:	7 land wherein they were strangers **c** not	3201
	37:	4 and **c** not speak peaceably unto him.	3201
	41:	8 *there* was none that **c** interpret them unto	NIH
	41:21	**c** not be known that they had eaten them;	NIH
	41:24	but *there* was none that **c** declare *it* to me.	NIH
	43:	7 **c** we certainly know that he would say,	NIH
	45:	1 Joseph **c** not refrain himself before all	3201
	45:	3 his brethren **c** not answer him; for they	3201
	48:10	were dim for age, *so that* he **c** not see.	3201
Ex	2:	3 when she **c** not longer hide him, she took	3201
	7:21	the Egyptians **c** not drink of the water of	3201
	7:24	for they **c** not drink of the water of	3201
	8:18	to bring forth lice, but they **c** not:	3201
	9:11	the magicians **c** not stand before Moses	3201
	12:39	were thrust out of Egypt, and **c** not tarry,	3201
	15:23	they **c** not drink of the waters of Marah,	3201
Nu	9:	6 that they **c** not keep the passover on that	3201
Jos	7:12	the children of Israel **c** not stand	3201
	15:63	children of Judah **c** not drive them out:	3201
	17:12	Yet the children of Manasseh **c** not drive	3201
Jdg	1:19	**c** not drive out the inhabitants of the	NIH
	2:14	they **c** not any longer stand before their	3201
	3:22	that he **c** not draw the dagger out of his	NIH
	6:27	of the city, **that** *he* **c** **not** do *it* by day,	4480
	12:	6 for he **c** not **frame** to pronounce *it* right.	3559
	14:14	not *in* three days expound the riddle.	3201
	17:	8 to sojourn where he **c** find *a place.*	NIH
	20:16	every one **c** sling stones at a hair *breadth,*	NIH
Ru	3:14	she rose up before one **c** know another.	NIH
1Sa	3:	2 eyes began *to wax* dim, *that* he **c** not see;	3201
	4:15	and his eyes were dim, that he **c** not see.	3201
	10:21	when they sought him, he **c** not be found.	NIH
	23:13	and went whithersoever they **c** go.	NIH
2Sa	3:10	faint that they **c** not go over the brook	NIH
	3:21	so faint that they **c** not follow David,	NIH
	1:10	I was sure that he **c** not live after *that* he	NIH
	3:11	he **c** not answer Abner a word again,	NIH
	17:20	**c** not find *them,* they returned to	NIH
	22:39	and wounded them, that they **c** not arise:	NIH
1Ki	3:	7 knowest how that David my father **c**	3201
	8:	5 that **c** not be told nor numbered for	NIH
	8:11	So that the priests **c** not stand to minister	3201
	13:	4 so that he **c** not pull it in again to him.	NIH
	14:	4 Ahijah **c** not see; for his eyes were set by	3201
2Ki	3:26	unto the king of Edom: but they **c** not.	3201
	4:40	in the pot. And they **c** not eat *thereof.*	3201
	16:	5 besieged Ahaz, but **c** not overcome *him.*	3201
1Ch	12:	2 use both the right hand and the left in	NIH
	12:	8 battle, that **c** handle shield and buckler,	NIH
	12:33	of war, fifty thousand, which **c** keep rank:	NIH
	12:38	All these men of war, that **c** keep rank,	NIH
	21:30	David **c** not go before it to inquire of God:	3201
2Ch	4:18	for the weight of the brass **c** not be found	NIH
	5:	6 which **c** not be told nor numbered for	NIH
	5:14	that the priests **c** not stand to minister by	3201
	7:	2 the priests **c** not enter into the house of	3201
	13:	7 tender hearted, and **c** not withstand them.	NIH
	14:13	that they **c** not recover themselves;	NIH
	20:25	more than they **c** carry away:	NIH
	25:	5 to war, that **c** handle spear and shield.	NIH
	25:15	which **c** not deliver their own people out	NIH
	29:34	that they **c** not flay all the burnt offerings:	3201

C

2Ch 30: 3 For they **c** not keep it at that time, 3201
 32:14 that **c** deliver his people out of mine hand, 3201
 34:12 all that **c** skill of instruments of musick. NIH
Ezr 2:59 they **c** not shew their fathers' house, 3201
 3:13 So that the people **c** not discern the noise NIH
 5: 5 that they **c** not cause them to cease, till NIH
Ne 7:61 they **c** not shew their fathers' house, 3201
 8: 2 and all that **c** hear with understanding, NIH
 8: 3 the women, and those that **c** understand; NIH
 13:24 **c** not speak in the Jews' language, 5234
Est 6: 1 On that night **c not** the king sleep, 5074
 7: 4 although the enemy **c** not countervail NIH
 9: 2 no man **c** withstand them; for the fear of NIH
Job 4:16 but I **c** not discern the form thereof; NIH
 16: 4 I also **c** speak as ye *do:* if your soul were in NIH
 16: 4 I **c** heap up words against you, NIH
 31:23 by reason of his highness I **c** not **endure.** 3201
Ps 37:36 yea, I sought him, but he **c** not be found. NIH
 55:12 I **c** have borne *it:* neither *was it* he that NIH
 73: 7 they have more than heart **c** wish. NIH
 78:44 and their floods, *that* they **c** not drink. NIH
SS 5: 6 I sought him, but I **c** not find him; I called NIH
Isa 5: 4 What **c** have been done more to my NIH
 7: 1 war against it, but **c** not prevail against it. 3201
 30: 5 They were all ashamed of a people *that* **c** NIH
 33:23 they **c** not well strengthen their mast, NIH
 33:23 their mast, they **c** not spread the sail: NIH
 41:28 when I asked of them, **c** answer a word. NIH
 46: 2 they **c** not deliver the burden, 3201
Jer 6:15 not at all ashamed, neither **c** they blush: 3045
 8:12 not at all ashamed, neither **c** they blush: 3045
 15: 1 *yet* my mind **c** not *be* toward this people: NIH
 20: 9 weary with forbearing, and I **c** not stay. 3201
 24: 2 which **c** not be eaten, they were so bad. NIH
 44:22 So that the Lord **c** no longer bear, 3201
La 4:14 so that men **c** not touch their garments. 3201
 4:17 watched for a nation *that* **c** not save *us.* NIH
Eze 31: 8 The cedars in the garden of God **c** not hide NIH
 47: 5 *and it was* a river that I **c** not pass over: 3201
 47: 5 swim in, a river that **c** not be passed over. NIH
Da 5: 8 men: but they **c** not read the writing, 3546
 5:15 they **c** not shew the interpretation of 3546
 6: 4 they **c** find none occasion nor fault; 3202
 8: 4 neither *was there any* that **c** deliver out of NIH
 8: 7 there was none that **c** deliver the ram out NIH
Hos 5:13 yet **c** he not heal you nor cure you of your 3201
Jnh 1:13 hard to bring *it* to the land; but they **c** not: 3201
Mt 17:16 to thy disciples, and they **c** not cure him. 1410
 17:19 and said, Why **c** not we cast him out? 1410
 26:40 What, **c** ye not watch with me one hour? 2480
 27:24 When Pilate saw that he **c** prevail nothing, NIG
Mk 1:45 that *Jesus* **c** no more openly enter 1410
 2: 4 And when they **c** not come nigh unto him 1410
 3:20 so that they **c** not so much as eat bread. 1410
 5: 3 and no *man* **c** bind him, no, not with 1410
 5: 4 in pieces: neither **c** any *man* tame him. 2480
 6: 5 And he **c** there do no mighty work, 1410
 6:19 and would have killed him; but she **c** not: 1410
 7:24 no *man* know *it:* but he **c** not be hid. 1410
 9:18 they should cast him out; and they **c** not. 2480
 9:28 privately, Why **c** not we cast him out? 1410
 14: 8 She hath done what she **c**: she is come NIG
Lk 1:22 he came out, he **c** not speak unto them: 1410
 5:19 when they **c** not find by what *way* they NIG
 6:48 upon that house, and **c** not shake it: 2480
 8:19 and **c** not come at him for the press. 1410
 8:43 physicians, neither **c** be healed of any, 2480
 9:40 disciples to cast him out; and they **c** not. 1410
 13:11 and **c** in no wise lift up *herself.* 1410
 14: 6 And they **c** not answer him again to these 2480
 19: 3 and **c** not for the press, because he was 1410
 19:48 And **c** not find what they might do: for all NIG
 20: 7 that *they* **c** not tell whence *it was.* NIG
 20:26 And **c** not take hold of his words 2480
Jn 9:33 *man* were not of God, he **c** do nothing. 1410
 11:37 **C** not this *man,* which opened the eyes of 1410
 12:39 Therefore they **c** not believe, because 1410
 21:25 I suppose that even the world itself **c** not 1410
Ac 4:14 with them, they **c** say nothing against *it.* 2192
 11:17 what was I, that I **c** withstand God? 1415
 13:39 ye **c** not be justified by the law of Moses. 1410
 21:34 when he **c** not know the certainty for 1410
 22:11 And when I **c** not see for the glory of that NIG
 25: 7 against Paul, which they **c** not prove. 2480
 27:15 and **c** not bear up into the wind, we let 1410
 27:43 commanded that they which **c** swim 1410
Ro 8: 3 For what the law **c not do,** in that it was 102
 9: 3 I **c** wish that myself were accursed from NIG
1Co 3: 1 **c** not speak unto you as unto spiritual, 1410
 3: 2 that *I* **c** not *receive* meat: for hitherto ye were not able NIG
2Co 3: 7 that the children of Israel **c** not stedfastly NIG
 3:13 that the children of Israel **c** not stedfastly NIG
 11: 1 Would *to God* you **c** bear with me a little NIG
Gal 3:21 for if there had been a law given which **c** 1410
1Th 3: 1 Wherefore when we **c** no longer forbear, NIG
 3: 5 For this cause, when I **c** no longer forbear, NIG
Heb 3:19 So we see that they **c** not enter in because 1410
 6:13 because he **c** swear by no greater, he sware NIG
 9: 9 that **c** not make him that did the service 1410
 12:20 (For they **c** not endure that which was 1410
Rev 7: 9 which no *man* **c** number, of all nations, 1410
 14: 3 and no *man* **c** learn *that* song but 1410

COULD NOT TALK See DUMB

COULDEST (5) [COULD]

Jer 3: 5 spoken and done evil *things* as thou **c.** 3201
Eze 16:28 with them, and yet **c** not be satisfied. NIH
Da 2:47 of secrets, seeing thou **c** reveal this secret. 3202
Mk 14:37 **c** not thou watch one hour? 2480
Jn 19:11 Thou **c** have no power *at all* against me, NIG

COULTER (1) [COULTERS]

1Sa 13:20 and his **c,** and his axe, and his mattock. 855

COULTERS (1) [COULTER]

1Sa 13:21 the **c,** and for the forks, and for the axes, 855

COUNCIL (23) [COUNCILS]

Ps 68:27 princes of Judah *and* their **c,** the princes 7277
Mt 5:22 Raca, shall be in danger of the **c:** 4892
 12:14 went out, and held a **c** against him, 4824
 26:59 the chief priests, and elders, and all the **c,** 4892
Mk 14:55 all the **c** sought for witness against Jesus 4892
 15: 1 the elders and scribes and the whole **c,** 4892
Lk 22:66 and led him into their **c,** saying, 4892
Jn 11:47 the chief priests and the Pharisees a **c,** 4892
Ac 4:15 commanded them to go aside out of the **c,** 4892
 5:21 called the **c** together, and all the senate 4892
 5:27 brought them, they set *them* before the **c:** 4892
 5:34 Then stood there up one in the **c,** 4892
 5:41 they departed from the presence of the **c,** 4892
 6:12 and caught him, and brought *him* to the **c,** 4892
 6:15 And all that sat in the **c,** looking stedfastly 4892
 22:30 the chief priests and all their **c** to appear, 4892
 23: 1 earnestly beholding the **c,** said, Men *and* 4892
 23: 6 he cried out in the **c,** Men *and* brethren, 4892
 23:15 ye with the **c** signify to the chief captain 4892
 23:20 bring down Paul to morrow into the **c,** 4892
 23:28 I brought him forth into their **c:** 4892
 24:20 doing in me, while I stood before the **c,** 4892
 25:12 when he had conferred with the **c,** 4824

COUNCILS (2) [COUNCIL]

Mt 10:17 for they will deliver you up to the **c,** 4892
Mk 13: 9 for they shall deliver you up to **c;** and in 4892

COUNSEL (143) [COUNSELLED, COUNSELLER,
COUNSELLERS, COUNSELS]

Ex 18:19 I will **give** thee **c,** and God shall be with 3289
Nu 27:21 who shall ask **c** for him after the judgment NIH
 31:16 of Israel, through the **c** of Balaam, 1697
Dt 32:28 For they *are* a nation void of **c,** neither *is* 6098
Jos 9:14 and asked not **c** at the mouth of the Lord. NIH
Jdg 18: 5 unto him, Ask **c,** we pray thee, of God, 6098
 20: 7 of Israel; give here your advice and **c.** 6098
 20:18 house of God, and asked **c** of God, NIH
 20:23 and asked **c** of the Lord, saying, NIH
1Sa 14:37 Saul asked **c** of God, Shall I go down after NIH
2Sa 15:31 turn the **c** of Ahithophel into foolishness. 6098
 15:34 mayest thou for me defeat the **c** of 6098
 16:20 Give **c** among you what we shall do. 6098
 16:23 the **c** of Ahithophel, which he counselled 6098
 16:23 all the **c** of Ahithophel both with David 6098
 17: 7 The **c** that Ahithophel hath **given** 3289+6098
 17:11 Therefore I **c** *that* all Israel be generally 3289
 17:14 The **c** of Hushai the Archite *is* better than 6098
 17:14 Archite *is* better than the **c** of Ahithophel. 6098
 17:14 to defeat the good **c** of Ahithophel, 6098
 17:15 thus did Ahithophel **c** Absalom and 3289
 17:23 when Ahithophel saw that his **c** was not 6098
 20:18 They shall surely ask **c** at Abel: NIH
1Ki 1:12 let me, I pray thee, **give** thee **c,** 3289+6098
 12: 8 **c** of the old men, which they
 had **given** 3289+6098
 12: 9 What **c give** ye that we may answer this 3289
 12:13 old men's **c** that they **gave** him; 3289+6098
 12:14 to them after the **c** of the young men, 6098
 12:28 Whereupon the king **took c,** and made 3289
2Ki 6: 8 **took c** with his servants, saying, In such 3289
 18:20 *I have* **c** and strength for the war. 6098
1Ch 10:13 also for asking **c** of *one that had* a familiar NIH
2Ch 10: 8 king Rehoboam **took c with** the old men 3289
 10: 9 What **c give** ye *me* to return answer to 3289
 10: 8 the **c** which the old men **gave** him, 3289+6098
 10: 8 **took c with** the young men that were 3289
 10:13 king Rehoboam forsook the **c** of the old 6098
 22: 5 He walked also after their **c,** and went 6098
 25:16 unto him, Art thou made of the king's **c?** 3289
 25:16 and hast not hearkened unto my **c.** 6098
 30: 2 For the king had **taken c,** and his princes, 3289
 30:23 the whole assembly **took c** to keep other 3289
 32: 3 He **took c** with his princes and his mighty 3289
Ezr 10: 3 according to the **c** of my lord, and of those 6098
 10: 8 according to the **c** of the princes and 6098
Ne 4:15 God had brought their **c** to nought, 6098
 6: 7 now therefore, and let us **take c** together. 3289
Job 5:13 the **c** of the froward is carried headlong. 6098
 10: 3 and shine upon the **c** of the wicked? 6098
 12:13 strength, he hath **c** and understanding. 6098
 18: 7 and his own **c** shall cast him down. 6098
 21:16 the **c** of the wicked is far from me. 6098
 22:18 but the **c** of the wicked is far from me. 6098
 29:21 and waited, and kept silence at my **c.** 6098
 38: 2 Who *is* this that darkeneth **c** by words 6098
 42: 3 Who *is* he that hideth **c** without 6098
Ps 1: 1 *is* the man that walketh not in the **c** 6098
 2: 2 the rulers **take c** together, against 3245
 13: 2 How long shall I take **c** in my soul, 6098
 14: 6 You have shamed the **c** of the poor, 6098

Ps 16: 7 bless the Lord, who hath **given** me **c:** 3289
 20: 4 to thine own heart, and fulfil all thy **c.** 6098
 31:13 while they **took c** together against me, 3245
 33:10 The Lord bringeth the **c** of the heathen 6098
 33:11 The **c** of the Lord standeth for ever, 6098
 55:14 We took sweet **c** together, *and* walked 5475
 64: 2 Hide me from the **secret** of the wicked; 5475
 71:10 they that lay wait for my soul **take c** 3289
 73:24 Thou shalt guide me with thy **c,** 6098
 83: 3 They have taken crafty **c** against thy 5475
 106:13 forgat his works; they waited not for his **c:** 6098
 106:43 they provoked *him* with their **c,** 6098
 107:11 and contemned the **c** of the most High: 6098
Pr 1:25 ye have set at nought all my **c,** 6098
 1:30 They would none of my **c:** they despised 6098
 8:14 **C** *is* mine, and sound wisdom: I *am* 6098
 11:14 Where no **c** *is,* the people fall: but in 8458
 12:15 but he that hearkeneth unto **c** *is* wise. 6098
 15:22 Without **c** purposes *are* disappointed: but 5475
 19:20 Hear **c,** and receive instruction, that thou 6098
 19:21 nevertheless the **c** of the Lord, that shall 6098
 20: 5 **C** in the heart of man *is* like deep water; 6098
 20:18 Every purpose is established by **c:** and 6098
 21:30 *is* no wisdom nor understanding nor **c** 6098
 24: 6 For by **wise c** thou shalt make thy war: 8458
 27: 9 sweetness of a man's friend by hearty **c.** 6098
Ecc 8: 2 I **c** thee to keep the king's commandment, NIH
Isa 5:19 let the **c** of the Holy One of Israel draw 6098
 7: 5 have **taken** evil **c** against thee, saying, 3289
 8:10 **Take c together,** and it shall come 5779+6098
 11: 2 understanding, the spirit of **c** and might, 6098
 16: 3 Take **c,** execute judgment; make thy 6098
 19: 3 and I will destroy the **c** thereof: 6098
 19:11 the **c** of the wise counsellers of Pharaoh is 6098
 19:17 because of the **c** of the Lord of hosts, 6098
 23: 8 Who hath **taken** this **c** against Tyre, 6098
 28:29 which is wonderful in **c,** *and* excellent in 6098
 29:15 seek deep to hide *their* **c** from the Lord, 6098
 30: 1 saith the Lord, that take **c,** but not of me; 6098
 36: 5 vain words) *I have* **c** and strength for war: 6098
 40:14 whom **took** he **c,** and *who* instructed 3289
 44:26 and performeth the **c** of his messengers; 6098
 45:21 *them* near; yea, let them **take c** together: 3289
 46:10 My **c** shall stand, and I will do all my 6098
 46:11 the man that executeth my **c** from a far 6098
Jer 18:18 nor **c** from the wise, nor the word from 6098
 18:23 thou knowest all their **c** against me to slay 6098
 19: 7 I will make void the **c** of Judah and 6098
 23:18 For who hath stood in the **c** of the Lord, 5475
 23:22 if they had stood in my **c,** and had caused 5475
 32:19 Great in **c,** and mighty in work: for thine 6098
 38:15 if I **give** thee **c,** wilt thou not hearken 3289
 49: 7 is **c** perished from the prudent? is their 6098
 49:20 Therefore hear the **c** of the Lord, that he 6098
 49:30 Babylon hath **taken c** against you, 3289+6098
 50:45 Therefore hear ye the **c** of the Lord, 6098
Eze 7:26 from the priest, and **c** from the ancients. 6098
 11: 2 and **give** wicked **c** in this city: 3289+6098
Da 2:14 Daniel answered with **c** and wisdom to 5843
 4:27 let my **c** be acceptable unto thee, 4431
Hos 4:12 My people ask **c** at their stocks, NIH
 10: 6 and Israel shall be ashamed of his own **c.** 6098
Mic 4:12 the Lord, neither understand they his **c:** 6098
Zec 6:13 the **c** of peace shall be between them 6098
Mt 22:15 took **c** how they might entangle him in 4824
 27: 1 elders of the people took **c** against Jesus 4824
 27: 7 And they took **c,** and bought with them 4824
 28:12 and had taken **c,** they gave large money 4824
Mk 3: 6 straightway took **c** with the Herodians 4824
Lk 7:30 lawyers rejected the **c** of God against 1012
 23:51 (The same had not consented to the **c** and 1012
Jn 11:53 took **c** together for to put him to death. 4823
 18:14 was he, which **gave c** to the Jews, 4823
Ac 2:23 being delivered by the determinate **c** and 1012
 4:28 and thy **c** determined before to be done. 1012
 5:33 cut *to the heart,* and took **c** to slay them. 1011
 5:38 for if this **c** or this work be of men, it will 1012
 9:23 were fulfilled, the Jews took **c** to kill him: 4823
 20:27 to declare unto you all the **c** of God. 1012
 27:42 And the soldiers' **c** was to kill 1012
Eph 1:11 all *things* after the **c** of his own will: 1012
Heb 6:17 heirs of promise the immutability of his **c,** 1012
Rev 3:18 I **c** thee to buy of me gold tried in the fire, 4823

COUNSELLED (4) [COUNSEL]

2Sa 16:23 of Ahithophel, which he **c** in those days, 3289
 17:15 of Israel; and thus and thus have I **c.** 3289
 17:21 for thus hath Ahithophel **c** against you. 3289
Job 26: 3 hast thou **c** *him* that hath no wisdom? 3289

COUNSELLER (14) [COUNSEL]

2Sa 15:12 David's **c,** from his city, *even* from Giloh, 3289
1Ch 26:14 Zechariah his son, a wise **c,** they cast lots; 3289
 27:32 Also Jonathan David's uncle *was* a **c,** 3289
 27:33 Ahithophel *was* the king's **c:** and 3289
2Ch 22: 3 for his mother *was* his **c** to do wickedly. 3289
Isa 3: 3 the honourable *man,* and the **c,** 3289
 9: 6 **C,** The mighty God, The everlasting 3289
 40:13 or *being* his **c** hath taught him? 376+6098
 41:28 amongst them, and *there was* no **c,** that, 3289
Mic 4: 9 thy **c** perished? for pangs have taken thee 3289
Na 1:11 evil against the Lord, a wicked **c.** 3289
Mk 15:43 Joseph of Arimathea, an honourable **c,** 1010
Lk 23:50 *there was* a man named Joseph, a **c;** 1010
Ro 11:34 mind of the Lord? or who hath been his **c?** 4825

COUNSELLERS (21) [COUNSEL]

2Ch	22: 4 for they were his **c** after the death of his	3289
Ezr	4: 5 hired **c** against them, to frustrate their	3289
	7:14 his seven **c**, to inquire concerning Judah	3272
	7:15 his **c** have freely offered unto the God of	3272
	7:28 his **c**, and before all the king's mighty	3289
	8:25 his **c**, and his lords, and all Israel *there*	3289
Job	3:14 With kings and **c** of the earth, which built	3289
	12:17 He leadeth **c** away spoiled, and maketh	3289
Ps	119:24 also *are* my delight and my **c**.	376+6098
Pr	11:14 but in the multitude of **c** *there is* safety.	3289
	12:20 imagine evil: but to the **c** of peace *is* joy.	3289
	15:22 in the multitude of **c** *they* are established.	3289
	24: 6 and in multitude of **c** *there is* safety.	3289
Isa	1:26 at the first, and thy **c** as at the beginning:	3289
	19:11 the counsel of the wise **c** of Pharaoh is	3289
Da	3: 2 the sheriffs, and all the rulers of	1884
	3: 3 the sheriffs, and all the rulers of	1884
	3:24 in haste, *and* spake, and said unto his **c**,	1907
	3:27 governors, and captains, and the king's **c**,	1907
	4:36 and my **c** and my lords sought unto me;	1907
	6: 7 and the princes, the **c** and the captains,	1907

COUNSELS (12) [COUNSEL]

Job	37:12 it is turned round about by his **c**:	8458
Ps	5:10 O God; let them fall by their own **c**;	4156
	81:12 lust: *and* they walked in their own **c**.	4156
Pr	1: 5 of understanding shall attain unto **wise c**:	8458
	12: 5 right: *but* the **c** of the wicked *are* deceit.	8458
	22:20 not I written to thee excellent things in **c**	4156
Isa	25: 1 *thy* **c** of old *are* faithfulness and truth.	6098
	47:13 art wearied in the multitude of thy **c**.	6098
Jer	7:24 walked in the **c** *and* in the imagination of	4156
Hos	11: 6 and devour *them*, because of their own **c**.	4156
Mic	6:16 the house of Ahab, and ye walk in their **c**;	4156
1Co	4: 5 and will make manifest the **c** of the hearts:	1012

COUNT (26) [COUNTED, COUNTETH, COUNTING]

Ex	12: 4 his eating shall **make** your **c** for the lamb.	3699
Lev	19:23 *c* the fruit thereof **as uncircumcised:**	6188+6190
	23:15 ye shall **c** unto you from the morrow after	5608
	25:27 let him **c** the years of the sale thereof,	2803
	25:52 he shall **c** with him, *and* according unto	2803
Nu	23:10 Who can **c** the dust of Jacob,	4487
1Sa	1:16 **C** not thine handmaid for a daughter of	5414
Job	19:15 and my maidens, **c** me for a stranger:	2803
	31: 4 not he see my ways, and **c** all my steps?	5608
Ps	87: 6 The LORD shall **c**, when he writeth *up*	5608
	139:18 I should **c** them, they are moe in number	5608
	139:22 I **c** them mine enemies.	1961+3807.1
Mic	6:11 Shall I **c** *them* **pure** with the wicked	2135
Ac	20:24 neither **c** I my life dear unto myself,	2192
Php	3: 8 and I **c** all *things* but loss for	2233
	3: 8 loss of all *things*, and do **c** *them* but dung,	2233
	3:13 I **c** not myself to have apprehended:	3049
2Th	1:11 that our God would **c** you **worthy** of *this*	515
	3:15 Yet **c** *him* not as an enemy,	2233
1Ti	6: 1 **c** their own masters worthy of all honour,	2233
Phm	1:17 If thou **c** me therefore a partner,	2192
Jas	1: 2 **c** *it* all joy when ye fall into divers	2233
	5:11 Behold, we **c** them **happy** which endure.	3106
2Pe	2:13 *as* they that **c** it pleasure to riot in the day	2233
	3: 9 *his* promise, as some *men* **c** slackness;	2233
Rev	13:18 Let him that hath understanding **c**	5585

COUNTED (40) [COUNT]

Ge	15: 6 and he **c** it to him *for* righteousness.	2803
	30:33 the sheep, that *shall be* **c** stolen with me.	NIH
	31:15 Are we not **c** of him strangers? for he hath	2803
Ex	38:21 of the tabernacle of Testimony, as it was **c**,	6485
Lev	25:31 shall be **c** as the fields of the country:	2803
Nu	18:30 shall be **c** unto the Levites as the increase	2803
Jos	13: 3 *which* is **c** to the Canaanite:	2803
1Ki	1:21 and my son Solomon shall be **c** offenders.	NIH
	3: 8 that cannot be numbered nor **c** for	5608
1Ch	21: 6 and Benjamin he not among them:	6485
	23:24 as they were **c** by number of names by	6485
Ne	13:13 for they were **c** faithful, and their office	2803
Job	18: 3 Wherefore are we **c** as beasts,	2803
	41:29 Darts are **c** as stubble: he laugheth at	2803
Ps	44:22 we are **c** as sheep for the slaughter.	2803
	88: 4 am **c** with them that go down into the pit:	2803
	106:31 was **c** unto him for righteousness unto	2803
Pr	17:28 fool, when he holdeth his peace, is **c** wise:	2803
	27:14 the morning, it shall be **c** a curse to him.	2803
Isa	5:28 their horses' hoofs shall be **c** like flint,	2803
	32:15 and the fruitful field be **c** for a forest.	2803
	33:18 receiver? where *is* he that **c** the towers?	5608
	40:15 and are **c** as the small dust of the balance:	2803
	40:17 they are **c** to him less than nothing,	2803
Hos	8:12 law, *but* they were **c** as a strange *thing*.	2803
Mt	14: 5 because they **c** him as a prophet.	2192
Mk	11:32 for all *men* **c** John, that he was a prophet	2192
Ac	5:41 rejoicing that they were **c worthy** to suffer	2661
	19:19 all *men*: and they **c** the price of them,	4860
Ro	2:26 shall not his uncircumcision be **c** for	3049
	4: 3 and it was **c** unto him for righteousness.	3049
	4: 5 ungodly, his faith is **c** for righteousness,	3049
	9: 8 the children of the promise are **c** for	3049
Php	3: 7 were gain to me, those I **c** loss for Christ.	2233
2Th	1: 5 that ye may be **c worthy** of the kingdom	2661
1Ti	1:12 hath enabled me, for that he **c** me faithful,	2233
	5:17 Let the elders that rule well be **c worthy** of	515

Heb	3: 3 For this *man* was **c worthy** of more glory	515
	7: 6 But he whose **descent** is not **c** from them	1075
	10:29 and hath **c** the blood of the covenant,	2233

COUNTENANCE (53) [COUNTENANCES]

Ge	4: 5 And Cain was very wroth, and his **c** fell.	6440
	4: 6 art thou wroth? and why is thy **c** fallen?	6440
	31: 2 Jacob beheld the **c** of Laban, and, behold,	6440
	31: 5 said unto them, I see your father's **c**,	6440
Ex	23: 3 Neither shalt thou **c** a poor *man* in his	1921
Nu	6:26 The LORD lift up his **c** upon thee,	6440
Dt	28:50 nation of fierce **c**, which shall not regard	6440
Jdg	13: 6 his **c** was like the countenance of an angel	4758
	13: 6 his countenance *was* like the **c** of an angel	4758
1Sa	1:18 and did eat, and her **c** was no more *sad*.	6440
	16: 7 Look not on his **c**, or on the height of his	4758
	16:12 *and* withal of a beautiful **c**, and goodly to	5869
	17:42 but a youth, and ruddy, and of a fair **c**.	4758
	25: 3 good understanding, and of a beautiful **c**:	8389
2Sa	14:27 was Tamar: she was a woman of a fair **c**.	4758
2Ki	8:11 he settled his **c** stedfastly, until *he* was	6440
Ne	2: 2 Why *is* thy **c** sad, seeing thou *art* not sick?	6440
	2: 3 should not my **c** be sad, when the city,	6440
Job	14:20 changest his **c**, and sendest him away.	6440
	29:24 and the light of my **c** they cast not down.	6440
Ps	4: 6 lift thou up the light of thy **c** upon us.	6440
	10: 4 The wicked, through the pride of his **c**,	639
	11: 7 his **c** doth behold the upright.	6440
	21: 6 hast made him exceeding glad with thy **c**.	6440
	42: 5 I shall yet praise him *for* the help of his **c**.	6440
	42:11 who *is* the health of my **c**, and my God.	6440
	43: 5 who *is* the health of my **c**, and my God.	6440
	44: 3 the light of thy **c**, because thou hadst a	6440
	80:16 they perish at the rebuke of thy **c**.	6440
	89:15 shall walk, O LORD, in the light of thy **c**.	6440
	90: 8 our secret *sins* in the light of thy **c**.	6440
Pr	15:13 A merry heart maketh a cheerful **c**: but	6440
	16:15 In the light of the king's **c** *is* life;	6440
	25:23 so *doth* an angry **c** a backbiting tongue.	6440
	27:17 so a man sharpeneth the **c** of his friend.	6440
Ecc	7: 3 for by the sadness of the **c** the heart is	6440
SS	2:14 let me see thy **c**, let me hear thy voice;	4758
	2:14 sweet *is* thy voice, and thy **c** *is* comely.	4758
	5:15 **c** *is* as Lebanon, excellent as the cedars.	4758
Isa	3: 9 The shew of their **c** doth witness against	6440
Eze	27:35 afraid, they shall be troubled in their **c**.	6440
Da	1:13 **c** of the children that eat *of* the portion	4758
	5: 6 king's **c** was changed, and his thoughts	2122
	5: 9 his **c** *was* changed in him, and his lords	2122
	5:10 trouble thee, nor let thy **c** be changed.	2122
	7:28 troubled me, and my **c** changed in me:	2122
	8:23 a king of fierce **c**, and understanding dark	6440
Mt	6:16 fast, be not as the hypocrites, of a **sad c**:	4659
	28: 3 His **c** was like lightning, and his raiment	2397
Lk	9:29 the fashion of his **c** was altered,	4383
Ac	2:28 thou shalt make me full of joy with thy **c**.	4383
2Co	3: 7 the face of Moses for the glory of his **c**;	4383
Rev	1:16 **c** *was* as the sun shineth in his strength.	3799

COUNTENANCES (2) [COUNTENANCE]

Da	1:13 let our **c** be looked upon before thee,	4758
	1:15 the end of ten days their **c** appeared fairer	4758

COUNTERVAIL (1)

Est	7: 4 although the enemy could not **c** the king's	7737

COUNTETH (3) [COUNT]

Job	19:11 he **c** me unto him as one *of* his enemies.	2803
	33:10 against me, he **c** me for his enemy,	2803
Lk	14:28 sitteth not down first, and **c** the cost,	5585

COUNTING (1) [COUNT]

Ecc	7:27 I found, saith the Preacher, **c** one by one,	NIH

COUNTRIES (55) [COUNTRY]

Ge	10:20 tongues, in their **c**, *and* in their nations.	776
	26: 3 I will give thee **c**, and I will perform	776
	26: 4 and will give unto thy seed all these **c**;	776
	41:57 all **c** came into Egypt to Joseph for to buy	776
Jos	13:32 *are* the **c** which Moses did distribute	NIH
	14: 1 *are* the **c** which the children of Israel	NIH
	17:11 of Megiddo and her towns, *even* three **c**.	5316
2Ki	18:35 Who are *they* among all the gods of the **c**,	776
1Ch	22: 5 of fame and of glory throughout all **c**:	776
	29:30 and over all the kingdoms of the **c**.	776
2Ch	11:23 his children throughout all the **c** of Judah	776
	12: 8 and the service of the kingdoms of the **c**.	776
	15: 5 *were* upon all the inhabitants of the **c**.	776
	20:29 of God was on all the kingdoms of *those* **c**,	776
	34:33 **c** that *pertained* to the children of Israel,	776
Ezr	3: 3 them because of the people of *those* **c**:	776
	4:20 which have ruled over all **c** beyond	NIH
Ps	110: 6 he shall wound the heads over many **c**.	776
Isa	8: 9 in pieces; and give ear, all ye of far **c**:	776
	37:18 have laid waste all the nations, and their **c**,	776
Jer	23: 3 out of all **c** whither I have driven them,	776
	23: 8 and from all **c** whither I had driven them;	776
	28: 8 of old prophesied both against many **c**,	776
	32:37 Behold, I *will* gather them out of all **c**,	776
	40:11 in Edom, and in all the **c**, heard that the	776
Eze	5: 5 the nations and **c** that *are* round about her.	776
	5: 6 my statutes more than the **c** that *are* round	776
	6: 8 when ye shall be scattered through the **c**.	776
	11:16 I have scattered them among the **c**,	776
	11:16 sanctuary in the **c** where they shall come.	776

Eze	11:17 assemble you out of the **c** where ye have	776
	12:15 the nations, and disperse them in the **c**.	776
	20:23 and disperse them through the **c**;	776
	20:32 as the families of the **c**, to serve wood and	776
	20:34 will gather you out of the **c** wherein ye are	776
	20:41 gather you out of the **c** wherein ye have	776
	22: 4 unto the heathen, and a mocking to all **c**.	776
	22:15 disperse thee in the **c**, and will consume	776
	25: 7 and I will cause thee to perish out of the **c**:	776
	29:12 in the midst of the **c** *that are* desolate,	776
	29:12 and will disperse them through the **c**.	776
	30: 7 they shall be desolate in the midst of the **c**	776
	30:23 and will disperse them through the **c**.	776
	30:26 nations, and disperse them among the **c**;	776
	32: 9 into the **c** which thou hast not known.	776
	34:13 gather them from the **c**, and will bring	776
	35:10 two nations and these two **c** shall be mine,	776
	36:19 and they were dispersed through the **c**:	776
	36:24 gather you out of all **c**, and will bring you	776
Da	9: 7 through all the **c** whither thou hast driven	776
	11:40 he shall enter into the **c**, and shall overflow	776
	11:41 and many **c** shall be overthrown:	NIH
	11:42 shall stretch forth his hand also upon the **c**:	776
Zec	10: 9 they shall remember me in **far c**;	4801
Lk	21:21 let not them that are in the **c** enter	5561

COUNTRY (179) [COUNTRIES, COUNTRYMEN]

Ge	12: 1 thee out of thy **c**, and from thy kindred,	776
	14: 7 smote all the **c** of the Amalekites,	7704
	19:28 the smoke of the **c** went up as the smoke	776
	20: 1 journeyed from thence toward the south **c**,	776
	24: 4 shalt go unto my **c**, and to my kindred,	776
	24:62 well Lahai-roi; for he dwelt in the south **c**.	776
	25: 6 he sent away, eastward, unto the east **c**.	776
	29:26 said, It must not be so done in our **c**,	4725
	30:25 go unto mine own place, and to my **c**.	776
	32: 3 unto the land of Seir, the **c** of Edom.	7704
	32: 9 Return unto thy **c**, and to thy kindred,	776
	34: 2 prince of the **c**, saw her, he took her,	776
	36: 6 went into the **c** from the face of his brother	776
	42:30 to us, and took us for spies of the **c**.	776
	42:33 the man, the lord of the **c**, said unto us,	776
	47:27 in the land of Egypt, in the **c** of Goshen;	776
Lev	16:29 *at all*, whether it be one of **your own c**,	249
	17:15 *beasts, whether it be* one of **your own c**,	249
	24:22 for the stranger, as for **one** of **your own c**:	249
	25:31 shall be counted as the fields of the **c**:	776
Nu	15:13 All that are **born of the c** shall do these	249
	20:17 Let us pass, I pray thee, through thy **c**:	776
	21:20 that *is* in the **c** of Moab, *to* the top of	7704
	32: 4 *Even* the **c** which the LORD smote before	776
	32:33 *even* the cities of the **c** round about.	776
Dt	3:14 Jair the son of Manasseh took all the **c** of	2256
	4:43 in the plain **c**, of the Reubenites;	776
	26: 3 that I am come unto the **c** which the LORD	776
Jos	2: 2 of the children of Israel to search out the **c**.	776
	2: 3 for they be come to search out all the **c**.	776
	2:24 for even all the inhabitants of the **c** do faint	776
	6:22 unto the two men that had spied out the **c**,	776
	6:27 his fame was *noised* throughout all the **c**.	776
	7: 2 unto them, saying, Go up and view the **c**.	776
	9: 6 men of Israel, We be come from a far **c**:	776
	9: 9 From a very far **c** thy servants are come	776
	9:11 all the inhabitants of our **c** spake to us,	776
	10:40 So Joshua smote all the **c** of the hills,	776
	10:41 all the **c** of Goshen, even unto Gibeon.	776
	11:16 all the south **c**, and all the land of Goshen,	NIH
	12: 7 these *are* the kings of the **c** which Joshua	776
	12: 8 in the south **c**, the Hittites, the Amorites,	NIH
	13: 6 All the inhabitants of the **hill c** from	2022
	13:21 *were* dukes of Sihon, dwelling in the **c**.	776
	17:15 *then* get thee up to the wood **c**,	NIH
	19:51 So they made an end of dividing the **c**.	776
	21:11 which *city* is Hebron, in the hill **c** of Judah,	NIH
	22: 9 to go unto the **c** of Gilead, to the land of	776
Jdg	8:28 the **c** was in quietness forty years in the	776
	11:21 of the Amorites, the inhabitants of that **c**.	776
	12:12 was buried in Aijalon in the **c** of Zebulun.	776
	16:24 the destroyer of our **c**, which slew many of	776
	18:14 men that went to spy out the **c** of Laish,	776
	20: 6 sent her throughout all the **c** of	7704
Ru	1: 1 went to sojourn in the **c** of Moab,	7704
	1: 2 they came *into* the **c** of Moab,	7704
	1: 6 that she might return from the **c** of Moab:	7704
	1: 6 for she had heard in the **c** of Moab how	7704
	1:22 which returned out of the **c** of Moab:	7704
	2: 6 back with Naomi out of the **c** of Moab,	7704
	4: 3 that is come again out of the **c** of Moab,	7704
1Sa	6: 1 the ark of the LORD was in the **c** of	7704
	6:18 *both* of fenced cities, and of **c** villages,	6521
	14:21 into the camp *from the* **c** round about,	NIH
	27: 5 give me a place in some town in the **c**,	776
	27: 7 the time that David dwelt in the **c** of	7704
	27:11 he dwelleth in the **c** of the Philistines,	7704
2Sa	15:23 all the **c** wept *with* a loud voice, and all	776
	18: 8 there scattered over the face of all the **c**:	776
	21:14 Jonathan his son buried they in the **c** of	776
1Ki	4:19 Geber the son of Uri *was* in the **c** of Gilead,	776
	4:19 *in* the **c** of Sihon king of the Amorites,	776
	4:30 wisdom of all the children of the **east c**,	6924
	8:41 cometh out of a far **c** for thy name's sake;	776
	10:13 So she turned and went to her own **c**,	776
	10:15 of Arabia, and *of* the governors of the **c**.	776
	11:21 me depart, that I may go to mine own **c**.	776
	11:22 thou seekest to go to thine own **c**?	776

C

1Ki 20:27 flocks of kids; but the Syrians filled the **c.** 776
 22:36 to his city, and every man to his own **c.** 776
2Ki 3:20 of Edom, and the **c** was filled with water. 776
 3:24 smiting the Moabites, even in their **c**⁵. 1886.3
 18:35 have delivered their **c** out of mine hand, 776
 20:14 Hezekiah said, They are come from a far **c,** 776
1Ch 8: 8 begat *children* in the **c** of Moab, 7704
 20: 1 wasted the **c** of the children of Ammon, 776
2Ch 6:32 is come from a far **c** for thy great name's 776
 9:14 governors of the **c** brought gold and silver 776
 26:10 both in the **low c**, and in the plains: 8219
 28:18 also had invaded the cities of the **low c** 8219
 30:10 from city to city through the **c** of Ephraim 776
Ne 12:28 both out of the **plain c** round about 3603
Pr 25:25 a thirsty soul, so *is* good news from a far **c.** 776
Isa 1: 7 Your *is* desolate, your cities *are* burnt 776
 13: 5 They come from a far **c**, from the end of 776
 22:18 and toss thee like a ball into a large **c:** 776
 39: 3 They are come from a far **c** unto me, 776
 46:11 that executeth my counsel from a far **c:** 776
Jer 2: 7 I brought you into a plentiful **c,** to eat 776
 4:16 *that* watchers come from a far **c,** 776
 6:20 Sheba, and the sweet cane from a far **c?** 776
 6:22 a people cometh from the north **c,** 776
 8:19 because of them that dwell in a far **c:** 776
 10:22 and a great commotion out of the north **c,** 776
 22:10 shall return no more, nor see his native **c.** 776
 22:26 into another **c,** where ye were not born; 776
 23: 8 of the house of Israel out of the north **c,** 776
 31: 8 I *will* bring them from the north **c,** 776
 32: 8 Anathoth, which *is* in the **c** of Benjamin: 776
 44: 1 at Noph, and in the **c** of Pathros, saying, 776
 46:10 in the north **c** by the river Euphrates. 776
 47: 4 the remnant of the **c** of Caphtor. 339
 48:21 judgment is come upon the plain **c;** 776
 50: 9 assembly of great nations from the north **c:** 776
 51: 9 and let us go every one into his own **c:** 776
Eze 20:38 I will bring them forth out of the **c** where 776
 20:42 the **c** *for* the which I lifted up mine hand 776
 25: 9 the glory of the **c**, Beth-jeshimoth, 776
 32:15 the **c** shall be destitute of that whereof it 776
 34:13 and in all the inhabited places of the **c.** 776
 47: 8 These waters issue out toward the east **c,** 1552
 47:22 they shall be unto you as **born in the c** 249
Hos 12:12 Jacob fled *into* the **c** of Syria, 7704
Jnh 1: 8 what *is* thy **c?** and of what people *art* thou? 776
 4: 2 this my saying, when I was yet in my **c?** 127
Zec 6: 6 *are* therein go forth into the north **c;** 776
 6: 6 the grisled go forth toward the south **c.** 776
 6: 8 that go toward the north **c** have quieted 776
 6: 8 have quieted my spirit in the north **c.** 776
 8: 7 I *will* save my people from the east **c,** 776
 8: 7 the east country, and from the west **c;** 776
Mt 2:12 departed into their own **c** another way. 5561
 8:28 other side into the **c** of the Gergesenes. 5561
 9:31 spread abroad his fame in all that **c.** 1093
 13:54 And when he was come into his own **c,** 3968
 13:57 save in his own **c,** and in his own house. 3968
 14:35 they sent out into all that **c round about,** 4066
 21:33 to husbandmen, and **went into a far c:** 589
 25:14 *is* as a man **travelling into a far c,** 589
Mk 5: 1 of the sea, into the **c** of the Gadarenes. 5561
 5:10 would not send them away out of the **c.** 5561
 5:14 fled, and told *it* in the city, and in the **c.** 68
 6: 1 from thence, and came into his own **c;** 3968
 6: 4 but in his own **c,** and among his own kin, 3968
 6:36 that they may go into the **c** round about, 68
 6:56 he entered, into villages, or cities, or **c,** 68
 12: 1 to husbandmen, and **went into a far c.** 589
 15:21 passed by, coming out of the **c,** the father 68
 16:12 as they walked, and went into the **c.** 68
Lk 1:39 and went into the **hill c** with haste, into a 3714
 1:65 abroad throughout all the **hill c** of Judea. 3714
 2: 8 in the same **c** shepherds **abiding** in the field, 63
 3: 3 And he came into all the **c about** Jordan, 4066
 4:23 done in Capernaum, do also here in thy **c.** 3968
 4:24 No prophet is accepted in his own **c.** 3968
 4:37 into every place of the **c round about.** 4066
 8:26 they arrived at the **c** of the Gadarenes, 5561
 8:34 went and told *it* in the city and in the **c.** 68
 8:37 **c** of the Gadarenes **round about** besought 4066
 9:12 may go into the towns and **c** round about, 68
 15:13 and took his journey into a far **c,** 5561
 15:15 and joined himself to a citizen of that **c;** 5561
 19:12 A certain nobleman went into a far **c** to 5561
 20: 9 and **went into a far c** for a long time. 589
 23:26 coming out of the **c,** and on him they laid 68
Jn 4:44 a prophet hath no honour in his own **c.** 3968
 11:54 thence unto a **c** near to the wilderness, 5561
 11:55 many went out of the **c** up to Jerusalem 5561
Ac 4:36 a Levite, *and* **of the c** of Cyprus, 1085
 7: 3 out of thy **c,** and from thy kindred, 1093
 12:20 their **c** was nourished by the king's 5561
 12:20 country was nourished by the king's NIG
 13: 7 was with the deputy *of the* **c,** Sergius NIG
 18:23 and went over *all* the **c** of Galatia and 5561
 27:27 deemed that they drew near to some **c;** 5561
Heb 11: 9 as *in* a strange **c,** dwelling in tabernacles NIG
 11:14 *things* declare plainly that they seek a **c.** 3968
 11:15 if they had been mindful of that **c** from NIG
 11:16 But now they desire a better **c,** that is, NIG

COUNTRYMEN (2) [COUNTRY, MAN]

2Co 11:26 *in* perils of robbers, *in* perils by *my own* **c,** 1085
1Th 2:14 have suffered like *things* of your own **c,** 4853

COUPLE (10) [COUPLED, COUPLETH, COUPLING, COUPLINGS]

Ex 26: 6 **c** the curtains together with the taches: 2266
 26: 9 thou shalt **c** five curtains by themselves, 2266
 26:11 **c** the tent **together**, that it may be one. 2266
 36:18 taches of brass to **c** the tent **together**, 2266
 39: 4 shoulderpieces for it, to **c** *it* **together:** 2266
Jdg 19: 3 his servant with him, and a **c** of asses: 6776
2Sa 13: 6 make me a **c** of cakes in my sight, that I 8147
 16: 1 with a **c** of asses saddled, and upon them 6776
Isa 21: 7 he saw a chariot *with* a **c** of horsemen, 6776
 21: 9 a chariot of men, *with* a **c** of horsemen. 6776

COUPLED (12) [COUPLE]

Ex 26: 3 The five curtains shall be **c together** one 2266
 26: 3 five curtains *shall be* **c** one to another. 2266
 26:24 they shall be **c together** beneath, 8382
 26:24 they shall be **c together** above 3162+8535
 36:10 he **c** the five curtains one unto another: 2266
 36:10 *the other* five curtains he **c** one unto 2266
 36:13 **c** the curtains one unto another with 2266
 36:16 he **c** five curtains by themselves, and six 2266
 36:29 were **c** beneath, and coupled together 8382
 36:29 **c** together at the head thereof, 1961+8535
 39: 4 by the two edges was it **c together.** 2266
1Pe 3: 2 your chaste conversation **c** with fear. NIG

COUPLETH (2) [COUPLE]

Ex 26:10 edge of the curtain which **c** the second. 2279
 36:17 edge of the curtain which **c** the second. 2279

COUPLING (10) [COUPLE]

Ex 26: 4 one curtain from the selvedge in the **c;** 2279
 26: 4 *another* curtain, in the **c** of the second. 4225
 26: 5 the curtain that *is* in the **c** of the second; 4225
 26:10 the one curtain that *is* outmost in the **c,** 2279
 28:27 over against *the other* thereof, 4225
 36:11 of one curtain from the selvedge in the **c** 4225
 36:11 of *another* curtain, in the **c** of the second. 4225
 36:12 curtain which *was* in the **c** of the second: 4225
 36:17 the uttermost edge of the curtain in the **c,** 4225
 39:20 of it, over against the *other* thereof, 4225

COUPLINGS (1) [COUPLE]

2Ch 34:11 timber for **c,** and to floor the houses which 4226

COURAGE (20) [COURAGEOUS, COURAGEOUSLY]

Nu 13:20 be ye of **good c**, and bring of the fruit of 2388
Dt 31: 6 Be strong and **of a good c**, fear not, nor be 553
 31: 7 of all Israel, Be strong and **of a good c,** 553
 31:23 and said, Be strong and **of a good c** 553
Jos 1: 6 Be strong and **of a good c:** for unto this 553
 1: 9 Be strong and **of a good c;** be not afraid, 553
 1:18 to death: only be strong and **of a good c.** 553
 2:11 neither did there remain any more **c** in 7307
 10:25 nor be dismayed, be strong and **of good c:** 553
2Sa 10:12 Be **of good c**, and let us play the men for 2388
1Ch 19:13 Be **of good c**, and let us behave ourselves 2388
 22:13 be strong, and **of good c;** dread not, 553
 28:20 Be strong and **of good c**, and do *it:* 2388
2Ch 15: 8 he **took c,** and put away the abominable 2388
Ezr 10: 4 *will be* with thee: be **of good c**, and do *it.* 2388
Ps 27:14 be **of good c**, and he shall strengthen 2388
 31:24 Be **of good c**, and he shall strengthen 2388
Isa 41: 6 *one* said to his brother, Be **of good c.** 2388
Da 11:25 his **c** against the king of the south with a 3824
Ac 28:15 Paul saw, he thanked God, and took **c.** 2294

COURAGEOUS (5) [COURAGE]

Jos 1: 7 Only be thou strong and very **c,** that *thou* 553
 23: 6 ye therefore very **c** to keep and to do all 2388
2Sa 13:28 I commanded you? be **c,** and be valiant. 2388
2Ch 32: 7 Be strong and **c**, be not afraid nor 553
Am 2:16 he that *is* **c** among the mighty shall 533+3820

COURAGEOUSLY (1) [COURAGE]

2Ch 19:11 Deal **c**, and the Lord shall be with 2388

COURSE (35) [COURSES]

1Ch 27: 1 every **c** were twenty and four thousand. 4256
 27: 2 Over the first **c** for the first month *was* 4256
 27: 2 in his **c** were twenty and four thousand. 4256
 27: 4 the **c** of the second month *was* Dodai 4256
 27: 4 and *of* his **c** *was* Mikloth also the ruler: 4256
 27: 4 in his **c** likewise *were* twenty and 4256
 27: 5 in his **c** *were* twenty and four thousand. 4256
 27: 6 and *in* his **c** *was* Ammizabad his son. 4256
 27: 7 in his **c** *were* twenty and four thousand. 4256
 27: 8 in his **c** *were* twenty and four thousand. 4256
 27: 9 in his **c** *were* twenty and four thousand. 4256
 27:10 in his **c** *were* twenty and four thousand. 4256
 27:11 in his **c** *were* twenty and four thousand. 4256
 27:12 in his **c** *were* twenty and four thousand. 4256
 27:13 in his **c** *were* twenty and four thousand. 4256
 27:14 in his **c** *were* twenty and four thousand. 4256
 27:15 in his **c** *were* twenty and four thousand. 4256
 28: 1 **companies** that ministered to the king
 by c, 4256
2Ch 5:11 sanctified, *and* did not *then* wait by **c:** 4256
Ezr 3:11 And they sung together by **c** in praising NIH
Ps 82: 5 the foundations of the earth are **out of c.** 4131
Jer 8: 6 every one turned to his **c,** as the horse 4794
 23:10 their **c** is evil, and their force *is* not right. 4794
Lk 1: 5 priest named Zacharias, of the **c** of Abia: 2183

Lk 1: 8 office before God in the order of his **c,** 2183
Ac 13:25 And as John fulfilled *his* **c,** he said, 1408
 16:11 **came with a straight c** to Samothracia, 2113
 20:24 so that *I* might finish my **c** with joy, 1408
 21: 1 we came with a **straight c** unto Cos, 2113
 21: 7 when we had finished *our* **c** from Tyre, 4144
1Co 14:27 at the most *by* three, and *that* **by c;** 303+3313
Eph 2: 2 ye walked according to the **c** of this world, 165
2Th 3: 1 that the word of the Lord may have **free c,** 5143
2Ti 4: 7 I have finished *my* **c,** I have kept the faith: 1408
Jas 3: 6 and setteth on fire the **c** of nature; 5164

COURSES (18) [COURSE]

Jdg 5:20 the stars in their **c** fought against Sisera. 4546
1Ki 5:14 to Lebanon, ten thousand a month *by* **c:** 2487
1Ch 23: 6 David divided them *into* **c** among the 4256
 27: 1 served the king in any matter of the **c,** 4256
 28:13 for the **c** of the priests and the Levites, 4256
 28:21 the **c** of the priests and the Levites, 4256
2Ch 8:14 the **c** of the priests to their service, 4256
 8:14 the porters also by their **c** at every gate: 4256
 23: 8 for Jehoiada the priest dismissed not the **c.** 4256
 31: 2 Hezekiah appointed the **c** of the priests 4256
 31: 2 of the priests and the Levites after their **c,** 4256
 31:15 set office, to give to their brethren by **c,** 4256
 31:16 in their charges according to their **c;** 4256
 31:17 and upward, in their charges by their **c;** 4256
 35: 4 after your **c,** according to the writing of 4256
 35:10 in their place, and the Levites in their **c,** 4256
Ezr 6:18 the Levites in their **c,** for the service of 4255
Isa 44: 4 the grass, as willows by the water **c.** 2988

COURT (122) [COURTS]

Ex 27: 9 thou shalt make the **c** of the tabernacle: 2691
 27: 9 *of* fine twined linen of an hundred 2691
 27:12 *for* the breadth of the **c** on the west side 2691
 27:13 the breadth of the **c** on the east side 2691
 27:16 for the gate of the **c** *shall be* a hanging of 2691
 27:17 All the pillars round about the **c** *shall be* 2691
 27:18 The length of the **c** *shall be* an hundred 2691
 27:19 and all the pins of the **c,** *shall be of* brass. 2691
 35:17 The hangings of the **c,** his pillars, 2691
 35:17 and the hanging for the door of the **c,** 2691
 35:18 and the pins of the **c,** and their cords, 2691
 38: 9 he made the **c:** on the south side 2691
 38: 9 hangings of the **c** *were* of fine twined 2691
 38:15 the other side of the **c** gate, on this hand 2691
 38:16 All the hangings of the **c** round about 2691
 38:17 all the pillars of the **c** were filleted *with* 2691
 38:18 the hanging for the gate of the **c** was 2691
 38:18 answerable to the hangings of the **c.** 2691
 38:20 and of the **c** round about, *were of* brass. 2691
 38:31 the sockets of the **c** round about, 2691
 38:31 the sockets of the **c** gate, and all the pins 2691
 38:31 and all the pins of the **c** round about. 2691
 39:40 The hangings of the **c,** his pillars, and his 2691
 39:40 the hanging for the **c** gate, his cords, 2691
 40: 8 thou shalt set up the **c** round about, 2691
 40: 8 and hang up the hanging at the **c** gate. 2691
 40:33 he reared up the **c** round about 2691
 40:33 and set up the hanging of the **c** gate. 2691
Lev 6:16 in the **c** of the tabernacle of 2691
 6:26 in the **c** of the tabernacle of 2691
Nu 3:26 the hangings of the **c,** and the curtain for 2691
 3:26 the curtain for the door of the **c,** which *is* 2691
 3:37 the pillars of the **c** round about, 2691
 4:26 the hangings of the **c,** and the hanging for 2691
 4:26 hanging for the door and the gate of the **c,** 2691
 4:32 the pillars of the **c** round about, 2691
2Sa 17:18 in Bahurim, which had a well in his **c** 2691
1Ki 6:36 he built the inner **c** *with* three rows of 2691
 7: 8 his house where he dwelt *had* another **c** 2691
 7: 9 and *so* on the outside toward the great **c.** 2691
 7:12 great **c** round about *was with* three rows 2691
 7:12 both for the inner **c** of the house of 2691
 8:64 **c** that *was* before the house of the Lord: 2691
2Ki 20: 4 Isaiah was gone out *into* the middle **c,** 2691
2Ch 4: 9 Furthermore he made the **c** of the priests, 2691
 4: 9 the great **c,** and doors for the court, 5835
 4: 9 doors for the **c,** and overlaid the doors of 5835
 6:13 and had set it in the midst of the **c:** 5835
 7: 7 **c** that *was* before the house of the Lord: 2691
 20: 5 the house of the Lord, before the new **c,** 2691
 24:21 king in the **c** of the house of the Lord. 2691
 29:16 into the **c** of the house of the Lord. 2691
Ne 3:25 house, that *was* by the **c** of the prison. 2691
Est 1: 5 the **c** of the garden of the king's palace; 2691
 2:11 Mordecai walked every day before the **c** 2691
 4:11 shall come unto the king into the inner **c,** 2691
 5: 1 stood in the inner **c** of the king's house, 2691
 5: 1 saw Esther the queen standing in the **c,** 2691
 6: 4 the king said, Who *is* in the **c?** 2691
 6: 4 Haman was come into the outward **c** 2691
 6: 5 him, Behold, Haman standeth in the **c.** 2691
Isa 34:13 a habitation of dragons, *and* a **c** for owls. 2681
Jer 19:14 he stood in the **c** of the Lord's house; 2691
 26: 2 Stand in the **c** of the Lord's house, 2691
 32: 2 Jeremiah the prophet was shut up in the **c** 2691
 32: 8 **c** of the prison according to the word of 2691
 32:12 before all the Jews that sat in the **c** of 2691
 33: 1 while he was yet shut up in the **c** of 2691
 36:10 the higher **c** *at* the entry of the new gate 2691
 36:20 they went in to the king into the **c,** 2691
 37:21 commit Jeremiah into the **c** of the prison, 2691
 37:21 Thus Jeremiah remained in the **c** of 2691

C

Jer 38: 6 that *was* in the **c** of the prison: 2691
38:13 Jeremiah remained in the **c** of the prison. 2691
38:28 So Jeremiah abode in the **c** of the prison 2691
39:14 took Jeremiah out of the **c** of the prison, 2691
39:15 he was shut up in the **c** of the prison, 2691
Eze 8: 7 And he brought me to the door of the **c**; 2691
8:16 he brought me into the inner **c** 2691
10: 3 went in; and the cloud filled the inner **c.** 2691
10: 4 was full of the brightness of 2691
10: 5 wings was heard *even* to the utter **c,** 2691
40:14 even unto the post of the **c** round about 2691
40:17 Then brought he me into the outward **c,** 2691
40:17 a pavement made for the **c** round about: 2691
40:19 unto the forefront of the inner **c** without, 2691
40:20 the gate of the outward **c** that looked 2691
40:23 the gate of the inner **c** *was* over against 2691
40:27 *there was* a gate in the inner **c** toward 2691
40:28 he brought me to the inner **c** by the south 2691
40:31 arches thereof *were* toward the utter **c**; 2691
40:32 he brought me into the inner **c** toward 2691
40:34 thereof *were* toward the outward **c**; 2691
40:37 posts thereof *were* toward the utter **c**; 2691
40:44 chambers of the singers in the inner **c,** 2691
40:47 So he measured the **c,** an hundred cubits 2691
41:15 inner temple, and the porches of the **c**; 2691
42: 1 he brought me forth into the utter **c,** 2691
42: 3 twenty *cubits* which *were* for the inner **c,** 2691
42: 3 the pavement which *was* for the utter **c,** 2691
42: 7 towards the utter **c** on the forepart of 2691
42: 8 that *were* in the utter **c** *was* fifty cubits: 2691
42: 9 as one goeth into them from the utter **c.** 2691
42:10 of the wall of the **c** toward the east, 2691
42:14 go out of the holy *place* into the utter **c,** 2691
43: 5 me up, and brought me into the inner **c**; 2691
44:17 they enter in at the gates of the inner **c,** 2691
44:17 they minister in the gates of the inner **c,** 2691
44:19 when they go forth into the utter **c,** 2691
44:19 *even* into the utter **c** to the people, 2691
44:21 when they enter into the inner **c.** 2691
44:27 unto the inner **c,** to minister in 2691
45:19 upon the posts of the gate of the inner **c.** 2691
46: 1 The gate of the inner **c** that looketh 2691
46:20 *they* bear *them* not out into the utter **c,** 2691
46:21 he brought me forth into the utter **c,** 2691
46:21 me to pass by the four corners of the **c**; 2691
46:21 every corner of the **c** *there was* a court. 2691
46:21 in every corner of the court *there was* a **c.** 2691
46:22 In the four corners of the **c** *there were* 2691
Am 7:13 *is* the king's chapel, and it *is* the king's **c.** 1004
Rev 11: 2 But the **c** which is without the temple 833

COURTEOUS (1) [COURTEOUSLY]
1Pe 3: 8 another, love as brethren, *be* pitiful, *be* **c**: 5391

COURTEOUSLY (2) [COURTEOUS]
Ac 27: 3 And Julius **c** entreated Paul, and gave *him* 5364
28: 7 received us, and lodged *us* three days **c.** 5390

COURTS (25) [COURT]
2Ki 21: 5 in the two **c** of the house of the Lord. 2691
23:12 in the two **c** of the house of the Lord, 2691
1Ch 23:28 in the **c,** and in the chambers, and in 2691
28: 6 son, he shall build my house and my **c**: 2691
28:12 of the **c** of the house of the Lord, 2691
2Ch 23: 5 the people *shall be* in the **c** of the house 2691
33: 5 in the two **c** of the house of the Lord. 2691
Ne 8:16 in their **c,** and in the courts of the house 2691
8:16 in the **c** of the house of God, and in 2691
13: 7 in preparing him a chamber in the **c** of 2691
Ps 65: 4 *unto thee, that* he may dwell *in* thy **c**: 2691
84: 2 yea, even fainteth for the **c** of the Lord: 2691
84:10 a day in thy **c** *is* better than a thousand. 2691
92:13 Lord shall flourish in the **c** of our God. 2691
96: 8 bring an offering, and come into his **c.** 2691
100: 4 *and* into his **c** with praise: 2691
116:19 In the **c** of the Lord's house, 2691
135: 2 in the **c** of the house of our God, 2691
Isa 1:12 required this at your hand, to tread my **c**? 2691
62: 9 shall drink it in the **c** of my holiness. 2691
Eze 9: 7 The house, and fill the **c** *with* the slain: 2691
42: 6 but had not pillars as the pillars of the **c**: 2691
46:22 the four corners of the court *there were* **c** 2691
Zec 3: 7 shalt also keep my **c,** and I will give thee 2691
Lk 7:25 and live delicately, are in **kings**' **c.** 933

COUSIN (1) [COUSINS]
Lk 1:36 And behold, thy **c** Elisabeth, she hath also 4773

COUSINS (1) [COUSIN]
Lk 1:58 her **c** heard how the Lord had shewed 4773

COVENANT (292) [COVENANT-BREAKERS, COVENANTED, COVENANTS]
Ge 6:18 with thee will I establish my **c**; 1285
9: 9 behold I establish my **c** with you and 1285
9:11 I will establish my **c** with you; neither 1285
9:12 This *is* the token of the **c** which I make 1285
9:13 it shall be for a token of a **c** between me 1285
9:15 I will remember my **c,** which *is* between 1285
9:16 that I may remember the everlasting **c** 1285
9:17 said unto Noah, This *is* the token of the **c,** 1285
15:18 In the same day the Lord made a **c** with 1285
17: 2 I will make my **c** between me and thee, 1285
17: 4 my **c** *is* with thee, and thou shalt be a 1285
17: 7 I will establish my **c** between me and thee 1285

Ge 17: 7 in their generations for an everlasting **c,** 1285
17: 9 Thou shalt keep my **c** therefore, thou, 1285
17:10 This *is* my **c,** which ye shall keep, 1285
17:11 it shall be a token of the **c** betwixt me and 1285
17:13 my **c** shall be in your flesh for an 1285
17:13 shall be in your flesh for an everlasting **c.** 1285
17:14 off from his people; he hath broken my **c.** 1285
17:19 I will establish my **c** for an 1285
17:19 covenant with him for an everlasting **c,** 1285
17:21 my **c** will I establish with Isaac, 1285
21:27 and both of them made a **c.** 1285
21:32 Thus they made a **c** at Beer-sheba: then 1285
26:28 and thee, and let us make a **c** with thee; 1285
31:44 come thou, let us make a **c,** I and thou; 1285
Ex 2:24 God remembered his **c** with Abraham, 1285
6: 4 I have also established my **c** with them, 1285
6: 5 bondage; and I have remembered my **c.** 1285
19: 5 keep my **c,** then ye shall be a peculiar 1285
23:32 Thou shalt make no **c** with them, nor 1285
24: 7 he took the book of the **c,** and read in 1285
24: 8 and said, Behold, the blood of the **c,** 1285
31:16 their generations, *for* a perpetual **c.** 1285
34:10 he said, Behold, I make a **c**: before all thy 1285
34:12 lest thou make a **c** with the inhabitants of 1285
34:15 Lest thou make a **c** with the inhabitants of 1285
34:27 of these words I have made a **c** with thee 1285
34:28 wrote upon the tables the words of the **c,** 1285
Lev 2:13 neither shalt thou suffer the salt of the **c** 1285
24: 8 the children of Israel *by* an everlasting **c.** 1285
26: 9 multiply you, and establish my **c** with you. 1285
26:15 commandments, *but* that ye break my **c**: 1285
26:25 that shall avenge the quarrel of *my* **c**: 1285
26:42 will I remember my **c** with Jacob, 1285
26:42 my **c** with Isaac, and also my covenant 1285
26:42 my **c** with Abraham will I remember; 1285
26:44 utterly, and to break my **c** with them: 1285
26:45 I will for their sakes remember the **c** of 1285
Nu 10:33 the ark of the **c** of the Lord went before 1285
14:44 nevertheless the ark of the **c** of the Lord, 1285
18:19 it *is* a salt for ever before the Lord 1285
25:12 Behold, I give unto him my **c** of peace: 1285
25:13 *even* the **c** of an everlasting priesthood; 1285
Dt 4:13 he declared unto you his **c,** which he 1285
4:23 lest ye forget the **c** of the Lord your 1285
4:31 nor forget the **c** of thy fathers which he 1285
5: 2 The Lord our God made a **c** with us in 1285
5: 3 The Lord made not this **c** with our 1285
7: 2 shalt make no **c** with them, nor shew 1285
7: 9 which keepeth **c** and mercy with them 1285
7:12 Lord thy God shall keep unto thee the **c** 1285
8:18 he may establish his **c** which he sware 1285
9: 9 *even* the tables of the **c** which the Lord 1285
9:11 tables of stone, *even* the tables of the **c** 1285
9:15 the two tables of the **c** *were* in my two 1285
10: 8 to bear the ark of the **c** of the Lord, 1285
17: 2 the Lord thy God, in transgressing his **c,** 1285
29: 1 These *are* the words of the **c,** which 1285
29: 1 beside the **c** which he made with them in 1285
29: 9 Keep therefore the words of this **c,** 1285
29:12 That thou shouldest enter into **c** with 1285
29:14 Neither with you only do I make this **c** 1285
29:21 according to all the curses of the **c** that 1285
29:25 Because they have forsaken the **c** of 1285
31: 9 which bare the ark of the **c** of the Lord, 1285
31:16 break my **c** which I have made with them 1285
31:20 and provoke me, and break my **c.** 1285
31:25 which bare the ark of the **c** of the Lord, 1285
31:26 put it in the side of the ark of the **c** of 1285
33: 9 have observed thy word, and kept thy **c.** 1285
Jos 3: 3 When ye see the ark of the **c** of the Lord 1285
3: 6 Take up the ark of the **c,** and pass over 1285
3: 6 they took up the ark of the **c,** 1285
3: 8 the priests that bear the ark of the **c** 1285
3:11 Behold, the ark of the **c,** *even* the Lord of 1285
3:14 the priests bearing the ark *of* the **c** before 1285
3:17 the priests that bare the ark *of* the **c** 1285
4: 7 off before the ark of the **c** of the Lord; 1285
4: 9 priests which bare the ark of the **c** stood: 1285
4:18 the priests that bare the ark of the **c** of 1285
6: 6 Take up the ark of the **c,** and let seven 1285
6: 8 the ark of the **c** of the Lord followed 1285
7:11 they have also transgressed my **c** which I 1285
7:15 he hath transgressed the **c** of the Lord, 1285
8:33 which bare the ark of the **c** of the Lord, 1285
23:16 When ye have transgressed the **c** of 1285
Jos 24: 25 So Joshua made a **c** with the people that 1285
Jdg 2: 1 I said, I will never break my **c** with you. 1285
2:20 my **c** which I commanded their fathers, 1285
20:27 (for the ark of the **c** of God *was* there in 1285
1Sa 4: 3 Let us fetch the ark of the **c** of the Lord 1285
4: 4 the ark of the **c** of the Lord of hosts, 1285
4: 4 *were* there with the ark of the **c** of God. 1285
4: 5 when the ark of the **c** of the Lord came 1285
11: 1 Make a **c** with us, and we will serve thee. 1285
11: 2 this *condition* will I make a **c** with you, NIH
18: 3 Jonathan and David made a **c,** because 1285
20: 8 thou hast brought thy servant into a **c** of 1285
20:16 So Jonathan made a **c** with the house of NIH
23:18 they two made a **c** before the Lord: and 1285
2Sa 15:24 with him, bearing the ark of the **c** of God: 1285
23: 5 he hath made with me an everlasting **c,** 1285
1Ki 3:15 stood before the ark of the **c** of the Lord. 1285
6:19 to set there the ark of the **c** of the Lord. 1285
8: 1 *they* might bring up the ark of the **c** of 1285
8: 6 the priests brought in the ark of the **c** of 1285

1Ki 8: 9 when the Lord made *a* **c** with NIH
8:21 wherein *is* the **c** of the Lord, which he 1285
8:23 keepest **c** and mercy with thy servants 1285
11:11 thou hast not kept my **c** and my statutes, 1285
19:10 the children of Israel have forsaken thy **c,** 1285
19:14 the children of Israel have forsaken thy **c,** 1285
20:34 *Ahab,* I will send thee away with *this* **c.** 1285
20:34 So he made a **c** with him, and sent him 1285
2Ki 11: 4 made a **c** with them, and took an oath of 1285
11:17 Jehoiada made a **c** between the Lord 1285
13:23 because of his **c** with Abraham, Isaac, 1285
17:15 his **c** that he made with their fathers, 1285
17:35 With whom the Lord had made a **c,** 1285
17:38 the **c** that I have made with you ye shall 1285
18:12 transgressed his **c,** *and* all that Moses 1285
23: 2 **c** which was found in the house of 1285
23: 3 made a **c** before the Lord, to walk after 1285
23: 3 to perform the words of this **c** that were 1285
23: 3 And all the people stood to the **c.** 1285
23:21 as it is written in the book of this **c.** 1285
1Ch 11: 3 David made a **c** with them in Hebron 1285
15:25 went to bring up the ark of the **c** of 1285
15:26 that bare the ark of the **c** of the Lord, 1285
15:28 Thus all Israel brought up the ark of the **c** 1285
15:29 *as* the ark of the **c** of the Lord came to 1285
16: 6 continually before the ark of the **c** of God. 1285
16:15 Be ye mindful always of his **c**; the word 1285
16:16 *Even of* the **c** which he made with NIH
16:17 a law, *and* to Israel *for* an everlasting **c,** 1285
16:37 So he left there before the ark of the **c** of 1285
17: 1 the ark of the **c** of the Lord *remaineth* 1285
22:19 to bring the ark of the **c** of the Lord, 1285
28: 2 of rest for the ark of the **c** of the Lord, 1285
28:18 and covered the ark of the **c** of the Lord. 1285
2Ch 5: 2 to bring up the ark of the **c** of the Lord 1285
5: 7 the priests brought in the ark of the **c** of 1285
5:10 when the Lord made *a* **c** with NIH
6:11 put the ark, wherein *is* the **c** of the Lord, 1285
6:14 which keepest **c,** and *shewest* mercy unto 1285
13: 5 *even* to him and to his sons *by* a **c** of salt? 1285
15:12 they entered into a **c** to seek the Lord 1285
21: 7 of the **c** that he had made with David, 1285
23: 1 the son of Zichri, into **c** with him. 1285
23: 3 the congregation made a **c** with the king 1285
23:16 Jehoiada made a **c** between him, 1285
29:10 Now *it is* in mine heart to make a **c** with 1285
34:30 **c** that was found in the house of 1285
34:31 made a **c** before the Lord, to walk after 1285
34:31 to perform the words of the **c** which are 1285
34:32 Jerusalem did according to the **c** of God, 1285
Ezr 10: 3 let us make a **c** with our God to put away 1285
Ne 1: 5 keepeth **c** and mercy for them that love 1285
9: 8 madest a **c** with him to give the land of 1285
9:32 terrible God, who keepest **c** and mercy, 1285
9:38 because of all this we **make** a sure **c,** 3772
13:29 the **c** of the priesthood, and of the Levites. 1285
Job 31: 1 I made a **c** with mine eyes; why then 1285
41: 4 Will he make a **c** with thee? wilt thou take 1285
Ps 25:10 truth and such as keep his **c** and 1285
25:14 fear him; and he will shew them his **c.** 1285
44:17 neither have we dealt falsely in thy **c.** 1285
50: 5 those that have made a **c** with me by 1285
50:16 thou shouldest take my **c** in thy mouth? 1285
55:20 at peace with him: he hath broken his **c.** 1285
74:20 Have respect unto the **c**: for the dark 1285
78:10 They kept not the **c** of God, and refused 1285
78:37 neither were they stedfast in his **c.** 1285
89: 3 I have made a **c** with my chosen, I have 1285
89:28 and my **c** *shall* stand fast with him. 1285
89:34 My **c** will I not break, nor alter the thing 1285
89:39 Thou hast made void the **c** of thy servant: 1285
103:18 To such as keep his **c,** and to those that 1285
105: 8 He hath remembered his **c** for ever, 1285
105: 9 Which **c** he made with Abraham, NIH
105:10 a law, *and* to Israel *for* an everlasting **c**: 1285
106:45 he remembered for them his **c,** 1285
111: 5 fear him: he will ever be mindful of his **c.** 1285
111: 9 he hath commanded his **c** for ever: holy 1285
132:12 If thy children will keep my **c** and 1285
Pr 2:17 youth, and forgetteth the **c** of her God. 1285
Isa 24: 5 the ordinance, broken the everlasting **c.** 1285
28:15 have made a **c** with death, and with hell 1285
28:18 your **c** with death shall be disannulled, 1285
33: 8 he hath broken the **c,** he hath despised 1285
42: 6 and give thee for a **c** of the people, 1285
49: 8 and give thee for a **c** of the people, 1285
54:10 shall the **c** of my peace be removed, 1285
55: 3 I will make an everlasting **c** with you, 1285
56: 4 that please me, and take hold of my **c**; 1285
56: 6 from polluting it, and taketh hold of my **c**; 1285
57: 8 thy bed, and made thee a **c** with them; NIH
59:21 As for me, this *is* my **c** with them, saith 1285
61: 8 I will make an everlasting **c** with them. 1285
Jer 3:16 no more, The ark of the **c** of the Lord: 1285
11: 2 Hear ye the words of this **c,** and speak 1285
11: 3 man that obeyeth not the words of this **c,** 1285
11: 6 Hear ye the words of this **c,** and do them. 1285
11: 8 bring upon them all the words of this **c,** 1285
11:10 the house of Judah have broken my **c** 1285
14:21 remember, break not thy **c** with us. 1285
22: 9 Because they have forsaken the **c** of 1285
31:31 that I will make a new **c** with the house 1285
31:32 Not according to the **c** that I made with 1285
31:32 which my **c** they brake, although I was a 1285
31:33 this *shall be* the **c** that I will make with 1285

C

Jer 32:40 I will make an everlasting **c** with them, 1285
33:20 If you can break my **c** of the day, and my 1285
33:20 my **c** of the night, and that there should 1285
33:21 may also my **c** be broken with David 1285
33:25 If my **c** be not with day and night, *and if* 1285
34: 8 after that the king Zedekiah had made a **c** 1285
34:10 the people, which had entered into the **c**, 1285
34:13 I make a **c** with your fathers in the day 1285
34:15 ye had made a **c** before me in the house 1285
34:18 give the men that have transgressed my **c**, 1285
34:18 of the **c** which they had made before me, 1285
50: 5 a perpetual **c** *that* shall not be forgotten, 1285
Eze 16: 8 unto thee, and entered into a **c** with thee, 1285
16:59 hast despised the oath in breaking the **c**. 1285
16:60 Nevertheless I will remember my **c** with 1285
16:60 I will establish unto thee an everlasting **c**. 1285
16:61 unto thee for daughters, but not by thy **c**. 1285
16:62 I will establish my **c** with thee; 1285
17:13 made a **c** with him, and hath taken an 1285
17:14 that by keeping of his **c** it might stand. 1285
17:15 such *things?* or shall he break the **c**, 1285
17:16 oath he despised, and whose **c** he brake, 1285
17:18 he despised the oath by breaking the **c**, 1285
17:19 and my **c** that he hath broken, 1285
20:37 I will bring you into the bond of the **c**: 1285
34:25 I will make with them a **c** of peace, 1285
37:26 Moreover I will make a **c** of peace with 1285
37:26 it shall be an everlasting **c** with them: 1285
44: 7 they have broken my **c** because of all your 1285
Da 9: 4 keeping the **c** and mercy to them that love 1285
9:27 he shall confirm the **c** with many *for* one 1285
11:22 be broken; yea also, the prince of the **c**. 1285
11:28 his heart *shall be* against the holy **c**; 1285
11:30 and have indignation against the holy **c**: 1285
11:30 with them that forsake the holy **c**. 1285
11:32 such as do wickedly against the **c** shall he 1285
Hos 2:18 in that day will I make a **c** for them with 1285
6: 7 they like men have transgressed the **c**: 1285
8: 1 because they have transgressed my **c**, 1285
10: 4 swearing falsely in making a **c**: 1285
12: 1 they do make a **c** with the Assyrians, 1285
Am 1: 9 and remembered not the brotherly **c**: 1285
Zec 9:11 by the blood of thy **c** I have sent forth thy 1285
11:10 that *I* might break my **c** which I had made 1285
Mal 2: 4 that my **c** might be with Levi, saith 1285
2: 5 My **c** was with him of life and peace; 1285
2: 8 ye have corrupted the **c** of Levi, saith 1285
2:10 by profaning the **c** of our fathers? 1285
2:14 she thy companion, and the wife of thy **c**. 1285
3: 1 even the messenger of the **c**, whom ye 1285
Lk 1:72 to our fathers, and to remember his holy **c**; 1242
Ac 3:25 of the **c** which God made with our fathers, 1242
7: 8 And he gave him the **c** of circumcision: 1242
Ro 11:27 For this *is* my **c** unto them, when I shall 1242
Gal 3:15 Though *it be* but a man's **c**, *yet if it be* 1242
3:17 And this I say, *that* the **c**, that was 1242
Heb 8: 6 much also he is the mediator of a better **c**, 1242
8: 7 For if that first **c** had been faultless, *then* NIG
8: 8 I will make a new **c** with the house of 1242
8: 9 Not according to the **c** that I made with 1242
8: 9 because they continued not in my **c**, and I 1242
8:10 For this *is* the **c** that I will make with 1242
8:13 A new **c**, he hath made the first old. NIG
9: 1 Then verily the first **c** had also ordinances NIG
9: 4 the ark of the **c** overlaid round about with 1242
9: 4 rod that budded, and the tables of the **c**; 1242
10:16 This *is* the **c** that I will make with them 1242
10:29 and hath counted the blood of the **c**, 1242
12:24 And to Jesus the mediator of the new **c**, 1242
13:20 through the blood of the everlasting **c**, 1242

COVENANT-BREAKERS (1) [BREAK, COVENANT]

Ro 1:31 Without understanding, **c**, without natural 802

COVENANTED (4) [COVENANT]

2Ch 7:18 as I have **c** with David thy father, 3772
Hag 2: 5 *According to* the word that I **c** with you 3772
Mt 26:15 And they **c** with him for thirty pieces of 2476
Lk 22: 5 they were glad, and **c** to give him money. 4934

COVENANTS (3) [COVENANT]

Ro 9: 4 and the **c**, and the giving of the law, 1242
Gal 4:24 for these are the two **c**; the one from 1242
Eph 2:12 and strangers from the **c** of promise, 1242

COVER (72) [COVERED, COVEREDST, COVEREST, COVERETH, COVERING, COVERINGS, COVERS, UNCOVER]

Ex 10: 5 they shall **c** the face of the earth, that *one* 3680
21:33 not **c** it, and an ox or an ass fall therein; 3680
25:20 and bowls thereof, to **c** withal: 5258
26:13 on this side and on that side, to **c** it. 3680
28:42 thou shalt make them linen breeches to **c** 3680
33:22 will I **c** thee with my hand while I pass by: 5526
37:16 and his bowls, and *his* covers to **c** withal, 5258
40: 3 Testimony, and **c** the ark with the vail. 5526
Lev 13:12 the leprosy **c** all the skin of *him that hath* 3680
16:13 that the cloud of the incense may **c** 3680
17:13 out the blood thereof, and **c** it with dust. 3680
Nu 4: 5 and the ark of Testimony with it: 3680
4: 7 and the bowls, and covers to **c** withal: 5262
4: 8 the same with a covering of badgers' 3680
4: 9 the candlestick of the light, and his 3680
4:11 **c** it with a covering of badgers' skins, 3680
4:12 **c** them with a covering of badgers' skins, 3680

Nu 22: 5 **c** the face of the earth, and they abide 3680
Dt 23:13 and **c** that which cometh from thee: 3680
33:12 the LORD shall **c** him all the day long, 2653
1Sa 24: 3 a cave; and Saul went in to **c** his feet: 5526
1Ki 7:18 to **c** the chapiters that *were* upon the top, 3680
7:41 to **c** the two bowls of the chapiters which 3680
7:42 to **c** the two bowls of the chapiters that 3680
2Ch 4:12 the two wreaths to **c** the two pommels of 3680
4:13 to to **c** the two pommels of the chapiters 3680
Ne 4: 5 **c** not their iniquity, and let not their sin 3680
Job 16: **c** not thou my blood, and let my cry have 3680
21:26 in the dust, and the worms shall **c** them. 3680
22:11 not see; and abundance of waters **c** thee. 3680
38:34 that abundance of waters may **c** thee? 3680
40:22 The shady trees **c** him *with* their shadow; 5526
Ps 91: 4 He shall **c** thee with his feathers, 5526
104: 9 *that* they turn not again to **c** the earth. 3680
109:29 let them **c** themselves with their own 5844
139:11 If I say, Surely the darkness shall **c** me; 7779
140: 9 let the mischief of their own lips **c** them. 3680
Isa 11: 9 of the LORD, as the waters **c** the sea. 3680
14:11 spread under thee, and the worms **c** thee. 4374
22:17 and will **surely** **c** thee. 5844+5844
26:21 her blood, and shall no more **c** her slain. 3680
30: 1 with a covering, but not of my Spirit, 5258
58: 7 thou seest the naked, that thou **c** him; 3680
59: 6 neither shall they **c** themselves with their 3680
60: 2 the darkness shall **c** the earth, 3680
60: 6 The multitude of camels shall **c** thee, 3680
Jer 46: 8 he saith, I will go up, *and* will **c** the earth; 3680
Eze 7:18 with sackcloth, and horror shall **c** them; 3680
12: 6 thou shalt **c** thy face, that thou see not 3680
12:12 he shall **c** his face, that he see not 3680
24: 7 it not upon the ground, to **c** it with dust; 3680
24:17 **c** not *thy* lips, and eat not the bread of 5844
24:22 ye shall not **c** *your* lips, nor eat the bread 5844
26:10 of his horses their dust shall **c** thee: 3680
26:19 upon thee, and great waters shall **c** thee; 3680
30:18 cloud shall **c** her, and her daughters shall 3680
32: 7 I will **c** the heaven, and make the stars 3680
32: 7 will **c** the sun with a cloud, and the moon 3680
37: 6 **c** you **with** skin, and put breath in you, 7159
38: 9 thou shalt be like a cloud to **c** the land, 3680
38:16 people of Israel, as a cloud to **c** the land; 3680
Hos 2: 9 and my flax *given* to **c** her nakedness. 3680
10: 8 they shall say to the mountains, **C** us; 3680
Ob 1:10 thy brother Jacob shame shall **c** thee, 3680
Mic 3: 7 they shall all **c** their lips; for *there is* no 5844
7:10 shame shall **c** her which said unto me, 3680
Hab 2:14 of the LORD, as the waters **c** the sea. 3680
2:17 For the violence of Lebanon shall **c** thee, 3680
Mk 14:65 and to **c** his face, and to buffet him, 4028
Lk 23:30 Fall on us; and to the hills, **C** us. 2572
1Co 11: 7 For a man indeed ought not to **c** his head, 2619
1Pe 4: 8 for charity shall **c** the multitude of sins. 2572

COVERED (105) [COVER]

Ge 7:19 *were* under the whole heaven, were **c**. 3680
7:20 waters prevail; and the mountains were **c**. 3680
9:23 and **c** the nakedness of their father; 3680
24:65 therefore she took a vail, and **c** herself. 3680
38:14 **c** her with a vail, and wrapped herself, 3680
38:15 to be a harlot; because she had **c** her face. 3680
Ex 8: 6 frogs came up, and **c** the land of Egypt. 3680
10:15 For they **c** the face of the whole earth, 3680
14:28 **c** the chariots, and the horsemen, and all 3680
15: 5 The depths have **c** them: they sank into 3680
15:10 didst blow with thy wind, the sea **c** them: 3680
16:13 even the quails came up, and **c** the camp: 3680
24:15 into the mount, and a cloud **c** the mount. 3680
24:16 mount Sinai, and the cloud **c** it six days: 3680
37: 9 **c** with their wings over the mercy seat, 5526
40:21 and **c** the ark of the Testimony; 3680
40:34 a cloud **c** the tent of the congregation, 3680
Lev 13:13 behold, *if* the leprosy have **c** all his flesh, 3680
Nu 4:20 go in to see when the holy *things* are **c**, 1104
7: 3 six **c** wagons, and twelve oxen; 6632
9:15 cloud **c** the tabernacle, *namely*, the tent 3680
9:16 the cloud **c** it *by day*, and the appearance 3680
16:42 the cloud **c** it, and the glory of the LORD 3680
Dt 32:15 art **c** *with fatness;* then he forsook God 3780
Jos 24: 7 brought the sea upon them, and **c** them; 3680
Jdg 4:18 into the tent, she **c** him with a mantle. 3680
4:19 of milk, and gave him drink, and **c** him. 3680
1Sa 19:13 *hair for* his bolster, and **c** it with a cloth. 3680
28:14 cometh up; and he *is* **c** with a mantle. 5844
2Sa 15:30 had his head **c**, and he went barefoot: 2645
15:30 all the people that *was* with him **c** every 2645
19: 4 the king **c** his face, and the king cried 3813
1Ki 1: 1 **c** him with clothes, but he gat no heat. 3680
6: 9 the house with beams and boards of 5603
6:15 *and* he **c** them on the inside with wood, 6823
6:15 **c** the floor of the house with planks of fir. 6823
6:20 and so **c** the altar *which was of* cedar. 6823
6:35 **c** *them* with gold fitted upon the carved 6823
7: 3 **c** with cedar above upon the beams, 5603
7: 7 *it was* **c** with cedar from one side of 5603
7: 7 the cherubims the ark and the staves 5526
2Ki 19: 1 **c** himself with sackcloth, and went *into* 3680
19: 2 the elders of the priests, **c** with sackcloth, 3680
1Ch 28:18 **c** the ark of the covenant of the LORD. 5526
2Ch 5: 8 the cherubims the ark and the staves 5526
Ne 3:15 and **c** it, and set up the doors thereof, 2926
Est 6:12 house mourning, and having his head **c**. 2645
7: 8 of the king's mouth, they **c** Haman's face. 2645

Job 23:17 *neither* hath he **c** the darkness from my 3680
31:33 If I **c** my transgressions as Adam, by 3680
Ps 32: 1 transgression *is* forgiven, whose sin *is* **c**. 3680
44:15 and the shame of my face hath **c** me, 3680
44:19 and **c** us with the shadow of death. 3680
65:13 the valleys also are **c** over with corn; 5848
68:13 yet shall ye be as **c** the wings of a dove 2645
69: 7 borne reproach; shame hath **c** my face. 3680
71:13 let them be **c** with reproach and 5844
80:10 The hills were **c** *with* the shadow of it, 3680
85: 2 of thy people, thou hast **c** all their sin. 3680
89:45 thou hast **c** him **with** shame. Selah. 5844
106:11 the waters **c** their enemies: there was not 3680
106:17 up Dathan, and **c** the company of Abiram. 3680
139:13 thou hast **c** me in my mother's womb. 5526
140: 7 thou hast **c** my head in the day of battle. 5526
Pr 24:31 *and* nettles had **c** the face thereof, 3680
26:23 a wicked heart *are like* a potsherd **c** with 6823
26:26 hatred is **c** by deceit, his wickedness 3680
Ecc 6: 4 and his name shall be **c** with darkness. 3680
Isa 6: 2 with twain he **c** his face, and with twain 3680
6: 2 with twain he **c** his feet, and with twain 3680
29:10 and your rulers, the seers hath he **c**. 3680
37: 1 **c** himself with sackcloth, and went *into* 3680
37: 2 the elders of the priests **c** with sackcloth, 3680
51:16 have **c** thee in the shadow of mine hand, 3680
61:10 he hath **c** me **with** the robe of 3271
Jer 14: 3 and confounded, and **c** their heads. 2645
14: 4 were ashamed, they **c** their heads. 2645
51:42 she is **c** with the multitude of the waves 3680
51:51 shame hath **c** our faces: for strangers are 3680
La 2: 1 **c** the daughter of Zion **with a cloud** in his 5743
3:16 gravel stones, he hath **c** me with ashes. 3728
3:43 Thou hast **c** with anger, and persecuted 5526
3:44 Thou hast **c** thyself with a cloud, that *our* 5526
Eze 1:11 one to another, and two **c** their bodies. 3680
1:23 which **c** on this *side*, and every one had 3680
1:23 two, which **c** on that *side*, their bodies. 3680
16: 8 my skirt over thee, and **c** thy nakedness: 3680
16:10 with fine linen, and I **c** thee *with* silk. 3680
18: 7 and hath **c** the naked with a garment; 3680
18:16 and hath **c** the naked with a garment, 3680
24: 8 the top of a rock, that *it* should not be **c**. 3680
27: 7 the isles of Elishah was that which **c** thee. 4374
31:15 I **c** the deep for him, and I restrained 3680
37: 8 upon them, and the skin **c** them above: 7159
41:16 the windows, and the windows *were* **c**; 3680
Jnh 3: 6 **c** him with sackcloth, and sat in ashes. 3680
3: 8 let man and beast be **c** with sackcloth, 3680
Hab 3: 3 His glory **c** the heavens, and the earth 3680
Mt 8:24 insomuch that the ship was **c** with 2572
10:26 for there is nothing **c**, that shall not be 2572
Lk 12: 2 For there is nothing **c**, that shall not be 4780
Ro 4: 7 are forgiven, and whose sins are **c**. 1943
1Co 11: 4 or prophesying, having *his* head **c**, 2596
11: 6 For if the woman be not **c**, let her also be 2619
11: 6 to be shorn or shaven, let her be **c**. 2619

COVEREDST (2) [COVER]

Ps 104: 6 Thou **c** it *with* the deep as *with* a garment: 3680
Eze 16:18 thy broidered garments, and **c** them: 3680

COVEREST (2) [COVER]

Dt 22:12 of thy vesture, wherewith thou **c** *thyself*. 3680
Ps 104: 2 **c** *thyself* with light as *with* a garment: 5844

COVERETH (27) [COVER]

Ex 29:13 shalt take all the fat that **c** the inwards, 3680
29:22 the fat that **c** the inwards, and the caul 3680
Lev 3: 3 the fat that **c** the inwards, and all the fat 3680
3: 9 the fat that **c** the inwards, and all the fat 3680
3:14 the fat that **c** the inwards, and all the fat 3680
4: 8 the fat that **c** the inwards, and all the fat 3680
7: 3 the rump, and the fat that **c** the inwards, 3680
9:19 which **c** *the inwards*, and the kidneys, 4374
Nu 22:11 of Egypt, which **c** the face of the earth: 3680
Jdg 3:24 he **c** his feet in *his* summer chamber. 5526
Job 9:24 he **c** the faces of the judges thereof; if not, 3680
15:27 Because he **c** his face with his fatness, 3680
36:30 light upon it, and **c** the bottom of the sea. 3680
36:32 With clouds he **c** the light; 3680
Ps 73: 6 as a chain; violence **c** them *as a* garment. 5848
109:19 Let it be unto him as the garment *which* **c** 5844
147: 8 Who **c** the heaven with clouds, 3680
Pr 10: 6 but violence **c** the mouth of the wicked. 3680
10:11 but violence **c** the mouth of the wicked. 3680
10:12 stirreth up strifes: but love **c** all sins. 3680
12:16 but a prudent *man* **c** shame. 3680
17: 9 He that **c** a transgression seeketh love; 3680
28:13 He that **c** his sins shall not prosper: but 3680
Jer 3:25 in our shame, and our confusion **c** us: 3680
Eze 28:14 Thou *art* the anointed cherub that **c**; 5526
Mal 2:16 for *one* **c** violence with his garment, 3680
Lk 8:16 **c** it with a vessel, or putteth *it* under a bed 2572

COVERING (48) [COVER]

Ge 8:13 Noah removed the **c** of the ark, 4372
20:16 he *is* to thee a **c** of the eyes, unto all 3682
Ex 22:27 For that *is* his **c** only, it *is* his raiment for 3682
25:20 the mercy seat with their wings, 5526
26: 7 goats' *hair* to be a **c** upon the tabernacle: 168
26:14 thou shalt make a **c** for the tent *of* rams' 4372
26:14 dyed red, and a **c** above of badgers' skins. 4372
35:11 his tent, and his **c**, his taches, 4372
35:12 *with* the mercy seat, and the vail of the **c**, 4539

C

Ex	36:19 made a **c** for the tent *of* rams' skins dyed	4372
	36:19 made a **c** of badgers' skins above *that.*	4372
	39:34 the **c** of rams' skins dyed red,	4372
	39:34 the **c** of badgers' skins, and the vail of	4539
	39:34 of badgers' skins, and the vail of the **c,**	4539
	40:19 and put the **c** of the tent above upon it;	4372
	40:21 the vail of the **c,** and covered the ark	4539
Lev	13:45 he shall **put a c** upon *his* upper lip,	5844
Nu	3:25 the **c** thereof, and the hanging for the door	4372
	4: 5 they shall take down the **c** vail,	4539
	4: 6 shall put thereon the **c** of badgers' skins,	3681
	4: 8 cover the same with a **c** of badgers' skins,	4372
	4:10 all the vessels thereof within a **c** of	4372
	4:11 cover it with a **c** of badgers' skins,	4372
	4:12 cover them with a **c** of badgers' skins,	4372
	4:14 they shall spread upon it a **c** of badgers'	3681
	4:15 his sons have made an end of **c**	3680
	4:25 his **c,** and the covering of the badgers'	4372
	4:25 of the badgers' skins that *is* above	4372
	16:38 let them make them broad plates *for* a **c**	6826
	16:39 they were made broad *plates for* a **c** of	6826
	19:15 hath no **c** bound upon it, *is* unclean.	6781
2Sa	17:19 and spread a **c** over the well's mouth,	4539
Job	22:14 Thick clouds *are* a **c** to him, that he seeth	5643
	24: 7 that *they have* no **c** in the cold.	3682
	26: 6 before him, and destruction hath no **c.**	3682
	31:19 want of clothing, or *any* poor without **c;**	3682
Ps	105:39 He spread a cloud for a **c;** and fire to give	4539
SS	3:10 thereof *of* gold, the **c** of it *of* purple,	4817
Isa	22: 8 discovered the **c** of Judah, and thou didst	4539
	25: 7 the face of the **c** cast over all people,	3875
	28:20 the **c** narrower than that *he* can wrap	4541
	30: 1 that cover *with* a **c,** but not of my Spirit,	4541
	30:22 Ye shall defile also the **c** of thy graven	6826
	50: 3 and I make sackcloth their **c.**	3682
Eze	28:13 precious stone *was* thy **c,** the sardius,	4540
	28:16 I will destroy thee, O **c** cherub, from	5526
Mal	2:13 **c** the altar of the LORD *with* tears, *with*	3680
1Co	11:15 to her: for *her* hair is given her for a **c.**	4018

COVERINGS (2) [COVER]

Pr	7:16 I have deckt my bed *with* **c of tapestry,**	4765
	31:22 She maketh herself **c of tapestry;**	4765

COVERS (3) [COVER]

Ex	25:29 and **c** thereof, and bowls thereof,	7184
	37:16 and his bowls, and *his* **c** to cover withal,	7184
Nu	4: 7 and the bowls, and the **c** to cover withal:	7184

COVERT (9)

1Sa	25:20 that she came down by the **c** of the hill,	5643
2Ki	16:18 the **c** for the sabbath that they had built	4329
Job	38:40 dens, *and* abide in the **c** to lie in wait?	5521
	40:21 shady trees, in the **c** of the reed, and fens.	5643
Ps	61: 4 I will trust in the **c** of thy wings. Selah.	5643
Isa	4: 6 and for a **c** from storm and from rain.	4563
	16: 4 be thou a **c** to them from the face of	5643
	32: 2 from the wind, and a **c** from the tempest;	5643
Jer	25:38 He hath forsaken his **c,** as the lion:	5520

COVET (8) [COVETED, COVETETH, COVETOUS, COVETOUSNESS]

Ex	20:17 Thou shalt not **c** thy neighbour's house,	2530
	20:17 thou shalt not **c** thy neighbour's wife,	2530
Dt	5:21 neither shalt thou **c** thy neighbour's house,	183
Mic	2: 2 they **c** fields, and take *them* by violence;	2530
Ro	7: 7 except the law had said, Thou shalt not **c.**	1937
	13: 9 not bear false witness, Thou shalt not **c;**	1937
1Co	12:31 **c earnestly** the best gifts: and yet shew	2206
	14:39 **c** to prophesy, and forbid not to speak	2206

COVETED (3) [COVET]

Jos	7:21 then I **c** them, and took them;	2530
Ac	20:33 I have **c** no *man's* silver, or gold,	1937
1Ti	6:10 while some **c after,** they have erred	3713

COVETETH (2) [COVET]

Pr	21:26 He **c greedily** all the day long: but	183+8378
Hab	2: 9 Woe to him that **c** an evil covetousness to	1214

COVETOUS (9) [COVET]

Ps	10: 3 blesseth the **c,** *whom* the LORD	1214
Lk	16:14 who were **c,** heard all these *things:* and	5366
1Co	5:10 or with the **c,** or extortioners,	4123
	5:11 or **c,** or an idolater, or a railer,	4123
	6:10 Nor thieves, nor **c,** nor drunkards,	4123
Eph	5: 5 nor unclean *person,* nor **c man** who is an	4123
1Ti	3: 3 lucre; but patient, not a brawler, not **c;**	866
2Ti	3: 2 **c,** boasters, proud, blasphemers,	5366
2Pe	2:14 they have exercised with **c practices;**	4124

COVETOUSNESS (19) [COVET]

Ex	18:21 such as fear God, men of truth, hating **c;**	1215
Ps	119:36 heart unto thy testimonies, and not to **c.**	1215
Pr	28:16 *but* he that hateth **c** shall prolong *his* days.	1215
Isa	57:17 For the iniquity of his **c** was I wroth,	1215
Jer	6:13 of them every one *is* **given to c;**	1214+1215
	8:10 least even unto the greatest is given to **c;**	1215
	22:17 and thine heart *are* not but for thy **c,**	1215
	51:13 end is come, *and* the measure of thy **c.**	1215
Eze	33:31 *but* their heart goeth after their **c.**	1215
Hab	2: 9 Woe to him that coveteth an evil **c** to his	1215
Mk	7:22 Thefts, **c, wickedness, deceit,**	4124
Lk	12:15 unto them, Take heed, and beware of **c:**	4124
Ro	1:29 fornication, wickedness, **c,** maliciousness;	4124
2Co	9: 5 as *a matter of* bounty, and not as *of* **c.**	4124

Eph	5: 3 But fornication, and all uncleanness, or **c,**	4124
Col	3: 5 and **c,** which is idolatry:	4124
1Th	2: 5 as ye know, nor a cloke of **c;**	4124
Heb	13: 5 *Let your* conversation *be* **without c;**	866
2Pe	2: 3 And through **c** shall they with feigned	4124

COW (6) [COW'S]

Lev	22:28 *whether it be* **c** or ewe, ye shall not kill it	7794
Nu	18:17 the firstling of a **c,** or the firstling of a	7794
Job	21:10 their **c** calveth, and casteth not her calf.	6510
Isa	7:21 that a man shall nourish a **young c,**	1241+5697
	11: 7 the **c** and the bear shall feed; their young	6510
Am	4: 3 every **c** *at that which is* before her;	NIH

COW'S (1) [COW]

Eze	4:15 I have given thee **c** dung for man's dung,	1241

COWS THAT HAVE CALVED See MILCH

COZ (1)

1Ch	4: 8 **C** begat Anub, and Zobebah,	6976

COZBI (2)

Nu	25:15 Midianitish woman that was slain *was* **C,**	3579
	25:18 the matter of **C,** the daughter of a prince	3579

COZEBA See CHOZEBA

CRACKLING (1)

Ecc	7: 6 For as the **c** of thorns under a pot, so *is*	6963

CRACKNELS (1)

1Ki	14: 3 **c,** and a cruse of honey, and go to him:	5350

CRAFT (6) [CRAFTINESS, CRAFTSMAN, CRAFTSMEN, CRAFTY, WITCHCRAFT, WITCHCRAFTS]

Da	8:25 through his policy also he shall cause **c** to	4820
Mk	14: 1 sought how they might take him by **c,**	1388
Ac	18: 3 And because *he* was of the **same c,**	3673
	19:25 know that by this **c** we have our wealth.	2039
	19:27 So *that* not only this our **c** is in danger to	3313
Rev	18:22 of whatsoever **c** *he be,* shall be found any	5078

CRAFTINESS (5) [CRAFT]

Job	5:13 He taketh the wise in their own **c:** and	6193
Lk	20:23 But he perceived their **c,** and said unto	3834
1Co	3:19 He taketh the wise in their own **c.**	3834
2Co	4: 2 not walking in **c,** nor handling the word	3834
Eph	4:14 by the sleight of men, and **cunning c,**	3834

CRAFTSMAN (2) [CRAFT, MAN]

Dt	27:15 the work of the hands of the **c,**	2796
Rev	18:22 no **c,** of whatsoever craft *he be,* shall be	5079

CRAFTSMEN (7) [CRAFT, MAN]

2Ki	24:14 captives, and all the **c** and smiths:	2796
	24:16 **c** and smiths a thousand, all *that were*	2796
1Ch	4:14 the valley of Charashim; for they were **c.**	2796
Ne	11:35 Lod, and Ono, the valley of **c.**	2791
Hos	13: 2 all of it the work of the **c:**	2796
Ac	19:24 Diana, brought no small gain unto the **c;**	5079
	19:38 Demetrius, and the **c** which are with him,	5079

CRAFTY (4) [CRAFT]

Job	5:12 He disappointeth the devices of the **c,**	6175
	15: 5 and thou choosest the tongue of the **c.**	6175
Ps	83: 3 They have **taken c** counsel against thy	6191
2Co	12:16 nevertheless, being **c,** I caught you with	3835

CRAG (1)

Job	39:28 upon the **c** of the rock, and the strong	8127

CRANE (2)

Isa	38:14 Like a **c** *or* a swallow, so did I chatter:	5483
Jer	8: 7 turtle and the **c** and the swallow observe	5483

CRASHING (1)

Zep	1:10 the second, and a great **c** from the hills.	7667

CRAVED (1) [CRAVETH]

Mk	15:43 boldly unto Pilate, and **c** the body of Jesus.	154

CRAVETH (1) [CRAVED]

Pr	16:26 for himself; for his mouth **c** it of him.	404

CREATE (8) [CREATED, CREATETH, CREATION, CREATOR, CREATURE, CREATURES]

Ps	51:10 **C** in me a clean heart, O God; and renew	1254
Isa	4: 5 the LORD will **c** upon every dwelling	1254
	45: 7 I form the light, and **c** darkness: I make	1254
	45: 7 I make peace, and **c** evil: I the LORD do	1254
	57:19 I **c** the fruit of the lips; Peace, peace to	1254
	65:17 behold, I **c** new heavens and a new earth:	1254
	65:18 and rejoice for ever *in that* which I **c:**	1254
	65:18 I **c** Jerusalem a rejoicing, and her people a	1254

CREATED (45) [CREATE]

Ge	1: 1 In the beginning God **c** the heaven and	1254
	1:21 God **c** great whales, and every living	1254
	1:27 So God **c** man in his own image,	1254
	1:27 own image, in the image of God **c** he him;	1254
	1:27 he him; male and female **c** he them.	1254
	2: 3 had rested from all his work which God **c**	1254
	2: 4 and of the earth when they were **c,**	1254
	5: 1 In the day God **c** man, in the likeness	1254
	5: 2 Male and female **c** he them;	1254

Ge	5: 2 Adam, in the day when they were **c.**	1254
	6: 7 I will destroy man whom I have **c** from	1254
Dt	4:32 since the day that God **c** man upon	1254
Ps	89:12 north and the south thou hast **c** them:	1254
	102:18 the people which *shall be* **c** shall praise	1254
	104:30 Thou sendest forth thy spirit, they are **c:**	1254
	148: 5 for he commanded, and they were **c.**	1254
Isa	40:26 behold who hath **c** these *things,* that	1254
	41:20 the Holy One of Israel hath **c** it.	1254
	42: 5 he that **c** the heavens, and stretched them	1254
	43: 1 now thus saith the LORD that **c** thee,	1254
	43: 7 for I have **c** him for my glory, I have	1254
	45: 8 spring up together; I the LORD have **c** it.	1254
	45:12 I have made the earth, and **c** man upon it:	1254
	45:18 For thus saith the LORD that **c**	1254
	45:18 he hath established it, he **c** it not in vain,	1254
	48: 7 They are **c** now, and not from	1254
	54:16 I have **c** the smith that bloweth the coals	1254
	54:16 and I have **c** the waster to destroy.	1254
Jer	31:22 for the LORD hath **c** a new *thing* in	1254
Eze	21:30 judge thee in the place where thou wast **c,**	1254
	28:13 in thee in the day that thou wast **c.**	1254
	28:15 in thy ways from the day that thou wast **c,**	1254
Mal	2:10 hath not one God **c** us? why do we deal	1254
Mk	13:19 the creation which God **c** unto this time,	2936
1Co	11: 9 Neither was the man **c** for the woman;	2936
Eph	2:10 **c** in Christ Jesus unto good works,	2936
	3: 9 in God, who **c** all *things* by Jesus Christ:	2936
	4:24 which after God is **c** in righteousness and	2936
Col	1:16 For by him were all *things* **c,** that are in	2936
	1:16 all *things* were **c** by him, and for him:	2936
	3:10 after the image of him that **c** him:	2936
1Ti	4: 3 which God hath **c** to be received with	2936
Rev	4:11 for thou hast **c** all *things,* and for thy	2936
	4:11 and for thy pleasure they are and were **c.**	2936
	10: 6 who **c** heaven, and the *things* that therein	2936

CREATETH (1) [CREATE]

Am	4:13 **c** the wind, and declareth unto man what	1254

CREATION (6) [CREATE]

Mk	10: 6 But from the beginning of the **c** God made	2937
	13:19 as was not from the beginning of the **c**	2937
Ro	1:20 For the invisible *things* of him from the **c**	2937
	8:22 For we know that the whole **c** groaneth	2937
2Pe	3: 4 as *they were* from the beginning of the **c.**	2937
Rev	3:14 witness, the beginning of the **c** of God;	2937

CREATOR (5) [CREATE]

Ecc	12: 1 Remember now thy **C** in the days of thy	1254
Isa	40:28 **C** of the ends of the earth, fainteth not,	1254
	43:15 your Holy One, the **c** of Israel, your King.	1254
Ro	1:25 and served the creature more than the **C,**	2936
1Pe	4:19 *to him* in well doing, as unto a faithful **C.**	2939

CREATURE (29) [CREATE]

Ge	1:20 abundantly the **moving c** that hath life,	5315
	1:21 and every living **c** that moveth,	5315
	1:24 Let the earth bring forth the living **c** after	5315
	2:19 whatsoever Adam called every living **c,**	5315
	9:10 with every living **c** that *is* with you,	5315
	9:12 you and every living **c** that *is* with you,	5315
	9:15 and you and every living **c** of all flesh;	5315
	9:16 every living **c** of all flesh that *is* upon	5315
Lev	11:46 every living **c** that moveth in the waters,	5315
	11:46 of every **c** that creepeth upon the earth:	5315
Eze	1:20 for the spirit of the **living c** *was* in	2416
	1:21 for the spirit of the **living c** *was* in	2416
	1:22 **living c** *was* as the colour of the terrible	2416
	10:15 This *is* the **living c** that I saw by the river	2416
	10:17 for the spirit of the **living c** *was* in them.	2416
	10:20 This *is* the **living c** that I saw under	2416
Mk	16:15 world, and preach the gospel to every **c.**	2937
Ro	1:25 and served the **c** more than the Creator,	2937
	8:19 the earnest expectation of the **c** waiteth	2937
	8:20 For the **c** was made subject to vanity,	2937
	8:21 Because the **c** itself also shall be delivered	2937
	8:39 Nor height, nor depth, nor any other **c,**	2937
2Co	5:17 if any *man* be in Christ, he *is* a new **c:**	2937
Gal	6:15 *thing,* nor uncircumcision, but a new **c.**	2937
Col	1:15 the invisible God, the firstborn of every **c:**	2937
	1:23 which was preached to every **c** which is	2937
1Ti	4: 4 For every **c** of God *is* good, and nothing to	2938
Heb	4:13 Neither is there any **c** *that is* not manifest	2937
Rev	5:13 And every **c** which is in heaven, and on	2938

CREATURES (12) [CREATE]

Isa	13:21 their houses shall be full *of* **doleful c;**	255
Eze	1: 5 thereof *came* the likeness of four **living c.**	2416
	1:13 As for the likeness of the **living c,**	2416
	1:13 it went up and down among the **living c;**	2416
	1:14 the **living c** ran and returned as	2416
	1:15 Now as I beheld the **living c,** behold one	2416
	1:15 one wheel upon the earth by the **living c,**	2416
	1:19 when the **living c** went, the wheels went	2416
	1:19 when the **living c** were lift up from	2416
	3:13 of the **living c** that touched one another,	2416
Jas	1:18 we should be a kind of firstfruits of his **c.**	2938
Rev	8: 9 And the third *part* of the **c** which were in	2938

CREDIT; CREDITED; CREDITS See IMPUTE; IMPUTED; IMPUTETH; IMPUTING

CREDITOR (3) [CREDITORS]

Dt	15: 2 Every **c** that lendeth *ought*	1167+3027+4874
2Ki	4: 1 **c** is come to take unto him my two sons	5383

C

Lk 7:41 There was a certain **c** which had two *1157*

CREDITORS (1) [CREDITOR]
Isa 50: 1 which of my **c** *is it* to whom I have sold *5383*

CREEK (1)
Ac 27:39 they discovered a certain **c** with a shore, *2859*

CREEP (7) [CREEPETH, CREEPING, CREPT]
Lev 11:20 All fowls that **c**, going upon *all* four, *8318*
 11:29 the creeping things that **c** upon the earth; *8317*
 11:31 *are* unclean to you among all that **c**: *8318*
 11:42 all creeping things that **c** upon the earth, *8317*
Ps 104:20 wherein all the beasts of the forest do **c** *7430*
Eze 38:20 all creeping things that **c** upon the earth, *7430*
2Ti 3: 6 For of this sort are they which **c** into *1744*

CREEPETH (14) [CREEP]
Ge 1:25 every **thing that c** upon the earth after his *7431*
 1:26 over every creeping thing that **c** upon *7430*
 1:30 to every *thing* that **c** upon the earth, *7430*
 7: 8 and of every *thing* that **c** upon the earth, *7430*
 7:14 every creeping thing that **c** upon the earth *7431*
 7:21 of every creeping thing that **c** upon *8317*
 8:17 of every creeping thing that **c** upon *7431*
 8:19 *and* whatsoever **c** upon the earth, *7430*
Lev 11:41 every creeping thing that **c** upon the earth *8317*
 11:43 abominable with any creeping thing that **c** *8317*
 11:44 *of* creeping thing that **c** upon the earth. *8317*
 11:46 every creature that **c** upon the earth: *8317*
 20:25 by any *manner of living thing* that **c** *on* *7430*
Dt 4:18 The likeness of any *thing* that **c** on *7430*

CREEPING (29) [CREEP]
Ge 1:24 **c thing**, and beast of the earth after his *7431*
 1:26 over every **c thing** that creepeth upon *7431*
 6: 7 and the **c thing**, and the fowls of the air; *7431*
 6:20 of every **c thing** of the earth after his kind, *7431*
 7:14 every **c thing** that creepeth upon the earth *7431*
 7:21 of every **c thing** that creepeth upon *8318*
 7:23 the **c things**, and the fowl of the heaven; *7431*
 8:17 of every **c thing** that creepeth *7431*
 8:19 every **c thing**, and every fowl, *7431*
Lev 5: 2 the carcase of unclean **c things**, and *if* it *8318*
 11:21 flying **c thing** that goeth upon *all* four, *8318*
 11:23 all *other* flying **c things**, which have four *8318*
 11:29 the **c things** that creep upon the earth; *8318*
 11:41 every **c thing** that creepeth upon the earth *8318*
 11:42 all **c things** that creep upon the earth, *8318*
 11:43 with any **c thing** that creepeth, *8318*
 11:44 *of* **c thing** that creepeth upon the earth. *8318*
 22: 5 Or whosoever toucheth any **c thing**, *8318*
Dt 14:19 every **c thing** that flieth *is* unclean unto *8318*
1Ki 4:33 of fowl, and of **c things**, and of fishes. *7431*
Ps 104:25 wherein *are* **things c** innumerable, *7431*
 148:10 all cattle; **c things**, and flying fowl: *7431*
Eze 8:10 behold every form of **c things**, *7431*
 38:20 all **c things** that creep upon the earth, *7431*
Hos 2:18 and *with* the **c things** of the ground; *7431*
Hab 1:14 as the **c things**, *that have* no ruler over *7431*
Ac 10:12 and **c things**, and fowls of the air. *2062*
 11: 6 and **c things**, and fowls of the air. *2062*
Ro 1:23 and fourfooted beasts, and **c things**. *2062*

CREPT (1) [CREEP]
Jude 1: 4 For there are certain men **c in unawares**, *3921*

CRESCENS (1)
2Ti 4:10 **C** to Galatia, Titus unto Dalmatia. *2913*

CRETANS See CRETES; CRETIANS

CRETE (5) [CRETES, CRETIANS]
Ac 27: 7 we sailed under **C**, over against Salmone; *2914*
 27:12 *which is* a haven of **C**, and lieth toward *2914*
 27:13 loosing *thence*, they sailed close by **C**. *2914*
 27:21 and not have loosed from **C**, and to have *2914*
Tit 1: 5 For this cause left I thee in **C**, that thou *2914*

CRETES (1) [CRETE]
Ac 2:11 and Arabians, we do hear them speak *2912*

CRETIANS (2) [CRETE]
Tit 1:12 said, The **C** *are* alway liars, evil beasts, *2912*
 3: S the first bishop of the church of the **C**, *2912*

CREW (5) [CROW]
Mt 26:74 not the man. And immediately *the* cock **c**. *5455*
Mk 14:68 went out into the porch; and *the* cock **c**. *5455*
 14:72 And the second time *the* cock **c**. *5455*
Lk 22:60 while he yet spake, the cock **c**. *5455*
Jn 18:27 denied again: and immediately *the* cock **c**. *5455*

CRIB (3)
Job 39: 9 be willing to serve thee, or abide by thy **c**? *18*
Pr 14: 4 Where no oxen *are*, the **c** *is* clean: but *18*
Isa 1: 3 his owner, and the ass his master's **c**: *18*

CRICKET See BEETLE

CRIED (199) [CRY]
Ge 27:34 he **c** with a great and exceeding bitter cry, *6817*
 39:14 to lie with me, and I **c** with a loud voice: *7121*
 39:15 he heard that I lifted up my voice and **c**, *7121*
 39:18 it came to pass, as I lift up my voice and **c**, *7121*
 41:43 and they **c** before him, Bow the knee: *7121*
 41:55 the people **c** to Pharaoh for bread: *6817*

Ge 45: 1 he **c**, Cause every man to go out from me. *7121*
Ex 2:23 they **c**, and their cry came up unto God *2199*
 5:15 of Israel came and **c** unto Pharaoh, *6817*
 8:12 Moses **c** unto the LORD because of *6817*
 14:10 the children of Israel **c** out unto *6817*
 15:25 he **c** unto the LORD; and the LORD *6817*
 17: 4 Moses **c** unto the LORD, saying, *6817*
Nu 11: 2 people **c** unto Moses; and when Moses *6817*
 12:13 Moses **c** unto the LORD, saying, Heal her *6817*
 14: 1 congregation lifted up their voice, and **c**; *5414*
 20:16 when we **c** unto the LORD, he heard our *6817*
Dt 22:24 the damsel, because she **c** not, *being* *6817*
 22:27 the betrothed damsel **c**, and *there was* *6817*
 26: 7 when we **c** unto the LORD God of our *6817*
Jos 24: 7 when they **c** unto the LORD, he put *6817*
Jdg 3: 9 when the children of Israel **c** unto *2199*
 3:15 when the children of Israel **c** unto *2199*
 4: 3 the children of Israel **c** unto the LORD: *6817*
 5:28 **c** through the lattice, Why is his chariot *2980*
 6: 6 the children of Israel **c** unto the LORD. *2199*
 6: 7 when the children of Israel **c** unto *2199*
 7:20 right hands to blow *withal:* and they **c**, *7121*
 7:21 and all the host ran, and **c**, and fled. *7321*
 9: 7 his voice, and **c**, and said unto them, *7121*
 10:10 the children of Israel **c** unto the LORD, *2199*
 10:12 ye **c** to me, and I delivered you out of *6817*
 18:23 they **c** unto the children of Dan. *7121*
1Sa 4:13 into the city, and told *it*, all the city **c** out. *2199*
 5:10 *to* Ekron, that the Ekronites **c** out, saying, *2199*
 7: 9 Samuel **c** unto the LORD for Israel; *2199*
 12: 8 your fathers **c** unto the LORD, then *2199*
 12:10 they **c** unto the LORD, and said, We have *2199*
 15:11 and he **c** unto the LORD all night. *2199*
 17: 8 he stood and **c** unto the armies of Israel, *7121*
 20:37 Jonathan **c** after the lad, and said, *Is* not *7121*
 20:38 Jonathan **c** after the lad, Make speed, *7121*
 24: 8 and **c** after Saul, saying, My lord the king. *7121*
 26:14 David **c** to the people, and to Abner the *7121*
 28:12 saw Samuel, she **c** with a loud voice: *2199*
2Sa 18:25 the watchman **c**, and told the king. *7121*
 19: 4 the king **c** *with* a loud voice, O my son *2199*
 20:16 **c** a wise woman out of the city, Hear, *7121*
 22: 7 called upon the LORD, and **c** to my God: *7121*
1Ki 13: 2 he **c** against the altar in the word of *7121*
 13: 4 which had **c** against the altar in Beth-el, *7121*
 13:21 he **c** unto the man of God that came from *7121*
 13:32 For the saying which he **c** by the word of *7121*
 17:20 he **c** unto the LORD, and said, O Lord *7121*
 17:21 **c** unto the LORD, and said, O LORD my *7121*
 18:28 they **c** loud, and cut themselves after their *7121*
 20:39 as the king passed by, he **c** unto the king: *6817*
 22:32 fight against him: and Jehoshaphat **c** out. *2199*
2Ki 2:12 Elisha saw *it*, and he **c**, My father, *6817*
 4: 1 there **c** a certain woman of the wives *6817*
 4:40 that they **c** out, and said, O thou man of *6817*
 6: 5 he **c**, and said, Alas, master, for it *was* *6817*
 6:26 there **c** a woman unto him, saying, Help, *6817*
 8: 5 **c** to the king for her house and for her *6817*
 11:14 rent her clothes, and **c**, Treason, Treason. *7121*
 18:28 **c** with a loud voice in the Jews' language, *7121*
 20:11 Isaiah the prophet **c** unto the LORD: and *7121*
1Ch 5:20 for they **c** to God in the battle, and he *2199*
2Ch 13:14 they **c** unto the LORD, and the priests *6817*
 14:11 Asa **c** unto the LORD his God, and said, *7121*
 18:31 Jehoshaphat **c** out, and the LORD helped *2199*
 32:18 **c** with a loud voice in the Jews' speech *7121*
 32:20 the son of Amoz, prayed and **c** *to* heaven. *2199*
Ne 9: 4 **c** with a loud voice unto the LORD their *2199*
 9:27 of their trouble, when they **c** unto thee, *6817*
 9:28 yet when they returned, and **c** unto thee, *2199*
Est 4: 1 city, and **c** *with* a loud and a bitter cry; *2199*
Job 29:12 Because I delivered the poor that **c**, *7768*
 30: 5 (they **c** after them as *after* a thief;) *7321*
 30:28 I stood up, *and* I **c** in the congregation. *7768*
Ps 3: 4 I **c** unto the LORD *with* my voice, *7121*
 18: 6 upon the LORD, and **c** unto my God: *7768*
 18:41 They **c**, but *there was* none to save *them:* *7768*
 22: 5 They **c** unto thee, and were delivered: *2199*
 22:24 but when he **c** unto him, he heard. *7768*
 30: 2 I **c** unto thee, and thou hast healed me. *7768*
 30: 8 I **c** to thee, O LORD; and unto *7121*
 31:22 of my supplications when I **c** unto thee. *7768*
 34: 6 This poor *man* **c**, and the LORD heard *7121*
 66:17 I **c** unto him *with* my mouth, and *he was* *7121*
 77: 1 I **c** unto God *with* my voice, *even unto* *6817*
 88: 1 I have **c** day *and* night before thee: *6817*
 88:13 unto thee have I **c**, O LORD; and in *7768*
 107: 6 they **c** unto the LORD in their trouble, *6817*
 107:13 they **c** unto the LORD in their trouble, *2199*
 119:145 I **c** with *my* whole heart; hear me, *7121*
 119:146 I **c** unto thee; save me, and I shall keep *7121*
 119:147 the dawning of the morning, and **c**: *7768*
 120: 1 In my distress I **c** unto the LORD, *7121*
 130: 1 Out of the depths have I **c** unto thee, *7121*
 138: 3 In the day when I **c** thou answeredst me, *7121*
 142: 1 I **c** unto the LORD *with* my voice; *2199*
 142: 5 I **c** unto thee, O LORD: I said, Thou *art* *2199*
Isa 6: 3 one **c** unto another, and said, Holy, holy, *7121*
 6: 4 door moved at the voice of him that **c**, *7121*
 21: 8 he **c**, A lion: My lord, I stand continually *7121*
 30: 7 therefore have I **c** concerning this, *7121*
 36:13 **c** with a loud voice in the Jews' language, *7121*
Jer 4:20 Destruction upon destruction is **c**; *7121*
 20: 8 I spake, I **c** out, I cried violence and spoil; *2199*
 20: 8 I spake, I cried out, I **c** violence and spoil; *7121*

La 2:18 Their heart **c** unto the Lord, O wall of; *6817*
 4:15 *unto them,* Depart ye; *it is* unclean; *7121*
Eze 9: 1 He also **c** in mine ears *with* a loud voice, *7121*
 9: 8 My face, and **c**, and said, Ah Lord God, *2199*
 10:13 was **c** unto them in my hearing, O wheel. *7121*
 11:13 **c** *with* a loud voice, and said, Ah Lord *2199*
Da 3: 4 a herald **c** aloud, To you it is commanded, *7123*
 4:14 He **c** aloud, and said thus, Hew down *7123*
 5: 7 king **c** aloud to bring in the astrologers, *7123*
 6:20 he **c** with a lamentable voice unto Daniel: *2200*
Hos 7:14 they have not **c** unto me with their heart, *2199*
Jnh 1: 5 **c** every man unto his god, and cast forth *2199*
 1:14 Wherefore they **c** unto the LORD, *7121*
 2: 2 I **c** by reason of mine affliction unto *7121*
 2: 2 out of the belly of hell **c** I, *7768*
 3: 4 he **c**, and said, Yet forty days, *7121*
Zec 1: 4 unto whom the former prophets have **c**, *7121*
 6: 8 he **c** upon me, and spake unto me, saying, *2199*
 7: 7 the LORD hath **c** by the former prophets, *7121*
 7:13 *that* as he **c**, and they would not hear; *7121*
 7:13 so they **c**, and I would not hear, saith *7121*
Mt 8:29 behold, they **c** out, saying, What have *2896*
 14:26 It is a spirit; and they **c** out for fear. *2896*
 14:30 to sink, he **c**, saying, Lord, save me. *2896*
 15:22 **c** unto him, saying, Have mercy on me, *2905*
 20:30 **c** out, saying, Have mercy on us, O Lord, *2896*
 20:31 they **c** the more, saying, Have mercy on *2896*
 21: 9 and that followed, **c**, saying, Hosanna to *2896*
 27:23 they **c** out the more, saying, Let him be *2896*
 27:46 about the ninth hour Jesus **c** with a loud *310*
 27:50 when he had **c** again with a loud voice, *2896*
Mk 1:23 man with an unclean spirit; and he **c** out, *349*
 1:26 and **c** with a loud voice, he came out of *2896*
 3:11 fell down before him, and **c**, saying, *2896*
 5: 7 And **c** with a loud voice, and said, *2896*
 6:49 supposed *it* had been a spirit, and **c** out: *349*
 9:24 straightway the father of the child **c** out, *2896*
 9:26 And *the spirit* **c**, and rent him sore, *2896*
 10:48 he **c** the more a great deal, *Thou* Son of *2896*
 11: 9 they that followed, **c**, saying, Hosanna; *2896*
 15:13 And they **c** out again, Crucify him. *2896*
 15:14 And they **c** out the more exceedingly, *2896*
 15:34 And at the ninth hour Jesus **c** with a loud *994*
 15:37 Jesus **c** with a loud voice, and gave up *863*
 15:39 that he so **c** out, and gave up the ghost, *2896*
Lk 4:33 unclean devil, and **c** out with a loud voice, *349*
 8: 8 And when he said these *things*, he **c**, *5455*
 8:28 he **c** out, and fell down before him, *349*
 9:38 man of the company **c** out, saying, Master, *310*
 16:24 And he **c** and said, Father Abraham, *5455*
 18:38 And he **c**, saying, Jesus, *thou* Son of David, *994*
 18:39 but he **c** *so* much the more, *Thou* Son of *2896*
 23:18 And they **c** out all at once, saying, *349*
 23:21 But they **c**, saying, Crucify *him*, crucify *2019*
 23:46 And when Jesus had **c** with a loud voice, *5455*
Jn 1:15 John bare witness of him, and **c**, saying, *2896*
 7:28 Then **c** Jesus in the temple as he taught, *2896*
 7:37 stood and **c**, saying, If any *man* thirst, *2896*
 11:43 with a loud voice, Lazarus, come forth. *2905*
 12:13 went forth to meet him, and **c**, Hosanna: *2896*
 12:44 Jesus **c** and said, He that believeth on me, *2896*
 18:40 they **c** all again, saying, Not this *man*, *2905*
 19: 6 and officers saw him, they **c** out, saying, *2905*
 19:12 but the Jews **c** out, saying, If thou let this *2896*
 19:15 But they **c** out, Away with *him*, away *2905*
Ac 7:57 Then they **c** out with a loud voice, *2896*
 7:60 and **c** with a loud voice, Lord, *2896*
 16:17 The same followed Paul and us, and **c**, *2896*
 16:28 But Paul **c** with a loud voice, saying, *5455*
 19:28 and **c** out, saying, Great *is* Diana of *2896*
 19:32 Some therefore **c** one *thing*, and some *2896*
 19:34 voice about the space of two hours **c** out, *2896*
 21:34 And some **c** one *thing*, some another, *994*
 22:23 And as they **c** out, and cast *off* their *2905*
 22:24 might know wherefore they **c** so *against* *2019*
 23: 6 **c** out in the council, Men *and* brethren, *2896*
 24:21 one voice, that I **c** standing among them, *2896*
Rev 6:10 And they **c** with a loud voice, saying, *2896*
 7: 2 he **c** with a loud voice to the four angels, *2896*
 7:10 And **c** with a loud voice, saying, Salvation *2896*
 10: 3 And **c** with a loud voice, as *when* a lion *2896*
 10: 3 when he had **c**, seven thunders uttered *2896*
 12: 2 And she being with child **c**, travailing in *2896*
 14:18 **c** with a loud cry to him that had the *5455*
 18: 2 And he **c** mightily with a strong voice, *2896*
 18:18 And **c** when they saw the smoke of her *2896*
 18:19 and **c**, weeping and wailing, saying, Alas, *2896*
 19:17 and he **c** with a loud voice, saying to all *2896*

CRIES (1) [CRY]
Jas 5: 4 **c** of them which have reaped are entered *995*

CRIEST (5) [CRY]
Ex 14:15 unto Moses, Wherefore **c** thou unto me? *6817*
1Sa 26:14 and said, Who *art* thou *that* **c** to the king? *7121*
Pr 2: 3 if thou **c** after knowledge, *and* liftest up *7121*
Isa 57:13 When thou **c**, let thy companies deliver *2199*
Jer 30:15 Why **c** thou for thine affliction? *2199*

CRIETH (17) [CRY]
Ge 4:10 the voice of thy brother's blood **c** unto me *6817*
Ex 22:27 pass, when he **c** unto me, that I will hear; *6817*
Job 24:12 city, and the soul of the wounded **c** out: *7768*
Ps 72:2 For he shall deliver the needy when he **c**; *7768*
 84: 2 and my flesh **c** out for the living God. *7442*

Pr 1:20 Wisdom **c** without; she uttereth her voice 7442
1:21 She **c** in the chief place of concourse, 7121
8: 3 She **c** at the gates, at the entry of the city, 7442
9: 3 she **c** upon the highest places of the city, 7121
Isa 26:17 is in pain, *and* **c** out in her pangs; 2199
40: 3 The voice of him that **c** in the wilderness, 7121
Jer 12: 8 forest; it **c** out against me: 5414+6963+871.1
Mic 6: 9 The LORD's voice **c** unto the city, 7121
Mt 15:23 saying, Send her away; for she **c** after us. 2896
Lk 9:39 spirit taketh him, and he suddenly **c** out; 2896
Ro 9:27 Esaias also **c** concerning Israel, Though 2896
Jas 5: 4 which is of you kept back by fraud, **c**: 2896

CRIME (2) [CRIMES]
Job 31:11 this *is* a **heinous c**; yea, it *is* an iniquity 2154
Ac 25:16 concerning the **c** laid *against* him. 1462

CRIMES (2) [CRIME]
Eze 7:23 the land is full *of* bloody **c**, and the city 4941
Ac 25:27 not withal to signify the **c** *laid* against him. 156

CRIMINAL; CRIMINALS See MALEFACTOR; MALEFACTORS

CRIMSON (5)
2Ch 2: 7 **c**, and blue, and that can skill to grave 3758
2:14 in blue, and in fine linen, and in **c**; 3758
3:14 **c**, and fine linen, and wrought cherubims 3758
Isa 1:18 though they be red like **c**, they shall be as 8438
Jer 4:30 Though thou clothest thyself with **c**, 8144

CRIPPLE (1)
Ac 14: 8 feet, being a **c** from his mother's womb, 5560

CRISPING (1)
Isa 3:22 and the wimples, and the **c** pins, 2754

CRISPUS (2)
Ac 18: 8 And **C**, the *chief* ruler of the synagogue, 2921
1Co 1:14 I baptized none of you, but **C** and Gaius; 2921

CROOKBACKT (1) [BACK, CROOKED]
Lev 21:20 Or **c**, or a dwarf, or that hath a blemish in 1384

CROOKED (14) [CROOKBACKT]
Dt 32: 5 *they* are a perverse and **c** generation. 6618
Job 26:13 his hand hath formed the **c** serpent. 1281
Ps 125: 5 for such as turn aside *unto* their **c ways**, 6128
Pr 2:15 Whose ways *are* **c**, and *they* froward in 6141
Ecc 1:15 *That which is* **c** cannot be made straight: 5791
7:13 *that* straight, which he hath **made c**? 5791
Isa 27: 1 even leviathan *that* **c** serpent; 6129
40: 4 the **c** shall be made straight, and the 6121
42:16 light before them, and **c things** straight. 4625
45: 2 and make the **c places** straight: 1921
59: 8 they have **made** them **c** paths: 6140
La 3: 9 hewn stone, he hath **made** my paths **c**. 5753
Lk 3: 5 and the **c** shall be made straight, 4646
Php 2:15 in the midst of a **c** and perverse nation, 4646

CROP (2) [CROPT]
Lev 1:16 shall pluck away his **c** with his feathers, 4760
Eze 17:22 will set *it*; I will **c off** from the top of his 6998

CROPT (1) [CROP]
Eze 17: 4 He **c off** the top of his young twigs, 6998

CROSS (28) [CROSSWAY]
Mt 10:38 And he that taketh not his **c**, 4716
16:24 take up his **c**, and follow me. 4716
27:32 name: him they compelled to bear his **c**. 4716
27:40 the Son of God, come down from the **c**. 4716
27:42 let him now come down from the **c**, 4716
Mk 8:34 and take up his **c**, and follow me. 4716
10:21 and come, take up the **c**, and follow me. 4716
15:21 of Alexander and Rufus, to bear his **c**. 4716
15:30 Save thyself, and come down from the **c**. 4716
15:32 King of Israel descend now from the **c**, 4716
Lk 9:23 him deny himself, and take up his **c** daily, 4716
14:27 And whosoever doth not bear his **c**, 4716
23:26 the country, and on him they laid the **c**, 4716
Jn 19:17 he bearing his **c** went forth into a place 4716
19:19 Pilate wrote a title, and put *it* on the **c**. 4716
19:25 Now there stood by the **c** of Jesus his 4716
19:31 remain upon the **c** on the sabbath day, 4716
1Co 1:17 lest the **c** of Christ should be made of 4716
1:18 For the preaching of the **c** is to them that 4716
Gal 5:11 then is the offence of the **c** ceased. 4716
6:12 suffer persecution for the **c** of Christ. 4716
6:14 save in the **c** of our Lord Jesus Christ, 4716
Eph 2:16 both unto God in one body by the **c**, 4716
Php 2: 8 unto death, even the death of the **c**. 4716
3:18 *they* are the enemies of the **c** of Christ: 4716
Col 1:20 made peace through the blood of his **c**, 4716
2:14 took it out of the way, nailing it to *his* **c**; 4716
Heb 12: 2 joy that was set before him endured the **c**, 4716

CROSSWAY (1) [CROSS]
Ob 1:14 shouldest thou have stood in the **c**, 6563

CROUCH (1) [CROUCHETH]
1Sa 2:36 **c** to him for a piece of silver and a morsel 7812

CROUCHETH (1) [CROUCH]
Ps 10:10 He **c**, *and* humbleth himself, that the poor 1794

CROW (7) [COCKCROWING, CREW]
Mt 26:34 That this night, before *the* cock **c**, 5455
26:75 which said unto him, Before *the* cock **c**, 5455
Mk 14:30 in this night, before *the* cock **c** twice, 5455
14:72 Before *the* cock **c** twice, thou shalt deny 5455
Lk 22:34 Peter, *the* cock shall not **c** this day, 5455
22:61 Before *the* cock **c**, thou shalt deny me 5455
Jn 13:38 I say unto thee, *The* cock shall not **c**, 5455

CROWING See COCKCROWING

CROWN (66) [CROWNED, CROWNEDST, CROWNEST, CROWNETH, CROWNING, CROWNS]
Ge 49:26 on the **c of the head** of him *that* was 6936
Ex 25:11 make upon it a **c** of gold round about. 2213
25:24 and make thereto a **c** *of* gold round about. 2213
25:25 thou shalt make a golden **c** to the border 2213
29: 6 head, and put the holy **c** upon the mitre. 5145
30: 3 thou shalt make unto it a **c** *of* gold round 2213
30: 4 shalt thou make to it under the **c** of it, 2213
37: 2 and made a **c** *of* gold to it round about. 2213
37:11 made thereunto a **c** *of* gold round about. 2213
37:12 made a **c** of gold for the border thereof 2213
37:26 also he made unto it a **c** *of* gold round 2213
37:27 made two rings of gold for it under the **c** 2213
39:30 they made the plate of the holy **c** *of* pure 5145
Lev 8: 9 did he put the golden plate, the holy **c**; 5145
21:12 for the **c** of the anointing oil of his God *is* 5145
Dt 33:20 teareth the arm with the **c of the head**. 6936
2Sa 1:10 and I took the **c** that *was* upon his head, 5145
12:30 he took their king's **c** from off his head, 5850
14:25 **c** of his **head** there was no blemish in 6936
2Ki 11:12 put the **c** upon him, and *gave him* 5145
1Ch 20: 2 David took the **c** of their king from off his 5850
2Ch 23:11 put upon him the **c**, and *gave him* 5145
Est 1:11 queen before the king with the **c** royal, 3804
2:17 so that he set the royal **c** upon her head, 3804
6: 8 the royal which is set upon his head: 3804
8:15 *with* a great **c** of gold, and *with* a garment 5850
Job 2: 7 boils from the sole of his foot unto his **c** 6936
19: 9 my glory, and taken the **c** *from* my head. 5850
31:36 my shoulder, *and* bind it *as* a **c** to me. 5850
Ps 21: 3 thou settest a **c** of pure gold on his head. 5850
89:39 thou hast profaned his **c** *by* casting *it* to 5145
132:18 but upon himself shall his **c** flourish. 5145
Pr 4: 9 a **c** of glory shall she deliver *to* thee. 5850
12: 4 A virtuous woman *is* a **c** to her husband: 5850
14:24 The **c** of the wise *is* their riches: *but* 5850
16:31 The hoary head *is* a **c** of glory, *if* it be 5850
17: 6 Children's children *are* the **c** of old men; 5850
27:24 doth the **c** *endure* to every generation? 5850
SS 3:11 king Solomon with the **c** where*with* 5850
Isa 3:17 **c of the head** of the daughters of Zion, 6936
28: 1 Woe to the **c** of pride, to the drunkards of 5850
28: 3 The **c** of pride, the drunkards of Ephraim, 5850
28: 5 the LORD of hosts be for a **c** of glory, 5850
62: 3 Thou shalt also be a **c** of glory in the hand 5850
Jer 13:18 Tahapanes have broken the **c** of thy **head**. 6936
13:18 come down, *even* the **c** of your glory. 5850
48:45 the of **c of the head** of the tumultuous ones. 6936
La 5:16 The **c** is fallen *from* our head: woe to 5850
Eze 16:12 and a beautiful **c** upon thine head. 5850
21:26 Remove the diadem, and take off the **c**: 5850
Zec 9:16 for *they shall be as* the stones of a **c**, 5145
Mt 27:29 And when they had platted a **c** of thorns, 4735
Mk 15:17 and platted a **c** of thorns, and put *it* about 4735
Jn 19: 2 And the soldiers platted a **c** of thorns, 4735
19: 5 wearing the **c** of thorns, and the purple 4735
1Co 9:25 Now they *do it* to obtain a corruptible **c**; 4735
Php 4: 1 my joy and **c**, so stand fast in the Lord, 4735
1Th 2:19 what *is* our hope, or joy, or **c** of rejoicing? 4735
2Ti 4: 8 Henceforth there is laid up for me a **c** of 4735
Jas 1:12 he is tried, he shall receive the **c** of life, 4735
1Pe 5: 4 ye shall receive a **c** of glory that fadeth not 4735
Rev 2:10 unto death; and I will give thee a **c** of life. 4735
3:11 which thou hast, that no *man* take thy **c**. 4735
6: 2 had a bow; and a **c** was given unto him: 4735
12: 1 and upon her head a **c** of twelve stars: 4735
14:14 having on his head a golden **c**, and in his 4735

CROWNED (6) [CROWN]
Ps 8: 5 and hast **c** him *with* glory and honour. 5849
Pr 14:18 but the prudent are **c** *with* knowledge. 3803
SS 3:11 mother **c** him in the day of his espousals, 5849
Na 3:17 Thy **c** *are* as the locusts, and thy captains 4502
2Ti 2: 5 *yet* is he not **c**, except he strive lawfully. 4737
Heb 2: 9 of death, **c** with glory and honour; 4737

CROWNEDST (1) [CROWN]
Heb 2: 7 thou **c** him with glory and honour, 4737

CROWNEST (1) [CROWN]
Ps 65:11 Thou **c** the year with thy goodness; 5849

CROWNETH (1) [CROWN]
Ps 103: 4 who **c** thee *with* lovingkindness and 5849

CROWNING (1) [CROWN]
Isa 23: 8 the **c** *city*, whose merchants *are* princes, 5849

CROWNS (9) [CROWN]
Eze 23:42 and beautiful **c** upon their heads. 5850
Zec 6:11 make **c**, and set *them* upon the head of 5850
6:14 the **c** shall be to Helem, and to Tobijah, 5850

Rev 4: 4 and they had on their heads **c** of gold. 4735
4:10 ever, and cast their **c** before the throne, 4735
9: 7 on their heads *were* as *it were* **c** like gold, 4735
12: 3 ten horns, and seven **c** upon his heads. 1238
13: 1 and upon his horns ten **c**, and upon his 1238
19:12 of fire, and on his head *were* many **c**; 1238

CRUCIBLE See FINING POT

CRUCIFIED (37) [CRUCIFY]
Mt 26: 2 and the Son of man is betrayed to be **c**. 4717
27:22 *They* all say unto him, Let him be **c**. 4717
27:23 cried out the more, saying, Let him be **c**. 4717
27:26 scourged Jesus, he delivered *him* to be **c**. 4717
27:35 And they **c** him, and parted his garments, 4717
27:38 Then were there two thieves **c** with him, 4957
27:44 The thieves also, which were **c** with 4957
28: 5 I know that ye seek Jesus, which was **c**. 4717
Mk 15:15 when he had scourged *him*, to be **c**. 4717
15:24 when they had **c** him, they parted his 4717
15:25 it was the third hour, and they **c** him. 4717
15:32 that were **c** with him reviled him. 4957
16: 6 Ye seek Jesus of Nazareth, which was **c**: 4717
Lk 23:23 loud voices, requiring that he might be **c**. 4717
23:33 there they **c** him, and the malefactors, 4717
24: 7 and be **c**, and the third day rise again. 4717
24:20 be condemned to death, and have **c** him. 4717
Jn 19:16 he him therefore unto them to be **c**. 4717
19:18 Where they **c** him, and two other with 4717
19:20 for the place where Jesus was **c** was nigh 4717
19:23 Then the soldiers, when they had **c** Jesus, 4717
19:32 and of the other which was **c** with him. 4957
19:41 in the place where he was **c** there was 4717
Ac 2:23 and by wicked hands have **c** and slain: 4362
2:36 whom ye have **c**, both Lord and Christ. 4717
4:10 whom ye **c**, whom God raised from 4717
Ro 6: 6 that our old man is **c** with *him*, that 4957
1Co 1:13 was Paul **c** for you? or were ye baptized 4717
1:23 But we preach Christ **c**, unto the Jews a 4717
2: 2 among you, save Jesus Christ, and him **c**. 4717
2: 8 they would not have **c** the Lord of glory. 4717
2Co 13: 4 For though he was **c** through weakness, 4957
Gal 2:20 I am **c** with Christ: nevertheless I live; 4957
3: 1 been evidently set forth, **c** among you? 4717
5:24 And they that are Christ's have **c** the flesh 4717
6:14 by whom the world is **c** unto me, and I 4717
Rev 11: 8 and Egypt, where also our Lord was **c**. 4717

CRUCIFY (16) [CRUCIFIED]
Mt 20:19 to **c** *him*: and the third day he shall rise 4717
23:34 and *some* of them ye shall kill and **c**; 4717
27:31 on him, and led him away to **c** *him*. 4717
Mk 15:13 And they cried out again, **C** him. 4717
15:14 cried out the more exceedingly, **C** him. 4717
15:20 clothes on him, and led him out to **c** him. 4717
15:27 And with him they **c** two thieves; the one 4717
Lk 23:21 they cried, saying, **C** *him*, crucify him. 4717
23:21 they cried, saying, Crucify *him*, **c** him. 4717
Jn 19: 6 **C** him, crucify *him*. Pilate saith unto 4717
19: 6 Crucify *him*, **c** *him*. Pilate saith unto 4717
19: 6 and **c** *him*: for I find no fault in him. 4717
19:10 knowest thou not that I have power to **c** 4717
19:15 Away with *him*, away with *him*, **c** him. 4717
19:15 Pilate saith unto them, Shall I **c** your King? 4717
Heb 6: 6 to themselves the Son of God **afresh**, 388

CRUDDLED (1)
Job 10:10 me out as milk, and **c** me like cheese? 7087

CRUEL (19) [CRUELLY, CRUELTY]
Ge 49: 7 *it was* fierce; and their wrath, for it was **c**: 7185
Ex 6: 9 for anguish of spirit, and for **c** bondage. 7186
Dt 32:33 poison of dragons, and the **c** venom of asps. 393
Job 30:21 Thou art become **c** to me: with thy strong 393
Ps 25:19 and they hate me *with* **c hatred**. 2555+8135
71: 4 the hand of the unrighteous and **c** *man*. 2556
Pr 5: 9 unto others, and thy years unto the **c**: 394
11:17 but *he that is* **c** troubleth his own flesh. 394
12:10 but the tender mercies of the wicked *are* **c**. 394
17:11 a **c** messenger shall be sent against him. 394
27: 4 Wrath *is* **c**, and anger *is* outrageous; 395
SS 8: 6 strong as death; jealousy *is* **c** as the grave: 7186
Isa 13: 9 **c** both *with* wrath and fierce anger, to lay 394
19: 4 will I give over into the hand of a **c** lord; 7186
Jer 6:23 and spear; they *are* **c**, and have no mercy; 394
30:14 *with* the chastisement of a **c one**, 394
50:42 they *are* **c**, and will not shew mercy: 394
La 4: 3 the daughter of my people *is* become **c**, 393
Heb 11:36 And others had trial of **c** mockings and NIG

CRUELLY (1) [CRUEL]
Eze 18:18 father, because he **c** oppressed, 6231+6233

CRUELTY (5) [CRUEL]
Ge 49: 5 instruments of **c** *are in* their habitations. 2555
Jdg 9:24 That the **c** *done* to the threescore and 2555
Ps 27:12 up against me, and such as breathe out **c**. 2555
74:20 of the earth are full *of* the habitations of **c**. 2555
Eze 34: 4 with force and with **c** have ye ruled them. 6531

CRUMBLES See NOUGHT

CRUMBS (3)
Mt 15:27 yet the dogs eat of the **c** which fall from 5589
Mk 7:28 under the table eat of the children's **c**. 5589
Lk 16:21 desiring to be fed with the **c** which fell 5589

C

CRUSE (9)

1Sa	26:11 and the **c** of water, and let us go.	6835
	26:12 and the **c** of water from Saul's bolster,	6835
	26:16 and the **c** of water that *was at* his bolster.	6835
1Ki	14: 3 and a **c** of honey, and go to him:	1228
	17:12 of meal in a barrel, and a little oil in a **c**:	6835
	17:14 not waste, neither shall the **c** of oil fail,	6835
	17:16 wasted not, neither did the **c** of oil fail,	6835
	19: 6 on the coals, and a **c** of water *at* his head.	6835
2Ki	2:20 Bring me a new **c**, and put salt therein.	6746

CRUSH (4) [CRUSHED, CRUSHT]

Job	39:15 forgetteth that the foot may **c** them,	2115
La	1:15 hath called an assembly against me to **c**	7665
	3:34 To **c** under his feet all the prisoners of	1792
Am	4: 1 oppress the poor, which **c** the needy,	7533

CRUSHED (6) [CRUSH]

Lev	22:24 which is bruised, or **c**, or broken, or cut;	3807
Dt	28:33 thou shalt be only oppressed and **c** alway:	7533
Job	4:19 in the dust, which are **c** before the moth?	1792
	5: 4 far from safety, and they are **c** in the gate,	1792
Isa	59: 5 that which is **c** breaketh out *into* a viper.	2116
Jer	51:34 he hath **c** me, he hath made me an empty	2000

CRUSHT (1) [CRUSH]

Nu	22:25 and **c** Balaam's foot against the wall:	3905

CRY (181) [CRIED, CRIES, CRIEST, CRIETH, CRYING]

Ge	18:20 Because the **c** of Sodom and Gomorrah is	2201
	18:21 done altogether according to the **c** of it,	6818
	19:13 of them is waxen great before the	6818
	27:34 cried with a great and exceeding bitter **c**,	6818
Ex	2:23 their **c** came up unto God by reason of	7775
	3: 7 have heard their **c** by reason of their	6818
	3: 9 the **c** of the children of Israel is come unto	6818
	5: 8 therefore they **c**, saying, Let us go *and*	6817
	11: 6 there shall be a great **c** throughout all	6818
	12:30 and there was a great **c** in Egypt;	6818
	22:23 they **c** at all unto me, I will surely 6817+6818	
	22:23 at all unto me, I will surely hear their **c**;	6818
	32:18 neither *is it* the voice of *them that* **c** for	6030
Lev	13:45 upper lip, and shall **c**, Unclean, unclean.	7121
Nu	16:34 round about them fled at the **c** of them:	6963
Dt	15: 9 he **c** unto the LORD against thee, and it be	7121
	24:15 lest he **c** against thee unto the LORD,	7121
Jdg	10:14 **c** unto the gods which ye have chosen;	2199
1Sa	5:12 and the **c** of the city went up *to* heaven.	7775
	7: 8 Cease not to **c** unto the LORD our God for	2199
	8:18 ye shall **c** out in that day because of your	2199
	9:16 because their **c** is come unto me.	6818
2Sa	19:28 have I yet to **c** any more unto the king?	2199
	22: 7 temple, and my **c** *did enter* into his ears.	7775
1Ki	8:28 to hearken unto the **c** and to the prayer,	7440
	18:27 Elijah mocked them, and said, **C** aloud:	7121
2Ki	8: 3 she went forth to **c** unto the king for her	6817
2Ch	6:19 to hearken unto the **c** and the prayer	7440
	13:12 sounding trumpets to **c alarm** against you.	7321
	20: 9 **c** unto thee in our affliction, then thou	2199
Ne	5: 1 there was a great **c** of the people and	6818
	5: 6 I was very angry when I heard their **c** and	2201
	9: 9 and heardest their **c** by the Red sea;	2201
Est	4: 1 and cried *with* a loud and a bitter **c**;	2201
	9:31 the matters of the fastings and their **c**.	2201
Job	16:18 my blood, and let my **c** have no place.	2201
	19: 7 I **c** out *of wrong*, but I am not heard:	6817
	19: 7 I **c** aloud, but *there is* no judgment.	7768
	27: 9 Will God hear his **c** when trouble cometh	6818
	30:20 I **c** unto thee, and thou dost not hear me:	7768
	30:24 grave, though *they* **c** in his destruction.	7769
	31:38 my land **c** against me, or that the furrows	2199
	34:28 that *they* cause the **c** of the poor to come	6818
	34:28 and he heareth the **c** of the afflicted.	6818
	35: 9 they **make** *the oppressed* to **c**:	2199
	35: 9 they **c** out by reason of the arm of	7768
	35:12 There they **c**, but none giveth answer,	6817
	36:13 wrath: they **c** not when he bindeth them.	7768
	38:41 when his young ones **c** unto God,	7768
Ps	5: 2 Hearken unto the voice of my **c**, my King,	7773
	9:12 he forgetteth not the **c** of the humble.	6818
	17: 1 the right, O LORD, attend unto my **c**,	7440
	18: 6 my **c** came before him, *even* into his ears.	7775
	22: 2 I **c** in the daytime, but thou hearest not;	7121
	27: 7 Hear, O LORD, *when* I **c with** my voice:	7121
	28: 1 Unto thee will I **c**, O LORD, my rock;	7121
	28: 2 of my supplications, when I **c** unto thee,	7768
	34:15 and his ears *are open* unto their **c**.	7775
	34:17 *The righteous* **c**, and the LORD heareth,	6817
	39:12 O LORD, and give ear unto my **c**;	7775
	40: 1 and he inclined unto me, and heard my **c**.	7775
	55:17 and at noon, will I pray, and **c aloud**:	1993
	56: 9 When I **c** *unto thee*, then shall mine	7121
	57: 2 I will **c** unto God most High; unto God	7121
	61: 1 Hear my **c**, O God; attend unto my prayer.	7440
	61: 2 From the end of the earth will I **c** unto	7121
	86: 3 unto me, O Lord: for I **c** unto thee daily.	7121
	88: 2 before thee: incline thine ear unto my **c**;	7440
	89:26 He shall **c** unto me, Thou *art* my Father,	7121
	102: 1 O LORD, and let my **c** come unto thee.	7775
	106:44 their affliction, when he heard their **c**:	7440
	107:19 they **c** unto the LORD in their trouble,	2199
	107:28 they **c** unto the LORD in their trouble,	6817
	119:169 Let my **c** come near before thee,	7440
	141: 1 LORD, I **c unto** thee: make haste unto	7121
	141: 1 give ear unto my voice, when I **c** unto	7121

Ps	142: 6 Attend unto my **c**; for I am brought very	7440
	145:19 he also will hear their **c**, and will save	7775
	147: 9 food, *and* to the young ravens which **c**.	7121
Pr	8: 1 Doth not wisdom **c**? and understanding	7121
	21:13 Whoso stoppeth his ears at the **c** of	2201
	21:13 he also shall **c** himself, but shall not be	7121
Ecc	9:17 more than the **c** of him that ruleth among	2201
Isa	5: 7 for righteousness, but behold a **c**.	6818
	4 the child shall have knowledge to **c**,	7121
	12: 6 **C** out and shout, thou inhabitant of Zion:	6670
	13:22 the wild beasts of the islands shall **c** in	6030
	14:31 **c**, O city; thou, whole Palestina,	2199
	15: 4 Heshbon shall **c**, and Elealeh: their voice	2199
	15: 4 the armed soldiers of Moab shall **c** out;	7321
	15: 5 My heart shall **c** out for Moab;	2199
	15: 5 they shall raise up a **c** of destruction.	2201
	15: 8 the **c** is gone round about the borders of	2201
	19:20 for they shall **c** unto the LORD because of	6817
	24:14 they shall **c aloud** from the sea.	6670
	29: 9 and wonder; **c** ye out, and cry:	8173
	29: 9 and wonder; cry ye out, and **c**:	8173
	30:19 gracious unto thee at the voice of thy **c**;	2199
	33: 7 Behold, their valiant ones shall **c** without:	6817
	34:14 and the satyr shall **c** to his fellow;	7121
	40: 2 **c** unto her, that her warfare is	7121
	40: 6 The voice said, **C**. And he said, What shall	7121
	40: 6 he said, What shall I **c**? All flesh *is* grass,	7121
	42: 2 He shall not **c**, nor lift up, nor cause his	6817
	42:13 he shall **c**, yea, roar; he shall prevail	7321
	42:14 will I **c** like a travailing woman; I will	6463
	43:14 the Chaldeans, whose **c** *is* in the ships.	7440
	46: 7 yea, *one* shall **c** unto him, yet can he not	6817
	54: 1 break forth *into* singing, and **c aloud**,	6670
	58: 1 **C** aloud, spare not, lift up thy voice like a	7121
	58: 9 thou shalt **c**, and he shall say, Here I *am*.	7768
	65:14 ye shall **c** for sorrow of heart,	6817
Jer	2: 2 Go and **c** in the ears of Jerusalem, saying,	7121
	3: 4 Wilt thou not from this time **c** unto me,	7121
	4: 5 **c**, gather together, and say,	7121
	7:16 neither lift up **c** nor prayer for them,	7440
	8:19 Behold the voice of the **c** of the daughter	7775
	11:11 though they shall **c** unto me, I will not	2199
	11:12 unto the gods unto whom they offer	2199
	11:14 neither lift up a **c** or prayer for them:	7440
	11:14 time that they **c** unto me for their trouble.	7121
	14: 2 and the **c** of Jerusalem is gone up.	6682
	14:12 When they fast, I will not hear their **c**;	7440
	18:22 Let a **c** be heard from their houses,	2201
	20:16 let him hear the **c** in the morning,	2201
	22:20 Go up to Lebanon, and **c**; and lift up thy	6817
	22:20 voice in Bashan, and **c** from the passages:	6817
	25:34 Howl, ye shepherds, and **c**;	2199
	25:36 A voice of the **c** of the shepherds,	6818
	31: 6 upon the mount Ephraim shall **c**,	7121
	46:12 thy shame, and thy **c** hath filled the land:	6682
	46:17 They did **c** there, Pharaoh king of Egypt *is*	7121
	47: 2 the men shall **c**, and all the inhabitants of	2199
	48: 4 her little ones have caused a **c** to be heard.	2201
	48: 5 the enemies have heard a **c** of destruction.	6818
	48:20 howl and **c**; tell ye *it* in Arnon, that Moab	2199
	48:31 for Moab, and I will **c** out for all Moab;	2199
	48:34 From the **c** of Heshbon *even* unto Elealeh,	2201
	49: 3 **c**, ye daughters of Rabbah, gird ye with	6817
	49:21 the **c**, the noise thereof was heard in	6818
	49:29 they shall **c** unto them, Fear *is* on every	7121
	50:46 and the **c** is heard among the nations.	2201
	51:54 A sound of a **c** *cometh* from Babylon,	2201
La	2:19 Arise, **c** out in the night: in the beginning	7442
	3: 8 Also when I **c** and shout, he shutteth out	2199
	3:56 not thine ear at my breathing, at my **c**.	7775
Eze	8:18 though they **c** in mine ears *with* a loud	7121
	9: 4 that **c** for all the abominations that be done	602
	21:12 **C** and howl, son of man: for it shall be	2199
	24:17 Forbear to **c**, make no mourning *for*	602
	26:15 sound of the fall, when the wounded **c**,	602
	27:28 shake at the sound of the **c** of thy pilots.	2201
	27:30 shall **c** bitterly, and shall cast up dust upon	2199
Hos	8: 2 Israel shall **c** unto me, My God, we know	2199
Joel	1:14 your God, and **c** unto the LORD,	2199
	1:19 O LORD, to thee will I **c**: for the fire hath	7121
	1:20 The beasts of the field also **c** unto thee:	6165
Am	3: 4 will a young lion **c** out of his den,	5414+6963
Jnh	1: 2 Nineveh, *that* great city, and **c** against it;	7121
	3: 8 with sackcloth, and **c** mightily unto God:	7121
Mic	3: 4 shall they **c** unto the LORD, but he will	2199
	3: 5 that bite with their teeth, and **c**, Peace;	7121
	4: 9 Now why dost thou **c** out aloud?	7321+7452
Na	2: 8 *shall they* **c**; but none shall look back.	NIH
Hab	1: 2 long shall I **c**, and thou wilt not hear?	7768
	1: 2 *even* **c** out unto thee *of* violence,	2199
	2:11 For the stone shall **c** out of the wall,	2199
Zep	1:10 *that there shall be* the noise of a **c** from	6818
	1:14 the mighty *man* shall **c** there bitterly.	6873
Zec	1:14 **C** thou, saying, Thus saith the LORD of	7121
	1:17 **C** yet, saying, Thus saith the LORD of	7121
Mt	12:19 He shall not strive, nor **c**; neither shall	2905
	25: 6 And at midnight there was a **c** made,	2906
Mk	10:47 began to **c** out, and say, Jesus, *thou* Son	2896
Lk	18: 7 which **c** day and night unto him, though	994
	19:40 the stones would immediately **c** out.	2896
Ac	23: 9 And there arose a great **c**: and the scribes	2906
Ro	8:15 of adoption, whereby we **c**, Abba, Father.	2896
Gal	4:27 break forth and **c**, thou that travailest not:	994
Rev	14:18 cried with a loud **c** to him that had	2906

CRYING	(31) [CRY]	
1Sa	4:14 when Eli heard the noise of the **c**, he said,	6818
2Sa	13:19 laid her hand on her head, and went on **c**.	2199
Job	39: 7 neither regardeth he the **c** of the driver.	8663
Ps	69: 3 I am weary of my **c**: my throat is dried;	7121
Pr	19:18 hope, and let not thy soul spare for his **c**.	4191
	30:15 hath two daughters, **c**, Give, give.	NIH
Isa	22: 5 the walls, and of **c** to the mountains.	7771
	24:11 There *is* a **c** for wine in the streets; all joy	6682
	65:19 no more heard in her, nor the voice of **c**.	2201
Jer	48: 3 A voice of **c** *shall be* from Horonaim,	6818
Zec	7: 7 *with* shoutings, **c**, Grace, grace unto it.	NIH
Mal	2:13 *with* tears, *with* weeping, and *with* **c** out,	603
Mt	3: 3 The voice of one **c** in the wilderness,	994
	9:27 **c**, and saying, *Thou* Son of David,	2896
	21:15 and the children **c** in the temple,	2896
Mk	1: 3 The voice of one **c** in the wilderness,	994
	5: 5 **c**, and cutting himself with stones.	2896
	15: 8 the multitude **c aloud** began to desire	310
Lk	3: 4 The voice of one **c** in the wilderness,	994
	4:41 And devils also came out of many, **c** out,	2896
Jn	1:23 I *am* the voice of one **c** in the wilderness,	994
Ac	8: 7 For unclean spirits, **c** with loud voice,	2896
	14:14 and ran in among the people, **c** out,	2896
	17: 6 brethren unto the rulers of the city, **c**,	994
	21:28 **C** out, Men of Israel, help: This is the	2896
	21:36 multitude of the people followed *after*, **c**,	2896
	25:24 **c** that he ought not to live any longer.	1916
Gal	4: 6 his Son into your hearts, **c**, Abba, Father.	2896
Heb	5: 7 and supplications with strong **c** and	2906
Rev	14:15 **c** with a loud voice to him that sat on	2896
	21: 4 be no more death, neither sorrow, nor **c**,	2906

CRYSTAL	(5)	
Job	28:17 The gold and the **c** cannot equal it: and	2137
Eze	1:22 creature *was* as the colour of the terrible **c**,	7140
Rev	4: 6 throne *there was* a sea of glass like unto **c**:	2930
	21:11 *even* like a jasper stone, **clear as c**;	2929
	22: 1 clear as **c**, proceeding out of the throne of	2930

CUB; CUBS See WHELP; WHELPS

CUBIT (45) [CUBITS]

Ge	6:16 ark, and in a **c** shalt thou finish it above;	520
Ex	25:10 a **c** and a half the breadth thereof,	520
	25:10 and a **c** and a half the height thereof.	520
	25:17 and a **c** and a half the breadth thereof,	520
	25:23 a **c** the breadth thereof, and a cubit and	520
	25:23 and a **c** and a half the height thereof.	520
	26:13 a **c** on the one side, and a cubit on	520
	26:13 on the other side of that which	520
	26:16 a **c** and a half *shall* be the breadth of one	520
	30: 2 A **c** *shall be* the length thereof, and a cubit	520
	30: 2 length thereof, and a **c** the breadth thereof;	520
	36:21 The breadth of a board one a **c** and a half.	520
	37: 1 a **c** and a half the breadth of it, and a cubit	520
	37: 1 of it, and a **c** and a half the height of it:	520
	37: 6 and one a **c** and a half the breadth thereof,	520
	37:10 a **c** the breadth thereof, and a cubit and	520
	37:10 and a **c** and a half the height thereof:	520
	37:25 length of it *was* a **c**, and the breadth of it	520
	37:25 of it *was* a cubit, and the breadth of it a **c**;	520
Dt	3:11 the breadth of it, after the **c** of a man.	520
Jdg	3:16 dagger which had two edges, of a **c** length	1574
1Ki	7:24 ten in a **c**, compassing the sea round about	520
	7:31 within the chapiter and above *was* a **c**:	520
	7:31 *after* the work of the base, a **c** and a half:	520
	7:32 the height of a wheel *was* a **c** and half a	520
	7:32 height of a wheel *was* a cubit and half a **c**.	520
	7:35 *there* a round compass of half a **c** high:	520
2Ch	4: 2 ten in a **c**, compassing the sea round about.	520
Eze	40: 5 measuring reed of six cubits *long* by the **c**	520
	40:12 the little chambers *was* one **c** *on this side*,	520
	40:12 and the space *was* one **c** on that side:	520
	40:42 a **c** and a half long, and a cubit and a half	520
	40:42 a **c** and a half broad, and one cubit high:	520
	40:42 a cubit and a half broad, and one **c** high:	520
	42: 4 ten cubits breadth inward, a way of one **c**;	520
	43:13 The **c** *is* a cubit and a hand breadth; even	520
	43:13 The cubit *is* a **c** and a hand breadth; even	520
	43:13 the bottom *shall be* a **c**, and the breadth	520
	43:13 the breadth a **c**, and the border thereof by	520
	43:14 *shall be* two cubits, and the breadth one **c**.	520
	43:14 *shall be* four cubits, and the breadth one **c**.	520
	43:17 and the border about it *shall be* half a **c**;	520
	43:17 the bottom thereof *shall be* a **c** about:	520
Mt	6:27 thought can add one **c** unto his stature?	4083
Lk	12:25 thought can add to his stature one **c**?	4083

CUBITS (213) [CUBIT]

Ge	6:15 length of the ark *shall be* three hundred **c**,	520
	6:15 the breadth of it fifty **c**, and the height of it	520
	6:15 it fifty cubits, and the height of it thirty **c**.	520
	7:20 Fifteen **c** upward did the waters prevail;	520
Ex	25:10 **two c** and a half *shall be* the length thereof,	520
	25:17 **two c** and a half *shall be* the length thereof,	520
	25:23 **two c** *shall be* the length thereof, and a	520
	26: 2 of one curtain *shall be* eight and twenty **c**,	520
	26: 2 and the breadth of one curtain four **c**:	520
	26: 8 The length of one curtain *shall be* thirty **c**,	520
	26: 8 and the breadth of one curtain four **c**:	520
	26:16 Ten **c** *shall be* the length of a board,	520
	27: 1 five **c** long, and five cubits broad;	520
	27: 1 five cubits long, and five **c** broad;	520
	27: 1 and the height thereof *shall be* three **c**.	520

C

Ex	27: 9 linen of an hundred **c** long for one side:	520
	27:11 *shall be* hangings of an hundred **c** long,	NIH
	27:12 the west side *shall be* hangings of fifty **c**:	520
	27:13 on the east side eastward *shall be* fifty **c**.	520
	27:14 of one side **c** shall be an hundred	520
	27:15 fifteen **c**: their pillars three,	NIH
	27:16 the court *shall be* a hanging of twenty **c**,	520
	27:18 length of the court *shall be* an hundred **c**,	520
	27:18 the height five **c** of fine twined linen,	520
	30: 2 **two c** *shall be* the height thereof:	520
	36: 9 of one curtain *was* twenty and eight **c**,	520
	36: 9 and the breadth of one curtain four **c**:	520
	36:15 The length of one curtain *was* thirty **c**,	520
	36:15 and four **c** *was* the breadth of one curtain:	520
	36:21 The length of a board *was* ten **c**,	520
	37: 1 **two c** and a half *was* the length of it,	520
	37: 6 **two c** and a half *was* the length thereof,	520
	37:10 **two c** *was* the length thereof, and a cubit	520
	37:25 and **two c** *was* the height of it;	520
	38: 1 five **c** *was* the length thereof, and five	520
	38: 1 and five **c** the breadth thereof;	520
	38: 1 and three **c** the height thereof.	520
	38: 9 *were* of fine twined linen, an hundred **c**:	520
	38:11 side *the hangings were* an hundred **c**,	520
	38:12 for the west side *were* hangings of fifty **c**,	520
	38:13 And for the east side eastward fifty **c**.	520
	38:14 of the *one* side *of the gate were* fifteen **c**;	520
	38:15 and that hand, *were* hangings of fifteen **c**;	520
	38:18 twenty **c** *was* the length, and the height in	520
	38:18 the height in the breadth *was* five **c**,	520
Nu	11:31 as it were **two c** *high* upon the face of	520
	35: 4 and outward a thousand **c** round about.	520
	35: 5 the city on the east side two thousand **c**,	520
	35: 5 *on* the south side two thousand **c**, and *on*	520
	35: 5 *on* the west side two thousand **c**, and *on*	520
	35: 5 and *on* the north side two thousand **c**;	520
Dt	3:11 nine **c** *was* the length thereof, and four	520
	3:11 four **c** the breadth of it, after the cubit of a	520
Jos	3: 4 it, about two thousand **c** by measure:	520
1Sa	17: 4 Gath, whose height *was* six **c** and a span.	520
1Ki	6: 2 the length thereof *was* threescore **c**,	520
	6: 2 breadth thereof twenty **c**, and the height	NIH
	6: 2 *cubits*, and the height thereof thirty **c**.	520
	6: 3 twenty **c** *was* the length thereof, according	520
	6: 3 ten **c** *was* the breadth thereof before	520
	6: 6 The nethermost chamber *was* five **c** broad,	520
	6: 6 the middle *was* six **c** broad, and the third	520
	6: 6 and the third *was* seven **c** broad:	520
	6:10 chambers against all the house, five **c** high:	520
	6:16 he built twenty **c** on the sides of the house,	520
	6:17 *is*, the temple before it, *was* forty **c** long.	520
	6:20 the oracle in the forepart *was* twenty **c** in	520
	6:20 twenty **c** in breadth, and twenty cubits in	520
	6:20 and twenty **c** in the height thereof:	520
	6:23 cherubims of olive tree, each ten **c** high.	520
	6:24 five **c** *was* the one wing of the cherub,	520
	6:24 and five **c** the other wing of the cherub:	520
	6:24 the uttermost part of the other *were* ten **c**.	520
	6:25 the other cherub *was* ten **c**: both	520
	6:26 The height of the one cherub *was* ten **c**,	520
	7: 2 the length thereof *was* an hundred **c**,	520
	7: 2 the breadth thereof fifty **c**, and the height	520
	7: 2 fifty cubits, and the height thereof thirty **c**,	520
	7: 6 the length thereof *was* fifty **c**,	520
	7: 6 cubits, and the breadth thereof thirty **c**:	520
	7:10 stones of ten **c**, and stones of eight cubits.	520
	7:10 stones ten cubits, and stones of eight **c**.	520
	7:15 pillars of brass, of eighteen **c** high apiece:	520
	7:15 line of twelve **c** did compass either of them	520
	7:16 the height of the one chapiter *was* five **c**,	520
	7:16 the height of the other chapiter *was* five **c**:	520
	7:19 *were* of lily work in the porch, four **c**).	520
	7:23 ten **c** from the one brim to the other:	520
	7:23 round all about, and his height *was* five **c**:	520
	7:23 line of thirty **c** did compass it round about.	520
	7:27 four **c** *was* the length of one base,	520
	7:27 four **c** the breadth thereof, and three	520
	7:27 thereof, and three **c** the height of it.	520
	7:38 every laver was four **c**: *and* upon every	520
2Ki	14:13 unto the corner gate, four hundred **c**.	520
	25:17 height of the one pillar *was* eighteen **c**,	520
	25:17 the height of the chapiter three **c**;	520
1Ch	11:23 five **c** *high*; and in the Egyptian's hand *was*	520
2Ch	3: 3 The length by **c** after the first measure was	520
	3: 3 after the first measure *was* threescore **c**,	520
	3: 3 cubits, and the breadth twenty **c**.	520
	3: 4 twenty **c**, and the height *was* an hundred	520
	3: 8 twenty **c**, and the breadth thereof twenty	520
	3: 8 and the breadth thereof twenty **c**.	520
	3:11 the wings of the cherubims *were* twenty **c**	520
	3:11 *one* wing of the one *cherub was* five **c**,	520
	3:11 the other wing *was* likewise five **c**,	520
	3:12 *one* wing of the other *cherub was* five **c**,	520
	3:12 the other wing *was* five **c** *also*, joining to	520
	3:13 spread themselves forth twenty **c**:	520
	3:15 house two pillars of thirty and five **c** high,	520
	3:15 *was* on the top of *each* of them *was* five **c**.	520
	4: 1 twenty **c** the length thereof,	520
	4: 1 twenty **c** the breadth thereof, and ten	520
	4: 1 thereof, and ten **c** the height thereof.	520
	4: 2 Also he made a molten sea of ten **c** from	520
	4: 2 in compass, and five **c** the height thereof;	520
	4: 2 line of thirty **c** did compass it round about.	520
	6:13 of five **c** long, and five cubits broad,	520
	6:13 five **c** broad, and three cubits high,	520

2Ch	6:13 three **c** high, and had set it in the midst of	520
	25:23 Ephraim to the corner gate, four hundred **c**.	520
Ezr	6: 3 the height thereof threescore **c**,	521
	6: 3 *and* the breadth thereof threescore **c**,	521
Ne	3:13 thousand **c** on the wall unto the dung gate.	520
Est	5:14 Let a gallows be made of fifty **c** high,	520
	7: 9 Behold also, the gallows fifty **c** high,	520
Jer	52:21 the height of one pillar *was* eighteen **c**;	520
	52:21 a fillet of twelve **c** did compass it;	520
	52:22 the height of one chapiter *was* five **c**;	520
Eze	40: 5 the man's hand a measuring reed of six **c**	520
	40: 7 between the little chambers *were* five **c**;	520
	40: 9 measured he the porch of the gate, eight **c**;	520
	40: 9 the posts thereof, two **c**; and the porch of	520
	40:11 the breadth of the entry of the gate, ten **c**;	520
	40:11 *and* the length of the gate, thirteen **c**.	520
	40:12 the little chambers *were* six **c** on this side,	520
	40:12 cubits on this side, and six **c** on that side.	520
	40:13 the breadth *was* five and twenty **c**,	520
	40:14 He made also posts *of* threescore **c**,	520
	40:15 the front of the gate inner *were* fifty **c**.	520
	40:19 an hundred **c** east*ward* and north*ward*.	520
	40:21 the length thereof *was* fifty **c**,	520
	40:21 and the breadth five and twenty **c**.	520
	40:23 measured from gate to gate an hundred **c**.	520
	40:25 the length *was* fifty **c**, and the breadth five	520
	40:25 and the breadth five and twenty **c**.	520
	40:27 to gate toward the south an hundred **c**.	520
	40:29 it *was* fifty **c** long, and five and	520
	40:29 cubits long, and five and twenty **c** broad.	520
	40:30 round about *were* five and twenty **c** long,	520
	40:30 and twenty cubits long, and five **c** broad.	520
	40:33 it *was* fifty **c** long, and five and	520
	40:33 cubits long, and five and twenty **c** broad.	520
	40:36 the length *was* fifty **c**, and the breadth five	520
	40:36 and the breadth five and twenty **c**.	520
	40:47 an hundred **c** long, and an hundred cubits	520
	40:47 an hundred **c** broad, foursquare;	520
	40:48 five **c** on this side, and five cubits on that	520
	40:48 cubits on this side, and five **c** on that side:	520
	40:48 the breadth of the gate *was* three **c** on this	520
	40:48 cubits on this side, and three **c** on that side.	520
	40:49 The length of the porch *was* twenty **c**,	520
	40:49 twenty cubits, and the breadth eleven **c**;	520
	41: 1 six **c** broad on the one side, and six cubits	520
	41: 1 one side, and six **c** broad on the other side,	520
	41: 2 the breadth of the door *was* ten **c**;	520
	41: 2 the sides of the door *were* five **c** on the one	520
	41: 2 the one side, and five **c** on the other side:	520
	41: 2 he measured the length thereof, forty **c**:	520
	41: 2 forty cubits: and the breadth, twenty **c**.	520
	41: 3 measured the post of the door, two **c**;	520
	41: 3 door, six **c**; and the breadth of the door,	520
	41: 3 and the breadth of the door, seven **c**.	520
	41: 4 he measured the length thereof, twenty **c**;	520
	41: 4 the breadth, twenty **c**, before the temple:	520
	41: 5 he measured the wall of the house, six **c**;	520
	41: 5 the breadth of *every* side chamber, four **c**,	520
	41: 8 chambers *were* a full reed of six great **c**.	520
	41: 9 for the side chamber without, *was* five **c**:	520
	41:10 **c** round about the house on every side.	520
	41:11 place that was left *was* five **c** round about.	520
	41:12 end toward the west *was* seventy **c** broad;	520
	41:12 the wall of the building *was* five **c** thick	520
	41:12 about, and the length thereof ninety **c**.	520
	41:13 measured the house, an hundred **c** long;	520
	41:13 with the walls thereof, an hundred **c** long;	520
	41:14 place toward the east, an hundred **c**.	520
	41:15 side and of the other side, an hundred **c**,	520
	41:22 The altar *of* wood *was* three **c** high,	520
	41:22 cubits high, and the length thereof two **c**;	520
	42: 2 Before the length of an hundred **c** *was*	520
	42: 2 the north door, and the breadth *was* fifty **c**.	520
	42: 3 Over against the twenty **c** which *were* for	NIH
	42: 4 before the chambers *was* a walk of ten **c**	520
	42: 7 chambers, the length thereof *was* fifty **c**.	520
	42: 8 that *were* in the utter court *was* fifty **c**:	520
	42: 8 before the temple *were* an hundred **c**.	520
	43:13 *are* the measures of the altar after the **c**:	520
	43:14 *even* to the lower settle *shall be* two **c**,	520
	43:14 *even* to the greater settle *shall be* four **c**,	520
	43:15 So the altar *shall be* four **c**; and from	520
	43:16 the altar *shall be* twelve **c** long, twelve	NIH
	43:17 the settle *shall be* fourteen **c** long and	NIH
	45: 2 **c** round about for the suburbs thereof.	NIH
	46:22 *there were* courts joined of forty **c** long	NIH
	47: 3 east*ward*, he measured a thousand **c**,	520
Da	3: 1 whose height *was* threescore **c**,	521
	3: 1 *and* the breadth thereof six **c**:	521
Zec	5: 2 the length thereof *is* twenty **c**,	520
	5: 2 cubits, and the breadth thereof ten **c**.	520
Jn	21: 8 from land, but as it were two hundred **c**,)	4083
Rev	21:17 an hundred *and* forty and four **c**,	4083

CUCKOW (2)

Lev	11:16 and the **c**, and the hawk after his kind,	7828
Dt	14:15 and the **c**, and the hawk after his kind,	7828

CUCUMBERS (2)

Nu	11: 5 the **c**, and the melons, and the leeks,	7180
Isa	1: 8 as a lodge in a **garden of c**, as a besieged	4750

CUD (11)

Lev	11: 3 *is* clovenfooted, *and* cheweth **c**, among	1625
	11: 4 shall ye not eat of them that chew the **c**,	1625

Lev	11: 4 he cheweth the **c**, but divideth not	1625
	11: 5 he cheweth the **c**, but divideth not	1625
	11: 6 he cheweth the **c**, but divideth not	1625
	11: 7 clovenfooted, yet he cheweth not the **c**;	1625
	11:26 is not clovenfooted, nor cheweth the **c**,	1625
Dt	14: 6 *and* cheweth the **c** amongst the beasts:	1625
	14: 7 ye shall not eat of them that chew the **c**,	1625
	14: 7 they chew the **c**, but divide not the hoof;	1625
	14: 8 divideth the hoof, yet *cheweth* not the **c**,	1625

CULTIVATED See TILLED; TILLER; TILLEST; TILLETH

CUMBERED (1) [CUMBRANCE]

Lk	10:40 But Martha was **c** about much serving,	4049

CUMBERETH (1) [CUMBRANCE]

Lk	13: 7 none: cut it down; why **c** it the ground?	2673

CUMBRANCE (1) [CUMBERETH, CUMBERED]

Dt	1:12 How can I myself alone bear your **c**,	2960

CUMI (1)

Mk	5:41 the hand, and said unto her, TALITHA **C**;	2891

CUMMIN (4)

Isa	28:25 scatter the **c**, and cast in the principal	3646
	28:27 is a cart wheel turned about upon the **c**;	3646
	28:27 with a staff, and the **c** with a rod.	3646
Mt	23:23 for ye pay tithe of mint and anise and **c**,	2951

CUN See CHUN

CUNNING (33) [CUNNINGLY]

Ge	25:27 Esau was a **c** hunter, a man of the field;	3045
Ex	26: 1 cherubims of **c** work shalt thou make	2803
	26:31 scarlet, and fine twined linen of **c** work:	2803
	28: 6 and fine twined linen, with **c** work.	2803
	28:15 the breastplate of judgment with **c** work;	2803
	31: 4 To devise **c works**, to work in gold,	4284
	35:33 of wood, to make any *manner of* **c** work.	4284
	35:35 the **c workman**, and of the embroiderer,	2803
	35:35 and of **those that devise c work**.	2803+4284
	36: 8 with cherubims of **c** work made he them.	2803
	36:35 with cherubims made he it of **c** work.	2803
	38:23 **c workman**, and an embroiderer in blue,	2803
	39: 3 and in the fine linen, with **c** work.	2803
	39: 8 he made the breastplate of **c** work, like	2803
1Sa	16:16 a man, who *is* a **c** player on a harp:	3045
	16:18 *that is* **c** in playing, and a mighty valiant	3045
1Ki	7:14 and to work all works in brass.	1847
1Ch	22:15 all *manner of* **c** men for every *manner of*	2450
	25: 7 *even* all that were **c**, was two hundred	995
2Ch	2: 7 now therefore a man to work in gold,	2450
	2: 7 can skill to grave with the **c** men that	2450
	2:13 now I have sent a **c** man, endued with	2450
	2:14 thy **c** men, and with the cunning men	2450
	2:14 the **c** men of my lord David thy father.	2450
	26:15 invented by **c** men, to be on the towers	2803
Ps	137: 5 Jerusalem, let my right hand forget her **c**.	NIH
SS	7: 1 the work of the hands of a **c workman**.	542
Isa	3: 3 the artificer, and the eloquent orator.	2450
	40:20 he seeketh unto him a **c** workman to	2450
Jer	9:17 send for **c women**, that they may come:	2450
	10: 9 they *are* all the work of **c** men.	2450
Da	1: 4 **c** in knowledge, and understanding	3045
Eph	4:14 by the sleight of men, and **c craftiness**,	3834

CUNNINGLY (1) [CUNNING]

2Pe	1:16 we have not followed **c devised** fables,	4679

CUP (68) [CUPBEARER, CUPBEARERS, CUPS]

Ge	40:11 Pharaoh's **c** *was* in my hand: and I took	3563
	40:11 I pressed them into Pharaoh's **c**, and I gave	3563
	40:11 and I gave the **c** into Pharaoh's hand.	3563
	40:13 shalt deliver Pharaoh's **c** into his hand;	3563
	40:21 and he gave the **c** into Pharaoh's hand:	3563
	44: 2 put my **c**, the silver cup, in the sack's	1375
	44: 2 put my cup, the silver **c**, in the sack's	1375
	44:12 and the **c** was found in Benjamin's sack.	1375
	44:16 and *he* also with whom the **c** is found.	1375
	44:17 the man in whose hand the **c** is found,	1375
2Sa	12: 3 drank of his own **c**, and lay in his bosom,	3563
1Ki	7:26 thereof was wrought like the brim of a **c**,	3563
2Ch	4: 5 it like the work of the brim of a **c**,	3563
Ps	11: 6 this *shall be* the portion of their **c**.	3563
	16: 5 portion of mine inheritance and of my **c**:	3563
	23: 5 my head with oil; my **c** runneth over.	3563
	73:10 waters of a full **c** are wrung out to them.	NIH
	75: 8 For in the hand of the Lord *there is* a **c**,	3563
	116:13 will take the **c** of salvation, and call upon	3563
Pr	23:31 when it giveth his colour in the **c**,	3563
Isa	51:17 at the hand of the Lord the **c** of his fury;	3563
	51:17 thou hast drunken the dregs of the **c** of	3563
	51:22 I have taken out of thine hand the **c** of	3563
	51:22 *even* the dregs of the **c** of my fury;	3563
Jer	16: 7 neither shall *men* give them the **c** of	3563
	25:15 Take the wine **c** of this fury at mine hand,	3563
	25:17 took I the **c** at the Lord's hand,	3563
	25:28 if they refuse to take the **c** at thine hand to	3563
	49:12 to drink of the **c** have assuredly drunken;	3563
	51: 7 Babylon *hath been* a golden **c** in	3563
La	4:21 the **c** also shall pass through unto thee:	3563
Eze	23:31 therefore will I give her **c** into thine hand.	3563
	23:32 Thou shalt drink of thy sister's **c** deep and	3563
	23:33 the **c** of astonishment and desolation,	3563
	23:33 *with* the **c** of thy sister Samaria.	3563

C

Hab	2:16 the c of the LORD's right hand shall be	3563
Zec	12: 2 I will make Jerusalem a c of trembling	5592
Mt	10:42 c of cold *water* only in the name of a	4221
	20:22 Are ye able to drink of the c that I shall	4221
	20:23 Ye shall drink indeed of my c,	4221
	23:25 for ye make clean the outside of the c and	4221
	23:26 cleanse first that *which is* within the c	4221
	26:27 And he took the c, and gave thanks,	4221
	26:39 if it be possible, let this c pass from me:	4221
	26:42 if this c may not pass away from me,	4221
Mk	9:41 For whosoever shall give you a c of water	4221
	10:38 can ye drink of the c that I drink of?	4221
	10:39 Ye shall indeed drink of the c that I drink	4221
	14:23 he took the c, and when he had given	4221
	14:36 unto thee; take away this c from me:	4221
Lk	11:39 Pharisees make clean the outside of the c	4221
	22:17 And he took *the* cup, and gave thanks,	4221
	22:20 Likewise also the c after supper, saying,	4221
	22:20 This c is the new testament in my blood,	4221
	22:42 if thou be willing, remove this c from me:	4221
Jn	18:11 the c which my Father hath given me,	4221
1Co	10:16 The c of blessing which we bless, is it not	4221
	10:21 Ye cannot drink the c of the Lord,	4221
	10:21 the cup of the Lord, and the c of devils:	4221
	11:25 After the same manner also *he took* the c,	4221
	11:25 This c is the new testament in my blood:	4221
	11:26 as ye eat this bread, and drink this c,	4221
	11:27 and drink *this* c of the Lord unworthily,	4221
	11:28 him eat of *that* bread, and drink of *that* c.	4221
Rev	14:10 mixture into the c of his indignation;	4221
	16:19 to give unto her the c of the wine of	4221
	17: 4 having a golden c in her hand full of	4221
	18: 6 in the c which she hath filled fill to her	4221

CUPBEARER (1) [BEAR, CUP]

Ne	1:11 sight of this man. For I was the king's c.	8248

CUPBEARERS (2) [BEAR, CUP]

1Ki	10: 5 his c, and his ascent *by* which he went up	8248
2Ch	9: 4 his c also, and their apparel; and his	8248

CUPS (6) [CUP]

1Ch	28:17 the fleshhooks, and the bowls, and the c:	7184
Isa	22:24 of small quantity, from the vessels of c,	101
Jer	35: 5 c, and I said unto them, Drink ye wine.	3563
	52:19 candlesticks, and the spoons, and the c;	4518
Mk	7: 4 *as* the washing of cups, and pots,	4221
	7: 8 of men, *as* the washing of pots and c:	4221

CURE (5) [CURED, CURES]

Jer	33: 6 I *will* bring it health and c, and I will cure	4832
	33: 6 I will c them, and will reveal unto them	7495
Hos	5:13 yet could he not heal you nor c you of	1455
Mt	17:16 to thy disciples, and they could not c him.	2323
Lk	9: 1 authority over all devils, and to c diseases.	2323

CURED (4) [CURE]

Jer	46:11 many medicines; *for* thou shalt not be c.	8585
Mt	17:18 and the child was c from that *very* hour.	2323
Lk	7:21 And in that *same* hour he c many of *their*	2323
Jn	5:10 therefore said unto him that was c,	2323

CURES (1) [CURE]

Lk	13:32 and I do c to day and to morrow,	2392

CURIOUS (10) [CURIOUSLY]

Ex	28: 8 c **girdle** of the ephod, which *is* upon it,	2805
	28:27 above the c **girdle** of the ephod.	2805
	28:28 that *it* may be above the c **girdle** of	2805
	29: 5 gird him with the c **girdle** of the ephod:	2805
	35:32 to devise c **works**, to work in gold,	4284
	39: 5 c **girdle** of his ephod, that *was* upon it,	2805
	39:20 above the c **girdle** of the ephod.	2805
	39:21 that *it* might be above the c **girdle** of	2805
Lev	8: 7 he girded him with the c **girdle** of the	2805
Ac	19:19 Many also of them which used c **arts**	4021

CURIOUSLY (1) [CURIOUS]

Ps	139:15 c wrought in the lowest parts of the earth	7551

CURRENT (1)

Ge	23:16 of silver, c *money* with the merchant.	5674

CURRY FAVOR See INTREAT; INTREATED; INTREATIES; INTREATY

CURSE (101) [ACCURSED, CURSED, CURSEDST, CURSES, CURSEST, CURSETH, CURSING, CURSINGS]

Ge	8:21 I will not again c the ground any more for	7043
	12: 3 bless thee, and c him that curseth thee:	779
	27:12 I shall bring a c upon me, and not a	7045
	27:13 said unto him, Upon me *be* thy c, my son:	7045
Ex	22:28 the gods, nor c the ruler of thy people.	779
Lev	19:14 Thou shalt not c the deaf, nor put a	7043
Nu	5:18 hand the bitter water that **causeth** the c:	779
	5:19 bitter water that **causeth the** c:	779
	5:21 The LORD make thee a c and an oath	423
	5:22 this water that **causeth the** c shall go into	779
	5:24 drink the bitter water that **causeth the** c	779
	5:24 the water that **causeth the** c shall enter	779
	5:27 the water that **causeth the** c shall enter	779
	5:27 the woman shall be a c among her people.	423
	22: 6 therefore, I pray thee, c me this people;	779
	22:11 now, c me them; peradventure I shall	6895
	22:12 go with them; thou shalt not c the people:	779

Nu	22:17 I pray thee, c me this people.	6895
	23: 7 c me Jacob, and come, defy Israel.	779
	23: 8 shall I c, whom God hath not cursed?	5344
	23:11 I took thee to c mine enemies,	6895
	23:13 see them all: and c them from thence.	6895
	23:25 c them at all, nor bless them at all.	5344+5344
	23:27 that thou mayest c me them from thence.	6895
	24:10 I called thee to c mine enemies,	6895
Dt	11:26 set before you this day a blessing and a c;	7045
	11:28 c, if ye will not obey the commandments	7045
	11:29 Gerizim, and the c upon mount Ebal.	7045
	23: 4 Beor of Pethor of Mesopotamia, to c thee.	7043
	23: 5 the LORD thy God turned the c into a	7045
	27:13 these shall stand upon mount Ebal to c;	7045
	29:19 when he heareth the words of this c,	423
	30: 1 the blessing and the c, which I have set	7045
Jos	6:18 the camp of Israel a c, and trouble it.	2764
	24: 9 called Balaam the son of Beor to c you:	7043
Jdg	5:23 c ye Meroz, said the angel of the LORD,	779
	5:23 c ye bitterly the inhabitants thereof;	779
	9:57 upon them came the c of Jotham the son	7045
2Sa	16: 9 Why should this dead dog c my lord	7043
	16:10 so let him c, because the LORD hath said	7043
	16:10 the LORD hath said unto him, C David.	7043
	16:11 *do it?* let him alone, and let him c,	7043
1Ki	2: 8 which cursed me *with* a grievous c in	7045
2Ki	22:19 *they* should become a desolation and a c,	7045
Ne	10:29 and entered into a c, and into an oath,	423
	13: 2 against them, that he should c them:	7043
	13: 2 howbeit our God turned the c into a	7045
Job	1:11 he hath, and he will c thee to thy face.	1288
	2: 5 his flesh, and he will c thee to thy face.	1288
	2: 9 still retain thine integrity? c God, and die.	1288
	3: 8 Let them c it that curse the day, who are	5344
	3: 8 Let them curse it that c the day, who are	779
	31:30 mouth to sin by wishing a c to his soul.)	423
Ps	62: 4 with their mouth, but they c inwardly.	7043
	109:28 Let them c, but bless thou: when they	7043
Pr	3:33 The c of the LORD *is* in the house of	3994
	11:26 withholdeth corn, the people shall c him:	5344
	24:24 him shall the people c, nations shall abhor	5344
	26: 2 so the c causeless shall not come.	7045
	27:14 morning, it shall be counted a c to him.	7045
	28:27 that hideth his eyes shall have many a c.	3994
	30:10 lest he c thee, and thou be found guilty.	7043
Ecc	7:21 lest thou hear thy servant c thee:	7043
	10:20 C not the king, no not in thy thought;	7043
	10:20 and c not the rich in thy bedchamber:	7043
Isa	8:21 c their king and their God,	7043
	24: 6 Therefore hath the c devoured the earth,	423
	34: 5 upon the people of my c, to judgment.	2764
	43:28 have given Jacob to the c, and Israel to	2764
	65:15 ye shall leave your name for a c unto my	7621
Jer	15:10 usury; *yet* every one of them doth c me.	7043
	24: 9 reproach and a proverb, a taunt and a c,	7045
	25:18 an astonishment, a hissing, and a c;	7045
	26: 6 will make this city a c to all the nations of	7045
	29:18 be a c, and an astonishment, and a hissing,	423
	42:18 of them shall be taken up a c by all	7045
	42:18 an astonishment, and a c, and a reproach;	7045
	44: 8 that *ye* might be a c and a reproach	7045
	44:12 an astonishment, and a c, and a reproach.	7045
	44:22 an astonishment, and a c, without an	7045
	49:13 a desolation, a reproach, a waste, and a c;	7045
La	3:65 Give them sorrow of heart, thy c unto	8381
Da	9:11 therefore the c is poured upon us,	423
Zec	5: 3 This *is* the c that goeth forth over the face	423
	8:13 *that* as ye were a c among the heathen,	7045
Mal	2: 1 I will even send a c upon you,	3994
	2: 2 curse you, and will c your blessings:	779
	3: 9 Ye *are* cursed with a c: for ye *have* robbed	3994
	4: 6 lest I come and smite the earth *with* a c.	2764
Mt	5:44 Love your enemies, bless them that c you,	2672
	26:74 Then began he to c and to swear, *saying,*	2653
Mk	14:71 But he began to c and to swear, *saying,* I	332
Lk	6:28 Bless them that c you, and pray for them	2672
Ac	23:12 and **bound** themselves **under a** c,	332
	23:14 **bound** ourselves **under a great** c,	331+332
Ro	12:14 which persecute you: bless, and c not.	2672
Gal	3:10 of the works of the law are under the c:	2671
	3:13 Christ hath redeemed us from the c of	2671
	3:13 curse of the law, being made a c for us:	2671
Jas	3: 9 and therewith c we men, which are made	2672
Rev	22: 3 And there shall be no more c: but	2652

CURSED (72) [CURSE]

Ge	3:14 thou *art* c above all cattle, and above	779
	3:17 c *is* the ground for thy sake; in sorrow	779
	4:11 now *art* thou c from the earth, which hath	779
	5:29 of the ground which the LORD hath c.	779
	9:25 said, C *be* Canaan; a servant of servants	779
	27:29 c *be* every one that curseth thee;	779
	49: 7 C *be* their anger, for *it was* fierce;	779
Lev	20: 9 hath c his father or his mother;	7043
	24:11 blasphemed the name *of the LORD*, and c.	7043
	24:14 Bring forth him that hath c without	7043
	24:23 they should bring forth him that had c	7043
Nu	22: 6 blessed, and *he* whom thou cursest is c.	779
	23: 8 How shall I curse, whom God hath not c?	6895
	24: 9 thee, and c *is* he that curseth thee.	779
Dt	7:26 thine house, lest thou be a c thing like it:	2764
	7:26 shalt utterly abhor it; for it *is* a c *thing.*	2764
	13:17 shall cleave nought of the c **thing** to	2764
	27:15 the man that maketh *any* graven or	779
	27:16 C *be* he that setteth light by his father or	779

Dt	27:17 C *be* he that removeth his neighbour's	779
	27:18 C *be* he that maketh the blind to wander	779
	27:19 C *be* he that perverteth the judgment of	779
	27:20 C *be* he that lieth with his father's wife;	779
	27:21 C *be* he that lieth with any *manner of*	779
	27:22 C *be* he that lieth with his sister,	779
	27:23 C *be* he that lieth with his mother in law.	779
	27:24 C *be* he that smiteth his neighbour	779
	27:25 C *be* he that taketh reward to slay an	779
	27:26 C *be* he that confirmeth not *all* the words	779
	28:16 C *shalt* thou *be* in the city, and cursed	779
	28:16 in the city, and c *shalt* thou *be* in the field.	779
	28:17 C *shall* be thy basket and thy store.	779
	28:18 C *shall* be the fruit of thy body, and the	779
	28:19 C *shalt* thou *be* when thou comest in,	779
	28:19 and c *shalt* thou *be* when thou goest out.	779
Jos	6:26 saying, C *be* the man before the LORD,	779
	9:23 therefore ye *are* c, and there shall none	779
Jdg	9:27 and did eat and drink, and c Abimelech.	7043
	21:18 C *be* he that giveth a wife to Benjamin.	779
1Sa	14:24 C *be* the man that eateth *any* food until	779
	14:28 C *be* the man that eateth *any* food *this*	779
	17:43 And the Philistine c David by his gods.	7043
	26:19 of men, c *be* they before the LORD;	779
2Sa	16: 5 he came forth, and c still as he came.	7043
	16: 7 thus said Shimei when he c, Come out,	7043
	16:13 as he went, and threw stones at him,	7043
	19:21 because he c the LORD's anointed?	7043
1Ki	2: 8 c me *with* a grievous curse in the day	7043
	2:24 and c them in the name of the LORD.	779
	9:34 Go, see now this c *woman,* and bury her:	779
Ne	13:25 c them, and smote certain of them,	7043
Job	1: 5 have sinned, and c God in their hearts.	1288
	3: 1 this opened Job his mouth, and c his day.	7043
	5: 3 root: but suddenly I c his habitation.	5344
	24:18 the waters; their portion is c in the earth:	7043
Ps	37:22 and they that be c of him shall be cut off.	7043
	119:21 Thou hast rebuked the proud *that are* c,	779
Ecc	7:22 that thou thyself likewise hast c others.	7043
Jer	11: 3 C *be* the man that obeyeth not the words	779
	17: 5 C *be* the man that trusteth in man,	779
	20:14 C *be* the day wherein I was born: let not	779
	20:15 C *be* the man who brought tidings to my	779
	48:10 C *be* he that doeth the work of the LORD	779
	48:10 c *be* he that keepeth back his sword from	779
Mal	1:14 c *be* the deceiver, which hath in his flock	779
	2: 2 yea, I have c them already, because ye do	779
	3: 9 Ye *are* c with a curse: for ye *have* robbed	779
Mt	25:41 Depart from me, ye c, into everlasting fire,	2672
Jn	7:49 people who knoweth not the law are c.	1944
Gal	3:10 c is every one that continueth not in all	1944
	3:13 C *is* every one that hangeth on a tree:	1944
2Pe	2:14 with covetous practices; c children:	2671

CURSEDST (2) [CURSE]

Jdg	17: 2 about which thou c, and spakest of also in	422
Mk	11:21 fig tree which thou c is withered away.	2672

CURSES (8) [CURSE]

Nu	5:23 the priest shall write these c in a book,	423
Dt	28:15 that all these c shall come upon thee,	7045
	28:45 all these c shall come upon thee,	7045
	29:20 all the c that are written in this book shall	423
	29:21 according to all the c of the covenant that	423
	29:27 to bring upon it all the c that are written	7045
	30: 7 the LORD thy God will put all these c upon	423
2Ch	34:24 *even* all the c that are written in the book	423

CURSEST (1) [CURSE]

Nu	22: 6 *is* blessed, and *he* whom thou c is cursed.	779

CURSETH (10) [CURSE]

Ge	12: 3 that bless thee, and curse him that c thee:	7043
	27:29 cursed *be* every one that c thee,	779
Ex	21:17 he that c his father, or his mother,	7043
Lev	20: 9 every one that c his father or his mother	7043
	24:15 Whosoever c his God shall bear his sin.	7043
Nu	24: 9 blesseth thee, and cursed *is* he that c thee.	779
Pr	20:20 Whoso c his father or his mother,	7043
	30:11 *There is* a generation *that* c their father,	7043
Mt	15: 4 He that c father or mother, let him die	2551
Mk	7:10 Whoso c father or mother, let him die	2551

CURSING (12) [CURSE]

Nu	5:21 shall charge the woman with an oath of c,	423
Dt	28:20 The LORD shall send upon thee c,	3994
	30:19 before you life and death, blessing and c:	7045
2Sa	16:12 will requite me good for his c this day.	7045
Ps	10: 7 His mouth is full of c and deceit and fraud:	423
	59:12 and for c and lying *which* they speak.	423
	109:17 As he loved c, so let it come *unto* him: as	7045
	109:18 As he clothed himself with c like as with	7045
Pr	29:24 he heareth c, and bewrayeth *it* not.	423
Ro	3:14 Whose mouth is full of c and bitterness:	685
Heb	6: 8 and briers *is* rejected, and *is* nigh unto c;	2671
Jas	3:10 same mouth proceedeth blessing and c.	2671

CURSINGS (1) [CURSE]

Jos	8:34 the words of the law, the blessings and c,	7045

CURTAIN (26) [CURTAINS]

Ex	26: 2 The length of one c *shall* be eight and	3407
	26: 2 and the breadth of one c four cubits:	3407
	26: 4 one c from the selvedge in the coupling;	3407
	26: 4 make in the uttermost edge of *another* c,	3407

C

Ex	26: 5	Fifty loops shalt thou make in the one **c**,	3407
	26: 5	the **c** that *is* in the coupling of the second;	3407
	26: 8	The length of one *shall be* thirty cubits,	3407
	26: 8	and the breadth of one **c** four cubits:	3407
	26: 9	shalt double the sixth in the forefront of	3407
	26:10	the one **c** that is outmost in the coupling,	3407
	26:10	fifty loops in the edge of the **c** which	3407
	26:12	the half **c** that remaineth, shall hang over	3407
	36: 9	The length of one **c** was twenty and	3407
	36: 9	and the breadth of one **c** four cubits:	3407
	36:11	made loops of blue on the edge of one **c**	3407
	36:11	made in the uttermost side of *another* **c**,	3407
	36:12	fifty loops made he in one **c**,	3407
	36:12	fifty loops made he in the edge of the **c**	3407
	36:12	second: the loops held one **c** to another.	NIH
	36:15	The length of one **c** was thirty cubits,	3407
	36:15	and four cubits *was* the breadth of one **c**:	3407
	36:17	uttermost edge of the **c** in the coupling,	3407
	36:17	loops made he upon the edge of the **c**	3407
Nu	3:26	the **c** for the door of the court, which *is*	4539
Ps	104: 2	who stretchest out the heavens like a **c**:	3407
Isa	40:22	that stretcheth out the heavens as a **c**,	1852

CURTAINS (31) [CURTAIN]

Ex	26: 1	tabernacle *with* ten **c** *of* fine twined linen,	3407
	26: 2	every one of the **c** shall have one measure.	3407
	26: 3	The five **c** shall be coupled together one to	3407
	26: 3	five **c** *shall be* coupled one to another.	3407
	26: 6	and couple the **c** together with the taches:	3407
	26: 7	thou shalt make **c** *of* goats' *hair* to be a	3407
	26: 7	the tabernacle: eleven **c** shalt thou make.	3407
	26: 8	the eleven **c** *shall be* all of one measure.	3407
	26: 9	thou shalt couple five **c** by themselves,	3407
	26: 9	six **c** by themselves, and shalt double	3407
	26:12	the remnant that remaineth of the **c** of	3407
	26:13	in the length of the **c** of the tent,	3407
	36: 8	made ten **c** *of* fine twined linen,	3407
	36: 9	four cubits: the **c** *were* all of one size.	3407
	36:10	he coupled the five **c** one unto another:	3407
	36:10	the *other* five **c** he coupled one unto	3407
	36:13	coupled the **c** one unto another with	3407
	36:14	he made **c** *of* goats' *hair* for the tent over	3407
	36:14	the tabernacle: eleven **c** he made them.	3407
	36:15	curtain: the eleven **c** *were* of one size.	3407
	36:16	he coupled five **c** by themselves, and six	3407
	36:16	by themselves, and six **c** by themselves.	3407
Nu	4:25	they shall bear the **c** of the tabernacle,	3407
2Sa	7: 2	but the ark of God dwelleth within **c**.	3407
1Ch	17: 1	covenant of the LORD *remaineth* under **c**.	3407
SS	1: 5	the tents of Kedar, as the **c** of Solomon.	3407
Isa	54: 2	let them stretch forth the **c** of thine	3407
Jer	4:20	my tents spoiled, *and* my **c** in a moment.	3407
	10:20	my tent any more, and to set up my **c**.	3407
	49:29	they shall take to themselves their **c**,	3407
Hab	3: 7	the **c** of the land of Midian did tremble.	3407

CUSH (8)

Ge	10: 6	**C**, and Mizraim, and Phut, and Canaan.	3568
	10: 7	the sons of **C**; Seba, and Havilah,	3568
	10: 8	begat Nimrod: he began to be a mighty	3568
1Ch	1: 8	Ham; **C**, and Mizraim, Put, and Canaan.	3568
	1: 9	the sons of **C**; Seba, and Havilah,	3568
	1:10	begat Nimrod: he began to be mighty	3568
Ps	7: T	concerning the words of **C** the Benjamite.	3568
Isa	11:11	from **C**, and from Elam, and from Shinar,	3568

CUSHAN (1)

Hab	3: 7	I saw the tents of **C** in affliction: *and*	3572

CUSHAN-RISHATHAIM See
CHUSHAN-RISHATHAIM

CUSHI (10)

2Sa	18:21	said Joab to **C**, Go tell the king what thou	3569
	18:21	And **C** bowed himself unto Joab, and ran.	3569
	18:22	let me, I pray thee, also run after **C**.	3569
	18:23	*by* the way of the plain, and overran **C**.	3569
	18:31	behold, **C** came; and Cushi said, Tidings,	3569
	18:31	and **C** said, Tidings, my lord the king:	3569
	18:32	the king said unto **C**, *Is* the young man	3569
	18:32	**C** answered, The enemies of my lord	3569
Jer	36:14	the son of **C**, unto Baruch, saying,	3569
Zep	1: 1	which came unto Zephaniah the son of **C**,	3569

CUSTODY (5)

Nu	3:36	under the **c** and charge of the sons of	6486
Est	2: 3	to the **c** of Hege the king's chamberlain,	3027
	2: 8	to the **c** of Hegai, that Esther was brought	3027
	2: 8	to the **c** of Hegai, keeper of the women,	3027
	2:14	to the **c** of Shaashgaz, the king's	3027

CUSTOM (20) [ACCUSTOMED, CUSTOMS]

Ge	31:35	thee; for the **c** of women *is* upon me.	1870
Jdg	11:39	knew no man. And it was a **c** in Israel,	2706
1Sa	2:13	the priests' **c** with the people was, *that*	4941
Ezr	3: 4	*according to* the **c**, as the duty of every	3509.1
	4:13	**c**, and *so* thou shalt endamage the	1983
	4:20	toll, tribute, and **c**, *was* paid unto them.	1983
	7:24	to impose toll, tribute, or **c**, upon them.	1983
Jer	32:11	was sealed *according to* the law and **c**,	2706
Mt	9: 9	Matthew, sitting at the **receipt of c**:	5058
	17:25	of whom do the kings of the earth take **c**	5056
Mk	2:14	*son* of Alpheus sitting at the **receipt of c**,	5058
Lk	1: 9	According to the **c** of the priest's office,	1485
	2:27	to do for him after the **c** of the law,	1480
	2:42	they went up to Jerusalem after the **c** of	1485

Lk	4:16	and, as his **c** was, he went into	1486
	5:27	named Levi, sitting at the **receipt of c**:	5058
Jn	18:39	But ye have a **c**, that I should release unto	4914
Ro	13: 7	tribute to whom tribute *is due;* **c** to whom	5056
	13: 7	whom tribute *is due;* custom to whom **c**;	5056
1Co	11:16	we have no such **c**, neither the churches	4914

CUSTOMS (7) [CUSTOM]

Lev	18:30	not *any one* of *these* abominable **c**,	2708
Jer	10: 3	For the **c** of the people *are* vain: for *one*	2708
Ac	6:14	shall change the **c** which Moses delivered	1485
	16:21	teach **c**, which are not lawful for us to	1485
	21:21	children, neither to walk after the **c**.	1485
	26: 3	*I know* thee to be expert in all **c** and	1485
	28:17	against the people, or **c** of our fathers,	1485

CUT (320) [CUTTEST, CUTTETH, CUTTING, CUTTINGS]

Ge	9:11	neither shall all flesh be **c off** any more	3772
	17:14	that soul shall be **c off** from his people;	3772
Ex	4:25	**c off** the foreskin of her son, and cast *it* at	3772
	9:15	and thou shalt be **c off** from the earth.	3582
	12:15	that soul shall be **c off** from Israel.	3772
	12:19	even that soul shall be **c off** from	3772
	23:23	and the Jebusites: and I will **c** them **off**.	3582
	29:17	thou shalt **c** the ram in pieces, and wash	5408
	30:33	shall even be **c off** from his people.	3772
	30:38	shall even be **c off** from his people.	3772
	31:14	that soul shall be **c off** from amongst his	3772
	34:13	their images, and **c down** their groves:	3772
	39: 3	**c** *it* into wires, to work *it* in the blue,	7112
Lev	1: 6	the burnt offering, and **c** it into his pieces.	5408
	1:12	he shall **c** it into his pieces, with his head	5408
	7:20	even that soul shall be **c off** from his	3772
	7:21	even that soul shall be **c off** from his	3772
	7:25	even the soul that eateth *it* shall be **c off**	3772
	7:27	even that soul shall be **c off** from his	3772
	8:20	he **c** the ram into pieces; and Moses	5408
	17: 4	that man shall be **c off** from among his	3772
	17: 9	even that man shall be **c off** from among	3772
	17:10	will **c** him **off** from among his people.	3772
	17:14	whosoever eateth it shall be **c off**.	3772
	18:29	shall be **c off** from among their people.	3772
	19: 8	that soul shall be **c off** from among his	3772
	20: 3	will **c** him **off** from among his people;	3772
	20: 5	will **c** him **off**, and all that go a whoring	3772
	20: 6	will **c** him **off** from among his people.	3772
	20:17	they shall be **c off** in the sight of their	3772
	20:18	both of them shall be **c off** from among	3772
	22: 3	that soul shall be **c off** from my presence:	3772
	22:24	is bruised, or crushed, or broken, or **c**;	3772
	23:29	he shall be **c off** from among his people.	3772
	26:30	**c down** your images, and cast your	3772
Nu	4:18	Ye not off the tribe of the families of	3772
	9:13	even the same soul shall be **c off** from	3772
	13:23	**c down** from thence a branch with one	3772
	13:24	children of Israel **c down** from thence.	3772
	15:30	that soul shall be **c off** from among his	3772
	15:31	that soul **utterly** be **c off**; 3772+3772	
	19:13	and that soul shall be **c off** from Israel:	3772
	19:20	that soul shall be **c off** from among	3772
Dt	7: 5	**c down** their groves, and burn their	1438
	12:29	When the LORD thy God shall **c off**	3772
	14: 1	ye shall not **c** yourselves, nor make *any*	1413
	19: 1	When the LORD thy God hath **c off**	3772
	19: 5	a stroke with the axe to **c down** the tree,	3772
	20:19	thou shalt not **c** them **down** (for the tree	3772
	20:20	thou shalt destroy and **c** them **down**;	3772
	23: 1	stones, or hath *his* privy member **c off**,	3772
	25:12	thou shalt **c off** her hand, thine eye shall	7112
Jos	3:13	the waters of Jordan shall be **c off** *from*	3772
	3:16	*even* the salt sea, failed, *and* were **c off**:	3772
	4: 7	the waters of Jordan were **c off** before	3772
	4: 7	the waters of Jordan were **c off**:	3772
	7: 9	and **c off** our name from the earth:	3772
	11:21	the Anakims from the mountains,	3772
	17:15	**c down** for thyself there in the land of	1254
	17:18	it *is* a wood, and thou shalt **c** it **down**:	1254
	23: 4	with all the nations that I have **c off**,	3772
Jdg	1: 6	and **c off** his thumbs and his great toes.	7112
	1: 7	their thumbs and their great toes **c off**,	7112
	6:25	and **c down** the grove that *is* by it:	3772
	6:26	of the grove which thou shalt **c down**.	3772
	6:28	the grove was **c down** that *was* by it,	3772
	6:30	he hath **c down** the grove that *was* by it.	3772
	9:48	**c down** a bough from the trees, and took	3772
	9:49	all the people likewise **c down** every man	3772
	20: 6	**c** her **in pieces**, and sent her throughout	5408
	21: 6	is one tribe **c off** from Israel this day.	1438
Ru	4:10	the name of the dead be not **c off** from	3772
1Sa	2:31	that I will **c off** thine arm, and the arm of	1438
	2:33	*whom* I shall not **c off** from mine altar,	3772
	5: 4	the palms of his hands *were* **c off** upon	3772
	17:51	slew him, and **c off** his head therewith.	3772
	20:15	thou shalt not **c off** thy kindness from	3772
	20:15	not when the LORD hath **c off**	3772
	24: 4	and **c off** the skirt of Saul's robe privily.	3772
	24: 5	because he had **c off** Saul's skirt.	3772
	24:11	for in that I **c off** the skirt of thy robe,	3772
	24:21	that thou wilt not **c off** my seed after me,	3772
	28: 9	how he hath **c off** those that have familiar	3772
	31: 9	they **c off** his head, and stripped off his	3772
2Sa	4:12	**c off** their hands and their feet,	7112
	7: 9	have **c off** all thine enemies out of thy	3772
	10: 4	**c off** their garments in the middle,	3772

2Sa	20:22	they **c off** the head of Sheba the son of	3772
1Ki	9: 7	will I **c off** Israel out of the land which I	3772
	11:16	until he had **c off** every male in Edom:)	3772
	13:34	even to **c** *it* **off**, and to destroy *it* from	3582
	14:10	will **c off** from Jeroboam *him that* pisseth	3772
	14:14	who shall **c off** the house of Jeroboam	3772
	18: 4	when Jezebel **c off** the prophets of	3772
	18:23	**c** it **in pieces**, and lay *it* on wood,	5408
	18:28	**c** themselves after their manner with	1413
	18:33	**c** the bullock **in pieces**, and laid *him* on	5408
	21:21	will **c off** from Ahab *him that* pisseth	3772
2Ki	6: 4	they came to Jordan, they **c down** wood.	1504
	6: 6	he **c down** a stick, and cast *it* in thither;	7094
	9: 8	I will **c off** from Ahab *him that* pisseth	3772
	10:32	days the LORD began to **c** Israel **short**:	7096
	16:17	king Ahaz **c off** the borders of the bases,	7112
	18: 4	**c down** the groves, and brake in pieces	3772
	18:16	At that time did Hezekiah **c off** *the gold*	7112
	19:23	will **c down** the tall cedar trees thereof,	3772
	23:14	**c down** the groves, and filled their places	3772
	24:13	**c in pieces** all the vessels of gold which	7112
1Ch	17: 8	have **c off** all thine enemies from before	3772
	19: 4	**c off** their garments in the midst hard by	3772
	20: 3	**c** *them* with saws, and with harrows of	7787
2Ch	2: 8	for I know that thy servants can skill to **c**	3772
	2:10	to thy servants, the hewers that **c** timber,	3772
	2:16	we will **c** wood out of Lebanon, as much	3772
	14: 3	down the images, and **c down** the groves:	1438
	15:16	Asa **c down** her idol, and stamped *it*, and	3772
	22: 7	whom the LORD had anointed to **c off**	3772
	26:21	for he was **c off** from the house of	1504
	28:24	**c in pieces** the vessels of the house of	7112
	31: 1	images *in pieces*, and **c down** the groves,	1438
	32:21	which **c off** all the mighty *men* of valour,	3582
	34: 4	*were* on high above them, he **c down**;	1438
	34: 7	**c down** all the idols throughout all the	1438
Job	4: 7	or where were the righteous **c off**?	3582
	6: 9	he would let loose his hand, and **c** me **off**!	1214
	8:12	it *is* yet in his greenness, *and* not **c down**,	6998
	8:14	Whose hope shall be **c off**, and whose	6990
	11:10	If he **c off**, and shut up, or gather	2498
	14: 2	forth like a flower, and is **c down**:	5243
	14: 7	if it be **c down**, that it will sprout again,	3772
	18:16	above shall his branch be **c off**.	5243
	21:21	of his months is **c off in the midst**?	2686
	22:16	Which were **c down** out of time,	7059
	22:20	Whereas our substance is not **c down**,	3582
	23:17	Because I was not **c off** before	6789
	24:24	and **c off** as the tops of the ears of corn.	5243
	30: 4	Who **c up** mallows by the bushes,	6998
	36:20	when people are **c off** in their place.	5927
Ps	12: 3	The LORD shall **c off** all flattering lips,	3772
	31:22	I am **c off** from before thine eyes:	1629
	34:16	to **c off** the remembrance of them from	3772
	37: 2	For they shall soon be **c down** like	5243
	37: 9	For evildoers shall be **c off**: but those that	3772
	37:22	they that be cursed of him shall be **c off**.	3772
	37:28	but the seed of the wicked shall be **c off**.	3772
	37:34	when the wicked are **c off**, thou shalt see	3772
	37:38	the end of the wicked shall be **c off**.	3772
	54: 5	mine enemies: **c** them **off** in thy truth.	6789
	58: 7	his arrows, let them be as **c in pieces**.	4135
	75:10	the horns of the wicked also will I **c off**;	1438
	76:12	He shall **c off** the spirit of princes: *he is*	1219
	80:16	*It is* burnt with fire, *it is* **c down**:	3683
	83: 4	and let us **c** them **off** from *being* a nation;	3582
	88: 5	and they are **c off** from thy hand.	1504
	88:16	goeth over me; thy terrors have **c** me **off**.	6789
	90: 6	the evening it is **c down**, and withereth.	4135
	90:10	for it is soon **c off**, and we fly away.	1468
	94:23	shall **c** them **off** in their own wickedness;	6789
	94:23	yea, the LORD our God shall **c** them **off**.	6789
	101: 5	slandereth his neighbour, him will I **c off**:	6789
	101: 8	that *I* may **c off** all wicked doers from	3772
	107:16	of brass, and **c** the bars of iron **in sunder**.	1438
	109:13	Let his posterity be **c off**; *and in*	3772
	109:15	that he may **c off** the memory of them	3772
	129: 4	hath **c asunder** the cords of the wicked.	7112
	143:12	of thy mercy **c off** mine enemies,	6789
Pr	2:22	the wicked shall be **c off** from the earth,	3772
	10:31	but the froward tongue shall be **c out**.	3772
	23:18	and thine expectation shall not be **c off**.	3772
	24:14	and thy expectation shall not be **c off**.	3772
Isa	9:10	the sycomores are **c down**, but we will	1438
	9:14	Therefore the LORD will **c off** from Israel	3772
	10: 7	to destroy and **c off** nations not a few.	3772
	10:34	he shall **c down** the thickets of the forest	5362
	11:13	the adversaries of Judah shall be **c off**:	3772
	14:12	*how* art thou **c down** to the ground,	1438
	14:22	**c off** from Babylon the name,	3772
	15: 2	*shall be* baldness, *and* every beard **c off**.	1438
	18: 5	he shall both **c off** the sprigs with pruning	3772
	18: 5	and take away *and* **c down** the branches.	8456
	22:25	be removed, and be **c down**, and fall;	1438
	22:25	burden that *was* upon it shall be **c off**:	3772
	29:20	and all that watch for iniquity are **c off**:	3772
	33:12	as thorns **c up** shall they be burnt in	3683
	37:24	I will **c down** the tall cedars thereof,	3772
	38:12	I have **c off** like a weaver my life: he will	7088
	38:12	he will **c** me **off** with pining sickness:	1214
	45: 2	of brass, and **c in sunder** the bars of iron:	1438
	48: 9	will I refrain for thee, that *I* **c** thee not **off**.	3772
	48:19	his name should not have been **c off** nor	3772
	51: 9	*Art* thou not it that hath **c** Rahab,	2672
	53: 8	for he was **c off** out of the land of	1504

D

Isa	55:13 an everlasting sign *that* shall not be **c off**.	3772
	56: 5 everlasting name, that shall not be **c off**	3772
	66: 3 a lamb, *as if* he **c off** a dog's **neck**;	6202
Jer	7:28 is perished, and is **c off** from their mouth.	3772
	7:29 **C off** thine hair, O *Jerusalem*, and cast *it*	1494
	9:21 to **c off** the children from without,	3772
	11:19 us **c off** from the land of the living,	3772
	16: 6 *men* lament for them, nor **c** themselves,	1413
	22: 7 they shall **c down** thy choice cedars,	3772
	25:37 the peaceable habitations are **c down**	1826
	34:18 when they **c** the calf in twain,	3772
	36:23 he **c** it with the penknife, and cast *it* into	7167
	41: 5 having **c** themselves, with offerings and	1413
	44: 7 to **c off** from you man and woman, child	3772
	44: 8 that ye might **c** yourselves **off**, and that	3772
	44:11 against you for evil, and to **c off** all Judah.	3772
	46:23 They shall **c down** her forest, saith	3772
	47: 4 *and* to **c off** from Tyrus and Zidon every	3772
	47: 5 with the remnant of	1820
	47: 5 their valley: how long wilt thou **c** thyself?	1413
	48: 2 and let us **c** it **off** from *being* a nation.	3772
	48: 2 Also thou shalt be **c down**, O Madmen;	1826
	48:25 The horn of Moab is **c off**, and his arm is	1438
	49:26 the men of war shall be **c off** in that day,	1826
	50:16 **C off** the sower from Babylon, and him	3772
	50:23 hammer of the whole earth **c asunder**	1438
	50:30 her men of war shall be **c off** in that day,	1826
	51: 6 be not **c off** in her iniquity; for this *is*	1826
	51:62 to **c** it **off**, that none shall remain in it,	3772
La	2: 3 hath **c off** in *his* fierce anger all the horn	1438
	3:53 They have **c off** my life in the dungeon,	6789
	3:54 over mine head; *then* I said, I am **c off**.	1504
Eze	6: 6 your images may be **c down**,	1438
	14: 8 I will **c** him **off** from the midst of my	3772
	14:13 and will **c off** man and beast from it:	3772
	14:17 so that I **c off** man and beast from it:	3772
	14:19 in blood, to **c off** from it man and beast:	3772
	14:21 to **c off** from it man and beast?	3772
	16: 4 day thou wast born thy navel was not **c**,	3772
	17: 9 and **c off** the fruit thereof, that it wither?	7082
	17:17 and building forts, to **c off** many persons:	3772
	21: 3 will **c off** from thee the righteous and	3772
	21: 4 that I will **c off** from thee the righteous	3772
	25: 7 I will **c** thee **off** from the people,	3772
	25:13 and will **c off** man and beast from it;	3772
	25:16 I will **c off** the Cherethims, and destroy	3772
	29: 8 and **c off** man and beast out of thee.	3772
	30:15 and I will **c off** the multitude of No.	3772
	31:12 have **c** him **off**, and have left him:	3772
	35: 7 **c off** from it him that passeth out and	3772
	37:11 hope is lost: we are **c off** for our parts.	1504
	39:10 neither **c down** *any* out of the forests;	2404
Da	2: 5 ye shall be **c** in pieces, and your houses	5648
	2:34 Thou sawest till that a stone was **c out**	1505
	2:45 was **c out** of the mountain without hands,	1505
	3:29 shall be **c** in pieces, and their houses shall	5648
	4:14 down the tree, and **c off** his branches,	7113
	9:26 and two weeks shall Messiah be **c off**,	3772
Hos	8: 6 made them idols, that they may be **c off**	3772
	10: 7 her king is **c off** as the foam upon	1820
	10:15 the king of Israel **utterly** be **c off**.	1820+1820
Joel	1: 5 new wine, for it is **c off** from your mouth.	3772
	1: 9 drink offering is **c off** from the house of	3772
	1:16 Is not the meat **c off** before our eyes,	3772
Am	1: 5 **c off** the inhabitant from the plain of	3772
	1: 8 I will **c off** the inhabitant from Ashdod,	3772
	2: 3 I will **c off** the judge from the midst	3772
	3:14 the horns of the altar shall be **c off**,	1438
	9: 1 **c** them in the head, all of them; and I will	1214
Ob	1: 5 if robbers by night, (how art thou **c off**!)	1820
	1: 9 mount of Esau may be **c off** by slaughter.	3772
	1:10 and thou shalt be **c off** for ever.	3772
	1:14 to **c off** those of his that did escape;	3772
Mic	5: 9 and all thine enemies shall be **c off**.	3772
	5:10 I will **c off** thy horses out of the midst	3772
	5:11 I will **c off** the cities of thy land,	3772
	5:12 I will **c off** witchcrafts out of thine hand;	3772
	5:13 Thy graven images also will I **c off**,	3772
Na	1:12 yet thus shall they be **c down**,	1494
	1:14 out of the house of thy gods will I **c off**	3772
	1:15 pass through thee; he is utterly **c off**.	3772
	2:13 I will **c off** thy prey from the earth,	3772
	3:15 the sword shall **c** thee **off**, it shall eat thee	3772
Hab	3:17 the flock shall be **c off** from the fold,	1504
Zep	1: 3 I will **c off** man from off the land, saith	3772
	1: 4 I will **c off** the remnant of Baal from this	3772
	1:11 for all the merchant people are **c down**;	1820
	1:11 down; all they that bear silver are **c off**.	3772
	3: 6 I have **c off** the nations: their towers are	3772
	3: 7 so their dwelling should not be **c off**,	3772
Zec	5: 3 every one that stealeth shall be **c off** *as*	5352
	5: 3 every one that sweareth shall be **c off** *as*	5352
	9: 6 and I will **c off** the pride of the Philistines.	3772
	9:10 I will **c off** the chariot from Ephraim,	3772
	9:10 and the battle bow shall be **c off**:	3772
	11: 8 Three shepherds also I **c off** in one month;	3582
	11: 9 that is to be **c off**, let it be **c off**;	3582
	11: 9 that is to be cut off, let it be **c off**;	3582
	11:10 my staff, *even* Beauty, and **c** it **asunder**,	1438
	11:14 I **c asunder** mine other staff, *even* Bands,	1438
	11:16 *which* shall not visit those that be **c off**,	3772
	12: 3 with it shall be **c** in pieces,	8295+8295
	13: 2 *that* I will **c off** the names of the idols out	3772
	13: 8 two parts therein shall be **c off** *and* die;	3772
	14: 2 residue of the people shall not be **c off**	3772

Mal	2:12 The LORD will **c off** the man that doth	3772
Mt	5:30 offend thee, **c** it **off**, and cast *it* from thee:	1581
	18: 8 **c** them **off**, and cast *them* from thee:	1581
	21: 8 others **c down** branches from the trees,	2875
	24:51 shall **c** him **asunder**, and appoint *him*	1371
Mk	9:43 And if thy hand offend thee, **c** it **off**: it is	609
	9:45 And if thy foot offend thee, **c** it **off**: it is	609
	11: 8 and others **c down** branches off the trees,	2875
	14:47 servant of the high priest, and **c off** his ear.	851
Lk	12:46 will **c** him **in sunder**, and will appoint	1371
	13: 7 **c** it **down**; why cumbereth it the ground?	1581
	13: 9 not, *then* after that thou shalt **c** it **down**.	1581
	22:50 of the high priest, and **c off** his right ear.	851
Jn	18:10 high priest's servant, and **c off** his ear.	609
	18:26 being *his* kinsman whose ear Peter **c off**,	609
Ac	5:33 When they heard *that*, they were **c to**	1282
	7:54 they heard these *things*, they were **c**	1282
	27:32 the soldiers **c off** the ropes of the boat,	609
Ro	9:28 the work, and **c** it **short** in righteousness:	4932
	11:22 otherwise thou also shalt be **c off**.	1581
	11:24 For if thou wert **c out** of the olive tree	1581
2Co	11:12 that I may **c off** occasion **from** them	1581
Gal	5:12 I would they were even **c off** which	609

CUTH (1) [CUTHAH]
2Ki	17:30 the men of **C** made Nergal, and the men	3575

CUTHAH (1) [CUTH]
2Ki	17:24 from **C**, and from Ava, and from Hamath,	3575

CUTTEST (1) [CUT]
Dt	24:19 thou **c down** thine **harvest** in	7105+7114

CUTTETH (6) [CUT]
Job	28:10 He **c out** rivers among the rocks;	1234
Ps	46: 9 the bow, and **c** the spear **in sunder**;	7112
	141: 7 as when one **c** and cleaveth *wood* upon	6398
Pr	26: 6 by the hand of a fool **c off** the feet,	7096
Jer	10: 3 for *one* **c** a tree out of the forest,	3772
	22:14 large chambers, and **c** him **out** windows;	7167

CUTTING (5) [CUT]
Ex	31: 5 in **c** of stones, to set *them*, and in carving	2799
	35:33 in the **c** of stones, to set *them*, and	2799
Isa	38:10 I said, in the **c off** of my days, I shall go to	1824
Hab	2:10 shame to thy house by **c off** many people,	7096
Mk	5: 5 crying, and **c** himself with stones.	2629

CUTTINGS (3) [CUT]
Lev	19:28 Ye shall not make any **c** in your flesh for	8296
	21: 5 nor **make any c** in their flesh.	8295+8296
Jer	48:37 upon all the hands shall be **c**, and upon	1417

CUZ See CHUZA

CYMBAL (1) [CYMBALS]
1Co	13: 1 become as sounding brass, or a tinkling **c**.	2950

CYMBALS (16) [CYMBAL]
2Sa	6: 5 on timbrels, and on cornets, and on **c**.	6767
1Ch	13: 8 and with **c**, and with trumpets.	4700
	15:16 psalteries and harps and **c**, sounding,	4700
	15:19 *were* appointed to sound with **c** of brass;	4700
	15:28 cornet, and with trumpets, and with **c**,	4700
	16: 5 harps; but Asaph made a sound with **c**;	4700
	16:42 and **c** for those that should make a sound,	4700
	25: 1 with harps, with psalteries, and with **c**:	4700
	25: 6 with **c**, psalteries, and harps,	4700
2Ch	5:12 having **c** and psalteries and harps	4700
	5:13 and **c** and instruments of musick,	4700
	29:25 Levites *in* the house of the LORD with **c**,	4700
Ezr	3:10 the Levites the sons of Asaph with **c**,	4700
Ne	12:27 *with* **c**, psalteries, and with harps.	4700
Ps	150: 5 Praise him upon the loud **c**: praise him	6767
	150: 5 praise him upon the high sounding **c**.	6767

CYPRESS (1)
Isa	44:14 cedars, and taketh the **c** and the oak,	8645

CYPRUS (8)
Ac	4:36 a Levite, *and* of the country of **C**,	2953
	11:19 and **C**, and Antioch, preaching the word	2954
	11:20 And some of them were men of **C** and	2953
	13: 4 and from thence they sailed to **C**.	2954
	15:39 Barnabas took Mark, and sailed unto **C**;	2954
	21: 3 when we had discovered **C**, we left it	2954
	21:16 and brought *with* them one Mnason of **C**,	2953
	27: 4 we sailed under **C**, because the winds	2954

CYRENE (4) [CYRENIAN, CYRENIANS]
Mt	27:32 they found a man of **C**, Simon by name:	2956
Ac	2:10 and in the parts of Libya about **C**,	2957
	11:20 some of them were men of Cyprus and **C**,	2956
	13: 1 Niger, and Lucius of **C**, and Manaen,	2956

CYRENIAN (2) [CYRENE]
Mk	15:21 And they compel one Simon a **C**,	2956
Lk	23:26 **C**, coming out of the country, and on him	2956

CYRENIANS (1) [CYRENE]
Ac	6: 9 and **C**, and Alexandrians, and of them of	2956

CYRENIUS (1)
Lk	2: 2 (*And* this taxing was first made when **C**	2958

CYRUS (23)
2Ch	36:22 Now in the first year of **C** king of Persia,	3566

2Ch	36:22 the LORD stirred up the spirit of **C** king	3566
	36:23 Thus saith **C** king of Persia,	3566
Ezr	1: 1 Now in the first year of **C** king of Persia,	3566
	1: 1 the LORD stirred up the spirit of **C** king	3566
	1: 2 Thus saith **C** king of Persia, The LORD	3566
	1: 7 **C** the king brought forth the vessels of	3566
	1: 8 those did **C** king of Persia bring forth	3566
	3: 7 according to the grant that they had of **C**	3566
	4: 3 as king **C** the king of Persia hath	3566
	4: 5 all the days of **C** king of Persia,	3566
	5:13 in the first year of **C** the king of Babylon	3567
	5:13 **C** made a decree to build this house of	3567
	5:14 did **C** the king take out of the temple	3567
	5:17 that a decree *was* made of **C** the king to	3567
	6: 3 In the first year of **C** the king the same	3567
	6: 3 **C** the king made a decree *concerning*	3567
	6:14 according to the commandment of **C**,	3566
Isa	44:28 That saith of **C**, *He is* my shepherd,	3566
	45: 1 to **C**, whose right hand I have holden,	3566
Da	1:21 *even* unto the first year of king **C**.	3566
	6:28 and in the reign of **C** the Persian.	3567
	10: 1 In the third year of **C** king of Persia	3566

D

DABAREH (1)
Jos	21:28 with her suburbs, **D** with her suburbs,	1705

DABBASHETH (1)
Jos	19:11 reached to **D**, and reached to the river	1708

DABBESHETH See DABBASHETH

DABERATH (2)
Jos	19:12 goeth out to **D**, and goeth up *to* Japhia,	1705
1Ch	6:72 with her suburbs, **D** with her suburbs,	1705

DAGGER (3)
Jdg	3:16 Ehud made him a **d** which had two edges,	2719
	3:21 took the **d** from his right thigh, and thrust	2719
	3:22 that he could not draw the **d** out of his	2719

DAGON (12) [BETH-DAGON, DAGON'S]
Jdg	16:23 to offer a great sacrifice unto **D** their god,	1712
1Sa	5: 2 they brought it *into* the house of **D**,	1712
	5: 2 into the house of Dagon, and set it by **D**.	1712
	5: 3 **D** *was* fallen upon his face to the earth	1712
	5: 3 took **D**, and set him in his place again.	1712
	5: 4 **D** *was* fallen upon his face to the ground	1712
	5: 4 the head of **D** and both the palms of his	1712
	5: 4 only *the stump of* **D** was left to him.	1712
	5: 5 Therefore neither the priests of **D**, nor any	1712
	5: 5 tread on the threshold of **D** in Ashdod	1712
	5: 7 is sore upon us, and upon **D** our god.	1712
1Ch	10:10 and fastened his head *in* the temple of **D**.	1712

DAGON'S (1) [DAGON]
1Sa	5: 5 Dagon, nor any that come *into* **D** house,	1712

DAILY (63) [DAY]
Ex	5:13 Fulfil your works, *your* **d**	3117+3117+871.1
	5:19 your bricks of *your* **d** task.	3117+3117+871.1
	16: 5 be twice as much as they gather **d**.	3117+3117
Nu	4:16 the **d** meat offering, and the anointing oil,	8548
	28:24 manner ye shall offer **d**, 3117+1886.1+3807.1	
	29: 6 the **d** burnt offering, and his meat offering,	8548
Jdg	16:16 she pressed him **d** 3117+3605+1886.1	
2Ki	25:30 a **d** rate for every day, all the days of his	3117
2Ch	31:16 *his* **d** portion for their service 3117+3117+871.1	
Ezr	3: 4 **d** burnt offerings by number, 3117+3117+871.1	
Ne	5:18 *for me* **d** was one ox	259+3117+3807.1
Est	3: 4 they spake unto him, 3117+1886.1+2050.1	
Ps	13: 2 in my soul, *having* sorrow in my heart **d**?	3119
	42:10 while they say unto me, 3117+3605+1886.1	
	56: 1 fighting **d** oppresseth me. 3117+3605+1886.1	
	56: 2 Mine enemies would **d** 3117+3605+1886.1	
	61: 8 that I may perform my vows.	3117+3117
	68:19 *who* **d** loadeth us *with* benefits,	3117+3117
	72:15 and **d** shall he be praised. 3117+3605+1886.1	
	74:22 *man* reproacheth thee **d**. 3117+3605+1886.1	
	86: 3 for I cry unto thee **d**. 3117+3605+1886.1	
	88: 9 LORD, I have called **d** upon 3117+3605+871.1	
	88:17 came round about me **d** 3117+3605+1886.1	
Pr	8:30 *with* him: and I was **d** *his* delight, 3117+3117	
	8:34 watching **d** at my gates, waiting at	3117+3117
Isa	58: 2 Yet they seek me **d**, and delight to	3117+3117
Jer	7:25 **d** rising up early and sending *them*:	3117
	20: 7 every one mocketh me. 3117+3605+1886.1	
	20: 8 unto me, and a derision, **d**. 3117+3605+1886.1	
	37:21 **d** a piece of bread out of 3117+1886.1+3807.1	
Eze	30:16 and Noph *shall* have distresses **d**.	3119
	45:23 **d** the seven days; 3117+1886.1+3807.1	
	45:23 goats **d** *for* a sin offering. 3117+1886.1+3807.1	
	46:13 Thou shalt **d** prepare a 3117+1886.1+3807.1	
Da	1: 5 the king appointed them a **d** 3117+3117+871.1	
	8:11 by him the **d** *sacrifice* was taken away,	8548

Da	8:12 host was given *him* against the **d** *sacrifice*	8548
	8:13 *be* the vision concerning the **d** *sacrifice,*	8548
	11:31 shall take away the **d** *sacrifice,* and	8548
	12:11 from the time *that* the **d** *sacrifice* shall be	8548
Hos	12: 1 he **d** increaseth lies and	3117+3605+1886.1
Mt	6:11 Give us this day our **d** bread.	1967
	26:55 I sat **d** with you teaching in	2250+2596
Mk	14:49 I was **d** with you in the temple	2250+2596
Lk	9:23 and take up his cross **d,**	2250+2596
	11: 3 Give us day by day our **d** bread.	1967
	19:47 And he taught **d** in the temple.	2250+2596
	22:53 When I was **d** with you in	2250+2596
Ac	2:46 continuing **d** with one accord in	2250+2596
	2:47 the Lord added to the church	2250+2596
	3: 2 whom they laid **d** at the gate of	2250+2596
	5:42 And **d** in the temple, and in every	2250+3956
	6: 1 their widows were neglected in the **d**	2522
	16: 5 faith, and increased in number **d.**	2250+2596
	17:11 and searched the scriptures **d,**	2250+2596
	17:17 in the market **d** with them	2250+2596+3956
	19: 9 **d** in the school of one Tyrannus.	2250+2596
1Co	15:31 in Christ Jesus our Lord, I die **d.**	2250+2596
2Co	11:28 that which cometh upon me **d,**	2250+2596
Heb	3:13 But exhort one another **d,**	1538+2250+2596
	7:27 Who needeth not **d,** as *those* high	2250+2596
	10:11 And every priest standeth **d**	2250+2596
Jas	2:15 or sister be naked, and destitute of **d** food,	2184

DAINTIES (3) [DAINTY]

Ge	49:20 *shall* be fat, and he shall yield royal **d.**	4574
Ps	141: 4 iniquity: and let me not eat of their **d.**	4516
Pr	23: 3 Be not desirous of his **d:** for they *are*	4303

DAINTY (3) [DAINTIES]

Job	33:20 life abhorreth bread, and his soul **d** meat.	8378
Pr	23: 6 evil eye, neither desire thou his **d** meats:	4303
Rev	18:14 all *things* which were **d** and goodly are	3045

DALAIAH (1)

1Ch	3:24 and Johanan, and **D,** and Anani, seven.	1806

DALE (2)

Ge	14:17 valley of Shaveh, which *is* the king's **d.**	6010
2Sa	18:18 himself a pillar, which *is* in the king's **d:**	6010

DALMANUTHA (1)

Mk	8:10 his disciples, and came into the parts of **D.**	1148

DALMATIA (1)

2Ti	4:10 Crescens to Galatia, Titus unto **D.**	1149

DALPHON (1)

Est	9: 7 And Parshandatha, and **D,** and Aspatha,	1813

DAM (5)

Ex	22:30 seven days it shall be with his **d;**	517
Lev	22:27 then it shall be seven days under the **d;**	517
Dt	22: 6 *the* **d** sitting upon the young, or upon	517
	22: 6 thou shalt not take the **d** with the young;	517
	22: 7 *But* thou shalt in any wise let the **d** go,	517

DAMAGE (6) [ENDAMAGE]

Ezr	4:22 should **d** grow to the hurt of the kings?	2257
Est	7: 4 enemy could not countervail the king's **d.**	5143
Pr	26: 6 a fool cutteth off the feet, *and* drinketh **d.**	2555
Da	6: 2 them, and the king should have no **d.**	5142
Ac	27:10 *this* voyage will be with hurt and much **d,**	2209
2Co	7: 9 that ye might **receive d** by us in nothing.	2210

DAMARIS (1)

Ac	17:34 and a woman named **D,** and others with	1152

DAMASCENES (1) [DAMASCUS]

2Co	11:32 **D** *with* a garrison, desirous to apprehend	1153

DAMASCUS (60) [DAMASCENES, SYRIA-DAMASCUS]

Ge	14:15 Hobah, which *is* on the left hand of **D.**	1834
	15: 2 steward of my house *is* this Eliezer of **D?**	1834
2Sa	8: 5 when the Syrians of **D** came to succour	1834
	8: 6 David put garrisons in Syria of **D:** and	1834
1Ki	11:24 slew *them* of Zobah: and they went to **D,**	1834
	11:24 and dwelt therein, and reigned in **D.**	1834
	15:18 king of Syria, that dwelt at **D,** saying,	1834
	19:15 return on thy way to the wilderness of **D:**	1834
	20:34 thou shalt make streets for thee in **D,** as	1834
2Ki	5:12 *Are* not Abana and Pharpar, rivers of **D,**	1834
	8: 7 Elisha came to **D;** and Ben-hadad the king	1834
	8: 9 even *of* every good thing of **D,**	1834
	14:28 and how he recovered **D,** and Hamath,	1834
	16: 9 for the king of Assyria went up against **D,**	1834
	16:10 king Ahaz went to **D** to meet	1834
	16:10 of Assyria, and saw an altar that *was* at **D:**	1834
	16:11 to all that king Ahaz had sent from **D:**	1834
	16:11 made *it* against king Ahaz came from **D.**	1834
	16:12 when the king was come from **D,** the king	1834
1Ch	18: 5 when the Syrians of **D** came to help	1834
2Ch	16: 2 king of Syria, that dwelt at **D,** saying,	1834
	24:23 all the spoil of them unto the king of **D.**	1834
	28: 5 of them captives, and brought *them* to **D.**	1834
	28:23 For he sacrificed unto the gods of **D,**	1834
SS	7: 4 of Lebanon which looketh toward **D.**	1834
Isa	7: 8 For the head of Syria *is* **D,** and the head	1834
	7: 8 *is* Damascus, and the head of **D** *is* Rezin:	1834
	8: 4 the riches of **D** and the spoil of Samaria	1834
	10: 9 Hamath as Arpad? *is* not Samaria as **D?**	1834

Isa	17: 1 The burden of **D.** Behold, Damascus *is*	1834
	17: 1 **D** *is* taken away from *being* a city,	1834
	17: 3 the kingdom from **D,** and the remnant of	1834
Jer	49:23 Concerning **D.** Hamath is confounded,	1834
	49:24 **D** is waxed feeble, *and* turneth herself to	1834
	49:27 I will kindle a fire in the wall of **D,**	1834
Eze	27:18 **D** *was* thy merchant in the multitude of	1834
	47:16 which *is* between the border of **D** and	1834
	47:17 the border of **D,** and the north northward,	1834
	47:18 from **D,** and from Gilead, and from the	1834
	48: 1 Hazar-enan, the border of **D** northward,	1834
Am	1: 3 three transgressions of **D,** and for four,	1834
	1: 5 I will break also the bar of **D,** and cut off	1834
	3:12 the corner of a bed, and in **D** *in* a couch.	1833
	5:27 I cause you to go into captivity beyond **D,**	1834
Zec	9: 1 Hadrach, and **D** *shall be* the rest thereof:	1834
Ac	9: 2 And desired of him letters to **D** to	1154
	9: 3 as *he* journeyed, he came near **D:** and	1154
	9: 8 him by the hand, and brought *him* into **D.**	1154
	9:10 And there was a certain disciple at **D,**	1154
	9:19 days with the disciples which were at **D.**	1154
	9:22 confounded the Jews which dwelt at **D,**	1154
	9:27 how he had preached boldly at **D** in	1154
	22: 5 and went to **D,** to bring them which were	1154
	22: 6 and was come nigh unto **D** about noon,	1154
	22:10 Lord said unto me, Arise, and go into **D;**	1154
	22:11 them that were with me, I came into **D.**	1154
	26:12 Whereupon as I went to **D** with authority	1154
	26:20 But shewed first unto them of **D,**	1154
2Co	11:32 In **D** the governor under Aretas the king	1154
Gal	1:17 into Arabia, and returned again unto **D.**	1154

DAMNABLE (1) [DAMNATION]

2Pe	2: 1 who privily shall bring in **d** heresies,	684

DAMNATION (11) [DAMNABLE, DAMNED]

Mt	23:14 therefore ye shall receive the greater **d.**	2917
	23:33 vipers, how can ye escape the **d** of hell?	2920
Mk	3:29 but is in danger of eternal **d.**	2920
	12:40 long prayers: these shall receive greater **d.**	2917
Lk	20:47 the same shall receive greater **d.**	2917
Jn	5:29 done evil, unto the resurrection of **d.**	2920
Ro	3: 8 that good may come? whose **d** is just.	2917
	13: 2 that resist shall receive to themselves **d.**	2917
1Co	11:29 eateth and drinketh **d** to himself,	2917
1Ti	5:12 Having **d,** because they have cast off *their*	2917
2Pe	2: 3 lingereth not, and their **d** slumbereth not.	684

DAMNED (4) [DAMNATION]

Mk	16:16 but he that believeth not shall be **d.**	2632
Ro	14:23 he that doubteth is **d** if he eat, because	2632
2Th	2:12 they all might be **d** who believed not	2919

DAMSEL (40) [DAMSEL'S, DAMSELS]

Ge	24:14 *that* the **d** to whom I shall say, Let down	5291
	24:16 the **d** *was* very fair to look upon, a virgin,	5291
	24:28 the **d** ran, and told *them of* her mother's	5291
	24:55 Let the **d** abide with us *a few* days,	5291
	24:57 We will call the **d,** and inquire at her	5291
	34: 3 he loved the **d,** and spake kindly unto	5291
	34: 3 the damsel, and spake kindly unto the **d.**	5291
	34: 4 saying, Get me this **d** to wife.	3207
	34:12 say unto me: but give me the **d** to wife.	5291
Dt	22:15 shall the father of the **d,** and her mother,	5291
	22:19 give *them* unto the father of the **d,**	5291
	22:20 tokens *of* virginity be not found for the **d:**	5291
	22:21 they shall bring out the **d** to the door of	5291
	22:23 If a **d** *that is* a virgin be betrothed unto a	5291
	22:24 the **d,** because she cried not, *being* in	5291
	22:25 if a man find a betrothed **d** in the field,	5291
	22:26 unto the **d** thou shalt do nothing; *there is*	5291
	22:26 *there is* in the **d** no sin *worthy* of death:	5291
	22:27 *and* the betrothed **d** cried, *and there was*	5291
	22:28 If a man find a **d** *that is* a virgin, which is	5291
Jdg	5:30 divided the prey; to every man a **d** *or* two;	7356
	19: 3 when the father of the **d** saw him,	5291
Ru	2: 5 was set over the reapers, Whose **d** *is* this?	5291
	2: 6 It is the Moabitish **d** that came back with	5291
1Ki	1: 3 So they sought for a fair **d** throughout all	5291
	1: 4 *was* very fair, and cherished the king,	5291
Mt	14:11 brought in a charger, and given to the **d:**	2877
	26:69 and a **d** came unto him, saying, Thou also	3814
Mk	5:39 and weep? the **d** is not dead, but sleepeth.	3813
	5:40 taketh the father and the mother of the **d,**	3813
	5:40 and entereth in where the **d** was lying.	3813
	5:41 And he took the **d** by the hand,	3813
	5:41 being interpreted, **D** (I say unto thee)	2877
	5:42 And straightway the **d** arose, and walked;	2877
	6:22 sat with *him,* the king said unto the **d,**	2877
	6:28 his head in a charger, and gave it to the **d:**	2877
	6:28 damsel: and the **d** gave it to her mother.	2877
Jn	18:17 Then saith the **d** that kept the door unto	3814
Ac	12:13 a **d** came to hearken, named Rhoda.	3814
	16:16 a certain **d** possessed with a spirit of	3814

DAMSEL'S (8) [DAMSEL]

Dt	22:15 bring forth *the tokens of* the **d** virginity	5291
	22:16 the **d** father shall say unto the elders,	5291
	22:29 unto the **d** father fifty *shekels* of silver,	5291
Jdg	19: 4 father in law, the **d** father, retained him;	5291
	19: 5 the **d** father said unto his son in law,	5291
	19: 6 for the **d** father had said unto the man,	5291
	19: 8 the **d** father said, Comfort thine heart,	5291
	19: 9 the **d** father, said unto him, Behold now,	5291

DAMSELS (3) [DAMSEL]

Ge	24:61 her **d,** and they rode upon the camels,	5291
1Sa	25:42 with five **d** of hers that went after her;	5291
Ps	68:25 among *them* were the **d** playing with	5959

DAN (72) [DAN-JAAN, DANITES, LESHEM, MAHANEH-DAN]

Ge	14:14 and eighteen, and pursued *them* unto **D.**	1835
	30: 6 a son: therefore called she his name **D.**	1835
	35:25 Rachel's handmaid; **D,** and Naphtali.	1835
	46:23 And the sons of **D;** Hushim.	1835
	49:16 **D** shall judge his people, as one of	1835
	49:17 **D** shall be a serpent by the way, an adder	1835
Ex	1: 4 **D,** and Naphtali, Gad, and Asher.	1835
	31: 6 the son of Ahisamach, of the tribe of **D:**	1835
	35:34 the son of Ahisamach, of the tribe of **D.**	1835
	38:23 of the tribe of **D,** an engraver,	1835
Lev	24:11 the daughter of Dibri, of the tribe of **D:)**	1835
Nu	1:12 Of **D;** Ahiezer the son of Ammishaddai.	1835
	1:38 Of the children of **D,** *by* their generations,	1835
	1:39 *even* of the tribe of **D,** were threescore	1835
	2:25 The standard of the camp of **D** *shall be* on	1835
	2:25 the captain of the children of **D** *shall be*	1835
	2:31 the camp of **D** *were* an hundred thousand	1835
	7:66 prince of the children of **D,** *offered:*	1835
	10:25 the camp of the children of **D** set forward,	1835
	13:12 Of the tribe of **D,** Ammiel the son of	1835
	26:42 *are* the sons of **D** after their families:	1835
	26:42 These *are* the families of **D** after their	1835
	34:22 prince of the tribe of the children of **D,**	1835
Dt	27:13 and Asher, and Zebulun, and **D,** and Naphtali.	1835
	33:22 of **D** he said, Dan *is* a lion's whelp: he	1835
	33:22 of Dan he said, **D** *is* a lion's whelp: he	1835
	34: 1 him all the land of Gilead, unto **D,**	1835
Jos	19:40 children of **D** according to their families.	1835
	19:47 the coast of the children of **D** went out	1835
	19:47 the children of **D** went up to fight against	1835
	19:47 and dwelt therein, and called Leshem, **D,**	1835
	19:47 Dan, after the name of **D** their father.	1835
	19:48 the children of **D** according to their families,	1835
	21: 5 out of the tribe of **D,** and out of the half	1835
	21:23 out of the tribe of **D,** Eltekeh with her	1835
Jdg	1:34 the Amorites forced the children of **D** into	1835
	5:17 why did **D** remain *in* ships?	1835
	13:25 to move him at times in the camp of **D,**	1835
	18: 2 the children of **D** sent of their family five	1835
	18:16 which *were* of the children of **D,** stood *by*	1835
	18:22 and overtook the children of **D.**	1835
	18:23 they cried unto the children of **D.**	1835
	18:25 the children of **D** said unto him, Let not	1835
	18:26 the children of **D** went their way: and	1835
	18:29 they called the name of the city **D,** after	1835
	18:29 after the name of **D** their father, who was	1835
	18:30 the children of **D** set up the graven image:	1835
	18:30 his sons were priests to the tribe of **D** until	1839
	20: 1 from **D** even to Beer-sheba, with the land	1835
1Sa	3:20 all Israel from **D** even to Beer-sheba knew	1835
2Sa	3:10 over Judah, from **D** even to Beer-sheba.	1835
	17:11 from **D** even to Beer-sheba, as the sand	1835
	24: 2 from **D** even to Beer-sheba, and number	1835
	24:15 there died of the people from **D** even to	1835
1Ki	4:25 his fig tree, from **D** even to Beer-sheba,	1835
	12:29 one in Beth-el, and the other put he in **D.**	1835
	12:30 to worship before the one, *even* unto **D.**	1835
	15:20 **D,** and Abel-beth-maachah, and all	1835
2Ki	10:29 that *were* in Beth-el, and that *were* in **D.**	1835
1Ch	2: 2 Joseph, and Benjamin, Naphtali, Gad,	1835
	21: 2 number Israel from Beer-sheba even to **D;**	1835
	27:22 Of **D,** Azareel the son of Jeroham.	1835
2Ch	2:14 son of a woman of the daughters of **D,**	1835
	16: 4 **D,** and Abel-maim, and all the store cities	1835
	30: 5 all Israel, from Beer-sheba even to **D,**	1835
Jer	4:15 For a voice declareth from **D,**	1835
	8:16 snorting of his horses was heard from **D:**	1835
Eze	27:19 **D** also and Javan going to and fro	1835
	48: 1 his sides east *and* west; a *portion for* **D.**	1835
	48: 2 by the border of **D,** from the east side	1835
	48:32 one gate of Benjamin, one gate of **D,**	1835
Am	8:14 of Samaria, and say, Thy god, O **D,** liveth;	1835

DANCE (8) [DANCED, DANCES, DANCING]

Jdg	21:21 if the daughters of Shiloh come out to **d** in	2342
Job	21:11 ones like a flock, and their children **d.**	7540
Ps	149: 3 Let them praise his name in the **d:**	4234
	150: 4 Praise him with the timbrel and **d:**	4234
Ecc	3: 4 laugh; a time to mourn, and a time to **d;**	7540
Isa	13:21 shall dwell there, and satyrs shall **d** there.	7540
Jer	31:13 the virgin rejoice in the **d,** both young	4234
La	5:15 is ceased; our **d** is turned into mourning.	4234

DANCED (6) [DANCE]

Jdg	21:23 of them that **d,** whom they caught:	2342
2Sa	6:14 David **d** before the LORD with all *his*	3769
Mt	11:17 have piped unto you, and ye have not **d;**	3738
	14: 6 the daughter of Herodias **d** before them,	3738
Mk	6:22 and pleased Herod and them that	3738
Lk	7:32 have piped unto you, and ye have not **d;**	3738

DANCES (6) [DANCE]

Ex	15:20 out after her with timbrels and with **d.**	4246
Jdg	11:34 to meet him with timbrels and with **d:**	4246
	21:21 of Shiloh come out to dance in **d,**	4246
1Sa	21:11 they not sing one to another of him in **d,**	4246
	29: 5 of whom they sang one to another in **d,**	4246
Jer	31: 4 shalt go forth in the **d** of them that make	4234

D

DANCING (7) [DANCE]

Ex	32:19 the camp, that he saw the calf, and the **d**:	4246
1Sa	18: 6 singing and **d**, to meet king Saul,	4246
	30:16 **d**, because of all the great spoil that they	2287
2Sa	6:14 David leaping and **d** before the Lord;	3769
1Ch	15:29 out at a window saw king David **d**	7540
Ps	30:11 hast turned for me my mourning into **d**	4234
Lk	15:25 to the house, he heard musick and **d**.	5525

DANDLED (1)

Isa	66:12 upon *her* sides, and be **d** upon *her* knees.	8173

DANGER (7) [DANGEROUS]

Mt	5:21 whosoever shall kill shall be **in d** of	1777
	5:22 a cause shall be **in d** of the judgment:	1777
	5:22 Raca, shall be **in d** of the council:	1777
	5:22 Thou fool, shall be **in d** of hell fire.	1777
Mk	3:29 but is **in d** of eternal damnation.	1777
Ac	19:27 So *that* not only this our craft is **in d** to be	2793
	19:40 For we are **in d** to be called in question	2793

DANGEROUS (1) [DANGER]

Ac	27: 9 and when sailing was now **d**, because	2000

DANIEL (83) [BELTESHAZZAR]

1Ch	3: 1 the second **D**, of Abigail the Carmelitess:	1840
Ezr	8: 2 of the sons of Ithamar; **D**: of the sons of	1840
Ne	10: 6 **D**, Ginnethon, Baruch,	1840
Eze	14:14 Noah, **D**, and Job, were in it, they should	1840
	14:20 **D**, and Job, were in it, as I live,	1840
	28: 3 Behold, thou *art* wiser than **D**; *there is* no	1840
Da	1: 6 Hananiah, Mishael, and Azariah:	1840
	1: 7 for he gave unto **D** *the name of*	1840
	1: 8 **D** purposed in his heart that he would not	1840
	1: 9 Now God had brought **D** into favour and	1840
	1:10 the prince of the eunuchs said unto **D**,	1840
	1:11 said **D** to Melzar, whom the prince of	1840
	1:11 the prince of the eunuchs had set over **D**,	1840
	1:17 **D** had understanding in all visions and	1840
	1:19 among them all was found none like **D**,	1840
	1:21 **D** continued *even* unto the first year of	1840
	2:13 they sought **D** and his fellows to be slain.	1841
	2:14 **D** answered with counsel and wisdom to	1841
	2:15 Then Arioch made the thing known to **D**,	1841
	2:16 **D** went in, and desired of the king that he	1841
	2:17 **D** went to his house, and made the thing	1841
	2:18 that **D** and his fellows should not perish	1841
	2:19 *was* the secret revealed unto **D** in a night	1841
	2:19 Then **D** blessed the God of heaven.	1841
	2:20 **D** answered and said, Blessed be the name	1841
	2:24 Therefore **D** went in unto Arioch,	1841
	2:25 Arioch brought in **D** before the king in	1841
	2:26 The king answered and said to **D**,	1841
	2:27 **D** answered in the presence of the king,	1841
	2:46 worshipped **D**, and commanded that *they*	1841
	2:47 The king answered unto **D**, and said, Of a	1841
	2:48 the king made **D** a great man, and gave	1841
	2:49 **D** requested of the king, and he set	1841
	2:49 but **D** *sat* in the gate of the king.	1841
	4: 8 at the last **D** came in before me,	1841
	4:19 **D**, whose name *was* Belteshazzar,	1841
	5:12 of doubts, were found in the same **D**,	1841
	5:12 now let **D** be called, and he will shew	1841
	5:13 was **D** brought in before the king.	1841
	5:13 *And* the king spake and said unto **D**,	1841
	5:13 and said unto Daniel, *Art* thou that **D**,	1841
	5:17 **D** answered and said before the king,	1841
	5:29 clothed **D** with scarlet, and *put* a chain	1841
	6: 2 three presidents; of whom **D** *was* first:	1841
	6: 3 this **D** was preferred above the presidents	1841
	6: 4 princes sought to find occasion against **D**	1841
	6: 5 shall not find any occasion against this **D**,	1841
	6:10 Now when **D** knew that the writing *was*	1841
	6:11 found **D** praying and making supplication	1841
	6:13 and said before the king, That **D**,	1841
	6:14 and set *his* heart on **D** to deliver him:	1841
	6:16 they brought **D**, and cast *him* into the den	1841
	6:16 *Now* the king spake and said unto **D**,	1841
	6:17 might not be changed concerning **D**.	1841
	6:20 he cried with a lamentable voice unto **D**:	1841
	6:20 the king spake and said to **D**, O Daniel,	1841
	6:20 the king spake and said to Daniel, O **D**,	1841
	6:21 said **D** unto the king, O king, live for ever.	1841
	6:23 commanded that *they* should take **D** up	1841
	6:23 So **D** was taken up out of the den,	1841
	6:24 brought those men which had accused **D**,	1841
	6:26 tremble and fear before the God of **D**:	1841
	6:27 who hath delivered **D** from the power of	1841
	6:28 So this **D** prospered in the reign of Darius,	1841
	7: 1 Belshazzar king of Babylon **D** had a dream	1777
	7: 2 **D** spake and said, I saw in my vision by	1841
	7:15 I **D** was grieved in my spirit in the midst	1841
	7:28 *for* me **D**, my cogitations much troubled	1841
	8: 1 *unto* me **D**, after that which appeared	1840
	8:15 when I, *even* I **D**, had seen the vision,	1840
	8:27 I **D** fainted, and was sick *certain* days;	1840
	9: 2 the first year of his reign I **D** understood	1840
	9:22 and talked with me, and said, O **D**,	1840
	10: 1 of Persia a thing was revealed unto **D**,	1840
	10: 2 In those days I **D** was mourning three full	1840
	10: 7 I **D** alone saw the vision: for the men that	1840
	10:11 he said unto me, O **D**, a man greatly	1840
	10:12 said he unto me, Fear not, **D**: for from	1840
	12: 4 thou, O **D**, shut up the words, and seal	1840
	12: 5 I **D** looked, and behold, there stood other	1840

Da	12: 9 he said, Go thy way, **D**: for the words *are*	1840
Mt	24:15 spoken of by **D** the prophet, stand in	1158
Mk	13:14 spoken of by **D** the prophet, standing	1158

DANITES (4) [DAN]

Jdg	13: 2 of the family of the **D**, whose name *was*	1839
	18: 1 those days the tribe of the **D** sought them	1839
	18:11 went from thence of the family of the **D**,	1839
1Ch	12:35 of the **D** expert in war twenty and	1839

DAN-JAAN (1) [DAN]

2Sa	24: 6 and they came to **D**, and about to Zidon,	1842

DANNAH (1)

Jos	15:49 **D**, and Kirjath-sannah, which *is* Debir,	1837

DAPPLED See GRISLED

DARA (1)

1Ch	2: 6 Ethan, and Heman, and Calcol, and **D**:	1873

DARDA (1)

1Ki	4:31 Heman, and Chalcol, and **D**, the sons of	1862

DARE (5) [DURST]

Job	41:10 None *is so* fierce that **d** stir him **up**: who	5782
Ro	5: 7 for a good *man* some would even **d** to die.	5111
	15:18 For I will not **d** to speak of any of *those*	5111
1Co	6: 1 any of you, having a matter against	5111
2Co	10:12 For we **d** not make *ourselves* of	5111

DARE; DARED See DURST

DARICS See DRAMS

DARING See DURST

DARIUS (25)

Ezr	4: 5 even until the reign of **D** king of Persia.	1867
	4:24 year of the reign of **D** king of Persia.	1868
	5: 5 them to cease, till the matter came to **D**:	1868
	5: 6 *this* side the river, sent unto **D** the king:	1868
	5: 7 written thus: Unto **D** the king, all peace.	1868
	6: 1 Then **D** the king made a decree, and search was	1868
	6:12 I **D** have made a decree; let it be done	1868
	6:13 according to that which **D** the king had	1868
	6:14 and **D**, and Artaxerxes king of Persia.	1868
	6:15 sixth year of the reign of **D** the king.	1868
Ne	12:22 the priests, to the reign of **D** the Persian.	1867
Da	5:31 the Median took the kingdom,	1868
	6: 1 It pleased **D** to set over the kingdom an	1868
	6: 6 said thus unto him, King **D**, live for ever.	1868
	6: 9 Wherefore king **D** signed the writing and	1868
	6:25 king **D** wrote unto all people, nations,	1868
	6:28 So this Daniel prospered in the reign of **D**,	1868
	9: 1 In the first year of **D** the son of Ahasuerus,	1867
	11: 1 Also I in the first year of **D** the Mede,	1867
Hag	1: 1 In the second year of **D** the king,	1867
	1:15 in the second year of **D** the king.	1867
	2:10 the ninth *month*, in the second year of **D**,	1867
Zec	1: 1 the eighth month, in the second year of **D**,	1867
	1: 7 the month Sebat, in the second year of **D**,	1867
	7: 1 came to pass in the fourth year of king **D**,	1867

DARK (43)

Ge	15:17 when the sun went down, and it was **d**,	5939
Lev	13: 6 *if* the plague be **somewhat d**,	3544
	13:21 lower than the skin, but *be* **somewhat d**;	3544
	13:26 than the *other* skin, but *be* **somewhat d**;	3544
	13:28 not in the skin, but it *be* **somewhat d**;	3544
	13:56 the plague *be* **somewhat d** after	3544
Nu	12: 8 even apparently, and not in **d** speeches;	2420
Jos	2: 5 when it was **d**, that the men went out:	2822
2Sa	22:12 **d** waters, *and* thick clouds of the skies.	2841
Ne	13:19 began to be **d** before the sabbath,	6751
Job	3: 9 Let the stars of the twilight thereof be **d**;	2821
	12:25 They grope *in* the **d** without light,	2822
	18: 6 The light shall be **d** in his tabernacle,	2821
	22:13 can he judge through the **d** cloud?	6205
	24:16 In the **d** they dig *through* houses,	2822
Ps	18:11 pavilion round about him *were* **d** waters	2824
	35: 6 Let their way be **d** and slippery: and let	2822
	49: 4 I will open my **d** saying upon the harp.	2420
	74:20 for the **d** places of the earth are full *of*	4285
	78: 2 in a parable: I will utter **d** sayings of old:	2420
	88:12 Shall thy wonders be known in the **d**?	2822
	105:28 He sent darkness, and **made** it **d**;	2821
Pr	1: 6 words of the wise, and their **d** sayings.	2420
	7: 9 in the evening, in the black and **d** night:	653
Isa	29:15 their works are in the **d**, and they say,	4285
	45:19 spoken in secret, in a **d** place of the earth:	2822
Jer	13:16 before your feet stumble upon the **d**	5399
La	3: 6 He hath set me in **d** places, as they that	4285
Eze	8:12 ancients of the house of Israel do in the **d**,	2822
	32: 7 the heaven, and **make** the stars thereof **d**;	6937
	32: 8 the bright lights of heaven will I **make d**	6937
	34:12 been scattered in the cloudy and **d** day.	6205
Da	8:23 understanding **d** sentences, shall stand	2420
Joel	2:10 the sun and the moon shall be **d**,	6937
Am	5: 8 **maketh** the day **d** *with* night:	2821
	5:20 even **very d**, and no brightness in it?	651
Mic	3: 6 it shall be **d** unto you, that *ye* shall not	2821
	3: 6 and the day shall be **d** over them.	6937
Zec	14: 6 *that* the light shall not be clear, nor **d**:	7087
Lk	11:36 therefore *be* full of light, having no part **d**,	4652
Jn	6:17 it was now **d**, and Jesus was not come	4653
	20: 1 when it was yet **d**, unto the sepulchre,	4653

DARKEN (1) [DARKENED, DARKENETH, DARKISH, DARKLY, DARKNESS]

Am	8: 9 and I will **d** the earth in the clear day:	2821

DARKENED (19) [DARKEN]

Ex	10:15 the whole earth, so that the land was **d**;	2821
Ps	69:23 Let their eyes be **d**, that *they* see not;	2821
Ecc	12: 2 light, or the moon, or the stars, be not **d**,	2821
	12: 3 those that look out of the windows be **d**,	2821
Isa	5:30 and the light is **d** in the heavens thereof.	2821
	9:19 wrath of the Lord of hosts is the land **d**,	6272
	13:10 the sun shall be **d** in his going forth,	2821
	24:11 all joy is **d**, the mirth of the land is gone.	6150
Eze	30:18 At Tehaphnehes also the day shall be **d**,	2821
Joel	3:15 The sun and the moon shall be **d**,	6937
Zec	11:17 his right eye shall be **utterly d**.	3543+3543
Mt	24:29 tribulation of those days shall the sun be **d**,	4654
Mk	13:24 the sun shall be **d**, and the moon shall not	4654
Lk	23:45 And the sun was **d**, and the vail of	4654
Ro	1:21 and their foolish heart was **d**.	4654
	11:10 Let their eyes be **d**, that *they* may not see,	4654
Eph	4:18 Having the understanding **d**,	4654
Rev	8:12 so as the third *part* of them was **d** and	4654
	9: 2 the air were **d** by reason of the smoke of	4654

DARKENETH (1) [DARKEN]

Job	38: 2 Who *is* this that **d** counsel by words	2821

DARKISH (1) [DARKEN]

Lev	13:39 spots in the skin of their flesh *be* **d** white;	3544

DARKLY (1) [DARKEN]

1Co	13:12 For now we see through a glass, **d**;	135+1722

DARKNESS (162) [DARKEN]

Ge	1: 2 and *was* upon the face of the deep.	2822
	1: 4 and God divided the light from the **d**.	2822
	1: 5 the light Day, and the **d** he called Night.	2822
	1:18 night, and to divide the light from the **d**:	2822
	15:12 and, lo, a horror of great **d** fell upon him.	2825
Ex	10:21 there may be **d** over the land of Egypt,	2822
	10:21 land of Egypt, even *which* may be felt.	2822
	10:22 was a thick **d** in all the land of Egypt	2822
	14:20 it was a cloud and **d** *to them*, but it gave	2822
	20:21 Moses drew near unto the **thick d** where	6205
Dt	4:11 with **d**, clouds, and thick darkness.	2822
	4:11 *with* darkness, clouds, and **thick d**,	6205
	5:22 of the cloud, and of the **thick d**, *with* a	6205
	5:23 heard the voice out of the midst of the **d**,	2822
	28:29 as the blind gropeth in **d**, and thou shalt	653
Jos	24: 7 he put **d** between you and the Egyptians,	3990
1Sa	2: 9 and the wicked shall be silent in **d**;	2822
2Sa	22:10 came down; and **d** *was* under his feet.	6205
	22:12 he made **d** pavilions round about him,	2822
	22:29 and the Lord will lighten my **d**.	2822
1Ki	8:12 said that he would dwell in the **thick d**.	6205
2Ch	6: 1 said that *he* would dwell in the **thick d**.	6205
Job	3: 4 Let that day be **d**; let not God regard it	2822
	3: 5 Let **d** and the shadow of death stain it;	6757
	3: 6 *As for* that night, let **d** seize upon it; let it	652
	5:14 They meet with **d** in the daytime,	2822
	10:21 *even* to the land of **d** and the shadow of	2822
	10:22 A land of **d**, as darkness *itself*; *and of*	5890
	10:22 A land of darkness, as *itself*; *and of*	652
	10:22 any order, and *where* the light is as **d**.	652
	12:22 He discovereth deep *things* out of **d**,	2822
	15:22 believeth not that *he* shall return out of **d**,	2822
	15:23 that the day of **d** is ready at his hand.	2822
	15:30 He shall not depart out of **d**; the flame	2822
	17:12 into day: the light *is* short, because of **d**.	2822
	17:13 house: I have made my bed in the **d**.	2822
	18:18 He shall be driven from light into **d**,	2822
	19: 8 pass, and he hath set **d** in my paths.	2822
	20:26 All **d** *shall* be hid in his secret places:	2822
	22:11 Or **d**, *that* thou canst not see;	2822
	23:17 Because I was not cut off before the **d**,	2822
	23:17 hath he covered the **d** from my face.	652
	28: 3 setteth an end to **d**, and searcheth out all	2822
	28: 3 the stones of **d**, and the shadow of death.	652
	29: 3 *and when* by his light I walked *through* **d**;	2822
	30:26 and when I waited for light, there came **d**.	652
	34:22 *There is* no **d**, nor shadow of death,	2822
	37:19 cannot order *our speech* by reason of **d**.	2822
	38: 9 and **thick d** a swaddling band for it,	6205
	38:19 and *as for* **d**, where *is* the place thereof,	2822
Ps	18: 9 came down; and **d** *was* under his feet.	6205
	18:11 He made **d** his secret place; his pavilion	2822
	18:28 the Lord my God will enlighten my **d**.	2822
	82: 5 will they understand; they walk on in **d**:	2825
	88: 6 in the lowest pit, in **d**, in the deeps.	4285
	88:18 from me, *and* mine acquaintance *into* **d**.	4285
	91: 6 *Nor* for the pestilence *that* walketh in **d**;	652
	97: 2 Clouds and *are* round about him:	6205
	104:20 Thou makest **d**, and it is night: wherein	2822
	105:28 He sent **d**, and made it dark;	2822
	107:10 as sit in **d** and in the shadow of death,	2822
	107:14 brought them out of **d** and the shadow	2822
	112: 4 the upright there ariseth light in the **d**:	2822
	139:11 If I say, Surely the **d** shall cover me;	2822
	139:12 Yea, the **d** hideth not from thee;	2822
	139:12 the **d** and the light *are* both alike *to thee*.	2825
	143: 3 he hath made me to dwell in **d**, as those	4285
Pr	2:13 of uprightness, to walk in the ways of **d**;	2822

Pr	4:19	The way of the wicked *is* as **d**: they know	653
	20:20	his lamp shall be put out in obscure **d**.	2822
Ecc	2:13	excelleth folly, as far as light excelleth **d**.	2822
	2:14	*are* in his head; but the fool walketh in **d**:	2822
	5:17	All his days also he eateth in **d**, and *he*	2822
	6: 4	departeth in **d**, and his name shall be	2822
	6: 4	and his name shall be covered with **d**.	2822
	11: 8	yet let him remember the days of **d**;	2822
Isa	5:20	that put **d** for light, and light for darkness;	2822
	5:20	that put darkness for light, and light for **d**;	2822
	5:30	behold **d** *and* sorrow, and the light is	2822
	8:22	behold trouble and **d**, dimness of anguish;	2825
	8:22	of anguish; and *they shall be* driven to **d**.	653
	9: 2	The people that walked in **d** have seen a	2822
	29:18	shall see out of obscurity, and out of **d**.	2822
	42: 7	them that sit in **d** out of the prison house.	2822
	42:16	I will make **d** light before them,	4285
	45: 3	I will give thee the treasures of **d**,	2822
	45: 7	form the light, and create **d**: I make peace,	2822
	47: 5	Sit thou silent, and get thee into **d**,	2822
	49: 9	to *them* that *are* in **d**, Shew yourselves.	2822
	50:10	that walketh *in* **d**, and hath no light?	2825
	58:10	in obscurity, and thy **d** *be* as the noonday:	653
	59: 9	for brightness, *but* we walk in **d**.	653
	60: 2	the **d** shall cover the earth,	2822
	60: 2	cover the earth, and **gross d** the people:	6205
Jer	2:31	a land of **d**? wherefore say my people,	3991
	13:16	before he **cause d**, and before your feet	2821
	13:16	shadow of death, *and* make *it* **gross d**.	6205
	23:12	be unto them as slippery *ways* in the **d**:	653
La	3: 2	and brought *me into* **d**, but not *into* light.	2822
Eze	32: 8	set up upon thy land, saith the Lord GOD.	2822
Da	2:22	*things*: he knoweth what *is* in the **d**,	2816
Joel	2: 2	A day of **d** and of gloominess, a day of	2822
	2: 2	a day of clouds and **thick d**,	6205
	2:31	The sun shall be turned into **d**,	2822
Am	4:13	that maketh the morning **d**,	5890
	5:18	the day of the LORD *is* **d**, and not light.	2822
	5:20	*Shall* not the day of the LORD *be* **d**,	2822
Mic	7: 8	when I sit in **d**, the LORD *shall be* a light	2822
Na	1: 8	and **d** shall pursue his enemies.	2822
Zep	1:15	desolation, a day of **d** and gloominess,	2822
	1:15	gloominess, a day of clouds and **thick d**,	6205
Mt	4:16	The people which sat in **d** saw great light;	4655
	6:23	be evil, thy whole body shall be **full of d**.	4652
	6:23	If therefore the light that is in thee be **d**,	4655
	6:23	in thee be darkness, how great *is* that **d**?	4655
	8:12	kingdom shall be cast out into outer **d**:	4655
	10:27	I tell you in **d**, *that* speak ye in light:	4653
	22:13	him away, and cast *him* into outer **d**,	4655
	25:30	ye the unprofitable servant into outer **d**:	4655
	27:45	from the sixth hour there was **d** over	4655
Mk	15:33	there was **d** over the whole land until	4655
Lk	1:79	To give light to them that sit in **d** and *in*	4655
	11:34	*thine eye* is evil, thy body also *is* **full of d**.	4652
	11:35	that the light which is in thee be not **d**.	4655
	12: 3	Therefore whatsoever ye have spoken in **d**	4653
	22:53	but this is your hour, and the power of **d**.	4655
	23:44	there was a **d** over all the earth until	4655
Jn	1: 5	the light shineth in **d**; and the darkness	4653
	1: 5	darkness; and the **d** comprehended it not.	4653
	3:19	men loved **d** rather than light, because	4653
	8:12	that followeth me shall not walk in **d**,	4653
	12:35	ye have the light, lest **d** come upon you:	4653
	12:35	for he that walketh in **d** knoweth not	4653
	12:46	believeth on me should not abide in **d**.	4653
Ac	2:20	The sun shall be turned into **d**,	4655
	13:11	there fell on him a mist and a **d**;	4655
	26:18	*and* to turn *them* from **d** to light,	4655
Ro	2:19	the blind, a light of them which are in **d**,	4655
	13:12	let us therefore cast off the works of **d**,	4655
1Co	4: 5	will bring to light the hidden *things* of **d**,	4655
2Co	4: 6	commanded the light to shine out of **d**,	4655
	6:14	and what communion hath light with **d**?	4655
Eph	5: 8	For ye were sometimes **d**, but now *are ye*	4655
	5:11	fellowship with the unfruitful works of **d**,	4655
	6:12	against the rulers of the **d** of this world,	4655
Col	1:13	hath delivered us from the power of **d**,	4655
1Th	5: 4	ye, brethren, are not in **d**, that *that* day	4655
	5: 5	the day: we are not of the night, nor of **d**.	4655
Heb	12:18	with fire, nor unto blackness, and **d**,	4655
1Pe	2: 9	you out of **d** into his marvellous light;	4655
2Pe	2: 4	hell, and delivered *them* into chains of **d**,	2217
	2:17	whom the mist of **d** is reserved for ever.	4655
1Jn	1: 5	that God is light, and in him is no **d** at all.	4653
	1: 6	walk in **d**, we lie, and do not the truth:	4655
	2: 8	because the **d** is past, and the true light	4653
	2: 9	hateth his brother, is in **d** *even* until now.	4653
	2:11	But he that hateth his brother is in **d**,	4653
	2:11	walketh in **d**, and knoweth not whither	4653
	2:11	because that **d** hath blinded his eyes.	4653
Jude	1: 6	under **d** unto the judgment of the great	2217
	1:13	whom is reserved the blackness of **d** for	4655
Rev	16:10	and his kingdom was **full of d**;	4656

DARKON (2)
Ezr	2:56	the children of **D**, the children of Giddel,	1874
Ne	7:58	The children of Jaala, the children of **D**,	1874

DARLING (2)
Ps	22:20	sword; my **d** from the power of the dog.	3173
	35:17	their destructions, my **d** from the lions.	3173

DART (3) [DARTS]
Job	41:26	the spear, the **d**, nor the habergeon.	4551

Pr	7:23	Till a **d** strike through his liver; as a bird	2671
Heb	12:20	be stoned, or thrust through with a **d**:	*1002*

DARTS (4) [DART]
2Sa	18:14	took three **d** in his hand, and thrust them	7626
2Ch	32: 5	and made **d** and shields in abundance.	7973
Job	41:29	**D** are counted as stubble: he laugheth at	8455
Eph	6:16	to quench all the fiery **d** of the wicked.	956

DASH (7) [DASHED, DASHETH]
2Ki	8:12	wilt **d** their children, and rip up their	7376
Ps	2: 9	thou shalt **d** them **in pieces** like a potter's	5310
	91:12	lest thou **d** thy foot against a stone.	5062
Isa	13:18	also shall **d** the young men **to pieces**;	7376
Jer	13:14	I will **d** them one against another, even	5310
Mt	4: 6	lest at any time thou **d** thy foot against a	4350
Lk	4:11	lest at any time thou **d** thy foot against a	4350

DASHED (5) [DASH]
Ex	15: 6	O LORD, hath **d in pieces** the enemy.	7492
Isa	13:16	Their children also shall be **d to pieces**	7376
Hos	10:14	the mother was **d in pieces** upon *her*	7376
	13:16	their infants shall be **d in pieces**,	7376
Na	3:10	young children also were **d in pieces** at	7376

DASHETH (2) [DASH]
Ps	137: 9	and **d** thy little ones against the stones.	5310
Na	2: 1	He that **d in pieces** is come up before thy	6327

DATHAN (10)
Nu	16: 1	the son of Levi, and **D** and Abiram,	1885
	16:12	Moses sent to call **D** and Abiram, the sons	1885
	16:24	the tabernacle of Korah, **D**, and Abiram.	1885
	16:25	rose up and went unto **D** and Abiram;	1885
	16:27	of Korah, **D**, and Abiram, on every side:	1885
	16:27	**D** and Abiram came out, and stood *in*	1885
	26: 9	of Eliab; Nemuel, and **D**, and Abiram.	1885
	26: 9	This *is that* **D** and Abiram, *which were*	1885
Dt	11: 6	what he did unto **D** and Abiram, the sons	1885
Ps	106:17	The earth opened and swallowed up **D**,	1885

DAUB (1) [DAUBED, DAUBING]
Eze	13:11	unto them which **d** *it with* untempered	2902

DAUBED (7) [DAUB]
Ex	2: 3	**d** it with slime and with pitch, and put	2560
Eze	13:10	lo, others **d** *it with* untempered *morter*:	2902
	13:12	*is* the daubing wherewith ye have **d**	2902
	13:14	that ye have **d** with untempered *morter*,	2902
	13:15	them that have **d** it with untempered	2902
	13:15	wall is no more, neither they that **d** it;	2902
	22:28	prophets have **d** them *with* untempered	2902

DAUBING (1) [DAUB]
Eze	13:12	Where *is* the **d** wherewith ye have daubed	2915

DAUGHTER (324) [DAUGHTER'S, DAUGHTERS]
Ge	11:29	Milcah, the **d** of Haran, the father of	1323
	11:31	Sarai his **d in law**, his son Abram's wife;	3618
	20:12	she *is* the **d** of my father, but not	1323
	20:12	of my father, but not the **d** of my mother;	1323
	24:23	Whose **d** *art* thou? tell me, I pray thee:	1323
	24:24	I *am* the **d** of Bethuel the son of Milcah,	1323
	24:47	I asked her, and said, Whose **d** *art* thou?	1323
	24:47	she said, The **d** of Bethuel, Nahor's son,	1323
	24:48	take my master's brother's **d** unto his son.	1323
	25:20	the **d** of Bethuel the Syrian of Padan-aram,	1323
	26:34	to wife Judith the **d** of Beeri the Hittite,	1323
	26:34	and Bashemath the **d** of Elon the Hittite:	1323
	28: 9	Mahalath the **d** of Ishmael Abraham's son,	1323
	29: 6	Rachel his **d** cometh with the sheep.	1323
	29:10	when Jacob saw Rachel the **d** of Laban his	1323
	29:18	thee seven years for Rachel thy younger **d**.	1323
	29:23	that he took Leah his **d**, and brought her	1323
	29:24	Laban gave unto his **d** Leah Zilpah his	1323
	29:28	and he gave him Rachel his **d** to wife *also*.	1323
	29:29	Laban gave to Rachel his **d** Bilhah his	1323
	30:21	afterwards she bare a **d**, and called her	1323
	34: 1	Dinah the **d** of Leah, which she bare unto	1323
	34: 3	his soul clave unto Dinah the **d** of Jacob,	1323
	34: 5	heard that he had defiled Dinah his **d**:	1323
	34: 7	folly in Israel in lying with Jacob's **d**;	1323
	34: 8	of my son Shechem longeth for your **d**:	1323
	34:17	will we take our **d**, and we will be gone.	1323
	34:19	because he had delight in Jacob's **d**:	1323
	36: 2	Adah the **d** of Elon the Hittite,	1323
	36: 2	Aholibamah the **d** of Anah the daughter	1323
	36: 2	Aholibamah the daughter of Anah the **d**	1323
	36: 3	Bashemath Ishmael's **d**, sister of Nebajoth	1323
	36:14	the **d** of Anah, daughter of Zibeon,	1323
	36:14	of Anah, of Zibeon, Esau's wife:	1323
	36:18	*that came* of Aholibamah the **d** of Anah,	1323
	36:25	Dishon, and Aholibamah the **d** of Anah.	1323
	36:39	the **d** of Matred, the daughter of Mezahab	1323
	36:39	the daughter of Matred, the **d** of Mezahab	1323
	38: 2	Judah saw there a **d** of a certain Canaanite	1323
	38:11	said Judah to Tamar his **d in law**, Remain	3618
	38:12	in process of time the **d** of Shuah Judah's	1323
	38:16	he knew not that she *was* his **d in law**:)	3618
	38:24	Tamar thy **d in law** hath played the harlot	3618
	41:45	he gave him to wife Asenath the **d** of	1323
	41:50	which Asenath the **d** of Poti-pherah priest	1323
	46:15	Jacob in Padan-aram, with his **d** Dinah:	1323
	46:18	whom Laban gave to Leah his **d**,	1323
	46:20	Asenath the **d** of Poti-pherah priest	1323
	46:25	which Laban gave to Rachel his **d**,	1323

Ex	1:16	but if it *be* a **d**, then she shall live.	1323
	1:22	the river, and every **d** ye shall save alive.	1323
	2: 1	of Levi, and took *to* wife a **d** of Levi.	1323
	2: 5	the **d** of Pharaoh came down to wash	1323
	2: 7	said his sister to Pharaoh's **d**, Shall I go	1323
	2: 8	Pharaoh's **d** said to her, Go. And the maid	1323
	2: 9	Pharaoh's **d** said unto her, Take this child	1323
	2:10	she brought him unto Pharaoh's **d**,	1323
	2:21	and he gave Moses Zipporah his **d**.	1323
	6:23	**d** of Amminadab, sister of Naashon,	1323
	20:10	thou, nor thy son, nor thy **d**,	1323
	21: 7	if a man sell his **d** to be a maidservant,	1323
	21:31	he have gored a son, or have gored a **d**,	1323
Lev	12: 6	purifying are fulfilled, for a son, or for a **d**,	1323
	18: 9	the **d** of thy father, or daughter of thy	1323
	18: 9	daughter of thy father, or **d** of thy mother,	1323
	18:10	The nakedness of thy son's **d**, or of thy	1323
	18:10	thy son's daughter, or of thy daughter's **d**,	1323
	18:11	The nakedness of thy father's wife's **d**,	1323
	18:15	uncover the nakedness of thy **d in law**:	3618
	18:17	the nakedness of a woman and her **d**,	1323
	18:17	neither shalt thou take her son's **d**,	1323
	18:17	or her daughter's **d**, to uncover her	1323
	19:29	Do not prostitute thy **d**, to cause her to	1323
	20:12	if a man lie with his **d in law**, both of	3618
	20:17	his father's, or his mother's, **daughter**,	1323
	20:17	or his mother's **d**, and see her nakedness,	1323
	21: 2	his son, and for his **d**, and for his brother,	1323
	21: 9	the **d** of any priest, if she profane herself	1323
	22:12	If the priest's **d** also be *married* unto a	1323
	22:13	If the priest's **d** be a widow, or divorced,	1323
	24:11	the **d** of Dibri, of the tribe of Dan:)	1323
Nu	25:15	that was slain *was* Cozbi, the **d** of Zur;	1323
	25:18	the **d** of a prince of Midian, their sister,	1323
	26:46	the name of the **d** of Asher *was* Sarah.	1323
	26:59	the **d** of Levi, whom *her mother* bare to	1323
	27: 8	cause his inheritance to pass unto his **d**.	1323
	27: 9	if he have no **d**, then ye shall give his	1323
	30:16	his wife, between the father and his **d**,	1323
	36: 8	every **d**, that possesseth an inheritance in	1323
Dt	5:14	thou, nor thy son, nor thy **d**, nor thy	1323
	7: 3	thy **d** thou shalt not give unto his son,	1323
	7: 3	nor his **d** shalt thou take unto thy son.	1323
	12:18	thy **d**, and thy manservant,	1323
	13: 6	or thy **d**, or the wife of thy bosom,	1323
	16:11	thy **d**, and thy manservant,	1323
	16:14	thy **d**, and thy manservant,	1323
	18:10	his son or his **d** to pass through the fire,	1323
	22:16	I gave my **d** unto this man to wife,	1323
	22:17	*her*, saying, I found not thy **d** a maid;	1323
	27:22	the **d** of his father, or the daughter of his	1323
	27:22	of his father, or the **d** of his mother.	1323
	28:56	and towards her son, and towards her **d**,	1323
Jos	15:16	to him will I give Achsah my **d** to wife.	1323
	15:17	and he gave him Achsah his **d** to wife.	1323
Jdg	1:12	to him will I give Achsah my **d** to wife.	1323
	1:13	and he gave him Achsah his **d** to wife.	1323
	11:34	his **d** came out to meet him with timbrels	1323
	11:34	beside her he had neither son nor **d**.	1323
	11:35	he rent his clothes, and said, Alas, my **d**,	1323
	11:40	of Jephthah the Gileadite four days in a	1323
	19:24	*is* my **d** a maiden, and his concubine;	1323
	21: 1	There shall not any of us give his **d** unto	1323
Ru	1:22	Ruth the Moabitess, her **d in law**,	3618
	2: 2	And she said unto her, Go, my **d**.	1323
	2: 8	Boaz unto Ruth, Hearest thou not, my **d**?	1323
	2:20	Naomi said unto her **d in law**, Blessed *be*	3618
	2:22	Naomi said unto Ruth her **d in law**,	3618
	2:22	*It is* good, my **d**, that thou go out with his	1323
	3: 1	My **d**, shall I not seek rest for thee, that it	1323
	3:10	Blessed *be* thou of the LORD, my **d**:	1323
	3:11	now, my **d**, fear not; I will do to thee all	1323
	3:16	in law, she said, Who *art* thou, my **d**?	1323
	3:18	said she, Sit still, my **d**, until thou know	1323
	4:15	for thy **d in law**, which loveth thee,	3618
1Sa	1:16	not thine handmaid for a **d** of Belial:	1323
	4:19	his **d in law**, Phinehas' wife, was with	3618
	14:50	wife *was* Ahinoam, the **d** of Ahimaaz:	1323
	17:25	will give him his **d**, and make his father's	1323
	18:17	said to David, Behold my elder **d** Merab,	1323
	18:19	Saul's **d** should have been given to David,	1323
	18:20	Michal Saul's **d** loved David: and they	1323
	18:27	And Saul gave him Michal his **d** to wife.	1323
	18:28	and *that* Michal Saul's **d** loved him.	1323
	25:44	Saul had given Michal his **d**, David's wife,	1323
2Sa	3: 3	Absalom the son of Maacah the **d** of	1323
	3: 7	whose name *was* Rizpah, the **d** of Aiah:	1323
	3:13	except thou first bring Michal Saul's **d**,	1323
	6:16	Michal Saul's **d** looked through a window	1323
	6:20	Michal the **d** of Saul came out to meet	1323
	6:23	Therefore Michal the **d** of Saul had no	1323
	11: 3	*Is* not this Bath-sheba, the **d** of Eliam,	1323
	12: 3	in his bosom, and was unto him as a **d**.	1323
	14:27	and one **d**, whose name *was* Tamar:	1323
	17:25	that went in to Abigail the **d** of Nahash,	1323
	21: 8	king took the two sons of Rizpah the **d**	1323
	21: 8	the five sons of Michal the **d** of Saul,	1323
	21:10	Rizpah the **d** of Aiah took sackcloth,	1323
	21:11	it was told David what Rizpah the **d** of	1323
1Ki	3: 1	took Pharaoh's **d**, and brought her into	1323
	4:11	which had Taphath the **d** of Solomon to	1323
	4:15	he also took Basmath the **d** of Solomon to	1323
	7: 8	made also a house for Pharaoh's **d**,	1323
	9:16	given *it for* a present unto his **d**,	1323
	9:24	Pharaoh's **d** came up out of the city of	1323

D

D

1Ki 11: 1 together with the **d** of Pharaoh, *women* 1323
15: 2 name *was* Maachah, the **d** of Abishalom. 1323
15:10 name *was* Maachah, the **d** of Abishalom. 1323
16:31 that he took *to* wife Jezebel the **d** of 1323
22:42 his mother's name *was* Azubah the **d** of 1323
2Ki 8:18 for the **d** of Ahab was his wife: and he did 1323
8:26 *was* Athaliah, the **d** of Omri king of Israel. 1323
9:34 and bury her: for she *is* a king's **d**. 1323
11: 2 Jehosheba, the **d** of king Joram, sister of 1323
14: 9 Give thy **d** to my son to wife: 1323
15:33 name *was* Jerusha, the **d** of Zadok. 1323
18: 2 name also *was* Abi, the **d** of Zachariah. 1323
19:21 The virgin the **d** of Zion hath despised 1323
19:21 the **d** of Jerusalem hath shaken her head 1323
21:19 the **d** of Haruz of Jotbah. 1323
22: 1 *was* Jedidah, the **d** of Adaiah of Boscath. 1323
23:10 his to pass through the fire to Molech. 1323
23:31 Hamutal, the **d** of Jeremiah of Libnah. 1323
23:36 Zebudah, the **d** of Pedaiah of Rumah. 1323
24: 8 the **d** of Elnathan of Jerusalem. 1323
24:18 Hamutal, the **d** of Jeremiah of Libnah. 1323
1Ch 1:50 **d** of Matred, the daughter of Mezahab. 1323
1:50 daughter of Matred, the **d** of Mezahab. 1323
2: 3 three were born unto him of the **d** of 1323
2: 4 Tamar his **d in law** bare him Pharez and 3618
2:21 afterward Hezron went in to the **d** of 1323
2:35 Sheshan gave his **d** to Jarha his servant to 1323
2:49 of Gibea: and the **d** of Caleb *was* Achsah. 1323
3: 2 Absalom the son of Maachah the **d** of 1323
3: 5 four, of Bath-shua the **d** of Ammiel: 1323
4:18 these *are* the sons of Bithiah the **d** of 1323
7:24 (And his **d** *was* Sherah, who built 1323
15:29 that Michal the **d** of Saul looking out at a 1323
2Ch 8:11 Solomon brought up the **d** of Pharaoh out 1323
11:18 Rehoboam took him Mahalath the **d** of 1323
11:18 Abihail the **d** of Eliab the son of Jesse; 1323
11:20 after her he took Maachah the **d** of 1323
11:21 Rehoboam loved Maachah the **d** of 1323
13: 2 mother's name also *was* Michaiah the **d** 1323
20:31 his mother's name *was* Azubah the **d** of 1323
21: 6 for he had the **d** of Ahab to wife: and 1323
22: 2 mother's name also *was* Athaliah the **d** 1323
22:11 Jehoshabeath, the **d** of the king, took 1323
22:11 So Jehoshabeath, the **d** of king Jehoram, 1323
25:18 Give thy **d** to my son to wife: 1323
27: 1 name also *was* Jerushah, the **d** of Zadok. 1323
29: 1 name *was* Abijah, the **d** of Zechariah. 1323
Ne 6:18 his son Johanan had taken the **d** of 1323
Est 2: 7 Hadassah, that *is*, Esther, his uncle's **d**: 1323
2: 7 mother were dead, took for his own **d**. 1323
2:15 the **d** of Abihail the uncle of Mordecai, 1323
2:15 who had taken *her* for his **d**, was come to 1323
9:29 the **d** of Abihail, and Mordecai the Jew, 1323
Ps 9:14 all thy praise in the gates of the **d** of Zion: 1323
45:10 O **d**, and consider, and incline thine ear; 1323
45:12 the **d** of Tyre *shall be there* with a gift; 1323
45:13 The king's **d** *is* all glorious within: 1323
137: 8 O **d** of Babylon, who art *to be* destroyed; 1323
SS 7: 1 are thy feet with shoes, O prince's **d**! 1323
Isa 1: 8 the **d** of Zion is left as a cottage in a 1323
10:30 Lift up thy voice, O **d** of Gallim: cause *it* 1323
10:32 hand *against* the mount of the **d** of Zion, 1323
16: 1 unto the mount of the **d** of Zion: 1323
22: 4 of the spoiling of the **d** of my people. 1323
23:10 thy land as a river, O **d** of Tarshish: 1323
23:12 O thou oppressed virgin, **d** of Zidon: 1323
37:22 The virgin, the **d** of Zion, hath despised 1323
37:22 the **d** of Jerusalem hath shaken her head 1323
47: 1 and sit in the dust, O virgin **d** of Babylon, 1323
47: 1 *there is* no throne, O **d** of the Chaldeans: 1323
47: 5 thee into darkness, O **d** of the Chaldeans: 1323
52: 2 bands of thy neck, O captive **d** of Zion. 1323
62:11 Say ye to the **d** of Zion, Behold, 1323
Jer 4:11 the wilderness toward the **d** of my people, 1323
4:31 the voice of the **d** of Zion, *that* bewaileth 1323
6: 2 I have likened the **d** of Zion *to* a comely 1323
6:14 have healed also the hurt of *the* **d** *of* NIH
6:23 as men for war against thee, O **d** of Zion. 1323
6:26 **d** of my people, gird *thee* with sackcloth, 1323
8:11 For they have healed the hurt of the **d** of 1323
8:19 Behold the voice of the cry of the **d** of my 1323
8:21 For the hurt of the **d** of my people am I 1323
8:22 is not the health of the **d** of my people 1323
9: 1 night for the slain of the **d** of my people! 1323
9: 7 for how shall I do for the **d** of my people? 1323
14:17 for the virgin **d** of my people is broken 1323
31:22 wilt thou go about, O thou backsliding **d**? 1323
46:11 and take balm, O virgin, **d** of Egypt: 1323
46:19 thou **d** dwelling in Egypt, furnish thyself 1323
46:24 The **d** of Egypt shall be confounded: 1323
48:18 Thou **d** that dost inhabit Dibon, come 1323
49: 4 thy flowing valley, O backsliding **d**? 1323
50:42 the battle, against thee, O **d** of Babylon. 1323
51:33 The **d** of Babylon *is* like a threshingfloor, 1323
52: 1 his mother's name *was* Hamutal the **d** of 1323
La 1: 6 from the **d** of Zion all her beauty is 1323
1:15 the **d** of Judah, *as in* a winepress. 1323
2: 1 How hath the Lord covered the **d** of Zion 1323
2: 2 wrath the strong holds of the **d** of Judah; 1323
2: 4 the eye, in the tabernacle of the **d** of Zion: 1323
2: 5 increased in the **d** of Judah mourning 1323
2: 8 to destroy the wall of the **d** of Zion: 1323
2:10 The elders of the **d** of Zion sit upon 1323
2:11 for the destruction of the **d** of my people; 1323
2:13 shall I liken to thee, O **d** of Zion? 1323

La 2:13 I may comfort thee, O virgin **d** of Zion? 1323
2:15 and wag their head at the **d** of Jerusalem, 1323
2:18 unto the Lord, O wall of the **d** of Zion, 1323
3:48 for the destruction of the **d** of my people. 1323
4: 3 the **d** of my people *is* become cruel, like 1323
4: 6 the punishment of the iniquity of the **d** 1323
4:10 in the destruction of the **d** of my people. 1323
4:21 Rejoice and be glad, O **d** of Edom, 1323
4:22 iniquity is accomplished, O **d** of Zion; 1323
4:22 he will visit thine iniquity, O **d** of Edom; 1323
Eze 14:20 they shall deliver neither son nor **d**; 1323
16:44 saying, As *is* the mother, *so is* her **d**. 1323
16:45 Thou *art* thy mother's **d**, that loatheth her 1323
22:11 another hath lewdly defiled his **d in law**; 3618
22:11 hath humbled his sister, his father's **d**. 1323
44:25 or for mother, or for son, or for **d**, 1323
Da 11: 6 for the king's **d** of the south shall come to 1323
11:17 he shall give him the **d** of women, 1323
Hos 1: 3 went and took Gomer the **d** of Diblaim; 1323
1: 6 she conceived again, and bare a **d**. 1323
Mic 1:13 she *is* the beginning of the sin to the **d** of 1323
4: 8 the flock, the strong hold of the **d** of Zion, 1323
4: 8 the kingdom shall come to the **d** of 1323
4:10 and labour to bring forth, O **d** of Zion, 1323
4:13 Arise and thresh, O **d** of Zion: for I will 1323
5: 1 gather thyself in troops, O **d** of troops: 1323
7: 6 the **d** riseth up against her mother, 1323
7: 6 the **d in law** against her mother in law; 3618
Zep 3:10 *even* the **d** of my dispersed, shall bring 1323
3:14 Sing, O **d** of Zion; shout, O Israel; be glad 1323
3:14 with all the heart, O **d** of Jerusalem. 1323
Zec 2: 7 that dwellest *with* the **d** of Babylon. 1323
2:10 Sing and rejoice, O **d** of Zion: for lo, 1323
9: 9 Rejoice greatly, O **d** of Zion; shout, 1323
9: 9 daughter of Zion; shout, O **d** of Jerusalem: 1323
Mal 2:11 and hath married the **d** of a strange god. 1323
Mt 9:18 saying, My **d** is even now dead: 2364
9:22 and when he saw her, he said, **D**, be of 2364
10:35 and the **d** against her mother, 2364
10:35 the **d in law** against her mother in law. 3565
10:37 or **d** more than me is not worthy of me. 2364
14: 6 the **d** of Herodias danced before them, 2364
15:22 my **d** is grievously vexed with a devil. 2364
15:28 her **d** was made whole from that *very* 2364
21: 5 Tell ye the **d** of Sion, Behold, thy King 2364
Mk 5:23 My **little d** lieth at the point of death: 2365
5:34 And he said unto her, **D**, thy faith hath 2364
5:35 *house certain* which said, Thy **d** is dead: 2364
6:22 when the **d** of the said Herodias came 2364
7:25 whose **young d** had an unclean spirit, 2365
7:26 he would cast forth the devil out of her **d**. 2364
7:29 go thy way; the devil is gone out of thy **d**. 2364
7:30 gone out, and *her* **d** laid upon the bed. 2364
Lk 2:36 prophetess, the **d** of Phanuel, of the tribe 2364
8:42 For he had one only **d**, about twelve years 2364
8:48 he said unto her, **D**, be of good comfort: 2364
8:49 *house*, saying to him, Thy **d** is dead; 2364
12:53 mother against the **d**, and the daughter 2364
12:53 daughter, and the **d** against the mother; 2364
12:53 the mother in law against her **d in law**, 3565
12:53 the **d in law** against her mother in law. 3565
13:16 And ought not this *woman*, being a **d** of 2364
Jn 12:15 Fear not, **d** of Sion: behold, thy King 2364
Ac 7:21 Pharaoh's **d** took him up, 2364
Heb 11:24 to be called the son of Pharaoh's **d**; 2364

DAUGHTER'S (3) [DAUGHTER]

Lev 18:10 thy son's daughter, or of thy **d** daughter, 1323
18:17 or her **d** daughter, to uncover her 1323
Dt 22:17 yet these *are* the tokens of my **d** virginity. 1323

DAUGHTERS (254) [DAUGHTER]

Ge 5: 4 hundred years: and he begat sons and **d**: 1323
5: 7 seven years, and begat sons and **d**: 1323
5:10 fifteen years, and begat sons and **d**: 1323
5:13 forty years, and begat sons and **d**: 1323
5:16 thirty years, and begat sons and **d**: 1323
5:19 hundred years, and begat sons and **d**: 1323
5:22 hundred years, and begat sons and **d**: 1323
5:26 and two years, and begat sons and **d**: 1323
5:30 and five years, and begat sons and **d**: 1323
6: 1 of the earth, and **d** were born unto them, 1323
6: 2 That the sons of God saw the **d** of men 1323
6: 4 the sons of God came in unto the **d** of 1323
11:11 five hundred years, and begat sons and **d**. 1323
11:13 three years, and begat sons and **d**. 1323
11:15 three years, and begat sons and **d**. 1323
11:17 thirty years, and begat sons and **d**. 1323
11:19 nine years, and begat sons and **d**. 1323
11:21 seven years, and begat sons and **d**. 1323
11:23 two hundred years, and begat sons and **d**. 1323
11:25 nineteen years, and begat sons and **d**. 1323
19: 8 have two **d** which have not known man; 1323
19:12 al, and whatsoever thou hast in the city, 1323
19:14 which married his **d**, and said, Up, get ye 1323
19:15 Arise, take thy wife, and thy two **d**, 1323
19:16 his wife, and upon the hand of his two **d**; 1323
19:30 in the mountain, and his two **d** with him; 1323
19:30 and he dwelt in a cave, he and his two **d**. 1323
19:36 Thus were both the **d** of Lot with child by 1323
24: 3 unto my son of the **d** of the Canaanites, 1323
24:13 the **d** of the men of the city come out to 1323
24:37 wife to my son of the **d** of the Canaanites, 1323
27:46 weary of my life because of the **d** of Heth; 1323
27:46 if Jacob take a wife of the **d** of Heth, 1323

Ge 27:46 as these *which are* of the **d** of the land, 1323
28: 1 Thou shalt not take a wife of the **d** of 1323
28: 2 take thee a wife from thence of the **d** of 1323
28: 6 Thou shalt not take a wife of the **d** of 1323
28: 8 Esau seeing that the **d** of Canaan pleased 1323
29:16 Laban had two **d**: the name of the elder 1323
30:13 Happy am I, for the **d** will call me blessed: 1323
31:26 carried away my **d**, as captives taken with 1323
31:28 not suffered me to kiss my sons and my **d**? 1323
31:31 wouldest take by force thy **d** from me. 1323
31:41 I served thee fourteen years for thy two **d**, 1323
31:43 *These are* my daughters, and *these* 1323
31:43 *These* daughters *are* my **d**, and *these* 1323
31:43 what can I do *this* day unto these my **d**, 1323
31:50 If thou shalt afflict my **d**, or if thou shalt 1323
31:50 if thou shalt take *other* wives beside my **d**, 1323
31:55 his sons and his **d**, and blessed them: 1323
34: 1 went out to see the **d** of the land. 1323
34: 9 *and* give your **d** unto us, and take our 1323
34: 9 unto us, and take our **d** unto you. 1323
34:16 will we give our **d** unto you, and we will 1323
34:16 will take your **d** to us, and we will dwell 1323
34:21 us take their **d** to us for wives, and let us 1323
34:21 us for wives, and let us give them our **d**. 1323
36: 2 Esau took his wives of the **d** of Canaan; 1323
36: 6 his **d**, and all the persons of his house, 1323
37:35 and all his **d** rose up to comfort him; 1323
46: 7 his **d**, and his sons' daughters, and all his 1323
46: 7 his sons' **d**, and all his seed brought he 1323
46:15 his sons and his **d** *were* thirty and three. 1323
Ex 2:16 Now the priest of Midian had seven **d**: 1323
2:20 he said unto his **d**, And where *is* he? why 1323
3:22 *them* upon your sons, and upon your **d**; 1323
6:25 Eleazar Aaron's son took him *one* of the **d** 1323
10: 9 our old, with our sons and with our **d**, 1323
21: 4 a wife, she have born him sons or **d**; 1323
21: 9 shall deal with her after the manner of **d**. 1323
32: 2 and of your **d**, and bring *them* unto me. 1323
34:16 thou take of their **d** unto thy sons, 1323
34:16 their **d** go a whoring after their gods, 1323
Lev 10:14 thou, and thy sons, and thy **d** with thee: 1323
26:29 and the flesh of your **d** shall ye eat. 1323
Nu 18:11 to thy sons and to thy **d** with thee, by a 1323
18:19 and thy sons and thy **d** with thee, 1323
21:29 his **d** into captivity with Sihon king of 1323
25: 1 commit whoredom with the **d** of Moab. 1323
26:33 the son of Hepher had no sons, but **d**: 1323
26:33 the names of the **d** of Zelophehad *were* 1323
27: 1 came the **d** of Zelophehad, the son of 1323
27: 1 these *are* the names of his **d**; Mahlah, 1323
27: 7 The **d** of Zelophehad speak right: thou 1323
36: 2 of Zelophehad our brother unto his **d**. 1323
36: 6 concerning the **d** of Zelophehad, 1323
36:10 so did the **d** of Zelophehad: 1323
36:11 Milcah, and Noah, the **d** of Zelophehad, 1323
Dt 12:12 your **d**, and your menservants, 1323
12:31 their **d** they have burnt in the fire to their 1323
23:17 There shall be no whore of the **d** of Israel, 1323
28:32 thy **d** *shall be* given unto another people, 1323
28:41 Thou shalt beget sons and **d**, but thou 1323
28:53 the flesh of thy sons and of thy **d**, which 1323
32:19 of the provoking of his sons, and of his **d**. 1323
Jos 7:24 his **d**, and his oxen, and his asses, and his 1323
17: 3 the son of Manasseh, had no sons, but **d**: 1323
17: 3 these *are* the names of his **d**, Mahlah, 1323
17: 6 Because the **d** of Manasseh had an 1323
Jdg 3: 6 they took their **d** to be their wives, 1323
3: 6 gave their **d** to their sons, and served their 1323
11:40 *That* the **d** of Israel went yearly to lament 1323
12: 9 thirty **d**, *whom* he sent abroad, and took 1323
12: 9 took in thirty **d** from abroad for his sons. 1323
14: 1 saw a woman in Timnath of the **d** of 1323
14: 2 have seen a woman in Timnath of the **d** of 1323
14: 3 *Is there* never a woman among the **d** of 1323
21: 7 we will not give them of our **d** to wives? 1323
21:18 we may not give them wives of our **d**: 1323
21:21 if the **d** of Shiloh come out to dance in 1323
21:21 catch you every man his wife of the **d** of 1323
Ru 1: 6 she arose with her **d in law**, that she 3618
1: 7 she was, and her two **d in law** with her; 3618
1: 8 Naomi said unto her two **d in law**, 3618
1:11 Naomi said, Turn again, my **d**: why will 1323
1:12 Turn again, my **d**, go *your way*; for I am 1323
1:13 my **d**; for it grieveth me much for your 1323
1Sa 1: 4 and to all her sons and her **d**, portions: 1323
2:21 and bare three sons and two **d**. 1323
8:13 he will take your **d** to be confectionaries, 1323
14:49 the names of his two **d** *were* these; 1323
30: 3 their wives, and their sons, and their **d**, 1323
30: 6 every man for his sons and for his **d**: 1323
30:19 great, neither sons nor **d**, neither spoil, 1323
2Sa 1:20 lest the **d** of the Philistines rejoice, lest 1323
1:20 lest the **d** of the uncircumcised triumph. 1323
1:24 Ye *d* of Israel, weep over Saul, 1323
5:13 there were yet sons and **d** born to David. 1323
13:18 for with such robes were the king's **d** *that* 1323
19: 5 the lives of thy sons and of thy **d**, 1323
2Ki 17:17 and their **d** to pass through the fire, 1323
1Ch 2:34 Now Sheshan had no sons, but **d**. 1323
4:27 Shimei had sixteen sons and six **d**; but his 1323
7:15 *was* Zelophehad: and Zelophehad had **d**. 1323
14: 3 and David begat moe sons and **d**. 1323
23:22 Eleazar died, and had no sons, but **d**: and 1323
25: 5 gave to Heman fourteen sons and three **d**. 1323
2Ch 2:14 The son of a woman of the **d** of Dan, 1323

2Ch	11:21 and eight sons, and threescore **d**.)	1323
	13:21 begat twenty and two sons, and sixteen **d**.	1323
	24: 3 him two wives; and he begat sons and **d**.	1323
	28: 8 **d**, and took also away much spoil from	1323
	29: 9 our sons and our **d** and our wives *are* in	1323
	31:18 their wives, and their sons, and their **d**,	1323
Ezr	2:61 which took a wife of the **d** of Barzillai	1323
	9: 2 For they have taken of their **d** for	1323
	9:12 therefore give not your **d** unto their sons,	1323
	9:12 neither take their **d** unto your sons, nor	1323
Ne	3:12 of the half part of Jerusalem, he and his **d**.	1323
	4:14 your sons, and your **d**, your wives,	1323
	5: 2 We, our sons, and our **d**, *are* many:	1323
	5: 5 our sons and our **d** to be servants,	1323
	5: 5 *some* of our **d** are brought unto bondage	1323
	7:63 which took one of the **d** of Barzillai	1323
	10:28 their wives, their sons, and their **d**,	1323
	10:30 that we would not give our **d** unto	1323
	10:30 of the land, nor take their **d** for our sons:	1323
	13:25 *saying*, Ye shall not give your **d** unto their	1323
	13:25 nor take their **d** unto your sons,	1323
Job	1: 2 born unto him seven sons and three **d**.	1323
	1:13 when his sons and his **d** *were* eating and	1323
	1:18 Thy sons and thy **d** *were* eating and	1323
	42:13 He had also seven sons and three **d**.	1323
	42:15 no women found *so* fair as the **d** of Job:	1323
Ps	45: 9 Kings' **d** *were* among thy honourable	1323
	48:11 let the **d** of Judah be glad, because of thy	1323
	97: 8 of Judah rejoiced, because of thy	1323
	106:37 their sons and their **d** unto devils,	1323
	106:38 the blood of their sons and of their **d**,	1323
	144:12 *that* our **d** *may be* as corner stones,	1323
Pr	30:15 The horseleach hath two **d**, *crying*, Give,	1323
	31:29 Many **d** have done virtuously,	1323
Ecc	12: 4 all the **d** of musick shall be brought low;	1323
SS	1: 5 black, but comely, O ye **d** of Jerusalem,	1323
	2: 2 among thorns, so *is* my love among the **d**.	1323
	2: 7 O ye **d** of Jerusalem, by the roes,	1323
	3: 5 O ye **d** of Jerusalem, by the roes,	1323
	3:10 paved *with* love, for the **d** of Jerusalem.	1323
	3:11 O ye **d** of Zion, and behold king Solomon	1323
	5: 8 I charge you, O **d** of Jerusalem, if ye find	1323
	5:16 and this *is* my friend, O **d** of Jerusalem.	1323
	6: 9 The saw her, and blessed her; *yea*,	1323
	8: 4 charge you, O **d** of Jerusalem, that ye stir	1323
Isa	3:16 Because the **d** of Zion are haughty,	1323
	3:17 the crown of the head of the **d** of Zion,	1323
	4: 4 washed away the filth of the **d** of Zion,	1323
	16: 2 the **d** of Moab shall be *at* the fords of	1323
	32: 9 ye careless **d**, give ear unto my speech.	1323
	43: 6 and my **d** from the ends of the earth;	1323
	49:22 **d** shall be carried upon *their* shoulders.	1323
	56: 5 and a name better than *of* sons and *of* **d**:	1323
	60: 4 and thy **d** shall be nursed at *thy* side.	1323
Jer	3:24 and their herds, their sons and their **d**.	1323
	5:17 *which* thy sons and thy **d** should eat:	1323
	7:31 to burn their sons and their **d** in the fire;	1323
	9:20 teach your **d** wailing, and every one her	1323
	11:22 their sons and their **d** shall die by famine:	1323
	14:16 their wives, nor their sons, nor their **d**:	1323
	16: 2 neither shalt thou have sons nor **d** in this	1323
	16: 3 concerning the **d** that are born in this	1323
	19: 9 flesh of their sons and the flesh of their **d**,	1323
	29: 6 Take ye wives, and beget sons and **d**;	1323
	29: 6 give your **d** to husbands, that they may	1323
	29: 6 husbands, that they may bear sons and **d**;	1323
	32:35 their **d** to pass through *the fire* unto	1323
	35: 8 we, our wives, our sons, nor our **d**;	1323
	41:10 *even* the king's **d**, and all the people that	1323
	43: 6 the king's **d**, and every person that	1323
	48:46 are taken captives, and thy **d** captives.	1323
	49: 2 and her **d** shall be burnt with fire:	1323
	49: 3 ye **d** of Rabbah, gird ye with sackcloth;	1323
La	3:51 mine heart because of all the **d** of my city.	1323
Eze	13:17 set thy face against the **d** of thy people,	1323
	14:16 they shall deliver neither sons nor **d**;	1323
	14:18 they shall deliver neither sons nor **d**,	1323
	14:22 shall be brought forth, *both* sons and **d**:	1323
	16:20 thou hast taken thy sons and thy **d**,	1323
	16:27 **d** of the Philistines, which are ashamed	1323
	16:46 she and her **d** that dwell at thy left hand:	1323
	16:46 at thy right hand, *is* Sodom and her **d**.	1323
	16:48 she nor her **d**, as thou hast done, thou	1323
	16:48 as thou hast done, thou and thy **d**.	1323
	16:49 of idleness was in her and in her **d**,	1323
	16:53 the captivity of Sodom and her **d**,	1323
	16:53 and the captivity of Samaria and her **d**,	1323
	16:55 When thy sisters, Sodom and her **d**,	1323
	16:55 her **d** shall return to their former estate,	1323
	16:55 thy **d** shall return to your former estate.	1323
	16:57 as *at* the time of *thy* reproach of the **d** of	1323
	16:57 round about her, the **d** of the Philistines,	1323
	16:61 I will give them unto thee for **d**, but not	1323
	23: 2 were two women, the **d** of one mother:	1323
	23: 4 were mine, and they bare sons and **d**.	1323
	23:10 took her sons and her **d**, and slew her	1323
	23:25 they shall take thy sons and thy **d**;	1323
	23:47 they shall slay their sons and their **d**,	1323
	24:21 your **d** whom ye have left shall fall by	1323
	24:25 set their minds, their sons and their **d**,	1323
	26: 6 her **d** which *are* in the field shall be slain	1323
	26: 8 He shall slay with the sword thy **d** in	1323
	30:18 her, and her **d** shall go into captivity.	1323
	32:16 the of the nations shall lament her:	1323
	32:18 *even* her, and the **d** of the famous nations,	1323

Hos	4:13 therefore your **d** shall commit whoredom,	1323
	4:14 will not punish your **d** when they commit	1323
Joel	2:28 your sons and your **d** shall prophesy,	1323
	3: 8 your **d** into the hand of the children of	1323
Am	7:17 thy sons and thy **d** shall fall by the sword,	1323
Lk	1: 5 and his wife *was* of the **d** of Aaron,	2364
	23:28 say, **D** of Jerusalem, weep not for me,	2364
Ac	2:17 and your sons and your **d** shall prophesy,	2364
	21: 9 And the same *man* had four **d**, virgins,	2364
2Co	6:18 and ye shall be my sons and **d**, saith	2364
1Pe	3: 6 whose **d** ye are, as long as ye do well,	5043

DAVID (1085) [DAVID'S]

Ru	4:17 he *is* the father of Jesse, the father of **D**.	1732
	4:22 And Obed begat Jesse, and Jesse begat **D**.	1732
1Sa	16:13 the spirit of the LORD came upon **D** from	1732
	16:19 said, Send me **D** thy son, which *is* with	1732
	16:20 and sent *them* by **D** his son unto Saul.	1732
	16:21 **D** came to Saul, and stood before him:	1732
	16:22 Let **D**, I pray thee, stand before me;	1732
	16:23 that **D** took a harp, and played with his	1732
	17:12 Now **D** *was* the son of that Ephrathite of	1732
	17:14 **D** *was* the youngest: and the three eldest	1732
	17:15 **D** went and returned from Saul to feed his	1732
	17:17 Jesse said unto **D** his son, Take now for	1732
	17:20 **D** rose up early in the morning, and left	1732
	17:22 **D** left his carriage in the hand of the	1732
	17:23 to the same words: and **D** heard *them*.	1732
	17:26 **D** spake to the men that stood by him,	1732
	17:28 Eliab's anger was kindled against **D**,	1732
	17:29 **D** said, What have I now done? *Is there*	1732
	17:31 the words were heard which **D** spake,	1732
	17:32 **D** said to Saul, Let no man's heart fail	1732
	17:33 Saul said to **D**, Thou art not able to go	1732
	17:34 **D** said unto Saul, Thy servant kept his	1732
	17:37 **D** said moreover, The LORD that	1732
	17:37 Saul said unto **D**, Go, and the LORD be	1732
	17:38 Saul armed **D** with his armour, and he	1732
	17:39 **D** girded his sword upon his armour,	1732
	17:39 for he had not proved *it*. And **D** said unto	1732
	17:39 for I have not proved *them*. And **D** put	1732
	17:41 Philistine came on and drew near unto **D**;	1732
	17:42 about, and saw **D**, he disdained him:	1732
	17:43 The Philistine said unto **D**, *Am* I a dog,	1732
	17:43 And the Philistine cursed **D** by his gods.	1732
	17:44 the Philistine said to **D**, Come to me,	1732
	17:45 said **D** to the Philistine, Thou comest to	1732
	17:48 and drew nigh to meet **D**, that David	1732
	17:48 that **D** hasted, and ran *toward* the army to	1732
	17:49 **D** put his hand in *his* bag, and took thence	1732
	17:50 So **D** prevailed over the Philistine with a	1732
	17:50 but *there was* no sword in the hand of **D**.	1732
	17:51 Therefore **D** ran, and stood upon	1732
	17:54 **D** took the head of the Philistine,	1732
	17:55 when Saul saw **D** go forth against	1732
	17:57 as **D** returned from the slaughter of	1732
	17:58 **D** answered, *I am* the son of thy servant	1732
	18: 1 of Jonathan was knit with the soul of **D**,	1732
	18: 3 Jonathan and **D** made a covenant, because	1732
	18: 4 gave it to **D**, and his garments, even to his	1732
	18: 5 **D** went out whithersoever Saul sent him,	1732
	18: 6 when **D** was returned from the slaughter	1732
	18: 7 his thousands, and **D** his ten thousands.	1732
	18: 8 They have ascribed unto **D** ten thousands,	1732
	18: 9 Saul eyed **D** from that day and forward.	1732
	18:10 **D** played with his hand, as at other times:	1732
	18:11 I will smite **D** even to the wall *with it*.	1732
	18:11 And **D** avoided out of his presence twice.	1732
	18:12 Saul was afraid of **D**, because the LORD	1732
	18:14 **D** behaved himself wisely in all his ways;	1732
	18:16 all Israel and Judah loved **D**, because	1732
	18:17 Saul said to **D**, Behold my elder daughter	1732
	18:18 **D** said unto Saul, Who *am* I? and what *is*	1732
	18:19 daughter should have been given to **D**,	1732
	18:20 Michal Saul's daughter loved **D**: and	1732
	18:21 Wherefore Saul said to **D**, Thou shalt *this*	1732
	18:22 Commune with **D** secretly, and say,	1732
	18:23 spake those words in the ears of **D**.	1732
	18:23 **D** said, Seemeth it to you a light *thing* to	1732
	18:24 told him, saying, On this manner spake **D**.	1732
	18:25 Saul said, Thus shall ye say to **D**, The king	1732
	18:25 Saul thought to make **D** fall by the hand of	1732
	18:26 when his servants told **D** these words,	1732
	18:26 it pleased **D** well to be the king's son in	1732
	18:27 Wherefore **D** arose and went, he and	1732
	18:27 **D** brought their foreskins, and they gave	1732
	18:28 and knew that the LORD *was* with **D**,	1732
	18:29 Saul was yet the more afraid of **D**;	1732
	18:30 *that* **D** behaved himself more wisely than	1732
	19: 1 to all his servants, that they should kill **D**.	1732
	19: 2 Jonathan Saul's son delighted much in **D**:	1732
	19: 2 Jonathan told **D**, saying, Saul my father	1732
	19: 4 Jonathan spake good of **D** unto Saul his	1732
	19: 4 the king sin against his servant, against **D**;	1732
	19: 5 innocent blood, to slay **D** without a cause?	1732
	19: 7 Jonathan called **D**, and Jonathan shewed	1732
	19: 7 Jonathan brought **D** to Saul, and he was in	1732
	19: 8 Went out, and fought with the	1732
	19: 9 in his hand: and **D** played with *his* hand.	1732
	19:10 Saul sought to smite **D** even to the wall	1732
	19:10 and **D** fled, and escaped that night.	1732
	19:12 So Michal let **D** down through a window:	1732
	19:14 when Saul sent messengers to take **D**,	1732
	19:15 Saul sent them *again* to see **D**,	1732
	19:18 So **D** fled, and escaped, and came to	1732

1Sa	19:19 Behold, **D** *is* at Naioth in Ramah.	1732
	19:20 Saul sent messengers to take **D**: and	1732
	19:22 and said, Where *are* Samuel and **D**?	1732
	20: 1 **D** fled from Naioth in Ramah, and came	1732
	20: 3 **D** sware moreover, and said, Thy father	1732
	20: 4 Jonathan unto **D**, Whatsoever thy soul	1732
	20: 5 **D** said unto Jonathan, Behold, to morrow	1732
	20: 6 **D** earnestly asked *leave* of me that he	1732
	20:10 said **D** to Jonathan, Who shall tell me?	1732
	20:11 Jonathan said unto **D**, Come, and let us	1732
	20:12 Jonathan said unto **D**, O LORD God of	1732
	20:12 *if there be* good toward **D**, and I then	1732
	20:15 of **D** every one from the face of the earth.	1732
	20:16 made a *covenant* with the house of **D**,	1732
	20:17 Jonathan caused **D** to swear again,	1732
	20:18 Jonathan said to **D**, To morrow is the	NIH
	20:24 So **D** hid himself in the field: and when	1732
	20:28 **D** earnestly asked *leave* of me *to go* to	1732
	20:33 it was determined of his father to slay **D**.	1732
	20:34 he was grieved for **D**, because his father	1732
	20:35 the field at the time appointed with **D**,	1732
	20:39 only Jonathan and **D** knew the matter.	1732
	20:41 **D** arose out of *a place* toward the south,	1732
	20:41 wept one with another, until **D** exceeded.	1732
	20:42 Jonathan said to **D**, Go in peace,	1732
	21: 1 came **D** to Nob to Ahimelech the priest:	1732
	21: 1 Ahimelech was afraid at the meeting of **D**,	1732
	21: 2 **D** said unto Ahimelech the priest,	1732
	21: 4 the priest answered **D**, and said, There is	1732
	21: 5 **D** answered the priest, and said unto him,	1732
	21: 8 **D** said unto Ahimelech, And is there not	1732
	21: 9 **D** said, There is none like that; give it me.	1732
	21:10 **D** arose, and fled that day for fear of Saul,	1732
	21:11 him, *Is* not this **D** the king of the land?	1732
	21:11 his thousands, and **D** his ten thousands?	1732
	21:12 **D** laid up these words in his heart,	1732
	22: 1 **D** therefore departed thence, and escaped	1732
	22: 3 **D** went thence *to* Mizpeh of Moab: and	1732
	22: 4 they dwelt with him all the while that **D**	1732
	22: 5 the prophet Gad said unto **D**, Abide not in	1732
	22: 5 **D** departed, and came *into* the forest of	1732
	22: 6 When Saul heard that **D** was discovered,	1732
	22:14 *so* faithful among all thy servants as **D**,	1732
	22:17 because their hand also *is* with **D**,	1732
	22:20 Abiathar, escaped, and fled after **D**.	1732
	22:21 Abiathar shewed **D** that Saul had slain	1732
	22:22 **D** said unto Abiathar, I knew *it* that day,	1732
	23: 1 they told **D**, saying, Behold, the Philistines	1732
	23: 2 Therefore **D** inquired of the LORD,	1732
	23: 2 the LORD said unto **D**, Go, and smite	1732
	23: 4 **D** inquired of the LORD yet again.	1732
	23: 5 So **D** and his men went *to* Keilah,	1732
	23: 5 So **D** saved the inhabitants of Keilah.	1732
	23: 6 the son of Ahimelech fled to **D** to Keilah,	1732
	23: 7 was told Saul that **D** was come to Keilah.	1732
	23: 8 *to* Keilah, to besiege **D** and his men.	1732
	23: 9 knew that Saul secretly practised	1732
	23:10 said **D**, O LORD God of Israel,	1732
	23:12 said **D**, Will the men of Keilah deliver me	1732
	23:13 **D** and his men, which *were* about six	1732
	23:13 it was told Saul that **D** was escaped from	1732
	23:14 **D** abode in the wilderness in strong holds,	1732
	23:15 **D** saw that Saul was come out to seek his	1732
	23:15 **D** *was* in the wilderness of Ziph in a	1732
	23:16 went to **D** *into* the wood,	1732
	23:18 **D** abode in the wood, and Jonathan went	1732
	23:19 Doth not **D** hide himself with us in strong	1732
	23:24 **D** and his men *were* in the wilderness of	1732
	23:25 men went to seek *him*. And they told **D**:	1732
	23:25 when Saul heard *that*, he pursued after **D**	1732
	23:26 **D** and his men on that side of the	1732
	23:26 **D** made haste to get away for fear of Saul;	1732
	23:26 for Saul and his men compassed **D** and his	1732
	23:28 Saul returned from pursuing after **D**,	1732
	23:29 **D** went up from thence, and dwelt in	1732
	24: 1 Behold, **D** *is* in the wilderness of En-gedi.	1732
	24: 2 to seek **D** and his men upon the rocks	1732
	24: 3 **D** and his men remained in the sides of	1732
	24: 4 men of **D** said unto him, Behold the day	1732
	24: 4 **D** arose, and cut off the skirt of Saul's	1732
	24: 7 stayed his servants with *these* words,	1732
	24: 8 **D** also rose afterward, and went out of	1732
	24: 8 **D** stooped *with his* face to the earth,	1732
	24: 9 **D** said to Saul, Wherefore hearest thou	1732
	24: 9 saying, Behold, **D** seeketh thy hurt?	1732
	24:16 when **D** had made an end of speaking	1732
	24:16 that Saul said, *Is* this thy voice, my son **D**?	1732
	24:17 he said to **D**, Thou *art* more righteous	1732
	24:22 **D** sware unto Saul. And Saul went home;	1732
	24:22 **D** and his men gat them up unto the hold.	1732
	25: 1 **D** arose, and went down to the wilderness	1732
	25: 4 **D** heard in the wilderness that Nabal did	1732
	25: 5 **D** sent out ten young men, and David said	1732
	25: 5 **D** said unto the young men, Get you up to	1732
	25: 8 hand unto thy servants, and to thy son **D**.	1732
	25: 9 to all those words in the name of **D**,	1732
	25:10 David's servants, and said, Who *is* **D**?	1732
	25:13 **D** said unto his men, Gird you on every	1732
	25:13 sword; and **D** also girded on his sword:	1732
	25:13 there went up after **D** about four hundred	1732
	25:14 **D** sent messengers out of the wilderness	1732
	25:20 **D** and his men came down against her;	1732
	25:21 **D** had said, Surely in vain have I kept	1732
	25:22 more also do God unto the enemies of **D**,	1732
	25:23 when Abigail saw **D**, she hasted,	1732

D

1Sa		
25:23	fell before **D** on her face,	1732
25:32	**D** said to Abigail, Blessed *be* the Lord	1732
25:35	So **D** received of her hand *that* which she	1732
25:39	**D** heard that Nabal was dead, he said,	1732
25:39	**D** sent and communed with Abigail, to	1732
25:40	when the servants of **D** were come to	1732
25:40	spake unto her, saying, **D** sent us unto	1732
25:42	she went after the messengers of **D**,	1732
25:43	**D** also took Ahinoam of Jezreel;	1732
26: 1	Doth not **D** hide himself in the hill of	1732
26: 2	to seek **D** in the wilderness of Ziph.	1732
26: 3	**D** abode in the wilderness, and he saw	1732
26: 4	therefore sent out spies,	1732
26: 5	**D** arose, and came to the place where Saul	1732
26: 5	**D** beheld the place where Saul lay,	1732
26: 6	answered **D** and said to Ahimelech	1732
26: 7	So **D** and Abishai came to the people by	1732
26: 8	said Abishai to **D**, God hath delivered	1732
26: 9	**D** said to Abishai, Destroy him not:	1732
26:10	**D** said furthermore, *As* the Lord liveth,	1732
26:12	So **D** took the spear and the cruse of water	1732
26:13	**D** went over *to* the *other* side, and stood	1732
26:14	**D** cried to the people, and to Abner the	1732
26:15	**D** said to Abner, *Art* not thou a *valiant*	1732
26:17	and said, *Is* this thy voice, my son **D**?	1732
26:17	**D** said, *It is* my voice, my lord, O king.	1732
26:21	return, my son **D**: for I will no more do	1732
26:22	**D** answered and said, Behold, the king's	1732
26:25	Saul said to **D**, Blessed *be* thou, my son	1732
26:25	said to David, Blessed *be* thou, my son **D**:	1732
26:25	So **D** went on his way, and Saul returned	1732
27: 1	**D** said in his heart, I shall now perish one	1732
27: 2	**D** arose, and he passed over with the six	1732
27: 3	**D** dwelt with Achish at Gath, he and	1732
27: 3	*even* **D** with his two wives, Ahinoam	1732
27: 4	it was told Saul that **D** was fled *to* Gath:	1732
27: 5	**D** said unto Achish, If I have now found	1732
27: 7	the time that **D** dwelt in the country of	1732
27: 8	**D** and his men went up, and invaded	1732
27: 9	smote the land, and left neither man	1732
27:10	**D** said, Against the south of Judah,	1732
27:11	**D** saved neither man nor woman alive,	1732
27:11	So did **D**, and so *will be* his manner all	1732
27:12	Achish believed **D**, saying, He hath made	1732
28: 1	Achish said unto **D**, Know thou assuredly,	1732
28: 2	**D** said to Achish, Surely thou shalt know	1732
28: 2	Achish said to **D**, Therefore will I make	1732
28:17	and given it to thy neighbour, *even* to **D**:	1732
29: 2	**D** and his men passed on in the rereward	1732
29: 3	*Is* not this **D**, the servant of Saul the king	1732
29: 5	*Is* not this **D**, of whom they sang one to	1732
29: 5	his thousands, and **D** his ten thousands?	1732
29: 6	Achish called **D**, and said unto him,	1732
29: 8	**D** said unto Achish, But what have I done?	1732
29: 9	Achish answered and said to **D**, I know	1732
29:11	**D** and his men rose up early to depart in	1732
30: 1	when **D** and his men were come to Ziklag	1732
30: 3	So **D** and his men came to the city,	1732
30: 4	**D** and the people that *were* with him lift	1732
30: 6	**D** was greatly distressed; for the people	1732
30: 6	**D** encouraged himself in the Lord his	1732
30: 7	**D** said to Abiathar the priest,	1732
30: 7	Abiathar brought thither the ephod to **D**.	1732
30: 8	**D** inquired at the Lord, saying, Shall I	1732
30: 9	So **D** went, he and the six hundred men	1732
30:10	**D** pursued, he and four hundred men:	1732
30:11	brought him to **D**, and gave him bread,	1732
30:13	**D** said unto him, To whom *belongest*	1732
30:15	**D** said to him, Canst thou bring me down	1732
30:17	**D** smote them from the twilight even unto	1732
30:18	**D** recovered all that the Amalekites had	1732
30:18	away: and **D** rescued his two wives.	1732
30:19	they had taken to them: **D** recovered all.	1732
30:20	**D** took all the flocks and the herds,	1732
30:21	**D** came to the two hundred men,	1732
30:21	so faint that they could not follow **D**,	1732
30:21	they went forth to meet **D**, and to meet	1732
30:21	**D** came near to the people, he saluted	1732
30:22	of those that went with **D**, and said,	1732
30:23	said **D**, Ye shall not do so, my brethren,	1732
30:26	**D** came to Ziklag, he sent of the spoil	1732
30:31	to all the places where **D** himself and	1732

2Sa		
1: 1	when **D** was returned from the slaughter	1732
1: 1	and **D** had abode two days in Ziklag;	1732
1: 2	*so* it was, when he came to **D**, that he fell	1732
1: 3	**D** said unto him, From whence comest	1732
1: 4	**D** said unto him, How went the matter?	1732
1: 5	**D** said unto the young man that told him,	1732
1:11	**D** took hold on his clothes, and rent them	1732
1:13	**D** said unto the young man that told him,	1732
1:14	**D** said unto him, How wast thou not	1732
1:15	**D** called one of the young men, and said,	1732
1:16	**D** said unto him, Thy blood *be* upon thy	1732
1:17	**D** lamented with this lamentation over	1732
2: 1	that **D** inquired of the Lord, saying,	1732
2: 1	**D** said, Whither shall I go up? And he	1732
2: 2	So **D** went up thither, and his two wives	1732
2: 3	men that *were* with him did **D** bring up,	1732
2: 4	they anointed **D** king over the house	1732
2: 4	they told **D**, saying, *That* the men of	1732
2: 5	**D** sent messengers unto the men of	1732
2:10	But the house of Judah followed **D**.	1732
2:11	the time that **D** was king in Hebron over	1732
2:13	the servants of **D**, went out,	1732
2:15	of Saul, and twelve of the servants of **D**.	1732

2Sa		
2:17	men of Israel, before the servants of **D**.	1732
2:31	servants of **D** had smitten of Benjamin,	1732
3: 1	the house of Saul and the house of **D**:	1732
3: 1	**D** waxed stronger and stronger,	1732
3: 2	unto **D** were sons born in Hebron: and	1732
3: 5	These were born to **D** in Hebron.	1732
3: 6	the house of Saul and the house of **D**,	1732
3: 8	not delivered thee into the hand of **D**,	1732
3: 9	as the Lord hath sworn to **D**, even so	1732
3:10	to set up the throne of **D** over Israel and	1732
3:12	Abner sent messengers to **D** on his behalf,	1732
3:14	**D** sent messengers to Ish-bosheth Saul's	1732
3:17	Ye sought for **D** in times past to be king	1732
3:18	do *it*: for the Lord hath spoken of **D**,	1732
3:18	By the hand of my servant **D** I will save	1732
3:19	Abner went also to speak in the ears of **D**	1732
3:20	So Abner came to **D** *to* Hebron,	1732
3:20	**D** made Abner and the men that *were*	1732
3:21	Abner said unto **D**, I will arise and go,	1732
3:21	**D** sent Abner away; and he went in peace.	1732
3:22	the servants of **D** and Joab came from	1732
3:22	Abner *was* not with **D** in Hebron; for he	1732
3:26	when Joab was come out from **D**, he sent	1732
3:26	from the well of Sirah: but **D** knew *it* not.	1732
3:28	afterward when **D** heard *it*, he said, I and	1732
3:31	**D** said to Joab, and to all the people that	1732
3:31	And king **D** *himself* followed the bier.	1732
3:35	all the people came to cause **D** to eat	1732
3:35	**D** sware, saying, So do God to me,	1732
4: 8	head of Ish-bosheth unto **D** to Hebron,	1732
4: 9	**D** answered Rechab and Baanah his	1732
4:12	**D** commanded *his* young men,	1732
5: 1	came all the tribes of Israel to **D** unto	1732
5: 3	**D** made a league with them in Hebron	1732
5: 3	and they anointed **D** king over Israel.	1732
5: 4	**D** *was* thirty years old when he *began* to	1732
5: 6	which spake unto **D**, saying, Except thou	1732
5: 6	thinking, **D** cannot come in hither.	1732
5: 7	Nevertheless **D** took the strong hold of	1732
5: 7	hold of Zion: the same *is* the city of **D**.	1732
5: 8	said on that day, Whosoever getteth up	1732
5: 9	**D** dwelt in the fort, and called it the city	1732
5: 9	in the fort, and called it the city of **D**.	1732
5: 9	**D** built round about from Millo and	1732
5:10	**D** went on, and grew great, and the Lord	1732
5:11	Hiram king of Tyre sent messengers to **D**,	1732
5:11	masons: and they built **D** a house.	1732
5:12	**D** perceived that the Lord had	1732
5:13	**D** took *him* mo concubines and wives out	1732
5:13	were yet sons and daughters born to **D**.	1732
5:17	that they had anointed **D** king over Israel,	1732
5:17	all the Philistines came up to seek **D**;	1732
5:17	**D** heard *of it*, and went down to the hold.	1732
5:19	**D** inquired of the Lord, saying, Shall I	1732
5:19	the Lord said unto **D**, Go up: for I will	1732
5:20	**D** came to Baal-perazim, and David smote	1732
5:20	and **D** smote them there, and said,	1732
5:21	and **D** and his men burnt them.	1732
5:23	when **D** inquired of the Lord, he said,	1732
5:25	**D** did so, as the Lord had commanded	1732
6: 1	**D** gathered together all the chosen *men* of	1732
6: 2	**D** arose, and went with all the people that	1732
6: 5	**D** and all the house of Israel played before	1732
6: 8	**D** was displeased, because the Lord had	1732
6: 9	**D** was afraid of the Lord that day,	1732
6:10	So **D** would not remove the ark of	1732
6:10	of the Lord unto him into the city of **D**:	1732
6:10	**D** carried it aside *into* the house of	1732
6:12	it was told king **D**, saying, The Lord	1732
6:12	So **D** went and brought up the ark of God	1732
6:12	*into* the city of **D** with gladness.	1732
6:14	**D** danced before the Lord with all *his*	1732
6:14	and **D** *was* girded *with* a linen ephod.	1732
6:15	**D** and all the house of Israel brought up	1732
6:16	ark of the Lord came *into* the city of **D**,	1732
6:16	saw king **D** leaping and dancing before	1732
6:17	in the midst of the tabernacle that **D** had	1732
6:17	**D** offered burnt offerings and	1732
6:18	as soon as **D** had made an end of offering	1732
6:20	**D** returned to bless his household.	1732
6:20	the daughter of Saul came out to meet **D**,	1732
6:21	**D** said unto Michal, *It was* before	1732
7: 5	Go and tell my servant **D**, Thus saith	1732
7: 8	so shalt thou say unto my servant **D**,	1732
7:17	this vision, so did Nathan speak unto **D**.	1732
7:18	went king **D** in, and sat before the Lord,	1732
7:20	what can **D** say more unto thee? for thou,	1732
7:26	let the house of thy servant **D** be	1732
8: 1	that **D** smote the Philistines,	1732
8: 1	**D** took Metheg-ammah out of the hand of	1732
8: 3	**D** smote also Hadadezer, the son of Rehob	1732
8: 4	**D** took from him a thousand *chariots*, and	1732
8: 4	houghed all the chariot *horses*, but	1732
8: 5	**D** slew of the Syrians two and	1732
8: 6	**D** put garrisons in Syria of Damascus:	1732
8: 6	the Syrians became servants to **D**,	1732
8: 6	the Lord preserved **D** whithersoever he	1732
8: 7	**D** took the shields of gold that were on	1732
8: 8	king **D** took exceeding much brass.	1732
8: 9	Toi king of Hamath heard that **D** had	1732
8:10	Toi sent Joram his son unto king **D**,	1732
8:11	Which also king **D** did dedicate unto	1732
8:13	**D** gat *him* a name when he returned from	1732
8:14	the Lord preserved **D** whithersoever he	1732
8:15	**D** reigned over all Israel; and David	1732

2Sa		
8:15	**D** executed judgment and justice unto all	1732
9: 1	**D** said, Is there yet *any* that is left of	1732
9: 2	they had called him unto **D**, the king	1732
9: 5	**D** sent, and fet him out of the house of	1732
9: 6	the son of Saul, was come unto **D**, he fell	1732
9: 6	**D** said, Mephibosheth. And he answered,	1732
9: 7	**D** said unto him, Fear not: for I will surely	1732
10: 2	said **D**, I will shew kindness unto Hanun	1732
10: 2	**D** sent to comfort him by the hand of his	1732
10: 3	Thinkest thou that **D** doth honour thy	1732
10: 3	hath not **D** *rather* sent his servants unto	1732
10: 5	When they told *it* unto **D**, he sent to meet	1732
10: 6	of Ammon saw that they stank before **D**,	1732
10: 7	when **D** heard *of it*, he sent Joab, and all	1732
10:17	when it was told **D**, he gathered all Israel	1732
10:17	Syrians set *themselves* in array against **D**,	1732
10:18	**D** slew *the men* of seven hundred	1732
11: 1	kings go forth *to* battle, that **D** sent Joab,	1732
11: 1	But **D** tarried *still* at Jerusalem.	1732
11: 2	that **D** arose from off his bed,	1732
11: 3	**D** sent and inquired after the woman.	1732
11: 4	**D** sent messengers, and took her;	1732
11: 5	sent and told **D**, and said, I *am* with child.	1732
11: 6	**D** sent to Joab, *saying*, Send me Uriah	1732
11: 6	the Hittite. And Joab sent Uriah to **D**.	1732
11: 7	**D** demanded *of him* how Joab did,	1732
11: 8	**D** said to Uriah, Go down to thy house,	1732
11:10	when they had told **D**, saying, Uriah went	1732
11:10	**D** said unto Uriah, Camest thou not from	1732
11:11	Uriah said unto **D**, The ark, and Israel,	1732
11:12	**D** said to Uriah, Tarry here to day also,	1732
11:13	when **D** had called him, he did eat and	1732
11:14	**D** wrote a letter to Joab, and sent it by	1732
11:17	*some* of the people of the servants of **D**;	1732
11:18	told **D** all the things concerning the war;	1732
11:22	shewed **D** all that Joab had sent him for.	1732
11:23	messenger said unto **D**, Surely the men	1732
11:25	**D** said unto the messenger, Thus shalt	1732
11:27	**D** sent and fet her to his house,	1732
11:27	the thing that **D** had done displeased	1732
12: 1	the Lord sent Nathan unto **D**. And he	1732
12: 7	Nathan said to **D**, Thou *art* the man.	1732
12:13	**D** said unto Nathan, I have sinned against	1732
12:13	Nathan said unto **D**, The Lord also hath	1732
12:15	the child that Uriah's wife bare unto **D**,	1732
12:16	**D** therefore besought God for the child;	1732
12:16	**D** fasted, and went in, and lay all night	1732
12:18	the servants of **D** feared to tell him that	1732
12:19	when **D** saw that his servants whispered,	1732
12:19	**D** perceived that the child was dead:	1732
12:19	therefore **D** said unto his servants,	1732
12:20	**D** arose from the earth, and washed,	1732
12:24	**D** comforted Bath-sheba his wife,	1732
12:27	Joab sent messengers to **D**, and said,	1732
12:29	And **D** gathered all the people together,	1732
12:31	So **D** and all the people returned *unto*	1732
13: 1	Absalom the son of **D** had a fair sister,	1732
13: 1	and Amnon the son of **D** loved her.	1732
13: 7	**D** sent home to Tamar, saying, Go now	1732
13:21	when king **D** heard of all these things,	1732
13:30	in the way, that tidings came to **D**, saying,	1732
13:37	And **D** mourned for his son every day.	NIH
13:39	*the soul of* king **D** longed to go forth unto	1732
15:13	there came a messenger to **D**, saying,	1732
15:14	**D** said unto all his servants that *were* with	1732
15:22	**D** said to Ittai, Go and pass over. And Ittai	1732
15:30	**D** went up by the ascent of *mount* Olivet,	1732
15:31	*one* told **D**, saying, Ahithophel *is* among	1732
15:31	**D** said, O Lord, I pray thee, turn	1732
15:32	that *when* **D** was come to the top of	1732
15:33	Unto whom **D** said, If thou passest on	1732
16: 1	**D** was a little past the top *of the hill,*	1732
16: 5	when king **D** came to Bahurim, behold,	1732
16: 6	he cast stones at **D**, and at all the servants	1732
16: 6	at David, and at all the servants of king **D**:	1732
16:10	the Lord hath said unto him, Curse **D**.	1732
16:11	**D** said to Abishai, and to all his servants,	1732
16:13	and his men went by the way, Shimei	1732
16:23	all the counsel of Ahithophel both with **D**	1732
17: 1	I will arise and pursue after **D** *this* night:	1732
17:16	therefore send quickly, and tell **D**, saying,	1732
17:17	told them; and they went and told king **D**.	1732
17:21	and told king **D**, and said unto David,	1732
17:21	said unto **D**, Arise, and pass quickly over	1732
17:22	**D** arose, and all the people that *were* with	1732
17:24	**D** came to Mahanaim. And Absalom	1732
17:27	to pass, when **D** was come to Mahanaim,	1732
17:29	for **D**, and for the people that *were* with	1732
18: 1	**D** numbered the people that *were* with	1732
18: 2	**D** sent forth a third part of the people	1732
18: 7	Israel were slain before the servants of **D**,	1732
18: 9	Absalom met the servants of **D**.	1732
18:24	**D** sat between the two gates: and	1732
19:11	king **D** sent to Zadok and to Abiathar	1732
19:16	with the men of Judah to meet king **D**.	1732
19:22	**D** said, What have I to do with you, ye	1732
19:43	and we have also more *right* in **D** than ye:	1732
20: 1	trumpet, and said, We have no part in **D**,	1732
20: 2	every man of Israel went up from after **D**,	1732
20: 3	**D** came to his house at Jerusalem,	1732
20: 6	**D** said to Abishai, Now shall Sheba the	1732
20:11	and he that *is* for **D**, *let* him *go* after Joab.	1732
20:21	his hand against the king, *even* against **D**:	1732
20:26	also the Jairite was a chief ruler about **D**.	1732
21: 1	there was a famine in the days of **D** three	1732

D

2Sa 21: 1	after year; and **D** inquired of the LORD.	1732
21: 3	Wherefore **D** said unto the Gibeonites,	1732
21: 7	between **D** and Jonathan the son of Saul.	1732
21:11	it was told **D** what Rizpah the daughter of	1732
21:12	**D** went and took the bones of Saul and	1732
21:15	**D** went down, and his servants with him,	1732
21:15	against the Philistines: and **D** waxed faint.	1732
21:16	a new *sword,* thought to have slain **D**.	1732
21:17	the men of **D** sware unto him, saying,	1732
21:21	the son of Shimea the brother of **D**	1732
21:22	fell by the hand of **D**, and by the hand of	1732
22: 1	spake unto the LORD the words of this	1732
22:51	unto **D**, and to his seed for evermore.	1732
23: 1	Now these *be* the last words of **D**,	1732
23: 1	**D** the son of Jesse said, and the man *who*	1732
23: 8	names of the mighty *men* whom **D** had:	1732
23: 9	*one* of the three mighty *men* with **D**,	1732
23:13	to **D** in the harvest time unto the cave	1732
23:14	**D** *was* then in a hold, and the garrison of	1732
23:15	**D** longed, and said, Oh that one would	1732
23:16	the gate, and took *it,* and brought *it* to **D**:	1732
23:23	*first* three. And **D** set him over his guard.	1732
24: 1	he moved **D** against them to say,	1732
24:10	**D** said unto the LORD, I have sinned	1732
24:11	For when **D** was up in the morning,	1732
24:12	Go and say unto **D**, Thus saith the LORD,	1732
24:13	So Gad came to **D**, and told him,	1732
24:14	**D** said unto Gad, I am in a great strait:	1732
24:17	**D** spake unto the LORD when he saw	1732
24:18	came that day to **D**, and said unto him,	1732
24:19	**D**, according to the saying of Gad, went	1732
24:21	**D** said, To buy the threshingfloor of thee,	1732
24:22	Araunah said unto **D**, Let my lord the	1732
24:24	So **D** bought the threshingfloor and	1732
24:25	**D** built there an altar unto the LORD,	1732
1Ki 1: 1	king **D** was old *and* stricken in years;	1732
1: 8	the mighty *men* which *belonged* to **D**,	1732
1:11	reign, and **D** our lord knoweth *it* not?	1732
1:13	Go and get thee in unto king **D**,	1732
1:28	king **D** answered and said, Call me	1732
1:31	and said, Let my lord king **D** live for ever.	1732
1:32	king **D** said, Call me Zadok the priest,	1732
1:37	greater than the throne of my lord king **D**.	1732
1:43	our lord king **D** hath made Solomon	1732
1:47	servants came to bless our lord king **D**,	1732
2: 1	Now the days of **D** drew nigh that *he*	1732
2:10	**D** slept with his fathers, and was buried	1732
2:10	fathers, and was buried in the city of **D**.	1732
2:11	the days that **D** reigned over Israel *were*	1732
2:12	sat Solomon upon the throne of **D** his	1732
2:24	set me on the throne of **D** my father,	1732
2:26	ark of the Lord GOD before **D** my father,	1732
2:32	my father **D** not knowing *thereof,* to wit,	1732
2:33	upon **D**, and upon his seed, and upon his	1732
2:44	is privy to, that thou didst to **D** my father:	1732
2:45	throne of **D** shall be established before	1732
3: 1	and brought her into the city of **D**,	1732
3: 3	walking in the statutes of **D** his father:	1732
3: 6	Thou hast shewed unto thy servant **D** my	1732
3: 7	thy servant king instead of **D** my father:	1732
3:14	as thy father **D** did walk, then I will	1732
5: 1	father: for Hiram was ever a lover of **D**.	1732
5: 3	Thou knowest how that **D** my father	1732
5: 5	as the LORD spake unto **D** my father,	1732
5: 7	which hath given unto **D** a wise son over	1732
6:12	thee, which I spake unto **D** thy father:	1732
7:51	Solomon brought in the *things* which **D**	1732
8: 1	of the LORD out of the city of **D**,	1732
8:15	which spake with his mouth unto **D** my	1732
8:16	but I chose **D** to be over my people Israel.	1732
8:17	it was in the heart of **D** my father to build	1732
8:18	the LORD said unto **D** my father,	1732
8:20	I am risen up in the room of **D** my father,	1732
8:24	hast kept with thy servant **D** my father	1732
8:25	keep with thy servant **D** my father that	1732
8:26	thou spakest unto thy servant **D** my	1732
8:66	that the LORD had done for **D** his servant,	1732
9: 4	**D** thy father walked, in integrity of heart,	1732
9: 5	as I promised to **D** thy father, saying,	1732
9:24	her house which *Solomon* had	1732
11: 4	his God, as *was* the heart of **D** his father.	1732
11: 6	fully after the LORD, as *did* **D** his father.	1732
11:12	I will not do it for **D** thy father's sake:	1732
11:13	will give one tribe to thy son for **D** my	1732
11:15	**D** was in Edom, and Joab the captain	1732
11:21	when Hadad heard in Egypt that **D** slept	1732
11:24	**D** slew them *of Zobah:* and they went	1732
11:27	repaired the breaches of the city of **D** his	1732
11:33	and my judgments, as *did* **D** his father.	1732
11:34	days of his life for **D** my servant's sake,	1732
11:36	that **D** my servant may have a light alway	1732
11:38	my commandments, as **D** my servant did;	1732
11:38	as I built for **D**, and will give Israel unto	1732
11:39	I will for this afflict the seed of **D**,	1732
11:43	and was buried in the city of **D** his father:	1732
12:16	saying, What portion have we in **D**?	1732
12:16	now see to thine own house, **D**. So Israel	1732
12:19	So Israel rebelled against the house of **D**,	1732
12:20	was none that followed the house of **D**,	1732
12:26	the kingdom return to the house of **D**:	1732
13: 2	a child *shall* be born unto the house of **D**,	1732
14: 8	the kingdom away from the house of **D**,	1732
14: 8	*yet* thou hast not been as my servant **D**,	1732
14:31	buried with his fathers in the city of **D**.	1732
15: 3	his God, as the heart of **D** his father.	1732

1Ki 15: 5	Because **D** did *that* which *was* right in	1732
15: 8	and they buried him in the city of **D**:	1732
15:11	the eyes of the LORD, as *did* **D** his father.	1732
15:24	buried with his fathers in the city of **D**	1732
22:50	buried with his fathers in the city of **D**	1732
2Ki 8:19	not destroy Judah for **D** his servant's sake,	1732
8:24	buried with his fathers in the city of **D**.	1732
9:28	sepulchre with his fathers in the city of **D**.	1732
12:21	him with his fathers in the city of **D**.	1732
14: 3	of the LORD, yet not like **D** his father:	1732
14:20	Jerusalem with his fathers in the city of **D**.	1732
15: 7	him with his fathers in the city of **D**:	1732
15:38	buried with his fathers in the city of **D**	1732
16: 2	of the LORD his God, like **D** his father.	1732
16:20	buried with his fathers in the city of **D**:	1732
17:21	For he rent Israel from the house of **D**;	1732
18: 3	according to all that **D** his father did.	1732
20: 5	saith the LORD, the God of **D** thy father,	1732
21: 7	of which the LORD said to **D**,	1732
22: 2	walked in all the way of **D** his father,	1732
1Ch 2:15	Ozem the sixth, **D** the seventh:	1732
3: 1	these were the sons of **D**, which were	1732
3: 9	*These were* all the sons of **D**, beside	1732
4:31	*were* their cities unto the reign of **D**.	1732
6:31	*are they* whom **D** set over the service	1732
7: 2	whose number *was* in the days of **D** two	1732
9:22	whom **D** and Samuel the seer did ordain	1732
10:14	the kingdom unto **D** the son of Jesse.	1732
11: 1	all Israel gathered themselves to **D** unto	1732
11: 3	**D** made a covenant with them in Hebron	1732
11: 3	they anointed **D** king over Israel,	1732
11: 4	**D** and all Israel went *to* Jerusalem, which	1732
11: 5	the inhabitants of Jebus said to **D**,	1732
11: 5	Nevertheless **D** took the castle of Zion,	1732
11: 5	the castle of Zion, which *is* the city of **D**.	1732
11: 6	**D** said, Whosoever smiteth the Jebusites	1732
11: 7	**D** dwelt in the castle; therefore they called	1732
11: 7	therefore they called it the city of **D**.	1732
11: 9	So **D** waxed greater and greater: for	1732
11:10	the chief of the mighty *men* whom **D** had,	1732
11:11	number of the mighty *men* whom **D** had;	1732
11:13	He was with **D** at Pas-dammim,	1732
11:15	captains went down to the rock to **D**,	1732
11:16	**D** *was* then in the hold, and the	1732
11:17	**D** longed, and said, Oh that one would	1732
11:18	the gate, and took *it,* and brought *it* to **D**:	1732
11:18	**D** would not drink *of* it, but poured it out	1732
11:25	*first* three: and **D** set him over his guard.	1732
12: 1	Now these *are* they that came to **D** to	1732
12: 8	**D** into the hold to the wilderness men of	1732
12:16	Benjamin and Judah to the hold unto **D**.	1732
12:17	**D** went out to meet them, and answered	1732
12:18	*and he said,* Thine *are we,* **D**, and on thy	1732
12:18	**D** received them, and made them captains	1732
12:19	there fell *some* of Manasseh to **D**, when	1732
12:21	they helped **D** against the band *of*	1732
12:22	at *that* time day by day there came to **D**	1732
12:23	*and* came to **D** to Hebron, to turn	1732
12:31	by name, to come and make **D** king.	1732
12:38	to Hebron, to make **D** king over all Israel:	1732
12:38	Israel *were of* one heart to make **D** king.	1732
12:39	there they were with **D** three days, eating	1732
13: 1	**D** consulted with the captains of	1732
13: 2	**D** said unto all the congregation of Israel,	1732
13: 5	So **D** gathered all Israel together,	1732
13: 6	**D** went up, and all Israel, to Baalah,	1732
13: 8	**D** and all Israel played before God with all	1732
13:11	**D** was displeased, because the LORD had	1732
13:12	**D** was afraid of God that day, saying,	1732
13:13	So **D** brought not the ark *home* to himself	1732
13:13	the ark *home* to himself to the city of **D**,	1732
14: 1	Hiram king of Tyre sent messengers to **D**,	1732
14: 2	**D** perceived that the LORD had	1732
14: 3	**D** took moe wives at Jerusalem: and	1732
14: 3	and **D** begat moe sons and daughters.	1732
14: 8	when the Philistines heard that **D** was	1732
14: 8	all the Philistines went up to seek **D**.	1732
14: 8	**D** heard *of it,* and went out against them.	1732
14:10	**D** inquired of God, saying, Shall I go up	1732
14:11	to Baal-perazim; and **D** smote them there.	1732
14:11	**D** said, God hath broken in upon mine	1732
14:12	**D** gave a commandment, and they were	1732
14:14	Therefore **D** inquired again of God;	1732
14:16	**D** therefore did as God commanded him:	1732
14:17	the fame of **D** went out into all lands;	1732
15: 1	*D* made him houses in the city of David,	NIH
15: 1	*David* made him houses in the city of **D**,	1732
15: 2	**D** said, None ought to carry the ark of	1732
15: 3	**D** gathered all Israel together to Jerusalem	1732
15: 4	**D** assembled the children of Aaron,	1732
15:11	**D** called for Zadok and Abiathar	1732
15:16	**D** spake to the chief of the Levites to	1732
15:25	So **D**, and the elders of Israel,	1732
15:27	**D** *was* clothed with a robe of fine linen,	1732
15:27	**D** also *had* upon him an ephod of linen.	1732
15:29	of the LORD came to the city of **D**,	1732
15:29	out at a window saw king **D** dancing	1732
16: 1	set it in the midst of the tent that **D** had	1732
16: 2	when **D** had made an end of offering	1732
16: 7	on that day **D** delivered first *this psalm* to	1732
16:43	and **D** returned to bless his house.	1732
17: 1	it came to pass, as **D** sat in his house,	1732
17: 1	that **D** said to Nathan the prophet,	1732
17: 2	Nathan said unto **D**, Do all that *is* in thine	1732
17: 4	Go and tell **D** my servant, Thus saith	1732

1Ch 17: 7	thus shalt thou say unto my servant **D**,	1732
17:15	this vision, so did Nathan speak unto **D**.	1732
17:16	the king came and sat before	1732
17:18	What can **D** *speak* more to thee for	1732
17:24	*let* the house of **D** thy servant *be*	1732
18: 1	that **D** smote the Philistines,	1732
18: 3	**D** smote Hadarezer king of Zobah unto	1732
18: 4	**D** took from him a thousand chariots,	1732
18: 4	also houghed all the chariot *horses,* but	1732
18: 5	**D** slew of the Syrians two and	1732
18: 6	**D** put *garrisons* in Syria-damascus;	1732
18: 6	Thus the LORD preserved **D**	1732
18: 7	**D** took the shields of gold that were on	1732
18: 8	of Hadarezer, brought **D** very much brass,	1732
18: 9	**D** had smitten all the host of Hadarezer	1732
18:10	He sent Hadoram his son to king **D**,	1732
18:11	Them also king **D** dedicated unto	1732
18:13	Thus the LORD preserved **D**	1732
18:14	So **D** reigned over all Israel, and executed	1732
18:17	the sons of **D** *were* chief about the king.	1732
19: 2	**D** said, I will shew kindness unto Hanun	1732
19: 2	**D** sent messengers to comfort him	1732
19: 2	So the servants of **D** came into the land of	1732
19: 3	Thinkest thou that **D** doth honour thy	1732
19: 5	and told **D** how the men were served.	1732
19: 6	they had made themselves odious to **D**,	1732
19: 8	when **D** heard *of it,* he sent Joab, and all	1732
19:17	it was told **D**; and he gathered all Israel,	1732
19:17	So when **D** had put the battle in array	1732
19:18	**D** slew of the Syrians seven thousand	1732
19:19	they made peace with **D**, and became his	1732
20: 1	**D** tarried at Jerusalem. And Joab smote	1732
20: 2	**D** took the crown of their king from off	1732
20: 3	dealt **D** with all the cities of the children	1732
20: 3	And all the people returned *to* Jerusalem	1732
20: 8	fell by the hand of **D**, and by the hand	1732
21: 1	and provoked **D** to number Israel.	1732
21: 2	**D** said to Joab and to the rulers of	1732
21: 5	sum of the number of the people unto **D**.	1732
21: 8	**D** said unto God, I have sinned greatly,	1732
21:10	Go and tell **D**, saying, Thus saith	1732
21:11	So Gad came to **D**, and said unto him,	1732
21:13	**D** said unto Gad, I am in a great strait:	1732
21:16	**D** lift up his eyes, and saw the angel of	1732
21:16	**D** and the elders *of Israel, who* were	1732
21:17	**D** said unto God, *Is it* not I *that*	1732
21:18	the LORD commanded Gad to say to **D**,	1732
21:18	that **D** should go up, and set up an altar	1732
21:19	**D** went up at the saying of Gad, which he	1732
21:21	And as **D** came to Ornan, Ornan looked	1732
21:21	Ornan looked and saw **D**, and went out	1732
21:21	bowed himself to **D** *with his* face to	1732
21:22	**D** said to Ornan, Grant me the place of	1732
21:23	And Ornan said unto **D**, Take *it* to thee,	1732
21:24	**D** said to Ornan, Nay; but I will verily	1732
21:25	So **D** gave to Ornan for the place six	1732
21:26	**D** built there an altar unto the LORD,	1732
21:28	At that time when **D** saw that the LORD	1732
21:30	**D** could not go before it to inquire of God:	1732
22: 1	**D** said, This *is* the house of the LORD	1732
22: 2	**D** commanded to gather together	1732
22: 3	**D** prepared iron in abundance for the nails	1732
22: 4	of Tyre brought much cedar wood to **D**.	1732
22: 5	said, Solomon my son *is* young and	1732
22: 5	**D** prepared abundantly before his death.	1732
22: 7	**D** said to Solomon, My son, *as for* me,	1732
22:17	**D** also commanded all the princes of Israel	1732
23: 1	So when **D** was old and full *of* days,	1732
23: 5	which I made, *said* **D**, to praise *therewith.*	NIH
23: 6	**D** divided them *into* courses among	1732
23:25	For **D** said, The LORD God of Israel hath	1732
23:27	For by the last words of **D**, the Levites	1732
24: 3	distributed them, both Zadok of the	1732
24:31	of Aaron in the presence of **D** the king,	1732
25: 1	Moreover **D** and the captains of the host	1732
26:26	of the dedicate *things,* which **D** the king,	1732
26:31	In the fortieth year of the reign of **D** they	1732
26:32	whom king **D** made rulers over	1732
27:18	Of Judah, Elihu, *one* of the brethren of **D**:	1732
27:23	**D** took not the number of them from	1732
27:24	in the account of the chronicles of king **D**.	1732
28: 1	**D** assembled all the princes of Israel,	1732
28: 2	Then **D** the king stood up upon his feet,	1732
28:11	**D** gave to Solomon his son the pattern of	1732
28:19	All *this, said* **D**, the LORD made me	NIH
28:20	**D** said to Solomon his son, Be strong and	1732
29: 1	Furthermore **D** the king said unto all	1732
29: 9	**D** the king also rejoiced *with* great joy.	1732
29:10	Wherefore **D** blessed the LORD before all	1732
29:10	**D** said, Blessed *be* thou, LORD God of	1732
29:20	**D** said to all the congregation, Now bless	1732
29:22	they made Solomon the son of **D** king	1732
29:23	the LORD as king instead of **D** his father,	1732
29:24	and all the sons likewise of king **D**,	1732
29:26	Thus **D** the son of Jesse reigned over all	1732
29:29	Now the acts of **D** the king, first and last,	1732
2Ch 1: 1	Solomon the son of **D** was strengthened	1732
1: 4	the ark of God had **D** brought up from	1732
1: 4	*to* the place which **D** had prepared for it:	1732
1: 8	Thou hast shewed great mercy unto **D** my	1732
1: 9	let thy promise unto **D** my father be	1732
2: 3	As thou didst deal with **D** my father,	1732
2: 7	whom **D** my father did provide.	1732
2:12	who hath given to **D** the king a wise son,	1732
2:14	with the cunning *men* of my lord **D** thy	1732

D

Ref	Text	Strong
2Ch 2:17	the numbering where*with* **D** his father	1732
3: 1	where the LORD appeared unto **D** his	1732
3: 1	in the place that **D** had prepared in	1732
5: 1	Solomon brought in *all the things* that **D**	1732
5: 2	of the LORD out of the city of **D**,	1732
6: 4	he spake with his mouth to my father **D**,	1732
6: 6	chosen **D** to be over my people Israel.	1732
6: 7	Now it was in the heart of **D** my father to	1732
6: 8	the LORD said to **D** my father,	1732
6:10	for I am risen up in the room of **D** my	1732
6:15	Thou which hast kept with thy servant **D**	1732
6:16	keep with thy servant **D** my father *that*	1732
6:17	thou hast spoken unto thy servant **D**.	1732
6:42	remember the mercies of **D** thy servant.	1732
7: 6	which **D** the king had made to praise	1732
7: 6	ever, when **D** praised by their ministry;	1732
7:10	that the LORD had shewed unto **D**,	1732
7:17	as **D** thy father walked, and do according	1732
7:18	according as I have covenanted with **D**	1732
8:11	**D** unto the house that he had built for her:	1732
8:11	My wife shall not dwell in the house of **D**	1732
8:14	according to the order of **D** his father,	1732
8:14	so had **D** the man of God commanded.	1732
9:31	he was buried in the city of **D** his father:	1732
10:16	saying, What portion have we in **D**?	1732
10:16	*and* now, **D**, see to thine own house.	1732
10:19	Israel rebelled against the house of **D** unto	1732
11:17	three years they walked in the way of **D**	1732
11:18	daughter of Jerimoth the son of **D** *to* wife,	1732
12:16	fathers, and was buried in the city of **D**:	1732
13: 5	the kingdom over Israel to **D** for ever,	1732
13: 6	the servant of Solomon the son of **D**,	1732
13: 8	of the LORD in the hand of the sons of **D**;	1732
14: 1	and they buried him in the city of **D**:	1732
16:14	he had made for himself in the city of **D**,	1732
17: 3	he walked in the first ways of his father **D**,	1732
21: 1	buried with his fathers in the city of **D**.	1732
21: 7	LORD would not destroy the house of **D**,	1732
21: 7	of the covenant that he had made with **D**,	1732
21:12	Thus saith the LORD God of **D** thy father,	1732
21:20	Howbeit they buried him in the city of **D**,	1732
23: 3	as the LORD hath said of the sons of **D**.	1732
23:18	whom **D** had distributed in the house of	1732
23:18	and with singing, as it was ordained by **D**.	1732
24:16	they buried him in the city of **D** among	1732
24:25	they buried him in the city of **D**,	1732
27: 9	and they buried him in the city of **D**:	1732
28: 1	the sight of the LORD, like **D** his father:	1732
29: 2	to all that **D** his father had done.	1732
29:25	according to the commandment of **D**,	1732
29:26	Levites stood with the instruments of **D**,	1732
29:27	the instruments ordained by **D** king of	1732
29:30	unto the LORD with the words of **D**,	1732
30:26	since the time of Solomon the son of **D**	1732
32: 5	repaired Millo *in* the city of **D**,	1732
32:30	down to the west *side* of the city of **D**.	1732
32:33	of the sepulchres of the sons of **D**:	1732
33: 7	of which God had said to **D** and	1732
33:14	this he built a wall without the city of **D**,	1732
34: 2	walked in the ways of his father,	1732
34: 3	he began to seek after the God of **D** his	1732
35: 3	the son of **D** king of Israel did build;	1732
35: 4	to the writing of **D** king of Israel,	1732
35:15	according to the commandment of **D**,	1732
Ezr 3:10	after the ordinance of **D** king of Israel.	1732
8: 2	Daniel: of the sons of **D**; Hattush.	1732
8:20	whom **D** and the princes had appointed	1732
Ne 3:15	the stairs that go down from the city of **D**.	1732
3:16	*the place* over against the sepulchres of **D**,	1732
12:24	according to the commandment of **D**	1732
12:36	the musical instruments of **D** the man	1732
12:37	they went up by the stairs of the city of **D**,	1732
12:37	up of the wall, above the house of **D**,	1732
12:45	according to the commandment of **D**,	1732
12:46	For in the days of **D** and Asaph of old	1732
Ps 3: T	A Psalm of **D**, when he fled from Absalom	1732
4: T	Musician on Neginoth, A Psalm of **D**.	1732
5: T	Musician upon Nehiloth, A Psalm of **D**.	1732
6: T	Neginoth upon Sheminith, A Psalm of **D**.	1732
7: T	Shiggaion of **D**, which he sang unto	1732
8: T	Musician upon Gittith, A Psalm of **D**.	1732
9: T	upon Muth-labben, A Psalm of **D**.	1732
11: T	To the chief Musician, *A Psalm* of **D**.	1732
12: T	Musician upon Sheminith, A Psalm of **D**.	1732
13: T	To the chief Musician, A Psalm of **D**.	1732
14: T	To the chief Musician, *A Psalm* of **D**.	1732
15: T	A Psalm of **D**.	1732
16: T	Michtam of **D**.	1732
17: T	A Prayer of **D**.	1732
18: T	To the chief Musician, *A Psalm* of **D**,	1732
18:50	to **D**, and to his seed for evermore.	1732
19: T	To the chief Musician, A Psalm of **D**.	1732
20: T	To the chief Musician, A Psalm of **D**.	1732
21: T	To the chief Musician, A Psalm of **D**.	1732
22: T	upon Aijeleth Shahar, A Psalm of **D**.	1732
23: T	A Psalm of **D**.	1732
24: T	A Psalm of **D**.	1732
25: T	*A Psalm* of **D**.	1732
26: T	A Psalm of **D**.	1732
27: T	*A Psalm* of **D**.	1732
28: T	A Psalm of **D**.	1732
29: T	A Psalm of **D**.	1732
30: T	Song *at* the dedication of the house of **D**.	1732
31: T	To the chief Musician, A Psalm of **D**.	1732
32: T	*A Psalm* of **D**, Maschil.	1732

Ref	Text	Strong
Ps 34: T	*A Psalm* of **D**, when he changed his	1732
35: T	*A Psalm* of **D**.	1732
36: T	*A Psalm* of **D** the servant of the LORD.	1732
37: T	*A Psalm* of **D**.	1732
38: T	A Psalm of **D**, to bring to remembrance.	1732
39: T	*even* to Jeduthun, A Psalm of **D**.	1732
40: T	To the chief Musician, A Psalm of **D**.	1732
41: T	To the chief Musician, A Psalm of **D**.	1732
51: T	To the chief Musician, A Psalm of **D**.	1732
52: T	chief Musician, Maschil, *A Psalm* of **D**,	1732
52: T	**D** is come to the house of Ahimelech.	1732
53: T	upon Mahalath, Maschil, *A Psalm* of **D**.	1732
54: T	Maschil, *A Psalm* of **D**, when the Ziphims	1732
54: T	to Saul, Doth not **D** hide himself with us?	1732
55: T	on Neginoth, Maschil, *A Psalm* of **D**.	1732
56: T	Michtam of **D**, when the Philistines took	1732
57: T	Musician, Al-taschith, Michtam of **D**,	1732
58: T	Musician, Al-taschith, Michtam of **D**.	1732
59: T	Musician, Al-taschith, Michtam of **D**;	1732
60: T	Michtam of **D**, to teach;	1732
61: T	Musician upon Neginah, *A Psalm* of **D**.	1732
62: T	Musician, to Jeduthun, A Psalm of **D**.	1732
63: T	A Psalm of **D**, when he was in	1732
64: T	To the chief Musician, A Psalm of **D**.	1732
65: T	chief Musician, A Psalm *and* Song of **D**.	1732
68: T	the chief Musician, A Psalm *or* Song of **D**.	1732
69: T	upon Shoshannim, *A Psalm* of **D**.	1732
70: T	To the chief Musician, *A Psalm* of **D**,	1732
72:20	The prayers of **D** the son of Jesse are	1732
78:70	He chose **D** also his servant, and took	1732
86: T	A Prayer of **D**.	1732
89: 3	I have sworn unto **D** my servant,	1732
89:20	I have found **D** my servant; with my holy	1732
89:35	by my holiness that I will not lie unto **D**.	1732
89:49	*which* thou swarest unto **D** in thy truth?	1732
101: T	A Psalm of **D**.	1732
103: T	*A Psalm* of **D**.	1732
108: T	A Song *or* Psalm of **D**.	1732
109: T	To the chief Musician, A Psalm of **D**.	1732
110: T	A Psalm of **D**.	1732
122: T	A Song of degrees of **D**.	1732
122: 5	judgment, the thrones of **D**.	1732
124: T	A Song of degrees of **D**.	1732
131: T	A Song of degrees of **D**.	1732
132: 1	remember **D**, *and* all his afflictions:	1732
132:11	The LORD hath sworn in truth unto **D**;	1732
132:17	There will I make the horn of **D** to bud:	1732
133: T	A Song of degrees of **D**.	1732
138: T	*A Psalm* of **D**.	1732
139: T	To the chief Musician, A Psalm of **D**.	1732
140: T	To the chief Musician, A Psalm of **D**.	1732
141: T	A Psalm of **D**.	1732
142: T	Maschil of **D**; A Prayer when he was in	1732
143: T	A Psalm of **D**.	1732
144: T	*A Psalm* of **D**.	1732
144:10	who delivereth **D** his servant from	1732
Pr 1: T	The proverbs of Solomon the son of **D**,	1732
Ecc 1: T	the son of **D**, king in Jerusalem.	1732
SS 4: 4	Thy neck *is* like the tower of **D** builded	1732
Isa 7: 2	it was told the house of **D**, saying, Syria is	1732
7:13	he said, Hear ye now, O house of **D**; *Is* it	1732
9: 7	upon the throne of **D**, and upon his	1732
16: 5	sit upon it in truth in the tabernacle of **D**,	1732
22: 9	seen also the breaches of the city of **D**,	1732
22:22	the key of the house of **D** will I lay upon	1732
29: 1	to Ariel, to Ariel, the city *where* **D** dwelt!	1732
38: 5	saith the LORD, the God of **D** thy father,	1732
55: 3	with you, *even* the sure mercies of **D**.	1732
Jer 17:25	and princes sitting upon the throne of **D**,	1732
21:12	O house of **D**, thus saith the LORD;	1732
22: 2	that sittest upon the throne of **D**, thou,	1732
22: 4	house kings sitting upon the throne of **D**,	1732
22:30	sitting upon the throne of **D**, and ruling	1732
23: 5	I will raise unto **D** a righteous Branch,	1732
29:16	king that sitteth upon the throne of **D**,	1732
30: 9	their king, whom I will raise up unto	1732
33:15	of righteousness to grow up unto **D**;	1732
33:17	**D** shall never want a man to sit upon	1732
33:21	covenant be broken with **D** my servant,	1732
33:22	will I multiply the seed of **D** my servant,	1732
33:26	**D** my servant, *so* that *I* will not take *any*	1732
36:30	have none to sit upon the throne of **D**:	1732
Eze 34:23	he shall feed them, *even* my servant **D**;	1732
34:24	and my servant **D** a prince among them;	1732
37:24	my servant **D** *shall be* king over them;	1732
37:25	servant **D** *shall be* their prince for ever.	1732
Hos 3: 5	the LORD their God, and **D** their king;	1732
Am 6: 5	themselves instruments of musick, like **D**;	1732
9:11	I raise up the tabernacle of **D** that is fallen,	1732
Zec 12: 7	that the glory of the house of **D** and	1732
12: 8	among them at that day shall be as **D**;	1732
12: 8	house of **D** *shall be* as God, as the angel	1732
12:10	I will pour upon the house of **D**,	1732
12:12	the family of the house of **D** apart,	1732
13: 1	be a fountain opened to the house of **D**	1732
Mt 1: 1	the son of **D**, the son of Abraham.	1138
1: 6	And Jesse begat **D** the king; and David	1138
1: 6	the king begat Solomon of *her that had*	1138
1:17	So all the generations from Abraham to **D**	1138
1:17	from **D** until the carrying away into	1138
1:20	saying, Joseph, *thou* son of **D**, fear not to	1138
9:27	crying, and saying, Thou Son of **D**,	1138
12: 3	unto them, Have ye not read what **D** did,	1138
12:23	amazed, and said, Is this the son of **D**?	1138
15:22	mercy on me, O Lord, *thou* Son of **D**;	1138

Ref	Text	Strong
Mt 20:30	Have mercy on us, O Lord, *thou* Son of **D**.	1138
20:31	Have mercy on us, O Lord, *thou* Son of **D**.	1138
21: 9	cried, saying, Hosanna to the Son of **D**:	1138
21:15	and saying, Hosanna to the Son of **D**;	1138
22:42	is he? They say unto him, *The Son* of **D**.	1138
22:43	How then doth **D** in spirit call him Lord,	1138
22:45	**D** then call him Lord, how is he his son?	1138
Mk 2:25	Have ye never read what **D** did, when he	1138
10:47	and say, Jesus, *thou* Son of **D**, have mercy	1138
10:48	*Thou* Son of **D**, have mercy on me.	1138
11:10	Blessed be the kingdom of our father **D**,	1138
12:35	the scribes that Christ is the Son of **D**?	1138
12:36	For **D** himself said by the Holy Ghost,	1138
12:37	**D** therefore himself calleth him Lord;	1138
Lk 1:27	name was Joseph, of the house of **D**;	1138
1:32	give unto him the throne of his father **D**:	1138
1:69	for us in the house of his servant **D**;	1138
2: 4	Nazareth, into Judea, unto the city of **D**,	1138
2: 4	he was of the house and lineage of **D**:)	1138
2:11	is born this day in the city of **D** a Saviour,	1138
3:31	son of Nathan, which was *the* son of **D**,	1138
6: 3	ye not read so much as this, what **D** did,	1138
18:38	And he cried, saying, Jesus, *thou* Son of **D**,	1138
18:39	cried *so* much the more, Thou Son of **D**,	1138
20:42	**D** himself saith in the book of Psalms,	1138
20:44	**D** therefore calleth him Lord, how is he	1138
Jn 7:42	That Christ cometh of the seed of **D**,	1138
7:42	of the town of Bethlehem, where **D** was?	1138
Ac 1:16	which the Holy Ghost by the mouth of **D**	1138
2:25	For **D** speaketh concerning him, I foresaw	1138
2:29	freely speak unto you of the patriarch **D**,	1138
2:34	For **D** is not ascended into the heavens:	1138
4:25	Who by the mouth of thy servant **D** hast	1138
7:45	the face of our fathers, unto the days of **D**;	1138
13:22	he raised up unto them **D** to be their king;	1138
13:22	and said, I have found **D** the *son* of Jesse,	1138
13:34	I will give you the sure mercies of **D**.	1138
13:36	For **D**, after he had served his own	1138
15:16	and will build again the tabernacle of **D**,	1138
Ro 1: 3	was made of the seed of **D** according	1138
4: 6	Even as **D** also describeth the blessedness	1138
11: 9	And **D** saith, Let their table be made a	1138
2Ti 2: 8	that Jesus Christ of the seed of **D**	1138
Heb 4: 7	saying in **D**, To day, after so long a time;	1138
11:32	**D** also, and Samuel, and *of* the prophets:	1138
Rev 3: 7	*he that is* true, he that hath the key of **D**,	1138
5: 5	the Lion of the tribe of Juda, the root of **D**,	1138
22:16	I am the root and the offspring of **D**,	1138

DAVID'S (54) [DAVID]

Ref	Text	Strong
1Sa 18:29	and Saul became **D** enemy continually.	1732
19:11	Saul also sent messengers unto **D** house,	1732
19:11	Michal **D** wife told him, saying, If thou	1732
20:16	even require *it* at the hand of **D** enemies.	1732
20:25	sat by Saul's side, and **D** place was empty.	1732
20:27	of the month, that **D** place was empty:	1732
23: 3	**D** men said unto him, Behold, we *be*	1732
24: 5	**D** heart smote him, because he had cut	1732
25: 9	when **D** young men came, they spake to	1732
25:10	Nabal answered **D** servants, and said,	1732
25:12	So **D** young men turned their way,	1732
25:44	**D** wife, to Phalti the son of Laish,	1732
26:17	Saul knew **D** voice, and said, *Is* this thy	1732
30: 5	**D** two wives were taken captives,	1732
30:20	*other* cattle, and said, This *is* **D** spoil.	1732
2Sa 2:30	there lacked of **D** servants nineteen men	1732
3: 5	the sixth, Ithream, by Eglah **D** wife.	1732
5: 8	and the blind, *that are* hated of **D** soul,	1732
8: 2	*so* the Moabites became **D** servants,	1732
8:14	and all they of Edom became **D** servants.	1732
8:18	Pelethites; and **D** sons were chief rulers.	1732
10: 2	**D** servants came *into* the land of	1732
10: 4	Wherefore Hanun took **D** servants,	1732
12: 5	**D** anger was greatly kindled against	1732
12:30	it was *set* on **D** head. And he brought	1732
13: 3	the son of Shimeah **D** brother:	1732
13:32	the son of Shimeah **D** brother, answered	1732
15:12	counsellor, from his city, *even* from	1732
15:37	So Hushai **D** friend came *into* the city,	1732
16:16	**D** friend, was come unto Absalom,	1732
19:41	and all **D** men with him, over Jordan?	1732
24:10	**D** heart smote him after that he had	1732
24:11	unto the prophet Gad, **D** seer, saying,	1732
1Ki 1:38	Solomon to ride upon king **D** mule,	1732
11:32	have one tribe for my servant **D** sake,	1732
15: 4	Nevertheless for **D** sake did the LORD his	1732
2Ki 11:10	hundreds did the priest give king **D** spears	1732
19:34	own sake, and for my servant **D** sake.	1732
20: 6	own sake, and for my servant **D** sake.	1732
1Ch 18: 2	the Moabites became **D** servants,	1732
18: 6	the Syrians became **D** servants,	1732
18:13	and all the Edomites became **D** servants.	1732
19: 4	Wherefore Hanun took **D** servants,	1732
20: 2	stones in it; and it was *set* upon **D** head:	1732
20: 7	Jonathan the son of Shimea **D** brother	1732
21: 9	LORD spake unto Gad, **D** seer, saying,	1732
27:31	the substance which *was* king **D**.	1732+3807.1
27:32	Also Jonathan **D** uncle *was* a counseller,	1732
2Ch 23: 9	shields, that *had been* king **D**,	1732+3807.1
Ps 145: T	**D** *Psalm of* praise.	1732
Isa 37:35	own sake, and for my servant **D** sake.	1732
Jer 13:13	even the kings that sit upon **D**	1732+3807.1
Lk 20:41	How say they that Christ is **D** son?	1138

DAWN (2) [DAWNING]

Mt	28: 1 as it began to **d** towards the first *day* of	2020
2Pe	1:19 until the day **d**, and the day star arise in	1306

DAWNING (5) [DAWN]

Jos	6:15 that they rose early about the **d** of the day,	5927
Jdg	19:26 came the woman in the **d** of the day,	6437
Job	3: 9 neither let it see the **d** of the day:	6079
	7: 4 tossings to and fro unto the **d of the day**.	5399
Ps	119:147 I prevented the **d of the morning**,	5399

DAY (1732) [BIRTHDAY, DAILY, DAY'S, DAYS, DAYS', DAYSMAN, DAYSPRING, DAYTIME, HOLYDAY, MIDDAY, NOONDAY, NOONDAYS, YESTERDAY]

Ge	1: 5 God called the light **D**, and the darkness	3117
	1: 5 and the morning were the first **d**.	3117
	1: 8 and the morning were the second **d**.	3117
	1:13 and the morning were the third **d**.	3117
	1:14 the heaven to divide the **d** from the night;	3117
	1:16 greater light to rule the **d**, and the lesser	3117
	1:18 to rule over the **d** and over the night,	3117
	1:19 and the morning were the fourth **d**.	3117
	1:23 and the morning were the fifth **d**.	3117
	1:31 and the morning were the sixth **d**.	3117
	2: 2 on the seventh **d** God ended his work	3117
	2: 2 rested on the seventh **d** from all his work	3117
	2: 3 God blessed the seventh **d**,	3117
	2: 4 in the **d** that the Lord God made	3117
	2:17 for in the **d** that thou eatest thereof thou	3117
	3: 5 For God doth know that in the **d** ye eat	3117
	3: 8 walking in the garden in the cool of the **d**:	3117
	4:14 hast driven me out *this* **d** from the face	3117
	5: 1 In the **d** that God created man,	3117
	5: 2 in the **d** when they were created.	3117
	7:11 the seventeenth **d** of the month,	3117
	7:11 the same **d** were all the fountains of	3117
	7:13 In the selfsame **d** entered Noah,	3117
	8: 4 on the seventeenth **d** of the month, upon	3117
	8: 5 in the tenth *month*, on the first **d** of	NIH
	8:13 the first *month*, the first **d** of the month,	NIH
	8:14 the seven and twentieth **d** of the month,	3117
	8:22 winter, and **d** and night shall not cease.	3117
	15:18 In the same **d** the Lord made a covenant	3117
	17:23 flesh of their foreskin in the selfsame **d**,	3117
	17:26 In the selfsame **d** was Abraham	3117
	18: 1 sat *in* the tent door in the heat of the **d**;	3117
	19:37 *is* the father of the Moabites unto *this* **d**.	3117
	19:38 of the children of Ammon unto *this* **d**.	3117
	21: 8 Abraham made a great feast the *same* **d**	3117
	21:26 neither yet heard I *of it*, but to **d**.	3117+1886.1
	22: 4 on the third **d** Abraham lift up his eyes,	3117
	22:14 as it is said to *this* **d**, In the mount of	3117
	24:12 send me good speed *this* **d**,	3117
	24:42 I came *this* **d** unto the well, and said,	3117
	25:31 Jacob said, Sell me *this* **d** thy birthright.	3117
	25:33 Jacob said, Swear to me *this* **d**;	3117
	26:32 it came to pass the same **d**, that Isaac's	3117
	26:33 name of the city *is* Beer-sheba unto *this* **d**.	3117
	27: 2 I am old, I know not the **d** of my death:	3117
	27:45 I be deprived also of you both *in* one **d**?	3117
	29: 7 he said, Lo, *it is* yet high **d**, neither *is it*	3117
	30:32 pass through all thy flock to **d**,	3117+1886.1
	30:35 he removed that **d** the he goats that were	3117
	31:22 it was told Laban on the third **d** that Jacob	3117
	31:39 *whether* stolen by **d**, or stolen by night.	3117
	31:40 I was in the **d**, the drought consumed	3117
	31:43 what can I do *this* **d** unto these my	3117
	31:48 *is* a witness between me and thee *this* **d**.	3117
	32:24 man with him until the breaking of the **d**.	7837
	32:26 he said, Let me go, for the **d** breaketh.	7837
	32:32 upon the hollow of the thigh, unto this **d**:	3117
	33:13 if *men* should overdrive them one **d**,	3117
	33:16 So Esau returned that **d** on his way unto	3117
	34:25 it came to pass on the third **d**, when they	3117
	35: 3 who answered me in the **d** of my distress,	3117
	35:20 *is* the pillar of Rachel's grave unto *this* **d**.	3117
	39:10 to pass, as she spake to Joseph **d** by day,	3117
	39:10 to pass, as she spake to Joseph day by **d**,	3117
	40: 7 Wherefore look ye *so* sadly to **d**?	3117+1886.1
	40:20 it came to pass the third **d**, *which* was	3117
	41: 9 I do remember my faults *this* **d**:	3117
	42:13 the youngest *is this* **d** with our father,	3117
	42:18 Joseph said unto them the third **d**,	3117
	42:32 the youngest *is this* **d** with our father in	3117
	47:23 I have bought you *this* **d** and your land	3117
	47:26 it a law over the land of Egypt unto this **d**,	3117
	48:15 which fed me all my life long unto this **d**,	3117
	48:20 he blessed them that **d**, saying, In thee	3117
	50:20 unto good, to bring to pass, as *it is* this **d**,	3117
Ex	2:13 when he went out the second **d**, behold,	3117
	2:18 *is it that* you are come so soon **d**?	3117+1886.1
	5: 6 Pharaoh commanded the same **d**	3117
	5:14 brick both yesterday and **to d**,	3117+1886.1
	6:28 it came to pass on the **d** *when* the Lord	3117
	8:22 I will sever in that **d** the land of Goshen,	3117
	10: 6 since the **d** that they were upon the earth	3117
	10: 6 that they were upon the earth unto this **d**.	3117
	10:13 an east wind brought the land all that **d**,	3117
	10:28 for in that **d** thou seest my face thou shalt	3117
	12: 3 In the tenth **d** of this month they shall take	NIH
	12: 6 ye shall keep it *up* until the fourteenth **d**	3117
	12:14 this **d** shall be unto you for a memorial;	3117
	12:15 even the first **d** ye shall put away leaven	3117
	12:15 from the first **d** until the seventh day,	3117

Ex	12:15 from the first day until the seventh **d**,	3117
	12:16 in the first **d** *there shall be* a holy	3117
	12:16 in the seventh **d** there shall be a holy	3117
	12:17 for in this selfsame **d** have I brought your	3117
	12:17 shall ye observe this **d** in your generations	3117
	12:18 In the first *month*, on the fourteenth **d** of	3117
	12:18 and twentieth **d** of the month at even.	3117
	12:41 even the selfsame **d** it came to pass,	3117
	12:51 it came to pass the selfsame **d**, that	3117
	13: 3 said unto the people, Remember this **d**,	3117
	13: 4 this **d** came ye out in the month Abib.	3117
	13: 6 in the seventh **d** *shall be* a feast to	3117
	13: 8 thou shalt shew thy son in that **d**, saying,	3117
	13:21 the Lord went before them **by d** in a	3119
	13:21 to give them light; to go **by d** and night:	3119
	13:22 took not away the pillar of the cloud **by d**,	3119
	14:13 which he will shew to you to **d**:	3117+1886.1
	14:13 whom ye have seen to **d**,	3117+1886.1
	14:30 Thus the Lord saved Israel that **d** out of	3117
	16: 1 on the fifteenth **d** of the second month	3117
	16: 4 a certain rate **every d**,	3117+3117+871.1
	16: 5 that on the sixth **d** they shall prepare *that*	3117
	16:22 *that* on the sixth **d** they gathered twice as	3117
	16:23 bake *that* which you will bake to **d**,	NIH
	16:25 Moses said, Eat that to **d**; for to	3117+1886.1
	16:25 **to d** *is* a sabbath unto the Lord:	3117+1886.1
	16:25 *is* a sabbath unto the Lord: **to d**	3117+1886.1
	16:26 on the seventh **d**, *which is* the sabbath,	3117
	16:27 the people on the seventh **d** for to gather,	3117
	16:29 he giveth you on the sixth **d** the bread of	3117
	16:29 man go out of his place on the seventh **d**.	3117
	16:30 So the people rested on the seventh **d**.	3117
	19: 1 the same **d** came they *into* the wilderness	3117
	19:10 sanctify them to **d** and to	3117+1886.1
	19:11 be ready against the third **d**: for the third	3117
	19:11 for the third **d** the Lord will come down	3117
	19:15 the people, Be ready against the third **d**:	3117
	19:16 it came to pass on the third **d** in	3117
	20: 8 Remember the sabbath **d**, to keep it holy.	3117
	20:10 the seventh **d** *is* the sabbath of the Lord	3117
	20:11 that in heaven, *is*, and rested the seventh **d**:	3117
	20:11 the Lord blessed the sabbath **d**,	3117
	21:21 if he continue a **d** or two,	3117
	22:30 on the eighth **d** thou shalt give it me.	3117
	23:12 and on the seventh **d** thou shalt rest:	3117
	24:16 the seventh **d** he called unto Moses out of	3117
	29:36 thou shalt offer every **d** a bullock *for* a sin	3117
	29:38 **by day** continually.	3117+1886.1+3807.1
	29:38 **day by d** continually.	3117+1886.1+3807.1
	31:15 doeth *any* work in the sabbath **d**,	3117
	31:17 on the seventh **d** he rested,	3117
	32:28 there fell of the people that **d** about three	3117
	32:29 yourselves **to d** to the Lord,	3117+1886.1
	32:29 he may bestow upon you a blessing *this* **d**.	3117
	32:34 nevertheless in the **d** when I visit, I will	3117
	34:11 thou that which I command thee *this* **d**:	3117
	34:21 but on the seventh **d** thou shalt rest:	3117
	35: 2 on the seventh **d** there shall be to you a	3117
	35: 2 a holy **d**, a sabbath of rest to the Lord:	NIH
	35: 3 your habitations upon the sabbath **d**.	3117
	40: 2 On the first **d** of the first month shalt thou	3117
	40:17 on the first **d** of the month, *that*	NIH
	40:37 they journeyed not till the **d** that it was	3117
	40:38 the Lord *was* upon the tabernacle **by d**,	3119
Lev	6: 5 in the **d** of his trespass offering.	3117
	6:20 the Lord in the **d** when he is anointed;	3117
	7:15 shall be eaten the same **d** that it is offered;	3117
	7:16 shall be eaten the *same* **d** that he offereth	3117
	7:17 on the third **d** shall be burnt with fire.	3117
	7:18 offerings be eaten at all on the third **d**,	3117
	7:35 the **d** *when* he presented them to minister	3117
	7:36 the **d** that he anointed them, *by* a statute	3117
	7:38 the **d** that he commanded the children of	3117
	8:34 As he hath done this **d**, *so* the Lord hath	3117
	8:35 of the tabernacle of the congregation **d**	3119
	9: 1 came to pass on the eighth **d**, *that* Moses	3117
	9: 4 **to d** the Lord will appear unto	3117+1886.1
	10:19 *this* **d** have they offered their sin offering	3117
	10:19 I had eaten the sin offering to **d**,	3117+1886.1
	12: 3 in the eighth **d** the flesh of his foreskin	3117
	13: 5 the priest shall look on him the seventh **d**:	3117
	13: 6 shall look on him again the seventh **d**:	3117
	13:27 priest shall look upon him the seventh **d**:	3117
	13:32 in the seventh **d** the priest shall look on	3117
	13:34 in the seventh **d** the priest shall look on	3117
	13:51 shall look on the plague on the seventh **d**:	3117
	14: 2 This shall be the law of the leper in the **d**	3117
	14: 9 it shall be on the seventh **d**, *that* he shall	3117
	14:10 the eighth **d** he shall take two he lambs	3117
	14:23 shall bring them on the eighth **d** for his	3117
	14:39 the priest shall come again the seventh **d**,	3117
	15:14 on the eighth **d** shall take to him two	3117
	15:29 on the eighth **d** she shall take unto her	3117
	16:29 the tenth **d** of the month, ye shall afflict	NIH
	16:30 For on that **d** shall *the priest* make an	3117
	19: 6 It shall be eaten the *same* **d** ye offer it,	3117
	19: 6 if ought remain until the third **d**, it shall	3117
	19: 7 if it be eaten at all on the third **d**, it *is*	3117
	22:27 from the eighth **d** and thenceforth it shall	3117
	22:28 not kill it and her young both in one **d**.	3117
	22:30 On the same **d** it shall be eaten up;	3117
	23: 3 seventh *is* the sabbath of rest, a holy	3117
	23: 5 the fourteenth **d** of the first month at even	NIH
	23: 6 on the fifteenth **d** of the same month *is*	3117
	23: 7 In the first **d** ye shall have a holy	3117

Lev	23: 8 in the seventh **d** *is* a holy convocation:	3117
	23:12 ye shall offer that **d** when ye wave	3117
	23:14 until the selfsame **d** that ye have brought	3117
	23:15 from the **d** that ye brought the sheaf of	3117
	23:21 ye shall proclaim on the selfsame **d**, *that* it	3117
	23:24 seventh month, in the first **d** of the month,	NIH
	23:27 Also on the tenth **d** of this seventh month	NIH
	23:27 month *there shall be* a **d** of atonement:	3117
	23:28 ye shall do no work in that same **d**: for it	3117
	23:28 for it *is* a **d** of atonement, to make an	3117
	23:29 that shall not be afflicted in that same **d**,	3117
	23:30 *it be* that doeth any work in that same **d**,	3117
	23:32 in the ninth **d** of the month at even,	NIH
	23:34 The fifteenth **d** of this seventh month	3117
	23:35 On the first **d** *shall be* a holy convocation:	3117
	23:36 the eighth **d** shall be a holy convocation	3117
	23:37 every thing **upon** his **d**:	3117+3117+871.1
	23:39 Also in the fifteenth **d** of the seventh	3117
	23:39 on the first **d** *shall be* a sabbath, and on	3117
	23:39 and on the eighth **d** *shall be* a sabbath.	3117
	23:40 ye shall take you on the first **d** the boughs	3117
	25: 9 on the tenth **d** of the seventh month,	NIH
	25: 9 in the **d** of atonement shall ye make	3117
	27:23 he shall give thine estimation in that **d**,	3117
Nu	1: 1 on the first **d** of the second month,	NIH
	1:18 on the first **d** of the second month,	NIH
	3: 1 Moses in the **d** that the Lord spake with	3117
	3:13 *for* on the **d** that I smote all the firstborn	3117
	6: 9 he shall shave his head in the **d** of his	3117
	6: 9 on the seventh **d** shall he shave it.	3117
	6:10 on the eighth **d** he shall bring two turtles,	3117
	6:11 and shall hallow his head that *same* **d**.	3117
	7: 1 it came to pass on the **d** that Moses had	3117
	7:10 of the altar in the **d** that it was anointed,	3117
	7:11 each prince on *his* **d**, for the dedicating of	3117
	7:12 he that offered his offering the first **d** was	3117
	7:18 the second **d** Nethaneel the son of Zuar,	3117
	7:24 On the third **d** Eliab the son of Helon,	3117
	7:30 The fourth **d** Elizur the son of Shedeur,	3117
	7:36 On the fifth **d** Shelumiel the son of	3117
	7:42 On the sixth **d** Eliasaph the son of Deuel,	3117
	7:48 On the seventh **d** Elishama the son of	3117
	7:54 On the eighth **d** *offered* Gamaliel the son	3117
	7:60 the ninth **d** Abidan the son of Gideoni,	3117
	7:66 On the tenth **d** Ahiezer the son of	3117
	7:72 the eleventh **d** Pagiel the son of Ocran,	3117
	7:78 On the twelfth **d** Ahira the son of Enan,	3117
	7:84 in the **d** when it was anointed,	3117
	8:17 on the **d** that I smote every firstborn in	3117
	9: 3 the fourteenth **d** of this month, at even,	3117
	9: 5 kept the passover on the fourteenth **d**	3117
	9: 6 could not keep the passover on that **d**:	3117
	9: 6 before Moses and before Aaron on that **d**:	3117
	9:11 The fourteenth **d** of the second month at	3117
	9:15 on the **d** that the tabernacle was reared	3117
	9:16 the cloud covered it *by* **d**,	NIH
	9:21 whether *it was* **by d** or by night that	3119
	10:10 in the **d** of your gladness, and in your	3117
	10:11 it came to pass on the twentieth **d** of	NIH
	10:34 cloud of the Lord *was* upon them **by d**,	3119
	11:19 Ye shall not eat one **d**, nor two days,	3117
	11:32 the people stood up all that **d**, and all *that*	3117
	11:32 the next **d**, and they gathered the quails:	3117
	14:14 **by d time** in a pillar of a cloud, and in a	3119
	14:34 *even* forty days, each **d** for a year, shall ye	3117
	15:23 from the **d** that the Lord commanded	3117
	15:32 that gathered sticks upon the sabbath **d**.	3117
	19:12 shall purify himself with it on the third **d**,	3117
	19:12 and on the seventh **d** he shall be clean:	3117
	19:12 if he purify not himself the third **d**, then	3117
	19:12 then the seventh **d** he shall not be clean.	3117
	19:19 sprinkle upon the unclean on the third **d**,	3117
	19:19 on the third day, and on the seventh **d**:	3117
	19:19 on the seventh **d** he shall purify him*self*,	3117
	22:30 ridden ever since *I was* thine unto this **d**?	3117
	25:18 which was slain in the **d** of the plague for	3117
	28: 3 without spot **d by day**,	3117+1886.1+3807.1
	28: 3 without spot **day by d**,	3117+1886.1+3807.1
	28: 9 the sabbath **d** two lambs of the first year	3117
	28:16 in the fourteenth **d** of the first month *is*	3117
	28:17 in the fifteenth **d** of this month *is* the feast:	3117
	28:18 In the first **d** *shall be* a holy convocation;	3117
	28:25 on the seventh **d** ye shall have a holy	3117
	28:26 Also in the **d** of the firstfruits, when ye	3117
	29: 1 month, on the first **d** of the month,	NIH
	29: 1 is a **d** of blowing the trumpets unto you.	3117
	29: 7 shall have on the tenth **d** of this seventh	NIH
	29:12 on the fifteenth **d** of the seventh month	3117
	29:17 on the second **d** *ye shall offer* twelve	3117
	29:20 on the third **d** eleven bullocks, two rams,	3117
	29:23 on the fourth **d** ten bullocks, two rams,	3117
	29:26 on the fifth **d** nine bullocks, two rams,	3117
	29:29 on the sixth **d** eight bullocks, two rams,	3117
	29:32 the seventh **d** seven bullocks, two rams,	3117
	29:35 On the eighth **d** ye shall have a solemn	3117
	30: 5 if her father disallow her in the **d** that he	3117
	30: 7 his peace at her in the **d** that he heard	3117
	30: 8 if her husband disallow her on the **d** that	3117
	30:12 made them void on the **d** he heard *them*;	3117
	30:14 hold his peace at her from **d** to day;	3117
	30:14 hold his peace at her from day to **d**;	3117
	30:14 he held his peace at her in the **d** that he	3117
	31:19 and your captives on the third **d**,	3117
	31:19 on the third day, and on the seventh **d**.	3117
	31:24 shall wash your clothes on the seventh **d**,	3117

D

Nu	33: 3 on the fifteenth **d** of the first month;	3117
	33:38 of Egypt, in the first **d** of the fifth month.	NIH
Dt	1: 3 month, on the first **d** of the month,	NIH
	1:10 you *are this* **d** as the stars of heaven for	3117
	1:33 way ye should go, and in a cloud **by d**.	3119
	1:39 *in that* **d** had no knowledge between	3117
	2:18 *through* Ar, the coast of Moab, *this* **d**:	3117
	2:22 and dwelt in their stead *even* unto this **d**:	3117
	2:25 This **d** will I begin to put the dread of thee	3117
	2:30 him into thy hand, as *appeareth* this **d**.	3117
	3:14 name, Bashan-havoth-jair, unto this **d**.	3117
	4: 4 God *are* alive every one of you *this* **d**.	3117
	4: 8 all this law, which I set before you *this* **d**?	3117
	4:10 *Specially* the **d** that thou stoodest before	3117
	4:15 ye saw no *manner of* similitude on the **d**	3117
	4:20 a people of inheritance, as *ye* are this **d**.	3117
	4:26 and earth to witness against you *this* **d**,	3117
	4:32 since the **d** that God created man upon	3117
	4:38 land *for* an inheritance, as *it is* this **d**.	3117
	4:39 Know therefore *this* **d**, and consider *it* in	3117
	4:40 which I command thee *this* **d**,	3117
	5: 1 which I speak in your ears *this* **d**,	3117
	5: 3 us, who *are* all of us here alive *this* **d**.	3117
	5:12 Keep the sabbath **d** to sanctify it,	3117
	5:14 the seventh *is* the sabbath of the LORD	3117
	5:15 commanded thee to keep the sabbath **d**.	3117
	5:24 we have seen this **d** that God doth talk	3117
	6: 6 words, which I command thee *this* **d**,	3117
	6:24 might preserve us alive, as *it is* at this **d**.	3117
	7:11 I command thee *this* **d**, to do them.	3117
	8: 1 command thee *this* **d** shall ye observe	3117
	8:11 statutes, which I command thee *this* **d**:	3117
	8:18 he sware unto thy fathers, as *it is* this **d**.	3117
	8:19 I testify against you *this* **d** that ye shall	3117
	9: 1 Thou art to pass over Jordan *this* **d**, to go	3117
	9: 3 Understand therefore *this* **d**, that	3117
	9: 7 from the **d** that thou didst depart out of	3117
	9:10 midst of the fire in the **d** of the assembly.	3117
	9:24 the LORD from the **d** that I knew you.	3117
	10: 4 midst of the fire in the **d** of the assembly:	3117
	10: 8 and to bless in his name, unto this **d**.	3117
	10:13 I command thee *this* **d** for thy good?	3117
	10:15 *even* you above all people, as *it is* this **d**.	3117
	11: 2 know you *this* **d**: for *I* speak not with	3117
	11: 4 LORD hath destroyed them unto this **d**;	3117
	11: 8 which I command you *this* **d**,	3117
	11:13 which I command you *this* **d**,	3117
	11:26 I set before you *this* **d** a blessing and	3117
	11:27 your God, which I command you *this* **d**:	3117
	11:28 of the way which I command you *this* **d**,	3117
	11:32 judgments which I set before you *this* **d**,	3117
	12: 8 after all the *things* that we do here *this* **d**,	3117
	13:18 which I command thee *this* **d**,	3117
	15: 5 which I command thee *this* **d**.	3117
	15:15 I command thee this thing **to d**. 3117+1886.1	
	16: 3 that thou mayest remember the **d** when	3117
	16: 4 which thou sacrificedst the first **d** at even,	3117
	16: 8 on the seventh **d** *shall* be a solemn	3117
	18:16 God in Horeb in the **d** of the assembly,	3117
	19: 9 which I command thee *this* **d**, to love	3117
	20: 3 you approach *this* **d** unto battle against	3117
	21:23 thou shalt in any wise bury him that **d**;	3117
	24:15 At his **d** thou shalt give *him* his hire,	3117
	26: 3 I profess *this* **d** unto the LORD thy God,	3117
	26:16 This **d** the LORD thy God hath	3117
	26:17 Thou hast avouched the LORD *this* **d** to	3117
	26:18 the LORD hath avouched thee *this* **d** to be	3117
	27: 1 which I command you *this* **d**.	3117
	27: 2 it shall be on the **d** when you shall pass	3117
	27: 4 which I command you *this* **d**, in mount	3117
	27: 9 *this* **d** thou art become the people of	3117
	27:10 statutes, which I command thee *this* **d**.	3117
	27:11 Moses charged the people the same **d**,	3117
	28: 1 which I command thee *this* **d**,	3117
	28:13 which I command thee *this* **d**, to observe	3117
	28:14 the words which I command thee *this* **d**,	3117
	28:15 his statutes which I command thee *this* **d**;	3117
	28:32 fail *with longing* for them all the **d** long:	3117
	28:66 thou shalt fear **d** and night, and shalt	3119
	29: 4 eyes to see, and ears to hear, unto this **d**.	3117
	29:10 Ye stand *this* **d** all of you before	3117
	29:12 LORD thy God maketh with thee *this* **d**:	3117
	29:13 That he may establish thee **to d** 3117+1886.1	
	29:15 with *him* that standeth here with us *this* **d**	3117
	29:15 with *him* that *is* not here with us *this* **d**.	3117
	29:18 whose heart turneth away *this* **d** from	3117
	29:28 cast them into another land, as *it is* this **d**.	3117
	30: 2 to all that I command thee *this* **d**,	3117
	30: 8 which I command thee *this* **d**.	3117
	30:11 which I command thee *this* **d**,	3117
	30:15 I have set before thee *this* **d** life and good,	3117
	30:16 In that I command thee *this* **d** to love	3117
	30:18 I denounce unto you *this* **d**, that ye shall	3117
	30:19 call heaven and earth to record *this* **d** against you,	3117
	31: 2 an hundred and twenty years old *this* **d**;	3117
	31:17 shall be kindled against them in that **d**,	3117
	31:17 so that they will say in that **d**, Are not	3117
	31:18 I will surely hide my face in that **d** for all	3117
	31:22 wrote this song the same **d**,	3117
	31:27 while I am yet alive with you *this* **d**,	3117
	32:35 for the **d** of their calamity *is* at hand,	3117
	32:46 words which I testify among you *this* **d**,	3117
	32:48 LORD spake unto Moses that selfsame **d**,	3117
	33:12 *the* LORD shall cover him all the **d** long,	3117
	34: 6 knoweth of his sepulchre unto this **d**.	3117

Jos	1: 8 thou shalt meditate therein **d** and night,	3119
	3: 7 This **d** will I begin to magnify thee in	3117
	4: 9 and they are there unto this **d**.	3117
	4:14 On that **d** the LORD magnified Joshua in	3117
	4:19 Jordan on the tenth **d** of the first month,	NIH
	5: 9 *This* **d** have I rolled away the reproach of	3117
	5: 9 of the place is called Gilgal unto this **d**.	3117
	5:10 kept the passover on the fourteenth **d** of	3117
	5:11 and parched *corn* in the selfsame **d**.	3117
	6: 4 the seventh ye shall compass the city	3117
	6:10 your mouth, until the **d** I bid you shout;	3117
	6:14 second **d** they compassed the city once,	3117
	6:15 came to pass on the seventh **d**, that they	3117
	6:15 rose early about the dawning of the **d**,	7837
	6:15 only on that **d** they compassed the city	3117
	6:25 she dwelleth in Israel *even* unto this **d**;	3117
	7:25 the LORD shall trouble thee this **d**.	3117
	7:26 him a great heap of stones unto this **d**.	3117
	7:26 The valley of Achor, unto this **d**.	3117
	8:25 *so* it was, *that* all that fell that **d**, both of	3117
	8:28 for ever, *even* a desolation unto this **d**.	3117
	8:29 of stones, *that remaineth* unto this **d**.	3117
	9:12 on the **d** we came forth to go unto you;	3117
	9:17 and came unto their cities on the third **d**.	3117
	9:27 Joshua made them that **d** hewers of wood	3117
	9:27 the altar of the LORD, *even* unto this **d**,	3117
	10:12 spake Joshua to the LORD in the **d** when	3117
	10:13 hasted not to go down about a whole **d**.	3117
	10:14 was no **d** like that before it or after it,	3117
	10:27 *which remain* until this very **d**.	3117
	10:28 that **d** Joshua took Makkedah, and smote	3117
	10:32 which took it on the second **d**, and smote	3117
	10:35 they took it on that **d**, and smote it with	3117
	10:35 *were* therein he utterly destroyed that **d**,	3117
	13:13 dwell among the Israelites until this **d**.)	3117
	14: 9 Moses sware on that **d**, saying, Surely	3117
	14:10 I *am* this **d** fourscore and five years old.	3117
	14:11 As yet I *am* as strong *this* **d** as *I was* in	3117
	14:11 day as *I was* in the **d** that Moses sent me:	3117
	14:12 whereof the LORD spake in that **d**;	3117
	14:12 for thou heardest in that **d** how	3117
	14:14 of Jephunneh the Kenezite unto this **d**,	3117
	15:63 children of Judah at Jerusalem unto this **d**,	3117
	16:10 dwell among the Ephraimites unto this **d**,	3117
	22: 3 brethren these many days unto this **d**,	3117
	22:16 to turn away *this* **d** from following	3117
	22:16 that ye might rebel *this* **d** against	3117
	22:17 which we are not cleansed until this **d**,	3117
	22:18 that ye must turn away *this* **d** from	3117
	22:18 ye rebel *this* **d** against the LORD, 3117+1886.1	
	22:22 against the LORD, (save us not this **d**,)	3117
	22:29 turn *this* **d** from following the LORD,	3117
	22:31 *This* **d** we perceive that the LORD *is*	3117
	23: 8 your God, as ye have done unto this **d**.	3117
	23: 9 *been* able to stand before you unto this **d**.	3117
	23:14 *this* **d** I am going the way of all the earth:	3117
	24:15 choose you *this* **d** whom you will serve;	3117
	24:25 made a covenant with the people that **d**,	3117
Jdg	1:21 of Benjamin in Jerusalem unto this **d**.	3117
	1:26 which *is* the name thereof unto this **d**.	3117
	3:30 So Moab was subdued that **d** under	3117
	4:14 for this *is* the **d** in which the LORD hath	3117
	4:23 So God subdued on that **d** Jabin the king	3117
	5: 1 and Barak the son of Abinoam on that **d**,	3117
	6:24 unto this **d** it *is* yet in Ophrah of	3117
	6:27 of the city, that *he* could not do *it* **by d**,	3119
	6:32 Therefore on that **d** he called him	3117
	9:18 risen up against my father's house *this* **d**,	3117
	9:19 with Jerubbaal and with his house this **d**,	3117
	9:45 fought against the city all that **d**;	3117
	10: 4 which are called Havoth-jair unto this **d**,	3117
	10:15 deliver us only, we pray thee, this **d**.	3117
	11:27 the LORD the Judge be judge *this* **d**	3117
	12: 3 are ye come up unto me this **d**,	3117
	13: 7 God from the womb to the **d** of his death.	3117
	13:10 unto me, that came unto me the *other* **d**.	3117
	14:15 it came to pass on the seventh **d**, that they	3117
	14:17 it came to pass on the seventh **d**, that he	3117
	14:18 the seventh **d** before the sun went down,	3117
	15:19 which *is* in Lehi unto this **d**.	3117
	16: 2 saying, In the morning, when it is **d**, we	216
	18: 1 **d** *all* their inheritance had not fallen unto	3117
	18:12 that place Mahaneh-dan unto this **d**:	3117
	18:30 until the **d** of the captivity of the land.	3117
	19: 5 it came to pass on the fourth **d**, when	3117
	19: 8 arose early in the morning on the fifth **d**	3117
	19: 9 the **d** draweth towards evening,	3117
	19: 9 behold, the **d** groweth to an end,	3117
	19:11 they *were* by Jebus, the **d** was far spent;	3117
	19:25 when the **d** began to spring, they let her	7837
	19:26 came the woman in the dawning of the **d**,	1242
	19:30 that the children of Israel came up out	3117
	19:30 up out of the land of Egypt unto this **d**:	3117
	20:21 the ground of the Israelites that **d** twenty	3117
	20:22 they put *themselves* in array the first **d**.	3117
	20:24 the children of Benjamin the second **d**.	3117
	20:25 against them out of Gibeah the second **d**,	3117
	20:26 fasted that **d** until even, and offered burnt	3117
	20:30 the children of Benjamin on the third **d**,	3117
	20:35 destroyed of the Benjamites that **d** twenty	3117
	20:46 So that all which fell that **d** of Benjamin	3117
	21: 3 there should be to **d** one tribe 3117+1886.1	
	21: 6 is one tribe cut off from Israel *this* **d**.	3117
Ru	2:19 Where hast thou gleaned **to d**? 3117+1886.1	
	2:19 whom I wrought **to d** *is* Boaz. 3117+1886.1	

Ru	3:18 until he have finished the thing *this* **d**.	3117
	4: 5 What **d** thou buyest the field of the hand	3117
	4: 9 all the people, Ye *are* witnesses *this* **d**,	3117
	4:10 gate of his place: ye *are* witnesses *this* **d**,	3117
	4:14 which hath not left thee *this* **d** without a	3117
1Sa	2:34 in one **d** they shall die both of them.	3117
	3:12 In that **d** I will perform against Eli all	3117
	4: 3 us **to d** before the Philistines? 3117+1886.1	
	4:12 *to* Shiloh the same **d** with his clothes	3117
	4:16 and I fled **to d** out of the army. 3117+1886.1	
	5: 5 threshold of Dagon in Ashdod unto this **d**.	3117
	6:15 sacrificed sacrifices the same **d** unto	3117
	6:16 they returned to Ekron the same **d**.	3117
	6:18 *which* stone *remaineth* unto this **d** in	3117
	7: 6 and fasted on that **d**, and said there,	3117
	7:10 thunder on that **d** upon the Philistines,	3117
	8: 8 **d** that I brought them up out of Egypt	3117
	8: 8 them up out of Egypt even unto this **d**,	3117
	8:18 ye shall cry out in that **d** because of your	3117
	8:18 and the LORD will not hear you in that **d**.	3117
	9:12 for he came **to d** to the city; 3117+1886.1	
	9:12 the people **to d** in the high place: 3117+1886.1	
	9:15 Samuel in his ear a **d** before Saul came,	3117
	9:19 for ye shall eat with me **to d**, 3117+1886.1	
	9:24 So Saul did eat with Samuel that **d**.	3117
	9:26 it came to pass about the spring of the **d**,	7837
	10: 2 thou art departed from me **to d**, 3117+1886.1	
	10: 9 and all those signs came to pass that **d**.	3117
	10:19 ye have *this* **d** rejected your God,	3117
	11:11 the Ammonites until the heat of the **d**:	3117
	11:13 shall not a man be put to death *this* **d**?	3117
	11:13 for **to d** the LORD hath wrought 3117+1886.1	
	12: 2 before you from my childhood unto this **d**.	3117
	12: 5 and his anointed *is* witness *this* **d**,	3117
	12:17 *Is it* not wheat harvest **to d**? 3117+1886.1	
	12:18 the LORD sent thunder and rain that **d**:	3117
	13:22 So it came to pass in the **d** of battle,	3117
	14: 1 Now it came to pass upon a **d**,	3117
	14:23 So the LORD saved Israel that **d**: and	3117
	14:24 the men of Israel were distressed that **d**:	3117
	14:28 be the man that eateth *any* food *this* **d**.	3117
	14:30 **to d** of the spoil of their enemies 3117+1886.1	
	14:31 they smote the Philistines that **d** from	3117
	14:33 roll a great stone unto me *this* **d**.	3117
	14:37 of Israel? But he answered him not that **d**.	3117
	14:38 and see wherein this sin hath been *this* **d**.	3117
	14:45 for he hath wrought with God this **d**.	3117
	15:28 the kingdom of Israel from thee *this* **d**,	3117
	15:35 more to see Saul until the **d** of his death:	3117
	16:13 came upon David from that **d** forward.	3117
	17:10 I defy the armies of Israel this **d**;	3117
	17:46 This **d** will the LORD deliver thee into	3117
	17:46 Philistines *this* **d** unto the fowls of the air,	3117
	18: 2 Saul took him that **d**, and would let him	3117
	18: 9 Saul eyed David from that **d** and forward.	3117
	18:21 Thou shalt *this* **d** be my son in law in	3117
	19:24 down naked all that **d** and all that night.	3117
	20: 5 in the fields unto the third **d** at even.	NIH
	20:12 the third **d**, and behold, *if there be* good	NIH
	20:26 Saul spake not any thing that **d**:	3117
	20:27 *which was* the second **d** of the month,	NIH
	20:27 neither yesterday, nor **to d**? 3117+1886.1	
	20:34 eat no meat the second **d** of the month:	3117
	21: 5 though it were sanctified *this* **d** in	3117
	21: 6 put hot bread in the **d** when it was taken	3117
	21: 7 of the servants of Saul *was* there that **d**,	3117
	21:10 fled that **d** for fear of Saul, and went to	3117
	22: 8 against me, to lie in wait, as at this **d**?	3117
	22:13 rise against me, to lie in wait, as at this **d**?	3117
	22:18 slew on that **d** fourscore and five persons	3117
	22:22 David said unto Abiathar, I knew *it* that **d**,	3117
	23:14 Saul sought him every **d**, but God	3117
	24: 4 Behold the **d** of which the LORD said	3117
	24:10 this **d** thine eyes have seen how that	3117
	24:10 **to d** into mine hand in the cave: 3117+1886.1	
	24:18 thou hast shewed *this* **d** how that thou	3117
	24:19 for that thou hast done unto me *this* **d**,	3117
	25: 8 we come in a good **d**: give, I pray thee,	3117
	25:16 were a wall unto us both by night and **d**,	3119
	25:32 Israel, which sent thee *this* **d** to meet me:	3117
	25:33 which hast kept me this **d** from coming to	3117
	26: 8 thine enemy into thine hand *this* **d**:	3117
	26:10 or his **d** shall come to die; or he shall	3117
	26:19 for they have driven me out *this* **d** from	3117
	26:21 my soul was precious in thine eyes *this* **d**:	3117
	26:23 delivered thee into *my* hand **to d**, 3117+1886.1	
	26:24 as thy life was much set by this **d** in mine	3117
	27: 1 I shall now perish one **d** by the hand of	3117
	27: 6 Achish gave him Ziklag that **d**: wherefore	3117
	27: 6 unto the kings of Judah unto this **d**.	3117
	27:10 have ye made a road **to d**? 3117+1886.1	
	28:18 the LORD done this thing unto thee this **d**.	3117
	28:20 for he had eaten no bread all the **d**, nor all	3117
	29: 3 in him since he fell *unto me* unto this **d**?	3117
	29: 6 I have not found evil in thee since the **d**	3117
	29: 6 day of thy coming unto me unto this **d**:	3117
	29: 8 long as I have been with thee unto this **d**,	3117
	30: 1 men were come to Ziklag on the third **d**,	3117
	30:17 even unto the evening of the **next d**:	4283
	30:25 was *so* from that **d** forward, that he made	3117
	30:25 and an ordinance for Israel unto this **d**.	3117
	31: 6 all his men, that *same* **d** together.	3117
2Sa	1: 2 It came even to pass on the third **d**, that	
	2:17 there was a very sore battle that **d**;	3117
	2:32 and they came to Hebron **at break of d**.	215

2Sa
3: 8 *this* d unto the house of Saul thy father, 3117
3: 8 that thou chargest me to d with a 3117+1886.1
3:35 David to eat meat while it was yet d, 3117
3:37 all Israel understood that d that it was not 3117
3:38 and a great *man* fallen this d in Israel? 3117
3:39 I *am* this d weak, though anointed king; 3117
4: 4 and were sojourners there until this d.) 3117
4: 5 came about the heat of the d to the house 3117
4: 8 avenged my lord the king this d of Saul, 3117
5: 8 David said on that d, Whosoever getteth 3117
6: 8 *name* of the place Perez-uzzah to this d. 3117
6: 9 David was afraid of the LORD that d, 3117
6:20 was the king of Israel to d, 3117+1886.1
6:20 who uncovered himself to d in 3117+1886.1
6:23 Saul had no child unto the d of her death. 3117
7: 6 even to this d, but have walked in a tent 3117
11:12 Tarry here to d also, 3117+1886.1
11:12 So Uriah abode in Jerusalem that d, 3117
12:18 it came to pass on the seventh d, that 3117
13: 4 *being* the king's son, lean from d to day? 1242
13: 4 *being* the king's son, lean from day to d? 1242
13:32 from the d that he forced his sister Tamar. 3117
13:37 And *David* mourned for his son every d. 3117
14:22 To d thy servant knoweth that I 3117+1886.1
15:20 should I *this* d make thee go up and 3117
16: 3 he said, To d shall the house of 3117+1886.1
16:12 will requite me good for his cursing this d. 3117
18: 7 there was there a great slaughter that d *of* 3117
18: 8 the wood devoured more people that d 3117
18:18 it is called unto this d, Absalom's place. 3117
18:20 Thou *shalt* not bear tidings this d, 3117
18:20 but thou shalt bear tidings another d: 3117
18:20 d thou shalt bear no tidings, because 3117
18:31 for the LORD hath avenged thee *this* d of 3117
19: 2 victory that d was *turned* into mourning 3117
19: 2 for the people heard say that d *how* 3117
19: 3 the people gat them by stealth that d *into* 3117
19: 5 Thou hast shamed this d the faces of all 3117
19: 5 which *this* d have saved thy life, 3117
19: 6 for thou hast declared *this* d, that thou 3117
19: 6 for *this* d I perceive, that if Absalom had 3117
19: 6 all we had died *this* d, then it had pleased 3117
19:19 d that my lord the king went out of 3117
19:20 I am come the first *this* d of all the house 3117
19:22 that ye should *this* d be adversaries unto 3117
19:22 there any man be put to death *this* d in 3117
19:22 do not I know that I *am* this d king over 3117
19:24 from the d the king departed until the day 3117
19:24 from the day the king departed until the d 3117
19:35 I *am* this d fourscore years old: *and* can I 3117
20: 3 So they were shut up unto the d of their 3117
21:10 the birds of the air to rest on them by d, 3119
22: 1 d *that* the LORD had delivered him out of 3117
22:19 They prevented me in the d of my 3117
23:10 the LORD wrought a great victory that d; 3117
24:18 Gad came that d to David, and said unto 3117

1Ki
1:25 For he is gone down *this* d, and hath slain 3117
1:30 stead; even so will I certainly do this d. 3117
1:48 hath given *one* to sit on my throne *this* d, 3117
1:51 to d that he will not slay his 3117+1886.1
2: 8 curse in the d when I went *to* Mahanaim: 3117
2:24 Adonijah shall be put to death *this* d. 3117
2:37 *that* on the d thou goest out, 3117
2:42 on the d thou goest out, and walkest 3117
3: 6 a son to sit on his throne, as *it is* this d. 3117
3:18 it came to pass the third d after that I was 3117
4:22 Solomon's provision for one d was thirty 3117
5: 7 and said, Blessed *be* the LORD *this* d, 3117
8: 8 without: and there they are unto this d. 3117
8:16 Since the d that I brought forth my people 3117
8:24 fulfilled *it* with thine hand, as *it is* this d. 3117
8:28 servant prayeth before thee to d: 3117+1886.1
8:29 be open toward this house night and d, 3117
8:59 be nigh unto the LORD our God and d 3119
8:61 to keep his commandments, as at this d. 3117
8:64 The same d did the king hallow the 3117
8:66 On the eighth d he sent the people away; 3117
9:13 called them the land of Cabul unto this d. 3117
9:21 levy a tribute of bondservice unto this d. 3117
10:12 almug trees, nor were seen unto this d. 3117
12: 7 wilt be a servant unto this people *this* d, 3117
12:12 the people came to Rehoboam the third d, 3117
12:12 saying, Come to me again the third d. 3117
12:19 against the house of David unto this d. 3117
12:32 on the fifteenth d of the month, like unto 3117
12:33 el the fifteenth d of the eighth month, 3117
13: 3 he gave a sign the same d, saying, This *is* 3117
13:11 man of God had done *that* d in Beth-el: 3117
14:14 shall cut off the house of Jeroboam that d: 3117
16:16 king over Israel that d in the camp. 3117
17:14 until the d *that* the LORD sendeth rain 3117
18:15 shew myself unto him to d. 3117+1886.1
18:36 let it be known *this* d that thou *art* God in 3117
20:13 I will deliver it into thine hand *this* d; 3117
20:29 in the seventh d the battle was joined: 3117
20:29 an hundred thousand footmen in one d. 3117
22: 5 at the word of the LORD to d. 3117+1886.1
22:25 Behold, thou shalt see in that d, 3117
22:35 the battle increased that d: and the king 3117

2Ki
2: 3 thy master from thy head to d? 3117+1886.1
2: 5 thy master from thy head to d? 3117+1886.1
2:22 So the waters were healed unto this d, 3117
4: 8 fell on a d, that Elisha passed to Shunem, 3117
4:11 it fell on a d, that he came thither, 3117
4:18 when the child was grown, it fell on a d, 3117

2Ki
4:23 wilt thou go to him to d? 3117+1886.1
6:28 that we may eat him to d, and we 3117+1886.1
6:29 said unto her on the next d, Give thy son, 3117
6:31 son of Shaphat shall stand on him this d. 3117
7: 9 this d *is* a day of good tidings, and we 3117
7: 9 this day *is* a day of good tidings, and we 3117
8: 6 all the fruits of the field since the d that 3117
8:22 from under the hand of Judah unto this d. 3117
10:27 and made it a draught house unto this d. 3117
14: 7 called the name of it Joktheel unto this d. 3117
15: 5 he was a leper unto the d of his death, 3117
16: 6 to Elath, and dwelt there unto this d. 3117
17:23 of their own land to Assyria unto this d. 3117
17:34 Unto this d they do after the former 3117
17:41 did their fathers, *so* do they unto this d. 3117
19: 3 This d *is* a day of trouble, and of rebuke, 3117
19: 3 This day *is* a d of trouble, and of rebuke, 3117
20: 5 on the third d thou shalt go up *unto* 3117
20: 8 *into* the house of the LORD the third d? 3117
20:17 fathers have laid up in store unto this d, 3117
21:15 since the d their fathers came forth out of 3117
21:15 came forth out of Egypt, even unto this d. 3117
25: 1 tenth month, in the tenth d of the month, NIH
25: 3 on the ninth d of the *fourth* month NIH
25: 8 month, on the seventh d of the month, NIH
25:27 the seven and twentieth d of the month, NIH
25:30 a daily rate for every d, all the days of his 3117

1Ch
4:41 destroyed them utterly unto this d, 3117
4:43 escaped, and dwelt there unto this d. 3117
5:26 Hara, and to the river Gozan, unto this d. 3117
9:33 for they were employed in *that* work d 3119
11:22 and slew a lion in a pit in a snowy d. 3117
12:22 For at *that* time d by day there came to 3117
12:22 For at *that* time day by day there came to 3117
13:11 that place is called Perez-uzza to this d. 3117
13:12 David was afraid of God that d, saying, 3117
16: 7 on that d David delivered first *this psalm* 3117
16:23 shew forth from d to day his salvation. 3117
16:23 shew forth from day to d his salvation. 3117
17: 5 I have not dwelt in a house since the d 3117
17: 5 day that I brought up Israel unto this d; 3117
26:17 northward four a, southward four a day, 3117
26:17 southward four a d, and toward Asuppim 3117
28: 7 and my judgments, as *at* this d. 3117
29: 5 is willing to consecrate his service *this* d 3117
29:21 the morrow after that d, *even* a thousand 3117
29:22 drink before the LORD on that d with 3117

2Ch
2: 3 he began to build in the second d *of* NIH
5: 9 seen without. And there it is unto this d. 3117
6: 5 Since the d that I brought forth my people 3117
6:15 fulfilled *it* with thine hand, as *it is* this d. 3117
6:20 eyes may be open upon this house d 3119
7: 9 in the eighth d they made a solemn 3117
7:10 twentieth d of the seventh month he sent 3117
8: 8 Solomon make to pay tribute until this d. 3117
8:13 after a certain rate every d, 3117+3117+871.1
8:14 duty of every d required: 3117+3117+871.1
8:16 of the foundation of the house of 3117
10:12 people came to Rehoboam the third d, 3117
10:12 saying, Come again to me on the third d. 3117
10:19 against the house of David unto this d. 3117
18: 4 at the word of the LORD to d. 3117+1886.1
18:34 shalt see on that d when thou shalt go 3117
18:34 battle increased that d: howbeit the king 3117
20:26 on the fourth d they assembled themselves 3117
20:26 The valley of Berachah, unto *this* d. 3117
21:10 from under the hand of Judah unto this d. 3117
21:15 fall out by reason of the sickness d by day. 3117
21:15 fall out by reason of the sickness day by d. 3117
24:11 Thus they did d by day, 3117
24:11 Thus they did day by d, 3117
26:21 Uzziah the king was a leper unto the d of 3117
28: 6 hundred and twenty thousand in one d, 3117
29:17 Now they began on the first d of the first NIH
29:17 on the eighth d of the month came they 3117
29:17 in the sixteenth d of the first month they 3117
30:15 killed the passover on the fourteenth d NIH
30:21 the priests praised the LORD d by day, 3117
30:21 the priests praised the LORD day by d, 3117
35: 1 killed the passover on the fourteenth d NIH
35:16 of the LORD was prepared the same d, 3117
35:21 I *come* not against thee this d, 3117
35:25 of Josiah in their lamentations to *this* d. 3117

Ezr
3: 4 duty of every d required; 3117+3117+871.1
3: 6 From the first d of the seventh month 3117
6: 9 let *it* be given them d by day without fail: 3118
6: 9 let *it* be given them day by d without fail: 3118
6:15 this house was finished on the third d of 3117
6:19 upon the fourteenth d of the first month. NIH
7: 9 upon the first d of the first month began NIH
7: 9 on the first d of the fifth month came he to NIH
8:31 Ahava on the twelfth d of the first month, 3117
8:33 Now on the fourth d was the silver and 3117
9: 7 we *been* in a great trespass unto this d; 3117
9: 7 and to confusion of face, as *it is* this d. 3117
9:15 for we remain *yet* escaped, as *it is* this d: 3117
10: 9 on the twentieth d of the month; NIH
10:13 neither *is this* a work of one d or two: 3117
10:16 sat down in the first d of the tenth month 3117
10:17 wives by the first d of the first month. 3117

Ne
1: 6 I pray before thee now, d and night, 3119
1:11 thy servant *this* d, and grant him mercy in 3117
2: 1 will they make an end in a d? will they 3117
4: 9 set a watch against them d and night, 3119
4:22 be a guard to us, and labour on the d. 3117

Ne
5:11 Restore, I pray you, to them, even *this* d, 3117
6:15 the twenty and fifth d of *the month* Elul, NIH
8: 2 upon the first d of the seventh month. 3117
8: 9 *This* d *is* holy unto the LORD your God; 3117
8:10 for *this* d *is* holy unto our Lord: neither 3117
8:11 Hold your peace, for the d *is* holy; 3117
8:13 on the second d were gathered together 3117
8:17 had not the children of Israel done so. 3117
8:18 Also d by day, from the first day unto 3117
8:18 Also day by d, from the first day unto 3117
8:18 by day, from the first d unto the last day, 3117
8:18 by day, from the first day unto the last d, 3117
8:18 on the eighth d *was* a solemn assembly, 3117
9: 1 fourth d of this month the children of 3117
9: 3 LORD their God one fourth *part* of the d; 3117
9:10 didst thou get thee a name, as *it is* this d. 3117
9:12 Moreover thou leddest them in the d by a 3119
9:19 of the cloud departed not from them by d, 3119
9:32 time of the kings of Assyria unto this d. 3117
9:36 we *are* servants this d, and *for* the land 3117
10:31 or any victuals on the sabbath d to sell, 3117
10:31 of them on the sabbath, or on the holy d: 3117
11:23 singers, due for every d. 3117+3117+871.1
12:43 Also that d they offered great sacrifices, 3117
12:47 every d his portion: 3117+3117+871.1
13: 1 On that d they read in the book of Moses 3117
13:15 brought *into* Jerusalem on the sabbath d: 3117
13:15 I testified *against them* in the d wherein 3117
13:17 this ye do, and profane the sabbath d? 3117
13:19 no burden be brought in on the sabbath d 3117
13:22 keep the gates, to sanctify the sabbath d. 3117

Est
1:10 On the seventh d, when the heart of 3117
1:18 say this d unto all the king's princes, 3117
2:11 every d Mordecai 3117+3117+3605+2050.1
3: 7 before Haman from d to day, 3117
3: 7 before Haman from day to d, 3117
3:12 on the thirteenth d of the first month, 3117
3:13 little children and women, in one d, 3117
3:13 *even* upon the thirteenth d of the twelfth NIH
3:14 that *they* should be ready against that d. 3117
4:16 eat nor drink three days, night or d; 3117
5: 1 Now it came to pass on the third d, 3117
5: 4 Haman come *this* d unto the banquet that 3117
5: 9 went Haman forth that d joyful and with 3117
7: 2 on the second d at the banquet of wine, 3117
8: 1 On that d did the king Ahasuerus give 3117
8: 9 on the three and twentieth d thereof; NIH
8:12 Upon one d in all the provinces of king 3117
8:12 upon the thirteenth d of the twelfth NIH
8:13 the Jews should be ready against that d 3117
8:17 joy and gladness, a feast and a good d. 3117
9: 1 on the thirteenth d of the same, 3117
9: 1 in the d that the enemies of the Jews 3117
9:11 On that d the number of those that were 3117
9:15 the fourteenth d also of the month Adar, 3117
9:17 On the thirteenth d of the month Adar; 3117
9:17 the fourteenth d of the same rested they, NIH
9:17 and made it a d of feasting and gladness. 3117
9:18 together on the thirteenth d thereof, NIH
9:18 on the fifteenth d of the same they rested, NIH
9:18 and made it a d of feasting and gladness. 3117
9:19 made the fourteenth d of the month Adar 3117
9:19 day of the month Adar a d *of* gladness NIH
9:19 a good d, and *of* sending portions one to 3117
9:21 that they should keep the fourteenth d of 3117
9:21 and the fifteenth d of the same, yearly, 3117
9:22 to joy, and from mourning into a good d: 3117

Job
1: 4 feasted in *their* houses, every one his d; 3117
1: 6 Now there was a d when the sons of God 3117
1:13 there was a d when his sons and 3117
2: 1 there was a d when the sons of God 3117
3: 1 opened Job his mouth, and cursed his d. 3117
3: 3 Let the d perish wherein I was born, 3117
3: 4 Let that d be darkness; let not God regard 3117
3: 5 it; let the blackness of the d terrify it. 3117
3: 8 Let them curse it that curse the d, who 3117
3: 9 neither let it see the dawning of the d: 7837
7: 4 and fro unto the **dawning of the** d. 5399
14: 6 he shall accomplish, as a hireling, his d. 3117
15:23 Where *is it?* he knoweth that the d 3117
17:12 They change the night into d: the light *is* 3117
18:20 come after *him* shall be astonied at his d, 3117
19:25 *that* he shall stand *at* the latter d *upon* NIH
20:28 *his* goods *shall* flow away in the d of his 3117
21:30 That the wicked is reserved to the d of 3117
21:30 they shall be brought forth to the d of 3117
23: 2 Even to d *is* my complaint bitter: 3117+1886.1
26:10 until the d and night come to an end. 216
38:23 of trouble, against the d of battle and war? 3117

Ps
1: 2 in his law doth he meditate d and night. 3119
2: 7 *art* my Son; *this* d have I begotten thee. 3117
7:11 God is angry *with the wicked* every d. 3117
18: T d *that* the LORD delivered him from 3117
18:18 They prevented me in the d of my 3117
19: 2 D unto day uttereth speech, and night 3119
19: 2 Day unto d uttereth speech, and night 3117
20: 1 The LORD hear thee in the d of trouble; 3117
25: 5 my salvation; on thee do I wait all the d. 3117
32: 3 old through my roaring all the d long. 3117
32: 4 For d and night thy hand was heavy upon 3119
35:28 *and of* thy praise all the d long. 3117
37:13 at him: for he seeth that his d is coming. 3117
38: 6 greatly; I go mourning all the d long. 3117
38:12 and imagine deceits all the d long. 3117
42: 3 My tears have been my meat d and night, 3119

D

D

Ps 44: 8 In God we boast all the **d** long, 3117
 44:22 for thy sake are we killed all the **d** long; 3117
 50:15 call upon me in the **d** of trouble: I will 3117
 55:10 **D** and night they go about it upon the 3119
 56: 5 Every **d** they wrest my words: all their 3117
 59:16 and refuge in the **d** of my trouble. 3117
 71: 8 thy praise *and with* thy honour all the **d**. 3117
 71:15 *and* thy salvation all the **d**; 3117
 71:24 talk of thy righteousness all the **d** long: 3117
 73:14 For all the **d** long have I been plagued, 3117
 74:16 The **d** *is* thine, the night also *is* thine: 3117
 77: 2 In the **d** of my trouble I sought the Lord: 3117
 78: 9 turned *back* in the **d** of battle. 3117
 78:42 *nor* the **d** when he delivered them from 3117
 81: 3 time appointed, on our solemn feast **d**. 3117
 84:10 For a **d** in thy courts *is* better than a 3117
 86: 7 In the **d** of my trouble I will call upon 3117
 88: 1 I have cried **d** *and* night before thee: 3117
 89:16 In thy name shall they rejoice all the **d** 3117
 91: 5 night; *nor* for the arrow *that* flieth **by d**; 3119
 92: T A Psalm *or* Song for the sabbath **d**. 3117
 95: T **To d** if ye will hear his voice, 3117+1886.1
 95: 8 *in* the **d** of temptation in the wilderness: 3117
 96: 2 shew forth his salvation from **d** to day. 3117
 96: 2 shew forth his salvation from day to **d**. 3117
 102: 2 Hide not thy face from me in the **d** *when* 3117
 102: 2 in the **d** *when* I call answer me speedily. 3117
 102: 8 Mine enemies reproach me all the **d**; 3117
 110: 3 Thy people *shall be* willing in the **d** of thy 3117
 110: 5 strike through kings in the **d** of his wrath. 3117
 118:24 This *is* the **d** *which* the Lord hath made; 3117
 119:91 They continue *this* **d** according to thine 3117
 119:97 I thy law! it *is* my meditation all the **d**. 3117
 119:164 Seven *times* a **d** do I praise thee because 3117
 121: 6 The sun shall not smite thee **by d**, 3119
 136: 8 The sun to rule by **d**: for his mercy 3117
 137: 7 children of Edom *in* the **d** of Jerusalem; 3117
 138: 3 In the **d** when I cried thou answeredst 3117
 139:12 from thee; but the night shineth as the **d**: 3117
 140: 7 thou hast covered my head in the **d** of 3117
 145: 2 Every **d** will I bless thee; and I will praise 3117
 146: 4 earth; in that *very* **d** his thoughts perish. 3117
Pr 4:18 more and more unto the perfect **d**. 3117
 6:34 he will not spare in the **d** of vengeance. 3117
 7:14 with me; *this* **d** have I payed my vows. 3117
 7:20 will come home at the **d** appointed. 3117
 11: 4 Riches profit not in the **d** of wrath: but 3117
 16: 4 even the wicked for the **d** of evil. 3117
 21:26 He coveteth greedily all the **d** long: but 3117
 21:31 The horse *is* prepared against the **d** of 3117
 22:19 I have made known to thee *this* **d**, even 3117
 23:17 *be* thou in the fear of the Lord all the **d** 3117
 24:10 *If* thou faint in the **d** of adversity, 3117
 27: 1 for thou knowest not what a **d** may bring 3117
 27:10 go *into* thy brother's house in the **d** 3117
 27:15 A continual dropping in a very rainy **d** 3117
Ecc 7: 1 the **d** of death than the day of one's birth. 3117
 7: 1 the day of death than the **d** of one's birth. 3117
 7:14 In the **d** of prosperity be joyful, but in 3117
 7:14 joyful, but in the **d** of adversity consider: 3117
 8: 8 neither *hath* he power in the **d** of death: 3117
 8:16 (for also *there is that* neither **d** nor night 3117
 12: 3 In the **d** when the keepers of the house 3117
SS 2:17 Until the **d** break, and the shadows flee 3117
 3:11 crowned him in the **d** of his espousals, 3117
 3:11 and in the **d** of the gladness of his heart. 3117
 4: 6 Until the **d** break, and the shadows flee 3117
 8: 8 what shall we do for our sister in the **d** 3117
Isa 2:11 the Lord alone shall be exalted in that **d**. 3117
 2:12 For the **d** of the Lord of hosts *shall be* 3117
 2:17 the Lord alone shall be exalted in that **d**. 3117
 2:20 that **d** a man shall cast his idols of silver, 3117
 3: 7 In that **d** shall he swear, saying, I will not 3117
 3:18 In that **d** the Lord will take away 3117
 4: 1 in that **d** seven women shall take hold of 3117
 4: 2 In that **d** shall the branch of the Lord be 3117
 4: 5 cloud and smoke **by d**, and the shining of 3119
 5:30 in that **d** they shall roar against them like 3117
 7:17 from the **d** that Ephraim departed from 3117
 7:18 it shall come to pass in that **d**, *that* 3117
 7:20 In the same **d** shall the Lord shave with a 3117
 7:21 it shall come to pass in that **d**, *that* a man 3117
 7:23 it shall come to pass in that **d**, *that* every 3117
 9: 4 of his oppressor, as *in* the **d** of Midian. 3117
 9:14 and tail, branch and rush, *in* one **d**. 3117
 10: 3 what will ye do in the **d** of visitation, 3117
 10:17 devour his thorns and his briers in one **d**; 3117
 10:20 it shall come to pass in that **d**, *that* 3117
 10:27 it shall come to pass in that **d**, *that* his 3117
 10:32 As yet shall *he* remain at Nob that **d**: 3117
 11:10 in that **d** there shall be a root of Jesse, 3117
 11:11 shall come to pass in that **d**, *that* the Lord 3117
 11:16 as it was to Israel in the **d** that he 3117
 12: 1 in that **d** thou shalt say, O Lord, I will 3117
 12: 4 in that **d** shall ye say, Praise the Lord, 3117
 13: 6 for the **d** of the Lord *is* at hand; 3117
 13: 9 Behold, the **d** of the Lord cometh, 3117
 13:13 of hosts, and in the **d** of his fierce anger. 3117
 14: 3 it shall come to pass in that **d** that the glory 3117
 17: 4 that it shall come to pass, *that* the glory 3117
 17: 7 At that **d** shall a man look to his Maker, 3117
 17: 9 In that **d** shall his strong cities be as a 3117
 17:11 the **d** shalt thou make thy plant to grow, 3117
 17:11 harvest *shall be* a heap in the **d** of grief 3117
 19:16 In that **d** shall Egypt be like unto women: 3117

Isa 19:18 In that **d** shall five cities in the land of 3117
 19:19 In that **d** shall there be an altar to 3117
 19:21 Egyptians shall know the Lord in that **d**, 3117
 19:23 In that **d** shall there be a highway out of 3117
 19:24 that **d** shall Israel be the third with Egypt 3117
 20: 6 inhabitant of this isle shall say in that **d**, 3117
 22: 5 For *it is* a **d** of trouble, and of treading 3117
 22: 8 thou didst look in that **d** to the armour of 3117
 22:12 in that **d** did the Lord God of hosts call to 3117
 22:20 it shall come to pass in that **d**, that I will 3117
 22:25 In that **d**, saith the Lord of hosts, 3117
 23:15 it shall come to pass in that **d**, that Tyre 3117
 24:21 it shall come to pass in that **d**, *that* 3117
 25: 9 it shall be said in that **d**, Lo, this *is* our 3117
 26: 1 that **d** shall this song be sung in the land 3117
 27: 1 In that **d** the Lord with his sore and 3117
 27: 2 In that **d** sing ye unto her, A vineyard of 3117
 27: 3 lest *any* hurt it, I will keep it night and **d**. 3117
 27: 8 he stayeth his rough wind in the **d** of 3117
 27:12 it shall come to pass in that **d**, *that* 3117
 27:13 shall come to pass in that **d**, *that* the great 3117
 28: 5 In that **d** shall the Lord of hosts be for a 3117
 28:19 shall it pass over, by **d** and by night: 3117
 28:24 Doth the plowman plow all **d** to sow? 3117
 29:18 in that **d** shall the deaf hear the words of 3117
 30:23 in that **d** shall thy cattle feed *in* large 3117
 30:25 streams of waters in the **d** of the great 3117
 30:26 in the **d** that the Lord bindeth up 3117
 31: 7 in that **d** every man shall cast away his 3117
 34: 8 For *it is* the **d** of the Lord's vengeance, 3117
 34:10 It shall not be quenched night nor **d**; 3119
 37: 3 This *is* a day of trouble, and of rebuke, 3117
 37: 3 This day *is* a **d** of trouble, and of rebuke, 3117
 38:12 **d** *even* to night wilt thou make an end 3117
 38:13 **d** *even* to night wilt thou make an end 3117
 38:19 he shall praise thee, as I *do this* **d**: 3117
 39: 6 fathers have laid up in store until this **d**, 3117
 43:13 before the **d** *was* I am he; and *there is* 3117
 47: 9 shall come to thee *in* a moment in one **d**, 3117
 48: 7 before the **d** when thou heardest them 3117
 49: 8 and in a **d** of salvation have I helped thee: 3117
 51:13 hast feared continually every **d** because of 3117
 52: 5 my name continually every **d** *is* 3117
 52: 6 *they shall know* in that **d** that I *am* he that 3117
 56:12 to morrow shall be as this **d**, 3117
 58: 3 in the **d** of your fast you find pleasure, 3117
 58: 4 ye shall not fast as *ye do this* **d**, to make 3117
 58: 5 a **d** for a man to afflict his soul? 3117
 58: 5 a fast, and an acceptable **d** to the Lord? 3117
 58:13 *from* doing thy pleasure on my holy **d**; 3117
 60:11 they shall not be shut **d** nor night; 3119
 60:19 The sun shall be no more thy light **by d**; 3119
 61: 2 and the **d** of vengeance of our God; 3117
 62: 6 *which* shall never hold their peace **d** nor 3117
 63: 4 For the **d** of vengeance *is* in mine heart, 3117
 65: 2 have spread out mine hands all the **d** unto 3117
 65: 5 in my nose, a fire that burneth all the **d**. 3117
 66: 8 the earth be made to bring forth in one **d**? 3117
Jer 1:10 I have this **d** set thee over the nations and 3117
 1:18 I have made thee *this* **d** a defenced city, 3117
 3:25 from our youth even unto this **d**, 3117
 4: 9 it shall come to pass at that **d**, saith 3117
 6: 4 for the **d** goeth away, for the shadows of 3117
 7:22 nor commanded them in the **d** that I 3117
 7:25 Since the **d** that your fathers came forth 3117
 7:25 forth out of the land of Egypt unto this **d**, 3117
 9: 1 that I might weep **d** and night for the slain 3119
 11: 4 Which I commanded your fathers in the **d** 3117
 11: 5 with milk and honey, as *it is* this **d**. 3117
 11: 7 that I brought them up out of the land 3117
 11: 7 *even* unto this **d**, rising early and 3117
 12: 3 and prepare them for the **d** of slaughter. 3117
 14:17 eyes run down *with* tears night and **d**, 3119
 15: 9 her sun is gone down while *it was* yet **d**: 3117
 16:13 shall ye serve other gods *and* night; 3119
 16:19 and my refuge in the **d** of affliction, 3117
 17:16 neither have I desired the woeful **d**; 3117
 17:17 me: thou *art* my hope in the **d** of evil. 3117
 17:18 bring upon them the **d** of evil, 3117
 17:21 bear no burden on the sabbath **d**, 3117
 17:22 out of your houses on the sabbath **d**, 3117
 17:22 any work, but hallow ye the sabbath **d**, 3117
 17:24 the gates of this city on the sabbath **d**, 3117
 17:24 hallow the sabbath **d**, to do no work 3117
 17:27 hearken not unto me to hallow the sabbath **d**, 3117
 17:27 the gates of Jerusalem on the sabbath **d**; 3117
 18:17 not the face, in the **d** of their calamity. 3117
 20:14 Cursed *be* the **d** wherein I was born: 3117
 20:14 let not the **d** wherein my mother bare me 3117
 25: 3 even unto this **d**, that *is* the three and 3117
 25:18 a hissing, and a curse; as *it is* this **d**; 3117
 25:33 the slain of the Lord shall be at that **d** 3117
 27:22 there shall they be until the **d** that I visit 3117
 30: 7 for that **d** *is* great, so that none *is* like it: 3117
 30: 8 For it shall come to pass in that **d**, saith 3117
 31: 6 For there shall be a **d**, *that* the watchmen 3117
 31:32 in the **d** *that* I took them by the hand, 3117
 31:35 which giveth the sun for a light **by d**, 3119
 32:20 *even* unto this **d**, and in Israel, 3117
 32:20 and hast made thee a name, as *at* this **d**; 3117
 32:31 my fury from the **d** that they built it even 3117
 32:31 the day that they built it even unto this **d**; 3117
 33:20 If you can break my covenant of the **d**, 3117
 33:20 there should not be **d** and night in their 3119
 33:25 If my covenant *be* not with **d** and night, 3119

Jer 34:13 a covenant with your fathers in the **d** 3117
 35:14 for unto this **d** they drink none, 3117
 36: 2 the nations, from the **d** I spake unto thee, 3117
 36: 2 from the days of Josiah, even unto this **d**. 3117
 36: 6 *in* the Lord's house upon the fasting **d**: 3117
 36:30 his dead body shall be cast out in the **d** to 3117
 38:28 until the **d** that Jerusalem was taken: 3117
 39: 2 fourth month, the ninth **d** of the month, NIH
 39:16 shall be *accomplished* in that **d** before 3117
 39:17 I will deliver thee in that **d**, saith 3117
 40: 4 I loose thee *this* **d** from the chains which 3117
 41: 4 it came to pass the second **d** after *he* had 3117
 42:19 that I have admonished you *this* **d**. 3117
 42:21 *now* I have *this* **d** declared *it* to you; 3117
 44: 2 *this* **d** they *are* a desolation, and no man 3117
 44: 6 they are wasted *and* desolate, as *at* this **d**. 3117
 44:10 They are not humbled *even* unto this **d**, 3117
 44:22 curse, without an inhabitant, as *at* this **d**. 3117
 44:23 evil is happened unto you, as *at* this **d**. 3117
 46:10 For this *is* the **d** of the Lord God of hosts, 3117
 46:10 a **d** of vengeance, *that he* may avenge him 3117
 46:21 the **d** of their calamity was come upon 3117
 47: 4 Because of the **d** that cometh to spoil all 3117
 48:41 mighty *men's* hearts in Moab at that **d** 3117
 49:22 shall **d** the heart of the mighty *men* 3117
 49:26 the men of war shall be cut off in that **d**, 3117
 50:27 for their **d** is come, the time of their 3117
 50:30 her men of war shall be cut off in that **d**, 3117
 50:31 for thy **d** is come, the time *that* I will visit 3117
 51: 2 for in the **d** of trouble they shall be against 3117
 52: 4 tenth month, in the tenth **d** of the month, NIH
 52: 6 fourth month, in the ninth **d** of the month, NIH
 52:11 put him in prison till the **d** of his death. 3117
 52:12 fifth month, in the tenth **d** of the month, NIH
 52:31 in the five and twentieth **d** of the month, NIH
 52:34 **every d** a portion until 3117+3117+871.1
 52:34 day a portion until the **d** of his death, 3117
La 1:12 afflicted *me* in the **d** of his fierce anger. 3117
 1:13 hath made me desolate *and* faint all the **d**. 3117
 1:21 thou wilt bring the **d** *that* thou hast called, 3117
 2: 1 remembered not his footstool in the **d** of 3117
 2: 7 the Lord, as *in* the **d** of a solemn feast. 3117
 2:16 certainly this *is* the **d** that we looked for; 3117
 2:18 tears run down like a river **d** and night: 3119
 2:21 hast slain *them* in the **d** of thine anger; 3117
 2:22 Thou hast called as *in* a solemn **d** my 3117
 2:22 that in the **d** of the Lord's anger none 3117
 3: 3 he turneth his hand *against me* all the **d**. 3117
 3:14 to all my people; *and* their song all the **d**. 3117
 3:57 Thou drewest near in the **d** that I called 3117
 3:62 and their device against me all the **d**. 3117
Eze 1: 1 in the fourth *month*, in the fifth **d** of NIH
 1: 2 In the fifth **d** of the month, which *was* NIH
 1:28 bow that is in the cloud in the **d** of rain, 3117
 2: 3 against me, *even* unto this very **d**. 3117
 4: 6 appointed thee **each d** for a year. 3117+3117
 4:10 eat *shall be* by weight, twenty shekels a **d**: 3117
 7: 7 of trouble *is* near, and not 3117
 7:10 Behold the **d**, behold, it is come: 3117
 7:12 The time is come, the **d** draweth near: 3117
 7:19 them in the **d** of the wrath of the Lord: 3117
 8: 1 in the sixth *month*, in the fifth **d** of NIH
 12: 3 and remove **by d** in their sight; 3119
 12: 4 shalt thou bring forth thy stuff **by d**, as 3119
 12: 7 I brought forth my stuff **by d**, as stuff for 3119
 13: 5 stand in the battle in the **d** of the Lord. 3117
 16: 4 in the **d** thou wast born thy navel was not 3117
 16: 5 thy person, in the **d** that thou wast born. 3117
 16:56 by thy mouth in the **d** of thy pride, 3117
 20: 1 the fifth *month*, the tenth **d** of the month, NIH
 20: 5 In the **d** when I chose Israel, and lifted up 3117
 20: 6 In the **d** that I lifted up mine hand unto 3117
 20:29 name thereof is called Bamah unto this **d**. 3117
 20:31 with all your idols, *even* unto *this* **d**: 3117
 21:25 wicked prince of Israel, whose **d** is come, 3117
 21:29 whose **d** is come, when *their* iniquity 3117
 22:24 nor rained upon in the **d** of indignation. 3117
 23:38 have defiled my sanctuary in the same **d**, 3117
 23:39 they came the same **d** into my sanctuary to 3117
 24: 1 tenth month, in the tenth **d** of the month, NIH
 24: 2 Son of man, write thee the name of the **d**, 3117
 24: 2 the name of the day, *even* of this same **d**: 3117
 24: 2 set himself against Jerusalem this same **d**. 3117
 24:25 *shall it* not *be* in the **d** when I take from 3117
 24:26 *That* he that escapeth in that **d** shall come 3117
 24:27 In that **d** shall thy mouth be opened to 3117
 26: 1 eleventh year, in the first **d** of the month, NIH
 26:18 Now shall the isles tremble *in* the **d** of thy 3117
 27:27 fall into the midst of the seas in the **d** 3117
 28:13 of thy pipes was prepared in thee in the **d** 3117
 28:15 Thou *wast* perfect in thy ways from the **d** 3117
 29: 1 In the tenth *month*, in the twelfth **d** of NIH
 29:17 in the first *month*, in the first **d** of NIH
 29:21 In that **d** will I cause the horn of the 3117
 30: 2 Lord God; Howl ye, Woe worth the **d**! 3117
 30: 3 For the **d** is near, even the day of 3117
 30: 3 even the **d** of the Lord *is* near, a cloudy 3117
 30: 3 the day of the Lord *is* near, a cloudy **d**; 3117
 30: 9 In that **d** shall messengers go forth from 3117
 30: 9 come upon them, as *in* the **d** of Egypt: 3117
 30:18 At Tehaphnehes also the **d** shall be 3117
 30:20 in the first *month*, in the seventh **d** of NIH
 31: 1 in the third *month*, in the first **d** of NIH
 31:15 In the **d** when he went down to the grave 3117
 32: 1 twelfth month, in the first **d** of the month, NIH

Eze	32:10 man for his own life, in the **d** of thy fall.	3117
	32:17 in the fifteenth **d** of the month,	NIH
	33:12 deliver him in the **d** of his transgression:	3117
	33:12 he shall not fall thereby in the **d** that he	3117
	33:12 his *righteousness* in the **d** that he sinneth.	3117
	33:21 in the tenth *month,* in the fifth **d** of	NIH
	34:12 a shepherd seeketh out his flock in the **d**	3117
	34:12 been scattered in the cloudy and dark **d**.	3117
	36:33 In the **d** that I have cleansed you	3117
	38:14 In that **d** when my people of Israel	3117
	38:19 Surely in that **d** there shall be a great	3117
	39: 8 this *is* the **d** whereof I have spoken.	3117
	39:11 it shall come to pass in that **d**, *that* I will	3117
	39:13 it shall be to them a renown the **d** that I	3117
	39:22 that I *am* the Lord their God from that **d**	3117
	40: 1 of the year, in the tenth **d** of the month,	NIH
	40: 1 in the selfsame **d** the hand of the Lord	3117
	43:18 the altar in the **d** when *they* shall make it,	3117
	43:22 on the second **d** thou shalt offer a kid of	3117
	43:25 Seven days shalt thou prepare every **d** a	3117
	43:27 *that* upon the eight **d**, and *so* forward,	3117
	44:27 in the **d** that he goeth into the sanctuary,	3117
	45:18 In the first *month,* in the first **d** of	NIH
	45:20 thou shalt do the seventh **d** of the month	NIH
	45:21 In the first *month,* in the fourteenth **d** of	3117
	45:22 upon that **d** shall the prince prepare for	3117
	45:25 In the seventh *month,* in the fifteenth **d** of	3117
	46: 1 in the **d** of the new moon it shall be	3117
	46: 4 **d** *shall be* six lambs without blemish,	3117
	46: 6 in the **d** of the new moon *it shall be* a	3117
	46:12 offerings, as he did on the sabbath **d**:	3117
	48:35 the name of the city from that **d** *shall be,*	3117
Da	6:10 kneeled upon his knees three times a **d**,	3118
	6:13 but maketh his petition three times a **d**.	3118
	9: 7 unto us confusion of faces, as *at* this **d**;	3117
	9:15 and hast gotten thee renown, as *at* this **d**;	3117
	10: 4 four and twentieth **d** of the first month,	3117
	10:12 from the first **d** that thou didst set thine	3117
Hos	1: 5 it shall come to pass at that **d**, that I will	3117
	1:11 land: for great *shall be* the **d** of Jezreel.	3117
	2: 3 set her as *in* the **d** that she was born,	3117
	2:15 as *in* the **d** when she came up out of	3117
	2:16 it shall be at that **d**, saith the Lord,	3117
	2:18 in that **d** will I make a covenant for them	3117
	2:21 it shall come to pass in that **d**, I will hear,	3117
	4: 5 Therefore shalt thou fall *in* the **d**,	3117
	5: 9 Ephraim shall be desolate in the **d** of	3117
	6: 2 in the third **d** he will raise us up,	3117
	7: 5 *In* the **d** of our king the princes have	3117
	9: 5 What will ye do in the solemn **d**, and in	3117
	9: 5 and in the **d** of the feast of the Lord?	3117
	10:14 as Shalman spoiled Beth-arbel in the **d** of	3117
Joel	1:15 Alas for the **d**! for the day of the Lord *is*	3117
	1:15 for the **d** of the Lord *is* at hand, and as a	3117
	2: 1 for the **d** of the Lord cometh, for *it is*	3117
	2: 2 A **d** of darkness and of gloominess, a day	3117
	2: 2 a **d** of clouds and of thick darkness,	3117
	2:11 for the **d** of the Lord *is* great and	3117
	2:31 and the terrible **d** of the Lord come.	3117
	3:14 for the **d** of the Lord *is* near in the valley	3117
	3:18 it shall come to pass in that **d**, *that*	3117
Am	1:14 with shouting in the **d** of battle,	3117
	1:14 with a tempest in the **d** of the whirlwind:	3117
	2:16 mighty shall flee away naked in that **d**,	3117
	3:14 That in the **d** that I shall visit	3117
	5: 8 and maketh the **d** dark *with* night:	3117
	5:18 Woe unto *you* that desire the **d** of	3117
	5:18 the **d** of the Lord is darkness,	3117
	5:20 *Shall* not the **d** of the Lord *be* darkness,	3117
	6: 3 Ye that put far away the evil **d**,	3117
	8: 3 of the temple shall be howlings in that **d**,	3117
	8: 9 it shall come to pass in that **d**, saith	3117
	8: 9 and I will darken the earth in the clear **d**:	3117
	8:10 *son,* and the end thereof as a bitter **d**.	3117
	8:13 In that **d** shall the fair virgins and young	3117
	9:11 In that **d** will I raise up the tabernacle of	3117
Ob	1: 8 Shall I not in that **d**, saith the Lord,	3117
	1:11 In the **d** that thou stoodest on the other	3117
	1:11 in the **d** that the strangers carried away	3117
	1:12 thou shouldest not have looked on the **d**	3117
	1:12 in the **d** that he became a stranger;	3117
	1:12 in the **d** of their destruction;	3117
	1:12 have spoken proudly in the **d** of distress.	3117
	1:13 of my people in the **d** of their calamity;	3117
	1:13 their affliction in the **d** of their calamity,	3117
	1:13 their substance in the **d** of their calamity;	3117
	1:14 of his that did remain in the **d** of distress.	3117
	1:15 For the **d** of the Lord *is* near upon all	3117
Jnh	4: 7 when the morning rose the next **d**,	4283
Mic	2: 4 In that **d** shall *one* take up a parable	3117
	3: 6 and the **d** shall be dark over them.	3117
	4: 6 In that **d**, saith the Lord, will I assemble	3117
	5:10 it shall come to pass in that **d**, saith	3117
	7: 4 the **d** of thy watchmen *and* thy visitation	3117
	7:11 *In* the **d** that thy walls are *to be* built,	3117
	7:11 in that **d** shall the decree be far removed.	3117
	7:12 *In that* **d** *also* he shall come even to thee	3117
Na	1: 7 *is* good, a strong hold in the **d** of trouble;	3117
	2: 3 torches in the **d** of his preparation,	3117
	3:17 which camp in the hedges in the cold **d**,	3117
Hab	3:16 that I might rest in the **d** of trouble:	3117
Zep	1: 7 for the **d** of the Lord *is* at hand: for	3117
	1: 8 it shall come to pass in the **d**	3117
	1: 9 In the same **d** also will I punish all those	3117
	1:10 it shall come to pass in that **d**, saith	3117

Zep	1:14 The great **d** of the Lord *is* near, *it is*	3117
	1:14 *even* the voice of the **d** of the Lord:	3117
	1:15 That **d** *is* a day of wrath, a day of trouble	3117
	1:15 That day *is* a **d** of wrath, a day of trouble	3117
	1:15 of trouble and distress, a day of	3117
	1:15 distress, a **d** of wasteness and desolation,	3117
	1:15 a **d** of darkness and gloominess,	3117
	1:15 a **d** of clouds and thick darkness,	3117
	1:16 A **d** of the trumpet and alarm against	3117
	1:18 them in the **d** of the Lord's wrath;	3117
	2: 2 bring forth, *before* the **d** pass as the chaff,	3117
	2: 2 before the **d** of the Lord's anger come	3117
	2: 3 it may be ye shall be hid in the **d** of	3117
	2: 4 shall drive out Ashdod at the **noon d**,	6672
	3: 8 until the **d** that I rise up to the prey:	3117
	3:11 In that **d** shalt thou not be ashamed for all	3117
	3:16 In that **d** it shall be said to Jerusalem,	3117
Hag	1: 1 sixth month, in the first **d** of the month,	3117
	1:15 four and twentieth **d** of the sixth month,	3117
	2: 1 in the one and twentieth **d** of the month,	NIH
	2:10 twentieth **d** of the ninth *month,* in	NIH
	2:15 consider from this **d** and upward,	3117
	2:18 Consider now from this **d** and upward,	3117
	2:18 twentieth **d** of the ninth *month,* even	3117
	2:18 that the foundation of the Lord's	3117
	2:19 brought forth: from this **d** will I bless *you.*	3117
	2:20 in the four and twentieth **d** of the month,	NIH
	2:23 In that **d**, saith the Lord of hosts, will I	3117
Zec	1: 7 and twentieth **d** of the eleventh *month,*	3117
	2:11 shall be joined to the Lord in that **d**,	3117
	3: 9 remove the iniquity of that land in one **d**.	3117
	3:10 In that **d**, saith the Lord of hosts,	3117
	4:10 For who hath despised the **d** of small	3117
	6:10 come thou the same **d**, and go *into*	3117
	7: 1 in the fourth **d** of the ninth month,	NIH
	8: 9 which *were* in the **d** *that* the foundation	3117
	9:12 even to **d** do I declare *that* I will	3117+1886.1
	9:16 them in that **d** as the flock of his people:	3117
	11:11 it was broken in that **d**: and so the poor of	3117
	12: 3 in that **d** will I make Jerusalem a	3117
	12: 4 In that **d**, saith the Lord, I will smite	3117
	12: 6 In that **d** will I make the governors of Judah	3117
	12: 8 In that **d** shall the Lord defend	3117
	12: 8 that is feeble among them at that **d** shall	3117
	12: 9 it shall come to pass in that **d**, *that* I will	3117
	12:11 In that **d** shall there be a great mourning	3117
	13: 1 In that **d** there shall be a fountain opened	3117
	13: 2 it shall come to pass in that **d**, saith	3117
	13: 4 it shall come to pass in that **d**, *that*	3117
	14: 1 the **d** of the Lord cometh, and thy spoil	3117
	14: 3 as when he fought in the **d** of battle.	3117
	14: 4 feet shall stand in that **d** upon the mount	3117
	14: 6 shall come to pass in that **d**, *that* the light	3117
	14: 7 it shall be one **d** which shall be known to	3117
	14: 7 be known to the Lord, not **d**, nor night:	3117
	14: 8 shall be in that **d**, *that* living waters shall	3117
	14: 9 in that **d** shall there be one Lord,	3117
	14:13 it shall come to pass in that **d**, *that* a great	3117
	14:20 In that **d** shall there be upon the bells of	3117
	14:21 In that **d** there shall be no more	3117
Mal	3: 2 who *may* abide the **d** of his coming? and	3117
	3:17 in that **d** when I make *up my* jewels;	3117
	4: 1 behold, the **d** cometh, that *shall* burn as	3117
	4: 1 the **d** that cometh shall burn them up,	3117
	4: 3 **d** that I *shall* do *this,* saith the Lord of	3117
	4: 5 of the great and dreadful **d** of the Lord:	3117
Mt	6:11 Give us **this d** our daily bread.	4594
	6:30 which **to d** is, and to morrow is cast into	4594
	6:34 Sufficient unto the **d** *is* the evil thereof.	2250
	7:22 Many will say to me in that **d**, Lord, Lord,	2250
	10:15 and Gomorrha in the **d** of judgment,	2250
	11:22 for Tyre and Sidon at the **d** of judgment,	2250
	11:23 it would have remained until **this d**.	4594
	11:24 the land of Sodom in the **d** of judgment,	2250
	12: 1 At that time Jesus went on the sabbath **d**	NIG
	12: 2 is not lawful to do upon the sabbath **d**.	NIG
	12: 8 Son of man is Lord even of the sabbath **d**.	NIG
	12:11 and if it fall into a pit on the sabbath **d**,	NIG
	12:36 they shall give account thereof in the **d** of	2250
	13: 1 The same **d** went Jesus out of the house,	2250
	16: 3 the morning, *It will be* foul weather **to d**:	4594
	16:21 be killed, and be raised *again* the third **d**.	2250
	17:23 the third **d** he shall be raised *again.* And	2250
	20: 2 agreed with the labourers for a penny a **d**,	2250
	20: 6 Why stand ye here all the **d** idle?	2250
	20:12 have borne the burden and heat of the **d**.	2250
	20:19 and the third **d** he shall rise again.	2250
	21:28 said, Son, go work **to d** in my vineyard.	4594
	22:23 The same **d** came to him the Sadducees,	2250
	22:46 durst any *man* from that **d** forth ask	2250
	24:20 in the winter, neither on the sabbath **d**:	NIG
	24:36 But of that **d** and hour knoweth no *man,*	2250
	24:38 until the **d** that Noe entered into the ark,	2250
	24:50 The lord of that servant shall come in a **d**	2250
	25:13 for ye know neither the **d** nor the hour	2250
	26: 5 Not on the feast **d**, lest there be an uproar	NIG
	26:17 Now the first **d** of the *feast of* unleavened	NIG
	26:29 until that **d** when I drink it new with you	2250
	27: 8 called, The field of blood, unto **this d**.	4594
	27:19 suffered many *things* **this d** in a dream	4594
	27:62 Now the **next d**, that followed the *day of*	1887
	27:62 that followed the **d** *of the* preparation,	1887
	27:64 sepulchre be made sure until the third **d**,	2250
	28: 1 as it began to dawn towards the first **d** of	NIG
	28:15 reported among the Jews until **this d**.	4594

D

Mk	1:21 straightway on the sabbath **d** he entered	NIG
	1:35 rising up a great while **before d**, he went	1773
	2:23 through the corn fields on the sabbath **d**;	NIG
	2:24 why do they on the sabbath **d** *that* which	NIG
	3: 2 he would heal him on the sabbath **d**;	NIG
	4:27 and rise night and **d**, and the seed should	2250
	4:35 the same **d**, when the even was come,	2250
	5: 5 And always, night and **d**, he was in	2250
	6: 2 And when the sabbath **d** was come,	NIG
	6:11 and Gomorrha in the **d** of judgment,	2250
	6:21 And when a convenient **d** was come,	2250
	6:35 And when the **d** was now far spent,	5610
	9:31 that he is killed, he shall rise the third **d**.	2250
	10:34 kill him: and the third **d** he shall rise	2250
	13:32 But of that **d** and *that* hour knoweth no	2250
	14: 2 Not on the feast **d**, lest there be an uproar	NIG
	14:12 And the first **d** of unleavened bread,	2250
	14:25 until that **d** that I drink it new in	2250
	14:30 unto thee, That **this d**, *even* in this night,	4594
	15:42 that is, the **d** before the sabbath,	4315
	16: 2 very early in the morning the first **d** of	NIG
	16: 9 when *Jesus* was risen early the first **d**	NIG
Lk	1:20 until the **d** that these *things* shall be	2250
	1:59 *that* on the eighth **d** they came to	2250
	1:80 was in the deserts till the **d** of his shewing	2250
	2:11 For unto you is born **this d** in the city of	4594
	2:37 *God* with fastings and prayers night and **d**.	2250
	4:16 went into the synagogue on the sabbath **d**,	2250
	4:21 This **d** is this scripture fulfilled in your	4594
	4:42 And when it was **d**, he departed and	2250
	5:17 And it came to pass on a certain **d**, as he	2250
	5:26 saying, We have seen strange *things* **to d**.	4594
	6: 7 whether he would heal on the sabbath **d**;	NIG
	6:13 when it was **d**, he called unto *him* his	2250
	6:23 Rejoice ye in that **d**, and leap *for joy:* for	2250
	7:11 it came to pass the **d** after, *that* he went	NIG
	8:22 it came to pass on a certain **d**, that he	2250
	9:12 And *when* the **d** began to wear away,	2250
	9:22 and be slain, and be raised the third **d**.	2250
	9:37 And it came to pass, *that* on the next **d**,	2250
	10:12 that it shall be more tolerable in that **d** for	2250
	11: 3 Give us **d** by **day** our daily bread.	2250+2596
	11: 3 Give us **day** by **d** our daily bread.	2250+2596
	12:28 which is **to d** in the field, and to morrow	4594
	12:46 The lord of that servant will come in a **d**	2250
	13:14 that Jesus had healed on the sabbath **d**,	NIG
	13:14 be healed, and not on the sabbath **d**.	2250
	13:16 loosed from this bond on the sabbath **d**?	2250
	13:31 The same **d** there came certain *of*	2250
	13:32 and I do cures **to d**, and to morrow,	4594
	13:32 and the third **d** I shall be perfected.	NIG
	13:33 Nevertheless I must walk **to d**,	4594
	13:33 and to morrow, and the **d** following:	NIG
	14: 1 Pharisees to eat bread on the sabbath **d**,	NIG
	14: 3 Is it lawful to heal on the sabbath **d**?	NIG
	14: 5 pull him out on the sabbath **d**?	2250
	16:19 linen, and fared sumptuously every **d**:	2250
	17: 4 trespass against thee seven times in a **d**,	2250
	17: 4 and seven times in a **d** turn again to thee,	2250
	17:24 so shall also the Son of man be in his **d**.	2250
	17:27 until the **d** that Noe entered into the ark,	2250
	17:29 the *same* **d** that Lot went out of Sodom	2250
	17:30 thus shall it be in the **d** when the Son	2250
	17:31 In that **d**, he which shall be upon	2250
	18: 7 which cry **d** and night unto him, though	2250
	18:33 death: and the third **d** he shall rise again.	2250
	19: 5 for **to d** I must abide at thy house.	4594
	19: 9 This **d** is salvation come to this house,	4594
	19:42 even thou, at least in this thy **d**,	2250
	21:34 and *so* that **d** come upon you unawares.	2250
	21:37 And in the **d** *time* he was teaching in	2250
	22: 7 Then came the **d** of unleavened bread,	2250
	22:34 Peter, *the* cock shall not crow **this d**,	4594
	22:66 And as soon as it was **d**, the elders of	2250
	23:12 And the same **d** Pilate and Herod were	2250
	23:43 **To d** shalt thou be with me in paradise.	4594
	23:54 And *that* **d** was the preparation,	2250
	23:56 rested the sabbath **d** according to	NIG
	24: 1 upon the first **d** of the week, very early	NIG
	24: 7 be crucified, and the third **d** rise again.	2250
	24:13 two of them went *that* same **d** to a village	2250
	24:21 **to d** is the third day since these *things*	4594
	24:21 to day is the third **d** since these *things*	2250
	24:29 towards evening, and the **d** is far spent.	2250
	24:46 and to rise from the dead the third **d**:	2250
Jn	1:29 The **next d** John seeth Jesus coming unto	1887
	1:35 Again the **next d** *after* John stood,	1887
	1:39 he dwelt, and abode with him that **d**:	2250
	1:43 The **d** *following* Jesus would go forth into	1887
	2: 1 And the third **d** there was a marriage in	2250
	2:23 in the feast **d**, many believed in his name,	NIG
	5: 9 and on the same **d** was the sabbath.	NIG
	5:10 him that was cured, It is the sabbath **d**:	NIG
	5:16 had done these *things* on the sabbath **d**.	NIG
	6:22 The **d** *following*, when the people which	1887
	6:39 but should raise it up *again* at the last **d**.	2250
	6:40 and I will raise him up *at* the last **d**.	2250
	6:44 and I will raise him up *at* the last **d**.	2250
	6:54 and I will raise him up *at* the last **d**.	2250
	7:22 ye on the sabbath **d** circumcise a man.	NIG
	7:23 If a man on the sabbath **d** receive	NIG
	7:23 man every whit whole on the sabbath **d**?	NIG
	7:37 In the last **d**, *that* great *day of* the feast,	2250
	7:37 *that* great **d** of the feast, Jesus stood and	NIG
	8:56 Your father Abraham rejoiced to see my **d**:	2250

D

Jn	9: 4 works of him that sent me, while it is **d**:	2250
	9:14 it was the sabbath **d** when Jesus made	2250
	9:16 because he keepeth not the sabbath **d**.	NIG
	11: 9 Are there not twelve hours in the **d**?	2250
	11: 9 any man walk in the **d**, he stumbleth not,	2250
	11:24 rise again in the resurrection at the last **d**.	2250
	11:53 Then from that **d** forth they took counsel	2250
	12: 7 against the **d** of my burying hath she kept	2250
	12:12 On the **next d** much people that were	1887
	12:48 the same shall judge him in the last **d**.	2250
	14:20 At that **d** ye shall know that I am in my	2250
	16:23 And in that **d** ye shall ask me nothing.	2250
	16:26 At that **d** ye shall ask in my name: and I	2250
	19:31 remain upon the cross on the sabbath **d**,	NIG
	19:31 (for that sabbath **d** was a high day,)	NIG
	19:31 (for that sabbath day was a high **d**,)	2250
	19:42 the Jews' preparation **d**; for the sepulchre	NIG
Ac	1: 2 Until the **d** in which he was taken up,	2250
	1:22 that same **d** that he was taken up from	2250
	2: 1 And when the **d** of Pentecost was fully	2250
	2:15 seeing it is but the third hour of the **d**.	2250
	2:20 great and notable of the Lord come:	2250
	2:29 and his sepulchre is with us unto this **d**.	2250
	2:41 the same **d** there were added unto them	2250
	4: 3 and put them in hold unto the **next d**:	839
	4: 9 If we this **d** be examined of the good	4594
	7: 8 and circumcised him the eighth **d**;	2250
	7:26 And the next **d** he shewed himself unto	2250
	9:24 they watched the gates **d** and night to	2250
	10: 3 about the ninth hour of the **d**,	2250
	10:40 Him God raised up the third **d**,	2250
	12:18 Now as soon as it was **d**, there was no	2250
	12:21 And upon a set **d** Herod, arrayed in royal	2250
	13:14 into the synagogue on the sabbath **d**,	2250
	13:27 prophets which are read every sabbath **d**,	NIG
	13:33 art my Son, this **d** have I begotten thee.	4594
	13:44 And the next sabbath **d** came almost	NIG
	14:20 the **next d** he departed with Barnabas to	1887
	15:21 read in the synagogues every sabbath **d**.	NIG
	16:11 Samothracia, and the next **d** to Neapolis;	2250
	16:35 And when it was **d**, the magistrates sent	2250
	17:31 Because he hath appointed a **d**,	2250
	20: 7 And upon the first **d** of the week, when	NIG
	20:11 even till **break of d**, so he departed.	827
	20:15 and came the next **d** over against Chios;	NIG
	20:15 and the next **d** we arrived at Samos,	NIG
	20:15 and the next **d** we came to Miletus.	NIG
	20:16 to be at Jerusalem the **d** of Pentecost.	2250
	20:18 from the first **d** that I came into Asia,	2250
	20:26 I take you to record this **d**,	2250+4594
	20:31 to warn every one night and **d** with tears.	2250
	21: 1 the **d** following into Rhodes, and from	NIG
	21: 7 the brethren, and abode with them one **d**.	2250
	21: 8 And the **next d** we that were of Paul's	1887
	21:18 And the **d** following Paul went in with us	NIG
	21:26 the next **d** purifying himself with them	NIG
	22: 3 zealous towards God, as ye all are this **d**.	4594
	23: 1 good conscience before God until this **d**.	2250
	23:12 And when it was **d**, certain of the Jews	2250
	24:21 I am called in question by you this **d**.	4594
	25: 6 the **next d** sitting in the judgment seat,	1887
	26: 2 I shall answer for myself this **d** before	4594
	26: 7 instantly serving God **d** and night, hope to	2250
	26:22 help of God, I continue unto this **d**,	2250
	26:29 but also all that hear me this **d**, were both	4594
	27: 3 And the next **d** we touched at Sidon.	NIG
	27:18 the next **d** lightened the ship;	NIG
	27:19 And the third **d** we cast out with our own	NIG
	27:29 out of the stern, and wished for the **d**.	2250
	27:33 And while the **d** was coming on, Paul	2250
	27:33 This is the fourteenth day that ye have	4594
	27:33 This day is the fourteenth that ye have	2250
	27:39 when it was **d**, they knew not the land:	2250
	28:13 and after one **d** the south wind blew,	2250
	28:13 and we came the **next d** to Puteoli:	1206
	28:23 And when they had appointed him a **d**,	2250
Ro	2: 5 unto thyself wrath against the **d** of wrath	2250
	2:16 In the **d** when God shall judge the secrets	2250
	8:36 For thy sake we are killed all the **d** long;	2250
	10:21 All **d** long have I stretched forth my hands	2250
	11: 8 they should not hear;) unto this **d**.	2250+4594
	13:12 The night is far spent, the **d** is at hand:	2250
	13:13 Let us walk honestly, as in the **d**; not in	2250
	14: 5 One man esteemeth one **d** above another:	2250
	14: 5 another esteemeth every **d** alike. Let every	2250
	14: 6 He that regardeth the **d**, regardeth it unto	2250
	14: 6 he that regardeth not the **d**, to the Lord	2250
1Co	1: 8 that ye may be blameless in the **d** of our	2250
	3:13 for the **d** shall declare it, because it shall	2250
	4:13 the offscouring of all things unto this **d**.	737
	5: 5 that the spirit may be saved in the **d** of	2250
	10: 8 fell in one **d** three and twenty thousand.	2250
	15: 4 that he rose again the third **d** according to	2250
	16: 2 Upon the first **d** of the week let every one	NIG
2Co	1:14 as ye also are ours in the **d** of the Lord	2250
	3:14 for until this **d** remaineth the same	2250+4594
	3:15 even unto this **d**, when Moses is read,	4594
	4:16 yet the inward man is renewed **d** by day.	2250
	4:16 yet the inward man is renewed day by **d**.	2250
	6: 2 the **d** of salvation have I succoured thee:	2250
	6: 2 behold, now is the **d** of salvation.)	2250
	11:25 a **night and a d** I have been in the deep;	3574

Eph	4:30 whereby ye are sealed unto the **d** of	2250
	6:13 ye may be able to withstand in the evil **d**,	2250
Php	1: 5 in the gospel from the first **d** until now;	2250
	1: 6 will perform it until the **d** of Jesus Christ:	2250
	1:10 and without offence till the **d** of Christ;	2250
	2:16 that I may rejoice in the **d** of Christ, that I	2250
	3: 5 Circumcised the **eighth d**, of the stock of	3637
Col	1: 6 since the **d** ye heard of it, and knew	2250
	1: 9 the **d** we heard it, do not cease to pray	2250
1Th	2: 9 for labouring night and **d**, because we	2250
	3:10 **d** praying exceedingly that we might see	2250
	5: 2 yourselves know perfectly that the **d** of	2250
	5: 4 that that **d** should overtake you as a thief.	2250
	5: 5 of light, and the children of the **d**:	2250
	5: 8 But let us, who are of the **d**, be sober,	2250
2Th	1:10 among you was believed) in that **d**.	2250
	2: 2 from us, as that the **d** of Christ is at hand.	2250
	2: 3 that that **d** not come, except there come	NIG
	3: 8 with labour and travail night and **d**,	2250
1Ti	5: in supplications and prayers night and **d**.	2250
2Ti	1: 3 of thee in my prayers night and **d**;	2250
	1:12 have committed unto him against that **d**.	2250
	1:18 he may find mercy of the Lord in that **d**:	2250
	4: 8 righteous judge, shall give me at that **d**:	2250
Heb	1: 5 art my Son, this **d** have I begotten thee?	4594
	3: 7 Ghost saith, **To d** if ye will hear his voice,	4594
	3: 8 in the **d** of temptation in the wilderness:	2250
	3:13 one another daily, while it is called **To d**;	4594
	3:15 it is said, **To d** if ye will hear his voice,	4594
	4: 4 certain place of the seventh **d** on this wise,	NIG
	4: 4 God did rest the seventh **d** from all his	2250
	4: 7 Again he limiteth a certain **d**, saying in	2250
	4: 7 saying in David, **To d**, after so long a time;	4594
	4: 7 As it is said, **To d** if ye will hear his voice,	4594
	4: 8 not afterward have spoken of another **d**.	2250
	5: 5 art my Son, this **d** have I begotten thee.	4594
	8: 9 when I took them by the hand to lead	2250
	10:25 the more, as ye see the **d** approaching.	2250
	13: 8 same yesterday, and **to d**, and for ever.	4594
Jas	4:13 **To d** or to morrow we will go into such a	4594
	5: 5 your hearts, as in a **d** of slaughter.	2250
1Pe	2:12 glorify God in the **d** of visitation.	2250
2Pe	1:19 until the **d** dawn, and the day star arise in	2250
	1:19 and the **d** star arise in your hearts:	5459
	2: 8 vexed his righteous soul from **d** to day	2250
	2: 8 vexed his righteous soul from day to **d**	2250
	2: 9 reserve the unjust unto the **d** of judgment	2250
	2:13 they that count it pleasure to riot in the **d**	2250
	3: 7 unto fire against the **d** of judgment	2250
	3: 8 not ignorant of this one thing, that one **d**	2250
	3: 8 and a thousand years as one **d**.	2250
	3:10 the **d** of the Lord will come as a thief in	2250
	3:12 hasting unto the coming of the **d** of God,	2250
1Jn	4:17 that we may have boldness in the **d** of	2250
Jude	6 darkness unto the judgment of the great **d**.	2250
Rev	1:10 I was in the spirit on the Lord's **d**,	2250
	4: 8 they rest not **d** and night, saying, Holy,	2250
	6:17 For the great **d** of his wrath is come;	2250
	7:15 and serve him **d** and night in his temple:	2250
	8:12 and the **d** shone not for a third part of it,	2250
	9:15 a **d**, and a month, and a year, for to slay	2250
	12:10 accused them before our God **d** and	2250
	14:11 and they have no rest **d** nor night,	2250
	16:14 to gather them to the battle of that great **d**	2250
	18: 8 Therefore shall her plagues come in one **d**,	2250
	20:10 shall be tormented **d** and night for ever	2250
	21:25 the gates of it shall not be shut at all by **d**:	2250

DAY'S (9) [DAY]

Nu	11:31 as it were a **d** journey on this side, and	3117
	11:31 as it were a **d** journey on the other side,	3117
1Ki	19: 4 he himself went a **d** journey into	3117
1Ch	16:37 as **every d** work required:	3117+3117+871.1
Est	9:13 morrow also according unto this **d** decree,	3117
Jnh	3: 4 Jonah began to enter into the city a **d**	3117
Lk	2:44 been in the company, went a **d** journey;	2250
Ac	1:12 a **sabbath d** journey.	2192+3598+4521
	9:40 to be called in question for this **d** uproar,	4594

DAYS (855) [DAY]

Ge	1:14 and for seasons, and for **d**, and years:	3117
	3:14 dust shalt thou eat all the **d** of thy life:	3117
	3:17 in sorrow shalt thou eat of it all the **d** of	3117
	5: 4 the **d** of Adam after he had begotten Seth	3117
	5: 5 all the **d** that Adam lived were nine	3117
	5: 8 all the **d** of Seth were nine hundred	3117
	5:11 all the **d** of Enos were nine hundred	3117
	5:14 all the **d** of Cainan were nine hundred	3117
	5:17 all the **d** of Mahalaleel were eight	3117
	5:20 all the **d** of Jared were nine hundred sixty	3117
	5:23 all the **d** of Enoch were three hundred	3117
	5:27 all the **d** of Methuselah were nine	3117
	5:31 all the **d** of Lamech were seven hundred	3117
	6: 3 yet his **d** shall be an hundred and	3117
	6: 4 There were giants in the earth in those **d**;	3117
	7: 4 For yet seven **d**, and I will cause it to rain	3117
	7: 4 cause it to rain upon the earth forty **d**	3117
	7:10 it came to pass after seven **d**, that	3117
	7:12 the rain was upon the earth forty **d** and	3117
	7:17 the flood was forty **d** upon the earth;	3117
	7:24 upon the earth an hundred and fifty **d**.	3117
	8: 3 and fifty **d** the waters were abated.	3117
	8: 6 it came to pass at the end of forty **d**,	3117
	8:10 he stayed yet other seven **d**; and again he	3117
	8:12 stayed yet other seven **d**; and sent forth	3117

Ge	9:29 all the **d** of Noah were nine hundred and	3117
	10:25 for in his **d** was the earth divided;	3117
	11:32 the **d** of Terah were two hundred and	3117
	14: 1 it came to pass in the **d** of Amraphel king	3117
	17:12 he that is eight **d** old shall be circumcised	3117
	21: 4 circumcised his son Isaac being eight **d**	3117
	21:34 sojourned in the Philistines' land many **d**.	3117
	24:55 Let the damsel abide with us a few **d**,	3117
	25: 7 these are the **d** of the years of Abraham's	3117
	25:24 when her **d** to be delivered were fulfilled,	3117
	26: 1 besides the first famine that was in the **d**	3117
	26:15 had digged in the **d** of Abraham his father,	3117
	26:18 they had digged in the **d** of Abraham	3117
	27:41 The **d** of mourning for my father are at	3117
	27:44 tarry with him a few **d**, until thy brother's	3117
	29:20 they seemed unto him but a few **d**,	3117
	29:21 Give me my wife, for my **d** are fulfilled,	3117
	30:14 Reuben went in the **d** of wheat harvest,	3117
	35:28 the **d** of Isaac were an hundred	3117
	35:29 unto his people, being old and full of **d**:	3117
	37:34 loins, and mourned for his son many **d**.	3117
	40:12 of it: The three branches are three **d**:	3117
	40:18 The three baskets are three **d**:	3117
	40:19 Yet within three **d** shall Pharaoh lift up	3117
	42:17 put them all together into ward three **d**.	3117
	47: 9 The **d** of the years of my pilgrimage are	3117
	47: 9 have the **d** of the years of my life been,	3117
	47: 9 have not attained unto the **d** of the years	3117
	47: 9 of my fathers in the **d** of their pilgrimage.	3117
	49: 1 that which shall befall you in the last **d**.	3117
	50: 3 forty **d** were fulfilled for him; for so	3117
	50: 3 are fulfilled the **d** of those which are	3117
	50: 3 mourned for him threescore and ten **d**.	3117
	50: 4 when the **d** of his mourning were past,	3117
	50:10 made a mourning for his father seven **d**.	3117
Ex	2:11 it came to pass in those **d**, when Moses	3117
	7:25 seven **d** were fulfilled, after that	3117
	10:22 darkness in all the land of Egypt three **d**:	3117
	10:23 rose any from his place for three **d**:	3117
	12:15 Seven **d** shall ye eat unleavened bread;	3117
	12:19 Seven **d** shall there be no leaven found in	3117
	13: 6 Seven **d** thou shalt eat unleavened bread,	3117
	13: 7 Unleavened bread shall be eaten seven **d**;	3117
	15:22 they went three **d** in the wilderness,	3117
	16:26 Six **d** ye shall gather it; but on the seventh	3117
	16:29 you on the sixth day the bread of **two d**;	3117
	20:11 For in six **d** the Lord made heaven and	3117
	20:12 that thy **d** may be long upon the land	3117
	22:30 seven **d** it shall be with his dam;	3117
	23:12 Six **d** thou shalt do thy work, and on	3117
	23:15 thou shalt eat unleavened bread seven **d**,	3117
	23:26 thy land: the number of thy **d** I will fulfil.	3117
	24:16 Sinai, and the cloud covered it six **d**:	3117
	24:18 Moses was in the mount forty **d** and	3117
	29:30 in his stead shall put them on seven **d**,	3117
	29:35 seven **d** shalt thou consecrate them.	3117
	29:37 Seven **d** thou shalt make an atonement	3117
	31:15 Six **d** may work be done; but in the	3117
	31:17 for in six **d** the Lord made heaven and	3117
	34:18 seven **d** thou shalt eat unleavened bread,	3117
	34:21 Six **d** thou shalt work, but on the seventh	3117
	34:28 he was there with the Lord forty **d** and	3117
	35: 2 Six **d** shall work be done, but on	3117
Lev	8:33 tabernacle of the congregation in seven **d**,	3117
	8:33 until the **d** of your consecration be at an	3117
	8:33 end: for seven **d** shall he consecrate you.	3117
	8:35 the congregation day and night seven **d**,	3117
	12: 2 she shall be unclean seven **d**; according to	3117
	12: 2 according to the **d** of the separation for	3117
	12: 4 blood of her purifying three and thirty **d**;	3117
	12: 4 until the **d** of her purifying be fulfilled.	3117
	12: 5 of her purifying threescore and six **d**.	3117
	12: 6 when the **d** of her purifying are fulfilled,	3117
	13: 4 shut up him that hath the plague seven **d**:	3117
	13: 5 the priest shall shut him up seven **d** more:	3117
	13:21 then the priest shall shut him up seven **d**:	3117
	13:26 then the priest shall shut him up seven **d**:	3117
	13:31 that hath the plague of the scall seven **d**:	3117
	13:33 up him that hath the scall seven **d** more:	3117
	13:46 All the **d** wherein the plague shall be in	3117
	13:50 shut up it that hath the plague seven **d**:	3117
	13:54 and he shall shut it up seven **d** more:	3117
	14: 8 shall tarry abroad out of his tent seven **d**.	3117
	14:38 house, and shut up the house seven **d**:	3117
	15:13 he shall number to himself seven **d** for his	3117
	15:19 be blood, she shall be put apart seven **d**:	3117
	15:24 upon him, he shall be unclean seven **d**;	3117
	15:25 many **d** out of the time of her separation,	3117
	15:25 all the **d** of the issue of her uncleanness	3117
	15:25 shall be as the **d** of her separation:	3117
	15:26 Every bed whereon she lieth all the **d** of	3117
	15:28 she shall number to herself seven **d**,	3117
	22:27 then it shall be seven **d** under the dam;	3117
	23: 3 Six **d** shall work be done: but the seventh	3117
	23: 6 seven **d** ye must eat unleavened bread.	3117
	23: 8 made by fire unto the Lord seven **d**:	3117
	23:16 seventh sabbath shall ye number fifty **d**;	3117
	23:34 of tabernacles for seven **d** unto the Lord.	3117
	23:36 Seven **d** ye shall offer an offering made by	3117
	23:39 shall keep a feast unto the Lord seven **d**:	3117
	23:40 before the Lord your God seven **d**.	3117
	23:41 feast unto the Lord seven **d** in the year.	3117
	23:42 Ye shall dwell in booths seven **d**; all that	3117

Nu	6: 4 All the **d** of his separation shall he eat	3117
	6: 5 All the **d** of the vow of his separation	3117
	6: 5 until the **d** be fulfilled, *in* the which he	3117
	6: 6 All the **d** that he separateth *himself* unto	3117
	6: 8 All the **d** of his separation he *is* holy unto	3117
	6:12 he shall consecrate unto the LORD the **d**	3117
	6:12 the **d** that were before shall be lost,	3117
	6:13 when the **d** of his separation are fulfilled:	3117
	9:19 tarried long upon the tabernacle many **d,**	3117
	9:20 when the cloud was a few **d** upon	3117
	9:22 Or *whether it were* **two d,** or a month,	3117
	10:10 in your **solemn d,** and in the beginnings	4150
	11:19 nor **two d,** nor five days, neither ten days,	3117
	11:19 nor two days, nor five **d,** neither ten days,	3117
	11:19 nor two days, nor five days, neither ten **d,**	3117
	11:19 five days, neither ten days, nor twenty **d;**	3117
	12:14 should she not be ashamed seven **d?**	3117
	12:14 her be shut out from the camp seven **d,**	3117
	12:15 was shut out from the camp seven **d:**	3117
	13:25 from searching of the land after forty **d.**	3117
	14:34 After the number of the **d** in which ye	3117
	14:34 *even* forty **d,** each day for a year, shall ye	3117
	19:11 *body* of any man shall be unclean seven **d.**	3117
	19:14 *is* in the tent, shall be unclean seven **d.**	3117
	19:16 man, or a grave, shall be unclean seven **d.**	3117
	20:29 they mourned for Aaron thirty **d,** *even* all	3117
	24:14 shall do to thy people in the latter **d.**	3117
	28:17 seven **d** shall unleavened bread be eaten.	3117
	28:24 shall offer daily, *throughout* the seven **d,**	3117
	29:12 shall keep a feast unto the LORD seven **d:**	3117
	31:19 do ye abide without the camp seven **d:**	3117
Dt	1:46 So ye abode in Kadesh many **d,**	3117
	1:46 according unto the **d** that ye abode *there.*	3117
	2: 1 and we compassed mount Seir many **d.**	3117
	4: 9 lest they depart from thy heart all the **d** of	3117
	4:10 they may learn to fear me all the **d** that	3117
	4:26 ye shall not prolong *your* **d** upon it,	3117
	4:30 *even* in the latter **d,** if thou turn to	3117
	4:32 For ask now of the **d** that are past,	3117
	4:40 that thou mayest prolong *thy* **d** upon	3117
	5:13 Six **d** thou shalt labour, and do all thy	3117
	5:16 that thy **d** may be prolonged, and that it	3117
	5:33 *that* ye may prolong *your* **d** in the land	3117
	6: 2 and thy son's son, all the **d** of thy life;	3117
	6: 2 thy life; and that thy **d** may be prolonged.	3117
	9: 9 I abode in the mount forty **d** and	3117
	9:11 it came to pass at the end of forty **d** and	3117
	9:18 as at the first, forty **d** and forty nights:	3117
	9:25 Thus I fell down before the LORD forty **d**	3117
	10:10 to the first time, forty **d** and forty nights;	3117
	11: 9 that ye may prolong *your* **d** in the land,	3117
	11:21 That your **d** may be multiplied,	3117
	11:21 be multiplied, and the **d** of your children,	3117
	11:21 as the **d** of heaven upon the earth.	3117
	12: 1 all the **d** that ye live upon the earth.	3117
	16: 3 seven **d** shalt thou eat unleavened bread	3117
	16: 3 of the land of Egypt all the **d** of thy life.	3117
	16: 4 seen with thee in all thy coast seven **d;**	3117
	16: 8 Six **d** thou shalt eat unleavened bread:	3117
	16:13 observe the feast of tabernacles seven **d,**	3117
	16:15 Seven **d** shalt thou keep a solemn feast	3117
	17: 9 unto the judge that shall be in those **d,**	3117
	17:19 he shall read therein all the **d** of his life:	3117
	17:20 to the end that he may prolong *his* **d** in	3117
	19:17 and the judges, which shall be in those **d;**	3117
	22: 7 and *that* thou mayest prolong *thy* **d.**	3117
	22:19 wife; he may not put her away all his **d.**	3117
	22:29 he may not put her away all his **d.**	3117
	23: 6 nor their prosperity all thy **d** for ever.	3117
	25:15 that thy **d** may be lengthened in the land	3117
	26: 3 go unto the priest that shall be in those **d,**	3117
	30:18 *that* ye shall not prolong *your* **d** upon	3117
	30:20 for he *is* thy life, and the length of thy **d:**	3117
	31:14 thy **d** approach that *thou* must die:	3117
	31:29 evil will befall you in the latter **d;** because	3117
	32: 7 Remember the **d** of old, consider the	3117
	32:47 through this thing ye shall prolong *your* **d**	3117
	33:25 and as thy **d,** *so shall* thy strength *be.*	3117
	34: 8 for Moses in the plains of Moab thirty **d:**	3117
	34: 8 so the **d** of weeping *and* mourning for	3117
Jos	1: 5 *to* stand before thee all the **d** of thy life:	3117
	1:11 for within three **d** ye shall pass over this	3117
	2:16 hide yourselves there three **d,** until	3117
	2:22 the mountain, and abode there three **d,**	3117
	3: 2 it came to pass after three **d,** that	3117
	4:14 as they feared Moses, all the **d** of his life.	3117
	6: 3 the city once. Thus shalt thou do six **d.**	3117
	6:14 returned *into* the camp: so they did six **d.**	3117
	9:16 it came to pass at the end of three **d** after	3117
	20: 6 of the high priest that shall be in those **d:**	3117
	22: 3 have not left your brethren these many **d**	3117
	24:31 Israel served the LORD all the **d** of	3117
	24:31 the **d** of the elders that overlived Joshua,	3117
Jdg	2: 7 the people served the LORD all the **d** of	3117
	2: 7 the **d** of the elders that outlived Joshua,	3117
	2:18 of their enemies all the **d** of the judge:	3117
	5: 6 In the **d** of Shamgar the son of Anath,	3117
	5: 6 In the **d** of Jael, the highways were	3117
	8:28 quietness forty years in the **d** of Gideon.	3117
	11:40 of Jephthah the Gileadite four **d** in a year.	3117
	14:12 it me *within* the seven **d** of the feast,	3117
	14:14 they could not *in* three **d** expound	3117
	14:17 she wept before him the seven **d,**	3117
	15:20 he judged Israel in the **d** of the Philistines	3117
	17: 6 In those **d** *there was* no king in Israel,	3117

Jdg	18: 1 In those **d** *there was* no king in Israel:	3117
	18: 1 in those **d** the tribe of the Danites sought	3117
	19: 1 it came to pass in those **d,** when *there*	3117
	19: 4 and he abode with him three **d:**	3117
	20:27 the covenant of God *was* there in those **d,**	3117
	20:28 son of Aaron, stood before it in those **d,)**	3117
	21:25 In those **d** *there was* no king in Israel:	3117
Ru	1: 1 Now it came to pass in the **d** when	3117
1Sa	1:11 I will give him unto the LORD all the **d** of	3117
	2:31 Behold, the **d** come, that I will cut off	3117
	3: 1 of the LORD was precious in those **d;**	3117
	7:13 against the Philistines all the **d** of Samuel.	3117
	7:15 Samuel judged Israel all the **d** of his life.	3117
	9:20 for thine asses that were lost three **d** ago,	3117
	10: 8 seven **d** shalt thou tarry, till I come to	3117
	13: 8 tarried seven **d,** according to the set time	3117
	13:11 *that* thou camest not within the **d**	3117
	14:52 against the Philistines all the **d** of Saul:	3117
	17:12 men *for* an old man in the **d** of Saul.	3117
	17:16 evening, and presented himself forty **d.**	3117
	18:26 son in law: and the **d** were not expired.	3117
	20:19 when thou hast **stayed three d,** *then*	8027
	21: 5 kept from us about **these three d,**	8032+8543
	25:10 there be many servants **now a d**	3117+1886.1
	25:28 evil hath not been found in thee *all* thy **d.**	3117
	25:38 it came to pass about ten **d** *after,* that	3117
	28: 1 it came to pass in those **d,** that	3117
	29: 3 which hath been with me these **d,**	3117
	30:12 drunk *any* water, three **d** and three nights.	3117
	30:13 let me, because three **d** agone I fell sick.	3117
	31:13 under a tree at Jabesh, and fasted seven **d.**	3117
2Sa	1: 1 and David had abode two **d** in Ziklag;	3117
	7:12 thy **d** be fulfilled, and thou shalt sleep	3117
	16:23 which he counselled in those **d,**	3117
	20: 4 me the men of Judah *within* three **d,**	3117
	21: 1 there was a famine in the **d** of David three	3117
	21: 9 and were put to death in the **d** of harvest,	3117
	21: 9 in the first **d,** in the beginning of barley	NIH
	24: 8 at the end of nine months and twenty **d.**	3117
1Ki	2: 1 Now the **d** of David drew nigh that *he*	3117
	2:11 the **d** that David reigned over Israel *were*	3117
	2:38 And Shimei dwelt in Jerusalem many **d.**	3117
	3: 2 unto the name of the LORD, until those **d.**	3117
	3:13 among the kings like unto thee all thy **d.**	3117
	3:14 did walk, then I will lengthen thy **d.**	3117
	4:21 and served Solomon all the **d** of his life.	3117
	4:25 even to Beer-sheba, all the **d** of Solomon.	3117
	8:40 That they may fear thee all the **d** that	3117
	8:65 seven **d** and seven days, *even* fourteen	3117
	8:65 seven days and *seven* days, *even* fourteen	3117
	8:65 and seven days, *even* fourteen **d.**	3117
	10:21 it was nothing accounted of in the **d** of	3117
	11:12 Notwithstanding in thy **d** I will not do it	3117
	11:25 he was an adversary to Israel all the **d** of	3117
	11:34 I will make him prince all the **d** of his life	3117
	12: 5 Depart yet *for* three **d,** then come again	3117
	14:20 the **d** which Jeroboam reigned *were* two	3117
	14:30 and Jeroboam all *their* **d.**	3117
	15: 5 he commanded him all the **d** of his life,	3117
	15: 6 and Jeroboam all the **d** of his life.	3117
	15:14 heart was perfect with the LORD all his **d.**	3117
	15:16 and Baasha king of Israel all their **d.**	3117
	15:32 and Baasha king of Israel all their **d.**	3117
	16:15 Judah did Zimri reign seven **d** in Tirzah.	3117
	16:34 In his **d** did Hiel the Bethelite build	3117
	17:15 and he, and her house, did eat *many* **d.**	3117
	18: 1 came to pass *after* many **d,** that the word	3117
	19: 8 went in the strength of that meat forty **d**	3117
	20:29 one over against the other seven **d.**	3117
	21:29 I will not bring the evil in his **d:**	3117
	21:29 in his son's **d** will I bring the evil upon his	3117
	22:46 which remained in the **d** of his father Asa,	3117
2Ki	2:17 they sought three **d,** but found him not.	3117
	8:20 In his **d** Edom revolted from under	3117
	10:32 In those **d** the LORD began to cut Israel	3117
	12: 2 *d* where *in* Jehoiada the priest instructed	3117
	13: 3 Ben-hadad the son of Hazael, all *their* **d.**	3117
	13:22 oppressed Israel all the **d** of Jehoahaz.	3117
	15:18 he departed not all his **d** from the sins of	3117
	15:29 In the **d** of Pekah king of Israel came	3117
	15:37 In those **d** the LORD began to send	3117
	18: 4 for unto those **d** the children of Israel did	3117
	20: 1 In those **d** was Hezekiah sick unto death.	3117
	20: 6 I will add unto thy **d** fifteen years;	3117
	20:17 the **d** come, that all that *is* in thine	3117
	20:19 not *good,* if peace and truth be in my **d?**	3117
	23:22 from the **d** of the judges that judged Israel,	3117
	23:22 nor *in* all the **d** of the kings of Israel, nor	3117
	23:29 In his **d** Pharaoh-nechoh king of Egypt	3117
	24: 1 In his **d** Nebuchadnezzar king of Babylon	3117
	25:29 continually before him all the **d** of his life.	3117
	25:30 for every day, all the **d** of his life.	3117
1Ch	1:19 because in his **d** the earth was divided:	8027
	4:41 these written by name came in the **d** of	3117
	5:10 in the **d** of Saul they made war with	3117
	5:17 in the **d** of Jotham king of Judah,	3117
	5:17 and in the **d** of Jeroboam king of Israel.	3117
	7: 2 whose number *was* in the **d** of David two	3117
	7:22 Ephraim their father mourned many **d,**	3117
	9:25 *were* to come after seven **d** from time to	3117
	10:12 the oak in Jabesh, and fasted seven **d.**	3117
	12:39 there they were with David three **d,**	3117
	13: 3 for we inquired not *at* it in the **d** of Saul.	3117
	17:11 when thy **d** be expired that *thou* must go	3117
	21:12 or else three **d** the sword of the LORD,	3117

1Ch	22: 9 and quietness unto Israel in his **d.**	3117
	23: 1 So when David was old and full of **d,**	3117
	29:15 our **d** on the earth *are* as a shadow,	3117
	29:28 old age, full of **d,** riches, and honour:	3117
2Ch	7: 8 time Solomon kept the feast seven **d,**	3117
	7: 9 kept the dedication of the altar seven **d,**	3117
	7: 9 altar seven days, and the feast seven **d.**	3117
	9:20 was *not* any thing accounted of in the **d**	3117
	10: 5 Come again unto me after three **d.**	3117
	13:20 recover strength again in the **d** of Abijah:	3117
	14: 1 In his **d** the land was quiet ten years.	3117
	15:17 the heart of Asa was perfect all his **d.**	3117
	20:25 were three **d** in gathering of the spoil,	3117
	21: 8 In his **d** the Edomites revolted from under	3117
	24: 2 the LORD all the **d** of Jehoiada the priest.	3117
	24:14 LORD continually all the **d** of Jehoiada.	3117
	24:15 old, and was full of **d** when he died;	3117
	26: 5 he sought God in the **d** of Zechariah,	3117
	29:17 the house of the LORD in eight **d;**	3117
	30:21 bread seven **d** with great gladness:	3117
	30:22 they did eat throughout the feast seven **d,**	3117
	30:23 took counsel to keep other seven **d:**	3117
	30:23 they kept *other* seven **d** *with* gladness.	3117
	32:24 In those **d** Hezekiah was sick to the death	3117
	32:26 not upon them in the **d** of Hezekiah.	3117
	34:33 *And* all his **d** they departed not from	3117
	35:17 the feast of unleavened bread seven **d.**	3117
	35:18 kept in Israel from the **d** of Samuel	3117
	36: 9 three months and ten **d** in Jerusalem:	3117
Ezr	4: 2 we do sacrifice unto him since the **d** of	3117
	4: 5 all the **d** of Cyrus king of Persia,	3117
	4: 7 in the **d** of Artaxerxes wrote Bishlam,	3117
	6:22 the feast of unleavened bread seven **d**	3117
	8:15 and there abode we in tents three **d:**	3117
	8:32 *to* Jerusalem, and abode there three **d.**	3117
	9: 7 Since the **d** of our fathers *have we been* in	3117
	10: 8 would not come within three **d,**	3117
	10: 9 together *unto* Jerusalem within three **d.**	3117
Ne	1: 4 mourned *certain* **d,** and fasted,	3117
	2:11 came to Jerusalem, and was there three **d.**	3117
	5:18 once in ten **d** store of all *sorts* of wine:	3117
	6:15 *day of the month* Elul, in fifty and two **d.**	3117
	6:17 Moreover in those **d** the nobles of Judah	3117
	8:17 for since the **d** of Jeshua the son of Nun	3117
	8:18 they kept the feast seven **d;** and on	3117
	12: 7 and of their brethren in the **d** of Jeshua.	3117
	12:12 in the **d** of Joiakim were priests, the chief	3117
	12:22 The Levites in the **d** of Eliashib, Joiada,	3117
	12:23 even until the **d** of Johanan the son of	3117
	12:26 These *were* in the **d** of Joiakim the son of	3117
	12:26 in the **d** of Nehemiah the governor,	3117
	12:46 For in the **d** of David and Asaph of old	3117
	12:47 all Israel in the **d** of Zerubbabel, and in	3117
	12:47 in the **d** of Nehemiah, gave the portions	3117
	13: 6 after certain **d** obtained I *leave* of the king:	3117
	13:15 In those **d** saw I in Judah *some* treading	3117
	13:23 those **d** also saw I Jews *that* had married	3117
Est	1: 1 it came to pass in the **d** of Ahasuerus,	3117
	1: 2 *That* in those **d,** when the king Ahasuerus	3117
	1: 4 honour of his excellent majesty many **d,**	3117
	1: 4 *even* an hundred and fourscore **d.**	3117
	1: 5 when these **d** were expired, the king	3117
	1: 5 both unto great and small, seven **d,**	3117
	2:12 were the **d** of their purifications	3117
	2:21 In those **d,** while Mordecai sat in the	3117
	4:11 to come in unto the king these thirty **d.**	3117
	4:16 neither eat nor drink three **d,** night or day;	3117
	9:22 As the **d** wherein the Jews rested from	3117
	9:22 that *they* should make them **d** of feasting	3117
	9:26 Wherefore they called these **d** Purim after	3117
	9:27 they would keep these two **d** according	3117
	9:28 *that* these **d** *should* be remembered and	3117
	9:28 that these **d** of Purim should not fail from	3117
	9:31 To confirm these **d** of Purim in their times	3117
Job	1: 5 when the **d** of *their* feasting were gone	3117
	2:13 down with him upon the ground seven **d**	3117
	3: 6 let it not be joined unto the **d** of the year,	3117
	7: 1 *are not* his **d** also like the days of a	3117
	7: 1 *are not* his days also like the **d** of a	3117
	7: 6 My **d** are swifter than a weaver's shuttle,	3117
	7:16 let me alone; for my **d** *are* vanity.	3117
	8: 9 because our **d** upon earth *are* a shadow:)	3117
	9:25 Now my **d** are swifter than a post: they	3117
	10: 5 *Are* thy **d** as the days of man? *are* thy	3117
	10: 5 *Are* thy days as the **d** of man? *are* thy	3117
	10: 5 the days of man? *are* thy years as man's **d,**	3117
	10:20 *Are not* my **d** few? cease then, and let me	3117
	12:12 and in length of **d** understanding.	3117
	14: 1 Man *that is* born of a woman *is* of few **d,**	3117
	14: 5 Seeing his **d** are determined, the number	3117
	14:14 shall he live *again?* all the **d** of my	3117
	15:20 wicked *man* travaileth with pain all his **d,**	3117
	17: 1 My breath is corrupt, my **d** are extinct,	3117
	17:11 My **d** are past, my purposes are broken off	3117
	21:13 They spend their **d** in wealth, and in a	3117
	24: 1 do they that know him not see his **d?**	3117
	29: 2 as *in the* **d** when God preserved me;	3117
	29: 4 As I was in the **d** of my youth, when	3117
	29:18 and I shall multiply *my* **d** as the sand.	3117
	30:16 the **d** of affliction have taken hold upon	3117
	30:27 not: the **d** of affliction prevented me.	3117
	32: 7 **D** should speak, and multitude of years	3117
	33:25 he shall return to the **d** of his youth:	3117
	36:11 serve *him,* they shall spend their **d** in	3117
	38:12 commanded the morning since thy **d;**	3117

D

Job 38:21 or *because* the number of thy **d** *is* great?	3117
42:17 So Job died, *being* old and full of **d**.	3117
Ps 21: 4 him, *even* length of **d** for ever and ever.	3117
23: 6 mercy shall follow me all the **d** of my life:	3117
27: 4 house of the LORD all the **d** of my life,	3117
34:12 loveth *many* **d**, that *he* may see good?	3117
37:18 The LORD knoweth the **d** of the upright:	3117
37:19 in the **d** of famine they shall be satisfied.	3117
39: 4 mine end, and the measure of my **d**,	3117
39: 5 thou hast made my **d** *as* a handbreadth;	3117
44: 1 work thou didst in their **d**, in the times	3117
49: 5 Wherefore should I fear in the **d** of evil,	3117
55:23 men shall not live out half their **d**;	3117
72: 7 In his **d** shall the righteous flourish;	3117
77: 5 I have considered the **d** of old, the years	3117
78:33 their **d** did he consume in vanity,	3117
89:29 ever, and his throne as the **d** of heaven.	3117
89:45 The **d** of his youth hast thou shortened?	3117
90: 9 all our **d** are passed away in thy wrath:	3117
90:10 The **d** of our years *are* threescore years	3117
90:12 So teach *us* to number our **d**, that we	3117
90:14 that we may rejoice and be glad all our **d**.	3117
90:15 Make us glad according to the **d** *wherein*	3117
94:13 *thou* mayest give him rest from the **d**	3117
102: 3 For my **d** are consumed like smoke,	3117
102:11 My **d** *are* like a shadow that declineth;	3117
102:23 strength in the way; he shortened my **d**.	3117
102:24 take me not away in the midst of my **d**:	3117
103:15 *As for* man, his **d** *are* as grass: as a flower	3117
109: 8 Let his **d** be few; *and* let another take his	3117
119:84 How many *are* the **d** of thy servant?	3117
128: 5 the good of Jerusalem all the **d** of thy life.	3117
143: 5 I remember the **d** of old; I meditate on all	3117
144: 4 his **d** *are* as a shadow that passeth away.	3117
Pr 3: 2 For length of **d**, and long life, and peace,	3117
3:16 Length of **d** *is* in her right hand; and in	3117
9:11 For by me thy **d** shall be multiplied,	3117
10:27 The fear of the LORD prolongeth **d**: but	3117
15:15 All the **d** of the afflicted *are* evil: but	3117
28:16 hateth covetousness shall prolong *his* **d**.	3117
31:12 him good and not evil all the **d** of her life.	3117
Ecc 2: 3 do under the heaven all the **d** of their life.	3117
2:16 *that* which now *is*, in the **d** to come	3117
2:23 For all his **d** *are* sorrows, and his travail	3117
5:17 All his **d** also he eateth in darkness,	3117
5:18 taketh under the sun all the **d** of his life,	3117
5:20 For he shall not much remember the **d** of	3117
6: 3 so that the **d** of his years be many,	3117
6:12 the **d** of his vain life which he spendeth	3117
7:10 What is *the* cause that the former **d** were	3117
7:15 All *things* have I seen in the **d** of my	3117
8:12 hundred *times*, and his **d** be prolonged,	NIH
8:13 neither shall he prolong *his* **d**, *which are*	3117
8:15 with him of his labour the **d** of his life,	3117
9: 9 lovest all the **d** of the life of thy vanity,	3117
9: 9 under the sun, all the **d** of thy vanity:	3117
11: 1 for thou shalt find it after many **d**.	3117
11: 8 yet let him remember the **d** of darkness;	3117
11: 9 let thy heart cheer thee in the **d** of thy	3117
12: 1 Remember now thy Creator in the **d** of	3117
12: 1 while the evil **d** come not, nor the years	3117
Isa 1: 1 and Jerusalem in the **d** of Uzziah,	3117
2: 2 it shall come to pass in the last **d**, *that*	3117
7: 1 it came to pass in the **d** of Ahaz the son	3117
7:17 thy father's house, **d** that have not come,	3117
13:22 come, and her **d** shall not be prolonged:	3117
23: 7 *city*, whose antiquity *is* of ancient **d**?	3117
23:15 according to the **d** of one king:	3117
24:22 and after many **d** shall they be visited.	3117
30:26 shall be sevenfold, as the light of seven **d**,	3117
32:10 Many **d** and years shall ye be troubled,	3117
38: 1 In those **d** was Hezekiah sick unto death.	3117
38: 5 behold, I will add unto thy **d** fifteen years.	3117
38:10 I said, in the cutting off of my **d**, I shall go	3117
38:20 of our life in the house of the LORD.	3117
39: 6 the **d** come, that all that *is* in thine	3117
39: 8 there shall be peace and truth in my **d**.	3117
51: 9 awake, as *in* the ancient **d**,	3117
53:10 he shall prolong *his* **d**, and the pleasure of	3117
60:20 and the **d** of thy mourning shall be ended.	3117
63: 9 them, and carried them all the **d** of old.	3117
63:11 he remembered the **d** of old, Moses,	3117
65:20 shall be no more thence an infant of **d**,	3117
65:20 nor an old man that hath not filled his **d**:	3117
65:22 for as the **d** of a tree *are* the days of my	3117
65:22 as the days of a tree *are* the **d** of my	3117
Jer 1: 2 of Josiah the son of Amon king of Judah	3117
1: 3 It came also in the **d** of Jehoiakim the son	3117
2:32 my people have forgotten me **d** without	3117
3: 6 The LORD said also unto me in the **d** of	3117
3:16 in the land, in those **d**, saith the LORD,	3117
3:18 In those **d** the house of Judah shall walk	3117
5:18 Nevertheless in those **d**, saith the LORD,	3117
6:11 taken, the aged *with* him *that* is full of **d**.	3117
7:32 Therefore, behold, the **d** come, saith	3117
9:25 Behold, the **d** come, saith the LORD,	3117
13: 6 it came to pass after many **d**, that	3117
16: 9 in your **d**, the voice of mirth, and the	3117
16:14 the **d** come, saith the LORD,	3117
17:11 shall leave him in the midst of his **d**,	3117
19: 6 the **d** come, saith the LORD,	3117
20:18 my **d** should be consumed with shame?	3117
22:30 a man *that* shall not prosper in his **d**:	3117
23: 5 Behold, the **d** come, saith the LORD,	3117
23: 6 In his **d** Judah shall be saved,	3117

Jer 23: 7 the **d** come, saith the LORD,	3117
23:20 the latter **d** ye shall consider it perfectly.	3117
25:34 for the **d** of your slaughter and of your	3117
26:18 the Morasthite prophesied in the **d**	3117
30: 3 For lo, the **d** come, saith the LORD, that I	3117
30:24 heart: in the latter **d** ye shall consider it.	3117
31:27 Behold, the **d** come, saith the LORD,	3117
31:29 In those **d** they shall say no more,	3117
31:31 Behold, the **d** come, saith the LORD,	3117
31:33 After those **d**, saith the LORD, I will put	3117
31:38 Behold, the **d** come, saith the LORD,	3117
32:14 that they may continue many **d**.	3117
33:14 Behold, the **d** come, saith the LORD,	3117
33:15 In those **d**, and at that time, will I cause	3117
33:16 In those **d** shall Judah be saved,	3117
35: 1 of Jehoiakim the son of Josiah king of	3117
35: 7 but all your **d** ye shall dwell in tents;	3117
35: 7 that ye may live many **d** in the land where	3117
35: 8 to drink no wine all our **d**, we, our wives,	3117
36: 2 from the **d** of Josiah, even unto this day.	3117
37:16 Jeremiah had remained there many **d**;	3117
42: 7 it came to pass after ten **d**, that the word	3117
46:26 as in the **d** of old, saith the LORD.	3117
48:12 the **d** come, saith the LORD,	3117
48:47 again the captivity of Moab in the latter **d**,	3117
49: 2 the **d** come, saith the LORD,	3117
49:39 it shall come to pass in the latter **d**, *that* I	3117
50: 4 In those **d**, and in that time, saith	3117
50:20 In those **d**, and in that time, saith	3117
51:47 behold, the **d** come, that I will do	3117
51:52 the **d** come, saith the LORD,	3117
52:33 eat bread before him all the **d** of his life.	3117
52:34 the day of his death, all the **d** of his life.	3117
La 1: 7 Jerusalem remembered in the **d** of her	3117
1: 7 things that she had in the **d** of old,	3117
2:17 that he had commanded in the **d** of old:	3117
4:18 our end is near, our **d** are fulfilled; for our	3117
5:21 we shall be turned; renew our **d** as of old.	3117
Eze 3:15 there astonished among them seven **d**.	3117
3:16 it came to pass at the end of seven **d**,	3117
4: 4 *according to* the number of the **d** that	3117
4: 5 according to the number of the **d**,	3117
4: 5 of the days, three hundred and ninety **d**:	3117
4: 6 the iniquity of the house of Judah forty **d**:	3117
4: 8 till thou hast ended the **d** of thy siege.	3117
4: 9 *according to* the number of thy **d** that	3117
4: 9 and ninety **d** shalt thou eat thereof.	3117
5: 2 when the **d** of the siege are fulfilled:	3117
12:22 The **d** are prolonged, and every vision	3117
12:23 The **d** are at hand, and the effect of every	3117
12:25 for in your **d**, O rebellious house, will I	3117
12:27 The vision that he seeth *is* for many **d** *to*	3117
16:22 hast not remembered the **d** of thy youth,	3117
16:43 thou hast not remembered the **d** of	3117
16:60 covenant with thee in the **d** of thy youth,	3117
22: 4 thou hast caused thy **d** to draw near,	3117
22:14 in the **d** that I shall deal with thee?	3117
23:19 in calling to remembrance the **d** of her	3117
38: 8 After many **d** thou shalt be visited: in	3117
38:16 it shall be in the latter **d**, and I will bring	3117
38:17 which prophesied in those **d** *many* years,	3117
43:25 Seven **d** shalt thou prepare every **d** a	3117
43:26 Seven **d** shall they purge the altar and	3117
43:27 when *these* **d** are expired, it shall be,	3117
44:26 they shall reckon unto him seven **d**.	3117
45:21 shall have the passover, a feast of seven **d**;	3117
45:23 seven **d** of the feast he shall prepare a	3117
45:23 rams without blemish daily the seven **d**;	3117
45:25 he do the like in the feast *of* the seven **d**,	3117
46: 1 the east shall be shut the six working **d**;	3117
Da 1:12 Prove thy servants, I beseech thee, ten **d**;	3117
1:14 in this matter, and proved them ten **d**.	3117
1:15 at the end of ten **d** their countenances	3117
1:18 Now at the end of the **d** that the king had	3117
2:28 what shall be in the latter **d**.	3117
2:44 in the **d** of these kings shall the God of	3117
4:34 at the end of the **d** I Nebuchadnezzar lift	3118
5:11 in the **d** of thy father light and	3118
6: 7 a petition of any God or man for thirty **d**,	3118
6:12 of any God or man within thirty **d**,	3118
7: 9 cast *down*, and the Ancient of **d** did sit,	3118
7:13 came to the Ancient of **d**, and they	3118
7:22 Until the Ancient of **d** came,	3118
8:14 two thousand and three hundred **d**; 1242+6153	
8:26 up the vision; for *it shall be* for many **d**.	3117
8:27 I Daniel fainted, and was sick *certain* **d**;	3117
10: 2 In those **d** I Daniel was mourning three	3117
10:13 of Persia withstood me one and twenty **d**:	3117
10:14 what shall befall thy people in the latter **d**:	3117
10:14 days: for yet the vision *is* for *many* **d**.	3117
11:20 within few **d** he shall be destroyed,	3117
11:33 by captivity, and by spoil, *many* **d**.	3117
12:11 *be* a thousand two hundred and ninety **d**.	3117
12:12 three hundred *and* five and thirty **d**.	3117
12:13 and stand in thy lot at the end of the **d**.	3117
Hos 1: 1 in the **d** of Uzziah, Jotham, Ahaz,	3117
1: 1 in the **d** of Jeroboam the son of Joash,	3117
2:11 her feast **d**, her new moons,	NIH
2:13 I will visit upon her the **d** of Baalim,	3117
2:15 as *in* the **d** of her youth, and as *in* the day	3117
3: 3 her, Thou shalt abide for me many **d**;	3117
3: 4 Israel shall abide many **d** without a king,	3117
3: 5 and his goodness in the latter **d**.	3117
6: 2 After **two d** will he revive us: in the third	3117
9: 7 The **d** of visitation are come, the days of	3117

Hos 9: 7 are come, the **d** of recompence are come;	3117
9: 9 *themselves*, as *in* the **d** of Gibeah:	3117
10: 9 thou hast sinned from the **d** of Gibeah:	3117
12: 9 as *in* the **d** of the solemn feast.	3117
Joel 1: 2 Hath this been in your **d**, or even in	3117
1: 2 days, or even in the **d** of your fathers?	3117
2:29 upon the handmaids in those **d** will I pour	3117
3: 1 For behold, in those **d**, and in that time,	3117
Am 1: 1 he saw concerning Israel in the **d** of	3117
1: 1 in the **d** of Jeroboam the son of Joash king	3117
4: 2 lo, the **d** shall come upon you, that he	3117
5:21 I despise your feast **d**, and I will not smell	NIH
8:11 Behold, the **d** come, saith the Lord GOD,	3117
9:11 and I will build it as *in* the **d** of old:	3117
9:13 Behold, the **d** come, saith the LORD,	3117
Jnh 1:17 Jonah was in the belly of the fish three **d**	3117
3: 4 Yet forty **d**, and Nineveh *shall be*	3117
Mic 1: 1 Micah the Morasthite in the **d** of Jotham,	3117
4: 1 in the last **d** it shall come to pass, *that*	3117
7:14 *in* Bashan and Gilead, as *in* the **d** of old.	3117
7:15 According to the **d** of thy coming out of	3117
7:20 sworn unto our fathers from the **d** of old.	3117
Hab 1: 5 for *I will* work a work in your **d**, *which* ye	3117
Zep 1: 1 of Josiah the son of Amon, king	3117
Hag 2:16 Since those *d* were, when *one* came to a	NIH
Zec 8: 6 of the remnant of this people in these **d**,	3117
8: 9 ye that hear in these **d** these words by	3117
8:10 For before these **d** there was no hire for	3117
8:11 residue of this people as *in* the former **d**,	3117
8:15 So again have I thought in these **d** to do	3117
8:23 In those **d** *it shall come to pass*, that ten	3117
14: 5 in the **d** of Uzziah king of Judah:	3117
Mal 3: 4 as *in* the **d** of old, and as in former years.	3117
3: 7 from the **d** of your fathers ye are gone	3117
Mt 2: 1 of Judea in the **d** of Herod the king,	2250
3: 1 In those **d** came John the Baptist,	2250
4: 2 And when he had fasted forty **d** and	2250
9:15 the **d** will come, when the bridegroom	2250
11:12 And from the **d** of John the Baptist until	2250
12: 5 how that on the sabbath **d** the priests in	NIG
12:10 Is it lawful to heal on the sabbath **d**?	NIG
12:12 it is lawful to do well on the sabbath **d**.	NIG
12:40 as Jonas was three **d** and three nights in	2250
12:40 so shall the Son of man be three **d** and	2250
15:32 they continue with me now three **d**,	2250
17: 1 And after six **d** Jesus taketh Peter, James,	2250
23:30 If we had been in the **d** of our fathers,	2250
24:19 and to them that give suck in those **d**!	2250
24:22 And except those **d** should be shortened,	2250
24:22 for the elect's sake those **d** shall be	2250
24:29 after the tribulation of those **d**	2250
24:37 But as the **d** of Noe *were*, so shall also	2250
24:38 For as in the **d** that were before the flood	2250
26: 2 Ye know that after two **d** *is* the feast of	2250
26:61 temple of God, and to build it in three **d**.	2250
27:40 and buildest *it* in three **d**, save thyself.	2250
27:63 yet alive, After three **d** I will rise again.	2250
Mk 1: 9 And it came to pass in those **d**, *that* Jesus	2250
1:13 he was there in the wilderness forty **d**,	2250
2: 1 he entered into Capernaum after *some* **d**;	2250
2:20 the **d** will come, when the bridegroom	2250
2:20 and then shall they fast in those **d**.	2250
2:26 God *in* the **d** of Abiathar the high priest,	1909
3: 4 Is it lawful to do good on the sabbath **d**,	NIG
8: 1 In those **d** the multitude being very great,	2250
8: 2 they have now been with me three **d**,	2250
8:31 and be killed, and after three **d** rise again.	2250
9: 2 after six **d** Jesus taketh with *him* Peter,	2250
13:17 and to them that give suck in those **d**!	2250
13:19 For *in* those **d** shall be affliction, such as	2250
13:20 that the Lord had shortened *those* **d**,	2250
13:20 he hath chosen, he hath shortened the **d**.	2250
13:24 in those **d**, after that tribulation, the sun	2250
14: 1 After two **d** was the *feast* of the passover,	2250
14:58 within three **d** I will build another made	2250
15:29 the temple, and buildest *it* in three **d**,	2250
Lk 1: 5 There was in the **d** of Herod, the king of	2250
1:23 it came to pass, *that*, as soon as the **d** of	2250
1:24 And after those **d** his wife Elisabeth	2250
1:25 hath the Lord dealt with me in the **d**	2250
1:39 And Mary arose in those **d**, and went into	2250
1:75 before him, all the **d** of our life.	2250
2: 1 And it came to pass in those **d**, *that* there	2250
2: 6 the **d** were accomplished that she should	2250
2:21 And when eight **d** were accomplished for	2250
2:22 And when the **d** of her purification	2250
2:43 when they had fulfilled the **d**, as they	2250
2:46 that after three **d** they found him in	2250
4: 2 Being forty **d** tempted of the devil. And in	2250
4: 2 And in those **d** he did eat nothing: and	2250
4:25 many widows were in Israel in the **d** of	2250
4:31 and taught them on the sabbath **d**.	NIG
5:35 the **d** will come, when the bridegroom	2250
5:35 and then shall they fast in those **d**	2250
6: 2 is not lawful to do on the sabbath **d**?	NIG
6: 9 Is it lawful on the sabbath **d** to do good,	NIG
6:12 it came to pass in those **d**, *that* he went	2250
9:28 And it came to pass about an eight **d** after	2250
9:36 told no *man* in those **d** any of *those things*	2250
13:14 There are six **d** in which *men* ought to	2250
15:13 And not many **d** after the younger son	2250
17:22 said unto the disciples, The **d** will come,	2250
17:22 ye shall desire to see one of the **d** of	2250
17:26 as it was in the **d** of Noe, so shall it be	2250
17:26 shall it be also in the **d** of the Son of man.	2250

Lk	17:28 Likewise also as it was in the **d** of Lot;	2250
	19:43 For the **d** shall come upon thee, that thine	2250
	20: 1 it came to pass, *that* on one of those **d**,	2250
	21: 6 *things* which ye behold, the **d** will come,	2250
	21:22 For these be the **d** of vengeance, that all	2250
	21:23 and to them that give suck, in those **d**,	2250
	23:29 behold, the **d** are coming, in the which	2250
	24:18 which are come to pass there in these **d**?	2250
Jn	2:12 and they continued there not many **d**.	2250
	2:19 temple, and in three **d** I will raise it up.	2250
	2:20 and wilt thou rear it up in three **d**?	2250
	4:40 with them: and he abode there two **d**.	2250
	4:43 Now after two **d** he departed thence,	2250
	11: 6 he abode two **d** *still* in the *same* place	2250
	11:17 he had *lien* in the grave four **d** already.	2250
	11:39 stinketh: for he hath been *dead* four **d**.	5066
	12: 1 Jesus **d** before the passover came	2250
	20:26 And after eight **d** again his disciples were	2250
Ac	1: 3 being seen of them forty **d**, and speaking	2250
	1: 5 with the Holy Ghost not many **d** hence.	2250
	1:15 in those **d** Peter stood up in the midst	2250
	2:17 And it shall come to pass in the last **d**,	2250
	2:18 I will pour out in those **d** of my Spirit;	2250
	3:24 have likewise foretold of these **d**.	2250
	5:36 For before these **d** rose up Theudas,	2250
	5:37 Judas of Galilee in the **d** of the taxing,	2250
	6: 1 And in those **d**, when the number of	2250
	7:41 And they made a calf in those **d**,	2250
	7:45 face of our fathers, unto the **d** of David;	2250
	9: 9 And he was three **d** without sight,	2250
	9:19 was Saul certain **d** with the disciples	2250
	9:23 And after that many **d** were fulfilled,	2250
	9:37 it came to pass in those **d**, that she was	2250
	9:43 that he tarried many **d** in Joppa with one	2250
	10:30 Four **d** ago I was fasting until this hour;	2250
	10:48 Then prayed they him to tarry certain **d**.	2250
	11:27 And in these **d** came prophets from	2250
	11:28 which came to pass in the **d** of Claudius	NIG
	12: 3 (Then were the **d** of unleavened bread.)	2250
	13:31 And he was seen many **d** of them which	2250
	13:41 I work a work in your **d**, a work which	2250
	15:36 some **d** after Paul said unto Barnabas,	2250
	16:12 we were in that city abiding certain **d**.	2250
	16:18 And this did she many **d**. But Paul,	2250
	17: 2 three sabbath **d** reasoned with them out	NIG
	20: 6 Philippi after the **d** of unleavened bread,	2250
	20: 6 and came unto them to Troas in five **d**;	2250
	20: 6 in five days; where we abode seven **d**.	2250
	21: 4 finding disciples, we tarried there seven **d**:	2250
	21: 5 And when we had accomplished *those* **d**,	2250
	21:10 as we tarried *there* many **d**, there came	2250
	21:15 after those **d** we took up our carriages,	2250
	21:26 to signify the accomplishment of the **d** of	2250
	21:27 when the seven **d** were almost ended,	2250
	21:38 which before these **d** madest an uproar,	2250
	24: 1 And after five **d** Ananias the high priest	2250
	24:11 twelve **d** since I went up to Jerusalem for	2250
	24:24 And after certain **d**, when Felix came with	2250
	25: 1 after three **d** he ascended from Cesarea to	2250
	25: 6 had tarried among them more than ten **d**,	2250
	25:13 And after certain **d** king Agrippa and	2250
	25:14 And when they had been there many **d**,	2250
	27: 7 And when we had sailed slowly many **d**,	2250
	27:20 when neither sun nor stars in many **d**	2250
	28: 7 and lodged *us* three **d** courteously.	2250
	28:12 at Syracuse, we tarried *there* three **d**.	2250
	28:14 were desired to tarry with them seven **d**:	2250
	28:17 that after three **d** Paul called the chief of	2250
Gal	1:18 see Peter, and abode with him fifteen **d**.	2250
	4:10 Ye observe **d**, and months, and times,	2250
Eph	5:16 the time, because the **d** are evil.	2250
Col	2:16 or of the new moon, or of the **sabbath d**:	4521
2Ti	3: 1 in the last **d** perilous times shall come.	2250
Heb	1: 2 Hath in these last **d** spoken unto us by *his*	2250
	5: 7 Who in the **d** of his flesh, when he had	2250
	7: 3 having neither beginning of **d**, nor end of	2250
	8: 8 *he* saith, Behold, the **d** come, saith	2250
	8:10 with the house of Israel after those **d**,	2250
	10:16 that I will make with them after those **d**,	2250
	10:32 But call to remembrance the former **d**,	2250
	11:30 after they were compassed about seven **d**.	2250
	12:10 For they verily for a few **d** chastened *us*	2250
Jas	5: 3 heaped treasure together for the last **d**.	2250
1Pe	3:10 For he that will love life, and see good **d**,	2250
	3:20 of God waited in the **d** of Noah,	2250
2Pe	3: 3 that there shall come in the last **d** scoffers,	2250
Rev	2:10 tried; and ye shall have tribulation ten **d**:	2250
	2:13 even in those **d** wherein Antipas *was* my	2250
	9: 6 And in those **d** shall men seek death,	2250
	10: 7 But in the **d** of the voice of the seventh	2250
	11: 3 thousand two hundred *and* threescore **d**,	2250
	11: 6 that it rain not in the **d** of their prophecy:	2250
	11: 9 nations shall see their dead bodies three **d**	2250
	11:11 after three **d** and a half the spirit of life	2250
	12: 6 thousand two hundred *and* threescore **d**.	2250

DAYS' (13) [DAY]

Ge	30:36 he set three **d** journey betwixt himself	3117
	31:23 and pursued after him seven **d** journey;	3117
Ex	3:18 three **d** journey into the wilderness,	3117
	5: 3 three **d** journey into the desert,	3117
	8:27 We will go three **d** journey into	3117
Nu	10:33 the mount of the LORD three **d** journey:	3117
	10:33 went before them *in* the three **d** journey,	3117
	33: 8 went three **d** journey in the wilderness of	3117

Dt	1: 2 (*There are* eleven **d** *journey* from Horeb	3117
1Sa	11: 3 said unto him, Give us seven **d** respite,	3117
2Sa	24:13 there be three **d** pestilence in thy land?	3117
2Ki	3: 9 they fetcht a compass of seven **d** journey:	3117
Jnh	3: 3 an exceeding great city of three **d** journey.	3117

DAYSMAN (1) [DAY, MAN]

Job	9:33 Neither is there *any* **d** betwixt us,	3198

DAYSPRING (2) [DAY, SPRING]

Job	38:12 *and* caused the **d** to know his place;	7837
Lk	1:78 the **d** from on high hath visited us,	395

DAYTIME (7) [DAY, TIME]

Job	5:14 They meet with darkness **in** the **d**,	3119
	24:16 they had marked for themselves **in** the **d**:	3119
Ps	22: 2 I cry in the **d**, but thou hearest not;	3119
	42: 8 command his lovingkindness in the **d**,	3119
	78:14 In the **d** also he led them with a cloud,	3119
Isa	4: 6 for a shadow **in** the **d** from the heat,	3119
	21: 8 continually upon the watchtower **in** the **d**	3119

DEACON (2) [DEACONS]

1Ti	3:10 then let them **use the office of** a **d**,	1247
	3:13 For they that have **used the office of** a **d**	1247

DEACONS (3) [DEACON]

Php	1: 1 are at Philippi, with the bishops and **d**:	1249
1Ti	3: 8 Likewise *must* the **d** *be* grave,	1249
	3:12 Let the **d** be the husbands of one wife,	1249

DEAD (364) [DIE]

Ge	20: 3 to him, Behold, thou *art but* a **d** man,	4191
	23: 3 Abraham stood up from before his **d**,	4191
	23: 4 that I may bury my **d** out of my sight.	4191
	23: 6 the choice of our sepulchres bury thy **d**;	4191
	23: 6 but that thou mayest bury thy **d**.	4191
	23: 8 If it be your mind that I should bury my **d**	4191
	23:11 of my people give I it thee: bury thy **d**.	4191
	23:13 take *it* of me, and I will bury my **d** there.	4191
	23:15 me and thee? bury therefore thy **d**.	4191
	42:38 for his brother is **d**, and he is left alone:	4191
	44:20 his brother is **d**, and he alone is left of his	4191
	50:15 brethren saw that their father was **d**,	4191
Ex	4:19 all the men are **d** which sought thy life.	4191
	9: 7 not one of the cattle of the Israelites **d**.	4191
	12:30 not a house where *there was* not one **d**.	4191
	12:33 in haste; for they said, We *be* all **d** men.	4191
	14:30 Israel saw the Egyptians **d** upon the sea	4191
	21:34 owner of them; and the **d** *beast* shall be	4191
	21:35 of it; and the **d** *ox* also they shall divide.	4191
	21:36 pay ox for ox; and the **d** shall be his own.	4191
Lev	11:31 doth touch them, when they be **d**,	4194
	11:32 when they are **d**, doth fall, it shall be	4194
	19:28 make any cuttings in your flesh for the **d**,	5315
	21: 1 shall none be defiled for the **d** among	5315
	21:11 Neither shall he go in to any **d** body,	5315
	22: 4 any *thing that is* unclean *by* the **d**,	5315
Nu	5: 2 issue, and whosoever is defiled by the **d**,	5315
	6: 6 the LORD he shall come at no **d** body.	4191
	6:11 that he sinned by the **d**, and shall hallow	5315
	6: 9 were defiled by the **d** **body** of a man,	5315
	9: 7 We *are* defiled by the **d** *body* of a man:	5315
	9:10 shall be unclean by reason of a **d** **body**,	5315
	12:12 Let her not be as one **d**, of whom the	4191
	16:48 he stood between the **d** and the living;	4191
	19:11 He that toucheth the **d** *body* of any man	4191
	19:13 Whosoever toucheth the **d** *body* of *any*	4191
	19:13 the dead *body* of *any* man that is **d**,	4191
	19:16 a **d** *body*, or a bone of a man, or a grave,	4191
	19:18 a bone, or one slain, or one **d**, or a grave:	4191
	20:29 the congregation saw that Aaron was **d**,	1478
Dt	2:16 and **d** from among the people,	4191
	14: 1 baldness between your eyes for the **d**.	4191
	14: 8 of their flesh, nor touch their **carcase**.	5038
	25: 5 the wife of the **d** shall not marry without	4191
	25: 6 in the name of his brother which is **d**,	4191
	26:14 *use*, nor given *ought* thereof for the **d**:	4191
Jos	1: 2 Moses my servant is **d**; now therefore	4191
Jdg	2:19 when the judge was **d**, *that* they returned	4194
	3:25 their lord *was* fallen down **d** on the earth.	4191
	4: 1 the sight of the LORD, when Ehud was **d**.	4191
	4:22 Sisera lay **d**, and the nail *was* in his	4191
	5:27 where he bowed, there he fell down **d**.	7703
	8:33 it came to pass, as soon as Gideon was **d**,	4191
	9:55 men of Israel saw that Abimelech was **d**,	4191
	16:30 So the **d** which he slew at his death were	4191
	20: 5 concubine have they forced, that she is **d**.	4191
Ru	1: 8 as ye have dealt with the **d**, and with me.	4191
	2:20 off his kindness to the living and to the **d**.	4191
	4: 5 of Ruth the Moabitess, the wife of the **d**,	4191
	4: 5 to raise up the name of the **d** upon his	4191
	4:10 to raise up the name of the **d** upon his	4191
	4:10 that the name of the **d** be not cut off from	4191
1Sa	4:17 are **d**, and the ark of God is taken.	4191
	4:19 father in law and her husband were **d**,	4191
	17:51 the Philistines saw their champion was **d**,	4191
	24:14 thou pursue? after a **d** dog, after a flea.	4191
	25:39 when David heard that Nabal was **d**,	4191
	28: 3 Now Samuel was **d**, and all Israel had	4191
	31: 5 his armourbearer saw that Saul was **d**,	4191
	31: 7 Saul and his sons were **d**, they forsook	4191
2Sa	1: 4 many of the people also are fallen and **d**;	4191
	1: 4 and Saul and Jonathan his son are also **d**.	4191
	1: 5 thou Saul and Jonathan his son be **d**?	4191

2Sa	2: 7 for your master Saul is **d**, and also	4191
	4: 1 Saul's son heard that Abner was **d** in	4191
	4:10 one told me, saying, Behold, Saul is **d**,	4191
	9: 8 thou shouldest look upon such a **d** dog	4191
	11:21 Thy servant Uriah the Hittite is **d** also.	4191
	11:24 *some* of the king's servants be **d**,	4191
	11:24 thy servant Uriah the Hittite is **d** also.	4191
	11:26 heard that Uriah her husband was **d**,	4191
	12:18 feared to tell him that the child was **d**:	4191
	12:18 if we tell him *that* the child is **d**?	4191
	12:19 David perceived that the child was **d**:	4191
	12:19 said unto his servants, Is the child **d**?	4191
	12:19 Is the child dead? And they said, He is **d**.	4191
	12:21 when the child was **d**, thou didst rise and	4191
	12:23 now he is **d**, wherefore should I fast?	4191
	13:32 men the king's sons; for Amnon only is **d**:	4191
	13:33 to think *that* all the king's sons are **d**:	4191
	13:33 king's sons are dead: for Amnon only is **d**.	4191
	13:39 concerning Amnon, seeing he was **d**.	4191
	14: 2 *that had* a long time mourned for the **d**:	4191
	14: 5 a widow woman, and mine husband is **d**.	4191
	16: 9 Why should this **d** dog curse my lord	4191
	18:20 no tidings, because the king's son is **d**.	4191
	19:10 whom we anointed over us, is **d** in battle.	4191
	19:28 but **d** men before my lord the king:	4194
1Ki	3:20 and laid her **d** child in my bosom.	4191
	3:21 to give my child suck, behold, it was **d**:	4191
	3:22 the living *is* my son, and the **d** *is* thy son.	4191
	3:22 the **d** *is* thy son, and the living *is* my son.	4191
	3:23 my son that liveth, and thy son *is* the **d**:	4191
	3:23 thy son *is* the **d**, and my son *is* the living.	4191
	11:21 that Joab the captain of the host was **d**,	4191
	13:31 When I am **d**, then bury me in	4191
	21:14 saying, Naboth is stoned, and is **d**.	4191
	21:15 and was **d**, that Jezebel said to Ahab,	4191
	21:15 for money: for Naboth is not alive, but **d**.	4191
	21:16 when Ahab heard that Naboth was **d**,	4191
2Ki	3: 5 it came to pass, when Ahab was **d**, that	4194
	4: 1 Thy servant my husband is **d**;	4191
	4:32 the child was **d**, *and* laid upon his bed.	4191
	8: 5 king how he had restored a **d** *body* to life,	4191
	11: 1 of Ahaziah saw that her son was **d**,	4191
	19:35 behold, they *were* all **d** corpses.	4191
	23:30 servants carried him *in a chariot* **d** from	4191
1Ch	1:44 when Bela was **d**, Jobab the son of Zerah	4191
	1:45 when Jobab was **d**, Husham of the land	4191
	1:46 when Husham was **d**, Hadad the son of	4191
	1:47 when Hadad was **d**, Samlah of Masrekah	4191
	1:48 when Samlah was **d**, Shaul of Rehoboth	4191
	1:49 when Shaul was **d**, Baal-hanan the son of	4191
	1:50 when Baal-hanan was **d**, Hadad reigned	4191
	2:19 when Azubah was **d**, Caleb took unto	4191
	2:24 that Hezron was **d** in Caleb-ephratah,	4194
	10: 5 his armourbearer saw that Saul was **d**,	4191
	10: 7 that Saul and his sons were **d**, then	4191
2Ch	20:24 they *were* **d** bodies fallen to the earth,	6297
	20:25 abundance both riches with the **d bodies**,	6297
	22:10 of Ahaziah saw that her son was **d**,	4191
Est	2: 7 when her father and mother were **d**,	4194
Job	1:19 fell upon the young men, and they are **d**;	4191
	26: 5 **D** things are formed from under the	7496
Ps	31:12 I am forgotten as a **d** *man* out of mind:	4191
	76: 6 and horse *are* cast into a **d** sleep.	7290
	79: 2 The **d** bodies of thy servants have they	5038
	88: 5 Free among the **d**, like the slain that lie in	4191
	88:10 Wilt thou shew wonders to the **d**? shall	4191
	88:10 shall the **d** arise *and* praise thee? Selah.	7496
	106:28 and ate the sacrifices of the **d**.	4191
	110: 6 he shall fill the places with the **d bodies**;	1472
	115:17 The **d** praise not the LORD, neither any	4191
	143: 3 darkness, as those that have been long **d**.	4191
Pr	2:18 unto death, and her paths unto the **d**.	7496
	9:18 But he knoweth not that the **d** *are* there;	7496
	21:16 shall remain in the congregation of the **d**.	7496
Ecc	4: 2 Wherefore I praised the **d** which are	4191
	4: 2 more than the living which are yet alive.	4191
	9: 3 they live, and after that *they* go to the **d**.	4191
	9: 4 for a living dog is better than a **d** lion.	4191
	9: 5 the **d** know not any thing, neither have	4191
	10: 1 **D** flies cause the ointment of	4194
Isa	8:19 unto their God? for the living to the **d**?	4191
	14: 9 it stirreth up the **d** for thee, *even* all	7496
	22: 2 not slain with the sword, nor **d** in battle.	4191
	26:14 *They are* **d**, they shall not live; *they are*	4191
	26:19 Thy **d** men shall live, *together with* my	4191
	26:19 *together with* my **d** body shall they arise.	5038
	26:19 herbs, and the earth shall cast out the **d**.	7496
	37:36 behold, they *were* all **d** corpses.	4191
	59:10 *we are* in desolate places as **d** *men*.	4191
Jer	16: 7 in mourning, to comfort them for the **d**;	4191
	22:10 Weep ye not for the **d**, neither bemoan	4191
	26:23 cast his **d** *body* into the graves of	5038
	31:40 the whole valley of the **d bodies**, and of	6297
	33: 5 to fill them with the **d bodies** of men,	6297
	34:20 their **d** bodies shall be for meat unto	5038
	36:30 his **d** *body* shall be cast out in the day to	5038
	41: 9 had cast all the **d** bodies of the men,	6297
La	3: 6 in dark places, as they that be **d** of old.	4191
Eze	6: 5 I will lay the **d** carcases of the children	6297
	24:17 to cry, make no mourning *for* the **d**,	4191
	44:25 they shall come at no **d** person to defile	4191
	44:31 not *of* any thing that **is d** of itself,	5038
Am	8: 3 *there shall be* many **d** bodies in every	6297
Hag	2:13 If *one that is* unclean *by* a **d** body touch	5315
Mt	2:19 when Herod was **d**, behold, an angel of	5053

D

Mt	2:20	for they are **d** which sought the young	2348
	8:22	Follow me; and let the **d** bury their dead.	3498
	8:22	Follow me; and let the dead bury their **d**.	3498
	9:18	saying, My daughter is even now **d**:	5053
	9:24	for the maid is not **d**, but sleepeth.	599
	10: 8	the lepers, raise the **d**, cast out devils:	3498
	11: 5	the **d** are raised up, and the poor have	3498
	14: 2	he is risen from the **d**; and therefore	3498
	17: 9	the Son of man be risen again from the **d**.	3498
	22:31	But as touching the resurrection of the **d**,	3498
	22:32	God is not the God of the **d**, but of	3498
	23:27	but are within full of **d** men's bones,	3498
	27:64	unto the people, He is risen from the **d**:	3498
	28: 4	keepers did shake, and became as **d** men.	3498
	28: 7	his disciples that he is risen from the **d**;	3498
Mk	5:35	*certain* which said, Thy daughter is **d**:	599
	5:39	weep? the damsel is not **d**, but sleepeth.	599
	6:14	John the Baptist was risen from the **d**,	3498
	6:16	whom I beheaded: he is risen from the **d**,	3498
	9: 9	till the Son of man were risen from the **d**,	3498
	9:10	what rising from the **d** should mean.	3498
	9:26	came out of *him*: and he was as **one d**;	3498
	9:26	dead; insomuch that many said, He is **d**.	599
	12:25	For when they shall rise from the **d**,	3498
	12:26	And as touching the **d**, that they rise:	3498
	12:27	He is not the God of the **d**, but the God	3498
	15:44	And Pilate marvelled if he were already **d**:	2348
	15:44	him whether he had been any while **d**.	599
Lk	7:12	behold, there was a **d man** carried out,	2348
	7:15	And he that was **d** sat up, and began to	3498
	7:22	cleansed, the deaf hear, the **d** are raised,	3498
	8:49	*house*, saying to him, Thy daughter is **d**;	2348
	8:52	said, Weep not; she is not **d**, but sleepeth.	599
	8:53	him to scorn, knowing that she was **d**.	599
	9: 7	of some, that John was risen from the **d**;	3498
	9:60	said unto him, Let the **d** bury their dead:	3498
	9:60	said unto him, Let the dead bury their **d**:	3498
	10:30	and departed, leaving *him* **half d**.	2253
	15:24	For this my son was **d**, and is alive again;	3498
	15:32	for this thy brother was **d**, and is alive	3498
	16:30	but if one went unto them from the **d**,	3498
	16:31	persuaded, though one rose from the **d**.	3498
	20:35	and the resurrection from the **d**,	3498
	20:37	Now that the **d** are raised, even Moses	3498
	20:38	For he is not a God of the **d**, but of	3498
	24: 5	Why seek ye the living among the **d**?	3498
	24:46	and to rise from the **d** the third day:	3498
Jn	2:22	When therefore he was risen from the **d**,	3498
	5:21	For as the Father raiseth up the **d**,	3498
	5:25	when the **d** shall hear the voice of the Son	3498
	6:49	eat manna in the wilderness, and are **d**.	599
	6:58	as your fathers did eat manna, and are **d**:	599
	8:52	Abraham is **d**, and the prophets;	599
	8:53	than our father Abraham, which is **d**?	599
	8:53	the prophets are **d**: whom makest thou	599
	11:14	said Jesus unto them plainly, Lazarus is **d**.	599
	11:25	in me, though he were **d**, *yet* shall he live:	599
	11:39	Martha, the sister of him that was **d**, saith	2348
	11:39	he stinketh: for he hath been *d* four days.	NIG
	11:41	*from the place* where the **d** was laid.	2348
	11:44	he that was **d** came forth, bound hand	2348
	12: 1	where Lazarus was which had been **d**,	2348
	12: 1	been dead, whom he raised from the **d**.	3498
	12: 9	whom he had raised from the **d**.	3498
	12:17	and raised him from the **d**, bare record.	3498
	19:33	and saw that he was **d** already, they brake	2348
	20: 9	that he must rise again from the **d**.	3498
	21:14	after that he was risen from the **d**.	3498
Ac	2:29	that he is both **d** and buried,	5053
	3:15	of life, whom God hath raised from the **d**;	3498
	4: 2	through Jesus the resurrection of the **d**.	3498
	4:10	crucified, whom God raised from the **d**,	3498
	5:10	and found her **d**, and, carrying *her* forth,	3498
	7: 4	And from thence, when his father was **d**,	599
	10:41	drink with him after he rose from the **d**.	3498
	10:42	of God *to be* the Judge of quick and **d**.	3498
	13:30	But God raised him from the **d**:	3498
	13:34	that he raised him up from the **d**,	3498
	14:19	out of the city, supposing he had been **d**.	2348
	17: 3	have suffered, and risen again from the **d**;	3498
	17:31	in that he hath raised him from the **d**.	3498
	17:32	they heard of the resurrection of the **d**,	3498
	20: 9	from the third loft, and was taken up **d**.	3498
	23: 6	resurrection of the **d** I am called in	3498
	24:15	that there shall be a resurrection of the **d**,	3498
	24:21	Touching the resurrection of the **d** I am	3498
	25:19	of one Jesus, *which was* **d**, whom Paul	2348
	26: 8	with you, that God should raise the **d**?	3498
	26:23	*be* the first *that* should rise from the **d**,	3498
	28: 6	have swollen, or fallen down **d** suddenly:	3498
Ro	1: 4	holiness, by the resurrection from the **d**:	3498
	4:17	who quickeneth the **d**, and calleth those	3498
	4:19	he considered not his own body now **d**,	3499
	4:24	that raised up Jesus our Lord from the **d**;	3498
	5:15	if through the offence of one many be **d**,	599
	6: 2	How shall we, that are **d** to sin, live any	599
	6: 4	like as Christ was raised up from the **d**	3498
	6: 7	For he that is **d** is freed from sin.	599
	6: 8	Now if we be **d** with Christ, we believe	599
	6: 9	being raised from the **d** dieth no more;	3498
	6:11	Likewise reckon ye also yourselves to be **d**	3498
	6:13	as *those that* are alive from the **d**,	3498
	7: 2	but if the husband be **d**, she is loosed from	599
	7: 3	if *her* husband be **d**, she is free from *that*	599
	7: 4	ye also are become **d** to the law by	2289

Ro	7: 4	*even* to him who is raised from the **d**,	3498
	7: 6	law, *that* being **d** wherein we were held;	599
	7: 8	For without the law sin *was* **d**.	3498
	8:10	*be* in you, the body *is* **d** because of sin;	3498
	8:11	raised up Jesus from the **d** dwell in you,	3498
	8:11	he that raised up Christ from the **d** shall	3498
	10: 7	to bring up Christ again from the **d**.)	3498
	10: 9	that God hath raised him from the **d**,	3498
	11:15	receiving *of them be*, but life from the **d**?	3498
	14: 9	that he might be Lord both of the **d** and	3498
1Co	7:39	but if her husband be **d**, she is at liberty to	2837
	15:12	be preached that he rose from the **d**,	3498
	15:12	you that there is no resurrection of the **d**?	3498
	15:13	But if there be no resurrection of the **d**,	3498
	15:15	raised not up, if so be that the **d** rise not.	3498
	15:16	For if the **d** rise not, then is not Christ	3498
	15:20	But now is Christ risen from the **d**,	3498
	15:21	man *came* also the resurrection of the **d**.	3498
	15:29	they do which are baptized for the **d**,	3498
	15:29	for the dead, if the **d** rise not at all?	3498
	15:29	why are they then baptized for the **d**?	3498
	15:32	what advantageth it me, if the **d** rise not?	3498
	15:35	*man* will say, How are the **d** raised up?	3498
	15:42	So also *is* the resurrection of the **d**. It is	3498
	15:52	and the **d** shall be raised incorruptible,	3498
2Co	1: 9	but in God which raiseth the **d**:	3498
	5:14	that if one died for all, then were all **d**:	599
Gal	1: 1	the Father, who raised him from the **d**;)	3498
	2:19	For I through the law am **d** to the law,	599
	2:21	*come* by the law, then Christ is **d** in vain.	599
Eph	1:20	when he raised him from the **d**,	3498
	2: 1	you hath he quickened, who were **d** in	3498
	2: 5	Even when we were **d** in sins,	3498
	5:14	and arise from the **d**, and Christ shall give	3498
Php	3:11	attain unto the resurrection of the **d**.	3498
Col	1:18	is the beginning, the firstborn from the **d**;	3498
	2:12	of God, who hath raised him from the **d**.	3498
	2:13	**d** in *your* sins and the uncircumcision	3498
	2:20	Wherefore if ye be **d** with Christ from	599
	3: 3	ye are **d**, and your life is hid with Christ	599
1Th	1:10	whom he raised from the **d**, *even* Jesus,	3498
	4:16	of God: and the **d** in Christ shall rise first:	3498
1Ti	5: 6	But she that liveth in pleasure is **d** while	2348
2Ti	2: 8	raised from the **d** according to my gospel:	3498
	4: 1	For if we be **d** with *him*, we shall also live	4880
	4: 1	the **d** at his appearing and his kingdom;	3498
Heb	6: 1	foundation of repentance from **d** works,	3498
	6: 2	of resurrection of the **d**, and of eternal	3498
	9:14	purge your conscience from **d** works to	3498
	9:17	a testament *is* of force after *men* are **d**:	3498
	11: 4	his gifts: and by it he being **d** yet speaketh.	3498
	11:12	him **as good as d**, *so many* as the stars	3499
	11:19	able to raise *him* up, even from the **d**;	3498
	11:35	Women received their **d** raised to life	3498
	13:20	that brought again from the **d** our Lord	3498
Jas	2:17	if it hath no works, is **d**, *being* alone.	3498
	2:20	vain man, that faith without works is **d**?	3498
	2:26	For as the body without the spirit is **d**,	3498
	2:26	is dead, so faith without works is **d** also.	3498
1Pe	1: 3	resurrection of Jesus Christ from the **d**,	3498
	1:21	that raised him up from the **d**, and gave	3498
	2:24	that we, being **d** to sins, should live unto	581
	4: 5	that is ready to judge the quick and the **d**.	3498
	4: 6	gospel preached also to *them that are* **d**,	3498
Jude	1:12	without fruit, twice **d**, plucked up by	599
Rev	1: 5	*and* the first begotten of the **d**,	3498
	1:17	And when I saw him, I fell at his feet as **d**.	3498
	1:18	I am he that liveth, and was **d**;	3498
	2: 8	and the last, which was **d**, and is alive;	3498
	3: 1	hast a name that thou livest, and art **d**.	3498
	11: 8	their **d bodies** *shall* lie in the street of	4430
	11: 9	nations shall see their **d bodies** three days	4430
	11: 9	shall not suffer their **d bodies** to be put in	4430
	11:18	thy wrath is come, and the time of the **d**,	3498
	14:13	Blessed *are* the **d** which die in the Lord	3498
	16: 3	and it became as the blood of a **d** man:	3498
	20: 5	But the rest of the **d** lived not again until	3498
	20:12	And I saw the **d**, small and great, stand	3498
	20:12	the **d** were judged out of those *things*	3498
	20:13	the sea gave up the **d** which were in it;	3498
	20:13	hell delivered up the **d** which were in	3498

DEADLY (7) [DIE]

1Sa	5:11	there was a **d** destruction throughout all	4194
Ps	17: 9	*from* my **d** enemies, *who* compass	5315+871.1
Eze	30:24	with the groanings of a **d wounded** man.	2491
Mk	16:18	if they drink any **d** thing, it shall not hurt	2286
Jas	3: 8	*it* is an unruly evil, full of **d** poison.	2287
Rev	13: 3	to death; and his **d** wound was healed:	2288
	13:12	first beast, whose **d** wound was healed.	2288

DEADNESS (1) [DIE]

| Ro | 4:19 | year old, neither *yet* the **d** of Sara's womb: | 3500 |

DEAF (15)

Ex	4:11	dumb, or **d**, or the seeing, or the blind?	2795
Lev	19:14	Thou shalt not curse the **d**, nor put a	2795
Ps	38:13	I, as a **d** *man*, heard not; and *I* was as a	2795
	58: 4	*they* are like the **d** *adder that* stoppeth	2795
Isa	29:18	in that day shall the **d** hear the words of	2795
	35: 5	and the ears of the **d** shall be unstopped.	2795
	42:18	Hear, ye **d**; and look, ye blind, that *ye*	2795
	42:19	or **d**, as my messenger *that* I send? who	2795
	43: 8	that have eyes, and the **d** that have ears.	2795
Mic	7:16	upon *their* mouth, their ears shall be **d**.	2790

Mt	11: 5	and the **d** hear, the dead are raised up,	2974
Mk	7:32	And they bring unto him one *that was* **d**,	2974
	7:37	maketh both the **d** to hear, and the dumb	2974
	9:25	*Thou* dumb and **d** spirit, I charge thee,	2974
Lk	7:22	the **d** hear, the dead are raised,	2974

DEAL (60) [DEALER, DEALERS, DEALEST, DEALETH, DEALING, DEALINGS, DEALS, DEALT]

Ge	19: 9	now will we **d** worse with thee, than	7489
	21:23	God that thou wilt not **d** falsely with me,	8266
	24:49	now if ye will **d** kindly and truly with my	6213
	32: 9	thy kindred, and I will **d** well with thee:	3190
	34:31	Should he **d** with our sister as with a	6213
	47:29	thigh, and **d** kindly and truly with me,	6213
Ex	1:10	Come on, let us **d** wisely with them;	2449
	8:29	let not Pharaoh **d** deceitfully any more	2048
	21: 9	he shall **d** with her after the manner of	6213
	23:11	In like manner thou shalt **d** with thy	6213
	29:40	with the one lamb a **tenth d** of flour	6213
Lev	14:21	one tenth **d** of fine flour mingled	259+6241
	19:11	Ye shall not steal, neither **d falsely**,	3584
Nu	11:15	if thou **d** thus with me, kill me, I pray	6213
	15: 4	**tenth d** of flour mingled with the fourth	6241
	28:13	a **several tenth d** of flour mingled	6241+6241
	28:21	A **several tenth d** shalt thou offer	6241+6241
	28:29	A **several tenth d** unto one lamb,	6241+6241
	29: 4	one **tenth d** for one lamb, throughout	6241
	29:10	A **several tenth d** for one lamb,	6241+6241
	29:15	a **several tenth d** to each lamb of	6241+6241
Dt	7: 5	thus shall ye **d** with them; ye shall destroy	6213
Jos	2:14	that we will **d** kindly and truly with	6213
Ru	1: 8	the Lord **d** kindly with you, as ye have	6213
1Sa	20: 8	Therefore thou shalt **d** kindly with thy	6213
2Sa	18: 5	**D** gently for my sake with the young man,	NIH
2Ch	2: 3	As thou didst **d** with David my father,	6213
	2: 3	to dwell therein, *even so d* with me.	NIH
	19:11	**D** courageously, and the Lord shall be	6213
Job	42: 8	lest *I* **d** with you *after your* folly, in that ye	6213
Ps	75: 4	I said unto the fools, **D** not **foolishly**: and	1984
	105:25	his people, to **d** subtilly with his servants.	5230
	119:17	**D** bountifully with thy servant, *that* I	1580
	119:124	**D** with thy servant according unto thy	6213
	142: 7	for thou shalt **d** bountifully with me.	1580
Pr	12:22	but they that **d** truly *are* his delight.	6213
Isa	26:10	land of uprightness will he **d unjustly**,	5765
	33: 1	shalt make an end to **d treacherously**,	898
	33: 1	they shall **d treacherously** with thee.	898
	48: 8	thou wouldest **d** very **treacherously**,	898+898
	52:13	Behold, my servant shall **d prudently**,	7919
	58: 7	*Is it* not to **d** thy bread to the hungry,	6536
Jer	18:23	**d** *thus* with them in the time of thine	6213
	21: 2	be that the Lord will **d** with us	6213
Eze	8:18	Therefore will I also **d** in fury: mine eye	6213
	16:59	I will even **d** with thee as thou hast done,	6213
	18: 9	and hath kept my judgments, to **d** truly;	6213
	22:14	in the days that I shall **d** with thee?	6213
	23:25	and they shall **d** furiously with thee:	6213
	23:29	they shall **d** with thee hatefully,	6213
	31:11	he shall **surely d** with him:	6213+6213
Da	1:13	and as thou seest, **d** with thy servants.	6213
	11: 7	and shall **d** against them, and shall prevail:	6213
Hab	1:13	thou upon them that **d treacherously**,	898
Mal	2:10	why do we **d treacherously** every man	898
	2:15	let none **d treacherously** against the wife	898
	2:16	your spirit, that ye **d** not **treacherously**,	898
Mk	7:36	the more a **great d** they published *it*;	4054
	10:48	he cried the more a **great d**, *Thou* Son	4183

DEALER (1) [DEAL]

| Isa | 21: 2 | the **treacherous d** dealeth treacherously, | 898 |

DEALERS (2) [DEAL]

| Isa | 24:16 | **treacherous d** have dealt treacherously; | 898 |
| | 24:16 | the **treacherous d** have dealt very | 898 |

DEALEST (2) [DEAL]

| Ex | 5:15 | Wherefore **d** thou thus with thy servants? | 6213 |
| Isa | 33: 1 | **d treacherously**, and they dealt not | 898 |

DEALETH (10) [DEAL]

Jdg	18: 4	Thus and thus **d** Micah with me,	6213
1Sa	23:22	is told me *that* he **d** very **subtilly**.	6191+6191
Pr	10: 4	becometh poor that **d** *with* a slack hand:	6213
	13:16	Every prudent *man* **d** with knowledge:	6213
	14:17	*He that is* soon angry **d** foolishly: and	6213
	21:24	is his name, who **d** in proud wrath.	6213
Isa	21: 2	the treacherous dealer **d treacherously**,	898
Jer	6:13	even unto the priest every one **d** falsely.	6213
	8:10	even unto the priest every one **d** falsely.	6213
Heb	12: 7	God **d** with you as with sons;	4374

DEALING (1) [DEAL]

| Ps | 7:16 | his **violent d** shall come down upon his | 2555 |

DEALINGS (2) [DEAL]

| 1Sa | 2:23 | for I hear of your evil **d** by all this people. | 1697 |
| Jn | 4: 9 | for the Jews **have** no **d** with | 4798 |

DEALS (19) [DEAL]

Lev	14:10	**three tenth d** of fine flour *for* a	6241+7969
	23:13	two **tenth d** of fine flour mingled with oil,	6241
	23:17	two wave loaves of two **tenth d**:	6241
	24: 5	two **tenth d** shall be *in* one cake.	6241
Nu	15: 6	**tenth d** *of* flour mingled with the third	6241
	15: 9	**tenth d** *of* flour mingled with half a hin	6241

D

Nu 28: 9 two **tenth d** *of* flour *for* a meat offering, 6241
28:12 three **tenth d** *of* flour *for* a meat offering, 6241
28:12 three **tenth d** *of* flour *for* a meat offering, 6241
28:20 three **tenth d** shall ye offer for a bullock, 6241
28:20 for a bullock, and two **tenth d** for a ram; 6241
28:28 three **tenth d** unto one bullock, two tenth 6241
28:28 one bullock, two **tenth d** unto one ram, 6241
29: 3 three **tenth d** for a bullock, *and* two tenth 6241
29: 3 for a bullock, *and* two **tenth d** for a ram, 6241
29: 9 three **tenth d** to a bullock, *and* two tenth 6241
29: 9 to a bullock, *and* two **tenth d** to one ram, 6241
29:14 three **tenth d** unto every bullock of 6241
29:14 two **tenth d** to each ram of the two rams, 6241

DEALT (57) [DEAL]
Ge 16: 6 when Sarai **d hardly with** her, she fled 6031
33:11 because God hath **d graciously** with me, 2603
43: 6 Israel said, Wherefore **d** ye *so* ill with me, 7489
Ex 1:20 Therefore God **d well** with the midwives; 3190
14:11 wherefore hast thou **d** thus with us, 6213
18:11 in the thing wherein they **d proudly** *he* 2102
21: 8 seeing he hath **d deceitfully** with her. 898
Jdg 9:16 if ye have **d well** with Jerubbaal and his 6213
9:19 If ye then have **d truly** and sincerely with 6213
9:23 men of Shechem **d treacherously** with 898
Ru 1: 8 as ye have **d** with the dead, and with me. 6213
1:20 for the Almighty hath **d very bitterly** with 4843
1Sa 24:18 day how that thou hast **d well** with me: 6213
25:31 when the Lᴏʀᴅ shall have **d well** with 3190
2Sa 6:19 he **d** among all the people, *even* among 2505
2Ki 12:15 on workmen: for they **d** faithfully. 6213
21: 6 and **d** with familiar spirits and wizards: 6213
22: 7 into their hand, because they **d** faithfully. 6213
1Ch 16: 3 he **d** to every one of Israel, both man and 2505
20: 3 and David with all the cities of the children 6213
2Ch 6:37 have done amiss, and have **d wickedly**; 7561
11:23 he **d wisely**, and dispersed of all his 995
33: 6 **d** with a familiar spirit, and with wizards: 6213
Ne 1: 7 We have **d very corruptly** against 2254+2254
9:10 for thou knewest that they **d proudly** 2102
9:16 they and our fathers **d proudly**, 2102
9:29 yet they **d proudly**, and hearkened not 2102
Job 6:15 brethren have **d deceitfully** as a brook, 898
Ps 13: 6 because he hath **d bountifully** with me. 1580
44:17 have we **d falsely** in thy covenant. 8266
78:57 and **d unfaithfully** like their fathers: 898
103:10 He hath not **d with** us after our sins; 6213
116: 7 for the Lᴏʀᴅ hath **d bountifully** with 1580
119:65 Thou hast **d well** with thy servant, 6213
119:78 for they **d perversely with** me without a 5791
147:20 He hath not **d** so with any nation: and 6213
Isa 24:16 treacherous dealers have **d treacherously**; 898
24:16 dealers have **d very treacherously**. 898+899
33: 1 and they **d** not **treacherously** with thee! 898
Jer 3:20 so have you **d treacherously** with me, 898
5:11 have **d very treacherously** against 898+898
12: 6 they have **d treacherously** with thee; 898
La 1: 2 her friends have **d treacherously** with her, 898
Eze 22: 7 in the midst of thee have they **d** by 6213
25:12 Because that Edom hath **d** against 6213
25:15 Because the Philistines have **d** by revenge, 6213
Hos 5: 7 They have **d treacherously** against 898
6: 7 have they **d treacherously** against me. 898
Joel 2:26 that hath **d** wondrously with you: 6213
Zec 1: 6 to our doings, so hath he **d** with us. 6213
Mal 2:11 Judah hath **d treacherously**, 898
2:14 against whom thou hast **d treacherously**: 898
Lk 1:25 Thus hath the Lord **d** with me in the days 4160
2:48 Son, why hast thou thus **d** with us? 4160
Ac 7:19 The same **d subtilly with** our kindred, 2686
25:24 multitude of the Jews have **d** with me, 1793
Ro 12: 3 according as God hath **d** to every man 3307

DEAR (7) [DEARLY]
Jer 31:20 *Is* Ephraim my **d** son? *is he* a pleasant 3357
Lk 7: 2 who was **d** unto him, was sick, and ready 1784
Ac 20:24 neither count I my life **d** unto myself, 5093
Eph 5: 1 therefore followers of God, as **d** children; 27
Col 1: 7 As ye also learned of Epaphras our **d** 27
1:13 hath translated *us* into the kingdom of his **d** 26
1Th 2: 8 our own souls, because ye were **d** unto us. 27

DEARLY (10) [DEAR]
Jer 12: 7 I have given the **d beloved** of my soul 3033
Ro 12:19 **D beloved**, avenge not yourselves, 27
1Co 10:14 my **d beloved**, flee from idolatry. 27
2Co 7: 1 therefore these promises, **d beloved**, 27
12:19 but *we do* all *things*, **d beloved**, for your 27
Php 4: 1 my brethren **d beloved** and longed for, 27
4: 1 so stand fast in the Lord, *my* **d beloved**. 27
2Ti 1: 2 To Timothy, *my* **d beloved** son: Grace, 27
Phm 1: 1 unto Philemon our **d beloved**, 27
1Pe 2:11 **D beloved**, I beseech *you* as strangers and 27

DEARTH (8)
Ge 41:54 the seven years of **d** began to come, 7458
41:54 the **d** was in all lands; but in all the land 7458
2Ki 4:38 *there was* a **d** in the land; and the sons of 7458
2Ch 6:28 If there be **d** in the land, if there be 7458
Ne 5: 3 that we might buy corn, because of the **d**. 7458
Jer 14: 1 that came to Jeremiah concerning the **d**. 1226
Ac 7:11 Now there came a **d** over all the land of 3042
11:28 be great **d** throughout all the world: 3042

DEATH (372) [DIE]
Ge 21:16 she said, Let me not see the **d** of the child. 4194
24:67 Isaac was comforted after his mother's **d**. NIH
25:11 it came to pass after the **d** of Abraham, 4194
26:11 his wife shall **surely** be **put to d**. 4191+4191
26:18 had stopped them after the **d** of Abraham. 4194
27: 2 I am old, I know not the day of my **d**: 4194
27: 7 bless thee before the Lᴏʀᴅ before my **d**. 4194
27:10 and that he may bless thee before his **d**. 4194
Ex 10:17 he may take away from me this **d** only. 4194
19:12 mount shall be **surely put to d**: 4191+4191
21:12 he die, shall be **surely put to d**. 4191+4191
21:15 mother, he shall be **surely put to d**. 4191+4191
21:16 hand, he shall be **surely put to d**. 4191+4191
21:17 mother, he shall **surely** be **put to d**. 4191+4191
21:29 and his owner also shall be **put to d**. 4191
22:19 a beast shall **surely** be **put to d**. 4191+4191
31:14 defileth it shall **surely** be **put to d**: 4191+4191
31:15 he shall **surely** be **put to d**. 4191+4191
35: 2 doeth work therein shall be **put to d**. 4191
Lev 16: 1 the Lᴏʀᴅ spake unto Moses after the **d** of 4194
19:20 they shall not be **put to d**, because she 4191
20: 2 he shall **surely** be **put to d**: 4191+4191
20: 9 mother shall be **surely put to d**: 4191+4191
20:10 adulteress **surely** be **put to d**. 4191+4191
20:11 of them shall **surely** be **put to d**: 4191+4191
20:12 of them shall **surely** be **put to d**; 4191+4191
20:13 they shall **surely** be **put to d**; their 4191+4191
20:15 beast, he shall **surely** be **put to d**: 4191+4191
20:16 they shall **surely** be **put to d**; their 4191+4191
20:27 a wizard, shall **surely** be **put to d**, 4191+4191
24:16 he shall **surely** be **put to d**, 4191
24:16 the name of the Lᴏʀᴅ, shall be **put to d**. 4191
24:17 any man shall **surely** be **put to d**; 4191+4191
24:21 that killeth a man, he shall be **put to d**. 4191
27:29 *but* shall **surely** be **put to d**. 4191+4191
Nu 1:51 that cometh nigh shall be **put to d**. 4191
3:10 that cometh nigh shall be **put to d**. 4191
3:38 that cometh nigh shall be **put to d**. 4191
15:35 The man shall be **surely put to d**: 4191+4191
16:29 If these *men* die the common **d** of all men, 4194
18: 7 that cometh nigh shall be **put to d**. 4191
23:10 Let me die the **d** of the righteous, 4194
35:16 murderer shall **surely** be **put to d**. 4191+4191
35:17 murderer shall **surely** be **put to d**. 4191+4191
35:18 murderer shall **surely** be **put to d**. 4191+4191
35:21 smote *him* shall **surely** be **put to d**; 4191+4191
35:25 he shall abide in it unto the **d** of the high 4194
35:28 of his refuge until the **d** of the high priest: 4194
35:28 after the **d** of the high priest the slayer 4194
35:30 murderer shall be **put to d** by the mouth 7523
35:31 the life of a murderer, which *is* guilty of **d**: 4191
35:31 but he shall be **surely put to d**. 4191+4191
35:32 dwell in the land, until the **d** of the priest. 4194
Dt 13: 5 that dreamer of dreams, shall be **put to d**; 4191
13: 9 shall be first upon him to **put** him to **d**, 4191
17: 6 he that is *worthy* of **d** be **put to death**; 4191
17: 6 he that is *worthy* of death be **put to d**; 4191
17: 6 of one witness he shall not be **put to d**. 4191
17: 7 shall be first upon him to **put** him to **d**, 4191
19: 6 whereas he *was* not worthy of **d**, 4194
21:22 a man have committed a sin worthy of **d**, 4194
21:22 he be *to be* **put to d**, and thou hang him 4191
22:26 *there is* in the damsel no sin *worthy* of **d**: 4194
24:16 The fathers not be **put to d** for 4191
24:16 neither shall the children be **put to d** for 4191
24:16 man shall be **put to d** for his own sin. 4191
30:15 *this* day life and good, and **d** and evil; 4194
30:19 *that* I have set before you life and **d**, 4194
31:27 and how much more after my **d**? 4194
31:29 For I know that after my **d** ye will utterly 4194
33: 1 blessed the children of Israel before his **d**. 4194
Jos 1: 1 Now after the **d** of Moses the servant of 4194
1:18 commandeth him, he shall be **put to d**: 4191
2:13 they have, and deliver our lives from **d**. 4194
20: 6 until the **d** of the high priest that shall be 4194
Jdg 1: 1 Now after the **d** of Joshua it came to pass, 4194
5:18 unto the **d** in the high places of the field. 4191
6:31 him be **put to d** whilst *it is* yet morning: 4191
13: 7 God from the womb to the day of his **d**. 4194
16:16 so that his soul was vexed unto **d**; 4194
16:30 So the dead which he slew at his **d** were 4194
20:13 that we may **put** them to **d**, and put 4191
21: 5 He shall **surely** be **put to d**. 4191+4191
Ru 1:17 also, *if ought* but **d** part thee and me. 4194
2:11 in law since the **d** of thine husband: 4194
1Sa 4:20 about the time of her **d** the *women* that 4191
11:12 the men, that we may **put** them to **d**. 4191
11:13 shall not a man be **put to d** this day: 4191
15:32 Surely the bitterness of **d** is past. 4194
15:35 no more to see Saul until the day of his **d**: 4194
20: 3 *there is* but a step between me and **d**. 4194
22:22 I have occasioned the **d** of all the persons NIH
2Sa 1: 1 Now it came to pass after the **d** of Saul, 4194
1:23 and in their **d** they were not divided: 4194
6:23 Saul had no child unto the day of her **d**. 4194
8: 2 *with* two lines measured he to **put to d**, 4191
15:21 whether in **d** or life, even there *also* will 4194
19:21 said, Not Shimei be **put to d** for this, 4191
19:22 shall there any man be **put to d** this day 4191
20: 3 they were shut up unto the day of their **d**, 4191
21: 9 and were **put to d** in the days of harvest, 4191
22: 5 When the waves of **d** compassed me, 4194
22: 6 me about; the snares of **d** prevented me: 4194

1Ki 2: 8 I will not **put** thee **to d** with the sword. 4191
2:24 Adonijah shall be **put to d** *this* day. 4191
2:26 thine own fields; for thou *art* worthy of **d**: 4194
2:26 I will not at this time **put** thee **to d**, 4191
11:40 and was in Egypt until the **d** of Solomon. 4194
2Ki 1: 1 Moab rebelled against Israel after the **d** of 4194
2:21 there shall not be from thence any more **d** 4194
4:40 O thou man of God, *there is* **d** in the pot. 4194
14: 6 The fathers shall not be **put to d** for 4191
14: 6 the children be **put to d** for the fathers; 4191
14: 6 man shall be **put to d** for his own sin. 4191
14:17 of Jehoash king of Israel 4194
15: 5 that he was a leper unto the day of his **d**, 4194
20: 1 In those days was Hezekiah sick unto **d**. 4191
1Ch 22: 5 David prepared abundantly before his **d**. 4194
2Ch 15:13 Lᴏʀᴅ God of Israel should be **put to d**, 4194
22: 4 they were his counsellers after the **d** of 4194
23: 7 into the house, he shall be **put to d**: 4191
24:17 Now after the **d** of Jehoiada came 4194
25:25 **d** of Joash son of Jehoahaz king of Israel 4194
26:21 the king was a leper unto the day of his **d**, 4194
32:24 In those days Hezekiah was sick to the **d**, 4191
32:33 of Jerusalem did him honour at his **d**. 4194
Ezr 7:26 whether *it be* unto **d**, or to banishment, 4193
Est 4:11 *there is* one law of his to **put** *him* to **d**, 4191
Job 3: 5 darkness and the **shadow of d** stain it; 6757
3:21 Which long for **d**, but it *cometh* not; 4194
5:20 In famine he shall redeem thee from **d**: 4194
7:15 *and* I rather than my life. 4194
10:21 land of darkness and the **shadow of d**, 6757
10:22 *and* of the **shadow of d**, without any 6757
12:22 bringeth out to light the **shadow of d**. 6757
16:16 and on mine eyelids *is* the **shadow of d**; 6757
18:13 even the firstborn of **d** shall devour his 4194
24:17 *is* to them even as the **shadow of d**: 6757
24:17 *are* in the terrors of the **shadow of d**. 6757
27:15 that remain of him shall be buried in **d**: 4194
28: 3 stones of darkness, and the **shadow of d**. 6757
28:22 Destruction and **d** say, We have heard 4194
30:23 For I know *that* thou wilt bring me *to* **d**, 4194
34:22 *There is* no darkness, nor **shadow of d**, 6757
38:17 the gates of **d** been opened unto thee? 4194
38:17 thou seen the doors of the **shadow of d**? 6757
Ps 6: 5 For in **d** *there is* no remembrance of thee: 4194
7:13 prepared for him the instruments of **d**; 4194
9:13 thou that liftest me up from the gates of **d**: 4194
13: 3 mine eyes, lest I sleep the *sleep* of **d**; 4194
18: 4 The sorrows of **d** compassed me, 4194
18: 5 me about: the snares of **d** prevented me. 4194
22:15 thou hast brought me into the dust of **d**. 4194
23: 4 through the valley of the **shadow of d**, 6757
33:19 To deliver their soul from **d**, and to keep 4194
44:19 and covered us with the **shadow of d**. 6757
48:14 ever: he will be our guide *even* unto **d**. 4191
49:14 shall feed *on* them; and the upright shall 4194
55: 4 and the terrors of **d** are fallen upon me. 4194
55:15 Let **d** seize upon them, *and* let them go 4194
56:13 For thou hast delivered my soul from **d**: 4194
68:20 Gᴏᴅ the Lord *belong* the issues from **d**. 4194
73: 4 For *there are* no bands in their **d**: but 4194
78:50 he spared not their soul from **d**, 4194
89:48 man *is he that* liveth, and shall not see **d**? 4194
102:20 those that are **appointed to d**; 1121+8546
107:10 as sit in darkness and in the **shadow of d**, 6757
107:14 out of darkness and the **shadow of d**, 6757
107:18 they draw near unto the gates of **d**. 4194
116: 3 The sorrows of **d** compassed me, 4194
116: 8 For thou hast delivered my soul from **d**, 4194
116:15 Precious in the sight of the Lᴏʀᴅ *is* the **d** 4194
118:18 but he hath not given me over unto **d**. 4194
Pr 2:18 For her house inclineth unto **d**, 4194
5: 5 Her feet go down to **d**; her steps take hold 4194
7:27 to hell, going down to the chambers of **d**. 4194
8:36 his own soul: all they that hate me love **d**. 4194
10: 2 but righteousness delivereth from **d**. 4194
11: 4 but righteousness delivereth from **d**. 4194
11:19 pursueth evil *pursueth it* to his own **d**. 4194
12:28 and in the pathway *thereof there is* no **d**. 4194
13:14 of life, to depart from the snares of **d**. 4194
14:12 but the end thereof *are* the ways of **d**. 4194
14:27 of life, to depart from the snares of **d**. 4194
14:32 but the righteous hath hope in his **d**. 4194
16:14 The wrath of a king *is as* messengers of **d**: 4194
16:25 but the end thereof *are* the ways of **d**. 4194
18:21 **D** and life *are* in the power of the tongue: 4194
21: 6 tossed to and fro of them that seek **d**. 4194
24:11 to deliver *them* that *are* drawn unto **d**, 4194
26:18 who casteth firebrands, arrows, and **d**, 4194
Ecc 7: 1 the day of **d** than the day of one's birth. 4194
7:26 I find more bitter than **d** the woman, 4194
8: 8 neither *hath he* power in the day of **d**: 4194
SS 8: 6 for love *is* strong as **d**; jealousy *is* cruel as 4194
Isa 9: 2 dwell in the land of the **shadow of d**, 6757
25: 8 He will swallow up **d** in victory; 4194
28:15 We have made a covenant with **d**, 4194
28:18 your covenant with **d** shall be disannulled, 4194
38: 1 In those days was Hezekiah sick unto **d**. 4191
38:18 praise thee, **d** can *not* celebrate thee: 4194
53: 9 the wicked, and with the rich in his **d**; 4194
53:12 he hath poured out his soul unto **d**: 4194
Jer 2: 6 land of drought, and of the **shadow of d**, 6757
8: 3 shall be chosen rather than life by all 4194
9:21 For *d* is come up into our windows, 4194
13:16 he turn it into the **shadow of d**, 6757
15: 2 Such as *are* for **d**, to death; and such as 4194

D

Ref	Text	Strong's
Jer	15: 2 Such as *are* for death, to d; and such as	4194
	18:21 and let their men be **put to d**;	2026+4194
	21: 8 you the way of life, and the way of d.	4194
	26:15 ye for certain, that if ye **put me to d**,	4191
	26:19 and all Judah **put** him **at all to d**?	4191+4191
	26:21 words, the king sought to **put him to d**.	4191
	26:24 the hand of the people to **put him to d**.	4191
	38: 4 beseech thee, let this man be **put to d**:	4191
	38:15 wilt thou not **surely put** me **to d**?	4191+4191
	38:16 made us this soul, I will not **put thee to d**,	4191
	38:25 from us, and we will not **put thee to d**;	4191
	43: 3 that *they* might **put** us **to d**, and carry us	4191
	43:11 *and deliver* such *as are* for d to death;	4194
	43:11 *and deliver* such *as are* for death to d;	4194
	52:11 and put him in prison till the day of his d.	4194
	52:27 **put** them **to d** in Riblah in the land of	4191
	52:34 every day a portion until the day of his d,	4194
La	1:20 sword bereaveth, at home *there is* as d.	4194
Eze	18:32 For I have no pleasure in the d of him that	4194
	31:14 for they are all delivered unto d,	4194
	33:11 I have no pleasure in the d of the wicked;	4194
Hos	13:14 of the grave; I will redeem them from d:	4194
	13:14 O d, I will be thy plagues; O grave, I will	4194
Am	5: 8 the **shadow of d** into the morning,	6757
Jnh	4: 9 said, I do well to be angry, *even* unto d.	4194
Hab	2: 5 *is* as d, and cannot be satisfied,	4194
Mt	2:15 And was there until the d of Herod: that it	5054
	4:16 and shadow of d light is sprung up.	2288
	10:21 brother shall deliver up the brother to d,	2288
	10:21 and cause them to be **put to d**.	2289
	14: 5 And when he would have **put** him **to d**,	615
	15: 4 father or mother, let him die the d.	2288
	16:28 standing here, which shall not taste of d,	2288
	20:18 and they shall condemn him to d,	2288
	26:38 soul is exceeding sorrowful, *even* unto d:	2288
	26:59 witness against Jesus, to **put him to d**;	2289
	26:66 They answered and said, He is guilty of d.	2288
	27: 1 counsel against Jesus to **put him to d**:	2289
Mk	5:23 daughter **lieth at the point of d**:	2079+2192
	7:10 father or mother, let him die the d.	2288
	9: 1 that stand here, which shall not taste of d,	2288
	10:33 and they shall condemn him to d,	2288
	13:12 the brother betray the brother to d,	2288
	13:12 and shall cause them to be **put to d**.	2289
	14: 1 might take him by craft, and **put** *him* **to d**.	615
	14:34 My soul is exceeding sorrowful unto d:	2288
	14:55 for witness against Jesus to **put him to d**;	2289
	14:64 they all condemned him to be guilty of d.	2288
Lk	1:79 sit in darkness and *in* the shadow of d,	2288
	2:26 *he* should not see d, before he had seen	2288
	9:27 standing here, which shall not taste of d,	2288
	18:33 they shall scourge *him*, and **put** him **to d**:	615
	21:16 of you shall they cause to be **put to d**.	2289
	22:33 go with thee, both into prison, and to d.	2288
	23:15 lo, nothing worthy of d is done unto him.	2288
	23:22 I have found no cause of d in him: I will	2288
	23:32 malefactors, led with him to be **put to d**.	337
	24:20 delivered him to be condemned to d,	2288
Jn	4:47 heal his son: for he was at the point of d:	599
	5:24 but is passed from d unto life.	2288
	8:51 man keep my saying, he shall never see d.	2288
	8:52 keep my saying, he shall never taste of d.	2288
	11: 4 This sickness is not unto d, but for	2288
	11:13 Howbeit Jesus spake of his d:	2288
	11:53 took counsel together for to **put** him **to d**.	615
	12:10 that they might **put** Lazarus also **to d**;	615
	12:33 he said, signifying what d he should die.	2288
	18:31 is not lawful for us to **put** any *man* **to d**:	615
	18:32 he spake, signifying what d he should die.	2288
	21:19 signifying by what d he should glorify	2288
Ac	2:24 raised up, having loosed the pains of d:	2288
	8: 1 And Saul was consenting unto his d.	336
	12:19 commanded that *they* should be **put to d**.	520
	13:28 And though they found no cause of d *in*	2288
	22: 4 And I persecuted this way unto the d,	2288
	22:20 and consenting unto his d, and kept	336
	23:29 nothing laid to his charge worthy of d	2288
	25:11 have committed any *thing* worthy of d,	2288
	25:25 he had committed nothing worthy of d,	2288
	26:10 and when they were **put to d**, I gave my	337
	26:31 This man doeth nothing worthy of d or	2288
	28:18 because there was no cause of d in me.	2288
Ro	1:32 commit such *things* are worthy of d,	2288
	5:10 we were reconciled to God by the d of his	2288
	5:12 sin entered into the world, and d by sin;	2288
	5:12 and so d passed upon all men, for that all	2288
	5:14 Nevertheless d reigned from Adam to	2288
	5:17 For if by one man's offence d reigned by	2288
	5:21 That as sin hath reigned unto d, even so	2288
	6: 3 into Jesus Christ were baptized into his d?	2288
	6: 4 we are buried with him by baptism into d:	2288
	6: 5 planted together in the likeness of his d,	2288
	6: 9 d hath no more dominion over him.	2288
	6:16 whether of sin unto d, or of obedience	2288
	6:21 for the end of those *things is* d.	2288
	6:23 For the wages of sin *is* d; but the gift of	2288
	7: 5 in our members to bring forth fruit unto d.	2288
	7:10 was *ordained* to life, I found *to be* unto d.	2288
	7:13 then that which is good made d unto me?	2288
	7:13 working d in me by that which is good;	2288
	7:24 shall deliver me from the body of this d?	2288
	8: 2 made me free from the law of sin and d.	2288
	8: 6 For to be carnally minded *is* d;	2288
	8:38 that neither d, nor life, nor angels,	2288
1Co	3:22 or d, or *things* present, or *things* to come;	2288

Ref	Text	Strong's
1Co	4: 9 apostles last, as *it were* **appointed to d**:	1935
	11:26 ye do shew the Lord's d till he come.	2288
	15:21 For since by man *came* d, by man *came*	2288
	15:26 last enemy *that* shall be destroyed *is* d.	2288
	15:54 is written, D is swallowed up in victory.	2288
	15:55 O d, where *is* thy sting? O grave, where	2288
	15:56 The sting of d *is* sin;	2288
2Co	1: 9 we had the sentence of d in ourselves,	2288
	1:10 Who delivered us from so great a d,	2288
	2:16 To the one we are the savour of d unto	2288
	2:16 one we are the savour of death unto d;	2288
	3: 7 But if the ministration of d, written *and*	2288
	4:11 are alway delivered unto d for Jesus' sake,	2288
	4:12 So then d worketh in us, but life in you.	2288
	7:10 but the sorrow of the world worketh d.	2288
Php	1:20 in my body, whether *it be* by life, or by d.	2288
	2: 8 and became obedient unto d,	2288
	2: 8 even unto death, even the d of the cross.	2288
	2:27 For indeed he was sick nigh unto d: but	2288
	2:30 the work of Christ he was nigh unto d,	2288
	3:10 being made conformable unto his d;	2288
Col	1:22 In the body of his flesh through d,	2288
2Ti	1:10 hath abolished d, and hath brought life	2288
Heb	2: 9 for the suffering of d, crowned with glory	2288
	2: 9 that he by the grace of God should taste d	2288
	2:14 that through d he might destroy him that	2288
	2:14 destroy him that had the power of d,	2288
	2:15 And deliver them who through fear of d	2288
	5: 7 him that was able to save him from d,	2288
	7:23 not suffered to continue by reason of d:	2288
	9:15 the new testament, that by means of d,	2288
	9:16 also of necessity be the d of the testator.	2288
	11: 5 was translated that *he* should not see d,	2288
Jas	1:15 when it is finished, bringeth forth d.	2288
	5:20 error of his way shall save a soul from d,	2288
1Pe	3:18 being **put to d** in the flesh,	2289
1Jn	3:14 know that we have passed from d unto	2288
	3:14 that loveth not *his* brother abideth in d.	2288
	5:16 his brother sin a sin *which* is not unto d,	2288
	5:16 give him life for them that sin not unto d.	2288
	5:16 There is a sin unto d: I do not say that he	2288
	5:17 is sin: and there is a sin not unto d.	2288
Rev	1:18 and have the keys of hell and of d.	2288
	2:10 be thou faithful unto d, and I will give	2288
	2:11 shall not be hurt of the second d.	2288
	2:23 And I will kill her children with d;	2288
	6: 8 and his name that sat on him *was* D,	2288
	6: 8 with d, and with the beasts of the earth.	2288
	9: 6 And in those days shall men seek d,	2288
	9: 6 desire to die, and d shall flee from them.	2288
	12:11 and they loved not their lives unto the d.	2288
	13: 3 one of his heads as *it were* wounded to d;	2288
	18: 8 in one day, d, and mourning, and famine;	2288
	20: 6 on such the second d hath no power,	2288
	20:13 and d and hell delivered up the dead	2288
	20:14 And d and hell were cast into the lake of	2288
	20:14 into the lake of fire. This is the second d.	2288
	21: 4 and there shall be no more d,	2288
	21: 8 and brimstone: which is the second d.	2288

DEATHS (4) [DIE]

Ref	Text	Strong's
Jer	16: 4 They shall die of grievous d; they shall not	4463
Eze	28: 8 thou shalt die the d of *them that* are slain	4463
	28:10 Thou shalt die the d of the uncircumcised	4194
2Co	11:23 in prisons more frequent, in d oft.	2288

DEBASE

Ref	Text	Strong's
Isa	57: 9 far off, and didst d thyself *even* unto hell.	8213

DEBATE (4) [DEBATES]

Ref	Text	Strong's
Pr	25: 9 D thy cause with thy neighbour *himself*;	7378
Isa	27: 8 it shooteth forth, thou wilt d with it:	7378
	58: 4 ye fast for strife and d, and to smite with	4683
Ro	1:29 full of envy, murder, d, deceit, malignity;	2054

DEBATES (1) [DEBATE]

Ref	Text	Strong's
2Co	12:20 lest *there be* d, envyings, wraths, strifes,	2054

DEBAUCHERY See LASCIVIOUSNESS

DEBIR (14) [KIRJATH-SANNAH, KIRJATH-SEPHER]

Ref	Text	Strong's
Jos	10: 3 and unto D king of Eglon, saying,	1688
	10:38 and all Israel with him, to D;	1688
	10:39 so he did to D, and to the king thereof;	1688
	11:21 from D, from Anab, and from all	1688
	12:13 The king of D, one; the king of Geder,	1688
	13:26 from Mahanaim unto the border of D;	1688
	15: 7 the border went up toward D from	1688
	15:15 went up thence to the inhabitants of D:	1688
	15:15 the name of D before *was* Kirjath-sepher.	1688
	15:49 and Kirjath-sannah, which *is* D,	1688
	21:15 her suburbs, and D with her suburbs,	1688
Jdg	1:11 he went against the inhabitants of D:	1688
	1:11 the name of D before *was* Kirjath-sepher.	1688
1Ch	6:58 with her suburbs, D with her suburbs,	1688

DEBORAH (10)

Ref	Text	Strong's
Ge	35: 8 D Rebekah's nurse died, and she was	1683
Jdg	4: 4 D, a prophetess, the wife of Lapidoth,	1683
	4: 5 she dwelt under the palm tree of D	1683
	4: 9 D arose, and went with Barak to Kedesh.	1683
	4:10 men at his feet: and D went up with him.	1683
	4:14 D said unto Barak, Up; for this *is* the day	1683
	5: 1 sang D and Barak the son of Abinoam on	1683
	5: 7 they ceased in Israel, until I D arose,	1683
	5:12 Awake, awake, D: awake, awake, utter a	1683

Ref	Text	Strong's
Jdg	5:15 the princes of Issachar *were* with D;	1683

DEBT (7) [DEBTOR, DEBTORS, DEBTS, INDEBTED]

Ref	Text	Strong's
1Sa	22: 2 every one that was in d, and every one	5378
2Ki	4: 7 pay thy d, and live thou and thy children	5386
Ne	10:31 and the **exaction of** every d.	3027+4853
Mt	18:27 loosed him, and forgave him the d.	1156
	18:30 him into prison, till he should pay the d.	3784
	18:32 I forgave thee all that d, because	3782
Ro	4: 4 reward not reckoned of grace, but of d.	3783

DEBTOR (4) [DEBT]

Ref	Text	Strong's
Eze	18: 7 *but* hath restored to the d his pledge,	2326
Mt	23:16 swear by the gold of the temple, he is a d.	3784
Ro	1:14 I am d both to the Greeks, and to	3781
Gal	5: 3 that he is a d to do the whole law.	3781

DEBTORS (5) [DEBT]

Ref	Text	Strong's
Mt	6:12 forgive us our debts, as we forgive our d.	3781
Lk	7:41 was a certain creditor which had two d:	5533
	16: 5 So he called every one of his lord's d unto	5533
Ro	8:12 Therefore, brethren, we are d, not to	3781
	15:27 pleased them verily; and their d they are.	3781

DEBTS (2) [DEBT]

Ref	Text	Strong's
Pr	22:26 *or* of them that are sureties for d.	4859
Mt	6:12 And forgive us our d, as we forgive our	3783

DECAPOLIS (3)

Ref	Text	Strong's
Mt	4:25 and *from* D, and *from* Jerusalem,	1179
Mk	5:20 began to publish in D how great *things*	1179
	7:31 through the midst of the coasts of D.	1179

DECAY (1) [DECAYED, DECAYETH]

Ref	Text	Strong's
Lev	25:35 and **fallen in** d with thee;	3027+4131

DECAYED (2) [DECAY]

Ref	Text	Strong's
Ne	4:10 strength of the bearers of burdens is d,	3782
Isa	44:26 and I will raise up the d places thereof:	2723

DECAYETH (3) [DECAY]

Ref	Text	Strong's
Job	14:11 the sea, and the flood d and drieth up:	2717
Ecc	10:18 By much slothfulness the building d;	4355
Heb	8:13 that which d and waxeth old *is* ready	3822

DECEASE (2) [DECEASED]

Ref	Text	Strong's
Lk	9:31 spake of his d which he should accomplish	1841
2Pe	1:15 d to have these *things* always in	1841

DECEASED (2) [DECEASE]

Ref	Text	Strong's
Isa	26:14 not live; *they are* d, they shall not rise:	7496
Mt	22:25 when he had married a wife, d, and,	5053

DECEIT (34) [DECEIVE]

Ref	Text	Strong's
Job	15:35 forth vanity, and their belly prepareth d.	4820
	27: 4 speak wickedness, nor my tongue utter d.	7423
	31: 5 vanity, or *if* my foot hath hasted to d;	4820
Ps	10: 7 mouth is full of cursing and d and fraud:	4820
	36: 3 words of his mouth *are* iniquity and d:	4820
	50:19 mouth to evil, and thy tongue frameth d.	4820
	55:11 d and guile depart not from her streets.	8496
	72:14 He shall redeem their soul from d and	8496
	101: 7 He that worketh d shall not dwell within	7423
	119:118 from thy statutes: for their d is falsehood.	8649
Pr	12: 5 *but* the counsels of the wicked *are* d.	4820
	12:17 forth righteousness: but a false witness d.	4820
	12:20 D *is* in the heart of them that imagine evil	4820
	14: 8 his way: but the folly of fools *is* d.	4820
	20:17 Bread of d *is* sweet to a man;	8267
	26:24 with his lips, and layeth up d within him;	4820
	26:26 *Whose* hatred is covered by d,	4860
Isa	53: 9 neither *was* any d in his mouth.	4820
Jer	5:27 full of birds, so *are* their houses full of d:	4820
	8: 5 they hold fast d, they refuse to return.	8649
	9: 6 Thine habitation *is* in the midst of d;	4820
	9: 6 through d they refuse to know me, saith	4820
	9: 8 *is* as an arrow shot out; it speaketh d:	4820
	14:14 thing of nought, and the d of their heart.	8649
	23:26 *they* are prophets of the d of their own	8649
Hos	11:12 with lies, and the house of Israel with d:	4820
	12: 7 the balances of d *are* in his hand:	4820
Am	8: 5 falsifying the balances by d?	4820
Zep	1: 9 masters' houses with violence and d.	4820
Mk	7:22 Thefts, covetousness, wickedness, d,	1388
Ro	1:29 full of envy, murder, debate, d, malignity;	1388
	3:13 with their tongues they have used d;	1387
Col	2: 8 spoil you through philosophy and vain d,	539
1Th	2: 3 For our exhortation *was* not of d, nor of	4106

DECEITFUL (21) [DECEIVE]

Ref	Text	Strong's
Ps	5: 6 LORD will abhor the bloody and d man.	4820
	35:20 they devise d matters against *them that*	4820
	43: 1 O deliver me from the d and unjust man.	4820
	52: 4 all devouring words, O thou d tongue.	4820
	55:23 d men shall not live out half their days;	4820
	78:57 they were turned aside like a d bow.	7423
	109: 2 mouth of the d are opened against me:	4820
	120: 2 from lying lips, *and* from a d tongue.	7423
Pr	11:18 The wicked worketh a d work: but to	8267
	14:25 but a d *witness* speaketh lies.	4820
	23: 3 of his dainties: for they *are* d meat.	3577
	27: 6 a friend; but the kisses of an enemy *are* d.	6280
	29:13 The poor and the d man meet together:	8501
	31:30 Favour *is* d, and beauty *is* vain: but	8267
Jer	17: 9 The heart *is* d above all *things*, and	6121
Hos	7:16 they are like a d bow: their princes shall	7423

Mic 6:11 and with the bag of **d** weights? 4820
 6:12 and their tongue *is* **d** in their mouth. 7423
Zep 3:13 neither shall a **d** tongue be found in their 8649
2Co 11:13 For such *are* false apostles, **d** workers, 1386
Eph 4:22 which is corrupt according to the **d** lusts; 539

DECEITFULLY (11) [DECEIVE]

Ge 34:13 and Hamor his father **d**, 4820+871.1
Ex 8:29 let not Pharaoh **deal d** any more in not 2048
 21: 8 power, seeing he hath **dealt d** with her. 898
Lev 6: 4 the thing which he hath **d gotten**, 6231+6233
Job 6:15 My brethren have **dealt d** as a brook, 898
 13: 7 wickedly for God? and talk **d** for him? 7423
Ps 24: 4 his soul unto vanity, nor sworn **d**. 4820+3807.1
 52: 2 like a sharp rasor, working **d**. 7423
Jer 48:10 *be* he that doeth the work of the LORD **d**, 7423
Da 11:23 league *made* with him he shall work **d** 4820
2Co 4: 2 nor **handling** the word of God **d**; 1389

DECEITFULNESS (3) [DECEIVE]

Mt 13:22 and the **d** of riches, choke the word, 539
Mk 4:19 and the **d** of riches, and the lusts of other 539
Heb 3:13 lest any of you be hardened through the **d** 539

DECEITS (2) [DECEIVE]

Ps 38:12 and imagine **d** all the day long. 4820
Isa 30:10 speak unto us smooth *things*, prophesy: 4123

DECEIVABLENESS (1) [DECEIVE]

2Th 2:10 And with all **d** of unrighteousness in them 539

DECEIVE (27) [DECEIT, DECEITFUL, DECEITFULLY, DECEITFULNESS, DECEITS, DECEIVABLENESS, DECEIVED, DECEIVER, DECEIVERS, DECEIVETH, DECEIVING, DECEIVINGS]

2Sa 3:25 that he came to **d** thee, and to know thy 6601
2Ki 4:28 of my lord? did I not say, Do not **d** me? 7952
 18:29 saith the king, Let not Hezekiah **d** you: 5377
 19:10 Let not thy God in whom thou trustest **d** 5377
2Ch 32:15 Now therefore let not Hezekiah **d** you, 5377
Pr 24:28 without cause; and **d** not with thy lips. 6601
Isa 36:14 saith the king, Let not Hezekiah **d** you: 5377
 37:10 in whom thou trustest, **d** thee, saying, 5377
Jer 9: 5 they will **d** every one his neighbour, 2048
 29: 8 that *be* in the midst of you, **d** you, 5377
 37: 9 **D** not yourselves, saying, The Chaldeans 5377
Zec 13: 4 shall they wear a rough garment to **d**: 3584
Mt 24: 4 them, Take heed that no *man* **d** you. 4105
 24: 5 saying, I am Christ; and shall **d** many. 4105
 24:11 false prophets shall rise, and shall **d** many. 4105
 24:24 *were* possible, they shall **d** the very elect. 4105
Mk 13: 5 to say, Take heed lest any *man* **d** you: 4105
 13: 6 saying, I am Christ; and shall **d** many. 4105
Ro 16:18 fair speeches the hearts of the simple. 1818
1Co 3:18 Let no *man* **d** himself. If any *man* among 1818
Eph 4:14 whereby they lie in wait to **d**; 4106
 5: 6 Let no *man* **d** you with vain words: for 538
2Th 2: 3 Let no *man* **d** you by any means: for *that* 1818
1Jn 1: 8 we **d** ourselves, and the truth is not in us. 4105
 3: 7 Little children, let no *man* **d** you: he that 4105
Rev 20: 3 that he should **d** the nations no more, 4105
 20: 8 And shall go out to **d** the nations which 4105

DECEIVED (34) [DECEIVE]

Ge 31: 7 your father hath **d** me, and changed my 2048
Lev 6: 2 by violence, or hath **d** his neighbour; 6231
Dt 11:16 your heart be not **d**, and ye turn aside, 6601
1Sa 19:17 Why hast thou **d** me so, and sent away 7411
 28:12 to Saul, saying, Why hast thou **d** me? 7411
2Sa 19:26 My lord, O king, my servant **d** me: 7411
Job 12:16 wisdom: the **d** and the deceiver *are* his. 7683
 15:31 Let not him that is **d** trust in vanity: 8582
 31: 9 If mine heart have been **d** by a woman, 6601
Pr 20: 1 and whosoever is **d** thereby is not wise. 7686
Isa 19:13 become fools, the princes of Noph are **d**; 5377
 44:20 a **d** heart hath turned him aside, that he 2048
Jer 4:10 thou hast **greatly d** this people 5377+5377
 20: 7 thou hast **d** me, and I was deceived: 6601
 20: 7 thou hast deceived me, and I was **d**: 6601
 49:16 terribleness hath **d** thee, *and* the pride 5377
La 1:19 I called for my lovers, *but* they **d** me: 7411
Eze 14: 9 if the prophet be **d** when he hath spoken 6601
 14: 9 I the LORD have **d** that prophet, 5377
Ob 1: 3 The pride of thine heart hath **d** thee, 5377
 1: 7 men that were at peace with thee have **d** 5377
Lk 21: 8 And he said, Take heed that ye be not **d**: 4105
Jn 7:47 them the Pharisees, Are ye also **d**? 4105
Ro 7:11 **d** me, and by it slew *me*. 1818
1Co 6: 9 not **d**: neither fornicators, nor idolaters, 4105
 15:33 Be not **d**: evil communications corrupt 4105
Gal 6: 7 Be not **d**; God is not mocked: 4105
1Ti 2:14 Adam was not **d**, but the woman being 538
 2:14 woman being **d** was in the transgression. 538
2Ti 3:13 and worse, deceiving, and being **d**. 4105
Tit 3: 3 disobedient, **d**, serving divers lusts and 4105
Rev 18:23 for by thy sorceries were all nations **d**. 4105
 19:20 with which he **d** them that had received 4105
 20:10 and the devil that **d** them was cast into 4105

DECEIVER (5) [DECEIVE]

Ge 27:12 feel me, and I shall seem to him as a **d**: 8591
Job 12:16 the: deceived and the **d** *are* his. 7686
Mal 1:14 cursed *be* the **d**, which hath in his flock 5230
Mt 27:63 Saying, Sir, we remember that that **d** said, 4108
2Jn 1: 7 in the flesh. This is a **d** and an antichrist. 4108

DECEIVERS (3) [DECEIVE]

2Co 6: 8 and good report: as **d**, and *yet* true; 4108
Tit 1:10 are many unruly and vain talkers and **d**, 5423
2Jn 1: 7 For many **d** are entered into the world, 4108

DECEIVETH (6) [DECEIVE]

Pr 26:19 So *is* the man *that* **d** his neighbour, 7411
Jn 7:12 others said, Nay; but he **d** the people. 4105
Gal 6: 3 when he is nothing, he **d** himself. 5422
Jas 1:26 not his tongue, but **d** his own heart, 538
Rev 12: 9 and Satan, which **d** the whole world: 4105
 13:14 And **d** them that dwell on the earth by 4105

DECEIVING (2) [DECEIVE]

2Ti 3:13 and worse, **d**, and being deceived. 4105
Jas 1:22 and not hearers only, **d** your own selves. 3884

DECEIVINGS (2) [DECEIVE]

2Pe 2:13 sporting themselves with their own **d** while 539

DECENCY See SHAMEFACEDNESS

DECENTLY (1)

1Co 14:40 Let all *things* be done **d** and in order. 2156

DECIDE See REPROOF; REPROVE

DECIDED (1) [DECISION]

1Ki 20:40 So *shall* thy judgment *be*; thyself hast **d** it. 2782

DECISION (2) [DECIDED]

Joel 3:14 Multitudes, multitudes in the valley of **d**: 2742
 3:14 of the LORD *is* near in the valley of **d**. 2742

DECK (2) [DECKED, DECKEDST, DECKEST, DECKETH, DECKT]

Job 40:10 **D** thyself now with majesty and 5710
Jer 10: 4 They **d** it with silver and with gold; 3302

DECKED (5) [DECK]

Eze 16:11 I **d** thee also *with* ornaments, and I put 5710
 16:13 Thus wast thou **d** *with* gold and silver; 5710
Hos 2:13 she **d** herself with her earrings and 5710
Rev 17: 4 **d** with gold and precious stone 5557+5558
 18:16 and **d** with gold, and precious stones, 5558

DECKEDST (2) [DECK]

Eze 16:16 thou **d** thy high places with divers colours, 6213
 23:40 and **d** thyself **with ornaments**, 5710+5716

DECKEST (1) [DECK]

Jer 4:30 thou **d** thee **with** ornaments of gold, 5710

DECKETH (1) [DECK]

Isa 61:10 a bridegroom **d** *himself* **with** ornaments, 3547

DECKT (1) [DECK]

Pr 7:16 have **d** my bed *with* coverings of tapestry, 7234

DECLARATION (4) [DECLARE]

Est 10: 2 and the **d** of the greatness of Mordecai, 6575
Job 13:17 my speech, and my **d** with your ears. 262
Lk 1: 1 of those things which are most surely 1335
2Co 8:19 the same Lord, and **d** *of* your ready mind: NIG

DECLARE (95) [DECLARATION, DECLARED, DECLARETH, DECLARING]

Ge 41:24 but *there was* none that could **d** *it* to me. 5046
Dt 1: 5 Moab, began Moses to **d** this law, saying, 874
Jos 20: 4 shall **d** his cause in the ears of the elders 1696
Jdg 14:12 if you can **certainly d** it me *within* 5046+5046
 14:13 if ye cannot **d** *it* me, then shall ye give me 5046
 14:15 that he may **d** unto us the riddle, lest we 5046
1Ki 22:13 the words of the prophets **d** good unto NIH
1Ch 16:24 **D** his glory among the heathen; 5608
2Ch 18:12 words of the prophets **d** good to the king NIH
Est 4: 8 to **d** *it* unto her, and to charge her that 5046
Job 12: 8 the fishes of the sea shall **d** unto thee. 5608
 15:17 and that which I have seen I will **d**; 5608
 21:31 Who shall **d** his way to his face? and 5046
 28:27 did he see it, and **d** it; he prepared it, yea, 5608
 31:37 I would **d** unto him the number of my 5046
 38: 4 the earth? **d**, if thou hast understanding. 5046
 38:18 of the earth? **d** if thou knowest it all. 5046
 40: 7 will demand of thee, and **d** thou unto me. 3045
 42: 4 will demand of thee, and **d** thou unto me. 3045
Ps 2: 7 I will **d** the decree: the LORD hath said 5608
 9:11 in Zion: **d** among the people his doings. 5046
 19: 1 The heavens **d** the glory of God; 5608
 22:22 I will **d** thy name unto my brethren: in 5608
 22:31 shall **d** his righteousness unto a people 5046
 30: 9 the dust praise thee? shall it **d** thy truth? 5046
 38:18 For I will **d** mine iniquity; I will be sorry 5046
 40: 5 *if* I would **d** and speak *of them*, they are 5046
 50: 6 the heavens shall **d** his righteousness: 5046
 50:16 What hast thou to do to **d** my statutes, 5608
 64: 9 shall fear, and shall **d** the work of God; 5046
 66:16 I will **d** what he hath done for my soul. 5608
 73:28 the Lord GOD, that *I* may **d** all thy works. 5608
 75: 1 thy name *is* near thy wondrous works **d**. 5046
 75: 9 I will **d** for ever; I will sing *praises* to 5608
 78: 6 should arise and **d** *them* to their children: 5608
 96: 3 **D** his glory among the heathen; 5608
 97: 6 The heavens **d** his righteousness, 5046
 102:21 To **d** the name of the LORD in Zion, 5608
 107:22 and **d** his works with rejoicing. 5608

Ps 118:17 but live, and **d** the works of the LORD. 5608
 145: 4 to another, and shall **d** thy mighty acts. 5046
 145: 6 terrible acts: and I will **d** thy greatness. 5608
Ecc 9: 1 all this I considered in my heart even to **d** 952
Isa 3: 9 they **d** their sin as Sodom, they hide *it* not. 5046
 12: 4 his name, **d** his doings among the people, 3045
 21: 6 set a watchman, let him **d** what he seeth. 5046
 41:22 end of them; or **d** us things for to come. 8085
 42: 9 are come to pass, and new *things* do I **d**: 5046
 42:12 the LORD, and **d** his praise in the islands. 5046
 43: 9 who among them can **d** this, and shew us 5046
 43:26 **d** thou, that thou mayest be justified. 5608
 44: 7 and shall **d** it, and set it in order for me, 5046
 45:19 I **d** things that are right. 5046
 48: 6 will not ye **d** *it*? I have shewed thee new 5046
 48:20 with a voice of singing **d** ye, tell this, 5046
 53: 8 who shall **d** his generation? for he was 7878
 57:12 I will **d** thy righteousness, and thy works; 5046
 66:19 they shall **d** my glory among the Gentiles. 5046
Jer 4: 5 **D** ye in Judah, and publish in Jerusalem; 5046
 5:20 **D** this in the house of Jacob, and publish 5046
 9:12 that he may **d** it, for what the land 5046
 31:10 and *it* in the isles afar off, and say, 5046
 38:15 said unto Zedekiah, If I **d** *it* unto thee, 5046
 38:25 **D** unto us now what thou hast said unto 5046
 42: 3 shall answer you, I will **d** *it* unto you; 5046
 42:20 shall say, so **d** unto us, and we will do *it*. 5046
 46:14 **D** ye in Egypt, and publish in Migdol, 5046
 50: 2 **D** ye among the nations, and publish, 5046
 50:28 to **d** in Zion the vengeance of the LORD 5046
 51:10 let us **d** in Zion the work of the LORD our 5608
Eze 12:16 that they may **d** all their abominations 5608
 23:36 yea, **d** unto them their abominations; 5046
 40: 4 all that thou seest to the house of Israel. 5046
Da 4:18 Belteshazzar, **d** the interpretation thereof, 560
Mic 1:10 **D** ye it not at Gath, weep ye not at all: 5046
 3: 8 to **d** unto Jacob his transgression, 5046
Zec 9:12 even to day do I **d** *that* I will render 5419
Mt 13:36 **D** unto us the parable of the tares of 5419
 15:15 and said unto him, **D** unto us this parable. 5419
Jn 17:26 will **d** *it*: that the love wherewith thou 1107
Ac 8:33 shall **d** his generation? for his life 1334
 13:32 we **d** unto you **glad tidings**, how that 2097
 13:41 wise believe, though a man **d** it unto you. 1555
 17:23 ye ignorantly worship, him **d** I unto you. 2605
 20:27 For I have not shunned to **d** unto you all 312
Ro 3:25 to **d** his righteousness for the remission of 1732
 3:26 To **d**, *I say*, at this time his righteousness; 1732
1Co 3:13 for the day shall **d** *it*, because it shall be 1213
 11:17 Now in this that I **d** *unto you* I praise *you* 3853
 15: 1 I **d** unto you the gospel which I preached 1107
Col 4: 7 All my state shall Tychicus **d** unto you, 1107
Heb 2:12 I will **d** thy name unto my brethren, 518
 11:14 they that say such *things* **d** plainly that 1718
1Jn 1: 3 we have seen and heard **d** we unto you, 518
 1: 5 and unto you, that God is light, and in 312

DECLARED (41) [DECLARE]

Ex 9:16 that my name may be **d** throughout all 5608
Lev 23:44 Moses **d** unto the children of Israel 1696
Nu 1:18 they **d** their **pedigrees** after their families 3205
 15:34 it was not **d** what should be done to him. 6567
Dt 4:13 he **d** unto you his covenant, which he 5046
2Sa 19: 6 thou hast **d** this day, that thou regardest 5046
Ne 8:12 had understood the words that were **d** 3045
Job 26: 3 how hast thou plentifully **d** the thing as it 3045
Ps 40:10 I have **d** thy faithfulness and thy salvation: 559
 71:17 hitherto have I **d** thy wondrous works. 5046
 77:14 hast **d** thy strength among the people. 3045
 88:11 thy lovingkindness be **d** in the grave? 5608
 119:13 With my lips have I **d** all the judgments of 5608
 119:26 I have **d** my ways, and thou heardest me: 5608
Isa 21: 2 A grievous vision is **d** unto me; 5046
 21:10 the God of Israel, have I **d** unto you. 5046
 41:26 Who hath **d** from the beginning, that we 5046
 43:12 I have **d**, and have saved, and I have 5046
 44: 8 and have **d** *it?* ye are even my witnesses. 8085
 45:21 who hath **d** this from ancient time? 5046
 48: 3 I have **d** the former *things* from 5046
 48: 5 I have even from the beginning **d** *it* to 5046
 48:14 which among them hath **d** these *things*? 5046
Jer 36:13 Michaiah **d** unto them all the words that 5046
 42:21 I have *this* day **d** *it* to you; but ye have 5046
Lk 8:47 she **d** unto him before all the people for 518
Jn 1:18 the bosom of the Father, he hath **d** *him*. 1834
 17:26 And I have **d** unto them thy name, 1107
Ac 9:27 **d** unto them how he had seen the Lord in 1334
 10: 8 And when he had **d** all *these things* unto 1834
 12:17 unto them how the Lord had brought 1334
 15: 4 they **d** all *things* that God had done with 312
 15:14 hath **d** how God at the first did visit 1834
 21:19 he *particularly* what *things* God had 1834
 25:14 Paul's cause unto the king, saying, 394
Ro 1: 4 And **d** *to be* the Son of God with power, 3724
 9:17 that my name might be **d** throughout all 1229
1Co 1:11 hath it been **d** unto me of you, 1213
2Co 3: 3 Forasmuch as ye are **manifestly d** to be 5319
Col 1: 8 Who also **d** unto us your love in the Spirit. 1213
Rev 10: 7 as he hath **d** to his servants the prophets. 2097

DECLARETH (4) [DECLARE]

Isa 41:26 that sheweth, yea, *there is* none that **d**, 8085
Jer 4:15 For a voice from Dan, 5046
Hos 4:12 their stocks, and their staff **d** unto them: 5046
Am 4:13 and **d** unto man what *is* his thought, 5046

D

D

DECLARING (4) [DECLARE]
Isa	46:10 **D** the end from the beginning,	5046
Ac	15: 3 Samaria, **d** the conversion of the Gentiles:	1555
	15:12 **d** what miracles and wonders God had	1834
1Co	2: 1 **d** unto you the testimony of God.	2605

DECLINE (5) [DECLINED, DECLINETH]
Ex	23: 2 neither shalt thou speak in a cause to **d**	5186
Dt	17:11 thou shalt not **d** from the sentence which	5493
Ps	119:157 *yet* do I not **d** from thy testimonies.	5186
Pr	4: 5 neither **d** from the words of my mouth.	5186
	7:25 Let not thine heart **d** to her ways, go not	7847

DECLINED (4) [DECLINE]
2Ch	34: 2 **d** neither *to* the right hand, nor *to* the left.	5493
Job	23:11 his steps, his way have I kept, and not **d**.	5186
Ps	44:18 neither have our steps **d** from thy way;	5186
	119:51 in derision: *yet* have I not **d** from thy law.	5186

DECLINETH (2) [DECLINE]
Ps	102:11 My days *are* like a shadow that **d**;	5186
	109:23 I am gone like the shadow when it **d**:	5186

DECREASE (2) [DECREASED]
Ps	107:38 and **suffereth** not their cattle to **d**.	4591
Jn	3:30 He must increase, but I *must* **d**.	1642

DECREASED (1) [DECREASE]
Ge	8: 5 the waters **d** continually until the tenth	2637

DECREE (49) [DECREED, DECREES]
2Ch	30: 5 So they established a **d** to make	1697
Ezr	5:13 Cyrus made a **d** to build this house of	2942
	5:17 that a **d** *was* made of Cyrus the king to	2942
	6: 1 Darius the king made a **d**, and search was	2942
	6: 3 **d** *concerning* the house of God at	2942
	6: 8 Moreover I make a **d** what ye shall do to	2942
	6:11 I have made a **d**, that whosoever shall	2942
	6:12 I Darius have made a **d**; let it be done	2942
	7:13 I make a **d**, that all they of the people of	2942
	7:21 make a **d** to all the treasurers which *are*	2942
Est	1:20 when the king's **d** which he shall make	6599
	2: 8 commandment and his **d** was heard,	1881
	3:15 the **d** was given in Shushan the palace.	1881
	4: 3 king's commandment and his **d** came,	1881
	4: 8 **d** that was given at Shushan to destroy	1881
	8:14 the **d** was given at Shushan the palace.	1881
	8:17 king's commandment and his **d** came,	1881
	9: 1 his **d** drew near to be put in execution,	1881
	9:13 morrow also according unto *this* day's **d**,	1881
	9:14 the **d** was given at Shushan; and they	1881
	9:32 the **d** of Esther confirmed these matters	3982
Job	22:28 Thou shalt also **d** a thing, and it shall be	1504
	28:26 When he made a **d** for the rain, and a way	2706
Ps	2: 7 I will declare the **d**: the LORD hath said	2706
	148: 6 he hath made a **d** which shall not pass.	2706
Pr	8:15 By me kings reign, and princes **d** justice.	2710
	8:29 When he gave to the sea his **d**, that	2706
Isa	10: 1 unto them that **d** unrighteous decrees,	2710
Jer	5:22 *for* the bound of the sea *by* a perpetual **d**,	2706
Da	2: 9 me the dream, *there is but* one **d** for you:	1882
	2:13 the **d** went forth that the wise *men*	1882
	2:15 Why *is* the **d** *so* hasty from the king?	1882
	3:10 Thou, O king, hast made a **d**, that every	2942
	3:29 Therefore I make a **d**, That every people,	2942
	4: 6 Therefore made I a **d** to bring in all	2942
	4:17 *This* matter *is* by the **d** of the watchers,	1510
	4:24 O king, and this *is* the **d** of the most High,	1510
	6: 7 to make a firm **d**, that whosoever shall	633
	6: 8 king, establish the **d**, and sign the writing,	633
	6: 9 king Darius signed the writing and the **d**.	633
	6:12 before the king concerning the king's **d**;	633
	6:12 Hast thou not signed a **d**, that every man	633
	6:13 nor the **d** that thou hast signed,	633
	6:15 Persians *is*, That no **d** nor statute which	633
	6:26 I make a **d**, That in every dominion of my	2942
Jnh	3: 7 published through Nineveh by the **d** of	2940
Mic	7:11 *in* that day shall the **d** be far removed.	2706
Zep	2: 2 Before the **d** bring forth, *before* the day	2706
Lk	2: 1 *that* there went out a **d** from Cesar	1378

DECREED (5) [DECREE]
Est	2: 1 she had done, and what was **d** against her.	1504
	9:31 as they had **d** for themselves and for their	6965
Job	38:10 brake up for it my **d** *place*, and set bars	2706
Isa	10:22 the consumption **d** shall overflow *with*	2782
1Co	7:37 in his heart that *he* will keep his virgin,	2919

DECREES (3) [DECREE]
Isa	10: 1 unto them that decree unrighteous **d**,	2711
Ac	16: 4 delivered them the **d** for to keep,	1378
	17: 7 these all do contrary to the **d** of Cesar,	1378

DEDAN (11) [DEDANIM]
Ge	10: 7 and the sons of Raamah; Sheba, and **D**.	1719
	25: 3 Jokshan begat Sheba, and **D**.	1719
	25: 3 the sons of **D** were Asshurim,	1719
1Ch	1: 9 And the sons of Raamah; Sheba, and **D**.	1719
	1:32 And the sons of Jokshan; Sheba, and **D**.	1719
Jer	25:23 **D**, and Tema, and Buz, and all *that are* in	1719
	49: 8 turn back, dwell deep, O inhabitants of **D**;	1719
Eze	25:13 and they of **D** shall fall by the sword.	1719
	27:15 The men of **D** *were* thy merchants;	1719
	27:20 **D** *was* thy merchant in precious clothes	1719
	38:13 and **D**, and the merchants of Tarshish,	1719

DEDANIM (1) [DEDAN]
Isa	21:13 ye lodge, O ye travelling companies of **D**.	1720

DEDANITES See DEDANIM

DEDICATE (11) [DEDICATED, DEDICATING, DEDICATION]
Dt	20: 5 die in the battle, and another man **d** it.	2596
2Sa	8:11 Which also king David did **d** unto	6942
2Ki	12:18 had **d**, and his own hallowed *things*,	6942
1Ch	26:20 and over the treasures of the **d** *things*.	6944
	26:26 of the **d** *things*, which David the king,	6944
	26:27 of the spoils won in battles did they **d**	6942
	26:28 of the treasuries of the **d** *things*:	6944
2Ch	2: 4 to **d** *it* to him, *and* to burn before him	6942
	24: 7 also all the **d** *things* of the house of	6944
	31:12 and the tithes and the **d** *things* faithfully:	6944
Eze	44:29 and every **d thing** in Israel shall be theirs.	2764

DEDICATED (17) [DEDICATE]
Dt	20: 5 hath built a new house, and hath not **d** it?	2596
Jdg	17: 3 I had **wholly d** the silver unto	6942+6942
2Sa	8:11 gold that he had **d** of all nations which he	6942
1Ki	7:51 the *things* which David his father had **d**;	6944
	8:63 all the children of Israel the house of	2596
	15:15 the *things* which his father had **d**, *into*	6944
	15:15 the *things* which himself had **d**, *into*	6944
2Ki	12: 4 All the money of the **d** *things* that is	6944
1Ch	18:11 Them also king David **d** unto the LORD,	6942
	26:26 and the captains of the host, had **d**.	6942
	26:28 Ner, and Joab the son of Zeruiah, had **d**;	6942
	26:28 whosoever had **d** *anything, it was* under	6942
2Ch	5: 1 *all* the *things* that David his father had **d**;	6944
	7: 5 and all the people the house of God.	2596
	15:18 of God the *things* that his father had **d**,	6944
	15:18 that he himself had **d**, silver, and gold,	6944
Heb	9:18 the first *testament* was **d** without blood.	1457

DEDICATING (2) [DEDICATE]
Nu	7:10 The princes offered *for* **d** of the altar in	2598
	7:11 prince on *his* day, for the **d** of the altar.	2598

DEDICATION (11) [DEDICATE]
Nu	7:84 This *was* the **d** of the altar, in the day	2598
	7:88 This *was* the **d** of the altar, after *that* it	2598
2Ch	7: 9 for they kept the **d** of the altar seven days,	2598
Ezr	6:16 kept the **d** of this house of God with joy,	2597
	6:17 offered at the **d** of this house of God an	2597
Ne	12:27 at the **d** of the wall of Jerusalem they	2598
	12:27 to keep the **d** with gladness, both with	2598
Ps	30: T *and* Song *at* the **d** of the house of David.	2598
Da	3: 2 to come to the **d** of the image which	2597
	3: 3 were gathered together unto the **d** of	2597
Jn	10:22 And it was at Jerusalem *the feast of* the **d**,	1456

DEED (19) [DEEDS]
Ge	44:15 What **d** *is* this that ye have done?	4639
Ex	9:16 **in very d** for this cause have I raised thee	199
Jdg	19:30 There was no such **d** done nor seen from	NIH
1Sa	25:34 For **in very d**, *as* the LORD God of Israel	199
	26: 4 understood that Saul was come in **very d**.	3559
2Sa	12:14 by this **d** thou hast given great occasion to	1697
2Ch	6:18 will God **in very d** dwell with men on	552
Est	1:17 For *this* **d** of the queen shall come abroad	1697
	1:18 which have heard of the **d** of the queen.	1697
Lk	23:51 consented to the counsel and **d** of them;)	4234
	24:19 which was a prophet mighty in **d** and	2041
Ac	4: 9 If we this day be examined of the **good d**	2108
Ro	15:18 the Gentiles obedient, by word and **d**,	2041
1Co	5: 2 that he hath done this **d** might be taken	2041
	5: 3 *concerning* him that hath so done this **d**,	NIG
2Co	10:11 such *will we be* also in **d** when we are	2041
Col	3:17 whatsoever ye do in word or **d**, *do* all	2041
Jas	1:25 work, this *man* shall be blessed in his **d**.	4162
1Jn	3:18 neither in tongue; but in **d** and in truth.	2041

DEEDS (33) [DEED]
Ge	20: 9 thou hast done **d** unto me that ought not	4639
1Ch	16: 8 make known his **d** among the people.	5949
2Ch	35:27 his **d**, first and last, behold, they *are*	1697
Ezr	9:13 all that is come upon us for our evil **d**,	4639
Ne	6:19 Also they reported his **good d** before me,	2896
	13:14 wipe not out my **good d** that I have done	2617
Ps	28: 4 Give them according to their **d**,	6467
	105: 1 make known his **d** among the people.	5949
Isa	59:18 according to *their* **d**, accordingly he will	1578
Jer	5:28 yea, they overpass the **d** of the wicked:	1697
	25:14 recompense them according to their **d**,	6467
Lk	11:48 ye bear witness that ye allow the **d** of	2041
	23:41 for we receive the due reward of our **d**:	4238
Jn	3:19 than light, because their **d** were evil.	2041
	3:20 to the light, lest his **d** should be reproved.	2041
	3:21 that his **d** may be made manifest, that	2041
	8:41 Ye do the **d** of your father. Then said they	2041
Ac	7:22 and was mighty in words and in **d**.	2041
	19:18 and confessed, and shewed their **d**.	4234
	24: 2 that **very worthy d** are done unto this	2735
Ro	2: 6 render to every *man* according to his **d**:	2041
	3:20 Therefore by the **d** of the law there shall	2041
	3:28 justified by faith without the **d** of the law.	2041
	8:13 ye through the Spirit do mortify the **d** of	4234
2Co	12:12 in signs, and wonders, and **mighty d**.	1411
Col	3: 9 ye have put off the old man with his **d**;	4234
2Pe	2: 8 from day to day with *their* unlawful **d**;)	2041
2Jn	1:11 him God speed is partaker of his evil **d**.	2041

3Jn	1:10 I will remember his **d** which he doeth,	2041
Jude	1:15 all the ungodly **d** which they have ungodly committed,	2041
Rev	2: 6 that thou hatest the **d** of the Nicolaitans,	2041
	2:22 except they repent of their **d**.	2041
	16:11 their sores, and repented not of their **d**.	2041

DEEMED (1)
Ac	27:27 about midnight the shipmen **d** that they	5282

DEEP (65) [DEEPER, DEEPLY, DEEPNESS, DEEPS, DEPTH, DEPTHS]
Ge	1: 2 and darkness *was* upon the face of the **d**.	8415
	2:21 the LORD God caused a **d** sleep to fall	8639
	7:11 all the fountains of the great **d** broken up,	8415
	8: 2 The fountains also of the **d** and	8415
	15:12 going down, a **d** sleep fell upon Abram;	8639
	49:25 blessings of the **d** that lieth under,	8415
Dt	33:13 and for the **d** that coucheth beneath,	8415
1Sa	26:12 a **d** sleep from the LORD was fallen upon	8639
Job	4:13 the night, when **d sleep** falleth on men.	8639
	12:22 He discovereth **d** *things* out of darkness,	6013
	33:15 night, when **d sleep** falleth upon men,	8639
	38:30 a stone, and the face of the **d** is frozen.	8415
	41:31 He maketh the **d** to boil like a pot:	4688
	41:32 *one* would think the **d** to be hoary.	8415
Ps	36: 6 thy judgments *are* a great **d**:	8415
	42: 7 **D** calleth unto deep at the noise of thy	8415
	42: 7 Deep calleth unto **d** at the noise of thy	8415
	64: 6 of every one of *them*, and the heart, *is* **d**.	6013
	69: 2 I sink in **d** mire, where *there is* no	4688
	69: 2 I am come into **d** waters, where the floods	4615
	69:14 that hate me, and out of the **d** waters.	4615
	69:15 neither let the **d** swallow me up, and let	4688
	80: 9 didst **cause** it **to take root**,	8327+8328
	92: 5 thy works! *and* thy thoughts are very **d**.	6009
	95: 4 In his hand *are* the **d** places of the earth:	4278
	104: 6 Thou coveredst it *with* the **d** as *with* a	8415
	107:24 of the LORD, and his wonders in the **d**.	4688
	135: 6 and in earth, in the seas, and all **d** places.	8415
	140:10 into **d** pits, *that* they rise not up again.	4113
Pr	8:28 he strengthened the fountains of the **d**:	8415
	18: 4 The words of a man's mouth *are as* **d**	6013
	19:15 Slothfulness casteth into a **d sleep**;	8639
	20: 5 in the heart of man *is like* a **d** water;	6013
	22:14 The mouth of strange *women is* a **d** pit:	6013
	23:27 For a whore *is* a **d** ditch; and a strange	6013
Ecc	7:24 **exceeding d**, who can find it out?	6013+6013
Isa	29:10 poured out upon you the spirit of **d** sleep,	8639
	29:15 Woe unto them that **seek d** to hide *their*	6009
	30:33 is prepared; he hath **made** it **d** *and* large:	6009
	44:27 That saith to the **d**, Be dry, and I will dry	6683
	51:10 dried the sea, the waters of the great **d**;	8415
	63:13 That led them through the **d**, as a horse	8415
Jer	49: 8 Flee ye, turn back, dwell **d**, O inhabitants	6009
	49:30 Flee, get you far off, dwell **d**, O ye	6009
Eze	23:32 Thou shalt drink *of* thy sister's cup **d** and	6013
	26:19 when *I* shall bring up the **d** upon thee,	8415
	31: 4 the **d** set him up on high with her rivers	8415
	31:15 I covered the **d** for him, and I restrained	8415
	32:14 will I **make** their waters **d**, and cause	8257
	34:18 to have drunk of the **d** waters, but ye	4950
Da	2:22 He revealeth the **d** and secret *things*: he	5994
	8:18 I was **in a d** sleep on my face toward	7290
	10: 9 was **in a d** sleep on my face, and my	7290
Am	7: 4 it devoured the great **d**, and did eat up a	8415
Jnh	2: 3 For thou hadst cast me *into* the **d**,	4688
Hab	3:10 the **d** uttered his voice, *and* lift up his	8415
Lk	5: 4 Launch out into the **d**, and let down your	899
	6:48 and digged **d**, and laid the foundation on a	900
	8:31 not command them to go out into the **d**.	12
Jn	4:11 nothing to draw with, and the well is **d**:	901
Ac	20: 9 Eutychus, being fallen into a **d** sleep:	901
Ro	10: 7 Or, Who shall descend into the **d**? (that is,	12
1Co	2:10 all *things*, yea, the **d** things of God.	899
2Co	8: 2 their **d** poverty abounded unto	899+2596
	11:25 a night and a day I have been in the **d**;	1037

DEEPER (9) [DEEP]
Lev	13: 3 the plague in sight *be* **d** than the skin of	6013
	13: 4 in sight *be* not **d** than the skin, and the	6013
	13:25 and it *be* in sight **d** than the skin;	6013
	13:30 behold, *if* it *be* in sight **d** than the skin;	6013
	13:31 it *be* not in sight **d** than the skin,	6013
	13:32 the scall *be* not in sight **d** than the skin,	6013
	13:34 the skin, nor *be* in sight **d** than the skin;	6013
Job	11: 8 **d** than hell; what canst thou know?	6013
Isa	33:19 a people of a **d** speech than *thou* canst	6012

DEEPLY (3) [DEEP]
Isa	31: 6 the children of Israel have revolted.	6009
Hos	9: 9 They have corrupted *themselves*, as in	6009
Mk	8:12 And he **sighed d** in his spirit, and saith,	389

DEEPNESS (1) [DEEP]
Mt	13: 5 sprung up, because *they* had no **d** of earth:	899

DEEPS (4) [DEEP]
Ne	9:11 persecutors thou threwest into the **d**,	4688
Ps	88: 6 in the lowest pit, in darkness, in the **d**.	4688
	148: 7 from the earth, ye dragons, and all **d**:	8415
Zec	10:11 and all the **d** of the river shall dry up:	4688

DEER (1)
Dt	14: 5 the **fallow d**, and the wild goat,	3180

DEFAMED (1) [DEFAMING]
1Co 4:13 **d**, we intreat: we are made as the filth 987

DEFAMING (1) [DEFAMED]
Jer 20:10 For I heard the **d** of many, fear on every 1681

DEFEAT (2)
2Sa 15:34 mayest thou for me **d** the counsel of 6565
 17:14 For the LORD had appointed to **d** 6565

DEFENCE (22) [DEFEND]
Nu 14: 9 their **d** is departed from them, 6738
2Ch 11: 5 Jerusalem, and built cities for **d** in Judah. 4692
Job 22:25 the Almighty shall be thy **d**, and thou shalt 1220
Ps 7:10 My **d** is of God, which saveth the upright 4043
 31: 2 strong rock, for a house of **d** to save me. 4686
 59: 9 will I wait upon thee: for God is my **d**. 4869
 59:16 for thou hast been my **d** and refuge in 4869
 59:17 God is my **d**, and the God of my mercy. 4869
 62: 2 is my rock and my salvation; *he is* my **d**; 4869
 62: 6 *he* is my **d**; I shall not be moved. 4869
 89:18 For the LORD *is* our **d**; and the Holy One 4043
 94:22 the LORD is my **d**; and my God *is* 4869
Ecc 7:12 wisdom *is* a **d**, *and* money *is* a defence; 6738
 7:12 wisdom *is* a defence, *and* money *is* a **d**: 6738
Isa 4: 5 night: for upon all the glory *shall be* a **d**. 2646
 19: 6 *and* the brooks of **d** shall be emptied and 4693
 33:16 his **place of d** *shall be* the munitions of 4869
Na 2: 1 shall thereof, and the **d** shall be prepared. 5526
Ac 19:33 would have **made** *his* **d** unto the people. 626
 22: 1 hear ye my **d** *which I make* now unto you. 627
Php 1: 7 *in* the **d** and confirmation of the gospel, 627
 1:17 that I am set for the **d** of the gospel. 627

DEFENCED (9) [DEFEND]
Isa 25: 2 made of a heap, *of* a **d** city a ruin: 1219
 27:10 Yet the **d** city *shall be* desolate, 1219
 36: 1 came up against all the **d** cities of Judah, 1219
 37:26 thou shouldest be to lay waste **d** cities 1219
Jer 1:18 I have made thee *this* day a **d** city, 4013
 4: 5 and let us go into the **d** cities. 4013
 8:14 let us enter into the **d** cities, and let us be 4013
 34: 7 for these **d** cities remained of the cities of 4013
Eze 21:20 to Judah in Jerusalem the **d**. 1219

DEFEND (11) [DEFENCE, DEFENCED, DEFENDED, DEFENDEST, DEFENDING]
Jdg 10: 1 after Abimelech there arose to **d** Israel 3467
2Ki 19:34 For I will **d** this city, to save it, for mine 1598
 20: 6 I will **d** this city for mine own sake, 1598
Ps 20: 1 the name of the God of Jacob **d** thee; 7682
 59: 1 **d** me from them that rise up against me. 7682
 82: 3 **D** the poor and fatherless: do justice to 8199
Isa 31: 5 so will the LORD of hosts **d** Jerusalem; 1598
 37:35 I will **d** this city to save it for mine own 1598
 38: 6 the king of Assyria: and I will **d** this city. 1598
Zec 9:15 The LORD of hosts shall **d** them; 1598
 12: 8 In that day shall the LORD **d** 1598

DEFENDED (2) [DEFEND]
2Sa 23:12 and **d** it, and slew the Philistines: 5337
Ac 7:24 **d** *him*, and avenged him that was 292

DEFENDEST (1) [DEFEND]
Ps 5:11 shout for joy, because thou **d** them: 5526+5921

DEFENDING (1) [DEFEND]
Isa 31: 5 also he will deliver *it*; and passing over 1598

DEFER (3) [DEFERRED, DEFERRETH]
Ecc 5: 4 vowest a vow unto God, **d** not to pay it; 309
Isa 48: 9 For my name's sake will I **d** mine anger, 748
Da 9:19 do; **d** not, for thine own sake, O my God: 309

DEFERRED (3) [DEFER]
Ge 34:19 the young man **d** not to do the thing, 309
Pr 13:12 Hope **d** maketh the heart sick: but *when* 4900
Ac 24:22 he **d** them, and said, When Lysias the chief 306

DEFERRETH (1) [DEFER]
Pr 19:11 The discretion of a man **d** his anger; and 748

DEFIED (6) [DEFY]
Nu 23: 8 shall I defy, *whom* the LORD hath not **d**? 2194
1Sa 17:36 seeing he hath **d** the armies of the living 2778
 17:45 of the armies of Israel, whom thou hast **d**. 2778
2Sa 21:21 when he **d** Israel, Jonathan the son of 2778
 23: 9 when they **d** the Philistines *that* were 2778
1Ch 20: 7 when he **d** Israel, Jonathan the son of 2778

DEFILE (39) [DEFILED, DEFILEDST, DEFILETH, UNDEFILED]
Lev 11:44 neither shall ye **d** yourselves with any 2930
 15:31 when they **d** my tabernacle that *is* among 2930
 18:20 neighbour's wife, to **d** thyself with her. 2930
 18:23 Neither shalt thou lie with any beast to **d** 2930
 18:24 **D** not you yourselves in any of these 2930
 18:28 land spue not you out also, when ye **d** it, 2930
 18:30 and that ye **d** not **yourselves** therein: 2930
 20: 3 to **d** my sanctuary, and to profane my 2930
 21: 4 *But* he shall not **d** himself, *being* a chief 2930
 21:11 nor **d** himself for his father, or for his 2930
 22: 8 is torn *with beasts*, he shall not eat to **d** 2930
Nu 5: 3 that they **d** not their camps, in the midst 2930
 35:34 **D** not therefore the land which ye shall 2930
2Ki 23:13 the children of Ammon, did the king **d**. 2930

SS 5: 3 have washed my feet; how shall I **d** them? 2936
Isa 30:22 Ye shall **d** also the covering of thy graven 2930
Jer 32:34 which is called by my name, to **d** it. 2930
Eze 7:22 for the robbers shall enter into it, and **d** it. 2490
 9: 7 **D** the house, and fill the courts with 2930
 20: 7 not yourselves with the idols of Egypt: 2930
 20:18 nor **d** yourselves with their idols: 2930
 22: 3 maketh idols against herself to **d** *herself*. 2930
 28: 7 and they shall **d** thy brightness. 2490
 33:26 and ye every one his neighbour's wife: 2930
 37:23 Neither shall they **d** themselves any more 2930
 43: 7 shall the house of Israel no more **d**, 2930
 44:25 they shall come at no dead person to **d** 2930
 44:25 had no husband, they may **d** themselves. 2930
Da 1: 8 himself with the portion of the king's 1351
 1: 8 the eunuchs that he might not **d** himself. 1351
Mt 15:18 forth from the heart; and they **d** the man. 2840
 15:20 These are *the things* which **d** a man: but 2840
Mk 7:15 a man, that entering into him can **d** him: 2840
 7:15 out of him, those are they that **d** the man. 2840
 7:18 entereth into the man, *it* cannot **d** him; 2840
 7:23 *things* come from within, and **d** the man. 2840
1Co 3:17 If any *man* **d** the temple of God, him shall 5351
1Ti 1:10 **them** that **d** themselves **with mankind**, 733
Jude 1: 8 Likewise also these *filthy* dreamers **d** 3392

DEFILED (71) [DEFILE]
Ge 34: 2 he took her, and lay with her, and **d** her. 6031
 34: 5 Jacob heard that he had **d** Dinah his 2930
 34:13 said, because he had **d** Dinah their sister. 2930
 34:27 the city, because they had **d** their sister. 2930
Lev 5: 3 *it be* that a man shall be **d** withal, 2930
 11:43 with them, that ye should be **d** thereby. 2930
 13:46 the plague *shall be* in him he shall be **d**; 2930
 15:32 seed goeth from him, and is **d** therewith; 2930
 18:24 nations are **d** which I cast out before you: 2930
 18:25 the land is **d**: therefore I do visit 2930
 18:27 *were* before you, and the land is **d**;) 2930
 19:31 seek after wizards, to be **d** by them: 2930
 21: 1 There shall none be **d** for the dead among 2930
 21: 3 had no husband; for her may he be **d**. 2930
Nu 5: 2 an issue, and whosoever is **d** by the dead: 2931
 5:13 she be **d**, and *there be* no witness against 2930
 5:14 he be jealous of his wife, and she be **d**: 2930
 5:14 be jealous of his wife, and she be not **d**: 2930
 5:20 if thou be **d**, and *some* man hath lain 2930
 5:27 *that*, if she be **d**, and have done trespass 2930
 5:28 if the woman be not **d**, but *be* clean; then 2930
 5:29 *another* instead of her husband, and is **d**; 2930
 6: 9 he hath **d** the head of his consecration; 2930
 6:12 be lost, because his separation was **d**. 2930
 9: 6 who were **d** by the dead body of a man, 2931
 9: 7 We *are* **d** by the dead body of a man: 2931
 19:20 he hath **d** the sanctuary of the LORD: 2930
Dt 21:23 that thy land be not **d**, which the LORD 2930
 22: 9 and the fruit of thy vineyard, be **d**. 6942
 24: 4 again to be his wife, after that she is **d**; 2930
2Ki 23: 8 the high places where the priests had 2930
 23:10 he **d** Topheth, which *is* in the valley of 2930
1Ch 5: 1 but, forasmuch as he **d** his father's bed, 2490
Ne 13:29 because they have **d** the priesthood, 1352
Job 16:15 upon my skin, and **d** my horn in the dust. 5953
Ps 74: 7 have **d** *by casting down* the dwelling 2490
 79: 1 thy holy temple have they **d**; they have 2930
 106:39 Thus were they **d** with their own works, 2930
Isa 24: 5 The earth also is **d** under the inhabitants 2610
 59: 3 For your hands are **d** with blood, 1351
Jer 2: 7 ye **d** my land, and made mine heritage an 2930
 3: 9 she **d** the land, and committed adultery 2610
 16:18 because they have **d** my land, they have 2490
 19:13 shall be **d** as the place of Tophet, because 2931
Eze 4:13 Israel eat their **d** bread among the 2931
 5:11 thou hast **d** my sanctuary with all thy 2930
 7:24 to cease; and their holy places shall be **d**. 2490
 18: 6 neither hath **d** his neighbour's wife, 2930
 18:11 mountains, and **d** his neighbour's wife, 2930
 18:15 of Israel, hath not **d** his neighbour's wife, 2930
 20:43 all your doings, wherein ye have been **d**; 2930
 22: 4 hast **d** *thyself* in thine idols which thou 2930
 22:11 hath lewdly **d** his daughter in law; 2930
 23: 7 doted: with all their idols she **d** herself. 2930
 23:13 I saw that she was **d**, *that* they took both 2930
 23:17 they **d** her with their whoredom, 2930
 23:38 have **d** my sanctuary in the same day, 2930
 28:18 Thou hast **d** thy sanctuaries by 2490
 36:17 they **d** it by their own way and by their 2930
 43: 8 they have even **d** my holy name by their 2930
Hos 5: 3 committest whoredom, *and* Israel is **d**. 2930
 6:10 *is* the whoredom of Ephraim, Israel is **d**. 2930
Mic 4:11 Let her be **d**, and let our eye look upon 2610
Mk 7: 2 some of his disciples eat bread with **d**, 2839
Jn 18:28 the judgment hall, lest they should be **d**; 3392
1Co 8: 7 and their conscience being weak is **d**. 3435
Tit 1:15 but unto them that are **d** and unbelieving 3392
 1:15 but even their mind and conscience is **d**. 3392
Heb 12:15 up trouble *you*, and thereby many be **d**; 3392
Rev 3: 4 Sardis, which have not **d** their garments; 3435
 14: 4 These are they which were not **d** with 3435

DEFILEDST (1) [DEFILE]
Ge 49: 4 then **d** thou *it*: he went up to my couch. 2490

DEFILETH (9) [DEFILE]
Ex 31:14 *every* one that **d** it shall surely be put to 2490
Nu 19:13 **d** the tabernacle of the LORD; 2930

Nu 35:33 wherein ye *are*: for blood it **d** the land: 2610
Mt 15:11 Not that which goeth into the mouth **d** a 2840
 15:11 cometh out of the mouth, this **d** a man. 2840
 15:20 to eat with unwashen hands **d** not a man. 2840
Mk 7:20 cometh out of the man, that **d** the man. 2840
Jas 3: 6 it **d** the whole body, and setteth on fire 4695
Rev 21:27 in no wise enter into it any *thing* that **d**, 2840

DEFORMED See CORRUPTION; SUPERFLUOUS

DEFRAUD (5) [DEFRAUDED]
Lev 19:13 shalt not **d** thy neighbour, neither rob 6231
Mk 10:19 **D** not, Honour thy father and mother. 650
1Co 6: 8 do wrong, and **d**, and that *your* brethren. 650
 7: 5 **D** you not one the other, except *it be* with 650
1Th 4: 6 beyond and **d** his brother in *any* matter: 4122

DEFRAUDED (4) [DEFRAUD]
1Sa 12: 3 or whom have I **d**? whom have I 6231
 12: 4 they said, Thou hast not **d** us, 6231
1Co 6: 7 do ye not rather *suffer yourselves* to be **d**? 650
2Co 7: 2 corrupted no *man*, we have **d** no *man*. 4122

DEFY (5) [DEFIED]
Nu 23: 7 curse me Jacob, and come, **d** Israel. 2194
 23: 8 or how shall I **d**, *whom* the LORD hath 2194
1Sa 17:10 I **d** the armies of Israel this day; 2778
 17:25 surely to **d** Israel is he come up: and it 2778
 17:26 that he should **d** the armies of the living 2778

DEGENERATE (1)
Jer 2:21 thou turned *into* the **d** plant of a strange 5494

DEGREE (7) [DEGREES]
1Ch 15:18 with them their brethren the **second d**, 4932
 17:17 according to the estate of a man of **high d**, 4609
Ps 62: 9 Surely **men of low d** *are* vanity, 120+1121
 62: 9 *and* **men of high d** *are* a lie: 376+1121
Lk 1:52 *their* seats, and exalted them of **low d**. 5011
1Ti 3:13 well purchase to themselves a good **d**, 898
Jas 1: 9 Let the brother of **low d** rejoice in that he 5011

DEGREES (24) [DEGREE]
2Ki 20: 9 shall the shadow go forward ten **d**, 4609
 20: 9 go forward ten degrees, or go back ten **d**? 4609
 20:10 thing for the shadow to go down ten **d**: 4609
 20:10 let the shadow return backward ten **d**. 4609
 20:11 he brought the shadow ten **d** backward, 4609
Ps 120: T A Song of **d**. 4609
 121: T A Song of **d**. 4609
 122: T A Song of **d** of David. 4609
 123: T A Song of **d**. 4609
 124: T A Song of **d** of David. 4609
 125: T A Song of **d**. 4609
 126: T A Song of **d**. 4609
 127: T A Song of **d** for Solomon. 4609
 128: T A Song of **d**. 4609
 129: T A Song of **d**. 4609
 130: T A Song of **d**. 4609
 131: T A Song of **d** of David. 4609
 132: T A Song of **d**. 4609
 133: T A Song of **d** of David. 4609
 134: T A Song of **d**. 4609
Isa 38: 8 I will bring again the shadow of the **d**, 4609
 38: 8 in the sun dial of Ahaz, ten **d** backward. 4609
 38: 8 So the sun returned ten **d**, by which 4609
 38: 8 degrees, by which it was gone down. 4609

DEHAVITES (1)
Ezr 4: 9 the Susanchites, the **D**, *and* the Elamites, 1723

DEITY See GODHEAD

DEKAR (1)
1Ki 4: 9 The son of **D**, in Makaz, and in Shaalbim, 1857

DELAIAH (6)
1Ch 24:18 The three and twentieth to **D**, the four 1806
Ezr 2:60 The children of **D**, the children of Tobiah, 1806
Ne 6:10 the son of **D** the son of Mehetabeel, 1806
 7:62 The children of **D**, the children of Tobiah, 1806
Jer 36:12 **D** the son of Shemaiah, and Elnathan 1806
 36:25 Nevertheless Elnathan and **D** and 1806

DELAY (3) [DELAYED, DELAYETH]
Ex 22:29 shalt not **d** *to offer the first of* thy ripe 309
Ac 9:38 desiring *him* that *he* would not **d** to come 3635
 25:17 were come hither, without any **d**, 311+4160

DELAYED (2) [DELAY]
Ex 32: 1 the people saw that Moses **d** to come 954
Ps 119:60 and **d** not to keep thy commandments. 4102

DELAYETH (2) [DELAY]
Mt 24:48 say in his heart, My lord **d** his coming; 5549
Lk 12:45 say in his heart, My lord **d** his coming; 5549

DELECTABLE (1)
Isa 44: 9 their *things* shall not profit; and they 2530

DELEGATION See AMBASSAGE

DELICACIES (1)
Rev 18: 3 rich through the abundance of her **d**. 4764

DELICATE (5) [DELICATELY, DELICATENESS, DELICATES, DELICIOUSLY]

Dt 28:54 very **d**, his eye shall be evil toward his　6028
28:56 The tender and **d** woman among you,　6028
Isa 47: 1 shalt no more be called tender and **d**.　6028
Jer 6: 2 of Zion to a comely and **d** woman.　6026
Mic 1:16 bald, and poll thee for thy **d** children;　8588

DELICATELY (4) [DELICATE]

1Sa 15:32 Agag came unto him **d**. And Agag said,　4574
Pr 29:21 He that **d bringeth up** his servant from a　6445
La 4: 5 They that did feed **d** are desolate　4574+3807.1
Lk 7:25 and live **d**, are in kings' courts.　5172

DELICATENESS (1) [DELICATE]

Dt 28:56 the sole of her foot upon the ground for **d**　6026

DELICATES (1) [DELICATE]

Jer 51:34 he hath filled his belly with my **d**, he hath　5730

DELICIOUSLY (2) [DELICATE]

Rev 18: 7 and **lived d**, so much torment and　4763
18: 9 fornication and **lived d** with her,　4763

DELIGHT (51) [DELIGHTED, DELIGHTEST, DELIGHTETH, DELIGHTS, DELIGHTSOME]

Ge 34:19 because he had **d** in Jacob's daughter:　2654
Nu 14: 8 If the Lord **d** in us, then he will bring us　2654
Dt 10:15 Only the Lord **had** a **d** in thy fathers to　2836
21:14 if thou have no **d** in her, then thou shalt　2654
1Sa 15:22 Hath the Lord **as great d** in burnt　2656
18:22 king hath **d** in thee, and all his servants　2654
2Sa 15:26 if he thus say, I have no **d** in thee;　2654
24: 3 doth my lord the king **d** in this thing?　2654
Est 2: 14 whom would the king **d** to do honour　2654
Job 22:26 shalt thou **have** thy **d** in the Almighty,　6026
27:10 Will he **d** himself in the Almighty? will he　6026
34: 9 profiteth a man nothing that he should **d**　7521
Ps 1: 2 his **d** is in the law of the Lord; and in his　2656
16: 3 to the excellent, in whom is all my **d**.　2656
37: 4 **D** thyself also in the Lord; and he shall　6026
37:11 shall **d** themselves in the abundance of　6026
40: 8 I to do thy will, O my God: yea, thy law　2654
62: 4 they **d** in lies: they bless with their mouth　7521
68:30 scatter thou the people that **d** in war.　2654
94:19 within me thy comforts **d** my soul.　8173
119:16 I will **d** myself in thy statutes: I will not　8173
119:24 Thy testimonies also are my **d** and　8191
119:35 of thy commandments; for therein do I **d**.　2654
119:47 I will **d** myself in thy commandments,　8173
119:70 heart is as fat as grease; but I **d** in thy law.　8173
119:77 that I may live: for thy law is my **d**.　8191
119:174 O Lord; and thy law is my **d**.　8191
Pr 1:22 the scorners **d** in their scorning,　2530
2:14 and **d** in the frowardness of the wicked;　1523
8:30 up with him: and I was daily his **d**,　8191
11: 1 to the Lord: but a just weight is his **d**.　7522
11:20 such as are upright in their way are his **d**.　7522
12:22 but they that deal truly are his **d**.　7522
15: 8 but the prayer of the upright is his **d**.　7522
16:13 Righteous lips are the **d** of kings;　7522
18: 2 A fool hath no **d** in understanding,　2654
19:10 **D** is not seemly for a fool; much less for a　8588
24:25 to them that rebuke him shall be **d**,　5276
29:17 rest; yea, he shall give **d** unto thy soul.　4574
SS 2: 3 sat down under his shadow **with great d**,　2530
Isa 1:11 I **d** not in the blood of bullocks.　2654
13:17 and as for gold, they shall not **d** in it.　2654
55: 2 good, and let your soul **d** itself in fatness.　6026
58: 2 seek me daily, and to know my ways,　2654
58: 2 they **take d** in approaching to God.　2654
58:13 call the sabbath a **d**, the holy of　6027
58:14 shalt thou **d** thyself in the Lord;　6026
Jer 6:10 them a reproach; they have no **d** in it.　2654
9:24 for in these things I **d**, saith the Lord.　2654
Mal 3: 1 messenger of the covenant, whom ye **d** in:　2655
Ro 7:22 For I **d** in the law of God after the inward　4913

DELIGHTED (12) [DELIGHT]

1Sa 19: 2 Jonathan Saul's son **d** much in David:　2654
2Sa 22:20 he delivered me, because he **d** in me.　2654
1Ki 10: 9 be the Lord thy God, which **d** in thee,　2654
2Ch 9: 8 which **d** in thee to set thee on his throne,　2654
Ne 9:25 and **d** themselves in thy great goodness.　5727
Est 2:14 except the king **d** in her, and that she　2654
Ps 18:19 he delivered me, because he **d** in me.　2654
22: 8 let him deliver him, seeing he **d** in him.　2654
109:17 as he **d** not in blessing, so let it be far　2654
Isa 65:12 and did choose that wherein I **d** not.　2654
66: 4 eyes, and chose that in which I **d** not.　2654
66:11 be **d** with the abundance of her glory.　6026

DELIGHTEST (1) [DELIGHT]

Ps 51:16 else would I give it: thou **d** not **in** burnt　7521

DELIGHTETH (14) [DELIGHT]

Est 6: 6 the man whom the king **d** to honour?　2654
6: 7 For the man whom the king **d** to honour,　2654
6: 9 man withal whom the king **d** to honour,　2654
6: 9 to the man whom the king **d** to honour.　2654
6:11 the man whom the king **d** to honour.　2654
Ps 37:23 by the Lord: and he **d** in his way.　2654
112: 1 that **d** greatly in his commandments.　2654
147:10 He **d** not in the strength of the horse:　2654
Pr 3:12 even as a father the son in whom he **d**.　7521

Isa 42: 1 uphold; mine elect, in whom my soul **d**;　7521
62: 4 for the Lord **d** in thee, and thy land shall　2654
66: 3 and their soul **d** in their abominations.　2654
Mic 7:18 his anger for ever, because he **d** in mercy.　2654
Mal 2:17 the sight of the Lord, and he **d** in them;　2654

DELIGHTFUL See GOODLIER; GOODLIEST; GOODLY

DELIGHTS (6) [DELIGHT]

2Sa 1:24 who clothed you in scarlet, with other **d**,　5730
Ps 119:92 Unless thy law had been my **d**, I should　8191
119:143 on me: yet thy commandments are my **d**.　8191
Pr 8:31 and my **d** were with the sons of men.　8191
Ecc 2: 8 and the **d** of the sons of men,　8588
SS 7: 6 and how pleasant art thou, O love, for **d**!　8588

DELIGHTSOME (1) [DELIGHT]

Mal 3:12 for ye shall be a **d** land, saith the Lord of　2656

DELILAH (6)

Jdg 16: 4 the valley of Sorek, whose name was **D**.　1807
16: 6 **D** said to Samson, Tell me, I pray thee,　1807
16:10 **D** said unto Samson, Behold, thou hast　1807
16:12 **D** therefore took new ropes, and bound　1807
16:13 **D** said unto Samson, Hitherto thou hast　1807
16:18 when **D** saw that he had told her all his　1807

DELIVER (296) [DELIVERANCE, DELIVERANCES, DELIVERED, DELIVEREDST, DELIVERER, DELIVEREST, DELIVERETH, DELIVERING, DELIVERY]

Ge 32:11 **D** me, I pray thee, from the hand of my　5337
37:22 their hands, to **d** him to his father again.　3807.1
40:13 thou shalt **d** Pharaoh's cup into his hand,　5414
42:34 true men: so will I **d** you your brother,　5414
42:37 him into my hand, and I will bring him　5414
Ex 3: 8 I am come down to **d** them out of the　5337
5:18 given you, yet shall ye **d** the tale of bricks.　5414
21:13 not in wait, but God **d** him into his hand;　579
22: 7 a man shall **d** unto his neighbour money　5414
22:10 If a man **d** unto his neighbour an ass,　5414
22:26 thou shalt **d** it unto him by that the sun　7725
23:31 for I will **d** the inhabitants of the land into　5414
Lev 26:26 they shall **d** you your bread **again** by　7725
Nu 21: 2 If thou wilt **indeed d** this people　5414+5414
35:25 the congregation shall **d** the slayer out of　5337
Dt 1:27 to **d** us into the hand of the Amorites,　5414
2:30 that he might **d** him into thy hand,　5414
3: 2 for I will **d** him, and all his people,　5414
7: 2 when the Lord thy God shall **d** them　5414
7:16 which the Lord thy God shall **d** thee;　5414
7:23 the Lord thy God shall **d** them unto thee,　5414
7:24 he shall **d** their kings into thine hand,　5414
19:12 him into the hand of the avenger of　5414
23:14 to **d** thee, and to give up thine enemies　5337
23:15 shalt not **d** unto his master the servant　5462
24:13 **In any case** thou shalt **d** him　7725+7725
25:11 the wife of the one draweth near for to **d**　5337
32:39 neither is there any that can **d** out of my　5337
Jos 2:13 they have, and **d** our lives from death.　5337
7: 7 to **d** us into the hand of the Amorites,　5414
8: 7 for the Lord your God will **d** it into your　5414
11: 6 will I **d** them **up** all slain before Israel:　5414
20: 5 shall not **d** the slayer **up** into his hand;　5462
Jdg 4: 7 and I will **d** him into thine hand.　5414
7: 7 and **d** the Midianites into thine hand:　5414
10:11 Did not I **d** you from the Egyptians,　5337
10:13 gods: wherefore I will **d** you no more.　3467
10:14 let them **d** you in the time of your　3467
10:15 thee; **d** us only, we pray thee, this day.　5337
11: 9 the Lord **d** them before me, shall I be　5414
11:30 If thou shalt **without fail d**　5414+5414
13: 5 he shall begin to **d** Israel out of the hand　3467
15:12 that we may **d** thee into the hand　5414
15:13 bind thee fast, and **d** thee into their hand;　5414
20:13 Now therefore **d** us the men, the children　5414
20:28 to morrow I will **d** them into thine hand.　5414
1Sa 4: 8 who shall **d** us out of the hand of these　5337
7: 3 he will **d** you out of the hand of　5337
7:14 the coasts thereof did Israel **d** out of　5337
12:10 now **d** us out of the hand of our enemies,　5337
12:21 vain things, which cannot profit nor **d**;　5337
14:37 wilt thou **d** them into the hand of Israel?　5414
17:37 he will **d** me out of the hand of this　5337
17:46 This day will the Lord **d** thee into mine　5462
23: 4 for I will **d** the Philistines into thine hand.　5414
23:11 Will the men of Keilah **d** me **up** into his　5462
23:12 Will the men of Keilah **d** me and my men　5462
23:12 And the Lord said, They will **d** thee **up**.　5462
23:20 our part shall be to **d** him into the king's　5462
24: 4 I will **d** thine enemy into thine hand,　5414
24:15 my cause, and **d** me out of thine hand.　8199
26:24 and let him **d** me out of all tribulation.　5337
28:19 Moreover the Lord will also **d** Israel　5414
28:19 the Lord also shall **d** the host of Israel　5414
30:15 nor **d** me into the hands of my master,　5462
2Sa 3:14 Saul's son, saying, **D** me my wife Michal,　5414
5:19 wilt thou **d** them into mine hand?　5414
5:19 I will **doubtless d** the Philistines　5414+5411
14: 7 they said, **D** him that smote his brother,　5414
14:16 to **d** his handmaid out of the hand of　5337
20:21 **d** him only, and I will depart from the city.　5414
1Ki 8:46 **d** them to the enemy, so that they carry　5414

1Ki 18: 9 that thou wouldest **d** thy servant into　5414
20: 5 Thou shalt **d** me thy silver, and thy gold,　5414
20:13 I will **d** it into thine hand this day;　5414
20:28 will I **d** all this great multitude into thine　5414
22: 6 for the Lord shall **d** it into the king's hand.　5414
22:12 for the Lord shall **d** it into the king's　5414
22:15 for the Lord shall **d** it into the hand of　5414
2Ki 3:10 to **d** them into the hand of Moab.　5414
3:13 will **d** them into the hand of Moab.　5414
3:18 will **d** the Moabites also into your hand.　5414
12: 7 but **d** it for the breaches of the house.　5414
17:39 he shall **d** you out of the hand of all your　5337
18:23 and I will **d** thee two thousand horses,　5414
18:29 for he shall not be able to **d** you out of his　5337
18:30 The Lord shall **surely d** us,　5337+5337
18:32 saying, The Lord will **d** us.　5337
18:35 that the Lord should **d** Jerusalem out of　5337
20: 6 I will **d** thee and this city out of the hand　5337
21:14 the hand into the hand of their enemies,　5414
22: 5 let them **d** it into the hand of the doers of　5414
1Ch 14:10 wilt thou **d** them into mine hand? And　5414
14:10 Go up; for I will **d** them into thine hand.　5414
16:35 us together, and **d** us from the heathen,　5337
2Ch 6:36 **d** them over before their enemies,　5414
18: 5 for God will **d** it into the king's hand.　5414
18:11 for the Lord shall **d** it into the hand of　5414
25:15 which could not **d** their own people out　5337
25:20 he might **d** them into the hand of their　5414
28:11 me therefore, and the **d** the captives **again**,　7725
32:11 The Lord our God shall **d** us out of　5337
32:13 able to **d** their lands out of mine hand?　5337
32:14 that could **d** his people out of mine hand,　5337
32:14 that your God should be able to **d** you out　5337
32:15 kingdom was able to **d** his people out of　5337
32:15 how much less shall your God **d** you out　5337
32:17 shall not the God of Hezekiah **d** his people　5337
Ezr 7:19 those **d** thou before the God of Jerusalem.　8000
Ne 9:28 many times didst thou **d** them according　5337
Job 5: 4 the gate, neither is there any to **d** them.　5337
5:19 He shall **d** thee in six troubles: yea,　5337
6:23 Or, **D** me from the enemy's hand? or,　4422
10: 7 is none that can **d** out of thine hand.　5337
22:30 He shall **d** the island of the innocent: and　4422
33:24 saith, **D** him from going down to the pit:　6308
33:28 He will **d** his soul from going into the pit,　6299
36:18 then a great ransom cannot **d** thee.　5186
Ps 6: 4 Return, O Lord, **d** my soul: O save me　2502
7: 1 let them that persecute me, and **d** me:　5337
7: 2 it in pieces, while there is none to **d**.　6403
17:13 **d** my soul from the wicked, which is thy　6403
22: 4 thee: they trusted, and thou didst **d** them.　6403
22: 8 He trusted on the Lord that he would **d**　6403
22: 8 let him **d** him, seeing he delighted in him.　5337
22:20 **D** my soul from the sword; my darling　5337
25:20 O keep my soul, and **d** me: let me not be　5337
27:12 **D** me not **over** unto the will of mine　5414
31: 1 be ashamed: **d** me in thy righteousness.　6403
31: 2 Bow down thine ear to me; **d** me speedily:　5337
31:15 **d** me from the hand of mine enemies,　5337
33:17 shall he **d** any by his great strength.　4422
33:19 To **d** their soul from death, and to keep　5337
37:40 the Lord shall help them, and **d** them:　6403
37:40 he shall **d** them from the wicked,　6403
39: 8 **D** me from all my transgressions: make　5337
40:13 Be pleased, O Lord, to **d** me: O Lord,　5337
41: 1 the Lord will **d** him in time of trouble.　4422
41: 2 thou wilt not **d** him unto the will of his　5414
43: 1 O **d** me from the deceitful and unjust man.　6403
50:15 I will **d** thee, and thou shalt glorify me.　2502
50:22 tear you in pieces, and there be none to **d**.　5337
51:14 **D** me from bloodguiltiness, O God,　5337
56:13 wilt not thou **d** my feet from falling, that　NIH
59: 1 **D** me from mine enemies, O my God:　5337
59: 2 **D** me from the workers of iniquity,　5337
69:14 **D** me out of the mire, and let me not sink:　5337
69:18 redeem it: **d** me because of mine enemies.　6299
70: 1 Make haste, O God, to **d** me; make haste　5337
71: 2 **D** me in thy righteousness, and cause me　5337
71: 4 **D** me, O my God, out of the hand of　6403
71:11 and take him; for there is none to **d** him.　5337
72:12 For he shall **d** the needy when he crieth;　5337
74:19 O **d** not the soul of thy turtledove unto	5414
79: 9 **d** us, and purge away our sins, for thy	5337
82: 4 **D** the poor and needy: rid them out of	6403
89:48 shall he **d** his soul from the hand of	4422
91: 3 Surely he shall **d** thee from the snare of	5337
91:14 his love upon me, therefore will I **d** him:	6403
91:15 in trouble; I will **d** him, and honour him.	2502
106:43 Many times did he **d** them;	5337
109:21 because thy mercy is good, **d** thou me.	5337
116: 4 O Lord, I beseech thee, **d** my soul.	4422
119:134 **D** me from the oppression of man: so will	6299
119:153 Consider mine affliction, and **d** me: for I	2502
119:154 Plead my cause, and **d** me: quicken my	1350
119:170 before thee: **d** me according to thy word.	5337
120: 2 **D** my soul, O Lord, from lying lips,	5337
140: 1 **D** me, O Lord, from the evil man:	2502
142: 6 **d** me from my persecutors; for they are	5337
143: 9 **D** me, O Lord, from mine enemies:	5337
144: 7 rid me, and **d** me out of great waters,	5337
144:11 me from the hand of strange children,	5337
Pr 2:12 To **d** thee from the way of the evil man,	5337
2:16 To **d** thee from the strange woman,	5337
4: 9 a crown of glory shall she **d** to thee.	4042
6: 3 Do this now, my son, and **d** thyself,	5337

Pr 6: 5 **D** thyself as a roe from the hand *of* — 5337
11: 6 The righteousness of the upright shall **d** — 5337
12: 6 the mouth of the upright shall **d** them. — 5337
19:19 if thou **d** *him*, yet thou must do *it* again. — 5337
23:14 the rod, and shalt **d** his soul from hell. — 5337
24:11 If thou forbear to **d** *them that are* drawn — 5337
Ecc 8: 8 neither shall wickedness **d** those that are — 4422
Isa 5:29 carry *it* away safe, and none shall **d** *it.* — 5337
19:20 and a great one, and he shall **d** them. — 5337
29:11 which *men* **d** to one that is learned, — 5414
31: 5 defending also he will **d** *it;* and — 5337
36:14 for he shall not be able to **d** you. — 5337
36:15 The Lord will **surely d** us: — 5337+5337
36:18 saying, The Lord will **d** us. — 5337+5337
36:20 that the Lord should **d** Jerusalem out of — 5337
38: 6 I will **d** thee and this city out of the hand — 5337
43:13 *there is* none that can **d** out of my hand: — 5337
44:17 and prayeth unto it, and saith, **D** me; — 5337
44:20 that he cannot **d** his soul, nor say, *Is there* — 5337
46: 2 they could not **d** the burden, — 4422
46: 4 will bear; even I will carry, and will **d** *you.* — 4422
47:14 shall not **d** themselves from the power — 5337
50: 2 or have I no power to **d**? behold, at my — 5337
57:13 thou criest, let thy companies **d** thee; — 5337
Jer 1: 8 for I *am* with thee to **d** thee, saith — 5337
1:19 I *am* with thee, saith the Lord, to **d** thee. — 5337
15: 9 the residue of them will I **d** to the sword — 5414
15:20 I *am* with thee to save thee and to **d** thee, — 5337
15:21 will I **d** thee out of the hand of the wicked, — 5337
18:21 **d** up their children to the famine, — 5414
20: 5 Moreover I will **d** all the strength of this — 5414
21: 7 I will **d** Zedekiah king of Judah, and his — 5414
21:12 **d** *him that is* spoiled out of the hand of — 5337
22: 3 **d** the spoiled out of the hand of — 5337
24: 9 I will **d** them to be removed into all — 5414
29:18 will **d** them to be removed to all — 5414
29:21 I will **d** them into the hand of — 5414
38:19 lest they **d** me into their hand, — 5414
38:20 They shall not **d** thee. Obey, I beseech — 5337
39:17 I will **d** thee in that day, saith the Lord: — 5337
39:18 For I will **surely d** thee, — 4422+4422
42:11 to save you, and to **d** you from his hand. — 5337
43: 3 to **d** us into the hand of the Chaldeans, — 5414
43:11 *and* **d** such *as are* for death to death; — NIH
46:26 I will **d** them into the hand of those that — 5414
51: 6 of Babylon, and **d** every man his soul: — 4422
51:45 **d** ye every man his soul from the fierce — 4422
La 5: 8 *there is* none that doth **d** *us* out of their — 6561
Eze 7:19 their gold shall not be able to **d** them in — 5337
11: 9 **d** you into the hands of strangers, — 5414
13:21 **d** my people out of your hand, — 5337
13:23 for I will **d** my people out of your hand: — 5337
14:14 they should **d** *but* their own souls by their — 5337
14:16 they shall **d** neither sons nor daughters; — 5337
14:18 they shall **d** neither sons nor daughters, — 5337
14:20 they shall **d** neither son nor daughter; — 5337
14:20 **d** their own souls by their righteousness. — 5337
21:31 **d** thee into the hand of brutish men, — 5414
23:28 I *will* **d** thee into the hand *of them* whom — 5414
25: 4 I *will* **d** thee to the men of the east for a — 5414
25: 7 and will **d** thee for a spoil to the heathen; — 5414
33: 5 he that taketh warning shall **d** his soul. — 4422
33:12 not **d** him in the day of his transgression: — 5337
34:10 for I will **d** my flock from their mouth, — 5337
34:12 will **d** them out of all places where they — 5337
Da 3:15 who *is* that God that shall **d** you out of — 7804
3:17 our God whom we serve *is* able to **d** us — 7804
3:17 he will **d** *us* out of thine hand, O king. — 7804
3:29 there is no other God that can **d** after this — 5338
6:14 and set *his* heart on Daniel to **d** him: — 7804
6:14 till the going down of the sun to **d** him. — 5338
6:16 thou servest continually, he will **d** thee. — 7804
6:20 able to **d** thee from the lions? — 7804
8: 4 *was there any* that could **d** out of his — 5337
8: 7 was none that could **d** the ram out of his — 5337
Hos 2:10 and none shall **d** her out of mine hand. — 5337
11: 8 *how* shall I **d** thee, Israel? how shall I — 4042
Am 1: 6 whole captivity, to **d** *them* **up** to Edom: — 5462
2:14 neither shall the mighty **d** himself: — 4422
2:15 *he that is* swift of foot shall not **d** *himself:* — 4422
2:15 shall he that rideth the horse **d** himself. — 4422
6: 8 I **d** up the city with all that is therein. — 5462
Jnh 4: 6 over his head, to **d** him from his grief. — 5337
Mic 5: 6 thus shall he **d** *us* from the Assyrian, — 5337
5: 8 and teareth in pieces, and none can **d**. — 5337
6:14 thou shalt take hold, but shalt not **d**; — 6403
Zep 1:18 **d** them in the day of the Lord's wrath; — 5337
Zec 2: 7 Deliver thyself, O Zion, that dwellest *with* — 4422
11: 6 I *will* **d** the men every one into his — 4672
11: 6 and out of their hand I will not **d** *them.* — 5337
Mt 5:25 lest at any time the adversary **d** thee to — 3860
5:25 and the judge **d** thee to the officer, — 3860
6:13 not into temptation, but **d** us from evil: — 4506
10:17 for they will **d** you **up** to the councils, — 3860
10:19 But when they **d** you **up**, take no thought — 3860
10:21 And the brother shall **d** **up** the brother to — 3860
20:19 And shall **d** him to the Gentiles to mock, — 3860
24: 9 Then shall they **d** you **up** to be afflicted, — 3860
26:15 ye give me, and I will **d** him unto you? — 3860
27:43 let him **d** him now, if he will have him: — 4506
Mk 10:33 to death, and shall **d** him to the Gentiles: — 3860
13: 9 for they shall **d** you **up** to councils; — 3860
13:11 when they shall lead *you*, and **d** you **up**, — 3860
Lk 11: 4 not into temptation; but **d** us from evil. — 4506
12:58 and the judge **d** thee to the officer, — 3860

Lk 20:20 *so they* might **d** him unto the power and — 3860
Ac 7:25 by his hand would **d** them: — 1325+4991
7:34 and am come down to **d** them. — 1807
21:11 shall **d** *him* into the hands of the Gentiles. — 3860
25:11 accuse me, no *man* may **d** me unto them. — 5483
25:16 is not the manner of the Romans to **d** any — 5483
Ro 7:24 who shall **d** me from the body of this — 4506
1Co 5: 5 To **d** such a one unto Satan for — 3860
2Co 1:10 us from so great a death, and doth **d**: — 4506
1:10 in whom we trust that he will yet **d** *us;* — 4506
Gal 1: 4 that he might **d** us from this present evil — 1807
2Ti 4:18 And the Lord shall **d** me from every evil — 4506
Heb 2:15 And *d* them who through fear of death — 525
2Pe 2: 9 The Lord knoweth *how to* **d** the godly — 4506

DELIVERANCE (16) [DELIVER]

Ge 45: 7 and to save your lives by a great **d**. — 6413
Jdg 15:18 Thou hast given this great **d** into the hand — 8668
2Ki 5: 1 by him the Lord had given **d** unto Syria: — 8668
13:17 The arrow of the Lord's **d**, — 8668
13:17 and the arrow of **d** from Syria: — 8668
1Ch 11:14 and the Lord saved *them by* a great **d**. — 8668
2Ch 12: 7 them, but I will grant them some **d**; — 6413
Ezr 9:13 and hast given us *such* **d** as this; — 6413
Est 4:14 *d* arise to the Jews from another place; — 2020
Ps 18:50 Great **d** giveth he to his king: — 3444
32: 7 shalt compass me about *with* songs of **d**. — 6405
Isa 26:18 we have not wrought any **d** *in* the earth; — 3444
Joel 2:32 in mount Zion and in Jerusalem shall be **d**, — 6413
Ob 1:17 upon mount Zion shall be **d**, and there — 6413
Lk 4:18 to preach **d** to the captives, and recovering — 859
Heb 11:35 and others were tortured, not accepting **d**; — 629

DELIVERANCES (1) [DELIVER]

Ps 44: 4 my King, O God: command **d** for Jacob. — 3444

DELIVERED (291) [DELIVER]

Ge 9: 2 of the sea; into your hand **are** they **d**. — 5414
14:20 which hath **d** thine enemies into thy hand. — 4042
25:24 when her days to be **d** were fulfilled, — 3205
32:16 he **d** *them* into the hand of his servants, — 5414
37:21 heard *it*, and he **d** him out of their hands; — 5337
Ex 1:19 **d** ere the midwives come in unto them. — 3205
2:19 An Egyptian **d** us out of the hand of — 5337
5:23 hast thou **d** thy people **at all**. — 5337+5337
12:27 he smote the Egyptians, and **d** our houses. — 5337
18: 4 and **d** me from the sword of Pharaoh: — 5337
18: 8 by the way, and *how* the Lord **d** them. — 5337
18: 9 whom he had **d** out of the hand of — 5337
18:10 who hath **d** you out of the hand of — 5337
18:10 who hath **d** the people from under the — 5337
Lev 6: 2 in *that which was* **d** him **to keep**, — 6487
6: 4 which was *d* him **to keep**, — 854+6485+6487
26:25 ye shall be **d** into the hand of the enemy. — 5414
Nu 21: 3 voice of Israel, and **d up** the Canaanites; — 5414
21:34 for I have **d** him into thy hand, and all his — 5414
31: 5 So there were **d** out of the thousands of — 4560
Dt 2:33 the Lord our God **d** him before us; — 5414
2:36 for us: the Lord our God **d** all unto us: — 5414
3: 3 So the Lord our God **d** into our hands — 5414
5:22 two tables of stone, and **d** them unto me. — 5414
9:10 the Lord **d** unto me two tables of stone — 5414
20:13 when the Lord thy God hath **d** it into — 5414
21:10 the Lord thy God hath **d** them into thine — 5414
31: 9 **d** it unto the priests the sons of Levi, — 5414
Jos 2:24 Truly the Lord hath **d** into our hands all — 5414
9:26 them out of the hand of the children of — 5337
10: 8 for I have **d** them into thine hand; — 5414
10:12 **d up** the Amorites before the children of — 5414
10:19 for the Lord your God hath **d** them into — 5414
10:30 the Lord **d** it also, and the king thereof, — 5414
10:32 the Lord **d** Lachish into the hand of — 5414
11: 8 the Lord **d** them into the hand of Israel, — 5414
21:44 the Lord **d** all their enemies into their — 5414
22:31 ye have **d** the children of Israel out of — 5337
24:10 you still: so I **d** you out of his hand. — 5337
24:11 Jebusites; and I have **d** them into your — 5414
Jdg 1: 2 behold, I have **d** the land into his hand. — 5414
1: 4 the Lord **d** the Canaanites and — 5414
2:14 he **d** them into the hands of spoilers that — 5414
2:16 which **d** them out of the hand of those — 3467
2:18 **d** them out of the hand of their enemies — 5414
2:23 neither **d** he them into the hand of Joshua. — 5414
3: 9 who **d** them, *even* Othniel the son of — 3467
3:10 the Lord **d** Chushan-rishathaim king of — 5414
3:28 for the Lord hath **d** your enemies — 5414
3:31 men with an ox goad; and he also **d** Israel. — 3467
4:14 the Lord hath **d** Sisera into thine hand: — 5414
5:11 *They that are* **d** from the noise of archers — NIH
6: 1 the Lord **d** them into the hand of Midian — 5414
6: 9 I **d** you out of the hand of the Egyptians, — 5337
6:13 and **d** us into the hands of the Midianites. — 5414
7: 9 the host; for I have **d** it into thine hand. — 5414
7:14 *for* into his hand hath God **d** Midian, — 5414
7:15 for the Lord hath **d** into your hand — 5414
8: 3 God hath **d** into your hands the princes of — 5414
8: 7 Therefore when the Lord hath **d** Zebah — 5414
8:22 thou hast **d** us from the hand of Midian. — 3467
8:34 who had **d** them out of the hands of all — 5337
9:17 and **d** you out of the hand of Midian: — 5337
10:12 to me, and I **d** you out of their hand. — 3467
11:21 the Lord God of Israel **d** Sihon and all — 5414
11:32 and the Lord **d** them into his hands. — 5414
12: 2 called you, ye **d** me not out of their hands. — 3467
12: 3 when I saw that ye **d** *me* not, I put my life — 3467

Jdg 12: 3 and the Lord **d** them into my hand: — 5414
13: 1 the Lord **d** them into the hand of — 5414
16:23 Our god hath **d** Samson our enemy into — 5414
16:24 god hath **d** into our hands our enemy, — 5414
1Sa 4:19 was with child, *near* to be **d**: — 3205
10:18 **d** you out of the hand of the Egyptians, — 5337
12:11 **d** you out of the hand of your enemies on — 5337
14:10 for the Lord hath **d** them into our hand: — 5414
14:12 for the Lord hath **d** them into the hand — 5414
14:48 **d** Israel out of the hands of them that — 5337
17:35 smote him, and **d** *it* out of his mouth: — 5337
17:37 The Lord that **d** me out of the paw of — 5234
23: 7 said, God hath **d** him into mine hand; — 5414
23:14 day, but God **d** him not into his hand. — 5414
24:10 **d** thee to day into mine hand in the cave: — 5414
24:18 forasmuch as when the Lord had **d** me — 5462
26: 8 God hath **d** thine enemy into thine hand — 5462
26:23 for the Lord **d** thee into *my* hand to day, — 5414
30:23 the company that came against us into — 5414
2Sa 3: 8 have not **d** thee into the hand of David, — 4672
10:10 the rest of the people he **d** into the hand — 5414
12: 7 and I **d** thee out of the hand of Saul, — 5337
16: 8 the Lord hath **d** the kingdom into — 5414
18:28 which hath **d up** the men that lift up their — 5462
19: 9 he is out of the hand of the Philistines, — 4422
21: 6 Let seven men of his sons be **d** unto us, — 5414
21: 9 **d** them into the hands of the Gibeonites, — 5414
22: 1 **d** him out of the hand of all his enemies, — 5337
22:18 He **d** me from my strong enemy, — 5337
22:20 he **d** me, because he delighted in me. — 2502
22:44 Thou also hast **d** me from the strivings of — 6403
22:49 thou hast **d** me from the violent man. — 5337
1Ki 3:17 I was **d** of a child with her in the house. — 3205
3:18 to pass the third day after that I was **d**, — 3205
3:18 delivered, that this woman was **d** also: — 3205
13:26 the Lord hath **d** him unto the lion, — 5414
15:18 and **d** them into the hand of his servants: — 5414
17:23 the house, and **d** him unto his mother: — 5414
2Ki 12:15 into whose hand they **d** the money to be — 5414
13: 3 he **d** them into the hand of Hazael king of — 5414
17:20 and **d** them into the hand of spoilers, — 5414
18:30 this city shall not be **d** into the hand of — 5414
18:33 **d** at all his land out of the hand of — 5337+5337
18:34 have they **d** Samaria out of mine hand? — 5337
18:35 have **d** their country out of mine hand, — 5337
19:10 Jerusalem shall not be **d** into the hand of — 5337
19:11 them utterly: and shalt thou be **d**? — 5337
19:12 Have the gods of the nations **d** them — 5337
22: 7 of the money that was **d** into their hand, — 5414
22: 9 have **d** it into the hand of them that do — 5414
22:10 Hilkiah the priest hath **d** me a book. — 5414
1Ch 5:20 the Hagarites were **d** into their hand, — 5414
11:14 and **d** it, and slew the Philistines; — 5337
16: 7 on that day David **d** first *this psalm* to — 5414
19:11 the rest of the people he **d** unto the hand — 5414
2Ch 13:16 and God **d** them into their hand. — 5414
16: 8 on the Lord, he **d** them into thine hand. — 5414
18:14 and they shall be **d** into your hand. — 5414
23: 9 Moreover Jehoiada the priest **d** to — 5414
24:24 the Lord **d** a very great host into their — 5414
28: 5 Wherefore the Lord his God **d** him into — 5414
28: 5 he was also **d** into the hand of the king of — 5414
28: 9 he hath **d** them into your hand, and ye — 5414
29: 8 Jerusalem, and he hath **d** them to trouble, — 5414
32:17 have not **d** their people out of mine hand, — 5337
34: 9 they **d** the money that was brought *into* — 5414
34:15 And Hilkiah **d** the book to Shaphan. — 5414
34:17 have **d** it into the hand of the overseers, — 5414
Ezr 5:14 they *were* **d** unto *one*, whose name *was* — 3052
8:31 he **d** us from the hand of the enemy, — 5337
8:36 they **d** the king's commissions unto — 5414
9: 7 been **d** into the hand of the kings of — 5414
Est 6: 9 horse be **d** to the hand of one of the king's — 5414
Job 16:11 God hath **d** me to the ungodly, — 5462
22:30 and it is **d** by the pureness of thine hands. — 4422
23: 7 so should I be **d** for ever from my judge. — 6403
29:12 Because I **d** the poor that cried, — 4422
Ps 7: 4 I have **d** him that without cause is mine — 2502
18: 1 **d** him from the hand of all his enemies, — 5337
18:17 He **d** me from my strong enemy, — 5337
18:19 he **d** me, because he delighted in me. — 2502
18:43 Thou hast **d** me from the strivings of — 6403
18:48 thou hast **d** me from the violent man. — 5337
22: 5 They cried unto thee, and were **d**: — 4422
33:16 a mighty *man* is not **d** by much strength. — 5337
34: 4 he heard me, and **d** me from all my fears. — 5337
54: 7 For he hath **d** me out of all trouble: and — 5337
55:18 He hath **d** my soul in peace from the — 6299
56:13 For thou hast **d** my soul from death: *wilt* — 5337
60: 5 That thy beloved may be **d**; save *with* thy — 2502
69:14 let me be **d** from them that hate me, — 5337
78:42 *nor* the day when he **d** them from — 6299
78:61 his strength into captivity, and his glory — 5674
81: 6 burden: his hands were **d** from the pots. — 5674
81: 7 Thou calledst in trouble, and I **d** thee; — 2502
86:13 thou hast **d** my soul from the lowest hell. — 5337
107: 6 *and* he **d** them out of their distresses. — 5337
107:20 and **d** them from their destructions. — 5337
108: 6 That thy beloved may be **d**: save *with* thy — 2502
116: 8 For thou hast **d** my soul from death, mine — 2502
Pr 11: 8 The righteous is **d** out of trouble, — 2502
11: 9 through knowledge shall the just be **d**. — 2502
11:21 the seed of the righteous shall be **d**. — 4422
28:26 but whoso walketh wisely, he shall be **d**. — 4422
Ecc 9:15 man, and he by his wisdom **d** the city; — 4422

D

Isa 20: 6 whither we flee for help to be **d** from | 5337
29:12 the book is **d** to *him* that is not learned, | 5414
34: 2 he hath **d** them to the slaughter. | 5414
36:15 this city shall not be **d** into the hand of | 5414
36:18 Hath any of the gods of the nations **d** his | 5337
36:19 and have they **d** Samaria out of my hand? | 5337
36:20 that have **d** their land out of my hand, | 5337
37:11 them utterly; and shalt thou be **d**? | 5337
37:12 Have the gods of the nations **d** them | 5337
38:17 hast in love to my soul *d it* from the pit | NIH
49:24 from the mighty, or the lawful captive **d**? | 4422
49:25 and the prey of the terrible shall be **d**: | 4422
66: 7 her pain came, she was **d** of a man child. | 4422

Jer 7:10 We are **d** to do all these abominations? | 5337
20:13 for he hath **d** the soul of the poor from | 5337
32: 4 **surely** be **d** into the hand of | 5414+5414
32:16 Now when I had **d** the evidence of | 5414
32:36 It shall be **d** into the hand of the king of | 5414
34: 3 shalt surely be taken, and be **d** into his hand; | 5414
37:17 thou shalt be **d** into the hand of the king | 5414
46:24 she shall be **d** into the hand of the people | 5414

La 1:14 fall, I shall not be able to rise up. *their*hand, | 5414
Eze 3:19 in his iniquity; but thou hast **d** thy soul. | 5337
3:21 he is warned; also thou hast **d** thy soul. | 5337
14:16 they only shall be **d**, but the land shall be | 5337
14:18 but they only shall be **d** themselves. | 5337
16:21 **d** them to cause them to pass through | 5414
16:27 **d** thee unto the will of them that hate | 5414
17:15 or shall he break the covenant, and be **d**? | 4422
23: 9 Wherefore I have **d** her into the hand of | 5414
31:11 him into the hand of the mighty one of | 5414
31:14 for they are all **d** unto death, to the nether | 5414
32:20 she is **d** *to* the sword: draw her and all | 5414
33: 9 in his iniquity; but thou hast **d** thy soul. | 5337
34:27 **d** them out of the hand of those that | 5337

Da 3:28 **d** his servants that trusted in him, | 7804
6:27 who hath **d** Daniel from the power of | 7804
12: 1 at that time thy people shall be **d**, every | 4422

Joel 2:32 call on the name of the LORD shall be **d**: | 4422
Am 1: 9 they **d up** the whole captivity to Edom, | 5462
9: 1 he that escapeth of them shall not be **d**. | 4422
Ob 1:14 neither shouldest thou have **d up** those of | 5462
Mic 4:10 go *even* to Babylon; there shalt thou be **d**; | 5337
Hab 2: 9 that *he* may be **d** from the power of evil! | 5337
Mal 3:15 yea, *they* that tempt God are even **d**. | 4422

Mt 11:27 All *things* are **d** unto me of my Father: | 3860
18:34 was wroth, and **d** him to the tormentors, | 3860
25:14 own servants, and **d** unto them his goods. | 3860
27: 2 and **d** him to Pontius Pilate the governor. | 3860
27:18 he knew that for envy they had **d** him. | 3860
27:26 scourged Jesus, he **d** *him* to be crucified. | 3860
27:58 Then Pilate commanded the body to be **d**. | 591

Mk 7:13 through your tradition, which ye have **d**: | 3860
9:31 Son of man is **d** into the hands of men, | 3860
10:33 the Son of man shall be **d** unto the chief | 3860
15: 1 carried *him* away, and **d** *him* to Pilate. | 3860
15:10 For he knew that the chief priests had **d** | 3860
15:15 released Barabbas unto them, and **d** Jesus, | 3860

Lk 1: 2 Even as they **d** *them* us, which from | 3860
1:57 full time came that she should be **d**; | 5088
1:74 that *we* being **d** out of the hand of our | 4506
2: 6 were accomplished that she should be **d**. | 5088
4: 6 for *that* is **d** unto me; and to whomsoever | 3860
4:17 And there was **d** unto him the book of | 1929
7:15 to speak. And he **d** him to his mother. | 1325
9:42 the child, and **d** him **again** to his father. | 591
9:44 the Son of man shall be **d** into the hands | 3860
10:22 All *things* are **d** to me of my Father: and | 3860
12:58 give diligence that *thou* mayest be **d** from | 525
18:32 For he shall be **d** unto the Gentiles, | 3860
19:13 **d** them ten pounds, and said unto them, | 1325
23:25 had desired; but he **d** Jesus to their will. | 3860
24: 7 The Son of man must be **d** into the hands | 3860
24:20 rulers **d** him to be condemned to death, | 3860

Jn 16:21 but as soon as she is **d** of the child, | 1080
18:30 we would not have **d** him **up** unto thee. | 3860
18:35 and the chief priests have **d** thee unto me: | 3860
18:36 that I should not be **d** to the Jews: | 3860
19:11 that **d** me unto thee hath the greater sin. | 3860
19:16 Then he **d** him therefore unto them to be | 3860

Ac 2:23 being **d** by the determinate counsel and | 1560
3:13 whom ye **d up**, and denied him in the | 3860
6:14 shall change the customs which Moses **d** | 1807
7:10 And **d** him out of all his afflictions, | 1807
12: 4 **d** *him* to four quaternions of soldiers to | 3860
12:11 and hath **d** me out of the hand of Herod, | 1807
15:30 the multitude together, they **d** the epistle: | 1929
16: 4 they **d** them the decrees for to keep, | 1929
23:33 Cesarea, and **d** the epistle to the governor, | 325
27: 1 they **d** Paul and certain other prisoners | 3860
28:16 centurion **d** the prisoners to the captain | 3860
28:17 *yet* was I **d** prisoner from Jerusalem into | 3860

Ro 4:25 was **d** for our offences, and was raised | 3860
6:17 *that* form of doctrine which was **d** you. | 3860
7: 6 now we are **d** from the law, *that* being | 2673
8:21 Because the creature itself also shall be **d** | 1659
8:32 but his own Son, but **d** him **up** for us all, | 3860
15:31 That I may be **d** from them that do not | 4506

1Co 11: 2 keep the ordinances, as I **d** *them* to you. | 3860
11:23 of the Lord *that* which also I **d** unto you, | 3860
15: 3 For I **d** unto you first *of all* that which I | 3860
15:24 when he shall have **d up** the kingdom to | 3860

2Co 1:10 Who **d** us from so great a death, | 4506
4:11 For we which live are alway **d** unto death | 3860

Col 1:13 hath **d** us from the power of darkness, | 4506

1Th 1:10 which **d** us from the wrath to come. | 4506
2Th 3: 2 And that we may be **d** from unreasonable | 4506
1Ti 1:20 whom I have **d** unto Satan, that they may | 3860
2Ti 4: 6 but of them all the Lord **d** me. | 4506
4:17 and I was **d** out of the mouth of the lion. | 4506
Heb 11:11 was **d** of a child when *she* was past age, | 5088
2Pe 2: 4 hell, and **d** them **into** chains of darkness, | 3860
2: 7 And **d** just Lot, vexed with the filthy | 4506
2:21 the holy commandment **d** unto them. | 3860
Jude 1: 3 faith which was once **d** unto the saints. | 3860
Rev 12: 2 travailing in birth, and pained to be **d**, | 5088
12: 4 the woman which was ready to be **d**, | 5088
20:13 hell **d up** the dead which were in them: | 1325

DELIVEREDST (3) [DELIVER]
Ne 9:27 Therefore thou **d** them into the hand of | 5414
Mt 25:20 saying, Lord, thou **d** unto me five talents: | 3860
25:22 said, Lord, thou **d** unto me two talents: | 3860

DELIVERER (10) [DELIVER]
Jdg 3: 9 the LORD raised up a **d** to the children of | 3467
3:15 the LORD raised them up a **d**, Ehud | 3467
18:28 *there* was no **d**, because *it* was far from | 5337
2Sa 22: 2 is my rock, and my fortress, and my **d**; | 6403
Ps 18: 2 is my rock, and my fortress, and my **d**; | 6403
40:17 thou *art* my help and my **d**; make no | 6403
70: 5 thou *art* my help and my **d**; O LORD, | 6403
144: 2 my high tower, and my **d**; my shield, | 6403
Ac 7:35 a **d** by the hand of the angel which | 3086
Ro 11:26 There shall come out of Sion the **D**, | 4506

DELIVEREST (2) [DELIVER]
Ps 35:10 which **d** the poor from him that is too | 5337
Mic 6:14 *that* which thou **d** will I give up to | 6403

DELIVERETH (13) [DELIVER]
Job 36:15 He **d** the poor in his affliction, | 2502
Ps 18:48 He **d** me from mine enemies: yea, | 6403
34: 7 about them that fear him, and **d** them. | 2502
34:17 and **d** them out of all their troubles. | 5337
34:19 but the LORD **d** him out of them all. | 5337
97:10 he **d** them out of the hand of the wicked. | 5337
144:10 who **d** David his servant from the hurtful | 6475
Pr 10: 2 but righteousness **d** from death. | 5337
11: 8 of wrath: but righteousness **d** from death. | 5337
14:25 A true witness **d** souls: but a deceitful | 5337
31:24 and **d** girdles unto the merchant. | 5414
Isa 5:29 for a prey, and none **d**; *for* a spoil, | 5337
Da 6:27 He **d** and rescueth, and he worketh signs | 7804

DELIVERING (3) [DELIVER]
Lk 21:12 you, **d** *you* **up** to *the* synagogues, | 3860
Ac 22: 4 binding and **d** into prisons both men and | 3860
26:17 **D** thee from the people, and *from* | 1807

DELIVERY (1) [DELIVER]
Isa 26:17 that draweth near the time of her **d**, is in | 3205

DELUSION (1) [DELUSIONS]
2Th 2:11 this cause God shall send them strong **d**, | 4106

DELUSIONS (1) [DELUSION]
Isa 66: 4 I also will choose their **d**, and will bring | 8586

DEMAND (4) [DEMANDED]
Job 38: 3 for I will **d** of thee, and answer thou me. | 7592
40: 7 will **d** of thee, and declare thou unto me. | 7592
42: 4 will **d** of thee, and declare thou unto me. | 7592
Da 4:17 and the **d** *by* the word of the holy ones: | 7595

DEMANDED (7) [DEMAND]
Ex 5:14 had set over them, were beaten, *and* **d**, | 559
2Sa 11: 7 David *of him* how Joab did, and how | 7592
Da 2:27 The secret which the king hath **d** cannot | 7593
Mt 2: 4 **d** of them where Christ should be born. | 4441
Lk 3:14 And the soldiers likewise **d** of him, saying, | 1905
17:20 And when he was **d** of the Pharisees, | 1905
Ac 21:33 **d** who he was, and what he had done. | 4441

DEMAS (3)
Col 4:14 the beloved physician, and **D**, greet you. | 1214
2Ti 4:10 For **D** hath forsaken me, having loved *this* | 1214
Phm 1:24 Marcus, Aristarchus, **D**, Lucas, | 1214

DEMETRIUS (3)
Ac 19:24 For a certain *man* named **D**, a silversmith, | 1216
19:38 Wherefore if **D**, and the craftsmen which | 1216
3Jn 1:12 **D** hath good report of all *men*, and of | 1216

DEMON; DEMONS See DEVIL; DEVILS

DEMONSTRATION (1)
1Co 2: 4 but in **d** of the Spirit and of power: | 585

DEN (19) [DENS]
Ps 10: 9 He lieth in wait secretly as a lion in his **d**: | 5520
Isa 11: 8 shall put his hand on the cockatrice' **d**. | 3975
Jer 7:11 become a **d** of robbers in your eyes? | 4631
9:11 Jerusalem heaps, *and* a **d** of dragons; | 4583
10:22 of Judah desolate, *and* a **d** of dragons. | 4583
Da 6: 7 King, he shall be cast into the **d** of lions. | 1358
6:12 O king, shall be cast into the **d** of lions? | 1358
6:16 and cast *him* into the **d** of lions. | 1358
6:17 and laid upon the mouth of the **d**; | 1358
6:19 and went in haste unto the **d** of lions. | 1358
6:20 when he came to the **d**, he cried with a | 1358

Da 6:23 *they* should take Daniel up out of the **d**. | 1358
6:23 So Daniel was taken up out of the **d**, | 1358
6:24 they cast *them* into the **d** of lions, them, | 1358
6:24 or ever they came at the bottom of the **d**, | 1358
Am 3: 4 will a young lion cry out of his **d**, if he | 4585
Mt 21:13 but ye have made it a **d** of thieves. | 4693
Mk 11:17 but ye have made it a **d** of thieves. | 4693
Lk 19:46 but ye have made it a **d** of thieves. | 4693

DENARII See PENCE

DENARIUS See PENNY

DENIED (19) [DENY]
Ge 18:15 Sarah **d**, saying, I laughed not; for she was | 3584
1Ki 20: 7 and for my gold; and I **d** him not. | 4513
Job 31:28 for I should have **d** the God *that is* above. | 3584
Mt 26:70 he **d** before *them* all, saying, I know not | 720
26:72 again he **d** with an oath, I do not know | 720
Mk 14:68 But he **d**, saying, I know not, neither | 720
14:70 he **d** *it* again. And a little after, they that | 720
Lk 8:45 When all **d**, Peter and they that were with | 720
12: 9 he that **denieth** me before men shall be **d** | 533
22:57 he **d** him, saying, Woman, I know him | 720
Jn 1:20 he confessed, and **d** not; but confessed, | 720
13:38 shall not crow, till thou hast **d** me thrice. | 533
18:25 of his disciples? He **d** *it*, and said, I am not. | 720
18:27 Peter then **d** again: and immediately *the* | 720
Ac 3:13 and **d** him in the presence of Pilate, | 720
3:14 But ye **d** the Holy One and the Just, | 720
1Ti 5: 8 he hath **d** the faith, and is worse than an | 720
Rev 2:13 fast my name, and hast not **d** my faith, | 720
3: 8 kept my word, and hast not **d** my name. | 720

DENIETH (4) [DENY]
Lk 12: 9 he that **d** me before men shall be denied | 720
1Jn 2:22 a liar but he that **d** that Jesus is the Christ? | 720
2:22 is antichrist, that **d** the Father and the Son. | 720
2:23 Whosoever **d** the Son, the same hath not | 720

DENOUNCE (1)
Dt 30:18 I **d** unto you *this* day, that ye shall surely | 5046

DENOUNCED See UPBRAID; UPBRAIDED; UPBRAIDETH

DENS (9) [DEN]
Jdg 6: 2 them the **d** which *are* in the mountains, | 4492
Job 37: 8 the beasts go into **d**, and remain in their | 695
38:40 When they couch in *their* **d**, *and* abide in | 4585
Ps 104:22 and lay them down in their **d**. | 4585
SS 4: 8 of Shenir and Hermon, from the lions' **d**, | 4585
Isa 32:14 forts and towers shall be for **d** for ever, | 4631
Na 2:12 his holes *with* prey, and his **d** *with* ravin. | 4585
Heb 11:38 and *in* dens and caves of the earth. | 4693
Rev 6:15 every free *man*, hid themselves in the **d** | 4693

DENY (24) [DENIED, DENIETH, DENYING]
Jos 24:27 a witness unto you, lest ye **d** your God. | 3584
1Ki 2:16 I ask one petition of thee, **d** me not. | 6440+7725
Job 8:18 shall **d** him, *saying*, I have not seen thee. | 3584
Pr 30: 7 of thee; **d** me not before I *die*: | 4513
30: 9 Lest I be full, and **d** *thee*, and say, Who *is* | 3584
Mt 10:33 But whosoever shall **d** me before men, | 720
10:33 him will I also **d** before my Father which *is* | 720
16:24 let him **d** himself, and take up his cross, | 533
26:34 cock crow, thou shalt **d** me thrice. | 533
26:35 I should die with thee, *yet* will I not **d** thee. | 533
26:75 the cock crow, thou shalt **d** me thrice. | 533
Mk 8:34 let him **d** himself, and take up his cross, | 533
14:30 cock crow twice, thou shalt **d** me thrice. | 533
14:31 die with thee, I will not **d** thee in any wise. | 533
14:72 cock crow twice, thou shalt **d** me thrice. | 533
Lk 9:23 let him **d** himself, and take up his cross | 533
20:27 which **d** that there is any resurrection; | 483
22:34 before that thou shalt thrice **d** that *thou* | 533
22:61 the cock crow, thou shalt **d** me thrice. | 533
Ac 4:16 dwell in Jerusalem; and we cannot **d** *it*. | 720
2Ti 2:12 we shall also reign with *him*: if we **d** *him*, | 720
2:12 if we deny *him*, he also will **d** us: | 720
2:13 he abideth faithful: he cannot **d** himself. | 720
Tit 1:16 in works they **d** *him*, being abominable, | 720

DENYING (4) [DENY]
2Ti 3: 5 form of godliness, but **d** the power thereof: | 720
Tit 2:12 Teaching us that **d** ungodliness and worldly | 720
2Pe 2: 1 even **d** the Lord that bought them, | 720
Jude 1: 4 **d** the only Lord God, and our Lord Jesus | 720

DEPART (125) [DEPARTED, DEPARTETH, DEPARTING, DEPARTURE]
Ge 13: 9 if *thou* **d** to the right hand, then I will go | NIH
49:10 The sceptre shall not **d** from Judah, nor a | 5493
Ex 8:11 the frogs shall **d** from thee, and from thy | 5493
8:29 the swarms *of flies* may **d** from Pharaoh, | 5493
18:27 Moses let his father in law **d**; and he went | 7971
21:22 so that her fruit *d from her*, and yet no | 3318
33: 1 **D**, *and* go up hence, thou and | 1980+4480
Lev 25:41 *then* shall he **d** from thee, *both* he and | 3318
Nu 10: 1 will **d** to mine own land, and to my | 1980
16:26 saying, **D**, I pray you, from the tents of | 5493
Dt 4: 9 lest they **d** from thy heart all the days of | 5493
9: 7 from the day that thou didst **d** out of | 3318
Jos 1: 8 This book of the law shall not **d** out of | 4185
24:28 Joshua **let** the people, every man unto | 7971
Jdg 6:18 **D** not hence, I pray thee, until I come | 4185

D

Jdg	7: 3 return and **d** early from mount Gilead.	6852
	19: 5 early in the morning, that he rose up to **d**:	1980
	19: 7 the man rose up to **d**, his father in law	1980
	19: 8 early in the morning on the fifth day to **d**:	1980
	19: 9 when the man rose up to **d**, he,	1980
1Sa	15: 6 Saul said unto the Kenites, Go, **d**, get you	5493
	22: 5 **d**, and get thee *into* the land of Judah.	1980
	29:10 up early in the morning, and have light, **d**.	1980
	29:11 his men rose up early to **d** in the morning,	1980
	30:22 that they may lead *them* away, and **d**.	1980
2Sa	7:15 my mercy shall not **d** away from him, as	5493
	11:12 day also, and to morrow I will let thee **d**.	7971
	12:10 the sword shall never **d** from thine house,	5493
	15:14 make speed to **d**, lest he overtake us	1980
	20:21 him only, and I will **d** from the city.	1980
	22:23 *as for* his statutes, I did not **d** from them.	5493
1Ki	11:21 Hadad said to Pharaoh, Let me **d**, that I	7971
	12: 5 **D** yet *for* three days, then come again to	1980
	12:24 the word of the LORD, and returned to **d**,	1980
	15:19 king of Israel, that he may **d** from me.	5927
2Ch	16: 3 king of Israel, that he may **d** from me.	5927
	18:31 and God moved them to **d** from him.	NIH
	35:15 they might not **d** from their service;	5493
Job	7:19 How long wilt thou not **d** from me, nor	8159
	15:30 He shall not **d** out of darkness; the flame	1540
	20:28 The increase of his house shall **d**,	5493
	21:14 Therefore they say unto God, **D** from us;	5493
	22:17 Which said unto God, **D** from us: and	5493
	28:28 and to **d** from evil *is* understanding.	5493
Ps	6: 8 **D** from me, all ye workers of iniquity;	5493
	34:14 **D** from evil, and do good; seek peace,	5493
	37:27 **D** from evil, and do good; and dwell for	5493
	55:11 and guile **d** not from her streets.	4185
	101: 4 A froward heart shall **d** from me: I will	5493
	119:115 **D** from me, ye evildoers: for I will keep	5493
	139:19 **d** from me therefore, ye bloody men.	5493
Pr	3: 7 fear the LORD, and **d** from evil.	5493
	3:21 My son, let not them **d** from thine eyes:	3868
	4:21 Let them not **d** from thine eyes; keep	3868
	5: 7 and **d** not from the words of my mouth.	5493
	13:14 of life, to **d** from the snares of death.	5493
	13:19 *it is* abomination to fools to **d** from evil.	5493
	14:27 of life, to **d** from the snares of death.	5493
	15:24 wise, that he may **d** from hell beneath.	5493
	16: 6 by the fear of the LORD *men* **d** from evil.	5493
	16:17 The highway of the upright *is* to **d** from	5493
	17:13 for good, evil shall not **d** from his house.	4185
	22: 6 and when he is old, he will not **d** from it.	5493
	27:22 *yet* will not his foolishness **d** from him.	5493
Isa	11:13 The envy also of Ephraim shall **d**,	5493
	14:25 shall his yoke **d** from off them,	5493
	14:25 and his burden **d** from off their shoulders.	5493
	52:11 **D** ye, depart ye, go ye out from thence,	5493
	52:11 Depart ye, **d** ye, go ye out from thence,	5493
	54:10 the mountains shall **d**, and the hills be	4185
	54:10 my kindness shall not **d** from thee,	4185
	59:21 shall not **d** out of thy mouth, nor out of	4185
Jer	6: 8 O Jerusalem, lest my soul **d** from thee;	3363
	17:13 they that **d** from me shall be written in	5493
	31:36 If those ordinances **d** from before me,	4185
	32:40 hearts, that *they* shall not **d** from me.	5493
	37: 9 Chaldeans shall **surely** **d** from us: 1980+1980	
	37: 9 surely depart from us: for they shall not **d**.	1980
	50: 3 they shall **d**, both man and beast.	1980
La	4:15 They cried unto them, **D** ye; *it is* unclean;	5493
	4:15 **d**, depart, touch not, when they fled away	5493
	4:15 depart, touch not, when they fled away	5493
Eze	16:42 my jealousy shall **d** from thee, and I will	5493
Hos	9:12 woe also to them when I **d** from them!	5493
Mic	2:10 Arise ye, and **d**; for this *is* not *your* rest:	1980
Zec	10:11 and the sceptre of Egypt shall **d away**.	5493
Mt	7:23 *you:* **d** from me, ye that work iniquity.	672
	8:18 he gave commandment to **d** unto the	565
	8:34 they besought *him* that he would **d** out of	3327
	10:14 when ye **d** out of that house or city,	1831
	14:16 Jesus said unto them, They need not **d**;	565
	25:41 **D** from me, ye cursed, into everlasting fire	4198
Mk	5:17 they began to pray him to **d** out of their	565
	6:10 there abide till ye **d** from that place.	1831
	6:11 nor hear you, when ye **d** thence,	1607
Lk	2:29 now lettest thou thy servant **d** in peace,	630
	4:42 him, that *he* should not **d** from them.	4198
	5: 8 down at Jesus' knees, saying, **D** from me;	1831
	8:37 about besought him to **d** from them;	565
	9: 4 ye enter into, there abide, and thence **d**.	1831
	12:59 I tell thee, thou shalt not **d** thence, till	1831
	13:27 **d** from me, all ye workers of iniquity.	868
	13:31 unto him, Get *thee* out, and **d** hence:	4198
	21:21 them which are in the midst of it **d** out;	1633
Jn	7: 3 unto him, **D** hence, and go into Judea,	3327
	13: 1 **d** out of this world unto the Father,	3327
	16: 7 but if I **d**, I will send him unto you.	4198
Ac	1: 4 commanded that *they* should not **d**	5563
	16:36 you go: now therefore **d**, and go in peace.	1831
	16:39 and desired *them* to **d** out of the city.	1831
	18: 2 Claudius had commanded all Jews to **d**	5563
	20: 7 unto them, ready to **d** on the morrow;	1826
	22:21 he said unto me, **D**: for I will send thee	4198
	23:22 chief captain then **let** the young man **d**,	630
	25: 4 that he himself would **d** shortly *thither*.	1607
	27:12 the more part advised to **d** thence also,	321
1Co	7:10 Let not the wife **d** from *her* husband.	5563
	7:11 and if she **d**, let her remain unmarried,	5563
	7:15 But if the unbelieving, let him depart.	5563
	7:15 But if the unbelieving depart, let him **d**.	5563

2Co	12: 8 the Lord thrice, that it might **d** from me.	868
Php	1:23 having a desire to **d**, and to be with Christ;	360
1Ti	4: 1 that in the latter times some shall **d from**	868
2Ti	2:19 nameth the name of Christ **d** from iniquity.	868
Jas	2:16 **D** in peace, be you warmed and filled;	5217

DEPARTED (217) [DEPART]

Ge	12: 4 So Abram **d**, as the LORD had spoken	1980
	12: 4 five years old when he **d** out of Haran.	3318
	14:12 dwelt in Sodom, and his goods, and **d**.	1980
	21:14 she **d**, and wandered in the wilderness of	1980
	24:10 camels of the camels of his master, and **d**;	1980
	26:17 Isaac **d** thence, and pitched his tent in	1980
	26:31 them away, and they **d** from him in peace.	1980
	31:40 by night; and my sleep **d** from mine eyes.	5074
	31:55 and Laban **d**, and returned unto his place.	1980
	37:17 man said, They are **d** hence; for I heard	5265
	42:26 their asses with the corn, and **d** thence.	1980
	45:24 So he sent his brethren away, and they **d**:	1980
Ex	19: 2 For they were **d** from Rephidim,	5265
	33:11 a young man, **d** not out of the tabernacle.	4185
	33:23 of Israel **d** from the presence of Moses.	3318
Lev	13:58 if the plague be **d** from them, then it shall	5493
Nu	10:33 they **d** from the mount of the LORD three	5265
	12: 9 was kindled against them; and he **d**.	1980
	12:10 the cloud **d** from off the tabernacle;	5493
	14: 9 their defence is **d** from them,	5493
	14:44 and Moses, **d** not out of the camp.	4185
	22: 7 the elders of Midian **d** with the rewards	1980
	33: 3 they **d** from Rameses in the first month,	5265
	33: 6 they **d** from Succoth, and pitched in	5265
	33: 8 they **d** from before *Pi*-hahiroth,	5265
	33:13 they **d** from Dophkah, and encamped in	5265
	33:15 they **d** from Rephidim, and pitched in	5265
	33:17 they **d** from Kibroth-hattaavah,	5265
	33:18 they **d** from Hazeroth, and pitched in	5265
	33:19 they **d** from Rithmah, and pitched at	5265
	33:20 they **d** from Rimmon-parez, and pitched	5265
	33:27 they **d** from Tahath, and pitched at Tarah.	5265
	33:30 they **d** from Hashmonah, and encamped	5265
	33:31 they **d** from Moseroth, and pitched in	5265
	33:35 they **d** from Ebronah, and encamped at	5265
	33:41 they **d** from mount Hor, and pitched in	5265
	33:42 they **d** from Zalmonah, and pitched in	5265
	33:43 they **d** from Punon, and pitched in Oboth.	5265
	33:44 they **d** from Oboth, and pitched in	5265
	33:45 they **d** from Iim, and pitched in	5265
	33:48 they **d** from the mountains of Abarim,	5265
Dt	1:19 when we **d** from Horeb, we went	5265
	24: 2 she is **d** out of his house, she may go	3318
Jos	2:21 she sent them away, and they **d**: and	1980
	2: 9 from the children of Israel out of Shiloh,	1980
Jdg	6:21 the angel of the LORD **d** out of his sight.	1980
	9:55 dead, they **d** every man unto his place.	1980
	16:20 he wist not that the LORD was **d** from	5493
	17: 8 the man **d** out of the city from	1980
	18: 2 the five men, and came to Laish,	1980
	18:21 they turned and **d**, and put the little ones	1980
	19:10 he rose up and **d**, and came over against	1980
	21:24 the children of Israel **d** thence at 1980+4480	
1Sa	4:21 saying, The glory is **d** from Israel:	1540
	4:22 she said, The glory is **d** from Israel: for	1540
	6: 6 did they not let the people go, and they **d**?	1980
	10: 2 When thou art **d** from me to day, then	1980
	15: 6 So the Kenites **d** from among	5493
	16:14 the spirit of the LORD **d** from Saul,	5493
	16:23 was well, and the evil spirit **d** from him.	5493
	18:12 was with him, and was **d** from Saul.	5493
	20:42 he arose and **d**: and Jonathan went *into*	1980
	22: 1 David therefore **d** thence, 1980+4480	
	22: 5 David **d**, and came *into* the forest of	1980
	23:13 arose and **d** out of Keilah,	3318
	28:15 God is **d** from me, and answereth me no	5493
	28:16 seeing the LORD is **d** from thee,	5493
2Sa	3:21 a flagon of **wine**. So all the people **d** every	1980
	11: 8 Uriah **d** out of the king's house,	3318
	12:15 Nathan **d** unto his house. And the LORD	1980
	17:21 it came to pass, after they were **d**, that	1980
	19:24 from the day the king until the day he	1980
	22:22 and have not **wickedly** **d** from my God.	7561
1Ki	12: 5 then come again to me. And the people **d**.	1980
	12:16 David. So Israel **d** unto their tents.	1980
	14:17 wife arose, and **d**, and came to Tirzah:	1980
	19:19 he **d** thence, and found Elisha the son of	1980
	20: 9 the messengers **d**, and brought him word	1980
	20:36 behold, as soon as thou art **d** from me,	1980
	20:36 as soon as he was **d** from him, a lion	1980
	20:38 So the prophet **d**, and waited for the king	1980
2Ki	1: 4 up, but shalt surely die. And Elijah **d**.	1980
	3: 3 made Israel to sin; he **d** not therefrom.	5493
	3: 27 they **d** from him, and returned to *their*	5265
	5: 5 he **d**, and took with him ten talents of	1980
	5:19 in peace. So he **d** from him a little way.	1980
	5:24 and he let the men go, and they **d**.	1980
	8:14 So he **d** from Elisha, and came to his	1980
	10:12 he arose and **d**, and came *to* Samaria.	935
	10:15 when he was **d** thence, he lighted 1980+4480	
	10:29 Israel to sin, Jehu **d** not from after them,	5493
	10:31 *for* he **d** not from the sins of Jeroboam,	5493
	13: 2 made Israel to sin; he **d** not therefrom.	5493
	13: 6 Nevertheless they **d** not from the sins of	5493
	13:11 he **d** not from all the sins of Jeroboam	5493
	14:24 he **d** not from all the sins of Jeroboam	5493
	15: 9 he **d** not from the sins of Jeroboam the	5493
	15:18 he **d** not all his days from the sins of	5493

2Ki	15:24 he **d** not from the sins of Jeroboam the	5493
	15:28 he **d** not from the sins of Jeroboam the	5493
	17:22 which he did; they **d** not from them;	5493
	18: 6 *and* **d** not from following him, but kept	5493
	19: 8 for he had heard that he was **d** from	5265
	19:36 So Sennacherib king of Assyria **d**,	5265
1Ch	16:43 all the people **d** every man to his house:	1980
	21: 4 Wherefore Joab **d**, and went throughout	3318
2Ch	8:15 they **d** not *from* the commandment of	5493
	10: 5 me after three days. And the people **d**.	1980
	20:32 way of Asa his father, and **d** not from it,	5493
	21:20 eight years, and **d** without being desired.	1980
	24:25 when they were **d** from him, (for they left	1980
	34:33 *And* all his days they **d** not from following	5493
Ezr	8:31 we **d** from the river of Ahava on the	
Ne	9:19 the pillar of the cloud **d** not from them by	5493
Ps	18:21 and have not **wickedly** **d** from my God.	7561
	34: T who drove him away, and he **d**.	1980
	105:38 Egypt was glad when they **d**: for the fear	3318
	119:102 I have not **d** from thy judgments: for thou	5493
Isa	7:17 from the day that Ephraim **d** from Judah;	5493
	37: 8 for he had heard that he was **d** from	5265
	37:37 So Sennacherib king of Assyria **d**,	5265
	38:12 Mine age is **d**, and is removed from me as	5265
Jer	29: 2 and the smiths, were **d** from Jerusalem;)	3318
	37: 5 tidings of them, they **d** from Jerusalem.	5927
	41:10 and **d** to go over to the Ammonites.	1980
	41:17 they **d**, and dwelt in the habitation of	1980
La	1: 6 the daughter of Zion all her beauty is **d**:	3318
Eze	6: 9 hath **d** from me, and with their eyes,	5493
	10:18 the glory of the LORD **d** from off	3318
Da	4:31 it is spoken; The kingdom is **d** from thee.	5709
Hos	10: 5 the glory thereof, because it is **d** from it.	1540
Mal	2: 8 ye are **d** out of the way; ye have caused	5493
Mt	2: 9 When they had heard the king, they **d**;	4198
	2:12 **d** into their own country another way.	402
	2:13 when they were **d**, behold, *the* angel of	402
	2:14 and his mother by night, and **d** into Egypt:	402
	4:12 John was cast into prison, he **d** into Galilee;	402
	9: 7 And he arose, and **d** to his house.	565
	9:27 And when Jesus **d** thence, two blind men	3855
	9:31 they, when they were **d**, spread abroad	1831
	11: 1 he **d** thence to teach and to preach in their	3327
	11: 7 And as they **d**, Jesus began to say unto	4198
	12: 9 And when he was **d** thence, he went into	3327
	13:53 had finished these parables, he **d** thence.	3332
	14:13 Jesus heard *of it*, he **d** thence by ship	402
	15:21 and **d** into the coasts of Tyre and Sidon.	402
	15:29 And Jesus **d** from thence, and came nigh	3327
	16: 4 And he left them, and **d**.	565
	17:18 rebuked the devil; and he **d** out of him:	1831
	19: 1 he **d** from Galilee, and came into the coasts	3332
	19:15 he laid *his* hands on them, and **d** thence.	4198
	20:29 And as they **d** from Jericho, a great	1607
	24: 1 Jesus went out, and **d** from the temple:	4198
	27: 5 and **d**, and went and hanged himself.	402
	27:60 stone to the door of the sepulchre, and **d**.	565
	28: 8 they **d** quickly from the sepulchre with	1831
Mk	1:35 **d** into a solitary place, and there prayed.	565
	1:42 immediately the leprosy **d** from him,	565
	5:20 he **d**, and began to publish in Decapolis	565
	6:32 And they **d** into a desert place by ship	565
	6:46 them away, he **d** into a mountain to pray.	565
	8:13 entering into the ship again **d** to the other	565
	9:30 And they **d** thence, and passed through	1831
Lk	1:23 accomplished, he **d** to his own house.	565
	1:38 to the word. And the angel **d** from her.	565
	2:37 which **d** not from the temple, but served	868
	4:13 temptation, he **d** from him for a season.	868
	4:42 day, he **d** and went into a desert place:	1831
	5:13 And immediately the leprosy **d** from him.	565
	5:25 and **d** to his own house, glorifying God.	565
	7:24 And when the messengers of John were **d**,	565
	8:35 the man, out of whom the devils were **d**,	1831
	8:38 besought him that *he* might be with	1831
	9: 6 And they **d**, and went through the towns,	1831
	9:33 And it came to pass, as they **d** from him,	1316
	10:30 wounded *him*, and **d**, leaving *him* half	565
	10:35 on the morrow when he **d**, he took out	1831
	24:12 linen clothes laid by themselves, and **d**,	565
Jn	4: 3 He left Judea, and **d** again into Galilee.	565
	4:43 Now after two days he **d** thence,	1831
	5:15 The man **d**, and told the Jews that it was	565
	6:15 he **d** again into a mountain himself alone.	402
	12:36 and **d**, and did hide himself from them.	565
Ac	5:41 and **d** from the presence of	4198
	10: 7 angel which spake unto Cornelius was **d**,	565
	11:25 Then **d** Barnabas to Tarsus, for to seek	1831
	12:10 and forthwith the angel **d** from him.	868
	12:17 And he **d**, and went into another place.	1831
	13: 4 forth by the Holy Ghost, **d** unto Seleucia;	2718
	13:14 But when they **d** from Perga, they came	1330
	14:20 the next day he **d** with Barnabas to Derbe.	1831
	15:38 *them*, who **d** from them from Pamphylia,	868
	15:39 sharp *between them*, that they **d asunder**	673
	15:40 And Paul chose Silas, and **d**,	1831
	16:40 the brethren, they comforted them, and **d**.	1831
	17:15 for to come to him with all speed, they **d**.	1826
	17:33 So Paul **d** from among them.	1831
	18: 1 After these *things* Paul **d** from Athens,	5563
	18: 7 he **d** thence, and entered into a certain	3327
	18:23 after he had spent some time *there*, he **d**,	1831
	19: 9 **d** from them, and separated the disciples,	868
	19:12 and the diseases **d** from them, and the evil	525
	20: 1 and **d** for to go into Macedonia.	1831

D

Ac 20:11 long while, *even* till break of day, so he **d**. 1831
21: 5 we **d** and went *our way;* and *they* all 1831
21: 8 day we that were of Paul's company **d**, 1831
22:29 Then straightway they **d** from him which 868
28:10 and when we **d**, they laded *us* with such 321
28:11 And after three months we **d** in a ship of 321
28:25 they **d**, after that Paul had spoken one 630
28:29 when he had said these *words*, the Jews **d**, 565
Php 4:15 of the gospel, when I **d** from Macedonia, 1831
2Ti 4:10 present world, and is **d** unto Thessalonica; 4198
Phm 1:15 For perhaps he therefore **d** for a season, 5563
Rev 6:14 And the heaven **d** as a scrole when it is 673
16:14 the fruits that thy soul lusted after are **d** 565
18:14 *were* dainty and goodly are **d** from thee, 565

DEPARTETH (8) [DEPART]
Job 27:21 east wind carrieth him away, and he **d**: 1980
Pr 14:16 A wise *man* feareth, and **d** from evil: but 5493
Ecc 6: 4 **d** in darkness, and his name shall be 1980
Isa 59:15 he *that* **d** from evil maketh himself a prey: 5493
Jer 3:20 Surely *as* a wife treacherously **d** from her 4480
17: 5 and whose heart **d** from the LORD. 5493
Na 3: 1 all full *of* lies *and* robbery; the prey **d** not; 4185
Lk 9:39 and bruising him hardly **d** from him. 672

DEPARTING (12) [DEPART]
Ge 35:18 pass, as her soul was **in d** (for she died) 3318
Ex 16: 1 after their **d** out of the land of Egypt. 3318
Isa 59:13 **d** away from our God, speaking 5253
Da 9: 5 even by **d** from thy precepts and from thy 5493
9:11 even by **d**, that *they* might not obey thy 5493
Hos 1: 2 great whoredom, **d** from the LORD. NIH
Mk 6:33 And the people saw them **d**, 5217
7:31 **d** from the coasts of Tyre and Sidon, 1831
Ac 13:13 John **d** from them returned to Jerusalem. 672
20:29 that after my **d** shall grievous wolves enter 867
Heb 3:12 heart of unbelief, in **d** from the living God. 868
11:22 made mention of the **d** of the children of 1841

DEPARTURE (2) [DEPART]
Eze 26:18 *are* in the sea shall be troubled at thy **d**. 3318
2Ti 4: 6 offered, and the time of my **d** is at hand. 359

DEPOSED (1)
Da 5:20 he was **d** from his kingly throne, 5182

DEPRAVED See REPROBATE; REPROBATES

DEPRIVE See SUBVERT

DEPRIVED (3)
Ge 27:45 why should I be **d** also of you both *in* one 7921
Job 39:17 Because God hath **d** her of wisdom, 5382
Isa 38:10 I am **d** of the residue of my years. 6485

DEPTH (12) [DEEP]
Job 28:14 The **d** saith, It *is* not in me: and the sea 8415
38:16 hast thou walked in the search of the **d**? 8415
Ps 33: 7 a heap: he layeth up the **d** in storehouses. 8415
Pr 8:27 he set a compass upon the face of the **d**: 8415
25: 3 the earth for **d**, and the heart of kings *is* 6011
Isa 7:11 ask it either in the **d**, or in the height 6009
Jnh 2: 5 the **d** closed me round about, the weeds 8415
Mt 18: 6 *that* he were drowned in the **d** of the sea. 3989
Mk 4: 5 it sprang up, because *it* had no **d** of earth: 899
Ro 8:39 Nor height, nor **d**, nor any other creature, 899
11:33 O the **d** of the riches both of the wisdom 899
Eph 3:18 the breadth, and length, and **d**, and height; 899

DEPTHS (17) [DEEP]
Ex 15: 5 The **d** have covered them: they sank into 8415
15: 8 the **d** were congealed in the heart of 8415
Dt 8: 7 **d** that spring out of the valleys and hills; 8415
Ps 68:22 I will bring *my* people again from the **d** of 4688
71:20 shalt bring me up again from the **d** of 8415
77:16 they were afraid: the **d** also were troubled. 8415
78:15 and gave *them* drink as *out of* the great **d**. 8415
106: 9 so he led them through the **d**, as *through* 8415
107:26 the heaven, they go down *again* to the **d**: 8415
130: 1 Out of the **d** have I cried unto thee, 4615
Pr 3:20 By his knowledge the **d** are broken up, 8415
8:24 *there were* no **d**, I was brought forth; 8415
9:18 *and that* her guests *are* in the **d** of hell. 6012
Isa 51:10 that hath made the **d** of the sea a way for 4615
Eze 27:34 broken by the seas in the **d** of the waters, 4615
Mic 7:19 thou wilt cast all their sins into the **d** of 4688
Rev 2:24 and which have not known the **d** of Satan, 899

DEPUTED (1) [DEPUTY]
2Sa 15: 3 *there is* no man **d** of the king to hear thee. NIH

DEPUTIES (3) [DEPUTY]
Est 8: 9 the **d** and rulers of the provinces which 6346
9: 3 and the **d**, and officers of the king, 6346
Ac 19:38 any *man*, the law is open, and there are **d**: 446

DEPUTY (5) [DEPUTED, DEPUTIES]
1Ki 22:47 then no king in Edom: a **d** *was* king. 5324
Ac 13: 7 Which was with the **d** *of* the country, 446
13: 8 seeking to turn away the **d** from the faith. 446
13:12 Then the **d**, when he saw what was done, 446
18:12 And when Gallio was the **d** of Achaia, 445

DERBE (4)
Ac 14: 6 ware of *it*, and fled unto Lystra and D, 1191
14:20 next day he departed with Barnabas to D. 1191

Ac 16: 1 came he to D and Lystra: and behold, 1191
20: 4 and Gaius **of D**, and Timotheus; 1190

DERIDE (1) [DERIDED, DERISION]
Hab 1:10 they shall **d** every strong hold; for they 7832

DERIDED (2) [DERIDE]
Lk 16:14 heard all these *things:* and they **d** him. 1592
23:35 And the rulers also with them **d** *him,* 1592

DERISION (15) [DERIDE]
Job 30: 1 *that are* younger than I have me in **d**, 7832
Ps 2: 4 the LORD shall have them in **d**. 3932
44:13 and a **d** to them that are round about us. 7047
59: 8 thou shalt **have** all the heathen in **d**. 3932
79: 4 and a **d** to them that are round about us. 7047
119:51 The proud have **had** me greatly **in d**: 3887
Jer 20: 7 I am in **d** daily, every one mocketh me. 7814
20: 8 made a reproach unto me, and a **d**, daily. 7047
48:26 in his vomit, and he also shall be in **d**. 7814
48:27 For was not Israel a **d** unto thee? was he 7814
48:39 shall Moab be a **d** and a dismaying to all 7814
La 3:14 I was a **d** to all my people; *and* their song 7814
Eze 23:32 shalt be laughed to scorn and had in **d**; 3933
36: 4 **d** to the residue of the heathen that *are* 3933
Hos 7:16 this *shall be* their **d** in the land of Egypt. 3933

DESCEND (10) [DESCENDED, DESCENDETH, DESCENDING, DESCENT]
Nu 34:11 the border shall **d**, and shall reach unto 3381
1Sa 26:10 die; or he shall **d** into battle, and perish. 3381
Ps 49:17 his glory shall not **d** after him. 3381
Isa 5:14 and that hell rejoiceth, shall **d** into it. 3381
Eze 26:20 thee down with them that **d** into the pit, 3381
31:16 to hell with them that **d** into the pit: 3381
Mk 15:32 Let Christ the King of Israel **d** now from 2597
Ac 11: 5 a trance I saw a vision, A certain vessel **d**, 2597
Ro 10: 7 Or, Who shall **d** into the deep? (that is, 2597
1Th 4:16 For the Lord himself shall **d** from heaven 2597

DESCENDED (19) [DESCEND]
Ex 19:18 the LORD **d** upon it in fire: 3381
33: 9 the cloudy pillar **d**, and stood *at* the door 3381
34: 5 the LORD **d** in the cloud, and stood with 3381
Dt 9:21 cast the dust thereof into the brook that **d** 3381
Jos 2:23 **d** from the mountain, and passed over, 3381
17: 9 the coast **d** *unto* the river Kanah, 3381
18:13 the border **d** to Ataroth-adar, near the hill 3381
18:16 **d** *to* the valley of Hinnom, to the side of 3381
18:16 of Jebusi on the south, and **d** *to* En-rogel, 3381
18:17 to the stone of Bohan the son of Reuben 3381
Ps 133: 3 *as* the dew that **d** upon the mountains of 3381
Pr 30: 4 Who hath ascended up *into* heaven, or **d**? 3381
Mt 7:25 And the rain **d**, and the floods came, 2597
7:27 And the rain **d**, and the floods came, 2597
28: 2 for *the* angel of the Lord **d** from heaven, 2597
Lk 3:22 and the Holy Ghost **d** in a bodily shape 2597
Ac 24: 1 Ananias the high priest **d** with the elders, 2597
Eph 4: 9 that he also **d** first into the lower parts of 2597
4:10 He that **d** is the same also that ascended 2597

DESCENDETH (1) [DESCEND]
Jas 3:15 This wisdom **d** not from above, 2718

DESCENDING (8) [DESCEND]
Ge 28:12 the angels of God ascending and **d** on it. 3381
Mt 3:16 he saw the Spirit of God **d** like a dove, 2597
Mk 1:10 and the Spirit like a dove **d** upon him: 2597
Jn 1:32 saw the Spirit **d** from heaven like a dove, 2597
1:33 Upon whom thou shalt see the Spirit **d**, 2597
1:51 ascending and **d** upon the Son of man. 2597
Ac 10:11 and a certain vessel **d** unto him, 2597
Rev 21:10 Jerusalem, **d** out of heaven from God, 2597

DESCENT (3) [DESCEND]
Lk 19:37 now at the **d** of the mount of Olives, 2600
Heb 7: 3 father, without mother, **without d**, 35
7: 6 he whose **d** is not **counted** from them 1075

DESCRIBE (4) [DESCRIBED, DESCRIBETH, DESCRIPTION]
Jos 18: 4 **d** it according to the inheritance of them; 3789
18: 6 therefore **d** the land *into* seven parts, 3789
18: 8 Joshua charged them that went to **d** 3789
18: 8 the land, and **d** it, and come again to me, 3789

DESCRIBED (2) [DESCRIBE]
Jos 18: 9 **d** it by cities into seven parts in a book, 3789
Jdg 8:14 he **d** unto him the princes of Succoth, 3789

DESCRIBETH (2) [DESCRIBE]
Ro 4: 6 Even as David also **d** the blessedness of 3004
10: 5 For Moses **d** the righteousness which is of 1125

DESCRIPTION (1) [DESCRIBE]
Jos 18: 6 seven parts, and bring the **d** hither to me, NIH

DESCRY (1)
Jdg 1:23 the house of Joseph **sent** to **d** Beth-el. 8446

DESERT (42) [DESERTS]
Ex 3: 1 he led the flock to the backside of the **d**, 4057
5: 3 three days' journey into the **d**, 4057
19: 2 were come *to* the **d** of Sinai, 4057
23:31 and from the **d** unto the river: 4057
Nu 20: 1 *into* the **d** of Zin in the first month; 4057

Nu 27:14 against my commandment in the **d** of Zin, 4057
33:16 they removed from the **d** of Sinai, 4057
Dt 32:10 He found him in a **d** land, and in the 4057
2Ch 26:10 Also he built towers in the **d**, 4057
Job 24: 5 as wild asses in the **d**, go they forth 4057
Ps 28: 4 of their hands; render to them their **d**. 1576
78:40 the wilderness, *and* grieve him in the **d!** 3452
102: 6 the wilderness: I am like an owl of the **d**. 2723
106:14 wilderness, and tempted God in the **d**. 3452
Isa 13:21 **wild beasts of the d** shall lie there; 6728
21: 1 The burden of the **d** of the sea. 4057
21: 1 *so* it cometh from the **d**, from a terrible 4057
34:14 The **wild beasts of the d** shall also meet 6728
35: 1 **d** shall rejoice, and blossom as the rose. 6160
35: 6 waters break out, and streams in the **d**. 6160
40: 3 make straight in the **d** a highway for our 6160
41:19 will set in the **d** the fir tree, *and* the pine, 6160
43:19 way in the wilderness, *and* rivers in the **d**. 3452
43:20 *and* rivers in the **d**, to give drink to my 3452
51: 3 and her **d** like the garden of the LORD; 6160
Jer 17: 6 For he shall be like the heath in the **d**, 6160
25:24 of the mingled people that dwell in the **d**, 4057
50:12 *shall be* a wilderness, a dry land, and a **d**. 6160
50:39 Therefore the **wild beasts of the d** with 6728
Eze 47: 8 go down into the **d**, and go into the sea: 6160
Mt 14:13 thence by ship into a **d** place apart: 2048
14:15 is a **d** place, and the time is now past; 2048
24:26 shall say unto you, Behold, he is in the **d**; 2048
Mk 1:45 into the city, but was without in **d** places: 2048
6:31 Come ye yourselves apart into a **d** place, 2048
6:32 And they departed into a **d** place by ship 2048
6:35 *This* is a **d** place, and now the time is far 2048
Lk 4:42 he departed and went into a **d** place: 2048
9:10 went aside privately into a **d** place 2048
9:12 get victuals: for we are here in a **d** place. 2048
Jn 6:31 Our fathers did eat manna in the **d**; as it is 2048
Ac 8:26 from Jerusalem unto Gaza, which is **d**. 2048

DESERTS (6) [DESERT]
Isa 48:21 not *when* he led them through the **d**: 2723
Jer 2: 6 through a land of **d** and of pits, through a 6160
Eze 7:27 and according to their **d** will I judge them; 4941
13: 4 thy prophets are like the foxes in the **d**. 2723
Lk 1:80 was in the **d** till the day of his shewing 2048
Heb 11:38 they wandered in **d**, and in mountains, 2047

DESERVE (1) [DESERVETH, DESERVING]
Ezr 9:13 hast punished us less than our iniquities **d**, NIH

DESERVETH (1) [DESERVE]
Job 11: 6 exacteth of thee *less* than thine iniquity **d**. NIH

DESERVING (1) [DESERVE]
Jdg 9:16 have done unto him according to the **d** of 1576

DESIRABLE (3) [DESIRE]
Eze 23: 6 and rulers, all of them **d** young men, 2531
23:12 upon horses, all of them **d** young men, 2531
23:23 all of them **d** young men, captains and 2531

DESIRE (111) [DESIRABLE, DESIRED, DESIREDST, DESIRES, DESIREST, DESIRETH, DESIRING, DESIROUS]
Ge 3:16 thy **d** *shall be* to thy husband, and he 8669
4: 7 unto thee *shall be* his **d**, and thou shalt 8669
Ex 10:11 and serve the LORD; for that you did **d**. 1245
34:24 shall any man **d** thy land, when thou 2530
Dt 5:21 Neither shalt thou **d** thy neighbour's wife, 2530
7:25 thou shalt not **d** the silver or gold *that is* 2530
18: 6 come with all the **d** of his mind unto 185
21:11 **hast a d** unto her, that thou wouldest 2836
Jdg 8:24 I would **d** a **request** of you, 7592+7596
1Sa 9:20 on whom *is* all the **d** of Israel? *Is it* not on 2532
23:20 down according to all the **d** of thy soul 185
2Sa 23: 5 for *this is* all my salvation, and all *my* **d**, 2656
1Ki 2:20 she said, I **d** one small petition of thee; 7592
5: 8 I will do all thy **d** concerning timber of 2656
5: 9 and thou shalt accomplish my **d**, 2656
5:10 and fir trees *according* to all his **d**. 2656
9: 1 all Solomon's **d** which he was pleased to 2837
9:11 and with gold, according to all his **d**,) 2656
10:13 gave unto the queen of Sheba all her **d**, 2656
2Ki 4:28 she said, Did I **d** a son of my lord? did I 7592
2Ch 9:12 gave to the queen of Sheba all her **d**, 2656
15:15 and sought him with their whole **d**; 7522
Ne 1:11 of thy servants, who **d** to fear thy name; 2655
Job 13: 3 the Almighty, and I **d** to reason with God. 2654
14:15 thou wilt **have** a **d** to the work of thine 3700
21:14 for we **d** not the knowledge of thy ways. 2654
31:16 If I have withheld the poor from *their* **d**, 2656
31:35 my **d** *is, that* the Almighty would answer 8420
33:32 answer me: speak, for I **d** to justify thee. 2654
34:36 **My d** *is that* Job may be tried unto the 15
36:20 **D** not the night, when people are cut off 7602
Ps 10: 3 For the wicked boasteth of his heart's **d**, 8378
10:17 thou hast heard the **d** of the humble: 8378
21: 2 Thou hast given him his heart's **d**, 8378
38: 9 Lord, all my **d** *is* before thee; 8378
40: 6 Sacrifice and offering thou didst not **d**; 2654
45:11 So shall the king greatly **d** thy beauty: 183
54: 7 mine eye hath seen *his* **d** upon mine NIH
59:10 God shall let me see my **d** upon mine NIH
70: 2 and put to confusion, that **d** my hurt. 2655
73:25 *there is* none upon earth that I **d** beside 2654
78:29 well filled: for he gave them their own **d**; 8378

Ps 92:11 Mine eye also shall see *my d* on mine — NIH
 92:11 mine ears shall hear *my d* of the wicked — NIH
 112: 8 until he see *his d* upon his enemies. — NIH
 112:10 away: the d of the wicked shall perish. — 8378
 118: 7 shall I see *my d* upon them that hate me. — NIH
 145:16 and satisfiest the d of every living thing. — 7522
 145:19 He will fulfil the d of them that fear him: — 7522
Pr 3:15 all the things thou canst d are not to be — 2656
 10:24 the d of the righteous shall be granted. — 8378
 11:23 The d of the righteous *is* only good: *but* — 8378
 13:12 *when* the d cometh, *it is* a tree of life. — 8378
 13:19 The d accomplished is sweet to the soul: — 8378
 18: 1 Through d a man, having separated — 8378
 19:22 The d of a man *is* his kindness: and a — 8378
 21:25 The d of the slothful killeth him; for his — 8378
 23: 6 evil eye, neither d thou his dainty meats: — 183
 24: 1 evil men, neither d to be with them. — 183
Ecc 6: 9 of the eyes than the wandering of the d: — 5315
 12: 5 shall be a burden, and d shall fail: — 35
SS 7:10 my beloved's, and his d *is* towards me. — 8669
Isa 26: 8 the d of *our* soul *is* to thy name, and to — 8378
 53: 2 *there is* no beauty that we should d him. — 2530
Jer 22:27 to the land whereunto they d to — 5315+5375
 42:22 in the place whither ye d to go *and* — 2654
 44:14 the which they **have** a d to return — 5315+5375
Eze 24:16 I take away from thee the d of thine eyes — 4261
 24:21 the d of your eyes, and that which your — 4261
 24:25 the d of their eyes, and that whereupon — 4261
Da 2:18 That *they* would d mercies of the God of — 1156
 11:37 nor the d of women, nor regard any god: — 2532
Hos 10:10 *It is* in my d that I should chastise them; — 185
Am 5:18 Woe unto *you* that the d of the LORD! — 183
Mic 7: 3 great *man*, he uttereth his mischievous *d*, — 5315
Hab 2: 5 enlargeth his d as hell, and *is* as death, — 5315
Hag 2: 7 and the d of all nations shall come: — 2532
Mk 9:35 saith unto them, If any *man* to be first, — 2309
 10:35 shouldest do for us whatsoever we shall d. — 154
 11:24 What *things* soever ye d, when ye pray, — 154
 15: 8 the multitude crying aloud began to d — 154
Lk 17:22 when ye shall d to see one of the days of — 1937
 20:46 which d to walk in long robes, — 2309
 22:15 With d I have desired to eat this passover — 1939
Ac 3:20 The Jews have agreed to d thee that thou — 2065
 28:22 we d to hear of thee what thou thinkest: — 515
Ro 10: 1 my heart's d and prayer to God for Israel — 2107
 15:23 a **great** d these many years to come — 1974
1Co 14: 1 d spiritual *gifts*, but rather that ye may — 2206
2Co 7: 7 when he told us your **earnest** d, your — 1972
 7:11 yea, *what* fear, yea, *what* **vehement** d, — 1972
 11:12 off occasion from them which d occasion; — 2309
 12: 6 For though I would d to glory, I shall not — 2309
Gal 4: 9 whereunto ye d again to be in bondage? — 2309
 4:20 I d to be present with you now, — 2309
 4:21 Tell me, ye that d to be under the law, — 2309
 6:12 As many as d to make a fair shew in — 2309
 6:13 but d to have you circumcised, that they — 2309
Eph 3:13 Wherefore I d that ye faint not at my — 154
Php 1:23 a d to depart, and to be with Christ; — 1939
 4:17 Not because I d a gift: but I desire fruit — 1934
 4:17 I d fruit that *may* abound to your account. — 1934
Col 1: 9 to d that ye might be filled *with* — 154
1Th 2:17 abundantly to see your face with great d. — 1939
1Ti 3: 1 If a man d the office of a bishop, — 3713
Heb 6:11 And we d that every one of you do shew — 1937
 11:16 But now they d a better *country*, that is, — 3713
Jas 4: 2 ye kill, and d to have, and cannot obtain: — 2206
1Pe 1:12 which *things* the angels d to look into. — 1937
 2: 2 the sincere milk of the word, — 1971
Rev 9: 6 shall d to die, and death shall flee from — 1937

DESIRED (50) [DESIRE]

Ge 3: 6 a tree to be d to make *one* wise, she took — 2530
1Sa 12:13 ye have chosen, *and* whom ye have d: — 7592
1Ki 9:19 that which Solomon d to build in — 2836+2837
2Ch 8: 6 Solomon d to build in Jerusalem, — 2836+2837
 11:23 in abundance. And he d many wives. — 7592
 21:20 eight years, and departed without being d. — 2532
Est 2:13 whatsoever she d was given her to go with — 559
Job 20:20 he shall not save of that which he d. — 2530
Ps 19:10 More to be d are *they* than gold, yea, — 2530
 27: 4 One *thing* have I d of the LORD, that will — 7592
 107:30 so he bringeth them unto their d haven. — 2656
 132:13 Zion; he hath d *it* for his habitation. — 183
 132:14 for ever: here will I dwell; for I have d it. — 183
Pr 8:11 all the things that may be d are not to be — 2656
 21:20 *There is* treasure to be d and oil in — 2530
Ecc 2:10 whatsoever mine eyes I d kept not from — 7592
Isa 1:29 be ashamed of the oaks which ye have d, — 2530
 26: 9 *With* my soul have I d thee in the night; — 183
Jer 17:16 neither have I d the woeful day; — 183
Da 2:16 d of the king that he would give him time, — 1156
 2:23 made known unto me now what we d — 2654
Hos 6: 6 For I d mercy, and not sacrifice; — 2654
Mic 7: 1 cluster to eat: my soul d the firstripe fruit. — 183
Zep 2: 1 yea, gather together, O nation not d; — 3700
Mt 13:17 righteous *men* have d to see *those things* — 1937
 16: 1 tempting d him that *he* would shew them — 1905
Mk 15: 6 one prisoner, whomsoever they d. — 154
Lk 7:36 And one of the Pharisees d him that he — 2065
 9: 9 of whom I hear such *things?* And he d to — 2212
 10:24 kings have d to see *those things* which ye — 2309
 22:15 With desire I have d to eat this passover — 1937
 22:31 Simon, behold, Satan hath d *to have* you, — 1809
 23:25 was cast into prison, whom they had d; — 154
Jn 12:21 d him, saying, Sir, we would see Jesus. — 2065

Ac 3:14 and d a murderer to be granted unto you; — 154
 7:46 d to find a tabernacle for the God of Jacob. — 154
 8:31 And he d Philip that he would come up — 3870
 9: 2 And d of him letters to Damascus to — 154
 12:20 king's chamberlain their friend, d peace; — 154
 13: 7 and Saul, and d to hear the word of God. — 1934
 13:21 afterward they d a king: and God gave — 154
 13:28 *yet* d they Pilate that he should be slain. — 154
 16:39 and d *them* to depart out of the city. — 2065
 18:20 When they d *him* to tarry longer time — 2065
 25: 3 And d favour against him, that he would — 154
 28:14 and were d to tarry with them seven days: — 3870
1Co 16:12 I greatly d him to come unto you with — 3870
2Co 8: 6 Insomuch that we d Titus, that as he had — 3870
 12:18 I d Titus, and with *him* I sent a brother. — 3870
1Jn 5:15 know that we have the petitions that we d — 154

DESIREDST (2) [DESIRE]

Dt 18:16 According to all that thou d of the LORD — 7592
Mt 18:32 thee all that debt, because thou d me: — 3870

DESIRES (3) [DESIRE]

Ps 37: 4 he shall give thee the d of thine heart. — 4862
 140: 8 Grant not, O LORD, the d of the wicked: — 3970
Eph 2: 3 fulfilling the d of the flesh and of the mind — 2307

DESIREST (2) [DESIRE]

Ps 51: 6 Behold, thou d truth in the inward parts: — 2654
 51:16 For thou d not sacrifice; else would I give — 2654

DESIRETH (17) [DESIRE]

Dt 14:26 strong drink, or for whatsoever thy soul d: — 7592
1Sa 2:16 *then* take *as much* as thy soul d; — 183
 18:25 king d not *any* dowry, but an hundred — 2656
 20: 4 Whatsoever thy soul d, I will even do *it* — 559
2Sa 3:21 mayest reign over all that thine heart d. — 183
1Ki 11:37 shalt reign according to all that thy soul d, — 183
Job 7: 2 As a servant **earnestly** d the shadow, — 7602
 23:13 and what his soul d, even *that* he doeth. — 183
Ps 34:12 What man *is he that* d life, *and* loveth — 2655
 68:16 *this is* the hill *which* God d to dwell in; — 2530
Pr 12:12 The wicked d the net of evil *men:* but — 2530
 13: 4 soul of the sluggard d, and *hath* nothing: — 183
 21:10 soul of the wicked d evil: his neighbour — 183
Ecc 6: 2 nothing for his soul of all that he d, — 183
Lk 5:39 having drunk old *wine* straightway d new: — 2309
 14:32 an ambassage, and d conditions of peace. — 2065
1Ti 3: 1 the office of a bishop, he d a good work. — 1937

DESIRING (12) [DESIRE]

Mt 9:18 stood without, d to speak with him. — 2212
 12:47 stand without, d to speak with thee. — 2212
 20:20 and a certain *thing* of him. — 154
Lk 8:20 thy brethren stand without, d to see thee. — 2309
 16:21 d to be fed with the crumbs which fell — 1937
Ac 9:38 d him that *he* would not delay to come to — 3870
 19:31 d him that *he* would not adventure — 3870
 25:15 the elders of the Jews informed *me,* d to — 154
2Co 5: 2 **earnestly** d to be clothed upon with our — 1971
1Th 3: 6 and d **greatly** to see us, as we also *to see* you: — 1971
1Ti 1: 7 D to be teachers of the law; — 2309
2Ti 1: 4 **Greatly** d to see thee, being mindful of — 1971

DESIROUS (6) [DESIRE]

Pr 23: 3 Be not d of his dainties: for they *are* — 183
Lk 23: 8 for he was d to see him of a long *season,* — 2309
Jn 16:19 Now Jesus knew that they were d to ask — 2309
2Co 11:32 with a garrison, d to apprehend me: — NIG
Gal 5:26 Let us not be d of vain glory, provoking — 2442
1Th 2: 8 So being **affectionately** d of you, we — 2442

DESOLATE (148) [DESOLATION, DESOLATIONS]

Ge 47:19 and not die, that the land be not d. — 3456
Ex 23:29 lest the land become d, and the beast of — 8077
Lev 26:22 number; and your *high* ways shall be d. — 8074
 26:33 land shall be d, and your cities waste. — 8077
 26:34 as long as it **lieth** d, and ye *be* in your — 8074
 26:35 As long as it **lieth** d it shall rest; because — 8074
 26:43 while she **lieth** d without them: — 8074
2Sa 13:20 So Tamar remained d *in* her brother — 8074
2Ch 36:21 *for* as long as *she* **lay** d she kept sabbath, — 8074
Job 3:14 which built d *places* for themselves; — 2723
 15:28 he dwelleth in d cities, *and* in houses — 3582
 15:34 the congregation of hypocrites *shall be* d, — 1565
 16: 7 thou hast **made** d all my company. — 8074
 30: 3 *into* the wilderness in former time d — 7722
 38:27 To satisfy the d and waste *ground;* and — 7722
Ps 25:16 mercy upon me; for I *am* d and afflicted. — 3173
 34:21 they that hate the righteous shall be d. — 816
 34:22 none of them that trust in him shall be d. — 8074
 40:15 Let them be d for a reward of their shame — 8074
 69:25 Let their habitation be d; *and* let none — 8074
 109:10 *their bread* also out of their d **places.** — 2723
 143: 4 within me; my heart within me is d. — 8074
Isa 1: 7 Your country *is* d, your cities *are* burnt — 8077
 1: 7 and it *is* d, as overthrown by strangers. — 8077
 3:26 she *being* d shall sit upon the ground. — 5352
 5: 9 Of a truth many houses shall be d, — 8047
 6:11 without man, and the land be utterly d, — 7582
 7:19 shall rest all of them in the d valleys, — 1327
 9:19 and fierce anger, to lay the land d: — 8047
 13:22 of the islands shall cry in their d *houses,* — 490
 15: 6 For the waters of Nimrim shall be d: for — 4923
 24: 6 earth, and they that dwell therein are d: — 816
 27:10 Yet the defenced city *shall be* d, — 910

Isa 49: 8 earth, to cause to inherit the d heritages; — 8074
 49:19 For thy waste and thy d **places,** — 8074
 49:21 am *I*, a captive, and removing to and fro? — 1565
 54: 1 for more *are* the children of the d than — 8074
 54: 3 and make the d cities to be inhabited. — 8074
 59:10 night; *we are* in d *places* as dead *men.* — 820
 62: 4 shall thy land any more be termed D: — 8077
Jer 2:12 be ye very d, saith the LORD. — 2717
 4: 7 forth from his place to make thy land d; — 8047
 4:27 LORD said, The whole land shall be d; — 8077
 6: 8 lest I make thee d, a land not inhabited. — 8077
 7:34 voice of the bride: for the land shall be d. — 2723
 9:11 I will make the cities of Judah d, — 8077
 10:22 to make the cities of Judah d, *and* a den — 8077
 10:25 and have made his habitation d. — 8074
 12:10 they have made my pleasant portion a d — 8077
 12:11 They have made it d, *and being* desolate — 8076
 12:11 *and being* d it mourneth unto me; — 8077
 12:11 the whole land is **made** d, because no — 8074
 16:18 To make their land d, *and* a perpetual — 8047
 19: 8 I will make this city d, and a hissing; — 8047
 25:38 their land is d because of the fierceness — 8047
 26: 9 this city shall be d without an inhabitant? — 2717
 32:43 ye say, It *is* d without man or beast; — 8077
 33:10 which ye say *shall be* d without man and — 2720
 33:10 that are d, without man, and without — 8074
 33:12 *is* d without man and without beast, — 2720
 44: 6 and they are wasted *and* d, as *at* this day. — 8077
 46:19 waste and d without an inhabitant. — 3341
 48: 9 for the cities thereof shall be d, without — 8047
 48:34 for the waters of Nimrim shall be d. — 4923
 49: 2 it shall be a heap, and her daughters — 8077
 49:20 surely he shall **make** their habitations d — 8074
 50: 3 which shall make her land d, and none — 8047
 50:13 not be inhabited, but it shall be wholly d: — 8077
 50:45 he shall **make** *their* habitation with — 8077
 51:26 thou shalt be d for ever, saith the LORD. — 8077
 51:62 nor beast, but that it shall be d for ever. — 8077
La 1: 4 all her gates are d: her priests sigh: — 8074
 1:13 he hath made me d *and* faint all the day. — 8074
 1:16 my children are d, because the enemy — 8074
 3:11 pulled me in pieces: he hath made me d. — 8074
 4: 5 They that did feed delicately are d — 8074
 5:18 Zion, which is d, the foxes walk upon it. — 8074
Eze 6: 4 your altars shall be d, and your images — 3456
 6: 6 laid waste, and the high places shall be d; — 8077
 6: 6 altars may be laid waste and **made** d, — 816
 6:14 hand upon them, and make the land d, — 8077
 6:14 more *than* the wilderness toward — 4923
 12:19 that her land may be d from all that is — 3456
 12:20 be laid waste, and the land shall be d; — 8077
 14:15 they spoil it, so that it be d, that no man — 8077
 14:16 shall be delivered, but the land be d. — 8077
 15: 8 I will make the land d, because they have — 8077
 19: 7 knew their d **palaces,** and he laid waste — 490
 19: 7 the land was d, and the fulness thereof, — 3456
 20:26 that I might make them d, to the end — 8074
 25: 3 against the land of Israel, when it was d; — 2723
 25:13 I will make it d from Teman; and they — 2723
 26:19 When I shall make thee a d city, like — 2717
 26:20 in *places* of old, with them that go — 2723
 29: 9 the land of Egypt shall be d and waste; — 8077
 29:10 the land of Egypt utterly waste *and* d, — 8077
 29:12 I will make the land of Egypt d in the — 8074
 29:12 in the midst of the countries *that are* d, — 8074
 29:12 *that are* laid waste shall be d forty years: — 8074
 30: 7 shall be d in the midst of the countries — 8074
 30: 7 in the midst of the countries *that are* d, — 8074
 30:14 will **make** Pathros d, and will set fire in — 8074
 32:15 When I shall make the land of Egypt d, — 8077
 33:28 I will lay the land most d, — 4923+8077+2050.1
 33:28 the mountains of Israel shall be d, that — 8074
 33:29 have laid the land most d — 4923+8077+2050.1
 35: 3 I will make thee most d, — 4923+8077+2050.1
 35: 4 thou shalt be d, and thou shalt know that — 8074
 35: 7 make mount Seir most d, — 8077+8077+2050.1
 35:12 saying, They are **laid** d, they are given us — 8074
 35:14 whole earth rejoiceth, I will make thee d. — 8074
 35:15 because it was d, so will I do unto thee: — 8074
 35:15 thou shalt be d, O mount Seir, — 8074
 36: 3 Because *they* have **made** *you* d, — 8074
 36: 4 to the d wastes, and to the cities that are — 8074
 36:34 the d land shall be tilled, whereas it lay — 8077
 36:34 whereas it lay d in the sight of all that — 8077
 36:35 This land that was d is become like — 8074
 36:35 The waste and d and ruined cities *are* — 8074
 36:36 ruined *places,* and plant that that was d: — 8074
 38:12 to turn thine hand upon the d **places** — 2723
Da 9:17 face to shine upon thy sanctuary that is d, — 8076
 9:27 of abominations he *shall* **make** it d, — 8074
 9:27 determined shall be poured upon the d. — 8074
 11:31 place the abomination that **maketh** d. — 8074
 12:11 the abomination that **maketh** d set up, — 8074
Hos 5: 9 Ephraim shall be d in the day of rebuke: — 8047
 13:16 Samaria shall become d; for she hath — 816
Joel 1:17 garners are **laid** d, the barns are broken — 8074
 1:18 yea, the flocks of sheep are **made** d. — 8074
 2: 3 and behind them a wilderness; — 8077
 2:20 will drive him into a land barren and d, — 8077
 3:19 and Edom shall be a d wilderness, — 8074
Am 7: 9 the high places of Isaac shall be d, — 8074
Mic 7:13 and all the idols thereof will I lay d. — 8074
 6:13 in **making** *thee* d because of thy sins. — 8074
 7:13 Notwithstanding the land shall be d — 8074
Zep 3: 6 their towers are d; I made their streets — 8074

D

Zec	7:14 the land was **d** after them, that no man	8074
	7:14 for they laid the pleasant land **d**.	8047
Mal	1: 4 we will return and build the **d** places,	2723
Mt	23:38 Behold, your house is left unto you **d**.	2048
Lk	13:35 Behold, your house is left unto you **d**:	2048
Ac	1:20 Let his habitation be **d**, and let no man	2048
Gal	4:27 for the **d** hath many moe children than	2048
1Ti	5: 5 and **d**, trusteth in God, and continueth in	3443
Rev	17:16 and shall make her **d** and naked, and shall	2049
	18:19 for in one hour is she **made d**.	2049

DESOLATION (46) [DESOLATE]

Lev	26:31 **bring** your sanctuaries **unto d**, and I will	8074
	26:32 I will **bring** the land **into d**: and	8074
Jos	8:28 it a heap for ever, *even* a **d** unto this day.	8077
2Ki	22:19 that *they* should become a **d** and a curse,	8047
2Ch	30: 7 therefore gave them up to **d**, as ye see.	8047
Job	30:14 in the **d** they rolled themselves *upon me*.	7722
Ps	73:19 How are they **brought** into **d**, as *in* a	8047
Pr	1:27 When your fear cometh as **d**,	7722
	3:25 neither of the **d** of the wicked, when it	7722
Isa	10: 3 and in the **d** *which* shall come from far?	7722
	17: 9 children of Israel: and there shall be **d**.	8077
	24:12 the city is left **d**, and the gate is smitten	8047
	47:11 **d** shall come upon thee suddenly,	7722
	51:19 **d**, and destruction, and the famine,	7701
	64:10 Zion is a wilderness, Jerusalem a **d**.	8077
Jer	2: 5 that this house shall become a **d**.	2723
	25:11 this whole land shall be a **d**,	2723
	25:18 to make them a **d**, an astonishment,	2723
	34:22 I will make the cities of Judah a **d**	8077
	44: 2 day they *are* a **d**, and no man dwelleth	2723
	44:22 therefore is your land a **d**, and an	2723
	49:13 that Bozrah shall become a **d**, a reproach,	8047
	49:17 Also Edom shall be a **d**: every one that	8047
	49:33 a dwelling for dragons, *and* a **d** for ever:	8077
	50:23 how is Babylon become a **d** among	8047
	51:29 to make the land of Babylon a **d** without	8047
	51:43 Her cities are a **d**, a dry land,	8047
La	3:47 snare is come upon us, **d** and destruction.	7612
Eze	7:27 the prince shall be clothed with **d**,	8077
	23:33 *with* the cup of astonishment and **d**,	8077
Da	8:13 daily *sacrifice*, and the transgression of **d**,	8074
Hos	12: 1 he daily increaseth lies and **d**; and they do	7701
Joel	3:19 Egypt shall be a **d**, and Edom shall be a	8077
Mic	6:16 that I should make thee a **d**,	8047
Zep	1:13 become a booty, and their houses a **d**:	8077
	1:15 and distress, a day of wasteness and **d**,	4875
	2: 4 Gaza shall be forsaken, and Ashkelon a **d**:	8077
	2: 9 of nettles, and saltpits, and a perpetual **d**:	8077
	2:13 will make Nineveh a **d**, *and* dry like a	8077
	2:14 the windows; **d** *shall be* in the thresholds:	2721
	2:15 how is she become a **d**, a place for beasts	8047
Mt	12:25 divided against itself is **brought to d**;	2049
	24:15 therefore shall see the abomination of **d**,	2050
Mk	13:14 when ye shall see the abomination of **d**,	2050
Lk	11:17 divided against itself is **brought to d**;	2049
	21:20 then know that the **d** thereof is nigh.	2050

DESOLATIONS (11) [DESOLATE]

Ezr	9: 9 repair the **d** thereof, and to give us a wall	2723
Ps	46: 8 what he hath made in the earth.	8047
	74: 3 Lift up thy feet unto the perpetual **d**;	4876
Isa	61: 4 they shall raise up the former **d**,	8074
	61: 4 waste cities, the **d** of many generations.	8074
Jer	25: 9 and a hissing, and perpetual **d**.	2723
	25:12 and will make it perpetual **d**.	8077
Eze	35: 9 will make thee perpetual **d**, and thy cities	8077
Da	9: 2 seventy years in the **d** of Jerusalem.	2723
	9:18 behold our **d**, and the city which is called	8074
	9:26 unto the end of the war **d** *are* determined.	8074

DESPAIR (3) [DESPAIRED]

1Sa	27: 1 Saul shall **d** of me, to seek me any more	2976
Ecc	2:20 **cause** my heart to **d** of all the labour	2976
2Co	4: 8 *we are* perplexed, but not in **d**;	1820

DESPAIRED (1) [DESPAIR]

2Co	1: 8 insomuch that we **d** even of life:	1820

DESPERATE (2) [DESPERATELY]

Job	6:26 the speeches of one that is **d**, *which* are	2976
Isa	17:11 a heap in the day of grief and of **d** sorrow.	605

DESPERATELY (1) [DESPERATE]

Jer	17: 9 deceitful above all *things*, and **d** wicked:	605

DESPISE (37) [DESPISED, DESPISERS, DESPISEST, DESPISETH, DESPISING]

Lev	26:15 if ye shall **d** my statutes, or if your soul	3988
1Sa	2:30 they that **d** me shall be lightly esteemed.	959
2Sa	19:43 why then did ye **d** us, that our advice	7043
Est	1:17 *they* shall **d** their husbands in their eyes,	959
Job	5:17 **d** not thou the chastening of the Almighty:	3988
	9:21 I not know my soul: I would **d** my life.	3988
	10: 3 that thou shouldest **d** the work of thine	3988
	31:13 If I did **d** the cause of my manservant or	3988
Ps	51:17 a contrite heart, O God, thou wilt not **d**.	959
	73:20 *thou* awakest, thou shalt **d** their image.	959
	102:17 the destitute, and not **d** their prayer.	959
Pr	1: 7 *but* fools **d** wisdom and instruction.	936
	3:11 **d** not the chastening of the LORD;	3988
	6:30 *Men* do not **d** a thief, if he steal to satisfy	936
	23: 9 for he will **d** the wisdom of thy words.	936
	23:22 and **d** not thy mother when she is old.	936

Isa	30:12 Because ye **d** this word, and trust in	3988
Jer	4:30 *thy* lovers will **d** thee, they will seek thy	3988
	23:17 They say still unto them that **d** me,	5006
La	1: 8 all that honoured her **d** her, because	2107
Eze	16:57 the Philistines, which **d** thee round about.	7590
	28:26 all those that **d** them round about them;	7590
Am	5:21 I **d** your feast *days*, and I will not smell in	3988
Mal	1: 6 hosts unto you, O priests, that **d** my name.	959
Mt	6:24 he will hold to the one, and **d** the other.	2706
	18:10 Take heed that ye **d** not one of these little	2706
Lk	16:13 he will hold to the one, and **d** the other.	2706
Ro	14: 3 Let not him that eateth **d** him that eateth	1848
1Co	11:22 to drink in? or ye the church of God,	2706
	16:11 Let no *man* therefore **d** him: but	1848
1Th	5:20 **D** not prophesyings.	1848
1Ti	4:12 Let no *man* **d** thy youth; but be thou an	2706
	6: 2 let them not **d** *them*, because they are	2706
Tit	2:15 with all authority. Let no *man* **d** thee.	4065
Heb	12: 5 **d** not thou the chastening of the Lord,	3643
2Pe	2:10 lust of uncleanness, and **d** government.	2706
Jude	1: 8 **d** dominion, and speak evil of dignities.	114

DESPISED (60) [DESPISE]

Ge	16: 4 her mistress was **d** in her eyes.	7043
	16: 5 she had conceived, I was **d** in her eyes:	7043
	25:34 went his way: thus Esau **d** *his* birthright.	959
Lev	26:43 even because they **d** my judgments,	3988
Nu	11:20 that ye have **d** the LORD which *is* among	3988
	14:31 they shall know the land which ye have **d**.	3988
	15:31 Because he hath **d** the word of the LORD,	959
Jdg	9:38 *is* not this the people that thou hast **d**? go	3988
1Sa	10:27 they **d** him, and brought him no presents.	959
2Sa	6:16 the LORD; and she **d** him in her heart.	959
	12: 9 Wherefore hast thou **d** the commandment	959
	12:10 because thou hast **d** me, and hast taken	959
2Ki	19:21 virgin the daughter of Zion hath **d** thee,	959
1Ch	15:29 and playing: and she **d** him in her heart.	959
2Ch	36:16 **d** his words, and misused his prophets,	959
Ne	2:19 and us, and said, What *is* this thing that ye	959
	4: 4 Hear, O our God; for we are **d**: and turn	939
Job	12: 5 a lamp **d** in the thought of him that is at	937
	19:18 Yea, young children **d** me; I arose,	3988
Ps	22: 6 a reproach of men, and **d** of the people.	959
	22:24 he hath not **d** nor abhorred the affliction	959
	53: 5 to shame, because God hath **d** them.	3988
	106:24 they **d** the pleasant land, they believed	3988
	119:141 I *am* small and **d**: *yet* do not I forget thy	959
Pr	1:30 none of my counsel: they **d** all my reproof.	5006
	5:12 hated instruction, and my heart **d** reproof;	5006
	12: 8 he that is of a perverse heart shall be **d**.	937
	12: 9 He that is **d**, and hath a servant, *is* better	7034
Ecc	9:16 nevertheless the poor *man's* wisdom *is* **d**,	959
SS	8: 1 I would kiss thee; yea, I should not be **d**.	936
Isa	5:24 and the word of the Holy One of Israel.	5006
	33: 8 he hath **d** the cities, he regardeth no man.	3988
	37:22 hath **d** thee, *and* laughed thee to scorn;	959
	53: 3 He is **d** and rejected of men; a man of	959
	53: 3 he was **d**, and we esteemed him not.	959
	60:14 all they that **d** thee shall bow themselves	5006
Jer	22:28 *Is* this man Coniah a **d** broken idol? *is* he a	959
	33:24 thus they have **d** my people, that *they*	5006
	49:15 among the heathen, *and* **d** among men.	959
La	2: 6 hath **d** in the indignation of his anger	5006
Eze	16:59 which hast **d** the oath in breaking	959
	17:16 whose oath he **d**, and whose covenant he	959
	17:18 Seeing he **d** the oath by breaking	959
	17:19 surely mine oath that he hath **d**,	959
	20:13 they **d** my judgments, which *if* a man do,	3988
	20:16 Because they **d** my judgments, and walked	3988
	20:24 had **d** my statutes, and had polluted my	3988
	22: 8 Thou hast **d** mine holy *things*, and hast	959
	28:24 *that are* round about them, that **d** them;	7590
Am	2: 4 because they have **d** the law of the LORD,	3988
Ob	1: 2 among the heathen: thou *art* greatly **d**.	959
Zec	4:10 For who hath **d** the day of small *things*?	936
Mal	1: 6 And ye say, Wherein have we **d** thy name?	959
Lk	18: 9 that they were righteous, and **d** other:	1848
Ac	19:27 goddess Diana should be **d**,	1519+3049+3762
1Co	1:28 and *things* which are **d**, hath God chosen,	1848
	4:10 strong; ye *are* honourable, but we *are* **d**.	820
Gal	4:14 which was in my flesh ye **d** not,	1848
Heb	10:28 He that **d** Moses' law died without mercy	114
Jas	2: 6 But ye have **d** the poor. Do not rich *men*	818

DESPISERS (2) [DESPISE]

Ac	13:41 Behold *ye* **d**, and wonder, and perish: for	2707
2Ti	3: 3 fierce, **d** of *those that are* good,	865

DESPISEST (1) [DESPISE]

Ro	2: 4 Or **d** thou the riches of his goodness and	2706

DESPISETH (19) [DESPISE]

Job	36: 5 not *any*: he is mighty in strength and	3988
Ps	69:33 heareth the poor, and **d** not his prisoners.	959
Pr	11:12 He that is void of wisdom **d** his neighbour:	936
	13:13 Whoso **d** the word shall be destroyed: but	959
	14: 2 but he that is perverse in his ways **d** him.	936
	14:21 He that **d** his neighbour sinneth: but he	936
	15: 5 A fool **d** his father's instruction: but he	5006
	15:20 glad father: but a foolish man **d** his mother.	959
	15:32 that refuseth instruction **d** his own soul:	3988
	19:16 own soul; *but* he that **d** his ways shall die.	959
	30:17 at *his* father, and to obey *his* mother,	959
Isa	33:15 he that **d** the gain of oppressions,	3988
	49: 7 *and* his Holy One, to whom man **d**,	960

Lk	10:16 he that **d** you despiseth me; and he that	114
	10:16 he that despiseth you **d** me; and he that	114
	10:16 he that **d** me despiseth him that sent me.	114
	10:16 he that despiseth **d** him that sent me.	114
1Th	4: 8 He therefore that **d**, despiseth not man,	114
	4: 8 that despiseth, **d** not man, but God,	114

DESPISING (1) [DESPISE]

Heb	12: 2 **d** the shame, and is set down at the right	2706

DESPITE (2) [DESPITEFUL, DESPITEFULLY]

Eze	25: 6 rejoiced in heart with all thy **d** against	7589
Heb	10:29 and hath **done** it unto the Spirit of grace?	1796

DESPITEFUL (2) [DESPITE]

Eze	25:15 have taken vengeance with a **d** heart,	7589
	36: 5 with **d** minds, to cast it out for a prey.	7589
Ro	1:30 haters of God, **d**, proud, boasters,	5197

DESPITEFULLY (3) [DESPITE]

Mt	5:44 and pray for them which **d** use you,	1908
Lk	6:28 and pray for them which **d** use you.	1908
Ac	14: 5 to **use** *them* **d**, and to stone them,	5195

DESTINY See END; EVENT; NUMBER; PATHS

DESTITUTE (8)

Ge	24:27 hath not **left** **d** my master of his mercy	5800
Ps	102:17 He will regard the prayer of the **d**,	6199
	141: 8 in thee is my trust; **leave** not my soul **d**.	6168
Pr	15:21 Folly *is* joy to *him that is* **d** of wisdom:	2638
Eze	32:15 the country shall be **d** of that whereof it	8074
1Ti	6: 5 and **d** of the truth, supposing that gain is	650
Heb	11:37 being **d**, afflicted, tormented;	5302
Jas	2:15 or sister be naked, and **d** of daily food,	3007

DESTROY (261) [DESTROYED, DESTROYER, DESTROYERS, DESTROYEST, DESTROYETH, DESTROYING, DESTRUCTION, DESTRUCTIONS]

Ge	6: 7 I will **d** man whom I have created from	4229
	6:13 and behold, I will **d** them with the earth.	7843
	6:17 to **d** all flesh, wherein *is* the breath of life,	7843
	7: 4 will I **d** from off the face of the earth.	4229
	9:11 shall there any more be a flood to **d**	7843
	9:15 no more become a flood to **d** all flesh.	7843
	18:23 Wilt thou also **d** the righteous with	5595
	18:24 wilt thou also **d** and not spare the place	5595
	18:28 wilt thou **d** all the city for *lack of* five?	7843
	18:28 I find there forty and five, I will not **d** *it*.	7843
	18:31 he said, I will not **d** *it* for twenty's sake.	7843
	18:32 And he said, I will not **d** *it* for ten's sake.	7843
	19:13 For we will **d** this place, because the cry	7843
	19:13 and the LORD hath sent us to **d** it.	7843
	19:14 this place; for the LORD will **d** this city.	7843
Ex	8: 9 to **d** the frogs from thee and thy houses,	3772
	12:13 the plague shall not be upon you to **d** *you*,	4889
	15: 9 draw my sword, my hand shall **d** them.	3423
	23:27 will **d** all the people to whom thou shalt	2000
	34:13 ye shall **d** their altars, break their images,	5422
Lev	23:30 same soul will I **d** from among his people.	6
	26:22 **d** your cattle, and make you few in	3772
	26:30 I will **d** your high places, and cut down	8045
	26:44 to **d** them **utterly**, and to break my	3615
Nu	21: 2 hand, then I will **utterly d** their cities.	2763
	24:17 of Moab, and **d** all the children of Sheth.	6979
	24:19 and shall **d** him that remaineth of the city.	6
	32:15 and ye shall **d** all this people.	7843
	33:52 **d** all their pictures, and destroy all their	6
	33:52 **d** all their molten images, and quite pluck	6
Dt	1:27 us into the hand of the Amorites, to **d** us.	8045
	2:15 to **d** them from among the host, until they	2000
	4:31 he will not forsake thee, neither **d** thee,	7843
	6:15 and **d** thee from off the face of the earth.	8045
	7: 2 shalt smite them, and **utterly d**	2763+2763
	7: 4 kindled against you, and **d** thee suddenly.	8045
	7: 5 ye shall **d** their altars, and break down	5422
	7:10 that hate him to their face, to **d** them:	6
	7:23 shalt **d** them *with* a mighty destruction,	1949
	7:24 shalt **d** their name from under heaven:	6
	9: 3 as a consuming fire he shall **d** them,	8045
	9: 3 thou drive them out, and **d** them quickly,	8045
	9:14 I may **d** them, and blot out their name	8045
	9:19 LORD was wroth against you to **d** you.	8045
	9:25 the LORD had said he would **d** you.	8045
	9:26 **d** not thy people and thine inheritance,	7843
	10:10 *and* the LORD would not **d** thee.	7843
	12: 2 Ye shall **utterly d** all the places, wherein	6+6
	12: 3 and the names of them out of that place.	6
	20:17 thou shalt **utterly d** them;	2763+2763
	20:19 thou shalt not **d** the trees thereof by	7843
	20:20 meat, thou shalt **d** and cut them down;	7843
	28:63 the LORD will rejoice over you to **d** you,	6
	31: 3 he will **d** these nations from before thee,	8045
	32:25 shall **d** both the young man and the virgin,	7921
	33:27 from before thee; and shall say, **D** *them*.	8045
Jos	7: 7 us into the hand of the Amorites, to **d** us?	6
	7:12 except ye **d** the accursed from amongst	8045
	9:24 to **d** all the inhabitants of the land from	8045
	11:20 he might **d** them **utterly**, *and* that they	2763
	11:20 no favour, but that *he* might **d** them,	8045
	22:33 to **d** the land wherein the children of	7843
Jdg	21:11 Ye shall **utterly d** every male,	2763
1Sa	15: 3 **utterly d** all that they have, and spare	2763
	15: 6 the Amalekites, lest I **d** you with them:	622
	15: 9 *was* good, and would not **utterly d** them:	2763

1Sa
15:18 and **utterly d** the sinners the Amalekites, 2763
23:10 come to Keilah, to **d** the city for my sake. 7843
24:21 that thou wilt not **d** my name out of my 8045
26: 9 David said to Abishai, **D** him not: for who 7843
26:15 for there came one of the people in to **d** 7843
2Sa
1:14 thine hand to **d** the LORD's anointed? 7843
14: 7 he slew; and we will **d** the heir also: 8045
14:11 the revengers of blood to **d** any more, 7843
14:11 to destroy any more, lest they **d** my son. 8045
14:16 of the hand of the man that would **d** me 8045
20:19 thou seekest to **d** a city and a mother in 4191
20:20 from me, that I should swallow up or **d**. 7843
22:41 that I might **d** them that hate me. 6789
24:16 out his hand upon Jerusalem to **d** it, 7843
1Ki
9:21 of Israel also were not able **utterly** to **d**, 2763
13:34 and to **d** it from off the face of the earth. 8045
16:12 Thus did Zimri **d** all the house of Baasha. 8045
2Ki
8:19 Yet the LORD would not **d** Judah for 7843
10:19 intent that he might **d** the worshippers of 6
13:23 Isaac, and Jacob, and would not **d** them, 7843
18:25 The LORD against this place to **d** it? 7843
18:25 to me, Go up against this land, and **d** it. 7843
24: 2 and sent them against Judah to **d** it, 6
1Ch 21:15 God sent an angel unto Jerusalem to **d** it: 7843
2Ch 12: 7 I will not **d** them, but I will grant 7843
12:12 that he would not **d** him altogether: 7843
20:23 utterly to slay and **d** them: and when they 8045
20:23 of Seir, every one helped to **d** another. 4889
21: 7 Howbeit the LORD would not **d** the house 7843
25:16 that God hath determined to **d** thee, 7843
35:21 who is with me, that he **d** thee not. 7843
Ezr
6:12 caused his name to dwell there all kings 4049
6:12 to **d** this house of God which is at 2255
Est
3: 6 wherefore Haman sought to **d** all the Jews 8045
3:13 **d**, to kill, and to cause to perish, all Jews, 8045
4: 7 king's treasuries for the Jews, to **d** them. 6
4: 8 that was given at Shushan to **d** them, 8045
8: 5 which he wrote to **d** the Jews which are 6
8:11 to **d**, to slay, and to cause to perish, 8045
9:24 had devised against the Jews to **d** them, 6
9:24 the lot, to consume them, and to **d** them; 6
Job
2: 3 me against him, to **d** him without cause. 1104
6: 9 Even that it would please God to **d** me: 1792
8:18 If he **d** him from his place, then it shall 1104
10: 8 together round about; yet thou dost **d** me. 1104
19:26 though after my skin worms **d** this body, 5362
Ps
5: 6 Thou shalt **d** them that speak leasing: 6
5:10 **D** thou them, O God; let them fall by their 816
18:40 that I might **d** them that hate me. 6789
21:10 Their fruit shalt thou **d** from the earth, 2040
28: 5 he shall **d** them, and not build them up. 2040
40:14 together that seek after my soul to **d** it; 5595
52: 5 God shall likewise **d** thee for ever, he 5422
55: 9 **D**, O Lord, and divide their tongues: for I 1104
63: 9 to **d** it, shall go into the lower parts of 7722
69: 4 that would **d** me, being mine enemies 6789
74: 8 in their hearts, Let us **d** them together: 3238
101: 8 I will early **d** all the wicked of the land; 8045
106:23 Therefore he said that he would **d** them, 8045
106:23 away his wrath, lest he should **d** them. 7843
106:34 They did not **d** the nations, 8045
118:10 in the name of the LORD will I **d** them. 4135
118:11 in the name of the LORD I will **d** them. 4135
118:12 for in the name of the LORD I will **d** 4135
119:95 The wicked have waited for me to **d** me: 6
143:12 and **d** all them that afflict my soul: 6
144: 6 shoot out thine arrows, and **d** them. 2000
145:20 love him: but all the wicked will he **d**. 8045
Pr
1:32 and the prosperity of fools shall **d** them. 6
11: 3 the perverseness of transgressors shall **d** 7703
15:25 The LORD will **d** the house of the proud: 5255
21: 7 The robbery of the wicked shall **d** them; 1641
Ecc
5: 6 thy voice, and **d** the work of thine hands? 2254
7:16 over wise: why shouldest thou **d** thyself? 8074
Isa
3:12 thee to err, and **d** the way of thy paths. 1104
10: 7 in his heart to **d** and cut off nations not 8045
11: 9 They shall not hurt nor **d** in all my holy 7843
11:15 the LORD shall **utterly d** the tongue of 2763
13: 5 of his indignation, to **d** the whole land. 2254
13: 9 he shall **d** the sinners thereof out of it. 8045
19: 3 and I will **d** the counsel thereof: 1104
23:11 city, to **d** the strong holds thereof. 8045
25: 7 he will **d** in this mountain the face of 1104
32: 7 he deviseth wicked devices to **d** the poor 2254
36:10 The LORD against this land to **d** it? 7843
36:10 me, Go up against this land, and **d** it. 7843
42:14 I will **d** and devour at once. 5395
51:13 of the oppressor, as if he were ready to **d**? 7843
54:16 and I have created the waster to **d**. 2254
65: 8 in the cluster, and one saith, **D** it not; 7843
65: 8 servants' sakes, that I may not **d** them all. 7843
65:25 They shall not hurt nor **d** in all my holy 7843
Jer
1:10 to **d**, and to throw down, to build, 6
5:10 Go ye up upon her walls, and **d**; 7843
6: 5 us go by night, and let us **d** her palaces. 7843
11:19 saying, Let us **d** the tree with the fruit 7843
12:17 will utterly pluck up and **d** that nation, 6
13:14 nor spare, nor have mercy, but **d** them. 7843
15: 3 the beasts of the earth, to devour and **d**. 7843
15: 6 out my hand against thee, and **d** thee; 7843
15: 7 them of children, I will **d** my people, 6
17:18 evil, and **d** them with double destruction. 7665
18: 7 to pluck up, and to pull down, and to **d** it; 6
23: 1 Woe be unto the pastors that **d** and scatter 6
25: 9 will **utterly d** them, and make them an 2763

Jer
31:28 to throw down, and to **d**, and to afflict; 6
36:29 shall certainly come and **d** this land, 7843
46: 8 I will **d** the city and the inhabitants 6
48:18 thee, and he shall **d** thy strong holds. 7843
49: 9 night, they will **d** till they have enough. 7843
49:38 **d** from thence the king and the princes, 6
50:21 waste and **utterly d** after them, saith 2763
50:26 cast her up as heaps, and **d** her **utterly**: 2763
51: 3 her young men; **d** ye **utterly** all her host. 7843
51:11 for his device is against Babylon, to **d** it; 7843
51:20 and with thee will I **d** kingdoms; 7843
La
2: 8 The LORD hath purposed to **d** the wall of 7843
3:66 **d** them in anger from under the heavens 8045
Eze
5:16 which I will send to **d** you: 7843
6: 3 upon you, and I will **d** your high places. 6
9: 8 wilt thou **d** all the residue of Israel in thy 7843
14: 9 will **d** him from the midst of my people 8045
21:31 the hand of brutish men, and skilful to **d**. 4889
22:27 shed blood, and to **d** souls, to get dishonest 6
22:30 me for the land, that I should not **d** it: 7843
25: 7 I will **d** thee; and thou shalt know that I 8045
25:15 despiteful heart, to **d** it for the old hatred; 4889
25:16 and the remnant of the sea coast. 6
26: 4 they shall **d** the walls of Tyrus, 7843
26:12 thy walls, and **d** thy pleasant houses: 5422
28:16 I will **d** thee, O covering cherub, from 6
30:11 nations, shall be brought to **d** the land: 7843
30:13 I will also **d** the idols, and I will cause 6
32:13 I will also **d** all the beasts thereof from 6
34:16 I will **d** the fat and the strong; I will feed 8045
43: 3 that I saw when I came to **d** the city: 7843
Da
2:12 to **d** all the wise men of Babylon. 7
2:24 the king had ordained to **d** the wise men 7
2:24 unto him; **D** not the wise men of Babylon: 7
4:23 saying, Hew the tree down, and **d** it; 2255
7:26 to consume and to **d** it unto the end. 7
8:24 he shall **d** wonderfully, and shall prosper, 7843
8:24 shall **d** the mighty and the holy people. 7843
8:25 in his heart, and by peace shall **d** many: 7843
9:26 the prince that shall come shall **d** the city 7843
11:26 of the portion of his meat shall **d** him, 7665
11:44 he shall go forth with great fury to **d**, 8045
Hos
2:12 I will **d** her vines and her fig trees, 8074
4: 5 thee in the night, and I will **d** thy mother. 1820
11: 9 anger, I will not return to **d** Ephraim: 7843
Am
9: 8 I will **d** it from off the face of the earth; 8045
9: 8 saving that I will not **utterly d** 8045+8045
Ob
1: 8 even the wise men out of Edom, 6
Mic
2:10 of you, even with a sore destruction. 2254
5:10 the midst of thee, and I will **d** thy chariots; 6
5:14 of the midst of thee: so will I **d** thy cities. 8045
Zep
2: 5 land of the Philistines, I will even **d** thee, 6
2:13 his hand against the north, and **d** Assyria; 6
Hag
2:22 I will **d** the strength of the kingdoms of 8045
Zec
12: 9 that I will seek to **d** all the nations that 8045
Mal
3:11 he shall not **d** the fruits of your ground; 7843
Mt
2:13 for Herod will seek the young child to **d** 622
5:17 Think not that I am come to **d** the law, 2647
5:17 I am not come to **d**, but to fulfil. 2647
10:28 fear him which is able to **d** both soul 622
12:14 against him, how they might **d** him. 622
21:41 He will miserably **d** those wicked men, 622
26:61 I am able to **d** the temple of God, 2647
27:20 that they should ask Barabbas, and **d** Jesus. 622
Mk
1:24 art thou come to **d** us? I know thee who 622
3: 6 against him, how they might **d** him. 622
9:22 into the fire, and into the waters, to **d** him: 622
11:18 heard it, and sought how they might **d** him: 622
12: 9 he will come and **d** the husbandmen, 622
14:58 will **d** this temple that is made with hands, 2647
Lk
4:34 art thou come to **d** us? I know thee who 622
6: 9 or to do evil? to save life, or to **d** it? 622
9:56 For the Son of man is not come to **d** men's 622
19:47 the chief of the people sought to **d** him, 622
20:16 He shall come and **d** these husbandmen, 622
Jn
2:19 **D** this temple, and in three days I will 3089
10:10 but for to steal, and to kill, and to **d**: 622
Ac
6:14 that this Jesus of Nazareth shall **d** this 2647
Ro
14:15 **D** not him with thy meat, for whom Christ 622
14:20 For meat **d** not the work of God. 2647
1Co
1:19 I will **d** the wisdom of the wise, 622
3:17 defile the temple of God, him shall God **d**; 5351
6:13 but God shall **d** both it and them. 2673
2Th
2: 8 shall **d** with the brightness of his coming: 2673
Heb
2:14 that through death he might **d** him that 2673
Jas
4:12 one lawgiver, who is able to save and to **d**: 622
1Jn
3: 8 that he might **d** the works of the devil. 3089
Rev
11:18 shouldest **d** them which destroy the earth. 1311
11:18 shouldest destroy them which **d** the earth. 1311

DESTROYED (167) [DESTROY]

Ge
7:23 every living substance was **d** which was 4229
7:23 heaven; and they were **d** from the earth: 4229
13:10 before the LORD **d** Sodom and 7843
19:29 pass, when God **d** the cities of the plain, 7843
34:30 slay me; and I shall be **d**, I and my house. 8045
Ex
10: 7 knowest thou not yet that Egypt is **d**? 6
22:20 the LORD only, he shall be **utterly d**. 2763
Nu
21: 3 and they **utterly d** them and their cities: 2763
Dt
1:44 chased you, as bees do, and **d** you in Seir, 3807
2:12 when they had **d** them from before them, 8045
2:21 the LORD **d** them before them; 8045
2:22 when he **d** the Horims from before them; 8045
2:23 **d** them, and dwelt in their stead.) 8045
2:34 **utterly d** the men, and the women, 2763

D

Dt
3: 6 we **utterly d** them, as we did unto Sihon 2763
4: 3 the LORD thy God hath **d** them from 8045
4:26 days upon it, but shall utterly be **d**. 8045+8045
7:20 left, and hide themselves from thee, be **d**. 6
7:23 with a mighty destruction, until they be **d**. 8045
7:24 stand before thee, until thou have **d** them. 8045
9: 8 LORD was angry with you to have **d** you. 6
9:20 was very angry with Aaron to have **d** him: 8045
11: 4 how the LORD hath **d** them unto this day; 6
12:30 after that they be **d** from before thee; 8045
28:20 until thou be **d**, and until thou perish 8045
28:24 it come down upon thee, until thou be **d**. 8045
28:45 and overtake thee, till thou be **d**; 8045
28:48 iron upon thy neck, until he have **d** thee. 8045
28:51 and the fruit of thy land, until thou be **d**: 8045
28:51 flocks of thy sheep, until he have **d** thee. 6
28:61 LORD bring upon thee, until thou be **d**. 8045
31: 4 and unto the land of them, whom he **d**. 8045
Jos
2:10 Sihon and Og, whom ye **utterly d**. 2763
6:21 they **utterly d** all that was in the city, 2763
8:26 until he had **utterly d** all the inhabitants 2763
10: 1 Joshua had taken Ai, and had **utterly d** it; 2763
10:28 the king thereof he **utterly d** them, 2763
10:35 the souls that were therein he **utterly d** 2763
10:37 **d** it **utterly**, and all the souls that were 2763
10:39 **utterly d** all the souls that were therein; 2763
10:40 but **utterly d** all that breathed, 2763
11:12 of the sword, and he **utterly d** them, 2763
11:14 until they had **d** them, neither left they 8045
11:21 Joshua **d** them **utterly** with their cities. 2763
23:15 he have **d** you from off this good land 8045
24: 8 their land; and I **d** them from before you. 8045
Jdg
1:17 that inhabited Zephath, and **utterly d** it: 2763
4:24 until they had **d** Jabin king of Canaan. 3772
6: 4 the increase of the earth, till thou come 7843
20:21 **down** to the ground of the Israelites 7843
20:25 **down** to the ground of the children of 7843
20:35 the children of Israel **d** of the Benjamites 7843
20:42 which came out of the cities they **d** in 7843
21:16 seeing the women are **d** out of Benjamin? 8045
21:17 that a tribe be not **d** out of Israel. 4229
1Sa
5: 6 **d** them, and smote them with emerods, 8074
15: 8 **utterly d** all the people with the edge of 2763
15: 9 was vile and refuse, that they **d utterly**. 2763
15:15 thy God; and the rest we have **utterly d**. 2763
15:20 and have **utterly d** the Amalekites. 2763
15:21 things which should have been **utterly d** 2764
2Sa
10: 1 they **d** the children of Ammon, 7843
21: 5 devised against us that we should be **d** 8045
22:38 have pursued mine enemies, and **d** them; 8045
24:16 said to the angel that **d** the people, It is 7843
1Ki
15:13 Asa her idol, and burnt it by the brook 3772
15:29 until he had **d** him, according unto 8045
2Ki
10:17 till he had **d** him, according to the saying 8045
10:28 Thus Jehu **d** Baal out of Israel. 8045
11: 1 dead, she arose and **d** all the seed royal. 6
13: 7 for the king of Syria had **d** them, 6
19:12 delivered them which my fathers have **d**; 7843
19:17 the kings of Assyria have **d** the nations 2717
19:18 and stone: therefore they have **d** them. 6
21: 3 places which Hezekiah his father had **d**; 6
21: 9 the LORD **d** before the children of Israel. 8045
1Ch
4:41 **d** them **utterly** unto this day, and dwelt 2763
5:25 of the land, whom God **d** before them. 8045
20: 1 And Joab smote Rabbah, and **d** it. 2040
21:12 or three months to be **d** before thy foes, 5595
21:15 said to the angel that **d**, It is enough, 7843
2Ch
14:13 for they were **d** before the LORD, 7665
15: 6 nation was **d** of nation, and city of city: 3807
20:10 they turned from them, and **d** them not; 8045
22:10 **d** all the seed royal of the house of Judah. 1696
24:23 **d** all the princes of the people from among 7843
31: 1 until they had **utterly d** them all. 3615
32:14 of those nations that my fathers **utterly d**, 2763
33: 9 whom the LORD had **d** before 8045
34:11 houses which the kings of Judah had **d**. 7843
36:19 and **d** all the goodly vessels thereof. 7843
Ezr
4:15 old time: for which cause was this city **d**. 2718
5:12 who **d** this house, and carried the people 5642
Est
3: 9 king, let it be written that they may be **d**: 6
4:14 but thou and thy father's house shall be **d**: 6
7: 4 to be **d**, to be slain, and to perish. 8045
9: 6 the Jews slew and **d** five hundred men. 6
9:12 and **d** five hundred men in Shushan the 6
Job
4:20 They are **d** from morning to evening: 3807
19:10 hath **d** me on every side, and I am gone: 5422
34:25 them in the night, so that they are **d**. 1792
Ps
9: 5 the heathen, thou hast **d** the wicked, 6
9: 6 thou hast **d** cities; their memorial is 5428
11: 3 If the foundations be **d**, what can 2040
37:38 the transgressors shall be **d** together: 8045
73:27 thou hast **d** all them that go a whoring 6789
78:38 forgave their iniquity, and **d** them not: 7843
78:45 devoured them; and frogs, which **d** them. 7843
78:47 He **d** their vines with hail, 2026
92: 7 it is that they shall be **d** for ever: 8045
137: 8 O daughter of Babylon, who art to be **d**; 7703
Pr
13:13 Whoso despiseth the word shall be **d**: 2254
13:20 but a companion of fools shall be **d**. 7489
13:23 there is that is **d** for want of judgment. 5595
29: 1 shall suddenly be **d**, and that without 7665
Isa
9:16 to err; and they that are led of them are **d**. 1104
10:27 the yoke shall be **d** because of 2254
14:17 as a wilderness, and **d** the cities thereof; 2040
14:20 because thou hast **d** thy land, and slain 7843

D

Isa	26:14 therefore hast thou visited and **d** them,	8045
	34: 2 he hath **utterly d** them, he hath delivered	2763
	37:12 delivered them which my fathers have **d**,	7843
	37:19 and stone: therefore they have **d**,	6
	48:19 name should not have been cut off nor **d**	8045
Jer	12:10 Many pastors have **d** my vineyard,	7843
	22:20 from the passages: for all thy lovers are **d**.	7665
	48: 4 Moab is **d**; her little ones have caused a	7665
	48: 8 also shall perish, and the plain shall be **d**,	8045
	48:42 Moab shall be **d** from *being* a people,	8045
	51: 8 Babylon is suddenly fallen and **d**: howl for	7665
	51:55 and **d** out of her the great voice;	6
La	2: 5 he hath **d** his strong holds,	7843
	2: 6 he hath **d** his places of the assembly:	7843
	2: 9 ground; he hath **d** and broken her bars:	6
Eze	26:17 thee, How art thou **d**, *that was* inhabited	6
	27:32 like the **d** in the midst of the sea?	1822
	30: 8 and *when* all her helpers shall be **d**.	7665
	32:12 and all the multitude thereof shall be **d**.	8045
Da	2:44 a kingdom, which shall never be **d**:	2255
	6:26 his kingdom *that* which shall not be **d**,	2255
	7:11 his body, and given to the burning flame.	7
	7:14 his kingdom *that* which shall not be **d**.	2255
	11:20 within few days he shall be **d**, neither in	7665
Hos	4: 6 My people are **d** for lack of knowledge,	1820
	10: 8 also of Aven, the sin of Israel, shall be **d**:	8045
	13: 9 O Israel, *thou* hast **d** thyself; but in me *is*	7843
Am	2: 9 Yet **d** I the Amorite before them,	8045
	2: 9 yet I **d** his fruit from above, and his roots	8045
Zep	3: 6 their cities are **d**, so that there is no man,	6658
Mt	22: 7 and those murderers, and burnt up their	622
Lk	17:27 ark, and the flood came, and **d** them all.	622
	17:29 brimstone from heaven, and **d** *them* all.	622
Ac	3:23 shall be **d** from among the people.	1842
	9:21 Is not this he that **d** them which called on	4199
	13:19 And when he had **d** seven nations in	2507
	19:27 and her magnificence should be **d**,	2507
Ro	6: 6 with *him*, that the body of sin might be **d**,	2673
1Co	10: 9 also tempted, and were **d** of serpents.	622
	10:10 murmured, and were **d** of the destroyer.	622
	15:26 The last enemy *that* shall be **d** *is* death.	2673
2Co	4: 9 but not forsaken; cast down, but not **d**;	622
Gal	1:23 now preacheth the faith which once he **d**.	4199
	2:18 For if I build again the *things* which I **d**,	2647
Heb	11:28 lest he that **d** the firstborn should touch	3645
2Pe	2:12 brute beasts, made to be taken and **d**,	5356
Jude	1: 5 Egypt, afterward **d** them that believed not.	622
Rev	8: 9 and the third *part* of the ships were **d**.	1311

DESTROYER (7) [DESTROY]

Ex	12:23 will not suffer the **d** to come in unto your	7843
Jdg	16:24 the **d** of our country, which slew many of	2717
Job	15:21 in prosperity the **d** shall come upon him.	7703
Ps	17: 4 I have kept *me* from the paths of the **d**.	6530
Pr	28:24 the same *is* the companion of a **d**.	376+4889
Jer	4: 7 and the **d** of the Gentiles is on his way;	7843
1Co	10:10 and were destroyed of the **d**.	3644

DESTROYERS (4) [DESTROY]

Job	33:22 near unto the grave, and his life to the **d**.	4191
Isa	49:17 thy **d** and they that made thee waste shall	2040
Jer	22: 7 I will prepare against thee, every one	7843
	50:11 O ye **d** of mine heritage, because ye are	8154

DESTROYEST (4) [DESTROY]

Job	14:19 of the earth; and thou **d** the hope of man.	6
Jer	51:25 saith the LORD, which **d** all the earth:	7843
Mt	27:40 Thou that **d** the temple, and buildest *it in*	2647
Mk	15:29 thou that **d** the temple, and buildest *it in*	2647

DESTROYETH (8) [DESTROY]

Dt	8:20 As the nations which the LORD **d** before	6
Job	9:22 therefore I said *it*, He **d** the perfect and	3615
	12:23 He increaseth the nations, and **d** them:	6
Pr	6:32 he that doeth it **d** his own soul.	7843
	11: 9 A hypocrite with *his* mouth **d** his	7843
	31: 3 nor thy ways to *that which* **d** kings.	4229
Ecc	7: 7 a wise *man* mad; and a gift **d** the heart.	6
	9:18 of war: but one sinner **d** much good.	6

DESTROYING (14) [DESTROY]

Dt	3: 6 **utterly d** the men, women, and children,	2763
	13:15 **d** it **utterly**, and all that *is* therein,	2763
Jos	11:11 **utterly d** *them*: there was not any left to	2763
2Ki	19:11 have done to all lands, by **d** them **utterly**:	2763
1Ch	21:12 the angel of the LORD **d** throughout all	7843
	21:15 as *he* was **d**, the LORD beheld,	7843
Isa	28: 2 *which* as a tempest of hail and **a** storm,	6986
	37:11 have done to all lands by **d** them **utterly**,	2763
Jer	2:30 devoured your prophets, like a **d** lion.	7843
	51: 1 of them that rise up against me, a **d** wind;	7843
	51:25 Behold, I *am* against thee, O **d** mountain,	4889
La	2: 8 he hath not withdrawn his hand from **d**:	1104
Eze	9: 1 even every man *with* his **d** weapon in his	4892
	20:17 mine eye spared them from **d**	7843

DESTRUCTION (94) [DESTROY]

Dt	7:23 shall destroy them *with* a mighty **d**,	4103
	32:24 with burning heat, and with bitter **d**:	6986
1Sa	5: 9 was against the city *with* a very great **d**:	4103
	5:11 there was a deadly **d** throughout all	4103
1Ki	20:42 a man whom I **appointed to utter d**,	2764
2Ch	22: 4 after the death of his father to his **d**.	7843
	22: 7 the **d** of Ahaziah was of God by coming to	8395
	26:16 strong, his heart was lifted up to *his* **d**:	7843

Est	8: 6 can I endure to see the **d** of my kindred?	13
	9: 5 **d**, and did what they would unto those	12
Job	5:21 neither shalt thou be afraid of **d** when it	7701
	5:22 At **d** and famine thou shalt laugh:	7701
	18:12 and *shall be* ready at his side.	343
	21:17 how oft cometh their **d** upon them!	343
	21:20 His eyes shall see his **d**, and he shall drink	3589
	21:30 the wicked is reserved to the day of **d**?	343
	26: 6 naked before him, and **d** hath no covering.	11
	28:22 And death say, We have heard the fame	11
	30:12 raise up against me the ways of their **d**.	343
	30:24 to the grave, though *they* cry in his **d**.	6365
	31: 3 *Is* not **d** to the wicked? and a strange	343
	31:12 For it *is* a fire *that* consumeth to **d**,	11
	31:23 For **d** from God *was* a terror to me,	343
	31:29 If I rejoiced at the **d** of him that hated me,	6365
Ps	35: 8 Let **d** come upon him at unawares;	7722
	35: 8 catch himself: into that *very* **d** let him fall.	7722
	55:23 shalt bring them down into the pit of **d**:	7845
	73:18 *places*: thou castedst them down into **d**.	4876
	88:11 in the grave? *or* thy faithfulness in **d**?	11
	90: 3 Thou turnest man to *d*; and sayest, Return	1793
	91: 6 *nor* for the **d** that wasteth at noonday.	6986
	103: 4 Who redeemeth thy life from **d**;	7845
Pr	1:27 and your **d** cometh as a whirlwind;	343
	10:14 but the mouth of the foolish *is* near **d**.	4288
	10:15 the **d** of the poor *is* their poverty.	4288
	10:29 but **d** *shall be* to the workers of iniquity.	4288
	13: 3 he that openeth wide his lips shall have **d**.	4288
	14:28 the want of people *is* the **d** of the prince.	4288
	15:11 Hell and **d** *are* before the LORD: how	11
	16:18 Pride *goeth* before **d**, and a haughty spirit	7667
	17:19 and he that exalteth his gate seeketh **d**.	6607
	18: 7 A fool's mouth *is* his **d**, and his lips *are*	4288
	18:12 Before **d** the heart of man is haughty,	7667
	21:15 but **d** *shall be* to the workers of iniquity.	4288
	24: 2 their heart studieth **d**, and their lips talk	7701
	27:20 Hell and **d** are never full; so the eyes of	10
	31: 8 of all such as are **appointed to d**.	1121+2475
Isa	1:28 **d** of the transgressors and of the sinners	7667
	10:25 shall cease, and mine anger in their **d**.	8399
	13: 6 it shall come as a **d** from the Almighty.	7701
	14:23 I will sweep it with the besom of **d**,	8045
	15: 5 of Horonaim they shall raise up a cry of **d**.	7667
	19:18 of hosts: one shall be called, The city of **d**.	2041
	24:12 and the gate is smitten *with* **d**.	7591
	49:19 thy desolate places, and the land of thy **d**,	2035
	51:19 and **d**, and the famine, and the sword:	7667
	59: 7 iniquity; wasting and **d** *are* in their paths.	7667
	60:18 land, wasting nor **d** within thy borders;	7667
Jer	4: 6 bring evil from the north, and a great **d**.	7667
	4:20 **D** upon destruction is cried; for the whole	7667
	4:20 Destruction upon **d** is cried; for the whole	7667
	6: 1 appeareth out of the north, and great **d**.	7667
	17:18 of evil, and destroy them with **d** double **d**.	7670
	46:20 *is* like a very fair heifer, *but* **d** cometh;	7171
	48: 3 *be* from Horonaim, spoiling and great **d**.	7667
	48: 5 the enemies have heard a cry of **d**.	7667
	50:22 of battle *is* in the land, and of great **d**.	7667
	51:54 great **d** from the land of the Chaldeans:	7667
La	2:11 for the daughter of my people;	7667
	3:47 snare is come upon us, desolation and **d**.	7667
	3:48 for the **d** of the daughter of my people.	7667
	4:10 they were their meat in the **d** of	7667
Eze	5:16 which shall be for *their* **d**, *and* which I	4889
	7:25 **D** cometh; and they shall seek peace,	7089
	32: 9 I shall bring thy **d** among the nations,	7667
Hos	7:13 **d** unto them! because they have	7701
	9: 6 For lo, they are gone because of **d**:	7701
	13:14 be thy plagues; O grave, I will be thy **d**:	6987
Joel	1:15 as a **d** from the Almighty shall it come.	7701
Ob	1:12 the children of Judah in the day of their **d**;	6
Mic	2:10 it shall destroy *you*, even with a sore **d**.	2256
Zec	14:11 in it, and there shall be no more **utter d**;	2764
Mt	7:13 that leadeth to **d**, and many there be	684
Ro	3:16 **D** and misery *are* in their ways:	4938
	9:22 the vessels of wrath fitted to **d**:	684
1Co	5: 5 To deliver such a one unto Satan for the **d**	3639
2Co	10: 8 and not for your **d**, I should not be	2506
	13:10 hath given me to edification, and not to **d**.	2506
Php	3:19 Whose end *is* **d**, whose God *is their* belly,	684
1Th	5: 3 sudden **d** cometh upon them, as travail	3639
2Th	1: 9 Who shall be punished *with* everlasting **d**	3639
1Ti	6: 9 which drown men in **d** and perdition.	3639
2Pe	2: 1 and bring upon themselves swift **d**.	684
	3:16 also the other scriptures, unto their own **d**.	684

DESTRUCTIONS (3) [DESTROY]

Ps	9: 6 enemy, **d** are come to a perpetual end:	2723
	35:17 rescue my soul from their **d**, my darling	7722
	107:20 and delivered *them* from their **d**.	7825

DETAIN (2) [DETAINED]

Jdg	13:15 I pray thee, let us **d** thee, until we shall	6113
	13:16 Though thou **d** me, I will not eat of thy	6113

DETAINED (1) [DETAIN]

1Sa	21: 7 *was* there that day, **d** before the LORD;	6113

DETER See FORBAD

DETERMINATE (1) [DETERMINE]

Ac	2:23 being delivered by the **d** counsel and	3724

DETERMINATION (1) [DETERMINE]

Zep	3: 8 for my **d** *is* to gather the nations, that I	4941

DETERMINE (1) [DETERMINATE, DETERMINATION, DETERMINED]		
Ex	21:22 him; and he shall pay as the judges **d**.	NIH

DETERMINED (30) [DETERMINE]

1Sa	20: 7 then be sure that evil is **d** by him.	3615
	20: 9 for if I knew certainly that evil were **d** by	3615
	20:33 whereby Jonathan knew that it was **d** of	3617
	25:17 for evil is **d** against our master,	3615
2Sa	13:32 from the day that he forced his	1961+7760
2Ch	2: 1 Solomon **d** to build a house for the name	559
	25:16 I know that God hath **d** to destroy thee,	3289
Est	7: 7 he saw that there was evil **d** against him	3615
Job	14: 5 Seeing his days *are* **d**, the number of his	2782
Isa	10:23 even **d**, *in* the midst of all the land.	2782
	19:17 of hosts, which he hath **d** against it.	3289
	28:22 even **d** upon the whole earth.	2782
Da	9:24 Seventy weeks are **d** upon thy people and	2782
	9:26 unto the end of the war desolations *are* **d**.	2782
	9:27 that **d** shall be poured upon the desolate.	2782
	11:36 for that that is **d** shall be done.	2782
Lk	22:22 truly the Son of man goeth, as it was **d**:	3724
Ac	3:13 of Pilate, when he was **d** to let *him* go.	2919
	4:28 and thy counsel **before** to be done.	4309
	11:29 to send relief unto the brethren which	3724
	15: 2 they **d** that Paul and Barnabas,	5021
	15:37 And Barnabas **d** to take with *them* John,	1011
	17:26 and hath **d** the times before appointed,	3724
	19:39 matters, it shall be **d** in a lawful assembly.	1956
	20:16 For Paul had **d** to sail by Ephesus, because	2919
	25:25 to Augustus, I have **d** to send him.	2919
	27: 1 when it was **d** that we should sail into	2919
1Co	2: 2 For I **d** not to know any *thing* among you,	2919
2Co	2: 1 But I **d** this with myself, that *I* would not	2919
Tit	3:12 to Nicopolis: for I have **d** there to winter.	2919

DETEST (1) [DETESTABLE]

Dt	7:26 *but* thou shalt **utterly d** it,	8262+8262

DETESTABLE (6) [DETEST]

Jer	16:18 inheritance with the carcases of their **d**	8251
Eze	5:11 my sanctuary with all thy **d things**,	8251
	7:20 *and* of their **d things** therein:	8251
	11:18 they shall take away all the **d things**	8251
	11:21 walketh after the heart of their **d things**	8251
	37:23 nor with their **d things**, nor with any of	8251

DEUEL (4) [REUEL]

Nu	1:14 Of Gad; Eliasaph the son of **D**.	1845
	7:42 On the sixth day Eliasaph the son of **D**,	1845
	7:47 *was* the offering of Eliasaph the son of **D**.	1845
	10:20 children of Gad *was* Eliasaph the son of **D**.	1845

DEVICE (10) [DEVICES]

2Ch	2:14 to find out every **d** which shall be put to	4284
Est	8: 3 his **d** that he had devised against the Jews.	4284
	9:25 commanded by letters *that* his wicked **d**,	4284
Ps	21:11 they imagined a **mischievous d**,	4209
	140: 8 further not his **wicked d**; *lest* they exalt	2162
Ecc	9:10 nor **d**, nor knowledge, nor wisdom,	2808
Jer	18:11 against you, and devise a **d** against you:	4284
	51:11 for his **d** *is* against Babylon, to destroy it;	4209
La	3:62 and their **d** against me all the day.	1902
Ac	17:29 silver, or stone, graven by art and man's **d**.	1761

DEVICES (16) [DEVICE]

Job	5:12 He disappointeth the **d** of the crafty,	4284
	21:27 the **d** *which* ye wrongfully imagine against	4209
Ps	10: 2 let them be taken in the **d** that they have	4284
	33:10 he maketh the **d** of the people of none	4284
	37: 7 the man who bringeth **wicked d** to pass.	4209
Pr	1:31 own way, and be filled with their own **d**.	4156
	12: 2 but a man of **wicked d** will he condemn.	4209
	14:17 and a man of **wicked d** is hated.	4209
	19:21 *There are* many **d** in a man's heart;	4284
Isa	32: 7 he deviseth **wicked d** to destroy the poor	2154
Jer	11:19 knew not that they had devised **d** against	4284
	18:12 will walk after our own **d**, and we will	4284
	18:18 and let us devise **d** against Jeremiah;	4284
Da	11:24 he shall forecast his **d** against the strong	4284
	11:25 for they shall forecast **d** against him.	4284
2Co	2:11 of us: for we are not ignorant of his **d**.	3540

DEVIL (61) [DEVILISH, DEVILS]

Mt	4: 1 into the wilderness to be tempted of the **d**.	1228
	4: 5 the **d** taketh him *up* into the holy city,	1228
	4: 8 the **d** taketh him *up* into an exceeding	1228
	4:11 Then the **d** leaveth him, and, behold,	1228
	9:32 to him a dumb man **possessed with a d**.	1139
	9:33 And when the **d** was cast out, the dumb	1140
	11:18 nor drinking, and they say, He hath a **d**.	1140
	12:22 unto him **one possessed with a d**,	1139
	13:39 The enemy that sowed them is the **d**;	1228
	15:22 daughter is grievously **vexed with a d**.	1139
	17:18 And Jesus rebuked the **d**; and he departed	1140
	25:41 prepared for the **d** and his angels:	1228
Mk	5:15 see him that was **possessed with the d**,	1139
	5:16 to him that was **possessed with the d**,	1139
	5:18 he that had been **possessed with the d**,	1139
	7:26 cast forth the **d** out of her daughter.	1140
	7:29 way; the **d** is gone out of thy daughter.	1140
	7:30 found the **d** gone out, and *her* daughter	1140
Lk	4: 2 Being forty days tempted of the **d**. And in	1228
	4: 3 the **d** said unto him, If thou be the Son	1228
	4: 5 And the **d**, taking him up into a high	1228

Lk 4: 6 And the **d** said unto him, All this power *1228*
4:13 And when the **d** had ended all *1228*
4:33 which had a spirit of an unclean **d**, *1140*
4:35 And when the **d** had thrown him in *1140*
7:33 drinking wine; and ye say, He hath a **d**. *1140*
8:12 then cometh the **d**, and taketh away *1228*
8:29 was driven of the **d** into the wilderness.) *1142*
9:42 the **d** threw him down, and tare *him*. And *1140*
11:14 And he was casting out a **d**, and it was *1140*
11:14 the **d** was gone out, the dumb spake; *1140*
Jn 6:70 chosen you twelve, and one of you is a **d**? *1228*
7:20 people answered and said, Thou hast a **d**: *1140*
8:44 Ye are of *your* father the **d**, and the lusts *1228*
8:48 that thou art a Samaritan, and hast a **d**? *1140*
8:49 Jesus answered, I have not a **d**; *1140*
8:52 him, Now we know that thou hast a **d**. *1140*
10:20 of them said, He hath a **d**, and is mad; *1139*
10:21 are not the words of him that **hath a d**. *1140*
10:21 Can a **d** open the eyes of the blind? *1140*
13: 2 having now put into the heart of Judas *1228*
Ac 10:38 healing all that were oppressed of the **d**; *1228*
13:10 and all mischief, *thou* child of the **d**, *1228*
Eph 4:27 Neither give place to the **d**. *1228*
6:11 be able to stand against the wiles of the **d**. *1228*
1Ti 3: 6 he fall into the condemnation of the **d**. *1228*
3: 7 fall into reproach and the snare of the **d**, *1228*
2Ti 2:26 themselves out of the snare of the **d**, *1228*
Heb 2:14 had the power of death, that is, the **d**; *1228*
Jas 4: 7 Resist the **d**, and he will flee from you. *1228*
1Pe 5: 8 because your adversary the **d**, as a roaring *1228*
1Jn 3: 8 He that committeth sin is of the **d**; *1228*
3: 8 for the **d** sinneth from the beginning. *1228*
3: 8 that he might destroy the works of the **d**. *1228*
3:10 are manifest, and the children of the **d**: *1228*
Jude 1: 9 when contending with the **d** he disputed *1228*
Rev 2:10 the **d** shall cast *some* of you into prison, *1228*
12: 9 called the **d**, and Satan, which deceiveth *1228*
12:12 for the **d** is come down unto you, *1228*
20: 2 which is the **d**, and Satan, and bound him *1228*
20:10 the **d** that deceived them was cast into *1228*

DEVILISH (1) [DEVIL]
Jas 3:15 not from above, but *is* earthly, sensual, **d**. *1141*

DEVILS (55) [DEVIL]
Lev 17: 7 shall no more offer their sacrifices unto **d**, *8163*
Dt 32:17 They sacrificed unto **d**, not *to* God; *7700*
2Ch 11:15 for the **d**, and for the calves which he had *8163*
Ps 106:37 their sons and their daughters unto **d**, *7700*
Mt 4:24 and those which were **possessed with d**, *1139*
7:22 name? and in thy name have cast out **d**? *1140*
8:16 him many *that were* **possessed with d**, *1139*
8:28 there met him two **possessed with d**, *1139*
8:31 the **d** besought him, saying, If thou cast *1142*
8:33 was befallen to the **possessed of the d**. *1139*
9:34 He casteth out the **d** through the prince of *1140*
9:34 out the devils through the prince of the **d**. *1140*
10: 8 the lepers, raise the dead, cast out **d**: *1140*
12:24 This *fellow* doth not cast out **d**, but by *1140*
12:24 but by Beelzebub the prince of the **d**. *1140*
12:27 if I by Beelzebub cast out **d**, by whom *1140*
12:28 if I cast out **d** by the Spirit of God, then *1140*
Mk 1:32 and them that were **possessed with d**. *1139*
1:34 of divers diseases, and cast out many **d**; *1140*
1:34 and suffered not the **d** to speak, because *1140*
1:39 throughout all Galilee, and cast out **d**. *1140*
3:15 to heal sicknesses, and to cast out **d**: *1140*
3:22 the prince of the **d** casteth he out devils. *1140*
3:22 the prince of the devils casteth he out **d**. *1140*
5:12 And all the **d** besought him, saying, *1142*
6:13 And they cast out many **d**, *1140*
9:38 we saw one casting out **d** in thy name, *1140*
16: 9 out of whom he had cast seven **d**. *1140*
16:17 In my name shall they cast out **d**; they *1140*
Lk 4:41 And also came out of many, crying out, *1140*
8: 2 out of whom went seven **d**, *1140*
8:27 which had **d** long time, and ware no *1140*
8:30 because many **d** were entered into him. *1140*
8:33 Then went the **d** out of the man, *1140*
8:35 man, out of whom the **d** were departed, *1140*
8:36 that was **possessed of the d** was healed. *1139*
8:38 Now the man out of whom the **d** were *1140*
9: 1 gave them power and authority over all **d**, *1140*
9:49 we saw one casting out **d** in thy name; *1140*
10:17 even the **d** are subject unto us through *1140*
11:15 He casteth out **d** through Beelzebub *1140*
11:15 He casteth out the chief of the **d**. *1140*
11:18 say that I cast out **d** through Beelzebub. *1140*
11:19 if I by Beelzebub cast out **d**, by whom *1140*
11:20 But if I with the finger of God cast out **d**, *1140*
13:32 I cast out **d**, and I do cures to day and *1140*
1Co 10:20 they sacrifice to **d**, and not to God: *1140*
10:20 not that ye should have fellowship with **d**. *1140*
10:21 the cup of the Lord, and the cup of **d**: *1140*
10:21 of the Lord's table, and of the table of **d**. *1140*
1Ti 4: 1 to seducing spirits, and doctrines of **d**; *1140*
Jas 2:19 well: the **d** also believe, and tremble. *1140*
Rev 9:20 that they should not worship **d**, and idols *1142*
16:14 For they are the spirits of **d**, working *1142*
18: 2 fallen, and is become the habitation of **d**, *1142*

DEVIOUS See FROWARD

DEVISE (16) [DEVISED, DEVISETH]
Ex 31: 4 To **d** cunning works, to work in gold, *2803*

Ex 35:32 to **d** curious works, to work in gold, *2803*
35:35 of those that **d** cunning work. *2803+4284*
2Sa 14:14 yet doth he **d** means, that *his* banished be *2803*
Ps 35: 4 and brought to confusion that **d** my hurt. *2803*
35:20 they **d** deceitful matters against *them that* *2803*
41: 7 against me: against me do they **d** my hurt. *2803*
Pr 3:29 **D** not evil against thy neighbour, seeing *2790*
14:22 Do they not err that **d** evil? but mercy *2790*
14:22 and truth *shall be* to them that **d** good. *2790*
16:30 He shutteth his eyes to **d** froward things: *2803*
Jer 18:11 against you, and **d** a device against you: *2803*
18:18 and let us **d** devices against Jeremiah: *2803*
Eze 11: 2 *are* the men that **d** mischief, and give *2803*
Mic 2: 1 Woe to them that **d** iniquity, and work *2803*
2: 3 Behold, against this family do I **d** an evil, *2803*

DEVISED (12) [DEVISE]
2Sa 21: 5 that **d** against us *that* we should be *1819*
1Ki 12:33 in the month which he had **d** of his own *908*
Est 8: 3 his device that he had **d** against the Jews. *2803*
8: 5 let it be written to reverse the letters **d** by *4284*
9:24 had **d** against the Jews to destroy them, *2803*
9:25 he **d** against the Jews, should return *2803*
Ps 31:13 against me, they **d** to take away my life. *2161*
Jer 11:19 I knew not that they had **d** devices *2803*
48: 2 in Heshbon they have **d** evil against it; *2803*
51:12 for the Lord hath both **d** and done that *2161*
La 2:17 Lord hath done *that* which he had **d**; *2161*
2Pe 1:16 For we have not followed **cunningly d** *4679*

DEVISETH (8) [DEVISE]
Ps 36: 4 He **d** mischief upon his bed; he setteth *2803*
52: 2 Thy tongue **d** mischiefs; like a sharp rasor *2803*
Pr 6:14 *is* in his heart, he **d** mischief continually; *2790*
6:18 A heart that **d** wicked imaginations, *2790*
16: 9 A man's heart **d** his way: but the Lord *2803*
24: 8 He that **d** to do evil shall be called a *2803*
Isa 32: 7 he **d** wicked devices to destroy the poor *3289*
32: 8 the liberal **d** liberal *things;* and by liberal *3289*

DEVOTE (1) [DEVOTED, DEVOTIONS]
Lev 27:28 that a man shall **d** unto the Lord of all *2763*

DEVOTED (7) [DEVOTE]
Lev 27:21 shall be holy unto the Lord, as a field **d**; *2764*
27:28 Notwithstanding no **d thing**, that a man *2764*
27:28 every **d thing** *is* most holy unto *2764*
27:29 None **d**, which shall be devoted of men, *2764*
27:29 None devoted, which shall be **d** of men, *2763*
Nu 18:14 Every thing **d** in Israel shall be thine. *2764*
Ps 119:38 unto thy servant, who *is* **d** to thy fear. *NIH*

DEVOTIONS (1) [DEVOTE]
Ac 17:23 For as I passed by, and beheld your **d**, *4574*

DEVOUR (71) [DEVOURED, DEVOURER, DEVOUREST, DEVOURETH, DEVOURING]
Ge 49:27 in the morning he shall **d** the prey, *398*
Dt 32:42 with blood, and my sword shall **d** flesh; *398*
Jdg 9:15 the bramble, and **d** the cedars of Lebanon. *398*
9:20 the men of Shechem, and the house of *398*
9:20 from the house of Millo, and **d** Abimelech. *398*
2Sa 2:26 Joab, and said, Shall the sword **d** for ever? *398*
2Ch 7:13 or if I command the locusts to **d** the land, *398*
Job 18:13 It shall **d** the strength of his skin: *even* *398*
18:13 *even* the firstborn of death shall **d** *398*
Ps 21: 9 up in his wrath, and the fire shall **d** them. *398*
50: 3 a fire shall **d** before him, and it shall be *398*
80:13 and the wild beast of the field doth **d** it. *7462*
Pr 30:14 to **d** the poor from off the earth, *398*
Isa 1: 7 strangers **d** it in your presence, and *it is* *398*
9:12 they shall **d** Israel with open mouth. *398*
9:18 it shall **d** the briers and thorns, *398*
10:17 shall burn and **d** his thorns and his briers *398*
26:11 the fire of thine enemies shall **d** them. *398*
31: 8 sword, not of a mean man, shall **d** him: *398*
33:11 your breath, *as* fire, shall **d** you. *398*
42:14 I will destroy and **d** at once. *7602*
56: 9 All ye beasts of the field, come to **d**, *yea*, *398*
Jer 2: 3 all that **d** him shall offend; evil shall come *398*
5:14 and this people wood, and it shall **d** them. *398*
12: 9 all the beasts of the field, come to **d**. *402*
12:12 for the sword of the Lord *shall* **d** from *398*
15: 3 the beasts of the earth, to **d** and destroy. *398*
17:27 it shall **d** the palaces of Jerusalem, *398*
21:14 and it shall **d** all things round about it. *398*
30:16 Therefore all they that **d** thee shall be *398*
46:10 the sword shall **d**, and it shall be satiate *398*
46:14 for the sword shall **d** round about thee. *398*
48:45 shall **d** the corner of Moab, and the crown *398*
50:32 cities, and it shall **d** all round about him. *398*
Eze 7:15 city, famine and pestilence shall **d** him. *398*
15: 7 *one* fire, and *another* fire shall **d** them; *398*
20:47 it shall **d** every green tree in thee, *398*
23:37 pass for them through the *fire*, to **d** *them*. *402*
28:18 shall **d** thee, and I will bring thee to ashes *398*
34:28 neither shall the beast of the land **d** them; *398*
36:14 Therefore thou shalt **d** men no more, *398*
Da 7: 5 they said thus unto it, Arise, **d** much flesh. *399*
7:23 shall **d** the whole earth, and shall tread it *399*
Hos 5: 7 now shall a month **d** them with their *398*
8:14 his cities, and it shall **d** the palaces thereof. *398*
11: 6 and **d**, because of their own counsels. *398*
13: 8 and there will I **d** them like a lion: *398*
Am 1: 4 which shall **d** the palaces of Ben-hadad. *398*

Am 1: 7 of Gaza, which shall **d** the palaces thereof: *398*
1:10 of Tyrus, which shall **d** the palaces thereof. *398*
1:12 which shall **d** the palaces of Bozrah. *398*
1:14 it shall **d** the palaces thereof, with shouting *398*
2: 2 and it shall **d** the palaces of Kerioth, *398*
2: 5 and it shall **d** the palaces of Jerusalem. *398*
5: 6 *it*, and *there be* none to quench *it* in *398*
Ob 1:18 and they shall kindle in them, and **d** them; *398*
Na 2:13 and the sword shall **d** thy young lions: *398*
3:13 thine enemies: the fire shall **d** thy bars. *398*
3:15 There shall the fire **d** thee; the sword shall *398*
Hab 3:14 rejoicing *was* as to **d** the poor secretly. *398*
Zec 9:15 they shall **d**, and subdue *with* sling stones; *398*
11: 1 O Lebanon, that the fire may **d** thy cedars. *398*
12: 6 they shall **d** all the people round about, *398*
Mt 23:14 ye **d widows' houses**, and for a pretence *2719*
Mk 12:40 Which **d widows' houses**, and for a *2719*
Lk 20:47 Which **d widows' houses**, and for a shew *2719*
2Co 11:20 if a man **d** *you*, if a man take *of you*, if a *2719*
Gal 5:15 if ye bite and **d** one another, take heed *2719*
Heb 10:27 which shall **d** the adversaries. *2068*
1Pe 5: 8 walketh about, seeking whom he may **d**: *2666*
Rev 12: 4 for to **d** her child as soon as it was born. *2719*

DEVOURED (53) [DEVOUR]
Ge 31:15 and hath **quite d** also our money. *398+398*
37:20 we will say, *Some* evil beast hath **d** him: *398*
37:33 is my son's coat; an evil beast hath **d** him; *398*
41: 7 the seven thin ears **d** the seven rank and *1104*
41:24 the thin ears **d** the seven good ears: *1104*
Lev 10: 2 them, and they died before the Lord. *398*
Nu 26:10 what time the fire **d** two hundred and *398*
Dt 31:17 they shall be **d**, and many evils and *398*
32:24 **d** with burning heat, and with bitter *3898*
2Sa 18: 8 the wood **d** more people that day than *398*
18: 8 more people that day than the sword *398*
22: 9 of his nostrils, and fire out of his mouth **d**: *398*
Ps 18: 8 of his nostrils, and fire out of his mouth **d**: *398*
78:45 sorts *of flies* among them, which **d** them; *398*
79: 7 For they have **d** Jacob, and laid waste his *398*
105:35 their land, and **d** the fruit of their ground. *398*
Isa 1:20 and rebel, ye shall be **d** *with* the sword: *398*
24: 6 Therefore hath the curse **d** the earth, *398*
Jer 2:30 your own sword hath **d** your prophets, like *398*
3:24 For shame hath **d** the labour of our fathers *398*
8:16 and have **d** the land, and all that is in it; *398*
10:25 have **d** him, and consumed him, and have made *398*
30:16 all they that devour thee shall be **d**; *398*
50: 7 All that found them have **d** them: and *398*
50:17 the king of Assyria hath **d** him; and last *398*
51:34 the king of Babylon hath **d** *398*
La 4:11 and it hath **d** the foundations thereof. *398*
Eze 15: 5 when the fire hath **d** it, and it is burned? *398*
16:20 hast thou sacrificed unto them to be **d**. *398*
19: 3 and it learned to catch the prey; it **d** men. *398*
19: 6 and learned to catch the prey, *and* **d** men. *398*
19:14 *which* hath **d** her fruit, so that she hath no *398*
22:25 they have **d** souls; they have taken *398*
23:25 and thy residue shall be **d** by the fire. *398*
33:27 open field will I give to the beasts to be **d**, *398*
39: 4 and *to* the beasts of the field to be **d**. *402*
Da 7: 7 it **d** and brake in pieces, and stamped *399*
7:19 *which* **d**, brake in pieces, and stamped *399*
Hos 7: 7 all hot as an oven, and have **d** their judges; *398*
7: 9 Strangers have **d** his strength, *398*
Joel 1:19 for the fire hath **d** the pastures of *398*
1:20 fire hath **d** the pastures of the wilderness. *398*
Am 4: 9 the palmerworm **d** *them:* yet have ye not *398*
7: 4 it **d** the great deep, and did eat up a part. *398*
Na 1:10 they shall be **d** as stubble fully dry. *398*
Zep 1:18 the whole land shall be **d** by the fire of his *398*
3: 8 for all the earth shall be **d** with the fire of *398*
Zec 9: 4 in the sea; and she shall be **d** with fire. *398*
Mt 13: 4 and the fowls came and **d** them **up**: *2719*
Mk 4: 4 and the fowls of the air came and **d** it **up**. *2719*
Lk 8: 5 down, and the fowls of the air **d** it. *2719*
15:30 which hath **d** thy living with harlots, *2719*
Rev 20: 9 from God out of heaven, and **d** them. *2719*

DEVOURER (1) [DEVOUR]
Mal 3:11 I will rebuke the **d** for your sakes, *398*

DEVOUREST (1) [DEVOUR]
Eze 36:13 Thou *land* **d** up men, and hast bereaved *398*

DEVOURETH (10) [DEVOUR]
2Sa 11:25 for the sword **d** one as well as another: *398*
Pr 19:28 and the mouth of the wicked **d** iniquity. *1104*
20:25 a snare to the man *who* **d** *that which is* *3216*
Isa 5:24 Therefore as the fire **d** the stubble, *398*
La 2: 3 like a flaming fire, *which* **d** round about. *398*
Eze 15: 4 the fire **d** both the ends of it, and the midst *398*
Joel 2: 3 A fire **d** before them; and behind them a *398*
2: 5 like the noise of a flame of fire that **d** *398*
Hab 1:13 holdest thy tongue when the wicked **d** *1104*
Rev 11: 5 out of their mouth, and **d** their enemies: *2719*

DEVOURING (6) [DEVOUR]
Ex 24:17 fire on the top of the mount in the eyes *398*
Ps 52: 4 Thou lovest all **d** words, O thou deceitful *1105*
Isa 29: 6 and tempest, and the flame of **d** fire. *398*
30:27 *of* indignation, and his tongue as a **d** fire: *398*
30:30 *with* the flame of a **d** fire, *with* scattering, *398*
33:14 Who among us shall dwell *with* the **d** fire? *398*

D

DEVOUT (9)

Lk	2:25 and the same man *was* just and **d**,	2126
Ac	2: 5 **d** men, out of every nation under heaven.	2126
	8: 2 And **d** men carried Stephen *to his burial,*	2126
	10: 2 A **d** *man,* and one that feared God with	2152
	10: 7 a **d** soldier of them that waited on him	2152
	13:50 But the Jews stirred up the **d** and	4576
	17: 4 and of the **d** Greeks a great multitude,	4576
	17:17 with the **d** *persons,* and in the market	4576
	22:12 Ananias, a **d** man according to the law,	2152

DEW (37)

Ge	27:28 God give thee of the **d** of heaven,	2919
	27:39 and of the **d** of heaven from above;	2919
Ex	16:13 in the morning the **d** lay round about	2919
	16:14 when the **d** that lay was gone up, behold,	2919
Nu	11: 9 the **d** fell upon the camp in the night,	2919
Dt	32: 2 the rain, my speech shall distil as the **d**,	2919
	33:13 for the **d**, and for the deep that coucheth	2919
	33:28 wine; also his heavens shall drop down **d**.	2919
Jdg	6:37 if the **d** be on the fleece only, and *it be*	2919
	6:38 wringed the **d** out of the fleece, a bowl	2919
	6:39 upon all the ground let there be **d**.	2919
	6:40 and there was **d** on all the ground.	2919
2Sa	1:21 mountains of Gilboa, *let there be* no **d**,	2919
	17:12 we *will* light upon him as the **d** falleth on	2919
1Ki	17: 1 there shall not be **d** nor rain these years,	2919
Job	29:19 and the **d** lay all night upon my branch.	2919
	38:28 or who hath begotten the drops of **d**?	2919
Ps	110: 3 the morning: thou hast the **d** of thy youth.	2919
	133: 3 As the **d** of Hermon, *and as the dew* that	2919
	133: 3 *the d* that descended upon the mountains	NIH
Pr	3:20 , and the clouds drop down the **d**.	2919
	19:12 lion; but his favour *is* as **d** upon the grass.	2919
SS	5: 2 for my head is filled *with* **d**, *and* my locks	2919
Isa	18: 4 like a cloud of **d** in the heat of harvest.	2919
	26:19 for thy **d** *is as* the dew of herbs,	2919
	26:19 for thy dew *is as* the **d** of herbs,	2919
Da	4:15 let it be wet with the **d** of heaven,	2920
	4:23 let it be wet with the **d** of heaven,	2920
	4:25 they shall wet thee with the **d** of heaven,	2920
	4:33 his body was wet with the **d** of heaven,	2920
	5:21 his body was wet with the **d** of heaven;	2920
Hos	6: 4 your goodness *is* as a morning cloud,	2919
	13: 3 and as the early **d** that passeth away,	2919
	14: 5 I will be as the **d** unto Israel: he shall	2919
Mic	5: 7 of many people as a **d** from the Lord,	2919
Hag	1:10 the heaven over you is stayed from **d**,	2919
Zec	8:12 and the heavens shall give their **d**;	2919

DIADEM (4)

Job	29:14 my judgment *was* as a robe and a **d**.	6797
Isa	28: 5 for a **d** of beauty, unto the residue of his	6843
	62: 3 and a royal **d** in the hand of thy God.	6797
Eze	21:26 Remove the **d**, and take off the crown:	4701

DIAL (2)

2Ki	20:11 by which it had gone down in the **d** of	4609
Isa	38: 8 which is gone down in the sun **d** of Ahaz,	4609

DIAMOND (4)

Ex	28:18 *shall* be an emerald, a sapphire, and a **d**.	3095
	39:11 an emerald, a sapphire, and a **d**.	3095
Jer	17: 1 a pen of iron, *and* with the point of a **d**:	8068
Eze	28:13 topaz, and the **d**, the beryl, the onyx,	3095

DIANA (5)

Ac	19:24 which made silver shrines for **D**,	735
	19:27 also that the temple of the great goddess **D**	735
	19:28 saying, Great *is* **D** of the Ephesians.	735
	19:34 cried out, Great *is* **D** of the Ephesians.	735
	19:35 is a worshipper of the great goddess **D**,	735

DIBLAH See DIBLATH

DIBLAIM (1)

Hos	1: 3 went and took Gomer the daughter of **D**;	1691

DIBLATH (1)

Eze	6:14 desolate than the wilderness toward **D**,	1689

DIBON (9) [DIBON-GAD]

Nu	21:30 Heshbon is perished even unto **D**,	1769
	32: 3 **D**, and Jazer, and Nimrah, and Heshbon,	1769
	32:34 the children of Gad built **D**, and Ataroth,	1769
Jos	13: 9 and all the plain of Medeba unto **D**;	1769
	13:17 **D**, and Bamoth-baal, and Beth-baal-meon,	1769
Ne	11:25 at **D**, and *in* the villages thereof,	1769
Isa	15: 2 and *to* **D**, the high places, to weep:	1769
Jer	48:18 Thou daughter that dost inhabit **D**,	1769
	48:22 upon **D**, and upon Nebo,	1769

DIBON-GAD (2) [DIBON, GAD]

Nu	33:45 they departed from Iim, and pitched in **D**.	1769
	33:46 they removed from **D**, and encamped in	1769

DIBRI (1)

Lev	24:11 the daughter of **D**, of the tribe of Dan:)	1704

DID (1006) [DO]

Ge	3: 6 eat, and gave also unto her husband	NIH
	3: 6 unto her with her; and he **d** eat.	NIH
	3:12 she gave me of the tree, and I **d** eat.	NIH
	3:13 The serpent beguiled me, and I **d** eat.	NIH
	3:21 to his wife **d** the Lord God make coats of	NIH
	6:22 Thus **d** Noah; according to all that God	6213

Ge	6:22 to all that God commanded him, so **d** he.	6213
	7: 5 Noah **d** according unto all that the Lord	6213
	7:20 Fifteen cubits upward **d** the waters prevail;	NIH
	11: 9 the Lord **d** there confound the language	NIH
	11: 9 from thence **d** the Lord scatter them	NIH
	18: 8 by them under the tree, and they **d** eat.	NIH
	18:13 Wherefore **d** Sarah laugh, saying,	NIH
	19: 3 **d** bake unleavened bread, and they did eat.	NIH
	19: 3 did bake unleavened bread, and they **d** eat.	NIH
	21: 1 the Lord **d** unto Sarah as he had spoken.	6213
	22: 1 that God **d** tempt Abraham, and said unto	NIH
	22:23 these eight Milcah **d** bear to Nahor,	NIH
	24:54 they **d** eat and drink, he and the men that	NIH
	25:28 Esau, because he **d** eat of *his* venison:	NIH
	25:34 he **d** eat and drink, and rose up,	NIH
	26:30 them a feast, and they **d** eat and drink.	NIH
	27:25 he brought *it* near to him, and he **d** eat:	NIH
	29:25 **d** not I serve with thee for Rachel?	NIH
	29:28 Jacob **d** so, and fulfilled her week: and	6213
	30:40 Jacob **d** separate the lambs, and set the	NIH
	30:41 whensoever the stronger cattle **d** conceive,	NIH
	31:46 heap: and they **d** eat there upon the heap.	NIH
	31:54 they **d** eat bread, and tarried all night in	NIH
	35: 5 they **d** not pursue after the sons of Jacob.	NIH
	38:10 *the thing* which he **d** displeased	6213
	38:11 as his brethren **d**. And Tamar went and	NIH
	39: 3 *that* the Lord made all that he **d** to	6213
	39: 6 he had, save the bread which he **d** eat.	NIH
	39:19 After this manner **d** thy servant to me;	NIH
	39:22 whatsoever they **d** there, he was the doer	6213
	39:23 Lord *was* with him, and *that* which he **d**,	6213
	40:17 the birds **d** eat them out of the basket	NIH
	40:23 **d** not the chief butler remember Joseph,	NIH
	41: 4 leanfleshed kine **d** eat up the seven well	NIH
	41:12 to each man according to his dream he **d**	NIH
	41:20 Ill favoured kine **d** eat up the first seven	NIH
	42:20 and ye shall not die. And they **d** so.	6213
	42:25 for the way: and thus **d** he unto them.	6213
	43: 3 The man **d** solemnly protest unto us,	NIH
	43:17 the man **d** as Joseph bade; and the man	6213
	43:30 for his bowels **d** yern upon his brother:	NIH
	43:32 which **d** eat with him, by themselves:	NIH
	44: 2 he **d** according to the word that Joseph	6213
	45: 5 for God **d** send me before you to preserve	NIH
	45:21 the children of Israel **d** so: and Joseph	6213
	47:22 **d** eat their portion which Pharaoh gave	NIH
	48:15 my fathers Abraham and Isaac **d** walk,	NIH
	50:12 his sons **d** unto him according as he	6213
	50:15 us all the evil which we **d** unto him.	1580
	50:16 Thy father **d** command before he died,	NIH
	50:17 and their sin; for they **d** unto thee evil:	1580
Ex	1:11 they **d** set over them taskmasters	NIH
	1:17 **d** not as the king of Egypt commanded	6213
	2:13 he said to **him that d** the wrong,	7563
	4:30 and **d** the signs in the sight of the people.	6213
	5: 8 they **d** make heretofore, you shall lay	NIH
	5:19 the officers of the children of Israel **d** see	NIH
	6: 8 *concerning* the which I **d** swear to give it	NIH
	7: 6 Aaron **d** as the Lord commanded them,	6213
	7: 6 as the Lord commanded them, so **d** they.	6213
	7:10 they **d** so as the Lord had commanded:	6213
	7:11 they also **d** in like manner with their	NIH
	7:20 Moses and Aaron **d** so, as the Lord	6213
	7:22 the magicians of Egypt **d** so with their	6213
	7:22 neither **d** he hearken unto them;	NIH
	7:23 neither **d** he set his heart to this also.	NIH
	8: 7 magicians **d** so with their enchantments,	6213
	8:13 the Lord **d** according to the word of	6213
	8:17 they **d** so; for Aaron stretched out his	6213
	8:18 magicians **d** so with their enchantments	6213
	8:24 the Lord **d** so; and there came a	6213
	8:31 the Lord **d** according to the word of	6213
	9: 6 the Lord **d** that thing on the morrow,	6213
	9: 7 and he **d** not let the people go.	NIH
	10:11 and serve the Lord; for that you **d** desire.	NIH
	10:15 they **d** eat every herb of the land, and all	NIH
	11:10 Aaron **d** all these wonders before Pharaoh:	NIH
	12:28 **d** as the Lord had commanded Moses	6213
	12:28 commanded Moses and Aaron, so **d** they.	6213
	12:35 the children of Israel **d** according to	6213
	12:50 Thus **d** all the children of Israel;	NIH
	12:50 commanded Moses and Aaron, so **d** they.	6213
	12:51 *that* the Lord **d** bring the children of	NIH
	13: 8 of that *which* the Lord **d** unto me when I	6213
	14: 4 know that I *am* the Lord. And they **d** so.	6213
	14:12 *Is* not this the word that we **d** tell thee in	NIH
	14:31 which the Lord **d** upon the Egyptians:	6213
	16: 3 *and* when we **d** eat bread to the full;	NIH
	16:17 the children of Israel **d** so, and gathered,	6213
	16:18 when they **d** mete *it* with an omer, he that	NIH
	16:24 it **d** not stink, neither was there any worm	NIH
	16:35 the children of Israel **d** eat manna forty	NIH
	16:35 they **d** eat manna, until they came unto	NIH
	17: 2 Wherefore the people **d** chide with Moses,	NIH
	17: 6 Moses **d** so in the sight of the elders of	6213
	17:10 So Joshua **d** as Moses had said to him,	6213
	18: 1 in law, and **d obeisance**, and kissed him;	7812
	18:14 Moses' father in law saw all that he **d**	NIH
	18:24 father in law, and **d** all that he had said.	6213
	19: 4 Ye have seen what I **d** unto the Egyptians,	6213
	24:11 also they saw God, and **d** eat and drink.	NIH
	32:12 say, For mischief **d** he bring them out,	6213
	32:21 What **d** this people unto thee, that thou	6213
	32:28 the children of Levi **d** according to	NIH

Ex	33: 4 and no man **d** put on him his ornaments.	NIH
	34:28 he **d** neither eat bread, nor drink water.	NIH
	35:24 Every one that **d** offer an offering of silver	NIH
	35:25 the women that were wise hearted **d** spin	NIH
	36:22 thus **d** he make for all the boards of	NIH
	36:29 thus he **d** to both of them in both	6213
	39: 3 they **d** beat the gold into thin plates,	NIH
	39:21 they **d** bind the breastplate by his rings	NIH
	39:32 the children of Israel **d** according to all	6213
	39:32 the Lord commanded Moses, so **d** they.	6213
	39:43 Moses **d** look upon all the work,	NIH
	40:16 Thus **d** Moses: according to all that	6213
	40:16 that the Lord commanded him, so **d** he.	6213
Lev	4:20 he shall do with the bullock as he **d** with	6213
	8: 4 Moses **d** as the Lord commanded him;	6213
	8: 9 he put the golden plate, the holy crown;	NIH
	8:36 his sons **d** all things which the Lord	6213
	9:14 he **d** wash the inwards and the legs,	NIH
	10: 7 they **d** according to the word of Moses.	6213
	16:15 do with that blood as he **d** with the blood	6213
	16:34 he **d** as the Lord commanded Moses.	6213
	24:23 the children of Israel **d** as the Lord	6213
	26:35 because it **d** not rest in your sabbaths,	NIH
	27:24 the possession of the land **d** belong.	NIH
Nu	1:54 the children of Israel **d** according to all	6213
	1:54 the Lord commanded Moses, so **d** they.	6213
	2:34 the children of Israel **d** according to all	6213
	4:37 Aaron **d** number according to	NIH
	4:41 Aaron **d** number according to	NIH
	5: 4 the children of Israel **d** so, and put them	6213
	5: 4 unto Moses, so **d** the children of Israel.	NIH
	7:18 the son of Zuar, prince of Issachar, **d** offer:	NIH
	7:24 prince of the children of Zebulun, **d** offer:	NIH
	7:30 prince of the children of Reuben, **d** offer:	NIH
	7:36 prince of the children of Simeon, **d** offer:	NIH
	8: 3 Aaron **d** so; he lighted the lamps thereof	6213
	8:20 to the Levites according unto all that	6213
	8:20 so **d** the children of Israel unto them.	6213
	8:22 the Levites, so **d** they unto them.	6213
	9: 5 so **d** the children of Israel.	NIH
	10:21 *the other* **d** set up the tabernacle against	NIH
	11: 5 the fish, which we **d** eat in Egypt freely;	NIH
	11:25 they prophesied, and **d** not cease.	NIH
	14:22 which I **d** in Egypt and in the wilderness,	6213
	14:37 Even *those* men that **d** bring up the evil	NIH
	17:11 Moses **d** *so:* as the Lord commanded	6213
	17:11 as the Lord commanded him, so **d** he.	6213
	20:27 Moses **d** as the Lord commanded: and	6213
	21:14 **What** he **d** in the Red sea, and *in*	2052
	22:37 **D** I not earnestly send unto thee to call	NIH
	23: 2 Balak **d** as Balaam had spoken; and Balak	6213
	23:30 Balak **d** as Balaam had said, and offered a	6213
	25: 2 the people **d** eat, and bowed down to	NIH
	27:22 Moses **d** as the Lord commanded him:	6213
	31:31 Eleazar the priest **d** as the Lord	6213
	32: 8 Thus **d** your fathers, when I sent them	6213
	36:10 so **d** the daughters of Zelophehad:	6213
Dt	1:30 according to all that he **d** for you in Egypt	6213
	1:32 Yet in this thing ye **d** not believe	NIH
	2:12 as Israel **d** unto the land of his possession,	6213
	2:22 As he **d** to the children of Esau,	6213
	2:29 Moabites which dwell in Ar, **d** unto me;)	6213
	3: 6 as we **d** unto Sihon king of Heshbon,	6213
	4: 3 Your eyes have seen what the Lord **d**	6213
	4: 4 ye that **d** cleave unto the Lord your God	NIH
	4:33 **D** *ever* people hear the voice of God	NIH
	4:34 God **d** for you in Egypt before your eyes?	6213
	5:23 (for the mountain **d** burn with fire,)	NIH
	7: 7 The Lord **d** not set his love upon you,	NIH
	7:18 what the Lord thy God **d** unto Pharaoh,	6213
	8: 3 knewest not, neither **d** thy fathers know;	NIH
	8: 4 neither **d** thy foot swell, these forty years.	NIH
	9: 9 I neither **d** eat bread nor drink water:	NIH
	9:18 I **d** neither eat bread, nor drink water,	NIH
	11: 3 which he **d** in the midst of Egypt unto	6213
	11: 4 what he **d** unto the army of Egypt,	6213
	11: 5 what he **d** unto you in the wilderness,	NIH
	11: 6 what he **d** unto Dathan and Abiram,	6213
	11: 7 all the great acts of the Lord which he **d**.	6213
	12:30 How **d** these nations serve their gods?	NIH
	24: 9 Remember what the Lord thy God **d**	NIH
	25:17 Remember what Amalek **d** unto thee by	6213
	29: 2 Ye have seen all that the Lord **d** before	6213
	31: 4 the Lord shall do unto them as he **d** to	6213
	32:12 *So* the Lord alone **d** lead him,	NIH
	32:38 Which **d** eat the fat of their sacrifices,	NIH
	33: 9 neither **d** he acknowledge his brethren,	NIH
	34: 9 and **d** as the Lord commanded Moses.	6213
Jos	2:10 what you **d** unto the two kings of	6213
	2:11 heard these **d** these *things,* our hearts **d** melt,	NIH
	2:11 neither **d** there remain any more courage	NIH
	4: 8 the children of Israel **d** so as Joshua	6213
	4:18 flowed over all his banks, as *they* **d** before.	NIH
	4:20 out of Jordan, **d** Joshua pitch in Gilgal.	NIH
	4:23 as the Lord your God **d** to the Red sea,	6213
	5: 4 this *is* the cause why Joshua **d** circumcise:	NIH
	5:11 they **d** eat of the old corn of the land on	NIH
	5:12 they **d** eat of the fruit of the land of	NIH
	5:14 **d** worship, and said unto him, What saith	NIH
	5:15 thou standest *is* holy. And Joshua **d** so.	6213
	6:14 *into* the camp: so they **d** six days.	6213
	9: 4 They **d** work wilily, and went and made	NIH
	9: 9 fame of him, and all that he **d** in Egypt,	6213
	9:10 all that he **d** to the two kings of	6213
	9:26 so **d** he unto them, and delivered them	6213

D

Jos
10:23 they **d** so, and brought forth those five — 6213
10:28 he **d** to the king of Makkedah as he did — 6213
10:28 he did to the king of Makkedah as he **d** — 6213
10:30 did unto the king thereof as he did unto — 6213
10:30 did unto the king thereof as he **d** unto — 6213
10:39 so he **d** to Debir, and to the king thereof; — 6213
10:42 and their land **d** Joshua take *at* one time, — NIH
11: 9 Joshua **d** unto them as the LORD bade — 6213
11:12 **d** Joshua take, and smote them with — NIH
11:13 save Hazor only; *that* **d** Joshua burn. — NIH
11:15 so **d** Moses command Joshua, and so — NIH
11:15 Moses command Joshua, and so **d** Joshua; — 6213
12: 6 Them **d** Moses the servant of the LORD — NIH
13:12 these *d* Moses smite, and cast them out. — NIH
13:22 **d** the children of Israel slay with the sword — NIH
13:32 These *are the countries* which Moses **d** — 6213
14: 5 so the children of Israel **d**, and they — 6213
17:13 tribute; but **d** not utterly drive them — NIH
22:20 **D** not Achan the son of Zerah commit a — NIH
22:33 **d** not intend to go up against them in — NIH
24: 5 to *that* which I **d** amongst them: — 6213
24:13 I have given you a land for which ye **d** not — NIH
24:17 which **d** those great signs in our sight, — 6213

Jdg
1:21 the children of Benjamin **d** not drive out — NIH
1:27 Neither **d** Manasseh drive out — NIH
1:28 tribute, and **d** not utterly drive them out. — NIH
1:29 **d** Ephraim drive out the Canaanites — NIH
1:30 **d** Zebulun drive out the inhabitants — NIH
1:31 **d** Asher drive out the inhabitants of — NIH
1:32 of the land: for they **d** not drive them out. — NIH
1:33 **d** Naphtali drive out the inhabitants — NIH
2: 7 works of the LORD, that he **d** for Israel. — 6213
2:11 the children of Israel **d** evil in the sight of — 6213
2:17 of the LORD; *but* they **d** not so. — NIH
2:22 as their fathers **d** keep *it*, or not. — NIH
3: 7 the children of Israel **d** evil in the sight of — 6213
3:12 the children of Israel **d** evil again in — 6213
3:16 he **d** gird it under his raiment upon his — NIH
4: 1 the children of Israel again **d** evil in — 6213
5:17 why **d** Dan remain *in* ships? — NIH
6: 1 the children of Israel **d** evil in the sight of — 6213
6:13 **D** not the LORD bring us up from Egypt? — NIH
6:20 and pour out the broth. And he **d** so. — 6213
6:27 and **d** as the LORD had said unto him: — 6213
6:27 not do *it* by day, that he **d** *it* by night. — 6213
6:40 God **d** so that night: for it was dry upon — 6213
8: 1 And they **d** chide with him sharply. — NIH
8:15 with whom ye **d** upbraid me, saying, — NIH
8:25 **d** cast therein every man the earrings of — NIH
9:27 **d** eat and drink, and cursed Abimelech. — NIH
9:56 which he **d** unto his father, in slaying his — 6213
9:57 all the evil of the men of Shechem **d** God — NIH
10: 6 the children of Israel **d** evil again in — 6213
10:11 **D** not I deliver you from the Egyptians, — NIH
10:12 and the Maonites, **d** oppress you; — NIH
11: 7 **D** not ye hate me, and expel me out of my — NIH
11:25 **d** he ever strive against Israel, or did he — NIH
11:25 or **d** he ever fight against them, — NIH
11:26 **d** ye not recover *them* within that time? — NIH
11:39 who **d** with her *according to* his vow — 6213
13: 1 the children of Israel **d** evil again in — 6213
13:19 *the angel* **d** wondrously; and Manoah and — 6213
13:21 the angel of the LORD **d** no more appear — NIH
14: 9 and he gave them, and they **d** eat: — NIH
15:11 As they **d** unto me, so have I done unto — 6213
16:21 brass; and he **d** grind in the prison house. — 1961
17: 6 every man **d** *that* which *was* right in his — 6213
19: 4 so they **d** eat and drink, and lodged there. — NIH
19: 6 **d** eat and drink both of them together: — NIH
19: 8 afternoon, and they **d** eat both of them. — NIH
19:21 washed their feet, and **d** eat and drink. — NIH
21:22 for ye **d** not give unto them at *this* time, — NIH
21:23 the children of Benjamin **d** so, — 6213
21:25 every man **d** *that* which *was* right in his — NIH

Ru
2:14 reached her parched *corn*, and she **d** eat, — 6213
2:19 blessed be he that **d** take knowledge of — NIH
3: 6 **d** according to all that her mother in law — 6213
4:11 which two **d** build the house of Israel: — NIH

1Sa
1: 7 *as he* **d** so year by year, when she went — 6213
1: 7 therefore she wept, and **d** not eat. — NIH
1:18 **d** eat, and her countenance was no more — NIH
2:11 the child **d** minister unto the LORD before — 1961
2:14 So they **d** in Shiloh unto all the Israelites — 6213
2:22 heard all that his sons **d** unto all Israel; — NIH
2:27 **D** I plainly appear unto the house of thy — NIH
2:28 **d** I choose him out of all the tribes of Israel — NIH
2:28 **d** I give unto the house of thy father all — NIH
3: 7 Now Samuel **d** not yet know the LORD, — NIH
3:19 **d** let none of his words fall to the ground. — NIH
4:20 she answered not, neither **d** she regard it. — NIH
6: 6 **d** they not let the people go, — NIH
6:10 the men **d** so; and took two milch kine, — 6213
7: 4 the children of Israel **d** put away Baalim — NIH
7:14 the coasts thereof **d** Israel deliver out of — NIH
9:24 So Saul **d** eat with Samuel that day. — NIH
12: 7 which he **d** to you and to your fathers. — 6213
13: 6 the people **d** hide themselves in caves, — NIH
14:32 and the people **d** eat *them* with the blood. — NIH
14:43 I **but** taste a little honey with — 2938+2938
15: 2 remember *that* which Amalek **d** to Israel, — 6213
16: 4 Samuel **d** *that* which the LORD spake, — 6213
19: 5 For he **d** put his life in his hand, — NIH
20:34 **d** eat no meat the second day of the month — NIH
21:11 **d** they not sing one to another of him in — NIH
22:15 **D** I then begin to inquire of God for him? — NIH

1Sa
22:17 when he fled, and **d** not shew it to me. — NIH
22:18 five persons that **d** wear a linen ephod. — NIH
25: 4 heard in the wilderness that Nabal **d** — NIH
27:11 So **d** David, and **d** not *will be* his manner all — 6213
28:24 and **d** bake unleavened bread thereof: — NIH
28:25 and before his servants; and they **d** eat. — NIH
30:11 David, and gave him bread, and he **d** eat; — NIH

2Sa
1: 2 that he fell to the earth, and **d** obeisance. — NIH
2: 3 his men that *were* with him **d** David bring — NIH
3:36 as whatsoever the king **d**, pleased all — 6213
5:25 David **d** so, as the LORD had commanded — 6213
7:17 this vision, so **d** Nathan speak unto David. — NIH
8:11 Which also king David **d** dedicate unto — NIH
9: 6 he fell on his face, and **d** reverence. — NIH
9:13 for he **d** eat continually at the king's table; — NIH
11: 7 demanded *of him* how Joab **d**, — 7965+3807.1
11: 7 how the people **d**, and how the — 7965+3807.1
11:13 called him, he **d** eat and drink before him; — NIH
11:20 *so* nigh unto the city when *ye* **d** fight? — NIH
11:21 **d** not a woman cast a piece of a millstone — NIH
12: 3 it **d** eat of his own meat, and drank of his — NIH
12: 6 because he **d** this thing, and because he — 6213
12:17 not, neither **d** he eat bread with them. — NIH
12:20 they set bread before him, and he **d** eat. — NIH
12:31 thus **d** he unto all the cities of the children — 6213
13: 8 cakes in his sight, and **d** bake the cakes. — NIH
13:29 the servants of Absalom **d** unto Amnon as — 6213
14: 4 and **d** obeisance, and said, Help, O king. — NIH
15: 6 on this manner **d** Absalom to all Israel that — 6213
17:15 and thus **d** Ahithophel counsel Absalom — NIH
19:19 **d** perversely the day that my lord the — 5753
19:28 among them that **d** eat at thine own table. — NIH
19:43 why then **d** ye despise us, that our advice — NIH
20: 6 Bichri do us more harm than **d** Absalom: — NIH
21: 6 of Saul, whom the LORD **d** choose. — NIH
22: 7 he **d** hear my voice out of his temple, — NIH
22: 7 temple, and my cry **d** *enter* into his ears. — NIH
22:11 he rode upon a cherub, and **d** fly: and — NIH
22:23 his statutes, I **d** not depart from them. — NIH
22:37 steps under me; so that my feet **d** not slip. — NIH
22:43 I beat them *as* small as the dust of — NIH
22:43 I **d** stamp them as the mire of the street, — NIH
22:43 of the street, *and* **d** spread them abroad. — NIH
23:17 These *things* **d** these three mighty *men*. — 6213
23:22 These *things* **d** Benaiah the son of — 6213
24:23 All *these things* **d** Araunah, *as* a king, — NIH

1Ki
1:16 and **d** obeisance unto the king. — 7812
1:31 **d** reverence to the king, and said, Let — 7812
2: 5 what Joab the son of Zeruiah **d** to me, — 6213
2: 5 he **d** to the two captains of the hosts — 6213
2:35 Zadok the priest **d** the king put in the — NIH
2:42 **D** I not make thee to swear by the LORD, — NIH
3: 4 thousand burnt offerings **d** Solomon offer — NIH
3:14 as thy father David **d** walk, then I will — NIH
3:21 it was not my son, which I **d** bear. — NIH
5:18 Hiram's builders **d** hew *them*, and — NIH
7:15 line of twelve cubits **d** compass either of — 6213
7:18 and so **d** he for the other chapter. — 6213
7:23 a line of thirty cubits **d** compass it round — NIH
7:46 In the plain of Jordan **d** the king cast them, — NIH
7:51 **d** he put among the treasures of the house — NIH
8: 4 even those **d** the priests and the Levites — NIH
8:64 The same day **d** the king hallow the — NIH
9:21 upon those **d** Solomon levy a tribute of — NIH
9:22 the children of Israel **d** Solomon make no — NIH
9:24 had built for her: then **d** he build Millo. — NIH
9:25 three times in a year **d** Solomon offer — NIH
10:29 **d** they bring *them* out by their means. — NIH
11: 6 Solomon **d** evil in the sight of the LORD, — 6213
11: 6 after the LORD, as *d* David his father. — NIH
11: 7 **d** Solomon build a high place for Chemosh — NIH
11: 8 likewise **d** he for all his strange wives, — 6213
11:16 (For six months **d** Joab remain there with — NIH
11:25 beside the mischief that Hadad *d*: and — NIH
11:33 and my judgments, as *d* David his father. — NIH
11:38 as David my servant **d**; — 6213
11:41 and all that he **d**, and his wisdom, — 6213
12: 9 Make the yoke which thy father **d** put — NIH
12:11 now whereas my father **d** lade you with a — NIH
12:32 offered upon the altar (so **d** he in Beth-el,) — 6213
13:19 **d** eat bread in his house, and drank water. — NIH
13:22 of the which the LORD **d** say to thee, — NIH
14: 4 Jeroboam's wife **d** so, and arose, — 6213
14:16 who **d** sin, and who made Israel to sin. — NIH
14:21 the city which the LORD **d** choose out of — 6213
14:22 Judah **d** evil in the sight of the LORD, — 6213
14:24 they **d** according to all the abominations — NIH
14:29 the acts of Rehoboam, and all that he **d**, — 6213
15: 4 Nevertheless for David's sake the LORD — NIH
15: 5 Because David **d** *that* which *was* right in — 6213
15: 7 of the acts of Abijam, and all that he **d**, — 6213
15:11 Asa **d** *that* which *was* right in the eyes of — 6213
15:11 eyes of the LORD, as *d* David his father. — NIH
15:23 that he **d**, and the cities which he built, — 6213
15:26 he **d** evil in the sight of the LORD, — 6213
15:28 of Asa king of Judah **d** Baasha slay him, — NIH
15:31 of the acts of Nadab, and all that he **d**, — 6213
15:34 he **d** evil in the sight of the LORD, — 6213
16: 5 of Baasha, and what he **d**, and his might, — 6213
16: 7 even for all the evil that he **d** in the sight — 6213
16:12 Thus **d** Zimri destroy all the house of — NIH
16:14 rest of the acts of Elah, and all that he **d**, — 6213
16:15 seventh year of Asa king of Judah **d** Zimri — NIH
16:19 in his sin which he **d**, to make Israel sin. — 6213
16:25 **d** worse than all that *were* before him. — NIH

1Ki
16:27 the rest of the acts of Omri which he **d**, — 6213
16:30 Ahab the son of Omri **d** evil in the sight — 6213
16:33 Ahab **d** more to provoke the LORD God — 6213
16:34 In his days **d** Hiel the Bethelite build — NIH
17: 5 according unto the word of the LORD: — 6213
17:15 and **d** according to the saying of Elijah: — 6213
17:15 and he, and her house, **d** eat *many* days. — NIH
17:16 wasted not, neither **d** the cruse of oil fail, — NIH
18:13 Was it not told my lord what I **d** when — 6213
18:34 they **d** *it* **the second time**. And he said, — 8138
18:34 third time. And they **d** *it* **the third time**. — 8027
19: 6 he **d** eat and drink, and laid him down — NIH
19: 8 **d** eat and drink, and went in the strength — NIH
19:21 and gave unto the people, and they **d** eat. — NIH
20:25 he hearkened unto their voice, and **d** so. — 6213
20:33 the men **d** diligently observe whether — NIH
20:33 **d** hastily catch *it:* and they said, Thy — NIH
21:11 **d** as Jezebel had sent unto them, *and* as it — 6213
21:13 Naboth **d** blaspheme God and the king. — NIH
21:25 which **d** sell himself to work wickedness — NIH
21:26 he **d** very abominably in following idols, — 6213
21:26 according to all *things* as **d** the Amorites, — 6213
22:18 **D** I not tell thee that he would prophesy — NIH
22:39 all that he **d**, and the ivory house which — 6213
22:52 he **d** evil in the sight of the LORD, — 6213

2Ki
1:18 rest of the acts of Ahaziah which he **d**, — 6213
2:18 unto them, **D** I not say unto you, Go not? — NIH
4: 1 thou knowest that thy servant **d** fear — 1961
4:28 she said, **D** I desire a son of my lord? did I — NIH
4:28 my lord? **d** I not say, Do not deceive me? — NIH
4:44 they **d** eat, and left *thereof*, according to — NIH
6: 6 cast *it* in thither; and the iron **d** swim. — NIH
6:29 So we boiled my son, and **d** eat him: and — NIH
7: 8 **d** eat and drink, and carried thence silver, — NIH
8: 2 and **d** after the saying of the man of God: — 6213
8:18 kings of Israel, as **d** the house of Ahab: — 6213
8:18 and he **d** evil in the sight of the LORD. — 6213
8:23 rest of the acts of Joram, and all that he **d**, — 6213
8:25 **d** Ahaziah the son of Jehoram king of — NIH
8:27 **d** evil in the sight of the LORD, as *did* — 6213
8:27 of the LORD, as *d* the house of Ahab: — NIH
9:27 *And they d* so at the going up to Gur, — NIH
9:34 come in, he **d** eat and drink, and said, — NIH
10:19 Jehu **d** *it* in subtilty, to the intent that *he* — 6213
10:34 Jehu, and all that he **d**, and all his might, — 6213
11: 3 And Athaliah *d* reign over the land. — NIH
11: 9 captains over the hundreds **d** according — 6213
11:10 to the captains over hundreds **d** the priest — NIH
12: 2 Jehoash **d** *that* which *was* right in the — 6213
12:11 into the hands of *them* that **d** the work, — 6213
12:19 rest of the acts of Joash, and all that he **d**, — 6213
13: 2 he **d** *that* which *was* evil in the sight of — 6213
13: 7 Neither **d** he leave *of the* people to — NIH
13: 8 and all that he **d**, and his might, — 6213
13:11 he **d** *that* which *was* evil in the sight of — 6213
13:12 all that he **d**, and his might where*with* he — 6213
13:25 Three times **d** Joash beat him, — NIH
14: 3 he **d** *that* which *was* right in the sight of — 6213
14: 3 he **d** according to all *things* as Joash his — 6213
14: 3 to all *things* as Joash his father **d**. — NIH
14: 4 as yet the people **d** sacrifice and — NIH
14:15 rest of the acts of Jehoash which he **d**, — 6213
14:24 he **d** *that* which *was* evil in the sight of — 6213
14:28 that he **d**, and his might, how he warred, — 6213
15: 3 he **d** *that* which *was* right in the sight of — 6213
15: 6 of the acts of Azariah, and all that he **d**, — 6213
15: 8 eighth year of Azariah king of Judah **d** — NIH
15: 9 he **d** *that* which *was* evil in the sight of — 6213
15:18 he **d** *that* which *was* evil in the sight of — 6213
15:21 the acts of Menahem, and all that he **d**, — 6213
15:24 he **d** *that* which *was* evil in the sight of — 6213
15:26 acts of Pekahiah, and all that he **d**, behold, — 6213
15:28 he **d** *that* which *was* evil in the sight of — 6213
15:31 acts of Pekah, and all that he **d**, behold, — 6213
15:34 he **d** *that* which *was* right in the sight of — 6213
15:34 he **d** according to all that his father Uzziah — 6213
15:36 of the acts of Jotham, and all that he **d**, — 6213
16: 2 **d** not *that* which *was* right in the sight of — 6213
16:16 Thus **d** Urijah the priest, according to all — 6213
16:19 the rest of the acts of Ahaz which he **d**, — 6213
17: 2 he **d** *that* which *was* evil in the sight of — 6213
17: 9 children of Israel **d** secretly *those* things — NIH
17:11 as **d** the heathen whom the LORD carried — NIH
17:14 that **d** not believe in the LORD their God. — 6213
17:22 in all the sins of Jeroboam which he **d**; — 6213
17:40 Howbeit they **d** not hearken, but they did — NIH
17:40 but they **d** after their former manner. — 6213
17:41 their fathers, *so* do they unto this day. — 6213
18: 3 he **d** *that* which *was* right in the sight of — 6213
18: 3 according to all that David his father **d**. — NIH
18: 4 unto those days the children of Israel **d** — 1961
18:11 the king of Assyria **d** carry away Israel — NIH
18:13 **d** Sennacherib king of Assyria come up — NIH
18:16 At that time **d** Hezekiah cut off *the gold* — 6213
21: 2 he **d** *that* which *was* evil in the sight of — 6213
21: 3 made a grove, as **d** Ahab king of Israel; — 6213
21: 9 the nations whom the LORD destroyed — NIH
21:11 wickedly above all that the Amorites **d**, — 6213
21:17 all that he **d**, and his sin that he sinned, — 6213
21:20 he **d** *that* which *was* evil in the sight of — 6213
21:20 of the LORD, as his father Manasseh **d**. — NIH
21:25 the rest of the acts of Amon which he **d**, — 6213
22: 2 he **d** *that* which *was* right in the sight of — 6213
23: 9 they **d** eat of the unleavened bread among — NIH
23:12 **d** the king beat down, and brake *them* — NIH

D

2Ki
23:13 the children of Ammon, **d** the king defile. NIH
23:19 **d** to them according to all the acts that 6213
23:24 and in Jerusalem, **d** Josiah put away, NIH
23:28 rest of the acts of Josiah, and all that he **d**, 6213
23:32 he **d** *that* which *was* evil in the sight of 6213
23:37 he **d** *that* which *was* evil in the sight of 6213
24: 3 of Manasseh, according to all that he **d**; 6213
24: 5 of the acts of Jehoiakim, and all that he **d**, 6213
24: 9 he **d** *that* which *was* evil in the sight of 6213
24:11 the city, and his servants **d** besiege it. NIH
24:19 he **d** *that* which *was* evil in the sight of 6213
25:11 **d** Nebuzar-adan the captain of the guard NIH
25:13 **d** the Chaldees break *in pieces,* and NIH
25:27 **d** lift up the head of Jehoiachin king of NIH
25:29 he **d** eat bread continually before him all NIH
1Ch
4:27 neither **d** all their family multiply, like to NIH
9:22 Samuel the seer **d** ordain in their set office. NIH
11:19 These *things* **d** these three mightiest. 6213
11:24 These *things* **d** Benaiah the son of 6213
14:16 David therefore **d** as God commanded 6213
15:13 For because ye **d** *it* not at the first, NIH
15:24 **d** blow with the trumpets before the ark NIH
17:15 this vision, so **d** Nathan speak unto David. NIH
23:24 the work for the service of the house 6213
26:27 Out of the spoils won in battles **d** they NIH
27:26 over them that **d** the work of the field for 6213
29:22 **d** eat and drink before the Lord on that NIH
2Ch
1: 7 In that night **d** God appear unto Solomon, NIH
2: 7 whom David my father **d** provide. NIH
4: 2 a line of thirty cubits **d** compass it round NIH
4: 3 of oxen, which **d** compass it round about: NIH
4:16 **d** Huram his father make to king Solomon NIH
4:17 In the plain of Jordan **d** the king cast them, NIH
5: 5 **d** the priests *and* the Levites bring up. NIH
5:11 *and* **d** not *then* wait by course: NIH
8: 8 them **d** Solomon make to pay tribute until NIH
8: 9 the children of Israel **d** Solomon make no NIH
10: 9 Ease somewhat the yoke that thy father **d** NIH
12:14 **d** evil, because he prepared not his heart 6213
13:20 Neither **d** Jeroboam recover strength again NIH
14: 2 Asa **d** *that* which *was* good and right in 6213
15: 4 when they in their trouble **d** turn unto NIH
15: 6 for God **d** vex them with all adversity. NIH
18:16 I **d** see all Israel scattered upon NIH
18:17 **D** I not tell thee *that* he would not NIH
19: 8 Moreover in Jerusalem **d** Jehoshaphat set NIH
20:35 after this **d** Jehoshaphat king of Judah join NIH
20:35 king of Israel, who **d** very wickedly: 6213
21: 6 of Israel, like as **d** the house of Ahab: 6213
21:10 The same time also **d** Libnah revolt from NIH
22: 4 Wherefore he **d** evil in the sight of 6213
23: 8 all Judah **d** according to all *things* that 6213
24: 2 Joash **d** *that* which *was* right in the sight 6213
24: 7 of the Lord **d** they bestow upon Baalim. NIH
24:11 Thus they **d** day by day, 6213
24:12 Jehoiada gave it to such as **d** the work of 6213
25: 2 he **d** *that* which *was* right in the sight of 6213
25: 4 **d** as it is written in the law in the book of NIH
25:12 ten thousand *left* alive **d** the children NIH
25:27 Now after the time that Amaziah **d** turn NIH
26: 4 he **d** *that* which *was* right in the sight of 6213
26: 4 to all that his father Amaziah **d**. 6213
26:22 first and last, **d** Isaiah the prophet, the son NIH
27: 2 he **d** *that* which *was* right in the sight of 6213
27: 2 according to all that his father Uzziah **d:** 6213
27: 2 the Lord. And the people **d** yet corruptly. NIH
27: 5 So much **d** the children of Ammon pay NIH
28: 1 he **d** not *that* which *was* right in the sight 6213
28:16 At that time **d** king Ahaz send unto NIH
28:22 in the time of his distress **d** he trespass yet NIH
29: 2 he **d** *that* which *was* right in the sight of 6213
29:19 which king Ahaz in his reign **d** cast away NIH
29:34 their brethren the Levites **d** help NIH
30:18 yet **d** they eat the passover otherwise than NIH
30:22 they **d** eat throughout the feast seven days, NIH
30:24 For Hezekiah king of Judah **d** give to NIH
31:20 thus **d** Hezekiah throughout all Judah, 6213
31:21 he **d** *it* with all his heart, and prospered. 6213
32: 3 without the city: and they **d** help him. NIH
32: 9 After this **d** Sennacherib king of Assyria NIH
32:33 the inhabitants of Jerusalem **d** him honour 6213
33: 2 **d** *that* which *was* evil in the sight of 6213
33:17 Nevertheless the people **d** sacrifice still in NIH
33:22 he **d** *that* which *was* evil in the sight of 6213
33:22 of the Lord, as **d** Manasseh his father: 6213
34: 2 he **d** *that* which *was* right in the sight of 6213
34: 6 so **d** he in the cities of Manasseh, NIH
34:12 the men **d** the work faithfully: and 6213
34:32 **d** according to the covenant of God, 6213
35: 3 the son of David king of Israel **d** build; NIH
35:12 of Moses. And so **d** *they* with the oxen. NIH
35:18 neither **d** all the kings of Israel keep such a NIH
36: 5 he **d** *that* which *was* evil in the sight of 6213
36: 8 his abominations which he **d**, 6213
36: 9 he **d** *that* which *was* evil in the sight of 6213
36:12 he **d** *that* which *was* evil in the sight of 6213
Ezr
1: 8 Even those **d** Cyrus king of Persia bring NIH
1:11 All *these* **d** Sheshbazzar bring up with NIH
5:14 those **d** Cyrus the king take out of NIH
6:13 the king had sent, so they **d** speedily. 5648
6:21 to seek the Lord God of Israel, **d** eat, NIH
10: 6 he **d** eat no bread, nor drink water: NIH
10:16 the children of the captivity **d** so. 6213
Ne
2:16 knew not whither I went, or what I **d**; 6213
2:16 the rulers, nor to the rest that **d** the work. 6213

Ne
3: 3 fish gate **d** the sons of Hassenaah build, NIH
5:13 the people **d** according to this promise. 6213
5:15 but so **d** not I, because of the fear of God. 6213
9:25 so they **d** eat, and were filled, NIH
9:28 had rest, they **d** evil again before thee: 6213
11:12 brethren that **d** the work of the house 6213
13: 7 understood of the evil that Eliashib **d** for 6213
13:10 Levites and the singers, that **d** the work, 6213
13:18 **D** not your fathers thus, and *did not* our 6213
13:18 **d** *not* our God bring all this evil upon us, NIH
13:26 **D** not Solomon king of Israel sin by these NIH
13:26 *nevertheless* even him **d** outlandish NIH
Est
1: 8 *was* according to the law; none **d** compel: NIH
1:21 the king **d** according to the word of 6213
2: 4 the thing pleased the king; and he **d** so. 6213
2:11 to know how Esther **d**, and what should 7965
2:20 for Esther the commandment of 6213
3: 1 After these things **d** king Ahasuerus NIH
3: 2 bowed not, nor **d** *him* reverence. NIH
3: 5 nor **d** him reverence, *then* was Haman NIH
4:17 according to all that Esther had 6213
5:12 Esther the queen **d** let no *man* come in NIH
8: 1 On that day **d** the king Ahasuerus give NIH
9: 5 **d** what they would unto those that hated 6213
9:24 in their hearts. Thus **d** Haman NIH
Job
1: 5 in their hearts. Thus **d** Job continually. NIH
2:10 In all this **d** not Job sin with his lips. NIH
3:11 *why* **d** I *not* give up the ghost when I NIH
3:12 Why **d** the knees prevent me? or why NIH
6:22 **D** I say, Bring unto me? or, Give a reward NIH
28:27 he **d** see it, and declare it; he prepared it, NIH
30:25 **D** not I weep for him that was in trouble? NIH
31:13 If I **d** despise the cause of my manservant NIH
31:15 **D** not he that made me in the womb make NIH
31:15 and **d** not one fashion us in the womb? NIH
31:32 The stranger **d** not lodge in the street: NIH
31:34 **D** I fear a great multitude, or did NIH
31:34 or **d** the contempt of families terrify me, NIH
42: 9 **d** according as the Lord commanded 6213
42:11 and **d** eat bread with him in his house: NIH
Ps
14: 2 see if there were *any* that **d** understand, NIH
18:10 he rode upon a cherub, and **d** fly: yea, NIH
18:10 yea, he **d** fly upon the wings of the wind. NIH
18:22 I **d** not put away his statutes from me. NIH
18:36 steps under me, that my feet **d** not slip. NIH
18:37 neither **d** I turn again till they were NIH
18:42 **d** I beat them small as the dust before NIH
18:42 I **d** cast them out as the dirt in the streets. NIH
31:11 they that **d** see me without fled from me. NIH
35:11 False witnesses **d** rise up; they laid to my NIH
35:15 *it* not; they **d** tear *me*, and ceased not: NIH
41: 9 whom I trusted, which **d** eat *of* my bread, NIH
44: 3 neither **d** their own arm save them: NIH
45: 9 hand **d** stand the queen in gold of Ophir. NIH
51: 5 and in sin **d** my mother conceive me. NIH
53: 2 to see if there were *any* that **d** understand, NIH
53: 2 *any* that did understand, that **d** seek God. NIH
55:12 me *that* **d** magnify *himself* against me; NIH
66: 6 flood on foot: there **d** we rejoice in him. NIH
68:12 Kings of armies **d** flee apace: and she that NIH
78:12 Marvellous things **d** he in the sight of 6213
78:25 Man **d** eat angels' food: he sent them meat NIH
78:29 So they **d** eat, and were well filled: for he NIH
78:33 Therefore their days **d** he consume in NIH
78:36 Nevertheless they **d** flatter him with their NIH
78:38 away, and **d** not stir up all his wrath. NIH
78:40 How oft **d** they provoke him in NIH
102:19 from heaven **d** the Lord behold the earth; NIH
105:35 **d** eat up all the herbs in their land, NIH
106:34 They **d** not destroy the nations, NIH
106:43 Many times **d** he deliver them; NIH
119:23 Princes also **d** sit *and* speak against me: NIH
119:23 *but* thy servant **d** meditate in thy statutes. NIH
135: 6 *that* **d** he in heaven, and in earth, 6213
139:16 Thine eyes **d** see my substance, yet being NIH
142: 1 *with* my voice unto the Lord **d** I make NIH
Pr
1:29 and **d** not choose the fear of the Lord: NIH
Isa
5:25 the hills **d** tremble, and their carcases NIH
6: 2 covered his feet, and with twain he **d** fly. NIH
9: 1 afterward **d** more grievously afflict *her* by NIH
10:10 whose graven images **d** excel *them* of NIH
13: 1 which Isaiah the son of Amoz **d** see. NIH
14:16 earth to tremble, that **d** shake kingdoms; NIH
20: 2 And he **d** so, walking naked and barefoot. 6213
22:12 in that day **d** the Lord God of hosts call to NIH
38:14 Like a crane *or* a swallow, so **d** I chatter: NIH
38:14 I **d** mourn as a dove: mine eyes fail *with* NIH
42:24 **d** not the Lord, he against whom we NIH
48: 3 I **d** them suddenly, and they came to pass. 6213
53: 4 yet we **d** esteem him stricken, smitten of NIH
58: 2 as a nation that **d** righteousness, 6213
65:12 because when I called, ye **d** not answer; NIH
65:12 when I spake, ye **d** not hear; but did evil NIH
65:12 **d** evil before mine eyes, and did choose 6213
65:12 and **d** choose *that* wherein I delighted not. NIH
66: 4 because when I called, none **d** answer; NIH
66: 4 did answer; when I spake, they **d** not hear: NIH
66: 4 they **d** evil before mine eyes, and chose 6213
Jer
7:12 see what I **d** to it for the wickedness of 6213
7:26 neck: they **d worse** than their fathers. 7489
11: 8 *them* to do; but they **d** them not. 6213
14: 6 the wild asses **d** stand in the high places, NIH
14: 6 eyes **d** fail, because *there* was no grass. NIH
15: 4 Judah, for *that* which he **d** in Jerusalem. 6213
15:16 Thy words were found, and I **d** eat them; NIH
22:15 **d** not thy father eat and drink, NIH

Jer
26:19 **D** Hezekiah king of Judah and all Judah NIH
26:19 he **d** not fear the Lord, and besought NIH
31:19 because I **d** bear the reproach of my youth. NIH
36: 8 Baruch the son of Neriah **d** according to 6213
37: 2 **d** hearken unto the words of the Lord, NIH
38:12 under the cords. And Jeremiah **d** so. 6213
41: 1 there they **d** eat bread together in Mizpah. NIH
44:19 **d** we make her cakes to worship her, NIH
44:21 **d** not the Lord remember them, NIH
46:15 because the Lord **d** drive them. NIH
46:17 They **d** cry there, Pharaoh king of Egypt *is* NIH
46:21 they **d** not stand, because the day of their NIH
52: 2 he **d** *that* which *was* evil in the eyes of 6213
52:21 a fillet of twelve cubits **d** compass it; NIH
52:33 he **d** continually eat bread before him all NIH
La
1: 7 hand of the enemy, and none **d** help her: NIH
1: 7 saw her, *and* **d** mock at her sabbaths. NIH
4: 5 They that **d** feed delicately are desolate in NIH
Eze
3: 3 I **d** eat *it*; and it was in my mouth as honey NIH
6:13 the place where they **d** offer sweet savour NIH
11:22 the cherubims lift up their wings, NIH
12: 7 I **d** so as I was commanded: I brought 6213
16:49 neither **d** she strengthen the hand of NIH
17: 7 this vine **d** bend her roots toward him, NIH
18:18 **d** *that* which *is* not good among his 6213
20: 8 they **d** not every man cast away NIH
20: 8 neither **d** they forsake the idols of Egypt: NIH
20:17 neither **d** I make an end of them in NIH
24:18 I **d** in the morning as I was commanded. 6213
27:25 The ships of Tarshish **d** sing of thee *in* thy NIH
31: 6 under his branches **d** all the beasts of NIH
34: 6 and none **d** search or seek *after* them. NIH
34: 8 **d** my shepherds search for my flock, NIH
43:22 as they **d** cleanse *it* with the bullock. NIH
46:12 offerings, as he **d** on the sabbath day: 6213
Da
1:15 in flesh than all the children which **d** NIH
3:24 **D** not we cast three men bound into NIH
4: 7 they **d** not make known unto me NIH
4:33 **d** eat grass as oxen, and his body was wet NIH
6:10 thanks before his God, as he **d** aforetime. 5648
7: 9 cast *down*, and the Ancient of days **d** sit, NIH
8: 4 he **d** according to his will, 6213
8:27 I rose up, and **d** the king's business; 6213
10: 3 neither **d** I anoint myself at all, till three NIH
Hos
2: 8 For she **d** not know that I gave her corn, NIH
9:17 because they **d** not hearken unto him: NIH
10: 9 children of iniquity **d** not overtake them. NIH
13: 5 I **d** know thee in the wilderness, in the NIH
Am
1:11 he **d** pursue his brother with the sword, NIH
1:11 **d** cast off all pity, and his anger did tear NIH
1:11 his anger **d** tear perpetually, and he kept NIH
5:19 As if a man **d** flee from a lion, and a bear NIH
7: 4 the great deep, and **d** eat up a part. NIH
Ob
1:14 to cut off those of his that **d** escape; NIH
1:14 of his that **d** remain in the day of distress. NIH
Jnh
3:10 he would do unto them; and he **d** it not. 6213
4: 8 it came to pass, when the sun **d** arise, NIH
Na
2:12 The lion **d** tear in pieces enough for his NIH
Hab
1: 1 burden which Habakkuk the prophet **d** NIH
3: 6 were scattered, the perpetual hills **d** bow: NIH
3: 7 curtains of the land of Midian **d** tremble. NIH
Hag
1: 9 ye brought *it* home, I **d** blow upon it. NIH
1:12 and the people **d** fear before the Lord. NIH
1:14 **d** work in the house of the Lord of 6213
Zec
1: 4 they **d** not hear, nor hearken unto me, NIH
1: 6 **d** they not take hold of your fathers? NIH
1:21 so that no man **d** lift up his head: NIH
7: 5 **d** ye at all fast *unto* me, *even* to me? NIH
7: 6 when ye **d** eat, and when ye **d** drink, NIH
7: 6 when ye did eat, and when ye **d** drink, NIH
7: 6 **d** not ye eat *for* yourselves, and drink *for* NIH
9: 3 And Tyrus **d** build herself a strong hold, NIH
Mal
2: 6 and **d** turn many away from iniquity. NIH
2:15 **d** not he make one? Yet had he the residue NIH
Mt
1:24 Then Joseph being raised from sleep **d** as 4160
2:22 when he heard that Archelaus **d** reign in NIG
9:19 and followed him, and *so* **d** his disciples. NIH
12: 3 them, Have ye not read what David **d,** 4160
12: 4 and **d** eat the shewbread, which was not NIG
13:58 And he **d** not many mighty works there, NIH
14:20 And they **d** all eat, and were filled: and NIG
15: 7 well **d** Esaias prophesy of you, saying, NIG
15:37 And they **d** all eat, and were filled: and NIG
15:38 And they that **d** eat were four thousand NIG
17: 2 and his face **d** shine as the sun, NIG
19: 7 Why **d** Moses then command to give a NIH
20: 5 the sixth and ninth hour, and **d** likewise. 4160
21: 6 and **d** as Jesus commanded them, 4160
21:15 saw the wonderful *things* that he **d,** 4160
21:25 unto us, Why **d** ye not then believe him? NIG
21:31 Whether of *them* twain **d** the will of *his* 4160
21:36 the first: and they **d** unto them likewise. 4160
21:42 them, **D** ye never read in the scriptures, NIG
25:44 or in prison, and **d** not minister unto thee? NIG
25:45 Inasmuch as ye **d** *it* not to one of the least 4160
25:45 of the least of these, ye **d** *it* not to me. 4160
26:12 on my body, she **d** *it* for my burial. 4160
26:19 And the disciples **d** as Jesus had appointed 4160
26:21 as they **d** eat, he said, Verily I say unto NIG
26:67 Then they **d** spit in his face, NIG
27: 9 they of the children of Israel **d** value; NIG
27:35 and upon my vesture they **d** cast lots. NIH
27:51 and the earth **d** quake, and the rocks rent; NIH
28: 4 And for fear of him the keepers **d** shake, NIG
28: 8 and **d** run to bring his disciples word. NIG

D

Mt	28:15 the money, and **d** as they were taught:	4160
Mk	1: 4 John **d** baptize in the wilderness,	1096
	1: 6 and he **d** eat locusts and wild honey;	NIG
	1:32 And at even, when the sun **d** set,	NIG
	2:25 Have ye never read what David **d**, when	4160
	2:26 and **d** eat the shewbread, which is not	NIG
	3: 8 they had heard what great *things* he **d**,	4160
	4: 8 and **d** yield fruit that sprang up and	NIG
	5:20 had done for him: and all *men* **d** marvel.	NIG
	6:20 he **d** many *things*, and heard him gladly.	4160
	6:42 And they **d** all eat, and were filled.	NIG
	6:44 And they that **d** eat *of* the loaves were	NIG
	8: 6 and they **d** set *them* before the people.	NIG
	8: 8 they **d** eat, and were filled: and they took	NIG
	10: 3 unto them, What **d** Moses command you?	NIG
	11:31 will say, Why then **d** ye not believe him?	NIG
	12:44 For all *they* **d** cast in of their abundance;	NIG
	12:44 she of her want **d** cast in all that she had,	NIG
	14:18 And as they sat and **d** eat, Jesus said,	NIG
	14:22 And as they **d** eat, Jesus took bread,	NIG
	14:59 so **d** their witness agree together.	NIG
	14:65 the servants **d** strike him with the palms	NIG
	15:19 And **d** spit upon him, and bowing *their* knees	NIG
Lk	4: 2 And in those days he **d** eat nothing: and	NIG
	6: 1 and **d** eat, rubbing *them* in *their* hands.	NIG
	6: 3 not read so much as this, what David **d**,	4160
	6: 4 God, and **d** take and eat the shewbread,	NIG
	6:10 And he **d** so: and his hand was restored	4160
	6:23 for in the like manner **d** their fathers unto	4160
	6:26 for so **d** their fathers to the false prophets.	4160
	6:49 which the stream **d** beat vehemently,	NIG
	7:38 **d** wipe *them* with the hairs of her head,	NIG
	9:15 they **d** so, and made *them* all sit down.	NIG
	9:17 And they **d** eat, and were all filled: and	4160
	9:43 every one at all *things* which Jesus **d**,	NIG
	9:53 And they **d** not receive him, because his	4160
	9:54 and consume them, even as Elias **d**?	4160
	11:40 **d** not he that made that *which is* without	NIG
	12:47 prepared not *himself*, neither **d** according	4160
	12:48 and **d** commit *things* worthy of stripes,	NIG
	15:16 belly with the husks that the swine **d** eat:	NIG
	17: 9 he **d** the *things* that were commanded	4160
	17:27 They **d** eat, they drank, they married	NIG
	17:28 They **d** eat, they drank, they bought,	NIG
	19:22 not down, and reaping that I **d** not sow:	NIG
	24:32 another, **D** not our heart burn within us,	1510
	24:43 And he took *it*, and **d** eat before them.	NIG
Jn	1:45 the prophets, **d** write, Jesus of Nazareth,	NIG
	2:11 This beginning of miracles **d** Jesus in Cana	4160
	2:23 when they saw the miracles which he **d**.	4160
	2:24 Jesus **d** not commit himself unto them,	NIG
	4:29 which told me all *things* that ever I **d**:	4160
	4:39 testified, He told me all that ever I **d**.	4160
	4:45 having seen all *the things* that he **d** at	4160
	4:54 *is* again the second miracle *that* Jesus **d**,	4160
	5:16 And therefore **d** the Jews persecute Jesus,	NIG
	6: 2 they saw his miracles which he **d** on them	4160
	6:14 they had seen the miracle that Jesus **d**,	4160
	6:23 unto the place where they **d** eat bread,	4160
	6:26 but because ye **d** eat of the loaves,	NIG
	6:31 Our fathers **d** eat manna in the desert; as it	NIG
	6:49 fathers **d** eat manna in the wilderness,	NIG
	6:58 not as your fathers **d** eat manna,	NIG
	7: 5 For neither **d** his brethren believe in him.	NIG
	7:19 **D** not Moses give you the law, and *yet*	NIG
	8:40 I have heard of God: this **d** not Abraham.	4160
	9: 2 saying, Master, who **d** sin, this *man*, or	NIG
	9:18 the Jews **d** not believe concerning him,	NIG
	9:22 if any *man* **d** confess that he *was* Christ,	NIG
	9:26 said they to him again, What **d** he to thee?	4160
	9:27 I have told you already, and ye **d** not hear:	NIG
	10: 8 robbers: but the sheep **d** not hear them.	NIG
	10:41 unto him, and said, John **d** no miracle:	4160
	11:45 and had seen the *things* which Jesus **d**,	4160
	12:36 departed, and **d** hide himself from them.	NIG
	12:42 of the Pharisees they **d** not confess *him*,	NIG
	15:24 them the works which none other *man* **d**,	4160
	18:15 followed Jesus, and *so* **d** another disciple:	NIG
	18:26 **D** not I see thee in the garden with him?	NIG
	18:34 of thyself, or **d** others tell *it* thee of me?	NIG
	19:24 and for my vesture they **d** cast lots.	4160
	19:24 These *things* therefore the soldiers **d**.	4160
	20: 4 and the other disciple **d** outrun Peter,	NIG
	20:30 And many other signs truly **d** Jesus in	4160
	21: 7 naked,) and **d** cast himself into the sea.	NIG
	21:25 are also many other *things* which Jesus **d**,	4160
Ac	2:22 which God **d** by him in the midst of you,	4160
	2:26 Therefore **d** my heart rejoice,	NIG
	2:31 in hell, neither his flesh **d** see corruption.	NIG
	2:40 And with many other words **d** he testify	NIG
	2:46 **d** eat *their* meat with gladness and	NIG
	3:17 I wot that through ignorance ye **d** *it*, as	4238
	3:17 wot that through ignorance ye **d** *it*, as **d**	NIG
	4:25 Why **d** the heathen rage, and the people	NIG
	5:28 **D** not we straitly command you that *you*	NIG
	6: 8 great wonders and miracles among	4160
	7:27 he that **d** his neighbour **wrong** thrust him	91
	7:35 the same **d** God send *to be* a ruler and	NIG
	7:51 Holy Ghost: as your fathers **d**, so *do* ye.	NIG
	8: 6 and seeing the miracles which he **d**.	4160
	9: 9 without sight, and neither **d** eat nor drink.	NIG
	9:36 good works and almsdeeds which she **d**.	4160
	10:39 which he **d** both in the land of the Jews,	4160
	10:41 **d** eat and drink with him after he rose	NIG
	11:17 as God gave them the like gift as he **d** unto	NIG

Ac	11:30 Which also they **d**, and sent it to the	4160
	12: 8 And so he **d**. And he said unto him,	4160
	14:17 without witness, in that he **d** good,	15
	15: 8 the Holy Ghost, even as *he* **d** unto us;	NIG
	16:18 hath declared how God at the first **d**	NIG
	16:18 And this **d** she many days. But Paul,	4160
	19:14 Jew, *and* chief of the priests, which **d** so.	4160
	21: 9 four daughters, virgins, which **d** prophesy.	NIG
	26:10 Which *thing* I also **d** in Jerusalem:	4160
	26:10 many of the saints **d** I shut up in prison,	NIG
	26:22 prophets and Moses **d** say should come:	NIG
Ro	1:26 even their women **d** change the natural	NIG
	1:28 even as they **d** not like to retain God in	NIG
	3: 3 For what if some **d** not believe? shall their	NIG
	5:20 sin abounded, grace **d** much more abound:	NIG
	7: 5 **d** work in our members to bring forth fruit	NIG
	8:29 For whom he **d** foreknow, he also **d**	NIG
	8:29 he also **d** predestinate *to be* conformed to	NIG
	8:30 Moreover whom he **d** predestinate, them	NIG
	10:19 But I say, **D** not Israel know? First Moses	NIG
1Co	4: 8 I would *to God* ye reign, that we also	1065
	10: 3 And **d** all eat the same spiritual meat;	NIG
	10: 4 and **d** all drink the same spiritual drink:	NIG
	15:27 which **d** put all *things* under him.	NIG
2Co	1:17 was thus minded, **d** I use lightness?	NIG
	2: 9 For to this end also **d** I write, that I might	NIG
	5:20 as though God **d** beseech *you* by us:	NIG
	7: 8 letter, I do not repent, though I **d** repent:	NIG
	7:12 I **d** *it* not for his cause that had done	NIG
	8: 5 And *this they* **d**, not as we hoped,	NIG
	12:16 But be it so, I **d** not burden you:	NIG
	12:17 **D** I make a gain of you by any of them	NIG
	12:18 **D** Titus make a gain of you? walked we	NIG
Gal	2:12 from James, he **d** eat with the Gentiles:	NIG
	4: 8 ye **d** **service** unto them which by nature	1398
	5: 7 Ye **d** run well; who did hinder you that *ye*	NIG
	5: 7 who **d** hinder you that *ye* should not obey	NIG
Php	4:14 that *ye* **d** communicate with my affliction.	NIG
	3: 8 Neither **d** we eat any *man's* bread for	NIG
1Ti	1:13 because I **d** *it* ignorantly in unbelief.	4160
2Ti	4:14 Alexander the coppersmith **d** me much	1731
Heb	3:16 some, when they had heard, **d** provoke:	NIG
	4: 2 but the word preached **d** not profit them,	NIG
	4: 4 God **d** rest the seventh day from all his	NIG
	4:10 from his own works, as God **d** from his.	NIG
	7:19 the bringing in of a better hope **d**;	NIG
	7:27 for this he **d** once, when he offered up	4160
	9: 6 could not make him that **d** the service	NIG
1Pe	1:11 of Christ which was in them **d** signify,	NIG
	1:12 but unto us they **d** minister the things,	NIG
	2:22 Who **d** no sin, neither was guile found in	4160
Rev	12: 4 of heaven, and **d** cast them to the earth:	NIG
	13:14 had the wound by a sword, and **d** live.	NIG
	19: 2 which **d** corrupt the earth with her	NIG
	21:23 for the glory of God **d** lighten it,	NIG

DIDST (123) [DO]

Ge	12:18 why **d** thou not tell me that she *was* thy	NIH
	18:15 And he said, Nay; but thou **d** laugh.	NIH
	20: 6 I know that thou **d** this in the integrity of	6213
	21:26 neither **d** thou tell me, neither yet heard I	NIH
	21:27 Wherefore **d** thou flee away secretly,	NIH
	21:27 **d** not tell me, that I might have sent thee	NIH
	31:39 my hand **d** thou require it, *whether* stolen	NIH
Ex	15:10 **d** blow with thy wind, the sea covered	NIH
	40:15 anoint them, as thou **d** anoint their father,	NIH
Nu	21:34 thou shalt do to him as thou **d** unto Sihon	6213
Dt	3: 2 shalt do unto him as thou **d** unto Sihon	6213
	9: 7 from the day that thou **d** depart out of	NIH
	32:14 thou **d** drink the pure blood of the grape.	NIH
	33: 8 whom thou **d** prove at Massah,	NIH
	33: 8 *with* whom thou **d** strive at the waters of	NIH
Jos	2:18 the window which thou **d** let us down by:	NIH
	8: 2 her king as thou **d** unto Jericho and	6213
Jdg	12: 1 and **d** not call us to go with thee?	NIH
	13: 8 the man of God which thou **d** send come	NIH
1Sa	3: 6 and said, Here *am* I; for thou **d** call me.	NIH
	3: 8 and said, Here *am* I; for thou **d** call me.	NIH
	15:19 **d** thou not obey the voice of the LORD,	NIH
	15:19 **d** fly upon the spoil, and didst evil in	NIH
	15:19 and **d** evil in the sight of the LORD?	6213
	19: 5 thou sawest *it*, and **d** rejoice: wherefore	NIH
	20:19 to the place where thou **d** hide thyself	NIH
	25:25 men of my lord, whom thou **d** send.	NIH
2Sa	11:10 **d** thou not go down unto thine house?	NIH
	12:12 For thou **d** *it* secretly: but I will do this	6213
	12:21 thou **d** fast and weep for the child,	NIH
	12:21 child was dead, thou **d** rise and eat bread.	NIH
	13:16 than the other that thou **d** unto me.	6213
	18:11 why **d** thou not smite him there to	NIH
	19:28 yet **d** thou set thy servant among them	NIH
1Ki	1:13 unto him, **D** not thou, my lord O king,	NIH
	2:44 privy to, that thou **d** to David my father:	6213
	8:18 thou **d** **well** that it was in thine heart.	2895
	8:53 For thou **d** separate them from among all	NIH
	20: 9 All that thou **d** send for to thy servant at	NIH
	21:10 Thou **d** blaspheme God and the king.	NIH
1Ch	17:22 thy people Israel **d** thou make thine own	NIH
2Ch	2: 3 As thou **d** deal with David my father,	NIH
	2: 3 **d** send him cedars to build him a house to	NIH
	6: 8 thou **d** **well** in that it was in thine heart:	2895
	16: 8 yet, because thou **d** rely on the LORD,	NIH
	20: 7 **d** drive out the inhabitants of this land	NIH
	34:27 and thou **d** humble thyself before God,	NIH
	34:27 **d** rend thy clothes, and weep before me;	NIH

Ne	9: 7 who **d** choose Abram, and broughtest him	NIH
	9: 9 see the affliction of our fathers in Egypt,	NIH
	9:10 So **d** thou get thee a name, as *it is* this day.	NIH
	9:11 thou **d** divide the sea before them,	NIH
	9:17 of thy wonders that thou **d** among them;	6213
	9:21 forty years **d** thou sustain them in	NIH
	9:22 nations, and **d** divide them into corners:	NIH
	9:28 many times **d** thou deliver them according	NIH
	9:30 Yet many years **d** thou forbear them,	NIH
	9:31 sake thou **d** not utterly consume them,	6213
	9:34 where*with* thou **d** testify against them.	NIH
Ps	22: 4 they trusted, and thou **d** deliver them.	NIH
	22: 9 thou **d** make me hope *when I was* upon	NIH
	30: 7 thou **d** hide thy face, *and* I was troubled.	NIH
	39: 9 opened not my mouth; because thou **d** *it*.	6213
	40: 6 Sacrifice and offering thou **d** not desire;	NIH
	44: 1 work thou **d** in their days, in the times	6466
	44: 2 thou **d** drive out the heathen *with* thy	NIH
	44: 2 thou **d** afflict the people, and cast them	NIH
	60:10 God, *which* **d** not go out with our armies?	NIH
	68: 7 thou **d** march through the wilderness;	NIH
	68: 9 Thou, O God, **d** send a plentiful rain,	NIH
	68: 9 whereby thou **d** confirm thine inheritance,	NIH
	73:18 Surely thou **d** set them in slippery *places*:	NIH
	74:13 Thou **d** divide the sea by thy strength:	NIH
	74:15 Thou **d** cleave the fountain and the flood:	NIH
	76: 8 Thou **d** cause judgment to be heard from	NIH
	80: 8 **d** cause it to take deep root, and it filled	NIH
Isa	14:12 the ground, which **d** weaken the nations!	NIH
	22: 8 thou **d** look in that day to the armour of	NIH
	47: 6 thou **d** shew them no mercy; upon	NIH
	47: 7 thou **d** not lay these *things* to thy heart,	NIH
	47: 7 neither **d** remember the latter end of it.	NIH
	48: 6 hidden *things*, and thou **d** not know them.	NIH
	54: 1 Sing, O barren, thou *that* **d** not bear;	NIH
	54: 1 aloud, thou *that* **d** not travail with child:	NIH
	57: 9 of increase thy perfumes, and didst send	NIH
	57: 9 **d** send thy messengers far off,	NIH
	57: 9 far off, and **d** debase *thyself* even unto hell.	NIH
	63:14 so **d** thou lead thy people, to make thyself	NIH
	64: 3 When thou **d** terrible things *which* we	6213
Jer	32:22 which thou **d** swear to their fathers to give	NIH
	36:17 How **d** thou write all these words at his	NIH
	45: 3 Thou **d** say, Woe is me now! for	NIH
La	1:10 thou **d** command *that* they should not	NIH
Eze	16:13 thou **d** eat fine flour, and honey, and oil:	NIH
	16:13 and thou **d** prosper into a kingdom.	NIH
	16:15 thou **d** trust in thine own beauty,	NIH
	16:16 of thy garments thou **d** take,	NIH
	16:17 and **d** commit whoredom with them,	NIH
	16:36 children, which thou **d** give unto them;	NIH
	23:40 for whom thou **d** wash *thyself*, paintedst	NIH
	27:33 thou **d** enrich the kings of the earth with	NIH
	29: 7 thou **d** break, and rent all their shoulder:	NIH
	35:15 As thou **d** rejoice at the inheritance of	NIH
Da	10:12 for from the first day that thou **d** set thine	NIH
Hos	10:13 because thou **d** trust in thy way,	NIH
Hab	3: 8 that thou **d** ride upon thine horses *and*	NIH
	3: 9 Selah. Thou **d** cleave the earth *with* rivers.	NIH
	3:12 Thou **d** march through the land in	NIH
	3:12 thou **d** thresh the heathen in anger.	NIH
	3:14 Thou **d** strike through with his staves	NIH
	3:15 Thou **d** walk through the sea *with* thine	NIH
Mt	13:27 Sir, **d** not thou sow good seed in thy field?	NIG
	14:31 of little faith, wherefore **d** thou doubt?	NIG
	20:13 **d** not thou agree with me for a penny?	NIG
Lk	7:46 Mine head with oil thou **d** not anoint:	NIG
	19:21 down, and reapest that thou **d** not sow.	NIG
Jn	17: 8 they have believed that thou **d** send me.	NIG
Ac	7:28 kill me, as thou **d** the Egyptian yesterday?	337
	11: 3 men uncircumcised, and **d** eat with them.	NIG
1Co	4: 7 what hast thou that thou **d** not receive?	NIG
	4: 7 now if thou **d** receive *it*, why dost thou	NIG
Heb	2: 7 **d** set him over the works of thy hands:	NIG
Rev	17: 7 said unto me, Wherefore **d** thou marvel?	NIG

DIDYMUS (3)

Jn	11:16 Then said Thomas, which is called **D**,	1324
	20:24 But Thomas, one of the twelve, called **D**,	1324
	21: 2 and Thomas called **D**, and Nathanael of	1324

DIE (321) [DEAD, DEADLY, DEADNESS, DEATH, DEATHS, DIED, DIEST, DIETH]

Ge	2:17 eatest thereof thou shalt **surely d**.	4191+4191
	3: 3 eat of it, neither shall ye touch it, lest ye **d**.	4191
	3: 4 the woman, Ye shall not **surely d**:	4191+4191
	6:17 *and* every thing that *is* in the earth shall **d**.	1478
	19:19 lest *some* evil take me, and I **d**.	4191
	20: 7 thou that thou shalt **surely d**,	4191+4191
	25:32 Esau said, Behold, I *am* at the point to **d**:	4191
	26: 9 unto him, Because I said, Lest I **d** for her.	4191
	27: 4 that my soul may bless thee before I **d**.	4191
	30: 1 unto Jacob, Give me children, or else I **d**.	4191
	33:13 them one day, all the flock will **d**.	4191
	38:11 for he said, Lest peradventure he **d** also,	4191
	42: 2 from thence; that we may live, and not **d**.	4191
	42:20 your words be verified, and ye shall not **d**.	4191
	43: 8 not **d**, both we, and thou, *and* also our	4191
	44: 9 both let him **d**, and we also will be my	4191
	44:22 leave his father, *his father* would **d**.	4191
	44:31 that the lad *is* not *with* us, that he will **d**:	4191
	45:28 yet alive: I will go and see him before I **d**.	4191
	46:30 Now let me **d**, since I have seen thy face,	4191
	47:15 for why should we **d** in thy presence?	4191
	47:19 Wherefore shall we **d** before thine eyes,	4191

D

Ge
47:19 give *us* seed, that we may live, and not **d**, 4191
47:29 the time drew nigh that Israel must **d**: 4191
48:21 Israel said unto Joseph, Behold, I **d**: but 4191
50: 5 father made me swear, saying, Lo, I **d**: 4191
50:24 Joseph said unto his brethren, I **d**: and 4191
Ex 7:18 the fish that *is* in the river shall **d**, 4191
9: 4 there shall nothing **d** of all *that is* 4191
9:19 come down upon them, and they shall **d**. 4191
10:28 *that* day thou seest my face thou shalt **d**. 4191
11: 5 the firstborn in the land of Egypt shall **d**, 4191
14:11 hast thou taken us away to **d** in 4191
14:12 than that we should **d** in the wilderness. 4191
20:19 but let not God speak with us, lest we **d**. 4191
21:12 He that smiteth a man, so that he **d**, shall 4191
21:14 take him from mine altar, that he may **d**. 4191
21:18 *his* fist, and he **d** not, but keepeth *his* bed: 4191
21:20 with a rod, and he **d** under his hand; 4191
21:28 ox gore a man or a woman, that they **d**: 4191
21:35 if one man's ox hurt another's, that he **d**; 4191
22: 2 breaking up, and be smitten that he **d**, 4191
22:10 it **d**, or be hurt, or driven away, no man 4191
22:14 hurt, or **d**, the owner thereof *being* not 4191
28:35 and when he cometh out, that he **d** not. 4191
28:43 *place;* that they bear not iniquity, and **d**: 4191
30:20 shall wash *with* water, that they **d** not; 4191
30:21 hands and their feet, that they **d** not: 4191
Lev 8:35 the charge of the LORD, that ye **d** not: 4191
10: 6 lest you **d**, and lest wrath come upon all 4191
10: 7 tabernacle of the congregation, lest you **d**: 4191
10: 9 tabernacle of the congregation, lest ye **d**: 4191
11:39 if any beast, of which ye may eat, **d**; he 4191
15:31 that they **d** not in their uncleanness, 4191
16: 2 which *is* upon the ark; that he **d** not: 4191
16:13 that *is* upon the Testimony, that he **d** not: 4191
20:20 shall bear their sin; they shall **d** childless. 4191
22: 9 for it, and **d** therefore, if they profane it: 4191
Nu 4:15 shall not touch *any* holy *thing,* lest they **d**. 4191
4:19 unto them, that they may live, and not **d**, 4191
4:20 the holy *things* are covered, lest they **d**. 4194
6: 7 his brother, or for his sister, when they **d**: 4194
6: 9 if any man **d** very suddenly by him, 4191+4191
14:35 shall be consumed, and there they shall **d**. 4191
16:29 If these *men* **d** the common death of all 4191
17:10 murmurings from me, that they **d** not. 4191
17:12 saying, Behold, we **d**, we perish, we all 1478
17:13 unto the tabernacle of the LORD shall **d**: 4191
18: 3 altar, that neither they, nor you also, **d**. 4191
18:22 congregation, lest they bear sin, and **d**. 4191
18:32 *things* of the children of Israel, lest ye **d**. 4191
20: 4 that we and our cattle should **d** there? 4191
20:26 gathered *unto* his people, and shall **d** 4191
21: 5 up out of Egypt to **d** in the wilderness? 4191
23:10 Let me **d** the death of the righteous, 4191
26:65 shall **surely d** in the wilderness. 4191+4191
27: 8 If a man **d**, and have no son, then ye shall 4191
35:12 that the manslayer **d** not, until he stand 4191
35:16 of iron, so that he **d**, he *is* a murderer: 4191
35:17 wherewith he may **d**, and he die, he *is* a 4191
35:17 he may die, and he **d**, he *is* a murderer: 4191
35:18 wherewith he may **d**, and he die, he *is* a 4191
35:18 he may die, and he **d**, he *is* a murderer: 4191
35:20 or hurl at him by laying of wait, that he **d**; 4191
35:21 smite him with his hand, that he **d**: 4191
35:23 wherewith *a man* may **d**, seeing *him* not, 4191
35:23 that he **d**, and *was* not his enemy, 4191
35:30 against *any* person to cause him to **d**. 4191
Dt 4:22 I *must* **d** in this land, I *must* not go over 4191
5:25 Now therefore why should we **d**? for this 4191
5:25 our God any more, then we shall **d**. 4191
13:10 shalt stone him with stones, that he **d**; 4191
17: 5 shalt stone him with stones, till they **d**; 4191
17:12 or unto the judge, even that man shall **d**: 4191
18:16 see this great fire any more, that I **d** not. 4191
18:20 of other gods, even that prophet shall **d**. 4191
19: 5 lighteth upon his neighbour, that he **d**; 4191
19:11 smite him mortally that he **d**, 4191
19:12 of the avenger of blood, that he may **d**. 4191
20: 5 lest he **d** in the battle, and another man 4191
20: 6 lest he **d** in the battle, and another man 4191
20: 7 lest he **d** in the battle, and another man 4191
21:21 city shall stone him with stones, that he **d**: 4191
22:21 city shall stone her with stones that she **d**: 4191
22:22 they shall both of them **d**, *both* the man 4191
22:24 shall stone them with stones that they **d**; 4191
22:25 the man only that lay with her shall **d**: 4191
24: 3 or if the latter husband, which took her 4191
24: 7 that thief shall **d**; and thou shalt put evil 4191
25: 5 and one of them **d**, and have no child, 4191
31:14 thy days approach that *thou* must **d**: 4191
32:50 **d** in the mount whither thou goest up, 4191
33: 6 Let Reuben live, and not **d**; and let *not* his 4191
Jos 20: 9 not **d** by the hand of the avenger of blood, 4191
Jdg 6:23 *be* unto thee; fear not: thou shalt not **d**. 4191
6:30 Bring out thy son, that he may **d**: 4191
13:22 We shall **surely d**, because we 4191+4191
15:18 now shall I **d** for thirst, and fall into 4191
16:30 said, Let me **d** with the Philistines. 4191
Ru 1:17 will I **d**, and there will I be buried: 4191
1Sa 2:33 all the increase of thine house shall **d** in 4191
2:34 in one day shall **d** both of them. 4191
12:19 unto the LORD thy God, that we **d** not: 4191
14:39 Jonathan my son, he shall **surely d**. 4191+4191
14:43 that *was* in mine hand, *and* lo, I must **d**. 4191
14:44 for thou shalt **surely d**, Jonathan. 4191+4191
14:45 people said unto Saul, Shall Jonathan **d**, 4191

1Sa 20: 2 unto him, God forbid; thou shalt not **d**: 4191
20:14 the kindness of the LORD, that I **d** not: 4191
20:31 him unto me, for he shall **surely d**. 1121+4194
22:16 Thou shalt **surely d**, Ahimelech, 4191+4191
26:10 or his day shall come to **d**; or he shall 4191
26:16 ye *are* **worthy to d**, because ye 1121+4194
28: 9 a snare for my life, to **cause me to d**? 4191
2Sa 11:15 from him, that he may be smitten, and **d**. 4191
12: 5 hath done this *thing* shall **surely d**: 1121+4194
12:13 hath put away thy sin; thou shalt not **d**. 4191
12:14 is born unto thee shall **surely d**. 4191+4191
14:14 For we **must needs d**, and *are* as 4191+4191
18: 3 neither if half of us **d**, will they care for us: 4191
19:23 king said unto Shimei, Thou shalt not **d**. 4191
19:37 that I may **d** in mine own city, 4191
1Ki 1:52 shall be found in him, he shall **d**. 4191
2: 1 days of David drew nigh that *he* should **d**; 4191
2:30 he said, Nay; but I will **d** here. 4191
2:37 for certain that thou shalt **surely d**: 4191+4191
2:42 that thou shalt **surely d**? 4191+4191
14:12 feet enter into the city, the child shall **d**. 4191
17:12 and my son, that we may eat it, and **d**. 4191
19: 4 he requested for himself that he might **d**; 4191
21:10 him out, and stone him, that he may **d**. 4191
2Ki 1: 4 art gone up, but shalt **surely d**. 4191+4191
1: 6 art gone up, but shalt **surely d**. 4191+4191
1:16 art gone up, but shalt **surely d**. 4191+4191
7: 3 to another, Why sit we here until we **d**? 4191
7: 4 famine *is* in the city, and we shall **d** there: 4191
7: 4 if we sit still here, we **d** also. 4191
7: 4 live; and if they kill us, we shall but **d**. 4191
8:10 shewed me that he shall **surely d**. 4191+4191
18:32 and of honey, that ye may live, and not **d**: 4191
20: 1 in order; for thou shalt **d**, and not live. 4191
2Ch 25: 4 The fathers shall not **d** for the children, 4191
25: 4 neither shall the children **d** for the fathers, 4191
25: 4 but every man shall **d** for his own sin. 4191
32:11 you to give over yourselves to **d** by famine 4191
Job 2: 9 retain thine integrity? curse God, and **d**. 4191
4:21 go away? they **d**, even without wisdom. 4191
12: 2 the people, and wisdom shall **d** with you. 4191
14: 8 and the stock thereof **d** in the ground; 4191
14:14 If a man **d**, shall he live *again?* all the days 4191
27: 5 till I **d** I will not remove my integrity from 1478
29:18 I shall **d** in my nest, and I shall multiply 1478
34:20 *In* a moment shall they **d**, and the people 4191
36:12 and they shall **d** without knowledge. 4191
36:14 They **d** in youth, and their life *is* among 4191
Ps 41: 5 When shall he **d**, and his name perish? 4191
49:10 For he seeth that wise men **d**, likewise 4191
79:11 thou those that are **appointed to d**; 1121+8546
82: 7 ye shall **d** like men, and fall like one of 4191
88:15 **ready to d** from *my* youth *up:* while I 1478
104:29 breath, they **d**, and return to their dust. 1478
118:17 not **d**, but live, and declare the works 4191
Pr 5:23 He shall **d** without instruction; and in 4191
10:21 many: but fools **d** for want of wisdom. 4191
15:10 way: *and* he that hateth reproof shall **d**. 4191
19:16 *but* he that despiseth his ways shall **d**. 4191
23:13 beatest him with the rod, he shall not **d**. 4191
30: 7 of thee; deny me *them* not before I **d**: 4191
Ecc 3: 2 A time to be born, and a time to **d**; 4191
7:17 why shouldest thou **d** before thy time? 4191
9: 5 For the living know that they shall **d**: but 4191
Isa 22:13 eat and drink; for to morrow we shall **d**. 4191
22:14 shall not be purged from you till ye **d**, 4191
22:18 there shalt thou **d**, and there the chariots 4191
38: 1 in order: for thou shalt **d**, and not live. 4191
51: 6 they that dwell therein shall **d** in like 4191
51:12 shouldest be afraid of a man *that* shall **d**, 4191
51:14 that he should not **d** in the pit, nor that 4191
65:20 for the child shall **d** an hundred years old; 4191
66:24 for their worm shall not **d**, neither shall 4191
Jer 11:21 of the LORD, that thou **d** not by our hand: 4191
11:22 the young men shall **d** by the sword; 4191
11:22 and their daughters shall **d** by famine: 4191
16: 4 They shall **d** of grievous deaths; they shall 4191
16: 6 the great and the small shall **d** in this land: 4191
20: 6 there thou shalt **d**, and shalt be buried 4191
21: 6 beast: they shall **d** of a great pestilence. 4191
21: 9 He that abideth in this city shall **d** by 4191
22:12 he shall **d** in the place whither they have 4191
22:26 ye were not born; and there shall ye **d**. 4191
26: 8 saying, Thou shalt **surely d**. 4191+4191
26:11 saying, This man *is* worthy to **d**; 4194
26:16 the prophets; This man *is* not worthy to **d**: 4194
27:13 Why will ye **d**, thou and thy people, 4191
28:16 *this* year thou *shalt* **d**, because thou hast 4191
31:30 every one shall **d** for his own iniquity: 4191
34: 4 of thee, Thou shalt not **d** by the sword: 4191
34: 5 *But* thou shalt **d** in peace: and with 4191
37:20 of Jonathan the scribe, lest I **d** there. 4191
38: 2 He that remaineth in this city shall **d** by 4191
38: 9 he is like to **d** for hunger in the place 4191
38:10 prophet out of the dungeon, before he **d**. 4191
38:24 of these words, and thou shalt not **d**. 4191
38:26 to return *to* Jonathan's house, to **d** there. 4191
42:16 you there *in* Egypt; and there ye shall **d**. 4191
42:17 they shall **d** by the sword, by the famine, 4191
42:22 certainly that ye shall **d** by the sword, 4191
44:12 they shall **d**, from the least even unto 4191
Eze 3:18 the wicked, Thou shalt **surely d**; 4191+4191
3:18 the same wicked man shall **d** in his 4191
3:19 his wicked way, he shall **d** in his iniquity; 4191
3:20 a stumblingblock before him, he shall **d**: 4191

Eze 3:20 he shall **d** in his sin, and his righteousness 4191
5:12 A third part of thee shall **d** with 4191
6:12 He that *is* far off shall **d** of the pestilence; 4191
6:12 and is besieged shall **d** by the famine: 4191
7:15 he that *is* in the field shall **d** with 4191
12:13 shall he not see it, though he shall **d** there. 4191
13:19 to slay the souls that should not **d**, 4191
17:16 him in the midst of Babylon he shall **d**. 4191
18: 4 *is* mine: the soul that sinneth, it shall **d**. 4191
18:13 he shall **surely d**; his blood shall be 4191+4191
18:17 he shall not **d** for the iniquity of his father, 4191
18:18 lo, even he shall **d** in his iniquity. 4191
18:20 The soul that sinneth, it shall **d**. The son 4191
18:21 right, he shall surely live, he shall not **d**. 4191
18:23 pleasure at all that the wicked should **d**? 4194
18:24 that he hath sinned, in them shall he **d**. 4191
18:26 his iniquity that he hath done shall he **d**. 4191
18:28 he shall surely live, he shall not **d**. 4191
18:31 for why will ye **d**, O house of Israel? 4191
28: 8 thou shalt **d** the deaths of *them that are* 4191
28:10 Thou shalt **d** the deaths of 4191
33: 8 wicked *man,* thou shalt **surely d**; 4191+4191
33: 8 that wicked *man* shall **d** in his iniquity; 4191
33: 9 from his way, he shall **d** in his iniquity; 4191
33:11 for why will ye **d**, O house of Israel? 4191
33:13 he hath committed, he shall **d** for it. 4191
33:14 the wicked, Thou shalt **surely d**; 4191+4191
33:15 he shall surely live, he shall not **d**. 4191
33:18 he shall even **d** thereby. 4191
33:27 and in the caves shall **d** of the pestilence. 4191
Am 2: 2 Moab shall **d** with tumult, with shouting, 4191
6: 9 ten men in one house, that they shall **d**. 4191
7:11 Jeroboam shall **d** by the sword, 4191
7:17 line; and thou shalt **d** in a polluted land: 4191
9:10 All the sinners of my people shall **d** by 4191
Jnh 4: 3 for *it is* better for me to **d** than to live. 4194
4: 8 and wished in himself to **d**, and said, 4191
4: 8 said, *It is* better for me to **d**, than to live. 4194
Hab 1:12 we shall not **d**. O LORD, thou hast 4191
Zec 11: 9 that that dieth, let it **d**; and that that is 4191
13: 8 two parts therein shall be cut off *and* **d**; 1478
Mt 15: 4 or mother, let him **d** the death. 5053
22:24 Saying, Master, Moses said, If a man **d**, 599
26:35 unto him, Though I should **d** with thee, 599
Mk 7:10 or mother, let him **d** the death. 5053
12:19 If a man's brother **d**, and leave *his* wife 599
14:31 If I should **d** with thee, I will not deny 4880
Lk 7: 2 dear unto him, was sick, and ready to **d**. 5053
20:28 If any man's brother **d**, having a wife, 599
20:28 having a wife, and he **d** without children, 599
20:36 Neither can they **d** any more: for they are 599
Jn 4:49 unto him, Sir, come down ere my child **d**. 599
6:50 that a man may eat thereof, and not **d**. 599
8:21 ye shall seek me, and shall **d** in your sins: 599
8:24 unto you, that ye shall **d** in your sins: 599
8:24 if ye believe not that I am *he,* ye shall **d** 599
11:16 Let us also go, that we may **d** with him. 599
11:26 and believeth in me shall never **d**. 599
11:50 that one man should **d** for the people, 599
11:51 he prophesied that Jesus should **d** for *that* 599
12:24 a corn of wheat fall into the ground and **d**, 599
12:24 but if it **d**, it bringeth forth much fruit. 599
12:33 he said, signifying what death he should **d**. 599
18:14 it was expedient that one man should **d** 622
18:32 spake, signifying what death he should **d**. 599
19: 7 and by our law he ought to **d**, because 599
21:23 brethren, that that disciple should not **d**: 599
21:23 yet Jesus said not unto him, He shall not **d**; 599
Ac 21:13 also to **d** at Jerusalem for the name of 599
25:11 thing worthy of death, I refuse not to **d**: 599
25:16 of the Romans to deliver any man to **d**, 684
Ro 5: 7 For scarcely for a righteous *man* will one **d**: 599
5: 7 for a good *man* some would even dare to **d**. 599
8:13 For if ye live after the flesh, ye shall **d**: but 599
14: 8 and whether we **d**, we die unto the Lord: 599
14: 8 and whether we die, we **d** unto the Lord: 599
14: 8 we live therefore, or **d**, we are the Lord's. 599
1Co 9:15 *it were* better for me to **d**, than that any 599
15:22 as in Adam all **d**, even so in Christ shall 599
15:31 I have in Christ Jesus our Lord, I **d** daily. 599
15:32 let us eat and drink; for to morrow we **d**. 599
15:36 thou sowest is not quickened, except it **d**: 599
2Co 7: 3 you are in our hearts to **d** and live with 4880
Php 1:21 For to me to live *is* Christ, and to **d** *is* gain. 599
Heb 7: 8 And here men that **d** receive tithes; 599
9:27 And as it is appointed unto men once to **d**, 599
Rev 3: 2 *things* which remain, that are ready to **d**: 599
9: 6 and shall desire to **d**, and death shall flee 599
14:13 Blessed *are* the dead which **d** in the Lord 599

DIED (201) [DIE]
Ge 5: 5 nine hundred and thirty years: and he **d**. 4191
5: 8 nine hundred and twelve years: and he **d**. 4191
5:11 nine hundred and five years: and he **d**. 4191
5:14 nine hundred and ten years: and he **d**. 4191
5:17 hundred ninety and five years: and he **d** 4191
5:20 hundred sixty and two years: and he **d**. 4191
5:27 hundred sixty and nine years: and he **d**. 4191
5:31 seventy and seven years: and he **d**. 4191
7:21 all flesh **d** that moved upon the earth, 1478
7:22 of life, of all that *was* in the dry *land,* **d**. 4191
9:29 nine hundred and fifty years: and he **d**. 4191
11:28 Haran **d** before his father Terah in the 4191
11:32 five years: and Terah **d** in Haran. 4191
23: 2 Sarah **d** in Kirjath-arba; the same *is* 4191

D

Ge	25: 8	**d** in a good old age, an old man, and full 4191
	25:17	he gave up the ghost and **d**; 4191
	25:18	he **d** in the presence of all his brethren. 5307
	35: 8	Deborah Rebekah's nurse **d**, and she was 4191
	35:18	as her soul was in departing (for she **d**) 4191
	35:19	Rachel **d**, and was buried in the way to 4191
	35:29	**d**, and was gathered unto his people, 4191
	36:33	Bela **d**, and Jobab the son of Zerah of 4191
	36:34	Jobab **d**, and Husham of the land of 4191
	36:35	Husham **d**, and Hadad the son of Bedad, 4191
	36:36	Hadad **d**, and Samlah of Masrekah 4191
	36:37	Samlah **d**, and Saul of Rehoboth *by* 4191
	36:38	Saul **d**, and Baal-hanan the son of Achbor 4191
	36:39	Baal-hanan the son of Achbor **d**, 4191
	38:12	the daughter of Shuah Judah's wife **d**; 4191
	46:12	Er and Onan in the land of Canaan. 4191
	48: 7	Rachel **d** by me in the land of Canaan in 4191
	50:16	Thy father did command before he **d**, 4194
	50:26	So Joseph **d**, *being* an hundred and 4191
Ex	1: 6	Joseph **d**, and all his brethren, and all 4191
	2:23	process of time, that the king of Egypt **d**: 4191
	7:21	the fish that *was* in the river **d**; and the 4191
	8:13	the frogs **d** out of the houses, out of 4191
	9: 6	the morrow, and all the cattle of Egypt **d**: 4191
	9: 6	of the cattle of the children of Israel **d** not 4191
	16: 3	Would to God we had **d** by the hand of 4191
Lev	10: 2	and they **d** before the Lord. 4191
	16: 1	they offered before the Lord, and **d**; 4191
	17:15	soul that eateth **that which d of itself,** 5038
Nu	3: 4	and Abihu **d** before the Lord, 4191
	14: 2	Would God that we had **d** in the land of 4191
	14: 2	would God we had **d** in this wilderness! 4191
	14:37	**d** by the plague before the Lord. 4191
	15:36	and stoned him with stones, and he **d**; 4191
	16:49	Now they that **d** in the plague were 4191
	16:49	beside them that **d** about the matter of 4191
	20: 1	Miriam **d** there, and was buried there. 4191
	20: 3	Would God that we had **d** when our 1478
	20: 3	when our brethren **d** before the Lord! 1478
	20:28	Aaron **d** there in the top of the mount: 4191
	21: 6	the people; and much people of Israel **d**. 4191
	25: 9	those that **d** in the plague were twenty 4191
	26:10	when that company **d**, what time the fire 4194
	26:11	Notwithstanding the children of Korah **d**. 4191
	26:19	and Er and Onan **d** in the land of Canaan. 4191
	26:61	Nadab and Abihu **d**, when they offered 4191
	27: 3	Our father **d** in the wilderness, and he 4191
	27: 3	but **d** in his own sin, and had no sons. 4191
Dt	10: 6	there Aaron **d**, and he was buried; 4191
	32:50	as Aaron thy brother **d** in mount Hor, 4191
	34: 5	So Moses the servant of the Lord **d** 4191
	34: 7	and twenty years old when he **d**: 4194
Jos	5: 4	of war, **d** in the wilderness by the way, 4191
	10:11	upon them unto Azekah, and they **d**: 4191
	10:11	*they were* moe which **d** with hailstones 4191
	24:29	**d**, *being* an hundred and ten years old. 4191
	24:33	Eleazar the son of Aaron **d**; and they 4191
Jdg	1: 7	brought him *to* Jerusalem, and there he **d**. 4191
	2: 8	**d**, *being* an hundred and ten years old. 4191
	2:21	the nations which Joshua left when he **d**: 4191
	3:11	And Othniel the son of Kenaz **d**. 4191
	4:21	for he was fast asleep and weary. So he **d**. 4191
	8:32	Gideon the son of Joash **d** in a good old 4191
	9:49	all the men of the tower of Shechem **d** 4191
	9:54	young man thrust him through, and he **d**. 4191
	10: 2	and **d**, and was buried in Shamir. 4191
	10: 5	And Jair **d**, and was buried in Camon. 4191
	12: 7	Jephthah the Gileadite, and was buried 4191
	12:10	**d** Ibzan, and was buried at Beth-lehem. 4191
	12:12	Elon the Zebulonite **d**, and was buried in 4191
	12:15	Abdon the son of Hillel the Pirathonite **d**, 4191
Ru	1: 3	Elimelech Naomi's husband; and she 4191
	1: 5	and Chilion **d** also both of them; 4191
1Sa	4:18	of the gate, and his neck brake, and he **d**: 4191
	5:12	the men that **d** not were smitten with 4191
	14:45	people rescued Jonathan, that he **d** not. 4191
	25: 1	Samuel **d**; and all the Israelites were 4191
	25:37	his heart **d** within him, and he became 4191
	25:38	that the Lord smote Nabal, that he **d**. 4191
	31: 5	likewise upon his sword, and **d** with him. 4191
	31: 6	So Saul **d**, and his three sons, 4191
2Sa	1:15	upon him. And he smote him that he **d**. 4191
	2:23	fell down there, and **d** in the same place: 4191
	2:23	where Asahel fell down and **d** stood still. 4191
	2:31	*that* three hundred and threescore men **d**. 4191
	3:27	him there *under* the fifth *rib*, that he **d**, 4191
	3:33	and said, **D** Abner as a fool dieth? 4191
	6: 7	error; and there he **d** by the ark of God. 4191
	10: 1	that the king of the children of Ammon **d**, 4191
	10:18	the captain of their host, who **d** there. 4191
	11:17	of Joab; and Uriah the Hittite **d** also. 4191
	11:21	him from the wall, that he **d** in Thebez? 4191
	12:18	pass on the seventh day, that the child **d**. 4191
	17:23	and was buried in the sepulchre of his 4191
	18:33	would God I had **d** for thee, O Absalom, 4191
	19: 6	all we had **d** *this* day, then it had pleased 4191
	20:10	strake him not again; and he **d**. 4191
	24:15	there **d** of the people from Dan even to 4191
1Ki	2:25	Jehoiada; and he fell upon him that he **d**. 4191
	2:46	went out, and fell upon him, that he **d**. 4191
	3:19	this woman's child in the night; 4191
	12:18	Israel stoned him with stones, that he **d**. 4191
	14:17	to the threshold of the door, the child **d**; 4191

1Ki	16:18	king's house over him with fire, and **d**, 4191
	16:22	of Ginath: so Tibni **d**, and Omri reigned. 4191
	21:13	and stoned him with stones, that he **d**. 4191
	22:35	chariot against the Syrians, and **d** at even: 4191
	22:37	the king **d**, and was brought *to* Samaria; 4191
2Ki	1:17	So he **d** according to the word of 4191
	4:20	he sat on her knees till noon, and *then* **d**. 4191
	7:17	and he **d**, as the man of God had said, 4191
	7:20	trode upon him in the gate, and he **d**. 4191
	8:15	and spread *it* on his face, so that he **d**: 4191
	9:27	And he fled *to* Megiddo, and **d** there. 4191
	12:21	his servants, smote him, and he **d**; 4191
	13:14	fallen sick of his sickness whereof he **d**. 4191
	13:20	Elisha **d**, and they buried him. 4191
	13:24	So Hazael king of Syria **d**; 4191
	23:34	and he came *to* Egypt, and **d** there. 4191
	25:25	that he **d**, and the Jews and the Chaldees 4191
1Ch	1:51	Hadad **d** also. And the dukes of Edom 4191
	2:30	Appaim: but Seled **d** without children. 4191
	2:32	Jonathan: and Jether **d** without children. 4191
	10: 5	he fell likewise on the sword, and **d**. 4191
	10: 6	So Saul **d**, and his three sons, and all his 4191
	10: 6	three sons, and all his house **d** together. 4191
	10:13	So Saul **d** for his transgression which he 4191
	13:10	to the ark: and there he **d** before God. 4191
	19: 1	the king of the children of Ammon **d**, 4191
	23:22	Eleazar **d**, and had no sons, but daughters 4191
	24: 2	Nadab and Abihu **d** before their father, 4191
	29:28	he **d** in a good old age, full of days, riches, 4191
2Ch	10:18	Israel stoned him with stones, that he **d**. 4191
	13:20	and the Lord struck him, and he **d**. 4191
	16:13	**d** in the one and fortieth year of his reign. 4191
	18:34	the time of the sun going down he **d**. 4191
	21: 9	so he **d** of sore diseases. And his people 4191
	24:15	old, and was full *of* days when he **d**; 4191
	24:15	and thirty years old when he **d**, 4194
	24:22	when he **d**, he said, The Lord look upon 4194
	24:25	and slew him on his bed, and he **d**: 4191
	35:24	he **d**, and was buried in *one* of 4191
Job	3:11	Why **d** I not from the womb? *why* did I 4191
	42:17	So Job **d**, *being* old and full of days. 4191
Isa	6: 1	In the year that king Uzziah **d** I saw also 4194
	14:28	In the year that king Ahaz **d** was this 4194
Jer	28:17	Hananiah the prophet **d** the same year in 4191
Eze	11:13	that Pelatiah the son of Benaiah **d**. 4191
	24:18	even my wife **d**; and I did in the morning 4191
Hos	13: 1	but when he offended in Baal, he **d**. 4191
Mt	22:27	And last of all the woman **d** also. 599
Mk	12:21	took her, and **d**, neither left he *any* seed: 599
	12:22	left no seed: last of all the woman **d** also. 599
Lk	16:22	And it came to pass that the beggar **d**, 599
	16:22	the rich *man* also, and was buried; 599
	20:29	first took a wife, and **d** without children. 599
	20:30	took her to wife, and he **d** childless. 599
	20:31	also: and they left no children, and **d**. 599
	20:32	Last of all the woman **d** also. 599
Jn	11:21	hadst been here, my brother had not **d**. 2348
	11:32	hadst been here, my brother had not **d**. 599
	11:37	that even this *man* should not have **d**? 599
Ac	7:15	into Egypt, and **d**, he, and our fathers, 5053
	9:37	in those days, that she was sick, and **d**: 599
Ro	5: 6	in due time Christ **d** for the ungodly. 599
	5: 8	while we were yet sinners, Christ **d** for us. 599
	6:10	For in that he **d**, he died unto sin once: 599
	6:10	For in that he died, he died unto sin once: 599
	7: 9	commandment came, sin revived, and I **d**. 599
	8:34	*It is* Christ that **d**, yea rather, that is risen 599
	14: 9	For to this end Christ both **d**, and rose, 599
	14:15	not him with thy meat, for whom Christ **d**. 599
1Co	8:11	weak brother perish, for whom Christ **d**? 599
	15: 3	how that Christ **d** for our sins according to 599
2Co	5:14	that if one **d** for all, then were all dead: 599
	5:15	And *that* he **d** for all, that they which live 599
	5:15	but unto him which **d** for them, 599
1Th	4:14	if we believe that Jesus **d** and rose again, 599
	5:10	Who **d** for us, that, whether we wake or 599
Heb	10:28	He that despised Moses' law **d** without 599
	11:13	These all **d** in faith, not having received 599
	11:22	By faith Joseph, when he **d**, made 5053
Rev	8: 9	which were in the sea, and had life, **d**; 599
	8:11	and many men of the waters, because 599
	16: 3	*man*: and every living soul **d** in the sea. 599

DIEST (1) [DIE]

Ru	1:17	Where thou **d**, will I die, and there will I 4191

DIET (2)

Jer	52:34	*for* his **d**, there was a continual diet given 737
	52:34	there was a continual given him of 737

DIETH (30) [DIE]

Lev	7:24	the fat of the **beast that d of itself,** 5038
	22: 8	**That which d of itself,** or is torn *with* 5038
Nu	19:14	This *is* the law, when a man **d** in a tent: 4191
Dt	14:21	shall not eat of any thing that **d of itself:** 5038
2Sa	3:33	and said, Died Abner as a fool **d**? 4194
1Ki	14:11	Him that **d** of Jeroboam in the city shall 4191
	14:11	him that **d** in the field shall the fowls of 4191
	16: 4	Him that **d** of Baasha in the city shall 4191
	16: 4	him that **d** of his in the fields shall 4191
	21:24	Him that **d** of Ahab in the city the dogs 4191
	21:24	him that **d** in the field shall the fowls of 4191
Job	14:10	man **d**, and wasteth away: yea, man 4191
	21:23	One **d** in his full strength, *being* wholly 4191
	21:25	another **d** in the bitterness of his soul, 4191

Ps	49:17	when he **d** he shall carry nothing away: 4194
Pr	11: 7	When a wicked *man*, *his* expectation 4194
Ecc	2:16	And how **d** the wise *man*? as the fool. 4191
	3:19	as the one **d**, so **d** the other; yea, 4194
	3:19	as the one dieth, so **d** the other; yea, 4194
Isa	50: 2	there *is* no water, and **d** for thirst. 4191
	59: 5	he that eateth of their eggs **d**, 4191
Eze	4:14	have not eaten *of* that which **d of itself**, 5038
	18:26	and committeth iniquity, and **d** in them; 4191
	18:32	no pleasure in the death of him that **d**, 4191
Zec	11: 9	that that **d**, let it die; and that that is to be 4191
Mk	9:44	Where their worm **d** not, and the fire is 5053
	9:46	Where their worm **d** not, and the fire is 5053
	9:48	Where their worm **d** not, and the fire is 5053
Ro	6: 9	being raised from the dead **d** no more; 599
	14: 7	liveth to himself, and no *man* **d** to himself. 599

DIFFER (1) [DIFFERENCE, DIFFERENCES, DIFFERETH, DIFFERING]

1Co	4: 7	For who **maketh** thee **to d** *from another?* 1252

DIFFERENCE (12) [DIFFER]

Ex	11: 7	doth **put a d** between the Egyptians 6395
Lev	10:10	*ye* may **put d** between holy and unholy, 914
	11:47	To **make a d** between the unclean and 914
	20:25	**put d** between clean beasts and unclean, 914
Eze	22:26	they have **put** no **d** between the holy 914
	22:26	neither have they shewed **d** between NIH
	44:23	they shall teach my people *the* **d** between NIH
Ac	15: 9	And **put** no **d** between us and them, 1252
Ro	3:22	all them that believe: for there is no **d**: 1293
	10:12	For there is no **d** between the Jew and 1293
1Co	7:34	There is **d** *also* **between** a wife and a 3307
Jude	1:22	of some have compassion, **making a d**: 1252

DIFFERENCES (1) [DIFFER]

1Co	12: 5	And there are **d** of administrations, 1243

DIFFERENT See DIVERS; DIVERSE

DIFFERETH (2) [DIFFER]

1Co	15:41	for *one* star **d** *from another* star in glory. 1308
Gal	4: 1	as he is a child, **d** nothing **from** a servant, 1308

DIFFERING (1) [DIFFER]

Ro	12: 6	gifts **d** according to the grace that is given 1313

DIG (13) [DIGGED, DIGGEDST, DIGGETH]

Ex	21:33	or if a man shall **d** a pit, and not cover it, 3738
Dt	8: 9	out of whose hills thou mayest **d** brass. 2672
	23:13	thou shalt **d** therewith, and shalt turn 2658
Job	3:21	and **d** for it more than for hid treasures; 2658
	6:27	and you **d** *a pit* for your friend. 3738
	11:18	thou shalt **d** *about thee*, and thou shalt 2658
	24:16	In the dark *they* **d** *through* houses, 2864
Eze	8: 8	unto me, Son of man, **d** now in the wall: 2864
	12: 5	**D** thou through the wall in their sight, 2864
	12:12	they shall **d** through the wall to carry out 2864
Am	9: 2	Though they **d** into hell, thence shall 2864
Lk	13: 8	also, till I shall **d** about it, and dung *it*: 4626
	16: 3	I cannot **d**; to beg I am ashamed. 4626

DIGGED (37) [DIG]

Ge	21:30	witness unto me, that I have **d** this well. 2658
	26:15	had **d** in the days of Abraham his father, 2658
	26:18	Isaac **d** again the wells of water, which 2658
	26:18	which they had **d** in the days of Abraham 2658
	26:19	Isaac's servants **d** in the valley, 2658
	26:21	they **d** another well, and strove for that 2658
	26:22	removed from thence, and **d** another well; 2658
	26:25	and there Isaac's servants **d** a well; 3738
	26:32	concerning the well which they had **d**, 2658
	49: 6	and in their selfwill they **d down** a wall. 6131
	50: 5	in my grave which I have **d** for me in 3738
Ex	7:24	all the Egyptians **d** round about the river 2658
Nu	21:18	The princes **d** the well, the nobles of 2658
	21:18	the well, the nobles of the people **d** it, 3738
	21: 1	wells **d**, which thou diggedst not, 2672
2Ki	19:24	I have **d**, and drunk strange waters, 6979
2Ch	26:10	towers in the desert, and **d** many wells: 2672
Ne	9:25	wells **d**, vineyards, and oliveyards, 2672
Ps	7:15	**d** it, and is fallen into the ditch *which* he 2658
	35: 7	*which* without cause they have **d** for my 2658
	57: 6	they have **d** a pit before me, into the midst 3738
	94:13	until the pit be **d** for the wicked. 3738
	119:85	The proud have **d** pits for me, which *are* 3738
Isa	5: 6	it shall not be pruned, nor **d**; but there 5737
	7:25	all hills that shall be **d** with the mattock, 5737
	37:25	I have **d**, and drunk water; and with 6979
	51: 1	to the hole of the pit *whence* ye are **d**. 5365
Jer	13: 7	**d**, and took the girdle from the place 2658
	18:20	for they have **d** a pit for my soul. 3738
	18:22	for they have **d** a pit to take me, 3738
Eze	8: 8	when I had **d** in the wall, behold a door. 2864
	12: 7	in the even I **d** through the wall with 2864
Mt	21:33	and **d** a winepress in it, and built a tower, 3736
	25:18	had received one went and **d** in the earth, 3736
Mk	12: 1	about *it*, and **d** *a place for* the winefat, 3736
Lk	6:48	**d** deep, and laid the foundation on a 4626
Ro	11: 3	thy prophets, and **d down** thine altars; 2679

DIGGEDST (1) [DIG]

Dt	6:11	which thou **d** not, vineyards and olive 2672

DIGGETH (3) [DIG]

Pr	16:27	An ungodly man **d up** evil: and in his lips 3738

Pr 26:27 Whoso **d** a pit shall fall therein: and he 3738
Ecc 10: 8 He that **d** a pit shall fall into it; 2658

DIGNITIES (2) [DIGNITY]
2Pe 2:10 they are not afraid to speak evil of **d**. *1391*
Jude 1: 8 despise dominion, and speak evil of **d**. *1391*

DIGNITY (4) [DIGNITIES]
Ge 49: 3 the excellency of **d**, and the excellency of 7613
Est 6: 3 **d** hath been done to Mordecai for this? 1420
Ecc 10: 6 Folly is set in great **d**, and the rich sit in 4791
Hab 1: 7 and their **d** shall proceed of themselves. 7613

DIKLAH (2)
Ge 10:27 And Hadoram, and Uzal, and **D**, 1853
1Ch 1:21 Hadoram also, and Uzal, and **D**, 1853

DILEAN (1)
Jos 15:38 And **D**, and Mizpeh, and Joktheel, 1810

DILIGENCE (10) [DILIGENT]
Pr 4:23 Keep thy heart with all **d**; for out of it *are* 4929
Lk 12:58 give **d** that *thou* mayest be delivered from 2039
Ro 12: 8 he that ruleth, with **d**; he that sheweth 4710
2Co 8: 7 and *in* all **d**, and *in* your love to us, 4710
2Ti 4: 9 **Do** thy **d** to come shortly unto me: 4704
 4:21 **Do** thy **d** to come before winter. 4704
Heb 6:11 **d** to the full assurance of hope unto the 4710
2Pe 1: 5 And beside this, giving all **d**, add to your 4710
 1:10 give **d** to make your calling and 4704
Jude 1: 3 when I gave all **d** to write unto you of 4710

DILIGENT (15) [DILIGENCE, DILIGENTLY]
Dt 19:18 the judges shall make **d** inquisition: and 3190
Jos 22: 5 take **d** heed to do the commandment and 3966
Ps 64: 6 out iniquities; they accomplish a **d** search: 2664
 77: 6 own heart; and my spirit **made d search**. 2664
Pr 10: 4 but the hand of the **d** maketh rich. 2742
 12:24 The hand of the **d** shall bear rule: but 2742
 12:27 but the substance of a **d** man *is* precious. 2742
 13: 4 but the soul of the **d** shall be made fat. 2742
 21: 5 The thoughts of the **d** *tend* only to 2742
 22:29 Seest thou a man **d** in his business? 4106
 27:23 Be thou **d to know** the state of thy 3045+3045
2Co 8:22 whom we have oftentimes proved **d** in 4707
 8:22 in many *things*, but now much more **d**, 4705
Tit 3:12 be **d** to come unto me to Nicopolis: 4704
2Pe 3:14 seeing that ye look for such *things*, be **d** 4704

DILIGENTLY (37) [DILIGENT]
Ex 15:26 If thou wilt **hearken** to the voice 8085+8085
Lev 10:16 Moses **d sought** the goat of the sin 1875+1875
Dt 4: 9 take heed to thyself, and keep thy soul **d**, 3966
 6: 7 shalt **teach** them **d** unto thy children, 8150
 6:17 shall **d keep** the commandments 8104+8104
 11:13 if you shall **hearken** unto my 8085+8085
 11:22 For if ye shall **d keep** all these 8104+8104
 13:14 thou inquire, and make search, and ask **d**; 3190
 17: 4 thou hast heard *of it*, and inquired **d**, 3190
 24: 8 *thou* observe **d**, and do according to all 3966
 28: 1 if thou shalt **hearken** unto 8085+8085
1Ki 20:33 Now the men did **d observe** whether *any* 5172
Ezr 7:23 let it be **d** done for the house of the God of 149
Job 13:17 **Hear d** my speech, 8085+8085
 21: 2 **Hear d** my speech, and let this be 8085+8085
Ps 37:10 thou shalt **d consider** his place, and it 995
 119: 4 commanded *us* to keep thy precepts **d**. 3966
Pr 7:15 **d to seek** thy face, and I have found thee. 7836
 11:27 that **d seeketh** good procureth favour: 7836
 23: 1 ruler, **consider d** what *is* before thee: 995+995
Isa 21: 7 he **hearkened d** with much heed: 7181+7182
 55: 2 **hearken d** unto me, and eat ye 8085+8085
Jer 2:10 consider **d**, and see if there be such a 3966
 12:16 if they will **d learn** the ways of my 3925+3925
 17:24 if **hearken** unto me, saith 8085+8085
Zec 6:15 if ye will **d obey** the voice of 8085+8085
Mt 2: 7 **inquired** of them **d** what time the star 198
 2: 8 said, Go and search **d** for the young child; 199
 2:16 which he had **d inquired** of the wise men. 198
Lk 15: 8 the house, and seek **d** till she find *it*? 1960
Ac 18:25 spake and taught **d** the *things* of the Lord, 199
1Ti 5:10 if she have **d followed** every good work. 1872
2Ti 1:17 was in Rome, he sought me out **very d**, 4706
Tit 3:13 the lawyer and Apollos on their journey **d**, 4709
Heb 11: 6 *that* he is a rewarder of them that **d seek** 1567
 12:15 **Looking d** lest any *man* fail of the grace 1983
1Pe 1:10 prophets have inquired and **searched d**, 1830

DILL See ANISE

DIM (9) [DIMNESS]
Ge 27: 1 his eyes were **d**, so that he could not see, 3543
 48:10 Now the eyes of Israel were **d** for age, 3513
Dt 34: 7 his eye was not **d**, nor his natural force 3543
1Sa 3: 2 his eyes began to wax **d**, he could not 3544
 4:15 his eyes were **d**, that he could not see. 6965
Job 17: 7 Mine eye also is **d** by reason of sorrow, 3543
Isa 32: 3 the eyes of them that see shall not be **d**, 8159
La 4: 1 How is the gold **become d**! *how* is the 6004
 5:17 is faint; for these *things* our eyes are **d**. 2821

DIMINISH (8) [DIMINISHED, DIMINISHING]
Ex 5: 8 upon them; you shall not *ought* thereof: 1639
 21:10 her duty of marriage, shall he not **d**. 1639
Lev 25:16 fewness of years thou shalt **d** the price of 4591
Dt 4: 2 neither shall you **d** *ought* from it, 1639

Dt 12:32 thou shalt not add thereto, nor **d** from it. 1639
Jer 26: 2 thee to speak unto them; **d** not a word: 1639
Eze 5:11 will I also **d** *thee;* neither shall mine eye 1639
 29:15 for I will **d** them, that *they* shall no more 4591

DIMINISHED (5) [DIMINISH]
Ex 5:11 *it:* yet not ought of your work *shall be* **d**. 1639
Pr 13:11 Wealth *gotten* by vanity shall be **d**: but 4591
Isa 21:17 *men* of the children of Kedar, shall be **d**: 4591
Jer 30:19 that ye may be increased there, and not **d**. 4591
Eze 16:27 have **d** thine ordinary *food*, and 1639

DIMINISHING (1) [DIMINISH]
Ro 11:12 the **d** of them the riches of the Gentiles; *2275*

DIMNAH (1)
Jos 21:35 **D** with her suburbs, Nahalal with her 1829

DIMNESS (2) [DIM]
Isa 8:22 behold trouble and darkness, **d** of anguish; 4588
 9: 1 Nevertheless the **d** shall not *be* such as 4155

DIMON (2)
Isa 15: 9 For the waters of **D** shall be full *of* blood; 1775
 15: 9 for I will bring more upon **D**, lions upon 1775

DIMONAH (1)
Jos 15:22 And Kinah, and **D**, and Adadah, 1776

DINAH (7) [DINAH'S]
Ge 30:21 bare a daughter, and called her name **D**. 1783
 34: 1 **D** the daughter of Leah, which she bare 1783
 34: 3 soul clave unto **D** the daughter of Jacob, 1783
 34: 5 Jacob heard that he had defiled **D** his 1783
 34:13 said, because he had defiled **D** their sister: 1783
 34:26 took **D** out of Shechem's house, 1783
 46:15 Jacob in Padan-aram, with his daughter **D**: 1783

DINAH'S (1) [DINAH]
Ge 34:25 Simeon and Levi, **D** brethren, took each 1783

DINAITES (1)
Ezr 4: 9 the **D**, the Apharsathchites, the Tarpelites, 1784

DINE (3) [DINED, DINNER]
Ge 43:16 for *these* men shall **d** with me at noon. 398
Lk 11:37 a certain Pharisee besought him to **d** with 709
Jn 21:12 Jesus saith unto them, Come *and* **d**. 709

DINED (1) [DINE]
Jn 21:15 So when they had **d**, Jesus saith to Simon 709

DINHABAH (2)
Ge 36:32 in Edom: and the name of his city *was* **D**. 1838
1Ch 1:43 of Beor: and the name of his city *was* **D**. 1838

DINNER (4) [DINE]
Pr 15:17 Better *is* a **d** of herbs where love is, than a 737
Mt 22: 4 are bidden, Behold, I have prepared my **d**: *712*
Lk 11:38 that he had not first washed before **d**. *712*
 14:12 When thou makest a **d** or a supper, call not *712*

DIONYSIUS (1)
Ac 17:34 among the which *was* **D** the Areopagite, *1354*

DIOTREPHES (1)
3Jn 1: 9 **D**, who loveth to have the preeminence *1361*

DIP (10) [DIPPED, DIPPETH, DIPT]
Ex 12:22 **d** *it* in the blood that *is* in the bason, 2881
Lev 4: 6 the priest shall **d** his finger in the blood, 2881
 4:17 the priest shall **d** his finger *in some* of 2881
 14: 6 **d** them and the living bird in the blood 2881
 14:16 the priest shall **d** his right finger in the oil 2881
 14:51 **d** them in the blood of the slain bird, 2881
Nu 19:18 **d** *it* in the water, and sprinkle *it* upon 2881
Dt 33:24 his brethren, and let him **d** his foot in oil. 2881
Ru 2:14 bread, and **d** thy morsel in the vinegar. 2881
Lk 16:24 he may **d** the tip of his finger in water, *911*

DIPPED (6) [DIP]
Ge 37:31 of the goats, and **d** the coat in the blood; 2881
Jos 3:15 the ark were **d** in the brim of the water, 2881
2Ki 5:14 and **d** *himself* seven times in Jordan, 2881
Ps 68:23 That thy foot may be **d** in the blood of 4272
Jn 13:26 I have **d** *it*. And when he had **dipped** *911*
 13:26 I have **dipped** *it*. And when he had **d** *1686*

DIPPETH (2) [DIP]
Mt 26:23 He that **d** *his* hand with me in the dish, *1686*
Mk 14:20 of the twelve, that **d** with me in the dish. *1686*

DIPT (4) [DIP]
Lev 9: 9 he **d** his finger in the blood, and put *it* 2881
1Sa 14:27 **d** *it* in a honeycomb, and put his hand to 2881
2Ki 8:15 **d** *it* in water, and spread *it* on his face, 2881
Rev 19:13 And he *was* clothed with a vesture **d** in *911*

DIRECT (10) [DIRECTED, DIRECTETH, DIRECTION, DIRECTLY]
Ge 46:28 unto Joseph, to **d** his face unto Goshen; 3384
Ps 5: 3 in the morning will I **d** *my prayer* unto 6186
Pr 3: 6 him, and he shall **d** thy paths. 3474
 11: 5 The righteousness of the perfect shall **d** 3474
Ecc 10:10 but wisdom *is* profitable to **d**. 3787
Isa 45:13 in righteousness, and I will **d** all his ways: 3474
 61: 8 I will **d** their work in truth, and I will 5414

Jer 10:23 *is* not in man that walketh to **d** his steps. 3559
1Th 3:11 Lord Jesus Christ, **d** our way unto you. *2720*
2Th 3: 5 And the Lord **d** your hearts into the love *2720*

DIRECTED (3) [DIRECT]
Job 32:14 Now he hath not **d** *his* words against me: 6186
Ps 119: 5 that my ways were **d** to keep thy statutes! 3559
Isa 40:13 Who hath **d** the spirit of the Lord, 8505

DIRECTETH (3) [DIRECT]
Job 37: 3 He **d** it under the whole heaven, 3474
Pr 16: 9 his way: but the Lord **d** his steps. 3559
 21:29 face: but *as for* the upright, he **d** his way. 995

DIRECTION (1) [DIRECT]
Nu 21:18 **by the d of** the lawgiver, with their 871:1

DIRECTLY (2) [DIRECT]
Nu 19: 4 sprinkle of her blood **d** before 413+5227
Eze 42:12 *even* the way **d** before the wall toward 1903

DIRT (3)
Jdg 3:22 out of his belly; and the **d** came out. 6574
Ps 18:42 I did cast them out as the **d** in the streets. 2916
Isa 57:20 whose waters cast up mire and **d**. 2916

DISABLED See IMPOTENT

DISALLOW (2) [DISALLOWED]
Nu 30: 5 if her father **d** her in the day that he 5106
 30: 8 if her husband **d** her on the day that he 5106

DISALLOWED (4) [DISALLOW]
Nu 30: 5 shall forgive her, because her father **d** her. 5106
 30:11 and held his peace at her, and *all* her not: 5106
1Pe 2: 4 indeed of men, but chosen of God, 593
 2: 7 the stone which the builders **d**, 593

DISANNUL (3) [DISANNULLED, DISANNULLETH, DISANNULLING]
Job 40: 8 Wilt thou also **d** my judgment? wilt thou 6565
Isa 14:27 who shall **d** *it?* and his hand *is* stretched 6565
Gal 3:17 hundred and thirty years after, cannot **d**, *208*

DISANNULLED (1) [DISANNUL]
Isa 28:18 your covenant with death shall be **d**, 3722

DISANNULLETH (1) [DISANNUL]
Gal 3:15 *be* confirmed, no *man* **d**, or added thereto. *114*

DISANNULLING (1) [DISANNUL]
Heb 7:18 For there is verily a **d** of the commandment *115*

DISAPPOINT (1) [DISAPPOINTED, DISAPPOINTETH]
Ps 17:13 Arise, O Lord, **d** him, cast him 6440+6923

DISAPPOINTED (1) [DISAPPOINT]
Pr 15:22 Without counsel purposes *are* **d**: but in 6565

DISAPPOINTETH (1) [DISAPPOINT]
Job 5:12 He **d** the devices of the crafty, so that their 6565

DISCERN (17) [DISCERNED, DISCERNER, DISCERNETH, DISCERNING]
Ge 31:32 before our brethren **d** thou what *is* thine 5234
 38:25 she said, **D**, I pray thee, whose *are* these, 5234
2Sa 14:17 so *is* my lord the king to **d** good and bad: 8085
 19:35 *and* can I **d** between good and evil? 3045
1Ki 3: 9 that I *may* **d** between good and bad: 995
 3:11 hast asked for thyself understanding to **d** 8085
Ezr 3:13 So that the people could not **d** the noise 5234
Job 4:16 but I could not **d** the form thereof: 5234
 6:30 cannot my taste **d** perverse things? 995
Eze 44:23 **cause** them **to d** between the unclean 5234
Jnh 4:11 that cannot **d** between their right hand 3045
Mal 3:18 **d** between the righteous and the wicked, 7200
Mt 16: 3 hypocrites, ye can **d** the face of the sky; *1252*
 16: 3 but can ye not **d** the signs of the times? NIG
Lk 12:56 ye can **d** the face of the sky and of *1381*
 12:56 how *is it that* ye do not **d** this time? 1381+1492
Heb 5:14 have their senses exercised to **d** both good *1253*

DISCERNED (4) [DISCERN]
Ge 27:23 **d** him not, because his hands were hairy, 5234
1Ki 20:41 the king of Israel **d** him that he *was* of 5234
Pr 7: 7 the simple ones, I **d** among the youths, 995
1Co 2:14 know *them*, because they are spiritually **d**. *350*

DISCERNER (1) [DISCERN]
Heb 4:12 and *is* a **d** of the thoughts and intents of *2924*

DISCERNETH (1) [DISCERN]
Ecc 8: 5 a wise *man's* heart **d** *both* time and 3045

DISCERNING (2) [DISCERN]
1Co 11:29 to himself, not **d** the Lord's body. *1252*
 12:10 to another prophecy; to another **d** of spirits; *1253*

DISCHARGE (1) [DISCHARGED]
Ecc 8: 8 *there is* no **d** in *that* war; neither shall 4917

DISCHARGED (1) [DISCHARGE]
1Ki 5: 9 will **cause** them **to be d** there, 5310

DISCIPLE (29) [DISCIPLES, DISCIPLES', FELLOW-DISCIPLES]

Mt	10:24 The **d** is not above *his* master,	3101
	10:25 *It is* enough for the **d** that he be as his	3101
	10:42 cup of cold *water* only in the name of a **d**,	3101
	27:57 who also himself was Jesus' **d**:	3100
Lk	6:40 The **d** is not above his master: but	3101
	14:26 and his own life also, he cannot be my **d**.	3101
	14:27 and come after me, cannot be my **d**.	3101
	14:33 not all that he hath, he cannot be my **d**.	3101
Jn	9:28 they reviled him, and said, Thou art his **d**;	3101
	18:15 followed Jesus, and *so did* another **d**:	3101
	18:15 that **d** was known unto the high priest,	3101
	18:16 Then went out *that* other **d**, which was	3101
	19:26 saw *his* mother, and the **d** standing by,	3101
	19:27 then saith he to the **d**, Behold thy mother.	3101
	19:27 And from that hour *that* **d** took her unto	3101
	19:38 being a **d** of Jesus, but secretly for fear of	3101
	20: 2 and to the other **d**, whom Jesus loved,	3101
	20: 3 *that* other **d**, and came to the sepulchre.	3101
	20: 4 and the other **d** did outrun Peter,	3101
	20: 8 went in also *that* other **d**, which came	3101
	21: 7 Therefore *that* **d** whom Jesus loved saith	3101
	21:20 seeth the **d** whom Jesus loved following;	3101
	21:23 the brethren, that that **d** should not die:	3101
	21:24 This is the **d** which testifieth of these	3101
Ac	9:10 And there was a certain **d** at Damascus,	3101
	9:26 of him, and believed not that he was a **d**.	3101
	9:36 Now there was at Joppa a certain **d** named	3102
	16: 1 and behold, a certain **d** was there,	3101
	21:16 an old **d**, with whom we should lodge.	3101

DISCIPLES (243) [DISCIPLE]

Isa	8:16 the testimony, seal the law among my **d**.	3928
Mt	5: 1 when he was set, his **d** came unto him:	3101
	8:21 And another of his **d** said unto him, Lord,	3101
	8:23 entered into a ship, his **d** followed him.	3101
	8:25 And his **d** came to *him*, and awoke him,	3101
	9:10 and sat down with him and his **d**.	3101
	9:11 the Pharisees saw *it*, they said unto his **d**,	3101
	9:14 Then came to him the **d** of John, saying,	3101
	9:14 the Pharisees fast oft, but thy **d** fast not?	3101
	9:19 and followed him, and *so did* his **d**.	3101
	9:37 saith he unto his **d**, The harvest truly	3101
	10: 1 he had called unto *him* his twelve **d**,	3101
	11: 1 made an end of commanding his twelve **d**,	3101
	11: 2 the works of Christ, he sent two of his **d**,	3101
	12: 1 and his **d** were a hungred, and began to	3101
	12: 2 thy **d** do *that* which is not lawful to do	3101
	12:49 he stretched forth his hand toward his **d**,	3101
	13:10 And the **d** came, and said unto him,	3101
	13:36 and his **d** came unto him, saying,	3101
	14:12 And his **d** came, and took up the body,	3101
	14:15 his **d** came to him, saying, *This* is a desert	3101
	14:19 and gave the loaves to *his* **d**,	3101
	14:19 *his* disciples, and the **d** to the multitude.	3101
	14:22 And straightway Jesus constrained his **d** to	3101
	14:26 And when the **d** saw him walking on	3101
	15: 2 Why do thy **d** transgress the tradition of	3101
	15:12 Then came his **d**, and said unto him,	3101
	15:23 And his **d** came and besought him, saying,	3101
	15:32 Then Jesus called his **d** unto *him*, and said,	3101
	15:33 And his **d** say unto him, Whence should	3101
	15:36 and brake *them*, and gave to his **d**,	3101
	15:36 his disciples, and the **d** to the multitude.	3101
	16: 5 And when his **d** were come to the other	3101
	16:13 he asked his **d**, saying, Whom do men say	3101
	16:20 charged he his **d** that they should tell	3101
	16:21 time forth began Jesus to shew unto his **d**,	3101
	16:24 Then said Jesus unto his **d**, If any *man* will	3101
	17: 6 And when the **d** heard *it*, they fell on their	3101
	17:10 And his **d** asked him, saying, Why then	3101
	17:13 Then the **d** understood that he spake unto	3101
	17:16 I brought him to thy **d**, and they could	3101
	17:19 Then came the **d** to Jesus apart,	3101
	18: 1 At the same time came the **d** unto Jesus,	3101
	19:10 His **d** say unto him, If the case of the man	3101
	19:13 them, and pray: and the **d** rebuked them.	3101
	19:23 Then said Jesus unto his **d**, Verily I say	3101
	19:25 his **d** heard *it*, they were exceedingly	3101
	20:17 took the twelve **d** apart in the way,	3101
	21: 1 mount of Olives, then sent Jesus two **d**,	3101
	21: 6 And the **d** went, and did as Jesus	3101
	21:20 And when the **d** saw *it*, they marvelled,	3101
	22:16 And they sent out unto him their **d** with	3101
	23: 1 spake Jesus to the multitude, and to his **d**,	3101
	24: 1 his **d** came to *him* for to shew him	3101
	24: 3 the **d** came unto him privately, saying,	3101
	26: 1 all these sayings, he said unto his **d**,	3101
	26: 8 But when his **d** saw *it*, they had	3101
	26:17 *of* unleavened bread the **d** came to Jesus,	3101
	26:18 keep the passover at thy house with my **d**.	3101
	26:19 the **d** did as Jesus had appointed them;	3101
	26:26 *it*, and brake *it*, and gave *it* to the **d**,	3101
	26:35 deny thee. Likewise also said all the **d**.	3101
	26:36 saith unto the **d**, Sit ye here, while I go	3101
	26:40 And he cometh unto the **d**,	3101
	26:45 Then cometh he to his **d**, and saith unto	3101
	26:56 Then all the **d** forsook him, and fled.	3101
	27:64 lest his **d** come by night, and steal him	3101
	28: 7 tell his **d** that he is risen from the dead;	3101
	28: 8 great joy; and did run to bring his **d** word.	3101
	28: 9 as they went to tell his **d**, behold, Jesus	3101
	28:13 His **d** came by night, and stole him *away*	3101
	28:16 Then the eleven **d** went *away* into Galilee,	3101

Mk	2:15 sat also together with Jesus and his **d**:	3101
	2:16 and sinners, they said unto his **d**,	3101
	2:18 the **d** of John and of the Pharisees used	3101
	2:18 Why do the **d** of John and of the Pharisees	3101
	2:18 of the Pharisees fast, but thy **d** fast not?	3101
	2:23 and his **d** began, as they went, to pluck	3101
	3: 7 But Jesus withdrew himself with his **d** to	3101
	3: 9 And he spake to his **d**, that a small ship	3101
	4:34 he expounded all *things* to his **d**.	3101
	5:31 And his **d** said unto him, Thou seest	3101
	6: 1 his own country; and his **d** follow him.	3101
	6:29 And when his **d** heard *of it*, they came	3101
	6:35 his **d** came unto him, and said, *This* is a	3101
	6:41 and gave *them* to his **d** to set before them;	3101
	6:45 And straightway he constrained his **d** to	3101
	7: 2 when they saw some of his **d** eat bread	3101
	7: 5 Why walk not thy **d** according to	3101
	7:17 his **d** asked him concerning the parable.	3101
	8: 1 Jesus called his **d** unto *him*, and saith unto	3101
	8: 4 his **d** answered him, From whence can	3101
	8: 6 and gave to his **d** to set before *them*; and	3101
	8:10 he entered into a ship with his **d**,	3101
	8:14 Now the **d** had forgotten to take bread,	NIG
	8:27 And Jesus went out, and his **d**, into	3101
	8:27 by the way he asked his **d**, saying unto	3101
	8:33 he had turned about and looked on his **d**,	3101
	8:34 called the people *unto him* with his **d** also,	3101
	9:14 when he came to *his* **d**, he saw a great	3101
	9:18 I spake to thy **d** that they should cast him	3101
	9:28 his **d** asked him privately, Why could not	3101
	9:31 For he taught his **d**, and said unto them,	3101
	10:10 And in the house his **d** asked him again of	3101
	10:13 *his* **d** rebuked those that brought *them*,	3101
	10:23 looked round about, and saith unto his **d**,	3101
	10:24 And the **d** were astonished at his words.	3101
	10:46 as he went out of Jericho with his **d** and	3101
	11:14 thee hereafter for ever. And his **d** heard *it*.	3101
	12:43 And he called unto *him* his **d**,	3101
	13: 1 one of his **d** saith unto him, Master,	3101
	14:12 his **d** said unto him, Where wilt thou *that*	3101
	14:13 And he sendeth forth two of his **d**,	3101
	14:14 where I shall eat the passover with my **d**?	3101
	14:16 And his **d** went forth, and came into	3101
	14:32 and he saith to his **d**, Sit ye here, while I	3101
	16: 7 tell his **d** and Peter that he goeth before	3101
Lk	5:30 and Pharisees murmured against his **d**,	3101
	5:33 Why do the **d** of John fast often,	3101
	5:33 and likewise the **d** of the Pharisees;	NIG
	6: 1 and his **d** plucked the ears of corn,	3101
	6:13 when it was day, he called unto *him* his **d**:	3101
	6:17 and the company of his **d**, and a great	3101
	6:20 he lifted up his eyes on his **d**, and said,	3101
	7:11 and many of his **d** went with him,	3101
	7:18 And the **d** of John shewed him of all these	3101
	7:19 John calling unto *him* two of his **d** sent	3101
	8: 9 And his **d** asked him, saying, What might	3101
	8:22 that he went into a ship with his **d**:	3101
	9: 1 Then he called his twelve **d** together,	3101
	9:14 And he said to his **d**, Make them sit down	3101
	9:16 gave to the **d** to set before the multitude.	3101
	9:18 was alone praying, his **d** were with him:	3101
	9:40 And I besought thy **d** to cast him out;	3101
	9:43 *things* which Jesus did, he said unto his **d**,	3101
	9:54 And when his **d** James and John saw *this*,	3101
	10:23 And he turned him unto *his* **d**,	3101
	11: 1 ceased, one of his **d** said unto him, Lord,	3101
	11: 1 teach us to pray, as John also taught his **d**.	3101
	12: 1 he began to say unto his **d** first *of all*,	3101
	12:22 And he said unto his **d**, Therefore I say	3101
	16: 1 And he said also unto his **d**, There was a	3101
	17: 1 said he unto the **d**, It is impossible but	3101
	17:22 And he said unto the **d**, The days will	3101
	18:15 when his **d** saw *it*, they rebuked them.	3101
	19:29 *the mount* of Olives, he sent two of his **d**,	3101
	19:37 the whole multitude of the **d** began to	3101
	19:39 said unto him, Master, rebuke thy **d**.	3101
	20:45 of all the people he said unto his **d**,	3101
	22:11 where I shall eat the passover with my **d**?	3101
	22:39 of Olives; and his **d** also followed him.	3101
	22:45 up from prayer, and was come to his **d**,	3101
Jn	1:35 day *after* John stood, and two of his **d**;	3101
	1:37 And the two **d** heard him speak,	3101
	2: 2 was called, and his **d**, to the marriage.	3101
	2:11 forth his glory; and his **d** believed on him.	3101
	2:12 his mother, and his brethren, and his **d**:	3101
	2:17 And his **d** remembered that it was written,	3101
	2:22 his **d** remembered that he had said this	3101
	3:22 Jesus and his **d** into the land of Judea;	3101
	3:25 a question between *some* of John's **d**	3101
	4: 1 Jesus made and baptized moe **d** than John,	3101
	4: 2 Jesus himself baptized not, but his **d**,)	3101
	4: 8 (For his **d** were gone away unto the city to	3101
	4:27 And upon this came his **d**,	3101
	4:31 In the mean while his **d** prayed him,	3101
	4:33 Therefore said the **d** one to another,	3101
	6: 3 a mountain, and there he sat with his **d**.	3101
	6: 8 One of his **d**, Andrew, Simon Peter's	3101
	6:11 he distributed to the **d**, and the disciples	3101
	6:11 and the **d** to them that were set down;	3101
	6:12 When they were filled, he said unto his **d**,	3101
	6:16 *now* come, his **d** went down unto the sea,	3101
	6:22 that one whereinto his **d** were entered,	3101
	6:22 Jesus went not with his **d** into the boat,	3101
	6:22 but *that* his **d** were gone away alone;	3101

Jn	6:24 neither his **d**, they also took shipping,	3101
	6:60 Many therefore of his **d**, when they had	3101
	6:61 When Jesus knew in himself that his **d**	3101
	6:66 From that *time* many of his **d** went back,	3101
	7: 3 thy **d** also may see the works that thou	3101
	8:31 in my word, *then* are ye my **d** indeed;	3101
	9: 2 And his **d** asked him, saying, Master,	3101
	9:27 you hear *it* again? will ye also be his **d**?	3101
	9:28 Thou art his disciple; but we are Moses' **d**.	3101
	11: 7 Then after that saith he to *his* **d**, Let us go	3101
	11: 8 *His* **d** say unto him, Master, the Jews of	3101
	11:12 Then said his **d**, Lord, if he sleep, he shall	3101
	11:54 there continued with his **d**.	3101
	12: 4 Then saith one of his **d**, Judas Iscariot,	3101
	12:16 These *things* understood not his **d** at	3101
	13:22 Then the **d** looked one on another,	3101
	13:23 was leaning on Jesus' bosom one of his **d**,	3101
	13:35 this shall all *men* know that ye are my **d**,	3101
	15: 8 ye bear much fruit; so shall ye be my **d**.	3101
	16:17 said *some* of his **d** among themselves,	3101
	16:29 His **d** said unto him, Lo, now speakest	3101
	18: 1 forth with his **d** over the brook Cedron,	3101
	18: 1 into the which he entered, and his **d**.	3101
	18:17 Art not thou also *one* of this man's **d**?	3101
	18:19 The high priest then asked Jesus of his **d**,	3101
	18:25 unto him, Art not thou also *one* of his **d**?	3101
	20:10 the **d** went away again unto their own	3101
	20:18 and told the **d** that she had seen the Lord,	3101
	20:19 the doors were shut where the **d** were	3101
	20:20 Then were the **d** glad, when they saw	3101
	20:25 The other **d** therefore said unto him,	3101
	20:26 And after eight days again his **d** were	3101
	20:30 truly did Jesus in the presence of his **d**,	3101
	21: 1 again to the **d** at the sea of Tiberias;	3101
	21: 2 *sons* of Zebedee, and two other of his **d**.	3101
	21: 4 but the **d** knew not that it was Jesus.	3101
	21: 8 And the other **d** came in a little ship;	3101
	21:12 And none of the **d** durst ask him, Who art	3101
	21:14 time *that* Jesus shewed himself to his **d**,	3101
Ac	1:15 days Peter stood up in the midst of the **d**,	3101
	6: 1 when the number of the **d** was multiplied,	3101
	6: 2 called the multitude of the **d** unto *them*,	3101
	6: 7 number of the **d** multiplied in Jerusalem	3101
	9: 1 and slaughter against the **d** of the Lord,	3101
	9:19 Then was Saul certain days with the **d**	3101
	9:25 Then the **d** took him by night, and let *him*	3101
	9:26 he assayed to join himself to the **d**:	3101
	9:38 and the **d** had heard that Peter was there,	3101
	11:26 the **d** were called Christians first in	3101
	11:29 Then the **d**, every man according to his	3101
	13:52 And the **d** were filled with joy, and with	3101
	14:20 Howbeit, as the **d** stood round about him,	3101
	14:22 Confirming the souls of the **d**,	3101
	14:28 there they abode long time with the **d**.	3101
	15:10 to put a yoke upon the neck of the **d**,	3101
	18:23 Phrygia in order, strengthening all the **d**.	3101
	18:27 exhorting the **d** to receive him:	3101
	19: 1 came to Ephesus: and finding certain **d**,	3101
	19: 9 departed from them, and separated the **d**,	3101
	19:30 in unto the people, the **d** suffered him not.	3101
	20: 1 Paul called unto *him* the **d**, and embraced	3101
	20: 7 when the **d** came together to break bread,	3101
	20:30 speaking perverse *things*, to draw away **d**	3101
	21: 4 finding **d**, we tarried there seven days:	3101
	21:16 There went with us also *certain* of the **d**	3101

DISCIPLES' (1) [DISCIPLE]

Jn	13: 5 and began to wash the **d** feet, and to wipe	3101

DISCIPLINE (1)

Job	36:10 He openeth also their ear to **d**,	4148

DISCLOSE (1)

Isa	26:21 the earth also shall **d** her blood,	1540

DISCOMFITED (9) [DISCOMFITURE]

Ex	17:13 Joshua **d** Amalek and his people with	2522
Nu	14:45 smote them, and **d** them, *even* unto	3807
Jos	10:10 the LORD **d** them before Israel,	2000
Jdg	4:15 the LORD **d** Sisera, and all *his* chariots,	2000
	8:12 and Zalmunna, and **d** all the host.	2729
1Sa	7:10 that day upon the Philistines, and **d** them;	2000
2Sa	22:15 scattered them; lightning, and **d** them.	2000
Ps	18:14 he shot out lightnings, and **d** them.	2000
Isa	31: 8 the sword, and his young men shall be **d**.	4522

DISCOMFITURE (1) [DISCOMFITED]

1Sa	14:20 his fellow, *and there was* a very great **d**.	4103

DISCONTENTED (1)

1Sa	22: 2 in debt, and every one *that was* **d**,	4751+5315

DISCONTINUE (1)

Jer	17: 4 shalt **d** from thine heritage that I gave	8058

DISCORD (2)

Pr	6:14 mischief continually; he soweth **d**.	4066
	6:19 and he that soweth **d** among brethren.	4066

DISCOURAGE (1) [DISCOURAGED]

Nu	32: 7 wherefore **d** ye the heart of the children of	5106

DISCOURAGED (6) [DISCOURAGE]

Nu	21: 4 soul of the people was much **d** because	7114
	32: 9 they **d** the heart of the children of Israel,	5106

D

D

Dt　1:21 said unto thee; fear not, neither be **d**,　2865
　　1:28 our brethren have **d** our heart, saying,　4549
Isa　42:　4 He shall not fail nor be **d**, till he have set　7533
Col　3:21 not your children *to* anger, lest they be **d**.　120

DISCOVER (12) [DISCOVERED, DISCOVERETH, DISCOVERING]
Dt　22:30 his father's wife, nor **d** his father's skirt.　1540
1Sa　14: 8 and we will **d** ourselves unto them.　1540
Job　41:13 Who can **d** the face of his garment? *or*　1540
Pr　18: 2 but that his heart may **d** itself.　1540
　　25: 9 and **d** not a secret *to* another:　1540
Isa　3:17 and the Lord will **d** their secret parts.　6168
Jer　13:26 Therefore will I **d** thy skirts upon thy face,　2834
La　4:22 O daughter of Edom; he will **d** thy sins.　1540
Eze　16:37 will **d** thy nakedness unto them, that they　1540
Hos　2:10 now will I **d** her lewdness in the sight of　1540
Mic　1:　6 and I will **d** the foundations thereof.　1540
Na　3:　5 I will **d** thy skirts upon thy face, and I will　1540

DISCOVERED (22) [DISCOVER]
Ex　20:26 that thy nakedness be not **d** thereon.　1540
Lev　20:18 he hath **d** her fountain, and she hath　6168
1Sa　14:11 both of them **d** themselves unto　1540
　　22:　6 When Saul heard that David was **d**,　3045
2Sa　22:16 the foundations of the world were **d**,　1540
Ps　18:15 the foundations of the world were **d** at　1540
Isa　22:　8 he **d** the covering of Judah, and thou　1540
　　57:　8 thou hast **d** *thyself to another* than me,　1540
Jer　13:22 greatness of thine iniquity are thy skirts **d**,　1540
La　2:14 they have not **d** thine iniquity, to turn　1540
Eze　13:14 so that the foundation thereof shall be **d**,　1540
　　16:36 thy nakedness **d** through thy whoredoms　1540
　　16:57 Before thy wickedness was **d**, as *at* the　1540
　　21:24 in that your transgressions are **d**, so that　1540
　　22:10 In thee have they **d** their father's　1540
　　23:10 These **d** her nakedness: they took her　1540
　　23:18 So she **d** her whoredoms,　1540
　　23:18 her whoredoms, and **d** her nakedness:　1540
　　23:29 nakedness of thy whoredoms shall be **d**,　1540
Hos　7:　1 the iniquity of Ephraim was **d**,　1540
Ac　21:　3 Now when we had **d** Cyprus, we left it　398
　　27:39 but they **d** a certain creek with a shore,　2657

DISCOVERETH (2) [DISCOVER]
Job　12:22 He **d** deep *things* out of darkness,　1540
Ps　29:　9 the hinds to calve, and **d** the forests:　2834

DISCOVERING (1) [DISCOVER]
Hab　3:13 by **d** the foundation unto the neck.　6168

DISCREDIT See DISANNUL; DISANNULLED

DISCREET (3) [DISCREETLY, DISCRETION]
Ge　41:33 let Pharaoh look out a man **d** and wise,　995
　　41:39 *there is* none so **d** and wise as thou *art*:　995
Tit　2:　5 *To be* **d**, chaste, keepers at home, good,　4998

DISCREETLY (1) [DISCREET]
Mk　12:34 And when Jesus saw that he answered **d**,　3562

DISCRETION (9) [DISCREET]
Ps　112:　5 lendeth: he will guide his affairs with **d**.　4941
Pr　1:　4 to the young man knowledge and **d**.　4209
　　2:11 **D** shall preserve thee, understanding shall　4209
　　3:21 thine eyes: keep sound wisdom and **d**:　4209
　　5:　2 *thou* mayest regard **d**, and *that* thy lips　4209
　　11:22 *so is* a fair woman which is without **d**.　2940
　　19:11 The **d** of a man deferreth his anger;　7922
Isa　28:26 For his God doth instruct him to **d**,　4941
Jer　10:12 hath stretched out the heavens by his **d**.　8394

DISDAINED (2)
1Sa　17:42 looked about, and saw David, he **d** him:　959
Job　30:　1 whose fathers I would have **d** to have set　3988

DISEASE (15) [DISEASED, DISEASES]
2Ki　1:　2 Ekron whether I shall recover of this **d**.　2483
　　8:　8 by him, saying, Shall I recover of this **d**?　2483
　　8:　9 to thee, saying, Shall I recover of this **d**?　2483
2Ch　16:12 until his **d** *was* exceeding *great:* yet in his　2483
　　16:12 yet in his **d** he sought not *to* the Lord,　2483
　　21:15 thou *shalt* have great sickness by **d** of thy　4245
　　21:18 him in his bowels with an incurable **d**.　2483
Job　30:18 By the great force *of* my **d** is my garment　NIH
Ps　38:　7 For my loins are filled *with* a loathsome **d**:　NIH
　　41:　8 An evil **d**, *say they*, cleaveth fast unto him:　1697
Ecc　6:　2 eateth it: this *is* vanity, and it *is* an evil **d**.　2483
Mt　4:23 and all *manner of* **d** among the people.　3119
　　9:35 and every **d** among the people.　3119
　　10:　1 *manner of* sickness and all *manner of* **d**.　3119
Jn　5:　4 was made whole of whatsoever he had.　3553

DISEASED (8) [DISEASE]
1Ki　15:23 time of his old age he was **d** in his feet.　2470
2Ch　16:12 ninth year of his reign was **d** in his feet,　2456
Eze　34:　4 The ye not strengthened,　2470
　　34:21 and pusht all the **d** with your horns,　2470
Mt　9:20 which was **d** with an issue of blood　131
　　14:35 brought unto him all that were **d**;　2192+2560
Mk　1:32 they brought unto him all that were **d**.　2560
Jn　6:　2 which he did on them that were **d**.　770

DISEASES (13) [DISEASE]
Ex　15:26 I will put none of *these* **d** upon thee,　4245
Dt　7:15 will put none of the evil **d** of Egypt,　4064

Dt　28:60 he will bring upon thee all the **d**　4064
2Ch　21:19 so he died of sore **d**. And his people made　8463
　　24:25 from him, (for they left him in great **d**,)　4251
Ps　103:　3 all thine iniquities; who healeth all thy **d**;　8463
Mt　4:24 sick people that were taken with divers **d**　3554
Mk　1:34 healed many *that were* sick of divers **d**,　3554
Lk　4:40 all they that had *any* sick with divers **d**　3554
　　6:17 to hear him, and to be healed of their **d**;　3554
　　9:　1 authority over all devils, and to cure **d**.　3554
Ac　19:12 the **d** departed from them, and the evil　3554
　　28:　9 which had **d** in the island, came,　769

DISFIGURE (1)
Mt　6:16 for they **d** their faces, that they may appear　853

DISGRACE (1)
Jer　14:21 do not **d** the throne of thy glory:　5034

DISGUISE (3) [DISGUISED, DISGUISETH]
1Ki　14:　2 his wife, Arise, I pray thee, and **d** thyself,　8138
　　22:30 I will **d** myself, and enter into the battle;　2664
2Ch　18:29 I will **d** myself, and will go to the battle;　2664

DISGUISED (5) [DISGUISE]
1Sa　28:　8 Saul **d** himself, and put on other raiment,　2664
1Ki　20:38 and **d** himself with ashes upon his face.　2664
　　22:30 the king of Israel **d** himself, and went into　2664
2Ch　18:29 So the king of Israel **d** himself;　2664
　　35:22 **d** himself, that *he* might fight with him,　2664

DISGUISETH (1) [DISGUISE]
Job　24:15 No eye shall see me: and **d** *his* face.　5643+7760

DISH (4) [DISHES, SNUFFDISHES]
Jdg　5:25 she brought forth butter in a lordly **d**.　5602
2Ki　21:13 wipe Jerusalem as *a man* wipeth a **d**,　6747
Mt　26:23 that dippeth *his* hand with me in the **d**,　5165
Mk　14:20 the twelve, that dippeth with me in the **d**.　5165

DISHAN (5)
Ge　36:21 Dishon, and Ezer, and **D**: these *are*　1789
　　36:28 The children of **D** *are* these; Uz, and Aran.　1789
　　36:30 Duke Dishon, duke Ezer, duke **D**: these　1789
1Ch　1:38 and Anah, and Dishon, and Ezer, and **D**.　1789
　　1:42 *and* Jakan. The sons of **D**; Uz, and Aran.　1789

DISHES (3) [DISH]
Ex　25:29 thou shalt make the **d** thereof,　7086
　　37:16 his **d**, and his spoons, and his bowls,　7086
Nu　4:　7 put thereon the **d**, and the spoons,　7086

DISHON (7)
Ge　36:21 **D**, and Ezer, and Dishan: these *are*　1787
　　36:25 **D**, and Aholibamah the daughter of Anah:　1787
　　36:26 these *are* the children of **D**; Hemdan,　1789
　　36:30 Duke **D**, duke Ezer, duke Dishan: these　1787
1Ch　1:38 and Anah, and **D**, and Ezer, and Dishan.　1787
　　1:41 The sons of Anah; **D**. And the sons of　1787
　　1:41 the sons of **D**; Amram, and Eshban,　1787

DISHONEST (2) [DISHONESTY]
Eze　22:13 I have smitten mine hand at thy **d** gain　1215
　　22:27 *and* to destroy souls, to **get d** gain.　1214+1215

DISHONESTY (1) [DISHONEST]
2Co　4:　2 But have renounced the hidden *things* of **d**,　152

DISHONOUR (11) [DISHONOUREST, DISHONOURETH]
Ezr　4:14 *it was* not meet for us to see the king's **d**,　6173
Ps　35:26 that magnify *themselves* against me.　3639
　　69:19 my reproach, and my shame, and my **d**:　3639
　　71:13 *with* reproach and **d** that seek my hurt.　3639
Pr　6:33 A wound and **d** shall he get;　7036
Jn　8:49 but I honour my Father, and ye do **d** me.　818
Ro　1:24 to **d** their own bodies between themselves:　818
　　9:21 vessel unto honour, and another unto **d**?　819
1Co　15:43 It is sown in **d**; it is raised in glory: it is　819
2Co　6:　8 By honour and, by evil report and　819
2Ti　2:20 earth; and some to honour, and some to **d**.　819

DISHONOUREST (1) [DISHONOUR]
Ro　2:23 through breaking the law **d** thou God?　818

DISHONOURETH (3) [DISHONOUR]
Mic　7:　6 the son **d** the father, the daughter riseth　5034
1Co　11:　4 having *his* head covered, **d** his head.　2617
　　11:　5 prophesieth with *her* head uncovered **d**　2617

DISINHERIT (1)
Nu　14:12 **d** them, and will make of thee a greater　3423

DISMAYED (31) [DISMAYING]
Dt　31:　8 forsake thee: fear not, neither be **d**.　2865
Jos　1:　9 be not afraid, neither be thou **d**:　2865
　　8:　1 unto Joshua, Fear not, neither be thou **d**:　2865
　　10:25 Fear not, nor be **d**, be strong and of good　2865
1Sa　17:11 they were **d**, and greatly afraid.　2865
2Ki　19:26 power, they were **d** and confounded.　2865
1Ch　22:13 of good courage; dread not, nor be **d**.　2865
　　28:20 courage, and do *it:* fear not, nor be **d**:　2865
2Ch　20:15 Be not afraid nor **d** by reason of this great　2865
　　20:17 fear not, nor be **d**; to morrow go out　2865
　　32:　7 be not afraid and **d** for the king of Assyria,　2865
Isa　21:　3 hearing *of it;* I was **d** at the seeing of it;　926
　　37:27 power, they were **d** and confounded:　2865

Isa　41:10 be not **d**; for I *am* thy God: I will　8159
　　41:23 that we may be **d**, and behold *it* together.　8159
Jer　1:17 be not **d** at their faces, lest I confound　2865
　　8:　9 *men* are ashamed, they are **d** and taken:　2865
　　10:　2 and be not **d** at the signs of heaven;　2865
　　10:　2 of heaven; for the heathen are **d** at them.　2865
　　17:18 let them be **d**, but let not me be dismayed　2865
　　17:18 let them be dismayed, but let not me be **d**　2865
　　23:　4 they shall fear no more, nor be **d**, neither　2865
　　30:10 saith the Lord; neither be **d**, O Israel:　2865
　　46:　5 Wherefore have I seen them **d** *and*　2844
　　46:27 my servant Jacob, and be not **d**, O Israel:　2865
　　48:　1 *and* taken: Misgab is confounded and **d**.　2865
　　49:37 For I will *cause* Elam *to be* before their　2865
　　50:36 her mighty *men;* and they shall be **d**.　2865
Eze　2:　6 of thy words, nor be **d** at their looks,　2865
　　3:　9 fear them not, neither be **d** at their looks,　2865
Ob　1:　9 thy mighty *men*, O Teman, shall be **d**,　2865

DISMAYING (1) [DISMAYED]
Jer　48:39 a derision and a **d** to all them about him.　4288

DISMISSED (3)
2Ch　23:　8 for Jehoiada the priest **d** not the courses.　6362
Ac　15:30 when they were **d**, they came to Antioch:　630
　　19:41 he had thus spoken, he **d** the assembly.　630

DISOBEDIENCE (6) [DISOBEDIENT, DISOBEYED]
Ro　5:19 For as by one man's **d** many were made　3876
2Co　10:　6 And having in a readiness to revenge all **d**,　3876
Eph　2:　2 that now worketh in the children of **d**:　543
　　5:　6 the wrath of God upon the children of **d**.　543
Col　3:　6 wrath of God cometh on the children of **d**:　543
Heb　2:　2 **d** received a just recompence of reward;　3876

DISOBEDIENT (13) [DISOBEDIENCE]
1Ki　13:21 who was **d** unto the word of the Lord,　4784
Ne　9:26 Nevertheless they were **d**,　4784
Lk　1:17 and the **d** to the wisdom of the just;　545
Ac　26:19 I was not **d** unto the heavenly vision:　545
Ro　1:30 inventors of evil *things*, **d** to parents,　545
1Ti　1:　9 a righteous *man*, but for the lawless and **d**,　506
2Ti　3:　2 **d** to parents, unthankful, unholy,　545
Tit　1:16 and unto every good work reprobate.　545
　　3:　3 **d**, deceived, serving divers lusts and　545
1Pe　2:　7 but unto them which be **d**, the stone　545
　　2:　8 *them* which stumble at the word, being **d**:　544
　　3:20 Which sometime were **d**, when once　544

DISOBEYED (1) [DISOBEDIENCE]
1Ki　13:21 Forasmuch as thou hast **d** the mouth of　4784

DISORDERLY (3)
2Th　3:　6 from every brother that walketh **d**,　814
　　3:　7 we **behaved** not ourselves **d** among you;　812
　　3:11 *there are* some which walk among you **d**,　814

DISPATCH (1)
Eze　23:47 stones, and **d** them with their swords;　1254

DISPENSATION (4)
1Co　9:17 a **d** *of the gospel* is committed unto me.　3622
Eph　1:10 That in the **d** of the fulness of times he　3622
　　3:　2 If ye have heard of the **d** of the grace of　3622
Col　1:25 according to the **d** of God which is given　3622

DISPERSE (8) [DISPERSED, DISPERSIONS]
1Sa　14:34 **D** yourselves among the people,　6327
Pr　15:　7 The lips of the wise **d** knowledge: but　2219
Eze　12:15 the nations, and **d** them in the countries.　2219
　　20:23 and **d** them through the countries;　2219
　　22:15 **d** thee in the countries, and will consume　2219
　　29:12 and will **d** them through the countries.　2219
　　30:23 and will **d** them through the countries.　2219
　　30:26 and them among the countries;　2219

DISPERSED (10) [DISPERSE]
2Ch　11:23 **d** of all his children throughout all　6555
Est　3:　8 **d** among the people in all the provinces of　6504
Ps　112:　9 He hath **d**, he hath given to the poor;　6340
Pr　5:16 Let thy fountains be **d** abroad, *and* rivers　6327
Isa　11:12 gather together the **d** of Judah from the　5310
Eze　36:19 and they were **d** through the countries:　2219
Zep　3:10 the daughter of my **d**, shall bring mine　6327
Jn　7:35 will he go unto the **d** among the Gentiles,　1290
Ac　5:37 all, *even* as many as obeyed him, were **d**.　1287
2Co　9:　9 (As it is written, He hath **d** abroad; he　4650

DISPERSIONS (1) [DISPERSE]
Jer　25:34 and of your **d** are accomplished.　8600

DISPLAYED (1)
Ps　60:　4 that *it* may be **d** because of the truth.　5127

DISPLEASE (5) [DISPLEASED, DISPLEASURE]
Ge　31:35 Let it not **d** my lord that I　2734+5869+871.1
Nu　22:34 now therefore, if it **d** thee,　5869+7489+871.1
1Sa　29:　7 **d** not the lords of　5869+6213+7451+871.1
2Sa　11:25 Let not this thing **d** thee,　3415+5869+871.1
Pr　24:18 the Lord see *it*, and it **d**　5869+7489+871.1

DISPLEASED (25) [DISPLEASE]
Ge　38:10 the thing which he did **d**　3415+5869+871.1
　　48:17 head of Ephraim, it **d** him:　3415+5869+871.1
Nu　11:　1 it **d** the Lord:　241+7451+871.1

Nu 11:10 Moses also was **d**. 5869+7489+871.1
1Sa 8: 6 the thing Samuel, 3415+5869+871.1
 18: 8 and the saying **d** him; 3415+5869+871.1
2Sa 6: 8 David was **d**, because the Lᴏʀᴅ had 2734
 11:27 had done the Lᴏʀᴅ. 3415+7489+871.1
1Ki 1: 6 his father had not **d** him at any time in 6087
 20:43 of Israel went to his house heavy and **d**, 2198
 21: 4 came into his house heavy and **d** because 2198
1Ch 13:11 David was **d**, because the Lᴏʀᴅ had 2734
 21: 7 God was **d** with this thing; 3415+5869+871.1
Ps 60: 1 thou hast scattered us, thou hast been **d**; 599
Isa 59:15 **d** him that *there was* no 3415+5869+871.1
Da 6:14 was sore **d** with himself, and set *his* heart 888
Jnh 4: 1 it **d** Jonah **exceedingly**, 1419+3415+7451
Hab 3: 8 Was the Lᴏʀᴅ **d** against the rivers? 2734
Zec 1: 2 The Lᴏʀᴅ hath been **sore d** with 7107+7110
 1:15 I am very **sore d** with the heathen 7107+7110
 1:15 for I was *but* a little **d**, and they helped 7107
Mt 21:15 to the Son of David; they were **sore d**, 23
Mk 10:14 But when Jesus saw *it*, he was **much d**, 23
 10:41 they began to be **much d** with James 23
Ac 12:20 Herod was **highly d** with them of Tyre 2371

DISPLEASURE (5) [DISPLEASE]
Dt 9:19 For I was afraid of the anger and **hot d**, 2534
Jdg 15: 3 the Philistines, though I do them a **d**. 7451
Ps 2: 5 in his wrath, and vex them in his **sore d**. 2740
 6: 1 neither chasten me in thy **hot d**. 2534
 38: 1 wrath: neither chasten me in thy **hot d**. 2534

DISPOSED (4) [DISPOSITION]
Job 34:13 earth? or who hath **d** the whole world? 7760
 37:15 Dost thou know when God **d** them, 7760
Ac 18:27 And when he was **d** to pass into Achaia, 1014
1Co 10:27 not bid you *to a feast*, and ye be **d** to go; 2309

DISPOSING (1) [DISPOSITION]
Pr 16:33 but the whole **d** thereof *is* of the Lᴏʀᴅ. 4941

DISPOSITION (1) [DISPOSED, DISPOSING]
Ac 7:53 Who have received the law by the **d** of 1296

DISPOSSESS (2) [DISPOSSESSED]
Nu 33:53 ye shall **d** *the inhabitants of* the land, 3423
Dt 7:17 *are* moe than I; how can I **d** them? 3423

DISPOSSESSED (2) [DISPOSSESS]
Nu 32:39 and the Amorite which *was* in it. 3423
Jdg 11:23 So now the Lᴏʀᴅ God of Israel hath **d** 3423

DISPUTATION (1) [DISPUTE]
Ac 15: 2 had no small dissension and **d** with them, 4803

DISPUTATIONS (1) [DISPUTE]
Ro 14: 1 faith receive you, *but* not to doubtful **d**. 1253

DISPUTE (1) [DISPUTATION, DISPUTATIONS, DISPUTED, DISPUTER, DISPUTING, DISPUTINGS]
Job 23: 7 There the righteous *might* **d** with him; 3198

DISPUTED (5) [DISPUTE]
Mk 9:33 What *was it that* ye **d** among yourselves 1260
 9:34 for by the way they had **d** among 1256
Ac 9:29 Lord Jesus, and **d** against the Grecians: 4802
 17:17 Therefore **d** he in the synagogue with 1256
Jude 1: 9 contending with the devil he **d** about 1256

DISPUTER (1) [DISPUTE]
1Co 1:20 where *is* the **d** of this world? hath not 4804

DISPUTING (5) [DISPUTE]
Ac 6: 9 of Cilicia and of Asia, **d** with Stephen. 4802
 15: 7 And when there had been much **d**, Peter 4803
 19: 8 **d** and persuading the *things* concerning 1256
 19: 9 **d** daily in the school of one Tyrannus, 1256
 24:12 they neither found me in the temple **d** 1256

DISPUTINGS (2) [DISPUTE]
Php 2:14 Do all *things* without murmurings and **d**: 1261
1Ti 6: 5 **Perverse d** of men of corrupt minds, 3859

DISQUALIFIED See CASTAWAY

DISQUALIFY See BEGUILE; BEGUILED; BEGUILING

DISQUIET (1) [DISQUIETED, DISQUIETNESS]
Jer 50:34 land, and **d** the inhabitants of Babylon. 7264

DISQUIETED (6) [DISQUIET]
1Sa 28:15 Why hast thou **d** me, to bring me up? 7264
Ps 39: 6 surely they are **d** in vain: he heapeth up 1993
 42: 5 *why* art thou **d** in me? hope thou in God: 1993
 42:11 why art thou **d** within me? hope thou in 1993
 43: 5 why art thou **d** within me? hope in God: 1993
Pr 30:21 For three *things* the earth is **d**, and for 7264

DISQUIETNESS (1) [DISQUIET]
Ps 38: 8 I have roared by reason of the **d** of my 5100

DISSEMBLED (3) [DISSEMBLERS, DISSEMBLETH]
Jos 7:11 **d** also, and they have put *it* even amongst 3584
Jer 42:20 For ye **d** in your hearts, when ye sent me 8582
Gal 2:13 And the other Jews **d** likewise **with** him; 4942

DISSEMBLERS (1) [DISSEMBLED]
Ps 26: 4 vain persons, neither will I go in with **d**. 5956

DISSEMBLETH (1) [DISSEMBLED]
Pr 26:24 He that hateth **d** with his lips, and layeth 5234

DISSENSION (3)
Ac 15: 2 and Barnabas had no small **d** and 4714
 23: 7 there arose a **d** between the Pharisees and 4714
 23:10 And when there arose a great **d**, the chief 4714

DISSENSIONS See SEDITIONS

DISSIMULATION (2)
Ro 12: 9 *Let* love *be* **without d**. Abhor *that which* 505
Gal 2:13 also was carried away with their **d**. 5272

DISSIPATION See SURFEITING

DISSOLVE (1) [DISSOLVED, DISSOLVEST, DISSOLVING]
Da 5:16 canst make interpretations, and **d** doubts: 8271

DISSOLVED (8) [DISSOLVE]
Ps 75: 3 and all the inhabitants thereof *are* **d**: 4127
Isa 14:31 cry, O city; thou, whole Palestina, *art* **d**: 4127
 24:19 the earth is **clean d**, the earth is 6565+6565
 34: 4 all the host of heaven shall be **d**, 4743
Na 2: 6 shall be opened, and the palace shall be **d**. 4127
2Co 5: 1 earthly house of *this* tabernacle were **d**, 2647
2Pe 3:11 then that all these *things shall* be **d**, 3089
 3:12 the heavens being on fire shall be **d**, 3089

DISSOLVEST (1) [DISSOLVE]
Job 30:22 me to ride *upon it*, and **d** my substance. 4127

DISSOLVING (1) [DISSOLVE]
Da 5:12 of hard sentences, and **d** of doubts, 8271

DISTAFF (1)
Pr 31:19 to the spindle, and her hands hold the **d**. 6418

DISTANT (1)
Ex 36:22 two tenons, **equally d** one from another: 7947

DISTIL (2)
Dt 32: 2 as the rain, my speech shall **d** as the dew, 5140
Job 36:28 do drop *and* **d** upon man abundantly. 7491

DISTINCTION (1) [DISTINCTLY]
1Co 14: 7 harp, except they give a **d** in the sounds, 1293

DISTINCTLY (1) [DISTINCTION]
Ne 8: 8 they read in the book in the law of God **d**, 6567

DISTORT See WREST

DISTRACTED (1) [DISTRACTION]
Ps 88:15 youth *up: while* I suffer thy terrors I am **d**. 6323

DISTRACTION (1) [DISTRACTED]
1Co 7:35 you may attend upon the Lord **without d**. 563

DISTRESS (33) [DISTRESSED, DISTRESSES]
Ge 35: 3 who answered me in the day of my **d**, 6869
 42:21 hear; therefore is this **d** come upon us. 6869
Dt 2: 9 Lᴏʀᴅ said unto me, **D** not the Moabites, 6696
 2:19 **d** them not, nor meddle with them: 6696
 28:53 wherewith thine enemies shall **d** thee: 6693
 28:55 wherewith thine enemies shall **d** thee in 6693
 28:57 wherewith thine enemy shall **d** thee in 6693
Jdg 11: 7 ye come unto me now when ye are in **d**? 6887
1Sa 22: 2 every one *that was* in **d**, and every one 4689
2Sa 22: 7 In my **d** I called upon the Lᴏʀᴅ, 6862
1Ki 1:29 that hath redeemed my soul out of all **d**, 6869
2Ch 28:22 in the time of his **d** did he trespass yet 6887
Ne 2:17 I unto them, Ye see the **d** that we *are* in, 7451
 9:37 at their pleasure, and we *are* in great **d**. 6869
Ps 4: 1 thou hast enlarged me *when I was* in **d**; 6862
 18: 6 In my **d** I called upon the Lᴏʀᴅ, 6862
 118: 5 I called upon the Lᴏʀᴅ in **d**: the Lᴏʀᴅ 4712
 120: 1 In my **d** I cried unto the Lᴏʀᴅ, 6869
Pr 1:27 when **d** and anguish cometh upon you: 6869
Isa 25: 4 a strength to the needy in his **d**, a refuge 6862
 29: 2 Yet I will **d** Ariel, and there shall be 6693
 29: 7 and her munition, and that **d** her, 6693
Jer 10:18 and will **d** them, that they may find *it so.* 6887
La 1:20 Behold, O Lᴏʀᴅ; for I *am* in **d**: my 6887
Ob 1:12 thou have spoken proudly in the day of **d**. 6869
 1:14 of his that did remain in the day of **d**. 6869
Zep 1:15 a day of trouble and **d**, a day of wasteness 4691
 1:17 I will **bring d** upon men, that they shall 6887
Lk 21:23 for there shall be great **d** in the land, 318
 21:25 and upon the earth **d** of nations, 4928
Ro 8:35 or **d**, or persecution, or famine, 4730
1Co 7:26 that this is good for the present **d**, 318
1Th 3: 7 over you in all our affliction and **d**, 318

DISTRESSED (11) [DISTRESS]
Ge 32: 7 Jacob was greatly afraid and **d**: and he 3334
Nu 22: 3 Moab was **d** because of the children of 6973
Jdg 2:15 unto them: and they were greatly **d**. 3334
 10: 9 of Ephraim; so that Israel was sore **d**. 3334
1Sa 13: 6 were in a strait, (for the people were **d**,) 5065
 14:24 the men of Israel were **d** that day: for Saul 5065
 28:15 Saul answered, I am sore **d**; 6887
 30: 6 David was greatly **d**; for the people spake 3334

DISTRESSES (8) [DISTRESS]
Ps 25:17 enlarged: O bring thou me out of my **d**. 4691
 107: 6 *and* he delivered them out of their **d**. 4691
 107:13 *and* he saved them out of their **d**. 4691
 107:19 trouble, he saveth them out of their **d**. 4691
 107:28 then he bringeth them out of their **d**. 4691
Eze 30:16 asunder, and Noph *shall have* **d** daily. 6862
2Co 6: 4 in afflictions, in necessities, in **d**, 4730
 12:10 in persecutions, in **d** for Christ's sake: 4730

DISTRIBUTE (5) [DISTRIBUTED, DISTRIBUTETH, DISTRIBUTING, DISTRIBUTION]
Jos 13:32 **d for inheritance** in the plains of Moab, 5157
2Ch 31:14 to **d** the oblations of the Lᴏʀᴅ, 5414
Ne 13:13 their office *was* to **d** unto their brethren. 2505
Lk 18:22 and **d** unto the poor, and thou shalt have 1239
1Ti 6:18 **ready to d**, willing to communicate; 2130

DISTRIBUTED (6) [DISTRIBUTE]
Jos 14: 1 of Israel, **d for inheritance** to them. 5157
1Ch 24: 3 David **d** them, both Zadok of the sons of 2505
2Ch 23:18 whom David had **d** in the house of 2505
Jn 6:11 he **d** to the disciples, and the disciples to 1239
1Co 7:17 But as God hath **d** to every man, 3307
2Co 10:13 of the rule which God hath **d** to us, 3307

DISTRIBUTETH (1) [DISTRIBUTE]
Job 21:17 upon them! *God* **d** sorrows in his anger. 2505

DISTRIBUTING (1) [DISTRIBUTE]
Ro 12:13 **D** to the necessity of saints; given to 2841

DISTRIBUTION (2) [DISTRIBUTE]
Ac 4:35 **d** was made unto every man according as 1239
2Co 9:13 *for your* liberal **d** unto them, and unto 2842

DITCH (6) [DITCHES]
Job 9:31 Yet shalt thou plunge me in the **d**, 7845
Ps 7:15 and is fallen into the **d** which he made. 7845
Pr 23:27 For a whore *is* a deep **d**; and a strange 7745
Isa 22:11 Ye made also a **d** between the two walls 4724
Mt 15:14 lead the blind, both shall fall into the **d**. 999
Lk 6:39 blind? shall they not both fall into the **d**? 999

DITCHES (1) [DITCH]
2Ki 3:16 Make this valley **full of d**. 1356+1356

DIVERS (37) [DIVERSE]
Dt 22: 9 Thou shalt not sow thy vineyard with **d** 3610
 22:11 shalt not wear a **garment of d sorts**, 8162
 25:13 not have in thy bag **d weights**, 68+68+2050.1
 25:14 in thine house **d measures**, 374+374+2050.1
Jdg 5:30 to Sisera a prey of **d colours**, a prey of 6648
 5:30 a prey of **d colours** of needlework, 6648
 5:30 of **d colours** of needlework on both sides, 6648
2Sa 13:18 *she had* a garment of **d colours** upon her: 6446
 13:19 rent her garment of **d colours** that *was* 6446
1Ch 29: 2 of **d colours**, and all *manner of* precious 7553
2Ch 16:14 **d kinds** *of* spices prepared by 2177
 21: 4 and *also* of the princes of Israel. NIH
 30:11 Nevertheless **d** of Asher and Manasseh 376
Ps 78:45 He sent **d sorts** *of* flies among them, 6157
 105:31 there came **d sorts** *of flies, and* lice in all 6157
Pr 20:10 **D weights**, *and* divers 68+68+2050.1
 20:10 *and* **d measures**, 374+374+2050.1
 20:23 **D weights** *are* an abomination 68+68+2050.1
Ecc 5: 7 and many words *there are also d* vanities: NIH
Eze 16:16 deckedst thy high places with **d colours**, 2921
 17: 3 full *of* feathers, which had **d colours**, 7553
Mt 4:24 people that were taken with **d diseases** 4164
 24: 7 pestilences, and earthquakes **in d** places. 2596
Mk 1:34 And he healed many *that were* sick of **d** 4164
 8: 3 by the way: for **d** of them came from far. 5100
 13: 8 there shall be earthquakes **in d** places, 2596
Lk 4:40 all they that had *any* sick with **d diseases** 4164
 21:11 great earthquakes shall be **in d** places, 2596
Ac 19: 9 But when **d** were hardened, 5100
1Co 12:10 of spirits; to another **d** kinds of tongues; NIG
2Ti 3: 6 laden with sins, led away with **d** lusts, 4164
Tit 3: 3 deceived, serving **d** lusts and pleasures, 4164
Heb 1: 1 in **d manners** spake in time past unto 3588
 2: 4 and with **d** miracles, and gifts of the Holy 4164
 9:10 and **d** washings, and carnal ordinances, 1313
 13: 9 Be not carried about with **d** and 4164
Jas 1: 2 count *it* all joy when ye fall into **d** 4164

DIVERSE (8) [DIVERS, DIVERSITIES]
Lev 19:19 not let thy cattle gender with a **d** kind: 3610
Est 1: 7 the vessels being **d** one from another,) 8138
 3: 8 their laws *are* **d** from all people; 8138
Da 7: 3 up from the sea, **d** one from another. 8133
 7: 7 *was* **d** from all the beasts that *were* before 8133
 7:19 which was **d** from all the others, 8133
 7:23 which shall be **d** from all kingdoms, 8133
 7:24 he shall be **d** from the first, and he shall 8133

DIVERSITIES (3) [DIVERSE]
1Co 12: 4 Now there are **d** of gifts, but the same 1243
 12: 6 And there are **d** of operations, but it is 1243
 12:28 helps, governments, **d** of tongues. 1085

D

D

DIVIDE (49) [DIVIDED, DIVIDER, DIVIDETH, DIVIDING, DIVISION, DIVISIONS]

Ge	1: 6	let it **d** the waters from the waters.	914
	1:14	of the heaven to **d** the day from the night;	914
	1:18	and to **d** the light from the darkness.	914
	49: 7	I will **d** them in Jacob, and scatter them in	2505
	49:27	the prey, and at night he shall **d** the spoil.	2505
Ex	14:16	out thine hand over the sea, and **d** it:	1234
	15: 9	I will overtake, I will **d** the spoil;	2505
	21:35	sell the live ox, and **d** the money of it;	2673
	21:35	of it; and the dead *ox* also they shall **d.**	2673
	26:33	the vail shall **d** unto you between the holy	914
Lev	1:17	wings thereof, *but* shall not **d** *it* **asunder:**	914
	5: 8	from his neck, but shall not **d** *it* **asunder:**	914
	11: 4	chew the cud, or of them that **d** the hoof:	6536
	11: 7	he **d** the hoof, and *be* clovenfooted,	6536
Nu	31:27	**d** the prey into **two parts;** between them	2673
	33:54	the land by lot for **an inheritance among**	5157
	34:17	the men which shall **d** the land unto you:	5157
	34:18	every tribe, to **d** the land **by inheritance.**	5157
	34:29	**d** the **inheritance unto** the children of	5157
Dt	14: 7	cud, or of them that **d** the cloven hoof:	6536
	14: 7	they chew the cud, but **d** not the hoof;	6536
	19: 3	**d** the coasts . . . , **into three parts,**	8027
Jos	1: 6	shalt thou **d for an inheritance** the land,	5157
	13: 6	only **d** thou it *by lot* unto the Israelites for	5307
	13: 7	**d** this land for an inheritance unto the	2505
	18: 5	they shall **d** it into seven parts: Judah shall	2505
	22: 8	**d** the spoil of your enemies with your	2505
2Sa	19:29	I have said, Thou and Ziba **d** the land.	2505
1Ki	3:25	**D** the living child in two, and give half to	1504
	3:26	Let it be neither mine nor thine, *but* **d** it.	1504
Ne	9:11	thou didst **d** the sea before them,	1234
	9:22	nations, and didst **d** them into corners:	2505
Job	27:17	and the innocent shall **d** the silver.	2505
Ps	55: 9	Destroy, O Lord, *and* **d** their tongues: for	6385
	60: 6	I will **d** Shechem, and mete out the valley	2505
	74:13	Thou didst **d** the sea by thy strength;	6565
	108: 7	I will **d** Shechem, and mete out the valley	2505
Pr	16:19	than to **d** the spoil with the proud.	2505
Isa	9: 3	*and* as *men* rejoice when they **d** the spoil.	2505
	53:12	Therefore will I **d** him *a portion* with the	2505
	53:12	and he shall **d** the spoil with the strong;	2505
Eze	5: 1	balances to weigh, and **d** *the hair.*	2505
	45: 1	when ye shall **d** *by lot* the land for	5307
	47:21	So shall ye **d** this land unto you according	2505
	47:22	*that* ye shall **d** it *by lot* for an inheritance	5307
	48:29	This *is* the land which ye shall **d** *by lot*	5307
Da	11:39	over many, and shall **d** the land for gain.	2505
Lk	12:13	that *he* **d** the inheritance with me.	3307
	22:17	Take this, and **d** *it* among yourselves:	1266

DIVIDED (69) [DIVIDE]

Ge	1: 4	and God **d** the light from the darkness.	914
	1: 7	**d** the waters which *were* under	914
	10: 5	By these were the isles of the Gentiles **d** in	6504
	10:25	for in his days was the earth **d;**	6385
	10:32	by these were the nations **d** in the earth	6504
	14:15	he himself against them, he and	2505
	15:10	**d** them in the midst, and laid each piece	1334
	15:10	against another: but the birds he **d** not.	1334
	32: 7	he **d** the people that *was* with him,	2673
	33: 1	he the children unto Leah,	2673
Ex	14:21	the sea dry *land,* and the waters were **d.**	1234
Nu	26:53	Unto these the land shall be **d** for an	2505
	26:55	Notwithstanding the land shall be **d** by lot	2505
	26:56	possession thereof be **d** between many	2505
	31:42	Moses **d** from the men that warred,	2673
Dt	4:19	which the Lord thy God hath **d** unto all	2505
	32: 8	High **d** to the nations their **inheritance,**	5157
Jos	14: 5	children of Israel did, and they **d** the land.	2505
	18:10	Joshua **d** the land unto the children of	2505
	19:51	**d** for an inheritance by lot in Shiloh	5157
	23: 4	I have **d** unto you *by lot* these nations that	5307
Jdg	5:30	have they *not* **d** the prey; to every man a	2505
	7:16	he **d** the three hundred men *into* three	2673
	9:43	**d** them into three companies, and laid	2673
	19:29	**d** her, *together* with her bones, into	5408
2Sa	1:23	and in their death they were not **d.**	6504
1Ki	16:21	were the people of Israel **d** into two parts:	2505
	18: 6	So they **d** the land between them to pass	2505
2Ki	2: 8	they **d** hither and thither, so that	2673
1Ch	1:19	because in his days the earth was **d:**	6385
	23: 6	David **d** them *into* courses among the	2505
	24: 4	the sons of Ithamar; and *thus* were they **d.**	2505
	24: 5	Thus were they **d** by lot, one *sort* with	2505
2Ch	35:13	**d** *them* **speedily** among all the people.	7323
Job	38:25	Who hath **d** a watercourse for	6385
Ps	68:12	she that tarried at home **d** the spoil.	2505
	78:13	He **d** the sea, and caused them to pass	1234
	78:55	**d** them an inheritance by line, and made	5307
	136:13	To him which **d** the Red sea into parts:	1504
Isa	33:23	the prey of a great spoil; the lame take	2505
	34:17	and his hand hath **d** it unto them by line:	2505
	51:15	that **d** the sea, whose waves roared:	7280
La	4:16	The anger of the Lord hath **d** them;	2505
Eze	37:22	neither shall they be **d** into two kingdoms	2673
Da	2:41	and part of iron, the kingdom shall be **d;**	6386
	5:28	Thy kingdom is **d,** and given to the Medes	6537
	11: 4	be **d** toward the four winds of heaven;	2673
Hos	10: 2	Their heart is **d;** now shall they be found	2505
Am	7:17	the sword, and thy land shall be **d** by line;	2505
Mic	2: 4	turning away he hath **d** our fields.	2505
Zec	14: 1	thy spoil shall be **d** in the midst of thee.	2505

Mt	12:25	Every kingdom **d** against itself is brought	3307
	12:25	or house **d** against itself shall not stand:	3307
	12:26	cast out Satan, he is **d** against himself;	3307
Mk	3:24	And if a kingdom be **d** against itself,	3307
	3:25	And if a house be **d** against a house,	3307
	3:26	be **d,** he cannot stand, but hath an end.	3307
	6:41	and the two fishes **d** he among *them* all.	3307
Lk	11:17	Every kingdom **d** against itself is brought	1266
	11:17	a house **d** against a house falleth.	NIG
	11:18	If Satan also be **d** against himself,	1266
	12:52	there shall be five in one house **d,**	1266
	12:53	The father shall be **d** against the son,	1266
	15:12	to *me.* And he **d** unto them *his* living.	1244
Ac	13:19	Canaan, he **d** their land to them **by lot.**	2624
	14: 4	But the multitude of the city was **d:** and	4977
	23: 7	the Sadducees: and the multitude was **d.**	4977
1Co	1:13	Is Christ **d?** was Paul crucified for you?	3307
Rev	16:19	And the great city was **d** into three parts,	NIG

DIVIDER (1) [DIVIDE]

Lk	12:14	who made me a judge or a **d** over you?	3312

DIVIDETH (10) [DIVIDE]

Lev	11: 4	he cheweth the cud, but **d** not the hoof;	6536
	11: 5	he cheweth the cud, but **d** not the hoof,	6536
	11: 6	he cheweth the cud, but **d** not the hoof:	6536
	11:26	*The carcases* of every beast which **d**	6536
Dt	14: 8	the swine, because it **d** the hoof,	6536
Job	26:12	He **d** the sea with his power, and by his	7280
Ps	29: 7	The voice of the Lord **d** the flames of	2672
Jer	31:35	which **d** the sea when the waves thereof	7280
Mt	25:32	as a shepherd **d** *his* sheep from the goats:	873
Lk	11:22	wherein he trusted, and **d** his spoils.	1239

DIVIDING (7) [DIVIDE]

Jos	19:49	**d** the land **for inheritance** by their coasts	5157
	19:51	So they made an end of **d** the country.	2505
Isa	63:12	**d** the water before them, to make himself	1234
Da	7:25	until a time and times and the **d** of time.	6387
1Co	12:11	**d** to every man severally as he will.	1244
2Ti	2:15	be ashamed, **rightly** **d** the word of truth.	3718
Heb	4:12	piercing even to the **d asunder** of soul	3311

DIVINATION (12) [DIVINE]

Nu	22: 7	with the **rewards of d** in their hand;	7081
	23:23	neither *is there* any **d** against Israel:	7081
Dt	18:10	or that **useth d,** *or* an observer of	7080+7081
2Ki	17:17	**used d** and enchantments,	7080+7081
Jer	14:14	prophesy unto you a false vision and **d,**	7081
Eze	12:24	nor flattering **d** within the house of Israel.	4738
	13: 6	They have seen vanity and lying **d,** saying,	7081
	13: 7	have ye not spoken a lying **d,** whereas ye	4738
	21:21	the head of the two ways, to **use d:**	7080+7081
	21:22	At his right hand was the **d** for Jerusalem,	7081
	21:23	it shall be unto them as a false **d** in their	7080
Ac	16:16	certain damsel possessed with a spirit of **d**	4436

DIVINATIONS (1) [DIVINE]

Eze	13:23	ye shall see no more vanity, nor divine **d:**	7081

DIVINE (11) [DIVINATION, DIVINATIONS, DIVINERS, DIVINETH, DIVINING]

Ge	44:15	such a man as I can **certainly d?**	5172+5172
1Sa	28: 8	**d** unto me by the familiar spirit,	7080
Pr	16:10	A **d sentence** *is* in the lips of the king:	7081
Eze	13: 9	prophets that see vanity, and that **d** lies:	7080
	13:23	see no more vanity, nor **d** divinations:	7080
	21:29	unto thee, whiles *they* **d** a lie unto thee,	7080
Mic	3: 6	be dark unto you, that *ye* shall not **d;**	7080
	3:11	and the prophets thereof **d** for money:	7080
Heb	9: 1	had also ordinances of **d service,**	2999
2Pe	1: 3	According as his **d** power hath given unto	2304
	1: 4	ye might be partakers of the **d** nature,	2304

DIVINE BEING See GODHEAD

DIVINERS (7) [DIVINE]

Dt	18:14	unto observers of times, and unto **d:**	7080
1Sa	6: 2	Philistines called for the priests and the **d,**	7080
Isa	44:25	the tokens of the liars, and maketh **d** mad;	7080
Jer	27: 9	nor to your **d,** nor to your dreamers, nor	7080
	29: 8	Let not your prophets and your **d,** that *be*	7080
Mic	3: 7	seers be ashamed, and the **d** confounded:	7080
Zec	10: 2	the **d** have seen a lie, and have told false	7080

DIVINETH (1) [DIVINE]

Ge	44: 5	and whereby **indeed** he **d?**	5172+5172

DIVINING (1) [DIVINE]

Eze	22:28	**d** lies unto them, saying, Thus saith	7080

DIVISION (6) [DIVIDE]

Ex	8:23	I will put a **d** between my people and thy	6304
2Ch	35: 5	*after* the **d** of the families of the Levites.	2515
Lk	12:51	on earth? I tell you, Nay; but rather **d:**	1267
Jn	7:43	So there was a **d** among the people	4978
	9:16	And there was a **d** among them.	4978
	10:19	There was a **d** therefore again among	4978

DIVISIONS (17) [DIVIDE]

Jos	11:23	Israel according to their **d** by their tribes.	4256
	12: 7	*for* a possession according to their **d;**	4256
	18:10	the children of Israel according to their **d.**	4256
Jdg	5:15	For the **d** of Reuben *there were* great	6390
	5:16	For the **d** of Reuben *there were* great	6390
1Ch	24: 1	Now *these are* the **d** of the sons of Aaron.	4256

1Ch	26: 1	Concerning the **d** of the porters: Of	4256
	26:12	Among these *were* the **d** of the porters,	4256
	26:19	These *are* the **d** of the porters among	4256
2Ch	35: 5	in the holy *place* according to the **d** of	6391
	35: 5	that they might give according to the **d** of	4653
Ezr	6:18	they set the priests in their **d,**	6392
Ne	11:36	of the Levites *were* **d** in Judah,	4256
Ro	16:17	mark them which cause **d** and offences	1370
1Co	1:10	and *that* there be no **d** among you;	4978
	3: 3	and strife, and **d,** are ye not carnal,	1370
	11:18	I hear that there be **d** among you;	4978

DIVISIVE PERSON See HERETICK

DIVORCE (1) [DIVORCED, DIVORCEMENT]

Jer	3: 8	put her away, and given her a bill of **d;**	3748

DIVORCED (4) [DIVORCE]

Lev	21:14	or a **d** woman, or profane, *or* a harlot,	1644
	22:13	or **d,** and have no child, and is returned	1644
Nu	30: 9	vow of a widow, and of her that is **d,**	1644
Mt	5:32	whosoever shall marry her that is **d**	630

DIVORCEMENT (6) [DIVORCE]

Dt	24: 1	let him write her a bill of **d,** and give *it* in	3748
	24: 3	write her a bill of **d,** and giveth *it* in her	3748
Isa	50: 1	*Where is* the bill of your mother's **d,**	3748
Mt	5:31	his wife, let him give her a **writing of d:**	647
	19: 7	then command to give a writing of **d,**	647
Mk	10: 4	Moses suffered to write a bill of **d,**	647

DIZAHAB (1)

Dt	1: 1	and Laban, and Hazeroth, and **D.**	1774

DO (1368) [DID, DIDST, DOER, DOERS, DOEST, DOETH, DOING, DOINGS, DONE, DOST, DOTH, UNDO]

Ge	6:17	bring a flood of waters upon the earth,	NIH
	9:13	I **d** set my bow in the cloud, and it shall	NIH
	11: 6	all one language; and this they begin to **d:**	6213
	11: 6	them, which they have imagined to **d.**	6213
	16: 6	in thy hand; **d** to her as it pleaseth thee.	6213
	18: 5	And they said, So **d,** as thou hast said.	6213
	18:17	hide from Abraham *that thing* which I **d;**	6213
	18:19	of the Lord, to **d** justice and judgment;	6213
	18:25	That be far from thee to **d** after this	6213
	18:25	not the Judge of all the earth **d** right?	6213
	18:29	he said, I will not **d** *it* for forty's sake.	6213
	18:30	said, I will not **d** *it,* if I find thirty there.	6213
	19: 7	I pray you, brethren, **d** not so **wickedly.**	7489
	19: 8	and ye to them as *is* good in your eyes:	6213
	19: 8	only unto these men **d** nothing;	6213
	19:22	for I cannot **d** any thing till thou be come	6213
	21:23	thou shalt **d** unto me, and to the land	6213
	22:12	lad, neither **d** thou any thing unto him:	6213
	24:42	if now thou **d** prosper my way which I go:	3426
	25:32	what profit shall this birthright **d** to me?	NIH
	26:29	That thou wilt **d** us no hurt, as we have	6213
	27:37	what shall I **d** now unto thee, my son?	6213
	27:46	the land, what good shall my life **d** me?	NIH
	30:31	if thou wilt **d** this thing for me, I will	6213
	31:16	whatsoever God hath said unto thee, **d.**	6213
	31:29	is in the power of my hand to **d** you hurt:	6213
	31:43	what can I **d** *this* day unto these my	6213
	32:12	I will **surely d** thee **good,**	3190+3190
	34:14	said unto them, We cannot **d** this thing,	6213
	34:19	young man deferred not to **d** the thing,	6213
	37:13	**D** not thy brethren feed the *flock* in	NIH
	39: 9	how then can I **d** this great wickedness,	6213
	39:11	that *Joseph* went into the house to **d** his	6213
	40: 8	*D* not interpretations **belong** to God?	NIH
	41: 9	I remember my faults *this* day:	NIH
	41:25	shewed Pharaoh what he *is* about to **d,**	6213
	41:28	What God *is* about to **d** he sheweth unto	6213
	41:34	Let Pharaoh **d** *this,* and let him appoint	6213
	41:55	Go unto Joseph; what he saith to you, **d.**	6213
	42: 1	sons, Why **d** ye look one upon another?	NIH
	42:18	unto them the third day, This **d,** and live;	6213
	42:22	saying, **D** not sin against the child;	NIH
	43:11	unto them, If *it must be* so now, **d** this;	6213
	44: 7	God forbid that thy servants should **d**	6213
	44:17	he said, God forbid that I should **d** so:	6213
	45:17	Say unto thy brethren, This **d** ye;	6213
	45:19	Now thou art commanded, this **d** ye;	6213
	47:30	And he said, I will **d** as thou hast said.	6213
Ex	1:16	When ye **d** the **office of a midwife** to	3205
	3:20	which I will **d** in the midst thereof:	6213
	4:15	and will teach you what ye shall **d.**	6213
	4:17	thine hand, wherewith thou shalt **d** signs.	6213
	4:21	see that thou **d** all *those* wonders before	6213
	5: 4	Wherefore **d** ye, Moses and Aaron,	NIH
	5:17	Let us go *and* **d sacrifice** to the Lord.	2076
	6: 1	Now shalt thou see what I will **d** to	6213
	8: 8	that they may **d sacrifice** unto the Lord.	2076
	8:26	Moses said, It is not meet so to **d;** for we	6213
	9: 5	To morrow the Lord shall **d** this thing in	6213
	15:26	wilt **d** that which is right in his sight,	6213
	17: 2	wherefore **d** ye tempt the Lord?	NIH
	17: 4	What shall I **d** unto this people?	NIH
	18:16	I make *them* know the statutes of God,	NIH
	18:20	walk, and the work that they must **d.**	6213
	18:23	If thou shalt **d** this thing,	6213
	19: 8	All that the Lord hath spoken we will **d.**	6213
	20: 9	shalt thou labour, and **d** all thy work:	6213
	20:10	*in it* thou shalt not **d** any work, thou,	6213

D

Ex	21: 7 shall not go out as the menservants d**s**.	3318
21:11 if he d not these three unto her, then	6213	
22:30 Likewise shalt thou d with thine oxen,	6213	
23: 2 shalt not follow a multitude to d evil;	NIH	
23:12 Six days thou shalt d thy work, and on	6213	
23:22 obey his voice, and d all that I speak;	6213	
23:24 nor serve them, nor d after their works:	6213	
24: 3 which the Lord hath said will we d.	6213	
24: 7 All that the Lord hath said will we d.	6213	
24:14 if any man have any matters to d, let him	NIH	
29: 1 is the thing that thou shalt d unto them	6213	
29:35 thus shalt thou d unto Aaron, and to his	6213	
29:41 shalt d thereto according to the meat	6213	
31:11 that I have commanded thee shall they d.	6213	
32:14 which he thought to d unto his people.	6213	
32:18 but the noise of them that sing d I hear.	NIH	
33: 5 that I may know what to d unto thee.	6213	
33:17 I will d this thing also that thou hast	6213	
34:10 before all thy people I will d marvels,	6213	
34:10 for it is a terrible thing that I will d with	6213	
34:15 d sacrifice unto their gods, and one call	NIH	
35: 1 hath commanded, that ye should d them.	6213	
35:19 to d service in the holy place, the holy	8334	
35:35 even them that d any work, and of	6213	
36: 2 him up to come unto the work to d it:	6213	
39: 1 to d service in the holy place, and made	NIH	
39:41 The clothes of service to d service in	NIH	
Lev	4: 2 be done), and shall d against any of them:	6213
4: 3 If the priest that is anointed d sin	6213	
4:20 he shall d with the bullock as he did with	6213	
4:20 for a sin offering, so shall he d with this:	6213	
5: 1 or known of it; if he d not utter it, then	7489	
5: 4 pronouncing with his lips to d evil, or to	7489	
5: 4 with his lips to do evil, or to d good,	3190	
8:34 so the Lord hath commanded to d,	6213	
9: 6 the Lord commanded that ye should d:	6213	
10: 9 D not drink wine nor strong drink, thou,	6213	
16:15 with that blood as he did with the blood	6213	
16:16 shall he d for the tabernacle of	6213	
16:29 d no work at all, whether it be one of	6213	
18: 3 of Egypt, wherein ye dwelt, shall ye not d:	6213	
18: 3 whither I bring you, shall ye not d:	6213	
18: 4 Ye shall d my judgments, and keep mine	6213	
18: 5 which if a man d, he shall live in them:	6213	
18:25 I d visit the iniquity thereof upon it,	NIH	
19:15 shall d no unrighteousness in judgment:	6213	
19:29 D not prostitute thy daughter, to cause	NIH	
19:35 shall d no unrighteousness in judgment,	6213	
19:37 and all my judgments, and d them:	6213	
20: 4 if the people of the land d any ways hide	NIH	
20: 8 ye shall keep my statutes, and d them:	6213	
20:22 and all my judgments, and d them:	6213	
21: 6 and the bread of their God, they d offer:	NIH	
21:15 his people: for I the Lord d sanctify him.	NIH	
21:23 for I the Lord d sanctify them.	NIH	
22: 9 profane it: I the Lord d sanctify them.	NIH	
22:16 things: for I the Lord d sanctify them.	NIH	
22:31 ye keep my commandments, and d them:	6213	
23: 3 shall d no work therein: it is the sabbath	6213	
23: 7 ye shall d no servile work therein.	6213	
23: 8 ye shall d no servile work therein: it shall	6213	
23:21 ye shall d no servile work therein: it shall	6213	
23:25 Ye shall d no servile work therein: but	6213	
23:28 ye shall d no work in that same day: for it	6213	
23:31 Ye shall d no manner of work: it shall be	6213	
23:35 ye shall d no servile work therein.	6213	
23:36 and ye shall d no servile work therein.	6213	
25:18 Wherefore ye shall d my statutes, and	6213	
25:18 and keep my judgments, and d them;	6213	
25:45 of the strangers that d sojourn among you,	NIH	
26: 3 keep my commandments, and d them;	6213	
26:14 and will not d all these commandments;	6213	
26:15 that ye will not d all my commandments,	6213	
26:16 I also will d this unto you; I will even	6213	
27:11 of which they d not offer a sacrifice unto	NIH	
Nu	2: 5 those that d pitch next unto him shall be	NIH
3: 7 to d the service of the tabernacle.	5647	
3: 8 Israel, to d the service of the tabernacle.	5647	
4: 3 to d the work in the tabernacle of	5647	
4:19 thus d unto them, that they may live,	6213	
4:23 to d the work in the tabernacle of	5647	
4:30 to d the work in the tabernacle of	5647	
4:37 all that might d service in the tabernacle	5647	
4:41 all that might d service in the tabernacle	5647	
4:47 every one that came to d the service of	5647	
5: 6 to d a trespass against the Lord,	4603+4604	
6:21 so he must d after the law of	6213	
7: 5 that they may be to d the service of	5647	
8: 7 thus shalt thou d unto them, to cleanse	6213	
8:15 the service of the tabernacle of	5647	
8:19 to d the service of the children of Israel in	5647	
8:22 after that went the Levites in to d their	5647	
8:26 to keep the charge, and shall d no service.	5647	
8:26 Thus shalt thou d unto the Levites	6213	
9:14 to the manner thereof, so shall he d:	6213	
10:29 thou with us, and we will d thee good:	2895	
10:32 that what goodness the Lord shall d	2895	
10:32 do unto us, the same will we d unto thee.	3190	
11:27 and Medad d prophesy in the camp.		
14:28 spoken in mine ears, so will I d to you:	6213	
14:35 I will surely d it unto all this evil	6213	
14:41 Wherefore now d ye transgress	NIH	
15:12 shall ye d to every one according to their	6213	
15:13 All that are born of the country shall d	6213	
15:14 unto the Lord; as ye d, so he shall do.	6213	

Nu	15:14 unto the Lord; as ye do, so he shall d.	6213
15:20 as ye d the heave offering of	NIH	
15:39 of the Lord, and d them;	6213	
15:40 d all my commandments, and be holy	6213	
16: 6 This d; Take you censers, Korah,	6213	
16: 9 bring you near to himself to d the service	5647	
16:28 Lord hath sent me to d all these works;	6213	
18: 6 to d the service of the tabernacle of	5647	
18:23 the Levites shall d the service of	5647	
21:34 shalt d to him as thou didst unto Sihon	6213	
22: 7 I will d whatsoever thou sayest unto me:	6213	
22:18 of the Lord my God, to d less or more.	6213	
22:20 I shall say unto thee, that shalt thou d.	6213	
22:30 was I ever wont to d so unto thee?	6213	
23:19 shall he not d it? or hath he spoken,	6213	
23:26 that the Lord speaketh, that I must d?	6213	
24:13 d either good or bad of mine own mind;	6213	
24:14 advertise thee what this people shall d	6213	
24:18 his enemies; and Israel shall d valiantly.	6213	
28:18 ye shall d no manner of servile work	6213	
28:25 ye shall d no servile work.	6213	
28:26 ye shall d no servile work:	6213	
29: 1 ye shall d no servile work:	6213	
29: 7 ye shall not d any work therein:	6213	
29:12 ye shall d no servile work, and ye shall	6213	
29:35 ye shall d no servile work therein:	6213	
29:39 These things ye shall d unto the Lord in	6213	
30: 2 he shall d according to all that proceedeth	6213	
31:19 ye abide without the camp seven days:	NIH	
32:20 said unto them, If ye will d this thing,	6213	
32:23 if ye will not d so, behold, ye have sinned	6213	
32:24 that which hath proceeded out of your	6213	
32:25 Thy servants will d as my lord	6213	
32:31 hath said unto thy servants, so will we d.	6213	
33:56 that I shall d unto you, as I thought to do	6213	
33:56 do unto you, as I thought to d unto them.	6213	
Dt	1:14 thou hast spoken is good for us to d.	6213
1:18 time all the things which ye should d.	6213	
1:44 as bees d, and destroyed you in Seir,	6213	
2: 9 shalt d unto him as thou didst unto	6213	
3:21 shalt the Lord d unto all the kingdoms	6213	
3:24 that can d according to thy works,	6213	
4: 1 for to d them, that ye may live, and go in	6213	
4: 5 that ye should d so in the land whither ye	6213	
4: 6 and d them; for this is your wisdom and	6213	
4:14 ye might d them in the land whither ye	6213	
4:25 shall d evil in the sight of the Lord thy	6213	
5: 1 may learn them, and keep, and d them.	6213	
5:13 thou shalt labour, and d all thy work:	6213	
5:14 in it thou shalt not d any work, thou,	6213	
5:27 unto thee; and we will hear it, and d it.	6213	
5:31 that they may d them in the land which I	6213	
5:32 Ye shall observe to d therefore as	6213	
6: 1 that ye might d them in the land whither	6213	
6: 3 observe to d it; that it may be well with	6213	
6:18 thou shalt d that which is right and good	6213	
6:24 the Lord commanded us to d all these	6213	
6:25 we observe to d all these commandments	6213	
7:11 I command thee this day, to d them.	6213	
7:12 these judgments, and keep, and d them,	6213	
7:19 shall the Lord thy God d unto all	6213	
8: 1 thee this day shall ye observe to d,	6213	
8:16 thee, to d thee good at thy latter end;	3190	
8:19 if thou d at all forget the Lord	7911+7911	
11:22 to d them, to love the Lord your God,	6213	
11:32 ye shall observe to d all the statutes and	6213	
12: 1 which ye shall observe to d in the land,	6213	
12: 4 Ye shall not d so unto the Lord your	6213	
12: 8 shall not d after all the things that we do	6213	
12: 8 shall not do after all the things that we d	6213	
12:14 thou shalt d that I command thee.	6213	
12:25 when thou shalt d that which is right in	6213	
12:30 their gods? even so will I d likewise.	6213	
12:31 Thou shalt not d so unto the Lord thy	6213	
12:32 soever I command you, observe to d it:	6213	
13:11 shall d no more any such wickedness as	6213	
13:18 to d that which is right in the eyes of	6213	
15: 5 to observe to d all these commandments	6213	
15:17 also unto thy maidservant thou shalt d	6213	
15:19 thou shalt d no work with the firstling of	5647	
16: 8 thy God: thou shalt d no work therein.	6213	
16:12 thou shalt observe and d these statutes.	6213	
17:10 thou shalt d according to the sentence,	6213	
17:10 shalt observe to d according to all	6213	
17:11 which they shall tell thee, thou shalt d:	6213	
17:12 the man that will d presumptuously,	6213	
17:13 and fear, and d no more presumptuously.	NIH	
17:19 of this law and these statutes, to d them:	6213	
18: 7 as all his brethren the Levites d, which	NIH	
18: 9 thou shalt not learn to d after	6213	
18:12 For all that d these things are an	6213	
18:14 thy God hath not suffered thee so to d.	NIH	
19: 9 keep all these commandments to d them,	6213	
19:19 shall ye d unto him, as he had thought to	6213	
20: 3 fear not, and d not tremble, neither be ye	NIH	
20:15 Thus shalt thou d unto all the cities	6213	
20:18 That they teach you not to d after all their	6213	
21: 9 when thou shalt d that which is right in	6213	
22: 3 In like manner shalt thou d with his ass;	6213	
22: 3 so shalt thou d with his raiment; and with	6213	
22: 3 thou hast found, shalt thou d likewise:	6213	
22: 5 for all that d so are abomination unto	6213	
22:26 unto the damsel thou shalt d nothing;	6213	
24: 8 d according to all that the priests	6213	
24: 8 them, so ye shall observe to d.	6213	

Dt	24:18 I command thee to d this thing.	6213
24:22 I command thee to d this thing.	6213	
25:16 For all that d such things, and all that do	6213	
25:16 such things, and all that d unrighteously,	6213	
26:16 hath commanded thee to d these statutes	6213	
26:16 keep and d them with all thine heart,	6213	
27:10 all his commandments and his statutes,	6213	
27:26 not all the words of this law to d them.	6213	
28: 1 to d all his commandments which I	6213	
28:13 thee this day, to observe and to d them:	6213	
28:15 to observe to d all his commandments and	6213	
28:20 that thou settest thine hand unto for to d,	6213	
28:58 If thou wilt not observe to d all the words	6213	
28:63 Lord rejoiced over you to d you good,	3190	
29: 9 the words of this covenant, and d them,	6213	
29: 9 that ye may prosper in all that ye d.	6213	
29:14 Neither with you only d I make this	NIH	
29:29 that we may d all the words of this law.	6213	
30: 5 he will d thee good, and multiply thee	3190	
30: 8 d all his commandments which I	6213	
30:12 it unto us, that we may hear it, and d it?	6213	
30:13 it unto us, that we may hear it, and d it?	6213	
30:14 and in thy heart, that thou mayest d it.	6213	
31: 4 the Lord shall d unto them as he did to	6213	
31: 5 ye may d unto them according unto all	6213	
31:12 observe to d all the words of this law:	6213	
31:29 ye will d evil in the sight of the Lord,	6213	
32: 6 D ye thus requite the Lord, O foolish	6213	
32:46 command your children to observe to d,	6213	
34:11 which the Lord sent him to d in the land	6213	
Jos	1: 2 unto the land which I d give to them,	NIH
1: 7 that thou mayest observe to d according	6213	
1: 8 that thou mayest observe to d according	6213	
1:16 All that thou commandest us we will d,	6213	
2:24 even all the inhabitants of the country d	NIH	
3: 5 for to morrow the Lord will d wonders	6213	
6: 3 the city once. Thus shalt thou d six days.	6213	
7: 9 what wilt thou d unto thy great name?	6213	
8: 2 thou shalt d to Ai and her king as thou	6213	
8: 8 commandment of the Lord shall ye d.	6213	
9:20 This we will d to them; we will even let	6213	
9:25 and right unto thee to d unto us,	6213	
9:25 and right unto thee to do unto us, d.	6213	
10:25 for thus shall the Lord d to all your	6213	
22: 5 take diligent heed to d the commandment	6213	
22:24 What have you to d with the Lord	3807.1	
22:27 that we might d the service of the Lord	5647	
23: 6 d all that is written in the book of the law	6213	
23:12 Else if ye d in any wise go back,	NIH	
24:13 oliveyards which ye planted not d ye eat.	NIH	
24:20 he will turn and d hurt,	7489	
Jdg	6:27 of the city, that he could not d it by day,	6213
7:17 unto them, Look on me, and d likewise:	6213	
7:17 it shall be that, as I d, so shall ye do.	6213	
7:17 it shall be that, as I d, so shall ye d.	6213	
8: 3 was I able to d in comparison of you?	6213	
9:33 mayest thou d to them as thou shalt find	6213	
9:48 What ye have seen me d, make haste,	6213	
9:48 me do, make haste, and d as I have done.	6213	
10:15 d thou unto us whatsoever seemeth good	6213	
11:10 if we d not so according to thy words.	6213	
11:12 saying, What hast thou to d with me,	NIH	
11:36 d to me according to that which hath	6213	
13: 8 teach us what we shall d unto the child	6213	
13:12 the child, and how shall we d unto him?	4639	
13:17 come to pass we may d thee honour?	3513	
14:10 a feast; for so used the young men to d.	6213	
15: 3 though I d them a displeasure.	6213	
15:10 to d to him as he hath done to us.	6213	
17:13 know I that the Lord will d me good,	3190	
18:14 D ye know that there is in these houses an	NIH	
18:14 now therefore consider what ye have to d.	6213	
18:18 said the priest unto them, What d ye?	6213	
19:23 nay, I pray you, d not so wickedly;	NIH	
19:23 is come into mine house, d not this folly.	6213	
19:24 d with them what seemeth good unto	6213	
19:24 but unto this man d not so vile a thing.	6213	
20: 9 this shall be the thing which we will d	6213	
20:10 victual for the people, that they may d,	6213	
21: 7 How shall we d for wives for them that	6213	
21:11 this is the thing that ye shall d, Ye shall	6213	
21:16 How shall we d for wives for them that	6213	
Ru	1:17 the Lord d so to me, and more also,	6213
2: 9 Let thine eyes be on the field that they d	NIH	
3: 4 and he will tell thee what thou shalt d.	6213	
3: 5 All that thou sayest unto me I will d.	6213	
3:11 I will d to thee all that thou requirest:	6213	
3:13 well; let him d the kinsman's part:	1350	
3:13 if he will not d the part of a kinsman to	1350	
3:13 will I d the part of a kinsman to thee,	1350	
4:11 d thou worthily in Ephratah, and be	6213	
1Sa	1:23 said unto her, D what seemeth thee good;	6213
2:23 he said unto them, Why d ye such things?	6213	
2:35 shall d according to that which is in my	6213	
3:11 Behold, I will d a thing in Israel,	6213	
3:17 God d so to thee, and more also, if thou	6213	
3:18 let him d what seemeth him good.	6213	
5: 8 What shall we d with the ark of the God	6213	
6: 2 What shall we d to the ark of the Lord?	6213	
6: 6 Wherefore then d ye harden your hearts,	NIH	
7: 3 If ye d return unto the Lord with all your	6213	
8: 8 other gods, so d they also unto thee.	6213	
10: 2 you, saying, What shall I d for my son?	6213	
10: 7 that thou d as occasion serve thee;	6213	
10: 8 to thee, and shew thee what thou shalt d.	6213	

D

1Sa 11:10 ye shall **d** with us all that seemeth good 6213
12:16 which the LORD will **d** before your eyes. 6213
12:25 if ye shall still **d** wickedly, ye shall 7489+7489
14: 7 said unto him, **D** all that *is* in thine heart; 6213
14:36 D whatsoever seemeth good unto thee. 6213
14:40 Saul, **D** what seemeth good unto thee. 6213
14:44 Saul answered, God **d** so and more also: 6213
16: 3 and I will shew thee what thou shalt **d:** 6213
20: 2 my father will **d** nothing *either* great or 6213
20: 4 thy soul desireth, I will even **d** *it* for thee. 6213
20:13 The LORD **d** so and much more to 6213
20:13 *but* if it please my father to **d** thee evil, NIH
20:30 **d** not I know that thou hast chosen the NIH
22: 3 till I know what God will **d** for me. 6213
24: 4 that thou mayest **d** to him as it shall seem 6213
24: 6 The LORD forbid that I should **d** this 6213
25:17 know and consider what thou wilt **d;** 6213
25:22 more also **d** God unto the enemies of 6213
26:21 for I will no more **d** thee **harm**, because 7489
26:25 thou shalt both **d great things,** 6213+6213
28: 2 thou shalt know what thy servant can **d.** 6213
28:15 make known unto me what I shall **d.** 6213
29: 3 What **d** these Hebrews *here?* And Achish NIH
30:23 said David, Ye shall not **d** so, my brethren, 6213
2Sa 3: 8 which against Judah **d** shew kindness *this* NIH
3: 9 So God **d** to Abner, and more also, 6213
3: 9 hath sworn to David, even so I **d** to him; 6213
3:18 **d** *it:* for the LORD hath spoken of David, 6213
3:35 So **d** God to me, and more also, 6213
7: 3 the king, Go, **d** all that *is* in thine heart; 6213
7:23 to **d** for you great things and terrible, 6213
7:25 for ever, and **d** as thou hast said. 6213
9:11 his servant, so shall thy servant **d.** 6213
10:12 the LORD **d** that which seemeth him 6213
11:11 *as* thy soul liveth, I will not **d** this thing. 6213
12: 9 of the LORD, to **d** evil in his sight? 6213
12:12 I will **d** this thing before all Israel, 6213
13: 2 Amnon thought it hard for him to **d** any 6213
13:12 Nay, my brother, **d** not force me; NIH
13:12 to be done in Israel: **d** not thou this folly. 6213
15: 4 come unto me, and I would **d** him justice. NIH
15: 5 when any man came nigh to *him* to **d** NIH
15:15 thy servants *are ready to* **d** whatsoever NIH
15:26 let him **d** to me as seemeth good unto 6213
16:10 the king said, What have I to **d** with you, NIH
16:11 much more now *may this* Benjamite **d** NIH
16:20 Give counsel among you what we shall **d.** 6213
17: 6 shall we **d** *after* his saying? if not; 6213
18:32 all that rise against thee to **d** *thee* hurt, NIH
19:13 God **d** so to me, and more also, if thou be 6213
19:18 and to **d** what he thought good. 6213
19:19 neither **d** thou remember *that* which thy NIH
19:22 David said, What have I to **d** with you, NIH
19:22 for **d** not I know that I am *this* day king NIH
19:27 **d** therefore what *is* good in thine eyes. 6213
19:37 **d** to him what shall seem good unto thee. 6213
19:38 I will **d** to him *that* which shall seem good 6213
19:38 shalt require of me, *that* will I **d** for thee. 6213
20: 6 Bichri **d** us more **harm** than *did* Absalom: 3415
20:17 handmaid. And he answered, I **d** hear. NIH
21: 3 the Gibeonites, What shall I **d** for you? 6213
21: 4 What you shall say, *that* will I **d** for you. 6213
23:17 from me, O LORD, that I may **d** this? 6213
24:12 one of them, that I may **d** *it* unto thee. 6213
1Ki 1:30 even so will I certainly **d** this day. 6213
2: 6 **D** therefore according to thy wisdom, 6213
2: 9 what thou oughtest to **d** unto him; 6213
2:23 God **d** so to me, and more also, 6213
2:31 **D** as he hath said, and fall upon him, 6213
2:38 the king hath said, so will thy servant **d.** 6213
3:28 of God *was* in him, to **d** judgment. 6213
5: 8 I will **d** all thy desire concerning timber 6213
8:32 **d,** and judge thy servants, condemning 6213
8:39 **d,** and give to every man according to his 6213
8:43 **d** according to all that the stranger calleth 6213
8:43 to fear thee, as **d** thy people Israel; NIH
9: 1 desire which he was pleased to **d,** 6213
9: 4 to **d** according to all that I have 6213
10: 9 he thee king, to **d** judgment and justice. 6213
11:12 Notwithstanding in thy days I will not **d** it 6213
11:33 to **d** *that* which *is* right in mine eyes, 6213
11:38 **d** that *is* right in my sight, to keep my 6213
12: 6 How **d** you advise that *I* may answer this NIH
12:27 If this people go up to **d** sacrifice in 6213
14: 8 **d** *that* only which *was* right in mine eyes; 6213
17:13 Fear not; go *and* **d** as thou hast said: 6213
17:18 What have I to **d** with thee, O thou man NIH
18:34 said, **D** *it* **the second time**. And they did 8138
18:34 said, **D** *it* **the third time**. And they did *it* 8027
19: 2 So let the gods **d** *to me,* and more also, 6213
20: 9 send for to thy servant at the first I will **d:** 6213
20: 9 this thing I may not **d.** 6213
20:10 The gods **d** so unto me, and more also, 6213
20:24 this thing, Take the kings away, 6213
22:22 and prevail also: go forth, and **d** so. 6213
2Ki 2: 9 unto Elisha, Ask what I shall **d** for thee, 6213
3:13 king of Israel, What have I to **d** with thee? NIH
4: 2 said unto her, What shall I **d** for thee? 6213
4:16 of God, **d** not lie unto thine handmaid. NIH
4:28 my lord? did I not say, **D** not deceive me? NIH
5:13 *if* the prophet had bid thee **d** *some* great NIH
6:15 Alas, my master, how shall we **d?** 6213
6:27 he said, *If* the LORD **d** not help thee, NIH
6:31 he said, God **d** so and more also to me, 6213

2Ki 7: 9 they said one to another, We **d** not well: 6213
8:12 Because I know the evil that thou wilt **d** 6213
8:13 a dog, that he should **d** this great thing? 6213
9:18 said, What hast thou to **d** with peace? NIH
9:19 What hast thou to **d** with peace? NIH
10: 5 and will **d** all that thou shalt bid us; 6213
10: 5 **d** thou *that* which *is* good in thine eyes. 6213
10:19 for I have a great sacrifice *to* **d** to Baal; NIH
11: 5 This *is* the thing that ye shall **d;** 6213
17:12 said unto them, Ye shall not **d** this thing. 6213
17:15 that *they* should not **d** like them. 6213
17:17 sold themselves to **d** evil in the sight of 6213
17:34 Unto this day they **d** after the former 6213
17:34 neither **d** they after their statutes, 6213
17:36 worship, and to him shall ye **d** sacrifice. NIH
17:37 you, ye shall observe to **d** for evermore; 6213
17:41 did their fathers, *so* **d** they unto this day. 6213
18:12 and would not hear *them,* nor **d** *them.* 6213
19:31 the zeal of the LORD *of hosts* shall **d** this. 6213
20: 9 that the LORD will **d** the thing that he 6213
21: 8 only if they will observe to **d** according to 6213
21: 9 Manasseh seduced them to **d** more evil 6213
22: 9 it into the hand of them that **d** the work, 6213
22:13 **d** according unto all that which is written 6213
1Ch 11:19 that *I* should **d** this *thing:* shall I drink 6213
12:32 the times, to know what Israel ought to **d;** 6213
13: 4 the congregation said that *they* would **d** 6213
16:21 He suffered no man to **d** them **wrong:** 6231
16:22 and **d** my prophets no **harm.** 7489
16:40 to **d** according to all that is written in NIH
17: 2 unto David, **D** all that *is* in thine heart; 6213
17:23 for ever, and **d** as thou hast said. 6213
19:13 let the LORD **d** *that* which *is* good in his 6213
21: 8 **d** **away** the iniquity of thy servant; 5674
21:10 one of them, that I may **d** *it* unto thee. 6213
21:23 let my lord the king **d** *that* which *is* good 6213
28: 7 if he be constant to **d** my commandments 6213
28:10 for the sanctuary: be strong, and **d** *it.* 6213
28:20 and of good courage, and **d** *it:* fear not, 6213
29:19 to **d** all *these things,* and to build 6213
2Ch 6:23 **d,** and judge thy servants, by requiting 6213
6:33 **d** according to all that the stranger calleth 6213
7:17 according to all that I have commanded 6213
9: 8 over them, to **d** judgment and justice. 6213
14: 4 and to **d** the law and the commandment. 6213
18:21 shalt also prevail: go out, and **d** *even* so. 6213
19: 6 said to the judges, Take heed what ye **d** 6213
19: 7 **d** *it:* for *there is* no iniquity with 6213
19: 9 Thus shall ye **d** in the fear of the LORD, 6213
19:10 this **d,** and ye shall not trespass. 6213
20:12 against us; neither know we what to **d:** 6213
22: 3 mother was his counsellor to **d** wickedly. 7561
23: 4 This *is* the thing that ye shall **d;** A third 6213
25: 8 thou *wilt* go, **d** *it,* be strong for the battle: 6213
25: 9 what *shall we* **d** for the hundred talents 6213
30:12 heart to **d** the commandment of the king 6213
32:10 Whereon **d** ye trust, that ye abide in NIH
33: 8 they will take heed to **d** all that I have 6213
33: 9 to err, *and* to **d** worse than the heathen, 6213
34:16 was committed to thy servants, they **d** *it.* 6213
34:21 to **d** after all that is written in this book. 6213
35: 6 that *they* may **d** according to the word of 6213
35:21 saying, What have I to **d** with thee, NIH
Ezr 4: 2 as ye **d;** and we **d** sacrifice unto him 2076
4: 2 we **d** **sacrifice** unto him since the days of 2076
4: 3 You have nothing to **d** with us to build a NIH
4:22 Take heed now that ye fail not to **d** this: 5648
6: 8 Moreover I make a decree what ye shall **d** 5648
7:10 to **d** *it,* and to teach in Israel statutes and 6213
7:18 to **d** with the rest of the silver and gold, 5648
7:18 and gold, *that* **d** after the will of your God. 5648
7:21 **d** make a decree to all the treasurers NIH
7:26 whosoever will not **d** the law of thy God, 5648
10: 4 with thee: be of good courage, and **d** *it.* 5648
10: 5 to swear that *they* should **d** according to 6213
10:11 God of your fathers, and **d** his pleasure: 6213
10:12 As thou hast said, so must we **d.** 6213
Ne 1: 9 keep my commandments, and **d** them; 6213
2:12 had put in my heart to **d** at Jerusalem: 6213
2:19 and said, What *is* this thing that ye **d?** 6213
4: 2 and said, What **d** these feeble Jews? 6213
5: 9 Also I said, It *is* not good that ye **d:** ought 6213
5:12 of them; so will we **d** as thou sayest. 6213
5:12 that *they* should **d** according to this 6213
6: 2 But they thought to **d** me mischief. 6213
6:13 **d** so, and sin, and *that* they might have 6213
9:24 *they* might **d** with them as they would. 6213
9:29 (which if a man **d,** he shall live in them;) 6213
10:29 all the commandments of the LORD our 6213
13:17 What evil thing *is* this that ye **d,** 6213
13:21 if ye **d** *so* **again,** I will lay hands on you. 8138
13:27 hearken unto you to **d** all this great evil, NIH
Est 1: 8 *they* should **d** according to every man's 6213
1:15 What shall we **d** unto the queen Vashti 6213
3:11 to **d** with them as it seemeth good to thee. 6213
4:11 **d** know, that whosoever, *whether* man or NIH
5: 5 that *he* may **d** as Esther hath said. 6213
5: 8 I will **d** to morrow as the king hath said. 6213
6: 6 To whom would the king delight to **d** 6213
6:10 and **d** *even* so to Mordecai the Jew, 6213
7: 5 that durst presume in his heart to **d** so? 6213
9:13 **d** to morrow also according unto *this* 6213
9:23 Jews undertook to **d** as they had begun, NIH
Job 6: 4 terrors of God **d** set *themselves* in array NIH
6:26 **D** ye imagine to reprove words, NIH

Job 7:20 what shall I **d** unto thee, O thou preserver 6466
9:13 the proud helpers **d** stoop under him. NIH
10: 2 I will say unto God, **D** not condemn me; NIH
11: 8 *It is* as high as heaven; what canst thou **d?** 6466
13: 2 What ye know, *the same* I know also. NIH
13: 9 man mocketh another, **d** ye *so* mock him? NIH
13:10 if ye **d** secretly accept persons. NIH
13:14 Wherefore **d** I take my flesh in my teeth, NIH
13:20 Only **d** not two *things* unto me: then will NIH
15: 3 speeches wherewith he can **d** no **good?** 3276
15:12 thee away? and what **d** thine eyes wink at, NIH
16: 4 I also could speak as ye **d:** if your soul NIH
17:10 *for* you all, **d** you return, and come now: NIH
19:22 Why **d** ye persecute me as God, and are NIH
20: 2 Therefore **d** my thoughts cause me to NIH
21: 7 Wherefore **d** the wicked live, become old, NIH
21:29 the way? and **d** ye not know their tokens, NIH
22:17 and what can the Almighty **d** for them? 6466
24: 1 *d* they that know him not see his days? NIH
31:14 What then shall I **d** when God riseth up? 6213
32: 9 neither **d** the aged understand judgment. NIH
34:10 from God, *that he should* **d** wickedness; NIH
34:12 Yea, surely God will not **d** wickedly, 7561
34:32 if I have done iniquity, I will **d** no **more.** 3254
36:28 Which the clouds **d** drop and distil upon NIH
37:12 that they may **d** whatsoever he 6467
37:24 Men **d** therefore fear him: he respecteth NIH
39: 1 canst thou mark when the hinds **d** calve? NIH
41: 8 him, remember the battle, **d** no **more.** 3254
42: 2 I know that thou **canst d** every *thing,* 3201
Ps 2: 1 Why **d** the heathen rage, and the people NIH
7: 1 O LORD my God, in thee **d** I put my trust: NIH
11: 3 be destroyed, what can the righteous **d?** 6466
12: 2 *and* with a double heart **d** they speak. NIH
16: 1 O God: for in thee **d** I put my trust. NIH
25: 1 Unto thee, O LORD, **d** I lift up my soul. NIH
25: 5 my salvation; on thee **d** I wait all the day. NIH
31: 1 In thee, O LORD, **d** I put my trust; let me NIH
34:10 The young lions **d** lack, and suffer hunger: NIH
34:14 Depart from evil, and **d** good; seek peace, 6213
34:16 of the LORD *is* against them that **d** evil, 6213
36: 3 he hath left off to be wise, *and* to **d** **good.** 3190
37: 3 Trust in the LORD, and **d** good; 6213
37: 8 fret not thyself in any wise to **d** **evil.** 7489
37:27 Depart from evil, and **d** good; and dwell 6213
38:15 For in thee, O LORD, **d** I hope: thou wilt NIH
40: 8 I delight to **d** thy will, O my God: yea, 6213
41: 7 against me **d** they devise my hurt. NIH
50:16 What hast thou to **d** to declare my 3807.1
51:18 **D** good in thy good pleasure unto Zion: 3190
56: 4 I will not fear what flesh can **d** unto me. 6213
56:11 I will not be afraid what man can **d** unto 6213
58: 1 **D** ye indeed speak righteousness, NIH
58: 1 **d** ye judge uprightly, O ye sons of men? NIH
60:12 Through God we shall **d** valiantly: for he 6213
64: 4 suddenly **d** they shoot at him, and fear not. NIH
71: 1 In thee, O LORD, **d** I put my trust: let me NIH
75: 1 Unto thee, O God, **d** we give thanks, NIH
75: 1 give thanks, *unto thee* **d** we give thanks: NIH
80:12 all they which pass by the way **d** pluck NIH
82: 3 **d** **justice** to the afflicted and needy. 6663
83: 9 **D** unto them as *unto* the Midianites; as *to* 6213
86: 4 for unto thee, O Lord, **d** I lift up my soul. NIH
89:50 I **d** bear in my bosom *the reproach of* NIH
92: 7 all the workers of iniquity **d** flourish; NIH
95:10 It *is* a people that **d** err in *their* heart, NIH
103:18 remember his commandments to **d** them. 6213
103:20 in strength, that **d** his commandments, 6213
103:21 ye ministers of his, that **d** his pleasure. 6213
104:20 wherein all the beasts of the forest **d** creep NIH
105:14 He suffered no man to **d** them **wrong:** 6231
105:15 and **d** my prophets no **harm.** 7489
107:23 in ships, that **d** business in great waters; 6213
108:13 Through God we shall **d** valiantly: for he 6213
109:21 **d** thou for me, O GOD the Lord, for thy 6213
111:10 a good understanding have all they that **d** 6213
118: 6 I will not fear: what can man **d** unto me? 6213
119: 3 They also **d** no iniquity: they walk in his 6466
119:21 which **d** err from thy commandments. NIH
119:35 commandments; for therein **d** I delight. NIH
119:83 the smoke; *yet* **d** I not forget thy statutes. NIH
119:109 in my hand: yet **d** I not forget thy law. NIH
119:113 I hate *vain* thoughts: but thy law **d** I love. NIH
119:132 as thou **usest** to **d** unto those that love 4941
119:141 despised: *yet* **d** I not forget thy precepts. NIH
119:153 and deliver me: for I **d** not forget thy law. NIH
119:157 *yet* **d** I not decline from thy testimonies. NIH
119:163 hate and abhor lying: *but* thy law **d** I love. NIH
119:164 Seven *times* a day **d** I praise thee because NIH
119:176 for I **d** not forget thy commandments. NIH
125: 4 **D** **good,** O LORD, unto *those that be* 2895
129: 8 Neither **d** they which go by say, NIH
130: 5 soul doth wait, and in his word **d** I hope. NIH
131: 1 I exercise myself in great *matters,* NIH
137: 6 If I **d** not remember thee, let my tongue NIH
139:21 **D** not I hate them, O LORD, that hate NIH
143: 8 in the morning; for in thee **d** I trust: NIH
143:10 Teach me to **d** thy will; for thou *art* my NIH
Pr 2:14 Who rejoice to **d** evil, *and* delight in 6213
3:27 it is in the power of thine hand to **d** 6213
6: 3 **D** this now, my son, and deliver thyself, 6213
6:30 *Men* **d** not despise a thief, if he steal to NIH
8:13 way, and the froward mouth, **d** I hate. NIH
10:23 *It is* as sport to a fool to **d** mischief: but a 6213
14:22 **D** they not err that devise evil? but mercy NIH

Pr
17: 7 not a fool: much less **d** lying lips a prince. NIH
19: 7 All the brethren of the poor **d** hate him: NIH
19: 7 how much more **d** his friends go far from NIH
19:19 yet thou must **d** it **again**. 3254+5750
20:30 so **d** stripes the inward parts of the belly. NIH
21: 3 To **d** justice and judgment *is* more 6213
21: 7 because they refuse to **d** judgment. 6213
21:15 *It is* joy to the just to **d** judgment: but 6213
24: 8 He that deviseth to **d evil** shall be called a 7489
24:29 I will **d** so to him as he hath done to me: 6213
25: 8 lest *thou know not* what to **d** in the end 6213
28:12 When righteous *men* **d** rejoice, *there is* NIH
31:12 She will **d** him good and not evil all 1580

Ecc
2: 3 which they should **d** under the heaven all 6213
2:11 on the labour that I had laboured to **d**: 6213
2:12 for what *can* the man **d** that cometh after NIH
3:12 *a man* to rejoice, and to **d** good in his life. 6213
4: 8 neither *saith he*, For whom **d** I labour, NIH
5: 1 for they consider not that *they* **d** evil. 6213
6: 6 he seen no good: **d** not all go to one place? NIH
8:11 sons of men is fully set in them to **d** evil. 6213
8:12 Though a sinner **d** evil an hundred *times,* 6213
9:10 Whatsoever thy hand findeth to **d**, *do it* 6213
9:10 hand findeth to do, **d** it with thy might; 6213
10:10 he not whet the edge, then must he put NIH
11: 5 *nor* how the bones **d** *grow* in the womb NIH

SS
1: 3 therefore **d** the virgins love thee. NIH
8: 8 what shall we **d** for our sister in the day 6213

Isa
1:16 from before mine eyes; cease to **d evil**; 7489
1:17 Learn to **d well**; seek judgment, relieve 3190
5: 5 will tell you what I *will* **d** to my vineyard: 6213
9:13 neither **d** they seek the LORD of hosts. NIH
10: 3 what will ye **d** in the day of visitation, 6213
10:11 her idols, so to Jerusalem and her idols? 6213
14:21 *that* they **d** not rise, nor possess the land, NIH
19:15 the head or tail, branch or rush, may **d**. 6213
19:21 that day, and shall **d** sacrifice and oblation; 5647
23: 4 neither **d** I nourish up young men, NIH
24: 4 haughty people of the earth **d** languish. NIH
24: 7 all the merryhearted **d** sigh. NIH
24:18 and the foundations of the earth **d** shake. NIH
27: 3 I the LORD **d** keep it; I will water it every NIH
28:21 that *he may* **d** his work, his strange work; NIH
29:13 with their lips **d** honour me, NIH
29:14 I will proceed to **d a marvellous work** 6381
37:32 the zeal of the LORD of hosts shall **d** this. 6213
38: 7 that the LORD will **d** this thing that he 6213
38:19 he shall praise thee, as I **d** *this* day: NIH
41:23 yea, **d good**, or do evil, that we may be 3190
41:23 yea, do good, or do **d evil**, that we may be 7489
42: 9 come to pass, and new *things* **d** I declare: NIH
42:16 These things will I **d** unto them, 6213
43:19 I will **d** a new *thing*; now it shall spring 6213
45: 7 create evil: I the LORD **d** all these *things.* 6213
46:10 shall stand, and I will **d** all my pleasure: 6213
46:11 to pass; I have purposed *it,* I will also **d** it. 6213
48:11 will I **d** *it:* for how should *my name* be 6213
48:14 he will **d** his pleasure on Babylon, 6213
55: 2 Wherefore **d** ye spend money for *that* NIH
56: 1 Keep ye judgment, and **d** justice: 6213
57: 4 against whom **d** ye sport yourselves? NIH
58: 4 ye shall not fast as *ye* **d** this day, to make NIH
64: 6 we all **d** fade as a leaf; and our iniquities, NIH
65: 8 so will I **d** for my servants' sakes, that *I* 6213

Jer
2: 8 and walked after *things that* **d** not profit. NIH
2:18 now what hast thou to **d** in the way of 6213
2:18 what hast thou to **d** in the way of Assyria, NIH
4:22 they *are* wise to **d evil**, but to do good 7489
4:22 but to **d good** they have no knowledge. 3190
4:30 when thou art spoiled, what wilt thou **d**? 6213
5:28 the right of the needy they not judge. NIH
5:31 and what will ye **d** in the end thereof? 6213
7:10 We are delivered to **d** all these 6213
7:14 Therefore will I **d** unto *this* house, which 6213
7:17 Seest thou not what they **d** in the cities of 6213
7:19 **D** they provoke me to anger? saith NIH
7:19 *d they* not *provoke* themselves to NIH
8: 8 How **d** ye say, We *are* wise, and the law NIH
8:14 Why **d** we sit still? assemble yourselves, NIH
9: 7 for how shall I **d** for the daughter of my 6213
10: 5 for they cannot **d evil**, neither also *is it in* 7489
10: 5 evil, neither also *is it* in them to **d good**. 3190
11: 4 Obey my voice, and **d** them, 6213
11: 6 the words of this covenant, and **d** them. 6213
11: 8 which I commanded *them* to **d**; 6213
11:15 What **hath** my beloved to **d** in mine 3807.1
12: 5 how wilt thou **d** in the swelling of Jordan? 6213
13:12 We not certainly know that every bottle NIH
13:23 *then* may ye also **d good**, that are 3190
13:23 do good, that are accustomed to **d evil**. 7489
14: 7 against us, **d** thou *it* for thy name's sake: 6213
14:21 **D** not abhor *us*, for thy name's sake, NIH
14:21 **d** not disgrace the throne of thy glory: NIH
17:22 neither **d** ye any work, but hallow ye 6213
17:24 the sabbath day, to **d** no work therein; 6213
18: 6 Israel, cannot I **d** with you as this potter? 6213
18: 8 will repent of the evil that I thought to **d** 6213
18:10 If it **d** evil in my sight, that *it* obey not my 6213
18:12 we will every one **d** the imagination of his 6213
19:12 Thus will I **d** unto this place, saith 6213
22: 3 **d** no **wrong**, do no violence, 3238
22: 3 do no wrong, **d** no **violence**, 2554
22: 4 For if ye **d** this thing **indeed**, then 6213+6213
22:15 **d** judgment and justice, *and then it was* 6213
22:17 for oppression, and for violence, to **d** *it.* 6213

Jer
23:24 **D** not I fill heaven and earth? saith NIH
23:32 **d** tell them, and cause my people to err by NIH
25: 6 of your hands; and I will **d** you no hurt. NIH
26: 3 which I purpose to **d** unto them because 6213
26:14 **d** with me as seemeth good and meet 6213
28: 6 the LORD **d** so: the LORD perform thy 6213
29:32 the good that I will **d** for my people, 6213
30: 6 **d** I see every man *with* his hands NIH
31:20 I earnestly remember him still: NIH
32:23 **d** all that thou commandedst them to **d**: 6213
32:35 that *they* should **d** this abomination, 6213
32:40 turn away from them, to **d** them **good**; 3190
32:41 I will rejoice over them to **d** them good, 2895
33: 9 which shall hear all the good that I **d** unto 6213
33:18 and to **d** sacrifice continually. 6213
36: 3 the evil which I purpose to **d** unto them; 6213
38: 5 for the king *is not he that* **can d** *any* thing 3201
39:12 and look well to him, and **d** him no harm; 6213
39:12 unto him even as he shall say unto thee. 6213
40:16 son of Kareah, Thou shalt not **d** this thing: 6213
42: 2 a few of many, as thine eyes **d** behold us:) NIH
42: 3 may walk, and the thing that we may **d**. 6213
42: 5 if we **d** not even according to all things 6213
42:20 so declare unto us, and we will **d** *it.* 6213
44: 4 this abominable thing that I hate. 6213
44:17 will **certainly d** whatsoever thing 6213+6213
50:15 upon her; as she hath done, **d** unto her. 6213
50:21 **d** according to all that I have commanded 6213
50:29 to all that she hath done, **d** unto her: 6213
51:47 that I will **d judgment** upon the graven 6485
51:52 that I will **d judgment** upon her graven 6485
51:55 when her waves **d** roar like great waters, NIH

La
1: 4 The ways of Zion **d** mourn, because NIH
1:22 **d** unto them, as thou hast done unto me 5953
2:11 Mine eyes **d** fail with tears, my bowels NIH

Eze
2: 4 I **d** send thee unto them; and thou shalt NIH
5: 9 will in thee that which I have not done, 6213
5: 9 whereunto I will not **d** any more the like, 6213
6:10 *that* I have not said in vain that *I* would **d** 6213
7:27 I will **d** unto them after their way, 6213
8: 6 Son of man, seest thou what they **d**? 6213
8: 9 the wicked abominations that they **d** 6213
8:12 of the house of Israel **d** in the dark, 6213
8:13 see great*er* abominations that they **d**. 6213
11:20 and keep mine ordinances, and **d** them: 6213
15: 3 wood be taken thereof to **d** *any* work? 6213
16: 5 pitied thee, to **d** any of these unto thee, 6213
18: 5 and **d** that which is lawful and right, 6213
18: 5 that which is lawful and right, he shall 6213
20:11 which *if* a man **d**, he shall even live in 6213
20:13 which *if* a man **d**, he shall even live in 6213
20:19 and keep my judgments, and **d** them; 6213
20:21 neither kept my judgments to **d** them, 6213
20:21 which *if* a man **d**, he shall even live in 6213
21:24 that in all your doings your sins **d** appear; NIH
22:14 the LORD have spoken *it,* and will **d** *it.* 6213
23:30 *I will* **d** these *things* unto thee, because 6213
23:48 all women may be taught not to **d** after 6213
24:14 I will **d** *it;* I will not go back, neither will 6213
24:22 shall **d** as I have done: ye shall not cover 6213
24:24 to all that he hath done shall ye **d**: 6213
25: 8 Because that Moab and Seir **d** say, Behold, NIH
25:14 they shall **d** in Edom according to mine 6213
33: 9 if he **d** not turn from his way, he shall die NIH
33:14 and **d** that which is lawful and right; 6213
33:19 **d** that which is lawful and right, he shall 6213
33:31 hear thy words, but they will not **d** them: 6213
33:32 they hear thy words, but they **d** them not. 6213
34: 2 Woe *be to* the shepherds of Israel that **d** 1961
35:11 I will even **d** according to thine anger, 6213
35:15 it was desolate, so will I **d** unto thee: 6213
36:11 will **d better** *unto* you than at your 2895
36:22 I **d** not *this* for your sakes, O house of 6213
36:27 ye shall keep my judgments, and **d** *them.* 6213
36:32 Not for your sakes **d** I *this,* saith the Lord 6213
36:36 the LORD have spoken *it,* and I will **d** *it*; 6213
36:37 of by the house of Israel, to **d** *it* for them; 6213
37:24 and observe my statutes, and **d** them. 6213
37:28 the heathen shall know that I the LORD **d** NIH
39:17 to my sacrifice that I **d** sacrifice for you, NIH
43:11 all the ordinances thereof, and **d** them. 6213
44:13 to **d the office of a priest** unto me, 3547
45:20 thou shalt **d** the seventh *day* of the month 6213
45:25 shall he **d** the like in the feast *of* the seven 6213

Da
3:14 and Abed-nego, **d** not ye serve my gods, NIH
4:26 shalt have known that the heavens **d** rule. NIH
9:18 for we **d** not present our supplications NIH
9:19 O Lord, forgive; O Lord, hearken and **d**; 6213
11: 3 dominion, and **d** according to his will. 6213
11:16 he that cometh against him shall **d** 6213
11:17 upright ones with him; thus shall he **d**: 6213
11:24 he shall **d** that which his fathers have not 6213
11:27 these kings' hearts *shall be* to **d mischief**, 4827
11:28 he shall **d exploits**, and return to his own 6213
11:30 so shall he **d**; he shall even return, 6213
11:32 such as **d wickedly** against the covenant 7561
11:32 the people that **d** know their God shall be NIH
11:32 their God shall be strong, and **d** *exploits.* NIH
11:36 the king shall **d** according to his will; 6213
11:39 Thus shall he **d** in the most strong holds 6213
12:10 tried; but the wicked shall **d wickedly**. 7561

Hos
4:18 their rulers *with* shame **d** love, Give ye. NIH
6: 4 O Ephraim, what shall I **d** unto thee? 6213
6: 4 Judah, what shall I **d** unto thee? for your 6213
7:10 they **d** not return to the LORD their God, NIH

Hos
7:15 yet **d** they imagine mischief against me. NIH
9: 5 What will ye **d** in the solemn day, 6213
10: 3 what then should a king **d** to us? 6213
10:15 So shall Beth-el **d** unto you because of NIH
12: 1 **d** make a covenant with the Assyrians, NIH
14: 8 What **have** I to **d** any more **with** idols? 3807.1

Joel
1:18 How **d** the beasts groan! the herds of NIH
2:21 rejoice: for the LORD will **d** great things. 6213
2:22 for the pastures of the wilderness **d** spring, NIH
2:22 fig tree and the vine **d** yield their strength. NIH
3: 4 Yea, and what have ye to **d** with me, 6213

Am
3: 7 Surely the Lord GOD will **d** nothing, 6213
3:10 For they know not to **d** right, saith 6213
4:12 Therefore thus will I **d** unto thee, O Israel: 6213
4:12 *and* because I will **d** this unto thee, 6213

Jnh
1:11 unto him, What shall we **d** unto thee, NIH
3:10 he had said that he would **d** unto them; 6213
4: 9 he said, I **d well** to be angry, *even* unto 3190

Mic
2: 3 against this family **d** I devise an evil, NIH
2: 7 **d** not my words do good to him that NIH
2: 7 do not my words **d good** to him that 3190
2:11 walking *in* the spirit and falsehood **d** lie, NIH
6: 8 to **d** justly, and to love mercy, and to walk 6213
7: 3 That *they* may **d** evil with both hands NIH

Na
1: 9 What **d** ye imagine against the LORD? NIH
1:12 in their heart, The LORD will not **d good**, 3190
1:12 will not do good, neither will he **d evil**. 7489
3: 5 the midst thereof; he will not **d** iniquity: 6213
3:13 The remnant of thee shall not **d** iniquity, 6213

Zep

Hag
2: 3 how **d** ye see it now? *is it* not in your eyes NIH
2:12 with his skirt **d** touch bread, or pottage, NIH

Zec
1: 5 and the prophets, **d** they live for ever? NIH
1: 6 Like as the LORD of hosts thought to **d** 6213
1:21 said I, What come these to **d**? And he 6213
5:10 with me, Whither **d** these bear the ephah? NIH
8:15 in these days to **d well** unto Jerusalem 3190
8:16 These *are* the things that ye shall **d**; 6213
9:12 even to day **d** I declare *that* I will render NIH
12: 7 the glory of the inhabitants of Jerusalem **d** NIH

Mal
1:10 **d** ye kindle *fire* on mine altar for nought. NIH
2: 2 because ye **d** not lay *it* to heart. NIH
2:10 why **d** we deal treacherously every man NIH
4: 1 all the proud, yea, and all that **d** wickedly, 6213
4: 3 I *shall* **d** *this,* saith the LORD of hosts. 6213

Mt
5: 6 Blessed *are* they which **d** hunger and NIG
5:15 Neither **d** men light a candle, and put it NIG
5:19 but whosoever shall **d** and teach *them*, 4160
5:44 **d** good to them that hate you, and pray 4160
5:46 **d** not even the publicans the same? 4160
5:47 what **d** ye more *than others?* do not even 4160
5:47 what do ye more *than others?* **d** not even 4160
6: 1 Take heed that *ye* **d** not your alms before 4160
6: 2 **d** not sound a trumpet before thee, NIG
6: 2 as the hypocrites **d** in the synagogues and 4160
6: 7 as the heathen **d**: for they think that they NIG
6:20 thieves **d** not break through nor steal: NIG
6:26 for they sow not, neither **d** they reap, NIG
6:28 grow; they toil not, neither **d** they spin: NIG
6:32 (For after all these *things* **d** the Gentiles NIG
7:12 ye would that men should **d** to you, 4160
7:12 should do to you, **d** ye even so to them: 4160
7:16 **D** *men* gather grapes of thorns, or figs of NIG
8: 9 to my servant, **D** this, and he doeth *it.* 4160
8:29 What have we to **d** with thee, Jesus, NIG
9:14 Why **d** we and the Pharisees fast oft, NIG
9:17 Neither **d** *men* put new wine into old NIG
9:28 Believe ye that I am able to **d** this? 4160
11: 3 should come, or **d** we look for another? NIG
11: 4 shew John again *those things* which ye **d** NIG
12: 2 thy disciples **d** *that* which is not lawful to 4160
12: 2 is not lawful to **d** upon the sabbath day. 4160
12:12 Wherefore it is lawful to **d** well on 4160
12:27 by whom **d** your children cast *them* out? NIG
12:50 For whosoever shall **d** the will of my 4160
13:13 they hear not, neither **d** they understand. NIG
13:41 that offend, and them which **d** iniquity; 4160
14: 2 mighty works **d** shew forth themselves in NIG
15: 2 Why **d** thy disciples transgress the tradition NIG
15: 3 Why **d** you also transgress NIG
15: 9 But in vain they **d** worship me, teaching NIG
15:17 **D** not ye yet understand, that whatsoever NIG
16: 9 **D** ye not yet understand, neither NIG
16:11 How *is it that* ye **d** not understand that I NIG
16:13 Whom **d** men say that I the Son of man NIG
17:25 of whom **d** the kings of the earth take NIG
18:10 in heaven their angels **d** always behold NIG
18:35 So likewise shall my heavenly Father **d** 4160
19:16 Good Master, what good *thing* shall I **d**, 4160
19:18 Jesus said, Thou shalt **d** no murder, NIG
20:13 and said, Friend, I **d** thee no wrong: NIG
20:15 Is it not lawful for me to **d** what I will 4160
20:32 said, What will ye *that* I shall **d** unto you? 4160
21:21 ye shall not only **d** this which is done to 4160
21:24 you by what authority I **d** these *things.* 4160
21:27 Neither tell I you by what authority I **d** 4160
21:40 what will he **d** unto those husbandmen? 4160
22:29 and said unto them, Ye **d** err, NIG
23: 3 they bid you observe, *that* observe and **d**; 4160
23: 3 and do; but **d** not ye after their works: 4160
23: 3 after their works: for they say, and **d** not. 4160
23: 5 all their works they **d** for to be seen of 4160
26:72 with an oath, I **d** not know the man. NIG
27:19 thou nothing to **d** with that just *man:* NIG
27:22 What shall I **d** then with Jesus which is 4160

Mk
1:24 what have we to **d** with thee, *thou* Jesus NIG

D

Mk	1:27 the unclean spirits, and they **d** obey him.	NIG
	2:18 Why **d** the disciples of John and of	NIG
	2:24 why **d** they on the sabbath day *that* which	4160
	3: 4 Is it lawful to **d good** on the sabbath days,	15
	3: 4 do good on the sabbath days, or to **d** evil?	2554
	3:35 For whosoever shall **d** the will of God,	4160
	5: 7 said, What have I to **d** with thee, Jesus,	NIG
	6: 5 And he could there **d** no mighty work,	4160
	6:14 mighty works **d** shew forth themselves in	NIG
	7: 7 Howbeit in vain **d** they worship me,	4160
	7: 8 and many other such like *things* ye **d**.	4160
	7:12 ye suffer him no more to **d** ought for	4160
	7:13 and many such like *things* **d** ye.	4160
	7:18 **D** ye not perceive, that whatsoever *thing*	NIG
	8:18 hear ye not? and **d** ye not remember?	NIG
	8:21 How *is it that* ye **d** not understand?	NIG
	8:27 unto them, Whom **d** men say that I am?	NIG
	9:22 thou canst **d** any *thing*, have compassion	4160
	9:39 there is no *man* which shall **d** a miracle	NIG
	10:17 what shall I **d** that I may inherit eternal	4160
	10:19 **D** not commit adultery, Do not kill,	NIG
	10:19 commit adultery, **D** not kill, Do not steal,	NIG
	10:19 commit adultery, Do not kill, **D** not steal,	NIG
	10:19 **D** not bear false witness, Defraud not,	NIG
	10:35 we would that thou shouldest **d** for us	4160
	10:36 What would ye that I should **d** for you?	4160
	10:51 What wilt thou *that* I should **d** unto thee?	4160
	11: 3 if any *man* say unto you, Why **d** ye this?	4160
	11: 5 unto them, What **d** ye, loosing the colt?	NIG
	11:26 But if ye **d** not forgive, neither will your	NIG
	11:28 who gave thee this authority to **d** these	4160
	11:29 I will tell you by what authority I **d** these	NIG
	11:33 Neither **d** I tell you by what authority I do	NIG
	11:33 Neither do I tell you by what authority I **d**	4160
	12: 9 therefore the lord of the vineyard **d**?	4160
	12:24 **D** ye not therefore err, because ye know	NIG
	12:27 of the living: ye therefore **d** greatly err.	4160
	13:11 ye shall speak, neither **d** ye premeditate:	NIG
	14: 7 whensoever ye will ye may **d** them good:	4160
	15: 8 *him to* **d** as he had ever done unto them.	NIG
	15:12 *that* I shall **d** *unto him* whom ye call	4160
Lk	2:27 to **d** for him after the custom of the law,	4160
	3:10 him, saying, What shall we **d** then?	4160
	3:11 he that hath meat, let him **d** likewise.	4160
	3:12 said unto him, Master, what shall we **d**?	4160
	3:14 of him, saying, And what shall we **d**?	4160
	3:14 he said unto them, **D** violence to no man,	4160
	4:23 in Capernaum, **d** also here in thy country.	4160
	4:34 what have we to **d** with thee, *thou* Jesus	NIG
	5:30 Why **d** ye eat and drink with publicans	NIG
	5:33 Why **d** the disciples of John fast often,	NIG
	6: 2 Why **d** ye *that* which is not lawful to do	4160
	6: 2 Why do ye *that* which is not lawful to **d**	4160
	6: 9 Is it lawful on the sabbath days to **d good**,	15
	6: 9 the sabbath days to do good, or to **d** evil?	2554
	6:11 with another what they might **d** to Jesus.	4160
	6:27 **d** good to them which hate you,	4160
	6:31 as ye would that men should **d** to you,	4160
	6:31 do to you, **d** ye also to them likewise.	4160
	6:33 if ye **d good** to them which do good to	15
	6:33 if ye do good to them which **d good** to	15
	6:33 have ye? for sinners also **d** *even* the same.	4160
	6:35 and **d** good, and lend, hoping for nothing	15
	6:44 For of thorns *men* **d** not gather figs, nor	NIG
	6:46 Lord, and **d** not *the things* which I say?	NIG
	7: 4 he was worthy for whom he should **d**	3930
	7: 8 to my servant, **D** this, and he doeth *it*.	4160
	8:21 which hear the word of God, and **d** it.	4160
	8:28 What have I to **d** with thee, Jesus,	NIG
	10:11 cleaveth on us, we **d** wipe off against you:	NIG
	10:25 what shall I **d** to inherit eternal life?	4160
	10:28 answered right: this **d**, and thou shalt live.	4160
	10:37 Jesus unto him, Go, and **d** thou likewise.	4160
	11:19 by whom **d** your sons cast *them* out?	NIG
	11:39 **d** ye Pharisees make clean the outside	NIG
	12: 4 after that have no more that *they* can **d**.	NIG
	12:17 saying, What shall I **d**, because I have no	NIG
	12:18 he said, This will I **d**: I will pull down	NIG
	12:26 be not able to **d** *that thing which is* least,	NIG
	12:30 For all these *things* **d** the nations of	NIG
	12:56 how *is it that* ye **d** not discern this time?	NIG
	13:32 and I **d** cures to day and to morrow,	2005
	15:29 Lo, these many years **d** I serve thee,	NIG
	16: 3 said within himself, What shall I **d**?	NIG
	16: 4 I am resolved what to **d**, that, when I am	NIG
	17:10 have done *that* which was our duty to **d**.	4160
	18:18 what shall I **d** to inherit eternal life?	4160
	18:20 **D** not commit adultery, Do not kill,	NIG
	18:20 commit adultery, **D** not kill, Do not steal,	NIG
	18:20 commit adultery, Do not kill, **D** not steal,	NIG
	18:20 Do not steal, **D** not bear false witness,	NIG
	18:41 What wilt thou *that* I shall **d** unto thee?	4160
	19:31 Why **d** ye loose *him?* thus shall ye say	NIG
	19:48 And could not find what they might **d**:	NIG
	20: 8 Neither tell I you by what authority I **d**	4160
	20:13 the lord of the vineyard, What shall I **d**?	4160
	20:15 the lord of the vineyard **d** unto them?	4160
	22:19 for you: this **d** in remembrance of me.	4160
	22:23 which of them it was that should **d** this	4238
	23:31 For if they **d** these *things* in a green tree,	4160
	23:34 for they know not what they **d**.	4160
	24:38 and why **d** thoughts arise in your hearts?	NIG
Jn	2: 4 Woman, what have I to **d** with thee?	NIG
	2: 5 Whatsoever he saith unto you, **d** it.	4160
	3: 2 for no *man* can **d** these miracles that thou	4160

Jn	3:11 We speak that we **d** know, and testify	NIG
	4:34 My meat is to **d** the will of him that sent	4160
	5:19 The Son can **d** nothing of himself,	4160
	5:19 himself, but what he seeth the Father **d**:	4160
	5:30 can of mine own self **d** nothing: as I hear,	4160
	5:36 the same works that I **d**, bear witness of	4160
	5:45 **D** not think that I will accuse you to	NIG
	6: 6 for he himself knew what he would **d**.	4160
	6:28 said they unto him, What shall we **d**,	4160
	6:38 not to **d** mine own will, but the will of	4160
	7: 4 If thou **d** *things*, shew thyself to	4160
	7:17 If any *man* will **d** his will, he shall know of	4160
	7:26 **D** the rulers know indeed that this is	NIG
	7:31 will he **d** moe miracles than these which	NIG
	8:11 said unto her, Neither **d** I condemn thee:	NIG
	8:28 I am *he*, and *that* I **d** nothing of myself,	4160
	8:29 I **d** always those *things* that please him.	4160
	8:38 ye **d** *that* which ye have seen with your	4160
	8:39 ye would **d** the works of Abraham.	4160
	8:41 Ye **d** the deeds of your father.	4160
	8:43 Why **d** ye not understand my speech?	NIG
	8:44 and the lusts of your father ye will **d**.	4160
	8:46 I say the truth, why **d** ye not believe me?	NIG
	8:49 honour my Father, and ye **d** dishonour me.	NIG
	9:15 upon mine eyes, and I washed, and **d** see.	NIG
	9:16 How can a man *that is* a sinner **d** such	4160
	9:33 were not of God, he could **d** nothing.	4160
	10:25 the works that I **d** in my Father's name,	4160
	10:32 for which of those works **d** ye stone me?	NIG
	10:37 If I **d** not the works of my Father,	4160
	10:38 But if I **d**, though ye believe not me,	4160
	11:12 Lord, if he sleep, he shall **d well**.	4982
	11:47 Pharisees a council, and said, What **d** we?	4160
	13: 7 What I **d** thou knowest not now;	4160
	13:15 that ye should **d** as I have done to you.	4160
	13:17 these *things*, happy are ye if ye **d** them.	4160
	13:27 unto him, That thou doest, **d** quickly.	4160
	14:12 the works that I **d** shall he do also;	4160
	14:12 the works that I do shall he **d** also;	4160
	14:12 and *greater works* than these shall he **d**;	4160
	14:13 ye shall ask in my name, that will I **d**,	4160
	14:14 ask any *thing* in my name, I will **d** *it*.	4160
	14:31 gave me commandment, *even* so I **d**.	4160
	15: 5 for without me ye can **d** nothing.	4160
	15:14 if ye **d** whatsoever I command you.	4160
	15:21 all these *things* will they **d** unto you for	4160
	16: 3 And these *things* will they **d** unto you,	4160
	16:19 **D** ye inquire among yourselves of that I	NIG
	16:31 Jesus answered them, **D** ye now believe?	NIG
	17: 4 the work which thou gavest me to **d**.	4160
	21:21 Jesus, Lord, and what *shall* this *man* **d**?	4160
Ac	1: 1 all that Jesus began both to **d** and teach,	4160
	2:11 we **d** hear them speak in our tongues	NIG
	2:37 Men *and* brethren, what shall we **d**?	4160
	4:16 Saying, What shall we **d** to these men?	4160
	4:28 For to **d** whatsoever thy hand and thy	4160
	5:35 heed to yourselves what ye intend to **d**	4238
	7:26 why **d** ye wrong one to another?	NIG
	7:51 ears, ye **d** always resist the Holy Ghost:	NIG
	7:51 Holy Ghost: as your fathers *did,* so **d** ye.	NIG
	9: 6 Lord, what wilt thou have me to **d**?	4160
	9: 6 it shall be told thee what thou must **d**.	4160
	10: 6 shall tell thee what thou oughtest to **d**.	4160
	14:15 why **d** ye these *things?* We also are men	4160
	15:29 if ye keep yourselves, ye shall **d** well.	4238
	15:36 word of the Lord, *and see* how they **d**.	2192
	16:20 Jews, **d** exceedingly trouble our city,	NIG
	16:28 a loud voice, saying, **D** thyself no harm:	4238
	16:30 and said, Sirs, what must I **d** to be saved?	4160
	16:37 and now **d** they thrust us out privily?	NIG
	17: 7 all **d** contrary to the decrees of Cesar,	4238
	19:36 to be quiet, and to **d** nothing rashly.	4238
	21:23 **D** therefore this that we say to thee:	4160
	22:10 And I said, What shall I **d**, Lord?	4160
	22:10 *things* which are appointed for thee to **d**.	4160
	23:21 But **d** not thou yield unto them: for there	4160
	24:10 I **d** the more cheerfully answer for myself:	NIG
	24:16 And herein **d** I exercise myself, to have	4160
	25: 9 willing to **d** the Jews a pleasure,	2698
	26: 9 that *I* ought to **d** many *things* contrary to	4238
	26:20 to God, and **d** works meet for repentance.	4238
Ro	1:28 **d** those *things* which are not convenient;	4160
	1:32 not only **d** the same, but have pleasure in	4160
	1:32 but have pleasure in them that **d** them.	4238
	2: 3 that judgest them which **d** such *things,*	4238
	2: 8 and **d** not obey the truth,	NIG
	2:14 **d** by nature the *things* contained in the	4160
	3: 8 Let us **d** evil, that good may come?	4160
	3:31 **D** we then make void the law through	NIG
	7:15 For *that* which I **d** I allow not: for what I	2716
	7:15 for what I would, that **d** I not; but what I	4238
	7:15 that do I not; but what I hate, that **d** I.	4160
	7:16 If then I **d** that which I would not,	4160
	7:17 Now then it is no more I that **d** it,	2716
	7:19 For the good that I would I **d** not: but	4160
	7:19 but the evil which I would not, that I **d**.	4238
	7:20 Now if I **d** that I would not, it is no more	4160
	7:20 it is no more I that **d** it, but sin that	2716
	7:21 then a law, that, when I would **d** good,	4160
	8: 3 For what the law could not **d**, in that it	102
	8: 5 For they that are after the flesh **d** mind	NIG
	8:13 if ye through the Spirit **d** mortify the deeds	NIG
	8:25 not, *then* **d** we with patience wait for *it*.	NIG
	12: 8 he that giveth, *let him* **d** *it* with simplicity;	NIG
	12:15 Rejoice with them that **d** rejoice,	NIG

Ro	13: 3 **d** *that which is* good, and thou shalt have	4160
	13: 4 But if thou **d** *that which is* evil, be afraid;	4160
	15:31 That I may be delivered from them that **d**	NIG
1Co	5:12 For **what have I to** **d** to judge them	1473+5101
	5:12 **d** not ye judge them that are within?	NIG
	6: 2 **D** ye not know that the saints shall judge	NIG
	6: 7 Why **d** ye not rather take wrong? why do	NIG
	6: 7 why **d** ye not rather *suffer yourselves* to be	NIG
	6: 8 you **d** wrong, and defraud, and that *your*	NIG
	7:36 need so require, let him **d** what he will,	4160
	9: 3 Mine answer to them that **d** examine me	NIG
	9:13 **D** ye not know that they which minister	NIG
	9:17 For if I **d** this *thing* willingly, I have a	4238
	9:23 And this I **d** for the gospel's sake, that I	4160
	9:25 they **d** *it* to obtain a corruptible crown;	NIG
	10:22 **D** we provoke the Lord to jealousy?	NIG
	10:31 ye eat, or drink, or whatsoever ye **d**,	4160
	10:31 ye do, **d** all to the glory of God.	4160
	11:24 for you: this **d** in remembrance of me.	4160
	11:25 this **d** ye, as oft as ye drink *it*, in	NIG
	11:26 ye **d** shew the Lord's death till he come.	NIG
	12:30 all speak with tongues? do all interpret?	NIG
	12:30 do all speak with tongues? **d** all interpret?	NIG
	15:29 Else what shall they **d** which are baptized	4160
	15:35 and with what body **d** they come?	NIG
	16: 1 to the churches of Galatia, even so **d** ye.	4160
	16: 5 for I **d** pass through Macedonia.	NIG
	16:10 worketh the work of the Lord, as I also **d**.	NIG
2Co	1:17 **d** I purpose according to the flesh,	NIG
	3: 1 **D** we begin again to commend ourselves?	NIG
	5: 4 For we that are in *this* tabernacle **d** groan,	NIG
	7: 8 letter, I **d** not repent, though I did repent:	NIG
	8: 1 we **d** you to wit of the grace of God	NIG
	8:10 not only to **d**, but also to be forward a	4160
	8:23 Whether *any* **d** *inquire* of Titus, *he is* my	NIG
	10: 3 in the flesh, we **d** not war after the flesh:	NIG
	10: 7 **D** ye look on *things* after the outward	NIG
	11: 8 taking wages *of them*, to **d** you service.	4314
	11:12 what I **d**, that I will do, that I may cut	4160
	11:12 what I do, that I will **d**, that I may cut	4160
	12:19 but *we* **d** all *things*, dearly beloved,	4160
	13: 7 Now I pray to God that ye **d** no evil;	4160
	13: 7 but that ye should **d** *that which is* honest,	4160
	13: 8 For we **can d** nothing against the truth,	1410
Gal	1:10 For if I now persuade men, or God?	NIG
	1:10 or **d** I seek to please men? for if I yet	NIG
	2:10 the same which I also was forward to **d**.	4160
	2:14 of Gentiles, and not **as d the Jews**,	2452
	2:14 thou the Gentiles to **live as d the Jews**?	2450
	2:21 I **d** not frustrate the grace of God: for if	NIG
	3:10 written in the book of the law to **d** them.	4160
	4:21 be under the law, **d** ye not hear the law?	NIG
	5: 3 that he is a debtor to **d** the whole law.	4160
	5:11 why **d** I yet suffer persecution?	NIG
	5:17 ye cannot **d** the *things* that ye would.	4160
	5:21 that they which **d** such *things* shall not	4238
	6:10 let us **d** good unto all *men*, especially	2038
Eph	3:20 Now unto him that is able to **d** exceeding	4160
	6: 9 ye masters, **d** the same *things* unto them,	4160
	6:21 *and how* I **d**, Tychicus, a beloved brother	4238
Php	1:18 I therein rejoice, yea, and will rejoice.	NIG
	2:13 both to will and to **d** of *his* good pleasure.	1754
	2:14 **D** all *things* without murmurings and	4160
	2:18 *For* the same *cause* **d** ye joy,	NIG
	3: 8 of all *things*, and **d** count *them but* dung,	NIG
	3:13 this one *thing I* **d**, forgetting those *things*	NIG
	4: 9 received, and heard, and seen in me, **d**:	4238
	4:13 I **can d** all *things* through Christ which	2480
Col	1: 9 since the day we heard *it*, **d** not cease to	NIG
	3:13 even as Christ forgave you, so also **d** ye.	NIG
	3:17 And whatsoever ye **d** in word or deed,	4160
	3:17 deed, **d** all in the name of the Lord Jesus,	4160
	3:23 And whatsoever ye **d**, **d** *it* heartily, as to	4160
	3:23 **d** *it* heartily, as to the Lord, and not unto	2038
1Th	3:12 all *men*, even as we **d** towards you:	NIG
	4:10 indeed ye **d** it towards all the brethren	NIG
	4:11 and to **d** your own *business*, and to work	4238
	5: 6 Therefore let us not sleep, as **d** others;	NIG
	5:11 and edify one another, even as also ye **d**.	4160
	5:24 *is* he that calleth you, who also will **d** *it*.	4160
2Th	3: 4 that ye both **d** and will do the things	4160
	3: 4 will **d** *the things* which we command	4160
1Ti	1: 4 than godly edifying which is in faith: *so* **d**.	NIG
	2: 2 rather **d** *them* **service**, because they are	1398
	6:18 they **d** good, that *they* be rich in good	14
2Ti	2:23 knowing that they **d** gender strifes.	NIG
	3: 8 so **d** these also resist the truth:	NIG
	4: 5 **d** the work of an evangelist, make full	NIG
	4: 9 **D** thy **diligence** to come shortly unto me:	4704
	4:21 **D** thy **diligence** to come before winter.	4704
Phm	1:14 But without thy mind would I **d** nothing;	NIG
	1:19 I will repay *it*: albeit I **d** not say to thee	NIG
	1:21 knowing that thou wilt also **d** more than	4160
Heb	3:10 and said, They **d** alway err in *their* heart;	NIG
	3: 4 For we which have believed **d** enter into	NIG
	4:13 eyes of him with whom we **have to d**.	3056
	6: 3 And this will we **d**, if God permit.	4160
	6:10 ministered to the saints, and **d** minister.	NIG
	6:11 we desire that every one of you **d** shew	NIG
	10: 7 it is written of me,) to **d** thy will, O God.	4160
	10: 9 said he, Lo, I come to **d** thy will, O God.	4160
	11: 3 were not made of *things* which **d** appear.	NIG
	11:29 Egyptians assaying to **d** were drowned.	2983
	13: 6 I will not fear what man shall **d** unto me.	NIG
	13:16 But to **d good** and to communicate forget	2140

Heb	13:17 that they may **d** it with joy, and not with	4160
	13:19 But I beseech *you* the rather to **d** this,	4160
	13:21 Make you perfect in every good work to **d**	4160
Jas	1:16 **D** not err, my beloved brethren.	NIG
	2: 6 **D** not rich *men* oppress you, and draw	NIG
	2: 7 **D** not they blaspheme *that* worthy name	NIG
	2: 8 love thy neighbour as thyself, ye **d** well;	4160
	2:11 **D** not commit adultery, said also, Do not	NIG
	2:11 not commit adultery, said also, **D** not kill.	NIG
	2:12 So speak ye, and so **d**, as they that shall	4160
	4: 5 **D** ye think that the scripture saith in vain,	NIG
	4:15 will, we shall live, and **d** this, or that.	NIG
	4:17 Therefore to him that knoweth to **d** good,	4160
	5:19 if any of you **d** err from the truth,	NIG
1Pe	1:21 Who by him **d** believe in God, that raised	NIG
	2:14 and *for* the praise of them that **d** well.	17
	2:20 but if, when ye **d** well, and suffer *for it,*	15
	3: 6 as long as ye **d** well, and are not afraid	15
	3:11 Let him eschew evil, and **d** good; let him	4160
	3:12 face of the Lord *is* against them that **d**	4160
	4:11 *let him* **d** *it* as of the ability which God	NIG
2Pe	1:10 if ye **d** these *things*, ye shall never fall:	4160
	1:19 whereunto ye **d** well that ye take heed,	4160
	3:16 as *they* **d** also the other scriptures,	NIG
1Jn	1: 6 in darkness, we lie, and **d** not the truth:	4160
	2: 3 hereby we **d** know that we know him,	NIG
	3:22 **d** those *things* that are pleasing in his	4160
	4:14 testify that the Father sent the Son *to be*	NIG
	5:16 I **d** not say that he shall pray for it.	NIG
3Jn	1: 6 after a godly sort, thou shalt **d** well:	4160
Rev	2: 5 fallen, and repent, and **d** the first works;	4160
	3: 9 say they are Jews, and are not, but **d** lie;	NIG
	3:18 *that* the shame of thy nakedness **d** not	NIG
	9:19 had heads, and with them they **d** hurt.	NIG
	13:14 had power to **d** in the sight of the beast;	4160
	14:13 and their works **d** follow them.	NIG
	19:10 And he said unto me, See *thou* **d** it not:	NIG
	21:24 the kings of the earth **d** bring their glory	NIG
	22: 9 Then saith he unto me, See *thou* **d** it not:	NIG
	22:14 *are* they that **d** his commandments,	4160

DO BEST See STUDY

DOCTOR (1) [DOCTORS]

Ac	5:34 a Pharisee, named Gamaliel, a **d of law**,	3547

DOCTORS (2) [DOCTOR]

Lk	2:46 sitting in the midst of the **d**, both hearing	1320
	5:17 of the law sitting *by*, which were come	3547

DOCTRINE (51) [DOCTRINES]

Dt	32: 2 My **d** shall drop as the rain, my speech	3948
Job	11: 4 My **d** *is* pure, and I am clean in thine	3948
Pr	4: 2 For I give you good **d**, forsake you not	3948
Isa	28: 9 whom shall he make to understand **d**?	8052
	29:24 and they that murmured shall learn **d**.	3948
Jer	10: 8 and foolish: the stock *is* a **d** of vanities.	4148
Mt	7:28 the people were astonished at his **d**:	1322
	16:12 but of the **d** of the Pharisees and *of*	1322
	22:33 heard *this*, they were astonished at his **d**.	1322
Mk	1:22 And they were astonished at his **d**: for he	1322
	1:27 What new **d** *is* this? for with authority	1322
	4: 2 by parables, and said unto them in his **d**,	1322
	11:18 all the people was astonished at his **d**,	1322
	12:38 And he said unto them in his **d**,	1322
Lk	4:32 And they were astonished at his **d**:	1322
Jn	7:16 My **d** is not mine, but his that sent me.	1322
	7:17 he shall know of the **d**, whether it be of	1322
	18:19 asked Jesus of his disciples, and of his **d**.	1322
Ac	2:42 continued stedfastly in the apostles' **d**	1322
	5:28 ye have filled Jerusalem with your **d**,	1322
	13:12 being astonished at the **d** of the Lord.	1322
	17:19 saying, May we know what this new **d**,	1322
Ro	6:17 *that* form of **d** which was delivered you.	1322
	16:17 offences contrary to the **d** which ye have	1322
1Co	14: 6 by knowledge, or by prophesying, or by **d**?	1322
	14:26 hath a **d**, hath a tongue, hath a revelation,	1322
Eph	4:14 and carried about with every wind of **d**,	1319
1Ti	1: 3 charge some that *they* **teach** no other **d**,	2085
	1:10 other *thing that* is contrary to sound **d**;	1319
	4: 6 up in the words of faith and of good **d**,	1319
	4:13 to reading, to exhortation, to **d**.	1319
	4:16 Take heed unto thyself, and unto the **d**;	1319
	5:17 they who labour in the word and **d**.	1319
	6: 1 of God and *his* **d** be not blasphemed.	1319
	6: 3 to the **d** which is according to godliness;	1319
2Ti	3:10 But thou hast fully known my **d**, manner	1319
	3:16 and *is* profitable for **d**, for reproof,	1322
	4: 2 exhort with all longsuffering and **d**.	1319
	4: 3 when they will not endure sound **d**;	1319
Tit	1: 9 that he may be able by sound **d** both to	1319
	1: 1 thou *the things* which become sound **d**:	1319
	2: 7 in *d* shewing uncorruptness, gravity,	1319
	2:10 that they may adorn the **d** of God our	1319
Heb	6: 1 Therefore leaving the principles of the **d**	3056
	6: 2 Of the **d** of baptisms, and of laying on of	1322
2Jn	1: 9 abideth not in the **d** of Christ, hath not	1322
	1: 9 He that abideth in the **d** of Christ, he hath	1322
	1:10 come unto you, and bring not this **d**,	1322
Rev	2:14 thou hast there them that hold the **d** of	1322
	2:15 So hast thou also them that hold the **d** of	1322
	2:24 as many as have not this **d**, and which	1322

DOCTRINES (5) [DOCTRINE]

Mt	15: 9 teaching for **d** the commandments of men	1319

Mk	7: 7 teaching for **d** the commandments of men	1319
Col	2:22 after the commandments and **d** of men?	1319
1Ti	4: 1 heed to seducing spirits, and **d** of devils;	1319
Heb	13: 9 carried about with divers and strange **d**.	1322

DODAI (1)

1Ch	27: 4 the course of the second month *was* **D**	1737

DODANIM (2)

Ge	10: 4 Elishah, and Tarshish, Kittim, and **D**.	1721
1Ch	1: 7 Elishah, and Tarshish, Kittim, and **D**.	1721

DODAVAH (1)

2Ch	20:37 Eliezer the son of **D** of Mareshah	1735

DODAVAHU See DODAVAH

DODO (5)

Jdg	10: 1 of Puah, the son of **D**, a man of Issachar;	1734
2Sa	23: 9 after him *was* Eleazar the son of **D**	1734
	23:24 Elhanan the son of **D** *of* Beth-lehem,	1734
1Ch	11:12 after him *was* Eleazar the son of **D**,	1734
	11:26 Elhanan the son of **D** of Beth-lehem,	1734

DOE See HIND

DOEG (6)

1Sa	21: 7 his name *was* **D**, an Edomite, the chiefest	1673
	22: 9 answered **D** the Edomite, which *was* set	1673
	22:18 king said to **D**, Turn thou, and fall upon	1673
	22:18 **D** the Edomite turned, and he fell upon	1673
	22:22 that day, when **D** the Edomite *was* there,	1673
Ps	52: T when **D** the Edomite came and told Saul,	1673

DOER (8) [DO]

Ge	39:22 they did there, he was the **d** of *it*.	6213
2Sa	3:39 the Lord shall reward the **d** of evil	6213
Ps	31:23 and plentifully rewardeth the proud **d**.	6213
Pr	17: 4 A **wicked d** giveth heed to false lips;	7489
2Ti	2: 9 as an **evil d**, *even* unto bonds;	2557
Jas	1:23 any be a hearer of the word, and not a **d**,	4163
	1:25 but a **d** of the work, this *man* shall be	4163
	4:11 thou art not a **d** of the law, but a judge.	4163

DOERS (6) [DO]

2Ki	22: 5 let them deliver it into the hand of the **d**	6213
	22: 5 let them give it to the **d** of the work	6213
Job	8:20 neither will he help the **evil d**:	7489
Ps	101: 8 *I* may cut off all wicked **d** from the city	6466
Ro	2:13 but the **d** of the law shall be justified.	4163
Jas	1:22 But be ye **d** of the word, and not hearers	4163

DOEST (45) [DO]

Ge	4: 7 If thou **d** well, *shalt thou* not be accepted?	NIH
	4: 7 if thou **d** not well, sin lieth at the door.	NIH
	21:22 God *is* with thee in all that thou **d**:	6213
Ex	18:14 *is* this thing that thou **d** to the people?	6213
	18:17 him, The thing that thou **d** is not good.	6213
Dt	12:28 when thou **d** *that which* is good and right	6213
	14:29 all the work of thine hand which thou **d**.	6213
	15:18 thy God shall bless thee in all that thou **d**.	6213
Jdg	11:27 but thou **d** me wrong to war against me:	6213
2Sa	3:25 coming in, and to know all that thou **d**.	6213
1Ki	2: 3 thou mayest prosper in all that thou **d**,	6213
	19: 9 unto him, What **d** thou here, Elijah?	3807.1
	19:13 and said, What **d** thou here, Elijah?	3807.1
	20:22 and mark, and see what thou **d**:	6213
Job	9:12 who will say unto him, What **d** thou?	6213
	35: 6 If thou sinnest, what **d** thou against him?	6466
	35: 6 be multiplied, what **d** thou unto him?	6213
Ps	49:18 praise thee, when thou **d** well to thyself.	3190
	77:14 Thou *art* the God that **d** wonders: thou	6213
	86:10 wondrous *things*: thou *art* God alone.	6213
	119:68 Thou *art* good, and **d** good; teach me thy	2895
Ecc	8: 4 and who may say unto him, What **d** thou?	6213
Jer	11:15 when thou **d** evil, then thou rejoicest.	7451
	15: 5 shall go aside to ask **how** thou **d**?	7965+3807.1
Eze	12: 9 said unto thee, What **d** thou?	6213
	16:30 seeing thou **d** all these *things*, the work	6213
	24:19 these *things are* to us, that thou **d** *so*?	6213
Da	4:35 his hand, or say unto him, What **d** thou?	5648
Jnh	4: 4 said the Lord, **D** thou well to be angry?	NIH
	4: 9 **D** thou well to be angry for the gourd?	NIH
Mt	6: 2 Therefore when thou **d** *thine* alms, do not	4160
	6: 3 when thou **d** alms, let not thy left hand	4160
	21:23 By what authority **d** thou these *things*?	4160
Mk	11:28 By what authority **d** thou these *things*?	4160
Lk	20: 2 by what authority **d** thou these *things*?	4160
Jn	2:18 unto us, seeing that thou **d** these *things*?	4160
	3: 2 man can do these miracles that thou **d**,	4160
	7: 3 also may see the works that thou **d**.	4160
	13:27 Jesus unto him, That thou **d**, do quickly.	4160
Ac	22:26 saying, Take heed what thou **d**:	4160
Ro	2: 1 for thou that judgest **d** the same *things*.	4238
	2: 3 which do such *things*, and **d** the same,	4160
Jas	2:19 that there is one God; thou **d** well:	4160
3Jn	1: 5 thou faithfully whatsoever thou **d**oest	4160
	1: 5 thou doest faithfully whatsoever thou **d**	2038

DOETH (93) [DO]

Ge	31:12 for I have seen all that Laban **d** unto thee.	6213
Ex	31:14 whosoever **d** *any* work therein, that soul	6213
	31:15 whosoever **d** *any* work in the sabbath	6213
	35: 2 whosoever **d** work therein shall be put to	6213
Lev	4:27 while he **d** somewhat against *any* of	6213
	6: 3 in any of all *these* that a man **d**, sinning	

Lev	23:30 whatsoever soul *it be* that **d** any work in	6213
Nu	15:30 the soul that **d** *ought* presumptuously,	6213
	24:23 Alas, who shall live when God **d** this!	7760
Job	5: 9 Which **d** great *things* and unsearchable;	6213
	9:10 Which **d** great *things* past finding out;	6213
	23:13 *what* his soul desireth, even *that* he **d**.	6213
	24:21 and **d** not **good** to the widow.	3190
	37: 5 great *things* **d** he, which we cannot	6213
Ps	1: 3 and whatsoever he **d** shall prosper.	6213
	14: 1 *there is* none that **d** good.	6213
	14: 3 *there is* none that **d** good, no, not one.	6213
	15: 3 his tongue, nor **d** evil to his neighbour,	6213
	15: 5 He that **d** these *things* shall never be	6213
	52: 1 *there is* none that **d** good.	6213
	53: 1 *there is* none that **d** good, no, not one.	6213
	72:18 of Israel, who only **d** wondrous *things*.	6213
	106: 3 *and* he that **d** righteousness at all times.	6213
	118:15 the right hand of the Lord **d** valiantly.	6213
	118:16 the right hand of the Lord **d** valiantly.	6213
	136: 4 To him who alone **d** great wonders:	6213
Pr	6:32 he *that* **d** it destroyeth his own soul.	6213
	11:17 The merciful man **d** good to his own soul:	1580
	15: 7 but the heart of the foolish **d** not so.	NIH
	17:21 He that begetteth a fool **d** it to his sorrow:	NIH
	17:22 A merry heart **d** good *like* a medicine:	3190
	28:17 A man that **d** violence to the blood of	6231
Ecc	2: 2 *It is* mad: and of mirth, What **d** it?	6213
	3:14 I know that, whatsoever God **d**, it shall	6213
	3:14 God **d** *it*, that *men* should fear before him	6213
	7:20 upon earth, that **d** good, and sinneth not.	6213
	8: 3 for he **d** whatsoever pleaseth him.	6213
Isa	56: 2 Blessed *is* the man *that* **d** this,	6213
Jer	48:10 Cursed *be* he that **d** the work of the Lord	6213
Eze	17:15 shall he escape that **d** such *things?* or	6213
	18:10 *that* **d** the like to *any* one of these *things*,	6213
	18:11 that **d** not any of those *duties*, but even	6213
	18:14 and considereth, and **d** not such like,	6213
	18:24 according to all the abominations that	6213
	18:24 the abominations that the wicked *man* **d**,	6213
	18:27 **d** that which is lawful and right, he shall	6213
Da	4:35 he **d** according to his will in the army of	5648
	9:14 *is* righteous in all his works which he **d**:	6213
Am	9:12 by my name, saith the Lord that **d** this.	6213
Mal	2:17 Every one that **d** evil *is* good in the sight	6213
Mt	6: 3 thy left hand know what thy right hand **d**:	4160
	7:21 he that **d** the will of my Father which is in	4160
	7:24 and **d** them, I will liken him unto a wise	4160
	7:26 and **d** them not, shall be likened unto a	4160
	8: 9 and to my servant, Do this, and he **d** it.	4160
Lk	6:47 me, and heareth my sayings, and **d** them,	4160
	6:49 he that heareth, and **d** not, is like a man	4160
	7: 8 and to my servant, Do this, and he **d** it.	4160
Jn	3:20 For every one that **d** evil hateth the light,	4238
	3:21 But he that **d** truth cometh to the light,	4160
	5:19 for what *things* soever he **d**, these also	4160
	5:19 he doeth, these also the Son likewise.	4160
	5:20 sheweth him all *things* that himself **d**:	4160
	7: 4 For *there is* no *man* that **d** any *thing* in	4160
	7:51 before it hear him, and know what he **d**?	4160
	9:31 of God, and **d** his will, him he heareth.	4160
	11:47 do we? for this man **d** many miracles.	4160
	14:10 that dwelleth in me, he **d** the works.	4160
	15:15 the servant knoweth not what his lord **d**:	4160
	16: 2 will think that he **d** God service.	4374
Ac	15:17 saith the Lord, who **d** all these *things*.	4160
	26:31 This man **d** nothing worthy of death or	4238
Ro	2: 9 upon every soul of man that **d** evil,	2716
	3:12 there is none that **d** good, no, not one.	4160
	10: 5 That the man which **d** those *things* shall	4160
	13: 4 to *execute* wrath upon him that **d** evil.	4238
1Co	6:18 sin that a man **d** is without the body;	4160
	7:37 heart that *he* will keep his virgin, **d** well.	4160
	7:38 that giveth *her* in marriage **d** well;	4160
	7:38 that giveth *her* not in marriage **d** better.	4160
Gal	3: 5 **d** he it by the works of the law, or by	NIG
	3:12 The man that **d** them shall live in them.	4160
Eph	6: 8 that whatsoever good *thing* any man **d**,	4160
Col	3:25 But he that **d** wrong shall receive *for*	91
Jas	4:17 to do good, and **d** *it* not, to him it is sin.	4160
1Jn	2:17 he that **d** the will of God abideth for ever.	4160
	2:29 ye know that every one which **d**	4160
	3: 7 he that **d** righteousness is righteous,	4160
	3:10 whosoever **d** not righteousness is not of	4160
3Jn	1:10 I will remember his deeds which he **d**,	4160
	1:11 He that **d** good is of God: but he that	15
	1:11 but he that **d** evil hath not seen God.	2554
Rev	13:13 he **d** great wonders, so that he maketh	4160

DOG (15) [DOG'S, DOGS]

Ex	11: 7 of Israel shall not a **d** move his tongue,	3611
Dt	23:18 the hire of a whore, or the price of a **d**,	3611
Jdg	7: 5 as a **d** lappeth, him shalt thou set by	3611
1Sa	17:43 the Philistine said unto David, *Am* I a **d**,	3611
	24:14 thou pursue? after a dead **d**, after a flea.	3611
2Sa	9: 8 thou shouldest look upon such a dead **d**	3611
	16: 9 Why should this dead **d** curse my lord	3611
2Ki	8:13 Hazael said, But what, *is* thy servant a **d**,	3611
Ps	22:20 my darling from the power of the **d**.	3611
	59: 6 they make a noise like a **d**, and go round	3611
	59:14 *and* let them make a noise like a **d**,	3611
Pr	26:11 As a **d** returneth to his vomit, *so* a fool	3611
	26:17 *is* like one that taketh a **d** by the ears.	3611
Ecc	9: 4 for a living **d** *is* better than a dead lion.	3611
2Pe	2:22 The **d** *is* turned to his own vomit again;	2965

D

DOG'S (2) [DOG]

2Sa	3: 8 of Ish-bosheth, and said, *Am* I a **d** head,	3611	
Isa	66: 3 sacrificeth a lamb, *as if* he cut off a **d** neck	3611	

DOGS (24) [DOG]

Ex	22:31 *beasts* in the field; ye shall cast it to the **d.**	3611
1Ki	14:11 of Jeroboam in the city shall the **d** eat;	3611
	16: 4 dieth of Baasha in the city shall the **d** eat;	3611
	21:19 In the place where **d** licked the blood of	3611
	21:19 blood of Naboth shall **d** lick thy blood,	3611
	21:23 The **d** shall eat Jezebel by the wall of	3611
	21:24 Him that dieth of Ahab in the city the **d**	3611
	22:38 the **d** licked up his blood; and they	3611
2Ki	9:10 the **d** shall eat Jezebel in the portion of	3611
	9:36 the portion of Jezreel shall **d** eat the flesh	3611
Job	30: 1 to have set with the **d** of my flock.	3611
Ps	22:16 For **d** have compassed me: the assembly	3611
	68:23 and the tongue of thy **d** in the same.	3611
Isa	56:10 they *are* all dumb **d**, they cannot bark;	3611
	56:11 *they are* greedy **d** *which* can never have	3611
Jer	15: 3 the **d** to tear, and the fowls of the heaven,	3611
Mt	7: 6 Give not that which is holy unto the **d**,	2965
	15:26 the children's bread, and to cast *it* to **d.**	2952
	15:27 yet the **d** eat of the crumbs which fall	2952
Mk	7:27 children's bread, and to cast *it* unto the **d.**	2952
	7:28 yet the **d** under the table eat of	2952
Lk	16:21 the **d** came and licked his sores.	2965
Php	3: 2 Beware of **d**, beware of evil workers,	2965
Rev	22:15 For without *are* **d**, and sorcerers,	2965

DOING (39) [DO]

Ge	31:28 thou hast now done foolishly in *so* **d.**	6213
	44: 5 he divineth? ye have done evil in *so* **d.**	6213
Ex	15:11 in holiness, fearful *in* praises, **d** wonders?	6213
Nu	20:19 without **d** *any* thing *else*, go through on	NIH
Dt	9:18 in wickedly in the sight of the Lord,	6213
1Ki	7:40 So Hiram made an end of **d** all the work	6213
	16:19 For his sins which he sinned in **d** evil in	6213
	22:43 **d** *that* which *was* right in the eyes of	6213
2Ki	21:16 in **d** *that* which *was* evil in the sight of	6213
1Ch	22:16 Arise *therefore*, and be **d**, and the Lord	6213
2Ch	20:32 **d** *that* which *was* right in the sight of	6213
Ezr	9: 1 **d** according to their abominations, *even*	NIH
Ne	6: 3 I *am* a great work, so that I cannot	6213
Job	33:22 *so* **d** my Maker would soon take me away.	4639
Ps	64: 9 for they shall wisely consider of his **d.**	4639
	66: 5 he *is* terrible *in his* **d** toward the children	5949
	118:23 This is the Lord's **d**; it is	854+4480
Isa	56: 2 and keepeth his hand from **d** any evil.	6213
	58:13 *from* thy pleasure on my holy day;	6213
	58:13 shalt honour him, not **d** thine own ways,	6213
Mt	21:42 This is the Lord's **d**, and it is marvellous	1096
	24:46 his lord when he cometh shall find so **d.**	4160
Mk	12:11 This was the Lord's **d**, and it is marvellous	1096
Lk	12:43 his lord when he cometh shall find so **d.**	4160
Ac	10:38 who went about **d** good, and healing all	2109
	24:20 say, if they have found any evil **d** in me,	92
Ro	2: 7 continuance in well **d** seek for glory	2041
	12:20 **d** thou shalt heap coals of fire on his head.	4160
2Co	8:11 perform the **d** of *it;* that as *there was* a	4160
Gal	6: 9 And let us not be weary in well **d**: for in	4160
Eph	6: 6 Christ, the will of God from the heart;	4160
	6: 7 With good will **d** service, as to the Lord,	1398
2Th	3:13 But ye, brethren, be not weary in well **d.**	2569
1Ti	4:16 for in **d** this thou shalt both save thyself,	4160
	5:21 before another, **d** nothing by partiality.	4160
1Pe	2:15 that with well **d** ye may put to silence	15
	3:17 ye suffer for well **d**, than for evil doing.	15
	3:17 ye suffer for well doing, than for evil **d**	2554
	4:19 the keeping of their souls to him in well **d**,	16

DOINGS (51) [DO]

Lev	18: 3 After the **d** of the land of Egypt, wherein	4639
	18: 3 after the **d** of the land of Canaan, whither	4639
Dt	28:20 because of the wickedness of thy **d**,	4611
Jdg	2:19 ceased not from their own **d**, nor from	4611
1Sa	25: 3 the man *was* churlish and evil in his **d**;	4611
2Ch	17: 4 and not after the **d** of Israel.	4639
Ps	9:11 in Zion: declare among the people his **d.**	5949
	77:12 also of all thy work, and talk of thy **d.**	5949
Pr	20:11 Even a child is known by his **d**, whether	4611
Isa	1:16 put away the evil of your **d** from before	4611
	3: 8 and their **d** *are* against the Lord,	4611
	3:10 *him:* for they shall eat the fruit of their **d.**	4611
	12: 4 his name, declare his **d** among the people,	5949
Jer	4: 4 quench *it*, because of the evil of your **d.**	4611
	4:18 thy **d** have procured these *things* unto	4611
	7: 3 Amend your ways and your **d**, and I will	4611
	7: 5 throughly amend your ways and your **d**;	4611
	11:18 know *it:* then thou shewedst me their **d.**	4611
	17:10 *and* according to the fruit of his **d.**	4611
	18:11 and make your ways and your **d** good.	4611
	21:12 quench *it*, because of the evil of your **d.**	4611
	21:14 you according to the fruit of your **d.**	4611
	23: 2 I will visit upon you the evil of your **d**,	4611
	23:22 evil way, and from the evil of their **d.**	4611
	25: 5 from the evil of your **d**, and dwell in	4611
	26: 3 unto them because of the evil of their **d.**	4611
	26:13 now amend your ways and your **d**,	4611
	32:19 and according to the fruit of his **d.**	4611
	35:15 amend your **d**, and go not after other gods	4611
	44:22 because of the evil of your **d**, *and* because	4611
Eze	14:22 and ye shall see their way and their **d.**	5949
	14:23 when ye see their ways and their **d:**	5949
	20:43 all your **d**, wherein ye have been defiled;	5949

Eze	20:44 according to your corrupt **d**, O ye house	5949
	21:24 so that in all your **d** your sins do appear;	5949
	24:14 according to thy **d**, shall they judge thee,	5949
	36:17 defiled it by their own way and by their **d:**	5949
	36:19 and according to their **d** I judged them.	5949
	36:31 your **d** that *were* not good, and shall lothe	4611
Hos	4: 9 for their ways, and reward them their **d.**	4611
	5: 4 They will not frame their **d** to turn unto	4611
	7: 2 now their own **d** have beset them about;	4611
	9:15 for the wickedness of their **d** I will drive	4611
	12: 2 according to his **d** will he recompense	4611
Mic	2: 7 these *his* **d?** do not my words do good	4611
	3: 4 have behaved themselves ill in their **d.**	4611
	7:13 that dwell therein, for the fruit of their **d.**	4611
Zep	3: 7 they rose early, *and* corrupted all their **d.**	5949
	3:11 shalt thou not be ashamed for all thy **d**,	5949
Zec	1: 4 your evil ways, and *from* your evil **d:**	4611
	1: 6 according to our **d**, so hath he dealt with	4611

DOLEFUL (2)

Isa	13:21 their houses shall be full of **d** creatures;	255
Mic	2: 4 lament with a **d** lamentation, *and* say,	5093

DOMINION (62) [DOMINIONS]

Ge	1:26 let them **have d** over the fish of the sea,	7287
	1:28 **have d** over the fish of the sea, and over	7287
	27:40 come to pass when thou shalt have the **d**,	7300
	37: 8 shalt thou **indeed have d** over us?	4910+4910
Nu	24:19 of Jacob shall come *he* that shall have a **d**,	7287
Jdg	5:13 he **made** him that remaineth **have d over**	7287
	5:13 the Lord **made** me **have d over**	7287
	14: 4 for at that time the Philistines **had d** over	4910
1Ki	4:24 he had **d** over all *the region* on *this* side	7287
	9:19 in Lebanon, and in all the land of his **d.**	4475
2Ki	20:13 was nothing in his house, nor in all his **d**,	4475
1Ch	4:22 had the **d** in Moab, and Jashubi-lehem.	1166
	18: 3 as he went to stablish his **d** by the river	3027
2Ch	8: 6 and throughout all the land of his **d**,	4475
	21: 8 revolted from under the **d** of Judah,	3027
Ne	9:28 so that they had the **d** over them:	7287
	9:37 also they have **d** over our bodies,	4910
Job	25: 2 **D** and fear *are* with him, he maketh peace	4910
	38:33 canst thou set the **d** thereof in the earth?	4896
Ps	8: 6 Thou **madest** him to **have d** over the	4910
	19:13 *sins;* let them not **have d** over me:	4910
	49:14 the upright shall **have d** over them in	7287
	72: 8 He shall **have d** also from sea to sea,	7287
	103:22 all his works in all places of his **d:**	4475
	114: 2 Judah was his sanctuary, *and* Israel his **d.**	4475
	119:133 and let not any iniquity **have d** over me.	7980
	145:13 **d** endureth throughout all generations.	4475
Isa	26:13 *other* lords besides thee have **had d over**	1166
	39: 2 was nothing in his house, nor in all his **d.**	4475
Jer	34: 1 the kingdoms of the earth of his **d**,	3027+4475
	51:28 rulers thereof, and all the land of his **d.**	4475
Da	4: 3 his **d** is from generation to generation,	7985
	4:22 and thy **d** to the end of the earth.	7985
	4:34 whose **d** *is* an everlasting dominion,	7985
	4:34 whose dominion *is* an everlasting **d**,	7985
	6:26 That in every **d** of my kingdom *men*	7985
	6:26 and his **d** *shall be* even unto the end.	7985
	7: 6 also four heads; and **d** *was* given to it.	7985
	7:12 the beasts, they had their **d** taken away:	7985
	7:14 there was given him **d**, and glory,	7985
	7:14 his **d** *is* an everlasting dominion,	7985
	7:14 his dominion *is* an everlasting **d**,	7985
	7:26 they shall take away his **d**, to consume	7985
	7:27 the kingdom and, the greatness of **d**	7985
	11: 3 that shall rule *with* great **d**,	4474
	11: 4 nor according to his **d** which he ruled:	4915
	11: 5 he shall be strong above him, and **have d;**	4910
	11: 5 his **d** *shall be* a great dominion.	4475
	11: 5 his dominion *shall be* a great **d.**	4474
Mic	4: 8 unto thee shall it come, even the first **d;**	4475
Zec	9:10 his **d** *shall be* from sea *even* to sea,	4915
Mt	20:25 of the Gentiles **exercise d over** them,	2634
Ro	6: 9 no more; death hath no more **d over** him.	2961
	6:14 For sin shall not have **d** over you: for ye	NIG
	7: 1 how that the law **hath d over** a man,	2961
2Co	1:24 Not for that we **have d over** your faith,	2961
Eph	1:21 and **d**, and every name that is named,	2963
1Pe	4:11 whom be praise and **d** for ever and ever.	2904
	5:11 To him *be* glory and **d** for ever and ever.	2904
Jude	1: 8 despise **d**, and speak evil of dignities.	2963
	1:25 *be* glory and majesty, and power,	2904
Rev	1: 6 to him *be* glory and **d** for ever and ever.	2904

DOMINIONS (2) [DOMINION]

Da	7:27 and all **d** shall serve and obey him.	7985
Col	1:16 or **d**, or principalities, or powers:	2963

DONE (565) [DO]

Ge	3:13 the woman, What *is this that* thou hast **d?**	6213
	3:14 Because thou hast **d** this, thou *art* cursed	6213
	4:10 he said, What hast thou **d?** the voice of	6213
	8:21 any more every *thing* living, as I have **d.**	6213
	9:24 what his younger son had **d** unto him.	6213
	12:18 What *is this that* thou hast **d** unto me?	6213
	18:21 see whether they have **d** altogether	6213
	20: 5 and innocency of my hands have I **d** this.	6213
	20: 9 said unto him, What hast thou **d** unto us?	6213
	20: 9 thou hast **d** deeds unto me that ought not	6213
	20: 9 deeds unto me that ought not to be **d.**	6213
	20:10 sawest thou, that thou hast **d** this thing?	6213
	21:23 according to the kindness that I have **d**	6213

Ge	21:26 I wot not who hath **d** this thing:	6213
	22:16 for because thou hast **d** this thing,	6213
	24:15 before he had **d** speaking, that behold,	3615
	24:19 she had **d** giving him drink, she said,	3615
	24:19 camels also, until they have **d** drinking.	3615
	24:22 to pass, as the camels had **d** drinking,	3615
	24:45 before I had **d** speaking in mine heart,	3615
	24:66 servant told Isaac all things that he had **d.**	6213
	26:10 What *is* this thou hast **d** unto us?	6213
	26:29 as we have **d** unto thee nothing but good,	6213
	27:19 I have **d** according as thou badest me:	6213
	27:45 he forget *that* which thou hast **d** to him:	6213
	28:15 until I have **d** *that* which I have spoken to	6213
	29:25 Laban, What *is this* thou hast **d** unto me?	6213
	29:26 It must not be so **d** in our country,	6213
	30:26 knowest my service which I have **d** thee.	5647
	31:26 Laban said to Jacob, What hast thou **d**,	6213
	31:28 thou hast now **d** foolishly *in so* doing.	5528
	34: 7 which thing ought not to be **d.**	6213
	40:15 also have I **d** nothing that they should	6213
	42:28 What *is this that* God hath **d** unto us?	6213
	44: 5 he divineth? ye have **d** evil *in so* doing.	7489
	44:15 What deed *is this* that ye have **d?**	6213
Ex	1:18 Why have ye **d** this thing, and have saved	6213
	2: 4 afar off, to wit what would be **d** to him.	6213
	3:16 and *seen* that which is **d** to you in Egypt:	6213
	5:23 in thy name, he hath **d evil** to this people;	7489
	10: 2 my signs which I have **d** amongst them;	7760
	12:16 no *manner of* work shall be **d** in them,	6213
	12:16 man must eat, that only may be **d** of you.	6213
	13: 8 *This is* **d** because of that which the Lord	NIH
	14: 5 they said, Why have we **d** this, that we	6213
	18: 1 heard of all that God had **d** for Moses,	6213
	18: 8 law all that the Lord had **d** unto Pharaoh	6213
	18: 9 which the Lord had **d** to Israel,	6213
	21:31 according to this judgment shall it be **d**	6213
	31:15 Six days may work be **d**; but in the	6213
	34:10 such as have not been **d** in all the earth,	1254
	34:33 *till* Moses had **d** speaking with them,	3615
	35: 2 Six days shall work be **d**, but on	6213
	39:43 they had **d** it as the Lord had	6213
	39:43 had commanded, *even* so had they **d** it:	6213
Lev	4: 2 *things* which ought not to be **d)**,	6213
	4:13 they have somewhat against any of	6213
	4:13 *concerning things* which should not be **d**,	6213
	4:22 somewhat through ignorance against	6213
	4:22 *concerning things* which should not be **d**,	6213
	4:27 *things* which ought not to be **d**,	6213
	5:16 **harm** that he hath **d** in the holy *thing,*	2398
	5:17 be by the commandments of the Lord;	6213
	6: 7 all that he hath **d** in trespassing therein.	6213
	8: 5 which the Lord commanded to be **d.**	6213
	8:34 As he hath **d** this day, *so* the Lord hath	6213
	11:32 vessel *it be*, wherein *any* work is **d**,	6213
	18:27 abominations have the men of the land **d**,	6213
Nu	19:22 the Lord for his sin which he hath **d:**	2398
	19:22 the sin which he hath **d** shall be forgiven	2398
	23: 3 Six days shall work be **d**: but the seventh	6213
	24:19 as he hath **d**, so shall it be done to him;	6213
	24:19 as he hath done, so shall it be **d** to him;	6213
	24:20 in a man, so shall it be **d** to him *again.*	5414
	5: 7 shall confess their sin which they have **d:**	6213
	5:27 **d trespass** against her husband,	4603+4604
	12:11 wherein we have **d foolishly**,	2973
	15:11 Thus shall it be **d** for one bullock,	6213
	15:34 it was not declared what should be **d** to	6213
	16:28 for *I have* not **d** *them* of mine own mind.	NIH
	22: 2 saw all that Israel had **d** to the Amorites.	6213
	22:28 unto Balaam, What have I **d** unto thee,	6213
	23:11 unto Balaam, What hast thou **d** unto me?	6213
	27: 4 father be **d away** from among his family,	1639
	32:13 that had evil in the sight of the Lord,	6213
Dt	3:21 your God hath **d** unto these two kings:	6213
	10:21 hath **d** for thee these great and terrible	6213
	12:31 he hateth, have they **d** unto their gods;	6213
	19:19 as he had thought to have **d** unto his	6213
	20:18 which they have **d** unto their gods;	6213
	25: 9 So shall it be **d** unto *that* man that will	6213
	26:14 have **d** according to all that thou hast	6213
	29:24 Wherefore hath the Lord **d** thus unto	6213
	32:27 is high, and the Lord hath not **d** all this.	6466
Jos	5: 8 when they had **d** circumcising all	8552
	7:19 tell me now what thou hast **d**; hide *it* not	6213
	7:20 God of Israel, and thus and thus have I **d:**	6213
	9: 3 heard what Joshua had **d** unto Jericho	6213
	9:24 because of you, and have **d** this thing,	6213
	10: 1 as he had **d** to Jericho and her king,	6213
	10: 1 her king, so he had **d** to Ai and her king;	6213
	10:32 according to all that he had **d** to Libnah.	6213
	10:35 according to all that he had **d** to Lachish.	6213
	10:37 according to all that he had **d** to Eglon;	6213
	10:39 as he had **d** to Hebron, so he did to Debir,	6213
	10:39 he had *also* to Libnah, and to her king.	6213
	22:24 if we have not *rather* **d** it for fear of *this*	6213
	23: 3 your God hath **d** unto all these nations	6213
	23: 8 your God, as ye have **d** unto this day.	6213
	24: 7 your eyes have seen what I have **d** in	6213
	24:20 after that he hath **d** you good.	3190
	24:31 of the Lord, that he had **d** for Israel.	6213
Jdg	1: 7 as I have **d**, so God hath requited me.	6213
	2: 2 not obeyed my voice: why have ye **d** this?	6213
	2:10 yet the works which he had **d** for Israel.	6213
	3:12 they had evil in the sight of the Lord.	6213
	6:29 one to another, Who hath **d** this thing?	6213
	6:29 Gideon the son of Joash hath **d** this thing.	6213

D

Jdg	8: 2 What have I **d** now in comparison of you?	6213
	9:16 if ye have **d** truly and sincerely,	6213
	9:16 have **d** unto him according to the	6213
	9:24 That the cruelty **d** to the threescore and	NIH
	9:48 me do, make haste, *and* do as I *have* **d.**	NIH
	11:37 her father, Let this thing be **d** for me:	6213
	14: 6 his father or his mother what he had **d.**	6213
	15: 6 the Philistines said, Who hath **d** this?	6213
	15: 7 Though ye have **d** this, yet will I be	6213
	15:10 come up, to do to him as he hath **d** to us.	6213
	15:11 what *is* this *that* thou hast **d** unto us?	6213
	15:11 they did unto me, so have I **d** unto them.	6213
	19:30 There was no such *deed* nor seen from	1961
	20:12 What wickedness *is* this that is **d** among	1961
Ru	2:11 that thou hast **d** unto thy mother in law	6213
	3: 3 until he shall have **d** eating and drinking.	3615
	3:16 she told her all that the man had **d** to her.	6213
1Sa	4:16 And he said, What is there **d**, my son?	1961
	6: 9 *then* he hath **d** us this great evil:	6213
	8: 8 **d** since the day that I brought them up	6213
	11: 7 Samuel, so shall it be **d** unto his oxen.	6213
	12:17 which ye have **d** in the sight of the LORD,	6213
	12:20 ye have **d** all this wickedness: yet turn	6213
	12:24 consider how **great things** he hath **d** for	1431
	13:11 Samuel said, What hast thou **d**? And Saul	6213
	13:13 said to Saul, Thou hast **d foolishly:**	5528
	14:43 to Jonathan, Tell me what thou hast **d.**	6213
	17:26 What shall be **d** to the man that killeth	6213
	17:27 So shall it be **d** to the man that killeth	6213
	17:29 David said, What have I now **d**? *Is there*	6213
	19:18 and told him all that Saul had **d** to him.	6213
	20: 1 and said before Jonathan, What have I **d**?	6213
	20:32 shall he be slain? what hath he **d**?	6213
	20:34 because his father had **d** him **shame.**	3637
	24:19 for that thou hast **d** unto me this day.	6213
	25:30 when the LORD shall have **d** to my lord	6213
	26:16 This thing *is* not good that thou hast **d.**	6213
	26:18 for what have I **d**? or what evil *is* in mine	6213
	28: 9 Behold, thou knowest what Saul hath **d,**	6213
	28:17 the LORD hath **d** to him, as he spake by	6213
	28:18 hath the LORD **d** this thing unto thee this	6213
	29: 8 said unto Achish, But what have I **d**?	6213
	31:11 that which the Philistines had **d** to Saul,	6213
2Sa	2: 6 kindness, because ye have **d** this thing.	6213
	3:24 to the king, and said, What hast thou **d**?	6213
	7:21 hast thou **d** all these great things,	6213
	11:27 the thing that David had **d** displeased	6213
	12: 5 the man that hath **d** this *thing* shall surely	6213
	12:21 What thing *is* this that thou hast **d**?	6213
	13:12 for no such thing ought to be **d** in Israel:	6213
	14:20 speech hath thy servant Joab **d** this thing:	6213
	14:21 Joab, Behold now, I have **d** this thing:	6213
	15:24 until all the people had **d** passing out of	8552
	16:10 then say, Wherefore hast thou **d** so?	6213
	21:11 of Aiah, the concubine of Saul, had **d.**	6213
	23:20 of Kabzeel, who had **d** many **acts,**	6467
	24:10 I have sinned greatly *in* that I have **d:**	6213
	24:10 of thy servant; for I have **d** very **foolishly.**	5528
	24:17 Lo, I have sinned, and I have **d wickedly:**	5753
	24:17 these sheep, what have they **d**? let thine	6213
1Ki	1: 6 at any time in saying, Why hast thou **d** so?	6213
	1:27 Is this thing **d** by my lord the king,	1961
	3:12 Behold, I have **d** according to thy word:	6213
	8:47 We have sinned, and have **d perversely,**	5753
	8:66 the LORD had **d** for David his servant,	6213
	9: 8 Why hath the LORD **d** thus unto this land,	6213
	11:11 Forasmuch as this is **d** of thee,	1961
	13:11 the man of God had **d** *that* day in Beth-el:	6213
	14: 9 hast **d** evil above all that were before thee	6213
	14:22 above all that their fathers had **d.**	6213
	15: 3 of his father, which he had **d** before him:	6213
	18:36 *that* I have **d** all these things at thy word.	6213
	19: 1 Ahab told Jezebel all that Elijah had **d,**	6213
	19:20 Go back again: for what have I **d** to thee?	6213
	22:53 according unto all that his father had **d.**	6213
2Ki	4:13 all this care; what *is* to be **d** for thee?	6213
	4:14 he said, What then *is* to be **d** for her?	6213
	5:13 wouldest thou not have **d** *it*? how much	6213
	7:12 shew you what the Syrians have **d** to us.	6213
	8: 4 all the great *things* that Elisha hath **d.**	6213
	10:10 for the LORD hath **d** *that* which he spake	6213
	10:30 Because thou hast **d well** in executing	2895
	10:30 hast **d** unto the house of Ahab according	6213
	15: 3 to all that his father Amaziah had **d:**	6213
	15: 9 sight of the LORD, as his fathers had **d:**	6213
	15:34 to all that his father Uzziah had **d.**	6213
	17: 4 king of Assyria, as *he had* **d** year by year:	NIH
	19:11 the kings of Assyria have **d** to all lands,	6213
	19:25 thou not heard long ago *how* I have **d**	6213
	20: 3 have **d** *that* which *is* good in thy sight.	6213
	21:11 Because Manasseh king of Judah hath **d**	6213
	21:11 hath **d wickedly** above all that	7489
	21:15 Because they have **d** *that* which *was* evil	6213
	23:17 proclaimed these things that thou hast **d**	6213
	23:19 to all the acts that he had **d** in Beth-el.	6213
	23:32 according to all that his fathers had **d.**	6213
	23:37 according to all that his fathers had **d.**	6213
	24: 9 according to all that his father had **d.**	6213
	24:19 according to all that Jehoiakim had **d.**	6213
1Ch	10:11 all that the Philistines had **d** to Saul,	6213
	11:22 man of Kabzeel, who had **d** many **acts;**	6467
	16:12 his marvellous works that he hath **d,**	6213
	17:19 own heart, hast thou **d** all this greatness,	6213
	21: 8 sinned greatly, because I have **d** this	6213
	21: 8 of thy servant; for I have **d** very **foolishly.**	5528

1Ch	21:17 have sinned and **d evil indeed;**	7489+7489
	21:17 *as for* these sheep, what have they **d**?	6213
2Ch	6:37 have **d amiss**, and have dealt wickedly;	5753
	7:21 Why hath the LORD **d** thus unto this land,	6213
	11: 4 man to his house, for this thing is **d** of me.	1961
	16: 9 Herein thou hast **d foolishly:** therefore	5528
	24:16 because he had **d** good in Israel,	6213
	24:22 which Jehoiada his father had **d** to him,	6213
	25:16 because thou hast **d** this, and hast not	6213
	29: 2 to all that David his father had **d.**	6213
	29: 6 **d** *that* which *was* evil in the eyes of	6213
	29:36 the people: for the thing was **d** suddenly.	NIH
	30: 5 they had not **d** *it* of a long *time in such*	6213
	32:13 my fathers have **d** unto all the people of	6213
	32:25 again according to the benefit **d** unto him;	NIH
	32:31 of the wonder that was **d** in the land,	NIH
Ezr	6:12 made a decree; let it be **d** with speed.	5648
	7:21 shall require of you, *it* be **d** speedily,	5648
	7:23 let it be diligently **d** for the house of	5648
	9: 1 when these *things* were **d**, the princes	3615
	10: 3 and let it be according to the law.	6213
Ne	5:19 *according to* all that I have **d** for this	6213
	6: 8 There are no such things **d** as thou sayest,	NIH
	6: 9 weakened from the work, that it be not **d.**	6213
	8:17 day had not the children of Israel **d** so.	6213
	9:33 for thou hast **d** right, but we have done	6213
	9:33 hast done right, but we have **d wickedly:**	7561
	13:14 wipe not out my good deeds that I have **d**	6213
Est	1:16 Vashti the queen hath not **d wrong** to	5753
	2: 1 what she had **d**, and what was decreed	6213
	4: 1 When Mordecai perceived all that was **d,**	6213
	6: 3 dignity hath been **d** to Mordecai for this?	6213
	6: 3 unto him, There is nothing **d** for him.	6213
	6: 6 What shall be **d** unto the man whom	6213
	6: 9 Thus shall it be **d** to the man whom	6213
	6:11 Thus shall it be **d** unto the man whom	6213
	9:12 what have they **d** in the rest of the king's	6213
	9:12 *is* thy request further? and it shall be **d.**	6213
	9:14 the king commanded it so to be **d**: and	6213
Job	21:31 and who shall repay him *what* he hath **d**?	6213
	34:29 whether *it be* **d** against a nation, or	NIH
	34:32 if I have **d** iniquity, I will do no more.	6466
Ps	7: 3 O LORD my God, if I have **d** this; if there	6213
	14: 1 they have **d abominable** works,	8581
	22:31 that *shall* be born, that he hath **d** this.	6213
	33: 4 *is* right; and all his works *are* **d** in truth.	NIH
	33: 9 it was **d**; he commanded, and it stood fast.	NIH
	40: 5 thy wonderful works *which* thou hast **d,**	6213
	50:21 *things* hast thou **d**, and I kept silence;	6213
	51: 4 have I sinned, and **d** *this* evil in thy sight:	6213
	52: 9 because thou hast **d** *it:* and I will wait on	6213
	53: 1 they, and have **d abominable** iniquity:	8581
	66:16 I will declare what he hath **d** for my soul.	6213
	71:19 high, who hast **d** great *things:* O God,	6213
	74: 3 all *that* the enemy hath **d wickedly** in	7489
	78: 4 and his wonderful works that he hath **d.**	6213
	98: 1 for he hath **d** marvellous *things:* his right	6213
	105: 5 his marvellous works that he hath **d;**	6213
	106: 6 committed iniquity, we have **d wickedly.**	7561
	106:21 which had **d** great *things* in Egypt;	6213
	109:27 *is* thy hand; *that* thou, LORD, hast **d** it.	6213
	111: 8 *and are* **d** in truth and uprightness.	6213
	115: 3 he hath **d** whatsoever he pleased.	6213
	119:121 I have **d** judgment and justice: leave me	6213
	119:166 thy salvation, and **d** thy commandments.	6213
	120: 3 or what shall be **d** unto thee, thou false	3254
	126: 2 The LORD hath **d** great things for them.	6213
	126: 3 The LORD hath **d** great things for us;	6213
Pr	3:30 without cause, if he have **d** thee no harm.	1580
	6:16 sleep not, except they have **d mischief;**	7489
	24:29 I will do so to him as he hath **d** to me:	6213
	30:20 and saith, I have **d** no wickedness.	6466
	30:32 If thou hast **d foolishly** in lifting up	5034
	31:29 Many daughters have **d** virtuously,	6213
Ecc	1: 9 which is & *is* that which shall be done:	6213
	1: 9 which is done is that which shall be **d:**	6213
	1:13 all *things* that are **d** under heaven:	6213
	1:14 I have seen all the works that are **d** under	6213
	2:12 *even* that which hath been already **d.**	6213
	4: 1 considered all the oppressions that *are* **d**	6213
	4: 3 who hath not seen the evil work that is **d**	6213
	8: 9 my heart unto every work that is **d**	6213
	8:10 forgotten in the city where they had so **d:**	6213
	8:14 is a vanity which is **d** upon the earth;	6213
	8:16 see the business that is **d** upon the earth:	6213
	8:17 find out the work that is **d** under the sun:	6213
	9: 3 This *is* an evil among all *things* that are **d**	6213
	9: 6 ever in any *thing* that is **d** under the sun.	6213
Isa	5: 4 What could have been **d** more to my	6213
	5: 4 to my vineyard, that I have not **d** in it?	6213
	10:11 as I have **d** unto Samaria and her idols,	6213
	10:13 By the strength of my hand I have **d** *it,*	6213
	12: 5 the LORD; for he hath **d** excellent things:	6213
	24:13 the gleaning grapes when the vintage is **d.**	3615
	25: 1 name; for thou hast **d** wonderful things;	6213
	33:13 Hear, ye *that are* far off, what I have **d;**	6213
	37:11 **d** to all lands by destroying them utterly;	6213
	37:26 thou not heard long ago, *how* I have **d** it;	6213
	38: 3 have **d** *that* which *is* good in thy sight.	6213
	38:15 himself hath **d** *it:* I shall go softly all my	6213
	41: 4 **d** *it*, calling the generations from	6213
	41:20 that the hand of the LORD hath **d** this,	6213
	44:23 for the LORD hath **d** *it:* shout, ye lower	6213
	46:10 times *the things* that are not *yet* **d,**	6213
	48: 5 Mine idol hath **d** them, and my graven	6213

Isa	53: 9 because he had **d** no violence, neither	6213
Jer	2:23 way in the valley, know what thou hast **d:**	6213
	3: 5 and **d** evil *things* as thou couldest.	6213
	3: 6 seen *that* which backsliding Israel hath **d**?	6213
	3: 7 I said after she had **d** all these *things,*	6213
	3:16 visit *it;* neither shall *that* be **d** any more.	6213
	5:13 not in them: thus shall it be **d** unto them.	6213
	7:13 because ye have **d** all these works,	6213
	7:14 and to your fathers, as I have **d** to Shiloh.	6213
	7:30 For the children of Judah have **d** evil in	6213
	8: 6 of his wickedness, saying, What have I **d**?	6213
	11:17 which they have **d** against themselves to	6213
	16:12 ye have **d** worse than your fathers;	6213
	18:13 of Israel hath **d** a very horrible thing.	6213
	22: 8 Wherefore hath the LORD **d** thus unto	6213
	30:15 I have **d** these things unto thee.	6213
	30:24 until he have **d** *it*, and until he have	6213
	31:37 the seed of Israel for all that they have **d,**	6213
	32:23 they have **d** nothing of all that thou	6213
	32:30 the children of Judah have only **d** evil	6213
	32:32 they have **d** to provoke me to anger,	6213
	34:15 now turned, and had **d** right in my sight,	6213
	35:10 according to all that Jonadab our father	6213
	35:18 **d** according unto all that he hath	6213
	38: 9 these men have **d** evil in all that they	7489
	38: 9 that they have **d** to Jeremiah the prophet,	6213
	40: 3 and **d** according as he hath said:	6213
	41:11 that Ishmael the son of Nethaniah had **d,**	6213
	42:10 for I repent me of the evil that I have **d**	6213
	44:17 as we have **d**, we, and our fathers,	6213
	48:19 and her that escapeth, *and* say, What is **d**?	1961
	50:15 upon her; as she hath **d**, do unto her.	6213
	50:29 according to all that she hath **d**, do unto	6213
	51:12 **d** *that* which he spake against	6213
	51:24 evil that they have **d** in Zion in your sight,	6213
	51:35 The violence **d** to me and *to* my flesh *be*	NIH
	52: 2 according to all that Jehoiakim had **d.**	6213
La	1:12 like unto my sorrow, which is **d** unto me,	5953
	1:21 they are glad that thou hast **d** *it:* thou wilt	6213
	1:22 as thou hast **d** unto me for all my	5953
	2:17 The LORD hath **d** *that* which he had	6213
	2:20 and consider to whom thou hast **d** this.	5953
Eze	3:20 his righteousness which he hath **d** shall	6213
	5: 7 neither have **d** according to the judgments	6213
	5: 9 I will do in thee that which I have not **d,**	6213
	9: 4 cry for all the abominations that be **d** in	6213
	9:11 I have **d** as thou hast commanded me.	6213
	11:12 have **d** after the manners of the heathen	6213
	12:11 like as I have **d**, so shall it be done unto	6213
	12:11 as I have done, so shall it be **d** unto them:	6213
	12:28 the word which I have spoken shall be **d,**	6213
	14:23 ye shall know that I have not **d** without	6213
	14:23 done without cause all that I have **d** in it,	6213
	16:47 their ways, nor *after* their abominations:	6213
	16:48 Lord GOD, Sodom thy sister hath not **d,**	6213
	16:48 as thou hast **d**, thou and thy daughters.	6213
	16:51 all thine abominations which thou hast **d.**	6213
	16:54 be confounded in all that thou hast **d,**	6213
	16:59 I will even deal with thee as thou hast **d,**	6213
	16:63 toward thee for all that thou hast **d,**	6213
	17:18 **d** all these *things*, he shall not escape.	6213
	17:24 I the LORD have spoken and have **d** *it.*	6213
	18:13 he hath **d** all these abominations; he shall	6213
	18:14 seeth all his father's sins which he hath **d,**	6213
	18:19 When the son hath **d** that which is lawful	6213
	18:19 and hath **d** them, he shall surely live.	6213
	18:22 in his righteousness that he hath **d** he	6213
	18:24 All his righteousness that he hath **d** shall	6213
	18:26 for his iniquity that he hath **d** shall he die.	6213
	23:38 Moreover this they have **d** unto me:	6213
	23:39 thus have they **d** in the midst of mine	6213
	24:22 ye shall do as I have **d**: ye shall not cover	6213
	24:24 according to all that he hath **d** shall ye do:	6213
	33:16 he hath **d** that which is lawful and right;	6213
	39: 8 Behold, it is come, and it is **d**, saith	1961
	39:24 according to their transgressions have I **d**	6213
	43:11 if they be ashamed of all that they have **d,**	6213
	44:14 and for all that shall be **d** therein.	6213
Da	6:22 also before thee, O king, have I **d** no hurt.	5648
	9: 5 and have **d wickedly**, and have rebelled,	7561
	9:12 under the whole heaven hath not been **d**	6213
	9:12 done as hath been **d** upon Jerusalem.	6213
	9:15 we have sinned, and have **d wickedly.**	7561
	11:24 do *that* which his fathers have not **d,**	6213
	11:36 for that that is determined shall be **d.**	6213
Hos	2: 5 that conceived them hath **d shamefully:**	954
Joel	2:20 come up, because he hath **d** great things.	6213
Am	3: 6 in a city, and the LORD hath not **d** *it*?	6213
Ob	1:15 as thou hast **d**, it shall be done unto thee;	6213
	1:15 as thou hast done, it shall be **d** unto thee:	6213
Jnh	1:10 said unto him, Why hast thou **d** this?	6213
	1:14 O LORD, hast **d** as it pleased thee.	6213
Mic	6: 3 O my people, what have I **d** unto thee?	6213
Zep	3: 7 *as* I have **d** these so many years?	6213
Zec	7: 3 as I have **d** these so many years?	6213
Mal	2:13 this have ye **d** again, covering the altar of	6213
Mt	1:22 all this was, & that it might be fulfilled	1096
	6:10 Thy will be **d** in earth, as *it is* in heaven.	1096
	7:22 in thy name many wonderful works?	4160
	8:13 as thou hast believed, *so* be it **d** unto thee.	1096
	11:20 wherein most of his mighty works were **d,**	1096
	11:21 for if the mighty works which were **d** in	1096
	11:21 had been **d** in Tyre and Sidon they would	1096
	11:23 mighty works, which have been **d** in thee,	1096
	11:23 been **d** in thee, had been **d** in Sodom,	1096

D

Mt	13:28	He said unto them, An enemy hath **d** this.	4160
	17:12	unto him whatsoever they listed.	4160
	18:19	it shall be **d** for them of my Father which	1096
	18:31	when his fellowservants saw what was **d**,	1096
	18:31	and told unto their lord all that was **d**.	1096
	21: 4	All this was **d**, that it might be fulfilled	1096
	21:21	ye shall not only do this which is **d** to	NIG
	21:21	and be thou cast into the sea; it shall be **d**.	1096
	23:23	these ought *ye* to have **d**, and not to leave	4160
	25:21	Well **d**, *thou* good and faithful servant:	NIG
	25:23	him, Well **d**, good and faithful servant;	NIG
	25:40	Inasmuch as ye have **d** *it* unto one of	4160
	25:40	these my brethren, ye have **d** *it* unto me.	4160
	26:13	shall also *this*, that this *woman* hath **d**,	4160
	26:42	from me, except I drink it, thy will be **d**.	1096
	26:56	But all this, that the scriptures of	4160
	27:23	governor said, Why, what evil hath he **d**?	4160
	27:54	and *those* things that were **d**, they feared	1096
	28:11	the chief priests all the *things* that were **d**.	1096
Mk	4:11	all *these things* are **d** in parables:	1096
	5:14	went out to see what it was that was **d**.	1096
	5:19	them how great *things* the Lord hath **d**	4160
	5:20	how great *things* Jesus had **d** for him:	4160
	5:32	about to see her that had **d** this *thing*.	1096
	5:33	knowing what was **d** in her, came and	1096
	6:30	told him all *things*, both what they had **d**,	4160
	7:37	saying, He hath **d** all *things* well:	4160
	9:13	they have **d** unto him whatsoever they	4160
	13:30	shall not pass, till all these *things* be **d**.	1096
	14: 8	She hath **d** what she could: is come	4160
	14: 9	also that she hath **d** shall be spoken of	4160
	15: 8	*him to do* as he had ever **d** unto them.	4160
	15:14	unto them, Why, what evil hath he **d**?	4160
Lk	1:49	For he *that is* mighty hath **d** to me great	4160
	3:19	and for all the evils which Herod had **d**,	1096
	4:23	we have heard **d** in Capernaum,	1096
	5: 6	And when they had this **d**, they inclosed	4160
	8:34	they that fed *them* saw what was **d**,	1096
	8:35	Then they went out to see what was **d**;	1096
	8:39	shew what great *things* God hath **d** unto	4160
	8:39	how great *things* Jesus had **d** unto him.	4160
	8:56	that they should tell no *man* what was **d**.	1096
	9: 7	tetrarch heard of all that was **d** by him:	1096
	9:10	returned, told him all that they had **d**.	4160
	10:13	if the mighty works had been **d** in Tyre	1096
	10:13	and Sidon, which have been **d** in you,	1096
	11: 2	Thy will be **d**, as in heaven, so in earth.	1096
	11:42	these ought *ye* to have **d**, and not to leave	4160
	13:17	all the glorious *things* that were **d** by him.	1096
	14:22	it is **d** as thou hast commanded,	1096
	16: 8	unjust steward, because he had **d** wisely:	4160
	17:10	when ye shall have **d** all those *things*	4160
	17:10	we have **d** *that* which was our duty to do.	4160
	22:42	nevertheless not my will, but thine, be **d**.	1096
	23: 8	he hoped to have seen some miracle **d** by	1096
	23:15	lo, nothing worthy of death is **d** unto him.	4238
	23:22	the third time, Why, what evil hath he **d**?	4160
	23:31	in a green tree, what shall be **d** in the dry?	1096
	23:41	but this *man* hath **d** nothing amiss.	4238
	23:47	Now when the centurion saw what was **d**,	1096
	23:48	beholding the *things* which were **d**,	1096
	24:21	is the third day since these *things* were **d**.	1096
	24:35	And they told what *things* were **d** in the	NIG
Jn	1:28	These *things* were **d** in Bethabara beyond	1096
	5:16	he had **d** these *things* on the sabbath day.	4160
	5:29	that have **d** good, unto the resurrection	4160
	5:29	and they that have **d** evil, unto	4238
	7:21	I have **d** one work, and ye all marvel.	4160
	7:31	than these which this *man* hath **d**?	4160
	11:46	and told them what *things* Jesus had **d**.	4160
	12:16	*that* they had **d** these *things* unto him.	4160
	12:18	for that they heard that he had **d** this	4160
	12:37	But though he had **d** so many miracles	4160
	13:12	them, Know ye what I have **d** to you?	4160
	13:15	that ye should do as I have **d** to you.	4160
	15: 7	what ye will, and it shall be **d** unto you.	1096
	15:24	If I had not **d** among them the works	4160
	18:35	delivered thee unto me: what hast thou **d**?	4160
	19:36	For these *things* were **d**, that the scripture	1096
Ac	2:43	and signs were **d** by the apostles.	1096
	4: 7	or by what name, have ye **d** this?	4160
	4: 9	of the good deed **d** to the impotent man,	NIG
	4:16	**d** by them *is* manifest to all them that	1096
	4:21	men glorified God for that which was **d**.	1096
	4:28	thy counsel determined before to be **d**.	1096
	4:30	wonders may be **d** by the name of thy	1096
	5: 7	wife, not knowing what was **d**, came in.	1096
	8:13	the miracles and signs which *were* **d**.	1096
	9:13	how much evil he hath **d** to thy saints at	4160
	10:16	This was **d** thrice: and the vessel was	1096
	10:33	and thou hast well **d** that thou art come.	4160
	11:10	And this was **d** three times: and all were	1096
	12: 9	wist not that it was true which was **d** by	1096
	13:12	when he saw what was **d**, believed,	1096
	14: 3	and wonders to be **d** by their hands.	1096
	14:11	when the people saw what Paul had **d**,	4160
	14:13	would have **d** sacrifice with the people.	NIG
	14:18	that *they* had not **d** sacrifice unto them.	2380
	14:27	they rehearsed all that God had **d** with	4160
	15: 4	declared all *things* that God had **d** with	4160
	21:14	saying, The will of the Lord be **d**.	1096
	21:33	who he was, and what he had **d**.	4160
	24: 2	that very worthy deeds are **d** unto this	1096
	25:10	to the Jews have I **d** no **wrong**, as thou	91
	26:26	for this *thing* was not **d** in a corner.	4238

Ac	28: 9	So when this was **d**, others also, which	1096
Ro	9:11	born, neither having **d** any good or evil,	4238
1Co	5: 2	he that hath **d** this deed might be taken	4160
	5: 3	*concerning* him that hath so **d** this *deed*,	2716
	9:15	*things*, that it should be so **d** unto me:	1096
	13:10	that which is in part shall be **d away**.	2673
	14:26	Let all *things* be **d** unto edifying.	1096
	14:40	Let all *things* be **d** decently and in order.	1096
	16:14	Let all your *things* be **d** with charity.	1096
2Co	3: 7	which *glory* was to be **d away**:	2673
	3:11	For if that which is **d away** *was* glorious,	2673
	3:14	which *vail* is **d away** in Christ.	2673
	5:10	that every one may receive the *things* **d** in	NIG
	5:10	according to that he hath **d**, whether *it be*	4238
	7:12	for his cause that had **d** the **wrong**,	91
Eph	5:12	*things* which are **d** of them in secret.	1096
	6:13	in the evil day, and having **d** all, to stand.	2716
Php	2: 3	*Let* nothing **be d** through strife or	NIG
	4:14	Notwithstanding ye have well **d**, that ye	4160
Col	3:25	receive *for* the **wrong** which he hath **d**:	91
	4: 9	unto you all *things* which *are* **d** here.	NIG
Tit	3: 5	works of righteousness which we have **d**,	4160
Heb	10:29	hath **d despite unto** the Spirit of grace?	1796
	10:36	that, after ye have **d** the will of God,	4160
Rev	16:17	of heaven, from the throne, saying, It is **d**.	1096
	21: 6	And he said unto me, It is **d**. I am Alpha	1096
	22: 6	*the things* which must shortly be **d**.	1096

DONKEY; DONKEYS See ASS; ASS'S; ASSES

DOOR (189) [DOORKEEPER, DOORKEEPERS, DOORS]

Ge	4: 7	if thou doest not well, sin lieth at the **d**.	6607
	6:16	the **d** of the ark shalt thou set in the side	6607
	18: 1	he sat *in* the tent in the heat of the day;	6607
	18: 2	he ran to meet them from the tent **d**,	6607
	18:10	Sarah heard *it* in the tent **d**, which *was*	6607
	19: 6	Lot went out at the **d** unto them,	6607
	19: 9	door unto them, and shut the **d** after him,	1817
	19: 9	*even* Lot, and came near to break the **d**.	1817
	19:10	into the house to them, and shut to the **d**.	1817
	19:11	they smote the men that *were* at the **d** of	6607
	19:11	they wearied themselves to find the **d**.	6607
	43:19	they communed with him *at* the **d** of	6607
Ex	12: 7	and on the **upper d post** of the houses,	4947
	12:22	none of you shall go out at the **d** of his	6607
	12:23	the Lord will pass over the **d**,	6607
	21: 6	he shall also bring him to the **d**, or unto	1817
	21: 6	bring him to the door, or unto the **d post**;	4201
	26:36	thou shalt make a hanging for the **d** of	6607
	29: 4	his sons thou shalt bring unto the **d** of	6607
	29:11	*by* the **d** of the tabernacle of the	6607
	29:32	*by* the **d** of the tabernacle of	6607
	29:42	**d** of the tabernacle of the congregation	6607
	33: 8	stood every man *at* his tent **d**,	6607
	33: 9	stood at the **d** of the tabernacle,	6607
	33:10	the cloudy pillar stand at the tabernacle **d**:	6607
	33:10	and worshipped, every man *in* his tent **d**.	6607
	35:15	the hanging for the **d** at the entering in of	6607
	35:17	and the hanging for the **d** of the court,	8179
	36:37	he made a hanging for the tabernacle **d** *of*	6607
	38: 8	assembled *at* the **d** of the tabernacle	6607
	38:30	therewith he made the sockets to the **d** of	6607
	39:38	and the hanging for the tabernacle **d**,	6607
	40: 5	the hanging of the **d** to the tabernacle.	6607
	40: 6	**d** of the tabernacle of the tent of	6607
	40:12	his sons unto the **d** of the tabernacle of	6607
	40:28	he set up the hanging at the **d** of	6607
	40:29	put the altar of burnt offering *by* the **d** of	6607
Lev	1: 3	**d** of the tabernacle of the congregation	6607
	1: 5	**d** of the tabernacle of the congregation.	6607
	3: 2	kill it at the **d** of the tabernacle of	6607
	4: 4	he shall bring the bullock unto the **d** of	6607
	4: 7	which *is* at the **d** of the tabernacle of	6607
	4:18	which *is* at the **d** of the tabernacle of	6607
	8: 3	**d** of the tabernacle of the congregation.	6607
	8: 4	**d** of the tabernacle of the congregation.	6607
	8:31	Boil the flesh *at* the **d** of the tabernacle of	6607
	8:33	ye shall not go out of the **d** of	6607
	8:35	Therefore shall ye abide *at* the **d** of	6607
	10: 7	ye shall not go out from the **d** of	6607
	12: 6	unto the **d** of the tabernacle of	6607
	14:11	*at* the **d** of the tabernacle of	6607
	14:23	unto the **d** of the tabernacle of	6607
	14:38	priest shall go out of the house to the **d**	6607
	15:14	come before the Lord unto the **d** of	6607
	15:29	to the **d** of the tabernacle of	6607
	16: 7	present them before the Lord *at* the **d** of	6607
	17: 4	not unto the **d** of the tabernacle	6607
	17: 5	unto the **d** of the tabernacle of	6607
	17: 6	**d** of the tabernacle of the congregation,	6607
	17: 9	not unto the **d** of the tabernacle	6607
	19:21	unto the **d** of the tabernacle of	6607
Nu	3:25	the hanging for the **d** of the tabernacle of	6607
	3:26	the curtain for the **d** of the court, which *is*	6607
	4:25	the hanging for the **d** of the tabernacle of	6607
	4:26	the hanging for the **d** of the gate of	6607
	6:10	to the **d** of the tabernacle of	6607
	6:13	he shall be brought unto the **d** of	6607
	6:18	**d** of the tabernacle of the congregation,	6607
	10: 3	**d** of the tabernacle of the congregation.	6607
	11:10	every man in the **d** of his tent:	6607
	12: 5	stood *in* the **d** of the tabernacle,	6607
	16:18	stood *in* the **d** of the tabernacle of	6607
	16:19	**d** of the tabernacle of the congregation:	6607

Nu	16:27	stood *in* the **d** of their tents,	6607
	16:50	Aaron returned unto Moses unto the **d** of	6607
	20: 6	**d** of the tabernacle of the congregation,	6607
	25: 6	who *were* weeping *before* the **d** of	6607
	27: 2	*by* the **d** of the tabernacle of	6607
Dt	11:20	thou shalt write them upon the **d** posts	4201
	15:17	thrust *it* through his ear unto the **d**,	1817
	22:21	they shall bring out the damsel to the **d** of	6607
	31:15	the pillar of the cloud stood over the **d** of	6607
Jos	19:51	*at* the **d** of the tabernacle of	6607
Jdg	4:20	Stand *in* the **d** of the tent, and it shall be,	6607
	9:52	went hard unto the **d** of the tower to burn	6607
	19:22	beat at the **d**, and spake to the master of	1817
	19:26	fell down *at* the **d** of the man's house	6607
	19:27	*was* fallen down *at* the **d** of the house,	6607
1Sa	2:22	**d** of the tabernacle of the congregation.	6607
2Sa	11: 9	Uriah slept *at* the **d** of the king's house	6607
	13:17	out from me, and bolt the **d** after her.	1817
	13:18	her out, and bolted the **d** after her.	1817
1Ki	6: 8	The **d** for the middle chamber *was* in	6607
	6:33	So also made he for the **d** of the temple	6607
	6:34	the two leaves of the one **d** *were* folding,	1817
	6:34	two leaves of the other **d** *were* folding.	1817
	14: 6	as she came in at the **d**, that he said,	6607
	14:17	when she came to the threshold of the **d**,	1004
	14:27	which kept the **d** of the king's house.	6607
2Ki	4: 4	thou shalt shut the **d** upon thee and	1817
	4: 5	shut the **d** upon her and upon her sons,	1817
	4:15	he had called her, she stood in the **d**.	6607
	4:21	and shut *the **d*** upon him, and went out.	NIH
	4:33	shut the **d** upon them twain,	1817
	5: 9	and stood *at* the **d** of the house of Elisha.	6607
	6:32	shut the **d**, and hold him fast at the door:	1817
	6:32	shut the door, and hold him fast at the **d**:	1817
	9: 3	Then open the **d**, and flee, and tarry not.	6607
	9:10	none to bury *her*. And he opened the **d**,	1817
	12: 9	the priests that kept the **d** put therein all	5592
	22: 4	which the keepers of the **d** have gathered	5592
	23: 4	the keepers of the **d**, to bring forth out of	5592
	25:18	and the three keepers of the **d**:	5592
1Ch	9:21	**d** of the tabernacle of the congregation.	6607
Ne	3:20	from the turning *of* the wall unto the **d** of	6607
	3:21	from the **d** of the house of Eliashib even	6607
Est	2:21	and Teresh, of those which kept the **d**,	5592
	6: 2	king's chamberlains, the keepers of the **d**,	5592
Job	31: 9	or *if* I have laid wait at my neighbour's **d**;	6607
	31:34	I kept silence, *and* went not out *of* the **d**	6607
Ps	141: 3	before my mouth; keep the **d** of my lips.	1817
Pr	5: 8	and come not nigh the **d** of her house:	6607
	9:14	For she sitteth at the **d** of her house, on a	6607
	26:14	*As* the **d** turneth upon his hinges,	1817
SS	5: 4	put in his hand by the hole of the **d**,	NIH
	8: 9	if she *be* a **d**, we will inclose her with	1817
Isa	6: 4	the posts of the **d** moved at the voice of	5592
Jer	35: 4	the son of Shallum, the keeper of the **d**:	5592
	52:24	and the three keepers of the **d**:	5592
Eze	8: 3	to the **d** of the inner gate that looketh	6607
	8: 7	he brought me to the **d** of the court;	6607
	8: 8	I had digged in the wall, behold a **d**.	6607
	8:14	he brought me to the **d** of the gate of	6607
	8:16	*at* the **d** of the temple of the Lord,	6607
	10:19	*every one* stood *at* the **d** of the east gate	6607
	11: 1	behold at the **d** of the gate five and	6607
	40:13	five and twenty cubits, **d** against door.	6607
	40:13	five and twenty cubits, door against **d**.	6607
	41: 2	the breadth of the **d** was ten cubits;	6607
	41: 2	the sides of the **d** *were* five cubits on	6607
	41: 3	measured the post of the **d**, two cubits;	6607
	41: 3	the **d**, six cubits; and the breadth of	6607
	41: 3	and the breadth of the **d**, seven cubits.	6607
	41:11	one **d** toward the north, and another door	6607
	41:11	north, and another **d** toward the south:	6607
	41:16	The **posts**, and the narrow windows,	5592
	41:16	on their three *stories*, over against the **d**,	5592
	41:17	To *that* above the **d**, even unto the inner	6607
	41:20	From the ground unto above the **d** *were*	6607
	41:24	two *leaves* for the one **d**, and two leaves	1817
	41:24	one door, and two leaves for the other **d**.	NIH
	42: 2	of an hundred cubits *was* the north **d**,	6607
	42:12	the south *was* a **d** in the head of the way,	6607
	46: 3	**d** of this gate before the Lord in	6607
	47: 1	he brought me again unto the **d** of	6607
Hos	2:15	and the valley of Achor for a **d** of hope:	6607
Am	9: 1	*lintel of the* **d**, that **lintel of the d**, that	3730
Mt	6: 6	thy closet, and when thou hast shut thy **d**,	2374
	25:10	him to the marriage: and the **d** was shut.	2374
	27:60	he rolled a great stone to the **d** of	2374
	28: 2	and rolled back the stone from the **d**,	2374
Mk	1:33	all the city was gathered together at the **d**.	2374
	2: 2	*them*, no, not so much as about the **d**:	2374
	11: 4	found the colt tied by the **d** without in a	2374
	15:46	rolled a stone unto the **d** of the sepulchre.	2374
	16: 3	shall roll us away the stone from the **d**	2374
Lk	11: 7	The **d** is now shut, and my children are	2374
	13:25	and hath shut to the **d**, and ye begin to	2374
	13:25	and to knock at the **d**, saying, Lord, Lord,	2374
Jn	10: 1	He that entereth not by the **d** into	2374
	10: 2	But he that entereth in by the **d** is	2374
	10: 7	I say unto you, I am the **d** of the sheep.	2374
	10: 9	I am the **d**: by me if any *man* enter in,	2374
	18:16	But Peter stood at the **d** without.	2374
	18:16	and spake unto her that **kept the d**,	2377
	18:17	saith the damsel that **kept the d** unto	2377
Ac	5: 9	have buried thy husband *are* at the **d**,	2374
	12: 6	*the* keepers before the **d** kept the prison.	2374

Ac 12:13 And as Peter knocked at the **d** of the gate, *2374*
 12:16 and when they had opened *the* **d**, NIG
 14:27 how he had opened *the* **d** of faith unto *2374*
1Co 16: 9 For a great **d** and effectual is opened unto *2374*
2Co 2:12 and a **d** was opened unto me of the Lord, *2374*
Col 4: 3 that God would open unto us a **d** of *2374*
Jas 5: 9 the judge standeth before the **d**. *2374*
Rev 3: 8 I have set before thee an open **d**, and no *2374*
 3:20 Behold, I stand at the **d**, and knock: if any *2374*
 3:20 and open the **d**, I will come in to him, *2374*
 4: 1 and behold, a **d** *was* opened in heaven: *2374*

DOORKEEPER (1) [DOOR, KEEP]

Ps 84:10 had rather be a **d** in the house of my God, *5605*

DOORKEEPERS (2) [DOOR, KEEP]

1Ch 15:23 and Elkanah *were* **d** for the ark. *7778*
 15:24 Obed-edom and Jehiah *were* **d** for the ark. *7778*

DOORS (71) [DOOR]

Jos 2:19 *that* whosoever shall go out of the **d** of thy *1817*
Jdg 3:23 shut the **d** of the parlour upon him, *1817*
 3:24 the **d** of the parlour *were* locked, *1817*
 3:25 he opened not the **d** of the parlour; *1817*
 11:31 that whatsoever cometh forth of the **d** of *1817*
 16: 3 took the **d** of the gate of the city, *1817*
 19:27 opened the **d** of the house, and went out *1817*
1Sa 3:15 opened the **d** of the house of the Lord. *1817*
 21:13 scrabled on the **d** of the gate, and let his *1817*
1Ki 6:31 for the entering of the oracle he made **d** *1817*
 6:32 The two **d** also *were* of olive tree; *1817*
 6:34 the two **d** *were* of fir tree: the two leaves *1817*
 7: 5 all the **d** and posts *were* square, with *6607*
 7:50 *of* gold, *both* for the **d** of the inner house, *1817*
 7:50 holy place, *and* for the **d** of the house, *1817*
2Ki 18:16 *from* the **d** of the temple of the Lord, *1817*
1Ch 22: 3 for the nails for the **d** of the gates, *1817*
2Ch 3: 7 thereof, and the **d** thereof, with gold; *1817*
 4: 9 **d** for the court, and overlaid the doors of *1817*
 4: 9 and overlaid the **d** of them with brass. *1817*
 4:22 inner **d** thereof for the most holy *place*, *1817*
 4:22 and the **d** of the house of the temple, *1817*
 23: 4 of the Levites, *shall be* porters of the **d**; *5592*
 28:24 shut up the **d** of the house of the Lord, *1817*
 29: 3 opened the **d** of the house of the Lord, *1817*
 29: 7 they have shut up the **d** of the porch, *1817*
 34: 9 which the Levites that kept the **d** had *5592*
Ne 3: 1 they sanctified it, and set up the **d** of it; *1817*
 3: 3 set up the **d** thereof, the locks thereof, *1817*
 3: 6 set up the **d** thereof, and the locks thereof *1817*
 3:13 they built it, and set up the **d** thereof, *1817*
 3:14 he built it, and set up the **d** thereof, *1817*
 3:15 and covered it, and set up the **d** thereof, *1817*
 6: 1 at that time I had not set up the **d** *1817*
 6:10 and let us shut the **d** of the temple: *1817*
 7: 1 I had set up the **d**, and the porters and *1817*
 7: 3 let them shut the **d**, and bar *them*: and *1817*
Job 3:10 Because it shut not up the **d** of my *1817*
 31:32 *but* I opened my **d** to the traveller. *1817*
 38: 8 Or *who* shut up the sea with **d**, when it *1817*
 38:10 *it* my decreed *place*, and set bars and **d**, *1817*
 38:17 hast thou seen the **d** of the shadow of *8179*
 41:14 Who can open the **d** of his face? his teeth *1817*
Ps 24: 7 ye lift up, ye everlasting **d**; and the King *6607*
 24: 9 even lift *them* up, ye everlasting **d**; *6607*
 78:23 from above, and opened the **d** of heaven, *1817*
Pr 8: 3 of the city, *at* the coming in at the **d**. *6607*
 8:34 at my gates, waiting at the posts of my **d**. *6607*
Ecc 12: 4 the **d** shall be shut in the streets, when *1817*
Isa 26:20 thy chambers, and shut thy **d** about thee: *1817*
 57: 8 Behind the **d** also and the posts hast thou *1817*
Eze 33:30 by the walls and in the **d** of the houses, *6607*
 41:11 the **d** of the side chambers *were* toward *6607*
 41:23 the temple and the sanctuary had two **d**. *1817*
 41:24 the **d** had two leaves *apiece*, two turning *1817*
 41:25 on the **d** of the temple, cherubims and *1817*
 42: 4 one cubit; and their **d** toward the north. *6607*
 42:11 to their fashions, and according to their **d**. *6607*
 42:12 according to the **d** of the chambers that *6607*
Mic 7: 5 keep the **d** of thy mouth from her that *6607*
Zec 11: 1 Open thy **d**, O Lebanon, that the fire may *1817*
Mal 1:10 **d** *for nought?* neither do ye kindle *fire on* *1817*
Mt 24:33 know that it is near, *even* at the **d**. *2374*
Mk 13:29 pass, know that it is nigh, *even* at the **d**. *2374*
Jn 20:19 when the **d** were shut where the disciples *2374*
 20:26 *then* came Jesus, the **d** being shut, *2374*
Ac 5:19 of the Lord by night opened the prison **d**, *2374*
 5:23 keepers standing without before the **d**: *2374*
 16:26 and immediately all the **d** were opened, *2374*
 16:27 seeing the prison **d** open, he drew out *2374*
 21:30 temple: and forthwith the **d** were shut. *2374*

DOPHKAH (2)

Nu 33:12 the wilderness of Sin, and encamped in **D**. *1850*
 33:13 they departed from **D**, and encamped in *1850*

DOR (7) [HAMMOTH-DOR]

Jos 11: 2 and in the borders of **D** on the west, *1756*
 12:23 The king of Dor in the coast of **D**, one; *1756*
 12:23 The king of Dor in the coast of **D**, one; *1756*
 17:11 the inhabitants of **D** and her towns, *1756*
Jdg 1:27 nor the inhabitants of **D** and her towns, *1756*
1Ki 4:11 son of Abinadab, *in* all the region of **D**; *1756*
1Ch 7:29 and her towns, **D** and her towns. *1756*

DORCAS (2)

Ac 9:36 which by interpretation is called **D**: *1393*
 9:39 the coats and garments which **D** made, *1393*

DOST (56) [DO]

Ge 32:29 Wherefore *is* it *that* thou **d** ask after my NIH
 44: 4 thou **d** overtake them, say unto them, NIH
Dt 9: 5 heart, thou **d** go to possess their land: NIH
 24:10 When thou **d** lend thy brother any thing, NIH
 24:11 man to whom thou **d** lend shall bring out NIH
Jdg 14:16 Thou **d** but hate me, and lovest me not: NIH
1Sa 24:14 whom **d** thou pursue? after a dead dog, NIH
 28:16 Wherefore then **d** thou ask of me, NIH
1Ki 2:22 why **d** thou ask Abishag the Shunammite NIH
 21: 7 **D** thou now govern the kingdom of Israel? NIH
2Ki 18:20 Now on whom **d** thou trust, that thou NIH
2Ch 6:26 from their sin, when thou **d** afflict them; NIH
Ne 2: 4 unto me, For what **d** thou make request? NIH
Job 2: 9 him, **D** thou still retain thine integrity? NIH
 7:21 why **d** thou not pardon my transgression, NIH
 10: 8 round about; yet thou **d** destroy me. NIH
 14: 3 **d** thou open thine eyes upon such a one, NIH
 14:16 my steps: **d** thou not watch over my sin? NIH
 15: 8 and **d** thou restrain wisdom to thyself? NIH
 30:20 I cry unto thee, and thou **d** not hear me: NIH
 33:13 Why **d** thou strive against him? for he NIH
 37:15 **D** thou know when God disposed them, NIH
 37:16 **D** thou know the balancings of the clouds, NIH
Ps 39:11 When thou with rebukes **d** correct man NIH
 43: 2 why **d** thou cast me off? why go I NIH
 44:12 **d** not increase *thy wealth* by their price. NIH
 99: 4 thou **d** establish equity, thou executest NIH
Pr 4: 8 to honour, when thou **d** embrace her. NIH
Ecc 7:10 for thou **d** not inquire wisely concerning NIH
SS 5: 9 *another* beloved, that thou **d** so charge us? NIH
Isa 26: 7 most upright, thou **d** weigh the path of the just. NIH
 36: 5 now on whom **d** thou trust, that thou NIH
Jer 32: 3 Wherefore **d** thou prophesy, and say, NIH
 40:14 **D** thou certainly know that Baalis the king NIH
 48:18 Thou daughter that **d** inhabit Dibon, NIH
La 5:20 Wherefore **d** thou forget us for ever, NIH
Eze 2: 6 and thou **d** dwell among scorpions: NIH
 32:19 Whom **d** thou pass in beauty? go down, NIH
 33: 8 if thou **d** not speak to warn the wicked NIH
Mic 4: 9 why **d** thou cry out aloud? *is there* no NIH
Hab 1: 3 Why **d** thou shew me iniquity, and cause NIH
Lk 10:40 **d** thou not care that my sister hath left me NIG
 23:40 rebuked him, saying, **D** not thou fear God, NIG
Jn 6:30 and believe thee? what **d** thou work? NIG
 9:34 born in sins, and **d** thou teach us? NIG
 9:35 **D** thou believe on the Son of God? NIG
 10:24 How long **d** thou make us to doubt? NIG
 13: 6 unto him, Lord, **d** thou wash my feet? NIG
Ro 2:21 *a man* should not steal, **d** thou steal? NIG
 2:22 commit adultery, **d** thou commit adultery? NIG
 2:22 abhorrest idols, **d** thou commit sacrilege? NIG
 2:27 and circumcision **d** transgress the law? NIG
 14:10 But why **d** thou judge thy brother? or why NIG
 14:10 or why **d** thou set at nought thy brother? NIG
1Co 4: 7 now if thou didst receive *it*, why **d** thou NIG
Rev 6:10 **d** thou not judge and avenge our blood on NIG

DOTE (1) [DOTED, DOTING]

Jer 50:36 sword *is* upon the liars; and they shall **d**: *2973*

DOTED (6) [DOTE]

Eze 23: 5 she **d** on her lovers, on the Assyrians *her* *5689*
 23: 7 of Assyria, and with all *on* whom she **d**. *5689*
 23: 9 hand of the Assyrians, upon whom she **d**. *5689*
 23:12 She **d** upon the Assyrians *her* neighbours, *5689*
 23:16 she **d** upon them, and sent messengers *5689*
 23:20 For she **d** upon their paramours, *5689*

DOTH (210) [DO]

Ge 3: 5 For God **d** know that in the day ye eat NIH
 27:42 as touching thee, **d** comfort himself, NIH
 45: 3 I *am* Joseph; **d** my father yet live? NIH
Ex 11: 7 that ye may know how that the Lord **d** NIH
 31:13 that I *am* the Lord that **d** sanctify you. NIH
 32:11 thy wrath wax hot against thy people, NIH
Lev 11:31 whosoever **d** touch them, when they be NIH
 11:32 they are dead, shall it fall, shall be unclean; NIH
 25:16 *the years* of the fruits **d** he sell unto thee. NIH
Nu 5:21 when the Lord **d** make thy thigh to rot, NIH
 16: 7 it shall be *that* the man whom the Lord **d** NIH
 36: 6 This *is* the thing, which the Lord **d** NIH
Dt 1:20 which the Lord our God **d** give unto us. NIH
 1:25 land which the Lord our God **d** give us. NIH
 1:31 as a man **d** bear his son, in all the way that NIH
 5:24 we have seen this day that God **d** talk with NIH
 8: 3 that he might make thee know that man **d** NIH
 8: 3 out of the mouth of the Lord **d** man live. NIH
 9: 4 Lord **d** drive them out from before thee. NIH
 9: 5 God **d** drive them out from before thee, NIH
 10:12 what **d** the Lord thy God require of thee, NIH
 10:18 **d** execute the judgment of the fatherless NIH
 16:19 for a gift **d** blind the eyes of the wise, NIH
 18:12 these abominations the Lord thy God **d** NIH
 20:16 which the Lord thy God **d** give thee *for* NIH
 31: 6 thy God, he *it is* that **d** go with thee; NIH
 31: 8 the Lord, he *it is* that **d** go before thee: NIH
Jos 1:18 Whosoever *he be* that **d** rebel against thy NIH
 20: 4 he that **d** flee unto one of those cities NIH
Jdg 4:20 any man **d** come and inquire of thee, NIH
Ru 3:11 for all the city of my people **d** know that NIH

9:13 he come, because he **d** bless the sacrifice; NIH
 23:19 **D** not David hide himself with us in strong NIH
 26: 1 **D** not David hide himself in the hill of NIH
 26:18 Wherefore **d** my lord thus pursue after his NIH
 26:20 as when *one* **d** hunt a partridge in NIH
2Sa 10: 3 Thinkest thou that David **d** honour thy NIH
 14:13 for the king **d** speak this thing as one NIH
 14:13 in that the king **d** not fetch *home* again NIH
 14:14 *again;* neither **d** God respect *any* person: NIH
 14:14 yet **d** he devise means, that *his* banished NIH
 19: 8 Behold, the king **d** sit in the gate. NIH
 19:20 For thy servant **d** know that I have sinned: NIH
 24: 3 why **d** my lord the king delight in this NIH
 24:24 my God of that which **d** cost me nothing. NIH
1Ki 1:11 that Adonijah the son of Haggith **d** reign, NIH
 1:13 why throne? why then **d** Adonijah reign? NIH
 22: 8 he **d** not prophesy good concerning me, NIH
2Ki 2:15 The spirit of Elijah **d** rest on Elisha. NIH
 5: 7 that this *man* **d** send unto me to recover a NIH
1Ch 19: 3 Thinkest thou that David **d** honour thy NIH
 21: 3 **d** my lord require this *thing?* why will he NIH
2Ch 6:33 as *d* thy people Israel, and may know that NIH
 32:11 **D** not Hezekiah persuade you to give over NIH
Job 1: 9 and said, **D** Job fear God for nought? NIH
 4:21 **D** not their excellency *which is* in them go NIH
 5: 6 neither **d** trouble spring out of the ground; NIH
 6: 5 **D** the wild ass bray when he hath grass? NIH
 6:25 but what **d** your arguing reprove? NIH
 8: 3 **D** God pervert judgment? or doth NIH
 8: 3 or **d** the Almighty pervert justice? NIH
 12:11 **D** not the ear try words? and the mouth NIH
 15:12 Why **d** thine heart carry thee away? and NIH
 16:13 my reins asunder, and **d** not spare; NIH
 17: 2 *d not* mine eye continue in their NIH
 22:13 thou sayest, How **d** God know? can he NIH
 23: 9 where he **d** work, but I cannot behold NIH
 24:19 *so* **d** the grave *those which* have sinned. NIH
 25: 3 and upon whom **d** not his light arise? NIH
 31: 4 **D** not he see my ways, and count all my NIH
 35:16 Therefore **d** Job open his mouth in vain; NIH
 36: 7 he **d** establish them for ever, and they are NIH
 39:26 **D** the hawk fly by thy wisdom, NIH
 39:27 **D** the eagle mount up at thy command, NIH
 41:18 *By* his neesings a light **d** shine, and his NIH
Ps 1: 2 in his law **d** he meditate day and night. NIH
 10: 2 The wicked in *his* pride **d** persecute NIH
 10: 8 in the secret places **d** he murder NIH
 10: 9 he **d** catch the poor, when he draweth NIH
 10:13 Wherefore **d** the wicked contemn God? NIH
 11: 7 his countenance **d** behold the upright. NIH
 29: 9 his temple **d** every one speak of *his* glory. NIH
 41:11 mine enemy **d** not triumph over me. NIH
 54: T To Saul, **D** not David hide himself with us? NIH
 59: 7 are in their lips: for who, *say they,* **d** hear? NIH
 68:33 lo, he **d** send out his voice, *and that a* NIH
 73:11 they say, How **d** God know? and is there NIH
 74: 1 *why* **d** thine anger smoke against the sheep NIH
 77: 8 for ever? **d** *his* promise fail for evermore? NIH
 80:13 The boar out of the wood **d** waste it, NIH
 80:13 and the wild beast of the field **d** devour it. NIH
 92: 6 neither **d** a fool understand this. NIH
 119:129 therefore **d** my soul keep them. NIH
 130: 5 my soul **d** wait, and in his word do I hope. NIH
 147: 2 The Lord **d** build up Jerusalem: NIH
Pr 6:16 These six *things* the Lord **d** hate: yea, NIH
 8: 1 **D** not wisdom cry? and understanding put NIH
 14:10 a stranger **d** not intermeddle with his joy. NIH
 22: 5 he that **d** keep his soul shall be far from NIH
 24:12 **d** not he that pondereth the heart consider NIH
 24:12 and he know *it?* and shall *not* he render NIH
 25:23 *d* an angry countenance a backbiting NIH
 26:14 his hinges, so **d** the slothful upon his bed. NIH
 27: 9 **d** the sweetness of a man's friend by NIH
 27:24 **d** the crown *endure* to every generation? NIH
 29: 6 snare: but the righteous **d** sing and rejoice. NIH
 30:11 their father, and **d** not bless their mother. NIH
 31:11 The heart of her husband **d** *safely* trust in NIH
Ecc 10: 1 **d** *a* little folly *him that is* in reputation for NIH
SS 6: 2 head, and his right hand **d** embrace me. NIH
Isa 1: 3 *but* Israel **d** not know, my people doth not NIH
 1: 3 doth not know, my people **d** not consider. NIH
 1:23 neither **d** the cause of the widow come NIH
 3: 1 **d** take away from Jerusalem and from NIH
 3: 9 The shew of their countenance **d** witness NIH
 10: 7 not so, neither **d** his heart think so; NIH
 28:24 **D** the plowman plow all day to sow? NIH
 28:24 **d** he open and break the clods of his NIH
 28:25 **d** he not cast abroad the fitches, NIH
 28:26 For his God **d** instruct him to discretion, NIH
 28:26 him to discretion, *and* **d** teach him. NIH
 30:33 like a stream of brimstone, **d** kindle it. NIH
 42:11 voice, the villages *that* Kedar **d** inhabit: NIH
 44:14 planteth an ash, and the rain **d** nourish *it.* NIH
 49:18 and bind them *on thee,* as a bride **d**. NIH
 52: 6 in that day that I *am* he that **d** speak: NIH
 59: 9 far from us, neither **d** justice overtake us: NIH
Jer 2:11 their glory for that which **d** not profit. NIH
 5:19 Wherefore **d** the Lord our God all these *6213*
 10: 7 for to thee **d** it appertain: forasmuch as NIH
 12: 1 Wherefore **d** the way of the wicked NIH
 14:10 therefore the Lord **d** not accept them; NIH
 15:10 usury; *yet* every one of them **d** curse me. NIH
 23:14 that none **d** return from his wickedness: NIH
 30: 6 see whether a man **d** travail with child? NIH
 31:10 and keep him as a shepherd **d** *his* flock. NIH

D

D

Jer 49: 1 why *then* d their king inherit Gad, NIH
51:43 neither d *any* son of man pass thereby. NIH
La 1: 1 How the city sit solitary, *that was* full of NIH
3:33 For he d not afflict willingly nor grieve NIH
3:39 Wherefore d a living man complain, a man NIH
5: 8 *there is* none that d deliver *us* out of their NIH
Eze 3:20 When a righteous *man* d turn from his NIH
3:21 he d not sin, he shall surely live, because NIH
18:19 d not the son bear the iniquity of the NIH
20:49 they say of me, D he not speak parables? NIH
Hos 4:14 the people *that* d not understand shall fall. NIH
5: 5 the pride of Israel d testify to his face: NIH
Mic 6: 8 what d the LORD require of thee, but to NIH
Hab 1: 4 is slacked, and judgment d never go forth: NIH
1: 4 for the wicked d compass about NIH
Zep 3: 5 every morning he d bring his judgment to NIH
Mal 2:12 The LORD will cut off the man that d 6213
Mt 6:19 where moth and rust d corrupt, NIG
6:20 where neither moth nor rust d corrupt, NIG
12:24 This *fellow* d not cast out devils, but by NIG
17:24 and said, D not your master pay tribute? NIG
18:12 d he not leave the ninety and nine, NIG
19: 9 whoso marrieth her *which* is put away d NIG
22:43 How then d David in spirit call him Lord, NIG
24:42 for ye know not what hour your Lord d NIG
26:46 behold, he is at hand that d betray me. NIG
Mk 2: 7 Why d this *man* thus speak blasphemies? NIG
2:22 else the new wine d burst the bottles, NIG
8:12 Why d this generation seek after a sign? NIG
Lk 1:46 Mary said, My soul d magnify the Lord, NIG
6:43 neither d a corrupt tree bring forth good NIG
11:36 as when the bright shining of a candle d NIG
13:15 d not each one of you on the sabbath NIG
13:34 as a hen d gather her brood under her NIG
14:27 And whosoever d not bear his cross, NIG
15: 4 d not leave the ninety and nine in NIG
15: 8 d not light a candle, and sweep the house, NIG
17: 9 D he thank that servant because he did NIG
22:26 and he that is chief, as he that d serve. NIG
Jn 2:10 Every man at the beginning d set forth NIG
6:61 he said unto them, D this offend you? NIG
7:51 D our law judge any man, before it hear NIG
9:19 was born blind? how then d he now see? NIG
10:17 Therefore d my Father love me, because NIG
Ac 4:10 *even* by him d this *man* stand here before NIG
8:36 *is* water; what d hinder me to be baptized? NIG
22: 5 As also the high priest d bear me witness, NIG
26:24 much learning d make thee mad. NIG
Ro 8:24 what a man seeth, why d he yet hope for? NIG
9:19 then unto me, Why d he yet find fault? NIG
14: 6 to the Lord he d not regard *it.* He that NIG
1Co 9: 9 out the corn. D God take care for oxen? NIG
11:14 D not even nature itself teach you, that, NIG
13: 5 D not behave itself unseemly, seeketh not NIG
15:50 neither d corruption inherit incorruption. NIG
2Co 1:10 us from so great a death, and d deliver: NIG
3: 9 much more d the ministration of NIG
Eph 5:13 for whatsoever d make manifest is light. NIG
Col 1: 6 and bringeth forth fruit, as *it* d also in you, NIG
1Th 2:11 every one of you, as a father d his children, NIG
2Th 2: 7 For the mystery of iniquity d already work: NIG
2Ti 2:17 And their word will eat as *d* a canker. NIG
Heb 1:11 and they all shall wax old as *d* a garment; NIG
12: 1 and the sin which d so easily beset *us,* and NIG
Jas 2:14 What *d* it profit, my brethren, though a NIG
2:16 *are* needful to the body; what *d* it profit? NIG
3:11 D a fountain send forth at the same place 3385
5: 6 killed the just; *and* he d not resist you. NIG
1Pe 3:11 The like figure whereunto *even* baptism d NIG
5:13 saluteth you; and so d Marcus my son. NIG
1Jn 3: 2 and it d not yet appear what we shall be: NIG
3: 9 Whosoever is born of God d not commit NIG
3Jn 1:10 neither d he himself receive the brethren, NIG
Rev 19:11 and in righteousness he d judge and NIG

DOTHAN (3)
Ge 37:17 for I heard *them* say, Let us go to D. 1886
37:17 after his brethren, and found them in D. 1886
2Ki 6:13 was told him, saying, Behold, *he is* in D. 1886

DOTING (1) [DOTE]
1Ti 6: 4 but d about questions and strifes of words, *3552*

DOUBLE (26) [DOUBLED, DOUBLETONGUED]
Ge 43:12 take d money in your hand; and the 4932
43:15 they took d money in their hand, 4932
Ex 22: 4 be ox, or ass, or sheep; he shall restore d. 8147
22: 7 if the thief be found, let him pay d. 8147
22: 9 he shall pay d unto his neighbour. 8147
26: 9 shalt d the sixth curtain in the forefront of 3717
39: 9 they made the breastplate d: 3717
Dt 15:18 for he hath been worth a d hired servant 4932
21:17 by giving him a d portion of all that he 8147
2Ki 2: 9 let a d portion of thy spirit be upon me. 8147
1Ch 12:33 they were not of d **heart**, 3820+3820+2050.1
Job 11: 6 wisdom, that *they are* d to that which is. 3718
41:13 who can come *to him* with his d bridle? 3718
Ps 12: 2 a d **heart** do they speak. 3820+3820+2050.1
Isa 40: 2 of the LORD's hand d for all her sins. 3718
61: 7 For your shame *you shall have* d; 4932
61: 7 in their land they shall possess the d: 4932
Jer 16:18 recompense their iniquity and their sin d; 4932
17:18 and destroy them *with* d destruction. 4932
Zec 9:12 to day do I declare *that* I will render d 4932
1Ti 5:17 rule be counted worthy of d honour, *1362*

Jas 1: 8 A d **minded** man *is* unstable in all his *1374*
4: 8 and purify your hearts, ye d **minded**. *1374*
Rev 18: 6 d unto her double according to her works: *1363*
18: 6 double unto her d according to her works: *1362*
18: 6 the cup which she hath filled fill to her d. *1362*

DOUBLED (4) [DOUBLE]
Ge 41:32 for that the dream was d unto Pharaoh 8138
Ex 28:16 Foursquare it shall be *being* d; a span 3717
39: 9 and a span the breadth thereof, *being* d 3717
Eze 21:14 let the sword be d the third time, 3717

DOUBLE-EDGED See TWOEDGED

DOUBLETONGUED (1) [DOUBLE, TONGUE]
1Ti 3: 8 not d, not given to much wine, not greedy *1351*

DOUBT (13) [DOUBTED, DOUBTETH, DOUBTFUL, DOUBTING, DOUBTLESS, DOUBTS]
Ge 37:33 is without d rent in pieces. 2963+2963
Dt 28:66 thy life shall hang in d before thee; 8511
Job 12: 2 No d but ye *are* the people, 551
Mt 14:31 thou of little faith, wherefore didst thou d? *1365*
21:21 I say unto you, If ye have faith, and not, *1252*
Mk 11:23 and shall not d in his heart, *1252*
Lk 11:20 no d the kingdom of God is come upon *686*
Jn 10:24 long dost thou make us to d? 142+3588+5590
Ac 2:12 and were in d, saying one to another, *1280*
28: 4 No d this is a murderer, whom, 3843
1Co 9:10 For our sakes, no d, *this* is written: that *1063*
Gal 4:20 change my voice; for I **stand** in d of you. 639
1Jn 2:19 they would *no* d have continued with us: NIG

DOUBTED (4) [DOUBT]
Mt 28:17 him, they worshipped him: but some d. *1365*
Ac 5:24 of them whereunto this would grow. *1280*
10:17 Now while Peter d in himself what *this* *1280*
25:20 because I d of such *manner* of questions, 639

DOUBTETH (1) [DOUBT]
Ro 14:23 And he that d is damned if he eat, *1252*

DOUBTFUL (2) [DOUBT]
Lk 12:29 ye shall drink, neither be ye of d mind. *3349*
Ro 14: 1 receive you, *but* not to d disputations. *1261*

DOUBTING (4) [DOUBT]
Jn 13:22 one on another, d of whom he spake. 639
Ac 10:20 *thee* down, and go with them, d nothing: *1252*
11:12 Spirit bade me go with them, nothing d. *1252*
1Ti 2: 8 holy hands, without wrath and d. *1261*

DOUBTLESS (7) [DOUBT]
Nu 14:30 D ye shall **not** come into the land, 518
2Sa 5:19 for I will d **deliver** the Philistines 5414+5414
Ps 126: 6 shall d **come again** with rejoicing, 935+935
Isa 63:16 D thou *art* our father, though Abraham be 3588
1Co 9: 2 unto others, yet d I am to you: 235+1005
2Co 12: 1 It is not expedient for me d to glory. *1211*
Php 3: 8 Yea d, and I count all *things but* loss for *3304*

DOUBTS (2) [DOUBT]
Da 5:12 of hard sentences, and dissolving of d, 7001
5:16 make interpretations, and dissolve d: 7001

DOUGH (8)
Ex 12:34 the people took their d before it was 1217
12:39 they baked unleavened cakes of the d, 1217
Nu 15:20 of the first of your d *for* a heave offering: 6182
15:21 Of the first of your d ye shall give unto 6182
Ne 10:37 we should bring the firstfruits of our d, 6182
Jer 7:18 the fire, and the women knead *their* d, 6182
Eze 44:30 give unto the priest the first of your d, 6182
Hos 7: 4 from raising after *he* hath kneaded the d, 1217

DOVE (18) [DOVE'S, DOVES, DOVES']
Ge 8: 8 Also he sent forth a d from him, to see if 3123
8: 9 d found no rest for the sole of her foot, 3123
8:10 again he sent forth the d out of the ark; 3123
8:11 the d came in to him in the evening; 3123
8:12 other seven days; and sent forth the d; 3123
Ps 55: 6 O that I had wings like a d, *for then* 3123
68:13 *shall* ye be as the wings of a d covered 3123
SS 2:14 O my d, *that art* in the clefts of the rock, 3123
5: 2 my sister, my love, my d, my undefiled: 3123
6: 9 My d, my undefiled *is but* one; she *is* 3123
Isa 38:14 I did mourn as a d: mine eyes fail *with* 3123
Jer 48:28 be like the d *that* maketh her nest in 3123
Hos 7:11 Ephraim also is like a silly d, without 3123
11:11 and as a d out of the land of Assyria: 3123
Mt 3:16 saw the Spirit of God descending like a d, *4058*
Mk 1:10 the Spirit like a d descending upon him: *4058*
Lk 3:22 in a bodily shape like a d upon him, *4058*
Jn 1:32 Spirit descending from heaven like a d, *4058*

DOVE'S (1) [DOVE]
2Ki 6:25 the fourth part of a kab of d dung for five 1686

DOVES (10) [DOVE]
SS 5:12 His eyes *are* as the eyes of d by the rivers 3123
Isa 59:11 roar all like bears, and mourn sore like d: 3123
60: 8 as a cloud, and as the d to their windows? 3123
Eze 7:16 shall be on the mountains like d of 3123
Na 2: 7 *shall* lead *her* as with the voice of d, 3123
Mt 10:16 wise as serpents, and harmless as d. *4058*

Mt 21:12 and the seats of them that sold d, *4058*
Mk 11:15 and the seats of them that sold d, *4058*
Jn 2:14 those that sold oxen and sheep and d, *4058*
2:16 said unto them that sold d, Take these *4058*

DOVES' (2) [DOVE]
SS 1:15 behold, thou *art* fair; thou *hast* d eyes. 3123
4: 1 fair; thou *hast* d eyes within thy locks: 3123

DOWN (1125) [DOWNSITTING, DOWNWARD]
Ge 11: 5 the LORD came d to see the city and 3381
11: 7 let us go d, and there confound their 3381
12:10 Abram went d into Egypt to sojourn 3381
15:11 the fowls came d upon the carcases, 3381
15:12 the sun was going d, a deep sleep fell 935
15:17 when the sun went d, and it was dark, 3381
18:21 I will go d now, and see whether they 3381
19: 4 before they lay d, the men of the city, 7901
19:33 he perceived not when she lay d, nor 7901
19:35 he perceived not when she lay d, nor 7901
23:12 sat her d over against *him* a good way off, 3427
23:12 Abraham bowed d himself before 7812
24:11 he made *his* camels to kneel d without 1288
24:14 Let d thy pitcher, I pray thee, that I may 5186
24:16 she went d to the well, and filled her 3381
24:18 let d her pitcher upon her hand, 3381
24:26 the man bowed d his head, 6915
24:45 she went d unto the well, and drew 3381
24:46 let d her pitcher from her *shoulder,* and 3381
24:48 I bowed d my **head,** and worshipped 6915
26: 2 unto him, and said, Go not d into Egypt; 3381
27:29 serve thee, and nations bow d to thee: 7812
27:29 and let thy mother's sons bow d to thee: 7812
28:11 pillows, and lay d in that place to sleep. 7901
37:10 thy brethren indeed come to bow d 7812
37:25 they sat d to eat bread: and they lift up 3427
37:25 and myrrh, going to carry *it* d to Egypt. 3381
37:35 For I will go d into the grave unto my son 3381
38: 1 that Judah went d from his brethren, 3381
39: 1 Joseph was brought d to Egypt; 3381
39: 1 which had brought him d thither. 3381
42: 2 get you d thither, and buy for us from 3381
42: 3 Joseph's ten brethren went d to buy corn 3381
42: 6 bowed d themselves before him *with* 7812
42:38 he said, My son shall not go d with you; 3381
42:38 ye bring d my gray hairs with sorrow 3381
43: 4 with us, we will go d and buy thee food: 3381
43: 5 thou wilt not send *him,* we will not go d: 3381
43: 7 that he would say, Bring your brother d? 3381
43:11 carry d the man a present, a little balm, 3381
43:15 went d to Egypt, and stood before Joseph. 3381
43:20 we came indeed d at the first 3381+3381
43:22 other money have we brought d in our 3381
43:28 they bowed d their **heads,** 6915
44:11 they speedily took d every man his sack 3381
44:21 unto thy servants, Bring him d unto me, 3381
44:23 Except your youngest brother come d 3381
44:26 we said, We cannot go d: if our youngest 3381
44:26 brother be with us, then will we go d: 3381
44:29 shall bring d my gray hairs with sorrow 3381
44:31 thy servants shall bring d the gray hairs 3381
45: 9 of all Egypt: come d unto me, tarry not: 3381
45:13 shall haste and bring d my father hither. 3381
46: 3 fear not to go d into Egypt; for I will there 3381
46: 4 I will go d with thee into Egypt; and I will 3381
49: 6 and in their selfwill they digged d a wall. 6131
49: 8 thy father's children shall bow d before 7812
49: 9 he stooped d, he couched as a lion, 3766
49:14 Issachar *is* a strong ass couching 7257
50:18 also went and fell d before his face; 5307
Ex 2: 5 the daughter of Pharaoh came d to wash 3381
2:15 land of Midian: and he sat d by a well. 3427
3: 8 I am come d to deliver them out of 3381
7:10 Aaron cast d his rod before Pharaoh, 7993
7:12 for they cast d every man his rod, 7993
9:19 the hail shall come d upon them, 3381
11: 8 these thy servants shall come d unto me, 3381
11: 8 bow d themselves unto me, saying, 7812
17:11 he let d his hand, Amalek prevailed. 5117
17:12 his hands were steady until the going d 935
19:11 for the third day the LORD will come d in 3381
19:14 Moses went d from the mount unto 3381
19:20 And the LORD came d upon mount Sinai, 3381
19:21 unto Moses, Go d, charge the people, 3381
19:24 get thee d, and thou shalt come up, thou, 3381
19:25 So Moses went d unto the people, 3381
20: 5 Thou shalt not bow d thyself to them, 7812
22:26 unto him by that the sun goeth d: 935
23:24 Thou shalt not bow d to their gods, 7812
23:24 and quite break d their images. 7665+7665
32: 1 delayed to come d out of the mount, 3381
32: 6 and the people sat d to eat and to drink, 3427
32: 7 LORD said unto Moses, Go, get thee d; 3381
32:15 went d from the mount, and the two 3381
34:13 break their images, and cut d their groves: 3772
34:29 when Moses came d from mount Sinai 3381
34:29 when he came d from the mount, 3381
Lev 9:22 came d from offering of the sin offering, 3381
11:35 ranges for pots, they shall be broken d: 5422
14:45 he shall break d the house, the stones 5422
18:23 stand before a beast to lie d thereto: 7250
19:16 shalt not go up and d *as* a talebearer 1980
20:16 lie d thereto, thou shalt kill the woman 7250
22: 7 And when the sun is d, he shall be clean, 935
26: 1 of stone in your land, to bow d unto it: 7812

D

Ref	Text	Num
Lev 26: 6	ye shall **lie d**, and none shall make *you*	7901
26:30	**cut d** your images, and cast your carcases	3772
Nu 1:51	forward, the Levites shall **take it d:**	3381
4: 5	they shall **take d** the covering vail,	3381
10:17	the tabernacle was **taken d**; and the sons	3381
11:17	I will **come d** and talk with thee there:	3381
11:25	the Lord **came d** in a cloud,	3381
12: 5	the Lord **came d** in the pillar of	3381
13:23	**cut d** from thence a branch with one	3772
13:24	the children of Israel **cut d** from thence.	3772
14:45	Amalekites **came d**, and the Canaanites	3381
16:30	them, and they **go d** quick into the pit;	3381
16:33	**went d** alive into the pit, and the earth	3381
20:15	How our fathers **went d** into Egypt,	3381
20:28	Moses and Eleazar **came d** from the	3381
21:15	the stream of the brooks that **goeth d** to	5186
22:27	of the Lord, she **fell d** under Balaam:	7257
22:31	he **bowed d** his head, and fell flat on his	6915
23:24	he shall not **lie d** until he eat *of* the prey,	7901
24: 9	he **lay d** as a lion, and as a great lion:	7901
25: 2	did eat, and **bowed d** to their gods.	7812
33:52	and **quite pluck d** all their high places:	8045
34:11	the coast shall **go d** from Shepham to	3381
34:12	the border shall **go d** to Jordan,	3381
Dt 1:25	**brought** *it* **d** unto us, and brought us	3381
5: 9	Thou shalt not **bow d** thyself unto them,	7812
6: 7	thou **liest d**, and when thou risest up.	7901
7: 5	**break d** their images, and cut down their	7665
7: 5	**cut d** their groves, and burn their graven	3772
9: 3	and he shall **bring them d** before thy face:	3665
9:12	Arise, **get thee d** quickly from hence;	3381
9:15	So I turned and **came d** from the mount,	3381
9:18	I **fell d** before the Lord, as at the first,	5307
9:25	Thus I **fell d** before the Lord forty days	5307
9:25	as I **fell d** *at the first;* because the Lord	5307
10: 5	myself and **came d** from the mount,	3381
10:22	Thy fathers **went d** into Egypt with	3381
11:19	thou **liest d**, and when thou risest up.	7901
11:30	by the way where the sun **goeth d**,	3996
12: 3	you shall **hew d** the graven images of	1438
16: 6	at the **going d** of the sun, *at* the season	935
19: 5	a stroke with the axe to **cut d** the tree,	3772
20:19	thou shalt not **cut them d** (for the tree of	3772
20:20	meat, thou shalt destroy and **cut them d**;	3772
21: 4	the elders of that city shall **bring d**	3381
22: 4	brother's ass or his ox **fall d** by the way,	5307
23:11	when the sun is d, he shall come into	935
24:13	the pledge again when the sun **goeth d**,	935
24:15	his hire, neither shall the sun **go d** upon it;	935
24:19	thou **cuttest d** thine **harvest** in	7105+7114
25: 2	that the judge shall **cause him to lie d**,	5307
26: 4	**set** it **d** before the altar of the Lord thy	3240
26: 5	he **went d** into Egypt, and sojourned	3381
26:15	**Look d** from thy holy habitation,	8259
28:24	from heaven shall it **come d** upon thee,	3381
28:43	high; and thou shalt **come d** very low.	3381
28:52	until thy high and fenced walls **come d**,	3381
33: 3	they **sat d** at thy feet; *every one* shall	8497
33:28	wine; also his heavens shall **drop d** dew.	6201
Jos 1: 4	unto the great sea *toward* the **going d** of	3996
2: 8	before they were **laid d**, she came up	7901
2:15	she **let them d** by a cord through	3381
2:18	the window which thou didst **let us d** by:	3381
3:13	*from* the waters that **come d** from above;	3381
3:16	the waters which **came d** from above	3381
3:16	those that **came d** toward the sea of	3381
4: 8	they lodged, and **laid them d** there.	3240
6: 5	the wall of the city shall **fall d** flat,	5307
6:20	that the wall **fell d** flat, so that the people	5307
7: 5	and smote them in the **going d:**	4174
8:29	as soon as the sun was **d**,	935
8:29	should **take** his carcase **d** from the tree,	3381
10:11	*and* in the **going d** to Beth-horon,	4174
10:11	that the Lord **cast d** great stones from	7993
10:13	and hasted not to **go d** about a whole day.	935
10:27	it came to pass at the time of the **going d**	935
10:27	they **took them d** off the trees,	3381
15:10	**went d** *to* Beth-shemesh, and passed on	3381
16: 3	**goeth d** westward to the coast of Japhleti,	3381
16: 7	it **went d** from Janohah to Ataroth,	3381
17:15	**cut d** for thyself there in the land of	1254
17:18	for it *is* a wood, and thou shalt **cut it d:**	1254
18:16	the border **came d** to the end of	3381
18:18	and **went d** unto Arabah:	3381
24: 4	Jacob and his children **went d** *into* Egypt.	3381
Jdg 1: 9	afterward the children of Judah **went d** to	3381
1:34	they would not suffer them to **come d** to	3381
2: 2	this land; you shall **throw d** their altars:	5422
2:19	to serve them, and to **bow d** unto them;	7812
3:25	their lord was **fallen d** dead on the earth.	5307
3:27	the children of Israel **went d** with him	3381
3:28	they **went d** after him, and took the fords	3381
4:14	So Barak **went d** from mount Tabor,	3381
4:15	so that Sisera **lighted d** off *his* chariot,	3381
5:11	shall the people of the Lord **go d** to	3381
5:14	out of Machir **came d** governors, and out	3381
5:21	O my soul, thou hast **trodden d** strength.	1869
5:27	At her feet he bowed, he fell, he **lay d:**	7901
5:27	where he bowed, there he **fell d** dead.	5307
6:25	**throw d** the altar of Baal that thy father	2040
6:25	and **cut d** the grove that *is* by it:	3772
6:26	wood of the grove which thou shalt **cut d.**	3772
6:28	the altar of Baal was **cast d**, and the grove	5422
6:28	the grove was **cut d** that *was* by it,	3772
6:30	because he hath **cast d** the altar of Baal,	5422

Ref	Text	Num
Jdg 6:30	he hath **cut d** the grove that *was* by it.	3772
6:31	because *one* hath **cast d** his altar.	5422
6:32	because he hath **thrown d** his altar.	5422
7: 4	**bring** them **d** unto the water, and I will	3381
7: 5	he **brought d** the people unto the water:	3381
7: 5	likewise every one that **boweth d** upon	3766
7: 6	all the rest of the people **bowed d** upon	3766
7: 9	unto him, Arise, **get thee d** unto the host;	3381
7:10	if thou fear to **go d**, go thou with Phurah	3381
7:10	**go** thou with Phurah thy servant *to*	3381
7:11	be strengthened to **go d** unto the host.	3381
7:11	**went he d** with Phurah his servant unto	3381
7:24	**Come d** against the Midianites,	3381
8: 9	again in peace, I will **break d** this tower.	5422
8:17	he **beat d** the tower of Penuel, and slew	5422
9:36	there **come** people **d** from the top of	3381
9:37	See there **come** people **d** by the middle of	3381
9:45	**beat d** the city, and sowed it *with* salt.	5422
9:48	**cut d** a bough from the trees, and took it,	3772
9:49	all the people likewise **cut d** every man	3772
11:37	I may go up and **go d** upon the mountains,	3381
14: 1	Samson **went d** *to* Timnath, and saw a	3381
14: 5	**went** Samson **d**, and his father and	3381
14: 7	he **went d**, and talked with the woman:	3381
14:10	So his father **went d** unto the woman:	3381
14:18	on the seventh day before the sun **went d**,	935
14:19	he **went d** *to* Ashkelon, and slew thirty	3381
15: 8	**went d** and dwelt in the top of the rock	3381
15:12	unto him, We are **come d** to bind thee,	3381
16:21	**brought him d** to Gaza, and bound him	3381
16:31	and all the house of his father **came d**,	3381
19: 6	they **sat d**, and did eat and drink both of	3427
19:14	the sun **went d** upon them *when they*	935
19:15	he **sat him d** in a street of the city:	3427
19:26	**fell d** *at* the door of the man's house	5307
19:27	the woman his concubine was **fallen d** at	5307
20:21	destroyed *d* to the ground of the Israelites	NIH
20:25	destroyed *d* to the ground of the children	NIH
20:32	*are* **smitten d** before us, as at the first.	5062
20:39	they are **smitten d** before us,	5062+5062
20:43	**trode** them **d** with ease over against	1869
Ru 3: 3	upon thee, and **get thee d** *to* the floor:	3381
3: 3	shall be, when he **lieth d**, that thou shalt	7901
3: 4	and uncover his feet, and **lay thee d**;	7901
3: 6	she **went d** *unto* the floor,	3381
3: 7	he went to **lie d** at the end of the heap *of*	7901
3: 7	and uncovered his feet, and **laid her d.**	7901
3:13	the Lord liveth: **lie d** until the morning.	7901
4: 1	Boaz up *to* the gate, and **sat him d** there:	3427
4: 1	*Ho*, such a one, turn aside, **sit d** here.	3427
4: 1	And he turned aside, and **sat d.**	3427
4: 2	elders of the city, and said, **Sit ye d** here.	3427
4: 2	said, Sit ye down here. And they **sat d.**	3427
1Sa 2: 6	he **bringeth d** *to* the grave,	3381
2: 2	when Eli *was* **laid d** in his place,	7901
3: 3	God *was*, and Samuel was **laid d** *to sleep;*	7901
3: 5	he said, I called not; **lie d** again. And he	7901
3: 5	he went again. And he went and **lay d.**	7901
3: 6	I called not, my son; **lie d** again.	7901
3: 9	Therefore Eli said unto Samuel, Go, **lie d:**	7901
3: 9	So Samuel went and **lay d** in his place.	7901
6:15	the Levites **took d** the ark of the Lord,	3381
6:18	whereon they **set d** the ark of the Lord:	3240
6:21	**come ye d**, *and* fetch it up to you.	3381
9:25	when they were **come d** from the high	3381
9:27	And as they were **going d** to the end of	3381
10: 5	**coming d** from the high place with a	3381
10: 8	thou shalt **go d** before me *to* Gilgal:	3381
10: 8	behold, I will **come d** unto thee, to offer	3381
13:12	Philistines will **come d** now upon me	3381
13:20	the Israelites **went d** *to* the Philistines,	3381
14:16	they went on **beating d** *one another.*	1986
14:36	Let us **go d** after the Philistines by night,	3381
14:37	of God, Shall I **go d** after the Philistines?	3381
15: 6	**get you d** from among the Amalekites,	3381
15:12	and passed on, and **gone d** to Gilgal.	3381
16:11	for we will not **sit d** till he come hither.	5437
17: 8	man for you, and let him **come d** to me.	3381
17:28	and he said, Why camest thou **d** hither?	3381
17:28	thou art **come d** that *thou* mightest see	3381
17:52	the wounded of the Philistines **fell d** by	5307
19:12	Michal **let** David **d** through a window:	3381
19:24	**lay d** naked all that day and all *that* night.	5307
20:19	*then* thou shalt **go d** quickly, and come	3381
20:24	come, the king **sat him d** to eat meat.	3427
21:13	and **let** his spittle **fall d** upon his beard.	3381
22: 1	his father's house heard *it*, they **went d**	3381
23: 4	and said, Arise, **go d** to Keilah:	3381
23: 6	he **came d** *with* an ephod in his hand.	3381
23: 8	to **go d** to Keilah, to besiege David and	3381
23:11	Will Saul **come d**, as thy servant hath	3381
23:11	And the Lord said, He will **come d.**	3381
23:20	**come d** according to all the desire of thy	3381
23:20	to all the desire of thy soul to **come d;**	3381
23:25	wherefore he **came d** *into* a rock,	3381
25: 1	and **went d** to the wilderness of Paran.	3381
25:20	that she **came d** by the covert of the hill,	3381
25:20	David and his men **came d** against her;	3381
26: 2	and **went d** to the wilderness of Ziph,	3381
26: 6	Who will **go d** with me to Saul to	3381
26: 6	And Abishai said, I will **go d** with thee.	3381
29: 4	And let him not **go d** with us to battle,	3381
30:15	Canst thou **bring** me **d** to this company?	3381
30:15	and I will **bring thee d** to this company.	3381
30:16	when he had **brought him d**, behold	3381

Ref	Text	Num
1Sa 30:24	as his part *is* that **goeth d** to the battle,	3381
31: 1	and **fell d** slain in mount Gilboa.	5307
2Sa 2:13	they **sat d**, the one on the one side of	3427
2:16	his fellow's side; so they **fell d** together:	5307
2:23	he **fell d** there, and died in the same	5307
2:23	as came to the place where Asahel **fell d**	5307
2:24	the sun **went d** when they were come to	935
3:35	taste bread, or ought else, till the sun **be d.**	935
5:17	David heard *of it*, and **went d** to the hold.	3381
8: 2	a line, **casting** them **d** to the ground;	7901
11: 8	**Go d** to thy house, and wash thy feet.	3381
11: 9	of his lord, and **went not d** to his house.	3381
11:10	saying, Uriah **went not d** unto his house,	3381
11:10	didst thou not **go d** unto thine house?	3381
11:13	of his lord, but **went not d** to his house.	3381
13: 5	**Lay thee d** on thy bed, and make thyself	7901
13: 6	So Amnon **lay d**, and made himself sick:	7901
13: 8	Amnon's house; and he was **laid d.**	7901
15:20	should I *this* day make thee **go up and d**	1980
15:24	they **set d** the ark of God;	3332
17:18	a well in his court; whither they **went d.**	3381
18:28	he **fell d** to the earth upon his face before	7812
19:16	came **d** with the men of Judah to meet	3381
19:18	Shimei the son of Gera **fell d** before	5307
19:20	Joseph to **go d** to meet my lord the king.	3381
19:24	Mephibosheth the son of Saul **came d** to	3381
19:31	Barzillai the Gileadite **came d** from	3381
20:15	with Joab battered the wall, to **throw** *it* **d.**	5307
21:15	David **went d**, and his servants with him,	3381
22:10	He bowed the heavens also, and **came d;**	3381
22:28	that thou mayest **bring** *them* **d.**	8213
22:48	that **bringeth d** the people under me,	3381
23:13	three of the thirty chief **went d**,	3381
23:20	he **went d** also and slew a lion in the	3381
23:21	he **went d** to him with a staff,	3381
1Ki 1:25	For he is **gone d** *this* day, and hath slain	3381
1:33	own mule, and **bring him d** to Gihon:	3381
1:38	**went d**, and caused Solomon to ride	3381
1:53	and they **brought him d** from the altar.	3381
2: 6	let not his hoar head **go d** to the grave in	3381
2: 8	he **came d** to meet me *at* Jordan,	3381
2: 9	his hoar head **bring** thou **d** *to the* grave	3381
2:19	**sat d** on his throne, and caused a seat to	3427
5: 9	My servants shall **bring** *them* **d** from	3381
8:33	thy people Israel be **smitten d** before	5062
17:23	**brought him d** out of the chamber into	3381
18:30	the altar of the Lord that was **broken d.**	2040
18:40	Elijah **brought** them **d** to the brook	3381
18:42	he **cast** himself **d** upon the earth,	1457
18:44	Prepare *thy chariot*, and **get thee d**,	3381
19: 4	and came and **sat d** under a juniper tree:	3427
19: 6	did eat and drink, and **laid** him **d** again.	7901
19:10	**thrown d** thine altars, and slain thy	2040
19:14	**thrown d** thine altars, and slain thy	2040
21: 4	he **laid** him **d** upon his bed,	7901
21:16	Ahab rose up to **go d** to the vineyard of	3381
21:18	Arise, **go d** to meet Ahab king of Israel,	3381
21:18	whither he is **gone d** to possess it.	3381
22: 2	Jehoshaphat the king of Judah **came d**	3381
22:36	the host about the **going d** of the sun,	935
2Ki 1: 2	Ahaziah **fell d** through a lattice in his	5307
1: 4	Thou shalt not **come d** from *that* bed on	3381
1: 6	thou shalt not **come d** from *that* bed on	3381
1: 9	man of God, the king hath said, **Come d.**	3381
1:10	let fire **come d** from heaven,	3381
1:10	there **came d** fire from heaven,	3381
1:11	thus hath the king said, **Come d** quickly.	3381
1:12	let fire **come d** from heaven,	3381
1:12	the fire of God **came d** from heaven,	3381
1:14	there **came** fire **d** from heaven,	3381
1:15	Lord said unto Elijah, **Go d** with him:	3381
1:15	and **went d** with him unto the king.	3381
1:16	thou shalt not **come d** off *that* bed on	3381
2: 2	not leave thee. So they **went d** to Beth-el.	3381
3:12	and the king of Edom **went d** to him.	3381
3:25	they **beat d** the cities, and *on* every good	2040
5:14	**went** he **d**, and dipped *himself* seven	3381
5:18	when I **bow d** myself in the house of	7812
5:21	he **lighted d** from the chariot to meet	5307
6: 4	they came to Jordan, they **cut d** wood.	1504
6: 6	he cut off a stick, and cast *it* in thither;	7094
6: 9	place; for thither the Syrians are **come d.**	5185
6:18	when they **came d** to him, Elisha prayed	3381
6:33	the messenger **came d** unto him:	3381
7:17	who spake when the king **came d** to him.	3381
8:29	**went d** to see Joram the son of Ahab in	3381
9:16	Ahaziah king of Judah was **come d** to see	3381
9:24	at his heart, and he **sunk d** in his chariot.	3766
9:33	he said, **Throw** her **d.** So they threw her	8058
9:33	So they threw her **d:** and *some* of her	8058
10:13	we **go d** to salute the children of the king	3381
10:27	they **brake d** the image of Baal,	5422
10:27	**brake d** the house of Baal, and made it a	5422
11: 6	of the house, that it be not **broken d.**	4535
11:18	*into* the house of Baal, and **brake** it **d;**	5422
11:19	they **brought d** the king from the house	3381
12:20	house of Millo, which **goeth d** *to* Silla.	3381
13:14	Joash the king of Israel **came d** unto him,	3381
13:21	when the man was **let d**, and touched	1980
14: 9	*was* in Lebanon, and **trode d** the thistle.	7429
14:13	brake the wall of Jerusalem from	6555
16:17	**took d** the sea from off the brasen oxen	3381
18: 4	**cut d** the groves, and brake in pieces	3772
19:16	Lord, **bow d** thine ear, and hear: open,	5186
19:23	will **cut d** the tall cedar trees thereof,	3772

D

2Ki 20:10 a light thing for the shadow to **go d** ten 5186
20:11 which it had **gone d** in the dial of Ahaz. 3381
21:13 wiping *it*, and turning *it* **upside**. 5921+6440
23: 5 he **put d** the idolatrous priests, whom 7673
23: 7 he **brake d** the houses of the sodomites, 5422
23: 8 **brake d** the high places of the gates that 5422
23:12 the king **beat d**, and brake *them* down 5422
23:12 **brake** *them* **d** from thence, and cast 7323
23:14 **cut d** the groves, and filled their places 3772
23:15 that altar and the high place he **brake d**, 5422
25:10 **brake** the walls of Jerusalem round 5422
1Ch 5:22 there **fell d** many slain, because the war 5307
7:21 they **came d** to take *away* their cattle. 3381
10: 1 and **fell d** slain in mount Gilboa. 5307
11:15 three of the thirty captains **went d** to 3381
11:22 he **went d** and slew a lion in a pit in a 3381
11:23 he **went d** to him with a staff, 3381
29:20 **bowed d** their **heads**, and worshipped 6915
2Ch 6:13 kneeled *d* upon his knees before all NIH
7: 1 the fire **came d** from heaven, 3381
7: 3 of Israel saw how the fire **came d**, 3381
13:17 there **fell d** slain of Israel five hundred 5307
14: 3 **brake d** the images, and **cut d** the groves: 7665
14: 3 down the images, and **cut d** the groves: 1438
15:16 Asa **cut d** her idol, and stamped *it*, and 3772
18: 2 after *certain* years he **went d** to Ahab to 3381
18:34 the time of the sun **going d** he died. 935
20:16 To morrow go ye **d** against them: behold, 3381
22: 6 **went d** to see Jehoram the son of Ahab at 3381
23:17 **brake** it **d**, and brake his altars and his 5422
23:20 **brought d** the king from the house of 3381
25: 8 God hath power to help, and to **cast d**. 3782
25:12 **cast** them **d** from the top of the rock, 7993
25:14 **bowed d** himself before them, 7812
25:18 *was* in Lebanon, and **trode d** the thistle. 7429
25:23 **brake d** the wall of Jerusalem from 6555
26: 6 **brake d** the wall of Gath, and the wall of 6555
31: 1 images *in pieces*, and **cut d** the groves, 1438
31: 1 **threw d** the high places and the altars out 5422
32:30 brought it straight **d** to the west 4295+3807.1
33: 3 which Hezekiah his father had **broken d**, 5422
34: 4 they **brake d** the altars of Baalim in his 5422
34: 4 that *were* on high above them, he **cut d**; 1438
34: 7 when he had **broken d** the altars and 5422
34: 7 **cut d** all the idols throughout all the land 1438
36: 3 the king of Egypt **put** him **d** at Jerusalem, 5493
36:19 **brake d** the wall of Jerusalem, 5422
Ezr 6:11 let timber be **pulled d** from his house, 5256
9: 3 and of my beard, and **sat d** astonied. 3427
10: 1 **casting** himself **d** before the house of 5307
10:16 **sat d** in the first day of the tenth month 3427
Ne 1: 3 the wall of Jerusalem also *is* **broken d**, 6555
1: 4 *that* I **sat d** and wept, and mourned 3427
2:13 were **broken d**, and the gates thereof 6555
3:15 unto the stairs that **go d** from the city of 3381
4: 3 he shall even **break d** their stone wall. 6555
6: 3 a great work, so that I cannot **come d**: 3381
6: 3 whilst I leave it, and **come d** to you? 3381
6:16 they were much **cast d** in their own eyes: 5307
9:13 Thou **camest d** also upon mount Sinai, 3381
Est 3:15 And the king and Haman **sat d** to drink; 3427
8: 3 **fell d** at his feet, and besought him with 5307
Job 1: 7 earth, and from **walking up and d** in it. 1980
1:20 **fell d** upon the ground, and worshipped, 5307
2: 2 earth, and from **walking up and d** in it. 1980
2: 8 and he **sat d** among the ashes. 3427
2:13 So they **sat d** with him upon the ground 3427
6:21 ye see *my* **casting d**, and are afraid. 2866
7: 4 When I **lie d**, I say, When shall I arise, 7901
7: 9 that **goeth d** *to* the grave shall come up 3381
7:19 let me alone till I **swallow d** my spittle? 1104
8:12 it *is* yet in his greenness, *and* not **cut d**, 6998
11:19 thou shalt **lie d**, and none shall make 7257
12:14 he **breaketh d**, and it cannot be built 2040
14: 2 cometh forth like a flower, and is **cut d**: 5243
14: 7 if it be **cut d**, that it will sprout again, 3772
14:12 So man **lieth d**, and riseth not: till 7901
17: 3 **Lay d** now, put me in a surety with thee; 7760
17:16 They shall **go d** *to* the bars of the pit, 3381
18: 7 and his own counsel shall **cast** him **d**. 7993
20:11 which shall **lie d** with him in the dust. 7901
20:15 He hath **swallowed d** riches, and he 1104
20:18 he restore, and shall not **swallow** *it* **d**: 1104
21:13 and in a moment **go d** *to* the grave. 2865
21:26 They shall **lie d** alike in the dust, 7901
22:16 Which were **cut d** out of time, 7059
22:20 Whereas our substance is not **cut d**, 3582
22:29 *men* are **cast d**, then thou shalt say, 8213
27:19 The rich *man* shall **lie d**, but he shall not 7901
29:24 light of my countenance they **cast** not **d**. 5307
31:10 and let others **bow d** upon her. 3766
32:13 God **thrusteth** him **d**, not man. 5086
33:24 Deliver him from **going d** *to* the pit: 3381
36:27 they **pour d** rain according to the vapour 2212
40:12 and **tread d** the wicked in their place. 1915
41: 1 tongue with a cord *which* thou **lettest d**? 8257
41: 9 shall *not* one be **cast d** even at the sight 2904
Ps 3: 5 I **laid** me **d** and slept; I awaked; 7901
4: 8 I will both **lay** me **d** in peace, and sleep: 7901
7: 5 let him **tread d** my life upon the earth, 7429
7:16 his violent dealing shall **come d** upon his 3381
9:15 The heathen are **sunk d** in the pit *that* 2883
14: 2 The Lord **looked d** from heaven upon 8259
17:11 they have set their eyes **bowing d** to 5186
17:13 O Lord, disappoint him, **cast** him **d**: 3766

Ps 18: 9 He bowed the heavens also, and **came d**: 3381
18:27 but with **high d** high looks. 8213
20: 8 They are **brought d** and fallen: but we 3766
22:29 all they that **go d** to the dust shall bow 3381
23: 2 He maketh me to **lie d** in green pastures: 7257
28: 1 I become like them that **go d** into the pit. 3381
30: 3 me alive, that I should not **go d** to the pit. 3381
30: 9 *there* in my blood, when I **go d** to the pit? 3381
31: 2 **Bow d** thine ear to me; deliver me 5186
35:14 I **bowed d** heavily, as one that mourneth 7817
36:12 they are **cast d**, and shall not be able to 1760
37: 2 For they shall soon be **cut d** like the grass, 5243
37:14 to **cast d** the poor and needy, *and* to slay 5307
37:24 he fall, he shall not be **utterly cast d**. 2904
38: 6 I am troubled; I am **bowed d** greatly; I go 7817
42: 5 Why art thou **cast d**, O my soul? 7817
42: 6 O my God, my soul is **cast d** within me: 7817
42:11 Why art thou **cast d**, O my soul? 7817
43: 5 Why art thou **cast d**, O my soul? and 7817
44: 5 thee will we **push d** our enemies: 5055
44:25 For our soul is **bowed d** to the dust: 7743
50: 1 rising of the sun unto the **going d** thereof. 3996
53: 2 God **looked d** from heaven upon 8259
55:15 *and* let them **go d** quick *into* hell: 3381
55:23 shalt **bring** them **d** into the pit of 3381
56: 7 in *thine* anger **cast d** the people, O God. 3381
57: 6 a net for my steps; my soul is **bowed d**: 3721
59:11 and **bring** them **d**, O Lord our shield. 3381
59:15 Let them **wander up and d** for meat, 5128
60:12 for he *it is that* shall **tread d** our enemies. 947
62: 4 They only consult to **cast** *him* **d** from his 5080
68: 9 He shall **come d** like rain upon the mown 3381
72:11 Yea, all kings shall **fall d** before him: 7812
73:18 thou **castedst** them **d** into destruction. 5307
74: 6 they **break d** the carved work thereof 1986
74: 7 have defiled *by* casting **d** the dwelling NIH
75: 7 he **putteth d** one, and setteth up another. 8213
78:16 and **caused** waters **to run d** like rivers. 3381
78:24 had **rained d** manna upon them to eat, 4305
78:31 and **smote d** the chosen *men* of Israel. 3766
80:12 hast thou *then* **broken d** her hedges, 6555
80:14 **look d** from heaven, and behold, 5027
80:16 *is* burnt with fire, *it is* **cut d**: they perish 3683
85:11 righteousness shall **look d** from heaven. 8259
86: 1 **Bow d** thine ear, O Lord, hear me: for I 5186
88: 4 I am counted with them that **go d** into 3381
89:23 I will **beat d** his foes before his face, 3807
89:40 Thou hast **broken d** all his hedges; 6555
89:44 and **cast** his throne **d** to the ground. 4048
90: 6 in the evening it is **cut d**, and withereth. 4135
95: 6 come, let us worship and **bow d**: let us 3766
102:10 for thou hast lifted me up, and **cast** me **d**. 7993
102:19 he hath **looked d** from the height of his 8259
104: 8 they **go d** *by* the valleys unto the place 3381
104:19 for seasons: the sun knoweth his **going d**. 3996
104:22 and **lay** them **d** in their dens. 7257
107:12 Therefore he **brought d** their heart with 3665
107:12 they **fell d**, and *there was* none to help. 3782
107:23 They that **go d** to the sea in ships, that do 3381
107:26 heaven, they **go d** *again* to the depths: 3381
108:13 for he *it is that* shall **tread d** our enemies. 947
109:23 I am **tossed up and d** as the locust. 5287
113: 3 the rising of the sun unto the **going d** 3996
115:17 neither any that **go d** into silence. 3381
119:118 Thou hast **trodden d** all them that err 5541
119:136 Rivers of waters **run d** mine eyes, because 3381
133: 2 that **ran d** upon the beard, *even* Aaron's 3381
133: 2 that **went d** to the skirts of his garments; 3381
137: 1 of Babylon, there we **sat d**, yea, we wept, 3427
139: 3 compassest my path and my **lying d**, 7252
143: 3 he hath **smitten** my life **d** to the ground; 1792
143: 7 lest I be like unto them that **go d** into 3381
144: 5 Bow thy heavens, O Lord, and **come d**: 3381
145:14 and raiseth up all those that be **bowed d**. 3721
146: 8 the Lord raiseth them that are **bowed d**: 3721
146: 9 way of the wicked he **turneth upside d**. 5791
147: 6 he **casteth** the wicked **d** to the ground. 8213
Pr 1:12 and whole, as those that **go d** into the pit: 3381
3:20 and the clouds **drop d** the dew. 7491
3:24 thou **liest d**, thou shalt not be afraid: 7901
3:24 thou shalt **lie d**, and thy sleep shall be 7901
5: 5 Her feet **go d** *to* death; her steps take 3381
7:26 For she hath **cast d** many wounded: yea, 5307
7:27 hell, **going d** to the chambers of death. 3381
14: 1 the foolish **plucketh** it **d** with her hands. 2040
18: 8 they **go d** *into* the innermost parts of 3381
21:22 **casteth d** the strength of the confidence 3381
22:17 **Bow d** thine ear, and hear the words of 5186
23:34 shalt be as he that **lieth d** in the midst 7901
24:31 the stone wall thereof was **broken d**. 2040
25:26 A righteous *man* **falling d** before 4131
25:28 own spirit *is* like a city *that is* **broken d**, 6555
26:22 they **go d** *into* the innermost parts of 3381
Ecc 1: 5 The sun **goeth d**, and hasteth to his place 935
3: 3 a time to **break d**, and a time to build *up*; 6555
SS 2: 3 **sat d** under his shadow with great delight, 3427
2: 1 My beloved is **gone d** into his garden, 3381
6:11 I **went d** into the garden of nuts to see 3381
7: 9 for my beloved, that **goeth d** sweetly, NIH
Isa 2: 9 the mean man **boweth d**, and the great 7817
2:11 the haughtiness of men shall be **bowed d**, 7817
2:17 the loftiness of man shall be **bowed d**, 7817
5: 5 *and* **break d** the wall thereof, and it shall 6555
5: 5 wall thereof, and it shall be **trodden d**: 4823
5:15 the mean man shall be **brought d**, 7817

Isa 9:10 The bricks are **fallen d**, but we will build 5307
9:10 the sycomores are **cut d**, but we will 1438
10: 4 Without me they shall **bow d** under 3766
10: 6 **tread** them **d** like the mire of 4823+7760
10:13 I have **put d** the inhabitants like a valiant 3381
10:33 the high ones of stature *shall be* **hewn d**, 1438
10:34 he shall **cut d** the thickets of the forest 5362
11: 6 and the leopard shall **lie d** with the kid; 7257
11: 7 their young ones shall **lie d** together: 7257
14: 8 of Lebanon, *saying*, Since thou art **laid d**, 7901
14:11 Thy pomp is **brought d** *to* the grave, 3381
14:12 *how* art thou **cut d** to the ground, 1438
14:15 Yet thou shalt be **brought d** to hell, 3381
14:19 sword, that **go d** to the stones of the pit; 3381
14:30 and the needy shall **lie d** in safety. 7257
16: 8 the lords of the heathen have **broken d** 1986
17: 2 which shall **lie d**, and none shall make 7257
18: 2 a nation meted out and **trodden d**, 4001
18: 5 and take away *and* **cut d** the branches. 8456
21: 3 I was **bowed d** at the hearing *of it*; I was 5753
22: 5 of **treading d**, and of perplexity by 4001
22: 5 **breaking d** the walls, and of crying to 6979
22:10 the houses have ye **broken d** to fortify 5422
22:19 and from thy state shall he **pull** thee **d**. 2040
22:25 place be removed, and be **cut d**, and fall; 1438
24: 1 turneth **upside d**, and scattereth abroad 6440
24:10 The city of confusion is **broken d**: 7665
24:19 The earth is **utterly broken d**, 7489+7489
25: 5 Thou shalt **bring d** the noise of strangers, 3665
25:10 Moab shall be **trodden d** under him, 1758
25:10 as straw is **trodden d** for the dunghill. 1758
25:11 he shall **bring d** their pride together with 8213
25:12 the high fort of thy walls shall he **bring d**, 7817
26: 5 he **bringeth d** them that dwell on high; 7817
26: 6 The foot shall **tread** it **d**, *even* the feet of 7429
27:10 there shall he **lie d**, and consume 7257
28: 2 shall **cast d** to the earth with the hand. 3240
28:18 then ye shall be **trodden d** by it. 4823
29: 4 thou shalt be **brought d**, *and* shalt speak 8213
29:16 Surely your **turning** of things **upside d** 2017
30: 2 That walk to **go d** *into* Egypt, and have 3381
30:30 shall shew the **lighting d** of his arm, 5183
30:31 the Lord shall the Assyrian be **beaten d**, 2865
31: 1 Woe to them that **go d** *to* Egypt for help; 3381
31: 3 he that is holpen shall **fall d**, and they all 5307
31: 4 shall the Lord of hosts **come d** to fight 3381
32:19 When it shall hail, **coming d** *on* the 3381
33: 9 Lebanon is ashamed *and* **hewn d**: Sharon 7060
33:20 a tabernacle *that* shall not be **taken d**; 6813
34: 4 all their host shall **fall d**, as the leaf falleth 5034
34: 5 it shall **come d** upon Idumea, and upon 3381
34: 7 the unicorns shall **come d** with them, 3381
37:24 I will **cut d** the tall cedars thereof, 3772
38: 8 which is **gone d** in the sun dial of Ahaz, 3381
38: 8 by which degrees it was **gone d**. 3381
38:18 they that **go d** into the pit cannot hope for 3381
42:10 ye that **go d** to the sea, and all that is 3381
43:14 have **brought d** all their nobles, 3381
43:17 shall **lie d** together, they shall not rise: 7901
44:14 *He* **heweth** him **d** cedars, and taketh 3772
44:15 it a graven image, and **falleth d** thereto. 5456
44:17 he **falleth d** unto it, and worshippeth *it*, 5456
44:19 shall I **fall d** to the stock of a tree? 5456
45: 8 **Drop d**, ye heavens, from above, 7491
45: 8 and let the skies **pour d** righteousness: 5140
45:14 over, and they shall **fall d** unto thee, 7812
46: 1 Bel **boweth d**, Nebo stoopeth, their idols 3766
46: 2 They stoop, they **bow d** together; 3766
46: 6 it a god: they **fall d**, yea, they worship. 5456
47: 1 **Come d**, and sit in the dust, O virgin 3381
49:23 they shall **bow d** to thee *with their* face 3381
50:11 of mine hand; ye shall **lie d** in sorrow. 7901
51:23 to thy soul, **Bow d**, that we may go over: 7812
52: 2 the dust; arise, *and* **sit d**, O Jerusalem: 3427
52: 4 My people **went d** aforetime *into* Egypt 3381
55:10 For as the rain **cometh d**, and the snow 3381
56:10 sleeping, **lying d**, loving to slumber. 7901
58: 5 *is it* to **bow d** his head as a bulrush, 3721
60:14 **bow** themselves **d** at the soles of thy feet; 7812
60:20 Thy sun shall no more **go d**; neither shall 935
63: 6 I will **tread d** the people in mine anger, 947
63: 6 I will **bring d** their strength to the earth. 3381
63:14 As a beast **goeth d** into the valley, 3381
63:15 **Look d** from heaven, and behold from 5027
63:18 our adversaries have **trodden d** thy 947
64: 1 the heavens, that thou wouldest **come d**, 3381
64: 1 that the mountains might **flow d** at thy 2151
64: 3 thou **camest d**, the mountains flowed 3381
64: 3 the mountains **flowed d** at thy presence. 2151
65:10 of Achor a **place** for the herds to **lie d** in, 3381
65:12 and ye shall all **bow d** to the slaughter: 3766
Jer 1:10 to **pull d**, and to destroy, and to throw 5422
1:10 and to **throw d**, to build, and to plant. 2040
3:25 We **lie d** in our shame, and our confusion 7901
4:26 all the cities thereof were **broken d** 5422
6: 6 **Hew** ye **d** trees, and cast a mount against 3772
6:15 time *that* I visit them they shall be **cast d**, 3782
8:12 of their visitation they shall be **cast d**, 3782
9:18 that our eyes may **run d** with tears, 3381
13:17 **run d** *with* tears, because the Lord's 3381
13:18 to the queen, Humble yourselves, **sit d**: 3427
13:18 for your principalities shall **come d**, 3381
14:17 Let mine eyes **run d** *with* tears night and 3381
15: 9 her sun is **gone d** while *it was* yet day: 935
18: 2 **go d** *to* the potter's house, and there I

Jer
18: 3 I **went d** to the potter's house, and 3381
18: 7 pluck up, and to **pull d**, and to destroy it; 5422
21:13 which say, Who shall **come d** against us? 5181
22: 1 **Go d** to the house of the king of Judah, 3381
22: 7 they shall **cut d** thy choice cedars, 3772
24: 6 I will build them, and not **pull** them **d;** 2040
25:37 peaceable habitations are **cut d** because 1826
26:10 **sat d** in the entry of the new gate of 3427
31:28 to **break d**, and to throw down, 5422
31:28 to **throw d**, and to destroy, and to afflict; 2040
31:40 nor **thrown d** any more for ever. 2040
33: 4 which are **thrown d** by the mounts, 5422
33:12 of shepherds **causing** their flocks **to lie d.** 7257
36:12 he **went d** into the king's house, into 3381
36:15 him, Sit **d** now, and read it in our ears. 3427
38: 6 they **let d** Jeremiah with cords. And in 7971
38:11 **let** them **d** by cords into the dungeon to 7971
39: 8 and **brake d** the walls of Jerusalem. 5422
42:10 not **pull** you **d**, and I will plant you, 2040
45: 4 that which I have built will I **break d**, 2040
46: 5 their mighty ones are **beaten d**, and are 3807
46:23 They shall **cut d** her forest, saith 3772
48: 2 Also thou shalt be **cut d**, O Madmen; 1826
48: 5 in the **going d** of Horonaim the enemies 4174
48:15 his chosen young men are **gone d** to 3381
48:18 **come d** from thy glory, and sit in thirst; 3381
48:20 Moab is confounded; for it is **broken d:** 2865
48:39 shall howl, saying, How is it **broken d!** 2865
49:16 I will **bring** thee **d** from thence, saith 3381
50:15 are fallen, her walls are **thrown d.** 2040
50:27 bullocks; let them **go d** to the slaughter; 3381
51:25 **roll** thee **d** from the rocks, and will make 1556
51:40 I will **bring** them **d** like lambs to 3381
52:14 **brake d** all the walls of Jerusalem round 5422

La
1: 9 end; therefore she **came d** wonderfully; 3381
1:16 mine eye **runneth d** with water, because 3381
2: 1 **cast d** from heaven unto the earth 7993
2: 2 he hath **thrown d** in his wrath the strong 2040
2: 2 he hath **brought** them **d** to the ground: 5060
2:10 virgins of Jerusalem **hang d** their heads 3381
2:17 he hath **thrown d**, and hath not pitied: 2040
2:18 let tears **run d** like a river day and night: 3381
3:48 Mine eye **runneth d** with rivers of water 3381
3:49 Mine eye **trickleth d**, and ceaseth not, 5064
3:50 Till the LORD **look d**, and behold from 8259
3:63 Behold their **sitting d**, and their rising up; 3427

Eze
1:13 it **went up and d** among the living 1980
1:24 when they stood, they **let d** their wings. 7503
1:25 they stood, and had **let d** their wings. 7503
6: 4 I will **cast d** your slain men before your 5307
6: 6 images may be **cut d**, and your works 1438
11:13 **fell I d** upon my face, and cried with a 5307
13:14 So will I **break d** the wall that ye have 2040
13:14 and **bring** it **d** to the ground, 5060
16:39 they shall **throw d** thine eminent place, 2040
16:39 and shall **break d** thy high places: 5422
17:24 I the LORD have **brought d** the high tree, 8213
19: 2 she **lay d** among lions, she nourished her 7257
19: 6 he **went up and d** among the lions, 1980
19:12 she was **cast d** to the ground, and the 7993
24:16 nor weep, neither shalt thy tears **run d.** 935
26: 4 walls of Tyrus, and **break d** her towers, 2040
26: 9 with his axes he shall **break d** thy towers. 5422
26:11 his horses shall he **tread d** all thy streets: 7429
26:11 thy strong garrisons shall **go d** to 3381
26:12 they shall **break d** thy walls, 2040
26:16 the princes of the sea shall **come d** from 3381
26:20 When I shall **bring** thee **d** with them that 3381
26:20 of old, with them that **go d** to the pit, 3381
27:29 of the sea, shall **come d** from their ships, 3381
28: 8 They shall **bring** thee **d** to the pit, 3381
28:14 thou hast **walked up and d** in the midst 1980
30: 4 and her foundations shall be **broken d.** 2040
30: 6 and the pride of her power shall **come d:** 3381
30:25 and the arms of Pharaoh shall **fall d**, 5307
31:12 all the people of the earth are **gone d** from 3381
31:14 of men, with them that **go d** to the pit. 3381
31:15 In the day when he **went d** to the grave I 3381
31:16 when I **cast** him **d** to hell with them that 3381
31:17 They also **went d** into hell with him unto 3381
31:18 shalt thou be **brought d** with the trees 3381
32:18 **cast** them **d**, even her, and the daughters 3381
32:18 earth, with them that **go d** into the pit. 3381
32:19 **go d**, and be thou laid with 3381
32:21 they are **gone d**, they lie uncircumcised, 3381
32:24 which are **gone d** uncircumcised into 3381
32:24 shame with them that **go d** to the pit. 3381
32:25 shame with them that **go d** to the pit: 3381
32:27 which are **gone d** to hell with their 3381
32:29 and with them that **go d** to the pit. 3381
32:30 which are **gone d** with the slain; 3381
32:30 bear their shame with them that **go d** to 3381
34:15 my flock, and I will **cause** them **to lie d,** 7257
34:18 must **tread d** with your feet the residue 7429
34:26 I will **cause** the shower **to come d** in his 3381
37: 1 **set** me **d** in the midst of the valley which 5117
38:20 the mountains shall be **thrown d**, 2040
39:10 neither **cut d** any out of the forests, 2404
47: 1 the waters **came d** from under from 3381
47: 8 **go d** into the desert, and go into the sea: 3381

Da
3: 5 ye **fall d** and worship the golden image 5308
3: 6 whoso **falleth** not **d** and worshippeth 5308
3: 7 **fell d** and worship the golden image 5308
3:10 shall **fall d** and worship the golden image: 5308
3:11 whoso **falleth** not **d** and worshippeth, 5308

Da
3:15 ye **fall d** and worship the image which I 5308
3:23 **fell d** bound into the midst of the burning 5308
4:13 and a holy one **came d** from heaven; 5182
4:14 **Hew d** the tree, and cut off his branches, 1414
4:23 and a holy one **coming d** from heaven, 5182
4:23 saying, **Hew** the tree **d**, and destroy it; 1414
5:19 he set up; and whom he would he **put d**. 8214
6:14 he laboured till the **going d** of the sun to 4606
7: 9 I beheld till the thrones were cast **d,** NIH
7:23 shall **tread** it **d**, and break it in pieces. 1759
8: 7 he **cast** him **d** to the ground, 7993
8:10 it **cast d** some of the host and of the stars 5307
8:11 and the place of his sanctuary was **cast d.** 7993
8:12 and it **cast d** the truth to the ground; 7993
11:12 and he shall **cast d** many ten thousands: 5307
11:26 shall overflow: and many shall **fall d** slain. 5307
2:18 and will **make** them **to lie d** safely. 7901

Hos
7:12 I will **bring** them **d** as the fowls of 3381
10: 2 shall **break d** their altars, he shall spoil 6202

Joel
1:17 are laid desolate, the barns are **broken d;** 2040
2:23 he will **cause to come d** for you the rain, 3381
3: 2 will **bring** them **d** into the valley of 3381
3:11 **cause** thy mighty ones **to come d,** 5181
3:13 come, **get** you **d;** for the press is full, 3381
3:18 the mountains shall **drop d** new wine, 5197

Am
2: 8 they **lay** themselves **d** upon clothes laid 5186
3:11 he shall **bring d** thy strength from thee, 3381
5:24 let judgment **run d** as waters, 1556
6: 2 **go d** to Gath of the Philistines: be they 3381
8: 9 that I will **cause to go d** at noon, 935
9: 2 up to heaven, thence will I **bring** them **d;** 3381

Ob
1: 3 Who shall **bring** me **d** to the ground? 3381
1: 4 thence will I **bring** thee **d**, saith 3381
1:16 they shall **swallow d**, and they shall be as 3886

Jnh
1: 3 of the LORD, and **went d** to Joppa; 3381
1: 3 paid the fare thereof, and **went d** into it, 3381
1: 5 was **gone d** into the sides of the ship; 3381
2: 6 **went d** to the bottoms of the mountains; 3381

Mic
1: 3 **come d** and tread upon the high places 3381
1: 4 as the waters that are poured **d** a steep 871.1
1: 6 I will **pour d** the stones thereof into 5064
1:12 evil **came d** from the LORD unto the gate 3381
3: 6 and the sun shall **go d** over the prophets, 935
5: 8 both **treadeth d**, and teareth in pieces, 7429
5:11 land, and **throw d** all thy strong holds: 2040
6:14 **casting d** shall be in the midst of thee; 3445
7:10 now shall she be **trodden d** as the mire 4823

Na
1: 6 and the rocks are **thrown d** by him. 5422
1:12 many, yet thus shall they be **cut d**, 1494

Zep
1:11 for all the merchant people are **cut d;** 1820
2: 7 in the houses of Ashkelon shall they **lie d** 7257
2:14 flocks shall **lie d** in the midst of her, 7257
2:15 desolation, a **place** for beasts **to lie d** in! 4769
3:13 for they shall feed and **lie d**, and none 7257

Hag
2:22 the horses and their riders shall **come d**, 3381

Zec
10: 5 shall be as mighty men, which **tread d** 947
10:11 the pride of Assyria shall be **brought d**, 3381
10:12 they shall **walk up and d** in his name, 1980
11: 2 for the forest of the vintage is **come d.** 3381

Mal
1: 4 They shall build, but I will **throw d;** 2040
1:11 **going d** of the same my name shall be 3996
4: 3 ye shall **tread d** the wicked; for they shall 6072

Mt
2:11 and **fell d**, and worshipped him: 4098
3:10 bringeth not forth good fruit is **hewn d,** 1581
4: 6 If thou be the Son of God, cast thyself **d:** 2736
4: 9 if thou wilt **fall d** and worship me. 4098
7:19 bringeth not forth good fruit is **hewn d,** 1581
8: 1 he was **come d** from the mountain, 2597
8:11 and shall **sit d** with Abraham, and Isaac, 347
8:32 the whole herd of swine ran violently **d** a 2596
9:10 and **sat d** with him and his disciples. 4873
11:23 unto heaven, shalt be **brought d** to hell: 2601
13:48 and **sat d**, and gathered the good into 2523
14:19 he commanded the multitude to **sit d** on 347
14:29 And when Peter was **come d** out of 2597
15:29 went up into a mountain, and **sat d** there. 2521
15:30 others, and cast them **d** at Jesus' feet; NIG
15:35 he commanded the multitude to **sit d** on 377
17: 9 And as they **came d** from the mountain, 2597
17:14 man, **kneeling d** to him, and saying, 1120
18:26 The servant therefore **fell d,** 4098
18:29 And his fellowservant **fell d** at his feet, 4098
21: 8 others **cut d** branches from the trees, 2875
24: 2 another, that shall not be **thrown d.** 2647
24:17 **come d** to take any thing out of his house 2597
26:20 even was come, he **sat d** with the twelve. 345
27: 5 And he **cast d** the pieces of silver in 4496
27:19 When he was **set d** on the judgment seat, 2521
27:36 And **sitting d** they watched him there; 2521
27:40 the Son of God, **come d** from the cross. 2597
27:42 let him now **come d** from the cross, 2597

Mk
1: 7 whose shoes I am not worthy to **stoop d** 2955
1:40 and **kneeling d** to him, and saying unto 1120
2: 4 they **let d** the bed wherein the sick of 5465
3:11 **fell d** before him, and cried, saying, 4363
3:22 And the scribes which **came d** from 2597
5:13 the herd ran violently **d** a steep place into 2596
5:33 and **fell d** before him, and told him 4363
6:39 he commanded them to **make** all **sit d** 347
6:40 And they **sat d** in ranks, by hundreds, 377
8: 6 he commanded the people to **sit d** on 377
9: 9 And as they **came d** from the mountain, 2597
9:35 And he **sat d**, and called the twelve, 2523
11: 8 and others **cut d** branches off the trees, 2875
13: 2 another, that shall not be **thrown d.** 2647

Mk
13:15 on the housetop not **go d** into the house, 2597
13:30 Save thyself, and **come d** from the cross. 2597
13:36 whether Elias will come to **take** him **d.** 2507
15:46 and **took** him **d**, and wrapped him in 2507

Lk
1:52 hath **put d** the mighty from their seats, 2507
2:51 And he **went d** with them, and came to 2597
3: 9 bringeth not forth good fruit is **hewn d,** 1581
4: 9 Son of God, cast thyself **d** from hence: 2736
4:20 he gave it again to the minister, and **sat d.** 2523
4:29 that they might **cast** him **d** headlong, 2630
4:31 And **came d** to Capernaum, a city of 2718
5: 3 he **sat d**, and taught the people out of 2523
5: 4 deep, and **let d** your nets for a draught. 5465
5: 5 at thy word I will **let d** the net. 5465
5: 8 When Simon Peter saw it, he **fell d** at 4363
5:19 **let** him **d** through the tiling with his 2524
5:29 and of others that sat **d** with them. 1510
6:17 And he **came d** with them, and stood in 2597
6:38 **pressed d**, and shaken together, and 4085
7:36 the Pharisee's house, and **sat d** to meat. 347
8: 5 and it was **trodden d**, and the fowls of 2662
8:23 there **came d** a storm of wind on the lake 2597
8:28 and **fell d** before him, and with a loud 4363
8:33 the herd ran violently **d** a steep place into 2596
8:41 and he **fell d** at Jesus' feet, 4098
8:47 trembling, and **falling d** before him, 4363
9:14 **Make** them **sit d** by fifties in a company. 2625
9:15 they did so, and **made** them all **sit d**. 347
9:37 when they were **come d** from the hill, 2718
9:42 the devil **threw** him **d**, and tare him. 4486
9:44 Let these sayings **sink d** into your ears: 5087
9:54 thou that we command fire to **come d** 2597
10:15 to heaven, shalt be **thrust d** to hell. 2601
10:30 A certain man **went d** from Jerusalem to 2597
10:31 And by chance there **came d** a certain 2597
11:37 him: and he went in, and **sat d** to meat. 377
12:18 I will **pull d** my barns, and build greater; 2507
12:37 and **make** them to **sit d** to meat, 347
13: 7 **cut** it **d;** why cumbereth it the ground? 1581
13: 9 if not, then after that thou shalt **cut** it **d.** 1581
13:29 and shall **sit d** in the kingdom of God. 347
14: 8 a wedding, **sit** not **d** in the highest room; 2625
14:10 bidden, go and **sit d** in the lowest room; 377
14:28 **sitteth** not **d** first, and counteth the cost, 2523
14:31 **sitteth** not **d** first, and consulteth 2523
16: 6 thy bill, and **sit d** quickly, and write fifty. 2523
17: 7 from the field, Go and **sit d** to meat? 377
17:16 And **fell d** on his face at his feet, 4098
17:31 let him not **come d** to take it away: 2597
18:14 this man **went d** to his house justified 2597
19: 5 Zaccheus, make haste, and **come d;** 2597
19: 6 and **came d**, and received him joyfully. 2597
19:21 thou takest up that thou **layedst** not **d**, 5087
19:22 taking up that I **laid** not **d**, and reaping 5087
21: 6 another, that shall not be **thrown d.** 2647
21:24 Jerusalem shall be **trodden d** of 377
22:14 he **sat d**, and the twelve apostles with 377
22:41 stone's cast, and **kneeled d**, 1119+3588+5087
22:44 drops of blood **falling d** to the ground. 2597
22:55 and were **set d** together, Peter sat down 4776
22:55 down together, Peter **sat d** among them. 2521
23:53 And he **took** it **d**, and wrapped it in linen, 2507
24: 5 and **bowed d** their faces to the earth, 2827
24:12 **stooping d**, he beheld the linen clothes 3879

Jn
2:12 After this he **went d** to Capernaum, he, 2597
3:13 but he that **came d** from heaven, even 2597
4:47 and besought him that he would **come d**, 2597
4:49 unto him, Sir, **come d** ere my child die. 2597
4:51 And as he was now **going d**, his servants 2597
5: 4 an angel went d at a certain season into 2597
5: 7 coming, another **steppeth d** before me. 2597
6:10 And Jesus said, **Make** the men **sit d**. 377
6:10 So the men **sat d**, in number about five 377
6:11 and the disciples to them that were **set d;** 345
6:16 his disciples **went d** unto the sea, 2597
6:33 the bread of God is he which **cometh d** 2597
6:38 I **came d** from heaven, not to do mine 2597
6:41 am the bread which **came d** from heaven. 2597
6:42 that he saith, I **came d** from heaven? 2597
6:50 This is the bread which **cometh d** from 2597
6:51 I am the living bread which **came d** from 2597
6:58 This is that bread which **came d** from 2597
8: 2 unto him; and he **sat d**, and taught them. 2523
8: 6 But Jesus stooped **d**, and with his finger 2736
8: 8 And again he stooped **d**, and wrote on 2736
10:15 and I **lay d** my life for the sheep. 5087
10:17 I **lay d** my life, that I might take it 5087
10:18 taketh it from me, but I **lay** it **d** of myself. 5087
10:18 I have power to **lay** it **d**, and I have 5087
11:32 and saw him, she **fell d** at his feet, 4098
13:12 and was **set d** again, he said unto them, 347
13:37 I will **lay d** my life for thy sake. 5087
13:38 Wilt thou **lay d** thy life for my sake? 5087
15:13 that a man **lay d** his life for his friends. 5087
19:13 **sat d** in the judgment seat in a place that 2523
20: 5 he **stooping d**, and looking in, 3879
20:11 she **stooped d**, and looked 3879

Ac
4:35 And laid them **d** at the apostles' feet: and NIG
5: 5 And Ananias hearing these words **fell d** 4098
5:10 Then **fell** she **d** straightway at his feet, 4098
7:15 So Jacob **went d** into Egypt, and died, 2597
7:34 and am **come d** to deliver them. 2597
7:58 the witnesses **laid d** their clothes at a 659
7:60 And he **kneeled d**, 1119+3588+5087
8: 5 Philip **went d** to the city of Samaria, 2718

D

D

Ac 8:15 Who, when they were **come d**, prayed 2597
8:26 that **goeth d** from Jerusalem unto Gaza, 2597
8:38 and they **went d** both into the water, 2597
9:25 let *him* d by the wall in a basket. 2524+5465
9:30 they **brought** him d to Cesarea, 2609
9:32 **came d** also to the saints which dwelt at 2718
9:40 and **kneeled d**, and prayed; 1119+3588+5087
10:11 at the four corners, and **let d** to the earth: 2524
10:20 and **get** *thee* d, and go with them, 2597
10:21 Peter **went d** to the men which were 2597
10:25 **fell d** at *his* feet, and worshipped *him*. 4098
11: 5 **let d** from heaven by four corners, 2524
12:19 And he **went d** from Judea to Cesarea, 2718
13:14 synagogue on the sabbath day, and **sat d**. 2523
13:29 they **took** *him* d from the tree, and laid 2507
14:11 The gods are **come d** to us in the likeness 2597
14:25 word in Perga, they **went d** into Attalia: 2597
15: 1 certain *men* which **came d** from Judea 2718
15:16 tabernacle of David, which is **fallen d**; 4098
16: 8 And they passing by Mysia **came d** to 2597
16:13 and we **sat d**, and spake unto the women 2523
16:29 and **fell d** before Paul and Silas, 4363
17: 6 that have **turned** the world **upside d** 387
18:22 the church, he **went d** to Antioch. 2597
19:35 of the *image* which **fell d** from **Jupiter**? 1356
20: 9 he **sunk d** with sleep, and fell down from 2702
20: 9 fell d from the third loft, and was taken 2736
20:10 And Paul **went d**, and fell on him, 2597
20:36 **kneeled d**, and prayed with 1119+3588+5087
21: 5 and we **kneeled d** on 1119+3588+5087
21:10 **came d** from Judea a certain prophet, 2718
21:32 and centurions, and **ran d** unto them: 2701
22:30 and **brought** Paul d, and set *him* before 2609
23:10 commanded the soldiers to **go d**, 2597
23:15 that he **bring** him d unto you to morrow, 2609
23:20 **bring d** Paul to morrow into the council, 2609
24:22 Lysias the chief captain shall **come d**, 2597
25: 5 **go d with** *me*, and accuse this man, 4782
25: 6 than ten days, he **went d** unto Cesarea; 2597
25: 7 the Jews which **came d** from Jerusalem 2597
27:27 as we were **driven up and d** in Adria, 1308
27:30 when they had **let d** the boat into the sea, 5465
28: 6 have swollen, or **fallen d** dead suddenly: 2667
Ro 10: 6 (that is, to **bring** Christ d *from above*:) 2609
10: 3 thy prophets, and **digged d** thine altars; 2679
11:10 may not see, and **bow d** their back alway. 4781
16: 4 Who have for my life **laid d** their own 5294
1Co 10: 7 The people **sat d** to eat and drink, 2523
14:25 **falling d** on *his* face he will worship God, 4098
15:24 when he shall have **put d** all rule and 2673
2Co 4: 9 not forsaken; **cast d**, but not destroyed; 2598
7: 6 that comforteth *those that are* **cast d**, 5011
10: 4 mighty through God to the **pulling** of 2506
10: 5 **Casting** d imaginations, and every high 2507
11:33 in a basket was I **let d** by the wall, 5465
Eph 2:14 **broken d** the middle wall of partition 3089
4:26 let not the sun **go d** upon your wrath: 1931
Heb 1: 3 **sat d** on the right hand of the Majesty on 2523
10:12 for ever, **sat d** on the right hand of God; 2523
11:30 By faith the walls of Jericho **fell d**, 4098
12: 2 is **set d** at the right hand of the throne of 2523
12:12 lift up the hands which **hang d**, 3935
Jas 1:17 and **cometh d** from the Father of lights, 2597
5: 4 labourers which have reaped *d* your fields, NIG
1Pe 1:12 with the Holy Ghost sent *d* from heaven; NIG
2Pe 2: 4 **cast** *them* **d to hell**, and delivered *them* 5020
1Jn 3:16 *of God*, because he **laid d** his life for us: 5087
3:16 ought to **lay d** *our* lives for the brethren. 5087
Rev 1:13 clothed with a garment d to the foot, 4158
3:12 which **cometh d** out of heaven from my 2597
3:21 am **set d** with my Father in his throne. 2523
4:10 twenty elders **fall d** before him that sat on 4098
5: 8 *and* twenty elders **fell d** before the Lamb, 4098
5:14 And the four *and* twenty elders **fell d** and 4098
10: 1 And I saw another mighty angel **come d** 2597
12:10 for the accuser of our brethren is **cast d**, 2598
12:12 for the devil is **come d** unto you, 2597
13:13 he maketh fire **come d** from heaven on 2597
18: 1 I saw another angel **come d** from heaven, 2597
18:21 shall *that* great city Babylon be thrown d, NIG
19: 4 twenty elders and the four beasts **fell d** 4098
20: 1 And I saw an angel **come d** from heaven, 2597
20: 9 and fire **came d** from God out of heaven, 2597
21: 2 **coming d** from God out of heaven, 2597
22: 8 I **fell d** to worship before the feet of 4098

DOWNSITTING (1) [DOWN, SIT]

Ps 139: 2 Thou knowest my d and mine uprising, 3427

DOWNWARD (5) [DOWN]

2Ki 19:30 Judah shall *yet* again take root d, 4295+3807.1
Ecc 3:21 spirit of the beast that goeth d 4295+3807.1
Isa 37:31 of Judah shall again take root d, 4295+3807.1
Eze 1:27 appearance of his loins even d, 4295+3807.1
8: 2 appearance of his loins even d, 4295+3807.1

DOWRY (4)

Ge 30:20 God hath endued me with a good d; 2065
34:12 Ask me never so much d and gift, 4119
Ex 22:17 he shall pay money according to the d of 4119
1Sa 18:25 king desireth not *any* d, but an hundred 4119

DRACHMAS See DRAMS

DRAG (2) [DRAGGING]

Hab 1:15 in their net, and gather them in their d: 4365
1:16 their net, and burn incense unto their d; 4365

DRAGGING (1) [DRAG]

Jn 21: 8 two hundred cubits,) d the net with fishes. 4951

DRAGON (19) [DRAGONS]

Ne 2:13 even before the d well, and to the dung 8577
Ps 91:13 and the d shalt thou trample under feet. 8577
Isa 27: 1 and he shall slay the d that *is* in the sea. 8577
51: 9 that hath cut Rahab, *and* wounded the d? 8577
Jer 51:34 he hath swallowed me up like a d, 8577
Eze 29: 3 the great d that lieth in the midst of his 8577
Rev 12: 3 and behold a great red d, having seven 1404
12: 4 the d stood before the woman which was 1404
12: 7 and his angels fought against the d; 1404
12: 7 dragon; and the d fought and his angels, 1404
12: 9 And the great d was cast *out*, that old 1404
12:13 when the d saw that he was cast unto 1404
12:16 swallowed up the flood which the d cast 1404
12:17 And the d was wroth with the woman, 1404
13: 2 the d gave him his power, and his seat, 1404
13: 4 And they worshipped the d which gave 1404
13:11 horns like a lamb, and he spake as a d. 1404
16:13 like frogs *come* out of the mouth of the d, 1404
20: 2 he laid hold on the d, *that* old serpent, 1404

DRAGONS (16) [DRAGON]

Dt 32:33 Their wine *is* the poison of d, and the 8577
Job 30:29 I am a brother to d, and a companion to 8577
Ps 44:19 thou hast sore broken us in the place of d, 8577
74:13 thou brakest the heads of the d in the 8577
148: 7 Lord from the earth, ye d, and all deeps: 8577
Isa 13:22 and in *their* pleasant palaces: 8577
34:13 it shall be a habitation of d, *and* a court 8577
35: 7 in the habitation of d, where each lay, 8577
43:20 field shall honour me, the d and the owls: 8577
Jer 9:11 make Jerusalem heaps, *and* a den of d; 8577
10:22 cities of Judah desolate, *and* a den of d. 8577
14: 6 they snuffed up the wind like d; 8577
49:33 Hazor shall be a dwelling for d, 8577
51:37 a dwelling place for d, an astonishment, 8577
Mic 1: 8 I will make a wailing like the d, 8577
Mal 1: 3 his heritage waste for the d of 8577

DRAMS (6)

1Ch 29: 7 five thousand talents and ten thousand d, 150
Ezr 2:69 and one thousand d *of* gold, 1871
8:27 twenty basons of gold, of a thousand d; 150
Ne 7:70 gave to the treasure a thousand d *of* gold, 1871
7:71 of the work twenty thousand d *of* gold, 1871
7:72 gave *was* twenty thousand d *of* gold, 1871

DRANK (18) [DRINK]

Ge 9:21 he of the wine, and was drunken; 8354
24:46 so I d, and she made the camels drink 8354
27:25 eat: and he brought him wine, and he d, 8354
Nu 20:11 the congregation d, and their beasts *also*. 8354
Dt 32:38 *and* d the wine of their drink offerings? 8354
2Sa 12: 3 of his own cup, and lay in his bosom, 8354
1Ki 13:19 did eat bread in his house, and d water. 8354
17: 6 in the evening; and he d of the brook. 8354
Da 1: 5 king's meat, and of the wine which he d: 4960
1: 8 meat, nor with the wine which he d: 4960
5: 1 lords, and d wine before the thousand. 8355
5: 3 his wives, and his concubines, d in them. 8355
5: 4 They d wine, and praised the gods of gold, 8355
Mk 14:23 he gave *it* to them: and they all d of it. 4095
Lk 17:27 They did eat, they d, they married *wives*, 4095
17:28 they did eat, they d, they bought, they sold, 4095
Jn 4:12 and of that himself, and his children, 4095
1Co 10: 4 for they d of *that* spiritual Rock that 4095

DRAUGHT (5)

2Ki 10:27 and made it a d **house** unto *this* day. 4280
Mt 15:17 into the belly, and is cast out into the d? 856
Mk 7:19 into the belly, and goeth out into the d, 856
Lk 5: 4 the deep, and let down your nets for a d 61
5: 9 at the d of the fishes which they had taken: 61

DRAVE (13) [DRIVE]

Ex 14:25 chariot wheels, that they d them heavily: 5090
Jos 16:10 they d not **out** the Canaanites that dwelt 3423
24:12 which d them **out** from before you, 1644
24:18 the Lord d out from before us all 1644
Jdg 1:19 he d out *the inhabitants of* the mountain; 3423
6: 9 them out from before you, and gave you 1644
1Sa 30:20 *which* they d before those *other* cattle, 5090
2Sa 6: 3 the sons of Abinadab, d the new cart. 5090
2Ki 16:28 Elath to Syria, and d the Jews from Elath: 5394
17:21 Jeroboam d Israel from following 5080
1Ch 13: 7 Abinadab: and Uzza and Ahio d the cart. 5090
Ac 7:45 whom God d out before the face of our 1856
18:16 And he d them from the judgment seat. 556

DRAW (76) [DRAWER, DRAWERS, DRAWETH, DRAWING, DRAWN, DREW, DREWEST]

Ge 24:11 *even* the time that *women* go out to d 7579
24:13 the men of the city come out to d water: 7579
24:19 she said, I will *d* water for thy camels 7579
24:20 ran again unto the well to d water, and 7579
24:43 *that* when the virgin cometh forth to d 7579
24:44 and I will also d for thy camels: 7579
Ex 3: 5 said, D not **nigh** hither: put off thy shoes 7126

Ex 12:21 D out and take you a lamb according to 4900
15: 9 I will d my sword, my hand shall destroy 7324
Lev 26:33 and will d out a sword after you: 7324
Jdg 3:22 that he could not d the dagger out of his 8025
4: 6 *saying*, Go and d toward mount Tabor, 4900
4: 7 I will d unto thee to the river Kishon 8025
9:54 said unto him, D thy sword, and slay me, 8025
19:13 let us d near to one of *these* places to 7126
20:32 d them from the city unto the highways. 5423
1Sa 9:11 they found young maidens going out to d 7579
14:36 the priest, Let us d near hither unto God. 7126
14:38 Saul said, D ye near hither, all the chief 5066
31: 4 D thy sword, and thrust me through 8025
2Sa 17:13 to that city, and we will d it into the river, 5498
1Ch 10: 4 D thy sword, and thrust me through 8025
Job 21:33 every man shall d after him, as *there are* 4900
40:23 he trusteth that he can d up Jordan into 1518
41: 1 Canst thou d out leviathan with a hook? 4900
Ps 28: 3 D me not **away** with the wicked, 4900
35: 3 D out also the spear, and stop the way 7324
69:18 D **nigh** unto my soul, *and* redeem it: 7126
73:28 *it is* good for me to d **near** to God: I have 7132
85: 5 wilt thou d out thine anger to all 4900
107:18 and they d **near** unto the gates of death. 5060
119:150 They d **nigh** that follow after mischief: 7126
Pr 20: 5 but a man of understanding will d it **out**. 1802
Ecc 12: 1 nor the years d **nigh**, when thou shalt say, 5060
SS 1: 4 D me, we will run after thee: the king 4900
Isa 5:18 Woe unto them that d iniquity with cords 4900
5:19 counsel of the Holy One of Israel d **nigh** 7126
12: 3 Therefore with joy shall ye d water out of 7579
29:13 Forasmuch as this people d **near** *me* with 5066
45:20 d **near** together, ye *that are* escaped of 5066
57: 3 d **near** hither, ye sons of the sorceress, 7126
57: 4 ye a wide mouth, *and* d **out** the tongue? 748
58:10 *if* thou d **out** thy soul to the hungry, 6329
66:19 Pul, and Lud, that d the bow, *to* Tubal, 4900
Jer 30:21 I will **cause** him to d **near**, and he shall 7126
46: 3 buckler and shield, and d **near** to battle. 5066
49:20 the least of the flock shall d them **out**: 5498
50:45 the least of the flock shall d them **out**: 5498
La 4: 3 Even the sea monsters d **out** the breast, 2502
Eze 5: 2 and I will d **out** a sword after them. 7324
5:12 and I will d **out** a sword after them. 7324
9: 1 **Cause** them that have charge over 7126
 the city to d **near**,
12:14 and I will d **out** the sword after them. 7324
21: 3 I will d **forth** my sword out of his sheath, 3318
22: 4 thou hast **caused** thy days to d **near**, 7126
28: 7 shall d their swords against the beauty 7324
30:11 they shall d their swords against Egypt, 7324
32:20 the sword: d her and all her multitudes. 4900
Joel 3: 9 men, let all the men of war d **near**; 5066
Na 3:14 D thee waters for the siege, fortify thy 7579
Hag 2:16 *one* came to the pressfat for to d 2834
Jn 2: 8 D out now, and bear unto the governor 501
4: 7 There cometh a woman of Samaria to d 501
4:11 thou hast nothing to d **with**, and the well 502
4:15 that I thirst not, neither come hither to d. 501
6:44 except the Father which hath sent me d 1670
12:32 from the earth, will d all *men* unto me. 1670
21: 6 now they were not able to d it for 1670
Ac 20:30 speaking perverse *things*, to d **away** 645
Heb 7:19 *did*; by the which we d **nigh** unto God. 1448
10:22 Let us d **near** with a true heart in full 4334
10:38 but if *any man* d **back**, my soul shall 5288
10:39 But we are not of *them* who d **back** 5289
Jas 2: 6 and d you before the judgment seats? 1670
4: 8 D **nigh** to God, and he will draw nigh to 1448
4: 8 nigh to God, and he will d **nigh** to you. 1448

DRAWER (1) [DRAW]

Dt 29:11 from the hewer of thy wood unto the d of 7579

DRAWERS (3) [DRAW]

Jos 9:21 and d of water unto all the congregation; 7579
9:23 and d of water for the house of my God. 7579
9:27 and d of water for the congregation, 7579

DRAWETH (12) [DRAW]

Dt 25:11 wife of the one d **near** for to deliver her 7126
Jdg 19: 9 Behold now, the day d towards evening, 7503
Job 24:22 He d also the mighty with his power: 4900
33:22 soul d **near** unto the grave, and his life 7126
Ps 10: 9 the poor, when he d him into his net. 4900
88: 3 and my life d **nigh** unto the grave. 5060
Isa 26:17 *that* d **near** the time of her delivery, 7126
Eze 7:12 The time is come, the day d **near**: let not 5060
Mt 15: 8 This people d **nigh** unto me with their 1448
Lk 21: 8 *saying*, I am *Christ*; and the time d **near**: 1448
21:28 your heads; for your redemption d **nigh**. 1448
Jas 5: 8 for the coming of the Lord d **nigh**. 1448

DRAWING (2) [DRAW]

Jdg 5:11 places of d water, there shall they 4857
Jn 6:19 on the sea, and d nigh unto the ship: 1096

DRAWN (28) [DRAW]

Nu 22:23 in the way, and his sword d in his hand: 8025
22:31 in the way, and his sword d in his hand, 8025
Dt 21: 3 *and* which hath not d in the yoke, 4900
30:17 shalt be d **away**, and worship other gods, 5080
Jos 5:13 against him with his sword d in his hand: 8025
8: 6 till we have d them from the city; for they 5423
8:16 and were d **away** from the city. 5423

D

Jos	15: 9 the border was **d** from the top of the hill	8388
	15: 9 the border was **d** to Baalah, which *is*	8388
	15:11 the border was **d** to Shicron,	8388
	18:14 the border was **d** *thence*, and	8388
	18:17 was **d** from the north, and went forth *to*	8388
Jdg	20:31 people, *and* were **d** *away* from the city;	
Ru	2: 9 *of* that which the young men have **d**.	7579
1Ch	21:16 having a **d** sword in his hand stretched	8025
Job	20:25 It *is*, and cometh out of the body; yea,	8025
Ps	37:14 The wicked have **d** out the sword,	6605
	55:21 softer than oil, yet *were* they **d** swords.	6609
Pr	24:11 to deliver *them that are* **d** *unto* death,	3947
Isa	21:15 from the **d** sword, and from the bent bow,	5203
	28: 9 from the milk, *and* from the breasts.	6267
Jer	22:19 **d** and cast forth beyond the gates of	5498
	31: 3 with lovingkindness have I **d** thee.	4900
La	2: 3 he hath **d** back his right hand from before	7725
Eze	21: 5 have I **forth** my sword out of his sheath:	3318
	21:28 even say thou, The sword, the sword *is* **d**:	6605
Ac	11:10 and all were **d** up again into heaven.	385
Jas	1:14 when he is **d** *away* of his own lust,	1828

DREAD (9) [DREADFUL]

Ge	9: 2 the **d** of you shall be upon every beast of	2844
Ex	15:16 Fear and **d** shall fall upon them;	6343
Dt	1:29 I said unto you, **D** not, neither be afraid	6206
	2:25 This day will I begin to put the **d** of thee	6343
	11:25 the **d** of you upon all the land that ye	4172
1Ch	22:13 of good courage; **d** not, nor be dismayed.	3372
Job	3:11 make you afraid? and his **d** fall upon you?	6343
	13:21 and let not thy **d** make me afraid.	367
Isa	8:13 him *be* your fear, and *let* him *be* your **d**.	6206

DREADFUL (9) [DREAD]

Ge	28:17 was afraid, and said, How **d** *is* this place!	3372
Job	15:21 A **d** sound *is* in his ears: in prosperity	6343
Eze	1:18 they were so high that they were **d**;	3374
Da	7: 7 **d** and terrible, and strong exceedingly;	1763
	7:19 exceeding **d**, whose teeth *were of* iron,	1763
	9: 4 and said, O Lord, the great and **d** God,	3372
Hab	1: 7 They *are* terrible and **d**: their judgment	3372
Mal	1:14 and my name *is* **d** among the heathen.	3372
	4: 5 of the great and **d** day of the Lord:	3372

DREAM (74) [DREAMED, DREAMER, DREAMERS, DREAMETH, DREAMS]

Ge	20: 3 God came to Abimelech in a **d** by night,	2472
	20: 6 God said unto him in a **d**, Yea, I know	2472
	31:10 mine eyes, and saw in a **d**, and, behold,	2472
	31:11 the angel of God spake unto me in a **d**,	2472
	31:24 God came to Laban the Syrian in a **d** by	2472
	37: 5 Joseph dreamed a **d**, and he told *it* his	2472
	37: 6 I pray you, this **d** which I have dreamed:	2472
	37: 9 he dreamed yet another **d**, and told it his	2472
	37: 9 said, Behold, I have dreamed a **d** more;	2472
	37:10 What *is* this **d** that thou hast dreamed?	2472
	40: 5 they dreamed a **d** both of them, each man	2472
	40: 5 of them, each man his **d** in one night,	2472
	40: 5 according to the interpretation of his **d**,	2472
	40: 8 We have dreamed a **d**, and *there is* no	2472
	40: 9 the chief butler told his **d** to Joseph,	2472
	40: 9 said to him, In my **d**, behold, a vine *was*	2472
	40:16 I also *was* in my **d**, and, behold,	2472
	41: 8 Pharaoh awoke, and behold, *it was* a **d**.	2472
	41: 8 Pharaoh told them his **d**; but *there was*	2472
	41:11 we dreamed a **d** in one night, I and he;	2472
	41:11 according to the interpretation of his **d**.	2472
	41:12 to each man according to his **d** he did	2472
	41:15 I have dreamed a **d**, and *there is* none	2472
	41:15 thou canst understand a **d** to interpret	2472
	41:17 Pharaoh said unto Joseph, In my **d**,	2472
	41:22 I saw in my **d**, and behold, seven ears	2472
	41:25 unto Pharaoh, The **d** of Pharaoh *is* one:	2472
	41:26 good ears *are* seven years: the **d** *is* one.	2472
	41:32 for that the **d** was doubled unto Pharaoh	2472
Nu	12: 6 a vision, *and* will speak unto him in a **d**.	2472
Jdg	7:13 *there was* a man that told a **d** unto his	2472
	7:13 and said, Behold, I dreamed a **d**, and lo,	2472
	7:15 when Gideon heard the telling of the **d**,	2472
1Ki	3: 5 appeared to Solomon in a **d** by night:	2472
	3:15 Solomon awoke; and behold, *it was* a **d**.	2472
Job	20: 8 He shall fly away as a **d**, and shall not be	2472
	33:15 In a **d**, *in* a vision of the night, when deep	2472
Ps	73:20 As a **d** when *one* awaketh; so, O Lord,	2472
	126: 1 of Zion, we were like them that **d**.	2492
Ecc	5: 3 For a **d** cometh through the multitude of	2472
Isa	29: 7 shall be as a **d** of a night vision.	2472
Jer	23:28 The prophet that hath a **d**, let him tell a	2472
	23:28 that hath a dream, let him tell a **d**;	2472
Da	2: 3 I have dreamed a **d**, and my spirit was	2472
	2: 3 my spirit was troubled to know the **d**.	
	2: 4 tell thy servants the **d**, and we will shew	2493
	2: 5 ye will not make known unto me the **d**,	2493
	2: 6 if ye shew the **d**, and the interpretation	2493
	2: 6 therefore shew me the **d**,	2493
	2: 7 Let the king tell his servants the **d**,	2493
	2: 9 ye will not make known unto me the **d**,	2493
	2: 9 therefore tell me the **d**, and I shall know	2493
	2:26 thou able to make known unto me the **d**	2493
	2:28 Thy **d**, and the visions of thy head upon	2493
	2:36 This *is* the **d**; and we will tell	2493
	2:45 the **d** *is* certain, and the interpretation	2493
	4: 5 I saw a **d** which made me afraid,	2493
	4: 6 unto me the interpretation of the **d**.	2493
	4: 7 I told the **d** before them; but they *did* not	2493

Da	4: 8 and before him I told the **d**, *saying*,	2493
	4: 9 my the visions of my **d** that I have seen,	2493
	4:18 This **d** I king Nebuchadnezzar have seen.	2493
	4:19 let not the **d**, or the interpretation thereof,	2493
	4:19 the **d** *be* to them that hate thee,	2493
	7: 1 king of Babylon Daniel had a **d**	2493
	7: 1 he wrote the **d**, *and* told the sum of	2493
Joel	2:28 your old men shall **d** dreams,	2492
Mt	1:20 of the Lord appeared unto him in a **d**,	3677
	2:12 And being warned of God in a **d** that *they*	3677
	2:13 of the Lord appeareth to Joseph in a **d**,	3677
	2:19 an angel of the Lord appeareth in a **d** to	3677
	2:22 being warned of God in a **d**,	3677
	27:19 have suffered many *things* this day in a **d**	3677
Ac	2:17 and your old men shall **d** dreams:	1797

DREAMED (20) [DREAM]

Ge	28:12 he **d**, and behold a ladder set up on	2492
	37: 5 Joseph **d** a dream, and he told *it* his	2492
	37: 6 I pray you, this dream which I have **d**:	2492
	37: 9 he **d** yet another dream, and told it his	2492
	37: 9 and said, Behold, I have **d** a dream more;	2492
	37:10 What *is* this dream that thou hast **d**?	2492
	40: 5 they **d** a dream both of them, each man	2492
	40: 8 We have **d** a dream, and *there is* no	2492
	41: 1 the end of two full years, that Pharaoh **d**:	2492
	41: 5 slept and he **d** the second time: and behold,	2492
	41:11 we **d** a dream in one night, I and he;	2492
	41:11 we **d** each man according to	2492
	41:15 I have **d** a dream, and *there is* none that	2492
	42: 9 remembered the dreams which he **d**	2492
Jdg	7:13 and said, Behold, I **d** a dream, and lo,	2492
Jer	23:25 name, saying, I have **d**, I have dreamed.	2492
	23:25 name, saying, I have dreamed, I have **d**.	2492
	29: 8 to your dreams which ye **cause to be d**.	2492
Da	2: 1 Nebuchadnezzar **d** dreams, wherewith	2492
	2: 3 I have **d** a dream, and my spirit was	2492

DREAMER (4) [DREAM]

Ge	37:19 this **d** cometh.	1167+2472+1886.1
Dt	13: 1 or a **d** of dreams, and giveth thee a sign	2492
	13: 3 of that prophet, or that **d** of dreams:	2492
	13: 5 that prophet, or that **d** of dreams, shall	2492

DREAMERS (2) [DREAM]

| Jer | 27: 9 nor to your diviners, nor to your **d**, nor to | 2472 |
| Jude | 1: 8 also these *filthy* **d** defile the flesh, | 1797 |

DREAMETH (2) [DREAM]

| Isa | 29: 8 shall even be as when a hungry *man* **d**, | 2492 |
| | 29: 8 or as when a thirsty *man* **d**, and, behold, | 2492 |

DREAMS (21) [DREAM]

Ge	37: 8 they hated him yet the more for his **d**,	2472
	37:20 we shall see what will become of his **d**.	2472
	41:12 told him, and he interpreted to us our **d**;	2472
	42: 9 Joseph remembered the **d** which he	2472
Dt	13: 1 or a dreamer of **d**, and giveth thee a sign	2472
	13: 3 of that prophet, or that dreamer of **d**:	2472
	13: 5 that prophet, or that dreamer of **d**, shall	2472
1Sa	28: 6 by d, nor by Urim, nor by prophets.	2472
	28:15 no more, neither by prophets, nor by **d**:	2472
Job	7:14 thou scarest me with **d**, and terrifiest me	2472
Ecc	5: 7 For in the multitude of **d** and many words	2472
Jer	23:27 which they tell every man to his **d**	2472
	23:32 I *am* against them that prophesy false **d**,	2472
	29: 8 neither hearken to your **d** which ye cause	2472
Da	1:17 had understanding in all visions and **d**.	2472
	2: 1 Nebuchadnezzar **d**, wherewith	2472
	2: 2 the Chaldeans, for to shew the king his **d**.	2472
	5:12 interpreting of **d**, and shewing of hard	2493
Joel	2:28 prophesy, your old men shall dream **d**,	2472
Zec	10: 2 have seen a lie, and have told false **d**;	2472
Ac	2:17 and your old men shall dream **d**:	1798

DREGS (3)

Ps	75: 8 the **d** thereof, all the wicked of the earth	8105
Isa	51:17 hast drunken the **d** of the cup of	6907
	51:22 *even* the **d** of the cup of my fury;	6907

DRESS (9) [DRESSED, DRESSER, DRESSETH, UNDRESSED, VINEDRESSERS]

Ge	2:15 put him into the garden of Eden to **d** it	5647
	18: 7 unto a young man; and he hasted to **d** it.	6213
Dt	28:39 **d** *them*, but shalt neither drink *of* the	5647
2Sa	12: 4 to **d** for the wayfaring man that was come	6213
	13: 5 give me meat, and **d** the meat in my sight,	6213
	13: 7 brother Amnon's house, and **d** him meat.	6213
1Ki	17:12 I may go in and **d** it for me and my son,	6213
	18:23 fire *under:* and I will **d** the other bullock,	6213
	18:25 one bullock for yourselves, and **d** *it* first;	6213

DRESSED (7) [DRESS]

Ge	18: 8 the calf which he had **d**, and set *it* before	6213
Lev	7: 9 *that is* **d** in the fryingpan, and in the pan,	6213
1Sa	25:18 five sheep **ready d**, and five measures of	6213
2Sa	12: 4 **d** it for the man that was come to him.	6213
	19:24 had neither **d** his feet, nor trimmed his	6213
1Ki	18:26 they **d** *it*, and called on the name of Baal	6213
Heb	6: 7 forth herbs meet for them by whom it is **d**,	1090

DRESSER (1) [DRESS]

| Lk | 13: 7 Then said he unto the **d** of his **vineyard**, | 289 |

DRESSETH (1) [DRESS]

| Ex | 30: 7 he **d** the lamps, he shall burn incense | 3190 |

DREW (85) [DRAW]

Ge	18:23 Abraham **d** near, and said, Wilt thou also	5066
	24:20 to draw *water*, and **d** for all his camels.	7579
	24:45 **d** water, and I said unto her, Let me drink	7579
	37:28 they **d** and lift up Joseph out of the pit,	4900
	38:29 to pass, as he **d** back his hand, that,	7725
	47:29 the time **d** *nigh* that Israel must die: and	7126
Ex	2:10 said, Because I **d** him out of the water.	4871
	2:16 they came and **d** *water*, and filled	1802
	2:19 also **d** water enough for us,	1802+1802
	14:10 Pharaoh **d** *nigh*, the children of Israel	7126
	20:21 Moses **d** near unto the thick darkness	5066
Lev	9: 5 all the congregation **d** near and	7126
Jos	8:11 **d** *nigh*, and came before the city,	5066
	8:26 For Joshua **d** not his hand **back**,	7725
Jdg	8:10 and twenty thousand men that **d** sword.	8025
	8:20 the youth **d** not his sword: for he feared,	8025
	20: 2 four hundred thousand footmen that **d**	8025
	20:15 and six thousand men that **d** sword,	8025
	20:17 hundred thousand men that **d** sword:	8025
	20:25 thousand men; all these **d** the sword.	8025
	20:35 an hundred men: all these **d** the sword.	8025
	20:37 the liers in wait **d** *themselves* **along**,	4900
	20:46 and five thousand men that **d** the sword;	8025
Ru	4: 8 the kinsman. So he **d** off his shoe.	8025
1Sa	7: 6 **d** water, and poured *it* out before	7579
	7:10 the Philistines **d** near to battle against	5066
	9:18 Saul **d** near to Samuel in the gate,	5066
	17:16 Philistine **d** near morning and evening,	5066
	17:40 his hand: and he **d** near to the Philistine.	5066
	17:41 came on and **d** near unto David;	7131
	17:48 and **d** nigh to meet David, that David	7126
	17:51 **d** it out of the sheath thereof, and slew	8025
2Sa	3:27 **d** *nigh*, and the people that *were*	5066
	18:25 And he came apace, and **d** near.	7131
	22:17 took me; he **d** me out of many waters;	4871
	23:16 **d** water out of the well of Beth-lehem,	7579
	24: 9 thousand valiant men that **d** the sword;	8025
1Ki	2: 1 Now the days of David **d** nigh that *he*	7126
	22:34 **d** out the staves, that the ends of	748
	22:34 a *certain* man **d** a bow at a venture,	4900
2Ki	3:26 took with him seven hundred men that **d**	8025
	9:24 And Jehu **d** a bow **with** his full strength,	3027+4390+871.1
1Ch	11:18 **d** water out of the well of Beth-lehem,	7579
	19:14 the people that *were* with him **d** nigh	5066
	19:16 **d** forth the Syrians that *were* beyond	3318
	21: 5 an hundred thousand men that **d** sword:	8025
	21: 5 and ten thousand men that **d** sword.	8025
2Ch	5: 9 they **d** out the staves of the ark, that the	748
	14: 8 bare shields and **d** bows, two hundred	1869
	18:33 a *certain* man **d** a bow at a venture,	4900
Est	5: 2 So Esther **d** near, and touched the top of	7126
	9: 1 his decree **d** near to be put in execution,	5060
Ps	18:16 he took me, he **d** me **out** of many waters;	4871
Isa	41: 5 the earth were afraid, **d** near, and came.	7126
Jer	38:13 So they **d** up Jeremiah with cords,	4900
Hos	11: 4 I **d** them with cords of a man, with bands	4900
Zep	3: 2 in the Lord; she **d** not **near** to her God.	7126
Mt	13:48 they **d** to shore, and sat down,	307
	21: 1 And when they **d** nigh unto Jerusalem,	1448
	21:34 And when the time of the fruit **d** near,	1448
	26:51 and **d** his sword, and stroke a servant of	645
Mk	6:53 land of Genesaret, and **d** to the **shore**.	4358
	14:47 And one of them that stood by **d** a sword,	4685
Lk	15: 1 Then **d** near unto him all the publicans	1448
	15:25 and as he came and **d** nigh to the **house**,	1448
	22: 1 the feast of unleavened bread **d** nigh,	1448
	22:47 and **d** near unto Jesus to kiss him.	1448
	23:54 the preparation, and the sabbath **d** **on**.	2020
	24:15 Jesus himself **d** near, and went with	1448
	24:28 And they **d** nigh unto the village,	1448
Jn	2: 9 the servants which **d** the water knew;)	501
	18:10 Then Simon Peter having a sword **d** it,	1670
	21:11 and the net to land full of great fishes,	1670
Ac	5:37 and **d** *away* much people after him:	808
	7:17 But when the time of the promise **d** nigh,	1448
	7:31 as he **d** near to behold *it*, the voice of	4334
	10: 9 their journey, and **d** nigh unto the city,	1448
	14:19 having stoned Paul, **d** *him* out of the city,	4951
	16:19 **d** *them* into the market-place unto	1670
	16:27 he **d** out his sword, and would have killed	4685
	17: 6 they **d** Jason and certain brethren unto	4951
	19:33 they **d** Alexander out of the multitude,	4264
	21:30 took Paul, and **d** him **out** of the temple:	1670
	27:27 that they **d** near to some country;	4317
Rev	12: 4 And his tail **d** the third *part* of the stars of	4951

DREWEST (1) [DRAW]

| La | 3:57 Thou **d** near in the day *that* I called upon | 7126 |

DRIED (39) [DRY]

Ge	8: 7 until the waters were **d** up from off	3001
	8:13 the waters were **d** up from off the earth:	2717
	8:14 day of the month, was the earth **d**.	3001
Lev	2:14 firstfruits green ears of corn **d** by the fire,	7033
Nu	6: 3 of grapes, nor eat moist grapes, or **d**.	3002
	11: 6 now our soul *is* **d** *away: there is* nothing	3002
Jos	2:10 For we have heard how the Lord **d** up	3001
	4:23 For the Lord your God **d** up the waters	3001
	4:23 which he **d** up from before us, until we	3001
	5: 1 I heard that the Lord had **d** up the waters	3001
Jdg	16: 7 seven green withs that were never **d**,	2717
	16: 8 seven green withs which had not been **d**,	2717
1Ki	13: 4 up, so that he could not pull it in again	3001

D

1Ki	17: 7 that the brook **d** up, because there had	3001
2Ki	19:24 with the sole of my feet have I **d** up all	2717
Job	18:16 His roots shall be **d** up beneath,	3001
	28: 4 they are **d** up, they are gone away from	1809
Ps	22:15 My strength is **d** up like a potsherd;	3001
	69: 3 my throat is **d**: mine eyes fail while I wait	2787
	106: 9 rebuked the Red sea also, and it was **d** up:	2717
Isa	5:13 and their multitude **d** up with thirst.	6704
	19: 5 and the river shall be wasted and **d** up:	3001
	19: 6 of defence shall be emptied and **d** up:	2717
	37:25 with the sole of my feet have I **d** up all	2717
	51:10 Art thou not it which hath **d** the sea,	2717
Jer	23:10 pleasant places of the wilderness are **d** up,	3001
	50:38 upon her waters; and they shall be **d** up:	2717
Eze	17:24 have **d** up the green tree, and have made	3001
	19:12 and the east wind **d** up her fruit:	3001
	37:11 Our bones are **d**, and our hope is lost:	3001
Hos	9:16 Ephraim is smitten, their root is **d** up,	3001
	13:15 dry, and his fountain shall be **d** up:	2717
Joel	1:10 the new wine is **d** up, the oil languisheth.	3001
	1:12 The vine is **d** up, and the fig tree	3001
	1:20 for the rivers of waters are **d** up,	3001
Zec	11:17 his arm shall be **clean d** up,	3001+3001
Mk	5:29 the fountain of her blood was **d** up;	*3583*
	11:20 they saw the fig tree **d** up from the roots.	*3583*
Rev	16:12 and the water thereof was **d** up, that	*3583*

DRIEDST (1) [DRY]

Ps	74:15 and the flood: thou **d** up mighty rivers.	3001

DRIETH (3) [DRY]

Job	14:11 the sea, and the flood decayeth and **d** up:	3001
Pr	17:22 medicine: but a broken spirit **d** the bones.	3001
Na	1: 4 and maketh it dry, and **d** up all the rivers:	2717

DRINK (369) [DRANK, DRINKERS, DRINKETH, DRINKING, DRINKS, DRUNK, DRUNKARD, DRUNKARDS, DRUNKEN, DRUNKENNESS]

Ge	19:32 let us **make** our father **d** wine, and we	8248
	19:33 they **made** their father **d** wine that night:	8248
	19:34 let us **make** him **d** wine this night also;	8248
	19:35 they **made** their father **d** wine that night	8248
	21:19 the bottle *with* water, and **gave** the lad **d**.	8248
	24:14 thy pitcher, I pray thee, that I may **d**:	8354
	24:14 **D**, and I will give thy camels drink also:	8354
	24:14 **Drink**, and I will give thy camels **d** also:	8248
	24:17 I pray thee, **d** a little water of thy pitcher.	1572
	24:18 she said, **D**, my lord: and she hasted,	8354
	24:18 pitcher upon her hand, and **gave** him **d**.	8248
	24:19 when she had done **giving** him **d**, she said,	8248
	24:43 **Give** me, I pray thee, a little water of thy pitcher to **d**;	8354
	24:44 Both **d** thou, and I will also draw for thy	8354
	24:45 and I said unto her, Let me **d**, I pray thee.	8248
	24:46 **D**, and I will give thy camels drink also:	8354
	24:46 **Drink**, and I will **give** thy camels **d** also:	8248
	24:46 I drank, and she **made** the camels **d** also.	8354
	24:54 they did eat and **d**, he and the men that	8354
	25:34 he did eat and **d**, and rose up, and went	8354
	26:30 made them a feast, and they did eat and **d**.	8354
	30:38 troughs when the flocks came to **d**,	8354
	30:38 should conceive when they came to **d**.	8354
	35:14 he poured a **d** offering thereon,	5262
Ex	7:18 the Egyptians shall lothe to **d** of the water	8354
	7:21 the Egyptians could not **d** of the water of	8354
	7:24 round about the river *for* water to **d**;	8354
	7:24 for they could not **d** of the water of	8354
	15:23 they could not **d** of the waters of Marah,	8354
	15:24 against Moses, saying, What shall we **d**?	8354
	17: 1 *there was* no water for the people to **d**.	8354
	17: 2 and said, Give us water that we may **d**.	8354
	17: 6 water out of it, that the people may **d**.	8354
	24:11 also they saw God, and did eat and **d**.	8354
	29:40 *part* of a hin of wine *for* a **d** offering.	5262
	29:41 according to the **d** offering thereof, for a	5262
	30: 9 neither shall ye pour a **d** offering thereon.	5262
	32: 6 and the people sat down to eat and to **d**,	8354
	32:20 and **made** the children of Israel **d** *of it.*	8354
	34:28 he did neither eat bread, nor **d** water.	8354
Lev	10: 9 Do not **d** wine nor strong drink, thou,	8354
	10: 9 Do not drink wine nor **strong d**, thou,	7941
	11:34 all **d** that may be drunk in every *such*	4945
	23:13 the **d** offering thereof *shall be of* wine,	5262
	23:18 their meat offering, and their **d** offerings,	5262
	23:37 meat offering, a sacrifice, and **d** offerings,	5262
Nu	5:24 he shall **cause** the woman to **d** the bitter	8248
	5:26 afterward shall **cause** the woman to **d**	8248
	5:27 when he hath **made** her to **d** the water,	8248
	6: 3 separate *himself* from wine and **strong d**,	7941
	6: 3 and shall **d** no vinegar of wine,	8354
	6: 3 vinegar of wine, or vinegar of **strong d**,	7941
	6: 3 neither shall he **d** any liquor of grapes,	8354
	6:15 their meat offering, and their **d** offerings.	5262
	6:17 also his meat offering, and his **d** offering.	5262
	6:20 and after *that* the Nazarite may **d** wine.	8354
	15: 5 **d offering** shalt thou prepare with the	5262
	15: 7 for a **d offering** thou shalt offer the third	5262
	15:10 thou shalt bring for a **d offering** half a hin	5262
	15:24 with his meat offering, and his **d offering**,	5262
	20: 5 neither *is there any* water to **d**.	8354
	20: 8 **give** the congregation and their beasts **d**.	8248
	20:17 will we **d** *of* the water of the wells:	8354
	20:19 if I and my cattle **d** *of* thy water, then I	8354
	21:22 we will not **d** *of* the waters of the well:	8354
	23:24 *of* the prey, and **d** the blood of the slain.	8354

Nu	28: 7 the **d offering** thereof *shall be* the fourth	5262
	28: 7 poured unto the Lord *for* a **d offering**.	5262
	28: 8 morning, and as the **d offering** thereof,	5262
	28: 9 with oil, and the **d offering** thereof:	5262
	28:10 burnt offering, and his **d offering**.	5262
	28:14 **d offerings** shall be half a hin of wine	5262
	28:15 burnt offering, and his **d offering**.	5262
	28:24 burnt offering, and his **d offering**.	5262
	28:31 without blemish) and their **d offerings**.	5262
	29: 6 his meat offering, and their **d offerings**,	5262
	29:11 meat offering of it, and their **d offerings**.	5262
	29:16 his meat offering, and his **d offering**.	5262
	29:18 and their **d offerings** for the bullocks,	5262
	29:19 offering thereof, and their **d offerings**.	5262
	29:21 and their **d offerings** for the bullocks,	5262
	29:22 and his meat offering, and his **d offering**.	5262
	29:24 and their **d offerings** for the bullocks,	5262
	29:25 and his meat offering, and his **d offering**.	5262
	29:27 and their **d offerings** for the bullocks,	5262
	29:28 and his meat offering, and his **d offering**.	5262
	29:30 and their **d offerings** for the bullocks,	5262
	29:31 and his meat offering, and his **d offering**.	5262
	29:33 and their **d offerings** for the bullocks,	5262
	29:34 and his meat offering, and his **d offering**.	5262
	29:37 and their **d offerings** for the bullock,	5262
	29:38 and his meat offering, and his **d offering**.	5262
	29:39 for your **d offerings**, and for your peace	5262
	33:14 where was no water for the people to **d**.	8354
Dt	2: 6 water of them for money, that ye may **d**.	8354
	2:28 give me water for money, that I may **d**:	8354
	9: 9 I neither did eat bread nor **d** water:	8354
	9:18 nor **d** water, because of all your sins	8354
	14:26 for **strong d**, or for whatsoever thy soul	7941
	28:39 but shalt neither **d** *of* the wine,	8354
	29: 6 neither have ye drunk wine or **strong d**;	7941
	32:14 thou didst **d** the pure blood of the grape.	8354
	32:38 *and* drank the wine of their **d offerings**?	5257
Jdg	4:19 **Give** me, I pray thee, a little water **to d**;	8248
	4:19 milk, and **gave** him **d**, and covered him.	8248
	7: 5 that boweth down upon his knees to **d**.	8354
	7: 6 bowed down upon their knees to **d** water.	8354
	9:27 and did eat and **d**, and cursed Abimelech.	8354
	13: 4 not wine nor strong drink, and eat not	8354
	13: 4 drink not wine nor **strong d**, and eat not	7941
	13: 7 **d** no wine nor strong drink, neither eat	8354
	13: 7 drink no wine nor **strong d**, neither eat	7941
	13:14 neither let her **d** wine or strong drink,	8354
	13:14 neither let her drink wine or **strong d**,	7941
	19: 4 so they did eat and **d**, and lodged there.	8354
	19: 6 and did eat and **d** both of them together:	8354
	19:21 they washed their feet, and did eat and **d**.	8354
Ru	2: 9 of *that* which the young men have	8354
1Sa	1:15 I have drunk neither wine nor **strong d**,	7941
	30:11 he did eat; and they **made** him **d** water;	8248
2Sa	11:11 to eat and to **d**, and to lie with my wife?	8354
	11:13 called him, he did eat and **d** before him;	8354
	16: 2 such as be faint in the wilderness may **d**.	8354
	19:35 thy servant taste what I eat or what I **d**?	8354
	23:15 that one would **give** me **d** *of* the water	8248
	23:16 nevertheless he would not **d** thereof,	8354
	23:17 therefore he would not **d** it.	8354
1Ki	1:25 they eat and **d** before him, and say,	8354
	13: 8 neither will I eat bread nor **d** water in	8354
	13: 9 saying, Eat no bread, nor **d** water,	8354
	13:16 neither will I eat bread nor **d** water with	8354
	13:17 shalt eat no bread nor **d** water there,	8354
	13:18 that he may eat bread and **d** water.	8354
	13:22 say to thee, Eat no bread, and **d** no water;	8354
	17: 4 it shall be, *that* thou shalt **d** of the brook;	8354
	17:10 a little water in a vessel, that I may **d**.	8354
	18:41 said unto Ahab, Get thee up, eat and **d**;	8354
	18:42 So Ahab went up to eat and to **d**.	8354
	19: 6 did eat and **d**, and laid him down again.	8354
	19: 8 did eat and **d**, and went in the strength of	8354
2Ki	3:17 that ye may **d**, *both* ye, and your cattle,	8354
	6:22 that they may eat and **d**, and go to their	8354
	7: 8 did eat and **d**, and carried thence silver,	8354
	9:34 come in, he did eat and **d**, and said,	8354
	16:13 poured his **d offering**, and sprinkled	5262
	16:15 meat offering, and their **d offerings**;	5262
	18:27 dung, and **d** their own piss with you?	8354
	18:31 ye every one the waters of his cistern:	8354
1Ch	11:17 that one would **give** me **d** *of* the water	8248
	11:18 David would not **d** *of* it, but poured it out	8354
	11:19 that *I should* do this *thing*: shall I **d**	8354
	11:19 Therefore he would not **d** it.	8354
	29:21 with their **d offerings**, and sacrifices in	5262
	29:22 **d** before the Lord on that day with great	8248
2Ch	28:15 gave them to eat and to **d**,	8248
	29:35 the **d offerings** for *every* burnt offering.	5262
Ezr	3: 7 meat, and **d**, and oil, unto them of Zidon,	4960
	7:17 their meat offering, and their **d offerings**,	5261
	10: 6 he did eat no bread, nor **d** water:	8354
Ne	8:10 the sweet, and send portions unto *them*	8354
	8:12 to **d**, and to send portions, and to make	8354
Est	1: 7 they **gave** *them* **d** in vessels of gold,	8248
	3:15 And the king and Haman sat down to **d**;	8354
	4:16 neither eat nor **d** three days, night or day;	8354
Job	1: 4 three sisters to eat and to **d** with them.	8354
	21:20 he shall **d** of the wrath of the Almighty.	8354
	22: 7 hast not **given** water to the weary to **d**,	8354
Ps	16: 4 their **d offerings** of blood will I not offer,	5262
	36: 8 thou shalt **make** them **d** *of* the river of	8248
	50:13 the flesh of bulls, or **d** the blood of goats?	8354
	60: 3 **made** us **to d** the wine *of* astonishment.	8248

Ps	69:21 in my thirst they **gave** me vinegar **to d**.	8248
	75: 8 earth shall wring *them* out, *and* **d** them.	8354
	78:15 **gave** *them* **d** as *out of* the great depths.	8354
	78:44 and their floods, *that* they could not **d**.	8354
	80: 5 **givest** them tears **to d** *in great* measure.	8248
	102: 9 and mingled my **d** with weeping,	8249
	104:11 They **give d** to every beast of the field:	8354
	110: 7 He shall **d** of the brook in the way:	8354
Pr	4:17 wickedness, and **d** the wine of violence.	8354
	5:15 **D** waters out of thine own cistern,	8354
	9: 5 and **d** of the wine which I have mingled.	8354
	20: 1 Wine *is* a mocker, **strong d** *is* raging:	7941
	23: 7 Eat and **d**, saith he to thee; but his heart	8354
	25:21 and if he *be* thirsty, **give** him water **to d**:	8248
	31: 4 O Lemuel, *it is* not for kings to **d** wine;	8354
	31: 4 to drink wine; nor for princes **strong d**:	7941
	31: 5 Lest they **d**, and forget the law,	8354
	31: 6 Give **strong d** unto him that is ready to	7941
	31: 7 Let him **d**, and forget his poverty,	8354
Ecc	2:24 *than* that he should eat and **d**, and *that*	8354
	3:13 also that every man should eat and **d**,	8354
	5:18 good and comely *for one* to eat and to **d**,	8354
	8:15 than to eat, and to **d**, and to be merry:	8354
	9: 7 and **d** thy wine with a merry heart;	8354
SS	5: 1 drink, yea, **d abundantly**, O beloved.	8354
	5: 1 drink, yea, drink **abundantly**, O beloved.	7937
	8: 2 I would **cause** thee to **d** of spiced wine,	8248
Isa	5:11 *that* they may follow **strong d**;	7941
	5:22 unto *them that are* mighty to **d** wine,	8354
	5:22 and men of strength to mingle **strong d**:	7941
	21: 5 table, watch *in* the watchtower, eat, **d**:	8354
	22:13 us eat and **d**; for to morrow we shall die.	8354
	24: 9 They shall not **d** wine with a song;	8354
	24: 9 **strong d** shall be bitter to them that drink	7941
	24: 9 drink shall be bitter to them that **d** it.	8354
	28: 7 and through **strong d** are out of the way;	7941
	28: 7 the prophet have erred through **strong d**,	7941
	28: 7 they are out of the way through **strong d**;	7941
	29: 9 they stagger, but not *with* **strong d**.	7941
	32: 6 he will cause the **d** of the thirsty to fail.	4945
	36:12 dung, and **d** their own piss with you?	8354
	36:16 **d** ye every one the waters of his own	8354
	43:20 to **give d** to my people, my chosen.	8248
	51:22 of my fury; thou shalt no more **d** it again:	8354
	56:12 and we will fill ourselves with **strong d**;	7941
	57: 6 to them hast thou poured a **d offering**,	5262
	62: 8 the sons of the stranger shall not **d** thy	8354
	62: 9 that have brought it together shall **d** it	8354
	65:11 that furnish the **d offering** unto *that*	4469
	65:13 servants shall **d**, but ye shall be thirsty:	8354
Jer	2:18 way of Egypt, to **d** the waters of Sihor?	8354
	2:18 of Assyria, to **d** the waters of the river?	8354
	7:18 to pour out **d offerings** unto other gods,	5262
	8:14 **given** us water of gall **to d**, because	8248
	9:15 and **give** them water of gall **to d**.	8248
	16: 7 **give** them the cup of consolation **to d** for	8248
	16: 8 feasting, to sit with them to eat and to **d**.	8354
	19:13 have poured out **d offerings** unto other	5262
	22:15 did not thy father eat and **d**,	8354
	23:15 and **make** them **d** the water of gall:	8354
	25:15 **cause** all the nations, to whom I send thee, **to d**	8354
	25:16 they shall **d**, and be moved, and be mad,	8354
	25:17 **made** all the nations to **d**, unto whom	8248
	25:26 the king of Sheshach shall **d** after them.	8354
	25:27 **D** ye, and be drunken, and spue, and fall,	8354
	25:28 refuse to take the cup at thine hand to **d**,	8354
	25:28 of hosts; Ye shall **certainly d**.	8354+8354
	32:29 poured out **d offerings** unto other gods,	5262
	35: 2 the chambers, and **give** them wine to **d**.	8248
	35: 5 cups, and I said unto them, **D** ye wine.	8354
	35: 6 they said, We will **d** no wine: for Jonadab	8354
	35: 6 saying, Ye shall **d** no wine, *neither* ye,	8354
	35: 8 to **d** no wine all our days, we, our wives,	8354
	35:14 he commanded his sons not to **d** wine,	8354
	35:14 for unto this day they **d** none.	8354
	44:17 to pour out **d offerings** unto her, as we	5262
	44:18 to pour out **d offerings** unto her, we	5262
	44:19 poured out **d offerings** unto her, did we	5262
	44:19 pour out **d offerings** unto her, without	5262
	44:25 and to pour out **d offerings** unto her:	5262
	49:12 they whose judgment *was* not to **d** of	8354
	49:12 but thou shalt **surely d** *of it.*	8354+8354
Eze	4:11 Thou shalt **d** also water by measure,	8354
	4:11 of a hin: from time to time shalt thou **d**.	8354
	4:16 they shall **d** water by measure,	8354
	12:18 **d** thy water with trembling and	8354
	12:19 and their water with astonishment,	8354
	20:28 and poured out there their **d offerings**.	5262
	23:32 Thou shalt **d** *of* thy sister's cup deep and	8354
	23:34 Thou shalt even **d** it and suck *it* out,	8354
	25: 4 eat thy fruit, and they shall **d** thy milk.	8354
	31:14 stand up in their height, all that **d** water:	8354
	31:16 and best of Lebanon, all that **d** water,	8354
	34:19 they **d** that which ye have fouled with	8354
	39:17 that ye may eat flesh, and **d** blood.	8354
	39:18 the blood of the princes of the earth,	8354
	39:19 ye be full, and **d** blood till *ye* be drunken,	8354
	44:21 Neither shall any priest **d** wine, when	8354
	45:17 **d offerings**, in the feasts, and in the new	5262
Da	1:10 hath appointed your meat and your **d**:	4960
	1:12 them **give** us pulse to eat, and water to **d**.	8354
	1:16 meat, and the wine that they should **d**;	4960
	5: 2 and his concubines, might **d** therein.	8355
Hos	2: 5 my wool and my flax, mine oil and my **d**.	8250

Hos	4:18 Their **d** is sour; they have committed	5435
Joel	1: 9 the **d** offering is cut off from the house of	5262
	1:13 the **d** offering is withholden from the	5262
	2:14 a **d** offering unto the Lord your God?	5262
	3: 3 sold a girl for wine, that they might **d**.	8354
Am	2: 8 they **d** the wine of the condemned *in*	8354
	2:12 ye **gave** the Nazarites wine to **d**;	8248
	4: 1 say to their masters, Bring, and let us **d**.	8354
	4: 8 wandered unto one city, to **d** water;	8354
	5:11 but ye shall not **d** wine of them.	8354
	6: 6 That **d** wine in bowls,	8354
	9:14 plant vineyards, and **d** the wine thereof;	8354
Ob	1:16 *so* shall all the heathen **d** continually, yea,	8354
	1:16 they shall **d**, and they shall swallow down,	8354
Jnh	3: 7 any thing: let them not feed, nor **d** water:	8354
Mic	2:11 unto thee of wine and of **strong d**.	7941
	6:15 and sweet wine, but shalt not **d** wine.	8354
Hab	2:15 unto him that **giveth** his neighbour **d**,	8248
	2:16 thou also, and let thy foreskin be	8354
Zep	1:13 vineyards, but not **d** the wine thereof.	8354
Hag	1: 6 ye, but ye are not filled with drink;	8354
	1: 6 ye drink, but ye are not **filled with d**;	7937
Zec	7: 6 ye did eat, and when ye did **d**, did not	8354
	7: 6 eat *for yourselves*, and **d** *for yourselves*?	8354
	9:15 they shall **d**, *and* make a noise as *through*	8354
Mt	6:25 what ye shall eat, or what ye shall **d**;	4095
	6:31 What shall we **d**? or, Wherewithal shall	4095
	10:42 whosoever shall **give** to **d** unto one of	4222
	20:22 ye able to **d** of the cup that I shall **drink**	4095
	20:22 ye able to drink *of* the cup that I shall **d**	4095
	20:23 Ye shall **d** indeed *of* my cup,	4095
	24:49 and to eat and **d** with the drunken;	4095
	25:35 I was thirsty, and ye **gave** me **d**: I was a	4222
	25:37 and fed *thee*? or thirsty, and **gave** thee **d**?	4222
	25:42 I was thirsty, and ye **gave** me no **d**:	4222
	26:27 and **gave** *it* to them, saying, **D** ye all of it;	4095
	26:29 I will not henceforth **d** of this fruit of	4095
	26:29 until that day when I **d** it new with you	4095
	26:42 from me, except I **d** it, thy will be done.	4095
	27:34 They gave him vinegar to **d** mingled with	4095
	27:34 he had tasted *thereof*, he would not **d**.	4095
	27:48 and put *it* on a reed, and **gave** him to **d**.	4222
Mk	9:41 **give** you a cup of water to **d** in my name,	4222
	10:38 can ye **d** of the cup that I drink *of*? and be	4095
	10:38 can ye drink *of* the cup that I **d** *of*? and be	4095
	10:39 shall indeed **d** of the cup that I drink *of*;	4095
	10:39 shall indeed drink *of* the cup that I **d** *of*;	4095
	14:25 I will **d** no more of the fruit of the vine,	4095
	14:25 that day that I **d** it new in the kingdom	4095
	15:23 they gave him to **d** wine mingled with	4095
	15:36 and **gave** him to **d**, saying, Let alone;	4222
	16:18 they **d** any deadly *thing*, it shall not hurt	4095
Lk	1:15 and shall **d** neither wine nor strong drink;	4095
	1:15 shall drink neither wine nor **strong d**;	4608
	5:30 ye eat and **d** with publicans and sinners?	4095
	5:33 of the Pharisees; but thine eat and **d**?	4095
	12:19 take thine ease, eat, **d**, *and* be merry.	4095
	12:29 what ye shall **d**, neither be ye of doubtful	4095
	12:45 and to eat and **d**, and to be drunken;	4095
	17: 8 and afterward thou shalt eat and **d**?	4095
	22:18 I will not **d** of the fruit of the vine,	4095
	22:30 eat and **d** at my table in my kingdom,	4095
Jn	4: 7 Jesus saith unto her, Give me to **d**.	4095
	4: 9 it *that* thou, being a Jew, askest **d** of me,	4095
	4:10 who it is that saith to thee, Give me to **d**;	4095
	6:53 and **d** his blood, ye have no life in you.	4095
	6:55 is meat indeed, and my blood is **d** indeed.	4213
	7:37 man thirst, let him come unto me, and **d**.	4095
	18:11 my Father hath given me, shall I not **d** it?	4095
Ac	9: 9 without sight, and neither did eat nor **d**.	4095
	10:41 **d** with him after he rose from the dead.	4844
	23:12 saying that *they* would neither eat nor **d**	4095
	23:21 they will neither eat nor **d** till they have	4095
Ro	12:20 feed him; if he thirst, **give** him **d**:	4222
	14:17 The kingdom of God is not meat and **d**,	4213
	14:21 good neither to eat flesh, nor to **d** wine,	4095
1Co	9: 4 Have we not power to eat and to **d**?	4095
	10: 4 And did all **d** the same spiritual drink;	4095
	10: 4 And did all drink the same spiritual **d**:	4188
	10: 7 The people sat down to eat and **d**,	4095
	10:21 Ye cannot **d** the cup of the Lord,	4095
	10:31 ye eat, or **d**, or whatsoever ye do,	4095
	11:22 have ye not houses to eat and to **d** *in?* or	4095
	11:25 as oft as ye **d** *it*, in remembrance of me.	4095
	11:26 often as ye eat this bread, and **d** this cup,	4095
	11:27 and **d** *this* cup of the Lord unworthily,	4095
	11:28 him eat of *that* bread, and **d** of *that* cup.	4095
	12:13 have been all **made to d** into one Spirit.	4222
	15:32 let us eat and **d**; for to morrow we die.	4095
Col	2:16 or in **d**, or in respect of a holyday, or of	4213
1Ti	5:23 **D** no longer **water**, but use a little wine	5202
Rev	14: 8 she **made** all nations **d** of the wine of	4222
	14:10 The same shall **d** of the wine of the wrath	4095
	16: 6 and thou hast given them blood to **d**;	4095

DRINKERS (1) [DRINK]

Joel	1: 5 howl, all ye **d** of wine, because of the	8354

DRINKETH (17) [DRINK]

Ge	44: 5 *Is* not this *it* in which my lord **d**,	8354
	44: 5 *and* **d** water of the rain of heaven:	8354
Job	6: 4 the poison whereof **d** up my spirit:	8354
	15:16 filthy *is* man, which **d** iniquity like water?	8354
	34: 7 is like Job, *who* **d** up scorning like water?	8354
	40:23 Behold, he **d** up a river, *and* hasteth not:	6231

Pr	26: 6 a fool cutteth off the feet, *and* **d** damage.	8354
Isa	29: 8 thirsty man dreameth, and behold, he **d**;	8354
	44:12 faileth: he **d** no water, and is faint.	8354
Mk	2:16 eateth and **d** with publicans and sinners?	4095
Jn	4:13 Whosoever **d** of this water shall thirst	4095
	4:14 But whosoever **d** of the water that I shall	4095
	6:54 flesh, and **d** my blood, hath eternal life;	4095
	6:56 and **d** my blood, dwelleth in me, and I in	4095
1Co	11:29 For he that eateth and **d** unworthily,	4095
	11:29 eateth and **d** damnation to himself,	4095
Heb	6: 7 For the earth which **d** in the rain that	4095

DRINKING (21) [DRINK]

Ge	24:19 thy camels also, until they have done **d**.	8354
	24:22 it came to pass, as the camels had done **d**,	8354
Ru	3: 3 until he have done eating and **d**:	8354
1Sa	30:16 eating and **d**, and dancing, because of all	8354
1Ki	4:20 eating and **d**, and making merry.	8354
	10:21 all king Solomon's **d** vessels *were of* gold,	4945
	16: 9 **d** himself drunk *in* the house of Arza	8354
	20:12 as he *was* **d**, he and the kings in	8354
	20:16 Ben-hadad *was* **d** himself drunk in the	8354
1Ch	12:39 were with David three days, eating and **d**:	8354
2Ch	9:20 all the **d** vessels of king Solomon *were of*	4945
Est	1: 8 the **d** *was* according to the law; none did	8360
Job	1:13 *d* wine in their eldest brother's house:	8354
	1:18 *d* wine in their eldest brother's house:	8354
Isa	22:13 killing sheep, eating flesh, and **d** wine:	8354
Mt	11:18 For John came neither eating nor **d**,	4095
	11:19 The Son of man came eating and **d**,	4095
	24:38 before the flood they were eating and **d**,	4095
Lk	7:33 came neither eating bread nor **d** wine;	4095
	7:34 The Son of man is come eating and **d**;	4095
	10: 7 eating and **d** such *things* as they give:	4095

DRINKS (1) [DRINK]

Heb	9:10 Which *stood* only in meats and **d**,	4188

DRIVE (57) [DRAVE, DRIVEN, DRIVER, DRIVETH, DRIVING, DROVE, OVERDRIVE]

Ex	6: 1 with a strong hand shall he **d** them *out* of	1644
	23:28 shall **d** out the Hivite, the Canaanite,	1644
	23:29 I will not **d** them out from before thee in	1644
	23:30 little I will **d** them out from before thee,	1644
	23:31 thou shalt **d** them out before thee.	1644
	33: 2 I will **d** out the Canaanite, the Amorite,	1644
	34:11 I **d** out before thee the Amorite,	1644
Nu	22: 6 and *that* I may **d** them out of the land:	1644
	22:11 able to overcome them, and **d** them out.	1644
	33:52 shall **d** out all the inhabitants of the land	3423
	33:55 if ye will not **d** out the inhabitants of	3423
Dt	4:38 To **d** out nations from before thee greater	3423
	9: 3 shalt thou **d** them out, and destroy them	3423
	9: 4 Lord doth **d** them out before thee.	3423
	9: 5 God doth **d** them out from before thee,	3423
	11:23 will the Lord **d** out all these nations	3423
	18:12 God doth **d** them out from before thee.	3423
Jos	3:10 he will **without fail d** out from	3423+3423
	13: 6 them will I **d** out from before the children	3423
	14:12 I shall *be able* to **d** them out, as the Lord	3423
	15:63 children of Judah could not **d** them out	3423
	17:12 the children of Manasseh could not **d** out	3423
	17:13 but did not **utterly d** them out.	3423+3423
	17:18 for thou shalt **d** out the Canaanites,	3423
	23: 5 and **d** them from out of your sight;	3423
	23:13 **d** out *any of* these nations from before	3423
Jdg	1:19 could not **d** out the inhabitants of	3423
	1:21 the children of Benjamin did not **d** out	3423
	1:27 did Manasseh **d** out *the inhabitants*	3423
	1:28 and did not **utterly d** them out.	3423+3423
	1:29 Neither did Ephraim **d** out the Canaanites	3423
	1:30 Neither did Zebulun **d** out the inhabitants	3423
	1:31 Neither did Asher **d** out the inhabitants	3423
	1:32 of the land: for they did not **d** them out.	3423
	1:33 did Naphtali **d** out the inhabitants	3423
	2: 3 I will not **d** them out from before you;	1644
	2:21 I also will not henceforth **d** out any from	3423
	11:24 our God shall **d** out from before us,	3423
2Ki	4:24 **D**, and go *forward*; slack not *thy* riding for	5090
2Ch	20: 7 didst **d** out the inhabitants of this land	3423
Job	18:11 on every side, and shall **d** him to his feet.	6327
	24: 3 They **d** away the ass of the fatherless,	5090
Ps	44: 2 How thou didst **d** out the heathen *with*	3423
	68: 2 smoke is driven away, so **d** *them* **away**:	5086
Pr	22:15 the rod of correction shall **d** it **far** from	7368
Isa	22:19 I will **d** thee from thy station, and from	1920
Jer	24: 9 curse, in all places whither I shall **d** them.	5080
	27:10 *that* I should **d** you out, and ye should	5080
	27:15 that I might **d** you out, and that ye might	5080
	46:15 stood not, because the Lord did **d** them.	1920
Eze	4:13 the Gentiles, whither I will **d** them.	5080
Da	4:25 That they *shall* **d** thee from men,	2957
	4:32 they *shall* **d** thee from men,	2957
Hos	9:15 doings I will **d** them **out** of mine house,	1644
Joel	2:20 will **d** him into a land barren and desolate,	5080
Zep	2: 4 they shall **d** out Ashdod at the noon day,	1644
Ac	27:15 into the wind, we **let** *her* **d**.	1929+5342

DRIVEN (49) [DRIVE]

Ge	4:14 thou hast **d** me out *this* day from the face	1644
Ex	10:11 they were **d** out from Pharaoh's presence.	1644
	22:10 be hurt, or **d** away, no man seeing	7617
Nu	32:21 until he hath **d** out his enemies from	3423
Dt	4:19 shouldest be **d** to worship them,	5080
	30: 1 whither the Lord thy God hath **d** thee,	5080

Dt	30: 4 If *any* of thine be **d** out unto the outmost	5080
Jos	23: 9 For the Lord hath **d** out from before you	3423
1Sa	26:19 for they have **d** me **out** *this* day from	1644
Job	6:13 in me? and is wisdom **d** *quite* from me?	5080
	13:25 Wilt thou break a leaf **d** to and fro? and	5086
	18:18 He shall be **d** from light into darkness,	1920
	30: 5 They were **d** **forth** from among men,	1644
Ps	40:14 let them be **d** backward and put to shame	5472
	68: 2 As smoke is **d** *away*, *so* drive *them* away:	5086
	114: 3 sea saw *it*, and fled: Jordan was **d** back.	5437
	114: 5 thou Jordan, *that* thou wast **d** back?	5437
Pr	14:32 The wicked is **d** away in his wickedness:	1760
Isa	8:22 anguish; and *they shall be* **d** to darkness.	5080
	19: 7 shall wither, be **d** away, and *be no more*.	5086
	41: 2 to his sword, *and as* **d** stubble to his bow.	5086
Jer	8: 3 in all the places whither I have **d** them,	5080
	16:15 from all the lands whither he had **d** them:	5080
	23: 2 **d** them away, and have not visited them:	5080
	23: 3 out of all countries whither I have **d** them,	5080
	23: 8 from all countries whither I had **d** them;	5080
	23:12 they shall be **d** on, and fall therein: for I	1760
	29:14 from all the places whither I have **d** you,	5080
	29:18 among all the nations whither I have **d**	5080
	32:37 whither I have **d** them in mine anger,	5080
	40:12 out of all places whither they were **d**,	5080
	43: 5 whither they had been **d**, to dwell in	5080
	46:28 of all the nations whither I have **d** thee:	5080
	49: 5 ye shall be **d** out every man right forth;	5080
	50:17 sheep; the lions have **d** *him* **away**:	5080
Eze	31:11 I have **d** him out for his wickedness;	1644
	34: 4 ye brought again that which was **d** away,	5080
	34:16 bring again that which was **d** away,	5080
Da	4:33 he *was* **d** from men, and did eat grass as	2957
	5:21 he *was* **d** from the sons of men;	2957
	9: 7 the countries whither thou hast **d** them,	5080
Hos	13: 3 the chaff *that* is **d** **with a whirlwind** out	5590
Mic	4: 6 I will gather her that is **d** out, and *her*	5080
Zep	3:19 halteth, and gather her that was **d** out;	5080
Lk	8:29 was **d** of the devil into the wilderness.	1643
Ac	27:17 the quicksands, strake sail, and so were **d**.	5342
	27:27 as we were **d** **up and down** in Adria,	1308
Jas	1: 6 is like a wave of the sea **d** **with the wind**	416
	3: 4 they be so great, and are **d** of fierce winds,	1643

DRIVER (2) [DRIVE]

1Ki	22:34 he said unto the **d** of his **chariot**,	7395
Job	39: 7 neither regardeth he the crying of the **d**.	5065

DRIVETH (4) [DRIVE]

2Ki	9:20 Jehu the son of Nimshi; for he **d** furiously.	5090
Ps	1: 4 *are* like the chaff which the wind **d** away.	5086
Pr	25:23 The north wind **d** away rain: so *doth* an	2342
Mk	1:12 And immediately the Spirit **d** him into	1544

DRIVING (4) [DRIVE]

Jdg	2:23 those nations, without **d** them out hastily;	3423
2Ki	9:20 the **d** *is* like the driving of Jehu the son of	4491
	9:20 the driving *is* like the **d** of Jehu the son of	4491
1Ch	17:21 by **d** out nations from before thy people,	1644

DROMEDARIES (3) [DROMEDARY]

1Ki	4:28 brought they unto the place where	7409
Est	8:10 riders on mules, camels, *and* young **d**:	7424
Isa	60: 6 cover thee, the **d** of Midian and Ephah;	1070

DROMEDARY (1) [DROMEDARIES]

Jer	2:23 *thou art* a swift **d** traversing her ways;	1072

DROP (15) [DROPPED, DROPPETH, DROPPING, DROPS]

Dt	32: 2 doctrine shall **d** as the rain, my speech	6201
	33:28 wine; also his heavens shall **d** **down** dew.	6201
Job	36:28 the clouds do **d** *and* distil upon man	5140
Ps	65:11 thy goodness; and thy paths **d** fatness.	7491
	65:12 **d** *upon* the pastures of the wilderness:	7491
Pr	3:20 and the clouds **d** down the dew.	7491
SS	4:11 O *my* spouse, **d** as the honeycomb:	5197
Isa	40:15 the nations *are* as a **d** of a bucket,	4752
	45: 8 **D** down, ye heavens, from above,	7491
Eze	20:46 *d* thy word toward the south,	5197
	21: 2 *d* thy word toward the holy places,	5197
Joel	3:18 the mountains shall **d** **down** new wine,	5197
Am	7:16 **d** not *thy word* against the house of Isaac.	5197
	9:13 the mountains shall **d** sweet wine,	5197

DROPPED (7) [DROP]

Jdg	5: 4 the earth trembled, and the heavens **d**,	5197
	5: 4 heavens dropped, the clouds also **d** water.	5197
1Sa	14:26 come into the wood, behold the honey **d**;	1982
2Sa	21:10 the beginning of harvest until water **d**	5413
Job	29:22 not again; and my speech **d** upon them.	5197
Ps	68: 8 the heavens also **d** at the presence of God:	5197
SS	5: 5 my hands **d** *with* myrrh, and my fingers	5197

DROPPETH (1) [DROP]

Ecc	10:18 of the hands the house **d** **through**.	1811

DROPPING (3) [DROP]

Pr	19:13 contentions of a wife *are* a continual **d**.	1812
	27:15 A **continual d** in a very rainy day	1812+2956
SS	5:13 lips *like* lilies, **d** sweet smelling myrrh.	5197

DROPS (4) [DROP]

Job	36:27 For he maketh small the **d** of water:	5198
	38:28 or who hath begotten the **d** of dew?	96

D

SS 5: 2 *and* my locks *with* the **d** of the night. 7447
Lk 22:44 his sweat was as it were great **d** of blood *2361*

DROPSY (1)

Lk 14: 2 certain man before him, which **had the d.** 5203

DROSS (8)

Ps 119:119 away all the wicked of the earth *like* **d:** 5509
Pr 25: 4 Take away the **d** from the silver, 5509
 26:23 *are* like a potsherd covered with silver **d.** 5509
Isa 1:22 Thy silver is become **d,** thy wine mixt 5509
 1:25 purely purge away thy **d,** and take away 5509
Eze 22:18 the house of Israel is to me become **d:** 5509
 22:18 the furnace; they are *even the* **d** *of* silver. 5509
 22:19 Because ye are all become **d,** 5509

DROUGHT (10)

Ge 31:40 **d** consumed me, and the frost by night; 2721
Dt 8:15 and **d,** where *there was* no water; 6774
Job 24:19 **D** and heat consume the snow waters: 6723
Ps 32: 4 my moisture is turned into the **d** of 2725
Isa 58:11 satisfy thy soul in **d,** and make fat thy 6710
Jer 2: 6 through a land of **d,** and of the shadow of 6723
 17: 8 shall not be careful in the year of **d,** 1226
 50:38 A **d** *is* upon her waters; and they shall be 2721
Hos 13: 5 in the wilderness, in the land of **great d.** 8514
Hag 1:11 I called *for* a **d** upon the land, and upon 2721

DROVE (13) [DRIVE, DROVES]

Ge 3:24 So he **d** out the man; and he placed at 1644
 15:11 upon the carcases, Abram **d** them **away.** 5380
 32:16 servants, **every d** by themselves; 5739+5739
 32:16 and put a space betwixt **d** and drove. 5739
 32:16 and put a space betwixt drove and **d.** 5739
 33: 8 What meanest thou by all this **d** which I 4264
Ex 2:17 the shepherds came and **d** them **away:** 1644
Nu 21:32 and **d** out the Amorites that *were* there. 3423
Jos 15:14 Caleb **d** thence the three sons of Anak, 3423
1Ch 8:13 who **d** away the inhabitants of Gath: 1272
Ps 34: T when he **d** him **away,** and he departed. 1644
Hab 3: 6 he beheld, and **d asunder** the nations; 5425
Jn 2:15 he **d** them all out of the temple, *1544*

DROVES (1) [DROVE]

Ge 32:19 and all that followed the **d,** saying, 5739

DROWN (2) [DROWNED]

SS 8: 7 quench love, neither can the floods **d** it: 7857
1Ti 6: 9 which **d** men in destruction and perdition. *1036*

DROWNED (5) [DROWN]

Ex 15: 4 his chosen captains also are **d** in the Red 2883
Am 8: 8 it shall be cast out and **d,** as *by* the flood 8257
 9: 5 and shall be **d,** as *by* the flood of Egypt. 8257
Mt 18: 6 that he were **d** in the depth of the sea. *2670*
Heb 11:29 the Egyptians assaying to do were **d.** *2666*

DROWSINESS (1)

Pr 23:21 and **d** shall clothe a man with rags. 5124

DRUNK (31) [DRINK]

Ge 43:34 And they **d,** and were merry with him. 8354
Lev 11:34 drink that may be **d** in every *such* vessel 8354
Dt 29: 6 neither have you **d** wine or strong drink: 8354
 32:42 I will **make** mine arrows **d** with blood, 7937
Jdg 15:19 when he had **d,** his spirit came again, 8354
Ru 3: 7 Boaz had eaten and **d,** and his heart 8354
1Sa 1: 9 had eaten in Shiloh, and after *they* had **d.** 8354
 1:15 I have **d** neither wine nor strong drink, 8354
 30:12 nor **d** *any* water, three days and 8354
2Sa 11:13 drink before him; and he **made** him **d:** 7937
1Ki 13:22 hast eaten bread and **d** water in the place, 8354
 13:23 he had eaten bread, and after he had **d,** 8354
 16: 9 drinking *himself* **d** *in* the house of Arza 7910
 20:16 Ben-hadad *was* drinking *himself* **d** in 7910
2Ki 6:23 when they had eaten and **d,** he sent them 8354
 19:24 I have digged and **d** strange waters, 8354
SS 5: 1 honey; I have **d** my wine with my milk: 8354
Isa 37:25 I have digged, and **d** water; and with 8354
 51:17 which hast **d** at the hand of the LORD 8354
 63: 6 **make** them **d** in my fury, and I will bring 7937
Jer 46:10 be satiate and **made d** with their blood: 7301
 51:57 I will **make d** her princes, and her wise 7937
Eze 34:18 to have **d** of the deep waters, but ye must 8354
Da 5:23 and thy concubines, *have* **d** wine in them; 8355
Ob 16 For as ye have **d** upon my holy mountain, 8354
Lk 5:39 No *man* also having **d** old *wine* *4095*
 13:26 We have eaten and **d** in thy presence, *4095*
Jn 2:10 when men have **well d,** then that which *3182*
Eph 5:18 be not **d** with wine, wherein is excess; *3182*
Rev 17: 2 **made d** with the wine of her fornication, *3184*
 18: 3 For all nations have **d** of the wine of *4095*

DRUNKARD (5) [DRINK]

Dt 21:20 obey our voice; *he is* a glutton, and a **d.** 5433
Pr 23:21 For the **d** and the glutton shall come to 5433
 26: 9 *As* a thorn goeth up into the hand of a **d,** 7910
Isa 24:20 The earth shall reel to and fro like a **d,** 7910
1Co 5:11 or a railer, or a **d,** or an extortioner; *3183*

DRUNKARDS (6) [DRINK]

Ps 69:12 and *I was* the song of the **d.** 7941+8354
Isa 28: 1 the crown of pride, to the **d** of Ephraim, 7910
 28: 3 The crown of pride, the **d** of Ephraim, 7910
Joel 1: 5 Awake, ye **d,** and weep; and howl, all ye 7910
Na 1:10 while they be drunken *as* **d,** they shall be 5435

1Co 6:10 nor covetous, nor **d,** nor revilers, *3183*

DRUNKEN (33) [DRINK]

Ge 9:21 he drank of the wine, and was **d;** 7937
1Sa 1:13 therefore Eli thought she had been **d.** 7910
 1:14 How long wilt thou be **d?** 7937
 25:36 *was* merry within him, for he *was* very **d:** 7910
Job 12:25 he maketh them to stagger like a **d** *man.* 7937
Ps 107:27 stagger like a **d** *man,* and are at their wit's 7910
Isa 19:14 as a **d** *man* staggereth in his vomit. 7910
 29: 9 are **d,** but not *with* wine; they stagger, 7937
 49:26 they shall be **d** with their own blood, 7937
 51:17 thou hast **d** the dregs of the cup of 8354
 51:21 thou afflicted, and **d,** but not with wine: 7937
Jer 23: 9 I am like a **d** man, and like a man whom 7910
 25:27 be **d,** and spue, and fall, and rise no more, 7937
 48:26 **Make** ye him **d:** for he magnified *himself* 7937
 49:12 drink of the cup have **assuredly d;** 8354+8354
 51: 7 LORD's hand, that **made** all the earth **d:** 7937
 51: 7 the nations have **d** of her wine; therefore 7937
 51:39 will **make** them **d,** that they may rejoice, 7937
La 3:15 he hath **made** me **d** with wormwood. 7301
 4:21 thou shalt be **d,** and shalt make thyself 7937
 5: 4 We have **d** our water for money; 8354
Eze 39:19 till ye be full, and drink blood till ye be **d,** 7943
Na 1:10 while they be **d** *as* drunkards, they shall 5433
 3:11 Thou also shalt be **d:** thou shalt be hid, 7937
Hab 2:15 bottle to *him,* and **makest** *him* **d** also, 7937
Mt 24:49 and to eat and drink with the **d;** *3184*
Lk 12:45 and to eat and drink, and to be **d;** *3182*
 17: 8 and serve me, till I have eaten and **d;** *4095*
Ac 2:15 For these are not **d,** as ye suppose, seeing *3184*
1Co 11:21 and one is hungry, and another is **d.** *3184*
1Th 5: 7 they that be **d** are drunken in the night. *3182*
 5: 7 they that be drunken are **d** in the night. *3184*
Rev 17: 6 I saw the woman **d** with the blood of *3184*

DRUNKENNESS (7) [DRINK]

Dt 29:19 of mine heart, to add **d** *to* thirst: 7302
Ecc 10:17 in due season, for strength, and not for **d.** 8358
Jer 13:13 all the inhabitants of Jerusalem, *with* **d.** 7943
Eze 23:33 Thou shalt be filled *with* **d** and sorrow, 7943
Lk 21:34 **d,** and cares of *this* life, *and so* that day *3178*
Ro 13:13 not in rioting and **d,** not in chambering *3178*
Gal 5:21 Envyings, murders, **d,** revellings, *3178*

DRUSILLA (1)

Ac 24:24 when Felix came with his wife **D,** *1409*

DRY (71) [DRIED, DRIEDST, DRIETH, DRYSHOD]

Ge 1: 9 unto one place, and let the **d** land *appear:* 3004
 1:10 God called the **d** *land* Earth; 3004
 7:22 of life, of all that *was* in the **d** *land,* died. 2724
 8:13 and behold, the face of the ground was **d.** 3004
Ex 4: 9 pour *it* upon the **d** *land:* and the water 3004
 4: 9 river shall become blood upon the **d** *land.* 3006
 14:16 the children of Israel shall go on **d** *ground* 3004
 14:21 made the sea **d** *land,* and the waters were 2724
 14:22 the midst of the sea upon the **d** *ground;* 3004
 14:29 the children of Israel walked upon **d** *land* 3004
 15:19 the children of Israel went on **d** *land* in 3004
Lev 7:10 meat offering, mingled with oil, and **d,** 2720
 13:30 *is* a **d scall,** *even* a leprosy upon the head 2720
Jos 3:17 firm on **d** *ground* in the midst of Jordan, 2724
 3:17 all the Israelites passed over on **d** *ground,* 2724
 4:18 **d** *land,* that the waters of Jordan returned 2724
 4:22 Israel came over this Jordan on **d** *land.* 3004
 9: 5 all the bread of their provision was **d** *and* 3001
 9:12 but now, behold, it is **d,** and it is mouldy: 3001
Jdg 6:37 *it be* **d** upon all the earth *beside,* then 2721
 6:39 let it now be **d** only upon the fleece, 2721
 6:40 for it was **d** upon the fleece only, 2721
2Ki 2: 8 so that they two went over on **d** *ground.* 2724
Ne 9:11 the midst of the sea on the **d** *land;* 3004
Job 12:15 withholdeth the waters, and they **d** up: 3001
 13:25 fro? and wilt thou pursue the **d** stubble? 3002
 15:30 the flame shall **d** up his branches, 3001
Ps 63: 1 a **d** and thirsty land, where no water is; 6723
 66: 6 He turned the sea into **d** *land:* they went 3004
 68: 6 but the rebellious dwell *in* a **d** *land.* 6707
 95: 5 and his hands formed the **d** *land.* 3006
 105:41 they ran in the **d** *places like* a river. 6723
 107:33 the watersprings into **d** *ground;* 4774
 107:35 and **d** ground into watersprings: 6723
Pr 17: 1 Better *is* a **d** morsel, 2720
Isa 25: 5 of strangers, as the heat in a **d** *place,* 6724
 32: 2 as rivers of water in a **d** *place,* 6724
 41:18 of water, and the **d** land springs of water. 6723
 42:15 and hills, and **d** up all their herbs; 3001
 42:15 rivers islands, and I will **d** up the pools. 3001
 44: 3 floods upon the **d** *ground:* I will pour my 3004
 44:27 deep, **Be d,** and I will dry up thy rivers: 2717
 44:27 deep, Be dry, and I will **d** up thy rivers: 3001
 50: 2 at my rebuke I **d** up the sea, I make 2717
 53: 2 and as a root out of a **d** ground: 6723
 56: 3 let the eunuch say, Behold, I am a **d** tree. 3002
Jer 4:11 A **d** wind of the high places in 6703
 50:12 *be* a wilderness, a **d** land, and a desert. 6723
 51:36 I will **d** up her sea, and make her springs 2717
 51:36 dry up her sea, and **make** her springs **d;** 3001
 51:43 a desolation, a **d** land, and a wilderness, 6723
Eze 17:24 have made the **d** tree to flourish: 3002
 19:13 the wilderness, in a **d** and thirsty ground. 6723
 20:47 every green tree in thee, and every **d** tree: 3002
 30:12 I will make the rivers **d,** and sell the land 2724

Eze 37: 2 the open valley; and lo, *they were* very **d.** 3002
 37: 4 and said unto them, O ye **d** bones, 3002
Hos 2: 3 set her like a **d** land, and slay her with 6723
 9:14 them a miscarrying womb and **d** breasts. 6784
 13:15 spring shall become **d,** and his fountain 3001
Jnh 1: 9 which hath made the sea and the **d** *land.* 3004
 2:10 it vomited out Jonah upon the **d** *land.* 3004
Na 1: 4 **maketh** it **d,** and drieth up all the rivers: 3001
 1:10 they shall be devoured as stubble fully **d.** 3002
Zep 2:13 a desolation, *and* **d** like a wilderness, 6723
Hag 2: 6 the earth, and the sea, and the **d** *land;* 2724
Zec 10:11 and all the deeps of the river shall **d** up: 3001
Mt 12:43 he walketh through **d** places, seeking rest, *504*
Lk 11:24 he walketh through **d** places, seeking rest, *504*
 23:31 a green tree, what shall be done in the **d?** *3584*
Heb 11: 2 **d** *land:* which the Egyptians assaying to *3584*

DRYSHOD (1) [DRY]

Isa 11:15 seven streams, and make *men* go over **d.** 5275

DUE (31) [DUES]

Lev 10:13 because it *is* thy **d,** and thy sons' due, 2706
 10:13 because it *is* thy due, and thy sons' **d,** 2706
 10:14 for *they be* thy **d,** and thy sons' due, 2706
 10:14 for *they be* thy due, and thy sons' **d,** 2706
 26: 4 I will give you rain in **d** season. 6256
Nu 28: 2 to offer unto me in their **d** season. 4150
Dt 11:14 *you* the rain of your land in his **d** season, 6256
 18: 3 shall be the priest's **d** from the people, 4941
 32:35 their foot shall slide in **d** time: NIH
1Ch 15:13 that we sought him not after the **d** order. 4941
 16:29 Give unto the LORD the glory **d** unto his NIH
Ne 11:23 *should* be for the singers, **d** for every day. 1697
Ps 29: 2 Give unto the LORD the glory **d** unto his NIH
 96: 8 Give unto the LORD the glory **d** unto his NIH
 104:27 mayest give *them* their meat in **d** season. 6256
 145:15 thou givest them their meat in **d** season. 6256
Pr 3:27 not good from **them** to whom it is **d,** 1167
 15:23 a word *spoken* in **d** season, 6256+2050.2
Ecc 10:17 thy princes eat in **d** season, for strength, 6256
Mt 18:34 till he should pay all that was **d** unto him. 3784
 24:45 to give them meat in **d** season? 2540
Lk 12:42 *them* their portion of meat in **d** season? 2540
 23:41 we receive the **d reward** of our deeds: 514
Ro 5: 6 in **d** time Christ died for the ungodly. 2596
 13: 7 tribute to whom tribute *is* **d;** custom to NIG
1Co 7: 3 Let the husband render unto the wife **d** 3784
 15: 8 of me also, as of one **born out of d time.** 1626
Gal 6: 9 for in **d** season we shall reap, if we faint 2398
1Ti 2: 6 a ransom for all, to be testified in **d** time. 2398
Tit 3: 1 But hath in **d** times manifested his word 2398
1Pe 5: 6 of God, that he may exalt you in **d** time: 2540

DUES (1) [DUE]

Ro 13: 7 Render therefore to all *their* **d:** tribute to 3782

DUKE (43) [DUKES]

Ge 36:15 **d** Teman, duke Omar, duke Zepho, 441
 36:15 duke Omar, **d** Zepho, duke Kenaz, 441
 36:15 duke Omar, duke Zepho, **d** Kenaz, 441
 36:15 duke Omar, duke Zepho, duke Kenaz, 441
 36:16 **D** Korah, duke Gatam, *and* duke Amalek: 441
 36:16 Duke Korah, **d** Gatam, *and* duke Amalek: 441
 36:16 Duke Korah, duke Gatam, *and* **d** Amalek: 441
 36:17 **d** Nahath, duke Zerah, duke Shammah, 441
 36:17 duke Nahath, **d** Zerah, duke Shammah, 441
 36:17 duke Nahath, duke Zerah, **d** Shammah, 441
 36:17 duke Zerah, duke Shammah, **d** Mizzah: 441
 36:18 **d** Jeush, duke Jaalam, duke Korah: 441
 36:18 duke Jeush, **d** Jaalam, duke Korah: 441
 36:18 duke Jeush, duke Jaalam, **d** Korah: 441
 36:29 **d** Lotan, duke Shobal, duke Zibeon, 441
 36:29 duke Lotan, **d** Shobal, duke Zibeon, 441
 36:29 duke Lotan, duke Shobal, **d** Zibeon, 441
 36:29 duke Shobal, **d** Zibeon, duke Anah, 441
 36:30 **D** Dishon, duke Ezer, duke Dishan: these 441
 36:30 Duke Dishon, **d** Ezer, duke Dishan: these 441
 36:30 Duke Dishon, duke Ezer, **d** Dishan: these 441
 36:40 **d** Timnah, duke Alvah, duke Jetheth, 441
 36:40 duke Timnah, **d** Alvah, duke Jetheth, 441
 36:40 duke Timnah, duke Alvah, **d** Jetheth, 441
 36:41 **D** Aholibamah, duke Elah, duke Pinon, 441
 36:41 Duke Aholibamah, **d** Elah, duke Pinon, 441
 36:41 Duke Aholibamah, duke Elah, **d** Pinon, 441
 36:42 **D** Kenaz, duke Teman, duke Mibzar, 441
 36:42 Duke Kenaz, **d** Teman, duke Mibzar, 441
 36:42 Duke Kenaz, duke Teman, **d** Mibzar, 441
 36:43 **D** Magdiel, duke Iram: these *be* the dukes 441
 36:43 Duke Magdiel, **d** Iram: these *be* the dukes 441
1Ch 1:51 **d** Timnah, duke Aliah, duke Jetheth, 441
 1:51 duke Timnah, **d** Aliah, duke Jetheth, 441
 1:51 duke Timnah, duke Aliah, **d** Jetheth, 441
 1:52 **D** Aholibamah, duke Elah, duke Pinon, 441
 1:52 Duke Aholibamah, **d** Elah, duke Pinon, 441
 1:52 Duke Aholibamah, duke Elah, **d** Pinon, 441
 1:53 **D** Kenaz, duke Teman, duke Mibzar, 441
 1:53 Duke Kenaz, **d** Teman, duke Mibzar, 441
 1:53 Duke Kenaz, duke Teman, **d** Mibzar, 441
 1:54 **D** Magdiel, duke Iram. These *are* the dukes 441
 1:54 Duke Magdiel, **d** Iram. These *are* the dukes 441

DUKES (15) [DUKE]

Ge 36:15 These *were* **d** of the sons of Esau: the sons 441
 36:16 these *are* the **d** that came of Eliphaz in 441
 36:17 these *are* the **d** that came of Reuel in the 441

Ge 36:18 these *were* the **d** that came of Aholibamah 441
36:19 Esau, who *is* Edom, and these *are* their **d**. 441
36:21 these *are* the **d** of the Horites, the children 441
36:29 These *are* the **d** that came of the Horites; 441
36:30 these *are* the **d** that came of Hori, 441
36:30 of Hori, among their **d** in the land of Seir. 441
36:40 these are the names of the **d** of Esau, 441
36:43 these *be* the **d** of Edom, according to their 441
Ex 15:15 the **d** of Edom shall be amazed; the mighty 441
Jos 13:21 Hur, and Reba, *which were* **d** of Sihon, 5257
1Ch 1:51 the **d** of Edom were; duke Timnah, 441
1:54 duke Iram. These *are* the **d** of Edom. 441

DULCIMER (3)
Da 3: 5 psaltery, **d**, and all kinds of musick, 5481
3:10 psaltery, and **d**, and all kinds of musick, 5481
3:15 psaltery, and **d**, and all kinds of musick, 5481

DULL (3)
Mt 13:15 *their* ears are **d** of hearing, and their eyes 917
Ac 28:27 *their* ears are **d** of hearing, and their eyes 917
Heb 5:11 to be uttered, seeing ye are **d** of hearing. 3576

DUMAH (4)
Ge 25:14 And Mishma, and **D**, and Massa, 1746
Jos 15:52 Arab, and **D**, and Eshean, 1746
1Ch 1:30 Mishma, and **D**, Massa, Hadad, and Tema, 1746
Isa 21:11 The burden of **D**. He calleth to me out of 1746

DUMB (29)
Ex 4:11 who maketh the **d**, or deaf, or the seeing, 483
Ps 38:13 as a **d** *man that* openeth not his mouth. 483
39: 2 I was **d** *with* silence, I held my peace, 481
39: 9 I was **d**, I opened not my mouth; because 481
Pr 31: 8 Open thy mouth for the **d** in the cause of 483
Isa 35: 6 leap as a hart, and the tongue of the **d** sing: 483
53: 7 as a sheep before her shearers is **d**, 481
56:10 they *are all* **d** dogs, they cannot bark; 483
Eze 3:26 thou shalt be **d**, and shalt not be to them 481
24:27 and thou shalt speak, and be no more 481
33:22 mouth was opened, and I was no more **d**. 481
Da 10:15 face toward the ground, and I **became d**. 481
Hab 2:18 his work trusteth therein, to make **d** idols? 483
2:19 Awake; to the **d** stone, Arise, it shall 1748
Mt 9:32 they brought to him a **d** man possessed 2974
9:33 when the devil was cast out, the **d** spake: 2974
12:22 one possessed with a devil, blind, and **d**: 2974
12:22 that the blind and **d** both spake and saw. 2974
15:30 blind, **d**, maimed, and many others, 2974
15:31 they saw the **d** to speak, the maimed 2974
Mk 7:37 both the deaf to hear, and the **d** to speak. 216
9:17 unto thee my son, which hath a **d** spirit: 216
9:25 *Thou* **d** *and deaf spirit, I charge thee,* 216
Lk 1:20 thou shalt be **d**, and not able to speak, 4623
11:14 he was casting out a devil, and it was **d**. 2974
11:14 the devil was gone out, the **d** spake; 2974
Ac 8:32 and like a lamb **d** before his shearer, 880
1Co 12: 2 carried away unto these **d** idols, *even* as ye 880
2Pe 2:16 the **d** ass speaking with man's voice forbad 880

DUNG (28) [DUNGHILL, DUNGHILLS]
Ex 29:14 of the bullock, and his skin, and his **d**, 6569
Lev 4:11 with his legs, and his inwards, and his **d**, 6569
8:17 and his hide, his flesh, and his **d**, 6569
16:27 their skins, and their flesh, and their **d**. 6569
Nu 19: 5 her flesh, and her blood, with her **d**, 6569
1Ki 14:10 as *a man* taketh away **d**, till it be all gone. 1557
2Ki 6:25 the fourth part of a kab of **dove's d** for 1686
9:37 the carcase of Jezebel shall be as **d** upon 1828
18:27 that *they* may eat their own **d**, and drink 6675
Ne 2:13 to the **d** port, and viewed the walls of 830
3:13 a thousand cubits on the wall unto the **d** 830
3:14 the **d** gate repaired Malchiah the son of 830
12:31 hand upon the wall toward the **d** gate: 830
Job 20: 7 he shall perish for ever like his own **d**: 1561
Ps 83:10 at En-dor: they became as **d** for the earth. 1828
Isa 36:12 that *they* may eat their own **d**, and drink 6675
Jer 8: 2 they shall be for **d** upon the face of 1828
9:22 Even the carcases of men shall fall as **d** 1828
16: 4 they shall be as **d** upon the face of 1828
25:33 buried; they shall be **d** upon the ground. 1828
Eze 4:12 shalt bake it with **d** that cometh out of 1561
4:15 I have given thee cow's **d** for man's dung, 6832
4:15 I have given thee cow's dung for man's **d**, 1561
Zep 1:17 out as dust, and their flesh as the **d**. 1561
Mal 2: 3 your seed, and spread **d** upon your faces, 6569
2: 3 *even* the **d** of your solemn feasts; 6569
Lk 13: 8 till I shall dig about it, and **d** *it*: 906+2874
Php 3: 8 of all *things,* and do count *them* but **d**, 4657

DUNGEON (13)
Ge 40:15 nothing that they should put me into the **d**. 953
41:14 and they brought him hastily out of the **d**: 953
Ex 12:29 of the captive that *was* in the **d**; 953+1004
Jer 38: 6 was entered into the **d**, 953+1004+1886.1
38: 6 cast him into the **d** of Malchiah the son of 953
38: 6 And in the **d** *there* was no water, but mire: 953
38: 7 heard that they had put Jeremiah in the **d**; 953
38: 9 prophet, whom they have cast into the **d**; 953
38:10 take up Jeremiah the prophet out of the **d** 953
38:11 let them down by cords into the **d** to 953
38:13 with cords, and took him up out of the **d**: 953
La 3:53 They have cut off my life in the **d**, and cast 953
3:55 upon thy name, O Lord, out of the low **d**. 953

DUNGHILL (7) [DUNG, HILL]
1Sa 2: 8 lifteth up the beggar from the **d**, to set 830
Ezr 6:11 let his house be made a **d** for this. 5122
Ps 113: 7 dust, *and* lifteth the needy out of the **d**; 830
Isa 25:10 *even* as straw is trodden down for the **d**. 4087
Da 2: 5 and your houses shall be made a **d**. 5122
3:29 and their houses shall be made a **d**. 5122
Lk 14:35 neither fit for the land, nor yet for the **d**; 2874

DUNGHILLS (1) [DUNG, HILL]
La 4: 5 that were brought up in scarlet embrace **d**. 830

DURA (1)
Da 3: 1 he set it up in the plain of **D**, 1757

DURABLE (2) [DURETH]
Pr 8:18 with me; *yea,* **d** riches and righteousness. 6276
Isa 23:18 to eat sufficiently, and for **d** clothing. 6266

DURETH (1) [DURABLE]
Mt 13:21 he not root in himself, but **d** for a while: 1510

DURST (9) [DARE]
Est 7: 5 that **d** presume in his heart to do so? 4390
Job 32: 6 and **d** not shew you mine opinion. 3372
Mt 22:46 neither **d** any *man* from that day forth ask 5111
Mk 12:34 no *man* after that **d** ask him any 5111
Lk 20:40 And after that they **d** not ask him any 5111
Jn 21:12 And none of the disciples **d** ask him, 5111
Ac 5:13 And of the rest **d** no *man* join himself to 5111
7:32 Then Moses trembled, and **d** not behold. 5111
Jude 1: 9 **d** not bring against *him* a railing 5111

DUST (108)
Ge 2: 7 the Lord God formed man *of* the **d** of 6083
3:14 **d** shalt thou eat all the days of thy life: 6083
3:19 for **d** thou *art,* and unto dust shalt thou 6083
3:19 thou *art,* and unto **d** shalt thou return. 6083
13:16 will make thy seed as the **d** of the earth: 6083
13:16 if a man can number the **d** of the earth, 6083
18:27 the Lord, which *am but* **d** and ashes: 6083
28:14 thy seed shall be as the **d** of the earth, 6083
Ex 8:16 out thy rod, and smite the **d** of the land, 6083
8:17 smote the **d** of the earth, and it became 6083
8:17 all of the land became lice 6083
9: 9 it shall become **small** in all the land of 80
Lev 14:41 they shall pour out the **d** that they scrape 6083
17:13 out the blood thereof, and cover it with **d**. 6083
Nu 5:17 the **d** that is in the floor of the tabernacle 6083
23:10 Who can count the **d** of Jacob, 6083
Dt 9:21 small, *even* until *it was as* small as **d**: 6083
9:21 I cast the **d** thereof into the brook that 6083
28:24 make the rain of thy land powder and **d**: 6083
32:24 with the poison of serpents of the **d**. 6083
Jos 7: 6 of Israel, and put **d** upon their heads. 6083
1Sa 2: 8 He raiseth up the poor out of the **d**, 6083
2Sa 16:13 and threw stones at him, and cast **d**. 6083
22:43 did I beat them *as* small as the **d** of 6083
1Ki 16: 2 Forasmuch as I exalted thee out of the **d**, 6083
18:38 the **d**, and licked up the water that *was* 6083
20:10 if the **d** of Samaria shall suffice for 6083
2Ki 13: 7 had made them like the **d** by threshing. 6083
23:12 cast the **d** of them into the brook Kidron. 6083
2Ch 1: 9 people like the **d** of the earth in multitude. 6083
34: 4 brake *in pieces,* and **made d** *of them,* 1854
Job 2:12 sprinkled **d** upon their heads toward 6083
4:19 whose foundation *is* in the **d**, which are 6083
5: 6 affliction cometh not forth of the **d**, 6083
7: 5 is clothed with worms and clods of **d**; 6083
7:21 for now shall I sleep in the **d**; 6083
10: 9 and wilt thou bring me into **d** again? 6083
14:19 which grow out of the **d** of the earth; 6083
16:15 my skin, and defiled my horn in the **d**. 6083
17:16 the pit, when *our* rest together *is* in the **d**. 6083
20:11 which shall lie down with him in the **d**. 6083
21:26 They shall lie down alike in the **d**, 6083
22:24 shalt thou lay up gold as **d**, and *the gold* 6083
27:16 Though he heap up silver as the **d**, 6083
28: 6 place of sapphires: and it hath **d** of gold. 6083
30:19 mire, and I am become like **d** and ashes. 6083
34:15 and man shall turn again unto **d**. 6083
38:38 When the **d** groweth into hardness, 6083
39:14 eggs in the earth, and warmeth them in **d**, 6083
40:13 Hide them in the **d** together; *and* bind 6083
42: 6 I abhor *myself,* and repent in **d** and ashes. 6083
Ps 7: 5 the earth, and lay mine honour in the **d**. 6083
18:42 did I beat them small as the **d** before 6083
22:15 thou hast brought me into the **d** of death. 6083
22:29 all they that go down to the **d** shall bow 6083
30: 9 Shall the **d** praise thee? shall it declare thy 6083
44:25 For our soul is bowed down to the **d**: 6083
72: 9 and his enemies shall lick the **d**. 6083
78:27 He rained flesh also upon them as **d**, 6083
102:14 in her stones, and favour the **d** thereof. 6083
103:14 our frame; he remembereth that we *are* **d**. 6083
104:29 breath, they die, and return to their **d**. 6083
113: 7 He raiseth up the poor out of the **d**, 6083
119:25 My soul cleaveth unto the **d**: quicken 6083
Pr 8:26 nor the highest part of the **d** of the world. 6083
Ecc 3:20 all are of the **d**, and all turn to dust again. 6083
3:20 all are of the dust, and all turn to **d** again. 6083
12: 7 shall the **d** return to the earth as it was: 6083
Isa 2:10 into the rock, and hide thee in the **d**, 6083
5:24 and their blossom shall go up as **d**: 80
25:12 *and* bring to the ground, *even* to the **d**. 6083

Isa 26: 5 the ground; he bringeth it *even* to the **d**. 6083
26:19 Awake and sing, ye that dwell in **d**: 6083
29: 4 thy speech shall be low out of the **d**, 6083
29: 4 and thy speech shall whisper out of the **d**, 6083
29: 5 of thy strangers shall be like small **d**, 80
34: 7 and their **d** shall be made fat with fatness. 6083
34: 9 the **d** thereof into brimstone, and the land 6083
40:12 comprehended the **d** of the earth in a 6083
40:15 are counted as the **small d** of the balance: 7834
41: 2 he gave *them* as the **d** *to* his sword, 6083
47: 1 Come down, and sit in the **d**, O virgin 6083
49:23 the earth, and lick up the **d** of thy feet; 6083
52: 2 Shake thyself from the **d**; arise, 6083
65:25 **d** *shall be* the serpent's meat. They shall 6083
La 2:10 they have cast up **d** upon their heads, 6083
3:29 He putteth his mouth in the **d**; if so be 6083
Eze 24: 7 it not upon the ground, to cover it with **d**; 6083
26: 4 I will also scrape her **d** from her, 6083
26:10 of his horses their **d** shall cover thee: 80
26:12 and thy **d** in the midst of the water. 6083
27:30 and shall cast up **d** upon their heads, 6083
Da 12: 2 of them that sleep in the **d** of the earth 127
Am 2: 7 That pant after the **d** of the earth on 6083
Mic 1:10 the house of Aphrah roll thyself *in the* **d**. 6083
7:17 They shall lick the **d** like a serpent, 6083
Na 1: 3 storm, and the clouds *are* the **d** of his feet. 80
3:18 thy nobles shall dwell *in the* **d**: thy people NIH
Hab 1:10 for they shall heap **d**, and take it. 6083
Zep 1:17 their blood shall be poured out as **d**, 6083
Zec 9: 3 heaped up silver as the **d**, and fine gold as 6083
Mt 10:14 or city, shake off the **d** of your feet. 2868
Mk 6:11 shake off the **d** under your feet for a 5522
Lk 9: 5 shake off the very **d** from your feet for a 2868
10:11 Even the very **d** of your city, 2868
Ac 13:51 But they shook off the **d** of their feet 2868
22:23 *off their* clothes, and threw **d** into the air, 2868
Rev 18:19 And they cast **d** on their heads, and cried, 5522

DUTIES (1) [DUTY]
Eze 18:11 doeth not any of those **d**, but even hath NIH

DUTY (8) [DUTIES]
Ex 21:10 her raiment, and her **d of marriage**, 5772
Dt 25: 5 **perform the d of a husband's brother** 2992
25: 7 **perform the d of my husband's brother.** 2992
2Ch 8:14 priests, as the **d** of every day **required**; 1697
Ezr 3: 4 custom, as the **d** of every day required; 1697
Ecc 12:13 for this *is* the whole **d** *of* man. NIH
Lk 17:10 have done that which was our **d** to do. 3784
Ro 15:27 **d** is also to minister unto them in carnal 3784

DWARF (1)
Lev 21:20 or a **d**, or that hath a blemish in his eye, 1851

DWELL (338) [DWELLED, DWELLERS, DWELLEST, DWELLETH, DWELLING, DWELLINGS, DWELT]
Ge 4:20 he was the father of such as **d** in tents, 3427
9:27 and he shall **d** in the tents of Shem; 7931
13: 6 to bear them, that they might **d** together: 3427
13: 6 great, so that they could not **d** together. 3427
16:12 he shall **d** in the presence of all his 7931
19:30 with him; for he feared to **d** in Zoar: 3427
20:15 *is* before thee: **d** where it pleaseth thee. 3427
24: 3 of the Canaanites, amongst whom I **d**: 3427
24:37 of the Canaanites, in whose land I **d**: 3427
26: 2 **d** in the land which I shall tell thee of: 7931
30:20 now will my husband **d with** me, because 2082
34:10 ye shall **d with** us: and the land shall be 3427
34:10 and trade you therein, and get you 3427
34:16 we will **d** with you, and we will become 3427
34:21 therefore let them **d** in the land, 3427
34:22 the men consent unto us for to **d** with us, 3427
34:23 unto them, and they will **d** with us. 3427
35: 1 Arise, go up to Beth-el, and **d** there: 3427
36: 7 more than that they might **d** together: 3427
46:34 And thou shalt **d** in the land of Goshen, 3427
47: 4 let thy servants **d** in the land of Goshen. 3427
47: 6 land **make** thy father and brethren to **d**; 3427
47: 6 dwell; in the land of Goshen let them **d**: 3427
49:13 Zebulun shall **d** at the haven of the sea; 7931
Ex 2:21 Moses was content to **d** with the man: 3427
8:22 in which my people **d**, that no swarms of 5975
15:17 *which* thou hast made for thee to **d** in, 3427
23:33 They shall not **d** in thy land, lest they 3427
25: 8 a sanctuary; that I may **d** amongst them. 7931
29:45 I will **d** amongst the children of Israel, 7931
29:46 land of Egypt, that I may **d** amongst them: 7931
Lev 13:46 he shall **d** alone; without the camp *shall* 3427
20:22 the land, whither I bring you to **d** therein, 3427
23:42 Ye shall **d** in booths seven days; all that 3427
23:42 that are Israelites born shall **d** in booths: 3427
23:43 **made** the children of Israel to **d** in booths 3427
25:18 and ye shall **d** in the land in safety. 3427
25:19 shall eat *your* fill, and **d** therein in safety. 3427
26: 5 bread to the full, and **d** in your land safely. 3427
26:32 your enemies which **d** therein shall be 3427
Nu 5: 3 not their camps, in the midst whereof I **d**. 7931
13:19 what the land *is* that they **d** in, whether 3427
13:19 cities *they be* that they **d** in, whether 3427
13:28 Nevertheless the people *be* strong that **d** 3427
13:29 The Amalekites **d** in the land of the south: 3427
13:29 and the Amorites, **d** in the mountains: 3427
13:29 the Canaanites **d** by the sea, and by 3427

D

Nu	14:30 which I sware to **make** you **d**	7931
	23: 9 the people shall **d** alone, and shall not be	7931
	32:17 our little ones shall **d** in the fenced cities	3427
	33:53 *the* inhabitants *of* the land, and **d** therein:	3427
	33:55 shall vex you in the land wherein ye **d**.	3427
	35: 2 of their possession cities to **d** in;	3427
	35: 3 the cities shall they have to **d** in;	3427
	35:32 he should come again to **d** in the land,	3427
	35:34 land which ye shall inhabit, wherein I **d**:	7931
	35:34 for I the LORD **d** among the children of	7931
Dt	2: 4 the children of Esau, which **d** in Seir;	3427
	2:29 (As the children of Esau which **d** in Seir,	3427
	2:29 Moabites which **d** in Ar, did unto me;)	3427
	11:30 which **d** in the champaign over against	3427
	11:31 and ye shall possess it, and **d** therein.	3427
	12:10 in the land which the LORD your God	3427
	12:10 round about, so that ye **d** in safety;	3427
	12:11 choose to **cause** his name to **d** there;	7931
	13:12 LORD thy God hath given thee to **d** there,	3427
	17:14 and shalt **d** therein, and shalt say,	3427
	23:16 He shall **d** with thee, *even* among you,	3427
	25: 5 brethren **d** together, and one of them die,	3427
	28:30 a house, and thou shalt not **d** therein:	3427
	30:20 that thou mayest **d** in the land which	3427
	33:12 The beloved of the LORD shall **d** in	7931
	33:12 and he shall **d** between his shoulders.	7931
	33:28 Israel then shall **d** in safety alone:	7931
Jos	9: 7 the Hivites, Peradventure ye **d** among us;	3427
	9:22 very far from you; when ye **d** among us?	3427
	10: 6 for all the kings of the Amorites that **d** in	3427
	13:13 the Maachathites **d** among the Israelites	3427
	14: 4 save cities to **d** in, with their suburbs for	3427
	15:63 the Jebusites **d** with the children of Judah	3427
	16:10 the Canaanites **d** among the Ephraimites	3427
	17:12 but the Canaanites would **d** in that land.	3427
	17:16 all the Canaanites that **d** in the land of	3427
	20: 4 him a place, that he may **d** among them.	3427
	20: 6 he shall **d** in that city, until he stand	3427
	21: 2 hand of Moses to give us cities to **d** in,	3427
	24:13 which ye built not, and ye **d** in them;	3427
	24:15 gods of the Amorites, in whose land ye **d**:	3427
Jdg	1:21 the Jebusites **d** with the children of	3427
	1:27 but the Canaanites would **d** in that land.	3427
	1:35 the Amorites would **d** in mount Heres in	3427
	6:10 gods of the Amorites, in whose land ye **d**;	3427
	9:41 that *they* should not **d** in Shechem.	3427
	17:10 **D** with me, and be unto me a father and	3427
	17:11 the Levite was content to **d** with the man;	3427
	18: 1 **d** *in*; for unto that day *all their* inheritance	3427
1Sa	12: 8 of Egypt, and **made** them **d** in this place.	3427
	27: 5 town in the country, that I may **d** there?	3427
	27: 5 for why should thy servant **d** in the royal	3427
2Sa	7: 2 I **d** in a house of cedar, but the ark of God	3427
	7: 5 thou build me a house for me to **d** in?	3427
	7:10 that they may **d** in a place of their own,	7931
1Ki	2:36 **d** there, and go not forth thence any	3427
	3:17 lord, I and this woman **d** in one house;	3427
	6:13 I will **d** among the children of Israel,	7931
	8:12 The LORD said that *he* would **d** in	7931
	8:13 I have surely built thee a house to **d** in,	2073
	8:27 But will God indeed **d** on the earth?	3427
	17: 9 which *belongeth* to Zidon, and **d** there:	3427
2Ki	4:13 answered, I **d** among mine own people.	3427
	6: 1 place where we **d** with thee is too strait	3427
	6: 2 make us a place there, where we may **d**.	3427
	17:27 let them go and **d** there, and let him teach	3427
	25:24 in the land, and serve the king of	3427
1Ch	17: 1 I **d** in a house of cedars, but the ark of	3427
	17: 4 Thou shalt not build me a house to **d** in:	3427
	17: 9 they shall **d** in their place, and shall be	7931
	23:25 that they may **d** in Jerusalem for ever:	3427
2Ch	2: 3 cedars to build him a house to **d** therein,	3427
	6: 1 The LORD hath said that *he* would **d** in	7931
	6:18 will God in very deed **d** with men on	3427
	8: 2 **caused** the children of Israel to **d** there.	3427
	8:11 My wife shall not **d** in the house of David	3427
	19:10 of your brethren that **d** in their cities,	3427
Ezr	4:17 *to* the rest of their companions that **d** in	3488
	6:12 the God that hath **caused** his name to **d**	7932
Ne	8:14 that the children of Israel should **d** in	3427
	11: 1 to bring one of ten to **d** in Jerusalem	3427
	11: 1 city, and nine parts *to* **d** in *other* cities.	NIH
	11: 2 that willingly offered themselves to **d** at	3427
Job	3: 5 of death stain it; let a cloud **d** upon it;	7931
	4:19 How much less *in* them that **d** in houses	7931
	11:14 let not wickedness **d** in thy tabernacles.	7931
	18:15 It shall **d** in his tabernacle, because *it is*	7931
	19:15 They that **d** in mine house,	1481
	30: 6 To **d** in the clifts of the valleys, *in* caves of	7931
Ps	4: 8 LORD, only **makest** me **d** in safety.	3427
	5: 4 neither shall evil **d** *with* thee.	1481
	15: 1 who shall **d** in thy holy hill?	7931
	23: 6 I will **d** in the house of the LORD for	3427
	24: 1 the world, and they that **d** therein.	3427
	25:13 His soul shall **d** at ease; and his seed shall	3885
	27: 4 that I may **d** in the house of the LORD all	3427
	37: 3 shalt thou **d** in the land, and verily thou	7931
	37:27 and do good; and **d** for evermore.	7931
	37:29 inherit the land, and **d** therein for ever.	7931
	65: 4 *unto* thee, *that* he may **d** in thy courts:	7931
	65: 8 They also that **d** in the uttermost parts are	3427
	68: 6 but the rebellious **d** *in* a dry *land*.	7931
	68:16 *this is* the hill *which* God desireth to **d** in;	3427
	68:16 yea, the LORD will **d** *in it* for ever.	7931
	68:18 that the LORD God might **d** *among* them.	7931

Ps	69:25 be desolate; *and* let none **d** in their tents.	3427
	69:35 that they may **d** there, and have it in	3427
	69:36 they that love his name shall **d** therein.	7931
	72: 9 They **that d in the wilderness** shall bow	6728
	78:55 **made** the tribes of Israel to **d** in their	7931
	84: 4 Blessed *are* they that **d** in thy house:	3427
	84:10 than to **d** in the tents of wickedness.	1752
	85: 9 fear him; that glory may **d** in our land.	7931
	98: 7 the world, and they that **d** therein.	3427
	101: 6 of the land, that *they* may **d** with me:	3427
	101: 7 He that worketh deceit shall not **d** within	3427
	107: 4 a solitary way; they found no city to **d** in.	4186
	107:34 for the wickedness of them that **d** therein.	3427
	107:36 there he **maketh** the hungry to **d**,	3427
	120: 5 *in* Mesech, *that* I **d** in the tents of Kedar!	7931
	132:14 here will I **d**; for I have desired it.	3427
	133: 1 pleasant *it is* for brethren to **d** together	3427
	139: 9 *and* **d** in the uttermost parts of the sea;	7931
	140:13 the upright shall **d** in thy presence.	3427
	143: 3 he hath **made** me to **d** in darkness,	3427
Pr	1:33 whoso hearkeneth unto me shall **d** safely,	7931
	2:21 For the upright shall **d** *in* the land,	7931
	8:12 I wisdom **d** *with* prudence, and find out	7931
	21: 9 better to **d** in a corner of the housetop,	3427
	21:19 better to **d** in the wilderness, than with	3427
	25:24 better to **d** in a corner of the housetop,	3427
Isa	6: 5 I **d** in the midst of a people of unclean lips:	3427
	9: 2 they that **d** in the land of the shadow of	3427
	11: 6 The wolf also shall **d** with the lamb,	1481
	13:21 owls shall **d** there, and satyrs shall dance	7931
	16: 4 Let mine outcasts **d** with thee, Moab;	1481
	22:13 it for **them that d in the wilderness**:	6728
	23:18 her merchandise shall be for them that **d**	3427
	24: 6 and they that **d** therein are desolate:	3427
	26: 5 he bringeth down them that **d** on high;	3427
	26:19 Awake and sing, ye that **d** in dust: for thy	7931
	30:19 the people shall **d** in Zion at Jerusalem:	3427
	32:16 judgment shall **d** in the wilderness,	7931
	32:18 people shall **d** in a peaceable habitation,	3427
	33:14 among us shall **d** *with* the devouring	1481
	33:14 who amongst us shall **d** *with* everlasting	1481
	33:16 He shall **d** on high: his place of defence	7931
	33:24 people that **d** therein *shall be* forgiven	3427
	34:11 the owl also and the raven shall **d** in it;	7931
	34:17 generation to generation shall they **d**	7931
	40:22 and spreadeth them out as a tent to **d** in:	3427
	49:20 for me: give place to me that I may **d**.	3427
	51: 6 that **d** therein shall die in like manner:	3427
	57:15 I **d** in the high and holy *place*, with him	7931
	58:12 the breach, The restorer of paths to **d** in.	3427
	65: 9 inherit it, and my servants shall **d** there.	7931
Jer	4:29 be forsaken, and not a man **d** therein.	3427
	7: 3 and I will **cause** you to **d** in this place.	7931
	7: 7 will I **cause** you to **d** in this place,	7931
	8:16 is in it; the city, and those that **d** therein.	3427
	8:19 because of them that **d** in a far country:	NIH
	9:26 utmost corners, that **d** in the wilderness:	3427
	12: 4 the wickedness of them that **d** therein?	3427
	20: 6 all that **d** in thine house shall go into	3427
	23: 6 shall be saved, and Israel shall **d** safely:	7931
	23: 8 and they shall **d** in their own land.	3427
	24: 8 and them that **d** in the land of Egypt:	3427
	25: 5 **d** in the land that the LORD hath given	3427
	27:11 and they shall till it, and **d** therein.	3427
	29: 5 **d** *in them*; and plant gardens, and eat	3427
	29:28 **d** *in them*; and plant gardens, and eat	3427
	29:32 he shall not have a man to **d** among this	3427
	31:24 there shall **d** in Judah itself, and *in* all	3427
	32:37 and I will **cause** them to **d** safely:	3427
	33:16 be saved, and Jerusalem shall **d** safely:	7931
	35: 7 but all your days ye shall **d** in tents;	3427
	35: 9 Nor to build houses for us to **d** in:	3427
	35:11 army of the Syrians: so we **d** at Jerusalem.	3427
	35:15 ye shall **d** in the land which I have given	3427
	40: 5 and **d** with him among the people:	3427
	40: 9 **d** in the land and serve the king of	3427
	40:10 I *will* **d** at Mizpah to serve the Chaldeans,	3427
	40:10 and in your cities that ye have taken.	3427
	42:13 if ye say, We will not **d** in this land,	3427
	42:14 hunger of bread; and there will we **d**:	3427
	43: 4 of the LORD, to **d** in the land of Judah.	3427
	43: 5 been driven, to **d** in the land of Judah:	1481
	44: 1 all the Jews which **d** in the land of Egypt,	3427
	44: 1 which **d** at Migdol, and at Tahpanhes,	3427
	44: 8 whither ye be gone to **d**, that ye might	1481
	44:13 I will punish them that **d** in the land of	3427
	44:14 they have a desire to return to **d** there:	3427
	44:26 all Judah that **d** in the land of Egypt;	3427
	47: 2 therein; the city, and them that **d** therein:	3427
	48: 9 be desolate, without any to **d** therein.	3427
	48:28 O ye that **d** in Moab, leave the cities,	3427
	48:28 **d** in the rock, and be like the dove *that*	7931
	49: 1 inherit Gad, and his people in his cities?	3427
	49: 8 Flee ye, turn back, **d** deep, O inhabitants	3427
	49:18 neither shall a son of man **d** in it.	1481
	49:30 Flee, get you far off, **d** deep, O ye	3427
	49:31 neither gates nor bars, *which* **d** alone.	7931
	49:33 abide there, nor *any* son of man **d** in it.	1481
	50: 3 land desolate, and none shall **d** therein:	3427
	50:39 wild beasts of the islands shall **d** *there*,	3427
	50:39 **dwell** *there*, and the owls shall **d** *there*,	3427
	50:40 neither shall any son of man **d** therein.	1481
	51: 1 against them that **d** in the midst of them,	3427
Eze	2: 6 and thou dost **d** among scorpions:	3427

Eze	12:19 of the violence of all them that **d** therein.	3427
	16:46 and her daughters that **d** at thy left hand:	3427
	17:23 under it shall **d** all fowl of every wing;	7931
	17:23 of the branches thereof shall they **d**.	7931
	28:25 shall they **d** in their land that I have given	3427
	28:26 they shall **d** safely therein, and shall build	3427
	28:26 yea, they shall **d** with confidence, when I	3427
	32:15 when I shall smite all them that **d** therein,	3427
	34:25 they shall **d** safely in the wilderness,	3427
	34:28 they shall **d** safely, and none shall make	3427
	36:28 ye shall **d** in the land that I gave to your	3427
	36:33 I will also **cause** *you* to **d** in the cities,	3427
	37:25 they shall **d** in the land that I have given	3427
	37:25 they shall **d** therein, *even* they,	3427
	38: 8 and they shall **d** safely all of them.	3427
	38:11 go *to* them that are at rest, that **d** safely,	3427
	38:12 and goods, that **d** in the midst of the land.	3427
	39: 6 among them that **d** carelessly in the isles:	3427
	39: 9 they that **d** in the cities of Israel shall go	3427
	43: 7 where I will **d** in the midst of the children	7931
	43: 9 and I will **d** in the midst of them for ever.	7931
Da	2:38 wheresoever the children of men **d**,	1753
	4: 1 languages, that **d** in all the earth;	1753
	6:25 languages, that **d** in all the earth;	1753
Hos	9: 3 They shall not **d** in the LORD's land;	3427
	12: 9 will yet **make** thee to **d** in tabernacles,	3427
	14: 7 They that **d** under his shadow shall return;	3427
Joel	3:20 Judah shall **d** for ever, and Jerusalem from	3427
Am	3:12 that **d** in Samaria in the corner of a bed,	3427
	5:11 of hewn stone, but ye shall not **d** in them;	3427
	9: 5 and all that **d** therein shall mourn:	3427
Mic	4:10 thou shalt **d** in the field, and thou shalt go	7931
	7:13 desolate because of them that **d** therein,	3427
	7:14 solitarily *in* the wood, in the midst	7931
Na	1: 5 yea, the world, and all that **d** therein.	3427
	3:18 thy nobles shall **d** *in the dust:* thy people	7931
Hab	2: 8 *of* the city, and *of* all that **d** therein.	3427
	2:17 *of* the city, and *of* all that **d** therein.	3427
Zep	1:18 riddance of all them that **d** in the land.	3427
Hag	1: 4 to **d** in your cieled houses, and this house	3427
Zec	2:10 I come, and I will **d** in the midst of thee,	7931
	2:11 I will **d** in the midst of thee, and thou	7931
	8: 3 and will **d** in the midst of Jerusalem:	7931
	8: 4 old women **d** in the streets of Jerusalem,	3427
	8: 8 and they shall **d** in the midst of Jerusalem:	7931
	9: 6 a bastard shall **d** in Ashdod, and I will cut	3427
	14:11 shall **d** in it, and there shall be no more	3427
Mt	12:45 himself, and they enter in and **d** there:	2730
Lk	11:26 himself; and they enter in, and **d** there:	2730
	21:35 that **d** on the face of the whole earth.	2521
Ac	1:20 be desolate, and let no man **d** therein:	2730
	2:14 of Judea, and all *ye* that **d** at Jerusalem,	2730
	4:16 manifest to all them that **d** in Jerusalem;	2730
	7: 4 him into this land, wherein ye now **d**.	2730
	13:27 For they that **d** at Jerusalem,	2730
	17:26 men for to **d** on all the face of the earth,	2730
	28:16 Paul was suffered to **d** by himself with a	3306
Ro	8: 9 if so be that the Spirit of God **d** in you.	3611
	8:11 raised up Jesus from the dead **d** in you,	3611
1Co	7:12 and she be pleased to **d** with him, let him	3611
	7:13 and *if* he be pleased to **d** with her, let her	3611
2Co	6:16 I will **d** in them, and walk in *them;* and	1774
Eph	3:17 That Christ may **d** in your hearts by faith;	2730
Col	1:19 *the Father* that in him should all fulness **d**;	2730
	3:16 Let the word of Christ **d** in you richly in	1774
1Pe	3: 7 **d** *with them* according to knowledge,	4924
1Jn	4:13 Hereby know we that we **d** in him,	3306
Rev	3:10 world, to try them that **d** upon the earth.	2730
	6:10 avenge our blood on them that **d** on	2730
	7:15 that sitteth on the throne shall **d** among	4637
	11:10 they that **d** upon the earth shall rejoice	2730
	12:12 ye heavens, and ye that **d** in them.	4637
	13: 6 tabernacle, and them that **d** in heaven.	4637
	13: 8 all that **d** upon the earth shall worship	2730
	13:12 them which **d** therein to worship the first	2730
	13:14 deceiveth them that **d** on the earth by	2730
	13:14 saying to them that **d** on the earth, that	2730
	14: 6 to preach unto them that **d** on the earth,	2730
	17: 8 and they that **d** on the earth shall wonder,	2730
	21: 3 he will **d** with them, and they shall be	4637

DWELLED (6) [DWELL]

Ge	13: 7 and the Perizzite **d** then in the land.	3427
	13:12 Abram **d** in the land of Canaan,	3427
	13:12 Lot **d** in the cities of the plain,	3427
	20: 1 **d** between Kadesh and Shur,	3427
Ru	1: 4 and they **d** there about ten years.	3427
1Sa	12:11 enemies on every side, and ye **d** safe.	3427

DWELLERS (3) [DWELL]

Isa	18: 3 of the world, and **d** on the earth, see ye,	7931
Ac	1:19 And it was known unto all the **d** at	2730
	2: 9 and the **d** in Mesopotamia, and in Judea,	2730

DWELLEST (19) [DWELL]

Dt	12:29 thou succeedest them, and **d** in their land;	3427
	19: 1 and **d** in their cities, and in their houses;	3427
	26: 1 and possessest it, and **d** therein;	3427
2Ki	19:15 which **d** *between* the cherubims, thou *art*	3427
Ps	80: 1 thou that **d** *between* the cherubims,	3427
	123: 1 mine eyes, O thou that **d** in the heavens.	3427
SS	8:13 that **d** in the gardens, the companions	3427
Isa	10:24 my people that **d** in Zion, be not afraid of	3427
	37:16 of Israel, that **d** *between* the cherubims,	3427
	47: 8 that **d** carelessly, that sayest in thine heart	3427

Jer	49:16 O thou that **d** in the clefts of the rock,	7931
	51:13 O thou that **d** upon many waters,	7931
La	4:21 of Edom, that **d** in the land of Uz;	3427
Eze	7: 7 unto thee, O thou that **d** in the land:	3427
	12: 2 thou **d** in the midst of a rebellious house,	3427
Ob	1: 3 thou that **d** in the clefts of the rock,	7931
Zec	2: 7 that **d** with the daughter of Babylon.	3427
Jn	1:38 being interpreted, Master,) where **d** thou?	*3306*
Rev	2:13 I know thy works, and where thou **d**,	*2730*

DWELLETH (58) [DWELL]

Lev	19:34 *But* the stranger that **d** with you shall be	1481
	25:39 thy brother *that* **d** by thee be waxen poor,	NIH
	25:47 and thy brother *that* **d** by him wax poor,	NIH
Nu	13:18 what it *is*; and the people that **d** therein,	3427
Dt	33:20 he **d** as a lion, and teareth the arm with	7931
Jos	6:25 she **d** in Israel *even* unto this day;	3427
	22:19 wherein the LORD's tabernacle **d**,	7931
1Sa	4: 4 of hosts, which **d** *between* the cherubims:	3427
	27:11 *will be* his manner all the while he **d** in	3427
2Sa	6: 2 of hosts that **d** *between* the cherubims.	3427
	7: 2 but the ark of God **d** within curtains.	3427
1Ch	13: 6 that **d** *between* the cherubims,	3427
Job	15:28 he **d** in desolate cities, *and* in houses	7931
	38:19 Where is the way *where* light **d**?	7931
	39:28 She **d** and abideth on the rock, upon	7931
Ps	9:11 *praises* to the LORD, which **d** in Zion:	3427
	26: 8 and the place *where* thine honour **d**.	4908
	91: 1 He that **d** in the secret place of the most	3427
	113: 5 unto the LORD our God, who **d** on high,	3427
	135:21 LORD out of Zion, which **d** *at* Jerusalem.	7931
Pr	3:29 seeing he **d** securely by thee.	3427
Isa	8:18 LORD of hosts, which **d** in mount Zion.	7931
	33: 5 The LORD *is* exalted; for he **d** on high:	7931
Jer	29:16 of all the people that **d** in this city,	3427
	44: 2 *are* a desolation, and no man **d** therein,	3427
	49:31 that **d** without care, saith the LORD,	3427
	51:43 a wilderness, a land wherein no man **d**,	3427
La	1: 3 she **d** among the heathen, she findeth no	3427
Eze	16:46 that **d** at thy right hand, *is* Sodom and	3427
	17:16 surely in the place *where* the king **d** that	NIH
	38:14 In that day when my people of Israel **d**	3427
Da	2:22 in the darkness, and the light **d** with him.	8271
Hos	4: 3 every one that **d** therein shall languish,	3427
Joel	3:21 not cleansed: for the LORD **d** in Zion.	7931
Am	8: 8 and every one mourn that **d** therein.	3427
Mt	23:21 sweareth by it, and by him that **d** therein.	*2730*
Jn	6:56 drinketh my blood, **d** in me, and I in him.	*3306*
	14:10 but the Father that **d** in me, he doeth	*3306*
	14:17 for he **d** with you, and shall be in you.	*3306*
Ac	7:48 Howbeit the most High **d** not in temples	*2730*
	17:24 earth, **d** not in temples made with hands;	*2730*
Ro	7:17 no more I that do it, but sin that **d** in me.	*3611*
	7:18 **d** no good *thing*: for to will is present with	*3611*
	7:20 no more I that do it, but sin that **d** in me.	*3611*
	8:11 mortal bodies by his Spirit that **d** in you.	*1774*
1Co	3:16 God, and *that* the Spirit of God **d** in you?	*3611*
Col	2: 9 in him **d** all the fulness of the Godhead	*2730*
2Ti	1:14 keep by the Holy Ghost which **d** in us.	*1774*
Jas	4: 5 the spirit that **d** in us lusteth to envy?	*2730*
2Pe	3:13 a new earth, wherein **d** righteousness.	*2730*
1Jn	3:17 from him, how **d** the love of God in him?	*3306*
	3:24 he that keepeth his commandments **d**	*3306*
	4:12 God in us, and his love is perfected in	*3306*
	4:15 Son of God, God **d** in him, and he in God.	*3306*
	4:16 and he that **d** in love dwelleth in God,	*3306*
	4:16 and he that dwelleth in love **d** in God,	*3306*
2Jn	1: 2 **d** in us, and shall be with us for ever.	*3306*
Rev	2:13 was slain among you, where Satan **d**.	*2730*

DWELLING (60) [DWELL]

Ge	10:30 their **d** was from Mesha, as thou goest	4186
	25:27 and Jacob *was* a plain man, **d** in tents.	3427
	27:39 thy **d** shall be the fatness of the earth,	4186
Lev	25:29 if a man sell a **d** house in a walled city,	4186
Nu	21:15 brooks that goeth down to the **d** of Ar,	3427
	24:21 Strong *is* thy **d place**, and thou puttest	4186
Jos	13:21 *were* dukes of Sihon, **d** in the country.	3427
1Ki	8:30 hear thou in heaven thy **d** place: and	3427
	8:39 hear thou *in* heaven thy **d** place,	3427
	8:43 Hear thou *in* heaven thy **d** place,	3427
	8:49 their supplication *in* heaven thy **d** place,	3427
	21: 8 that *were* in his city, **d** with Naboth.	3427
2Ki	17:25 *so* it was at the beginning of their **d** there,	3427
1Ch	6:32 they ministered before the **d place** of	4908
	6:54 Now these *are* their **d places** throughout	4186
2Ch	6: 2 for thee, and a place for thy **d** for ever.	3427
	6:21 hear thou from thy **d** place, *even* from	4908
	6:30 hear thou from heaven thy **d** place,	3427
	6:33 *even* from thy **d** place, and do according	3427
	6:39 *even* from thy **d** place, their prayer and	3427
	30:27 their prayer came *up* to his **holy d** place,	6944
	36:15 on his people, and on his **d place**:	4583
Job	8:22 the **d place** of the wicked shall come to	168
	21:28 and where *are* the **d places** of the wicked?	4908
Ps	49:11 and their **d places** to all generations;	4908
	49:14 shall consume *in* the grave from their **d**.	2073
	52: 5 pluck thee out of thy **d place**, and root	168
	74: 7 the **d place** of thy name to the ground.	4908
	76: 2 is his tabernacle, and his **d place** in Zion.	4585
	79: 7 Jacob, and laid waste his **d place**.	5116
	90: 1 thou hast been our **d place** in all	4583
	91:10 neither shall *any* plague come nigh thy **d**.	168
Pr	21:20 to be desired and oil in the **d** of the wise;	5116
	24:15 O wicked *man,* against the **d** of	5116

Isa	4: 5 the LORD will create upon every **d** place	4349
	18: 4 I will consider in my **d** place like a clear	4349
Jer	30:18 and have mercy on his **d** places;	4908
	46:19 O thou daughter **d** in Egypt, furnish	3427
	49:33 Hazor shall be a **d** for dragons,	4583
	51:30 they have burnt her **d** places; her bars	4908
	51:37 a **d** place for dragons, an astonishment,	4583
Eze	6: 6 In all your **d** places the cities shall be laid	4186
	37:23 I will save them out of all their **d places**,	4186
	38:11 all of them **d** without walls,	3427
	48:15 *place* for the city, for **d**, and for suburbs:	4186
Da	2:11 the gods, whose **d** is not with flesh.	4070
	4:25 thy **d** shall be with the beasts of the field,	4070
	4:32 thy **d** *shall* be with the beasts of the field:	4070
	5:21 and his **d** *was* with the wild asses:	4070
Joel	3:17 that I *am* the LORD your God in Zion,	7931
Na	2:11 Where *is* the **d** of the lions, and the	4583
Hab	1: 6 possess the **d** places *that are* not theirs.	4908
Zep	3: 7 so their **d** should not be cut off,	4583
Mk	5: 3 Who had *his* **d** among the tombs;	*2731*
Ac	2: 5 And there were **d** at Jerusalem Jews,	*2730*
	19:17 all the Jews and Greeks also at Ephesus;	*2730*
1Co	4:11 buffeted, and **have no certain d** place;	*790*
1Ti	6:16 **d** in the light which no *man* can approach	*3611*
Heb	11: 9 as *in* a strange *country*, **d** in tabernacles	*2730*
2Pe	2: 8 (For *that* righteous *man* **d** among them,	*1460*

DWELLINGS (17) [DWELL]

Ex	10:23 the children of Israel had light in their **d**.	4186
Lev	3:17 your generations throughout all your **d**,	4186
	7:26 *it be* of fowl or of beast, in any of your **d**.	4186
	23: 3 *is* the sabbath of the LORD in all your **d**.	4186
	23:14 throughout your generations in all your **d**.	4186
	23:21 in all your **d** throughout your generations.	4186
	23:31 throughout your generations in all your **d**.	4186
Nu	35:29 throughout your generations in all your **d**.	4186
Job	18:19 his people, nor *any* remaining in his **d**.	4033
	18:21 Surely such *are* the **d** of the wicked,	4908
	39: 6 the wilderness, and the barren *land* his **d**.	4908
Ps	55:15 for wickedness *is* in their **d**,	4033
	87: 2 gates of Zion more than all the **d** of Jacob.	4908
Isa	32:18 and in sure **d**, and in quiet resting places;	4908
Jer	9:19 the land, because our **d** have cast *us* out.	4908
Eze	25: 4 palaces in thee, and make their **d** in thee:	4908
Zep	2: 6 the sea coast shall be **d** *and* cottages for	5116

DWELT (226) [DWELL]

Ge	4:16 in the land of Nod, on the east of Eden.	3427
	11: 2 in the land of Shinar; and they **d** there.	3427
	11:31 and they came unto Haran, and **d** there.	3427
	13:18 came and **d** in the plain of Mamre,	3427
	14: 7 the Amorites, that **d** in Hazezon-tamar.	3427
	14:12 who **d** in Sodom, and his goods,	3427
	14:13 he **d** in the plain of Mamre the Amorite,	7931
	16: 3 after Abram had **d** ten years in the land	3427
	19:29 overthrew the cities in the which Lot **d**.	3427
	19:30 **d** in the mountain, and his two daughters	3427
	19:30 he **d** in a cave, he and his two daughters.	3427
	21:20 **d** in the wilderness, and became an	3427
	21:21 he **d** in the wilderness of Paran: and	3427
	22:19 and Abraham **d** at Beer-sheba.	3427
	23:10 Ephron **d** amongst the children of Heth:	3427
	24:62 for he **d** in the south country.	3427
	25:11 and Isaac **d** by the well Lahai-roi.	3427
	25:18 they **d** from Havilah unto Shur, that *is*	7931
	26: 6 And Isaac **d** in Gerar:	3427
	26:17 tent in the valley of Gerar, and **d** there.	3427
	35:22 when Israel **d** in that land, that Reuben	7931
	36: 8 Thus **d** Esau in mount Seir: Esau *is* Edom.	3427
	37: 1 Jacob **d** in the land wherein his father was	3427
	38:11 Tamar went and **d** in her father's house.	3427
	47:27 Israel **d** in the land of Egypt, in the	3427
	50:22 Joseph **d** in Egypt, he, and his father's	3427
Ex	2:15 of Pharaoh, and **d** in the land of Midian:	3427
	12:40 who **d** in Egypt, *was* four hundred and	3427
Lev	18: 3 of Egypt, wherein ye **d**, shall ye not do:	3427
	26:35 rest in your sabbaths, when ye **d** upon it.	3427
Nu	14:25 and the Canaanites **d** in the valley.)	3427
	14:45 the Canaanites which **d** in that hill,	3427
	20:15 and we have **d** in Egypt a long time;	3427
	21: 1 Arad the Canaanite, which **d** *in* the south,	3427
	21:25 Israel **d** in all the cities of the Amorites,	3427
	21:31 Thus Israel **d** in the land of the Amorites.	3427
	21:34 of the Amorites, which **d** at Heshbon.	3427
	31:10 they burnt all their cities wherein they **d**,	4186
	32:40 the son of Manasseh; and he **d** therein.	3427
	33:40 **d** in the south in the land of Canaan,	3427
Dt	1: 4 which **d** in Heshbon, and Og the king of	3427
	1: 4 of Bashan, which **d** at Astaroth in Edrei:	3427
	1: 6 Ye have **d** long enough in this mount:	3427
	1:44 the Amorites, which **d** in that mountain,	3427
	2: 8 which **d** in Seir, through the way of	3427
	2:10 (The Emims **d** therein in times past,	3427
	2:12 The Horims also **d** in Seir beforetime;	3427
	2:12 from before them, and **d** in their stead;	3427
	2:20 giants **d** therein in old time;	3427
	2:21 succeeded them, and **d** in their stead:	3427
	2:22 to the children of Esau, which **d** in Seir,	3427
	2:22 and **d** in their stead *even* unto this day:	3427
	2:23 Avims which **d** in Hazerim, *even* unto	3427
	2:23 destroyed them, and **d** in their stead.)	3427
	3: 2 of the Amorites, which **d** at Heshbon.	3427
	4:46 who **d** at Heshbon, whom Moses and	3427
	8:12 hast built goodly houses, and **d** *therein;*	3427
	29:16 (For ye know how we have **d** in the land	3427

Dt	33:16 the good will of him that **d** in the bush:	7931
Jos	2:15 the town wall, and she **d** upon the wall.	3427
	7: 7 and **d** on the *other* side Jordan!	3427
	9:16 and *that* they **d** among them.	3427
	12: 2 who **d** in Heshbon, *and* ruled from Aroer,	3427
	12: 4 giants, that **d** at Ashtaroth and at Edrei,	3427
	16:10 drave not out the Canaanites that **d** in	3427
	19:47 and **d** therein, and called Leshem, Dan,	3427
	19:50 and he built the city, and **d** therein.	3427
	21:43 and they possessed it, and **d** therein.	3427
	22:33 the children of Reuben and Gad **d**	3427
	24: 2 Your fathers **d** on the *other* side of	3427
	24: 7 and ye **d** in the wilderness a long season.	3427
	24: 8 which **d** on the *other* side Jordan;	3427
	24:18 even the Amorites which **d** in the land:	3427
Jdg	1: 9 that **d** in the mountain, and in the south,	3427
	1:10 went against the Canaanites that **d** in	3427
	1:16 and they went and **d** among the people.	3427
	1:29 drive out the Canaanites that **d** in Gezer;	3427
	1:29 the Canaanites **d** in Gezer among them.	3427
	1:30 the Canaanites **d** among them,	3427
	1:32 the Asherites **d** among the Canaanites,	3427
	1:33 among the Canaanites, the inhabitants	3427
	3: 3 and the Hivites that **d** in mount Lebanon,	3427
	3: 5 the children of Israel **d** among	3427
	4: 2 which **d** in Harosheth of the Gentiles.	3427
	4: 5 she **d** under the palm tree of Deborah	3427
	8:11 went up *by* the way of them that **d**	7931
	8:29 of Joash went and **d** in his own house.	3427
	9:21 and fled, and went to Beer, and **d** there,	3427
	9:41 Abimelech **d** at Arumah: and Zebul thrust	3427
	10: 1 and he **d** in Shamir in mount Ephraim.	3427
	11: 3 his brethren, and **d** in the land of Tob:	3427
	11:26 While Israel **d** in Heshbon and her towns,	3427
	15: 8 and **d** in the top of the rock Etam.	3427
	18: 7 that *were* therein, how they **d** careless,	3427
	18:28 And they built a city, and **d** therein,	3427
	21:23 and repaired the cities, and **d** in them.	3427
Ru	2:23 and **d** with her mother in law.	3427
1Sa	19:18 he and Samuel went and **d** in Naioth.	3427
	22: 4 they **d** with him all the while that David	3427
	23:29 and **d** in strong holds at En-gedi.	3427
	27: 3 David **d** with Achish at Gath, he and	3427
	27: 7 the time that David **d** in the country of	3427
	31: 7 and the Philistines came and **d** in them.	3427
2Sa	2: 3 and they **d** in the cities of Hebron.	3427
	5: 9 David **d** in the fort, and called it the city	3427
	7: 6 Whereas I have not **d** in *any* house since	3427
	9:12 that **d** in the house of Ziba *were* servants	4186
	9:13 Mephibosheth **d** in Jerusalem: for he did	3427
	14:28 So Absalom **d** two full years in Jerusalem,	3427
1Ki	2:38 And Shimei **d** in Jerusalem many days.	3427
	4:25 Judah and Israel **d** safely, every man	3427
	7: 8 his house where he **d** *had* another court	3427
	9:16 slain the Canaanites that **d** in the city,	3427
	11:24 and **d** therein, and reigned in Damascus.	3427
	12: 2 king Solomon, and Jeroboam in Egypt;)	3427
	12:17 *as for* the children of Israel which **d** in	3427
	12:25 in mount Ephraim, and **d** therein;	3427
	13:11 Now there **d** an old prophet in Beth-el;	3427
	13:25 told *it* in the city where the old prophet **d**.	3427
	15:18 king of Syria, that **d** at Damascus, saying,	3427
	15:21 left off building of Ramah, and **d** in Tirzah.	3427
	17: 5 for he went and **d** by the brook Cherith,	3427
2Ki	13: 5 the children of Israel **d** in their tents,	3427
	15: 5 day of his death, and **d** in a several house.	3427
	16: 6 came *to* Elath, and **d** there unto this day.	3427
	17:24 and **d** in the cities thereof.	3427
	17:28 from Samaria came and **d** in Beth-el,	3427
	17:29 nation in their cities wherein they **d**.	3427
	19:36 went and returned, and **d** at Nineveh.	3427
	22:14 (now she **d** in Jerusalem in the college;)	3427
1Ch	2:55 the families of the scribes which **d** at	3427
	4:23 those that **d** *amongst* plants and hedges;	3427
	4:23 there they **d** with the king for his work.	3427
	4:28 they **d** at Beer-sheba, and Moladah,	3427
	4:40 for *they* had **d** there of old.	3427
	4:41 unto this day, and **d** in their rooms:	3427
	4:43 were escaped, and **d** there unto this day.	3427
	5: 8 the son of Joel, who **d** in Aroer, even unto	3427
	5:10 they **d** in their tents throughout all the	3427
	5:11 the children of Gad **d** over against them,	3427
	5:16 they **d** in Gilead in Bashan, and in her	3427
	5:22 they **d** in their steads until the captivity.	3427
	5:23 children of the half tribe of Manasseh **d**	3427
	7:29 In these **d** the children of Joseph the son	3427
	8:28 chief *men.* These **d** in Jerusalem.	3427
	8:29 at Gibeon **d** the father of Gibeon;	3427
	8:32 these also **d** with their brethren in	3427
	9: 2 Now the first inhabitants that **d** in their	NIH
	9: 3 In Jerusalem **d** of the children of Judah,	3427
	9:16 that **d** in the villages of the Netophathites.	3427
	9:34 their generations; these **d** at Jerusalem.	3427
	9:35 In Gibeon **d** the father of Gibeon, Jehiel,	3427
	9:38 they also **d** with their brethren at	3427
	10: 7 and the Philistines came and **d** in them.	3427
	11: 7 David **d** in the castle; therefore they called	3427
	17: 5 For I have not **d** in a house since the day	3427
2Ch	10:17 *as for* the children of Israel that **d** in	3427
	11: 5 Rehoboam **d** in Jerusalem, and built cities	3427
	16: 2 king of Syria, that **d** at Damascus, saying,	3427
	19: 4 Jehoshaphat **d** at Jerusalem: and he went	3427
	20: 8 they **d** therein, and have built thee a	3427
	26: 7 against the Arabians that **d** in Gur-baal,	3427
	26:21 and **d** *in* a several house, *being* a leper;	3427

D

2Ch 28:18 and the villages thereof: and they **d** there. 3427
30:25 of Israel, and that **d** in Judah, rejoiced. 3427
31: 4 **d** in Jerusalem to give the portion of 3427
31: 6 and Judah, that **d** in the cities of Judah, 3427
34:22 (now she **d** in Jerusalem in the college:) 3427
Ezr 2:70 **d** in their cities, and all Israel in their 3427
Ne 3:26 Moreover the Nethinims in Ophel, 3427
4:12 when the Jews which **d** by them came, 3427
7:73 and all Israel, in their cities; 3427
11: 1 the rulers of the people **d** at Jerusalem: 3427
11: 3 chief of the province that **d** in Jerusalem: 3427
11: 3 in the cities of Judah **d** every one in his 3427
11: 4 at Jerusalem **d** certain of the children of 3427
11: 6 All the sons of Perez that **d** at Jerusalem 3427
11:21 the Nethinims in Ophel: and Ziha and 3427
11:25 some of the children of Judah **d** at 3427
11:30 they **d** from Beer-sheba unto the valley of 2583
11:31 children also of Benjamin from Geba **d** NIH
13:16 There **d** men of Tyre also therein, which 3427
Est 9:19 villages, that **d** in the unwalled towns, 3427
Job 22: 8 the earth; and the honourable man **d** in it. 3427
29:25 and sat chief, and **d** as a king in the army, 7931
Ps 68:10 Thy congregation hath **d** therein: thou, 7931
74: 2 this mount Zion, wherein thou hast **d**. 7931
94:17 my help, my soul had almost **d** in silence. 7931
120: 6 My soul hath long **d** with him that hateth 7931
Isa 13:20 neither shall it be **d** in from generation to 7931
29: 1 to Ariel, to Ariel, the city where David **d!** 2583
33: and went and returned, and **d** at Nineveh. 3427
Jer 2: 6 passed through, and where no man **d?** 3427
35:10 we have **d** in tents, and have obeyed, 3427
39:14 him home: so he **d** among the people. 3427
40: 6 **d** with him among the people that were 3427
41:17 and **d** in the habitation of Chimham, 3427
44:15 even all the people that **d** in the land of 3427
50:39 neither shall it be **d** in from generation to 7931
Eze 3:15 that **d** by the river of Chebar, and I sat 3427
31: 6 and under his shadow **d** all great nations. 3427
31:17 that **d** under his shadow in the midst of 3427
36:17 when the house of Israel **d** in their own 3427
37:25 my servant, wherein your fathers have **d**; 3427
39:26 when they **d** safely in their land, 3427
Da 4:12 the fowls of the heaven **d** in the boughs 1753
4:21 under which the beasts of the field **d**, 1753
Zep 2:15 This is the rejoicing city that **d** carelessly, 3427
Mt 2:23 he came and **d** in a city called Nazareth. 2730
4:13 he came and **d** in Capernaum, 2730
Lk 1:65 And fear came on all that **d** round about 4039
13: 4 sinners above all men that **d** in Jerusalem? 2730
Jn 1:14 and among us, (and we beheld his glory, 4637
1:39 They came and saw where he **d**, 3306
Ac 7: 2 in Mesopotamia, before he **d** in Charran, 2730
7: 4 land of the Chaldeans, and **d** in Charran: 2730
9:22 the Jews which **d** at Damascus, 2730
9:32 down also to the saints which **d** at Lydda. 2730
9:35 all that **d** at Lydda and Saron saw him, 2730
11:29 relief unto the brethren which **d** in Judea: 2730
13:17 they **d** as strangers in the land of Egypt, 3940
19:10 that all they which **d** in Asia heard 2730
22:12 good report of all the Jews which **d** there, 2730
28:30 And Paul two whole years in his own 3306
2Ti 1: 5 which **d** first in thy grandmother Lois, 1774
Rev 11:10 two prophets tormented them that **d** 2730

DYED (7) [DYING]

Ex 25: 5 rams' skins **d** red, and badgers' skins, 119
26:14 covering for the tent of rams' skins **d** red, 119
35: 7 rams' skins **d** red, and badgers' skins, 119
36:19 covering for the tent of rams' skins **d** red, 119
39:34 the covering of rams' skins **d** red, 119
Isa 63: 1 Edom, with **d** garments from Bozrah? 2556
Eze 23:15 **exceeding in d** attire upon their 2871+5628

DYING (6) [DYED]

Nu 17:13 shall die: shall we be consumed with **d?** 1478
Mk 12:20 the first took a wife, and **d** left no seed. 599
Lk 8:42 about twelve years of age, and she lay a **d.** 599
2Co 4:10 Always bearing about in the body the **d** of 3500
6: 9 as **d**, and behold, we live; as chastened, 599
Heb 11:21 By faith Jacob, when he was a **d**, 599

DYSENTERY See FLUX

E

EACH (51)

Ge 15:10 and laid **e** piece one against another: 376
34:25 took **e man** his sword, and came upon 376
40: 5 of them, **e man** his dream in one night, 376
40: 5 **e man** according to the interpretation of 376
41:11 we dreamed **e man** according to 376
41:12 to **e man** according to his dream he did 376
45:22 To all of them he gave **e man** changes of 376

Ex 18: 7 they asked **e** other of their welfare; 376
30:34 shall there be **a like** weight: 905+905+871.1
Lev 24: 7 thou shalt put pure frankincense upon **e** NIH
Nu 1:44 one was for the house of his fathers. 376+376
7: 3 for two of the princes, and for **e** one an ox: NIH
7:11 **e** prince on his day, for the dedicating of 259
7:85 **E** charger of silver weighing an hundred 259
7:85 and thirty shekels, **e** bowl seventy: 259
14:34 even forty days, for **e** day for a year, shall ye 3117
16:17 thou also, and Aaron, **e** of you his censer. 376
17: 6 **e** prince one, according to their 3807.1
29:14 two tenth deals to **e** ram of the two rams, 259
29:15 several tenth deal to **e** lamb of the fourteen 259
Jos 18: 4 Give out from among you three men for **e** NIH
22:14 of **e** chief house a prince throughout all 259
22:14 **e one** was a head of the house of their 376
Jdg 8:18 one resembled the children of a king. NIH
21:22 we reserved not to **e man** his wife in 376
Ru 1: 8 in law, Go, return **e** to her mother's house: 802
1: 9 **e** of you in the house of her husband. 802
1Ki 4: 7 **e man** his month in a year made provision. 259
6:23 cherubims of olive tree, **e** ten cubits 2050.2
22:10 Jehoshaphat the king of Judah sat **e** on his 376
2Ki 9:21 in his chariot, and they went out against 376
15:20 of **e man** fifty shekels of silver, to give to 259
1Ch 20: 6 six on **e** hand, and six on **e** foot: and NIH
20: 6 six on **e** hand, and six on **e** foot: and NIH
2Ch 3:15 chapter that was on the top of **e** of them NIH
4:13 two rows of pomegranates on **e** wreath, 259
9:18 on **e** side 2088+2088+4480+4480+2050.1
Ne 13:24 the language of **e** people. 5971+5971+2050.1
Ps 85:10 and peace have kissed **e** other. NIH
Isa 2:20 which they made **e** one for himself to NIH
6: 2 **e one** had six wings; with twain he NIH
35: 7 where **e** lay, shall be grass with reeds 1886.3
57: 2 beds, **e one** walking in his uprightness. NIH
Eze 4: 6 appointed thee **e day** for a year. 3117+3117
40:16 and upon **e** post were palm trees. NIH
40:48 measured **e** post of the porch, five cubits NIH
Lk 13:15 doth not **e one** of you on the sabbath 1538
Ac 2: 3 as of fire, and it sat upon **e** of them. 1520+1538
Php 2: 3 in lowliness of mind let **e** esteem other 240
2Th 1: 3 one of you all towards **e** other aboundeth; 240
Rev 4: 8 the four beasts had **e** of them six wings 1527

EAGERNESS See FORWARDNESS

EAGLE (23) [EAGLE'S, EAGLES, EAGLES']

Lev 11:13 the **e**, and the ossifrage, and the ospray, 5404
11:18 the swan, and the pelican, and the **gier e**, 7360
Dt 14:12 the **e**, and the ossifrage, and the ospray, 5404
14:17 and the **gier e**, and the cormorant, 7360
28:49 end of the earth, as swift as the **e** flieth; 5404
32:11 As an **e** stirreth up her nest, fluttereth 5404
Job 9:26 ships: as the **e** that hasteth to the prey. 5404
39:27 Doth the **e** mount up at thy command, 5404
Pr 23: 5 they fly away as an **e** toward heaven. 5404
30:19 The way of an **e** in the air; the way of a 5404
Jer 48:40 he shall fly as an **e**, and shall spread his 5404
49:16 shouldest make thy nest as high as the **e**, 5404
49:22 he shall come up and fly as the **e**, 5404
Eze 1:10 side; they four also had the face of an **e**. 5404
10:14 of a lion, and the fourth the face of an **e**. 5404
17: 3 A great **e** with great wings, longwinged, 5404
17: 7 There was also another great **e** with great 5404
Hos 8: 1 He shall come as an **e** against the house 5404
Ob 1: 4 Though thou exalt thyself as the **e**, 5404
Mic 1:16 enlarge thy baldness as the **e**; 5404
Hab 1: 8 they shall fly as the **e** that hasteth to eat. 5404
Rev 4: 7 the fourth beast was like a flying **e**. 105
12:14 woman were given two wings of a great **e**, 105

EAGLE'S (2) [EAGLE]

Ps 103: 5 so that thy youth is renewed like the **e**. 5404
Da 7: 4 The first was like a lion, and had **e** wings: 5403

EAGLES (7) [EAGLE]

2Sa 1:23 were swifter than **e**, they were stronger 5404
Pr 30:17 pick it out, and the young **e** shall eat it. 5404
Isa 40:31 they shall mount up with wings as **e**; 5404
Jer 4:13 horses are swifter than **e**. Woe unto us! 5404
La 4:19 Our persecutors are swifter than the **e** of 5404
Mt 24:28 there will the **e** be gathered together. 105
Lk 17:37 Wheresoever the body is, thither will the **e** 105

EAGLES' (2) [EAGLE]

Ex 19: 4 how I bare you on **e** wings, 5404
Da 4:33 till his hairs were grown like **e** feathers, 5403

EAR (120) [EARED, EARING, EARRING, EARRINGS, EARS]

Ex 9:31 for the barley was in the **e**, and the flax 24
15:26 wilt **give e** to his commandments, 238
21: 6 his master shall bore his **e** through with an 241
29:20 put it upon the tip of the right **e** of Aaron, 241
29:20 upon the tip of the right **e** of his sons, 241
Lev 8:23 put it upon the tip of Aaron's right **e**, 241
8:24 of the blood upon the tip of their right **e**, 241
14:14 of the right **e** of him that is to be cleansed, 241
14:17 of the right **e** of him that is to be cleansed, 241
14:25 put it upon the tip of the right **e** of him 241
14:28 of the right **e** of him that is to be cleansed, 241
Dt 1:45 to your voice, nor **give e** unto you. 238
15:17 and thrust it through his **e** unto the door, 241
32: 1 **Give e**, O ye heavens, and I will speak; 238
Jdg 5: 3 **give e**, O ye princes; I, even I, will sing 238

1Sa 8:12 will set them to **e** his ground, and to reap 2790
9:15 Now the LORD had told Samuel in his **e** 241
2Ki 19:16 LORD, bow down thine **e**, and hear: open, 241
2Ch 24:19 against them: but they would not **give e**. 238
Ne 1: 6 Let thine **e** now be attentive, and mine 241
1:11 let now thine **e** be attentive to the prayer 241
9:30 yet would they not **give e**: therefore 238
Job 4:12 to me, and mine **e** received a little thereof. 241
12:11 Doth not the **e** try words? and the mouth 241
13: 1 mine eye hath seen all this, mine **e** hath 241
29:11 When the **e** heard me, then it blessed me; 241
29:21 Unto me men **gave e**, and waited, 8085
32:11 I **gave e** to your reasons, whilst you 238
34: 2 ye wise men; and **give e** unto me, 241
34: 3 the **e** trieth words, as the mouth tasteth 241
36:10 He openeth also their **e** to discipline, 241
42: 5 have heard of thee by the hearing of the **e**: 241
Ps 5: 1 **Give e** to my words, O LORD, consider my 238
10:17 their heart, thou wilt cause thine **e** to hear: 238
17: 1 attend unto my cry, **give e** unto my prayer, 238
17: 6 incline thine **e** unto me, and hear my 241
31: 2 Bow down thine **e** to me; deliver me 241
39:12 O LORD, and **give e** unto my cry; 238
45:10 and consider, and incline thine **e**; 241
49: 1 **give e**, all ye inhabitants of the world: 238
49: 4 will incline mine **e** to a parable: I will open 241
54: 2 O God; **give e** to the words of my mouth. 238
55: 1 **Give e** to my prayer, O God; and hide not 238
58: 4 are like the deaf adder that stoppeth her **e**; 241
71: 2 incline thine **e** unto me, and save me. 241
77: 1 with my voice; and he **gave e** unto me. 238
78: 1 **Give e**, O my people, to my law: 238
80: 1 **Give e**, O Shepherd of Israel, thou that 238
84: 8 my prayer: **give e**, O God of Jacob. Selah. 238
86: 1 Bow down thine **e**, O LORD, hear me: for I 241
86: 6 **Give e**, O LORD, unto my prayer; 238
88: 2 before thee: incline thine **e** unto my cry; 241
94: 9 He that planted the **e**, shall he not hear? 241
102: 2 I am in trouble; incline thine **e** unto me, 241
116: 2 Because he hath inclined his **e** unto me, 241
141: 1 **give e** unto my voice, when I cry unto 238
143: 1 O LORD, **give e** to my supplications; 238
Pr 2: 2 So that thou incline thine **e** unto wisdom, 241
4:20 my words; incline thine **e** to my sayings. 241
5: 1 and bow thine **e** to my understanding; 241
5:13 inclined mine **e** to them that instructed 241
15:31 The **e** that heareth the reproof of life 241
17: 4 and a liar **giveth e** to a naughty tongue. 241
18:15 and the **e** of the wise seeketh knowledge. 241
20:12 The hearing **e**, and the seeing eye, 241
22:17 Bow down thine **e**, and hear the words of 241
25:12 so is a wise reprover upon an obedient **e**. 241
28: 9 He that turneth away his **e** from hearing 241
Ecc 1: 8 with seeing, nor the **e** filled with hearing. 241
Isa 1: 2 Hear, O heavens, and **give e**, O earth: 238
1:10 **give e** unto the law of our God, ye people 238
8: 9 pieces; and **give e**, all ye of far countries: 238
28:23 **Give ye e**, and hear my voice; hearken, 238
30:24 the young asses that **e** the ground shall 5647
32: 9 careless daughters, **give e** unto my speech. 238
37:17 Incline thine **e**, O LORD, and hear; 241
42:23 Who among you will **give e** to this? 238
48: 8 that time that thine **e** was not opened: 241
50: 4 he wakeneth mine **e** to hear as the learned. 241
50: 5 The Lord GOD hath opened mine **e**, 241
51: 4 and **give e** unto me, O my nation: 238
55: 3 Incline your **e**, and come unto me: hear, 241
59: 1 neither his **e** heavy, that it cannot hear: 241
64: 4 nor **perceived by the e**, neither hath the 238
Jer 6:10 their **e** is uncircumcised, and they cannot 241
7:24 nor inclined their **e**, but walked in 241
7:26 inclined their **e**, but hardened their neck: 241
9:20 let your **e** receive the word of his mouth, 241
11: 8 nor inclined their **e**, but walked every one 241
13:15 Hear ye, and **give e**; be not proud: 238
17:23 neither inclined their **e**, but made their 241
25: 4 hearkened, nor inclined your **e** to hear. 241
34:14 not unto me, neither inclined their **e**. 241
35:15 have not inclined your **e**, nor hearkened 241
44: 5 nor inclined their **e** to turn from their 241
La 3:56 hide not thine **e** at my breathing, at my 241
Da 9:18 O my God, incline thine **e**, and hear; 241
Hos 5: 1 Israel; and **give e**, O house of the king; 238
Joel 1: 2 Hear this, ye old men, and **give e**, all ye 238
Am 3:12 of the lion two legs, or a piece of an **e**; 241
Mt 10:27 and what ye hear in the **e**, that preach ye 3775
26:51 of the high priest's, and smote off his **e**. 5621
Mk 4:28 first the blade, then the **e**, after that the 4719
4:28 the ear, after that the full corn in the **e**. 4719
14:47 of the high priest, and cut off his **e**. 5621
Lk 12: 3 that which ye have spoken in the **e** in 3775
22:50 of the high priest, and cut off his right **e**. 5621
22:51 And he touched his **e**, and healed him. 5621
Jn 18:10 priest's servant, and cut off his right **e**. 5621
18:26 being his kinsman whose **e** Peter cut off, 5621
1Co 2: 9 is written, Eye hath not seen, nor **e** heard, 3775
12:16 And if the **e** shall say, Because I am not 3775
Rev 2: 7 He that hath an **e**, let him hear what 3775
2:11 He that hath an **e**, let him hear what 3775
2:17 He that hath an **e**, let him hear what 3775
2:29 He that hath an **e**, let him hear what 3775
3: 6 He that hath an **e**, let him hear what 3775
3:13 He that hath an **e**, let him hear what 3775
3:22 He that hath an **e**, let him hear what 3775
13: 9 If any man have an **e**, let him hear. 3775

EARED (1) [EAR]

Dt 21: 4 which is neither **e** nor sown, and shall 5647

EARING (2) [EAR]

Ge 45: 6 *in* the which *there shall* neither *be* **e** nor 2758
Ex 34:21 in **e** *time* and in harvest thou shalt rest. 2758

EARLIER See HERETOFORE

EARLY (86)

Ge	19: 2 ye shall **rise up e**, and go on your ways.	7925
	19:27 Abraham **gat up e** in the morning to	7925
	20: 8 Therefore Abimelech **rose e** in	7925
	21:14 Abraham **rose up e** in the morning,	7925
	22: 3 Abraham **rose up e** in the morning,	7925
	28:18 Jacob **rose up e** in the morning,	7925
	31:55 **e** in the morning Laban **rose up**,	7925
Ex	8:20 **Rise up e** in the morning, and stand	7925
	9:13 **Rise up e** in the morning, and stand	7925
	24: 4 **rose up e** in the morning, and builded an	7925
	32: 6 they **rose up e** on the morrow,	7925
	34: 4 Moses **rose up e** in the morning,	7925
Nu	14:40 they **rose up e** in the morning,	7925
Jos	3: 1 Joshua **rose e** in the morning;	7925
	6:12 Joshua **rose e** in the morning,	7925
	6:15 that they **rose e** about the dawning of	7925
	7:16 So Joshua **rose up e** in the morning,	7925
	8:10 Joshua **rose up e**, and numbered	7925
	8:14 Ai saw *it*, that they hasted and **rose up e**,	7925
Jdg	6:28 when the men of the city **arose e** in	7925
	6:38 for he **rose up e** on the morrow,	7925
	7: 1 **rose up e**, and pitched beside the well of	7925
	7: 3 and **depart e** from mount Gilead.	6852
	9:33 thou shalt **rise e**, and set upon the city:	7925
	19: 5 when they **arose e** in the morning, that	7925
	19: 8 he **arose e** in the morning on the fifth	7925
	19: 9 to morrow **get** you **e** on your way, that	7925
	21: 4 that the people **rose e**, and built there an	7925
1Sa	1:19 they **rose up e** in the morning,	7925
	5: 3 when they of Ashdod **arose e** on	7925
	5: 4 they **arose e** on the morrow morning,	7925
	9:26 they **arose e**: and it came to pass about	7925
	15:12 when Samuel **rose e** to meet Saul in	7925
	17:20 David **rose e** in the morning,	7925
	29:10 Wherefore now **rise up e** in the morning	7925
	29:10 as soon as ye **be up e** in the morning,	7925
	29:11 men **rose up e** to depart in the morning,	7925
2Sa	15: 2 Absalom **rose up e**, and stood beside	7925
2Ki	3:22 they **rose up e** in the morning, and the	7925
	6:15 the servant of the man of God was risen **e**,	7925
	19:35 when they **arose e** in the morning,	7925
2Ch	20:20 they **rose e** in the morning, and went	7925
	29:20 Hezekiah the king **rose e**, and gathered	7925
Job	1: 5 **rose up e** in the morning, and offered	7925
Ps	5: 3 God shall help her, *and that* right **e**.	1242
	57: 8 and harp: I *myself* will awake **e**.	7837
	63: 1 God, thou *art* my God; **e** will I **seek**	7836
	78:34 they returned and **inquired e after** God.	7836
	90:14 O satisfy us **e** *with* thy	1242+871.1+1886.1
	101: 8 I will **e** destroy all	1242+1886.1+3807.1
	108: 2 and harp: I *myself* will awake **e**.	7837
	127: 2 *It is* vain for you to rise up **e**, to sit up late,	7925
Pr	1:28 they shall **seek** me **e**, but they shall not	7836
	8:17 and those that **seek** me **e** shall find me.	7836
	27:14 **rising e** in the morning, it shall be	7925
SS	7:12 Let us **get up e** to the vineyards; let us see	7925
Isa	5:11 Woe unto them that **rise up e** in	7836
	26: 9 my spirit within me will I **seek** thee **e**:	7836
	37:36 when they **arose e** in the morning,	7925
Jer	7:13 **rising up e** and speaking, but ye heard	7925
	7:25 daily **rising up e** and sending *them*:	7925
	11: 7 **rising e** and protesting, saying, Obey my	7925
	25: 3 spoken unto you, **rising e** and speaking;	7925
	25: 4 **rising e** and sending; but ye have	7925
	26: 5 both **rising up e**, and sending *them*, but	7925
	29:19 **rising up e** and sending *them*; but ye	7925
	32:33 **rising up e** and teaching *them*, yet they	7925
	35:14 spoken unto you, **rising e** and speaking;	7925
	35:15 **rising up e** and sending *them*, saying,	7925
	44: 4 **rising e** and sending *them*, saying,	7925
Da	6:19 the king arose **very e** in the morning,	8238
Hos	5:15 in their affliction they will **seek** me **e**.	7836
	6: 4 and as the **e** dew *it* goeth away.	7925
	13: 3 and as the **e** dew that passeth away,	7925
Zep	3: 7 **rose e**, *and* corrupted all their doings.	7925
Mt	20: 1 which went out **e** **in the morning**	260+4404
Mk	16: 2 very **e** in the morning the first *day* of	4404
	16: 9 when *Jesus* was risen **e** the first *day* of	4404
Lk	21:38 all the people **came e** **in the morning**	3719
	24: 1 very **e** **in the morning**, they came	901+3722
	24:22 which were **e** at the sepulchre;	3721
Jn	8: 2 And **e** **in the morning** he came again into	3722
	18:28 unto the hall of judgment: and it was **e**;	4405
	20: 1 of the week cometh Mary Magdalene **e**,	4404
Ac	5:21 temple **e** **in the morning**,	3588+3722+5259
Jas	5: 7 until he receive the **e** and latter rain.	4406

EARNEST (8) [EARNESTLY]

Ro 8:19 For the **e expectation** of the creature 603
2Co 1:22 and given the **e** of the Spirit in our hearts. 728
 5: 5 who also hath given unto us the **e** of 728
 7: 7 when he told us your **e desire**, your 1972
 8:16 which put the same **e care** into the heart 4710
Eph 1:14 Which is the **e** of our inheritance, until 728
Php 1:20 According to my **e expectation** and 603

Heb 2: 1 Therefore we ought to give the **more e** 4056

EARNESTLY (16) [EARNEST]

Nu 22:37 I not **e send** unto thee to call thee? 7971+7971
1Sa 20: 6 David **e asked** *leave* of me that *he* 7592+7592
 20:28 David **e asked** *leave* of me *to go to* 7592+7592
Ne 3:20 After him Baruch the son of Zabbai **e** 2734
Job 7: 2 As a servant **e desireth** the shadow, 7602
Jer 11: 7 For I **e protested** unto your fathers 5749+5749
 31:20 I do **e remember** him still: 2142+2142
Mic 7: 3 may do evil with both hands **e**, 3190+3807.1
Lk 22:44 And being in an agony he prayed **more e**: 1617
 22:56 **e looked** upon him, and said, This *man* 816
Ac 3:12 why **look** ye *so* **e** on us, as though by our 816
 23: 1 **e beholding** the council, said, Men *and* 816
1Co 12:31 But **covet e** the best gifts: and yet shew I 2206
2Co 5: 2 **e desiring** to be clothed upon with our 1971
Jas 5:17 he **prayed e** that it might not rain: 4335+4336
Jude 1: 3 exhort *you* that ye should **e contend for** 1864

EARNESTNESS See FORWARDNESS

EARNETH (2)

Hag 1: 6 he that **e wages** earneth wages *to put it* 7936
 1: 6 he that earneth wages **e wages** *to put it* 7936

EARRING (5) [EAR, RING]

Ge 24:22 that the man took a golden **e** of half a 5141
 24:30 when he saw the **e** and bracelets upon his 5141
 24:47 put the **e** upon her face, and the bracelets 5141
Job 42:11 of money, and every one an **e** of gold. 5141
Pr 25:12 *As* an **e** of gold, and an ornament of fine 5141

EARRINGS (12) [EAR, RING]

Ge 35: 4 and *all their* **e** which *were* in their ears; 5141
Ex 32: 2 said unto them, Break off the golden **e**, 5141
 32: 3 all the people brake off the golden **e** 5141
 35:22 and **e**, and rings, and tablets, 5141
Nu 31:50 chains, and bracelets, rings, **e**, and tablets 5694
Jdg 8:24 you would give me every man the **e** of 5141
 8:24 (For they had golden **e**, because they 5141
 8:25 cast therein every man the **e** of his prey. 5141
 8:26 weight of the golden **e** that he requested 5141
Isa 3:20 the headbands, and the tablets, and the **e**, 3908
Eze 16:12 in thine ears, and a beautiful crown 5694
Hos 2:13 she decked herself with her **e** and 5141

EARS (151) [EAR]

Ge	20: 8 and told all these things in their **e**:	241
	35: 4 all *their* earrings which *were* in their **e**;	241
	41: 5 seven **e of corn** came up upon one stalk,	7641
	41: 6 seven thin **e** blasted with the east	7641
	41: 7 The seven thin **e** devoured the seven rank	7641
	41: 7 **e** devoured the seven rank and full **e**.	7641
	41:22 seven **e** came up in one stalk, full and	7641
	41:23 seven **e**, withered, thin, *and* blasted with	7641
	41:24 the thin **e** devoured the seven good ears:	7641
	41:24 thin ears devoured the seven good **e**:	7641
	41:26 the seven good **e** *are* seven years:	7641
	41:27 the seven empty **e** blasted with the east	7641
	44:18 speak a word in my lord's **e**, and let not	241
	50: 4 I pray you, in the **e** of Pharaoh, saying,	241
Ex	10: 2 that thou mayest tell in the **e** of thy son,	241
	11: 2 Speak now in the **e** of the people,	241
	17:14 a book, and rehearse *it* in the **e** of Joshua:	241
	32: 2 which *are* in the **e** of your wives, of your	241
	32: 3 the golden earrings which *were* in their **e**,	241
Lev	2:14 firstfruits **green e of corn** dried by the fire,	24
	2:14 the fire, *even* corn beaten out **of full e**.	3759
	23:14 nor parched *corn*, nor **green e**,	3759
Nu	11:18 for you have wept in the **e** of the Lord,	241
	14:28 as ye have spoken in mine **e**, so will I do	241
Dt	5: 1 which I speak in your **e** *this* day,	241
	23:25 thou mayest pluck the **e** with thine hand;	4425
	29: 4 eyes to see, and **e** to hear, unto this day.	241
	31:28 that I may speak these words in their **e**,	241
	31:30 spake in the **e** of all the congregation	241
	32:44 spake all the words of this song in the **e** of	241
Jos	20: 4 declare his cause in the **e** of the elders	241
Jdg	7: 3 go to, proclaim in the **e** of the people,	241
	9: 2 in the **e** of all the men of Shechem,	241
	9: 3 mother's brethren spake of him in the **e**	241
	9: 7 spakest of also in mine **e**, behold,	241
Ru	2: 2 glean **e of corn** after *him* in whose sight I	7641
1Sa	3:11 both the **e** of every one that heareth	241
	8:21 he rehearsed them in the **e** of the Lord.	241
	11: 4 and told the tidings in the **e** of the people:	241
	15:14 then this bleating of the sheep in mine **e**,	241
	18:23 Saul's servants spake those words in the **e**	241
2Sa	3:19 Abner also spake in the **e** of Benjamin:	241
	3:19 Abner went also to speak in the **e** of David	241
	7:22 to all that we have heard with our **e**.	241
	22: 7 temple, and my cry *did enter* into his **e**.	241
2Ki	4:42 and **full e of corn** in the husk thereof.	3759
	18:26 in the **e** of the people that *are* on the wall.	241
	19:28 and thy tumult is come up into mine **e**,	241
	21:12 heareth of it, both his **e** shall tingle.	241
	23: 2 he read it in their **e** all the words of the book	241
1Ch	17:20 to all that we have heard with our **e**.	241
2Ch	6:40 *let* thine **e** be attent unto the prayer *that is*	241
	7:15 mine **e** attent unto the prayer *that is* made	241
	34:30 he read in their **e** all the words of the book	241
Ne	8: 3 the **e** of all the people *were* attentive unto	241
Job	13:17 speech, and my declaration with your **e**.	241
	15:21 A dreadful sound *is* in his **e**: in prosperity	241
	24:24 and cut off as the tops of the **e of corn**.	7641

Job	28:22 have heard the fame thereof with our **e**.	241
	33:16 he openeth the **e** of men, and sealeth their	241
	36:15 and openeth their **e** in oppression.	241
Ps	18: 6 my cry came before him, even in his **e**.	241
	34:15 and his **e** *are* open unto their cry.	241
	40: 6 didst not desire; mine **e** hast thou opened:	241
	44: 1 We have heard with our **e**, O God,	241
	78: 1 incline your **e** to the words of my mouth.	241
	92:11 mine **e** shall hear my *desire* of the wicked	241
	115: 6 They have **e**, but they hear not: noses have	241
	130: 2 let thine **e** be attentive to the voice of my	241
	135:17 They have **e**, but they hear not; neither is	241
Pr	21:13 stoppeth his **e** at the cry of the poor,	241
	23: 9 Speak not in the **e** of a fool: for he will	241
	23:12 and thine **e** to the words of knowledge.	241
	26:17 him, *is like* one that taketh a dog by the **e**.	241
Isa	5: 9 In mine **e** *said* the Lord of hosts, Of a	241
	6:10 make their **e** heavy, and shut their eyes;	241
	6:10 hear with their **e**, and understand *with*	241
	11: 3 neither reprove after the hearing of his **e**:	241
	17: 5 the corn, and reapeth the **e** *with* his arm;	7641
	17: 5 it shall be as he that gathereth **e** in	7641
	22:14 it was revealed in mine **e** *by* the Lord of	241
	30:21 thine **e** shall hear a word behind thee,	241
	32: 3 and the **e** of them that hear shall hearken.	241
	33:15 that stoppeth his **e** from hearing of blood,	241
	35: 5 and the **e** of the deaf shall be unstopped.	241
	36:11 in the **e** of the people that *are* on the wall.	241
	37:29 is come up into mine **e**, therefore will I put	241
	42:20 opening the **e**, but he heareth not.	241
	43: 8 that have eyes, and the deaf that have **e**.	241
	49:20 lost the other, shall say again in thine **e**,	241
Jer	2: 2 Go and cry in the **e** of Jerusalem, saying,	241
	5:21 and see not; which have **e**, and hear not:	241
	19: 3 whosoever heareth, his **e** shall tingle.	241
	26:11 this city, as ye have heard with your **e**.	241
	26:15 you to speak all these words in your **e**.	241
	28: 7 now this word that I speak in thine **e**,	241
	28: 7 in thine ears, and in the **e** of all the people.	241
	29:29 the priest read this letter in the **e**	241
	36: 6 the words of the Lord in the **e** of	241
	36: 6 also thou shalt read them in the **e** of all	241
	36:10 Lord's house, in the **e** of all the people.	241
	36:13 when Baruch read the book in the **e** of	241
	36:14 thou hast read in the **e** of the people,	241
	36:15 him, Sit down now, and read it in our **e**.	241
	36:15 it in our ears. So Baruch read *it* in their **e**.	241
	36:20 and told all the words in the **e** of the king.	241
	36:21 Jehudi read it in the **e** of the king, and in	241
	36:21 in the **e** of all the princes which stood	241
Eze	3:10 in thine heart, and hear with thine **e**.	241
	8:18 they cry in mine **e** *with* a loud voice,	241
	9: 1 He cried also in mine **e** *with* a loud voice,	241
	12: 2 see not; they have **e** to hear, and hear not:	241
	16:12 earrings in thine **e**, and a beautiful crown,	241
	23:25 they shall take away thy nose and thine **e**;	241
	24:26 to cause *thee* to hear *it* with thine **e**?	241
	40: 4 hear with thine **e**, and set thine heart upon	241
	44: 5 hear with thine **e** all that I say unto thee	241
Mic	7:16 upon *their* mouth, their **e** shall be deaf.	241
Zec	7:11 stopped their **e**, that *they* should not hear.	241
Mt	11:15 He that hath **e** to hear, let him hear.	3775
	12: 1 and began to pluck the **e of corn**,	4719
	13: 9 Who hath **e** to hear, let him hear.	3775
	13:15 and *their* **e** are dull of hearing,	3775
	13:15 see with *their* eyes, and hear with *their* **e**,	3775
	13:16 for they see: and your **e**, for they hear.	3775
	13:43 Who hath **e** to hear, let him hear.	3775
	28:14 if this **come** to the governor's **e**,	191+1909
Mk	2:23 as they went, to pluck the **e of corn**.	4719
	4: 9 He that hath **e** to hear, let him hear.	3775
	4:23 If any *man* have **e** to hear, let him hear.	3775
	7:16 If any *man* have **e** to hear, let him hear.	3775
	7:33 and put his fingers into his **e**, and he spit,	3775
	7:35 And straightway his **e** were opened,	189
	8:18 and having **e**, hear ye not? and do ye not	3775
Lk	1:44 voice of thy salutation sounded in mine **e**,	3775
	4:21 day is this scripture fulfilled in your **e**.	3775
	6: 1 and his disciples plucked the **e of corn**,	4719
	8: 8 He that hath **e** to hear, let him hear.	3775
	9:44 Let these sayings sink down into your **e**:	3775
	14:35 He that hath **e** to hear, let him hear.	3775
Ac	7:51 and uncircumcised in heart and **e**,	3775
	7:57 stopped their **e**, and ran upon him with	3775
	11:22 **e** of the church which was in Jerusalem:	3775
	17:20 bringest certain strange *things* to our **e**:	189
	28:27 and *their* **e** are dull of hearing,	3775
	28:27 hear with *their* **e**, and understand with	3775
Ro	11: 8 not see, and **e** that *they* should not hear;)	3775
2Ti	4: 3 to themselves teachers, having itching **e**;	189
	4: 4 And they shall turn away *their* **e** from	189
Jas	5: 4 entered into the **e** of the Lord of sabaoth.	3775
1Pe	3:12 and his **e** *are* open unto their prayers:	3775

EARTH (987) [EARTHEN, EARTHLY, EARTHQUAKE, EARTHQUAKES, EARTHY]

Ge 1: 1 God created the heaven and the **e**. 776
 1: 2 the **e** was without form, and void; 776
 1:10 God called the dry *land* **E**; and the 776
 1:11 God said, Let the **e** bring forth grass, 776
 1:11 kind, whose seed *is* in itself, upon the **e**: 776
 1:12 the **e** brought forth grass, *and* herb 776
 1:15 of the heaven to give light upon the **e**: 776
 1:17 of the heaven to give light upon the **e**, 776
 1:20 fowl *that* may fly above the **e** in the open 776

E

E

Ge	1:22 in the seas, and let fowl multiply in the *e.* 776
	1:24 Let the *e.* bring forth the living creature 776
	1:24 and beast of the *e.* after his kind: 776
	1:25 God made the beast of the *e.* after his kind, 776
	1:25 every thing that creepeth upon the *e.* after 127
	1:26 over all the *e.*, and over every creeping 776
	1:26 creeping thing that creepeth upon the *e.* 776
	1:28 and replenish the *e.*, and subdue it: 776
	1:28 every living thing that moveth upon the *e.* 776
	1:29 which *is* upon the face of all the *e,* 776
	1:30 to every beast of the *e,* and to every fowl 776
	1:30 to every *thing* that creepeth upon the *e,* 776
	2: 1 Thus the heavens and the *e* were finished, 776
	2: 4 and of the *e* when they were created, 776
	2: 4 in the day that the Lord God made the *e* 776
	2: 5 plant of the field before it was in the *e,* 776
	2: 5 God had not caused it to rain upon the *e,* 776
	2: 6 there went up a mist from the *e,* 776
	4:11 now *art* thou cursed from the *e,* which 127
	4:12 and a vagabond shalt thou be in the *e.* 776
	4:14 me out *this* day from the face of the *e;* 127
	4:14 shall be a fugitive and a vagabond in the *e;* 776
	6: 1 men began to multiply on the face of the *e,* 127
	6: 4 There were giants in the *e* in those days; 776
	6: 5 the wickedness of man *was* great in the *e,* 776
	6: 6 the Lord that he had made man on the *e,* 776
	6: 7 I have created from the face of the *e;* 127
	6:11 The *e* also was corrupt before God, 776
	6:11 and the *e* was filled *with* violence. 776
	6:12 God looked upon the *e,* and behold, it was 776
	6:12 all flesh had corrupted his way upon the *e.* 776
	6:13 for the *e* is filled *with* violence through 776
	6:13 and behold, I will destroy them with the *e.* 776
	6:17 I, do bring a flood of waters upon the *e,* 776
	6:17 *and* every *thing* that *is* in the *e* shall die. 776
	6:20 of every creeping thing of the *e* after his 127
	7: 3 keep seed alive upon the face of all the *e.* 776
	7: 4 I will cause it to rain upon the *e* forty days 776
	7: 4 will I destroy from off the face of the *e.* 127
	7: 6 when the flood of waters was upon the *e.* 776
	7: 8 of every *thing* that creepeth upon the *e,* 127
	7:10 the waters of the flood were upon the *e.* 776
	7:12 the rain was upon the *e* forty days and 776
	7:14 creeping thing that creepeth upon the *e,* 776
	7:17 And the flood was forty days upon the *e;* 776
	7:17 up the ark, and it was lift up above the *e.* 776
	7:18 and were increased greatly upon the *e;* 776
	7:19 waters prevailed exceedingly upon the *e;* 776
	7:21 all flesh died that moved upon the *e,* 776
	7:21 creeping thing that creepeth upon the *e,* 776
	7:23 and they were destroyed from the *e:* 776
	7:24 waters prevailed upon the *e* an hundred 776
	8: 1 and God made a wind to pass over the *e,* 776
	8: 3 the waters returned from off the *e* 776
	8: 7 the waters were dried up from off the *e.* 776
	8: 9 waters *were* on the face of the whole *e:* 776
	8:11 that the waters were abated from off the *e.* 776
	8:13 the waters were dried up from off the *e:* 776
	8:14 day of the month, was the *e* dried. 776
	8:17 creeping thing that creepeth upon the *e;* 776
	8:17 that they may breed abundantly in the *e,* 776
	8:17 and be fruitful, and multiply upon the *e.* 776
	8:19 *and* whatsoever creepeth upon the *e,* 776
	8:22 While the *e* remaineth, seedtime and 776
	9: 1 fruitful, and multiply, and replenish the *e.* 776
	9: 2 of you shall be upon every beast of the *e,* 776
	9: 2 upon all that moveth *upon* the *e,* 127
	9: 7 bring forth abundantly in the *e,* 776
	9:10 and of every beast of the *e* with you; 776
	9:10 go out of the ark, to every beast of the *e.* 776
	9:11 there any more be a flood to destroy the *e.* 776
	9:13 token of a covenant between me and the *e.* 776
	9:14 to pass, when I bring a cloud over the *e,* 776
	9:16 creature of all flesh that *is* upon the *e.* 776
	9:17 me and all flesh that *is* upon the *e.* 776
	9:19 and of them was the whole *e* overspread. 776
	10: 8 he began to be a mighty *one* in the *e.* 776
	10:25 for in his days was the *e* divided; 776
	10:32 by these were the nations divided in the *e* 776
	11: 1 the whole *e* was *of* one language, and *of* 776
	11: 4 abroad upon the face of the whole *e.* 776
	11: 8 from thence upon the face of all the *e:* 776
	11: 9 there confound the language of all the *e:* 776
	11: 9 them abroad upon the face of all the *e.* 776
	12: 3 in thee shall all families of the *e* be blessed. 127
	13:16 I will make thy seed as the dust of the *e:* 776
	13:16 that if a man can number the dust of the *e,* 776
	14:19 most high God, possessor of heaven and *e,* 776
	14:22 high God, the possessor of heaven and *e,* 776
	18:18 all the nations of the *e* shall be blessed in 776
	18:25 Shall not the Judge of all the *e* do right? 776
	19:23 The sun was risen upon the *e* when Lot 776
	19:31 *is* not a man in the *e* to come in unto us 776
	19:31 in unto us after the manner of all the *e:* 776
	22:18 in thy seed shall all the nations of the *e* be 776
	24: 3 the God of heaven, and the God of the *e,* 776
	24:52 the Lord, *bowing himself* to the *e.* 776
	26: 4 in thy seed shall all the nations of the *e* be 776
	26:15 had stopped them, and filled them *with e.* 6083
	27:28 the fatness of the *e,* and plenty of corn and 776
	27:39 thy dwelling shall be the fatness of the *e,* 776
	28:12 a ladder set up on the *e,* and the top 776
	28:14 thy seed shall be as the dust of the *e,* 776
	28:14 in thy seed shall all the families of the *e* be 127
	37:10 to bow down ourselves to thee to the *e?* 776

Ge	41:47 in the seven plenteous years the *e* brought 776
	41:56 the famine was over all the face of the *e:* 776
	42: 6 before him *with* their faces to the *e.* 776
	43:26 and bowed themselves to him to the *e.* 776
	45: 7 to preserve you a posterity in the *e,* 776
	48:12 he bowed himself with his face to the *e.* 776
	48:16 grow into a multitude in the midst of the *e.* 776
Ex	8:17 smote the dust of the *e,* and it became lice 776
	8:22 that I *am* the Lord in the midst of the *e.* 776
	9:14 that *there is* none like me in all the *e.* 776
	9:15 and thou shalt be cut off from the *e.* 776
	9:16 may be declared throughout all the *e.* 776
	9:29 that thou mayest know how that the *e is* 776
	9:33 and the rain was not poured upon the *e.* 776
	10: 5 they shall cover the face of the *e,* that *one* 776
	10: 5 that *one* cannot be able to see the *e:* 776
	10: 6 the day that they were upon the *e* unto 127
	10:15 For they covered the face of the whole *e,* 776
	15:12 out thy right hand, the *e* swallowed them. 776
	19: 5 me above all people: for all the *e is* mine. 776
	20: 4 or that *is* in heaven above, or that *is* in 776
	20: 4 or that *is* in the water under the *e:* 776
	20:11 *in* six days the Lord made heaven and *e,* 776
	20:24 An altar of *e* thou shalt make unto me, 127
	31:17 in six days the Lord made heaven and *e,* 776
	32:12 to consume them from the face of the *e?* 127
	33:16 the people that *are* upon the face of the *e.* 127
	34: 8 bowed his head toward the *e,* 776
	34:10 such as have not been done in all the *e,* 776
Lev	11: 2 eat among all the beasts that *are* on the *e.* 776
	11:21 above their feet, to leap withal upon the *e;* 776
	11:29 the creeping things that creep upon the *e;* 776
	11:41 creeping thing that creepeth upon the *e,* 776
	11:42 all creeping things that creep upon the *e,* 776
	11:44 *of* creeping thing that creepeth upon the *e.* 776
	11:46 of every creature that moveth upon the *e.* 776
	15:12 the vessel of *e,* that he toucheth which 2789
	26:19 your heaven as iron, and your *e* as brass: 776
Nu	11:31 two cubits *high* upon the face of the *e.* 776
	12: 3 men which *were* upon the face of the *e.)* 127
	14:21 all the *e* shall be filled *with* the glory of 776
	16:30 the *e* open her mouth, and swallow them 127
	16:32 the *e* opened her mouth, 776
	16:33 into the pit, and the *e* closed upon them: 127
	16:34 they said, Lest the *e* swallow us up *also.* 776
	22: 5 they cover the face of the *e,* and they abide 776
	22:11 of Egypt, which covereth the face of the *e:* 776
	26:10 the *e* opened her mouth, 776
Dt	3:24 for what God *is there* in heaven or in *e,* 776
	4:10 all the days that they shall live upon the *e,* 127
	4:17 The likeness of any beast that *is* on the *e,* 776
	4:18 fish that *is* in the waters beneath the *e:* 776
	4:26 and *e* to witness against you *this* day, 776
	4:32 the day that God created man upon the *e,* 776
	4:36 and upon *e* he shewed thee his great fire; 776
	4:39 in heaven above, and upon the *e* beneath: 776
	4:40 thou mayest prolong *thy* days upon the *e,* 127
	5: 8 or that *is* in the *e* beneath, or that *is* in 776
	5: 8 or that *is* in the waters beneath the *e:* 776
	6:15 and destroy thee from off the face of the *e.* 127
	7: 6 all people that *are* upon the face of the *e.* 127
	10:14 God, the *e* also, with all that therein *is.* 776
	11: 6 how the *e* opened her mouth, 776
	11:21 them, as the days of heaven upon the *e.* 776
	12: 1 all the days that ye live upon the *e.* 127
	12:16 ye shall pour it upon the *e* as water. 776
	12:19 Levite as long as thou livest upon the *e.* 127
	12:24 thou shalt pour it upon the *e* as water. 776
	13: 7 from the *one* end of the *e* even unto the 776
	13: 7 the earth even unto the *other* end of the *e;* 776
	14: 2 above all the nations that *are* upon the *e.* 127
	26: 2 take of the first of all the fruit of the *e,* 127
	28: 1 set thee on high above all nations of the *e:* 776
	28:10 all people of the *e* shall see that thou art 776
	28:23 and the *e* that *is* under thee *shall be* iron. 776
	28:25 be removed into all the kingdoms of the *e.* 776
	28:26 unto the beasts of the *e,* and no man shall 776
	28:49 from the end of the *e, as swift* as the eagle 776
	28:64 from the *one* end of the *e* even unto 776
	30:19 and *e* to record *this* day against you, 776
	31:28 call heaven and *e* to record against them. 776
	32: 1 and hear, O *e,* the words of my mouth. 776
	32:13 made him ride on the high places of the *e,* 776
	32:22 shall consume the *e* with her increase, 776
	33:16 for the precious things of the *e* and 776
	33:17 the people together *to* the ends of the *e:* 776
Jos	2:11 God in heaven above, and in *e* beneath. 776
	3:11 the Lord of all the *e* passeth over before 776
	3:13 the Lord of all the *e,* shall rest in the waters 776
	4:24 That all the people of the *e* might know 776
	5:14 Joshua fell on his face to the *e,* 776
	7: 6 fell to the *e* upon his face before the ark of 776
	7: 9 round, and cut off our name from the *e:* 776
	7:21 *are* hid in the *e* in the midst of my tent, 776
Jdg	3:25 their lord *was* fallen down dead on the *e.* 776
	5: 4 the *e* trembled, and the heavens dropped, 776
	6: 4 destroyed the increase of the *e,* till thou 776
	6:37 *it be* dry upon all the *e beside,* then shall I 776
	18:10 is no want of any thing that *is* in the *e.* 776
1Sa	2: 8 for the pillars of the *e are* the Lord's, 776
	2:10 the Lord shall judge the ends of the *e:* 776
	4: 5 a great shout, so that the *e* rang again. 776
	4:12 his clothes rent, and *with e* upon his head. 127
	5: 3 Dagon *was* fallen upon his face to the *e* 776

1Sa	14:15 they also trembled, and the *e* quaked: 776
	17:46 of the air, and to the wild beasts of the *e;* 776
	17:46 that all the *e* may know that there is a God 776
	17:49 and he fell upon his face to the *e.* 776
	20:15 cut off David every one from the face of the *e.* 127
	24: 8 David stooped *with his* face to the *e,* 776
	25:41 herself *on her* face to the *e,* and said, 776
	26: 8 with the spear even to the *e* at once, 776
	26:20 not my blood fall to the *e* before the face 776
	28:13 Saul, I saw gods ascending out of the *e.* 776
	28:20 Saul fell straightway all along on the *e,* 776
	28:23 he arose from the *e,* and sat upon the bed. 776
	30:16 *they were* spread abroad upon all the *e,* 776
2Sa	1: 2 with his clothes rent, and *e* upon his head: 127
	1: 2 that he fell to the *e,* and did obeisance. 776
	4:11 your hand, and take you away from the *e?* 776
	7: 9 name of the great *men* that *are* in the *e.* 776
	7:23 what one nation in the *e is* like thy people, 776
	12:16 and went in, and lay all night upon the *e.* 776
	12:17 *went* to him, to raise him up from the *e:* 776
	12:20 David arose from the *e,* and washed, 776
	13:31 and tare his garments, and lay on the *e:* 776
	14: 7 *neither* name nor remainder upon the *e.* 127
	14:11 shall not one hair of thy son fall to the *e.* 776
	14:20 God, to know all *things* that *are* in the *e.* 776
	15:32 with his coat rent, and *e* upon his head: 127
	18: 9 taken up between the heaven and the *e;* 776
	18:28 he fell down to the *e* upon his face before 776
	22: 8 the *e* shook and trembled; the foundations 776
	22:43 I beat them *as* small as the dust of the *e,* 776
	23: 4 the tender grass *springing* out of the *e* by 776
1Ki	1:31 Bath-sheba bowed *with her* face to the *e,* 776
	1:40 so that the *e* rent with the sound of them. 776
	1:52 there shall not a hair of him fall to the *e:* 776
	2: 2 I go the way of all the *e:* be thou strong 776
	4:34 from all kings of the *e,* which had heard of 776
	8:23 in heaven above, or on *e* beneath, 776
	8:27 But will God indeed dwell on the *e?* 776
	8:43 all people of the *e* may know thy name, 776
	8:53 them from among all the people of the *e,* 776
	8:60 That all the people of the *e* may know that 776
	10:23 exceeded all the kings of the *e* for riches 776
	10:24 all the *e* sought to Solomon, to hear his 776
	13:34 and to destroy *it* from off the face of the *e.* 127
	17:14 day that the Lord sendeth rain upon the *e.* 127
	18: 1 unto Ahab; and I will send rain upon the *e.* 127
	18:42 cast himself down upon the *e,* and put his 776
2Ki	5:15 I know that *there is* no God in all the *e,* 776
	5:17 to thy servant two mules' burden of *e?* 127
	10:10 Know now that there shall fall unto the *e* 776
	19:15 thou alone, of all the kingdoms of the *e;* 776
	19:15 of the earth; thou hast made heaven and *e.* 776
	19:19 that all the kingdoms of the *e* may know 776
1Ch	1:10 he began to be mighty upon the *e.* 776
	1:19 because in his days the *e* was divided; 776
	16:14 our God; his judgments *are* in all the *e.* 776
	16:23 Sing unto the Lord, all the *e;* shew forth 776
	16:30 Fear before him, all the *e:* the world also 776
	16:31 the heavens be glad, and let the *e* rejoice: 776
	16:33 because he cometh to judge the *e.* 776
	17: 8 name of the great *men* that *are* in the *e.* 776
	17:21 what one nation in the *e is* like thy people 776
	21:16 the angel of the Lord stand between the *e* 776
	22: 8 thou hast shed much blood upon the *e* in 776
	29:11 and in the *e is* thine; thine *is* the kingdom, 776
	29:15 our days on the *e are* as a shadow, 776
2Ch	1: 9 people like the dust of the *e* in multitude. 776
	2:12 God of Israel, that made heaven and *e,* 776
	6:14 God like thee in the heaven, nor in the *e;* 776
	6:18 in very deed dwell with men on the *e?* 776
	6:33 all people of the *e* may know thy name, 776
	9:22 Solomon passed all the kings of the *e* in 776
	9:23 all the kings of the *e* sought the presence 776
	16: 9 run to and fro throughout the whole *e,* 776
	20:24 they *were* dead bodies fallen to the *e,* 776
	32:19 as against the gods of the people of the *e,* 776
	36:23 All the kingdoms of the *e* hath the Lord 776
Ezr	1: 2 hath given me all the kingdoms of the *e;* 776
	5:11 the servants of the God of heaven and *e,* 772
Ne	9: 1 and with sackclothes, and *e* upon them. 127
	9: 6 the *e,* and all *things* that *are* therein, 776
Job	1: 7 From going to and fro in the *e,* 776
	1: 8 *there is* none like him in the *e,* a perfect 776
	2: 2 From going to and fro in the *e,* 776
	2: 3 *there is* none like him in the *e,* a perfect 776
	3:14 With kings and counsellors of the *e,* 776
	5:10 Who giveth rain upon the *e,* 776
	5:22 shalt thou be afraid of the beasts of the *e.* 776
	5:25 and thine offspring as the grass of the *e.* 776
	7: 1 not an appointed time to man upon *e?* 776
	8: 9 because our days upon *e are* a shadow:) 776
	8:19 way, and out of the *e* shall others grow. 6083
	9: 6 Which shaketh the *e* out of her place, 776
	9:24 The *e* is given into the hand of the wicked: 776
	11: 9 The measure thereof *is* longer than the *e,* 776
	12: 8 Or speak to the *e,* and it shall teach thee: 776
	12:15 sendeth them out, and they overturn the *e.* 776
	12:24 heart of the chief of the people of the *e,* 776
	14: 8 Though the root thereof wax old in the *e,* 776
	14:19 things which grow out of the dust of the *e;* 776
	15:19 Unto whom alone the *e* was given, 776
	15:29 prolong the perfection thereof upon the *e.* 776
	16:18 O *e,* cover not thou my blood, and let my 776
	18: 4 shall the *e* be forsaken for thee? and shall 776
	18:17 His remembrance shall perish from the *e,* 776

Job	19:25 he shall stand *at* the latter *day* upon the **e**:	6083
	20: 4 this of old, since man was placed upon **e**,	776
	20:27 and the **e** shall rise up against him.	
	22: 8 But *as for* the mighty man, he had the **e**;	
	24: 4 the poor of the **e** hide themselves together.	
	24:18 the waters; their portion is cursed in the **e**:	
	26: 7 *and* hangeth the **e** upon nothing.	
	28: 2 Iron is taken out of the **e**, and brass *is*	6083
	28: 5 *As for* the **e**, out of it cometh bread:	776
	28:24 For he looketh to the ends of the **e**,	
	30: 6 *in* caves of the **e**, and *in* the rocks.	6083
	30: 8 of base men: they were viler than the **e**.	
	34:13 Who hath given him a charge over the **e**?	
	35:11 teacheth us more than the beasts of the **e**,	
	37: 3 and his lightning unto the ends of the **e**.	
	37: 6 For he saith to the snow, Be thou *on* the **e**;	
	37:12 them upon the face of the world in the **e**.	
	37:17 when he quieteth the **e** by the south *wind*?	
	38: 4 thou when I laid the foundations of the **e**?	776
	38:13 That *it* might take hold of the ends of the **e**,	776
	38:18 Hast thou perceived the breadth of the **e**?	776
	38:24 *which* scattereth the east wind upon the **e**?	776
	38:26 cause it to rain on the **e**, *where* no man *is;*	776
	38:33 thou set the dominion thereof in the **e**?	776
	39:14 Which leaveth her eggs in the **e**,	776
	41:33 Upon **e** there is not his like, who is made	6083
Ps	2: 2 The kings of the **e** set themselves,	776
	2: 8 the uttermost parts of the **e** *for* thy	776
	2:10 ye kings: be instructed, ye judges of the **e**.	776
	7: 5 let him tread down my life upon the **e**,	776
	8: 1 how excellent *is* thy name in all the **e**!	776
	8: 9 how excellent *is* thy name in all the **e**!	776
	10:18 the man of the **e** may no more oppress.	776
	12: 6 *as* silver tried in a furnace of **e**,	776
	16: 3 *But* to the saints that *are* in the **e**, and *to*	776
	17:11 have set their eyes bowing down to the **e**;	776
	18: 7 the **e** shook and trembled; the foundations	776
	19: 4 Their line is gone out through all the **e**,	776
	21:10 Their fruit shalt thou destroy from the **e**,	776
	22:29 All *they that be* fat upon **e** shall eat and	776
	24: 1 The **e** *is* the LORD'S, and the fulness	776
	25:13 at ease; and his seed shall inherit the **e**.	776
	33: 5 the **e** is full *of* the goodness of the LORD.	776
	33: 8 Let all the **e** fear the LORD: let all	776
	33:14 looketh upon all the inhabitants of the **e**.	776
	34:16 off the remembrance of them from the **e**.	776
	37: 9 upon the LORD, they shall inherit the **e**.	776
	37:11 meek shall inherit the **e**; and shall delight	776
	37:22 as be blessed of him shall inherit the **e**;	776
	41: 2 *and* he shall be blessed upon the **e**:	776
	44:25 to the dust: our belly cleaveth unto the **e**.	776
	45:16 thou mayest make princes in all the **e**.	776
	46: 2 though the **e** be removed, and though	776
	46: 6 he uttered his voice, the **e** melted.	776
	46: 8 what desolations he hath made in the **e**.	776
	46: 9 wars to cease unto the end of the **e**;	776
	46:10 the heathen, I will be exalted in the **e**.	776
	47: 2 is terrible; *he is* a great King over all the **e**.	776
	47: 7 For God *is* the King of all the **e**: sing ye	776
	47: 9 for the shields of the **e** *belong* unto God:	776
	48: 2 the joy of the whole **e**, *is* mount Zion,	776
	48:10 so *is* thy praise unto the ends of the **e**:	776
	50: 1 called the **e** from the rising of the sun unto	776
	50: 4 and to the **e**, that *he* may judge his people.	776
	57: 5 heavens; *let* thy glory *be* above all the **e**.	776
	57:11 heavens; *let* thy glory *be* above all the **e**.	776
	58: 2 weigh the violence of your hands in the **e**.	776
	58:11 verily he is a God that judgeth in the **e**.	776
	59:13 God ruleth in Jacob unto the ends of the **e**.	776
	60: 2 Thou hast made the **e** to tremble;	776
	61: 2 From the end of the **e** will I cry unto thee,	776
	63: 9 *it*, shall go into the lower parts of the **e**.	776
	65: 5 *art* the confidence of all the ends of the **e**,	776
	65: 9 Thou visitest the **e**, and waterest it:	776
	66: 4 All the **e** shall worship thee, and shall sing	776
	67: 2 That thy way may be known upon **e**,	776
	67: 4 and govern the nations upon **e**.	776
	67: 6 shall the **e** yield her increase; *and* God,	776
	67: 7 and all the ends of the **e** shall fear him.	776
	68: 8 The **e** shook, the heavens also dropped at	776
	68:32 Sing unto God, ye kingdoms of the **e**;	776
	69:34 Let the heaven and **e** praise him, the seas,	776
	71:20 me up again from the depths of the **e**.	776
	72: 6 mown grass: as showers that water the **e**.	776
	72: 8 and from the river unto the ends of the **e**.	776
	72:16 There shall be a handful of corn in the **e**	776
	72:16 of the city shall flourish like grass of the **e**.	776
	72:19 let the whole **e** be filled *with* his glory;	776
	73: 9 and their tongue walketh through the **e**.	776
	73:25 *is* none upon **e** *that* I desire beside thee.	776
	74:12 working salvation in the midst of the **e**.	776
	74:17 Thou hast set all the borders of the **e**:	776
	74:20 for the dark places of the **e** are full *of*	776
	75: 3 The **e** and all the inhabitants thereof *are*	776
	75: 8 the wicked of the **e** shall wring *them* out,	776
	76: 8 from heaven; the **e** feared, and was still,	776
	76: 9 to judgment, to save all the meek of the **e**.	776
	76:12 princes: *he is* terrible to the kings of the **e**.	776
	77:18 the world: the **e** trembled and shook.	776
	78:69 the **e** which he hath established for ever.	776
	79: 2 flesh of thy saints unto the beasts of the **e**.	776
	82: 5 the foundations of the **e** are out of course.	776
	82: 8 Arise, O God, judge the **e**: for thou shalt	776
	83:10 at En-dor: they became *as* dung for the **e**.	127
	83:18 *art* the most High over all the **e**.	776

Ps	85:11 Truth shall spring out of the **e**;	776
	89:11 The heavens *are* thine, the **e** also *is* thine:	776
	89:27 firstborn, higher than the kings of the **e**.	776
	90: 2 or ever thou hadst formed the **e** and	776
	94: 2 Lift up thyself, thou judge of the **e**: render	776
	95: 4 In his hand *are* the deep places of the **e**.	776
	96: 1 a new song: sing unto the LORD, all the **e**.	776
	96: 9 of holiness: fear before him, all the **e**.	776
	96:11 the heavens rejoice, and let the **e** be glad;	776
	96:13 he cometh, for he cometh to judge the **e**:	776
	97: 1 The LORD reigneth; let the **e** rejoice;	776
	97: 4 the world: the **e** saw, and trembled.	776
	97: 5 at the presence of the Lord of the whole **e**.	776
	97: 9 For thou, LORD, *art* High above all the **e**:	776
	98: 3 the ends of the **e** have seen the salvation	776
	98: 4 a joyful noise unto the LORD, all the **e**:	776
	98: 9 the LORD; for he cometh to judge the **e**:	776
	99: 1 the cherubims; let the **e** be moved.	776
	102:15 and all the kings of the **e** thy glory.	776
	102:19 from heaven did the LORD behold the **e**;	776
	102:25 old hast thou laid the foundation of the **e**:	776
	103:11 For as the heaven is high above the **e**,	776
	104: 5 *Who* laid the foundations of the **e**, *that* it	776
	104: 9 *that* they turn not again to cover the **e**.	776
	104:13 the **e** is satisfied with the fruit of thy works.	776
	104:14 that *he* may bring forth food out of the **e**;	776
	104:24 made them all: the **e** is full *of* thy riches.	776
	104:30 and thou renewest the face of the **e**.	127
	104:32 He looketh on the **e**, and it trembleth:	776
	104:35 Let the sinners be consumed out of the **e**,	776
	105: 7 our God: his judgments *are* in all the **e**.	776
	106:17 The **e** opened and swallowed up Dathan,	776
	108: 5 the heavens: and thy glory above all the **e**;	776
	109:15 cut off the memory of them from the **e**.	776
	112: 2 His seed shall be mighty upon **e**:	776
	113: 6 *things that are* in heaven, and in the **e**?	776
	114: 7 thou **e**, at the presence of the Lord,	776
	115:15 of the LORD which made heaven and **e**.	776
	115:16 the **e** hath he given to the children of men.	776
	119:19 I *am* a stranger in the **e**: hide not thy	776
	119:64 The **e**, O LORD, is full *of* thy mercy:	776
	119:87 They had almost consumed me upon **e**;	776
	119:90 thou hast established the **e**, and it abideth.	776
	119:119 Thou puttest away all the wicked of the **e**	776
	121: 2 from the LORD, which made heaven and **e**.	776
	124: 8 of the LORD, who made heaven and **e**.	776
	134: 3 made heaven and **e** bless thee out of Zion.	776
	135: 6 and in **e**, in the seas, and all deep places.	776
	135: 7 vapours to ascend from the ends of the **e**;	776
	136: 6 To him that stretched out the **e** above	776
	138: 4 All the kings of the **e** shall praise thee,	776
	139:15 wrought in the lowest parts of the **e**.	776
	140:11 not an evil speaker be established in the **e**:	776
	141: 7 one cutteth and cleaveth *wood* upon the **e**.	776
	146: 4 breath goeth forth, he returneth to his **e**;	127
	146: 6 and **e**, the sea, and all that therein is:	776
	147: 8 with clouds, who prepareth rain for the **e**,	776
	147:15 sendeth forth his commandment *upon* **e**:	776
	148: 7 Praise the LORD from the **e**, ye dragons,	776
	148:11 Kings of the **e**, and all people; princes,	776
	148:11 all people; princes, and all judges of the **e**:	776
	148:13 his glory *is* above the **e** and heaven.	776
Pr	2:22 the wicked shall be cut off from the **e**,	776
	3:19 The LORD by wisdom hath founded the **e**;	776
	8:16 and nobles, *even* all the judges of the **e**.	776
	8:23 from the beginning, or ever the **e** was.	776
	8:26 While as yet he had not made the **e**,	776
	8:29 he appointed the foundations of the **e**:	776
	8:31 Rejoicing in the habitable part of his **e**;	776
	8:31 but the wicked shall not inhabit the **e**.	776
	11:31 righteous shall be recompensed in the **e**:	776
	17:24 the eyes of a fool *are* in the ends of the **e**.	776
	25: 3 the **e** for depth, and the heart of kings *is*	776
	30: 4 who hath established all the ends of the **e**?	776
	30:14 to devour the poor from off the **e**,	776
	30:16 the **e** *that* is not filled *with* water;	776
	30:21 For three *things* the **e** is disquieted,	776
	30:24 be four *things which are* little upon the **e**,	776
	31: 2 but the **e** abideth for ever.	
Ecc	1: 4 but the **e** abideth for ever.	776
	3:21 of the beast that goeth downward to the **e**?	776
	5: 2 for God *is* in heaven, and thou upon **e**:	776
	5: 9 Moreover the profit of the **e** *is* for all:	776
	7:20 *there is* not a just man upon **e**, that doeth	776
	8:14 There is a vanity which is done upon the **e**;	776
	8:16 to see the business that is done upon the **e**:	776
	10: 7 and princes walking as servants upon the **e**.	776
	11: 2 knowest not what evil shall be upon the **e**.	776
	11: 3 *of* rain, they empty *themselves* upon the **e**:	776
	12: 7 shall the dust return to the **e** as it was:	776
SS	2:12 The flowers appear on the **e**; the time of	776
Isa	1: 2 Hear, O heavens, and give ear, O **e**:	776
	2:19 into the caves of the **e**, for fear of	6083
	2:19 when he ariseth to shake terribly the **e**.	776
	2:21 when he ariseth to shake terribly the **e**.	776
	4: 2 the fruit of the **e** *shall be* excellent and	776
	5: 8 may be placed alone in the midst of the **e**!	776
	5:26 will hiss unto them from the end of the **e**:	776
	6: 3 of hosts: the whole **e** *is* full of his glory.	776
	8:22 they shall look unto the **e**;	776
	10:14 eggs *that are* left, have I gathered all the **e**;	776
	11: 4 reprove with equity for the meek of the **e**:	776
	11: 4 he shall smite the **e** with the rod of his	776
	11: 9 for the **e** shall be full *of* the knowledge of	776
	11:12 of Judah from the four corners of the **e**.	776
	12: 5 excellent things: this *is* known in all the **e**.	776

Isa	13:13 and the **e** shall remove out of her place,	776
	14: 7 The whole **e** is at rest, *and* is quiet:	776
	14: 9 for thee, *even* all the chief ones of the **e**;	776
	14:16 *saying, Is* this the man that made the **e** to	776
	14:26 purpose that is purposed upon the whole **e**:	776
	18: 3 of the world, and dwellers on the **e**, see ye,	776
	18: 6 the mountains, and to the beasts of the **e**:	776
	18: 6 all the beasts of the **e** shall winter upon	776
	23: 8 traffickers *are* the honourable of the **e**?	776
	23: 9 into contempt all the honourable of the **e**.	776
	23:17 of the world upon the face of the **e**.	127
	24: 1 the LORD maketh the **e** empty,	776
	24: 4 The **e** mourneth *and* fadeth away,	776
	24: 4 the haughty people of the **e** do languish.	776
	24: 5 The **e** also is defiled under the inhabitants	776
	24: 6 Therefore hath the curse devoured the **e**,	776
	24: 6 the inhabitants of the **e** are burned,	776
	24:16 From the uttermost part of the **e** have we	776
	24:17 *are* upon thee, O inhabitant of the **e**.	776
	24:18 and the foundations of the **e** do shake.	776
	24:19 The **e** is utterly broken down, the earth is	776
	24:19 the **e** is clean dissolved, the earth is moved	776
	24:19 dissolved, the **e** is moved exceedingly.	776
	24:20 The **e** shall reel to and fro like a drunkard,	776
	24:21 and the kings of the **e** upon the earth.	127
	24:21 and the kings of the earth upon the **e**.	127
	25: 8 shall he take away from off all the **e**:	776
	26: 9 for when thy judgments *are* in the **e**,	776
	26:15 removed *it* far *unto* all the ends of the **e**.	776
	26:18 not wrought any deliverance in the **e**;	776
	26:19 of herbs, and the **e** shall cast out the dead.	776
	26:21 the inhabitants of the **e** for their iniquity:	776
	26:21 the **e** also shall disclose her blood,	776
	28: 2 shall cast down to the **e** with the hand.	776
	28:22 even determined upon the whole **e**.	776
	30:23 bread of the increase of the **e**, and it shall	127
	33: 9 The **e** mourneth and languisheth: Lebanon	776
	34: 1 let the **e** hear, and all that is therein;	776
	37:16 thou alone, of all the kingdoms of the **e**:	776
	37:16 of the earth: thou hast made heaven and **e**.	776
	37:20 all the kingdoms of the **e** may know that	776
	40:12 the dust of the **e** in a measure,	776
	40:21 understood *from* the foundations of the **e**?	776
	40:22 *It is* he that sitteth upon the circle of the **e**,	776
	40:23 he maketh the judges of the **e** as vanity.	776
	40:28 Creator of the ends of the **e**, fainteth not,	776
	41: 5 The ends of the **e** were afraid, drew near,	776
	41: 9 whom I have taken from the ends of the **e**,	776
	42: 4 till he have set judgment in the **e**:	776
	42: 5 he that spread forth the **e**, and that which	776
	42:10 his praise from the end of the **e**, ye that	776
	43: 6 and my daughters from the ends of the **e**;	776
	44:23 done *it:* shout, ye lower parts of the **e**:	776
	44:24 that spreadeth abroad the **e** by myself;	776
	45: 8 let the **e** open, and let them bring forth	776
	45: 9 potsherd *strive* with the potsherds of the **e**.	127
	45:12 have made the **e**, and created man upon it:	776
	45:18 God himself that formed the **e** and made it;	776
	45:19 spoken in secret, in a dark place of the **e**:	776
	45:22 and be ye saved, all the ends of the **e**:	776
	48:13 also hath laid the foundation of the **e**,	776
	48:20 tell this, utter it *even* to the end of the **e**;	776
	49: 6 be my salvation unto the end of the **e**.	776
	49: 8 covenant of the people, to establish the **e**,	776
	49:13 joyful, O **e**; and break forth *into* singing,	776
	49:23 down to thee *with their* face toward the **e**,	776
	51: 6 the heavens, and look upon the **e** beneath:	776
	51: 6 the **e** shall wax old like a garment,	776
	51:13 and laid the foundations of the **e**;	776
	51:16 lay the foundations of the **e**, and say unto	776
	52:10 all the ends of the **e** shall see the salvation	776
	54: 5 The God of the whole **e** shall he be called.	776
	54: 9 of Noah should no more go over the **e**;	776
	55: 9 For *as* the heavens are higher than the **e**,	776
	55:10 watereth the **e**, and maketh it bring forth	776
	58:14 thee to ride upon the high places of the **e**,	776
	60: 2 the darkness shall cover the **e**,	776
	61:11 For as the **e** bringeth forth her bud,	776
	62: 7 till he make Jerusalem a praise in the **e**.	776
	63: 6 I will bring down their strength to the **e**.	776
	65:16 That he who blesseth himself in the **e** shall	776
	65:16 he that sweareth in the **e** shall swear by	776
	65:17 behold, I create new heavens and a new **e**:	776
	66: 1 *is* my throne, and the **e** *is* my footstool:	776
	66: 8 the **e** be made to bring forth in one day?	776
	66:22 For as the new heavens and the new **e**,	776
Jer	4:23 I beheld the **e**, and, lo, *it was* without form,	776
	4:28 this shall the **e** mourn, and the heavens	776
	6:19 Hear, O **e**: behold, I will bring evil upon	776
	6:22 shall be raised from the sides of the **e**.	776
	7:33 of the heaven, and for the beasts of the **e**;	776
	8: 2 shall be for dung upon the face of the **e**.	127
	9: 3 are not valiant for the truth upon the **e**;	776
	9:24 judgment, and righteousness, in the **e**:	776
	10:10 at his wrath the **e** shall tremble,	776
	10:11 that have not made the heavens and the **e**,	778
	10:11 *even* they shall perish from the **e**,	772
	10:12 He hath made the **e** by his power, he hath	776
	10:13 vapours to ascend from the ends of the **e**;	776
	14: 4 there was no rain in the **e**, the plowmen	776
	15: 3 the beasts of the **e**, to devour and destroy.	776
	15: 4 to be removed into all kingdoms of the **e**,	776
	15:10 and a man of contention to the whole **e**!	776
	16: 4 shall be as dung upon the face of the **e**:	127

E

Jer 16: 4 of heaven, and for the beasts of the e. 776
16:19 come unto thee from the ends of the e, 776
17:13 depart from me shall be written in the e, 776
19: 7 of the heaven, and for the beasts of the e, 776
22:29 O e, earth, earth, hear the word of 776
22:29 O earth, e, earth, hear the word of 776
22:29 O earth, earth, e, hear the word of 776
23: 5 execute judgment and justice in the e. 776
23:24 Do not I fill heaven and e? saith the LORD. 776
24: 9 into all the kingdoms of the e for their hurt, 776
25:26 world, which are upon the face of the e, 127
25:29 a sword upon all the inhabitants of the e, 776
25:30 grapes, against all the inhabitants of the e. 776
25:31 noise shall come even to the ends of the e; 776
25:32 shall be raised up from the coasts of the e. 776
25:33 the e even unto the other end of the earth: 776
25:33 the earth even unto the other end of the e. 776
26: 6 this city a curse to all the nations of the e. 776
27: 5 I have made the e, the man and the beast 776
28:16 I will cast thee from off the face of the e. 127
29:18 to be removed to all the kingdoms of the e, 776
31: 8 and gather them from the coasts of the e, 776
31:22 LORD hath created a new thing in the e, 776
31:37 the foundations of the e searched out 776
32:17 the e by thy great power and stretched out 776
33: 9 an honour before all the nations of the e, 776
33:25 appointed the ordinances of heaven and e; 776
34: 1 all the kingdoms of the e of his dominion. 776
34:17 be removed into all the kingdoms of the e. 776
34:20 of the heaven, and to the beasts of the e. 776
44: 8 a reproach among all the nations of the e? 776
46: 8 he saith, I will go up, and will cover the e; 776
49:21 The e is moved at the noise of their fall, 776
50:23 How is the hammer of the whole e cut 776
50:41 shall be raised up from the coasts of the e. 776
50:46 At the noise of the taking of Babylon the e 776
51: 7 LORD's hand, that made all the e drunken: 776
51:15 He hath made the e by his power, hath 776
51:16 vapours to ascend from the ends of the e: 776
51:25 saith the LORD, which destroyest all the e: 776
51:41 how is the praise of the whole e surprised! 776
51:48 heaven and the e, and all that is therein, 776
51:49 so at Babylon shall fall the slain of all the e. 776
La 2: 1 down from heaven unto the e the beauty 776
2:11 are troubled, my liver is poured upon the e, 776
2:15 of beauty, The joy of the whole e? 776
3:34 under his feet all the prisoners of the e, 776
4:12 The kings of the e, and all the inhabitants 776
Eze 1:15 behold one wheel upon the e by the living 776
1:19 the living creatures were lift up from the e, 776
1:21 when those were lifted up from the e, 776
7:21 prey, and to the wicked of the e for a spoil; 776
8: 3 the spirit lift me up between the e and 776
8:12 seeth us not; the LORD hath forsaken the e. 776
9: 9 The LORD hath forsaken the e, 776
10:16 lift up their wings to mount up from the e, 776
10:19 and mounted up from the e in my sight: 776
26:20 shall set thee in the low parts of the e, 776
27:33 thou didst enrich the kings of the e with 776
28:18 I will bring thee to ashes upon the e in 776
31:12 all the people of the e are gone down from 776
31:14 to the nether parts of the e, in the midst of 776
31:16 be comforted in the nether parts of the e, 776
31:18 of Eden unto the nether parts of the e. 776
32: 4 will fill the beasts of the whole e with thee. 776
32:18 unto the nether parts of the e, with them 776
32:24 into the nether parts of the e, 776
34: 6 was scattered upon all the face of the e, 776
34:27 the e shall yield her increase, and they 776
35:14 When the whole e rejoiceth, I will make 776
38:20 all creeping things that creep upon the e, 127
38:20 the men that are upon the face of the e, 127
39:14 those that remain upon the face of the e, 776
39:18 drink the blood of the princes of the e, 776
43: 2 and the e shined with his glory. 776
Da 2:10 is not a man upon the e that can shew 3007
2:35 a great mountain, and filled the whole e. 772
2:39 brass, which shall bear rule over all the e. 772
4: 1 languages, that dwell in all the e; 772
4:10 a tree in the midst of the e, and the height 772
4:11 the sight thereof to the end of all the e: 772
4:15 leave the stump of his roots in the e, 772
4:15 be with the beasts in the grass of the e: 772
4:20 heaven, and the sight thereof to all the e; 772
4:22 and thy dominion to the end of the e. 772
4:23 the stump of the roots thereof in the e, 772
4:35 all the inhabitants of the e are reputed as 772
4:35 and among the inhabitants of the e: 772
6:25 languages, that dwell in all the e; 772
6:27 and wonders in heaven and in e, 772
7: 4 it was lifted up from the e, and made stand 772
7:17 four kings, which shall arise out of the e. 772
7:23 beast shall be the fourth kingdom upon e, 772
7:23 shall devour the whole e, and shall tread it 772
8: 5 from the west on the face of the whole e, 776
12: 2 of them that sleep in the dust of the e 6083
Hos 2:18 and the sword and the battle out of the e, 776
2:21 the heavens, and they shall hear the e; 776
2:22 the e shall hear the corn, and the wine, 776
2:23 I will sow her unto me in the e; and I will 776
6: 3 as the latter and former rain unto the e. 776
Joel 2:10 The e shall quake before them; the heavens 776
2:30 shew wonders in the heavens and in the e, 776
3:16 and the heavens and the e shall shake: 776
Am 2: 7 That pant after the dust of the e on the 776

Am 3: 2 have I known of all the families of the e: 127
3: 5 Can a bird fall in a snare upon the e, 776
3: 5 shall one take up a snare from the e, 127
4:13 treadeth upon the high places of the e, 776
5: 7 and leave off righteousness in the e, 776
5: 8 poureth them out upon the face of the e: 776
8: 9 and I will darken the e in the clear day: 776
9: 6 and hath founded his troop in the e, 776
9: 6 poureth them out upon the face of the e: 776
9: 8 I will destroy it from off the face of the e; 127
9: 9 yet shall not the least grain fall upon the e. 776
Jnh 2: 6 the e with her bars was about me for ever: 776
Mic 1: 2 hearken, O e, and all that therein is: 776
1: 3 and tread upon the high places of the e. 776
4:13 substance unto the Lord of the whole e. 776
5: 4 shall he be great unto the ends of the e. 776
6: 2 and ye strong foundations of the e: 776
7: 2 The good man is perished out of the e: 776
7:17 out of their holes like worms of the e: 776
Na 1: 5 the e is burnt at his presence, yea, 776
2:13 I will cut off thy prey from the e, 776
Hab 2:14 the e shall be filled with the knowledge 776
2:20 let all the e keep silence before him. 776
3: 3 heavens, and the e was full of his praise. 776
3: 6 He stood, and measured the e: he beheld, 776
3: 9 Selah. Thou didst cleave the e with rivers. 776
Zep 2: 3 Seek ye the LORD, all ye meek of the e, 776
2:11 for he will famish all the gods of the e; 776
3: 8 for all the e shall be devoured with the fire 776
3:20 and a praise among all people of the e, 776
Hag 1:10 dew, and the e is stayed from her fruit. 776
2: 6 and the e, and the sea, and the dry land; 776
2:21 I will shake the heavens and the e; 776
Zec 1:10 hath sent to walk to and fro through the e. 776
1:11 We have walked to and fro through the e, 776
1:11 behold, all the e sitteth still, and is at rest. 776
4:10 which run to and fro through the whole e. 776
4:14 that stand by the Lord of the whole e. 776
5: 3 goeth forth over the face of the whole e: 776
5: 6 This is their resemblance through all the e. 776
5: 9 they lift up the wings between the e and 776
5: 9 from standing before the Lord of all the e. 776
6: 7 they might walk to and fro through the e: 776
6: 7 ye hence, walk to and fro through the e. 776
6: 7 So they walked to and fro through the e. 776
9:10 from the river even to the ends of the e. 776
12: 1 layeth the foundation of the e, 776
12: 3 though all the people of the e be gathered 776
14: 9 And the LORD shall be king over all the e: 776
14:17 the e unto Jerusalem to worship the King, 776
Mal 4: 6 lest I come and smite the e with a curse. 776
Mt 5: 5 are the meek: for they shall inherit the e. 1093
5:13 Ye are the salt of the e: but if the salt have 1093
5:18 Till heaven and e pass, one jot or one tittle 1093
5:35 Nor by the e; for it is his footstool: neither 1093
6:10 Thy will be done in e, as it is in heaven. 1093
6:19 not up for yourselves treasures upon e, 1093
9: 6 Son of man hath power on e to forgive 1093
10:34 not that I am come to send peace on e: 1093
11:25 Lord of heaven and e, because thou hast 1093
12:40 and three nights in the heart of the e. 1093
12:42 of the e to hear the wisdom of Solomon; 1093
13: 5 stony places, where they had not much e: 1093
13: 5 because they had no deepness of e: 1093
16:19 whatsoever thou shalt bind on e shall be 1093
16:19 whatsoever thou shalt loose on e shall be 1093
17:25 whom do the kings of the e take custom 1093
18:18 Whatsoever ye shall bind on e shall be 1093
18:18 whatsoever ye shall loose on e shall be 1093
18:19 That if two of you shall agree on e as 1093
23: 9 And call no man your father upon the e: 1093
23:35 all the righteous blood shed upon the e, 1093
24:30 then shall all the tribes of the e mourn, 1093
24:35 Heaven and e shall pass away, 1093
25:18 received one went and digged in the e, 1093
25:25 and went and hid thy talent in the e: 1093
27:51 and the e did quake, and the rocks rent; 1093
28:18 is given unto me in heaven and in e. 1093
Mk 2:10 Son of man hath power on e to forgive 1093
4: 5 stony ground, where it had not much e; 1093
4: 5 it sprang up, because it had no depth of e: 1093
4:28 For the e bringeth forth fruit of herself; 1093
4:31 which, when it is sown in the e, 1093
4:31 is less than all the seeds that be in the e: 1093
9: 3 so as no fuller on e can white them. 1093
13:27 from the uttermost part of the e to 1093
13:31 Heaven and e shall pass away: 1093
Lk 2:14 and on e peace, good will towards men. 1093
5:24 of man hath power upon e to forgive sins, 1093
6:49 a foundation built a house upon the e; 1093
10:21 thee, O Father, Lord of heaven and e, 1093
11: 2 Thy will be done, as in heaven, so in e. 1093
11:31 she came from the utmost parts of the e 1093
12:49 I am come to send fire on the e; 1093
12:51 ye that I am come to give peace on e? 1093
12:56 discern the face of the sky and of the e; 1093
16:17 And it is easier for heaven and e to pass, 1093
18: 8 man cometh, shall he find faith on the e? 1093
21:25 and upon the e distress of nations, 1093
21:26 those things which are coming on the e: 3625
21:33 Heaven and e shall pass away: 1093
21:35 that dwell on the face of the whole e. 1093
23:44 there was a darkness over all the e until 1093
24: 5 and bowed down their faces to the e, 1093
Jn 3:31 is above all: he that is of the e is earthly, 1093

Jn 3:31 the earth is earthly, and speaketh of the e: 1093
12:32 I, if I be lifted up from the e, will draw 1093
17: 4 I have glorified thee on the e: I have 1093
Ac 1: 8 and unto the uttermost part of the e. 1093
2:19 heaven above, and signs in the e beneath; 1093
3:25 shall all the kindreds of the e be blessed. 1093
4:24 and e, and the sea, and all that in them are, 1093
4:26 The kings of the e stood up, and the rulers 1093
7:49 is my throne, and e is my footstool: 1093
8:33 for his life is taken from the e. 1093
9: 4 And he fell to the e, and heard a voice 1093
9: 8 And Saul arose from the e; and when his 1093
10:11 at the four corners, and let down to the e: 1093
10:12 all manner of fourfooted beasts of the e, 1093
11: 6 and saw fourfooted beasts of the e, 1093
13:47 be for salvation unto the ends of the e. 1093
14:15 and e, and the sea, and all things that are 1093
17:24 seeing that he is Lord of heaven and e, 1093
17:26 men for to dwell on all the face of the e, 1093
22:22 said, Away with such a fellow from the e: 1093
26:14 And when we were all fallen to the e, 1093
Ro 9:17 might be declared throughout all the e. 1093
9:28 short work will the Lord make upon the e. 1093
10:18 their sound went into all the e, 1093
1Co 8: 5 in heaven or in e, (as there be gods 1093
10:26 For the e is the Lord's, and the fulness 1093
10:28 conscience sake: for the e is the Lord's, 1093
15:47 The first man is of the e, earthy: the 1093
Eph 1:10 which are in heaven, and which are on e; 1093
3:15 whole family in heaven and e is named, 1093
4: 9 first into the lower parts of the e? 1093
6: 3 and thou mayest live long on the e. 1093
Php 2:10 things in e, and things under the earth; 1919
2:10 things in earth, and things under the e; 2709
Col 1:16 and that are in e, visible and invisible, 1093
1:20 I say, whether they be things in e, 1093
3: 2 on things above, not on things on the e. 1093
3: 5 your members which are upon the e; 1093
2Ti 2:20 and of silver, but also of wood and of e; 3749
Heb 1:10 hast laid the foundation of the e; 1093
6: 7 For the e which drinketh in the rain that 1093
8: 4 For if he were on e, he should not be a 1093
11:13 were strangers and pilgrims on the e. 1093
11:38 and in dens and caves of the e. 1093
12:25 not who refused him that spake on e, 1093
12:26 Whose voice then shook the e: but now 1093
12:26 Yet once more I shake not the e only, 1093
Jas 5: 5 Ye have lived in pleasure on the e, 1093
5: 7 waiteth for the precious fruit of the e, 1093
5:12 neither by heaven, neither by the e, 1093
5:17 rained not on the e by the space of three 1093
5:18 rain, and the e brought forth her fruit. 1093
2Pe 3: 5 and the e standing out of the water and 1093
3: 7 the heavens and the e, which are now, 1093
3:10 the e also and the works that are therein 1093
3:13 look for new heavens and a new e, 1093
1Jn 5: 8 And there are three that bear witness in e, 1093
Rev 1: 5 And the prince of the kings of the e. 1093
1: 7 all kindreds of the e shall wail because 1093
3:10 world, to try them that dwell upon the e. 1093
5: 3 heaven, nor in e, neither under the earth, 1093
5: 3 heaven, nor in earth, neither under the e, 1093
5: 6 spirits of God sent forth into all the e. 1093
5:10 and priests: and we shall reign on the e. 1093
5:13 and on the e, and under the earth, 1093
5:13 under the e, and such as are in the sea, 1093
6: 4 that sat thereon to take peace from the e, 1093
6: 8 unto them over the fourth part of the e, 1093
6: 8 with death, and with the beasts of the e. 1093
6:10 our blood on them that dwell on the e? 1093
6:13 And the stars of heaven fell unto the e, 1093
6:15 And the kings of the e, and the great men, 1093
7: 1 standing on the four corners of the e, 1093
7: 1 holding the four winds of the e, that 1093
7: 1 that the wind should not blow on the e, 1093
7: 2 to whom it was given to hurt the e and 1093
7: 3 Saying, Hurt not the e, neither the sea, 1093
8: 5 with fire of the altar, and cast it into the e: 1093
8: 7 blood, and they were cast upon the e: 1093
8:13 to the inhabiters of the e by reason of 1093
9: 1 I saw a star fall from heaven unto the e: 1093
9: 3 came out of the smoke locusts upon the e: 1093
9: 3 as the scorpions of the e have power. 1093
9: 4 they should not hurt the grass of the e, 1093
10: 2 upon the sea, and his left foot on the e, 1093
10: 5 upon the e lifted up his hand to heaven, 1093
10: 6 and the e, and the things that therein are, 1093
10: 8 standeth upon the sea and upon the e. 1093
11: 4 standing before the God of the e. 1093
11: 6 to smite the e with all plagues, as often 1093
11:10 they that dwell upon the e shall rejoice 1093
11:10 tormented them that dwell on the e. 1093
11:18 destroy them which destroy the e. 1093
12: 4 of heaven, and did cast them to the e: 1093
12: 9 he was cast out into the e, and his angels 1093
12:12 Woe to the inhabiters of the e and of 1093
12:13 dragon saw that he was cast unto the e, 1093
12:16 the e helped the woman, and the earth 1093
12:16 and the e opened her mouth, 1093
13: 8 all that dwell upon the e shall worship 1093
13:11 another beast coming up out of the e; 1093
13:12 and causeth the e and them which dwell 1093
13:13 from heaven on the e in the sight of men, 1093
13:14 deceiveth them that dwell on the e by 1093
13:14 saying to them that dwell on the e, that 1093

Rev 14: 3	which were redeemed from the **e**.	*1093*
14: 6	to preach unto them that dwell on the **e**,	*1093*
14: 7	and **e**, and the sea, and the fountains of	*1093*
14:15	to reap; for the harvest of the **e** is ripe.	*1093*
14:16	on the cloud thrust in his sickle on the **e**;	*1093*
14:16	sickle on the earth; and the **e** was reaped.	*1093*
14:18	gather the clusters of the vine of the **e**,	*1093*
14:19	the angel thrust in his sickle into the **e**,	*1093*
14:19	and gathered the vine of the **e**, and cast *it*	*1093*
16: 1	the vials of the wrath of God upon the **e**.	*1093*
16: 2	and poured out his vial upon the **e**;	*1093*
16:14	which go forth unto the kings of the **e** and	*1093*
16:18	as was not since men were upon the **e**,	*1093*
17: 2	With whom the kings of the **e** have	*1093*
17: 2	the inhabiters of the **e** have been made	*1093*
17: 5	AND ABOMINATIONS OF THE **E.**	*1093*
17: 8	they that dwell on the **e** shall wonder,	*1093*
17:18	which reigneth over the kings of the **e**.	*1093*
18: 1	and the **e** was lightened with his glory.	*1093*
18: 3	the kings of the **e** have committed	*1093*
18: 3	the merchants of the **e** are waxed rich	*1093*
18: 9	And the kings of the **e**, who have	*1093*
18:11	And the merchants of the **e** *shall* weep	*1093*
18:23	merchants were the great men of the **e**;	*1093*
18:24	and of all that were slain upon the **e**.	*1093*
19: 2	which did corrupt the **e** with her	*1093*
19:19	and the kings of the **e**, and their armies,	*1093*
20: 8	which are in the four quarters of the **e**,	*1093*
20: 9	they went up on the breadth of the **e**,	*1093*
20:11	whose face the **e** and the heaven fled	*1093*
21: 1	And I saw a new heaven and a new **e**:	*1093*
21: 1	and the first **e** were passed away;	*1093*
21:24	the kings of the **e** do bring their glory and	*1093*

EARTHEN (10) [EARTH]

Lev 6:28	the **e** vessel wherein it is sodden shall be	2789
11:33	every **e** vessel, whereinto *any* of them	2789
14: 5	killed in an **e** vessel over running water:	2789
14:50	he shall kill the one of the birds in an **e**	2789
Nu 5:17	the priest shall take holy water in an **e**	2789
2Sa 17:28	**e** vessels, and wheat, and barley,	3335
Jer 19: 1	Go and get a potter's **e** bottle, and *take it*	2789
32:14	put them in an **e** vessel, that they may	2789
La 4: 2	how are they esteemed as **e** pitchers,	2789
2Co 4: 7	But we have this treasure in **e** vessels,	3749

EARTHLY (5) [EARTH]

Jn 3:12	If I have told you **e** *things*, and ye believe	*1919*
3:31	he that is of the earth is **e**,	*1093+1537+3588*
2Co 5: 1	For we know that if our **e** house of *this*	*1919*
Php 3:19	*is* in their shame, who mind **e** *things*.)	*1919*
Jas 3:15	not from above, but *is* **e**, sensual, devilish.	*1919*

EARTHQUAKE (16) [EARTH, QUAKE]

1Ki 19:11	after the wind an **e**; *but* the LORD *was* not	7494
19:11	*but* the LORD *was* not in the **e**:	7494
19:12	after the **e** a fire; *but* the LORD *was* not in	7494
Isa 29: 6	with **e**, and great noise, *with* storm and	7494
Am 1: 1	Joash king of Israel, two year before the **e**.	7494
Zec 14: 5	as ye fled from before the **e** in the days	7494
Mt 27:54	saw the **e**, and *those* things that were	4578
28: 2	And behold, there was a great **e**:	4578
Ac 16:26	And suddenly there was a great **e**,	4578
Rev 6:12	the sixth seal, and lo, there was a great **e**;	4578
8: 5	thunderings, and lightnings, and an **e**.	4578
11:13	And the same hour was there a great **e**,	4578
11:13	the **e** were slain of men seven thousand:	4578
11:19	and thunderings, and an **e**, and great hail.	4578
16:18	and there was a great **e**, such as was not	4578
16:18	the earth, so mighty an **e**, *and* so great.	4578

EARTHQUAKES (3) [EARTH, QUAKE]

Mt 24: 7	and pestilences, and **e** in divers places.	4578
Mk 13: 8	and there shall be **e** in divers places,	4578
Lk 21:11	And great **e** shall be in divers places,	4578

EARTHY (4) [EARTH]

1Co 15:47	first man *is* of the earth, **e**: the second	5517
15:48	As *is* the **e**, such *are they* also that are	5517
15:48	the earthy, such *they* also *that are* **e**:	5517
15:49	And as we have borne the image of the **e**,	5517

EASE (20) [EASED, EASIER, EASILY, EASY]

Dt 23:13	shall be, when thou wilt **e** thyself abroad,	3427
28:65	among these nations shalt thou **find** no **e**,	7280
Jdg 20:43	trode them down **with e** over against	4496
2Ch 10: 4	**e** thou **somewhat** the grievous servitude	7043
10: 9	**E somewhat** the yoke that thy father did	7043
Job 7:13	my couch shall **e** my complaint;	5375
12: 5	in the thought of him that is **at e**.	7600
16:12	was **at e**, but he hath broken me asunder:	7961
21:23	full strength, *being* wholly **at e** and quiet.	7946
Ps 25:13	His soul shall dwell **at e**; and his seed	2896
123: 4	*with* the scorning of those that are **at e**,	7600
Isa 1:24	I will **e** me of mine adversaries,	5162
32: 9	Rise up, ye women that are **at e**, hear my	7600
32:11	Tremble, ye *women* that are **at e**;	7600
Jer 46:27	be in rest and **at e**, and none shall make	7599
48:11	Moab hath been **at e** from his youth,	7599
Eze 23:42	a voice of a multitude being **at e** *was* with	7961
Am 6: 1	Woe to them *that are* **at e** in Zion,	7600
Zec 1:15	displeased with the heathen *that are* **at e**:	7600
Lk 12:19	**take** thine **e**, eat, drink, *and* be merry.	*373*

EASED (2) [EASE]

Job 16: 6	*though* I forbear, what am I?	*4480+1980*
2Co 8:13	For *I mean* not that other *men* be **e**,	*425*

EASIER (8) [EASE]

Ex 18:22	so shall it be **e** for thyself,	*4480+7043*
Mt 9: 5	For whether is **e**, to say, *Thy* sins be	*2123*
19:24	It is **e** for a camel to go through the eye of	*2123*
Mk 2: 9	Whether is it **e** to say to the sick of	*2123*
10:25	It is **e** for a camel to go through the eye of	*2123*
Lk 5:23	Whether is **e**, to say, Thy sins be forgiven	*2123*
16:17	And it is **e** for heaven and earth to pass,	*2123*
18:25	For it is **e** for a camel to go through a	*2123*

EASILY (2) [EASE]

1Co 13: 5	is not **e provoked**, thinketh no evil;	*3947*
Heb 12: 1	and the sin which doth so **e beset** *us*,	*2139*

EAST (157) [EASTWARD]

Ge 2:14	that *is it* which goeth **toward** the **e**	6926
3:24	he placed at the **e** of the garden of Eden	6924
4:16	in the land of Nod, on the **e** of Eden.	6926
10:30	thou goest unto Sephar, a mount of the **e**.	6924
11: 2	to pass, as they journeyed from the **e**,	6924
12: 8	unto a mountain on the **e** of Beth-el,	6924
12: 8	Beth-el on the west, and Hai on the **e**:	6924
13:11	the plain of Jordan; and Lot journeyed **e**:	6924
25: 6	yet lived, eastward, unto the **e** country.	6924
28:14	the **e**, and to the north, and to the south:	6924
29: 1	came into the land of the people of the **e**.	6924
41: 6	blasted with the **e wind** sprang up after	6921
41:23	thin, *and* blasted with the **e**, **wind**,	6921
41:27	**e wind** shall be seven years of famine.	6921
Ex 10:13	the LORD brought an **e wind** upon	6921
10:13	the **e wind** brought the locusts.	6921
14:21	go *back* by a strong **e** wind all *that* night,	6921
27:13	the breadth of the court on the **e** side	6924
38:13	the **e** side eastward fifty cubits.	6924+1886.5
Lev 1:16	cast it beside the altar on the **e part**,	6924
Nu 2: 3	on the **e side** toward the rising of the sun	6924
3:38	before the tabernacle toward the **e**,	6924
10: 5	the camps that lie on the **e parts** shall go	6924
23: 7	out of the mountains of the **e**,	6924
34:10	ye shall point out your **e** border	6924+1886.5
34:11	Shepham *to* Riblah, on the **e side** of Ain;	6924
35: 5	the city *on* the **e** side two thousand cubits,	6924
Jos 4:19	in Gilgal, in the **e** border of Jericho.	4217
7: 2	on the **e side** of Beth-el, and spake unto	6924
11: 3	*And* to the Canaanite on the **e** and on	4217
12: 1	Hermon, and all the plain on the **e**;	4217
12: 3	the plain to the sea of Cinneroth on the **e**,	4217
12: 3	sea of the plain, *even* the salt sea on the **e**,	4217
15: 5	the **e** border *was* the salt sea,	6924+1886.5
16: 1	unto the water of Jericho on the **e**,	4217
16: 5	on the **e side** was Ataroth-addar,	4217
16: 6	and passed by it on the **e** *to* Janohah;	4217
17:10	on the north, and in Issachar on the **e**.	4217
18: 7	their inheritance beyond Jordan on the **e**,	4217
18:20	was the border of it on the **e**	6924+1886.5
19:13	on the **e** to Gittah-hepher,	4217+6924+1886.5
Jdg 6: 3	the Amalekites, and the children of the **e**,	6924
6:33	the children of the **e** were gathered	6924
7:12	all the children of the **e** lay along in	6924
8:10	of all the hosts of the children of the **e**:	6924
8:11	that dwelt in tents on the **e** of Nobah	6924
11:18	by the **e side** of the land of Moab,	4217+8121
21:19	the **e** side of the highway	4217+8121+1886.1
1Ki 4:30	all the children of the **e country**,	6924
7:25	the south, and three looking toward the **e**:	4217
1Ch 4:39	*even* unto the **e side** of the valley, to seek	4217
5:10	dwelt in their tents throughout all the **e**	4217
6:78	Jordan *by* Jericho, on the **e** side of Jordan,	4217
9:24	toward the **e**, west, north, and south.	4217
12:15	*both* toward the **e**, and toward the west.	4217
2Ch 4: 4	south, and three looking toward the **e**:	4217
4:10	set the sea on the right side of the **e end**,	6924
5:12	stood *at* the **e** end of the altar,	4217
29: 4	gathered them together into the **e** street,	4217
31:14	the Levite, the porter toward the **e**,	4217
Ne 3:26	over against the water gate toward the **e**,	4217
3:29	of Shechaniah, the keeper of the **e** gate.	4217
Job 1: 3	was the greatest of all the men of the **e**.	6924
15: 2	and fill his belly *with* the **e wind**?	6921
27:21	The **e wind** carrieth him away,	6921
38:24	scattereth the **e wind** upon the earth?	6921
Ps 48: 7	the ships of Tarshish with an **e** wind.	6921
75: 6	For promotion *cometh* neither from the **e**,	4161
78:26	caused an **e wind** to blow in the heaven:	6921
103:12	As far as the **e** is from the west, *so* far	4217
107: 3	from the **e**, and from the west, from	4217
Isa 2: 6	because they be replenished from the **e**,	6924
11:14	they shall spoil them of the **e** together;	6924
27: 8	his rough wind in the day of the **e wind**.	6921
41: 2	raised up the righteous *man* from the **e**,	4217
43: 5	I will bring thy seed from the **e**,	4217
46:11	Calling a ravenous bird from the **e**,	4217
Jer 18:17	I will scatter them as *with* an **e** wind	6921
19: 2	which *is by* the entry of the **e** gate,	2777
31:40	corner of the horse gate towards the **e**,	4217
49:28	up to Kedar, and spoil the men of the **e**.	6924
Eze 8:16	to the LORD, and their faces towards the **e**;	6924
8:16	they worshipped the sun towards the **e**.	6924
10:19	*every one* stood *at* the door of the **e** gate	6931
11: 1	brought me unto the **e** gate of	6931
11:23	which *is* on the **e** side of the city.	6924
Eze 17:10	wither, when the **e** wind toucheth it?	6921
19:12	and the **e** wind dried up her fruit:	6921
25: 4	I *will* deliver thee to the men of the **e** for	6924
25:10	the men of the **e** with the Ammonites,	6924
27:26	the **e** wind hath broken thee in the midst	6921
39:11	the valley of the passengers *on* the **e** of	6926
40: 6	gate which looketh toward the **e**,	6921+1886.5
40:22	of the gate that looketh towards the **e**;	6921
40:23	gate toward the north, and toward the **e**;	6921
40:32	me into the inner court toward the **e**:	6921
40:44	one at the side of the **e** gate *having*	6921
41:14	of the separate place toward the **e**,	6921
42: 9	chambers *was* the entry on the **e side**,	6921
42:10	of the wall of the court toward the **e**,	6921
42:12	way directly before the wall toward the **e**,	6921
42:15	the gate whose prospect *is* toward the **e**,	6921
42:16	measured the **e** side with the measuring	6921
43: 1	*even* the gate that looketh toward the **e**:	6921
43: 2	God of Israel came from the way of the **e**:	6921
43: 4	the glory whose prospect *is* toward the **e**.	6921
43:17	and his stairs *shall* look toward the **e**.	6921
44: 1	sanctuary which looketh *toward* the **e**;	6921
45: 7	from the **e** side eastward:	6924+1886.5
45: 7	the west border unto the **e** border.	6921+1886.5
46: 1	it shall be shut the six working days;	6921
46:12	the gate that looketh *toward* the **e**,	6921
47: 1	forefront of the house *stood toward* the **e**,	6921
47: 8	These waters issue out toward the **e**	6930
47:18	the side ye shall measure from Hauran,	6921
47:18	*by* Jordan, from the border unto the **e** sea.	6931
47:18	east sea. And *this is* the **e** side.	6921+1886.5
48: 1	these are his sides **e** *and* west; a *portion*	6921
48: 2	from the **e** side unto the west side,	6921
48: 3	the **e** side even unto the west	6921+1886.5
48: 4	the **e** side unto the west side,	6921+1886.5
48: 5	the **e** side unto the west side,	6921+1886.5
48: 6	from the **e** side even unto the west side,	6921
48: 7	from the **e** side unto the west side,	6921
48: 8	Judah, from the **e** side unto the west side,	6921
48: 8	the **e** side unto the west:	6921+1886.5
48:10	toward the **e** ten thousand *in* breadth,	6921
48:16	on the **e** side four thousand and	6921
48:17	and toward the **e** two hundred and fifty,	6921
48:21	the oblation toward the **e** border,	6921+1886.5
48:23	the **e** side unto the west side,	6921+1886.5
48:24	the **e** side unto the west side,	6921+1886.5
48:25	the **e** side unto the west side,	6921+1886.5
48:26	the **e** side unto the west side,	6921+1886.5
48:27	the **e** side unto the west side,	6921+1886.5
48:32	at the **e** side four thousand and	6921+1886.5
Da 8: 9	toward the **e**, and toward the pleasant	4217
11:44	tidings out of the **e** and out of the north	4217
Hos 12: 1	on wind, and followeth after the **e wind**:	6921
13:15	*his* brethren, an **e** wind shall come,	6921
Joel 2:20	with his face toward the **e** sea,	6931
Am 8:12	the north even to the **e**, they shall run	4217
Jnh 4: 5	sat on the **e** side of the city, and there	6924
4: 8	that God prepared a vehement **e** wind;	6921
Hab 1: 9	their faces shall sup up *as* the **e wind**,	6921
Zec 8: 7	I *will* save my people from the **e** country,	4217
14: 4	which *is* before Jerusalem on the **e**,	4217
14: 4	and cleave in the midst thereof toward the **e**	4217
Mt 2: 1	there came wise men from the **e** to	395
2: 2	for we have seen his star in the **e**,	395
2: 9	and lo, the star, which they saw in the **e**,	395
8:11	That many shall come from the **e** and west,	395
24:27	For as the lightning cometh out of the **e**,	395
Lk 13:29	And they shall come from the **e**,	395
Rev 7: 2	another angel ascending from the **e**,	395+2246
16:12	that the way of the kings of the **e**	395+2246
21:13	On the **e** three gates; on the north three	395

EASTER (1)

Ac 12: 4	intending after **E** to bring him forth to	*3957*

EASTWARD (40) [EAST]

Ge 2: 8	the LORD God planted a garden **e**	4480+6924
13:14	southward, and **e**, and westward:	6924+1886.5
25: 6	he yet lived, **e**, unto the east country.	6924
Ex 27:13	east side **e** shall be fifty cubits.	4217+1886.5
38:13	for the east side **e** fifty cubits.	4217+1886.5
Lev 16:14	his finger upon the mercy seat **e**;	6924+1886.5
Nu 3:38	tabernacle of the congregation **e**,	4217+1886.5
32:19	fallen to us on *this* side Jordan **e**.	4217+1886.5
34: 3	outmost coast of the salt sea **e**:	6924+1886.5
34:11	side of the sea of Chinnereth **e**:	6924+1886.5
34:15	*this* side Jordan *near* Jericho **e**,	4217+1886.5
Dt 3:17	salt sea, under Ashdoth-pisgah **e**.	4217+1886.5
3:27	**e**, and behold *it* with thine eyes:	4217+1886.5
4:49	all the plain on *this* side Jordan **e**,	4217+1886.5
Jos 11: 8	and unto the valley of Mizpeh **e**;	4217+1886.5
13: 8	I gave them, beyond Jordan **e**,	4217+1886.5
13:27	on the *other* side Jordan **e**.	4217+1886.5
13:32	*other* side Jordan, *by* Jericho, **e**.	4217+1886.5
16: 6	the border went about **e** *unto*	4217+1886.5
19:12	turned from Sarid **e** *toward*	6924+1886.5
20: 8	*other* side Jordan *by* Jericho **e**,	4217+1886.5
1Sa 13: 5	pitched in Michmash, **e** from Beth-aven.	6926
1Ki 7:39	house **e** over against the south.	4217+1886.5
17: 3	turn thee **e**, and hide thyself by	6924+1886.5
2Ki 10:33	From Jordan **e**, all the land	4217+8121+1886.1
13:17	he said, Open the window **e**.	6924+1886.5
1Ch 5: 9	he inhabited unto the entering in **e**	4217+1886.5
7:28	**e** Naaran, and westward	4217+1886.1+3807.1
9:18	*waited* in the king's gate **e**:	4217+1886.5

1Ch	26:14 the lot **e** fell to Shelemiah.	4217+1886.5
	26:17 **E** were six Levites, northward four a day,	4217
Ne	12:37 of David, even unto the water gate **e**.	4217
Eze	11: 1 Lord's house, which looketh **e**:	6921+1886.5
	40:10 **e** were three on this side,	1870+6921+1886.1
	40:19 an hundred cubits **e** and north*ward*.	6921
	45: 7 and from the east side **e**:	6921+1886.5
	47: 1 the threshold of the house **e**:	6921+1886.5
	47: 2 utter gate *by* the way that looketh **e**;	6921
	47: 3 **e**, he measured a thousand cubits,	6921
	48:18 *portion shall be* ten thousand **e**,	6921+1886.5

EASY (4) [EASE]

Pr	14: 6 knowledge *is* **e** unto him that	7043
Mt	11:30 For my yoke *is* **e**, and my burden is light.	5543
1Co	14: 9 by the tongue words **e to be understood**,	2154
Jas	3:17 peaceable, gentle, *and* **e to be intreated**,	2138

EAT (655) [ATE, EATEN, EATER, EATERS, EATEST, EATETH, EATING, MOTHEATEN, MOTH-EATEN]

Ge	2:16 of the garden thou mayest **freely** **e**.	398+398
	2:17 of good and evil, thou shalt not **e** of it:	398
	3: 1 Ye shall not **e** of every tree of the garden?	398
	3: 2 We may **e** of the fruit of the trees of	398
	3: 3 God hath said, Ye shall not **e** of it,	398
	3: 5 For God doth know that in the day ye **e**	398
	3: 6 did **e**, and gave also unto her husband with	398
	3: 6 unto her husband with her; and he did **e**.	398
	3:11 thee that thou shouldest not **e**?	398
	3:12 me, she gave me of the tree, and I did **e**.	398
	3:13 The serpent beguiled me, and I did **e**.	398
	3:14 dust shalt thou **e** all the days of thy life:	398
	3:17 saying, Thou shalt not **e** of it:	398
	3:17 in sorrow shalt thou **e** *of* it all the days of	398
	3:18 and thou shalt **e** the herb of the field;	398
	3:19 In the sweat of thy face shalt thou **e** bread,	398
	3:22 of the tree of life, and **e**, and live for ever:	398
	9: 4 *which is* the blood thereof, shall you not **e**.	398
	18: 8 by them under the tree, and they did **e**.	398
	19: 3 did bake unleavened bread, and they did **e**.	398
	24:33 there was set *meat* before him to **e**:	398
	24:33 he said, I will not **e**, until I have told mine	398
	24:54 they did **e** and drink, he and the men that	398
	25:28 because he did **e** of *his* venison:	6310+871.1
	25:34 he did **e** and drink, and rose up, and went	398
	26:30 them a feast, and they did **e** and drink.	398
	27: 4 as I love, and bring *it* to me, that I may **e**;	398
	27: 7 that I may **e**, and bless thee before	398
	27:10 that he may **e**, and that he may bless thee	398
	27:19 arise, I pray thee, sit and **e** of my venison,	398
	27:25 to me, and I will **e** of my son's venison,	398
	27:25 he brought *it* near to him, and he did **e**:	398
	27:31 my father arise, and **e** of his son's venison,	398
	28:20 will give me bread to **e**, and raiment to put	398
	31:46 a heap: and they did **e** there upon the heap.	398
	31:54 mount, and called his brethren to **e** bread:	398
	31:54 they did **e** bread, and tarried all night in	398
	32:32 Therefore the children of Israel **e** not *of*	398
	37:25 they sat down to **e** bread: and they lift up	398
	39: 6 he had, save the bread which he did **e**.	398
	40:17 the birds did **e** them out of the basket upon	398
	40:19 and the birds shall **e** thy flesh from off thee.	398
	41: 4 leanfleshed kine did **e up** the seven well	398
	41:20 the ill favoured kine did **e up** the first seven	398
	43:25 they heard that they should **e** bread.	398
	43:32 which did **e** with him, by themselves:	398
	43:32 the Egyptians might not **e** bread with	398
	45:18 of Egypt, and ye shall **e** the fat of the land.	398
	47:22 did **e** their portion which Pharaoh gave	398
Ex	2:20 the man? call him, that he may **e** bread.	398
	10: 5 they shall **e** the residue of that which is	398
	10: 5 shall **e** every tree which groweth for you	398
	10:12 **e** every herb of the land, *even* all that	398
	10:15 they did **e** every herb of the land, and all	398
	12: 7 post of the houses, wherein they shall **e** it.	398
	12: 8 they shall **e** the flesh in that night, roast	398
	12: 8 *and* with bitter *herbs* they shall **e** it.	398
	12: 9 **E** not of it raw, nor sodden at all with	398
	12:11 thus shall ye **e** it; *with* your loins girded,	398
	12:11 in your hand; and ye shall **e** it in haste:	398
	12:15 Seven days shall ye **e** unleavened bread;	398
	12:16 save *that* which every man must **e**, that	398
	12:18 ye shall **e** unleavened bread, until the one	398
	12:20 Ye shall **e** nothing leavened; in all your	398
	12:20 all your habitations shall ye **e** unleavened	398
	12:43 There shall no stranger **e** thereof:	398
	12:44 circumcised him, then shall he **e** thereof.	398
	12:45 and a hired servant shall not **e** thereof.	398
	12:48 no uncircumcised person shall **e** thereof.	398
	13: 6 Seven days thou shalt **e** unleavened bread,	398
	16: 3 *and* when we did **e** bread to the full;	398
	16: 8 shall give you in the evening flesh to **e**,	398
	16:12 At even ye shall **e** flesh, and in the morning	398
	16:15 bread which the Lord hath given you to **e**.	402
	16:25 Moses said, **E** that to day; for to day *is* a	398
	16:35 the children of Israel did **e** manna forty	398
	16:35 they did **e** manna, until they came unto	398
	18:12 to **e** bread with Moses' father in law before	398
	22:31 neither shall ye **e** *any* flesh *that* is torn *of*	398
	23:11 lie still; that the poor of thy people may **e**:	398
	23:11 they leave the beasts of the field shall **e**.	398
	23:15 thou shalt **e** unleavened bread seven days,	398
	24:11 also they saw God, and did **e** and drink.	398
	29:32 and his sons shall **e** the flesh of the ram,	398
	29:33 they shall **e** those *things* wherewith	398

Ex	29:33 a stranger shall not **e** *thereof*, because	398
	32: 6 the people sat down to **e** and to drink,	398
	34:15 *one* call thee, and thou **e** of his sacrifice;	398
	34:18 seven days thou shalt **e** unleavened bread,	398
	34:28 he did neither **e** bread, nor drink water.	398
Lev	3:17 *that* ye **e** neither fat nor blood.	398
	6:16 thereof shall Aaron and his sons **e**:	398
	6:16 of the congregation shall they **e** it.	398
	6:18 among the children of Aaron shall **e** of it.	398
	6:26 The priest that offereth it for sin shall **e** it:	398
	6:29 All the males among the priests shall **e**	398
	7: 6 male among the priests shall **e** thereof:	398
	7:19 the flesh, all that be clean shall **e** thereof.	398
	7:21 **e** of the flesh of the sacrifice of peace	398
	7:23 Ye shall **e** no *manner* fat, of ox, or of sheep,	398
	7:24 but ye shall **e** in no wise of it.	398+398+3808
	7:26 Moreover ye shall **e** no *manner of* blood,	398
	8:31 **e** it with the bread that *is* in the basket	398
	8:31 Aaron and his sons shall **e** it.	398
	10:12 and **e** it without leaven beside the altar:	398
	10:13 ye shall **e** it in the holy place, because it *is*	398
	10:14 heave shoulder shall ye **e** in a clean place;	398
	11: 2 are the beasts which ye shall **e** among	398
	11: 3 among the beasts, that shall ye **e**.	398
	11: 4 Nevertheless these shall ye not **e** of them	398
	11: 8 Of their flesh shall ye not **e**,	398
	11: 9 shall ye **e** of all that *are* in the waters:	398
	11: 9 the seas, and in the rivers, them shall ye **e**.	398
	11:11 ye shall not **e** of their flesh, but you shall	398
	11:21 Yet these may ye **e** of every flying creeping	398
	11:22 *Even* these of them ye may **e**; the locust	398
	11:39 if any beast, of which ye may **e**, die;	402
	11:42 creep upon the earth, them ye shall not **e**;	398
	17:12 of Israel, No soul of you shall **e** blood,	398
	17:12 that sojourneth among you **e** blood.	398
	17:14 Ye shall **e** the blood of no *manner of* flesh:	398
	19:25 the fifth year shall ye **e** of the fruit thereof,	398
	19:26 Ye shall not **e** *any thing* with the blood:	398
	21:22 He shall **e** the bread of his God, *both* of	398
	22: 4 he shall not **e** of the holy *things*, until he	398
	22: 6 not **e** of the holy *things*, unless he wash	398
	22: 7 shall afterward **e** of the holy *things*;	398
	22: 8 is torn *with beasts*, he shall not **e** to defile	398
	22:10 There shall no stranger **e** *of* the holy *thing*.	398
	22:10 hired servant, shall not **e** *of* the holy *thing*,	398
	22:11 he shall **e** of it, and he that is born in his	398
	22:11 born in his house: they shall **e** of his meat.	398
	22:12 she may not **e** of an offering of the holy	398
	22:13 her youth, she shall **e** of her father's meat:	398
	22:13 but there shall no stranger **e** thereof.	398
	22:14 if a man **e** *of* the holy *thing* unwittingly,	398
	22:16 when they **e** their holy *things*: for I	398
	23: 6 seven days ye must **e** unleavened bread.	398
	23:14 ye shall **e** neither bread, nor parched *corn*,	398
	24: 9 and they shall **e** it in the holy place:	398
	25:12 ye shall **e** the increase thereof out of	398
	25:19 ye shall **e** *your* fill, and dwell therein in	398
	25:20 say, What shall we **e** the seventh year?	398
	25:22 and **e** *yet* of old fruit until the ninth year;	398
	25:22 until her fruits come in ye shall **e** *of* the old	398
	26: 5 ye shall **e** your bread to the full, and dwell	398
	26:10 ye shall **e** old store, and bring forth the old	398
	26:16 seed in vain, for your enemies shall **e** it.	398
	26:26 and ye shall **e**, and not be satisfied.	398
	26:29 ye shall **e** the flesh of your sons,	398
	26:29 and the flesh of your daughters shall ye **e**.	398
	26:38 the land of your enemies shall **e** you **up**.	398
Nu	6: 3 grapes, nor **e** moist grapes, or dried.	398
	6: 4 All the days of his separation shall he **e**	398
	9:11 *and* **e** it with unleavened bread, and	398
	11: 4 and said, Who shall **give** us flesh to **e**?	398
	11: 5 the fish, which we did **e** in Egypt freely;	398
	11:13 saying, Give us flesh, that we may **e**.	398
	11:18 against to morrow, and ye shall **e** flesh:	398
	11:18 Who shall **give** us flesh to **e**?	398
	11:18 Lord will give you flesh, and ye shall **e**.	398
	11:19 Ye shall not **e** one day, nor two days,	398
	11:21 flesh, that they may **e** a whole month.	398
	15:19 *that* when ye **e** of the bread of the land,	398
	18:10 In the most holy *place* shalt thou **e** it;	398
	18:10 shalt thou eat it; every male shall **e** it:	398
	18:11 one *that is* clean in thy house shall **e** of	398
	18:13 one *that is* clean in thine house shall **e**	398
	18:31 ye shall **e** it in every place, ye and	398
	23:24 shall not lie down until he **e** *of* the prey,	398
	24: 8 he shall **e up** the nations his enemies,	398
	25: 2 the people did **e**, and bowed down to their	398
Dt	2: 6 meat of them for money, that ye may **e**;	398
	2:28 shalt sell me meat for money, that I may **e**;	398
	4:28 neither see, nor hear, nor **e**, nor smell.	398
	8: 9 A land wherein thou shalt **e** bread without	398
	9: 9 I neither did **e** bread nor drink water:	398
	9:18 I did neither **e** bread, nor drink water,	398
	11:15 thy cattle, that thou mayest **e** and be full.	398
	12: 7 there ye shall **e** before the Lord your God,	398
	12:15 thou mayest kill and **e** flesh in all thy gates,	398
	12:15 the unclean and the clean may **e** thereof,	398
	12:16 Only ye shall not **e** the blood; ye shall pour	398
	12:17 mayest not **e** within thy gates the tithe	398
	12:18 thou must **e** them before the Lord thy	398
	12:20 I will **e** flesh, because thy soul longeth to	398
	12:20 flesh, because thy soul longeth to **e** flesh;	398
	12:20 thou mayest **e** flesh, whatsoever thy soul	398
	12:21 shalt **e** in thy gates whatsoever thy soul	398
	12:22 the hart is eaten, so thou shalt **e** them:	398

Dt	12:22 and the clean shall **e** of them alike.	398
	12:23 Only be sure that thou **e** not the blood:	398
	12:23 thou mayest not **e** the life with the flesh.	398
	12:24 Thou shalt not **e** it; thou shalt pour it upon	398
	12:25 Thou shalt not **e** it; that it may go well	398
	12:27 Lord thy God, and thou shalt **e** the flesh.	398
	14: 3 Thou shalt not **e** any abominable *thing*.	398
	14: 4 These *are* the beasts which ye shall **e**:	398
	14: 6 the cud amongst the beasts: that ye shall **e**.	398
	14: 7 Nevertheless these ye shall not **e** of them	398
	14: 8 ye shall not **e** of their flesh, nor touch their	398
	14: 9 ye shall **e** of all that *are* in the waters:	398
	14: 9 all that have fins and scales shall ye **e**:	398
	14:10 hath not fins and scales ye may not **e**;	398
	14:11 Of all clean birds ye shall **e**.	398
	14:12 these *are they* of which ye shall not **e**:	398
	14:20 *But* of all clean fowls ye may **e**.	398
	14:21 Ye shall not **e** of any thing that dieth of	398
	14:21 that *is* in thy gates, that he may **e** it;	398
	14:23 And thou shalt **e** before the Lord thy God,	398
	14:26 thou shalt **e** there before the Lord thy	398
	14:29 shall come, and shall **e** and be satisfied;	398
	15:20 Thou shalt **e** it before the Lord thy God	398
	15:22 Thou shalt **e** it within thy gates:	398
	15:22 and the clean *person shall* **e** it alike,	NIH
	15:23 Only thou shalt not **e** the blood thereof;	398
	16: 3 Thou shalt **e** no leavened bread with it;	398
	16: 3 seven days shalt thou **e** unleavened bread	398
	16: 7 **e** *it* in the place which the Lord thy God	398
	16: 8 Six days thou shalt **e** unleavened bread:	398
	18: 1 they shall **e** the offerings of the Lord	398
	18: 8 They shall have like portions to **e**, beside	398
	20: 6 die in the battle, and another man **e** of it.	2490
	20:14 thou shalt **e** the spoil of thine enemies,	398
	20:19 thou mayest **e** of them, and thou shalt not	398
	23:24 thou mayest **e** grapes thy fill at thine own	398
	26:12 that they may **e** within thy gates,	398
	27: 7 shalt **e** there, and rejoice before the Lord	398
	28:31 thine eyes, and thou shalt not **e** thereof:	398
	28:33 a nation which thou knowest not **e up**;	398
	28:39 gather the grapes; for the worms shall **e**	398
	28:51 shall **e** the fruit of thy cattle, and the fruit	398
	28:53 thou shalt **e** the fruit of thine own body,	398
	28:55 the flesh of his children whom he shall **e**:	398
	28:57 for she shall **e** them for want of all *things*	398
	32:13 that he might **e** the increase of the fields;	398
	32:38 Which did **e** the fat of their sacrifices,	398
Jos	5:11 they did **e** of the old corn of the land on	398
	5:12 did **e** of the fruit of the land of Canaan	398
	24:13 oliveyards which ye planted not do ye **e**.	398
Jdg	9:27 did **e** and drink, and cursed Abimelech.	398
	13: 4 strong drink, and **e** not any unclean *thing*:	398
	13: 7 neither **e** any unclean *thing*: for the child	398
	13:14 She may not **e** of any *thing* that cometh of	398
	13:14 nor **e** any unclean *thing*: all that I	398
	13:16 thou detain me, I will not **e** of thy bread:	398
	14: 9 and he gave them, and they did **e**:	398
	19: 4 so they did **e** and drink, and lodged there.	398
	19: 6 and did **e** and drink both of them together:	398
	19: 8 afternoon, and they did **e** both of them.	398
	19:21 washed their feet, and did **e** and drink.	398
Ru	2:14 **e** of the bread, and dip thy morsel in	398
	2:14 reached her parched *corn*, and she did **e**,	398
1Sa	1: 7 therefore she wept, and did not **e**.	398
	1:18 did **e**, and her countenance was no more	398
	2:36 offices, that *I* may **e** a piece of bread.	398
	9:13 before he go up to the high place to **e**:	398
	9:13 for the people will not **e** until he come,	398
	9:13 *and* afterwards they **e** that be bidden.	398
	9:19 ye shall **e** with me to day, and to morrow	398
	9:24 that which is left; set *it* before thee, *and* **e**:	398
	9:24 So Saul did **e** with Samuel that day.	398
	14:32 and the people did **e** *them* with the blood.	398
	14:33 the Lord, in that they **e** with the blood.	398
	14:34 man his sheep, and slay *them* here, and **e**;	398
	20:24 come, the king sat him down to **e** meat.	398
	20:34 **e** no meat the second day of the month:	398
	28:22 **e**, that thou mayest have strength,	398
	28:23 he refused, and said, I will not **e**. But his	398
	28:25 and before his servants; and they did **e**.	398
	30:11 David, and gave him bread, and he did **e**;	398
2Sa	3:35 **cause** David to **e** meat while it was yet	1262
	7 thou shalt **e** bread at my table continually.	398
	9:10 that thy master's son may have food to **e**:	398
	9:10 thy master's son shall **e** bread	398
	9:11 *said* the king, he shall **e** at my table,	398
	9:13 for he did **e** continually at the king's table;	398
	11:11 to **e** and to drink, and to lie with my wife?	398
	11:13 called him, he did **e** and drink before him;	398
	12: 3 it did **e** of his own meat, and drank of his	398
	12:17 neither did he **e** bread with them.	1262
	12:20 they set bread before him, and he did **e**.	398
	12:21 was dead, thou didst rise and **e** bread.	398
	13: 5 that I may see *it*, and **e** *it* at her hand.	398
	13: 6 in my sight, that I may **e** at her hand.	1262
	13: 9 *them* out before him; but he refused to **e**.	398
	13:10 the chamber, that I may **e** of thine hand.	1262
	13:11 she had brought *them* unto him to **e**,	398
	16: 2 and summer fruit for the young men to **e**;	398
	17:29 for the people that *were* with him, to **e**:	398
	19:28 among them that did **e** at thine own table.	398
	19:35 can thy servant taste what I **e** or what I	398
1Ki	1:25 they **e** and drink before him, and say,	398
	2: 7 let them be of *those* that **e** at thy table:	398
	13: 8 neither will I **e** bread nor drink water in	398

1Ki	13: 9 **E** no bread, nor drink water,	398
	13:15 him, Come home with me, and **e** bread.	398
	13:16 neither will I **e** bread nor drink water with	398
	13:17 shalt **e** no bread nor drink water there,	398
	13:18 that he may **e** bread and drink water.	398
	13:19 did **e** bread in his house, and drank water.	398
	13:22 to me, Come home with me, and **e** bread;	398
	13:22 the place, of the which the LORD did say to him, Eat no bread, and drink no water:	398
	14:11 of Jeroboam in the city shall the dogs **e**;	398
	14:11 dieth in the field shall the fowls of the air **e**:	398
	16: 4 dieth of Baasha in the city shall the dogs **e**;	398
	16: 4 his in the fields shall the fowls of the air **e**.	398
	17:12 me and my son, that we may **e** it, and die.	398
	17:15 and he, and her house, did **e** *many* days.	398
	18:19 four hundred, which **e** *at* Jezebel's table.	398
	18:41 said unto Ahab, Get thee up, **e** and drink;	398
	18:42 So Ahab went up to **e** and to drink.	398
	19: 5 him, and said unto him, Arise *and* **e**.	398
	19: 6 he did **e** and drink, and laid him down	398
	19: 7 and touched him, and said, Arise *and* **e**;	398
	19: 8 did **e** and drink, and went in the strength	398
	19:21 and gave unto the people, and they did **e**.	398
	21: 4 away his face, and would **e** no bread.	398
	21: 7 *and* **e** bread, and let thine heart be merry:	398
	21:23 The dogs shall **e** Jezebel by the wall of	398
	21:24 dieth of Ahab in the city shall the dogs **e**;	398
	21:24 in the field shall the fowls of the air **e**.	398
2Ki	4: 8 and she constrained him to **e** bread.	398
	4: 8 passed by, he turned in thither to **e** bread.	398
	4:40 So they poured out for the men to **e**.	398
	4:40 in the pot. And they could not **e** *thereof*.	398
	4:41 Pour out for the people, that they may **e**.	398
	4:42 Give unto the people, that they may **e**.	398
	4:43 again, Give the people, that they may **e**.	398
	4:43 They shall **e**, and shall leave *thereof*.	398
	4:44 they did **e**, and left *thereof*, according to	398
	6:22 that they may **e** and drink, and go to their	398
	6:28 that we may **e** him to day, and we will eat	398
	6:28 to day, and we will **e** my son to morrow.	398
	6:29 So we boiled my son, and did **e** him:	398
	6:29 day, Give thy son, that we may **e** him:	398
	7: 2 *it* with thine eyes, but shalt not **e** thereof.	398
	7: 8 did **e** and drink, and carried thence silver,	398
	7:19 *it* with thine eyes, but shalt not **e** thereof.	398
	9:10 the dogs shall **e** Jezebel in the portion of	398
	9:34 come in, he did **e** and drink, and said,	398
	9:36 In the portion of Jezreel shall dogs **e**	398
	18:27 that *they* may **e** their own dung, and drink	398
	18:31 *then* ye every man of his own vine,	398
	19:29 Ye shall **e** *this* year such things as grow of	398
	19:29 plant vineyards, and **e** the fruits thereof.	398
	23: 9 they did **e** of the unleavened bread among	398
	25:29 he did **e** bread continually before him all	398
1Ch	29:22 did **e** and drink before the LORD on that	398
2Ch	28:15 **gave** them to **e** and to drink,	398
	30:18 yet did they **e** the passover otherwise than	398
	30:22 they did **e** throughout the feast seven days,	398
	31:10 *we* have had enough to **e**, and have left	398
Ezr	2:63 they should not **e** of the most holy *things*	398
	6:21 to seek the LORD God of Israel, did **e**,	398
	9:12 **e** the good of the land, and leave *it* for an	398
	10: 6 he did **e** no bread, nor drink water:	398
Ne	5: 2 we take up corn *for them*, that we may **e**,	398
	7:65 that they should not **e** of the most holy	398
	8:10 Go *your way*, **e** the fat, and drink the	398
	8:12 all the people went their *way* to **e**,	398
	9:25 so they did **e**, and were filled,	398
	9:36 gavest unto our fathers to **e** the fruit	398
Est	4:16 **e** nor drink three days, night or day;	398
Job	1: 4 sent and called for their three sisters to **e**	398
	3:24 For my sighing cometh before I **e**,	3899
	31: 8 *Then* let me sow, and let another **e**; yea,	398
	42:11 and did **e** bread with him in his house:	398
Ps	14: 4 who **e up** my people *as* they eat bread,	398
	14: 4 who eat up my people *as* they **e** bread,	398
	22:26 The meek shall **e** and be satisfied: they	398
	22:29 All *they that be* fat upon earth shall **e** and	398
	27: 2 my foes, came upon me to **e up** my flesh,	398
	41: 9 whom I trusted, which did **e** *of* my bread,	398
	50:13 I **e** the flesh of bulls, or drink the blood	398
	53: 4 who **e up** my people *as* they eat bread:	398
	53: 4 who eat up my people *as* they **e** bread:	398
	78:24 had rained down manna upon them to **e**,	398
	78:25 Man did **e** angels' food: he sent them meat	398
	78:29 So they did **e**, and were well filled: for he	398
	102: 4 like grass; so that I forget to **e** my bread.	398
	105:35 did **e up** all the herbs in their land,	398
	127: 2 to sit up late, to **e** the bread of sorrows;	398
	128: 2 For thou shalt **e** the labour of thine hands:	398
	141: 4 and let me not **e** of their dainties.	3898
Pr	1:31 Therefore shall they **e** of the fruit of their	398
	4:17 For they **e** the bread of wickedness,	3898
	9: 5 **e** of my bread, and drink of the wine	3898
	13: 2 man shall **e** good by the fruit of *his* mouth:	398
	13: 2 the soul of the transgressors shall **e**	NIH
	18:21 they that love it shall **e** the fruit thereof.	398
	23: 1 When thou sittest to **e** with a ruler,	3898
	23: 6 **E** thou not the bread of *him that hath* an	3898
	23: 7 **E** and drink, saith he to thee; but his heart	398
	24:13 My son, **e** thou honey, because *it is* good;	398
	25:16 **e** so much as is sufficient for thee, lest thou	398
	25:21 enemy *be* hungry, give him bread to **e**;	398
	25:27 *It is* not good to **e** much honey: so *for men*	398
	27:18 Whoso keepeth the fig tree shall **e** the fruit	398
	30:17 pick it out, and the young eagles shall **e** it.	398
Ecc	2:24 that he should **e** and drink, and *that he*	398

Ecc	2:25 For who can **e**, or who else can hasten	398
	3:13 also that every man should **e** and drink,	398
	5:11 they are increased that **e** them:	398
	5:12 *man is* sweet, whether he **e** little or much:	398
	5:18 good and comely *for one* to **e** and to drink,	398
	5:19 hath given him power to **e** thereof,	398
	6: 2 yet God giveth him not power to **e** thereof,	398
	8:15 than to **e**, and to drink, and to be merry:	398
	9: 7 Go *thy way*, **e** thy bread with joy,	398
	10:16 a child, and thy princes **e** in the morning.	398
	10:17 thy princes **e** in due season, for strength,	398
SS	4:16 into his garden, and **e** his pleasant fruits.	398
	5: 1 **e**, O friends; drink, yea, drink abundantly,	398
Isa	1:19 obedient, ye shall **e** the good of the land:	398
	3:10 *it shall be* well *with him*: for they shall **e**	398
	4: 1 We will **e** our own bread, and wear our	398
	5:17 places of the fat ones shall strangers **e**.	398
	7:15 Butter and honey shall he **e**, that he may	398
	7:22 milk *that they* shall give he shall **e** butter:	398
	7:22 honey shall every one **e** that is left in	398
	9:20 he shall **e** on the left hand, and they shall	398
	9:20 they shall **e** every man the flesh of his own	398
	11: 7 and the lion shall **e** straw like the ox.	398
	21: 5 table, watch *in* the watchtower, **e**, drink:	398
	22:13 let us **e** and drink; for to morrow we shall	398
	23:18 to **e** sufficiently, and for durable clothing.	398
	30:24 the young asses that ear the ground shall **e**	398
	36:12 that *they* may **e** their own dung, and drink	398
	36:16 **e** ye every one *of* his vine, and every one	398
	37:30 Ye shall **e** *this* year such as growth of	398
	37:30 plant vineyards, and **e** the fruit thereof.	398
	50: 9 as a garment; the moth shall **e** them **up**.	398
	51: 8 the moth shall **e** them **up** like a garment,	398
	51: 8 and the worm shall **e** them like wool:	398
	55: 1 come ye, buy, and **e**; yea, come, buy wine	398
	55: 2 ye *that which is* good, and let your soul	398
	61: 6 ye shall **e** the riches of the Gentiles,	398
	62: 9 they that have gathered it shall **e** it,	398
	65: 4 which **e** swine's flesh, and broth of	398
	65:13 my servants shall **e**, but ye shall be hungry:	398
	65:21 plant vineyards, and **e** the fruit of them.	398
	65:22 they shall not plant, and another **e**:	398
	65:25 and the lion shall **e** straw like the bullock:	398
Jer	2: 7 to **e** the fruit thereof and the goodness	398
	5:17 shall **e up** thine harvest, and thy bread,	398
	5:17 thy sons and thy daughters should **e**:	398
	5:17 they shall **e up** thy flocks and thine herds:	398
	5:17 they shall **e up** thy vines and thy fig trees:	398
	7:21 offerings unto your sacrifices, and **e** flesh.	398
	15:16 Thy words were found, and I did **e** them;	398
	16: 8 feasting, to sit with them to **e** and to drink.	398
	19: 9 will **cause** them to **e** the flesh of their sons	398
	19: 9 shall **e** every one the flesh of his friend	398
	22:15 did not thy father **e** and drink,	398
	22:22 The wind shall **e up** all thy pastors,	7462
	29: 5 and plant gardens, and **e** the fruit of them;	398
	29:28 and plant gardens, and **e** the fruit of them;	398
	31: 5 and shall **e** *them* **as common things**.	2490
	41: 1 there they did **e** bread together in Mizpah.	398
	52:33 he did continually **e** bread before him all	398
La	2:20 Shall the women **e** their fruit, *and* children	398
Eze	2: 8 open thy mouth, and **e** that I give thee.	398
	3: 1 unto me, Son of man, **e** that thou findest;	398
	3: 1 **e** this roll, and go speak unto the house of	398
	3: 2 mouth, and **caused** me to **e** that roll.	398
	3: 3 **cause** thy belly to **e**, and fill thy bowels	398
	3: 3 did I **e** *it*; and it was in my mouth as honey	398
	4: 9 and ninety days shalt thou **e** thereof.	398
	4:10 thy meat which thou shalt **e** *shall be* by	398
	4:10 a day: from time to time shalt thou **e** it.	398
	4:12 thou shalt **e** it *as* barley cakes, and thou	398
	4:13 thus shall the children of Israel **e** their	398
	4:16 shall **e** bread by weight, and with care;	398
	12:18 **e** thy bread with quaking, and drink thy	398
	12:19 They shall **e** their bread with carefulness,	398
	16:13 thou didst **e** fine flour, and honey, and oil:	398
	22: 9 in thee they **e** upon the mountains:	398
	24:17 not thy lips, and **e** not the bread of men.	398
	24:22 not cover *your* lips, nor **e** the bread of men.	398
	25: 4 they shall **e** thy fruit, and they shall drink	398
	33:25 Ye **e** with the blood, and lift up your eyes	398
	34: 3 Ye **e** the fat, and ye clothe you with	398
	34:19 they **e** that which ye have trodden with	7462
	39:17 that ye may **e** flesh, and drink blood.	398
	39:18 Ye shall **e** the flesh of the mighty,	398
	39:19 ye shall **e** fat till *ye* be full, and drink blood	398
	42:13 the most holy *things*: there shall they lay	398
	44: 3 he shall sit in it to **e** bread before	398
	44:29 They shall **e** the meat offering, and the sin	398
	44:31 The priests shall not **e** of any thing that is	398
Da	1:12 let them give us pulse to **e**, and water to	398
	1:13 the countenance of the children that **e** *of*	398
	1:15 which did **e** the portion of the king's meat.	398
	4:25 they shall **make** thee to **e** grass as oxen,	2939
	4:32 they shall **make** thee to **e** grass as oxen,	2939
	4:33 did **e** grass as oxen, and his body was wet	399
Hos	2:12 and the beasts of the field shall **e** them.	398
	4: 8 They **e up** the sin of my people, and they	398
	4:10 For they shall **e**, and not have enough:	398
	8:13 and **e** *it; but* the LORD accepteth them not;	398
	9: 3 and they shall **e** unclean *things* in Assyria;	398
	9: 4 all that **e** thereof shall be polluted:	398
Joel	2:26 ye shall **e in plenty**, and be satisfied,	398+398

Am	6: 4 **e** the lambs out of the flock, and the calves	398
	7: 4 the great deep, and did **e up** a part.	398
	7:12 and there **e** bread, and prophesy there:	398
	9:14 also make gardens, and **e** the fruit of them.	398
Ob	1: 7 *they that* **e** thy bread have laid a wound	NIH
Mic	3: 3 Who also **e** the flesh of my people,	398
	6:14 Thou shalt **e**, but not be satisfied;	398
Na	1: 7 *there is* no cluster to **e**: my soul desired	398
	3:15 it shall **e thee up** like the cankerworm;	398
Hab	1: 8 they shall fly as the eagle *that* hasteth to **e**.	398
Hag	1: 6 ye **e**, but ye have not enough; ye drink,	398
Zec	7: 6 when ye did **e**, and when ye did drink,	398
	7: 6 did not ye **e** *for yourselves*, and drink *for*	398
	11: 9 the rest **e** every one the flesh of another.	398
	11:16 he shall **e** the flesh of the fat, and tear their	398
Mt	6:25 what ye shall **e**, or what ye shall drink;	5315
	6:31 take no thought, saying, What shall we **e**?	5315
	12: 1 began to pluck the ears of corn, and to **e**.	2068
	12: 4 and did **e** the shewbread, which was not	5315
	12: 4 which was not lawful for him to **e**,	5315
	14:16 They need not depart; give ye them to **e**.	5315
	14:20 And they did all **e**, and were filled:	5315
	15: 2 they wash not their hands when they **e**	2068
	15:20 to **e** with unwashen hands defileth not a	5315
	15:27 yet the dogs **e** of the crumbs which fall	2068
	15:32 now three days, and have nothing to **e**:	5315
	15:37 And they did all **e**, and were filled:	5315
	15:38 And they that did **e** were four thousand	2068
	24:49 and to **e** and drink with the drunken;	2068
	26:17 we prepare for thee to **e** the passover?	5315
	26:21 as they did **e**, he said, Verily I say unto	2068
	26:26 gave *it* to the disciples, and said, Take, **e**;	5315
Mk	1: 6 and he did **e** locusts and wild honey;	2068
	2:16 Pharisees saw him **e** with publicans and	2068
	2:26 and did **e** the shewbread, which is not	5315
	2:26 is not lawful to **e** but for the priests,	5315
	3:20 that they could not so much as **e** bread.	2068
	5:43 that *something* should be given her to **e**.	5315
	6:31 and they had no leisure so much as to **e**.	2068
	6:36 for they have nothing to **e**.	5315
	6:37 and said unto them, Give ye them to **e**.	5315
	6:37 pennyworth of bread, and give them to **e**?	5315
	6:42 And they did all **e**, and were filled.	5315
	6:44 And they that did **e** of the loaves were	5315
	7: 2 when they saw some of his disciples **e**	2068
	7: 3 except they wash *their* hands oft, **e** not,	2068
	7: 4 market, except they wash, they **e** not.	2068
	7: 5 but **e** bread with unwashen hands?	2068
	7:28 yet the dogs under the table **e** of	2068
	8: 1 and having nothing to **e**, Jesus called his	5315
	8: 2 me three days, and have nothing to **e**:	5315
	8: 8 So they did **e**, and were filled:	5315
	11:14 No man **e** fruit of thee hereafter for ever.	5315
	14:12 prepare that thou mayest **e** the passover?	5315
	14:14 where I shall **e** the passover with my	5315
	14:18 And as they sat and did **e**, Jesus said,	2068
	14:22 And as they did **e**, Jesus took bread,	2068
	14:22 and gave to them, and said, Take, **e**:	5315
Lk	4: 2 And in those days he did **e** nothing:	5315
	5:30 Why do ye **e** and drink with publicans	2068
	5:33 of the Pharisees; but thine **e** and drink?	2068
	6: 1 and did **e**, rubbing *them* in *their* hands.	2068
	6: 4 God, and did take and **e** the shewbread,	5315
	6: 4 it is not lawful to **e** but for the priests	5315
	7:36 desired him that he would **e** with him.	5315
	9:13 he said unto them, Give ye them to **e**.	5315
	9:17 And they did **e**, and were all filled:	5315
	10: 8 **e** such *things* as are set before you:	5315
	12:19 take thine ease, **e**, drink, *and* be merry.	5315
	12:22 no thought for your life, what ye shall **e**;	5315
	12:29 seek not ye what ye shall **e**, or what ye	5315
	12:45 and to **e** and drink, and to be drunken;	2068
	14: 1 Pharisees to **e** bread on the sabbath day,	5315
	14:15 Blessed *is* he that shall **e** bread in	5315
	15:16 belly with the husks that the swine did **e**:	2068
	15:23 and kill *it*; and let us **e**, and be merry:	5315
	17: 8 and afterward thou shalt **e** and drink?	5315
	17:27 They did **e**, they drank, they married	2068
	17:28 they did **e**, they drank, they bought,	2068
	22: 8 prepare us the passover, that we may **e**.	5315
	22:11 where I shall **e** the passover with my	5315
	22:15 With desire I have desired to **e** this	5315
	22:16 unto you, I will not any more **e** thereof,	5315
	22:30 ye may **e** and drink at my table in my	2068
	24:43 And he took *it*, and did **e** before them.	5315
Jn	4:31 disciples prayed him, saying, Master, **e**.	5315
	4:32 I have meat to **e** that ye know not of.	5315
	4:33 Hath any *man* brought him *ought* to **e**?	5315
	6: 5 shall we buy bread, that these may **e**?	5315
	6:23 unto the place where they did **e** bread,	5315
	6:26 but because ye did **e** of the loaves,	5315
	6:31 Our fathers did **e** manna in the desert;	5315
	6:31 He gave them bread from heaven to **e**.	5315
	6:49 fathers did **e** manna in the wilderness,	5315
	6:50 from heaven, that a man may **e** thereof,	5315
	6:51 if any *man* **e** of this bread, he shall live for	5315
	6:52 How can this *man* give us *his* flesh to **e**?	5315
	6:53 Except ye **e** the flesh of the Son of man,	5315
	6:58 not as your fathers did **e** manna,	5315
	18:28 but that they might **e** the passover.	5315
Ac	2:46 did **e** *their* meat with gladness and	3335
	9: 9 without sight, and neither did **e** nor drink.	5315
	10:13 a voice to him, Rise, Peter; kill, and **e**.	5315
	10:41 did **e** and drink with him after he rose	4906
	11: 3 uncircumcised, and didst **e** **with** them.	4906

E

Ac	11: 7 saying unto me, Arise, Peter; slay and e.	5315	
	23:12 that *they* would neither e nor drink	5315	
	23:14 that *we* will e nothing until we have slain	1089	
	23:21 that *they* will neither e nor drink till they	5315	
	27:35 when he had broken *it*, he began to e.	2068	
Ro	14: 2 one believeth that *he* may e all *things*;	5315	
	14:21 for to e flesh, nor to drink	5315	
	14:23 And he that doubteth is damned if he e,	5315	
1Co	5:11 extortioner; **with** such a one no no to e.	4906	
	8: 7 e *it* as a thing offered unto an idol;	2068	
	8: 8 for neither, if we e, are we the better;	5315	
	8: 8 neither, if we e not, are we the worse.	5315	
	8:10 e those things which are offered to idols;	2068	
	8:13 I will e no flesh while the world standeth,	5315	
	9: 4 Have we not power to e and to drink?	5315	
	10: 3 And did all e the same spiritual meat;	5315	
	10: 7 The people sat down to e and drink,	2068	
	10:18 are not they which e *of* the sacrifices	2068	
	10:25 is sold in the shambles, *that* e,	2068	
	10:27 whatsoever is set before you, e, asking no	2068	
	10:28 e not for his sake that shewed *it*, and	2068	
	10:31 Whether therefore ye e, or drink,	2068	
	11:20 place, *this* is not to e the Lord's supper.	2068	
	11:22 have ye not houses to e and to drink *in*?	2068	
	11:24 thanks, he brake *it*, and said, Take, e:	5315	
	11:26 For as often as ye e this bread,	2068	
	11:27 Wherefore whosoever shall e this bread,	2068	
	11:28 so let him e of *that* bread, and drink of	2068	
	11:33 brethren, when ye come together to e,	5315	
	11:34 if any *man* hunger, let him e at home;	2068	
	15:32 let us e and drink; for to morrow we die.	5315	
Gal	2:12 from James, he did e with the Gentiles:	4906	
2Th	3: 8 Neither did we e any *man's* bread for	5315	
	3:10 any would not work, neither should he e.	2068	
	3:12 they work, and e their own bread.	2068	
2Ti	2:17 And their word will e as doth a	2192+3542	
Heb	13:10 they have no right to e whereof serve	5315	
Jas	5: 3 and shall e your flesh as *it were* fire:	5315	
Rev	2: 7 To him that overcometh will I give to e of	5315	
	2:14 to e things sacrificed unto idols,	5315	
	2:17 To him that overcometh will I give to e of	5315	
	2:20 and to e things sacrificed unto idols.	5315	
	10: 9 And he said unto me, Take *it*, and e *it* up;	2719	
	17:16 shall e her flesh, and burn her with fire.	5315	
	19:18 That ye may e the flesh of kings,	5315	

EATEN (104) [EAT]

Ge	3:11 Hast thou e of the tree, whereof I	398	
	3:17 hast e of the tree, of which I commanded	398	
	6:21 take thou unto thee of all food that is e,	398	
	14:24 only that which the young men have e,	398	
	27:33 I have e of all before thou camest,	398	
	31:38 and the rams of thy flock have I not e.	398	
	41:21 when they had e them,	413+935+7130	
	41:21 be known that they had e them;	413+935+7130	
	43: 2 when they had e up the corn which they	398	
Ex	12:46 In one house shall it be e; thou shalt not	398	
	13: 3 *place:* there shall no leavened bread be e.	398	
	13: 7 Unleavened bread be seven days;	398	
	21:28 surely stoned, and his flesh shall not be e;	398	
	22: 5 shall **cause** a field or vineyard to be e,	1197	
	29:34 fire: it shall not be e, because it *is* holy.	398	
Lev	6:16 *with* unleavened bread shall it be e in	398	
	6:23 be wholly *burnt:* it shall not be e.	398	
	6:26 in the holy place shall it be e, in the court	398	
	6:30 *withal* in the holy *place,* shall be e:	398	
	7: 6 shall be e in the holy place: it *is* most holy.	398	
	7:15 shall be the same day that it is offered;	398	
	7:16 it shall be e the *same* day that he offereth	398	
	7:16 morrow also the remainder of it shall be e:	398	
	7:18 offerings be e **at all** on the third day,	398+398	
	7:19 toucheth any unclean *thing* shall not be e;	398	
	10:17 Wherefore have ye not e the sin offering in	398	
	10:18 **indeed** have e it in the holy *place,*	398+398	
	10:19 *if* I had e the sin offering to day, should it	398	
	11:13 shall not be e, they *are* an abomination.	398	
	11:34 Of all meat which may be e, that on which	398	
	11:41 *shall* be an abomination; it shall not be e.	398	
	11:47 between the beast that may be e and	398	
	11:47 be eaten and the beast that may not be e.	398	
	17:13 catcheth *any* beast or fowl that may be e;	398	
	19: 6 It shall be e the *same* day ye offer it,	398	
	19: 7 if it be e **at all** on the third day, it *is*	398+398	
	19:23 uncircumcised unto you: it shall not be e	398	
	22:30 On the same day it shall be e up; ye shall	398	
Nu	28:17 seven days shall unleavened bread be e.	398	
Dt	6:11 when thou shalt have e and be full;	398	
	8:10 When thou hast e and art full, then thou	398	
	8:12 Lest *when* thou hast e and art full,	398	
	12:22 Even as the roebuck and the hart is e,	398	
	14:19 *is* unclean unto you: they shall not be e.	398	
	20: 6 a vineyard, and hath not *yet* e of it?	2490	
	26:14 I have not e thereof in my mourning,	398	
	29: 6 have not e bread, neither have you drunk	398	
	31:20 they shall have e and filled *themselves,*	398	
Jos	5:12 after they had e of the old corn of the land;	398	
Ru	3: 7 when Boaz had e and drunk, and his heart	398	
1Sa	1: 9 So Hannah rose up after *they* had e in	398	
	14:30 if haply the people had e **freely** to day	398+398	
	28:20 for he had e no bread all the day, nor all	398	
	30:12 he had e, his spirit came again to him:	398	
	30:12 he had e no bread, nor drunk *any* water,	398	
2Sa	19:42 have we e **at all** of the king's *cost?*	398+398	
1Ki	13:22 hast e bread and drunk water in the place,	398	
	13:23 he had e bread, and after he had drunk,	398	

1Ki	13:28 the lion had not e the carcase, nor torn	398	
2Ki	6:23 when they had e and drunk, he sent them	398	
Ne	5:14 my brethren have not e the bread of	398	
Job	6: 6 Can that which is unsavoury be e without	398	
	31:17 Or have e my morsel myself alone,	398	
	31:17 and the fatherless hath not e thereof;	398	
	31:39 I have e the fruits thereof without money,	398	
Ps	69: 9 For the zeal of thine house hath e me **up**;	398	
	102: 9 For I have e ashes like bread,	398	
Pr	9:17 sweet, and bread *e* in secret is pleasant.	NIH	
	23: 8 The morsel *which* thou hast e shalt thou	398	
SS	5: 1 I have e my honeycomb with my honey;	398	
Isa	3:14 for ye have e **up** the vineyard; the spoil of	1197	
	5: 5 the hedge thereof, and it shall be e **up**;	1197	
	6:13 a tenth, and *it* shall return, and shall be e:	1197	
	44:19 e *it:* and shall I make the residue thereof an	398	
Jer	10:25 for they have e **up** Jacob, and devoured	398	
	24: 2 which could not be e, they were so bad.	398	
	24: 3 very evil, that cannot be e, they are so evil.	398	
	24: 8 figs, which cannot be e, they are so evil;	398	
	29:17 vile figs, that cannot be e, they are so evil.	398	
	31:29 The fathers have e a sour grape,	398	
Eze	4:14 have I not e *of* that which dieth of itself,	398	
	18: 2 The fathers have e sour grapes,	398	
	18: 6 *And* hath not e upon the mountains,	398	
	18:11 but even hath e upon the mountains,	398	
	18:15 *That* hath not e upon the mountains,	398	
	34:18 unto you to have e **up** the good pasture,	7462	
	45:21 seven days; unleavened bread shall be e.	398	
Hos	10:13 reaped iniquity; ye have e the fruit of lies:	398	
Joel	1: 4 palmerworm hath left hath the locust e;	398	
	1: 4 locust hath left hath the cankerworm e;	398	
	1: 4 cankerworm hath left hath the caterpillar e.	398	
	2:25 to you the years that the locust hath e,	398	
Mt	14:21 And they that had e were about five	2068	
Mk	8: 9 And they that had e were about four	5315	
Lk	13:26 We have e and drunk in thy presence,	5315	
	17: 8 and serve me, till I have e and drunken;	5315	
Jn	2:17 The zeal of thine house hath e me **up**.	2719	
	6:13 and above unto them that had e.	977	
Ac	10:10 became very hungry, and would have e:	1089	
	10:14 I have never e any *thing that* is common	5315	
	12:23 and he was e of worms, and gave up	4662	
	20:11 and e, and talked a long while,	1089	
	27:38 And when they had e **enough**,	2880+5160	
Rev	10:10 and as soon as I had e it, my belly was	5315	

EATER (3) [EAT]

Jdg	14:14 Out of the e came forth meat, and out of	398	
Isa	55:10 give seed to the sower, and bread to the e:	398	
Na	3:12 they shall even fall into the mouth of the e.	398	

EATERS (1) [EAT]

Pr	23:20 amongst *riotous* e of flesh:	2151	

EATEST (3) [EAT]

Ge	2:17 in the day that thou e thereof thou shalt	398	
1Sa	1: 8 why e thou not? and why is thy heart	398	
1Ki	21: 5 is thy spirit so sad, that thou e no bread?	398	

EATETH (56) [EAT]

Ex	12:15 for whosoever e leavened bread from	398	
	12:19 for whosoever e that which is leavened,	398	
Lev	7:18 the soul that e of it shall bear his iniquity.	398	
	7:20 the soul that e *of* the flesh of the sacrifice	398	
	7:25 For whosoever e the fat of the beast,	398	
	7:25 even the soul that e *it* shall be cut off from	398	
	7:27 Whatsoever soul *it be* that e any manner	398	
	11:40 that e of the carcase of it shall wash his	398	
	14:47 that e in the house shall wash his clothes.	398	
	17:10 among you, that e any *manner of* blood;	398	
	17:10 even set my face against *that* soul that e	398	
	17:14 whosoever e it shall be cut off.	398	
	17:15 every soul e that which died of itself,	398	
	19: 8 Therefore *every one* that e it shall bear his	398	
Nu	13:32 *is* a land that e **up** the inhabitants thereof;	398	
1Sa	14:24 Cursed *be* the man that e *any* food until	398	
	14:28 Cursed *be* the man that e *any* food this	398	
Job	5: 5 Whose harvest the hungry e **up**, and taketh	398	
	21:25 of his soul, and never e with pleasure.	398	
	40:15 I made with thee; he e grass as an ox.	398	
Ps	106:20 into the similitude of an ox that e grass.	398	
Pr	13:25 The righteous e to the satisfying of his soul:	398	
	30:20 she e, and wipeth her mouth, and saith,	398	
	31:27 and e not the bread of idleness.	398	
Ecc	4: 5 his hands together, and e his own flesh.	398	
	5:17 All his days also he e in darkness,	398	
	6: 2 power to eat thereof, but a stranger e it:	398	
Isa	28: 4 while it is yet in his hand he e it **up**.	1104	
	29: 8 hungry *man* dreameth, and, behold, he e;	398	
	44:16 part thereof he e flesh; he roasteth roast,	398	
	59: 5 he that e of their eggs dieth, and *that*	398	
Jer	31:30 every man that e the sour grape, his teeth	398	
Mt	9:11 Why e your Master with publicans and	2068	
Mk	2:16 How *is it* that he e and drinketh with	2068	
	14:18 One of you which e with me shall betray	2068	
Lk	15: 2 *man* receiveth sinners, and e with them.	4906	
Jn	6:54 e my flesh, and drinketh my blood,	5176	
	6:56 that e my flesh, and drinketh my blood,	5176	
	6:57 so he that e me, even he shall live by me.	5176	
	6:58 he that e of this bread shall live for ever.	5176	
	13:18 He that e bread with me hath lift up his	5176	
Ro	14: 2 all *things:* another, who is weak, e herbs.	2068	
	14: 3 Let not him that e despise him that eateth	2068	
	14: 3 Let not him that e despise him that e	2068	

Ro	14: 3 let not him which e not judge him that	2068	
	14: 3 him which eateth not judge him that e	2068	
	14: 6 the Lord he doth not regard *it*. He that e,	2068	
	14: 6 e to the Lord, for he giveth God thanks;	2068	
	14: 6 he that e not, to the Lord he eateth not,	2068	
	14: 6 to the Lord he e not, and giveth God	2068	
	14:20 *it is* evil for *that* man who e with offence.	2068	
	14:23 damned if he eat, because *he* e not of faith:	NIG	
1Co	9: 7 a vineyard, and e not of the fruit thereof?	2068	
	9: 7 a flock, and e not of the milk of the flock?	2068	
	11:29 For he that e and drinketh unworthily,	2068	
	11:29 and drinketh damnation to himself,	2068	

EATING (27) [EAT]

Ex	12: 4 every man according to his e shall make	400	
	16:16 Gather of it every man according to his e,	400	
	16:18 gathered every man according to his e.	400	
	16:21 every man according to his e:	400	
Jdg	14: 9 went on e, and came to his father and	398	
Ru	3: 3 until he shall have done e and drinking.	398	
1Sa	14:34 sin not against the Lᴏʀᴅ in e with	398	
	30:16 e and drinking, and dancing, because of all	398	
1Ki	1:41 heard *it* as they had made an end of e.	398	
	4:20 e and drinking, and making merry.	398	
2Ki	4:40 they were e of the pottage, that they cried	398	
1Ch	12:39 with David three days, e and drinking:	398	
Job	1:13 when his sons and his daughters *were* e	398	
	1:18 Thy sons and thy daughters *were* e and	398	
	20:23 and shall rain *it* upon him while he is e.	3894	
Isa	22:13 killing sheep, e flesh, and drinking wine:	398	
	66:17 e swine's flesh, and the abomination,	398	
Am	7: 2 *that* when they had made an end of e	398	
Mt	11:18 For John came neither e nor drinking,	2068	
	11:19 The Son of man came e and drinking,	2068	
	24:38 that were before the flood they were e	5176	
	26:26 And as they were e, Jesus took bread,	2068	
Lk	7:33 For John the Baptist came neither e bread	2068	
	7:34 The Son of man is come e and drinking;	2068	
	10: 7 e and drinking such *things* as they give:	2068	
1Co	8: 4 the e of those things that are offered in	1035	
	11:21 For in e every one taketh before *other* his	5315	

EBAL (8)

Ge	36:23 Manahath, and E, Shepho, and Onam.	5858	
Dt	11:29 and the curse upon mount E.	5858	
	27: 4 in mount E, and thou shalt plaister them	5858	
	27:13 these shall stand upon mount E to curse;	5858	
Jos	8:30 unto the Lᴏʀᴅ God of Israel in mount E,	5858	
	8:33 and half of them over against mount E;	5858	
1Ch	1:22 And E, and Abimael, and Sheba,	5858	
	1:40 Manahath, and E, Shephi, and Onam.	5858	

EBED (6)

Jdg	9:26 Gaal the son of E came with his brethren,	5651	
	9:28 Gaal the son of E said, Who *is* Abimelech,	5651	
	9:30 city heard the words of Gaal the son of E,	5651	
	9:31 Gaal the son of E and his brethren be	5651	
	9:35 Gaal the son of E went out, and stood *in*	5651	
Ezr	8: 6 E the son of Jonathan, and with him fifty	5651	

EBED-MELECH (6)

Jer	38: 7 Now when E the Ethiopian, one of	5663	
	38: 8 E went forth out of the king's house,	5663	
	38:10 the king commanded E the Ethiopian,	5663	
	38:11 So E took the men with him, and went	5663	
	38:12 the Ethiopian said unto Jeremiah,	5663	
	39:16 Go and speak to E the Ethiopian, saying,	5663	

EBEN-EZER (3)

1Sa	4: 1 Philistines to battle, and pitched beside E:	72	
	5: 1 of God, and brought it from E unto Ashdod.	72	
	7:12 and Shen, and called the name of it E,	72	

EBENY (1)

Eze	27:15 thee *for* a present horns of ivory and e.	1894	

EBER (13) [HEBER]

Ge	10:21 the father of all the children of E,	5677	
	10:24 Arphaxad begat Salah; and Salah begat E.	5677	
	10:25 unto E were born two sons: the name of	5677	
	11:14 And Salah lived thirty years, and begat E:	5677	
	11:15 Salah lived after he begat E four hundred	5677	
	11:16 E lived four and thirty years,	5677	
	11:17 E lived after he begat Peleg four hundred	5677	
Nu	24:24 shall afflict E, and he also shall perish for	5677	
1Ch	1:18 begat Shelah, and Shelah begat E.	5677	
	1:19 unto E were born two sons: the name of	5677	
	1:25 E, Peleg, Rehu,	5677	
	8:12 E, and Misham, and Shamed, who built	5677	
Ne	12:20 Of Sallai, Kallai; of Amok, E;	5677	

EBEZ See ABEZ

EBIASAPH (3)

1Ch	6:23 his son, and E his son, and Assir his son,	43	
	6:37 the son of Assir, the son of E, the son of	43	
	9:19 the son of E, the son of Korah,	43	

EBRONAH (2)

Nu	33:34 from Jotbathah, and encamped at E.	5684	
	33:35 they departed from E, and encamped at	5684	

ECBATANA See ACHMETHA

ED (1)

Jos	22:34 the children of Gad called the altar *E:* for it	NIH	

EDAR (1)
Ge 35:21 spread his tent beyond the tower of **E**. 5740

EDEN (20)
Ge 2: 8 God planted a garden eastward in **E**; 5731
 2:10 a river went out of **E** to water the garden; 5731
 2:15 put him into the garden of **E** to dress it 5731
 3:23 God sent him forth from the garden of **E**, 5731
 3:24 he placed at the east of the garden of **E** 5731
 4:16 dwelt in the land of Nod, on the east of **E**. 5731
2Ki 19:12 the children of **E** which *were* in Thelasar? 5729
2Ch 29:12 the son of Zimmah, and **E** the son of Joah: 5731
 31:15 next him *were* **E**, and Miniamin, 5731
Isa 37:12 the children of **E** which *were* in Telassar? 5729
 51: 3 and he will make her wilderness like **E**, 5731
Eze 27:23 Haran, and Canneh, and **E**, the merchants 5729
 28:13 Thou hast been in **E** the garden of God; 5731
 31: 9 so that all the trees of **E**, that *were* in 5731
 31:16 all the trees of **E**, the choice and best of 5731
 31:18 and in greatness among the trees of **E**? 5731
 31:18 trees of **E** unto the nether parts of the 5731
 36:35 desolate is become like the garden of **E**; 5731
Joel 2: 3 the land *is* as the garden of **E** before them, 5731
Am 1: 5 holdeth the sceptre from the house of **E**: 5729

EDER (3)
Jos 15:21 were Kabzeel, and **E**, and Jagur, 5740
1Ch 23:23 Mahli, and **E**, and Jeremoth, three. 5740
 24:30 of Mushi; Mahli, and **E**, and Jerimoth. 5740

EDGE (56) [EDGES, TWOEDGED]
Ge 34:26 Shechem his son with the **e** of the sword, 6310
Ex 13:20 in Etham, in the **e** of the wilderness. 7097
 17:13 and his people with the **e** of the sword. 6310
 26: 4 shalt make loops of blue upon the **e** of 8193
 26: 4 shalt thou make in the uttermost **e** 8193
 26: 5 fifty loops shalt thou make in the **e** of 7097
 26:10 thou shalt make fifty loops on the **e** of 8193
 26:10 fifty loops in the **e** of the curtain which 8193
 36:11 he made loops of blue on the **e** of one 8193
 36:12 fifty loops made he in the **e** of the curtain 7097
 36:17 made fifty loops upon the uttermost **e** of 8193
 36:17 fifty loops made he upon the **e** of 8193
Nu 21:24 Israel smote him with the **e** of the sword, 6310
 33: 6 which *is* in the **e** of the wilderness. 7097
 33:37 mount Hor, in the **e** of the land of Edom. 7097
Dt 13:15 of that city with the **e** of the sword, 6310
 13:15 cattle thereof, with the **e** of the sword. 6310
 20:13 male thereof with the **e** of the sword: 6310
Jos 6:21 sheep, and ass, with the **e** of the sword. 6310
 8:24 *when* they were all fallen on the **e** of 6310
 8:24 and smote it with the **e** of the sword. 6310
 10:28 smote it with the **e** of the sword, 6310
 10:30 he smote it with the **e** of the sword, 6310
 10:32 smote it with the **e** of the sword, and all 6310
 10:35 smote it with the **e** of the sword, and all 6310
 10:37 smote it with the **e** of the sword, 6310
 10:39 they smote them with the **e** of the sword, 6310
 11:11 that *were* therein with the **e** of the sword, 6310
 11:12 smote them with the **e** of the sword, 6310
 11:14 every man they smote with the **e** of 6310
 13:27 unto the **e** of the sea of Cinnereth on 7097
 19:47 smote it with the **e** of the sword, 6310
Jdg 1: 8 smitten it with the **e** of the sword, 6310
 1:25 smote the city with the **e** of the sword, 6310
 4:15 with the **e** of the sword before Barak; 6310
 4:16 all the host of Sisera fell upon the **e** of 6310
 18:27 smote them with the **e** of the sword, 6310
 20:37 smote all the city with the **e** of the sword. 6310
 20:48 smote them with the **e** of the sword, 6310
 21:10 of Jabesh-gilead with the **e** of the sword, 6310
1Sa 15: 8 utterly destroyed all the people with the **e** 6310
 22:19 smote he with the **e** of the sword, 6310
 22:19 asses, and sheep, with the **e** of the sword. 6310
2Sa 15:14 smite the city with the **e** of the sword. 6310
2Ki 10:25 they smote them with the **e** of the sword; 6310
Job 1:15 they have slain the servants with the **e** of 6310
 1:17 slain the servants with the **e** of the sword; 6310
Ps 89:43 Thou hast also turned the **e** of his sword, 6697
Ecc 10:10 he do not whet the **e**, then must he put 6440
Jer 21: 7 shall smite them with the **e** of the sword; 6310
 31:29 and the children's teeth are **set on e**. 6949
 31:30 sour grape, his teeth shall be **set on e**. 6949
Eze 18: 2 and the children's teeth are **set on e**? 6949
 43:13 the border thereof by the **e** thereof round 8193
Lk 21:24 And they shall fall by the **e** of the sword, 4750
Heb 11:34 of fire, escaped the **e** of the sword, 4750

EDGES (4) [EDGE]
Ex 28: 7 *thereof* joined at the two **e** thereof; 7098
 39: 4 by the two **e** was it coupled together. 7098
Jdg 3:16 made him a dagger which had two **e**, 6310
Rev 2:12 which hath the sharp sword **with two e**; 1366

EDIFICATION (4) [EDIFY]
Ro 15: 2 please *his* neighbour for *his* good to **e**. 3619
1Co 14: 3 that prophesieth speaketh unto men *to* **e**, 3619
2Co 10: 8 which the Lord hath given us for **e**, 3619
 13:10 power which the Lord hath given me to **e**, 3619

EDIFIED (2) [EDIFY]
Ac 9:31 and Galilee and Samaria, and were **e**; 3618
1Co 14:17 givest thanks well, but the other is not **e**. 3618

EDIFIETH (3) [EDIFY]
1Co 8: 1 Knowledge puffeth up, but charity **e**. 3618
 14: 4 that speaketh in an *unknown* tongue **e** 3618
 14: 4 but he that prophesieth **e** *the* church. 3618

EDIFY (3) [EDIFICATION, EDIFIED, EDIFIETH, EDIFYING]
Ro 14:19 and *things* wherewith one may **e** another. 3619
1Co 10:23 are lawful for me, but all *things* **e** not. 3618
1Th 5:11 and **e** one another, even as also ye do. 3618

EDIFYING (8) [EDIFY]
1Co 14: 5 interpret, that the church may receive **e**. 3619
 14:12 that ye may excel to the **e** of the church. 3619
 14:26 Let all *things* be done unto **e**. 3619
2Co 12:19 do all *things*, dearly beloved, for your **e**. 3619
Eph 4:12 ministry, for the **e** of the body of Christ: 3619
 4:16 maketh increase of the body unto the **e** of 3619
 4:29 but that which *is* good to the use of **e**, 3619
1Ti 1: 4 rather than godly **e** which is in faith: 3622

EDOM (87) [EDOMITE, EDOMITES, ESAU]
Ge 25:30 *am* faint: therefore was his name called **E**. 123
 32: 3 unto the land of Seir, the country of **E**. 123
 36: 1 *are* the generations of Esau, who *is* **E**. 123
 36: 8 Thus dwelt Esau in mount Seir: Esau *is* **E**. 123
 36:16 *that came* of Eliphaz in the land of **E**; 123
 36:17 dukes *that came* of Reuel in the land of **E**; 123
 36:19 Esau, who *is* **E**, and these *are* their dukes. 123
 36:21 the children of Seir in the land of **E**. 123
 36:31 *are* the kings that reigned in the land of **E**, 123
 36:32 Bela the son of Beor reigned in **E**: 123
 36:43 these *be* the dukes of **E**, according to their 123
Ex 15:15 the dukes of **E** shall be amazed; the mighty 123
Nu 20:14 from Kadesh unto the king of **E**, 123
 20:18 **E** said unto him, Thou shalt not pass by 123
 20:20 **E** came out against him with much people, 123
 20:21 Thus **E** refused to give Israel passage 123
 20:23 by the coast of the land of **E**, saying, 123
 21: 4 of the Red sea, to compass the land of **E**: 123
 24:18 **E** shall be a possession, Seir also shall be a 123
 33:37 in mount Hor, in the edge of the land of **E**. 123
 34: 3 wilderness of Zin along by the coast of **E**, 123
Jos 15: 1 *even* to the border of **E**, the wilderness of 123
 15:21 the coast of **E** southward were Kabzeel, 123
Jdg 5: 4 when thou marchedst out of the field of **E**, 123
 11:17 Israel sent messengers unto the king of **E**, 123
 11:17 the king of **E** would not hearken *thereto*. 123
 11:18 compassed the land of **E**, and the land of 123
1Sa 14:47 against **E**, and against the kings of Zobah, 123
2Sa 8:14 he put garrisons in **E**; throughout all Edom 123
 8:14 throughout all **E** put he garrisons, 123
 8:14 and all they of **E** became David's servants. 123
1Ki 9:26 the shore of the Red sea, in the land of **E**. 123
 11:14 Edomite: he *was* of the king's seed in **E**. 123
 11:15 when David was in **E**, and Joab the captain 123
 11:15 after he had smitten every male in **E**; 123
 11:16 until he had cut off every male in **E**:) 123
 22:47 *There* was then no king in **E**: a deputy *was* 123
2Ki 3: 8 The way through the wilderness of **E**. 123
 3: 9 and the king of Judah, and the king of **E**: 123
 3:12 and the king of **E** went down to him. 123
 3:20 there came water by the way of **E**, 123
 3:26 to break through *even* unto the king of **E**: 123
 8:20 In his days **E** revolted from under the hand 123
 8:22 **E** revolted from under the hand of Judah 123
 14: 7 He slew of **E** in the valley of salt ten 123
 14:10 hast indeed smitten **E**, and thine heart 123
1Ch 1:43 **E** before *any* king reigned over the children 123
 1:51 the dukes of **E** were; duke Timnah, 123
 1:54 duke Iram. These *are* the dukes of **E**. 123
 18:11 from **E**, and from Moab, and from 123
 18:13 he put garrisons in **E**; and all the Edomites 123
2Ch 8:17 to Eloth, at the sea side in the land of **E**. 123
 25:20 because they sought after the gods of **E**. 123
Ps 60: T smote **E** in the valley of salt twelve 123
 60: 8 washpot; over **E** will I cast out my shoe: 123
 60: 9 the strong city? who will lead me into **E**? 123
 83: 6 The tabernacles of **E**, and the Ishmaelites; 123
 108: 9 washpot; over **E** will I cast out my shoe; 123
 108:10 the strong city? who will lead me into **E**? 123
 137: 7 the children of **E** *in* the day of Jerusalem; 123
Isa 11:14 shall lay their hand upon **E** and Moab; 123
 63: 1 Who *is* this *that* cometh from **E**, with 123
Jer 9:26 **E**, and the children of Ammon, and Moab, 123
 25:21 **E**, and Moab, and the children of Ammon, 123
 27: 3 send them to the king of **E**, and to the king 123
 40:11 in **E**, and that *were* in all the countries, 123
 49: 7 Concerning **E**, thus saith the Lᴏʀᴅ of 123
 49:17 Also **E** shall be a desolation: every one that 123
 49:20 of the Lᴏʀᴅ, that he hath taken against **E**; 123
 49:22 **E** be as the heart of a woman in her pangs. 123
La 4:21 Rejoice and be glad, O daughter of **E**, 123
 4:22 will visit thine iniquity, O daughter of **E**; 123
Eze 25:12 Because that **E** hath dealt against the 123
 25:13 I will also stretch out mine hand upon **E**, 123
 25:14 will lay my vengeance upon **E** by the hand 123
 25:14 they shall do in **E** according to mine anger 123
 32:29 There *is* **E**, her kings, and all her princes, 123
Da 11:41 *even* **E**, and Moab, and the chief of 123
Joel 3:19 and **E** shall be a desolate wilderness, 123
Am 1: 6 whole captivity, to deliver *them* up to **E**: 123
 1: 9 they delivered up the whole captivity to **E**, 123
 1:11 For three transgressions of **E**, and for four, 123
 2: 1 burnt the bones of the king of **E** into lime: 123

EDOMITE (7) [EDOM]
Dt 23: 7 Thou shalt not abhor an **E**; for he *is* thy 130
1Sa 21: 7 his name *was* Doeg, an **E**, the chiefest of 130
 22: 9 answered Doeg the **E**, which *was* set over 130
 22:18 Doeg the **E** turned, and he fell upon 130
 22:22 *it* that day, when Doeg the **E** *was* there, 130
1Ki 11:14 an adversary unto Solomon, Hadad the **E**: 130
Ps 52: T when Doeg the **E** came and told Saul, 130

EDOMITES (13) [EDOM]
Ge 36: 9 of Esau the father of the **E** in mount Seir: 123
 36:43 he *is* Esau the father of the **E**. 123
1Ki 11: 1 Ammonites, **E**, Zidonians, *and* Hittites; 130
 11:17 certain of **E** of his father's servants with him, 130
2Ki 8:21 smote the **E** which compassed him about, 123
1Ch 18:12 **E** in the valley of salt eighteen thousand. 123
 18:13 and all the **E** became David's servants. 123
2Ch 21: 8 In his days the **E** revolted from under 123
 21: 9 smote the **E** which compassed him in, 123
 21:10 So the **E** revolted from under the hand of 123
 25:14 was come from the slaughter of the **E**, 130
 25:19 Thou sayest, Lo, thou hast smitten the **E**; 123
 28:17 again the **E** had come and smitten Judah, 130

EDREI (8)
Nu 21:33 he, and all his people, to the battle *at* **E**. 154
Dt 1: 4 of Bashan, which dwelt at Astaroth in **E**: 154
 3: 1 he and all his people, to battle *at* **E**. 154
 3:10 and all Bashan, unto Salchah and **E**, 154
Jos 12: 4 giants, that dwelt at Ashtaroth and at **E**, 154
 13:12 which reigned in Ashtaroth and in **E**, 154
 13:31 Gilead, and Ashtaroth, and **E**, cities of 154
 19:37 And Kedesh, and **E**, and En-hazor, 154

EFFECT (14) [EFFECTED, EFFECTUAL, EFFECTUALLY]
Nu 30: 8 she bound her soul, of **none e**: 6565
2Ch 34:22 college:) and they spake to her to that **e**. NIH
Ps 33:10 **maketh** the devices of the people of **none e**. 5106
Isa 32:17 the **e** of righteousness quietness and 5656
Jer 48:30 *it shall* not *be* so; his lies shall not so **e** *it*. 6213
Eze 12:23 are at hand, and the **e** of every vision. 1697
Mt 15: 6 made the commandment of God of **none e** 208
Mk 7:13 Making the word of God of **none e** 208
Ro 3: 3 **make** the faith of God **without e**? 2673
 4:14 and the promise **made of none e**: 2673
 9: 6 the word of God hath **taken none e**. 1601
1Co 1:17 of Christ should be **made of none e**. 2758
Gal 3:17 *it* should **make** the promise of **none e**. 2673
 5: 4 Christ is **become of no e** unto you, 2673

EFFECTED (1) [EFFECT]
2Ch 7:11 in his own house, he **prosperously e**. 6743

EFFECTUAL (6) [EFFECT]
1Co 16: 9 For a great door and **e** is opened unto me, 1756
2Co 1: 6 which is **e** in the enduring of the same 1754
Eph 3: 7 unto me by the **e working** of his power. 1753
 4:16 to the **e working** in the measure 1753
Phm 1: 6 **e** by the acknowledging of every good 1756
Jas 5:16 The **e fervent** prayer of a righteous *man* 1754

EFFECTUALLY (2) [EFFECT]
Gal 2: 8 (For he that **wrought e** in Peter to 1754
1Th 2:13 which **e worketh** also in you that believe. 1754

EFFEMINATE (1)
1Co 6: 9 nor idolaters, nor adulterers, nor **e**, 3120

EGG (2) [EGGS]
Job 6: 6 or is there *any* taste in the white of an **e**? 2495
Lk 11:12 Or if he shall ask an **e**, will he offer him a 5609

EGGS (2) [EGG]
Dt 22: 6 or **e**, and the dam sitting upon the young, 1000
 22: 6 sitting upon the young, or upon the **e**, 1000
Job 39:14 Which leaveth her **e** in the earth, 1000
Isa 10:14 as *one* gathereth *that are* left, have I 1000
 59: 5 They hatch cockatrice' **e**, and weave 1000
 59: 5 he that eateth of their **e** dieth, 1000
Jer 17:11 As the partridge sitteth *on* **e**, NIH

EGLAH (2)
2Sa 3: 5 the sixth, Ithream, by **E** David's wife. 5698
1Ch 3: 3 Abital: the sixth, Ithream by **E** his wife. 5698

EGLAIM (1)
Isa 15: 8 howling thereof unto **E**, and the howling 97

EGLON (13)
Jos 10: 3 and unto Debir king of **E**, saying, 5700
 10: 5 the king of Lachish, the king of **E**, 5700
 10:23 the king of Lachish, *and* the king of **E**, 5700
 10:34 from Lachish Joshua passed unto **E**, 5700
 10:36 Joshua went up from **E**, and all Israel 5700
 10:37 according to all that he had done to **E**; 5700
 12:12 The king of **E**, one; the king of Gezer, 5700
 15:39 Lachish, and Bozkath, and **E**, 5700
Jdg 3:12 the Lᴏʀᴅ strengthened **E** the king of 5700

E

Am 9:12 That they may possess the remnant of **E**, 123
Ob 1: 1 Thus saith the Lord Gᴏᴅ concerning **E**, 123
 1: 8 even destroy the wise *men* out of **E**, 123
Mal 1: 4 Whereas **E** saith, We are impoverished, 123

E

Jdg	3:14 So the children of Israel served **E** the king	5700
	3:15 sent a present unto **E** the king of Moab.	5700
	3:17 he brought the present unto **E** king of	5700
	3:17 king of Moab: and **E** *was* a very fat man.	5700

EGYPT (611) [EGYPTIAN, EGYPTIAN'S, EGYPTIANS]

Ge	12:10 Abram went down into **E** to sojourn	4714
	12:11 when he was come near to enter into **E**,	4714
	12:14 that, when Abram was come into **E**,	4714
	13: 1 Abram went up out of **E**, he, and his wife,	4714
	13:10 like the land of **E**, as thou comest unto	4714
	15:18 from the river of **E** unto the great river,	4714
	21:21 took him a wife out of the land of **E**.	4714
	25:18 that *is* before **E**, as thou goest towards	4714
	26: 2 unto him, and said, Go not down into **E**;	4714
	37:25 and myrrh, going to carry *it* down to **E**.	4714
	37:28 of silver: and they brought Joseph into **E**.	4714
	37:36 the Medanites sold him into **E** unto	4714
	39: 1 Joseph was brought down to **E**;	4714
	40: 1 *that* the butler of the king of **E** and *his*	4714
	40: 1 had offended their lord the king of **E**.	4714
	40: 5 the butler and the baker of the king of **E**,	4714
	41: 8 and called for all the magicians of **E**,	4714
	41:19 as I never saw in all the land of **E** for	4714
	41:29 great plenty throughout all the land of **E**:	4714
	41:30 plenty shall be forgotten in the land of **E**;	4714
	41:33 and wise, and set him over the land of **E**.	4714
	41:34 take up the fifth *part* of the land of **E** in	4714
	41:36 of famine, which shall be in the land of **E**;	4714
	41:41 See, I have set thee over all the land of **E**.	4714
	41:43 he made him *ruler* over all the land of **E**.	4714
	41:44 lift up his hand or foot in all the land of **E**.	4714
	41:45 Joseph went out over *all* the land of **E**.	4714
	41:46 when he stood before Pharaoh king of **E**,	4714
	41:46 and went throughout all the land of **E**.	4714
	41:48 which were in the land of **E**, and laid up	4714
	41:53 that was in the land of **E**, were ended.	4714
	41:54 but in all the land of **E** there was bread.	4714
	41:55 when all the land of **E** was famished,	4714
	41:56 the famine waxed sore in the land of **E**.	4714
	41:57 all countries came into **E** to Joseph for to	4714
	42: 1 when Jacob saw that there was corn in **E**,	4714
	42: 1 I have heard that there is corn in **E**:	4714
	42: 3 ten brethren went down to buy corn in **E**.	4714
	43: 2 the corn which they had brought out of **E**,	4714
	43:15 went down to **E**, and stood before Joseph.	4714
	45: 4 Joseph your brother, whom ye sold into **E**.	4714
	45: 8 and a ruler throughout all the land of **E**.	4714
	45: 9 God hath made me lord of all **E**:	4714
	45:13 shall tell my father of all my glory in **E**,	4714
	45:18 I will give you the good of the land of **E**,	4714
	45:19 take you wagons out of the land of **E** for	4714
	45:20 for the good of all the land of **E** *is* yours.	4714
	45:23 ten asses laden with the good things of **E**,	4714
	45:25 they went up out of **E**, and came *into*	4714
	45:26 and he *is* governor over all the land of **E**.	4714
	46: 3 fear not to go down into **E**; for I will there	4714
	46: 4 I will go down with thee into **E**; and I will	4714
	46: 6 came into **E**, Jacob, and all his seed with	4714
	46: 7 all his seed brought he with him into **E**.	4714
	46: 8 which came into **E**, Jacob and his sons:	4714
	46:20 unto Joseph in the land of **E** were born	4714
	46:26 All the souls that came with Jacob into **E**,	4714
	46:27 were born him in **E**, *were* two souls:	4714
	46:27 which came into **E**, *were* threescore and	4714
	47: 6 The land of **E** *is* before thee; in the best of	4714
	47:11 gave them a possession in the land of **E**,	4714
	47:13 so that the land of **E** and *all* the land of	4714
	47:14 money that was found in the land of **E**,	4714
	47:15 when money failed in the land of **E**,	4714
	47:20 Joseph bought all the land of **E** for	4714
	47:21 borders of **E** even to the *other* end	4714
	47:26 Joseph made it a law over the land of **E**	4714
	47:27 Israel dwelt in the land of **E**, in the	4714
	47:28 Jacob lived in the land of **E** seventeen	4714
	47:29 with me; bury me not, I pray thee, in **E**:	4714
	47:30 thou shalt carry me out of **E**, and bury me	4714
	48: 5 were born unto thee in the land of **E**	4714
	48: 5 of Egypt before I came unto thee into **E**,	4714
	50: 7 and all the elders of the land of **E**,	4714
	50:14 Joseph returned into **E**, he,	4714
	50:22 Joseph dwelt in **E**, he, and his father's	4714
	50:26 and he was put in a coffin in **E**.	4714
Ex	1: 1 the children of Israel, which came into **E**;	4714
	1: 5 seventy souls: for Joseph was in **E** *already*.	4714
	1: 8 Now there arose up a new king over **E**,	4714
	1:15 the king of **E** spake to the Hebrew	4714
	1:17 not as the king of **E** commanded them,	4714
	1:18 the king of **E** called for the midwives,	4714
	2:23 in process of time, that the king of **E** died:	4714
	3: 7 the affliction of my people which *are* in **E**,	4714
	3:10 my people the children of Israel out of **E**.	4714
	3:11 bring forth the children of Israel out of **E**?	4714
	3:12 hast brought forth the people out of **E**,	4714
	3:16 and *seen* that which is done to you in **E**:	4714
	3:17 will bring you up out of the affliction of **E**	4714
	3:18 unto the king of **E**, and you shall say unto	4714
	3:19 I am sure that the king of **E** will not let	4714
	3:20 smite **E** with all my wonders which I will	4714
	4:18 return unto my brethren which *are* in **E**,	4714
	4:19 unto Moses in Midian, Go, return *into* **E**:	4714
	4:20 an ass, and he returned to the land of **E**:	4714
	4:21 When thou goest to return into **E**,	4714
	5: 4 king of **E** said unto them, Wherefore do	4714
	5:12 of **E** to gather stubble instead of straw.	4714

Ex	6:11 Go in, speak unto Pharaoh king of **E**,	4714
	6:13 of Israel, and unto Pharaoh king of **E**,	4714
	6:13 the children of Israel out of the land of **E**.	4714
	6:26 the land of **E** according to their armies.	4714
	6:27 they which spake to Pharaoh king of **E**,	4714
	6:27 to bring out the children of Israel from **E**:	4714
	6:28 LORD spake unto Moses in the land of **E**,	4714
	6:29 speak thou unto Pharaoh king of **E** all	4714
	7: 3 signs and my wonders in the land of **E**.	4714
	7: 4 that I may lay my hand upon **E**,	4714
	7: 4 out of the land of **E** by great judgments.	4714
	7: 5 when I stretch forth mine hand upon **E**,	4714
	7:11 now the magicians of **E**, they also did in	4714
	7:19 out thine hand upon the waters of **E**,	4714
	7:19 be blood throughout all the land of **E**,	4714
	7:21 was blood throughout all the land of **E**.	4714
	7:22 the magicians of **E** did so with their	4714
	8: 5 frogs to come up upon the land of **E**.	4714
	8: 6 out his hand over the waters of **E**;	4714
	8: 6 frogs came up, and covered the land of **E**.	4714
	8: 7 and brought up frogs upon the land of **E**.	4714
	8:16 become lice throughout all the land of **E**.	4714
	8:17 became lice throughout all the land of **E**.	4714
	8:24 houses, and into all the land of **E**:	4714
	9: 4 the cattle of Israel and the cattle of **E**:	4714
	9: 6 the morrow, and all the cattle of **E** died:	4714
	9: 9 become small dust in all the land of **E**,	4714
	9: 9 upon beast, throughout all the land of **E**.	4714
	9:18 such as hath not been in **E** since	4714
	9:22 that there may be hail in all the land of **E**,	4714
	9:23 of the field, throughout all the land of **E**.	4714
	9:24 all the land of **E** since it became a nation.	4714
	9:25 hail smote throughout all the land of **E**	4714
	10: 2 what things I have wrought in **E**, and my	4714
	10: 7 knowest thou not yet that **E** is destroyed?	4714
	10:12 Stretch out thine hand over the land of **E**	4714
	10:12 they may come up upon the land of **E**,	4714
	10:13 stretched forth his rod over the land of **E**,	4714
	10:14 the locusts went up over all the land of **E**,	4714
	10:14 of Egypt, and rested in all the coasts of **E**:	4714
	10:15 of the field, through all the land of **E**:	4714
	10:19 not one locust in all the coasts of **E**.	4714
	10:21 there may be darkness over the land of **E**,	4714
	10:22 darkness in all the land of **E** three days:	4714
	11: 1 plague *more* upon Pharaoh, and upon **E**;	4714
	11: 3 Moses *was* very great in the land of **E**,	4714
	11: 4 will I go out into the midst of **E**:	4714
	11: 5 all the firstborn in the land of **E** shall die,	4714
	11: 6 a great cry throughout all the land of **E**,	4714
	11: 9 may be multiplied in the land of **E**.	4714
	12: 1 unto Moses and Aaron in the land of **E**,	4714
	12:12 For I will pass through the land of **E** this	4714
	12:12 smite all the firstborn in the land of **E**,	4714
	12:12 against all the gods of **E** I will execute	4714
	12:13 destroy *you*, when I smite the land of **E**.	4714
	12:17 brought your armies out of the land of **E**:	4714
	12:27 the houses of the children of Israel in **E**,	4714
	12:29 smote all the firstborn in the land of **E**,	4714
	12:30 and there was a great cry in **E**;	4714
	12:39 dough which they brought forth out of **E**,	4714
	12:39 because they were thrust out of **E**,	4714
	12:40 who dwelt in **E**, *was* four hundred and	4714
	12:41 of the LORD went out from the land of **E**.	4714
	12:42 for bringing them out of the land of **E**:	4714
	12:51 Israel out of the land of **E** by their armies.	4714
	13: 3 this day, *in* which ye came out from **E**,	4714
	13: 8 did unto me when I came forth out of **E**.	4714
	13: 9 hath the LORD brought thee out of **E**.	4714
	13:14 of hand the LORD brought us out from **E**,	4714
	13:15 slew all the firstborn in the land of **E**,	4714
	13:16 hand the LORD brought us forth out of **E**.	4714
	13:17 when they see war, and they return to **E**:	4714
	13:18 went up harnessed out of the land of **E**.	4714
	14: 5 it was told the king of **E** that the people	4714
	14: 7 all the chariots of **E**, and captains over	4714
	14: 8 hardened the heart of Pharaoh king of **E**,	4714
	14:11 Because *there were* no graves in **E**,	4714
	14:11 thus with us, to carry us forth out of **E**?	4714
	14:12 this the word that we did tell thee in **E**,	4714
	16: 1 after their departing out of the land of **E**.	4714
	16: 3 by the hand of the LORD in the land of **E**,	4714
	16: 6 hath brought you out from the land of **E**:	4714
	16:32 I brought you forth out of the land of **E**.	4714
	17: 3 this that hast brought us up out of **E**,	4714
	18: 1 the LORD had brought Israel out of **E**;	4714
	19: 1 Israel were gone forth out of the land of **E**,	4714
	20: 2 have brought thee out of the land of **E**,	4714
	22:21 for ye were strangers in the land of **E**.	4714
	23: 9 seeing ye were strangers in the land of **E**.	4714
	23:15 for in it thou camest out from **E**:	4714
	29:46 brought them forth out of the land of **E**,	4714
	32: 1 that brought us up out of the land of **E**,	4714
	32: 4 brought thee up out of the land of **E**.	4714
	32: 7 thou broughtest out of the land of **E**,	4714
	32: 8 have brought thee up out of the land of **E**.	4714
	32:11 out of the land of **E** with great power,	4714
	32:23 that brought us up out of the land of **E**,	4714
	33: 1 thou hast brought up out of the land of **E**,	4714
	34:18 the month Abib thou camest out from **E**.	4714
Lev	11:45 that bringeth you up out of the land of **E**,	4714
	18: 3 After the doings of the land of **E**,	4714
	19:34 for ye were strangers in the land of **E**:	4714
	19:36 which brought you out of the land of **E**.	4714
	22:33 That brought you out of the land of **E**,	4714

Lev	23:43 when I brought them out of the land of **E**:	4714
	25:38 brought you forth out of the land of **E**,	4714
	25:42 whom I brought forth out of the land of **E**:	4714
	25:55 whom I brought forth out of the land of **E**:	4714
	26:13 brought you out of the land of **E**,	4714
	26:45 whom I brought forth out of the land of **E**	4714
Nu	1: 1 after they were come out of the land of **E**,	4714
	3:13 **E** I hallowed unto me all the firstborn in	4714
	8:17 I smote every firstborn in the land of **E**,	4714
	9: 1 after they were come out of the land of **E**,	4714
	11: 5 the fish, which we did eat in **E** freely;	4714
	11:18 for *it was* well with us in **E**: therefore	4714
	11:20 saying, Why came we forth out of **E**?	4714
	13:22 was built seven years before Zoan in **E**.)	4714
	14: 2 God that we had died in the land of **E**!	4714
	14: 3 were it not better for us to return into **E**?	4714
	14: 4 make a captain, and let us return into **E**.	4714
	14:19 this people, from **E** even until now.	4714
	14:22 which I did in **E** and in the wilderness,	4714
	15:41 which brought you out of the land of **E**,	4714
	20: 5 have ye made us to come up out of **E**,	4714
	20:15 How our fathers went down into **E**,	4714
	20:15 and we have dwelt in **E** a long time;	4714
	20:16 and hath brought us forth out of **E**:	4714
	21: 5 have ye brought us up out of **E** to	4714
	22: 5 there is a people come out from **E**:	4714
	22:11 Behold, *there is* a people come out of **E**,	4714
	23:22 God brought them out of **E**; he hath as it	4714
	24: 8 God brought him forth out of **E**; he hath	4714
	26: 4 which went forth out of the land of **E**.	4714
	26:59 whom *her mother* bare to Levi in **E**:	4714
	32:11 none of the men that came up out of **E**,	4714
	33: 1 which went forth out of the land of **E**	4714
	33:38 of Israel were come out of the land of **E**,	4714
	34: 5 compass from Azmon unto the river of **E**,	4714
Dt	1:27 hath brought us forth out of the land of **E**,	4714
	1:30 according to all that he did for you in **E**	4714
	4:20 *even* out of **E**, to be unto him a people of	4714
	4:34 God did for you in **E** before your eyes?	4714
	4:37 his sight with his mighty power out of **E**;	4714
	4:45 of Israel, after they came forth out of **E**,	4714
	4:46 after they were come forth out of **E**:	4714
	5: 6 which brought thee out of the land of **E**,	4714
	5:15 that thou wast a servant in the land of **E**,	4714
	6:12 brought thee forth out of the land of **E**,	4714
	6:21 son, We were Pharaoh's bondmen in **E**;	4714
	6:21 the LORD brought us out of **E** with a	4714
	6:22 and wonders, great and sore, upon **E**,	4714
	7: 8 from the hand of Pharaoh king of **E**.	4714
	7:15 will put none of the evil diseases of **E**,	4714
	7:18 God did unto Pharaoh, and unto all **E**;	4714
	8:14 brought thee forth out of the land of **E**,	4714
	9: 7 thou didst depart out of the land of **E**,	4714
	9:12 **E** have corrupted *themselves;* they are	4714
	9:26 which thou hast brought forth out of **E**	4714
	10:19 for ye were strangers in the land of **E**.	4714
	10:22 Thy fathers went down into **E** with	4714
	11: 3 which he did in the midst of **E** unto	4714
	11: 3 of Egypt unto Pharaoh the king of **E**,	4714
	11: 4 what he did unto the army of **E**, unto	4714
	11:10 *is* not as the land of **E**, from whence ye	4714
	13: 5 which brought you out of the land of **E**,	4714
	13:10 which brought thee out of the land of **E**,	4714
	15:15 thou wast a bondman in the land of **E**,	4714
	16: 1 God brought thee forth out of **E** by night.	4714
	16: 3 for thou camest forth out of the land of **E**	4714
	16: 3 out of the land of **E** all the days of thy life.	4714
	16:12 that thou wast a bondman in **E**:	4714
	17:16 nor cause the people to return to **E**,	4714
	20: 1 brought thee up out of the land of **E**.	4714
	23: 4 in the way, when ye came forth out of **E**;	4714
	24: 9 after that ye were come forth out of **E**.	4714
	24:18 that thou wast a bondman in **E**,	4714
	24:22 thou wast a bondman in the land of **E**:	4714
	25:17 when ye were come forth out of **E**;	4714
	26: 5 he went down into **E**, and sojourned	4714
	26: 8 the LORD brought us out of **E** with	4714
	28:27 LORD will smite thee with the botch of **E**,	4714
	28:60 will bring upon thee all the diseases of **E**,	4714
	28:68 the LORD shall bring thee *into* **E** again	4714
	29: 2 your eyes in the land of **E** unto Pharaoh,	4714
	29:16 how we have dwelt in the land of **E**;	4714
	29:25 brought them forth out of the land of **E**:	4714
	34:11 him to do in the land of **E** to Pharaoh,	4714
Jos	2:10 Red sea for you, when you came out of **E**;	4714
	5: 4 All the people that came out of **E**,	4714
	5: 4 by the way, after they came out of **E**.	4714
	5: 5 by the way as they came forth out of **E**.	4714
	5: 6 which came out of **E**, were consumed,	4714
	5: 9 rolled away the reproach of **E** from off	4714
	9: 9 the fame of him, and all that he did in **E**,	4714
	13: 3 From Sihor, which *is* before **E**, even unto	4714
	15: 4 and went out *unto* the river of **E**,	4714
	15:47 unto the river of **E**, and the great sea,	4714
	24: 4 Jacob and his children went down *into* **E**.	4714
	24: 5 Moses also and Aaron, and I plagued **E**,	4714
	24: 6 I brought your fathers out of **E**:	4714
	24: 7 eyes have seen what I have done in **E**:	4713
	24:14 on the *other* side of the flood, and in **E**;	4714
	24:17 up and our fathers out of the land of **E**,	4714
	24:32 the children of Israel brought up out of **E**,	4714
Jdg	2: 1 I made you to go up out of **E**,	4714
	2:12 which brought them out of the land of **E**,	4714
	6: 8 I brought you up from **E**, and brought you	4714

E

Jdg
6:13 Did not the LORD bring us up from **E**? 4714
11:13 when they came up out of **E**, from Arnon 4714
11:16 when Israel came up from **E**. 4714
19:30 up out of the land of **E** unto this day: 4714

1Sa
2:27 when they were in **E** in Pharaoh's house? 4714
8: 8 them up out of **E** even unto this day, 4714
10:18 I brought up Israel out of **E**, 4714
12: 6 your fathers up out of the land of **E**. 4714
12: 8 When Jacob was come *into* **E**, 4714
12: 8 which brought forth your fathers out of **E**, 4714
15: 2 in the way, when he came up from **E**. 4714
15: 6 of Israel, when they came up out of **E**. 4714
15: 7 comest *to* Shur, that *is* over against **E**. 4714
27: 8 goest to Shur, even unto the land of **E**. 4714
30:13 he said, I *am* a young man **of E**, servant 4713

2Sa
7: 6 brought up the children of Israel out of **E**, 4714
7:23 which thou redeemedst to thee from **E**, 4714

1Ki
3: 1 made affinity with Pharaoh king of **E**, 4714
4:21 the Philistines, and unto the border of **E**: 4714
4:30 the east country, and all the wisdom of **E**. 4714
6: 1 of Israel were come out of the land of **E**, 4714
8: 9 when they came out of the land of **E**. 4714
8:16 I brought forth my people Israel out of **E**, 4714
8:21 he brought them out of the land of **E**: 4714
8:51 which thou broughtest forth out of **E**, 4714
8:53 thou broughtest our fathers out of **E**, 4714
8:65 entering in of Hamath unto the river of **E**, 4714
9: 9 forth their fathers out of the land of **E**, 4714
9:16 *For* Pharaoh king of **E** had gone up, 4714
10:28 Solomon had horses brought out of **E**, 4714
10:29 went out of **E** for six hundred *shekels* of 4714
11:17 father's servants with him, to go *into* **E**; 4714
11:18 they came *to* **E**, unto Pharaoh king of 4714
11:18 came to Egypt, unto Pharaoh king of **E**; 4714
11:21 when Hadad heard in **E** that David slept 4714
11:40 Jeroboam arose, and fled *into* **E**, 4714
11:40 unto Shishak king of **E**, and was in Egypt 4714
11:40 and was in **E** until the death of Solomon. 4714
12: 2 the son of Nebat, who was yet in **E**, 4714
12: 2 king Solomon, and Jeroboam dwelt in **E**;) 4714
12:28 brought thee up out of the land of **E**. 4714
14:25 *that* Shishak king of **E** came up against 4714

2Ki
17: 4 he had sent messengers to So king of **E**, 4714
17: 7 had brought them up out of the land of **E**, 4714
17: 7 from under the hand of Pharaoh king of **E**, 4714
17:36 who brought you up out of the land of **E** 4714
18:21 upon **E**, on which if a man lean, it will 4714
18:21 *is* Pharaoh king of **E** unto all that trust on 4714
18:24 put thy trust on **E** for chariots and 4714
21:15 the day their fathers came forth out of **E**, 4714
23:29 In his days Pharaoh-nechoh king of **E** 4714
23:34 took Jehoahaz *away:* and he came to **E**, 4714
24: 7 the king of **E** came not again any more out 4714
24: 7 unto the river Euphrates all that 4714
24: 7 all that pertained to the king of **E**. 4714
25:26 of the armies, arose, and came to **E**: 4714

1Ch
13: 5 from Shihor of **E** even unto the entering 4714
17:21 whom thou hast redeemed out of **E**? 4714

2Ch
1:16 Solomon had horses brought out of **E**, 4714
1:17 brought forth out of **E** a chariot for six 4714
5:10 of Israel, when they came out of **E**. 4714
6: 5 **E** I chose no city among all the tribes of 4714
7: 8 entering in of Hamath unto the river of **E**. 4714
7:22 brought them forth out of the land of **E**, 4714
9:26 of the Philistines, and to the border of **E**. 4714
9:28 brought unto Solomon horses out of **E**, 4714
10: 2 Jeroboam the son of Nebat, who *was* in **E**, 4714
10: 2 heard *it,* that Jeroboam returned out of **E**. 4714
12: 2 king of **E** came up against Jerusalem, 4714
12: 3 number that came with him out of **E**; 4714
12: 9 So Shishak king of **E** came up against 4714
20:10 when they came out of the land of **E**, 4714
26: 8 abroad even to the entering in of **E**: 4714
35:20 Necho king of **E** came up to fight against 4714
36: 3 the king of **E** put him down at Jerusalem, 4714
36: 4 the king of **E** made Eliakim his brother 4714
36: 4 his brother, and carried him to **E**. 4714

Ne
9: 9 didst see the affliction of our fathers in **E**, 4714
9:18 is thy God that brought thee up out of **E**, 4714

Ps
68:31 Princes shall come out of **E**; Ethiopia shall 4714
78:12 in the land of **E**, *in* the field of Zoan. 4714
78:43 How he had wrought his signs in **E**, 4714
78:51 smote all the firstborn in **E**; the chief of 4714
80: 8 Thou hast brought a vine out of **E**: 4714
81: 5 when he went out through the land of **E**: 4714
81:10 which brought thee out of the land of **E**: 4714
105:23 Israel also came *into* **E**; 4714
105:38 **E** was glad when they departed: for the 4714
106: 7 fathers understood not thy wonders in **E**; 4714
106:21 which had done great *things* in **E**, 4714
114: 1 When Israel went out of **E**, the house of 4714
135: 8 smote the firstborn in **E**, both of man 4714
135: 9 O **E**, upon Pharaoh, and upon all his 4714
136:10 To him that smote **E** in their firstborn: 4714

Pr
7:16 *with* carved *works, with* fine linen of **E**. 4714

Isa
7:18 *is* in the uttermost part of the rivers of **E**, 4714
10:24 staff against thee, after the manner of **E**. 4714
10:26 so shall he lift it up after the manner of **E**. 4714
11:11 from **E**, and from Pathros, and from Cush, 4714
11:16 day that he came up out of the land of **E**. 4714
19: 1 The burden of **E**. Behold, the LORD 4714
19: 1 upon a swift cloud, and shall come *into* **E**: 4714
19: 1 the idols of **E** shall be moved at his 4714
19: 1 the heart of **E** shall melt in the midst of it. 4714
19: 3 spirit of **E** shall fail in the midst thereof; 4714

Isa
19:12 the LORD of hosts hath purposed upon **E**. 4714
19:13 they have also seduced **E**, *even they that* 4714
19:14 they have caused **E** to err in every work 4714
19:15 Neither shall there be *any* work for **E**, 4714
19:16 In that day shall **E** be like unto women: 4714
19:17 the land of Judah shall be a terror unto **E**, 4714
19:18 In that day shall five cities in the land of **E** 4714
19:19 to the LORD in the midst of the land of **E**, 4714
19:20 unto the LORD of hosts in the land of **E**: 4714
19:21 the LORD shall be known to **E**, 4714
19:22 the LORD shall smite **E**: *he* shall smite 4714
19:23 there be a highway out of **E** to Assyria, 4714
19:23 the Assyrian shall come into **E**, 4714
19:24 In that day shall Israel be the third with **E** 4714
19:25 Blessed *be* **E** my people, and Assyria 4714
20: 3 and wonder upon **E** and upon Ethiopia; 4714
20: 4 buttocks uncovered, *to* the shame of **E**. 4714
20: 5 their expectation, and of **E** their glory. 4714
23: 5 As *at* the report concerning **E**, so shall 4714
27:12 channel of the river unto the stream of **E**, 4714
27:13 the outcasts in the land of **E**, 4714
30: 2 That walk to go down *into* **E**, and have 4714
30: 2 Pharaoh, and to trust in the shadow of **E**, 4714
30: 3 trust in the shadow of **E** *your* confusion. 4714
31: 1 Woe to them that go down *to* **E** for help; 4714
36: 6 in the staff of this broken reed, on **E**; 4714
36: 6 Pharaoh king of **E** to all that trust in him. 4714
36: 9 put thy trust on **E** for chariots and 4714
43: 3 I gave **E** *for* thy ransom, Ethiopia and 4714
45:14 The labour of **E**, and merchandise of 4714
52: 4 My people went down aforetime *into* **E** to 4714

Jer
2: 6 that brought us up out of the land of **E**, 4714
2:18 what hast thou to do in the way of **E**, 4714
2:36 thou also shalt be ashamed of **E**, as thou 4714
7:22 that I brought them out of the land of **E**, 4714
7:25 forth out of the land of **E** unto this day, 4714
9:26 **E**, and Judah, and Edom, and the children 4714
11: 4 I brought them forth out of the land of **E**, 4714
11: 7 I brought them up out of the land of **E**, 4714
16:14 the children of Israel out of the land of **E**; 4714
23: 7 the children of Israel out of the land of **E**; 4714
24: 8 and them that dwell in the land of **E**: 4714
25:19 Pharaoh king of **E**, and his servants, and 4714
26:21 he was afraid, and fled, and went into **E**; 4714
26:22 Jehoiakim the king sent men *into* **E**, 4714
26:22 and *certain* men with him into **E**. 4714
26:23 they fet forth Urijah out of **E**, 4714
31:32 to bring them out of the land of **E**, 4714
32:20 set signs and wonders in the land of **E**, 4714
32:21 Israel out of the land of **E** with signs, 4714
34:13 I brought forth out of the land of **E**, 4714
37: 5 Pharaoh's army was come forth out of **E**: 4714
37: 7 shall return *to* **E** into their own land. 4714
41:17 is by Beth-lehem, to go to enter *into* **E**, 4714
42:14 we will go *into* the land of **E**, where we 4714
42:15 If ye wholly set your faces to enter *into* **E**, 4714
42:16 shall overtake you there in the land of **E**; 4714
42:16 shall follow close after you there in **E**; 4714
42:17 their faces to go *into* **E** to sojourn there; 4714
42:18 upon you, when ye shall enter *into* **E**: 4714
42:19 O ye remnant of Judah; Go ye not *into* **E**: 4714
43: 2 to say, Go not *into* **E** to sojourn there: 4714
43: 7 So they came *into* the land of **E**: for they 4714
43:11 he shall smite the land of **E**, 4714
43:12 a fire in the houses of the gods of **E**; 4714
43:12 he shall array himself with the land of **E**, 4714
43:13 of Beth-shemesh, that *is* in the land of **E**; 4714
44: 1 all the Jews which dwell in the land of **E**, 4714
44: 8 incense unto other gods in the land of **E**, 4714
44:12 to go into the land of **E** to sojourn there, 4714
44:12 all be consumed, *and* fall in the land of **E**; 4714
44:13 punish them that dwell in the land of **E**, 4714
44:14 which are gone into the land of **E** to 4714
44:15 all the people that dwelt in the land of **E**, 4714
44:24 all Judah that *are* in the land of **E**: 4714
44:26 all Judah that dwell in the land of **E**; 4714
44:26 of any man of Judah in all the land of **E**, 4714
44:27 land of **E** shall be consumed by the sword 4714
44:28 of the land of **E** *into* the land of Judah, 4714
44:28 that are gone into the land of **E** to sojourn 4714
44:30 I *will* give Pharaoh-hophra king of **E** into 4714
46: 2 Against **E**, against the army of 4714
46: 2 the army of Pharaoh-necho king of **E**, 4714
46: 8 **E** riseth up like a flood, and *his* waters are 4714
46:11 take balm, O virgin, the daughter of **E**: 4714
46:13 should come and smite the land of **E**. 4714
46:14 Declare ye in **E**, and publish in Migdol, 4714
46:17 there, Pharaoh King of **E** *is but* a noise; 4714
46:19 O thou daughter dwelling in **E**, 4714
46:20 **E** *is like* a very fair heifer, 4714
46:24 The daughter of **E** shall be confounded; 4714
46:25 Pharaoh, and **E**, with their gods, 4714

Eze
17:15 him in sending his ambassadors *into* **E**, 4714
19: 4 him with chains unto the land of **E**. 4714
20: 5 known unto them in the land of **E**, 4714
20: 6 to bring them forth of the land of **E** into a 4714
20: 7 defile not yourselves with the idols of **E**: 4714
20: 8 neither did they forsake the idols of **E**: 4714
20: 8 against them in the midst of the land of **E**. 4714
20: 9 bringing them forth out of the land of **E**. 4714
20:10 them to go forth out of the land of **E**, 4714
20:36 fathers in the wilderness of the land of **E**, 4714
23: 3 they committed whoredoms in **E**; 4714
23: 8 left she her whoredoms *brought* from **E**: 4714
23:19 she had played the harlot in the land of **E**. 4714

Eze
23:27 whoredom *brought* from the land of **E**: 4714
23:27 unto them, nor remember **E** any more. 4714
27: 7 Fine linen with broidered work from **E** 4714
29: 2 set thy face against Pharaoh king of **E**, 4714
29: 2 prophesy against him, and against all **E**: 4714
29: 3 I *am* against thee, Pharaoh king of **E**, 4714
29: 6 the inhabitants of **E** shall know that I *am* 4714
29: 9 the land of **E** shall be desolate and waste; 4714
29:10 I will make the land of **E** utterly waste 4714
29:12 I will make the land of **E** desolate in 4714
29:14 I will bring again the captivity of **E**, 4714
29:19 I *will* give the land of **E** unto 4714
29:20 I have given him the land of **E** *for his* 4714
30: 4 the sword shall come upon **E**, 4714
30: 4 when the slain shall fall in **E**, and they 4714
30: 6 They also that uphold **E** shall fall; 4714
30: 8 when I have set a fire in **E**, and when all 4714
30: 9 shall come upon them, as *in* the day of **E**: 4714
30:10 will also make the multitude of **E** to cease 4714
30:11 they shall draw their swords against **E**, 4714
30:13 shall be no more a prince of the land of **E**: 4714
30:13 and I will put a fear in the land of **E**. 4714
30:15 pour my fury upon Sin, the strength of **E**; 4714
30:16 I will set fire in **E**: Sin shall have great 4714
30:18 when I shall break there the yokes of **E**: 4714
30:19 Thus will I execute judgments in **E**: 4714
30:21 broken the arm of Pharaoh king of **E**; 4714
30:22 I *am* against Pharaoh king of **E**, 4714
30:25 he shall stretch it out upon the land of **E**. 4714
31: 2 speak unto Pharaoh king of **E**, and to his 4714
32: 2 up a lamentation for Pharaoh king of **E**, 4714
32:12 they shall spoil the pomp of **E**, and all 4714
32:15 When I shall make the land of **E** desolate, 4714
32:16 *even* for **E**, and for all her multitude, 4714
32:18 wail for the multitude of **E**, and cast them 4714

Da
9:15 out of the land of **E** with a mighty hand, 4714
11: 8 shall also carry captives *into* **E** their gods, 4714
11:42 and the land of **E** shall not escape. 4714
11:43 and over all the precious *things* of **E**: 4714

Hos
2:15 when she came up out of the land of **E**. 4714
7:11 they call to **E**, they go to Assyria. 4714
7:16 *shall be* their derision in the land of **E**. 4714
8:13 and visit their sins: they shall return *to* **E**. 4714
9: 3 Ephraim shall return *to* **E**, and they shall 4714
9: 6 shall gather them up, Memphis shall 4714
11: 1 I loved him, and called my son out of **E**. 4714
11: 5 He shall not return into the land of **E**, 4714
11:11 They shall tremble as a bird out of **E**, 4714
12: 1 the Assyrians, and oil is carried into **E**. 4714
12: 9 will yet make thee to dwell in 4714
12:13 the LORD brought Israel out of **E**, 4714
13: 4 *am* the LORD thy God from the land of **E**, 4714

Joel
3:19 **E** shall be a desolation, and Edom shall 4714

Am
2:10 Also I brought you up from the land of **E**, 4714
3: 1 which I brought up from the land of **E**, 4714
3: 9 in the palaces in the land of **E**, and say, 4714
4:10 you the pestilence after the manner of **E**: 4714
8: 8 out and drowned, as *by* the flood of **E**. 4714
9: 5 shall be drowned, as *by* the flood of **E**. 4714
9: 7 I brought up Israel out of the land of **E**? 4714

Mic
6: 4 For I brought thee up out of the land of **E**, 4714
7:15 **E** will I shew unto him marvellous *things*. 4714

Na
3: 9 Ethiopia and **E** were her strength, 4714

Hag
2: 5 with you when ye came out of **E**, 4714

Zec
10:10 bring them again also out of the land of **E**, 4714
10:11 and the sceptre of **E** shall depart away. 4714
14:18 if the family of **E** go not up, and come not, 4714
14:19 This shall be the punishment of **E**, 4714

Mt
2:13 into **E**, and be thou there until I 125
2:14 his mother by night, and departed into 125
2:15 saying, Out of **E** have I called my son. 125
2:19 Lord appeareth in a dream to Joseph in **E**, 125

Ac
2:10 **E**, and in the parts of Libya about Cyrene, 125
7: 9 moved with envy, sold Joseph into **E**: 125
7:10 wisdom in the sight of Pharaoh king of **E**: 125
7:10 he made him governor over **E** and all his 125
7:11 there came a dearth over all the land of **E** 125
7:12 when Jacob heard that there was corn in **E**, 125
7:15 So Jacob went down into **E**, and died, 125
7:17 the people grew and multiplied in **E**, 125
7:34 the affliction of my people which is in **E**, 125
7:34 And now come, I will send thee into **E**. 125
7:36 shewed wonders and signs in the land of **E**, 125
7:39 in their hearts turned *back again* into **E**, 125
7:40 which brought us out of the land of **E**, 125
13:17 *they* dwelt as strangers in the land of **E**, 125

Heb
3:16 not all that came out of **E** by Moses. 125
8: 9 the hand to lead them out of the land of **E**; 125
11:26 greater riches than the treasures in **E**: 125
11:27 By faith he forsook **E**, not fearing the wrath 125

Jude
1: 5 saved the people out of the land of **E**, 125

Rev
11: 8 which spiritually is called Sodom and **E**, 125

EGYPTIAN (23) [EGYPT]

Ge
16: 1 *children:* and she had a handmaid, an **E**, 4713
16: 3 Abram's wife took Hagar her maid the **E**, 4713
21: 9 Sarah saw the son of Hagar the **E**, 4713
25:12 Abraham's son, whom Hagar the **E**, 4713
39: 1 of Pharaoh, captain of the guard, an **E**, 4713
39: 2 he was in the house of his master the **E**. 4713

Ex
1:19 Hebrew women *are* not as the **E** women; 4713
2:11 spied an **E** smiting a Hebrew, *one* of his 4713
2:12 he slew the **E**, and hid him in the sand. 4713
2:14 thou to kill me, as thou killedst the **E**? 4713
2:19 An **E** delivered us out of the hand of 4713

E

Lev 24:10 Israelitish woman, whose father *was* an E, 4713
Dt 23: 7 thou shalt not abhor an E; because 4713
1Sa 30:11 they found an E in the field, 376+4713
2Sa 23:21 he slew an E, a goodly man; 4713
 23:21 the E had a spear in his hand; but he went 4713
1Ch 2:34 a servant, an E, whose name *was* Jarha. 4713
 11:23 slew an E, a man of *great* 376+4713+1886.1
Isa 11:15 utterly destroy the tongue of the E sea; 4714
 19:23 the E into Assyria, and the Egyptians shall 4714
Ac 7:24 him that was oppressed, and smote the E: 124
 7:28 kill me, as thou diddst the E yesterday? 124
 21:38 Art not thou *that* E, which before these 124

EGYPTIAN'S (4) [EGYPT]

Ge 39: 5 that the Lord blessed the E house for 4713
2Sa 23:21 plucked the spear out of the E hand, 4713
1Ch 11:23 in the E hand *was* a spear like a weaver's 4713
 11:23 pluckt the spear out of the E hand, 4713

EGYPTIANS (98) [EGYPT]

Ge 12:12 when the E shall see thee, that they shall 4714
 12:14 E beheld the woman that she *was* very 4713
 41:55 Pharaoh said unto all the E, Go unto 4714
 41:56 all the storehouses, and sold unto the E; 4714
 43:32 for the E, which did eat with him, 4713
 43:32 the E might not eat bread with 4713
 43:32 for that *is* an abomination unto the E. 4713
 45: 2 the E and the house of Pharaoh heard. 4714
 46:34 shepherd *is* an abomination unto the E. 4714
 47:15 all the E came unto Joseph, and said, 4714
 47:20 the E sold every man his field, because 4714
 50: 3 the E mourned for him threescore and 4714
 50:11 This *is* a grievous mourning to the E: 4714
Ex 1:13 the E made the children of Israel to serve 4714
 3: 8 to deliver them out of the hand of the E, 4714
 3: 9 oppression wherewith the E oppress 4714
 3:21 this people favour in the sight of the E: 4714
 3:22 your daughters; and ye shall spoil the E. 4714
 6: 5 of Israel, whom the E keep in bondage; 4714
 6: 6 you out from under the burdens of the E, 4714
 6: 7 you out from under the burdens of the E. 4714
 7: 5 the E shall know that I *am* the Lord, 4714
 7:18 the E shall lothe to drink of the water of 4714
 7:21 the E could not drink of the water of 4714
 7:24 all the E digged round about the river *for* 4714
 8:21 the houses of the E shall be full of swarms 4714
 8:26 of the E to the Lord our God: 4714
 8:26 we sacrifice the abomination of the E 4714
 9:11 upon the magicians, and upon all the E. 4714
 10: 6 thy servants, and the houses of all the E; 4714
 11: 3 the people favour in the sight of the E. 4714
 11: 7 doth put a difference between the E 4714
 12:23 Lord will pass through to smite the E; 4714
 12:27 when he smote the E, and delivered our 4714
 12:30 he, and all his servants, and all the E; 4714
 12:33 the E were urgent upon the people, that 4714
 12:35 they borrowed of the E jewels of silver, 4714
 12:36 the people favour in the sight of the E, 4714
 12:36 *as they required.* And they spoiled the E. 4714
 14: 4 that the E may know that I *am* the Lord. 4714
 14: 9 the E pursued after them (all the horses 4714
 14:10 and behold, the E marched after them; 4714
 14:12 Let us alone, that we may serve the E? 4714
 14:12 *it had been* better for us to serve the E, 4714
 14:13 for the E whom ye have seen to day, 4714
 14:17 I will harden the hearts of the E, 4714
 14:18 the E shall know that I *am* the Lord, 4714
 14:20 it came between the camp of the E and 4714
 14:23 the E pursued, and went in after them to 4714
 14:24 the host of the E through the pillar of fire 4714
 14:24 the cloud, and troubled the host of the E, 4714
 14:25 that the E said, Let us flee from the face 4714
 14:25 the Lord fighteth for them against the E. 4714
 14:26 the waters may come again upon the E, 4714
 14:27 the E fled against it; and the Lord 4714
 14:27 the Lord overthrew the E in the midst of 4714
 14:30 Israel that day out of the hand of the E, 4714
 14:30 Israel saw the E dead upon the sea shore. 4714
 14:31 work which the Lord did upon the E: 4714
 15:26 which I have brought upon the E: 4714
 18: 8 Pharaoh and to the E for Israel's sake, 4714
 18: 9 he had delivered out of the hand of the E. 4714
 18:10 delivered you out of the hand of the E, 4714
 18:10 the people from under the hand of the E. 4714
 19: 4 Ye have seen what I did unto the E, 4714
 32:12 Wherefore should the E speak, and say, 4714
Nu 14:13 the E shall hear *it,* (for thou broughtest up 4714
 20:15 and the E vexed us, and our fathers: 4714
 33: 3 with a high hand in the sight of all the E. 4714
 33: 4 For the E buried all *their* firstborn, which 4714
Dt 26: 6 the E evil entreated us, and afflicted us, 4713
Jos 24: 6 the E pursued after your fathers with 4714
 24: 7 he put darkness between you and the E, 4714
Jdg 6: 9 I delivered you out of the hand of the E, 4714
 10:11 *Did not I deliver you* from the E, 4714
1Sa 4: 8 *are* the Gods that smote the E with all 4714
 6: 6 the E and Pharaoh hardened their hearts? 4714
 10:18 delivered you out of the hand of the E, 4714
2Ki 7: 6 and the kings of the E, to come upon us. 4714
Ezr 9: 1 the Moabites, the E, and the Amorites. 4713
Isa 19: 2 I will set the E against the Egyptians: 4714
 19: 2 I will set the Egyptians against the E, 4714
 19: 4 the E will I give over into the hand of a 4714
 19:21 the E shall know the Lord in that day, 4714
 19:23 and the E shall serve *with* the Assyrians. 4714

Isa 20: 4 king of Assyria lead away the E prisoners, 4714
 30: 7 For the E shall help in vain, and to no 4714
 31: 3 Now the E *are* men, and not God; 4714
Jer 43:13 the houses of the gods of the E shall he 4714
La 5: 6 We have given the hand *to* the E, *and to* 4714
Eze 16:26 with the E thy neighbours, 1121+4714
 23:21 in bruising thy teats by the E for the paps 4714
 29:12 I will scatter the E among the nations, 4714
 29:13 the end of forty years will I gather the E 4714
 30:23 I will scatter the E among the nations, 4714
 30:26 I will scatter the E among the nations, 4714
Ac 7:22 was learned in all the wisdom of the E, 124
Heb 11:29 which the E assaying to do were drowned. 124

EHI (1)

Ge 46:21 Ashbel, Gera, and Naaman, E, and Rosh, 278

EHUD (10)

Jdg 3:15 E the son of Gera, a Benjamite, a man 164
 3:16 E made him a dagger which had two edges, 164
 3:20 E came unto him; and he was sitting in a 164
 3:20 E said, I have a message from God unto 164
 3:21 E put forth his left hand, and took the 164
 3:23 E went forth through the porch, and shut 164
 3:26 E escaped while they tarried, and passed 164
 4: 1 the sight of the Lord, when E was dead. 164
1Ch 7:10 E, and Chenaanah, and Zethan, 164
 8: 6 these *are* the sons of E: these *are* the heads 261

EIGHT (81) [EIGHTH]

Ge 5: 4 had begotten Seth were e hundred years: 8083
 5: 7 Seth lived after he begat Enos e hundred 8083
 5:10 lived after he begat Cainan e hundred 8083
 5:13 Cainan lived after he begat Mahalaleel e 8083
 5:16 Mahalaleel lived after he begat Jared e 8083
 5:17 all the days of Mahalaleel were e hundred 8083
 5:19 lived after he begat Enoch e hundred 8083
 17:12 he that is e days old shall be circumcised 8083
 21: 4 circumcised his son Isaac being e 8083
 22:23 these e Milcah did bear to Nahor, 8083
Ex 26: 2 The length of one curtain *shall be* e and 8083
 26:25 they shall be e boards, and their sockets 8083
 36: 9 of one curtain *was* twenty and e cubits, 8083
 36:30 there were e boards; and their sockets 8083
Nu 2:24 and e thousand and an hundred, 8083
 3:28 *were* e thousand and six hundred, 8083
 4:48 were e thousand and five hundred and 8083
 7: 8 e oxen he gave unto the sons of Merari, 8083
 29:29 on the sixth day e bullocks, two rams, 8083
 35: 7 to the Levites *shall be* forty and e cities: 8083
Dt 2:14 the brook Zered, *was* thirty and e years; 8083
Jos 31:41 *were* forty and e cities with their suburbs. 8083
Jdg 3: 8 Israel served Chushan-rishathaim e years. 8083
 12:14 ten ass colts: and he judged Israel e years. 8083
1Sa 4:15 Now Eli *was* ninety and e years old; 8083
 17:12 name *was* Jesse; and he had e sons: 8083
2Sa 23: 8 *he lift up his spear* against e hundred, 8083
 24: 9 there were in Israel e hundred thousand 8083
1Ki 7:10 of ten cubits, and stones of e cubits. 8083
2Ki 8:17 and he reigned e years in Jerusalem. 8083
 10:36 Israel in Samaria *was* twenty and e years. 8083
 22: 1 Josiah *was* e years old when he *began* to 8083
1Ch 12:24 spear *were* six thousand and e hundred, 8083
 12:30 Ephraim twenty thousand and e hundred, 8083
 12:35 and e thousand and six hundred. 8083
 16:38 with their brethren, threescore and e 8083
 23: 3 man by man, was thirty and e thousand. 8083
 24: 4 among the sons of Ithamar according to 8083
 25: 7 was two hundred fourscore and e. 8083
2Ch 11:21 begat twenty and e sons, 8083
 13: 3 with e hundred thousand chosen men, 8083
 21: 5 and he reigned e years in Jerusalem. 8083
 21:20 he reigned in Jerusalem e years, 8083
 29:17 the house of the Lord in days; 8083
 34: 1 Josiah *was* e years old when he *began* to 8083
 36: 9 Jehoiachin *was* e years old when he 8083
Ezr 2: 6 two thousand e hundred and twelve. 8083
 2:16 of Ater of Hezekiah, ninety and e. 8083
 2:23 of Anathoth, an hundred twenty and e. 8083
 2:41 of Asaph, an hundred twenty and e. 8083
 8:11 Bebai, and with him twenty and e males. 8083
Ne 7:11 thousand and e hundred *and* eighteen. 8083
 7:13 of Zattu, e hundred forty and five. 8083
 7:15 of Binnui, six hundred forty and e. 8083
 7:16 of Bebai, six hundred twenty and e. 8083
 7:21 of Ater of Hezekiah, ninety and e. 8083
 7:22 of Hashum, three hundred twenty and e. 8083
 7:26 Netophah, an hundred fourscore and e. 8083
 7:27 of Anathoth, an hundred twenty and e. 8083
 7:44 of Asaph, an hundred forty and e. 8083
 7:45 of Shobai, an hundred thirty and e. 8083
 11: 6 hundred threescore and e valiant men. 8083
 11: 8 Sallai, nine hundred twenty and e. 8083
 11:12 work of the house *were* e hundred 8083
 11:14 *men* of valour, an hundred twenty and e; 8083
Ecc 11: 2 Give a portion to seven, and also to e; 8083
Jer 41:15 escaped from Johanan with e men, 8083
 52:29 captive from Jerusalem e hundred thirty 8083
Eze 40: 9 the porch of the gate, e cubits; 8083
 40:31 and the going up to it *had* e steps. 8083
 40:34 side: and the going up to it *had* e steps. 8083
 40:37 side: and the going up to it *had* e steps. 8083
 40:41 e tables, whereupon they slew *their* 8083
 43:27 *that* upon the e day, and *so* forward, 8066
Mic 5: 5 seven shepherds, and e principal men. 8083

Lk 2:21 And when e days were accomplished for 3638
 9:28 And it came to pass about an e days after 3638
Jn 5: 5 which had an infirmity thirty *and* e years. 3638
 20:26 And after e days again his disciples were 3638
Ac 9:33 which had kept his bed e years, and was 3638
1Pe 3:20 that is, e souls were saved by water. 3638

EIGHTEEN (22) [EIGHTEENTH]

Ge 14:14 three hundred and e, 6240+8083
Jdg 3:14 Eglon the king of Moab e years. 6240+8083
 10: 8 e years, all the children of Israel 6240+8083
 20:25 of Israel again e thousand men; 6240+8083
 20:44 there fell of Benjamin e thousand 6240+8083
2Sa 8:13 valley of salt, *being* e thousand 6240+8083
1Ki 7:15 *of* brass, e cubits high apiece: 6240+8083
2Ki 24: 8 Jehoiachin *was* e years old when 6240+8083
 25:17 The height of the one pillar *was* e 6240+8083
1Ch 12:31 of the half tribe of Manasseh e 6240+8083
 18:12 in the valley of salt e thousand. 6240+8083
 26: 9 sons and brethren, strong men, e. 6240+8083
 29: 7 *of* brass e thousand 505+7239+8083+2050.1
2Ch 11:21 (for he took e wives, 6240+8083
Ezr 8: 9 him two hundred and e males. 6240+8083
 8:18 with his sons and his brethren, e; 6240+8083
Ne 7:11 and eight hundred *and* e. 6240+8083
Jer 52:21 height of one pillar *was* e cubits; 6240+8083
Eze 48:35 *It was* round about e thousand 6240+8083
Lk 13: 4 e, upon whom the tower 1176+2532+3638
 13:11 a spirit of infirmity e years, 1176+2532+3638
 13:16 Satan hath bound, lo *these* e 1176+2532+3638

EIGHTEENTH (11) [EIGHTEEN]

1Ki 15: 1 in the e year of king Jeroboam 6240+8083
2Ki 22: 3 it came to pass in the e year of king 6240+8083
 23:23 in the e year of king Josiah, 6240+8083
1Ch 24:15 to Hezir, the e to Aphses, 6240+8083
 25:25 The e to Hanani, *he,* his sons, 6240+8083
2Ch 13: 1 in the e year of king Jeroboam 6240+8083
 34: 8 Now in the e year of his reign, 6240+8083
 35:19 In the e year of the reign of Josiah 6240+8083
Jer 32: 1 *was* the e year of Nebuchadrezzar. 6240+8083
 52:29 In the e year of Nebuchadrezzar he 6240+8083

EIGHTH (38) [EIGHT]

Ex 22:30 dam; on the e day thou shalt give it me. 8066
Lev 9: 1 it came to pass on the e day, *that* Moses 8066
 12: 3 in the e day the flesh of his foreskin shall 8066
 14:10 on the e day he shall take two he lambs 8066
 14:23 he shall bring them on the e day for his 8066
 15:14 on the e day he shall take to him two 8066
 15:29 on the e day she shall take unto her two 8066
 22:27 from the e day and thenceforth it shall be 8066
 23:36 on the e day shall be a holy convocation 8066
 23:39 and on the e day *shall be* a sabbath. 8066
 25:22 ye shall sow the e year, and eat *yet* of old 8066
Nu 6:10 on the e day he shall bring two turtles, 8066
 7:54 On the e day *offered* Gamaliel the son of 8066
 29:35 On the e day ye shall have a solemn 8066
1Ki 6:38 in the month Bul, which *is* the e month, 8066
 8:66 On the e day he sent the people away: 8066
 12:32 Jeroboam ordained a feast in the e month, 8066
 12:33 Beth-el the fifteenth day of the e month, 8066
 16:29 year of Asa king of Judah *began* Ahab 8083
2Ki 15: 8 year of Azariah king of Judah did 8083
 24:12 king of Babylon took him in the e year 8083
1Ch 12:12 Johanan the e, Elzabad the ninth, 8066
 24:10 The seventh to Hakkoz, the e to Abijah, 8066
 25:15 The e *to* Jeshaiah, *he,* his sons, 8066
 26: 5 Issachar the seventh, Peulthai the e: 8066
 27:11 The e *captain* for the eighth month *was* 8066
 27:11 *captain* for the e month *was* 8066
2Ch 7: 9 the e day they made a solemn assembly: 8066
 29:17 on the e day of the month came they to 8083
 34: 3 For in the e year of his reign, while he 8083
Ne 8:18 on the e day *was* a solemn assembly, 8066
Zec 1: 1 In the e month, in the second year of 8066
Lk 1:59 *that* on the e day they came to circumcise 3590
Ac 7: 8 Isaac, and circumcised him the e day; 3590
Php 3: 5 Circumcised the e day, of the stock of 3637
2Pe 2: 5 saved Noah the e *person,* a preacher of 3590
Rev 17:11 even he is the e, and is of the seven, 3590
 21:20 the e, beryl; the ninth, a topaz; the tenth, 3590

EIGHTIETH (1) [EIGHTY]

1Ki 6: 1 e year after the children of Israel were 8084

EIGHTY (3) [EIGHTIETH, FOURSCORE]

Ge 5:25 Methuselah lived an hundred e and seven 8084
 5:26 after he begat Lamech seven hundred e 8084
 5:28 Lamech lived an hundred e and two years 8084

EITHER (41)

Ge 31:24 Take heed that thou speak not to Jacob e 4480
 31:29 heed that thou speak not to Jacob e good 4480
Lev 10: 1 took e[S] of them his censer, and put fire 376
 13:49 e in the warp, or in the woof, or in any 176
 13:51 e in the warp, or in the woof, or in a skin, 176
 13:53 e in the warp, or in the woof, or in any 176
 13:57 e in the warp, or in the woof, or in any 176
 13:58 e warp, or woof, or whatsoever thing of 176
 13:59 e in the warp, or woof, or any thing of 176
 22:23 E a bullock or a lamb that hath any 2050.1
 25:49 E his uncle, or his uncle's son, may redeem 176
Nu 6: 2 When e man or woman shall separate NIH

Nu	22:26 where *was* no way to turn *e* to the right	NIH
	24:13 to do *e* good or bad of mine own mind;	NIH
Dt	17: 3 *e* the sun, or moon, or any of the host	2050.1
	28:51 *also* shall not leave thee *e* corn, wine,	NIH
Jdg	9: 2 that all the sons of Jerubbaal, *which are*	518
1Sa	2 my father will do nothing *e* great or small,	NIH
	25:31 that thou hast shed blood causeless,	2050.1
	30: 2 *e* great or small, but carried *them* away,	4480
1Ki	7:15 a line of twelve cubits did compass *e* of	8145
	10:19 **on e side** on 2088+2088+4480+4480+2050.1	
	18:27 he is talking, or he is pursuing, or he is	3588
1Ch	21:12 *E* three years' famine; or three months to	518
2Ch	18: 9 Jehoshaphat king of Judah sat *e*[S] of them	376
Ecc	9: 1 no man knoweth *e* love or hatred *by* all	1571
	11: 6 this or that, or whether they both	1886.2
Isa	7:11 ask it *e* in the depth, or in the height	NIH
	17: 8 have made, *e* the groves, or the images.	2050.1
Eze	21:16 other, *e* on the right hand, or on the left,	NIH
Mt	6:24 for *e* he will hate the one, and love	2228
	12:33 *E* make the tree good, and his fruit good;	2228
Lk	6:42 *E* how canst thou say to thy brother,	2228
	15: 8 *E* what woman having ten pieces of silver	2228
	16:13 for *e* he will hate the one, and love	2228
Jn	19:18 with him, **on e side one,** 1782+1782+2532	
Ac	17:21 but *e* to tell, or to hear some new *thing*.)	NIG
1Co	14: 6 I shall speak to you *e* by revelation,	2228
Php	3:12 already attained, *e* were already perfect:	2228
Jas	3:12 *e* a vine, figs? so *can* no fountain *both*	2228
Rev	22: 2 and **of e side** of the river, 1782+1782+2532	

EKER (1)

1Ch	2:27 Jerahmeel were, Maaz, and Jamin, and *E*.	6134

EKRON (22) [EKRONITES]

Jos	13: 3 even unto the borders of *E* northward,	6138
	15:11 the border went out unto the side of *E*	6138
	15:45 *E*, with her towns and her villages:	6138
	15:46 From *E* even unto the sea, all that *lay*	6138
	19:43 And Elon, and Thimnathah, and *E*,	6138
Jdg	1:18 thereof, and *E* with the coast thereof.	6138
1Sa	5:10 Therefore they sent the ark of God to *E*.	6138
	5:10 to pass, as the ark of God came *to E*,	6138
	6:16 seen *it*, they returned to *E* the same day.	6138
	6:17 for Askelon one, for Gath one, for *E* one;	6138
	7:14 restored to Israel, from *E* even unto Gath;	6138
	17:52 come *to* the valley, and to the gates of *E*.	6138
	17:52 to Shaaraim, even unto Gath, and unto *E*.	6138
2Ki	1: 2 inquire of Baal-zebub the god of *E*	6138
	1: 3 go to inquire of Baal-zebub the god of *E*?	6138
	1: 6 to inquire of Baal-zebub the god of *E*?	6138
	1:16 to inquire of Baal-zebub the god of *E*,	6138
Jer	25:20 and *E*, and the remnant of Ashdod:	6138
Am	1: 8 and I will turn mine hand against *E*:	6138
Zep	2: 4 at the noon day, and *E* shall be rooted up.	6138
Zec	9: 5 *shall see it*, and be very sorrowful, and *E*;	6138
	9: 7 a governor in Judah, and *E* as a Jebusite.	6138

EKRONITES (2) [EKRON]

Jos	13: 3 the Eshkalonites, the Gittites, and the *E*;	6139
1Sa	5:10 came *to* Ekron, that the *E* cried out,	6139

ELADAH (1)

1Ch	7:20 his son, and *E* his son, and Tahath his son,	497

ELAH (17)

Ge	36:41 Duke Aholibamah, duke *E*, duke Pinon,	425
1Sa	17: 2 pitched by the valley of *E*, and set the battle	425
	17:19 the men of Israel, *were* in the valley of *E*,	425
	21: 9 whom thou slewest in the valley of *E*,	425
1Ki	4:18 Shimei the son of *E*, in Benjamin:	414
	16: 6 Tirzah: and *E* his son reigned in his stead.	425
	16: 8 sixth year of Asa king of Judah *began E*	425
	16:13 the sins of *E* his son, *by* which they sinned,	425
	16:14 Now the rest of the acts of *E*, and all that	425
2Ki	15:30 Hoshea the son of *E* made a conspiracy	425
	17: 1 to reign in Samaria over Israel nine years.	425
	18: 1 third year of Hoshea son of *E* king of Israel,	425
	18: 9 year of Hoshea son of *E* king of Israel,	425
1Ch	1:52 Duke Aholibamah, duke *E*, duke Pinon,	425
	4:15 the son of Jephunneh; Iru, *E*, and Naam:	425
	4:15 and Naam: and the sons of *E*, even Kenaz.	425
	9: 8 and *E* the son of Uzzi, the son of Michri,	425

ELAM (28) [ELAMITES]

Ge	10:22 *E*, and Asshur, and Arphaxad, and Lud,	5867
	14: 1 Chedorlaomer king of *E*, and Tidal king of	5867
	14: 9 With Chedorlaomer the king of *E*,	5867
1Ch	1:17 *E*, and Asshur, and Arphaxad, and Lud,	5867
	8:24 And Hananiah, and *E*, and Antothijah,	5867
	26: 3 *E* the fifth, Jehohanan the sixth,	5867
Ezr	2: 7 children of *E*, a thousand two hundred	5867
	2:31 children of the other *E*, a thousand two	5867
	8: 7 of the sons of *E*; Jeshaiah the son of	5867
	10: 2 *one* of the sons of *E*, answered and	5867
	10:26 of the sons of *E*; Mattaniah, Zechariah,	5867
Ne	7:12 children of *E*, a thousand two hundred	5867
	7:34 children of the other *E*, a thousand two	5867
	10:14 Parosh, Pahath-moab, *E*, Zatthu, Bani,	5867
	12:42 and Malchijah, and *E*, and Ezer.	5867
Isa	11:11 from *E*, and from Shinar,	5867
	21: 2 Go up, O *E*: besiege, O Media;	5867
	22: 6 *E* bare the quiver with chariots and men	5867
Jer	25:25 all the kings of *E*, and all the kings of	5867
	49:34 *E* in the beginning of the reign of	5867
	49:35 I *will* break the bow of *E*, the chief	5867

Jer	49:36 upon *E* will I bring the four winds from	5867
	49:36 whither the outcasts of *E* shall not come.	5867
	49:37 For I will cause *E* to be dismayed before	5867
	49:38 I will set my throne in *E*, and will destroy	5867
	49:39 *that* I will bring again the captivity of *E*,	5867
Eze	32:24 There *is E* and all her multitude round	5867
Da	8: 2 the palace, which *is* in the province of *E*;	5867

ELAMITES (2) [ELAM]

Ezr	4: 9 the Susanchites, the Dehavites, *and the* *E*,	5962
Ac	2: 9 and *E*, and the dwellers in Mesopotamia,	1639

ELAPSED See EXPIRED

ELASAH (2)

Ezr	10:22 Ishmael, Nethaneel, Jozabad, and *E*.	501
Jer	29: 3 By the hand of *E* the son of Shaphan,	501

ELATH (5) [ELOTH]

Dt	2: 8 through the way of the plain from *E*,	359
2Ki	14:22 He built *E*, and restored it to Judah, after	359
	16: 6 that time Rezin king of Syria recovered *E*	359
	16: 6 Elath to Syria, and drave the Jews from *E*:	359
	16: 6 the Syrians came *to E*, and dwelt there	359

EL-BERITH See BERITH; GOD

EL-BETH-EL (1) [BETH-EL]

Ge	35: 7 built there an altar, and called the place *E*:	416

ELDAAH (2)

Ge	25: 4 Epher, and Hanoch, and Abidah, and *E*.	420
1Ch	1:33 Epher, and Henoch, and Abida, and *E*.	420

ELDAD (2)

Nu	11:26 the name of the one *was E*, and the name	419
	11:27 *E* and Medad do prophesy in the camp.	419

ELDER (20) [OLD]

Ge	10:21 the brother of Japheth the *e*, even to him	1419
	25:23 and the *e* shall serve the younger.	7227
	27:42 these words of Esau her *e* son were told	1419
	29:16 name of the *e* *was* Leah, and the name	1419
1Sa	18:17 To David, Behold my *e* daughter Merab,	1419
1Ki	2:22 for he *is* mine *e* brother; even for 1419+4480	
Job	15:10 very aged men, much *e* than thy father.	3117
	32: 4 because they *were e* than 2205+3117+3807.1	
Eze	16:46 thine *e* sister *is* Samaria, she and	1419
	16:61 thy sisters, thine *e* and thy younger:	1419
	23: 4 the names of them *were* Aholah the *e*,	1419
Lk	15:25 Now his *e* son was in the field: and as he	4245
Ro	9:12 unto her, The *e* shall serve the younger.	3187
1Ti	5: 1 Rebuke not an *e*, but intreat *him* as a	4245
	5: 2 The *e* *women* as mothers; the younger as	4245
	5:19 Against an *e* receive not an accusation,	4245
1Pe	5: 1 who am **also an** *e*, and a witness of	4850
	5: 5 *ye* younger, submit yourselves unto the *e*.	4245
2Jn	1: 1 The *e* unto the elect lady and her children	4245
3Jn	1: 1 The *e* unto the wellbeloved Gaius,	4245

ELDERS (179) [OLD]

Ge	50: 7 the *e* of his house, and all the elders of	2205
	50: 7 and all the *e* of the land of Egypt,	2205
Ex	3:16 gather the *e* of Israel together, and say	2205
	3:18 thou shalt come, thou and the *e* of Israel,	2205
	4:29 gathered together all the *e* of the children	2205
	12:21 Moses called for all the *e* of Israel,	2205
	17: 5 and take with thee of the *e* of Israel;	2205
	17: 6 Moses did so in the sight of the *e* of Israel.	2205
	18:12 Aaron came, and all the *e* of Israel, to eat	2205
	19: 7 and called for the *e* of the people,	2205
	24: 1 and Abihu, and seventy of the *e* of Israel;	2205
	24: 9 and Abihu, and seventy of the *e* of Israel:	2205
	24:14 he said unto the *e*, Tarry ye here for us,	2205
Lev	4:15 the *e* of the congregation shall lay their	2205
	9: 1 and his sons, and the *e* of Israel;	2205
Nu	11:16 Gather unto me seventy men of the *e* of	2205
	11:16 whom thou knowest to be the *e* of	2205
	11:24 gathered the seventy men of the *e* of	2205
	11:25 upon him, and gave *it* unto the seventy *e*:	2205
	11:30 him into the camp, he and the *e* of Israel.	2205
	16:25 Abiram; and the *e* of Israel followed him.	2205
	22: 4 Moab said unto the *e* of Midian, Now	2205
	22: 7 the *e* of Moab and the elders of Midian	2205
	22: 7 the *e* of Midian departed with the	2205
Dt	5:23 all the heads of your tribes, and your *e*;	2205
	19:12 the *e* of his city shall send and fetch him	2205
	21: 2 thy *e* and thy judges shall come forth,	2205
	21: 3 even the *e* of that city shall take a heifer,	2205
	21: 4 *e* of that city shall bring down the heifer	2205
	21: 6 all the *e* of that city, *that are* next unto	2205
	21:19 and bring him out unto the *e* of his city,	2205
	21:20 they shall say unto the *e* of his city,	2205
	22:15 virginity unto the *e* of the city in the gate:	2205
	22:16 the damsel's father shall say unto the *e*,	2205
	22:17 they shall spread the cloth before the *e* of	2205
	22:18 the *e* of that city shall take *that* man and	2205
	25: 7 wife go up to the gate unto the *e*,	2205
	25: 8 the *e* of his city shall call him,	2205
	25: 9 come unto him in the presence of the *e*,	2205
	27: 1 Moses with the *e* of Israel commanded	2205
	29:10 *e*, and your officers, *with* all the men	2205
	31: 9 of the LORD, and unto all the *e* of Israel.	2205
	31:28 Gather unto me all the *e* of your tribes,	2205
	32: 7 shew thee; thy *e*, and they will tell thee.	2205
Jos	7: 6 he and the *e* of Israel, and put dust upon	2205

Jos	8:10 and went up, he and the *e* of Israel,	2205
	8:33 and their *e*, and officers, and their judges,	2205
	9:11 Wherefore our *e* and all the inhabitants of	2205
	20: 4 shall declare his cause in the ears of the *e*	2205
	23: 2 *and* for their *e*, and for their heads,	2205
	24: 1 called for the *e* of Israel, and for their	2205
	24:31 all the days of the *e* that overlived Joshua,	2205
Jdg	2: 7 all the days of the *e* that outlived Joshua,	2205
	8:14 the *e* thereof, *even* threescore	2205
	8:16 he took the *e* of the city, and thorns of	2205
	11: 5 the *e* of Gilead went to fetch Jephthah	2205
	11: 7 Jephthah said unto the *e* of Gilead, Did	2205
	11: 8 the *e* of Gilead said unto Jephthah,	2205
	11: 9 Jephthah said unto the *e* of Gilead, If ye	2205
	11:10 the *e* of Gilead said unto Jephthah,	2205
	11:11 Jephthah went with the *e* of Gilead,	2205
	21:16 the *e* of the congregation said, How shall	2205
Ru	4: 2 he took ten men of the *e* of the city,	2205
	4: 4 and before the *e* of my people.	2205
	4: 9 Boaz said unto the *e*, and *unto* all	2205
	4:11 gate, and the *e*, said, We *are* witnesses.	2205
1Sa	4: 3 come into the camp, the *e* of Israel said,	2205
	8: 4 all the *e* of Israel gathered themselves	2205
	11: 3 the *e* of Jabesh said unto him, Give us	2205
	15:30 before the *e* of my people,	2205
	16: 4 the *e* of the town trembled at his coming,	2205
	30:26 he sent of the spoil unto the *e* of Judah,	2205
2Sa	3:17 Abner had communication with the *e* of	2205
	5: 3 So all the *e* of Israel came to the king to	2205
	12:17 the *e* of his house arose, *and went* to him	2205
	17: 4 Absalom well, and all the *e* of Israel.	2205
	17:15 counsel Absalom and the *e* of Israel;	2205
	19:11 Speak unto the *e* of Judah, saying,	2205
1Ki	8: 1 Solomon assembled the *e* of Israel,	2205
	8: 3 all the *e* of Israel came, and the priests	2205
	20: 7 the king of Israel called all the *e* of	2205
	20: 8 all the *e* and all the people said unto him,	2205
	21: 8 the letters unto the *e* and to the nobles	2205
	21:11 *even* the *e* and the nobles who were	2205
2Ki	6:32 sat in his house, and the *e* sat with him;	2205
	6:32 messenger came to him, he said to the *e*,	2205
	10: 1 to the *e*, and to them that brought up	2205
	10: 5 the *e* also, and the bringers up *of*	2205
	19: 2 the scribe, and the *e* of the priests,	2205
	23: 1 they gathered unto him all the *e* of Judah	2205
1Ch	11: 3 Therefore came all the *e* of Israel to	2205
	15:25 the *e* of Israel, and the captains over	2205
	21:16 the *e* *of Israel, who were* clothed in	2205
2Ch	5: 2 Solomon assembled the *e* of Israel,	2205
	5: 4 all the *e* of Israel came; and the Levites	2205
	34:29 gathered together all the *e* of Judah and	2205
Ezr	5: 5 the eye of their God was upon the *e* of	7868
	5: 9 asked we those *e*, *and* said unto them	7868
	6: 7 the *e* of the Jews build this house of God	7868
	6: 8 *e* of these Jews for the building of this	7868
	6:14 the *e* of the Jews builded,	7868
	10: 8 to the counsel of the princes and the *e*,	2205
	10: 8 to the *e* of every city,	2205
Ps	107:32 and praise him in the assembly of the *e*.	2205
Pr	31:23 when he sitteth among the *e* of the land.	2205
Isa	37: 2 of the priests covered with sackcloth,	2205
Jer	26:17 rose up certain of the *e* of the land,	2205
	29: 1 the *e* which were carried away captives,	2205
La	1:19 and mine *e* gave up the ghost in the city,	2205
	2:10 The *e* of the daughter of Zion sit upon	2205
	4:16 of the priests, they favoured not the *e*.	2205
	5:12 the faces of *e* were not honoured.	2205
	5:14 The *e* have ceased from the gate,	2205
Eze	8: 1 and the *e* of Judah sat before me,	2205
	14: 1 came certain of the *e* of Israel unto me,	2205
	20: 1 *that* certain of the *e* of Israel came to	2205
	20: 3 speak unto the *e* of Israel, and say unto	2205
Joel	1:14 gather the *e* *and* all the inhabitants of	2205
	2:16 assemble the *e*, gather the children,	2205
Mt	15: 2 disciples transgress the tradition of the *e*?	4245
	16:21 and suffer many *things* of the *e* and	4245
	21:23 the *e* of the people came unto him as he	4245
	26: 3 and the scribes, and the *e* of the people,	4245
	26:47 from the chief priests and *e* of the people.	4245
	26:57 the scribes and the *e* were assembled.	4245
	26:59 chief priests, and *e*, and all the council,	4245
	27: 1 of the people took counsel against Jesus	4245
	27: 3 pieces of silver to the chief priests and *e*,	4245
	27:12 he was accused of the chief priests and *e*,	4245
	27:20 persuaded the multitude that they	4245
	27:41 mocking *him*, with the scribes and *e*	4245
	28:12 when they were assembled with the *e*,	4245
Mk	7: 3 eat not, holding the tradition of the *e*.	4245
	7: 5 according to the tradition of the *e*,	4245
	8:31 many *things*, and be rejected of the *e*,	4245
	11:27 chief priests, and the scribes, and the *e*,	4245
	14:43 chief priests and the scribes and the *e*.	4245
	14:53 chief priests and the *e* and the scribes.	4245
	15: 1 priests held a consultation with the *e*	4245
Lk	7: 3 Jesus, he sent unto him the *e* of the Jews,	4245
	9:22 and be rejected of the *e* and chief priests	4245
	20: 1 the scribes came upon *him* with the *e*,	4245
	22:52 and captains of the temple, and the *e*,	4245
	22:66 the *e* of the people and the chief priests	4244
Ac	4: 5 that their rulers, and *e*, and scribes,	4245
	4: 8 Ye rulers of the people, and *e* of Israel,	4245
	4:23 chief priests and *e* had said unto them.	4245
	6:12 the *e*, and the scribes, and came upon	4245
	11:30 sent it to the *e* by the hands of Barnabas	4245
	14:23 And when they had ordained them *e* in	4245

Ac	15: 2	the apostles and **e** about this question.	4245
	15: 4	*of* the apostles and **e**, and they declared	4245
	15: 6	came together for to consider of this	4245
	15:22	Then pleased it the apostles and **e**, with	4245
	15:23	The apostles and **e** and brethren *send*	4245
	16: 4	apostles and **e** which were at Jerusalem.	4245
	20:17	Ephesus, and called the **e** of the church.	4245
	21:18	us unto James; and all the **e** were present.	4245
	22: 5	witness, and all the **estate of the e**:	4244
	23:14	And they came to the chief priests and **e**,	4245
1Ti	24: 1	the high priest descended with the **e**,	4245
	25:15	the **e** of the Jews informed *me*, desiring	4245
	5:17	the **e** that rule well be counted worthy	4245
Tit	1: 5	and ordain **e** in every city, as I had	4245
Heb	11: 2	For by it the **e** obtained a good report.	4245
Jas	5:14	let him call for the **e** of the church;	4245
1Pe	5: 1	The **e** which are among you I exhort,	4245
Rev	4: 4	the seats I saw four and twenty **e** sitting,	4245
	4:10	twenty **e** fall down before him that sat on	4245
	5: 5	one of the **e** saith unto me, Weep not:	4245
	5: 6	the four beasts, and in the midst of the **e**,	4245
	5: 8	*and* twenty **e** fell down before the Lamb,	4245
	5:11	the throne and the beasts and the **e**:	4245
	5:14	And the four *and* twenty **e** fell down and	4245
	7:11	and *about* the **e** and the four beasts,	4245
	7:13	one of the **e** answered, saying unto me,	4245
	11:16	the four and twenty **e**, which sat before	4245
	14: 3	and before the four beasts, and the **e**:	4245
	19: 4	And the four and twenty **e** and the four	4245

ELDEST (14) [OLD]

Ge	24: 2	Abraham said unto his **e** servant of his	2205
	27: 1	called Esau his **e** son, and said unto him,	1419
	27:15	Rebekah took goodly raiment of her **e** son	1419
	44:12	began at the **e**, and left at the youngest:	1419
Nu	1:20	Israel's **e son**, *by* their generations,	1060
	26: 5	Reuben, the **e son** of Israel: the children	1060
1Sa	17:13	the three sons of Jesse went *and*	1419
	17:14	youngest: and the three **e** followed Saul.	1419
	17:28	Eliab his **e** brother heard when he spake	1419
2Ki	3:27	took his **e** son that should have reigned	1060
2Ch	21: 3	Arabians to the camp had slain all the **e**.	7223
Job	1:13	drinking wine in their **e** brother's house:	1060
	1:18	drinking wine in their **e** brother's house:	1060
Jn	8: 9	beginning at the **e**, *even* unto the last:	4245

ELEAD (1)

1Ch	7:21	and Shuthelah his son, and Ezer, and **E**,	496

ELEADAH See ELADAH

ELEALEH (5)

Nu	32: 3	and **E**, and Shebam, and Nebo, and Beon,	500
	32:37	built Heshbon, and **E**, and Kirjathaim,	500
Isa	15: 4	Heshbon shall cry, and **E**: their voice shall	500
	16: 9	thee *with* my tears, O Heshbon, and **E**:	500
Jer	48:34	From the cry of Heshbon *even* unto **E**,	500

ELEASAH (4)

1Ch	2:39	Azariah begat Helez, and Helez begat **E**,	501
	2:40	**E** begat Sisamai, and Sisamai begat	501
	8:37	Rapha *was* his son, **E** his son, Azel his son:	501
	9:43	Rephaiah his son, **E** his son, Azel his son.	501

ELEAZAR (74)

Ex	6:23	him Nadab, and Abihu, **E**, and Ithamar.	499
	6:25	**E** Aaron's son took him *one* of the	499
	28: 1	Nadab and Abihu, **E** and Ithamar,	499
Lev	10: 6	unto **E** and unto Ithamar his sons,	499
	10:12	unto **E** and unto Ithamar his sons that	499
	10:16	he was angry with **E** and Ithamar the sons	499
Nu	3: 2	the firstborn, and Abihu, **E**, and Ithamar.	499
	3: 4	**E** and Ithamar ministered in the priest's	499
	3:32	**E** the son of Aaron the priest *shall be* chief	499
	4:16	the office of **E** the son of Aaron the priest	499
	16:37	Speak unto **E** the son of Aaron the priest,	499
	16:39	**E** the priest took the brasen censers,	499
	19: 3	ye shall give her unto **E** the priest, that he	499
	19: 4	**E** the priest shall take of her blood with his	499
	20:25	Take Aaron and **E** his son, and bring them	499
	20:26	garments, and put them upon **E** his son:	499
	20:28	garments, and put them upon **E** his son;	499
	20:28	Moses and **E** came down from the mount.	499
	25: 7	when Phinehas, the son of **E**, the son of	499
	25:11	Phinehas, the son of **E**, the son of Aaron	499
	26: 1	and unto **E** the son of Aaron the priest,	499
	26: 3	The priest spake with them in the plains	499
	26:60	born Nadab, and Abihu, **E**, and Ithamar.	499
	26:63	were numbered by Moses and **E** the priest,	499
	27: 2	before **E** the priest, and before the princes	499
	27:19	set him before **E** the priest, and before all	499
	27:21	he shall stand before **E** the priest, who	499
	27:22	set him before **E** the priest, and before all	499
	31: 6	them and Phinehas the son of **E** the priest,	499
	31:12	**E** the priest, and unto the congregation of	499
	31:13	**E** the priest, and all the princes of	499
	31:21	**E** the priest said unto the men of war	499
	31:26	thou, and **E** the priest, and the chief fathers	499
	31:29	of their half, and give *it* unto **E** the priest,	499
	31:31	**E** the priest did as the LORD commanded	499
	31:41	unto **E** the priest, as the LORD commanded	499
	31:51	and **E** the priest took the gold of them,	499
	31:54	**E** the priest took the gold of the captains	499
	32: 2	to **E** the priest, and unto the princes of	499
	32:28	So concerning them Moses commanded **E**	499
	34:17	**E** the priest, and Joshua the son of Nun.	499

Dt	10: 6	**E** his son ministered in the priest's office	499
Jos	14: 1	which **E** the priest, and Joshua the son of	499
	17: 4	And they came near before **E** the priest,	499
	19:51	which **E** the priest, and Joshua the son of	499
	21: 1	the fathers of the Levites unto **E** the priest,	499
	22:13	of Gilead, Phinehas the son of **E** the priest,	499
	22:31	Phinehas the son of **E** the priest said unto	499
	22:32	Phinehas the son of **E** the priest,	499
	24:33	**E** the son of Aaron died; and they buried	499
Jdg	20:28	Phinehas, the son of **E**, the son of Aaron,	499
1Sa	7: 1	sanctified **E** his son to keep the ark of	499
2Sa	23: 9	after him *was* **E** the son of Dodo	499
1Ch	6: 3	Nadab, and Abihu, **E**, and Ithamar.	499
	6: 4	**E** begat Phinehas, Phinehas begat Abishua,	499
	6:50	**E** his son, Phinehas his son, Abishua his	499
	9:20	Phinehas the son of **E** was the ruler over	499
	11:12	after him *was* **E** the son of Dodo,	499
	23:21	and Mushi. The sons of Mahli; **E**, and Kish.	499
	23:22	**E** died, and had no sons, but daughters:	499
	24: 1	Nadab, and Abihu, **E**, and Ithamar.	499
	24: 2	**E** and Ithamar executed the priest's	499
	24: 3	both Zadok of the sons of **E**,	499
	24: 4	the sons of **E** than of the sons of Ithamar,	499
	24: 4	Among the sons of **E** *there were* sixteen	499
	24: 5	were of the sons of **E**, and of the sons of	499
	24: 6	one principal household being taken for **E**,	499
	24:28	Of Mahli *came* **E**, who had no sons.	499
Ezr	7: 5	the son of Phinehas, the son of **E**,	499
	8:33	and with him *was* **E** the son of Phinehas;	499
	10:25	and **E**, and Malchijah, and Benaiah.	499
Ne	12:42	**E**, and Uzzi, and Jehohanan,	499
Mt	1:15	And Eliud begat **E**; and Eleazar begat	1648
	1:15	begat Matthan; and Matthan begat	1648

ELECT (17) [ELECT'S, ELECTED, ELECTION, ELECTS']

Isa	42: 1	mine **e**, *in whom* my soul delighteth;	972
	45: 4	Jacob my servant's sake, and Israel mine **e**,	972
	65: 9	mine **e** shall inherit it, and my servants	972
	65:22	mine **e** shall long enjoy the work of their	972
Mt	24:24	possible, *they shall* deceive the very **e**.	1588
	24:31	they shall gather together his **e** from	1588
Mk	13:22	to seduce, if *it were* possible, even the **e**.	1588
	13:27	shall gather together his **e** from the four	1588
Lk	18: 7	And shall not God avenge his own **e**,	1588
Ro	8:33	lay any thing to the charge of God's **e**?	1588
Col	3:12	as the **e** of God, holy and beloved,	1588
1Ti	5:21	the Lord Jesus Christ, and the **e** angels,	1588
Tit	1: 1	according to the faith of God's **e**,	1588
1Pe	1: 2	**E** according to the foreknowledge of God	1588
	2: 6	in Sion a chief corner stone, **e**, precious;	1588
2Jn	1: 1	elder unto the **e** lady and her children,	1588
	1:13	The children of thy **e** sister greet thee.	1588

ELECT'S (2) [ELECT]

Mt	24:22	the **e** sake those days shall be shortened.	1588
Mk	13:20	but for the **e** sake, whom he hath chosen,	1588

ELECTED (1) [ELECT]

1Pe	5:13	**e together with** you, saluteth you;	4899

ELECTION (6) [ELECT]

Ro	9:11	that the purpose of God according to **e**	1589
	11: 5	is a remnant according to the **e** of grace.	1589
	11: 7	the **e** hath obtained *it*, and the rest were	1589
	11:28	as touching the **e**, *they are* beloved for	1589
1Th	1: 4	brethren beloved, your **e** of God.	1589
2Pe	1:10	diligence to make your calling and **e** sure:	1589

ELECTS' (1) [ELECT]

2Ti	2:10	Therefore I endure all *things* for the **e**	1588

ELEGANT See GORGEOUS

EL-ELOHE-ISRAEL (1) [ISRAEL]

Ge	33:20	he erected there an altar, and called it **E**.	415

ELEMENTS (4)

Gal	4: 3	in bondage under the **e** of the world:	4747
	4: 9	turn ye again to the weak and beggarly **e**,	4747
2Pe	3:10	and the **e** shall melt with fervent heat,	4747
	3:12	and the **e** shall melt with fervent heat?	4747

ELEPH (1)

Jos	18:28	Zelah, **E**, and Jebusi, which *is* Jerusalem,	507

ELEUZAI (1)

1Ch	12: 5	**E**, and Jerimoth, and Bealiah,	498

ELEVEN (24) [ELEVENTH]

Ge	32:22	his **e** sons, and passed over the ford	259+6240
	37: 9	the stars made obeisance to me.	259+6240
Ex	26: 7	**e** curtains shalt thou make.	6240+6249
	26: 8	**e** curtains *shall be all* of one	6240+6249
	36:14	**e** curtains he made them.	6240+6249
	36:15	the **e** curtains *were* of one size.	6240+6249
Nu	29:20	on the third day **e** bullocks,	6240+6249
Dt	1: 2	*are* days' *journey* from Horeb	259+6240
Jos	15:51	Giloh; **e** cities with their villages.	259+6240
Jdg	16: 5	**e hundred** *pieces* of silver.	505+3967+2050.1
	17: 2	The **e hundred** *shekels*	505+3967+2050.1
	17: 3	**e hundred** *shekels* of silver	505+3967+2050.1
2Ki	23:36	and he reigned **e** years in Jerusalem.	259+6240
	24:18	and he reigned **e** years in Jerusalem.	259+6240
2Ch	36: 5	and he reigned **e** years in Jerusalem:	259+6240
	36:11	and reigned **e** years in Jerusalem.	259+6240
Jer	52: 1	and he reigned **e** years in Jerusalem.	259+6240

Eze	40:49	and the breadth **e** cubits;	6240+6249
Mt	28:16	Then the **e** disciples went *away* unto	1733
Mk	16:14	Afterward he appeared unto the **e** as they	1733
Lk	24: 9	and told all these *things* unto the **e**,	1733
	24:33	and found the **e** gathered together,	1733
Ac	1:26	and he was numbered with the **e** apostles.	1733
	2:14	Peter, standing up with the **e**, lift up his	1733

ELEVENTH (20) [ELEVEN]

Nu	7:72	On the **e** day Pagiel the son of	6240+6249
Dt	1: 3	in the **e** month, on the first *day* of	6240+6249
1Ki	6:38	in the **e** year, in the month Bul,	259+6240
2Ki	9:29	in the **e** year of Joram the son of	259+6240
	25: 2	city was besieged unto the **e** year	6240+6249
1Ch	12:13	the tenth, Machbanai the **e**.	6240+6249
	24:12	The **e** to Eliashib, the twelfth to	6240+6249
	25:18	The **e** *to* Azareel, *he,* his sons,	6240+6249
	27:14	The **e** *captain* for the eleventh	6240+6249
	27:14	eleventh *captain* for the **e** month	6240+6249
Jer	1: 3	unto the end of the **e** year of	6240+6249
	39: 2	*And* in the **e** year of Zedekiah,	6240+6249
	52: 5	the city was besieged unto the **e**	6240+6249
Eze	26: 1	it came to pass in the **e** year,	6240+6249
	30:20	it came to pass in the **e** year,	259+6240
	31: 1	it came to pass in the **e** year,	259+6240
Zec	1: 7	and twentieth day of the **e** month,	6240+6249
Mt	20: 6	And about the **e** hour he went out,	1734
	20: 9	came that *were hired* about the **e** hour,	1734
Rev	21:20	the **e**, a jacinth; the twelfth, an amethyst.	1734

ELHANAN (4)

2Sa	21:19	where **E** the son of Jaare-oregim,	445
	23:24	thirty; **E** the son of Dodo *of* Beth-lehem,	445
1Ch	11:26	of Joab, **E** the son of Dodo of Beth-lehem,	445
	20: 5	**E** the son of Jair slew Lahmi the brother of	445

ELI (34) [ELI'S, ELOI]

1Sa	1: 3	the two sons of **E**, Hophni and Phinehas.	5941
	1: 9	Now **E** the priest sat upon a seat by a post	5941
	1:12	the LORD, that **E** marked her mouth.	5941
	1:13	**E** thought she had been drunken.	5941
	1:14	**E** said unto her, How long wilt thou be	5941
	1:17	**E** answered and said, Go in peace:	5941
	1:25	a bullock, and brought the child to **E**.	5941
	2:11	unto the LORD before **E** the priest.	5941
	2:12	Now the sons of **E** *were* sons of Belial;	5941
	2:20	**E** blessed Elkanah and his wife, and said,	5941
	2:22	Now **E** was very old, and heard all that	5941
	2:27	there came a man of God unto **E**,	5941
	3: 1	ministered unto the LORD before **E**.	5941
	3: 2	when **E** *was* laid down in his place,	5941
	3: 5	he ran unto **E**, and said, Here *am* I;	5941
	3: 6	Samuel arose and went to **E**, and said,	5941
	3: 8	he arose and went to **E**, and said, Here	5941
	3: 8	**E** perceived that the LORD had called	5941
	3: 9	Therefore **E** said unto Samuel,	5941
	3:12	In that day I will perform against **E** all	5941
	3:14	I have sworn unto the house of **E**,	5941
	3:15	And Samuel feared to shew **E** the vision.	5941
	3:16	**E** called Samuel, and said, Samuel, my	5941
	4: 4	the two sons of **E**, Hophni and Phinehas,	5941
	4:11	the two sons of **E**, Hophni and Phinehas,	5941
	4:13	**E** sat upon a seat *by* the wayside watching	5941
	4:14	when **E** heard the noise of the crying,	5941
	4:15	Now **E** was ninety and eight years old;	5941
	4:16	the man said unto **E**, I *am* he that came	5941
	14: 3	the son of Phinehas, the son of **E**,	5941
1Ki	2:27	he spake concerning the house of **E**	5941
Mt	27:46	saying, **E, ELI, LAMA SABACHTHANI?**	2241
	27:46	saying, **ELI, E, LAMA SABACHTHANI?**	2241

ELI'S (1) [ELI]

1Sa	3:14	that the iniquity of **E** house shall not be	5941

ELIAB (20) [ELIAB'S]

Nu	1: 9	Of Zebulun; **E** the son of Helon.	446
	2: 7	**E** the son of Helon *shall be* captain of	446
	7:24	On the third day **E** the son of Helon,	446
	7:29	this *was* the offering of **E** the son of Helon.	446
	10:16	of Zebulun *was* **E** the son of Helon.	446
	16: 1	and Abiram, the sons of **E**, and On,	446
	16:12	to call Dathan and Abiram, the sons of **E**:	446
	26: 8	And the sons of Pallu; **E**.	446
	26: 9	And the sons of **E**; Nemuel, and Dathan,	446
Dt	11: 6	unto Dathan and Abiram, the sons of **E**,	446
1Sa	16: 6	were come, that he looked on **E**, and said,	446
	17:13	went to the battle were **E** the firstborn,	446
	17:28	**E** his eldest brother heard when he spake	446
1Ch	2:13	Jesse begat his firstborn **E**, and Abinadab	446
	6:27	**E** his son, Jeroham his son, Elkanah his	446
	12: 9	the first, Obadiah the second, **E** the third,	446
	15:18	**E**, and Benaiah, and Maaseiah,	446
	15:20	Unni, and **E**, and Maaseiah, and Benaiah,	446
	16: 5	and **E**, and Benaiah, and Obed-edom:	446
2Ch	11:18	Abihail the daughter of **E** the son of Jesse;	446

ELIAB'S (1) [ELIAB]

1Sa	17:28	and **E** anger was kindled against David,	446

ELIADA (3)

2Sa	5:16	And Elishama, and **E**, and Eliphalet.	450
1Ch	3: 8	And Elishama, and **E**, and Eliphelet, nine.	450
2Ch	17:17	**E** a mighty *man* of valour, and with him	450

ELIADAH (1)
1Ki 11:23 up *another* adversary, Rezon the son of E, 450

ELIAH (2)
1Ch 8:27 Jaresiah, and E, and Zichri, the sons of 452
Ezr 10:26 and Jehiel, and Abdi, and Jeremoth, and E. 452

ELIAHBA (2)
2Sa 23:32 the Shaalbonite, *of* the sons of Jashen, 455
1Ch 11:33 the Baharumite, E the Shaalbonite, 455

ELIAKIM (15) [JEHOIAKIM]
2Ki 18:18 came out to them E the son of Hilkiah, 471
18:26 said E the son of Hilkiah, and Shebna, 471
18:37 came E the son of Hilkiah, which *was* over 471
19: 2 he sent E, which *was* over the household, 471
23:34 Pharaoh-nechoh made E the son of Josiah 471
2Ch 36: 4 the king of Egypt made E his brother king 471
Ne 12:41 E, Maaseiah, Miniamin, Michaiah, 471
Isa 22:20 that I will call my servant E the son of 471
36: 3 came forth unto him E, Hilkiah's son, 471
36:11 said E and Shebna and Joah unto 471
36:22 came E, the son of Hilkiah, that *was* over 471
37: 2 he sent E, who *was* over the household, 471
Mt 1:13 and Abiud begat E; and Eliakim begat 1662
1:13 Abiud begat Eliakim; and E begat Azor; 1662
Lk 3:30 *the* son of Jonan, which was *the* son of E, 1662

ELIAM (2)
2Sa 11: 3 *Is* not this Bath-sheba, the daughter of E, 463
23:34 E the son of Ahithophel the Gilonite, 463

ELIAS (30) [ELIJAH]
Mt 11:14 And if ye will receive *it*, this is E, 2243
16:14 some, E; and others, Jeremias, or one of 2243
17: 3 unto them Moses and E talking with him. 2243
17: 4 thee, and one for Moses, and one for E. 2243
17:10 say the scribes that E must first come? 2243
17:11 E truly shall first come, and restore all 2243
17:12 That E is come already, and they knew 2243
27:47 heard *that*, said, This *man* calleth for E. 2243
27:49 see whether E will come to save him 2243
Mk 6:15 Others said, That it is E. And others said, 2243
8:28 but some *say*, E; and others, One of 2243
9: 4 And there appeared unto them E with 2243
9: 5 thee, and one for Moses, and one for E. 2243
9:11 Why say the scribes that E must first 2243
9:12 E verily cometh first, and restoreth all 2243
9:13 E is indeed come, and they have done 2243
15:35 they heard *it*, said, Behold, he calleth E. 2243
15:36 see whether E will come to take him 2243
Lk 1:17 before him in the spirit and power of E, 2243
4:25 widows were in Israel in the days of E, 2243
4:26 But unto none of them was E sent, 2243
9: 8 And of some, that E had appeared; 2243
9:19 some *say*, E; and others *say*, that one of 2243
9:30 him two men, which were Moses and E: 2243
9:33 thee, and one for Moses, and one for E: 2243
9:54 and consume them, even as E did? 2243
Jn 1:21 Art thou E? And he saith, I am not. 2243
1:25 *that* Christ, nor E, neither *that* prophet? 2243
Ro 11: 2 Wot ye not what the scripture saith of E? 2243
Jas 5:17 E was a man subject to like passions as we 2243

ELIASAPH (6)
Nu 1:14 Of Gad; E the son of Deuel. 460
2:14 the captain of the sons of Gad *shall be* E 460
3:24 the Gershonites *shall be* E the son of Lael. 460
7:42 On the sixth day E the son of Deuel, 460
7:47 this *was* the offering of E the son of Deuel. 460
10:20 children of Gad *was* E the son of Deuel. 460

ELIASHIB (17)
1Ch 3:24 E, and Pelaiah, and Akkub, and Johanan, 475
24:12 The eleventh to E, the twelfth to Jakim, 475
Ezr 10: 6 into the chamber of Johanan the son of E: 475
10:24 Of the singers also; E: and of the porters, 475
10:27 Elioenai, E, Mattaniah, and Jeremoth, 475
10:36 Vaniah, Meremoth, E, 475
Ne 3: 1 the high priest rose up with his brethren 475
3:20 the door of the house of E the high priest. 475
3:21 from the door of the house of E even to 475
3:21 Eliashib even to the end of the house of E. 475
12:10 Joiakim also begat E, and Eliashib begat 475
12:10 also begat Eliashib, and E begat Joiada, 475
12:22 The Levites in the days of E, Joiada, 475
12:23 until the days of Johanan the son of E. 475
13: 4 this, E the priest, having the oversight 475
13: 7 of the evil that E did for Tobiah, 475
13:28 sons of Joiada, the son of E the high priest, 475

ELIATHAH (2)
1Ch 25: 4 Hanani, E, Giddalti, and Romamti-ezer, 448
25:27 The twentieth to E, *he*, his sons, 448

ELIDAD (1)
Nu 34:21 the tribe of Benjamin, E the son of Chislon. 449

ELIEHOENAI See ELIHOENAI

ELIEL (10)
1Ch 5:24 E, and Azriel, and Jeremiah, and Hodaviah, 447
6:34 of Jeroham, the son of E, the son of Toah, 447
8:20 And Elienai, and Zilthai, and E, 447
8:22 And Ishpan, and Heber, and E, 447
11:46 E the Mahavite, and Jeribai, and Joshaviah, 447

11:47 E, and Obed, and Jasiel the Mesobaite. 447
12:11 Attai the sixth, E the seventh, 447
15: 9 E the chief, and his brethren fourscore; 447
15:11 Joel, Shemaiah, and E, and Amminadab, 447
2Ch 31:13 E, and Ismachiah, and Mahath, 447

ELIENAI (1)
1Ch 8:20 And E, and Zilthai, and Eliel, 462

ELIEZER (15)
Ge 15: 2 the steward of my house *is* this E of 461
Ex 18: 4 the name of the other *was* E; for the God 461
1Ch 7: 8 and Eliezer, and Elioenai, and Omri, and Jerimoth, 461
15:24 and Zechariah, and Benaiah, and E, 461
23:15 The sons of Moses *were*, Gershom, and E. 461
23:17 the sons of E *were*, Rehabiah the chief. 461
23:17 E had none other sons; but the sons of 461
26:25 his brethren by E; Rehabiah his son, 461
27:16 the ruler of the Reubenites *was* E the son 461
2Ch 20:37 the son of Dodavah of Mareshah 461
Ezr 8:16 sent I for E, for Ariel, for Shemaiah, 461
10:18 Maaseiah, and E, and Jarib, and Gedaliah. 461
10:23 same *is* Kelita,) Pethahiah, Judah, and E. 461
10:31 E, Ishijah, Malchiah, Shemaiah, Shimeon, 461
Lk 3:29 *the son of* Jose, which was *the son of* E, 1663

ELIHOENAI (1)
Ezr 8: 4 E the son of Zerahiah, and with him two 454

ELIHOREPH (1)
1Ki 4: 3 E and Ahiah, the sons of Shisha, scribes; 456

ELIHU (11)
1Sa 1: 1 the son of E, the son of Tohu, the son of 453
1Ch 12:20 Michael, and Jozabad, and E, and Zilthai, 453
26: 7 *were* strong men, E, and Semachiah. 453
27:18 Of Judah, E, *one* of the brethren of David: 453
Job 32: 2 was kindled the wrath of E the son of 453
32: 4 Now E had waited till Job had spoken, 453
32: 5 When E saw that *there was* no answer in 453
32: 6 the son of Barachel the Buzite answered 453
34: 1 Furthermore E answered and said, 453
35: 1 E spake moreover, and said, 453
36: 1 E also proceeded, and said, 453

ELIJAH (69) [ELIAS]
1Ki 17: 1 E the Tishbite, *who was* of the inhabitants 452
17:13 E said unto her, Fear not; go *and* do as 452
17:15 and did according to the saying of E: 452
17:16 word of the LORD, which he spake by E. 452
17:18 said unto E, What have I to do with thee, 452
17:22 the LORD heard the voice of E; 452
17:23 E took the child, and brought him down 452
17:23 his mother: and he said, See, thy son liveth. 452
17:24 the woman said to E, Now *by* this I know 452
18: 1 that the word of the LORD came to E 452
18: 2 E went to shew himself unto Ahab. 452
18: 7 Obadiah was in the way, behold E met 452
18: 7 his face, and said, *Art* thou that my lord E? 452
18: 8 I *am*: go, tell thy lord, Behold, E *is* here. 452
18:11 Go, tell thy lord, Behold, E *is* here. 452
18:14 Behold, E *is* here: and he shall slay me. 452
18:15 E said, *As* the LORD of hosts liveth, before 452
18:16 and told him: and Ahab went to meet E. 452
18:17 it came to pass, when Ahab saw E, 452
18:21 E came unto all the people, and said, 452
18:22 said E unto the people, I, *even* I only, 452
18:25 E said unto the prophets of Baal, 452
18:27 that E mocked them, and said, Cry aloud: 452
18:30 E said unto all the people, Come near unto 452
18:31 E took twelve stones, according to 452
18:36 that E the prophet came near, and said, 452
18:40 E said unto them, Take the prophets of 452
18:40 brought them down to the brook Kishon, 452
18:41 said unto Ahab, Get thee up, eat and 452
18:42 E went up to the top of Carmel; and he 452
18:46 the hand of the LORD was on E; 452
19: 1 Ahab told Jezebel all that E had done, 452
19: 2 Jezebel sent a messenger unto E, saying, 452
19: 9 said unto him, What doest thou here, E? 452
19:13 when E heard *it*, that he wrapped his face 452
19:13 him, and said, What doest thou here, E? 452
19:19 E passed by, and cast his mantle upon 452
19:20 ran after E, and said, Let me, I pray thee, 452
19:21 and went after E, and ministered unto him. 452
21:17 the word of the LORD came to E 452
21:20 Ahab said to E, Hast thou found me, 452
21:28 the word of the LORD came to E 452
2Ki 1: 3 the angel of the LORD said to E 452
1: 4 but shalt surely die. And E departed. 452
1: 8 his loins. And he said, It *is* E the Tishbite. 452
1:10 E answered and said to the captain of fifty, 452
1:12 E answered and said unto them, If I *be* a 452
1:13 and came and fell on his knees before E, 452
1:15 the angel of the LORD said unto E, 452
1:17 word of the LORD which E had spoken. 452
2: 1 when the LORD would take up E *into* 452
2: 1 that E went with Elisha from Gilgal. 452
2: 2 E said unto Elisha, Tarry here, I pray thee; 452
2: 4 said unto him, Elisha, tarry here, I pray 452
2: 6 E said unto him, Tarry, I pray thee, here; 452
2: 8 E took his mantle, and wrapt *it* together, 452
2: 9 were gone over, that E said unto Elisha, 452
2:11 E went up by a whirlwind *into* heaven. 452
2:13 He took up also the mantle of E that fell 452

2Ki 2:14 he took the mantle of E that fell from him, 452
2:14 and said, Where *is* the LORD God of E? 452
2:15 said, The spirit of E doth rest on Elisha. 452
3:11 which poured water on the hands of E. 452
9:36 which he spake by his servant E 452
10:10 done *that* which he spake by his servant E. 452
10:17 saying of the LORD, which he spake to E. 452
2Ch 21:12 there came a writing to him from E 452
Ezr 10:21 E, and Shemaiah, and Jehiel, and Uzziah. 452
Mal 4: 5 I *will* send you E the prophet before 452

ELIKA (1)
2Sa 23:25 Shammah the Harodite, E the Harodite, 470

ELIM (6) [BEER-ELIM]
Ex 15:27 they came to E, where *were* twelve wells 362
16: 1 they took their journey from E, and all 362
16: 1 of Sin, which *is* between E and Sinai, 362
Nu 33: 9 removed from Marah, and came unto E: 362
33: 9 and in E *were* twelve fountains of water, 362
33:10 they removed from E, and encamped by 362

ELIMELECH (4) [ELIMELECH'S]
Ru 1: 2 the name of the man *was* E, and the name 458
1: 3 E Naomi's husband died; and she was left, 458
2: 1 a mighty man of wealth, of the family of E; 458
2: 3 unto Boaz, who *was* of the kindred of E. 458

ELIMELECH'S (2) [ELIMELECH]
Ru 4: 3 a parcel of land, which *was* our brother E: 458
4: 9 that I have bought all that *was* E, and all 458

ELIOENAI (8)
1Ch 3:23 E, and Hezekiah, and Azrikam, three. 454
3:24 the sons of E *were*, Hodaiah, and Eliashib, 454
4:36 E, and Jaakobah, and Jeshohaiah, 454
7: 8 E, and Omri, and Jerimoth, and Abiah, 454
26: 3 fifth, Jehohanan the sixth, E the seventh. 454
Ezr 10:22 E, Maaseiah, Ishmael, Nethaneel, Jozabad, 454
10:27 Elioenai, E, Eliashib, Mattaniah, and Jeremoth, 454
Ne 12:41 Eliakim, Maaseiah, Miniamin, Michaiah, E, 454

ELIPHAL (1)
1Ch 11:35 son of Sacar the Hararite, E the son of Ur, 465

ELIPHALET (2)
2Sa 5:16 And Elishama, and Eliada, and E. 467
1Ch 14: 7 And Elishama, and Beeliada, and E. 467

ELIPHAZ (15)
Ge 36: 4 Adah bare to Esau E; and Bashemath bare 464
36:10 E the son of Adah the wife of Esau, 464
36:11 the sons of E were Teman, Omar, Zepho, 464
36:12 Timna was concubine to E Esau's son; 464
36:12 Esau's son; and she bare to E Amalek: 464
36:15 the sons of E the firstborn *son* of Esau; 464
36:16 these *are* the dukes *that came* of E: 464
1Ch 1:35 E, Reuel, and Jeush, and Jaalam, and Korah. 464
1:36 The sons of E; Teman, and Omar, Zephi, 464
Job 2:11 E the Temanite, and Bildad the Shuhite, 464
4: 1 Then E the Temanite answered and said, 464
15: 1 Then answered E the Temanite, and said, 464
22: 1 Then E the Temanite answered and said, 464
42: 7 the LORD said to E the Temanite, 464
42: 9 So E the Temanite and Bildad the Shuhite 464

ELIPHELEH (2)
1Ch 15:18 E, and Mikneiah, and Obed-edom, 466
15:21 E, and Mikneiah, and Obed-edom, 466

ELIPHELEHU See ELIPHELEH

ELIPHELET (6)
2Sa 23:34 E the son of Ahasbai, the son of 467
1Ch 3: 6 Ibhar also, and Elishama, and E, 467
3: 8 And Elishama, and Eliada, and E, nine. 467
8:39 Jehush the second, and E the third. 467
Ezr 8:13 E, Jeiel, and Shemaiah, and with them 467
10:33 Zabad, E, Jeremai, Manasseh, *and* Shimei. 467

ELISABETH (8) [ELISABETH'S]
Lk 1: 5 daughters of Aaron, and her name *was* E. 1665
1: 7 because that E was barren, and they both 1665
1:13 and thy wife E shall bear thee a son, 1665
1:24 And after those days his wife E conceived, 1665
1:36 And behold, thy cousin E, she hath also 1665
1:40 into the house of Zacharias, and saluted E. 1665
1:41 And it came to pass *that*, when E heard 1665
1:41 and E was filled with the Holy Ghost: 1665

ELISABETH'S (1) [ELISABETH]
Lk 1:57 Now E full time came that she should be 1665

ELISEUS (1) [ELISHA]
Lk 4:27 in Israel in the time of E the prophet; 1666

ELISHA (58) [ELISEUS]
1Ki 19:16 the son of Shaphat of Abel-meholah shalt 477
19:17 from the sword of Jehu shall E slay. 477
19:19 and found E the son of Shaphat, 477
2Ki 2: 1 that Elijah went with E from Gilgal. 477
2: 2 Elijah said unto E, Tarry here, I pray thee; 477
2: 2 And E said *unto him*, As the LORD liveth, 477
2: 3 that *were* at Beth-el came forth to E, 477
2: 4 said unto him, E, tarry here, I pray thee; 477
2: 5 prophets that *were* at Jericho came to E, 477

E

2Ki 2: 9 were gone over, that Elijah said unto **E**, 477
2: 9 **E** said, I pray thee, let a double portion of 477
2:12 **E** saw *it*, and he cried, My father, my 477
2:14 parted hither and thither: and **E** went over. 477
2:15 said, The spirit of Elijah doth rest on **E** 477
2:19 the men of the city said unto **E**, Behold, 477
2:22 to the saying of **E** which he spake. 477
3:11 and said, Here *is* **E** the son of Shaphat, 477
3:13 **E** said unto the king of Israel, What have I 477
3:14 **E** said, *As* the LORD of hosts liveth, before 477
4: 1 wives of the sons of the prophets unto **E**, 477
4: 2 **E** said unto her, What shall I do for thee? 477
4: 8 it fell on a day, that **E** passed to Shunem, 477
4:17 bare a son at that season that **E** had said 477
4:32 when **E** was come into the house, behold, 477
4:38 came again to Gilgal: and *there was a* 477
5: 8 when the man of God had heard that 477
5: 9 and stood *at* the door of the house of **E**. 477
5:10 **E** sent a messenger unto him, saying, 477
5:20 the servant of **E** the man of God, said, 477
5:25 **E** said unto him, Whence *comest thou*, 477
6: 1 the sons of the prophets said unto **E**, 477
6:12 **E**, the prophet that *is* in Israel, telleth 477
6:17 **E** prayed, and said, LORD, I pray thee, 477
6:17 horses and chariots of fire round about **E**. 477
6:18 **E** prayed unto the LORD, and said, 477
6:18 with blindness according to the word of **E**. 477
6:19 **E** said unto them, This *is* not the way, 477
6:20 come *into* Samaria, that **E** said, LORD, 477
6:21 the king of Israel said unto **E**, when he saw 477
6:31 if the head of **E** the son of Shaphat shall 477
6:32 **E** sat in his house, and the elders sat with 477
7: 1 **E** said, Hear ye the word of the LORD; 477
8: 1 spake **E** unto the woman, whose son he 477
8: 4 all the great *things* that **E** hath done. 477
8: 5 this *is* her son, whom **E** restored to life. 477
8: 7 **E** came *to* Damascus; and Ben-hadad 477
8:10 **E** said unto him, Go, say unto him, 477
8:13 **E** answered, The LORD hath shewed me 477
8:14 So he departed from **E**, and came to his 477
8:14 who said to him, What said **E** to thee? 477
9: 1 **E** the prophet called one of the children of 477
13:14 Now **E** was fallen sick of his sickness 477
13:15 **E** said unto him, Take bow and arrows. 477
13:16 and **E** put his hands upon the king's hands. 477
13:17 he opened *it*. Then **E** said, Shoot. And he 477
13:20 **E** died, and they buried him. 477
13:21 they cast the man into the sepulchre of **E**: 477
13:21 and touched the bones of **E**, he revived, 477

ELISHAH (3)
Ge 10: 4 **E**, and Tarshish, Kittim, and Dodanim. 473
1Ch 1: 7 **E**, and Tarshish, Kittim, and Dodanim. 473
Eze 27: 7 purple from the isles of **E** was that which 473

ELISHAMA (17)
Nu 1:10 of Ephraim; **E** the son of Ammihud. 476
2:18 captain of the sons of Ephraim *shall be* **E** 476
7:48 the seventh day **E** the son of Ammihud, 476
7:53 this *was* the offering of **E** the son of 476
10:22 over his host *was* **E** the son of Ammihud. 476
2Sa 5:16 And **E**, and Eliada, and Eliphelet. 476
2Ki 25:25 the son of **E**, of the seed royal, came, 476
1Ch 2:41 begat Jekamiah, and Jekamiah begat **E**. 476
3: 6 Ibhar also, and **E**, and Eliphelet, 476
3: 8 And **E**, and Eliada, and Eliphelet, nine. 476
7:26 his son, Ammihud his son, **E** his son, 476
14: 7 And **E**, and Beeliada, and Eliphelet. 476
2Ch 17: 8 and with them **E** and Jehoram, priests, 476
Jer 36:12 *even* **E** the scribe, and Delaiah the son of 476
36:20 they laid up the roll in the chamber of **E** 476
36:21 he took it out of **E** the scribe's chamber. 476
41: 1 Ishmael the son of Nethaniah the son of **E**, 476

ELISHAPHAT (1)
2Ch 23: 1 **E** the son of Zichri, into covenant with him 478

ELISHEBA (1)
Ex 6:23 Aaron took him **E**, daughter of Amminadab 472

ELISHUA (2)
2Sa 5:15 Ibhar also, and **E**, and Nepheg, and Japhia, 474
1Ch 14: 5 And Ibhar, and **E**, and Elpalet, 474

ELIUD (2)
Mt 1:14 Sadoc begat Achim; and Achim begat **E**; *1664*
1:15 And **E** begat Eleazar; and Eleazar begat *1664*

ELIZABETH See ELISABETH

ELIZAPHAN (4)
Nu 3:30 the Kohathites *shall be* **E** the son of Uzziel. 469
34:25 children of Zebulun, **E** the son of Parnach. 469
1Ch 15: 8 Of the sons of **E**; Shemaiah the chief, 469
2Ch 29:13 And of the sons of **E**; Shimri, and Jeiel: 469

ELIZUR (5)
Nu 1: 5 *the tribe of* Reuben; **E** the son of Shedeur. 468
2:10 of Reuben *shall be* **E** the son of Shedeur. 468
7:30 On the fourth day **E** the son of Shedeur, 468
7:35 this *was* the offering of **E** the son of 468
10:18 over his host *was* **E** the son of Shedeur. 468

ELKANAH (21)
Ex 6:24 sons of Korah; Assir, and **E**, and Abiasaph: 511
1Sa 1: 1 of mount Ephraim, and his name *was* **E**, 511

1Sa 1: 4 when the time was that **E** offered, he gave 511
1: 8 said **E** her husband to her, Hannah, 511
1:19 **E** knew Hannah his wife; and the LORD 511
1:21 the man **E**, and all his house, went up to 511
1:23 **E** her husband said unto her, Do what 511
2:11 **E** went to Ramah to his house. And the 511
2:20 Eli blessed **E** and his wife, and said, 511
1Ch 6:23 his son, and Ebiasaph his son, 511
6:25 And the sons of **E**; Amasai, and Ahimoth. 511
6:26 *As for* **E**: the sons of Elkanah; Zophai his 511
6:26 the sons of **E**; Zophai his son, 511
6:27 Eliab his son, Jeroham his son, **E** his son. 511
6:34 The son of **E**, the son of Jeroham, the son 511
6:35 The son of Zuph, the son of **E**, the son of 511
6:36 The son of **E**, the son of Joel, the son of 511
9:16 and Berechiah the son of Asa, the son of **E**, 511
12: 6 **E**, and Jesiah, and Azareel, and Joezer, 511
15:23 and **E** *were* doorkeepers for the ark. 511
2Ch 28: 7 the house, and **E** that *was* next to the king. 511

ELKOSHITE (1)
Na 1: 1 The book of the vision of Nahum the **E**. 512

ELLASAR (2)
Ge 14: 1 Arioch king of **E**, Chedorlaomer king of 495
14: 9 king of Shinar, and Arioch king of **E**; 495

ELMADAM See ELMODAM

ELMODAM (1)
Lk 3:28 was *the son* of **E**, which was *the son* *1678*

ELMS (1)
Hos 4:13 under oaks and poplars and **e**, because 424

ELNAAM (1)
1Ch 11:46 the sons of **E**, and Ithmah the Moabite, 493

ELNATHAN (7)
2Ki 24: 8 the daughter of **E** of Jerusalem. 494
Ezr 8:16 for **E**, and for Jarib, and for Elnathan, 494
8:16 for **E**, and for Nathan, and for Zechariah, 494
8:16 Joiarib, and for **E**, *men* of understanding. 494
Jer 26:22 *namely*, **E** the son of Achbor, 494
36:12 **E** the son of Achbor, and Gemariah the son 494
36:25 Nevertheless **E** and Delaiah and 494

ELOI (2) [ELI]
Mk 15:34 saying, **E**, **ELOI**, *1682*
15:34 saying, **ELOI**, **E**, *1682*

ELON (7) [ELON-BETH-HANAN, ELONITES]
Ge 26:34 Bashemath the daughter of **E** the Hittite: 356
36: 2 Adah the daughter of **E** the Hittite, 356
46:14 sons of Zebulun; Sered, and **E**, and Jahleel. 440
Nu 26:26 of **E**, the family of the Elonites: of Jahleel, 356
Jos 19:43 And **E**, and Thimnathah, and Ekron, 356
Jdg 12:11 after him **E**, a Zebulonite, judged Israel; 356
12:12 **E** the Zebulonite died, and was buried in 356

ELON-BETH-HANAN (1) [ELON, HANAN]
1Ki 4: 9 in Shaalbim, and Beth-shemesh, and **E**: 358

ELONITES (1) [ELON]
Nu 26:26 of Elon, the family of the **E**: of Jahleel, 440

ELOQUENT (3)
Ex 4:10 I *am* not **e**, neither heretofore, 376+1697
Isa 3: 3 and the cunning artificer, and the **e** orator. 995
Ac 18:24 an **e** man, *and* mighty in the scriptures, 3052

ELOTH (3) [ELATH]
1Ki 9:26 which *is* beside **E**, on the shore of the Red 359
2Ch 8:17 to **E**, at the sea side in the land of Edom. 359
26: 2 He built **E**, and restored it to Judah, after 359

ELPAAL (3)
1Ch 8:11 And of Hushim he begat Abitub, and **E**. 508
8:12 The sons of **E**; Eber, and Misham, 508
8:18 and Jezliah, and Jobab, the sons of **E**; 508

ELPALET (1)
1Ch 14: 5 And Ibhar, and Elishua, and **E**, 467

EL-PARAN (1) [PARAN]
Ge 14: 6 unto **E**, which *is* by the wilderness. 364

ELPELET See ELPALET

ELSE (48)
Ge 30: 1 unto Jacob, Give me children, or **e** I die. 369
42:16 by the life of Pharaoh surely ye *are* 518+3808
Ex 8:21 **E**, if thou wilt not let my people go, 3588
10: 4 if thou refuse to let my people go, 3588
Nu 20:19 without *doing any* thing **e**, go through on NIH
Dt 4:35 he *is* God; *there is* none **e** besides him. 5750
4:39 upon the earth beneath: *there is* none **e**. 5750
Jos 23:12 **E** if ye do in any wise go back, 3588
Jdg 7:14 This *is* nothing **e** save the sword of 369+1115
2Sa 3:35 If I taste bread, or **ought e**, 3605+3972
15:14 for we shall not **e** escape from Absalom: NIH
1Ki 8:60 the LORD *is* God, *and that there is* none **e**. 5750
20:39 life, or **e** thou shalt pay a talent of silver. 176
20:39 or **e**, if it please thee, I will give thee NIH
1Ch 21:12 or **e** three days the sword of 518+2050.1
2Ch 23: 7 whosoever **e** cometh into the house, NIH
Ne 2: 2 this *is* nothing **e** but sorrow of heart. NIH

Ps 51:16 **e** would I give *it*: thou delightest not in 2050.1
Ecc 2:25 who **e** can hasten *hereunto*, more than I? 4310
Isa 45: 5 I *am* the LORD, and *there is* none **e**, 5750
45: 6 I *am* the LORD, and *there is* none **e**. 5750
45:14 and *there is* none **e**, *there is* no God. 5750
45:18 I *am* the LORD; and *there is* none **e**. 5750
45:21 *is* no God **e** beside me; 1107+4480+5750
45:22 for I *am* God, and *there is* none **e**. 5750
46: 9 for I *am* God, and *there is* none **e**; I *am* 5750
47: 8 thine heart, I *am*, and **none e** besides me; 657
47:10 thine heart, I *am*, and **none e** besides me. 657
Joel 2:27 I *am* the LORD your God, and none **e**: 5750
Mt 6:24 **or e** he will hold to the one, and despise 2228
9:17 **e** the bottles break, and the wine runneth 1490
12:29 **Or e** how can one enter into a strong 2228
12:33 **or e** make the tree corrupt, and his fruit 2228
Mk 2:21 **e** the new piece that filled it up taketh 1490
2:22 **e** the new wine doth burst the bottles, 1490
Lk 5:37 **e** the new wine will burst the bottles, 1490
14:32 **Or e**, while the other is yet a great way 1490
16:13 **or e** he will hold to the one, and despise 2228
Jn 14:11 **or e** believe me for the very works' sake. 1490
Ac 17:21 were there spent their time in nothing **e**, 2087
24:20 **Or e** let these same *here* say, if they have 2228
Ro 2:15 accusing or **e** excusing one another;) 2532
1Co 7:14 **e** were your children unclean; 686+1893
14:16 **e** when thou shalt bless with the spirit, 1893
15:29 **E** what shall they do which are baptized 1893
Php 1:27 I come and see you, or **e** be absent, NIG
Rev 2: 5 **or e** I *will* come unto thee quickly, 1490
2:16 **or e** I *will* come unto thee quickly, 1490

ELTEKEH (2)
Jos 19:44 And **E**, and Gibbethon, and Baalath, 514
21:23 out of the tribe of Dan, **E** with her suburbs, 514

ELTEKON (1)
Jos 15:59 Maarath, and Beth-anoth, and **E**; six cities 515

ELTOLAD (2)
Jos 15:30 And **E**, and Chesil, and Hormah, 513
19: 4 And **E**, and Bethul, and Hormah, 513

ELUL (1)
Ne 6:15 in the twenty and fifth *day* of *the month* **E**, 435

ELYMAS (1)
Ac 13: 8 But **E** the sorcerer (for so is his name by 1681

ELZABAD (2)
1Ch 12:12 Johanan the eighth, **E** the ninth, 443
26: 7 Othni, and Rephael, and Obed, **E**, 443

ELZAPHAN (2)
Ex 6:22 sons of Uzziel; Mishael, and **E**, and Zithri. 469
Lev 10: 4 Moses called Mishael and **E**, the sons of 469

EMBALM (1) [EMBALMED]
Ge 50: 2 his servants the physicians to **e** his father: 2590

EMBALMED (3) [EMBALM]
Ge 50: 2 his father: and the physicians **e** Israel. 2590
50: 3 are fulfilled the days of those which are **e**: 2590
50:26 they **e** him, and he was put in a coffin in 2590

EMBOLDENED (1) [BOLD]
1Co 8:10 **e** to eat those things which are offered to 3618

EMBOLDENETH (1) [BOLD]
Job 16: 3 or what **e** thee that thou answerest? 4834

EMBRACE (8) [EMBRACED, EMBRACING]
2Ki 4:16 to the time of life, thou shalt **e** a son. 2263
Job 24: 8 and **e** the rock for want of a shelter. 2263
Pr 4: 8 thee to honour, when thou dost **e** her. 2263
5:20 and the bosom of a stranger? 2263
Ecc 3: 5 a time to **e**, and a time to refrain from 2263
SS 2: 6 my head, and his right hand doth **e** me. 2263
8: 3 my head, and his right hand should **e** me. 2263
La 4: 5 they that were brought up in scarlet **e** 2263

EMBRACED (5) [EMBRACE]
Ge 29:13 **e** him, and kissed him, and brought him 2263
33: 4 **e** him, and fell on his neck, and kissed 2263
48:10 and he kissed them, and **e** them. 2263
Ac 20: 1 and **e** *them*, and departed for to go into 782
Heb 11:13 were persuaded *of them*, and **e** *them*, 782

EMBRACING (2) [EMBRACE]
Ecc 3: 5 to embrace, and a time to refrain from **e**; 2263
Ac 20:10 down, and fell on him, and **e** *him* said, 4843

EMBROIDER (1) [EMBROIDERER]
Ex 28:39 thou shalt **e** the coat of fine linen, 7660

EMBROIDERED See DIVERS; DIVERSE

EMBROIDERER (2) [EMBROIDER]
Ex 35:35 of the **e**, in blue, and in purple, in scarlet, 7551
38:23 an **e** in blue, and in purple, and in scarlet, 7551

EMERALD (5) [EMERALDS]
Ex 28:18 the second row *shall be an* **e**, a sapphire, 5306
39:11 an **e**, a sapphire, and a diamond. 5306
Eze 28:13 the **e**, and the carbuncle, and gold: 5306
Rev 4: 3 about the throne, in sight like unto an **e**. 4664
21:19 the third, a chalcedony; the fourth, an **e**; 4665

EMERALDS (1) [EMERALD]
Eze 27:16 they occupied in thy fairs with **e**, purple, 5306

EMERODS (8)
Dt	28:27 with the **e**, and with the scab, and with	6076
1Sa	5: 6 smote them with **e**, *even* Ashdod and	2914
	5: 9 and they had **e** in their secret parts.	2914
	5:12 that died not were smitten with the **e**:	2914
	6: 4 Five golden **e**, and five golden mice,	2914
	6: 5 ye shall make images of your **e**,	2914
	6:11 mice of gold and the images of their **e**.	2914
	6:17 *are* the golden **e** which the Philistines	2914

EMIMS (3)
Ge	14: 5 in Ham, and the **E** in Shaveh Kiriathaim,	368
Dt	2:10 (The **E** dwelt therein in times past,	368
	2:11 Anakims; but the Moabites call them **E**.	368

EMINENT (4) [PREEMINENCE]
Eze	16:24 thou hast also built unto thee an **e place**,	1354
	16:31 In that thou buildest thine **e place** in	1354
	16:39 they shall throw down thine **e place**,	1354
	17:22 will plant *it* upon a high mountain and **e**:	8524

EMISSION See COPULATION

EMITES See EMIMS

EMMANUEL (1) [IMMANUEL]
Mt 1:23 forth a son, and they shall call his name **E**, *1694*

EMMAUS (1)
Lk 24:13 went *that* same day to a village called **E**, *1695*

EMMOR (1) [HAMOR]
Ac 7:16 of the sons of **E** the *father* of Sychem. *1697*

EMPIRE (1)
Est 1:20 shall be published throughout all his **e**, 4438

EMPLOY (1) [EMPLOYED, EMPLOYMENT]
Dt 20:19 to **e** *them* in the siege: 935+4480+6440

EMPLOYED (2) [EMPLOY]
1Ch	9:33 they were **e** in *that* work day and night.	5921
Ezr	10:15 Jahaziah the son of Tikvah were **e** about	5975

EMPLOYMENT (1) [EMPLOY]
Eze 39:14 they shall sever out men of **continual e**, 8548

EMPTIED (8) [EMPTY]
Ge	24:20 **e** her pitcher into the trough, and ran	6168
	42:35 it came to pass as they **e** their sacks,	7324
2Ch	24:11 high priest's officer came and **e** the chest,	6168
Ne	5:13 even thus be he shaken out, and **e**.	7386
Isa	19: 6 *and* the brooks of defence shall be **e** and	1809
	24: 3 The land shall be **utterly e**,	1238+1238
Jer	48:11 and hath not been **e** from vessel to vessel,	7324
Na	2: 2 for the emptiers have **e** them **out,**	1238

EMPTIERS (1) [EMPTY]
Na 2: 2 for the **e** have emptied them out, 1238

EMPTINESS (1) [EMPTY]
Isa 34:11 the line of confusion, and the stones of **e**. 922

EMPTY (38) [EMPTIED, EMPTIERS, EMPTINESS]
Ge	31:42 surely thou hadst sent me away now **e**.	7387
	37:24 the pit *was* **e**, *there was* no water in it.	7386
	41:27 seven **e** ears blasted with the east wind	7386
Ex	3:21 pass, that, when ye go, ye shall not go **e**:	7387
	23:15 and none shall appear before me **e**:	7387
	34:20 and none shall appear before me **e**.	7387
Lev	14:36 the priest shall command that they **e**	6437
Dt	15:13 thee, thou shalt not let him go away **e**:	7387
	16:16 they shall not appear before the LORD **e**:	7387
Jdg	7:16 with **e** pitchers, and lamps within	7386
Ru	1:21 the LORD hath brought me *home* again **e**:	7387
	3:17 to me, Go not **e** unto thy mother in law.	7387
1Sa	6: 3 the ark of the God of Israel, send it not **e**;	7387
	20:18 be missed, because thy seat will be **e**.	6485
	20:25 by Saul's side, and David's place was **e**.	6485
	20:27 of the month, that David's place was **e**:	6485
2Sa	1:22 and the sword of Saul returned not **e**.	7387
2Ki	4: 3 of all thy neighbours, *even* **e** vessels;	7386
Job	22: 9 Thou hast sent widows away **e**,	7387
	26: 7 stretcheth out the north over the **e place**,	8414
Ecc	11: 3 of rain, they **e** *themselves* upon the earth:	7324
Isa	24: 1 the LORD **maketh** the earth **e**,	1238
	29: 8 eateth; but he awaketh, and his soul *is* **e**:	7386
	32: 6 to **make e** the soul of the hungry,	7324
Jer	14: 3 water; they returned *with* their vessels **e**;	7387
	48:12 shall **e** his vessels, and break their bottles.	7324
	51: 2 that shall fan her, and shall **e** her land:	1238
	51:34 crushed me, he hath made me an **e** vessel,	7385
Eze	24:11 set it **e** upon the coals thereof, that the	7386
Hos	10: 1 Israel *is* an **e** vine, he bringeth forth fruit	1238
Na	2:10 She *is* **e**, and void, and waste: and the	950
Hab	1:17 Shall they therefore **e** their net,	7324
Zec	4:12 the golden *oil* out of themselves?	7324
Mt	12:44 he findeth *it* **e**, swept, and garnished.	4980
Mk	12: 3 and beat *him*, and sent *him* away **e**.	2756
Lk	1:53 and the rich he hath sent **e** away.	2756
	20:10 beat him, and sent *him* away **e**.	2756
	20:11 *him* shamefully, and sent *him* away **e**.	2756

EMULATION (1) [EMULATIONS]
Ro 11:14 If by any means I may **provoke to e** them *3863*

EMULATIONS (1) [EMULATION]
Gal 5:20 variance, **e**, wrath, strife, seditions, 2205

ENABLED (1)
1Ti 1:12 who hath **e** me, for that he counted me *1743*

ENAM (1)
Jos 15:34 and En-gannim, Tappuah, and **E**, 5879

ENAN (5) [HAZAR-ENAN]
Nu	1:15 Of Naphtali; Ahira the son of **E**.	5881
	2:29 of Naphtali *shall be* Ahira the son of **E**.	5881
	7:78 On the twelfth day Ahira the son of **E**,	5881
	7:83 this *was* the offering of Ahira the son of **E**.	5881
	10:27 of Naphtali *was* Ahira the son of **E**.	5881

ENCAMP (11) [CAMP]
Ex	14: 2 that they turn and **e** before Pi-hahiroth,	2583
	14: 2 before it shall ye **e** by the sea.	2583
Nu	1:50 and shall **e** round about the tabernacle.	2583
	2:17 as they **e**, so shall they set forward,	2583
	2:27 those that **e** by him *shall be* the tribe of	2583
	3:38 those that **e** before the tabernacle toward	2583
	10:31 as thou knowest how we are to **e**	2583
2Sa	12:28 and **e** against the city, and take it:	2583
Job	19:12 and **e** round about my tabernacle.	2583
Ps	27: 3 Though a host should **e** against me,	2583
Zec	9: 8 I will **e about** mine house because of	2583

ENCAMPED (33) [CAMP]
Ex	13:20 **e** in Etham, in the edge of the wilderness.	2583
	15:27 trees: and they **e** there by the waters.	2583
	18: 5 where he **e** *at* the mount of God:	2583
Nu	33:10 removed from Elim, and **e** by the Red sea.	2583
	33:11 Red sea, and **e** in the wilderness of Sin.	2583
	33:12 the wilderness of Sin, and **e** in Dophkah.	2583
	33:13 departed from Dophkah, and **e** in Alush.	2583
	33:14 removed from Alush, and **e** at Rephidim,	2583
	33:17 Kibroth-hattaavah, and **e** at Hazeroth.	2583
	33:24 from mount Shapher, and **e** in Haradah.	2583
	33:26 from Makheloth, and **e** at Tahath.	2583
	33:30 from Hashmonah, and **e** at Moseroth.	2583
	33:32 from Bene-jaakan, and **e** at Hor-hagidgad.	2583
	33:34 from Jotbathah, and **e** at Ebronah.	2583
	33:35 from Ebronah, and **e** at Ezion-gaber.	2583
	33:46 and **e** in Almon-diblathaim.	2583
Jos	4:19 in Gilgal, in the east border of Jericho.	2583
	5:10 the children of Israel **e** in Gilgal,	2583
	10: 5 **e** before Gibeon, and made war against it.	2583
	10:31 and **e** against it, and fought against it:	2583
	10:34 they **e** against it, and fought against it:	2583
Jdg	6: 4 they **e** against them, and destroyed	2583
	9:50 and **e** against Thebez, and took it.	2583
	10:17 were gathered together, and **e** in Gilead.	2583
	10:17 themselves together, and **e** in Mizpeh.	2583
	20:19 up in the morning, and **e** against Gibeah.	2583
1Sa	4: 1 came up, and **e** against Eben-ezer:	2583
	13:16 but the Philistines **e** in Michmash.	2583
2Sa	11:11 of my lord, are **e** in the open fields;	2583
1Ki	16:15 The people *were* **e** against Gibbethon,	2583
	16:16 The people that *were* **e** heard say, Zimri	2583
1Ch	11:15 the host of the Philistines **e** in the valley	2583
2Ch	32: 1 **e** against the fenced cities, and thought to	2583

ENCAMPETH (2) [CAMP]
Ps	34: 7 The angel of the LORD **e** round about	2583
	53: 5 the bones of him that **e** *against* thee:	2583

ENCAMPING (1) [CAMP]
Ex 14: 9 overtook them **e** by the sea, 2583

ENCHANTER (1) [ENCHANTERS, ENCHANTMENT, ENCHANTMENTS]
Dt 18:10 an observer of times, or an **e**, or a witch, 5172

ENCHANTERS (1) [ENCHANTER]
Jer 27: 9 nor to your **e**, nor to your sorcerers, 6049

ENCHANTMENT (3) [ENCHANTER]
Lev	19:26 neither shall ye **use e**, nor observe times.	5172
Nu	23:23 Surely *there is* no **e** against Jacob, neither	5173
Ecc	10:11 Surely the serpent will bite without **e**;	3908

ENCHANTMENTS (10) [ENCHANTER]
Ex	7:11 they also did in like manner with their **e**.	3858
	7:22 magicians of Egypt did so with their **e**:	3909
	8: 7 the magicians did so with their **e**,	3909
	8:18 so with their **e** to bring forth lice,	3909
Nu	24: 1 to seek for **e**, but he set his face toward	5173
2Ki	17:17 divination and **e**, and sold themselves	5172
	21: 6 **used e**, and dealt with familiar spirits and	5172
2Ch	33: 6 **used e**, and used witchcraft, and dealt	5172
Isa	47: 9 *and* for the great abundance of thine **e**.	2267
	47:12 Stand now with thine **e**, and with	2267

ENCLOSE See INCLOSE

ENCOUNTERED (1)
Ac 17:18 the Epicureans, and of the Stoicks, **e** him. *4820*

ENCOURAGE (4) [ENCOURAGED]
Dt	1:38 **e** him: for he shall cause Israel to inherit	2388
	3:28 and **e** him, and strengthen him:	2388

2Sa	11:25 city, and overthrow it: and **e** thou him.	2388
Ps	64: 5 They **e** themselves *in* an evil matter:	2388

ENCOURAGED (5) [ENCOURAGE]
Jdg	20:22 the people the men of Israel **e** themselves,	2388
1Sa	30: 6 but David **e** himself in the LORD his God.	2388
2Ch	31: 4 that they might be **e** in the law of	2388
	35: 2 **e** them to the service of the house of	2388
Isa	41: 7 So the carpenter **e** the goldsmith,	2388

END (307) [ENDED, ENDETH, ENDING, ENDLESS, ENDS]
Ge	6:13 The **e** of all flesh is come before me;	7093
	8: 3 after the **e** of the hundred and fifty days	7097
	8: 6 it came to pass at the **e** of forty days,	7093
	23: 9 he hath, which *is* in the **e** of his field;	7097
	27:30 soon as Isaac had **made an e** of blessing	3615
	41: 1 it came to pass at the **e** of two full years,	7093
	47:21 he removed them to cities from *one* **e** of	7097
	47:21 of Egypt even to the *other* **e** thereof.	7097
	49:33 Jacob had **made an e** of commanding	3615
Ex	8:22 *of flies* shall be there; **to the e**	4616+3807.1
	12:41 came to pass at the **e** of the four hundred	7093
	23:16 ingathering, *which is* in the **e** of the year,	3318
	25:18 make one cherub on the one **e**,	7098
	25:19 and the other cherub on the other **e**:	7098
	26:28 of the boards shall reach from **e** to end.	7097
	26:28 of the boards shall reach from end to **e**.	7097
	31:18 when he had **made an e** of communing	3615
	34:22 the feast of ingathering *at* the year's **e**.	8622
	36:33 the boards from the one **e** to the other.	7097
	37: 8 One cherub on the **e** on this side,	7098
	37: 8 cherub on the *other* **e** on that side:	7098
Lev	8:33 the days of your consecration be at an **e**:	4390
	16:20 when he hath **made an e** of reconciling	3615
	17: 5 **To the e** that the children of	4616+3807.1
Nu	4:15 his sons have **made an e** of covering	3615
	16:31 he had **made an e** of speaking all these	3615
	23:10 righteous, and let my **last e** be like his!	319
	24:20 his *latter* **e** *shall be* that he perish for ever.	319
Dt	8:16 to do thee good at thy **latter e**;	319
	9:11 it came to pass at the **e** of forty days and	7093
	11:12 of the year even unto the **e** of the year.	319
	13: 7 from the one **e** of the earth even unto	7097
	13: 7 earth even unto the *other* **e** of the earth;	7097
	14:28 At the **e** of three years thou shalt bring	7097
	15: 1 At the **e** of *every* seven years thou shalt	7093
	17:16 to return to Egypt, **to the e** that	4616+3807.1
	17:20 *to* the left: **to the e** that he may	4616+3807.1
	20: 9 when the officers have **made an e** of	3615
	26:12 When thou hast **made an e** of tithing all	3615
	28:49 the **e** of the earth, *as swift* as the eagle	7097
	28:64 from the *one* **e** of the earth even unto	7097
	31:10 saying, At the **e** of *every* seven years,	7093
	31:24 when Moses had **made an e** of writing	3615
	32:20 I will see what their **e** *shall be*: for they	319
	32:29 *that* they would consider their **latter e**!	319
	32:45 Moses **made an e** of speaking all these	3615
Jos	8:24 when Israel had **made an e** of slaying all	3615
	9:16 it came to pass at the **e** of three days after	7097
	10:20 the children of Israel had **made an e** of	3615
	15: 5 the salt sea, *even* unto the **e** of Jordan.	7097
	15: 8 *is* at the **e** of the valley of the giants	7097
	18:15 the south quarter *was* from the **e** of	7097
	18:16 the border came down to the **e** of	7097
	18:19 of the salt sea at the south **e** of Jordan:	7097
	19:49 When they had **made an e** of dividing	3615
	19:51 they **made an e** of dividing the country.	3615
Jdg	3:18 when he had **made an e** to offer	3615
	6:21 the angel of the LORD put forth the **e** of	7097
	11:39 it came to pass at the **e** of two months,	7093
	15:17 when he had **made an e** of speaking,	3615
	19: 9 behold, the day **groweth** to an **e**,	2583
Ru	2:23 Boaz to glean unto the **e** of barley harvest	3615
	3: 7 he went to lie down at the **e** of the heap	7097
	3:10 in the **latter e** than at the beginning,	314
1Sa	3:12 when I begin, I will also **make an e**.	3615
	9:27 *And* as they were going down to the **e** of	7097
	10:13 when he had **made an e** of prophesying,	3615
	13:10 that as soon as he had **made an e** of	3615
	14:27 wherefore he put forth the **e** of the rod	7097
	14:43 taste a little honey with the **e** of the rod	7097
	18: 1 he had **made an e** of speaking unto Saul,	3615
	24:16 when David had **made an e** of speaking	3615
2Sa	2:23 wherefore Abner with the **hinder e** of	310
	2:26 that it will be bitterness in the **latter e**?	314
	6:18 soon as David had **made an e** of offering	3615
	11:19 When thou hast **made an e** of telling	3615
	13:36 as soon as he had **made an e** of speaking,	3615
	14:26 (for it was at every year's **e** that he polled	7093
	24: 8 they came *to* Jerusalem at the **e** of nine	7097
1Ki	1:41 heard *it* as they had **made an e** of eating.	3615
	2:39 it came to pass at the **e** of three years,	7093
	3: 1 he had **made an e** of building his own	3615
	7:40 Hiram **made an e** of doing all the work	3615
	8:54 *that* when Solomon had **made an e** of	3615
	9:10 it came to pass at the **e** of twenty years,	7097
2Ki	8: 3 it came to pass at the seven years' **e**,	7097
	10:21 the house of Baal was full from one **e** to	6310
	10:25 as soon as he had **made an e** of offering	3615
	18:10 at the **e** of three years they took it:	7097
	21:16 till he had filled Jerusalem from one **e** to	6310
1Ch	16: 2 when David had **made an e** of offering	3615
2Ch	4:10 set the sea on the right side of the **east e**,	6924
	5:12 stood *at* the east **e** of the altar,	NIH

2Ch	7: 1 Now when Solomon had **made an e** of	3615
	8: 1 it came to pass at the **e** of twenty years,	7093
	20:16 ye shall find them at the **e** of the brook,	5490
	20:23 when they had **made an e** of	3615
	21:19 process of time, after the **e** of two years,	7093
	24:10 into the chest, until *they* had **made an e.**	3615
	24:23 it came to pass at the **e** of the year, *that*	8622
	29:17 day of the first month they **made an e.**	3615
	29:29 when *they* had **made an e** of offering,	3615
Ezr	9:11 which have filled it from one **e** to another	6310
	10:17 they **made an e** with all the men that	3615
Ne	3:21 even to the **e** of the house of Eliashib.	8503
	4: 2 will they **make an e** in a day? will they	3615
Job	6:11 what *is* mine **e**, that I should prolong my	7093
	8: 7 yet thy **latter e** should greatly increase.	319
	16: 3 Shall vain words **have an e?**	7093
	18: 2 How long *will it be ere* you make an **e** of	7078
	26:10 until the day and night **come to an e.**	8503
	28: 3 setteth an **e** to darkness, and searcheth	7093
	34:36 desire *is that* Job may be tried unto the **e**	5331
	42:12 So the LORD blessed the **latter e** of Job	319
Ps	7: 9 wickedness of the wicked **come to an e;**	1584
	9: 6 destructions are **come to** a perpetual **e:**	8552
	19: 4 and their words to the **e** of the world.	7097
	19: 6 going forth *is* from the **e** of the heaven,	7097
	30:12 **To the e that** *my* glory may sing	4616+3807.1
	37:37 the upright: for the **e** of *that* man *is* peace.	319
	37:38 the **e** of the wicked shall be cut off.	319
	39: 4 make me to know mine **e**, and the	7093
	46: 9 He maketh wars to cease unto the **e** of	7097
	61: 2 From the **e** of the earth will I cry unto	7097
	73:17 of God; *then* understood I their **e.**	319
	102:27 the same, and thy years shall have no **e.**	8552
	107:27 and are at their **wit's e.**	1104+2451+3605
	119:33 statutes; and I shall keep it *unto* the **e.**	6118
	119:96 I have seen an **e** of all perfection:	7093
	119:112 thy statutes alway, *even unto* the **e.**	6118
Pr	5: 4 her **e** is bitter as wormwood, sharp as a	319
	14:12 but the **e** thereof *are* the ways of death.	319
	14:13 end of the **e** of that mirth *is* heaviness.	319
	16:25 but the **e** thereof *are* the ways of death.	319
	19:20 that thou mayest be wise in thy **latter e.**	319
	20:21 but the **e** thereof shall not be blessed.	319
	23:18 For surely there is an **e;**	319
	25: 8 lest *thou know not* what to do in the **e**,	319
Ecc	3:11 God maketh from the beginning to the **e**,	5490
	4: 8 yet *is there* no **e** of all his labour; neither	7093
	4:16 *There is* no **e** of all the people, *even* of all	7093
	7: 2 for that *is* the **e** of all men; and the living	5490
	7: 8 Better *is* the **e** of a thing than the	319
	7:14 to the **e** that man should find nothing	1700
	10:13 the **e** of his talk *is* mischievous madness.	319
	12:12 of making many books *there* is no **e;**	7093
Isa	2: 7 neither *is there any* **e** of their treasures;	7097
	2: 7 neither *is there any* **e** of their chariots;	7097
	5:26 hiss unto them from the **e** of the earth:	7097
	7: 3 at the **e** of the conduit of the upper pool	7097
	9: 7 and peace *there shall be* no **e**,	7093
	13: 5 from the **e** of the heaven, *even* the LORD,	7097
	16: 4 for the extortioner is at an **e**, the spoiler	656
	23:15 after the **e** of seventy years shall Tyre sing	7093
	23:17 it shall come to pass after the **e** of seventy	7093
	33: 1 when thou shalt **make an e** to deal	5239
	38:12 day *even* to night wilt thou **make an e**	7999
	38:13 day *even* to night wilt thou **make an e**	7999
	41:22 and know the **latter e** of them;	319
	42:10 *and* his praise from the **e** of the earth,	7097
	45:17 **world without e.**	5703+5704+5769
	46:10 Declaring the **e** from the beginning,	319
	47: 7 neither didst remember the **latter e** of it.	319
	48:20 tell this, utter it to the **e** of the earth;	7097
	49: 6 *thou* mayest be my salvation unto the **e**	7097
	62:11 the LORD hath proclaimed unto the **e** of	7097
Jer	1: 3 the **e** of the eleventh year of Zedekiah	8552
	3: 5 will he keep *it* to the **e?** Behold, thou hast	5331
	4:27 be desolate; yet will I not make a **full e.**	3617
	5:10 and destroy; but make not a **full e:**	3617
	5:18 I will not make a **full e** with you.	3617
	5:31 *it so:* and what will ye do in the **e** thereof?	319
	12: 4 they said, He shall not see our **last e.**	319
	12:12 **e** of the land even to the *other* end of	7097
	12:12 the land even to the *other* **e** of the land:	7097
	17:11 of his days, and at his **e** shall be a fool.	319
	25:33 **e** of the earth even unto the *other* end of	7097
	25:33 earth even unto the *other* **e** of the earth:	7097
	26: 8 Jeremiah had **made an e** of speaking	3615
	29:11 not of evil, to give you an expected **e.**	319
	30:11 though I make a **full e** of all nations	3617
	30:11 yet will I not make a **full e** of thee:	3617
	31:17 there is hope in thine **e**, saith the LORD,	319
	34:14 At the **e** of seven years let ye go every	7093
	43: 1 *that* when Jeremiah had **made an e** of	3615
	44:27 the famine, until there be an **e** of them.	3615
	46:28 for I will make a **full e** of all the nations	3617
	46:28 I will not make a **full e** of thee,	3617
	51:13 thine **e** is come, *and* the measure of thy	7093
	51:31 of Babylon that his city is taken at *one* **e**,	7097
	51:63 when thou hast **made an e** of reading	3615
La	1: 9 she remembereth not her **last e;** therefore	319
	4:18 our **e** is near, our days are fulfilled; for our	7093
	4:18 our days are fulfilled; for our **e** is come.	7093
Eze	3:16 it came to pass at the **e** of seven days,	7097
	7: 2 An **e**, the end is come upon the four	7093
	7: 2 the **e** is come upon the four corners of	7093
	7: 3 Now *is* the **e** come upon thee, and I will	7093

Eze	7: 6 An **e** is come, the end is come:	7093
	7: 6 An end is come, the end is come:	7093
	11:13 *wilt* thou make a **full e** of the remnant of	3617
	20:17 neither did I make an **e** of them in	3617
	20:26 make them desolate, **to the e**	4616+3807.1
	21:25 is come, when iniquity *shall have* an **e**,	7093
	21:29 when *their* iniquity *shall have* an **e.**	7093
	29:13 At the **e** of forty years will I gather	7093
	31:14 for that none of all the **e**	4616+3807.1
	35: 5 in the time *that their* iniquity *had* an **e:**	7093
	39:14 after the **e** of seven months shall they	7097
	41:12 **e** toward the west *was* seventy cubits	6285
	42:15 when he had **made an e** of measuring	3615
	43:23 thou hast **made an e** of cleansing *it,*	3615
	48: 1 From the north *to* the coast of the way	7097
Da	1: 5 at the **e** thereof they might stand before	7117
	1:15 at the **e** of ten days their countenances	7117
	1:18 Now at the **e** of the days that the king	7117
	4:11 the sight thereof to the **e** of all the earth:	5491
	4:22 thy dominion to the **e** of the earth.	5491
	4:29 At the **e** of twelve months he walked in	7118
	4:34 at the **e** of the days I Nebuchadnezzar lift	7118
	6:26 his dominion *shall be even* unto the **e.**	5491
	7:26 to consume and to destroy *it* unto the **e.**	5491
	7:28 Hitherto *is* the **e** of the matter. *As for* me	5491
	8:17 for at the time of the **e** *shall be* the vision.	7093
	8:19 shall be in the **last e** of the indignation:	319
	8:19 for at the time appointed the **e** *shall be.*	7093
	9:24 to **make an e** of sins, and to make	8552
	9:26 the **e** thereof *shall be* with a flood,	7093
	9:26 unto the **e** of the war desolations *are*	7093
	11: 6 in the **e** of years they shall join themselves	7093
	11:27 yet the **e** *shall be* at the time appointed.	7093
	11:35 *them* white, *even* to the time of the **e:**	7093
	11:40 at the time of the **e** shall the king of	7093
	11:45 yet he shall come to his **e**, and none shall	7093
	12: 4 seal the book, *even* to the time of the **e:**	7093
	12: 6 How long *shall it be to* the **e** of these	7093
	12: 8 lord, what *shall be* the **e** of these *things?*	7093
	12: 9 closed up and sealed till the time of the **e.**	7093
	12:13 go thou thy way till the **e** *be:* for thou	7093
	12:13 and stand in thy lot at the **e** of the days.	7093
Am	3:15 the great houses shall **have an e**, saith	5486
	5:18 **to what e** *is* it for you? the day	4100+3807.1
	7: 2 *that* when they had **made an e** of eating	3615
	8: 2 The **e** is come upon my people *of* Israel;	7093
	8:10 only *son*, and the **e** thereof as a bitter day.	319
Ob	1: 9 **to the e** that every one of	4616+3807.1
Na	1: 8 will make an **utter e** of the place thereof,	3617
	1: 9 he *will* make an **utter e:** affliction shall	3617
	2: 9 for *there is* none **e** of the store *and* glory	7097
	3: 3 and *there is* none **e** of *their* corpses:	7097
	3: 3 but at the **e** they shall speak, and not lie:	7093
Mt	10:22 he that endureth to the **e** shall be saved.	5056
	11: 1 Jesus had **made an e** of commanding	5055
	13:39 the harvest is the **e** of the world;	4930
	13:40 fire; so shall it be in the **e** of this world.	4930
	13:49 So shall it be at the **e** of the world:	4930
	24: 3 of thy coming, and of the **e** of the world?	4930
	24: 6 must come to pass, but the **e** is not yet.	5056
	24:13 But he that shall endure unto the **e**,	5056
	24:14 all nations; and then shall the **e** come.	5056
	24:31 from one **e** of heaven to the other.	206
	26:58 and sat with the servants, to see the **e.**	5056
	28: 1 In the **e** of the sabbath, as it began to	3796
	28:20 you alway, *even* unto the **e** of the world.	4930
Mk	3:26 divided, he cannot stand, but hath an **e.**	5056
	13: 7 must needs be; but the **e** *shall* not *be* yet.	5056
	13:13 he that shall endure unto the **e**, the same	5056
Lk	1:33 and of his kingdom there shall be no **e.**	5056
	18: 1 he spake a parable unto them *to* this **e**,	NIG
	21: 9 come to pass; but the **e** *is* not by and by.	5056
	22:37 for the *things* concerning me have an **e.**	5056
Jn	13: 1 in the world, he loved them unto the **e.**	5056
	18:37 To this **e** was I born, and for this cause	1519
Ac	7:19 **to the e** *they* might not live.	1519+3588
Ro	1:11 **to the e** you may be established;	1519+3588
	4:16 **to the e** the promise might be sure	1519+3588
	6:21 for the **e** of those *things* is death.	5056
	6:22 unto holiness, and the **e** everlasting life.	5056
	10: 4 For Christ *is* the **e** of the law for	5056
	14: 9 For to this **e** Christ both died,	1519+3778
1Co	1: 8 Who shall also confirm you unto the **e**,	5056
	15:24 Then *cometh* the **e**, when he shall have	5056
2Co	1:13 trust you shall acknowledge even to the **e;**	5056
	2: 9 For to this **e** also did I write, that I	1519+3778
	3:13 look to the **e** of that which is abolished:	5056
	11:15 whose **e** shall be according to their works.	5056
Eph	3:21 ages, **world without e.**	165+165+3588+3588
Php	3:19 Whose **e** *is* destruction, whose God *is*	5056
1Th	3:13 **To the e** *he* may stablish your	1519+3588
1Ti	1: 5 the **e** of the commandment is charity	5056
Heb	3: 6 the rejoicing of the hope firm unto the **e.**	5056
	3:14 of *our* confidence stedfast unto the **e;**	5056
	6: 8 unto cursing; whose **e** *is* to be burned.	5056
	6:11 to the full assurance of hope unto the **e:**	5056
	6:16 oath for confirmation *is* to them an **e** of	4009
	7: 3 neither beginning of days, nor **e** of life;	5056
	9:26 now once in the **e** of the world hath he	4930
	13: 7 considering the **e** of *their* conversation.	1545
Jas	5:11 of Job, and have seen the **e** of the Lord;	5056
1Pe	1: 9 Receiving the **e** of your faith, *even*	5056
	1:13 hope to the **e** for the grace that is *to be*	5049
	4: 7 But the **e** of all *things* is at hand: be ye	5056
	4:17 what *shall* the **e** *be* of them that obey not	5056

2Pe	2:20 the latter **e** is worse with them than	NIG
Rev	2:26 and keepeth my works unto the **e**,	5056
	21: 6 and Omega, the beginning and the **e.**	5056
	22:13 the beginning and the **e**, the first and	5056

ENDAMAGE (1) [DAMAGE]
Ezr	4:13 so thou shalt **e** the revenue of the kings.	5142

ENDANGER (1) [ENDANGERED]
Da	1:10 shall ye **make** *me* **e** my head to the king.	2325

ENDANGERED (1) [ENDANGER]
Ecc	10: 9 he that cleaveth wood shall be **e** thereby.	5533

ENDEAVOUR (1) [ENDEAVOURED, ENDEAVOURING, ENDEAVOURS]
2Pe	1:15 Moreover I will **e** that you may be able	4704

ENDEAVOURED (2) [ENDEAVOUR]
Ac	16:10 immediately we **e** to go into Macedonia,	2212
1Th	2:17 **e** the more abundantly to see your face	4704

ENDEAVOURING (1) [ENDEAVOUR]
Eph	4: 3 **E** to keep the unity of the Spirit in the	4704

ENDEAVOURS (1) [ENDEAVOUR]
Ps	28: 4 according to the wickedness of their **e:**	4611

ENDED (21) [END]
Ge	2: 2 on the seventh day God **e** his work which	3615
	41:53 that was in the land of Egypt, were **e.**	3615
	47:18 When that year was **e**, they came unto	8552
Dt	31:30 the words of this song, until they were **e.**	8552
	34: 8 *and* mourning for Moses were **e.**	8552
Ru	2:21 until they have **e** all my harvest.	3615
2Sa	20:18 counsel at Abel: and so they **e** the matter.	8552
1Ki	7:51 So was **e** all the work that king Solomon	7999
2Ch	29:34 till the work was **e**, and until the *other*	3615
Job	31:40 instead of barley. The words of Job are **e.**	8552
Ps	72:20 prayers of David the son of Jesse are **e.**	3615
Isa	60:20 and the days of thy mourning shall be **e.**	7999
Jer	8:20 the summer is **e**, and we are not saved.	3615
Eze	4: 8 till thou hast **e** the days of thy siege.	3615
Mt	7:28 to pass, when Jesus had **e** these sayings,	4931
Lk	4: 2 and when they were **e**, he afterward	4931
	4:13 And when the devil had **e** all	4931
	7: 1 Now when he had **e** all his sayings in	4137
Jn	13: 2 And supper being **e**, the devil having now	1096
Ac	19:21 After these *things* were **e**, Paul purposed	4137
	21:27 And when the seven days were almost **e**,	4931

ENDETH (1) [END]
Isa	24: 8 the noise of them that rejoice **e**, the joy of	2308

ENDING (1) [END]
Rev	1: 8 and Omega, the beginning and the **e**,	5056

ENDLESS (2) [END]
1Ti	1: 4 give heed to fables and **e** genealogies,	562
Heb	7:16 but after the power of an **e** life.	179

ENDOR, EN-DOR (3) [ENDOR]
Jos	17:11 the inhabitants of **E** and her towns,	5874
1Sa	28: 7 *is* a woman that hath a familiar spirit at **E.**	5874
Ps	83:10 perished at **E:** they became *as* dung	5874

ENDOW (1)
Ex	22:16 shall **surely e** her to be his wife.	4117+4117

ENDS (51) [END]
Ex	25:18 them, in the two **e** of the mercy seat.	7098
	25:19 make the cherubims on the two **e** thereof.	7098
	28:14 two chains of *pure* gold at the **e;**	4020
	28:22 at the **e** of wreathen work of *pure* gold.	1383
	28:23 shalt put the two rings on the two **e** of	7098
	28:24 *which are* on the two **e** of the breastplate.	7098
	28:25 *other* two **e** of the two wreathen *chains*	7098
	28:26 thou shalt put them upon the two **e** of	7098
	37: 7 he them, on the two **e** of the mercy seat;	7098
	37: 8 he the cherubims on the two **e** thereof.	7098
	38: 5 cast four rings for the four **e** of the grate	7099
	39:15 upon the breastplate chains **at the e**,	1383
	39:16 put the two rings in the two **e** of	7098
	39:17 the two rings on the **e** of the breastplate.	7098
	39:18 the two **e** of the two wreathen *chains*	7098
	39:19 put *them* on the two **e** of the breastplate,	7098
Dt	33:17 the people together *to* the **e** of the earth:	657
1Sa	2:10 the LORD shall judge the **e** of the earth;	657
1Ki	8: 8 that the **e** of the staves were seen out in	7218
2Ch	5: 9 the **e** of the staves were seen from the ark	7218
Job	28:24 For he looketh to the **e** of the earth,	7098
	37: 3 and his lightning unto the **e** of the earth.	3671
	38:13 it might take hold of the **e** of the earth,	3671
Ps	19: 6 heaven, and his circuit unto the **e** of it:	7098
	22:27 All the **e** of the world shall remember	7098
	48:10 so *is* thy praise unto the **e** of the earth:	7099
	59:13 God ruleth in Jacob unto the **e** of the earth.	657
	65: 5 *who art* the confidence of all the **e** of	7099
	67: 7 and all the **e** of the earth shall fear him.	657
	72: 8 and from the river unto the **e** of the earth.	657
	98: 3 the **e** of the earth have seen the salvation	657
	135: 7 vapours to ascend from the **e** of the earth;	7097
Pr	17:24 the eyes of a fool *are* in the **e** of the earth.	7097
	30: 4 hath established all the **e** of the earth?	657
Isa	26:15 hadst removed *it* far *unto* all the **e** of	7099
	40:28 the Creator of the **e** of the earth,	7098

E

Isa 41: 5 the **e** of the earth were afraid, drew near, 7098
41: 9 *Thou* whom I have taken from the **e** of 7098
43: 6 and my daughters from the **e** of the earth; 7097
45:22 and be ye saved, all the **e** of the earth 657
52:10 the **e** of the earth shall see the salvation of 657
Jer 10:13 causeth the vapours to ascend from the **e** 7097
16:19 Gentiles shall come unto thee from the **e** 657
25:31 A noise shall come *even* to the **e** of 7097
51:16 causeth the vapours to ascend from the **e** 7097
Eze 15: 4 the fire devoureth both the **e** of it, 7098
Mic 5: 4 for now shall he be great unto the **e** of 657
Zec 9:10 from the river *even* to the **e** of the earth. 657
Ac 13:47 be for salvation unto the **e** of the earth, 2078
Ro 10:18 and their words unto the **e** of the world. 4009
1Co 10:11 upon whom the **e** of the world are come. 5056

ENDUED (5)
Ge 30:20 God hath **e** me with a good dowry; 2064
2Ch 2:12 **e** with prudence and understanding, 3045
2:13 **e** with understanding, of Huram my 3045
Lk 24:49 until ye be **e** with power from on high. 1746
Jas 3:13 and **e** with knowledge amongst you? NIG

ENDURE (29) [ENDURED, ENDURETH, ENDURING]
Ge 33:14 and the children be **able to e**, 7272+3807.1
Ex 18:23 *so*, thou shalt be able to **e**, 5975
Est 8: 6 For how can I **e** to see the evil that shall 3201
8: 6 how can I **e** to see the destruction of my 3201
Job 8:15 he shall hold it fast, but it shall not **e** 6965
31:23 by reason of his highness I **could** not **e**. 3201
Ps 9: 7 the LORD shall **e** for ever: he hath 3427
30: 5 weeping may **e** for a night, but joy 3885
72: 5 as long as the sun and moon **e**, 6440+3807.1
72:17 His name shall **e** for ever: his name shall 1961
89:29 His seed also will I make **to e** for ever, NIH
89:36 His seed shall **e** for ever, and his throne as 1961
102:12 thou, O LORD, shalt **e** for ever; 3427
102:26 They shall perish, but thou shalt **e**: yea, 5975
104:31 The glory of the LORD shall **e** for ever: 1961
Pr 27:24 and doth the crown **e** to every generation? NIH
Eze 22:14 Can thine heart **e**, or can thine hands be 5975
Mt 24:13 he that shall **e** unto the end, the same 5278
Mk 4:17 in themselves, and so **e** but for a time; 1510
13:13 he that shall **e** unto the end, the same 5278
2Th 1: 4 persecutions and tribulations that ye **e**: 430
2Ti 2: 3 Thou therefore **e hardness**, as a good 2553
2:10 I **e** all **things** for the elect's sakes, 5278
4: 3 the time will come when they will not **e** 430
4: 5 watch thou in all **things**, **e afflictions**, 2553
Heb 12: 7 If ye **e** chastening, God dealeth with you 5278
12:20 (For they could not **e** that which was 5342
Jas 5:11 Behold, we count them happy which **e**. 5278
1Pe 2:19 a man for conscience toward God **e** grief, 5297

ENDURED (8) [ENDURE]
Ps 81:15 but their time should have **e** for ever. 1961
Ro 9:22 **e** with much longsuffering *the* vessels of 5342
2Ti 3:11 at Lystra; what persecutions I **e**: 5297
Heb 6:15 And so, after he had **patiently e**, 3114
10:32 ye **e** a great fight of afflictions; 5278
11:27 for he **e**, as seeing *him who is* invisible. 2594
12: 2 who for the joy that was set before him **e** 5278
12: 3 consider him that **e** such contradiction 5278

ENDURETH (59) [ENDURE]
1Ch 16:34 for *he is* good; for his mercy **e** for ever. NIH
16:41 the LORD, because his mercy **e** for ever; NIH
2Ch 5:13 For *he is* good; for his mercy **e** for ever. NIH
7: 3 For *he is* good; for his mercy **e** for ever. NIH
7: 6 because his mercy **e** for ever, when David NIH
20:21 Praise the LORD; for his mercy **e** for ever. NIH
Ezr 3:11 for his mercy **e** for ever towards Israel. NIH
Ps 30: 5 his anger **e** but a moment; in his favour NIH
52: 1 O mighty *man?* the goodness of God **e** NIH
72: 7 of peace **so long as** the moon **e**. 1097+5704
100: 5 his truth **e** to all generations. NIH
106: 1 for *he is* good: for his mercy **e** for ever. NIH
107: 1 for *he is* good: for his mercy **e** for ever. NIH
111: 3 glorious: and his righteousness **e** for ever. 5975
111:10 *his* commandments; his praise **e** for ever. 5975
112: 3 house: and his righteousness **e** for ever. NIH
112: 9 to the poor; his righteousness **e** for ever; 5975
117: 2 the truth of the LORD **e** for ever. Praise ye NIH
118: 1 he *is* good: because his mercy **e** for ever. NIH
118: 2 Israel now say, that his mercy **e** for ever. NIH
118: 3 Aaron now say, that his mercy **e** for ever. NIH
118: 4 the LORD say, that his mercy **e** for ever. NIH
118:29 for *he is* good: for his mercy **e** for ever. NIH
119:160 every one of thy righteous judgments *e* for NIH
135:13 Thy name, O LORD, *e* for ever; NIH
136: 1 for *he is* good: for his mercy **e** for ever. NIH
136: 2 the God of gods: for his mercy **e** for ever. NIH
136: 3 the Lord of lords: for his mercy **e** for ever. NIH
136: 4 great wonders: for his mercy **e** for ever. NIH
136: 5 the heavens: for his mercy **e** for ever. NIH
136: 6 the waters: for his mercy **e** for ever. NIH
136: 7 great lights: for his mercy **e** for ever: NIH
136: 8 to rule by day: for his mercy **e** for ever: NIH
136: 9 to rule by night: for his mercy **e** for ever: NIH
136:10 in their firstborn: for his mercy **e** for ever: NIH
136:11 among them: for his mercy **e** for ever. NIH
136:12 out arm: for his mercy **e** for ever. NIH
136:13 sea into parts: for his mercy **e** for ever. NIH
136:14 the midst of it: for his mercy **e** for ever. NIH

Ps 136:15 in the Red sea: for his mercy **e** for ever. NIH
136:16 the wilderness: for his mercy **e** for ever. NIH
136:17 great kings: for his mercy **e** for ever: NIH
136:18 famous kings: for his mercy **e** for ever: NIH
136:19 of the Amorites: for his mercy **e** for ever: NIH
136:20 king of Bashan: for his mercy **e** for ever: NIH
136:21 for an heritage: for his mercy **e** for ever. NIH
136:22 Israel his servant: for his mercy **e** for ever. NIH
136:23 in our low estate: for his mercy **e** for ever. NIH
136:24 from our enemies: for his mercy **e** for ever. NIH
136:25 food to all flesh: for his mercy **e** for ever. NIH
136:26 God of heaven: for his mercy **e** for ever. NIH
138: 8 thy mercy, O LORD, **e** for ever: NIH
145:13 dominion *e* throughout all generations. NIH
Jer 33:11 LORD *is* good; for his mercy **e** for ever: NIH
Mt 10:22 but he that **e** to the end shall be saved. 5278
Jn 6:27 *that* meat which **e** unto everlasting life, 3306
1Co 13: 7 all *things*, hopeth all *things*, **e** all *things*. 5278
Jas 1:12 Blessed *is* the man that **e** temptation: 5278
1Pe 1:25 But the word of the Lord **e** for ever. 3306

ENDURING (3) [ENDURE]
Ps 19: 9 The fear of the LORD *is* clean, **e** for ever: 5975
2Co 1: 6 which is effectual in the **e** of the same 5281
Heb 10:34 in heaven a better and an **e** substance. 3306

EN-EGLAIM (1)
Eze 47:10 stand upon it from En-gedi even unto **E**; 5882

ENEMIES (267) [ENEMY]
Ge 14:20 hath delivered thine **e** into thy hand. 6862
22:17 thy seed shall possess the gate of his **e**; 341
49: 8 thy hand *shall* be in the neck of thine **e**; 341
Ex 1:10 they join also unto our **e**, and fight 8130
23:22 I will be an enemy unto thine **e**, 341
23:27 I will make all thine **e** turn their backs 341
23:25 naked unto *their* shame amongst their **e**:) 6965
Lev 26: 7 ye shall chase your **e**, and they shall fall 341
26: 8 your **e** shall fall before you by the sword. 341
26:16 your seed in vain, for your **e** shall eat it. 341
26:17 and ye shall be slain before your **e**; 341
26:32 your **e** which dwell therein shall be 341
26:36 into their hearts in the lands of their **e**; 341
26:37 have no power to stand before your **e**. 341
26:38 and the land of your **e** shall eat you up. 341
26:41 brought them into the land of their **e**; 341
26:44 that, when they be in the land of their **e**, 341
Nu 10: 9 God, and ye shall be saved from your **e**. 341
10:35 LORD, and let thine **e** be scattered; 341
14:42 that ye be not smitten before your **e**. 341
23:11 I took thee to curse mine **e**, and behold, 341
24: 8 he shall eat up the nations his **e**, 6862
24:10 I called thee to curse mine **e**, and behold, 341
24:18 Seir also shall be a possession for his **e**; 341
32:21 until he hath driven out his **e** from before 341
Dt 1:42 lest ye be smitten before your **e**. 341
6:19 To cast out all thine **e** from before thee, 341
12:10 *when* he giveth you rest from all your **e** 341
20: 1 thou goest out to battle against thine **e**, 341
20: 3 *this* day unto battle against your **e**: 341
20: 4 to fight for you against your **e**, to save you. 341
20:14 thou shalt eat the spoil of thine **e**, which 341
21:10 thou goest forth to war against thine **e**, 341
23: 9 When the host goeth forth against thine **e**, 341
23:14 and to give up thine **e** before thee; 341
25:19 given thee rest from all thine **e** round 341
28: 7 The LORD shall cause thine **e** that rise up 341
28:25 cause thee *to be* smitten before thine **e**: 341
28:31 thy sheep *shall be* given unto thine **e**, 341
28:48 Therefore shalt thou serve thine **e** which 341
28:53 wherewith thine **e** shall distress thee: 341
28:55 wherewith thine **e** shall distress thee in all 341
28:68 there ye shall be sold unto your **e** for 341
30: 7 God will put all these curses upon thine **e**, 341
32:31 even our **e** themselves *being* judges. 341
32:41 I will render vengeance to mine **e**, 6862
33: 7 be thou a help *to him* from his **e**. 6862
33:29 thine **e** shall be found liars unto thee; 341
Jos 7: 8 Israel turneth *their* backs before their **e**! 341
7:12 of Israel could not stand before their **e**, 341
7:12 *but* turned *their* backs before their **e**, 341
7:13 thou canst not stand before thine **e**, until 341
10:13 had avenged themselves upon their **e**. 341
10:19 *but* pursue after your **e**, and smite 341
10:25 for thus shall the LORD do to all your **e** 341
21:44 there stood not a man of all their **e** before 341
21:44 the LORD delivered all their **e** into their 341
22: 8 the spoil of your **e** with your brethren. 341
23: 1 rest unto Israel from all their **e** round 341
Jdg 2:14 sold them into the hands of their **e** round 341
2:14 could not any longer stand before their **e** 341
2:18 delivered them out of the hand of their **e** 341
3:28 for the LORD hath delivered your **e** 341
5:31 So let all thine **e** perish, O LORD: 341
8:34 of the hands of all their **e** on every side: 341
11:36 hath taken vengeance for thee of thine **e**, 341
1Sa 2: 1 my mouth is enlarged over mine **e**; 341
4: 3 it may save us out of the hand of our **e**. 341
12:10 now deliver us out of the hand of our **e**, 341
12:11 delivered you out of the hand of your **e** on 341
14:24 that I may be avenged on mine **e**. 341
14:30 of the spoil of their **e** which they found? 341
14:47 fought against all his **e** on every side, 341
18:25 Philistines, to be avenged of the king's **e**. 341
20:15 not when the LORD hath cut off the **e** of 341

1Sa 20:16 even require *it* at the hand of David's **e**. 341
25:22 and more also do God unto the **e** of David, 341
25:26 now let thine **e**, and they that seek evil to 341
25:29 the souls of thine **e**, them shall he sling out 341
29: 8 that I may not go fight against the **e** of my 341
30:26 a present for you of the spoil of the **e** 341
2Sa 3:18 and out of the hand of all their **e**. 341
5:20 The LORD hath broken forth upon mine **e** 341
7: 1 given him rest round about from all his **e**; 341
7: 9 have cut off all thine **e** out of thy sight, 341
7:11 have caused thee to rest from all thine **e**. 341
12:14 to the **e** of the LORD to blaspheme, 341
18:19 that the LORD hath avenged him of his **e**. 341
18:32 The **e** of my lord the king, and all that rise 341
19: 6 In that thou lovest thine **e**, and hatest thy 8130
19: 9 The king saved us out of the hand of our **e**, 341
22: 1 delivered him out of the hand of all his **e**, 341
22: 4 be praised: so shall I be saved from mine **e**. 341
22:38 I have pursued mine **e**, and destroyed 341
22:41 hast also given me the necks of mine **e**, 341
22:49 that bringeth me forth from mine **e**: thou 341
24:13 that thou flee three months before thine **e**, 6862
1Ki 3:11 thyself, nor hast asked the life of thine **e**; 341
8:48 with all their soul, in the land of their **e**, 341
2Ki 17:39 deliver you out of the hand of all your **e**. 341
21:14 and deliver them into the hand of their **e**; 341
21:14 become a prey and a spoil to all their **e**; 341
1Ch 12:17 if *ye be come* to betray me to mine **e**, 6862
14:11 God hath broken in upon mine **e** by mine 341
17: 8 have cut off all thine **e** from before thee, 341
17:10 Moreover I will subdue all thine **e**. 341
21:12 while that the sword of thine **e** overtaketh 341
22: 9 him rest from all his **e** round 341
2Ch 1:11 wealth, or honour, nor the life of thine **e**, 8130
6:28 if their **e** besiege them in the cities of their 341
6:34 If thy people go out to war against their **e** 341
6:36 deliver them *over* before their **e**, 341
20:27 had made them to rejoice over their **e**. 341
20:29 the LORD fought against the **e** of Israel. 341
25:20 deliver them into the hand *of their* **e**, NIH
Ne 4:15 our **e** heard that it was known unto us, 341
5: 9 of the reproach of the heathen our **e**? 341
6: 1 Geshem the Arabian, and the rest of our **e**, 341
6:16 that when all our **e** heard *thereof*, and all 341
9:27 deliveredst them into the hand of their **e**, 6862
9:27 saved them out of the hand of their **e**. 6862
9:28 leftest thou them in the hand of their **e**, 341
Est 8:13 that day to avenge themselves on their **e**. 341
9: 1 in the day that the **e** of the Jews hoped to 341
9: 5 Thus the Jews smote all their **e** *with* 341
9:16 had rest from their **e**, and slew of their foes 341
9:22 days wherein the Jews rested from their **e**, 341
Job 19:11 he counteth me unto him as *one of* his **e**. 6862
Ps 3: 7 for thou hast smitten all mine **e** *upon* 341
5: 8 in thy righteousness because of mine **e**; 8324
6: 7 it waxeth old because of all mine **e**. 6887
6:10 Let all mine **e** be ashamed and sore vexed: 341
7: 6 up thyself because of the rage of mine **e**: 6887
8: 2 thou ordained strength because of thine **e**, 6887
9: 3 mine **e** are turned back, they shall fall 341
10: 5 *as for* all his **e**, he puffeth at them. 6887
17: 9 my deadly **e**, *who* compass me about. 341
18: 1 I delivered him from the hand of all his **e**, 341
18: 3 praised: so shall I be saved from mine **e**. 341
18:37 I have pursued mine **e**, and overtaken 341
18:40 hast also given me the necks of mine **e**; 341
18:48 He delivereth me from mine **e**: yea, 341
21: 8 Thine hand shall find out all thine **e**: 341
23: 5 table before me in the presence of mine **e**: 6887
25: 2 ashamed, let not mine **e** triumph over me. 341
25:19 Consider mine **e**; for they are many; 341
27: 2 the wicked, *even* mine **e** and my foes, 6862
27: 6 lifted up above mine **e** round about me: 341
27:11 me in a plain path, because of mine **e**. 8324
27:12 me not over unto the will of mine **e**: 6862
31:11 I was a reproach among all mine **e**, 6887
31:15 deliver me from the hand of mine **e**, 341
35:19 Let not them that are mine **e** wrongfully 341
37:20 the **e** of the LORD *shall be* as the fat of 341
38:19 mine **e** *are* lively, *and* they are strong; 341
41: 2 wilt not deliver him unto the will of his **e**. 341
41: 5 Mine **e** speak evil of me, When shall he 341
42:10 sword in my bones, mine **e** reproach me; 6887
44: 5 Through thee will we push down our **e**: 6862
44: 7 thou hast saved us from our **e**, and hast 6862
45: 5 *are* sharp in the heart of the king's **e**; 341
54: 5 He shall reward evil unto mine **e**: cut 8324
54: 7 eye hath seen *his desire* upon mine **e**. 341
56: 2 Mine **e** would daily swallow *me* up: 8324
56: 9 I cry unto *thee*, then shall mine **e** turn 341
59: 1 Deliver me from mine **e**, O my God: 341
59:10 shall let me see *my desire* upon mine **e**. 8324
60:12 for he *it is that* shall tread down our **e**. 6862
66: 3 shall thine **e** submit themselves unto thee. 341
68: 1 Let God arise, let his **e** be scattered: let 341
68:21 God shall wound the head of his **e**, 341
68:23 foot may be dipped in the blood of *thine* **e**, 341
69: 4 *being* mine **e** wrongfully, are mighty: 341
69:18 redeem it: deliver me because of mine **e**. 341
71:10 For mine **e** speak against me; and they that 341
72: 9 before him; and his **e** shall lick the dust. 341
74: 4 Thine **e** roar in the midst of thy 6887
74:23 Forget not the voice of thine **e**: the tumult 6887
78:53 not: but the sea overwhelmed their **e**. 341
78:66 he smote his **e** in the hinder parts: he put 6862

E

Ps 80: 6 and our **e** laugh among themselves. 341
81:14 I should soon have subdued their **e**, 341
83: 2 lo, thine **e** make a tumult: and they that 341
89:10 thou hast scattered thine **e** with thy strong 341
89:42 thou hast made all his **e** to rejoice. 341
89:51 Wherewith thine **e** have reproached, 341
92: 9 For lo, thine **e**, O LORD, for lo, 341
92: 9 O LORD, for lo, thine **e** shall perish; 341
92:11 eye also shall see *my desire* on mine **e**, 7790
97: 3 and burneth up his **e** round about. 6862
102: 8 Mine **e** reproach me all the day; 341
105:24 and made them stronger than their **e**. 6862
106:11 the waters covered their **e**: there was not 6862
106:42 Their **e** also oppressed them, and they 341
108:13 for he *it is that* shall tread down our **e**. 6862
110: 1 hand, until I make thine **e** thy footstool. 341
110: 2 of Zion: rule thou in the midst of thine **e**. 341
112: 8 afraid, until he see *his desire* upon his **e**. 6862
119:98 hast made me wiser than mine **e**: 341
119:139 because mine **e** have forgotten thy words. 6862
119:157 Many *are* my persecutors and mine **e**; 6862
127: 5 but they shall speak with the **e** in the gate. 341
132:18 His **e** will I clothe with shame: 341
136:24 redeemed us from our **e**: for his mercy 6862
138: 7 thine hand against the wrath of mine **e**, 341
139:20 *and* thine **e** take *thy name* in vain. 6145
139:22 *with* perfect hatred: I count them mine **e**. 341
143: 9 Deliver me, O LORD, from mine **e**: I flee 341
143:12 thy mercy cut off mine **e**, and destroy all 341
Pr 16: 7 he maketh even his **e** to be at peace with 341
Isa 1:24 adversaries, and avenge me of mine **e**: 341
9:11 Rezin against him, and join his **e** together; 341
26:11 yea, the fire of thine **e** shall devour them. 6862
42:13 yea, roar; he shall prevail against his **e**. 341
59:18 to his adversaries, recompence to his **e**; 341
62: 8 give thy corn *to be* meat for thine **e**; 341
66: 6 LORD that rendereth recompence to his **e**. 341
66:14 and *his* indignation towards his **e**. 341
Jer 12: 7 beloved of my soul into the hand of her **e**. 341
15: 9 will I deliver to the sword before their **e**, 341
15:14 I will make *thee* to pass with thine **e** into 341
17: 4 will cause thee to serve thine **e** in the land 341
19: 7 them to fall by the sword before their **e**, 341
19: 9 wherewith they **e**, and they that seek 341
20: 4 they shall fall by the sword of their **e**, 341
20: 5 Judah will I give into the hand of their **e**, 341
21: 7 into the hand of their **e**, and into the hand 341
34:20 even give them into the hand of their **e**, 341
34:21 princes will I give into the hand of their **e**, 341
44:30 king of Egypt into the hand of his **e**, 341
48: 5 for in the going down of Horonaim the **e** 6862
49:37 cause Elam to be dismayed before their **e**, 341
La 1: 2 with her, they are become her **e**. 341
1: 5 adversaries are the chief, her **e** prosper; 341
1:21 all mine **e** have heard of my trouble; 341
2:16 All thine **e** have opened their mouth 341
3:46 All our **e** have opened their mouths 341
3:52 Mine **e** chased me sore, like a bird, 341
Eze 39:23 and gave them into the hand of their **e**: 6862
Da 4:19 and the interpretation thereof to thine **e**, 6146
Am 9: 4 they go into captivity before their **e**, 341
Mic 4:10 redeem thee from the hand of thine **e**. 341
5: 9 and all thine **e** shall be cut off. 341
7: 6 a man's *are* the men of his own house. 341
Na 1: 2 and he reserveth *wrath* for his **e**. 341
1: 8 and darkness shall pursue his **e**. 341
3:13 land shall be set wide open unto thine **e**: 341
Zec 10: 5 *their* **e** in the mire of the streets in the NIH
Mt 5:44 I say unto you, Love your **e**, bless them 2190
22:44 hand, till I make thine **e** thy footstool? 2190
Mk 12:36 hand, till I make thine **e** thy footstool. 2190
Lk 1:71 That *we* should be saved from our **e**, 2190
1:74 of our **e** might serve him without fear, 2190
6:27 I say unto you which hear, Love your **e**, 2190
6:35 love ye your **e**, and do good, and lend, 2190
19:27 But those mine **e**, which would not that 2190
19:43 thine **e** shall cast a trench about thee, 2190
20:43 Till I make thine **e** thy footstool. 2190
Ro 5:10 if, when we were **e**, we were reconciled 2190
11:28 the gospel, *they are* **e** for your sakes: 2190
1Co 15:25 till he hath put all **e** under his feet. 2190
Php 3:18 *that they are* the **e** of the cross of Christ: 2190
Col 1:21 and in *your* mind by wicked works, 2190
Heb 1:13 until I make thine **e** thy footstool? 2190
10:13 From henceforth expecting till his **e** be 2190
Rev 11: 5 of their mouth, and devoureth their **e**: 2190
11:12 in a cloud; and their **e** beheld them. 2190

ENEMIES' (3) [ENEMY]

Lev 26:34 it lieth desolate, and ye *be* in your **e** land; 341
26:39 pine away in their iniquity in your **e** lands; 341
Eze 39:27 gathered them out of their **e** lands, 341

ENEMY (107) [ENEMIES, ENEMIES', ENEMY'S]

Ex 15: 6 O LORD, hath dashed in pieces the **e**. 341
15: 9 The **e** said, I will pursue, I will overtake, 341
23:22 I will be an **e** unto thine enemies, 340
Lev 26:25 shall be delivered into the hand of the **e**. 341
Nu 10: 9 if ye go *to war* in your land against the **e** 6862
35:23 upon him, that he die, and *was* not his **e**, 341
Dt 28:57 wherewith thine **e** shall distress thee in 341
32:27 it not that I feared the wrath of the **e**, 341
32:42 the beginning of revenges upon the **e**. 341
33:27 he shall thrust out the **e** from before thee; 341
Jdg 16:23 Our god hath delivered Samson our **e** into 341

Jdg 16:24 god hath delivered into our hands our **e**. 341
1Sa 2:32 thou shalt see an **e** *in my* habitation, in all 6862
18:29 thou Saul became David's **e** continually. 341
19:17 and sent away mine **e**, that he is escaped? 341
24: 4 I will deliver thine **e** into thine hand, 341
24:19 For if a man find his **e**, will he let him go 341
26: 8 God hath delivered thine **e** into thine hand 341
28:16 from thee, and is become thine **e**? 6145
2Sa 4: 8 of Ish-bosheth the son of Saul thine **e**, 341
22:18 He delivered me from my strong **e**, 341
1Ki 8:33 Israel be smitten down before the **e**, 341
8:37 if their **e** besiege them in the land of their 341
8:44 thy people go out to battle against their **e**, 341
8:46 deliver them to the **e**, so that they carry 341
8:46 them away captives unto the land of the **e**, 341
21:20 to Elijah, Hast thou found me, O mine **e**? 341
2Ch 6:24 Israel be put to the worse before the **e**, 341
25: 8 God shall make thee fall before the **e**. 341
26:13 power, to help the king against the **e**. 341
Ezr 8:22 the hand of the **e** in the way: 341
8:31 he delivered us from the hand of the **e**, 341
Est 3:10 of Hammedatha the Agagite, the Jews' **e**. 6887
7: 4 although the **e** could not countervail 6862
7: 6 adversary and **e** *is* this wicked Haman. 341
8: 1 Haman the Jews' **e** unto Esther the queen. 6887
9:10 the **e** of the Jews, slew they; 6887
9:24 the Agagite, the **e** of all the Jews, 6887
Job 13:24 thou my face, and holdest me for thine **e**? 341
16: 9 mine **e** sharpeneth his eyes upon me. 6862
27: 7 Let mine **e** be as the wicked, and he that 341
33:10 against me, he counteth me for his **e**, 341
Ps 7: 4 him that without cause is mine **e**:) 6887
7: 5 Let the **e** persecute my soul, and take *it*; 341
8: 2 *thou* mightest still the **e** and the avenger. 341
9: 6 O thou **e**, destructions are come to a 341
13: 2 how long shall mine **e** be exalted over me? 341
13: 4 Lest mine **e** say, I have prevailed against 341
18:17 He delivered me from my strong **e**, 341
31: 8 hast not shut me up into the hand of the **e**: 341
41:11 because mine **e** doth not triumph over me. 341
42: 9 because of the oppression of the **e**? 341
43: 2 because of the oppression of the **e**? 341
44:10 Thou makest us to turn back from the **e**: 6862
44:16 by reason of the **e** and avenger. 341
55: 3 Because of the voice of the **e**, because of 341
55:12 For *it was* not an **e** *that* reproached me; 341
61: 3 for me, *and* a strong tower from the **e**. 341
64: 1 preserve my life from fear of the **e**. 341
74: 3 *even* all *that* the **e** hath done wickedly in 341
74:10 shall the **e** blaspheme thy name for ever? 341
74:18 *that* the **e** hath reproached, O LORD, 341
78:42 day when he delivered them from the **e**. 6862
89:22 The **e** shall not exact upon him; nor the 341
106:10 redeemed them from the hand of the **e**. 341
107: 2 hath redeemed from the hand of the **e**; 6862
143: 3 For the **e** hath persecuted my soul; 341
Pr 24:17 Rejoice not when thine **e** falleth, and let 341
25:21 If thine **e** *be* hungry, give him bread 8130
27: 6 but the kisses of an **e** *are* deceitful. 8130
Isa 59:19 When the **e** shall come in like a flood, 6862
63:10 therefore he was turned to be their **e**, 341
Jer 6:25 for the sword of the **e** *and* fear *is* on every 341
15:11 I will cause the **e** to entreat thee *well* 341
18:17 them as with an east wind before the **e**; 341
30:14 wounded thee *with* the wound of an **e**, 341
31:16 shall come again from the land of the **e**. 341
44:30 Zedekiah, his **e**, and that sought his life. 341
La 1: 5 are gone *into* captivity before the **e**. 6862
1: 7 her people fell into the hand of the **e**, 341
1: 9 for he **e** hath magnified *himself*. 341
1:16 are desolate, because the **e** prevailed. 341
2: 3 back his right hand from before the **e**, 341
2: 4 He hath bent his bow like an **e**: *he* stood 341
2: 5 The Lord was as an **e**: he hath swallowed 341
2: 7 he hath given up into the hand of the **e** 341
2:17 he hath caused *thine* **e** to rejoice over thee, 341
2:22 and brought up hath mine **e** consumed. 341
4:12 the **e** should have entered into the gates of 341
Eze 36: 2 Because the **e** hath said against you, Aha, 341
Hos 8: 3 *thing that is* good: the **e** shall pursue him. 341
Mic 2: 8 Even of late my people is risen up as an **e**: 341
7: 8 Rejoice not against me, O mine **e**: when I 341
7:10 she *that is* mine **e** shall see *it*, and 341
Na 3:11 also shalt seek strength because of the **e**. 341
Zep 3:15 thy judgments, he hath cast out thine **e**: 341
Mt 5:43 love thy neighbour, and hate thine **e**. 2190
13:25 his **e** came and sowed tares among 2190
13:28 He said unto them, An **e** hath done 444+2190
13:39 The **e** that sowed them is the devil; 2190
Lk 10:19 scorpions, and over all the power of the **e**: 2190
Ac 13:10 of the devil, *thou* **e** of all righteousness, 2190
Ro 12:20 Therefore if thine **e** hunger, feed him; 2190
1Co 15:26 The last **e** *that* shall be destroyed *is* death. 2190
Gal 4:16 Am I therefore become your **e**, because 2190
2Th 3:15 Yet count *him* not as an **e**, 2190
Jas 4: 4 will be a friend of the world is the **e** of 2190

ENEMY'S (3) [ENEMY]

Ex 23: 4 If thou meet thine **e** ox or his ass going 341
Job 2: Or, Deliver me from the **e** hand? 6862
Ps 78:61 captivity, and his glory into the **e** hand; 6862

ENGAGED (1)

Jer 30:21 who *is* this that **e** his heart to approach 6148

EN-GANNIM (3)

Jos 15:34 And Zanoah, and, **E**, Tappuah, and Enam, 5873
19:21 and **E**, and En-haddah, and Beth-pazzez; 5873
21:29 with her suburbs, **E** with her suburbs; 5873

EN-GEDI (6)

Jos 15:62 Nibshan, and the city of salt, and **E**; 5872
1Sa 23:29 thence, and dwelt in strong holds at **E**. 5872
24: 1 Behold, David *is* in the wilderness of **E**. 5872
2Ch 20: 2 they *be* in Hazazon-tamar, which *is* **E**. 5872
SS 1:14 cluster of camphire in the vineyards of **E**. 5872
Eze 47:10 that the fishers shall stand upon it from **E** 5872

ENGINES (2)

2Ch 26:15 he made in Jerusalem **e**, invented by 2810
Eze 26: 9 he shall set **e** of war against thy walls, 4239

ENGRAFTED (1)

Jas 1:21 and receive with meekness the **e** word, 1721

ENGRAVE (2) [ENGRAVEN, ENGRAVER, ENGRAVINGS]

Ex 28:11 thou **e** the two stones with the names 6605
Zec 3: 9 behold, I *will* **e** the graving thereof, 6605

ENGRAVED See GRAVED; GRAVEN

ENGRAVEN (1) [ENGRAVE]

2Co 3: 7 written *and* **e** in stones, was glorious, 1795

ENGRAVER (3) [ENGRAVE]

Ex 28:11 *With* the work of an **e** in stone, *like* 2796
35:35 of the **e**, and of the cunning workman, 2796
38:23 an **e**, and a cunning workman, 2796

ENGRAVINGS (5) [ENGRAVE]

Ex 28:11 engraver in stone, *like* the **e** of a signet, 6603
28:21 to their names, *like* the **e** of a signet; 6603
28:36 grave upon it, *like* the **e** of a signet, 6603
39:14 *like* the **e** of a signet, every one with his 6603
39:30 upon it a writing, *like to* the **e** of a signet, 6603

EN-HADDAH (1)

Jos 19:21 and En-gannim, and **E**, and Beth-pazzez; 5876

EN-HAKKORE (1)

Jdg 15:19 wherefore he called the name thereof **E**, 5875

ENHANCE See ABOUNDED; ABOUNDETH

EN-HAZOR (1)

Jos 19:37 And Kedesh, and Edrei, and **E**, 5877

ENJOIN (1) [ENJOINED]

Phm 1: 8 I might be much bold in Christ to **e** 2004

ENJOINED (3) [ENJOIN]

Est 9:31 and Esther the queen had **e** them, 5921+6965
Job 36:23 Who hath **e** him his way? or who can say, 6485
Heb 9:20 the testament which God hath **e** unto you. 1781

ENJOY (14) [ENJOYED]

Lev 26:34 shall the land **e** her sabbaths, as long as it 7521
26:34 shall the land rest, and **e** her sabbaths, 7521
26:43 be left of them, and shall **e** her sabbaths, 7521
Nu 36: 8 the children of Israel may **e** every man 3423
Dt 28:41 but thou shalt not **e** them; 1961+3807.1
Jos 1:15 unto the land of your possession, and **e** it, 3423
Ecc 2: 1 thee with mirth, therefore **e** pleasure: 7200
2:24 *that* he should **make** his soul **e** good in 7200
3:13 drink, and the good of all his labour, 7200
5:18 **e** the good of all his labour that he taketh 7200
Isa 65:22 mine elect shall **long e** the work of their 1086
Ac 24: 2 Seeing that by thee we **e** great quietness, 5177
1Ti 6:17 who giveth us richly all *things* to **e**; 619
Heb 11:25 than to **e** the pleasures of sin for a season; 2192

ENJOYED (1) [ENJOY]

2Ch 36:21 until the land had **e** her sabbaths: 7521

ENLARGE (10) [ENLARGED, ENLARGEMENT, ENLARGETH, ENLARGING]

Ge 9:27 God shall **e** Japheth, and he shall dwell in 6601
Ex 34:24 nations before thee, and **e** thy borders: 7337
Dt 12:20 When the LORD thy God shall **e** thy 7337
19: 8 if the LORD thy God thy coast, as he 7337
1Ch 4:10 **e** my coast, and that thine hand might be 7235
Ps 119:32 when thou shalt **e** my heart. 7337
Isa 54: 2 **E** the place of thy tent, and let them 7337
Am 1:13 at Gilead, that *they* might **e** their border: 7337
Mic 1:16 thy baldness as the eagle; 7337
Mt 23: 5 and **e** the borders of their garments, 3170

ENLARGED (11) [ENLARGE]

1Sa 2: 1 my mouth is over mine enemies; 7337
2Sa 22:37 Thou hast **e** my steps under me; so that 7337
Ps 4: 1 thou hast **e** me *when I was* in distress; 7337
18:36 Thou hast **e** my steps under me, that my 7337
25:17 The troubles of my heart are **e**: O bring 7337
Isa 5:14 Therefore hell hath **e** herself, 7337
57: 8 thou hast **e** thy bed, and made thee *a* 7337
60: 5 and thine heart shall fear, and be **e**; 7337
2Co 6:11 mouth is open unto you, our heart is **e**. 4115
6:13 speak as unto *my* children,) be ye also **e**. 4115
10:15 that *we* shall be **e** by you according to our 3170

ENLARGEMENT (1) [ENLARGE]
Est 4:14 *then* shall there **e** and deliverance arise to 7305

ENLARGETH (3) [ENLARGE]
Dt 33:20 of Gad he said, Blessed *be* he that **e** Gad: 7337
Job 12:23 he **e** the nations, and straiteneth them 7849
Hab 2: 5 who **e** his desire as hell, and *is* as death, 7337

ENLARGING (1) [ENLARGE]
Eze 41: 7 *there was* an **e**, and a winding about still 7337

ENLIGHTEN (1) [LIGHT]
Ps 18:28 the LORD my God will **e** my darkness. 5050

ENLIGHTENED (6) [LIGHT]
1Sa 14:27 hand to his mouth; and his eyes were **e**. 215
14:29 mine eyes have been **e**, because I tasted 215
Job 33:30 the pit, to be **e** with the light of the living. 215
Ps 97: 4 his lightnings the world: the earth saw, 215
Eph 1:18 The eyes of your understanding being **e**; 5461
Heb 6: 4 impossible for those who were once **e**, 5461

ENLIGHTENING (1) [LIGHT]
Ps 19: 8 of the LORD *is* pure, **e** the eyes, 215

EN-MISHPAT (1)
Ge 14: 7 came to **E**, which *is* Kadesh, and smote all 5880

ENMITY (8)
Ge 3:15 I will put **e** between thee and the woman, 342
Nu 35:21 in **e** smite him with his hand, that he die: 342
35:22 if he thrust him suddenly without **e**, 342
Lk 23:12 for before they were at **e** between 2189
Ro 8: 7 Because the carnal mind *is* **e** against God: 2189
Eph 2:15 Having abolished in his flesh the **e**, 2189
2:16 by the cross, having slain the **e** thereby: 2189
Jas 4: 4 the friendship of the world is **e** with God? 2189

ENOCH (12) [HENOCH]
Ge 4:17 his wife; and she conceived, and bare **E**: 2585
4:17 of the city, after the name of his son, **E**. 2585
4:18 unto **E** was born Irad: and Irad begat 2585
5:18 and two years, and he begat **E**: 2585
5:19 Jared lived after he begat **E** eight hundred 2585
5:21 **E** lived sixty and five years, 2585
5:22 walked with God after he begat 2585
5:23 all the days of **E** were three hundred sixty 2585
5:24 **E** walked with God: and he *was* not; 2585
Lk 3:37 was *the son* of **E**, which was *the son* 1802
Heb 11: 5 By faith **E** was translated that *he* should 1802
Jude 1:14 And **E** also, the seventh from Adam, 1802

ENOS (7) [ENOSH]
Ge 4:26 called his name **E**; then began *men* to call 583
5: 6 an hundred and five years, and begat **E**: 583
5: 7 Seth lived after he begat **E** eight hundred 583
5: 9 And **E** lived ninety years, and begat Cainan: 583
5:10 lived after he begat Cainan eight hundred 583
5:11 all the days of **E** were nine hundred and 583
Lk 3:38 was *the son* of **E**, which was *the son* 1800

ENOSH (1) [ENOS]
1Ch 1: 1 Adam, Sheth, **E**, 583

ENOUGH (32)
Ge 24:25 We have both straw and provender **e**, 7227
33: 9 Esau said, I have **e**, my brother; keep that 7227
33:11 graciously with me, and because I have **e**. 3605
34:21 behold, *it is* **large** **e** for them; 3027+7342
45:28 Israel said, *It is* **e**; Joseph my son *is* yet 7227
Ex 2:19 also **drew water** for us, 1802+1802
9:28 Intreat the LORD (for *it is* **e**) that there be 7227
36: 5 The people bring much more than **e** for 1767
Dt 1: 6 Ye have dwelt **long e** in this mount: 7227
2: 3 Ye have compassed this mountain **long e**: 7227
Jos 17:16 of Joseph said, The hill is not **e** for us: 4672
2Sa 24:16 angel that destroyed the people, *It is* **e**: 7227
1Ki 19: 4 said, *It is* **e**; now, O LORD, take away my 7227
1Ch 21:15 destroyed, *It is* **e**, stay now thine hand. 7227
2Ch 31:10 have **had e** to eat, and have left plenty. 7646
Pr 27:27 *thou shalt have* goats' milk **e** for thy food, 7646
28:19 after vain *persons* shall **have** poverty **e**. 7646
30:15 yea, four *things* say not, *It is* **e**: 1952
30:16 and the fire *that* saith not, *It is* **e**. 1952
Isa 56:11 are greedy dogs *which* can never have **e**, 7654
Jer 49: 9 by night, they will destroy till they have **e**. 1767
Hos 4:10 For they shall eat, and not **have e**: 7646
Ob 1: 5 they have not stolen till they had **e**? 1767
Na 2:12 lion did tear in pieces **e** for his whelps, 1767
Hag 1: 6 *ye* eat, but ye have not **e**; *ye* drink, 7654
Mal 3:10 *there shall* not *be* room **e** to receive it. 1767
Mt 10:25 *It is* **e** for the disciple that he be as his 713
25: 9 *Not so*; lest there be not **e** for us and you: 714
Mk 14:41 *it is* **e**, the hour is come; behold, the Son 568
Lk 15:17 my father's **have** bread **e** and to spare, 4052
22:38 swords. And he said unto them, *It is* **e**. 2425
Ac 27:38 And when they had **eaten e**, 2880+5160

ENRICH (2) [RICH]
1Sa 17:25 the king will **e** him *with* great riches, 6238
Eze 27:33 thou didst **e** the kings of the earth with 6238

ENRICHED (2) [RICH]
1Co 1: 5 That in every *thing* ye are **e** by him, in all 4148
2Co 9:11 Being **e** in every *thing* to all bountifulness, 4148

ENRICHEST (1) [RICH]
Ps 65: 9 thou greatly **e** it *with* the river of God, 6238

EN-RIMMON (1)
Ne 11:29 And at **E**, and at Zareah, and at Jarmuth, 5884

EN-ROGEL (4)
Jos 15: 7 and the goings out thereof were at **E**: 5883
18:16 Jebusi on the south, and descended *to* **E**, 5883
2Sa 17:17 Now Jonathan and Ahimaaz stayed by **E**; 5883
1Ki 1: 9 which *is* by **E**, and called all his brethren 5883

ENSAMPLE (3) [ENSAMPLES]
Php 3:17 which walk so as ye have us for an **e**. 5179
2Th 3: 9 to make ourselves an **e** unto you to follow 5179
2Pe 2: 6 making *them* an **e** unto those that after 5262

ENSAMPLES (3) [ENSAMPLE]
1Co 10:11 all these *things* happened unto them for **e**: 5179
1Th 1: 7 So that ye were **e** to all that believe in 5179
1Pe 5: 3 *God's* heritage, but being **e** to the flock. 5179

EN-SHEMESH (2)
Jos 15: 7 the border passed towards the waters of **E**, 5885
18:17 went forth to **E**, and went forth toward 5885

ENSIGN (8) [ENSIGNS]
Nu 2: 2 with the **e** of their father's house: 226
Isa 5:26 he will lift up an **e** to the nations from far, 5251
11:10 which shall stand for an **e** of the people; 5251
11:12 And he shall set up an **e** for the nations, 5251
18: 3 *he* lifteth up an **e** on the mountains; 5251
30:17 top of a mountain, and as an **e** on a hill. 5251
31: 9 his princes shall be afraid of the **e**, saith 5251
Zec 9:16 a crown, **lifted up as an e** upon his land. 5264

ENSIGNS (1) [ENSIGN]
Ps 74: 4 they set up their **e** *for* signs. 226

ENSNARED (1) [SNARE]
Job 34:30 hypocrite reign not, lest the people be **e**. 4170

ENSUE (1)
1Pe 3:11 and do good; let him seek peace, and **e** it. 1377

ENSURE See SURETY

ENTANGLE (1) [ENTANGLED, ENTANGLETH]
Mt 22:15 took counsel how they might **e** him in *his* 3802

ENTANGLED (3) [ENTANGLE]
Ex 14: 3 They *are* **e** in the land, the wilderness 943
Gal 5: 1 be not **e** again with the yoke of bondage. 1758
2Pe 2:20 they are again **e** therein, and overcome, 1707

ENTANGLETH (1) [ENTANGLE]
2Ti 2: 4 No *man* that warreth **e** himself **with** 1707

EN-TAPPUAH (1)
Jos 17: 7 the right hand unto the inhabitants of **E**. 5887

ENTER (149) [ENTERED, ENTERETH, ENTERING, ENTRANCE, ENTRANCES]
Ge 12:11 when he was come near to **e** into Egypt, 935
Ex 40:35 Moses was not able to **e** into the tent of 935
Nu 4: 3 until fifty years old, all that **e** into the host, 935
4:23 all that **e** in to perform the service, to do 935
5:24 the water that causeth the curse shall **e** 935
5:27 the water that causeth the curse shall **e** 935
20:24 he shall not **e** into the land which I have 935
Dt 23: 1 shall not **e** into the congregation of 935
23: 2 A bastard shall not **e** into the congregation 935
23: 2 even *to* his tenth generation shall he not **e** 935
23: 3 Moabite shall not **e** into the congregation 935
23: 3 **e** into the congregation of the LORD for 935
23: 8 children that are begotten of them shall **e** 935
29:12 That thou shouldest **e** into covenant with 5674
Jos 10:19 suffer them not to **e** into their cities: 935
Jdg 18: 9 slothful to go, *and* to **e** to possess the land. 935
2Sa 22: 7 his temple, and my cry *did* **e** into his ears. NIH
1Ki 14: 12 when thy feet **e** into the city, the child 935
22:30 will disguise myself, and **e** into the battle; 935
2Ki 7: 4 We will **e** *into* the city, then the famine *is* 935
11: 5 A third *part* of you that **e** in on the sabbath 935
19:23 I will **e** *into* the lodgings of his borders, 935
2Ch 7: 2 the priests could not **e** into the house of 935
23:19 *was* unclean in any thing should **e** **in**. 935
30: 8 into his sanctuary, which he hath 935
Ne 2: 8 city, and for the house that I shall **e** into. 935
Est 4: 2 none might **e** into the king's gate clothed 935
Job 22: 4 will he **e** with thee into judgment? 935
34:23 that *he* should **e** into judgment with God. 1980
Ps 37:15 Their sword shall **e** into their own heart, 935
45:15 they shall **e** into the king's palace. 935
95:11 wrath that they should not **e** into my rest. 935
100: 4 **E** *into* his gates with thanksgiving, 935
118:20 the LORD, into which the righteous shall **e**. 935
143: 2 nor **e** into judgment with thy servant: for in 935
Pr 4:14 **E** not into the path of the wicked, 935
18: 6 A fool's lips **e** into contention, 935
23:10 and **e** not into the fields of the fatherless: 935
Isa 2:10 **E** into the rock, and hide thee in the dust, 935
3:14 The LORD will **e** into judgment with 935
26: 2 nation which keepeth the truth may **e** **in**. 935
26:20 **e** thou into thy chambers, and shut thy 935
37:24 and I will **e** into the height of his border, 935

Isa 57: 2 He shall **e** *into* peace: they shall rest in 935
59:14 is fallen in the street, and equity cannot **e**. 935
Jer 7: 2 that **e** in at these gates to worship 935
8:14 let us **e** into the defenced cities, and let us 935
14:18 if I **e** *into* the city, then behold them that 935
16: 5 **E** not *into* the house of mourning, 935
17:20 of Jerusalem, that **e** in by these gates: 935
17:25 shall there **e** into the gates of this city kings 935
21:13 or who shall **e** into our habitations? 935
22: 2 and thy people that **e** in by these gates: 935
22: 4 shall there **e** in by the gates of this house 935
41:17 *is* by Beth-lehem, to go to **e** into Egypt, 935
42:15 If ye wholly set your faces to **e** *into* Egypt, 935
42:18 upon you, when ye shall **e** *into* Egypt: 935
La 1:10 they should not **e** into thy congregation. 935
3:13 hath **caused** the arrows of his quiver to **e** 935
Eze 7:22 secret *place*: for the robbers shall **e** into it, 935
13: 9 neither shall they **e** into the land of Israel: 935
20:38 and they shall not **e** into the land of Israel: 935
26:10 chariots, when he shall **e** into thy gates, 935
26:10 as men **into** a city wherein is made a 3996
37: 5 I *will* **cause** breath **to e** into you, and ye 935
42:14 When the priests **e** *therein*, then shall they 935
44: 2 not be opened, and no man shall **e** in by it; 935
44: 3 he shall **e** by the way of the porch of *that* 935
44: 9 in flesh, shall **e** into my sanctuary, 935
44:16 They shall **e** into my sanctuary, 935
44:17 when they **e** in at the gates of the inner 935
44:21 wine, when they **e** into the inner court. 935
46: 2 the prince shall **e** by the way of the porch 935
46: 8 when the prince shall **e**, he shall go in *by* 935
Da 11: 7 shall **e** into the fortress of the king of 935
11:17 He shall also set his face to **e** with 935
11:24 He shall **e** peaceably even upon the fattest 935
11:40 he shall **e** into the countries, 935
11:41 He shall **e** also into the glorious land, 935
Hos 11: 9 of thee: and I will not **e** into the city. 935
Joel 2: 9 they shall **e** in at the windows like a thief. 935
Am 5: 5 to Gilgal, and pass not *to* Beer-sheba: 935
Jnh 3: 4 Jonah began to **e** into the city a day's 935
Zec 5: 4 and it shall **e** into the house of the thief, 935
Mt 5:20 ye shall in no case **e** into the kingdom of 1525
6: 6 thou into thy closet, and when thou hast shut 1525
7:13 **E** ye **in** at the strait gate: for wide *is* 1525
7:21 Lord, shall **e** into the kingdom of heaven; 1525
10: 5 into *any* city of the Samaritans ye not: 1525
10:11 into whatsoever city or town ye shall **e**, 1525
12:29 Or else how can one **e** into a strong *man's* 1525
12:45 himself, and they **e** in and dwell there: 1525
18: 3 ye shall not **e** into the kingdom of heaven. 1525
18: 8 it is better for thee to **e** into life halt or 1525
18: 9 it is better for thee to **e** into life with one 1525
19:17 but if thou wilt **e** into life, keep 1525
19:23 That a rich *man* shall hardly **e** into 1525
19:24 for a rich *man* to **e** into the kingdom of 1525
25:21 *things*: **e** thou into the joy of thy lord. 1525
25:23 *things*: **e** thou into the joy of thy lord. 1525
26:41 and pray, that ye **e** not into temptation: 1525
Mk 1:45 *Jesus* could no more openly **e** into the city 1525
3:27 No *man* can **e** into a strong *man's* house, 1525
5:12 into the swine, that we may **e** into them. 1525
6:10 In what place soever ye **e** into a house, 1525
9:25 come out of him, and **e** no more into him. 1525
9:43 it is better for thee to **e** into life maimed, 1525
9:45 it is better for thee to **e** halt into life, 1525
9:47 it is better for thee to **e** into the kingdom 1525
10:15 God as a little child, he shall not **e** therein. 1525
10:23 How hardly shall they that have riches **e** 1525
10:24 in riches to **e** into the kingdom of God! 1525
10:25 for a rich *man* to **e** into the kingdom of 1525
13:15 neither **e** *therein*, to take any *thing* out of 1525
14:38 and pray, lest ye **e** into temptation. 1525
Lk 7: 6 for I am not worthy that thou shouldest **e** 1525
8:16 that they which **e** in may see the light. 1531
8:32 that he would suffer them to **e** into them. 1525
9: 4 And whatsoever house ye **e** into, 1525
10: 5 And into whatsoever house ye **e**, first say, 1525
10: 8 And into whatsoever city ye **e**, 1525
10:10 But into whatsoever city ye **e**, 1525
11:26 and they **e** in, and dwell there: 1525
13:24 Strive to **e** in at the strait gate: for many, 1525
13:24 will seek to **e** in, and shall not be able. 1525
18:17 as a little child shall in no wise **e** therein. 1525
18:24 How hardly shall they that have riches **e** 1525
18:25 for a rich *man* to **e** into the kingdom of 1525
21:21 let not them that are in the countries **e** 1525
22:40 Pray that ye **e** not into temptation. 1525
22:46 rise and pray, lest ye **e** into temptation. 1525
24:26 these *things*, and to **e** into his glory? 1525
Jn 3: 4 he **e** the second time into his mother's 1525
3: 5 he cannot **e** into the kingdom of God. 1525
10: 9 by me if any *man* **e** in, he shall be saved, 1525
Ac 14:22 that we must through much tribulation **e** 1525
20:29 shall grievous wolves **e** in among you, 1525
Heb 3:11 my wrath, They shall not **e** into my rest. 1525
3:18 he that *they* should not **e** into his rest, 1525
3:19 we see that they could not **e** in because 1525
4: 3 we which have believed do **e** into rest, 1525
4: 3 in my wrath, if they shall **e** into my rest: 1525
4: 5 *place* again, If they shall **e** into my rest. 1525
4: 6 It remaineth that some **must e** therein, 1525
4:11 Let us labour therefore to **e** into that rest, 1525
10:19 boldness to **e** into the holiest by the blood 1529
Rev 15: 8 and no *man* was able to **e** into the temple, 1525
21:27 And there shall in no wise **e** into it any 1525

E

Rev 22:14 may e in through the gates into the city. 1525

ENTERED (107) [ENTER]

Ge	7:13 In the selfsame day e Noah, and Shem,	935
	19: 3 turned in unto him, and e into his house;	935
	19:23 sun was risen upon the earth when Lot e	935
	31:33 of Leah's tent, and e into Rachel's tent.	935
	43:30 he e into his chamber, and wept there.	935
Ex	33: 9 to pass, as Moses e into the tabernacle,	935
Jos	2: 3 to thee, which are e into thine house:	935
	8:19 they e into the city, and took it,	935
	10:20 the rest which remained them e into	935
Jdg	6: 5 and they e into the land to destroy it.	935
	9:46 e into a hold of the house of the god	935
2Sa	10:14 also before Abishai, and e into the city.	935
2Ki	7: 8 e into another tent, and carried thence	935
	9:31 as Jehu e in at the gate, she said,	935
1Ch	19:15 Abishai his brother, and e into the city.	935
2Ch	12:11 when the king e into the house of	935
	15:12 they e into a covenant to seek the LORD	935
	27: 2 howbeit he e not into the temple of	935
	32: 1 e into Judah, and encamped against	935
Ne	2:15 e by the gate of the valley, and so returned.	935
	10:29 and e into a curse, and into an oath,	935
Job	38:16 Hast thou e into the springs of the sea?	935
	38:22 Hast thou e into the treasures of the snow?	935
Jer	2: 7 when ye e, ye defiled my land,	935
	9:21 and is e into our palaces, to cut off	935
	34:10 the people, which had e into the covenant,	935
	37:16 When Jeremiah was e into the dungeon,	935
La	1:10 she hath seen that the heathen e into her	935
	4:12 the enemy should have e into the gates of	935
Eze	2: 2 spirit e into me when he spake unto me,	935
	3:24 spirit e into me, and set me upon my feet,	935
	16: 8 thee, and e into a covenant with thee,	935
	36:20 when they e unto the heathen, whither	935
	41: 6 e into the wall which was of the house	935
	44: 2 hath e in by it, therefore it shall be shut.	935
Ob	1:11 foreigners e into his gates, and cast lots	935
	1:13 Thou shouldest not have e into the gate of	935
Hab	3:16 rottenness e into my bones, and I trembled	935
Mt	8: 5 And when Jesus was e into Capernaum,	1525
	8:23 And when he was e into a ship,	1684
	9: 1 And he e into a ship, and passed over,	1684
	12: 4 How he e into the house of God,	1525
	24:38 until the day that Noe e into the ark,	1525
Mk	1:21 straightway on the sabbath day he e into	1525
	1:29 they e into the house of Simon and	2064
	2: 1 again he e into Capernaum after some	1525
	3: 1 And he e again into the synagogue;	1525
	4: 1 that he e into a ship, and sat in the sea;	1684
	5:13 spirits went out, and e into the swine:	1525
	6:56 And whithersoever he e, into villages,	1531
	7:17 And when he was e into the house from	1525
	7:24 and e into a house, and would have no	1525
	8:10 And straightway he e into a ship with his	1684
	11: 2 as soon as ye be e into it, ye shall find a	1531
	11:11 And Jesus e into Jerusalem, and into	1525
Lk	1:40 And e into the house of Zacharias,	1525
	4:38 the synagogue, and e into Simon's house.	1525
	5: 3 And e into one of the ships, which was	1684
	6: 6 that he e into the synagogue and taught:	1525
	7: 1 of the people, he e into Capernaum.	1525
	7:44 I e into thine house, thou gavest me no	1525
	8:30 because many devils were e into him.	1525
	8:33 out of the man, and e into the swine:	1525
	9:34 and they feared as they e into the cloud.	1525
	9:52 and e into a village of the Samaritans,	1525
	10:38 they went, that he e into a certain village:	1525
	11:52 ye e not in yourselves, and them that	1525
	17:12 as he e into a certain village, there met	1525
	17:27 until the day that Noe e into the ark,	1525
	19: 1 And Jesus e and passed through Jericho.	1525
	22: 3 e Satan into Judas surnamed Iscariot,	1525
	22:10 Behold, when ye are e into the city,	1525
	24: 3 And they e in, and found not the body of	1525
	24: 3 and ye are e into their labours.	1525
Jn	4:38 And ye are e into their labours.	1525
	6:17 And e into a ship, and went over the sea	1684
	6:22 that one whereinto his disciples were e,	1684
	13:27 And after the sop Satan e into him.	1525
	18: 1 into the which he e, and his disciples.	1525
	18:33 Pilate e into the judgment hall again,	1525
	21: 3 forth, and e into a ship immediately;	305
Ac	3: 2 ask alms of them that e into the temple;	1531
	3: 8 walked, and e with them into the temple,	1525
	5:21 And when they heard that, they e into	1525
	9:17 went his way, and e into the house;	1525
	10:24 the morrow after they e into Cesarea.	1525
	11: 8 hath at any time e into my mouth.	1525
	11:12 and we e into the man's house:	1525
	16:40 the prison, and e into the house of Lydia:	1525
	18: 7 and e into a certain man's house,	2064
	18:19 but he himself e into the synagogue,	1525
	19:30 And when Paul would have e in unto	1525
	21: 8 e into the house of Philip the evangelist,	1525
	21:26 next day purifying himself with them e	1524
	23:16 went and e into the castle, and told Paul.	1525
	25:23 and were e into the place of hearing,	1525
	28: 8 to whom Paul e in, and prayed, and laid	1525
Ro	5:12 as by one man sin e into the world,	1525
	5:20 Moreover the law e, that the offence	3922
1Co	2: 9 neither have e into the heart of man,	305
Heb	4: 6 to whom it was first preached e not in	1525
	4:10 For he that is e into his rest, he also hath	1525
	6:20 Whither the forerunner is for us e,	1525

Heb	9:12 by his own blood he e in once into the	1525
	9:24 For Christ is not e into the holy places	1525
Jas	5: 4 cries of them which have reaped are e	1525
2Jn	1: 7 For many deceivers are e into the world,	1525
Rev	11:11 a half the spirit of life from God e into	1525

ENTERETH (20) [ENTER]

Nu	4:30 every one that e into the service, to do	935
	4:35 years old, every one that e into the service,	935
	4:39 years old, every one that e into the service,	935
	4:43 years old, every one that e into the service,	935
2Ch	31:16 unto every one that e into the house of	935
Pr	2:10 When wisdom e into thine heart,	935
	17:10 A reproof e more into a wise man than an	5181
Eze	21:14 which e into their privy chambers.	2314
	42:12 wall toward the east, as one e into.	935
	46: 9 he that e in by the way of the north gate to	935
	46: 9 he that e by the way of the south gate shall	935
Mt	15:17 whatsoever e in at the mouth goeth into	1531
Mk	5:40 and e in where the damsel was lying.	1531
	7:18 whatsoever thing from without e at	1531
	7:19 Because it e not into his heart, but into	1531
Lk	22:10 follow him into the house where he e in.	1525
Jn	10: 1 He that e not by the door into	1525
	10: 2 But he that e in by the door is the shepherd	1525
Heb	6:19 and which e into that within the vail;	1525
	9:25 as the high priest e into the holy place	1525

ENTERING (46) [ENTER]

Ex	35:15 the hanging for the door at the e in of	6607
Jos	8:29 cast it at the e of the gate of the city,	6607
	13: 5 mount Hermon unto the e into Hamath.	935
	20: 4 shall stand at the e of the gate of the city,	6607
Jdg	3: 3 from mount Baal-hermon unto the e in of	935
	9:35 and stood in the e of the gate of the city:	6607
	9:40 wounded, even unto the e of the gate.	6607
	9:44 and stood in the e of the gate of the city:	6607
	18:16 the priest stood in the e of the gate with	6607
1Sa	23: 7 by town that hath gates and bars.	935
2Sa	10: 8 the battle in array at the e in of the gate:	6607
	11:23 we were upon them even unto the e of	6607
1Ki	6:31 for the e of the oracle he made doors of	6607
	8:65 from the e in of Hamath unto the river of	935
	19:13 out, and stood in the e in of the cave.	6607
2Ki	7: 3 there were four leprous men at the e in	6607
	10: 8 Lay ye them in two heaps at the e in of	6607
	14:25 restored the coast of Israel from the e of	935
	23: 8 e in of the gate of Joshua the governor of	6607
	23:11 at the e in of the house of the LORD,	935
1Ch	5: 9 eastward he inhabited unto the e in of	935
	13: 5 from Shihor of Egypt even unto the e of	935
2Ch	7: 8 from the e in of Hamath unto the river of	935
	18: 9 they sat in a void place at the e in of	6607
	23: 4 A third part of you e on the sabbath,	935
	23:13 the king stood at his pillar at the e in,	3996
	23:15 when she was come to the e of the horse	3996
	26: 8 name spread abroad even to the e in of	935
	33:14 even to the e in at the fish gate,	935
Isa	23: 1 waste, so that there is no house, no e in:	935
Jer	1:15 shall set every one his throne at the e	6607
	17:27 even e in at the gates of Jerusalem on	935
Eze	44: 5 mark well the e of the house,	3996
Am	6:14 they shall afflict you from the e in of	935
Mt	23:13 neither suffer ye them that are e to go in.	1525
Mk	4:19 and the lusts of other things e in, choke	1531
	7:15 a man, that e into him can defile him:	1531
	8:13 e into the ship again departed to the other	1684
	16: 5 And e into the sepulchre, they saw a	1525
Lk	11:52 and them that were e in ye hindered.	1525
	19:30 which at your e ye shall find a colt tied,	1531
Ac	8: 3 havock of the church, e into every house,	1531
	27: 2 And e into a ship of Adramyttium,	1910
1Th	1: 9 what manner of e in we had unto you,	1529
Heb	4: 1 a promise being left us of e into his rest,	1525

ENTERPRISE (1)

Job	5:12 that their hands cannot perform their e.	8454

ENTERTAIN (1) [ENTERTAINED]

Heb	13: 2 Be not forgetful to e strangers: for	5381

ENTERTAINED (1) [ENTERTAIN]

Heb	13: 2 for thereby some have e angels unawares.	3579

ENTICE (8) [ENTICED, ENTICETH, ENTICING]

Ex	22:16 if a man e a maid that is not betrothed,	6601
Dt	13: 6 e thee secretly, saying, Let us go and	5496
Jdg	14:15 said unto Samson's wife, E thy husband,	6601
	16: 5 E him, and see wherein his great strength	6601
2Ch	18:19 Who shall e Ahab king of Israel, that he	6601
	18:20 before the LORD, and said, I will e him.	6601
	18:21 Thou shalt e him, and thou shalt also	6601
Pr	1:10 son, if sinners e thee, consent thou not.	6601

ENTICED (3) [ENTICE]

Job	31:27 heart hath been secretly e, or my mouth	6601
Jer	20:10 saying, Peradventure he will be e,	6601
Jas	1:14 he is drawn away of his own lust, and e.	1185

ENTICETH (1) [ENTICE]

Pr	16:29 A violent man e his neighbour,	6601

ENTICING (2) [ENTICE]

1Co	2: 4 my preaching was not with e words of	3981
Col	2: 4 man should beguile you with e words.	4086

ENTIRE (1)

Jas	1: 4 that ye may be perfect and e,	3648

ENTRANCE (11) [ENTER]

Nu	34: 8 your border unto the e of Hamath.	935
Jdg	1:24 the e into the city, and we will shew thee	3996
	1:25 when he shewed them the e into the city,	3996
1Ki	18:46 and ran before Ahab to the e of Jezreel.	935
	12:10 into a void place in the e of the gate of the	6607
1Ch	4:39 they went to the e of Gedor, even unto	3996
2Ch	12:10 that kept the e of the king's house.	6607
Ps	119:130 The e of thy words giveth light; it giveth	6608
Eze	40:15 from the face of the gate of the e unto	2978
1Th	2: 1 brethren, know our e in unto you,	1529
2Pe	1:11 an e shall be ministered unto you	1529

ENTRANCES (1) [ENTER]

Mic	5: 6 and the land of Nimrod in the e thereof:	6607

ENTREAT (2) [ENTREATED, ENTREATETH, INTREAT]

Jer	15:11 I will cause the enemy to e thee well	6293
Ac	7: 6 and e them evil four hundred years.	2559

ENTREATED (9) [ENTREAT]

Ge	12:16 he e Abram well for her sake: and he had	3190
Ex	5:22 wherefore hast thou so evil e this people?	7489
Dt	26: 6 the Egyptians evil e us, and afflicted us,	7489
Mt	22: 6 and e them spitefully, and slew them.	5195
Lk	18:32 mocked, and spitefully e, and spitted on:	5195
	20:11 e him shamefully, and sent him away	818
Ac	7:19 evil e our fathers, so that they cast out	2559
	27: 3 And Julius courteously e Paul,	5530
1Th	2: 2 and were shamefully e, as ye know,	5195

ENTREATETH (1) [ENTREAT]

Job	24:21 He evil e the barren that beareth not:	7462

ENTREATY See INTREAT; INTREATED; INTREATIES; INTREATY

ENTRIES (1) [ENTRY]

Eze	40:38 e thereof were by the posts of the gates,	6607

ENTRY (15) [ENTRIES]

2Ki	16:18 in the house, and the king's e without,	3996
1Ch	9:19 host of the LORD, were keepers of the e.	3996
2Ch	4:22 the e of the house, the inner doors	6607
Pr	8: 3 She crieth at the gates, at the e of the city,	6310
Jer	19: 2 which is by the e of the east gate,	6607
	26:10 sat down in the e of the new gate of	6607
	36:10 the higher court at the e of the new gate	6607
	38:14 third e that is in the house of the LORD:	3996
	43: 9 which is at the e of Pharaoh's house in	6607
Eze	8: 5 the altar this image of jealousy in the e.	872
	27: 3 O thou that art situate at the e of the sea,	3997
	40:11 he measured the breadth of the e of	6607
	40:40 as one goeth up to the e of the north gate,	6607
	42: 9 from under these chambers was the e on	3996
	46:19 After, he brought me through the e,	3996

ENVIED (6) [ENVY]

Ge	26:14 of servants: and the Philistims e him.	7065
	30: 1 Jacob no children, Rachel e her sister;	7065
	37:11 brethren e him; but his father observed	7065
Ps	106:16 They e Moses also in the camp,	7065
Ecc	4: 4 that for this a man is e of his neighbour.	7068
Eze	31: 9 that were in the garden of God, e him.	7065

ENVIES (1) [ENVY]

1Pe	2: 1 hypocrisies, and e, and all evil speakings,	5355

ENVIEST (1) [ENVY]

Nu	11:29 Moses said unto him, E thou for my sake?	7065

ENVIETH (1) [ENVY]

1Co	13: 4 suffereth long, and is kind; charity e not;	2206

ENVIOUS (4) [ENVY]

Ps	37: 1 neither be thou e against the workers of	7065
	73: 3 For I was e at the foolish, when I saw	7065
Pr	24: 1 Be not thou e against evil men,	7065
	24:19 of evil men, neither be thou e at	7065

ENVIRON (1)

Jos	7: 9 land shall hear of it, and shall e us round,	5437

ENVY (20) [ENVIED, ENVIES, ENVIEST, ENVIETH, ENVIOUS, ENVYING, ENVYINGS]

Job	5: 2 foolish man, and e slayeth the silly one.	7068
Pr	3:31 E thou not the oppressor, and choose	7065
	14:30 flesh: but e the rottenness of the bones.	7068
	23:17 Let not thine heart e sinners: but be thou	7065
	27: 4 but who is able to stand before e?	7068
Ecc	9: 6 their love, and their hatred, and their e,	7068
Isa	11:13 The e also of Ephraim shall depart,	7065
	11:13 Ephraim shall not e Judah, and Judah	7065
	26:11 and be ashamed for their e at the people;	7068
Eze	35:11 according to thine e which thou hast used	7068
Mt	27:18 For he knew that for e they had delivered	5355
Mk	15:10 the chief priests had delivered him for e.	5355
Ac	7: 9 And the patriarchs, moved with e,	2206
	13:45 they were filled with e, and spake against	2205
	17: 5 Jews which believed not, moved with e,	2206
Ro	1:29 full of e, murder, debate, deceit,	5355
Php	1:15 Some indeed preach Christ even of e and	5355

1Ti	6:	4 whereof cometh **e**, strife, railings,	5355
Tit	3:	3 living in malice and **e**, hateful,	5355
Jas	4:	5 the spirit that dwelleth in us lusteth to **e**?	5355

ENVYING (5) [ENVY]

Ro	13:13	and wantonness, not in strife and **e**.	2205
1Co	3:	3 for whereas *there is* among you **e**,	2205
Gal	5:26	provoking one another, **e** one another.	5354
Jas	3:14	But if ye have bitter **e** and strife in your	2205
	3:16	where **e** and strife *is,* there is confusion	2205

ENVYINGS (2) [ENVY]

2Co	12:20	**e**, wraths, strifes, backbitings,	2205
Gal	5:21	**E**, murders, drunkenness, revellings,	5355

EPAPHRAS (3)

Col	1:	7 As ye also learned of **E** our dear	1889
	4:12	**E**, who is *one* of you, a servant of Christ,	1889
Phm	1:23	There salute thee **E**, my fellowprisoner in	1889

EPAPHRODITUS (3)

Php	2:25	I supposed it necessary to send to you **E**,	1891
	4:18	received of **E** the *things which were*	1891
	4:	8 **S** to the Philippians from Rome by **E**.	1891

EPENETUS (1)

Ro	16:	5 Salute my wellbeloved **E**, who is	1866

EPHAH (39)

Ge	25:	4 **E**, and Epher, and Hanoch, and Abidah,	5891
Ex	16:36	Now an omer *is* the tenth *part* of an **e**.	374
Lev	5:11	*part* of an **e** of fine flour for a sin offering;	374
	6:20	tenth *part* of an **e** of fine flour *for* a meat	374
	19:36	just weights, a just **e**, and a just hin, shall	374
Nu	5:15	the tenth *part* of an **e** of barley meal;	374
	28:	5 a tenth *part* of an **e** *of* flour for a meat	374
Jdg	6:19	kid, and unleavened *cakes of* an **e** of flour:	374
Ru	2:17	gleaned: and it was about an **e** of barley.	374
1Sa	1:24	and one **e** of flour, and a bottle of wine,	374
	17:17	Take now for thy brethren an **e** of this	374
1Ch	1:33	**E**, and Epher, and Henoch, and Abida,	5891
	2:46	**E**, Caleb's concubine, bare Haran,	5891
	2:47	Geshan, and Pelet, and **E**, and Shaaph.	5891
Isa	5:10	and the seed of a homer shall yield an **e**.	374
	60:	6 the dromedaries of Midian and **E**;	5891
Eze	45:10	just balances, and a just **e**, and a just bath.	374
	45:11	The **e** and the bath shall be of one measure,	374
	45:11	homer, and the **e** the tenth *part* of a homer:	374
	45:13	the sixth *part* of an **e** of a homer of wheat,	374
	45:13	shall give the sixth part of an **e** of a homer	374
	45:24	he shall prepare a meat offering *of* an **e** for	374
	45:24	**e** for a ram, and a hin of oil for an ephah.	374
	45:24	ephah for a ram, and a hin of oil for an **e**.	374
	46:	5 the meat offering *shall be* an **e** for a ram,	374
	46:	5 be able to give, and a hin of oil to an **e**.	374
	46:	7 an **e** for a bullock, and an ephah for a ram,	374
	46:	7 an **e** for a ram, and for the lambs	374
	46:	7 shall attain unto, and a hin of oil to an **e**.	374
	46:11	meat offering shall be an **e** to a bullock,	374
	46:11	an **e** to a ram, and to the lambs as he is	374
	46:11	he is able to give, and a hin of oil to an **e**.	374
	46:14	the sixth *part* of an **e**, and the third *part* of	374
Am	8:	5 making the **e** small, and the shekel great,	374
Zec	5:	6 he said, This *is* an **e** that goeth forth.	374
	5:	7 a woman that sitteth in the midst of the **e**.	374
	5:	8 he cast it into the midst of the **e**; and he	374
	5:	9 they lift up the **e** between the earth and	374
	5:10	with me, Whither do these bear the **e**?	374

EPHAI (1)

Jer	40:	8 the sons of **E** the Netophathite,	5778

EPHER (4)

Ge	25:	4 **E**, and Hanoch, and Abidah, and Eldaah.	6081
1Ch	1:33	**E**, and Henoch, and Abida, and Eldaah.	6081
	4:17	Jether, and Mered, and **E**, and Jalon:	6081
	5:24	even **E**, and Ishi, and Eliel, and Azriel,	6081

EPHES-DAMMIM (1)

1Sa	17:	1 between Shochoh and Azekah, in **E**.	658

EPHESIAN (1) [EPHESUS]

Ac	21:29	with him in the city Trophimus an **E**,	2180

EPHESIANS (5) [EPHESUS]

Ac	19:28	cried out, saying, Great *is* Diana of the **E**.	2180
	19:34	hours cried out, Great *is* Diana of the **E**.	2180
	19:35	of the **E** is a worshipper of the great	2180
Eph	6:	**S** Written from Rome unto the **E** by	2180
2Ti	4:	**S** the first bishop of the church of the **E**,	2180

EPHESUS (17) [EPHESIAN, EPHESIANS]

Ac	18:19	And he came to **E**, and left them there:	2181
	18:21	if God will. And he sailed from **E**.	2181
	18:24	*and* mighty in the scriptures, came to **E**.	2181
	19:	1 through the upper coasts came to **E**:	2181
	19:17	the Jews and Greeks also dwelling at **E**;	2181
	19:26	that not alone at **E**, but almost throughout	2181
	19:35	appeased the people, he said, *Ye* men of **E**,	2180
	20:16	For Paul had determined to sail by **E**,	2181
	20:17	And from Miletus he sent to **E**,	2181
1Co	15:32	of men I have fought with beasts at **E**,	2181
	16:	8 But I will tarry at **E** until Pentecost.	2181
Eph	1:	1 to the saints which are at **E**, and to	2181
1Ti	1:	3 As I besought thee to abide *still* at **E**,	2181
2Ti	1:18	many *things* he ministered *unto me* at **E**,	2181

2Ti	4:12	And Tychicus have I sent to **E**.	2181
Rev	1:11	unto **E**, and unto Smyrna,	2181
	2:	1 Unto the angel of the church of **E** write;	2179

EPHLAL (2)

1Ch	2:37	Zabad begat **E**, and Ephlal begat Obed,	654
	2:37	Zabad begat Ephlal, and **E** begat Obed,	654

EPHOD (52)

Ex	25:	7 stones to be set in the **e**, and in	646
	28:	4 an **e**, and a robe, and a broidered coat,	646
	28:	6 they shall make the **e** *of* gold, *of* blue,	646
	28:	8 curious girdle of the **e**, which *is* upon it,	642
	28:12	for stones of memorial unto the children	646
	28:15	after the work of the **e** thou shalt make it;	646
	28:25	put *them* on the shoulderpieces of the **e**	646
	28:26	which *is* in the side of the **e** inward.	646
	28:27	shalt put them on the two sides of the **e**.	646
	28:27	above the curious girdle of the **e**.	646
	28:28	unto the rings of the **e** with a lace of blue,	646
	28:28	*it* may be above the curious girdle of the **e**,	646
	28:28	the breastplate be not loosed from the **e**.	646
	28:31	shalt make the robe of the **e** all of blue.	646
	29:	5 the robe of the **e**, and the ephod,	646
	29:	5 the **e**, and the breastplate, and gird him	646
	29:	5 gird him with the curious girdle of the **e**:	646
	35:	9 stones to be set for the **e**, and for	646
	35:27	to be set, for the **e**, and for the breastplate;	646
	39:	2 he made the **e** *of* gold, blue, and purple,	646
	39:	5 curious girdle of his **e**, that *was* upon it,	642
	39:	7 he put them on the shoulders of the **e**,	646
	39:	8 *of* cunning work, like the work of the **e**;	646
	39:18	put them on the shoulderpieces of the **e**,	646
	39:19	which *was* on the side of the **e** inward.	646
	39:20	put them on the two sides of the **e**	646
	39:20	above the curious girdle of the **e**.	646
	39:21	unto the rings of the **e** with a lace of blue,	646
	39:21	might be above the curious girdle of the **e**,	646
	39:21	breastplate might not be loosed from the **e**;	646
	39:22	he made the robe of the **e** *of* woven work,	646
Lev	8:	7 put the **e** upon him, and he girded him	646
	8:	7 girded him with the curious girdle of the **e**,	646
Nu	34:23	of Manasseh, Hanniel the son of **E**.	641
Jdg	8:27	Gideon made an **e** thereof, and put it in	646
	17:	5 house an **e**, and teraphim,	646
	18:14	ye know that there is in these houses an **e**,	646
	18:17	the **e**, and the teraphim, and the molten	646
	18:18	the **e**, and the teraphim, and the molten	646
	18:20	he took the **e**, and the teraphim,	646
1Sa	2:18	*being* a child, girded *with* a linen **e**.	646
	2:28	to burn incense, to wear an **e** before me?	646
	14:	3 the LORD's priest in Shiloh, wearing an **e**.	646
	21:	9 it *is here* wrapt in a cloth behind the **e**:	646
	22:18	and five persons that did wear a linen **e**.	646
	23:	6 that he came down *with* an **e** in his hand.	646
	23:	9 to Abiathar the priest, Bring hither the **e**.	646
	30:	7 I pray thee, bring me hither the **e**.	646
	30:	7 Abiathar brought thither the **e** to David.	646
2Sa	6:14	and David *was* girded *with* a linen **e**.	646
1Ch	15:27	David also *had* upon him an **e** of linen.	646
Hos	3:	4 and without an **e**, and *without* teraphim:	646

EPHPHATHA (1)

Mk	7:34	saith unto him, **E**, that is, Be opened.	2188

EPHRAIM (172) [EPHRAIM'S, EPHRAIMITE, EPHRAIMITES]

Ge	41:52	name of the second called he **E**: For God	669
	46:20	land of Egypt were born Manasseh and **E**,	669
	48:	1 with him his two sons, Manasseh and **E**.	669
	48:	5 now thy two sons, **E** and Manasseh,	669
	48:13	**E** in his right hand toward Israel's left	669
	48:17	laid his right hand upon the head of **E**,	669
	48:20	God make thee as **E** and as Manasseh:	669
	48:20	Manasseh: and he set **E** before Manasseh.	669
Nu	1:10	of **E**; Elishama the son of Ammihud:	669
	1:32	*namely,* of the children of **E**, by their	669
	1:33	*even* of the tribe of **E**, *were* forty thousand	669
	2:18	of the camp of **E** according to their armies:	669
	2:18	the captain of the sons of **E** *shall be*	669
	2:24	All that were numbered of the camp of **E**	669
	7:48	prince of the children of **E**, *offered:*	669
	10:22	standard of the camp of the children of **E**	669
	13:	8 Of the tribe of **E**, Oshea the son of Nun.	669
	26:28	after their families *were* Manasseh and **E**.	669
	26:35	These *are* the sons of **E** after their families:	669
	26:37	These *are* the families of the sons of **E**	669
	34:24	the prince of the tribe of the children of **E**,	669
Dt	33:17	*they are* the ten thousands of **E**, and they	669
	34:	2 land of **E**, and Manasseh, and all the land	669
Jos	14:	4 Joseph were two tribes, Manasseh and **E**:	669
	16:	4 Manasseh and **E**, took their inheritance.	669
	16:	5 the border of the children of **E** according to	669
	16:	8 tribe of the children of **E** by their families.	669
	16:	9 the separate cities for the children of **E**	669
	17:	8 of Manasseh *belonged* to the children of **E**;	669
	17:	9 these cities of **E** *are* among the cities of	669
	17:15	giants, if mount **E** be too narrow for thee.	669
	17:17	to **E** and to Manasseh, saying, Thou *art*	669
	19:50	he asked, *even* Timnath-serah in mount **E**:	669
	20:	7 Shechem in mount **E**, and Kirjath-arba,	669
	21:	5 by lot out of the families of the tribe of **E**,	669
	21:20	the cities of their lot out of the tribe of **E**.	669
	21:21	Shechem with her suburbs in mount **E**,	669
	24:30	which *is* in mount **E**, on the north side of	669

Jos	24:33	his son, which was given him in mount **E**.	669
Jdg	1:29	Neither did **E** drive out the Canaanites that	669
	2:	9 in the mount of **E**, on the north side	669
	3:27	he blew a trumpet in the mountain of **E**,	669
	4:	5 between Ramah and Beth-el in mount **E**:	669
	5:14	Out of **E** *was there* a root of them against	669
	7:24	sent messengers throughout all mount **E**,	669
	7:24	all the men of **E** gathered themselves	669
	8:	1 the men of **E** said unto him, Why hast	669
	8:	2 *Is* not the gleaning of the grapes of **E** better	669
	10:	1 and he dwelt in Shamir in mount **E**.	669
	10:	9 and against the house of **E**;	669
	12:	1 the men of **E** gathered themselves together,	669
	12:	4 all the men of Gilead, and fought with **E**:	669
	12:	4 the men of Gilead smote **E**, because	669
	12:	4 Ye Gileadites *are* fugitives of **E** among	669
	12:15	was buried in Pirathon in the land of **E**,	669
	17:	1 there was a man of mount **E**, whose name	669
	17:	8 came *to* mount **E** to the house of Micah,	669
	18:	2 who when they came *to* mount **E**,	669
	18:13	they passed thence *unto* mount **E**,	669
	19:	1 Levite sojourning on the side of mount **E**,	669
	19:16	field at even, which *was* also of mount **E**;	669
	19:18	toward the side of mount **E**;	669
1Sa	1:	1 of mount **E**, and his name *was* Elkanah,	669
	9:	4 he passed through mount **E**,	669
	14:22	which had hid themselves in mount **E**,	669
2Sa	2:	9 over **E**, and over Benjamin, and over all	669
	13:23	in Baal-hazor, which *is* beside **E**:	669
	18:	6 and the battle was in the wood of **E**;	669
	20:21	a man of mount **E**, Sheba the son of Bichri	669
1Ki	4:	8 their names: The son of Hur, in mount **E**:	669
	12:25	Jeroboam built Shechem in mount **E**,	669
2Ki	5:22	**E** two young men of the sons of	669
	14:13	from the gate of **E** unto the corner gate,	669
1Ch	6:66	cities of their coasts out of the tribe of **E**.	669
	6:67	Shechem in mount **E** with her suburbs;	669
	7:20	sons of **E**; Shuthelah, and Bered his son,	669
	7:22	And **E** their father mourned many days,	669
	9:	3 and of the children of **E**, and Manasseh,	669
	12:30	of the children of **E** twenty thousand and	669
	27:10	Helez the Pelonite, of the children of **E**:	669
	27:14	the Pirathonite, of the children of **E**:	669
	27:20	Of the children of **E**, Hoshea the son of	669
2Ch	13:	4 which *is* in mount **E**, and said, Hear me,	669
	15:	8 cities which he had taken from mount **E**,	669
	15:	9 the strangers with them out of **E** and	669
	17:	2 in the cities of **E**, which Asa his father had	669
	19:	4 the people from Beer-sheba to mount **E**,	669
	25:	7 Israel, *to wit, with* all the children of **E**.	669
	25:10	the army that was come to him out of **E**,	669
	25:23	from the gate of **E** to the corner gate,	669
	28:	7 Zichri, a mighty *man* of **E**, slew Maaseiah	669
	28:12	certain of the heads of the children of **E**,	669
	30:	1 and wrote letters also to **E** and Manasseh,	669
	30:10	from city to city through the country of **E**	669
	30:18	*even* many of **E**, and Manasseh, Issachar,	669
	31:	1 and Benjamin, in **E** also and Manasseh,	669
	34:	6 and in the cities of Manasseh, and **E**,	669
	34:	9 gathered of the hand of Manasseh and **E**,	669
Ne	8:16	and in the street of the gate of **E**.	669
	12:39	from above the gate of **E**, and above the	669
Ps	60:	7 mine; **E** also *is* the strength of mine head;	669
	78:	9 The children of **E**, *being* armed,	669
	78:67	of Joseph, and chose not the tribe of **E**:	669
	80:	2 Before **E** and Benjamin and Manasseh stir	669
	108:	8 mine; **E** also *is* the strength of mine head;	669
Isa	7:	2 saying, Syria is confederate with **E**.	669
	7:	5 Because Syria, **E**, and the son of Remaliah,	669
	7:	8 and five years shall **E** be broken,	669
	7:	9 the head of **E** *is* Samaria, and the head of	669
	7:17	from the day that **E** departed from Judah;	669
	9:	9 *even* **E** and the inhabitant of Samaria,	669
	9:21	Manasseh, **E**; and Ephraim, Manasseh:	669
	9:21	Manasseh, Ephraim; and **E**, Manasseh:	669
	11:13	The envy also of **E** shall depart,	669
	11:13	**E** shall not envy Judah, and Judah shall not	669
	11:13	not envy Judah, and Judah shall not vex **E**.	669
	17:	3 The fortress also shall cease from **E**,	669
	28:	1 the crown of pride, to the drunkards of **E**,	669
	28:	3 The crown of pride, the drunkards of **E**,	669
Jer	4:15	and publisheth affliction from mount **E**.	669
	7:15	your brethren, *even* the whole seed of **E**.	669
	31:	6 the watchmen upon the mount **E** shall	669
	31:	9 a father to Israel, and **E** *is* my firstborn.	669
	31:18	I have surely heard **E** bemoaning himself	669
	31:20	*Is* **E** my dear son? *is* he a pleasant child?	669
	50:19	his soul shall be satisfied upon mount **E**	669
Eze	37:16	stick of **E**, and *for* all the house of Israel	669
	37:19	which *is* in the hand of **E**, and the tribes of	669
	48:	5 side unto the west side, a *portion for* **E**.	669
	48:	6 by the border of **E**, from the east side even	669
Hos	4:17	**E** *is* joined to idols: let him alone.	669
	5:	3 I know **E**, and Israel is not hid from me:	669
	5:	3 now, O **E**, thou committest whoredom,	669
	5:	5 shall Israel and **E** fall in their iniquity:	669
	5:	9 **E** shall be desolate in the day of rebuke:	669
	5:11	**E** *is* oppressed *and* broken in judgment,	669
	5:12	Therefore *will* I be unto **E** as a moth,	669
	5:13	When **E** saw his sickness, and Judah *saw*	669
	5:13	went **E** to the Assyrian, and sent to king	669
	5:14	I *will* be unto **E** as a lion, and as a young	669
	6:	4 O **E**, what shall I do unto thee? O Judah,	669
	6:10	*is* the whoredom of **E**, Israel is defiled.	669
	7:	1 the iniquity of **E** was discovered,	669

E

E

Hos 7: 8 **E**, he hath mixed himself among the 669
 7: 8 among the people; **E** is a cake not turned. 669
 7:11 **E** also is like a silly dove, without heart: 669
 8: 9 ass alone by himself: **E** hath hired lovers. 669
 8:11 Because **E** hath made many altars to sin, 669
 9: 3 **E** shall return to Egypt, and they shall eat 669
 9: 8 The watchman of **E** was with my God: 669
 9:11 As for **E**, their glory shall fly away like a 669
 9:13 **E**, as I saw Tyrus, is planted in a pleasant 669
 9:13 **E** shall bring forth his children to 669
 9:16 **E** is smitten, their root is dried up, they 669
 10: 6 **E** shall receive shame, and Israel shall be 669
 10:11 **E** is as a heifer that is taught, and loveth 669
 10:11 I will make **E** to ride; Judah shall plow, 669
 11: 3 I taught **E** also to go, taking them by their 669
 11: 8 How shall I give thee up, **E**? how shall I 669
 11: 9 mine anger, I will not return to destroy **E**: 669
 11:12 **E** compasseth me about with lies, 669
 12: 1 **E** feedeth on wind, and followeth after 669
 12: 8 **E** said, Yet I am become rich, I have found 669
 12:14 **E** provoked him to anger most bitterly: 669
 13: 1 When **E** spake trembling, he exalted 669
 13:12 The iniquity of **E** is bound up; his sin is hid. 669
 14: 8 **E** shall say, What have I to do any more 669
Ob 1:19 they shall possess the fields of **E**, 669
Zec 9:10 I will cut off the chariot from **E**, 669
 9:13 filled the bow with **E**, and raised up thy 669
 10: 7 they of **E** shall be like a mighty man, and 669
Jn 11:54 into a city called **E**, and there continued 2187

EPHRAIM'S (4) [EPHRAIM]

Ge 48:14 laid it upon **E** head, who was the younger, 669
 48:17 to remove it from **E** head unto Manasseh's 669
 50:23 Joseph saw **E** children of the third 669
Jos 17:10 Southward it was **E**, 669+3807.1

EPHRAIMITE (1) [EPHRAIM]

Jdg 12: 5 of Gilead said unto him, Art thou an **E**? 673

EPHRAIMITES (5) [EPHRAIM]

Jos 16:10 the Canaanites dwell among the **E** unto 669
Jdg 12: 4 are fugitives of Ephraim among the **E**, 669
 12: 5 took the passages of Jordan before the **E**: 669
 12: 5 when those **E** which were escaped said, 669
 12: 6 there fell at that time of the **E** forty and 669

EPHRAIN (1)

2Ch 13:19 and **E** with the towns thereof. 6085

EPHRATAH (5) [CALEB-EPHRATAH, EPHRATH]

Ru 4:11 do thou worthily in **E**, and be famous in 672
1Ch 2:50 of Caleb the son of Hur, the firstborn of **E**; 672
 4: 4 firstborn of **E**, the father of Beth-lehem. 672
Ps 132: 6 Lo, we heard of it at **E**: we found it in 672
Mic 5: 2 thou, Beth-lehem **E**, though thou be little 672

EPHRATH (5) [EPHRATAH, EPHRATHITE, EPHRATHITES]

Ge 35:16 there was but a little way to come to **E**: 672
 35:19 died, and was buried in the way to **E**, 672
 48: 7 there was but a little way to come unto **E**: 672
 48: 7 I buried her there in the way of **E**; 672
1Ch 2:19 took unto him **E**, which bare him Hur. 672

EPHRATHITE (3) [EPHRATH]

1Sa 1: 1 the son of Tohu, the son of Zuph, an **E**: 673
 17:12 Now David was the son of that **E** of 673
1Ki 11:26 an **E** of Zereda, Solomon's servant, 673

EPHRATHITES (1) [EPHRATH]

Ru 1: 2 and Chilion, **E** of Beth-lehem-judah. 673

EPHRON (13)

Ge 23: 8 and intreat for me to **E** the son of Zohar, 6085
 23:10 **E** dwelt amongst the children of Heth: 6085
 23:10 **E** the Hittite answered Abraham in 6085
 23:13 he spake unto **E** in the audience of 6085
 23:14 **E** answered Abraham, saying unto him, 6085
 23:16 Abraham hearkened unto **E**; 6085
 23:16 Abraham weighed to **E** the silver, which 6085
 23:17 the field of **E**, which was in Machpelah, 6085
 25: 9 in the field of **E** the son of Zohar 6085
 49:29 cave that is in the field of **E** the Hittite, 6085
 49:30 Abraham bought with the field of **E** 6085
 50:13 of a buryingplace of **E** the Hittite, 6085
Jos 15: 9 and went out to the cities of mount **E** 6085

EPICUREANS (1)

Ac 17:18 Then certain philosophers of the **E**, 1946

EPISTLE (19) [EPISTLES]

Ac 15:30 multitude together, they delivered the **e**: 1992
 23:33 and delivered the **e** to the governor, 1992
Ro 16:22 I Tertius, who wrote this **e**, salute you in 1992
1Co 5: 9 I wrote unto you in an **e** not to company 1992
 16: S The first **e** to the Corinthians was written NIG
2Co 3: 2 Ye are our **e** written in our hearts, known 1992
 3: 3 to be the **e** of Christ ministered by us, 1992
 7: 8 for I perceive that the same **e** hath made 1992
 13: S The second **e** to the Corinthians was NIG
Col 4:16 And when this **e** is read amongst you, 1992
 4:16 that ye likewise read the **e** from Laodicea. NIG
1Th 5:27 charge you by the Lord that this **e** be read 1992
 5: S The first **e** unto the Thessalonians was NIG
2Th 2:15 taught, whether by word, or by our **e**. 1992
 3:14 if any man obey not our word by this **e**, 1992

2Th 3:17 own hand, which is the token in every **e**: 1992
 3: S The second **e** to the Thessalonians was NIG
2Ti 4: S The second **e** unto Timotheus, ordained NIG
2Pe 3: 1 This second **e**, beloved, I now write unto 1992

EPISTLES (2) [EPISTLE]

2Co 3: 1 some others, **e** of commendation to you, 1992
2Pe 3:16 As also in all his **e**, speaking in them of 1992

EQUAL (21) [EQUALITY, EQUALLY, EQUALS, UNEQUAL]

Job 28:17 The gold and the crystal cannot **e** it: 6186
 28:19 The topaz of Ethiopia shall not **e** it, 6186
Ps 17: 2 thine eyes behold the things that are **e**. 4339
 55:13 a man mine **e**, my guide, 6187+3509.1
Pr 26: 7 The legs of the lame are not **e**: so is a 1809
Isa 40:25 then will ye liken me, or shall I be **e**? 7737
 46: 5 **make** me, and compare me, that we 7737
La 2:13 what shall I **e** to thee, that I may comfort 7737
Eze 18:25 Yet ye say, The way of the Lord is not **e**. 8505
 18:25 O house of Israel; Is not my way **e**? 8505
 18:29 of Israel, The way of the Lord is not **e**. 8505
 18:29 O house of Israel, are not my ways **e**? 8505
 33:17 people say, The way of the Lord is not **e**. 8505
 33:17 but as for them, their way is not **e**. 8505
 33:20 Yet ye say, The way of the Lord is not **e**. 8505
Mt 20:12 and thou hast made them **e** unto us, 2470
Lk 20:36 for they are unto the angels; and are 2465
Jn 5:18 his Father, making himself **e** with God. 2470
Php 2: 6 thought it not robbery to be **e** with God: 2470
Col 4: 1 your servants that which is just and **e**; 2471
Rev 21:16 and the breadth and the height of it are **e**. 2470

EQUALITY (2) [EQUAL]

2Co 8:14 But by an **e**, that now at this time your 2471
 8:14 supply for your want: that there may be **e**: 2471

EQUALLY (1) [EQUAL]

Ex 36:22 two tenons, **e** distant one from another: 7947

EQUALS (1) [EQUAL]

Gal 1:14 above many my **e** in mine own nation, 4915

EQUITY (10)

Ps 98: 9 judge the world, and the people with **e**. 4339
 99: 4 thou dost establish **e**, thou executest 4339
Pr 1: 3 of wisdom, justice, and judgment, and **e**; 4339
 2: 9 and judgment, and **e**; 4339
 17:26 is not good, nor to strike princes for **e**. 3476
Ecc 2:21 in wisdom, and in knowledge, and in **e**; 3788
Isa 11: 4 reprove with **e** for the meek of the earth: 4334
 59:14 is fallen in the street, and **e** cannot enter. 5229
Mic 3: 9 that abhor judgment, and pervert all **e**. 3477
Mal 2: 6 he walked with me in peace and **e**, 4334

ER (11)

Ge 38: 3 and bare a son; and he called his name **E**. 6147
 38: 6 Judah took a wife for **E** his firstborn, 6147
 38: 7 **E**, Judah's firstborn, was wicked in 6147
 46:12 **E**, and Onan, and Shelah, and Pharez, 6147
 46:12 **E** and Onan died in the land of Canaan. 6147
Nu 26:19 The sons of Judah were **E** and Onan: 6147
 26:19 **E** and Onan died in the land of Canaan. 6147
1Ch 2: 3 sons of Judah; **E**, and Onan, and Shelah: 6147
 2: 3 **E**, the firstborn of Judah, was evil in 6147
 4:21 son of Judah were, **E** the father of Lecah, 6147
Lk 3:28 son of Elmodam, which was the son of **E**, 2262

ERAN (1) [ERANITES]

Nu 26:36 of **E**, the family of the Eranites. 6197

ERANITES (1) [ERAN]

Nu 26:36 of Shuthelah: of Eran, the family of the **E**. 6198

ERASTUS (3)

Ac 19:22 ministered unto him, Timotheus and **E**; 2037
Ro 16:23 **E** the chamberlain of the city saluteth you, 2037
2Ti 4:20 **E** abode at Corinth: but Trophimus have 2037

ERE (10)

Ex 1:19 delivered **e** the midwives come 2962+871.1
Nu 11:33 yet between their teeth, **e** it was chewed, 2962
 14:11 how long will it be **e** they believe me, 3808
1Sa 3: 3 **e** the lamp of God went out in the temple 2962
2Sa 2:26 **e** thou bid the people return from 3808
2Ki 6:32 but **e** the messenger came to him, 2962+871.1
Job 18: 2 How long will it be **e** you make an end of NIH
Jer 47: 6 how long will it be **e** thou be quiet? 3808
Hos 8: 5 how long will it be **e** they attain to 3808
Jn 4:49 unto him, Sir, come down **e** my child die. 4250

ERECH (1)

Ge 10:10 **E**, and Accad, and Calneh, in the land of 751

ERECTED (1)

Ge 33:20 he **e** there an altar, and called it 5324

ERI (2) [ERITES]

Ge 46:16 and Ezbon, **E**, and Arodi, and Areli. 6179
Nu 26:16 the Oznites: of **E**, the family of the Erites: 6179

ERITES (1) [ERI]

Nu 26:16 of the Oznites: of Eri, the family of the **E**: 6180

ERR (24) [ERRED, ERRETH, ERROR, ERRORS]

2Ch 33: 9 **made** Judah and the inhabitants of Jerusalem to **e**, 8582
Ps 95:10 It is a people that do **e** in their heart, 8582
 119:21 which do **e** from thy commandments. 7686
 119:118 Thou hast trodden down all them that **e** 7686
Pr 14:22 Do they not **e** that devise evil? but mercy 8582
 19:27 to hear the instruction that causeth to **e** 7686
Isa 3:12 they which lead thee **cause** thee to **e**, 8582
 9:16 leaders of this people **cause** them to **e**; 8582
 19:14 have **caused** Egypt to **e** in every work 8582
 28: 7 in vision, they stumble in judgment. 7686
 30:28 jaws of the people, **causing** them to **e**. 8582
 35: 8 though fools, shall not **e** therein. 8582
 63:17 hast thou **made** us to **e** from thy ways, 8582
Jer 23:13 Baal, and **caused** my people Israel to **e**. 8582
 23:32 **cause** my people to **e** by their lies, 8582
Hos 4:12 of whoredoms hath **caused** them to **e**, 8582
Am 2: 4 and their lies **caused** them to **e**, 8582
Mic 3: 5 the prophets that **make** my people **e**, 8582
Mt 22:29 and said unto them, Ye do **e**, 4105
Mk 12:24 Do ye not therefore, because ye know 4105
 12:27 of the living: ye therefore do greatly **e**. 4105
Heb 3:10 and said, They do alway **e** in their heart; 4105
Jas 1:16 Do not **e**, my beloved brethren. 4105
 5:19 if any of you do **e** from the truth, 4105

ERRAND (3)

Ge 24:33 I will not eat, until I have told mine **e**. 1697
Jdg 3:19 said, I have a secret **e** unto thee, O king: 1697
2Ki 9: 5 he said, I have an **e** to thee, O captain. 1697

ERRED (12) [ERR]

Lev 5:18 concerning his ignorance wherein he **e** 7683
Nu 15:22 if ye have **e**, and not observed all these 7686
1Sa 26:21 played the fool, and have **e** exceedingly. 7686
Job 6:24 cause me to understand wherein I have **e**. 7686
 19: 4 be it indeed that I have **e**, mine error 7686
Ps 119:110 for me: yet I **e** not from thy precepts. 8582
Isa 28: 7 they also have **e** through wine, 7686
 28: 7 the prophet have **e** through strong drink, 7686
 29:24 They also that **e** in spirit shall come to 8582
1Ti 6:10 they have **e** from the faith, 635
 6:21 Which some professing have **e** concerning 795
2Ti 2:18 Who concerning the truth have **e**, saying 795

ERRETH (2) [ERR]

Pr 10:17 but he that refuseth reproof **e**. 8582
Eze 45:20 day of the month for every one that **e**, 7686

ERROR (13) [ERR]

2Sa 6: 7 God smote him there for his **e**; and there 7944
Job 19: 4 erred, mine **e** remaineth with myself. 4879
Ecc 5: 6 thou before the angel, that it was an **e**: 7684
 10: 5 as an **e** which proceedeth from the ruler: 7684
Isa 32: 6 and to utter an **e** against the Lord, 8442
Da 6: 4 neither was there any **e** or fault found in 7960
Mt 27:64 so the last **e** shall be worse than the first. 4106
Ro 1:27 recompence of their **e** which was meet. 4106
Jas 5:20 of his way shall save a soul from death, 4106
2Pe 2:18 clean escaped from them who live in **e**. 4106
 3:17 being led away with the **e** of the wicked, 4106
1Jn 4: 6 we the spirit of truth, and the spirit of **e**. 4106
Jude 1:11 ran greedily after the **e** of Balaam for 4106

ERRORS (4) [ERR]

Ps 19:12 Who can understand his **e**? cleanse thou 7691
Jer 10:15 They are vanity, and the work of **e**: 8595
 51:18 They are vanity, the work of **e**: in the 8595
Heb 9: 7 for himself, and for the **e** of the people: 51

ESAI (1) [ISAIAH]

2Ki 19: 2 to **E** the prophet the son of Amoz. 3470

ESAIAS (21) [ISAIAH]

Mt 3: 3 he that was spoken of by the prophet **E**, 2268
 4:14 which was spoken by **E** the prophet, 2268
 8:17 which was spoken by **E** the prophet, 2268
 12:17 which was spoken by **E** the prophet, 2268
 13:14 And in them is fulfilled the prophecy of **E**, 2268
 15: 7 well did **E** prophesy of you, saying, 2268
Mk 7: 6 Well hath **E** prophesied of you hypocrites, 2268
Lk 3: 4 in the book of the words of **E** the prophet, 2268
 4:17 unto him the book of the prophet **E**. 2268
Jn 1:23 the way of the Lord, as said the prophet **E**. 2268
 12:38 That the saying of **E** the prophet might be 2268
 12:39 not believe, because that **E** said again, 2268
 12:41 things said **E**, when he saw his glory, 2268
Ac 8:28 sitting in his chariot read **E** the prophet. 2268
 8:30 him, and heard him read the prophet **E**, 2268
 28:25 Well spake the Holy Ghost by **E** 2268
Ro 9:27 **E** also crieth concerning Israel, Though 2268
 9:29 And as **E** said before, Except the Lord of 2268
 10:16 For **E** saith, Lord, who hath believed our 2268
 10:20 But **E** is very bold, and saith, I was found 2268
 15:12 again **E** saith, There shall be a root of 2268

ESARHADDON, ESAR-HADDON (3) [ESARHADDON]

2Ki 19:37 And **E** his son reigned in his stead. 634
Ezr 4: 2 do sacrifice unto him since the days of **E** 634
Isa 37:38 and **E** his son reigned in his stead. 634

ESAU (88) [EDOM, ESAU'S]

Ge 25:25 garment; and they called his name **E**. 6215

E

Ge		
25:27	**E** was a cunning hunter, a man of the	6215
25:28	Isaac loved **E**, because he did eat of *his*	6215
25:29	came from the field, and he *was* faint:	6215
25:30	**E** said to Jacob, Feed me, I pray thee,	6215
25:32	**E** said, Behold, I *am* at the point to die:	6215
25:34	Jacob gave **E** bread and pottage of lentiles;	6215
25:34	his way: thus **E** despised his birthright.	6215
26:34	**E** was forty years old when he took to	6215
27: 1	he called **E** his eldest son, and said unto	6215
27: 5	Rebekah heard when Isaac spake to **E** his	6215
27: 5	**E** went to the field to hunt for venison,	6215
27: 6	heard thy father speak unto **E** thy brother,	6215
27:11	**E** my brother *is* a hairy man, and I *am* a	6215
27:15	took goodly raiment of her eldest son **E**,	6215
27:19	said unto his father, I *am* **E** thy firstborn;	6215
27:21	whether thou *be* my very son **E** or not.	6215
27:22	but the hands *are* the hands of **E**.	6215
27:24	he said, *Art* thou my very son **E**? And he	6215
27:30	**E** his brother came in from his hunting.	6215
27:32	he said, I *am* thy son, thy firstborn **E**.	6215
27:34	when **E** heard the words of his father,	6215
27:37	Isaac answered and said unto **E**, Behold,	6215
27:38	**E** said unto his father, Hast thou but one	6215
27:38	And **E** lift up his voice, and wept.	6215
27:41	**E** hated Jacob because of the blessing	6215
27:41	**E** said in his heart, The days of mourning	6215
27:42	these words of **E** her elder son were told	6215
27:42	said unto him, Behold, thy brother **E**,	6215
28: 6	When **E** saw that Isaac had blessed Jacob,	6215
28: 8	seeing that the daughters of Canaan	6215
28: 9	went **E** unto Ishmael, and took unto	6215
32: 3	Jacob sent messengers before him to **E** his	6215
32: 4	Thus shall ye speak unto my lord **E**;	6215
32: 6	We came to thy brother **E**, and also he	6215
32:11	hand of my brother, from the hand of **E**:	6215
32:13	to his hand a present for **E** his brother;	6215
32:17	When **E** my brother meeteth thee,	6215
32:18	it *is* a present sent unto my lord **E**.	6215
32:19	On this manner shall you speak unto **E**,	6215
33: 1	**E** came, and with him four hundred men.	6215
33: 4	**E** ran to meet him, and embraced him,	6215
33: 9	**E** said, I have enough, my brother;	6215
33:15	**E** said, Let me now leave with thee *some*	6215
33:16	So **E** returned that day on his way unto	6215
35: 1	fleddest from the face of **E** thy brother.	6215
35:29	and his sons **E** and Jacob buried him.	6215
36: 1	Now these *are* the generations of **E**, who	6215
36: 2	**E** took his wives of the daughters of	6215
36: 4	Adah bare to **E** Eliphaz;	6215
36: 5	these *are* the sons of **E**, which were born	6215
36: 6	**E** took his wives, and his sons, and his	6215
36: 8	dwelt **E** in mount Seir: Esau *is* Edom.	6215
36: 8	dwelt Esau in mount Seir: **E** *is* Edom.	6215
36: 9	these *are* the generations of **E** the father	6215
36:10	Eliphaz the son of Adah the wife of **E**,	6215
36:10	Reuel the son of Bashemath the wife of **E**.	6215
36:14	she bare to **E** Jeush, and Jaalam,	6215
36:15	These *were* dukes of the sons of **E**:	6215
36:15	the sons of Eliphaz the firstborn *son* of **E**;	6215
36:19	These *are* the sons of **E**, who *is* Edom,	6215
36:40	the names of the dukes *that came* of **E**,	6215
36:43	he *is* **E** the father of the Edomites.	6215
Dt 2: 4	coast of your brethren the children of **E**,	6215
2: 5	I have given mount Seir unto **E** *for* a	6215
2: 8	by from our brethren the children of **E**,	6215
2:12	the children of **E** succeeded them,	6215
2:22	he did to the children of **E**, which dwelt	6215
2:29	(As the children of **E** which dwell in Seir,	6215
Jos 24: 4	I gave unto Isaac Jacob and **E**: and I gave	6215
24: 4	I gave unto **E** mount Seir, to possess it;	6215
1Ch 1:34	The sons of Isaac; **E** and Israel.	6215
1:35	The sons of **E**; Eliphaz, Reuel, and Jeush,	6215
Jer 49: 8	I will bring the calamity of **E** upon him,	6215
49:10	I have made **E** bare, I have uncovered his	6215
Ob 1: 6	How are the things *of* **E** searched out!	6215
1: 8	understanding out of the mount of **E**?	6215
1: 9	the end that every one of the mount of **E**	6215
1:18	the house of **E** for stubble, and they shall	6215
1:18	not be *any* remaining of the house of **E**;	6215
1:19	*of* the south shall possess the mount of **E**;	6215
1:21	on mount Zion to judge the mount of **E**;	6215
Mal 1: 2	*was* not **E** Jacob's brother? saith	6215
1: 3	I hated **E**, and laid his mountains and his	6215
Ro 9:13	Jacob have I loved, but **E** have I hated.	2269
Heb 11:20	and **E** concerning *things* to come.	2269
12:16	any fornicator, or profane *person*, as **E**,	2269

ESAU'S (12) [ESAU]

Ge		
25:26	and his hand took hold on **E** heel;	6215
27:23	hands were hairy, as his brother **E** hands:	6215
28: 5	of Rebekah, Jacob's and **E** mother.	6215
36:10	These *are* the names of **E** sons; Eliphaz	6215
36:12	Timna was concubine to Eliphaz **E** son;	6215
36:12	these *were* the sons of Adah **E** wife.	6215
36:13	these *were* the sons of Bashemath **E** wife.	6215
36:14	of Anah, daughter of Zibeon, **E** wife:	6215
36:17	these *are* the sons of Reuel **E** son;	6215
36:17	these *are* the sons of Bashemath **E** wife.	6215
36:18	these *are* the sons of Aholibamah **E** wife;	6215
36:18	Aholibamah the daughter of Anah, **E** wife.	6215

ESCAPE (59) [ESCAPED, ESCAPETH, ESCAPING]

Ge		
19:17	forth abroad, that he said, **E** for thy life;	4422
19:17	**e** to the mountain, lest thou be	4422

Ge		
19:19	cannot **e** to the mountain, lest *some* evil	4422
19:20	let me **e** thither, (*is* it not a little one?)	4422
19:22	Haste thee, **e** thither; for I cannot do any	4422
32: 8	the *other* company which is left shall **e**.	4422
Jos 8:22	so that *they* let none of them remain or **e**.	6412
1Sa 27: 1	**speedily e** into the land of	4422+4422
27: 1	coast of Israel: so shall I **e** out of his hand.	4422
2Sa 15:14	we shall not *else* **e** from Absalom:	1961+6413
20: 6	he get him fenced cities, and **e** us.	5337+5869
1Ki 18:40	prophets of Baal; let not one of them **e**.	6412
2Ki 9:15	let none go forth *nor* **e** out of the city to	4422
10:24	whom I *have* brought into your hands **e**,	4422
19:31	and **they** that **e** out of mount Zion:	6413
Ezr 9: 8	to leave us a **remnant to e**, and to give us	6413
Est 4:13	Think not with thyself that *thou* shalt **e** *in*	4422
Job 11:20	they shall not **e**, and their hope *shall* be	4498
Ps 55: 8	I would hasten my **e** from the windy	4655
56: 7	*Shall* they **e** by iniquity? in *thine* anger	6405
71: 2	in thy righteousness, and **cause** me to **e**:	6403
141:10	into their own nets, whilst that I withal **e**.	5674
Pr 19: 5	and *he* that speaketh lies shall not **e**.	4422
Ecc 7:26	whoso pleaseth God shall **e** from her;	4422
Isa 20: 6	the king of Assyria: and how shall we **e**?	6413
37:32	and **they** that **e** out of mount Zion:	6413
66:19	I will send those that **e** of them unto the	6412
Jer 11:11	which they shall not be able to **e**;	3318
25:35	to flee, nor the principal of the flock to **e**.	6413
32: 4	Zedekiah king of Judah shall not **e** out of	4422
34: 3	thou shalt not **e** out of his hand,	4422
38:18	and thou shalt not **e** out of their hand.	4422
38:23	thou shalt not **e** out of their hand,	4422
42:17	**e** from the evil that I *will* bring upon	4422
44:14	shall **e** or remain, that *they* should	1961+6412
44:14	for none shall return but such as shall **e**.	6405
44:28	Yet a small number that **e** the sword shall	6412
46: 6	swift flee away, nor the mighty *man* **e**;	4422
48: 8	come upon every city, and no city shall **e**:	4422
50:28	that flee and **e** out of the land of Babylon,	6405
50:29	against it round about; let none thereof **e**:	6413
Eze 6: 8	that ye may have *some* that shall **e**	6412
6: 9	they that **e** of you shall remember me	6412
7:16	they that **e** of them shall escape,	6412
7:16	they that escape of them shall **e**,	6403
17:15	shall he **e** that doeth such *things?* or	4422
17:18	hath done all these *things*, he shall not **e**.	4422
Da 11:41	these shall **e** out of his hand, *even* Edom,	4422
11:42	and the land of Egypt shall not **e**.	6413
Joel 2: 3	and nothing shall **e** them.	1961+6413
Ob 1:14	to cut off those of his that did **e**;	6412
Mt 23:33	how can ye **e** the damnation of hell?	5343
Lk 21:36	that ye may be accounted worthy to **e** all	1628
Ac 27:42	lest any of *them* should swim out, and **e**.	1309
Ro 2: 3	that thou shalt **e** the judgment of God?	1628
1Co 10:13	with the temptation also make a **way to e**	1545
1Th 5: 3	a *woman* with child; and they shall not **e**.	1628
Heb 2: 3	How shall we **e**, if we neglect so	1628
12:25	much more *shall not* we **e**, if we turn	NIG

ESCAPED (58) [ESCAPE]

Ge		
14:13	came one that had **e**, and told Abram	6412
Ex 10: 5	shall eat the residue of that **which is e**	6413
Nu 21:29	he hath given his sons that **e**,	6412
Dt 23:15	which is **e** from his master unto thee:	5337
Jdg 3:26	Ehud **e** while they tarried, and passed	4422
3:26	beyond the quarries, and **e** unto Seirath.	4422
3:29	all men of valour; and there **e** not a man.	4422
12: 5	When those Ephraimites which were **e**	6412
21:17	for **them** that be **e** of Benjamin,	6413
1Sa 14:41	Jonathan were taken: but the people **e**.	3318
19:10	and David fled, and **e** that night.	4422
19:12	a window: and he went, and fled, and **e**.	4422
19:17	and sent away mine enemy, that he is **e**?	4422
19:18	**e**, and came to Samuel to Ramah,	4422
22: 1	thence, and **e** to the cave Adullam:	4422
22:20	named Abiathar, **e**, and fled after David.	4422
23:13	it was told Saul that David was **e** from	4422
30:17	there **e** not a man of them, save four	4422
2Sa 1: 3	him, Out of the camp of Israel am I **e**.	4422
4: 6	and Rechab and Baanah his brother **e**.	4422
1Ki 20:20	Ben-hadad the king of Syria **e** on a horse	4422
2Ki 19:30	remnant that is **e** of the house of Judah	6413
19:37	they **e** *into* the land of Armenia.	4422
1Ch 4:43	the rest of the Amalekites that were **e**,	6413
2Ch 16: 7	is the host of the king of Syria **e** out of	4422
20:24	bodies fallen to the earth, and none **e**.	6413
30: 6	that are **e** out of the hand of the kings of	6413
36:20	them that had **e** from the sword carried	7611
Ezr 9:15	for we remain *yet* **e**, as *it is* this day:	6413
Ne 1: 2	them concerning the Jews that had **e**,	6413
Job 1:15	and I only am **e** alone to tell thee.	4422
1:16	and I only am **e** alone to tell thee.	4422
1:17	and I only am **e** alone to tell thee.	4422
1:19	dead; and I only am **e** alone to tell thee.	4422
19:20	and I am **e** with the skin of my teeth.	4422
Ps 124: 7	Our soul is **e** as a bird out of the snare of	4422
124: 7	the snare is broken, and we are **e**.	4422
Isa 4: 2	and comely for **them** that are **e** of Israel.	6413
10:20	and **such as are e** of the house of Jacob,	6413
37:31	remnant **that is e** of the house of Judah	6413
37:38	and they **e** *into* the land of Armenia.	4422
45:20	near together, ye *that are* **e** of the nations:	6412
Jer 41:15	Ishmael the son of Nethaniah **e** from	4422
51:50	Ye that have **e** the sword, go *away*, stand	6405
La 2:22	the Lord's anger none **e** nor remained:	6412
Eze 24:27	thy mouth be opened to him which is **e**,	6412

Eze 33:21	**one that** had **e** out of Jerusalem came	6412
33:22	in the evening, afore he **that** was **e** came;	6412
Jn 10:39	to take him: but he **e** out of their hand,	1831
Ac 27:44	came to pass, that *they* all **safe** to land.	1295
28: 1	when they were **e**, then they knew that	1295
28: 4	whom, though he hath **e** the sea,	1295
2Co 11:33	I let down by the wall, and **e** his hands.	1628
Heb 11:34	violence of fire, **e** the edge of the sword,	5343
12:25	if they **e** not who refused him that spake	5343
2Pe 1: 4	having **e** the corruption that is in the world	668
2:18	that were clean **e** from them who live	668
2:20	For if after they have **e** the pollutions of	668

ESCAPETH (6) [ESCAPE]

1Ki 19:17	*that* him that **e** the sword of Hazael shall	4422
19:17	him that **e** from the sword of Jehu shall	4422
Isa 15: 9	lions upon **him that e** of Moab,	6413
Jer 48:19	and her that **e**, and say, What is done?	4422
Eze 24:26	he that **e** in that day shall come unto	6412
Am 9: 1	he that **e** of them shall not be delivered.	6412

ESCAPING (1) [ESCAPE]

| Ezr 9:14 | that *there should be* no remnant nor **e**? | 6413 |

ESCHEW (1) [ESCHEWED, ESCHEWETH]

| 1Pe 3:11 | Let him **e** evil, and do good; let him seek | 1578 |

ESCHEWED (1) [ESCHEW]

| Job 1: 1 | and one that feared God, and **e** evil. | 5493 |

ESCHEWETH (2) [ESCHEW]

Job 1: 8	one that feareth God, and **e** evil?	5493
2: 3	one that feareth God, and **e** evil?	5493

ESCORT See FETCH; FETCHED

ESEK (1)

| Ge 26:20 | he called the name of the well **E**; because | 6230 |

ESHAN See ESHEAN

ESHBAAL (2) [ISH-BOSHETH]

1Ch 8:33	and Malchishua, and Abinadab, and **E**.	792
9:39	and Malchishua, and Abinadab, and **E**.	792

ESHBAN (2)

Ge 36:26	Hemdan, and **E**, and Ithran, and Cheran.	790
1Ch 1:41	Amram, and **E**, and Ithran, and Cheran.	790

ESHCOL (6)

Ge 14:13	brother of **E**, and brother of Aner:	812
14:24	went with me, Aner, **E**, and Mamre;	812
Nu 13:23	came unto the brook of **E**, and cut down	812
13:24	The place was called the brook **E**, because	812
32: 9	when they went up unto the valley of **E**,	812
Dt 1:24	came unto the valley of **E**, and searched it	812

ESHEAN (1)

| Jos 15:52 | Arab, and Dumah, and **E**, | 824 |

ESHEK (1)

| 1Ch 8:39 | the sons of **E** his brother *were*, Ulam his | 6232 |

ESHKALONITES (1) [ASHKELON]

| Jos 13: 3 | the **E**, the Gittites, and the Ekronites; | 832 |

ESHTAOL (7)

Jos 15:33	in the valley, **E**, and Zoreah, and Ashnah,	847
19:41	was Zorah, and **E**, and Ir-shemesh,	847
Jdg 13:25	in the camp of Dan, between Zorah and **E**.	847
16:31	**E** in the buryingplace of Manoah his father.	847
18: 2	men of valour, from Zorah and from **E**,	847
18: 8	came unto their brethren *to* Zorah and **E**:	847
18:11	of Zorah and out of **E**, six hundred men	847

ESHTAOLITES See ESHTAULITES

ESHTAULITES (1)

| 1Ch 2:53 | of them came the Zareathites, and the **E**. | 848 |

ESHTEMOA (6)

Jos 21:14	with her suburbs, and **E** with her suburbs,	851
1Sa 30:28	Siphmoth, and to *them* which *were* in **E**,	851
1Ch 4:17	and Shammai, and Ishbah the father of **E**.	851
4:19	the Garmite, and **E** the Maachathite.	851
6:57	and Jattir, and **E**, with their suburbs,	851

ESHTEMOH (1)

| Jos 15:50 | And Anab, and **E**, and Anim, | 851 |

ESHTON (2)

1Ch 4:11	begat Mehir, which *was* the father of **E**.	850
4:12	**E** begat Beth-rapha, and Paseah,	850

ESLI (1)

| Lk 3:25 | *son* of Naum, which was the *son* of **E**, | 2069 |

ESPECIALLY (5) [SPECIAL]

Ps 31:11	am among my neighbours, and a fear to	3966
Ac 26: 3	**E** *because I know* thee to be expert in all	3122
Gal 6:10	us do good unto all *men*, **e** unto them	3122
1Ti 5: 8	they who labour in the word and	3122
2Ti 4:13	and the books, *but* **e** the parchments.	3122

ESPIED (2) [SPY]

Ge 42:27	ass provender in the inn, he **e** his money;	7200
Eze 20: 6	of Egypt into a land that I had **e** for them,	8446

ESPOUSALS (2) [ESPOUSED]
SS 3:11 mother crowned him in the day of his **e**, 2861
Jer 2: 2 kindness of thy youth, the love of thine **e**, 3623

ESPOUSED (5) [ESPOUSALS]
2Sa 3:14 which I **e** to me for an hundred foreskins 781
Mt 1:18 as his mother Mary was **e** to Joseph, *3423*
Lk 1:27 To a virgin **e** to a man whose name was *3423*
 2: 5 To be taxed with Mary his **e** wife, *3423*
2Co 11: 2 I have **e** you to one husband, that *I* may *718*

ESPY (2) [SPY]
Jos 14: 7 from Kadesh-barnea to **e** *out* the land; 7270
Jer 48:19 of Aroer, stand by the way and **e**; 6822

ESROM (3) [HEZRON]
Mt 1: 3 and Phares begat **E**; and Esrom begat *2074*
 1: 3 Phares begat Esrom; and **E** begat Aram; *2074*
Lk 3:33 *the son of* Aram, which was *the son of* **E**, *2074*

ESTABLISH (41) [ESTABLISHED, ESTABLISHETH, ESTABLISHMENT]
Ge 6:18 with thee will I **e** my covenant; 6965
 9: 9 behold I **e** my covenant with you and 6965
 9:11 I will **e** my covenant with you; neither 6965
 17: 7 I will **e** my covenant between me and 6965
 17:19 I will **e** my covenant with him for an 6965
 17:21 my covenant will I **e** with Isaac, 6965
Lev 26: 9 and **e** my covenant with you. 6965
Nu 30:13 her husband may **e** it, or her husband 6965
Dt 8:18 he may **e** his covenant which he sware 6965
 28: 9 The LORD shall **e** thee a holy people unto 6965
 29:13 he may **e** thee to day for a people unto 6965
1Sa 1:23 weaned him; only the LORD **e** his word. 6965
2Sa 7:12 of thy bowels, and I will **e** his kingdom. 3559
 7:25 **e** *it* for ever, and do as thou hast said. 6965
1Ki 9: 5 I will **e** the throne of thy kingdom upon 6965
 4 his son after him, and to **e** Jerusalem: 5975
1Ch 22:10 I will **e** the throne of his kingdom over 3559
 28: 7 Moreover I will **e** his kingdom for ever, 3559
2Ch 9: 8 to **e** them for ever, therefore made he 5975
Job 36: 7 he doth **e** them for ever, and they are 3427
Ps 7: 9 wicked come to an end; but **e** the just: 3559
 48: 8 of our God: God will **e** it for ever. Selah. 3559
 87: 5 and the Highest himself shall **e** her. 3559
 89: 2 thy faithfulness shalt thou **e** in the very 3559
 90:17 **e** thou the work of our hands upon us; 3559
 90:17 yea, the work of our hands **e** thou it. 3559
 99: 4 dost **e** equity, thou executest judgment 3559
Pr 15:25 but he will **e** the border of the widow. 5324
Isa 49: 8 a covenant of the people, to **e** the earth, 6965
 62: 7 he **e**, and till he make Jerusalem a praise 3559
Jer 33: 2 the LORD that formed it, to **e** it; 3559
Eze 16:60 I will **e** unto thee an everlasting covenant. 6965
 16:62 I will **e** my covenant with thee; 6965
Da 6: 7 consulted together to **e** a royal statute, 6966
 6: 8 king, the decree, and sign the writing, 6966
 11:14 shall exalt themselves to **e** the vision; 5975
Am 5:15 the good, and **e** judgment in the gate: 3322
Ro 3:31 God forbid: yea, we **e** the law. 2476
 10: 3 going about to **e** their own righteousness, 2476
1Th 3: 2 to **e** you, and to comfort you concerning 4741
Heb 10: 9 away the first, that he may **e** the second. 2476

ESTABLISHED (68) [ESTABLISH]
Ge 9:17 which I have **e** between me and all flesh 6965
 41:32 *it is* because the thing *is* **e** by God, 3559
Ex 6: 4 I have also **e** my covenant with them, 6965
 15:17 O Lord, *which* thy hands have **e**. 3559
Dt 32: 6 hath he *not* made thee, and **e** thee? 3559
1Sa 3:20 Samuel *was* **e** to be a prophet of the LORD. 539
 13:13 for now would the LORD have **e** thy 3559
 24:20 *that* the kingdom of Israel shall be **e** in 6965
2Sa 5:12 David perceived that the LORD had **e** him 3559
 7:26 let the house of thy servant David be **e** 3559
1Ki 2:12 his father; and his kingdom was **e** greatly. 3559
 2:24 hath **e** me, and set me on the throne 3559
 2:45 the throne of David shall be **e** before 3559
 2:46 kingdom was **e** in the hand of Solomon. 3559
1Ch 17:14 and his throne shall be **e** for evermore. 3559
 17:23 and concerning his house be **e** for ever, 539
 17:24 Let it even be **e**, that thy name may be 539
 17:24 *let* the house of David thy servant *be* **e** 3559
2Ch 1: 9 let thy promise unto David my father be **e**: 539
 12: 1 when Rehoboam had **e** the kingdom, 3559
 20:20 in the LORD your God, so shall ye be **e**; 539
 25: 3 to pass, when the kingdom was **e** to him, 2388
 30: 5 So they **e** a decree to make proclamation 5975
Job 21: 8 Their seed is **e** in their sight with them, 3559
 22:28 decree a thing, and it shall be **e** unto thee: 6965
Ps 24: 2 it upon the seas, and **e** it upon the floods. 3559
 40: 2 set my feet upon a rock, and **e** my goings. 3559
 78: 5 For he **e** a testimony in Jacob, 6965
 78:69 like the earth which he hath **e** for ever. 3245
 89:21 With whom my hand shall be **e**: mine 3559
 89:37 It shall be **e** for ever as the moon, and *as* 3559
 93: 2 Thy throne is **e** of old: thou *art* from 3559
 96:10 the world also shall be **e** *that* it shall not 3559
 102:28 and their seed shall be **e** before thee. 3559
 112: 8 His heart *is* **e**, he shall not be afraid, 5564
 119:90 thou **e** the earth, and it abideth. 3559
 140:11 Let not an evil speaker be **e** in the earth: 3559
Pr 3:19 by understanding hath he **e** the heavens. 3559
 4:26 path of thy feet, and let all thy ways be **e**. 3559
 8:28 When he **e** the clouds above: when *he* 553

Pr 12: 3 A man shall not be **e** by wickedness: 3559
 12:19 The lip of truth shall be **e** for ever: 3559
 15:22 in the multitude of counsellers *they* are **e**. 6965
 16: 3 the LORD, and thy thoughts shall be **e**. 3559
 16:12 for the throne is **e** by righteousness. 3559
 20:18 Every purpose is **e** by counsel: 3559
 24: 3 builded; and by understanding it is **e**: 3559
 25: 5 and his throne shall be **e** in righteousness. 3559
 29:14 the poor, his throne shall be **e** for ever. 3559
 30: 4 who hath **e** all the ends of the earth? 6965
Isa 2: 2 shall be **e** in the top of the mountains, 3559
 7: 9 ye will not believe, surely ye shall not be **e**. 539
 16: 5 in mercy shall the throne be **e**: and he 3559
 45:18 he hath **e** it, he created it not in vain, 3559
 54:14 In righteousness shalt thou be **e**: thou 3559
Jer 10:12 he hath **e** the world by his wisdom, 3559
 30:20 their congregation shall be **e** before me, 3559
 51:15 he hath **e** the world by his wisdom, 3559
Da 4:36 I was **e** in my kingdom, 8627
Mic 4: 1 shall be **e** in the top of the mountains, 3559
Hab 1:12 thou hast **e** them for correction. 3245
Zec 5:11 it shall be **e**, and set there upon her own 3559
Mt 18:16 or three witnesses every word may be **e**. 2476
Ac 16: 5 And so were the churches **e** in the faith, 4732
Ro 1:11 spiritual gift, to the end you may be **e**; 4741
2Co 13: 1 or three witnesses shall every word be **e**. 2476
Heb 8: 6 which was **e** upon better promises. 3549
 13: 9 For *it is* a good *thing* that the heart be **e** 950

ESTABLISHETH (2) [ESTABLISH]
Nu 30:14 he **e** all her vows, or all her bonds, 6965
Da 6:15 statute which the king **e** may be changed. 6966

ESTABLISHMENT (1) [ESTABLISH]
2Ch 32: 1 the **e** *thereof*, Sennacherib king of Assyria 571

ESTATE (17) [ESTATES]
1Ch 17:17 hast regarded me according to the **e** of a 8448
Est 1:19 let the king give her *royal* **e** unto another 4438
Ps 136:23 Who remembered us in our low **e**: 8216
Ecc 1:16 I am **come to great e**, and have gotten 1431
 3:18 I said in my heart concerning the **e** of 1700
Eze 16:55 return to their **former e**, and Samaria 6927
 16:55 daughters shall return to their **former e**, 6927
 16:55 daughters shall return to your **former e**, 6927
Da 11: 7 of her roots shall *one* stand up *in* his **e**, 3653
 11:20 shall stand up in his **e** a raiser of taxes *in* 3653
 11:21 in his **e** shall stand up a vile person, 3653
 11:38 in his **e** shall he honour the God of forces: 3653
Lk 1:48 For he hath regarded the **low e** of his 5014
Ac 22: 5 witness, and all the **e of the elders**: 4244
Ro 12:16 *things,* but condescend to *men* of **low e**. 5011
Col 4: 8 that he might know your **e**, 4012
Jude 1: 6 the angels which kept not their **first e**, 746

ESTATES (2) [ESTATE]
Eze 36:11 I will settle you after your **old e**, 6927
Mk 6:21 high captains, and chief *e* of Galilee; NIG

ESTEEM (5) [ESTEEMED, ESTEEMETH, ESTEEMING]
Job 36:19 Will he **e** thy riches? *no,* not gold, nor all 6186
Ps 119:128 **e** all *thy* precepts concerning 3474
 all *things* **to be right**;
Isa 53: 4 we did **e** him stricken, smitten of God, 2803
Php 2: 3 in lowliness of mind *let* each **e** other 2233
1Th 5:13 to **e** them very highly in love for their 2233

ESTEEMED (11) [ESTEEM]
Dt 32:15 and **lightly e** the Rock of his salvation. 5034
1Sa 18:23 that they despise to be **lightly e**. 7043
 18:23 that I am a poor man, and **lightly e**? 7034
Job 23:12 have **e** the words of his mouth more 6845
Pr 17:28 he that shutteth his lips *is* **e** a man of NIH
Isa 29:16 down shall be **e** as the potter's clay: 2803
 29:17 the fruitful field shall be **e** as a forest? 2803
 53: 3 he was despised, and we **e** him not. 2803
La 4: 2 how are they **e** as earthen pitchers, 2803
Lk 16:15 for that which is **highly e** amongst men 5308
1Co 6: 4 set them to judge who are **least e** in 1848

ESTEEMETH (4) [ESTEEM]
Job 41:27 He **e** iron as straw, *and* brass as rotten 2803
Ro 14: 5 One man **e** one day above another: 2919
 14: 5 another **e** every day *alike.* Let every man 2919
 14:14 but to him that **e** any *thing* to be unclean, 3049

ESTEEMING (1) [ESTEEM]
Heb 11:26 **E** the reproach of Christ greater riches 2233

ESTHER (53) [ESTHER'S, HADASSAH]
Est 2: 7 Hadassah, that *is,* **E**, his uncle's daughter: 635
 2: 8 that **E** was brought *also* unto the king's 635
 2:10 **E** had not shewed her people nor her 635
 2:11 to know how **E** did, and what should 635
 2:15 Now when the turn of **E**, the daughter of 635
 2:15 **E** obtained favour in the sight of all them 635
 2:16 So **E** was taken unto king Ahasuerus into 635
 2:17 the king loved **E** above all the women, 635
 2:20 **E** had not *yet* shewed her kindred nor her 635
 2:20 for **E** did the commandment of Mordecai, 635
 2:22 to Mordecai, who told *it* unto **E** the queen; 635
 2:22 **E** certified the king *thereof* in Mordecai's 635
 4: 5 called **E** for Hatach, *one* of the king's 635
 4: 8 to shew *it* unto **E**, and to declare *it* 635
 4: 9 and told **E** the words of Mordecai. 635
 4:10 Again **E** spake unto Hatach, and gave him 635

Est 4:13 Mordecai commanded to answer **E**, 635
 4:15 **E** bade *them* return Mordecai *this answer*: 635
 4:17 did according to all that **E** had commanded 635
 5: 1 **E** put on *her* royal *apparel*, and stood in 635
 5: 2 the king saw **E** the queen standing in 635
 5: 2 the king held out to **E** the golden sceptre 635
 5: 2 So **E** drew near, and touched the top of 635
 5: 3 king unto her, What wilt thou, queen **E**? 635
 5: 4 **E** answered, If *it seem* good unto the king, 635
 5: 5 make haste, that *he* may do as **E** hath said. 635
 5: 5 Haman came to the banquet that **E** had 635
 5: 6 king said unto **E** at the banquet of wine, 635
 5: 7 Then answered **E**, and said, My petition 635
 5:12 **E** the queen did let *no man* come in with 635
 6:14 unto the banquet that **E** had prepared. 635
 7: 1 Haman came to banquet with **E** the queen. 635
 7: 2 king said again unto **E** on the second day 635
 7: 2 of wine, What *is* thy petition, queen **E**? 635
 7: 3 **E** the queen answered and said, If I have 635
 7: 5 and said unto **E** the queen, 635
 7: 6 **E** said, The adversary and enemy *is* this 635
 7: 7 to make request for his life to **E** the queen; 635
 7: 8 Haman was fallen upon the bed whereon **E** 635
 8: 1 Haman the Jews' enemy unto **E** the queen. 635
 8: 1 for **E** had told what he *was* unto her. 635
 8: 2 **E** set Mordecai over the house of Haman. 635
 8: 3 **E** spake yet again before the king, 635
 8: 4 king held out the golden sceptre toward **E**. 635
 8: 4 So **E** arose, and stood before the king, 635
 8: 7 the king Ahasuerus said unto **E** the queen 635
 8: 7 I have given **E** the house of Haman, 635
 9:12 the king said unto **E** the queen, The Jews 635
 9:13 said **E**, If it please the king, let it be granted 635
 9:25 when *E* came before the king, NIH
 9:29 **E** the queen, the daughter of Abihail, 635
 9:31 and **E** the queen had enjoined them, 635
 9:32 the decree of **E** confirmed these matters of 635

ESTHER'S (3) [ESTHER]
Est 2:18 his princes and his servants, *even* **E** feast; 635
 4: 4 So **E** maids and her chamberlains came 635
 4:12 And they told to Mordecai **E** words. 635

ESTIMATE (2) [ESTIMATION, ESTIMATIONS]
Lev 27:14 the priest shall **e** it, whether it be good or 6186
 27:14 as the priest shall **e** it, so shall it stand. 6186

ESTIMATION (23) [ESTIMATE]
Lev 5:15 with thy **e** *by* shekels of silver, after 6187
 5:18 with thy **e**, for a trespass offering, unto 6187
 6: 6 with thy **e**, for a trespass offering, unto 6187
 27: 2 persons *shall be* for the LORD by thy **e**. 6187
 27: 3 thy **e** shall be, of the male from twenty 6187
 27: 3 even thy **e** shall be fifty shekels of silver, 6187
 27: 4 female, then thy **e** shall be thirty shekels. 6187
 27: 5 thy **e** shall be of the male twenty shekels, 6187
 27: 6 thy **e** shall be of the male five shekels of 6187
 27: 6 for the female thy **e** *shall be* three shekels 6187
 27: 7 thy **e** shall be fifteen shekels, and for 6187
 27: 8 if he be poorer than thy **e**, then he shall 6187
 27:13 shall add a fifth *part* thereof unto thy **e**. 6187
 27:15 fifth *part* of the money of thy **e** unto it, 6187
 27:16 thy **e** shall be according to the seed 6187
 27:17 of jubile, according to thy **e** it shall stand. 6187
 27:18 jubile, and it shall be abated from thy **e**. 6187
 27:19 fifth *part* of the money of thy **e** unto it, 6187
 27:23 shall reckon unto him the worth of thy **e**, 6187
 27:23 he shall give thine **e** in that day, *as* a holy 6187
 27:27 he shall redeem *it* according to thine **e**, 6187
 27:27 then it shall be sold according to thy **e**. 6187
Nu 18:16 according to thine **e**, *for* the money of five 6187

ESTIMATIONS (1) [ESTIMATE]
Lev 27:25 all thy **e** shall be according to the shekel 6187

ESTRANGED (5)
Job 19:13 mine acquaintance are verily **e** from me. 2114
Ps 58: 3 The wicked are **e** from the womb: they go 2114
 78:30 They were not **e** from their lust. 2114
Jer 19: 4 have **e** this place, and have burnt incense 5234
Eze 14: 5 they are all **e** from me through their idols. 2114

ETAM (5)
Jdg 15: 8 and dwelt in the top of the rock **E**. 5862
 15:11 of Judah went to the top of the rock **E**, 5862
1Ch 4: 3 these *were* the father of **E**; Jezreel, 5862
 4:32 their villages *were*, **E**, and Ain, Rimmon, 5862
2Ch 11: 6 built even Beth-lehem, and **E**, and Tekoa, 5862

ETERNAL (47) [ETERNITY]
Dt 33:27 The **e** God *is thy* refuge, and underneath 6924
Isa 60:15 *thee*, I will make thee an **e** excellency, 5769
Mt 19:16 *thing* shall I do, that I may have **e** life? 166
 25:46 but the righteous into life **e**. 166
Mk 3:29 but is in danger of **e** damnation: 166
 10:17 what shall I do that I may inherit **e** life? 166
 10:30 and in the world to come **e** life. 166
Lk 10:25 Master, what shall I do to inherit **e** life? 166
 18:18 what shall I do to inherit **e** life? 166
Jn 3:15 in him should not perish, but have **e** life. 166
 4:36 and gathereth fruit unto life **e**: 166
 5:39 for in them ye think ye have **e** life: 166
 6:54 flesh, and drinketh my blood, hath **e** life; 166
 6:68 shall we go? thou hast the words of **e** life. 166
 10:28 And I give unto them **e** life; and they shall 166

Jn	12:25	life in this world shall keep it unto life **e**.	166
	17: 2	he should give **e** life to as many as thou	166
	17: 3	this is life **e**, that they might know thee	166
Ac	13:48	many as were ordained to **e** life believed.	166
Ro	1:20	are made, *even* his **e** power and Godhead;	126
	2: 7	glory and honour and immortality, **e** life:	166
	5:21	unto **e** life by Jesus Christ our Lord.	166
	6:23	gift of God *is* **e** life through Jesus Christ	166
2Co	4:17	far more exceeding *and* **e** weight of glory;	166
	4:18	but the *things* which are not seen *are* **e**.	166
	5: 1	not made with hand, **e** in the heavens.	166
Eph	3:11	According to the **e** purpose which he	165
1Ti	1:17	Now unto the King **e**, immortal, invisible,	165
	6:12	the good fight of faith, lay hold on **e** life,	166
	6:19	to come, that they may lay hold on **e** life.	166
2Ti	2:10	which is in Christ Jesus with **e** glory.	166
Tit	1: 2	hope of **e** life, which God, that cannot lie,	166
	3: 7	made heirs according to the hope of **e** life.	166
Heb	5: 9	became the author of **e** salvation unto all	166
	6: 2	resurrection of the dead, and of **e** judgment.	166
	9:12	*place*, having obtained **e** redemption *for us.*	166
	9:14	who through the **e** Spirit offered himself	166
	9:15	might receive the promise of **e** inheritance	166
1Pe	5:10	hath called us into his **e** glory by Christ	166
1Jn	1: 2	witness, and shew unto you *that* **e** life,	166
	2:25	that he hath promised us, *even* **e** life.	166
	3:15	ye know that no murderer hath **e** life	166
	5:11	God hath given to us **e** life, and this life	166
	5:13	that ye may know that ye have **e** life,	166
	5:20	This is the true God, and **e** life.	166
Jude	1: 7	suffering the vengeance of **e** fire.	166
	1:21	mercy of our Lord Jesus Christ unto **e** life.	166

ETERNITY (1) [ETERNAL]

Isa	57:15	the high and lofty One that inhabiteth **e**,	5703

ETH KAZIN See ITTAH-KAZIN

ETHAM (4)

Ex	13:20	encamped in **E**, in the edge of	864
Nu	33: 6	departed from Succoth, and pitched in **E**,	864
	33: 7	they removed from **E**, and turned again	864
	33: 8	three days' journey in the wilderness of **E**,	864

ETHAN (8)

1Ki	4:31	than **E** the Ezrahite, and Heman,	387
1Ch	2: 6	and **E**, and Heman, and Calcol, and Dara:	387
	2: 8	And the sons of **E**; Azariah.	387
	6:42	The son of **E**, the son of Zimmah, the son	387
	6:44	**E** the son of Kishi, the son of Abdi, the son	387
	15:17	their brethren, **E** the son of Kushaiah;	387
	15:19	So the singers, Heman, Asaph, and **E**,	387
Ps	89: T	Maschil of **E** the Ezrahite.	387

ETHANIM (1)

1Ki	8: 2	king Solomon at the feast in the month **E**,	388

ETHBAAL (1)

1Ki	16:31	the daughter of **E** king of the Zidonians,	856

ETHER (2)

Jos	15:42	Libnah, and **E**, and Ashan,	6281
	19: 7	Ain, Remmon, and **E**, and Ashan;	6281

ETHIOPIA (20) [ETHIOPIAN, ETHIOPIANS]

Ge	2:13	*is it* that compasseth the whole land of **E**.	3568
2Ki	19: 9	when he heard say of Tirhakah king of **E**,	3568
Est	1: 1	from India even unto **E**, *over* an hundred	3568
	8: 9	provinces which *are* from India unto **E**,	3568
Job	28:19	The topaz of **E** shall not equal it,	3568
Ps	68:31	**E** shall soon stretch out her hands unto	3568
	87: 4	behold Philistia, and Tyre, with **E**;	3568
Isa	18: 1	which *is* beyond the rivers of **E**:	3568
	20: 3	sign and wonder upon Egypt and upon **E**;	3568
	20: 5	and ashamed of **E** their expectation,	3568
	37: 9	heard say concerning Tirhakah king of **E**,	3568
	43: 3	Egypt *for* thy ransom, **E** and Seba for thee.	3568
	45:14	merchandise of **E** and of the Sabeans,	3568
Eze	29:10	tower of Syene even unto the border of **E**.	3568
	30: 4	great pain shall be in **E**, when the slain	3568
	30: 5	**E**, and Libya, and Lydia, and all	3568
	38: 5	Persia, **E**, and Libya with them; all of	3568
Na	3: 9	**E** and Egypt *were* her strength, and *it was*	3568
Zep	3:10	beyond the rivers of **E** my suppliants,	3568
Ac	8:27	behold, a man of **E**, an eunuch of great	128

ETHIOPIAN (8) [ETHIOPIA]

Nu	12: 1	of the **E** woman whom he had married:	3569
	12: 1	for he had married an **E** woman.	3569
2Ch	14: 9	there came out against them Zerah the **E**	3569
Jer	13:23	Can the **E** change his skin, or the leopard	3569
	38: 7	Now when Ebed-melech the **E**, one of	3569
	38:10	the king commanded Ebed-melech the **E**,	3569
	38:12	Ebed-melech the **E** said unto Jeremiah,	3569
	39:16	Go and speak to Ebed-melech the **E**,	3569

ETHIOPIANS (13) [ETHIOPIA]

2Ch	12: 3	the Lubims, the Sukkiims, and the **E**.	3569
	14:12	So the LORD smote the **E** before Asa,	3569
	14:12	and before Judah; and the **E** fled.	3569
	14:13	**E** were overthrown, that they could not	3569
	16: 8	Were not the **E** and the Lubims a huge	3569
	21:16	and of the Arabians, that *were* near the **E**:	3569
Isa	20: 4	the **E** captives, young and old, naked and	3568
Jer	46: 9	the **E** and the Libyans that handle	3568
Eze	30: 9	me in ships to make the careless **E** afraid,	3568

Da	11:43	Libyans and the **E** shall *be* at his steps.	3569
Am	9: 7	*Are* ye not as children of the **E** unto me,	3569
Zep	2:12	Ye **E** also, ye *shall be* slain by my sword.	3569
Ac	8:27	authority under Candace queen of the **E**,	128

ETHNAN (1)

1Ch	4: 7	of Helah *were*, Zereth, and Jezoar, and **E**.	869

ETHNI (1)

1Ch	6:41	The son of **E**, the son of Zerah, the son of	867

EUBULUS (1)

2Ti	4:21	**E** greeteth thee, and Pudens, and Linus,	2103

EUNICE (1)

2Ti	1: 5	thy grandmother Lois, and thy mother **E**;	2131

EUNUCH (7) [EUNUCHS]

Isa	56: 3	neither let the **e** say, Behold, I *am* a dry	5631
Jer	52:25	He took also out of the city an **e**, which	5631
Ac	8:27	an **e** of great authority under Candace	2135
	8:34	the **e** answered Philip, and said, I pray	2135
	8:36	he said, See, *here is* water; what doth	2135
	8:38	into the water, both Philip and the **e**;	2135
	8:39	away Philip, that the **e** saw him no more:	2135

EUNUCHS (20) [EUNUCH]

2Ki	9:32	there looked out to him two *or* three **e**.	5631
	20:18	they shall be **e** in the palace of the king of	5631
Isa	39: 7	they shall be **e** in the palace of the king of	5631
	56: 4	For thus saith the LORD unto the **e** that	5631
Jer	29: 2	the queen, and the **e**, the princes of Judah	5631
	34:19	the **e**, and the priests, and all the people	5631
	38: 7	of the **e** which *was* in the king's house,	5631
	41:16	the women, and the children, and the **e**,	5631
Da	1: 3	spake unto Ashpenaz the master of his **e**,	5631
	1: 7	whom the prince of the **e** gave names;	5631
	1: 8	he requested of the prince of the **e** that	5631
	1: 9	and tender love with the prince of the **e**.	5631
	1:10	the prince of the **e** said unto Daniel, I fear	5631
	1:11	whom the prince of the **e** had set over	5631
	1:18	the prince of the **e** brought them in before	5631
Mt	19:12	For there are *some* **e**, which were so	2135
	19:12	and there are *some* **e**, which were made	2135
	19:12	eunuchs, which were **made e** of men:	2134
	19:12	and there be **e**, which have made	2135
	19:12	which have **made** themselves **e** for	2134

EUODIAS (1)

Php	4: 2	I beseech **E**, and beseech Syntyche,	2136

EUPHRATES (21)

Ge	2:14	east of Assyria. And the fourth river *is* **E**.	6578
	15:18	of Egypt unto the great river, the river **E**:	6578
Dt	1: 7	unto the great river, the river **E**.	6578
	11:24	and Lebanon, from the river, the river **E**,	6578
Jos	1: 4	the river **E**, all the land of the Hittites,	6578
2Sa	8: 3	went to recover his border at the river **E**.	6578
2Ki	23:29	against the king of Assyria to the river **E**:	6578
	24: 7	**E** all that pertained to the king of Egypt.	6578
1Ch	5: 9	in of the wilderness from the river **E**:	6578
	18: 3	to stablish his dominion by the river **E**.	6578
2Ch	35:20	came up to fight against Carchemish by **E**:	6578
Jer	13: 4	go to **E**, and hide it there in a hole of	6578
	13: 5	So I went, and hid it by **E**, as the LORD	6578
	13: 6	go to **E**, and take the girdle from thence,	6578
	13: 7	went to **E**, and digged, and took the girdle	6578
	46: 2	which was by the river **E** in Carchemish,	6578
	46: 6	and fall toward the north by the river **E**.	6578
	46:10	in the north country by the river **E**.	6578
	51:63	stone to it, and cast it into the midst of **E**:	6578
Rev	9:14	which are bound in the great river **E**.	2166
	16:12	poured out his vial upon the great river **E**;	2166

EUROCLYDON (1)

Ac	27:14	against it a tempestuous wind, called **E**.	2148

EUTYCHUS (1)

Ac	20: 9	a window a certain young man named **E**,	2161

EVANGELIST (2) [EVANGELISTS]

Ac	21: 8	we entered into the house of Philip the **e**,	2099
2Ti	4: 5	do the work of an **e**, make full proof of	2099

EVANGELISTS (1) [EVANGELIST]

Eph	4:11	and some, **e**; and some, pastors and	2099

EVE (4)

Ge	3:20	Adam called his wife's name **E**; because	2332
	4: 1	Adam knew **E** his wife; and she	2332
2Co	11: 3	as the serpent beguiled **E** through his	2096
1Ti	2:13	For Adam was first formed, then **E**.	2096

EVEN (1395) [EVENING, EVENINGS, EVENINGTIDE, EVENTIDE]

Ge	6:17	behold, I, **e** I, do bring a flood of waters	NIH
	9: 3	**e** as the green herb have I given you all	NIH
	10: 9	**E** as Nimrod the mighty hunter before	NIH
	10:19	and Admah, and Zeboim, **e** unto Lasha.	5704
	10:21	the elder, **e** to him were *children* born.	1571
	13: 3	went on his journeys from the south **e**	2050.1
	13:10	as the garden of the LORD,	NIH
	14:23	That I will not *take* from a thread **e** to	2050.1
	19: 1	there came two angels to Sodom at **e**;	6153
	19: 4	the men of the city, **e** the men of Sodom,	NIH
	19: 9	**e** Lot, and came near to break the door.	NIH

Ge	20: 5	she, **e** she herself said, He *is* my brother:	1571
	21:10	not be heir with my son, **e** with Isaac.	NIH
	23: 7	of the land, **e** to the children of Heth.	NIH
	23:10	**e** of all that went in *at* the gate of his city,	NIH
	24:11	**e** the time that *women* go out to draw	NIH
	26:28	**e** betwixt us and thee, and let us make a	NIH
	27:34	father, Bless me, **e** me also, O my father.	NIH
	27:38	bless me, **e** me also, O my father.	NIH
	34:29	and spoiled **e** all that *was* in the house.	2050.1
	35:14	he talked with him, **e** a pillar of stone:	NIH
	37:18	off, **e** before he came near unto them,	2050.1
	42:28	is restored; and lo, *it is* **e** in my sack:	1571
	44:18	thy servant: for thou *art* **e** as Pharaoh.	3644
	46:18	these she bare unto Jacob, **e** sixteen souls.	2050.1
	46:34	about cattle from our youth **e** until now,	2050.1
	47: 2	**e** five men, and presented them unto	2050.1
	47:21	of Egypt **e** to the *other* end thereof.	2050.1
	49:22	fruitful bough, **e** a fruitful bough by a well;	NIH
	49:25	**E** by the God of thy father, who shall help	NIH
Ex	3: 1	came to the mountain of God, **e** to Horeb.	NIH
	4:16	he shall be to thee instead of a mouth,	NIH
	4:22	Israel *is* my son, **e** my firstborn:	NIH
	4:23	behold, I slay thy son, **e** thy firstborn.	NIH
	9:18	the foundation thereof **e** until now.	2050.1
	10:12	of the land, **e** all that the hail hath left.	NIH
	10:21	of Egypt, **e** darkness *which* may be felt.	2050.1
	11: 5	**e** unto the firstborn of the maidservant	NIH
	12:15	the first day ye shall put away leaven out	389
	12:18	on the fourteenth day of the month at **e**,	6153
	12:18	one and twentieth day of the month at **e**.	6153
	12:19	**e** that soul shall be cut off from	NIH
	12:38	and flocks, and herds, **e** very much cattle.	NIH
	12:41	**e** the selfsame day it came to pass,	871.1
	14:23	**e** all Pharaoh's horses, his chariots,	NIH
	16: 6	At **e**, then ye shall know that the LORD	6153
	16:12	At **e** ye shall eat flesh,	996+6153+1886.1
	16:13	that at **e** the quails came up,	6153
	18:14	stand by thee from morning unto **e**?	6153
	23:31	I will set thy bounds from the Red sea **e**	2050.1
	25: 9	so shall ye make *it*.	2050.1
	25:19	**e** of the mercy seat shall ye make	NIH
	27: 5	that the net may be **e** to the midst of	5704
	28: 1	**e** Aaron, Nadab and Abihu, Eleazar and	NIH
	28: 8	**e** of gold, of blue, and purple, and scarlet,	NIH
	28:17	it settings of stones, **e** four rows of stones:	NIH
	28:42	from the loins **e** unto the thighs they	2050.1
	29:27	**e** of that which *is* for Aaron, and of *that*	NIH
	29:28	**e** their heave offering unto the LORD.	NIH
	29:39	lamb thou shalt offer **at e**:	996+6153+1886.1
	29:41	lamb thou shalt offer **at e**,	996+6153+1886.1
	30: 8	Aaron lighteth the lamps **at e**.	996+6153+1886.1
	30:21	**e** to him and to his seed throughout their	NIH
	30:23	**e** two hundred and fifty *shekels*, and	NIH
	30:33	shall **e** be cut off from his people.	2050.1
	30:38	shall **e** be cut off from his people.	2050.1
	32:29	**e** every man upon his son, and upon his	3588
	35:35	**e** of them that do any work, and of those	NIH
	36: 2	**e** every one whose heart stirred him up to	NIH
	37: 3	**e** two rings upon the one side of it,	2050.1
	37: 9	**e** to the mercy seatward were the faces of	NIH
	38:21	**e** of the tabernacle of Testimony, as it was	NIH
	38:24	holy *place*, **e** the gold of the offering,	2050.1
	39:37	**e** *with* the lamps to be set in order, and all	NIH
	39:43	had commanded, **e** so had they done it:	NIH
Lev	1: 2	the cattle, **e** of the herd, and of the flock.	NIH
	2:14	by the fire, **e** corn beaten out of full ears.	NIH
	3:14	**e** an offering made by fire unto the LORD;	NIH
	4:12	**E** the whole bullock shall he carry forth	2050.1
	4:17	times before the LORD, **e** before the vail.	NIH
	5:12	**e** a memorial thereof, and burn *it* on	NIH
	6: 5	he shall **e** restore it in the principal,	2050.1
	6:15	**e** the memorial of it, unto the LORD.	NIH
	7: 8	**e** the priest shall have to himself the skin	NIH
	7:20	**e** that soul shall be cut off from his	2050.1
	7:21	**e** that soul shall be cut off from his	2050.1
	7:25	**e** the soul that eateth *it* shall be cut off	2050.1
	7:27	**e** that soul shall be cut off from his	2050.1
	8: 9	also upon the mitre, **e** upon his forefront,	NIH
	11:11	shall be **e** an abomination unto you:	2050.1
	11:22	**E** these of them ye may eat; the locust	NIH
	11:24	of them shall be unclean until the **e**.	6153
	11:25	his clothes, and be unclean until the **e**.	6153
	11:27	their carcase shall be unclean until the **e**.	6153
	11:28	his clothes, and be unclean until the **e**.	6153
	11:31	they be dead, shall be unclean until the **e**.	6153
	11:32	and it shall be unclean until the **e**.	6153
	11:39	thereof shall be unclean until the **e**.	6153
	11:40	his clothes, and be unclean until the **e**.	6153
	11:40	his clothes, and be unclean until the **e**.	6153
	13:12	the plague from his head **e** to his foot,	2050.1
	13:18	in which, **e** in the skin thereof, was a boil,	NIH
	13:30	**e** a leprosy upon the head or beard.	NIH
	13:38	flesh bright spots, **e** white bright spots;	NIH
	14: 9	**e** all his hair he shall shave off:	2050.1
	14:31	as he is able to get, the one *for* a sin	NIH
	14:46	it is shut up shall be unclean until the **e**.	6153
	15: 5	in water, and be unclean until the **e**.	6153
	15: 6	in water, and be unclean until the **e**.	6153
	15: 7	in water, and be unclean until the **e**.	6153
	15: 8	in water, and be unclean until the **e**.	6153
	15:10	under him shall be unclean until the **e**:	6153
	15:10	in water, and be unclean until the **e**.	6153
	15:11	in water, and be unclean until the **e**.	6153
	15:16	in water, and be unclean until the **e**.	6153
	15:17	with water, and be unclean until the **e**.	6153

E

Lev		
15:18	in water, and be unclean until the **e**.	6153
15:19	toucheth her shall be unclean until the **e**.	6153
15:21	in water, and be unclean until the **e**.	6153
15:22	in water, and be unclean until the **e**.	6153
15:23	it, he shall be unclean until the **e**.	6153
15:27	in water, and be unclean until the **e**.	6153
16:32	on the linen clothes, **e** the holy garments:	NIH
17: 5	**e** that they may bring them unto	2050.1
17: 9	**e** that man shall be cut off from among	2050.1
17:10	I will **e** set my face against *that* soul that	2050.1
17:13	he shall **e** pour out the blood thereof,	2050.1
17:15	in water, and be unclean until the **e**:	6153
18: 9	**e** their nakedness thou shalt not uncover.	NIH
18:10	their nakedness thou shalt not uncover:	NIH
18:29	the souls that commit *them* shall be	2050.1
19:21	**e** a ram for a trespass offering.	NIH
20: 6	I will **e** set my face against that soul,	2050.1
20:10	**e** he that committeth adultery with his	
22: 6	touched *any* such shall be unclean until **e**,	6153
23: 2	holy convocations, **e** these *are* my feasts.	NIH
23: 4	feasts of the LORD, **e** holy convocations,	NIH
23: 5	the fourteenth *day* of the first month at **e**	6153
23:16	**E** to the morrow after the seventh	5704
23:18	drink offerings, **e** an offering made by fire,	NIH
23:32	in the ninth *day* of the month at **e**,	6153
23:32	from **e** unto even, shall ye celebrate your	6153
23:32	from even unto **e**, shall ye celebrate your	6153
24: 7	**e** an offering made by fire unto the LORD.	NIH
26:16	I will **e** appoint over you terror,	2050.1
26:28	I, **e** I, will chastise you seven *times* for	637
26:34	**e** then shall the land rest, and enjoy her	
26:43	because they despised my judgments,	2050.1
27: 3	the male from twenty years old **e** unto	2050.1
27: 3	**e** thy estimation shall be fifty shekels of	2050.1
27: 5	if *it be* from five years old **e** unto twenty	2050.1
27: 6	if *it be* from a month old **e** unto five	2050.1
27:18	**e** unto the year of the jubile, and it shall	NIH
27:23	estimation, **e** unto the year of the jubile:	NIH
27:24	**e** to him to whom the possession of	NIH
27:32	**e** of whatsoever passeth under the rod,	NIH

Nu		
1:21	**e** of the tribe of Reuben, *were* forty and	NIH
1:23	**e** of the tribe of Simeon, *were* fifty and	NIH
1:25	**e** of the tribe of Gad, *were* forty and	NIH
1:27	**e** of the tribe of Judah, *were* threescore	NIH
1:29	**e** of the tribe of Issachar, *were* fifty and	NIH
1:31	**e** of the tribe of Zebulun, *were* fifty and	NIH
1:33	**e** of the tribe of Ephraim, *were* forty	NIH
1:35	**e** of the tribe of Manasseh, *were* thirty	NIH
1:37	**e** of the tribe of Benjamin, *were* thirty and	NIH
1:39	**e** of the tribe of Dan, *were* threescore and	NIH
1:41	**e** of the tribe of Asher, *were* forty and	NIH
1:43	**e** of the tribe of Naphtali, *were* fifty and	NIH
1:46	**E** all they that were numbered were six	2050.1
3:22	**e** those that were numbered of them *were*	NIH
3:38	**e** before the tabernacle of the congregation	NIH
3:47	Thou shalt **e** take five shekels apiece by	2050.1
4: 3	and upward **e** until fifty years old,	2050.1
4:14	**e** the censers, the fleshhooks,	NIH
4:30	upward **e** unto fifty years old shalt thou	2050.1
4:35	and upward **e** until fifty years old,	2050.1
4:39	and upward **e** unto fifty years old,	2050.1
4:40	**E** those that were numbered of them,	2050.1
4:43	and upward **e** unto fifty years old,	2050.1
4:44	**E** those that were numbered of them	2050.1
4:47	and upward **e** unto fifty years old,	2050.1
4:48	**E** those that were numbered were	2050.1
5: 8	unto the LORD, **e** to the priest;	NIH
5:26	the memorial thereof, and burn *it* upon	NIH
6: 4	tree, from the kernels **e** to the husk.	2050.1
7:10	**e** the princes offered their offering	2050.1
8: 8	**e** fine flour mingled with oil,	NIH
8:16	**e** instead of the firstborn of all the children	NIH
9: 3	In the fourteenth day of this month, at **e**,	6153
9: 5	first month at **e** in the wilderness of Sinai:	6153
9:11	fourteenth day of the second month at **e**	6153
9:13	the same soul shall be cut off from	2050.1
9:15	at **e** there was upon the tabernacle as it	6153
9:21	when the cloud abode from **e** unto	6153
11:20	*But* **e** a whole month, until it come out at	5704
12: 8	**e** apparently, and not in dark speeches;	NIH
14:19	this people, from Egypt **e** until now.	2050.1
14:34	**e** forty days, each day for a year, shall ye	NIH
14:34	**e** forty years, and ye shall know my breach	NIH
14:37	**E** those men that did bring up the evil	2050.1
14:45	and discomfited them, **e** unto Hormah.	NIH
15:23	**E** all that the LORD hath commanded you	NIH
16: 5	**E** to morrow the LORD will shew who *are*	NIH
16: 5	**e** him whom he hath chosen will he	2050.1
17: 6	to their fathers' houses, **e** twelve rods:	NIH
18:21	**e** the service of the tabernacle of	NIH
18:26	it for the LORD, **e** a tenth *part* of the tithe.	NIH
18:29	**e** the hallowed *part* thereof out of it.	NIH
19: 7	and the priest shall be unclean until the **e**.	6153
19: 8	in water, and shall be unclean until the **e**:	6153
19:10	his clothes, and be unclean until the **e**:	6153
19:19	*himself* in water, and shall be clean at **e**.	6153
19:21	of separation shall be unclean until **e**.	6153
19:22	that toucheth *it* shall be unclean until **e**.	6153
20: 1	of Israel, the whole congregation,	NIH
20:22	the whole congregation, journeyed from	NIH
20:29	Aaron thirty days, **e** all the house of Israel.	NIH
21:24	Jabbok, **e** unto the children of Ammon:	NIH
21:26	all his land out of his hand, **e** unto Arnon.	NIH
21:30	Heshbon is perished **e** *unto* Dibon,	5704
21:30	we have laid *them* waste **e** *unto* Nophah,	5704

Nu		
25:13	**e** the covenant of an everlasting priesthood	NIH
25:14	**e** that was slain with the Midianitish	
27:21	Israel with him, **e** all the congregation.	2050.1
28: 4	lamb shalt thou offer at **e**;	996+6153+1886.1
28: 8	lamb shalt thou offer at **e**:	996+6153+1886.1
31:47	**E** of the children of Israel's half,	2050.1
31:51	the gold of them, **e** all wrought jewels.	NIH
32: 4	**E** the country which the LORD smote	NIH
32:33	**e** to the children of Gad, and to the	NIH
32:33	**e** the cities of the country round about.	NIH
33:49	from Beth-jesimoth **e** unto Abel-shittim in	NIH
34: 2	**e** the land of Canaan with the coasts	NIH
34: 6	shall **e** have the great sea for a border:	NIH
36:10	**E** as the LORD commanded	834+3509.1

Dt		
1:44	destroyed you in Seir, **e** unto Hormah.	NIH
2:22	and dwelt in their stead **e** unto this day:	NIH
2:23	**e** unto Azzah, the Caphtorims, which	NIH
2:36	city that *is* by the river, **e** unto Gilead,	2050.1
3:16	unto the Gadites I gave from Gilead **e**	2050.1
3:16	and the border, **e** unto the river Jabbok,	2050.1
3:17	the coast *thereof*, from Chinnereth **e**	2050.1
3:17	the salt sea, under Ashdoth-pisgah	NIH
4: 5	**e** as the LORD my God	834+3509.1
4:13	you to perform, **e** ten commandments;	NIH
4:19	and the stars, **e** all the host of heaven,	NIH
4:20	**e** out of Egypt, to be unto him a people of	NIH
4:24	God *is* a consuming fire, **e** a jealous God.	NIH
4:30	in the latter days, if thou turn to	NIH
4:48	**e** unto mount Sion, which *is* Hermon,	2050.1
4:49	**e** unto the sea of the plain, under	NIH
5: 3	with us, **e** us, who *are* all of us here alive	NIH
5:23	**e** all the heads of your tribes,	NIH
9: 9	**e** the tables of the covenant which	NIH
9:11	of stone, **e** the tables of the covenant.	NIH
9:21	very small, **e** until *it was as* small as dust:	NIH
10:15	**e** you above all people, as *it is* this day.	NIH
11:12	from the beginning of the year **e** unto	2050.1
11:24	**e** unto the uttermost sea shall your	NIH
12: 5	**e** unto his habitation shall ye seek,	NIH
12:22	**E** as the roebuck and the hart is eaten,	389
12:30	serve their gods? **e** so will I do likewise.	2050.1
12:31	for **e** their sons and their daughters they	1571
13: 7	from the *one* end of the earth **e** unto	2050.1
16: 3	bread therewith, **e** the bread of affliction;	NIH
16: 4	which thou sacrificedst the first day at **e**,	6153
16: 6	thou shalt sacrifice the passover at **e**,	6153
17: 5	**e** that man or *that* woman, and shalt stone	NIH
17:12	or unto the judge, *that* man shall die:	2050.1
18:20	of other gods, **e** that prophet shall die.	2050.1
20:14	that is in the city, **e** all the spoil thereof,	NIH
21: 3	**e** the elders of that city shall take a	2050.1
22:26	and slayeth him, **e** so *is* this matter:	3651
23: 2	**e** to his tenth generation shall he not enter	1571
23: 3	**e** to their tenth generation shall they not	1571
23:16	He shall dwell with thee, **e** among you,	1571
23:18	for **e** both these *are* abomination unto	1571
23:23	**e** a freewill offering, according as thou	NIH
25:18	**e** all that were feeble behind thee,	NIH
26: 9	**e** a land that floweth with milk and honey.	NIH
28:59	**e** great plagues, and of long continuance,	NIH
28:64	from the *one* end of the earth **e** unto	2050.1
28:64	fathers have known, **e** wood and stone.	NIH
28:67	thou shalt say, Would God it were **e**!	6153
28:67	at **e** thou shalt say, Would God it were	6153
29:24	**E** all nations shall say, Wherefore hath	2050.1
31:21	imagination which they go about, **e** now,	NIH
32:31	**e** our enemies themselves *being* judges.	2050.1
32:39	**e** I, *am* he, and *there is* no god with me:	NIH
33: 4	**e** the inheritance of the congregation of	NIH

Jos		
1: 2	give to them, **e** to the children of Israel.	NIH
1: 4	and this Lebanon **e** unto the great river,	2050.1
2: 1	Go view the land, **e** Jericho.	2050.1
2:24	for **e** all the inhabitants of the country do	1571
3:11	the Lord of all the earth passeth over	NIH
3:16	the salt sea, failed, *and* were cut off:	NIH
5: 4	*that* were males, **e** all the men of war,	NIH
5:10	of the month at **e** in the plains of Jericho.	6153
6:17	**e** it, and all that *are* therein, to the LORD:	NIH
6:25	she dwelleth in Israel **e** unto this day;	NIH
7: 5	they chased them *from* before the gate **e**	NIH
7:11	they have **e** taken of the accursed thing,	1571
7:11	they have put *it* **e** amongst their own stuff.	1571
8: 4	in wait against the city, **e** behind the city:	NIH
8:11	the *people* of war that *were* with him,	NIH
8:13	**e** all the host that *was* on the north of	NIH
8:25	*were* twelve thousand, **e** all the men of Ai.	NIH
8:28	heap for ever, **e** a desolation unto this day.	NIH
9:20	We will **e** let them live, lest wrath be	NIH
9:27	for the altar of the LORD, **e** unto this day,	NIH
10:41	smote them from Kadesh-barnea **e**	2050.1
10:41	the country of Goshen, **e** unto Gibeon.	2050.1
11: 4	**e** as the sand that *is* upon the sea shore in	NIH
11:17	**E** from the mount Halak, that goeth up *to*	NIH
11:17	**e** unto Baal-gad in the valley of Lebanon	2050.1
12: 2	half Gilead, **e** unto the river Jabbok,	2050.1
12: 3	sea of the plain, **e** the salt sea on the east,	NIH
12: 7	from Baal-gad in the valley of Lebanon **e**	2050.1
13: 3	**e** unto the borders of Ekron northward,	2050.1
13: 8	**e** as Moses the servant of the LORD gave	NIH
13:24	**e** unto the children of Gad according to	NIH
13:27	**e** unto the edge of the sea of Cinnereth on	NIH
13:31	**e** to the one half of the children of Machir	NIH
14:10	**e** since the LORD spake this word unto	NIH
14:11	**e** so *is* my strength now, for war, both	2050.1
15: 1	**e** to the border of Edom, the wilderness of	NIH

Jos		
15: 5	*was* the salt sea, **e** unto the end of Jordan.	NIH
15:13	the city of Arba the father of Anak,	NIH
15:46	From Ekron **e** unto the sea, all that *lay*	2050.1
16: 5	the border of their inheritance on	2050.1
17:11	and her towns, **e** three countries.	NIH
17:17	**e** to Ephraim and to Manasseh, saying,	NIH
19: 1	**e** for the tribe of the children of Simeon	NIH
19:28	Hammon, and Kanah, **e** unto great Zidon,	NIH
19:32	**e** for the children of Naphtali according to	NIH
19:50	**e** Timnath-serah in mount Ephraim:	NIH
21:20	they had **e** the cities of their lot out of	2050.1
23: 4	cut off, **e** *unto* the great sea westward.	2050.1
23:12	**e** these that remain among you,	NIH
24: 2	**e** Terah, the father of Abraham,	NIH
24:12	you, **e** the two kings of the Amorites;	NIH
24:18	the Amorites which dwelt in the land:	2050.1

Jdg		
3: 1	**e** as many *of Israel* as had not known all	NIH
3: 9	them, **e** Othniel the son of Kenaz,	NIH
4:13	**e** nine hundred chariots of iron, and all	NIH
5: 3	ye princes; I, **e** I, will sing unto the LORD;	NIH
5: 5	**e** that Sinai from before the LORD God of	NIH
5:11	**e** the righteous acts *towards* the	NIH
5:15	Deborah; **e** Issachar, *and* also Barak:	2050.1
6: 3	the east, **e** they came up against them;	2050.1
6:25	**e** the second bullock of seven years old,	2050.1
7:22	his fellow, **e** throughout all the host;	2050.1
8:14	**e** threescore and seventeen men.	NIH
8:19	my brethren, **e** the sons of my mother:	NIH
8:27	and put it in his city, **e** in Ophrah:	NIH
9:40	wounded, **e** unto the entering of the gate.	NIH
11:13	from Arnon **e** unto Jabbok,	2050.1
11:22	from Arnon **e** unto Jabbok, and from	2050.1
11:22	and from the wilderness **e** unto Jordan.	2050.1
11:33	**e** till thou come *to* Minnith,	2050.1
11:33	**e** twenty cities, and unto the plain of	NIH
11:36	enemies, **e** of the children of Ammon.	NIH
18:15	**e** unto the house of Micah, and saluted	6153
19:16	man from his work out of the field at **e**,	6153
20: 1	from Dan **e** to Beer-sheba, with the land	2050.1
20: 2	of all the people, **e** of all the tribes of Israel,	NIH
20:23	and wept before the LORD until **e**,	6153
20:26	fasted that day until **e**, and offered burnt	6153
20:33	**e** out of the meadows of Gibeah.	NIH
21: 2	abode there till **e** before God, and lift up	2050.1

Ru		
2: 7	hath continued **e** *from* the morning	227+4480
2:15	Let her glean **e** among the sheaves,	1571
2:17	So she gleaned in the field until **e**,	6153

1Sa		
3:20	all Israel from Dan **e** to Beer-sheba knew	2050.1
5: 6	Ashdod and the coasts thereof.	NIH
6:18	unto the great *stone* of Abel,	2050.1
6:19	**e** he smote of the people fifty thousand	2050.1
7:14	to Israel, from Ekron **e** unto Gath;	2050.1
8: 8	**e** them up out of Egypt **e** unto this day,	2050.1
8:14	**e** the best *of them*, and give *them* to his	NIH
14:21	**e** they also *turned* to be with	2050.1
14:22	**e** they also followed hard after them in	2050.1
17:40	bag which he had, **e** in a scrip;	2050.1
17:52	**e** unto Gath, and unto Ekron.	NIH
18: 4	**e** to his sword, and to his bow, and to	2050.1
18:11	I will smite David **e** to the wall *with it*.	2050.1
19:10	Saul sought to smite David **e** to the wall	2050.1
20: 4	thy soul desireth, I will **e** do *it* for thee.	2050.1
20: 5	myself in the fields unto the third *day* at **e**.	6153
20:16	*saying*, Let the LORD **e** require *it* at	NIH
20:25	as at other times, **e** upon a seat by the wall:	NIH
25:25	regard this man of Belial, **e** Nabal:	5921
25:27	let it **e** be given unto the young men	2050.1
26: 8	with the spear **e** to the earth at once,	2050.1
27: 3	**e** David with his two wives, Ahinoam	NIH
27: 8	goest to Shur, **e** unto the land of Egypt.	2050.1
28: 3	buried him in Ramah, **e** in his own city.	2050.1
28:17	and given it to thy neighbour, **e** to David:	NIH
30:17	David smote them from the twilight **e**	2050.1
30:26	the elders of Judah, **e** to his friends,	NIH

2Sa		
1: 2	It came **e** to pass on the third day, that	2050.1
1:12	wept, and fasted until **e**, for Saul,	6153
2: 5	your lord, **e** unto Saul, and have buried	NIH
3: 9	hath sworn to David, **e** so I do to him;	3588
3:10	over Judah, from Dan **e** to Beer-sheba.	NIH
3:15	**e** from Phaltiel the son of Laish.	NIH
6: 5	**e** on harps, and on psalteries.	2050.1
6:19	**e** among the whole multitude of Israel,	NIH
7: 6	**e** to this day, but have walked in a tent	2050.1
7:23	**e** like Israel, whom God went to redeem	NIH
8: 2	**e** with two lines measured he to put to	2050.1
10: 4	**e** to their buttocks, and sent them away.	NIH
11:13	at **e** he went out to lie on his bed with	6153
11:23	we were upon them **e** unto the entering	NIH
14:25	from the sole of his foot **e** to the crown	2050.1
15:12	from his city, **e** from Giloh,	NIH
15:21	or life, **e** there *also* will thy servant be.	3588
17:11	from Dan **e** to Beer-sheba, as the sand	2050.1
18: 5	with the young man, **e** with Absalom.	NIH
19:11	Israel is come to the king, **e** to his house.	NIH
19:14	men of Judah, **e** as the heart of one man;	NIH
19:32	a very aged man, **e** fourscore years old:	NIH
20: 2	their king, from Jordan **e** to Jerusalem.	2050.1
20:21	his hand against the king, **e** against David:	NIH
22:42	**e** unto the LORD, but he answered them	2050.1
23: 4	sun riseth, **e** a morning without clouds;	NIH
24: 2	from Dan **e** to Beer-sheba, and number	2050.1
24: 7	out to the south of Judah, **e** to Beer-sheba.	NIH
24:15	the morning **e** to the time appointed:	2050.1
24:15	there died of the people from Dan **e** to	NIH

1Ki		
1:26	**e** me thy servant, and Zadok the priest,	NIH

E

1Ki
1:30 **E** as I sware unto thee by the L<small>ORD</small> God 3588
1:30 my stead; **e so** will I certainly do this day. 3588
1:37 **e so** be he with Solomon, and make his 3651
1:48 throne *this* day, mine eyes **e** seeing *it.* 2050.1
2:22 **e** for him, and for Abiathar the priest, 2050.1
4:12 **e** unto *the* place *that is* beyond Jokneam: NIH
4:24 from Tiphsah **e** to Azzah, over all 2050.1
4:25 his fig tree, from Dan **e** to Beer-sheba, 2050.1
4:29 **e** as the sand that *is* on the sea shore. NIH
4:33 from the cedar tree that *is* in Lebanon **e** 2050.1
6:16 he built *them* for it within, *even* for 2050.1
6:16 **e** for the oracle, *even* for the most holy NIH
6:16 for the oracle, **e** for the most holy *place.* NIH
7: 7 he might judge, **e** the porch of judgment: NIH
7: 9 **e** from the foundation unto the coping, 2050.1
7:10 **e** great stones, stones of ten cubits, NIH
7:42 **e** two rows *of* pomegranates for one NIH
7:51 **e** the silver, and the gold, and the vessels, NIH
8: 4 **e** those did the priests and the Levites 2050.1
8: 6 to the most holy *place,* **e** under the wings NIH
8:29 **e** toward the place of which thou hast said, NIH
8:39 (for thou, **e** thou only, knowest the hearts NIH
8:65 seven days and seven days, **e** fourteen days. NIH
11:26 **e** he lift up *his* hand against the king. 2050.1
11:35 and will give it unto thee, **e** ten tribes. NIH
12:27 **e** unto Rehoboam king of Judah, NIH
12:30 to worship before the one, **e** unto Dan. NIH
12:33 **e** in the month which he had devised of NIH
13:34 **e** to cut *it* off, and to destroy *it* from off 2050.1
14:14 of Jeroboam that day: but what? **e** now. 1571
14:26 of the king's house; he **e** took away all: 2050.1
15:13 **e** her he removed from *being* queen, NIH
15:28 **E** in the third year of Asa king of Judah 2050.1
16: 7 **e** for all the evil that he did in the sight 2050.1
18:22 I, **e I** only, remain a prophet of the L<small>ORD</small>; NIH
18:26 of Baal from morning **e** until noon, 2050.1
19:10 I, **e I** only, am left; and they seek my life, NIH
19:14 I, **e I** only, am left; and they seek my life, NIH
20: 3 thy children, **e** the goodliest, *are* mine. NIH
20:14 **E** by the young men of the princes of NIH
20:15 **e** all the children of Israel, *being* seven NIH
21:11 **e** the elders and the nobles who *were* NIH
21:13 **e** against Naboth, in the presence of NIH
21:19 Naboth shall dogs lick thy blood, **e** thine. 1571
22:35 chariot against the Syrians, and died at **e:** 6153

2Ki
3:24 smiting the Moabites, **e** in their country. 2050.1
3:26 to break through **e** unto the king of Edom: NIH
4: 3 of all thy neighbours, **e** empty vessels; NIH
5:22 **e now** there be come to me from 2088+6258
7: 6 noise of horses, **e** the noise of a great host: NIH
7: 7 the camp as it *was,* and fled for their life. NIH
7:13 I say, they *are* **e** as all the multitude of 2050.1
8: 6 day that she left the land, **e** until now. 2050.1
8: 9 **e** of every good thing of Damascus, 2050.1
9: 4 young man, the young man the prophet, NIH
9: 6 the people of the L<small>ORD</small>, **e** over Israel. NIH
9:20 he came **e** unto them, and cometh not 5704
10: 3 Look **e** out the best and meetest of your 2050.1
10:14 the shearing house, **e** two and forty men; NIH
10:33 the river Arnon, **e** Gilead and Bashan. 2050.1
11: 2 they hid him, **e** him and his nurse, NIH
11: 5 be keepers of the watch of the king's 2050.1
11: 7 **e** they shall keep the watch of the house 2050.1
12: 4 **e** the money of every one that passeth NIH
14:10 fall, **e** thou, and Judah with thee? NIH
14:29 with his fathers, **e** with the kings of Israel; NIH
15:20 **e** of all the mighty *men* of wealth, of each NIH
17:16 two calves, and made a grove, NIH
18: 8 **e** unto Gaza, and the borders thereof, NIH
18:10 **e** in the sixth year of Hezekiah, that *is* NIH
18:21 **e** upon Egypt, on which if a man lean, NIH
19:15 thou *art* the God, **e** thou alone, of all NIH
19:19 that thou *art* the L<small>ORD</small> God, **e** thou only. NIH
19:22 on high? **e** against the Holy One of Israel. NIH
20:14 come from a far country, **e** from Babylon. NIH
21:15 came forth out of Egypt, **e** unto this day. 2050.1
22:16 **e** all the words of the book which the king NIH
24:14 **e** ten thousand captives, and all NIH
24:16 **e** seven thousand, and craftsmen and NIH
24:16 **e** them the king of Babylon brought 2050.1
25:22 **e** over them he made Gedaliah the son 2050.1
25:23 **e** Ishmael the son of Nethaniah, NIH

1Ch
2:23 and the towns thereof, **e** threescore cities. NIH
4:15 Naam: and the sons of Elah, **e** Kenaz. 2050.1
4:39 **e** unto the east *side* of the valley, to seek NIH
4:42 **e** of the sons of Simeon, five hundred NIH
5: 8 in Aroer, **e** unto Nebo and Baal-meon: 2050.1
5:24 **e** Epher, and Ishi, and Eliel, and Azriel, NIH
5:26 **e** the Reubenites, and the Gadites, 3807.1
6:39 **e** Asaph the son of Berachiah, the son of NIH
10:13 **e** against the word of the L<small>ORD</small>, which he NIH
11: 2 in time past, **e** when Saul was king, 1571
11: 8 **e** from Millo round about: 5704+2050.1
12: 2 of a bow, **e** of Saul's brethren of Benjamin. NIH
12:40 **even** Issachar and Zebulun and Naphtali, NIH
13: 5 from Shihor of Egypt **e** unto the entering 2050.1
14:16 from Gibeon **e** to Gazer. 5704+2050.1
16:16 **E** of the covenant which he made with NIH
16:19 *but* few, **e** a few, and strangers in it. 3509.1
17: 7 sheepcote, **e** from following the sheep, NIH
17:24 Let it be established, that thy name NIH
17:24 *is* the God of Israel, **e** a God to Israel: NIH
20: 3 **E so** dealt David with all the cities of 2050.1
21: 2 Israel from Beer-sheba **e** to Dan; 2050.1
21:12 **e** the pestilence, in the land, and the 2050.1

21:17 **e** I *it is* that have sinned and done evil 2050.1
23:24 the chief of the fathers, as they were NIH
23:30 and praise the L<small>ORD</small>, and likewise at **e**; 6153
24:31 **e** the principal fathers over against their NIH
25: 7 **e** all that were cunning, was two hundred NIH
26:12 **e** among the chief men, *having* wards one NIH
26: 2 **e** of Laadan the Gershonite, *were* Jehieli. NIH
26:31 **e** among the Hebronites, according to NIH
28:15 **E** the weight for the candlesticks of gold 2050.1
28:19 upon me, **e** all the works of *this* pattern. NIH
28:20 L<small>ORD</small> God, **e** my God, *will* be with thee; NIH
28:21 **e** they shall be with thee for all the service NIH
29: 4 **E** three thousand talents of gold, of the NIH
29:21 **e** a thousand bullocks, a thousand rams, NIH

2Ch
2: 3 to dwell therein, **e so** deal with me. NIH
2: 9 **E** to prepare me timber in abundance: 2050.1
5: 9 The most holy *place,* **e** under the wings NIH
5:13 It came **e** to pass, as the trumpeters and 2050.1
5:13 *with* a cloud, **e** the house of the L<small>ORD</small>; NIH
6:21 from thy dwelling place, **e** from heaven; NIH
6:33 **e** from thy dwelling place, and do NIH
6:39 **e** from thy dwelling place, their prayer NIH
8:10 two hundred and fifty, that bare rule NIH
8:13 **E** after a certain rate every day, offering 2050.1
8:13 **e** in the feast of unleavened bread, NIH
9:26 river **e** unto the land of the Philistines, 2050.1
11: 6 He built **e** Beth-lehem, and Etam, 2050.1
13: 3 **e** four hundred thousand chosen men: NIH
13: 5 **e** to him and to his sons *by* a covenant of NIH
17: 7 **e** to Ben-hail, and to Obadiah, NIH
17: 8 **e** Shemaiah, and Nethaniah, and Zebadiah, NIH
18:13 what my God saith, that will I speak. 3588
18:21 shalt also prevail: go out, and do **e** so. NIH
18:34 his chariot against the Syrians until the **e**: 6153
19:10 ye shall **e** warn them that they trespass 2050.1
20: 4 **e** out of all the cities of Judah they came 1571
24:14 **e** vessels to minister, and to offer *withal,* NIH
25:13 from Samaria **e** unto Beth-horon, 2050.1
25:19 fall, **e** thou, and Judah with thee? NIH
26: 8 his name spread abroad **e** to the entering 5704
26:19 the leprosy **e** rose up in his forehead NIH
28:10 *are there* not *with* you, **e** with you, NIH
28:27 they buried him in the city, **e** in Jerusalem: NIH
30: 5 all Israel, from Beer-sheba **e** to Dan, 2050.1
30:10 and Manasseh **e** unto Zebulun: 2050.1
30:18 **e** many of Ephraim, and Manasseh, NIH
30:27 to his holy dwelling place, **e** unto heaven. NIH
31:16 **e** unto every one that entereth into the NIH
33:14 **e** to the entering in at the fish gate, 2050.1
34: 6 Ephraim, and Simeon, **e** unto Naphtali, 2050.1
34:11 **E** to the artificers and builders gave they 2050.1
34:24 **e** all the curses that are written in the NIH
34:27 have **e** heard *thee* also, saith the L<small>ORD</small>. NIH
34:33 to serve, **e** to serve the L<small>ORD</small> their God. NIH

Ezr
1: 8 **E** those did Cyrus king of Persia bring 2050.1
3: 3 **e** burnt offerings morning and evening. NIH
4: 5 **e** until the reign of Darius king of Persia. 2050.1
4:11 unto him, **e** unto Artaxerxes the king: NIH
5: 1 name of the God of Israel, **e** unto them. NIH
5:16 since that time **e** until now *hath it been* 2050.3
6: 8 **e** of the tribute beyond the river, NIH
7:11 **e** a scribe of the words of NIH
7:21 I, **e I** Artaxerxes the king, do make a NIH
8:25 **e** the offering of the house of our God, NIH
8:26 I weighed unto their hand six 2050.1
9: 1 **e** of the Canaanites, the Hittites, NIH

Ne
2:13 **e** before the dragon well, and to the 2050.1
3: 1 **e** unto the tower of Meah they 2050.1
3:10 of Harumaph, **e** over against his house. 2050.1
3:21 from the door of the house of Eliashib **e** 2050.1
3:24 turning *of the wall,* **e** unto the corner. 2050.1
3:27 that lieth out, **e** unto the wall of Ophel. NIH
4: 3 said, **E** *that* which they build, if a fox go 1571
4: 3 he shall **e** break down their stone wall. 2050.1
4:13 I **e** set the people after *their* families 2050.1
5: 8 and will you **e** sell your brethren? NIH
5:11 Restore, I pray you, to them, **e** this day, 3509.1
5:13 **e** thus be he shaken out, and emptied. 2050.1
5:14 from the twentieth year **e** unto the two 2050.1
5:15 yea, **e** their servants bare rule over 1571
8:13 **e** to understand the words of the law. 2050.1
9: 6 Thou, **e** thou, *art* L<small>ORD</small> alone; thou hast NIH
12:23 **e** until the days of Johanan the son of 2050.1
12:37 David, **e** unto the water gate east*ward.* NIH
12:38 from beyond the tower of the furnaces **e** 2050.1
12:39 tower of Meah, **e** unto the sheep gate. 2050.1
12:43 of Jerusalem was heard **e afar off.** 4480+7350
13:26 nevertheless did outlandish women 1571

Est
1: 1 from India **e** unto Ethiopia, *over* an 2050.1
1: 4 **e** an hundred and fourscore days. NIH
2:18 and his servants, **e** Esther's feast; NIH
3: 6 of Ahasuerus, **e** the people of Mordecai. NIH
3:13 upon the thirteenth *day* of the twelfth 5704
4: 2 came **e** before the king's gate: for none 5704
5: 3 it shall be **e** given thee to the half of 2050.1
5: 6 **e** to the half of the kingdom it shall be 5704
6:10 said, and do **e** so to Mordecai the Jew, NIH
7: 2 performed, **e** to the half of the kingdom. NIH

Job
4: 8 **E** as I have seen, they that plow 834+3509.1
4:21 go away? they die, **e** without wisdom. 2050.1
5: 5 taketh it **e** out of the thorns, and the NIH
6: 9 **E** that it would please God to destroy 2050.1
10:21 to the land of darkness and the shadow NIH
15:26 He runneth upon him, **e** on *his* neck, NIH
17: 5 the eyes of his children shall fail. 2050.1

17:11 are broken off, **e** the thoughts of my heart. NIH
18:13 **e** the firstborn of death shall devour his. NIH
21: 6 **E** when I remember I am afraid, 2050.1
23: 2 **E** to day *is* my complaint bitter: my stroke 1571
23: 3 find him! *that* I might come **e** to his seat! NIH
23:13 what his soul desireth, **e** *that* he doeth. 2050.1
24:17 the morning *is* to them **e** as the shadow 3162
25: 5 Behold **e** to the moon, and it shineth not; NIH
28: 4 **e** the waters forgotten of the foot: NIH
31: 6 Let me be weighed in an **e** balance, 6664
34:17 Shall **e** he that hateth right govern? 637
36:16 **E so** would he have removed thee out NIH
41: 9 shall *not one* be cast down **e** at the sight 1571
42:16 and his sons' sons, **e** four generations. NIH

Ps
18: 6 my cry came before him, **e** into his ears. NIH
18:41 *there was* none to save *them:* **e** unto NIH
21: 4 it him, **e** length of days for ever and ever. 2050.1
24: 9 **e** lift *them* up, ye everlasting doors; 2050.1
26:12 My foot standeth in an **e** place; 4334
27: 2 the wicked, **e** mine enemies and my foes, NIH
35:23 **e** unto my cause, my God and my Lord. NIH
39: T **e** to Jeduthun, A Psalm of David. NIH
39: 2 silence, I held my peace, **e** from good; NIH
40: 3 song in my mouth, **e** praise unto our God: NIH
45:12 the rich among the people shall intreat NIH
47: 9 **e** the people of the God of Abraham: NIH
48:14 ever: he will be our guide **e** unto death. NIH
50: 1 **e** the L<small>ORD</small>, hath spoken, and called NIH
50: 7 testify against thee: I *am* God, **e** thy God. NIH
55:19 afflict them, **e** he that abideth of old. 2050.1
57: 4 and I lie **e** among them that are set on fire, NIH
57: 4 **e** the sons of men, whose teeth *are* spears NIH
59:12 words of their lips let them **e** be taken 2050.1
64: 3 bows *to* shoot their arrows, **e** bitter words: NIH
65: 4 of thy house, **e** of thy holy temple. NIH
67: 6 and God, *our* own God, shall bless us. NIH
68: 8 **e** Sinai itself *was* moved at the presence of NIH
68:17 twenty thousand, **e** thousands of angels: NIH
68:19 *who* daily loadeth us *with benefits,* **e** NIH
68:24 **e** the goings of my God, my King, NIH
68:26 **e** the Lord, from the fountain of Israel. NIH
71:16 of thy righteousness, **e** of thine only. NIH
71:22 with the psaltery, **e** thy truth, O my God: NIH
73: 1 to Israel, **e** to such as are of a clean heart. NIH
74: 3 **e** all *that* the enemy hath done wickedly NIH
74:11 thou thy hand, **e** thy right hand? 2050.1
76: 7 Thou, **e** thou, *art* to be feared: and who NIH
77: 1 *with* my voice, **e** unto God *with* my voice; NIH
78: 6 the children *which* should be born; NIH
78:54 **e** to this mountain, *which* his right hand NIH
84: 2 yea, **e** fainteth for the courts of the L<small>ORD</small>: 1571
84: 3 **e** thine altars, O L<small>ORD</small> of hosts, my King, NIH
90: 2 **e** from everlasting to everlasting, 2050.1
90:11 according to thy fear, *so is* thy wrath. 2050.1
91: 9 refuge, **e** the most High, thy habitation; NIH
105:17 **e** Joseph, *who* was sold for a servant: NIH
105:20 the ruler of the people, and let him go NIH
106: 7 provoked *him* at the sea, **e** at the Red sea. NIH
106:38 the blood of their sons and of their NIH
107:43 will observe these *things,* **e** they shall 2050.1
108: 1 I will sing and give praise, **e** *with* my glory. 637
109:16 he might **e** slay the broken in heart. 2050.1
113: 8 **e** with the princes of his people. NIH
115:16 The heaven, **e** the heavens, NIH
118:27 with cords, **e** unto the horns of the altar. NIH
119:41 O L<small>ORD</small>, **e** thy salvation, according to thy NIH
119:112 thy statutes alway, **e** unto the end. NIH
121: 8 from this time forth, **e** for evermore. NIH
125: 2 his people from henceforth **e** for ever. 2050.1
131: 2 mother: my soul *is* **e** as a weaned child. NIH
133: 2 down upon the beard, **e** Aaron's beard: NIH
133: 3 the blessing, **e** life for evermore. NIH
136:22 **E** an heritage unto Israel his servant: NIH
137: 7 Rase it, rase *it,* **e** to the foundation thereof. 1571
139:10 **E** there shall thy hand lead me, 1571
139:11 **e** the night *shall be* light about me. 2050.1
146:10 **e** thy God, O Zion, unto all generations. NIH
148:14 **e** of the children of Israel, a people near NIH

Pr
2:16 **e** from the stranger *which* flattereth with 2050.1
3:12 **e** as a father the son *in whom* he NIH
8:16 and nobles, **e** all the judges of the earth. NIH
14:13 **E** in laughter the heart is sorrowful; 1571
14:20 The poor is hated **e** of his own neighbour: 1571
16: 4 the wicked for the day of evil. 1571
16: 7 he maketh **e** his enemies to be at peace 1571
17:15 **e** they both *are* abomination to the L<small>ORD</small>. 1571
17:28 A fool, when he holdeth his peace, 1571
20:11 **E** a child is known by his doings, 1571
20:12 the L<small>ORD</small> hath made **e** both of them. 1571
22:19 made known to thee *this* day, **e** to thee. 637
23:15 be wise, my heart shall rejoice, **e** mine. 1571
28: 9 law, **e** his prayer *shall be* abomination. 1571
30: 1 of Agur the son of Jakeh, **e** the prophecy: NIH
30: 1 spake unto Ithiel, **e** unto Ithiel and Ucal. NIH

Ecc
2:12 **e** that which hath been already done. NIH
2:15 to the fool, so it happeneth **e** to me; NIH
3:19 **e** one thing befalleth them: 2050.1
4:16 of all that have been before them: NIH
7:25 of folly, **e** of foolishness and madness: 2050.1
9: 1 For all this I considered in my heart **e** to 2050.1
11: 5 **e so** thou knowest not the works of God 3602
12:10 written *was* upright, **e** words of truth. NIH

SS
4: 2 *are* like a flock of *sheep that are* **e shorn,** 7094

Isa
1: 6 the sole of the foot **e** unto the head 2050.1
1:13 *it is* iniquity, **e** the solemn meeting. 2050.1

E

Isa
4: 3 *e* every one that is written among the NIH
5: 9 *e* great and fair, without inhabitant. NIH
7: 6 king in the midst of it, *e* the son of Tabeal: NIH
7:17 departed from Judah; *e* the king of Assyria. NIH
7:23 it shall *e* be for briers and thorns. NIH
8: 7 *e* the king of Assyria, and all his glory: NIH
8: 8 and go over, he shall reach *e* to the neck; NIH
9: 7 with justice from henceforth *e* for ever. 2050.1
9: 9 *e* Ephraim and the inhabitant of Samaria, NIH
10:21 the remnant of Jacob, unto the mighty NIH
10:23 *e* determined, *in* the midst of all 2050.1
13: 3 *e* them that rejoice in my highness. NIH
13: 5 *e* the Lord, and the weapons of his NIH
13:12 *e* a man than the golden wedge of 2050.1
14: 9 for thee, *e* all the chief ones of the earth; NIH
14:18 of the nations, *e* all of them, lie in glory, NIH
15: 4 their voice shall be heard *e* unto Jahaz. NIH
16: 6 of his haughtiness, and his pride, NIH
16: 8 are come *e* unto Jazer, they wandered NIH
18: 2 *e* in vessels of bulrushes upon the 2050.1
19:13 *e they that are* the stay of the tribes NIH
19:22 and they shall return *e* to the Lord, NIH
19:24 *e* a blessing in the midst of the land: NIH
20: 4 *e* with *their* buttocks uncovered, 2050.1
22:15 *e* unto Shebna, which *is* over the house, NIH
22:24 of cups, *e* to all the vessels of flagons. 2050.1
23: 4 *e* the strength of the sea, saying, I travail NIH
24:15 *e* the name of the Lord God of Israel in NIH
24:16 we heard songs, *e* glory to the righteous. NIH
25: 5 *e* the heat with the shadow of a cloud: NIH
25:10 *e* as straw is trodden down for the NIH
25:12 *and* bring to the ground, *e* to the dust. NIH
26: 5 it low; he layeth it low, *e* to the ground; NIH
26: 5 to the ground; he bringeth it *e* to the dust. NIH
26: 6 *e* the feet of the poor, and the steps of NIH
27: 1 *e* leviathan *that* crooked serpent; 2050.1
28:22 *e* determined upon the whole earth. 2050.1
29: 7 *e* all that fight against her and 2050.1
29: 8 It shall *e* be as when a hungry *man* NIH
29:14 *e* a marvellous work and a wonder: NIH
32: 7 *e* when the needy speaketh right. 2050.1
35: 2 rejoice *e* with joy and singing; 637
35: 4 vengeance, *e* God *with* a recompence; NIH
37:16 thou *art* the God, *e* thou alone, of all NIH
37:20 know that thou *art* the Lord, *e* thou only. NIH
37:23 on high? *e* against the Holy One of Israel. NIH
38:11 the Lord, in the land of the living: NIH
38:12 from day *e* to night wilt thou make an end NIH
38:13 from day *e* to night wilt thou make an end NIH
39: 3 a far country unto me, *e* from Babylon. NIH
40:30 E the youths shall faint and be weary, 2050.1
41: 3 *e by* the way *that* he had not gone with his NIH
41:12 them, *e* them that contended with thee: NIH
41:28 *e* amongst them, and *there was* no 2050.1
43: 7 E every one that is called by my name: NIH
43:11 I, *e I, am* the Lord; and beside me *there* NIH
43:19 I will *e* make a way in the wilderness, 637
43:25 I, *e I, am* he that blotteth out thy NIH
44: 8 declared *it? ye* are *e* my witnesses. 2050.1
44:17 he maketh a god, *e* his graven image: NIH
44:28 *e* saying to Jerusalem, Thou shalt be 2050.1
45: 4 I have *e* called thee by thy name: NIH
45:12 I, *e* my hands, have stretched out NIH
45:24 to him shall *men* come; and all that are NIH
46: 4 *e* to *your* old age I *am* he; and *even* to NIH
46: 4 *e* to hoar hairs will I carry *you: I* have NIH
46: 4 I will carry, and will deliver *you.* 2050.1
47:15 *e* thy merchants, from thy youth: NIH
48: 5 I have *e* from the beginning declared *it* 2050.1
48: 6 *e* hidden *things,* and thou didst not 2050.1
48: 7 *e* before the day when thou heardest 2050.1
48:11 For mine own sake, *e* for mine own sake, NIH
48:15 I, *e I,* have spoken; yea, I have called him: NIH
48:20 tell this, utter it *e* to the end of the earth; NIH
49:10 *e* by the springs of water shall he guide 2050.1
49:19 shall *e* now be too narrow by reason of 3588
49:25 E the captives of the mighty shall be taken 1571
51:12 I, *e I, am* he that comforteth you: who *art* NIH
51:22 the dregs of the cup of my fury; NIH
55: 3 with you, *e* the sure mercies of David. NIH
56: 5 E unto them will I give in mine house 2050.1
56: 7 E them will I bring to my holy mountain, 2050.1
57: 6 *e* to them hast thou poured a drink 1571
57: 7 *e* thither wentest thou up to offer sacrifice. 1571
57: 9 far off, and didst debase *thyself* unto hell. NIH
57:11 have not I held my peace *e* of old, 2050.1
65: 6 *e* recompense into their bosom, 2050.1
66: 2 *e* to *him that is* poor and of a contrite NIH

Jer
3:25 from our youth *e* unto this day, 2050.1
4:12 E a full wind from those *places* shall NIH
6:11 for *e* the husband with the wife shall be 1571
6:13 For from the least of them *e* unto 2050.1
6:13 from the prophet *e* unto the priest 2050.1
6:19 *e* the fruit of their thoughts, because NIH
7:11 Behold, *e* I have seen *it,* saith the Lord. 1571
7:15 brethren, *e* the whole seed of Ephraim. NIH
7:25 I have *e* sent unto you all my servants NIH
8:10 *e* unto the greatest is given to 2050.1
8:10 from the prophet *e* unto the priest every 2050.1
9:15 Behold, I will *e* feed them, *even* this people, NIH
9:22 E the carcases of men shall fall as dung 2050.1
10:11 *e* they shall perish from the earth, NIH
11: 7 *e* unto this day, rising early and protesting, NIH
11:13 *e* altars to burn incense unto Baal. NIH
11:23 of Anathoth, *e* the year of their visitation. NIH

Jer
12: 6 For *e* thy brethren, and the house of thy 1571
12: 6 *e* they have dealt treacherously with thee; 1571
12:12 the land *e* to the *other* end of the land: 2050.1
13:10 worship them, shall *e* be as this girdle, 2050.1
13:13 *e* the kings that sit upon David's throne, 2050.1
13:14 *e* the fathers and the sons together, 2050.1
13:18 come down, *e* the crown of your glory. 2050.1
15:13 *that* for all thy sins, *e* in all thy borders. 2050.1
16: 5 the Lord, *e* lovingkindness and mercies. 2050.1
17: 4 thou, *e* thyself, shalt discontinue from 2050.1
17:10 *e* to give every man according to his 2050.1
17:27 *e* entering in at the gates of Jerusalem 2050.1
19:11 E so will I break this people and this city, 3602
19:12 and make this city as Tophet: NIH
21: 5 *e* in anger, and in fury, and in great 2050.1
22:25 *e* into the hand of Nebuchadrezzar 2050.1
23:12 *e* the year of their visitation, saith 2050.1
23:19 forth *in* fury, *e* a grievous whirlwind: NIH
23:33 I will *e* forsake you, saith the Lord. 2050.1
23:34 I will *e* punish that man and his house. 2050.1
23:39 behold, I, *e* I, will utterly forget 2050.1
24: 2 good figs, *e* like the figs *that are* first ripe: NIH
25: 3 unto this day, that *is* the three and 2050.1
25:13 *e* all that is written in this book, which NIH
25:31 A noise shall come *e* to the ends of NIH
25:33 earth *e* unto the *other* end of the earth: 2050.1
28: 6 E the prophet Jeremiah said, Amen: 2050.1
28:11 E so will I break the yoke of 3602
29:23 *e* I know, and *am* a witness, saith 2050.1
30: 7 it *is e* the time of Jacob's trouble: NIH
31: 2 *e* Israel when *I* went to cause him to rest. NIH
31:19 yea, *e* confounded, because I did bear 2050.1
31:21 highway, *e* the way *which* thou wentest: NIH
32: 9 the money, *e* seventeen shekels of silver. NIH
32:20 *even* unto this day, and in Israel, NIH
32:31 my fury from the day that they built it *e* 2050.1
33:10 *e* in the cities of Judah, and in the streets NIH
33:24 hath chosen, he hath *e* cast them off? 2050.1
34:20 I will *e* give them into the hand of their 2050.1
36: 2 from the days of Josiah, *e* unto this day. 2050.1
36:12 *e* Elishama the scribe, and Delaiah the son NIH
39: 3 *e* Nergal-sharezer, Samgar-nebo, NIH
39:12 *e as* he shall say unto thee. 834+3651+3509.1
39:14 They sent, and took Jeremiah out of 2050.1
40: 7 *were* in the fields, *e* they and their men, NIH
40: 8 *e* Ishmael the son of Nethaniah, 2050.1
40:12 E all the Jews returned out of all places 2050.1
41: 1 of the king, *e* ten men with him, 2050.1
41: 3 *e* with Gedaliah at Mizpah, NIH
41: 5 and from Samaria, *e* fourscore men, NIH
41:10 the king's daughters, and all the people NIH
41:16 *e* mighty men of war, and the women, NIH
42: 1 all the people from the least *e* unto 2050.1
42: 2 the Lord thy God, *e* for all this remnant, NIH
42: 5 if we do **not** *e* according to all things *for* 3808
42: 8 all the people from the least *e* to 2050.1
43: 1 I had sent him to them, *e* all these words; NIH
43: 6 E men, and women, and children, NIH
43: 7 the Lord: thus came they *e* to Tahpanhes. NIH
44:10 They are not humbled *e* unto this day, NIH
44:12 they shall *e* be consumed by the sword, NIH
44:12 from the least *e* unto the greatest, 2050.1
44:15 *e* all the people that dwelt in the land 2050.1
45: 4 I *will* pluck up, *e* this whole land. 2050.1
46:25 *e* Pharaoh, and *all* them that trust in 2050.1
48:32 the sea, they reach *e* to the sea of Jazer: NIH
48:34 From the cry of Heshbon *e* unto Elealeh, NIH
48:34 *and e* unto Jahaz, have they uttered their NIH
48:34 from Zoar *e* unto Horonaim, *as* a heifer of NIH
48:44 for I will bring upon it, *e* upon Moab, NIH
49:37 *e* my fierce anger, saith the Lord; NIH
50: 7 the habitation of justice, *e* the Lord, 2050.1
50:21 *e* against it, and against the inhabitants of NIH
51: 9 unto heaven, and is lifted up *e* to the skies. NIH
51:56 *e* upon Babylon, and her mighty *men* are NIH
51:60 *e* all these words that are written against NIH

La
4: 3 E the sea monsters draw out the breast, 1571

Eze
1:27 from the appearance of his loins *e* 2050.1
1:27 from the appearance of his loins *e* 2050.1
2: 3 against me, *e* unto this very day. 2050.1
4: 1 and pourtray upon it *the* city, *e* Jerusalem: NIH
4:13 E thus shall the children of Israel eat their 3602
4:14 for from my youth up *e* till now have I 2050.1
5: 8 Behold, I, *e I, am* against thee, 1571
6: 3 I, *e I, will* bring a sword upon you, NIH
7:14 blown the trumpet, *e* to make all ready; 2050.1
8: 2 from the appearance of his loins 2050.1
8: 2 from his loins *e* upward, 2050.1
8: 6 *e* the great abominations that the house NIH
9: 1 *e* every man *with* his destroying weapon 2050.1
10: 2 *e* under the cherub, and fill thine hand NIH
10: 5 wings was heard *e* to the utter court, 2050.1
10:12 *e* the wheels that they four had. NIH
11:15 Son of man, thy brethren, *e* thy brethren, NIH
11:17 I will *e* gather you from the people, 2050.1
12: 4 thou shalt go forth at *e* in their sight, 6153
12: 7 in the *e* I digged through the wall with 6153
13:10 because they have seduced my people 2050.1
13:13 I will *e* rent *it with* a stormy wind in NIH
13:20 *e* the souls that ye hunt to catch *them* fly. NIH
14:10 *e as* the punishment of him that seeketh 3509.1
14:22 *e* concerning all that I have brought upon NIH
16:19 thou hast *e* set it before them for a 2050.1
16:37 I will *e* gather them round about 2050.1
16:59 will *e* deal with thee as thou hast done, 2050.1

Eze
17: 9 *e* without great power or many people 2050.1
17:16 *e* with him in the midst of Babylon he NIH
17:19 *e* it will I recompense upon his own 2050.1
18:11 but *e* hath eaten upon the mountains, 1571
18:18 lo, *e* he shall die in his iniquity. 2050.1
20:11 *if* a man do, he shall *e* live in them: 2050.1
20:13 *if* a man do, he shall *e* live in them: 2050.1
20:21 *if* a man do, he shall *e* live in them: 2050.1
20:31 with all your idols, *e* unto *this* day: NIH
21:13 what if *the sword* contemn *e* the rod? 1571
21:28 *e* say thou, The sword, the sword *is* 2050.1
22: 4 draw near, and art come *e* unto thy years: NIH
22:18 the furnace; they are *e the* dross *of* silver. NIH
23:34 Thou shalt *e* drink it and suck *it* out, 2050.1
24: 2 the name of the day, *e* of this same day: NIH
24: 4 *e* every good piece, the thigh, NIH
24: 9 I will *e* make the pile for fire great. 1571
24:18 at *e* my wife died; and I did in the 6153
29:10 the tower of Syene *e* unto the border 2050.1
30: 3 *e* the day of the Lord *is* near, a cloudy 2050.1
32: 6 thou swimmest, *e* to the mountains; NIH
32:16 *e* for Egypt, and for all her multitude, NIH
32:18 *e* her, and the daughters of the famous NIH
32:31 *e* Pharaoh and all his army slain by NIH
32:32 *e* Pharaoh and all his multitude, saith NIH
33:18 he shall *e* die thereby. 2050.1
34:11 Behold, I, *e I,* will both search my sheep, NIH
34:20 Behold, I, *e I,* will judge between the fat NIH
34:23 he shall feed them, *e* my servant David; NIH
34:30 that they, *e* the house of Israel, *are* my NIH
35: 6 hated blood, *e* blood shall pursue thee. 2050.1
35:11 I will *e* do according to thine anger, 2050.1
35:15 O mount Seir, and all Idumea, *e* all of it: NIH
36: 2 *e* the ancient high places are ours in 2050.1
36:10 upon you, all the house of Israel, *e* all of it: NIH
36:12 men to walk upon you, *e* my people Israel; NIH
37:19 *e* with the stick of Judah, and make them NIH
37:25 *e* they, and their children, NIH
38: 4 *armour, e* a great company *with* bucklers NIH
39:17 *e* a great sacrifice upon the mountains of NIH
40:14 *e* unto the post of the court round about 2050.1
41:17 *e* unto the inner house, and without, 2050.1
42:12 *e* the way directly before the wall toward NIH
43: 1 *e* the gate that looketh toward the east: NIH
43: 3 *e* according to the vision that I saw when NIH
43: 8 they have *e* defiled my holy name by 2050.1
43:13 *e* the bottom *shall be* a cubit, 2050.1
43:14 from the bottom *upon* the ground *e* to NIH
43:14 from the lesser settle *e* to the greater settle NIH
44: 6 to the house of Israel, Thus saith the NIH
44: 7 in my sanctuary, to pollute it, *e* my house, NIH
44:10 idols; they shall *e* bear their iniquity. 2050.1
44:19 *e* into the utter court to the people, NIH
47:10 upon it from En-gedi *e* unto En-eglaim; 2050.1
47:19 from Tamar *e* to the waters of strife *in* NIH
48: 3 from the east side *e* unto the west side, 2050.1
48: 6 from the east side *e* unto the west side, NIH
48:10 them, *e* for the priests, shall be *this* holy NIH
48:28 the border shall be *e* from Tamar unto 2050.1

Da
1:21 Daniel continued *e* unto the first year of NIH
2:43 another, *e* as iron is not mixed with clay. 1888
4:15 *e* with a band of iron and brass, 2050.3
4:23 *e* with a band of iron and brass, 2050.3
5:14 I have *e* heard of thee, that the spirit of 2050.3
6:26 and his dominion *shall be e* unto the end. NIH
7:11 I beheld *e till* the beast *was* slain, NIH
7:18 kingdom for ever, *e* for ever and ever. 2050.3
7:20 *e* of that horn that had eyes, and a 2050.3
8: 1 *e unto* me Daniel, after that which NIH
8:10 it waxed great, *e* to the host of heaven; NIH
8:11 he magnified *himself e* to the prince of NIH
8:15 when I, *e I* Daniel, had seen the vision, NIH
9: 5 *e* by departing from thy precepts and 2050.1
9:11 *e* by departing, that *they* might not obey 2050.1
9:21 speaking in prayer, *e* the man Gabriel, 2050.1
9:25 and the wall, *e* in troublous times. 2050.1
9:27 *e* until the consummation, 2050.1
11: 1 *e I,* stood to confirm and to strengthen NIH
11: 4 be pluckt up, *e* for others besides those. 2050.1
11:10 return, and be stirred up, *e* to his fortress. NIH
11:11 with him, *e* with the king of the north: NIH
11:24 He shall enter peaceably *e* upon 2050.1
11:24 against the strong holds, *e* for a time. 2050.1
11:30 he shall *e* return, and have intelligence 2050.1
11:35 *them* white, *e* to the time of the end: NIH
11:41 *e* Edom, and Moab, and the chief of 2050.1
12: 1 as never was since there was a nation *e* NIH
12: 4 seal the book, *e* to the time of the end: NIH

Hos
2:20 I will *e* betroth thee unto me in 2050.1
5:14 I, *e I,* will tear and go away; I will take NIH
9:16 yet will I slay *e* the beloved *fruit* of their NIH
12: 5 E the Lord God of hosts; the Lord 2050.1

Joel
1: 2 your days, or *e* in the days of your fathers? 518
1:12 all the trees of the field, are withered: NIH
2: 2 after it, *e* to the years of many generations. NIH
2:12 turn ye *e* to me with all your heart, NIH
2:14 *e* a meat offering and a drink offering unto NIH

Am
2:11 *Is it* not *e* thus, O ye children of Israel? 637
3:11 An adversary *there* shall be *e* round 2050.1
5: 1 a lamentation, O house of Israel. NIH
5:20 very dark, and no brightness in it? 2050.1
8: 4 to make the poor of the land to fail, 2050.1
8:12 the north *e* to the east, they shall run NIH
8:14 they shall fall, and never rise up again. 2050.1

Ob
1: 7 have brought thee *e* to the border: NIH

Ob
1: 8 e destroy the wise *men* out of Edom, 2050.1
1:11 e thou *wast* as one of them. 1571
1:20 that of the Canaanites, e unto Zarephath; NIH

Jnh
2: 5 waters compassed me about, e to the soul: 2050.1
3: 5 from the greatest of them e to the least NIH
4: 9 said, I do well to be angry, e unto death. NIH

Mic
1: 9 the gate of my people, e to Jerusalem. NIH
2: 2 his house, e a man and his heritage. 2050.1
2: 8 E of late my people is risen up as an 2050.1
2:10 it shall destroy *you*, e *with* a sore 2050.1
2:11 he shall e be the prophet of this people. 2050.1
3: 4 he will e hide his face from them at 2050.1
3: 5 they e prepare war against him. 2050.1
4: 7 mount Zion from henceforth, e for ever. 2050.1
4: 8 thee shall it come, the first dominion; 2050.1
4:10 the field, and thou shalt go e to Babylon; NIH
7:12 *In* that day *also* he shall come e to thee 2050.1
7:12 from the fortress e to the river, NIH

Na
2:11 e the old lion, walked, *and* the lion's NIH
3:12 shall e fall into the mouth of the eater. 2050.1

Hab
1: 2 e cry out unto thee *of* violence, NIH
3: 9 *to* the oaths of the tribes, e *thy* word. NIH
3:13 e for salvation with thine anointed; NIH

Zep
1:14 e the voice of the day of the LORD: NIH
1:18 he shall make e a speedy riddance of all 389
2: 5 of the Philistines, I will e destroy thee, 2050.1
2: 9 e the breeding of nettles, and saltpits, NIH
2:11 his place, e all the isles of the heathen. NIH
3: 8 mine indignation, e all my fierce anger: NIH
3:10 e the daughter of my dispersed, shall bring NIH
3:15 the king of Israel, e the LORD, *is* in NIH
3:20 At that time will I bring you *again,* e in 2050.1

Hag
2:18 twentieth day of the ninth *month,* e from NIH

Zec
3: 2 e the LORD that hath chosen Jerusalem 2050.1
6:10 of Heldai, of Tobijah, and of Jedaiah, NIH
6:13 E he shall build the temple of 2050.1
7: 1 day of the ninth month, e in Chisleu; NIH
7: 5 seventh *month,* e those seventy years, 2050.1
7: 5 did ye at all fast *unto* me, e to me? NIH
8:23 e shall take hold of the skirt of him that 2050.1
9: 7 he that remaineth, e he, *shall be* for our 1571
9:10 his dominion *shall be* from sea e to sea, NIH
9:10 from the river e to the ends of the earth. NIH
9:12 e to day do I declare *that* I will render 1571
11: 7 of slaughter, e you, O poor of the flock. NIH
11:10 my staff, e Beauty, and cut it asunder, NIH
11:14 I cut asunder mine other staff, e Bands, NIH
12: 6 again in her own place, e in Jerusalem. NIH
14:16 e go up from year to year to worship 2050.1
14:17 of hosts, e upon them shall be no rain. 2050.1

Mal
1:10 *is there* e among you that would shut 1571
1:11 For from the rising of the sun e unto 2050.1
1:12 fruit thereof, e his meat, *is* contemptible. NIH
2: 2 I will e send a curse upon you, 2050.1
2: 3 e the dung of your solemn feasts; NIH
3: 1 e the messenger of the covenant, 2050.1
3: 7 E from the days of your fathers ye are 3807.1
3: 9 ye *have* robbed me, e this whole nation. 2050.1
3:15 *they that* tempt God are e delivered. 2050.1

Mt
5:46 do not e the publicans the same? 2532
5:47 what do ye more *than others?* do not e 2532
5:48 e as your Father which is in heaven is 5618
6:29 That e Solomon in all his glory was **not** 3761
7:12 should do to you, do ye so to them: 2532
7:17 E so every good tree bringeth forth good NIG
8:16 When the e was come, they brought unto 3798
8:27 that e the winds and the sea obey him? 2532
9:18 saying, My daughter is e **now** dead: 737
11:26 E so, Father: for so it seemed good in thy 3483
12: 8 the Son of man is Lord e of the sabbath 2532
12:45 E so shall it be also unto this wicked NIG
13:12 from him shall be taken away e that he 2532
15:28 be it unto thee e as thou wilt. NIG
18:14 E so it is not the will of your Father which NIG
18:33 thy fellowservant, e as I had pity on thee? 2504
20: 8 So when e was come, the lord of 3798
20:14 I will give unto this last, e as unto thee. 2532
20:28 E as the Son of man came not to be 5618
23: 8 for one is your Master, e Christ; NIG
23:10 for one is your Master, e Christ. NIG
23:28 E so ye also outwardly appear righteous NIG
23:37 e as a hen gathereth her chickens 3739+5158
24:27 of the east, and shineth e unto the west; NIG
24:33 know that it is near, e at the doors. NIG
25:29 shall be taken away e *that* which he hath. 2532
26:20 Now when the e was come, he sat down 3798
26:38 soul is exceeding sorrowful, e unto death: NIG
27:57 When the e was come, there came a rich 3798
28:20 alway, e unto the end of the world. NIG

Mk
1:27 with authority commandeth he e 2532
1:32 And at e, when the sun did set, 1096+3798
4:25 from him shall be taken away e *that* which he 3798
4:35 And the same day, when the e was come, 3798
4:36 they took him e as he was in the ship. NIG
4:41 that e the wind and the sea obey him? 2532
6: 2 that e such mighty works are wrought by 2532
6:47 And when e was come, the ship was in 3798
10:45 For e the Son of man came not to be 2532
11: 6 And they said unto them e **as** Jesus had 2531
11:19 And when e was come, he went out of 3796
12:44 did cast in all that she had, e all her living. 2532
13:22 to seduce, if *it were* possible, e the elect. 2532
13:29 to pass, know that it is nigh, e at the doors. NIG
13:35 at e, or at midnight, or at the 3796
14:30 unto thee, That this day, e in this night, NIG

Mk
14:54 off, e into the palace of the high priest: 2193
15:42 And now when the e was come, because 3798

Lk
1: 2 E as they delivered *them* unto us, 2531
1:15 Holy Ghost, e from his mother's womb. 2089
2:15 Let us now go e unto Bethlehem, NIG
6:33 have ye? for sinners also do e the same. NIG
8:18 from him shall be taken e *that* which he 2532
8:25 he commandeth e the winds and water, 2532
9:54 and consume them, e as Elias did? 2532
10:11 E the *very* dust of your city, which 2532
10:17 e the devils are subject unto us through 2532
10:21 e so, Father; for so it seemed good in thy 3483
12: 7 But e the *very* hairs of your head are all 2532
12:41 thou this parable unto us, or e to all? 2532
12:57 why e of yourselves judge ye not what *is* 2532
17:30 E thus shall it be in the day when 2596+5024
18:11 unjust, adulterers, or e as this publican. 2532
19:26 e that he hath shall be taken away from 2532
19:32 and found e as he had said unto them. 2531
19:37 e now at the descent of the mount of NIG
19:42 If thou hadst known, e thou, at least 2532
19:44 And shall **lay** thee e **with the ground,** 1474
20:37 are raised, e Moses shewed at the bush, 2532
24:24 and found *it* e so as the women had said: 2532

Jn
1:12 God, e to them that believe on his name: NIG
3:13 e the Son of man which is in heaven. NIG
3:14 e so must the Son of man be lifted up: 2532
5:21 and quickeneth *them;* e so the Son 2532
5:23 the Son, e as they honour the Father. 2531
5:45 accuseth you, e Moses, in whom ye trust. NIG
6:16 And when e was *now* come, his disciples 3798
6:57 he that eateth me, e he shall live by me. 2548
8: 9 beginning at the eldest, e unto the last: NIG
8:25 E the same that I said unto you *from* 2532
8:41 fornication; we have one Father, e God. 2532
8:43 e because ye cannot hear my word. NIG
10:15 knoweth me, e so know I the Father: NIG
11:22 But I know, that e now, whatsoever thou 2532
11:37 caused that e this *man* should not have 2532
12:50 e as the Father said unto me, so I speak. 2531
14:17 E the Spirit of truth; whom the world NIG
14:31 Father gave me commandment, e so I do. 2532
15:10 e as I have kept my Father's 2531
15:26 e the Spirit of truth, which proceedeth NIG
17:14 of the world, e as I am not of the world. 2531
17:16 of the world, e as I am not of the world. 2531
17:18 e so have I also sent them into the world. 2504
17:22 that they may be one, e as we are one: 2531
20:21 *my* Father hath sent me, e *so* send I you. 2504
21:25 I suppose that e the world itself could not NIG

Ac
2:39 as many as the Lord our God shall call. NIG
4:10 e by him doth this *man* stand here before NIG
5:37 and all, e as many as obeyed him, 2532
5:39 lest haply ye be found e to fight against 2532
9:17 said, Brother Saul, the Lord, e Jesus, NIG
10:41 e to us, who did eat and drink with him NIG
11: 5 by four corners; and it came e to me: NIG
12:15 she constantly affirmed that it was e so. NIG
15: 8 the Holy Ghost, e as he did unto us; 2548
20:11 e till break of day, so he departed. NIG
22:17 e while I prayed in the temple, I was in a 2532
26:11 persecuted *them* e unto strange. 2193+2532
27:25 e as it was told me. 2596+3739+3779+5158

Ro
1:13 you also, e as among other Gentiles. 2532
1:20 made, e his eternal power and Godhead; NIG
1:26 for e their women did change the natural 5037
1:28 And e as they did not like to retain God 2532
3:22 E the righteousness of God *which is* by 1161
4: 6 E as David also describeth the blessedness 2509
4:17 e God, who quickeneth the dead, 2532
5: 7 for a good *man* some would e dare to die. 2532
5:14 e over them that had not sinned after 2532
5:18 e so by the righteousness of one *the free* 2532
5:21 e so might grace reign through 2532
6: 4 e so we also should walk in newness of NIG
6:19 e so now yield your members servants to NIG
7: 4 e to him who is raised from the dead, NIG
8:23 e we ourselves groan within ourselves, 2532
8:34 that is risen *again*, who is e at the right 2532
9:10 conceived by one, e by our father Isaac; NIG
9:17 E for this same purpose have I raised thee NIG
9:24 E us, whom he hath called, not of the 2532
9:30 e the righteousness which is of faith. 1161
10: 8 e in thy mouth, and in thy heart: NIG
11: 5 E so then at *this* present time also there NIG
11:31 E so have these also now not believed, 2532
15: 3 For e Christ pleased not himself; but, as 2532
15:16 e the gospel of our Lord Jesus Christ. 2532

1Co
1: 6 E as the testimony of Christ was 2531
2: 7 e the hidden *wisdom,* which God NIG
2:11 e so the *things* of God knoweth no *man,* 2532
3: 1 as unto carnal, e as unto babes in Christ. NIG
3: 5 e as the Lord gave to every man? 2532
4:11 E unto this present hour we both hunger, 891
5: 7 For e Christ our passover is sacrificed for 2532
7: 7 I would that all men were e as I myself. 2532
7: 8 It is good for them if they abide e as I. 2504
9:14 E so hath the Lord ordained that they 2532
10:33 E as I please all *men* in all *things,* not 2504
11: 1 followers of me, e as I also *am* of Christ. 2531
11: 5 e all one as if she 846+1520+2532+3588
11:12 man, e so *is* the man also by the woman; NIG
11:14 Doth **not** e nature itself teach you, that, 3761
12: 2 unto *these* dumb idols, e as ye were led. NIG

1Co
13:12 then shall I know e as also I am known. 2531
14: 7 *And* e *things* without life giving sound, 3676
14:12 E so ye, forasmuch as ye are zealous of 2532
15:22 e so in Christ shall all be made alive. 2532
15:24 up the kingdom to God, e the Father; 2532
16: 1 to the churches of Galatia, e so do ye. 2532

2Co
1: 3 e the Father of our Lord Jesus Christ, 2532
1: 8 insomuch that we despaired e of life: 2532
1:13 trust you shall acknowledge e to the end; 2532
1:14 e as ye also *are* ours in the day of the 2509
1:19 e by me and Silvanus and Timotheus, NIG
3:10 For e that which was made glorious had 2532
3:15 But e unto this day, when Moses is read, NIG
3:18 to glory, e as by the Spirit of the Lord. NIG
7:14 e so our boasting, which *I made* before 2532
10: 7 as he *is* Christ's, e so *are* we Christ's. 2532
10:13 to us, a measure to reach e unto you. 2532
11:12 they glory, they may be found e as we. 2532
13: 9 and this also we wish, e your perfection. NIG

Gal
2:16 we have believed in Jesus Christ, 2532
3: 6 E as Abraham believed God, and it was 2531
4: 3 E so we, when we were children, were 2532
4:14 me as an angel of God, e as Christ Jesus. NIG
4:29 was *born* after the Spirit, e so *it is* now. 2532
5:12 I would they were e cut off which trouble 2532
5:14 e in *this;* Thou shalt love thy neighbour as NIG

Eph
1:10 heaven, and which are on earth; e in him: NIG
2: 3 nature the children of wrath, e as others. 2532
2: 5 E when we were dead in sins, 2532
2:15 e the law of commandments *contained* in NIG
4: 4 e as ye are called in one hope of your 2531
4:15 *in* all *things,* which is the head, e Christ: NIG
4:32 e as God for Christ's sake hath forgiven 2531
5:12 For it is a shame e to speak of those *things* 2532
5:23 e as Christ *is* the head of the church: 2532
5:25 e as Christ also loved the church, 2531
5:29 cherisheth it, e as the Lord the church: 2531
5:33 in particular so love his wife e as himself; 5613

Php
1: 7 E as it is meet for me to think this of you 2531
1:15 Some indeed preach Christ e of envy and 2532
2: 8 unto death, e the death of the cross. 1161
3:15 God shall reveal e this unto you. 2532
3:18 you often, and now tell you e weeping, 2532
3:21 able to subdue all *things* unto himself. 2532
4:16 For e in Thessalonica ye sent once and 2532

Col
1:14 his blood, e the forgiveness of sins: NIG
1:26 E the mystery which hath been hid from NIG
3:13 e as Christ forgave you, so also *do ye.* 2531

1Th
1:10 whom he raised from the dead, e Jesus, NIG
2: 2 But e after that we had suffered before, NIG
2: 4 in trust with the gospel, e so we speak; NIG
2: 7 e as a nurse cherisheth her children: NIG
2:14 e as they have of the Jews: 2531
2:18 come unto you, e I Paul, once and again; 3303
2:19 *Are* not e ye in the presence of our Lord 2532
3: 4 e as it came to pass, and ye know. 2532
3:12 towards all *men,* e as we *do* towards you: 2532
3:13 e our Father, at the coming of our Lord 2532
4: 3 is the will of God, e your sanctification, 2532
4: 5 e as the Gentiles which know not God: 2532
4:13 e as others which have no hope. 2531
4:14 e so them also which sleep in Jesus will NIG
4:18 and edify one another, e as also ye do. 2531

2Th
2: 9 E him, whose coming is after the working NIG
2:16 God, e our Father, which hath loved us, 2532
3: 1 and be glorified, e as *it is* with you; 2532
3:10 For e when we were with you, this we 2532

1Ti
3:11 E so *must their* wives *be* grave, 5615
6: 3 e the *words* of our Lord Jesus Christ, 2532

2Ti
2: 9 trouble, as an evil doer, e unto bonds; NIG

Tit
1:12 e a prophet of their own, said, 2532
1:15 e their mind and conscience is defiled. 2532

Phm
1: owest unto me e thine own self besides. 2532

Heb
1: 9 therefore God, e thy God, hath anointed NIG
4:12 piercing e **to** the dividing asunder of soul 891
5:14 e those who by reason of use have their NIG
6:20 the forerunner is for us entered, e Jesus, NIG
7: 4 e the patriarch Abraham gave the tenth of 2532
11:12 Therefore sprang there e of one, and him 2532
11:19 *was* able to raise *him* up, e from the dead; 2532

Jas
2:17 E so faith, if it hath not works, is dead, 2532
3: 5 E so the tongue is a little member, 2532
3: 9 Therewith bless we God, e the Father; 2532
4: 1 e of your lusts that war in your members? 2532
4:14 It is e a vapour, that appeareth for a little 1063

1Pe
1: 9 of your faith, e the salvation of *your* souls. NIG
2: 8 e to them which stumble at the word, NIG
2:21 For e hereunto were ye called: because NIG
3: 4 e the ornament of a meek and quiet spirit, NIG
3: 6 E as Sara obeyed Abraham, calling him NIG
3:21 The like figure whereunto e baptism doth NIG
4:10 e so minister the same one to another, NIG

2Pe
1:14 e as our Lord Jesus Christ hath shewed 2532
2: 1 e as there shall be false teachers among 2532
2: 1 e denying the Lord that bought them, 2532
3:15 e as our beloved brother Paul also 2532

1Jn
2: 6 himself also so to walk, e as he walked. 2531
2: 9 his brother, is in darkness e until now. NIG
2:18 e now are there many antichrists; 2532
2:25 that he hath promised us, e eternal life. NIG
2:27 and is no lie, e as it hath taught you, 2531
3: 3 in him purifieth himself, e as he is pure. 2531
3: 7 is righteous, e as he is righteous. 2531
4: 3 and e now already is it in the world. NIG
5: 4 that overcometh the world, e our faith. NIG

E

1Jn 5: 6 came by water and blood, *e* Jesus Christ;	NIG
5:20 him *that is* true, *e* in his Son Jesus Christ.	2531
3Jn 1: 2 and be in health, *e* as thy soul prospereth.	2531
1: 3 *is* in thee, *e* as thou walkest in the truth.	2531
Jude 1: 7 *E* as Sodom and Gomorrha, and the cities	NIG
1:23 hating *e* the garment spotted by the flesh.	2532
Rev 1: 7 shall wail because of him. **E** so, Amen.	3483
2:13 *e* where Satan's seat *is:* and thou holdest	NIG
2:13 *e* in *those* days wherein Antipas *was* my	2532
2:27 to shivers: *e* as I received of my Father.	2504
3: 4 Thou hast a few names in Sardis,	2532
3:21 *e* as I also overcame, and am set down	NIG
6:13 *e* as a fig tree casteth her untimely figs,	NIG
14:20 *e* unto the horse bridles, by the space of a	NIG
16: 7 **E** so, Lord God Almighty, true and	3483
17:11 *e* he is the eighth, and is of the seven,	2532
18: 6 Reward her *e* as she rewarded you,	2532
21:11 *e* like a jasper stone, clear as crystal;	NIG
22:20 Amen. **E** so, come, Lord Jesus.	3483

EVENING (60) [EVEN]

Ge 1: 5 the *e* and the morning were the first day.	6153
1: 8 the *e* and the morning were the second	6153
1:13 the *e* and the morning were the third day.	6153
1:19 the *e* and the morning were the fourth	6153
1:23 the *e* and the morning were the fifth day.	6153
1:31 the *e* and the morning were the sixth day.	6153
8:11 the dove came in to him in the *e;* and lo,	6153
24:11 by a well of water at the time of the *e,*	6153
29:23 came to pass in the *e,* that he took Leah	6153
30:16 Jacob came out of the field in the *e.*	6153
Ex 12: 6 congregation of Israel shall kill it in the *e.*	6153
16: 8 LORD shall give you in the *e* flesh to eat,	6153
18:13 by Moses from the morning unto the *e.*	6153
27:21 his sons shall order it from *e* to morning	6153
Lev 24: 3 shall Aaron order it from the *e* unto	6153
Dt 23:11 when *e* cometh on, he shall wash	6153
Jos 10:26 were hanging upon the trees until the *e.*	6153
Jdg 19: 9 Behold now, the day draweth towards *e,*	6150
1Sa 14:24 be the man that eateth *any* food until *e,*	6153
17:16 the Philistine drew near morning and *e,*	6150
30:17 twilight even unto the *e* of the next day:	6153
1Ki 17: 6 morning, and bread and flesh in the *e;*	6153
18:29 *the time* of the offering of the *e* sacrifice,	NIH
18:36 *the time* of the offering of the *e* sacrifice,	NIH
2Ki 16:15 the *e* meat offering, and the king's burnt	6153
1Ch 16:40 burnt offering continually morning and *e,*	6153
2Ch 2: 4 *for* the burnt offerings morning and *e,*	6153
13:11 every morning and **every** *e*	6153+6153+871.1+871.1+1886.1
13:11 to burn **every** *e:*	6153+6153+871.1+871.1+1886.1+1886.1
31: 3 for the morning and *e* burnt offerings,	6153
Ezr 3: 3 *even* burnt offerings morning and *e.*	6153
9: 4 and I sat astonied until the *e* sacrifice.	6153
9: 5 at the *e* sacrifice I arose up from my	6153
Est 2:14 In the *e* she went, and on the morrow	6153
Job 4:20 They are destroyed from morning to *e:*	6153
Ps 55:17 **E**, and morning, and at noon, will I pray,	6153
59: 6 They return at *e:* they make a noise like a	6153
59:14 at *e* let them return; *and* let them make a	6153
65: 8 outgoings of the morning and *e* to rejoice.	6153
90: 6 in the *e* it is cut down, and withereth.	6153
104:23 his work and to his labour until the *e.*	6153
141: 2 lifting up of my hands *as* the *e* sacrifice.	6153
Pr 7: 9 in the *e,* in the black and dark night;	6153
Ecc 11: 6 and in the *e* withhold not thine hand:	6153
Jer 6: 4 the shadows of the *e* are stretched out.	6153
Eze 33:22 hand of the LORD was upon me in the *e,*	6153
46: 2 but the gate shall not be shut until the *e.*	6153
Da 8:26 the vision of the *e* and the morning	6153
9:21 touched me about the time of the *e*	6153
Hab 1: 8 and are more fierce than the *e* wolves:	6153
Zep 2: 7 of Ashkelon shall they lie down in the *e:*	6153
3: 3 *are* roaring lions; her judges *are e* wolves;	6153
Zec 14: 7 to pass, *that* at *e* time it shall be light.	6153
Mt 14:15 And when it was *e,* his disciples came to	3798
14:23 and when the *e* was come, he was there	3798
16: 2 and said unto them, When it is *e,* ye say,	3798
Mk 14:17 And in the *e* he cometh with the twelve.	3798
Lk 24:29 it is towards *e,* and the day is far spent.	2073
Jn 20:19 the same day at *e,* being the first *day*	3798
Ac 28:23 *out* of the prophets, from morning till *e.*	2073

EVENINGS (1) [EVEN]

Jer 5: 6 *and* a wolf of the *e* shall spoil them,	6160

EVENINGTIDE (2) [EVEN]

2Sa 11: 2 it came to pass in an *e,* that David	6153+6256
Isa 17:14 behold at *e* trouble; *and* before	6153+6256

EVENT (3)

Ecc 2:14 I myself perceived also that one *e*	4745
9: 2 *there is* one *e* to the righteous, and to	4745
9: 3 the sun, that *there is* one *e* unto all:	4745

EVENTIDE (5) [EVEN]

Ge 24:63 out to meditate in the field at the *e:*	6153+6437
Jos 7: 6 before the ark of the LORD until the *e,*	6153
8:29 hanged on a tree until *e:*	6153+6256+1886.1
Mk 11:11 and now the *e* was come,	3588+3798+5610
Ac 4: 3 hold unto the next day: for it was now *e.*	2073

EVER (476) [EVERLASTING, EVERMORE, HOWSOEVER, SOEVER, WHATSOEVER, WHENSOEVER, WHEREINSOEVER, WHERESOEVER, WHITHERSOEVER, WHOMSOEVER, WHOSOEVER]

Ge 3:22 of the tree of life, and eat, and live for *e:*	5769
13:15 to thee will I give it, and to thy seed for *e.*	5769
43: 9 me bear the blame for *e:*	3117+3605+1886.1
44:32 blame to my father for *e.*	3117+3605+1886.1
Ex 3:15 this *is* my name for *e,* and this *is* my	5769
12:14 shall keep it a feast by an ordinance **for e.**	5769
12:17 in your generations by an ordinance **for e.**	5769
12:24 an ordinance to thee and to thy sons for *e.*	5769
14:13 ye shall see them again no more for *e.*	5769
15:18 The LORD shall reign for *e* and ever.	5769
15:18 The LORD shall reign for ever and *e.*	5703
19: 9 I speak with thee, and believe thee for *e*	5769
21: 6 with an aul; and he shall serve him for *e.*	5769
27:21 it shall be a statute for *e* unto their	5769
28:43 it shall be a statute for *e* unto him and his	5769
29:28 his sons' by a statute for *e* from	5769
30:21 it shall be a statute for *e* to them, *even* to	5769
31:17 me and the children of Israel for *e.*	5769
32:13 your seed, and they shall inherit *it* for *e.*	5769
Lev 6:13 The fire shall *e* be burning upon the altar;	8548
6:18 *It* shall be a statute for *e* in your	5769
6:22 *it is* a statute for *e* unto the LORD; it shall	5769
7:34 unto his sons by a statute for *e* from	5769
7:36 *by* a statute for *e* throughout their	5769
10: 9 *it shall be* a statute for *e* throughout your	5769
10:15 thy sons' with thee, by a statute for *e;*	5769
16:29 *this* shall be a statute for *e* unto you:	5769
16:31 shall afflict your souls, *by* a statute for *e.*	5769
17: 7 This shall be a statute for *e* unto them	5769
23:14 *it shall be* a statute for *e* throughout your	5769
23:21 for *e* in all your dwellings throughout	5769
23:31 *It shall be* a statute for *e* throughout your	5769
23:41 *It shall be* a statute for *e* in your	5769
24: 3 *it shall be* a statute for *e* throughout your	5769
25:23 The land shall not be sold for *e:* for the	6783
25:30 *e* to him that bought it throughout his	6783
25:46 they shall be your bondmen for *e:*	5769
Nu 10: 8 shall be to you for an ordinance for *e*	5769
15:15 an ordinance for *e* in your generations:	5769
18: 8 and to thy sons, by an ordinance for *e*	5769
18:11 daughters with thee, by a statute for *e.*	5769
18:19 daughters with thee, by a statute for *e.*	5769
18:19 *it is* a covenant of salt for *e* before	5769
18:23 *it shall be* a statute for *e* throughout your	5769
19:10 among them, for a statute for *e.*	5769
22:30 which thou hast ridden *e* **since**	4480+5750
22:30 was I *e* **wont** to do so unto thee?	5532+5532
24:20 latter end *shall be* that he perish for *e.*	5703
24:24 afflict Eber, and he also shall perish for *e.*	5703
Dt 4:33 Did *e* people hear the voice of God	5769
4:40 thy God giveth thee, for *e.*	3117+3605+1886.1
5:29 and with their children for *e!*	5769+3807.1
12:28 and with thy children after thee for *e,*	5769
13:16 shall be a heap for *e;* it shall not be built	5769
15:17 door, and he shall be thy servant for *e.*	5769
18: 5 him and his sons for *e.*	3117+3605+1886.1
19: 9 and to walk in his ways;	3117+3605+1886.1
23: 3 into the congregation of the LORD for *e:*	5769
23: 6 nor their prosperity all thy days for *e.*	5769
28:46 for a wonder, and upon thy seed for *e.*	5769
29:29 *belong* unto us and to our children for *e,*	5769
32:40 my hand to heaven, and say, I live for *e.*	5769
Jos 4: 7 memorial unto the children of Israel for *e.*	5769
4:24 the LORD your God **for e.**	3117+3605+1886.1
8:28 Joshua burnt Ai, and made it a heap for *e,*	5769
14: 9 thy children's for *e,* because thou hast	5769
Jdg 11:25 did he *e* **strive** against Israel,	7378+7378
11:25 or did he *e* **fight** against them,	3898+3898
1Sa 1:22 before the LORD, and there abide for *e.*	5769
2:30 thy father, should walk before me for *e:*	5769
2:32 man in thine house for *e.*	3117+3605+1886.1
2:35 mine anointed for *e.*	3117+3605+1886.1
3:13 for *e* for the iniquity which he knoweth;	5769
3:14 be purged with sacrifice nor offering for *e.*	5769
13:13 established thy kingdom upon Israel for *e.*	5769
20:15 cut off thy kindness from my house for *e:*	5769
20:23 the LORD *be* between thee and me for *e.*	5769
20:42 and between my seed and thy seed for *e.*	5769
27:12 therefore he shall be my servant for *e.*	5769
28: 2 keeper of mine head for *e.*	3117+3605+1886.1
2Sa 2:26 and said, Shall the sword devour for *e?*	5331
3:28 *e* from the blood of Abner the son of Ner:	5769
7:13 stablish the throne of his kingdom for *e.*	5769
7:16 thy kingdom shall be stablished for *e*	5769
7:16 thy throne shall be established for *e.*	5769
7:24 Israel to be a people unto thee for *e;*	5769
7:25 establish *it* for *e,* and do as thou hast said.	5769
7:26 let thy name be magnified for *e,* saying,	5769
7:29 that *it* may continue for *e* before thee:	5769
7:29 the house of thy servant be blessed for *e.*	5769
1Ki 1:31 said, Let my lord king David live for *e.*	5769
2:33 and upon the head of his seed for *e.*	5769
2:33 shall there be peace for *e* from the LORD.	5769
2:45 be established before the LORD for *e.*	5769
5: 1 was *e* a lover of David.	3117+3605+1886.1
8:13 a settled place for thee to abide in for *e.*	5769
9: 3 hast built, to put my name there for *e;*	5769
9: 3 throne of thy kingdom upon Israel for *e,*	5769
10: 9 because the LORD loved Israel for *e,*	5769
11:39 of David, but not for *e.*	3117+3605+1886.1
12: 7 will be thy servants for *e.*	3117+3605+1886.1
2Ki 5:27 cleave unto thee, and unto thy seed for *e.*	5769

2Ki 21: 7 Israel, will I put my name for *e:*	5769+3807.1
1Ch 15: 2 of God, and to minister unto him for *e.*	5769
16:34 *he is* good; for his mercy *endureth* for *e.*	5769
16:36 Blessed *be* the LORD God of Israel for *e*	5769
16:36 *be* the LORD God of Israel for ever and *e.*	5769
16:41 because his mercy *endureth* for *e;*	5769
17:12 house, and I will stablish his throne for *e.*	5769
17:14 in mine house and in my kingdom for *e:*	5769
17:22 didst thou make thine own people for *e;*	5769
17:23 concerning his house be established for *e,*	5769
17:24 that thy name may be magnified for *e,*	5769
17:27 servant, that *it* may be before thee for *e:*	5769
17:27 O LORD, and *it shall be* blessed for *e.*	5769
22:10 throne of his kingdom over Israel for *e.*	5769
23:13 most holy *things,* he and his sons for *e,*	5769
23:13 unto him, and to bless in his name for *e.*	5769
23:25 may dwell in Jerusalem for *e:*	5769+3807.1
28: 4 of my father to be king over Israel for *e:*	5769
28: 7 I will establish his kingdom for *e,*	5769
28: 8 for your children after you for *e.*	5703
28: 9 forsake him, he will cast thee off for *e.*	5703
29:10 God of Israel our father, for *e* and ever.	5769
29:10 God of Israel our father, for ever and *e.*	5769
29:18 keep this for *e* in the imagination of	5769
2Ch 2: 4 This *is* an ordinance for *e* to Israel.	5769
5:13 *he is* good; for his mercy *endureth* for *e:*	5769
6: 2 thee, and a place for thy dwelling **for e.**	5769
7: 3 *he is* good; for his mercy *endureth* **for e,**	5769
7: 6 because his mercy *endureth* for *e,*	5769
7:16 that my name may be there for *e:*	5769
9: 8 establish them for *e,* therefore made he	5769
10: 7 will be thy servants for *e.*	3117+3605+1886.1
13: 5 the kingdom over Israel to David for *e,*	5769
20: 7 it to the seed of Abraham thy friend for *e?*	5769
20:21 the LORD; for his mercy *endureth* for *e.*	5769
21: 7 him and to his sons **for e.**	3117+3605+1886.1
30: 8 which he hath sanctified for *e.*	5769
33: 4 In Jerusalem shall my name be for *e.*	5769
33: 7 tribes of Israel, will I put my name for *e:*	5865
Ezr 3:11 his mercy *endureth* for *e* towards Israel.	5769
9:12 nor seek their peace or their wealth for *e.*	5769
9:12 *it* for an inheritance to your children for *e.*	5769
Ne 2: 3 said unto the king, Let the king live for *e:*	5769
9: 5 *and* bless the LORD your God for *e* and	5769
9: 5 bless the LORD your God for ever and *e:*	5769
13: 1 come into the congregation of God for *e;*	5769
Job 4: 7 Remember, I pray thee, who *e* perished,	NIH
4:20 they perish for *e* without *any* regarding *it.*	5331
14:20 Thou prevailest for *e* against him,	5331
19:24 an iron pen and lead in the rock for *e!*	5703
20: 7 he shall perish for *e* like his own dung:	5331
23: 7 should I be delivered for *e* from my judge.	5331
36: 7 he doth establish them for *e,* and they are	5331
41: 4 wilt thou take him for a servant for *e?*	5769
Ps 5:11 let them *e* shout for joy, because	5769+3807.1
9: 5 hast put out their name for *e* and ever.	5769
9: 5 hast put out their name for ever and *e.*	5703
9: 7 the LORD shall endure for *e:* he hath	5769
9:18 of the poor shall *not* perish for *e.*	5331
10:16 The LORD *is* King for *e* and ever:	5769
10:16 The LORD *is* King for ever and *e:*	5703
12: 7 preserve them from this generation for *e.*	5769
13: 1 for *e?* how long wilt thou hide thy face	5331
19: 9 fear of the LORD *is* clean, enduring for *e:*	5703
21: 4 *it* him, *even* length of days for *e* and ever.	5769
21: 4 *it* him, *even* length of days for ever and *e.*	5703
21: 6 thou hast made him most blessed for *e:*	5703
22:26 that seek him: your heart shall live for *e.*	5769
23: 6 in the house of the LORD for *e.*	753+3117
25: 6 for they *have been e* of old.	4480+5769
25:15 Mine eyes *are e* towards the LORD; for he	8548
28: 9 feed them also, and lift them up for *e.*	5769
29:10 yea, the LORD sitteth King for *e.*	5769
30:12 God, I will give thanks unto thee for *e.*	5769
33:11 The counsel of the LORD standeth for *e,*	5769
37:18 and their inheritance shall be for *e.*	5769
37:26 *He is e* merciful,	3117+3605+1886.1
37:28 not his saints; they are preserved for *e.*	5769
37:29 inherit the land, and dwell therein for *e.*	5703
41:12 and settest me before thy face for *e.*	5769
44: 8 the day long, and praise thy name for *e.*	5769
44:23 O Lord? arise, cast *us* not off for *e.*	5331
45: 2 therefore God hath blessed thee for *e.*	5769
45: 6 Thy throne, O God, *is* for *e* and ever:	5769
45: 6 Thy throne, O God, *is* for ever and *e:*	5703
45:17 the people praise thee for *e* and ever.	5769
45:17 the people praise thee for ever and *e.*	5703
48: 8 our God: God will establish it for *e.*	5769
48:14 For this God *is* our God for *e* and ever:	5769
48:14 For this God *is* our God for ever and *e.*	5703
49: 8 soul is precious, and it ceaseth for *e:)*	5769
49: 9 That he should still live for *e, and* not see	5331
49:11 *is, that* their houses *shall* continue for *e,*	5769
51: 3 and my sin *is* before me.	8548
52: 5 God shall likewise destroy thee for *e,*	5331
52: 8 I trust in the mercy of God for *e* and ever.	5769
52: 8 I trust in the mercy of God for ever and *e.*	5703
52: 9 I will praise thee for *e,* because thou hast	5769
61: 4 I will abide in thy tabernacle **for e:** I will	5769
61: 7 He shall abide before God **for e:**	5769
61: 8 So will I sing praise unto thy name for *e,*	5703
66: 7 He ruleth by his power for *e;* his eyes	5769
68:16 yea, the LORD will dwell in it for *e.*	5331
72:17 His name shall endure for *e:* his name	5769
72:19 And blessed *be* his glorious name for *e:*	5769

Ps 73:26 of my heart, and my portion for **e**. 5769
74: 1 O God, why hast thou cast *us* off for **e**? 5769
74:10 the enemy blaspheme thy name for **e**? 5331
74:19 not the congregation of thy poor for **e**. 5331
75: 9 I will declare for **e**; I will sing *praises* to 5769
77: 7 Will the Lord cast off for **e**? and will he 5769
77: 8 Is his mercy clean gone for **e**? doth *his* 5331
78:69 earth which he hath established for **e**. 5769
79: 5 thou be angry, for **e**? shall thy jealousy 5331
79:13 of thy pasture will give thee thanks for **e**: 5769
81:15 but their time should have endured for **e**. 5769
83:17 them be confounded and troubled for **e**; 5703
85: 5 Wilt thou be angry with us for **e**? 5769
89: 1 sing of the mercies of the Lord **for e**. 5769
89: 2 I have said, Mercy shall be built up for **e**: 5769
89: 4 Thy seed will I stablish for **e**, and build 5769
89:29 His seed also will I make *to endure* for **e**, 5703
89:36 His seed shall endure for **e**, and his throne 5769
89:37 It shall be established **for e** as the moon, 5769
89:46 thou hide thyself, for **e**? shall thy wrath 5331
90: 2 or **e** thou hadst formed the earth and NIH
92: 7 *it is* that they shall be destroyed for **e**: 5703
93: 5 thine house, O Lord, for **e**. 753+3117
102:12 thou, O Lord, shalt endure for **e**; 5769
103: 9 neither will he keep *his* anger for **e**. 5769
104: 5 not be removed **for e**. 5703+5769+2050.1
104:31 The glory of the Lord shall endure for **e**: 5769
105: 8 He hath remembered his covenant for **e**, 5769
106: 1 *he* is good: for his mercy *endureth* for **e**. 5769
107: 1 *he* is good: for his mercy *endureth* for **e**. 5769
110: 4 Thou *art* a priest for **e** after the order of 5769
111: 3 and his righteousness endureth for **e**. 5703
111: 5 will **e** be mindful of his covenant. 5769+3807.1
111: 8 stand fast for **e** and ever, *and are* done 5703
111: 8 They stand fast for ever and **e**, 5769+3807.1
111: 9 he hath commanded his covenant for **e**: 5769
111:10 his praise endureth for **e**. 5703
112: 3 and his righteousness endureth for **e**. 5769
112: 6 Surely he shall not be moved for **e**: 5769
112: 9 poor; his righteousness endureth for **e**; 5703
117: 2 the truth of the Lord *endureth* for **e**. 5769
118: 1 good: because his mercy *endureth* for **e**. 5769
118: 2 now say, that his mercy *endureth* for **e**. 5769
118: 3 now say, that his mercy *endureth* for **e**. 5769
118: 4 Lord say, that his mercy *endureth* for **e**. 5769
118:29 *he* is good: for his mercy *endureth* for **e**. 5769
119:44 So shall I keep thy law continually for **e** 5769
119:44 I keep thy law continually for ever and **e**. 5703
119:89 For **e**, O Lord, thy word *is* settled in 5769
119:98 for they *are* **e** with me. 5769+3807.1
119:111 have I taken as an heritage for **e**: 5769
119:152 of old that thou hast founded them for **e**. 5769
119:160 thy righteous judgments *endureth* for **e**. 5769
125: 1 cannot be removed, *but* abideth for **e**. 5769
125: 2 his people from henceforth even for **e**. 5769
131: 3 in the Lord from henceforth and for **e**. 5769
132:14 This *is* my rest for **e**: here will I dwell; 5703
135:13 Thy name, O Lord, *endureth* for **e**; 5769
136: 1 *he* is good: for his mercy *endureth* for **e**. 5769
136: 2 God of gods: for his mercy *endureth* for **e**. 5769
136: 3 of lords: for his mercy *endureth* for **e**. 5769
136: 4 for his mercy *endureth* for **e**. 5769
136: 5 heavens: for his mercy *endureth* for **e**. 5769
136: 6 the waters: for his mercy *endureth* for **e**. 5769
136: 7 great lights: for his mercy *endureth* for **e**. 5769
136: 8 rule by day: for his mercy *endureth* for **e**. 5769
136: 9 by night: for his mercy *endureth* for **e**. 5769
136:10 firstborn: for his mercy *endureth* for **e**: 5769
136:11 from: for his mercy *endureth* for **e**: 5769
136:12 out arm: for his mercy *endureth* for **e**: 5769
136:13 into parts: for his mercy *endureth* for **e**: 5769
136:14 midst of it: for his mercy *endureth* for **e**: 5769
136:15 Red sea: for his mercy *endureth* for **e**: 5769
136:16 for his mercy *endureth* for **e**: 5769
136:17 great kings: for his mercy *endureth* for **e**: 5769
136:18 kings: for his mercy *endureth* for **e**: 5769
136:19 Amorites: for his mercy *endureth* for **e**: 5769
136:20 of Bashan: for his mercy *endureth* for **e**: 5769
136:21 an heritage: for his mercy *endureth* for **e**: 5769
136:22 his servant: for his mercy *endureth* for **e**: 5769
136:23 low estate: for his mercy *endureth* for **e**: 5769
136:24 enemies: for his mercy *endureth* for **e**: 5769
136:25 to all flesh: for his mercy *endureth* for **e**. 5769
136:26 of heaven: for his mercy *endureth* for **e**. 5769
138: 8 thy mercy, O Lord, *endureth* for **e**: 5769
145: 1 and I will bless thy name for **e** and ever. 5769
145: 1 and I will bless thy name for ever and **e**. 5769
145: 2 and I will praise thy name for **e** and ever. 5769
145: 2 and I will praise thy name for ever and **e**. 5769
145:21 let all flesh bless his holy name for **e** and 5769
145:21 flesh bless his holy name for ever and **e**. 5703
146: 6 that therein is: which keepeth truth for **e**: 5769
146:10 The Lord shall reign for **e**, *even* thy 5769
148: 6 hath also stablished them for **e** and ever: 5703
148: 6 hath also stablished them for ever and **e**. 5769
Pr 8:23 the beginning, or **e** the earth was. 4480+6924
12:19 The lip of truth shall be established for **e**: 5703
27:24 riches *are* not for **e**: and doth the crown 5769
29:14 his throne shall be established for **e**. 5703
Ecc 1: 4 but the earth abideth for **e**. 5769
2:16 of the wise more than of the fool for **e**; 5769
3:14 whatsoever God doeth, it shall be for **e**: 5769
6: 4 have they any more a portion for **e**. 5769
12: 6 **Or e** the silver cord be loosed, 834+3808+5704
SS 6:12 **Or e** I was aware, my soul made me *like* 3808

Isa 9: 7 with justice from henceforth even for **e**. 5769
26: 1 for the Lord for **e**: for in 5703
28:28 he will not **e** be threshing 5331+3807.1
30: 8 that it may be for the time to come for **e** 5703
30: 8 be for the time to come for ever and **e**: 5769
32:14 forts and towers shall be for dens for **e**, 5769
32:17 and assurance for **e**. 5769
33:20 one of the stakes thereof shall **e** 5331+3807.1
34:10 the smoke thereof shall go up for **e**: 5769
34:10 none shall pass through it for **e** and ever. 5331
34:10 none shall pass through it for ever and **e**. 5331
34:17 they shall possess it for **e**, from generation 5769
40: 8 but the word of our God shall stand for **e**. 5769
47: 7 thou saidst, I shall be a lady for **e**: 5703+5769
51: 6 my salvation shall be for **e**, 5769
51: 8 my righteousness shall be for **e**, 5769
57:16 For I will not contend for **e**, neither will I 5769
59:21 the Lord, from henceforth and for **e**. 5769
60:21 shall inherit the land for **e**, the branch 5769
64: 9 O Lord, neither remember iniquity for **e**: 5703
65:18 and rejoice for **e** *in that* which I create: 5703
Jer 3: 5 Will he reserve *his anger* for **e**? will he 5769
3:12 the Lord, *and* I will not keep *anger* for **e**. 5769
7: 7 gave to your fathers, for **e** and ever. 4480+5769
7: 7 gave to your fathers, for ever and **e**. 5704+5769
17: 4 fire in mine anger, *which* shall burn for **e**. 5769
17:25 and this city shall remain for **e**. 5769
25: 5 you and to your fathers for **e** and ever: 5769
25: 5 and to your fathers for ever and **e**: 5704+5769
31:36 a nation before me **for e**. 3117+3605+1886.1
31:40 nor thrown down any more for **e**. 5769
32:39 *they* may fear me **for e**, 3117+3605+1886.1
33:11 *is* good; for his mercy *endureth* for **e**: 5769
35: 6 no wine, *neither* ye, nor your sons for **e**: 5769
35:19 to stand before me for **e**. 3117+3605+1886.1
49:33 for dragons, *and* a desolation for **e**: 5769
50:39 it shall be no more inhabited for **e**; 5331
51:26 thou shalt be desolate **for e**, saith 5769
51:62 beast, but that it shall be desolate **for e**. 5769
La 3:31 For the Lord will not cast off for **e**: 5769
5:19 Thou, O Lord, remainest for **e**; 5769
5:20 Wherefore dost thou forget us for **e**, 5331
Eze 37:25 and their children's children for **e**: 5769
37:25 servant David *shall* be their prince for **e**. 5769
43: 7 the midst of the children of Israel for **e**, 5769
43: 9 I will dwell in the midst of them for **e**. 5769
Da 2: 4 to the king in Syriack, O king, live for **e**: 5957
2:20 be the name of God for **e** and ever: 0.2+5957
2:20 name of God for ever and **e**: 0.2+5705+5957
2:44 these kingdoms, and it shall stand for **e**. 5957
3: 9 king Nebuchadnezzar, O king, live for **e**. 5957
4:34 and honoured him that liveth **for e**, 0.2+5957
5:10 queen spake and said, O king, live for **e**: 5957
6: 6 thus unto him, King Darius, live for **e**. 5957
6:21 Daniel unto the king, O king, live for **e**. 5957
6:24 or **e** they came at the bottom of the den. 3809
6:26 stedfast for **e**, and his kingdom *that* which 5957
7:18 possess the kingdom for **e**, even for ever 5957
7:18 the kingdom for ever, even for **e** and ever. 5957
7:18 the kingdom for ever, even for ever and **e**. 5957
12: 3 many to righteousness as the stars for **e** 5769
12: 3 righteousness as the stars for ever and **e**. 5703
12: 7 sware by him that liveth **for e** that *it shall* 5769
Hos 2:19 I will betroth thee unto me for **e**, yea, 5769
Joel 2: 2 there hath not been **e** 4480+5769+1886.1
3:20 Judah shall dwell for **e**, and Jerusalem 5769
Am 1:11 and he kept his wrath **for e** 5331
Ob 1:10 cover thee, and thou shalt be cut off for **e**. 5769
Jnh 2: 6 earth *with* her bars *was* about me for **e**: 5769
Mic 2: 9 have ye taken *away* my glory for **e**. 5769
4: 5 in the name of the Lord our God for **e** 5769
4: 5 of the Lord our God for ever and **e**. 5703
4: 7 mount Zion from henceforth, even for **e**. 5769
7:18 he retaineth not his anger for **e**, because 5703
Zec 1: 5 and the prophets, do they live for **e**? 5769
Mal 1: 4 whom the Lord hath indignation for **e**. 5769
Mt 6:13 and the power, and the glory, for **e**. 165
21:19 no fruit grow on thee henceforward for **e**. 165
24:21 the world to this time, no, **nor e** shall be. 3364
Mk 11:14 No *man* eat fruit of thee hereafter for **e**. 165
15: 8 him to do as he had *e* done unto them. 104
Lk 1:33 he shall reign over the house of Jacob for **e**; 165
1:55 to Abraham, and to his seed for **e**. 165
15:31 thou art **e** with me, and all that I have is 3842
Jn 4:29 which told me all *things* **that e** I did: 3745
4:39 which testified, He told me all that **e** I did. 3745
6:51 *man* eat of this bread, he shall live for **e**: 165
6:58 he that eateth *of* this bread shall live for **e**. 165
8:35 the servant abideth not in the house for **e**: 165
8:35 ever: *but* the son abideth **e**. 165+1519+3588
10: 8 All that **e** came before me are thieves and 3745
12:34 out of the law that Christ abideth for **e**: 165
14:16 that he may abide with you for **e**; 165
18:20 I **e** taught in the synagogue, and in 3842
Ac 23:15 we, or **e** he come near, are ready 3588+4253
Ro 1:25 than the Creator, who is blessed for **e**. 165
9: 5 came, who is over all, God blessed for **e**. 165
11:36 *are* all *things*: to whom *be* glory for **e**. 165
16:27 *be* glory through Jesus Christ for **e**. 165
2Co 9: 9 the poor: his righteousness remaineth for **e**. 165
Gal 1: 5 To whom *be* glory for **e** and ever. Amen. 165
1: 5 To whom *be* glory for ever and **e**. Amen. 165
Eph 5:29 For no *man* **e** yet hated his own flesh; 4218
Php 4:20 and our Father *be* glory for **e** and ever. 165
4:20 and our Father *be* glory for ever and **e**. 165

1Th 4:17 and so shall we **e** be with the Lord. 3842
5:15 any; but **e** follow *that which is* good, 3842
1Ti 1:17 *be* honour and glory for **e** and ever. 165
1:17 *be* honour and glory for ever and **e**. 165
2Ti 3: 7 **E** learning, and never able to come to 3842
4:18 to whom *be* glory for **e** and ever. Amen. 165
4:18 to whom *be* glory for ever and **e**. Amen. 165
Phm 1:15 that thou shouldest receive him **for e**; 166
Heb 1: 8 Thy throne, O God, *is* for **e** and ever: 165
1: 8 Thy throne, O God, *is* for ever and **e**: 165
6:20 a priest for **e** after the order of Melchisedec. 165
6:20 made a high priest for **e** after the order of 165
7:17 Thou *art* a priest for **e** after the order of 165
7:21 Thou *art* a priest for **e** after the order of 165
7:24 because he continueth **e**, 165+1519+3588
7:25 seeing he **e** liveth to make intercession for 3842
10:12 one sacrifice for sins **for e**, 1330+1519+3588
10:14 **for e** them that are sanctified. 1330+1519+3588
13: 8 the same yesterday, and to day, and for **e**. 165
13:21 to whom *be* glory for **e** and ever. 165
13:21 to whom *be* glory for ever and **e**. 165
1Pe 1:23 of God, which liveth and abideth for **e**. 165
1:25 But the word of the Lord endureth for **e**. 165
4:11 be praise and dominion for **e** and ever. 165
4:11 be praise and dominion for ever and **e**. 165
5:11 him *be* glory and dominion for **e** and ever. 165
5:11 him *be* glory and dominion for ever and **e**. 165
2Pe 2:17 the mist of darkness is reserved for **e**. 165+2250
3:18 *be* glory both now and for **e**. Amen. 165+2250
1Jn 2:17 he that doeth the will of God abideth for **e**. 165
2Jn 1: 2 dwelleth in us, and shall be with us for **e**. 165
Jude 1:13 is reserved the blackness of darkness for **e**. 165
1:25 power, both now and **e**. 165+1519+3588+3956
Rev 1: 6 him *be* glory and dominion for **e** and ever. 165
1: 6 him *be* glory and dominion for ever and **e**. 165
4: 9 on the throne, who liveth for **e** and ever, 165
4: 9 on the throne, who liveth for ever and **e**, 165
4:10 and worship him that liveth for **e** and ever, 165
4:10 and worship him that liveth for ever and **e**, 165
5:13 throne, and unto the Lamb **for e** and ever. 165
5:13 throne, and unto the Lamb for ever and **e**. 165
5:14 and worshipped him that liveth for **e** and 165
5:14 worshipped him that liveth for ever and **e**. 165
7:12 and might, *be* unto our God for **e** and ever. 165
7:12 and might, *be* unto our God for ever and **e**. 165
10: 6 sware by him that liveth for **e** and ever, 165
10: 6 sware by him that liveth for ever and **e**, 165
11:15 Christ; and he shall reign for **e** and ever. 165
11:15 Christ; and he shall reign for ever and **e**. 165
14:11 smoke of their torment ascendeth up for **e** 165
14:11 their torment ascendeth up for ever and **e**: 165
15: 7 wrath of God, who liveth for **e** and ever. 165
15: 7 wrath of God, who liveth for ever and **e**. 165
19: 3 And her smoke rose up for **e** and ever. 165
19: 3 And her smoke rose up for ever and **e**. 165
20:10 be tormented day and night for **e** and ever. 165
20:10 be tormented day and night for ever and **e**. 165
22: 5 and they shall reign for **e** and ever. 165
22: 5 and they shall reign for ever and **e**. 165

EVERLASTING (97) [EVER]

Ge 9:16 that I may remember the **e** covenant 5769
17: 7 in their generations for an **e** covenant, 5769
17: 8 the land of Canaan, for an **e** possession; 5769
17:13 covenant shall be in your flesh for an **e** 5769
17:19 my covenant with him for an **e** covenant, 5769
21:33 on the name of the Lord, the **e** God. 5769
48: 4 to thy seed after thee *for an* **e** possession. 5769
49:26 unto the utmost bound of the **e** hills: 5769
Ex 40:15 for their anointing shall surely be an **e** 5769
Lev 16:34 this shall be an **e** statute unto you, 5769
24: 8 the children of Israel *by* an **e** covenant. 5769
Nu 25:13 *even* the covenant of an **e** priesthood; 5769
Dt 33:27 refuge, and underneath *are* the **e** arms: 5769
2Sa 23: 5 yet he hath made with me an **e** covenant, 5769
1Ch 16:17 for a law, *and* to Israel *for* an **e** covenant, 5769
Ps 7: 7 be ye lift up, ye **e** doors; and the King of 5769
24: 9 lift *them* up, ye **e** doors; and the King 5769
41:13 *be* the Lord God of Israel from **e**, 5769
41:13 God of Israel from everlasting, and to **e**. 5769
90: 2 and the world, even from **e** to everlasting, 5769
90: 2 and the world, even from everlasting to **e**, 5769
93: 2 is established of old: thou *art* from **e**. 5769
100: 5 his mercy *is* **e**; and his truth 5769+3807.1
103:17 the mercy of the Lord *is* from **e** to 5769
103:17 everlasting to **e** upon them that fear him, 5769
105:10 for a law, *and* to Israel *for* an **e** covenant: 5769
106:48 *be* the Lord God of Israel from **e** 5769
106:48 Lord God of Israel from everlasting to **e**: 5769
112: 6 the righteous shall be in **e** remembrance. 5769
119:142 Thy righteousness *is* an **e** 5769+3807.1
119:144 of thy testimonies *is* **e**: 5769+3807.1
139:24 way in me, and lead me in the way **e**. 5769
145:13 Thy kingdom *is* an **e** kingdom, 3605+5769
Pr 8:23 I was set up from **e**, from the beginning, 5769
10:25 but the righteous *is* an **e** foundation. 5769
Isa 9: 6 The mighty God, The **e** Father, 5703
24: 5 the ordinance, broken the **e** covenant. 5769
26: 4 for in the Lord JEHOVAH *is* **e** strength: 5769
33:14 who amongst us shall dwell with **e** 5769
35:10 with songs and joy upon their heads: 5769
40:28 thou not heard, *that* the **e** God, the Lord, 5769
45:17 be saved in the Lord with an **e** salvation: 5769
51:11 and joy *shall* be upon their head: 5769
54: 8 with **e** kindness will I have mercy on thee 5769

E

Isa	55: 3 I will make an **e** covenant with you,	5769
	55:13 for an **e** sign *that* shall not be cut off.	5769
	56: 5 I will give them an **e** name, that shall not	5769
	60:19 the Lord shall be unto thee an **e** light,	5769
	60:20 for the Lord shall be thine **e** light,	5769
	61: 7 the double: **e** joy shall be unto them.	5769
	61: 8 I will make an **e** covenant with them.	5769
	63:12 before them, to make himself an **e** name?	5769
	63:16 our redeemer; thy name *is* from **e**.	5769
Jer	10:10 he *is* the living God, and an **e** king:	5769
	20:11 *their* **e** confusion shall never be forgotten.	5769
	23:40 I will bring an **e** reproach upon you,	5769
	31: 3 I have loved thee *with* an **e** love;	5769
	32:40 I will make an **e** covenant with them:	5769
Eze	16:60 I will establish unto them an **e** covenant.	5769
	37:26 it shall be an **e** covenant with them:	5769
Da	4: 3 his kingdom *is* an **e** kingdom,	5957
	4:34 whose dominion *is* an **e** dominion,	5957
	7:14 his dominion *is* an **e** dominion, which	5957
	7:27 whose kingdom *is* an **e** kingdom,	5957
	9:24 to bring in **e** righteousness, and to seal up	5769
	12: 2 some to **e** life, and some to shame *and*	5769
	12: 2 and some to shame *and* **e** contempt.	5769
Mic	5: 2 *have been* from of old, from **e**.	3117+5769
Hab	1:12 *Art* thou not from **e**, O Lord my God,	6924
	3: 6 the **e** mountains were scattered,	5703
	3: 6 perpetual hills did bow: his ways *are* **e**.	5769
Mt	18: 8 two hands or two feet to be cast into **e** fire.	*166*
	19:29 an hundredfold, and shall inherit **e** life.	*166*
	25:41 Depart from me, ye cursed, into **e** fire,	*166*
	25:46 these shall go away into **e** punishment:	*166*
Lk	16: 9 they may receive you into **e** habitations.	*166*
	18:30 time, and in the world to come life **e**.	*166*
Jn	3:16 in him should not perish, but have **e** life.	*166*
	3:36 He that believeth on the Son hath **e** life:	*166*
	4:14 him a well of water springing up into **e** life.	*166*
	5:24 hath **e** life, and shall not come into	*166*
	6:27 for *that* meat which endureth unto **e** life,	*166*
	6:40 and believeth on him, may have **e** life:	*166*
	6:47 you, He that believeth on me hath **e** life.	*166*
	12:50 I know that his commandment is life **e**:	*166*
Ac	13:46 and judge yourselves unworthy of **e** life,	*166*
Ro	6:22 your fruit unto holiness, and the end **e** life.	*166*
	16:26 according to the commandment of the **e**	*166*
Gal	6: 8 to the Spirit shall of the Spirit reap life **e**.	*166*
2Th	1: 9 Who shall be punished *with* **e** destruction	*166*
	2:16 and hath given *us* **e** consolation and	*166*
1Ti	1:16 should hereafter believe on him to life **e**.	*166*
	6:16 to whom *be* honour and power **e**. Amen.	*166*
Heb	13:20 through the blood of the **e** covenant,	*166*
2Pe	1:11 abundantly into the **e** kingdom of our Lord	*166*
Jude	1: 6 hath reserved in **e** chains under darkness	*126*
Rev	14: 6 having the **e** gospel to preach unto them	*166*

EVERMORE (26) [EVER]

Dt	28:29 and spoiled **e**,	3117+3605+1886.1
2Sa	22:51 unto David, and to his seed for **e**.	5769
2Ki	17:37 shall observe to do **for e**;	3117+3605+1886.1
1Ch	17:14 and his throne shall be established for **e**.	5769
Ps	16:11 thy right hand *there are* pleasures **for e**.	5331
	18:50 to David, and to his seed for **e**.	5769
	37:27 from evil, and do good; and dwell for **e**.	5769
	77: 8 doth *his* promise fail for **e**?	1755+1755+2050.1
	86:12 heart: and I will glorify thy name for **e**.	5769
	89:28 My mercy will I keep for him for **e**,	5769
	89:52 Blessed *be* the Lord for **e**. Amen,	5769
	92: 8 But thou, Lord, *art most* high for **e**.	5769
	105: 4 and his strength: seek his face **e**.	8548
	106:31 righteousness unto all generations for **e**.	5769
	113: 2 the Lord from this time forth and for **e**.	5769
	115:18 the Lord from this time forth and for **e**.	5769
	121: 8 in from this time forth, and *even* for **e**.	5769
	132:12 also shall sit upon thy throne for **e**.	5703
	133: 3 commanded the blessing, *even* life for **e**.	5769
Eze	37:26 my sanctuary in the midst of them for **e**.	5769
	37:28 shall be in the midst of them for **e**.	5769
Jn	6:34 they unto him, Lord, **e** give us this bread.	*3842*
2Co	11:31 is blessed for **e**, knoweth that I lie not.	*165*
1Th	5:16 Rejoice **e**.	*3842*
Heb	7:28 *maketh* the Son, who is consecrated for **e**.	*165*
Rev	1:18 and behold, I am alive for **e**, Amen;	*165+165*

EVERY (1238)

Ge	1:21 and **e** living creature that moveth,	3605
	1:21 kind, and **e** winged fowl after his kind:	3605
	1:25 **e** thing that creepeth upon the earth after	3605
	1:26 over **e** creeping thing that creepeth upon	3605
	1:28 over **e** living thing that moveth upon	3605
	1:29 I have given you **e** herb bearing seed,	3605
	1:29 upon the face of all the earth, and **e** tree,	3605
	1:30 to **e** beast of the earth, and to every fowl	3605
	1:30 to **e** beast of the air, and to every thing	3605
	1:30 to **e** thing that creepeth upon the earth,	3605
	1:30 *is* life, I have given **e** green herb for meat:	3605
	1:31 God saw **e** thing that he had made,	3605
	2: 5 **e** plant of the field before it was in	3605
	2: 5 and **e** herb of the field before it grew:	3605
	2: 9 to grow **e** tree that is pleasant to the sight,	3605
	2:16 Of **e** tree of the garden thou mayest freely	3605
	2:19 Lord God formed **e** beast of the field,	3605
	2:19 beast of the field, and **e** fowl of the air;	3605
	2:19 Adam called **e**[S] living creature,	2050.2
	2:20 fowl of the air, and to **e** beast of the field;	3605
	3: 1 Ye shall not eat of **e** tree of the garden?	3605
	3:14 all cattle, and above **e** beast of the field;	3605

Ge	3:24 a flaming sword which **turned e** way,	2015
	4:14 that **e** one that findeth me shall slay me.	3605
	4:22 instructor of **e** artificer in brass and iron:	3605
	6: 5 *that* **e** imagination of the thoughts of his	3605
	6:17 and **e** thing *that is* in the earth shall die.	3605
	6:19 of **e** living *thing* of all flesh, two of every	3605
	6:19 two of **e** *sort* shalt thou bring into the ark,	3605
	6:20 of **e** creeping thing of the earth after his	3605
	6:20 two of **e** sort shall come unto thee,	3605
	7: 2 Of **e** clean beast thou shalt take to thee by	3605
	7: 4 **e** living substance that I have made will I	3605
	7: 8 of **e** *thing* that creepeth upon the earth,	3605
	7:14 beast after his kind, and all the cattle	3605
	7:14 **e** creeping thing that creepeth upon	3605
	7:14 fowl after his kind, every bird of every	3605
	7:14 fowl after his kind, **e** bird of every sort.	3605
	7:14 fowl after his kind, every bird of every	3605
	7:14 fowl after his kind, every bird of **e** sort.	3605
	7:21 of **e** creeping thing that creepeth upon	3605
	7:21 that creepeth upon the earth, and **e** man:	3605
	7:23 **e** living substance was destroyed which	3605
	8: 1 **e** living thing, and all the cattle that *was*	3605
	8:17 Bring forth with thee **e** living thing that *is*	3605
	8:17 of **e** creeping thing that creepeth upon	3605
	8:19 **E** beast, every creeping thing,	3605
	8:19 **e** creeping thing, and every fowl,	3605
	8:19 **e** fowl, *and* whatsoever creepeth upon	3605
	8:20 took of **e** clean beast, and of every clean	3605
	8:20 clean fowl, and offered burnt offerings	3605
	8:21 will I again smite any more **e** thing	3605
	9: 2 the dread of you shall be upon **e** beast of	3605
	9: 2 **e** fowl of the air, upon all that moveth	3605
	9: 3 **E** moving thing that liveth shall be meat	3605
	9: 5 at the hand of **e** beast will I require it,	3605
	9: 5 at the hand of **e**[S] man's brother will I	2050.2
	9:10 with **e** living creature that *is* with you,	3605
	9:10 and of **e** beast of the earth with you;	3605
	9:10 go out of the ark, to **e** beast of the earth.	3605
	9:12 and **e** living creature that *is* with you,	3605
	9:15 and you and **e** living creature of all flesh;	3605
	9:16 **e** living creature of all flesh that *is* upon	3605
	10: 5 **e** one after his tongue, after their families,	376
	13:10 Jordan, that it *was* well watered **e** where,	3605
	16:12 his hand *will be* against **e** man,	3605
	16:12 man, and **e** man's hand against him;	3605
	17:10 **E** man *child* among you shall be	3605
	17:12 **e** man *child* in your generations, he that is	3605
	17:23 **e** male among the men of Abraham's	3605
	19: 4 and young, all the people from **e** quarter:	7097
	20:13 at **e** place whither we shall come, say of	3605
	27:29 cursed *be* **e** one that curseth thee,	NIH
	30:33 **e** one that *is* not speckled and	3605
	30:35 *and* **e** one that had *some* white in it,	3605
	32:16 servants, **e** drove by themselves;	5739+5739
	34:15 Ye will be as we *be*, that **e** male of you	3605
	34:22 if **e** male among us be circumcised,	3605
	34:23 and **e** beast of theirs *be* ours?	3605
	34:24 **e** male was circumcised, all that went out	3605
	41:48 field, which *was* round about **e**[S] city,	1886.1
	42:25 to restore **e**[S] man's money into his sack,	1992.1
	42:35 **e**[S] man's bundle of money *was* in his	2050.2
	43:21 **e** man's money *was* in the mouth of his	NIH
	44: 1 put **e** man's money in his sack's mouth.	376
	44:11 they speedily took down **e** man his sack to	376
	44:11 to the ground, and opened **e** man his sack.	376
	44:13 laded **e** man his ass, and returned to the	376
	45: 1 he cried, Cause **e** man to go out from me.	3605
	46:34 for **e** shepherd *is* an abomination unto	3605
	47:20 for the Egyptians sold **e** man his field,	376
	49:28 **e** one according to his blessing he blessed	376
Ex	1: 1 **e** man and his household came with Jacob.	376
	1:22 **E** son that is born ye shall cast into	3605
	1:22 river, and **e** daughter ye shall save alive.	3605
	3:22 **e** woman shall borrow of her neighbour,	NIH
	7:12 For they cast down **e** man his rod,	376
	9:19 *for upon* **e** man and beast which shall be	3605
	9:22 upon beast, and upon **e** herb of the field,	3605
	9:25 the hail smote **e** herb of the field, and	3605
	9:25 of the field, and brake **e** tree of the field.	3605
	10: 5 shall eat **e** tree which groweth for you out	3605
	10:12 eat **e** herb of the land, *even* all that the	3605
	10:15 they did eat **e** herb of the land, and all	3605
	11: 2 let **e** man borrow of his neighbour,	376
	11: 2 **e** woman of her neighbour, jewels of	802
	12: 3 they shall take to them **e** man a lamb,	376
	12: 4 **e** man according to his eating shall make	376
	12:16 save *that* which **e** man must eat, that only	3605
	12:44 **e** man's servant that is bought for money,	3605
	13:12 **e** firstling that cometh of a beast which	3605
	13:13 **e** firstling of an ass thou shalt redeem with	3605
	14: 7 of Egypt, and captains over **e** one of them.	3605
	16: 4 gather a certain rate **e** day,	3117+3117+871.1
	16:16 Gather of it **e** man according to his eating,	376
	16:16 an omer for **e** man, *according to*	1538
	16:16 take ye **e** man for *them* which *are* in his	376
	16:18 gathered **e** man according to his eating.	376
	16:21 they gathered it **e** morning,	1242+1242+871.1+1886.1+1886.1
	16:21 **e** man according to his eating:	376
	16:29 abide ye **e** man in his place, let no man go	376
	18:22 *that* **e** great matter they shall bring unto	3605
	18:22 but **e** small matter they shall judge:	3605
	18:26 **e** small matter they judged themselves.	3605
	25: 2 of **e** man that giveth it willingly with his	3605
	26: 2 **e** one of the curtains shall have one	3605
	27:18 **fifty e** where,	2572+2572+871.1+1886.1

Ex	28:21 **e** one with his name shall they be	376
	29:36 thou shalt offer **e** day a bullock *for* a sin	3807.1
	30: 7 burn thereon sweet incense **e** morning:	1242+1242+871.1+871.1+1886.1+1886.1
	30:12 they give **e** man a ransom for his soul	376
	30:13 **e** one that passeth among them that are	3605
	30:14 **E** one that passeth among them that are	3605
	31:14 **e** one that defileth it shall surely be put to	NIH
	32:27 Put **e** man his sword by his side, *and* go in	376
	32:27 slay **e** man his brother, and every man his	376
	32:27 **e** man his companion, and every man his	376
	32:27 his companion, and **e** man his neighbour.	376
	32:29 even **e** man upon his son, and upon his	376
	33: 7 *that* **e** one which sought the Lord went	3605
	33: 8 stood **e** man *at* his tent door,	376
	33:10 and worshipped, **e** man *in* his tent door.	376
	34:19 **e** firstling amongst thy cattle, *whether* ox	3605
	35:10 **e** wise hearted among you shall come,	3605
	35:21 **e** one whose heart stirred him up,	3605
	35:21 **e** one whom his spirit made willing,	3605
	35:22 **e** man that offered *offered* an offering of	3605
	35:23 **e** man, with whom was found blue,	3605
	35:24 **E** one that did offer an offering of silver	3605
	35:24 **e** man, with whom was found shittim	3605
	35:29 **e** man and woman, whose heart made	3605
	36: 1 and Aholiab, and **e** wise hearted man,	3605
	36: 2 and Aholiab, and **e** wise hearted man,	3605
	36: 2 *even* **e** one whose heart stirred him up to	3605
	36: 3 free offerings **e** morning.	1242+1242+871.1+1886.1+1886.1
	36: 4 came **e** man from his work which	376+376
	36: 8 wise hearted *man* among them that	3605
	36:30 *of* silver, under **e** board two sockets.	259
	38:26 A bekah for **e** man, *that is*, half a shekel,	1886.1
	38:26 for **e** one that went to be numbered,	3605
	39:14 **e** one with his name, according to the	376
Lev	2:13 **e** oblation of thy meat offering shalt thou	3605
	6:12 burn wood on it **e** morning,	1242+1242+871.1+871.1+1886.1+1886.1
	6:18 **e** one that toucheth them shall be holy.	3605
	6:23 For **e** meat offering for the priest shall be	3605
	7: 6 **E** male among the priests shall eat thereof:	3605
	7:10 **e** meat offering, mingled with oil, and dry,	3605
	11:15 **E** raven after his kind;	3605
	11:21 Yet these may ye eat of **e** flying creeping	3605
	11:26 *The* carcases of **e** beast which divideth	3605
	11:26 **e** one that toucheth them shall be	3605
	11:33 **e** earthen vessel, whereinto *any* of them	3605
	11:34 drink that may be drunk in **e** *such* vessel	3605
	11:35 **e** thing whereupon *any part* of their	3605
	11:41 **e** creeping thing that creepeth upon	3605
	11:46 of **e** living creature that moveth in the	3605
	11:46 **e** creature that creepeth upon the earth:	3605
	15: 4 **E** bed, whereon he lieth that hath the	3605
	15: 4 **e** thing, whereon he sitteth, shall be	3605
	15:12 **e** vessel of wood shall be rinsed in water.	3605
	15:17 **e** garment, and every skin, whereon is	3605
	15:17 every garment, and **e** skin, whereon is	3605
	15:20 **e** *thing* that she lieth upon in her	3605
	15:20 **e** *thing* also that she sitteth upon shall be	3605
	15:26 **E** bed whereon she lieth all the days of	3605
	17:15 **e** soul that eateth that which died of itself,	3605
	19: 3 Ye shall fear **e** man his mother,	376
	19: 8 Therefore **e** one that eateth it shall bear	NIH
	19:10 neither shalt thou gather **e** grape of thy	NIH
	20: 9 For **e** one that curseth his father or	376+376
	23:37 drink offerings, **e** thing upon his day:	1697
	24: 8 **e** sabbath he shall set it in order	3117+3117+7676+7676+871.1+871.1+1886.1+1886.1
	25:10 ye shall return **e** man unto his possession,	376
	25:10 and ye shall return **e** man unto his family.	376
	25:13 ye shall return **e** man unto his possession.	376
	27:28 **e** devoted thing *is* most holy unto	3605
Nu	1: 2 of *their* names, **e** male by their polls;	3605
	1: 4 there shall be a man of **e**[S] tribe;	1886.1
	1: 4 **e** one head of the house of his fathers.	NIH
	1:20 **e** male from twenty years old and upward,	3605
	1:22 **e** male from twenty years old and upward,	3605
	1:52 **e** man by his own camp, and every man	376
	1:52 **e** man by his own standard, throughout	376
	2: 2 **E** man of the children of Israel shall pitch	376
	2:17 **e** man in his place by their standards.	376
	2:34 they set forward, **e** one after their families,	3605
	3:15 **e** male from a month old and upward	3605
	4:19 appoint them **e** one to his service and	376+376
	4:30 **e** one that entereth into the service, to do	3605
	4:35 **e** one that entereth into the service,	3605
	4:39 **e** one that entereth into the service,	3605
	4:43 **e** one that entereth into the service,	3605
	4:47 **e** one that came to do the service of	3605
	4:49 **e** one according to his service,	376+376
	5: 2 that they put out of the camp **e** leper,	3605
	5: 2 **e** one that hath an issue, and whosoever	3605
	5: 9 **e** offering of all the holy *things* of	3605
	5:10 **e** man's hallowed *things* shall be his:	3605
	7: 5 to **e** man according to his service.	376
	8:16 instead of such, as open **e** womb,	3605
	8:17 on the day that I smote **e** firstborn in	3605
	11:10 families, **e** man in the door of his tent:	376
	13: 2 of **e** tribe of their fathers shall ye send a	NIH
	13: 2 send a man, **e** one a ruler among them.	3605
	15:12 shall ye do to **e** one according to their	NIH
	16: 3 **e** one of them, and the Lord *is* among	3605
	16:17 take **e** man his censer, and put incense in	376
	16:17 bring ye before the Lord **e** man his	376

Nu
16:18 they took **e** man his censer, and put fire 376
16:27 Korah, Dathan, and Abiram, on **e** side: 5439
17: 2 take **e** one of them a rod according to NIH
17: 2 write thou **e** man's name upon his rod. 376
17: 6 **e** one of their princes gave him a rod 3605
17: 9 and they looked, and took **e** man his rod. 376
18: 7 your priest's office for **e** thing of the altar, 3605
18: 9 oblation of theirs, every meat offering 3605
18: 9 **e** meat offering of theirs, and every sin 3605
18: 9 sin offering of theirs, and every trespass 3605
18: 9 of theirs, and **e** trespass offering of theirs, 3605
18:10 place shalt thou eat it; **e** male shall eat it: 3605
18:11 **e** one that is clean in thy house shall eat 3605
18:13 **e** one that is clean in thine house shall 3605
18:14 **E** thing devoted in Israel shall be thine. 3605
18:15 **E** thing that openeth the matrix in all 3605
18:29 Out of all your gifts ye shall offer **e** heave 3605
18:31 ye shall eat it in **e** place, ye and 3605
19:15 **e** open vessel, which hath no covering 3605
21: 8 come to pass, that **e** one that is bitten, 3605
23: 2 and Balaam offered on **e** altar a bullock NIH
23: 4 I have offered upon **e** altar a bullock and NIH
23:14 and offered a bullock and a ram on **e** altar. NIH
23:30 and offered a bullock and a ram on **e** altar. NIH
25: 5 Slay ye **e** one his men that were joined 376
26:54 to **e** one shall his inheritance be given 376
28:10 burnt offering of **e** sabbath, 7676+7676+871.1
28:14 **e** month throughout 2320+2320+871.1
28:21 A several tenth deal shalt thou offer for **e** 259
29:14 three tenth deals unto **e** bullock of 259
30: 4 **e** bond wherewith she hath bound her 3605
30: 9 **e** vow of a widow, and of her that is 3605
30:11 **e** bond wherewith she bound her soul 3605
30:13 **E** vow, and every binding oath to afflict 3605
30:13 **e** binding oath to afflict the soul, 3605
31: 4 Of **e** tribe a thousand, throughout all 1886.1
31: 5 a thousand of **e** tribe, twelve thousand NIH
31: 6 a thousand of **e** tribe, them and Phinehas NIH
31:17 therefore kill **e** male among the little ones, 3605
31:17 kill **e** woman that hath known man by 3605
31:23 **E** thing that may abide the fire, ye shall 3605
31:50 what **e** man hath gotten, of jewels of gold, 376
31:53 war had taken spoil, **e** man for himself.) 376
32:18 have inherited **e** man his inheritance. 376
32:27 **e** man armed for war, before the Lord to 3605
32:29 **e** man armed to battle, before the Lord, 3605
33:54 **e** man's *inheritance* shall be in the place 834
34:18 shall take one prince of **e** tribe, to divide 259
35: 8 **e** one shall give of his cities unto the 376
35:15 **e** one that killeth *any* person unawares 3605
36: 7 **e** one of the children of Israel shall keep 376
36: 8 **e** daughter, that possesseth an inheritance 3605
36: 8 the children of Israel may enjoy **e** man 376
36: 9 **e** one of the tribes of the children of Israel 376

Dt
1:16 judge righteously between **e** man and his NIH
1:22 ye came near unto me **e** one of you, 3605
1:41 ye had girded on **e** man his weapons 3605
2:34 the women, and the little ones, of **e** city, 3605
3: 6 the men, women, and children, of **e** city. 3605
3:20 shall ye return **e** man unto his possession, 376
4: 4 your God are alive **e** one of you *this* day. 3605
3: 3 by **e** *word* that proceedeth out of the 3605
11:24 **E** place whereon the soles of your feet 3605
12: 2 upon the hills, and under **e** green tree: 3605
12: 8 **e** man whatsoever *is* right in his own eyes. 376
12:13 burnt offerings in **e** place that thou seest: 3605
12:31 for **e** abomination to the Lord, which he 3605
13:16 all the spoil thereof **e** whit, for the Lord 3632
14: 6 beast that parteth the hoof, 3605
14:14 And **e** raven after his kind, 3605
14:19 **e** creeping thing that flieth *is* unclean unto 3605
15: 1 At the end of **e** seven years thou shalt NIH
15: 2 **E** creditor that lendeth aught unto his 3605
16:17 **E** man *shall give* as he is able, according to 376
19: 3 three parts, that **e** slayer may flee thither. 3605
20:13 thou shalt smite **e** male thereof with 3605
21: 5 by their word shall **e** controversy and 3605
21: 5 every controversy **e** stroke be tried: 3605
23: 9 then keep thee from **e** wicked thing. 3605
24:16 **e** man shall be put to death for his own sin. 376
26:11 thou shalt rejoice in **e** good *thing* which 3605
28:61 sickness, and every plague, which *is* 3605
28:61 every sickness, and **e** plague, which *is* 3605
30: 9 thee plenteous in **e** work of thine hand, 3605
31:10 saying, At the end of **e** seven years, NIH
33: 3 thy feet; **e** one shall receive of thy words. NIH

Jos
1: 3 **E** place that the sole of your foot shall 3605
3:12 the tribes of Israel, out of **e** tribe a man. 3807.1
4: 2 out of the people, out of **e** tribe a man, NIH
4: 4 children of Israel, out of **e** tribe a man: NIH
4: 5 take ye up **e** man of you a stone upon his 376
4:10 until **e** thing was finished that the Lord 3605
6: 5 the people shall ascend up **e** man straight 376
6:20 **e** man straight before him, and they took 376
11:14 **e** man they smote with the edge of 376
21:42 These **cities** were **e** one with their 5892+5892
24:28 people depart, **e** man unto his inheritance. 376

Jdg
2: 6 the children of Israel went **e** man unto his 376
5:30 the prey; to **e** man a damsel or two; 7218
7: 5 **E** one that lappeth of the water with his 3605
7: 5 likewise **e** one that boweth down upon 3605
7: 7 let all the *other* people go **e** man unto his 376
7: 8 he sent all the *rest of* Israel **e** man to his 376
7:16 he put a trumpet in **e** man's hand, 3605
7:18 blow ye the trumpets also on **e** side of all 5439

Jdg
7:21 they stood **e** man in his place round about 376
7:22 the Lord set **e** man's sword against his 376
8:24 that you would give me **e** man the earrings 376
8:25 did cast therein **e** man the earrings of his 376
8:34 of all their enemies on **e** side: 4480+5439
9:49 all the people likewise cut down **e** man 376
9:55 they departed **e** man unto his place. 376
16: 5 will give thee **e** one *of us* eleven hundred 376
17: 6 **e** man did *that* which *was* right in his own 376
20:16 **e** one could sling stones at a hair *breadth*, 3605
20:48 as well the men of **e** city, as the beast, NIH
21:11 Ye shall utterly destroy **e** male, 3605
21:11 and **e** woman that hath lien by man. 3605
21:21 catch you **e** man his wife of the daughters 376
21:24 **e** man to his tribe and to his family, 376
21:24 they went out from thence **e** man to his 376
21:25 **e** man did *that* which *was* right in his own 376

1Sa
2:36 that **e** one that is left in thine house shall 3605
3:11 which both the ears of **e** one that heareth 3605
3:18 Samuel told him **e** whit, and hid nothing 3605
4:10 and they fled **e** man into his tent: 376
8:22 men of Israel, Go ye **e** man unto his city. 376
10:25 all the people away, **e** man to his house. 376
12:11 of the hand of your enemies on **e** side; 5439
13: 2 the rest of the people he sent **e** man to his 376
13:20 sharpen **e** man his share, and his coulter, 376
14:20 **e** man's sword was against his fellow, 376
14:34 Bring me hither **e** man his ox, 376
14:34 **e** man his sheep, and slay *them* here, 376
14:34 all the people brought **e** man his ox with 376
14:47 fought against all his enemies on **e** side, 5439
15: 9 **e** thing *that was* vile and refuse, that they 3605
20:15 of David **e** one from the face of the earth. 376
22: 2 **e** one *that was* in distress, and every one 3605
22: 2 **e** one that was in debt, and every one 3605
22: 2 in debt, and **e** one *that was* discontented, 3605
22: 7 will the son of Jesse give **e** one of you 3605
23:14 Saul sought him **e** day, but God delivered 3605
25:10 that break away **e** man from his master. 376
25:13 his men, Gird you on **e** man his sword. 376
25:13 you on **e** man his sword; 376
26:23 The Lord render to **e** man his 376
27: 3 and his men, **e** man with his household, 376
30: 6 **e** man for his sons and for his daughters: 376
30:22 save to **e** man his wife and his children, 376

2Sa
3: 1 bring up, **e** man with his household; 376
2:16 they caught **e** one his fellow by the head, 376
2:27 morning the people had gone up **e** one 376
6:19 to **e** one a cake of bread, and a good piece 376
6:19 all the people departed **e** one to his house. 376
13: 9 And they went out **e** man from him. 3605
13:29 **e** man gat him up upon his mule, and fled. 376
13:37 And David mourned for his son **e** day. 3605
14:26 (for it was at **e** **year's** end 3117+3117+3807.1
15: 4 that **e** man which hath *any* suit or 3605
15:30 *was* with him covered **e** man his head, 376
15:36 by them ye shall send unto me **e** thing 376
18:17 and all Israel fled **e** one to his tent. 376
19: 8 for Israel had fled **e** man to his tent. 376
20: 1 son of Jesse: **e** man to his tents, O Israel. 376
20: 2 So **e** man of Israel went up from after 3605
20:12 he saw that **e** one that came by him 376
20:22 retired from the city, **e** man to his tent. 376
21:20 that had on e⁵ hand six fingers, 2050.2
21:20 on e⁵ foot six toes, four and twenty in 2050.2

1Ki
1:49 and rose up, and went **e** man his way. 376
4:25 **e** man under his vine and under his fig 376
4:27 king Solomon's table, **e** man *in* his month: 376
4:28 **e** man according to his charge. 376
5: 3 wars which were **about** him on **e** side, 5437
5: 4 my God hath given me rest on **e** side, 5439
7:30 **e** base had four brasen wheels, and plates 259
7:30 molten, at the side of **e** addition. 259
7:36 according to the proportion of **e** one, 376
7:38 **e** laver was four cubits: *and* upon every 376
7:38 e⁵ one of the ten bases one laver. 4350+1886.1
8:38 which shall know **e** man the plague of his 3605
8:39 and give to **e** man according to his ways, 376
9: 8 **e** one that passeth by it shall be 3605
10:25 they brought **e** man his present, vessels of 376
11:15 after he had smitten **e** male in Edom; 3605
11:16 until he had cut off **e** male in Edom: 3605
12:24 return **e** man to his house; for this thing is 376
14:23 on **e** high hill, and under every green tree. 3605
14:23 on every high hill, and under **e** green tree. 3605
19:18 and **e** mouth which hath not kissed him. 3605
20:20 they slew **e** one his man: and the Syrians 376
20:24 **e** man out of his place, and put captains in 376
22:17 them return **e** man to his house in peace. 376
22:28 he said, Hearken, O people, **e** one of you. 3605
22:36 **E** man to his city, and every man to his 376
22:36 to his city, and **e** man to his own country. 376

2Ki
3:19 ye shall smite **e** fenced city, 3605
3:19 **e** choice city, and shall fell every good 3605
3:19 shall fell **e** good tree, and stop all wells of 3605
3:19 and mar **e** good piece of land with stones. 3605
3:25 on **e** good piece of land cast every man 376
3:25 every good piece of land cast **e** man his 376
6: 2 take thence **e** man a beam, and let us 376
8: 9 even of **e** good thing of Damascus, 376
9:13 took his garment, and put *it* under 376
11: 8 **e** man with his weapons in his hand; 376
11: 9 took **e** man his men that were to come in 376
11:11 **e** man with his weapons in his hand, 376
12: 4 *even* the money that **e** one passeth 376

2Ki
12: 4 the money that **e** man is set at, NIH
12: 5 to them, **e** man of his acquaintance. 376
14: 6 **e** man shall be put to death for his own sin. 376
14:12 and they fled **e** man to their tents. 376
16: 4 and on the hills, and under **e** green tree. 3605
17:10 them up images and groves in **e** high hill, 3605
17:10 in every high hill, and under **e** green tree: 3605
17:29 **e** nation made gods of their 1471+1471
17:29 **e** nation in their cities wherein 1471+1471
18:31 then eat ye **e** man of his own vine, 376
18:31 **e** one of his fig tree, and drink ye every 376
18:31 drink ye **e** one the waters of his cistern: 376
23:35 **e** one according to his taxation, to give *it* 376
25: 9 great **man's** house burnt he with fire. 3605
25:30 a daily rate for **e** day, all the days of his 871.1

1Ch
9:27 the opening *thereof* **e** morning 1242+1242+1886.1+1886.1+3807.1+3807.1
9:32 to prepare *it* **e** sabbath. 7676+7676
13: 1 and hundreds, *and* with **e** leader. 3605
13: 2 send **abroad** unto our brethren **e** where, 6555
16: 3 he dealt to **e** one of Israel, both man and 3605
16: 3 to **e** one a loaf of bread, and a good piece 376
16:37 as **e** **day's** work required: 3117+3117+871.1
16:43 all the people departed **e** man to his house: 376
22:15 *manner of* cunning *men* for **e** *manner of* 3605
22:18 he *not* given you rest on **e** side? 4480+5439
23:30 **e** morning to thank and praise the Lord, 1242+1242+871.1+871.1+1886.1+1886.1
26:13 of their fathers, for **e** gate. 8179+8179+2050.1
26:32 **e** matter pertaining to God, 3605
27: 1 **e** course *were* twenty and four thousand. 259
28:14 of **e** kind of service: 5656+5656+2050.1
28:15 weight for **e** candlestick, 4501+4501+2050.1
28:15 the use of **e** candlestick. 4501+4501+2050.1
28:16 of shewbread, for **e** table; 7979+7979+2050.1
28:17 by weight for **e** bason; 3713+3713+2050.1
28:17 for **e** bason of silver: 3713+3713+2050.1
28:21 **e** willing skilful *man*, for any *manner of* 3605

2Ch
1: 2 the judges, and **e** governor in all Israel, 3605
2:14 to find out **e** device which shall be put to 3605
6:29 when **e** one shall know his own sore and 376
6:30 render unto **e** man according unto all his 376
7:21 shall be an astonishment to **e** one that 3605
8:13 after a certain rate **e** day, 3117+3117+871.1
8:14 the duty of **e** day required: 3117+3117+871.1
8:14 by their courses at **e** gate: 8179+8179+2050.1
9:21 **e** three years once came the ships of 3807.1
9:24 they brought **e** man his present, vessels of 376
10:16 **e** man to your tents, O Israel: *and* now, 376
11: 4 return **e** man to his house; for this thing is 376
11:12 in several city *he put* shields and spears, 3605
11:23 of Judah and Benjamin, unto **e** fenced city: 3605
13:11 burn unto the Lord **e** morning 1242+1242+871.1+871.1+1886.1+1886.1
13:11 **e** evening burnt sacrifices 6153+6153+871.1+871.1+1886.1+1886.1
13:11 to burn **e** evening: 6153+6153+871.1+871.1+1886.1+1886.1
14: 7 he hath given us rest on **e** side. 4480+5439
18:16 therefore **e** man to his house in peace. 376
20:23 of Seir, **e** man helped to destroy another. 376
20:27 **e** man of Judah and Jerusalem, 3605
23: 7 **e** man with his weapons in his hand; 376
23: 8 took **e** man his men that were to come in 376
23:10 **e** man having his weapon in his hand, 376
25: 4 but **e** man shall die for his own sin. 376
25:22 Israel, and they fled **e** man to his tent. 376
28: 4 and on the hills, and under **e** green tree. 3605
28:24 he made him altars in **e** corner of 3605
28:25 in **e** several city of Judah he made high 3605
29:35 the drink offerings for **e** burnt offering. NIH
30:17 passovers for **e** one *that was* not clean, 3605
30:18 The good Lord pardon **e** one 3605
31: 1 **e** man to his possession, into their own 376
31: 2 **e** man according to his service, the priests 376
31:16 unto **e** one that entereth into the house 3605
31:19 in several city, the men that were 3605
31:21 in **e** work that he began in the service of 3605
32:22 and guided them on **e** side. 4480+5439
35:15 porters *waited* at **e** gate; 8179+8179+2050.1

Ezr
2: 1 and Judah, **e** one unto his city; 376
3: 4 the duty of **e** day required; 3117+3117+871.1
3: 5 of **e** one that willingly offered a freewill 3605
5: 5 **e** one to his place, and place *them* in NIH
8:34 By number *and* by weight of **e** one: 3605
9: 4 were assembled unto me **e** one that 3605
10:14 them the elders of **e** city, 5892+5892+2050.1

Ne
3:28 the priests, **e** one over against his house. 376
4:15 all of us to the wall, **e** one unto his work. 376
4:17 *e one* with one of his hands wrought in NIH
4:18 **e** one had his sword girded by his side, 376
4:22 Let **e** one with his servant lodge within 376
4:23 *saving that* **e** one put them off *for* washing. 376
5: 7 You exact usury, **e** one of his brother. 376
5:13 So God shake out **e** man from his house, 3605
7: 3 **e** one in his watch, and every one *to be* 376
7: 3 and **e** one *to be* over against his house. 376
7: 6 and to Judah, **e** one unto his city; 376
8:16 **e** one upon the roof of his house, and in 376
10:28 **e** one having knowledge, 3605
10:31 seventh year, and the exaction of **e** debt. 3605
11: 3 in the cities of Judah dwelt in his 376
11:20 cities of Judah, **e** one in his inheritance. 376
11:23 the singers, due **for e** day. 3117+3117+871.1
12:47 porters, **e** day his portion: 3117+3117+871.1

E

E

Ne 13:10 did the work, were fled **e one** to his field. 376
13:30 and the Levites, **e** one in his business; 376
Est 1: 8 to **e man's** pleasure. 376+376+2050.1
1:22 into **e province** according 4082+4082+2050.1
1:22 to **e people** after their 5971+5971+2050.1
1:22 that **e** man should bear rule in his own 3605
1:22 according to the language of **e** people. 2050.2
2:11 walked **e day** 3117+3117+3605+2050.1
2:12 Now when **e maid's** turn 5291+5291+2050.1
2:13 thus came **e** maiden unto the king; NIH
3:12 were over **e province**, 4082+4082+2050.1
3:12 the rulers of **e people** of 5971+5971+2050.1
3:12 **e province** according to 4082+4082+2050.1
3:12 **e people** after their 5971+5971+2050.1
3:14 **e province** was 3605+4082+4082+2050.1
4: 3 in **e province**, 3605+4082+4082+2050.1
6:13 his friends **e thing** that had befallen him. 3605
8: 9 **e province** according to 4082+4082+2050.1
8: 9 unto **e people** after their 5971+5971+2050.1
8:11 **e city** to gather 3605+5892+5892+2050.1
8:13 **e province** was 3605+4082+4082+2050.1
8:17 in **e province**, 3605+4082+4082+2050.1
8:17 in **e city**, 3605+5892+5892+2050.1
9:27 time **e year**; 3605+8141+8141+2050.1
9:28 **e generation**, 1755+1755+3605+2050.1
9:28 **e family**, every province, 4940+4940+2050.1
9:28 **e province**, and every city 4082+4082+2050.1
9:28 every province, and **e city** 5892+5892+2050.1
Job 1: 4 and feasted in their houses, **e one** NIH
1:10 about all that he hath **on e side**? 4480+5439
2:11 they came **e one** from his own place; 376
2:12 they rent **e one** his mantle, 376
7:18 that thou shouldest visit him **e** morning, 3807.1
7:18 every morning, and try him **e** moment? 3807.1
12:10 In whose hand is the soul of **e** living 3605
18:11 Terrors shall make him afraid **on e side**, 5439
19:10 He hath destroyed me **on e side**, and I 5439
20:22 **e** hand of the wicked shall come upon 3605
21:33 **e** man shall draw after him, as there are 3605
24: 6 They reap **e one** his corn in the field: NIH
28:10 and his eye seeth **e** precious thing. 3605
34:11 cause **e man** to find according to his ways. 376
36:25 **E** man may see it; man may behold it afar 3605
37: 7 He sealeth up the hand of **e** man; that all 3605
39: 8 and he searcheth after **e** green thing. 3605
40:11 **e one** that is proud, and abase him. 3605
40:12 Look on **e one** that is proud, and bring 3605
42: 2 I know that thou canst do **e thing**, and 3605
42:11 **e** man also gave him a piece of money, 376
42:11 of money, and **e one** an earring of gold. 3605
Ps 7:11 and God is angry with the wicked **e** day. 3605
12: 2 speak vanity **e one** with his neighbour: 376
12: 8 wicked walk **on e side**, when the vilest 5439
29: 9 his temple doth **e one** speak of his glory. 3605
31:13 fear was **on e side**: while they 4480+5439
32: 6 For this shall **e one** that is godly pray unto 3605
39: 5 verily **e man** at his best state is altogether 3605
39: 6 Surely **e man** walketh in a vain shew: 3605
39:11 like a moth: surely **e** man is vanity. Selah. 3605
50:10 For **e** beast of the forest is mine, 3605
53: 3 **E one** of them is gone back, they are 3605
56: 5 **E** day they wrest my words: all their 3605
58: 8 melteth, let **e one** of them pass away: NIH
62:12 thou renderest to **e** man according to his NIH
63:11 **e one** that sweareth by him shall glory: 3605
64: 6 the inward thought of **e one** of them, 376
65:12 and the little hills rejoice **on e side**. 2296
68:30 till **e one** submit himself with pieces of NIH
69:34 the seas, and **e** thing that moveth therein. 3605
71:18 and thy power to **e one** that is to come. 3605
71:21 my greatness, and comfort me **on e side**. 5437
73:14 plagued, and chastened **e** morning. 3807.1
84: 7 **e one** of them in Zion appeareth before NIH
92: 2 the morning, and thy faithfulness **e** night, 871.1
104:11 They give drink to **e** beast of the field: 3605
115: 8 so is **e one** that trusteth in them. 3605
119:101 I have refrained my feet from **e** evil way, 3605
119:104 therefore I hate **e** false way. 3605
119:128 things to be right; and I hate **e** false way. 3605
119:160 **e one** of thy righteous judgments 3605
128: 1 Blessed is **e one** that feareth the LORD; 3605
135:18 so is **e one** that trusteth in them. 3605
145: 2 **E** day will I bless thee; and I will praise 3605
145:16 and satisfiest the desire of **e** living thing. 3605
150: 6 Let **e** thing that hath breath praise 3605
Pr 1:19 So are the ways of **e one** that is greedy of 3605
2: 9 judgment, and equity; yea, **e** good path. 3605
3:18 and happy is **e** one that retaineth her. NIH
7:12 the streets, and lieth in wait at **e** corner.) 3605
13:16 **E** prudent man dealeth with knowledge: 3605
14: 1 **E** wise woman buildeth her house: NIH
14:15 The simple believeth **e** word: 3605
15: 3 The eyes of the LORD are in **e** place, 3605
16: 5 **E one** that is proud in heart is an 3605
19: 6 **e man** is a friend to him that giveth gifts. 3605
20: 3 from strife: but **e** fool will be meddling. 3605
20: 6 Most men will proclaim **e one** his own 376
20:18 **e** purpose is established by counsel: NIH
21: 2 **E** way of a man is right in his own eyes: NIH
21: 5 but of **e one** that is hasty only to want. NIH
24:12 not he render to **e** man according to his NIH
24:26 **E** man shall kiss his lips that giveth a right NIH
27: 7 to the hungry soul **e** bitter thing is sweet. 3605
27:24 endure to **e generation**? 1755+1755+2050.1
29:26 **e** man's judgment cometh from the LORD. NIH

Pr 30: 5 **E** word of God is pure: he is a shield unto 3605
Ecc 3: 1 To **e** thing there is a season, and a time to 3605
3: 1 a time to **e** purpose under the heaven: 3605
3:11 hath made **e** thing beautiful in his time: 3605
3:13 also that **e** man should eat and drink, 3605
3:17 for there is a time there for **e** purpose and 3605
3:17 there for every purpose and for **e** work. 3605
4: 1 I considered all travail, and **e** right work, 3605
5:19 **E** man also to whom God hath given 3605
8: 6 Because to **e** purpose there is time and 3605
8: 9 applied my heart unto **e** work that is done 3605
10: 3 and he saith to **e one** that he is a fool. 3605
10:15 of the foolish wearieth **e one** of them, 5105.2
12:14 For God shall bring **e** work into judgment, 3605
12:14 with secret thing, whether it be good, 3605
SS 3: 8 **e man** hath his sword upon his thigh 376
4: 2 whereof **e one** beareth twins, and none is 3605
6: 6 whereof **e one** beareth twins, and there is 3605
8:11 **e one** for the fruit thereof was to bring a 376
Isa 1:23 **e one** loveth gifts, and followeth after 3605
2:12 of hosts shall be upon **e one** that is proud 3605
2:12 and lofty, and upon **e one** that is lifted up; 3605
2:15 upon **e** high tower, and upon every fenced 3605
2:15 every high tower, and upon **e** fenced wall, 3605
3: 5 **e one** by another, and every one by his 376
3: 5 by another, and **e one** by his neighbour: 376
3:12 **e one** that is written among the living 3605
4: 3 the LORD will create upon **e** dwelling 3605
7:22 honey shall **e one** eat that is left in the 3605
7:23 to pass in that day, that **e** place shall be, 3605
9: 5 battle of the warrior is with confused 3605
9:17 for **e one** is a hypocrite and an evildoer, 3605
9:17 an evildoer, and **e** mouth speaketh folly. 3605
9:20 they shall eat **e** man the flesh of his own 376
13: 7 be faint, and **e** man's heart shall melt: 3605
13: 7 they shall **e** man turn to his own people, 376
13:14 and flee **e one** into his own land. 376
13:15 **E one** that is found shall be thrust 3605
13:15 **e one** that is joined unto them shall fall 3605
14:18 lie in glory, **e one** in his own house. 376
15: 3 in their streets, **e one** shall howl, weeping 3605
16: 7 Moab howl for Moab, **e one** shall howl: 3605
19: 2 they shall fight **e one** against his brother, 376
19: 2 brother, and **e one** against his neighbour; 376
19: 7 **e thing** sown by the brooks, shall wither, 3605
19:14 they have caused Egypt to err in **e** work 3605
19:17 **e one** that maketh mention thereof shall 376
24:10 **e** house is shut up, that no man may come 3605
27: 3 I will water it **e moment**: 7281+3807.1
30:25 there shall be upon **e** high mountain, 3605
30:25 upon **e** high hill, rivers and streams of 3605
30:32 in **e** place where the grounded staff shall 3605
31: 7 For in that day **e** man shall cast away his 376
33: 2 be thou their arm **e** morning, 3807.1
34:15 also be gathered, **e one** with her mate. 802
36:16 eat ye **e one** of his vine, and every one of 376
36:16 one of his fig tree, and drink ye every 376
36:16 ye **e one** the waters of his own cistern; 376
40: 4 **E** valley shall be exalted, 3605
40: 4 **e** mountain and hill shall be made low: 3605
41: 6 They helped **e** his neighbour; 376
41: 6 **e** one said to his brother, Be of good NIH
43: 7 Even **e one** that is called by my name: 3605
44:23 mountains, O forest, and **e** tree therein: 3605
45:23 That unto me **e** knee shall bow, 3605
45:23 knee shall bow, **e** tongue shall swear. 3605
47:15 they shall wander **e one** to his quarter; 376
51:13 hast feared continually **e** day because of 3605
52: 5 name continually **e** day is blasphemed. 3605
53: 6 we have turned **e one** to his own way; 376
54:17 **e** tongue that shall rise against thee in 3605
55: 1 Ho, **e one** that thirsteth, come ye to 3605
56: 6 **e one** that keepeth the sabbath from 3605
56:11 **e one** for his gain, from his quarter. 376
57: 5 Inflaming yourselves with idols under **e** 3605
58: 6 go free, and that ye break **e** yoke? 3605
Jer 1:15 shall set **e one** his throne at the entering 3605
2:20 when upon **e** high hill and under every 3605
2:20 and under **e** green tree thou wanderest, 3605
3: 6 she is gone up upon **e** high mountain and 3605
3: 6 high mountain and under **e** green tree, 3605
3:13 ways to the strangers under **e** green tree, 3605
4:29 **e** city shall be forsaken, and not a man 3605
5: 6 **e one** that goeth out thence shall be torn 3605
5: 8 **e one** neighed after his neighbour's wife. 376
6: 3 they shall feed **e one** in his place. 376
6:13 of them **e one** is given to covetousness; 3605
6:13 the prophet even unto the priest **e one** 3605
6:25 of the enemy and fear is **on e side**. 4480+5439
8: 6 **e one** turned to his course, as the horse 3605
8:10 **e one** from the least even unto the 3605
8:10 the prophet even unto the priest **e one** 3605
9: 4 Take ye heed **e one** of his neighbour, 376
9: 4 for brother will utterly supplant, 3605
9: 4 neighbour will walk with slanders. 3605
9: 5 they will deceive **e one** his neighbour, 376
9:20 and **e one** her neighbour lamentation. 802
10:14 **E** man is brutish in his knowledge: 3605
10:14 **e** founder is confounded by the graven 3605
11: 8 walked **e one** in the imagination of their 3605
12: 4 mourn, and the herbs of **e** field wither, 3605
12:15 **e man** to his heritage, and every man to 376
12:15 to his heritage, and **e** man to his land. 376
13:12 Israel, **E** bottle shall be filled with wine: 3605

Jer 13:12 Do we not certainly know that **e** bottle 3605
15:10 usury; yet **e** one of them doth curse me. 3605
16:12 ye walk **e one** after the imagination of his 376
16:16 they shall hunt them from **e** mountain, 3605
16:16 from **e** hill, and out of the holes of 3605
17:10 even to give **e man** according to his ways, 376
18:11 return ye now **e one** from his evil way, 376
18:12 will **e one** do the imagination of his evil 376
18:16 **e one** that passeth thereby shall be 3605
19: 8 **e one** that passeth thereby shall be 3605
19: 9 they shall eat **e one** the flesh of his friend 376
20: 7 I am in derision daily, **e one** mocketh me. 376
20:10 defaming of many, fear **on e side**. 4480+5439
22: 7 against thee, **e one** with his weapons; 376
22: 8 they shall say **e man** to his neighbour, 376
23:17 they say unto **e one** that walketh after 3605
23:27 which they tell **e man** to his neighbour, 376
23:30 that steal my words **e one** from his 376
23:35 Thus shall ye say **e one** to his neighbour, 376
23:35 **e one** to his brother, What hath the LORD 376
23:36 for **e man's** word shall be his 376+3807.1
25: 5 Turn ye again now **e one** from his evil 376
26: 3 and turn **e man** from his evil way, 376
29:26 **e** man that is mad, and maketh himself 3605
30: 6 wherefore do I see **e** man with his hands 3605
30:16 all thine adversaries, **e one** of them, 3605
31:25 and I have replenished **e** sorrowful soul. 3605
31:30 **e one** shall die for his own iniquity: 376
31:30 **e** man that eateth the sour grape, his teeth 3605
31:34 they shall teach no more **e man** his 376
31:34 **e** man his brother, saying, Know 376
32:19 to give **e one** according to his ways, 376
34: 9 That **e man** should let his manservant, 376
34: 9 **e man** his maidservant, being a Hebrew 376
34:10 that **e one** should let his manservant, 376
34:10 and **e one** his maidservant, go free, 376
34:14 At the end of seven years let ye go **e** man 376
34:15 in proclaiming liberty **e man** to his 376
34:16 caused **e man** his servant, and every man 376
34:16 man his servant, and **e man** his handmaid, 376
34:17 **e one** to his brother, and every man to his 376
34:17 to his brother, and **e man** to his neighbour: 376
35:15 Return ye now **e man** from his evil way, 376
36: 3 that they may return **e man** from his evil 376
36: 7 and will return **e one** from his evil way: 376
37:10 yet should they rise up **e man** in his tent, 376
43: 6 **e** person that Nebuzar-adan the captain of 3605
47: 4 and Zidon **e** helper that remaineth: 3605
48: 8 the spoiler shall come upon **e** city, 3605
48:37 For **e** head shall be bald, and every beard 3605
48:37 head shall be bald, and **e** beard clipt: 3605
49: 5 ye shall be driven out **e man** right forth; 376
49:17 **e one** that goeth by it shall be astonished, 3605
49:29 cry unto them, Fear is **on e side**. 4480+5439
50:13 **e one** that goeth by Babylon shall be 3605
50:16 sword they shall turn **e one** to his people, 376
50:16 and they shall flee **e one** to his own land. 376
50:42 **e one** put in array, like a man to the battle, NIH
51: 6 of Babylon, and deliver **e man** his soul: 376
51: 9 and let us go **e one** into his own country: 376
51:17 **E** man is brutish by his knowledge; 376
51:17 **e** founder is confounded by the graven 3605
51:29 for **e** purpose of the LORD shall be NIH
51:45 deliver ye **e man** his soul from the fierce 376
51:56 are taken, **e one** of their bows is broken: 376
52:34 **e day** a portion until the 3117+3117+871.1
La 2:19 that faint for hunger in the top of **e** street. 3605
3:23 They are new **e** morning: great is thy 3807.1
4: 1 are poured out in the top of **e** street. 3605
Eze 1: 6 **e one** had four faces, and every one had NIH
1: 6 had four faces, and **e one** had four wings. 259
1: 9 they went **e one** straight forward. 376
1:11 two wings of **e one** were joined one to 376
1:12 they went **e one** straight forward: whither 376
1:23 **e one** had two, which covered on this 376
1:23 covered on this side, and **e one** had two, 376
6:13 upon **e** high hill, in all the tops of 3605
6:13 under **e** green tree, and under every thick 3605
6:13 every green tree, and under **e** thick oak, 3605
7:16 of them mourning, **e one** for his iniquity. 376
8:10 behold **e** form of creeping things, 3605
8:11 with **e man** his censer in his hand; 376
8:12 **e** man in the chambers of his imagery? 376
9: 1 **e man** with his destroying weapon in 376
9: 2 **e man** a slaughter weapon in his hand; 376
10:14 **e** one had four faces: the first face was NIH
10:19 **e one** stood at the door of the east gate of NIH
10:21 **E one** had four faces apiece, and every one 259
10:21 four faces apiece, and **e one** four wings; 259
10:22 they went **e one** straight forward. 376
11: 5 that come into your mind, **e one** of them. NIH
12:14 I will scatter toward **e** wind all that are 3605
12:22 days are prolonged, and **e** vision faileth? 3605
12:23 are at hand, and the effect of **e** vision. 3605
13:18 kerchiefs upon the head of **e** stature 3605
14: 4 **E man** of the house of Israel that 376+3605
14: 7 For **e** one of the house of Israel, 376+3605
16:15 pouredst out thy fornications on **e one** 3605
16:24 hast made thee a high place in **e** street. 3605
16:25 Thou hast built thy high place at **e** head 3605
16:25 hast opened thy feet to **e one** that passed 3605
16:31 thine eminent place in the head of **e** way, 3605
16:31 and makest thine high place in **e** street; 3605
16:33 thee **on e side** for thy whoredom. 4480+5439
16:44 **e one** that useth proverbs shall use this 3605

Eze 17:23 under it shall dwell all fowl of **e** wing; 3605
18:30 of Israel, **e** one according to his ways, 376
19: 8 the nations set against him **on e side** 5439
20: 7 Cast ye away **e man** the abominations of 376
20: 8 they did not **e man** cast away 376
20:28 saw **e** high hill, and all the thick trees, 3605
20:39 serve ye **e** his idols, and hereafter 376
20:47 it shall devour **e** green tree in thee, 3605
20:47 every green tree in thee, and **e** dry tree: 3605
21: 7 **e** heart shall melt, and all hands shall be 3605
21: 7 **e** spirit shall faint, and all knees shall be 3605
21:10 contemneth the rod of my son, *as* **e** tree. 3605
22: 6 **e one** were in thee to their power to shed 376
23:22 bring them against thee **on e side**; 4480+5439
24: 4 *even* **e** good piece, the thigh, 3605
26:16 shall tremble at moment, NIH
28:13 **e** precious stone *was* thy covering, NIH
28:23 by the sword upon her **on e side**; 4480+5439
29:18 **e** head *was* made bald, and every shoulder 3605
29:18 made bald, and **e** shoulder *was* peeled: 3605
32:10 they shall tremble at moment, every NIH
32:10 **e** man for his own life, in the day of thy 376
33:20 I will judge you **e** one after his ways. 376
33:26 and ye defile **e** one his neighbour's wife: 376
33:30 **e** one to his brother, saying, Come, I pray 376
34: 6 all the mountains, and upon **e** high hill: 3605
34: 8 my flock became meat to **e** beast of 3605
36: 3 and swallowed you up **on e side**, 4480+5439
37:21 will gather them **on e side**, 4480+5439
38:20 and **e** wall shall fall to the ground. 3605
38:21 **e** man's sword shall be against his brother. 376
39: 4 give thee unto the ravenous birds of **e** 3605
39:17 Speak unto **e** feathered fowl, and to every 3605
39:17 to **e** beast of the field, 3605
39:17 gather yourselves **on e side** to my 4480+5439
40: 7 And **e** little chamber *was* one reed long, NIH
41: 5 the breadth of **e** side chamber, four cubits, NIH
41: 5 round about the house **on e side**. 5439
41:10 round about the house **on e side**. 5439+5439
41:18 a cherub; and **e** cherub had two faces; NIH
43:25 Seven days shalt thou prepare **e** day a 3807.1
44: 5 with **e** going forth of the sanctuary. 3605
44:29 **e** dedicate thing in Israel shall be theirs. 3605
44:30 of all *things*, and **e** oblation of all, 3605
44:30 of **e** sort of your oblations, shall be 3605
45:20 *day* of the month for **e** one that erreth, 376
46:13 thou shalt prepare it **e** morning. 1242+1242+871.1+871.1+1886.1+1886.1
46:14 a meat offering for it **e** morning, 1242+1242+871.1+871.1+1886.1+1886.1
46:15 **e** morning for a continual burnt offering. 1242+1242+871.1+871.1+1886.1+1886.1
46:18 that my people be not scattered **e** man 376
46:21 **e corner** of the court *there was* a 4740+4740
47: 9 *that* **e** thing that liveth, which moveth, 3605
47: 9 **e** thing shall live whither the river 3605

Da 3:10 that **e** man that shall hear the sound of 3606
3:29 That **e** people, nation, and language, 3606
6:12 that **e** man that shall ask *a petition* of any 3606
6:26 That in **e** dominion of my kingdom *men* 3606
11:36 magnify himself above **e** god, 3605
12: 1 **e** one that *shall* be found written in 3605

Hos 4: 3 **e** one that dwelleth therein shall languish 3605
9: 1 hast loved a reward upon **e** cornfloor. 3605

Joel 2: 7 and they shall march **e** one on his ways, 3605
2: 8 they shall walk **e** one in his path: 1397

Am 2: 8 upon clothes laid to pledge by **e** altar, 3605
4: 3 **e** cow at that which is before her; 802
4: 4 bring your sacrifices **e** morning, NIH
8: 3 *shall* be many dead bodies in **e** place; 3605
8: 8 and **e** one mourn that dwelleth therein? 3605
8:10 upon all loins, and baldness upon **e** head; 3605

Ob 1: 9 the end that **e** one of the mount of Esau 376

Jnh 1: 5 cried **e** man unto his god, and cast forth 376
1: 7 And they said **e** one to his fellow, Come, 376
3: 8 let them turn **e** one from his evil way, 376

Mic 4: 4 they shall sit **e** man under his vine and 376
4: 5 For all people will walk **e** one in the name 376
7: 2 they hunt **e man** his brother *with* a net. 376

Hab 1:10 they shall deride **e** strong hold; for they 3605

Zep 2:11 shall worship him, *even* **e** one from his place, 376
2:15 **e** one that passeth by her shall hiss, 3605
3: 5 **e** morning doth he bring his judgment 1242+1242+871.1+871.1+1886.1+1886.1

Zec 3:19 fame in *the* land where they have been put 3605
1: 9 and ye run **e man** unto his own house. 376
2:14 so *is* **e** work of their hands; and *that* 376
2:22 **e** one by the sword of his brother. 376

Zec 3:10 shall ye call **e man** his neighbour, under 376
5: 3 for **e one** that stealeth shall be cut off *as* 3605
5: 3 **e** one that sweareth shall be cut off *as on* 3605
7: 9 and compassions **e man** to his brother: 376
8: 4 **e man** with his staff in his hand for very 376
8:10 Let not all men **e** one against his neighbour. 376
8:16 Speak ye **e man** the truth to his neighbour; 376
10: 1 showers of rain, to **e** one grass in the field. 3605
10: 4 out of him **e** oppressor together. 3605
11: 6 I *will* deliver the men **e** one into his 376
11: 6 let the rest eat **e** one the flesh of another. 802
12: 4 I will smite **e** horse with astonishment, 3605
12: 4 will smite **e** horse of the people with 3605
12:12 land shall mourn, **e family** apart; 4940+4940
12:14 **e family** apart, and their wives 4940+4940
13: 4 the prophets shall be ashamed **e one** of 376
14:13 they shall lay hold **e** one of his hand on 376

Zec 14:16 *that* **e one** that is left of all the nations 3605
14:21 **e** pot in Jerusalem and in Judah shall be 3605

Mal 1:11 in **e** place incense *shall* be offered unto 3605
2:10 why do we deal treacherously **e man** 376
2:17 **E** one that doeth evil *is* good in the sight 3605

Mt 3:10 **e** tree which bringeth not forth good fruit 3956
4: 4 **e** word that proceedeth out of the mouth 3956
7: 8 For **e one** that asketh receiveth; and he 3956
7:17 so **e** good tree bringeth forth good fruit; 3956
7:19 **E** tree that bringeth not forth good fruit is 3956
7:21 Not **e one** that saith unto me, Lord, Lord, 3956
7:26 And **e one** that heareth these sayings of 3956
8:33 told **e** thing, and what was befallen in 3956
9:35 and healing **e** sickness and every disease 3956
9:35 and **e** disease among the people. 3956
12:25 **E** kingdom divided against itself is 3956
12:25 and **e** city or house divided against itself 3956
12:36 That **e** idle word that men shall speak, 3956
13:47 cast into the sea, and gathered of **e** kind: 3956
13:52 Therefore **e** scribe *which is* instructed 3956
15:13 But he answered and said, **E** plant, 3956
16:27 he shall reward **e man** according to his 1538
18:16 witnesses **e** word may be established. 3956
18:35 if ye from your hearts forgive not **e** one 1538
19: 3 a man to put away his wife for **e** cause? 3956
19:29 And **e one** that hath forsaken houses, 3956
20: 9 hour, they received **e man** a penny. 303
20:10 they likewise received **e man** a penny. 303
25:15 to **e man** according to his several ability; 1538
25:29 For unto **e one** that hath shall be given, 3956
26:22 began **e one** of them to say unto him, 1538

Mk 1:45 and they came to him **from e quarter**. 3836
7:14 Hearken unto me **e one** of you, 3956
8:25 he was restored, and saw **e** *man* clearly. 537
9:49 For **e one** shall be salted with fire, 3956
9:49 and **e** sacrifice shall be salted with salt. 3956
13:34 and to **e man** his work, and commanded 1538
15:24 lots upon them, what **e** man should take. 5101
16:15 and preach the gospel to **e** creature. 3956
16:20 they went forth, and preached **e** where, 3837

Lk 2: 3 went to be taxed, **e one** into his own city. 1538
2:23 **E** male that openeth the womb shall be 3956
2:41 Now his parents went to Jerusalem **e** year 2596
3: 5 **E** valley shall be filled, and every 3956
3: 5 and **e** mountain and hill shall be brought 3956
3: 9 **e** tree therefore which bringeth not forth 3956
4: 4 by bread alone, but by **e** word of God. 3956
4:37 the fame of him went out into **e** place 3956
4:40 and he laid *his* hands on **e** one of them, 1538
5:17 were come out of **e** town of Galilee, 3956
6:30 Give to **e man** that asketh of thee; 3956
6:40 **e one** *that is* perfect shall be as his master 3956
6:44 For **e** tree is known by his own fruit. 1538
8: 1 he went throughout **e** city and village, 2596
8: 4 and were come to him out of **e** city, 2596
9: 6 the gospel, and healing **e** where. 3837
9:43 while they wondered **e one** at all *things* 3956
10: 1 and two before his face into **e** city and 3956
11: 4 we also forgive **e one** *that is* indebted to 3956
11:10 For **e one** that asketh receiveth; and he 3956
11:17 **E** kingdom divided against itself is 3956
16: 5 So he called **e** one of his lord's debtors 1538
16:16 is preached, and **e man** presseth into it. 3956
16:19 fine linen, and fared sumptuously **e** day: 2596
18:14 for **e one** that exalteth himself shall be 3956
19:15 he might know how much **e man** had 5101
19:26 unto **e one** which hath shall be given; 3956
19:43 thee round, and keep thee in **on e side**, 3840

Jn 1: 9 which lighteth **e man** *that* cometh into 3956
2:10 **E** man at the beginning doth set forth 3956
3: 8 so is **e one** that is born of the Spirit. 3956
3:20 For **e one** that doeth evil hateth the light, 3956
6: 7 that **e one** of them may take a little. 1538
6:40 that **e one** which seeth the Son, 3956
6:45 **E** *man* therefore that hath heard, 3956
7:23 I have made a man **e whit** whole on 3650
7:53 And **e man** went unto his own house. 1538
13:10 save to wash *his* feet, but is clean **e whit**: 3650
15: 2 **E** branch in me that beareth not fruit he 3956
15: 2 *e branch* that beareth fruit, he purgeth 3956
16:32 **e** man to his own, and shall leave me 1538
18:37 **E one** that is of the truth heareth my 3956
19:23 and made four parts, to **e** soldier a part; 1538
21:25 which, if they should be written **e** one, 2596

Ac 2: 5 men, out of **e** nation under heaven. 3956
2: 6 that **e** man heard them speak in his own 1538
2: 8 And how hear we **e man** in our own 1538
2:38 be baptized **e one** of you in the name of 1538
2:43 And fear came upon **e** soul: 3956
2:45 them to all *men*, as **e** man had need. 5100
3:23 And it shall come to pass, *that* **e** soul, 3956
3:26 in turning away **e one** of you from *his* 1538
4:35 distribution was made unto **e man** 1538
5:16 spirits: and they were healed **e** one. 537
5:42 and **in e house**, they ceased not to 2596+3624
8: 3 the church, entering into **e house**, 2596+3624
8: 4 went **e where** preaching the word. 1330
11:29 But in **e** nation he that feareth him, 3956
11:29 **e man** according to his ability, 1538
13:27 which are read **e** sabbath day, 2596+3956
14:23 ordained them elders in **e** church, 1577+2596
15:21 For Moses of old time hath in **e** city 2596
15:21 being read in the synagogues **e** 2596+3956
15:36 visit our brethren in **e** city where we 3956
16:26 and **e one's** bands were loosed. 3956

Ac 17:27 though he be not far from **e** one 1538
17:30 now commandeth all men **e** where to 3837
18: 4 he reasoned in the synagogue **e** 2596+3956
20:23 that the Holy Ghost witnesseth in **e** 2596
20:31 three years I ceased not to warn **e** one 1538
21:26 should be offered for **e** one of them. 1538
21:28 that teacheth all *men* **e** where against 3837
22:19 beat in **e** synagogue them that believed 2596
26:11 And I punished them oft in **e** synagogue, 3956
28: 2 and received us **e** one, because of 3956
28:22 know that **e where** it is spoken against. 3837

Ro 1:16 unto salvation to **e** one that believeth; 3956
2: 6 will render to **e** *man* according to his 1538
2: 9 upon **e** soul of man that doeth evil, 3956
2:10 and peace, to **e** man that worketh good, 3956
3: 2 Much **e** way: chiefly, because that unto 3956
3: 4 let God be true, but **e** man a liar; as it 3956
3:19 that **e** mouth may be stopped, and all 3956
10: 4 for righteousness to **e** one that believeth. 3956
12: 3 unto me, to **e** *man* that is among you, 3956
12: 3 according as God hath dealt to **e** man 3956
12: 5 are **e** one members one of another. 2596+3588
13: 1 Let **e** soul be subject unto the higher 3956
14: 5 another esteemeth **e** day *alike*. Let every 3956
14: 5 **e** man be fully persuaded in his own 1538
14:11 that **e** knee shall bow to me, and every tongue 3956
14:11 to me, and **e** tongue shall confess to God. 3956
14:12 **e** one of us shall give account of himself 1538
15: 2 Let **e** one of us please *his* neighbour for 1538

1Co 1: 2 with all that in **e** place call upon the name 3956
1: 5 That in **e** *thing* ye are enriched by him, 3956
1:12 that **e** one of you saith, I am of Paul; 1538
3: 5 even as the Lord gave to **e** man? 1538
3: 8 **e man** shall receive his own reward 1538
3:10 But let **e man** take heed how he buildeth 1538
3:13 **E man's** work shall be made manifest: 1538
3:13 fire shall try **e man's** work of what sort 1538
4: 5 and then shall **e man** have praise of God. 1538
4:17 as I teach **e where** in every church. 3837
4:17 as I teach every where in **e** church. 3956
6:18 **E** sin that a man doeth is without the 3956
7: 2 let **e man** have his own wife, and 1538
7: 2 and let **e woman** have her own husband. 1538
7: 7 But **e man** hath his proper gift of God, 1538
7:17 But as God hath distributed to **e** man, 1538
7:17 as the Lord hath called **e** one, so let him 1538
7:20 Let **e man** abide in the same calling 1538
7:24 Brethren, let **e man**, wherein he is called, 1538
8: 7 Howbeit *there is* not in **e** man that 3956
9:25 And **e** *man* that striveth for the mastery is 3956
10:24 his own, but **e** man another's *wealth*. 3956
11: 3 know, that the head of **e** man is Christ; 3956
11: 4 **E** man praying or prophesying, having *his* 3956
11: 5 But **e** woman that prayeth or 3956
11:21 in eating **e one** taketh before *other* his 1538
12: 7 Spirit is given to **e** man to profit withal. 1538
12:11 dividing to **e** man severally as he will. 1538
12:18 now hath God set the members one of **e** 1538
14:26 **e** one of you hath a psalm, hath a 1538
15:23 But **e** man in his own order: Christ 1538
15:30 And why stand we in jeopardy **e** hour? 3956
15:38 pleased him, and to **e** seed his own body. 1538
16: 2 Upon the first *day* of the week let **e** one 1538
16:16 and to **e** one that helpeth with *us*, and 3956

2Co 2:14 savour of his knowledge by us in **e** place. 3956
4: 2 to **e** man's conscience in the sight of God. 3956
4: 8 *We are* troubled on **e** side, yet not 3956
5:10 that **e** one may receive the *things done* 1538
7: 5 we were troubled on **e** side; without 3956
8: 7 as ye abound in **e** *thing, in* faith, 3956
9: 7 **E** man according as he purposeth in *his* 1538
9: 8 all *things*, may abound to **e** good work: 3956
9:11 Being enriched in **e** *thing* to all 3956
10: 5 high *thing* that exalteth itself against 3956
10: 5 bringing into captivity **e** thought to 3956
13: 1 witnesses shall **e** word be established. 3956

Gal 3:10 Cursed *is* **e** one that continueth not in 3956
3:13 Cursed *is* **e** one that hangeth on a tree: 3956
5: 3 For I testify again to **e** man that is 3956
6: 4 But let **e man** prove his own work, 1538
6: 5 For **e man** shall bear his own burden. 1538

Eph 1:21 dominion, and name that is named, 3956
4: 7 But unto **e** one of us is given grace 1538
4:14 carried about with **e** wind of doctrine, 3956
4:16 by that which is **e** joint supplieth, 3956
4:16 working in the measure of **e** part, 1520+1538
4:25 speak **e man** truth with his neighbour: 1538
5:24 the wives *be* to their own husbands in **e** 3956
5:33 Nevertheless let **e** one of you in particular 1538

Php 1: 3 I thank my God upon **e** remembrance of 3956
1: 4 Always in **e** prayer of mine for you all 3956
1:18 notwithstanding, **e** way, whether in 3956
2: 4 Look not **e man** on his own *things*, but 1538
2: 4 but **e** man also on the *things* of others. 1538
2: 9 given him a name which is above **e** name: 3956
2:10 That at the name of Jesus **e** knee should 3956
2:11 *that* **e** tongue should confess that Jesus 3956
4: 6 but in **e** *thing* by prayer and supplication 3956
4:12 **e where** and in all *things* I am instructed 3956
4:21 Salute **e** saint in Christ Jesus. 3956

Col 1:10 being fruitful in **e** good work, 3956
1:15 invisible God, the firstborn of **e** creature: 3956
1:23 which was preached to **e** creature which 3956
1:28 warning **e** man, and teaching every man 3956
1:28 and teaching **e** man in all wisdom; 3956

E

Col	1:28	we may present *e* man perfect in Christ	3956
	4: 6	know how ye ought to answer *e* man.	1538
1Th	1: 8	also in *e* place your faith to God-ward is	3956
	2:11	and comforted and charged *e* one of you,	1538
	4: 4	That *e* one of you should know how to	1538
	5:18	In *e* thing give thanks: for this *is* the will	3956
2Th	1: 3	the charity of *e* one of you all towards	1538
	2:17	stablish you in *e* good word and work.	3956
	3: 6	ye withdraw yourselves from *e* brother	3956
	3:17	hand, which is the token in *e* epistle:	3956
1Ti	2: 8	I will therefore that men pray *e* where,	3956
	4: 4	For *e* creature of God *is* good,	3956
	5:10	if she have diligently followed *e* good	3956
2Ti	2:19	Let *e* one that nameth the name of Christ	3956
	2:21	*and* prepared unto *e* good work.	3956
	4:18	And the Lord shall deliver me from *e* evil	3956
Tit	1: 5	and ordain elders in *e* city, as I had	2596
	1:16	and unto *e* good work reprobate.	3956
	3: 1	to be ready to *e* good work,	3956
Phm	1: 6	*e* good *thing* which is in you in Christ	3956
Heb	2: 2	and transgression and	3956
	2: 9	grace of God should taste death for *e* man.	3956
	3: 4	For *e* house is builded by some *man;* but	3956
	5: 1	For *e* high priest taken from among men	3956
	5:13	For *e* that useth milk *is* unskilful in	3956
	6:11	And we desire that *e* one of you do shew	3956
	8: 3	For *e* high priest is ordained to offer gifts	3956
	8:11	And they shall not teach *e* man his	1538
	8:11	and *e* man his brother, saying, Know	1538
	9: 7	*went* the high priest alone once *e* year,	NIG
	9:19	For when Moses had spoken *e* precept to	3956
	9:25	holy *place e* year with blood of others;	2596
	10: 3	remembrance *again made* of sins *e* year.	2596
	10:11	And *e* priest standeth daily ministering	3956
	12: 1	let us lay aside *e* weight, and the sin	3956
	12: 6	and scourgeth *e* son whom he receiveth.	3956
	13:21	Make you perfect in *e* good work to do	3956
Jas	1:14	But *e* man is tempted, when he is drawn	1538
	1:17	*E* good gift and every perfect gift is from	3956
	1:17	good gift and *e* perfect gift is from above,	3956
	1:19	let *e* man be swift to hear, slow to speak,	3956
	3: 7	For *e* kind of beasts, and of birds,	3956
	3:16	there *is* confusion and *e* evil work.	3956
1Pe	1:17	judgeth according to *e* man's work,	1538
	2:13	Submit yourselves to *e* ordinance of man	3956
	3:15	ready always to *give* an answer to *e* man	3956
	4:10	As *e* man hath received the gift, *even so*	1538
1Jn	2:29	ye know that *e* one which doeth	3956
	3: 3	And *e* man that hath this hope in him	3956
	4: 1	believe not *e* spirit, but try the spirits	3956
	4: 2	*E* spirit that confesseth that Jesus Christ is	3956
	4: 3	And *e* spirit that confesseth not that Jesus	3956
	4: 7	and *e* one that loveth is born of God,	3956
	5: 1	*e* one that loveth him that begat loveth	3956
Rev	1: 7	and *e* eye shall see him, and they *also*	3956
	2:23	I will give unto *e* one of you according to	1538
	5: 8	having *e* one *of them* harps,	1538
	5: 9	us to God by thy blood out of *e* kindred,	3956
	5:13	And *e* creature which is in heaven,	3956
	6:11	white robes were given unto *e* one of	1538
	6:14	*e* mountain and island were moved out	3956
	6:15	and the mighty *men,* and *e* bondman,	3956
	6:15	free *man,* hid themselves in the dens	3956
	14: 6	and to *e* nation, and kindred, and tongue,	3956
	16: 3	and living soul died in the sea.	3956
	16:20	*e* island fled *away,* and the mountains	3956
	16:21	*e* stone about the weight of a talent:	NIG
	18: 2	and the hold of *e* foul spirit, and a cage of	3956
	18: 2	and a cage of *e* unclean and hateful bird.	3956
	18:17	And *e* shipmaster, and all the company in	3956
	20:13	were judged *e* man according to their	1538
	21:21	*e* several gate was of one pearl:	3956
	22: 2	yielded her fruit *e* month:	1520+1538+2596
	22:12	to give *e* man according as his work shall	1538
	22:18	For I testify unto *e* *man* that heareth	3956

EVI (2)

| Nu | 31: 8 | namely, **E**, and Rekem, and Zur, and Hur, | 189 |
| Jos | 13:21 | **E**, and Rekem, and Zur, and Hur, | 189 |

EVIDENCE (7) [EVIDENCES]

Jer	32:10	I subscribed the *e,* and sealed *it,* and	5612
	32:11	So I took the *e* of the purchase, *both* that	5612
	32:12	I gave the *e* of the purchase unto Baruch	5612
	32:14	*e* of the purchase, both which is sealed,	5612
	32:14	which is sealed, and this *e* which is open;	5612
	32:16	Now when I had delivered the *e* of	5612
Heb	11: 1	*things* hoped for, the *e* of things not seen.	1650

EVIDENCES (2) [EVIDENCE]

| Jer | 32:14 | these *e,* this evidence of the purchase, | 5612 |
| | 32:44 | subscribe *e,* and seal *them,* and | 5612 |

EVIDENT (5) [EVIDENTLY]

Job	6:28	look upon me; for *it is e* unto you if I lie.	6440
Gal	3:11	by the law in the sight of God, *it is e:*	1212
Php	1:28	which is to them an *e* token of perdition,	1732
Heb	7:14	*it is e* that our Lord sprang out of Juda;	4271
	7:15	And it is yet far more *e:* for that after	2612

EVIDENTLY (2) [EVIDENT]

| Ac | 10: 3 | He saw in a vision *e,* about the ninth hour | 5320 |
| Gal | 3: 1 | eyes Jesus Christ hath been *e* **set forth,** | 4270 |

EVIL (613) [EVILDOER, EVILDOERS, EVILS]

Ge	2: 9	and the tree of knowledge of good and *e.*	7451
	2:17	the tree of the knowledge of good and *e,*	7451
	3: 5	ye shall be as gods, knowing good and *e.*	7451
	3:22	as one of us, to know good and *e:*	7451
	6: 5	of his heart *was* only *e* continually.	7451
	8:21	the imagination of man's heart *is e* from	7451
	19:19	lest some *e* take me, and I die:	7451
	37: 2	Joseph brought unto his father their *e*	7451
	37:20	say, Some *e* beast hath devoured him:	7451
	37:33	son's coat; an *e* beast hath devoured him;	7451
	44: 4	Wherefore have ye rewarded *e* for good?	7451
	44: 5	he divineth? ye have **done** *e* in so doing.	7489
	44:34	peradventure I see the *e* that shall come	7451
	47: 9	have the days of the years of my life	7451
	48:16	Angel which redeemed me from all *e,*	7451
	50:15	will certainly requite us all the *e* which	7451
	50:17	and their sin; for they did unto thee *e:*	7451
	50:20	But as for you, ye thought *e* against me;	7451
Ex	5:19	*that* they *were* in *e* case, after it was said,	7451
	5:22	hast thou so *e* **entreated** this people?	7489
	5:23	thy name, he hath **done** *e* to this people;	7489
	10:10	little ones: look *to it;* for *e* is before you.	7451
	23: 2	shalt not follow a multitude to do *e;*	7451
	32:12	and repent of *this e* against thy people.	7451
	32:14	the Lord repented of the *e* which he	7451
	33: 4	when the people heard these *e* tidings,	7451
Lev	5: 4	pronouncing with *his* lips to do *e,*	7489
	26: 6	*e* beasts out of the land,	7451
Nu	13:32	they brought up an *e* **report** of the land	1681
	14:27	How long *shall I bear* with this *e*	7451
	14:35	I will surely do it unto all this *e*	7451
	14:37	Even *those* men that did bring up the *e*	7451
	20: 5	of Egypt, to bring us in unto this *e* place?	7451
	32:13	that had done *e* in the sight of the Lord,	7451
Dt	1:35	of this *e* generation see that good land,	7451
	1:39	had no knowledge between good and *e,*	7451
	4:25	shall do *e* in the sight of the Lord thy	7451
	7:15	will put none of the *e* diseases of Egypt,	7451
	13: 5	shalt thou put the *e* away from the midst	7451
	15: 9	thine eye be *e* against thy poor brother,	7451
	17: 1	is blemish, *or* any *e* **favouredness:**	1697+7451
	17: 7	So thou shalt put the *e* away from among	7451
	17:12	and thou shalt put away the *e* from Israel.	7451
	19:19	thou put the *e* away from among you.	7451
	19:20	henceforth commit no more any such *e*	7451
	21:21	shalt thou put *e* away from among you;	7451
	22:14	bring up an *e* name upon her, and say,	7451
	22:19	hath brought up an *e* name upon a virgin	7451
	22:21	shalt thou put *e* away from among you.	7451
	22:22	so shalt thou put away *e* from Israel.	7451
	22:24	thou shalt put away *e* from among you.	7451
	24: 7	thou shalt put *e* away from among you.	7451
	26: 6	the Egyptians *e* **entreated** us,	7489
	28:54	his eye shall be *e* toward his brother,	3415
	28:56	her eye shall be *e* towards the husband of	3415
	29:21	the Lord shall separate him unto *e* out of	7451
	30:15	*this* day life and good, and death and *e;*	7451
	31:29	*e* will befall you in the latter days;	7451
	31:29	ye will do *e* in the sight of the Lord,	7451
Jos	23:15	shall the Lord bring upon you all *e*	7451
	24:15	if it seem *e* unto you to serve the Lord,	7489
Jdg	2:11	the children of Israel did *e* in the sight of	7451
	2:15	hand of the Lord was against them for *e,*	7451
	3: 7	the children of Israel did *e* in the sight of	7451
	3:12	the children of Israel did *e* again in	7451
	3:12	they had done *e* in the sight of the Lord.	7451
	4: 1	the children of Israel again did *e* in	7451
	6: 1	the children of Israel did *e* in the sight of	7451
	9:23	God sent an *e* spirit between Abimelech	7451
	9:57	all the *e* of the men of Shechem did God	7451
	10: 6	the children of Israel did *e* again in	7451
	13: 1	the children of Israel did *e* again in	7451
	20:13	to death, and put away *e* from Israel.	7451
	20:34	but they knew not that *e* *was* near them.	7451
	20:41	for they saw that *e* was come upon them.	7451
1Sa	2:23	for I hear of your *e* dealings by all this	7451
	6: 9	*then* he hath done us this great *e:*	7451
	12:19	for we have added unto all our sins *this e,*	7451
	15:19	and didst *e* in the sight of the Lord?	7451
	16:14	an *e* spirit from the Lord troubled him.	7451
	16:15	an *e* spirit from God troubleth thee.	7451
	16:16	when the *e* spirit from God is upon thee,	7451
	16:23	the *e* spirit from God was upon Saul,	NIH
	16:23	and the *e* spirit departed from him.	7451
	18:10	the *e* spirit from God came upon Saul,	7451
	19: 9	the *e* spirit from the Lord was upon	7451
	20: 7	be sure that *e* is determined by him.	7451
	20: 9	for if I knew certainly that *e* were	7451
	20:13	*but* if it please my father to do thee *e,*	7451
	24:11	that *there is* neither *e* nor transgression	7451
	24:17	good, whereas I have rewarded thee *e.*	7451
	25: 3	man *was* churlish and *e in* his doings:	7451
	25:17	for *e* is determined against our master,	7451
	25:21	and he hath requited me *e* for good.	7451
	25:26	they that seek *e* to my lord, be as Nabal.	7451
	25:28	*e* hath not been found in thee *all* thy days.	7451
	25:39	Nabal, and hath kept his servant from *e:*	7451
	26:18	have I done? or what *e is* in mine hand?	7451
	29: 6	I have not found *e* in thee since the day	7451
2Sa	3:39	the Lord shall reward the doer of *e*	7451
	12: 9	of the Lord, to do *e* in his sight?	7451
	12:11	I will raise up *e* against thee out of thine	7451
	13:16	this *e* in sending me away *is* greater than	7451

2Sa	15:14	bring *e* upon us, and smite the city with	7451
	17:14	to the intent that the Lord might bring *e*	7451
	19: 7	*will be* worse unto thee than all the *e*	7451
	19:35	and can I discern between good and *e?*	7451
	24:16	the Lord repented him of the *e,*	7451
1Ki	5: 4	*that there is* neither adversary nor *e.*	7451
	9: 9	the Lord brought upon them all this *e.*	7451
	11: 6	Solomon did *e* in the sight of the Lord,	7451
	13:33	Jeroboam returned not from his *e* way,	7451
	14: 9	done *e* above all that were before thee:	7489
	14:10	will bring *e* upon the house of Jeroboam,	7451
	14:22	And Judah did *e* in the sight of the Lord,	7451
	15:26	he did *e* in the sight of the Lord,	7451
	15:34	he did *e* in the sight of the Lord,	7451
	16: 7	even for all the *e* that he did in the sight	7451
	16:19	For his sins which he sinned in doing *e* in	7451
	16:25	Omri wrought *e* in the eyes of the Lord,	7451
	16:30	Ahab the son of Omri did *e* in the sight of	7451
	17:20	hast thou also **brought** *e* upon the widow	7489
	21:20	hast sold thyself to work *e* in the sight	7451
	21:21	I will bring *e* upon thee, and will take	7451
	21:29	me, I will not bring the *e* in his days:	7451
	21:29	in his son's days will I bring the *e* upon	7451
	22: 8	not prophesy good concerning me, but *e.*	7451
	22:18	prophesy no good concerning me, but *e?*	7451
	22:23	the Lord hath spoken *e* concerning thee.	7451
	22:52	he did *e* in the sight of the Lord,	7451
2Ki	3: 2	he wrought *e* in the sight of the Lord;	7451
	6:33	he said, Behold, this *e is* of the Lord;	7451
	8:12	Because I know the *e* that thou wilt do	7451
	8:18	and he did *e* in the sight of the Lord.	7451
	8:27	did *e* in the sight of the Lord, as *did*	7451
	13: 2	he did *e* which *was* in the sight of	7451
	13:11	he did *that* which *was* in the sight of	7451
	14:24	he did *that* which *was* in the sight of	7451
	15: 9	he did *that* which *was* in the sight of	7451
	15:18	he did *that* which *was* in the sight of	7451
	15:24	he did *that* which *was* in the sight of	7451
	15:28	he did *that* which *was* in the sight of	7451
	17: 2	he did *that* which *was* in the sight of	7451
	17:13	Turn ye from your *e* ways, and keep my	7451
	17:17	sold themselves to do *e* in the sight of	7451
	21: 2	he did *that* which *was* in the sight of	7451
	21: 9	Manasseh seduced them to do more *e*	7451
	21:12	I *am* bringing *such e* upon Jerusalem and	7451
	21:15	they have done *that* which *was e*	7451
	21:16	in doing *that* which *was e* in the sight of	7451
	21:20	he did *that* which *was e* in the sight of	7451
	22:20	thine eyes shall not see all the *e* which I	7451
	23:32	he did *that* which *was e* in the sight of	7451
	23:37	he did *that* which *was e* in the sight of	7451
	24: 9	he did *that* which *was e* in the sight of	7451
	24:19	he did *that* which *was e* in the sight of	7451
1Ch	2: 3	of Judah, was *e* in the sight of the Lord;	7451
	4:10	that thou wouldest keep *me* from *e,*	7451
	7:23	because it went *e* with his house.	7451
	21:15	he repented him of the *e,* and said to	7451
	21:17	have sinned and **done e indeed;**	7489+7489
2Ch	7:22	hath he brought all this *e* upon them.	7451
	12:14	did *e,* because he prepared not his heart	7451
	18: 7	prophesied good unto me, but always *e:*	7451
	18:17	would not prophesy good unto me, but *e?*	7451
	18:22	and the Lord hath spoken *e* against thee.	7451
	20: 9	If, *when e* cometh upon us, *as* the sword,	7451
	21: 6	he wrought *that* which *was e* in the eyes	7451
	22: 4	Wherefore he did *e* in the sight of	7451
	29: 6	done *that* which *was e* in the eyes of	7451
	33: 2	did *that* which *was e* in the sight of	7451
	33: 6	he wrought much *e* in the sight of	7451
	33:22	he did *that* which *was e* in the sight of	7451
	34:24	I will bring *e* upon this place, and upon	7451
	34:28	neither shall thine eyes see all the *e* that	7451
	36: 5	he did *that* which *was e* in the sight of	7451
	36: 9	he did *that* which *was e* in the sight of	7451
	36:12	he did *that* which *was e* in the sight of	7451
Ezr	9:13	after all that is come upon us for our *e*	7451
Ne	6:13	they might have *matter* for an *e* report,	7451
	9:28	had rest, they did *e* again before thee:	7451
	13: 7	understood of the *e* that Eliashib did for	7451
	13:17	What *e* thing *is* this that ye do,	7451
	13:18	*did not* our God bring all this *e* upon us,	7451
	13:27	hearken unto you to do all this great *e,*	7451
Est	7: 7	for he saw that there was *e* determined	7451
	8: 6	For how can I endure to see the *e* that	7451
Job	1: 1	one that feared God, and escheweth *e.*	7451
	1: 8	one that feareth God, and escheweth *e?*	7451
	2: 3	one that feareth God, and escheweth *e?*	7451
	2:10	hand of God, and shall we not receive *e?*	7451
	2:11	of all this *e* that was come upon him,	7451
	5:19	yea, in seven *there* shall no *e* touch thee.	7451
	8:20	*man,* neither will he help the *e* **doers:**	7489
	24:21	he **entreateth** the barren *that* beareth	7462
	28:28	and to depart from *e is* understanding.	7451
	30:26	came unto me: and when I waited for	7451
	31:29	or lift up myself when I found him:	7451
	35:12	because of the pride of *e* men.	7451
	42:11	comforted him over all the *e* that	7451
Ps	5: 4	neither shall *e* dwell *with* thee.	7451
	7: 4	I have rewarded *e* *unto* him that was at	7451
	10:15	the *e* man: seek out his wickedness	7451
	15: 3	his tongue, nor doeth *e* to his neighbour,	7451
	21:11	For they intended *e* against thee:	7451
	23: 4	of the shadow of death, I will fear no *e:*	7451
	34:13	Keep thy tongue from *e,* and thy lips from	7451

E

Ps
34:14 Depart from **e**, and do good; seek peace, 7451
34:16 of the LORD *is* against them that do **e**, 7451
34:21 **E** shall slay the wicked: and they that hate 7451
35:12 They rewarded me for good to 7451
36: 4 way *that is* not good; he abhorreth not **e**. 7451
37: 8 fret not thyself in any wise to do **e**. 7489
37:19 They shall not be ashamed in the time: 7451
37:27 Depart from **e**, and do good; and dwell 7451
38:20 They also that render **e** for good are mine 7451
40:14 and put to shame that wish me **e**. 7451
41: 5 Mine enemies speak **e** of me, When shall 7451
41: 8 An **e** disease, *say they,* cleaveth fast unto 1100
49: 5 Wherefore should I fear in the days of **e**, 7451
50:19 givest thy mouth to **e**, and thy tongue 7451
51: 4 I sinned, and done *this* **e** in thy sight: 7451
52: 3 Thou lovest **e** more than good; 7451
54: 5 He shall reward **e** unto mine enemies: 7451
56: 5 all their thoughts *are* against me for **e**. 7451
64: 5 encourage themselves *in* an **e** matter: 7451
78:49 *by* sending **e** angels *among them.* 7451
90:15 *and* the years *wherein* we have seen **e**. 7451
91:10 There shall no **e** befall thee, neither shall 7451
97:10 Ye that love the LORD, hate **e**: 7451
109: 5 And they have rewarded me **e** for good, 7451
109:20 and of them that speak **e** against my soul. 7451
112: 7 He shall not be afraid of **e** tidings: 7451
119:101 have refrained my feet from every **e** way, 7451
121: 7 The LORD shall preserve thee from all **e**: 7451
140: 1 Deliver me, O LORD, from the **e** man: 7451
140:11 Let not an **e** speaker be established 376+3956
140:11 **e** shall hunt the violent man to overthrow 7451
141: 4 Incline not my heart to any **e** thing, 7451

Pr
1:16 For their feet run to **e**, and make haste to 7451
1:33 and shall be quiet from fear of **e**. 7451
2:12 deliver thee from the way of the **e** man, 7451
2:14 Who rejoice to do **e**, *and* delight in 7451
3: 7 fear the LORD, and depart from **e**. 7451
3:29 Devise not **e** against thy neighbour, 7451
4:14 and go not in the way of **e** men. 7451
4:27 nor *to* the left: remove thy foot from **e**. 7451
5:14 I was almost in all **e** in the midst of 7451
6:24 To keep thee from the **e** woman, from 7451
8:13 The fear of the LORD *is* to hate **e**: pride, 7451
8:13 the **e** way, and the froward mouth, do I 7451
11:19 he that pursueth **e** *pursueth it* to his own 7451
12:12 The wicked desireth the net of **e** men: 7451
12:20 *is* in the heart of them that imagine **e**: 7451
12:21 There shall no **e** happen to the just: 205
13:19 *is* abomination to fools to depart from **e**. 7451
13:21 **E** pursueth sinners: but to the righteous 7451
14:16 A wise *man* feareth, and departeth from **e**: 7451
14:19 The **e** bow before the good; and the 7451
14:22 Do they not err that devise **e**? but mercy 7451
15: 3 place, beholding the **e** and the good. 7451
15:15 All the days of the afflicted *are* **e**: 7451
15:28 the mouth of the wicked poureth out **e** 7451
16: 4 even the wicked for the day of **e**. 7451
16: 6 the fear of the LORD *men* depart from **e**. 7451
16:17 of the upright *is* to depart from **e**: 7451
16:27 An ungodly man diggeth up **e**: and in his 7451
16:30 moving his lips he bringeth **e** to pass. 7451
17:11 An **e** *man* seeketh only rebellion: 7451
17:13 Whoso rewardeth **e** for good, evil shall 7451
17:13 good, **e** shall not depart from his house. 7451
19:23 he shall not be visited with **e**. 7451
20: 8 scattereth *away* all **e** with his eyes. 7451
20:22 Say not thou, I will recompense **e**; 7451
20:30 blueness of a wound cleanseth away **e**: 7451
21:10 The soul of the wicked desireth **e**: 7451
22: 3 A prudent *man* foreseeth the **e**, 7451
23: 6 thou not the bread of *him that hath* an **e** 7451
24: 1 Be not thou envious against **e** men, 7451
24: 8 He that deviseth to do **e** shall be called a 7489
24:19 of **e** men, neither be thou envious at 7489
24:20 there shall be no reward to the **e** *man;* 7451
27:12 A prudent *man* foreseeth the **e**, 7451
28: 5 **E** men understand not judgment: 7451
28:10 the righteous to go astray in an **e** way, 7451
28:22 He that hasteth to be rich hath an **e** eye, 7451
29: 6 In the transgression of an **e** man *there is* 7451
30:32 or if thou hast **thought**, *lay* thine hand 2161
31:12 good and not **e** all the days of her life. 7451

Ecc
2:21 This also *is* vanity and a great **e**. 7451
4: 3 hath not seen the **e** work that is done 7451
5: 1 for they consider not that *they* do **e**. 7451
5:13 There is a sore **e** *which* I have seen under 7451
5:14 those riches perish by **e** travail: 7451
5:16 this also *is* a sore **e**, *that* in all points as 7451
6: 1 There is an **e** which I have seen under 7451
6: 2 this *is* vanity, and it *is* an **e** disease. 7451
8: 3 stand not in an **e** thing; for he doeth 7451
8: 5 the commandment shall feel no **e** thing: 7451
8:11 Because sentence *against* an **e** work is 7451
8:11 sons of men is fully set in them to do **e**. 7451
8:12 Though a sinner do **e** an hundred *times,* 7451
9: 3 *is* an **e** among all *things* that are done 7451
9: 3 the heart of the sons of men is full of **e**, 7451
9:12 as the fishes that are taken in an **e** net, 7451
9:12 *are* the sons of men snared in an **e** time, 7451
10: 5 There is an **e** *which* I have seen under 7451
11: 2 for thou knowest not what **e** shall be 7451
11:10 thy heart, and put away **e** from thy flesh: 7451
12: 1 while the **e** days come not, nor the years 7451
12:14 whether *it be* good, or whether *it be* **e**. 7451

Isa
1:16 put away the **e** of your doings from before 7455
1:16 from before mine eyes; cease to do **e**; 7489
3: 9 they have rewarded **e** unto themselves. 7451
5:20 Woe unto them that call **e** good, 7451
5:20 them that call evil good, and good **e**; 7451
7: 5 have taken **e** counsel against thee, saying, 7451
7:15 that he may know to refuse the **e**, 7451
7:16 the child shall know to refuse the **e**, 7451
13:11 I will punish the world for *their* **e**, 7451
31: 2 will bring **e**, and will not call back his 7451
32: 7 The instruments also of the churl *are* **e**: 7451
33:15 and shutteth his eyes from seeing **e**; 7451
41:23 yea, do good, or do **e**, that we may be 7489
45: 7 I make peace, and create **e**: I the LORD 7451
47:11 Therefore shall **e** come upon thee; 7451
56: 2 and keepeth his hand from doing any **e**. 7451
57: 1 is taken away from the **e** *to come.* 7451
59: 7 Their feet run to **e**, and they make haste 7451
59:15 he *that* departeth from **e** maketh himself 7451
65:12 did **e** before mine eyes, and did choose 7451
66: 4 they did **e** before mine eyes, and chose 7451

Jer
1:14 Out of the north an **e** shall break forth 7451
2: 3 **e** shall come upon them, saith the LORD. 7451
2:19 and see that *it is* an **e** *thing* and bitter, 7451
3: 5 and done *things* as thou couldest. 7451
3:17 after the imagination of their **e** heart. 7451
4: 4 because of the **e** of your doings. 7455
4: 6 I will bring **e** from the north, and a great 7451
4:22 they *are* wise to do **e**, but to do good 7489
5:12 *It is* not he; neither shall **e** come upon us; 7451
6: 1 for **e** appeareth out of the north, 7451
6:19 behold, I will bring **e** upon this people, 7451
7:24 and in the imagination of their **e** heart, 7451
7:30 For the children of Judah have done **e** in 7451
8: 3 of them that remain of this **e** family, 7451
9: 3 for they proceed from **e** to evil, and they 7451
9: 3 for they proceed from evil to **e**, and they 7451
10: 5 for they cannot do **e**, neither also *is it* in 7489
11: 8 one in the imagination of their **e** heart: 7451
11:11 Behold, I *will* bring **e** upon them, 7451
11:15 when thou **doest** **e**, then thou rejoicest. 7451
11:17 hath pronounced **e** against thee, 7451
11:17 for the **e** of the house of Israel and of 7451
11:23 for I will bring **e** upon the men of 7451
12:14 Thus saith the LORD against all mine **e** 7451
13:10 This **e** people, which refuse to hear my 7451
13:23 do good, that are accustomed to do **e**. 7489
15:11 to entreat thee *well* in the time of **e**, 7451
16:10 pronounced all this great **e** against us? 7451
16:12 one after the imagination of his **e** heart, 7451
17:17 thou *art* my hope in the day of **e**. 7451
17:18 bring upon them the day of **e**, 7451
18: 8 I have pronounced, turn from their **e**, 7451
18: 8 I will repent of the **e** that I thought to do 7451
18:10 If it do **e** in my sight, that *it* obey not my 7451
18:11 I frame **e** against you, and devise a device 7451
18:11 return ye now every one from his **e** way, 7451
18:12 one do the imagination of his **e** heart. 7451
18:20 Shall **e** be recompensed for good? 7451
19: 3 Behold, I *will* bring **e** upon this place, 7451
19:15 upon all her towns all the **e** that I have 7451
21:10 I have set my face against this city for **e**, 7451
21:12 because of the **e** of your doings. 7455
23: 2 I will visit upon you the **e** of your doings, 7451
23:10 course is **e**, and their force is not right. 7451
23:12 I will bring **e** upon them, *even* the year 7451
23:17 his own heart, No **e** shall come upon you. 7451
23:22 should have turned them from their **e** 7451
23:22 evil way, and from the **e** of their doings. 7455
24: 3 the **e**, very evil, that cannot be eaten, 7451
24: 3 the evil, very **e**, that cannot be eaten, 7451
24: 3 that cannot be eaten, they are so **e**. 7451
24: 8 as the figs, which cannot be eaten, 7451
24: 8 which cannot be eaten, they are so **e**; 7455
25: 5 Turn ye again now every one from his **e** 7451
25: 5 from the **e** of your doings, and dwell in 7451
25:29 I begin to **bring** **e** on the city which is 7489
25:32 **e** *shall* go forth from nation to nation, 7451
26: 3 and turn every man from his **e** way, 7451
26: 3 that I may repent me of the **e**, which I 7451
26: 3 them because of the **e** of their doings. 7455
26:13 the LORD will repent him of the **e** that he 7451
26:19 the LORD repented him of the **e** which he 7451
26:19 Thus *might* we procure great **e** against 7451
28: 8 of war, and of **e**, and of pestilence. 7451
29:11 thoughts of peace, and not of **e**, 7451
29:17 figs, that cannot be eaten, they are so **e**. 7455
32:23 thou hast caused all this **e** to come upon 7451
32:30 the children of Judah have only done **e** 7451
32:32 of all the **e** of the children of Israel 7451
32:42 as I have brought all this great **e** upon 7451
35:15 Return ye now every man from his **e** way, 7451
35:17 the **e** that I have pronounced against 7451
36: 3 the **e** which I purpose to do unto them; 7451
36: 3 they may return every man from his **e** 7451
36: 7 will return every one from his **e** way: 7451
36:31 all the **e** that I have pronounced against 7451
38: 9 these men have **done** **e** in all that they 7489
39:16 I *will* bring my words upon this city for **e**, 7451
40: 2 LORD thy God hath pronounced this **e** 7451
41:11 heard of all the **e** that Ishmael the son of 7451
42: 6 Whether *it be* good, or whether *it be* **e**, 7451
42:10 for I repent me of the **e** that I have done 7451
42:17 escape from the **e** that I *will* bring upon 7451
44: 2 Ye have seen all the **e** that I have brought 7451
44: 7 Wherefore commit ye *this* great **e** against 7451
44:11 I will set my face against you for **e**, 7451
44:17 of victuals, and were well, and saw no **e**. 7451
44:22 because of the **e** of your doings, 7455
44:23 therefore this is happened unto you, 7451
44:27 I *will* watch over them for **e**, and not for 7451
44:29 words shall surely stand against you for **e**: 7451
45: 5 for behold, I *will* bring **e** upon all flesh, 7451
48: 2 in Heshbon they have devised **e** against it; 7451
49:23 for they have heard **e** tidings: they are 7451
49:37 I will bring **e** upon them, *even* my fierce 7451
51:24 to all the inhabitants of Chaldea all their **e** 7451
51:60 So Jeremiah wrote in a book all the **e** that 7451
51:64 shall not rise from the **e** that I *will* bring 7451
52: 2 he did *that* which *was* **e** in the eyes of 7451

La
3:38 mouth of the most High proceedeth not **e** 7451

Eze
5:16 I shall send upon them the **e** arrows 7451
5:17 will I send upon you famine and **e** beasts, 7451
6:10 in vain that I *would* do this **e** unto them. 7451
6:11 for all the **e** abominations of the house 7451
7: 5 An **e**, an only evil, behold, is come. 7451
7: 5 An evil, an only **e**, behold, is come. 7451
14:22 shall be comforted concerning the **e** that 7451
33:11 turn ye, turn ye from your **e** ways; 7451
34:25 will cause the **e** beasts to cease out of 7451
36:31 shall ye remember your own **e** ways, 7451
38:10 mind, and thou shalt think an **e** thought: 7451

Da
9:12 judged us, by bringing upon us a great **e**: 7451
9:13 law of Moses, all this **e** is come upon us: 7451
9:14 hath the LORD watched upon the **e**, 7451

Joel
2:13 kindness, and repenteth him of the **e**. 7451

Am
3: 6 shall there be **e** in a city, and the LORD 7451
5:13 silence in that time; for it *is* an **e** time. 7451
5:14 Seek good, and not **e**, that ye may live: 7451
5:15 Hate the **e**, and love the good, 7451
6: 3 Ye that put far away the **e** day, 7451
9: 4 I will set mine eyes upon them for **e**, 7451
9:10 The **e** shall not overtake nor prevent us. 7451

Jnh
1: 7 that we may know for whose cause this **e** 7451
1: 8 for whose cause this **e** is upon us; 7451
3: 8 let them turn every one from his **e** way, 7451
3:10 that they turned from their **e** way; 7451
3:10 God repented of the **e**, that he had said 7451
4: 2 kindness, and repentest thee of the **e**. 7451

Mic
1:12 came down from the LORD unto 7451
2: 1 and work **e** upon their beds! 7451
2: 3 this family do I devise an **e**, 7451
2: 3 shall ye go haughtily: for this time *is* **e**. 7451
3: 2 Who hate the good, and love the 7451
3:11 among us? none **e** can come upon us. 7451
7: 3 That *they* may do **e** with both hands 7451

Na
1:11 that imagineth **e** against the LORD, 7451

Hab
1:13 *Thou art* of purer eyes than to behold **e**, 7451
2: 9 to him that coveteth an **e** covetousness 7451
2: 9 *he* may be delivered from the power of **e**! 7451

Zep
1:12 will not do good, neither will he do **e**. 7489
3:15 of thee: thou shalt not see **e** any more. 7451

Zec
1: 4 Turn ye now from your **e** ways, 7451
1: 4 your evil ways, and *from* your **e** doings: 7451
7:10 let none of you imagine **e** against his 7451
8:17 let none of you imagine **e** in your hearts 7451

Mal
1: 8 ye offer the blind for sacrifice, *is it* not **e**? 7451
1: 8 if ye offer the lame and sick, *is it* not **e**? 7451
2:17 Every one that doeth **e** *is* good in the 7451

Mt
5:11 shall say all manner of **e** against you 4190
5:37 is more than these cometh of **e**. 4190
5:39 But I say unto you, That ye resist not **e**: 4190
5:45 he maketh his sun to rise on the **e** and 4190
6:13 into temptation, but deliver us from **e**: 4190
6:23 if thine eye be **e**, thy whole body shall 4190
6:34 Sufficient unto the day *is* the **e** thereof. 2549
7:11 ye then, being **e**, know how to give good 4190
7:17 but a corrupt tree bringeth forth **e** fruit. 4190
7:18 A good tree cannot bring forth **e** fruit, 4190
9: 4 Wherefore think ye **e** in your hearts? 4190
12:34 of vipers, how can ye, being **e**, 4190
12:35 an **e** man out of the evil treasure bringeth 4190
12:35 an evil man out of the **e** treasure bringeth 4190
12:35 evil treasure bringeth forth **e** *things*. 4190
12:39 An **e** and adulterous generation seeketh 4190
15:19 For out of the heart proceed **e** thoughts, 4190
20:15 I *will* with mine own? Is thine eye **e**, 4190
24:48 if that **e** servant shall say in his heart, 2556
27:23 said, Why, what **e** hath he done? 2556

Mk
3: 4 do good on the sabbath days, or to **do** **e**? 2554
7:21 proceed **e** thoughts, adulteries, 2556
7:22 an **e** eye, blasphemy, pride, foolishness: 4190
7:23 All these **e** *things* come from within, 4190
9:39 my name, that can lightly **speak** **e** of me. 2551
15:14 unto them, Why, what **e** hath he done? 2556

Lk
6: 9 do good on the sabbath days, or to **do** **e**? 2554
6:22 and cast out your name as **e**, 4190
6:35 is kind unto the unthankful and *to the* **e**. 4190
6:45 an **e** man out of the evil treasure of his 4190
6:45 an evil man out of the **e** treasure of his 4190
6:45 his heart bringeth forth that which is **e**: 4190
7:21 and plagues, and of **e** spirits; 4190
8: 2 which had been healed of **e** spirits and 4190
11: 4 into temptation; but deliver us from **e**. 4190
11:13 ye then, being **e**, know how to give good 4190
11:29 he began to say, This is an **e** generation: 4190
11:34 but when *thine* eye is **e**, thy body also *is* 4190
16:25 likewise Lazarus **e** *things*: but now he 2556
23:22 third time, Why, what **e** hath he done? 2556

Jn
3:19 than light, because their deeds were **e**. 4190
3:20 every one that doeth **e** hateth the light, 5337

E

Jn 5:29 and they that have done **e**, unto | 5337
7: 7 testify of it, that the works thereof are **e** | 4190
17:15 thou shouldest keep them from the **e**. | 4190
18:23 Jesus answered him, If I have spoken, | 2560
18:23 I have spoken evil, bear witness of the **e**; | 2556
Ac 7: 6 and **entreat** *them* **e** four hundred years. | 2559
7:19 and **e entreated** our fathers, so that *they* | 2559
9:13 how much **e** he hath done to thy saints at | 2556
14: 2 **made** their minds **e affected** against | 2559
19: 9 **spake e** of *that* way before the multitude, | 2551
19:12 and the **e** spirits went out of them. | 4190
19:13 had **e** spirits the name of the Lord Jesus, | 4190
19:15 And the **e** spirit answered and said, Jesus | 4190
19:16 the man in whom the **e** spirit was leapt | 4190
23: 5 Thou shalt not speak **e** of the ruler of thy | 2560
23: 9 strove, saying, We find no **e** in this man: | 2556
24:20 if they have found any **e doing** in me, | 92
Ro 1:30 inventors of **e** things, disobedient to | 2556
2: 9 upon every soul of man that doeth **e**, | 2556
3: 8 Let us do **e**, that good may come? | 2556
7:19 but the **e** which I would not, that I do. | 2556
7:21 I would do good, **e** is present with me. | 2556
9:11 neither having done any good or **e**, | 2556
12: 9 Abhor *that* which is **e**; cleave to *that* | 4190
12:17 Recompense to no *man* **e** for evil. | 2556
12:17 Recompense to no *man* evil for **e**. | 2556
12:21 Be not overcome of **e**, but overcome evil | 2556
12:21 of evil, but overcome **e** with good. | 2556
13: 3 not a terror to good works, but to the **e**. | 2556
13: 4 But if thou do *that* which is **e**, be afraid; | 2556
13: 4 to **execute** wrath upon him that doeth **e**. | 2556
14:16 Let not then your good be **e spoken of:** | 987
14:20 *is* **e** for *that* man who eateth with offence. | 2556
16:19 *which is* good, and simple concerning **e**. | 2556
1Co 10: 6 to the intent we should not lust after **e** | 2556
10:30 why am I **e spoken** of for *that for* which | 987
13: 5 is not easily provoked, thinketh no **e**; | 2556
15:33 **e** communications corrupt good manners. | 2556
2Co 6: 8 dishonour, by **e report** and good report: | 1426
13: 7 I pray to God that ye do no **e**; not that | 2556
Gal 1: 4 he might deliver us from *this* present **e** | 4190
Eph 4:31 anger, and clamour, and **e speaking**, | 988
5:16 the time, because the days are **e**. | 4190
6:13 that ye may be able to withstand in the **e** | 4190
Php 3: 2 Beware of dogs, beware of **e** workers, | 2556
Col 3: 5 **e** concupiscence, and covetousness, | 2556
1Th 5:15 See that none render **e** for evil unto any | 2556
5:15 See that none render evil for **e** unto any | 2556
5:22 Abstain from all appearance of **e**. | 4190
2Th 3: 3 shall stablish you, and keep *you* from **e**. | 4190
1Ti 6: 4 cometh envy, strife, railings, **e** surmisings, | 4190
6:10 For the love of money is the root of all **e**: | 2556
2Ti 2: 9 as an **e doer**, *even* unto bonds; | 2557
3:13 But **e** men and seducers shall wax worse | 4190
4:14 the coppersmith did me much **e**: | 2556
4:18 the Lord shall deliver me from every **e** | 4190
Tit 1:12 *are* alway liars, **e** beasts, slow bellies. | 2556
2: 8 having no **e** *thing* to say of you. | 5337
3: 2 To **speak e** of no *man*, to be no brawlers, | 987
Heb 3:12 lest there be in any of you an **e** heart of | 4190
5:14 exercised to discern both good and **e**. | 2556
10:22 having *our* hearts sprinkled from an **e** | 4190
Jas 1:13 for God cannot be tempted with **e**, | 2556
2: 4 and are become judges of **e** thoughts? | 4190
3: 8 *it is* an unruly **e**, full of deadly poison. | 2556
3:16 *is*, there *is* confusion and every **e** work. | 5337
4:11 **Speak** not **e** of one another, brethren. | 2635
4:11 He that **speaketh e** of *his* brother, | 2635
4:11 **speaketh e** of the law, and judgeth the | 2635
4:16 in your boastings: all such rejoicing is **e**. | 4190
1Pe 2: 1 and envies, and all **e speakings**, | 2636
3: 9 Not rendering **e** for evil, or railing for | 2556
3: 9 Not rendering evil for **e**, or railing for | 2556
3:10 let him refrain his tongue from **e**, | 2556
3:11 Let him eschew **e**, and do good; let him | 2556
3:12 face of the Lord *is* against them that do **e**. | 2556
3:16 that, whereas they **speak e** of you, as of | 2635
3:17 *ye* suffer for well doing, than for **e doing**. | 2554
4: 4 same excess of riot, **speaking e** *of you:* | 987
4:14 on their part he is **e spoken of**, but on | 987
2Pe 2: 2 the way of truth shall be **e spoken of**. | 987
2:10 they are not afraid to **speak e** of dignities. | 987
2:12 **speak e** of *the things* that they understand | 987
1Jn 3:12 Because his own works were **e**, and his | 4190
2Jn 1:11 him God speed is partaker of his **e** deeds. | 4190
3Jn 1:11 follow not *that which is* **e**, but *that which* | 2556
1:11 but he that **doeth e** hath not seen God. | 2554
Jude 1: 8 despise dominion, and **speak e** of dignities. | 987
1:10 But these **speak e** of those *things* which | 987
Rev 2: 2 thou canst not bear *them* which are **e**: | 2556

EVILDOER (2) [EVIL]

Isa 9:17 for every one *is* a hypocrite and an **e**, | 7489
1Pe 4:15 *as* an **e**, or as a busybody in other men's | 2555

EVILDOERS (13) [EVIL]

Ps 26: 5 I have hated the congregation of **e**; | 7489
37: 1 Fret not thyself because of **e**, neither be | 7489
37: 9 For **e** shall be cut off: but those that wait | 7489
94:16 Who will rise up for me against the **e**? | 7489
119:115 Depart from me, ye **e**: for I will keep | 7489
Isa 1: 4 a seed of **e**, children that are corrupters: | 7489
14:20 the seed of **e** shall never be renowned. | 7489
31: 2 but will arise against the house of the **e**, | 7489
Jer 20:13 the soul of the poor from the hand of **e**. | 7489

Jer 23:14 they strengthen also the hands of **e**, | 7489
1Pe 2:12 that, whereas they speak against you as **e**, | 2555
2:14 are sent by him for the punishment of **e**, | 2555
3:16 whereas they speak evil of you, as of **e**, | 2555

EVIL-MERODACH (2)

2Ki 25:27 *day* of the month, *that* **E** king of Babylon, | 192
Jer 52:31 *that* **E** king of Babylon in the *first* year of | 192

EVILS (9) [EVIL]

Dt 31:17 many **e** and troubles shall befall them; | 7451
31:17 Are not these **e** come upon us, because | 7451
31:18 all the **e** which they shall have wrought, | 7451
31:21 when many **e** and troubles are befallen | 7451
Ps 40:12 For innumerable **e** have compassed me | 7451
Jer 2:13 For my people have committed two **e**; | 7451
Eze 6: 9 they shall lothe themselves for the **e** | 7451
20:43 for all your **e** that ye have committed. | 7451
Lk 3:19 and for all the **e** which Herod had done, | 4190

EWE (7) [EWES]

Ge 21:28 Abraham set seven **e lambs** of the flock | 3535
21:29 Mean these seven **e lambs** which | 3535
21:30 For *these* seven **e lambs** shalt thou take | 3535
Lev 14:10 one **e lamb** of the first year without | 3535
22:28 *whether it be* cow or **e**, ye shall not kill it | 7716
Nu 6:14 one **e lamb** of the first year without | 3535
2Sa 12: 3 save one little **e lamb**, which he had | 3535

EWES (3) [EWE]

Ge 31:38 thy **e** and thy she goats have not cast | 7353
32:14 goats, two hundred **e**, and twenty rams, | 7353
Ps 78:71 From following the *e* great with young he | NIH

EXACT (8) [EXACTED, EXACTETH, EXACTION, EXACTIONS, EXACTORS]

Dt 15: 2 he shall not **e** it of his neighbour, | 5065
15: 3 Of a foreigner thou mayest **e** *it again:* but | 5065
Ne 5: 7 rulers, and said unto them, You **e** usury, | 5378
5:10 might **e** of them money and corn: | 5383
5:11 the wine, and the oil, that ye **e** of them. | 5383
Ps 89:22 The enemy shall not **e** upon him; | 5378
Isa 58: 3 you find pleasure, and **e** all your labours. | 5065
Lk 3:13 **E** no more than that which is appointed | 4238

EXACTED (2) [EXACT]

2Ki 15:20 Menahem **e** the money of Israel, *even* of | 3318
23:35 he **e** the silver and the gold of the people | 5065

EXACTETH (1) [EXACT]

Job 11: 6 that God **e** of thee *less* than thine iniquity | 5382

EXACTION (1) [EXACT]

Ne 10:31 and the **e** of every **debt**. | 3027+4853

EXACTIONS (1) [EXACT]

Eze 45: 9 justice, take away your **e** from my people, | 1646

EXACTORS (1) [EXACT]

Isa 60:17 officers peace, and thine **e** righteousness. | 5065

EXALT (26) [EXALTED, EXALTEST, EXALTETH]

Ex 15: 2 my father's God, and I will **e** him. | 7311
1Sa 2:10 his king, and the horn of his anointed. | 7311
Job 17: 4 shalt thou not **e** *them*. | 7311
Ps 34: 3 with me, and let us **e** his name together. | 7311
37:34 and he shall **e** thee to inherit the land: | 7311
66: 7 let not the rebellious **e** themselves. Selah. | 7311
92:10 my horn shalt thou **e** like *the horn of* an | 7311
99: 5 **E** ye the LORD our God, and worship at | 7311
99: 9 **E** the LORD our God, and worship at his | 7311
107:32 Let them **e** him also in the congregation | 7311
118:28 praise thee: *thou art* my God, I will **e** thee. | 7311
140: 8 his wicked device; *lest* they **e** themselves. | 7311
Pr 4: 8 **E** her, and she shall promote thee: she | 5549
Isa 13: 2 **e** the voice unto them, shake the hand, | 7311
14:13 I will **e** my throne above the stars of God: | 7311
25: 1 I will **e** thee, I will praise thy name; | 7311
Eze 21:26 **e** him that is low, and abase *him that is* | 1361
29:15 neither shall it **e** itself any more above | 5375
31:14 the waters **e** themselves for their height, | 1361
Da 11:14 also the robbers of thy people shall **e** | 5375
11:36 he shall **e** himself, and magnify himself | 7311
Hos 11: 7 the most High, none at all would **e** *him*. | 7311
Ob 1: 4 Though thou **e** *thyself* as the eagle, | 1361
Mt 23:12 And whosoever shall **e** himself shall be | 5312
2Co 11:20 if a man take *of you,* if a man **e** himself, | 1869
1Pe 5: 6 of God, that he may **e** you in due time: | 5312

EXALTED (64) [EXALT]

Nu 24: 7 than Agag, and his kingdom shall be **e**. | 5375
1Sa 2: 1 the LORD, mine horn is **e** in the LORD: | 7311
2Sa 5:12 that he had **e** his kingdom for his people | 5375
22:47 be the God of the rock of my salvation. | 7311
1Ki 1: 5 Adonijah the son of Haggith **e** himself, | 5375
14: 7 Forasmuch as I **e** thee from among | 7311
16: 2 Forasmuch as I **e** thee out of the dust, | 7311
2Ki 19:22 against whom hast thou **e** *thy* voice, | 7311
1Ch 29:11 and *thou* art **e** as head **above** all. | 5375
Ne 9: 5 which *is* above all blessing and praise. | 7311
Job 5:11 those which mourn may be **e** to safety. | 7682
24:24 They are **e** for a little while, but are gone | 7426
36: 7 establish them for ever, and they are **e**. | 1361
Ps 12: 8 on every side, when the vilest men are **e**. | 7311
13: 2 long shall mine enemy be **e** over me? | 7311
18:46 and let the God of my salvation be **e**. | 7311

Ps 21:13 Be thou **e**, LORD, in thine own strength: | 7311
46:10 I will be among the heathen, I will be | 7311
46:10 the heathen, I will be **e** in the earth. | 7311
47: 9 earth *belong* unto God: he is greatly **e**. | 5927
57: 5 Be thou **e**, O God, above the heavens; | 7311
57:11 Be thou **e**, O God, above the heavens; | 7311
75:10 the horns of the righteous shall be **e**. | 7311
89:16 and in thy righteousness shall they be **e**. | 7311
89:17 and in thy favour our horn shall be **e**. | 7311
89:19 I have **e** one chosen out of the people. | 7311
89:24 and in my name shall his horn be **e**. | 7311
97: 9 all the earth: thou art **e** far above all gods. | 5927
108: 5 Be thou **e**, O God, above the heavens; | 7311
112: 9 for ever; his horn shall be **e** with honour. | 7311
118:16 The right hand of the LORD is **e**: the right | 7426
Pr 11: 11 By the blessing of the upright the city is **e**: | 7311
Isa 2: 2 and *shall be* **e** above the hills; | 5375
2:11 and the LORD alone shall be **e** in that day. | 7682
2:17 and the LORD alone shall be **e** in that day. | 7682
5:16 the LORD of hosts shall be **e** in judgment, | 1361
12: 4 make mention that his name is **e**. | 7682
30:18 unto you, and therefore will he be **e**, | 7311
33: 5 The LORD *is* **e**; for he dwelleth on high: | 7682
33:10 I rise, saith the LORD; now will I be **e**; | 7426
37:23 against whom hast thou **e** *thy* voice, | 7311
40: 4 Every valley shall be **e**, and every | 5375
49:11 a way, and my highways shall be **e**. | 7311
52:13 shall be **e** and extolled, and be very high. | 7311
Eze 17:24 have **e** the low tree, have dried up the | 1361
19:11 stature was **e** among the thick branches, | 1361
31: 5 Therefore his height was **e** above all | 1361
Hos 13: 1 spake trembling, he **e** *himself* in Israel; | 5375
13: 6 they were filled, and their heart was **e**; | 7311
Mic 4: 1 and it *shall be* **e** above the hills; | 5375
Mt 11:23 Capernaum, which art **e** unto heaven, | 5312
23:12 he that shall humble himself shall be **e**. | 5312
Lk 1:52 *their* seats, and **e** them of low degree. | 5312
10:15 Capernaum, which art **e** to heaven, | 5312
14:11 and he that humbleth himself shall be **e**. | 5312
18:14 and he that humbleth himself shall be **e**. | 5312
Ac 2:33 being by the right hand of God **e**, | 5312
5:31 Him hath God **e** with his right hand *to be* | 5312
13:17 **e** the people when *they* dwelt as strangers | 5312
2Co 11: 7 in abasing myself that you might be **e**, | 5312
12: 7 And lest I should be **e above measure** | 5229
12: 7 lest I should be **e above measure**, | 5229
Php 2: 9 Wherefore God also hath **highly e** him, | 5251
Jas 1: 9 of low degree rejoice in that he is **e**: | 5311

EXALTEST (1) [EXALT]

Ex 9:17 As yet **e** thou thyself against my people, | 5549

EXALTETH (9) [EXALT]

Job 36:22 God **e** by his power: who teacheth | 7682
Ps 148:14 He also **e** the horn of his people, | 7311
Pr 14:29 but *he that is* hasty of spirit **e** folly. | 7311
14:34 Righteousness **e** a nation: but sin *is* a | 7311
17:19 he that **e** his gate seeketh destruction. | 1361
Lk 14:11 For whosoever **e** himself shall be abased; | 5312
18:14 for every one that **e** himself shall be | 5312
2Co 10: 5 every high thing that **e** itself against | 1869
2Th 2: 4 and **e** himself above all that is called God, | 5229

EXAMINATION (1) [EXAMINE]

Ac 25:26 O king Agrippa, that, after I had, | 351

EXAMINE (5) [EXAMINATION, EXAMINED, EXAMINING]

Ezr 10:16 day of the tenth month to **e** the matter. | 1875
Ps 26: 2 **E** me, O LORD, and prove me; try my | 974
1Co 9: 3 Mine answer to them that do **e** me is this: | 350
11:28 But let a man **e** himself, and so let him eat | 1381
2Co 13: 5 **E** yourselves, whether ye be in the faith; | 3985

EXAMINED (6) [EXAMINE]

Lk 23:14 and behold, I, having **e** *him* before you, | 350
Ac 4: 9 If we this day be **e** of the good deed done | 350
12:19 he the keepers, and commanded that | 350
22:24 and bade that he should be **e** by scourging; | 426
22:29 from whom should have **e** him: | 426
28:18 Who, when they had **e** me, would have let | 350

EXAMINING (1) [EXAMINE]

Ac 24: 8 by **e** of whom thyself mayest take | 350

EXAMPLE (8) [EXAMPLES]

Mt 1:19 and not willing to **make** her a **publick e**, | 3856
Jn 13:15 I have given you an **e**, that ye should do | 5262
1Ti 4:12 but be thou an **e** of the believers, in word, | 5179
Heb 4:11 lest any *man* fall after the same **e** of | 5262
8: 5 Who serve unto the **e** and shadow of | 5262
Jas 5:10 an **e** of suffering affliction, | 5262
1Pe 2:21 Christ also suffered for us, leaving us an **e**, | 5261
Jude 1: 7 after strange flesh, are set forth for an **e**, | 1164

EXAMPLES (1) [EXAMPLE]

1Co 10: 6 these *things* were our **e**, to the intent | 5179

EXCEED (4) [EXCEEDED, EXCEEDEST, EXCEEDETH, EXCEEDING, EXCEEDINGLY]

Dt 25: 3 Forty stripes he may give him, *and* not **e**: | 3254
25: 3 *if* he should **e**, and beat him above these | 3254
Mt 5:20 **e** *the righteousness* of the scribes | 4052+4183
2Co 3: 9 ministration of righteousness **e** in glory, | 4052

EXCEEDED (3) [EXCEED]

1Sa 20:41 wept one with another, until David **e**. 1431
1Ki 10:23 So king Solomon **e** all the kings of 1431+4480
Job 36: 9 and their transgressions that they have **e**. 1396

EXCEEDEST (1) [EXCEED]

2Ch 9: 6 told me: *for* thou **e** the fame that I heard. 3254

EXCEEDETH (1) [EXCEED]

1Ki 10: 7 and prosperity **e** the fame which I heard. 3254

EXCEEDING (59) [EXCEED]

Ge 15: 1 I *am* thy shield, *and* thy **e** great reward. 3966
 17: 6 I will make thee **e** fruitful, 3966+3966+871.1
 27:34 cried with a great and **e** bitter cry, 3966+5704
Ex 1: 7 and waxed **e** mighty; 3966+3966+871.1
 19:16 and the voice of the trumpet **e** loud; 3966
Nu 14: 7 to search it, *is* an **e** good land. 3966+3966
1Sa 2: 3 Talk no more so **e** proudly; let *not* 1364+1364
2Sa 8: 8 king David took **e** much brass. 3966
 12: 2 rich *man* had **e** many flocks and herds: 3966
1Ki 4:29 and understanding **e** much, 3966+3966
 7:47 because they were **e** many: 3966+3966
1Ch 20: 2 he brought also **e** much spoil *out of* 3966
 22: 5 the LORD *must be* **e** magnifical, 4605+1886.5
2Ch 11:12 spears, and made them **e** strong, 3966+7235
 14:14 for there was **e** much spoil in them. NIH
 16:12 until his disease *was* **e** 4605+1886.5+3807.1
 32:27 Hezekiah had **e** much riches and honour: 3966
Ps 21: 6 thou hast made him **e** glad with thy 871.1
 43: 4 unto the altar of God, unto God my **e** joy: 8057
 119:96 *but* thy commandment *is* **e** broad. 3966
Pr 30:24 the earth, but they *are* **e** wise: 2449+2450
Ecc 7:24 and **e** deep, who can find it out? 6013+6013
Jer 48:29 heard the pride of Moab; *he is* **e** proud: 3966
Eze 9: 9 Israel and Judah *is* **e** great, 3966+3966+871.1
 16:13 thou wast **e** beautiful, 3966+3966+871.1
 23:15 **e** in dyed attire upon their heads, 2871+5628
 37:10 up upon their feet, an **e** great army. 3966+3966
 47:10 as the fish of the great sea, **e** many. 3966
Da 3:22 *was* urgent, and the furnace **e** hot, 3493
 6:23 was the king **e** glad for him, 7690
 7:19 *was* dreadful, whose teeth *were of* iron, 3493
 8: 9 which waxed **e** great, toward the south, 3499
Jnh 3: 3 Now Nineveh was an **e** great city 430+3807.1
 4: 6 Jonah was **e** glad of the 1419+8055+8057
Mt 2:10 the star, they rejoiced *with* **e** great joy. 4970
 2:16 was **e** wroth, and sent forth, and slew all 3029
 4: 8 the devil taketh him *up* into an **e** high 3029
 5:12 Rejoice, and be **e** glad: for great *is* your 21
 8:28 **e** fierce, so that no *man* might pass by 3029
 17:23 be raised *again*. And they were **e** sorry. 4970
 26:22 And they were **e** sorrowful, 4970
 26:38 My soul is **e** sorrowful, *even* unto death: 4036
Mk 6:26 the king was **e** sorry; *yet* for his oaths' 4036
 9: 3 raiment became shining, **e** white as snow; 3029
 14:34 My soul is **e** sorrowful unto death: 4036
Lk 23: 8 when Herod saw Jesus, he was **e** glad: 3029
Ac 7:20 was born, and was **e** fair, 791+2316+3588
Ro 7:13 might become **e** sinful. 2596+5234
2Co 4:17 for us a **far more** 1519+2596+5236+5236
 7: 4 I am **e** joyful in all our tribulation. 5248
 9:14 long after you for the **e** grace of God 5235
Eph 1:19 *what is* the greatness of his power to 5235
 2: 7 **e** riches of his grace in *his* kindness 5235
 3:20 Now unto him that is able to do **e** 5228
1Ti 1:14 the grace of our Lord was **e abundant** 5250
1Pe 4:13 revealed, ye may be glad also with **e joy**. 21
2Pe 1: 4 Whereby are given unto us **e great** and 3176
Jude 1:24 before the presence of his glory with **e joy**, 20
Rev 16:21 for the plague thereof was **e** great. 4970

EXCEEDINGLY (39) [EXCEED]

Ge 7:19 waters prevailed **e** upon the earth; 3966+3966
 13:13 and sinners before the LORD **e**. 3966
 16:10 I will **multiply** thy seed, that it 7235+7235
 17: 2 and will multiply thee **e**. 3966+3966+871.1
 17:20 will multiply him **e**; 3966+3966+871.1
 27:33 Isaac trembled very **e**, and said, Who? 1419
 30:43 man increased, and had much 3966+3966
 47:27 and grew, and multiplied **e**. 3966
1Sa 26:21 played the fool, and have erred **e**. 3966+7235
2Sa 13:15 Amnon **hated** her **e**; 1419+3966+8130+8135
2Ki 10: 4 they were **e** afraid, and said, 3966+3966
1Ch 29:25 **e** in the sight of all Israel, 4605+1886.5+3807.1
2Ch 1: 1 and magnified him **e**. 4605+1886.5+3807.1
 17:12 waxed great **e**; 4605+5704+1886.5+3807.1
 26: 8 himself **e**. 4605+5704+1886.5+3807.1
Ne 2:10 it **grieved** them **e** 1419+7451+7489
Est 4: 4 was the queen **e** grieved; and she sent 3966
Job 3:22 **rejoice e**, *and are* glad, 413+1524+8056
Ps 68: 3 yea, let them be **e rejoice**. 7797+8057+871.1
 106:14 **lusted e** in the wilderness, 183+8378
 119:167 kept thy testimonies; and *I* love them **e**. 3966
 123: 3 for we are filled *with* contempt. 7227
 123: 4 Our soul is **e** filled *with* the scorning of 7227
Isa 24:19 the earth is **moved e**. 4131+4131
Da 7: 7 dreadful and terrible, and strong **e**; 3493
Jnh 1:10 were the men **e afraid**, 1419+3372+3374
 1:16 the men **feared** the LORD **e**, 1419+3372+3374
 4: 1 it **displeased** Jonah **e**, 1419+3415+7451
Mt 19:25 When his disciples heard *it*, they were **e** 4970
Mk 4:41 they feared **e**, and said one to another, 3173
 15:14 And they cried out the **more e**, Crucify 4056
Ac 16:20 being Jews, do **e trouble** our city, 1613

Ac 26:11 being **e** mad against them, I persecuted 4057
 27:18 And we being **e** tossed with a tempest, 4971
2Co 7:13 **e** the more joyed we for the joy of Titus, 4056
Gal 1:14 being **more e** zealous of the traditions of 4056
1Th 3:10 **e** that *we* might see your 1537+4053+5228
2Th 1: 3 because that your faith **groweth e**, 5232
Heb 12:21 Moses said, I **e fear** and quake;) 1510+1630

EXCEL (5) [EXCELLED, EXCELLENCY, EXCELLENT, EXCELLEST, EXCELLETH]

Ge 49: 4 Unstable as water, thou shalt not **e**; 3498
1Ch 15:21 with harps on the Sheminith to **e**. 5329
Ps 103:20 ye his angels, that **e** in strength, 1368
Isa 10:10 whose graven images did **e** *them of* 4480
1Co 14:12 ye may **e** to the edifying of the church. 4052

EXCELLED (1) [EXCEL]

1Ki 4:30 Solomon's wisdom **e** the wisdom of all 7235

EXCELLENCY (26) [EXCEL]

Ge 49: 3 of dignity, and the excellency of 3499
 49: 3 excellency of dignity, and the **e** of power: 3499
Ex 15: 7 in the greatness of thine **e** thou hast 1347
Dt 33:26 in thy help, and in his **e** *on* the sky. 1346
 33:29 thy help, and who *is* the sword of thy **e**! 1346
Job 4:21 Doth not their **e** *which is* in them go 3499
 13:11 Shall not his **e** make you afraid? 7613
 20: 6 Though his **e** mount up to the heavens, 7863
 37: 4 he thundereth with the voice of his **e**; 1347
 40:10 Deck thyself now with majesty and **e**; 1363
Ps 47: 4 for us, the **e** of Jacob whom he loved. 1347
 62: 4 only consult to cast *him* down from his **e**: 7613
 68:34 his **e** *is* over Israel, and his strength *is* in 1346
Ecc 7:12 the **e** of knowledge *is, that* wisdom giveth 3504
Isa 13:19 kingdoms, the beauty of the Chaldees' **e**, 1347
 35: 2 the **e** of Carmel and Sharon, they shall see 1926
 35: 2 glory of the LORD, *and* the **e** of our God. 1926
 60:15 I will make thee an eternal **e**, 1347
Eze 24:21 the **e** of your strength, the desire of your 1347
Am 6: 8 abhor the **e** of Jacob, and hate his palaces: 1347
 8: 7 The LORD hath sworn by the **e** of Jacob, 1347
Na 2: 2 For the LORD hath turned *away* the **e** of 1347
 2: 2 the excellency of Jacob, as the **e** of Israel: 1347
1Co 2: 1 came not with **e** of speech or of wisdom, 5247
2Co 4: 7 that the **e** of the power may be of God, 5236
Php 3: 8 loss for the **e** of the knowledge of Christ 5242

EXCELLENT (34) [EXCEL]

Est 1: 4 the honour of his **e** majesty many days, 8597
Job 37:23 he *is* **e** in power, and *in* judgment, 7689
Ps 8: 1 Lord, how **e** *is* thy name in all the earth! 117
 8: 9 Lord, how **e** *is* thy name in all the earth! 117
 16: 3 *to* the **e**, in whom *is* all my delight. 117
 36: 7 How **e** *is* thy lovingkindness, O God! 3368
 76: 4 *and* **e** than the mountains of prey. 117
 141: 5 *it shall be* an **e** oil, *which* shall not break 7218
 148:13 for his name alone *is* **e**; his glory *is* above 7682
 150: 2 praise him according to his **e** greatness. 7230
Pr 8: 6 Hear, for I will speak of **e things**; 5057
 12:26 righteous *is* more **e** than his neighbour: 8446
 17: 7 **E** speech becometh not a fool: much less 3499
 17:27 a man of understanding is of an **e** spirit. 3368
 22:20 Have not I written to thee **e things** 7991
SS 5:15 *is* as Lebanon, **e** as the cedars. 977
Isa 4: 2 fruit of the earth *shall be* **e** and comely 1347
 12: 5 the LORD; for he hath done **e things**: 1348
 28:29 wonderful in counsel, *and* **e** in working. 1431
Eze 16: 7 thou art come to **e ornaments**: 5716+5716
Da 2:31 This great image, whose brightness *was* **e**, 3493
 4:36 and **e** majesty was added unto me. 3493
 5:12 Forasmuch as an **e** spirit, and knowledge, 3493
 5:14 and **e** wisdom is found in thee. 3493
 6: 3 princes, because an **e** spirit *was* in him; 3493
Lk 1: 3 unto thee in order, **most e** Theophilus, 2903
Ac 23:26 Claudius Lysias unto the **most e** governor 2903
Ro 2:18 and approvest the *things* that are **more e**, 1308
1Co 12:31 yet shew I unto you a **more e** way. 2596+5236
Php 1:10 That ye may approve *things* that are **e**; 1308
Heb 1: 4 by inheritance obtained a **more e** 1313
 8: 6 But now hath he obtained a **more e** 1313
 11: 4 By faith Abel offered unto God a **more e** 4183
2Pe 1:17 such a voice to him from the **e** glory, 3169

EXCELLEST (1) [EXCEL]

Pr 31:29 have done virtuously, but thou **e** them all. 5927

EXCELLETH (3) [EXCEL]

Ecc 2:13 I saw that wisdom **e** folly, as far as light 3504
 2:13 excelleth folly, as far as light **e** darkness. 3504
2Co 3:10 this respect, by reason of the glory that **e**. 5235

EXCEPT (74) [EXCEPTED]

Ge 31:42 **E** the God of my father, the God of 3884
 32:26 will not let thee go, **e** thou bless me. 518+3588
 42:15 your youngest brother come hither. 518+3588
 43: 3 see my face, **e** your brother *be* with you. 1115
 43: 5 see my face, **e** your brother *be* with you. 1115
 43:10 For we had lingered, surely now we had 3884
 44:23 **E** your youngest brother come down 518+3808
 44:26 your youngest brother **be** with us. 369
 47:26 *that* Pharaoh should have the fifth *part*; **e** 7535
Nu 16:13 thou make thyself altogether a 1571+3588
Dt 32:30 their Rock had sold them, 518+3588+3808
Jos 7:12 **e** ye destroy the accursed from 518+3808
1Sa 25:34 kept me back from hurting thee, **e** 3588+3884

2Sa 3: 9 So do God to Abner, and more also, **e**, 3588
 3:13 thou first bring Michal Saul's 518+3588
 5: 6 **E** thou take away the blind and 518+3588
2Ki 4:24 not *thy* riding for me, **e** I bid thee. 518+3588
Est 2:14 the king delighted in her, 518+3807.1
 4:11 such to whom the king shall hold 905+3807.1
Ps 127: 1 **E** the LORD build the house, 518+3808
 127: 1 **e** the LORD keep the city, 518+3808
Pr 4:16 sleep not, **e** they have done mischief; 518+3808
Isa 1: 9 **E** the LORD of hosts had left unto us a 3884
Da 2:11 the gods, whose dwelling is not with 3861
 3:28 nor worship any god, **e** their own God. 3861
 6: 5 we find *it* against him concerning the 3861
Am 3: 3 two walk together, **e** they be agreed? 518+1115
Mt 5:20 That **e** your righteousness shall exceed 3362
 12:29 **e** he first bind the strong *man?* and then 3362
 18: 3 **E** ye be converted, and become as little 3362
 19: 9 **e** *it be* for fornication, and shall marry 1508
 24:22 And **e** those days should be shortened, 1508
 26:42 from me, **e** I drink it, thy will be done. 3362
Mk 3:27 **e** he will first bind the strong *man;* 3362
 7: 3 **e** they wash *their* hands oft, eat not, 3362
 7: 4 the market, **e** they wash, they eat not. 3362
 13:20 And **e** that the Lord had shortened *those* 1508
Lk 9:13 **e** we should go and buy meat for all this 1509
 13: 3 **e** ye repent, ye shall all likewise perish. 3362
 13: 5 **e** ye repent, ye shall all likewise perish. 3362
Jn 3: 2 that thou doest, **e** God be with him. 3362
 3: 3 I say unto thee, **E** a man be born again, 3362
 3: 5 **E** a man be born of water and *of* the Spirit 3362
 3:27 **e** it be given him from heaven. 3362
 4:48 **E** ye see signs and wonders, ye will not 3362
 6:44 **e** the Father which hath sent me draw 3362
 6:53 **E** ye eat the flesh of the Son of man, 3362
 6:65 **e** it were given unto him of my Father. 3362
 12:24 **E** a corn of wheat fall into the ground and 3362
 15: 4 **e** it abide in the vine; 3362
 15: 4 vine; no more can ye, **e** ye abide in me. 3362
 19:11 **e** it were given thee from above: 1508
 20:25 **E** I shall see in his hands the print of 3362
Ac 8: 1 of Judea and Samaria, **e** the apostles. 4133
 8:31 How can I, **e** some *man* should guide me? 3362
 15: 1 **E** ye be circumcised after the manner 3362
 24:21 **E** it be for this one voice, that I cried 2228
 26:29 altogether such as I am, **e** these bonds. 3924
 27:31 to the soldiers, **E** these abide in the ship, 3362
Ro 7: 7 **e** the law had said, Thou shalt not covet. 1508
 9:29 **E** the Lord of sabaoth had left us a seed, 1508
 10:15 how shall they preach, **e** they be sent? 3362
1Co 7: 5 **e** *it be* with consent for a time, 302+1509
 14: 5 he interpret, that the 1487+1622+3361
 14: 6 **e** I shall speak to you either by revelation, 3362
 14: 7 **e** they give a distinction in 1437+3361
 14: 9 **e** ye utter by the tongue words easy to be 3362
 15:36 thou sowest is not quickened, **e** it die: 3362
2Co 12:13 **e** *it be* that I myself was not burdensome 1508
 13: 5 Jesus Christ is in you, **e** ye be reprobates? 1509
2Th 2: 3 for *that day shall not come,* **e** there come 3362
2Ti 2: 5 *yet* is he not crowned, **e** he strive lawfully. 3362
Rev 2: 5 candlestick out of his place, **e** thou repent. 3362
 2:22 **e** they repent of their deeds. 3362

EXCEPTED (1) [EXCEPT]

1Co 15:27 put under *him, it is* manifest that he is **e**, 1622

EXCESS (4)

Mt 23:25 but within they are full of extortion and **e**. 192
Eph 5:18 And be not drunk with wine, wherein is **e**; 810
1Pe 4: 3 lusts, **e of wine**, revellings, banquetings, 3632
 4: 4 run not with *them* to the same **e** of riot, 401

EXCESSIVE See OVERMUCH

EXCHANGE (6) [EXCHANGERS]

Ge 47:17 Joseph gave them bread in **e** for horses, NIH
Lev 27:10 then it and the **e** thereof shall be holy. 8545
Job 28:17 the **e** of it *shall not be for* jewels of fine 8545
Eze 48:14 they shall not sell of it, neither **e**, 4171
Mt 16:26 or what shall a man give **in e for** his soul? 465
Mk 8:37 Or what shall a man give **in e for** his soul? 465

EXCHANGERS (1) [EXCHANGE]

Mt 25:27 therefore to have put my money to the **e**, 5133

EXCLUDE (1) [EXCLUDED]

Gal 4:17 yea, they would **e** you, that you might 1576

EXCLUDED (1) [EXCLUDE]

Ro 3:27 It is **e**. By what law? of works? Nay: 1576

EXCUSE (3) [EXCUSED, EXCUSING]

Lk 14:18 all with one **consent** began to **make e**. 3868
Ro 1:20 and Godhead; so that they are **without e**: 379
2Co 12:19 think you that we **e** ourselves unto you? 626

EXCUSED (2) [EXCUSE]

Lk 14:18 go and see it: I pray thee have me **e**. 3868
 14:19 I go to prove them: I pray thee have me **e**. 3868

EXCUSING (1) [EXCUSE]

Ro 2:15 while accusing or else **e** one another;) 626

EXECRATION (2)

Jer 42:18 ye shall be an **e**, and an astonishment, 423
 44:12 they shall be an **e**, *and* an astonishment, 423

E

EXECUTE (32) [EXECUTED, EXECUTEDST, EXECUTEST, EXECUTETH, EXECUTING, EXECUTION, EXECUTIONER]

Ex	12:12 against all the gods of Egypt I will **e**	6213
Nu	5:30 the priest shall **e** upon her all this law.	6213
	8:11 that they may **e** the service of the Lord.	5647
Dt	10:18 He doth **e** the judgment of the fatherless	6213
1Ki	6:12 **e** my judgments, and keep all my	6213
Ps	119:84 when wilt thou **e** judgment on them that	6213
	149: 7 To **e** vengeance upon the heathen;	6213
	149: 9 To **e** upon them the judgment written:	6213
Isa	16: 3 Take counsel, **e** judgment; make thy	6213
Jer	7: 5 if you **throughly e** judgment	6213+6213
	21:12 **E** judgment in the morning,	1777
	22: 3 **E** ye judgment and righteousness,	6213
	23: 5 shall **e** judgment and justice in the earth.	6213
	33:15 he shall **e** judgment and righteousness in	6213
Eze	5: 8 will **e** judgments in the midst of thee in	6213
	5:10 I will **e** judgments in thee, and the whole	6213
	5:15 when I shall **e** judgments in thee in anger	6213
	11: 9 and will **e** judgments among you.	6213
	16:41 **e** judgments upon thee in the sight of	6213
	25:11 I will **e** judgments upon Moab;	6213
	25:17 I will **e** great vengeance upon them with	6213
	30:14 fire in Zoan, and will **e** judgments in No.	6213
	30:19 Thus will I **e** judgments in Egypt:	6213
	45: 9 and spoil, and **e** judgment and justice,	6213
Hos	11: 9 will not **e** the fierceness of mine anger,	6213
Mic	5:15 I will **e** vengeance in anger and fury upon	6213
	7: 9 plead my cause, and **e** judgment for me:	6213
Zec	7: 9 **E** true judgment, and shew mercy and	8199
	8:16 **e** **the judgment** of truth and peace	4941+8199
Jn	5:27 hath given him authority to **e** judgment	4160
Ro	13: 4 revenger to **e** wrath upon him that doeth	NIG
Jude	1:15 To **e** judgment upon all, and to convince	4160

EXECUTED (20) [EXECUTE]

Nu	33: 4 upon their gods also the Lord **e**	6213
Dt	33:21 he **e** the justice of the Lord,	6213
2Sa	8:15 David **e** judgment and justice unto all his	6213
1Ch	6:10 (he **it is** that **e the priest's office** in	3547
	18:14 **e** judgment and justice among all his	6213
	24: 2 Eleazar and Ithamar **e the priest's office**.	3547
2Ch	24:24 So they **e** judgment against Joash.	6213
Ezr	7:26 let judgment be **e** speedily upon him,	5648
Ps	106:30 stood up Phinehas, and **e** judgment:	6419
Ecc	8:11 **against** an evil work is not **e** speedily,	6213
Jer	23:20 until he have **e**, and till he have	6213
Eze	11:12 neither **e** my judgments, but have done	6213
	18: 8 hath **e** true judgment between man and	6213
	18:17 hath **e** my judgments, hath walked in my	6213
	20:24 Because they had not **e** my judgments,	6213
	23:10 for they had **e** judgment upon her.	6213
	28:22 when I shall have **e** judgments in her,	6213
	28:26 when I have **e** judgments upon all those	6213
	39:21 shall see my judgment that I have **e**,	6213
Lk	1: 8 **that** while he **e the priest's office** before	2407

EXECUTEDST (1) [EXECUTE]

1Sa	28:18 nor **e** his fierce wrath upon Amalek,	6213

EXECUTEST (1) [EXECUTE]

Ps	99: 4 thou **e** judgment and righteousness in	6213

EXECUTETH (6) [EXECUTE]

Ps	9:16 is known **by** the judgment **which** he **e**:	6213
	103: 6 The Lord **e** righteousness and	6213
	146: 7 Which **e** judgment for the oppressed:	6213
Isa	46:11 the man that **e** my counsel from a far	NIH
Jer	5: 1 a man, if there be **any** that **e** judgment,	6213
Joel	2:11 he **is** strong that **e** his word: for the day	6213

EXECUTING (3) [EXECUTE]

2Ki	10:30 Because thou hast done well in **e** **that**	6213
2Ch	11:14 from **e the priest's office** unto the Lord:	3547
	22: 8 that when Jehu was **e** **judgment** upon	8199

EXECUTION (1) [EXECUTE]

Est	9: 1 and his decree drew near to be **put in e**,	6213

EXECUTIONER (1) [EXECUTE]

Mk	6:27 And immediately the king sent an **e**,	4688

EXEMPTED (1)

1Ki	15:22 throughout all Judah; none **was e**:	5355

EXERCISE (11) [EXERCISED, EXERCISETH]

Ps	131: 1 neither do I **e** myself in great **matters**, or	1980
Jer	9:24 that I **am** the Lord which **e**	6213
Mt	20:25 of the Gentiles **e dominion over** them,	2634
	20:25 **that are** great **e authority upon** them.	2715
Mk	10:42 over the Gentiles **e lordship over** them;	2634
	10:42 their great ones **e authority upon** them.	2715
Lk	22:25 The kings of the Gentiles **e lordship over**	2961
	22:25 that **e authority upon** them are called	1850
Ac	24:16 And herein do I **e** myself, to have always	778
1Ti	4: 7 and **e** thyself **rather** unto godliness.	1128
	4: 8 For bodily **e** profiteth little:	1129

EXERCISED (6) [EXERCISE]

Ecc	1:13 to the sons of man to be **e** therewith.	6031
	3:10 given to the sons of men to be **e** in it.	6031
Eze	22:29 **e robbery**, and have vexed the	1497+1498
Heb	5:14 have their senses **e** to discern both good	1128
	12:11 unto them which are **e** thereby.	1128

2Pe	2:14 heart they have **e** with covetous practices;	1128

EXERCISETH (1) [EXERCISE]

Rev	13:12 And he **e** all the power of the first beast	4160

EXHORT (16) [EXHORTATION, EXHORTED, EXHORTETH, EXHORTING]

Ac	2:40 many other words did he testify and **e**,	3870
	27:22 And now I **e** you to be of good cheer:	3867
2Co	9: 5 Therefore I thought it necessary to **e**	3870
1Th	4: 1 brethren, and **e** you by the Lord Jesus,	3870
	5:14 Now we **e** you, brethren, warn **them** that	3870
2Th	3:12 and **e** by our Lord Jesus Christ,	3870
1Ti	1: 1 **e** therefore that, first of all, supplications,	3870
	6: 2 of the benefit. These **things** teach and **e**.	3870
2Ti	4: 2 **e** with all longsuffering and doctrine.	3870
Tit	1: 9 may be able by sound doctrine both to **e**	3870
	2: 6 Young **men** likewise **e** to be sober minded.	3870
	2: 9 **E** servants to be obedient unto their own	NIG
	2:15 and **e**, and rebuke with all authority.	3870
Heb	3:13 But **e** one another daily, while it is called	3870
1Pe	5: 1 The elders which are among you I **e**,	3870
Jude	1: 3 **e** **you** that **ye** should earnestly contend for	3870

EXHORTATION (10) [EXHORT]

Lk	3:18 many other **things** in his **e** preached he	3870
Ac	13:15 if ye have **any** word of **e** for the people,	3874
	20: 2 had **given** them much **e**, he came	3056+3870
Ro	12: 8 Or he that exhorteth, on **e**: he that giveth,	3874
1Co	14: 3 men **to** edification, and **e**, and comfort.	3874
2Co	8:17 For indeed he accepted the **e**;	3874
1Th	2: 3 For our **e was** not of deceit, nor of	3874
1Ti	4:13 attendance to reading, to **e**, to doctrine.	3874
Heb	12: 5 ye have forgotten the **e** which speaketh	3874
	13:22 brethren, suffer the word of **e**:	3874

EXHORTED (3) [EXHORT]

Ac	11:23 grace of God, was glad, and **e** **them** all,	3870
	15:32 **e** the brethren with many words,	3870
1Th	2:11 As you know how we **e** and comforted	3870

EXHORTETH (1) [EXHORT]

Ro	12: 8 he that **e**, on exhortation: he that giveth,	3870

EXHORTING (4) [EXHORT]

Ac	14:22 and **e** **them** to continue in the faith,	3870
	18:27 **e** the disciples to receive him:	4389
Heb	10:25 **e** one another: and so much the more,	3870
1Pe	5:12 **e**, and testifying that this is the true grace	3870

EXILE (2)

2Sa	15:19 for thou **art** a stranger, and also an **e**.	1540
Isa	51:14 The **captive e** hasteneth that **he** may be	6808

EXORCISTS (1)

Ac	19:13 Then certain of the vagabond Jews, **e**,	1845

EXPANSE See FIRMAMENT

EXPECTATION (14) [EXPECTED, EXPECTING]

Ps	9:18 the **e** of the poor shall **not** perish for ever.	8615
	62: 5 only upon God; for my **e** is from him.	8615
Pr	10:28 but the **e** of the wicked shall perish.	8615
	11: 7 a wicked man dieth, his **e** shall perish:	8615
	11:23 good: **but** the **e** of the wicked **is** wrath.	8615
	23:18 is an end; and thine **e** shall not be cut off.	8615
	24:14 be a reward, and thy **e** shall not be cut off.	8615
Isa	20: 5 be afraid and ashamed of Ethiopia their **e**,	4007
	20: 6 say in that day, Behold, such **is** our **e**,	4007
Zec	9: 5 for her **e** shall be ashamed; and the king	4007
Lk	3:15 And as the people were in **e**, and all **men**	4328
Ac	12:11 **from** all the **e** of the people of the Jews.	4329
Ro	8:19 For the **earnest e** of the creature waiteth	603
Php	1:20 According to my **earnest e** and **my** hope,	603

EXPECTED (1) [EXPECTATION]

Jer	29:11 and not of evil, to give you an **e** end.	8615

EXPECTING (2) [EXPECTATION]

Ac	3: 5 them, **e** to receive something of them.	4328
Heb	10:13 henceforth **e** till his enemies be made	1551

EXPEDIENT (7)

Jn	11:50 Nor consider that it is **e** for us, that one	4851
	16: 7 the truth; It is **e** for you that I go away:	4851
	18:14 that it was **e** that one man should die for	4851
1Co	6:12 lawful unto me, but all **things** are not **e**:	4851
	10:23 lawful unto me, but all **things** are not **e**:	4851
2Co	8:10 for this is **e** for you, who have begun	4851
	12: 1 It is not **e** for me doubtless to glory. I will	4851

EXPEL (2) [EXPELLED]

Jos	23: 5 he shall **e** them from before you,	1920
Jdg	11: 7 and **e** me out of my father's house?	1644

EXPELLED (4) [EXPEL]

Jos	13:13 (Nevertheless the children of Israel **e** not	3423
Jdg	1:20 and he thence the three sons of Anak.	3423
2Sa	14:14 that **his** banished be not **e** from him.	5080
Ac	13:50 Barnabas, and **e** them out of their coasts.	1544

EXPENCES (2)

Ezr	6: 4 let the **e** be given out of the king's house:	5313
	6: 8 forthwith **e** be given unto these men,	5313

EXPERIENCE (4)

Ge	30:27 tarry: **for** I have **learned by e** that	5172

Ecc	1:16 my heart **had** great **e** of wisdom and	7200
Ro	5: 4 And patience, **e**; and experience, hope:	1382
	5: 4 And patience, experience; and **e**, hope:	1382

EXPERIMENT (1)

2Co	9:13 Whiles by the **e** of this ministration they	1382

EXPERT (6)

1Ch	12:33 **e** in war, with all instruments of war,	6186
	12:35 of the Danites **e** in war twenty and	6186
	12:36 forth to battle, **e** in war, forty thousand.	6186
SS	3: 8 They all hold swords, **being e** in war:	3925
Jer	50: 9 arrows **shall be** as of a mighty **e man;**	7919
Ac	26: 3 **I know** thee to be **e** in all customs and	1109

EXPERT BUILDER See MASTERBUILDER

EXPIRED (9)

1Sa	18:26 son in law: and the days were not **e**.	4390
2Sa	11: 1 it came to pass, after the year was **e**,	8666
1Ch	17:11 when thy days be **e** that **thou** must go	4390
	20: 1 it came to pass, after the year was **e**,	8666
2Ch	36:10 the year was **e**, king Nebuchadnezzar	8666
Est	1: 5 when these days were **e**, the king made a	4390
Eze	43:27 when **these** days are **e**, it shall be, **that**	3615
Ac	7:30 And when forty years were **e**,	4137
Rev	20: 7 And when the thousand years are **e**, Satan	5055

EXPLOITS (2)

Da	11:28 he shall do **e**, and return to his own land.	NIH
	11:32 know their God shall be strong, and do **e**.	NIH

EXPLORE See ESPIED; ESPY

EXPOSE See REPROOF; REPROVE

EXPOUND (1) [EXPOUNDED]

Jdg	14:14 they could not **in** three days **e** the riddle.	5046

EXPOUNDED (6) [EXPOUND]

Jdg	14:19 **garments** unto them which **e** the riddle.	5046
Mk	4:34 **were** alone, he **e** all **things** to his disciples.	1956
Lk	24:27 he **e** unto them in all the scriptures	1329
Ac	11: 4 and **e** **it** by order unto them, saying,	1620
	18:26 **e** unto him the way of God more perfectly.	1620
	28:23 whom he **e** and testified the kingdom of	1620

EXPRESS (1) [EXPRESSED, EXPRESSLY]

Heb	1: 3 and the **e image** of his person,	5481

EXPRESSED (6) [EXPRESS]

Nu	1:17 Aaron took these men which are **e** by	5344
1Ch	12:31 which were **e** by name, to come and	5344
	16:41 that were chosen, who were **e** by name,	5344
2Ch	28:15 the men which were **e** by name rose up,	5344
	31:19 city, the men that were **e** by name,	5344
Ezr	8:20 all of them were **e** by name.	5344

EXPRESSLY (3) [EXPRESS]

1Sa	20:21 If I **say** unto the lad, Behold,	559+559
Eze	1: 3 The word of the Lord came **e**	1961+1961
1Ti	4: 1 the Spirit speaketh **e**, that in the latter	4490

EXTEND (2) [EXTENDED, EXTENDETH]

Ps	109:12 Let there be none to **e** mercy **unto** him:	4900
Isa	66:12 I will **e** peace to her like a river,	5186

EXTENDED (2) [EXTEND]

Ezr	7:28 hath **e** mercy unto me before the king,	5186
	9: 9 hath **e** mercy unto us in the sight of	5186

EXTENDETH (1) [EXTEND]

Ps	16: 2 **art** my Lord: my goodness **e** not to thee;	NIH

EXTINCT (2)

Job	17: 1 My breath is corrupt, my days are **e**,	2193
Isa	43:17 they are **e**, they are quenched as tow.	1846

EXTINGUISHED See EXTINCT

EXTOL (4) [EXTOLLED]

Ps	30: 1 I will **e** thee, O Lord; for thou hast lifted	7311
	68: 4 **e** him that rideth upon the heavens by his	5549
	145: 1 I will **e** thee, my God, O king; and I will	7311
Da	4:37 and **e** and honour the King of heaven,	7313

EXTOLLED (2) [EXTOL]

Ps	66:17 my mouth, and he was **e** with my tongue.	7311
Isa	52:13 shall be exalted and **e**, and be very high.	5375

EXTORTION (2) [EXTORTIONER, EXTORTIONERS]

Eze	22:12 greedily gained of thy neighbours by **e**,	6233
Mt	23:25 but within they are full of **e** and excess.	724

EXTORTIONER (3) [EXTORTION]

Ps	109:11 Let the **e** catch all that he hath; and let	5383
Isa	16: 4 for the **e** is at an end, the spoiler ceaseth,	4160
1Co	5:11 idolater, or a railer, or a drunkard, or an **e**;	727

EXTORTIONERS (3) [EXTORTION]

Lk	18:11 that I am not as other men **are**, **e**, unjust,	727
1Co	5:10 with the covetous, or **e**, or with idolaters;	727
	6:10 nor drunkards, nor revilers, nor **e**,	727

EXTREME (1) [EXTREMITY]

Dt	28:22 with an **e burning**, and with the sword,	2746

EXTREMITY (1) [EXTREME]

Job 35:15 anger; yet he knoweth *it* not in great **e**: 6580

EYE (116) [EYE'S, EYEBROWS, EYED, EYELIDS, EYES, EYESALVE, EYESERVICE, EYESIGHT, EYEWITNESSES]

Ex 21:24 **E** for eye, tooth for tooth, hand for hand, 5869
21:24 Eye for **e**, tooth for tooth, hand for hand, 5869
21:26 if a man smite the **e** of his servant, 5869
21:26 or the **e** of his maid, that it perish; 5869
Lev 21:20 that hath a blemish in his **e**, or be scurvy, 5869
24:20 for breach, **e** for eye, tooth for tooth: 5869
24:20 for breach, eye for **e**, tooth for tooth: 5869
Dt 7:16 thine **e** shall have no pity upon them: 5869
13: 8 neither shall thine **e** pity him, neither 5869
15: 9 thine **e** be evil against thy poor brother, 5869
19:13 Thine **e** shall not pity him, but thou shalt 5869
19:21 thine **e** shall not pity; *but* life *shall go* for 5869
19:21 **e** for eye, tooth for tooth, hand for hand, 5869
19:21 eye for **e**, tooth for tooth, hand for hand, 5869
25:12 cut off her hand, thine **e** shall not pity 5869
28:54 his **e** shall be evil toward his brother, 5869
28:56 her **e** shall be evil towards the husband of 5869
32:10 he kept him as the apple of his **e**. 5869
34: 7 his **e** was not dim, nor his natural force 5869
1Sa 24:10 *mine* **e** spared thee; and I said, I will not NIH
2Sa 22:25 according to my cleanness in his **sight**. 5869
Ezr 5: 5 the **e** of their God was upon the elders of 5870
Job 7: 7 *is* wind: mine **e** shall no more see good. 5869
7: 8 The **e** of him that hath seen me shall see 5869
10:18 given up the ghost, and no **e** had seen me! 5869
13: 1 mine **e** hath seen all *this*, mine ear hath 5869
16:20 *but* mine **e** poureth out *tears* unto God. 5869
17: 2 *doth not* mine **e** continue in their 5869
17: 7 Mine **e** also is dim by reason of sorrow, 5869
20: 9 The **e** also *which* saw him shall *see him* 5869
24:15 The **e** also of the adulterer waiteth for 5869
24:15 the twilight, saying, No **e** shall see me: 5869
28: 7 and which the vulture's **e** hath not seen: 5869
28:10 and his **e** seeth every precious thing. 5869
29:11 the **e** saw *me*, it gave witness to me: 5869
42: 5 of the ear: but now mine **e** seeth thee. 5869
Ps 6: 7 Mine **e** is consumed because of grief; 5869
17: 8 Keep me as the apple of the **e**, hide me 5869
31: 9 mine **e** is consumed with grief, yea, my 5869
32: 8 shalt go: I will guide thee with mine **e**. 5869
33:18 the **e** of the LORD *is* upon them that fear 5869
35:19 let them wink *with* the **e** that hate 5869
35:21 *and* said, Aha, aha, our **e** hath seen *it*. 5869
54: 7 mine **e** hath seen *his desire* upon mine 5869
88: 9 Mine **e** mourneth by reason of affliction: 5869
92:11 Mine **e** also shall see *my desire* on mine 5869
94: 9 he that formed the **e**, shall he not see? 5869
Pr 7: 2 live; and my law as the apple of thine **e**. 5869
10:10 that winketh *with* the **e** causeth sorrow: 5869
20:12 The hearing ear, and the seeing **e**, 5869
22: 9 that hath a bountiful **e** shall be blessed; 5869
23: 6 not the bread of *him that hath* an evil **e**, 5869
28:22 He that hasteth to be rich *hath* an evil **e**, 5869
30:17 The **e** *that* mocketh at *his* father, 5869
Ecc 1: 8 man cannot utter *it*: the **e** is not satisfied 5869
4: 8 neither is his **e** satisfied *with* riches; 5869
Isa 13:18 womb; their **e** shall not spare children. 5869
52: 8 for they shall see **e** to eye, when 5869
52: 8 for they shall see eye to **e**, when 5869
64: 4 neither hath the **e** seen, O God, 5869
Jer 13:17 mine **e** shall weep sore, and run down 5869
La 1:16 mine **e**, mine eye runneth down *with* 5869
1:16 mine **e** runneth down *with* water, 5869
2: 4 slew all *that were* pleasant to the **e**: 5869
2:18 no rest; let not the apple of thine **e** cease. 5869
3:48 Mine **e** runneth down *with* rivers of water 5869
3:49 Mine **e** trickleth down, and ceaseth not, 5869
3:51 Mine **e** affecteth mine heart because of all 5869
Eze 5:11 diminish *thee;* neither shall mine **e** spare, 5869
7: 4 mine **e** shall not spare thee, neither will I 5869
7: 9 mine **e** shall not spare, neither will I have 5869
8:18 mine **e** shall not spare, neither will I have 5869
9: 5 let not your **e** spare, neither have ye pity: 5869
9:10 *as for* me also, mine **e** shall not spare, 5869
16: 5 None **e** pitied thee, to do any of these 5869
20:17 Nevertheless mine **e** spared them from 5869
Mic 4:11 be defiled, and let our **e** look upon Zion. 5869
Zec 2: 8 toucheth you toucheth the apple of his **e**. 5869
11:17 *be* upon his arm, and upon his right **e**: 5869
11:17 and his right **e** shall be utterly darkened. 5869
Mt 5:29 if thy right **e** offend thee, pluck it out, 3788
5:38 An **e** for an eye, and a tooth for a tooth: 3788
5:38 An eye for an **e**, and a tooth for a tooth. 3788
6:22 The light of the body is the **e**: if therefore 3788
6:22 if therefore thine **e** be single, thy whole 3788
6:23 if thine **e** be evil, thy whole body shall 3788
7: 3 thou the mote that is in thy brother's **e**, 3788
7: 3 not the beam that is in thine own **e**? 3788
7: 4 Let me pull out the mote out of thine **e**; 3788
7: 4 and, behold, a beam *is* in thine own **e**? 3788
7: 5 cast out the beam out of thine own **e**; 3788
7: 5 cast out the mote out of thy brother's **e**. 3788
18: 9 And if thine **e** offend thee, pluck it out, 3788
18: 9 for thee to enter into life with **one** **e**, 3442
19:24 is easier for a camel to go through the **e** 5169
20:15 I will with mine own? Is thine **e** evil, 3788
Mk 7:22 an evil **e**, blasphemy, pride, foolishness: 3788
9:47 And if thine **e** offend thee, pluck it out: 3788

EYE'S (1) [EYE]

Mk 9:47 into the kingdom of God with **one** **e**, 3442
10:25 It is easier for a camel to go through the **e** 5168
Lk 6:41 thou the mote that is in thy brother's **e**, 3788
6:41 not the beam that is in thine own **e**? 3788
6:42 let me pull out the mote that is in thine **e**, 3788
6:42 not the beam that is in thine own **e**? 3788
6:42 cast out first the beam out of thine own **e**, 3788
6:42 out the mote that is in thy brother's **e**. 3788
11:34 The light of the body is the **e**: 3788
11:34 therefore when thine **e** is single, 3788
11:34 when *thine* **e** is evil, thy body also *is* full NIG
18:25 for a camel to go through a needle's **e**, 5168
1Co 2: 9 is written, **E** hath not seen, nor ear heard, 3788
12:16 Because I am not the **e**, I am not of 3788
12:17 If the whole body *were* an **e**, where *were* 3788
12:21 the **e** cannot say unto the hand, I have 3788
15:52 In a moment, in the twinkling of an **e**, 3788
Rev 1: 7 and every **e** shall see him, and they also 3788

EYE'S (1) [EYE]

Ex 21:26 he shall let him go free for his **e** sake. 5869

EYEBROWS (1) [EYE, BROW]

Lev 14: 9 his head and his beard and his **e**, 1354+5869

EYED (2) [EYE]

Ge 29:17 Leah was tender **e**; but Rachel was 5869
1Sa 18: 9 Saul **e** David from that day and forward. 5770

EYELIDS (9) [EYE]

Job 16:16 and on mine **e** *is* the shadow of death; 6079
41:18 his eyes *are* like the **e** of the morning. 6079
Ps 11: 4 his eyes behold, his **e** try, the children of 6079
132: 4 sleep to mine eyes, *or* slumber to mine **e**, 6079
Pr 4:25 and let thine **e** look straight before thee. 6079
6: 4 to thine eyes, nor slumber to thine **e**. 6079
6:25 neither let her take thee with her **e**. 6079
30:13 are their eyes! and their **e** are lifted up. 6079
Jer 9:18 tears, and our **e** gush out with waters. 6079

EYES (501) [EYE]

Ge 3: 5 your **e** shall be opened, and ye shall be as 5869
3: 6 that it *was* pleasant to the **e**, and a tree to 5869
3: 7 the **e** of them both were opened, 5869
6: 8 Noah found grace in the **e** of the LORD. 5869
13:10 Lot lifted up his **e**, and beheld all the plain 5869
13:14 Lift up now thine **e**, and look from 5869
16: 4 her mistress was despised in her **e**. 5869
16: 5 had conceived, I was despised in her **e**: 5869
18: 2 he lift up his **e** and looked, and lo, 5869
19: 8 and do ye to them as *is* good in your **e**: 5869
20:16 behold, he *is* to thee a covering of the **e**, 5869
21:19 God opened her **e**, and she saw a well of 5869
22: 4 on the third day Abraham lift up his **e**, 5869
22:13 Abraham lifted up his **e**, and looked, 5869
24:63 he lift up his **e**, and saw, and behold, 5869
24:64 Rebekah lift up her **e**, and when she saw 5869
27: 1 his **e** were dim, so that he could not see, 5869
30:27 if I have found favour in thine **e**, 5869
30:41 that Jacob laid the rods before the **e** of 5869
31:10 I lifted up mine **e**, and saw in a dream, 5869
31:12 he said, Lift up now thine **e**, and see, 5869
31:40 and my sleep departed from mine **e**. 5869
33: 1 Jacob lifted up his **e**, and looked, 5869
33: 5 he lift up his **e**, and saw the women and 5869
34:11 Let me find grace in your **e**, and what ye 5869
37:25 they lift up their **e** and looked, 5869
39: 7 that his master's wife cast her **e** upon 5869
41:37 this was good in the **e** of Pharaoh, 5869
41:37 Pharaoh, and in the **e** of all his servants. 5869
42:24 and bound him before their **e**. 5869
43:29 he lift up his **e**, and saw his brother 5869
44:21 unto me, that I may set mine **e** upon him. 5869
45:12 your **e** see, and the eyes of my brother 5869
45:12 see, and the **e** of my brother Benjamin, 5869
46: 4 Joseph shall put his hand upon thine **e**. 5869
47:19 Wherefore shall we die before thine **e**, 5869
48:10 Now the **e** of Israel were dim for age, 5869
49:12 *His* **e** *shall* be red with wine, and *his* 5869
50: 4 If now I have found grace in your **e**, 5869
Ex 5:21 be abhorred in the **e** of Pharaoh, 5869
5:21 in the **e** of his servants, to put a sword in 5869
8:26 of the Egyptians before their **e**, 5869
13: 9 for a memorial between thine **e**, that 5869
13:16 and for frontlets between thine **e**: 5869
14:10 the children of Israel lift up their **e**, 5869
24:17 mount in the **e** of the children of Israel. 5869
Lev 4:13 thing be hid from the **e** of the assembly, 5869
20: 4 do any ways hide their **e** from the man, 5869
26:16 shall consume the **e**, and cause sorrow 5869
Nu 5:13 it be hid from the **e** of her husband, 5869
10:31 and thou mayest be to us instead of **e**. 5869
11: 6 at all, beside *this* manna, *before* our **e**. 5869
15:39 not after your own heart and your own **e**, 5869
16:14 wilt thou put out the **e** of these men? 5869
20: 8 and speak ye unto the rock before their **e**; 5869
20:12 to sanctify me in the **e** of the children of 5869
22:31 the LORD opened the **e** of Balaam, 5869
24: 2 Balaam lift up his **e**, and he saw Israel 5869
24: 3 and the man whose **e** are open hath said: 5869
24: 4 *into* a trance, but having his **e** open: 5869
24:15 and the man whose **e** are open hath said: 5869
24:16 *into* a trance, but having his **e** open: 5869
27:14 to sanctify me at the water before their **e**: 5869
33:55 remain in the **e**, and *shall be* pricks in your **e**, 5869

Dt 1:30 he did for you in Egypt before your **e**; 5869
3:21 Thine **e** have seen all that the LORD your 5869
3:27 lift up thine **e** westward, and northward, 5869
3:27 eastward, and behold *it* with thine **e**: 5869
4: 3 Your **e** have seen what the LORD did 5869
4: 9 lest thou forget the things which thine **e** 5869
4:19 lest thou lift up thine **e** unto heaven, 5869
4:34 God did for you in Egypt before your **e**? 5869
6: 8 they shall be as frontlets between thine **e**. 5869
6:22 and upon all his household, before our **e**: 5869
7:19 The great temptations which thine **e** saw, 5869
9:17 two hands, and brake them before your **e**. 5869
10:21 terrible *things*, which thine **e** have seen. 5869
11: 7 your **e** have seen all the great acts of 5869
11:12 the **e** of the LORD thy God *are* always 5869
11:18 they may be as frontlets between your **e**. 5869
12: 8 man whatsoever *is* right in his own **e**. 5869
13:18 to do *that which is* right in the **e** of 5869
14: 1 nor make *any* baldness between your **e** 5869
16:19 for a gift doth blind the **e** of the wise, 5869
21: 7 this blood, neither have our **e** seen *it*. 5869
24: 1 to pass that she find no favour in his **e**, 5869
28:31 Thine ox *shall be* slain before thine **e**, 5869
28:32 thine **e** shall look, and fail *with longing* 5869
28:34 the sight of thine **e** which thou shalt see. 5869
28:65 and failing of **e**, and sorrow of mind: 5869
28:67 the sight of thine **e** which thou shalt see. 5869
29: 2 your **e** in the land of Egypt unto Pharaoh, 5869
29: 3 The great temptations which thine **e** have 5869
29: 4 **e** to see, and ears to hear, unto this day. 5869
34: 4 I have caused thee to see *it* with thine **e**, 5869
Jos 5:13 that he lift up his **e** and looked, 5869
23:13 in your sides, and thorns in your **e**, 5869
24: 7 your **e** have seen what I have done in 5869
Jdg 16:21 put out his **e**, and brought him down to 5869
16:28 avenged of the Philistines for my two **e**. 5869
17: 6 did *that which was* right in his own **e**. 5869
19:17 when he had lift up his **e**, he saw a 5869
21:25 did *that which was* right in his own **e**. 5869
Ru 2: 9 thine **e** *be* on the field that they do reap, 5869
2:10 Why have I found grace in thine **e**, 5869
1Sa 2:33 *shall be* to consume thine **e**, and to grieve 5869
2: his **e** began to wax dim, *that* he could not 5869
4:15 and his **e** were dim, that he could not see. 5869
6:13 they lifted up their **e**, and saw the ark, 5869
11: 2 that *I* may thrust out all your right **e**, 5869
12: 3 *any* bribe to blind mine **e** therewith? 5869
12:16 which the LORD will do before your **e**. 5869
14:27 to his mouth; and his **e** were enlightened. 5869
14:29 how mine **e** have been enlightened, 5869
20: 3 that I have found grace in thine **e**; 5869
20:29 now, if I have found favour in thine **e**, 5869
24:10 this day thine **e** have seen how that 5869
25: 8 let the young men find favour in thine **e**: 5869
26:21 my soul was precious in thine **e** this day: 5869
26:24 life was much set by this day in mine **e**, 5869
26:24 let my life be much set by in the **e** of 5869
27: 5 If I have now found grace in the **e** of 5869
2Sa 6:20 who uncovered himself to day in the **e** of 5869
12:11 and I will take thy wives before thine **e**, 5869
13:34 man that kept the watch lift up his **e**, 5869
15:25 if I shall find favour in the **e** of the LORD, 5869
18:24 lift up his **e**, and looked, and behold a 5869
19:27 do therefore what *is* good in thine **e**. 5869
22:28 thine **e** *are* upon the haughty, *that* thou 5869
24: 3 *that* the **e** of my lord the king may see *it*: 5869
1Ki 1:20 O king, the **e** of all Israel *are* upon thee, 5869
1:48 my throne *this* day, mine **e** even seeing *it*. 5869
8:29 That thine **e** may be open toward this 5869
8:52 That thine **e** may be open unto 5869
9: 3 mine **e** and mine heart shall be there 5869
10: 7 I came, and mine **e** had seen *it*: 5869
11:33 to do *that which is* right in mine **e**, 5869
14: 4 for his **e** were set by reason of his age. 5869
14: 8 do *that* only *which was* right in mine **e**, 5869
15: 5 *which was* right in the **e** of the LORD, 5869
15:11 Asa did *that which was* right in the **e** of 5869
16:25 Omri wrought evil in the **e** of the LORD, 5869
20: 6 *that* whatsoever *is* pleasant in thine **e**, 5869
22:43 doing *that which was* right in the **e** of 5869
2Ki 4:34 his **e** upon his eyes, and his hands upon 5869
4:34 his eyes upon his **e**, and his hands upon 5869
4:35 seven times, and the child opened his **e**. 5869
6:17 said, LORD, I pray thee, open his **e**, 5869
6:17 the LORD opened the **e** of the young man; 5869
6:20 open the **e** of these *men*, that they may 5869
6:20 the LORD opened their **e**, and they saw; 5869
7: 2 shalt see *it* with thine **e**, but shalt not 5869
7:19 shalt see *it* with thine **e**, but shalt not 5869
10: 5 do thou *that which is* good in thine **e**. 5869
10:30 in executing *that which is* right in mine **e**, 5869
19:16 open, LORD, thine **e**, and see: 5869
19:22 *thy* voice, and lift up thine **e** on high? 5869
22:20 thine **e** shall not see all the evil which I 5869
25: 7 slew the sons of Zedekiah before his **e**, 5869
25: 7 put out the **e** of Zedekiah, and bound him 5869
1Ch 13: 4 for the thing was right in the **e** of all 5869
17:17 this was a small thing in thine **e**, O God; 5869
21:16 David lift up his **e**, and saw the angel of 5869
21:23 the king do *that which is* good in his **e**: 5869
2Ch 6:20 That thine **e** may be open upon this house 5869
6:40 thine **e** be open, and *let* thine ears *be* 5869
7:15 Now mine **e** shall be open, and mine ears 5869
7:16 mine **e** and mine heart shall be there 5869
9: 6 I came, and mine **e** had seen *it*: 5869

2Ch 14: 2 and right in the **e** of the Lᴏʀᴅ his God: 5869
16: 9 For the **e** of the Lᴏʀᴅ run to and 5869
20:12 we what to do: but our **e** *are* upon thee. 5869
21: 6 wrought *that which was* evil in the **e** of 5869
29: 6 done *that* which *was* evil in the **e** of 5869
29: 8 and to hissing, as ye see with your **e**. 5869
34:28 neither shall thine **e** see all the evil that I 5869
Ezr 3:12 of this house was laid before their **e**, 5869
9: 8 our God may lighten our **e**, and give us 5869
Ne 1: 6 ear now be attentive, and thine **e** open, 5869
6:16 were much cast down in their own **e**: 5869
Est 1:17 shall despise their husbands in their **e**, 5869
8: 5 before the king, and I *be* pleasing in his **e**, 5869
Job 2:12 when they lift up their **e** afar off, 5869
3:10 nor hid sorrow from mine **e**. 5869
4:16 an image *was* before mine **e**, *there was* 5869
7: 8 see me no *more:* thine **e** *are* upon me, 5869
10: 4 Hast thou **e** of flesh? or seest thou as man 5869
11: 4 *is* pure, and I am clean in thine **e**. 5869
11:20 the **e** of the wicked shall fail, and they 5869
14: 3 dost thou open thine **e** upon such a one, 5869
15:12 thee away? and what do thine **e** wink at, 5869
16: 9 mine enemy sharpeneth his **e** upon me. 5869
17: 5 even the **e** of his children shall fail. 5869
19:27 and mine **e** shall behold, and not another; 5869
21: 8 and their offspring before their **e**. 5869
21:20 His **e** shall see his destruction, and he 5869
24:23 he resteth; yet his **e** *are* upon their ways. 5869
27:19 gathered: he openeth his **e**, and he *is* not. 5869
28:21 Seeing it is hid from the **e** of all living, 5869
29:15 I was **e** to the blind, and feet *was* I to 5869
31: 1 I made a covenant with mine **e**; why then 5869
31: 7 heart walked after mine **e**, and *if any* 5869
31:16 or have caused the **e** of the widow to fail; 5869
32: 1 because he *was* righteous in his own **e**. 5869
34:21 For his **e** *are* upon the ways of man, 5869
36: 7 He withdraweth not his **e** from 5869
39:29 the prey, *and her* **e** behold afar off. 5869
40:24 He taketh it with his **e**: *his* nose pierceth 5869
41:18 his **e** *are* like the eyelids of the morning. 5869
Ps 10: 8 his **e** are privily set against the poor. 5869
11: 4 his **e** behold, his eyelids try, the children 5869
13: 3 lighten mine **e**, lest I sleep the *sleep of* 5869
15: 4 In whose **e** a vile *person* is contemned; 5869
17: 2 thine **e** behold the things that are equal. 5869
17:11 they have set their **e** bowing down to 5869
19: 8 of the Lᴏʀᴅ *is* pure, enlightening the **e**. 5869
25:15 Mine **e** *are* ever towards the Lᴏʀᴅ; for he 5869
26: 3 For thy lovingkindness *is* before mine **e**: 5869
31:22 haste, I am cut off from before thine **e**: 5869
34:15 The **e** of the Lᴏʀᴅ *are* upon 5869
36: 1 *that there is* no fear of God before his **e**. 5869
36: 2 For he flattereth himself in his own **e**, 5869
38:10 as for the light of mine **e**, it also is gone 5869
50:21 and set *them* in order before thine **e**. 5869
66: 7 power for ever; his **e** behold the nations: 5869
69: 3 mine **e** fail while I wait for my God. 5869
69:23 Let their **e** be darkened, that *they* see not; 5869
73: 7 Their **e** stand out with fatness: they have 5869
77: 4 Thou holdest mine **e** waking: I am *so* 5869
91: 8 Only with thine **e** shalt thou behold and 5869
101: 3 I will set no wicked thing before mine **e**: 5869
101: 6 Mine **e** *shall be* upon the faithful of 5869
115: 5 speak not: **e** have they, but they see not: 5869
116: 8 **e** from tears, *and* my feet from falling. 5869
118:23 Lᴏʀᴅ's doing; it is marvellous in our **e**. 5869
119:18 Open thou mine **e**, that I may behold 5869
119:37 Turn away mine **e** from beholding vanity; 5869
119:82 Mine **e** fail for thy word, saying, When 5869
119:123 Mine **e** fail for thy salvation, and for 5869
119:136 Rivers of waters run down mine **e**, 5869
119:148 Mine **e** prevent the *night* watches, that *I* 5869
121: 1 I will lift up mine **e** unto the hills, 5869
123: 1 Unto thee lift I up mine **e**, O thou that 5869
123: 2 as the **e** of servants *look* unto the hand of 5869
123: 2 as the **e** of a maiden unto the hand of her 5869
123: 2 so our **e** *wait* upon the Lᴏʀᴅ our God, 5869
131: 1 my heart is not haughty, nor mine **e** lofty: 5869
132: 4 I will not give sleep to mine **e**, 5869
135:16 speak not; **e** have they, but they see not; 5869
139:16 Thine **e** did see my substance, yet being 5869
141: 8 mine **e** *are* unto thee, O God the Lord: 5869
145:15 The **e** of all wait upon thee; and thou 5869
146: 8 The Lᴏʀᴅ openeth the **e** of the blind: NIH
Pr 3: 7 Be not wise in thine own **e**: fear 5869
3:21 My son, let not them depart from thine **e**: 5869
4:21 Let them not depart from thine **e**; 5869
4:25 Let thine **e** look right on, and let thine 5869
5:21 For the ways of man *are* before the **e** of 5869
6: 4 Give not sleep to thine **e**, nor slumber to 5869
6:13 He winketh with his **e**, he speaketh with 5869
10:26 as smoke to the **e**, so *is* the sluggard to 5869
12:15 The way of a fool *is* right in his own **e**: 5869
15: 3 The **e** of the Lᴏʀᴅ *are* in every place, 5869
15:30 The light of the **e** rejoiceth the heart: 5869
16: 2 the ways of a man *are* clean in his own **e**; 5869
16:30 He shutteth his **e** to devise froward things 5869
17: 8 gift *is as* a precious stone in the **e** of him 5869
17:24 the **e** of a fool *are* in the ends of the earth. 5869
20: 8 scattereth *away* all evil with his **e**. 5869
20:13 open thine **e**, *and* thou shalt be satisfied 5869
21: 2 way of a man *is* right in his own **e**: 5869
21:10 his neighbour findeth no favour in his **e**. 5869
22:12 The **e** of the Lᴏʀᴅ preserve knowledge, 5869
23: 5 Wilt thou set thine **e** upon that which is 5869

Pr 23:26 and let thine **e** observe my ways. 5869
23:29 without cause? who hath redness of **e**? 5869
23:33 Thine **e** shall behold strange *women,* and 5869
25: 7 of the prince whom thine **e** have seen. 5869
27:20 so the **e** of man are never satisfied. 5869
28:27 he that hideth his **e** shall have many a 5869
29:13 the Lᴏʀᴅ lighteneth both their **e**. 5869
30:12 a generation *that are* pure in their own **e**, 5869
30:13 a generation, O how lofty are their **e**! 5869
Ecc 2:10 whatsoever mine **e** desired I kept not 5869
2:14 The wise man's **e** *are* in his head; 5869
5:11 the beholding *of them* with their **e**? 5869
6: 9 Better *is* the sight of the **e** than 5869
8:16 day nor night seeth sleep with his **e**:) 5869
11: 7 a pleasant *thing it is* for the **e** to behold 5869
11: 9 of thine heart, and in the sight of thine **e**: 5869
SS 1:15 behold, thou *art* fair; thou *hast* doves' **e**. 5869
4: 1 fair; thou *hast* doves' **e** within thy locks: 5869
4: 9 ravished my heart with one of thine **e**, 5869
5:12 His **e** *are* as *the eyes of* doves by the rivers 5869
5:12 His eyes *are as the* **e** *of* doves by the rivers NIH
6: 5 Turn away thine **e** from me, for they have 5869
7: 4 thine **e** *like the fish*pools in Heshbon, 5869
8:10 was I in his **e** as one that found favour. 5869
Isa 1:15 your hands, I will hide mine **e** from you: 5869
1:16 evil of your doings from before mine **e**; 5869
3: 8 the Lᴏʀᴅ, to provoke the **e** of his glory. 5869
3:16 with stretched forth necks and wanton **e**, 5869
5:15 and the **e** of the lofty shall be humbled: 5869
5:21 unto *them that are* wise in their own **e**, 5869
6: 5 for mine **e** have seen the King, the Lᴏʀᴅ 5869
6:10 make their ears heavy, and shut their **e**; 5869
6:10 lest they see with their **e**, and hear with 5869
11: 3 he shall not judge after the sight of his **e**, 5869
13:16 shall be dashed to pieces before their **e**; 5869
17: 7 his **e** shall have respect to the Holy One of 5869
29:10 of deep sleep, and hath closed your **e**: 5869
29:18 **e** of the blind shall see out of obscurity, 5869
30:20 but thine **e** shall see thy teachers: 5869
32: 3 the **e** of them that see shall not be dim, 5869
33:15 and shutteth his **e** from seeing evil; 5869
33:17 Thine **e** shall see the king in his beauty: 5869
33:20 thine **e** shall see Jerusalem a quiet 5869
35: 5 Then the **e** of the blind shall be opened, 5869
37:17 and hear; open thine **e**, O Lᴏʀᴅ, and see: 5869
37:23 *thy* voice, and lifted up thine **e** on high? 5869
38:14 mine **e** fail *with looking* upward: 5869
40:26 Lift up your **e** on high, and behold who 5869
42: 7 To open the blind **e**, to bring out 5869
43: 8 Bring forth the blind people that have **e**, 5869
44:18 for he hath shut their **e**, that *they* cannot 5869
49: 5 yet shall I be glorious in the **e** of 5869
49:18 Lift up thine **e** round about, and behold: 5869
51: 6 Lift up your **e** to the heavens, 5869
52:10 his holy arm in the **e** of all the nations; 5869
59:10 blind, and we grope as if *we had* no **e**: 5869
60: 4 Lift up thine **e** round about, and see: 5869
65:12 did evil before mine **e**, and did choose 5869
65:16 and because mine **e** are hid from mine **e**. 5869
66: 4 they did evil before mine **e**, and chose 5869
Jer 3: 2 Lift up thine **e** unto the high places, 5869
5: 3 O Lᴏʀᴅ, *are* not thine **e** upon the truth? 5869
5:21 have **e**, and see not; which have ears, 5869
7:11 become a den of robbers in your **e**? 5869
9: 1 mine **e** a fountain of tears, that I might 5869
9:18 that our **e** may run down with tears, 5869
13:20 Lift up your **e**, and behold them that 5869
14: 6 **e** did fail, because *there* was no grass. 5869
14:17 Let mine **e** run down *with* tears night and 5869
16: 9 cause to cease out of this place in your **e**, 5869
16:17 For mine **e** *are* upon all their ways: they 5869
16:17 neither is their iniquity hid from mine **e**. 5869
20: 4 thine **e** *shall behold it;* and I will give all 5869
22:17 thine **e** and thine heart *are* not but for thy 5869
24: 6 For I will set mine **e** upon them for good, 5869
29:21 and he shall slay them before your **e**; 5869
31:16 from weeping, and thine **e** from tears: 5869
32: 4 to mouth, and his **e** shall behold his eyes: 5869
32: 4 to mouth, and his **e** shall behold his **e** 5869
32:19 for thine **e** *are* open upon all the ways of 5869
34: 3 thine **e** shall behold the eyes of the king 5869
34: 3 thine eyes shall behold the **e** of the king 5869
39: 6 sons of Zedekiah in Riblah before his **e**: 5869
39: 7 Moreover he put out Zedekiah's **e**, 5869
42: 2 A few of many, as thine **e** do behold us:) 5869
52: 2 he did *that* which *was* evil in the **e** of 5869
52:10 slew the sons of Zedekiah before his **e**: 5869
52:11 put out the **e** of Zedekiah; and the king 5869
La 2:11 Mine **e** do fail with tears, my bowels are 5869
4:17 our **e** as yet failed for our vain help: 5869
5:17 is faint; for these *things* our **e** are dim. 5869
Eze 1:18 rings *were* full *of* **e** round about them 5869
6: 9 hath departed from me, and with their **e**, 5869
8: 5 lift up thine **e** now the way towards 5869
8: 5 So I lift up mine **e** the way toward 5869
10:12 the wheels, *were* full *of* **e** round about, 5869
12: 2 which have **e** to see, and see not; 5869
12:12 that he see not the ground with his **e**. 5869
18: 6 neither hath lift up his **e** to the idols of 5869
18:12 and hath lift up his **e** to the idols, 5869
18:15 neither hath lift up his **e** to the idols of 5869
20: 7 every man the abominations of his **e**, 5869
20: 8 cast away the abominations of their **e**, 5869
20:24 and their **e** were after their fathers' idols. 5869
21: 6 and with bitterness sigh before their **e**. 5869

Eze 22:26 have hid their **e** from my sabbaths, 5869
23:16 as soon as she saw them with her **e**, 5869
23:27 thou shalt not lift up thine **e** unto them, 5869
23:40 thou didst wash *thyself,* paintedst thy **e**, 5869
24:16 take away from thee the desire of thine **e** 5869
24:21 the desire of your **e**, and that which your 5869
24:25 the desire of their **e**, and that whereupon 5869
33:25 lift up your **e** toward your idols, 5869
36:23 I shall be sanctified in you before their **e**. 5869
37:20 shall be in thine hand before their **e**. 5869
38:16 sanctified in thee, O Gog, before their **e**. 5869
38:23 I will be known in the **e** of many nations, 5869
40: 4 behold with thine **e**, and hear with thine 5869
44: 5 behold with thine **e**, and hear with thine 5869
Da 4:34 lift up mine **e** unto heaven, 5870
7: 8 in this horn *were* like the eyes of man, 5870
7: 8 in this horn *were* eyes like the **e** of man, 5870
7:20 even *of* that horn that had **e**, and a mouth 5870
8: 3 I lifted up mine **e**, and saw, and behold, 5869
8: 5 goat *had* a notable horn between his **e**. 5869
8:21 the great horn that *is* between his **e** *is* 5869
9:18 open thine **e**, and behold our desolations, 5869
10: 5 I lift up mine **e**, and looked, and behold, 5869
10: 6 his **e** as lamps of fire, and his arms and 5869
Hos 13:14 repentance shall be hid from mine **e**. 5869
Joel 1:16 Is not the meat cut off before our **e**, *yea,* 5869
Am 9: 4 I will set mine **e** upon them for evil, 5869
9: 8 the **e** of the Lord Gᴏᴅ *are* upon the sinful 5869
Mic 7:10 mine **e** shall behold her: now shall she be 5869
Hab 1:13 *Thou art* of purer **e** than to behold evil, 5869
Zep 3:20 I turn back your captivity before your **e**, 5869
Hag 2: 3 *is it* not in your **e** in comparison of it as 5869
Zec 1:18 lift I up mine **e**, and saw, and behold four 5869
2: 1 I lift up mine **e** again, and looked, 5869
3: 9 upon one stone *shall be* seven **e**: 5869
4:10 they *are the* **e** of the Lᴏʀᴅ, which run to 5869
5: 1 lift up mine **e**, and looked, and behold 5869
5: 5 Lift up now thine **e**, and see what *is* this 5869
5: 9 lift I up mine **e**, and looked, and behold, 5869
6: 1 lift up mine **e**, and looked, and behold, 5869
8: 6 If it be marvellous in the **e** of the remnant 5869
8: 6 should it also be marvellous in my **e**? 5869
9: 1 when the **e** of man, as of all the tribes of 5869
9: 8 for now have I seen with mine **e**. 5869
12: 4 open mine **e** upon the house of Judah, 5869
14:12 their **e** shall consume away in their holes, 5869
Mal 1: 5 your **e** shall see, and ye shall say, 5869
Mt 9:29 Then touched he their **e**, saying, 3788
9:30 And their **e** were opened; and Jesus 3788
13:15 *of* hearing, and their **e** have closed; 3788
13:15 at any time they should see with *their* **e**, 3788
13:16 But blessed *are* your **e**, for they see: 3788
17: 8 when they had lift up their **e**, they saw 3788
18: 9 than having two **e** to be cast into hell 3788
20:33 Lord, that our **e** may be opened. 3788
20:34 compassion *on them,* and touched their **e**: 3788
20:34 and immediately their **e** received sight, 3788
21:42 doing, and it is marvellous in our **e**? 3788
26:43 them asleep again: for their **e** were heavy. 3788
Mk 8:18 Having **e**, see ye not? and having ears, 3659
8:23 when he had spit on his **e**, and put *his* 3788
8:25 that he put *his* hands again upon his **e**, 3788
9:47 having two **e** to be cast into hell fire: 3788
12:11 doing, and it is marvellous in our **e**? 3788
14:40 asleep again, (for their **e** were heavy,) 3788
Lk 2:30 For mine **e** have seen thy salvation, 3788
4:20 And the **e** of all *them that were* in 3788
6:20 And he lifted up his **e** on his disciples, 3788
10:23 Blessed *are* the **e** which see the things 3788
16:23 And in hell he lift up his **e**, being in 3788
18:13 not lift up so much as *his* **e** unto heaven, 3788
19:42 but now they are hid from thine **e**. 3788
24:16 their **e** were holden that *they* should not 3788
24:31 And their **e** were opened, and they knew 3788
Jn 4:35 Lift up your **e**, and look on the fields; 3788
6: 5 When Jesus then lift up his **e**, 3788
9: 6 he anointed the **e** of the blind man with 3788
9:10 unto him, How were thine **e** opened? 3788
9:11 and anointed mine **e**, and said unto me, 3788
9:14 Jesus made the clay, and opened his **e**. 3788
9:15 He put clay upon mine **e**, and I washed, 3788
9:17 thou of him, that he hath opened thine **e**? 3788
9:21 or who hath opened his **e**, we know not: 3788
9:26 did he to thee? how opened he thine **e**? 3788
9:30 he is, and *yet* he hath opened mine **e**. 3788
9:32 opened the **e** of one that was born blind. 3788
10:21 Can a devil open the **e** of the blind? 3788
11:37 Could not this *man,* which opened the **e** 3788
11:41 And Jesus lift up his **e**, and said, Father, 3788
12:40 He hath blinded their **e**, and hardened 3788
12:40 that they should not see with their **e**, 3788
17: 1 and lift up his **e** to heaven, and said, 3788
Ac 3: 4 fastening his **e** upon him with John, said, 816
9: 8 and when his **e** were opened, he saw no 3788
9:18 And immediately there fell from his **e** as it 3788
9:40 And she opened her **e**: and when she saw 3788
11: 6 the which when I had fastened mine **e**, 816
13: 9 with the Holy Ghost, set his **e** on him, 816
26:18 To open their **e**, *and* to turn *them* from 3788
28:27 of hearing, and their **e** have they closed; 3788
28:27 lest they should see with *their* **e**, 3788
Ro 3:18 There is no fear of God before their **e**. 3788
11: 8 *that they* should not see, and ears that 3788
11:10 Let their **e** be darkened, that *they* may not 3788
Gal 3: 1 before whose **e** Jesus Christ hath been 3788

Gal 4:15 ye would have plucked out your own **e**, 3788
Eph 1:18 The **e** of your understanding being 3788
Heb 4:13 opened unto the **e** of him with whom we 3788
1Pe 3:12 the **e** of the Lord *are* over the righteous. 3788
2Pe 2:14 Having **e** full of adultery and that cannot 3788
1Jn 1: 1 heard, which we have seen with our **e**, 3788
 2:11 because that darkness hath blinded his **e**. 3788
 2:16 and the lust of the **e**, and the pride of life, 3788
Rev 1:14 as snow; and his **e** *were* as a flame of fire; 3788
 2:18 who hath his **e** like unto a flame of fire, 3788
 3:18 anoint thine **e** with eyesalve, that thou 3788
 4: 6 *were* four beasts full of **e** before and 3788
 4: 8 about *him*; and *they were* full of **e** within. 3788
 5: 6 slain, having seven horns and seven **e**, 3788
 7:17 God shall wipe away all tears from their **e**. 3788
 19:12 His **e** *were* as a flame of fire, and on his 3788
 21: 4 God shall wipe away all tears from their **e**; 3788

EYESALVE (1) [EYE]
Rev 3:18 and anoint thine eyes *with* **e**, that thou 2854

EYESERVICE (2) [EYE, SERVE]
Eph 6: 6 Not with **e**, as menpleasers; but as 3787
Col 3:22 not with **e**, as menpleasers; 3787

EYESIGHT (1) [EYE, SEE]
Ps 18:24 to the cleanness of my hands in his **e**. 5869

EYEWITNESSES (2) [EYE, WITNESS]
Lk 1: 2 which from the beginning were **e**, 845
2Pe 1:16 Jesus Christ, but were **e** of his majesty. 2030

EZBAI (1)
1Ch 11:37 Hezro the Carmelite, Naarai the son of **E**, 229

EZBON (2)
Ge 46:16 Shuni, and **E**, Eri, and Arodi, and Areli. 675
1Ch 7: 7 E, and Uzzi, and Uzziel, and Jerimoth, 675

EZEKIAS (2) [HEZEKIAH]
Mt 1: 9 Joatham begat Achaz; and Achaz begat **E**; 1478
 1:10 And **E** begat Manasses; 1478

EZEKIEL (2)
Eze 1: 3 LORD came expressly unto **E** the priest, 3168
 24:24 Thus **E** is unto you a sign: according to all 3168

EZEL (1) [BETH-EZEL]
1Sa 20:19 *in hand,* and shalt remain by the stone **E**. 237

EZEM (1)
1Ch 4:29 And at Bilhah, and at **E**, and at Tolad, 6107

EZER (10)
Ge 36:21 Dishon, and **E**, and Dishan: these *are* 687
 36:27 The children of **E** *are* these; Bilhan, 687
 36:30 Duke Dishon, duke **E**, duke Dishan: 687
1Ch 1:38 Anah, and Dishon, and **E**, and Dishan. 687
 1:42 The sons of **E**; Bilhan, and Zavan, 687
 4: 4 of Gedor, and **E** the father of Hushah. 5829
 7:21 and Shuthelah his son, and **E**, and Elead, 5827
 12: 9 **E** the first, Obadiah the second, Eliab 5829
Ne 3:19 next to him repaired **E** the son of Jeshua, 5829
 12:42 and Malchijah, and Elam, and **E**. 5829

EZION-GABER (3) [EZION-GEBER]
Nu 33:35 from Ebronah, and encamped at **E**. 6100
 33:36 they removed from **E**, and pitched in 6100
Dt 2: 8 from **E**, we turned and passed *by* the way 6100

EZION-GEBER (4) [EZION-GABER]
1Ki 9:26 king Solomon made a navy *of ships* in **E**, 6100
 22:48 went not; for the ships were broken at **E**. 6100
2Ch 8:17 Solomon to **E**, and to Eloth, at the sea 6100
 20:36 Tarshish: and they made the ships in **E**. 6100

EZNITE (1)
2Sa 23: 8 the captains; the same *was* Adino the **E**: 6112

EZRA (26)
1Ch 4:17 the sons of **E** were, Jether, and Mered, 5834
Ezr 7: 1 the son of Seraiah, the son of Azariah, 5830
 7: 6 This **E** went up from Babylon; and he 5830
 7:10 For **E** had prepared his heart to seek 5830
 7:11 king Artaxerxes gave unto **E** the priest, 5830
 7:12 king of kings, unto **E** the priest, 5831
 7:21 that whatsoever **E** the priest, the scribe of 5831
 7:25 thou, **E**, after the wisdom of thy God, 5831
 10: 1 When **E** had prayed, and when he had 5830
 10: 2 sons of Elam, answered and said unto **E**, 5830
 10: 5 arose **E**, and made the chief priests, 5830
 10: 6 rose up from before the house of God, 5830
 10:10 **E** the priest stood up, and said unto them, 5830
 10:16 **E** the priest, *with* certain chief of 5830
Ne 8: 1 they spake unto **E** the scribe to bring 5830
 8: 2 **E** the priest brought the law before 5830
 8: 4 **E** the scribe stood upon a pulpit of wood, 5830
 8: 5 **E** opened the book in the sight of all 5830
 8: 6 **E** blessed the LORD, the great God. 5830
 8: 9 **E** the priest the scribe, and the Levites 5830
 8:13 and the Levites, unto **E** the scribe, 5830
 12: 1 and Jeshua: Seraiah, Jeremiah, **E**, 5830
 12:13 **E**, Meshullam; of Amariah, Jehohanan; 5830
 12:26 governor, and of **E** the priest, the scribe. 5830
 12:33 And Azariah, **E**, and Meshullam, 5830
 12:36 man of God, and **E** the scribe before them. 5830

EZRAHITE (3)
1Ki 4:31 than Ethan the **E**, and Heman, and Chalcol, 250
Ps 88: T Maschil of Heman the **E**. 250
 89: T Maschil of Ethan the **E**. 250

EZRI (1)
1Ch 27:26 of the ground *was* **E** the son of Chelub: 5836

F

FABLES (5)
1Ti 1: 4 Neither give heed to **f** and 3454
 4: 7 But refuse profane and old wives' **f**, 3454
2Ti 4: 4 from the truth, and shall be turned unto **f**. 3454
Tit 1:14 Not giving heed to Jewish **f**, 3454
2Pe 1:16 we have not followed cunningly devised **f**, 3454

FACE (416) [FACES]
Ge 1: 2 and darkness *was* upon the **f** of the deep. 6440
 1: 2 and the Spirit of God moved upon the **f** of 6440
 1:29 which *is* upon the **f** of all the earth, 6440
 2: 6 and watered the whole **f** of the ground. 6440
 3:19 In the sweat of thy **f** shalt thou eat bread, 639
 4:14 hast driven me out *this* day from the **f** 6440
 4:14 from thy **f** shall I be hid; and I shall be a 6440
 6: 1 when men began to multiply on the **f** of 6440
 6: 7 I have created from the **f** of the earth; 6440
 7: 3 to keep seed alive upon the **f** of all 6440
 7: 4 will I destroy from off the **f** of the earth. 6440
 7:18 the ark went upon the **f** of the waters. 6440
 7:23 which *was* upon the **f** of the ground, 6440
 8: 8 were abated from off the **f** of the ground; 6440
 8: 9 for the waters *were* on the **f** of the whole 6440
 8:13 and behold, the **f** of the ground was dry. 6440
 11: 4 lest we be scattered abroad upon the **f** of 6440
 11: 8 from thence upon the **f** of all the earth: 6440
 11: 9 them abroad upon the **f** of all the earth. 6440
 16: 6 dealt hardly with her, she fled from her **f**. 6440
 16: 8 I flee from the **f** of my mistress Sarai. 6440
 17: 3 Abram fell on his **f**: and God talked with 6440
 17:17 Abraham fell upon his **f**, and laughed, 6440
 19: 1 he bowed himself with his **f** toward 639
 19:13 cry of them is waxen great before the **f** 6440
 24:47 I put the earring upon her **f**, and the 639
 30:33 it shall come for my hire before thy **f**: 6440
 31:21 and set his **f** *toward* the mount Gilead. 6440
 32:20 before me, and afterward I will see his **f**; 6440
 32:30 for I have seen God **f** to face, and my life 6440
 32:30 for I have seen God face to **f**, and my life 6440
 33:10 for therefore I have seen thy **f**, as though I 6440
 33:10 as though I had seen the **f** of God, 6440
 35: 1 fleddest from the **f** of Esau thy brother. 6440
 35: 7 when he fled from the **f** of his brother. 6440
 36: 6 went into the country from the **f** of his 6440
 38:15 a harlot; because she had covered her **f**. 6440
 41:56 the famine was over all the **f** of the earth: 6440
 43: 3 saying, Ye shall not see my **f**, except your 6440
 43: 5 man said unto us, Ye shall not see my **f**, 6440
 43:31 he washed his **f**, and went out, 6440
 44:23 with you, ye shall see my **f** no more. 6440
 44:26 for we may not see the man's **f**, except 6440
 46:28 unto Joseph, to direct his **f** unto Goshen; 6440
 46:30 since I have seen thy **f**, because thou 6440
 48:11 Joseph, I had not thought to see thy **f**: 6440
 48:12 he bowed himself with his **f** to the earth. 639
 50: 1 Joseph fell upon his father's **f**, 6440
 50:18 also went and fell down before his **f**; 6440
Ex 2:15 Moses fled from the **f** of Pharaoh, 6440
 3: 6 Moses hid his **f**; for he was afraid to look 6440
 10: 5 they shall cover the **f** of the earth, that 5869
 10:15 For they covered the **f** of the whole earth, 5869
 10:28 take heed to thyself, see my **f** no more; 6440
 10:28 for in *that* day thou seest my **f** thou shalt 6440
 10:29 well, I will see thy **f** again no more. 6440
 14:19 of the cloud went from **before** their **f**, 6440
 14:25 Let us flee from the **f** of Israel; 6440
 16:14 upon the **f** of the wilderness *there lay* a 6440
 32:12 to consume them from the **f** of the earth? 6440
 33:11 the LORD spake unto Moses **f** to face, 6440
 33:11 the LORD spake unto Moses face to **f**, 6440
 33:16 from all the people that *are* upon the **f** of 6440
 33:20 he said, Thou canst not see my **f**: for there 6440
 33:23 my back parts: but my **f** shall not be seen. 6440
 34:29 that Moses wist not that the skin of his **f** 6440
 34:30 Moses, behold, the skin of his **f** shone; 6440
 34:33 speaking with them, he put a vail on his **f**. 6440
 34:35 the children of Israel saw the **f** of Moses, 6440
 34:35 of Moses, that the skin of Moses' **f** shone: 6440
 34:35 Moses put the vail upon his **f** again, until 6440
Lev 13:41 off from the part of *his head toward* his **f**, 6440
 17:10 I will even set my **f** against *that* soul 6440
 19:32 honour the **f** of the old man, and fear thy 6440
 20: 3 I will set my **f** against that man, 6440
 20: 5 I will set my **f** against that man, 6440
 20: 6 I will even set my **f** against that soul, 6440

Lev 26:17 I will set my **f** against you, and ye shall be 6440
Nu 6:25 The LORD make his **f** shine upon thee, 6440
 11:31 as it were two cubits *high* upon the **f** 6440
 12: 3 above all the men which *were* upon the **f** 6440
 12:14 If her father had but spit in her **f**, 6440
 14:14 that thou LORD *art* seen **f** to face, 5869
 14:14 that thou LORD *art* seen face to **f**, 5869
 16: 4 when Moses heard *it*, he fell upon his **f**: 6440
 19: 3 and *one* shall slay her before his **f**: 6440
 22: 5 cover the **f** of the earth, and they abide 5869
 22:11 Egypt, which covereth the **f** of the earth: 5869
 22:31 down his head, and fell flat on his **f**. 639
 24: 1 but he set his **f** toward the wilderness. 6440
Dt 1:17 you shall not be afraid of the **f** of man; 6440
 5: 4 The LORD talked with you **f** to face in 6440
 5: 4 The LORD talked with you face to **f** in 6440
 6:15 destroy thee from off the **f** of the earth. 6440
 7: 6 above all people that *are* upon the **f** of 6440
 7:10 repayeth them that hate him to his **f**, 6440
 7:10 hateth him, he will repay him to his **f**. 6440
 8:20 which the LORD destroyeth before your **f**, 6440
 9: 3 he shall bring them down before his **f**: 6440
 25: 2 to be beaten before his **f**, according to his 6440
 25: 9 and spit in his **f**, and shall answer and say, 6440
 28: 7 up against thee *to be* smitten before thy **f** 6440
 28:31 *be* violently taken away from before thy **f**, 6440
 31: 5 LORD shall give them up before your **f**, 6440
 31:17 I will hide my **f** from them, and they shall 6440
 31:18 I will surely hide my **f** in that day for all 6440
 32:20 he said, I will hide my **f** from them, I will 6440
 34:10 whom the LORD knew **f** to face, 6440
 34:10 whom the LORD knew face to **f**, 6440
Jos 5:14 Joshua fell on his **f** to the earth, 6440
 7: 6 fell to the earth upon his **f** before the ark 6440
 7:10 wherefore liest thou thus upon thy **f**? 6440
Jdg 6:22 I have seen an angel of the LORD face to **f**. 6440
 6:22 have seen an angel of the LORD face to **f**. 6440
 6:22 fell on her **f**, and bowed herself to 639
Ru 2:10 fell on her **f**, and bowed herself to 639
1Sa 5: 3 Dagon *was* fallen upon his **f** to the earth 6440
 5: 4 Dagon *was* fallen upon his **f** to the ground 6440
 17:49 and he fell upon his **f** to the earth. 6440
 20:15 of David every one from the **f** of the earth. 6440
 20:41 fell on his **f** to the ground, 639
 24: 8 David stooped *with his* **f** to the earth, 639
 25:23 fell before David on her **f**, 639
 25:41 bowed herself *on her* **f** to the earth, 639
 26:20 fall to the earth before the **f** of the LORD: 6440
 28:14 and he stooped *with his* **f** to the ground, 639
2Sa 2:22 should I hold up my **f** to Joab thy brother? 6440
 3:13 of thee, that is, Thou shalt not see my **f**, 6440
 3:13 when thou comest to see my **f**. 6440
 9: 6 he fell on his **f**, and did reverence. 6440
 14: 4 she fell on her **f** to the ground, 639
 14:22 Joab fell to the ground on his **f**, 639
 14:24 his own house, and let him not see my **f**. 6440
 14:24 his own house, and saw not the king's **f**. 6440
 14:28 in Jerusalem, and saw not the king's **f**. 6440
 14:32 now therefore let me see the king's **f**; 6440
 14:33 bowed himself on his **f** to the ground 639
 18: 8 the battle was there scattered over the **f** 6440
 18:28 he fell down to the earth upon his **f** before 639
 19: 4 the king covered his **f**, and the king cried 6440
 24:20 himself before the king *on* his **f** upon 639
1Ki 1:23 bowed himself before the king with his **f** 639
 1:31 Bath-sheba bowed *with her* **f** to the earth, 639
 8:14 the king turned his **f** about, and blessed 6440
 13: 6 Intreat now the **f** of the LORD thy God, 6440
 13:34 to destroy *it* from off the **f** of the earth. 6440
 18: 7 he knew him, and fell on his **f**, and said, 6440
 18:42 the earth, and put his **f** between his knees, 6440
 19:13 Elijah heard *it*, that he wrapped his **f** 6440
 20:38 disguised himself with ashes upon his **f**. 5869
 20:41 and took the ashes away from his **f**; 5869
 21: 4 turned away his **f**, and would eat no 6440
2Ki 4:29 and lay my staff upon the **f** of the child. 6440
 4:31 and laid the staff upon the **f** of the child; 6440
 8:15 and spread *it* on his **f**, so that he died: 6440
 9:30 Jezebel heard *of it;* and she painted her **f**, 5869
 9:32 he lift up his **f** to the window, and said, 6440
 9:37 the **f** of the field in the portion of Jezreel; 6440
 12:17 and Hazael set his **f** to go up to Jerusalem. 6440
 13:14 wept over his **f**, and said, O my father, 6440
 14: 8 Come, let us look one another in the **f**. 6440
 14:11 one another *in* the **f** at Beth-shemesh, 6440
 18:24 wilt thou turn away the **f** of one captain 6440
 20: 2 he turned his **f** to the wall, and prayed 6440
1Ch 16:11 and his strength, seek his **f** continually. 6440
 21:21 bowed himself to David *with his* **f** to 639
2Ch 6: 3 the king turned his **f**, and blessed the 6440
 6:42 turn not away the **f** of thine anointed: 6440
 7:14 seek my **f**, and turn from their wicked 6440
 20:18 Jehoshaphat bowed his head *with his* **f** to 639
 25:17 Come, let us see one another *in* the **f**. 6440
 25:21 they saw one another *in* the **f**, *both* he 6440
 30: 9 and will not turn away *his* **f** from you, 6440
 32:21 he returned with shame of **f** to his own 6440
 35:22 Nevertheless Josiah would not turn his **f** 6440
Ezr 9: 6 and blush to lift up my **f** to thee, 6440
 9: 7 and to a spoil, and to confusion of **f**, 6440
Est 1:14 which saw the king's **f**, *and* which sat 6440
 7: 8 king's mouth, they covered Haman's **f**. 6440
Job 1:11 he hath, and he will curse thee to thy **f**. 6440
 2: 5 his flesh, and he will curse thee to thy **f**. 6440
 4:15 a spirit passed before my **f**; the hair of my 6440
 11:15 then shalt thou lift up thy **f** without spot; 6440

F

Job 13:24 Wherefore hidest thou thy **f**, 6440
15:27 Because he covereth his **f** with his fatness, 6440
16: 8 rising up in me beareth witness to my **f**, 6440
16:16 My **f** is foul with weeping, and on mine 6440
21:31 Who shall declare his way to his **f**? 6440
22:26 and shalt lift up thy **f** unto God. 6440
23:17 hath he covered the darkness from my **f**. 6440
24:15 No eye shall see me: and disguiseth *his* **f**. 6440
26: 9 He holdeth back the **f** of *his* throne, 6440
30:10 far from me, and spare not to spit in my **f**. 6440
33:26 he shall see his **f** with joy: for he will 6440
34:29 he hideth *his* **f**, who then can behold 6440
37:12 them upon the **f** of the world in the earth. 6440
38:30 a stone, and the **f** of the deep is frozen. 6440
41:13 Who can discover the **f** of his garment? 6440
41:14 Who can open the doors of his **f**? 6440
Ps 5: 8 make thy way straight before my **f**. 6440
10:11 he hideth his **f**; he will never see *it*. 6440
13: 1 how long wilt thou hide thy **f** from me? 6440
17:15 me, I will behold thy **f** in righteousness: 6440
21:12 upon thy strings against the **f** of them. 6440
22:24 neither hath he hid his **f** from him; 6440
24: 6 that seek him, that seek thy **f**, O Jacob. 6440
27: 8 *When thou saidst,* Seek ye my **f**; my heart 6440
27: 8 said unto thee, Thy **f**, LORD, will I seek. 6440
27: 9 Hide not thy **f** *far* from me; put not thy 6440
30: 7 thou didst hide thy **f**, *and* I was troubled. 6440
31:16 Make thy **f** to shine upon thy servant: 6440
34:16 The **f** of the LORD *is* against them that do 6440
41:12 and settest me before thy **f** for ever. 6440
44:15 and the shame of my **f** hath covered me, 6440
44:24 Wherefore hidest thou thy **f**, 6440
51: 9 Hide thy **f** from my sins, and blot out all 6440
67: 1 *and* cause his **f** to shine upon us; Selah. 6440
69: 7 reproach; shame hath covered my **f**. 6440
69:17 hide not thy **f** from thy servant; for I am 6440
80: 3 again, O God, and cause thy **f** to shine; 6440
80: 7 O God *of* hosts, and cause thy **f** to shine; 6440
80:19 LORD God *of* hosts, cause thy **f** to shine; 6440
84: 9 and look upon the **f** of thine anointed. 6440
88:14 my soul? *why* hidest thou thy **f** from me? 6440
89:14 mercy and truth shall go before thy **f**. 6440
89:23 I will beat down his foes before his **f**, 6440
102: 2 Hide not thy **f** from me in the day *when* I 6440
104:15 *and* oil to make *his* **f** to shine, 6440
104:29 Thou hidest thy **f**, they are troubled: 6440
104:30 and thou renewest the **f** of the earth. 6440
105: 4 and his strength: seek his **f** evermore. 6440
119:135 Make thy **f** to shine upon thy servant; 6440
132:10 turn not away the **f** of thine anointed. 6440
143: 7 hide not thy **f** from me, lest I be like unto 6440
Pr 7:13 and with an impudent **f** said unto him, 6440
7:15 diligently to seek thy **f**, and I have found 6440
8:27 when he set a compass upon the **f** of 6440
21:29 A wicked man hardeneth his **f**: but *as for* 6440
24:31 *and* nettles had covered the **f** thereof, 6440
27:19 As *in* water *answereth* to face, so the 6440
27:19 As *in* water face *answereth* to **f**, so the 6440
Ecc 8: 1 a man's wisdom maketh his **f** to shine, 6440
8: 1 and the boldness of his **f** shall be changed. 6440
Isa 6: 2 with twain he covered his **f**, and with 6440
8:17 that hideth his **f** from the house of Jacob, 6440
14:21 nor fill the **f** of the world *with* cities. 6440
16: 4 be thou a covert to them from the **f** of 6440
23:17 of the world upon the **f** of the earth. 6440
25: 7 he will destroy in this mountain the **f** of 6440
27: 6 bud, and fill the **f** of the world *with* fruit. 6440
28:25 When he hath made plain the **f** thereof, 6440
29:22 neither shall his **f** now wax pale. 6440
36: 9 wilt thou turn away the **f** of one captain 6440
38: 2 Hezekiah turned his **f** toward the wall, 6440
49:23 they shall bow down to thee *with their* **f** 639
50: 6 I hid not my **f** from shame and spitting. 6440
50: 7 therefore have I set my **f** like a flint, 6440
54: 8 In a little wrath I hid my **f** from thee for a 6440
59: 2 and your sins have hid *his* **f** from you, 6440
64: 7 for thou hast hid thy **f** from us, 6440
65: 3 me to anger continually to my **f**; 6440
Jer 1:13 and the **f** thereof *is* towards the north. 6440
2:27 *their* back unto me, and not *their* **f**: 6440
4:30 though thou rentest thy **f** with painting, 5869
8: 2 they shall be for dung upon the **f** of 6440
13:26 will I discover thy skirts upon thy **f**, 6440
16: 4 they shall be as dung upon the **f** 6440
16:17 they are not hid from my **f**, neither is their 6440
18:17 I will shew them the back, and not the **f**, 6440
21:10 For I have set my **f** against this city for evil, 6440
22:25 the hand *of them* whose **f** thou fearest, 6440
25:26 which *are* upon the **f** of the earth: 6440
28:16 I will cast thee from off the **f** of the earth: 6440
32:31 that *I* should remove it from before my **f**, 6440
32:33 turned unto me the back, and not the **f**, 6440
33: 5 for all whose wickedness I have hid my **f** 6440
44:11 I will set my **f** against you for evil, 6440
La 2:19 out thine heart like water before the **f** 6440
3:35 turn aside the right of a man before the **f** 6440
Eze 1:10 four had the **f** of a man, and the face of 6440
1:10 man, and the **f** of a lion, on the right side: 6440
1:10 four had the **f** of an ox on the left side; 6440
1:10 they four also had the **f** of an eagle. 6440
1:28 I saw *it*, I fell upon my **f**, and I heard 6440
3: 8 have made thy **f** strong against their faces, 6440
3:23 by the river of Chebar; and I fell on my **f**. 6440
4: 3 set thy **f** against it, and it shall be besieged 6440
4: 7 Therefore thou shalt set thy **f** toward 6440

Eze 6: 2 set thy **f** towards the mountains of Israel, 6440
7:22 My **f** will I turn also from them, 6440
9: 8 that I fell upon my **f**, and cried, and said, 6440
10:14 the first *was* the face of a cherub, 6440
10:14 the first face *was* the **f** of a cherub, 6440
10:14 the second *was* the face of a man, 6440
10:14 the second face *was* the **f** of a man, 6440
10:14 the third the **f** of a lion, and the fourth 6440
10:14 of a lion, and the fourth the **f** of an eagle. 6440
11:13 fell I down upon my **f**, and cried with a 6440
12: 6 thou shalt cover thy **f**, that thou see not 6440
12:12 he shall cover his **f**, that he see not 6440
13:17 set thy **f** against the daughters of thy 6440
14: 3 of their iniquity before their **f**: 6440
14: 4 stumblingblock of his iniquity before his **f**, 6440
14: 7 stumblingblock of his iniquity before his **f**, 6440
14: 8 I will set my **f** against that man, 6440
15: 7 I will set my **f** against them; they shall go 6440
15: 7 The LORD, when I set my **f** against them. 6440
20:35 and there will I plead with you **f** to face. 6440
20:35 and there will I plead with you face to **f**. 6440
20:46 set thy **f** toward the south, and drop *thy* 6440
21: 2 set thy **f** toward Jerusalem, and drop *thy* 6440
21:16 on the left, whithersoever thy **f** *is* set. 6440
25: 2 set thy **f** against the Ammonites, 6440
28:21 set thy **f** against Zidon, 6440
29: 2 set thy **f** against Pharaoh king of Egypt, 6440
34: 6 my flock was scattered upon all the **f** of 6440
35: 2 set thy **f** against mount Seir, 6440
38: 2 Son of man, set thy **f** against Gog, the land 6440
38:18 *that* my fury shall come up in my **f**. 639
38:20 the men that *are* upon the **f** of the earth, 6440
39:14 those that remain upon the **f** of the earth, 6440
39:23 therefore hid I my **f** from them, 6440
39:24 done unto them, and hid my **f** from them. 6440
39:29 Neither will I hide my **f** any more from 6440
40:15 from the **f** of the gate of the entrance unto 6440
40:15 of the porch of the inner gate *were* fifty 6440
41:14 Also the breadth of the **f** of the house, 6440
41:19 that the **f** of a man *was* toward the palm 6440
41:19 the **f** of a young lion toward the palm tree 6440
41:21 *were* squared, *and* the **f** of the sanctuary; 6440
41:25 *there were* thick planks upon the **f** of the 6440
43: 3 by the river Chebar; and I fell upon my **f**. 6440
44: 4 house of the LORD: and I fell upon my **f**, 6440
Da 2:46 the king Nebuchadnezzar fell upon his **f**, 600
8: 5 a he goat came from the west on the **f** of 6440
8:17 he came, I was afraid, and fell upon my **f**: 6440
8:18 I was in a deep sleep on my **f** toward 6440
9: 3 I set my **f** unto the Lord God, to seek *by* 6440
9: 8 O Lord, to us *belongeth* confusion of **f**, 6440
9:17 cause thy **f** to shine upon thy sanctuary 6440
10: 6 his **f** as the appearance of lightning, 6440
10: 9 was I in a deep sleep on my **f**, and my face 6440
10: 9 on my face, and my **f** toward the ground. 6440
10:15 I set my **f** toward the ground, and I 6440
11:17 He shall also set his **f** to enter with 6440
11:18 After this shall he turn his **f** unto the isles, 6440
11:19 he shall turn his **f** towards the fort of his 6440
Hos 5: 5 the pride of Israel doth testify to his **f**: 6440
5:15 acknowledge their offence, and seek my **f**: 6440
7: 2 beset them about; they are before my **f**. 6440
7:10 the pride of Israel testifieth to his **f**: 6440
Joel 2: 6 Before their **f** the people shall be much 6440
2:20 with his **f** toward the east sea, 6440
Am 5: 8 poureth them out upon the **f** of the earth: 6440
9: 6 poureth them out upon the **f** of the earth: 6440
9: 8 I will destroy it from off the **f** of the earth; 6440
Mic 3: 4 he will even hide his **f** from them at that 6440
Na 2: 1 dasheth in pieces is come up before thy **f**: 6440
3: 5 I will discover thy skirts upon thy **f**, 6440
Zec 5: 3 *is* the curse that goeth forth over the **f** 6440
Mt 6:17 anoint thine head, and wash thy **f**; 4383
11:10 Behold, I send my messenger before thy **f**, 4383
16: 3 ye can discern the **f** of the sky; 4383
17: 2 and his **f** did shine as the sun, 4383
17: 6 the disciples heard *it*, they fell on their **f**, 4383
18:10 the **f** of my Father which is in heaven. 4383
26:39 and fell on his **f**, and prayed, saying, 4383
26:67 Then did they spit in his **f**, 4383
Mk 1: 2 Behold, I send my messenger before thy **f**, 4383
14:65 and to cover his **f**, and to buffet him, 4383
Lk 1:76 for thou shalt go before the **f** of the Lord 4383
2:31 thou hast prepared before the **f** of all 4383
5:12 who seeing Jesus fell on *his* **f**, 4383
7:27 Behold, I send my messenger before thy **f**, 4383
9:51 he stedfastly set his **f** to go to Jerusalem, 4383
9:52 And sent messengers before his **f**: 4383
9:53 his **f** was *as though* he would go to 4383
10: 1 and two before his **f** into every city and 4383
12:56 ye can discern the **f** of the sky and of 4383
17:16 And fell down on *his* **f** at his feet, 4383
21:35 that dwell on the **f** of the whole earth. 4383
22:64 they stroke him on the **f**, and asked him, 4383
Jn 11:44 and his **f** was bound about with a napkin. 3799
Ac 2:25 I foresaw the Lord always **before** my **f**, 1799
6:15 saw his **f** as it had been the face of an 4383
6:15 saw his face as it had been the **f** of an 4383
7:45 whom God drave out before the **f** of our 4383
17:26 men for to dwell on all the **f** of the earth, 4383
20:25 kingdom of God, shall see my **f** no more. 4383
20:38 that they should see his **f** no more. 4383
25:16 have the accusers **f to face**, 2596+4383
25:16 have the accusers **face to f**, 2596+4383
1Co 13:12 through a glass, darkly; but then **f** to face: 4383

1Co 13:12 through a glass, darkly; but then face to **f**: 4383
14:25 falling down on *his* **f** he will worship God, 4383
2Co 3: 7 **f** of Moses for the glory of his 4383
3:13 not as Moses, *which* put a vail over his **f**, 4383
3:18 with open **f** beholding as in a glass 4383
4: 6 of the glory of God in the **f** of Jesus Christ. 4383
11:20 exalt himself, if a man smite you on the **f**. 4383
Gal 1:22 And was unknown by **f** unto the churches 4383
2:11 I withstood him to the **f**, because he was 4383
Col 2: 1 *for* as many as have not seen my **f** in 4383
1Th 2:17 abundantly to see your **f** with great desire. 4383
3:10 exceedingly that *we* might see your **f**, 4383
Jas 1:23 is like unto a man beholding his natural **f** 4383
1Pe 3:12 the **f** of the Lord *is* against them that do 4383
2Jn 1:12 and speak **f** to face, that our joy may be 4750
1:12 and speak face to **f**, that our joy may be 4750
3Jn 1:14 see thee, and we shall speak **f** to face. 4750
1:14 see thee, and we shall speak face to **f**. 4750
Rev 1: 7 and the third beast had a **f** as a man, 4383
6:16 hide us from the **f** of him that sitteth on 4383
10: 1 his **f** was *as it were* the sun, and his feet 4383
12:14 and half a time, from the **f** of the serpent. 4383
20:11 whose **f** the earth and the heaven fled 4383
22: 4 they shall see his **f**; and his name *shall* 4383

FACES (73) [FACE]

Ge 9:23 their **f** *were* backward, and they saw not 6440
18:22 the men **turned** their **f** from thence, 6437
30:40 set the **f** of the flocks toward 6440
42: 6 before him *with* their **f** to the earth. 639
Ex 19: 7 laid before their **f** all these words which 6440
20:20 that his fear may be before your **f**, that ye 6440
25:20 and their **f** *shall look* one to another; 6440
25:20 toward the mercy seat shall the **f** of 6440
37: 9 mercy seat, with their **f** one to another; 6440
37: 9 *even* to the mercy seatward were the **f** of 6440
Lev 9:24 they shouted, and fell on their **f**. 6440
Nu 14: 5 fell on their **f** before all the assembly 6440
16:22 they fell upon their **f**, and said, O God, 6440
16:45 in a moment. And they fell upon their **f**. 6440
20: 6 congregation, and they fell upon their **f**: 6440
Jdg 13:20 on *it*, and fell on their **f** to the ground. 6440
18:23 they turned their **f**, and said unto Micah, 6440
2Sa 19: 5 Thou hast shamed *this* day the **f** of all thy 6440
1Ki 2:15 all Israel set their **f** on me, that *I* should 6440
18:39 all the people saw *it*, they fell on their **f**: 6440
1Ch 12: 8 whose **f** *were* like the faces of lions, 6440
12: 8 whose faces *were* like the **f** of lions, 6440
21:16 clothed in sackcloth, fell upon their **f**. 6440
2Ch 3:13 on their feet, and their **f** *were* inward. 6440
7: 3 they bowed themselves *with their* **f** to 639
Ne 8: 6 worshipped the LORD *with their* **f** to 639
Job 9:24 he covereth the **f** of the judges thereof; 6440
40:13 dust together; *and* bind their **f** in secret. 6440
Ps 34: 5 and their **f** were not ashamed. 6440
83:16 Fill their **f** *with* shame; that they may seek 6440
Isa 3:15 to pieces, and grind the **f** of the poor? 6440
13: 8 one at another; their **f** *shall be* as flames. 6440
25: 8 GOD will wipe away tears from off all **f**; 6440
53: 3 we hid as it were *our* **f** from him; he was 6440
Jer 1: 8 Be not afraid of their **f**: for I *am* with thee 6440
1:17 be not dismayed at their **f**, lest I confound 6440
5: 3 they have made their **f** harder than a rock; 6440
7:19 to the confusion of their own **f**? 6440
30: 6 travail, and all **f** are turned into paleness? 6440
42:15 If ye wholly set your **f** to enter *into* Egypt, 6440
42:17 set their **f** to go *into* Egypt to sojourn 6440
44:12 that have set their **f** to go *into* the land of 6440
50: 5 shall ask the way *to* Zion with their **f** 6440
51:51 shame hath covered our **f**: for strangers 6440
La 5:12 the **f** of elders were not honoured. 6440
Eze 1: 6 *every* one had four **f**, and every one had 6440
1: 8 and they four had their **f** and their wings. 6440
1:10 As for the likeness of their **f**, they four had 6440
1:11 Thus *were* their **f**: and their wings *were* 6440
1:15 by the living creatures, with his four **f**. 6440
3: 8 have made thy face strong against their **f**, 6440
7:18 shame *shall be* upon all **f**, 6440
8:16 of the LORD, and their **f** towards the east; 6440
10:14 *every* one had four **f**: the first face *was* 6440
10:21 Every one had four **f** apiece, and every 6440
10:22 the likeness of their **f** *was* the same faces 6440
10:22 the likeness of their faces *was* the same **f** 6440
14: 6 turn away your **f** from all your 6440
20:47 all **f** from the south to the north shall be 6440
41:18 a cherub; and *every* cherub had two **f**; 6440
Da 1:10 for why should he see your **f** worse liking 6440
9: 7 but unto us confusion of **f**, as *at* this day; 6440
Joel 2: 6 much pained: all **f** shall gather blackness. 6440
Na 2:10 the **f** of them all gather blackness. 6440
Hab 1: 9 their **f** shall sup up *as* the east wind, 6440
Mal 2: 3 your seed, and spread dung upon your **f**, 6440
Mt 6:16 for they disfigure their **f**, that they may 4383
Lk 24: 5 and bowed down *their* **f** to the earth, 4383
Rev 7:11 and fell before the throne on their **f**, 4383
9: 7 and their **f** *were* as the faces of men. 4383
9: 7 and their faces *were* as the **f** of men. 4383
11:16 fell upon their **f**, and worshipped God, 4383

FADE (6) [FADETH, FADING]

2Sa 22:46 Strangers shall **f away**, and they shall be 5034
18:45 The strangers shall **f away**, and be afraid 5034
Isa 64: 6 we all do **f** as a leaf; and our iniquities, 5034
Jer 8:13 figs on the fig tree, and the leaf shall **f**; 5034

F

Eze 47:12 all trees for meat, whose leaf shall not *f*, 5034
Jas 1:11 shall the rich *man* **f** away in his ways. *3133*

FADETH (7) [FADE]

Isa 1:30 For ye shall be as an oak whose leaf **f**, 5034
　24: 4 The earth mourneth *and* **f** away, 5034
　24: 4 the world languisheth *and* **f** away, 5034
　40: 7 The grass withereth, the flower **f**: 5034
　40: 8 The grass withereth, the flower **f**. 5034
1Pe 1: 4 and undefiled, and that **f** not away, *263*
　5: 4 receive a crown of glory that **f** not away. *262*

FADING (2) [FADE]

Isa 28: 1 whose glorious beauty *is* a **f** flower, 5034
　28: 4 shall be a **f** flower, *and* as the hasty fruit 5034

FAIL (64) [FAILED, FAILETH, FAILING]

Ge 47:16 I will give you for your cattle, if money **f**. 656
Dt 28:32 *with* **longing** for them all the day long: 3616
　31: 6 he will not **f** thee, nor forsake thee. 7503
　31: 8 he will be with thee, he will not **f** thee, 7503
Jos 1: 5 I will not **f** thee, nor forsake thee. 7503
　3:10 he will **without** **f** drive out from 3423+3423
Jdg 11:30 If thou shalt **without** **f** deliver 5414+5414
1Sa 2:16 Let me not **f** to burn the fat 6999+6999
　17:32 Let no man's heart **f** because of him; 5307
　30: 8 I should not **f** to sit with the king 3427+3427
　30: 8 and **without** **f** recover *all*. 5337+5337
2Sa 3:29 let there not **f** from the house of Joab one 3772
1Ki 2: 4 all their soul, there shall not **f** thee 3772
　8:25 There shall not **f** thee a man in my sight 3772
　9: 5 There shall not **f** thee a man upon 3772+3807.1
　17:14 not waste, neither shall the cruse of oil **f**, 2637
　17:16 wasted not, neither did the cruse of oil **f**, 2638
1Ch 28:20 he will not **f** thee, nor forsake thee, 7503
2Ch 6:16 There shall not **f** thee a man in my sight 3772
　7:18 There shall not **f** thee a man *to be* ruler in 3772
Ezr 4:22 Take heed now that ye **f** not to do this: 7960
　6: 9 let *it* be given them day by day without **f**: 7960
Est 6:10 let nothing **f** of all that thou hast spoken. 5307
　9:27 unto them, so as it should not **f**, 5674
　9:28 these days of Purim should not **f** from 5674
Job 11:20 the eyes of the wicked shall **f**, 3615
　14:11 the waters **f** from the sea, and the flood 235
　17: 5 even the eyes of his children shall **f**. 3615
　31:16 have **caused** the eyes of the widow **to f**; 3615
Ps 12: 1 for the faithful **f** from among the children 6461
　69: 3 mine eyes **f** while *I* wait for my God. 3615
　77: 8 for ever? doth *his* promise **f** for evermore? 8266
　89:33 from him, nor **suffer** my faithfulness **to f**. 8266
　119:82 Mine eyes **f** for thy word, saying, 3615
　119:123 Mine eyes **f** for thy salvation, and for 3615
Pr 22: 8 vanity: and the rod of his anger shall **f**. 3615
Ecc 12: 5 shall be a burden, and desire shall **f**: 6565
Isa 19: 3 the spirit of Egypt shall **f** in the midst 1238
　19: 5 waters shall **f** from the sea, and the river 5405
　21:16 and all the glory of Kedar shall **f**: 3615
　31: 3 fall down, and they all shall **f** together. 3615
　32: 6 he will **cause** the drink of the thirsty **to f**, 2637
　32:10 ye careless *women*: for the vintage shall **f**, 3615
　34:16 no one of these shall **f**, none shall want 5737
　38:14 mine eyes **f** *with looking* upward: 1809
　42: 4 He shall not **f** nor be discouraged, till he 3543
　51:14 die in the pit, nor that his bread should **f**. 2637
　57:16 for the spirit should **f** before me, 5848
　58:11 like a spring of water, whose waters **f** not. 3576
Jer 14: 6 eyes did **f**, because *there was* no grass. 3615
　15:18 me as a liar, *and as* waters that **f**? 539+3808
　48:33 I have **caused** wine **to f** from the wine 7673
La 2:11 Mine eyes do **f** with tears, my bowels are 3615
　3:22 because his compassions **f** not. 3615
Hos 9: 2 them, and the new wine shall **f** in her. 3584
Am 8: 4 even to **make** the poor of the land **to f**, 7673
Hab 3:17 labour of the olive shall **f**, and the fields 3584
Lk 16: 9 when ye **f**, they may receive you into *1587*
　16:17 to pass, than one tittle of the law to **f**. *4098*
　22:32 I have prayed for thee, that thy faith **f** not: *1587*
1Co 13: 8 whether *there be* prophecies, they shall **f**; 2673
Heb 1:12 art the same, and thy years shall not **f**. *1587*
　11:32 for the time would **f** me to tell of Gedeon, *1952*
　12:15 Looking diligently lest any *man* **f** of *5302*

FAILED (12) [FAIL]

Ge 42:28 their heart **f** *them*, and they were afraid, 3318
　47:15 when money **f** in the land of Egypt, 8552
Jos 3:16 *even* the salt sea, **f**, *and* were cut off: 8552
　21:45 There **f** not ought of any good thing 5307
　23:14 that not one thing hath **f** of all the good 5307
　23:14 you, *and* not one thing hath **f** thereof. 5307
1Ki 8:56 there hath not **f** one word of all his good 5307
Job 19:14 My kinsfolk have **f**, and my familiar 2308
Ps 142: 4 refuge **f** me; no man cared for my soul. 6+4480
SS 5: 6 my soul when he spake: I sought him, 3318
Jer 51:30 they became as women: 5405
La 4:17 for us, our eyes as yet **f** for our vain help: 3615

FAILETH (19) [FAIL]

Ge 47:15 we die in thy presence? for the money **f**. 656
Job 21:10 their bull gendereth, and **f** not; their cow 1602
Ps 31:10 my strength **f** because of mine iniquity, 3782
　38:10 My heart panteth, my strength **f** me: as 5800
　40:12 of mine head: therefore my heart **f** me. 5800
　71: 9 forsake me not when my strength **f**. 3615
　73:26 My flesh and my heart **f**: *but* God *is* 3615
　109:24 through fasting; and my flesh **f** of fatness. 3584

Ps 143: 7 my spirit **f**: hide not thy face from me, 3615
Ecc 10: 3 his wisdom **f** *him*, and he saith to every 2638
Isa 15: 6 the grass **f**, there is no green thing. 3615
　40:26 for that he *is* strong in power; not one **f**. 5737
　41:17 *is* none, *and* their tongue **f** for thirst, 5405
　44:12 yea, he is hungry, and his strength **f**: 369
　59:15 truth **f**; and he that departeth from evil 5737
Eze 12:22 The days are prolonged, and every vision **f**? 6
Zep 3: 5 he bring his judgment to light, he **f** not; 5737
Lk 12:33 a treasure in the heavens that **f** not, *413*
1Co 13: 8 Charity never **f**: *1601*

FAILING (2) [FAIL]

Dt 28:65 and **f** of eyes, and sorrow of mind: 3631
Lk 21:26 Men's **hearts f** them for fear, *674*

FAIN (2)

Job 27:22 he **would f** flee out of his hand. 1272+1272
Lk 15:16 And he **would f** have filled his belly with *1937*

FAINT (41) [FAINTED, FAINTEST, FAINTETH, FAINTHEARTED, FAINTNESS]

Ge 25:29 Esau came from the field, and he *was* **f**: 5889
　25:30 with that same red *pottage*; for I *am* **f**: 5889
Dt 20: 3 let not your hearts **f**, fear not, and do not 7401
　20: 8 lest his brethren's heart **f** as well as his 4549
　25:18 thee, when thou *wast* **f** and weary; 5889
Jos 2: 9 all the inhabitants of the land because 4127
　2:24 all the inhabitants of the country do **f** 4127
Jdg 8: 4 that *were* with him, **f**, yet pursuing *them*. 5889
　8: 5 they *be* **f**, and I am pursuing after Zebah 5889
1Sa 14:28 *any* food *this* day. And the people were **f**. 5774
　14:31 to Aijalon: and the people were very **f**. 5774
　30:10 **f** that they could not go over the brook 6296
　30:21 so **f** that they could not follow David, 6296
2Sa 16: 2 that such as be **f** in the wilderness may 3287
　21:15 the Philistines: and David **waxed f**. 5774
Pr 24:10 *If* thou **f** in the day of adversity, 7503
Isa 1: 5 head *is* sick, and the whole heart **f**. 1742
　13: 7 Therefore shall all hands be **f**, 7503
　29: 8 behold, *he is* **f**, and his soul hath appetite: 5889
　40:29 He giveth power to the **f**; and to *them* 3287
　40:30 Even the youths shall **f** and be weary, 3286
　40:31 be weary; *and* they shall walk, and not **f**. 3286
　44:12 he drinketh no water, and is **f**. 3286
Jer 8:18 against sorrow, my heart *is* **f** in me. 1742
　51:46 lest your heart **f**, and ye fear for the 7401
La 1:13 hath made me desolate *and* **f** all the day. 1739
　1:22 for my sighs *are* many, and my heart *is* **f**. 1742
　2:19 that **f** for hunger in the top of every street. 5848
　5:17 For this our heart is **f**; for these *things* our 1739
Eze 21: 7 every spirit shall **f**, and all knees shall be 3543
　21:15 that *their* heart may **f**, and *their* ruins be 4127
Am 8:13 the fair virgins and young men **f** for thirst. 5968
Mt 15:32 them away fasting, lest they **f** in the way. *1590*
Mk 8: 3 their own houses, they will **f** by the way: *1590*
Lk 18: 1 *men* ought always to pray, and not to **f**; *1573*
2Co 4: 1 as we have received mercy, we **f** not; *1573*
　4:16 For which cause we **f** not; but though our *1573*
Gal 6: 9 in due season we shall reap, if we **f** not. *1590*
Eph 3:13 Wherefore I desire that ye **f** not at my *1573*
Heb 12: 3 lest ye be wearied and **f** in your minds. *1590*
　12: 5 nor **f** when thou art rebuked of him: *1590*

FAINTED (12) [FAINT]

Ge 45:26 *Jacob's* heart **f**, for he believed them not. 6313
　47:13 all the land of Canaan **f** by reason of 3856
Ps 27:13 I *had* **f**, unless I had believed to see NIH
　107: 5 Hungry and thirsty, their soul **f** in them. 5848
Isa 51:20 Thy sons have **f**, they lie at the head of all 5968
Jer 45: 3 I **f** in my sighing, and I find no rest. 3021
Eze 31:15 and all the trees of the field **f** for him. 5969
Da 8:27 I Daniel **f**, and was sick *certain* days; 1961
Jnh 2: 7 When my soul **f** within me I remembered 5848
　4: 8 that he **f**, and wished in himself to die, 5968
Mt 9:36 with compassion on them, because they **f**, *1590*
Rev 2: 3 name's sake hast laboured, and hast not **f**. 2577

FAINTEST (1) [FAINT]

Job 4: 5 now it is come upon thee, and thou **f**; 3811

FAINTETH (4) [FAINT]

Ps 84: 2 yea, even **f** for the courts of the LORD: 3615
　119:81 My soul **f** for thy salvation: *but* I hope in 3615
Isa 10:18 they shall be as when a standard-bearer **f**. 4549
　40:28 ends of the earth, **f** not, neither is weary? 3286

FAINTHEARTED (3) [FAINT, HEART]

Dt 20: 8 *there that is* fearful and **f**? 3824+7390+1886.1
Isa 7: 4 neither be **f** for the two tails of 3824+7401
Jer 49:23 they are **f**; *there is* sorrow on the sea; 4127

FAINTNESS (1) [FAINT]

Lev 26:36 **f** into their hearts in the lands of their 4816

FAIR (53) [FAIRER, FAIREST, FAIRS]

Ge 6: 2 the daughters of men that they *were* **f**; 2896
　12:11 I know thou *art* a **f** woman to look 3303
　12:14 beheld the woman that she *was* very **f**. 3303
　24:16 the damsel *was* very **f** to look upon, 2896
　26: 7 because she *was* **f** to look upon. 2896
1Sa 17:42 youth, and ruddy, and of a **f** countenance. 3303
2Sa 13: 1 that Absalom the son of David had a **f** 3303
　14:27 she was a woman of a **f** countenance. 3303
1Ki 1: 3 So they sought for a **f** damsel throughout 3303
　1: 4 the damsel *was* very **f**, and cherished 3303

Est 1:11 her beauty: for she *was* **f** to look on. 2896
　2: 2 Let there be **f** young virgins sought 2896+4758
　2: 3 **f** young virgins unto Shushan 2896+4758
　2: 7 and the maid *was* **f** and beautiful; 3303+8389
Job 37:22 **F** weather cometh out of the north: 2091
　42:15 women found so **f** as the daughters of Job: 3303
Pr 7:21 With her much **f** speech she caused him 3948
　11:22 *is* a woman which is without discretion. 3300
　26:25 When he speaketh **f**, believe him not: 2603
SS 1:15 Behold, thou *art* **f**, my love; behold, 3303
　1:15 thou *art* fair, my love; behold, thou *art* **f**; 3303
　1:16 Behold, thou *art* **f**, my beloved, yea, 3303
　2:10 my love, my **f** one, and come away. 3303
　2:13 Arise, my love, my **f** one, and come away 3303
　4: 1 Behold, thou *art* **f**, my love; behold, 3303
　4: 1 thou *art* fair, my love; behold, thou *art* **f**; 3303
　4: 7 Thou *art* all **f**, my love; *there is* no spot in 3303
　4:10 How **f** is thy love, my sister, *my* spouse! 3303
　6:10 **f** as the moon, clear as the sun, 3303
　7: 6 How **f** and how pleasant art thou, O love, 3303
Isa 5: 9 *even* great and **f**, without inhabitant. 2896
　54:11 I will lay thy stones with **fair colours**, 6320
Jer 4:30 in vain shalt thou **make** thyself **f**; 3302
　11:16 A green olive tree, **f**, *and* of goodly fruit: 3303
　12: 6 though they speak **f** words unto thee. 2896
　46:20 Egypt *is* like a **very f** heifer, 3304
Eze 16:17 Thou hast also taken thy **f** jewels of my 8597
　16:39 take thy **f** jewels, and leave thee naked 8597
　23:26 of thy clothes, and take away thy **f** jewels. 8597
　31: 3 Assyrian *was* a cedar in Lebanon with **f** 3303
　31: 7 was he **f** in his greatness, in the length 3302
　31: 9 I have made him **f** by the multitude of his 3303
Da 4:12 The leaves thereof *were* **f**, and the fruit 8209
　4:21 Whose leaves *were* **f**, and the fruit thereof 8209
Hos 10:11 *corn*; but I passed over upon her **f** neck: 2898
Am 8:13 In that day shall the **f** virgins and young 3303
Zec 3: 3 set upon it a **f** mitre upon his head. 2889
　3: 5 So they set a **f** mitre upon his head, 2889
Mt 16: 2 it is evening, ye say, *It will be* **f weather**: 2105
Ac 7:20 born, and was **exceeding f**, 791+2316+3588
　27: 8 a place *which is* called The **f** havens; 2568
Ro 16:18 **f** speeches deceive the hearts of the 2129
Gal 6:12 As many as desire to **make a f shew** in 2146

FAIRER (3) [FAIR]

Jdg 15: 2 is not her younger sister **f** than she? 2896
Ps 45: 2 Thou art **f** than the children of men: 3302
Da 1:15 ten days their countenances appeared **f** 2896

FAIREST (3) [FAIR]

SS 1: 8 thou know not, O thou **f** among women, 3303
　5: 9 beloved, O thou **f** among women? 3303
　6: 1 beloved gone, O thou **f** among women? 3303

FAIRS (6) [FAIR]

Eze 27:12 iron, tin, and lead, they traded in thy **f**. 5801
　27:14 of Togarmah traded in thy **f** with horses 5801
　27:16 they occupied in thy **f** with emeralds, 5801
　27:19 Javan going to and fro occupied in thy **f**: 5801
　27:22 they occupied in thy **f** with chief of all 5801
　27:27 Thy riches, and thy **f**, thy merchandise, 5801

FAITH (246) [FAITHFUL, FAITHFULLY, FAITHFULNESS, FAITHLESS, UNFAITHFUL]

Dt 32:20 children in whom *is* no **f**. 529
Hab 2: 4 in him: but the just shall live by his **f**. 530
Mt 6:30 much more **clothe** you, O ye of **little f**? 3640
　8:10 have not found so great **f**, no not in Israel. 4102
　8:26 Why are ye fearful, O ye of **little f**? 3640
　9: 2 Jesus seeing their **f** said unto the sick of 4102
　9:22 comfort; thy **f** hath made thee whole. 4102
　9:29 According to your **f** be it unto you. 4102
　14:31 and said unto him, O thou of **little f**, 3640
　15:28 said unto her, O woman, great *is* thy **f**: 4102
　16: 8 he said unto them, O ye of **little f**, 3640
　17:20 If ye have **f** as a grain of mustard seed, 4102
　17:21 say unto you, If ye have **f**, and doubt not, 4102
　23:23 of the law, judgment, mercy, and **f**: 4102
Mk 2: 5 When Jesus saw their **f**, he said unto 4102
　4:40 so fearful? how *is it that* you have no **f**? 4102
　5:34 Daughter, thy **f** hath made thee whole; 4102
　10:52 Go thy way; thy **f** hath made thee whole. 4102
　11:22 saith unto them, Have **f** in God. 4102
Lk 5:20 when he saw their **f**, he said unto him, 4102
　7: 9 not found so great **f**, no, not in Israel. 4102
　7:50 said to the woman, Thy **f** hath saved thee; 4102
　8:25 And he said unto them, Where is your **f**? 4102
　8:48 thy **f** hath made thee whole; go in peace.) 4102
　12:28 more **will** he **clothe** you, O ye of **little f**? 3640
　17: 5 said unto the Lord, Increase our **f**. 4102
　17: 6 If ye had **f** as a grain of mustard seed, 4102
　17:19 go **thy way**: thy **f** hath made thee whole. 4102
　18: 8 man cometh, shall he find **f** on the earth? 4102
　18:42 Receive thy sight: thy **f** hath saved thee. 4102
　22:32 I have prayed for thee, that thy **f** fail not: 4102
Ac 3:16 And his name through **f** in his name hath 4102
　3:16 the **f** which is by him hath given him this 4102
　6: 5 a man full of **f** and of the Holy Ghost, 4102
　6: 7 of the priests were obedient to the **f**. 4102
　6: 8 Stephen, full of **f** and power, did great 4102
　11:24 and full of the Holy Ghost and of **f**: 4102
　13: 8 to turn away the deputy from the **f**. 4102
　14: 9 and perceiving that he had **f** to be healed, 4102
　14:22 *and* exhorting *them* to continue in the **f**, 4102
　14:27 how he had opened *the* door of **f** unto 4102

F

Ac 15: 9 and them, purifying their hearts by f. 4102
16: 5 so were the churches established in the f, 4102
20:21 and f toward our Lord Jesus Christ. 4102
24:24 and heard him concerning the f in Christ. 4102
26:18 which are sanctified by f that is in me. 4102
Ro 1: 5 for obedience to the f among all nations, 4102
1: 8 that your f is spoken of throughout 4102
1:12 with you by the mutual f both of you 4102
1:17 of God revealed from f to faith: 4102
1:17 of God revealed from faith to f: 4102
1:17 as it is written, The just shall live by f. 4102
3: 3 shall their unbelief make the f of God 4102
3:22 God *which is* by f of Jesus Christ unto all 4102
3:25 *to be* a propitiation through f in his blood, 4102
3:27 of works? Nay: but by the law of f. 4102
3:28 justified by f without the deeds of the law. 4102
3:30 which shall justify the circumcision by f, 4102
3:30 by faith, and uncircumcision through f. 4102
3:31 Do we then make void the law through f? 4102
4: 5 his f is counted for righteousness. 4102
4: 9 we say that f was reckoned to Abraham 4102
4:11 a seal of the righteousness of the f which 4102
4:12 who also walk in the steps of *that* f of our 4102
4:13 law, but through the righteousness of f. 4102
4:14 f is made void, and the promise made of 4102
4:16 Therefore *it is* of f, that *it might be* by 4102
4:16 to that also which is of the f of Abraham; 4102
4:19 being not weak in f, he considered not 4102
4:20 but was strong in f, giving glory to God; 4102
5: 1 Therefore being justified by f, we have 4102
5: 2 By whom also we have access by f into 4102
9:30 even the righteousness which is of f. 4102
9:32 Because *they* sought it not by f, but as *it* 4102
10: 6 But the righteousness which is of f 4102
10: 8 that is, the word of f, which we preach; 4102
10:17 So then f *cometh* by hearing, 4102
11:20 were broken off, and thou standest by f. 4102
12: 3 hath dealt to every man the measure of f. 4102
12: 6 *prophesy* according to the proportion of f; 4102
14: 1 Him that is weak in the f receive you, 4102
14:22 Hast thou f? have *it* to thyself before God. 4102
14:23 if he eat, because *he eateth* not of f. 4102
14:23 of faith: for whatsoever *is* not of f is sin. 4102
16:26 to all nations for the obedience of f. 4102
1Co 2: 5 your f should not stand in the wisdom 4102
12: 9 To another f by the same Spirit; to 4102
13: 2 and though I have all f, so that *I* could 4102
13:13 And now abideth f, hope, charity, 4102
15:14 preaching vain, and your f *is* also vain. 4102
15:17 And if Christ be not raised, your f *is* vain; 4102
16:13 Watch ye, stand fast in the f, quit you like 4102
2Co 1:24 for that we have dominion over your f, 4102
1:24 are helpers of your joy: for by f ye stand. 4102
4:13 We having the same spirit of f, 4102
5: 7 (For we walk by f, not by sight:) 4102
8: 7 as ye abound in every *thing, in* f, 4102
10:15 having hope, when your f is increased, 4102
13: 5 yourselves, whether ye be in the f; 4102
Gal 1:23 preacheth the f which once he destroyed. 4102
2:16 but by the f of Jesus Christ, even we have 4102
2:16 we might be justified by the f of Christ, 4102
2:20 the flesh I live by the f of the Son of God, 4102
3: 2 works of the law, or by the hearing of f? 4102
3: 5 works of the law, or by the hearing of f? 4102
3: 7 ye therefore that they which are of f, 4102
3: 8 God would justify the heathen through f, 4102
3: 9 which be of f are blessed with faithful 4102
3:11 *it is* evident for, The just shall live by f. 4102
3:12 And the law is not of f: but, The man that 4102
3:14 the promise of the Spirit through f. 4102
3:22 the promise by f of Jesus Christ might 4102
3:23 But before f came, we were kept under 4102
3:23 shut up unto the f which should 4102
3:24 Christ, that we might be justified by f. 4102
3:25 But after that f is come, we are no longer 4102
3:26 For ye are all the children of God by f in 4102
5: 5 wait for the hope of righteousness by f. 4102
5: 6 but f which worketh by love. 4102
5:22 longsuffering, gentleness, goodness, f, 4102
6:10 unto them who are of the household of f. 4102
Eph 1:15 after I heard of your f in the Lord Jesus, 4102
2: 8 For by grace are ye saved through f; 4102
3:12 access with confidence by the f of him. 4102
3:17 That Christ may dwell in your hearts by f; 4102
4: 5 One Lord, one f, one baptism, 4102
4:13 Till we all come in the unity of the f, 4102
6:16 Above all, taking the shield of f, 4102
6:23 and love with f, from God the Father and 4102
Php 1:25 you all for your furtherance and joy of f; 4102
1:27 one mind striving together for the f of 4102
2:17 upon the sacrifice and service of your f, 4102
3: 9 but that which is through the f of Christ, 4102
3: 9 the righteousness which is of God by f: 4102
Col 1: 4 Since we heard of your f in Christ Jesus, 4102
1:23 If ye continue in the f grounded and 4102
2: 5 and the stedfastness of your f in Christ. 4102
2: 7 built up in him, and stablished in the f, 4102
2:12 through the f of the operation of God, 4102
1Th 1: 3 without ceasing your work of f, 4102
1: 8 also in every place your f to God-ward is 4102
3: 2 and to comfort you concerning your f: 4102
3: 5 no longer forbear, I sent to know your f, 4102
3: 6 and brought us good tidings of your f and 4102
3: 7 in all our affliction and distress, by your f: 4102
3:10 perfect that which is lacking in your f? 4102

1Th 5: 8 putting on the breastplate of f and love; 4102
2Th 1: 3 because that your f groweth exceedingly, 4102
1: 4 and f in all your persecutions and 4102
1:11 goodness, and the work of f with power: 4102
3: 2 and wicked men: for all *men* have not f. 4102
1Ti 1: 2 Timothy, *my* own son in the f: Grace, 4102
1: 4 rather than godly edifying which is in f: 4102
1: 5 *of* a good conscience, and *of* f unfeigned: 4102
1:14 our Lord was exceeding abundant with f 4102
1:19 Holding f, and a good conscience; 4102
1:19 concerning f have made shipwrack: 4102
2: 7 a teacher of the Gentiles in f and verity. 4102
2:15 if they continue in f and charity and 4102
3: 9 Holding the mystery of the f in a pure 4102
3:13 great boldness in the f which is in Christ 4102
4: 1 latter times some shall depart from the f, 4102
4: 6 nourished up in the words of f and of 4102
4:12 in charity, in spirit, in f, in purity. 4102
5: 8 he hath denied the f, and is worse than 4102
5:12 because they have cast off *their* first f. 4102
6:10 they have erred from the f, 4102
6:11 godliness, f, love, patience, meekness. 4102
6:12 Fight the good fight of f, lay hold on 4102
6:21 professing have erred concerning the f. 4102
2Ti 1: 5 the unfeigned f that is in thee, 4102
1:13 in f and love which is in Christ Jesus. 4102
2:18 past already; and overthrow the f of some. 4102
2:22 follow righteousness, f, charity, peace, 4102
3: 8 minds, reprobate concerning the f. 4102
3:10 f, longsuffering, charity, patience, 4102
3:15 salvation through f which is in Christ 4102
4: 7 have finished *my* course, I have kept the f: 4102
Tit 1: 1 according to the f of God's elect, 4102
1: 4 *mine* own son after the common f: 4102
1:13 that they may be sound in the f; 4102
2: 2 grave, temperate, sound in f, in charity, 4102
3:15 Greet them that love us in the f. Grace 4102
Phm 1: 5 Hearing of thy love and f, which thou 4102
1: 6 That the communication of thy f may 4102
Heb 4: 2 not being mixed with f in them that 4102
6: 1 from dead works, and of f towards God, 4102
6:12 but followers of them who through f and 4102
10:22 with a true heart in full assurance of f, 4102
10:38 the just shall live by f: but if *any man* 4102
11: 1 f is the substance of *things* hoped for, 4102
11: 3 Through f we understand that the worlds 4102
11: 4 By f Abel offered unto God a more 4102
11: 5 By f Enoch was translated that he should 4102
11: 6 without *it is* impossible to please *him:* 4102
11: 7 By f Noah, being warned of God of *things* 4102
11: 7 heir of the righteousness which is by f. 4102
11: 8 By f Abraham, when he was called to go 4102
11: 9 By f he sojourned in the land of promise, 4102
11:11 Through f also Sara herself received 4102
11:13 These all died in f, not having received 4102
11:17 By f Abraham, when he was tried, 4102
11:20 By f Isaac blessed Jacob and Esau 4102
11:21 By f Jacob, when he was a dying, 4102
11:22 By f Joseph, when he died, made mention 4102
11:23 By f Moses, when he was born, was hid 4102
11:24 By f Moses, when he was come to years, 4102
11:27 By f he forsook Egypt, not fearing 4102
11:28 Through f he kept the passover, 4102
11:29 By f they passed through the Red sea as by 4102
11:30 By f the walls of Jericho fell down, 4102
11:31 By f the harlot Rahab perished not with 4102
11:33 Who through f subdued kingdoms, 4102
11:39 having obtained a good report through f, 4102
12: 2 unto Jesus the author and finisher of *our* f; 4102
13: 7 whose f follow, considering the end of 4102
Jas 1: 3 Knowing *this,* that the trying of your f 4102
1: 6 But let him ask in f, nothing wavering; 4102
2: 1 have not the f of our Lord Jesus Christ, 4102
2: 5 chosen the poor of this world rich in f, 4102
2:14 though a man say *he* hath f, and have not 4102
2:14 and have not works? can f save him? 4102
2:17 Even so f, if it hath not works, is dead, 4102
2:18 may say, Thou hast f, and I have works: 4102
2:18 shew me thy f without thy works, and I 4102
2:18 and I will shew thee my f by my works. 4102
2:20 O vain man, that f without works is dead? 4102
2:22 Seest thou how f wrought with his works, 4102
2:22 and by works was f made perfect? 4102
2:24 a man is justified, and not by f only. 4102
2:26 is dead, so f without works is dead also. 4102
5:15 And the prayer of f shall save the sick, 4102
1Pe 1: 5 f unto salvation ready to be revealed in 4102
1: 7 That the trial of your f, *being* much more 4102
1: 9 Receiving the end of your f, *even* 4102
1:21 that your f and hope might be in God. 4102
5: 9 Whom resist stedfast in the f, knowing 4102
2Pe 1: 1 to them that have obtained like precious f 4102
1: 5 giving all diligence, add to your f virtue; 4102
1Jn 5: 4 that overcometh the world, *even* our f. 4102
Jude 1: 3 which was once delivered unto the 4102
1:20 up yourselves on your most holy f, 4102
Rev 2:13 fast my name, and hast not denied my f, 4102
2:19 thy works, and charity, and service, and f, 4102
3:10 is the patience and the f of the saints. 4102
14:12 commandments of God, and the f of Jesus 4102

FAITHFUL (82) [FAITH]
Nu 12: 7 Moses *is* not so, who *is* f in all mine house. 539
Dt 7: 9 he *is* God, the f God, which keepeth 539
1Sa 2:35 I will raise me up a f priest, *that* shall do 539

1Sa 22:14 *is so* f among all thy servants as David, 539
2Sa 20:19 *of them that are* peaceable *and* f in Israel: 539
Ne 7: 2 for he *was* a f man, and feared God above 571
9: 8 foundest his heart f before thee, 539
13:13 they were counted f, and their office *was* 539
Ps 12: 1 for the f fail from among the children of 539
31:23 *for* the LORD preserveth the f, 529
89:37 as the moon, and *as* a f witness in heaven. 539
101: 6 Mine eyes *shall be* upon the f of the land, 539
119:86 All thy commandments *are* f: 530
119:138 hast commanded *are* righteous and very f. 530
Pr 11:13 that is of a f spirit concealeth the matter. 539
13:17 into mischief: but a f ambassador *is* health. 529
14: 5 A f witness will not lie: but a false witness 529
20: 6 own goodness: but a f man who can find? 529
25:13 *so is* a f messenger to them that send him: 539
27: 6 F *are* the wounds of a friend; but the kisses 539
28:20 A f man shall abound with blessings. 530
Isa 1:21 How is the f city become an harlot! 539
1:26 The city of righteousness, the f city. 539
8: 2 I took unto me f witnesses to record, Uriah 539
49: 7 because of the LORD that *is* f, 539
Jer 42: 5 The LORD be a true and f witness between us, 539
Da 6: 4 forasmuch as he *was* f, neither was there 540
Hos 11:12 ruleth with God, and is f with the saints. 539
Mt 24:45 Who then is a f and wise servant, whom 4103
25:21 Well *done, thou* good and f servant: 4103
25:21 thou hast been f over a few *things,* I will 4103
25:23 unto him, Well *done,* good and f servant; 4103
25:23 thou hast been f over a few *things,* I will 4103
Lk 12:42 Who then is *that* f and wise steward, 4103
16:10 He that is f in *that which is* least is faithful 4103
16:10 He that is faithful in *that which* is least is f 4103
16:11 ye have not been f in the unrighteous 4103
16:12 And if ye have not been f in that which is 4103
19:17 because thou hast been f in a very little, 4103
Ac 16:15 If ye have judged me to be f to the Lord, 4103
1Co 1: 9 God *is* f, by whom ye were called unto 4103
4: 2 in stewards, that a man be found f. 4103
4:17 who is my beloved son, and f in the Lord, 4103
7:25 hath obtained mercy of the Lord to be f. 4103
10:13 but God *is* f, who will not suffer you to be 4103
Gal 3: 9 they which be of faith are blessed with f 4103
Eph 1: 1 at Ephesus, and to the f in Christ Jesus: 4103
6:21 brother and f minister in the Lord, 4103
Col 1: 2 f brethren in Christ which are at Colosse: 4103
1: 7 who is for you a f minister of Christ; 4103
4: 7 and a f minister and fellowservant in 4103
4: 9 With Onesimus, a f and beloved brother, 4103
1Th 5:24 F *is* he that calleth you, who also will do 4103
2Th 3: 3 But the Lord is f, who shall stablish you, 4103
1Ti 1:12 enabled me, for that he counted me f, 4103
1:15 *This is* a f saying, and worthy of all 4103
3:11 not slanderers, sober, f in all *things.* 4103
4: 9 *This is* a f saying and worthy of all 4103
6: 2 because they are f and beloved, 4103
2Ti 2: 2 the same commit thou to f men, who 4103
2:11 *is* a f saying: For if we be dead with *him,* 4103
2:13 If we believe not, *yet* he abideth f: 4103
Tit 1: 6 having f children not accused of riot or 4103
1: 9 Holding fast the f word as *he* hath been 4103
3: 8 *This is* a f saying, and these *things* I will 4103
Heb 2:17 f high priest *in things* pertaining to God, 4103
3: 2 Who was f to him that appointed him, 4103
3: 2 as also Moses *was* f in all his house. NIG
3: 5 And Moses verily *was* f in all his house, 4103
10:23 (for he *is* f that promised;) 4103
11:11 she judged him f who had promised. 4103
1Pe 4:19 *to him* in well doing, as unto a f Creator. 4103
5:12 By Silvanus, a f brother unto you, as I 4103
1Jn 1: 9 he is f and just to forgive us *our* sins, 4103
Rev 1: 5 *is* the f witness, *and* the first begotten 4103
2:10 be thou f unto death, and I will give thee 4103
2:13 days wherein Antipas *was* my f martyr, 4103
3:14 saith the Amen, the f and true witness, 4103
17:14 with him *are* called, and chosen, and f. 4103
19:11 he that sat upon him *was* called F and 4103
21: 5 Write: for these words are true and f. 4103
22: 6 unto me, These sayings *are* f and true: 4103

FAITHFULLY (8) [FAITH]
2Ki 12:15 on workmen: for they dealt f. 530+871.1
22: 7 their hand, because they dealt f. 530+871.1
2Ch 19: 9 ye do in the fear of the LORD, f, 530+871.1
31:12 the tithes and the dedicate *things* f: 530+871.1
34:12 the men did the work f: 530+871.1
Pr 29:14 The king that f judgeth the poor, his throne 571
Jer 23:28 hath my word, let him speak my word f. 571
3Jn 1: 5 thou doest f whatsoever thou doest to 4103

FAITHFULNESS (19) [FAITH]
1Sa 26:23 to every man his righteousness and his f: 530
Ps 5: 9 For *there* is no f in their mouth; 3559
36: 5 *and* thy f *reacheth* unto the clouds. 530
40:10 I have declared thy f and thy salvation: 530
88:11 in the grave? *or* thy f in destruction? 530
89: 1 with my mouth will I make known thy f to 530
89: 2 f shalt thou establish in the very heavens. 530
89: 5 thy f also in the congregation of the saints. 530
89: 8 unto thee? or *to* thy f round about thee? 530
89:24 my f and my mercy *shall be* with him: 530
89:33 take from him, nor suffer my f to fail. 530
92: 2 in the morning, and thy f every night, 530
119:75 right, and *that* thou in f hast afflicted me. 530
119:90 Thy f *is* unto all generations: thou hast 530

Ps 143: 1 thy f answer me, *and* in thy righteousness. 530
Isa 11: 5 of his loins, and the girdle of his reins. 530
25: 1 *thy* counsels of old *are* f *and* truth. 530
La 3:23 *They are* new every morning: great *is* thy f. 530
Hos 2:20 I will even betroth thee unto me in f: 530

FAITHLESS (4) [FAITH]

Mt 17:17 and said, O f and perverse generation, 571
Mk 9:19 answereth him, and saith, O f generation, 571
Lk 9:41 said, O f and perverse generation, 571
Jn 20:27 *it* into my side: and be not f, but believing. 571

FALL (252) [FALLEN, FALLEST, FALLETH, FALLING, FELL]

Ge 2:21 the LORD God **caused** a deep sleep **to f** 5307
43:18 f upon us, and take us for bondmen, 5307
45:24 them, See that ye f not **out** by the way. 7264
49:17 so that his rider shall f backward. 5307
Ex 5: 3 lest he f **upon** us with pestilence, 6293
15:16 Fear and dread shall f upon them; 5307
21:33 not cover it, and an ox or an ass f therein; 5307
Lev 11:32 they are dead, doth f, it shall be unclean; 5307
11:37 if *any part* of their carcase f upon any 5307
11:38 *any part* of their carcase f thereon, it *shall* 5307
19:29 lest the land f **to whoredom**, and the 2181
26: 7 and they shall f before you by the sword. 5307
26: 8 your enemies shall f before you by 5307
26:36 and they shall f when none pursueth. 5307
26:37 they shall f one upon another, as it were 3782
Nu 11:31 from the sea, and let *them* f by the camp, 5203
14: 3 to f by the sword, *that* our wives and 5307
14:29 Your carcases shall f in this wilderness; 5307
14:32 they shall f in this wilderness. 5307
14:43 before you, and ye shall f by the sword: 5307
34: 2 (this *is* the land that shall f unto you for 5307
Dt 22: 4 ass or his ox f **down** by the way, 5307
22: 8 thine house, if any man f from thence. 5307
Jos 6: 5 the wall of the city shall f **down** flat, 5307
Jdg 8:21 Zalmunna said, Rise thou, and f upon us: 6293
15:12 that ye will not f **upon** me yourselves. 6293
15:18 and f into the hand of the uncircumcised? 5307
Ru 2:16 **let** f also *some* of the
handfuls **of purpose** 7997+7997
3:18 until thou know how the matter will f: 5307
1Sa 3:19 did let none of his words f to the ground. 5307
14:45 there shall not one hair of his head f to 5307
18:25 Saul thought to **make** David f by the 5307
21:13 and **let** his spittle f **down** upon his beard. 3381
22:17 hand to f upon the priests of the LORD. 6293
22:18 Doeg, Turn thou, and f upon the priests. 6293
26:20 let not my blood f to the earth before 5307
2Sa 1:15 and said, Go near, *and* f upon him. 6293
14:11 there shall not one hair of thy son f to 5307
24:14 let us f now into the hand of the LORD; 5307
24:14 and let me not f into the hand of man. 5307
1Ki 1:52 there shall not a hair of him f to the earth: 5307
2:29 son of Jehoiada, saying, Go, f upon him. 6293
2:31 hath said, and f upon him, and bury him; 6293
22:20 that he may go up and f at Ramoth-gilead? 5307
2Ki 7: 4 and let us f unto the host of the Syrians: 5307
10:10 now that there shall f unto the earth 5307
14:10 that thou shouldest f, *even* thou, 5307
19: 7 I will **cause** him to f by the sword in his 5307
1Ch 12:19 will f to his master Saul to *the jeopardy* 5307
21:13 let me f now into the hand of the LORD; 5307
21:13 but let me not f into the hand of man. 5307
2Ch 18:19 he may go up and f at Ramoth-gilead? 5307
21:15 until thy bowels **f out** by reason of 3318
25: 8 God shall **make** thee f before the enemy: 3782
25:19 that thou shouldest f, *even* thou, 5307
Est 6:13 before whom thou hast begun to f, 5307+5307
6:13 but shalt **surely** f before him. 5307+5307
Job 13:11 you afraid? and his dread f upon you? 5307
31:22 *Then* let mine arm f from *my* shoulder 5307
Ps 5:10 O God; let them f by their own counsels; 5307
9: 3 they shall f and perish at thy presence. 3782
10:10 that the poor may f by his strong *ones*. 5307
35: 8 into that *very* destruction let him f. 5307
37:24 Though he f, he shall not be utterly cast 5064
45: 5 *whereby* the people f under thee. 5307
63:10 They shall f by the sword: they shall be a 5064
64: 8 they shall **make** their own tongue **to f** 3782
72:11 Yea, all kings shall f **down** before him: 7812
78:28 he let *it* f in the midst of their camp, 5307
82: 7 like men, and f like one of the princes. 5307
91: 7 A thousand shall f at thy side, 5307
118:13 Thou hast thrust sore at me that *I* might f: 5307
140:10 Let burning coals f upon them: let them 4131
141:10 Let the wicked f into their own nets, 5307
145:14 The LORD upholdeth all that f, 5307
Pr 4:16 taken away, unless they **cause** *some* to f. 3782
10: 8 but a prating fool shall f. 3832
10:10 causeth sorrow: but a prating fool shall f. 3832
11: 5 the wicked shall f by his own wickedness. 5307
11:14 Where no counsel *is,* the people f: 5307
11:28 He that trusteth in his riches shall f: 5307
16:18 and a haughty spirit before a f. 3783
22:14 he that is abhorred of the LORD shall f 5307
24:16 but the wicked shall f into mischief. 3782
26:27 Whoso diggeth a pit shall f therein: 5307
28:10 he f himself into his own pit: 5307
28:14 but he that hardeneth his heart shall f into 5307
28:18 *he that* is perverse in *his* ways shall f at 5307
29:16 but the righteous shall see their f. 4658
Ecc 4:10 For if they f, the one will lift up his fellow: 5307

Ecc 10: 8 He that diggeth a pit shall f into it; 5307
11: 3 if the tree f toward the south, or toward 5307
Isa 3:25 Thy men shall f by the sword, 5307
8:15 f, and be broken, and be snared, 5307
10: 4 and they shall f under the slain. 5307
10:34 and Lebanon shall f by a mighty one. 5307
13:15 one that is joined *unto* them shall f by 5307
22:25 be removed, and be cut down, and f; 5307
24:18 the noise of the fear shall f into the pit; 5307
24:20 upon it; and it shall f, and not rise again. 5307
28:13 backward, and be broken, and snared, 3782
30:13 shall be to you as a breach ready to f, 5307
30:25 of the great slaughter, when the towers f. 5307
31: 3 both he that helpeth shall f, and he that is 3782
31: 3 he that is holpen shall f **down**, and they 5307
31: 8 shall the Assyrian f with the sword, not of 5307
34: 4 all their host shall f **down**, as the leaf 5034
37: 7 I will **cause** him to f by the sword in his 5307
40:30 and the young men shall **utterly** f: 3782+3782
44:19 shall I f **down** to the stock of a tree? 5456
45:14 and they shall f **down** unto thee, 7812
46: 6 it a god: they f **down**, yea, they worship. 5456
47:11 mischief shall f upon thee; thou shalt not 5307
54:15 together against thee shall f for thy sake. 5307
Jer 3:12 will not **cause** mine anger to f upon you: 5307
6:15 they shall f among them that fall: 5307
6:15 they shall fall among them that f: 5307
6:21 and the sons together shall f upon them; 3782
8: 4 the LORD; Shall they f, and not arise? 5307
8:12 shall they f among them that fall: 5307
8:12 shall they fall among them that f: 5307
9:22 Even the carcases of men shall f as dung 5307
15: 8 I have **caused** him to f upon it suddenly, 5307
19: 7 will **cause** them to f by the sword before 5307
20: 4 they shall f by the sword of their enemies, 5307
23:12 they shall be driven on, and f therein: 5307
23:19 it shall **grievously** upon the head of 2342
25:27 spue, and f, and rise no more, because 5307
25:34 And ye shall f like a pleasant vessel. 5307
30:23 it shall f **with pain** upon the head of 2342
37:14 *It is* false; I f not **away** to the Chaldeans. 5307
39:18 thou shalt not f by the sword, but thy life 5307
44:12 be consumed, *and* f in the land of Egypt; 5307
46: 6 f toward the north by the river Euphrates. 5307
46:16 He made many to f, yea, one fell upon 3782
48:44 He that fleeth from the fear shall f into 5307
49:21 The earth is moved at the noise of their f, 5307
49:26 Therefore her young men f in her 5307
50:30 Therefore shall her young men f in 5307
50:32 the most proud shall stumble and f, 5307
51: 4 Thus the slain shall f in the land of 5307
51:44 unto him: yea, the wall of Babylon shall f. 5307
51:47 and all her slain shall f in the midst of her. 5307
51:49 *hath caused* the slain of Israel to f, 5307
51:49 at Babylon shall f the slain of all the earth. 5307
La 1:14 he hath **made** my strength to f, the Lord 3782
Eze 5:12 a third *part* shall f by the sword round 5307
6: 7 the slain shall f in the midst of you, 5307
6:11 they shall f by the sword, by the famine, 5307
6:12 *he* that *is* near shall f by the sword; 5307
11:10 Ye shall f by the sword; I will judge you 5307
11:11 *it with* untempered *morter,* that it shall f: 5307
13:11 O great hailstones, shall f; and a stormy 5307
13:14 it shall f, and ye shall be consumed in 5307
17:21 his fugitives with all his bands shall f by 5307
23:25 and thy remnant shall f by the sword: 5307
24: 6 it out piece by piece; let no lot f upon it. 5307
24:21 your daughters whom ye have left shall f 5307
25:13 and they of Dedan shall f by the sword. 5307
26:15 not the isles shake at the sound of thy f, 4658
26:18 shall the isles tremble *in* the day of thy f; 4658
27:27 shall f into the midst of the seas in the day 5307
27:34 thy company in the midst of thee shall f. 5307
29: 5 thou shalt f upon the open fields; thou 5307
30: 4 when the slain shall f in Egypt, 5307
30: 5 in league, shall f with them by the sword. 5307
30: 6 They also that uphold Egypt shall f; 5307
30: 6 from the tower of Syene shall they f in it 5307
30:17 and of Phi-beseth shall f by the sword: 5307
30:22 will **cause** the sword to f out of his hand. 5307
30:25 and the arms of Pharaoh shall f **down**; 5307
31:16 the nations to shake at the sound of his f, 4658
32:10 man for his sake, in the day of thy f. 4658
32:12 mighty will I **cause** thy multitude to f, 5307
32:20 They shall f in the midst of *them that* are 5307
33:12 he shall not f thereby in the day that he 3782
33:27 *they* that are in the wastes shall f by 5307
35: 8 shall they f *that are* slain with the sword. 5307
36:15 neither shalt thou **cause** thy nations to f 3782
38:20 the steep places shall f, and every wall 5307
38:20 and every wall shall f to the ground. 5307
39: 3 will **cause** thine arrows to f out of thy 5307
39: 4 Thou shalt f upon the mountains of Israel, 5307
39: 5 Thou shalt f upon the open field: for I 5307
44:12 **caused** the house of Israel **to f** into 4383
47:14 this land shall f unto you for inheritance. 5307
Da 3: 5 ye f **down** and worship the golden image 5308
3:10 shall f **down** and worship the golden 5308
3:15 ye f **down** and worship the image which 5308
11:14 to establish the vision; but they shall f. 3782
11:19 he shall stumble and f, and not be found. 5307
11:26 and many shall f **down** slain. 5307
11:33 they shall f by the sword, and by flame, 3782
11:34 when they shall f, they shall be holpen 3782
11:35 *some* of them of understanding shall f, 3782

Hos 4: 5 Therefore shalt thou f in the day, 3782
4: 5 the prophet also shall f with thee *in* 3782
4:14 people *that* doth not understand shall f. 3832
5: 5 Israel and Ephraim in their iniquity; 3782
5: 5 iniquity; Judah also shall f with them. 3782
7:16 their princes shall f by the sword for 5307
10: 8 Cover us; and to the hills, F on us. 5307
13:16 they shall f by the sword: their infants 5307
14: 9 but the transgressors shall f therein. 3782
Joel 2: 8 they f upon the sword, they shall not 5307
Am 3: 5 Can a bird f in a snare upon the earth, 5307
3:14 altar shall be cut off, and f to the ground. 5307
7:17 and thy daughters shall f by the sword, 5307
8:14 even they shall f, and never rise up again. 5307
9: 9 shall not the least grain f *upon* the earth. 5307
Mic 7: 8 when I f, I shall arise; when I sit in 5307
Na 3:11 shalt thou even f into the mouth of 5307
Mt 4: 9 if thou wilt f **down** and worship me. 4098
7:27 and it fell: and great was the f of it. 4431
10:29 one of them shall not f on the ground 4098
12:11 and if it f into a pit on the sabbath day, 1706
15:14 lead the blind, both shall f into the ditch. 4098
15:27 the dogs eat of the crumbs which f from 4098
21:44 And whosoever shall f on this stone shall 4098
21:44 but on whomsoever it shall f, it will grind 4098
24:29 and the stars shall f from heaven, 4098
Mk 13:25 And the stars of heaven shall f, 1601
Lk 2:34 this *child* is set for the f and rising again 4431
6:39 shall they not both f into the ditch? 4098
8:13 and in time of temptation f **away**. 868
10:18 I beheld Satan as lightning f from heaven. 4098
20:18 Whosoever shall f upon that stone shall 4098
20:18 but on whomsoever it shall f, it will grind 4098
21:24 And they shall f by the edge of the sword, 4098
23:30 begin to say to the mountains, F on us; 4098
Jn 12:24 Except a corn of wheat f into the ground 4098
Ac 27:17 fearing lest they should f into 1601
27:32 of the ropes of the boat, and let her f **off**. 1601
27:34 for there shall not a hair f from the head 4098
Ro 11:11 Have they stumbled that they should f? 4098
11:11 through their f salvation *is come* unto 3900
11:12 Now if the f of them *be* the riches of 3900
14:13 or an **occasion to f** in *his* brother's way. 4625
1Co 10:12 thinketh he standeth take heed lest he f. 4098
1Ti 3: 6 lest being lifted up with pride he f into 1706
3: 7 lest he f into reproach and the snare of 1706
6: 9 they that will be rich f into temptation 4098
Heb 4:11 lest any *man* f after the same example of 4098
6: 6 If they shall f **away**, to renew *them* again 3895
10:31 *It is* a fearful *thing* to f into the hands of 1706
Jas 1: 2 count *it* all joy when ye f **into** divers 4045
5:12 nay, nay; lest ye f into condemnation. 4098
2Pe 1:10 for if ye do these *things,* ye shall never f: 4417
3:17 wicked, f from your own stedfastness. 1601
Rev 4:10 twenty elders f **down** before him that sat 4098
6:16 F on us, and hide us from the face of him 4098
9: 1 I saw a star f from heaven unto the earth: 4098

FALLEN (79) [FALL]

Ge 4: 6 wroth? and why is thy countenance f? 5307
Lev 13:40 the man whose **hair** is f off his head, he 4803
13:41 he that hath his **hair** f off from the part 4803
25:35 and f in decay with thee; 3027+4131
Nu 32:19 inheritance is f to us on *this* side Jordan 935
Jos 2: 9 that your terror is f upon us, and that all 5307
8:24 *when* they were all f on the edge of 5307
Jdg 3:25 their lord *was* f **down** dead on the earth. 5307
18: 1 f unto them among the tribes of Israel. 5307
19:27 the woman his concubine was f **down** at 5307
1Sa 5: 3 Dagon *was* f upon his face to the earth 5307
5: 4 Dagon *was* f upon his face to the ground 5307
26:12 a deep sleep from the LORD was f upon 5307
31: 8 and his three sons f in mount Gilboa. 5307
2Sa 1: 4 many of the people also are f and dead; 5307
1:10 that he could not live after *that* he was f: 5307
1:12 Israel; because they were f by the sword. 5307
1:19 thy high places: how are the mighty f! 5307
1:25 How are the mighty f in the midst of 5307
1:27 How are the mighty f, and the weapons 5307
3:38 and a great *man* f this day in Israel? 5307
22:39 not arise: yea, they are f under my feet. 5307
2Ki 13:14 Now Elisha was f **sick** of his sickness 2470
1Ch 10: 8 Saul and his sons f in mount Gilboa. 5307
2Ch 20:24 they *were* dead bodies f to the earth, 5307
29: 9 our fathers have f by the sword, 5307
Est 7: 8 Haman was f upon the bed whereon 5307
Job 1:16 The fire of God is f from heaven, 5307
Ps 7:15 and is f into the ditch *which* he made. 5307
16: 6 lines are f unto me in pleasant *places;* 5307
18:38 not able to rise: they are f under my feet. 5307
20: 8 They are brought down and f: but we are 5307
36:12 There are the workers of iniquity f. 5307
55: 4 and the terrors of death are f upon me. 5307
57: 6 into the midst whereof they are f 5307
69: 9 them that reproached thee are f upon me. 5307
Isa 3: 8 For Jerusalem is ruined, and Judah is f: 5307
9:10 The bricks are f **down**, but we will build 5307
14:12 How art thou f from heaven, O Lucifer, 5307
16: 9 thy summer fruits and for thy harvest is f. 5307
21: 9 he answered and said, Babylon is f, 5307
21: 9 and said, Babylon is fallen, is f; 5307
26:18 have the inhabitants of the world f. 5307
59:14 truth is f in the street, and equity cannot 3782
Jer 38:19 I am afraid of the Jews that are f to 5307
46:12 the mighty, *and* they are f both together. 5307

F

Jer	48:32 the spoiler is **f** upon thy summer fruits	5307
	50:15 her foundations are **f**, her walls are	5307
	51: 8 Babylon is suddenly **f** and destroyed:	5307
La	2:21 and my young men are **f** by the sword;	5307
	5:16 The crown is **f** *from* our head: woe unto	5307
Eze	13:12 Lo, when the wall is **f**, shall it not be said	5307
	31:12 and in all the valleys his branches are **f**,	5307
	32:22 him: all of them slain, **f** by the sword,	5307
	32:23 all of them slain, **f** by the sword,	5307
	32:24 grave, all of them slain, **f** by the sword,	5307
	32:27 shall not lie with the mighty *that are* **f**	5307
Hos	7: 7 devoured their judges; all their kings are **f**:	5307
	14: 1 thy God; for thou hast **f** by thine iniquity.	3782
Am	5: 2 The virgin of Israel is **f**; she shall no more	5307
	9:11 I raise up the tabernacle of David that is **f**,	5307
Zec	11: 2 Howl, fir tree; for the cedar is **f**; because	5307
Lk	14: 5 you shall have an ass or an ox **f** into a pit,	1706
Ac	8:16 (For as yet he was **f** upon none of	1968
	15:16 the tabernacle of David, which is **f** down;	4098
	20: 9 Eutychus, being **f** into a deep sleep;	2702
	26:14 And when we were all **f** to the earth,	2667
	27:29 Then fearing lest we should have **f** upon	1601
	28: 6 have swollen, or **f** down dead suddenly:	2667
1Co	15: 6 unto this present, but some are **f** asleep.	2837
	15:18 they also which are **f** asleep in Christ	2837
Gal	5: 4 justified by the law; ye are **f** from grace.	1601
Php	1:12 **f** out rather unto the furtherance of	2064
Rev	2: 5 therefore from whence thou art **f**,	1601
	14: 8 saying, Babylon is **f**, *that* great	4098
	14: 8 Babylon is fallen, is **f**, *that* great city,	4098
	17:10 five are **f**, and one is, *and* the other is not	4098
	18: 2 saying, Babylon the great is **f**, is fallen,	4098
	18: 2 **f**, and is become the habitation of devils,	4098

FALLEST (1) [FALL]
Jer	37:13 Thou **f** away to the Chaldeans.	5307

FALLETH (28) [FALL]
Ex	1:10 to pass, that, when there **f** out any war,	7122
Lev	11:33 earthen vessel, whereinto *any* of them **f**,	5307
	11:35 *part* of their carcase **f** shall be unclean;	5307
Nu	33:54 shall be in the place where his lot **f**;	3318
2Sa	3:29 that **f** on the sword, or that lacketh bread.	5307
	3:34 as a *man* **f** before wicked men,	5307
	17:12 we *will* light upon him as the dew **f** on	5307
Job	4:13 of the night, when deep sleep **f** on men,	5307
	33:15 the night, when deep sleep **f** upon men,	5307
Pr	13:17 A wicked messenger **f** into mischief:	5307
	17:20 he that hath a perverse tongue **f** into	5307
	24:16 For a just *man* **f** seven *times*, and riseth	5307
	24:17 Rejoice not when thine enemy **f**, and let	5307
Ecc	4:10 woe to him *that is* alone when he **f**;	5307
	9:12 evil time, when it **f** suddenly upon them.	5307
	11: 3 *in* the place where the tree **f**, there it shall	5307
Isa	34: 4 as the leaf **f** off from the vine, and as a	5034
	44:15 it a graven image, and **f** down thereto.	5456
	44:17 he **f** down unto it, and worshippeth *it*,	5456
Jer	21: 9 **f** to the Chaldeans that besiege you,	5307
Da	3: 6 whoso **f** not **down** and worshippeth shall	5308
	3:11 whoso **f** not **down** and worshippeth, *that*	5308
Mt	17:15 for ofttimes he **f** into the fire, and oft into	4098
Lk	11:17 and a house *divided* against a house **f**.	4098
	15:12 give me the portion of goods that **f** to *me.*	1911
Ro	14: 4 to his own master he standeth or **f**. Yea,	4098
Jas	1:11 and the flower thereof **f**, and the grace of	1601
1Pe	1:24 and the flower thereof **f** away:	1601

FALLING (15) [FALL]
Nu	24: 4 **f** *into a trance*, but having his eyes open:	5307
	24:16 **f** *into a trance*, but having his eyes open:	5307
Job	4: 4 Thy words have upholden him that was **f**,	3782
	14:18 surely the mountain **f** cometh to nought,	5307
Ps	56:13 *wilt* not *thou* deliver my feet from **f**, that *I*	1762
	116: 8 mine eyes from tears, *and* my feet from **f**.	1762
Pr	25:26 righteous *man* **f** down before the wicked	4131
Isa	34: 4 the vine, and as a *fig* from the fig tree.	5034
Lk	8:47 came trembling, and **f** down before him,	4363
	22:44 drops of blood **f** down to the ground.	2597
Ac	1:18 and **f** headlong, he burst asunder	1096+4248
	27:41 And **f** into a place where two seas met,	4045
1Co	14:25 **f** down on *his* face he will worship God,	4098
2Th	2: 3 *come*, except there come a **f** away first,	646
Jude	1:24 unto him that is able to keep you from **f**,	679

FALLOW (3)
Dt	14: 5 the **f** deer, and the wild goat,	3180
Jer	4: 3 Break up your **f** ground, and sow not	5215
Hos	10:12 reap in mercy; break up your **f** ground:	5215

FALLOWDEER (1)
1Ki	4:23 and roebucks, and **f**, and fatted fowl.	3180

FALSE (64) [FALSEHOOD, FALSELY, FALSIFYING]
Ex	20:16 not bear **f** witness against thy	8267
	23: 1 Thou shalt not raise a **f** report: put not	7723
	23: 7 Keep thee far from a **f** matter;	8267
Dt	5:20 Neither shalt thou bear **f** witness against	7723
	19:16 If a **f** witness rise up against any man to	2555
	19:18 *if* the witness *be* a **f** witness,	8267
2Ki	9:12 they said, It is **f**; tell us now. And he said,	8267
Job	36: 4 For truly my words *shall* not *be* **f**:	8267
Ps	27:12 for **f** witnesses are risen up against me,	8267
	35:11 **F** witnesses did rise up; they laid to my	2555
	119:104 therefore I hate every **f** way.	8267
	119:128 *things* to be right; *and* I hate every **f** way.	8267

Ps	120: 3 shall be done unto thee, thou **f** tongue?	7423
Pr	6:19 A **f** witness *that* speaketh lies, and he that	8267
	11: 1 A **f** balance *is* abomination to the LORD:	4820
	12:17 righteousness: but a **f** witness deceit.	8267
	14: 5 will not lie: but a **f** witness will utter lies.	8267
	17: 4 A wicked doer giveth heed to **f** lips;	205
	19: 5 A **f** witness shall not be unpunished,	8267
	19: 9 A **f** witness shall not be unpunished,	8267
	20:23 the LORD; and a **f** balance *is* not good.	4820
	21:28 A **f** witness shall perish: but the man that	3577
	25:14 Whoso boasteth himself of a **f** gift *is like*	8267
	25:18 A man that beareth **f** witness against his	8267
Jer	14:14 they prophesy unto you a **f** vision and	8267
	23:32 I *am* against them that prophesy **f** dreams,	8267
	37:14 said Jeremiah, It *is* **f**; I fall not away to	8267
La	2:14 have seen for thee **f** burdens and causes	7723
Eze	21:23 it shall be unto them as a **f** divination in	7723
Zec	8:17 against his neighbour; and love no **f** oath:	8267
	10: 2 have seen a lie, and have told **f** dreams;	7723
Mal	3: 5 against **f** swearers, and against those that	8267
Mt	7:15 Beware of **f** prophets, which come to you	5578
	15:19 adulteries, fornications, thefts, **f** witness,	5577
	19:18 not steal, Thou shalt not **bear f witness**,	5576
	24:11 And many **f** prophets shall rise,	5578
	24:24 For there shall arise **f** Christs,	5580
	24:24 **f** prophets, and shall shew great signs	5578
	26:59 council, sought **f** witness against Jesus,	5577
	26:60 yea, though many **f** witnesses came,	5575
	26:60 At the last came two **f** witnesses,	5575
Mk	10:19 Do not bear **f** witness, Defraud not,	5576
	13:22 For **f** Christs and false prophets shall rise,	5580
	13:22 For false Christs and **f** prophets shall rise,	5578
	14:56 For many bare **f** witness against him,	5576
	14:57 and bare **f** witness against him, saying,	5576
Lk	6:26 for so did their fathers to the **f** prophets.	5578
	18:20 Do not steal, Do not **bear f witness**,	5576
	19: 8 taken any *thing* from any *man*	
	by **f** accusation,	4811
Ac	6:13 And set up **f** witnesses, which said,	5571
	13: 6 a prophet, a Jew, whose name *was*	5578
Ro	13: 9 not steal, Thou shalt not **bear f witness**,	5576
1Co	15:15 we are found **f** witnesses of God;	5575
2Co	11:13 such *are* **f** apostles, deceitful workers,	5570
	11:26 in the sea, *in* perils among **f** brethren;	5569
Gal	2: 4 of **f** brethren unawares brought in,	5569
2Ti	3: 3 **f** accusers, incontinent, fierce,	1228
Tit	2: 3 not **f** accusers, not given to much wine,	1228
2Pe	2: 1 But there were **f** prophets also among	5578
	2: 1 even as there shall be **f** teachers among	5572
1Jn	4: 1 many **f** prophets are gone out into	5578
Rev	16:13 and out of the mouth of the **f** prophet,	5578
	19:20 with him the **f** prophet that wrought	5578
	20:10 where the beast and the **f** prophet *are,*	5578

FALSEHOOD (14) [FALSE]
2Sa	18:13 I should have wrought **f** against	8267
Job	21:34 seeing *in* your answers there remaineth **f**?	4604
Ps	7:14 conceived mischief, and brought forth **f**.	8267
	119:118 err from thy statutes: for their deceit *is* **f**.	8267
	144: 8 and their right hand *is* a right hand of **f**.	8267
	144:11 and their right hand *is* a right hand of **f**:	8267
Isa	28:15 and under **f** have we hid ourselves:	8267
	57: 4 not children of transgression, a seed of **f**,	8267
	59:13 and uttering from the heart words of **f**.	8267
Jer	10:14 for his molten image *is* **f**, and *there is* no	8267
	13:25 thou hast forgotten me, and trusted in **f**.	8267
	51:17 for his molten image *is* **f**, and *there is* no	8267
Hos	7: 1 for they commit **f**; and the thief cometh	8267
Mic	2:11 If a man walking *in* the spirit and **f** do lie,	8267

FALSELY (21) [FALSE]
Ge	21:23 by God that thou wilt not **deal f** with me,	8266
Lev	6: 3 lieth concerning it, and sweareth **f**;	5921+8267
	6: 5 which he hath sworn **f**;	8267+1886.1+3807.1
	19:11 shall not steal, neither **deal f**, neither lie	3584
	19:12 not swear by my name **f**,	8267+1886.1+3807.1
Dt	19:18 and hath testified **f** against his brother;	8267
Ps	44:17 neither have we **dealt f** in thy covenant.	8266
Jer	5: 2 surely they swear **f**.	8267+1886.1+3807.1
	5:31 The prophets prophesy **f**,	8267+871.1+1886.1
	6:13 even unto the priest every one dealeth **f**.	8267
	7: 9 and swear **f**, and burn	8267+1886.1+3807.1
	8:10 even unto the priest every one dealeth **f**.	8267
	29: 9 For they prophesy **f** unto you in my name:	8267
	40:16 this thing: for thou speakest **f** of Ishmael.	8267
	43: 2 saying unto Jeremiah, Thou speakest **f**:	8267
Hos	10: 4 swearing **f** in making a covenant:	7723
Zec	5: 4 the house of him that sweareth **f** by my	8267
Mt	5:11 shall say all manner of evil against you **f**,	5574
Lk	3:14 violence to no man, neither **accuse** *any* **f**;	4811
1Ti	6:20 and oppositions of science **f** so **called**:	5581
1Pe	3:16 they may be ashamed that **f accuse** your	1908

FALSIFYING (1) [FALSE]
Am	8: 5 shekel great, and **f** the balances by deceit?	5791

FALTERS See PANTED; PANTETH

FAME (24) [FAMOUS]
Ge	45:16 the **f** *thereof* was heard *in* Pharaoh's	6963
Nu	14:15 nations which have heard the **f** of thee	8088
Jos	6:27 his **f** was *noised* throughout all the	8089
	9: 9 for we have heard the **f** of him, and all	8089
	1Ki 4:31 and his **f** was in all nations round about.	8034
	10: 1 when the queen of Sheba heard of the **f**	8088

1Ki	10: 7 prosperity exceedeth the **f** which I heard.	8052
1Ch	14:17 the **f** of David went out into all lands;	8034
	22: 5 of **f** and of glory throughout all countries:	8034
2Ch	9: 1 when the queen of Sheba heard of the **f**	8088
	9: 6 *for* thou exceedest the **f** that I heard.	8052
Est	4: 1 Mordecai perceived all that was done,	8089
Job	28:22 have heard the **f** thereof with our ears.	8088
Isa	66:19 the isles afar off, that have not heard my **f**,	8088
Jer	6:24 We have heard the **f** thereof: our hands	8089
Zep	3:19 **f** in every land where they have been put	8034
Mt	4:24 And his **f** went throughout all Syria:	5345
	9:26 And the **f** hereof went abroad into all that	5345
	9:31 spread abroad his **f** in all that country.	1310
	14: 1 that time Herod the tetrarch heard of the **f**	189
Mk	1:28 And immediately his **f** spread abroad	189
Lk	4:14 there went out a **f** of him through all	5345
	4:37 the **f** of him went out into every place	2279
	5:15 *much* the more went there a **f** abroad of	3056

FAMILIAR (18) [FAMILIARS]
Lev	19:31 Regard not them that have **f** spirits,	178
	20: 6 that turneth after such as have **f** spirits,	178
	20:27 A man also or woman that hath a **f** spirit,	178
Dt	18:11 or a consulter with **f** spirits, or a wizard,	178
1Sa	28: 3 Saul had put away those that had **f** spirits,	178
	28: 7 Seek me a woman that hath a **f** spirit, that	178
	28: 7 *there is* a woman that hath a **f** spirit at	178
	28: 8 divine unto me by the **f** spirit, and bring	178
	28: 9 he hath cut off those that have **f** spirits,	178
2Ki	21: 6 and dealt with **f** spirits and wizards:	178
	23:24 Moreover the *workers with* **f** spirits,	178
1Ch	10:13 asking *counsel of one that had a* **f** spirit,	178
2Ch	33: 6 and dealt with a **f** spirit, and with wizards:	178
Job	19:14 and my **f friends** have forgotten me.	3045
Ps	41: 9 Yea, mine own **f friend**, in whom I	376+7965
Isa	8:19 Seek unto them that have **f** spirits,	178
	19: 3 to them that have **f** spirits, and to	178
	29: 4 as of one that hath a **f** spirit, out of	178

FAMILIARS (1) [FAMILIAR]
Jer	20:10 All my **f** watched for my halting,	582+7965

FAMILIES (174) [FAMILY]
Ge	10: 5 his tongue, after their **f**, in their nations.	4940
	10:18 afterward were the **f** of the Canaanites	4940
	10:20 after their **f**, after their tongues, in their	4940
	10:31 after their **f**, after their tongues, in their	4940
	10:32 These *are* the **f** of the sons of Noah,	4940
	12: 3 in thee shall all the **f** of the earth be blessed.	4940
	28:14 in thy seed shall all the **f** of the earth be	4940
	36:40 according to their **f**, after their places,	4940
	47:12 *with* bread, according to *their* **f**.	2945
Ex	6:14 and Carmi: these *be* the **f** of Reuben.	4940
	6:15 these *are* the **f** of Simeon.	4940
	6:17 Libni, and Shimi, according to their **f**.	4940
	6:19 these *are* the **f** of Levi according to their	4940
	6:24 Abiasaph: these *are* the **f** of the Korhites.	4940
	6:25 fathers of the Levites according to their **f**.	4940
	12:21 and take you a lamb according to your **f**,	4940
Lev	25:45 ye buy, and of their **f** that *are* with you,	4940
Nu	1: 2 after their **f**, by the house of their fathers,	4940
	1:18 they declared their pedigrees after their **f**,	4940
	1:20 *by* their generations, after their **f**,	4940
	1:22 *by* their generations, after their **f**,	4940
	1:24 of Gad, *by* their generations, after their **f**,	4940
	1:26 Judah, *by* their generations, after their **f**,	4940
	1:28 *by* their generations, after their **f**,	4940
	1:30 *by* their generations, after their **f**,	4940
	1:32 *by* their generations, after their **f**,	4940
	1:34 *by* their generations, after their **f**,	4940
	1:36 *by* their generations, after their **f**,	4940
	1:38 of Dan, *by* their generations, after their **f**,	4940
	1:40 Asher, *by* their generations, after their **f**,	4940
	1:42 after their **f**, by the house of their fathers,	4940
	2:34 they set forward, every one after their **f**,	4940
	3:15 after the house of their fathers, by their **f**:	4940
	3:18 names of the sons of Gershon by their **f**;	4940
	3:19 the sons of Kohath by their **f**; Amram,	4940
	3:20 the sons of Merari by their **f**; Mahli,	4940
	3:20 These *are* the **f** of the Levites according	4940
	3:21 these *are* the **f** of the Gershonites.	4940
	3:23 The **f** of the Gershonites shall pitch	4940
	3:27 these *are* the **f** of the Kohathites.	4940
	3:29 The **f** of the sons of Kohath shall pitch on	4940
	3:30 chief of the house of the father of the **f**	4940
	3:33 of the Mushites: these *are* the **f** of Merari.	4940
	3:35 chief of the house of the father of the **f**	4940
	3:39 throughout their **f**, all the males from a	4940
	4: 2 after their **f**, by the house of their fathers,	4940
	4:18 Cut ye not off the tribe of the **f** of	4940
	4:22 the houses of their fathers, by their **f**;	4940
	4:24 This *is* the service of the **f** of	4940
	4:28 This *is* the service of the **f** of the sons of	4940
	4:29 thou shalt number them after their **f**,	4940
	4:33 This *is* the service of the **f** of the sons of	4940
	4:34 the sons of the Kohathites after their **f**,	4940
	4:36 that were numbered of them by their **f**	4940
	4:37 were numbered of the **f** of the Kohathites,	4940
	4:38 throughout their **f**, and by the house of	4940
	4:40 throughout their **f**, by the house of their	4940
	4:41 *are* they that were numbered of the **f** of	4940
	4:42 those that were numbered of the **f** of	4940
	4:42 throughout their **f**, by the house of their	4940
	4:44 that were numbered of them after their **f**,	4940
	4:45 *be* those that were numbered of the **f**	4940

Nu	4:46 after their **f**, and after the house of their	4940
	11:10 heard the people weep throughout their **f**,	4940
	26: 7 These *are* the **f** of the Reubenites:	4940
	26:12 The sons of Simeon after their **f**:	4940
	26:14 These *are* the **f** of the Simeonites, twenty	4940
	26:15 The children of Gad after their **f**:	4940
	26:18 These *are* the **f** of the children of Gad	4940
	26:20 the sons of Judah after their **f** were,	4940
	26:22 These *are* the **f** of Judah according to	4940
	26:23 *Of* the sons of Issachar after their **f**:	4940
	26:25 These *are* the **f** of Issachar according to	4940
	26:26 *Of* the sons of Zebulun after their **f**:	4940
	26:27 These *are* the **f** of the Zebulunites	4940
	26:28 The sons of Joseph after their **f** were	4940
	26:34 These *are* the **f** of Manasseh, and those	4940
	26:35 *are* the sons of Ephraim after their **f**:	4940
	26:37 These *are* the sons of Ephraim	4940
	26:37 These *are* the sons of Joseph after their **f**.	4940
	26:38 The sons of Benjamin after their **f**: of Bela,	4940
	26:41 *are* the sons of Benjamin after their **f**:	4940
	26:42 These *are* the sons of Dan after their **f**:	4940
	26:42 These *are* the **f** of Dan after their families.	4940
	26:42 These *are* the families of Dan after their **f**.	4940
	26:43 All the **f** of the Shuhamites, according to	4940
	26:44 *Of* the children of Asher after their **f**:	4940
	26:47 These *are* the **f** of the sons of Asher	4940
	26:48 *Of* the sons of Naphtali after their **f**:	4940
	26:50 These *are* the **f** of Naphtali according to	4940
	26:50 families of Naphtali according to their **f**:	4940
	26:57 numbered of the Levites after their **f**:	4940
	26:58 These *are* the **f** of the Levites: the family	4940
	27: 1 of the **f** of Manasseh the son of Joseph:	4940
	33:54 by lot for an inheritance among your **f**:	4940
	36: 1 the chief fathers of the **f** of the children of	4940
	36: 1 of the **f** of the sons of Joseph, came near,	4940
	36:12 *And* they were married into the **f** of	4940
Jos	7:14 shall come according to the **f** *thereof;*	4940
	13:15 Reuben *inheritance* according to their **f**.	4940
	13:23 of the children of Reuben after their **f**.	4940
	13:24 the children of Gad according to their **f**.	4940
	13:28 the children of Gad after their **f**,	4940
	13:29 of the children of Manasseh by their **f**.	4940
	13:31 half of the children of Machir by their **f**.	4940
	15: 1 tribe of the children of Judah by their **f**;	4940
	15:12 of Judah round about according to their **f**.	4940
	15:20 the children of Judah according to their **f**.	4940
	16: 5 was *thus:* even the border of their	4940
	16: 8 tribe of the children of Ephraim by their **f**.	4940
	17: 2 of the children of Manasseh by their **f**;	4940
	17: 2 of Manasseh the son of Joseph by their **f**.	4940
	18:11 of Benjamin came up according to their **f**:	4940
	18:20 thereof round about, according to their **f**.	4940
	18:21 Benjamin according to their **f** were	4940
	18:28 children of Benjamin according to their **f**.	4940
	19: 1 children of Simeon according to their **f**:	4940
	19: 8 children of Simeon according to their **f**.	4940
	19:10 children of Zebulun according to their **f**:	4940
	19:16 children of Zebulun according to their **f**,	4940
	19:17 children of Issachar according to their **f**.	4940
	19:23 the children of Issachar according to their **f**,	4940
	19:24 the children of Asher according to their **f**,	4940
	19:31 the children of Asher according to their **f**.	4940
	19:32 children of Naphtali according to their **f**:	4940
	19:39 children of Naphtali according to their **f**,	4940
	19:40 the children of Dan according to their **f**:	4940
	19:48 the children of Dan according to their **f**,	4940
	21: 4 lot came out for the **f** of the Kohathites:	4940
	21: 5 by lot out of the **f** of the tribe of Ephraim,	4940
	21: 6 by lot out of the **f** of the tribe of Issachar,	4940
	21: 7 The children of Merari by their **f** had out	4940
	21:10 of Aaron, *being* of the **f** of the Kohathites,	4940
	21:20 the **f** of the children of Kohath, the Levites	4940
	21:26 of the children of Kohath that remained.	4940
	21:27 of Gershon, of the **f** of the Levites,	4940
	21:33 **f** were thirteen cities with their suburbs.	4940
	21:34 unto the **f** of the children of Merari, the	4940
	21:40 cities for the **f** of Merari by their **f**,	4940
	21:40 which were remaining of the **f** of	4940
1Sa	9:21 my family the least of all the **f** of the tribe	4940
	10:21 tribe of Benjamin to come near by their **f**,	4940
1Ch	2:53 the **f** of Kirjath-jearim; the Ithrites,	4940
	2:55 the **f** of the scribes which dwelt at Jabez;	4940
	4: 2 These *are* the Zorathites.	4940
	4: 8 and the **f** of Aharhel the son of Harum.	4940
	4:21 the **f** of the house of them that wrought	4940
	4:38 by *their* names *were* princes in their **f**:	4940
	5: 7 brethren by **f**, when the genealogy	4940
	6:19 these *are* the **f** of the Levites according to	4940
	6:54 sons of Aaron, of the **f** of the Kohathites:	4940
	6:60 All their cities throughout their **f** *were*	4940
	6:62 the sons of Gershon throughout their **f**	4940
	6:63 throughout their **f**, out of the tribe of	4940
	6:66 the *residue* of the **f** of the sons of Kohath	4940
	7: 5 their brethren among all the **f** of Issachar	4940
2Ch	35: 5 of the fathers of your brethren the	1004
	35: 5 *after* the division of the **f** of the Levites.	1+1004
	35:12 to the divisions of the **f** of the people,	1+1004
Ne	4:13 I even set the people after *their* **f** with	4940
Job	31:34 or did the contempt of *their* **f** terrify me, that I	4940
Ps	68: 6 God setteth the solitary in **f**: he bringeth	1004
	107:41 and maketh *him* like a flock.	4940
Jer	1:15 I will call all the **f** of the kingdoms of	4940
	2: 4 Jacob, and all the **f** of the house of Israel:	4940
	10:25 and upon the **f** that call not on thy name:	4940
	25: 9 I will send and take all the **f** of the north,	4940

Jer	31: 1 I will be the God of all the **f** of Israel,	4940
	33:24 The two **f** which the Lord hath chosen,	4940
Eze	20:32 as the **f** of the countries, to serve wood	4940
Am	3: 2 You only have I known of all the **f** of	4940
Na	3: 4 and **f** through her witchcrafts.	4940
Zec	14:17 All the **f** that remain, every family apart,	4940
	14:17 whoso will not come up of *all* the **f** of	

FAMILY (123) [FAMILIES]

Lev	20: 5 against his **f**, and will cut him off, and all	4940
	25:10 and ye shall return every man unto his **f**.	4940
	25:41 shall return unto his own **f**, and unto	4940
	25:47 by thee, or to the stock of the stranger's **f**:	4940
	25:49 *any* that is nigh of kin unto him of his **f**	4940
Nu	3:21 Of Gershon *was* the **f** of the Libnites,	4940
	3:21 of the Libnites, and the **f** of the Shimites:	4940
	3:27 of Kohath *was* the **f** of the Amramites,	4940
	3:27 the **f** of the Izeharites, and the family of	4940
	3:27 the **f** of the Hebronites, and the family of	4940
	3:27 Hebronites, and the **f** of the Uzzielites:	4940
	3:33 Of Merari *was* the **f** of the Mahlites,	4940
	3:33 the Mahlites, and the **f** of the Mushites:	4940
	26: 5 *whom cometh* the **f** of the Hanochites:	4940
	26: 5 of Pallu, the **f** of the Palluites:	4940
	26: 6 Of Hezron, the **f** of the Hezronites:	4940
	26: 6 of Carmi, the **f** of the Carmites.	4940
	26:12 of Nemuel, the **f** of the Nemuelites:	4940
	26:12 of Jamin, the **f** of the Jaminites: of Jachin,	4940
	26:12 of Jachin, the **f** of the Jachinites:	4940
	26:13 Of Zerah, the **f** of the Zarhites: of Shaul,	4940
	26:13 of Shaul, the **f** of the Shaulites.	4940
	26:15 of Zephon, the **f** of the Zephonites:	4940
	26:15 of Haggi, the **f** of the Haggites: of Shuni,	4940
	26:15 of Shuni, the **f** of the Shunites:	4940
	26:16 Of Ozni, the **f** of the Oznites: of Eri,	4940
	26:16 of the Oznites: of Eri, the **f** of the Erites:	4940
	26:17 Of Arod, the **f** of the Arodites: of Areli,	4940
	26:17 the Arodites: of Areli, the **f** of the Arelites.	4940
	26:20 of Shelah, the **f** of the Shelanites:	4940
	26:20 of Pharez, the **f** of the Pharzites: of Zerah,	4940
	26:20 of Zerah, the **f** of the Zarhites.	4940
	26:21 of Hezron, the **f** of the Hezronites:	4940
	26:21 of Hamul, the **f** of the Hamulites.	4940
	26:23 *of* Tola, the **f** of the Tolaites: of Pua,	4940
	26:23 the Tolaites: of Pua, the **f** of the Punites:	4940
	26:24 Of Jashub, the **f** of the Jashubites:	4940
	26:24 of Shimron, the **f** of the Shimronites.	4940
	26:26 of Sered, the **f** of the Sardites: of Elon,	4940
	26:26 of Elon, there *are* the Elonites: of Jahleel,	4940
	26:26 of Jahleel, the **f** of the Jahleelites.	4940
	26:29 of Machir, the **f** of the Machirites:	4940
	26:29 of Gilead *come* the **f** of the Gileadites.	4940
	26:30 *of* Jeezer, the **f** of the Jeezerites: of Helek,	4940
	26:30 of Helek, the **f** of the Helekites:	4940
	26:31 of Asriel, the **f** of the Asrielites:	4940
	26:31 *of* Shechem, the **f** of the Shechemites:	4940
	26:32 *of* Shemida, the **f** of the Shemidaites:	4940
	26:32 and *of* Hepher, the **f** of the Hepherites.	4940
	26:35 of Shuthelah, the **f** of the Shuthalhites:	4940
	26:35 Becher, the **f** of the Bachrites: of Tahan,	4940
	26:35 of Tahan, the **f** of the Tahanites.	4940
	26:36 Shuthelah: of Eran, the **f** of the Eranites.	4940
	26:38 of Bela, the **f** of the Belaites: of Ashbel,	4940
	26:38 of Ashbel, the **f** of the Ashbelites:	4940
	26:38 of Ahiram, the **f** of the Ahiramites:	4940
	26:39 of Shupham, the **f** of the Shuphamites:	4940
	26:39 of Hupham, the **f** of the Huphamites.	4940
	26:40 Ard, the **f** of the Ardites: *and* of Naaman,	4940
	26:40 *and* of Naaman, the **f** of the Naamites.	4940
	26:42 of Shuham, the **f** of the Shuhamites.	4940
	26:44 of Jimna, the **f** of the Jimnites: of Jesui,	4940
	26:44 of Jesui, the **f** of the Jesuites: of Beriah,	4940
	26:44 Jesuites: of Beriah, the **f** of the Beriites.	4940
	26:45 of Heber, the **f** of the Heberites:	4940
	26:45 of Malchiel, the **f** of the Malchielites.	4940
	26:48 Jahzeel, the **f** of the Jahzeelites: of Guni,	4940
	26:48 of Guni, the **f** of the Gunites:	4940
	26:49 Of Jezer, the **f** of the Jezerites: of Shillem,	4940
	26:49 of Shillem, the **f** of the Shillemites.	4940
	26:57 of Gershon, the **f** of the Gershonites:	4940
	26:57 of Kohath, the **f** of the Kohathites:	4940
	26:57 of Merari, the **f** of the Merarites.	4940
	26:58 of the Libnites, the family of	4940
	26:58 of the Libnites, the **f** of the Hebronites,	4940
	26:58 the **f** of the Mahlites, the family of	4940
	26:58 of the Mahlites, the **f** of the Mushites,	4940
	26:58 of the Mushites, the **f** of the Korahites.	4940
	27: 4 father be done away from among his **f**,	4940
	27:11 his kinsman that is next to him of his **f**,	4940
	36: 6 only to the **f** of the tribe of their father	4940
	36: 8 shall be wife unto one of the **f** of the tribe	4940
	36:12 in the tribe of the **f** of their father.	4940
Dt	29:18 among you man, or woman, or **f**, or tribe,	4940
Jos	7:14 the **f** which the Lord shall take shall	4940
	7:17 he brought the **f** of Judah; and he took	4940
	7:17 Judah; and he took the **f** of the Zarhites:	4940
	7:17 he brought the **f** of the Zarhites man by	4940
Jdg	1:25 but they let go the man and all his **f**.	4940
	6:15 my **f** *is* poor in Manasseh, and I *am* the	504
	9: 1 with all the **f** of the house of his mother's	4940
	13: 2 of the **f** of the Danites, whose name *was*	4940
	17: 7 out of Beth-lehem-judah of the **f** of Judah,	4940
	18: 2 children of Dan sent of their **f** five men	4940
	18:11 there went from thence of the **f** of	4940
	18:19 be a priest unto a tribe and a **f** in Israel?	4940

Jdg	21:24 every man to his tribe and to his **f**,	4940
Ru	2: 1 man of wealth, of the **f** of Elimelech;	4940
1Sa	9:21 my **f** the least of all the families of the	4940
	10:21 the **f** of Matri was taken, and Saul the son	4940
	18:18 what *is* my life, *or* my father's **f** in Israel,	4940
	20: 6 *is* a yearly sacrifice there for all the **f**.	4940
	20:29 for our **f** hath a sacrifice in the city;	4940
2Sa	14:7 whole **f** is risen against thine handmaid,	4940
	16: 5 came out a man of the **f** of the house	4940
1Ch	4:27 neither did all their **f** multiply, like to	4940
	6:61 which were left of the **f** of *that* tribe,	4940
	6:70 for the **f** of the remnant of the sons of	4940
	6:71 out of the **f** of the half tribe of Manasseh,	4940
	13:14 the ark of God remained with the **f** of	1004
Est	9:28 **every f**, every province,	4940+4940+2050.1
Jer	3:14 two of a **f**, and I will bring you *to* Zion:	4940
	8: 3 residue of them that remain of this evil **f**,	4940
Am	3: 1 against the whole **f** which I brought up	4940
Mic	2: 3 Behold, against this **f** do I devise an evil,	4940
Zec	12:12 land shall mourn, **every f** apart;	4940+4940
	12:12 the **f** of the house of David apart,	4940
	12:12 the **f** of the house of Nathan apart,	4940
	12:13 The **f** of the house of Levi apart,	4940
	12:13 the **f** of Shimei apart, and their wives	4940
	12:14 **every f** apart, and their wives	4940+4940
	14:18 if the **f** of Egypt go not up, and come not,	4940
Eph	3:15 Of whom the whole **f** in heaven and earth	3965

FAMINE (96) [FAMINES]

Ge	12:10 was a **f** in the land: and Abram went	7458
	12:10 for the **f** *was* grievous in the land.	7458
	26: 1 there was a **f** in the land, besides the first	7458
	26: 1 besides the first **f** that was in the days of	7458
	41:27 the east wind shall be seven years of **f**.	7458
	41:30 shall arise after them seven years of **f**;	7458
	41:30 Egypt; and the **f** shall consume the land;	7458
	41:31 in the land by reason of that **f** following;	7458
	41:36 to the land against the seven years of **f**,	7458
	41:36 that the land perish not through the **f**.	7458
	41:50 born two sons before the years of **f** came,	7458
	41:56 the **f** was over all the face of the earth:	7458
	41:56 and the **f** waxed sore in the land of Egypt.	7458
	41:57 because that the **f** was *so* sore in all lands.	7458
	42: 5 for the **f** was in the land of Canaan.	7458
	42:19 go ye, carry corn *for* the **f** of your houses:	7459
	42:33 take *food* for the **f** of your households,	7459
	43: 1 And the **f** *was* sore in the land.	7458
	45: 6 For these two years *hath* the **f** *been* in	7458
	45:11 for yet *there are* five years of **f**; lest thou,	7458
	47: 4 for the **f** *is* sore in the land of Canaan:	7458
	47:13 for the **f** *was* very sore, so that the land of	7458
	47:13 land of Canaan fainted by reason of the **f**.	7458
	47:20 field, because the **f** prevailed over them:	7458
Ru	1: 1 ruled, that there was a **f** in the land.	7458
2Sa	21: 1 there was a **f** in the days of David three	7458
	24:13 Shall seven years of **f** come unto thee in	7458
1Ki	8:37 If there be in the land, if there be	7458
	18: 2 And *there was* a sore **f** in Samaria.	7458
2Ki	6:25 there was a great **f** in Samaria: and	7458
	7: 4 the **f** *is* in the city, and we shall die there:	7458
	8: 1 for the Lord hath called for a **f**;	7458
	25: 3 the ninth *day* of the *fourth* month the **f**	7458
1Ch	21:12 Either three years' **f**; or three months to	7458
2Ch	20: 9 the sword, judgment, or pestilence, or **f**,	7458
	32:11 you to give over yourselves to die by **f**	7458
Job	5:20 In **f** he shall redeem thee from death:	7458
	5:22 At destruction and **f** thou shalt laugh:	3720
	30: 3 For want and **f** *they were* solitary; flying	3720
Ps	33:19 from death, and to keep them alive in **f**.	7458
	37:19 and in the days of **f** they shall be satisfied.	7459
	105:16 Moreover, he called for a **f** upon the land:	7458
Isa	14:30 I will kill thy root with **f**, and he shall slay	7458
	51:19 and destruction, and the **f**, and the sword:	7458
Jer	5:12 upon us; neither shall we see sword nor **f**:	7458
	11:22 sons and their daughters shall die by **f**:	7458
	14:12 and by the **f**, and by the pestilence.	7458
	14:13 not see the sword, neither shall ye have **f**;	7458
	14:15 Sword and **f** shall not be in this land;	7458
	14:15 and **f** shall those prophets be consumed.	7458
	14:16 because of the **f** and the sword;	7458
	14:18 then behold them that are sick with **f**:	7458
	15: 2 such as *are* for the **f**, to the famine;	7458
	15: 2 such as *are* for the famine, to the **f**;	7458
	16: 4 shall be consumed by the sword, and by **f**;	7458
	18:21 deliver up their children to the **f**,	7458
	21: 7 from the sword, and from the **f**,	7458
	21: 9 and by the **f**, and by the pestilence:	7458
	24:10 the **f**, and the pestilence, among them,	7458
	27: 8 and with the **f**, and with the pestilence,	7458
	27:13 the sword, by the **f**, and by the pestilence,	7458
	29:17 the **f**, and the pestilence, and will make	7458
	29:18 with the **f**, and with the pestilence,	7458
	32:24 and *of* the **f**, and *of* the pestilence:	7458
	32:36 and by the **f**, and by the pestilence;	7458
	34:17 the sword, to the pestilence, and to the **f**;	7458
	38: 2 the sword, by the **f**, and by the pestilence:	7458
	42:16 the **f**, whereof ye were afraid, shall follow	7458
	42:17 the sword, by the **f**, and by the pestilence:	7458
	42:22 by the **f**, and by the pestilence, in the	7458
	44:12 be consumed by the sword, *and* by the **f**:	7458
	44:12 the greatest, by the sword and by the **f**:	7458
	44:13 the sword, by the **f**, and by the pestilence:	7458
	44:18 consumed by the sword and by the **f**.	7458
	44:27 be consumed by the sword and by the **f**,	7458
	52: 6 the **f** was sore in the city, so that there	7458

F

F

La 5:10 like an oven because of the terrible **f**. 7458
Eze 5:12 with **f** shall they be consumed in the 7458
5:16 shall send upon them the evil arrows of **f**, 7458
5:16 I *will* increase the **f** upon you, 7458
5:17 So will I send upon you **f** and evil beasts, 7458
6:11 the sword, by the **f**, and by the pestilence. 7458
6:12 and is besieged shall die by the **f**: 7458
7:15 and the pestilence and the **f** within: 7458
7:15 the city, **f** and pestilence shall devour him. 7458
12:16 from the **f**, and from the pestilence; 7458
14:13 will send **f** upon it, and will cut off man 7458
14:21 the **f**, and the noisome beast, 7458
36:29 will increase the **f**, and lay no **f** upon you. 7458
36:30 that ye receive no more reproach of **f** 7458
Am 8:11 Lord GOD, that I will send a **f** in the land, 7458
8:11 not a **f** of bread, nor a thirst for water, 7458
Lk 4:25 when great **f** was throughout all the land; 3042
15:14 there arose a mighty **f** in that land; 3042
Ro 8:35 or **f**, or nakedness, or peril, or sword? 3042
Rev 18: 8 in one day, death, and mourning, and **f**; 3042

FAMINES (3) [FAMINE]
Mt 24: 7 and there shall be **f**, and pestilences, 3042
Mk 13: 8 and there shall be **f** and troubles: 3042
Lk 21:11 be in divers places, and **f**, and pestilences; 3042

FAMISH (2) [FAMISHED]
Pr 10: 3 not **suffer** the soul of the righteous **to f**: 7456
Zep 2:11 for he will **f** all the gods of the earth; 7329

FAMISHED (2) [FAMISH]
Ge 41:55 when all the land of Egypt was **f**, 7456
Isa 5:13 their honourable men *are* **f**, 7458

FAMOUS (10) [FAME]
Nu 16: 2 **f** in the congregation, men of renown: 7148
26: 9 Abiram, *which were* **f** in the congregation, 7148
Ru 4:11 Ephratah, and be **f** in Beth-lehem: 7121+8034
4:14 kinsman, that his name may be **f** in Israel. 7121
1Ch 5:24 **f** men, *and* heads of the house of their 8034
12:30 mighty *men* of valour, **f** throughout 376+8034
Ps 74: 5 *A man* was **f** according as he had lifted up 3045
136:18 slew **f** kings: for his mercy *endureth* for 117
Eze 23:10 she became **f** among women; for they had 8034
32:18 her, and the daughters of the **f** nations, 117

FAN (8) [FANNERS]
Isa 30:24 winnowed with the shovel and with the **f**. 4214
41:16 Thou shalt **f** them, and the wind shall 2219
Jer 4:11 of my people, not to **f**, nor to cleanse, 2219
15: 7 I will **f** them with a fan in the gates of 2219
15: 7 I will fan them with a **f** in the gates of 4214
51: 2 that shall **f** her, and shall empty her land: 2219
Mt 3:12 Whose **f** *is* in his hand, and he will 4425
Lk 3:17 Whose **f** *is* in his hand, and he will 4425

FANNERS (1) [FAN]
Jer 51: 2 send unto Babylon **f**, that shall fan her, 2114

FAR (173) [AFAR, FURTHER]
Ge 18:25 That be **f** from thee to do after this 2486
18:25 be as the wicked, **that be f** from thee, 2486
44: 4 *and* not yet **f** off, Joseph said unto his 7368
Ex 8:28 only you shall not go **very f** away: 7368+7368
23: 7 **Keep** thee **f** from a false matter; 7368
Nu 2: **f** off about the tabernacle of 4480+5048
Dt 12:21 to put his name there be too **f** from thee, 7350
13: 7 nigh unto thee, or **f** off from thee, 7350
14:24 *or* if the place be too **f** from thee, which 7350
20:15 the cities *which are* very **f** off from thee, 7350
28:49 shall bring a nation against thee from **f**, 7350
29:22 the stranger that shall come from a **f** land, 7350
30:11 *is* not hidden from thee, neither *is* it **f** off. 7350
Jos 3:16 *and* rose up *upon* a heap very **f**, 7368
8: 4 **go** not very **f** from the city, but be ye all 7368
9: 6 of Israel, We be come from a **f** country: 7350
9: 9 From a very **f** country thy servants are 7350
9:22 saying, We are very **f** from you; 7350
Jdg 9:17 adventured his life **f**, 4480+5048
18: 7 they *were* **f** from the Zidonians, and had 7350
18:28 because it *was* **f** from Zidon, and they had 7350
19:11 they *were* by Jebus, the day was **f** spent; 3966
1Sa 2:30 now the LORD saith, **Be it f** from me; 2486
20: 9 Jonathan said, **F** be it from thee: for if I 2486
22:15 **be it f** from me: let not the king impute 2486
2Sa 15:17 and tarried *in* a place that was **f** off. 4801
20:20 Joab answered and said, **F** be it, far be it 2486
20:20 and said, Far be it, **f** be it from me, 2486
23:17 he said, **Be it f** from me, O LORD, that I 2486
1Ki 8:41 cometh out of a **f** country for thy name's 7350
8:46 unto the land of the enemy, **f** or near; 7350
2Ki 20:14 They are come from a **f** country, 7350
2Ch 6:32 is come from a **f** country for thy great 7350
6:36 them away captives unto a land **f** off 7350
26:15 spread **f** abroad; 4480+5704+7350+3807.1
Ezr 6: 6 *are* beyond the river, be ye **f** from thence: 7352
Ne 4:19 upon the wall, one **f** from another. 7350
Est 9:20 of the king Ahasuerus, *both* nigh and **f**, 7350
Job 5: 4 His children are **f** from safety, and they 7368
11:14 **put** it **f** away, and let not wickedness 7368
13:21 **Withdraw** thine hand **f** from me: 7368
19:13 He hath **put** my brethren **f** from me, 7368
21:16 the counsel of the wicked is **f** from me. 7368
22:18 the counsel of the wicked is **f** from me. 7368
22:23 **put away** iniquity **f** from thy tabernacles, 7368

Job 30:10 they **flee f** from me, and spare not to spit 7368
34:10 **f** be it from God, *that he should do* 2486
Ps 10: 5 judgments *are* **f** above out of his sight: 4791
22: 1 why art thou so **f** from helping me, 7350
22:11 **Be** not **f** from me; for trouble *is* near; 7368
22:19 be not thou **f** *from me*, O LORD: O my 7368
27: 9 Hide not thy face **f** from me; put not thy NIH
35:22 not silence: O Lord, be not **f** from me. 7368
38:21 O LORD: O my God, be not **f** from me. 7368
55: 7 Lo, *then* would I wander **f** off, 7368
71:12 O God, be not **f** from me: O my God, 7368
73:27 they that are **f** from thee shall perish: 7369
88: 8 Thou hast **put away** mine acquaintance **f** 7368
88:18 Lover and friend hast thou **put f** from me, 7368
97: 9 earth: thou art exalted **f** above all gods. 3966
103:12 As **f** as the east is from the west, so **f** 7350
103:12 **f** hath he **removed** our transgressions 7368
109:17 not in blessing, so let it be **f** from him. 7368
119:150 after mischief: they are **f** from thy law. 7350
119:155 Salvation *is* **f** from the wicked: for they 7350
Pr 4:24 and perverse lips **put f** from thee. 7368
5: 8 **Remove** thy way **f** from her, and come 7368
15:29 The LORD *is* **f** from the wicked: 7350
19: 7 how much more do his friends **go f** from 7368
22: 5 he that doth **keep** his soul shall be **f** from 7350
22:15 the rod of correction shall **drive** it **f** from 7368
25:25 so *is* good news from a **f** country. 4801
27:10 neighbour *that is* near than a brother **f** off. 7350
30: 8 **Remove f** from me vanity and lies: give 7350
31:10 for her price *is* **f** above rubies. 7350
Ecc 2:13 as **f** as light excelleth darkness. 3509.1
7:23 I said, I will be wise; but it *was* **f** from me. 7350
7:24 That which is **f** off, and exceeding deep, 7350
Isa 5:26 will lift up an ensign to the nations from **f**, 7350
6:12 the LORD have **removed** men **f** away, 7368
8: 9 pieces; and give ear, all ye of **f** countries: 4801
10: 3 in the desolation *which* shall come from **f**? 4801
13: 5 They come from a **f** country, from the end 4801
17:13 they shall flee **f** off, and shall be 4480+4801
19: 6 they shall **turn** the rivers **f** away; 2186
22: 3 bound together, *which* have fled from **f**. 7350
26:15 thou hadst **removed** *it* **f** unto the ends 7368
29:13 have **removed** their heart **f** from me, 7368
30:27 the name of the LORD cometh from **f**, 4801
33:13 Hear, ye *that are* **f** off, what I have done; 7350
33:17 shall behold the land that is **very f** off. 4801
39: 3 They are come from a **f** country unto me, 7350
43: 6 bring my sons from **f**, and my daughters 7350
46:11 man that executeth my counsel from a **f** 4801
46:12 that *are* **f** from righteousness: 7350
46:13 it shall not be **f** off, and my salvation shall 7368
49:12 Behold, these shall come from **f**: and lo, 4801
49:19 that swallowed thee up shall be **f** away. 7368
54:14 thou shalt be **f** from oppression; for thou 7368
57: 9 didst send thy messengers **f** off, 4480+7350
57:19 peace to *him* that is **f** off, and to *him* that 7350
59: 9 Therefore is judgment **f** from us, 7368
59:11 none; for salvation, *but* it is **f** off from us. 7368
60: 4 thy sons shall come from **f**, 7350
60: 9 to bring thy sons from **f**, their silver and 7350
Jer 2: 5 that they are **gone f** from me, 7368
4:16 that watchers come from a **f** country, 4801
5:15 Lo, I will bring a nation upon you from **f**, 4801
6:20 and the sweet cane from a **f** country? 4801
8:19 because of them that dwell in a **f** country: 4801
12: 2 in their mouth, and **f** from their reins. 7350
25:26 **f** and near, one with another, and all 7350
27:10 you, to **remove** you **f** from your land; 7368
48:24 the cities of the land of Moab, **f** or near. 7350
48:47 **Thus f** *is* the judgment of Moab. 2008+5704
49:30 Flee, **get you f** off, dwell deep, O ye 3966
51:64 **Thus f** *are* the words of Jeremiah. 2008+5704
La 1:16 that *should* **relieve** my soul is **f** from me: 7368
3:17 thou hast **removed** my soul **f** off from 2186
Eze 6:12 He that is **f** off shall die of the pestilence; 7350
7:20 therefore have I set it **f** from them. 5079
8: 6 that *I* should **go f** off from my sanctuary? 7368
11:15 have said, **Get** ye **f** from the LORD: 7368
11:16 Although I have **cast** them **f** off among 7368
12:27 he prophesieth of the times *that are* **f** off. 7350
22: 5 *that be* **f** from thee, shall mock thee, 7350
23:40 that ye have sent for men to come from **f**, 4801
43: 9 **put away** their whoredom, and the 7368
carcases of their kings, **f** 7368
44:10 Levites that are **gone away f** from me, 7368
Da 9: 7 all Israel, *that are* near, and *that are* **f** off, 7350
11: 2 the fourth shall be **f** richer than *they* all: 1419
Joel 2:20 I will **remove f** off from you the northern 7368
3: 6 that *ye* might **remove** them **f** from their 7350
3: 8 sell them to the Sabeans, to a people **f** off: 7350
Am 6: 3 Ye that **put f** away the evil day, 5077
Mic 4: 7 her that was **cast f** off a strong nation: 1972
7:11 that day shall the decree be **f** removed. 7368
Hab 1: 8 and their horsemen shall come from **f**; 7368
Zec 6:15 *they that are* **f** off shall come and build in 7350
10: 9 they shall **remember** me in **f** countries; 4801
Mt 8:30 *their* lips, but their heart is **f** from me. 4206
16:22 saying, **Be** it **f** from thee, Lord: 2436
21:33 **husbandman**, and **went** into a **f** country: 589
25:14 *is* as a man **travelling** into a **f** country, 589
Mk 6:35 And when the day was now **f** spent, 4183
6:35 place, and now the time *is* **f** passed: 4183
7: 6 *their* lips, but their heart is **f** from me. 4206
8: 3 the way: for divers of them came **from f**. 3113
12: 1 **husbandman**, and **went** into a **f** country. 589

Mk 12:34 Thou art not **f** from the kingdom of God. 3112
13:34 *of man is* as a man **taking** a **f** journey, 590
Lk 7: 6 And when he was now not **f** from 3112
15:13 and took his journey into a **f** country, 3117
19:12 A certain nobleman went into a **f** country 3117
20: 9 **went** into a **f** country for a long time. 589
22:51 and said, Suffer ye **thus f**. 2193+2827
24:29 and the day is **f** spent. 2235+2827
24:50 And he led them out **as f** as to Bethany, 2193
Jn 21: 8 (for they were not **f** from land, but as it 3112
Ac 11:19 about Stephen travelled **as f** as Phenice, 2193
11:22 that *he* should go **as f** as Antioch. 2193
17:27 though he be not **f** from every one 3112
22:21 for I will send thee **f** hence unto 3112
28:15 they came to meet us **as f** as Appii forum, 891
Ro 13:12 The night is **f** spent, the day is at hand: 4298
2Co 4:17 a **f** more **exceeding** 1519+2596+5236+5236
10:14 for we are come **as f** as to you also in 891
Eph 1:21 **F** above all principality, and power, 5231
2:13 **f** off are made nigh by the blood of Christ. 3112
4:10 also that ascended up **f** above all heavens, 5231
Php 1:23 to be with Christ; *which is* **f** better: 3123+4183
Heb 7:15 And it is yet **f** more evident: for that after 4054
2Pe 1: 9 and **cannot see f** off, and hath forgotten 3467

FARE (3) [FARED, FAREWELL, SEAFARING, WAYFARING]
1Sa 17:18 look how thy brethren **f**, and take their 7965
Jnh 1: 3 so he paid the **f** thereof, and went down 7939
Ac 15:29 ye shall do well. **F** ye **well**. 4517

FARED (1) [FARE]
Lk 16:19 fine linen, and **f** sumptuously every day: 2165

FAREWELL (4) [FARE]
Lk 9:61 but let me first go **bid** them **f**, which are at 657
Ac 18:21 **bade** them **f**, saying, I must by all means 657
23:30 before them what *they* had against him. **F**. 4517
2Co 13:11 Finally, brethren, **f**. Be perfect, be of good 5463

FARM (1)
Mt 22: 5 light of *it*, and went their ways, one to his **f**, 68

FARMED See TILLAGE

FARMER See HUSBANDMAN

FARTHER (1)
Mk 10: 1 into the coasts of Judea by the **f** side 4008

FARTHEST See OUTGOINGS; UTTERMOST

FARTHING (3) [FARTHINGS]
Mt 5:26 till thou hast **paid** the uttermost **f**. 2835
10:29 Are not two sparrows sold for a **f**? 787
Mk 12:42 she threw in two mites, which make a **f**. 2835

FARTHINGS (1) [FARTHING]
Lk 12: 6 Are not five sparrows sold for two **f**, 787

FASHION (13) [FASHIONED, FASHIONETH, FASHIONING, FASHIONS]
Ge 6:15 this *is* the **f** which thou shalt make it of: NIH
Ex 26:30 **f** thereof which was shewed thee in 4941
37:19 bowls **made after the f** of almonds 8246
1Ki 6:38 and according to all the **f** of it. 4941
2Ki 16:10 king Ahaz sent to Urijah the priest the **f** of 1823
Job 31:15 and did not one **f** us in the womb? 3559
Eze 43:11 the **f** thereof, and the goings out thereof, 8498
Mk 2:12 saying, We never saw *it* on this **f**. 3779
Lk 9:29 the **f** of his countenance was altered, 1491
Ac 7:44 that he should make it according to the **f** 5179
1Co 7:31 as not abusing *it*: for the **f** of this world 4976
Php 2: 8 being found in **f** as a man, he humbled 4976
Jas 1:11 and the grace of the **f** of it perisheth: 4383

FASHIONED (7) [FASHION]
Ex 32: 4 **f** it with a graving tool, after he had made 6696
Job 10: 8 **made** me and I **f** together round about; 6213
Ps 119:73 Thy hands have **made** me and **f** me: 3559
139:16 *which* in continuance were **f**, when *as yet* 3335
Isa 22:11 neither had respect unto him that **f** it long 3335
Eze 16: 7 *thy* breasts are **f**, and thine hair is grown, 3559
Php 3:21 it may be **f like unto** his glorious body, 4832

FASHIONETH (3) [FASHION]
Ps 33:15 He **f** their hearts alike; he considereth all 3335
Isa 44:12 it with hammers, and worketh it with 3335
45: 9 Shall the clay say to him that **f** it, 3335

FASHIONING (1) [FASHION]
1Pe 1:14 not **f** yourselves **according to** the former 4964

FASHIONS (1) [FASHION]
Eze 42:11 goings out *were* both according to their **f**, 4941

FAST (85) [FASTED, FASTEST, FASTING, FASTINGS]
Ge 20:18 For the LORD had **f closed up** all 6113+6113
Jdg 4:21 for he was **f asleep** and weary. 7290
15:13 we will **bind** thee **f**, and deliver thee 631+631
16:11 If they **bind** me **f** with new ropes that 631+631
Ru 2: 8 but **abide** here **f** by my maidens: 1692
2:21 Thou shalt **keep f** by my young men, 1692
2:23 So she **kept f** by the maidens of Boaz to 1692
2Sa 12:21 thou didst **f** and weep for the child, 6684
12:23 now he is dead, wherefore should I **f**? 6684
1Ki 21: 9 Proclaim a **f**, and set Naboth on high 6685

1Ki	21:12 They proclaimed a f, and set Naboth on	6685
2Ki	6:32 shut the door, and **hold** him f at the door:	6685
2Ch	20: 3 and proclaimed a f throughout all Judah.	6685
Ezr	5: 8 this work goeth f on, and prospereth in	629
	8:21 I proclaimed a f there, at the river Ahava,	6685
Est	4:16 ye f me for me, and neither eat nor drink	6684
	4:16 I also and my maidens will f likewise;	6684
Job	2: 3 still he **holdeth** f his integrity,	2388
	8:15 he shall **hold** it f, but it shall not prosper	2388
	27: 6 My righteousness I **hold** f, and will not	2388
	38:38 and the clods **cleave f together?**	1692
Ps	5: 9 was *done;* he commanded, and it **stood f.**	5975
	38: 2 For thine arrows **stick** f in me,	5181
	41: 8 disease, *say they,* **cleaveth** f unto him:	3332
	65: 6 Which by his strength **setteth** f	3559
	89:28 and my covenant *shall* **stand** f with him.	539
	111: 8 They **stand** f for ever and ever,	5564
Pr	4:13 **Take** f **hold** of instruction; let *her* not go:	2388
Isa	58: 3 in the day of your f you find pleasure,	6685
	58: 4 ye f for strife and debate, and to smite	6684
	58: 4 ye shall not f as *ye do this* day, to make	6685
	58: 5 Is it such a f that I have chosen? a day for	6685
	58: 5 ashes *under him?* wilt thou call this a f,	6685
	58: 6 *Is* not this the f that I have chosen?	6685
Jer	8: 5 they **hold** f deceit, they refuse to return.	2388
	14:12 When they f, I will not hear their cry;	6684
	36: 9 *that* they proclaimed a f before the LORD	6685
	46:14 say ye, **Stand** f, and prepare thee;	6685
	48:16 near to come, and his affliction hasteth f.	3966
	50:33 all that took them captives **held** them f;	2388
Joel	1:14 Sanctify ye a f, call a solemn assembly,	6685
	2:15 sanctify a f, call a solemn assembly:	6685
Jnh	1: 5 of the ship; and he lay, and was f **asleep.**	7290
	3: 5 and proclaimed a f, and put on sackcloth,	6685
Zec	7: 5 ye f at all f unto me, *even* to me?	6684+6684
	8:19 The f of the fourth *month,* and the fast of	6685
	8:19 of the fourth *month,* and the f of the fifth,	6685
	8:19 the f of the seventh, and the fast of	6685
	8:19 fast of the seventh, and the f of the tenth,	6685
Mt	6:16 Moreover when ye f, be not as	3522
	6:16 that they may appear unto men to f.	3522
	6:18 That thou appear not unto men to f,	3522
	9:14 Why do we and the Pharisees f oft,	3522
	9:14 Pharisees fast oft, but thy disciples f not?	3522
	9:15 be taken from them, and then shall they f.	3522
	26:48 I shall kiss, *that same is* he: **hold** him f.	2902
Mk	2:18 of John and of the Pharisees used to f:	3522
	2:18 disciples of John and of the Pharisees f,	3522
	2:18 the Pharisees fast, but thy disciples f not?	3522
	2:19 Can the children of the bridechamber f,	3522
	2:19 bridegroom with them, they cannot f.	3522
	2:20 and then shall they f in those days.	3522
Lk	5:33 Why do the disciples of John f often,	3522
	5:34 make the children of the bridechamber f,	3522
	5:35 and then shall they f in those days.	3522
	18:12 I f twice in the week, I give tithes of all	3522
Ac	16:24 and **made** their feet f in the stocks,	805
	27: 9 because the f was now already past, Paul	3521
	27:41 and the forepart **stuck** f,	2043
1Co	16:13 Watch ye, **stand** f in the faith, quit you	4739
Gal	5: 1 **Stand** f therefore in the liberty wherewith	4739
Php	1:27 your affairs, that ye **stand** f in one spirit,	4739
	4: 1 joy and crown, so **stand** f in the Lord,	4739
1Th	3: 8 now we live, if ye **stand** f in the Lord.	4739
	5:21 all *things;* **hold** f *that* which is good.	2722
2Th	2:15 **stand** f, and hold the traditions which ye	4739
2Ti	1:13 **Hold** f the form of sound words,	2192
Tit	1: 9 **Holding** f the faithful word as *he* hath	472
Heb	3: 6 if we **hold** f the confidence and	2722
	4:14 Son of God, let us **hold** f *our* profession.	2902
	10:23 Let us **hold** f the profession of *our* hope	2722
Rev	2:13 seat *is:* and thou **holdest** f my name,	2902
	2:25 But *that* which ye have *already* hold f till	2902
	3: 3 and heard, and **hold** f, and repent.	5083
	3:11 **hold** *that* f which thou hast, that no *man*	2902

FASTED (15) [FAST]

Jdg	20:26 f that day until even, and offered burnt	6684
1Sa	7: 6 and f on that day, and said there,	6684
	31:13 under a tree at Jabesh, and f seven days.	6684
2Sa	1:12 wept, and f until even, for Saul,	6684
	12:16 David f, and went in, and lay all	6684+6685
	12:22 the child *was* yet alive, I f and wept:	6684
1Ki	21:27 f, and lay in sackcloth, and went softly.	6684
1Ch	10:12 the oak in Jabesh, and f seven days.	6684
Ezr	8:23 So we f and besought our God for this:	6684
Ne	1: 4 and prayed before the God of heaven,	6684
Isa	58: 3 Wherefore have we f, *say they,* and	6684
Zec	7: 5 When ye f and mourned in the fifth and	6684
Mt	4: 2 And when he had f forty days and	3522
Ac	13: 2 and f, the Holy Ghost said, Separate me	3522
	13: 3 And when they had f and prayed,	3522

FASTEN (5) [FASTENED, FASTENING]

Ex	28:14 and f the wreathen chains to the ouches,	5414
	28:25 *chains* thou shalt f in the two ouches,	5414
	39:31 of blue, to f *it* on high upon the mitre;	5414
Isa	22:23 I will f him *as* a nail in a sure place;	8628
Jer	10: 4 they f it with nails and with hammers,	2388

FASTENED (18) [FASTEN]

Ex	39:18 *chains* they f in the two ouches,	5414
	40:18 f his sockets, and set up the boards	5414
Jdg	4:21 into his temples, and f *it* into the ground:	6795
	16:14 she f *it* with the pin, and	8628

1Sa	31:10 they f his body to the wall of Beth-shan.	8628
2Sa	20: 8 upon it a girdle with a sword f upon his	6775
1Ki	6: 6 the *beams* should not be f in the walls of	270
1Ch	10:10 and f his head *in* the temple of Dagon.	8628
2Ch	9:18 which were f to the throne, and stays on	270
Est	1: 6 blue *hangings,* f with cords of fine linen	270
Ecc	12:11 as nails f *by* the masters of assemblies,	5193
Isa	22:25 shall the nail that is f in the sure place be	8628
	41: 7 he f it with nails, *that* it should not be	2388
Eze	40:43 *were* hooks, an hand broad, f round about:	3559
Lk	4:20 were in the synagogue were f on him.	816
Ac	11: 6 Upon the which when I had f mine **eyes,**	816
	28: 3 a viper out of the heat, and f on his hand.	2510

FASTENING (1) [FASTEN]

Ac	3: 4 f his **eyes** upon him with John, said,	816

FASTEST (1) [FAST]

Mt	6:17 thou, when thou f, anoint thine head,	3522

FASTING (17) [FAST]

Ne	9: 1 children of Israel were assembled with f,	6685
Est	4: 3 Jews, and f, and weeping, and wailing;	6685
Ps	35:13 I humbled my soul with f; and my prayer	6685
	69:10 I wept, and *chastened* my soul with f,	6685
	109:24 My knees are weak through f; and my	6685
Jer	36: 6 *in* the LORD's house upon the f day:	6685
Da	6:18 went to his palace, and passed the night f:	2908
	9: 3 with f, and sackcloth, and ashes:	6685
Joel	2:12 with f, and with weeping,	6685
Mt	15:32 and I will not send them away f, lest they	3523
	17:21 kind goeth not out but by prayer and f.	3521
Mk	8: 3 And if I send them away f to their own	3523
	9:29 forth by nothing, but by prayer and f.	3521
Ac	10:30 Four days ago I was f until this hour;	3522
	14:23 and had prayed with f, they commended	3521
	27:33 day that ye have tarried and continued f,	777
1Co	7: 5 that ye may give yourselves to f and	3521

FASTINGS (4) [FAST]

Est	9:31 seed, the matters of the f and their cry.	6685
Lk	2:37 but served *God* with f and prayers night	3521
2Co	6: 5 in tumults, in labours, in watchings, in f;	3521
	11:27 in hunger and thirst, in f often, in cold	3521

FAT (130) [FATFLESHED, FATLING, FATLINGS, FATNESS, FATS, FATTED, FATTER, FATTEST]

Ge	4: 4 firstlings of his flock and of the f thereof.	2459
	41: 4 eat up the seven well favoured and f kine.	1277
	41:20 kine did eat up the first seven f kine:	1277
	45:18 of Egypt, and ye shall eat the f of the land.	2459
	49:20 Out of Asher his bread *shall be* f,	8082
Ex	23:18 neither shall the f of my sacrifice remain	2459
	29:13 thou shalt take all the f that covereth	2459
	29:13 the f that *is* upon them, and burn *them*	2459
	29:22 Also thou shalt take of the ram the f and	2459
	29:22 the f that covereth the inwards, and the	2459
	29:22 the f that *is* upon them, and the right	2459
Lev	1: 8 shall lay the parts, the head, and the f,	6309
	1:12 it into his pieces, with his head and his f:	6309
	3: 3 the f that covereth the inwards, and all	2459
	3: 3 and all the f that *is* upon the inwards,	2459
	3: 4 two kidneys, and the f that *is on* them,	2459
	3: 9 f thereof, *and* the whole rump, it	2459
	3: 9 the f that covereth the inwards, and all	2459
	3: 9 and all the f that *is* upon the inwards,	2459
	3:10 two kidneys, and the f that *is* upon them,	2459
	3:14 the f that covereth the inwards, and all	2459
	3:14 and all the f that *is* upon the inwards,	2459
	3:15 two kidneys, and the f that *is* upon them,	2459
	3:16 a sweet savour: all the f *is* the LORD's.	2459
	3:17 *that* ye eat neither f nor blood.	2459
	4:20 he shall take off from it all the f of	2459
	4: 8 the f that covereth the inwards, and all	2459
	4: 8 and all the f that *is* upon the inwards,	2459
	4: 9 two kidneys, and the f that *is* upon them,	2459
	4:19 shall take all his f from him, and burn *it*	2459
	4:26 he shall burn all his f upon the altar,	2459
	4:26 as the f of the sacrifice of peace offerings	2459
	4:31 he shall take away all the f thereof,	2459
	4:31 the f is taken away from off the sacrifice	2459
	4:35 he shall take away all the f thereof,	2459
	4:35 as the f of the lamb is taken away from	2459
	6:12 he shall burn thereon the f of the peace	2459
	7: 3 he shall offer of it all the f thereof;	2459
	7: 3 and the f that covereth the inwards,	2459
	7: 4 two kidneys, and the f that *is on* them,	2459
	7:23 shall eat no *manner* f, of ox, or of sheep,	2459
	7:24 the f of the beast that dieth of itself,	2459
	7:24 the f of that which is torn *with beasts,*	2459
	7:25 For whosoever eateth of the f of the beast,	2459
	7:30 the f with the breast, it shall he bring,	2459
	7:31 the priest shall burn the f upon the altar:	2459
	7:33 the f, shall have the right shoulder for *his*	2459
	8:16 took all the f that *was* upon the inwards,	2459
	8:16 f, and Moses burned *it* upon the altar.	2459
	8:20 burnt the head, and the pieces, and the f.	6309
	8:25 took the f, and the rump, and all the fat	2459
	8:25 all the f that *was* upon the inwards,	2459
	8:25 and their f, and the right shoulder:	2459
	8:26 put *them* on the f, and upon the right	2459
	9:10 the f, and the kidneys, and the caul above	2459
	9:19 the f of the bullock and of the ram,	2459
	9:20 put the f upon the breasts, and he burnt	2459

Lev	9:20 and he burnt the f upon the altar:	2459
	9:24 the altar the burnt offering and the f:	2459
	10:15 with the offerings made by fire of the f,	2459
	16:25 the f of the sin offering shall he burn upon	2459
	17: 6 burn the f for a sweet savour unto	2459
Nu	13:20 what the land *is,* whether it *be* f or lean,	8082
	18:17 shalt burn their f *for* an offering made by	2459
Dt	31:20 and filled *themselves,* and **waxen** f;	1878
	32:14 with f of lambs, and rams of the breed of	2459
	32:14 and goats, with the f of kidneys of wheat;	2459
	32:15 Jeshurun **waxed** f, and kicked: thou art	8080
	32:15 thou art **waxed** f, thou art grown thick,	8080
	32:38 Which did eat the f of their sacrifices,	2459
Jdg	3:17 of Moab: and Eglon *was* a very f man.	1277
	3:22 the f closed upon the blade, so that he	2459
1Sa	2:15 Also before they burnt the f, the priest's	2459
	2:16 Let them not fail to burn the f presently,	2459
	2:29 to **make** yourselves f with the chiefest of	1254
	15:22 *and* to hearken than the f of rams.	2459
	28:24 the woman had a f calf in the house;	4770
2Sa	1:22 of the slain, from the f of the mighty,	2459
1Ki	1: 9 and f **cattle** by the stone of Zoheleth,	4806
	1:19 and f **cattle** and sheep in abundance,	4806
	1:25 hath slain oxen and f **cattle** and sheep in	4806
	4:23 Ten f oxen, and twenty oxen out of	1277
	8:64 the f of the peace offerings:	2459
	8:64 and the f of the peace offerings.	2459
1Ch	4:40 found f pasture and good, and the land	8082
2Ch	7: 7 the f of the peace offerings, because	2459
	7: 7 and the meat offerings, and the f.	2459
	29:35 with the f of the peace offerings,	2459
	35:14 of burnt offerings and the f until night;	2459
Ne	8:10 *your* way, eat the f, and drink the sweet,	4924
	9:25 a f land, and possessed houses full of *all*	8082
	9:25 **became** f, and delighted themselves in	8080
	9:35 and f land which thou gavest before them,	8082
Job	15:27 and maketh **collops** of f on *his* flanks.	6371
Ps	17:10 They are inclosed *in* their own f: *with*	2459
	22:29 All *they that be* f upon earth shall eat and	1879
	37:20 the enemies of the LORD *shall be* as the f	3368
	92:14 in old age; they shall be f and flourishing;	1879
	119:70 Their heart is as f as grease; *but* I delight	2954
Pr	11:25 The liberal soul shall be **made** f:	1878
	13: 4 the soul of the diligent shall be **made** f.	1878
	15:30 *and* a good report **maketh** the bones f.	1878
	28:25 his trust in the LORD shall be **made** f.	1878
Isa	1:11 offerings of rams, and the f of fed beasts;	2459
	5:17 the waste places of the f **ones** shall	4220
	6:10 **Make** the heart of this people f,	8080
	10:16 of hosts, send among his f **ones** leanness;	4924
	25: 6 make unto all people a feast of f **things,**	8081
	25: 6 on the lees, of f **things** full of marrow,	8081
	28: 1 which *are* on the head of the f valleys of	8081
	28: 4 which *is* on the head of the f valley,	8081
	30:23 the earth, and it shall be f and plenteous;	1879
	34: 6 it is **made** f with fatness, *and* with	1878
	34: 6 goats, with the f of the kidneys of rams:	2459
	34: 7 and their dust **made** f with fatness.	1878
	43:24 neither *hast* thou filled me with the f of	2459
	58:11 soul in drought, and **make** f thy bones:	2502
Jer	5:28 They are **waxen** f, they shine: yea,	8080
	50:11 ye are **grown** f as the heifer at grass,	6335
Eze	34: 3 Ye eat the f, and ye clothe you with	2459
	34:14 *in* a pasture shall they feed upon	8082
	34:16 I will destroy the f and the strong; I will	8082
	34:20 will judge between the f cattle and	1274
	39:19 ye shall eat f till *ye* be full, and drink	2459
	44: 7 the f and the blood, and they have broken	2459
	44:15 stand before me to offer unto me the f	2459
	45:15 out of the f **pastures** of Israel;	4945
Am	5:22 the peace offerings of your f **beasts.**	4806
Hab	1:16 because by them their portion *is* f,	8082
Zec	11:16 he shall eat the flesh of the f, and tear	1277

FATAL MISTAKE See DISSEMBLED; DISSIMULATION

FATE See END; EVENT; WAY

FATFLESHED (2) [FAT, FLESH]

Ge	41: 2 seven well favoured kine and f;	1277+1320
	41:18 seven kine, f and well favoured;	1277+1320

FATHER (979) [FATHER'S, FATHERLESS, FATHERS, FATHERS', FOREFATHERS]

Ge	2:24 Therefore shall a man leave his f and his	1
	4:20 he was the f of such as dwell in tents,	1
	4:21 he was the f of all such as handle the harp	1
	9:18 and Japheth: and Ham *is* the f of Canaan.	1
	9:22 Ham, the f of Canaan, saw the nakedness of	1
	9:22 saw the nakedness of his f, and told his two	1
	9:23 and covered the nakedness of their f:	1
	10:21 Shem also, the f of all the children of Eber,	1
	11:28 Haran died before his f Terah in the land of	1
	11:29 the f of Milcah, and the father of Iscah.	1
	11:29 the father of Milcah, and the f of Iscah.	1
	17: 4 and thou shalt be a f of many nations.	1
	17: 5 for a f of many nations have I made thee.	1
	19:31 Our f is old, and *there is* not a man in the	1
	19:32 let us make our f drink wine, and we will lie	1
	19:32 him, that we may preserve seed of our f.	1
	19:33 And they made their f drink wine that night:	1
	19:33 and the firstborn went in, and lay with her f;	1
	19:34 Behold, I lay yesternight with my f:	1
	19:34 him, that we may preserve seed of our f.	1

F

Ge	19:35 they made their **f** drink wine that night also: 1
19:36 the daughters of Lot with child by their **f**. 1	
19:37 same *is* the **f** of the Moabites unto *this* day. 1	
19:38 the same *is* the **f** of the children of Ammon 1	
20:12 she *is* the daughter of my **f**, but not 1	
22: 7 Isaac spake unto Abraham his **f**, and said, 1	
22: 7 unto Abraham his father, and said, My **f**: 1	
22:21 Buz his brother, and Kemuel the **f** of Aram, 1	
26: 3 the oath which I sware unto Abraham thy **f**; 1	
26:15 had digged in the days of Abraham his **f**, 1	
26:18 they had digged in the days of Abraham his **f**; 1	
26:18 the names by which his **f** had called them. 1	
26:24 and said, I *am* the God of Abraham thy **f**: 1	
27: 6 I heard thy **f** speak unto Esau thy brother, 1	
27: 9 and I will make them savoury meat for thy **f**, 1	
27:10 thou shalt bring *it* to thy **f**, that he may eat, 1	
27:12 My **f** peradventure will feel me, and I shall 1	
27:14 made savoury meat, such as his **f** loved. 1	
27:18 And he came unto his **f**, and said, My father: 1	
27:18 And he came unto his father, and said, My **f**: 1	
27:19 Jacob said unto his **f**, I *am* Esau thy firstborn; 1	
27:22 Jacob went near unto Isaac his **f**; and he felt 1	
27:26 And his **f** Isaac said unto him, Come near 1	
27:30 gone out from the presence of Isaac his **f**, 1	
27:31 brought *it* unto his **f**, and said unto his father, 1	
27:31 said unto his **f**, Let my father arise, and eat of 1	
27:31 Let my **f** arise, and eat of his son's venison, 1	
27:32 And Isaac his **f** said unto him, Who *art* thou? 1	
27:34 when Esau heard the words of his **f**, he cried 1	
27:34 said unto his **f**, Bless me, *even* me also, O my 1	
27:34 father, Bless me, *even* me also, O my **f**. 1	
27:38 Esau said unto his **f**, Hast thou but one 1	
27:38 his father, Hast thou but one blessing, my **f**? 1	
27:38 bless me, *even* me also, O my **f**. And Esau lift 1	
27:39 And Isaac his **f** answered and said unto him, 1	
27:41 of the blessing wherewith his **f** blessed him: 1	
27:41 The days of mourning for my **f** are at hand; 1	
28: 2 to the house of Bethuel thy mother's **f**; 1	
28: 7 And that Jacob obeyed his **f** and his mother, 1	
28: 8 daughters of Canaan pleased not Isaac his **f**; 1	
28:13 I *am* the LORD God of Abraham thy **f**, 1	
29:12 Rebekah's son: and she ran and told her **f**. 1	
31: 5 but the God of my **f** hath been with me. 1	
31: 6 that with all my power I have served your **f**. 1	
31: 7 your **f** hath deceived me, and changed my 1	
31: 9 God hath taken away the cattle of your **f**, 1	
31:16 the riches which God hath taken from our **f**, 1	
31:18 for to go to Isaac his **f** in the land of Canaan. 1	
31:29 the God of your **f** spake unto me yesternight, 1	
31:35 she said to her **f**, Let it not displease my lord 1	
31:42 Except the God of my **f**, the God of Abraham, 1	
31:53 Nahor, the God of their **f**, judge betwixt us. 1	
31:53 And Jacob sware by the fear of his **f** Isaac. 1	
32: 9 God of my **f** Abraham, and God of my father 1	
32: 9 of my father Abraham, and God of my **f** Isaac, 1	
33:19 Shechem's **f**, for an hundred pieces of money. 1	
34: 4 And Shechem spake unto his **f** Hamor, saying, 1	
34: 6 Hamor the **f** of Shechem went out unto Jacob 1	
34:11 Shechem said unto her **f** and unto her 1	
34:13 and Hamor his **f** deceitfully. 1	
34:19 more honourable than all the house of his **f**. 1	
35:18 name Ben-oni: but his **f** called him Benjamin. 1	
35:27 And Jacob came unto Isaac his **f** unto Mamre, 1	
36: 9 these *are* the generations of Esau the **f** of 1	
36:24 as he fed the asses of Zibeon his **f**. 1	
36:43 he *is* Esau the **f** of the Edomites. 1	
37: 1 Jacob dwelt in the land wherein his **f** was a 1	
37: 2 and Joseph brought unto his **f** their evil report. 1	
37: 4 when his brethren saw that their **f** loved him 1	
37:10 And he told *it* to his **f**, and to his brethren; 1	
37:10 his **f** rebuked him, and said unto him, What 1	
37:11 envied him; but his **f** observed the saying. 1	
37:22 of their hands, to deliver him to his **f** again. 1	
37:32 many colours, and they brought *it* to their **f**; 1	
37:35 my son mourning. Thus his **f** wept for him. 1	
38:13 Behold his **f in law** goeth up to Timnath 2524	
38:25 she sent to her **f in law**, saying, 2524	
42:13 the youngest *is this* day with our **f**, and one 1	
42:29 they came unto Jacob their **f** unto the land of 1	
42:32 We *be* twelve brethren, sons of our **f**; one *is* 1	
42:32 the youngest *is this* day with our **f** in the land 1	
42:35 they and their **f** saw the bundles of money, 1	
42:36 Jacob their **f** said unto them, Me have ye 1	
42:37 Reuben spake unto his **f**, saying, Slay my two 1	
43: 2 said unto them, Go again, buy us a 1	
43: 7 and of our kindred, saying, *Is* your **f** yet alive? 1	
43: 8 Judah said unto Israel his **f**, Send the lad with 1	
43:11 their **f** Israel said unto them, If *it must be* 1	
43:23 your God, and the God of your **f**, hath given 1	
43:27 said, *Is* your **f** well, the old man of whom ye 1	
43:28 Thy servant our **f** *is* in good health, he *is* yet 1	
44:17 as for you, get you up in peace unto your **f**. 1	
44:19 his servants, saying, Have ye a **f**, or a brother? 1	
44:20 We have a **f**, an old man, and a child of *his* 1	
44:20 is left of his mother, and his **f** loveth him. 1	
44:22 said unto my lord, The lad cannot leave his **f**: 1	
44:22 for *if* he should leave his **f**, *his father* would 1	
44:22 he should leave his father, *his f* would die. NIH	
44:24 when we came up unto thy servant my **f**, 1	
44:25 our **f** said, Go again, *and* buy us a little food. 1	
44:27 thy servant my **f** said unto us, Ye know that 1	
44:30 therefore when I come to thy servant my **f**, 1	
44:31 of thy servant our **f** with sorrow to the grave. 1	
44:32 servant became surety for the lad unto my **f**, 1	
44:32 then I shall bear the blame to my **f** for ever. 1	

Ge	44:34 For how shall I go up to my **f**, and the lad *be* 1
44:34 I see the evil that shall come on my **f**. 1	
45: 3 his brethren, I *am* Joseph; doth my **f** yet live? 1	
45: 8 he hath made me a **f** to Pharaoh, and lord of 1	
45: 9 and go up to my **f**, and say unto him, 1	
45:13 you shall tell my **f** of all my glory in Egypt, 1	
45:13 ye shall haste and bring down my **f** hither. 1	
45:18 take your **f** and your households, 1	
45:19 for your wives, and bring your **f**, and come. 1	
45:23 to his **f** he sent after this manner; ten asses 1	
45:23 and bread and meat for his **f** by the way. 1	
45:25 *into* the land of Canaan unto Jacob their **f**, 1	
45:27 carry him, the spirit of Jacob their **f** revived: 1	
46: 1 offered sacrifices unto the God of his **f** Isaac. 1	
46: 3 he said, I *am* God, the God of thy **f**: fear not 1	
46: 5 and the sons of Israel carried Jacob their **f**, 1	
46:29 went up to meet Israel his **f**, to Goshen, 1	
47: 1 My **f** and my brethren, and their flocks, 1	
47: 5 Thy **f** and thy brethren are come unto thee: 1	
47: 6 the best of the land make thy **f** and brethren 1	
47: 7 Joseph brought in Jacob his **f**, and set him 1	
47:11 And Joseph placed his **f** and his brethren, 1	
47:12 And Joseph nourished his **f**, and his brethren, 1	
48: 1 that *one* told Joseph, Behold, thy **f** *is* sick: 1	
48: 9 And Joseph said unto his **f**, They *are* my sons, 1	
48:17 when Joseph saw that his **f** laid his right hand 1	
48:18 And Joseph said unto his **f**, Not so, my father: 1	
48:18 And Joseph said unto his father, Not so, my **f**: 1	
48:19 And his **f** refused, and said, I know *it*, my son, 1	
49: 2 sons of Jacob; and hearken unto Israel your **f**. 1	
49:25 *Even* by the God of thy **f**, who shall help thee; 1	
49:26 The blessings of thy **f** have prevailed above 1	
49:28 and this *is it* that thy **f** spake unto them, 1	
50: 2 his servants the physicians to embalm his **f**: 1	
50: 5 My **f** made me swear, saying, Lo, I die: in my 1	
50: 5 and bury my **f**, and I will come again. 1	
50: 6 Pharaoh said, Go up, and bury thy **f**, 1	
50: 7 Joseph went up to bury his **f**: and with him 1	
50:10 and he made a mourning for his **f** seven days. 1	
50:14 and all that went up with him to bury his **f**, 1	
50:14 to bury his father, after he had buried his **f**. 1	
50:15 when Joseph's brethren saw that their **f** was 1	
50:16 Thy **f** did command before he died, saying, 1	
50:17 trespass of the servants of the God of thy **f**. 1	
Ex	2:18 when they came to Reuel their **f**, he said, 1
3: 1 kept the flock of Jethro his **f in law**, 2859	
3: 6 Moreover he said, I *am* the God of thy **f**, 1	
4:18 and returned to Jethro his **f in law**, 2859	
18: 1 the priest of Midian, Moses' **f in law**, 2859	
18: 1 Jethro, Moses' **f in law**, took Zipporah, 2859	
18: 4 for the God of my **f**, *said he, was* mine help, 1	
18: 5 Jethro, Moses' **f in law**, came with his 2859	
18: 6 I thy **f in law** Jethro am come unto thee, 2859	
18: 7 Moses went out to meet his **f in law**, 2859	
18: 8 Moses told his **f in law** all that the LORD 2859	
18:12 Jethro, Moses' **f in law**, took a burnt 2859	
18:12 to eat bread with Moses' **f in law** before 2859	
18:14 when Moses' **f in law** saw all that he did 2859	
18:15 Moses said unto his **f in law**, Because 2859	
18:17 Moses' **f in law** said unto him, The thing 2859	
18:24 hearkened to the voice of his **f in law**, 2859	
18:27 Moses let his **f in law** depart; and he 2859	
20:12 Honour thy **f** and thy mother: that thy days 1	
21:15 he that smiteth his **f**, or his mother, shall be 1	
21:17 he that curseth his **f**, or his mother, shall 1	
22:17 If her **f** utterly refuse to give her unto him, 1	
40:15 shalt anoint them, as thou didst anoint their **f**, 1	
Lev	18: 7 The nakedness of thy **f**, or the nakedness of 1
18: 9 the daughter of thy **f**, or daughter of thy 1	
18:11 begotten of thy **f**, she *is* thy sister, thou shalt 1	
19: 3 his mother, and his **f**, and keep my sabbaths: 1	
20: 9 For every one that curseth his **f** or his mother 1	
20: 9 he hath cursed his **f** or his mother; his blood 1	
21: 2 for his **f**, and for his son, and for his daughter, 1	
21: 9 by playing the whore, she profaneth her **f**: 1	
21:11 nor defile himself for his **f**, or for his mother; 1	
24:10 whose *f* was an Egyptian, 1121	
Nu	3: 4 the priest's office in the sight of Aaron their **f**. 1
3:24 the chief of the house of the **f** of 1	
3:30 the chief of the house of the **f** of the families 1	
3:35 the chief of the house of the **f** of the families 1	
6: 7 He shall not make himself unclean for his **f**, 1	
10:29 of Raguel the Midianite, Moses' **f in law**, 2859	
11:12 as a **nursing f** beareth the sucking child, 539	
12:14 unto Moses, If her **f** had but spit in her face, 1	
18: 2 the tribe of thy **f**, bring thou with thee, that 1	
27: 3 Our **f** died in the wilderness, and he was not 1	
27: 4 Why should the name of our **f** be done away 1	
27: 4 a possession among the brethren of our **f**. 1	
27: 7 thou shalt cause the inheritance of their **f** to 1	
27:11 if his **f** have no brethren, then ye shall give 1	
30: 4 her **f** hear her vow, and her bond wherewith 1	
30: 4 her soul, and her **f** shall hold his peace at her: 1	
30: 5 her **f** disallow her in the day that he heareth; 1	
30: 5 forgive her, because her **f** disallowed her. 1	
30:16 and his wife, between the **f** and his daughter, 1	
36: 6 only to the family of the tribe of their **f** shall 1	
36: 8 unto one of the family of the tribe of her **f**, 1	
36:12 remained in the tribe of the family of their **f**. 1	
Dt	5:16 Honour thy **f** and thy mother, as the LORD 1
21:13 bewail her **f** and her mother a full month: 1	
21:18 which will not obey the voice of his **f**, 1	
21:19 shall his **f** and his mother lay hold on him, 1	
22:15 shall the **f** of the damsel, and her mother, 1	
22:16 And the damsel's **f** shall say unto the elders, 1	

Dt	22:19 give *them* unto the **f** of the damsel, because 1
22:29 give unto the damsel's **f** fifty *shekels* of silver, 1	
26: 5 A Syrian ready to perish *was* my **f**, and he 1	
27:16 Cursed *be* he that setteth light by his **f** or 1	
27:22 the daughter of his **f**, or the daughter of his 1	
32: 6 is not he thy **f** *that* hath bought thee? hath he 1	
32: 7 ask thy **f**, and he will shew thee; thy elders, 1	
33: 9 Who said unto his **f** and to his mother, I have 1	
Jos	2:13 *that* ye will save alive my **f**, and my mother, 1
2:18 and thou shalt bring thy **f**, and thy mother, 1	
6:23 her **f**, and her mother, and her brethren, 1	
15:13 the city of Arba the **f** of Anak, which *city* 1	
15:18 that she moved him to ask of her **f** a field: 1	
17: 1 the firstborn of Manasseh, the **f** of Gilead: 1	
17: 4 an inheritance among the brethren of their **f**. 1	
19:47 Dan, after the name of Dan their **f**. 1	
21:11 gave them the city of Arbah the **f** of Anak, 1	
24: 2 the **f** of Abraham, and the father of Nachor: 1	
24: 2 the father of Abraham, and the **f** of Nachor: 1	
24: 3 I took your **f** Abraham from the *other* side of 1	
24:32 **f** of Shechem for an hundred pieces of silver: 1	
Jdg	1:14 that she moved him to ask of her **f** a field: 1
1:16 children of the Kenite, Moses' **f in law**, 2859	
4:11 children of Hobab the **f in law** of Moses, 2859	
6:25 throw down the altar of Baal that thy **f** hath, 1	
8:32 was buried in the sepulchre of Joash his **f**, 1	
9: 1 all the family of the house of his mother's **f**, 1	
9:17 (For my **f** fought for you, and adventured his 1	
9:28 serve the men of Hamor the **f** of Shechem: 1	
9:56 which he did unto his **f**, in slaying his seventy 1	
11:36 she said unto him, My **f**, *if* thou hast opened 1	
11:37 she said unto her **f**, Let this thing be done for 1	
11:39 of two months, that she returned unto her **f**, 1	
14: 2 and told his **f** and his mother, and said, 1	
14: 3 his **f** and his mother said unto him, *Is there* 1	
14: 3 And Samson said unto his **f**, Get her for me; 1	
14: 4 his **f** and his mother knew not that it *was* of 1	
14: 5 his **f** and his mother, *to* Timnath, and came 1	
14: 6 he told not his **f** or his mother what he had 1	
14: 9 came to his **f** and mother, and he gave them, 1	
14:10 So his **f** went down unto the woman: 1	
14:16 I have not told *it* my **f** nor my mother, and 1	
15: 1 But her **f** would not suffer him to go in. 1	
15: 2 her **f** said, I verily thought that thou hadst 1	
15: 6 came up, and burnt her and her **f** with fire. 1	
16:31 and all the house of his **f** came down, 1	
16:31 Eshtaol in the buryingplace of Manoah his **f**. 1	
17:10 unto me a **f** and a priest, and I will give thee 1	
18:19 and go with us, and be to us a **f** and a priest: 1	
18:29 after the name of Dan their **f**, who was born 1	
19: 3 the **f** of the damsel saw him, he rejoiced 1	
19: 4 his **f in law**, the damsel's father, 2859	
19: 4 father in law, the damsel's **f**, retained him; 1	
19: 5 the damsel's **f** said unto his son in law, 1	
19: 6 for the damsel's **f** had said unto the man, 1	
19: 7 rose up to depart, his **f in law** urged him: 2859	
19: 8 and the damsel's **f** said, Comfort thine heart, 1	
19: 9 concubine, and his servant, his **f in law**, 2859	
19: 9 the damsel's **f**, said unto him, Behold now, 1	
Ru	2:11 and *how* thou hast left thy **f** and thy mother, 1
4:17 he *is* the **f** of Jesse, the father of David. 1	
4:17 he *is* the father of Jesse, the **f** of David. 1	
1Sa	2:25 they hearkened not unto the voice of their **f**, 1
2:27 Did I plainly appear unto the house of thy **f**, 1	
2:28 did I give unto the house of thy **f** all 1	
2:30 *that* thy house, and the house of thy **f**, 1	
4:19 that her **f in law** and her husband were 2524	
4:21 because of her **f in law** and her husband. 2524	
9: 3 the asses of Kish Saul's **f** were lost. 1	
9: 5 lest my **f** leave *caring* for the asses, 1	
10: 2 and lo, thy **f** hath left the care of the asses, 1	
10:12 place answered and said, But who *is* their **f**? 1	
14: 1 *is* on the other side. But he told not his **f**. 1	
14:27 Jonathan heard not when his **f** charged 1	
14:28 Thy **f** straitly charged the people with an oath 1	
14:29 said Jonathan, My **f** hath troubled the land: 1	
14:51 Kish *was* the **f** of Saul; and Ner the father of 1	
14:51 and Ner the **f** of Abner *was* the son of Abiel. 1	
19: 2 saying, Saul my **f** seeketh to kill thee: 1	
19: 3 stand beside my **f** in the field where thou *art*, 1	
19: 3 and I will commune with my **f** of thee; 1	
19: 4 Jonathan spake good of David unto Saul his **f**, 1	
20: 1 what *is* my sin before thy **f**, that he seeketh 1	
20: 2 my **f** will do nothing *either* great or small, 1	
20: 2 why should my **f** hide this thing from me? 1	
20: 3 Thy **f** certainly knoweth that I have found 1	
20: 6 If thy **f** at all miss me, then say, 1	
20: 8 for why shouldest thou bring me to thy **f**? 1	
20: 9 were determined by my **f** to come upon thee, 1	
20:10 or what *if* thy **f** answer thee roughly? 1	
20:12 when I have sounded my **f** about to morrow 1	
20:13 if it please my **f** *to do* thee evil, then I will 1	
20:13 be with thee, as he hath been with my **f**. 1	
20:32 Jonathan answered Saul his **f**, and said 1	
20:33 that it was determined of his **f** to slay David. 1	
20:34 David, because his **f** had done him shame. 1	
22: 3 Let my **f** and my mother, I pray thee, 1	
22:15 his servant, *nor* to all the house of my **f**: 1	
23:17 for the hand of Saul my **f** shall not find thee; 1	
23:17 unto thee; and that also Saul my **f** knoweth. 1	
24:11 Moreover, my **f**, see, yea see the skirt of thy 1	
2Sa	2:32 and buried him in the sepulchre of his **f**, 1
3: 8 *this* day unto the house of Saul thy **f**, 1	
6:21 which chose me before thy **f**, and before all 1	
7:14 I will be his **f**, and he shall be my son. If he 1	

F

Ref	Text	
2Sa 9: 7	will restore thee all the land of Saul thy **f**;	1
10: 2	Nahash, as his **f** shewed kindness unto me.	1
10: 2	him by the hand of his servants for his **f**.	1
10: 3	Thinkest thou that David doth honour thy **f**,	1
13: 5	when thy **f** cometh to see thee, say unto him,	1
16: 3	of Israel restore me the kingdom of my **f**:	1
16:21	shall hear that thou art abhorred of thy **f**,	1
17: 8	thou knowest thy **f** and his men, that they	1
17: 8	thy **f** *is* a man of war, and will not lodge	1
17:10	for all Israel knoweth that thy **f** *is* a mighty	1
17:23	and was buried in the sepulchre of his **f**.	1
19:37	*be buried* by the grave of my **f** and of my	1
21:14	in Zelah, in the sepulchre of Kish his **f**:	1
1Ki 1: 6	his **f** had not displeased him at any time in	1
2:12	sat Solomon upon the throne of David his **f**;	1
2:24	and set me on the throne of David my **f**,	1
2:26	the ark of the Lord God before David my **f**,	1
2:26	hast been afflicted in all where*in* my **f** was	1
2:31	from me, and from the house of my **f**.	1
2:32	my **f** David not knowing *thereof, to wit,*	1
2:44	is privy to, that thou didst to David my **f**:	1
3: 3	walking in the statutes of David his **f**:	1
3: 6	hast shewed unto thy servant David my **f**	1
3: 7	made thy servant king Jered of David my **f**:	1
3:14	as thy **f** David did walk, then I will lengthen	1
5: 1	had anointed him king in the room of his **f**.	1
5: 3	Thou knowest how that David my **f** could	1
5: 5	as the Lord spake unto David my **f**, saying,	1
6:12	with thee, which I spake unto David thy **f**:	1
7:14	his **f** *was* a man of Tyre, a worker in brass:	1
7:51	the *things* which David his **f** had dedicated;	1
8:15	spake with his mouth unto David my **f**,	1
8:17	it was in the heart of David my **f** to build a	1
8:18	the Lord said unto David my **f**, Whereas it	1
8:20	and I am risen up in the room of David my **f**,	1
8:24	Who hast kept with thy servant David my **f**	1
8:25	keep with thy servant David my **f** that thou	1
8:26	thou spakest unto thy servant David my **f**.	1
9: 4	as David thy **f** walked, in integrity of heart,	1
9: 5	as I promised to David thy **f**, saying,	1
11: 4	his God, as *was* the heart of David his **f**.	1
11: 6	not fully after the Lord, as *did* David his **f**.	1
11:27	the breaches of the city of David his **f**.	1
11:33	and my judgments, as *did* David his **f**:	1
11:43	and was buried in the city of David his **f**:	1
12: 4	Thy **f** made our yoke grievous: now therefore	1
12: 4	make thou the grievous service of thy **f**,	1
12: 6	that stood before Solomon his **f** while he *yet*	1
12: 9	Make the yoke which thy **f** did put upon us	1
12:10	Thy **f** made our yoke heavy, but make thou	1
12:11	now whereas my **f** did lade you with a heavy	1
12:11	my **f** hath chastised you with whips, but I	1
12:14	My **f** made your yoke heavy, and I will add	1
12:14	my **f** *also* chastised you with whips, but I	1
13:11	unto the king, them they told also to their **f**.	1
13:12	their **f** said unto them, What way went he?	1
15: 3	he walked in all the sins of his **f**, which he	1
15: 3	Lord his God, as the heart of David his **f**.	1
15:11	in the eyes of the Lord, as *did* David his **f**.	1
15:15	he brought in *the* things which his **f** had	1
15:19	and thee, *and* between my **f** and thy father:	1
15:19	and thee, *and* between my father and thy **f**:	1
15:24	with his fathers in the city of David his **f**:	1
15:26	walked in the way of his **f**, and in his sin	1
19:20	kiss my **f** and my mother, and *then* I will	1
20:34	The cities, which my **f** took from thy father,	1
20:34	The cities, which my father took from thy **f**;	1
20:34	thee in Damascus, as my **f** made in Samaria.	1
22:43	he walked in all the ways of Asa his **f**,	1
22:46	which remained in the days of his **f** Asa,	1
22:50	with his fathers in the city of David his **f**:	1
22:52	walked in the way of his **f**, and in the way of	1
22:53	Israel, according unto all that his **f** had done.	1
2Ki 2:12	Elisha saw *it*, and he cried, My **f**, my father,	1
2:12	Elisha saw *it*, and he cried, My father, my **f**,	1
3: 2	but not like his **f**, and like his mother:	1
3: 2	he put away the image of Baal that his **f** had	1
3:13	get thee to the prophets of thy **f**, and to	1
4:18	day, that he went out to his **f** to the reapers.	1
4:19	he said unto his **f**, My head, my head.	1
5:13	near, and spake unto him, and said, My **f**,	1
6:21	said unto Elisha, when he saw them, My **f**,	1
9:25	I and thou rode together after Ahab his **f**,	1
13:14	over his face, and said, O my **f**, my father,	1
13:14	over his face, and said, O my father, my **f**,	1
13:25	out of the hand of Jehoahaz his **f** by war.	1
14: 3	sight of the Lord, yet not like David his **f**:	1
14: 3	did according to all *things* as Joash his **f** did.	1
14: 5	his servants which had slain the king his **f**.	1
14:21	and made him king instead of his **f** Amaziah.	1
15: 3	according to all that his **f** Amaziah had done;	1
15:34	he did according to all that his **f** Uzziah had	1
15:38	with his fathers in the city of David his **f**.	1
16: 2	sight of the Lord his God, like David his **f**.	1
18: 3	according to all that David his **f** did.	1
20: 5	Thus saith the Lord, the God of David thy **f**,	1
21: 3	places which Hezekiah his **f** had destroyed;	1
21:20	the sight of the Lord, as his **f** Manasseh did.	1
21:21	he walked in all the way that his **f** walked *in*,	1
21:21	and served the idols that his **f** served,	1
22: 2	and walked in all the way of David his **f**,	1
23:34	son of Josiah king in the room of Josiah his **f**,	1
24: 9	according to all that his **f** had done.	1
1Ch 2:17	and the **f** of Amasa *was* Jether the Ishmeelite.	1
2:21	in to the daughter of Machir the **f** of Gilead,	1

Ref	Text	
1Ch 2:23	these *belonged to* the sons of Machir the **f**	1
2:24	Abiah Hezron's wife bare him Ashur the **f** of	1
2:42	Mesha his firstborn, which *was* the **f** of Ziph;	1
2:42	and the sons of Mareshah the **f** of Hebron.	1
2:44	And Shema begat Raham, the **f** of Jorkoam:	1
2:45	*was* Maon: and Maon *was* the **f** of Beth-zur.	1
2:49	She bare also Shaaph the **f** of Madmannah,	1
2:49	Sheva the **f** of Machbenah, and the father of	1
2:49	the father of Machbenah, and the **f** of Gibea:	1
2:50	of Ephratah; Shobal the **f** of Kirjath-jearim,	1
2:51	Salma the **f** of Beth-lehem, Hareph the father	1
2:51	Beth-lehem, Hareph the **f** of Beth-gader.	1
2:52	And Shobal the **f** of Kirjath-jearim had sons;	1
2:55	of Hemath, the **f** of the house of Rechab.	1
4: 3	And these *were of* the **f** of Etam; Jezreel,	1
4: 4	Penuel the **f** of Gedor, and Ezer the father of	1
4: 4	father of Gedor, and Ezer the **f** of Hushah.	1
4: 4	firstborn of Ephratah, the **f** of Beth-lehem.	1
4: 5	Ashur the **f** of Tekoa had two wives, Helah	1
4:11	begat Mehir, which *was* the **f** of Eshton.	1
4:12	and Paseah, and Tehinnah the **f** of Irnahash.	1
4:14	begat Joab, the **f** of the valley of Charashim;	1
4:17	and Shammai, and Ishbah the **f** of Eshtemoa.	1
4:18	his wife Jehudijah bare Jered the **f** of Gedor,	1
4:18	Heber the **f** of Socho, and Jekuthiel the father	1
4:18	of Socho, and Jekuthiel the **f** of Zanoah.	1
4:19	the **f** of Keilah the Garmite, and Eshtemoa	1
4:21	the son of Judah *were*, Er the **f** of Lecah,	1
4:21	Laadah the **f** of Mareshah, and the families	1
7:14	concubine the Aramitess bare Machir the **f**	1
7:22	And Ephraim their **f** mourned many days,	1
7:31	and Malchiel, who *is* the **f** of Birzavith.	1
8:29	at Gibeon dwelt the **f** of Gibeon; whose	1
9:19	his brethren, of the house of his **f**,	1
9:35	And in Gibeon dwelt the **f** of Gibeon, Jehiel,	1
17:13	I will be his **f**, and he shall be my son:	1
19: 2	because his **f** shewed kindness to me.	1
19: 2	messengers to comfort him concerning his **f**.	1
19: 3	Thinkest thou that David doth honour thy **f**,	1
22:10	and he shall be my son, and I *will be* his **f**;	1
24: 2	But Nadab and Abihu died before their **f**,	1
24:19	to their manner, under Aaron their **f**,	1
25: 3	six, under the hands of their **f** Jeduthun,	1
25: 6	All these *were* under the hands of their **f** for	1
26: 6	that ruled throughout the house of their **f**:	1
26:10	the firstborn, yet his **f** made him the chief;)	1
28: 4	house of my **f** to be king over Israel for ever:	1
28: 4	and of the house of Judah, the house of my **f**;	1
28: 4	among the sons of my **f** he liked me to make	1
28: 6	chosen him to be my son, and I will be his **f**.	1
28: 9	know thou the God of thy **f**, and serve him	1
29:10	Lord God of Israel our **f**, for ever and ever.	1
29:23	of the Lord as king instead of David his **f**,	1
2Ch 1: 8	hast shewed great mercy unto David my **f**,	1
1: 9	thy promise unto David my **f** be established:	1
2: 3	As thou didst deal with David my **f**,	1
2: 7	in Jerusalem, whom David my **f** did provide.	1
2:14	his **f** *was* a man of Tyre, skilful to work in	1
2:14	the cunning *men* of my lord David thy **f**.	1
2:17	after the numbering where*with* David his **f**	1
3: 1	where the Lord appeared unto David his **f**,	1
4:16	did Huram his **f** make to king Solomon for	1
5: 1	*all the things* that David his **f** had dedicated;	1
6: 4	he spake with his mouth to my **f** David,	1
6: 7	it was in the heart of David my **f** to build	1
6: 8	the Lord said to David my **f**, Forasmuch as	1
6:10	for I am risen up in the room of David my **f**,	1
6:15	David my **f** *that* which thou hast promised	1
6:16	keep with thy servant David my **f** *that* which	1
7:17	as David thy **f** walked, and do according to	1
7:18	as I have covenanted with David thy **f**,	1
8:14	according to the order of David his **f**,	1
9:31	and he was buried in the city of David his **f**:	1
10: 4	Thy **f** made our yoke grievous: now therefore	1
10: 4	somewhat the grievous servitude of thy **f**,	1
10: 6	before Solomon his **f** while he *yet* lived,	1
10: 9	Ease somewhat the yoke that thy **f** did put	1
10:10	Thy **f** made our yoke heavy, but make thou	1
10:11	whereas my **f** put a heavy yoke upon you,	1
10:11	my **f** chastised you with whips, but I *will*	1
10:14	My **f** made your yoke heavy, but I will add	1
10:14	my **f** chastised you with whips, but I *will*	1
15:18	of God *the things* that his **f** had dedicated,	1
16: 3	as *there was* between my **f** and thy father:	1
16: 3	as *there was* between my father and thy **f**.	1
17: 2	cities of Ephraim, which Asa his **f** had taken.	1
17: 3	he walked in the first ways of his **f** David,	1
17: 4	sought to the Lord God of his **f**,	1
20:32	he walked in the way of Asa his **f**,	1
21: 3	And their **f** gave them great gifts of silver,	1
21: 4	Jehoram was risen up to the kingdom of his **f**,	1
21:12	Thus saith the Lord God of David thy **f**,	1
21:12	not walked in the ways of Jehoshaphat thy **f**,	1
22: 4	after the death of his **f** to his destruction.	1
24:22	which Jehoiada his **f** had done to him,	1
25: 3	his servants that had killed the king his **f**.	1
26: 1	made him king in the room of his **f** Amaziah.	1
26: 4	according to all that his **f** Amaziah did.	1
27: 2	according to all that his **f** Uzziah did:	1
28: 1	in the sight of the Lord, like David his **f**:	1
29: 2	according to all that David his **f** had done.	1
33: 3	which Hezekiah his **f** had broken down,	1
33:22	the sight of the Lord, as did Manasseh his **f**:	1
33:22	images which Manasseh his **f** had made,	1
33:23	as Manasseh his **f** had humbled himself;	1

Ref	Text	
2Ch 34: 2	walked in the ways of David his **f**,	1
34: 3	he began to seek after the God of David his **f**:	1
Est 2: 7	she had neither **f** nor mother, and the maid	1
2: 7	when her **f** and mother were dead,	1
Job 15:10	and very aged men, much elder than thy **f**.	1
17:14	I have said to corruption, Thou *art* my **f**:	1
29:16	I *was* a **f** to the poor: and the cause *which* I	1
31:18	as *with* a **f**, and I have guided her from my	1
38:28	Hath the rain a **f**? or who hath begotten	1
42:15	their **f** gave them inheritance among their	1
Ps 27:10	When my **f** and my mother forsake me, then	1
68: 5	A **f** of the fatherless, and a judge of	1
89:26	Thou *art* my **F**, my God, and the rock of my	1
103:13	Like as a **f** pitieth *his* children, *so* the Lord	1
Pr 1: 8	hear the instruction of thy **f**, and forsake not	1
3:12	even as a **f** the son *in whom* he delighteth.	1
4: 1	the instruction of a **f**, and attend to know	1
10: 1	A wise son maketh a glad **f**: but a foolish son	1
15:20	A wise son maketh a glad **f**: but a foolish	1
17:21	to his sorrow: and the **f** of a fool hath no joy.	1
17:25	A foolish son *is* a grief to his **f**,	1
19:13	A foolish son *is* the calamity of his **f**:	1
19:26	He that wasteth *his* **f**, *and* chaseth away *his*	1
20:20	Whoso curseth his **f** or his mother, his lamp	1
23:22	Hearken unto thy **f** that begat thee,	1
23:24	The **f** of the righteous shall greatly rejoice:	1
23:25	Thy **f** and thy mother shall be glad, and she	1
28: 7	is a companion of riotous *men* shameth his **f**.	1
28:24	Whoso robbeth his **f** or his mother, and saith,	1
29: 3	Whoso loveth wisdom rejoiceth his **f**:	1
30:11	*There is* a generation *that* curseth their **f**,	1
30:17	The eye *that* mocketh at *his* **f**, and despiseth	1
Isa 3: 6	take hold of his brother *of* the house of his **f**,	1
8: 4	My **f**, and my mother, the riches of	1
9: 6	The mighty God, The everlasting **f**,	1
22:21	shall be a **f** to the inhabitants of Jerusalem,	1
38: 5	Thus saith the Lord, the God of David thy **f**,	1
38:19	the **f** to the children shall make known thy	1
43:27	Thy first **f** hath sinned, and thy teachers have	1
45:10	Woe unto him that saith unto *his* **f**,	1
51: 2	Look unto Abraham your **f**, and unto Sarah	1
58:14	feed thee with the heritage of Jacob thy **f**:	1
63:16	Doubtless thou *art* our **f**, though Abraham be	1
63:16	thou, O Lord, *art* our **f**, our redeemer;	1
64: 8	O Lord, thou *art* our **f**; we *are* the clay,	1
Jer 2:27	Saying to a stock, Thou *art* my **f**; and to a	1
3: 4	My **f**, thou *art* the guide of my youth?	1
3:19	I said, Thou shalt call me, My **f**; and shalt	1
12: 6	even thy brethren, and the house of thy **f**,	1
16: 7	the cup of consolation to drink for their **f**	1
20:15	*be* the man who brought tidings to my **f**,	1
22:11	which reigned instead of Josiah his **f**,	1
22:15	did not thy **f** eat and drink, and do judgment	1
31: 9	for I am a **f** to Israel, and Ephraim *is* my	1
35: 6	for Jonadab the son of Rechab our **f**	1
35: 8	Rechab our **f** in all that he hath charged us,	1
35:10	done according to all that Jonadab our **f**	1
35:16	have performed the commandment of their **f**,	1
35:18	obeyed the commandment of Jonadab your **f**,	1
Eze 16: 3	**f** *was* an Amorite, and thy mother a Hittite.	1
16:45	mother *was* a Hittite, and your **f** an Amorite.	1
18: 4	as the soul of the **f**, so also the soul of the son	1
18:17	he shall not die for the iniquity of his **f**,	1
18:18	*As for* his **f**, because he cruelly oppressed,	1
18:19	doth not the son bear the iniquity of the **f**?	1
18:20	The son shall not bear the iniquity of the **f**,	1
18:20	shall the **f** bear the iniquity of the son:	1
22: 7	In thee have they set light by **f** and mother;	1
44:25	dead person to defile *themselves*: but for **f**,	1
Da 5: 2	silver vessels which his **f** Nebuchadnezzar	2
5:11	in the days of thy **f** light and understanding	2
5:11	the king Nebuchadnezzar thy **f**, the king,	2
5:11	the king, *I say,* thy **f**, made master of	2
5:13	whom the king my **f** brought out of Jewry?	2
5:18	most high God gave Nebuchadnezzar thy **f**	2
Am 2: 7	man and his **f** will go in unto the *same* maid,	1
Mic 7: 6	For the son dishonoureth the **f**, the daughter	1
Zec 13: 3	his **f** and his mother that begat him shall say	1
13: 3	his **f** and his mother that begat him shall	1
Mal 1: 6	A son honoureth *his* **f**, and a servant his	1
1: 6	if then I *be* a **f**, where *is* mine honour?	1
2:10	Have we not all one **f**? hath not one God	1
Mt 2:22	reign in Judea in the room of his **f** Herod,	3962
3: 9	We have Abraham to our **f**:	3962
4:21	brother, in a ship with Zebedee their **f**,	3962
4:22	they immediately left the ship and their **f**,	3962
5:16	and glorify your **F** which is in heaven.	3962
5:45	That ye may be the children of your **F**	3962
5:48	even as your **F** which is in heaven is	3962
6: 1	otherwise ye have no reward of your **F**	3962
6: 4	thy **F** which seeth in secret himself shall	3962
6: 6	thy door, pray to thy **F** which is in secret;	3962
6: 6	thy **F** which seeth in secret shall reward	3962
6: 8	for your **F** knoweth what *things* ye have	3962
6: 9	Our **F** which art in heaven, Hallowed be	3962
6:14	your heavenly **F** will also forgive you:	3962
6:15	will your **F** forgive your trespasses.	3962
6:18	to fast, but unto thy **F** which is in secret:	3962
6:18	and thy **F**, which seeth in secret,	3962
6:26	yet your heavenly **F** feedeth them.	3962
6:32	for your heavenly **F** knoweth that ye	3962
7:11	how much more shall your **F** which is in	3962
7:21	he that doeth the will of my **F** which is in	3962
8:21	Lord, suffer me first to go and bury my **f**.	3962
10:20	Spirit of your **F** which speaketh in you.	3962

F

Mt	10:21	the brother to death, and the **f** the child:	3962
	10:29	not fall on the ground without your **F**.	3962
	10:32	him will I confess also before my **F** which	3962
	10:33	him will I also deny before my **F** which is	3962
	10:35	to set a man at variance against his **f**,	3962
	10:37	He that loveth **f** or mother more than me	3962
	11:25	answered and said, I thank thee, O **F**,	3962
	11:26	Even so, **F**: for so it seemed good in thy	3962
	11:27	All things are delivered unto me of my **F**:	3962
	11:27	and no man knoweth the Son, but the **F**;	3962
	11:27	neither knoweth any man the **F**, save	3962
	12:50	For whosoever shall do the will of my **F**	3962
	13:43	forth as the sun in the kingdom of their **F**.	3962
	15: 4	saying, Honour thy **f** and mother:	3962
	15: 4	He that curseth **f** or mother, let him die	3962
	15: 5	shall say to his **f** or his mother,	3962
	15: 6	honour not his **f** or his mother, he shall	3962
	15:13	which my heavenly **F** hath not planted,	3962
	16:17	unto thee, but my **F** which is in heaven.	3962
	16:27	in the glory of his **F** with his angels:	3962
	18:10	the face of my **F** which is in heaven.	3962
	18:14	it is not the will of your **F** which is	3962
	18:19	it shall be done for them of my **F** which is	3962
	18:35	So likewise shall my heavenly **F** do also	3962
	19: 5	For this cause shall a man leave **f** and	3962
	19:19	Honour thy **f** and thy mother: and,	3962
	19:29	or **f**, or mother, or wife, or children,	3962
	20:23	to them for whom it is prepared of my **F**.	3962
	21:31	of them twain did the will of his **f**?	3962
	23: 9	And call no man your **f** upon the earth:	3962
	23: 9	for one is your **F**, which is in heaven.	3962
	24:36	not the angels of heaven, but my **F** only.	3962
	25:34	his right hand, Come, ye blessed of my **F**,	3962
	26:39	on his face, and prayed, saying, O my **F**,	3962
	26:42	second time, and prayed, saying, O my **F**,	3962
	26:53	thou that I cannot now pray to my **F**,	3962
	28:19	baptizing them in the name of the **F**,	3962
Mk	1:20	they left their **f** Zebedee in the ship with	3962
	5:40	he taketh the **f** and the mother of	3962
	7:10	Moses said, Honour thy **f** and thy mother;	3962
	7:10	Whoso curseth **f** or mother, let him die	3962
	7:11	say, If a man shall say to his **f** or mother,	3962
	7:12	suffer him no more to do ought for his **f**	3962
	8:38	when he cometh in the glory of his **F**	3962
	9:21	And he asked his **f**, How long is it ago	3962
	9:24	straightway the **f** of the child cried out,	3962
	10: 7	For this cause shall a man leave his **f** and	3962
	10:19	Defraud not, Honour thy **f** and mother.	3962
	10:29	or **f**, or mother, or wife, or children,	3962
	11:10	Blessed be the kingdom of our **f** David,	3962
	11:25	that your **F** also which is in heaven may	3962
	11:26	neither will your **F** which is in heaven	3962
	13:12	the brother to death, and the **f** the son;	3962
	13:32	are in heaven, neither the Son, but the **F**.	3962
	14:36	And he said, Abba, **F**, all things are	3962
	15:21	the **f** of Alexander and Rufus, to bear his	3962
Lk	1:32	give unto him the throne of his **f** David:	3962
	1:59	him Zacharias, after the name of his **f**.	3962
	1:62	And they made signs to his **f**, how he	3962
	1:67	And his **f** Zacharias was filled with	3962
	1:73	oath which he sware to our **f** Abraham,	3962
	2:48	thy **f** and I have sought thee sorrowing.	3962
	3: 8	We have Abraham to our **f**:	3962
	6:36	merciful, as your **F** also is merciful.	3962
	8:51	and the **f** and the mother of the maiden.	3962
	9:42	child, and delivered him again to his **f**.	3962
	9:59	Lord, suffer me first to go and bury my **f**.	3962
	10:21	said, I thank thee, O **F**, Lord of heaven	3962
	10:21	even so, **F**; for so it seemed good in thy	3962
	10:22	All things are delivered to me of my **F**:	3962
	10:22	knoweth who the Son is, but the **F**;	3962
	10:22	and who the **F** is, but the Son, and he to	3962
	11: 2	ye pray, say, Our **F** which art in heaven,	3962
	11:11	shall ask bread of any of you that is a **f**,	3962
	11:13	much more shall your heavenly **F** give	3962
	12:30	your **F** knoweth that ye have need of	3962
	12:53	The **f** shall be divided against the son,	3962
	12:53	against the son, and the son against the **f**;	3962
	14:26	and hate not his **f**, and mother, and wife,	3962
	15:12	And the younger of them said to his **f**,	3962
	15:12	the younger of them said to his **f**ather, **F**,	3962
	15:18	I will arise and go to my **f**, and will say	3962
	15:18	go to my father, and will say unto him, **F**,	3962
	15:20	And he arose, and came to his **f**.	3962
	15:20	his **f** saw him, and had compassion,	3962
	15:21	the son said unto him, **F**, I have sinned	3962
	15:22	But the **f** said to his servants, Bring forth	3962
	15:27	and thy **f** hath killed the fatted calf,	3962
	15:28	came his **f** out and intreated him.	3962
	15:29	And he answering said to his **f**,	3962
	16:24	And he cried and said, **F** Abraham,	3962
	16:27	Then he said, I pray thee therefore, **f**,	3962
	16:30	And he said, Nay, **f** Abraham: but if one	3962
	18:20	witness, Honour thy **f** and thy mother.	3962
	22:29	as my **F** hath appointed unto me;	3962
	22:42	Saying, **F**, if thou be willing, remove this	3962
	23:34	Then said Jesus, **F**, forgive them; for they	3962
	23:46	he said, **F**, into thy hands I commend my	3962
	24:49	I send the promise of my **F** upon you:	3962
Jn	1:14	the glory as of the only begotten of the **F**,)	3962
	1:18	which is in the bosom of the **F**, he hath	3962
	3:35	The **F** loveth the Son, and hath given all	3962
	4:12	Art thou greater than our **f** Jacob,	3962
	4:21	nor yet at Jerusalem, worship the **F**.	3962
	4:23	worshippers shall worship the **F** in spirit	3962

Jn	4:23	for the **F** seeketh such to worship him.	3962
	4:53	the **f** knew that it was at the same hour,	3962
	5:17	answered them, My **F** worketh hitherto,	3962
	5:18	but said also that God was his **F**,	3962
	5:19	of himself, but what he seeth the **F** do:	3962
	5:20	For the **F** loveth the Son, and sheweth	3962
	5:21	For as the **F** raiseth up the dead,	3962
	5:22	For the **F** judgeth no man, but	3962
	5:23	the Son, even as they honour the **F**.	3962
	5:23	honoureth not the **F** which hath sent him.	3962
	5:26	For as the **F** hath life in himself; so hath	3962
	5:30	but the will of the **F** which hath sent me.	3962
	5:36	for the works which the **F** hath given me	3962
	5:36	witness of me, that the **F** hath sent me.	3962
	5:37	And the **F** himself, which hath sent me,	3962
	5:45	not think that I will accuse you to the **F**:	3962
	6:27	unto you: for him hath God the **F** sealed.	3962
	6:32	my **F** giveth you the true bread from	3962
	6:37	All that the **F** giveth me shall come to me;	3962
	6:42	of Joseph, whose **f** and mother we know?	3962
	6:44	the **F** which hath sent me draw him:	3962
	6:45	hath heard, and hath learned of the **F**,	3962
	6:46	Not that any man hath seen the **F**, save	3962
	6:46	he which is of God, he hath seen the **F**.	3962
	6:57	As the living **F** hath sent me, and I live by	3962
	6:57	**F**ather hath sent me, and I live by the **F**:	3962
	6:65	except it were given unto him of my **F**.	3962
	8:16	but I and the **F** that sent me.	3962
	8:18	the **F** that sent me beareth witness of me.	3962
	8:19	Then said they unto him, Where is thy **F**?	3962
	8:19	Ye neither know me, nor my **F**:	3962
	8:19	ye should have known my **F** also.	3962
	8:27	not that he spake to them of the **F**.	3962
	8:28	but as my **F** hath taught me, I speak these	3962
	8:29	The **F** hath not left me alone; for I do	3962
	8:38	speak that which I have seen with my **F**:	3962
	8:38	do that which ye have seen with your **f**.	3962
	8:39	and said unto him, Abraham is our **f**.	3962
	8:41	Ye do the deeds of your **f**.	3962
	8:41	of fornication; we have one **F**, even God.	3962
	8:42	If God were your **F**, ye would love me:	3962
	8:44	Ye are of your **f** the devil, and the lusts of	3962
	8:44	devil, and the lusts of your **f** ye will do.	3962
	8:44	of his own: for he is a liar, and the **f** of it.	3962
	8:49	but I honour my **F**, and ye do dishonour	3962
	8:53	Art thou greater than our **f** Abraham,	3962
	8:54	it is my **F** that honoureth me; of whom ye	3962
	8:56	Your **f** Abraham rejoiced to see my day:	3962
	10:15	As the **F** knoweth me, even so know I	3962
	10:15	knoweth me, even so know I the **F**:	3962
	10:17	doth my **F** love me, because I lay	3962
	10:18	commandment have I received of my **F**.	3962
	10:29	My **F**, which gave them me, is greater	3962
	10:30	I and my **F** are one.	3962
	10:32	works have I shewed you from my **F**;	3962
	10:36	ye of him, whom the **F** hath sanctified,	3962
	10:37	If I do not the works of my **F**, believe me	3962
	10:38	believe, that the **F** is in me, and I in him.	3962
	11:41	And Jesus lift up his eyes, and said, **F**,	3962
	12:26	man serve me, him will my **F** honour.	3962
	12:27	**F**, save me from this hour: but for this	3962
	12:28	**F**, glorify thy name. Then came there a	3962
	12:49	but the **F** which sent me, he gave me a	3962
	12:50	even as the **F** said unto me, so I speak.	3962
	13: 1	depart out of this world unto the **F**,	3962
	13: 3	Jesus knowing that the **F** had given all	3962
	14: 6	no man cometh unto the **F**, but by me.	3962
	14: 7	ye should have known my **F** also:	3962
	14: 8	Lord, shew us the **F**, and it sufficeth us.	3962
	14: 9	he that hath seen me hath seen the **F**;	3962
	14: 9	how sayest thou then, Shew us the **F**?	3962
	14:10	Believest thou not that I am in the **F**,	3962
	14:10	that I am in the Father, and the **F** in me?	3962
	14:10	but the **F** that dwelleth in me, he doeth	3962
	14:11	Believe me that I am in the **F**,	3962
	14:11	that I am in the Father, and the **F** in me:	3962
	14:12	shall he do; because I go unto my **F**.	3962
	14:13	do, that the **F** may be glorified in the Son.	3962
	14:16	I will pray the **F**, and he shall give you	3962
	14:20	that day ye shall know that I am in my **F**,	3962
	14:21	he that loveth me shall be loved of my **F**,	3962
	14:23	my **F** will love him, and we will come	3962
	14:26	whom the **F** will send in my name,	3962
	14:28	because I said, I go unto the **F**:	3962
	14:28	the Father: for my **F** is greater than I.	3962
	14:31	the world may know that I love the **F**;	3962
	14:31	as the **F** gave me commandment, even	3962
	15: 1	true vine, and my **F** is the husbandman.	3962
	15: 8	Herein is my **F** glorified, that ye bear	3962
	15: 9	As the **F** hath loved me, so have I loved	3962
	15:15	for all things that I have heard of my **F** I	3962
	15:16	that whatsoever ye shall ask of the **F** in	3962
	15:23	He that hateth me hateth my **F** also.	3962
	15:24	both seen and hated both me and my **F**.	3962
	15:26	whom I will send unto you from the **F**,	3962
	15:26	which proceedeth from the **F**, he shall	3962
	16: 3	because they have not known the **F**,	3962
	16:10	because I go to my **F**, and ye see me no	3962
	16:15	All things that the **F** hath are mine:	3962
	16:16	ye shall see me, because I go to the **F**.	3962
	16:17	shall see me: and, Because I go to the **F**?	3962
	16:23	ye shall ask the **F** in my name,	3962
	16:25	but I shall shew you plainly of the **F**.	3962
	16:26	unto you, that I will pray the **F** for you:	3962
	16:27	For the **F** himself loveth you, because	3962

Jn	16:28	I came forth from the **F**, and am come	3962
	16:28	again, I leave the world, and go to the **F**.	3962
	16:32	I am not alone, because the **F** is with me.	3962
	17: 1	to heaven, and said, **F**, the hour is come;	3962
	17: 5	And now, O **F**, glorify thou me with thine	3962
	17:11	Holy **F**, keep through thine own name	3962
	17:21	as thou, **F**, art in me, and I in thee, that	3962
	17:24	**F**, I will that they also, whom thou hast	3962
	17:25	O righteous **F**, the world hath not known	3962
	18:11	the cup which my **F** hath given me, shall	3962
	18:13	for he was **f** in law to Caiaphas, which	3995
	20:17	not; for I am not yet ascended to my **F**:	3962
	20:17	I ascend unto my **F**, and your Father;	3962
	20:17	I ascend unto my Father, and your **F**;	3962
	20:21	my **F** hath sent me, even so send I you.	3962
Ac	1: 4	but wait for the promise of the **F**, which,	3962
	1: 7	which the **F** hath put in his own power.	3962
	2:33	having received of the **F** the promise of	3962
	7: 2	The God of glory appeared unto our **f**	3962
	7: 4	and from thence, when his **f** was dead,	3962
	7:14	and called his **f** Jacob to him, and all his	3962
	7:16	of the sons of Emmor the **f** of Sychem.	NIG
	16: 1	and believed; but his **f** was a Greek:	3962
	16: 3	for they knew all that his **f** was a Greek.	3962
	28: 8	that the **f** of Publius lay sick of a fever and	3962
Ro	1: 7	Grace to you and peace from God our **F**,	3962
	4: 1	shall we say then that Abraham our **f**,	3962
	4:11	that he might be the **f** of all them that	3962
	4:12	the **f** of circumcision to them who are	3962
	4:12	the steps of that faith of our **f** Abraham,	3962
	4:16	faith of Abraham; who is the **f** of us all,	3962
	4:17	I have made thee a **f** of many nations,)	3962
	4:18	that he might become the **f** of many	3962
	6: 4	up from the dead by the glory of the **F**,	3962
	8:15	of adoption, whereby we cry, Abba, **F**.	3962
	9:10	conceived by one, even by our **f** Isaac;	3962
	15: 6	even the **F** of our Lord Jesus Christ.	3962
1Co	1: 3	from God our **F**, and from the Lord Jesus	3962
	8: 6	But to us there is but one God, the **F**,	3962
	15:24	up the kingdom to God, even the **F**;	3962
2Co	1: 2	be to you and peace from God our **F**,	3962
	1: 3	even the **F** of our Lord Jesus Christ,	3962
	1: 3	the **F** of mercies, and the God of all	3962
	6:18	And will be a **F** unto you, and ye shall be	3962
	11:31	The God and **F** of our Lord Jesus Christ,	3962
Gal	1: 1	man, but by Jesus Christ, and God the **F**,	3962
	1: 3	and peace from God the **F**,	3962
	1: 4	according to the will of God and our **F**:	3962
	4: 2	until the time appointed of the **f**.	3962
	4: 6	his Son into your hearts, crying, Abba, **F**.	3962
Eph	1: 2	from God our **F**, and from the Lord Jesus	3962
	1: 3	the God and **F** of our Lord Jesus Christ,	3962
	1:17	of our Lord Jesus Christ, the **F** of glory,	3962
	2:18	both have access by one Spirit unto the **F**.	3962
	3:14	For this cause I bow my knees unto the **F**	3962
	4: 6	One God and **F** of all, who is above all,	3962
	5:20	the **F** in the name of our Lord Jesus Christ	3962
	5:31	For this cause shall a man leave his **f** and	3962
	6: 2	Honour thy **f** and mother; (which is the t	3962
	6:23	from God the **F** and the Lord Jesus Christ.	3962
Php	1: 2	from God our **F**, and from the Lord Jesus	3962
	2:11	Christ is Lord, to the glory of God the **F**.	3962
	2:22	the proof of him, that, as a son with the **f**,	3962
	4:20	and our **F** be glory for ever and ever.	3962
Col	1: 2	from God our **F** and the Lord Jesus Christ.	3962
	1: 3	to God and the **F** of our Lord Jesus Christ,	3962
	1:12	Giving thanks unto the **F**, which hath	3962
	1:19	For it pleased the **F** that in him should all	NIG
	2: 2	of the mystery of God and of the **F**,	3962
	3:17	giving thanks to God and the **F** by him.	3962
1Th	1: 1	the Thessalonians which is in God the **F**	3962
	1: 1	God our **F**, and the Lord Jesus Christ.	3962
	1: 3	Christ, in the sight of God and our **F**;	3962
	2:11	every one of you, as a **f** doth his children,	3962
	3:11	God himself and our **F**, and our Lord	3962
	3:13	our **F**, at the coming of our Lord Jesus	3962
2Th	1: 1	of the Thessalonians in God our **F**	3962
	1: 2	God our **F** and the Lord Jesus Christ.	3962
	2:16	God, even our **F**, which hath loved us,	3962
1Ti	1: 2	God our **F** and Jesus Christ our Lord.	3962
	5: 1	not an elder, but intreat him as a **f**;	3962
2Ti	1: 2	God the **F** and Christ Jesus our Lord.	3962
Tit	1: 4	God the **F** and the Lord Jesus Christ	3962
Phm	1: 3	God our **F** and the Lord Jesus Christ.	3962
Heb	1: 5	I will be to him a **F**, and he shall be to me	3962
	7: 3	**Without f**, without mother, without,	540
	7:10	For he was yet in the loins of his **f**,	3962
	12: 7	for what son is he whom the **f** chasteneth	3962
	12: 9	be in subjection unto the **F** of spirits,	3962
Jas	1:17	and cometh down from the **F** of lights,	3962
	1:27	undefiled before God and the **F** is this,	3962
	2:21	not Abraham our **f** justified by works,	3962
	3: 9	Therewith bless we God, even the **F**;	3962
1Pe	1: 2	to the foreknowledge of God the **F**,	3962
	1: 3	the God and **F** of our Lord Jesus Christ,	3962
	1:17	And if ye call on the **F**, who without	3962
2Pe	1:17	For he received from God the **F** honour	3962
1Jn	1: 2	was with the **F**, and was manifested	3962
	1: 3	and truly our fellowship is with the **F**,	3962
	2: 1	man sin, we have an advocate with the **F**,	3962
	2:13	because ye have known the **F**.	3962
	2:15	the world, the love of the **F** is not in him.	3962
	2:16	of life, is not of the **F**, but is of the world.	3962
	2:22	antichrist, that denieth the **F** and the Son.	3962
	2:23	denieth the Son, the same hath not the **F**:	3962

F

1Jn 2:23 that acknowledgeth the Son hath the **F** — NIG
2:24 shall continue in the Son, and in the **F**. 3962
3: 1 what manner of love the **F** hath bestowed 3962
4:14 do testify that the **F** sent the Son *to be* 3962
5: 7 the **F**, the Word, and the Holy Ghost: 3962
2Jn 1: 3 from God the **F**, and from the Lord Jesus 3962
1: 3 the Son of the **F**, in truth and love. 3962
1: 4 received a commandment from the **F**. 3962
1: 9 Christ, he hath both the **F** and the Son. 3962
Jude 1: 1 to them that are sanctified by God the **F**, 3962
Rev 1: 6 us kings and priests unto God and his **F**; 3962
2:27 to shivers: even as I received of my **F**. 3962
3: 5 but I will confess his name before my **F**, 3962
3:21 am set down with my **F** in his throne. 3962

FATHER'S (144) [FATHER]

Ge 9:23 and they saw not their **f** nakedness. 1
12: 1 and from thy kindred, and from thy **f** house, 1
20:13 when God caused me to wander from my **f** 1
24: 7 which took me from my **f** house, and from 1
24:23 there room in thy **f** house for us to lodge in? 1
24:38 thou shalt go unto my **f** house, and to my 1
24:40 for my son of my kindred, and of my **f** house: 1
26:15 For all the wells which his **f** servants had 1
28:21 So that I come again to my **f** house in peace; 1
29: 9 Rachel came with her **f** sheep: 1+3807.1
29:12 Jacob told Rachel that he *was* her **f** brother, 1
31: 1 hath taken all that *was* our **f**; 1+3807.1
31: 1 of *that* which *was* of our **f** hath he 1+3807.1
31: 5 said unto them, I see your **f** countenance, 1
31:14 or inheritance for us in our **f** house? 1
31:19 stolen the images that *were* her **f**. 1+3807.1
31:30 because thou sore longedst after thy **f** house, 1
35:22 and lay with Bilhah his **f** concubine. 1
37: 2 and with the sons of Zilpah, his **f** wives: 1
37:12 his brethren went to feed their **f** flock in 1
38:11 Remain a widow *at* thy **f** house, till Shelah 1
38:11 And Tamar went and dwelt *in* her **f** house. 1
41:51 me forget all my toil, and all my **f** house. 1
46:31 unto his **f** house, I will go up, 1
46:31 say unto him, My brethren, and my **f** house, 1
47:12 and all his **f** household, *with* bread, 1
48:17 he held up his **f** hand, to remove it from 1
49: 4 because thou wentest up to thy **f** bed; then 1
49: 8 thy **f** children shall bow down before thee. 1
50: 1 Joseph fell upon his **f** face, and wept upon 1
50: 8 of Joseph, and his brethren, and his **f** house: 1
50:22 Joseph dwelt in Egypt, he, and his **f** house: 1
Ex 2:16 and filled the troughs to water their **f** flock. 1
6:20 Amram took him Jochebed his **f** sister to 1733
15: 2 a habitation; my **f** God, and I will exalt him. 1
Lev 16:32 to minister in the priest's office in his **f** stead, 1
18: 8 The nakedness of thy **f** wife shalt thou not 1
18: 8 shalt thou not uncover: it *is* thy **f** nakedness. 1
18:11 The nakedness of thy **f** wife's daughter, 1
18:12 shalt not uncover the nakedness of thy **f** 1
18:12 father's sister: she *is* thy **f** near kinswoman. 1
18:14 shalt not uncover the nakedness of thy **f** 1
20:11 the man that lieth with his **f** wife hath 1
20:11 father's wife hath uncovered his **f** nakedness: 1
20:17 his **f** daughter, or his mother's daughter, 1
20:19 of thy mother's sister, nor of thy **f** sister: 1
22:13 no child, and is returned unto her **f** house, 1
22:13 as *in* her youth, she shall eat of her **f** meat: 1
Nu 2: 2 standard, with the ensign of their **f** house: 1
18: 1 thy **f** house with thee shall bear the iniquity 1
27: 7 of an inheritance among their **f** brethren; 1
27:10 shall give his inheritance unto his **f** brethren. 1
30: 3 *by* a bond, *being* in her **f** house in her youth; 1
30:16 *being yet* in her youth *in* her **f** house. 1
36:11 were married unto their **f brothers'** sons: 1730
Dt 22:21 the damsel to the door of her **f** house, 1
22:21 in Israel, to play the whore *in* her **f** house: 1
22:30 A man shall not take his **f** wife, nor discover 1
22:30 take his father's wife, nor discover his **f** skirt. 1
27:20 Cursed *be* he that lieth with his **f** wife; 1
27:20 wife; because he uncovereth his **f** skirt. 1
Jos 2:12 that ye will also shew kindness unto my **f** 1
2:18 and thy brethren, and all thy **f** household, 1
6:25 and her **f** household, and all that she had; 1
Jdg 6:15 Manasseh, and I *am* the least in my **f** house. 1
6:25 said unto him, Take thy **f** young bullock, 1
6:27 he feared his **f** household, and the men 1
9: 5 And he went unto his **f** house at Ophrah, 1
9:18 ye are risen up against my **f** house *this* day, 1
11: 2 him, Thou shalt not inherit in our **f** house; 1
11: 7 hate me, and expel me out of my **f** house? 1
14:15 lest we burn thee and thy **f** house with fire: 1
14:19 was kindled, and he went up *to* his **f** house. 1
19: 2 went away from him unto her **f** house to 1
19: 3 she brought him *into* her **f** house: and when 1
1Sa 2:31 cut off thine arm, and the arm of thy **f** house, 1
9:20 *Is it* not on thee, and on all thy **f** house? 1
17:15 returned from Saul to feed his **f** sheep *at* 1
17:25 and make his **f** house free in Israel. 1
17:34 Thy servant kept his **f** sheep, 1+3807.1
18: 2 let him go no more home *to* his **f** house. 1
18:18 and what *is* my life, *or* my **f** family in Israel, 1
22: 1 all his **f** house heard *it*, they went down 1
22:11 the son of Ahitub, and all his **f** house, 1
22:16 Ahimelech, thou, and all thy **f** house. 1
22:22 the *death* of all the persons of thy **f** house. 1
24:21 thou wilt not destroy my name out of my **f** 1
2Sa 3: 7 Wherefore hast thou gone in unto my **f** 1
3:29 on the head of Joab, and on all his **f** house; 1

2Sa 9: 7 shew thee kindness for Jonathan thy **f** sake, 1
14: 9 the iniquity *be* on me, and on my **f** house: 1
15:34 as I *have been* thy **f** servant hitherto, so *will* 1
16:19 as I have served in thy **f** presence, so will I 1
16:21 unto Absalom, Go in unto thy **f** concubines, 1
16:22 Absalom went in unto his **f** concubines in 1
19:28 For all *of* my **f** house were but dead men 1
24:17 be against me, and against my **f** house. 1
1Ki 11:12 thy days I will not do it for David thy **f** sake: 1
11:17 certain Edomites of his **f** servants with him, 1
12:10 little *finger* shall be thicker than my **f** loins. 1
18:18 and thy **f** house, in that ye have forsaken 1
2Ki 10: 3 set *him* on his **f** throne, and fight for your 1
23:30 him, and made him king in his **f** stead. 1
24:17 Mattaniah his **f brother** king in his stead, 1730
1Ch 5: 1 but, forasmuch as he defiled his **f** bed, 1
12:28 and *of* his **f** house twenty and two captains. 1
21:17 Lord my God, be on me, and on my **f** house; 1
23:11 in one reckoning, according to *their* **f** house. 1
2Ch 2:13 endued with understanding, of Huram my **f**, 1
10:10 little *finger* shall be thicker than my **f** loins. 1
21:13 also hast slain thy brethren of thy **f** house, 1
36: 1 made him king in his **f** stead in Jerusalem. 1
Ne 1: 6 both I and my **f** house have sinned. 1
Est 4:14 but thou and thy **f** house shall be destroyed: 1
Ps 45:10 forget also thine own people, and thy **f** house; 1
Pr 4: 3 For I was my **f** son, tender and 1+3807.1
6:20 keep thy **f** commandment, and forsake not 1
13: 1 A wise son *heareth his* **f** instruction: 1
15: 5 A fool despiseth his **f** instruction: but he that 1
27:10 own friend, and thy **f** friend, forsake not; 1
Isa 7:17 upon thy people, and upon thy **f** house, 1
22:23 shall be for a glorious throne to his **f** house. 1
22:24 they shall hang upon him all the glory of his **f** 1
Jer 35:14 drink none, but obey their **f** commandment: 1
Eze 18:14 that seeth all his **f** sins which he hath done, 1
22:10 thee have they discovered their **f** nakedness: 1
22:11 thee hath humbled his sister, his **f** daughter. 1
Mt 26:29 I drink it new with you in my **F** kingdom. 3962
Lk 2:49 wist ye not that I must be about my **F** 3962
9:26 and *in his* **F**, and of the holy angels. 3962
12:32 for it is your **F** good pleasure to give you 3962
15:17 How many hired *servants* of my **f** have 3962
16:27 thou wouldest send him to my **f** house: 3962
Jn 2:16 make not my **F** house a house of 3962
5:43 I am come in my **F** name, and ye receive 3962
6:39 And this is the **F** will which hath sent me, 3962
10:25 the works that I do in my **F** name, they 3962
10:29 no *man* is able to pluck *them* out of my **F** 3962
14: 2 In my **F** house are many mansions: if *it* 3962
14:24 is not mine, but the **F** which sent me. 3962
15:10 even as I have kept my **F** commandments, 3962
Ac 7:20 nourished up in his **f** house three months: 3962
1Co 5: 1 that one should have *his* **f** wife. 3962
Rev 14: 1 having his **F** name written in their 3962

FATHERLESS (43) [FATHER]

Ex 22:22 Ye shall not afflict any widow, or **f child**. 3490
22:24 shall be widows, and your children **f**. 3490
Dt 10:18 He doth execute the judgment of the **f** 3490
14:29 the stranger, and the **f**, and the widow, 3490
16:11 the stranger, and the **f**, and the widow, 3490
16:14 the stranger, and the **f**, and the widow, 3490
24:17 the judgment of the stranger, *nor* of the **f**; 3490
24:19 the stranger, for the **f**, and for the widow: 3490
24:20 the stranger, for the **f**, and for the widow. 3490
24:21 the stranger, for the **f**, and for the widow. 3490
26:12 the stranger, the **f**, and the widow, 3490
26:13 the stranger, to the **f**, and to the widow, 3490
27:19 judgment of the stranger, **f**, and widow. 3490
Job 6:27 ye overwhelm the **f**, and you dig a *pit* for 3490
22: 9 and the arms of the **f** have been broken. 3490
24: 3 drive away the ass of the **f**, they take 3490
24: 9 pluck the **f** from the breast, and take a 3490
29:12 the **f**, and *him that had* none to help him. 3490
31:17 and the **f** hath not eaten thereof; 3490
31:21 If I have lift up my hand against the **f**, 3490
Ps 10:14 unto thee; thou art the helper of the **f**. 3490
10:18 To judge the **f** and the oppressed, that 3490
68: 5 A father of the **f**, and a judge of 3490
82: 3 Defend the poor and **f**: do justice to 3490
94: 6 and the stranger, and murder the **f**. 3490
109: 9 his children be **f**, and his wife a widow. 3490
109:12 let there be any to favour his **f children**. 3490
146: 9 strangers; he relieveth the **f** and widow: 3490
Pr 23:10 and enter not into the fields of the **f**: 3490
Isa 1:17 judge the **f**, plead for the widow. 3490
1:23 judge not the **f**, neither doth the cause 3490
9:17 neither shall have mercy on their **f** and 3490
10: 2 their prey, and *that* they may rob the **f**! 3490
Jer 5:28 the cause of the **f**, yet they prosper; 3490
7: 6 the **f**, and the widow, and shed not 3490
22: 3 to the stranger, the **f**, nor the widow, 3490
49:11 Leave thy **f children**, I will preserve 3490
La 5: 3 We are orphans and **f**, our mothers *are* 1+369
Eze 22: 7 in thee have they vexed the **f** 3490
Hos 14: 3 our gods: for in thee the **f** findeth mercy. 3490
Zec 7:10 nor the **f**, the stranger, nor the poor; 3490
Mal 3: 5 the **f**, and that turn aside the stranger 3490
Jas 1:27 visit the **f** and widows in their affliction, 3737

FATHERS (538) [FATHER]

Ge 15:15 thou shalt go to thy **f** in peace; thou shalt be 1
31: 3 Return unto the land of thy **f**, and to thy 1
46:34 even until now, both we, *and* also our **f**: 1

Ge 47: 3 *are* shepherds, both we, *and* also our **f**. 1
47: 9 life of my **f** in the days of their pilgrimage. 1
48:15 before whom my **f** Abraham and Isaac did 1
48:16 and the name of my **f** Abraham and Isaac; 1
48:21 and bring you again unto the land of your **f**. 1
49:29 bury me with my **f** in the cave that *is* in 1
Ex 3:13 The God of your **f** hath sent me unto you; 1
3:15 The Lord God of your **f**, the God of 1
3:16 and say unto them, The Lord God of your **f**, 1
4: 5 may believe that the Lord God of their **f**, 1
6:25 these *are* the heads of the **f** of the Levites 1
10: 6 which neither thy **f**, nor thy fathers' fathers 1
10: 6 thy fathers, nor thy fathers' **f** have seen, 1
12: 3 according to the house of *their* **f**, a lamb for 1
13: 5 which he sware unto thy **f** to give thee, 1
13:11 as he sware unto thee and to thy **f**, 1
20: 5 the iniquity of the **f** upon the children 1
34: 7 the iniquity of the **f** upon the children, 1
Lev 25:41 unto the possession of his **f** shall he return. 1
26:39 in the iniquities of their **f** shall they pine 1
26:40 their iniquity, and the iniquity of their **f**, 1
Nu 1: 2 after their families, by the house of their **f**, 1
1: 4 every one head of the house of his **f**. 1
1:16 princes of the tribes of their **f**, heads of 1
1:18 house of their **f**, according to the number 1
1:20 after their families, by the house of their **f**, 1
1:22 after their families, by the house of their **f**, 1
1:24 after their families, by the house of their **f**, 1
1:26 after their families, by the house of their **f**, 1
1:28 after their families, by the house of their **f**, 1
1:30 after their families, by the house of their **f**, 1
1:32 after their families, by the house of their **f**, 1
1:34 after their families, by the house of their **f**, 1
1:36 after their families, by the house of their **f**, 1
1:38 after their families, by the house of their **f**, 1
1:40 after their families, by the house of their **f**, 1
1:42 after their families, by the house of their **f**, 1
1:44 each one was for the house of his **f**. 1
1:45 by the house of their **f**, from twenty years 1
1:47 the Levites after the tribe of their **f** were not 1
2:32 the children of Israel by the house of their **f**: 1
2:34 families, according to the house of their **f**. 1
3:15 the children of Levi after the house of their **f**, 1
3:20 the Levites according to the house of their **f**, 1
4: 2 after their families, by the house of their **f**, 1
4:22 throughout the houses of their **f**, by their 1
4:29 after their families, by the house of their **f**, 1
4:34 their families, and after the house of their **f**, 1
4:38 their families, by the house of their **f**, 1
4:40 by the house of their **f**, were two thousand 1
4:42 their families, by the house of their **f**, 1
4:46 their families, and after the house of their **f**, 1
7: 2 princes of Israel, heads of the house of their **f**, 1
11:12 the land which thou swarest unto their **f**? 1
13: 2 of every tribe of their **f** shall ye send a man, 1
14:18 of the **f** upon the children unto the third 1
14:23 not see the land which I sware unto their **f**, 1
17: 2 a rod according to the house of *their* **f**, 1
17: 2 according to the house of their **f** twelve rods: 1
17: 3 *shall be* for the head of the house of their **f**. 1
20:15 How our **f** went down into Egypt, and we 1
20:15 and the Egyptians vexed us, and our **f**: 1
26:55 according to the names of the tribes of their **f** 1
31:26 the priest, and the chief **f** of the congregation: 1
32: 8 Thus did your **f**, when I sent them from 1
32:28 chief of the tribes of the children of Israel: 1
33:54 according to the tribes of your **f** ye shall 1
34:14 of Reuben according to the house of their **f**, 1
34:14 of Gad according to the house of their **f**, 1
36: 1 the chief **f** of the families of the children of 1
36: 1 princes, the chief **f** of the children of Israel: 1
36: 3 be taken from the inheritance of our **f**, 1
36: 4 from the inheritance of the tribe of our **f**: 1
36: 7 to the inheritance of the tribe of his **f**. 1
36: 8 enjoy every man the inheritance of his **f**. 1
Dt 1: 8 the land which the Lord sware unto your **f**, 1
1:11 (The Lord God of your **f** make you a 1
1:21 possess *it*, as the Lord God of thy **f** hath said 1
1:35 good land, which I sware to give unto your **f**, 1
4: 1 which the Lord God of your **f** giveth you. 1
4:31 forget the covenant of thy **f** which he sware 1
4:37 because he loved thy **f**, therefore he chose 1
5: 3 The Lord made not this covenant with our **f**, 1
5: 9 visiting the iniquity of the **f** upon the children 1
6: 3 as the Lord God of thy **f** hath promised thee, 1
6:10 thee into the land which he sware unto thy **f**, 1
6:18 good land which the Lord sware unto thy **f**, 1
6:23 give us the land which he sware unto our **f**. 1
7: 8 the oath which he had sworn unto your **f**, 1
7:12 and the mercy which he sware unto thy **f**: 1
7:13 in the land which he sware unto thy **f** to give 1
8: 1 the land which the Lord sware unto your **f**. 1
8: 3 thou knewest not, neither did thy **f** know; 1
8:16 which thy **f** knew not, that he might humble 1
8:18 his covenant which he sware unto thy **f**, 1
9: 5 the word which the Lord sware unto thy **f**, 1
10:11 which I sware unto their **f** to give unto them. 1
10:15 Only the Lord had a delight in thy **f** to love 1
10:22 Thy **f** went down into Egypt with threescore 1
11: 9 which the Lord sware unto your **f** to give 1
11:21 the land which the Lord sware unto your **f** 1
12: 1 which the Lord God of thy **f** giveth thee to 1
13: 6 which thou hast not known, thou, nor thy **f**; 1
13:17 multiply thee, as he hath sworn unto thy **f**; 1

F

Dt 19: 8 as he hath sworn unto thy **f**, and give thee all 1
19: 8 land which he promised to give unto thy **f**; 1
24:16 **f** shall not be put to death for the children, 1
24:16 shall the children be put to death for the **f**: 1
26: 3 the Lord sware unto our **f** for to give us. 1
26: 7 when we cried unto the Lord God of our **f**, 1
26:15 as thou swearest unto our **f**, a land that 1
27: 3 as the Lord God of thy **f** hath promised thee. 1
28:11 in the land which the Lord sware unto thy **f** 1
28:36 a nation which neither thou nor thy **f** have 1
28:64 which neither thou nor thy **f** have known, 1
29:13 as he hath sworn unto thy **f**, to Abraham, 1
29:25 the covenant of the Lord God of their **f**, 1
30: 5 thee into the land which thy **f** possessed, 1
30: 5 do thee good, and multiply thee above thy **f**. 1
30: 9 over thee for good, as he rejoiced over thy **f**: 1
30:20 in the land which the Lord sware unto thy **f**, 1
31: 7 Lord hath sworn unto their **f** to give them; 1
31:16 Behold, thou shalt sleep with thy **f**; 1
31:20 into the land which I sware unto their **f**, 1
32:17 came newly up, whom your **f** feared not. 1
Jos 1: 6 which I sware unto their **f** to give them. 1
4: 6 when your children ask *their* **f** in time NIH
4:21 When your children shall ask their **f** in time 1
5: 6 which the Lord sware unto their **f** that he 1
14: 1 the heads of the tribes of the children 1
18: 3 which the Lord God of your **f** hath given 1
19:51 the heads of the tribes of the children 1
21: 1 came near the heads of the **f** of the Levites 1
21: 1 unto the heads of the **f** of the tribes of 1
21:43 the land which he sware to give unto their **f**; 1
21:44 according to all that he sware unto their **f**: 1
22:14 each one *was* a head of the house of their **f** 1
22:28 Your **f** dwelt on the *other* side of the flood in 1
24: 2 Your **f** dwelt on the *other* side of the flood in 1
24: 6 I brought your **f** out of Egypt: and you came 1
24: 6 Egyptians pursued after your **f** with chariots 1
24:14 put away the gods which your **f** served on 1
24:15 whether the gods which your **f** served that 1
24:17 us up and our **f** out of the land of Egypt, 1
Jdg 2: 1 you unto the land which I sware unto your **f**; 1
2:10 that generation were gathered unto their **f**, 1
2:12 And they forsook the Lord God of their **f**, 1
2:17 out of the way which their **f** walked in, 1
2:19 and corrupted *themselves* more than their **f**, 1
2:20 my covenant which I commanded their **f**, 1
2:22 to walk therein, as their **f** did keep *it*, or not. 1
3: 4 which he commanded their **f** by the hand of 1
6:13 *be* all his miracles which our **f** told us of, 1
21:22 when their **f** or their brethren come unto us 1
1Sa 12: 6 brought your **f** up out of the land of Egypt. 1
12: 7 the Lord, which he did to you and to your **f**. 1
12: 8 your **f** cried unto the Lord, then the Lord 1
12: 8 which brought forth your **f** out of Egypt, 1
12:15 be against you, as *it was* against your **f**. 1
2Sa 7:12 thou shalt sleep with thy **f**, I will set up thy 1
1Ki 1:21 when my lord the king shall sleep with his **f**, 1
2:10 So David slept with his **f**, and was buried in 1
8: 1 the chief of the **f** of the children of Israel, 1
8:21 of the Lord, which he made with our **f**, 1
8:34 unto the land which thou gavest unto their **f**. 1
8:40 live in the land which thou gavest unto our **f**. 1
8:48 which thou gavest unto their **f**, the city 1
8:53 when thou broughtest our **f** out of Egypt, 1
8:57 our God be with us, as he was with our **f**: 1
8:58 his judgments, which he commanded our **f**. 1
9: 9 who brought forth their **f** out of the land of 1
11:21 heard in Egypt that David slept with his **f**, 1
11:43 Solomon slept with his **f**, and was buried in 1
13:22 shall not come unto the sepulchre of thy **f**. 1
14:15 which he gave to their **f**, and shall scatter 1
14:20 slept with his **f**, and Nadab his son reigned 1
14:22 committed, above all that their **f** had done. 1
14:31 Rehoboam slept with his **f**, and was buried 1
14:31 was buried with his **f** in the city of David. 1
15: 8 Abijam slept with his **f**; and they buried him 1
15:12 removed all the idols that his **f** had made. 1
15:24 Asa slept with his **f**, and was buried with his 1
15:24 was buried with his **f** in the city of David his 1
16: 6 So Baasha slept with his **f**, and was buried in 1
16:28 So Omri slept with his **f**, and was buried in 1
19: 4 away my life; for I *am* not better than my **f**. 1
21: 3 I should give the inheritance of my **f** unto 1
21: 4 I will not give the inheritance of my **f**. 1
22:40 Ahab slept with his **f**; and Ahaziah his son 1
22:50 Jehoshaphat slept with his **f**, and was buried 1
22:50 was buried with his **f** in the city of David his 1
2Ki 8:24 Joram slept with his **f**, and was buried with 1
8:24 was buried with his **f** in the city of David: 1
9:28 buried him in his sepulchre with his **f** 1
10:35 Jehu slept with his **f**: and they buried him in 1
12:18 Jehoram, and Ahaziah, kings of Judah, 1
12:21 buried him with his **f** in the city of David: 1
13: 9 Jehoahaz slept with his **f**; and they buried 1
13:13 Joash slept with his **f**; and Jeroboam sat upon 1
14: 6 shall not be put to death for the children, 1
14: 6 nor the children be put to death for the **f**; 1
14:16 Jehoash slept with his **f**, and was buried in 1
14:20 buried at Jerusalem with his **f** in the city 1
14:22 to Judah, after that the king slept with his **f**. 1
14:29 Jeroboam slept with his **f**, *even* with the 1
15: 7 So Azariah slept with his **f**; and they buried 1
15: 7 buried him with his **f** in the city of David: 1
15: 9 in the sight of the Lord, as his **f** had done: 1
15:22 Menahem slept with his **f**; and Pekahiah his 1

2Ki 15:38 Jotham slept with his **f**, and was buried with 1
15:38 was buried with his **f** in the city of David his 1
16:20 Ahaz slept with his **f**, and was buried with 1
16:20 was buried with his **f** in the city of David: 1
17:13 to all the law which I commanded your **f**, 1
17:14 their necks, like to the neck of their **f**, 1
17:15 and his covenant that he made with their **f**, 1
17:41 as did their **f**, *so* do they unto this day. 1
19:12 delivered them which my **f** have destroyed; 1
20:17 which thy **f** have laid up in store unto this 1
20:21 Hezekiah slept with his **f**: and Manasseh his 1
21: 8 more out of the land which I gave their **f**; 1
21:15 since the day their **f** came forth out of Egypt, 1
21:18 Manasseh slept with his **f**, and was buried in 1
21:22 And he forsook the Lord God of his **f**, 1
22:13 our **f** have not hearkened unto the words of 1
22:20 I will gather thee unto thy **f**, and thou shalt 1
23:32 according to all that his **f** had done. 1
23:37 according to all that his **f** had done. 1
24: 6 So Jehoiakim slept with his **f**: 1
1Ch 4:38 and the house of their **f** increased greatly. 1
5:13 their brethren of the house of their **f** were, 1
5:15 the son of Guni, chief of the house of their **f**. 1
5:24 these *were* the heads of the house of their **f**, 1
5:24 men, *and* heads of the house of their **f**. 1
5:25 they transgressed against the God of their **f**, 1
6:19 families of the Levites according to their **f**. 1
7: 4 their generations, after the house of their **f**, 1
7: 7 heads of the house of *their* **f**, mighty *men* of 1
7: 9 heads of the house of their **f**, mighty *men* of 1
7:11 by the heads of *their* **f**, mighty *men* of valour, 1
8: 6 these *are* the heads of the **f** of the inhabitants 1
8:10 These *were* his sons, heads of the **f**. 1
8:13 who *were* heads of the **f** of the inhabitants of 1
8:28 *were* heads of the **f**, by their generations, 1
9: 9 All these men *were* chief of the **f** in the 1
9: 9 chief of the fathers in the house of their **f**. 1
9:13 heads of the house of their **f**, a thousand and 1
9:19 and their **f**, *being* over the host of the Lord, 1
9:33 *are* the singers, chief of the **f** of the Levites, 1
9:34 These chief **f** of the Levites *were* chief 1
12:17 the God of our **f** look *thereon*, and rebuke *it*. 1
12:30 famous throughout the house of their **f**. 1
15:12 Ye *are* the chief of the **f** of the Levites: 1
17:11 expired that *thou* must go *to be* with thy **f**, 1
23: 9 These *were* the chief of the **f** of Laadan. 1
23:24 the sons of Levi after the house of their **f**, 1
23:24 the chief of the **f**, as they were counted by 1
24: 4 sixteen chief *men* of the house of *their* **f**, 1
24: 4 of Ithamar according to the house of their **f**. 1
24: 6 *before* the chief of the **f** of the priests and 1
24:30 sons of the Levites after the house of their **f**. 1
24:31 the chief of the **f** of the priests and Levites, 1
24:31 the principal **f** over against their younger 1
26:13 to the house of their **f**, for every gate. 1
26:21 chief **f**, *even* of Laadan the Gershonite, 1
26:26 the chief **f**, the captains over thousands and 1
26:31 according to the generations of his **f**. 1
26:32 two thousand and seven hundred chief **f**, 1
27: 1 *to wit*, the chief **f** and captains of thousands 1
29: 6 the chief of the **f** and princes of the tribes of 1
29:15 before thee, and sojourners, as *were* all our **f**: 1
29:18 God of Abraham, Isaac, and of Israel, our **f**, 1
29:20 blessed the Lord God of their **f**, 1
2Ch 1: 2 every governor in all Israel, the chief of the **f**. 1
5: 2 the chief of the **f** of the children of Israel, 1
6:25 which thou gavest to them and to their **f**. 1
6:31 in the land which thou gavest unto our **f**. 1
6:38 which thou gavest unto their **f**, and *toward* 1
7:22 they forsook the Lord God of their **f**, 1
9:31 Solomon slept with his **f**, and he was buried 1
11:16 to sacrifice unto the Lord God of their **f**, 1
12:16 Rehoboam slept with his **f**, and was buried 1
13:12 fight ye not against the Lord God of your **f**; 1
13:18 they relied upon the Lord God of their **f**. 1
14: 1 Abijah slept with his **f**, and they buried him 1
14: 4 Judah to seek the Lord God of their **f**, 1
15:12 the Lord God of their **f** with all their heart 1
16:13 And Asa slept with his **f**, and died in the one 1
17:14 of them according to the house of their **f**: 1
19: 4 them back unto the Lord God of their **f**. 1
19: 8 the priests, and of the chief of the **f** of Israel, 1
20: 6 said, O Lord God of our **f**, *art* not thou God 1
20:33 prepared their hearts unto the God of their **f**. 1
21: 1 Now Jehoshaphat slept with his **f**, 1
21: 1 was buried with his **f** in the city of David. 1
21:10 he had forsaken the Lord God of his **f**. 1
21:19 no burning for him, like the burning of his **f**. 1
23: 2 the chief of Israel, and they came to 1
24:18 left the house of the Lord God of their **f**, 1
24:24 they had forsaken the Lord God of their **f**. 1
25: 4 saying, The **f** shall not die for the children, 1
25: 4 neither shall the children die for the **f**, 1
25: 5 according to the houses of *their* **f**, 1
25:28 buried him with his **f** in the city of Judah. 1
26: 2 to Judah, after that the king slept with his **f**. 1
26:12 The whole number of the chief of the **f** of 1
26:23 Uzziah slept with his **f**, and they buried him 1
26:23 they buried him with his **f** in the field of 1
27: 9 Jotham slept with his **f**, and they buried him 1
28: 6 they had forsaken the Lord God of their **f**. 1
28: 9 the Lord God of your **f** was wroth with 1
28:25 provoked to anger the Lord God of his **f**. 1
28:27 Ahaz slept with his **f**, and they buried him in 1
29: 5 the house of the Lord God of your **f**, 1

2Ch 29: 6 For our **f** have trespassed, and done *that* 1
29: 9 our **f** have fallen by the sword, and our sons 1
30: 7 be not ye like your **f**, and like your brethren, 1
30: 7 trespassed against the Lord God of their **f**, 1
30: 8 as your **f** *were*, *but* yield yourselves unto 1
30:19 his heart to seek God, the Lord God of his **f**, 1
30:22 confession to the Lord God of their **f**. 1
31:17 of the priests by the house of their **f**, 1
32:13 my **f** have done unto all the people of *other* 1
32:14 of those nations that my **f** utterly destroyed, 1
32:15 of mine hand, and out of the hand of my **f**: 1
32:33 Hezekiah slept with his **f**, and they buried 1
33: 8 of the land which I have appointed for your **f**; 1
33:12 himself greatly before the God of his **f**, 1
33:20 Manasseh slept with his **f**, and they buried 1
34:21 our **f** have not kept the word of the Lord, 1
34:28 I will gather thee to thy **f**, and thou shalt be 1
34:32 to the covenant of God, the God of their **f**. 1
34:33 from following the Lord, the God of their **f**. 1
35: 4 prepare *yourselves* by the houses of your **f**, 1
35: 5 families of the **f** of your brethren the people, 1
35:24 was buried in *one of* the sepulchres of his **f**. 1
36:15 the Lord God of their **f** sent to them by his 1
Ezr 1: 5 rose up the chief of the **f** of Judah and 1
2:68 *some* of the chief of the **f**, when they came to 1
3:12 of the priests and Levites and chief of the **f**, 1
4: 2 and to the chief of the **f**, and said unto them, 1
4: 3 and the rest of the chief of the **f** of Israel, 1
4:15 be made in the book of the records of thy **f**: 2
5:12 that our **f** had provoked the God of heaven 2
7:27 Blessed *be* the Lord God of our **f**, 1
8: 1 These *are* now the chief of their **f**, and *this is* 1
8:28 offering unto the Lord God of your **f**. 1
8:29 and the Levites, and chief of the **f** of Israel, 1
9: 7 Since the days of our **f** *have* we *been* in a 1
10:11 confession unto the Lord God of your **f**, 1
10:16 Ezra the priest, *with* certain chief of the **f**, 1
10:16 after the house of their **f**, and all of them by 1
Ne 7:70 some of the chief of the **f** gave unto the work. 1
7:71 of the chief of the **f** gave to the treasure 1
8:13 together the chief of the **f** of all the people, 1
9: 2 their sins, and the iniquities of their **f**. 1
9: 9 And didst see the affliction of our **f** in Egypt, 1
9:16 they and our **f** dealt proudly, and hardened 1
9:23 which thou hadst promised to their **f**, 1
9:32 and on our **f**, and on all thy people, 1
9:34 princes, our priests, nor our **f**, kept thy law, 1
9:36 the land that thou gavest unto our **f** to eat 1
10:34 after the houses of our **f**, at times appointed 1
11:13 his brethren, chief of the **f**, two hundred forty 1
12:12 of Joiakim were priests, the chief of the **f**: 1
12:22 and Jaddua, *were* recorded chief of the **f**, 1
12:23 The sons of Levi, the chief of the **f**, 1
13:18 Did not your **f** thus, and *did not* our God 1
Job 8: 8 and prepare *thyself* to the search of their **f**, 1
15:18 Which wise *men* have told from their **f**, 1
30: 1 whose **f** I would have disdained to have set 1
Ps 22: 4 Our **f** trusted in thee: they trusted, 1
39:12 with thee, *and* a sojourner, as all my **f** *were*. 1
44: 1 with our ears, O God, our **f** have told us, 1
45:16 Instead of thy **f** shall be thy children, 1
49:19 He shall go to the generation of his **f**; they 1
78: 3 heard and known, and our **f** have told us. 1
78: 5 a law in Israel, which he commanded our **f**, 1
78: 8 might not be as their **f**, a stubborn and 1
78:12 things did he in the sight of their **f**, 1
78:57 *back*, and dealt unfaithfully like their **f**: 1
95: 9 When your **f** tempted me, proved me, 1
106: 6 We have sinned with our **f**, we have 1
106: 7 Our **f** understood not thy wonders in Egypt; 1
109:14 Let the iniquity of his **f** be remembered with 1
Pr 17: 6 old men; and the glory of children *are* their **f**. 1
19:14 House and riches *are* the inheritance of **f**: 1
22:28 the ancient landmark, which thy **f** have set. 1
Isa 14:21 for his children for the iniquity of their **f**; 1
37:12 delivered them which my **f** have destroyed, 1
39: 6 which thy **f** have laid up in store until this 1
49:23 kings shall be thy **nursing f**, 539
64:11 beautiful house, where our **f** praised thee, 1
65: 7 and the iniquities of your **f** together, 1
Jer 2: 5 What iniquity have your **f** found in me, 1
3:18 I have given for an inheritance unto your **f**. 1
3:24 shame hath devoured the labour of our **f** 1
3:25 we and our **f**, from our youth even unto this 1
6:21 the **f** and the sons together shall fall upon 1
7: 7 in the land that I gave to your **f**, for ever and 1
7:14 the place which I gave to you and to your **f**, 1
7:18 the **f** kindle the fire, and the women knead 1
7:22 For I spake not unto your **f**, nor commanded 1
7:25 Since the day that your **f** came forth out of 1
7:26 their neck: they did worse than their **f**. 1
9:14 and after Baalim, which their **f** taught them: 1
9:16 whom neither they nor their **f** have known: 1
11: 4 Which I commanded your **f** in the day that I 1
11: 5 the oath which I have sworn unto your **f**, 1
11: 7 I earnestly protested unto your **f** in the day 1
11:10 my covenant which I made with their **f**. 1
13:14 even the **f** and the sons together, saith 1
14:20 our wickedness, *and* the iniquity of our **f**: 1
16: 3 their **f** that begat them in this land; 1
16:11 Because your **f** have forsaken me, saith 1
16:12 ye have done worse than your **f**; for behold, 1
16:13 land that ye know not, *neither* ye nor your **f**; 1
16:15 again into their land that I gave unto their **f**. 1
16:19 Surely our **f** have inherited lies, vanity, 1

Jer	17:22 ye the sabbath day, as I commanded your f.	1
	19: 4 whom neither they nor their f have known,	1
	23:27 as their f have forgotten my name for Baal.	1
	23:39 the city that I gave you and your f, *and cast*	1
	24:10 the land that I gave unto them and to their f.	1
	25: 5 unto you and to your f for ever and ever:	1
	30: 3 to return to the land that I gave to their f,	1
	31:29 The f have eaten a sour grape,	1
	31:32 their f in the day *that* I took them by the	1
	32:18 recompensest the iniquity of the f into	1
	32:22 thou didst swear to their f to give them,	1
	34: 5 with the burnings of thy f, the former kings	1
	34:13 I made a covenant with your f in the day	1
	34:14 your f hearkened not unto me, neither	1
	35:15 land which I have given to you and to your f:	1
	44: 3 they knew not, *neither* they, you, nor your f.	1
	44: 9 Have ye forgotten the wickedness of your f,	1
	44:10 that I set before you and before your f.	1
	44:17 we, and our f, our kings, and our princes,	1
	44:21 ye, and your f, your kings, and our princes,	1
	47: 3 the f shall not look back to *their* children for	1
	50: 7 of justice, even the LORD, the hope of their f.	1
La	5: 7 Our f have sinned, *and are* not; *and* we	1
Eze	2: 3 and their f have transgressed against me,	1
	5:10 the f shall eat the sons in the midst	1
	5:10 midst of thee, and the sons shall eat their f;	1
	18: 2 The f have eaten sour grapes,	1
	20: 4 them to know the abominations of their f:	1
	20:18 Walk ye not in the statutes of your f,	1
	20:27 Yet *in* this your f have blasphemed me, in	1
	20:30 Are ye polluted after the manner of your f?	1
	20:36 as I pleaded with your f in the wilderness	1
	20:42 I lifted up mine hand to give it to your f.	1
	36:28 shall dwell in the land that I gave to your f;	1
	37:25 my servant, wherein your f have dwelt;	1
	47:14 I lifted up mine hand to give it unto your f:	1
Da	2:23 and praise thee, O thou God of my f,	2
	9: 6 and our f, and to all the people of the land.	1
	9: 8 to our f, because we have sinned against	1
	9:16 and for the iniquities of our f, Jerusalem and	1
	11:24 he shall do *that* which his f have not done,	1
	11:24 his fathers have not done, nor his fathers' f;	1
	11:37 Neither shall he regard the God of his f,	1
	11:38 a god whom his f knew not shall he honour	1
Hos	9:10 I saw your f as the firstripe in the fig tree at	1
Joel	1: 2 in your days, or even in the days of your f?	1
Am	2: 4 to err, after the which their f have walked:	1
Mic	7:20 thou hast sworn unto our f from the days	1
Zec	1: 2 LORD hath been sore displeased with your f.	1
	1: 4 Be ye not as your f, unto whom the former	1
	1: 5 Your f, where *are* they? and the prophets,	1
	1: 6 prophets, did they not take hold of your f?	1
	8:14 when your f provoked me to wrath, saith	1
Mal	2:10 brother, by profaning the covenant of our f?	1
	3: 7 from the days of your f ye are gone away	1
	4: 6 shall turn the heart of the f to the children,	1
	4: 6 heart of the children to their f, lest I come	1
Mt	23:30 If we had been in the days of our f,	3962
	23:32 Fill ye up then the measure of your f.	3962
Lk	1:17 to turn the hearts of the f to the children,	3962
	1:55 (As he spake to our f), to Abraham,	3962
	1:72 To perform the mercy *promised* to our f,	3962
	6:23 for in the like manner did their f unto	3962
	6:26 for so did their f to the false prophets.	3962
	11:47 of the prophets, and your f killed them.	3962
	11:48 witness that ye allow the deeds of your f:	3962
Jn	4:20 Our f worshipped in this mountain;	3962
	6:31 Our f did eat manna in the desert; as it is	3962
	6:49 Your f did eat manna in the wilderness,	3962
	6:58 not as your f did eat manna, and are dead:	3962
	7:22 not because it is of Moses, but of the f;	3962
Ac	3:13 of Isaac, and of Jacob, the God of our f,	3962
	3:22 Moses truly said unto the f, A prophet	3962
	3:25 covenant which God made with our f,	3962
	5:30 The God of our f raised up Jesus, whom	3962
	7: 2 he said, Men, brethren, and f, hearken;	3962
	7:11 and our f found no sustenance.	3962
	7:12 was corn in Egypt, he sent out our f first.	3962
	7:15 down into Egypt, and died, he, and our f,	3962
	7:19 and evil entreated our f, so that *they* cast	3962
	7:32 *Saying*, I *am* the God of thy f, the God of	3962
	7:38 to him in the mount Sina, and *with* our f:	3962
	7:39 To whom our f would not obey,	3962
	7:44 Our f had the tabernacle of Witness in	3962
	7:45 also our f that came after brought in	3962
	7:45 God drave out before the face of our f,	3962
	7:51 the Holy Ghost: as your f *did*, so *do* ye.	3962
	7:52 Which of the prophets have not your f	3962
	13:17 God of this people of Israel chose our f,	3962
	13:32 the promise which was made unto the f,	3962
	13:36 was laid unto his f, and saw corruption:	3962
	15:10 which neither our f nor we were able to	3962
	22: 1 Men, brethren, and f, hear ye my defence	3962
	22: 3 to the perfect manner of the law of the f,	3971
	22:14 said, The God of our f hath chosen thee,	3962
	24:14 call heresy, so worship I the God of my f,	3971
	26: 6 of the promise made of God unto our f:	3962
	28:17 against the people, or customs of our f,	3971
	28:25 Ghost by Esaias the prophet unto our f,	3962
Ro	9: 5 Whose *are* the f, and of whom as	3962
	15: 8 to confirm the promises made unto the f:	3962
1Co	4:15 in Christ, yet *have* ye not many f:	3962
	10: 1 how that all our f were under the cloud,	3962
Gal	1:14 zealous of the traditions of my f.	3967
Eph	6: 4 And, ye f, provoke not your children to	3962

Col	3:21 F, provoke not your children *to* anger,	3962
1Ti	1: 9 for **murderers of** f and murderers of	3964
Heb	1: 1 in time past unto the f by the prophets,	3962
	3: 9 When your f tempted me, proved me,	3962
	8: 9 f in the day when I took them by the	3962
	12: 9 Furthermore we have had f of our flesh	3962
1Pe	1:18 **received by tradition from** your f;	3970
2Pe	3: 4 for since the f fell asleep, all *things*	3962
1Jn	2:13 f, because ye have known him that is	3962
	2:14 f, because ye have known him that is	3962

FATHERS' (14) [FATHER]

Ex	6:14 These *be* the heads of their f houses:	1
	10: 6 thy fathers, nor thy f fathers have seen,	1
Nu	17: 6 according to their f houses, *even* twelve	1
	26: 2 old and upward, throughout their f house,	1
	32:14 behold, ye are risen up in your f stead,	1
1Ch	7: 2 Jibsam, and Shemuel, heads of their f house,	1
	7:40 heads of their f house, choice *and* mighty	1
Ezr	2:59 they could not shew their f house,	1
Ne	2: 3 the place of my f sepulchres, *lieth* waste,	1
	2: 5 unto the city of my f sepulchres, that I may	1
	7:61 they could not shew their f house, nor their	1
Eze	20:24 and their eyes were after their f idols.	1
Da	11:24 his fathers have not done, nor his f fathers;	1
Ro	11: they *are* beloved for the f sakes.	3962

FATHOMS (2)

Ac	27:28 And sounded, and found *it* twenty f:	3712
	27:28 they sounded again, and found *it* fifteen f.	3712

FATLING (1) [FAT]

Isa	11: 6 and the young lion and the f together;	4806

FATLINGS (5) [FAT]

1Sa	15: 9 of the f, and the lambs, and all *that was*	4932
2Sa	6:13 gone six paces, he sacrificed oxen and f.	4806
Ps	66:15 I will offer unto thee burnt sacrifices of f,	4220
Eze	39:18 of bullocks, all of them f of Bashan.	4806
Mt	22: 4 my oxen and *my* f are killed, and all	4619

FATNESS (17) [FAT]

Ge	27:28 f of the earth, and plenty of corn and	4924
	27:39 thy dwelling shall be the f of the earth,	4924
Dt	32:15 thou art covered *with* f; then he forsook	NIH
Jdg	9: 9 tree said unto them, Should I leave my f,	1880
Job	15:27 Because he covereth his face with his f,	2459
	36:16 be set on thy table *should be* full *of* f.	1880
Ps	36: 8 satisfied with the f of thy house;	1880
	63: 5 shall be satisfied as *with* marrow and f;	1880
	65:11 with thy goodness; and thy paths drop f.	1880
	73: 7 Their eyes stand out with f: they have	2459
	109:24 through fasting; and my flesh faileth of f.	8081
Isa	17: 4 and the f of his flesh shall wax lean.	4924
	34: 6 it is made fat with f, *and* with the blood	2459
	34: 7 blood, and their dust made fat with f.	2459
	55: 2 good, and let your soul delight itself in f.	1880
Jer	31:14 I will satiate the soul of the priests with f,	1880
Ro	11:17 partakest of the root and f of the olive tree	4096

FATS (2) [FAT]

Joel	2:24 the f shall overflow *with* wine and oil.	3342
	3:13 for the press is full, the f overflow;	3342

FATTED (4) [FAT]

1Ki	4:23 and roebucks, and fallowdeer, and f fowl.	75
Jer	46:21 *are* in the midst of her like f bullocks;	4770
Lk	15:23 And bring hither the f calf, and kill *it;*	4618
	15:27 and thy father hath killed the f calf,	4618
	15:30 thou hast killed for him the f calf.	4618

FATTER (1) [FAT]

Da	1:15 f in flesh than all the children which did	1277

FATTEST (2) [FAT]

Ps	78:31 slew the f of them, and smote down	4924
Da	11:24 even upon the f **places** of the province;	4924

FAULT (19) [FAULTLESS, FAULTS, FAULTY]

Ex	5:16 beaten; but the f is in thine own people.	2398
Dt	25: 2 according to his f, by a *certain* number.	7564
1Sa	29: 3 I have found no f in him since he fell	NIH
2Sa	3: 8 that thou chargest me to day with a f	5771
Ps	59: 4 and prepare themselves without *my* f:	5771
Da	6: 4 they could find none occasion nor f;	7844
	6: 4 was there any error or f found in him.	7844
Mt	18:15 go and tell him his f between thee and	1651
Mk	7: 2 with unwashen, hands, they **found** f.	3201
Lk	23: 4 and *to* the people, I find no f in this man.	158
	23:14 found no f in this man *touching those*	158
Jn	18:38 saith unto them, I find in him no f *at all.*	156
	19: 4 that ye may know that I find no f in him.	156
	19: 6 and crucify *him:* for I find no f in him.	156
Ro	9:19 then unto me, Why doth he yet **find** f?	3201
1Co	6: 7 therefore there is utterly a f among you,	2275
Gal	6: 1 Brethren, if a man be overtaken in a f,	3900
Heb	8: 8 For **finding** f with them, he saith, Behold,	3201
Rev	14: 5 for they are **without** f before the throne of	299

FAULTLESS (2) [FAULT]

Heb	8: 7 For if that first *covenant* had been f, *then*	273
Jude	1:24 to present *you* faultless before the presence of his	299

FAULTS (4) [FAULT]

Ge	41: 9 I do remember my f *this* day:	2399
Ps	19:12 *his* errors? cleanse thou me from secret f.	NIH

Jas	5:16 Confess *your* f one to another, and pray	3900
1Pe	2:20 is it, if, when ye be buffeted for your f,	264

FAULTY (2) [FAULT]

2Sa	14:13 doth speak this thing as one **which is** f,	818
Hos	10: 2 is divided; now shall they be **found** f:	816

FAVORITISM See RESPECTER

FAVOUR (70) [FAVOURABLE, FAVOURED, FAVOUREDNESS, FAVOUREST, FAVOURETH, WELLFAVOURED]

Ge	18: 3 Lord, if now I have found f in thy sight,	2580
	30:27 pray thee, if I have found f in thine eyes,	2580
	39:21 gave him f in the sight of the keeper of	2580
Ex	3:21 I will give this people f in the sight of	2580
	11: 3 the LORD gave the people f in the sight of	2580
	12:36 the LORD gave the people f in the sight of	2580
Nu	11:11 wherefore have I not found f in thy sight,	2580
	11:15 out of hand, if I have found f in thy sight;	2580
Dt	24: 1 it come to pass that she find no f in his	2580
	28:50 of the old, nor **shew** f to the young:	2603
	33:23 satisfied with f, and full *with* the blessing	7522
Jos	11:20 that they might have no f, but that *he*	8467
Ru	2:13 Let me find f in thy sight, my lord;	2580
1Sa	2:26 was **in** f both with the LORD,	2896
	16:22 for he hath found f in my sight.	2580
	20:29 and now, if I have found f in thine eyes,	2580
	25: 8 Wherefore let the young men find f in	2580
	29: 6 the lords of thee not.	2896+5869+871.1
2Sa	15:25 if I shall find f in the eyes of the LORD,	2580
1Ki	11:19 found great f in the sight of Pharaoh,	2580
Ne	2: 5 if thy servant have **found** f in thy sight,	3190
Est	2:15 Esther obtained f in the sight of all them	2580
	2:17 in his sight more than all the virgins;	2617
	5: 2 the court, *that* she obtained f in his sight:	2580
	5: 8 If I have found f in the sight of the king,	2580
	7: 3 and said, If I have found f in thy sight,	2580
	8: 5 if I have found f in his sight, and the	2580
Job	10:12 Thou hast granted me life and f,	2617
Ps	5:12 *with* f wilt thou compass him as *with* a	7522
	30: 5 *but* a moment; in his f *is* life:	7522
	30: 7 by thy f thou hast made my mountain to	7522
	35:27 and be glad, that f my righteous cause:	2655
	44: 3 because thou **hadst** a f unto them.	7521
	45:12 the people shall **intreat** thy f.	2470+6440
	89:17 and in thy f our horn shall be exalted.	7522
	102:13 for the time to f her, yea, the set time,	2603
	102:14 in her stones, and f the dust thereof.	2603
	106: 4 the f *that thou bearest* unto thy people:	7522
	109:12 neither let there be any to f his fatherless	2603
	112: 5 A good man **sheweth** f, and lendeth:	2603
	119:58 I intreated thy f with *my* whole heart:	6440
Pr	3: 4 shalt thou find f and good understanding	2580
	8:35 and shall obtain f of the LORD.	7522
	11:27 that diligently seeketh good procureth f:	7522
	12: 2 A good *man* obtaineth f of the LORD:	7522
	13:15 Good understanding giveth f: but the way	2580
	14: 9 at sin: but among the righteous *there is* f.	7522
	14:35 The king's f *is* toward a wise servant:	7522
	16:15 and his f *is* as a cloud of the latter rain.	7522
	18:22 good *thing*, and obtaineth f of the LORD.	7522
	19: 6 Many will intreat the f of the prince:	6440
	19:12 a lion; but his f *is* as dew upon the grass.	7522
	21:10 his neighbour **findeth** no f in his eyes.	2603
	22: 1 *and* loving f rather than silver and gold.	2580
	28:23 afterwards shall find more f than he that	2580
	29:26 Many seek the ruler's f; but *every* man's	6440
	31:30 F is deceitful, and beauty *is* vain:	2580
Ecc	9:11 of understanding, nor yet f to men of skill;	2580
SS	8:10 then was I in his eyes as one that found f.	7965
Isa	26:10 Let **be shewed** to the wicked, *yet* will	2603
	27:11 that formed them will **shew** them no f.	2603
	60:10 but in my f have I had mercy on thee.	7522
Jer	16:13 and night; where I will not shew you f.	2594
Da	1: 9 Now God had brought Daniel into f and	2617
Lk	1:30 Mary: for thou hast found f with God.	5485
	2:52 and stature, and in f with God and man.	5485
Ac	2:47 and having f with all the people.	5485
	7:10 gave him f and wisdom in the sight of	5485
	7:46 Who found f before God, and desired to	5485
	25: 3 And desired f against him, that he would	5485

FAVOURABLE (4) [FAVOUR]

Jdg	21:22 unto them, Be f unto them for our sakes:	2603
Job	33:26 pray unto God, and he will be f unto him:	7521
Ps	77: 7 off for ever? and will he be f no more?	7521
	85: 1 LORD, thou hast been f unto thy land:	7521

FAVOURED (14) [FAVOUR]

Ge	29:17 but Rachel was beautiful and well f.	4758
	39: 6 Joseph was a goodly *person*, and well f.	4758
	41: 2 came up out of the river seven well f	4758
	41: 3 out of the river, ill f and leanfleshed,	4758
	41: 4 the ill f and leanfleshed kine did eat up	4758
	41: 4 kine did eat up the seven well f	4758
	41:18 river seven kine, fatfleshed and well f;	8389
	41:19 poor and very ill f and leanfleshed,	8389
	41:20 the ill f kine did eat up the first seven fat	7451
	41:21 they *were* still ill f, as at the beginning.	4758
	41:27 ill f kine that came up after them *are*	7451
La	4:16 of the priests, they f not the elders.	2603
Da	1: 4 well f, and skilful in all wisdom,	4758
Lk	1:28 and said, Hail, *thou that art* **highly** f,	5487

F

FAVOUREDNESS (1) [FAVOUR]

Dt 17: 1 wherein is blemish, *or* any **evil f**: 1697+7451

FAVOUREST (1) [FAVOUR]

Ps 41:11 By this I know that thou **f** me, because 2654

FAVOURETH (1) [FAVOUR]

2Sa 20:11 He that **f** Joab, and he that *is* for David, 2654

FEAR (400) [AFRAID, FEARED, FEAREST, FEARETH, FEARFUL, FEARFULLY, FEARFULNESS, FEARING, FEARS]

Ge 9: 2 the **f** of you and the dread of you shall be 4172
15: 1 Abram in a vision, saying, **F** not, Abram: 3372
20:11 Surely the **f** of God *is* not in this place; 3374
21:17 **f** not; for God hath heard the voice of 3372
26:24 **f** not, for I *am* with thee, and will bless 3372
31:42 and the **f** of Isaac, had been with me, 6343
31:53 Jacob sware by the **f** of his father Isaac. 6343
32:11 for I **f** him, lest he will come and smite 3372
35:17 that the midwife said unto her, **F** not; 3372
42:18 third day, This do, and live; *for* I **f** God: 3372
43:23 he said, Peace *be* to you, **f** not: your God, 3372
46: 3 **f** not to go down into Egypt; for I will 3372
50:19 Joseph said unto them, **F** not: for *am* I in 3372
50:21 Now therefore ye **f** not: I will nourish you 3372
Ex 9:30 I know that ye will not yet **f** the LORD 3372
14:13 **F** ye not, stand still, and see the salvation 3372
15:16 **F** and dread shall fall upon them; 367
18:21 such as **f** God, men of truth, 3373
20:20 Moses said unto the people, **F** not: for 3372
20:20 that his **f** may be before your faces, that ye 3374
23:27 send my **f** before thee, and will destroy 367
Lev 19: 3 Ye shall **f** every man his mother, 3372
19:14 before the blind, but shalt **f** thy God: 3372
19:32 the face of the old man, and **f** thy God: 3372
25:17 one another; but thou shalt **f** thy God: 3372
25:36 **f** thy God; that thy brother may live with 3372
25:43 over him with rigour; but shalt **f** thy God. 3372
Nu 14: 9 neither **f** ye the people of the land; 3372
14: 9 and the LORD *is* with us: **f** them not. 3372
21:34 the LORD said unto Moses, **F** him not: 3372
Dt 1:21 unto thee; **f** not, neither be discouraged. 3372
2:25 the **f** of thee upon the nations *that are* 3374
3: 2 the LORD said unto me, **F** him not: for I 3372
3:22 Ye shall not **f** them: for the LORD your 3372
4:10 they may learn to **f** me all the days that 3372
5:29 that they would **f** me, and keep all my 3372
6: 2 That thou mightest **f** the LORD thy God, 3372
6:13 Thou shalt **f** the LORD thy God, 3372
6:24 to **f** the LORD our God, for our good 3372
8: 6 God, to walk in his ways, and to **f** him. 3372
10:12 to **f** the LORD thy God, to walk in all his 3372
10:20 Thou shalt **f** the LORD thy God; him shalt 3372
11:25 *for* the LORD your God shall lay the **f** of 6343
13: 4 **f** him, and keep his commandments, 3372
13:11 **f**, and shall do no more any such 3372
14:23 that thou mayest learn to **f** the LORD thy 3372
17:13 and **f**, and do no more presumptuously. 3372
17:19 that he may learn to **f** the LORD his God, 3372
19:20 **f**, and shall henceforth commit no more 3372
20: 3 **f** not, and do not tremble, neither be ye 3372
21:21 you; and all Israel shall hear, and **f**. 3372
28:58 *thou* mayest **f** this glorious and fearful 3372
28:66 thou shalt **f** day and night, and shalt have 6342
28:67 for the **f** of thine heart wherewith thou 6343
28:67 fear of thine heart wherewith thou shalt **f**, 6342
31: 6 Be strong and of a good courage, **f** not, 3372
31: 8 forsake thee: **f** not, neither be dismayed. 3372
31:12 The LORD your God, and observe to do 3372
31:13 and learn to **f** the LORD your God, 3372
Jos 4:24 that ye might **f** the LORD your God for 3372
8: 1 **F** not, neither be thou dismayed: 3372
10: 8 the LORD said unto Joshua, **F** them not: 3372
10:25 **F** not, nor be dismayed, be strong and 3372
22:24 if we have not *rather* done it for **f** of *this* 1674
24:14 Now therefore **f** the LORD, and serve him 3372
Jdg 4:18 Turn in, my lord, turn in to me; **f** not. 3372
6:10 **f** not the gods of the Amorites, in whose 3372
6:23 said unto him, Peace *be* unto thee; **f** not: 3372
7:10 if thou **f** to go down, go thou with Phurah 3372
9:21 for **f** of Abimelech his brother. 4480+6440
Ru 3:11 now, my daughter, **f** not; I will do to thee 3372
1Sa 4:20 that stood by her said *unto her*, **F** not; 3372
11: 7 the **f** of the LORD fell on the people, 6343
12:14 If ye will **f** the LORD, and serve him, 3372
12:20 Samuel said unto the people, **F** not: 3372
12:24 Only **f** the LORD, and serve him in truth 3372
21:10 fled that day for **f** of Saul, and went to 6440
22:23 Abide thou with me, **f** not: for he that 3372
23:17 he said unto him, **F** not: for the hand of 3372
23:26 made haste to get away for **f** of Saul; 6440
2Sa 9: 7 David said unto him, **F** not: for I will 3372
13:28 Smite Amnon; then kill him; **f** not: 3372
23: 3 men *must be* just, ruling *in the* **f** of God. 3374
1Ki 8:40 That they may **f** thee all the days that 3372
8:43 name, to **f** thee, as *do* thy people Israel; 3372
17:13 Elijah said unto her, **F** not; go *and* do as 3372
18:12 *I* thy servant **f** the LORD from my youth. 3372
2Ki 4: 1 thou knowest thy servant did **f** 3373
6:16 answered, **F** not: for *they* that *be* with us 3372
17:28 taught them how they should **f** the LORD, 3372
17:34 they **f** not the LORD, neither do they after 3373
17:35 saying, Ye shall not **f** other gods, 3372
17:36 him shall ye **f**, and him shall ye worship, 3372

2Ki 17:37 evermore; and ye shall not **f** other gods, 3372
17:38 not forget; neither shall ye **f** other gods. 3372
17:39 the LORD your God ye shall **f**; 3372
25:24 **F** not to be the servants of the Chaldees: 3372
1Ch 14:17 the LORD brought the **f** of him upon all 6343
16:30 **F** before him, all the earth: the world also 2342
28:20 and of good courage, and do *it:* **f** not, 3372
2Ch 6:31 they may **f** thee, to walk in thy ways, 3372
6:33 **f** thee, as *doth* thy people Israel, and may 3372
14:14 for the **f** of the LORD came upon them: 6343
17:10 the **f** of the LORD fell upon all 6343
19: 7 Wherefore now let the **f** of the LORD be 6343
19: 9 Thus shall ye do in the **f** of the LORD, 3374
20:17 **f** not, nor be dismayed; to morrow go out 3372
20:29 the **f** of God was on all the kingdoms of 6343
Ezr 3: 3 for **f** *was* upon them because of the people 367
Ne 1:11 of thy servants, who desire to **f** thy name: 3372
5: 9 ought ye not to walk in the **f** of our God 3374
5:15 but so did not I, because of the **f** of God. 3374
6:14 prophets, that would have **put me in f**. 3372
6:19 *And* Tobiah sent letters to **put me in f**. 3372
Est 8:17 for the **f** of the Jews fell upon them 6343
9: 2 for the **f** of them fell upon all people. 6343
9: 3 because the **f** of Mordecai fell upon them. 6343
Job 1: 9 and said, Doth Job **f** God for nought? 3372
4: 6 *Is* not this thy **f**, thy confidence, thy hope; 3374
4:14 **F** came upon me, and trembling, 6343
6:14 but he forsaketh the **f** of the Almighty. 3374
9:34 away from me, and let not his **f** terrify me: 367
9:35 would I speak, and not **f** him; but *it is* 3372
11:15 thou shalt be steadfast, and shalt not **f**. 3372
15: 4 thou castest off **f**, and restrainest prayer 3374
21: 9 Their houses *are* safe from **f**, neither *is* 6343
22: 4 Will he reprove thee for **f** of thee? will he 3374
22:10 about thee, and sudden **f** troubleth thee; 6343
25: 2 Dominion and **f** *are* with him, he maketh 6343
28:28 Behold, the **f** of the Lord, that *is* wisdom; 3374
31:34 Did I **f** a great multitude, or did 6206
37:24 Men do therefore **f** him: he respecteth not 3372
39:16 not hers: her labour *is* in vain without **f**; 6343
39:22 He mocketh at **f**, and is not affrighted; 6343
41:33 is not his like, who is made without **f**. 2844
Ps 2:11 Serve the LORD with **f**, and rejoice with 3374
5: 7 in thy **f** will I worship toward thy holy 3374
9:20 Put them in **f**, O LORD: *that* the nations 4172
14: 5 There were they **in great f**: for 6342+6343
15: 4 but he honoureth them that **f** the LORD. 3373
19: 9 The **f** of the LORD *is* clean, enduring for 3374
22:23 Ye that **f** the LORD, praise him; all ye 3373
22:23 and **f** him, all ye the seed of Israel. 1481
22:25 will pay my vows before them that **f** him. 3373
23: 4 of the shadow of death, I will **f** no evil: 3372
25:14 the LORD *is* with them that **f** him; 3373
27: 1 light and my salvation; whom shall I **f**? 3372
27: 3 encamp against me, my heart shall not **f**: 3372
31:11 and a **f** to mine acquaintance: 6343
31:13 **f** *was* on every side: while they took 4032
31:19 thou hast laid up for them that **f** thee; 3373
33: 8 Let all the earth **f** the LORD: let all 3372
33:18 the eye of the LORD *is* upon them that **f** 3373
34: 7 encampeth round about them that **f** him, 3373
34: 9 O **f** the LORD, ye his saints: for *there is* 3372
34: 9 for *there is* no want to them that **f** him. 3373
34:11 I will teach you the **f** of the LORD. 3374
36: 1 *that* there *is* no **f** of God before his eyes. 6343
40: 3 many shall see *it*, and **f**, and shall trust in 3372
46: 2 Therefore will not we **f**, though the earth 3372
48: 6 **f** took hold upon them there, *and* pain, 7461
49: 5 Wherefore should I **f** in the days of evil, 3372
52: 6 shall see, and **f**, and shall laugh at him: 3372
53: 5 There were they **in great f**, 6342+6343
53: 5 were they in great fear, *where* no **f** was: 6343
55:19 no changes, therefore they **f** not God. 3372
56: 4 I will not **f** what flesh can do unto me. 3372
60: 4 Thou hast given a banner to them that **f** 3373
61: 5 *me* the heritage of those that **f** thy name. 3373
64: 1 preserve my life from **f** of the enemy. 6343
64: 4 suddenly do they shoot at him, and **f** not. 3372
64: 9 all men shall **f**, and shall declare the work 3372
66:16 all ye that **f** God, and I will declare what 3373
67: 7 and all the ends of the earth shall **f** him. 3372
72: 5 They shall **f** thee as long as the sun and 3372
85: 9 his salvation *is* nigh them that **f** him; 3373
86:11 thy truth: unite my heart to **f** thy name. 3372
90:11 even according to thy **f**, *so is* thy wrath. 3374
96: 9 of holiness: **f** before him, all the earth. 2342
102:15 So the heathen shall **f** the name of 3372
103:11 is his mercy toward them that **f** him: 3373
103:13 *so* the LORD pitieth them that **f** him. 3373
103:17 to everlasting upon them that **f** him, 3373
105:38 for the **f** of them fell upon them. 6343
111: 5 hath given meat unto them that **f** him: 3373
111:10 The **f** of the LORD *is* the beginning of 3374
115:11 Ye that **f** the LORD, trust in the LORD: 3373
115:13 He will bless them that **f** the LORD, *both* 3373
118: 4 Let them now that **f** the LORD say, 3373
118: 6 The LORD *is* on my side; I will not **f**: 3372
119:38 thy servant, who *is* devoted to thy **f**. 3374
119:39 Turn away my reproach which I **f**: 3025
119:63 I *am* a companion of all *them* that **f** thee, 3372
119:74 that **f** thee will be glad when they see 3373
119:79 Let those that **f** thee turn unto me, 3373
119:120 My flesh trembleth for **f** of thee; and I am 6343
135:20 ye that **f** the LORD, bless the LORD. 3373
145:19 will fulfil the desire of them that **f** him: 3373

Ps 147:11 The LORD taketh pleasure in them that **f** 3373
Pr 1: 7 The **f** of the LORD *is* the beginning of 3374
1:26 I will mock when your **f** cometh; 6343
1:27 When your **f** cometh as desolation, 6343
1:29 and did not choose the **f** of the LORD: 3374
1:33 and shall be quiet from **f** of evil. 6343
2: 5 shalt thou understand the **f** of the LORD, 3374
3: 7 **f** the LORD, and depart from evil. 3372
3:25 Be not afraid of sudden **f**, neither of 6343
8:13 The **f** of the LORD *is* to hate evil: pride, 3374
9:10 The **f** of the LORD *is* the beginning of 3374
10:24 The **f** of the wicked, it shall come *upon* 4034
10:27 The **f** of the LORD prolongeth days: 3374
14:26 In the **f** of the LORD *is* strong confidence: 3374
14:27 The **f** of the LORD *is* a fountain of life, 3374
15:16 Better *is* little with the **f** of the LORD than 3374
15:33 The **f** of the LORD *is* the instruction of 3374
16: 6 by the **f** of the LORD *men* depart from 3374
19:23 The **f** of the LORD *tendeth* to life: 3374
20: 2 The **f** of a king *is* as the roaring of a lion: 367
22: 4 *and* the **f** of the LORD *are* riches, 3374
23:17 *be* thou in the **f** of the LORD all the day 3374
24:21 My son, **f** thou the LORD and the king: 3372
29:25 The **f** of man bringeth a snare: 2731
Ecc 3:14 God doeth *it*, that *men* should **f** before 3372
5: 7 *are* also *divers* vanities: but **f** thou God. 3372
8:12 that it shall be well with them that **f** God, 3373
8:12 them that fear God, which **f** before him: 3372
12:13 **F** God, and keep his commandments: 3372
SS 3: 8 upon his thigh *because* of **f** in the night. 6343
Isa 2:10 for **f** of the LORD, and for the glory of his 6343
2:19 for **f** of the LORD, and for the glory of his 6343
2:21 for **f** of the LORD, and for the glory of his 6343
7: 4 **f** not, neither be fainthearted for the two 3372
7:25 there shall not come thither the **f** of briers 3374
8:12 neither **f** ye their **f**, nor be afraid. 3372
8:12 neither fear ye their **f**, nor be afraid. 4172
8:13 *let* him **f** your **f**, and *let* him *be* your 4172
11: 2 of knowledge and of the **f** of the LORD; 3374
11: 3 quick understanding in the **f** of the LORD: 3374
14: 3 from thy **f**, and from the hard bondage 7267
19:16 it shall be afraid and **f** because of 6342
21: 4 pleasure hath he turned into **f** unto me. 2731
24:17 **F**, and the pit, and the snare, *are* upon 6343
24:18 he who fleeth from the noise of the **f** 6343
25: 3 city of the terrible nations shall **f** thee. 3372
29:13 **f** towards me is taught *by* the precept 3374
29:23 of Jacob, and shall **f** the God of Israel. 6206
31: 9 he shall pass over *to* his strong hold for **f**, 4032
33: 6 the **f** of the LORD *is* his treasure. 3374
35: 4 that are of a fearful heart, Be strong, **f** not: 3372
41:10 **F** thou not; for I *am* with thee: be not 3372
41:13 thy right hand, saying unto thee, **F** not; 3372
41:14 **F** not, thou worm Jacob, *and* ye men of 3372
43: 1 and he that formed thee, O Israel, **F** not: 3372
43: 5 **F** not: for I *am* with thee: I will bring thy 3372
44: 2 **F** not, O Jacob, my servant; 3372
44: 8 **F** ye not, neither be afraid: have not I told 6342
44:11 let them stand *up*; *yet* they shall **f**, 6342
51: 7 **f** ye not the reproach of men, neither be 3372
54: 4 **F** not; for thou shalt not be ashamed: 3372
54:14 far from oppression; for thou shalt not **f**: 3372
59:19 So shall they **f** the name of the LORD 3372
60: 5 flow *together*, and thine heart shall **f**, 6342
63:17 *and* hardened our heart from thy **f**? 3374
Jer 2:19 *that* my **f** *is* not in thee, saith the Lord 6345
5:22 **F** ye not me? saith the LORD: will ye not 3372
5:24 Let us now **f** the LORD our God, 3372
6:25 of the enemy *and* **f** *is* on every side. 4032
10: 7 Who would not **f** thee, O King of nations? 3372
20:10 the defaming of many, **f** on every side. 4032
23: 4 they shall **f** no more, nor be dismayed, 3372
26:19 did he not **f** the LORD, and besought 3373
30: 5 voice of trembling, of **f**, and not of peace. 6343
30:10 Therefore **f** thou not, O my servant Jacob, 3372
32:39 one way, that *they* may **f** me for ever, 3372
32:40 I will put my **f** in their hearts, that *they* 3374
33: 9 shall **f** and tremble for all the goodness 6342
35:11 let us go *to* Jerusalem for **f** of the army of 6440
35:11 and for **f** of the army of the Syrians: 6440
37:11 from Jerusalem for **f** of Pharaoh's army, 6440
40: 9 saying, **F** not to serve the Chaldeans: 3372
41: 9 it which Asa the king had made for **f** of 6440
42:11 **f** not of him of whom ye are afraid: be not 3372
46:27 **f** not thou, O my servant Jacob, and be 3372
46:28 **F** thou not, O Jacob my servant, saith 3372
48:43 **F**, and the pit, and the snare, *shall be* 6343
48:44 He that fleeth from the **f** shall fall into 6343
49: 5 Behold, I will bring a **f** upon thee, saith 6343
49:24 **f** hath seized on *her:* anguish and 7374
49:29 shall cry unto them, **F** *is* on every side. 4032
50:16 for **f** of the oppressing sword they shall 6440
51:46 ye **f** for the rumour that shall be heard in 3372
La 3:47 **F** and a snare is come upon us, desolation 6343
3:57 *that* I called upon thee: thou saidst, **F** not. 3372
Eze 3: 9 **f** them not, neither be dismayed at their 3372
30:13 and I will put a **f** in the land of Egypt. 3374
Da 1:10 I **f** my lord the king, who hath appointed 3373
6:26 and **f** before the God of Daniel: 1763
10:12 said unto me, **F** not, Daniel: for from 3372
10:19 said, O man greatly beloved, **f** not: 3372
Hos 3: 5 shall **f** the LORD and his goodness in 6342
10: 5 The inhabitants of Samaria shall **f** because 1481
Joel 2:21 **F** not, O land; be glad and rejoice: 3372
Am 3: 8 The lion hath roared, who will not **f**? 3372

Jnh	1: 9 I f the LORD, the God of heaven,	3373
Mic	7:17 our God, and shall f because of thee.	3373
Zep	3: 7 I said, Surely thou wilt f me, thou wilt	3372
	3:16 it shall be said to Jerusalem, **F** thou not:	3372
Hag	1:12 and the people did f before the LORD.	3372
	2: 5 my spirit remaineth among you: f ye not.	3372
Zec	8:13 f not, *but* let your hands be strong.	3372
	8:15 and to the house of Judah: f ye not.	3372
	9: 5 Ashkelon shall see *it*, and f; Gaza also	3372
Mal	1: 6 if I *be* a master, where *is* my f? saith	4172
	2: 5 I gave them to him *for* the f wherewith	4172
	3: 5 the stranger *from his right*, and f not me,	3372
	4: 2 unto you that f my name shall the Sun of	3373
Mt	1:20 f not to take unto *thee* Mary thy wife:	5399
	10:26 **F** them not therefore: for there is nothing	5399
	10:28 And f not them which kill the body,	5399
	10:28 rather f him which is able to destroy both	5399
	10:31 **F** ye not therefore, ye are of more value	5399
	14:26 It is a spirit; and they cried out for f.	5401
	21:26 if we shall say, Of men; we f the people;	5399
	28: 4 And for f of him the keepers did shake,	5401
	28: 5 and said unto the women, **F** not ye:	5399
	28: 8 quickly from the sepulchre with f	5401
Lk	1:12 he was troubled, and f fell upon him.	5401
	1:13 the angel said unto him, **F** not, Zacharias:	5399
	1:30 And the angel said unto her, **F** not, Mary:	5399
	1:50 And his mercy *is* on them that f him from	5399
	1:65 And f came on all that dwelt round about	5401
	1:74 our enemies might serve him **without** f,	870
	2:10 And the angel said unto them, **F** not:	5399
	5:10 And Jesus said unto Simon, **F** not;	5399
	5:26 and were filled with f, saying,	5401
	7:16 And there came a f on all:	5401
	8:37 for they were taken with great f:	5401
	8:50 heard *it*, he answered him, saying, **F** not:	5399
	12: 5 But I will *forewarn* you whom you shall f:	5399
	12: 5 **F** him, which after *he* hath killed hath	5399
	12: 5 cast into hell; yea, I say unto you, **F** him.	5399
	12: 7 **F** not therefore: ye are of more value than	5399
	12:32 **F** not, little flock; for it is your Father's	5399
	18: 4 Though I f not God, nor regard man;	5399
	21:26 Men's hearts failing them for f,	5401
	23:40 him, saying, Dost not thou f God,	5399
Jn	7:13 no *man* spake openly of him for f	5401
	12:15 **F** not, daughter of Sion: behold, thy King	5399
	19:38 of Jesus, but secretly for f of the Jews,	5401
	20:19 were assembled for f of the Jews,	5401
Ac	2:43 And f came upon every soul:	5401
	5: 5 great f came on all them that heard these	5401
	5:11 And great f came upon all the church,	5401
	9:31 and walking in the f of the Lord, and in	5401
	13:16 Men of Israel, and *ye* that f God,	5399
	19:17 and f fell on them all, and the name of	5401
	27:24 Saying, **F** not, Paul; thou must be brought	5399
Ro	3:18 There is no f of God before their eyes.	5401
	8:15 received the spirit of bondage again to f;	5401
	11:20 by faith. Be not high-minded, but f:	5399
	13: 7 to whom fear; honour to whom honour.	5401
	13: 7 fear to whom f; honour to whom honour.	5401
1Co	2: 3 and in f, and in much trembling.	5401
	16:10 see that he may be with you **without** f:	870
2Co	7: 1 spirit, perfecting holiness in the f of God.	5401
	7:11 yea, *what* indignation, yea, *what* f, yea,	5401
	7:15 how with f and trembling you received	5401
	11: 3 But I f, lest by any means, as the serpent	5399
	12:20 For I f, lest, when I come, I shall not find	5399
Eph	5:21 yourselves one to another in the f of God.	5401
	6: 5 with f and trembling, in singleness of	5401
Php	1:14 more bold to speak the word **without** f.	870
	2:12 work out your own salvation with f and	5401
1Ti	5:20 before all, that others also may f.	2192+5401
2Ti	1: 7 For God hath not given us the spirit of f;	1167
Heb	2:15 And deliver them who through f of death	5401
	4: 1 Let us therefore f, lest, a promise being	5399
	11: 7 **moved with** f, prepared an ark to	2125
	12:21 **exceedingly** f and quake;)	1510+1630
	12:28 acceptably with reverence and **godly** f:	2124
	13: 6 I will not f what man shall do unto me.	5399
1Pe	1:17 pass the time of your sojourning *here* in f:	5401
	2:17 the brotherhood. **F** God. Honour the king.	5399
	2:18 *be* subject to *your* masters with all f;	5401
	3: 2 your chaste conversation *coupled* with f.	5401
	3:15 hope that is in you with meekness and f:	5401
1Jn	4:18 There is no f in love; but perfect love	5401
	4:18 fear in love; but perfect love casteth out f:	5401
	4:18 because f hath torment. He that feareth is	5401
Jude	1:12 with *you*, feeding themselves **without** f:	870
	1:23 others save with f, pulling *them* out of	5401
Rev	1:17 hand upon me, saying unto me, **F** not;	5399
	2:10 **F** none of *those things* which thou shalt	5399
	11:11 great f fell upon them which saw them.	5401
	11:18 them that f thy name, small and great;	5399
	14: 7 loud voice, **F** God, and give glory to him;	5399
	15: 4 Who shall not f thee, O Lord,	5399
	18:10 Standing afar off for the f of her torment,	5401
	18:15 stand afar off for the f of her torment,	5401
	19: 5 ye that f him, both small and great.	5399

FEARED (74) [FEAR]

Ge	19:30 with him; for he f to dwell in Zoar:	3372
	26: 7 for he f to say, *She is* my wife; lest,	3372
Ex	1:17 midwives f God, and did not as the king	3372
	1:21 to pass, because the midwives f God,	3372
	2:14 Moses f, and said, Surely *this* thing is	3372
	9:20 He that f the word of the LORD amongst	3373

Ex	14:31 the people f the LORD, and believed	3372
Dt	25:18 *wast* faint and weary; and he f not God.	3373
	32:17 came newly up, whom your fathers f not.	8175
	32:27 it not that I f the wrath of the enemy,	1481
Jos	4:14 they f him, as they feared Moses,	3372
	4:14 they feared him, as they f Moses,	3372
	10: 2 That they f greatly, because Gibeon *was*	3372
Jdg	6:27 because he f his father's household,	3372
	8:20 for he f, because he *was* yet a youth.	3372
1Sa	3:15 And Samuel f to shew Eli the vision.	3372
	12:18 all the people greatly f the LORD and	3372
	14:26 to his mouth: for the people f the oath.	3372
	15:24 because I f the people, and obeyed their	3372
2Sa	3:11 Abner a word again, because he f him.	3372
	10:19 So the Syrians f to help the children of	3372
	12:18 the servants of David f to tell him that	3372
1Ki	1:50 Adonijah f because of Solomon, and arose	3372
	3:28 the king had judged; and they f the king:	3372
	18: 3 (Now Obadiah f the LORD greatly:	3373
2Ki	17: 7 king of Egypt, and had f other gods,	3372
	17:25 dwelling there, *that* they f not the LORD:	3372
	17:32 So they f the LORD, and made unto	3373
	17:33 They f the LORD, and served their own	3373
	17:41 So these nations f the LORD, and served	3373
1Ch	16:25 praised: he also *is* to be f above all gods.	3372
2Ch	20: 3 Jehoshaphat f, and set himself to seek	3372
Ne	7: 2 a faithful man, and f God above many.	3372
Job	1: 1 and **one that** f God, and eschewed evil.	3373
	3:25 the thing which I **greatly** f is come	6342+6343
Ps	76: 7 Thou, *even* thou, *art* to be f: and who	3372
	76: 8 from heaven; the earth f, and was still,	3372
	76:11 presents unto him that ought to be f:	4172
	78:53 he led them on safely, so that they f not:	6342
	89: 7 God *is* greatly to be f in the assembly of	6206
	96: 4 to be praised: he *is* to be f above all gods.	3372
	130: 4 with thee, that thou mayest be f.	3372
Isa	41: 5 isles saw *it*, and f; the ends of the earth	3372
	51:13 hast f continually every day because of	6342
	57:11 of whom hast thou been afraid or f,	3372
Jer	3: 8 yet her treacherous sister Judah f not,	3372
	42:16 come to pass, *that* the sword, which ye f,	3373
	44:10 neither have they f, nor walked in my law,	3372
Eze	11: 8 Ye have f the sword; and I will bring a	3372
Da	5:19 languages, trembled and f before him:	1763
Hos	3: 3 have no king, because we f not the LORD:	3372
Jnh	1:16 f the LORD **exceedingly**,	1419+3372+3374
Mal	2: 5 to him *for* the fear wherewith he f me,	3372
	3:16 they that f the LORD spake often one to	3373
	3:16 before him for them that f the LORD,	3373
Mt	14: 5 he f the multitude, because they counted	5399
	21:46 the multitude, because they took	5399
	27:54 that were done, they f greatly, saying,	5399
Mk	4:41 they f exceedingly, and said one	5399+5401
	6:20 For Herod f John, knowing that he *was* a	5399
	11:18 for they f him, because all the people was	5399
	11:32 if we shall say, Of men; they f the people:	5399
	12:12 to lay hold on him, but f the people:	5399
Lk	9:34 and they f as they entered into the cloud.	5399
	9:45 not: and they f to ask him of that saying.	5399
	18: 2 which f not God, neither regarded man:	5399
	19:21 For I f thee, because thou art an austere	5399
	20:19 lay hands on him; and they f the people:	5399
	22: 2 they might kill him; for they f the people.	5399
Jn	9:22 spake his parents, because they f the Jews:	5399
Ac	5:26 for they f the people, lest they should	5399
	10: 2 and one that f God with all his house,	5399
	16:38 they f, when they heard that they were	5399
Heb	5: 7 from death, and was heard in that he f;	2124

FEAREST (3) [FEAR]

Ge	22:12 for now I know that thou f God,	3373
Isa	57:11 my peace even of old, and thou f me not?	3372
Jer	22:25 into the hand *of them* whose face thou f,	3016

FEARETH (20) [FEAR]

1Ki	1:51 Behold, Adonijah f king Solomon:	3372
Job	1: 8 **one that** f God, and escheweth evil?	3373
	2: 3 **one that** f God, and escheweth evil?	3373
Ps	25:12 What man *is* he that f the LORD?	3373
	112: 1 Blessed *is* the man *that* f the LORD,	3373
	128: 1 Blessed *is* every one that f the LORD;	3373
	128: 4 that thus shall the man be blessed that f	3373
Pr	13:13 he that f the commandment shall be	3372
	14: 2 He that walketh in his uprightness f	3373
	14:16 A wise *man* f, and departeth from evil:	3373
	28:14 Happy *is* the man that f alway: but he	6342
	31:30 *but* a woman that f the LORD, she shall	3373
Ecc	7:18 he that f God shall come forth of them	3373
	8:13 a shadow; because he f not before God.	3373
	9: 2 he that sweareth, as he that f an oath.	3373
Isa	50:10 Who *is* among you that f the LORD,	3373
Ac	10:22 and one that f God, and of good report	5399
	10:35 But in every nation he that f him,	5399
	13:26 and whosoever among you f God,	5399
1Jn	4:18 He that f is not made perfect in love.	5399

FEARFUL (11) [FEAR]

Ex	15:11 in holiness, f *in* praises, doing wonders?	3372
Dt	20: 8 What man *is there* that is f and	3373
	28:58 mayest fear this glorious and f name,	3372
Jdg	7: 3 Whosoever *is* f and afraid, let him	3373
Isa	35: 4 to them that are of a f heart, Be strong,	4116
Mt	8:26 Why are ye f, O ye of little faith?	1169
Mk	4:40 And he said unto them, Why are ye so f?	1169
Lk	21:11 and f sights and great signs shall be	5400

Heb	10:27 But a certain f looking for of judgment	5398
	10:31 *It is* a f *thing* to fall into the hands of	5398
Rev	21: 8 But the f, and unbelieving,	1169

FEARFULLY (1) [FEAR]

Ps	139:14 for I am f and wonderfully made:	3372

FEARFULNESS (3) [FEAR]

Ps	55: 5 F and trembling are come upon me,	3374
Isa	21: 4 My heart panted, f affrighted me:	6427
	33:14 are afraid; f hath surprised the hypocrites.	7461

FEARING (8) [FEAR]

Jos	22:25 our children cease from f the LORD:	3372
Mk	5:33 But the woman f and trembling,	5399
Ac	23:10 lest Paul should have been pulled in	2125
	27:17 f lest they should fall into the quicksands,	5399
	27:29 Then f lest we should have fallen upon	5399
Gal	2:12 f them which were of the circumcision.	5399
Col	3:22 but in singleness of heart, f God:	5399
Heb	11:27 forsook Egypt, not f the wrath of the king:	5399

FEARS (4) [FEAR]

Ps	34: 4 me, and delivered me from all my f.	4035
Ecc	12: 5 f *shall be* in the way, and the almond	2849
Isa	66: 4 and will bring their f upon them;	4035
2Co	7: 5 without *were* fightings, within *were* f.	5401

FEAST (123) [FEASTED, FEASTING, FEASTS]

Ge	19: 3 he made them a f, and did bake	4960
	21: 8 Abraham made a great f the *same* day	4960
	26:30 he made them a f, and they did eat and	4960
	29:22 all the men of the place, and made a f.	4960
	40:20 that he made a f unto all his servants:	4960
Ex	5: 1 that they may **hold a** f unto me in	2287
	10: 9 for we *must* hold a f unto the LORD.	2282
	12:14 you shall keep it a f by an ordinance for	2287
	12:14 you shall **keep** it a f by an ordinance for	2287
	12:17 shall observe the f of unleavened bread;	NIH
	13: 6 In the seventh day *shall be* a f to	2282
	23:14 Three times thou shalt **keep** a f unto me	2287
	23:15 shalt keep the f of unleavened bread:	2282
	23:16 the f of harvest, the firstfruits of thy	2282
	23:16 the f of ingathering, *which is* in the end	2282
	32: 5 and said, To morrow *is* a f to the LORD.	2282
	34:18 The f of unleavened bread shalt thou	2282
	34:22 thou shalt observe the f of weeks,	2282
	34:22 and the f of ingathering *at* the year's end.	2282
	34:25 neither shall the sacrifice of the f	2282
Lev	23: 6 the f of unleavened bread unto the LORD:	2282
	23:34 the f of tabernacles *for* seven days unto	2282
	23:39 ye shall keep a f unto the LORD seven	2282
	23:41 ye shall **keep** it a f unto the LORD	2282+2287
Nu	28:17 in the fifteenth day of this month *is* the f:	2282
	29:12 ye shall **keep a** f unto the LORD	2282+2287
Dt	16:10 thou shalt keep the f of weeks unto	2282
	16:13 Thou shalt observe the f of tabernacles	2282
	16:14 thou shalt rejoice in thy f, thou,	2282
	16:15 Seven days shalt thou **keep a solemn** f	2287
	16:16 in the f of unleavened bread, and in	2282
	16:16 in the f of weeks, and in the feast of	2282
	16:16 feast of weeks, and in the f of tabernacles:	2282
	31:10 the year of release, in the f of tabernacles,	2282
Jdg	14:10 Samson made there a f; for so used	4960
	14:12 it me *within* the seven days of the f,	4960
	14:17 him the seven days, while their f lasted:	4960
	21:19 *there is* a f of the LORD in Shiloh yearly	2282
1Sa	25:36 behold, he held a f in his house, like	4960
	25:36 a feast in his house, like the f of a king;	4960
2Sa	3:20 and the men that *were* with him a f.	4960
1Ki	3:15 and made a f to all his servants.	4960
	8: 2 Solomon at the f in the month Ethanim,	2282
	8:65 that time Solomon held a f, and all Israel	2282
	12:32 Jeroboam ordained a f in the eighth	2282
	12:32 like unto the f that *is* in Judah,	2282
	12:33 ordained a f unto the children of Israel:	2282
2Ch	5: 3 in the f which *was* in the seventh month.	2282
	7: 8 Also at the same time Solomon kept the f	2282
	7: 9 the altar seven days, and the f seven days.	2282
	8:13 even in the f of unleavened bread,	2282
	8:13 in the f of weeks, and in the feast of	2282
	8:13 feast of weeks, and in the f of tabernacles:	2282
	30:13 of unleavened bread in the second	2282
	30:21 of unleavened bread seven days with	2282
	30:22 they did eat throughout the f seven days,	4150
	35:17 of unleavened bread seven days.	2282
Ezr	3: 4 They kept also the f of tabernacles, as it is	2282
	6:22 kept the f of unleavened bread seven days	2282
Ne	8:14 in booths in the f of the seventh month:	2282
	8:18 they kept the f seven days; and on	2282
Est	1: 3 he made a f unto all his princes and	4960
	1: 5 the king made a f unto all the people that	4960
	1: 9 Also Vashti the queen made a f for	4960
	2:18 king made a great f unto all his princes	4960
	2:18 and his servants, *even* Esther's f;	4960
	8:17 had joy and gladness, a f and a good day.	4960
Ps	81: 3 the time appointed, on our **solemn** f day.	2282
Pr	15:15 *is* of a merry heart *hath* a continual f.	4960
Ecc	10:19 A f is made for laughter, and wine	3899
Isa	25: 6 make unto all people a f of fat things,	4960
	25: 6 a f of wines on the lees, of fat things full	4960
La	2: 7 of the LORD, as *in* the day of a **solemn** f.	4150
Eze	45:21 shall have the passover, a f of seven days;	2282
	45:23 seven days of the f he shall prepare a	2282
	45:25 shall he do the like in the f *of* the seven	2282

F

Da 5: 1 Belshazzar the king made a great **f** to a — 3900
Hos 2:11 her **f** days, her new moons, — 2282
 9: 5 and in the day of the **f** of the LORD? — 2282
 12: 9 as in the days of the **solemn f**. — 4150
Am 5:21 I despise your **f** days, and I will not smell — 2282
Zec 14:16 of hosts, and to keep the **f** of tabernacles. — 2282
 14:18 come not up to keep the **f** of tabernacles. — 2282
 14:19 come not up to keep the **f** of tabernacles. — 2282
Mt 26: 2 Ye know that after two days is the **f** of — NIG
 26: 5 Not on the **f** day, lest there be an uproar — 1859
 26:17 Now the first day of the **f** of unleavened — NIG
 27:15 Now at that the governor was wont to — 1859
Mk 14: 1 After two days was the **f** of the passover, — NIG
 14: 2 Not on the **f** day, lest there be an uproar — 1859
 15: 6 Now at that **f** he released unto them one — 1859
Lk 2:41 every year at the **f** of the passover. — 1859
 2:42 up to Jerusalem after the custom of the f. — 1859
 5:29 And Levi made him a great **f** in his own — 1403
 14:13 But when thou makest a **f**, call the poor, — 1403
 22: 1 Now the **f** of unleavened bread drew nigh, — 1859
 23:17 he must release one unto them at the f.) — 1859
Jn 2: 8 and bear unto the **governor of the f.** — 755
 2: 9 the **ruler of the f** had tasted the water — 755
 2: 9 **governor of the f** called the bridegroom, — 755
 2:23 in the **f** day, many believed in his name, — 1859
 4:45 things that he did at Jerusalem at the **f**: — 1859
 4:45 at the feast: for they also went unto the **f**. — 1859
 5: 1 After this there was a **f** of the Jews; — 1859
 6: 4 the passover, a **f** of the Jews, was nigh. — 1859
 7: 2 the Jews' **f** of tabernacles was at hand. — 1859
 7: 8 Go ye up unto this f: I go not up yet unto — 1859
 7: 8 I go not up yet unto this f; for my time is — 1859
 7:10 went he also up unto the **f**, not openly, — 1859
 7:11 the Jews sought him at the **f**, and said, — 1859
 7:14 about the midst of the **f** Jesus went up — 1859
 7:37 that great day of the **f**, Jesus stood and — 1859
 10:22 And it was at Jerusalem the **f** of — NIG
 11:56 think ye, that he will not come to the **f**? — 1859
 12:12 day much people that were come to the **f**, — 1859
 12:20 them that came up to worship at the **f**: — 1859
 13: 1 Now before the **f** of the passover, — 1859
 13:29 things that we have need of against the **f**; — 1859
Ac 18:21 I must by all means keep this **f** that — 1859
1Co 5: 8 Therefore let us **keep the f**, not with old — 1858
 10:27 of them that believe not bid you to a **f**, — NIG
2Pe 2:13 own deceivings while they **f with you**; — 4910
Jude 1:12 **f with** you, feeding themselves without — 4910

FEASTED (1) [FEAST]
Job 1: 4 his sons went and **f** in their houses, — 4960+6213

FEASTING (7) [FEAST]
Est 9:17 and made it a day of **f** and gladness. — 4960
 9:18 and made it a day of **f** and gladness. — 4960
 9:19 the month Adar a day of gladness and **f**, — 4960
 9:22 that they should make them days of **f** and — 4960
Job 1: 5 when the days of their **f** were gone about, — 4960
Ecc 7: 2 of mourning, than to go to the house of **f**: — 4960
Jer 16: 8 Thou shalt not also go into the house of **f**, — 4960

FEASTS (32) [FEAST]
Lev 23: 2 unto them, Concerning the **f** of the LORD, — 4150
 23: 2 holy convocations, even these are my **f**. — 4150
 23: 4 These are the **f** of the LORD, even holy — 4150
 23:37 These are the **f** of the LORD, which ye — 4150
 23:44 the children of Israel the **f** of the LORD. — 4150
Nu 15: 3 a freewill offering, or in your **solemn f**, — 4150
 29:39 ye shall do unto the LORD in your **set f**, — 4150
1Ch 23:31 moons, and on the **set f**, by number, — 4150
2Ch 2: 4 on the **solemn f** of the LORD our God. — 4150
 8:13 the new moons, and on the **solemn f**, — 4150
 31: 3 for the new moons, and for the **set f**, — 4150
Ezr 3: 5 of all the **set f** of the LORD that were — 4150
Ne 10:33 for the **set f**, and for the holy things, and — 4150
Ps 35:16 With hypocritical mockers in **f**, — 4580
Isa 1:14 and your **appointed f** my soul hateth: — 4150
 5:12 tabret, and pipe, and wine, are in their **f**: — 4150
Jer 51:39 In their heat I will make their **f**, and I will — 4960
La 1: 4 because none come to the **solemn f**. — 4150
 2: 6 the LORD hath caused the **solemn f** and — 4150
Eze 36:38 the flock of Jerusalem in her **solemn f**; — 4150
 45:17 in the **f**, and in the new moons, and in — 2282
 46: 9 come before the LORD in the **solemn f**, — 4150
 46:11 in the **f** and in the solemnities the meat — 2282
Hos 2:11 and her sabbaths, and all her **solemn f**. — 4150
Am 5:21 I will turn your **f** into mourning, — 2282
Na 1:15 O Judah, keep thy **solemn f**, perform thy — 2282
Zec 8:19 of Judah joy and gladness, and cheerful **f**; — 4150
Mal 2: 3 faces, even the dung of your **solemn f**; — 2282
Mt 23: 6 And love the uppermost rooms at **f**, — 1173
Mk 12:39 and the uppermost rooms at **f**, — 1173
Lk 20:46 the synagogues, and the chief rooms at **f**; — 1173
Jude 1:12 These are spots in your **f of charity** when — 26

FEATHERED (2) [FEATHERS]
Ps 78:27 and fowls like as the sand of the sea: — 3671
Eze 39:17 Speak unto every **f** fowl, and to every — 3671

FEATHERS (7) [FEATHERED]
Lev 1:16 he shall pluck away his crop with his **f**, — 5133
Job 39:13 or wings and **f** unto the ostrich? — 5133
Ps 68:13 with silver, and her **f** with yellow gold. — 84
 91: 4 He shall cover thee with his **f**, and under — 84
Eze 17: 3 longwinged, full of **f**, which had divers — 5133
 17: 7 great eagle with great wings and many **f**: — 5133

Da 4:33 till his hairs were grown like eagles' **f**, — NIH

FED (31) [FEED]
Ge 30:36 and Jacob **f** the rest of Laban's flocks. — 7462
 36:24 as he **f** the asses of Zibeon his father. — 7462
 41: 2 and fatfleshed; and they **f** in a meadow. — 7462
 41:18 well favoured; and they **f** in a meadow. — 7462
 47:17 he **f** them with bread for all their cattle — 5095
 48:15 the God which **f** me all my life long unto — 7462
Ex 16:32 wherewith I have **f** you in the wilderness, — 398
Dt 8: 3 thee to hunger, and **f** thee with manna, — 398
 8:16 Who **f** thee in the wilderness with manna, — 398
2Sa 20: 3 **f** them, but went not in unto them. — 3557
1Ki 18: 4 a cave, and **f** them with bread and water.) — 3557
 18:13 a cave, and **f** them with bread and water? — 3557
1Ch 27:29 the herds that **f** in Sharon was Shitrai — 7462
Ps 37: 3 in the land, and verily thou shalt be — 7462
 78:72 So he **f** them according to the integrity of — 7462
 81:16 He should have **f** them also with the finest — 398
Isa 1:11 offerings of rams, and the fat of **f beasts**; — 4806
Jer 5: 7 when I had **f** them **to the full**, they then — 7650
 5: 8 They were as **f** horses in the morning: — 2109
Eze 16:19 and oil, and honey, wherewith I **f** thee, — 1277
 34: 3 you with the wool, ye kill them that are **f**: — 1277
 34: 8 the shepherds themselves, and fed not — 7462
 34: 8 fed themselves, and **f** not my flock; — 7462
Da 4:12 boughs thereof, and all flesh was **f** of it. — 2110
 5:21 they **f** him with grass like oxen, — 2939
Zec 11: 7 the other I called Bands; and I **f** the flock. — 7462
Mt 25:37 thee? or thirsty, and gave thee drink? — 5142
Mk 5:14 the swine fled, and told it in — 1006
Lk 8:34 they that **f** them saw what was done, — 1006
 16:21 desiring to be **f** with the crumbs which — 5526
1Co 3: 2 have **f** you with milk, and not with meat: — 4222

FEEBLE (20) [FEEBLEMINDED, FEEBLENESS, FEEBLER]
Ge 30:42 the cattle were **f**, he put them not in: — 5848
Dt 25:18 all that were **f** behind thee, when thou — 2826
1Sa 2: 5 she that hath many children is **waxed f**. — 535
2Sa 4: 1 his hands were **f**, and all the Israelites — 7503
2Ch 28:15 carried all the **f** of them upon asses, — 3782
Ne 4: 2 Samaria, and said, What do these **f** Jews? — 537
Job 4: 4 and thou hast strengthened the **f** knees. — 3766
Ps 38: 8 I am **f** and sore broken: I have roared by — 6313
 105:37 there was not one **f** person among their — 3782
Pr 30:26 The conies are but a **f** folk, yet — 3808+6099
Isa 16:14 remnant shall be very small and **f**. — 3524+3808
 35: 3 the weak hands, and confirm the **f** knees. — 3782
Jer 6:24 our hands **wax f**: anguish hath taken — 7503
 49:24 Damascus is **waxed f**, and turneth — 7503
 50:43 report of them, and his hands **waxed f**: — 7503
Eze 7:17 All hands shall be **f**, and all knees shall be — 7503
 21: 7 all hands shall be **f**, and every spirit shall — 7503
Zec 12: 8 he that is **f** among them at that day shall — 3782
1Co 12:22 which seem to be **more f**, are necessary: — 772
Heb 12:12 hands which hang down, and the **f** knees; — 3886

FEEBLEMINDED (1) [FEEBLE, MIND]
1Th 5:14 unruly, comfort the **f**, support the weak, — 3642

FEEBLENESS (1) [FEEBLE]
Jer 47: 3 look back to their children for **f** of hands; — 7510

FEEBLER (1) [FEEBLE]
Ge 30:42 so the **f** were Laban's, and the stronger — 5848

FEED (81) [FED, FEEDEST, FEEDETH, FEEDING, FOOD]
Ge 25:30 Esau said to Jacob, **F** me, I pray thee, — 3938
 29: 7 water ye the sheep, and go and **f** them. — 7462
 30:31 for me, I will again **f** and keep thy flock: — 7462
 37:12 his brethren went to **f** their father's flock — 7462
 37:13 Do not thy brethren **f** the flock in — 7462
 37:16 I pray thee, where they **f** their flocks. — 7462
 46:32 for their **trade** hath been to **f cattle**; — 376+4735
Ex 22: 5 beast, and shall **f** in another man's field; — 1197
 22: 5 neither let the flocks nor herds **f** before — 7462
1Sa 17:15 returned from Saul to **f** his father's sheep — 7462
2Sa 5: 2 Thou shalt **f** my people Israel, — 7462
 7: 7 I commanded to **f** my people Israel, — 7462
 19:33 and I will **f** thee with me in Jerusalem. — 3557
1Ki 17: 4 I have commanded the ravens to **f** thee — 7462
 22:27 **f** him with bread of affliction and with — 398
1Ch 11: 2 Thou shalt **f** my people Israel, — 7462
 17: 6 whom I commanded to **f** my people, — 7462
2Ch 18:26 **f** him with bread of affliction and — 398
Job 24: 2 violently take away flocks, and **f** thereof: — 7462
 24:20 the worm shall **f sweetly** on him; — 4988
Ps 28: 9 **f** them also, and lift them up for ever. — 7462
 49:14 death shall **f** on them; and the upright — 7462
 78:71 he brought him to **f** Jacob his people, — 7462
Pr 10:21 The lips of the righteous **f** many: — 7462
 30: 8 **f** me with food convenient for me: — 2963
SS 1: 8 **f** thy kids beside the shepherds' tents. — 7462
 4: 5 that are twins, which **f** among the lilies. — 7462
 6: 2 to **f** in the gardens, and to gather lilies. — 7462
Isa 5:17 shall the lambs **f** after their manner, — 7462
 11: 7 the cow and the bear shall **f**; their young — 7462
 14:30 the firstborn of the poor shall **f**, — 7462
 27:10 there shall the calf **f**, and there shall he lie — 7462
 30:23 in that day shall thy cattle **f** in large — 7462
 40:11 He shall **f** his flock like a shepherd: he — 7462
 49: 9 shall **f** in the ways, and their pastures — 7462
 49:26 I will **f** them that oppress thee with their — 398

Isa 58:14 **f** thee with the heritage of Jacob thy father: — 398
 61: 5 strangers shall stand and **f** your flocks, — 7462
 65:25 The wolf and the lamb shall **f** together, — 7462
Jer 3:15 which shall **f** you with knowledge and — 7462
 6: 3 they shall **f** every one in his place. — 7462
 9:15 Behold, I will **f** them, even this people, — 398
 23: 2 Israel against the pastors that **f** my people; — 7462
 23: 4 shepherds over them which shall **f** them: — 7462
 23:15 I will **f** them with wormwood, — 398
 50:19 he shall **f** on Carmel and Bashan, — 7462
La 4: 5 They that did **f** delicately are desolate in — 398
Eze 34: 2 be to the shepherds of Israel that do **f** — 7462
 34: 2 should not the shepherds **f** the flocks? — 7462
 34: 3 them that are fed: but ye **f** not the flock. — 7462
 34:10 neither shall the shepherds **f** themselves — 7462
 34:13 them upon the mountains of Israel by — 7462
 34:14 I will **f** them in a good pasture, — 7462
 34:14 in a fat pasture shall they **f** upon — 7462
 34:15 I will **f** my flock, and I will cause them to — 7462
 34:16 the strong; I will **f** them with judgment. — 7462
 34:23 he shall **f** them, even my servant David; — 7462
 34:23 he shall **f** them, and he shall be their — 7462
Da 11:26 they that **f** of the portion of his meat shall — 398
Hos 4:16 now the LORD will **f** them as a lamb in a — 7462
 9: 2 and the winepress shall not **f** them, — 7462
Jnh 3: 7 any thing: let them not **f**, nor drink water: — 7462
Mic 5: 4 and **f** in the strength of the LORD, — 7462
 7:14 Thy people with thy rod, the flock of — 7462
 7:14 let them **f** in Bashan and Gilead, as in — 7462
Zep 2: 7 house of Judah; they shall **f** thereupon: — 7462
 3:13 for they shall **f** and lie down, and none — 7462
Zec 11: 4 my God; **F** the flock of the slaughter; — 7462
 11: 7 I will **F** the flock of slaughter, even you, — 7462
 11: 9 I will not **f** you: that that dieth, let it — 7462
 11:16 is broken, nor **f** that that standeth still: — 3557
Lk 15:15 and he sent him into his fields to **f** swine. — 1006
Jn 21:15 He saith unto him, **F** my lambs. — 1006
 21:16 He saith unto him, **F** my sheep. — 4165
 21:17 Jesus saith unto him, **F** my sheep. — 1006
Ac 20:28 to **f** the church of God, which he hath — 4165
Ro 12:20 Therefore if thine enemy hunger, **f** him; — 5595
1Co 13: 3 And though I **bestow** all my goods to **f** — 5595
1Pe 5: 2 **F** the flock of God which is among you, — 4165
Rev 7:17 is in the midst of the throne shall **f** them, — 4165
 12: 6 that they should **f** her there a thousand — 5142

FEEDEST (2) [FEED]
Ps 80: 5 Thou **f** them with the bread of tears; — 398
SS 1: 7 thou whom my soul loveth, where thou **f**, — 7462

FEEDETH (8) [FEED]
Pr 15:14 but the mouth of fools **f on** foolishness. — 7462
SS 2:16 mine, and I am his: he **f** among the lilies. — 7462
 6: 3 my beloved is mine: he **f** among the lilies. — 7462
Isa 44:20 He **f on** ashes: a deceived heart hath — 7462
Hos 12: 1 Ephraim **f on** wind, and followeth after — 7462
Mt 6:26 barns; yet your heavenly Father **f** them. — 5142
Lk 12:24 storehouse nor barn; and God **f** them: — 5142
1Co 9: 7 who a flock, and eateth not of the milk — 4165

FEEDING (9) [FEED]
Ge 37: 2 old, was **f** the flock with his brethren; — 7462
Job 1:14 plowing, and the asses **f** beside them: — 7462
Eze 34:10 and cause them to cease from **f** the flock; — 7462
Na 2:11 off from the **f place** of the young lions, where — 4829
Mt 8:30 off from them a herd of many swine **f**. — 1006
Mk 5:11 the mountains a great herd of swine **f**. — 1006
Lk 17: 7 having a servant plowing or **f cattle**, — 4165
Jude 1:12 feast with you, **f** themselves without fear: — 4165

FEEL (7) [FEELING, FELT]
Ge 27:12 My father peradventure will **f** me, — 4959
 27:21 I pray thee, that I may **f** thee, my son, — 4184
Jdg 16:26 Suffer me that I may **f** the pillars — 4184
Job 20:20 Surely he shall not **f** quietness in his belly, — 3045
Ps 58: 9 Before your pots can **f** the thorns, he shall — 995
Ecc 8: 5 Whoso keepeth the commandment shall **f** — 3045
Ac 17:27 if haply they might **f** after him, — 5584

FEELING (2) [FEEL]
Eph 4:19 Who being **past f** have given themselves — 524
Heb 4:15 be **touched with the f** of our infirmities; — 4834

FEET (256) [FOOT]
Ge 18: 4 wash your **f**, and rest yourselves under — 7272
 19: 2 wash your **f**, and ye shall rise up early, — 7272
 24:32 water to wash his **f**, and the men's feet — 7272
 24:32 and the men's that were with him. — 7272
 43:24 them water, and they washed their **f**; — 7272
 49:10 nor a lawgiver from between his **f**, — 7272
 49:33 he gathered up his **f** into the bed, — 7272
Ex 3: 5 put off thy shoes from off thy **f**, — 7272
 4:25 of her son, and cast it at his **f**, and said, — 7272
 12:11 your shoes on your **f**, and your staff in — 7272
 24:10 there was under his **f** as it were a paved — 7272
 25:26 four corners that are on the four **f** thereof. — 7272
 30:19 shall wash their hands and their **f** threat: — 7272
 30:21 they shall wash their hands and their **f**, — 7272
 37:13 corners that were in the four **f** thereof. — 7272
 40:31 washed their hands and their **f** thereat: — 7272
Lev 8:24 and upon the great toes of their right **f**: — 7272
 11:21 which have legs above their **f**, to leap — 7272
 11:23 have four **f**, shall be an abomination — 7272
 11:42 whatsoever hath more **f** among all — 7272

F

Nu 20:19	*doing any* thing *else,* go through on my f. 7272
Dt 2:28	only I will pass through on my f; 7272
28:57	one that cometh out from between her f, 7272
33: 3	they sat down at thy f; *every one* shall 7272
Jos 3:13	as soon as the soles of the f of the priests 7272
3:15	the f of the priests that bare the ark were 7272
4: 3	out of the place where the priests' f stood 7272
4: 9	in the place where the f of the priests 7272
4:18	the soles of the priests' f were lift up unto 7272
9: 5	old shoes and clouted upon their f, 7272
10:24	put your f upon the necks of these kings. 7272
10:24	and put their f upon the necks of them. 7272
14: 9	the land whereon thy f have trodden 7272
Jdg 3:24	Surely he covereth his f in *his* summer 7272
4:10	went up with ten thousand men at his f: 7272
4:15	off *his* chariot, and fled away on his f. 7272
4:17	Howbeit Sisera fled away on his f to 7272
5:27	At her f he bowed, he fell, he lay down: 7272
5:27	her f he bowed, he fell: where he bowed, 7272
19:21	washed their f, and did eat and drink. 7272
Ru 3: 4	in, and uncover his f, and lay thee down. 4772
3: 7	and uncovered his f, and laid her down. 4772
3: 8	and behold, a woman lay at his f. 4772
3:14	she lay *at* his f until the morning: 4772
1Sa 2: 9	He will keep the f of his saints, 7272
14:13	up upon his hands and upon his f, 7272
24: 3	a cave; and Saul went in to cover his f: 7272
25:24	fell at his f, and said, Upon me, my lord, 7272
25:41	to wash the f of the servants of my lord. 7272
2Sa 3:34	not bound, nor thy f put into fetters: 7272
4: 4	had a son that *was* lame of *his* f. 7272
4:12	cut off their hands and their f, 7272
9: 3	hath yet a son, which *is* lame on *his* f. 7272
9:13	king's table; and *was* lame on both his f. 7272
11: 8	Go down to thy house, and wash thy f. 7272
19:24	had neither dressed his f, nor trimmed his 7272
22:10	down; and darkness *was* under his f. 7272
22:34	He maketh my f like hinds' *feet:* and 7272
22:34	He maketh my feet like hinds' *f,* NIH
22:37	steps under me; so that my f did not slip. 7166
22:39	not arise: yea, they are fallen under my f. 7272
1Ki 2: 5	and in his shoes that *were* on his f. 7272
5: 3	Lord put them under the soles of his f. 7272
14: 6	so, when Ahijah heard the sound of her f, 7272
14:12	when thy f enter into the city, the child 7272
15:23	of his old age he was diseased in his f. 7272
2Ki 4:27	to the hill, she caught him by the f: 7272
4:37	fell at his f, and bowed herself to 7272
6:32	*is* not the sound of his master's f behind 7272
9:35	and the f, and the palms of *her* hands. 7272
13:21	Elisha, he revived, and stood up on his f. 7272
19:24	with the sole of my f have I dried up all 6471
21: 8	Neither will I make the f of Israel move 7272
1Ch 28: 2	David the king stood up upon his f, 7272
2Ch 3:13	they stood on their f, and their faces 7272
16:12	year of his reign was diseased in his f, 7272
Ne 9:21	waxed not old, and their f swelled not. 7272
Est 8: 3	fell down at his f, and besought him with 7272
Job 12: 5	He that is ready to slip with *his f is as a* 7272
13:27	Thou puttest my f also in the stocks, 7272
13:27	settest a print upon the heels of my f. 7272
18: 8	For he is cast into a net by his own f, 7272
18:11	every side, and shall drive him to his f. 7272
29:15	eyes to the blind, and f *was* I to the lame. 7272
30:12	they push away my f, and they raise up 7272
33:11	He putteth my f in the stocks, he marketh 7272
Ps 8: 6	thou hast put all *things* under his f: 7272
18: 9	down: and darkness *was* under his f, 7272
18:33	He maketh my f like hinds' *feet,* and 7272
18:33	He maketh my feet like hinds' *f,* NIH
18:36	steps under me, that my f did not slip. 7166
18:38	able to rise: they are fallen under my f. 7272
22:16	they pierced my hands and my f. 7272
25:15	for he shall pluck my f out of the net. 7272
31: 8	thou hast set my f in a large room. 7272
40: 2	set my f upon a rock, *and* established my 7272
47: 3	under us, and the nations under our f. 7272
56:13	*wilt* not thou deliver my f from falling, 7272
58:10	he shall wash his f in the blood of 6471
66: 9	and suffereth not our f to be moved. 7272
73: 2	*as for* me, my f were almost gone; 6471
74: 3	Lift up thy f unto the perpetual 7272
91:13	the dragon shalt thou **trample under** f. 7429
105:18	Whose f they hurt with fetters: he was 7272
115: 7	f *have* they, but they walk not: 7272
116: 8	eyes from tears, *and* my f from falling. 7272
119:59	and turned my f unto thy testimonies. 7272
119:101	I have refrained my f from every evil way, 7272
119:105	Thy word *is* a lamp unto my f, and a light 7272
122: 2	Our f shall stand within thy gates, 7272
Pr 1:16	For their f run to evil, and make haste to 7272
4:26	Ponder the path of thy f, and let all thy 7272
5: 5	Her f go down *to* death; her steps take 7272
6:13	with his eyes, he speaketh with his f, 7272
6:18	f that be swift in running to mischief, 7272
6:28	go upon hot coals, and his f not be burnt? 7272
7:11	stubborn; her f abide not in her house: 7272
19: 2	and he that hasteth with *his* f, sinneth. 7272
26: 6	by the hand of a fool cutteth off the f, 7272
29: 5	his neighbour spreadeth a net for his f. 6471
SS 5: 3	I have washed my f; how shall I defile 7272
7: 1	How beautiful are thy f with shoes, 6471
Isa 3:16	and making a tinkling with their f: 7272
3:18	of *their* tinkling ornaments *about their f,* NIH

Isa 6: 2	with twain he covered his f, and with 7272
7:20	of Assyria, the head, and the hair of the f: 7272
14:19	of the pit; as a carcase **trodden under f.** 947
23: 7	own f shall carry her afar off to sojourn. 7272
26: 6	*even* the f of the poor, *and* the steps of 7272
28: 3	of Ephraim, shall be trodden under f: 7272
32:20	that send forth *thither* the f of the ox and 7272
37:25	with the sole of my f have I dried up all 6471
41: 3	the way *that* he had not gone with his f. 7272
49:23	the earth, and lick up the dust of thy f; 7272
52: 7	beautiful upon the mountains are the f 7272
59: 7	Their f run to evil, and they make haste 7272
60:13	I will make the place of my f glorious. 7272
60:14	themselves down at the soles of thy f; 7272
Jer 13:16	before your f stumble upon the dark 7272
14:10	they have not refrained their f, therefore 7272
18:22	a pit to take me, and hid snares for my f. 7272
38:22	thy f are sunk in the mire, *and* they are 7272
La 1:13	he hath spread a net for my f, he hath 7272
3:34	To crush under his f all the prisoners of 7272
Eze 1: 7	their f *were* straight feet; and the sole of 7272
1: 7	their feet *were* straight f; and the sole of 7272
1: 7	the sole of their f *was* like the sole of a 7272
2: 1	upon thy f, and I will speak unto thee. 7272
2: 2	set me upon my f, that I heard him that 7272
3:24	set me upon my f, and spake with me, 7272
16:25	opened thy f to every one that passed 7272
24:17	put on thy shoes upon thy f, and cover 7272
24:23	your heads, and your shoes upon your f: 7272
25: 6	stamped with the f, and rejoiced in heart 7272
32: 2	troubledst the waters with thy f. 7272
34:18	must tread down with your f the residue 7272
34:18	but ye must foul the residue with your f? 7272
34:19	that which ye have trodden with your f; 7272
34:19	that which ye have fouled with your f. 7272
37:10	they lived, and stood up upon their f, 7272
43: 7	and the place of the soles of my f, 7272
Da 2:33	of iron, his f part of iron and part of clay. 7271
2:34	smote the image upon his f *that were* 7271
2:41	whereas thou sawest the f and toes, part 7271
2:42	*as* the toes of the f *were* part of iron, 7271
7: 4	made stand upon the f as a man, 7271
7: 7	and stamped the residue with the f of it: 7271
7:19	and stamped the residue with his f; 7271
10: 6	and his f like in colour to polished brass, 4772
Na 1: 3	and the clouds *are* the dust of his f. 7272
1:15	Behold upon the mountains the f of him 7272
Hab 3: 5	and burning coals went forth at his f. 7272
3:19	he will make my f like hinds' *feet,* and 7272
3:19	he will make my feet like hinds' *f,* NIH
Zec 14: 4	his f shall stand in that day upon the 7272
14:12	away while they stand upon their f, 7272
Mal 4: 3	in the day that I *shall* do *this,* saith 7272
Mt 7: 6	lest they trample them under their f, 4228
10:14	or city, shake off the dust of your f. 4228
15:30	and cast them *down* at Jesus' f; 4228
18: 8	or two f to be cast into everlasting fire. 4228
18:29	And his fellowservant fell down at his f, 4228
28: 9	And they came and held him by the f, 4228
Mk 5:22	and when he saw him, he fell at his f, 4228
6:11	shake off the dust under your f for a 4228
7:25	heard of him, and came and fell at his f: 4228
9:45	than having two f to be cast into hell, 4228
Lk 1:79	to guide our f into the way of peace. 4228
7:38	And stood at his f behind him weeping, 4228
7:38	and began to wash his f with tears, 4228
7:38	and kissed his f, and anointed *them* with 4228
7:44	thou gavest me no water for my f: 4228
7:44	but she hath washed my f with tears, 4228
7:45	I came in hath not ceased to kiss my f. 4228
7:46	this *woman* hath anointed my f with 4228
8:35	sitting at the f of Jesus, clothed, and in 4228
8:41	and he fell down at Jesus' f, 4228
9: 5	shake off the very dust from your f for a 4228
10:39	which also sat at Jesus' f, and heard his 4228
15:22	a ring on his hand, and shoes on *his* f: 4228
17:16	And fell down on *his* face at his f, 4228
24:39	Behold my hands and my f, that it is I 4228
24:40	he shewed them *his* hands and *his* f. 4228
Jn 11: 2	and wiped his f with her hair, 4228
11:32	and saw him, she fell down at his f, 4228
12: 3	anointed the f of Jesus, and wiped his 4228
12: 3	of Jesus, and wiped his f with her hair: 4228
13: 5	and began to wash the disciples' f, 4228
13: 6	unto him, Lord, dost thou wash my f? 4228
13: 8	unto him, Thou shalt never wash my f 4228
13: 9	not my f only, but also *my* hands and 4228
13:10	is washed needeth not save to wash *his* f, 4228
13:12	So after he had washed their f, 4228
13:14	Lord and Master, have washed your f; 4228
13:14	ye also ought to wash one another's f. 4228
20:12	one at the head, and the other at the f, 4228
Ac 3: 7	and immediately his f and ankle bones 939
4:35	And laid *them down* at the apostles' f: 4228
4:37	the money, and laid *it* at the apostles' f. 4228
5: 2	certain part, and laid *it* at the apostles' f. 4228
5: 9	the f of them which have buried thy 4228
5:10	Then fell she down straightway at his f, 4228
7:33	to him, Put off *thy* shoes from thy f: 4228
7:58	down their clothes at a young man's f, 4228
10:25	and fell down at his f, 4228
13:25	whose shoes of *his* f I am not worthy to 4228
13:51	But they shook off the dust of their f 4228
14: 8	a certain man at Lystra, impotent in *his* f, 4228
14:10	with a loud voice, Stand upright on thy f. 4228

Ac 16:24	and made their f fast in the stocks. 4228
21:11	and bound his *own* hands and f, and said, 4228
22: 3	yet brought up in this city at the f of 4228
26:16	But rise, and stand upon thy f: for I have 4228
Ro 3:15	Their f *are* swift to shed blood: 4228
10:15	beautiful *are the* f of them that preach 4228
16:20	shall bruise Satan under your f shortly. 4228
1Co 15:25	again the head to the f, I have no need 4228
15:25	till he hath put all enemies under his f. 4228
15:27	For he hath put all *things* under his f. 4228
Eph 1:22	And hath put all *things* under his f, 4228
6:15	And your f shod with the preparation of 4228
1Ti 5:10	if she have washed the saints' f, 4228
Heb 2: 8	put all *things* in subjection under his f. 4228
12:13	And make straight paths for your f, lest 4228
Rev 1:15	And his f like unto fine brass, as if they 4228
1:17	when I saw him, I fell at his f as dead. 4228
2:18	flame of fire, and his f *are* like fine brass; 4228
3: 9	them to come and worship before thy f, 4228
10: 1	*it were* the sun, and his f as pillars of fire: 4228
11:11	into them, and they stood upon their f; 4228
12: 1	and the moon under her f, and upon her 4228
13: 2	and his f *were* as *the feet* of a bear, 4228
13: 2	and his feet *were* as the f of a bear, NIG
19:10	And I fell at his f to worship him. 4228
22: 8	I fell down to worship before the f of 4228

FEIGN (3) [FEIGNED, FEIGNEDLY, FEIGNEST, UNFEIGNED]
2Sa 14: 2	f thyself **to be a mourner,** and put on 56
1Ki 14: 2	that she shall f herself **to be another** 5234
Lk 20:20	which *should* f themselves just *men,* that 5271

FEIGNED (3) [FEIGN]
1Sa 21:13	f himself **mad** in their hands, 1984
Ps 17: 1	my prayer, *that goeth* not out of f lips. 4820
2Pe 2: 3	through covetousness shall they with f 4112

FEIGNEDLY (1) [FEIGN]
Jer 3:10	whole heart, but f, saith the Lord. 8267+871.1

FEIGNEST (2) [FEIGN]
1Ki 14: 6	why f thou thyself **to be another?** 5234
Ne 6: 8	but thou f them out of thine own heart. 908

FELIX (8) [FELIX']
Ac 23:24	and bring *him* safe unto F the governor. 5344
23:26	excellent governor F *sendeth* greeting. 5344
24: 3	*it* always, and in all places, most noble F, 5344
24:22	And when F heard these *things,* having 5344
24:24	when F came with his wife Drusilla, 5344
24:25	and judgment to come, F trembled, 5344
24:27	willing to shew the Jews a pleasure, 5344
25:14	There is a certain man left in bonds by F: 5344

FELIX' (1) [FELIX]
Ac 24:27	years Porcius Festus came into F room: 5344

FELL (243) [FALL, FELLED, FELLER, FELLEST, FELLING]
Ge 4: 5	was very wroth, and his countenance f. 5307
14:10	Sodom and Gomorrah fled, and f there; 5307
15:12	going down, a deep sleep f upon Abram; 5307
15:12	lo, a horror of great darkness f upon him. 5307
17: 3	Abram f on his face: and God talked with 5307
17:17	Abraham f upon his face, and laughed, 5307
33: 4	and f on his neck, and kissed him: 5307
44:14	and they f before him on the ground. 5307
45:14	he f upon his brother Benjamin's neck, 5307
46:29	he f on his neck, and wept on his neck a 5307
50: 1	Joseph f upon his father's face, 5307
50:18	also went and f down before his face; 5307
Ex 32:28	there f of the people that day about three 5307
Lev 9:24	they shouted, and f on their faces. 5307
16: 9	the goat upon which the Lord's lot f, 5927
16:10	on which the lot f to be the scapegoat, 5927
Nu 11: 4	that *was* among them f a lusting: 183+8378
11: 9	the dew f upon the camp in the night, 3381
11: 9	camp in the night, the manna f upon it. 3381
14: 5	Aaron f on their faces before all 5307
16: 4	when Moses heard *it,* he f upon his face: 5307
16:22	they f upon their faces, and said, O God, 5307
16:45	for a moment. And they f upon their faces. 5307
20: 6	and they f upon their faces: 5307
22:27	of the Lord, she f down under Balaam: 7257
22:31	down his head, and f **flat** on his face. 7812
Dt 9:18	I f down before the Lord, as at the first, 5307
9:25	Thus I f down before the Lord forty 5307
9:25	as I f down *at the first;* because the Lord 5307
Jos 5:14	Joshua f on his face to the earth, 5307
6:20	the wall f down flat, so that the people 5307
7: 6	f to the earth upon his face before the ark 5307
8:25	*so it was,* that all that f that day, both of 5307
11: 7	Merom suddenly; and they f upon them. 5307
16: 1	the lot of the children of Joseph f from 3318
17: 5	there f ten portions to Manasseh, beside 2256
22:20	wrath f on all the congregation of Israel? 1961
Jdg 4:16	all the host of Sisera f upon the edge of 5307
5:27	At her feet he bowed, he f, he lay down: 5307
5:27	her feet he bowed, he f: where he bowed, 5307
5:27	where he bowed, there he f down dead. 5307
7:13	and smote it that it f, and overturned it, 5307
8:10	there f an hundred and twenty thousand 5307
12: 6	there f at that time of the Ephraimites 5307
13:20	on *it,* and f on their faces to the ground. 5307

F

Jdg	16:30	the house *f* upon the lords, and upon all	5307
	19:26	*f* down *at* the door of the man's house	5307
	20:44	there *f* of Benjamin eighteen thousand	5307
	20:46	So that all which *f* that day of Benjamin	5307
Ru	2:10	she *f* on her face, and bowed herself to	5307
1Sa	4:10	for there *f* of Israel thirty thousand	5307
	4:18	that he *f* from off the seat backward by	5307
	11: 7	And the fear of the Lord *f* on the people,	5307
	14:13	they *f* before Jonathan;	5307
	17:49	and he *f* upon his face to the earth.	5307
	17:52	the wounded of the Philistines **down** by	5307
	20:41	*f* on his face to the ground,	5307
	22:18	he *f* upon the priests, and slew on that	6293
	25:23	*f* before David on her face,	5307
	25:24	*f* at his feet, and said, Upon me, my lord,	5307
	28:20	Saul *f* straightway all along on the earth,	5307
	29: 3	I have found no *fault* in him since he *f*	5307
	30:13	because three days agone I *f* **sick**.	2470
	31: 1	and *f* **down** slain in mount Gilboa.	5307
	31: 4	Saul took a sword, and *f* upon it.	5307
	31: 5	he *f* likewise upon his sword, and died	5307
2Sa	1: 2	that he *f* to the earth, and did obeisance.	5307
	2:16	fellow's side; so they *f* **down** together:	5307
	2:23	he *f* **down** there, and died in the same	5307
	2:23	came to the place where Asahel *f* **down**	5307
	4: 4	haste to flee, that he *f*, and became lame.	5307
	9: 6	he *f* on his face, and did reverence.	5307
	11:17	there *f some* of the people of the servants	5307
	13: 2	vexed, that he *f* **sick** for his sister Tamar;	2470
	14: 4	she *f* on her face to the ground,	5307
	14:22	Joab *f* to the ground on his face,	5307
	18:28	he *f* **down** to the earth upon his face	7812
	19:18	Shimei the son of Gera *f* **down** before	5307
	20: 8	thereof; and as he went forth it *f* **out**.	5307
	21: 9	they *f all* seven together, and were put to	5307
	21:22	*f* by the hand of David, and by the hand	5307
1Ki	2:25	Jehoiada; and he *f* upon him that he died.	6293
	2:32	who *f* **upon** two men more righteous	6293
	2:34	went up, and *f* upon him, and slew him:	6293
	2:46	went out, and *f* upon him, that he died.	6293
	14: 1	time Abijah the son of Jeroboam *f* **sick**.	2470
	17:17	the mistress of the house, *f* **sick**;	2470
	18: 7	he knew him, and *f* on his face, and said,	5307
	18:38	the fire of the Lord *f*, and consumed	5307
	18:39	when all the people saw *it*, they *f* on their	5307
	20:30	there a wall *f* upon twenty and	5307
2Ki	1: 2	Ahaziah *f* **down** through a lattice in his	5307
	1:13	came and *f* on his knees before Elijah,	3766
	2:13	took up also the mantle of Elijah that *f*	5307
	2:14	he took the mantle of Elijah that *f* from	5307
	3:19	shall *f* every good tree, and stop all wells	5307
	4: 8	it *f* on a day, that Elisha passed to	1961
	4:11	it *f* on a day, that he came thither,	1961
	4:18	when the child was grown, it *f* on a day,	1961
	4:37	at his feet, and bowed herself to	5307
	6: 5	a beam, the axe head *f* into the water:	5307
	6: 6	the man of God said, Where *f* it? And he	5307
	7:20	so it *f* out unto him: for the people trode	1961
	25:11	the fugitives that *f* **away** to the king of	5307
1Ch	5:10	with the Hagarites, who *f* by their hand:	5307
	5:22	For there *f* **down** many slain, because	5307
	10: 1	and *f* **down** slain in mount Gilboa.	5307
	10: 4	So Saul took a sword, and *f* upon it.	5307
	10: 5	he *f* likewise on the sword, and died.	5307
	12:19	there *f some* of Manasseh to David,	5307
	12:20	there *f* to him of Manasseh, Adnah,	5307
	20: 8	they *f* by the hand of David, and by	5307
	21:14	there *f* of Israel seventy thousand men.	5307
	21:16	clothed in sackcloth, *f* upon their faces.	5307
	26:14	the lot eastward *f* to Shelemiah. Then *for*	5307
	27:24	because there *f* wrath for it against Israel;	1961
2Ch	13:17	there *f* **down** slain of Israel five hundred	5307
	15: 9	they *f* to him out of Israel in abundance,	5307
	17:10	the fear of the Lord *f* upon all	1961
	20:18	the inhabitants of Jerusalem *f* before	5307
	21:19	his bowels *f* **out** by reason of his sickness:	3318
	25:13	upon the cities of Judah, from Samaria	6584
Ezr	9: 5	I *f* upon my knees, and spread out my	3766
Est	8: 3	*f* **down** at his feet, and besought him	5307
	8:17	for the fear of the Jews *f* upon them.	5307
	9: 2	for the fear of them *f* upon all people.	5307
	9: 3	the fear of Mordecai *f* upon them.	5307
Job	1:15	the Sabeans *f* *upon them*, and took them	5307
	1:17	upon the camels, and have carried them	6584
	1:19	upon the young men, and they are dead;	5307
	1:20	*f* **down** upon the ground, and worshipped	5307
Ps	27: 2	to eat up my flesh, they stumbled and *f*.	5307
	78:64	Their priests *f* by the sword;	5307
	105:38	for the fear of them that *f* upon them.	5307
	107:12	they *f* **down**, and *there was* none to help.	3782
Jer	39: 9	those that *f* **away**, that fell to him, with	5307
	39: 9	those that fell away, that *f* to him, with	5307
	46:16	many to fall, yea, one *f* upon another:	5307
	52:15	those that *f* **away**, that fell to the king of	5307
	52:15	that *f* to the king of Babylon, and the rest	5307
La	1: 7	when her people *f* into the hand of	5307
	5:13	grind, and the children *f* under the wood.	3782
Eze	1:28	I saw *it*, I *f* upon my face, and I	5307
	3:23	by the river of Chebar: and I *f* on my face.	5307
	8: 1	that the hand of the Lord God *f* there	5307
	9: 8	that I *f* upon my face, and cried, and said,	5307
	11: 5	the Spirit of the Lord *f* upon me,	5307
	11:13	*f* **down** upon my face, and cried *with* a	5307
	39:23	their enemies: so they all *f* by the sword.	5307
	43: 3	the river Chebar: and I *f* upon my face.	5307

Eze	44: 4	house of the Lord: and I *f* upon my face.	5307
Da	2:46	the king Nebuchadnezzar *f* upon his face,	5308
	3: 7	*f* **down** *and* worshipped the golden image	5308
	3:23	*f* **down** bound into the midst of the	5308
	4:31	there *f* a voice from heaven, *saying*,	5308
	7:20	came up, and before whom three *f*;	5308
	8:17	came, I was afraid, and *f* upon my face:	5308
	10: 7	a great quaking *f* upon them, so that they	5307
Jnh	1: 7	they cast lots, and the lot *f* upon Jonah.	5307
Mt	2:11	and *f* **down**, and worshipped him:	4098
	7:25	and beat upon that house; and it *f* not:	4098
	7:27	and beat upon that house; and it *f*:	4098
	13: 4	*seeds f* by the way side, and the fowls	4098
	13: 5	Some *f* upon stony *places*, where they	4098
	13: 7	And some *f* among thorns; and the thorns	4098
	13: 8	But other *f* into good ground,	4098
	17: 6	when the disciples heard *it*, they *f* on	4098
	18:26	The servant therefore *f* **down**,	4098
	18:29	And his fellowservant *f* **down** at his feet,	4098
	26:39	and on his face, and prayed, saying,	4098
Mk	3:11	*f* **down** before him, and cried, saying,	4363
	4: 4	some *f* by the way side, and the fowls of	4098
	4: 5	some *f* on stony ground, where it had	4098
	4: 7	some *f* among thorns, and the thorns	4098
	4: 8	other *f* on good ground, and did yield	4098
	5:22	and when he saw him, he *f* at his feet,	4098
	5:33	and *f* **down** before him, and told him	4363
	7:25	heard of him, and came and *f* at his feet:	4363
	9:20	and he *f* on the ground,	4098
	14:35	and *f* on the ground, and prayed that, if it	4098
Lk	1:12	was troubled, and fear *f* upon him.	1968
	5: 8	When Simon Peter saw *it*, he *f* **down** at	4363
	5:12	who seeing Jesus *f* on *his* face,	4098
	6:49	beat vehemently, and immediately it *f*;	4098
	8: 5	as he sowed, some *f* by the way side;	4098
	8: 6	And some *f* upon a rock; and as soon as it	4098
	8: 7	And some *f* among thorns; and the thorns	4098
	8: 8	other *f* on good ground, and sprang up,	4098
	8:14	And that which *f* among thorns are they,	4098
	8:23	But as they sailed he *f* **asleep**:	879
	8:28	he *f* **down** before him, and with a loud	4363
	8:41	and he *f* **down** at Jesus' feet,	4098
	10:30	*f* **among** thieves, which stripped him of	4045
	10:36	was neighbour unto him that *f* among	1706
	13: 4	upon whom the tower in Siloam *f*,	4098
	15:20	ran, and *f* on his neck, and kissed him.	1968
	16:21	crumbs which *f* from the rich *man's* table:	4098
	17:16	And *f* **down** on *his* face at his feet,	4098
Jn	11:32	and saw him, she *f* **down** at his feet,	4098
	18: 6	they went backward, and *f* to the ground.	4098
Ac	1:25	from which Judas **by transgression** *f*,	3845
	1:26	and the lot *f* upon Matthias; and he was	4098
	5: 5	Ananias hearing these words *f* **down**,	4098
	5:10	Then *f* she **down** straightway at his feet,	4098
	7:60	And when he had said this, he *f* **asleep**.	2837
	9: 4	And he *f* to the earth, and heard a voice	4098
	9:18	immediately there *f* from his eyes as it	634
	10:10	while they made ready, he *f* into a trance,	1968
	10:25	and *f* **down** at *his* feet,	4098
	10:44	the Holy Ghost *f* on all them which	1968
	11:15	to speak, the Holy Ghost *f* on them,	1968
	12: 7	And his chains *f* **off** from *his* hands.	1601
	13:11	And immediately there *f* **on** him a	1968
	13:36	*f* **on sleep**, and was laid unto his fathers,	2837
	16:29	and *f* **down** before Paul and Silas,	4363
	19:17	and fear *f* **on** them all, and the name	1968
	19:35	of the *image* which *f* **down from Jupiter**?	1356
	20: 9	and *f* **down** from the third loft,	4098
	20:10	and *f* **on** him, and embracing *him* said,	1968
	20:37	and *f* **on** Paul's neck, and kissed him,	1968
	22: 7	I *f* **unto** the ground, and heard a voice	4098
Ro	11:22	them which *f*, severity; but toward thee,	4098
	15: 3	of them that reproached thee *f* on me.	1968
1Co	10: 8	*f* in one day three and twenty thousand.	4098
Heb	3:17	whose carcases *f* in the wilderness?	4098
	11:30	By faith the walls of Jericho *f* **down**,	4098
2Pe	3: 4	for since the fathers *f* **asleep**, all *things*	2837
Rev	1:17	when I saw him, I *f* at his feet as dead.	4098
	5: 8	twenty elders *f* **down** before the Lamb,	4098
	5:14	And the four *and* twenty elders *f* **down**	4098
	6:13	And the stars of heaven *f* unto the earth,	4098
	7:11	and *f* before the throne on their faces,	4098
	8:10	and there *f* a great star from heaven,	4098
	8:10	and it *f* upon the third *part* of the rivers,	4098
	11:11	great fear *f* upon them which saw them.	4098
	11:13	and the tenth *part* of the city *f*, and in	4098
	11:16	*f* upon their faces, and worshipped God,	4098
	16: 2	and there *f* a noisome and grievous sore	1096
	16:19	three parts, and the cities of the nations *f*:	4098
	16:21	there *f* upon men a great hail out of	2597
	19: 4	and the four beasts *f* **down** and	4098
	19:10	And I *f* at his feet to worship him. And he	4098
	22: 8	I *f* **down** to worship before the feet of	4098

FELLED (1) [FELL]

2Ki	3:25	wells of water, and *f* all the good trees:	5307

FELLER (1) [FELL]

Isa	14: 8	art laid down, no *f* is come up against us.	3772

FELLEST (1) [FELL]

2Sa	3:34	*man* falleth before wicked men, so *f* thou.	5307

FELLING (1) [FELL]

2Ki	6: 5	as one was *f* a beam, the axe head fell into	5307

FELLOES (1)

1Ki	7:33	their naves, and their *f*, and their spokes,	2839

FELLOW (27) [FELLOW'S, FELLOW-DISCIPLES, FELLOWCITIZENS, FELLOWHEIRS, FELLOWHELPER, FELLOWHELPERS, FELLOWLABOURER, FELLOWLABOURERS, FELLOWPRISONER, FELLOWPRISONERS, FELLOWS, FELLOWSERVANT, FELLOWSERVANTS, FELLOWSHIP, FELLOWSOLDIER, FELLOWWORKERS, WORKFELLOW, YOKEFELLOW]

Ge	19: 9	they said *again*, This one *f* came in to	NIH
Ex	2:13	the wrong, Wherefore smitest thou thy *f*?	7453
Jdg	7:13	*was* a man that told a dream unto his *f*,	7453
	7:14	his *f* answered and said, This *is* nothing	7453
	7:22	set every man's sword against his *f*,	7453
1Sa	14:20	every man's sword was against his *f*,	7453
	21:15	that ye have brought this *f* to play the mad	NIH
	21:15	shall this *f* come into my house?	NIH
	25:21	Surely in vain have I kept all that this *f*	NIH
	29: 4	Make *this* return, that he may go again	376
2Sa	2:16	they caught every one his *f* by the head,	7453
1Ki	22:27	Put this *f* in the prison, and feed him with	NIH
2Ki	9:11	wherefore came this mad *f* to thee?	NIH
2Ch	18:26	Put this *f* in the prison, and feed him	NIH
Ecc	4:10	For if they fall, the one will lift up his *f*:	2270
Isa	34:14	the island, and the satyr shall cry to his *f*;	7453
Jnh	1: 7	And they said every one to his *f*, Come,	7453
Zec	13: 7	and against the man *that is* my *f*,	5997
Mt	12:24	This *f* doth not cast out devils, but by	NIG
	26:61	And said, This *f* said, I am able to destroy	NIG
	26:71	This *f* was also with Jesus of Nazareth.	NIG
Lk	22:59	Of a truth this *f* also was with him:	NIG
	23: 2	We found this *f* perverting the nation,	NIG
Jn	9:29	*as for* this *f*, we know not from whence	NIG
Ac	18:13	This *f* persuadeth men to worship God	NIG
	22:22	said, Away with such a *f* from the earth:	NIG
	24: 5	For we have found this man a pestilent *f*,	NIG

FELLOW'S (1) [FELLOW]

2Sa	2:16	head, and *thrust* his sword in his *f* side;	7453

FELLOWCITIZENS (1) [FELLOW, CITIZEN]

Eph	2:19	*f* with the saints, and of the household	4847

FELLOW-DISCIPLES (1) [DISCIPLE, FELLOW]

Jn	11:16	called Didymus, unto *his f*, Let us also go,	4827

FELLOWHEIRS (1) [FELLOW, HEIR]

Eph	3: 6	That the Gentiles should be *f*, and of	4789

FELLOWHELPER (1) [FELLOW, HELP]

2Co	8:23	*he is* my partner and *f* concerning you:	4904

FELLOWHELPERS (1) [FELLOW, HELP]

3Jn	1: 8	that we might be *f* to the truth.	4904

FELLOWLABOURER (2) [FELLOW, LABOUR]

1Th	3: 2	and our *f* in the gospel of Christ,	4904
Phm	1: 1	unto Philemon *our* dearly beloved, and *f*,	4904

FELLOWLABOURERS (2) [FELLOW, LABOUR]

Php	4: 3	with Clement also, and *with* other my *f*,	4904
Phm	1:24	Marcus, Aristarchus, Demas, Lucas, my *f*.	4904

FELLOWPRISONER (2) [FELLOW, PRISON]

Col	4:10	Aristarchus my *f* saluteth you,	4869
Phm	1:23	salute thee Epaphras, my *f* in Christ Jesus;	4869

FELLOWPRISONERS (1) [FELLOW, PRISON]

Ro	16: 7	and Junia, my kinsmen, and my *f*,	4869

FELLOWS (13) [FELLOW]

Jdg	11:37	and bewail my virginity, I and my *f*.	7464
	18:25	lest angry *f* run upon thee, and thou lose	376
2Sa	6:20	one of the vain *f* shamelessly uncovereth	NIH
Ps	45: 7	thee *with* the oil of gladness above thy *f*.	2270
Isa	44:11	Behold, all his *f* shall be ashamed:	2270
Eze	37:19	the tribes of Israel his *f*, and will put them	2270
Da	2:13	they sought Daniel and his *f* to be slain.	2269
	2:18	his *f* should not perish with the rest of	2269
	7:20	whose look *was* more stout than his *f*.	2273
Zec	3: 8	thou, and thy *f* that sit before thee:	7453
Mt	11:16	in the markets, and calling unto their *f*,	2083
Ac	17: 5	took unto *them* certain lewd *f* of the baser	435
Heb	1: 9	thee *with* the oil of gladness above thy *f*.	3353

FELLOWSERVANT (6) [FELLOW, SERVE]

Mt	18:29	And his *f* fell down at his feet,	4889
	18:33	thou also have had compassion on thy *f*,	4889
Col	1: 7	As ye also learned of Epaphras our dear *f*,	4889
	4: 7	and a faithful minister and *f* in the Lord:	4889
Rev	19:10	I am thy *f*, and of thy brethren that have	4889
	22: 9	for I am thy *f*, and of thy brethren	4889

FELLOWSERVANTS (4) [FELLOW, SERVE]

Mt	18:28	servant went out, and found one of his *f*,	4889
	18:31	So when his *f* saw what was done,	4889
	24:49	And shall begin to smite *his f*, and to eat	4889
Rev	6:11	until their *f* also and their brethren,	4889

FELLOWSHIP (17) [FELLOW]

Lev	6: 2	or in *f*, or in a thing taken away by	3027+8667
Ps	94:20	Shall the throne of iniquity have *f* **with**	2266
Ac	2:42	stedfastly in the apostles' doctrine and *f*,	2842

1Co	1: 9	by whom ye were called unto the f of his	2842
	10:20	I would not that ye should have f with	2844
2Co	6:14	for what f hath righteousness with	3352
	8: 4	take upon *us* the f of the ministering to	2842
Gal	2: 9	to me and Barnabas the right hands of f;	2842
Eph	3: 9	And to make all *men* see what *is* the f of	2842
	5:11	And **have** no f with the unfruitful works	4790
Php	1: 5	For your f in the gospel from the first day	2842
	2: 1	if any f of the Spirit, if any bowels and	2842
	3:10	resurrection, and the f of his sufferings,	2842
1Jn	1: 3	you, that ye also may have f with us:	2842
	1: 3	truly our f is with the Father, and with	2842
	1: 6	If we say that we have f with him,	2842
	1: 7	have f one with another, and the blood	2842

FELLOWSOLDIER (2) [FELLOW, SOLDIER]

Php	2:25	and f, but your messenger, and he that	4961
Phm	1: 2	and Archippus our f, and to the church in	4961

FELLOWWORKERS (1) [FELLOW, WORK]

Col	4:11	These only *are* my f unto the kingdom of	4904

FELT (5) [FEEL]

Ge	27:22	he f him, and said, The voice *is* Jacob's	4959
Ex	10:21	of Egypt, even darkness *which* may be f.	4959
Pr	23:35	they have beaten me, *and* I f it not:	3045
Mk	5:29	she f in *her* body that she was healed of	1097
Ac	28: 5	off the beast into the fire, and f no harm.	3958

FEMALE (24)

Ge	1:27	male and f created he them.	5347
	5: 2	Male and f created he them;	5347
	6:19	alive with thee; they shall be male and f.	5347
	7: 2	take to thee by sevens, the male and his f:	802
	7: 2	*are* not clean by two, the male and his f.	802
	7: 3	Of the air by sevens, the male and the f;	5347
	7: 9	Noah into the ark, the male and the f,	5347
	7:16	went in, went in male and f of all flesh,	5347
Lev	3: 1	whether *it be* a male or f, he shall offer it	5347
	3: 6	or f, he shall offer it without blemish.	5347
	4:28	a kid of the goats, a f without blemish,	5347
	4:32	he shall bring it a f without blemish.	5347
	5: 6	a f from the flock, a lamb or a kid of	5347
	12: 7	law for her that hath born a male or a f.	5347
	27: 4	if it be a f, then thy estimation shall be	5347
	27: 5	twenty shekels, and for the f ten shekels.	5347
	27: 6	for the f thy estimation *shall be* three	5347
	27: 7	fifteen shekels, and for the f ten shekels.	5347
Nu	5: 3	Both male and f shall ye put out, without	5347
Dt	4:16	of any figure, the likeness of male or f,	5347
	7:14	shall not be male or f **barren** among you,	6135
Mt	19: 4	at the beginning made them male and f,	2338
Mk	10: 6	the creation God made them male and f.	2338
Gal	3:28	bond nor free, there is neither male nor f:	2338

FEMALE SLAVES See WOMENSERVANTS

FENCE (1) [FENCED]

Ps	62: 3	wall *shall ye be, and as* a tottering f.	1447

FENCED (38) [FENCE]

Nu	32:17	our little ones shall dwell in the f cities	4013
	32:36	Beth-nimrah, and Beth-haran, f cities:	4013
Dt	3: 5	All these cities *were* f *with* high walls,	1219
	9: 1	thyself, cities great and f up to heaven,	1219
	28:52	until thy high and f walls come down,	1219
Jos	10:20	remained of them entered into f cities.	4013
	14:12	and *that* the cities *were* great *and* f:	1219
	19:35	f cities *are* Ziddim, Zer, and Hammath,	4013
1Sa	6:18	*both* of f cities, and of country villages,	4013
2Sa	20: 6	lest he get him f cities, and escape us.	1219
	23: 7	the man *that* shall touch them must be f	4390
2Ki	3:19	ye shall smite every f city, and every	4013
	10: 2	and horses, a f city also, and armour;	4013
	17: 9	from the tower of the watchmen to the f	4013
	18: 8	from the tower of the watchmen to the f	4013
	18:13	come up against all the f cities of Judah,	1219
	19:25	that thou shouldest be to lay waste f cities	1219
2Ch	8: 5	f cities, with walls, gates, and bars;	4692
	11:10	*are* in Judah and in Benjamin, f cities.	4694
	11:23	of Judah and Benjamin, unto every f city:	4694
	12: 4	he took the f cities which *pertained* to	4694
	14: 6	he built f cities in Judah: for the land had	4694
	17: 2	he placed forces in all the f cities of Judah,	1219
	17:19	besides *those* whom the king put in the f	4013
	19: 5	set judges in the land throughout all the f	1219
	21: 3	of precious things, with f cities in Judah:	4694
	32: 1	encamped against the f cities,	1219
	33:14	put captains of war in all the f cities of	1219
Job	10:11	and hast f me with bones and sinews.	7753
	19: 8	He hath f **up** my way that I cannot pass,	1443
Isa	2:15	every high tower, and upon every f wall,	1219
	5: 2	he f it, and gathered out the stones	5823
Jer	5:17	they shall impoverish thy f cities,	4013
	15:20	will make thee unto this people a f brasen	1219
Eze	36:35	desolate and ruined cities *are become* f,	1219
Da	11:15	a mount, and take the **most** f cities:	4013
Hos	8:14	and Judah hath multiplied f cities;	1219
Zep	1:16	the trumpet and alarm against the f cities,	1219

FENS (1)

Job	40:21	trees, in the covert of the reed, and f.	1207

FERRET (1)

Lev	11:30	the f, and the chameleon, and the lizard,	604

FERRY (1)

2Sa	19:18	there went over a f **boat** to carry over	5679

FERVENT (7) [FERVENTLY]

Ac	18:25	and being f in the spirit, he spake and	2204
Ro	12:11	in business; f in spirit; serving the Lord;	2204
2Co	7: 7	your mourning, your f **mind** toward me;	2205
Jas	5:16	The **effectual** f prayer of a righteous *man*	1754
1Pe	4: 8	above all *things* have f charity among	1618
2Pe	3:10	and the elements shall melt with f **heat**,	2741
	3:12	and the elements shall melt with f **heat**?	2741

FERVENTLY (2) [FERVENT]

Col	4:12	always **labouring** f for you in prayers,	75
1Pe	1:22	*ye* love one another with a pure heart f:	1619

FESTERING See BLAINS; SCAB; SCABBED; SCURVY

FESTIVAL; FESTIVALS See SOLEMNITIES; SOLEMNITY

FESTUS (12) [FESTUS']

Ac	24:27	But after two years Porcius F came into	5347
	25: 1	Now when F was come into the province,	5347
	25: 4	But F answered, that Paul should be kept	5347
	25: 9	But F, willing to do the Jews a pleasure,	5347
	25:12	Then F, when he had conferred with	5347
	25:13	Bernice came unto Cesarea to salute F.	5347
	25:14	F declared Paul's cause unto the king,	5347
	25:22	Then Agrippa said unto F, I would also	5347
	25:24	And F said, King Agrippa, and all men	5347
	26:24	F said with a loud voice, Paul, thou art	5347
	26:25	But he said, I am not mad, most noble F;	5347
	26:32	Then said Festus unto F, This man	5347

FESTUS' (1) [FESTUS]

Ac	25:23	at F commandment Paul was brought	5347

FET (9) [FETCH]

2Sa	9: 5	f him out of the house of Machir, the son	3947
	11:27	David sent and f her to his house,	622
1Ki	7:13	Solomon sent and f Hiram out of Tyre.	3947
	9:28	f from thence gold, four hundred and	3947
2Ki	11: 4	and the rulers over hundreds,	5375
2Ch	12:11	the guard came and f them,	5375
Jer	26:23	they f **forth** Urijah out of Egypt,	3318
	36:21	So the king sent Jehudi to f the roll:	3947
Ac	28:13	And from thence we f **a compass**,	4022

FETCH (30) [FET, FETCHED, FETCHETH, FETCHT]

Ge	18: 5	I will f a morsel of bread, and comfort ye	3947
	27: 9	f me from thence two good kids of	3947
	27:13	only obey my voice, and go f me *them*.	3947
	27:45	I will send, and f thee from thence:	3947
	42:16	let him f your brother, and ye shall be	3947
Ex	2: 5	among the flags, she sent her maid to f it.	3947
Nu	20:10	must we f you water out of this rock?	3318
	34: 5	border shall f **a compass** from Azmon	5437
Dt	19:12	of his city shall send and f him thence,	3947
	24:10	thou shalt not go into his house to f his	5670
	24:19	the field, thou shalt not go again to f it:	3947
	30: 4	thee, and from thence will he f thee:	3947
Jdg	11: 5	elders of Gilead went to f Jephthah out	3947
	20:10	to f victual for the people, that *they* may	3947
1Sa	4: 3	Let us f the ark of the covenant of	3947
	6:21	come ye down, *and* f it **up** to you.	5927
	16:11	Samuel said unto Jesse, Send and f him:	3947
	20:31	Wherefore now send and f him unto me,	3947
	26:22	one of the young men come over and f it.	3947
2Sa	5:23	but f **a compass** behind them,	5437
	14:13	that the king doth not f **home again** his	7725
	14:20	To f **about** *this* form of speech hath thy	5437
1Ki	17:10	called to her, and said, F me, I pray thee,	3947
	17:11	as she was going to f *it*, he called to her,	3947
2Ki	6:13	where he *is*, that I may send and f him.	3947
2Ch	18: 8	said, F quickly Micaiah the son of Imla.	4116
Ne	8:15	and f olive branches, and pine branches,	935
Job	36: 3	I will f my knowledge from afar,	5375
Isa	56:12	*say they*, I will f wine, and we will fill	3947
Ac	16:37	let them come themselves and f us **out**.	1806

FETCHED (7) [FETCH]

Ge	18: 4	be f, and wash your feet,	3947
	27:14	and f, and brought *them* to his mother:	3947
Jos	15: 3	up to Adar, and f **a compass** to Karkaa:	5437
Jdg	18:18	f the carved image, the ephod,	3947
1Sa	7: 1	f **up** the ark of the Lord, and brought it	5927
	10:23	they ran and f him thence: and when he	3947
2Sa	4: 6	*as though* they would have f wheat;	3947

FETCHETH (1) [FETCH]

Dt	19: 5	his hand f **a stroke** with the axe to cut	5080

FETCHT (4) [FETCH]

Ge	18: 7	f a calf tender and good, and gave *it* unto	3947
2Sa	14: 2	f thence a wise woman, and said unto her,	3947
2Ki	3: 9	they f **a compass** of seven days' journey:	5437
2Ch	1:17	they f **up**, and brought forth out of Egypt	5927

FETTERS (11)

Jdg	16:21	to Gaza, and bound him with f **of brass**;	5178
2Sa	3:34	*were* not bound, nor thy feet put into f:	5178
2Ki	25: 7	bound him with f **of brass**, and carried	5178
2Ch	33:11	bound him with f, and carried him to	5178
	36: 6	bound him in f, to carry him to Babylon.	5178
Job	36: 8	if *they be* bound in f, *and* be holden in	2131

Ps	105:18	Whose feet they hurt with f: he was laid	3525
	149: 8	chains, and their nobles with f of iron;	3525
Mk	5: 4	that he had been often bound with f	3976
	5: 4	by him, and the f broken in pieces:	3976
Lk	8:29	he was kept bound with chains and in f;	3976

FEVER (9)

Dt	28:22	and with a f, and with an inflammation,	6920
Mt	8:14	his wife's mother laid, and **sick of a f**.	4445
	8:15	he touched her hand, and the f left her:	4446
Mk	1:30	But Simon's wife's mother lay **sick of a f**,	4445
	1:31	and immediately the f left her,	4446
Lk	4:38	wife's mother was taken with a great f;	4446
	4:39	And he stood over her, and rebuked the f;	4446
Jn	4:52	Yesterday at the seventh hour the f left	4446
Ac	28: 8	the father of Publius lay sick of a f and	4446

FEW (65) [FEWER, FEWEST, FEWNESS]

Ge	24:55	Let the damsel abide with us a f days,	NIH
	27:44	tarry with him a f days, until thy brother's	259
	29:20	they seemed unto him *but* a f days,	259
	34:30	I *being* f in number, they shall gather	4962
	47: 9	f and evil have the days of the years of	4592
Lev	25:52	but f years unto the year of jubile,	4592
	26:22	your cattle, and **make** you f **in number**;	4591
Nu	9:20	when the cloud was a f days upon	4557
	13:18	they be strong or weak, f or many;	4592
	26:54	to f thou shalt give the less inheritance:	4592
	26:56	thereof be divided between many and f.	4592
	35: 8	from *them that have* f ye shall give few:	4592
	35: 8	from *them that have* few ye shall **give**	4591
Dt	4:27	ye shall be left f in number among	4962
	26: 5	sojourned there with a f,	4592+4962
	28:62	be left f in number, whereas ye	4592
	33: 6	and not die; and let *not* his men be f	4557
Jos	7: 3	to labour thither; for they *are* but f.	4592
1Sa	14: 6	to the Lord to save by many or by f	4592
	17:28	with whom hast thou left those f sheep in	4592
2Ki	4: 3	*even* empty vessels; borrow not a f.	4591
1Ch	16:19	When ye were *but* f, even a few,	4557+4962
	16:19	*but* few, even a f, and strangers in it.	4592
2Ch	29:34	the priests were *too* f, so that they could	4592
Ne	2:12	in the night, I and *some* f men with me;	4592
	7: 4	the people *were* f therein, and the houses	4592
Job	10:20	*Are* not my days f? cease then, and let me	4592
	14: 1	Man *that is* born of a woman *is* of f days,	7116
	16:22	When a f years are come, then I shall go	4557
Ps	105:12	When they were *but a f* men in number;	NIH
	105:12	in number; yea, *very* f, and strangers in it.	4592
	109: 8	Let his days be f; *and* let another take his	4592
Ecc	5: 2	upon earth: therefore let thy words be f	4592
	9:14	*was* a little city, and f men within it;	4592
	12: 3	the grinders cease because they are f,	4591
Isa	10: 7	to destroy and cut off nations not a f.	4592
	10:19	the rest of the trees of his forest shall be f,	4557
	24: 6	of the earth are burned, and f men left.	4213
Jer	30:19	multiply them, and they shall not be f;	4591
	42: 2	(for we are left *but* a f of many, as thine	4592
Eze	5: 3	shalt also take thereof a f in number,	4592
	12:16	I will leave a f men of them from	4557
Da	11:20	within f days he shall be destroyed,	259
Mt	7:14	unto life, and f there be that find it.	3641
	9:37	truly is plenteous, but the labourers *are* f;	3641
	15:34	And they said, Seven, and a f little fishes.	3641
	20:16	first last: for many be called, but f chosen.	3641
	22:14	For many are called, but f are chosen.	3641
	25:21	thou hast been faithful over a f things, I	3641
	25:23	thou hast been faithful over a f things, I	3641
Mk	6: 5	save that he laid *his* hands upon a f sick	3641
	8: 7	And they had a f small fishes:	3641
Lk	10: 2	truly *is* great, but the labourers *are* f:	3641
	12:48	shall be beaten with f **stripes**. For unto	3641
	13:23	unto him, Lord, are there f that be saved?	3641
Ac	17: 4	and of the chief women not a f.	3641
	17:12	which were Greeks, and of men, not a f.	3641
	24: 4	hear us of thy clemency a f **words**.	4935
Eph	3: 3	the mystery; (as I wrote afore in f *words*,	3641
Heb	12:10	For they verily for a f days chastened *us*	3641
	13:22	for I have written a letter unto you in f	1024
1Pe	3:20	the ark was a preparing, wherein f, that is,	3641
Rev	2:14	But I have a f *things* against thee, because	3641
	2:20	Notwithstanding I have a f *things* against	3641
	3: 4	Thou hast a f names even in Sardis,	3641

FEWER (1) [FEW]

Nu	33:54	to the f ye shall give the less inheritance:	4592

FEWEST (1) [FEW]

Dt	7: 7	any people; for ye *were* the f of all people:	4592

FEWNESS (1) [FEW]

Lev	25:16	according to the f of years thou shalt	4591

FIDELITY (1)

Tit	2:10	Not purloining, but shewing all good f;	4102

FIELD (290) [FIELDS]

Ge	2: 5	every plant of the f before it was in	7704
	2: 5	and every herb of the f before it grew:	7704
	2:19	God formed every beast of the f,	7704
	2:20	fowl of the air, and to every beast of the f;	7704
	3: 1	of the f which the Lord God had made.	7704
	3:14	all cattle, and above every beast of the f;	7704
	3:18	thee; and thou shalt eat the herb of the f;	7704
	4: 8	it came to pass, when they were in the f,	7704

F

F

Ref	Text	Strong's
Ge 23: 9	he hath, which *is* in the end of his f;	7704
23:11	the f give I thee, and the cave that *is*	7704
23:13	I will give *thee* money for the f; take *it* of	7704
23:17	the f of Ephron, which *was* in Machpelah,	7704
23:17	the f, and the cave which *was* therein,	7704
23:17	and all the trees that *were* in the f,	7704
23:19	cave of the f of Machpelah before Mamre:	7704
23:20	the f, and the cave that *is* therein, were	7704
24:63	Isaac went out to meditate in the f at	7704
24:65	What man *is* this that walketh in the f to	7704
25: 9	in the f of Ephron the son of Zohar	7704
25:10	The f which Abraham purchased of	7704
25:27	was a cunning hunter, a man of the f;	7704
25:29	Esau came from the f, and he *was* faint:	7704
27: 3	out to the f, and take me *some* venison;	7704
27: 5	Esau went to the f to hunt for venison,	7704
27:27	the smell of my son *is* as the smell of a f	7704
29: 2	and behold a well in the f, and lo,	7704
30:14	found mandrakes in the f, and brought	7704
30:16	Jacob came out of the f in the evening,	7704
31: 4	and Leah to the f unto his flock,	7704
33:19	he bought a parcel of a f, where he had	7704
34: 5	now his sons were with his cattle in the f:	7704
34: 7	the sons of Jacob came out of the f when	7704
34:28	in the city, and that which *was* in the f,	7704
36:35	who smote Midian in the f of Moab,	7704
37: 7	we *were* binding sheaves in the f, and lo,	7704
37:15	and behold, *he was* wandering in the f:	7704
39: 5	all that he had in the house, and in the f.	7704
41:48	the food of the f, which *was* round about	7704
47:20	for the Egyptians sold every man his f,	7704
47:24	for seed of the f, and for your food,	7704
49:29	cave that *is* in the f of Ephron the Hittite,	7704
49:30	In the cave that *is* in the f of Machpelah,	7704
49:30	which Abraham bought with the f of	7704
49:32	The purchase of the f and of the cave that	7704
50:13	buried him in the cave of the f of	7704
50:13	which Abraham bought with the f for a	7704
Ex 1:14	and in all manner of service in the f:	7704
9: 3	LORD is upon thy cattle which *is* in the f,	7704
9:19	thy cattle, and all that thou hast in the f;	7704
9:19	and beast which shall be found in the f,	7704
9:21	left his servants and his cattle in the f.	7704
9:22	upon beast, and upon every herb of the f,	7704
9:25	all the land of Egypt all that *was* in the f,	7704
9:25	the hail smote every herb of the f,	7704
9:25	of the field, and brake every tree of the f.	7704
10: 5	tree which groweth for you out of the f:	7704
10:15	in the herbs of the f, through all the land	7704
16:25	to day ye shall not find it in the f.	7704
22: 5	If a man shall cause a f or vineyard to be	7704
22: 5	beast, and shall feed in another man's f;	7704
22: 5	of the best of his own f, and of the best of	7704
22: 6	of corn, or the standing corn, or the f,	7704
22:31	*any* flesh *that is* torn *of beasts* in the f;	7704
23:11	they leave the beasts of the f shall eat.	7704
23:16	labours, which thou hast sown in the f:	7704
23:16	hast gathered in thy labours out of the f.	7704
23:29	the beast of the f multiply against thee.	7704
Lev 14: 7	let the living bird loose into the open f.	7704
17: 5	which they offer in the open f, even that	7704
19: 9	shalt not wholly reap the corners of thy f,	7704
19:19	shalt not sow thy f with mingled seed:	7704
23:22	of the corners of thy f when thou reapest,	7704
25: 3	Six years thou shalt sow thy f, and six	7704
25: 4	thou shalt neither sow thy f, nor prune	7704
25:12	shall eat the increase thereof out of the f.	7704
25:34	the f of the suburbs of their cities may not	7704
26: 4	and the trees of the f shall yield their fruit.	7704
27:16	LORD *some part* of a f of his possession,	7704
27:17	If he sanctify his f from the year of jubile,	7704
27:18	if he sanctify his f after the jubile, then	7704
27:19	if he that sanctified the f will in any wise	7704
27:20	If he will not redeem the f, or if he have	7704
27:20	or if he have sold the f to another man,	7704
27:21	the f, when it goeth out in the jubile,	7704
27:21	be holy unto the LORD, as a f devoted;	7704
27:22	if a *man* sanctify unto the LORD a f	7704
27:24	In the year of the jubile the f shall return	7704
27:28	and beast, and of the f of his possession,	7704
Nu 22: 4	as the ox licketh up the grass of the f.	7704
22:23	aside out of the way, and went into the f:	7704
23:14	he brought him *into* the f of Zophim,	7704
Dt 5:21	f, or his manservant, or his maidservant,	7704
7:22	lest the beasts of the f increase upon thee.	7704
14:22	that the f bringeth forth year by year.	7704
20:19	down (for the tree of the f *is* man's *life*)	7704
21: 1	lying in the f, *and* it be not known who	7704
22:25	if a man find a betrothed damsel in the f,	7704
22:27	he found her in the f, *and* the betrothed	7704
24:19	thou cuttest down thine harvest in thy f,	7704
24:19	hast forgot a sheaf in the f, thou shalt not	7704
28: 3	city, and blessed *shalt* thou *be* in the f.	7704
28:16	the city, and cursed *shalt* thou *be* in the f.	7704
28:38	Thou shalt carry much seed out *into* the f,	7704
Jos 8:24	of slaying all the inhabitants of Ai in the f,	7704
15:18	she moved him to ask of her father a f:	7704
Jdg 1:14	she moved him to ask of her father a f:	7704
5: 4	thou marchedst out of the f of Edom,	7704
5:18	unto the death in the high places of the f.	7704
9:32	that *is* with thee, *and* lie in wait in the f:	7704
9:42	that the people went out *into* the f;	7704
9:43	laid wait in the f, and looked, and behold,	7704
13: 9	again unto the woman as she sat in the f:	7704
19:16	man from his work out of the f at even,	7704

Ref	Text	Strong's
Jdg 20:31	the other to Gibeah in the f, about thirty	7704
Ru 2: 2	Let me now go *to* the f, and glean ears of	7704
2: 3	and gleaned in the f after the reapers:	7704
2: 3	her hap was to light on a part of the f	7704
2: 8	Go not to glean in another f, neither go	7704
2: 9	*thine* eyes *be* on the f that they do reap,	7704
2:17	So she gleaned in the f until even,	7704
2:22	that they meet thee not in *any* other f.	7704
4: 5	What day thou buyest the f of the hand of	7704
1Sa 4: 2	they slew of the army in the f about four	7704
6:14	the cart came into the f of Joshua,	7704
6:18	*stone remaineth* unto this day in the f	7704
11: 5	Saul came after the herd out of the f;	7704
14:15	host, in the f, and among all the people:	7704
17:44	fowls of the air, and to the beasts of the f.	7704
19: 3	I stand beside my father in the f where	7704
20:11	Come, and let us go out *into* the f.	7704
20:11	they went out both of them *into* the f.	7704
20:24	So David hid himself in the f: and when	7704
20:35	Jonathan went out *into* the f at the time	7704
30:11	they found an Egyptian in the f,	7704
2Sa 10: 8	Maacah, *were* by themselves in the f.	7704
11:23	came out unto us *into* the f, and we were	7704
14: 6	they two strove together in the f,	7704
14:30	Joab's f is near mine, and he hath barley	2513
14:30	And Absalom's servants set the f on fire.	2513
14:31	Wherefore have thy servants set my f on	2513
17: 8	as a bear robbed of her whelps in the f:	7704
18: 6	So the people went out *into* the f against	7704
20:12	Amasa out of the highway *into* the f,	7704
21:10	by day, nor the beasts of the f by night.	7704
1Ki 11:29	and they two *were* alone in the f:	7704
14:11	him that dieth in the f shall the fowls of	7704
21:24	him that dieth in the f shall the fowls of	7704
2Ki 4:39	one went out into the f to gather herbs,	7704
7:12	of the camp to hide themselves in the f,	7704
8: 6	all the fruits of the f since the day that	7704
9:25	cast him in the portion of the f of Naboth	7704
9:37	the face of the f in the portion of Jezreel;	7704
18:17	which *is* in the highway of the fuller's f.	7704
19:26	they were *as* the grass of the f, and *as*	7704
1Ch 1:46	who smote Midian in the f of Moab,	7704
19: 9	were come *were* by themselves in the f:	7704
27:26	over them that did the work of the f for	7704
2Ch 26:23	buried him with his fathers in the f of	7704
31: 5	honey, and of all the increase of the f,	7704
Ne 13:10	did the work, were fled every one to his f.	7704
Job 5:23	shalt be in league with the stones of the f:	7704
5:23	the beasts of the f shall be at peace with	7704
24: 6	They reap *every one* his corn in the f:	7704
40:20	where all the beasts of the f play.	7704
Ps 8: 7	and oxen, yea, and the beasts of the f;	7704
50:11	and the wild beasts of the f *are* mine.	7704
78:12	in the land of Egypt, *in* the f of Zoan.	7704
78:43	Egypt, and his wonders in the f of Zoan:	7704
80:13	and the wild beast of the f doth devour it.	7704
96:12	Let the f be joyful, and all that *is* therein:	7704
103:15	as a flower of the f, so he flourisheth.	7704
104:11	They give drink to every beast of the f:	7704
Pr 24:27	and make it fit for thyself in the f;	7704
24:30	I went by the f of the slothful, and by	7704
27:26	and the goats *are* the price of the f.	7704
31:16	She considereth a f, and buyeth it: with	7704
Ecc 5: 9	for all: the king *himself* is served by the f.	7704
SS 2: 7	by the roes, and by the hinds of the f,	7704
3: 5	by the roes, and by the hinds of the f,	7704
7:11	my beloved, let us go forth *into* the f;	7704
Isa 5: 8	*that* lay f to field, till *there be* no place,	7704
5: 8	*that* lay field to f, till *there be* no place,	7704
7: 3	upper pool in the highway of the fuller's f;	7704
10:18	and of his **fruitful** f, both soul and body:	7704
16:10	taken away, and joy out of the **plentiful** f;	3759
29:17	Lebanon shall be turned into a **fruitful** f,	3759
29:17	the **fruitful** f shall be esteemed as a forest?	3759
32:15	the wilderness be a **fruitful** f,	3759
32:15	and the **fruitful** f be counted for a forest.	3759
32:16	and righteousness remain in the **fruitful** f.	3759
36: 2	upper pool in the highway of the fuller's f.	7704
37:27	they were *as* the grass of the f, and *as*	7704
40: 6	goodliness thereof *is* as the flower of the f.	7704
43:20	The beast of the f shall honour me,	7704
55:12	all the trees of the f shall clap *their* hands.	7704
56: 9	All ye beasts of the f, come to devour,	7704
Jer 4:17	As keepers of a f, are they against her	7704
6:25	Go not forth *into* the f, nor walk by	7704
7:20	upon the trees of the f, and upon the fruit	7704
9:22	of men shall fall as dung upon the open f,	7704
12: 4	and the herbs of every f wither,	7704
12: 9	come ye, assemble all the beasts of the f,	7704
14: 5	hind also calved in the f, and forsook *it,*	7704
14:18	I go forth *into* the f, then behold the slain	7704
17: 3	O my mountain in the f, I will give thy	7704
18:14	*which cometh* from the rock of the f?	7704
26:18	Zion shall be plowed *like* a f,	7704
27: 6	the beasts of the f have I given him also to	7704
28:14	I have given him the beasts of the f also.	7704
32: 7	Buy thee my f that *is* in Anathoth:	7704
32: 8	unto me, Buy my f, I pray thee, that *is*	7704
32: 9	bought the f of Hanameel my uncle's son,	7704
32:25	Buy thee the f for money,	7704
35: 9	neither have we vineyard, nor f, nor seed:	7704
41: 8	for we have treasures in the f, of wheat,	7704
48:33	gladness is taken from the **plentiful** f,	3759
La 4: 9	through for *want* of the fruits of the f.	7704
Eze 7:15	that *is* in the f shall die with the sword;	7704

Ref	Text	Strong's
Eze 16: 5	thou wast cast out in the open f,	7704
16: 7	thee to multiply as the bud of the f,	7704
17: 5	of the land, and planted it in a fruitful f;	7704
17:24	all the trees of the f shall know that I	7704
20:46	prophesy against the forest of the south f;	7704
26: 6	her daughters which *are* in the f shall be	7704
26: 8	with the sword thy daughters in the f:	7704
29: 5	given thee for meat to the beasts of the f.	776
31: 4	her little rivers unto all the trees of the f.	7704
31: 5	was exalted above all the trees of the f,	7704
31: 6	his branches did all the beasts of the f	7704
31:13	all the beasts of the f shall be upon his	7704
31:15	and all the trees of the f fainted for him.	7704
32: 4	I will cast thee forth upon the open f,	7704
33:27	him that *is* in the open f will I give to	7704
34: 5	became meat to all the beasts of the f,	7704
34: 8	flock became meat to every beast of the f,	7704
34:27	the tree of the f shall yield her fruit,	7704
36:30	fruit of the tree, and the increase of the f,	7704
38:20	the beasts of the f, and all creeping things	7704
39: 4	and *to* the beasts of the f to be devoured.	7704
39: 5	Thou shalt fall upon the open f: for I have	7704
39:10	that they shall take no wood out of the f,	7704
39:17	to every beast of the f,	7704
Da 2:38	the beasts of the f and the fowls of	1251
4:12	the beasts of the f had shadow under it,	1251
4:15	and brass, in the tender grass of the f;	1251
4:21	under which the beasts of the f dwelt,	1251
4:23	and brass, in the tender grass of the f;	1251
4:23	*let* his portion *be* with the beasts of the f,	1251
4:25	dwelling shall be with the beasts of the f:	1251
4:32	dwelling *shall* be with the beasts of the f:	1251
Hos 2:12	and the beasts of the f shall eat them.	7704
2:18	covenant for them with the beasts of the f,	7704
4: 3	the beasts of the f, and with the fowls	7704
10: 4	up as hemlock in the furrows of the f.	7704
Joel 1:10	The f is wasted, the land mourneth;	7704
1:11	because the harvest of the f is perished.	7704
1:12	*even* all the trees of the f, are withered:	7704
1:19	the flame hath burnt all the trees of the f.	7704
1:20	The beasts of the f cry also unto thee:	7704
2:22	Be not afraid, ye beasts of the f:	7704
Mic 1: 6	I will make Samaria as a heap of the f,	7704
3:12	shall Zion for your sake be plowed *as* a f,	7704
4:10	thou shalt dwell in the f, and thou shalt go	7704
Zec 10: 1	of rain, to every one grass in the f.	7704
Mal 3:11	vine cast her fruit before the time in the f,	7704
Mt 6:28	Consider the lilies of the f, how they grow;	68
6:30	if God so clothe the grass of the f,	68
13:24	a man which sowed good seed in his f:	68
13:27	Sir, didst not thou sow good seed in thy f?	68
13:31	which a man took, and sowed in his f:	68
13:36	unto us the parable of the tares of the f.	68
13:38	The f is the world; the good seed are	68
13:44	of heaven is like unto treasure hid in a f;	68
13:44	selleth all that he hath, and buyeth that f.	68
24:18	let him which is in the f return back to	68
24:40	Then shall two be in the f; the one shall be	68
27: 7	bought with them the potter's f, to bury	68
27: 8	Wherefore that f was called, The field of	68
27: 8	was called, The f of blood, unto this day.	68
27:10	gave them for the potter's f, as the Lord	68
Mk 13:16	let him that is in the f not turn back again	68
Lk 2: 8	same country shepherds abiding in the f,	5561
12:28	is to day in the f, and to morrow is cast	68
15:25	Now his elder son was in the f: and as he	68
17: 7	he is come from the f, Go and sit down	68
17:31	he that is in the f, let him likewise not	68
17:36	Two *men* shall be in the f; the one shall be	68
Ac 1:18	Now this *man* purchased a f with the	5564
1:19	insomuch as that f is called in their proper	5564
1:19	Aceldama, that is to say, The f of blood.	5564

FIELD COMMANDER See RABSHAKEH

FIELDS (60) [FIELD]

Ref	Text	Strong's
Ex 8:13	out of the villages, and out of the f.	7704
Lev 14:53	living bird out of the city into the open f,	7704
25:31	shall be counted as the f of the country:	7704
27:22	which *is* not of the f of his possession;	7704
Nu 16:14	given us inheritance of f and vineyards:	7704
19:16	that is slain with a sword in the open f,	7704
20:17	We will not pass through the f,	7704
21:22	we will not turn into the f, or into	7704
Dt 11:15	I will send grass in thy f for thy cattle,	7704
32:13	that he might eat the increase of the f;	7704
32:32	vine of Sodom, and of the f of Gomorrah:	7709
Jos 21:12	of the f of the city, and the villages thereof,	7704
Jdg 9:27	they went out *into* the f, and gathered	7704
9:44	upon all *the people* that *were* in the f,	7704
1Sa 8:14	he will take your f, and your vineyards,	7704
20: 5	that I may hide myself in the f unto the	7704
22: 7	the son of Jesse give every one of you f	7704
25:15	with them, when we were in the f:	7704
2Sa 1:21	*there be* rain upon you, nor f of offerings:	7704
11:11	of my lord, are encamped in the open f;	7704
1Ki 2:26	Get thee *to* Anathoth, unto thine own f;	7704
2Ki 23: 4	that dieth of his in the f shall the fowls	7704
23: 4	burnt them without Jerusalem in the f of	7709
1Ch 6:56	the f of the city, and the villages thereof,	7704
16:32	let the f rejoice, and all that *is* therein.	7704
27:25	the storehouses in the f, in the cities,	7704
2Ch 31:19	*were* in the f of the suburbs of their	7704
Ne 11:25	for the villages, with their f, *some* of	7704
11:30	f thereof, *at* Azekah, and *in* the villages	7704

Ne	12:29 and out of the **f** of Geba and Azmaveth:	7704
	12:44 gather into them out of the **f** of the cities	7704
Job	5:10 the earth, and sendeth waters upon the **f**:	2351
Ps	107:37 sow the **f**, and plant vineyards, which	7704
	132: 6 we found it in the **f** of the wood.	7704
Pr	8:26 yet he had not made the earth, nor the **f**,	2351
	24:30 and enter not into the **f** of the fatherless;	7704
Isa	16: 8 the **f** of Heshbon languish, *and* the vine	7709
	32:12 for the pleasant **f**, for the fruitful vine.	7704
Jer	6:12 others, *with their* **f** and wives together;	7704
	8:10 their **f** to them that *shall* inherit *them:* for	7704
	13:27 thine abominations on the hills in the **f**.	7704
	31:40 and all the **f** unto the brook of Kidron,	7709
	32:15 Houses and **f** and vineyards shall be	7704
	32:43 **f** shall be bought in this land, whereof ye	7704
	32:44 *Men* shall buy **f** for money,	7704
	39:10 them vineyards and **f** at the same time.	3010
	40: 7 captains of the forces which *were* in the **f**,	7704
	40:13 captains of the forces that *were* in the **f**,	7704
Eze	29: 5 thou shalt fall upon the open **f**; thou shalt	7704
Hos	12:11 altars *are* as heaps in the furrows of the **f**.	7704
Ob	1:19 and they shall possess the **f** of Ephraim,	7704
	1:19 fields of Ephraim, and the **f** of Samaria:	7704
Mic	2: 2 they covet **f**, and take *them* by violence;	7704
	2: 4 turning away he hath divided our **f**.	7704
Hab	3:17 shall fail, and the **f** shall yield no meat;	7709
Mk	2:23 that he went through the **corn f** on	4702
Lk	6: 1 the first, that he went through the **corn f**;	4702
	15:15 and he sent him into his **f** to feed swine.	68
Jn	4:35 Lift up your eyes, and look on the **f**;	5561
Jas	5: 4 labourers which have reaped *down* your **f**,	5561

FIERCE (41) [FIERCENESS, FIERCER, FIERY]

Ge	49: 7 Cursed *be* their anger, for *it was* **f**;	5794
Ex	32:12 Turn from thy **f** wrath, and repent of *this*	2740
Nu	25: 4 that the anger of the LORD may be	2740
	32:14 to augment yet the **f** anger of the LORD	2740
Dt	28:50 A nation of **f** countenance, which shall	5794
1Sa	20:34 Jonathan arose from the table in **f** anger,	2750
	28:18 nor executedst his **f** wrath upon Amalek,	2740
2Ch	28:11 for the **f** wrath of the LORD *is* upon you.	2740
	28:13 great, and *there is* **f** wrath against Israel.	2740
	29:10 that his **f** wrath may turn away from us.	2740
Ezr	10:14 until the **f** wrath of our God for this	2740
Job	4:10 the voice of the **f lion**, and the teeth of	7826
	10:16 Thou huntest me as a **f lion**: and again	7826
	28: 8 not trodden it, nor the **f lion** passed by it.	7826
	41:10 None *is so* **f** that dare stir him up: who	393
Ps	88:16 Thy **f wrath** goeth over me; thy terrors	2740
Isa	7: 4 for the **f** anger of Rezin with Syria,	2750
	13: 9 cruel both *with* wrath and **f** anger, to lay	2740
	13:13 of hosts, and in the day of his **f** anger.	2740
	19: 4 a king shall rule over them, saith the	5794
	33:19 Thou shalt not see a **f** people, a people of	3267
Jer	4: 8 for the **f** anger of the LORD is not turned	2740
	4:26 presence of the LORD, *and* by his **f** anger.	2740
	12:13 because of the **f** anger of the LORD.	2740
	25:37 because of the **f** anger of the LORD.	2740
	25:38 the oppressor, and because of his **f** anger.	2740
	30:24 The **f** anger of the LORD shall not return,	2740
	49:37 *even* my **f** anger, saith the LORD;	2740
	51:45 deliver ye every man his soul from the **f**	2740
La	1:12 hath afflicted *me* in the day of his **f** anger.	2740
	2: 3 He hath cut off in *his* **f** anger all the horn	2750
	4:11 he hath poured out his **f** anger,	2740
Da	8:23 a king of **f** countenance,	5794
Jnh	3: 9 repent, and turn away from his **f** anger,	2740
Hab	1: 8 and are more **f** than the evening wolves:	2300
Zep	2: 2 before the **f** anger of the LORD come	2740
	3: 8 mine indignation, *even* all my **f** anger:	2740
Mt	8:28 exceeding **f**, so that no *man* might pass by	5467
Lk	23: 5 And they were the **more f**, saying,	2001
2Ti	3: 3 false accusers, incontinent, **f**,	434
Jas	3: 4 they be so great, and are driven of **f** winds,	4642

FIERCENESS (12) [FIERCE]

Dt	13:17 that the LORD may turn from the **f** of his	2740
Jos	7:26 So the LORD turned from the **f** of his	2740
2Ki	23:26 turned not from the **f** of his great wrath,	2740
2Ch	30: 8 that the **f** of his wrath may turn away	7494
Job	39:24 swalloweth the ground with **f** and rage:	7494
Ps	78:49 cast upon them the **f** of his anger, wrath,	2740
	85: 3 thou hast turned *thyself* from the **f** of	2740
Jer	25:38 because of the **f** of the oppressor,	2740
Hos	11: 9 I will not execute the **f** of mine anger,	2740
Na	1: 6 who can abide in the **f** of his anger?	2740
Rev	16:19 give unto her the cup of the wine of the **f**	2372
	19:15 he treadeth the winepress of the **f** and	2372

FIERCER (1) [FIERCE]

2Sa	19:43 words of the men of Judah were **f** than	7185

FIERY (20) [FIERCE]

Nu	21: 6 the LORD sent **f** serpents among	8314
	21: 8 Make thee a **f** *serpent,* and set it upon a	8314
Dt	8:15 *wherein were* **f** serpents, and scorpions,	8314
	33: 2 from his right hand *went* a **f** law for them.	784
Ps	21: 9 Thou shalt make them as a **f** oven in the	784
Isa	14:29 and his fruit *shall be* a **f** flying **serpent**.	8314
	30: 6 old lion, the viper and **f** flying **serpent**,	8314
Da	3: 6 cast into the midst of a burning **f** furnace.	5135
	3:11 cast into the midst of a burning **f** furnace.	5135
	3:15 into the midst of a burning **f** furnace;	5135
	3:17 to deliver us from the burning **f** furnace,	5135
	3:20 to cast *them* into the burning **f** furnace.	5135

Da	3:21 were cast into the midst of the burning **f**	5135
	3:23 into the midst of the burning **f** furnace.	5135
	3:26 to the mouth of the burning **f** furnace,	5135
	7: 9 his throne *was* like the **f** flame,	5135
	7:10 A **f** stream issued and came forth from	5135
Eph	6:16 to quench all the **f** darts of the wicked.	4448
Heb	10:27 looking for of judgment and **f** indignation,	4442
1Pe	4:12 think it not strange concerning the **f trial**	4451

FIFTEEN (24) [FIFTEENTH]

Ge	5:10 Cainan eight hundred and **f** years,	2568+6240
	7:20 cubits upward did the waters	2568+6240
	25: 7 **threescore and f** years.	2568+7657+2050.1
Ex	27:14 side *of the gate shall be* **f** cubits:	2568+6240
	27:15 **f** *cubits:* their pillars three,	2568+6240
	38:14 one side of the gate *were* **f** cubits;	2568+6240
	38:15 hand, *were* hangings of **f** cubits;	2568+6240
	38:25 **threescore and f**	2568+7657+2050.1+2050.1
Lev	27: 7 thy estimation shall be **f** shekels,	2568+6240
Nu	31:37 *and* **threescore and f**	2568+7657+2050.1
Jdg	8:10 about **f** thousand *men,* all that	2568+6240
2Sa	9:10 Ziba had **f** sons and twenty	2568+6240
	19:17 his **f** sons and his twenty servants	2568+6240
1Ki	7: 3 *lay* on forty five pillars, **f** *in* a row.	2568+6240
2Ki	14:17 of Jehoahaz king of Israel **f** years.	2568+6240
	20: 6 I will add unto thy days **f** years;	2568+6240
2Ch	25:25 of Jehoahaz king of Israel **f** years.	2568+6240
Isa	38: 5 I will add unto thy days **f** years.	2568+6240
Eze	45:12 twenty shekels, **f** shekels,	2568+6235+2050.1
Hos	3: 2 I bought her to me for **f** *pieces of*	2568+6240
Jn	11:18 nigh unto Jerusalem, about **f** furlongs off:	1178
Ac	7:14 kindred, **threescore and f** souls.	1440+4002
	27:28 sounded again, and found *it* **f** fathoms.	1178
Gal	1:18 to see Peter, and abode with him **f** days.	1178

FIFTEENTH (18) [FIFTEEN]

Ex	16: 1 on the **f** day of the second month	2568+6240
Lev	23: 6 on the **f** day of the same month *is*	2568+6240
	23:34 The **f** day of this seventh month	2568+6240
	23:39 Also in the **f** day of the seventh	2568+6240
Nu	28:17 the **f** day of this month *is* the feast:	2568+6240
	29:12 the **f** day of the seventh month ye	2568+6240
	33: 3 on the **f** day of the first month;	2568+6240
1Ki	12:32 on the **f** day of the month, like	2568+6240
	12:33 the **f** day of the eighth month,	2568+6240
2Ki	14:23 In the **f** year of Amaziah the son of	2568+6240
1Ch	24:14 The **f** to Bilgah, the sixteenth to	2568+6240
	25:22 The **f** to Jeremoth, *he,* his sons,	2568+6240
2Ch	15:10 in the **f** year of the reign of Asa.	2568+6240
Est	9:18 the **f** day of the same they rested,	2568+6240
	9:21 and the **f** day of the same, yearly,	2568+6240
Eze	32:17 in the **f** *day* of the month,	2568+6240
	45:25 In the seventh *month,* in the **f** day	2568+6240
Lk	3: 1 Now in the **f** year of the reign of Tiberius	4003

FIFTH (61) [FIVE]

Ge	1:23 and the morning were the **f** day.	2549
	30:17 she conceived, and bare Jacob the **f** son.	2549
	41:34 **take up** the **f** *part* of the land of Egypt in	2567
	47:24 you shall give the **f** *part* unto Pharaoh,	2549
	47:26 that Pharaoh should have the **f** *part;*	2569
Lev	5:16 holy *thing,* and shall add the **f** *part*	2549
	6: 5 shall add the **f** *part* more thereto, *and* give	2549
	19:25 in the **f** year shall ye eat of the fruit	2549
	22:14 he shall put the **f** *part* thereof unto it,	2549
	27:13 he shall add a **f** *part* thereof unto thy	2549
	27:15 he shall add the **f** *part* of the money of thy	2549
	27:19 he shall add the **f** *part* of the money of thy	2549
	27:27 and shall add a **f** *part* of it thereto:	2549
	27:31 he shall add thereto the **f** *part* thereof.	2549
Nu	5: 7 add unto it the **f** *part* thereof, and give *it*	2549
	7:36 On the **f** day Shelumiel the son of	2549
	29:26 on the **f** day nine bullocks, two rams,	2549
	33:38 of Egypt, in the first *day* of the **f** month.	2549
Jos	19:24 the **f** lot came out for the tribe of	2549
Jdg	19: 8 arose early in the morning on the **f** day	2549
2Sa	2:23 **f** *rib,* that the spear came out behind him;	2570
	3: 4 and the **f**, Shephatiah the son of Abital;	2549
	3:27 smote him there *under* the **f** *rib,* that he	2570
	4: 6 smote him under the **f** *rib:* and Rechab	2570
	20:10 so he smote him therewith in the **f** *rib,*	2570
1Ki	6:31 *and* side posts *were* a **f** *part of* the wall.	2549
	14:25 it came to pass in the **f** year of king	2549
2Ki	25: 8 in the **f** month, on the seventh *day*	2549
1Ch	2:14 Nethaneel the fourth, Raddai the **f**,	2549
	3: 3 The **f**, Shephatiah of Abital: the sixth,	2549
	8: 2 Nohah the fourth, and Rapha the **f**.	2549
	12:10 Mishmannah the fourth, Jeremiah the **f**,	2549
	24: 9 The **f** to Malchijah, the sixth to Mijamin,	2549
	25:12 The **f** *to* Nethaniah, *he,* his sons,	2549
	26: 3 Elam the **f**, Jehohanan the sixth,	2549
	26: 4 Sacar the fourth, and Nethaneel the **f**,	2549
	27: 8 The **f** captain for the fifth month *was*	2549
	27: 8 The fifth captain for the **f** month *was*	2549
2Ch	12: 2 that in the **f** year of king Rehoboam	2549
Ezr	7: 8 he came *to* Jerusalem in the **f** month,	2549
	7: 9 on the first *day* of the **f** month came he	2549
Ne	6: 5 the **f** time with an open letter in his hand;	2549
	6:15 the twenty and **f** *day* of the *month* Elul,	2568
Jer	1: 3 away of Jerusalem captive in the **f** month.	2549
	28: 1 in the fourth year, *and* in the **f** month,	2549
	36: 9 it came to pass in the **f** year of Jehoiakim	2549
	52:12 Now in the **f** month, in the tenth *day* of	2549
Eze	1: 1 in the fourth *month,* in the **f** *day*	2568

F

Eze	1: 2 In the **f** day of the month, which *was*	2568
	1: 2 which *was* the **f** year of king Jehoiachin's	2549
	8: 1 in the sixth *month,* in the **f** *day* of	2568
	20: 1 the **f** *month,* the tenth *day* of the month,	2549
	33:21 in the tenth *month,* in the **f** *day* of	2568
Zec	7: 3 Should I weep in the **f** month,	2549
	7: 5 When ye fasted and mourned in the **f** and	2549
	8:19 of the fourth *month,* and the fast of the **f**,	2549
Rev	6: 9 And when he had opened the **f** seal, I saw	3991
	9: 1 And the **f** angel sounded, and I saw a star	3991
	16:10 And the **f** angel poured out his vial upon	3991
	21:20 The **f**, sardonyx; the sixth, sardius;	3991

FIFTIES (8) [FIFTY]

Ex	18:21 hundreds, rulers of **f**, and rulers of tens.	2572
	18:25 hundreds, rulers of **f**, and rulers of tens.	2572
Dt	1:15 captains over **f**, and captains over tens,	2572
1Sa	8:12 over thousands, and captains of **f**;	2572
2Ki	1:14 burnt up the two captains of the former **f**	2572
	1:14 captains of the former fifties with their **f**:	2572
Mk	6:40 sat down in ranks, by hundreds, and by **f**.	4004
Lk	9:14 Make them sit down by **f** in a company.	4004

FIFTIETH (4) [FIFTY]

Lev	25:10 ye shall hallow the **f** year,	2572
	25:11 A jubile shall that **f** year be unto you:	2572
2Ki	15:23 In the **f** year of Azariah king of Judah	2572
	15:27 **f** year of Azariah king of Judah Pekah	2572

FIFTY (157) [FIFTIES, FIFTIETH]

Ge	6:15 the breadth of it **f** cubits, and the height	2572
	7:24 upon the earth an hundred and **f** days.	2572
	8: 3 and **f** days the waters were abated.	2572
	9:28 after the flood three hundred and **f** years.	2572
	9:29 of Noah were nine hundred and **f** years:	2572
	18:24 Peradventure there be **f** righteous within	2572
	18:24 not spare the place for the **f** righteous that	2572
	18:26 If I find in Sodom **f** righteous within	2572
	18:28 Peradventure there shall lack five of the **f**	2572
Ex	26: 5 **F** loops shalt thou make in the one	2572
	26: 5 loops shalt thou make in the edge of the	2572
	26: 6 thou shalt make **f** taches of gold,	2572
	26:10 thou shalt make **f** loops on the edge of	2572
	26:10 **f** loops in the edge of the curtain which	2572
	26:11 thou shalt make **f** taches of brass,	2572
	27:12 west side *shall be* hangings of **f** cubits:	2572
	27:13 the east side eastward *shall be* **f** cubits.	2572
	27:18 **f every where**,	2572+2572+871.1+1886.1
	30:23 *even* two hundred and **f** *shekels,* and	2572
	30:23 sweet calamus two hundred and **f** *shekels*	2572
	36:12 **F** loops made he in one curtain,	2572
	36:12 **f** loops made he in the edge of the curtain	2572
	36:13 he made **f** taches of gold, and coupled	2572
	36:17 he made **f** loops upon the uttermost edge	2572
	36:17 **f** loops made he upon the edge of	2572
	36:18 made **f** taches of brass to couple the tent	2572
	38:12 the west side *were* hangings of **f** cubits,	2572
	38:13 And for the east side eastward **f** cubits.	2572
	38:26 and five hundred and **f** *men.*	2572
Lev	23:16 seventh sabbath shall ye number **f** days;	2572
	27: 3 even thy estimation shall be **f** shekels of	2572
	27:16 homer of barley seed *shall be* valued at **f**	2572
Nu	1:23 *were* **f** and nine thousand and	2572
	1:25 and five thousand six hundred and **f**.	2572
	1:29 **f** and four thousand and four hundred.	2572
	1:31 *were* **f** and seven thousand and	2572
	1:43 *were* **f** and three thousand and	2572
	1:46 three thousand and five hundred and **f**.	2572
	2: 6 **f** and four thousand and four hundred.	2572
	2: 8 *were* **f** and seven thousand and	2572
	2:13 *were* **f** and nine thousand and	2572
	2:15 and five thousand and six hundred and **f**.	2572
	2:16 **f** and one thousand and four hundred and	2572
	2:16 one thousand and four hundred and **f**,	2572
	2:30 *were* **f** and three thousand and	2572
	2:31 **f** and seven thousand and six hundred.	2572
	2:32 three thousand and five hundred and **f**.	2572
	4: 3 old and upward even until **f** years old,	2572
	4:23 until **f** years old shalt thou number	2572
	4:30 upward even unto **f** years old shalt thou	2572
	4:35 old and upward even unto **f** years old,	2572
	4:36 were two thousand seven hundred and **f**.	2572
	4:39 old and upward even unto **f** years old,	2572
	4:43 old and upward even unto **f** years old,	2572
	4:47 old and upward even unto **f** years old,	2572
	8:25 from the age of **f** years they shall cease	2572
	16: 2 hundred and **f** princes of the assembly,	2572
	16:17 his censer, two hundred and **f** censers;	2572
	16:35 and **f** men that offered incense.	2572
	26:10 fire devoured two hundred and **f** men:	2572
	26:34 **f** and two thousand and seven hundred.	2572
	26:47 *who were* **f** and three thousand and	2572
	31:30 thou shalt take one portion of **f**,	2572
	31:47 Moses took one portion of **f**, *both* of man	2572
	31:52 thousand seven hundred and **f** shekels.	2572
Dt	22:29 the damsel's father **f** *shekels* of silver,	2572
Jos	7:21 a wedge of gold of **f** shekels weight, then	2572
1Sa	6:19 even he smote of the people **f** thousand	2572
2Sa	15: 1 and horses, and **f** men to run before him.	2572
	24:24 and the oxen for **f** shekels of silver.	2572
1Ki	1: 5 horsemen, and **f** men to run before him.	2572
	7: 2 breadth thereof **f** cubits, and the height	2572
	7: 6 the length thereof *was* **f** cubits,	2572
	9:23 five hundred and **f**, which bare rule over	2572
	10:29 silver, and a horse for an hundred and **f**:	2572

F

1Ki	18: 4 hid them *by* f in a cave, and fed them	2572
	18:13 Lord's prophets *by* f in a cave,	2572+2572
	18:19 the prophets of Baal four hundred and f,	2572
	18:22 prophets *are* four hundred and f men.	2572
2Ki	1: 9 the king sent unto him a captain of f with	2572
	1: 9 sent unto him a captain of fifty with his f.	2572
	1:10 answered and said to the captain of f,	2572
	1:10 heaven, and consume thee and thy f.	2572
	1:10 heaven, and consumed him and his f.	2572
	1:11 him another captain of f with his fifty.	2572
	1:11 him another captain of fifty with his f.	2572
	1:12 heaven, and consume thee and thy f.	2572
	1:12 heaven, and consumed him and his f.	2572
	1:13 he sent again a captain of the third f with	2572
	1:13 again a captain of the third fifty with his f.	2572
	1:13 the third captain of f went up, and came	2572
	1:13 life, and the life of these f thy servants,	2572
	2: 7 And f men of the sons of the prophets	2572
	2:16 there be with thy servants f strong men;	2572
	2:17 sent therefore f men; and they sought	2572
	13: 7 the people to Jehoahaz but f horsemen,	2572
	15: 2 he reigned two and f years in Jerusalem.	2572
	15:20 of each man f shekels of silver, to give to	2572
	15:25 and with him f men of the Gileadites:	2572
	21: 1 and reigned f and five years in Jerusalem.	2572
1Ch	5:21 *of* their camels f thousand, and *of* sheep	2572
	5:21 *of* sheep two hundred and f thousand,	2572
	8:40 and sons' sons, an hundred and f.	2572
	9: 9 nine hundred and f and six.	2572
	12:33 war, f thousand, which could keep rank:	2572
2Ch	1:17 silver, and a horse for an hundred and f:	2572
	2:17 f thousand and three thousand and	2572
	3: 9 the weight of the nails *was* f shekels of	2572
	8:10 two hundred and f, that bare rule over	2572
	8:18 thence four hundred and f talents of gold,	2572
	26: 3 he reigned f and two years in Jerusalem.	2572
	33: 1 he reigned f and five years in Jerusalem.	2572
Ezr	2: 7 a thousand two hundred f and four.	2572
	2:14 of Bigvai, two thousand f and six.	2572
	2:15 of Adin, four hundred f and four.	2572
	2:22 The men of Netophah, f and six.	2572
	2:29 The children of Nebo, f and two.	2572
	2:30 of Magbish, an hundred f and six.	2572
	2:31 a thousand two hundred f and four.	2572
	2:37 children of Immer, a thousand f and two.	2572
	2:60 of Nekoda, six hundred f and two.	2572
	8: 3 genealogy of the males an hundred and f.	2572
	8: 6 son of Jonathan, and with him f males.	2572
	8:26 hand six hundred and f talents *of* silver,	2572
Ne	5:17 an hundred and f of the Jews and rulers,	2572
	6:15 *day of the month* Elul, in f and two days.	2572
	7:10 children of Arah, six hundred f and two.	2572
	7:12 a thousand two hundred f and four.	2572
	7:20 children of Adin, six hundred f and five.	2572
	7:33 The men of the other Nebo, f and two.	2572
	7:34 a thousand two hundred f and four.	2572
	7:40 children of Immer, a thousand f and two.	2572
	7:70 f basons, five hundred and thirty priests'	2572
Est	5:14 Let a gallows be made of f cubits high,	2572
	7: 9 Behold also, the gallows f cubits high,	2572
Isa	3: 3 The captain of f, and the honourable	2572
Eze	40:15 the porch of the inner gate *were* f cubits.	2572
	40:21 the length thereof *was* f cubits,	2572
	40:25 length *was* f cubits, and the breadth five	2572
	40:29 *it was* f cubits long, and five and	2572
	40:33 *it was* f cubits long, and five and	2572
	40:36 length *was* f cubits, and the breadth five	2572
	42: 2 north door, and the breadth *was* f cubits.	2572
	42: 7 The length thereof *was* f cubits.	2572
	42: 8 that *were* in the utter court *was* f cubits:	2572
	45: 2 f cubits round about *for* the suburbs	2572
	48:17 be toward the north two hundred and f,	2572
	48:17 be toward the south two hundred and f,	2572
	48:17 the toward the east two hundred and f,	2572
	48:17 and toward the west two hundred and f.	2572
Hag	2:16 for to draw out f *vessels out of* the press,	2572
Lk	7:41 five hundred pence, and the other f.	4004
	16: 6 bill, and sit down quickly, and write f.	4004
Jn	8:57 Thou art not yet f years old, and hast	4004
	21:11 great fishes, an hundred and f *and* three:	4004
Ac	13:20 *the space of* four hundred and f years,	4004
	19:19 *it* f thousand *pieces* of silver.	3461+4002

FIG (41) [FIGS]

Ge	3: 7 they sewed f leaves together,	8384
Dt	8: 8 vines, and f trees, and pomegranates;	8384
Jdg	9:10 the trees said to the f tree, Come thou,	8384
	9:11 the f tree said unto them, Should I	8384
1Ki	4:25 man under his vine and under his f tree,	8384
2Ki	18:31 every one of his f tree, and drink ye	8384
Ps	105:33 smote their vines also and their f trees;	8384
Pr	27:18 keepeth the f tree shall eat the fruit	8384
SS	2:13 The f tree putteth forth her green figs,	8384
Isa	34: 4 vine, and as a falling *f* from the fig tree.	NIH
	34: 4 vine, and as a falling *fig* from the f tree.	8384
	36:16 every one of his f tree, and drink ye	8384
Jer	5:17 shall eat up thy vines and thy f trees:	8384
Hos	8:13 nor figs on the f tree, and the leaf shall	8384
	2:12 I will destroy her vines and her f trees,	8384
	9:10 the firstripe in the f tree at her first time:	8384
Joel	1: 7 my vine waste, and barked my f tree:	8384
	1:12 is dried up, and the f tree languisheth;	8384
	2:22 the f tree and the vine do yield their	8384
Am	4: 9 and your vineyards and your f trees and	8384
Mic	4: 4 man under his vine and under his f tree;	8384

Na	3:12 All thy strong holds *shall be like* f trees	8384
Hab	3:17 Although the f tree shall not blossom,	8384
Hag	2:19 the f tree, and the pomegranate,	8384
Zec	3:10 under the vine and under the f tree.	8384
Mt	21:19 And when he saw a f tree in the way,	4808
	21:19 And presently the f tree withered away.	4808
	21:20 How soon is the f tree withered away!	4808
	21:21 only do this which is done to the f tree,	4808
	24:32 Now learn a parable of the f tree; When	4808
Mk	11:13 And seeing a f tree afar off having leaves,	4808
	11:20 saw the f tree dried up from the roots.	4808
	11:21 the f tree which thou cursedst is withered	4808
	13:28 learn a parable of the f tree; When her	4808
Lk	13: 6 A certain *man* had a f tree planted in his	4808
	13: 7 years I come seeking fruit on this f tree,	4808
	21:29 Behold the f tree, and all the trees;	4808
Jn	1:48 thou wast under the f tree, I saw thee.	4808
	1:50 saw thee under the f tree, believest thou?	4808
Jas	3:12 Can the f tree, my brethren, bear olive	4808
Rev	6:13 *even* as a f tree casteth her untimely figs,	4808

FIGHT (107) [FIGHTETH, FIGHTING, FIGHTINGS, FOUGHT]

Ex	1:10 f against us, and *so* get them up out of	3898
	14:14 The Lord shall f for you, and ye shall	3898
	17: 9 us out men, and go out, f with Amalek:	3898
Dt	1:30 which goeth before you, he shall f for you,	3898
	1:41 against the Lord, we will go up and f,	3898
	1:42 Say unto them, Go not up, neither f;	3898
	2:32 he and all his people, to f at Jahaz.	4421
	3:22 for the Lord your God he shall f for you.	3898
	20: 4 to f for you against your enemies, to save	3898
	20:10 When thou comest nigh unto a city to f	3898
Jos	9: 2 to f with Joshua and with Israel, with one	3898
	10:25 do to all your enemies against whom ye f	3898
	11: 5 at the waters of Merom, to f against Israel.	3898
	19:47 the children of Dan went up to f against	3898
Jdg	1: 1 the Canaanites first, to f against them?	3898
	1: 3 that we may f against the Canaanites,	3898
	1: 9 went down to f against the Canaanites,	3898
	8: 1 thou wentest to f with the Midianites?	3898
	9:38 go out, I pray now, and f with them.	3898
	10: 9 passed over Jordan to f also against Judah,	3898
	10:18 man *is* he that will begin to f against	3898
	11: 6 we may f with the children of Ammon.	3898
	11: 8 f against the children of Ammon,	3898
	11: 9 If ye bring me *home* again to f against	3898
	11:12 that thou art come against me to f in my	3898
	11:25 or did he *ever* f against them,	3898+3898
	11:32 the children of Ammon to f against them;	3898
	12: 1 Wherefore passedst thou over to f against	3898
	12: 3 up unto me this day, to f against me?	3898
	20:20 in array to f against them at Gibeah.	4421
1Sa	4: 9 to you: quit yourselves like men, and f.	3898
	8:20 and go out before us, and f our battles.	3898
	13: 5 themselves together to f with Israel,	3898
	15:18 f against them until they be consumed.	3898
	17: 9 If he be able to f with me, and *to* kill me,	3898
	17:10 give me a man, that we may f together.	3898
	17:20 as the host was going forth to the f,	4634
	17:32 servant will go and f with this Philistine.	3898
	17:33 to go against this Philistine to f with him:	3898
	18:17 valiant for me, and f the Lord's battles.	3898
	23: 1 the Philistines f against Keilah,	3898
	28: 1 together for warfare, to f with Israel.	3898
	29: 8 that I may not go f against the enemies of	3898
2Sa	11:20 so nigh unto the city when *ye* did f?	3898
1Ki	12:21 to f against the house of Israel,	3898
	12:24 nor f against your brethren the children of	3898
	20:23 let us f against them in the plain,	3898
	20:25 we will f against them in the plain,	3898
	20:26 and went up to Aphek, to f against Israel.	4421
	22:31 saying, F neither with small nor great,	3898
	22:32 they turned aside to f against him:	3898
2Ki	3:21 the kings were come up to f against thee:	3898
	10: 3 and f for your master's house.	3898
	19: 9 Behold, he is come out to f against thee:	3898
2Ch	11: 1 to f against Israel, that *he* might bring	3898
	11: 4 not go up, nor f against your brethren:	3898
	13:12 f ye not against the Lord God of your	3898
	18:30 saying, F ye not with small or great,	3898
	18:31 Therefore they compassed about him to f:	3898
	20:17 Ye shall not need to f in this *battle:* set	3898
	32: 2 that he was purposed to f against	4421
	32: 8 our God to help us, and to f our battles.	3898
	35:20 Necho king of Egypt came up to f against	3898
	35:22 that *he* might f with him, and hearkened	3898
	35:22 and came to f in the valley of Megiddo.	3898
Ne	4: 8 to come *and* to f against Jerusalem,	3898
	4:14 and terrible, and f for your brethren,	3898
	4:20 ye thither unto us: our God shall f for us.	3898
Ps	35: 1 f against them that fight against me.	3898
	35: 1 fight against them that f against me,	3898
	56: 2 for *they* be many that f against me,	3898
	144: 1 my hands to war, *and* my fingers to f:	4421
Isa	19: 2 they shall f every one against his brother,	3898
	29: 7 the multitude of all the nations that f	6633
	29: 7 all that f against her and her munition,	6638
	29: 8 the nations be, that f against mount Zion.	6633
	30:32 and in battles of shaking will he f with it.	3898
	31: 4 shall the Lord of hosts come down to f	6633
Jer	1:19 shall f against thee; but they shall not	3898
	15:20 shall f against thee, but they shall not	3898
	21: 4 ye f against the king of Babylon,	3898
	21: 5 I myself will f against you with an	3898

Jer	32: 5 ye f with the Chaldeans, ye shall not	3898
	32:24 that f against it, because of the sword,	3898
	32:29 that f against this city, shall come and	3898
	33: 5 They come to f with the Chaldeans, but	3898
	34:22 they shall f against it, and take it,	3898
	37: 8 f against this city, and take it, and burn it	3898
	37:10 army of the Chaldeans that f against you,	3898
	41:12 went to f with Ishmael the son of	3898
	51:30 mighty *men* of Babylon have forborn to f,	3898
Da	10:20 now will I return to f with the prince of	3898
	11:11 shall come forth and f with him, *even*	3898
Zec	10: 5 they shall f, because the Lord *is* with	3898
	14: 3 go forth, and f against those nations,	3898
	14:14 Judah also shall f at Jerusalem;	3898
Jn	18:36 of this world, then would my servants f,	75
Ac	5:39 haply ye be found even to f against God.	2314
	23: 9 spoken to him, let us not f against God.	2313
1Co	9:26 so f I, not as one that beateth the air:	4438
1Ti	6:12 F the good fight of faith, lay hold on eternal	75
	6:12 Fight the good fight of faith, lay hold on eternal	73
2Ti	4: 7 I have fought a good f, I have finished *my*	73
Heb	10:32 ye endured a great f of afflictions;	119
	11:34 were made strong, waxed valiant in f,	4171
Jas	4: 2 ye f and war, yet ye have not, because ye	3164
Rev	2:16 will f against them with the sword of my	4170

FIGHTETH (3) [FIGHT]

Ex	14:25 for the Lord f for them against	3898
Jos	23:10 he *it is* that f for you, as he hath promised	3898
1Sa	25:28 my lord the battles of the Lord,	3898

FIGHTING (3) [FIGHT]

1Sa	17:19 in the valley of Elah, f with the Philistines.	3898
2Ch	26:11 Moreover Uzziah had a host of f	4421+6213
Ps	56: 1 swallow me up; he f daily oppresseth me.	3898

FIGHTINGS (2) [FIGHT]

2Co	7: 5 troubled on every *side;* without *were* f,	3163
Jas	4: 1 whence *come* wars and f among you?	3163

FIGS (25) [FIG]

Nu	13:23 of the pomegranates, and of the f.	8384
	20: 5 or of f, or vines, or of pomegranates;	8384
1Sa	25:18 two hundred cakes *of* f, and laid *them* on	NIH
	30:12 they gave him a piece of a cake *of* f,	NIH
2Ki	20: 7 Isaiah said, Take a lump of f. And they	8384
1Ch	12:40 cakes *of* f, and bunches of raisins,	NIH
Ne	13:15 grapes, and f, and all *manner of* burdens,	8384
SS	2:13 The fig tree putteth forth her **green** f,	6291
Isa	38:21 Let them take a lump of f, and lay *it* for a	8384
Jer	8:13 f on the fig tree, and the leaf shall fade;	8384
	24: 1 baskets of f *were* set before the temple	8384
	24: 2 One basket *had* very good f, *even* like	8384
	24: 2 figs, *even* like the f *that are* first ripe:	8384
	24: 2 the other basket *had* very naughty f,	8384
	24: 3 And I said, F; the good figs, very good;	8384
	24: 3 the good f, very good; and the evil,	8384
	24: 5 Like these good f, so will I acknowledge	8384
	24: 8 as the evil f, which cannot be eaten,	8384
	29:17 and will make them like vile f,	8384
Na	3:12 *shall be like* fig trees with the **firstripe** f:	1061
Mt	7:16 gather grapes of thorns, or f of thistles?	4810
Mk	11:13 but leaves; for the time of f was not *yet.*	4810
Lk	6:44 For of thorns *men* do not gather f, nor of	4810
Jas	3:12 either a vine, f? so *can* no fountain both	4810
Rev	6:13 *even* as a fig tree casteth her **untimely** f,	3653

FIGURE (7) [FIGURES]

Dt	4:16 similitude of any f, the likeness of male	5566
Isa	44:13 maketh it after the f of a man, according	8403
Ro	5:14 who is the f of *him* that was to come.	5179
1Co	4: 6 I have in a f transferred to myself and	3345
Heb	9: 9 Which *was* a f for the time *then* present,	3850
	11:19 from whence also he received him in a f.	3850
1Pe	3:21 The **like** f whereunto *even* baptism doth	499

FIGURES (3) [FIGURE]

1Ki	6:29 about with **carved** f of cherubims	4734+6603
Ac	7:43 which ye made to worship them:	5179
Heb	9:24 with hands, *which are* the f of the true;	499

FILE (1)

1Sa	13:21 Yet they had a f for the mattocks,	6310+6477

FILIGREE See OUCHES

FILL (49) [FILLED, FILLEDST, FILLEST, FILLING, FULL, FULLY, FULNESS]

Ge	1:22 f the waters in the seas, and let fowl	4390
	42:25 Joseph commanded to f their sacks *with*	4390
	44: 1 saying, F the men's sacks *with* food,	4390
Ex	10: 6 they shall f thy houses, and the houses of	4390
	16:32 F an omer of it to be kept for your	4393
Lev	25:19 ye shall eat *your* f, and dwell therein in	7648
Dt	23:24 thou mayest eat grapes thy f at thine own	7648
1Sa	16: 1 f thine horn *with* oil, and go, I will send	4390
1Ki	18:33 F four barrels *with* water, and pour *it* on	4390
Job	8:21 Till he f thy mouth *with* laughing,	4390
	15: 2 and f his belly *with* the east wind?	4390
	20:23 *When* he is about to f his belly, *God* shall	4390
	23: 4 and f my mouth *with* arguments.	4390
	38:39 f the appetite of the young lions,	4390
	41: 7 Canst thou f his skin *with* barbed irons?	4390
Ps	81:10 open thy mouth wide, and I will f it.	4390
	83:16 f their faces *with* shame; that they may	4390
	110: 6 shall f the places *with* the dead bodies;	4390

Pr 1:13 we shall **f** our houses **with** spoil: — 4390
7:18 us **take** our **f** of love until the morning: — 7301
8:21 and I will **f** their treasures. — 4390
Isa 8: 8 the stretching out of his wings shall **f** — 4393
14:21 nor **f** the face of the world **with** cities. — 4390
27: 6 and **f** the face of the world **with** fruit. — 4390
56:12 we will **f** ourselves **with** strong drink: — 5433
Jer 13:13 I will **f** all the inhabitants of this land, — 4390
23:24 Do not I **f** heaven and earth? saith — 4392
33: 5 is to them **with** the dead bodies of men, — 4390
51:14 saying, Surely I will **f** thee **with** men, — 4390
Eze 3: 3 **f** thy bowels **with** this roll that I give thee. — 4390
7:19 satisfy their souls, neither **f** their bowels: — 4390
9: 7 the house, and **f** the courts **with** the slain: — 4390
10: 2 thine hand **with** coals of fire from — 4390
24: 4 the shoulder; **f** it **with** the choice bones. — 4390
30:11 Egypt, and **f** the land **with** the slain. — 4390
32: 4 I will **f** the beasts of the whole earth **with** — 7646
32: 5 and the valleys **with** thy height. — 4390
35: 8 I will **f** his mountains **with** his slain *men*: — 4390
Zep 1: 9 **f** their masters' houses **with** violence — 4390
Hag 2: 7 I will **f** this house **with** glory, saith — 4390
Mt 9:16 for that which is put in to **f** it up taketh — 4138
15:33 wilderness, as to **f** so great a multitude? — 5526
23:32 **F** ye **up** then the measure of your fathers. — 4137
Jn 2: 7 unto them, **F** the waterpots with water. — 1072
Ro 15:13 Now the God of hope **f** you **with** all joy — 4137
Eph 4:10 all heavens, that he might **f** all *things*.) — 4137
Col 1:24 **f up** that which is behind of the afflictions — 466
1Th 2:16 might be saved, to **f** up their sins alway: — 378
Rev 18: 6 in the cup which she hath filled **f** to her — 2767

FILLED (159) [FILL]
Ge 6:11 and the earth was **f** **with** violence. — 4390
6:13 for the earth is **f** **with** violence through — 4390
21:19 **f** the bottle **with** water, and gave the lad — 4390
24:16 the well, and **f** her pitcher, and came up. — 4390
26:15 had stopped them, and **f** them **with** earth. — 4390
Ex 1: 7 and the land was **f** **with** them. — 4390
2:16 the troughs to water their father's flock. — 4390
16:12 in the morning ye shall be **f** **with** bread; — 7646
28: 3 whom I have **f** **with** the spirit of wisdom, — 4390
31: 3 I have **f** him **with** the spirit of God, — 4390
35:31 he hath **f** him **with** the spirit of God, — 4390
35:35 Them hath he **f** **with** wisdom of heart, — 4390
40:34 the glory of the LORD **f** the tabernacle. — 4390
40:35 the glory of the LORD **f** the tabernacle. — 4390
Nu 14:21 all the earth shall be **f** **with** the glory of — 4390
Dt 26:12 they may eat within thy gates, and be **f**; — 7646
31:20 and *themselves*, and waxen fat; — 7646
Jos 9:13 bottles of wine, which we **f**, *were* new; — 4390
1Ki 7:14 was **f** **with** wisdom, and understanding, — 4390
8:10 that the cloud **f** the house of the LORD, — 4390
8:11 for the glory of the LORD had **f** the house — 4390
18:35 and he **f** the trench also **with** water. — 4390
20:27 of kids; but the Syrians **f** the country. — 4390
2Ki 3:17 yet that valley shall be **f** **with** water, that — 4390
3:20 Edom, and the country was **f** **with** water. — 4390
3:25 of land cast every man his stone, and **f** it; — 4390
21:16 till he had **f** Jerusalem from one end to — 4390
23:14 and **f** their places **with** the bones of men. — 4390
24: 4 for he **f** Jerusalem **with** innocent blood; — 4390
2Ch 5:13 that *then* the house was **f** **with** a cloud, — 4390
5:14 for the glory of the LORD had **f** the house — 4390
7: 1 and the glory of the LORD **f** the house. — 4390
7: 2 the glory of the LORD had **f** — 4390
16:14 him in the bed which was **f** **with** sweet — 4390
Ezr 9:11 which have **f** it from one end to another — 4390
Ne 9:25 were **f**, and became fat, — 7646
Job 3:15 had gold, who **f** their houses **with** silver: — 4390
16: 8 thou hast **f** me **with wrinkles**, which is a — 7059
22:18 Yet he **f** their houses **with** good *things*: — 4390
Ps 38: 7 For my loins are **f** **with** a loathsome — 4390
71: 8 Let my mouth be **f** **with** thy praise *and* — 4390
72:19 let the whole earth be **f** **with** his glory; — 4390
78:29 So they did eat, and were well **f**; for he — 7646
80: 9 it to take deep root, and it **f** the land. — 4390
104:28 openest thine hand, they are **f** **with** good. — 7646
123: 3 for we are exceedingly **f** **with** contempt. — 7646
123: 4 soul is exceedingly **f** **with** the scorning — 7646
126: 2 was our mouth **f** **with** laughter, — 4390
Pr 1:31 way, and be **f** **with** their own devices. — 7646
3:10 So shall thy barns be **f** **with** plenty, — 4390
5:10 Lest strangers be **f** **with** thy wealth; — 7646
12:21 but the wicked shall be **f** **with** mischief. — 4390
14:14 The backslider in heart shall be **f** **with** his — 7646
18:20 with the increase of his lips shall he be **f**. — 7646
20:17 his mouth shall be **f** **with** gravel. — 4390
24: 4 by knowledge shall the chambers be **f** — 4390
25:16 lest thou be **f** there**with**, and vomit it. — 7646
30:16 the earth *that* is not **f** **with** water; — 7646
30:22 and a fool when he is **f** **with** meat; — 4390
Ecc 1: 8 **with** seeing, nor the ear **f** **with** hearing. — 4390
6: 3 his soul be not **f** **with** good, and also *that* — 4390
6: 7 his mouth, and yet the appetite is not **f**. — 4390
SS 5: 2 for my head is **f** **with** dew, *and* my locks — 4390
Isa 6: 1 and lifted up, and his train **f** the temple. — 4392
6: 4 cried, and the house was **f** **with** smoke. — 4390
21: 3 Therefore my loins are **f** **with** pain: — 4390
33: 5 he hath **f** Zion **with** judgment and — 4390
34: 6 The sword of the LORD is **f** **with** blood, — 4390
43:24 neither hast thou **f** me **with** the fat of thy — 7301
65:20 nor an old man that hath not **f** his days: — 4390
Jer 13:12 Israel, Every bottle shall be **f** **with** wine: — 4390
13:12 that every bottle shall be **f** **with** wine? — 4390

Jer 15:17 for thou hast **f** me **with** indignation. — 4390
16:18 they have **f** mine inheritance **with** — 4390
19: 4 have **f** this place **with** the blood of — 4390
41: 9 the son of Nethaniah **f** it **with them** — 4390
46:12 of thy shame, and thy cry hath **f** the land: — 4390
51: 5 though their land was **f** **with** sin against — 4390
51:34 he hath **f** his belly **with** my delicates, — 4390
La 3:15 He hath **f** me **with** bitterness, he hath — 7646
3:30 smiteth him: he is **f** full **with** reproach. — 7646
Eze 8:17 for they have **f** the land **with** violence, — 4390
10: 3 went in; and the cloud **f** the inner court. — 4390
10: 4 the house was **f** **with** the cloud, — 4390
11: 6 have **f** the streets thereof **with** the slain. — 4390
23:33 Thou shalt be **f** **with** drunkenness and — 4390
28:16 have **f** the midst of thee **with** violence, — 4390
36:38 shall the waste cities be **f** **with** flocks of — 4392
39:20 Thus ye shall be **f** at my table **with** horses — 7646
43: 5 the glory of the LORD **f** the house. — 4390
44: 4 the glory of the LORD **f** the house of — 4390
Da 2:35 a great mountain, and **f** the whole earth. — 4391
Hos 13: 6 According to their pasture, so were they **f**; — 7646
13: 6 they were **f**, and their heart was exalted; — 7646
Na 2:12 **f** his holes **with** prey, and his dens **with** — 4390
Hab 2:14 the earth shall be **f** **with** the knowledge — 4390
2:16 Thou art **f** **with** shame for glory: drink — 7646
Hag 1: 6 ye drink, but ye are not **f with drink**; — 7937
Zec 9:13 **f** the bow **with** Ephraim, and raised up — 4390
9:15 they shall be **f** **like** bowls, and *as* — 4390
Mt 5: 6 after righteousness: for they shall be **f**. — 5526
14:20 And they did all eat, and were **f**: — 5526
15:37 And they did all eat, and were **f**: — 5526
27:48 and **f** *it* **with** vinegar, and put *it* on a reed, — 4130
Mk 2:21 the new *piece that* **f** it up taketh away — 4138
6:42 And they did all eat, and were **f**. — 5526
7:27 said unto her, Let the children first be **f**: — 5526
8: 5 So they did eat, and were **f**: and they took — 5526
15:36 one ran and **f** a spunge *full* of vinegar, — 1072
Lk 1:15 and he shall be **f** **with** the Holy Ghost, — 4130
1:41 and Elisabeth was **f** **with** the Holy Ghost: — 4130
1:53 He hath **f** the hungry with good *things*; — 1705
1:67 And his father Zacharias was **f** **with** — 4130
2:40 waxed strong in spirit, **f** **with** wisdom: — 4137
3: 5 Every valley shall be **f**, and every — 4137
4:28 they heard these *things*, were **f** with — 4130
5: 7 **f** both the ships, so that they began to — 4130
5:26 glorified God, and were **f** **with** fear, — 4130
6:11 And they were **f** **with** madness; — 4130
6:21 for ye shall be **f**. Blessed *are ye* that weep — 5526
8:23 and they were **f** **with water**, and were in — 4845
9:17 And they did eat, and were **f**: — 5526
14:23 *them* to come in, that my house may be **f**. — 1072
15:16 And he would fain have **f** his belly with — 1072
Jn 2: 7 And they **f** them up to the brim. — 1072
6:12 When they were **f**, he said unto his — 1705
6:13 twelve baskets with the fragments of — 1072
6:26 ye did eat of the loaves, and were **f**. — 5526
12: 3 the house was **f** **with** the odour of — 4137
16: 6 unto you, sorrow hath **f** your heart. — 4137
19:29 they **f** a spunge with vinegar, and put it — 4130
Ac 2: 2 it all the house where they were sitting. — 4137
2: 4 And they were all **f** **with** the Holy Ghost, — 4130
3:10 and they were **f** **with** wonder and — 4130
4: 8 Then Peter, **f** **with** the Holy Ghost, — 4130
4:31 and they were all **f** **with** the Holy Ghost, — 4130
5: 3 why hath Satan **f** thine heart to lie to — 4137
5:17 and were **f** **with** indignation, — 4130
5:28 ye have **f** Jerusalem **with** your doctrine, — 4130
9:17 thy sight, and be **f** **with** the Holy Ghost. — 4130
13: 9 **f** with the Holy Ghost, set his eyes on — 4130
13:45 they were **f** **with** envy, and spake against — 4130
13:52 And the disciples were **f** **with** joy, — 4137
19:29 And the whole city was **f** **with** confusion: — 4130
Ro 1:29 Being **f with** all unrighteousness, — 4137
15:14 are full of goodness, **f** **with** all knowledge, — 4137
15:24 if first I be somewhat **f** **with** your — 1705
2Co 7: 4 I am **f with** comfort, I am exceeding joyful — 4137
Eph 3:19 that ye might be **f with** all the fulness of — 4137
5:18 wherein is excess; but be **f with** the Spirit — 4137
Php 1:11 Being **f** with the fruits of righteousness, — 4137
Col 1: 9 to desire that ye might be **f with** — 4137
2Ti 1: 4 of thy tears, that I may be **f** with joy; — 4137
Jas 2:16 Depart in peace, be you warmed and **f**; — 5526
Rev 8: 5 and **f** it with fire of the altar, and cast *it* — 1072
15: 1 for in them is **f up** the wrath of God. — 5055
15: 8 And the temple was **f** with smoke from — 1072
18: 6 in the cup which she hath **f** fill to her — 2767
19:21 and all the fowls were **f** with their flesh. — 5526

FILLEDST (2) [FILL]
Dt 6:11 full of all good *things*, which thou **f** not, — 4390
Eze 27:33 forth out of the seas, thou **f** many people; — 7646

FILLEST (1) [FILL]
Ps 17:14 whose belly thou **f** with thy hid *treasure*: — 4390

FILLET (1) [FILLETED, FILLETH, FILLETS]
Jer 52:21 a **f** of twelve cubits did compass it; — 2339

FILLETED (3) [FILLET]
Ex 27:17 about the court shall be **f** with silver; — 2836
38:17 the pillars of the court *were* **f** with — 2836
38:28 and overlaid their chapiters, and **f** them. — 2836

FILLETH (6) [FILLET]
Job 9:18 take my breath, but **f** me **with** bitterness. — 7646

Ps 84: 6 make it a well; the rain also **f** the pools. — 5844
107: 9 and the hungry soul **f** with goodness. — 4390
129: 7 Where**with** the mower **f** not his hand; — 4390
147:14 and **f** thee **with** the finest of the wheat. — 7646
Eph 1:23 body, the fulness of him that **f** all in all. — 4137

FILLETS (8) [FILLET]
Ex 27:10 of the pillars and their **f** *shall be* of silver. — 2838
27:11 hooks of the pillars and their **f** *of* silver; — 2838
36:38 their chapiters and their **f** with gold: — 2838
38:10 of the pillars and their **f** *were of* silver. — 2838
38:11 hooks of the pillars and their **f** *of* silver; — 2838
38:12 hooks of the pillars and their **f** *of* silver; — 2838
38:17 hooks of the pillars and their **f** *of* silver; — 2838
38:19 of their chapiters and their **f** *of* silver. — 2838

FILLING (1) [FILL]
Ac 14:17 our hearts **with** food and gladness. — 1705

FILTH (4) [FILTHINESS, FILTHY]
Isa 4: 4 away the **f** of the daughters of Zion, — 6675
Na 3: 6 I will cast **abominable f** upon thee, — 8251
1Co 4:13 we are made as the **f** of the world, — 4027
1Pe 3:21 (not the putting away of the **f** of the flesh, — 4509

FILTHINESS (16) [FILTH]
2Ch 29: 5 and carry forth the **f** out of the holy *place*. — 5079
Ezr 6:21 from the **f** of the heathen of the land, — 2932
9:11 an unclean land with the **f** of the people — 5079
Pr 30:12 and *yet* is not washed from their **f**. — 6675
Isa 28: 8 For all tables are full of vomit *and* **f**, — 6675
La 1: 9 Her **f** *is* in her skirts; she remembereth — 2932
Eze 16:36 Because thy **f** was poured out, — 5178
22:15 and will consume thy **f** out of thee. — 2932
24:11 and *that* the **f** of it may be molten in it, — 2932
24:13 In thy **filthiness** *is* lewdness: because I have — 2932
24:13 thou shalt not be purged from thy **f** any — 2932
36:25 from all your **f**, and from all your idols, — 2932
2Co 7: 1 let us cleanse ourselves from all **f** of — 3436
Eph 5: 4 Neither **f**, nor foolish talking, nor jesting, — 151
Jas 1:21 Wherefore lay apart all **f** and superfluity — 4507
Rev 17: 4 of abominations and **f** of her fornication: — 168

FILTHY (17) [FILTH]
Job 15:16 much more abominable and **f** *is* man, — 444
Ps 14: 3 aside, they are *all* together become **f**: — 444
53: 3 gone back, they are altogether become **f**; — 444
Isa 64: 6 and all our righteousnesses *are* as **f** rags; — 5708
Zep 3: 1 Woe to her that is **f** and polluted, — 4754
Zec 3: 3 Joshua was clothed with **f** garments, — 6674
3: 4 Take away the **f** garments from him. — 6674
Col 3: 8 **f communication** out of your mouth. — 148
1Ti 3: 3 to wine, no striker, not **greedy of lucre**; — 146
3: 8 to much wine, not **greedy of lucre**; — 146
Tit 1: 7 to wine, no striker, not **given to f lucre**; — 146
1:11 which they ought not, for **f** lucre's sake. — 150
1Pe 5: 2 not **for f lucre**, but of a ready mind; — 147
2Pe 2: 7 with the **f** conversation of the wicked: — 766
Jude 1: 8 Likewise also these **f** dreamers defile — NIG
Rev 22:11 and he which is **f**, let him be filthy still: — 4510
22:11 and he which is filthy, let him be **f** still: — 4510

FINALLY (6)
2Co 13:11 **F**, brethren, farewell. Be perfect, be of — 3062
Eph 6:10 **F**, my brethren, be strong in — 3062+3588
Php 3: 1 **F**, my brethren, rejoice in the Lord. — 3062+3588
4: 8 **F**, brethren, whatsoever *things* are — 3062+3588
2Th 3: 1 **F**, brethren, pray for us, that — 3062+3588
1Pe 3: 8 *be ye* all of one mind, — 3588+5056

FIND (156) [FINDEST, FINDETH, FINDING, FOUND]
Ge 18:26 If I **f** in Sodom fifty righteous within — 4672
18:28 said, If I **f** there forty and five, I will not — 4672
18:30 he said, I will not do *it*, if I **f** thirty there. — 4672
19:11 they wearied themselves to **f** the door. — 4672
32: 5 my lord, that I may **f** grace in thy sight. — 4672
32:19 you speak unto Esau, when you **f** him. — 4672
33: 8 *are* to **f** grace in the sight of my lord. — 4672
33:15 let me **f** grace in the sight of my lord. — 4672
34:11 Let me **f** grace in your eyes, and what ye — 4672
38:22 to Judah, and said, I cannot **f** her; — 4672
41:38 Can we **f** *such a one* as this *is*, a man in — 4672
47:25 let us **f** grace in the sight of my lord, — 4672
Ex 5:11 get you straw where you can **f** *it*: yet not — 4672
16:25 to day ye shall not **f** it in the field. — 4672
33:13 thee, that I may **f** grace in thy sight: — 4672
Nu 32:23 and be sure your sin will **f** you **out**. — 4672
35:27 the revenger of blood **f** him without — 4672
Dt 4:29 thou shalt **f** *him*, if thou seek him with all — 4672
22:23 a man **f** her in the city, and lie with her; — 4672
22:25 if a man **f** a betrothed damsel in the field, — 4672
22:28 if a man **f** a damsel *that is* a virgin, which — 4672
24: 1 it come to pass that she **f** no favour in his — 4672
28:65 among these nations shalt thou **f** no **ease**, — 7280
Jdg 9:33 thou do to them as thou shalt **f** occasion. — 4672
14:12 **f** *it* **out**, then I will give you thirty sheets — 4672
17: 8 to sojourn where he could **f** *a place*: — 4672
17: 9 I go to sojourn where I may **f** *a place*. — 4672
Ru 1: 9 The LORD grant you that you may **f** rest, — 4672
2: 2 after *him* in whose sight I shall **f** grace. — 4672
2:13 Let me **f** favour in thy sight, my lord; — 4672
1Sa 1:18 Let thine handmaid **f** grace in thy sight. — 4672
9:13 *into* the city, ye shall straightway **f** him, — 4672
9:13 you up; for about *this* time ye shall **f** him. — 4672

F

F

1Sa	10: 2	shalt **f** two men by Rachel's sepulchre	4672
	20:21	send a lad, *saying*, Go, **f** out the arrows.	4672
	20:36	Run, **f** out now the arrows which I shoot.	4672
	23:17	for the hand of Saul my father shall not **f**	4672
	24:19	if a man **f** his enemy, will he let him go	4672
	25: 8	Wherefore let the young men **f** favour in	4672
2Sa	15:25	if I shall **f** favour in the eyes of the LORD,	4672
	16: 4	I humbly beseech thee *that* I may **f** grace	4672
	17:20	could not **f** *them*, they returned to	4672
1Ki	18: 5	peradventure we may **f** grass to save	4672
	18:12	come and tell Ahab, and he cannot **f** thee,	4672
2Ch	2:14	to **f** out every device which shall be put	2803
	20:16	ye shall **f** them at the end of the brook,	4672
	30: 9	your children *shall* **f** compassion before	NIH
	32: 4	kings of Assyria come, and **f** much water?	4672
Ezr	4:15	so shalt thou **f** in the book of the records,	7912
	7:16	gold that thou canst **f** in all the province	7912
Job	3:22	are glad, when they can **f** the grave?	4672
	11: 7	Canst thou *by* searching **f** out God?	4672
	11: 7	canst thou **f** out the Almighty unto	4672
	17:10	for I cannot **f** *one* wise *man* among you.	4672
	23: 3	that I knew where I might **f** him! *that* I	4672
	34:11	**cause** every man **to f** according to *his*	4672
	37:23	the Almighty, we cannot **f** him **out:**	4672
Ps	10:15	seek out his wickedness *till* thou **f** none.	4672
	17: 3	thou hast tried me, *and* shalt **f** nothing;	4672
	21: 8	Thine hand shall **f** out all thine enemies:	4672
	21: 8	thy right hand shall **f** out those that hate	4672
	132: 5	Until I **f** out a place for the LORD,	4672
Pr	1:13	We shall **f** all precious substance, we	4672
	1:28	seek me early, but they shall not **f** me:	4672
	2: 5	the LORD, and **f** the knowledge of God.	4672
	3: 4	So shalt thou **f** favour and	4672
	4:22	For they *are* life unto those that **f** them,	4672
	8: 9	and right to them that **f** knowledge.	4672
	8:12	and **f** out knowledge of witty inventions.	4672
	8:17	and those that seek me early shall **f** me.	4672
	16:20	He that handleth a matter wisely shall **f**	4672
	19: 8	that keepeth understanding shall **f** good.	4672
	20: 6	but a faithful man who can **f**?	4672
	28:23	afterwards shall **f** more favour than he	4672
	31:10	can **f** a virtuous woman? for her price	4672
Ecc	3:11	that no man can **f** out the work that God	4672
	7:14	to the end that man should **f** nothing after	4672
	7:24	and exceeding deep, who can **f** it **out?**	4672
	7:26	I **f** more bitter than death the woman,	4672
	7:27	one by one, to **f** out the account:	4672
	7:28	Which yet my soul seeketh, but I **f** not:	4672
	8:17	that a man cannot **f** out the work that is	4672
	8:17	seek it out, yet he shall not **f** *it*;	4672
	8:17	know *it*, yet shall he not be able to **f** *it*.	4672
	11: 1	for thou shalt **f** it after many days.	4672
	12:10	The Preacher sought to **f** out acceptable	4672
SS	5: 6	I sought him, but I could not **f** him;	4672
	5: 8	if ye **f** my beloved, that ye tell him, that I	4672
	8: 1	I should **f** thee without, I would kiss	4672
Isa	34:14	rest there, and **f** for herself a place of rest.	4672
	41:12	shalt seek them, and shalt not **f** them,	4672
	58: 3	in the day of your fast you **f** pleasure,	4672
Jer	2:24	in her month they shall **f** her.	4672
	5: 1	broad places thereof, if ye can **f** a man,	4672
	6:16	and ye shall **f** rest for your souls.	4672
	10:18	will distress them, that they may **f** *it so.*	4672
	29:13	**f** me, when ye shall search for me with all	4672
	45: 3	I fainted in my sighing, and I **f** no rest.	4672
La	1: 6	princes are become like harts *that* **f** no	4672
	2: 9	law *is* no *more*; her prophets also **f** no	4672
Da	6: 4	princes sought to **f** occasion against Daniel	7912
	6: 4	they could **f** none occasion nor fault;	7912
	6: 5	We shall not **f** any occasion against this	7912
	6: 5	except we **f** *it* against him concerning	7912
Hos	2: 6	a wall, that she shall not **f** her paths.	4672
	2: 7	shall not **f** *them*: then shall she say, I will	4672
	5: 6	they shall not **f** *him*; he hath withdrawn	4672
	12: 8	all my labours they shall **f** none iniquity	4672
Am	8:12	the word of the LORD, and shall not **f** *it*.	4672
Mt	7: 7	seek, and ye shall **f;** knock, and it shall be	2147
	7:14	unto life, and few there be that **f** it.	2147
	10:39	that loseth his life for my sake shall **f** it.	2147
	11:29	heart: and ye shall **f** rest unto your souls.	2147
	16:25	will lose his life for my sake shall **f** it.	2147
	17:27	his mouth, thou shalt **f** a piece of money:	2147
	18:13	And if so be that he **f** it, verily I say unto	2147
	21: 2	and straightway ye shall **f** an ass tied,	2147
	22: 9	the highways, and as many as ye shall **f,**	2147
	24:46	whom his lord when he cometh shall **f** so	2147
Mk	11: 2	ye shall **f** a colt tied, whereon never man	2147
	11:13	if haply he might **f** any *thing* thereon:	2147
	13:36	Lest coming suddenly he **f** you sleeping.	2147
Lk	2:12	Ye shall **f** *the* babe wrapped in swaddling	2147
	5:19	And when they could not **f** by what *way*	2147
	6: 7	they might **f** an accusation against him.	2147
	11: 9	seek, and ye shall **f;** knock, and it shall be	2147
	12:37	whom the lord when he cometh shall **f**	2147
	12:38	come in the third watch, and **f** *them* so,	2147
	12:43	whom his lord when he cometh shall **f** so	2147
	13: 7	seeking fruit on this fig tree, and **f** none:	2147
	15: 4	go after that which is lost, until he **f** it?	2147
	15: 8	the house, and seek diligently till she **f** it?	2147
	18: 8	man cometh, shall he **f** faith on the earth?	2147
	19:30	at your entering ye shall **f** a colt tied,	2147
	19:48	And could not **f** what they might do: for	2147
	23: 4	and *to* the people, I **f** no fault in this man.	2147
Jn	7:34	and shall not **f** me: and where I am,	2147
	7:35	will he go, that we shall not **f** him?	2147

Jn	7:36	and shall not **f** me: and where I am,	2147
	10: 9	and shall go in and out, and **f** pasture.	2147
	18:38	saith unto them, I **f** in him no fault *at all.*	2147
	19: 4	that ye may know that I **f** no fault in him.	2147
	19: 6	and crucify *him*: for I **f** no fault in him.	2147
	21: 6	the right side of the ship, and ye shall **f.**	2147
Ac	7:46	desired to **f** a tabernacle for the God of	2147
	17:27	**f** *him*, though he be not far from every	2147
	23: 9	strove, saying, We **f** no evil in this man:	2147
Ro	7:18	*how* to perform that which is good I **f** not.	2147
	7:21	I then a law, that, when I would do good,	2147
	9:19	then unto me, Why doth he yet **f** fault?	3201
2Co	9: 4	**f** you unprepared, we (that we say not,	2147
	12:20	I shall not **f** you such as I would, and	2147
2Ti	1:18	The Lord grant unto him that *he* may **f**	2147
Heb	4:16	and **f** grace to help in time of need.	2147
Rev	9: 6	shall men seek death, and shall not **f** it;	2147
	18:14	and thou shalt **f** them no more at all.	2147

FINDEST (2) [FIND]

Ge	31:32	With whomsoever thou **f** thy gods, let	4672
Eze	3: 1	said unto me, Son of man, eat that thou **f;**	4672

FINDETH (27) [FIND]

Ge	4:14	*that* every one that **f** me shall slay me.	4672
Job	33:10	Behold, he **f** occasions against me,	4672
Ps	119:162	at thy word, as one that **f** great spoil.	4672
Pr	3:13	Happy *is* the man that **f** wisdom,	4672
	8:35	For whoso **f** me findeth life,	4672
	8:35	For whoso **f** me findeth life,	4672
	14: 6	A scorner seeketh wisdom, and **f** it not:	NIH
	17:20	He that hath a froward heart **f** no good:	4672
	18:22	*Whoso* **f** a wife findeth a good *thing,* and	4672
	18:22	*Whoso* findeth a wife **f** a good *thing,* and	4672
	21:10	his neighbour **f** no **favour** in his eyes.	2603
	21:21	after righteousness and mercy **f** life,	4672
Ecc	9:10	Whatsoever thy hand **f** to do, do *it* with	4672
La	1: 3	among the heathen, she **f** no rest:	4672
Hos	14: 3	gods: for in thee the fatherless **f** mercy.	7355
Mt	7: 8	asketh receiveth; and he that seeketh **f:**	2147
	10:39	He that **f** his life shall lose it: and he that	2147
	12:43	dry places, seeking rest, and **f** none.	2147
	12:44	he **f** *it* empty, swept, and garnished.	2147
	26:40	and **f** them asleep, and saith unto Peter,	2147
Mk	14:37	**f** them sleeping, and saith unto Peter,	2147
Lk	11:10	and he that seeketh **f;** and to him that	2147
	11:25	he come, he **f** *it* swept and garnished.	2147
Jn	1:41	He first **f** his own brother Simon,	2147
	1:43	and **f** Philip, and saith unto him,	2147
	1:45	Philip **f** Nathanael, and saith unto him,	2147
	5:14	Afterward Jesus **f** him in the temple,	2147

FINDING (10) [FIND]

Ge	4:15	upon Cain, lest any **f** him should kill him.	4672
Job	9:10	Which doeth great *things* past **f** out; yea,	2714
Isa	58:13	thine own ways, nor **f** thine own pleasure,	4672
Lk	11:24	and **f** none, he saith, I will return unto	2147
Ac	4:21	**f** nothing how they might punish them,	2147
	19: 1	came to Ephesus: and **f** certain disciples,	2147
	21: 2	And **f** a ship sailing over unto Phenicia,	2147
	21: 4	**f** disciples, we tarried there seven days:	429
Ro	11:33	his judgments, and his ways **past f** out!	421
Heb	8: 8	For **f** fault with them, *he* saith, Behold,	3201

FINE (113) [FINER, FINEST, FINING]

Ge	18: 6	Make ready quickly three measures of **f**	5560
	41:42	arrayed him in vestures of **f linen,** and	8336
Ex	25: 4	and scarlet, and **f linen,** and goats' *hair,*	8336
	26: 1	*with* ten curtains of **f** twined **linen,**	8336
	26:31	**f** twined **linen** *of* cunning work:	8336
	26:36	purple, and scarlet, and **f** twined **linen,**	8336
	27: 9	**f** twined **linen** of an hundred cubits long	8336
	27:16	purple, and scarlet, and **f** twined **linen,**	8336
	27:18	the height five cubits of **f** twined **linen,**	8336
	28: 5	and purple, and scarlet, and **f linen.**	8336
	28: 6	*of* purple, *of* scarlet, and **f** twined **linen.**	8336
	28: 8	purple, and scarlet, and **f** twined **linen.**	8336
	28:15	and *of* scarlet, and *of* **f** twined **linen,**	8336
	28:39	thou shalt embroider the coat of **f linen,**	8336
	28:39	thou shalt make the mitre of **f linen,**	8336
	35: 6	and scarlet, and **f linen,** and goats' *hair,*	8336
	35:23	**f linen,** and goats' *hair,* and red skins of	8336
	35:25	of purple, *and* of scarlet, and of **f linen.**	8336
	35:35	scarlet, and in **f linen,** and of the weaver,	8336
	36: 8	made ten curtains of **f** twined **linen,**	8336
	36:35	purple, and scarlet, and **f** twined **linen,**	8336
	36:37	purple, and scarlet, and **f** twined **linen,**	8336
	38: 9	of the court *were* of **f** twined **linen,**	8336
	38:16	round about *were* of **f** twined **linen.**	8336
	38:18	purple, and scarlet, and **f** twined **linen:**	8336
	38:23	and in purple, and in scarlet, and **f linen.**	8336
	39: 2	purple, and scarlet, and **f** twined **linen.**	8336
	39: 3	and in the scarlet, and in the **f linen,**	8336
	39: 5	purple, and scarlet, and **f** twined **linen;**	8336
	39: 8	purple, and scarlet, and **f** twined **linen.**	8336
	39:27	made coats of **linen** *of* woven work	8336
	39:28	a mitre of **f linen,** and goodly bonnets *of*	8336
	39:28	goodly bonnets *of* **f linen,** and linen	8336
	39:28	and linen breeches *of* **f** twined **linen,**	8336
	39:29	a girdle of **f** twined **linen,** and blue,	8336
Lev	2: 1	the LORD, his offering shall be *of* **f flour;**	5560
	2: 4	*it shall be* unleavened cakes of **f flour**	5560
	2: 5	it shall be *of* **f flour** unleavened,	5560
	2: 7	it shall be made *of* **f flour** with oil.	5560
	5:11	of an ephah of **f flour** for a sin offering;	5560

Lev	6:20	the tenth *part* of an ephah of **f flour** *for* a	5560
	7:12	cakes mingled with oil, of **f flour,** fried.	5560
	14:10	three tenth deals of **f flour** *for* a meat	5560
	14:21	one tenth deal of **f flour** mingled with oil	5560
	23:13	tenth deals of **f flour** mingled with oil,	5560
	23:17	shall be *of* **f flour;** they shall be baken	5560
	24: 5	thou shalt take **f flour,** and bake twelve	5560
Nu	6:15	cakes *of* **f flour** mingled with oil,	5560
	7:13	both of them *were* full *of* **f flour** mingled	5560
	7:19	both of them full *of* **f flour** mingled with	5560
	7:25	both of them full *of* **f flour** mingled with	5560
	7:31	both of them full *of* **f flour** mingled with	5560
	7:37	both of them full *of* **f flour** mingled with	5560
	7:43	both of them full *of* **f flour** mingled with	5560
	7:49	both of them full *of* **f flour** mingled with	5560
	7:55	both of them full *of* **f flour** mingled with	5560
	7:61	both of them full *of* **f flour** mingled with	5560
	7:67	both of them full *of* **f flour** mingled with	5560
	7:73	both of them full *of* **f flour** mingled with	5560
	7:79	both of them full *of* **f flour** mingled with	5560
	8: 8	*even* **f flour** mingled with oil,	5560
1Ki	4:22	for one day was thirty measures of **f flour,**	5560
2Ki	7: 1	a measure of **f flour** *be sold* for a shekel,	5560
	7:16	So a measure of **f flour** was *sold* for a	5560
	7:18	and a measure of **f flour** for a shekel,	5560
1Ch	4:21	the house of them that wrought **f linen,**	948
	9:29	the **f flour,** and the wine, and the oil,	5560
	15:27	David *was* clothed with a robe of **f linen,**	948
	23:29	for the **f flour** for meat offering, and for	5560
2Ch	2:14	in blue, and in **f linen,** and in crimson;	948
	3: 5	which he overlaid with **f** gold,	2896
	3: 8	he overlaid it with **f** gold, *amounting* to	2896
	3:14	**f linen,** and wrought cherubims thereon.	948
Ezr	8:27	two vessels of **f** copper, precious	2896+6668
Est	1: 6	*hangings*, fastened with cords of **f linen**	948
	8:15	and *with* a garment of **f linen** and purple:	948
Job	28:17	it *shall not be for* jewels of **f** gold.	2212
	28:17	of it *shall not be for* jewels of **f** gold.	6337
	31:24	or have said to the **f** gold, *Thou art* my	3800
Ps	19:10	*they* than gold, yea, than much **f** gold:	6337
	119:127	above gold; yea, above **f** gold.	6337
Pr	3:14	silver, and the gain thereof than **f** gold.	2742
	7:16	*with* carved *works*, with **f linen** of Egypt.	330
	8:19	fruit *is* better than gold, yea, than **f** gold;	6337
	25:12	ornament of **f** gold, *so is* a wise reprover	3800
	31:24	She maketh **f linen,** and selleth *it;* and	5466
SS	5:11	His head *is as* the most **f** gold, his locks	6337
	5:15	of marble, set upon sockets of **f** gold:	6337
Isa	3:23	the **f linen,** and the hoods, and the vails.	5466
	13:12	make a man more precious than **f** gold;	6337
	19: 9	Moreover they that work in **f** flax,	8305
La	4: 1	is the most **f** gold changed! the stones	3800
	4: 2	sons of Zion, comparable to **f** gold,	6337
Eze	16:10	and I girded thee about with **f linen,**	8336
	16:13	thy raiment *was* of **f linen,** and silk,	8336
	16:13	thou didst eat **f flour,** and honey, and oil:	5560
	16:19	**f flour,** and oil, and honey, *wherewith* I	5560
	27: 7	**F linen** with broidered work from Egypt	8336
	27:16	and **f linen,** and coral, and agate.	948
	46:14	of a hin of oil, to temper with the **f flour;**	5560
Da	2:32	This image's head *was* of **f** gold, his breast	2869
	10: 5	whose loins *were* girded with **f** gold of	3800
Zec	9: 3	and **f** gold as the mire of the streets.	2742
Mk	15:46	he bought **f linen,** and took him down,	4616
Lk	16:19	which was clothed in purple and **f linen,**	1040
Rev	1:15	And his feet like unto **f** brass, as if they	5474
	2:18	flame of fire, and his feet *are* like **f** brass;	5474
	18:12	and **f linen,** and purple, and silk,	1040
	18:13	oil, and **f flour,** and wheat, and beasts,	4585
	18:16	that was clothed in **f linen,** and purple,	1039
	19: 8	that she should be arrayed in **f linen,**	1039
	19: 8	the **f linen** is the righteousness of saints.	1039
	19:14	clothed in **f linen,** white and clean.	1039

FINER (1) [FINE]

Pr	25: 4	there shall come forth a vessel for the **f.**	6884

FINERY See BRAVERY

FINEST (2) [FINE]

Ps	81:16	He should have fed them also with the **f**	2459
	147:14	and filleth thee *with* the **f** of the wheat.	2459

FINGER (26) [FINGERS]

Ex	8:19	said unto Pharaoh, This *is* the **f** of God:	676
	29:12	upon the horns of the altar with thy **f,**	676
	31:18	tables of stone, written with the **f** of God.	676
Lev	4: 6	the priest shall dip his **f** in the blood,	676
	4:17	priest shall dip his **f** *in* of the blood,	676
	4:25	of the blood of the sin offering with his **f,**	676
	4:30	shall take of the blood thereof with his **f,**	676
	4:34	of the blood of the sin offering with his **f,**	676
	8:15	horns of the altar round about with his **f,**	676
	9: 9	he dipt his **f** in the blood, and put it upon	676
	14:16	the priest shall dip his right **f** in the oil that	676
	14:16	shall sprinkle of the oil with his **f** seven	676
	14:27	the priest shall sprinkle with his right **f**	676
	16:14	sprinkle *it* with his **f** upon the mercy seat	676
	16:14	sprinkle of the blood with his **f** seven times.	676
	16:19	of the blood upon it with his **f** seven times,	676
Nu	19: 4	the priest shall take of her blood with his **f,**	676
Dt	9:10	tables of stone written with the **f** of God;	676
1Ki	12:10	My little *f* shall be thicker than my father's	NIH
2Ch	10:10	My little *f* shall be thicker than my father's	NIH
Isa	58: 9	the putting forth of the **f,**	676

Lk	11:20	But if I with the f of God cast out devils,	1147
	16:24	that he may dip the tip of his f in water,	1147
Jn	8: 6	and with *his* f wrote on the ground,	1147
	20:25	and put my f into the print of the nails,	1147
	20:27	Reach hither thy f, and behold my hands;	1147

FINGERS (15) [FINGER]

2Sa	21:20	that had on every hand six f, and on every	676
1Ch	20: 6	whose f **and toes** *were* four and twenty,	676
Ps	8: 3	the work of thy f, the moon and the stars,	676
	144: 1	my hands to war, *and* my f to fight:	676
Pr	6:13	with his feet, he teacheth with his f;	676
	7: 3	Bind them upon thy f, write them upon	676
SS	5: 5	my f *with* sweet smelling myrrh, upon	676
Isa	2: 8	*that* which their own f have made:	676
	17: 8	neither shall respect *that* which his f have	676
	59: 3	with blood, and your f with iniquity;	676
Jer	52:21	and the thickness thereof *was* four f:	676
Da	5: 5	In the same hour came forth f of a man's	677
Mt	23: 4	will not move them with *one* of their f.	1147
Mk	7:33	and put his f into his ears, and he spit,	1147
Lk	11:46	touch not the burdens with one of your f.	1147

FINING (2) [FINE]

Pr	17: 3	The f **pot** *is* for silver, and the furnace for	4715
	27:21	*As* the f **pot** for silver, and the furnace for	4715

FINISH (11) [FINISHED, FINISHER]

Ge	6:16	ark, and in a cubit shalt thou f it above;	3615
Da	9:24	f the transgression, and to make an end	3607
Zec	4: 9	his hands shall also f *it;* and thou shalt	1214
Lk	14:28	cost, whether he have sufficient to f it?	535
	14:29	is not able to f *it,* all that behold *it* begin	1615
	14:30	began to build, and was not able to f	1615
Jn	4:34	of him that sent me, and to f his work.	5048
	5:36	which the Father hath given me to f,	5048
Ac	20:24	so that *I* might f my course with joy,	5048
Ro	9:28	For he will f the work, and cut *it* short in	4931
2Co	8: 6	would also f in you the same grace also.	2005

FINISHED (42) [FINISH]

Ge	2: 1	Thus the heavens and the earth were f,	3615
Ex	39:32	of the tent of the congregation f:	3615
	40:33	of the court gate. So Moses f the work.	3615
Dt	31:24	of this law in a book, until they were f,	8552
Jos	4:10	until every thing was f that the LORD	8552
Ru	3:18	in rest, until he have f the thing *this* day.	3615
1Ki	6: 9	So he built the house, and f it;	3615
	6:14	So Solomon built the house, and f it.	3615
	6:22	with gold, until *he* had f all the house:	8552
	6:38	was the house f throughout all the parts	3615
	7: 1	thirteen years, and he f all his house.	3615
	7:22	work: so was the work of the pillars f.	8552
	9: 1	when Solomon had f the building of	3615
	9:25	*was* before the LORD. So he f the house.	7999
1Ch	27:24	he f not, because there fell wrath for it	3615
	28:20	*thou* hast f all the work for the service	3615
2Ch	4:11	Huram f the work that he was to make	3615
	5: 1	made for the house of the LORD was f:	7999
	7:11	Thus Solomon f the house of the LORD,	3615
	8:16	the house of the LORD, and until it was f.	3615
	24:14	when they had f *it,* they brought the rest	3615
	29:28	*continued* until the burnt offering was f.	3615
	31: 1	Now when all this was f, all Israel that	3615
	31: 7	heaps, and f *them* in the seventh month.	3615
Ezr	5:16	it *been* in building, and yet *it* is not f.	8000
	6:14	f *it,* according to the commandment of	3635
	6:15	this house was f on the third day of	3319
Ne	6:15	So the wall was f in the twenty and	7999
Da	5:26	God hath numbered thy kingdom, and f	8000
	12: 7	the holy people, all these *things* shall be f.	3615
Mt	13:53	*that* when Jesus had f these parables,	5055
	19: 1	*that* when Jesus had f these sayings,	5055
	26: 1	pass, when Jesus had f all these sayings,	5055
Jn	17: 4	I **have** f the work which thou gavest me	5048
	19:30	had received the vinegar, he said, It is f:	5055
Ac	21: 7	when we had f *our* course from Tyre,	1274
2Ti	4: 7	I have f *my* course, I have kept the faith:	5055
Heb	4: 3	although the works were f from	1096
Jas	1:15	and sin, when it is f, bringeth forth death.	658
Rev	10: 7	to sound, the mystery of God should be f,	5055
	11: 7	when they shall have f their testimony,	5055
	20: 5	not again until the thousand years were f.	5055

FINISHER (1) [FINISH]

Heb	12: 2	unto Jesus the author and f of *our* faith;	5051

FINS (5)

Lev	11: 9	hath f and scales in the waters,	5579
	11:10	all that have not f nor scales in the seas,	5579
	11:12	Whatsoever hath no f nor scales in	5579
Dt	14: 9	all that have f and scales shall ye eat:	5579
	14:10	whatsoever hath not f and scales ye may	5579

FIR (21)

2Sa	6: 5	*manner of instruments made of* f wood,	1265
1Ki	5: 8	of cedar, and concerning timber of f.	1265
	5:10	and f trees *according to* all his desire.	1265
	6:15	the floor of the house with planks of f,	1265
	6:34	two doors *were* of f tree: the two leaves	1265
	9:11	Solomon with cedar trees and f trees,	1265
2Ki	19:23	thereof, *and* the choice f **trees** thereof:	1265
2Ch	2: 8	f **trees**, and algum trees, out of Lebanon:	1265
	3: 5	the greater house he cieled with f tree,	1265
Ps	104:17	*as for* the stork, the f **trees** *are* her house.	1265

SS	1:17	our house *are* cedar, *and* our rafters of f.	1266
Isa	14: 8	the f **trees** rejoice at thee, *and* the cedars	1265
	37:24	*and* the choice f **trees** thereof:	1265
	41: 9	I will set in the desert the f **tree**,	1265
	55:13	up the thorn shall come up the f **tree**,	1265
	60:13	the f **tree**, the pine tree, and the box	1265
Eze	27: 5	all thy *ship* boards of f trees of Senir:	1265
	31: 8	the f **trees** were not like his boughs.	1265
Hos	14: 8	I *am* like a green f **tree**. From me is thy	1265
Na	2: 3	the f **trees** shall be terribly shaken.	1265
Zec	11: 2	Howl, f **tree**; for the cedar is fallen;	1265

FIRE (549) [FIREBRAND, FIREBRANDS, FIREPANS, FIRES]

Ge	19:24	and f from the LORD out of heaven;	784
	22: 6	he took the f in his hand, and a knife;	784
	22: 7	And he said, Behold the f and the wood:	784
Ex	3: 2	in a flame of f out of the midst of a bush:	784
	3: 2	the bush burned with f, and the bush was	784
	9:23	hail, and the f ran along upon the ground;	784
	9:24	and f mingled with the hail, very grievous,	784
	12: 8	roast with f, and unleavened bread;	784
	12: 9	sodden at all with water, but roast with f,	784
	12:10	until the morning ye shall burn with f.	784
	13:21	by night in a pillar of f, to give them light;	784
	13:22	nor the pillar of f by night, *from* before	784
	14:24	of the Egyptians through the pillar of f	784
	19:18	the LORD descended upon it in f:	784
	22: 6	If f break out, and catch in thorns, so that	784
	22: 6	kindled the f shall surely make restitution.	1200
	24:17	on the top of the mount in the eyes of	784
	29:14	shalt thou burn with f without the camp:	784
	29:18	an **offering made by** f unto the LORD.	801
	29:25	it *is* an **offering made by** f unto the LORD.	801
	29:34	then thou shalt burn the remainder with f:	784
	29:41	an **offering made by** f unto the LORD.	801
	30:20	to burn **offering made by** f unto	801
	32:20	burnt *it* in the f, and ground *it* to powder,	784
	32:24	I cast it into the f, and there came out this	784
	35: 3	Ye shall kindle no f throughout your	784
	40:38	f was on it by night, in the sight of all	784
Lev	1: 7	sons of Aaron the priest shall put f upon	784
	1: 8	and lay the wood in order upon the f	784
	1: 8	in order upon the wood that *is* on the f	784
	1: 9	a burnt sacrifice, an **offering made by** f,	801
	1:12	that *is* on the f which *is* upon the altar:	784
	1:13	a burnt sacrifice, an **offering made by** f,	801
	1:17	altar, upon the wood that *is* upon the f:	784
	1:17	a burnt sacrifice, an **offering made by** f,	801
	2: 2	*to be* an **offering made by** f, of a sweet	801
	2: 3	of the **offerings** of the LORD **made by** f.	801
	2: 9	it *is* an **offering made by** f, of a sweet	801
	2:10	of the **offerings** of the LORD **made by** f.	801
	2:11	*in* any **offering** of the LORD **made by** f.	801
	2:14	firstfruits green ears of corn dried by the f,	784
	2:16	it *is* an **offering made by** f unto the LORD:	801
	3: 3	an **offering made by** f unto the LORD;	801
	3: 5	which *is* upon the wood that *is* on the f:	784
	3: 5	it *is* a **offering made by** f, of a sweet	801
	3: 9	an **offering made by** f unto the LORD;	801
	3:11	it *is* the food of the **offering made by** f	801
	3:14	*even* an **offering made by** f unto	801
	3:16	it *is* the food of the **offering made by** f	801
	4:12	and burn him on the wood with f:	784
	4:35	according to the **offerings made by** f	801
	5:12	according to the **offerings made by** f	801
	6: 9	and the f of the altar shall be burning in it.	784
	6:10	the ashes which the f hath consumed	784
	6:12	the f upon the altar shall be burning in it;	784
	6:13	The f shall ever be burning upon the altar;	784
	6:17	their portion of my **offerings made by** f;	801
	6:18	of the **offerings** of the LORD **made by** f:	801
	6:30	shall be eaten: it shall be burnt in the f.	784
	7: 5	*for* an **offering made by** f unto the LORD:	801
	7:17	on the third day shall be burnt with f.	784
	7:19	shall not be eaten; it shall be burnt with f:	784
	7:25	which *men* offer an **offering made by** f	801
	7:30	the **offerings** of the LORD **made by** f,	801
	7:35	of the **offerings** of the LORD **made by** f,	801
	8:17	dung, he burnt with f without the camp;	784
	8:21	*and* an **offering made by** f unto the LORD;	801
	8:28	it *is* an **offering made by** f unto the LORD.	801
	8:32	and of the bread shall ye burn with f.	784
	9:11	hide he burnt with f without the camp.	784
	9:24	there came a f out from before the LORD,	784
	10: 1	put f therein, and put incense thereon,	784
	10: 1	offered strange f before the LORD,	784
	10: 2	there went out f from the LORD,	784
	10:12	of the **offerings** of the LORD **made by** f,	801
	10:13	of the **sacrifices** of the LORD **made by** f:	801
	10:15	with the **offerings made by** f of the fat,	801
	13:52	a fretting leprosy; it shall be burnt in the f.	784
	13:55	it *is* unclean; thou shalt burn it in the f;	784
	13:57	burn that wherein the plague *is* with f.	784
	16:12	take a censer full of burning coals of f	784
	16:13	he shall put the incense upon the f before	784
	16:27	they shall burn in the f their skins, and	784
	18:21	of thy seed pass through *the* f to Molech,	NIH
	19: 6	the third day, it shall be burnt in the f.	784
	20:14	shall be burnt with f, both he and they;	784
	21: 6	for the **offerings** of the LORD **made by** f,	801
	21: 9	her father: she shall be burnt with f.	784
	21:21	the **offerings** of the LORD **made by** f:	801
	22:22	nor make an **offering** of the LORD **by** f of them upon	801
	22:27	**offering made by** f unto the LORD.	801+7133

Lev	23: 8	ye shall offer an **offering made by** f unto	801
	23:13	an **offering made by** f unto the LORD *for*	801
	23:18	offerings, *even* an **offering made by** f,	801
	23:25	ye shall offer an **offering made by** f unto	801
	23:27	offer an **offering made by** f unto	801
	23:36	an **offering made by** f unto the LORD:	801
	23:36	ye shall offer an **offering made by** f unto	801
	23:37	to offer an **offering made by** f unto	801
	24: 7	*even* an **offering made by** f unto	801
	24: 9	of the **offerings** of the LORD **made by** f,	801
Nu	3: 4	when they offered strange f before	784
	6:18	put *it* in the f which *is* under the sacrifice	784
	9:15	tabernacle as it were the appearance of f,	784
	9:16	it *by day*, and the appearance of f by night.	784
	11: 1	the f of the LORD burnt among them,	784
	11: 2	unto the LORD, the f was quenched.	784
	11: 3	the f of the LORD burnt among them,	784
	14:14	of a cloud, and in a pillar of f by night.	784
	15: 3	will make an **offering by** f unto the LORD,	801
	15:10	an **offering made by** f, of a sweet savour	801
	15:13	in offering an **offering made by** f, of a	801
	15:14	offer an **offering made by** f, of a sweet	801
	15:25	a **sacrifice made by** f unto the LORD,	801
	16: 7	put f therein, and put incense in them	784
	16:18	put f in them, and laid incense thereon,	784
	16:35	there came out a f from the LORD,	784
	16:37	the burning, and scatter thou the f yonder;	784
	16:46	put f therein from off the altar, and put on	784
	18: 9	the most holy *things, reserved* from the f:	784
	18:17	burn their fat *for* an **offering made by** f,	801
	21:28	there is a f gone out of Heshbon, a flame	784
	26:10	what time the f devoured two hundred	784
	26:61	when they offered strange f before	784
	28: 2	my bread for my **sacrifices made by** f,	801
	28: 3	This *is* the **offering made by** f which ye	801
	28: 6	a **sacrifice made by** f unto the LORD.	801
	28: 8	thou shalt offer *it*, a **sacrifice made by** f,	801
	28:13	a **sacrifice made by** f unto the LORD.	801
	28:19	ye shall offer a **sacrifice made by** f *for* a	801
	28:24	the meat of the **sacrifice made by** f,	801
	29: 6	a **sacrifice made by** f unto the LORD.	801
	29:13	a burnt offering, a **sacrifice made by** f,	801
	29:36	a burnt offering, a **sacrifice made by** f,	801
	31:10	and all their goodly castles, with f.	784
	31:23	Every thing that may abide the f, ye shall	784
	31:23	ye shall make *it* go through the f, and it	784
	31:23	all that abideth not the f ye shall make go	784
Dt	1:33	a place to pitch your tents *in*, in f by night,	784
	4:11	the mountain burnt with f unto the midst	784
	4:12	spake unto you out of the midst of the f:	784
	4:15	you in Horeb out of the midst of the f:	784
	4:24	For the LORD thy God *is* a consuming f,	784
	4:33	of God speaking out of the midst of the f,	784
	4:36	upon earth he shewed thee his great f;	784
	4:36	his words out of the midst of the f.	784
	5: 4	in the mount out of the midst of the f,	784
	5: 5	for ye were afraid by reason of the f,	784
	5:22	in the mount out of the midst of the f,	784
	5:23	(for the mountain did burn with f,)	784
	5:24	heard his voice out of the midst of the f:	784
	5:25	for this great f will consume us: if we hear	784
	5:26	God speaking out of the midst of the f,	784
	7: 5	and burn their graven images with f.	784
	7:25	images of their gods shall ye burn with f:	784
	9: 3	*as* a consuming f he shall destroy them,	784
	9:10	midst of the f in the day of the assembly.	784
	9:15	the mount, and the mount burned with f:	784
	9:21	burnt it with f, and stamped it, *and* ground	784
	10: 4	midst of the f in the day of the assembly:	784
	12: 3	their pillars, and burn their groves with f;	784
	12:31	their daughters they have burnt in the f to	784
	13:16	shalt burn with f the city, and all the spoil	784
	18: 1	eat the **offerings** of the LORD **made by** f,	801
	18:10	son or his daughter to pass through the f,	784
	18:16	neither let me see this great f any more,	784
	32:22	a f is kindled in my anger, and shall burn	784
	32:22	set on f the foundations of the mountains.	3857
Jos	6:24	they burnt the city with f, and all that *was*	784
	7:15	the accursed thing shall be burnt with f,	784
	7:25	him *with* stones, and burned them with f,	784
	8: 8	the city, *that* ye shall set the city on f:	784
	8:19	took it, and hasted and set the city on f.	784
	11: 6	horses, and burn their chariots with f.	784
	11: 9	horses, and burnt their chariots with f.	784
	11:11	left to breathe: and he burnt Hazor with f.	784
	13:14	**sacrifices** of the LORD God of Israel	
		made by f	801
Jdg	1: 8	edge of the sword, and set the city on f.	784
	6:21	and there rose up f out of the rock,	784
	9:15	let f come out of the bramble, and devour	784
	9:20	let f come out from Abimelech,	784
	9:20	let f come out from the men of Shechem,	784
	9:49	the hold, and set the hold on f upon them;	784
	9:52	the door of the tower to burn it with f.	784
	12: 1	will burn thine house upon thee with f.	784
	14:15	burn thee and thy father's house with f:	784
	15: 5	when he had set the brands on f, he let	784
	15: 6	up, and burnt her and her father with f.	784
	15:14	became as flax that was burnt with f,	784
	16: 9	of tow is broken when it toucheth the f.	784
	18:27	of the sword, and burnt the city with f.	784
	20:48	they set on f all the cities that they came	784
1Sa	2:28	**offerings made by** f of the children of	801
	30: 1	and smitten Ziklag, and burnt it with f;	784
	30: 3	the city, and, behold, *it was* burnt with f;	784

F

1Sa 30:14 of Caleb; and we burnt Ziklag with **f.**	784
2Sa 14:30 he hath barley there; go and set it on **f.**	784
14:30 And Absalom's servants set the field on **f.**	784
14:31 have thy servants set my field on **f**?	784
22: 9 nostrils, and **f** out of his mouth devoured:	784
22:13 before him were coals of **f** kindled.	784
23: 7 shall be utterly burnt with **f** in the same	784
1Ki 9:16 burnt it with **f,** and slain the Canaanites	784
16:18 burnt the king's house over him with **f,**	784
18:23 put no **f** under: and I will dress the other	784
18:23 and lay it on wood, and put no **f** under:	784
18:24 God that answereth by **f,** let him be God.	784
18:25 the name of your gods, but put no **f** under:	784
18:38 the **f** of the LORD fell, and consumed	784
19:12 after the earthquake a **f**; but the LORD was	784
19:12 a fire; but the LORD was not in the **f**:	784
19:12 in the fire: and after the **f** a still small voice.	784
2Ki 1:10 let **f** come down from heaven,	784
1:10 there came down **f** from heaven,	784
1:12 let **f** come down from heaven,	784
1:12 the **f** of God came down from heaven,	784
1:14 there came **f** down from heaven,	784
2:11 there appeared a chariot of **f,** and horses	784
2:11 horses of **f,** and parted them both asunder;	784
6:17 and chariots of **f** round about Elisha.	784
8:12 their strong holds wilt thou set on **f,**	784
16: 3 and made his son to pass through the **f,**	784
17:17 and their daughters to pass through the **f,**	784
17:31 the Sepharvites burnt their children in **f** to	784
19:18 have cast their gods into the **f**: for they	784
21: 6 And he made his son pass through the **f,**	784
23:10 daughter to pass through the **f** to Molech.	784
23:11 and the chariots of the sun with **f.**	784
25: 9 every great man's house burnt he with **f.**	784
1Ch 14:12 and they were burnt with **f.**	784
21:26 he answered him from heaven by **f** upon	784
2Ch 7: 1 the **f** came down from heaven,	784
7: 3 all the children of Israel saw how the **f**	784
28: 3 burnt his children in the **f** after	784
33: 6 caused his children to pass through the **f**	784
35:13 they roasted the passover with **f** according	784
36:19 burnt all the palaces thereof with **f,**	784
Ne 1: 3 the gates thereof are burnt with **f.**	784
2: 3 and the gates thereof are consumed with **f**?	784
2:13 the gates thereof were consumed with **f,**	784
2:17 and the gates thereof are burnt with **f**:	784
9:12 in the night by a pillar of **f,** to give them	784
9:19 neither the pillar of **f** by night, to shew	784
Job 1:16 The **f** of God is fallen from heaven,	784
15:34 **f** shall consume the tabernacles of bribery,	784
18: 5 and the spark of his **f** shall not shine.	784
20:26 a **f** not blown shall consume him; it shall	784
22:20 but the remnant of them the **f** consumeth.	784
28: 5 and under it is turned up as it were **f.**	784
31:12 For it is a **f** that consumeth to destruction,	784
41:19 go burning lamps, and sparks of **f** leap out.	784
Ps 11: 6 **f** and brimstone, and a horrible tempest:	784
18: 8 nostrils, and **f** out of his mouth devoured:	784
18:12 clouds passed, hail-stones and coals of **f.**	784
18:13 gave his voice; hail-stones and coals of **f.**	784
21: 9 in his wrath, and the **f** shall devour them.	784
29: 7 voice of the LORD divideth the flames of **f.**	784
39: 3 me, while I was musing the **f** burned:	784
46: 9 in sunder; he burneth the chariot in the **f.**	784
50: 3 a **f** shall devour before him, and it shall be	784
57: 4 I lie even among them that are set on **f,**	3857
66:12 we went through **f** and through water:	784
68: 2 as wax melteth before the **f,** so let	784
74: 7 They have cast **f** into thy sanctuary,	784
78:14 a cloud, and all the night with a light of **f.**	784
78:21 so a **f** was kindled against Jacob,	784
78:63 The **f** consumed their young men;	784
79: 5 for ever? shall thy jealousy burn like **f**?	784
80:16 is burnt with **f,** it is cut down: they perish	784
83:14 As the **f** burneth a wood, and as the flame	784
83:14 as the flame **setteth** the mountains on **f**;	3857
89:46 for ever? shall thy wrath burn like **f**?	784
97: 3 A **f** goeth before him, and burneth up his	784
104: 4 his angels spirits; his ministers a flaming **f**:	784
105:32 hail for rain, and flaming **f** in their land.	784
105:39 a covering; and **f** to give light in the night.	784
106:18 **f** was kindled in their company; the flame	784
118:12 they are quenched as the **f** of thorns;	784
140:10 let them be cast into the **f**; into deep pits,	784
148: 8 **F,** and hail; snow, and vapour; stormy	784
Pr 6:27 Can a man take **f** in his bosom,	784
16:27 evil: and in his lips there is as a burning **f.**	784
25:22 For thou shalt heap **coals of f** upon his	1513
26:20 Where no wood is, there the **f** goeth out:	784
26:21 coals are to burning coals, and wood to **f**;	784
30:16 and the **f** that saith not, It is enough.	784
SS 8: 6 the coals thereof are coals of **f,** which hath	784
Isa 1: 7 is desolate, your cities are burnt with **f**:	784
4: 5 and the shining of a flaming **f** by night:	784
5:24 Therefore as the **f** devoureth	784+3956
9: 5 but this shall be with burning and fuel of **f.**	784
9:18 For wickedness burneth as the **f**: it shall	784
9:19 and the people shall be as the fuel of the **f**:	784
10:16 kindle a burning like the burning of a **f.**	784
10:17 the light of Israel shall be for a **f,**	784
26:11 the **f** of thine enemies shall devour them.	784
27:11 the women come, and **set** them on **f**:	215
29: 6 and tempest, and the flame of devouring **f.**	784
30:14 of it a sheard to take **f** from the hearth,	784
30:27 and his tongue as a devouring **f**:	784

Isa 30:30 with the flame of a devouring **f,**	784
30:33 the pile thereof is **f** and much wood;	784
31: 9 whose **f** is in Zion, and his furnace in	217
33:11 your breath, as **f,** shall devour you.	784
33:12 thorns cut up shall they be burnt in the **f.**	784
33:14 among us shall dwell with the devouring **f**?	784
37:19 have cast their gods into the **f**: for they	784
42:25 it hath **set** him **on f** round about, yet he	3857
43: 2 when thou walkest through the **f,** thou	784
44:16 He burneth part thereof in the **f**; with part	784
44:16 saith, Aha, I am warm, I have seen the **f**:	217
44:19 to say, I have burnt part of it in the **f,**	784
47:14 shall be as stubble; the **f** shall burn them;	784
47:14 be a coal to warm at, nor **f** to sit before it.	217
50:11 Behold, all ye that kindle a **f,** that compass	784
50:11 walk in the light of your **f,** and in the	784
54:16 the smith that bloweth the coals in the **f,**	784
64: 2 As when the melting **f** burneth, the fire	784
64: 2 burneth, the **f** causeth the waters to boil,	784
64:11 fathers praised thee, is burnt up with **f**:	784
65: 5 in my nose, a **f** that burneth all the day.	784
66:15 the LORD will come with **f,** and with his	784
66:15 with fury, and his rebuke with flames of **f.**	784
66:16 For by **f** and by his sword will the LORD	784
66:24 not die, neither shall their **f** be quenched;	784
Jer 4: 4 lest my fury come forth like **f,** and burn	784
5:14 I will make my words in thy mouth **f,**	784
6: 1 and set up a **sign** of **f** in Beth-haccerem:	4864
6:29 are burnt, the lead is consumed of the **f**;	784
7:18 the fathers kindle the **f,** and the women	784
7:31 their sons and their daughters in the **f**;	784
11:16 a great tumult he hath kindled **f** upon it,	784
15:14 a **f** is kindled in mine anger, which shall	784
17: 4 for ye have kindled a **f** in mine anger,	784
17:27 then will I kindle a **f** in the gates thereof,	784
19: 5 burn their sons with **f** for burnt offerings	784
20: 9 word was in mine heart as a burning **f**	784
21:10 of Babylon, and he shall burn it with **f.**	784
21:12 lest my fury go out like **f,** and burn that	784
21:14 and I will kindle a **f** in the forest thereof,	784
22: 7 choice cedars, and cast them into the **f.**	784
23:29 Is not my word like as a **f**? saith the LORD;	784
29:22 the king of Babylon roasted in the **f**;	784
32:29 come and set **f** on this city, and burn it	784
32:35 their daughters to pass through the **f** unto	NIH
34: 2 of Babylon, and he shall burn it with **f**:	784
34:22 against it, and take it, and burn it with **f**:	784
36:22 there was a **f** on the hearth burning	NIH
36:23 cast it into the **f** that was on the hearth,	784
36:23 until all the roll was consumed in the **f**	784
36:32 Jehoiakim king of Judah had burnt in the **f**:	784
37: 8 this city, and take it, and burn it with **f.**	784
37:10 man in his tent, and burn this city with **f.**	784
38:17 and this city shall not be burnt with **f**:	784
38:18 shall burn it with **f,** and thou shalt not	784
38:23 shalt cause this city to be burnt with **f.**	784
39: 8 with **f,** and brake down the walls of	784
43:12 I will kindle a **f** in the houses of the gods	784
43:13 gods of the Egyptians shall he burn with **f.**	784
48:45 but a **f** shall come forth out of Heshbon,	784
49: 2 and her daughters shall be burnt with **f.**	784
49:27 I will kindle a **f** in the wall of Damascus,	784
50:32 I will kindle a **f** in his cities, and it shall	784
51:32 the reeds they have burnt with **f,** and	784
51:58 her high gates shall be burnt with **f**;	784
51:58 the folk in the **f,** and they shall be weary.	784
52:13 houses of the great men, burnt he with **f**:	784
La 1:13 From above hath he sent **f** into my bones,	784
2: 3 he burned against Jacob like a flaming **f,**	784
2: 4 of Zion: he poured out his fury like **f.**	784
4:11 hath kindled a **f** in Zion, and it hath	784
Eze 1: 4 a **f** infolding itself, and a brightness was	784
1: 4 colour of amber, out of the midst of the **f.**	784
1:13 appearance was like burning coals of **f,**	784
1:13 the **f** was bright, and out of the fire went	784
1:13 and out of the **f** went forth lightning.	784
1:27 the appearance of **f** round about within it,	784
1:27 I saw as it were the appearance of **f,**	784
5: 2 Thou shalt burn with **f** a third part in	217
5: 4 cast them into the midst of the **f,**	784
5: 4 midst of the fire, and burn them in the	784
5: 4 for thereof shall a **f** come forth into all	784
8: 2 and lo, a likeness as the appearance of **f**:	784
8: 2 appearance of his loins even downward, **f,**	784
10: 2 fill thine hand with coals of **f** from between	784
10: 6 saying, Take **f** from between the wheels,	784
10: 7 the **f** that was between the cherubims,	784
10: 7 Behold, it is cast into the **f** for fuel; the fire	784
15: 4 the **f** devoureth both the ends of it,	784
15: 5 when the **f** hath devoured it, and it is	784
15: 6 which I have given to the **f** for fuel, so will	784
15: 7 shall go out from one **f,** and another fire	784
15: 7 one fire, and another shall devour them;	784
16:21 cause them to pass through the **f** for them?	NIH
16:41 And they shall burn thine houses with **f,**	784
19:12 and withered; the **f** consumed them.	784
19:14 **f** is gone out of a rod of her branches,	784
20:26 that they caused to pass through the **f** all	NIH
20:31 ye make your sons to pass through the **f,**	784
20:47 I will kindle a **f** in thee, and it shall devour	784
21:31 will blow against thee in the **f** of my wrath,	784
21:32 Thou shalt be for fuel to the **f**; thy blood	784
22:20 to blow the **f** upon it, to melt it; so will I	784
22:21 and blow upon you in the **f** of my wrath,	784
22:31 I have consumed them with the **f** of my	784

Eze 23:25 and thy residue shall be devoured by the **f.**	784
23:37 to pass for them through the **f,** to devour	NIH
23:47 and burn up their houses with **f.**	784
24: 9 I will even make the **pile for f** great.	4071
24:10 Heap on wood, kindle the **f,** consume	784
24:12 forth out of her: her scum shall be in the **f.**	784
28:14 and down in the midst of the stones of **f.**	784
28:16 from the midst of the stones of **f.**	784
28:18 will I bring forth a **f** from the midst of thee,	784
30: 8 when I have set a **f** in Egypt, and when all	784
30:14 will set **f** in Zoan, and will execute	784
30:16 I will set **f** in Egypt: Sin shall have great	784
36: 5 Surely in the **f** of my jealousy have I spoken	784
38:19 and in the **f** of my wrath have I spoken,	784
38:22 and great hailstones, **f,** and brimstone.	784
39: 6 I will send a **f** on Magog, and among them	784
39: 9 shall **set on f** and burn the weapons,	1197
39: 9 they shall burn them with **f** seven years:	784
39:10 for they shall burn the weapons with **f**:	784
Da 3:22 flame of the **f** slew those men that took	5135
3:24 three men bound into the midst of the **f**?	5135
3:25 walking in the midst of the **f,** and they	5135
3:26 came forth of the midst of the **f.**	5135
3:27 upon whose bodies the **f** had no power,	5135
3:27 nor the smell of **f** had passed on them.	5135
7: 9 fiery flame, and his wheels as burning **f.**	5135
Hos 7: 6 in the morning it burneth as a flaming **f.**	784
8:14 I will send a **f** upon his cities, and it shall	784
Joel 1:19 for the **f** hath devoured the pastures of	784
1:20 the **f** hath devoured the pastures of	784
2: 3 A **f** devoureth before them; and behind	784
2: 5 like the noise of a flame of **f** that devoureth	784
2:30 earth, blood, and **f,** and pillars of smoke.	784
Am 1: 4 I will send a **f** into the house of Hazael,	784
1: 7 I will send a **f** on the wall of Gaza,	784
1:10 I will send a **f** on the wall of Tyrus,	784
1:12 I will send a **f** upon the Teman, which	784
1:14 I will kindle a **f** in the wall of Rabbah,	784
2: 2 I will send a **f** upon Moab, and it shall	784
2: 5 I will send a **f** upon Judah, and it shall	784
5: 6 lest he break out like **f** in the house of	784
7: 4 the Lord GOD called to contend by **f,**	784
Ob 1:18 the house of Jacob shall be a **f,** and the	784
Mic 1: 4 as wax before the **f,** and as the waters that	784
1: 7 the hires thereof shall be burnt with the **f,**	784
Na 1: 6 his fury is poured out like **f,** and the rocks	784
3:13 thine enemies: the **f** shall devour thy bars.	784
3:15 There shall the **f** devour thee; the sword	784
Hab 2:13 that the people shall labour in the very **f,**	784
Zep 1:18 whole land shall be devoured by the **f** of	784
3: 8 all the earth shall be devoured with the **f**	784
Zec 2: 5 will be unto her a wall of **f** round about,	784
3: 2 is not this a brand pluckt out of the **f**?	784
9: 4 the sea; and she shall be devoured with **f.**	784
11: 1 that the **f** may devour thy cedars.	784
12: 6 Judah like a hearth of **f** among the wood,	784
12: 6 the wood, and like a torch of **f** in a sheaf;	784
13: 9 I will bring the third **part** through the **f,**	784
Mal 1:10 do ye kindle **f** on mine altar for nought.	NIH
3: 2 for he is like a refiner's **f,** and like fullers'	784
Mt 3:10 fruit is hewn down, and cast into the	4442
3:11 you with the Holy Ghost, and with **f**:	4442
3:12 burn up the chaff with unquenchable **f.**	4442
5:22 Thou fool, shall be in danger of hell **f.**	4442
7:19 fruit is hewn down, and cast into the **f.**	4442
13:40 the tares are gathered and burnt in the **f**;	4442
13:42 And shall cast them into a furnace of **f**:	4442
13:50 And shall cast them into the furnace of **f**:	4442
17:15 for ofttimes he falleth into the **f,**	4442
18: 8 or two feet to be cast into everlasting **f.**	4442
18: 9 having two eyes to be cast into hell **f.**	4442
25:41 from me, ye cursed, into everlasting **f,**	4442
Mk 9:22 And ofttimes it hath cast him into the **f,**	4442
9:43 into the **f** that never shall be quenched:	4442
9:44 dieth not, and the **f** is not quenched.	4442
9:45 into the **f** that never shall be quenched:	4442
9:46 dieth not, and the **f** is not quenched.	4442
9:47 having two eyes to be cast into hell **f**:	4442
9:48 dieth not, and the **f** is not quenched.	4442
9:49 For every one shall be salted with **f,**	4442
14:54 servants, and warmed himself at the **f.**	5457
Lk 3: 9 fruit is hewn down, and cast into the **f.**	4442
3:16 you with the Holy Ghost and with **f**:	4442
3:17 chaff he will burn with **f** unquenchable.	4442
9:54 thou that we command **f** to come down	4442
12:49 I am come to send **f** on the earth;	4442
17:29 that Lot went out of Sodom it rained	4442
22:55 when they had kindled a **f** in the midst	4442
22:56 maid beheld him as he sat by the **f,**	5457
Jn 15: 6 and cast them into the **f,** and they are	4442
18:18 stood there, who had made a **f of coals**	439
21: 9 they saw a **f of coals** there, and fish laid	439
Ac 2: 3 unto them cloven tongues like as of **f,**	4442
2:19 blood, and **f,** and vapour of smoke:	4442
7:30 angel of the Lord in a flame of **f** in a bush.	4442
28: 2 they kindled a **f,** and received us every	4443
28: 3 laid them on the **f,** there came a viper	4443
28: 5 And he shook off the beast into the **f,**	4442
Ro 12:20 doing thou shalt heap coals of **f** on his	4442
1Co 3:13 because it shall be revealed by **f**;	4442
3:13 the **f** shall try every man's work of what	4442
3:15 he himself shall be saved; yet so as by **f.**	4442
2Th 1: 8 In flaming **f,** taking vengeance on them	4442
Heb 1: 7 and his ministers a flame of **f.**	4442

Heb	11:34	Quenched the violence of **f**, escaped	4442
	12:18	that burned with **f**, nor unto blackness,	4442
	12:29	For our God *is* a consuming **f**.	4442
Jas	3: 5	how great a matter a little **f** kindleth.	4442
	3: 6	And the tongue *is* a **f**, a world of iniquity:	4442
	3: 6	and **setteth on f** the course of nature;	5394
	3: 6	course of nature; and it is **set on f** of hell.	5394
	5: 3	and shall eat your flesh as *it were* **f**:	4442
1Pe	1: 7	though it be tried with **f**, might be found	4442
2Pe	3: 7	unto **f** against the day of judgment	4442
	3:12	wherein the heavens being **on f** shall be	4448
Jude	1: 7	suffering the vengeance of eternal **f**.	4442
	1:23	save with fear, pulling *them* out of the **f**;	4442
Rev	1:14	snow; and his eyes *were* as a flame of **f**;	4442
	2:18	who hath his eyes like unto a flame of **f**,	4442
	3:18	thee to buy of me gold tried in the **f**,	4442
	4: 5	*were* seven lamps of **f** burning before	4442
	8: 5	and filled it with **f** of the altar, and cast	4442
	8: 7	followed hail and **f** mingled with blood,	4442
	8: 8	*it were* a great mountain burning with **f**	4442
	9:17	having breastplates of **f**, and of jacinth,	4447
	9:17	out of their mouths issued **f** and smoke	4442
	9:18	by the **f**, and by the smoke, and by	4442
	10: 1	*it were* the sun, and his feet as pillars of **f**:	4442
	11: 5	**f** proceedeth out of their mouth,	4442
	13:13	that he maketh **f** come down from heaven	4442
	14:10	and he shall be tormented with **f** and	4442
	14:18	from the altar, which had power over **f**;	4442
	15: 2	as *it were* a sea of glass mingled with **f**:	4442
	16: 8	was given unto him to scorch men with **f**.	4442
	17:16	shall eat her flesh, and burn her with **f**.	4442
	18: 8	and she shall be utterly burnt with **f**.	4442
	19:12	His eyes *were* as a flame of **f**, and on his	4442
	19:20	*These* both were cast alive into a lake of **f**	4442
	20: 9	**f** came down from God out of heaven,	4442
	20:10	deceived them was cast into the lake of **f**	4442
	20:14	and hell were cast into the lake of **f**.	4442
	20:15	the book of life was cast into the lake of **f**	4442
	21: 8	part in the lake which burneth with **f**	4442

FIREBRAND (2) [FIRE, BRAND]

| Jdg | 15: 4 | put a **f** in the midst between two tails. | 3940 |
| Am | 4:11 | ye were as a **f** pluckt out of the burning: | 181 |

FIREBRANDS (3) [FIRE, BRAND]

Jdg	15: 4	took **f**, and turned tail to tail, and put a	3940
Pr	26:18	As a mad *man* who casteth **f**, arrows,	2131
Isa	7: 4	for the two tails of these smoking **f**,	181

FIREPANS (4) [FIRE, PAN]

Ex	27: 3	his basons, and his fleshhooks, and his **f**:	4289
	38: 3	the basons, *and* the fleshhooks, and the **f**	4289
2Ki	25:15	the **f**, and the bowls, *and* such *things* as	4289
Jer	52:19	the **f**, and the bowls, and the caldrons,	4289

FIRES (1) [FIRE]

| Isa | 24:15 | Wherefore glorify ye the LORD in the **f**, | 217 |

FIRKINS (1)

| Jn | 2: 6 | the Jews, containing two or three **f** apiece. | 3355 |

FIRM (7)

Jos	3:17	**f** on dry *ground* in the midst of Jordan,	3559
	4: 3	the place where the priests' feet stood **f**,	3559
Job	41:23	they are **f** in themselves; they cannot be	3332
	41:24	His heart is as **f** as a stone; yea, as hard as	3332
Ps	73: 4	in their death: but their strength *is* **f**.	1277
Da	6: 7	to **make** a decree, that whosoever shall	8631
Heb	3: 6	the rejoicing of the hope **f** unto the end.	949

FIRMAMENT (17)

Ge	1: 6	Let there be a **f** in the midst of the waters,	7549
	1: 7	God made the **f**, and divided the waters	7549
	1: 7	the waters which *were* under the **f**	7549
	1: 7	from the waters which *were* above the **f**:	7549
	1: 8	God called the **f** Heaven. And the evening	7549
	1:14	Let there be lights in the **f** of the heaven	7549
	1:15	them be for lights in the **f** of the heaven	7549
	1:17	God set them in the **f** of the heaven to	7549
	1:20	above the earth in the open **f** of heaven.	7549
Ps	19: 1	God; and the **f** sheweth his handywork.	7549
	150: 1	praise him in the **f** of his power.	7549
Eze	1:22	the likeness of the **f** upon the heads of	7549
	1:23	under the **f** *were* their wings straight,	7549
	1:25	was a voice from the **f** that *was* over	7549
	1:26	above the **f** that *was* over their heads	7549
	10: 1	in the **f** that *was* above the head of	7549
Da	12: 3	wise shall shine as the brightness of the **f**;	7549

FIRST (436) [FIRSTBEGOTTEN, FIRSTBORN, FIRSTFRUIT, FIRSTFRUITS, FIRSTLING, FIRSTLINGS, FIRSTRIPE]

Ge	1: 5	evening and the morning were the **f** day.	259
	2:11	The name of the **f** *is* Pison: that *is* it which	259
	8: 5	in the tenth *month*, on the **f** day of	259
	8:13	to pass in the six hundredth and **f** year,	259
	8:13	the **f** *month*, the first *day* of the month,	7223
	8:13	the **f** *month*, the **f** *day* of the month,	259
	13: 4	altar, which he had made there at the **f**:	7223
	25:25	the **f** came out red, all over like a hairy	7223
	26: 1	besides the **f** famine that was in the days	7223
	28:19	name of that city was called Luz at the **f**.	7223
	38:28	a scarlet thread, saying, This came out **f**.	7223
	41:20	ill favoured kine did eat up the **f** seven	7223
	43:18	in our sacks at the **f** *time* are we brought	8462
	43:20	came indeed down at the **f** *time* to buy	8462

Ex	4: 8	neither hearken to the voice of the **f** sign,	7223
	12: 2	it *shall be* the **f** month of the year to you.	7223
	12: 5	be without blemish, a male of the **f** year:	1121
	12:15	the **f** day ye shall put away leaven out	7223
	12:15	from the **f** day until the seventh day,	7223
	12:16	in the **f** day *there shall be* an holy	7223
	12:18	In the **f** *month*, on the fourteenth day of	7223
	22:29	Thou shalt not delay *to offer* the **f** of thy	NIH
	23:19	The **f** of the firstfruits of thy land thou	7225
	28:17	the **f** *row* shall *be* a sardius, a topaz,	NIH
	28:17	and a carbuncle: this *shall be* the **f** row.	259
	29:38	two lambs of the **f** year day by day	1121
	34: 1	thee two tables of stone like unto the **f**:	7223
	34: 1	tables the words that were in the **f** tables,	7223
	34: 4	two tables of stone like unto the **f**;	7223
	34:26	The **f** of the firstfruits of thy land thou	7225
	39:10	the **f** *row* was a sardius, a topaz,	NIH
	39:10	and a carbuncle: this *was* the **f** row.	259
	40: 2	On the **f** day of the first month shalt thou	7223
	40: 2	On the first day of the **f** month shalt thou	259
	40:17	came to pass in the **f** month in the second	7223
	40:17	the **f** *day* of the month, *that* the tabernacle	7223
Lev	4:21	and burn him as he burned the **f** bullock:	7223
	5: 8	offer *that* which *is* for the sin offering **f**,	7223
	9: 3	a calf and a lamb, both of the **f** year,	1121
	9:15	and slew it, and offered it for sin, as the **f**:	7223
	12: 6	she shall bring a lamb of the **f** year for a	1121
	14:10	one ewe lamb of the **f** year without	1323
	23: 5	In the fourteenth *day* of the **f** month	7223
	23: 7	In the **f** day ye shall have a holy	7223
	23:12	**f** year for a burnt offering unto the LORD.	1121
	23:18	seven lambs without blemish of the **f** year,	1121
	23:19	two lambs of the **f** year for a sacrifice of	1121
	23:24	seventh month, in the **f** *day* of the month,	259
	23:35	On the **f** day *shall be* a holy convocation:	7223
	23:39	on the **f** day *shall be* a sabbath, and on	7223
	23:40	ye shall take you on the **f** day the boughs	7223
Nu	1: 1	on the **f** *day* of the second month,	259
	1:18	on the **f** *day* of the second month,	259
	2: 9	their armies. *These* shall **f** set forth.	7223
	6:12	shall bring a lamb of the **f year** for	1121+8141
	6:14	one he lamb of the **f year** without	1121+8141
	6:14	one ewe lamb of the **f year** without	1323+8141
	7:12	he that offered his offering the **f** day	7223
	7:15	one ram, one lamb of the **f year**:	1121+8141
	7:17	he goats, one lamb of the **f year**:	1121+8141
	7:21	one ram, one lamb of the **f year**:	1121+8141
	7:23	he goats, one lamb of the **f year**:	1121+8141
	7:27	one ram, one lamb of the **f year**:	1121+8141
	7:29	he goats, one lamb of the **f year**:	1121+8141
	7:33	one ram, one lamb of the **f year**:	1121+8141
	7:35	he goats, one lamb of the **f year**:	1121+8141
	7:39	one ram, one lamb of the **f year**:	1121+8141
	7:41	he goats, one lamb of the **f year**:	1121+8141
	7:45	one ram, one lamb of the **f year**:	1121+8141
	7:47	he goats, five lambs of the **f year**:	1121+8141
	7:51	one ram, one lamb of the **f year**:	1121+8141
	7:53	he goats, five lambs of the **f year**:	1121+8141
	7:57	one ram, one lamb of the **f year**:	1121+8141
	7:59	he goats, five lambs of the **f year**:	1121+8141
	7:63	one ram, one lamb of the **f year**:	1121+8141
	7:65	he goats, five lambs of the **f year**:	1121+8141
	7:69	one ram, one lamb of the **f year**:	1121+8141
	7:71	he goats, five lambs of the **f year**:	1121+8141
	7:75	one ram, one lamb of the **f year**:	1121+8141
	7:77	he goats, five lambs of the **f year**:	1121+8141
	7:81	one ram, one lamb of the **f year**:	1121+8141
	7:83	he goats, five lambs of the **f year**:	1121+8141
	7:87	the lambs of the **f year** twelve,	1121+8141
	7:88	the lambs of the **f year** sixty.	1121+8141
	9: 1	the **f** month of the second year after	7223
	9: 5	**f** month at even in the wilderness of Sinai	7223
	10:13	they **f** took their journey according to	7223
	10:14	In the **f** *place* went the standard of the	7223
	13:20	Now the time *was* the time of the **f** ripe	1061
	15:20	Ye shall offer up a cake *of the* **f** of your	7225
	15:21	Of the **f** of your dough ye shall give unto	7225
	15:27	he shall bring a she goat of the **f** year for a	1323
	18:13	*And* whatsoever is **f** ripe in the land,	1061
	20: 1	*into* the desert of Zin in the **f** month:	7223
	24:20	and said, Amalek *was* the **f** of the nations;	7225
	28: 3	two lambs of the **f** year without	1121+8141
	28: 9	the sabbath day two lambs of the **f** year	1121
	28:11	lambs of the **f year** without spot;	1121+8141
	28:16	in the fourteenth day of the **f** month *is*	7223
	28:18	In the **f** day *shall be* a holy convocation;	7223
	28:19	and seven lambs of the **f year**:	1121+8141
	28:27	one ram, seven lambs of the **f year**;	1121+8141
	29: 1	seventh month, on the **f** *day* of the month,	259
	29: 2	lambs of the **f year** without blemish:	1121+8141
	29: 8	and seven lambs of the **f year**;	1121+8141
	29:13	and fourteen lambs of the **f year**;	1121+8141
	29:17	lambs of the **f year** without spot:	1121+8141
	29:20	fourteen lambs of the **f year**	1121+8141
	29:23	fourteen lambs of the **f year**	1121+8141
	29:26	lambs of the **f year** without spot:	1121+8141
	29:29	fourteen lambs of the **f year**	1121+8141
	29:32	fourteen lambs of the **f year**	1121+8141
	29:36	lambs of the **f year** without	1121+8141
	33: 3	departed from Rameses in the **f** month,	7223
	33: 3	on the fifteenth day of the **f** month;	7223
	33:38	of Egypt, in the **f** *day* of the fifth month.	259
Dt	1: 3	eleventh month, on the **f** *day* of the month,	259
	9:18	as at the **f**, forty days and forty nights:	7223
	9:25	as I fell down at the **f**, because the LORD	NIH

Dt	10: 1	thee two tables of stone like unto the **f**,	7223
	10: 2	were in the **f** tables which thou brakest,	7223
	10: 3	two tables of stone like unto the **f**,	7223
	10: 4	according to the **f** writing, the ten	7223
	10:10	according to the **f** time, forty days and	7223
	11:14	the **f** rain and the latter rain, that thou	3138
	13: 9	thine hand shall be **f** upon him to put him	7223
	16: 4	which thou sacrificedst the **f** day at even,	7223
	17: 7	The hands of the witnesses shall be **f**	7223
	18: 4	oil, and the **f** of the fleece of thy sheep,	7225
	26: 2	thou shalt take of the **f** of all the fruit	7225
	33:21	he provided the **f** *part* for himself,	7225
Jos	4:19	of Jordan on the tenth day of the **f** month,	7223
	8: 5	as at the **f**, that we will flee before them,	7223
	8: 6	will say, *They* flee before us, as at the **f**:	7223
	21:10	of Levi, had: for theirs was the **f** lot.	7223
Jdg	1: 1	go up for us against the Canaanites **f**,	8462
	18:29	the name of the city *was* Laish at the **f**.	8462
	20:18	Which of us shall go up **f**	8462+871.1+1886.1
	20:18	Judah *shall go up* **f**.	8462+871.1+1886.1
	20:22	they put *themselves* in array the **f** day.	7223
	20:32	are smitten down before us, as at **f**:	7223
	20:39	smitten down before us, as in the **f** battle.	7223
1Sa	14:14	that **f** slaughter, which Jonathan and	7223
	14:35	the same was the **f** altar that he built unto	2490
2Sa	3:13	bring Michal Saul's daughter,	6440+3807.1
	17: 9	overthrown at the **f**,	8462
	19:20	I am come the **f** this day of all the house	7223
	19:43	that our advice should not be **f** had in	7223
	21: 9	in the **f** *days*, in the beginning of barley	7223
	23:19	howbeit he attained not unto the **f** three.	NIH
	23:23	thirty, but he attained not to the **f** three.	NIH
1Ki	16:23	**f** year of Asa king of Judah *began* Omri to	259
	17:13	me thereof a little cake **f**,	7223+871.1+1886.1
	18:25	one bullock for yourselves, and dress *it* **f**;	7223
	20: 9	send for to thy servant at the **f** I will do:	7223
	20:17	of the princes of the provinces went out **f**;	7223
1Ch	9: 2	Now the **f** inhabitants that *dwelt* in their	7223
	11: 6	Whosoever smiteth the Jebusites **f** shall be	7223
	11: 6	So Joab the son of Zeruiah went **f** up,	7223
	11:21	howbeit he attained not to the **f** three.	NIH
	11:25	the thirty, but attained not to the **f** three:	NIH
	12: 9	Ezer the **f**, Obadiah the second, Eliab	7218
	12:15	that went over Jordan in the **f** month,	7223
	15:13	For because ye *did it* not at the **f**,	7223
	16: 7	on that day David delivered **f** *this* psalm	7218
	23:19	Jeriah the **f**, Amariah the second,	7218
	23:20	Micah the **f**, and Jesiah the second.	7218
	24: 7	Now the **f** lot came forth to Jehoiarib,	7218
	24:21	the sons of Rehabiah, the **f** *was* Isshiah.	7218
	24:23	the sons *of* Hebron; Jeriah the **f**, Amariah	NIH
	25: 9	Now the **f** lot came forth for Asaph to	7223
	27: 2	Over the **f** course for the first month *was*	7223
	27: 3	Over the first course for the **f** month *was*	7223
	27: 3	the captains of the host for the **f** month.	7223
	29:29	acts of David the king, **f** and last, behold,	7223
2Ch	3: 3	The length *by* cubits after the **f** measure	7223
	9:29	the rest of the acts of Solomon, **f** and last,	7223
	12:15	Now the acts of Rehoboam, **f** and last,	7223
	16:11	behold, the acts of Asa, **f** and last,	7223
	17: 3	walked in the **f** ways of his father David,	7223
	20:34	rest of the acts of Jehoshaphat, **f** and last,	7223
	25:26	of the acts of Amaziah, **f** and last, behold,	7223
	26:22	**f** and last, did Isaiah the prophet, the son	7223
	28:26	and of all his ways, **f** and last, behold,	7223
	29: 3	He in the **f** year of his reign, in the first	7223
	29: 3	the first year of his reign, in the **f** month,	7223
	29:17	Now they began on the **f** *day* of the first	259
	29:17	Now they began on the first *day* of the **f**	7223
	29:17	in the sixteenth day of the **f** month they	7223
	35: 1	on the fourteenth *day* of the **f** month.	7223
	35:27	his deeds, **f** and last, behold, they *are*	7223
	36:22	Now in the **f** year of Cyrus king of Persia,	259
Ezr	1: 1	Now in the **f** year of Cyrus king of Persia,	259
	3: 6	From the **f** day of the seventh month	259
	3:12	*were* ancient men that had seen the **f**	7223
	5:13	in the **f** year of Cyrus the king of Babylon	2298
	6: 3	In the **f** year of Cyrus the king *the same*	2298
	6:19	upon the fourteenth *day* of the **f** month.	7223
	7: 9	upon the **f** *day* of the first month began	7223
	7: 9	upon the first *day* of the **f** month began	7223
	7: 9	on the **f** of the fifth month came he to	259
	8:31	Ahava on the twelfth *day* of the **f** month,	7223
	10:16	sat down in the **f** day of the tenth month	259
	10:17	wives by the **f** day of the first month.	259
	10:17	wives by the first day of the **f** month.	7223
Ne	7: 5	of them which came up at the **f**,	7223
	8: 2	upon the **f** day of the seventh month.	259
	8:18	by day, from the **f** day unto the last day,	7223
Est	1:14	*and* which sat the **f** in the kingdom;)	7223
	3: 7	In the **f** month, that *is*, the month Nisan,	7223
	3:12	on the thirteenth day of the **f** month,	7223
Job	15: 7	*Art* thou the **f** man *that* was born?	7223
	42:14	he called the name of the **f**, Jemima;	259
Pr	18:17	*that is* **f** in his own cause *seemeth* just;	7223
Isa	1:26	And I will restore thy judges as at the **f**,	7223
	9: 1	when at the **f** he lightly afflicted the land	7223
	41: 4	I the LORD, the **f**, and with the last; I *am*	7223
	41:27	The **f** *shall say* to Zion, Behold,	7223
	43:27	Thy **f** father hath sinned, and thy teachers	7223
	44: 6	I *am* the **f**, and I *am* the last; and besides	7223
	48:12	I *am* he; I *am* the **f**, I also *am* the last.	7223
	60: 9	the ships of Tarshish **f**, to bring thy sons	7223
Jer	4:31	as of her that **bringeth forth** her **f** child,	1069
	7:12	where I set my name at the **f**, and see	7223

Jer	16:18 f I will recompense their iniquity and	7223
	24: 2 figs, *even* like the figs *that are* f ripe:	1073
	25: 1 that *was* the f year of Nebuchadrezzar	7224
	33: 7 to return, and will build them, as at the f.	7223
	33:11 return the captivity of the land as at the f,	7223
	36:28 the former words that were in the f roll,	7223
	50:17 f the king of Assyria hath devoured him,	7223
	52:31 Evil-merodach king of Babylon in the *f*	NIH
Eze	10:14 f face *was* the face of a cherub,	259
	26: 1 eleventh year, in the f *day* of the month,	259
	29:17 the f *month*, in the first *day* of the month,	7223
	29:17 the first *month*, in the first *day* of the	259
	30:20 in the f *month*, in the seventh *day* of	7223
	31: 1 third *month*, in the f *day* of the month,	259
	32: 1 twelfth month, in the f *day* of the	259
	40:21 were after the measure of the f gate:	7223
	44:30 the f of all the firstfruits of all *things*, and	7225
	44:30 ye shall also give unto the priest the f of	7225
	45:18 In the f *month*, in the first *day*	7223
	45:18 the first *month*, in the f *day* of the	259
	45:21 In the f *month*, in the fourteenth *day* of	7223
	46:13 *of* a lamb of the f year without blemish:	1121
Da	1:21 Daniel continued *even* unto the f year of	259
	6: 2 three presidents; of whom Daniel *was* f:	2298
	7: 1 In the f year of Belshazzar king of Babylon	2298
	7: 4 The f *was* like a lion, and had eagle's	6933
	7: 8 before whom there were three of the f	6933
	7:24 he shall be diverse from the f, and he	6933
	8: 1 that which appeared unto me at the f.	8462
	8:21 horn that *is* between his eyes *is* the f king.	7223
	9: 1 In the f year of Darius the son of	259
	9: 2 the f year of his reign I Daniel understood	259
	10: 4 four and twentieth day of the f month,	7223
	10:12 from the f day that thou didst set thine	7223
	11: 1 Also I in the f year of Darius the Mede,	259
Hos	2: 7 I will go and return to my f husband;	7223
	9:10 as the firstripe in the fig tree at her f *time*:	7225
Joel	2:23 and the latter rain in the f *month*.	7223
Am	6: 7 they go captive with the f that go captive,	7218
Mic	4: 8 thee shall it come, even the f dominion;	7223
Hag	1: 1 sixth month, in the f day of the month,	259
	2: 3 you that saw this house in her f glory?	7223
Zec	6: 2 In the f chariot *were* red horses; and in	7223
	12: 7 Loʀᴅ also shall save the tents of Judah f,	7223
	14:10 gate unto the place of the f gate,	7223
Mt	5:24 f be reconciled to thy brother, and then	4412
	6:33 But seek ye f the kingdom of God,	4412
	7: 5 f cast out the beam out of thine own eye;	4412
	8:21 suffer me f to go and bury my father.	4412
	10: 2 The f, Simon, who is called Peter,	4413
	12:29 except he f bind the strong *man?* and	4412
	12:45 last *state* of that man is worse than the f.	4413
	13:30 Gather ye together f the tares,	4412
	17:10 say the scribes that Elias must f come?	4412
	17:11 Elias truly shall f come, and restore all	4413
	17:27 and take up the fish that f cometh up;	4412
	19:30 But many *that are* f shall be last;	4413
	19:30 first shall be last; and *the* last *shall be* f.	4413
	20: 8 beginning from the last unto the f.	4413
	20:10 But when the f came, they supposed that	4413
	20:16 So the last shall be f, and the first last:	4413
	20:16 So the last shall be first, and the f last:	4413
	21:28 and he came to the f, and said, Son,	4413
	21:31 They say unto him, The f. Jesus saith unto	4413
	21:36 he sent other servants moe than the f:	4413
	22:25 when he, when he had married a *wife*,	4413
	22:38 This is the f and great commandment.	4413
	23:26 cleanse f that *which is* within the cup and	4412
	26:17 Now the f *day* of the *feast of* unleavened	4413
	27:64 so the last error shall be worse than the f.	4413
	28: 1 as it began to dawn towards the f *day* of	1520
Mk	3:27 except he will f bind the strong *man;* and	4412
	4:28 the blade, then the ear, after that the full	4412
	7:27 said unto her, Let the children f be filled:	4412
	9:11 Why say the scribes that Elias must f	4412
	9:12 Elias verily cometh f, and restoreth all	4412
	9:35 saith unto them, If any *man* desire to be f,	4413
	10:31 But many *that are* f shall be last;	4413
	10:31 *that are* first shall be last; and the last f.	4413
	12:20 and the f took a wife, and dying left no	4413
	12:28 Which is the f commandment of all?	4413
	12:29 The f of all the commandments *is*, Hear,	4413
	12:30 thy strength: this *is* the f commandment.	4413
	13:10 the gospel must f be published among	4412
	14:12 And the f day of unleavened bread,	4413
	16: 2 very early in the morning the f *day* of	1520
	16: 9 when *Jesus* was risen early the f *day*	4413
	16: 9 he appeared f to Mary Magdalene, out of	4412
Lk	1: 3 of all *things* from the very f,	509
	2: 2 this taxing was f made when Cyrenius	4413
	6: 1 pass on the **second** sabbath **after the f**,	1207
	6:42 cast out f the beam out of thine own eye,	4412
	9:59 suffer me f to go and bury my father.	4412
	9:61 let me f go bid them farewell, which are	4412
	10: 5 ye enter, f say, Peace be to this house.	4412
	11:26 last *state* of that man is worse than the f.	4413
	11:38 that he had not f washed before dinner.	4412
	12: 1 he began to say unto his disciples *of all,*	4412
	13:30 there are last which shall be f, and there	4413
	13:30 first, and there *are* f which shall be last.	4413
	14:18 The f said unto him, I have bought a piece	4413
	14:28 sitteth not down f, and counteth the cost,	4412
	14:31 sitteth not down f, and consulteth	4412
	16: 5 debtors unto *him*, and said unto the f,	4413
	17:25 But f must he suffer many *things*, and	4412

Lk	19:16 Then came the f, saying, Lord, thy pound	4413
	20:29 and the f took a wife, and died without	4413
	21: 9 for these *things* must f come to pass;	4412
	24: 1 upon the f *day* of the week, very early	1520
Jn	1:41 He f findeth his own brother Simon,	4413
	5: 4 f after the troubling of the water stepped	4413
	8: 7 among you, let him f cast a stone at her.	4413
	10:40 into the place where John at f baptized;	4412
	12:16 understood not his disciples at the f:	4412
	18:13 And led him away to Annas; for he was	4413
	19:32 brake the legs of the f, and of the other	4413
	19:39 which at the f came to Jesus by night,	4412
	20: 1 The f *day* of the week cometh Mary	1520
	20: 4 outrun Peter, and came f to the sepulchre.	4413
	20: 8 came f to the sepulchre, and he saw,	4413
	20:19 at evening, being the f *day* of the week,	1520
Ac	3:26 Unto you f God, having raised up his Son	4412
	7:12 corn in Egypt, he sent out our fathers f.	4412
	11:26 the disciples were called Christians f in	4413
	12:10 they were past the f and the second	4413
	13:24 When John had f preached before his	4296
	13:46 of God should f have been spoken to you:	4412
	15:14 Simeon hath declared how God at the f	4412
	20: 7 And upon the f *day* of the week, when	1520
	20:18 from the f day that I came into Asia,	4413
	26: 4 was at the f among mine own nation	746
	26:20 But shewed f unto them of Damascus,	4412
	26:23 he *should be* the f that should rise from	4413
	27:43 should cast *themselves* f into the sea,	4413
Ro	1: 8 f, I thank my God through Jesus Christ	4412
	1:16 to the Jew f, and *also* to the Greek.	4412
	2: 9 of the Jew f, and *also* to the Gentile;	4412
	2:10 to the Jew f, and *also* to the Gentile;	4412
	10:19 F Moses saith, I will provoke you to	4413
	11:35 Or who hath f **given** to him, and it shall	4272
	15:24 *if* I be somewhat filled with your	4412
1Co	11:18 For f of all, when ye come together in	4412
	12:28 apostles, secondarily prophets,	4412
	14:30 that sitteth *by*, let the f hold his peace.	4413
	15: 3 For I delivered unto you f *of all* that	1722+4413
	15:45 The f man Adam was made a living soul;	4413
	15:46 Howbeit *that was* not f *which is* spiritual,	4412
	15:47 The f man *is* of the earth, earthy:	4413
	16: 2 Upon the f *day* of the week let every one	1520
	16: S The f *epistle* to the Corinthians was	4413
2Co	8: 5 but f gave their own selves to the Lord,	4412
	8:12 For if there be f a willing mind, *it is*	4295
Gal	4:13 I preached the gospel unto you at the f.	4387
Eph	1:12 of his glory, who f **trusted** in Christ:	4276
	4: 9 he also descended f into the lower parts	4412
	6: 2 (which is the f commandment with	4413
Php	1: 5 your fellowship in the gospel from the f	4413
1Th	4:16 God: and the dead in Christ shall rise f:	4412
	5: S The f *epistle* unto the Thessalonians was	4413
2Th	2: 3 *come*, except there come a falling away f,	4412
1Ti	1:16 that in me f Jesus Christ might shew forth	4413
	2: 1 I exhort therefore that, f of all,	4412
	2:13 For Adam was f formed, then Eve.	4413
	3:10 And let these also f be proved; then	4412
	5: 4 let them learn f to shew piety at home,	4412
	5:12 because they have cast off *their* f faith.	4413
	6: S The f to Timothy was written from	4413
2Ti	1: 5 which dwelt f in thy grandmother Lois,	4412
	2: 6 husbandman that laboureth must be f	4413
	4:16 At my f answer no *man* stood with me,	4413
	4: S ordained the f bishop of the church of	4413
Tit	3:10 A man *that is* a heretick after the f and	1520
	3: S ordained the f bishop of the church of	4413
Heb	2: 3 which at the f began to be spoken by	746
	4: 6 to whom it was f preached entered not	4387
	5:12 be the f principles of the oracles of God;	746
	7: 2 f being by interpretation King of	4412
	7:27 f for his own sins, *and* then for	4387
	8: 7 For if that f *covenant* had been faultless,	4413
	8:13 A new *covenant*, he hath made the f old.	4413
	9: 1 Then verily the f *covenant* had also	4413
	9: 2 the f, wherein *was* the candlestick,	4413
	9: 6 the priests went always into the f	4413
	9: 8 as the f tabernacle was yet standing:	4413
	9:15 that were under the f testament,	4413
	9:18 Whereupon neither the f *testament* was	4413
	10: 9 taketh away the f, that he may establish	4413
Jas	3:17 But the wisdom that is from above is f	4412
1Pe	4:17 if *it* f begin at us, what *shall* the end *be*	4412
2Pe	1:20 Knowing this f, that no prophecy of	4412
	3: 3 Knowing this f, that there shall come in	4412
1Jn	4:19 We love him, because he f loved us.	4412
Jude	1: 6 the angels which kept not their f *estate*,	746
Rev	1: 5 and the f **begotten** of the dead,	4416
	1:11 I am Alpha and Omega, the f and the last:	4413
	1:17 unto me, Fear not; I am the f and the last:	4413
	2: 4 because thou hast left thy f love.	4413
	2: 5 art fallen, and repent, and do the f works;	4413
	2: 8 These *things* saith the f and the last,	4413
	2:19 and the last *to be* more than the f.	4413
	4: 1 the f voice which I heard *was* as *it were*	4413
	4: 7 And the f beast *was* like a lion,	4413
	8: 7 The f angel sounded, and there followed	4413
	13:12 And he exerciseth all the power of the f	4413
	13:12 which dwell therein to worship the f	4413
	16: 2 And the f went, and poured out his vial	4413
	20: 5 were finished. This *is* the f resurrection.	4413
	20: 6 holy *is* he that hath part in the f	4413
	21: 1 for the f heaven and the first earth were	4413
	21: 1 the f earth were passed away;	4413

Rev	21:19 The f foundation *was* jasper; the second,	4413
	22:13 and the end, the f and the last.	4413

FIRSTBEGOTTEN (1) [FIRST, BEGET]

Heb	1: 6 when he bringeth in the f into the world,	4416

FIRSTBORN (117) [FIRST, BEAR]

Ge	10:15 And Canaan begat Sidon his f, and Heth,	1060
	19:31 the f said unto the younger, Our father *is*	1067
	19:33 the f went in, and lay with her father;	1067
	19:34 that the f said unto the younger, Behold,	1067
	19:37 f bare a son, and called his name Moab:	1067
	22:21 Huz his f, and Buz his brother,	1060
	25:13 the f of Ishmael, Nebajoth; and Kedar,	1060
	27:19 said unto his father, I *am* Esau thy f;	1060
	27:32 And he said, I *am* thy son, thy f Esau.	1060
	29:26 to give the younger before the f.	1067
	35:23 Jacob's f, and Simeon, and Levi,	1060
	36:15 the sons of Eliphaz the f *son* of Esau,	1060
	38: 6 Judah took a wife for Er his f, whose	1060
	38: 7 Er, Judah's f, was wicked in the sight of	1060
	41:51 Joseph called the name of the f Manasseh	1060
	43:33 the f according to his birthright,	1060
	46: 8 Jacob and his sons: Reuben, Jacob's f,	1060
	48:14 hands wittingly; for Manasseh *was* the f.	1060
	48:18 for this *is* the f; put thy right hand upon	1060
	49: 3 Reuben, thou *art* my f, my might,	1060
Ex	4:22 the Loʀᴅ, Israel *is* my son, *even* my f:	1060
	4:23 behold, I will slay thy son, *even* thy f.	1060
	6:14 The sons of Reuben the f of Israel;	1060
	11: 5 all the f in the land of Egypt shall die,	1060
	11: 5 from the f of Pharaoh that sitteth upon	1060
	11: 5 *even* unto the f of the maidservant that *is*	1060
	11: 5 *is* behind the mill; and all the f of beasts.	1060
	12:12 will smite all the f in the land of Egypt,	1060
	12:29 that at midnight the Loʀᴅ smote all the f	1060
	12:29 from the f of Pharaoh that sat on his	1060
	12:29 of the captive that *was* in the dungeon;	1060
	12:29 in the dungeon; and all the f of cattle.	1060
	13: 2 Sanctify unto me all the f,	1060
	13:13 all the f of man amongst thy children	1060
	13:15 that the Loʀᴅ slew all the f in the land of	1060
	13:15 both the f of man, and the firstborn of	1060
	13:15 the firstborn of man, and the f of beast:	1060
	13:15 but all the f of my children I redeem.	1060
	22:29 the f of thy sons shalt thou give unto me.	1060
	34:20 All the f of thy sons thou shalt redeem:	1060
Nu	3: 2 Nadab the f, and Abihu, Eleazar,	1060
	3:12 that openeth the matrix among	1060
	3:13 Because all the f *are* mine; *for* on the day	1060
	3:13 *for* on the day that I smote all the f in	1060
	3:13 I hallowed unto me all the f in Israel,	1060
	3:40 Number all the f of the males of	1060
	3:41 instead of all the f among the children of	1060
	3:42 all the f among the children of Israel.	1060
	3:43 all the f males by the number of names,	1060
	3:45 Take the Levites instead of all the f	1060
	3:46 thirteen of the f of the children of Israel,	1060
	3:50 Of the f of the children of Israel took he	1060
	8:16 *even instead* of the f of all the children of	1060
	8:17 For all the f of the children of Israel *are*	1060
	8:17 the day that I smote every f in the land	1060
	8:18 I have taken the Levites for all the f of	1060
	18:15 nevertheless the f of man shalt thou	1060
	33: 4 For the Egyptians buried all *their* f, which	1060
Dt	21:15 and *if* the f son be hers that was hated;	1060
	21:16 **make** the son of the beloved f before	1069
	21:16 son of the hated, *which is* indeed the f:	1060
	21:17 the son of the hated for the f,	1060
	21:17 of his strength; the right of the f *is* his.	1062
	25: 6 f which she beareth shall succeed	1060
Jos	6:26 shall lay the foundation thereof in his f,	1060
	17: 1 for he *was* the f of Joseph; *to wit*, for	1060
	17: 1 *to wit*, for Machir the f of Manasseh,	1060
Jdg	8:20 said unto Jether his f, Up, *and* slay them.	1060
1Sa	8: 2 Now the name of his f was Joel;	1060
	14:49 *were* these; the name of the f Merab,	1067
	17:13 that went to the battle *were* Eliab the f,	1060
2Sa	3: 2 his f was Amnon, of Ahinoam	1060
1Ki	16:34 the foundation thereof in Abiram his f,	1060
1Ch	1:13 And Canaan begat Zidon his f, and Heth,	1060
	1:29 The f of Ishmael, Nebajoth; then Kedar,	1060
	2: 3 Er, of Judah, was evil in the sight of	1060
	2:13 Jesse begat his f Eliab, and Abinadab	1060
	2:25 sons of Jerahmeel the f of Hezron were,	1060
	2:25 Ram the f, and Bunah, and Oren,	1060
	2:27 the sons of Ram the f of Jerahmeel were,	1060
	2:42 brother of Jerahmeel *were*, Mesha his f,	1060
	2:50 Caleb the son of Hur, the f of Ephratah;	1060
	3: 1 the f Amnon, of Ahinoam the Jezreelitess;	1060
	3:15 the sons of Josiah *were*, the f Johanan,	1060
	4: 4 f of Ephratah, the father of Beth-lehem.	1060
	5: 1 Now the sons of Reuben the f of Israel,	1060
	5: 1 the firstborn of Israel, (for he *was* the f,)	1060
	5: 3 *I say*, of Reuben the f of Israel *were*,	1060
	6:28 sons of Samuel; the f Vashni, and Abiah.	1060
	8: 1 Now Benjamin begat Bela his f, Ashbel	1060
	8:30 his f son Abdon, and Zur, and Kish,	1060
	8:39 of Eshek his brother *were*, Ulam his f,	1060
	9: 5 the Shilonites; Asaiah the f, and his sons.	1060
	9:31 who *was* the f of Shallum the Korahite,	1060
	9:36 his f son Abdon, then Zur, and Kish,	1060
	26: 2 of Meshelemiah *were*, Zechariah the f,	1060
	26: 4 sons of Obed-edom *were*, Shemaiah the f,	1060
	26:10 the chief, (for *though* he was not the f,	1060

2Ch	21: 3 gave he to Jehoram; because he *was* the f.	1060
Ne	10:36 Also the f of our sons, and of our cattle,	1060
Job	18:13 *even* the f of death shall devour his	1060
Ps	78:51 smote all the f in Egypt; the chief of *their*	1060
	89:27 Also I will make him *my* f, higher than	1060
	105:36 He smote also all the f in their land,	1060
	135: 8 Who smote the f of Egypt, both of man	1060
	136:10 To him that smote Egypt in their f: for his	1060
Isa	14:30 the f of the poor shall feed, and the needy	1060
Jer	31: 9 am a father to Israel, and Ephraim *is* my f.	1060
Mic	6: 7 shall I give my f *for* my transgression,	1060
Zec	12:10 him, as one that is in bitterness for *his* f.	1060
Mt	1:25 not till she had brought forth her f son:	4416
Lk	2: 7 And she brought forth her f son,	4416
Ro	8:29 that he might be the f amongst many	4416
Col	1:15 the invisible God, the f of every creature:	4416
	1:18 is the beginning, the f from the dead;	4416
Heb	11:28 lest he that destroyed the f should touch	4416
	12:23 the general assembly, and church of the f,	4416

FIRSTFRUIT (2) [FIRST, FRUIT]

Dt	18: 4 The f *also* of thy corn, of thy wine,	7225
Ro	11:16 For if the f *be* holy, the lump *is* also holy:	536

FIRSTFRUITS (32) [FIRST, FRUIT]

Ex	23:16 the feast of harvest, the f of thy labours,	1061
	23:19 The first of the f of thy land thou shalt	1061
	34:22 of the f of wheat harvest, and the feast of	1061
	34:26 The first of the f of thy land thou shalt	1061
Lev	2:12 *As* for the oblation of the f, ye shall offer	7225
	2:14 if thou offer a meat offering of *thy* f unto	1061
	2:14 thy f green ears of corn dried by the fire,	1061
	23:10 ye shall bring a sheaf of the f of your	7225
	23:17 *they are* the f unto the LORD.	1061
	23:20 f *for* a wave offering before the LORD,	1061
Nu	18:12 the f them which they shall offer unto	7225
	28:26 Also in the day of the f, when ye bring a	1061
Dt	26:10 I have brought the f of the land,	6529+7225
2Ki	4:42 brought the man of God bread of the f,	1061
2Ch	31: 5 Israel brought in abundance the f of corn,	7225
Ne	10:35 to bring the f of our ground,	1061
	10:35 the f all fruit of all trees, year by year,	1061
	10:37 *that* we should bring the f of our dough,	7225
	12:44 the offerings, for the f, and for the tithes,	7225
	13:31 at times appointed, and for the f.	1061
Pr	3: 9 and with the f of all thine increase:	7225
Jer	2: 3 unto the LORD, *and* the f of his increase:	7225
Eze	20:40 the f of your oblations, with all your holy	7225
	44:30 the first of all the f of all *things*, and	1061
	48:14 nor alienate the f of the land:	7225
Ro	8:23 also, which have the f of the Spirit,	536
	16: 5 who is the f of Achaia unto Christ.	536
1Co	15:20 *and* become the f of them that slept.	536
	15:23 Christ the f; afterward they that are Christ's	536
	16:15 that it is the f of Achaia, and *that* they have	536
Jas	1:18 we should be a kind of f of his creatures.	536
Rev	14: 4 *being* the f unto God and to the Lamb.	536

FIRSTLING (14) [FIRST]

Ex	13:12 every f that cometh of a beast which thou	6363
	13:13 every f of an ass thou shalt redeem with a	6363
	34:19 every f amongst thy cattle, *whether* ox or	6363
	34:20 the f of an ass thou shalt redeem with a	6363
Lev	27:26 Only the f of the beasts, which should be	1060
	27:26 which should be the LORD'S f, no man	1069
Nu	18:15 the f of unclean beasts shalt thou redeem.	1060
	18:17 the f of a cow, or the firstling of a sheep,	1060
	18:17 the f of a sheep, or the firstling of a goat,	1060
	18:17 or the f of a goat, thou shalt not redeem;	1060
Dt	15:19 All the f males that come of thy herd and	1060
	15:19 thou shalt do no work with the f of thy	1060
	15:19 thy bullock, nor shear the f of thy sheep.	1060
	33:17 His glory *is* like the f of his bullock,	1060

FIRSTLINGS (6) [FIRST]

Ge	4: 4 he also brought of the f of his flock and	1062
Nu	3:41 cattle of the Levites instead of all the f	1060
Dt	12: 6 the f of your herds and of your flocks:	1062
	12:17 oil, or the f of thy herds or of thy flock,	1062
	14:23 the f of thy herds and of thy flocks;	1062
Ne	10:36 and the f of our herds and of our flocks,	1062

FIRSTRIPE (3) [FIRST, RIPE]

Hos	9:10 I saw your fathers as the f in the fig tree	1063
Mic	7: 1 cluster to eat: my soul desired the f **fruit**.	1063
Na	3:12 holds *shall be like* fig trees with the f **figs**:	1061

FISH (35) [FISH'S, FISHER'S, FISHERMEN, FISHERS, FISHES, FISHHOOKS, FISHING, FISHPOOLS]

Ge	1:26 let them have dominion over the f of	1710
	1:28 have dominion over the f of the sea,	1710
Ex	7:18 the f that *is* in the river shall die,	1710
	7:21 the f that *was* in the river died; and the	1710
Nu	11: 5 We remember the f, which we did eat in	1710
	11:22 shall all the f of the sea be gathered	1709
Dt	4:18 the likeness of any f that *is* in the waters	1710
2Ch	33:14 even to the entering in at the f gate,	1709
Ne	3: 3 the f gate did the sons of Hassenaah build	1709
	12:39 above the f gate, and the tower of	1709
	13:16 which brought f, and all *manner of* ware,	1709
Job	41: 7 barbed irons? or his head with f spears?	1709
Ps	8: 8 the f of the sea, *and whatsoever* passeth	1709
	105:29 their waters into blood, and slew their f	1710
Isa	19:10 all that make sluces *and* ponds for f.	5315
	50: 2 f stinketh, because *there* is no water,	1710

Jer	16:16 saith the LORD, and they shall f them;	1770
Eze	29: 4 I will cause the f of thy rivers to stick	1710
	29: 4 all the f of thy rivers shall stick unto thy	1710
	29: 5 thee and all the f of thy rivers:	1710
	47: 9 there shall be a very great multitude of f,	1710
	47:10 their f shall be according to their kinds,	1710
	47:10 as the f of the great sea, exceeding many.	1710
Jnh	1:17 Now the LORD had prepared a great f	1709
	1:17 Jonah was in the belly of the f three days	1709
	2:10 the LORD spake unto the f,	1709
Zep	1:10 *shall be* the noise of a cry from the f gate,	1709
Mt	7:10 if he ask a f, will he give him a serpent?	2486
	17:27 and take up the f that first cometh up;	2486
Lk	11:11 if he ask a f, will he for a fish give him a	2486
	11:11 a fish, will he for a f give him a serpent?	2486
	24:42 they gave him a piece of a broiled f,	2486
Jn	21: 9 coals there, and f laid thereon, and bread.	3795
	21:10 Bring of the f which ye have now caught.	3795
	21:13 and giveth them, and f likewise.	3795

FISH'S (1) [FISH]

Jnh	2: 1 unto the LORD his God out of the f belly,	1710

FISHER'S (1) [FISH]

Jn	21: 7 he girt *his* f coat unto him, (for he was	1903

FISHERMEN (1) [FISH, MAN]

Lk	5: 2 but the f were gone out of them,	231

FISHERS (7) [FISH]

Isa	19: 8 The f also shall mourn, and all they that	1771
Jer	16:16 Behold, I will send for many f, saith	1771
Eze	47:10 the f shall stand upon it from En-gedi	1728
Mt	4:18 casting a net into the sea: for they were f.	231
	4:19 Follow me, and I will make you f of men.	231
Mk	1:16 casting a net into the sea: for they were f.	231
	1:17 and I will make you to become f of men.	231

FISHES (27) [FISH]

Ge	9: 2 the earth, and upon all the f of the sea;	1709
1Ki	4:33 of fowl, and of creeping things, and of f.	1709
Job	12: 8 the f of the sea shall declare unto thee.	1709
Ecc	9:12 as the f that are taken in an evil net,	1709
Eze	38:20 So that the f of the sea, and the fowls of	1709
Hos	4: 3 the f of the sea also shall be taken away.	1709
Hab	1:14 makest men as the f of the sea,	1709
Zep	1: 3 the f of the sea, and the stumblingblocks	1709
Mt	14:17 We have here but five loaves, and two f.	2486
	14:19 the two f, and looking up to heaven,	2486
	15:34 And they said, Seven, and a few **little** f.	2485
	15:36 And he took the seven loaves and the f,	2486
Mk	6:38 they knew, they say, Five, and two f.	2486
	6:41 had taken the five loaves and the two f,	2486
	6:41 and the two f divided he among *them* all.	2486
	6:43 baskets full of the fragments, and of the f.	2486
	8: 7 they had a few **small** f: and he blessed,	2485
Lk	5: 6 they inclosed a great multitude of f:	2486
	5: 9 at the draught of the f which they had	2486
	9:13 have no more but five loaves and two f;	2486
	9:16 he took the five loaves and the two f,	2486
Jn	6: 9 hath five barley loaves, and two **small** f:	3795
	6:11 likewise of the f as much as they would.	3795
	21: 6 not able to draw it for the multitude of f.	2486
	21: 8 hundred cubits,) dragging the net with f.	2486
	21:11 and drew the net to land full of great f,	2486
1Co	15:39 beasts, another of f, *and* another of birds.	2486

FISHHOOKS (1) [FISH, HOOK]

Am	4: 2 and your posterity with f.	1729+5518

FISHING (1) [FISH]

Jn	21: 3 Simon Peter saith unto them, I go a f.	232

FISHPOOLS (1) [FISH, POOL]

SS	7: 4 thine eyes *like* the f in Heshbon,	1295

FIST (2)

Ex	21:18 or with *his* f, and he die not, but keepeth	106
Isa	58: 4 and to smite with the f of wickedness;	106

FISTS (1) [HOOK]

Pr	30: 4 who hath gathered the wind in his f?	2651

FIT (9) [FITLY, FITTED, FITTETH]

Lev	16:21 send *him* away by the hand of a f man	6261
1Ch	7:11 two hundred *soldiers*, f to go out f for war	NIH
	12: 8 and men of war f for the battle, that could	NIH
Job	34:18 *Is it* f to say to a king, *Thou art* wicked?	NIH
Pr	24:27 and **make** it f for thyself in the field;	6257
Lk	9:62 looking back, is f for the kingdom of God.	2111
	14:35 It is neither f for the land, nor yet for	2111
Ac	22:22 earth: for it is not f that he should live.	2520
Col	3:18 your own husbands, as it is f in the Lord.	433

FITCHES (4)

Isa	28:25 doth he not cast abroad the f,	7100
	28:27 the f are not threshed with a threshing	7100
	28:27 the f are beaten out with a staff,	7100
Eze	4: 9 f, and put them in one vessel,	3698

FITLY (4) [FIT]

Pr	25:11 word f spoken *is like* apples of gold	212+5921
SS	5:12 of waters, washed with milk, *and* f set.	4402
Eph	2:21 f **framed together** groweth unto a holy	4883
	4:16 whom the whole body f **joined together**	4883

FITTED (3) [FIT]

1Ki	6:35 covered *them* with gold f upon the carved	3474
Pr	22:18 they shall withal be f in thy lips.	3559
Ro	9:22 *the* vessels of wrath f to destruction:	2675

FITTETH (1) [FIT]

Isa	44:13 he f it with planes, and he marketh it out	6213

FITTING See SEEMLY

FIVE (345) [FIFTH]

Ge	5: 6 Seth lived an hundred and f years,	2568
	5:11 of Enos were nine hundred and f years:	2568
	5:15 Mahalaleel lived sixty and f years,	2568
	5:17 were eight hundred ninety and f years:	2568
	5:21 Enoch lived sixty and f years,	2568
	5:23 were three hundred sixty and f years:	2568
	5:30 Lamech lived after he begat Noah f	2568
	5:30 Noah five hundred ninety and f years,	2568
	5:32 Noah was f hundred years old:	2568
	11:11 Shem lived after he begat Arphaxad f	2568
	11:12 Arphaxad lived f and thirty years,	2568
	11:32 of Terah were two hundred and f years:	2568
	12: 4 f years old when he departed out of	2568
	14: 9 Arioch king of Ellasar; four kings with f.	2568
	18:28 Peradventure there shall lack of the fifty	2568
	18:28 wilt thou destroy all the city for *lack of* f?	2568
	18:28 said, If I find there forty and f, I will not	2568
	43:34 Benjamin's mess was f times so much as	2568
	45: 6 yet *there are* f years, *in* the which *there*	2568
	45:11 for yet *there are* f years of famine;	2568
	45:22 *pieces of* silver, and f changes of raiment.	2568
	47: 2 *even* f men, and presented them unto	2568
Ex	22: 1 he shall restore f oxen for an ox,	2568
	26: 3 The f curtains shall be coupled together	2568
	26: 3 *other* f curtains *shall be* coupled one to	2568
	26: 9 shalt couple f curtains by themselves,	2568
	26:26 f for the boards of the one side of	2568
	26:27 f bars for the boards of the other side of	2568
	26:27 f bars for the boards of the side of	2568
	26:37 thou shalt make for the hanging f pillars	2568
	26:37 thou shalt cast f sockets of brass for them.	2568
	27: 1 f cubits long, and five cubits broad;	2568
	27: 1 five cubits long, and f cubits broad;	2568
	27:18 the height f cubits *of* fine twined linen,	2568
	30:23 of pure myrrh f hundred *shekels*, and	2568
	30:24 cassia f hundred *shekels*, after the shekel	2568
	36:10 coupled the f curtains one unto another:	2568
	36:10 *the other* f curtains he coupled one unto	2568
	36:16 he coupled f curtains by themselves,	2568
	36:31 for the boards of the one side of	2568
	36:32 f bars for the boards of the other side of	2568
	36:32 f bars for the boards of the tabernacle for	2568
	36:38 the f pillars of it with their hooks:	2568
	36:38 gold: but their f sockets *were of* brass.	2568
	38: 1 f cubits *was* the length thereof,	2568
	38: 1 and f cubits the breadth thereof;	2568
	38:18 the height in the breadth *was* f cubits,	2568
	38:26 and f hundred and fifty *men*.	2568
	38:28 f *shekels* he made hooks for the pillars,	2568
Lev	26: 8 of you shall chase an hundred,	2568
	27: 5 if *it be* from f years old even unto twenty	2568
	27: 6 *it be* from a month old even unto f years	2568
	27: 6 estimation shall be of the male f shekels	2568
Nu	1:21 forty and six thousand and f hundred.	2568
	1:25 and f thousand six hundred and fifty.	2568
	1:33 *were* forty thousand and f hundred.	2568
	1:37 *were* thirty and f thousand and	2568
	1:41 forty and one thousand and f hundred.	2568
	1:46 three thousand and f hundred and fifty.	2568
	2:11 forty and six thousand and f hundred.	2568
	2:15 forty and f thousand and six hundred	2568
	2:19 *were* forty thousand and f hundred.	2568
	2:23 *were* thirty and f thousand and	2568
	2:28 forty and one thousand and f hundred.	2568
	2:32 three thousand and f hundred and fifty.	2568
	3:22 them *were* seven thousand and f hundred.	2568
	3:47 shalt even take f shekels **apiece**	2568+2568
	3:50 f *shekels*, after the shekel of the sanctuary	2568
	4:48 and f hundred and fourscore.	2568
	7:17 oxen, f rams, five he goats, five lambs	2568
	7:17 oxen, five rams, f he goats, five lambs	2568
	7:17 five he goats, f lambs of the first year:	2568
	7:23 oxen, f rams, five he goats, five lambs	2568
	7:23 oxen, five rams, f he goats, five lambs	2568
	7:23 five he goats, f lambs of the first year:	2568
	7:29 oxen, f rams, five he goats, five lambs	2568
	7:29 oxen, five rams, f he goats, five lambs	2568
	7:29 five he goats, f lambs of the first year:	2568
	7:35 oxen, f rams, five he goats, five lambs	2568
	7:35 oxen, five rams, f he goats, five lambs	2568
	7:35 five he goats, f lambs of the first year:	2568
	7:41 oxen, f rams, five he goats, five lambs	2568
	7:41 oxen, five rams, f he goats, five lambs	2568
	7:41 five he goats, f lambs of the first year:	2568
	7:47 oxen, f rams, five he goats, five lambs	2568
	7:47 oxen, five rams, f he goats, five lambs	2568
	7:47 five he goats, f lambs of the first year:	2568
	7:53 oxen, f rams, five he goats, five lambs	2568
	7:53 oxen, five rams, f he goats, five lambs	2568
	7:53 five he goats, f lambs of the first year:	2568
	7:59 oxen, f rams, five he goats, five lambs	2568
	7:59 oxen, five rams, f he goats, five lambs	2568
	7:59 five he goats, f lambs of the first year:	2568
	7:65 oxen, f rams, five he goats, five lambs	2568

F

Nu	7:65 oxen, five rams, **f** he goats, five lambs	2568
	7:65 five he goats, **f** lambs of the first year:	2568
	7:71 oxen, **f** rams, five he goats, five lambs	2568
	7:71 oxen, five rams, **f** he goats, five lambs	2568
	7:71 five he goats, **f** lambs of the first year:	2568
	7:77 oxen, **f** rams, five he goats, five lambs	2568
	7:77 oxen, five rams, **f** he goats, five lambs	2568
	7:77 five he goats, **f** lambs of the first year:	2568
	7:83 oxen, **f** rams, five he goats, five lambs	2568
	7:83 oxen, five rams, **f** he goats, five lambs	2568
	7:83 five he goats, **f** lambs of the first year:	2568
	8:24 from twenty and **f** years old and	2568
	11:19 two days, nor **f** days, neither ten days,	2568
	18:16 *for* the money of **f** shekels,	2568
	26:18 of them, forty thousand and **f** hundred.	2568
	26:22 and sixteen thousand and **f** hundred.	2568
	26:27 threescore thousand and **f** hundred.	2568
	26:37 thirty and two thousand and **f** hundred.	2568
	26:41 forty and **f** thousand and six hundred.	2568
	26:50 and **f** thousand and four hundred.	2568
	31: 8 and Hur, and Reba, **f** kings of Midian:	2568
	31:28 soul of **f** hundred, *both* of the persons,	2568
	31:32 seventy thousand and **f** thousand sheep,	2568
	31:36 thirty thousand and **f** hundred sheep:	2568
	31:39 asses *were* thirty thousand and **f** hundred;	2568
	31:43 and seven thousand and **f** hundred sheep,	2568
	31:45 And thirty thousand asses and **f** hundred,	2568
Jos	8:12 took about **f** thousand men, and set them	2568
	10: 5 Therefore the **f** kings of the Amorites,	2568
	10:16 these **f** kings fled, and hid themselves in a	2568
	10:17 The **f** kings are found hid in a cave at	2568
	10:22 bring out those **f** kings unto me out of	2568
	10:23 brought forth those **f** kings unto him out	2568
	10:26 slew them, and hanged them on **f** trees:	2568
	13: 3 **f** lords of the Philistines; the Gazathites,	2568
	14:10 alive, as he said, these forty and **f** years,	2568
	14:10 I *am this* day fourscore and **f** years old.	2568
Jdg	3: 3 Namely, **f** lords of the Philistines,	2568
	18: 2 the children of Dan sent of their family **f**	2568
	18: 7 the **f** men departed, and came to Laish,	2568
	18:14 answered the **f** men that went to spy out	2568
	18:17 the **f** men that went to spy out the land	2568
	20:35 and **f** thousand and an hundred men:	2568
	20:45 they gleaned of them in the highways **f**	2568
	20:46 and **f** thousand men that drew the sword;	2568
1Sa	6: 4 **F** golden emerods, and five golden mice,	2568
	6: 4 Five golden emerods, and **f** golden mice,	2568
	6:16 the **f** lords of the Philistines had seen	2568
	6:18 of the Philistines *belonging* to the **f** lords,	2568
	17: 5 the weight of the coat *was* **f** thousand	2568
	17:40 chose him **f** smooth stones out of the	2568
	21: 3 give me **f** loaves of bread in mine hand,	2568
	22:18 and **f** persons that did wear a linen ephod.	2568
	25:18 **f** sheep ready dressed, and five measures	2568
	25:18 **f** measures of parched *corn,* and an	2568
	25:42 with **f** damsels of hers that went after her;	2568
2Sa	4: 4 was **f** years old when the tidings came of	2568
	21: 8 the **f** sons of Michal the daughter of Saul,	2568
	24: 9 men of Judah *were* **f** hundred thousand	2568
1Ki	4:32 and his songs were a thousand and **f.**	2568
	6: 6 The nethermost chamber *was* **f** cubits	2568
	6:10 against all the house, **f** cubits high:	2568
	6:24 **f** cubits *was* the one wing of the cherub,	2568
	6:24 and **f** cubits the other wing of the cherub:	2568
	7: 3 that *lay* on forty **f** pillars, fifteen *in* a row.	2568
	7:16 height of the one chapiter *was* **f** cubits,	2568
	7:16 the height of the other chapiter *was* **f**	2568
	7:23 all about, and his height *was* **f** cubits:	2568
	7:39 put **f** bases on the right side of the house,	2568
	7:39 and **f** on the left side of the house:	2568
	7:49 **f** on the right side, and five on the left,	2568
	7:49 **f** on the left, before the oracle, with	2568
	9:23 **f** hundred and fifty, which bare rule over	2568
	22:42 and **f** years old when he *began* to reign,	2568
	22:42 reigned twenty and **f** years in Jerusalem.	2568
2Ki	6:25 fourth part of a kab of dove's dung for **f**	2568
	7:13 I pray thee, **f** of the horses that remain,	2568
	13:19 shouldest have smitten **f** or six times;	2568
	14: 2 and **f** years old when he *began* to reign,	2568
	15:33 **F** and twenty years old was he when he	2568
	18: 2 **f** years old was he when he *began* to	2568
	19:35 an hundred fourscore and **f** thousand:	2568
	21: 1 reigned fifty and **f** years in Jerusalem.	2568
	23:36 and **f** year old when he *began* to reign;	2568
	25:19 **f** men of them that were in the king's	2568
1Ch	2: 4 and Zerah. All the sons of Judah *were* **f.**	2568
	2: 6 and Calcol, and Dara: **f** of them in all.	2568
	3:20 Berechiah, and Hasadiah, Jushabhesed, **f.**	2568
	4:32 Rimmon, and Tochen, and Ashan, **f** cities:	2568
	4:42 **f** hundred men, went to mount Seir,	2568
	7: 3 Michael, and Obadiah, and Joel, Ishiah, **f:**	2568
	7: 7 Uzzi, and Uzziel, and Jerimoth, and Iri, **f;**	2568
	11:23 **f** cubits *high;* and in the Egyptian's hand	2568
	29: 7 house of God of gold **f** thousand talents	2568
2Ch	3:11 *one* wing of the one cherub *was* **f** cubits,	2568
	3:11 the other wing *was* likewise **f** cubits,	2568
	3:12 wing of the other cherub *was* **f** cubits,	2568
	3:12 other wing *was* **f** cubits *also,* joining to	2568
	3:15 two pillars of thirty and **f** cubits high,	2568
	3:15 on the top of *each* of them was **f** cubits.	2568
	4: 2 compass, and **f** cubits the height thereof;	2568
	4: 6 on the right hand, and five on the left,	2568
	4: 6 and **f** on the left, to wash in them:	2568
	4: 7 on the right hand, and five on the left.	2568
	4: 7 five on the right hand, and **f** on the left.	2568

2Ch	4: 8 **f** on the right side, and five on the left.	2568
	4: 8 five on the right side, and **f** on the left.	2568
	6:13 of **f** cubits long, and five cubits broad,	2568
	6:13 cubits broad, and three cubits high,	2568
	13:17 there fell down slain of Israel **f** hundred	2568
	15:19 there was no *more* war unto the **f** and	2568
	20:31 and **f** years old when he *began* to reign,	2568
	20:31 reigned twenty and **f** years in Jerusalem.	2568
	25: 1 and **f** years old *when* he *began* to reign,	2568
	26:13 and seven thousand and **f** hundred,	2568
	27: 1 and **f** years old when he *began* to reign,	2568
	27: 8 He was **f** and twenty years old when he	2568
	29: 1 Hezekiah *began* to reign *when* he was **f**	2568
	33: 1 he reigned fifty and **f** years in Jerusalem.	2568
	35: 9 passover *offerings* **f** thousand *small cattle,*	2568
	35: 9 *small cattle,* and **f** hundred oxen.	2568
	36: 5 and **f** years old when he *began* to reign,	2568
Ezr	1:11 silver *were* **f** thousand and four hundred.	2568
	2: 5 of Arah, seven hundred seventy and **f.**	2568
	2: 8 of Zattu, nine hundred forty and **f.**	2568
	2:20 The children of Gibbar, ninety and **f.**	2568
	2:33 and Ono, seven hundred twenty and **f.**	2568
	2:34 of Jericho, three hundred forty and **f.**	2568
	2:66 six; their mules, two hundred forty and **f;**	2568
	2:67 Their camels, four hundred thirty and **f;**	2568
	2:69 **f** thousand pound *of* silver,	2568
Ne	7:13 of Zattu, eight hundred forty and **f.**	2568
	7:20 children of Adin, six hundred fifty and **f.**	2568
	7:25 The children of Gibeon, ninety and **f.**	2568
	7:36 of Jericho, three hundred forty and **f.**	2568
	7:67 and **f** singing *men* and singing *women.*	2568
	7:68 six: their mules, two hundred forty and **f;**	2568
	7:69 *Their* camels, four hundred thirty and **f:**	2568
	7:70 **f** hundred and thirty priests' garments.	2568
Est	9: 6 Jews slew and destroyed **f** hundred men.	2568
	9:12 destroyed **f** hundred men in Shushan	2568
	9:16 slew of their foes seventy and **f** thousand,	2568
Job	1: 3 **f** hundred yoke of oxen, and five hundred	2568
	1: 3 hundred she asses, and a very great	2568
Isa	7: 8 and **f** years shall Ephraim be broken,	2568
	17: 6 **f** in the outmost fruitful branches thereof,	2568
	19:18 that day shall **f** cities in the land of Egypt	2568
	30:17 of one; at the rebuke of **f** shall ye flee:	2568
	37:36 an hundred and fourscore and **f** thousand:	2568
Jer	52:22 the height of one chapiter *was* **f** cubits,	2568
	52:30 Jews seven hundred forty and **f** persons:	2568
	52:31 in the **f** and twentieth *day* of the month,	2568
Eze	8:16 the altar, *were* about **f** and twenty men,	2568
	11: 1 behold at the door of the gate **f** and	2568
	40: 1 the **f** and twentieth year of our captivity,	2568
	40: 7 between the little chambers *were* **f** cubits;	2568
	40:13 The breadth *was* **f** and twenty cubits,	2568
	40:21 and the breadth **f** and twenty cubits.	2568
	40:25 and the breadth **f** and twenty cubits.	2568
	40:29 long, and **f** and twenty cubits broad.	2568
	40:30 the arches round about *were* **f** and	2568
	40:30 twenty cubits long, and **f** cubits broad.	2568
	40:33 long, and **f** and twenty cubits broad.	2568
	40:36 and the breadth **f** and twenty cubits.	2568
	40:48 **f** cubits on this side, and five cubits on	2568
	40:48 on this side, and **f** cubits on that side:	2568
	41: 2 the sides of the door *were* **f** cubits on	2568
	41: 2 one side, and **f** cubits on the other side:	2568
	41: 9 the side chamber without, *was* **f** cubits:	2568
	41:11 breadth of the place that was left *was* **f**	2568
	41:12 the wall of the building *was* **f** cubits thick	2568
	42:16 **f** hundred reeds, with the measuring reed	2568
	42:17 measured the north side, **f** hundred reeds,	2568
	42:18 **f** hundred reeds, with the measuring reed.	2568
	42:19 measured **f** hundred reeds with	2568
	42:20 **f** hundred *reeds* long, and five hundred	2568
	42:20 *reeds* long, and **f** hundred broad,	2568
	45: 1 the length *shall be* the length of **f** and	2568
	45: 2 Of this there shall be for the sanctuary **f**	2568
	45: 2 **f** hundred *in* breadth, square round about;	2568
	45: 3 shalt thou measure the length of **f**	2568
	45: 5 the **f** and twenty thousand of length,	2568
	45: 6 shall appoint the possession of the city **f**	2568
	45: 6 and **f** and twenty thousand long,	2568
	45:12 **f** and twenty shekels, fifteen shekels,	2568
	48: 8 be the offering which ye shall offer of **f**	2568
	48: 9 ye shall offer unto the Lᴏʀᴅ *shall be* of **f**	2568
	48:10 toward the north **f** and twenty thousand	2568
	48:10 toward the south **f** and twenty thousand	2568
	48:13 the Levites *shall have* **f** and	2568
	48:13 all the length *shall be* **f** and	2568
	48:15 the **f** thousand, that are left in the breadth	2568
	48:15 are left in the breadth over against the **f**	2568
	48:16 north side four thousand and **f** hundred,	2568
	48:16 south side four thousand and **f** hundred,	2568
	48:16 east side four thousand and **f** hundred,	2568
	48:16 west side four thousand and **f** hundred.	2568
	48:20 All the oblation *shall be* **f** and	2568
	48:21 thousand by **f** and twenty thousand:	2568
	48:21 over against the **f** and twenty thousand of	2568
	48:21 westward over against the **f** and	2568
	48:30 four thousand and **f** hundred measures.	2568
	48:32 east side four thousand and **f** hundred	2568
	48:33 four thousand and **f** hundred measures:	2568
	48:34 west side four thousand and **f** hundred,	2568
Da	12:12 thousand and **f** and thirty days.	2568
Mt	14:17 have here but **f** loaves, and two fishes.	4002
	14:19 and took the **f** loaves, and the two fishes,	4002
	14:21 had eaten were about **f** thousand men,	4000
	16: 9 neither remember the **f** loaves of the five	4002

Mt	16: 9 the five loaves of the **f** thousand,	4000
	25: 2 And **f** of them were wise, and five *were*	4002
	25: 2 of them were wise, and **f** *were* foolish.	4002
	25:15 unto one he gave **f** talents, to another	4002
	25:16 Then he that had received the **f** talents	4002
	25:16 the same, and made *them* other **f** talents.	4002
	25:20 he that had received **f** talents came and	4002
	25:20 talents came and brought other **f** talents,	4002
	25:20 Lord, thou deliveredst unto me **f** talents:	4002
	25:20 I have gained besides them **f** talents moe.	4002
Mk	6:38 they knew, they say, **F**, and two fishes.	4002
	6:41 And when he had taken the **f** loaves and	4002
	6:44 the loaves were about **f** thousand men.	4000
	8:19 When I brake the **f** loaves among five	4002
	8:19 brake the five loaves among **f** thousand,	4000
Lk	1:24 and hid herself **f** months, saying,	4002
	7:41 the one ought **f** hundred pence,	4001
	9:13 have no more but **f** loaves and two fishes;	4002
	9:14 For they were about **f** thousand men.	4000
	9:16 Then he took the **f** loaves and the two	4002
	12: 6 Are not **f** sparrows sold for two farthings,	4002
	12:52 from henceforth there shall be **f** in one	4002
	14:19 I have bought **f** yoke of oxen, and I go to	4002
	16:28 For I have **f** brethren; that he may testify	4002
	19:18 Lord, thy pound hath gained **f** pounds.	4002
	19:19 likewise to him, Be thou also over **f** cities.	4002
Jn	4:18 thou hast had **f** husbands; and he whom	4002
	5: 2 tongue Bethesda, having **f** porches.	4002
	6: 9 which hath **f** barley loaves, and two small	4002
	6:10 sat down, *in* number about **f** thousand.	4000
	6:13 with the fragments of the **f** barley loaves,	4002
	6:19 So when they had rowed about **f** and	4002
Ac	4: 4 the number of the men was about **f**	4002
	20: 6 and came unto them to Troas in **f** days;	4002
	24: 1 And after **f** days Ananias the high priest	4002
1Co	14:19 in the church I had rather speak **f** words	4002
	15: 6 he was seen of above **f** hundred brethren	4001
2Co	11:24 Of the Jews **f** times received I forty	3999
Rev	9: 5 that they should be tormented **f** months:	4002
	9:10 their power *was* to hurt men **f** months.	4002
	17:10 **f** are fallen, and one is, *and* the other is	4002

FIXED (5)

Ps	57: 7 My heart is **f**, O God, my heart is fixed:	3559
	57: 7 My heart is fixed, O God, my heart is **f:**	3559
	108: 1 O God, my heart is **f;** I will sing and	3559
	112: 7 his heart is **f**, trusting in the Lᴏʀᴅ.	3559
Lk	16:26 between us and you there is a great gulf **f:**	4741

FLAG (1) [FLAGS]

Job	8:11 can the **f** grow without water?	260

FLAGON (2) [FLAGONS]

2Sa	6:19 and a good piece *of* flesh, and a **f** *of* wine.	809
1Ch 16:	3 and a good piece *of* flesh, and a **f** *of* wine.	809

FLAGONS (3) [FLAGON]

SS	2: 5 Stay me with **f**, comfort me with apples:	809
Isa	22:24 vessels of cups, even to all the vessels of **f.**	5035
Hos	3: 1 look to other gods, and love of **f** wine.	809

FLAGS (3) [FLAG]

Ex	2: 3 she laid *it* in the **f** by the river's brink.	5488
	2: 5 she saw the ark among the **f**, she sent	5488
Isa	19: 6 dried up: the reeds and **f** shall wither.	5488

FLAGSTAFF See BEACON

FLAKES (1)

Job	41:23 The **f** of his flesh are joined together:	4651

FLAME (34) [FLAMES, FLAMING]

Ex	3: 2 in a **f** of fire out of the midst of a bush:	3827
Nu	21:28 of Heshbon, a **f** from the city of Sihon:	3852
Jdg	13:20 when the **f** went up toward heaven from	3851
	13:20 the Lᴏʀᴅ ascended in the **f** of the altar.	3851
	20:38 they should make a great **f** with smoke	4864
	20:40 the **f** began to arise up out of the city	4864
	20:40 of the city ascended up to heaven.	3632
Job	15:30 the **f** shall dry up his branches, and by	7957
	41:21 and a **f** goeth out of his mouth.	3851
Ps	83:14 and as the **f** setteth the mountains on fire;	3852
	106:18 their company; the **f** burnt up the wicked.	3852
SS	8: 6 of fire, *which hath* a **most vehement** **f.**	7957
Isa	5:24 the **f** consumeth the chaff, *so* their root	3852
	10:17 be for a fire, and his Holy One for a **f:**	3852
	29: 6 and tempest, and the **f** of devouring fire.	3851
	30:30 *with* the **f** of a devouring fire,	3851
	43: 2 neither shall the **f** kindle upon thee.	3852
	47:14 themselves from the power of the **f:**	3852
Jer	48:45 a **f** from the midst of Sihon,	3852
Eze	20:47 the flaming **f** shall not be quenched,	7957
Da	3:22 the **f** of the fire slew those men that took	7631
	7: 9 his throne *was* like the fiery **f**,	7631
	7:11 destroyed, and given to the burning **f.**	785
	11:33 by **f**, by captivity, and by spoil, *many* days.	3852
Joel	1:19 the **f** hath burnt all the trees of the field.	3852
	2: 3 them; and behind them a **f** burneth:	3852
	2: 5 like the noise of a **f** of fire that devoureth	3851
Ob	1:18 the house of Joseph a **f**, and the house of	3852
Lk	16:24 my tongue; for I am tormented in this **f.**	5395
Ac	7:30 an angel of the Lord in a **f** of fire in a bush.	5395
Heb	1: 7 angels spirits, and his ministers a **f** of fire.	5395
Rev	1:14 as snow; and his eyes *were* as a **f** of fire;	5395
	2:18 who hath his eyes like unto a **f** of fire,	5395
	19:12 His eyes *were* as a **f** of fire, and on his	5395

FLAMES (3) [FLAME]
Ps 29: 7 The voice of the LORD divideth the f of 3852
Isa 13: 8 one at another; their faces *shall be as* f. 3851
 66:15 with fury, and his rebuke with f of fire. 3851

FLAMING (9) [FLAME]
Ge 3:24 f sword which turned every way, to keep 3858
Ps 104: 4 his angels spirits; his ministers a f fire: 3857
 105:32 them hail *for* rain, *and* f fire in their land. 3852
Isa 4: 5 day, and the shining of a f fire by night: 3852
La 2: 3 he burned against Jacob like a f fire, 3852
Eze 20:47 the f flame shall not be quenched, 3852
Hos 7: 6 *in* the morning it burneth as a f fire. 3852
Na 2: 3 chariots *shall be* with f torches in the day 784
2Th 1: 8 In f fire, taking vengeance on them that *5395*

FLANKS (6)
Lev 3: 4 which *is* by the f, and the caul above 3689
 3:10 which *is* by the f, and the caul above 3689
 3:15 which *is* by the f, and the caul above 3689
 4: 9 which *is* by the f, and the caul above 3689
 7: 4 which *is* by the f, and the caul *that is* 3689
Job 15:27 maketh collops of fat on his f. 3689

FLASH (1)
Eze 1:14 as the appearance of a f of lightning. 965

FLASK See BOX; VIAL; VIALS

FLAT (4)
Lev 21:18 or he that hath a f nose, or any thing 2763
Nu 22:31 down his head, and **fell** on his face. 7812
Jos 6: 5 the wall of the city shall fall down f, 8478
 6:20 the wall fell down f, so that the people 8478

FLATTER (2) [FLATTERETH, FLATTERIES, FLATTERING, FLATTERY]
Ps 5: 9 open sepulchre; they f with their tongue. 2505
 78:36 Nevertheless they did f him with their 6601

FLATTERETH (6) [FLATTER]
Ps 36: 2 For he f himself in his own eyes, until his 2505
Pr 2:16 *even* from the stranger which f with her 2505
 7: 5 the stranger *which* f with her words. 2505
 20:19 meddle not with him that f with his lips. 6601
 28:23 favour him that f with the tongue. 2505
 29: 5 man that f his neighbour spreadeth a net 2505

FLATTERIES (3) [FLATTER]
Da 11:21 peaceably, and obtain the kingdom by f. 2519
 11:32 against the covenant shall he corrupt by f: 2514
 11:34 but many shall cleave to them with f. 2519

FLATTERING (8) [FLATTER]
Job 32:21 neither let me **give f titles** unto man. 3655
 32:22 For I know not to **give f titles;** *in so* 3655
Ps 12: 2 *with* f lips *and* with a double heart 2513
 12: 3 The LORD shall cut off all f lips, 2513
Pr 7:21 of her lips she forced him. 2506
 26:28 by it; and a f mouth worketh ruin. 2509
Eze 12:24 divination within the house of Israel. 2509
1Th 2: 5 For neither at any time used we f words, *2850*

FLATTERY (2) [FLATTER]
Job 17: 5 He *that* speaketh f to *his* friends, 2506+3807.1
Pr 6:24 from the f of the tongue of a strange 2513

FLAWLESS See UNDEFILED

FLAX (11)
Ex 9:31 the f and the barley was smitten: 6594
 9:31 *was* in the ear, and the f *was* bolled. 6594
Jos 2: 6 hid them with the stalks of f, which she 6593
Jdg 15:14 arms became as f *that* was burnt with fire, 6593
Pr 31:13 f, and worketh willingly with her hands. 6593
Isa 19: 9 Moreover they that work in fine f, 6593
 42: 3 and the smoking f shall he not quench: 6594
Eze 40: 3 a line of f in his hand, and a measuring 6593
Hos 2: 5 wool and my f, mine oil and my drink. 6593
 2: 9 and my f *given* to cover her nakedness. 6593
Mt 12:20 and smoking f shall he not quench, *3043*

FLAY (1) [FLAYED]
Lev 1: 6 he shall f the burnt offering, and cut it 6584
2Ch 29:34 they could not f all the burnt offerings. 6584
Mic 3: 3 my people, and f their skin from off them; 6584

FLAYED (1) [FLAY]
2Ch 35:11 from their hands, and the Levites f *them.* 6584

FLEA (2)
1Sa 24:14 thou pursue? after a dead dog, after a f. 6550
 26:20 the king of Israel is come out to seek a f, 6550

FLED (148) [FLEE]
Ge 14:10 the kings of Sodom and Gomorrah f, 5127
 14:10 that remained f to the mountain. 5127
 16: 6 dealt hardly with her, she f from her face. 1272
 31:20 Syrian, in that he told him not that he f. 1272
 31:21 he f with all that he had; and he rose up, 1272
 31:22 Laban on the third day that Jacob was f. 1272
 35: 7 when he f from the face of his brother. 1272
 39:12 in her hand, and f, and got him out. 5127
 39:13 his garment in her hand, and was f forth, 5127
 39:15 garment with me, and f, and got him out. 5127
 39:18 he left his garment with me, and f out. 5127

Ex 2:15 Moses f from the face of Pharaoh, 1272
 4: 3 a serpent; and Moses f from before it. 5127
 14: 5 told the king of Egypt that the people f: 1272
 14:27 the Egyptians f against it; and the LORD 5127
Nu 16:34 all Israel that *were* round about them f at 5127
 35:25 to the city of his refuge, whither he was f: 1272
 35:26 of the city of his refuge, whither he was f; 5127
 35:32 shall take no satisfaction for him that is f 5127
Jos 7: 4 and they f before the men of Ai. 5127
 8:15 and f *by* the way of the wilderness. 5127
 8:20 the people that f to the wilderness turned 5127
 10:11 as they f from before Israel, *and* were in 5127
 10:16 these five kings f, and hid themselves in a 5127
 20: 6 house, unto the city from whence he f. 5127
Jdg 1: 6 Adoni-bezek f; and they pursued after 5127
 4:15 off *his* chariot, and f **away** on his feet. 5127
 4:17 Howbeit Sisera f **away** on his feet to 5127
 7:21 and all the host ran, and cried, and f. 5127
 7:22 the host f to Beth-shittah in Zererath, 5127
 8:12 when Zebah and Zalmunna f, he pursued 5127
 9:21 f, and went to Beer, and dwelt there, 1272
 9:40 he f before him, and many were 5127
 9:51 thither f all the men and women, 5127
 11: 3 Jephthah f from his brethren, and dwelt 1272
 20:45 f toward the wilderness unto the rock of 5127
 20:47 f to the wilderness unto the rock Rimmon, 5127
1Sa 4:10 and they f every man into his tent: 5127
 4:16 the army, and I f to day out of the army. 5127
 4:17 Israel is f before the Philistines, 5127
 14:22 when they heard that the Philistines f, 5127
 17:24 man, f from him, and were sore afraid. 5127
 17:51 saw their champion was dead, they f. 5127
 19: 8 a great slaughter; and they f from him. 5127
 19:10 and David f, and escaped that night. 5127
 19:12 window: and he went, and f, and escaped. 1272
 19:18 So David f, and escaped, and came to 1272
 20: 1 David f from Naioth in Ramah, and came 1272
 21:10 that day for fear of Saul, and went to 1272
 22:17 because they knew when he f, and did 1272
 22:20 escaped, and f after David. 1272
 23: 6 when Abiathar the son of Ahimelech f to 1272
 27: 4 it was told Saul that David was f *to* Gath: 1272
 30:17 men, which rode upon camels, and f. 5127
 31: 1 the men of Israel f from before 5127
 31: 7 saw that the men of Israel f, and that Saul 5127
 31: 7 were dead, they forsook the cities, and f; 5127
2Sa 1: 4 That the people are f from the battle, 5127
 4: 3 the Beerothites f to Gittaim, 1272
 4: 4 Jezreel, and his nurse took him up, and f: 5127
 10:13 against the Syrians: and they f before him. 5127
 10:14 of Ammon saw that the Syrians were f, 5127
 10:14 then f they also before Abishai, 5127
 10:18 the Syrians f before Israel; and David slew 5127
 13:29 man gat him up upon his mule, and f. 5127
 13:34 Absalom f. And the young man that kept 1272
 13:37 Absalom f, and went to Talmai, the son 1272
 13:38 So Absalom f, and went to Geshur, 1272
 18:17 and all Israel f every one to his tent. 5127
 19: 8 for Israel had f every man to his tent. 5127
 19: 9 now he is f out of the land for Absalom. 1272
 23:11 and the people f from the Philistines. 5127
1Ki 2: 7 for so they came to me when I f because 1272
 2:28 Joab f unto the tabernacle of the LORD, 5127
 2:29 it was told king Solomon that Joab was f 5127
 11:17 That Hadad f, he and certain Edomites of 1272
 11:23 which f from his lord Hadadezer king of 1272
 11:40 Jeroboam arose, and f into Egypt, 1272
 12: 2 (for he was f from the presence 1272
 20:20 the Syrians f; and Israel pursued them: 5127
 20:30 the rest f to Aphek, into the city; 5127
 20:30 Ben-hadad f, and came into the city, into 5127
2Ki 3:24 the Moabites, so that they f before them: 5127
 7: 7 Wherefore they arose and f in the twilight, 5127
 7: 7 the camp as it *was,* and f for their life. 5127
 8:21 and the people f into their tents. 5127
 9:10 bury *her.* And he opened the door, and f. 5127
 9:23 f, and said to Ahaziah, There is treachery, 5127
 9:27 *this,* he f *by* the way of the garden house. 5127
 9:27 And he f *to* Megiddo, and died there. 5127
 14:12 and they f every man to their tents. 5127
 14:19 he f to Lachish; but they sent after him to 5127
 25: 4 all the men of war f by night *by* the way NIH
1Ch 10: 1 the men of Israel f from before 5127
 10: 7 that *were* in the valley saw that they f, 5127
 10: 7 then they forsook their cities, and f: 5127
 11:13 the people f from before the Philistines. 5127
 19:14 unto the battle; and they f before him. 5127
 19:15 of Ammon saw that the Syrians were f, 5127
 19:15 they likewise f before Abishai his brother, 5127
 19:18 Syrians f before Israel; and David slew 5127
2Ch 10: 2 whither he had f from the presence of 1272
 13:16 the children of Israel f before Judah: 5127
 14:12 and before Judah; and the Ethiopians f, 5127
 25:22 and they f every man to his tent. 5127
 25:27 him in Jerusalem, and he f to Lachish: 5127
Ne 13:10 the work, were f every one to his field. 5127
Ps 3: 1 T David, when he f from Absalom his son. 1272
 31:11 they that did see me without f from me. 5074
 57: T David, when he f from Saul in the cave. 1272
 104: 7 At thy rebuke they f; at the voice of thy 5127
 114: 3 The sea saw *it,* and f: Jordan was driven 5127
Isa 10:29 Ramah is afraid; Gibeah of Saul is f. 5127
 21:14 prevented with their bread him that f. 5074
 21:15 they f from the swords, from the drawn 5074
 22: 3 All thy rulers are f together, they are 5074

Isa 22: 3 bound together, *which* have f from far. 1272
 33: 3 At the noise of the tumult the people f; 5074
Jer 4:25 and all the birds of the heavens were f; 5074
 9:10 fowl of the heavens and the beast are f; 5074
 26:21 he was afraid, and f, and went *into* Egypt; 1272
 39: 4 they f, and went forth out of the city by 1272
 46: 5 are f **apace,** and look not back: 4498+5127
 46:21 are turned back, *and* are f **away** together; 5127
 48:45 They that f stood under the shadow of 5127
 52: 7 all the men of war f, and went forth out of 1272
La 4:15 when they f **away** and wandered; 5132
Da 10: 7 so that they f to hide themselves. 1272
Hos 7:13 for they have f from me: destruction unto 5074
 12:12 Jacob f *into* the country of Syria, 1272
Jnh 1:10 For the men knew that he f from 1272
 4: 2 Therefore I f before unto Tarshish: for I 1272
Zec 14: 5 like as ye f from before the earthquake in 5127
Mt 8:33 And they that kept *them,* f, and went their 5343
 26:56 Then all the disciples forsook him, and f. 5343
Mk 5:14 And they that fed the swine f, and told *it* 5343
 14:50 And they all forsook him, and f. 5343
 14:52 the linen cloth, and f from them naked. 5343
 16: 8 out quickly, and f from the sepulchre; 5343
Lk 8:34 they f, and went and told *it* in the city 5343
Ac 7:29 Then f Moses at this saying, and was a 5343
 14: 6 ware of *it,* and f unto Lystra and Derbe, 2703
 16:27 supposing that the prisoners had been f. 1628
 19:16 so that *they* f **out** of that house naked 1628
Heb 6:18 who have f **for refuge** to lay hold upon 2703
Rev 12: 6 And the woman f *into* the wilderness, 5343
 16:20 And every island f *away,* and 5343
 20:11 face the earth and the heaven f *away;* 5343

FLEDDEST (2) [FLEE]
Ge 35: 1 that appeared unto thee when thou f from 1272
Ps 114: 5 What ailed thee, O thou sea, that thou f? 5127

FLEE (105) [FLED, FLEDDEST, FLEEING, FLEETH]
Ge 16: 8 I f from the face of my mistress Sarai. 1272
 19:20 this city *is* near to run, and it *is* a little 5127
 27:43 thou to Laban my brother to Haran; 1272
 31:27 Wherefore didst thou f **away** secretly, 1272
Ex 9:20 **made** his servants and his cattle f 5127
 14:13 Let us f from the face of Israel; 5127
 21:13 appoint thee a place whither he shall f. 5127
Lev 26:17 and ye shall f when none pursueth you. 5127
 26:36 they shall f, as fleeing from a sword; 5127
Nu 10:35 and let them that hate thee f before thee. 5127
 24:11 Therefore now f thou to thy place: 1272
 35: 6 for the manslayer, that he may f thither: 5127
 35:11 the slayer may f thither, which killeth 5127
 35:15 any person unawares may f thither. 5127
Dt 4:42 That the slayer might f thither, which 5127
 19: 3 parts, that every slayer may f thither. 5127
 19: 4 which shall f thither, that he may live: 5127
 19: 5 shall f unto one of those cities, and live: 5127
 28: 7 one way, and f before thee seven ways. 5127
 28:25 and f seven ways before them: 5127
Jos 8: 5 as at the first, that we will f before them, 5127
 8: 6 will say, They f before us, as at the first: 5127
 8: 6 the first: therefore we will f before them, 5127
 8:20 they had no power to f this way or 5127
 20: 3 and unwittingly may f thither: 5127
 20: 4 he that doth f unto one of those cities 5127
 20: 9 any person at unawares might f thither, 5127
Jdg 20:32 Let us f, and draw them from the city 5127
2Sa 4: 4 as she made haste to f, that he fell, 5127
 15:14 with him at Jerusalem, Arise, and let us f; 1272
 17: 2 all the people that *are* with him shall f; 5127
 18: 3 for if we f **away,** they will not care 5127+5127
 19: 3 ashamed steal away when they f in battle. 5127
 24:13 wilt thou f three months before thine 5127
1Ki 12:18 him to his chariot, to f to Jerusalem. 1272
2Ki 9: 3 Then open the door, and f, and tarry not. 1272
2Ch 10:18 him to his chariot, to f to Jerusalem. 1272
Ne 6:11 I said, Should such a man as I f? 1272
Job 9:25 a post: they f **away,** they see no good. 1272
 20:24 He shall f from the iron weapon, 1272
 27:22 he would **fain** f out of his hand. 1272+4422
 30:10 they f **far** from me, and spare not to spit 7368
 41:28 The arrow cannot **make** him f. 1272
Ps 11: 1 to my soul, F *as* a bird *to* your mountain? 5110
 64: 8 all that see them shall f **away.** 5074
 68: 1 let them also that hate him f before him. 5127
 68:12 Kings of armies did f **apace:** 5074+5074
 139: 7 or whither shall I f from thy presence? 1272
 143: 9 mine enemies: I f unto thee **to hide** me. 3680
Pr 28: 1 The wicked f when no man pursueth: 5127
 28:17 the blood of *any* person shall f to the pit; 5127
SS 2:17 the shadows f **away,** turn, my beloved, 5127
 4: 6 the day break, and the shadows f **away,** 5127
Isa 10: 3 to whom will ye f for help? and where 5127
 10:31 of Gebim **gather** themselves to f. 5756
 13:14 and f every one into his own land. 5127
 15: 5 his fugitives *shall* flee unto Zoar, a heifer of NIH
 17:13 they shall f far off, and shall be chased as 5127
 20: 6 whither we f for help to be delivered 5127
 30:16 ye said, No; for we will f upon horses; 5127
 30:16 will flee upon horses; therefore shall ye f 5127
 30:17 One thousand *shall* f at the rebuke of one; NIH
 30:17 of one; at the rebuke of five shall ye f: 5127
 31: 8 he shall f from the sword, and his young 5127
 35:10 and sorrow and sighing shall f **away.** 5127
 48:20 of Babylon, f ye from the Chaldeans, 1272
 51:11 *and* sorrow and mourning shall f **away.** 5127

F

F

Jer	4:29 The whole city shall **f** for the noise of	1272
	6: 1 **gather** yourselves **to f** out of the midst of	5756
	25:35 the shepherds shall have no **way to f**,	4498
	46: 6 Let not the swift **f away**, nor the mighty	5127
	48: 6 **F**, save your lives, and be like the heath	5127
	48: 9 unto Moab, that it may **f** and get away:	5323
	49: 8 **F** ye, turn back, dwell deep, O inhabitants	5127
	49:24 turneth herself to **f**, and fear hath seized	5127
	49:30 **F**, get you far off, dwell deep, O ye	5127
	50:16 they shall **f** every one to his own land.	5127
	50:28 The voice of them that **f** and escape out	5127
	51: 6 **F** out of the midst of Babylon,	5127
Am	2:16 mighty shall **f away** naked in that day,	5127
	5:19 As if a man did **f** from a lion, and a bear	5127
	7:12 go, **f** thee away into the land of Judah,	1272
	9: 1 he that fleeth of them shall not **f away**,	5127
Jnh	1: 3 Jonah rose up to **f** unto Tarshish from	1272
Na	2: 8 yet they *shall* **f away**. Stand, stand,	5127
	3: 7 all they that look upon thee shall **f** from	5074
	3:17 *but* when the sun ariseth they **f away**,	5074
Zec	2: 6 and **f** from the land of the north,	5127
	14: 5 ye shall **f** *to* the valley of the mountains;	5127
	14: 5 yea, ye shall **f**, like as ye fled from before	5127
Mt	2:13 into Egypt, and be thou there until	*5343*
	3: 7 who hath warned you to **f** from the wrath	*5343*
	10:23 you in this city, **f** ye into another:	*5343*
	24:16 Then let them which be in Judea **f** into	*5343*
Mk	13:14 them that be in Judea **f** to the mountains:	*5343*
Lk	3: 7 who hath warned you to **f** from the wrath	*5343*
	21:21 Then let them which are in Judea **f** to	*5343*
Jn	10: 5 will they not follow, but will **f** from him:	*5343*
Ac	27:30 as the shipmen were about to **f** out of	*5343*
1Co	6:18 **F** fornication. Every sin that a man doeth	*5343*
	10:14 my dearly beloved, **f** from idolatry.	*5343*
1Ti	6:11 **f** these *things*; and follow **after**	*5343*
2Ti	2:22 **F** also youthful lusts:	*5343*
Jas	4: 7 Resist the devil, and he will **f** from you.	*5343*
Rev	9: 6 desire to die, and death shall **f** from them.	*5343*

FLEECE (9)

Dt	18: 4 thy oil, and the first of the **f** of thy sheep,	1488
Jdg	6:37 Behold, I will put a **f** of wool in the floor;	1492
	6:37 *and* if the dew be on the **f** only, and *it be*	1492
	6:38 thrust the **f** together, and wringed the	1492
	6:38 wringed the dew out of the **f**, a bowl full	1492
	6:39 I pray thee, but *this* once with the **f**;	1492
	6:39 let it now be dry only upon the **f**,	1492
	6:40 for it was dry upon the **f** only,	1492
Job	31:20 *if* he were *not* warmed with the **f** of my	1488

FLEEING (2) [FLEE]

Lev	26:36 they shall flee, as **f** from a sword;	4499
Dt	4:42 **f** unto one of these cities he might live:	5127

FLEET See NAVY

FLEETH (8) [FLEE]

Dt	19:11 that he die, and **f** into one of these cities:	5127
Job	14: 2 he **f** also as a shadow, and continueth not.	1272
Isa	24:18 *that* he who **f** from the noise of the fear	5127
Jer	48:19 ask him that **f**, and her that escapeth,	5127
	48:44 that **f** from the fear shall fall into the pit;	5127
Am	9: 1 he that **f** of them shall not flee away,	5127
Jn	10:12 coming, and leaveth the sheep, and **f**:	*5343*
	10:13 The hireling **f**, because he is a hireling,	*5343*

FLEETING See FLEE; FLEETH; FRAIL; VANITIES; VANITY

FLESH (420) [FATFLESHED, FLESHHOOK, FLESHHOOKS, FLESHLY, FLESHY, LEANFLESHED]

Ge	2:21 ribs, and closed up the **f** instead thereof;	1320
	2:23 now bone of my bones, and **f** of my flesh:	1320
	2:23 now bone of my bones, and flesh of my **f**:	1320
	2:24 unto his wife: and they shall be one **f**.	1320
	6: 3 strive with man, for that he also *is* **f**:	1320
	6:12 for all **f** had corrupted his way upon	1320
	6:13 The end of all **f** is come before me;	1320
	6:17 destroy all **f**, wherein *is* the breath of life,	1320
	6:19 of every living *thing* of all **f**, two of every	1320
	7:15 and two of all **f**, wherein *is* the breath	1320
	7:16 went in, went in male and female of all **f**,	1320
	7:21 all **f** died that moved upon the earth,	1320
	8:17 of all **f**, *both* of fowl, and of cattle,	1320
	9: 4 **f** with the life thereof, *which is* the blood	1320
	9:11 neither shall all **f** be cut off any more by	1320
	9:15 and you and every living creature of all **f**;	1320
	9:15 no more become a flood to destroy all **f**.	1320
	9:16 every living creature of all **f** that *is* upon	1320
	9:17 me and all **f** that *is* upon the earth.	1320
	17:11 ye shall circumcise the **f** of your foreskin;	1320
	17:13 my covenant shall be in your **f** for an	1320
	17:14 The uncircumcised man *child* whose **f** of	1320
	17:23 circumcised the **f** of their foreskin in	1320
	17:24 when he was circumcised *in* the **f** of his	1320
	17:25 when he was circumcised in the **f** of his	1320
	29:14 to him, Surely thou *art* my bone and my **f**.	1320
	37:27 upon him; for he *is* our brother *and* our **f**.	1320
	40:19 and the birds shall eat thy **f** from off thee.	1320
Ex	4: 7 behold, it was turned again as his *other* **f**.	1320
	12: 8 they shall eat the **f** in that night, roast with	1320
	12:46 thou shalt not carry forth *ought* of the **f**	1320
	16: 3 we sat by the **f** pots, *and* when we did	1320
	16: 8 shall give you in the evening **f** to eat,	1320
	16:12 At even ye shall eat **f**, and in the morning	1320
	21:28 surely stoned, and his **f** shall not be eaten;	1320

Ex	22:31 neither shall ye eat *any* **f** *that is* torn *of*	1320
	29:14 the **f** of the bullock, and his skin, and his	1320
	29:31 and seethe his **f** in the holy place.	1320
	29:32 and his sons shall eat the **f** of the ram,	1320
	29:34 if *ought* of the **f** of the consecrations,	1320
	30:32 Upon man's **f** shall it not be poured,	1320
Lev	4:11 all his **f**, with his head, and with his legs,	1320
	6:10 *his* linen breeches shall he put upon his **f**,	1320
	6:27 Whatsoever shall touch the **f** thereof shall	1320
	7:15 the **f** of the sacrifice of his peace offerings	1320
	7:17 the remainder of the **f** of the sacrifice on	1320
	7:18 if *any* of the **f** of the sacrifice of his peace	1320
	7:19 the **f** that toucheth any unclean *thing* shall	1320
	7:19 *as for* the **f**, all that be clean shall eat	1320
	7:20 the soul that eateth *of* the **f** of the sacrifice	1320
	7:21 eat of the **f** of the sacrifice of peace	1320
	8:17 and his hide, his **f**, and his dung,	1320
	8:31 Boil the **f** *at* the door of the tabernacle of	1320
	8:32 that which remaineth of the **f** and of	1320
	9:11 the **f** and the hide he burnt with fire	1320
	11: 8 Of their **f** shall ye not eat, and their carcase	1320
	11:11 ye shall not eat of their **f**, but you shall	1320
	12: 3 in the eighth day the **f** of his foreskin shall	1320
	13: 2 When a man shall have in the skin of his **f**	1320
	13: 2 it be in the skin of his **f** like the plague of	1320
	13: 3 look on the plague in the skin of the **f**:	1320
	13: 3 in sight be deeper than the skin of his **f**,	1320
	13: 4 bright spot *be* white in the skin of his **f**,	1320
	13:10 and *there be* quick raw **f** in the rising;	1320
	13:11 It *is* an old leprosy in the skin of his **f**,	1320
	13:13 *if* the leprosy have covered all his **f**,	1320
	13:14 when raw **f** appeareth in him, he shall be	1320
	13:15 the priest shall see the raw **f**,	1320
	13:15 *for* the raw **f** *is* unclean: it *is* a leprosy.	1320
	13:16 Or if the raw **f** turn again, and be changed	1320
	13:18 The **f** also, in which, *even* in the skin	1320
	13:24 Or if there be *any* **f**, in the skin whereof	1320
	13:24 the quick **f** that burneth have a white	NIH
	13:38 woman have in the skin of their **f** bright	1320
	13:39 *if* the bright spots in the skin of their **f** *be*	1320
	13:43 the leprosy appeareth in the skin of the **f**,	1320
	14: 9 also he shall wash his **f** in water,	1320
	15: 2 any man hath a running issue out of his **f**,	1320
	15: 3 his **f** run with his issue, or his flesh	1320
	15: 3 or his **f** be stopped from his issue, it *is* his	1320
	15: 7 he that toucheth of him that hath	1320
	15:13 bathe his **f** in running water, and shall be	1320
	15:16 he shall wash all his **f** in water,	1320
	15:19 an issue, *and* her issue in her **f** be blood,	1320
	16: 4 shall have the linen breeches upon his **f**,	1320
	16: 4 therefore he wash his **f** in water,	1320
	16:24 he shall wash his **f** with water in the holy	1320
	16:26 bathe his **f** in water, and afterward come	1320
	16:27 fire their skins, and their **f**, and their dung.	1320
	16:28 bathe his **f** in water, and afterward he	1320
	17:11 For the life of the **f** *is* in the blood:	1320
	17:14 For it *is* the life of all **f**; the blood of it *is*	1320
	17:14 Ye shall eat the blood of no *manner of* **f**:	1320
	17:14 for the life of all **f** *is* the blood thereof:	1320
	17:16 if he wash *them* not, nor bathe his **f**; then	1320
	19:28 shall not make any cuttings in your **f** for	1320
	21: 5 nor make any cuttings in their **f**.	1320
	22: 6 *things*, unless he wash his **f** with water.	1320
	26:29 shall eat the **f** of your sons, and the flesh	1320
	26:29 and the **f** of your daughters shall ye eat.	1320
Nu	8: 7 them shave all their **f**, and let them wash	1320
	11: 4 and said, Who shall give us **f** to eat?	1320
	11:13 Whence should I have **f** to give unto all	1320
	11:13 me, saying, Give us **f**, that we may eat.	1320
	11:18 against to morrow, and ye shall eat **f**:	1320
	11:18 saying, Who shall give us **f** to eat?	1320
	11:18 therefore the Lᴏʀᴅ will give you **f**,	1320
	11:21 hast said, I will give them **f**, that they	1320
	11:33 while the **f** *was* yet between their teeth,	1320
	12:12 of whom the **f** is half consumed when he	1320
	16:22 said, O God, the God of the spirits of all **f**,	1320
	18:15 thing that openeth the matrix in all **f**,	1320
	18:18 the **f** of them shall be thine, as the wave	1320
	19: 5 skin, and her **f**, and her blood, with her	1320
	19: 7 he shall bathe his **f** in water,	1320
	19: 8 bathe his **f** in water, and shall be unclean	1320
	27:16 the Lᴏʀᴅ, the God of the spirits of all **f**,	1320
Dt	5:26 For who *is there* of all **f**, that hath heard	1320
	12:15 thou mayest kill and eat **f** in all thy gates,	1320
	12:20 I will eat **f**, because thy soul longeth to eat	1320
	12:20 flesh, because thy soul longeth to eat **f**;	1320
	12:20 thou mayest eat **f**, whatsoever thy soul	1320
	12:23 thou mayest not eat the life with the **f**.	1320
	12:27 the **f** and the blood, upon the altar of	1320
	12:27 Lᴏʀᴅ thy God, and thou shalt eat the **f**.	1320
	14: 8 ye shall not eat of their **f**, nor touch their	1320
	16: 4 neither shall there *any thing* of the **f**,	1320
	28:53 the **f** of thy sons and of thy daughters,	1320
	28:55 of the **f** of his children whom he shall eat:	1320
	32:42 with blood, and my sword shall devour **f**;	1320
Jdg	6:19 the **f** he put in a basket, and he put the	1320
	6:20 Take the **f** and the unleavened *cakes*,	1320
	6:21 touched the **f** and the unleavened *cakes*;	1320
	6:21 consumed the **f** and the unleavened	1320
	8: 7 I will tear your **f** with the thorns of	1320
	9: 2 also that I *am* your bone and your **f**.	1320
1Sa	2:13 servant came, while the **f** was in seething,	1320
	2:15 sacrificed, Give **f** to roast for the priest;	1320
	2:15 for he will not have sodden of thee,	1320
	17:44 I will give thy **f** unto the fowls of the air,	1320

1Sa	25:11 my **f** that I have killed for my shearers,	2878
2Sa	5: 1 Behold, we *are* thy bone and thy **f**.	1320
	6:19 a good piece *of* **f**, and a flagon *of* wine.	NIH
	19:12 my brethren, ye *are* my bones and my **f**:	1320
	19:13 *Art* thou not *of* my bone, and *of* my **f**?	1320
1Ki	17: 6 brought him bread and **f** in the morning,	1320
	17: 6 and bread and **f** in the evening;	1320
	19:21 boiled their **f** with the instruments of	1320
	21:27 put sackcloth upon his **f**, and fasted,	1320
2Ki	4:34 and the **f** of the child waxed warm.	1320
	5:10 thy **f** shall come again to thee,	1320
	5:14 his **f** came again like unto the flesh of a	1320
	5:14 his flesh came again like unto the **f** of a	1320
	6:30 he had sackcloth within upon his **f**.	1320
	9:36 the portion of Jezreel shall dogs eat the **f**	1320
1Ch	11: 1 Behold, we *are* thy bone and thy **f**.	1320
	16: 3 a good piece *of* **f**, and a flagon *of* wine.	NIH
2Ch	32: 8 With him *is* an arm of **f**; but with us *is*	1320
Ne	5: 5 Yet now our **f** *is* as the flesh of our	1320
	5: 5 Yet now our flesh *is* as the **f** of our	1320
Job	2: 5 touch his bone and his **f**, and he will	1320
	4:15 before my face; the hair of my **f** stood up:	1320
	6:12 the strength of stones? or *is* my **f** of brass?	1320
	7: 5 My **f** is clothed with worms and clods of	1320
	10: 4 Hast thou eyes of **f**? or seest thou as man	1320
	10:11 Thou hast clothed me with skin and **f**,	1320
	13:14 Wherefore do I take my **f** in my teeth,	1320
	14:22 his **f** upon him shall have pain, and his	1320
	19:20 My bone cleaveth to my skin and to my **f**,	1320
	19:22 as God, and are not satisfied with my **f**?	1320
	19:26 this *body*, yet in my **f** shall I see God:	1320
	21: 6 and trembling taketh hold on my **f**.	1320
	31:31 said not, O that we had of his **f**!	1320
	33:21 His **f** is consumed away, that it cannot be	1320
	33:25 His **f** shall be fresher than a child's:	1320
	34:15 All **f** shall perish together, and man shall	1320
	41:23 The flakes of his **f** are joined together:	1320
Ps	16: 9 rejoiceth: my **f** also shall rest in hope.	1320
	27: 2 my foes, came upon me to eat up my **f**,	1320
	38: 3 *There is* no soundness in my **f** because	1320
	38: 7 and *there is* no soundness in my **f**.	1320
	50:13 Will I eat the **f** of bulls, or drink the blood	1320
	56: 4 I will not fear what **f** can do unto me.	1320
	63: 1 my **f** longeth for thee, in a dry and	1320
	65: 2 hearest prayer, unto thee shall all **f** come.	1320
	73:26 My **f** and my heart faileth: *but God is*	7607
	78:20 can he provide **f** for his people?	7607
	78:27 He rained *also* upon them as dust,	7607
	78:39 For he remembered that they *were but* **f**;	1320
	79: 2 the **f** of thy saints unto the beasts of	1320
	84: 2 and my **f** crieth out for the living God.	1320
	109:24 fasting; and my **f** faileth of fatness.	1320
	119:120 My **f** trembleth for fear of thee; and I am	1320
	136:25 Who giveth food to all **f**: for his mercy	1320
	145:21 let all **f** bless his holy name for ever and	1320
Pr	4:22 that find them, and health to all their **f**.	1320
	5:11 when thy **f** and thy body are consumed,	1320
	11:17 but *he that is* cruel troubleth his own **f**.	7607
	14:30 A sound heart *is* the life of the **f**:	1320
	23:20 amongst riotous eaters of **f**:	1320
Ecc	4: 5 his hands together, and eateth his own **f**.	1320
	5: 6 Suffer not thy mouth to cause thy **f** to sin;	1320
	11:10 thy heart, and put away evil from thy **f**:	1320
	12:12 and much study *is* a weariness of the **f**.	1320
Isa	9:20 they shall eat every man the **f** of his own	1320
	17: 4 and the fatness of his **f** shall wax lean.	1320
	22:13 killing sheep, eating **f**, and drinking wine:	1320
	31: 3 not God; and their horses **f**, and not spirit.	1320
	40: 5 be revealed, and all **f** shall see *it* together:	1320
	40: 6 All **f** *is* grass, and all the goodliness	1320
	44:16 with part thereof he eateth **f**; he roasteth	1320
	44:19 I have roasted, and eaten *it*: and shall I	1320
	49:26 them that oppress thee with their own **f**;	1320
	49:26 all **f** shall know that I the Lᴏʀᴅ *am* thy	1320
	58: 7 thou hide not thyself from thine own **f**?	1320
	65: 4 which eat swine's **f**, and broth of	1320
	66:16 his sword will the Lᴏʀᴅ plead with all **f**	1320
	66:17 eating swine's **f**, and the abomination,	1320
	66:23 shall all **f** come to worship before me,	1320
	66:24 and they shall be an abhorring unto all **f**.	1320
Jer	7:21 offerings unto your sacrifices, and eat **f**.	1320
	11:15 and the holy **f** is passed from thee?	1320
	12:12 end of the land: no **f** *shall* have peace.	1320
	17: 5 maketh **f** his arm, and whose heart	1320
	19: 9 I will cause them to eat the **f** of their sons	1320
	19: 9 of their sons and the **f** of their daughters,	1320
	19: 9 they shall eat every one the **f** of his friend	1320
	25:31 with the nations, he *will* plead with all **f**;	1320
	45: 5 for behold, I *will* bring evil upon all **f**,	1320
	51:35 done to me and *to* my **f** *be* upon Babylon,	7607
La	3: 4 My **f** and my skin hath he made old;	1320
Eze	4:14 neither came there abominable **f** into my	1320
	11: 3 this *city is* the caldron, and we *be* the **f**.	1320
	11: 7 they *are* the **f**, and this *city is* the caldron:	1320
	11:11 neither shall ye be the **f** in the midst	1320
	11:19 I will take the stony heart out of their **f**,	1320
	11:19 their flesh, and will give them a heart of **f**:	1320
	16:26 the Egyptians thy neighbours, great of **f**;	1320
	20:48 all **f** shall see that I the Lᴏʀᴅ have	1320
	21: 4 against all **f** from the south to the north:	1320
	21: 5 That all **f** may know that I the Lᴏʀᴅ have	1320
	23:20 whose **f** *is* as the flesh of asses,	1320
	23:20 whose flesh *is* as the **f** of asses,	1320
	24:10 consume the **f**, and spice it well, and let	1320

Eze	32: 5 I will lay thy **f** upon the mountains,	1320
	36:26 take away the stony heart out of your **f**,	1320
	36:26 your flesh, and I will give you a heart of **f**.	1320
	37: 6 will bring up **f** upon you, and cover you	1320
	37: 8 the sinews and the **f** came up upon them,	1320
	39:17 Israel, that ye may eat **f**, and drink blood.	1320
	39:18 Ye shall eat the **f** of the mighty,	1320
	40:43 upon the tables *was* the **f** of the offering.	1320
	44: 7 uncircumcised in **f**, to be in my sanctuary,	1320
	44: 9 in heart, nor uncircumcised in **f**,	1320
Da	1:15 fatter in **f** than all the children which did	1320
	2:11 the gods, whose dwelling is not with **f**.	1321
	4:12 the boughs thereof, and all **f** was fed of it.	1321
	7: 5 said thus unto it, Arise, devour much **f**.	1321
	10: 3 neither came **f** nor wine in my mouth,	1320
Hos	8:13 They sacrifice **f** *for* the sacrifices of mine	1320
Joel	2:28 that I will pour out my spirit upon all **f**;	1320
Mic	3: 2 off them, and their **f** from off their bones;	7607
	3: 3 Who also eat the **f** of my people,	7607
	3: 3 as for the pot, and as **f** within the caldron.	1320
Zep	1:17 out as dust, and their **f** as the dung.	3894
Hag	2:12 If one bear holy **f** in the skirt of his	1320
Zec	2:13 Be silent, O all **f**, before the Lord: for he	1320
	11: 9 let the rest eat every one the **f** of another.	1320
	11:16 he shall eat the **f** of the fat, and tear their	1320
	14:12 Their **f** *shall* consume away while they	1320
Mt	16:17 for **f** and blood hath not revealed *it* unto	4561
	19: 5 to his wife: and they twain shall be one **f**?	4561
	19: 6 they are no more twain, but one **f**.	4561
	24:22 be shortened, there should no **f** be saved:	4561
	26:41 spirit indeed *is* willing, but the **f** *is* weak.	4561
Mk	10: 8 And they twain shall be one **f**: so then	4561
	10: 8 then they are no more twain, but one **f**.	4561
	13:20 *those* days, no **f** should be saved:	4561
	14:38 The spirit truly *is* ready, but the **f** *is* weak.	4561
Lk	3: 6 And all **f** shall see the salvation of God.	4561
	24:39 for a spirit hath not **f** and bones, as ye see	4561
Jn	1:13 not of blood, nor of the will of the **f**,	4561
	1:14 And the Word was made **f**,	4561
	3: 6 That which is born of the **f** is flesh;	4561
	3: 6 That which is born of the flesh is **f**;	4561
	6:51 and the bread that I will give is my **f**,	4561
	6:52 How can this *man* give us *his* **f** to eat?	4561
	6:53 Except ye eat the **f** of the Son of man,	4561
	6:54 eateth my **f**, and drinketh my blood,	4561
	6:55 For my **f** is meat indeed,	4561
	6:56 that eateth my **f**, and drinketh my blood,	4561
	6:63 that quickeneth; the **f** profiteth nothing:	4561
	8:15 Ye judge after the **f**; I judge no *man*.	4561
	17: 2 As thou hast given him power over all **f**,	4561
Ac	2:17 I will pour out of my Spirit upon all **f**:	4561
	2:26 moreover also my **f** shall rest in hope:	4561
	2:30 of the fruit of his loins, according to the **f**,	4561
	2:31 in hell, neither his **f** did see corruption.	4561
Ro	1: 3 of the seed of David according to the **f**;	4561
	2:28 which is outward in the **f**:	4561
	3:20 there shall no **f** be justified in his sight:	4561
	4: 1 as pertaining to the **f**, hath found?	4561
	6:19 of men because of the infirmity of your **f**:	4561
	7: 5 For when we were in the **f**, the motions	4561
	7:18 For I know that in me (that is, in my **f**,)	4561
	7:25 law of God; but with the **f** the law of sin.	4561
	8: 1 in Christ Jesus who walk not after the **f**,	4561
	8: 3 not do, in that it was weak through the **f**,	4561
	8: 3 his own Son in the likeness of sinful **f**,	4561
	8: 3 and for sin, condemned sin in the **f**:	4561
	8: 4 who walk not after the **f**, but after	4561
	8: 5 For they that are after the **f** do mind	4561
	8: 5 after the flesh do mind the *things* of the **f**;	4561
	8: 8 they that are in the **f** cannot please God.	4561
	8: 9 But ye are not in the **f**, but in the Spirit,	4561
	8:12 we are debtors, not to the **f**,	4561
	8:12 not to the flesh, to live after the **f**.	4561
	8:13 For if ye live after the **f**, ye shall die:	4561
	9: 3 my kinsmen according to the **f**:	4561
	9: 5 of whom as concerning the **f** Christ *came*,	4561
	9: 8 *They* which *are* the children of the **f**,	4561
	11:14 to emulation *them* which *are* my **f**,	4561
	13:14 and make not provision for the **f**, to *fulfil*	4561
	14:21 good neither to eat **f**, nor to drink wine,	2907
1Co	1:26 how that not many wise *men* after the **f**,	4561
	1:29 That no **f** should glory in his presence.	4561
	5: 5 unto Satan for the destruction of the **f**,	4561
	6:16 body? for two, saith *he*, shall be one **f**.	4561
	7:28 such shall have trouble in the **f**:	4561
	8:13 I will eat no **f** while the world standeth,	2907
	10:18 Behold Israel after the **f**: are not they	4561
	15:39 All **f** *is* not the same flesh: but *there is*	4561
	15:39 All flesh *is* not the same **f**: but *there is*	4561
	15:39 but *there is* one *kind* of **f** of men,	4561
	15:39 another **f** of beasts, another of fishes,	4561
	15:50 **f** and blood cannot inherit the kingdom	4561
2Co	1:17 purpose, do I purpose according to the **f**,	4561
	4:11 might be made manifest in our mortal **f**.	4561
	5:16 henceforth know we no *man* after the **f**:	4561
	5:16 though we have known Christ after the **f**	4561
	7: 1 ourselves from all filthiness of the **f**	4561
	7: 5 our **f** had no rest, but we were troubled	4561
	10: 2 of us as if we walked according to the **f**.	4561
	10: 3 though we walk in the **f**, we do not war	4561
	10: 3 in the flesh, we do not war after the **f**:	4561
	11:18 Seeing that many glory after the **f**, I will	4561
	12: 7 there was given to me a thorn in the **f**,	4561
Gal	1:16 immediately I conferred not with **f** and	4561
	2:16 by the works of the law shall no **f** be	4561

Gal	2:20 *the* life which I now live in the **f** I live by	4561
	3: 3 are ye now made perfect by the **f**?	4561
	4:13 Ye know how through infirmity of the **f** I	4561
	4:14 And my temptation which was in my **f** ye	4561
	4:23 of the bondwoman was born after the **f**;	4561
	4:29 that was born after the **f** persecuted him	4561
	5:13 *use* not liberty for an occasion to the **f**,	4561
	5:16 and ye shall not fulfil the lust of the **f**.	4561
	5:17 For the **f** lusteth against the Spirit,	4561
	5:17 the Spirit, and the Spirit against the **f**:	4561
	5:19 Now the works of the **f** are manifest,	4561
	5:24 have crucified the **f** with the affections	4561
	6: 8 he that soweth to his **f** shall of the flesh	4561
	6: 8 he that soweth to his flesh shall of the **f**	4561
	6:12 as desire to make a fair shew in the **f**,	4561
	6:13 that they may glory in your **f**.	4561
Eph	2: 3 in times past in the lusts of our **f**,	4561
	2: 3 fulfilling the desires of the **f** and of	4561
	2:11 ye *being* in time passed Gentiles in the **f**,	4561
	2:11 the Circumcision in the **f** made by hands;	4561
	2:15 Having abolished in his **f** the enmity,	4561
	5:29 For no *man* ever yet hated his own **f**;	4561
	5:30 of his body, of his **f**, and of his bones.	4561
	5:31 his wife, and they two shall be one **f**.	4561
	6: 5 *that are your* masters according to the **f**,	4561
	6:12 For we wrestle not against **f** and blood,	4561
Php	1:22 But if *I* live in the **f**, this *is* the fruit of my	4561
	1:24 Nevertheless to abide in the **f** *is* more	4561
	3: 3 and have no confidence in the **f**.	4561
	3: 4 I *might* also have confidence in the **f**.	4561
	3: 4 he hath *whereof he* might trust in the **f**,	4561
Col	1:22 In the body of his **f** through death,	4561
	1:24 of Christ in my **f** for his body's sake,	4561
	2: 1 many as have not seen my face in the **f**;	4561
	2: 5 For though I be absent in the **f**, yet am I	4561
	2:11 in putting off the body of the sins of the **f**,	4561
	2:13 sins and the uncircumcision of your **f**,	4561
	2:23 in any honour to the satisfying of the **f**.	4561
	3:22 *things your* masters according to the **f**;	4561
1Ti	3:16 God was manifest in the **f**, justified in	4561
Phm	1:16 unto thee, both in the **f**, and in the Lord?	4561
Heb	2:14 then as the children are partakers of **f** and	4561
	5: 7 Who in the days of his **f**, when he had	4561
	9:13 sanctifieth to the purifying of the **f**:	4561
	10:20 through the vail, that is to say, his **f**;	4561
	12: 9 Furthermore we have had fathers of our **f**	4561
Jas	5: 3 and shall eat your **f** as *it were* fire:	4561
1Pe	1:24 For all **f** *is* as grass, and all the glory of	4561
	3:18 being put to death in the **f**,	4561
	3:21 (not the putting away of the filth of the **f**,	4561
	4: 1 as Christ hath suffered for us in the **f**,	4561
	4: 1 that hath suffered in the **f** hath ceased	4561
	4: 2 of *his* time in the **f** to the lusts of men,	4561
	4: 6 be judged according to men in the **f**,	4561
2Pe	2:10 But chiefly them that walk after the **f** in	4561
	2:18 they allure through the lusts of the **f**,	4561
1Jn	2:16 the lust of the **f**, and the lust of the eyes,	4561
	4: 2 Jesus Christ is come in the **f** is of God:	4561
	4: 3 Jesus Christ is come in the **f** is not of God:	4561
2Jn	1: 7 not that Jesus Christ is come in the **f**.	4561
Jude	1: 7 and going after strange **f**, are set forth for	4561
	1: 8 also these *filthy* dreamers defile the **f**,	4561
	1:23 hating even the garment spotted by the **f**.	4561
Rev	17:16 and shall eat her **f**, and burn her with fire.	4561
	19:18 ye may eat the **f** of kings, and the flesh	4561
	19:18 the **f** of captains, and the flesh of	4561
	19:18 of mighty *men*, and the **f** of horses,	4561
	19:18 flesh of mighty *men*, and the **f** of horses,	4561
	19:18 and the **f** of all *men*, both free and bond,	4561
	19:21 and all the fowls were filled with their **f**.	4561

FLESHHOOK (2) [FLESH, HOOK]

1Sa	2:13 with a **f** of three teeth in his hand;	4207
	2:14 all that the **f** brought up the priest took	4207

FLESHHOOKS (5) [FLESH, HOOK]

Ex	27: 3 his basons, and his **f**, and his firepans:	4207
	38: 3 the basons, *and* the **f**, and the firepans:	4207
Nu	4:14 the **f**, and the shovels, and the basons,	4207
1Ch	28:17 Also pure gold *for* the **f**, and the bowls,	4207
2Ch	4:16 and the **f**, and all their instruments,	4207

FLESHLY (3) [FLESH]

2Co	1:12 with **f** wisdom, but by the grace of God,	4559
Col	2:18 not seen, vainly puft up by his **f** mind,	4561
1Pe	2:11 and pilgrims, abstain from **f** lusts,	4559

FLESHY (1) [FLESH]

2Co	3: 3 tables of stone, but in **f** tables of the heart.	4560

FLEW (2) [FLY]

1Sa	14:32 people **f** upon the spoil, and took sheep,	5860
Isa	6: 6 **f** one of the seraphims unto me, having a	5774

FLIES (10) [FLY]

Ex	8:21 I will send swarms *of* **f** upon thee,	NIH
	8:21 the Egyptians shall be full of swarms *of* **f**,	NIH
	8:22 that no swarms *of* **f** shall be there;	NIH
	8:24 there came a grievous swarm *of* **f** into	NIH
	8:24 corrupted by reason of the swarm *of* **f**.	NIH
	8:29 the swarms *of* **f** may depart from Pharaoh,	NIH
	8:31 removed the swarms *of* **f** from Pharaoh,	NIH
Ps	78:45 He sent divers sorts *of* **f** among them,	NIH
	105:31 there came divers sorts *of* **f**, *and* lice in all	NIH
Ecc	10: 1 Dead **f** cause the ointment of	2070

FLIETH (5) [FLY]

Dt	4:17 the likeness of any winged fowl that **f** in	5774
	14:19 every creeping thing that **f** *is* unclean	5775
	28:49 of the earth, as *swift* as the eagle **f**;	1675
Ps	91: 5 by night; *nor* for the arrow *that* **f** by day;	5774
Na	3:16 the cankerworm spoileth, and **f** **away**.	5774

FLIGHT (8) [FLY]

Lev	26: 8 of you shall **put** ten thousand **to f**:	7291
Dt	32:30 two **put** ten thousand **to f**, except their	5127
1Ch	12:15 they **put to f** all *them* of the valleys,	1272
Isa	52:12 shall not go out with haste, nor go by **f**;	4499
Am	2:14 Therefore the **f** shall perish from the swift,	4498
Mt	24:20 pray ye that your **f** be not in the winter,	5437
Mk	13:18 And pray ye that your **f** be not in	5437
Heb	11:34 turned to **f** the armies of the aliens.	2827

FLINT (4) [FLINT]

Dt	8:15 thee forth water out of the rock of **f**;	2496
Ps	114: 8 the **f** into a fountain of waters.	2496
Isa	5:28 their horses' hoofs shall be counted like **f**,	6864
	50: 7 therefore have I set my face like a **f**,	2496
Eze	3: 9 As an adamant harder than **f** have I made	6864

FLINTY (1) [FLINT]

Dt	32:13 out of the rock, and oil out of the **f** rock;	2496

FLIXE (1)

Ac	28: 8 lay sick of a fever and of a **bloody f**:	1420

FLOAT See FLOTES; SWIM

FLOCK (111) [FLOCKS]

Ge	4: 4 he also brought of the firstlings of his **f**	6629
	21:28 Abraham set seven ewe lambs of the **f** by	6629
	27: 9 Go now to the **f**, and fetch me from	6629
	29:10 watered the **f** of Laban his mother's	6629
	30:31 for me, I will again feed *and* keep thy **f**:	6629
	30:32 I will pass through all thy **f** to day,	6629
	30:40 and all the brown in the **f** of Laban,	6629
	31: 4 and Leah to the field unto his **f**,	6629
	31:38 and the rams of thy **f** have I not eaten.	6629
	33:13 overdrive them one day, all the **f** will die.	6629
	37: 2 was feeding the **f** with his brethren;	6629
	37:12 brethren went to feed their father's **f** in	6629
	37:13 not thy brethren feed *the* **f** in Shechem?	NIH
	38:17 he said, I will send *thee* a kid from the **f**.	6629
Ex	2:16 the troughs to water their father's **f**.	6629
	2:17 and helped them, and watered their **f**.	6629
	2:19 water enough for us, and watered the **f**.	6629
	3: 1 Now Moses kept the **f** of Jethro his father	6629
	3: 1 he led the **f** to the backside of the desert,	6629
Lev	1: 2 the cattle, *even* of the herd, and of the **f**.	6629
	3: 6 peace offering unto the Lord *be* of the **f**,	6629
	5: 6 a female from the **f**, a lamb or a kid of	6629
	5:18 bring a ram without blemish out of the **f**,	6629
	6: 6 a ram without blemish out of the **f**, with	6629
	27:32 the tithe of the herd, or of the **f**,	6629
Nu	15: 3 unto the Lord, of the herd, or of the **f**:	6629
Dt	12: 7 or the firstlings of thy herds or of thy **f**,	6629
	12:21 thou shalt kill of thy herd and of thy **f**,	6629
	15:14 shalt furnish him liberally out of thy **f**,	6629
	15:19 of thy **f** thou shalt sanctify unto the Lord	6629
	16: 2 the Lord thy God, *of* the **f** and the herd,	6629
1Sa	17:34 and a bear, and took a lamb out of the **f**:	5739
2Sa	12: 4 he spared to take of his own **f** and of his	6629
2Ch	35: 7 to the people, *of* the **f**, lambs and kids,	6629
Ezr	10:19 *they* offered a ram of the **f** for their	6629
Job	21:11 They send forth their little ones like a **f**,	6629
	30: 1 to have set with the dogs of my **f**.	6629
Ps	77:20 leddest thy people like a **f** by the hand	6629
	78:52 guided them in the wilderness like a **f**.	5739
	80: 1 of Israel, thou that leadest Joseph like a **f**;	6629
	107:41 and maketh *him* families like a **f**.	6629
SS	1: 7 where thou makest *thy* **f** to rest at noon:	NIH
	1: 8 go thy way forth by the footsteps of the **f**,	6629
	4: 1 thy hair *is* as a **f** of goats, that appear from	5739
	4: 2 Thy teeth *are* like a **f** of *sheep that are*	6629
	6: 5 thy hair *is* as a **f** of goats that appear from	5739
	6: 6 Thy teeth *are* as a **f** of sheep which go up	5739
Isa	40:11 He shall feed his **f** like a shepherd: he	5739
	63:11 out of the sea with the shepherd of his **f**?	6629
Jer	13:17 the Lord's **f** is carried away captive.	5739
	13:20 where *is* the **f** *that* was given thee,	5739
	13:20 flock *that* was given thee, thy beautiful **f**?	6629
	23: 2 Ye have scattered my **f**, and driven them	6629
	23: 3 I will gather the remnant of my **f** out of all	6629
	25:34 *in* the ashes, ye principal of the **f**:	6629
	25:35 flee, nor the principal of the **f** to escape.	6629
	25:36 and a howling of the principal of the **f**,	6629
	31:10 and keep him as a shepherd *doth* his **f**.	5739
	31:12 for the young of the **f** and of the herd:	6629
	49:20 Surely the least of the **f** shall draw them	6629
	50:45 Surely the least of the **f** shall draw them	6629
	51:23 pieces with thee the shepherd and his **f**;	5739
Eze	24: 5 Take the choice of the **f**, and burn also	6629
	34: 3 them that are fed: but *ye* feed not the **f**.	6629
	34: 6 my **f** was scattered upon all the face of	6629
	34: 8 surely because my **f** became a prey,	6629
	34: 8 my **f** became meat to every beast of	6629
	34: 8 neither did my shepherds search for my **f**,	6629
	34: 8 fed themselves, and fed not my **f**;	6629
	34:10 I will require my **f** at their hand,	6629
	34:10 cause them to cease from feeding the **f**;	6629
	34:10 for I will deliver my **f** from their mouth,	6629

Eze	34:12 As a shepherd seeketh out his **f** in the day	5739
	34:15 I will feed my **f**, and I will cause them to	6629
	34:17 *as for* you, O my **f**, thus saith the Lord	6629
	34:19 *as for* my **f**, they eat that which ye have	6629
	34:22 Therefore will I save my **f**, and they shall	6629
	34:31 ye my **f**, the flock of my pasture, *are* men,	6629
	34:31 the **f** of my pasture, *are* men, *and* I *am*	6629
	36:37 I will increase them with men like a **f**	6629
	36:38 As the holy **f**, as the flock of Jerusalem in	6629
	36:38 as the **f** of Jerusalem in her solemn feasts;	6629
	43:23 and a ram out of the **f** without blemish.	6629
	43:25 and a ram out of the **f**, without blemish.	6629
	45:15 lamb out of the **f**, out of two hundred,	6629
Am	6: 4 eat the lambs out of the **f**, and the calves	6629
	7:15 the Lord took me as I followed the **f**,	6629
Jnh	3: 7 nor beast, herd nor **f**, taste any thing:	6629
Mic	2:12 in the midst of their fold:	5739
	4: 8 thou, O tower of the **f**, the strong hold of	6629
	7:14 with thy rod, the **f** of thine heritage,	6629
Hab	3:17 the **f** shall be cut off from the fold,	6629
Zec	9:16 them in that day as the **f** of his people:	6629
	10: 2 therefore they went their way as a **f**,	6629
	10: 3 for the Lord of hosts hath visited his **f**	5739
	11: 4 my God; Feed the **f** of the slaughter;	6629
	11: 7 I will feed the **f** of slaughter, *even* you,	6629
	11: 7 of slaughter, *even* you, O poor of the **f**.	6629
	11: 7 the other I called Bands; and I fed the **f**.	6629
	11:11 the poor of the **f** that waited upon me	6629
	11:17 to the idol shepherd that leaveth the **f!**	6629
Mal	1:14 which hath in his **f** a male, and voweth,	5739
Mt	26:31 sheep of the **f** shall be scattered abroad.	4167
Lk	2: 8 keeping watch over their **f** by night.	4167
	12:32 Fear not, little **f**; for it is your Father's	4168
Ac	20:28 therefore unto yourselves, and to all the **f**,	4168
	20:29 enter in among you, not sparing the **f**.	4168
1Co	9: 7 or who feedeth a **f**, and eateth not of	4167
	9: 7 flock, and eateth not of the milk of the **f?**	4167
1Pe	5: 2 Feed the **f** of God which is among you,	4168
	5: 3 but being ensamples to the **f**.	4168

FLOCKS (80) [FLOCK]

Ge	13: 5 with Abram, had **f**, and herds, and tents.	6629
	24:35 he hath given him **f**, and herds, and silver,	6629
	26:14 For he had possession of **f**,	6629
	29: 2 lo, there *were* three **f** of sheep lying by it;	5739
	29: 2 for out of that well they watered the **f**:	5739
	29: 3 thither were all the **f** gathered:	5739
	29: 8 until all the **f** be gathered together,	5739
	30:36 and Jacob fed the rest of Laban's **f**.	6629
	30:38 **f** in the gutters in the watering troughs	6629
	30:38 troughs when the **f** came to drink,	6629
	30:39 the **f** conceived before the rods,	6629
	30:40 the faces of the **f** toward the ringstraked,	6629
	30:40 he put his own **f** by themselves,	5739
	32: 5 **f**, and menservants, and womenservants:	6629
	32: 7 the **f**, and herds, and the camels, into two	6629
	33:13 the **f** and herds with young *are* with me:	6629
	37:14 with thy brethren, and well with the **f**;	6629
	37:16 me, I pray thee, where they feed *their* **f**.	NIH
	45:10 thy **f**, and thy herds, and all that thou hast:	6629
	46:32 they have brought their **f**, and their herds,	6629
	47: 1 their **f**, and their herds, and all that they	6629
	47: 4 thy servants have no pasture for their **f**;	6629
	47:17 for the **f**, and for the cattle of	4735+6629
	50: 8 little ones, and their **f**, and their herds,	6629
Ex	10: 9 with our **f** and with our herds will we go;	6629
	10:24 only let your **f** and your herds be stayed:	6629
	12:32 take your **f** and your herds, as ye have	6629
	12:38 and **f**, and herds, *even* very much cattle.	6629
	34: 3 neither let the **f** nor herds feed before that	6629
Lev	1:10 if his offering *be* of the **f**, *namely*, of	6629
	5:15 Lord a ram without blemish out of the **f**,	6629
Nu	11:22 Shall the **f** and the herds be slain for them	6629
	31: 9 and all their **f**, and all their goods.	4735
	31:30 of the beeves, of the asses, and of the **f**,	6629
	32:26 our wives, our **f**, and all our cattle,	4735
Dt	7:13 of thy kine, and the **f** of thy sheep,	6251
	8:13 *when* thy herds and thy **f** multiply, and	6629
	12: 6 the firstlings of your herds and of your **f**:	6629
	14:23 and the firstlings of thy herds and of thy **f**;	6629
	28: 4 of thy kine, and the **f** of thy sheep.	6251
	28:18 of thy kine, and the **f** of thy sheep.	6251
	28:51 increase of thy kine, or **f** of thy sheep,	6251
Jdg	5:16 to hear the bleatings of the **f?**	5739
1Sa	30:20 David took all the **f** and the herds,	6629
2Sa	12: 2 The rich *man* had exceeding many **f** and	6629
1Ki	20:27 before them like two **little** **f** of kids;	2835
1Ch	4:39 of the valley, to seek pasture for their **f**.	6629
	4:41 *there* was pasture there for their **f**.	6629
	27:31 over the **f** *was* Jaziz the Hagerite.	6629
2Ch	17:11 Arabians brought him **f**, seven thousand	6629
	32:28 for all *manner* of beasts, and cotes for **f**.	5739
	32:29 possessions of **f** and herds in abundance:	6629
Ne	10:36 the firstlings of our herds and of our **f**,	6629
Job	24: 2 they violently take away **f**,	5739
Ps	65:13 The pastures are clothed with the **f**;	6629
	78:48 the hail, and their **f** to hot thunderbolts.	4735
Pr	27:23 thou diligent to know the state of thy **f**,	6629
SS	1: 7 turneth aside by the **f** of thy companions?	5739
Isa	17: 2 they shall be for **f**, which shall lie down,	5739
	32:14 for ever, a joy of wild asses, a pasture of **f**;	5739
	60: 7 All the **f** of Kedar shall be gathered	6629
	61: 5 strangers shall stand and feed your **f**,	6629
	65:10 Sharon shall be a fold of **f**, and the valley	6629
Jer	3:24 their **f** and their herds, their sons and	6629

Jer	5:17 they shall eat up thy **f** and thine herds:	6629
	6: 3 The shepherds with their **f** shall come	5739
	10:21 and all their **f** shall be scattered.	4830
	31:24 and they *that* go forth with **f**,	5739
	33:12 of shepherds causing *their* **f** to lie down.	6629
	33:13 shall the **f** pass again under the hands of	6629
	49:29 their **f** shall they take *away*: they shall	6629
	50: 8 and be as the he goats before the **f**.	6629
Eze	25: 5 the Ammonites a couching place for **f**:	6629
	34: 2 should not the shepherds feed the **f?**	6629
	36:38 the waste cities be filled with **f** of men:	6629
Hos	5: 6 They shall go with their **f** and with their	6629
Joel	1:18 yea, the **f** of sheep are made desolate.	5739
Mic	5: 8 as a young lion among the **f** of sheep:	5739
Zep	2: 6 cottages for shepherds, and folds for **f**.	6629
	2:14 **f** shall lie down in the midst of her,	5739

FLOG; FLOGGED; FLOGGING; FLOGGINGS
See SCOURGES; SCOURGETH; SCOURGING;
SCOURGINGS; STRIPE; STRIPES

FLOOD (43) [FLOODS, WATERFLOOD]

Ge	6:17 do bring a **f** of waters upon the earth,	3999
	7: 6 *was* six hundred years old when the **f**	3999
	7: 7 the ark, because of the waters of the **f**.	3999
	7:10 the waters of the **f** were upon the earth.	3999
	7:17 the **f** was forty days upon the earth;	3999
	9:11 be cut off any more by the waters of a **f**;	3999
	9:11 neither shall there any more be a **f** to	3999
	9:15 the waters shall no more become a **f** to	3999
	9:28 Noah lived after the **f** three hundred and	3999
	10: 1 and unto them were sons born after the **f**.	3999
	10:32 the nations divided in the earth after the **f**.	3999
	11:10 and begat Arphaxad two years after the **f**:	3999
Jos	24: 2 fathers dwelt on the *other* side of the **f**	5104
	24: 3 Abraham from the *other* side of the **f**,	5104
	24:14 fathers served on the *other* side of the **f**,	5104
	24:15 that *were* on the *other* side of the **f**:	5104
Job	14:11 the sea, and the **f** decayeth and drieth up:	5104
	22:16 foundation was overflown *with* a **f**:	5104
	28: 4 The **f** breaketh out from the inhabitant;	5158
Ps	29:10 The Lord sitteth upon the **f**; yea,	3999
	66: 6 dry *land*: they went through the **f** on foot:	5104
	74:15 Thou didst cleave the fountain and the **f**:	5158
	90: 5 Thou carriest them **away as with a f**.	2229
Isa	28: 2 as a **f** of mighty waters overflowing,	2230
	59:19 When the enemy shall come in like a **f**,	5104
Jer	46: 7 Who *is this that* cometh up as a **f**,	2975
	46: 8 Egypt riseth up like a **f**, and *his* waters are	2975
	47: 2 shall be an overflowing **f**,	5158
Da	9:26 the end thereof *shall be* with a **f**,	7858
	11:22 the arms of a **f** shall they be overflown	7858
Am	8: 8 it shall rise up wholly as a **f**; and it shall	2975
	8: 8 out and drowned, as *by* the **f** of Egypt.	2975
	9: 5 it shall rise up wholly like a **f**; and shall be	2975
	9: 5 and shall be drowned, as *by* the **f** of Egypt.	2975
Na	1: 8 with an overrunning **f** he will make an	7858
Mt	24:38 For as in the days that were before the **f**	2627
	24:39 And knew not until the **f** came,	2627
Lk	6:48 and when the **f** arose, the stream beat	4132
	17:27 and the **f** came, and destroyed *them* all.	2627
2Pe	2: 5 bringing in the **f** upon the world of	2627
Rev	12:15 his mouth water as a **f** after the woman,	4215
	12:15 cause her to be **carried away of the f**,	4216
	12:16 swallowed up the **f** which the dragon cast	4215

FLOODS (19) [FLOOD]

Ex	15: 8 the **f** stood upright as a heap, *and the*	5140
2Sa	22: 5 the **f** of ungodly men made me afraid;	5158
Job	20:17 the **f**, the brooks of honey and butter.	5104
	28:11 He bindeth the **f** from overflowing;	5104
Ps	18: 4 the **f** of ungodly men made me afraid.	5158
	24: 2 the seas, and established it upon the **f**.	5104
	32: 6 surely in the **f** of great waters they shall	7858
	69: 2 deep waters, where the overflow me.	7641
	78:44 and their **f**, *that* they could not drink.	5140
	93: 3 The **f** have lifted up, O Lord, the floods	5104
	93: 3 O Lord, the **f** have lifted up their voice;	5104
	93: 3 up their voice; the **f** lift up their waves.	5104
	98: 8 Let the **f** clap *their* hands: let the hills **be**	5104
SS	8: 7 quench love, neither can the **f** drown it:	5104
Isa	44: 3 **f** upon the dry *ground*: I will pour my	5140
Eze	31:15 I restrained the **f** thereof, and the great	5104
Jnh	2: 3 the seas; and the **f** compassed me about:	5104
Mt	7:25 and the **f** came, and the winds blew,	4215
	7:27 and the **f** came, and the winds blew,	4215

FLOODWATERS See WATERFLOOD

FLOOR (19) [BARNFLOOR, CORNFLOOR,
FLOORS, THRESHINGFLOOR,
THRESHINGFLOORS]

Ge	50:11 saw the mourning in the **f** of Atad, they	1637
Nu	5:17 the dust that is in the **f** of the tabernacle	7172
Dt	15:14 out of thy **f**, and out of thy winepress:	1637
Jdg	6:37 I will put a fleece of wool in the **f**;	1637
Ru	3: 3 upon thee, and get thee down *to* the **f**:	1637
	3: 6 she went down *unto* the **f**,	1637
	3:14 be known that a woman came *into* the **f**.	1637
1Ki	6:15 both the **f** of the house, and the walls of	7172
	6:15 covered the **f** of the house with planks of	7172
	6:16 both the **f** and the walls with boards of	7172
	6:30 the **f** of the house he overlaid with gold,	7172
	7: 7 cedar from one side of the **f** to the other.	7172
2Ch	34:11 to **f** the houses which the kings of Judah	7136

Isa	21:10 O my threshing, and the corn of my **f**:	1637
Hos	9: 2 The **f** and the winepress shall not feed	1637
	13: 3 is driven with a whirlwind out of the **f**,	1637
Mic	4:12 shall gather them as the sheaves into the **f**.	1637
Mt	3:12 and he will throughly purge his **f**,	257
Lk	3:17 and he will throughly purge his **f**,	257

FLOORS (1) [FLOOR]

Joel	2:24 the **f** shall be full *of* wheat, and the fats	1637

FLOTES (2)

1Ki	5: 9 I will convey them by sea *in* **f** unto	1702
2Ch	2:16 will bring it to thee *in* **f** by sea *to* Joppa;	7513

FLOUR (58)

Ex	29: 2 of wheaten **f** shalt thou make them.	5560
	29:40 the one lamb a tenth deal of **f** mingled	5560
Lev	2: 1 the Lord, his offering shall be *of* **f**;	5560
	2: 2 he shall take thereout his handful of the **f**	5560
	2: 4 *it shall be* unleavened cakes of **fine f**	5560
	2: 5 it shall be *of* **fine f** unleavened,	5560
	2: 7 it shall be made *of* **fine f**:	5560
	5:11 of an ephah of **fine f** for a sin offering;	5560
	6:15 of the **f** of the meat offering, and of the oil	5560
	6:20 the tenth *part* of an ephah of **fine f** for a	5560
	7:12 cakes mingled with oil, of **fine f**, fried.	5560
	14:10 three tenth deals of **fine f** for a meat	5560
	14:21 one tenth deal of **fine f** mingled with oil	5560
	23:13 two tenth deals of **fine f** mingled with oil,	5560
	23:17 they shall be *of* **fine f**; they shall be baken	5560
	24: 5 thou shalt take **fine f**, and bake twelve	5560
Nu	6:15 cakes of **fine f** mingled with oil,	5560
	7:13 both of them *were* full *of* **fine f** mingled	5560
	7:19 of them full *of* **fine f** mingled with oil	5560
	7:25 of them full *of* **fine f** mingled with oil	5560
	7:31 of them full *of* **fine f** mingled with oil	5560
	7:37 of them full *of* **fine f** mingled with oil	5560
	7:43 of them full *of* **fine f** mingled with oil	5560
	7:49 of them full *of* **fine f** mingled with oil	5560
	7:55 of them full *of* **fine f** mingled with oil	5560
	7:61 of them full *of* **fine f** mingled with oil	5560
	7:67 of them full *of* **fine f** mingled with oil	5560
	7:73 of them full *of* **fine f** mingled with oil	5560
	7:79 of them full *of* **fine f** mingled with oil	5560
	8: 8 *even* **fine f** mingled with oil,	5560
	15: 4 mingled with the fourth *part* of a hin of	5560
	15: 6 mingled with the third *part* of a hin of oil.	5560
	15: 9 deals of **f** mingled with half a hin of oil.	5560
	28: 5 a tenth *part* of an ephah of **f** for a meat	5560
	28: 9 two tenth deals of **f** for a meat offering,	5560
	28:12 three tenth deals of **f** for a meat offering,	5560
	28:12 two tenth deals of **f** for a meat offering,	5560
	28:13 a several tenth deal of **f** mingled with oil	5560
	28:20 their meat offering *shall be of* **f** mingled	5560
	28:28 their meat offering *of* **f** mingled with oil,	5560
	29: 3 their meat offering *of* **f** mingled with oil,	5560
	29: 9 their meat offering *of* **f** mingled with oil,	5560
	29:14 their meat offering *shall be of* **f** mingled	5560
Jdg	6:19 and unleavened cakes *of* an ephah of **f**:	7058
1Sa	1:24 one ephah of **f**, and a bottle of wine,	7058
	28:24 took **f**, and kneaded *it*, and did bake	7058
2Sa	13: 8 took **f**, and kneaded *it*, and made cakes	1217
	17:28 and parched *corn*, and beans, and	7058
1Ki	4:22 for one day was thirty measures of **fine f**,	5560
2Ki	7: 1 a measure of **fine f** *be sold* for a shekel,	5560
	7:16 So a measure of **fine f** was *sold* for a	5560
	7:18 a measure of **fine f** for a shekel,	5560
1Ch	9:29 the **fine f**, and the wine, and the oil,	5560
	23:29 for the **fine f** for meat offering, and for	5560
Eze	16:13 thou didst eat **fine f**, and honey, and oil:	5560
	16:19 **fine f**, and oil, and honey, *wherewith* I	5560
	46:14 of a hin of oil, to temper with the **fine f**;	5560
Rev	18:13 and oil, and **fine f**, and wheat, and beasts,	4585

FLOURISH (13) [FLOURISHED, FLOURISHETH,
FLOURISHING]

Ps	72: 7 In his days shall the righteous **f**;	6524
	72:16 *they* of the city shall **f** like grass of	6692
	92: 7 and when all the workers of iniquity do **f**;	6692
	92:12 The righteous shall **f** like the palm tree:	6524
	92:13 the Lord shall **f** in the courts of our God.	6524
	132:18 but upon himself shall his crown **f**.	6692
Pr	11:28 but the righteous shall **f** as a branch.	6524
	14:11 but the tabernacle of the upright shall **f**.	6524
Ecc	12: 5 almond tree shall **f**, and the grasshopper	5340
SS	7:12 let us see if the vine **f**, *whether* the tender	6524
Isa	17:11 morning shalt thou **make** thy seed to **f**:	6524
	66:14 and your bones shall **f** like an herb:	6524
Eze	17:24 tree, and have **made** the dry tree to **f**:	6524

FLOURISHED (2) [FLOURISH]

SS	6:11 *and* to see whether the vine **f**,	6524
Php	4:10 at the last your care of me hath **f again**;	330

FLOURISHETH (2) [FLOURISH]

Ps	90: 6 In the morning it **f**, and groweth up;	6692
	103:15 as grass: as a flower of the field, so he **f**.	6692

FLOURISHING (2) [FLOURISH]

Ps	92:14 fruit in old age; they shall be fat and **f**;	7488
Da	4: 4 at rest in mine house, and **f** in my palace:	7487

FLOW (13) [FLOWED, FLOWETH, FLOWING,
OVERFLOW]

Job	20:28 *his* goods shall **f** away in the day of his	5064
Ps	147:18 his wind to blow, *and* the waters **f**.	5140

SS	4:16 *that* the spices thereof may **f out**.	5140
Isa	2: 2 the hills; and all nations shall **f** unto it.	5102
	48:21 he **caused** the waters **to f** out of the rock	5140
	60: 5 **f** *together*, and thine heart shall fear,	5102
	64: 1 that the mountains might **f down** at thy	2151
Jer	31:12 shall **f together** to the goodness of	5102
	51:44 the nations shall not **f** *together* any more	5102
Joel	3:18 hills shall **f with** milk, and all the rivers	1980
	3:18 all the rivers of Judah shall **f with** waters,	1980
Mic	4: 1 above the hills; and people shall **f** unto it.	5102
Jn	7:38 out of his belly shall **f** rivers of living	4482

FLOWED (3) [FLOW]

Jos	4:18 **f** over all his banks, as *they did* before.	1980
Isa	64: 3 the mountains **f down** at thy presence.	2151
La	3:54 Waters **f** over mine head; *then* I said,	6687

FLOWER (20) [FLOWERS]

Ex	25:33 *with* a knop and a **f** in one branch;	6525
	25:33 in the other branch, *with* a knop and a **f**:	6525
	37:19 of almonds in one branch, a knop, and a **f**;	6525
	37:19 in another branch, a knop and a **f**:	6525
1Sa	2:33 thine house shall die **in the f** of their *age*.	376
Job	14: 2 He cometh forth like a **f**, and is cut down:	6731
	15:33 vine, and shall cast off his **f** as the olive.	5328
Ps	103:15 as a **f** of the field, so he flourisheth.	6731
Isa	18: 5 and the sour grape is ripening in the **f**,	5328
	28: 1 whose glorious beauty *is* a fading **f**,	6731
	28: 4 shall be a fading **f**, and as the hasty fruit	6733
	40: 6 all the goodliness thereof *is* as the **f** of	6731
	40: 7 The grass withereth, the **f** fadeth: because	6731
	40: 8 The grass withereth, the **f** fadeth:	6731
Na	1: 4 Carmel, and the **f** of Lebanon languisheth.	6525
1Co	7:36 if she **pass the f of** her *age*,	1510+5230
Jas	1:10 as the **f** of the grass he shall pass away.	438
	1:11 and the **f** thereof falleth, and the grace of	438
1Pe	1:24 and all the glory of man as the **f** of grass.	438
	1:24 the **f** thereof falleth away:	438

FLOWERS (17) [FLOWER]

Ex	25:31 his bowls, his knops, and his **f**,	6525
	25:34 almonds, *with* their knops and their **f**.	6525
	37:17 branch, his bowls, his knops, and his **f**,	6525
	37:20 made like almonds, his knops, and his **f**:	6525
Lev	15:24 her **f** be upon him, he shall be unclean	5079
	15:33 of her that is sick of her **f**, and of him that	5079
Nu	8: 4 unto the **f** thereof, *was* beaten work:	6525
1Ki	6:18 *was* carved with knops and open **f**:	6731
	6:29 of cherubims and palm trees and open **f**,	6731
	6:32 of cherubims and palm trees and open **f**,	6731
	6:35 and palm trees and open **f**:	6731
	7:26 like the brim of a cup, *with* **f** of lilies:	6525
	7:49 with the **f**, and the lamps, and the tongs	6525
2Ch	4: 5 work of the brim of a cup, *with* **f** of lilies;	6525
	4:21 the **f**, and the lamps, and the tongs, *made*	6525
SS	2:12 The **f** appear on the earth; the time of	5339
	5:13 cheeks *are* as a bed of spices, *as* sweet **f**:	4026

FLOWETH (12) [FLOW]

Lev	20:24 a land that **f** with milk and honey:	2100
Nu	13:27 and surely it **f** with milk and honey,	2100
	14: 8 a land which **f** with milk and honey.	2100
	16:13 us up out of a land that **f** with milk	2100
	16:14 brought us into a land that **f** with milk	2100
Dt	6: 3 *in* the land that **f** with milk and honey.	2100
	11: 9 a land that **f** with milk and honey.	2100
	26: 9 *even* a land that **f** with milk and honey.	2100
	26:15 a land that **f** with milk and honey.	2100
	27: 3 a land that **f** with milk and honey;	2100
	31:20 their fathers, that **f** with milk and honey;	2100
Jos	5: 6 a land that **f** with milk and honey.	2100

FLOWING (12) [FLOW]

Ex	3: 8 large, unto a land **f** with milk and honey;	2100
	3:17 unto a land **f** with milk and honey.	2100
	13: 5 give thee, a land **f** with milk and honey,	2100
	33: 3 Unto a land **f** with milk and honey: for I	2100
Pr	18: 4 the wellspring of wisdom *as* a **f** brook.	5042
Isa	66:12 the glory of the Gentiles like a **f** stream:	7857
Jer	11: 5 give them a land **f** with milk and honey,	2100
	18:14 shall the cold **f** waters that come from	5140
	32:22 give them, a land **f** with milk and honey;	2100
	49: 4 thy **f** valley, O backsliding daughter?	2100
Eze	20: 6 **f** with milk and honey, which *is* the glory	2100
	20:15 land which I had given *them*, **f** with milk	2100

FLUTE (4)

Da	3: 5 **f**, harp, sackbut, psaltery, dulcimer,	4953
	3: 7 **f**, harp, sackbut, psaltery, and all kinds of	4953
	3:10 **f**, harp, sackbut, psaltery, and dulcimer,	4953
	3:15 **f**, harp, sackbut, psaltery, and dulcimer,	4953

FLUTTERETH (1)

Dt	32:11 **f** over her young, spreadeth abroad her	7363

FLY (25) [FLEW, FLIES, FLIETH, FLIGHT, FLYING]

Ge	1:20 fowl *that* may **f** above the earth in the	5774
1Sa	15:19 didst **f** upon the spoil, and didst evil in	5860
2Sa	22:11 he rode upon a cherub, and did **f**:	5774
Job	5: 7 born unto trouble, as the sparks **f** upward.	5774
	20: 8 He shall **f** away as a dream, and shall not	5774
	39:26 Doth the hawk **f** by thy wisdom,	82
Ps	18:10 he rode upon a cherub, and did **f**: yea,	5774
	18:10 yea, he did **f** upon the wings of the wind.	1675
	55: 6 *for then* would I **f away**, and be at rest.	5774
	90:10 for it is soon cut off, and we **f away**.	5774

Pr	23: 5 they **f away** as an eagle *toward* heaven.	5774
Isa	6: 2 covered his feet, and with twain he did **f**.	5774
	7:18 *that* the LORD shall hiss for the **f** that *is* in	2070
	11:14 they shall **f** upon the shoulders of	5774
	60: 8 Who *are* these *that* **f** as a cloud, and as	5774
Jer	48:40 he shall **f** as an eagle, and shall spread his	1675
	49:22 he shall come up and **f** as the eagle,	1675
Eze	13:20 ye there hunt the souls to **make** *them* **f**,	6524
	13:20 the souls that ye hunt to **make** *them* **f**.	6524
Da	9:21 the beginning, being **caused to f** swiftly,	3286
Hos	9:11 their glory shall **f away** like a bird,	5774
Hab	1: 8 shall **f** as the eagle *that* hasteth to eat.	5774
Rev	12:14 that she might **f** into the wilderness,	4072
	14: 6 And I saw another angel **f** in the midst of	4072
	19:17 saying to all the fowls that **f** in the midst	4072

FLYING (12) [FLY]

Lev	11:21 Yet these may ye eat of every **f** creeping	5775
	11:23 all *other* **f** creeping things, which have	5775
Job	30: 3 **f** into the wilderness in former time	6207
Ps	148:10 all cattle; creeping things, and **f** fowl:	3671
Pr	26: 2 as the swallow by **f**, so the curse causeless	5774
Isa	14:29 and his fruit *shall be* a fiery **f** serpent.	5774
	30: 6 and old lion, the viper and fiery **f** serpent,	5774
	31: 5 As birds **f**, so will the LORD of hosts	5774
Zec	5: 1 eyes, and looked, and behold, a **f** roll.	5774
	5: 2 I answered, I see a **f** roll; the length	5774
Rev	4: 7 and the fourth beast *was* like a **f** eagle.	4072
	8:13 heard an angel **f** through the midst of	4072

FOAL (3) [FOALS]

Ge	49:11 Binding his **f** unto the vine, and his ass's	5895
Zec	9: 9 an ass, and upon a colt the **f** of an ass.	1121
Mt	21: 5 upon an ass, and a colt the **f** of an ass.	5207

FOALS (1) [FOAL]

Ge	32:15 and ten bulls, twenty she asses, and ten **f**.	5895

FOAM (1) [FOAMETH, FOAMING]

Hos	10: 7 her king is cut off as the **f** upon the water.	7110

FOAMETH (2) [FOAM]

Mk	9:18 and he **f**, and gnasheth with his teeth,	875
Lk	9:39 and it teareth him that he **f** again,	876+3326

FOAMING (2) [FOAM]

Mk	9:20 and he fell on the ground, and wallowed **f**.	875
Jude	1:13 waves of the sea, **f out** their own shame;	1890

FODDER (1)

Job	6: 5 he hath grass? or loweth the ox over his **f**?	1098

FOES (7)

1Ch	21:12 three months to be destroyed before thy **f**,	6862
Est	9:16 slew of their **f** seventy and five thousand,	8130
Ps	27: 2 the wicked, *even* mine enemies and my **f**,	341
	30: 1 and hast not made my **f** to rejoice over me.	341
	89:23 I will beat down his **f** before his face,	6862
Mt	10:36 And a man's **f** *shall be* they of his own	2190
Ac	2:35 Until I make thy **f** thy footstool.	2190

FOLD (9) [FOLDEN, FOLDETH, FOLDING, FOLDS, SHEEPFOLD, SHEEPFOLDS]

Isa	13:20 neither shall the shepherds **make** their **f**	7257
	65:10 Sharon shall be a **f** of flocks, and the valley	5116
Eze	34:14 high mountains of Israel shall their **f** be:	5116
	34:14 there shall they lie in a good **f**, and *in* a fat	5116
Mic	2:12 as the flock in the midst of their **f**:	1699
Hab	3:17 the flock shall be cut off from the **f**,	4356
Jn	10:16 other sheep I have, which are not of this **f**:	833
	10:16 there shall be one **f**, *and* one shepherd.	4167
Heb	1:12 And as a vesture shalt thou them **up**,	1667

FOLDEN (1) [FOLD]

Na	1:10 For while *they be* **f together** *as* thorns,	5440

FOLDETH (1) [FOLD]

Ecc	4: 5 The fool **f** his hands **together**,	2263

FOLDING (4) [FOLD]

1Ki	6:34 the two leaves of the one door *were* **f**,	1550
	6:34 the two leaves of the other door *were* **f**.	1550
Pr	6:10 a little **f** of the hands to sleep:	2264
	24:33 a little **f** of the hands to sleep:	2264

FOLDS (5) [FOLD]

Nu	32:24 for your little ones, and **f** for your sheep;	1448
	32:36 fenced cities: and **f** for sheep.	1448
Ps	50: 9 of thy house, *nor* he goats out of thy **f**.	4356
Jer	23: 3 and will bring them again to their **f**;	5116
Zep	2: 6 cottages for shepherds, and **f** for flocks.	1448

FOLK (5) [FOLKS, KINSFOLK, KINSFOLKS]

Ge	33:15 Let me now leave with thee *some* of the **f**	5971
Pr	30:26 The conies *are but* a feeble **f**, yet make	5971
Jer	51:58 the **f** in the fire, and they shall be weary.	3816
Mk	6: 5 that he laid *his* hands upon a few sick **f**,	NIG
Jn	5: 3 these lay a great multitude of impotent **f**,	NIG

FOLKS (1) [FOLK]

Ac	5:16 bringing sick **f**, and *them* which were vexed	NIG

FOLLOW (86) [FOLLOWED, FOLLOWEDST, FOLLOWERS, FOLLOWETH, FOLLOWING]

Ge	24: 5 not be willing to **f** me unto this land:	310+1980
	24: 8 if the woman will not be willing to **f**	310+1980

Ge	24:39 the woman will not **f** me.	310+1980
	44: 4 said unto his steward, Up, **f** after the men;	7291
Ex	11: 8 and all the people that **f** thee:	7272+871.1
	14: 4 Pharaoh's heart, that he shall **f** after them;	7291
	14:17 the Egyptians, and they shall **f** them:	310+935
	21:22 depart *from her*, and yet no mischief **f**:	1961
	21:23 if *any* mischief **f**, then thou shalt give life	1961
	23: 2 Thou shalt not **f** a multitude to *do*	310+1961
Dt	16:20 That which is altogether just shalt thou **f**,	7291
	18:22 if the thing **f** not, nor come to pass, that *is*	1961
Jdg	3:28 he said unto them, **F** after me:	7291
	8: 5 of bread unto the people that **f** me;	7272+871.1
	8: 5 their hearts inclined to **f** Abimelech; for	310
1Sa	25:27 young men that **f** my lord.	1980+7272+871.1
	25:42 that they could not **f** David,	310+1980
2Sa	17: 9 is a slaughter among the people that **f**	310
1Ki	18:21 if the LORD *be* God, **f** him;	310+1980
	18:21 if Baal, *then* **f** him. And the people	310+1980
	19:20 my mother, and *then* I will **f** thee.	310+1980
	20:10 for all the people that **f** me,	7272+871.1
2Ki	6:19 **f** me, and I will bring you to the man	310+1980
Ps	23: 6 mercy shall **f** me all the days of my life:	7291
	38:20 because I **f** *the thing that* good *is*.	7291
	45:14 the virgins her companions that **f** her *shall*	7291
	94:15 and all the upright in heart shall **f** it.	310
	119:150 They draw nigh that **f** after mischief:	7291
Isa	5:11 the morning, *that* they may **f** strong drink;	7291
	51: 1 to me, ye that **f** after righteousness,	7291
Jer	17:16 have not hastened from *being* a pastor to **f**	310
	42:16 shall **f close** after you there *in* Egypt;	1692
Eze	13: 3 that **f** their own spirit, and have seen	310+1980
Hos	2: 7 she shall **f** after her lovers, but she shall	7291
	6: 3 we know, *if* we **f** on to know the LORD:	7291
Mt	4:19 **F** me, and I will make you fishers	1205+3694
	8:19 I will **f** thee whithersoever thou goest.	190
	8:22 But Jesus said unto him, **F** me; and let	190
	9: 9 and he saith unto him, **F** me. And he arose,	190
	16:24 and take up his cross, and **f** me.	190
	19:21 treasure in heaven: and come *and* **f** me.	190
Mk	2:14 of custom, and said unto him, **F** me.	190
	5:37 And he suffered no *man* to **f** him,	4870
	6: 1 his own country; and his disciples **f** him.	190
	8:34 and take up his cross, and **f** me.	190
	10:21 and come, take up the cross, and **f** me.	190
	14:13 a man bearing a pitcher of water: **f** him.	190
	16:17 And these signs shall **f** them that believe;	3877
Lk	5:27 of custom: and he said unto him, **F** me.	190
	9:23 and take up his cross daily, and **f** me.	190
	9:57 I will **f** thee whithersoever thou goest.	190
	9:59 he said unto another, **F** me. But he said,	190
	9:61 And another also said, Lord, I will **f** thee;	190
	17:23 see there: go not after *them*, nor **f** *them*.	1377
	18:22 have treasure in heaven: and come, **f** me.	190
	22:10 **f** him into the house where he entereth in.	190
	22:49 which were about him saw what would **f**,	1510
Jn	1:43 findeth Philip, and saith unto him, **F** me.	190
	10: 4 he goeth before them, and the sheep **f** him:	190
	10: 5 And a stranger will they not **f**, but will flee	190
	10:27 my voice, and I know them, and they **f** me:	190
	12:26 If any *man* serve me, let him **f** me;	190
	13:36 Whither I go, thou canst not **f** me now;	190
	13:36 me now; but thou shalt **f** me afterwards.	190
	13:37 unto him, Lord, why cannot I **f** thee now?	190
	21:19 had spoken this, he saith unto him, **F** me.	190
	21:22 I come, what *is that* to thee? **f** thou me.	190
Ac	3:24 from Samuel and those that **f** after,	2517
	12: 8 Cast thy garment about thee, and **f** me.	190
Ro	14:19 **f** after the *things* which make for peace,	1377
1Co	14: 1 **F** after charity, and desire spiritual *gifts*,	1377
Php	3:12 I **f** after, if that I may apprehend *that* for	1377
1Th	5:15 any *man*; but ever **f** *that which* is good,	1377
2Th	3: 7 yourselves know how *ye* ought to **f** us:	3401
	3: 9 ourselves an ensample unto you to **f** us.	3401
1Ti	5:24 to judgment; and some men they **f** after.	1872
	6:11 flee these *things*; and **f** after righteousness,	1377
2Ti	2:22 but **f** righteousness, faith, charity, peace,	1377
Heb	12:14 **F** peace with all *men*, and holiness,	1377
	13: 7 whose faith **f**, considering the end of *their*	3401
1Pe	1:11 and the glory **that should f**.	3326+3778
	2:21 us an example, that ye should **f** his steps:	1872
2Pe	2: 2 And many shall **f** their pernicious ways;	1811
3Jn	1:11 **f** not *that which* is evil, but *that which* is	3401
Rev	14: 4 These are they which **f** the Lamb	190
	14:13 their labours; and their works do **f** them.	190

FOLLOWED (108) [FOLLOW]

Ge	24:61 upon the camels, and **f** the man:	310+1980
	32:19 and all that **f** the droves, saying,	310+1980
Nu	14:24 spirit with him, and hath **f** me fully,	310
	16:25 and the elders of Israel **f** him.	310+1980
	32:11 because they have not wholly **f** me:	310
	32:12 of Nun: for they have wholly **f** the LORD.	310
Dt	1:36 because he hath wholly **f** the LORD.	310
	4: 3 for all the men that **f** Baal-peor,	310+1980
Jos	6: 8 of the covenant of the LORD **f** them.	310+1980
	14: 8 but I wholly **f** the LORD my God.	310
	14: 9 thou hast wholly **f** the LORD my God.	310
	14:14 that he wholly **f** the LORD God of Israel.	310
Jdg	2:12 the land of Egypt, and **f** other gods,	310+1980
	9: 4 and light persons, which **f** him.	310
	9:49 Abimelech, and put *them* to the	310+1980
1Sa	13: 7 Gilgal, and all the people **f** him trembling.	310+1980
	14:22 even they also **f hard** after them in	1692
	17:13 Jesse went and **f** Saul to the battle:	310+1980
	17:14 and the three eldest **f** Saul.	310+1980

F

F

1Sa 31: 2 the Philistines f **hard** upon Saul and upon 1692
2Sa 1: 6 and horsemen f **hard after h**im. 1692
 2:10 But the house of Judah f David. 310+1961
 3:31 And king David himself f the bier. 310+1980
 11: 8 f him a mess of meat from the king. 310+3318
 17:23 Ahithophel saw that his counsel was not f, 6213
 20: 2 after David, and f Sheba the son of Bichri: 310
1Ki 12:20 there was none that f the house of David, 310
 14: 8 and who f me with all his heart, 310+1980
 16:21 half of the people f Tibni the son of 310+1961
 16:21 to make him king; and half f Omri. 310
 16:22 the people that f Omri prevailed against 310
 16:22 the people that f Tibni the son of Ginath: 310
 18:18 the Lord, and thou hast f Baalim. 310+1980
 20:19 of the city, and the army which f them. 310
2Ki 3: 9 and for the cattle that f them. 7272+871.1
 4:30 leave thee. And he arose, and f her. 310+1980
 5:21 So Gehazi f after Naaman. And when 7291
 9:27 Jehu f after him, and said, Smite him also 7291
 13: 2 f the sins of Jeroboam the son of 310+1980
 17:15 they f vanity, and became vain, 310+1980
1Ch 10: 2 the Philistines f **hard** after Saul, 1692
Ne 4:23 nor the men of the guard which f me, 310
Ps 68:25 the players on instruments f after; NIH
Eze 10:11 the place whither the head looked they f 1980
Am 7:15 the Lord took me as I f the flock, 310
Mt 4:20 they straightway left their nets, and f him. 190
 4:22 left the ship and their father, and f him. 190
 4:25 And there f him great multitudes of people 190
 8: 1 from the mountain, great multitudes f him. 190
 8:10 and said to them that f, Verily I say unto 190
 8:23 was entered into a ship, his disciples f him. 190
 9: 9 Follow me. And he arose, and f him. 190
 9:19 and f him, and so did his disciples. 190
 9:27 two blind men f him, crying, and saying, 190
 12:15 and great multitudes f him, and he healed 190
 14:13 when the people had heard thereof, they f 190
 19: 2 And great multitudes f him; and he healed 190
 19:27 Behold, we have forsaken all, and f thee; 190
 19:28 That ye which have f me, 190
 20:29 from Jericho, a great multitude f him. 190
 20:34 their eyes received sight, and they f him. 190
 21: 9 that f, cried, saying, Hosanna to the Son 190
 26:58 Peter f him afar off unto the high priest's 190
 27:55 which f Jesus from Galilee, ministering unto 190
 27:62 that f the day of the preparation, 1510+3326
Mk 1:18 they forsook their nets, and f him. 190
 1:36 and they that were with him f after him. 2614
 2:14 Follow me. And he arose and f him. 190
 2:15 for there were many, and they f him. 190
 3: 7 and a great multitude from Galilee f him, 190
 5:24 and much people f him, and thronged him. 190
 10:28 Lo, we have left all, and have f thee. 190
 10:32 and as they f, they were afraid. 190
 10:52 received his sight, and f Jesus in the way. 190
 11: 9 and they that f, cried, saying, Hosanna; 190
 14:51 And there f him a certain young man, 190
 14:54 And Peter f him afar off, even into 190
 15:41 Galilee, f him, and ministered unto him;) 190
Lk 5:11 ships to land, they forsook all, and f him. 190
 5:28 And he left all, rose up, and f him. 190
 7: 9 and said unto the people that f him, 190
 9:11 And the people, when they knew it, f him: 190
 18:28 Peter said, Lo, we have left all, and f thee. 190
 18:43 his sight, and f him, glorifying God: 190
 22:39 of Olives; and his disciples also f him. 190
 22:54 the high priest's house. And Peter f afar off. 190
 23:27 And there f him a great company of people, 190
 23:49 and the women that f him from Galilee, 4870
 23:55 f after, and beheld the sepulchre. 2628
Jn 1:37 disciples heard him speak, and they f Jesus. 190
 1:40 and f him, was Andrew, Simon Peter's 190
 6: 2 And a great multitude f him, because 190
 11:31 rose up hastily and went out, f her, saying, 190
 18:15 Simon Peter f Jesus, and so did another 190
Ac 12: 9 And he went out, and f him; and wist not 190
 13:43 religious proselytes f Paul and Barnabas; 190
 16:17 The same f Paul and us, and cried, saying, 2628
 21:36 For the multitude of the people f after, 190
Ro 9:30 which f not after righteousness, 1377
 9:31 which f after the law of righteousness, 1377
1Co 10: 4 for they drank of that spiritual Rock that f 190
1Ti 5:10 if she have **diligently** f every good work. 1872
2Pe 1:16 we have not f cunningly devised fables, 1811
Rev 6: 8 on him was Death, and Hell f with him. 190
 8: 7 and there f hail and fire mingled with 1096
 14: 8 And there f another angel, saying, 190
 14: 9 And the third angel f them, saying with a 190
 19:14 the armies which were in heaven f him 190

FOLLOWEDST (1) [FOLLOW]
Ru 3:10 inasmuch as thou f not young men, 310+1980

FOLLOWERS (8) [FOLLOW]
1Co 4:16 Wherefore I beseech you, be ye f of me. 3402
 11: 1 Be ye f of me, even as I also am of Christ. 3402
Eph 5: 1 Be ye therefore f of God, as dear children; 3402
Php 3:17 be f **together** of me, and mark them 4831
1Th 1: 6 And ye became f of us, and of the Lord, 3402
 2:14 became f of the churches of God which in 3402
Heb 6:12 but f of them who through faith and 3402
1Pe 3:13 harm you, if ye be f of that which is good? 3402

FOLLOWETH (15) [FOLLOW]
2Ki 11:15 him that f her kill with the sword. 310+935

2Ch 23:14 whoso f her, let him be slain with 310+935
Ps 63: 8 My soul f **hard** after thee: thy right hand 1692
Pr 12:11 he that f vain persons is void of 7291
 15: 9 he loveth him that f after righteousness. 7291
 21:21 He that f **after** righteousness and 7291
 28:19 he that f **after** vain persons shall have 7291
Isa 1:23 one loveth gifts, and f after rewards: 7291
Eze 16:34 none f thee to commit whoredoms: 310
Hos 12: 1 on wind, and f the east wind: 7291
Mt 10:38 and f after me, is not worthy of me. 190
Mk 9:38 out devils in thy name, and he f not us: 190
 9:38 we forbad him, because he f not us. 190
Lk 9:49 we forbad him, because he f not with us. 190
Jn 8:12 he that f me shall not walk in darkness, 190

FOLLOWING (43) [FOLLOW]
Ge 41:31 the land by reason of that famine f; 310+3651
Dt 7: 4 For they will turn away thy son from f me, 310
 12:30 thyself that thou be not snared by f them, 310
Jos 22:16 to turn away this day from f the Lord, 310
 22:18 that ye must turn away this day from f 310
 22:23 we have built us an altar to turn from f 310
 22:29 turn this day from f the Lord, to build an 310
Jdg 2:19 in f other gods to serve them, 310+1980
Ru 1:16 leave thee, or to return from f after thee: 310
1Sa 12:14 over you continue the Lord your God: 310
 12:20 yet turn not aside from f the Lord, 310
 14:46 Saul went up from f the Philistines. 310
 15:11 he is turned back from f me, and hath not 310
 24: 1 when Saul was returned from f 310
2Sa 2:19 the right hand nor to the left from f Abner. 310
 2:21 Asahel would not turn aside from f of him. 310
 2:22 again to Asahel, Turn thee aside from f me: 310
 2:26 ere thou bid the people return from their 310
 2:27 had gone up every one from f his brother. 310
 2:30 Joab returned from f Abner: and when he 310
 7: 8 the sheep, to be ruler over my people, 310
1Ki 1: 7 priest: and they f Adonijah helped him. 310
 9: 6 if you shall at all turn from f me, you or 310
 21:26 he did very abominably in f idols, 310+1980
2Ki 17:21 Jeroboam drave Israel from f the Lord, 310
 18: 6 and departed not from f him, but kept his 310
1Ch 17: 7 from the sheepcote, even from f the sheep, 310
2Ch 25:27 f the Lord they made a conspiracy against 310
 34:33 And all his days they departed not from f 310
Ps 48:13 that ye may tell it to the generation f. 314
 78:71 From the ewes great with young he 310
 109:13 the generation f let their name be blotted 312
Mk 16:20 and confirming the word with signs f. 1872
Lk 13:33 to day, and to morrow, and the day f: 2192
Jn 1:38 and saw them f, and saith unto them, 190
 1:43 The day f Jesus would go forth into 1887
 6:22 The day f, when the people which stood 1887
 20: 6 Then cometh Simon Peter f him, 190
 21:20 seeth the disciple whom Jesus loved f; 190
Ac 21: 1 the day f unto Rhodes, and from thence 1836
 21:18 And the day f Paul went in with us unto 1966
 23:11 And the night f the Lord stood by him, 1966
2Pe 2:15 f the way of Balaam the son of Bosor, 1811

FOLLY (37) [FOOL]
Ge 34: 7 he had wrought f in Israel in lying with 5039
Dt 22:21 because she hath wrought f in Israel, 5039
Jos 7:15 and because he hath wrought f in Israel. 5039
Jdg 19:23 is come into mine house, do not this f. 5039
 20: 6 have committed lewdness and f in Israel. 5039
 20:10 according to all the f that they have 5039
1Sa 25:25 Nabal is his name, and f is with him: 5039
2Sa 13:12 to be done in Israel: do not thou this f. 5039
Job 4:18 and his angels he charged with f: 8417
 24:12 crieth out: yet God layeth not f to them. 8604
 42: 8 lest I deal with you after your f, in that ye 5039
Ps 49:13 their way is their f: yet their posterity 3689
 85: 8 saints: but let them not turn again to f. 3690
Pr 5:23 in the greatness of his f he shall go astray. 200
 13:16 knowledge: but a fool layeth open his f. 200
 14: 8 his way: but the f of fools is deceit. 200
 14:18 The simple inherit f: but the prudent are 200
 14:24 riches: but the foolishness of fools is f. 200
 14:29 but he that is hasty of spirit exalteth f. 200
 15:21 F is joy to him that is destitute of wisdom: 200
 16:22 hath it: but the instruction of fools is f. 200
 17:12 meet a man, rather than a fool in his f. 200
 18:13 a matter before he heareth it, it is f 200
 26: 4 Answer not a fool according to his f, 200
 26: 5 Answer a fool according to his f, lest he be 200
 26:11 to his vomit, so a fool returneth to his f. 200
Ecc 1:17 wisdom, and to know madness and f: 5531
 2: 3 to lay hold on f, till I might see what was 5531
 2:12 to behold wisdom, and madness, and f: 5531
 2:13 I saw that wisdom excelleth f, as far as 5531
 7:25 things, and to know the wickedness of f, 3689
 10: 1 doth a little f him that is in reputation for 5531
 10: 6 F is set in great dignity, and the rich sit in 5529
Isa 9:17 an evildoer, and every mouth speaketh f. 5039
Jer 23:13 I have seen f in the prophets of Samaria; 8604
2Co 11: 1 you could bear with me a little in my f: 877
2Ti 3: 9 for their f shall be manifest unto all men, 454

FOOD (55) [FEED]
Ge 2: 9 is pleasant to the sight, and good for f; 3978
 3: 6 woman saw that the tree was good for f, 3978
 6:21 take thou unto thee of all f that is eaten, 3978
 6:21 and it shall be for f for thee, and for them. 402
 41:35 them gather all the f of those good years 400

Ge 41:35 Pharaoh, and let them keep f in the cities. 400
 41:36 that f shall be for store to the land against 400
 41:48 he gathered up all the f of the seven years, 400
 41:48 of Egypt, and laid up the f in the cities: 400
 41:48 the f of the field, which was round about 400
 42: 7 said, From the land of Canaan to buy f. 400
 42:10 lord, but to buy f are thy servants come. 400
 42:33 take f for the famine of your households, NIH
 43: 2 said unto them, Go again, buy us a little f 400
 43: 4 with us, we will go down and buy thee f: 400
 43:20 indeed down at the first time to buy f: 400
 43:22 we brought down in our hands to buy f: 400
 44: 1 Fill the men's sacks with f, as much 400
 44:25 said, Go again, and buy us a little f. 400
 47:24 your f, and for them of your households, 398
 47:24 your f, and for your little ones. 398
Ex 21:10 If he take him another wife; her f, 7607
Lev 3:11 it is the f of the offering made by fire unto 3899
 3:16 it is the f of the offering made by fire for a 3899
 19:23 have planted all manner of trees for f, 3978
 22: 7 eat of the holy things; because it is his f. 3899
Dt 10:18 the stranger, in giving him f and raiment. 3899
1Sa 14:24 Cursed be the man that eateth any f until 3899
 14:24 So none of the people tasted any f. 3899
 14:28 Cursed be the man that eateth any f this 3899
2Sa 9:10 that thy master's son may have f to eat: 3899
1Ki 5: 9 my desire, in giving f for my household, 3899
 5:11 measures of wheat for f to his household, 4361
Job 23:12 of his mouth more than my necessary f. NIH
 24: 5 the wilderness yieldeth f for them and 3899
 38:41 Who provideth for the raven his f? 6718
 40:20 Surely the mountains bring him forth f, 944
Ps 78:25 Man did eat angels' f: he sent them meat 3899
 104:14 that he may bring forth f out of the earth; 3899
 136:25 Who giveth f to all flesh: for his mercy 3899
 146: 7 which giveth f to the hungry. The Lord 3899
 147: 9 He giveth to the beast his f, and to 3899
Pr 6: 8 and gathereth her f in the harvest. 3978
 13:23 Much f is in the tillage of the poor: 400
 27:27 shalt have goats' milk enough for thy f, 3899
 27:27 for the f of thy household, and for 3899
 28: 3 like a sweeping rain which leaveth no f. 3899
 30: 8 feed me with f convenient for me: 3899
 31:14 she bringeth her f from afar. 3899
Eze 16:27 have diminished thine ordinary f, NIH
 48:18 increase thereof shall be for f unto them 3899
Ac 14:17 filling our hearts with f and gladness. 5160
2Co 9:10 the sower both minister bread for your f, 1035
1Ti 6: 8 And having f and raiment let us be 1305
Jas 2:15 sister be naked, and destitute of daily f, 5160

FOOL (66) [FOLLY, FOOL'S, FOOLISH, FOOLISHLY, FOOLISHNESS, FOOLS, FOOLS']
1Sa 26:21 I have **played the f**, and have erred 5528
2Sa 3:33 and said, Died Abner as a f dieth? 5036
Ps 14: 1 The f hath said in his heart, There is no 5036
 49:10 the f and the brutish person perish, 3684
 53: 1 The f hath said in his heart, There is no 5036
 92: 6 neither doth a f understand this. 3684
Pr 7:22 or as a f to the correction of the stocks; 191
 10: 8 but a prating f shall fall. 191
 10:10 causeth sorrow: but a prating f shall fall. 191
 10:18 and he that uttereth a slander, is a f. 3684
 10:23 It is as sport to a f to do mischief: but a 3684
 11:29 the f shall be servant to the wise of heart. 191
 12:15 The way of a f is right in his own eyes: 191
 13:16 but a f layeth open his folly. 3684
 14:16 evil: but the f rageth, and is confident. 3684
 15: 5 A f despiseth his father's instruction: 191
 17: 7 Excellent speech becometh not a f: 5036
 17:10 wise man than an hundred stripes into a f. 3684
 17:12 meet a man, rather than a f in his folly. 3684
 17:16 is there a price in the hand of a f 3684
 17:21 that begetteth a f doeth it to his sorrow: 3684
 17:21 sorrow: and the father of a f hath no joy. 5036
 17:24 eyes of a f are in the ends of the earth. 3684
 17:28 Even a f, when he holdeth his peace, 191
 18: 2 A f hath no delight in understanding, 3684
 19: 1 he that is perverse in his lips, and is a f. 3684
 19:10 Delight is not seemly for a f; much less for 3684
 20: 3 from strife: but every f will be meddling. 191
 23: 9 Speak not in the ears of a f: for he will 3684
 24: 7 Wisdom is too high for a f: he openeth 191
 26: 1 harvest, so honour is not seemly for a f. 3684
 26: 4 Answer not a f according to his folly, 3684
 26: 5 Answer a f according to his folly, lest he 3684
 26: 6 by the hand of a f cutteth off the feet, 3684
 26: 8 a sling, so is he that giveth honour to a f. 3684
 26:10 formed all things both rewardeth the f, 3684
 26:11 to his vomit, so a f returneth to his folly. 3684
 26:12 there is more hope of a f than of him. 3684
 27:22 Though thou shouldest bray a f in a mortar 191
 28:26 He that trusteth in his own heart is a f: 3684
 29:11 A f uttereth all his mind: but a wise man 3684
 29:20 there is more hope of a f than of him. 3684
 30:22 and a f when he is filled with meat; 5036
Ecc 2:14 his head; but the f walketh in darkness: 3684
 2:15 As it happeneth to the f, so it happeneth 3684
 2:16 of the wise more than of the f for ever; 3684
 2:16 And how dieth the wise man? as the f. 3684
 2:19 whether he shall be a wise man or a f? 5530
 4: 5 The f foldeth his hands together, 3684
 6: 8 For what hath the wise more than the f? 3684
 7: 6 under a pot, so is the laughter of the f: 3684
 10: 3 when he that is a f walketh by the way, 5530

Ecc 10: 3 and he saith to every one *that* he *is* a f. 5530
10:12 but the lips of a f will swallow up himself. 3684
10:14 A f also is full of words: a man cannot tell 5036
Jer 17:11 of his days, and at his end shall be a f. 5036
Hos 9: 7 Israel shall know *it:* the prophet *is* a f, 191
Mt 5:22 but whosoever shall say, Thou, f, shall be 3474
Lk 12:20 But God said unto him, Thou f, this night 878
1Co 3:18 let him become a f, that he may be wise. 3474
15:36 Thou f, *that* which thou sowest is not 878
2Co 11:16 I say again, Let no *man* think me a f; 878
11:16 if otherwise, yet as a f receive me, that I 878
11:23 (I speak as a f) I *am* more; in labours more 3912
12: 6 I would desire to glory, I shall not be a f; 878
12:11 I am become a f in glorying; ye have 878

FOOL'S (6) [FOOL]

Pr 12:16 f wrath is presently known: but a prudent 191
18: 6 f lips enter into contention, 3684
18: 7 A f mouth *is* his destruction, and his lips 3684
27: 3 but a f wrath *is* heavier than them both. 191
Ecc 5: 3 a f voice *is known* by multitude of words. 3684
10: 2 at his right hand; but a f heart at his left. 3684

FOOLISH (52) [FOOL]

Dt 32: 6 the LORD, O f people and unwise? 5036
32:21 I will provoke them to anger with a f 5036
Job 2:10 Thou speakest as one of the f *women* 5036
5: 2 For wrath killeth the **f man,** 191
5: 3 I have seen the f taking root: but suddenly 191
Ps 5: 5 The f shall not stand in thy sight: 1984
39: 8 make me not the reproach of the f. 5036
73: 3 For I was envious at the f, *when* I saw 1984
73:22 So f *was* I, and ignorant: I was *as* a beast 1198
74:18 *that* the f people have blasphemed thy 5036
74:22 remember how the f *man* reproacheth 5036
Pr 9: 6 Forsake the f, and live; and go in the way 6612
9:13 A f woman *is* clamorous: *she is* simple, 3687
10: 1 but a f son *is* the heaviness of his mother. 3684
10:14 but the mouth of the f *is* near destruction. 191
14: 1 the f plucketh it down with her hands. 200
14: 3 In the mouth of the f *is* a rod of pride: 191
14: 7 Go from the presence of a f man, 3684
15: 7 but the heart of the f *doeth* not so. 3684
15:20 but a f man despiseth his mother. 3684
17:25 A f son *is* a grief to his father, 3684
19:13 A f son *is* the calamity of his father: 3684
21:20 of the wise; but a f man spendeth it up. 3684
29: 9 If a wise man contendeth with a f man, 191
Ecc 4:13 and a wise child than an old and f king, 3684
7:17 not over much wicked, neither be thou f: 5530
10:15 The labour of the f wearieth every one of 3684
Isa 44:25 and **maketh** their knowledge f; 5528
Jer 4:22 my people *is* f, they have not known me; 191
5: 4 I said, Surely these *are* poor; they are f: 2973
5:21 O f people, and without understanding; 5530
10: 8 they are altogether brutish and f: the stock 3688
10:14 have seen vain and f **things** for thee: 8602
Eze 13: 3 Woe unto the f prophets, that follow their 5036
Zec 11:15 Take unto thee yet the instruments of a f 196
Mt 7:26 them not, shall be likened unto a f man, 3474
25: 2 five of them were wise, and five *were* f. 3474
25: 3 They that *were* f took their lamps, 3474
25: 8 And the f said unto the wise, Give us of 3474
Ro 1:21 and their f heart was darkened. 801
2:20 An instructor of the f, a teacher of babes, 878
10:19 people, *and* by a f nation I will anger you. 801
1Co 1:20 hath not God **made** f the wisdom of this 3471
1:27 But God hath chosen the f **things** of 3474
Gal 3: 1 O f Galatians, who hath bewitched you, 453
3: 3 Are ye so f? having begun in the Spirit, 453
Eph 5: 4 filthiness, nor f **talking,** nor jesting, 3473
1Ti 6: 9 a snare, and *into* many f and hurtful lusts, 3474
2Ti 2:23 But f and unlearned questions avoid, 453
Tit 3: 3 For we ourselves were sometimes f, 453
3: 9 But avoid f questions, and genealogies, 3474
1Pe 2:15 may put to silence the ignorance of f men: 878

FOOLISHLY (12) [FOOL]

Ge 31:28 thou hast now **done** f in *so* doing. 5528
Nu 12:11 wherein we have **done** f, and wherein 2973
1Sa 13:13 Samuel said to Saul, Thou hast **done** f: 5528
2Sa 24:10 of thy servant; for I have **done** very f. 5528
1Ch 21: 8 of thy servant; for I have **done** very f. 5528
2Ch 16: 9 Herein thou hast **done** f: therefore 5528
Job 1:22 all this Job sinned not, nor charged God f. 8604
Ps 75: 4 I said unto the fools, **Deal** not f: and to 1984
Pr 14:17 He that is soon angry dealeth f: and a man 200
30:32 If thou hast **done** f in lifting up thyself, 5034
2Co 11:17 it not after the Lord, but as *it were* f, 877+1722
11:21 any is bold, (I speak f,) 877+1722

FOOLISHNESS (20) [FOOL]

2Sa 15:31 **turn** the counsel of Ahithophel **into** f. 5528
Ps 38: 5 *are* corrupt because of my f; 200
69: 5 God, thou knowest my f; and my sins are 200
Pr 12:23 but the heart of fools proclaimeth f. 200
14:24 is their riches: *but the* f of fools is folly. 200
15: 2 but the mouth of fools poureth out f. 200
15:14 but the mouth of fools feedeth on f. 200
19: 3 The f of man perverteth his way: 200
22:15 F is bound in the heart of a child; *but the* 200
24: 9 The thought of f is sin: and the scorner *is* 200
27:22 a pestle, *yet* will not his f depart from him. 200
Ecc 7:25 of folly, even of f *and* madness; 5531
10:13 beginning of the words of his mouth *is* f: 5531

Mk 7:22 an evil eye, blasphemy, pride, f: 877
1Co 1:18 of the cross is to them that perish f; 3472
1:21 pleased God by the f of preaching to save 3472
1:23 a stumblingblock, and unto the Greeks f; 3472
1:25 Because the f of God is wiser than men; 3472
2:14 for they are f unto him: neither can he 3474
3:19 the wisdom of this world is f with God. 3472

FOOLS (42) [FOOL]

2Sa 13:13 thou shalt be as one of the f in Israel. 5036
Job 12:17 away spoiled, and **maketh** the judges f. 1984
30: 8 *They were* children of f, yea, children of 5036
Ps 75: 4 I said unto the f, Deal not foolishly: 1984
94: 8 people: and ye f, when will ye be wise? 3684
107:17 F because of their transgression, and 191
Pr 1: 7 *but* f despise wisdom and instruction. 191
1:22 in their scorning, and f hate knowledge? 3684
1:32 and the prosperity of f shall destroy them. 3684
3:35 but shame shall be the promotion of f. 3684
8: 5 and, ye f, be ye of an understanding heart. 3820
10:21 feed many: but f die for want of wisdom. 191
12:23 but the heart of f proclaimeth foolishness. 3684
13:19 it *is* abomination to f to depart from evil. 3684
13:20 but a companion of f shall be destroyed. 3684
14: 8 his way: but the folly of f *is* deceit. 3684
14: 9 F make a mock at sin: but among 191
14:24 riches: *but* the foolishness of f *is* folly. 3684
14:33 *that* which is in the midst of f is made 3684
15: 2 the mouth of f poureth out foolishness. 3684
15:14 but the mouth of f feedeth on foolishness. 3684
16:22 hath it: but the instruction of f is folly. 191
19:29 for scorners, and stripes for the back of f. 3684
26: 7 equal: so *is* a parable in the mouth of f. 3684
26: 9 so *is* a parable in the mouth of f. 3684
Ecc 5: 1 to hear, than to give the sacrifice of f: 3684
5: 4 not to pay it; for *he hath* no pleasure in f: 3684
7: 4 but the heart of f *is* in the house of mirth. 3684
7: 5 than for a man to hear the song of f. 3684
7: 9 for anger resteth in the bosom of f. 3684
9:17 than the cry of him that ruleth among f. 3684
Isa 19:11 the princes of Zoan *are* f, the counsel 191
19:13 The princes of Zoan are become f, 2973
35: 8 the wayfaring men, though f, shall not err 191
Mt 23:17 Ye f and blind: for whether *is* greater, 3474
23:19 Ye f and blind: for whether *is* greater, 3474
Lk 11:40 Ye f, did not he that made that *which is* 878
24:25 O f, and slow of heart to believe all that 453
Ro 1:22 *themselves* to be wise, they became f, 3471
1Co 4:10 We *are* f for Christ's sake, but ye *are* wise 3474
2Co 11:19 For ye suffer f gladly, seeing ye *yourselves* 878
Eph 5:15 walk circumspectly, not as f, but as wise, 781

FOOLS' (1) [FOOL]

Pr 26: 3 bridle for the ass, and a rod for the f back. 3684

FOOT (95) [AFOOT, BAREFOOT, BROKENFOOTED, CLOVENFOOTED, FEET, FOOTMEN, FOOTSTEPS, FOOTSTOOL, FOURFOOTED]

Ge 8: 9 dove found no rest for the sole of her f, 7272
41:44 up his hand or f in all the land of Egypt. 7272
Ex 12:37 about six hundred thousand **on** f that 7273
21:24 tooth for tooth, hand for hand, f for foot, 7272
21:24 tooth for tooth, hand for hand, foot for f, 7272
29:20 upon the great toe of their right f, 7272
30:18 his f *also of* brass, to wash *withal:* and 3653
30:28 all his vessels, and the laver and his f. 3653
31: 9 all his furniture, and the laver and his f, 3653
35:16 and all his vessels, the laver and his f. 3653
38: 8 the laver *of* brass, and the f of it *of* brass, 3653
39:39 and all his vessels, the laver and his f, 3653
40:11 thou shalt anoint the laver and his f, 3653
Lev 8:11 his vessels, both the laver and his f, 3653
8:23 and upon the great toe of his right f. 7272
13:12 the plague from his head even to his f, 7272
14:14 and upon the great toe of his right f: 7272
14:17 and upon the great toe of his right f: 7272
14:25 and upon the great toe of his right f: 7272
14:28 and upon the great toe of his right f, 7272
Nu 22:25 and crusht Balaam's f against the wall: 7272
Dt 2: 5 no, not so much as a f breadth; 3709+7272
8: 4 neither did thy f swell, these forty years. 7272
11:10 wateredst *it* with thy f, as a garden of 7272
19:21 tooth for tooth, hand for hand, f for foot. 7272
19:21 tooth for tooth, hand for hand, foot for f. 7272
25: 9 loose his shoe from off his f, and spit in 7272
28:35 from the sole of thy f unto the top of thy 7272
28:56 of her f upon the ground for delicateness 7272
28:65 neither shall the sole of thy f have rest: 7272
29: 5 and thy shoe is not waxen old upon thy f. 7272
32:35 their f shall slide in *due* time: 7272
33:24 his brethren, and let him dip his f in oil. 7272
Jos 1: 3 Every place that the sole of your f shall 7272
5:15 Joshua, Loose thy shoe from off thy f; 7272
Jdg 5:15 he was sent on f into the valley. 7272
2Sa 2:18 and Asahel *was* as light of f as a wild roe. 7272
14:25 from the sole of his f even to the crown 7272
21:20 on every f six toes, four and twenty in 7272
2Ki 9:33 on the horses: and he **trode** her **under** f. 7429
1Ch 20: 6 six *on each* hand, and six *on each* f. NIH
2Ch 33: 8 Neither will I any more remove the f of 7272
Job 2: 7 boils from the sole of his f unto his crown. 7272
23:11 My f hath held his steps, his way have I 7272
28: 4 *even* the waters forgotten of the f: 7272
31: 5 vanity, or *if* my f hath hasted to deceit; 7272

Job 39:15 forgetteth that the f may crush them, 7272
Ps 9:15 in the net which they hid is their own f 7272
26:12 My f standeth in an even place: 7272
36:11 Let not the f of pride come against me, 7272
38:16 when my f slippeth, they magnify 7272
66: 6 *land:* they went through the flood on f: 7272
68:23 That thy f may be dipped in the blood of 7272
91:12 lest thou dash thy f against a stone. 7272
94:18 When I said, My f slippeth; thy mercy, 7272
121: 3 He will not suffer thy f to be moved: 7272
Pr 1:15 with them; refrain thy f from their path: 7272
3:23 way safely, and thy f shall not stumble. 7272
3:26 and shall keep thy f from being taken. 7272
4:27 nor to the left: remove thy f from evil. 7272
25:17 Withdraw thy f from thy neighbour's 7272
25:19 *is like* a broken tooth, and a f out of joint. 7272
Ecc 5: 1 Keep thy f when thou goest to the house 7272
Isa 1: 6 From the sole of the f even unto the head 7272
14:25 upon my mountains **tread** him **under** f, 947
18: 7 a nation meted out and **trodden under** f, 4001
20: 2 thy loins, and put off thy shoe from thy f. 7272
26: 6 The f shall tread it down, *even* the feet of 7272
41: 2 called him to his f, gave the nations before 7272
58:13 If thou turn away thy f from the sabbath, 7272
Jer 2:25 Withhold thy f from being unshod, 7272
La 1:15 The Lord hath **trodden under** f all my 5541
Eze 6:11 thine hand, and stamp with thy f, and say, 7272
25:16 after the f of my 2:10 they have **trodden** my portion **under** f, 947
29:11 No of man shall pass through it, nor foot 7272
29:11 nor f of beast shall pass through it, 7272
32:13 neither shall the f of man trouble them 7272
Da 8:13 and the host to be **trodden under** f? 4823
Am 2:15 he that is swift of f shall not deliver 7272
Mt 4: 6 lest at any time thou dash thy f against a 4228
5:13 out, and to be **trodden under** f of men. 2662
14:13 they followed him on f out of the cities. 3979
18: 8 if thy hand or thy f offend thee, 4228
22:13 Bind him hand and f, and take him away, 4228
Mk 9:45 And if thy f offend thee, cut it off: it is 4228
Lk 4:11 lest at any time thou dash thy f against a 4228
Jn 11:44 bound hand and f with graveclothes: 4228
Ac 7: 5 in it, no, not so much as to set his f on: 4228
1Co 12:15 If the f shall say, Because I am not 4228
Heb 10:29 hath **trodden under** f the Son of God, 2662
Rev 1:13 clothed with a garment **down to the** f, 4158
10: 2 and he set his right f upon the sea,
10: 2 upon the sea, and *his* left f on the earth, NIG
11: 2 holy city shall they **tread under** f forty 3961

FOOTHILLS See VALE

FOOTMEN (12) [FOOT, MAN]

Nu 11:21 whom I *am, are* six hundred thousand f; 7273
Jdg 20: 2 hundred thousand f that drew sword 376+7273
1Sa 4:10 for there fell of Israel thirty thousand f. 7273
15: 4 two hundred thousand f, and ten 7273
22:17 the king said unto the f that stood about 7323
2Sa 8: 4 and twenty thousand f: 376+7273
1Ki 20:29 Syrians an hundred thousand f in one day. 7273
2Ki 13: 7 and ten chariots, and ten thousand f; 7273
1Ch 18: 4 and twenty thousand f: 376+7273
19:18 thousand f, and killed Shophach 376+7273
Jer 12: 5 If thou hast run with the f, and they have 7273

FOOTSTEPS (4) [FOOT, STEP]

Ps 17: 5 my goings in thy paths, *that* my f slip not. 6471
77:19 great waters, and thy f are not known. 6119
89:51 wherewith they have reproached the f of 6119
SS 1: 8 go thy way forth by the f of the flock, 6119

FOOTSTOOL (16) [FOOT, STOOL]

1Ch 28: 2 for the f of our God, and had made 1916+7272
2Ch 9:18 with a f of gold, which were fastened to 3534
Ps 99: 5 our God, and worship at his f; 1916+7272
110: 1 make thine enemies thy f. 1916+7272+3807.1
132: 7 we will worship at his f. 1916+7272
Isa 66: 1 is my throne, and the earth *is* my f: 1916+7272
La 2: 1 remembered not his f in the day of 1916+7272
Mt 5:35 Nor by the earth; for it is his f: neither by 5286
22:44 hand, till I make thine enemies thy f? 5286
Mk 12:36 hand, till I make thine enemies thy f. 5286
Lk 20:43 Till I make thine enemies thy f. 5286
Ac 2:35 Until I make thy foes thy f. 5286
7:49 Heaven *is* my throne, and earth *is* my f: 5286
Heb 1:13 until I make thine enemies thy f? 5286
10:13 expecting till his enemies be made his f. 5286
Jas 2: 3 Stand thou there, or sit here under my f: 5286

FOR (8985) [FORASMUCH, FORSOMUCH] See Index of Articles, Etc.

FORAGING See BETIMES

FORASMUCH (42) [AS, FOR, MUCH]

Ge 41:39 F as God hath shewed thee all this, *there* 310
Nu 10:31 f as thou knowest how we 3588+3651+5921
Dt 12:12 he hath no part nor inheritance with 3588
17:16 f as the LORD hath said unto you, 2050.1
Jos 17:14 f as the LORD hath blessed me 834+5704
Jdg 11:36 f as the LORD hath taken vengeance for 310
1Sa 24:18 f as we have sworn both of us in the name 834
24:18 f as when the LORD had delivered me into 834
2Sa 19:30 f as my lord the king is come *again* in peace 310
1Ki 11:11 F as this is done of thee, and thou 834+3282

F

1Ki	13:21	**F as** thou hast disobeyed the mouth	3282+3588
	14: 7	**F as** I exalted thee from among	834+3282
	16: 2	**F as** I exalted thee out of the dust,	834+3282
2Ki	1:16	**F as** thou hast sent messengers to	834+3282
1Ch	5: 1	but, **f as** he defiled his father's bed,	871.1
2Ch	6: 8	**F as** it was in thine heart to build a	834+3282
Ezr	7:14	**F as** *thou art* sent of the	1768+3606+6903
Isa	29:13	**F as** this people draw near *me* with their	3588
Jer	10: 6	**F as** *there is* none like unto thee,	4480
	10: 7	**f as** among all the wise *men* of the	3588
Da	2:40	**F as** iron breaketh in pieces	1768+3606+6903
	2:41	**F as** thou sawest the iron	1768+3606+6903
	2:45	**F as** thou sawest that the	1768+3606+6903
	4:18	**F as** all the wise *men* of my	1768+3606+6903
	5:12	**F as** an excellent spirit,	1768+3606+6903
	6: 4	**F as** he *was* faithful,	1768+3606+6903
	6:22	**F as** before him innocency	1768+3606+6903
Am	5:11	**F** therefore as your treading *is*	3651+3807.1
Mt	18:25	But **f** as he had not to pay, his lord	NIG
Lk	1: 1	**F as** many have taken in hand to set forth	1895
Ac	9:38	**And f as** Lydda was nigh to Joppa,	1161
	11:17	**F** then as God gave them the like gift as	1487
	15:24	**F as** we have heard, that certain which	1894
	17:29	**F** then as we are the offspring of God,	3767
	24:10	**F** as I know that thou hast been of many	NIG
1Co	1: 1	**f** as he is the image and glory of God:	NIG
	14:12	**f as** ye are zealous of spiritual *gifts*, seek	1893
	15:58	**f** as you know that your labour is not in	NIG
2Co	3: 3	**F as** ye are manifestly declared to be	NIG
Heb	2:14	**F** then as the children are partakers of	1893
1Pe	1:18	**F** as ye know that ye were not redeemed	NIG
	4: 1	**F** then as Christ hath suffered for us in	3767

FORBAD (5) [FORBID]

Dt	2:37	nor *unto* whatsoever the LORD our God **f**	6680
Mt	3:14	But John **f** him, saying, I have need to be	1254
Mk	9:38	we **f** him, because he followeth not us.	2967
Lk	9:49	and we **f** him, because he followeth not	2967
2Pe	2:16	dumb ass speaking with man's voice **f**	2967

FORBARE (3) [FORBEAR]

1Sa	23:13	escaped from Keilah; and he **f** to go forth.	2308
2Ch	25:16	the prophet **f**, and said, I know that God	2308
Jer	41: 8	So he **f**, and slew them not among their	2308

FORBEAR (22) [FORBARE, FORBEARANCE, FORBEARETH, FORBEARING, FORBORN]

Ex	23: 5	wouldest **f** to help him, thou shalt surely	2308
Dt	23:22	if thou shalt **f** to vow, it shall be no sin in	2308
1Ki	22: 6	Ramoth-gilead to battle, or shall I **f**?	2308
	22:15	Ramoth-gilead to battle, or shall we **f**?	2308
2Ch	18: 5	go to Ramoth-gilead to battle, or shall I **f**?	2308
	18:14	go to Ramoth-gilead to battle, or shall I **f**?	2308
	25:16	**f**; why shouldest thou be smitten? Then	2308
	35:21	**f** thee from meddling with God, who *is*	2308
Ne	9:30	Yet many years didst thou **f** them,	4900+5921
Job	16: 6	and *though* I **f**, what am I eased?	2308
Pr	24:11	If thou **f** to deliver *them that are* drawn	2820
Jer	40: 4	thee to come with me *into* Babylon, **f**:	2308
Eze	2: 5	they will hear, or whether they will **f**,	2308
	2: 7	they will hear, or whether they will **f**:	2308
	3:11	they will hear, or whether they will **f**.	2308
	3:27	hear; and he that forbeareth, let him **f**:	2308
	24:17	**F** to cry, make no mourning for the dead,	1826
Zec	11:12	good, give *me* my price; and if not, **f**.	2308
1Co	9: 6	have not we power to **f** working?	3361
2Co	12: 6	but *now* I **f**, lest any man should think of	5339
1Th	3: 1	Wherefore when we could no longer **f**,	4722
	3: 5	For this cause, when I could no longer **f**,	4722

FORBEARANCE (2) [FORBEAR]

Ro	2: 4	of his goodness and **f** and longsuffering;	463
	3:25	of sins that are past, through the **f** of God;	463

FORBEARETH (2) [FORBEAR]

Nu	9:13	in a journey, and **f** to keep the passover,	2308
Eze	3:27	him hear; and he that **f**, let him forbear:	2310

FORBEARING (5) [FORBEAR]

Pr	25:15	By long **f** is a prince persuaded, and a soft	639
Jer	20: 9	I was weary with **f**, and I could not stay.	3557
Eph	4: 2	with longsuffering, **f** one another in love;	430
	6: 9	the same *things* unto them, **f** threatening:	447
Col	3:13	**F** one another, and forgiving one another,	430

FORBID (37) [FORBAD, FORBIDDEN, FORBIDDETH, FORBIDDING]

Ge	44: 7	**God f** that thy servants should do	2486
	44:17	he said, **God f** that I should do so:	2486
Nu	11:28	and said, My lord Moses, **f** them.	3607
Jos	22:29	**God f** that we should rebel against	2486
	24:16	**God f** that we should forsake the LORD,	2486
1Sa	12:23	**God f** that I should sin against the LORD	2486
	14:45	**God f**: *as* the LORD liveth, there shall not	2486
	20: 2	said unto him, **God f**; thou shalt not die:	2486
	24: 6	The LORD **f** that I should do this thing	2486
	26:11	The LORD **f** that I should stretch forth	2486
1Ki	21: 3	Naboth said to Ahab, The LORD **f** it me,	2486
1Ch	11:19	My God **f** it me, that I should do this	2486
Job	27: 5	**God f** that I should justify you: till I die I	2486
Mt	19:14	and **f** them not, to come unto me:	2967
Mk	9:39	But Jesus said, **F** him not: for there is no	2967
	10:14	to come unto me, and **f** them not:	2967
Lk	6:29	that taketh away thy cloke **f** not *to take*	2967
	9:50	Jesus said unto him, **F** *him* not: for he	2967

Lk	18:16	to come unto me, and **f** them not:	2967
	20:16	they heard *it*, they said, **God f.**	1096+3361
Ac	10:47	Can any man **f** water, that these should	2967
	24:23	he should **f** none of his acquaintance to	2967
Ro	3: 4	**God f:** yea, let God be true,	1096+3361
	3: 6	**God f:** for then how shall God	1096+3361
	3:31	**God f:** yea, we establish the law.	1096+3361
	6: 2	**God f.** How shall we, that are dead	1096+3361
	6:15	the law, but under grace? **God f.**	1096+3361
	7: 7	**God f.** Nay, I had not known sin,	1096+3361
	7:13	**God f.** But sin, that it might appear	1096+3361
	9:14	unrighteousness with God? **God f.**	1096+3361
	11: 1	**God f.** For I also am an Israelite,	1096+3361
	11:11	that they should fall? **God f:**	1096+3361
1Co	6:15	the members of an harlot? **God f.**	1096+3361
	14:39	and **f** not to speak with tongues.	2967
Gal	2:17	Christ the minister of sin? **God f.**	1096+3361
	3:21	**God f:** for if there had been a law	1096+3361
	6:14	But **God f** that I should glory,	1096+3361

FORBIDDEN (3) [FORBID]

Lev	5:17	commit any *of these things* which are **f** to	3808
Dt	4:23	which the LORD thy God hath **f** thee.	6680
Ac	16: 6	were **f** of the Holy Ghost to preach	2967

FORBIDDETH (1) [FORBID]

3Jn	1:10	**f** them that would, and casteth *them* out	2967

FORBIDDING (4) [FORBID]

Lk	23: 2	**f** to give tribute to Cesar, saying that he	2967
Ac	28:31	with all confidence, **no** man **f** him.	209
1Th	2:16	**F** us to speak to the Gentiles that they	2967
1Ti	4: 3	to marry, *and commanding* to abstain	2967

FORBORN (1) [FORBEAR]

Jer	51:30	mighty *men* of Babylon have **f** to fight,	2308

FORCE (19) [FORCED, FORCES, FORCIBLE, FORCING]

Ge	31:31	Peradventure thou wouldest **take by f**	1497
Dt	22:25	and the man **f** her, and lie with her:	2388
	34: 7	was not dim, nor his **natural f** abated.	3893
1Sa	2:16	*it me* now: and if not, I will take *it* by **f**.	2394
2Sa	13:12	Nay, my brother, do not **f** me;	6031
Ezr	4:23	and made them to cease by **f** and power.	153
Est	7: 8	Will he **f** the queen also before me in	3533
Job	30:18	the great **f** of *my disease* is my garment	3581
	40:16	and his **f** *is* in the navel of his belly.	202
Jer	18:21	out their *blood* by the **f** of the sword;	3027
	23:10	course is evil, and their **f** *is* not right.	1369
	48:45	the shadow of Heshbon because of the **f:**	3581
Eze	34: 4	with **f** and with cruelty have ye ruled	2394
	35: 5	**f** of the sword in the time of their	3027
Am	2:14	the strong shall not strengthen his **f**,	3581
Mt	11:12	and the violent **take** it **by f.**	726
Jn	6:15	that they would come and **take** him **by f**,	726
Ac	23:10	and to **take** him **by f** from among them,	726
Heb	9:17	For a testament *is* of **f** after *men* are dead:	949

FORCED (7) [FORCE]

Jdg	1:34	the Amorites **f** the children of Dan into	3905
	20: 5	concubine have they **f**, that she is dead.	6031
1Sa	13:12	I myself therefore, and offered a burnt	662
2Sa	13:14	stronger than she, **f** her, and lay with her.	6031
	13:22	because he had **f** his sister Tamar.	6031
	13:32	from the day that he **f** his sister Tamar.	6031
Pr	7:21	with the flattering of her lips she **f** him.	5080

FORCES (16) [FORCE]

2Ch	17: 2	placed **f** in all the fenced cities of Judah,	2428
Job	36:19	no, not gold, nor all the **f** of strength.	3981
Isa	60: 5	**f** of the Gentiles shall come unto thee.	2428
	60:11	that *men* may bring unto thee the **f** of	2428
Jer	40: 7	*Now* when all the captains of the **f** which	2428
	40:13	all the captains of the **f** that *were* in	2428
	41:11	the captains of the **f** that *were* with him,	2428
	41:13	the captains of the **f** that *were* with him,	2428
	41:16	the captains of the **f** that *were* with him,	2428
	42: 1	all the captains of the **f**, and Johanan	2428
	42: 8	all the captains of the **f** which *were* with	2428
	43: 4	all the captains of the **f**, and all the people,	2428
	43: 5	all the captains of the **f**, took all	2428
Da	11:10	and shall assemble a multitude of great **f:**	2428
	11:38	in his estate shall he honour the God of **f:**	4581
Ob	1:11	the strangers carried away captive his **f**,	2428

FORCIBLE (1) [FORCE]

Job	6:25	How **f** are right words! but what doth	4834

FORCING (2) [FORCE]

Dt	20:19	shalt not destroy the trees thereof by **f**	5080
Pr	30:33	so the **f** of wrath bringeth forth strife.	4330

FORD (1) [FORDS]

Ge	32:22	eleven sons, and passed over the **f** Jabbok.	4569

FORDS (3) [FORD]

Jos	2: 7	after them the way to Jordan unto the **f**:	4569
Jdg	3:28	took the **f** of Jordan toward Moab,	4569
Isa	16: 2	the daughters of Moab *are* at the **f** of	4569

FORECAST (2)

Da	11:24	he shall **f** his devices **against** the strong	2803
	11:25	he shall **f** devices against him.	2803

FOREFATHERS (2) [FATHER]

Jer	11:10	turned back to the iniquities of their **f**,	1+7223
2Ti	1: 3	whom I serve from *my* **f** with pure	4269

FOREFRONT (10) [FRONT]

Ex	26: 9	double the sixth curtain in the **f**	4136+6440
	28:37	upon the **f** of the mitre it shall be.	4136+6440
Lev	8: 9	also upon the mitre, *even* upon his **f**,	6440
1Sa	14: 5	The **f** of the one *was* situate northward	8127
2Sa	11:15	Set ye Uriah in the **f** of the hottest	4136+6440
2Ki	16:14	from the **f** of the house, from between	6440
2Ch	20:27	and Jehoshaphat in the **f** of them,	7218
Eze	40:19	measured the breadth from the **f**	6440+3807.1
	40:19	gate unto the **f** of the inner court without,	6440
	47: 1	before the house *stood toward* the east,	6440

FOREHEAD (16) [HEAD]

Ex	28:38	it shall be upon Aaron's **f**, that Aaron may	4696
	28:38	it shall be always upon his **f**, that they	4696
Lev	13:41	of *his head toward* his face, he *is* **f** bald:	1371
	13:42	bald head, or **bald f**, a white reddish sore;	1372
	13:42	sprung up in his bald head, or his **bald f**,	1372
	13:43	in his **bald f**, as the leprosy appeareth in	1372
1Sa	17:49	slang *it*, and smote the Philistine in his **f**,	4696
	17:49	forehead, that the stone sunk into his **f**;	4696
2Ch	26:19	the leprosy even rose up in his **f** before	4696
	26:20	he was leprous in his **f**, and they thrust	4696
Jer	3: 3	thou hadst a whore's **f**, thou refusedst to	4696
Eze	3: 8	and thy **f** strong against their foreheads.	4696
	3: 9	harder than flint have I made thy **f:**	4696
	16:12	I put a jewel on thy **f**, and earrings in	639
Rev	14: 9	receive *his* mark in his **f**, or in his hand,	3359
	17: 5	And upon her **f** *was* a name written,	3359

FOREHEADS (8) [HEAD]

Eze	3: 8	and thy forehead strong against their **f**.	4696
	9: 4	set a mark upon the **f** of the men that sigh	4696
Rev	7: 3	sealed the servants of our God in their **f**.	3359
	9: 4	which have not the seal of God in their **f**.	3359
	13:16	a mark in their right hand, or in their **f:**	3359
	14: 1	his Father's name written in their **f**.	3359
	20: 4	had received *his* mark upon their **f**,	3359
	22: 4	his face; and his name *shall be* in their **f**.	3359

FOREIGN See OUTLANDISH; STRANGE

FOREIGNER (2) [FOREIGNERS]

Ex	12:45	A **f** and a hired servant shall not eat	8453
Dt	15: 3	Of a **f** thou mayest exact *it again*: but	5237

FOREIGNERS (2) [FOREIGNER]

Ob	1:11	entered *into* his gates, and cast lots upon	5237
Eph	2:19	therefore ye are no more strangers and **f**,	3941

FOREKNEW (1) [KNOW]

Ro	11: 2	hath not cast away his people which he **f**.	4267

FOREKNOW (1) [KNOW]

Ro	8:29	whom he did **f**, he also did predestinate	4267

FOREKNOWLEDGE (2) [KNOW]

Ac	2:23	by the determinate counsel and **f** of God,	4268
1Pe	1: 2	Elect according to the **f** of God the Father,	4268

FOREMOST (3)

Ge	32:17	he commanded the **f**, saying, When Esau	7223
	33: 2	he put the handmaids and their children **f**,	7223
2Sa	18:27	Me thinketh the running of the **f** *is* like	7223

FOREORDAINED (1) [ORDAIN]

1Pe	1:20	Who verily was **f** before the foundation of	4267

FOREPART (5) [PART]

Ex	28:27	towards the **f** thereof, over against *the*	6440
	39:20	toward the **f** of it, over against	4136+6440
1Ki	6:20	the oracle in the **f** *was* twenty cubits in	6440
Eze	42: 7	towards the utter court on the **f** of	6440
Ac	27:41	and the stuck fast,	4408

FORERUNNER (1) [RUN]

Heb	6:20	Whither the **f** is for us entered, *even* Jesus,	4274

FORESAIL See MAINSAIL

FORESAW (1) [SEE]

Ac	2:25	I **f** the Lord always before my face, for he	4308

FORESEEING (1) [SEE]

Gal	3: 8	**f** that God would justify the heathen	4275

FORESEETH (2) [SEE]

Pr	22: 3	A prudent *man* **f** the evil,	7200
	27:12	A prudent *man* **f** the evil,	7200

FORESHIP (1) [SHIP]

Ac	27:30	they would have cast anchors out of the **f**,	4408

FORESKIN (9) [SKIN]

Ge	17:11	ye shall circumcise the flesh of your **f**;	6190
	17:14	whose flesh of his **f** is not circumcised,	6190
	17:23	circumcised the flesh of their **f** in	6190
	17:24	he was circumcised in the flesh of his **f**.	6190
	17:25	he was circumcised in the flesh of his **f**.	6190
Ex	4:25	cut off the **f** of her son, and cast *it* at his	6190
Lev	12: 3	in the eighth day the flesh of his **f** shall be	6190
Dt	10:16	Circumcise therefore the **f** of your heart,	6190
Hab	2:16	thou also, and let thy **f** be **uncovered**:	6188

FORESKINS (5) [SKIN]

Jos	5: 3	the children of Israel at the hill of the f.	6190
1Sa	18:25	but an hundred f of the Philistines,	6190
	18:27	David brought their f, and they gave	6190
2Sa	3:14	I espoused to me for an hundred f of	6190
Jer	4: 4	take away the f of your heart, ye men of	6190

FOREST (38) [FORESTS]

1Sa	22: 5	and came *into* the f of Hareth.	3293
1Ki	7: 2	built also the house of the f of Lebanon;	3293
	10:17	the king put them *in* the house of the f of	3293
	10:21	all the vessels of the house of the f of	3293
2Ki	19:23	his borders, *and into* the f of his Carmel.	3293
2Ch	9:16	the king put them *in* the house of the f of	3293
	9:20	all the vessels of the house of the f of	3293
Ne	2: 8	unto Asaph the keeper of the king's f,	6508
Ps	50:10	For every beast of the f *is* mine,	3293
	104:20	wherein all the beasts of the f do creep	3293
Isa	9:18	shall kindle in the thickets of the f,	3293
	10:18	shall consume the glory of his f, and of	3293
	10:19	the rest of the trees of his f shall be few,	3293
	10:34	shall cut down the thickets of the f with	3293
	21:13	In the f in Arabia shall ye lodge, O ye	3293
	22: 8	day to the armour of the house of the f.	3293
	29:17	the fruitful field shall be esteemed as a f?	3293
	32:15	and the fruitful field be counted for a f.	3293
	32:19	When it shall hail, coming down *on* the f;	3293
	37:24	of his border, *and* the f of his Carmel.	3293
	44:14	for himself among the trees of the f:	3293
	44:23	ye mountains, O f, and every tree therein:	3293
	56: 9	come to devour, *yea,* all ye beasts in the f.	3293
Jer	5: 6	Wherefore a lion out of the f shall slay	3293
	10: 3	*one* cutteth a tree out of the f, the work	3293
	12: 8	heritage is unto me as a lion in the f.	3293
	21:14	I will kindle a fire in the f thereof,	3293
	26:18	of the house as the high places of a f.	3293
	46:23	They shall cut down her f, saith	3293
Eze	15: 2	branch which is among the trees of the f?	3293
	15: 6	As the vine tree among the trees of the f,	3293
	20:46	prophesy against the f of the south field;	3293
	20:47	say to the f of the south, Hear the word of	3293
Hos	2:12	I will make them a f, and the beasts of	3293
Am	3: 4	Will a lion roar in the f, when he hath no	3293
Mic	3:12	of the house as the high places of the f.	3293
	5: 8	people as a lion among the beasts of the f,	3293
Zec	11: 2	for the f of the vintage is come down.	3293

FORESTS (3) [FOREST]

2Ch	27: 4	and in the f he built castles and towers.	2793
Ps	29: 9	the hinds to calve, and discovereth the f:	3295
Eze	39:10	field, neither cut down *any* out of the f;	3293

FORETELL (1) [TELL]

2Co	13: 2	f *you,* as if I were present the second *time;*	4302

FORETOLD (2) [TELL]

Mk	13:23	ye heed: behold, I have f you all *things.*	4302
Ac	3:24	spoken, have likewise f of these days.	4293

FOREWARN (1) [WARN]

Lk	12: 5	But I will f you whom you shall fear:	5263

FOREWARNED (1) [WARN]

1Th	4: 6	such, as we also have f you and testified.	4302

FORFEITED (1)

Ezr	10: 8	all his substance should be f,	2763

FORGAT (8) [FORGET]

Ge	40:23	chief butler remember Joseph, but f him.	7911
Jdg	3: 7	the Lord their God, and served Baalim	7911
1Sa	12: 9	when they f the Lord their God, he sold	7911
Ps	78:11	f his works, and his wonders that he had	7911
	106:13	They soon f his works; they waited not	7911
	106:21	They f God their saviour, which had done	7911
La	3:17	my soul far off from peace: I f prosperity.	5382
Hos	2:13	her lovers, and f me, saith the Lord.	7911

FORGAVE (9) [FORGIVE]

Ps	78:38	f *their* iniquity, and destroyed *them* not:	3722
Mt	18:27	and loosed him, and f him the debt.	863
	18:32	f thee all that debt, because thou desiredst	863
Lk	7:42	nothing to pay, he **frankly** f *them* both.	5483
	7:43	I suppose that *he,* to whom he f most.	5483
2Co	2:10	for if I f any *thing,* to whom I forgave *it,*	5483
	2:10	for if I forgave any *thing,* to whom I f *it,*	5483
	2:10	for your sakes f *I it* in the person of Christ;	NIG
Col	3:13	even as Christ f you, so also *do* ye.	5483

FORGAVEST (2) [FORGIVE]

Ps	32: 5	and thou f the iniquity of my sin.	5375
	99: 8	thou wast a God that f them, though thou	5375

FORGED (1) [FORGERS]

Ps	119:69	The proud have f a lie against me: *but* I	2950

FORGERS (1) [FORGED]

Job	13: 4	ye *are* f of lies, ye *are* all physicians of no	2950

FORGET (54) [FORGAT, FORGETFUL, FORGETFULNESS, FORGETTEST, FORGETTETH, FORGETTING]

Ge	27:45	he f *that* which thou hast done to him:	7911
	41:51	*said he,* hath **made** me f all my toil,	5382
Dt	4: 9	lest thou f the things which thine eyes	7911
	4:23	lest ye f the covenant of the Lord your	7911

Dt	4:31	nor f the covenant of thy fathers which he	7911
	6:12	*Then* beware lest thou f the Lord,	7911
	8:11	Beware that thou f not the Lord thy	7911
	8:14	lifted up, and thou f the Lord thy God,	7911
	8:19	if thou **do at all** f the Lord thy	7911+7911
	9: 7	Remember, *and* f not, how thou	7911
	25:19	from under heaven; thou shalt not f *it.*	7911
1Sa	1:11	not f thine handmaid, but wilt give unto	7911
2Ki	17:38	that I have made with you ye shall not f;	7911
Job	8:13	So *are* the paths of all that f God;	7911
	9:27	If I say, I will f my complaint, I will leave	7911
	11:16	Because thou shalt f *thy* misery,	7911
	24:20	The womb shall f him; the worm shall	7911
Ps	9:17	into hell, *and* all the nations that f God.	7913
	10:12	God, lift up thine hand: f not the humble.	7911
	13: 1	How long wilt thou f me, O Lord?	7911
	45:10	f also thine own people, and thy father's	7911
	50:22	consider this, ye that f God, lest I tear	7911
	59:11	Slay them not, lest my people f:	7911
	74:19	f not the congregation of thy poor for ever.	7911
	74:23	F not the voice of thine enemies:	7911
	78: 7	not f the works of God, but keep his	7911
	102: 4	so that I f to eat my bread.	7911
	103: 2	O my soul, and f not all his benefits:	7911
	119:16	in thy statutes: I will not f thy word.	7911
	119:83	in the smoke; *yet* do I not f thy statutes.	7911
	119:93	I will never f thy precepts: for with them	7911
	119:109	in my hand: yet do I not f thy law.	7911
	119:141	and despised: *yet* do not I f thy precepts.	7911
	119:153	and deliver me: for I do not f thy law.	7911
	119:176	for I do not f thy commandments.	7911
	137: 5	If I f thee, O Jerusalem, let my right hand	7911
	137: 5	let my right hand *her* cunning.	7911
Pr	3: 1	My son, f not my law; but let thine heart	7911
	4: 5	f *it* not; neither decline from the words of	7911
	31: 5	f the law, and pervert the judgment of	7911
	31: 7	his poverty, and remember his misery	7911
Isa	49:15	Can a woman f her sucking child, that	7911
	49:15	yea, they may f, yet will I not forget thee.	7911
	49:15	yea, they may forget, yet will I not f thee.	7911
	54: 4	for thou shalt f the shame of thy youth,	7911
	65:11	that f my holy mountain, that prepare a	7913
Jer	2:32	Can a maid f her ornaments, *or* a bride	7911
	23:27	Which think to **cause** my people to f my	7911
	23:39	will **utterly** f you, and I will forsake	5377+5382
La	5:20	Wherefore dost thou f us for ever,	7911
Hos	4: 6	law of thy God, I will also f thy children.	7911
Am	8: 7	Surely I will never f any of their works.	7911
Heb	6:10	For God *is* not unrighteous to f your work	1950
	13:16	But to do good and to communicate f not:	1950

FORGETFUL (2) [FORGET]

Heb	13: 2	be not f to entertain strangers: for thereby	1950
Jas	1:25	continueth *therein,* he being not a f hearer	1953

FORGETFULNESS (1) [FORGET]

Ps	88:12	and thy righteousness in the land of f?	5388

FORGETTEST (2) [FORGET]

Ps	44:24	*and* f our affliction and our oppression?	7911
Isa	51:13	the Lord thy Maker, that hath stretched	7911

FORGETTETH (4) [FORGET]

Job	39:15	f that the foot may crush them, or *that*	7911
Ps	9:12	he f not the cry of the humble.	7911
Pr	2:17	her youth, and f the covenant of her God.	7911
Jas	1:24	straightway f what manner of *man* he was.	1950

FORGETTING (1) [FORGET]

Php	3:13	one *thing I do,* f those *things* which are	1950

FORGIVE (56) [FORGAVE, FORGAVEST, FORGIVEN, FORGIVENESS, FORGIVENESSES, FORGIVETH, FORGIVING, FORGOT, FORGOTTEN]

Ge	50:17	F, I pray thee now, the trespass of thy	5375
	50:17	the trespass of the servants of the God	5375
Ex	10:17	Now therefore f, I pray thee, my sin only	5375
	32:32	now, if thou wilt f their sin—; and if not,	5375
Nu	30: 5	the Lord shall f her, because her father	5545
	30: 8	of none effect: and the Lord shall f her.	5545
	30:12	them void; and the Lord shall f her.	5545
Jos	24:19	he will not f your transgressions nor your	5375
1Sa	25:28	thee, f the trespass of thine handmaid:	5545
1Ki	8:30	dwelling place: and when thou hearest, f.	5545
	8:34	f the sin of thy people Israel,	5545
	8:36	f the sin of thy servants, and of thy people	5545
	8:39	f, and do, and give to every man	5545
	8:50	f thy people that have sinned against thee,	5545
2Ch	6:21	from heaven; and when thou hearest, f.	5545
	6:25	f the sin of thy people Israel,	5545
	6:27	f the sin of thy servants, and of thy people	5545
	6:30	f, and render unto every man according	5545
	6:39	f thy people which have sinned against	5545
	7:14	will f their sin, and will heal their land.	5545
Ps	25:18	and my pain; and f all my sins.	5375
	86: 5	For thou, Lord, *art* good, and **ready to f;**	5546
Isa	2: 9	humbleth himself; therefore f them not.	5375
Jer	18:23	against me to slay *me:* f not their iniquity,	3722
	31:34	for I will f their iniquity, and I will	5545
	36: 3	that I may f their iniquity and their sin.	5545
	9:19	O Lord, hear; O Lord, f; O Lord, hearken	5545
Am	7: 2	I said, O Lord God, f, I beseech thee:	5545
Mt	6:12	And f us our debts, as we forgive our	863
	6:12	forgive us our debts, as we f our debtors.	863

Mt	6:14	For if ye f men their trespasses,	863
	6:14	your heavenly Father will also f you:	863
	6:15	But if ye f not men their trespasses,	863
	6:15	neither will your Father f your trespasses.	863
	9: 6	Son of man hath power on earth to f sins,	863
	18:21	my brother sin against me, and I f him?	863
	18:35	if ye from your hearts f not every one his	863
Mk	2: 7	who can f sins but God only?	863
	2:10	Son of man hath power on earth to f sins,	863
	11:25	And when ye stand praying, f, if ye have	863
	11:25	is in heaven may f you your trespasses.	863
	11:26	But if ye do not f, neither will your Father	863
	11:26	will your Father which is in heaven f	863
Lk	5:21	Who can f sins, but God alone?	863
	5:24	of man hath power upon earth to f sins,	863
	6:37	be condemned: f, and ye shall be forgiven:	630
	11: 4	And f us our sins; for we also forgive every	863
	11: 4	we also f every one *that* is indebted to us.	863
	17: 3	rebuke him; and if he repent, f him.	863
	17: 4	to thee, saying, I repent; thou shalt f him.	863
	23:34	Then said Jesus, Father, f them; for they	863
2Co	2: 7	So that contrariwise ye *ought* rather to f	5483
	2:10	To whom ye f any *thing,* I forgive also:	5483
	2:10	To whom ye forgive any *thing,* I f also:	NIG
	2:13	not burdensome to you? f me this wrong.	5483
1Jn	1: 9	he is faithful and just to f us *our* sins,	863

FORGIVEN (42) [FORGIVE]

Lev	4:20	for them, and it shall be f them.	5545
	4:26	concerning his sin, and it shall be f him.	5545
	4:31	atonement for him, and it shall be f him.	5545
	4:35	hath committed, and it shall be f him.	5545
	5:10	he had sinned, and it shall be f him.	5545
	5:13	in one of these, and it shall be f him:	5545
	5:16	trespass offering, and it shall be f him.	5545
	5:18	and wist *it* not, and it shall be f him.	5545
	6: 7	it shall be f him for any *thing* of all that	5545
	19:22	sin which he hath done shall be f him.	5545
Nu	14:19	as thou hast f this people, from Egypt	5375
	15:25	children of Israel, and it shall be f them;	5545
	15:26	it shall be f all the congregation of	5545
	15:28	atonement for him; and it shall be f him.	5545
Dt	21: 8	And the blood shall be f them.	3722
Ps	32: 1	Blessed *is* he whose transgression *is* f,	5375
	85: 2	Thou hast f the iniquity of thy people,	5375
Isa	33:24	people that dwell therein shall be f their	5375
Mt	9: 2	Son, be of good cheer; thy sins be f thee.	863
	9: 5	is easier, to say, *Thy* sins be f thee;	863
	12:31	of sin and blasphemy shall be f unto men:	863
	12:31	the *Holy* Ghost shall not be f unto men.	863
	12:32	against the Son of man, it shall be f him:	863
	12:32	it shall not be f him, neither in this world,	863
Mk	2: 5	sick of the palsy, Son, thy sins be f thee.	863
	2: 9	to the sick of the palsy, *Thy* sins be f thee;	863
	3:28	All sins shall be f unto the sons of men,	863
	4:12	and *their* sins should be f them.	863
Lk	5:20	he said unto him, Man, thy sins are f thee.	863
	5:23	is easier, to say, Thy sins be f thee;	863
	6:37	be condemned: forgive, and ye shall be f:	630
	7:47	thee, Her sins, which are many, are f;	863
	7:47	to whom little is f, *the same* loveth little.	863
	7:48	And he said unto her, Thy sins are f.	863
	12:10	against the Son of man, it shall be f him:	863
	12:10	against the Holy Ghost it shall not be f.	863
Ac	8:22	perhaps the thought of thine heart may be f	863
Ro	4: 7	Blessed *are they* whose iniquities are f,	863
Eph	4:32	even as God for Christ's sake hath f you.	5483
Col	2:13	with him, having f you all trespasses;	5483
Jas	5:15	have committed sins, they shall be f him.	863
1Jn	2:12	*your* sins are f you for his name's sake.	863

FORGIVENESS (7) [FORGIVE]

Ps	130: 4	*there is* f with thee, that thou mayest be	5547
Mk	3:29	against the Holy Ghost hath never f,	859
Ac	5:31	to give repentance to Israel, and f of sins.	859
	13:38	this *man* is preached unto you the f of sins:	859
	26:18	that they may receive f of sins,	859
Eph	1: 7	the f of sins, according to the riches of his	859
Col	1:14	through his blood, *even* the f of sins:	859

FORGIVENESSES (1) [FORGIVE]

Da	9: 9	the Lord our God *belong* mercies and f,	5547

FORGIVETH (2) [FORGIVE]

Ps	103: 3	Who f all thine iniquities; who healeth all	5545
Lk	7:49	Who is this that f sins also?	863

FORGIVING (4) [FORGIVE]

Ex	34: 7	f iniquity and transgression and sin,	5375
Nu	14:18	f iniquity and transgression, and by no	5375
Eph	4:32	to another, tenderhearted, f one another,	5483
Col	3:13	Forbearing one another, and f one another	5483

FORGOT (1) [FORGIVE]

Dt	24:19	hast f a sheaf in the field, thou shalt not	7911

FORGOTTEN (46) [FORGIVE]

Ge	41:30	all the plenty shall be f in the land of	7911
Dt	26:13	commandments, neither have I f *them:*	7911
	31:21	it shall not be f out of the mouths of	7911
	32:18	and hast f God that formed thee.	7911
Job	19:14	and my familiar friends have f me.	7911
	28: 4	inhabitant; *even the waters* f of the foot:	7911
Ps	9:18	For the needy shall not alway be f:	7911
	10:11	He hath said in his heart, God hath f:	7911

Ps 31:12 I am f as a dead man out of mind: I am 7911
42: 9 unto God my rock, Why hast thou f me? 7911
44:17 yet have we not f thee, neither have we 7911
44:20 If we have f the name of our God, 7911
77: 9 Hath God f to be gracious? hath he in 7911
119:61 have robbed me: but I have not f thy law. 7911
119:139 because mine enemies have f thy words. 7911
Ecc 2:16 now is, in the days to come shall all be f. 7911
8:10 they were f in the city where they had so 7911
9: 5 a reward; for the memory of them is f. 7911
Isa 17:10 Because thou hast f the God of thy 7911
23:15 that Tyre shall be f seventy years, 7911
23:16 the city, thou harlot that hast been f; 7911
42:21 O Israel, thou shalt not be f of me. 5382
49:14 forsaken me, and my Lord hath f me. 7911
65:16 because the former troubles are f, 7911
Jer 2:32 yet my people have f me days without 7911
3:21 and they have f the LORD their God. 7911
13:25 because thou hast f me, and trusted in 7911
18:15 Because my people hath f me, they have 7911
20:11 everlasting confusion shall never be f. 7911
23:27 as their fathers have f my name for Baal. 7911
23:40 a perpetual shame, which shall not be f. 7911
30:14 All thy lovers have f thee; they seek thee 7911
44: 9 Have ye f the wickedness of your fathers, 7911
50: 5 a perpetual covenant that shall not be f. 7911
50: 6 to hill, they have f their resting place. 7911
La 2: 6 **caused** the solemn feasts and sabbaths to be f 7911
Eze 22:12 and hast f me, saith the Lord GOD. 7911
23:35 thou hast f me, and cast me behind 7911
Hos 4: 6 seeing thou hast f the law of thy God, 7911
8:14 For Israel hath f his Maker, 7911
13: 6 was exalted; therefore have they f me. 7911
Mt 16: 5 the other side, they had f to take bread. 1950
Mk 8:14 Now *the disciples* had f to take bread, 1950
Lk 12: 6 and not one of them is f before God? 1950
Heb 12: 5 And ye have f the exhortation which 1585
2Pe 1: 9 f that *he* was purged from his old 2983+3024

FORKS (1)
1Sa 13:21 for the f, and for the axes, 7053+7969

FORM (24) [FORMED, FORMER, FORMETH, FORMS]
Ge 1: 2 the earth was **without** f, and void; 8414
1Sa 28:14 he said unto her, What f is he of? 8389
2Sa 14:20 To fetch about *this* f of speech hath thy 6440
2Ch 4: 7 candlesticks of gold according to their f, 4941
Job 4:16 but I could not discern the f thereof: 4758
Isa 45: 7 I f the light, and create darkness: I make 3335
52:14 and his f more than the sons of men: 8389
53: 2 he hath no f nor comeliness; and when 8389
Jer 4:23 and lo, it was **without** f, and void; 8414
Eze 8: 3 he put forth the f of a hand, and took me 8403
8:10 behold every f of creeping things, 8403
10: 8 there appeared in the cherubims the f of 8403
43:11 shew them the f of the house, 6699
43:11 that they may keep the whole f thereof, 6699
Da 2:31 thee; and the f thereof *was* terrible. 7299
3:19 the f of his visage was changed against 6755
3:25 the f of the fourth *is* like the Son of God. 7299
Mk 16:12 that he appeared in another f unto two 3444
Ro 2:20 which hast the f of knowledge and of 3446
6:17 ye have obeyed from the heart *that* f of 5179
Php 2: 6 Who, being in the f of God, thought it not 3444
2: 7 and took *upon him* the f of a servant, 3444
2Ti 1:13 Hold fast the f of sound words, which 5296
3: 5 Having a f of godliness, but denying 3446

FORMED (33) [FORM]
Ge 2: 7 the LORD God f man *of* the dust of 3335
2: 8 there he put the man whom he had f. 3335
2:19 out of the ground the LORD God f every 3335
Dt 32:18 and hast forgotten God that f thee. 2342
2Ki 19:25 *and* of ancient times that I have f it? 3335
Job 26: 5 Dead *things* are f from under the waters, 2342
26:13 his hand hath f the crooked serpent. 2342
33: 6 in God's stead: I also am f out of the clay. 7169
Ps 90: 2 ever thou hadst f the earth and the world, 2342
94: 9 hear? he that f the eye, shall he not see? 3335
95: 5 he made it: and his hands f the dry *land.* 3335
Pr 26:10 The great *God* that f all *things* both 2342
Isa 27:11 he that f them will shew them no favour. 3335
37:26 *and* of ancient times, that I have f it? 3335
43: 1 O Jacob, and he that f thee, O Israel, 3335
43: 7 created him for my glory, I have f him; 3335
43:10 before me there was no God f, neither 3335
43:21 This people have I f for myself; they shall 3335
44: 2 f thee from the womb, *which* will help 3335
44:10 Who hath f a god, or molten a graven 3335
44:21 I have f thee; thou *art* my servant: 3335
44:24 and he that f thee from the womb, 3335
45:18 God himself that f the earth and made it; 3335
45:18 it not in vain, he f it to be inhabited: 3335
49: 5 saith the LORD that f me from the womb 3335
54:17 No weapon that is f against thee shall 3335
Jer 1: 5 Before I f thee in the belly I knew thee; 3335
33: 2 the LORD that f it, to establish it; 3335
Am 7: 1 he f grasshoppers in the beginning of 3335
Ro 9:20 Shall the thing say to him that formed *it,* 4110
9:20 the thing formed say to him that f *it,* 4111
Gal 4:19 in birth again until Christ be f in you, 3445
1Ti 2:13 For Adam was first f, then Eve. 4111

FORMER (50) [FORM]
Ge 40:13 after the f manner when thou wast his 7223
Nu 21:26 had fought against the f king of Moab, 7223
Dt 24: 4 Her f husband, which sent her away, 7223
Ru 4: 7 this *was the manner* in f time 6440+3807.1
1Sa 17:30 people answered him again after the f 7223
2Ki 17:34 up the two captains of the f fifties 7223
17:34 Unto this day they do after the f manners: 7223
17:40 but they did after their f manner. 7223
Ne 5:15 the f governors that *had been* before me 7223
Job 8: 8 of the f age, and prepare *thyself* to 7223
8: 3 *into* the wilderness **in** f time desolate 570
Ps 79: 8 O remember not against us f iniquities: 7223
89:49 Lord, where *are* thy f lovingkindnesses, 7223
Ecc 1:11 *There is* no remembrance of f *things;* 7223
1:11 What is the cause that the f days were 7223
Isa 41:22 let them shew the f *things,* what they be, 7223
42: 9 the f *things* are come to pass, 7223
43: 9 shew us f *things?* let them bring forth 7223
43:18 Remember ye not the f *things,* neither 7223
46: 9 Remember the f *things* of old: for I *am* 7223
48: 3 I have declared the f *things* from 7223
61: 4 they shall raise up the f desolations, 7223
65: 7 will I measure their f work into their 7223
65:16 because the f troubles are forgotten, 7223
65:17 the f shall not be remembered, nor come 7223
Jer 5:24 both the f and the latter, in his season: 3138
10:16 for he *is* the f of all *things;* and Israel *is* 3335
34: 5 the f kings which were before thee, 7223
36:28 write in it all the f words that were in 7223
51:19 for he *is* the f of all *things:* and Israel *is* 3335
Eze 16:55 shall return to their f **estate**, and Samaria 6927
16:55 daughters shall return to their f **estate**, 6927
16:55 daughters shall return to your f **estate**. 6927
Da 11:29 set forth a multitude greater than the f, 7223
11:29 but it shall not be as the f, or as the latter. 7223
Hos 6: 3 as the latter *and* f rain *unto* the earth. 3384
Joel 2:23 for he hath given you the f **rain** 4175
2:23 the f **rain**, and the latter rain in the first 4175
Hag 2: 9 latter house shall be greater than of the f, 7223
Zec 1: 4 unto whom the f prophets have cried, 7223
7: 7 the LORD hath cried by the f prophets, 7223
7:12 hath sent in his spirit by the f prophets: 7223
8:11 the residue of this people as *in* the f days, 7223
14: 8 half of them toward the f sea, and half of 6931
Mal 3: 4 as *in* the days of old, and as *in* f years. 6931
Ac 1: 1 The f treatise have I made, O Theophilus, 4413
Eph 4:22 That ye put off concerning the f 4387
Heb 10:32 But call to remembrance the f days, 4387
1Pe 1:14 fashioning yourselves according to the f 4387
Rev 21: 4 pain: for the f *things* are passed away. 4413

FORMETH (2) [FORM]
Am 4:13 he that f the mountains, and createth 3335
Zec 12: 1 and f the spirit of man within him. 3335

FORMS (2) [FORM]
Eze 43:11 all the f thereof, and all the ordinances 6699
43:11 all the f thereof, and all the laws thereof: 6699

FORNICATION (36) [FORNICATIONS, FORNICATOR, FORNICATORS]
2Ch 21:11 **caused** the inhabitants of Jerusalem **to commit** f, 2181
Isa 23:17 shall **commit** f with all the kingdoms of 2181
Eze 16:26 Thou hast also **committed** f with 2181
16:29 Thou hast moreover multiplied thy f in 8457
Mt 5:32 saving for the cause of f, causeth her to 4202
19: 9 except it be for f, and shall marry another, 4202
Jn 8:41 said to them, We be not born of f; 4202
Ac 15:20 and *from* f, and *from* things strangled, 4202
15:29 and from things strangled, and from f: 4202
21:25 blood, and from strangled, and from f. 4202
Ro 1:29 f, wickedness, covetousness, 4202
1Co 5: 1 It is reported commonly *that there is* f 4202
5: 1 and such f as is not so much as named 4202
6:13 the body *is* not for f, but for the Lord; 4202
6:18 Flee f. Every sin that a man doeth is 4202
6:18 he that **committeth** f sinneth against his 4203
7: 2 Nevertheless, to avoid f, let every man 4202
7: 2 Neither let us **commit** f, as some of them 4203
2Co 12:21 not repented of the uncleanness and f and 4202
Gal 5:19 f, uncleanness, lasciviousness, 4202
Eph 5: 3 f, and all uncleanness, or covetousness, 4202
Col 3: 5 f, uncleanness, inordinate affection, 4202
1Th 4: 3 that ye should abstain from f: 4202
Jude 1: 7 like manner **giving** themselves **over to** f, 1608
Rev 2:14 sacrificed unto idols, and to **commit** f. 4203
2:20 and to seduce my servants to **commit** f, 4203
2:21 And I gave her space to repent of her f; 4202
9:21 nor of their f, nor of their thefts. 4202
14: 8 drink of the wine of the wrath of her f. 4202
17: 2 the kings of the earth have **committed** f, 4203
17: 2 been made drunk with the wine of her f. 4202
17: 4 of abominations and filthiness of her f: 4202
18: 3 drunk of the wine of the wrath of her f, 4202
18: 3 the kings of the earth have **committed** f, 4203
18: 9 who have **committed** f and 4203
19: 2 which did corrupt the earth with her f, 4202

FORNICATIONS (3) [FORNICATION]
Eze 16:15 pouredst out thy f on every one that 8457
Mt 15:19 adulteries, f, thefts, false witness, 4202
Mk 7:21 evil thoughts, adulteries, f, murders, 4202

FORNICATOR (2) [FORNICATION]
1Co 5:11 if any *man that is* called a brother be a f: 4205
Heb 12:16 Lest there *be* any f, or profane *person,* as 4205

FORNICATORS (3) [FORNICATION]
1Co 5: 9 you in an epistle not to company with f: 4205
5:10 not altogether with the f of this world, 4205
6: 9 neither f, nor idolaters, nor adulterers, 4205

FORSAKE (58) [FORSAKEN, FORSAKETH, FORSAKING, FORSOOK, FORSOOKEST]
Dt 4:31 he will not f thee, neither destroy thee, 7503
12:19 Take heed to thyself that thou f not 5800
14:27 *is* within thy gates; thou shalt not f him; 5800
31: 6 thee; he will not fail thee, nor f thee. 5800
31: 8 he will not fail thee, neither f thee: 5800
31:16 will f me, and break my covenant which 5800
31:17 will f them, and I will hide my face from 5800
Jos 1: 5 with thee: I will not fail thee, nor f thee. 5800
24:16 God forbid that we should f the LORD, 5800
24:20 If ye f the LORD, and serve strange gods, 5800
Jdg 9:11 Should I f my sweetness, and my good 2308
1Sa 12:22 For the LORD will not f his people for his 5800
1Ki 6:13 of Israel, and will not f my people Israel. 5800
8:57 fathers: let him not leave us, nor f us: 5203
2Ki 21:14 will f the remnant of mine inheritance, 5800
1Ch 28: 9 thou f him, he will cast thee off for ever. 5800
28: 20 he will not fail thee, nor f thee, until 5800
2Ch 7:19 f my statutes and my commandments, 5800
15: 2 you; but if ye f him, he will forsake you. 5800
15: 2 you; but if ye forsake him, he will f you. 5800
Ezr 8:22 his wrath *is* against all them that f him. 5800
Ne 9:31 not utterly consume them, nor f them; 5800
10:39 and we will not f the house of our God. 5800
Job 20:13 *Though* he spare it, and f it not; but keep 5800
Ps 27: 9 leave me not, neither f me, O God of my 5800
27:10 When my father and my mother f me, 5800
37: 8 Cease from anger, and f wrath: fret not 5800
38:21 F me not, O LORD: O my God, be not far 5800
71: 9 age; f me not when my strength faileth. 5800
71:18 am old and grayheaded, O God, f me not; 5800
89:30 If his children f my law, and walk not in 5800
94:14 people, neither will he f his inheritance. 5800
119: 8 will keep thy statutes: O f me not utterly. 5800
119:53 because of the wicked that f thy law. 5800
138: 8 f not the works of thine own hands. 7503
Pr 1: 8 father, and f not the law of thy mother: 5203
3: 1 Let not mercy and truth f thee: bind them 5800
4: 2 give you good doctrine, f you not my law. 5800
4: 6 F her not, and she shall preserve thee: 5800
6:20 and f not the law of thy mother: 5203
9: 6 F the foolish, and live; and go in the way 5800
27:10 own friend, and thy father's friend, f not; 5800
28: 4 They that f the law praise the wicked: 5800
Isa 1:28 they that f the LORD shall be consumed, 5800
41:17 *I* the God of Israel will not f them. 5800
42:16 will I do unto them, and not f them. 5800
55: 7 Let the wicked f his way, 5800
65:11 ye *are* they that f the LORD, that forget 5800
Jer 17:13 all that f thee shall be ashamed, 5800
23:33 I will even f you, saith the LORD. 5203
23:39 I will f you, and the city that I gave you 5203
51: 9 f her, and let us go every one into his own 5800
La 5:20 forget us for ever, *and* f us so long time? 5800
Eze 20: 8 neither did they f the idols of Egypt: 5800
Da 11:30 have intelligence with them that f the 5800
Jnh 2: 8 They that observe lying vanities f their 5800
Ac 21:21 are among the Gentiles to f Moses, 575+646
Heb 13: 5 said, I will never leave thee, nor f thee. 1459

FORSAKEN (76) [FORSAKE]
Dt 28:20 of thy doings, whereby thou hast f me. 5800
29:25 Because they have f the covenant of 5800
Jdg 6:13 now the LORD hath f us, and delivered us 5203
10:10 both because we have f our God, 5800
10:13 Yet ye have f me, and served other gods: 5800
1Sa 8: 8 wherewith they have f me, and served 5800
12:10 because we have f the LORD, 5800
1Ki 11:33 Because that they have f me, 5800
18:18 in that ye have f the commandments of 5800
19:10 for the children of Israel have f thy 5800
19:14 the children of Israel have f thy covenant, 5800
2Ki 22:17 Because they have f me, and have burnt 5800
2Ch 12: 5 Ye have f me, and *therefore* have I also 5800
13:10 LORD *is* our God, and we have not f him; 5800
13:11 of the LORD our God; but ye have f him. 5800
21:10 he have f the LORD God of his fathers. 5800
24:20 because ye have f the LORD, he hath also 5800
24:20 forsaken the LORD, he hath also f you. 5800
24:24 they had f the LORD God of their fathers. 5800
28: 6 they had f the LORD God of their fathers. 5800
29: 6 have f him, and have turned away their 5800
34:25 Because they have f me, and have burned 5800
Ezr 9: 9 yet our God hath not f us in our bondage, 5800
9:10 for we have f thy commandments, 5800
Ne 13:11 and said, Why is the house of God f? 5800
Job 18: 4 shall the earth be f for thee? and shall 5800
20:19 he hath oppressed *and* hath f the poor; 5800
Ps 9:10 LORD, hast not f them that seek thee. 5800
22: 1 My God, my God, why hast thou f me? 5800
37:25 have I not seen the righteous f, nor his 5800
71:11 Saying, God hath f him: persecute and 5800
Isa 1: 4 they have f the LORD, they have 5800
2: 6 thou hast f thy people the house 5203
7:16 the land that thou abhorrest shall be f of 5800

F

Isa 17: 2 The cities of Aroer are f: they shall be for — 5800
17: 9 In that day shall his strong cities be as a f — 5800
27:10 and the habitation f, and left like a — 7971
32:14 Because the palaces shall be f; — 5203
49:14 The Lord hath f me, and my Lord hath — 5800
54: 6 the Lord hath called thee as a woman f — 5800
54: 7 For a small moment have I f thee; — 5800
60:15 Whereas thou hast been f and hated, — 5800
62: 4 Thou shalt no more be termed F; — 5800
62:12 shalt be called, Sought out, A city not f. — 5800
Jer 1:16 who have f me, and have burnt incense — 5800
2:13 they have f me the fountain of living — 5800
2:17 in that thou hast the Lord thy God, — 5800
2:19 that thou hast the Lord thy God, — 5800
4:29 every city shall be f, and not a man dwell — 5800
5: 7 thy children have f me, and sworn by — 5800
5:19 Like as ye have f me, and served strange — 5800
7:29 and f the generation of his wrath. — 5203
9:13 Because they have f my law which I set — 5800
9:19 because we have f the land, because — 5800
12: 7 I have f mine house, I have left mine — 5800
15: 6 Thou hast f me, saith the Lord, thou art — 5203
16:11 Because your fathers have f me, saith — 5800
16:11 have f me, and have not kept my law; — 5800
17:13 because they have f the Lord, — 5800
18:14 that come from another place be f? — 5428
19: 4 Because they have f me, — 5800
22: 9 Because they have f the covenant of — 5800
25:38 He hath f his covert, as the lion: for their — 5800
51: 5 Israel hath not been f, nor Judah of his — 488
Eze 8:12 seeth us not; the Lord hath f the earth. — 5800
9: 9 The Lord hath f the earth, — 5800
36: 4 the cities that are f, which became a prey — 5800
Am 5: 2 she is f upon her land; there is none to — 5203
Zep 2: 4 For Gaza shall be f, and Ashkelon a — 5800
Mt 19:27 Behold, we have f all, and followed thee; — 863
19:29 And every one that hath f houses, — 863
27:46 My God, my God, why hast thou f me? — 1459
Mk 15:34 My God, my God, why hast thou f me? — 1459
2Co 4: 9 Persecuted, but not f; cast down, — 1459
2Ti 4:10 For Demas hath f me, having loved this — 1459
2Pe 2:15 Which have f the right way, and are gone — 2641

FORSAKETH (6) [FORSAKE]
Job 6:14 friend; but he f the fear of the Almighty. — 5800
Ps 37:28 loveth judgment, and f not his saints; — 5800
Pr 2:17 Which f the guide of her youth, — 5800
15:10 Correction is grievous unto him that f — 5800
28:13 and f them shall have mercy. — 5800
Lk 14:33 whosoever he be of you that f not all that — 657

FORSAKING (2) [FORSAKE]
Isa 6:12 there be a great f in the midst of the land. — 5805
Heb 10:25 The not the assembling of ourselves together, — 1459

FORSOMUCH (2) [FOR, MUCH, SO]
Isa 8: 6 F as this people refuseth the waters — 3282+3588
Lk 19: 9 f as he also is a son of Abraham. — 2530

FORSOOK (24) [FORSAKE]
Dt 32:15 then he f God which made him, — 5203
Jdg 2:12 And they f the Lord God of their fathers, — 5800
2:13 they f the Lord, and served Baal and — 5800
10: 6 and f the Lord, and served not him. — 5800
1Sa 31: 7 sons were dead, they f the cities, and fled; — 5800
1Ki 9: 9 Because they f the Lord their God, — 5800
12: 8 he f the counsel of the old men, which — 5800
12:13 the old men's counsel that they gave — 5800
2Ki 21:22 he f the Lord God of his fathers, — 5800
1Ch 10: 7 dead, then they f their cities, and fled: — 5800
2Ch 7:22 Because they f the Lord God of their — 5800
10: 8 he f the counsel which the old men gave — 5800
10:13 king Rehoboam the counsel of the old — 5800
12: 1 he f the law of the Lord, and all Israel — 5800
Ps 78:60 So that he f the tabernacle of Shiloh, — 5203
119:87 me upon earth; but I f not thy precepts. — 5800
Isa 58: 2 and f not the ordinance of their God: — 5800
Jer 14: 5 and f it, because there was no grass. — 5800
Mt 26:56 Then all the disciples f him, and fled. — 863
Mk 1:18 And straightway they f their nets, — 863
14:50 And they all f him, and fled. — 863
Lk 5:11 had brought their ships to land, they f all, — 863
2Ti 4:16 no man stood with me, but all men f me: — 1459
Heb 11:27 By faith he f Egypt, not fearing the wrath — 2641

FORSOOKEST (2) [FORSAKE]
Ne 9:17 and of great kindness, and f them not. — 5800
9:19 Yet thou in thy manifold mercies f them — 5800

FORSWEAR (1) [SWEAR]
Mt 5:33 Thou shalt not f thyself, but shalt perform — 1964

FORT (6) [FORTIFIED, FORTIFY, FORTRESS, FORTRESSES, FORTS]
2Sa 5: 9 So David dwelt in the f, and called it — 4686
Isa 25:12 the fortress of the high f thy walls shall — 4869
Eze 4: 2 build a f against it, and cast a mount — 1785
21:22 gates, to cast a mount, and to build a f. — 1785
26: 8 he shall make a f against thee, and cast a — 1785
Da 11:19 he shall turn his face towards the f of his — 4581

FORTH (888) [HENCEFORTH]
Ge 1:11 God said, Let the earth bring f grass, — 1876
1:12 earth brought f grass, and herb yielding — 3318
1:20 Let the waters bring f abundantly — 8317+8318
1:21 which the waters brought f abundantly, — 8317

Ge 1:24 Let the earth bring f the living creature — 3318
3:16 in sorrow thou shalt bring f children; — 3205
3:18 and thistles shall it bring f to thee; — 6779
3:22 lest he put f his hand, and take also of — 7971
3:23 Therefore the Lord God sent him f from — 7971
8: 7 he sent f a raven, which went forth to — 7971
8: 7 forth a raven, which went f to and fro, — 3318
8: 8 Also he sent f a dove from him, to see if — 7971
8: 9 he put f his hand, and took her, — 7971
8:10 again he sent f the dove out of the ark; — 7971
8:12 yet other seven days; and sent f the dove; — 7971
8:16 Go f of the ark, thou, and thy wife, — 3318
8:17 Bring f with thee every living thing that — 3318
8:18 Noah went f, and his sons, and his wife, — 3318
8:19 after their kinds, went f out of the ark. — 3318
9: 7 bring f abundantly in the earth, — 8317
9:18 that went f of the ark, were Shem, — 3318
10:11 Out of that land went f Asshur, — 3318
11:31 they went f with them from Ur of — 3318
12: 5 went f to go into the land of Canaan; — 3318
14:18 Melchizedek king of Salem brought f — 3318
15: 4 that shall come f of thine own — 3318
15: 5 he brought him f abroad, and said, — 3318
19:10 the men put f their hand, and pulled Lot — 7971
19:16 they brought him f, and set him without — 3318
19:17 when they had brought them f abroad, — 3318
22:10 Abraham stretched f his hand, and took — 7971
24:43 that when the virgin cometh f to draw — 3318
24:45 Rebekah came f with her pitcher on her — 3318
24:53 the servant brought f jewels of silver, — 3318
30:39 brought f cattle ringstraked, speckled, — 3205
38:24 Bring her f, and let her be burnt. — 3318
38:25 When she was brought f, she sent to her — 3318
38:29 she said, How hast thou broken f? — 6555
39:13 his garment in her hand, and was fled f, — 2351
40:10 it budded, and her blossoms shot f; — 5927
40:10 the clusters thereof brought f ripe grapes: — 1310
41:47 years the earth brought f by handfuls. — 6213
42:15 By the life of Pharaoh ye shall not go f — 3318
Ex 3:10 that thou mayest bring f my people — 3318
3:11 that I should bring f the children of Israel — 3318
3:12 thou hast brought f the people out of — 3318
4: 4 Put f thine hand, and take it by the tail. — 7971
4: 4 he put f his hand, and caught it, — 7971
4:14 behold, he cometh f to meet thee: — 3318
5:20 in the way, as they came f from Pharaoh: — 3318
7: 4 bring f mine armies, and my people — 3318
7: 5 when I stretch f mine hand upon Egypt, — 5186
8: 3 the river shall bring f frogs abundantly, — 8317
8: 5 Stretch f thine hand with thy rod over — 5186
8:18 so with their enchantments to bring f lice, — 3318
8:20 he cometh f to the water; and say unto — 3318
9: 8 be a boil breaking f with blains upon — 6524
9:10 it became a boil breaking f with blains — 6524
9:22 Stretch f thine hand toward heaven, — 5186
9:23 Moses stretched f his rod toward heaven — 5186
10:13 Moses stretched f his rod over the land — 5186
10:22 Moses stretched f his hand toward — 5186
12:31 and get you f from amongst my people, — 3318
12:39 dough which they brought f out of Egypt, — 3318
12:46 thou shalt not carry f ought of the flesh — 3318
13: 8 did unto me when I came f out of Egypt. — 3318
13:16 the Lord brought us f out of Egypt. — 3318
14:11 thus with us, to carry us f out of Egypt? — 3318
14:27 Moses stretched f his hand over the sea, — 5186
15: 7 thou sentest f thy wrath, which — 7971
15:13 Thou in thy mercy hast led f the people — 5148
16: 3 for ye have brought us f into this — 3318
16:32 when I brought you f from the land of — 3318
19: 1 the children of Israel were gone f out — 3318
19:17 Moses brought f the people out of — 3318
19:22 lest the Lord break f upon them. — 6555
19:24 the Lord, lest he break f upon them. — 6555
25:20 cherubims shall stretch f their wings on — 6566
29:46 that brought them f out of the land of — 3318
32:11 thou hast brought f out of the land — 3318
Lev 4:12 Even the whole bullock shall he carry f — 3318
4:21 he shall carry f the bullock without — 3318
6:11 carry f the ashes without the camp unto — 3318
14: 3 the priest shall go f out of the camp; — 3318
14:45 he shall carry them f out of the city into — 3318
16:24 come f, and offer his burnt offering, — 3318
16:27 shall one carry f without the camp; — 3318
22:27 is brought f, then it shall be seven days — 3205
24:14 Bring f him that hath cursed without — 3318
24:23 that they should bring f him that had — 3318
25:21 it shall bring f fruit for three years. — 6213
25:38 which brought you f out of the land of — 3318
25:42 I brought f out of the land of Egypt: — 3318
25:55 are my servants whom I brought f out — 3318
26:10 bring f the old because of the new. — 3318
26:13 which brought you f out of the land of — 3318
26:45 I brought f out of the land of Egypt — 3318
Nu 1: 3 all that are able to go f to war in Israel: — 3318
1:20 upward, all that were able to go f to war; — 3318
1:22 upward, all that were able to go f to war; — 3318
1:24 upward, all that were able to go f to war; — 3318
1:26 upward, all that were able to go f to war; — 3318
1:28 upward, all that were able to go f to war; — 3318
1:30 upward, all that were able to go f to war; — 3318
1:32 upward, all that were able to go f to war; — 3318
1:34 upward, all that were able to go f to war; — 3318
1:36 upward, all that were able to go f to war; — 3318
1:38 upward, all that were able to go f to war; — 3318
1:40 upward, all that were able to go f to war; — 3318

Nu 1:42 upward, all that were able to go f to war; — 3318
1:45 all that were able to go f to war in Israel; — 3318
2: 9 their armies. These shall first set f. — 5265
2:16 And they shall set f in the second rank. — 5265
11:20 saying, Why came we f out of Egypt? — 3318
11:31 there went f a wind from the Lord, — 5265
12: 5 and Miriam: and they both came f. — 3318
17: 8 brought f buds, and bloomed blossoms — 3318
19: 3 he may bring her f without the camp, — 3318
20: 8 it shall give f his water, and thou shalt — 5414
20: 8 thou shalt bring f to them water out of — 3318
20:16 and hath brought us f out of Egypt: — 3318
24: 6 the valleys are they spread f, as gardens — 5186
24: 8 God brought him f out of Egypt; he hath — 3318
26: 4 which went f out of the land of Egypt. — 3318
31:13 went f to meet them without the camp. — 3318
33: 1 which went f out of the land of Egypt — 3318
34: 4 going f thereof shall be from the south — 8444
34: 8 goings f of the border shall be to Zedad: — 8444
Dt 1:27 he hath brought us f out of the land of — 3318
2:23 which came f out of Caphtor, — 3318
4:20 brought you f out of the iron furnace, — 3318
4:45 of Israel, after they came f out of Egypt, — 3318
4:46 after they were come f out of Egypt: — 3318
6:12 which brought thee f out of the land of — 3318
8:14 which brought thee f out of the land of — 3318
8:15 who brought thee f water out of the rock — 3318
9:12 for thy people which thou hast brought f — 3318
9:26 which thou hast brought f out of Egypt — 3318
14:22 that the field bringeth f year by year. — 3318
14:28 the end of three years thou shalt bring f — 3318
16: 1 God brought thee f out of Egypt by night. — 3318
16: 3 for thou camest f out of the land of Egypt — 3318
16: 3 camest f out of the land of Egypt all — 3318
16: 6 at the season that thou camest f out of — 3318
17: 5 thou bring f that man or that woman, — 3318
21: 2 thy elders and thy judges shall come f, — 3318
21:10 When thou goest f to war against thine — 3318
22:15 bring f the tokens of the damsel's — 3318
23: 4 in the way, when ye came f out of Egypt; — 3318
23: 9 When the host goeth f against thine — 3318
23:12 the camp, whither thou shalt go f abroad: — 3318
24: 9 after that ye were come f out of Egypt. — 3318
25:11 putteth f her hand, and taketh him by — 7971
25:17 when ye were come f out of Egypt; — 3318
26: 8 the Lord brought us f out of Egypt with — 3318
29:25 brought them f out of the land of Egypt: — 3318
33: 2 he shined f from mount Paran, and he — 3313
33:14 the precious fruits brought f by the sun, — NIH
33:14 for the precious things put f by the moon, — 1645
Jos 2: 3 Bring f the men that are come to thee, — 3318
5: 5 by the way as they came f out of Egypt, — 3318
8: 9 Joshua therefore sent them f: and they — 7971
9:12 on the day we came f to go unto you; — 3318
10:23 brought f those five kings unto him out — 3318
18:11 the coast of their lot came f between — 3318
18:17 went f to En-shemesh, and went forth — 3318
18:17 En-shemesh, and went f toward Geliloth, — 3318
19: 1 the second lot came f to Simeon, even — 3318
Jdg 1:24 spies saw a man come f out of the city, — 3318
3:21 Ehud put f his left hand, and took — 7971
3:23 Ehud went f through the porch, — 3318
5:25 she brought f butter in a lordly dish. — 7126
5:31 as the sun when he goeth f in his might. — 3318
6: 8 brought you f out of the house of — 3318
6:18 bring f my present, and set it before thee. — 3318
9: 8 trees went f on a time to anoint — 1980+1980
9:43 the people were come f out of the city; — 3318
11:31 that whatsoever cometh f of the doors of — 3318
14:12 I will now put f a riddle unto you: — 2330
14:13 Put f thy riddle, that we may hear it. — 2330
14:14 Out of the eater came f meat, and out of — 3318
14:14 and out of the strong came f sweetness. — 3318
14:16 thou hast put f a riddle unto the children — 2330
15:15 put f his hand, and took it, and slew a — 7971
19:22 Bring f the man that came into thine — 3318
19:25 concubine, and brought her f unto them; — 2351
20:21 the children of Benjamin came f out of — 3318
20:25 Benjamin went f against them out of — 3318
20:33 the liers in wait of Israel came f out of — 1518
Ru 1: 7 Wherefore she went f out of the place — 3318
2:18 she brought f, and gave to her that she — 3318
1Sa 11: 7 Whosoever cometh not f after Saul and — 3318
12: 8 brought f your fathers out of Egypt, — 3318
14:11 the Hebrews come f out of the holes — 3318
14:27 wherefore he put f the end of the rod that — 7971
17:20 as the host was going f to the fight, — 3318
17:55 when Saul saw David go f against — 3318
18:30 the princes of the Philistines went f: — 3318
18:30 it came to pass, after they went f, — 3318
22: 3 I pray thee, come f, and be with you, — 3318
22:17 the servants of the king would not put f — 7971
23:13 from Keilah; and he forbare to go f. — 3318
24: 6 to stretch f mine hand against him, — 7971
24:10 will not put f mine hand against my lord; — 7971
26: 9 for who can stretch f his hand against — 7971
26:11 The Lord forbid that I should stretch f — 7971
26:23 I would not stretch f mine hand against — 7971
30:21 they went f to meet David, and to meet — 3318
2Sa 1:14 Wast thou not afraid to stretch f thine — 7971
5:20 The Lord hath broken f upon mine — 6555
6: 6 Uzzah put f his hand to the ark of God, — 7971
11: 1 at the time when kings go f to battle, that — 3318
12:30 he brought f the spoil of the city in great — 3318

F

2Sa	12:31 **brought f** the people that *were* therein, 3318
	13:39 *the soul of* king David longed to **go f** unto 3318
	15: 5 he **put f** his hand, and took him, 7971
	15:16 the king **went f**, and all his household 3318
	15:17 the king **went f**, and all the people after 3318
	16: 5 he **came f**, and cursed still as he came. 3318
	16:11 my son, which **came f** of my bowels, 3318
	18: 2 David **sent f** a third part of the people 7971
	18: 2 **surely go f** with you myself also. 3318+3318
	18: 3 the people answered, Thou shalt not **go f**: 3318
	18:12 *yet* would I not **put f** mine hand against 7971
	19: 7 **go f**, and speak comfortably unto thy 3318
	19: 7 for I swear by the LORD, if thou **go not f**, 3318
	20: 8 thereof; and as he **went f** it fell out. 3318
	22:20 He **brought** me **f** also into a large place: 3318
	22:49 that **bringeth** me **f** from mine enemies: 3318
1Ki	2:30 unto him, Thus saith the king, **Come f**. 3318
	2:36 and **go not f** thence any whither. 3318
	6:27 they **stretched f** the wings of 6566
	8: 7 the cherubims **spread f** *their* two wings 6566
	8:16 Since the day that I **brought f** my people 3318
	8:19 thy son that shall **come f** out of thy loins, 3318
	8:22 and **spread f** his hands *toward* heaven: 6566
	8:38 **spread f** his hands towards this house: 6566
	8:51 which thou **broughtest f** out of Egypt, 3318
	9: 7 **brought f** their fathers out of the land 3318
	13: 4 that he **put f** his hand from the altar, 7971
	13: 4 which he **put f** against him, dried up, 7971
	19:11 **Go f**, and stand upon the mount before 3318
	20:33 Ben-hadad **came f** to him; and he caused 3318
	21:13 Then they **carried** him **f** out of the city, 3318
	22:21 there **came f** a spirit, and stood before 3318
	22:22 I will **go f**, and I will be a lying spirit in 3318
	22:22 and prevail also: **go f**, and do so. 3318
2Ki	2: 3 that *were* at Beth-el **came f** to Elisha, 3318
	2:21 he **went f** unto the spring of the waters, 3318
	2:23 **came f** little children out of the city, 3318
	2:24 **came f** two she bears out of the wood, 3318
	6:15 **gone f**, behold, a host compassed the city 3318
	8: 3 she **went f** to cry unto the king for her 3318
	9:11 Jehu **came f** to the servants of his lord: 3318
	9:15 let none **go f** *nor* escape out of the city to 3318
	10:22 **Bring f** vestments for all the worshippers 3318
	10:22 And he **brought** them **f** vestments. 3318
	10:25 Go in, *and* slay them; let none **come f**. 3318
	10:26 **brought f** the images **out** of the house 3318
	11: 7 two parts of all you that **go f** on 3318
	11:12 he **brought f** the king's son, and put 3318
	11:15 them, **Have** her **f** without the ranges: 3318
	18: 7 he prospered whithersoever he **went f**: 3318
	19: 3 and *there is* not strength to **bring f**. 3205
	19:31 For out of Jerusalem shall **go f** a remnant, 3318
	21:15 since the day their fathers **came f** out of 3318
	23: 4 to **bring f** out of the temple of the LORD 3318
1Ch	12:33 Of Zebulun, such as **went f** to battle, 3318
	12:36 such as **went f** to battle, expert in war, 3318
	13: 9 Uzza **put f** his hand to hold the ark; 7971
	14:11 mine hand like the **breaking f** of waters: 6556
	14:15 for God is **gone f** before thee to smite 3318
	16:23 **shew f** from day to day his salvation. 1319
	19:16 **drew f** the Syrians that *were* beyond 3318
	20: 1 *battle*, Joab **led f** the power of the army, 5090
	24: 7 Now the first lot **came f** to Jehoiarib, 3318
	25: 9 Now the first lot **came f** for Asaph to 3318
	26:16 and Hosah *the* lot came *f* westward, NIH
2Ch	1:17 **brought f** out of Egypt a chariot for six 3318
	3:13 **spread** themselves **f** twenty cubits: 6566
	5: 8 For the cherubims **spread f** *their* wings 6566
	6: 5 Since the day that I **brought f** my people 3318
	6: 9 son which shall **come f** out of thy loins, 3318
	6:12 of Israel, and **spread f** his hands: 6566
	6:13 and **spread f** his hands towards heaven, 6566
	6:29 shall **spread f** his hands in this house: 6566
	7:22 which **brought** them **f** out of the land of 3318
	20:20 and **went f** into the wilderness of Tekoa: 3318
	20:20 as they **went f**, Jehoshaphat stood and 3318
	21: 9 Jehoram **went f** with his princes, and all 5674
	23:14 said unto them, **Have** her **f** of the ranges: 3318
	25: 5 thousand choice *men*, able to **go f** to war, 3318
	25:11 **led f** his people, and went *to* the valley of 5090
	26: 6 he **went f** and warred against 3318
	29: 5 **carry f** the filthiness out of the holy *place*. 3318
	29:23 they **brought f** the he goats for the sin 5066
	32:21 they that **came f** of his own bowels slew 3329
Ezr	1: 7 Also Cyrus the king **brought f** the vessels 3318
	1: 7 Nebuchadnezzar had **brought f** out 3318
	1: 8 those did Cyrus king of Persia **bring f** 3318
	6: 5 which Nebuchadnezzar **took f** out of 5312
Ne	4:16 it came to pass from that time *f*, *that* 4480
	8:15 **Go f** *unto* the mount, and fetch olive 3318
	8:16 So the people **went f**, and brought *them*, 3318
	9: 7 **broughtest** him **f** out of Ur of 3318
	9:15 **broughtest f** water for them out of Tobiah 3318
	13: 8 I cast *f* all the household stuff of Tobiah 7993
	13:21 **From** that time **f** came they no *more* on 4480
Est	4: 6 So Hatach **went f** to Mordecai unto 3318
	5: 9 **went** Haman **f** that day joyful and with a 3318
Job	1:11 **put f** thine hand now, and touch all that 7971
	1:12 only upon himself **put not f** thine hand. 7971
	1:12 So Satan **went f** from the presence of 3318
	2: 5 **put f** thine hand now, and touch his bone 7971
	2: 7 So **went** Satan **f** from the presence of 3318
	5: 6 Although affliction **cometh** not **f** of 3318
	8:16 and his branch **shooteth f** in his garden, 3318
	10:18 hast thou **brought** me **f** out of the womb? 3318

Job	11:17 thou shalt **shine f**, thou shalt be as 5774
	14: 2 He **cometh f** like a flower, and is cut 3318
	14: 9 will bud, and **bring f** boughs like a plant. 6213
	15:35 they conceive mischief, and bring f 3205
	21:11 They **send f** their little ones like a flock, 7971
	21:30 shall be **brought f** to the day of wrath. 2986
	23:10 he hath tried me, I shall **come f** as gold. 3318
	24: 5 in the desert, **go** they **f** to their work; 3318
	28: 1 He **putteth f** his hand upon the rock; 7971
	28:11 thing that is hid **bringeth** he **f** to light. 3318
	30: 5 They were **driven f** from among men, 1644
	38: 8 the sea with doors, when it **brake f**, 1518
	38:27 **cause** the bud of the tender herb
	to spring f? 6779
	38:32 Canst thou **bring f** Mazzaroth in his 3318
	39: 1 when the wild goats of the rock **bring f**? 3205
	39: 2 thou the time when they **bring f**? 3205
	39: 3 they **bring f** their young ones, 6398
	39: 4 they **go f**, and return not unto them. 3318
	40:20 Surely the mountains **bring** him **f** food, 5375
Ps	1: 3 that **bringeth f** his fruit in his season, 5414
	7:14 and **brought f** falsehood. 3205
	9: 1 I will **shew f** all thy marvellous works. 5608
	9:14 I may **shew f** all thy praise in the gates 5608
	17: 2 my sentence **come f** from thy presence; 3318
	18:19 He **brought** me **f** also into a large place; 3318
	19: 6 His **going f** *is* from the end of the heaven, 4161
	37: 6 he shall **bring f** thy righteousness as 3318
	44: 9 shame; and **goest** not **f** with our armies. 3318
	51:15 and my mouth shall **shew f** thy praise. 5046
	55:20 He hath **put f** his hands against such as 7971
	57: 3 God shall **send f** his mercy and his truth. 7971
	66: 2 **Sing f** the honour of his name: make his 2167
	68: 7 when thou **wentest f** before thy people, 3318
	71:15 My mouth shall **shew f** thy righteousness 5608
	78:52 **made** his own people to **go f** like sheep, 5265
	79:13 will **shew f** thy praise to all generations. 5608
	80: 1 dwellest *between* the cherubims, **shine f**. 3313
	88: 8 *I am* shut up, and I cannot **come f**. 3318
	90: 2 Before the mountains were **brought f**, 3205
	92: 2 To **shew f** thy lovingkindness in 5046
	92:14 They shall still **bring f** fruit in old age; 5107
	96: 2 **shew f** his salvation from day to day. 1319
	104:14 that *he* may **bring f** food out of the earth; 3318
	104:20 all the beasts of the forest do creep *f*. NIH
	104:23 Man **goeth f** unto his work and to his 3318
	104:30 **sendest f** thy spirit, they are created: 7971
	105:30 land **brought f** frogs **in abundance**, 8317
	105:37 He **brought** them **f** also with silver and 3318
	105:43 he **brought f** his people with joy, 3318
	106: 2 the LORD? *who* can **shew f** all his praise? 8085
	107: 7 he **led** them **f** by the right way, that *they* 1869
	108:11 not thou, O God, **go f** with our hosts? 3318
	113: 2 be the name of the LORD from **this time f** 6258
	115:18 we will bless the LORD from **this time f** 6258
	121: 8 and thy coming in from **this time f**, 6258
	125: 3 lest the righteous **put f** their hands unto 7971
	125: 5 the LORD shall **lead** them **f** with 1980
	126: 6 He that **goeth f** and weepeth, 1980+1980
	138: 7 thou shalt **stretch f** thine hand against 7971
	141: 2 Let my prayer be **set f** before thee *as* 3559
	143: 6 I **stretch f** my hands unto thee: my soul 6566
	144: 6 **Cast f** lightning, and scatter them: 1299+1300
	144:13 our sheep may **bring f** thousands and 503
	146: 4 breath **goeth f**, he returneth to his earth; 3318
	147: 15 He **sendeth f** his commandment *upon* 7971
	147:17 He **casteth f** his ice like morsels: who can 7993
Pr	7:15 Therefore **came** I **f** to meet thee, 3318
	8: 1 and understanding **put f** her voice? 5414
	8:24 *there were* no depths, I was **brought f**; 2342
	8:25 before the hills was I **brought f**: 2342
	9: 3 She hath **sent f** her maidens: she crieth 7971
	10:31 The mouth of the just **bringeth f** wisdom: 5107
	12:17 *He that* speaketh truth **sheweth f** 5046
	25: 4 there shall **come f** a vessel for the finer. 3318
	25: 6 **Put** not **f** thyself in the presence of 1921
	25: 8 **Go** not **f** hastily to strive, lest *thou know* 3318
	27: 1 knowest not what a day may **bring f**. 3205
	30:27 king, yet **go** they **f** all of them by bands; 3318
	30:33 Surely the churning of milk **bringeth f** 3318
	30:33 wringing of the nose **bringeth f** blood: 3318
	30:33 so forcing of wrath **bringeth f** strife. 3318
	31:20 she **reacheth f** her hands to the needy. 7971
Ecc	2: 6 water therewith the wood that **bringeth f** 6779
	5:15 As he **came f** of his mother's womb, 3318
	7:18 for he that feareth God shall **come f** of 3318
	10: 1 **cause** the ointment of the apothecary
	to send f 5042
SS	1: 3 thy name *is as* ointment **poured f**, 7324
	1: 8 **go** thy **way f** by the footsteps of the flock, 3318
	1:12 my spikenard **sendeth f** the smell thereof. 5414
	2: 9 our wall, he looketh **f** at the windows, 4480
	2:13 The fig tree **putteth f** her green figs, 2590
	3:11 **Go f**, O ye daughters of Zion, 3318
	6:10 *is* she that **looketh f** as the morning, 8259
	7:11 my beloved, let us **go f** *into* the field, 3318
	7:12 appear, *and* the pomegranates **bud f**: 5340
	8: 5 there thy mother **brought** thee **f**: there 2254
	8: 5 there she **brought** thee *f* that bare thee. 2254
Isa	1:15 when ye **spread f** your hands, I will hide 6566
	2: 3 out of Zion shall **go f** the law, 3318
	3:16 walk with **stretched f** necks and 5186
	5: 2 he looked that *it* should **bring f** grapes, 6213
	5: 2 forth grapes, and it **brought f** wild grapes. 6213
	5: 4 I looked that *it* should **bring f** grapes, 6213

Isa	5: 4 forth grapes, **brought** it **f** wild grapes? 6213
	5:25 hath **stretched f** his hand against him, 5186
	7: 3 **Go f** now to meet Ahaz, thou, 3318
	7:25 it shall be for the **sending f** of oxen, 4916
	11: 1 there shall **come f** a rod out of the stem 3318
	13:10 the sun shall be darkened in his **going f**, 3318
	14: 7 *and is* quiet: they **break f into** singing. 6476
	14:29 for out of the serpent's root shall **come f** 3318
	23: 4 I travail not, nor **bring f children**, 3205
	25:11 he shall **spread f** his hands in the midst 6566
	25:11 he that swimmeth **spreadeth f** *his hands* 6566
	26:18 pain, we have as it were **brought f** wind; 3205
	27: 8 In measure, when it **shooteth f**, thou wilt 7971
	28:19 From the time that it **goeth f** it shall take 5674
	28:29 This also **cometh f** from the LORD of 3318
	31: 4 when a multitude of shepherds is **called f** 7121
	32:20 that **send f** *thither* the feet of the ox and 7971
	33:11 conceive chaff, ye shall **bring f** stubble: 3205
	34: 1 world, and all things **that come f** of it. 6631
	36: 3 **came f** unto him Eliakim, Hilkiah's son, 3318
	37: 3 and *there is* not strength to **bring f**. 3205
	37: 9 He is **come f** to make war with thee. 3318
	37:32 For out of Jerusalem shall **go f** a remnant, 3318
	37:36 the angel of the LORD **went f**, 3318
	41: 2 **bring f** thy strong *reasons*, saith the 5066
	41:21 Let them **bring** *them* **f**, and shew us 5066
	42: 1 he shall **bring f** judgment to the Gentiles. 3318
	42: 3 he shall **bring f** judgment unto truth. 3318
	42: 5 he that **spread f** the earth, and that 7554
	42: 9 before they **spring f** I tell you of them. 6779
	42:13 The LORD shall **go f** as a mighty *man*, he 3318
	43: 8 **Bring f** the blind people that have eyes, 3318
	43: 9 shew us former *things*? let them **bring f** 5414
	43:17 Which **bringeth f** the chariot and horse, 3318
	43:19 will do a new *thing*; now it shall **spring f**; 6779
	43:21 for myself; they shall **shew f** my praise. 5608
	44:23 **break f into** singing, ye mountains, 6476
	44:24 that **stretcheth f** the heavens alone; 5186
	45: 8 let them **bring f** salvation, 6509
	45:10 the woman, What hast thou **brought f**? 2342
	48: 1 are **come f** out of the waters of Judah, 3318
	48: 3 **went f** out of my mouth, and I shewed 3318
	48:20 **Go** ye **f** of Babylon, flee ye from 3318
	49: 9 *thou* mayest say to the prisoners, **Go f**; 3318
	49:13 and **break f into** singing, O mountains: 6476
	49:17 that made thee waste shall **go f** of thee. 3318
	51: 5 my salvation is **gone f**, and mine arms 3318
	51:13 that hath **stretched f** the heavens, 5186
	51:18 all the sons *whom* she hath **brought f**; 3205
	52: 9 **Break f into** joy, sing together, ye waste 6476
	54: 1 **break f into** singing, and cry aloud, 6476
	54: 2 let them **stretch f** the curtains of thine 5186
	54: 3 for thou shalt **break f on** the right hand 6555
	54:16 **bringeth f** an instrument for his work; 3318
	55:10 earth, and **maketh** it **bring f** and bud, 3205
	55:11 shall my word be that **goeth f** out of my 3318
	55:12 ye shall **go** out with joy, and be **led f** with peace: 2986
	55:12 the hills shall **break f** before you *into* 6476
	58: 8 shall thy light **break f** as the morning, 1234
	58: 8 and thine health shall **spring f** speedily: 6779
	58: 9 the **putting f** of the finger, 7971
	59: 4 conceive mischief, and **bring f** iniquity. 3205
	60: 6 they shall **shew f** the praises of the LORD. 1319
	61:11 For as the earth **bringeth f** her bud, 3318
	61:11 **causeth** the things that are sown in it
	to spring f; 6779
	61:11 **cause** righteousness and praise **to spring f** 6779
	62: 1 until the righteousness thereof **go f** as 3318
	65: 9 I will **bring f** a seed out of Jacob, 3205
	65:23 labour in vain, nor **bring f** for trouble; 3205
	66: 7 Before she travailed, she **brought f**, 3205
	66: 8 the earth be made to **bring f** in one day? 2342
	66: 8 Zion travailed, she **brought f** her children. 3205
	66: 9 to the birth, and not **cause to bring f**? 3205
	66: 9 shall I **cause to bring f**, and shut 3205
	66:24 shall **go f**, and look upon the carcases 3318
Jer	1: 5 before thou **camest f** out of the womb I 3318
	1: 9 the LORD **put f** his hand, and touched my 7971
	1:14 of the north an evil shall **break f** upon 6605
	2:27 and to a stone, Thou hast **brought** me **f**: 3205
	2:37 thou shalt **go f** from him, and thine hands 3318
	4: 4 lest my fury **come f** like fire, and burn 3318
	4: 7 he is **gone f** from his place to make thy 3318
	4:31 as of her that **bringeth f** her first child, 1069
	6:25 **Go** not **f** into the field, nor walk by 3318
	7:25 Since the day that your fathers **came f** 3318
	10:13 **bringeth f** the wind out of his treasures. 3318
	10:20 my children are **gone f** *of* me, and they 3318
	10:20 *is* none to **stretch f** my tent any more, 5186
	11: 4 I **brought** them **f** out of the land of Egypt, 3318
	12: 2 they grow, yea, they **bring f** fruit: thou 6213
	14:18 I **go f** *into* the field, then behold the slain 3318
	15: 1 *them* out of my sight, and let them **go f**. 3318
	15: 2 say unto thee, Whither shall we **go f**? 3318
	15:19 if thou **take f** the precious from the vile, 3318
	17:22 Neither **carry f** a burden out of your 3318
	19: 2 **go f** unto the valley of the son of Hinnom, 3318
	20: 3 that Pashur **brought f** Jeremiah out of 3318
	20:18 Wherefore **came** I **f** out of the womb to 3318
	22:11 his father, which **went f** out of this place; 3318
	22:19 and **cast f** beyond the gates of Jerusalem. 7993
	23:15 is profaneness **gone f** into all the land. 3318
	23:19 a whirlwind of the LORD is **gone f** *in* 3318
	25:32 evil *shall* **go f** from nation to nation, 3318
	26:23 they **fet f** Urijah out of Egypt, 3318

F

Jer	29:16	*of* your brethren that are not **gone f** with	3318
	30:23	the whirlwind of the LORD **goeth f** *with*	3318
	31: 4	shalt **go f** in the dances of them that make	3318
	31:24	and they *that* **go f** with flocks.	5265
	31:39	the measuring line shall yet **go f** over	3318
	32:21	hast **brought f** thy people Israel out of	3318
	34:13	I **brought** them **f** out of the land of Egypt,	3318
	37: 5	Pharaoh's army was **come f** out of Egypt:	3318
	37: 7	which is **come f** to help you,	3318
	37:12	Jeremiah **went f** out of Jerusalem to go	3318
	38: 2	that **goeth f** to the Chaldeans shall live;	3318
	38: 8	Ebed-melech **went f** out of the king's	3318
	38:17	If thou wilt **assuredly go f** unto	3318+3318
	38:18	if thou wilt not **go f** to the king of	3318
	38:21	if thou refuse to **go f**, this *is* the word that	3318
	38:22	**brought f** to the king of Babylon's princes	3318
	39: 4	and **went f** out of the city by night,	3318
	41: 6	Ishmael the son of Nethaniah **went f**	3318
	42:18	my fury hath been **poured f** upon	5413
	42:18	so shall my fury be **poured f** upon you,	5413
	43:12	and he shall **go f** from thence in peace.	3318
	44: 6	my fury and mine anger was **poured f**,	5413
	44:17	thing **goeth f** out of our own mouth,	3320
	46: 4	and **stand f** with *your* helmets;	3320
	46: 9	chariots; and let the mighty *men* **come f**;	3318
	48: 7	Chemosh shall **go f** into captivity *with* his	3318
	48:45	a fire shall **go f** out of the midst of Heshbon,	3318
	49: 5	be driven out every man **right f**;	6440+3807.1
	50: 8	**go f** out of the land of the Chaldeans,	3318
	50:25	hath **brought f** the weapons of his	3318
	51:10	The LORD hath **brought f** our	3318
	51:16	**bringeth f** the wind out of his treasures.	3318
	51:44	I will **bring f** out of his mouth that which	3318
	52: 7	**went f** out of the city by night *by* the way	3318
	52:31	Judah, and **brought** him **f** out of prison;	3318
La	1:17	Zion **spreadeth f** her hands, *and there is*	6566
Eze	1:13	and out of the fire **went f** lightning.	3318
	1:22	**stretched f** over their heads above.	5186
	3:22	**go f** into the plain, and I will there talk	3318
	3:23	I arose, and **went f** into the plain:	3318
	5: 4	*for* thereof shall a fire **come f** into all	3318
	7:10	the morning is **gone f**; the rod hath	3318
	8: 3	he **put f** the form of a hand, and took me	7971
	9: 7	**go ye f**. And they went forth, and slew in	3318
	9: 7	And they **went f**, and slew in the city.	3318
	10: 7	*one* cherub **stretched f** his hand from	7971
	11: 7	I will **bring** you **f** out of the midst of it.	3318
	12: 4	shalt thou **bring f** thy stuff by day in their	3318
	12: 4	thou shalt **go f** at even in their sight, as	3318
	12: 4	their sight, as they that **go f** into captivity.	4161
	12: 6	shoulders, *and* **carry** *it* **f** in the twilight:	3318
	12: 7	I **brought f** my stuff by day, as stuff for	3318
	12: 7	I **brought** *it* **f** in the twilight, *and* I bare *it*	3318
	12:12	shoulder in the twilight, and shall **go f**:	3318
	14:22	be left a remnant that shall be **brought f**,	3318
	14:22	*shall* **come** f unto you, and ye shall see	3318
	16:14	thy renown **went f** among the heathen	3318
	17: 2	**put f** a riddle, and speak a parable	2330+2420
	17: 6	**brought f** branches, and shot forth sprigs.	6213
	17: 6	brought forth branches, and **shot f** sprigs.	7971
	17: 7	and **shot f** her branches toward him,	7971
	17: 8	that *it* might **bring f** branches, and that *it*	6213
	17:23	it shall **bring f** boughs, and bear fruit,	5375
	18: 8	He *that* hath not **given f** upon usury,	5414
	18:13	Hath **given f** upon usury, and hath taken	5414
	20: 6	to **bring** them **f** of the land of Egypt into	3318
	20: 9	**bringing** them **f** out of the land of Egypt.	3318
	20:10	Wherefore I **caused** them **to go f** out of	3318
	20:22	in whose sight I **brought** them **f**.	3318
	20:38	I will **bring** them **f** of the country	3318
	21: 3	will **draw f** my sword out of his sheath,	3318
	21: 4	shall my sword **go f** out of his sheath	3318
	21: 5	have **drawn f** my sword out of his sheath:	3318
	21:19	both twain shall **come f** out of one land:	3318
	24:12	and her great scum **went f** not **f** out of her:	3318
	27: 7	*which* thou **spreadest f** to be thy sail;	4666
	27:10	helmet in thee; they **set f** thy comeliness.	5414
	27:33	When thy wares **went f** out of the seas,	3318
	28:18	will I **bring f** a fire from the midst of thee,	3318
	29:21	**cause** the horn of the house of Israel	
		to **bud f**,	6779
	30: 9	In that day shall messengers **go f** from me	3318
	31: 5	the multitude of waters, when he **shot f**.	7971
	31: 6	beasts of the field **bring f** their *young*,	3205
	32: 2	thou **camest f** with thy rivers,	1518
	32: 4	I will **cast** thee **f** upon the open field,	2904
	33:30	hear what *is* the word that **cometh f** from	3318
	36: 8	ye shall **shoot f** your branches,	5414
	36:20	the LORD, and are **gone f** out of his land.	3318
	38: 4	I will **bring** thee **f**, and all thine army,	3318
	38: 8	it is **brought f** out of the nations,	3318
	39: 9	that dwell in the cities of Israel shall **go f**,	3318
	42: 1	he **brought** me into the utter court,	3318
	42:15	he **brought** me **f** toward the gate whose	3318
	44: 5	with every **going f** of the sanctuary.	4161
	44:19	when they **go f** into the utter court,	3318
	46: 2	shall **go f**; but the gate shall not be shut	3318
	46: 8	and he shall **go f** by the way thereof.	3318
	46: 9	shall **go f** by the way of the north gate:	3318
	46: 9	he came in, but shall **go f** over against it.	3318
	46:10	go in; and when they **go f**, shall go forth.	3318
	46:10	go in; and when they go forth, shall **go f**.	3318
	46:12	he shall **go f**; and after his going forth *one*	3318
	46:12	after his **going f** *one* shall shut the gate.	3318
	46:21	he **brought** me **f** into the utter court,	3318

Eze	47: 3	**went f** east*ward*, he measured a thousand	3318
	47: 8	*which* being **brought f** into the sea,	3318
	47:10	they shall be a **place to spread f** nets;	4894
	47:12	it shall **bring f** new fruit according to his	1069
Da	2:13	the decree **went f** that the wise *men*	5312
	2:14	which was **gone f** to slay the wise *men* of	5312
	3:26	**come f**, and come *hither*. Then Shadrach,	5312
	3:26	Abed-nego, **came f** of the midst of the fire.	5312
	5: 5	In the same hour **came f** fingers of a	5312
	7:10	issued and **came f** from before him:	5312
	8: 9	out of one of them **came f** a little horn,	3318
	9:15	that hast **brought** thy people **f** out of	3318
	9:22	I am now **come f** to give thee skill and	3318
	9:23	supplications the commandment **came f**,	3318
	9:25	from the **going f** of the commandment	4161
	10:20	I am **gone f**, lo, the prince of Grecia	3318
	11:11	shall **come f** and fight with him, *even*	3318
	11:11	he shall **set f** a great multitude;	5975
	11:13	shall **set f** a multitude greater than	5975
	11:42	He shall **stretch f** his hand also upon	7971
	11:44	he shall **go f** with great fury to destroy,	3318
Hos	6: 3	his **going f** *is* prepared as the morning;	4161
	6: 5	judgments *are as* the light *that* **goeth f**.	3318
	9:13	Ephraim *shall* **bring f** his children to	3318
	9:16	yea, though they **bring f**, yet will I slay	3205
	10: 1	he **bringeth f** fruit unto himself:	7737
	13:13	the place of the **breaking f** of children.	4866
	14: 5	the lily, and **cast f** his roots as Lebanon.	5221
Joel	2:16	let the bridegroom **go f** of his chamber,	3318
	3:18	a fountain shall **come f** of the house of	3318
Am	5: 3	which **went f** by an hundred shall leave	3318
	7:17	surely go into captivity **f** of his land.	4480+5921
	8: 3	they shall **cast** *them* **f** with silence.	7993
	8: 5	the sabbath, that we may **set f** wheat,	6605
Jnh	1: 5	**cast f** the wares that *were* in the ship into	2904
	1:12	Take me up, and **cast** me **f** into the sea;	2904
	1:15	Jonah, and **cast** him **f** into the sea:	2904
Mic	1: 3	the LORD **cometh f** out of his place,	3318
	1:11	the inhabitant of Zaanan **came** not **f** *in*	3318
	4: 2	the law shall **go f** of Zion, and the word	3318
	4:10	Be in pain, and **labour to bring f**,	1518
	4:10	for now shalt thou **go f** out of the city,	3318
	5: 2	*yet* out of thee shall he **come f** unto me	3318
	5: 2	whose *goings f* *have been* from of old,	4163
	5: 3	*that* she which travaileth hath **brought f**:	3205
	7: 9	he will **bring** me **f** to the light, *and* I shall	3318
Hab	1: 4	is slacked, and judgment doth never **go f**:	3318
	3: 5	and burning coals **went f** at his feet.	3318
	3:13	Thou **wentest f** for the salvation of thy	3318
Zep	2: 2	Before the decree **bring f**, *before* the day	3205
Hag	1:11	upon *that which* the ground **bringeth f**,	3318
	2:19	and the olive tree, hath not **brought f**:	5375
Zec	1:16	line shall be **stretched f** upon Jerusalem.	5186
	2: 3	the angel that talked with me **went f**,	3318
	2: 6	*come f*, and flee from the land of the north	NIH
	3: 8	I will **bring f** my servant the BRANCH.	935
	4: 7	he shall **bring f** the headstone *thereof*	3318
	5: 3	This *is* the curse that **goeth f** over the	3318
	5: 4	I will **bring** it **f**, saith the LORD of hosts,	3318
	5: 5	the angel that talked with me **went f**,	3318
	5: 5	eyes, and see what *is* this that **goeth f**.	3318
	5: 6	he said, This *is* an ephah that **goeth f**.	3318
	6: 5	*which* **go f** from standing before the Lord	3318
	6: 6	The black horses which *are* therein **go f**	3318
	6: 6	white **go f** after them; and the grisled **go**	3318
	6: 6	the grisled **go f** toward the south country.	3318
	6: 7	the bay **went f**, and sought to go that	3318
	9:11	the blood of thy covenant I have **sent f**	7971
	9:14	and his arrow shall **go f** as the lightning:	3318
	10: 4	Out of him **came f** the corner, out of	3318
	12: 1	which **stretcheth f** the heavens,	5186
	14: 2	half of the city shall **go f** into captivity,	3318
	14: 3	shall the LORD **go f**, and fight against	3318
Mal	4: 2	ye shall **go f**, and grow up as calves of	3318
Mt	1:21	she shall **bring f** a son, and thou shalt	5088
	1:23	shall **bring f** a son, and they shall call	5088
	1:25	And knew her not till she had **brought f**	5088
	2:16	and **sent f**, and slew all the children that	649
	3: 8	**Bring f** therefore fruits meet for	4160
	3:10	tree which **bringeth f** not good fruit	4160
	7:17	so every good tree **bringeth f** good fruit;	4160
	7:17	but a corrupt tree **bringeth f** evil fruit.	4160
	7:18	A good tree cannot **bring f** evil fruit,	4160
	7:18	neither *can* a corrupt tree **bring f** good	4160
	7:19	Every tree that **bringeth** not **f** good fruit	4160
	8: 3	Jesus **put f** *his* hand, and touched him,	1614
	9: 2	as Jesus **passed f** from thence, he saw	3855
	9:25	But when the people were **put f**, he went	1544
	9:38	that he will **send f** labourers into his	1544
	10: 5	These twelve Jesus **sent f**,	649
	10:16	I **send** you **f** as sheep in the midst of	649
	12:13	saith he to the man, **Stretch f** thine hand.	1614
	12:13	And he **stretched** *it* **f**; and it was restored	1614
	12:20	till he **send f** judgment unto victory.	1544
	12:35	of the heart **bringeth f** good *things*:	1544
	12:35	of the evil treasure **bringeth f** evil *things*.	1544
	12:49	And he **stretched f** his hand toward his	1614
	13: 3	saying, Behold, a sower **went f** to sow;	1831
	13: 8	fell into good ground, and **brought f** fruit,	1325
	13:23	and **bringeth f**, some an hundred*fold*,	4160
	13:24	Another parable **put** he **f** unto them,	3908
	13:26	**brought f** fruit, then appeared the tares	4160
	13:31	Another parable **put** he **f** unto them,	3908
	13:41	The Son of man shall **send f** his angels,	649
	13:43	shall the righteous **shine f** as the sun	1584

Mt	13:49	the angels shall **come f**, and sever	1831
	13:52	which **bringeth f** out of his treasure	1544
	14: 2	works do **shew f** themselves **in** him.	1754
	14:14	And Jesus **went f**, and saw a great	1831
	14:31	And immediately Jesus **stretched f** *his*	1614
	15:18	out of the mouth **come f** from the heart;	1831
	16:21	From *that* time he began Jesus to shew	5119
	21:43	given to a nation **bringing f** the fruits	4160
	22: 3	And **sent f** his servants to call them that	649
	22: 4	Again, he **sent f** other servants, saying,	649
	22: 7	and he **sent f** his armies,	3992
	22:46	neither durst any *man* from that day **f** ask	NIG
	24:26	Behold, he is in the desert; **go** not **f**:	1831
	24:32	**putteth f** leaves, ye know that summer	1631
	25: 1	and **went f** to meet the bridegroom.	1831
Mk	1:38	preach there also: for therefore **came** I **f**.	1831
	1:41	**put f** *his* hand, and	1614
	2:12	up the bed, and **went f** before *them* all;	1715
	2:13	And he **went f** again by the sea side;	1831
	3: 3	the withered hand, Stand **f**.	1519+3319+3588
	3: 5	saith unto the man, **Stretch f** thine hand.	1614
	3: 6	And the Pharisees **went f**,	1831
	3:14	and that he might **send** them **f** to preach,	649
	4: 8	**brought f**, some thirty, and some sixty,	5342
	4:20	word, and receive *it*, and **bring f fruit**,	2592
	4:28	For the earth **bringeth f fruit** of herself;	2592
	4:29	But when the fruit is **brought f**,	3860
	6: 7	began to **send** them **f** by two and two;	649
	6:14	works do **shew f** themselves in him.	1754
	6:17	Herod himself had **sent f** and laid hold	649
	6:24	she **went f**, and said unto her mother,	1831
	7:26	she besought him that he would **cast f**	1544
	8:11	And the Pharisees **came f**, and began to	1831
	9:29	This kind can **come f** by nothing, but by	1831
	10:17	And when he was **gone f** into the way,	1607
	11: 1	Olives, he **sendeth f** two of his disciples,	649
	13:28	**putteth f** leaves, ye know that summer	1631
	14:13	And he **sendeth f** two of his disciples,	649
	14:16	And his disciples **went f**, and came into	1831
	16:20	And they **went f**, and preached every	1831
Lk	1: 1	set **f** in order a declaration of those things	392
	1:31	and **bring f** a son, and shalt call his name	5088
	1:57	be delivered; and she **brought f** a son.	1080
	2: 7	And she **brought f** her firstborn son,	5088
	3: 7	said to the multitude that **came f** to	1607
	3: 8	**Bring f** therefore fruits worthy of	4160
	3: 9	which **bringeth** not **f** good fruit is hewn	4160
	5:13	And he **put f** *his* hand, and touched him,	1614
	5:27	after these *things* he **went f**, and saw a	1831
	6: 8	Rise up, and **stand f** in the midst.	NIG
	6: 8	in the midst. And he arose and stood **f**.	NIG
	6:10	he said unto the man, **Stretch f** thy hand.	1614
	6:43	a good tree **bringeth** not **f** corrupt fruit;	4160
	6:43	neither doth a corrupt tree **bring f** good	4160
	6:45	his heart **bringeth f** that which is good;	4393
	6:45	of his heart **bringeth f** that which is evil:	4393
	7:17	this rumour of him **went f** throughout	1831
	8:14	**go f**, and are choked with cares and riches	NIG
	8:15	keep *it*, and **bring f fruit** with patience.	2592
	8:22	side of the lake. And they **launched f**.	321
	8:27	when he **went f** to land, there met him	1831
	10: 2	that he would **send f** labourers into his	1544
	10: 3	I **send** you **f** as lambs among wolves.	649
	12:16	a certain rich man **brought f** plentifully:	2164
	12:37	to meat, and will **come f** and serve them.	3928
	14: 7	he **put f** a parable to those which were	3004
	15:22	**Bring f** the best robe, and put *it* on him;	1627
	20: 9	let it **f** to husbandmen, and went into a	1554
	20:20	And they watched *him*, and **sent f** spies,	649
	21:30	When they now **shoot f**, ye see and	4261
	22:53	ye **stretched f** no hands against me:	1614
Jn	1:43	The day following Jesus would **go f** into	1831
	2:10	Every man at the beginning doth **set f**	5087
	2:11	of Galilee, and **manifested f** his glory;	5319
	5:29	And shall **come f**; they that have done	1607
	8:42	for I **proceeded f** and came from God;	1831
	10: 4	And when he **putteth f** his own sheep,	1544
	11:43	cried with a loud voice, Lazarus, **come f**.	1854
	11:44	he that was dead **came f**, bound hand	1831
	11:53	Then from that day f they took counsel	NIG
	12:13	and **went f** to meet him, and cried,	1831
	12:24	but if it die, it **bringeth f** much fruit.	5342
	15: 2	purgeth it, that it may **bring f** more fruit.	5342
	15: 5	I in him, the same **bringeth f** much fruit:	5342
	15: 6	he is cast **f** as a branch, and is withered;	1854
	15:16	that you should go and **bring f fruit**,	5342
	16:28	I **came f** from the Father, and am come	1831
	16:30	this we believe that thou **camest f** from	1831
	18: 1	he **went f** with his disciples over the brook	1831
	18: 4	**went f**, and said unto them, Whom seek	1831
	19: 4	Pilate therefore **went f** again,	1854
	19: 4	unto them, Behold, I bring him **f** to you,	1854
	19: 5	Then **came** Jesus **f**, wearing the crown of	1831
	19:13	he brought Jesus **f**, and sat down in	1854
	19:17	And he bearing his cross **went f** into a	1831
	20: 3	Peter therefore **went f**, and *that other*	1831
	21: 3	They **went f**, and entered into a ship	1831
	21:18	thou shalt **stretch f** thy hands,	1614
Ac	1:26	And they **gave f** their lots; and the lot fell	1325
	2:33	he hath **shed f** this, which ye now see	1632
	4:30	By **stretching f** thine hand to heal;	1614
	5:10	And found her dead, and, **carrying** *her* **f**,	1627
	5:15	Insomuch that *they* **brought f** the sick	1627
	5:19	doors, and **brought** them **f**, and said,	1806
	5:34	commanded to put the apostles **f** a little	1854

Ac 7: 7 and after that shall they **come** f, · 1831
 9:30 to Cesarea, and **sent** him f to Tarsus. · 1821
 9:40 But Peter **put** *them* all f, · 1544
 11:22 they **sent** f Barnabas, that *he* should go · 1821
 12: 1 **stretched** f *his* hands to vex certain of · 1911
 12: 4 intending after Easter to **bring** him f to · 321
 12: 6 when Herod would have **brought** him f, · 4254
 13: 4 So they, being **sent** f by the Holy Ghost, · 1599
 16: 3 Him would Paul have to **go** f with him; · 1831
 17:18 *some*, He seemeth to be a **setter** f of · 2604
 21: 2 Phenicia, we went aboard, and **set** f. · 321
 23:28 I **brought** him f into their council: · 2609
 24: 2 when he was called f, Tertullus began · NIG
 25:17 and commanded the man to be brought f. · NIG
 25:23 Festus' commandment Paul was brought f. · NIG
 25:26 Wherefore I have **brought** him f before · 4254
 26: 1 Then Paul **stretched** f the hand, · 1614
 26:25 but **speak** *the* words of truth and · 669
 27:21 But after long abstinence Paul stood f in · NIG
Ro 3:25 Whom God hath **set** f *to be* a propitiation · 4388
 7: 4 that we should **bring** f **fruit** unto God. · 2592
 7: 5 did work in our members to **bring** f **fruit** · 2592
 8:19 All day long have I **stretched** f my hands · 1600
1Co 4: 9 I think that God hath **set** f us the apostles · 584
 16:11 but **conduct** him f in peace, that he may · 4311
Gal 3: 1 Jesus Christ hath been **evidently set** f, · 4270
 4: 4 God **sent** f his Son, made of a woman, · 1821
 4: 6 God hath **sent** f the Spirit of his Son into · 1821
 4:27 **break** f and cry, thou that travailest not: · 4486
Php 2:16 **Holding** f the word of life; that I may · 1907
 3:13 **reaching** f unto those *things which are* · 1901
Col 1: 6 **bringeth** f **fruit**, as *it doth* also in you, · 2592
1Ti 1:16 that in me first Jesus Christ might **shew** f · 1731
Heb 1:14 **sent** f to minister for them who shall be · 649
 6: 7 **bringeth** f meet for them by whom · 5088
 13:13 Let us **go** f therefore unto him without · 1831
Jas 1:15 lust hath conceived, it **bringeth** f **sin**: · 5088
 1:15 when it is finished, **bringeth** f **death**. · 616
 3:11 Doth a fountain **send** f at the same place · 1032
 5:18 rain, and the earth **brought** f her fruit. · 985
1Pe 2: 9 that ye should **shew** f the praises of him · 1804
3Jn 1: 7 for his name's sake they **went** f, · 1831
Jude 1: 7 strange flesh, are **set** f for an example, · 4295
Rev 5: 6 are the seven spirits of God **sent** f into · 649
 6: 2 he **went** f conquering, and to conquer. · 1831
 12: 5 she **brought** f a man child, who was to · 5088
 12:13 persecuted the woman which **brought** f · 5088
 16:14 which **go** f unto the kings of the earth and · 1607

FORTHWITH (10)

Ezr 6: 8 f expences be given unto these men, · 629
Mt 13: 5 *f they sprung up, because they* had no · 2112
 26:49 And f he came to Jesus, and said, Hail, · 2112
Mk 1:29 And f, when they were come out of · 2112
 1:43 charged him, and f sent him away; · 2112
 5:13 And Jesus gave them leave. · 2112
Jn 19:34 and f came there out blood and water. · 2112
Ac 9:18 and he received sight f, and arose, · 3916
 12:10 and f the angel departed from him. · 2112
 21:30 of the temple: and f the doors were shut. · 2112

FORTIETH (4) [FORTY]

Nu 33:38 in the f year after the children of Israel · 705
Dt 1: 3 came to pass in the f year, in the eleventh · 705
1Ch 26:31 In the f year of the reign of David they · 705
2Ch 16:13 and died in the one and f year of his reign. · 705

FORTIFIED (4) [FORT]

2Ch 11:11 he f the strong holds, and put captains in · 2388
 26: 9 at the turning *of the wall*, and f them. · 2388
Ne 3: 8 and they f Jerusalem unto the broad wall. · 5800
Mic 7:12 *from* the f cities, and from the fortress · 4693

FORTIFY (6) [FORT]

Jdg 9:31 and behold, they f the city against thee. · 6696
Ne 4: 2 will they f themselves? will they sacrifice? · 5800
Isa 22:10 the houses have ye broken down to f · 1219
Jer 51:53 though she should f the height of her · 1219
Na 2: 1 *thy* loins strong, f *thy* power mightily. · 553
 3:14 waters for the siege, f thy strong holds: · 2388

FORTRESS (15) [FORT]

2Sa 22: 2 *is* my rock, and my f, and my deliverer; · 4686
Ps 18: 2 *is* my rock, and my f, and my deliverer; · 4686
 31: 3 For thou *art* my rock and my f; therefore · 4686
 71: 3 save me; for thou *art* my rock and my f. · 4686
 91: 2 of the LORD, *He is* my refuge and my f: · 4686
 144: 2 My goodness, and my f; my high tower, · 4686
Isa 17: 3 The f also shall cease from Ephraim, · 4013
 25:12 the f of the high fort of thy walls shall he · 4013
Jer 6:27 *for* a tower *and* a f among my people, · 4013
 10:17 out of the land, O inhabitant of the f. · 4692
 16:19 f, and my refuge in the day of affliction, · 4581
Da 11: 7 shall enter into the f of the king of · 4581
 11:10 he return, and be stirred up, *even* to his f. · 4581
Am 5: 9 that the spoiled shall come against the f, · 4013
Mic 7:12 from the f even to the river, and from sea · 4693

FORTRESSES (2) [FORT]

Isa 34:13 nettles and brambles in the f thereof: · 4013
Hos 10:14 thy people, and all thy f shall be spoiled, · 4013

FORTS (6) [FORT]

2Ki 25: 1 and they built f against it round about. · 1785
Isa 29: 3 a mount, and I will raise f against thee. · 4694

Isa 32:14 the f and towers shall be for dens for ever, · 6076
Jer 32: 4 and built f against it round about. · 1785
Eze 17:17 casting up mounts, and building f, to cut · 1785
 33:27 *they* that *be* in the f and in the caves shall · 4679

FORTUNATUS (2)

1Co 16:17 coming of Stephanas and **F** and Achaicus, · 5415
 16: S and **F**, and Achaicus, and Timotheus. · 5415

FORTY (157) [FORTIETH, FORTY'S]

Ge 5:13 Mahalaleel eight hundred and f years, · 705
 7: 4 I will cause it to rain upon the earth f days · 705
 7: 4 rain upon the earth forty days and f nights; · 705
 7:12 the rain was upon the earth f days and · 705
 7:12 was upon the earth forty days and f nights. · 705
 7:17 And the flood was f days upon the earth; · 705
 8: 6 it came to pass at the end of f days, · 705
 18:28 he said, If I find there f and five, I will not · 705
 18:29 Peradventure there shall be f found there. · 705
 25:20 Isaac was f years old when he took · 705
 26:34 Esau was f years old when he took to wife · 705
 32:15 f kine, and ten bulls, twenty she asses, · 705
 47:28 the whole age of Jacob was an hundred f · 705
 50: f days were fulfilled for him; for so · 705
Ex 16:35 the children of Israel did eat manna f years, · 705
 24:18 Moses was in the mount f days and · 705
 24:18 was in the mount forty days and f nights. · 705
 26:19 thou shalt make f sockets of silver under · 705
 26:21 their f sockets *of* silver; two sockets under · 705
 34:28 he was there with the LORD f days and · 705
 34:28 with the LORD forty days and f nights; · 705
 36:24 f sockets of silver he made under the · 705
 36:26 their f sockets *of* silver; two sockets under · 705
Lev 25: 8 seven sabbaths of years shall be unto thee f · 705
Nu 1:21 *were* f and six thousand and five hundred. · 705
 1:25 *were* f and five thousand six hundred and · 705
 1:33 *were* f thousand and five hundred. · 705
 1:41 *were* f and one thousand and five hundred. · 705
 2:11 *were* f and six thousand and five hundred. · 705
 2:15 *were* f and five thousand and six hundred · 705
 2:19 them, *were* f thousand and five hundred. · 705
 2:28 *were* f and one thousand and five hundred. · 705
 13:25 from searching of the land after f days. · 705
 14:33 shall wander in the wilderness f years, · 705
 14:34 *even* f days, each day for a year, shall ye · 705
 14:34 *even* f years, and ye shall know my breach · 705
 26: 7 that were numbered of them were f and · 705
 26:18 of them, f thousand and five hundred. · 705
 26:41 that were numbered of them *were* f and · 705
 26:50 that were numbered of them *were* f and · 705
 32:13 he made them wander in the wilderness f · 705
 35: 6 to them ye shall add f and two cities. · 705
 35: 7 hich ye shall give to the Levites *shall be* f · 705
Dt 2: 7 these f years the LORD thy God *hath* been · 705
 8: 2 led thee these f years in the wilderness, · 705
 8: 4 neither did thy foot swell, these f years. · 705
 9: 9 abode in the mount f days and forty nights, · 705
 9: 9 abode in the mount forty days and f nights, · 705
 9:11 it came to pass at the end of f days and · 705
 9:11 pass at the end of forty days and f nights, · 705
 9:18 as at the first, f days and forty nights: · 705
 9:18 as at the first, forty days and f nights: · 705
 9:25 Thus I fell down before the LORD f days · 705
 9:25 before the LORD forty days and f nights, · 705
 10:10 to the first time, f days and forty nights; · 705
 10:10 to the first time, forty days and f nights; · 705
 25: 3 **F** stripes he may give him, *and* not exceed: · 705
 29: 5 I have led you f years in the wilderness: · 705
Jos 4:13 About f thousand prepared for war passed · 705
 5: 6 for the children of Israel walked f years in · 705
 14: 7 **F** years old *was* I when Moses the servant · 705
 14:10 me alive, as he said, these f and five years, · 705
 21:41 possession of the children of Israel *were* f · 705
Jdg 3:11 the land had rest f years. And Othniel · 705
 5: 8 or spear seen among f thousand in Israel? · 705
 5:31 in his might. And the land had rest f years. · 705
 8:28 the country was in quietness f years. And · 705
 12: 6 there fell at that time of the Ephraimites f · 705
 12:14 he had f sons and thirty nephews, that rode · 705
 13: 1 into the hand of the Philistines f years. · 705
1Sa 4:18 heavy. And he had judged Israel f years. · 705
 17:16 and evening, and presented himself f days. · 705
2Sa 2:10 Ish-bosheth Saul's son *was* f years old when · 705
 5: 4 he *began* to reign, *and* he reigned f years. · 705
 10:18 f thousand horsemen, and smote Shobach · 705
 15: 7 it came to pass after f years, that Absalom · 705
1Ki 2:11 that David reigned over Israel *were* f years. · 705
 4:26 Solomon had f thousand stalls of horses for · 705
 6:17 *is*, the temple before it, was f cubits *long*. · 705
 7: 3 that *lay* on f pillars, fifteen *in* a row. · 705
 7:38 one laver contained f baths: *and* every · 705
 11:42 in Jerusalem over all Israel *was* f years. · 705
 14:21 Rehoboam *was* f and one years old when · 705
 15:10 f and one years reigned he in Jerusalem. · 705
 19: 8 went in the strength of that meat f days · 705
 19: 8 and f nights unto Horeb the mount of God. · 705
2Ki 2:24 and tare f and two children of them. · 705
 8: 9 camels' burden, and came and stood · 705
 10:14 of the shearing house, *even* two and f men; · 1980
 12: 1 reign; and f years reigned he in Jerusalem. · 705
 14:23 in Samaria, *and reigned* f and one years. · 705
1Ch 5:18 four and f thousand seven hundred and · 705
 12:36 forth to battle, expert in war, f thousand. · 705
 19:18 f thousand footmen, and killed Shophach · 705
 29:27 the time that he reigned over Israel *was* f · 705

2Ch 9:30 reigned in Jerusalem over all Israel f years. · 705
 12:13 and f years old when he *began* to reign, · 705
 22: 2 **F** and two years old *was* Ahaziah when he · 705
 24: 1 reign, and he reigned f years in Jerusalem. · 705
Ezr 2: 8 children of Zattu, nine hundred and five. · 705
 2:10 children of Bani, six hundred f and two. · 705
 2:24 The children of Azmaveth, f and two. · 705
 2:25 Beeroth, seven hundred and f and three. · 705
 2:34 of Jericho, three hundred f and five. · 705
 2:38 a thousand two hundred f and seven. · 705
 2:64 *was* f and **two thousand** · 505+702+7239
 2:66 six; their mules, two hundred f and five; · 705
Ne 5:15 and wine, beside f shekels of silver; · 705
 7:13 children of Zattu, eight hundred f and five. · 705
 7:15 children of Binnui, six hundred f and eight. · 705
 7:28 The men of Beth-azmaveth, f and two. · 705
 7:29 and Beeroth, seven hundred f and three. · 705
 7:36 of Jericho, three hundred f and five. · 705
 7:41 a thousand two hundred f and seven. · 705
 7:44 children of Asaph, an hundred f and eight. · 705
 7:62 children of Nekoda, six hundred f and two. · 705
 7:66 *was* f and **two thousand** · 505+702+7239
 7:67 had two hundred f and five singing *men* · 705
 7:68 six; their mules, two hundred f and five; · 705
 9:21 f years didst thou sustain them in · 705
 11:13 of the fathers, two hundred f and two: · 705
Job 42:16 After this lived Job an hundred f years, · 705
Ps 95:10 F years long was I grieved with *this* · 705
Jer 52:30 away captive *of* the Jews seven hundred f · 705
Eze 4: 6 the iniquity of the house of Judah f days: · 705
 29:11 neither shall it be inhabited f years. · 705
 29:12 *that are* laid waste shall be desolate f years: · 705
 29:13 At the end of f years will I gather · 705
 41: 2 he measured the length thereof, f cubits: · 705
 46:22 *there* were courts joined *of* f cubits long · 705
Am 2:10 led you f years through the wilderness, · 705
 5:25 and offerings in the wilderness f years, · 705
Jnh 3: 4 Yet f days, and Nineveh *shall be* · 705
Mt 4: 2 And when he had fasted f days and · 5062
 4: 2 he had fasted forty days and f nights, · 5062
Mk 1:13 he was there in the wilderness f days, · 5062
Lk 4: 2 Being f days tempted of the devil. And in · 5062
Jn 2:20 **F** and six years was this temple in building · 5062
Ac 1: 3 being seen of them f days, and speaking of · 5062
 4:22 For the man was above f years old, · 5063
 7:23 when he was full f years old, it came · 5063
 7:30 And when f years were expired, · 5062
 7:36 Red sea, and in the wilderness f years. · 5062
 7:42 sacrifices *by the space of* f years in · 5063
 13:18 And about the time of f years suffered he · 5063
 13:21 tribe of Benjamin, *by the space of* f years. · 5062
 23:13 they were more than f which had made · 5062
 23:21 in wait for him of them moe than f men, · 5062
2Co 11:24 Of the Jews five times received I f *stripes* · 5062
Heb 3: 9 proved me, and saw my works f years. · 5062
 3:17 But with whom was he grieved f years? · 5062
Rev 7: 4 *there were* sealed an hundred *and* f *and* · 5062
 11: 2 the holy city shall they tread under foot f · 5062
 13: 5 power was given unto him to continue f · 5062
 14: 1 and with him an hundred f *and* · 5062
 14: 3 but the hundred *and* f *and* four thousand, · 5062
 21:17 an hundred *and* f *and* four cubits, · 5062

FORTY'S (1) [FORTY]

Ge 18:29 And he said, I will not do *it* for f sake. · 705

FORUM (1)

Ac 28:15 they came to meet us as far as Appii f, · 5410

FORWARD (47) [FORWARDNESS, HENCEFORWARD]

Ge 26:13 went f, and grew until he became · 1980+1980
Ex 14:15 unto the children of Israel, that they **go** f: · 5265
Nu 1:51 when the tabernacle **setteth** f, the Levites · 5265
 2:17 **set** f *with* the camp of the Levites in · 5265
 2:17 as they encamp, so shall they **set** f, · 5265
 2:24 And they shall **go** f in the third rank. · 5265
 2:34 they **set** f, every one after their families, · 5265
 4: 5 the camp **setteth** f, Aaron shall come, · 5265
 4:15 of the sanctuary, as the camp is to **set** f; · 5265
 10: 5 camps that lie on the east parts shall **go** f. · 5265
 10:17 of Gershon and the sons of Merari **set** f, · 5265
 10:18 the standard of the camp of Reuben **set** f · 5265
 10:21 Kohathites **set** f, bearing the sanctuary: · 5265
 10:22 Ephraim **set** f according to their armies: · 5265
 10:25 of the camp of the children of Dan **set** f, · 5265
 10:28 to their armies, when they **set** f. · 5265
 10:35 when the ark **set** f, that Moses said, · 5265
 21:10 the children of Israel **set** f, and pitched in · 5265
 22: 1 the children of Israel **set** f, and pitched in · 5265
 32:19 with them on *yonder* side Jordan, or f; · 1973
Jdg 9:44 **rushed** f, and stood *in* the entering of · 6584
1Sa 10: 3 shalt thou go on f from thence, · 1973
 16:13 came upon David from that day f. · 4605+1886.5
 18: 9 And Saul eyed David from that day and f. · 1973
 30:25 it was *so* from that day f, that he · 4605+1886.5
2Ki 3:24 they **went** f smiting the Moabites, even in · 935
 4:24 Drive, and go f; slack not *thy* riding for · NIH
 20: 9 shall the shadow **go** f ten degrees, · 1980
1Ch 23: 4 four thousand *were* to **set** f the work of · 5329
2Ch 34:12 of the sons of the Kohathites, to **set** *it* f; · 5329
Ezr 3: 8 to **set** f the work of the house of · 5329
 3: 9 to **set** f the workmen in the house of God: · 5329
Job 23: 8 I go f, but he *is* not *there*; and backward, · 6924
 30:13 They mar my path, they **set** f my calamity, · 3276

Jer	7:24 and went backward, and not f.　6440+3807.1
Eze	1: 9 went every one **straight f:**　413+5676+6440
	1:12 went every one **straight f:**　413+5676+6440
	10:22 went every one **straight f:**　413+5676+6440
	39:22 the LORD their God from that day and f.　1973
	43:27 shall be, *that* upon the eighth day, and *so* f,　1973
Zec	1:15 and they **helped** the affliction.　5826
Mk	14:35 And he **went** f a little, and fell on　4281
Ac	19:33 of the multitude, the Jews **putting** him f.　4261
2Co	8:10 not only to do, but also to be f a year ago.　2309
	8:17 but being **more** f, of his own accord he　4707
Gal	2:10 poor; the same which I also was f to do.　4704
3Jn	1: 6 whom if thou **bring f** on their **journey**　4311

FORWARDNESS (2) [FORWARD]

2Co	8: 8 but by occasion of the f of others,　4710
	9: 2 For I know the f of your **mind**, for which　4288

FOUGHT (64) [FIGHT]

Ex	17: 8 and f with Israel in Rephidim.　3898
	17:10 had said to him, and f with Amalek:　3898
Nu	21: 1 he f against Israel, and took *some* of them　3898
	21:23 and he came to Jahaz, and f against Israel.　3898
	21:26 had f against the former king of Moab,　3898
Jos	10:14 voice of a man: for the LORD f for Israel.　3898
	10:29 *unto* Libnah, and f against Libnah:　3898
	10:31 and encamped against it, and f against it:　3898
	10:34 they encamped against it, and f against it:　3898
	10:36 unto Hebron; and f against it:　3898
	10:38 Israel with him, to Debir; and f against it:　3898
	10:42 the LORD God of Israel f for Israel.　3898
	23: 3 for the LORD your God *is* he that hath f　3898
	24: 8 *other* side Jordan; and they f with you:　3898
	24:11 the men of Jericho f against you,　3898
Jdg	1: 5 they f against him, and they slew　3898
	1: 8 Now the children of Judah had f against　3898
	5:19 kings came *and* f, then fought the kings　3898
	5:19 f the kings of Canaan in Taanach by　3898
	5:20 They f from heaven; the stars in their　3898
	5:20 the stars in their courses f against Sisera.　3898
	9:17 (For my father f for you,　3898
	9:39 men of Shechem, and f with Abimelech.　3898
	9:45 Abimelech f against the city all that day;　3898
	9:52 f against it, and went hard unto the door　3898
	11:20 and pitched in Jahaz, and f against Israel.　3898
	12: 4 the men of Gilead, and f with Ephraim:　3898
1Sa	4:10 the Philistines f, and Israel was smitten,　3898
	12: 9 king of Moab, and they f against them.　3898
	14:47 f against all his enemies on every side,　3898
	19: 8 f with the Philistines, and slew them *with*　3898
	23: 5 f with the Philistines, and brought away　3898
	31: 1 Now the Philistines f against Israel:　3898
2Sa	2:28 Israel no more, neither f they any more.　3898
	8:10 because he had f against Hadadezer,　3898
	10:17 in array against David, and f with him.　3898
	11:17 of the city went out, and f with Joab:　3898
	12:26 Joab f against Rabbah of the children of　3898
	12:27 I have f against Rabbah, and have taken　3898
	12:29 to Rabbah, and f against it, and took it.　3898
	21:15 with him, and f **against** the Philistines:　3898
2Ki	8:29 when he f against Hazael king of Syria.　3898
	9:15 when he f with Hazael king of Syria.)　3898
	12:17 went up, and f against Gath, and took it:　3898
	13:12 might where*with* he f against Amaziah　3898
	14:15 how he f with Amaziah king of Judah,　3898
1Ch	10: 1 Now the Philistines f against Israel;　3898
	18:10 because he had f against Hadarezer,　3898
	19:17 array against the Syrians, they f with him.　3898
	19:18 seven thousand *men which f in* chariots,　NIH
2Ch	20:29 when they had heard that the LORD f　3898
	22: 6 when he had f against Hazael king of Syria.　3898
	27: 5 He f also with the king of the Ammonites,　3898
Ps	109: 3 hatred; and f against me without a cause.　3898
Isa	20: 1 and f against Ashdod, and took it;　3898
	63:10 to be their enemy, *and* he f against them.　3898
Jer	34: 1 f against Jerusalem, and against all　3898
	34: 7 the king of Babylon's army f against　3898
Zec	14: 3 as when he f in the day of battle.　3898
	14:12 the people that have f against Jerusalem,　6633
1Co	15:32 of men I have f **with beasts** at Ephesus,　2341
2Ti	4: 7 I have f a good fight, I have finished *my*　75
Rev	12: 7 and his angels f against the dragon;　4170
	12: 7 dragon; and the dragon f and his angels　4170

FOUL (5) [FOULED, FOULEDST]

Job	16:16 My face is f with weeping, and on mine　2560
Eze	34:18 but ye must f the residue with your feet?　7515
Mt	16: 3 the morning, *It will be* f **weather** to day:　5494
Mk	9:25 he rebuked the f spirit, saying unto him,　169
Rev	18: 2 the hold of every f spirit, and a cage of　169

FOULED (1) [FOUL]

Eze	34:19 they drink **that which** ye have f with　4833

FOULEDST (1) [FOUL]

Eze	32: 2 the waters with thy feet, and f their rivers.　7515

FOUND (403) [FIND, FOUNDATION, FOUNDATIONS, FOUNDED, FOUNDER, FOUNDEST]

Ge	2:20 for Adam there was not f a help meet for　4672
	6: 8 Noah f grace in the eyes of the LORD.　4672
	8: 9 the dove f no rest for the sole of her foot,　4672
	11: 2 that they f a plain in the land of Shinar;　4672
	16: 7 the angel of the LORD f her by a fountain　4672

Ge	18: 3 if now I have f favour in thy sight,　4672
	18:29 Peradventure there shall be forty f there.　4672
	18:30 Peradventure there shall be thirty f there.　4672
	18:31 Peradventure there shall be twenty f　4672
	18:32 Peradventure ten shall be f there.　4672
	19:19 thy servant hath f grace in thy sight,　4672
	26:19 and f there a well of springing water.　4672
	26:32 and said unto him, We have f water.　4672
	27:20 How is it *that* thou hast f *it so* quickly,　4672
	30:14 f mandrakes in the field, and brought　4672
	30:27 pray thee, if I have f favour in thine eyes,　4672
	31:33 maidservants' tents; but he f *them* not.　4672
	31:34 searched all the tent, but f *them* not.　4672
	31:35 And he searched, but f not the images.　4672
	31:37 hast thou f of all thy household stuff?　4672
	33:10 if now I have f grace in thy sight, then　4672
	36:24 this *was* that Anah that f the mules in　4672
	37:15 a *certain* man f him, and, behold, *he was*　4672
	37:17 after his brethren, and f them in Dothan.　4672
	37:32 to their father; and said, This have we f:　4672
	38:20 from the woman's hand: but he f her not.　4672
	38:23 I sent this kid, and thou hast not f her.　4672
	39: 4 Joseph f grace in his sight, and he served　4672
	44: 8 which we f in our sacks' mouths,　4672
	44: 9 With whom*soever* of thy servants it be f,　4672
	44:10 he with whom it is f shall be my servant;　4672
	44:12 and the cup was f in Benjamin's sack.　4672
	44:16 God hath f **out** the iniquity of thy　4672
	44:16 and *he* also with whom the cup is f.　4672
	44:17 *but* the man in whose hand the cup is f,　4672
	47:14 gathered up all the money that was f　4672
	47:29 If now I have f grace in thy sight, put,　4672
	50: 4 If now I have f grace in your eyes, speak,　4672
Ex	9:19 and beast which shall be f in the field,　4672
	12:19 Seven days shall there be no leaven f in　4672
	15:22 days in the wilderness, and f no water.　4672
	16:27 day for to gather, and they f none.　4672
	21:16 and selleth him, or if he be f in his hand,　4672
	22: 2 If a thief be f breaking up, and be smitten　4672
	22: 4 the theft be **certainly** f in his hand　4672+4672
	22: 7 if the thief be f, let him pay double.　4672
	22: 8 If the thief be not f, then the master of　4672
	33:12 and thou hast also f grace in my sight.　4672
	33:13 I pray thee, if I have f grace in thy sight,　4672
	33:16 and thy people have f grace in thy sight?　4672
	33:17 for thou hast f grace in my sight,　4672
	34: 9 If now I have f grace in thy sight, O Lord,　4672
	35:23 with whom was f blue, and purple,　4672
	35:24 with whom was f shittim wood for any　4672
Lev	6: 3 Or have f that which was lost,　4672
	6: 4 him to keep, or the lost *thing* which he f,　4672
Nu	11:11 wherefore have I not f favour in thy sight;　4672
	11:15 out of hand, if I have f favour in thy sight;　4672
	15:32 they f a man that gathered sticks upon　4672
	15:33 they that f him gathering sticks brought　4672
	32: 5 said they, if we have f grace in thy sight,　4672
Dt	17: 2 If there be f among you, within any of thy　4672
	18:10 There shall not be f among you *any one*　4672
	20:11 that all the people that is f therein shall be　4672
	21: 1 If *one* be f slain in the land which　4672
	22: 3 which he hath lost, and thou hast f, shalt　4672
	22:14 when I came to her, I f her not a maid:　4672
	22:17 *her*, saying, I f not thy daughter a maid;　4672
	22:20 the tokens of *virginity* be not f for　4672
	22:22 If a man be f lying with a woman married　4672
	22:27 For he f her in the field, *and* the betrothed　4672
	22:28 on her, and lie with her, and they be f;　4672
	24: 1 he hath f some uncleanness in her:　4672
	24: 7 If a man be f stealing any of his brethren　4672
	32:10 f him in a desert land, and in the waste　4672
	33:29 thine enemies shall be f **liars** unto thee;　3584
Jos	2:22 throughout all the way, but f *them* not.　4672
	10:17 The five kings are f hid in a cave at　4672
Jdg	1: 5 they f Adoni-bezek in Bezek:　4672
	6:17 if now I have f grace in thy sight, then　4672
	14:18 my heifer, ye had not f **out** my riddle.　4672
	15:15 he f a new jawbone of an ass, and put　4672
	21:12 they f among the inhabitants of　4672
Ru	2:10 him, Why have I f grace in thine eyes,　4672
1Sa	9: 4 the land of Shalisha, but they f *them* not:　4672
	9: 4 of the Benjamites, but they f *them* not.　4672
	9:11 they f young maidens going out to draw　4672
	9:20 set not thy mind on them; for they are f.　4672
	10: 2 asses which thou wentest to seek are f:　4672
	10:16 He told us plainly that the asses were f.　4672
	10:21 when they sought him, he could not be f.　4672
	12: 5 that ye have not f ought in my hand.　4672
	13:19 Now there was no smith f throughout all　4672
	13:22 that there was neither sword nor spear f　4672
	13:22 and with Jonathan his son was there f.　4672
	14:30 of the spoil of their enemies which they f?　4672
	16:22 me; for he hath f favour in my sight.　4672
	20: 3 Thy father certainly knoweth that I have f　4672
	20:29 and now, if I have f favour in thine eyes,　4672
	25:28 evil hath not been f in thee *all* thy days.　4672
	27: 5 If I have now f grace in thine eyes,　4672
	29: 3 I have f no *fault* in him since he fell *unto*　4672
	29: 6 for I have not f evil in thee since the day　4672
	29: 8 what hast thou f in thy servant so long as　4672
	30:11 they f an Egyptian in the field,　4672
	31: 8 they f Saul and his three sons fallen in　4672
2Sa	7:27 hath thy servant f in his heart to pray this　4672
	14:22 To day thy servant knoweth that I have f　4672
	17:12 him in some place where he shall be f,　4672
	17:13 until there be not one small stone f there.　4672

1Ki	1: 3 f Abishag a Shunammite, and brought her　4672
	1:52 wickedness shall be f in him, he shall die.　4672
	7:47 neither was the weight of the brass f **out**.　2713
	11:19 Hadad f great favour in the sight of　4672
	11:29 the prophet Ahijah the Shilonite f him　4672
	13:14 of God, and f him sitting under an oak:　4672
	13:28 he went and f his carcase cast in the way,　4672
	14:13 in him there is f *some* good thing toward　4672
	18:10 and nation, that they f thee not.　4672
	19:19 and f Elisha the son of Shaphat,　4672
	20:36 from him, a lion f him, and slew him.　4672
	20:37 he f another man, and said, Smite me,　4672
	21:20 to Elijah, Hast thou f me, O mine enemy?　4672
	21:20 I have f *thee*: because thou hast sold　4672
2Ki	2:17 and they sought three days, but f him not.　4672
	4:39 f a wild vine, and gathered thereof wild　4672
	9:35 but they f no more of her than the skull,　4672
	12: 5 wheresoever any breach shall be f.　4672
	12:10 told the money that was f in the house of　4672
	12:18 all the gold that was f in the treasures of　4672
	14:14 all the vessels that were f in the house of　4672
	16: 8 gold that was f in the house of the LORD,　4672
	17: 4 the king of Assyria f conspiracy in Hoshea:　4672
	18:15 gave *him* all the silver that was f　4672
	19: 8 f the king of Assyria warring against　4672
	20:13 and all that was f in his treasures.　4672
	22: 8 I have f the book of the law in the house　4672
	22: 9 the money that was f in the house,　4672
	22:13 the words of this book that is f:　4672
	23: 2 which is f in the house of the LORD.　4672
	23:24 the priest f *in* the house of the LORD.　4672
	25:19 which were f in the city, and the principal　4672
	25:19 people of the land that were f in the city:　4672
1Ch	4:40 they f fat pasture and good, and the land　4672
	4:41 the habitations that were f there,　4672
	10: 8 they f Saul and his sons fallen in mount　4672
	17:25 thy servant hath f *in his heart* to pray　4672
	20: 2 f it to weigh a talent of gold, and *there*　4672
	24: 4 there were moe chief men f of the sons of　4672
	26:31 there were f among them mighty *men* of　4672
	28: 9 if thou seek him, he will be f of thee;　4672
	29: 8 they with whom *precious* stones were f　4672
2Ch	2:17 they were f an hundred and fifty thousand　4672
	4:18 the weight of the brass could not be f **out**.　2713
	15: 2 if ye seek him, he will be f of you; but if　4672
	15: 4 Israel, and sought him, he was f of them.　4672
	15:15 their whole desire; and he was f of them:　4672
	19: 3 Nevertheless there are good things f in　4672
	20:25 they f among them in abundance both　4672
	21:17 carried away all the substance that was f　4672
	22: 8 f the princes of Judah, and the sons of　4672
	25: 5 f them three hundred thousand choice　4672
	25:24 all the vessels that were f in the house of　4672
	29:16 out all the uncleanness that they f　4672
	34:14 Hilkiah the priest f a book of the law of　4672
	34:15 I have f the book of the law in the house　4672
	34:17 that was f in the house of the LORD,　4672
	34:21 the words of the book that is f:　4672
	34:30 that was f *in* the house of the LORD.　4672
	36: 8 he did, and that which was f in him,　4672
Ezr	2:62 by genealogy, but they were not f:　4672
	4:19 it is f that this city of old time *hath* made　7912
	6: 2 there was f at Achmetha, in the palace　7912
	8:15 and f there none of the sons of Levi.　4672
	10:18 among the sons of the priests there were f　4672
Ne	2: 5 if thy servant have f **favour** in thy sight,　3190
	5: 8 they their peace, and f nothing to answer.　4672
	7: 5 I f a register of the genealogy of them　4672
	7: 5 came up at the first, and f written therein,　4672
	7:64 reckoned by genealogy, but it was not f:　4672
	8:14 they f written in the law which the LORD　4672
	13: 1 therein was f written, that the Ammonite　4672
Est	2:23 was made of the matter, it was f **out**;　4672
	5: 8 If I have f favour in the sight of the king,　4672
	6: 2 it was f written, that Mordecai had told of　4672
	7: 3 and said, If I have f favour in thy sight,　4672
	8: 5 If I have f favour in his sight, and the　4672
Job	19:28 seeing the root of the matter is f in me;　4672
	20: 8 fly away as a dream, and shall not be f:　4672
	28:12 where shall wisdom be f? and where *is*　4672
	28:13 neither is it f in the land of the living.　4672
	31:29 or lift up myself when evil f him:　4672
	32: 3 because they had f no answer, and *yet*　4672
	32:13 ye should say, We have f **out** wisdom:　4672
	33:24 going down *to* the pit: I have f a ransom.　4672
	42:15 in all the land were no women f *so* fair as　4672
Ps	32: 6 thee in a time when thou mayest be f:　4672
	36: 2 until his iniquity be f to be hateful.　4672
	37:36 yea, I sought him, but he could not be f.　4672
	69:20 none; and for comforters, but I f none.　4672
	76: 5 none of the men of might have f their　4672
	84: 3 sparrow hath f a house, and the swallow　4672
	89:20 I have f David my servant; with my holy　4672
	107: 4 a solitary way; they f no city to dwell in.　4672
	116: 3 gat hold upon me: I f trouble and sorrow.　4672
	132: 6 we f it in the fields of the wood.　4672
Pr	6:31 if he be f, he shall restore sevenfold;　4672
	7:15 to seek thy face, and I have f thee.　4672
	10:13 him that hath understanding wisdom is f:　4672
	16:31 if it be f in the way of righteousness.　4672
	24:14 when thou hast f *it*, then there shall be a　4672
	25:16 Hast thou f honey? eat so much as is　4672
	30: 6 lest he reprove thee, and thou be f **a liar**.　3576
	30:10 lest he curse thee, and thou be f **guilty**.　816
Ecc	7:27 Behold, this have I f, saith the Preacher,　4672

F

Ecc	7:28 one man among a thousand have I f;	4672
	7:28 a woman among all those have I not f.	4672
	7:29 Lo, this only have I f, that God hath made	4672
	9:15 Now there was f in it a poor wise man,	4672
SS	3: 1 soul loveth: I sought him, but I f him not.	4672
	3: 2 soul loveth: I sought him, but I f him not.	4672
	3: 3 watchmen that go about the city f me:	4672
	3: 4 but I f *him* whom my soul loveth:	4672
	5: 7 watchmen that went about the city f	4672
	8:10 was I in his eyes as one that f favour.	4672
Isa	10:10 As my hand hath f the kingdoms of	4672
	10:14 my hand hath f as a nest the riches of	4672
	13:15 one that is f shall be thrust through;	4672
	22: 3 all that are f in thee are bound together,	4672
	30:14 that there shall not be f in the bursting of	4672
	35: 9 shall go up therein, it shall not be f there;	4672
	37: 8 f the king of Assyria warring against	4672
	39: 2 and all that was f in his treasures:	4672
	51: 3 joy and gladness shall be f therein,	4672
	55: 6 Seek ye the LORD while he may be f,	4672
	57:10 thou hast f the life of thine hand;	4672
	65: 1 I am f of *them that* sought me not:	4672
	65: 8 As the new wine is f in the cluster,	4672
Jer	2: 5 What iniquity have your fathers f in me,	4672
	2:26 As the thief is ashamed when he is f,	4672
	2:34 in thy skirts is the blood of the souls	4672
	2:34 I have not f it by secret search, but upon	4672
	5:26 For among my people are f wicked *men*:	4672
	11: 9 A conspiracy is f among the men of Judah,	4672
	14: 3 they came to the pits, *and* f no	4672
	15:16 Thy words were f, and I did eat them;	4672
	23:11 in my house have I f their wickedness,	4672
	29:14 I will be f of you, saith the LORD:	4672
	31: 2 people which were left of the sword f	4672
	41: 3 the Chaldeans that were f there,	4672
	41: 8 ten men were f among them that said	4672
	41:12 f him by the great waters that *are* in	4672
	48:27 was he f among thieves? for since thou	4672
	50: 7 All that f them have devoured them:	4672
	50:20 the sins of Judah, and they shall not be f:	4672
	50:24 thou art f, and also caught, because	4672
	52:25 king's person, which were f in the city;	4672
	52:25 land, that were f in the midst of the city.	4672
La	2:16 looked for; we have f, we have seen it.	4672
Eze	22:30 that *I* should not destroy it: but I f none.	4672
	26:21 yet shalt thou never be f again, saith	4672
	28:15 wast created, till iniquity was f in thee.	4672
Da	1:19 among them all was none like Daniel,	4672
	1:20 he f them ten times better than all	4672
	2:25 I have f a man of the captives of Judah,	7912
	2:35 them away, that no place was f for them:	7912
	5:11 the wisdom of the gods, was f in him;	7912
	5:12 of doubts, were f in the same Daniel,	7912
	5:14 and excellent wisdom is f in thee.	7912
	5:27 in the balances, and art f wanting.	7912
	6: 4 was there any error or fault f in him.	7912
	6:11 f Daniel praying and making supplication	7912
	6:22 forasmuch as before him innocency was f	7912
	6:23 no manner of hurt was f upon him,	7912
	11:19 he shall stumble and fall, and not be f.	4672
	12: 1 every one that *shall* be f written in	4672
Hos	9:10 I f Israel like grapes in the wilderness;	4672
	10: 2 is divided; now shall they be **faulty**:	816
	12: 4 he f him *in* Beth-el, and there he spake	4672
	12: 8 become rich, I have f me **out** substance:	4672
	14: 8 a green fir tree. From me is thy fruit f.	4672
Jnh	1: 3 Joppa; and he f a ship going to Tarshish:	4672
Mic	1:13 for the transgressions of Israel were f in	4672
Zep	3:13 neither shall a deceitful tongue be f in	4672
Zec	10:10 and *place* shall not be f for them.	4672
Mal	2: 6 and iniquity was not f in his lips:	4672
Mt	1:18 she was f with child of the Holy Ghost.	2147
	2: 8 when ye have f *him*, bring me word again,	2147
	8:10 I have not f so great faith, no not in Israel.	2147
	13:44 the which when a man hath f, he hideth,	2147
	13:46 when he had f one pearl of great price,	2147
	18:28 went out, and f one of his fellowservants,	2147
	20: 6 and f others standing idle, and saith unto	2147
	21:19 he came to it, and f nothing thereon,	2147
	22:10 gathered together all as many as they f,	2147
	26:43 And he came and f them asleep again:	2147
	26:60 But f none: yea, though many false	2147
	26:60 false witnesses came, *yet* f they none.	2147
	27:32 they f a man of Cyrene, Simon by name:	2147
Mk	1:37 And when they had f him, they said unto	2147
	7: 2 say, with unwashen, hands, they f **fault**.	3201
	7:30 she f the devil gone out, and *her* daughter	2147
	11: 4 f the colt tied by the door without in a	2147
	11:13 he came to it, and f nothing but leaves;	2147
	14:16 the city, and f as he had said unto them:	2147
	14:40 when he returned, he f them asleep again,	2147
	14:55 Jesus to put him to death; and f none.	2147
Lk	1:30 Mary: for thou hast f favour with God.	2147
	2:16 f Mary, and Joseph, and the babe lying	429
	2:45 when they f him not, they turned back	2147
	2:46 *that* after three days they f him in	2147
	4:17 he f the place where it was written,	2147
	7: 9 have not f so great faith, no, not in Israel.	2147
	7:10 the servant whole that had been sick.	2147
	8:35 and came to Jesus, and f the man, out of	2147
	9:36 the voice was past, Jesus was f alone.	2147
	13: 6 and sought fruit thereon, and f none:	2147
	15: 5 And when he hath f *it*, he layeth *it* on his	2147
	15: 6 for I have f my sheep which was lost.	2147
	15: 9 And when she hath f *it*, she calleth *her*	2147

Lk	15: 9 for I have f the piece which I had lost.	2147
	15:24 and is alive again; he was lost, and is	2147
	15:32 and is alive again; and was lost, and is f.	2147
	17:18 There are not f that returned to give glory	2147
	19:32 and f even as he had said unto them.	2147
	22:13 went, and f as he had said unto them:	2147
	22:45 disciples, he f them sleeping for sorrow,	2147
	23: 2 We f this *fellow* perverting the nation,	2147
	23:14 have f no fault in this man *touching those*	2147
	23:22 I have f no cause of death in him: I will	2147
	24: 2 And they f the stone rolled away from	2147
	24: 3 and f not the body of the Lord Jesus.	2147
	24:23 And when they f not his body, they came,	2147
	24:24 and *it* even so as the women had said:	2147
	24:33 and f the eleven gathered together,	2147
Jn	1:41 him, We have f the Messias, which is,	2147
	1:45 and saith unto him, We have f him,	2147
	2:14 And f in the temple those that sold oxen	2147
	6:25 when they had f him on the other side	2147
	9:35 when he had f him, he said unto him,	2147
	11:17 he f that he had *lien* in the grave four	2147
	12:14 And Jesus, when he had f a young ass,	2147
Ac	5:10 and f her dead, and, carrying *her* forth,	2147
	5:22 f them not in the prison, they returned,	2147
	5:23 The prison truly f we shut with all safety,	2147
	5:23 we had opened, we f no *man* within.	2147
	5:39 haply ye be f even to fight against God.	2147
	7:11 and our fathers f no sustenance.	2147
	7:46 Who f favour before God, and desired to	2147
	8:40 But Philip was f at Azotus:	2147
	9: 2 that if he f any of *this* way, whether they	2147
	9:33 And there he f a certain man named	2147
	10:27 and f many *that were* come together.	2147
	11:26 And when he had f him, he brought him	2147
	12:19 and f *him* not, he examined the keepers,	2147
	13: 6 they f a certain sorcerer, a false prophet,	2147
	13:22 and said, I have f David the *son of* Jesse,	2147
	13:28 And though they f no cause of death *in*	2147
	17: 6 when they f them not, they drew Jason	2147
	17:23 f an altar with this inscription,	2147
	18: 2 And f a certain Jew named Aquila, born	2147
	19:19 and f *it* fifty thousand *pieces* of silver.	2147
	24: 5 For we have f this man a pestilent *fellow*,	2147
	24:12 And they neither f me in the temple	2147
	24:18 Whereupon certain Jews from Asia f me	2147
	24:20 if they have f any evil doing in me,	2147
	25:25 when I f that he had committed nothing	2638
	27: 6 And there the centurion f a ship of	2147
	27:28 And sounded, and f *it* twenty fathoms.	2147
	27:28 sounded again, and f *it* fifteen fathoms.	2147
	28:14 Where we f brethren, and were desired to	2147
Ro	4: 1 father, as pertaining to the flesh, hath f?	2147
	7:10 was *ordained* to life, I f *to be* unto death.	2147
	10:20 saith, I was f of them that sought me not;	2147
1Co	4: 2 in stewards, that a man be f faithful.	2147
	15:15 Yea, and we are f false witnesses of God;	2147
2Co	2:13 spirit, because I f not Titus my brother:	2147
	5: 3 be that being clothed we shall not be f	2147
	7:14 which *I* made before Titus, is f a truth.	1096
	11:12 they glory, they may be f even as we.	2147
	12:20 I shall be f unto you such as ye would	2147
Gal	2:17 ourselves also are f sinners, *is* therefore	2147
Php	2: 8 And being f in fashion as a man,	2147
	3: 9 And be f in him, not having mine own	2147
1Ti	3:10 the office of a deacon, being f blameless.	NIG
2Ti	1:17 sought me out very diligently, and f *me*.	2147
Heb	11: 5 was not f, because God had translated	2147
	12:17 for he f no place of repentance, though he	2147
1Pe	1: 7 might be f unto praise and honour and	2147
	2:22 no sin, neither was guile f in his mouth:	2147
2Pe	3:14 diligent that ye may be f of him in peace,	2147
2Jn	4 I rejoiced greatly that I f of thy children	2147
Rev	2: 2 and are not, and hast f them liars:	2147
	3: 2 for I have not f thy works perfect before	2147
	5: 4 because no *man* was f worthy to open	2147
	12: 8 neither was their place f any more in	2147
	14: 5 And in their mouth was f no guile: for	2147
	16:20 fled *away*, and the mountains were not f.	2147
	18:21 down, and shall be f no more at all.	2147
	18:22 of whatsoever craft *he be*, shall be f any	2147
	18:24 And in her was f the blood of prophets,	2311
	20:11 and there was f no place for them.	2147
	20:15 And whosoever was not f written in	2147

FOUNDATION (54) [FOUND]

Ex	9:18 such as hath not been in Egypt since the f	3245
Jos	6:26 he shall **lay** the f thereof in his firstborn,	3245
1Ki	5:17 hewed stones, to **lay the f** of the house.	3245
	6:37 was the f of the house of the LORD **laid**,	3245
	7: 9 even from the f unto the coping, and *so*	4527
	7:10 the f *was of* costly stones, *even* great	3245
	16:34 he **laid** the f thereof in Abiram his	3245
2Ch	8:16 the day of the f of the house of the LORD,	4143
	23: 5 and a third *part* at the gate of the f:	3247
	31: 7 In the third month they began to **lay** the f	3245
Ezr	3: 6 of the temple of the LORD was	
	not *yet* **laid**.	3245
	3:10 when the builders **laid** the f of the temple	3245
	3:11 the f of the house of the LORD was **laid**.	3245
	3:12 when the f of this house was **laid** before	3245
	5:16 laid the f of the house of God which *is* in	787
Job	4:19 whose f *is* in the dust, which are crushed	3247
	22:16 whose f was overflown *with* a flood;	3247
Ps	87: 1 His f *is* in the holy mountains.	3248
	102:25 Of old hast thou **laid** the f of the earth:	3245

Ps	137: 7 Rase *it*, rase *it, even* to the f thereof.	3247
Pr	10:25 but the righteous *is* an everlasting	3247
Isa	28:16 I **lay** in Zion **for a** f a stone, a tried	3245
	28:16 a precious corner *stone*, a **sure f**:	3245+4143
	44:28 and *to* the temple, Thy f shall be **laid**.	3245
	48:13 hath also **laid** the f of the earth,	3245
Eze	13:14 so that the f thereof shall be discovered,	3247
Hab	3:13 by discovering the f unto the neck.	3247
Hag	2:18 that the f of the LORD'S temple was **laid**,	3245
Zec	4: 9 The hands of Zerubbabel have **laid** the f	3245
	8: 9 f of the house of the LORD of hosts	
	was **laid**,	3245
	12: 1 **layeth** the f of the earth, and formeth	3245
Mt	13:35 been kept secret from the f of the world.	2602
	25:34 prepared for you from the f of the world:	2602
Lk	6:48 and digged deep, and laid the f on a rock:	2310
	6:49 is like a man that without a f built a house	2310
	11:50 which was shed from the f of the world,	2602
	14:29 after he hath laid the f, and is not able to	2310
Jn	17:24 for thou lovedst me before the f of	2602
Ro	15:20 lest I should build upon another *man's* f:	2310
1Co	3:10 I have laid the f, and another buildeth	2310
	3:11 other f can no *man* lay than that is laid,	2310
	3:12 Now if any *man* build upon this f gold,	2310
Eph	1: 4 us in him before the f of the world,	2602
	2:20 And are built upon the f of the apostles	2310
1Ti	6:19 Laying up in store for themselves a good f	2310
2Ti	2:19 Nevertheless the f of God standeth sure,	2310
Heb	1:10 the beginning hast **laid the** f of the earth;	2311
	4: 3 the works were finished from the f	2602
	6: 1 not laying again the f of repentance from	2310
	9:26 must he often have suffered since the f of	2602
1Pe	1:20 Who verily was foreordained before the f	2602
Rev	13: 8 of the Lamb slain from the f of the world.	2602
	17: 8 in the book of life from the f of the world,	2602
	21:19 The first f *was* jasper; the second,	2310

FOUNDATIONS (32) [FOUND]

Dt	32:22 and set on fire the f of the mountains.	4144
2Sa	22: 8 the f of heaven moved and shook,	4146
	22:16 the f of the world were discovered,	4146
Ezr	4:12 set up the walls *thereof*, and joined the f.	787
	6: 3 and *let* the f thereof be strongly laid;	787
Job	38: 4 Where wast thou when I **laid** the f	3245
	38: 6 Whereupon are the f thereof fastened?	134
Ps	11: 3 the f be destroyed, what can the righteous	8356
	18: 7 the f also of the hills moved and	4146
	18:15 the f of the world were discovered at thy	4146
	82: 5 all the f of the earth are out of course.	4144
	104: 5 *Who* laid the f of the earth, *that* it should	4349
Pr	8:29 when he appointed the f of the earth:	4144
Isa	16: 7 for the f of Kir-haresheth shall ye mourn;	808
	24:18 are open, and the f of the earth do shake.	4146
	40:21 have ye not understood *from* the f of the	4146
	51:13 the heavens, and **laid** the f of the earth,	3245
	51:16 **lay** the f of the earth, and say unto Zion,	3245
	54:11 fair colours, and **lay** thy f with sapphires.	3245
	58:12 thou shalt raise up the f of many	4146
Jer	31:37 the f of the earth searched out beneath,	4146
	50:15 her f are fallen, her walls are thrown	803
	51:26 a stone for a corner, nor a stone for f;	4146
La	4:11 Zion, and it hath devoured the f thereof.	3247
Eze	30: 4 and her f shall be broken down.	3247
	41: 8 f of the side chambers *were* a full reed	4155
Mic	1: 6 valley, and I will discover the f thereof.	3247
	6: 2 and ye strong f of the earth:	4146
Ac	16:26 so that the f of the prison were shaken:	2310
Heb	11:10 For he looked for a city which hath f,	2310
Rev	21:14 And the wall of the city had twelve f,	2310
	21:19 And the f of the wall of the city *were*	2310

FOUNDED (10) [FOUND]

Ps	24: 2 For he hath f it upon the seas,	3245
	89:11 and the fulness thereof, thou hast f them.	3245
	104: 8 the place which thou hast f for them.	3245
	119:152 have known of old that thou hast f them	3245
Pr	3:19 The LORD by wisdom hath f the earth;	3245
Isa	14:32 That the LORD hath f Zion, and the poor	3245
	23:13 *till* the Assyrian f it for them that dwell in	3245
Am	9: 6 and hath f his troop in the earth;	3245
Mt	7:25 and it fell not: for it was f upon a rock.	2311
Lk	6:48 not shake it: for it was f upon a rock.	2311

FOUNDER (5) [FOUND]

Jdg	17: 4 gave them to the f, who made thereof a	6884
Jer	6:29 of the fire; the f melteth in vain:	6884
	10: 9 the workman, and of the hands of the f:	6884
	10:14 f is confounded by the graven image:	6884
	51:17 f is confounded by the graven image:	6884

FOUNDEST (1) [FOUND]

Ne	9: 8 f his heart faithful before thee,	4672

FOUNTAIN (33) [FOUNTAINS]

Ge	16: 7 the angel of the LORD found her by a f of	5869
	16: 7 wilderness, by the f in the way to Shur.	5869
Lev	11:36 Nevertheless a f or pit, *wherein there is*	4599
	20:18 he hath discovered her f, and she hath	4726
	20:18 she hath uncovered the f of her blood:	4726
Dt	33:28 the f of Jacob *shall be* upon a land of corn	5869
Jos	15: 9 hill unto the f of the water of Nephtoah,	4599
1Sa	29: 1 the Israelites pitched by a f which *is* in	5869
Ne	2:14 I went on to the gate of the f, and to	5869
	3:15 gate of the f repaired Shallun the son of	5869
	12:37 the f gate, which *was* over against them,	5869

Ps 36: 9 For with thee *is* the **f** of life: in thy light 4726
 68:26 *even* the Lord, from the **f** of Israel. 4726
 74:15 Thou didst cleave the **f** and the flood: 4599
 114: 8 standing water, the flint into a **f** of waters. 4599
Pr 5:18 Let thy **f** be blessed: and rejoice with 4726
 13:14 The law of the wise *is* a **f** of life, to depart 4726
 14:27 The fear of the Lord *is* a **f** of life, 4726
 25:26 down before the wicked *is as* a troubled **f**, 4599
Ecc 12: 6 or the pitcher be broken at the **f**, 4002
SS 4:12 *my* spouse; a spring shut up, a **f** sealed. 4599
 4:15 A **f** of gardens, a well of living waters, 4599
Jer 2:13 they have forsaken me the **f** of living 4726
 6: 7 As a **f** casteth out her waters, so she 953
 9: 1 mine eyes a **f** of tears, that I might weep 4726
 17:13 forsaken the Lord, the **f** of living waters. 4726
Hos 13:15 become dry, and his **f** shall be dried up: 4599
Joel 3:18 a **f** shall come forth of the house of 4599
Zec 13: 1 In that day there shall be a **f** opened to 4726
Mk 5:29 And straightway the **f** of her blood was *4077*
Jas 3:11 Doth a **f** send forth at the same place *4077*
 3:12 *can* no **f** both yield salt water and fresh. *4077*
Rev 21: 6 I will give unto him that is athirst of the **f** *4077*

FOUNTAINS (15) [FOUNTAIN]

Ge 7:11 the same day were all the **f** of the great 4599
 8: 2 The **f** also of the deep and the windows 4599
Nu 33: 9 in Elim *were* twelve **f** of water, 5869
Dt 8: 7 of **f** and depths that spring out of 5869
1Ki 18: 5 unto all **f** of water, and unto all brooks: 4599
2Ch 32: 3 mighty *men* to stop the waters of the **f** 4599
 32: 4 stopt all the **f**, and the brook that ran 4599
Pr 5:16 Let thy **f** be dispersed abroad, *and* rivers 4599
 8:24 when *there were* no **f** abounding with 4599
 8:28 when *he* strengthened the **f** of the deep: 5869
Isa 41:18 and **f** in the midst of the valleys: 4599
Rev 7:17 shall lead them unto living **f** of waters: *4077*
 8:10 of the rivers, and upon the **f** of waters; *4077*
 14: 7 earth, and the sea, and the **f** of waters. *4077*
 16: 4 his vial upon the rivers and **f** of waters; *4077*

FOUR (328) [FOURFOLD, FOURFOOTED, FOURSCORE, FOURSQUARE, FOURTH]

Ge 2:10 it was parted, and became into **f** heads. 702
 11:13 Arphaxad lived after he begat Salah **f** 702
 11:15 Salah lived after he begat Eber **f** hundred 702
 11:16 Eber lived **f** and thirty years, 702
 11:17 Eber lived after he begat Peleg **f** hundred 702
 14: 9 Arioch king of Ellasar; **f** kings with five. 702
 15:13 they shall afflict them **f** hundred years; 702
 23:15 land *is worth* **f** hundred shekels of silver; 702
 23:16 **f** hundred shekels of silver, current *money* 702
 32: 6 to meet thee, and **f** hundred men with him. 702
 33: 1 Esau came, and with him **f** hundred men. 702
 47:24 **f** parts shall be your own, for seed of 702
Ex 12:40 in Egypt, *was* **f** hundred and thirty years. 702
 12:41 it came to pass at the end of the **f** hundred 702
 22: 1 five oxen for an ox, and **f** sheep for a sheep. 702
 25:12 And thou shalt cast **f** rings of gold for it, 702
 25:12 and put *them* in the **f** corners thereof; 702
 25:26 thou shalt make for it **f** rings of gold, 702
 25:26 put the rings in the **f** corners that *are on* 702
 25:26 four corners that *are on* the **f** feet thereof. 702
 25:34 the candlestick *shall be* **f** bowls made like 702
 26: 2 and the breadth of one curtain **f** cubits: 702
 26: 8 and the breadth of one curtain **f** cubits: 702
 26:32 thou shalt hang it upon **f** pillars of shittim 702
 26:32 *be of* gold, upon the **f** sockets of silver. 702
 27: 2 thou shalt make the horns of it upon the **f** 702
 27: 4 upon the net shalt thou make **f** brasen rings 702
 27: 4 four brasen rings in the **f** corners thereof. 702
 27:16 their pillars *shall be* **f**, and their sockets 702
 27:16 pillars *shall be* four, and their sockets **f**. 702
 28:17 settings of stones, *even* **f** rows of stones: 702
 36: 9 the breadth of one curtain **f** cubits: 702
 36:15 **f** cubits *was* the breadth of one curtain: 702
 36:36 made thereunto **f** pillars of shittim *wood,* 702
 36:36 and he cast for them **f** sockets of silver. 702
 37: 3 he cast for it **f** rings of gold, *to be set* by 702
 37: 3 of gold, *to be set* by the **f** corners of it; 702
 37:13 he cast for it **f** rings of gold, and put 702
 37:13 put the rings upon the **f** corners that *were* 702
 37:13 four corners that *were* in the **f** feet thereof. 702
 37:20 in the candlestick *were* **f** bowls made like 702
 38: 2 he made the horns thereof on the **f** corners 702
 38: 5 he cast **f** rings for the four ends of the grate 702
 38: 5 he cast four rings for the **f** ends of the grate 702
 38:19 pillars *were* **f**, and their sockets *of* brass 702
 38:19 *were* four, and their sockets *of* brass **f**; 702
 38:29 and two thousand and **f** hundred shekels. 702
 39:10 they set in it **f** rows of stones: the *first* row 702
Lev 11:20 All fowls that creep, going upon *all* **f**, 702
 11:21 flying creeping thing that goeth upon *all* **f**, 702
 11:23 which have **f** feet, *shall be* an abomination 702
 11:27 among all *manner of* beasts that go on *all* **f**, 702
 11:42 whatsoever goeth upon *all* **f**, 702
Nu 1:29 fifty and **f** thousand and four hundred. 702
 1:29 fifty and four thousand and **f** hundred. 702
 1:31 fifty and seven thousand and **f** hundred. 702
 1:37 thirty and five thousand and **f** hundred. 702
 1:43 thirty and three thousand and **f** hundred. 702
 2: 6 fifty and **f** thousand and four hundred. 702
 2: 6 fifty and four thousand and **f** hundred. 702
 2: 8 fifty and seven thousand and **f** hundred. 702
 2: 9 and six thousand and **f** hundred, 702
 2:16 and one thousand and **f** hundred and fifty, 702

Nu 2:23 thirty and five thousand and **f** hundred. 702
 2:30 fifty and three thousand and **f** hundred. 702
 7: 7 oxen he gave unto the sons of Gershon, 702
 7: 8 **f** wagons and eight oxen he gave unto 702
 7:85 **f** hundred *shekels*, after the shekel of 702
 7:88 peace offerings *were* twenty and **f** bullocks, 702
 25: 9 in the plague *were* twenty and **f** thousand. 702
 26:25 and **f** thousand and three hundred. 702
 26:43 and **f** thousand and four hundred. 702
 26:43 and four thousand and **f** hundred. 702
 26:47 fifty and three thousand and **f** hundred. 702
 26:50 forty and five thousand and **f** hundred. 702
Dt 3:11 **f** cubits the breadth of it, after the cubit of 702
 22:12 Thou shalt make thee fringes upon the **f** 702
Jos 19: 7 and Ashan; **f** cities and their villages: 702
 21:18 and Almon with her suburbs; **f** cities. 702
 21:22 and Beth-horon with her suburbs; **f** cities. 702
 21:24 Gath-rimmon with her suburbs; **f** cities. 702
 21:29 En-gannim with her suburbs; **f** cities. 702
 21:31 and Rehob with her suburbs; **f** cities. 702
 21:35 Nahalal with her suburbs; **f** cities. 702
 21:37 and Mephaath with her suburbs; **f** cities. 702
 21:39 Jazer with her suburbs; **f** cities in all. 702
Jdg 9:34 they laid wait against Shechem *in* **f** 702
 11:40 of Jephthah the Gileadite **f** days in a year. 702
 19: 2 was there **f** whole months. 702
 20: 2 hundred thousand footmen that drew 702
 20:17 numbered **f** hundred thousand men that 702
 20:47 and abode in the rock Rimmon **f** months. 702
 21:12 of Jabesh-gilead **f** hundred young virgins, 702
1Sa 4: 2 they slew of the army in the field about **f** 702
 22: 2 there were with him about **f** hundred men. 702
 25:13 there went up after David about **f** hundred 702
 27: 7 the Philistines was a full year and **f** months. 702
 30:10 David pursued, he and **f** hundred men: 702
 30:17 save **f** hundred young men, which rode 702
2Sa 21:20 foot six toes, **f** and twenty *in* number; 702
 21:22 These **f** were born to the giant in Gath, 702
1Ki 6: 1 it came to pass in the **f** hundred and 702
 7: 2 thirty cubits, upon **f** rows of cedar pillars, 702
 7:19 *were* of lily work in the porch, **f** cubits). 702
 7:27 **f** cubits *was* the length of one base, 702
 7:27 **f** cubits the breadth thereof, and three 702
 7:30 every base had **f** brasen wheels, and plates 702
 7:30 the corners thereof had undersetters: 702
 7:32 under the borders *were* **f** wheels; 702
 7:34 *were* **f** undersetters to the four corners 702
 7:34 *were* four undersetters to the **f** corners 702
 7:38 every laver was **f** cubits: *and* upon every 702
 7:42 **f** hundred pomegranates for the two 702
 9:28 **f** hundred and twenty talents, and brought 702
 10:26 he had a thousand and **f** hundred chariots, 702
 15:33 over all Israel in Tirzah, twenty and **f** years. 702
 18:19 the prophets of Baal **f** hundred and fifty, 702
 18:19 and the prophets of the groves **f** hundred, 702
 18:22 Baal's prophets *are* **f** hundred and fifty men. 702
 18:33 Fill **f** barrels *with* water, and pour *it* on 702
 22: 6 about **f** hundred men, and said unto them, 702
2Ki 7: 3 there were **f** leprous men *at* the entering in 702
 14:13 unto the corner gate, **f** hundred cubits. 702
1Ch 3: 5 and Shobab, and Nathan, and Solomon, **f**, 702
 5:18 *were* **f** and forty thousand seven hundred 702
 7: 1 and Puah, Jashub, and Shimron, **f**. 702
 7: 7 and two thousand and thirty and **f**. 702
 9:24 In **f** quarters were the porters, toward 702
 9:26 For these Levites, the **f** chief porters, *were* 702
 12:26 Of the children of Levi **f** thousand and 702
 20: 6 whose fingers and toes *were* **f** and twenty, 702
 21: 5 Judah *was* **f** hundred threescore and 702
 21:20 and his **f** sons with him hid themselves. 702
 23: 4 **f** thousand *were* to set forward the work of 702
 23: 5 Moreover **f** thousand *were* porters; 702
 23: 5 **f** thousand praised the Lord with 702
 23:10 Beriah. These **f** *were* the sons of Shimei. 702
 23:12 Amram, Izhar, Hebron, and Uzziel, **f**. 702
 24:18 to Delaiah, the **f** and twentieth to Maaziah. 702
 25:31 The **f** and twentieth to Romamti-ezer, **f**, 702
 26:17 northward **f** a day, southward four a day, 702
 26:17 southward **f** a day, and toward Asuppim 702
 26:18 **f** at the causeway, *and* two at Parbar. 702
 27: 1 every course *were* twenty and **f** thousand. 702
 27: 2 in his course *were* twenty and **f** thousand. 702
 27: 4 likewise *were* twenty and **f** thousand. 702
 27: 5 in his course *were* twenty and **f** thousand. 702
 27: 7 in his course *were* twenty and **f** thousand. 702
 27: 8 in his course *were* twenty and **f** thousand. 702
 27: 9 in his course *were* twenty and **f** thousand. 702
 27:10 in his course *were* twenty and **f** thousand. 702
 27:11 in his course *were* twenty and **f** thousand. 702
 27:12 in his course *were* twenty and **f** thousand. 702
 27:13 in his course *were* twenty and **f** thousand. 702
 27:14 in his course *were* twenty and **f** thousand. 702
 27:15 in his course *were* twenty and **f** thousand. 702
2Ch 1:14 he had a thousand and **f** hundred chariots, 702
 4:13 **f** hundred pomegranates on the two 702
 8:18 took thence **f** hundred and fifty talents of 702
 9:25 Solomon had **f** thousand stalls for horses 702
 13: 3 *even* **f** hundred thousand chosen men: 702
 18: 5 together *of* prophets **f** hundred men, 702
 25:23 to the corner gate, **f** hundred cubits. 702
Ezr 1:10 silver basons of a second sort **f** hundred 702
 1:11 of silver *were* five thousand and **f** hundred. 702
 2: 7 Elam, a thousand two hundred fifty and **f**. 702
 2:15 children of Adin, **f** hundred fifty and four. 702
 2:15 children of Adin, four hundred fifty and **f**. 702

Ezr 2:31 a thousand two hundred fifty and **f**. 702
 2:40 of the children of Hodaviah, seventy and **f**. 702
 2:67 Their camels, **f** hundred thirty and five; 702
 6:17 two hundred rams, **f** hundred lambs; 703
Ne 6: 4 they sent unto me **f** times after this sort; 702
 7:12 Elam, a thousand two hundred fifty and **f**. 702
 7:23 of Bezai, three hundred twenty and **f**. 702
 7:34 a thousand two hundred fifty and **f**. 702
 7:43 of the children of Hodevah, seventy and **f**. 702
 7:69 *Their* camels, **f** hundred thirty and five: 702
 11: 6 at Jerusalem *were* **f** hundred threescore 702
 11:18 city *were* two hundred fourscore and **f**. 702
Job 1:19 smote the **f** corners of the house, and it fell 702
 42:16 and his sons' sons, *even* **f** generations. 702
Pr 30:15 *yea,* **f** *things* say not, *It is* enough: 702
 30:18 for me, yea, **f** which I know not: 702
 30:21 disquieted, and for **f** *which* it cannot bear: 702
 30:24 There be **f** *things which are* little upon 702
 30:29 which go well, yea, **f** are comely in going: 702
Isa 11:12 of Judah from the **f** corners of the earth. 702
 17: 6 **f** or five in the outmost fruitful branches 702
Jer 15: 3 I will appoint over them **f** kinds, saith 702
 36:23 when Jehudi had read three or **f** leaves, 702
 49:36 upon Elam will I bring the **f** winds from 702
 49:36 four winds from the **f** quarters of heaven, 702
 52:21 and the thickness thereof *was* **f** fingers: 702
 52:30 all the persons *were* **f** thousand and 702
Eze 1: 5 *came* the likeness of **f** living creatures. 702
 1: 6 every one had **f** faces, and every one had 702
 1: 6 had four faces, and every one had **f** wings. 702
 1: 8 a man under their wings on their **f** sides; 702
 1: 8 and they **f** had their faces and their wings. 702
 1:10 they **f** had the face of a man, and the face 702
 1:10 they **f** had the face of an ox on the left side; 702
 1:10 side; they **f** also had the face of an eagle. 702
 1:15 by the living creatures, with his **f** faces. 702
 1:16 they **f** had one likeness: and their 702
 1:17 they went, they went upon their **f** sides: 702
 1:18 rings *were* full *of* eyes round about them **f**. 702
 7: 2 the end is come upon the **f** corners of 702
 10: 9 behold the **f** wheels by the cherubims, 702
 10:10 their appearances, they **f** had one likeness, 702
 10:11 they went, they went upon their **f** sides: 702
 10:12 about, *even* the wheels that they **f** had. 702
 10:14 every one had **f** faces: the first face *was* 702
 10:21 Every one had **f** faces **apiece**, and 702+702
 10:21 four faces apiece, and every one **f** wings; 702
 14:21 How much more when I send my **f** sore 702
 37: 9 Come from the **f** winds, O breath, 702
 40:41 **F** tables *were* on this side, and four tables 702
 40:41 **f** tables on that side, by the side of the gate; 702
 40:42 the **f** tables *were* of hewn stone for the 702
 41: 5 the breadth of *every* side chamber, **f** cubits, 702
 42:20 He measured it by the **f** sides: it had a wall 702
 43:14 *even* to the greater settle *shall be* **f** cubits, 702
 43:15 the altar *shall be* **f** cubits; and from 702
 43:15 from the altar and upward *shall be* **f** horns. 702
 43:16 broad, square in the **f** squares thereof. 702
 43:17 and fourteen broad in the **f** squares thereof; 702
 43:20 put *it* on the **f** horns of it, and on the four 702
 43:20 on the **f** corners of the settle, and upon 702
 45:19 upon the **f** corners of the settle of the altar, 702
 46:21 caused me to pass by the **f** corners of 702
 46:22 In the **f** corners of the court there were 702
 46:22 these **f** corners *were* of one measure. 702
 46:23 round about them **f**, and *it was* made *with* 702
 48:16 the north side **f** thousand and five hundred, 702
 48:16 the south side **f** thousand and five hundred, 505
 48:16 the east side **f** thousand and five hundred, 702
 48:16 the west side **f** thousand and five hundred. 702
 48:30 **f** thousand and five hundred measures. 702
 48:32 the east side **f** thousand and five hundred: 702
 48:33 the south side **f** thousand and five hundred 702
 48:34 *At* the west side **f** thousand and 702
Da 1:17 As for these **f** children, God gave them 702
 3:25 answered and said, Lo, I see **f** men loose, 703
 7: 2 the **f** winds of the heaven strove upon 703
 7: 3 **f** great beasts came up from the sea, 703
 7: 6 which had upon the back of it **f** wings of a 703
 7: 6 the beast had also **f** heads; and dominion 703
 7:17 great beasts, which *are* **f**, *are* four kings, 703
 7:17 great beasts, which *are* four, *are* **f** kings, 703
 8: 8 it came up **f** notable ones toward the four 702
 8: 8 it came up four notable ones toward the **f** 702
 8:22 being broken, whereas **f** stood up for it, 702
 8:22 **f** kingdoms shall stand up out of the nation, 702
 10: 4 the **f** and twentieth day of the first month, 702
 11: 4 shall be divided toward the **f** winds of 702
Am 1: 3 transgressions of Damascus, and for **f**, 702
 1: 6 For three transgressions of Gaza, and for **f**, 702
 1: 9 For three transgressions of Tyrus, and for **f**, 702
 1:11 For three transgressions of Edom, and for **f**, 702
 1:13 for **f**, I will not turn away the *punishment* 702
 2: 1 For three transgressions of Moab, and for **f**, 702
 2: 4 For three transgressions of Judah, and for **f**, 702
 2: 6 For three transgressions of Israel, and for **f**, 702
Hag 1:15 In the **f** and twentieth day of the sixth 702
 2:10 In the **f** and twentieth *day* of the ninth 702
 2:18 from the **f** and twentieth day of the ninth 702
 2:20 of the Lord came unto Haggai in the **f** 702
Zec 1: 7 the **f** and twentieth day of the eleventh 702
 1:18 mine eyes, and saw, and behold **f** horns. 702
 1:20 And the Lord shewed me **f** carpenters. 702
 2: 6 I have spread you abroad as the **f** winds 702
 6: 1 came **f** chariots out from between two 702

F

Zec	6: 5 These *are* the f spirits of the heavens,	702
Mt	15:38 they that did eat were f thousand men,	5070
	16:10 the seven loaves of the f thousand,	5070
	24:31 together they shall gather from the f winds,	5064
Mk	2: 3 sick of the palsy, *which was* borne of f.	5064
	8: 9 that had eaten were about f thousand:	5070
	8:20 And when the seven among f thousand,	5070
	13:27 shall gather together his elect from the f	5064
Lk	2:37 a widow of about fourscore and f years,	5064
Jn	4:35 There are yet f months, and *then* cometh	5072
	11:17 found that he had lien in the grave f days	5064
	11:39 he stinketh: for he hath been *dead* f days.	5066
	19:23 took his garments, and made f parts,	5064
Ac	5:36 about f hundred, joined themselves.	5071
	7: 6 and entreat *them* evil f hundred years.	5071
	10:11 as it had been a great sheet knit at the f	5064
	10:30 F days ago I was fasting until this hour;	5067
	11: 5 let down from heaven by f corners;	5064
	12: 4 delivered *him* to f quaternions of soldiers	5064
	13:20 judges about the space of f hundred	5071
	21: 9 the same *man* had f daughters, virgins,	5064
	21:23 have f men which have a vow on them;	5064
	21:38 out into the wilderness f thousand	5070
	27:29 they cast f anchors out of the stern,	5064
Gal	3:17 which was f hundred and thirty years	5071
Rev	4: 4 And round about the throne *were* f and	5064
	4: 4 and upon the seats I saw f and	5064
	4: 6 *were* f beasts full of eyes before and	5064
	4: 8 And the f beasts had each of them six	5064
	4:10 The f and twenty elders fall down before	5064
	5: 6 the midst of the throne and of the f beasts,	5064
	5: 8 the f beasts and four and twenty elders	5064
	5: 8 the four beasts and *and* twenty elders	5064
	5:14 And the f beasts said, Amen. And the four	5064
	5:14 And the f *and* twenty elders fell down	5064
	6: 1 one of the f beasts saying, Come and see.	5064
	6: 6 And I heard a voice in the midst of the f	5064
	7: 1 And after these *things* I saw f angels	5064
	7: 1 standing on the f corners of the earth,	5064
	7: 1 holding the f winds of the earth, that	5064
	7: 2 he cried with a loud voice to the f angels,	5064
	7: 4 f thousand of all the tribes of the children	5064
	7:11 and *about* the elders and the f beasts,	5064
	9:13 I heard a voice from the horns of	5064
	9:14 Loose the f angels which are bound in	5064
	9:15 And the f angels were loosed, which were	5064
	11:16 And the f and twenty elders, which sat	5064
	14: 1 an hundred forty *and* f thousand,	5064
	14: 3 and before the f beasts, and the elders:	5064
	14: 3 but the hundred *and* forty *and* f thousand,	5064
	15: 7 one of the f beasts gave unto the seven	5064
	19: 4 the f and twenty elders and the four	5064
	19: 4 twenty elders and the f beasts fell down	5064
	20: 8 which are in the f quarters of the earth,	5064
	21:17 an hundred *and* forty *and* f cubits,	5064

FOURFOLD (2) [FOUR]

2Sa	12: 6 he shall restore the lamb f, because he did	702
Lk	19: 8 man by false accusation, I restore *him* f.	5073

FOURFOOTED (3) [FOUR, FOOT]

Ac	10:12 Wherein were all *manner of* f beasts of	5074
	11: 6 and saw f beasts of the earth,	5074
Ro	1:23 birds, and f beasts, and creeping things.	5074

FOURSCORE (36) [EIGHTY, FOUR]

Ge	16:16 Abram *was* f and six years old, when	8084
	35:28 of Isaac were an hundred and f years.	8084
Ex	7: 7 Moses *was* f years old,	8084
	7: 7 Aaron f and three years old, when they	8084
Nu	2: 9 f thousand and six thousand and	8084
	4:48 eight thousand and five hundred and f	8084
Jos	14:10 now lo, I *am* this day f and five years old.	8084
Jdg	3:30 of Israel. And the land had rest f years.	8084
1Sa	22:18 slew on that day f and five persons that	8084
2Sa	19:32 was a very aged man, *even* f years old:	8084
	19:35 I *am* this day f years old: *and* can I	8084
1Ki	5:15 and f thousand hewers in the mountains,	8084
	12:21 f thousand chosen *men,* which were	8084
2Ki	6:25 until an ass's head was *sold* for f *pieces*	8084
	10:24 Jehu appointed f men without, and said,	8084
	19:35 the camp of the Assyrians an hundred f	8084
1Ch	7: 5 reckoned in all by their genealogies f and	8084
	15: 9 Eliel the chief, and his brethren f:	8084
	25: 7 cunning, was two hundred f and eight.	8084
2Ch	2: 2 f thousand to hew in the mountain,	8084
	2:18 f thousand *to be* hewers in the mountain,	8084
	11: 1 f thousand chosen *men,* which were	8084
	14: 8 drew bows, two hundred and f thousand:	8084
	17:15 with him two hundred and f thousand.	8084
	17:18 f thousand ready prepared for the war.	8084
	26:17 with him f priests of the Lord, *that were*	8084
Ezr	8: 8 the son of Michael, and with him f males.	8084
Ne	7:26 and Netophah, an hundred f and eight.	8084
	11:18 in the holy city *were* two hundred f	8084
Est	1: 1 many days, *even* an hundred and f days.	8084
Ps	90:10 if by reason of strength *they be* f years,	8084
SS	6: 8 concubines, and virgins without number.	8084
Isa	37:36 an hundred and f and five thousand:	8084
Jer	41: 5 and from Samaria, *even* f men,	8084
Lk	2:37 And she *was* a widow of about f and	3589
	16: 7 said unto him, Take thy bill, and write f.	3589

FOURSQUARE (10) [FOUR, SQUARE]

Ex	27: 1 and five cubits broad; the altar shall be f:	7251
Ex	28:16 F it shall be *being* doubled; a span *shall*	7251
	30: 2 a cubit the breadth thereof; f shall it be:	7251
	37:25 *was* f; and two cubits *was* the height of it;	7251
	38: 1 *was* f; and three cubits the height thereof.	7251
	39: 9 was f; they made the breastplate double:	7251
1Ki	7:31 gravings with their borders, f, not round.	7251
Eze	40:47 long, and an hundred cubits broad, f;	7251
	48:20 ye shall offer the holy oblation f, with	7243
Rev	21:16 And the city lieth f, and the length is as	5068

FOURTEEN (26) [FOURTEENTH]

Ge	31:41 I served thee f years for thy two	702+6240
	46:22 born to Jacob: all the souls *were* f.	702+6240
Nu	1:27 were **threescore and f**	702+7657+2050.1
	2: 4 were **threescore and f**	702+7657+2050.1
	16:49 died in the plague were f thousand	702+6240
	29:13 and f lambs of the first year;	702+6240
	29:15 deal to each lamb of the f lambs:	702+6240
	29:17 f lambs of the first year without spot	702+6240
	29:20 f lambs of the first year without	702+6240
	29:23 f lambs of the first year without	702+6240
	29:26 f lambs of the first year without spot	702+6240
	29:29 f lambs of the first year without	702+6240
	29:32 f lambs of the first year without	702+6240
Jos	15:36 f cities with their villages.	702+6240
	18:28 Kirjath; f cities with their villages.	702+6240
1Ki	8:65 and seven days, *even* f days.	702+6240
1Ch	25: 5 God gave to Heman f sons and	702+6240
2Ch	13:21 married f wives, and begat twenty	702+6240
Job	42:12 for he had f thousand sheep,	702+6240
Eze	43:17 the settle *shall be* f cubits long and	702+6240
	43:17 f broad in the four squares thereof;	702+6240
Mt	1:17 from Abraham to David *are* f generations;	1180
	1:17 away into Babylon *are* f generations;	1180
	1:17 into Babylon unto Christ *are* f generations.	1180
2Co	12: 2 I knew a man in Christ above f years ago,	1180
Gal	2: 1 Then f years after I went up again to	1180

FOURTEENTH (25) [FOURTEEN]

Ge	14: 5 in the f year came Chedorlaomer,	702+6240
Ex	12: 6 ye shall keep it *up* until the f day of	702+6240
	12:18 In the first *month,* on the f day of	702+6240
Lev	23: 5 In the f *day* of the first month at	702+6240
Nu	9: 3 In the f day of this month, at even,	702+6240
	9: 5 they kept the passover on the f day	702+6240
	9:11 The f day of the second month at	702+6240
	28:16 in the f day of the first month *is*	702+6240
Jos	5:10 kept the passover on the f day of	702+6240
2Ki	18:13 Now in the f year of king Hezekiah	702+6240
1Ch	24:13 to Huppah, the f to Jeshebeab,	702+6240
	25:21 The f to Mattithiah, he, his sons,	702+6240
2Ch	30:15 they killed the passover on the f *day*	702+6240
	35: 1 they killed the passover on the f *day*	702+6240
Ezr	6:19 upon the f *day* of the first month.	702+6240
Est	9:15 on the f day also of the month Adar,	702+6240
	9:17 on the f day of the same rested they,	702+6240
	9:18 *day* thereof, and on the f thereof;	702+6240
	9:19 made the f day of the month Adar *a*	702+6240
	9:21 that they should keep the f day of	702+6240
Isa	36: 1 Now it came to pass in the f year of	702+6240
Eze	40: 1 f year that the city was smitten,	702+6240
	45:21 In the first *month,* in the f day of	702+6240
Ac	27:27 when the f night was come, as we were	5065
	27:33 This day is the f day that ye have tarried	5065

FOURTH (84) [FOUR]

Ge	1:19 and the morning were the f day.	7243
	2:14 of Assyria. And the f *river is* Euphrates.	7243
	15:16 *in* the f generation they shall come hither	7243
Ex	20: 5 and f *generation* of them that hate me;	7256
	28:20 the f row a beryl, and an onyx, and a	7243
	29:40 with the f *part* of a hin of beaten oil;	7253
	29:40 the f *part* of a hin of wine *for a* drink	7243
	34: 7 unto the third and to the f *generation.*	7256
Lev	19:24 in the f year all the fruit thereof shall be	7243
	23:13 *shall be* of wine, the f *part* of a hin.	7243
Nu	7:30 On the f day Elizur the son of Shedeur,	7243
	14:18 children unto the third and f *generation.*	7256
	15: 4 mingled with the f *part* of a hin of oil.	7243
	15: 5 the f *part* of a hin *of* wine for a drink	7243
	23:10 and the number *of* the f *part* of Israel?	7255
	28: 5 mingled with the f *part* of a hin of beaten	7243
	28: 7 drink offering thereof *shall be* the f *part*	7243
	28:14 a ram, and a f *part* of a hin unto a lamb:	7243
	29:23 on the f day ten bullocks, two rams,	7243
Dt	5: 9 and f *generation* of them that hate me,	7256
Jos	19:17 *And* the f lot came out to Issachar,	7243
Jdg	19: 5 it came to pass on the f day, when they	7243
1Sa	9: 8 I have here at hand the f *part* of a shekel	7253
2Sa	3: 4 the f, Adonijah the son of Haggith;	7243
1Ki	6: 1 the f year of Solomon's reign over Israel,	7243
	6:33 posts of olive tree, a f *part* of the wall.	7243
	6:37 In the f year was the foundation of	7243
	22:41 Judah in the f year of Ahab king of Israel.	702
2Ki	6:25 the f *part* of a kab of dove's dung for five	7255
	10:30 children of the f *generation* shall sit on	7243
	15:12 throne of Israel in the f *generation.*	7243
	18: 9 it came to pass in the f year of king	7243
	25: 3 the ninth *day* of the f month the famine	NIH
1Ch	2:14 Nethaneel the f, Raddai the fifth,	7243
	3: 2 the f, Adonijah the son of Haggith:	7243
	3:15 the third Zedekiah, the f Shallum.	7243
	8: 2 Nohah the f, and Rapha the fifth.	7243
	12:10 Mishmannah the f, Jeremiah the fifth,	7243
1Ch	23:19 Jahaziel the third, and Jekameam the f.	7243
	24: 8 The third to Harim, the f to Seorim,	7243
	24:23 Jahaziel the third, Jekameam the f.	7243
	25:11 The f to Izri, *he,* his sons, and his	7243
	26: 2 Zebadiah the third, Jathniel the f,	7243
	26: 4 and Sacar the f, and Nethaneel the fifth,	7243
	26:11 Tebaliah the third, Zechariah the f:	7243
	27: 7 The f captain for the fourth month *was*	7243
	27: 7 fourth captain for the f month *was*	7243
2Ch	3: 2 second month, in the f year of his reign.	702
	20:26 on the f day they assembled themselves	7243
Ezr	8:33 Now on the f day was the silver and	7243
Ne	9: 1 f day of this month the children of Israel	702
	9: 3 the Lord their God one f *part* of the day;	7243
	9: 3 another f *part* they confessed,	7243
Jer	25: 1 f year of Jehoiakim the son of Josiah king	7243
	28: 1 In the f year, *and* in the fifth month,	7243
	36: 1 it came to pass in the f year of Jehoiakim	7243
	39: 2 f year, in the fourth month, the day of	7243
	45: 1 the f year of Jehoiakim the son of Josiah	7243
	46: 2 f year of Jehoiakim the son of Josiah king	7243
	51:59 *into* Babylon in the f year of his reign.	7243
	52: 6 in the f month, in the ninth *day* of	7243
Eze	1: 1 in the f month, in the fifth *day* of	7243
	10:14 of a lion, and the f the face of an eagle.	7243
Da	2:40 the f kingdom shall be strong as iron:	7244
	3:25 the form of the f *is* like the Son of God.	7244
	7: 7 behold, a f beast, dreadful and terrible,	7244
	7:19 I would know the truth of the f beast,	7244
	7:23 The f beast shall be the fourth kingdom	7244
	7:23 The fourth beast shall be the f kingdom	7244
	11: 2 and the f shall be far richer than *they* all:	7243
Zec	6: 3 in the f chariot grisled and bay horses.	7243
	6: 1 I came to pass in the f year of king Darius,	702
	7: 1 Zechariah in the f *day* of the ninth month,	702
	8:19 The fast of the f *month,* and the fast of	7243
Mt	14:25 And in the f watch of the night Jesus went	5067
Mk	6:48 about the f watch of the night he cometh	5067
Rev	4: 7 and the f beast *was* like a flying eagle.	5067
	6: 7 when he had opened the f seal, I heard	5067
	6: 7 I heard the voice of the f beast say, Come	5067
	6: 8 power was given unto them over the f	5067
	8:12 the f angel sounded, and the third *part*	5067
	16: 8 And the f angel poured out his vial upon	5067
	21:19 the third, a chalcedony; the f, an emerald;	5067

FOWL (31) [FOWLER, FOWLERS, FOWLS]

Ge	1:20 f *that* may fly above the earth in the open	5775
	1:21 and every winged f after his kind:	5775
	1:22 in the seas, and let f multiply in the earth.	5775
	1:26 over the f of the air, and over the cattle,	5775
	1:28 over the f of the air, and over every living	5775
	1:30 to every f of the air, and to every *thing*	5775
	2:19 beast of the field, and every f of the air;	5775
	2:20 to the f of the air, and to every beast of	5775
	7:14 every f after his kind, every bird of every	5775
	7:21 *both* of f, and of cattle, and of beast,	5775
	7:23 creeping things, and the f of the heaven;	5775
	8:17 *both* of f, and of cattle, and of every	5775
	8:19 every f, *and* whatsoever creepeth upon	5775
	8:20 every clean f, and offered burnt offerings	5775
	9: 2 upon every f of the air, upon all that	5775
	9:10 of the f, of the cattle, and of every beast of	5775
Lev	7:26 whether it be of f or of beast, in any of	5775
	11:46 of the f, and of every living creature that	5775
	17:13 catcheth *any* beast or f that may be eaten;	5775
	20:25 or by f, or by any *manner of living thing*	5775
Dt	4:17 the likeness of any winged f that flieth in	6833
1Ki	4:23 roebucks, and fallowdeer, and fatted f,	1257
	4:33 of f, and of creeping things, and of fishes.	5775
Job	28: 7 *There is* a path which no f knoweth,	5861
Ps	8: 8 The f of the air, and the fish of the sea,	6833
	148:10 all cattle; creeping things, and flying f:	6833
Jer	9:10 both the f of the heavens and the beast	5775
Eze	17:23 under it shall dwell all f of every wing;	6833
	39:17 Speak unto every feathered f, and to every	6833
	44:31 of itself, or torn, whether it be f or beast.	5775
Da	7: 6 had upon the back of it four wings of a f;	5776

FOWLER (3) [FOWL]

Ps	91: 3 shall deliver thee from the snare of the f,	3353
Pr	6: 5 and as a bird from the hand of the f.	3353
Hos	9: 8 prophet *is* a snare of a f in all his ways,	3352

FOWLERS (1) [FOWL]

Ps	124: 7 escaped as a bird out of the snare of the f:	3369

FOWLS (55) [FOWL]

Ge	6: 7 the creeping thing, and the f of the air;	5775
	6:20 Of f after their kind, and of cattle after	5775
	7: 3 Of f also of the air by sevens, the male	5775
	7: 8 Of f, and of every *thing* that creepeth upon	5775
	15:11 when the f came down upon the carcases,	5861
Lev	1:14 for his offering to the Lord *be* of f,	5775
	11:13 ye shall have in abomination among the f;	5775
	11:20 All f that creep, going upon *all* four,	5775
	20:25 and between unclean f and clean:	5775
Dt	14:20 *But* of all clean f ye may eat.	5775
	28:26 thy carcase shall be meat unto all f of	5775
1Sa	17:44 I will give thy flesh unto the f of the air,	5775
	17:46 Philistines this day unto the f of the air,	5775
1Ki	14:11 him that dieth in the field shall the f	5775
	16: 4 that dieth of his in the fields shall the f	5775
	21:24 him that dieth in the field shall the f of	5775
Ne	5:18 also were prepared for me, and once in	6833

Job	12: 7 the **f** of the air, and they shall tell thee:	5775
	28:21 and kept close from the **f** of the air.	5775
	35:11 maketh us wiser than the **f** of heaven?	5775
Ps	50:11 I know all the **f** of the mountains;	5775
	78:27 and feathered like as the sand of the sea:	5775
	79: 2 given *to be* meat unto the **f** of the heaven,	5775
	104:12 By them shall the **f** of the heaven have	5775
Isa	18: 6 They shall be left together unto the **f** of	5861
	18: 6 the **f** shall summer upon them, and all	5861
Jer	7:33 shall be meat for the **f** of the heaven,	5775
	15: 3 the **f** of the heaven, and the beasts of	5775
	16: 4 their carcases shall be meat for the **f** of	5775
	19: 7 I give to be meat for the **f** of the heaven,	5775
	34:20 be for meat unto the **f** of the heaven,	5775
Eze	29: 5 of the field and to the **f** of the heaven.	5775
	31: 6 All the **f** of heaven made their nests in his	5775
	31:13 Upon his ruin shall all the **f** of the heaven	5775
	32: 4 cause all the **f** of the heaven to remain	5775
	38:20 the **f** of the heaven, and the beasts of	5775
Da	2:38 the **f** of the heaven hath he given into	5776
	4:12 the **f** of the heaven dwelt in the boughs	6853
	4:14 under it, and the **f** from his branches:	6853
	4:21 upon whose branches the **f** of the heaven	6853
Hos	2:18 the **f** of heaven, and *with* the creeping	5775
	4: 3 of the field, and with the **f** of heaven;	5775
	7:12 I will bring them down as the **f** of	5775
Zep	3: 1 I will consume the **f** of the heaven,	5775
Mt	6:26 Behold the **f** of the air: for they sow not,	4071
	13: 4 and the **f** came and devoured them up:	4071
Mk	4: 4 and the **f** of the air came and devoured it	4071
	4:32 that the **f** of the air may lodge under	4071
Lk	8: 5 and the **f** of the air devoured it.	4071
	12:24 how much more are ye better than the **f**?	4071
	13:19 the **f** of the air lodged in the branches of it.	4071
Ac	10:12 and creeping things, and **f** of the air.	4071
	11: 6 and creeping things, and **f** of the air.	4071
Rev	19:17 saying to all the **f** that fly in the midst of	3732
	19:21 and all the **f** were filled with their flesh.	3732

FOX (2) [FOXES]

Ne	4: 3 Even *that* which they build, if a **f** go up,	7776
Lk	13:32 Go ye, and tell that **f**, Behold, I cast out	258

FOXES (8) [FOX]

Jdg	15: 4 Samson went and caught three hundred **f**,	7776
Ps	63:10 by the sword: they shall be a portion for **f**.	7776
SS	2:15 Take us the **f**, the little foxes, that spoil	7776
	2:15 Take us the foxes, the little **f**, that spoil	7776
La	5:18 which is desolate, the **f** walk upon it.	7776
Eze	13: 4 thy prophets are like the **f** in the deserts.	7776
Mt	8:20 The **f** have holes, and the birds of the air	258
Lk	9:58 **F** have holes, and birds of the air *have* nests	258

FRAGMENT See SHERD; SHERDS

FRAGMENTS (7)

Mt	14:20 took up of the **f** that remained twelve	2801
Mk	6:43 they took up twelve baskets full of the **f**,	2801
	8:19 how many baskets full of **f** took ye up?	2801
	8:20 how many baskets full of **f** took ye up?	2801
Lk	9:17 there was taken up of **f** that remained to	2801
Jn	6:12 Gather up the **f** that remain, that nothing	2801
	6:13 filled twelve baskets with the **f** of the five	2801

FRAGRANT See SWEETSMELLING

FRAIL (1)

Ps	39: 4 what it *is; that* I may know how **f** I *am*.	2310

FRAME (5) [FRAMED, FRAMETH]

Jdg	12: 6 for he **could** not **f** to pronounce *it* right.	3559
Ps	103:14 For he knoweth our **f**; he remembereth	3336
Jer	18:11 I **f** evil against you, and devise a device	3335
Eze	40: 2 which *was* as the **f** of a city on the south.	4011
Hos	5: 4 They will not **f** their doings to turn unto	5414

FRAMED (4) [FRAME]

Isa	29:16 shall the **thing f** say of him that framed it,	3336
	29:16 shall the thing framed say of him that **f** it,	3335
Eph	2:21 In whom all the building **fitly f together**	4883
Heb	11: 3 the worlds were **f** by the word of God,	2675

FRAMETH (2) [FRAME]

Ps	50:19 thy mouth to evil, and thy tongue **f** deceit.	6775
	94:20 with thee, which **f** mischief by a law?	3335

FRANKINCENSE (17) [INCENSE]

Ex	30:34 galbanum; *these* sweet spices with pure **f**:	3828
Lev	2: 1 shall pour oil upon it, and put **f** thereon:	3828
	2: 2 of the oil thereof, with all the **f** thereof;	3828
	2:15 shalt put oil upon it, and lay **f** thereon:	3828
	2:16 of the oil thereof, with all the **f** thereof:	3828
	5:11 it, neither shall he put *any* **f** thereon:	3828
	6:15 all the **f** which *is* upon the meat offering,	3828
	24: 7 thou shalt put pure **f** upon *each* row, that	3828
Nu	5:15 pour no oil upon it, nor put **f** thereon;	3828
1Ch	9:29 and the oil, and the **f**, and the spices.	3828
Ne	13: 5 the **f**, and the vessels, and the tithes of	3828
	13: 9 of God, with the meat offering and the **f**.	3828
SS	3: 6 perfumed *with* myrrh and **f**, with all	3828
	4: 6 mountain of myrrh, and to the hill of **f**.	3828
	4:14 calamus and cinnamon, with all trees of **f**;	3828
Mt	2:11 unto him gifts; gold, and **f**, and myrrh.	3030
Rev	18:13 and **f**, and wine, and oil, and fine flour,	3030

FRANKLY (1)

Lk	7:42 nothing to pay, he **f forgave** *them* both.	5483

FRAUD (2)

Ps	10: 7 mouth is full *of* cursing and deceit and **f**:	8496
Jas	5: 4 which is of you **kept back by f**, crieth:	650

FRAY (3)

Dt	28:26 the earth, and no man shall **f** them **away**.	2729
Jer	7:33 of the earth; and none shall **f** them **away**.	2729
Zec	1:21 these are come to **f** them, to cast out	2729

FRECKLED (1)

Lev	13:39 it *is* a **f** spot *that* groweth in the skin:	933

FREE (59) [FREED, FREEDOM, FREELY, FREEMAN, FREEWILL, FREEWOMAN]

Ex	21: 2 the seventh he shall go out **f** for nothing.	2670
	21: 5 and my children; I will not go out **f**:	2670
	21:11 then shall she go out **f** without money.	2600
	21:26 he shall let him go **f** for his eye's sake.	2670
	21:27 he shall let him go **f** for his tooth's sake.	2670
	36: 3 yet unto him **f offerings** every morning.	5071
Lev	19:20 be put to death, because she was not **f**.	2666
Nu	5:19 be thou **f** from this bitter water that	5352
	5:28 she shall be **f**, and shall conceive seed.	5352
Dt	15:12 the seventh year thou shalt let him go **f**	2670
	15:13 when thou sendest him out **f** from thee,	2670
	15:18 thou sendest him away **f** from thee;	2670
	24: 5 *but* he shall be **f** at home one year,	5355
1Sa	17:25 and make his father's house **f** in Israel.	2670
1Ch	9:33 *who* remaining in the chambers *were* **f**:	6362
2Ch	29:31 as many as were of a **f** heart burnt	5081
Job	3:19 and the servant *is* **f** from his master.	2670
	39: 5 Who hath sent out the wild ass **f**?	2670
Ps	51:12 and uphold me *with thy* **f** spirit.	5081
	88: 5 **F** among the dead, like the slain that lie	2670
	105:20 the ruler of the people, and let him go **f**.	6605
Isa	58: 6 let the oppressed go **f**, and *that* ye break	2670
Jer	34: 9 *being* a Hebrew or a Hebrewess, go **f**;	2670
	34:10 and every one his maidservant, go **f**,	2670
	34:11 whom they had let go **f**, to return,	2670
	34:14 six years, thou shalt let him go **f** from	2670
Am	4: 5 and proclaim *and* publish the **f offerings**:	5071
Mt	15: 6 he shall be **f**. Thus have ye made	NIG
	17:26 saith unto him, Then are the children **f**.	1658
Mk	7:11 mightest be profited by me; *he shall be* **f**.	NIG
Jn	8:32 the truth, and the truth shall **make** you **f**.	1659
	8:33 how sayest thou, Ye shall be made **f**?	1658
	8:36 If the Son therefore shall **make** you **f**,	1659
	8:36 shall make you free, ye shall be **f** indeed.	1658
Ac	22:28 And Paul said, But I was **f** born.	NIG
Ro	5:15 But not as the offence, so also *is* the **f gift**.	5486
	5:16 the **f gift** *is* of many offences unto	5486
	5:18 by the righteousness of one *the* **f gift** came	NIG
	6:18 Being then **made f** from sin, ye became	1659
	6:20 of sin, ye were **f** from righteousness.	1658
	6:22 But now being **made f** from sin,	1659
	7: 3 husband be dead, she is **f** from *that* law;	1658
	8: 2 Jesus hath **made** me **f** from the law of sin	1659
1Co	7:21 but if thou mayest be made **f**, use *it* rather.	1658
	7:22 that is called, *being* **f**, is Christ's servant.	1658
	9: 1 I not **f**? have I not seen Jesus Christ our	1658
	9:19 For though I be **f** from all *men*, yet have I	1658
	12:13 or Gentiles, whether *we be* bond or **f**;	1658
Gal	3:28 nor Greek, there is neither bond nor **f**,	1658
	4:26 Jerusalem which is above is **f**, which is	1658
	4:31 children of *the* bondwoman, but of the **f**.	1658
	5: 1 liberty wherewith Christ hath **made** us **f**,	1659
Eph	6: 8 of the Lord, whether *he be* bond or **f**.	1658
Col	3:11 barbarian, Scythian, bond nor **f**:	1658
2Th	3: 1 that the word of the Lord may have **f**	NIG
1Pe	2:16 As **f**, and not using *your* liberty for a cloke	1658
Rev	6:15 every **f** *man*, hid themselves in the dens	1658
	13:16 and great, rich and poor, **f** and bond,	1658
	19:18 and the flesh of all *men*, both **f** and bond,	1658

FREED (2) [FREE]

Jos	9:23 there shall none of you be **f** from being	3772
Ro	6: 7 For he that is dead is **f** from sin.	1344

FREEDMEN See LIBERTINES

FREEDOM (2) [FREE]

Lev	19:20 and not at all redeemed, nor **f** given her;	2668
Ac	22:28 With a great sum obtained I this **f**.	4174

FREELY (17) [FREE]

Ge	2:16 tree of the garden thou mayest **f eat**:	398+398
Nu	11: 5 the fish, which we did eat in Egypt **f**;	2600
1Sa	14:30 if haply the people had **eaten f** to day	398+398
Ezr	2:68 **offered f** for the house of God to set it up	5068
	7:15 counsellers have **f offered** unto the God	5069
Ps	54: 6 I will **f** sacrifice unto thee: I will	5071+871.1
Hos	14: 4 heal their backsliding, I will love them **f**:	5071
Mt	10: 8 out devils: **f** ye have received, freely give.	1432
	10: 8 out devils: freely ye have received, **f** give.	1432
Ac	2:29 let *me* **f** speak unto you of	3326+3954
	26:26 these *things*, before whom also I speak **f**:	3955
Ro	3:24 Being justified **f** by his grace through	1432
	8:32 how shall he not with him also **f give** us	5483
1Co	2:12 the *things* that are **f given** to us of God.	1432
2Co	11: 7 have preached to you the gospel of God **f**?	1432
Rev	21: 6 of the fountain of the water of life **f**.	1432
	22:17 let him take the water of life **f**.	1432

FREEMAN (1) [FREE, MAN]

1Co	7:22 in the Lord, *being* a servant, is the Lord's **f**:	558

FREEWILL (17) [FREE, WILL]

Lev	22:18 all his vows, and for all his **f offerings**,	5071
	22:21 or a **f offering** in beeves or sheep, it shall	5071
	22:23 that mayest thou offer *for* a **f offering**;	5071
	23:38 vows, and beside all your **f offerings**,	5071
Nu	15: 3 in a **f offering**, or in your solemn feasts,	5071
	29:39 besides your vows, and your **f offerings**,	5071
Dt	12: 6 your **f offerings**, and the firstlings of your	5071
	12:17 nor thy **f offerings**, or heave offering of	5071
	16:10 a tribute of a **f offering** of thine hand,	5071
	23:23 *even* a **f offering**, according as thou hast	5071
2Ch	31:14 the east, *was* over the **f offerings** of God,	5071
Ezr	1: 4 the **f offering** for the house of God	5071
	3: 5 offered a **f offering** unto the LORD.	5071
	7:13 which *are* **minded of** their **own f** to go	5069
	7:16 with the **f offering** of the people, and of	5069
	8:28 the gold *are* a **f offering** unto the LORD	5071
Ps	119:108 the **f offerings** of my mouth, O LORD,	5071

FREEWOMAN (3) [FREE, WOMAN]

Gal	4:22 the one by a bondmaid, the other by a **f**.	1658
	4:23 the flesh; but the of the **f** *was* by promise.	1658
	4:30 shall not be heir with the son of the **f**.	1658

FREQUENT (1)

2Co	11:23 in prisons **more f**, in deaths oft.	4056

FRESH (4) [AFRESH, FRESHER]

Nu	11: 8 and the taste of it was as the taste of **f** oil.	3955
Job	29:20 My glory *was* **f** in me, and my bow was	2319
Ps	92:10 an unicorn: I shall be anointed with **f** oil.	7488
Jas	3:12 no fountain *both* yield salt water and **f**.	1099

FRESHER (1) [FRESH]

Job	33:25 His flesh shall be **f** than a child's: he shall	7375

FRET (7) [FRETTED, FRETTETH, FRETTING]

Lev	13:55 it *is* **f** inward, *whether* it *be* bare within	6356
1Sa	1: 6 for to **make** her **f**, because the LORD had	7481
Ps	37: 1 **F** not thyself because of evildoers,	2734
	37: 7 **f** not thyself because of him who	2734
	37: 8 **f** not thyself in any wise to do evil.	2734
Pr	24:19 **F** not thyself because of evil *men*, neither	2734
Isa	8:21 shall **f** themselves, and curse their king	7107

FRETTED (1) [FRET]

Eze	16:43 hast **f** me in all these *things*; behold	7264

FRETTETH (1) [FRET]

Pr	19: 3 his way: and his heart **f** against the LORD.	2196

FRETTING (3) [FRET]

Lev	13:51 the plague *is* a **f** leprosy; it *is* unclean.	3992
	13:52 for it *is* a **f** leprosy; it shall be burnt in	3992
	14:44 the house, it *is* a **f** leprosy in the house:	3992

FRIED (2) [FRYINGPAN]

Lev	7:12 cakes mingled with oil, of fine flour, **f**.	7246
1Ch	23:29 for that which is **f**, and for all *manner of*	7246

FRIEND (53) [FRIENDLY, FRIENDS, FRIENDSHIP]

Ge	38:12 he and his **f** Hirah the Adullamite.	7453
	38:20 Judah sent the kid by the hand of his **f**	7453
Ex	33:11 face to face, as a man speaketh unto his **f**.	7453
Dt	13: 6 or the wife of thy bosom, or thy **f**,	7453
Jdg	14:20 companion, whom he had used as his **f**.	7462
2Sa	13: 3 Amnon had a **f**, whose name *was* Jonadab	7453
	15:37 So Hushai David's **f** came *into* the city,	7463
	16:16 David's **f**, was come unto Absalom,	7453
	16:17 to Hushai, *Is* this thy kindness to thy **f**?	7453
	16:17 why wentest thou not with thy **f**?	7453
1Ki	4: 5 was principal officer, *and* the king's **f**:	7463
2Ch	20: 7 gavest it to the seed of Abraham thy **f** for	157
Job	6:14 afflicted pity *should be shewed* from his **f**;	7453
	6:27 the fatherless, and you dig a *pit* for your **f**.	7453
Ps	35:14 myself as though he had been my **f**	7453
	41: 9 mine own **familiar f**, in whom I	376+7965
	88:18 Lover and **f** hast thou put far from me,	7453
Pr	6: 1 My son, if thou be surety for thy **f**, *if* thou	7453
	6: 3 thou art come into the hand of thy **f**;	7453
	6: 3 go, humble thyself, and make sure thy **f**.	7453
	17:17 A **f** loveth at all times, and a brother is	7453
	17:18 becometh surety in the presence of his **f**.	7453
	18:24 is a **f** *that* sticketh closer than a brother.	157
	19: 6 every *man* is a **f** to him that giveth gifts.	7453
	22:11 the grace of his lips the king *shall be* his **f**.	7453
	27: 6 Faithful *are* the wounds of a **f**; but the	157
	27: 9 *doth* the sweetness of a man's **f** by hearty	7453
	27:10 Thine own **f**, and thy father's friend,	7453
	27:10 own friend, and thy father's **f**, forsake not;	7453
	27:14 He that blesseth his **f** with a loud voice,	7453
	27:17 man sharpeneth the countenance of his **f**.	7453
SS	5:16 This *is* my beloved, and this *is* my **f**,	7453
Isa	41: 8 I have chosen, the seed of Abraham my **f**.	157
Jer	6:21 the neighbour and his **f** shall perish.	7453
	19: 9 they shall eat every one the flesh of his **f**	7453
Hos	3: 1 Go yet, love a woman beloved of *her* **f**,	7453
Mic	7: 5 Trust ye not in a **f**, put ye not confidence	7453
Mt	11:19 a winebibber, a **f** of publicans and sinners.	5384
	20:13 them, and said, **F**, I do thee no wrong;	2083
	22:12 he saith unto him, **F**, how camest thou	2083
	26:50 And Jesus said unto him, **F**, wherefore art	2083
Lk	7:34 a winebibber, a **f** of publicans and sinners.	5384

F

Lk 11: 5 Which of you shall have a **f**, and shall go 5384
11: 5 say unto him, **F**, lend me three loaves; 5384
11: 6 For a **f** of mine in *his* journey is come to 5384
11: 8 because he is his **f**, yet because of his 5384
14:10 he may say unto thee, **F**, go up higher: 5384
Jn 3:29 the **f** of the bridegroom, which standeth 5384
11:11 saith unto them, Our **f** Lazarus sleepeth; 5384
19:12 let this *man* go, thou art not Cesar's **f**: 5384
Ac 12:20 **made** Blastus the king's chamberlain
their **f**, 3982
Jas 2:23 and he was called the **F** of God. 5384
4: 4 will be a **f** of the world is the enemy of 5384

FRIENDLY (3) [FRIEND]
Jdg 19: 3 **f** unto her, *and* to bring her again, 3820+5921
Ru 2:13 that thou hast spoken **f** unto thine 3820+5921
Pr 18:24 that hath friends must **shew** himself **f**. 7462

FRIENDS (49) [FRIEND]
Ge 26:26 Ahuzzath *one* of his **f**, and Phichol the 4828
1Sa 30:26 the elders of Judah, *even* to his **f**, saying, 7453
2Sa 3: 8 to his **f**, and have not delivered thee into 4828
19: 6 lovest thine enemies, and hatest thy **f**; 157
1Ki 16:11 wall, neither *of* his kinsfolks, nor *of* his **f**. 7453
Est 5:10 he sent and called for his **f**, and Zeresh his 157
5:14 said Zeresh his wife and all his **f** unto him, 157
6:13 all his **f** every *thing* that had befallen him. 157
Job 2:11 Now when Job's three **f** heard of all this 7453
16:20 My **f** scorn me: *but* mine eye poureth out 7453
17: 5 He *that* speaketh flattery to *his* **f**, even 7453
19:14 and my **familiar f** have forgotten me. 3045
19:19 All my inward **f** abhorred me: 4962
19:21 upon me, have pity upon me, O ye my **f**; 7453
32: 3 Also against his three **f** was his wrath 7453
42: 7 against thee, and against thy two **f**: 7453
42:10 captivity of Job, when he prayed for his **f**: 7453
Ps 38:11 and my **f** stand aloof from my sore; 7453
Pr 14:20 own neighbour: but the rich *hath* many **f**. 157
16:28 and a whisperer separateth **chief f**. 441
17: 9 that repeateth a matter separateth **very f**. 441
18:24 A man that hath **f** must shew himself 7453
19: 4 Wealth maketh many **f**; but the poor is 7453
19: 7 how much more do his **f** go far from him! 4828
SS 5: 1 eat, O **f**; drink, yea, drink abundantly, 7453
Jer 20: 4 thee a terror to thyself, and to all thy **f**; 157
20: 6 shalt be buried there, thou, and all thy **f**, 157
38:22 Thy **f** have set thee on, 376+7965
La 1:2 all her **f** have dealt treacherously with her, 7453
Zec 13: 6 I was wounded *in* the house of my **f**. 157
Mk 3:21 when his **f** heard *of it*, they went 3588+3844
5:19 Go home to thy **f**, and tell them how great NIG
Lk 7: 6 the centurion sent **f** to him, saying unto 5384
12: 4 And I say unto you my **f**, Be not afraid of 5384
14:12 makest a dinner or a supper, call not thy **f**, 5384
15: 6 he calleth together *his* **f** and neighbours, 5384
15: 9 when she hath found *it*, she calleth her **f** 5384
15:29 a kid, that I might make merry with my **f**: 5384
16: 9 Make to yourselves **f** of the mammon of 5384
21:16 and brethren, and kinsfolks, and **f**, 5384
23:12 Pilate and Herod were made **f** together: 5384
Jn 15:13 that a man lay down his life for his **f**. 5384
15:14 Ye are my **f**, if ye do whatsoever I 5384
15:15 I have called you **f**; for all *things* that I 5384
Ac 10:24 called together his kinsmen and near **f**. 5384
19:31 of Asia, which were his **f**, sent unto him, 5384
27: 3 gave *him* liberty to go unto *his* **f** to refresh 5384
3Jn 1:14 Our **f** salute thee. Greet the friends by 5384
1:14 friends salute thee. Greet the **f** by name. 5384

FRIENDSHIP (2) [FRIEND]
Pr 22:24 **Make** no **f** with an angry man; and with 7462
Jas 4: 4 know ye not that the **f** of the world is 5373

FRIGHTENED See ABASE; ABASED; ABASING

FRINGE (2) [FRINGES]
Nu 15:38 that they put upon the **f** of the borders a 6734
15:39 shall be unto you for a **f**, that ye may look 6734

FRINGES (2) [FRINGE]
Nu 15:38 bid them that they make them **f** in 6734
Dt 22:12 Thou shalt make thee **f** upon the four 1434

FRO (25)
Ge 8: 7 forth a raven, which went forth to and **f**, 7725
2Ki 4:35 and walked in the house to and **f**, 259+2008
2Ch 16: 9 For the eyes of the LORD **run to and f** 7751
Job 1: 7 From **going to and f** in the earth, 7751
2: 2 From **going to and f** in the earth, 7751
7: 4 I am full of **tossings to and f** unto 5076
13:25 Wilt thou break a leaf **driven to and f**? 5086
Ps 107:27 They **reel to and f**, and stagger like a 2287
Pr 21: 6 a lying tongue *is* a vanity **tossed to and f** 5086
Isa 24:20 The earth shall **reel to and f** like a 5128+5128
33: 4 as the **running to and f** of locusts shall he 4944
49:21 a captive, and **removing to and f**? 5493
Jer 5: 1 **Run** ye to and **f** through the streets of 7751
49: 3 lament, and **run to and f** by the hedges; 7751
Eze 27:19 **going to and f** occupied in thy fairs: 235+4480
Da 12: 4 many shall **run to and f**, and knowledge 7751
Joel 2: 9 They shall **run to and f** in the city; 8264
Am 8:12 they shall **run to and f** to seek the word 7751
Zec 1:10 the LORD hath sent to **walk to and f** 1980
1:11 We have **walked to and f** through 1980
4:10 which **run to and f** through the whole 7751
6: 7 to go that *they* might **walk to and f** 1980

Zec 6: 7 Get ye hence, **walk to and f** through 1980
6: 7 they **walked to and f** through the earth. 1980
Eph 4:14 **tossed to and f**, and carried about with 2831

FROGS (14)
Ex 8: 2 behold, I will smite all thy borders with **f**: 6854
8: 3 the river shall bring forth **f** abundantly, 6854
8: 4 the **f** shall come up *both* on thee, 6854
8: 5 **f** to come up upon the land of Egypt. 6854
8: 6 the **f** came up, and covered the land of 6854
8: 7 and brought up **f** upon the land of Egypt. 6854
8: 8 that he may take away the **f** from me, 6854
8: 9 to destroy the **f** from thee and thy houses, 6854
8:11 the **f** shall depart from thee, and from thy 6854
8:12 of the **f** which he had brought against 6854
8:13 the **f** died out of the houses, out of 6854
Ps 78:45 and **f**, which destroyed them. 6854
105:30 Their land brought forth **f** in abundance, 6854
Rev 16:13 I saw three unclean spirits like **f** *come* 944

FROM (3660) [THEREFROM] See Index of Articles, Etc.

FRONT (2) [FOREFRONT]
2Sa 10: 9 When Joab saw that the **f** of the battle 6440
2Ch 3: 4 the porch that *was* **in** the **f** of 5921+6440

FRONTIERS (1)
Eze 25: 9 from his cities which *are* on his **f**, 7097

FRONTLETS (3)
Ex 13:16 thine hand, and for **f** between thine eyes: 2903
Dt 6: 8 and they shall be as **f** between thine eyes. 2903
11:18 that they may be as **f** between your eyes. 2903

FROST (6) [HOARFROST]
Ge 31:40 drought consumed me, and the **f** by night; 7140
Ex 16:14 *as* small as the **hoar f** on the ground. 3713
Job 37:10 By the breath of God **f** is given: 7140
38:29 **hoary f** of heaven, who hath gendered 3713
Ps 78:47 with hail, and their sycomore trees with **f**. 2602
Jer 36:30 day to the heat, and in the night to the **f**. 7140

FROWARD (21) [FROWARDLY, FROWARDNESS]
Dt 32:20 *shall be*: for they *are* a **very f** generation, 8419
2Sa 22:27 with the **f** thou wilt shew thyself 6141
Job 5:13 the counsel of the **f** is carried headlong, 6617
Ps 18:26 with the **f** thou wilt shew thyself froward. 6141
18:26 with the **froward** thou wilt **shew** thyself **f**. 6617
101: 4 A **f** heart shall depart from me: I will not 6141
Pr 2:12 from the man that speaketh **f things**; 8419
2:15 *are* crooked, and *they* **f** in their paths: 3868
3:32 For the **f** *is* abomination to the LORD: 3868
4:24 Put away from thee a **f** mouth, 6143
6:12 a wicked man, walketh *with* a **f** mouth. 6143
8: 8 *there is* nothing **f** or perverse in them. 6617
8:13 the evil way, and the **f** mouth, do I hate. 8419
10:31 but the **f** tongue shall be cut out. 8419
11:20 *They that are* of a **f** heart *are* abomination 6141
16:28 A **f** man soweth strife: and a whisperer 8419
16:30 He shutteth his eyes to devise **f** things: 8419
17:20 that hath a **f** heart findeth no good: 6141
21: 8 The way of man *is* **f** and strange: but *as* 2019
22: 5 Thorns *and* snares *are* in the way of the **f**: 6141
1Pe 2:18 to the good and gentle, but also to the **f**. 4646

FROWARDLY (1) [FROWARD]
Isa 57:17 and he went on **f** in the way of his heart. 7726

FROWARDNESS (3) [FROWARD]
Pr 2:14 evil, *and* delight in the **f** of the wicked; 8419
6:14 **F** *is* in his heart, he deviseth mischief 8419
10:32 but the mouth of the wicked speaketh **f**. 8419

FROZEN (1)
Job 38:30 a stone, and the face of the deep is **f**. 3920

FRUIT (208) [FIRSTFRUIT, FIRSTFRUITS, FRUITFUL, FRUITS, UNFRUITFUL]
Ge 1:11 *and* the **f** tree yielding fruit after his kind, 6529
1:11 *and* the fruit tree yielding **f** after his kind, 6529
1:12 tree yielding **f**, whose seed *was* in itself, 6529
1:29 the which *is* the **f** of a tree yielding seed; 6529
3: 2 We may eat of the **f** of the trees of 6529
3: 3 the **f** of the tree which *is* in the midst of 6529
3: 6 she took of the **f** thereof, and did eat, 6529
4: 3 that Cain brought of the **f** of the ground 6529
30: 2 who hath withheld from thee the **f** of 6529
Ex 10:15 the **f** of the trees which the hail had left: 6529
21:22 so that her **f** depart *from her*, and yet no 3206
Lev 19:23 ye shall count the **f** thereof as 6529
19:24 in the fourth year all the **f** thereof shall be 6529
19:25 the fifth year shall ye eat of the **f** thereof, 6529
23:39 ye have gathered in the **f** of the land, 8393
25: 3 thy vineyard, and gather in the **f** thereof; 8393
25:19 the land shall yield her **f**, and ye shall eat 6529
25:21 It shall bring forth **f** for three years. 8393
25:22 and eat *yet* of old **f** until the ninth year; 8393
26: 4 the trees of the field shall yield their **f**. 6529
27:30 *or* of the **f** of the tree, *is* the LORD's: 6529
Nu 13:20 and bring of the **f** of the land. 6529
13:26 and shewed them the **f** of the land. 6529
13:27 milk and honey; and this *is* the **f** of it. 6529
Dt 1:25 took of the **f** of the land in their hands, 6529
7:13 he will also bless the **f** of thy womb, 6529
7:13 the **f** of thy land, thy corn, and thy wine, 6529

Dt 11:17 no rain, and *that* the land yield not her **f**; 2981
22: 9 the **f** of thy vineyard be defiled. 4395
22: 9 and the **f** of thy vineyard, be defiled. 8393
26: 2 That thou shalt take of the first of all the **f** 6529
28: 4 Blessed *shall be* the **f** of thy body, 6529
28: 4 the **f** of thy ground, and the fruit of thy 6529
28: 4 **f** of thy ground, and the **f** of thy cattle, 6529
28:11 in the **f** of thy body, and in the fruit of thy 6529
28:11 of thy **f** of thy cattle, and in the fruit of thy 6529
28:11 of thy cattle, and in the **f** of thy ground, 6529
28:18 Cursed *shall be* the **f** of thy body, 6529
28:18 the **f** of thy land, the increase of thy kine, 6529
28:33 The **f** of thy land, and all thy labours, 6529
28:40 the oil; for thine olive shall cast *his* **f**. NIH
28:42 of thy land shall the locust consume. 6529
28:51 shall eat the **f** of thy cattle, and the fruit 6529
28:51 of thy cattle, and the **f** of thy land, 6529
28:51 of thy land, until thou be destroyed: 6529
28:53 thou shalt eat the **f** of thine own body, 6529
30: 9 the **f** of thy body, and in the fruit of thy, 6529
30: 9 in the **f** of thy cattle, and in the fruit of 6529
30: 9 cattle, and in the **f** of thy land, for good: 6529
Jos 5:12 did eat of the **f** of the land of Canaan 8393
Jdg 9:11 my good **f**, and go to be promoted over 8570
2Sa 16: 2 and **summer f** for the young men to eat; 7019
2Ki 19:30 take root downward, and bear **f** upward. 6529
Ne 9:25 and oliveyards, and **f** trees in abundance; 3978
9:36 gavest unto our fathers to eat the **f** thereof 6529
10:35 the firstfruits of all **f** of all trees, year by 6529
10:37 the **f** of all *manner of* trees, of wine and 6529
Ps 1: 3 that bringeth forth his **f** in his season; 6529
21:10 Their **f** shalt thou destroy from the earth, 6529
72:16 the **f** thereof shall shake like Lebanon: 6529
92:14 They shall still **bring forth f** in old age; 5107
104:13 the earth is satisfied with the **f** of thy 6529
105:35 and devoured the **f** of their ground. 6529
127: 3 *and* the **f** of the womb *is his* reward. 6529
132:11 Of the **f** of thy body will I set upon thy 6529
Pr 1:31 Therefore shall they eat of the **f** of their 6529
8:19 My **f** *is* better than gold, yea, than fine 6529
10:16 *tendeth* to life: the **f** of the wicked to sin. 8393
11:30 The **f** of the righteous *is* a tree of life; 6529
12:12 but the root of the righteous yieldeth **f**. NIH
12:14 man shall be satisfied *with* good by the **f** 6529
13: 2 man shall eat good by the **f** of *his* mouth: 6529
18:20 A man's belly shall be satisfied with the **f** 6529
18:21 they that love it shall eat the **f** thereof. 6529
27:18 Whoso keepeth the fig tree shall eat the **f** 6529
31:16 with the **f** of her hands she planteth a 6529
31:31 Give her of the **f** of her hands; and let her 6529
SS 2: 3 and his **f** *was* sweet to my taste. 6529
8:11 every one for the **f** thereof was to bring a 6529
8:12 that keep the **f** thereof two hundred. 6529
Isa 3:10 for they shall eat the **f** of their doings. 6529
4: 2 the **f** of the earth *shall be* excellent and 6529
10:12 I will punish the **f** of the stout heart of 6529
13:18 they shall have no pity on the **f** of 6529
14:29 and his **f** *shall be* a fiery flying serpent. 6529
27: 6 bud, and fill the face of the world *with* **f**. 8570
27: 9 and this *is* all the **f** to take away his sin; 6529
28: 4 and *as* the **hasty f** before the summer; 1061
37:30 and plant vineyards, and eat the **f** thereof. 6529
37:31 take root downward, and bear **f** upward. 6529
57:19 I create the **f** of the lips; Peace, peace to 5108
65:21 plant vineyards, and eat the **f** of them. 6529
Jer 2: 7 to eat the **f** thereof and the goodness 6529
6:19 *even* the **f** of their thoughts, because 6529
7:20 the field, and upon the **f** of the ground; 6529
11:16 A green olive tree, fair, *and* of goodly **f**: 6529
11:19 saying, Let us destroy the tree with the **f** 3899
12: 2 they grow, yea, they bring forth **f**: thou 6529
17: 8 neither shall cease from yielding **f**. 6529
17:10 and according to the **f** of his doings. 6529
21:14 I will punish you according to the **f** of 6529
29: 5 and plant gardens, and eat the **f** of them; 6529
29:28 and plant gardens, and eat the **f** of them. 6529
32:19 and according to the **f** of his doings: 6529
La 2:20 Shall the women eat their **f**, *and* children 6529
Eze 17: 8 that it might bear **f**, that *it* might be a 6529
17: 9 and cut off the **f** thereof, that it wither? 6529
17:23 and bear **f**, and be a goodly cedar: 6529
19:12 and the east wind dried up her **f**: 6529
19:14 hath devoured her **f**, so that she hath 6529
25: 4 they shall eat thy **f**, and they shall drink 6529
34:27 the tree of the field shall yield her **f**, 6529
36: 8 and yield your **f** to my people of Israel; 6529
36:11 beast; and they shall increase and **bring f**: 6509
36:30 I will multiply the **f** of the tree, 6529
47:12 neither shall the **f** thereof be consumed: 6529
47:12 it shall **bring forth new f** according to his 1069
47:12 the **f** thereof shall be for meat, and the leaf 6529
Da 4:12 the **f** thereof much, and in it *was* meat for 4
4:14 shake off his leaves, and scatter his **f**: 4
4:21 the **f** thereof much, and in it *was* meat for 4
Hos 9:16 their root is dried up, they shall bear no **f**: 6529
9:16 yet will I slay *even* the beloved **f** of their NIH
10: 1 he bringeth forth **f** unto himself: 6529
10: 1 according to the multitude of his **f** he 6529
10:13 iniquity; ye have eaten the **f** of lies: 6529
14: 8 a green fir tree. From me is thy **f** found. 6529
Joel 2:22 for the tree beareth her **f**, the fig tree and 6529
Am 2: 9 yet I destroyed his **f** from above, 6529
6:12 and the **f** of righteousness into hemlock: 6529
7:14 herdman, and a gatherer of **sycomore f**: 8256
8: 1 and behold, a basket of **summer f**. 7019
8: 2 I said, A basket of **summer f**. Then said 7019

Am	9:14	also make gardens, and eat the **f** of them.	6529
Mic	6: 7	the **f** of my body *for* the sin of my soul?	
	7: 1	to eat: my soul desired the **firstripe f.**	1063
	7:13	dwell therein, for the **f** of their doings.	6529
Hab	3:17	blossom, neither *shall* **f** be in the vines;	2981
Hag	1:10	and the earth is stayed *from* her **f.**	2981
Zec	8:12	the vine shall give her **f,** and the ground	6529
Mal	1:12	**f** thereof, *even* his meat,	5108
	3:11	vine **cast** her **f before** the **time** in the	7921
Mt	3:10	tree **which** bringeth not forth good **f**	2590
	7:17	so every good tree bringeth forth good **f;**	2590
	7:17	but a corrupt tree bringeth forth evil **f.**	2590
	7:18	A good tree cannot bring forth evil **f,**	2590
	7:18	*can* a corrupt tree bring forth good **f.**	2590
	7:19	Every tree that bringeth not forth good **f**	2590
	12:33	Either make the tree good, and his **f** good;	2590
	12:33	make the tree corrupt, and his **f** corrupt:	2590
	12:33	corrupt: for the tree is known by *his* **f.**	2590
	13: 8	fell into good ground, and brought forth **f,**	2590
	13:23	understandeth *it;* which also **beareth f,**	2592
	13:26	brought forth **f,** then appeared the tares	2590
	21:19	Let no **f** grow on thee henceforward for	2590
	21:34	And when the time of the **f** drew near,	2590
	26:29	I will not drink henceforth of this **f** of	1081
Mk	4: 7	and choked it, and it yielded no **f.**	2590
	4: 8	and did yield **f** that sprang up and	2590
	4:20	word, and receive *it,* and **bring forth f,**	2592
	4:28	For the earth **bringeth forth f** of herself;	2592
	4:29	But when the **f** is brought forth,	2590
	11:14	No *man* eat of thee hereafter for ever.	2590
	12: 2	the husbandmen of the **f** of the vineyard.	2590
	14:25	I will drink no more of the **f** of the vine,	1081
Lk	1:42	and blessed *is* the **f** of thy womb.	2590
	3: 9	which bringeth not forth good **f** is hewn	2590
	6:43	a good tree bringeth not forth corrupt **f;**	2590
	6:43	doth a corrupt tree bring forth good **f.**	2590
	6:44	For every tree is known by his own **f.**	2590
	8: 8	and sprang up, and bare **f** an hundredfold.	2590
	8:14	of *this* life, and bring no **f** to perfection.	NIG
	8:15	keep *it,* and **bring forth f** with patience.	2592
	13: 6	and he came and sought **f** thereon,	2590
	13: 7	*these* three years I come seeking **f** on this	2590
	13: 9	And if it bear **f,** *well:* and if not, *then*	2590
	20:10	that they should give him of the **f** of	2590
	22:18	I will not drink of the **f** of the vine,	1081
Jn	4:36	and gathereth **f** unto life eternal:	2590
	12:24	but if it die, it bringeth forth much **f.**	2590
	15: 2	Every branch in me that beareth not **f** he	2590
	15: 2	every **branch** that beareth **f,** he purgeth	2592
	15: 2	purgeth it, that it may bring forth more **f.**	2590
	15: 4	As the branch cannot bear **f** of itself,	2590
	15: 5	I in him, the same bringeth forth much **f:**	2590
	15: 8	My Father glorified, that ye bear much **f;**	2590
	15:16	that you should go and bring forth **f,**	2590
	15:16	forth **fruit,** and *that* your **f** should remain:	2590
Ac	2:30	that of the **f** of his loins, according to	2590
Ro	1:13	that I might have some **f** among you also,	2590
	6:21	What **f** had ye then *in those things*	2590
	6:22	ye have your **f** unto holiness, and the end	2590
	7: 4	that we should **bring forth f** unto God.	2592
	7: 5	work in our members to **bring forth f**	2592
	15:28	and have sealed to them this **f,**	2590
1Co	9: 7	vineyard, and eateth not of the **f** thereof?	2590
Gal	5:22	But the **f** of the Spirit is love, joy, peace,	2590
Eph	5: 9	(For the **f** of the Spirit *is* in all goodness	2590
Php	1:22	live in the flesh, this *is* the **f** of my labour:	2590
	4:17	desire **f** that *may* abound to your account.	2590
Col	1: 6	**bringeth forth f,** as *it doth* also in you,	2592
Heb	12:11	**f** of righteousness unto them which are	2590
	13:15	the **f** of *our* lips giving thanks to his name.	2590
Jas	3:18	the **f** of righteousness is sown in peace	2590
	5: 7	husbandman waiteth for the precious **f**	2590
	5:18	rain, and the earth brought forth her **f.**	2590
Jude	1:12	trees whose **f withereth,** without fruit,	5352
	1:12	**without f,** twice dead, plucked up by	175
Rev	22: 2	*of* fruits, *and* yielded her **f** every month:	2590

FRUITFUL (35) [FRUIT]

Ge	1:22	Be **f,** and multiply, and fill the waters in	6509
	1:28	Be **f,** and multiply, and replenish the earth	6509
	8:17	and be **f,** and multiply upon the earth.	6509
	9: 1	Be **f,** and multiply, and replenish the earth	6509
	9: 7	you, be ye **f,** and multiply; bring forth	6509
	17: 6	I will **make** thee exceeding **f,** and I will	6509
	17:20	will **make** him **f,** and will multiply him	6509
	26:22	for us, and we shall be **f** in the land.	6509
	28: 3	and **make** thee **f,** and multiply thee,	6509
	35:11	be **f** and multiply; a nation and a company	6509
	41:52	God hath **caused** me **to be f** in the land	6509
	48: 4	I will **make** thee **f,** and multiply thee,	6509
	49:22	Joseph *is* a **f bough,** *even* a fruitful	1121+6509
	49:22	*even* a **f bough** by a well;	1121+6509
Ex	1: 7	the children of Israel were **f,**	6509
Lev	26: 9	**make** you **f,** and multiply you,	6509
Ps	107:34	A **f** land into barrenness,	6529
	128: 3	Thy wife *shall be* as a **f** vine by the sides	6509
	148: 9	all hills; **f** trees, and all cedars:	6529
Isa	5: 1	hath a vineyard in a **very f** hill;	1121+8081
	10:18	and of his **f field,** both soul and body:	3759
	17: 6	or five and his **f** branches thereof,	6509
	29:17	Lebanon shall be turned into a **f field,**	3759
	29:17	the **f field** shall be esteemed as a forest?	3759
	32:12	for the pleasant fields, for the **f** vine.	6509
	32:15	the wilderness be a **f field,** and the fruitful	3759
	32:15	and the **f field** be counted for a forest.	3759

Isa	32:16	and righteousness remain in the **f field.**	3759
Jer	4:26	lo, the **f place** *was* a wilderness, and all	3759
	23: 3	folds; and they shall be **f** and increase.	6509
Eze	17: 5	seed of the land, and planted it in a **f field;**	2233
	19:10	she was **f** and full of branches by reason	6509
Hos	13:15	Though he be **f** among *his* brethren,	6500
Ac	14:17	gave us rain from heaven, and **f** seasons,	2593
Col	1:10	being **f** in every good work,	2592

FRUITS (42) [FRUIT]

Ge	43:11	take of the **best f** in the land in your	2173
Ex	22:29	not delay *to offer the first of* thy **ripe f,**	4395
	23:10	thy land, and shalt gather in the **f** thereof:	8393
Lev	25:15	unto the number of years of the **f**	8393
	25:16	the *years* of the **f** doth he sell unto thee.	8393
	25:22	until her **f** come in ye shall eat *of* the old	8393
	26:20	shall the trees of the land yield their **f.**	6529
Dt	33:14	the precious **f** brought forth by the sun,	8393
2Sa	9:10	thou shalt bring in the **f,** that thy master's	NIH
	16: 1	an hundred of **summer f,** and a bottle of	7019
2Ki	8: 6	all the **f** of the field since the day that she	8393
	19:29	and plant vineyards, and eat the **f** thereof.	6529
Job	31:39	I have eaten the **f** thereof without money,	3581
Ps	107:37	which may yield **f** of increase.	6529
Ecc	2: 5	and I planted trees in them of all *kind* of **f:**	6529
SS	4:13	orchard of pomegranates, with pleasant **f;**	6529
	4:16	into his garden, and eat his pleasant **f.**	6529
	6:11	down into the garden of nuts to see the **f**	3
	7:13	at our gates *are* all *manner of* pleasant **f,**	NIH
Isa	16: 9	for the shouting for thy **summer f** and	7019
	33: 9	and Bashan and Carmel shake off their **f.**	NIH
Jer	40:10	**summer f,** and oil, and put *them* in your	7019
	40:12	gathered wine and **summer f** very much.	7019
	48:32	the spoiler is fallen upon thy **summer f**	7019
La	4: 9	stricken through for *want of* the **f** of	8570
Mic	7: 1	when they have gathered the **summer f,**	7019
Mal	3:11	he shall not destroy the **f** of your ground;	6529
Mt	3: 8	forth therefore **f** meet for repentance:	2590
	7:16	Ye shall know them by their **f.** Do *men*	2590
	7:20	Wherefore by their **f** ye shall know them.	2590
	21:34	that *they* might receive the **f** of it.	2590
	21:41	which shall render him the **f** in their	2590
	21:43	given to a nation bringing forth the **f**	2590
Lk	3: 8	therefore **f** worthy of repentance,	2590
	12:17	I have no room where to bestow my **f?**	2590
	12:18	and there will I bestow all my **f** and	1081
2Co	9:10	and increase the **f** of your righteousness;)	1081
Php	1:11	Being filled with the **f** of righteousness,	2590
2Ti	2: 6	laboureth must be first partaker of the **f.**	2590
Jas	3:17	full of mercy and good **f,** without partiality	2590
Rev	18:14	And the **f** that thy soul lusted after are	3703
	22: 2	which bare twelve *manner of* **f,**	2590

FRUSTRATE (1) [FRUSTRATETH]

Ezr	4: 5	to **f** their purpose, all the days of Cyrus	6565
Gal	2:21	I do not **f** the grace of God: for if	114

FRUSTRATED See NOUGHT; VEX; VEXATION; VEXED

FRUSTRATETH (1) [FRUSTRATE]

Isa	44:25	That **f** the tokens of the liars,	6565

FRUSTRATION See VANITIES; VANITY

FRYINGPAN (2) [FRIED, PAN]

Lev	2: 7	oblation *be* a meat offering *baken* in the **f,**	4802
	7: 9	all *that* is dressed in the **f,** and in the pan,	4802

FUEL (5)

Isa	9: 5	but *this* shall be with burning *and* **f** of fire.	3980
	9:19	and the people shall be as the **f** of the fire;	3980
Eze	15: 4	Behold, it is cast into the fire for **f;** the fire	402
	15: 6	which I have given to the fire for **f,** so will	402
	21:32	Thou shalt be for **f** to the fire; thy blood	402

FUGITIVE (2) [FUGITIVES]

Ge	4:12	a **f** and a vagabond shalt thou be in	5128
	4:14	I shall be a **f** and a vagabond in the earth;	5128

FUGITIVES (4) [FUGITIVE]

Jdg	12: 4	Ye Gileadites *are* **f** of Ephraim among	6412
2Ki	25:11	the **f** that fell away to the king of Babylon,	5307
Isa	15: 5	his **f** *shall flee* unto Zoar, a heifer of three	1280
Eze	17:21	all his **f** with all his bands shall fall by	4015

FULFIL (24) [FULFILLED, FULFILLING]

Ge	29:27	**f** her week, and we will give thee this	4390
Ex	5:13	**F** your works, *your* daily tasks, as when	3615
	23:26	thy land: the number of thy days I will **f.**	4390
1Ki	2:27	that he might **f** the word of the LORD,	4390
1Ch	22:13	if thou takest heed to **f** the statutes and	6213
2Ch	36:21	To **f** the word of the LORD by the mouth	4390
	36:21	sabbath, to **f** threescore and ten years.	4390
Job	39: 2	thou number the months *that* they **f?**	4390
Ps	20: 4	to thine own heart, and **f** all thy counsel.	4390
	20: 5	our banners: the LORD **f** all thy petitions.	4390
	145:19	He will **f** the desire of them that fear him:	6213
Mt	3:15	for thus it becometh us to **f** all	4137
	5:17	I am not come to destroy, but to **f.**	4137
Ac	13:22	mine own heart, which shall **f** all my will.	4160
Ro	2:27	it **f** the law, judge thee, who by the letter	5055
	13:14	for the flesh, to **f** the lusts *thereof.*	NIG
Gal	5:16	and ye shall not **f** the lust of the flesh.	5055
	6: 2	burdens, and so **f** the law of Christ.	378
Php	2: 2	**F** ye my joy, that ye be likeminded,	4137

Col	1:25	given to me for you, to **f** the word of God;	4137
	4:17	hast received in the Lord, that thou **f** it.	4137
2Th	1:11	**f** all the good pleasure of *his* goodness,	4137
Jas	2: 8	If ye **f** the royal law according to	5055
Rev	17:17	For God hath put in their hearts to **f** his	4160

FULFILLED (82) [FULFIL]

Ge	25:24	when her days to be delivered were **f,**	4390
	29:21	Give *me* my wife, for my days are **f,** that	4390
	29:28	Jacob did so, and **f** her week: and he gave	4390
	50: 3	forty days were **f** for him; for so	4390
	50: 3	**f** the days of those which are	4390
Ex	5:14	Wherefore have ye not **f** your task in	3615
	7:25	seven days were **f,** after *that* the LORD	4390
Lev	12: 4	until the days of her purifying be **f.**	4390
	12: 6	when the days of her purifying are **f,** for	4390
Nu	6: 5	until the days be **f,** in the which he	4390
	6:13	when the days of his separation are **f:**	4390
2Sa	7:12	when thy days be **f,** and thou shalt sleep	4390
	14:22	in that the king hath **f** the request of his	6213
1Ki	8:15	and hath with his hand **f** *it,* saying,	4390
	8:24	hast **f** *it* with thine hand, as *it is* this day.	4390
2Ch	6: 4	who hath with his hands **f** *that* which he	4390
	6:15	hast **f** *it* with thine hand, as *it is* this day.	4390
Ezr	1: 1	by the mouth of Jeremiah might be **f,**	3615
Job	36:17	thou hast **f** the judgment of the wicked:	4390
Jer	44:25	mouths, and **f** with your hand, saying,	4390
La	2:17	hath **f** his word that he had commanded	1214
	4:18	end is near, our days are **f;** for our end	4390
Eze	5:13	the city, when the days of the siege are **f:**	4390
Da	4:33	The same hour was the thing **f** upon	5487
	10: 3	at all, till three whole weeks were **f.**	4390
Mt	1:22	that it might be **f** which was spoken of	4137
	2:15	that it might be **f** which was spoken of	4137
	2:17	Then was it **f** that which was spoken by	4137
	2:23	that it might be **f** which was spoken by	4137
	4:14	That it might be **f** which was spoken by	4137
	5:18	in no wise pass from the law, till all be **f.**	1096
	8:17	That it might be **f** which was spoken by	4137
	12:17	That it might be **f** which was spoken by	4137
	13:14	And in them is **f** the prophecy of Esaias,	378
	13:35	That it might be **f** which was spoken by	4137
	21: 4	that it might be **f** which was spoken by	4137
	24:34	shall not pass, till all these *things* be **f.**	1096
	26:54	*But* how then shall the scriptures be **f,**	4137
	26:56	the scriptures of the prophets might be **f.**	4137
	27: 9	Then was **f** that which was spoken by	4137
	27:35	that it might be **f** which was spoken by	4137
Mk	1:15	And saying, The time is **f,**	4137
	13: 4	the sign when all these *things* shall be **f?**	4931
	14:49	took me not: but the scriptures must be **f.**	4137
	15:28	And the scripture was **f,** which saith,	4137
Lk	1:20	words, which shall be **f** in their season.	4137
	2:43	And when they had **f** the days, as they	5048
	4:21	This day is this scripture **f** in your ears.	4137
	21:22	all *things* which are written may be **f.**	4137
	21:24	until the times of the Gentiles be **f.**	4137
	21:32	generation shall not pass away, till all be **f.**	1096
	22:16	until it be **f** in the kingdom of God.	4137
	24:44	yet with you, that all *things* must be **f,**	4137
Jn	3:29	this my joy therefore is **f.**	4137
	12:38	saying of Esaias the prophet might be **f,**	4137
	13:18	but that the scripture may be **f,** He that	4137
	15:25	might be **f** that is written in their law,	4137
	17:12	of perdition; that the scripture might be **f.**	4137
	17:13	that they might have my joy **f** in	4137
	18: 9	the saying might be **f,** which he spake,	4137
	18:32	That the saying of Jesus might be **f,**	4137
	19:24	that the scripture might be **f,** which saith,	4137
	19:28	that the scripture might be **f,** saith, I thirst.	5048
	19:36	were done, that the scripture should be **f,**	4137
Ac	1:16	this scripture must needs have been **f,**	4137
	3:18	that Christ should suffer, he hath so **f.**	4137
	9:23	And after that many days were **f,** the Jews	4137
	12:25	when they had **f** their ministry,	4137
	13:25	And as John **f** his course, he said,	4137
	13:27	they have **f** *them* in condemning *him.*	4137
	13:29	when they had **f** all that was written of	5055
	13:33	God hath **f** the same unto us their children	1603
	14:26	grace of God for the work which they **f.**	4137
Ro	8: 4	righteousness of the law might be **f** in us,	4137
	13: 8	for he that loveth another hath **f** the law.	4137
2Co	10: 6	disobedience, when your obedience is **f.**	4137
Gal	5:14	For all the law is **f** in one word, *even* in	4137
Jas	2:23	And the scripture was **f** which saith,	4137
Rev	6:11	should be killed as they *were,* should be **f.**	4137
	15: 8	seven plagues of the seven angels were **f.**	5055
	17:17	beast, until the words of God shall be **f.**	5055
	20: 3	till the thousand years should be **f:**	5055

FULFILLING (3) [FULFIL]

Ps	148: 8	and vapour; stormy wind **f** his word:	6213
Ro	13:10	therefore love *is* the **f** of the law.	4138
Eph	2: 3	**f** the desires of the flesh and of the mind;	4160

FULL (260) [FILL]

Ge	14:10	of Siddim *was* **f** of slimepits;	875+875+2564
	15:16	the iniquity of the Amorites *is* not yet **f.**	8003
	25: 8	**f** *of years;* and was gathered to his people.	7649
	35:29	unto his people, *being* old and **f** of days:	7649
	41: 1	to pass at the end of **two f years,**	3117+8141
	41: 7	ears devoured the seven rank and **f** ears.	4392
	41:22	ears came up in one stalk, **f** and good:	4392
	43:21	of his sack, our money in **f weight:**	4948
Ex	8:21	the houses of the Egyptians be **f** of	4390

F

Ex	16: 3 *and* when we did eat bread to the **f**;	7648
	16: 8 to eat, and in the morning bread to the **f**;	7646
	16:33 put an omer **f** of manna therein, and lay it	4393
	22: 3 *for* he should **make f restitution**;	7999+7999
Lev	2:14 the fire, *even* **corn** beaten out of **f ears**.	3759
	16:12 shall take a censer **f** of burning coals of	4393
	16:12 his hands of sweet incense beaten small,	4393
	19:29 and the land **become f** of wickedness.	4390
	25:29 is sold; *within a* **f** *year* may he redeem it.	3117
	25:30 be not redeemed within the space of a **f**	8549
	26: 5 ye shall eat your bread to the **f**, and dwell	7648
Nu	7:13 both of them *were* **f** *of* fine flour mingled	4392
	7:14 spoon of ten *shekels* of gold, **f** *of* incense:	4392
	7:19 both of them **f** *of* fine flour mingled with	4392
	7:20 One spoon of gold of ten *shekels*, **f** *of*	4392
	7:25 both of them **f** *of* fine flour mingled with	4392
	7:26 One golden spoon of ten *shekels*, **f** *of*	4392
	7:31 both of them **f** *of* fine flour mingled with	4392
	7:32 One golden spoon of ten *shekels*, **f** *of*	4392
	7:37 both of them **f** *of* fine flour mingled with	4392
	7:38 One golden spoon of ten *shekels*, **f** *of*	4392
	7:43 both of them **f** *of* fine flour mingled with	4392
	7:44 One golden spoon of ten *shekels*, **f** *of*	4392
	7:49 both of them **f** *of* fine flour mingled with	4392
	7:50 One golden spoon of ten *shekels*, **f** *of*	4392
	7:55 both of them **f** *of* fine flour mingled with	4392
	7:56 One golden spoon of ten *shekels*, **f** *of*	4392
	7:61 both of them **f** *of* fine flour mingled with	4392
	7:62 One golden spoon of ten *shekels*, **f** *of*	4392
	7:67 both of them **f** *of* fine flour mingled with	4392
	7:68 One golden spoon of ten *shekels*, **f** *of*	4392
	7:73 both of them **f** *of* fine flour mingled with	4392
	7:74 both of them **f** *of* fine flour mingled with	4392
	7:79 both of them **f** *of* fine flour mingled with	4392
	7:80 One golden spoon of ten *shekels*, **f** *of*	4392
	7:86 **f** *of* incense, *weighing* ten *shekels* apiece,	4392
	22:18 Balak would give me his house **f** *of* silver	4393
	24:13 Balak would give me his house **f** *of* silver	4393
Dt	6:11 houses **f** *of* all good *things*, which thou	4392
	6:11 when thou shalt have eaten and be **f**;	7646
	8:10 When thou hast eaten and art **f**, then	7646
	8:12 Lest *when* thou hast eaten and art **f**,	7646
	11:15 thy cattle, that thou mayest eat and be **f**.	7646
	21:13 father and her mother a **f month**:	3117+3391
	33:23 and **f** *with* the blessing of the LORD:	4392
	34: 9 Joshua the son of Nun was **f** *of* the spirit	4392
Jdg	6:38 dew out of the fleece, a bowl **f** *of* water.	4393
	16:27 the house was **f** *of* men and women;	4392
Ru	1:21 I went out **f**, and the LORD hath brought	4392
	2:12 a **f** reward be given thee of the LORD	8003
1Sa	2: 5 *that were* **f** have hired out themselves	7649
	18:27 and they **gave** them in **f tale** to the king,	4392
	27: 7 the country of the Philistines was a **f year**	3117
2Sa	8: 2 death, and *with* one **f** line to keep alive.	4393
	13:23 it came to pass after **two f years**,	3117+8141
	14:28 So Absalom dwelt **two f years** in	3117+8141
	23:11 where was a piece of ground **f** *of* lentiles:	4392
2Ki	3:16 Make this valley **f** *of* **ditches**.	1356+1356
	4: 4 and thou shalt set aside *that* which *is* **f**.	4392
	4: 6 it came to pass, when the vessels were **f**,	4390
	4:39 gathered thereof wild gourds his lap **f**,	4393
	4:42 and **f ears of corn** in the husk thereof.	3759
	6:17 the mountain was **f** *of* horses and	4390
	7:15 all the way *was* **f** *of* garments and vessels,	4392
	9:24 **drew** a bow with	
	his **f strength**,	3027+4390+871.1
	10:21 the house of Baal was **f** from one end to	4390
	15:13 he reigned a **f month** in Samaria.	3117+3391
1Ch	11:13 where was a parcel of ground **f** *of* barley,	4392
	21:22 thou shalt grant it me for the **f** price:	4392
	21:24 Nay; but I will verily buy *it* for the **f** price:	4392
	23: 1 So when David was old and **f** *of* days,	7646
	29:28 old age, **f** *of* days, riches, and honour:	7649
2Ch	24:15 old, and was **f** *of* days when he died;	7646
Ne	9:25 and possessed houses **f** *of* all goods,	4392
Est	3: 5 reverence, *then* was Haman **f** *of* wrath.	4390
	5: 9 he was **f** *of* indignation against Mordecai.	4390
Job	5:26 Thou shalt come to *thy* grave in a **f age**,	3624
	7: 4 I am **f** *of* tossings to and fro unto	7646
	10:15 *I am* **f** *of* confusion; therefore see thou	7649
	11: 2 and should a man **f** *of* **talk** be justified?	8193
	14: 1 a woman *is* of few days, and **f** *of* trouble.	7649
	20:11 His bones are **f** *of* the sin *of* his youth,	4390
	21:23 One dieth in his **f** strength, *being* wholly	8537
	21:24 His breasts are **f** *of* milk, and his bones are	4390
	32:18 For I am **f** *of* matter, the spirit within me	4390
	36:16 be set on thy table *should be* **f** *of* fatness.	4390
	42:17 So Job died, *being* old and **f** *of* days.	7649
Ps	10: 7 His mouth is **f** *of* cursing and deceit and	4390
	17:14 thy hid *treasure*: they are **f** *of* children,	7646
	26:10 and their right hand is **f** *of* bribes.	4390
	29: 4 the voice of the LORD *is* **f** *of* **majesty**.	1926
	33: 5 the earth is **f** *of* the goodness of	4390
	48:10 thy right hand is **f** *of* righteousness.	
	65: 9 *with* the river of God, *which is* **f** *of* water:	4392
	69:20 my heart; and I am **f** *of* **heaviness**:	5136
	73:10 waters of a **f** *cup* are wrung out to them.	4392
	74:20 for the dark places of the earth are **f** *of*	4390
	75: 8 it is **f** *of* mixture; but he poureth out of	4392
	78:25 angels' food: he sent them meat to the **f**.	7648
	78:38 he, *being* **f** *of* **compassion**, forgave *their*	7349
	86:15 *art* a God **f** *of* **compassion**, and gracious,	7349
	88: 3 For my soul is **f** *of* troubles: and my life	7646
	104:16 The trees of the LORD are **f** *of* sap;	7646
	104:24 made them all: the earth is **f** *of* thy riches.	4390

Ps	111: 4 LORD *is* gracious and **f** *of* **compassion**.	7349
	112: 4 and **f** *of* **compassion**, and righteous.	7349
	119:64 The earth, O LORD, is **f** *of* thy mercy:	4390
	127: 5 Happy *is* the man that hath his quiver **f** *of*	4390
	144:13 *That* our garners *may be* **f**, affording all	4392
	145: 8 LORD *is* gracious, and **f** *of* **compassion**;	7349
Pr	17: 1 than a house **f** *of* sacrifices with strife.	4392
	27: 7 The **f** soul loatheth a honeycomb; but *to*	7649
	27:20 Hell and destruction are never **f**; so the	7646
	30: 9 Lest I be **f**, and deny *thee*, and say, Who	7646
Ecc	1: 7 rivers run into the sea; yet the sea *is* not **f**;	4392
	1: 8 All things *are* **f** *of* **labour**; man cannot	3023
	4: 6 than both the hands **f** *with* travail and	4393
	9: 3 the heart of the sons of men is **f** *of* evil,	4390
	10:14 A fool also is **f** *of* words: a man cannot	7235
	11: 3 If the clouds be **f** *of* rain, they empty	4390
Isa	1:11 I am **f** *of* the burnt offerings of rams,	7646
	1:15 I will not hear: your hands are **f** *of* blood.	4390
	1:21 *was* **f** *of* judgment; righteousness lodged	4392
	2: 7 Their land also is **f** *of* silver and gold,	4390
	2: 7 their land is also **f** *of* horses, neither *is*	4390
	2: 8 Their land also is **f** *of* idols; they worship	4390
	6: 3 of hosts: the whole earth is **f** *of* his glory.	4393
	11: 9 for the earth shall be **f** *of* the knowledge	4390
	13:21 houses shall be **f** *of* doleful creatures;	4390
	15: 9 For the waters of Dimon shall be **f** *of*	4390
	22: 2 Thou *that art* **f** *of* stirs, a tumultuous city,	4392
	22: 7 *that* thy choicest valleys shall be **f** *of*	4390
	25: 6 on the lees, of fat things **f** *of* **marrow**,	4229
	28: 8 For all tables are **f** *of* vomit *and* filthiness,	4390
	30:27 lips are **f** *of* indignation, and his tongue	4390
	51:20 *they are* **f** *of* the fury of the LORD,	4392
Jer	4:12 a **f** wind from those *places* shall come	4392
	4:27 be desolate; yet will I not make a **f end**.	3617
	5: 7 when I had **fed** them **to the f**, they then	7650
	5:10 and destroy; but make not a **f end**:	3617
	5:18 I will not make a **f end** with you.	3617
	5:27 As a cage *is* **f** *of* birds, so *are* their houses	4392
	5:27 *of* birds, so *are* their houses **f** *of* deceit:	4392
	6:11 Therefore I am **f** *of* the fury of the LORD;	4390
	6:11 the aged with *him that is* **f** *of* days.	4392
	23:10 For the land is **f** *of* adulterers; for because	4390
	28: 3 Within **two f years** *will* I bring	3117+8141
	28:11 within the space of **two f years**.	3117+8141
	30:11 though I make a **f end** of all nations	3617
	30:11 yet will I not make a **f end** of thee:	3617
	35: 5 house of the Rechabites pots **f** *of* wine,	4392
	46:28 for I will make a **f end** of all the nations	3617
	46:28 I will not make a **f end** of thee,	3617
La	1: 1 the city sit solitary, *that was* **f** *of* people!	7227
	3:30 smiteth him: he is **filled f** with reproach.	7646
Eze	1:18 their rings *were* **f** *of* eyes round about	4392
	7:23 for the land is **f** *of* bloody crimes,	4390
	7:23 crimes, and the city is **f** *of* violence.	4390
	9: 9 the land is **f** *of* blood, and the city full *of*	4390
	9: 9 *of* blood, and the city **f** *of* perverseness:	4390
	10: 4 the court was **f** *of* the brightness of	4390
	10:12 the wheels, *were* **f** *of* eyes round about,	4392
	11:13 wilt thou make a **f end** of the remnant of	3617
	17: 3 longwinged, **f** *of* feathers, which had	4392
	19:10 **f** *of* branches by reason of many waters.	6058
	28:12 **f** *of* wisdom, and perfect in beauty.	4392
	32: 6 and the rivers shall be **f** *of* thee.	4390
	32:15 shall be destitute of that whereof it was **f**,	4393
	37: 1 midst of the valley which *was* **f** *of* bones,	4392
	39:19 ye shall eat fat till *ye* be **f**, and drink blood	7654
	41: 8 chambers *were* a **f** reed of six great cubits.	4393
Da	3:19 was Nebuchadnezzar **f** *of* fury,	4391
	8:23 the transgressors are **come to the f**,	8552
	10: 2 was mourning three **f weeks**.	3117+7620
Joel	2:24 the floors shall be **f** *of* wheat, and the fats	4390
	3:13 for the press is **f**, the fats overflow;	4390
Am	2:13 as a cart is pressed *that is* **f** *of* sheaves.	4392
Mic	3: 8 truly I am **f** *of* power by the spirit of	4390
	6:12 For the rich *men* thereof are **f** *of* violence,	4390
Na	3: 1 it is all **f** *of* lies *and* robbery; the prey	4392
Hab	3: 3 and the earth was **f** *of* his praise.	4390
Zec	8: 5 the streets of the city shall be **f** *of* boys	4390
Mt	6:22 thy whole body shall be **f** *of* light.	5460
	6:23 thy whole body shall be **f** *of* darkness.	4652
	13:48 Which, when it was **f**, they drew to shore,	4137
	14:20 fragments that remained twelve baskets **f**.	4134
	15:37 broken *meat* that was left seven baskets **f**.	4134
	23:25 but within they are **f** *of* extortion and	1073
	23:27 but are within **f** *of* dead *men's* bones,	1073
	23:28 but within ye are **f** *of* hypocrisy and	3324
Mk	4:28 the ear, after that the **f** corn in the ear.	4134
	4:37 beat into the ship, so that it was now **f**.	1072
	6:43 And they took up twelve baskets **f** *of*	4134
	7: 9 **F** well ye reject the commandment of	2573
	8:19 how many baskets **f** *of* fragments took ye	4134
	8:20 how many baskets **f** *of* fragments took ye	4138
	15:36 one ran and filled a spunge **f** *of* vinegar,	NIG
Lk	1:57 Now Elisabeth's **f** time **came** that she	4130
	4: 1 And Jesus being **f** *of* the Holy Ghost	4134
	5:12 a certain city, behold a man **f** *of* leprosy:	4134
	6:25 Woe unto you that are **f**! for ye shall	1705
	11:34 is single, thy whole body also is **f** *of* **light**;	5460
	11:34 *eye* is evil, thy body also *is* **f** *of* **darkness**.	4652
	11:36 If thy whole body therefore *be* **f** *of* **light**,	5460
	11:36 no part dark, the whole shall be **f** *of* **light**,	5460
	11:39 but your inward part is **f** *of* ravening and	1073
	16:20 which was laid at his gate, **f** *of* **sores**,	1669
Jn	1:14 of the Father,) **f** *of* grace and truth.	4134
	7: 8 this feast; for my time is not yet **f come**.	4137

Jn	15:11 in you, and *that* your joy might be **f**.	4137
	16:24 ye shall receive, that your joy may be **f**.	4137
	19:29 Now there was set a vessel **f** *of* vinegar:	3324
	21:11 and drew the net to land **f** *of* great fishes,	3324
Ac	2:13 These men are **f** *of* new wine.	3325
	2:28 thou shalt **make** me **f** *of* joy with thy	4137
	6: 3 **f** *of* the Holy Ghost and wisdom, whom	4134
	6: 5 a man **f** *of* faith and of the Holy Ghost,	4134
	6: 8 And Stephen, **f** *of* faith and power,	4134
	7:23 when he was **f** forty years old, it came	4137
	7:55 But he, being **f** *of* the Holy Ghost,	4134
	9:36 this *woman* was **f** *of* good works and	4134
	11:24 and of the Holy Ghost and of faith:	4134
	13:10 O **f** *of* all subtilty and all mischief,	4134
	19:28 heard *these sayings*, they were **f** *of* wrath,	4134
Ro	1:29 **f** *of* envy, murder, debate, deceit,	3324
	3:14 mouth is **f** *of* cursing and bitterness:	1073
	15:14 brethren, that ye also are **f** *of* goodness,	3324
1Co	4: 8 Now ye are **f**, now ye are rich, ye have	2880
Php	2:26 was **f** *of* **heaviness**, because that ye had	85
	4:12 in all *things* I am instructed both to be **f**	5526
	4:18 I am **f**, having received of Epaphroditus	4137
Col	2: 2 unto all riches of the **f assurance** of	4136
2Ti	4: 5 **make f proof** of thy ministry.	4135
Heb	5:14 meat belongeth to *them that are* of **f age**,	5046
	6:11 to the **f assurance** of hope unto the end:	4136
	10:22 with a true heart in **f assurance** of faith,	4136
Jas	3: 8 *it is* an unruly evil, **f** *of* deadly poison.	3324
	3:17 **f** *of* mercy and good fruits,	3324
1Pe	1: 8 with joy unspeakable and **f** *of* **glory**:	1392
2Pe	2:14 Having eyes **f** *of* adultery and that cannot	3324
1Jn	1: 4 we unto you, that your joy may be **f**.	4137
2Jn	1: 8 but *that* we receive a **f** reward.	4134
	1:12 speak face to face, that our joy may be **f**.	4137
Rev	4: 6 *were* four beasts **f** *of* eyes before and	1073
	4: 8 about *him;* and *they were* **f** *of* eyes within:	1073
	5: 8 and golden vials **f** *of* odours, which are	1073
	15: 7 seven golden vials **f** *of* the wrath of God,	1073
	16:10 and his kingdom was **f** *of* **darkness**;	4656
	17: 3 **f** *of* names of blasphemy, having seven	1073
	17: 4 having a golden cup in her hand **f** *of*	1073
	21: 9 the seven vials **f** *of* the seven last plagues,	1073

FULLER (1) [FULLER'S, FULLERS']

Mk	9: 3 so as no **f** on earth can white *them*.	1102

FULLER'S (3) [FULLER]

2Ki	18:17 which *is* in the highway of the **f** field.	3526
Isa	7: 3 upper pool in the highway of the **f** field;	3526
	36: 2 upper pool in the highway of the **f** field.	3526

FULLERS' (1) [FULLER]

Mal	3: 2 he is like a refiner's fire, and like **f** sope:	3526

FULLY (13) [FILL]

Nu	7: 1 came to pass on the day that Moses had **f**	3615
	14:24 spirit with him, and hath followed me **f**,	4392
Ru	2:11 her, It hath **f been shewed** me,	5046+5046
1Ki	11: 6 went not **f** after the LORD, as *did* David	4390
Ecc	8:11 heart of the sons of men is **f** set in them	4390
Na	1:10 they shall be devoured as stubble **f** dry.	4392
Ac	2: 1 when the day of Pentecost was **f come**,	4845
Ro	4:21 being **f persuaded**, that what he had	4135
	14: 5 man be **f persuaded** in his own mind.	4135
	15:19 I have **f** preached the gospel of Christ.	4137
2Ti	3:10 But thou hast **f known** my doctrine,	3877
	4:17 by me the preaching might be **f known**,	4135
Rev	14:18 vine of the earth; for her grapes are **f ripe**.	187

FULNESS (25) [FILL]

Nu	18:27 and as the **f** *of* the winepress.	4395
Dt	33:16 precious things of the earth and **f** thereof,	4393
1Ch	16:32 Let the sea roar, and the **f** thereof:	4393
Job	20:22 In the **f** of his sufficiency he shall be in	4390
Ps	16:11 in thy presence *is* **f** of joy; at thy right	7648
	24: 1 earth *is* the LORD's, and the **f** thereof;	4393
	50:12 for the world *is* mine, and the **f** thereof.	4393
	89:11 *as* for the world and the **f** thereof, thou	4393
	96:11 be glad; let the sea roar, and the **f** thereof.	4393
	98: 7 Let the sea roar, and the **f** thereof;	4393
Eze	16:49 **f** *of* bread, and abundance of idleness was	7653
	19: 7 the land was desolate, and the **f** thereof,	4393
Jn	1:16 And of his **f** have all we received,	4138
Ro	11:12 of the Gentiles; how much more their **f**?	4138
	11:25 until the **f** of the Gentiles be come in.	4138
	15:29 I shall come in the **f** of the blessing of	4138
1Co	10:26 the earth *is* the Lord's, and the **f** thereof.	4138
	10:28 the earth *is* the Lord's, and the **f** thereof:	4138
Gal	4: 4 But when the **f** of the time was come,	4138
Eph	1:10 That in the dispensation of the **f** of times	4138
	1:23 his body, the **f** of him that filleth all in all.	4138
	3:19 ye might be filled with all the **f** of God.	4138
	4:13 unto the measure of the stature of the **f** of	4138
Col	1:19 the *Father* that in him should all **f** dwell;	4138
	2: 9 For in him dwelleth all the **f** of	4138

FURBISH (1) [FURBISHED]

Jer	46: 4 **f** the spears, *and* put on the brigandines.	4838

FURBISHED (5) [FURBISH]

Eze	21: 9 A sword, a sword is sharpened, and also **f**:	4803
	21:10 a sore slaughter; *it is* **f** that it may glitter:	4803
	21:11 hath given it to be **f**, that *it* may be	4803
	21:11 this sword is sharpened, and it *is* **f**, to give	4803
	21:28 for the slaughter *it is* **f**, to consume	4803

FURIOUS (6) [FURY]
Pr	22:24	and with a **f** man thou shalt not go:	2534
	29:22	and a **f** man aboundeth in transgression.	2534
Eze	5:15	thee in anger and in fury and in **f** rebukes.	2534
	25:17	vengeance upon them with **f** rebukes,	2534
Da	2:12	this cause the king was angry and very **f**,	7108
Na	1: 2	the LORD revengeth, and *is* **f**;	1167+2534

FURIOUSLY (2) [FURY]
2Ki	9:20	the son of Nimshi; for he driveth **f**.	7697+871.1
Eze	23:25	and they shall deal **f** with thee:	2534+871.1

FURLONGS (5)
Lk	24:13	was from Jerusalem *about* threescore **f**.	4712
Jn	6:19	rowed about five and twenty or thirty **f**,	4712
	11:18	nigh unto Jerusalem, about fifteen **f** off:	4712
Rev	14:20	the space of a thousand *and* six hundred **f**.	4712
	21:16	the city with the reed, twelve thousand **f**.	4712

FURNACE (30) [FURNACES]
Ge	15:17	behold a smoking **f**, and a burning lamp	8574
	19:28	the country went up as the smoke of a **f**.	3536
Ex	9: 8	Take to you handfuls of ashes of the **f**,	3536
	9:10	they took ashes of the **f**, and stood before	3536
	19:18	thereof ascended as the smoke of a **f**,	3536
Dt	4:20	brought you forth out of the iron **f**, *even*	3564
1Ki	8:51	of Egypt, from the midst of the **f** of iron:	3564
Ps	12: 6	silver tried in a **f** of earth, purified seven	5948
Pr	17: 3	fining pot *is* for silver, and the **f** for gold:	3564
	27:21	the fining pot for silver, and the **f** for gold;	3564
Isa	31: 9	fire *is* in Zion, and his **f** in Jerusalem.	8574
	48:10	I have chosen thee in the **f** of affliction.	3564
Jer	11: 4	from the iron **f**, saying, Obey my voice,	3564
Eze	22:18	and iron, and lead, in the midst of the **f**,	3564
	22:20	and lead, and tin, into the midst of the **f**,	3564
	22:22	As silver is melted in the midst of the **f**,	3564
Da	3: 6	be cast into the midst of a burning fiery **f**.	861
	3:11	be cast into the midst of a burning fiery **f**.	861
	3:15	hour into the midst of a burning fiery **f**;	861
	3:17	able to deliver us from the burning fiery **f**,	861
	3:19	commanded that *they* should heat the **f**	861
	3:20	*and* to cast *them* into the burning fiery **f**.	861
	3:21	cast into the midst of the burning fiery **f**.	861
	3:22	*was* urgent, and the **f** exceeding hot,	861
	3:23	bound into the midst of the burning fiery **f**.	861
	3:26	near to the mouth of the burning fiery **f**,	861
Mt	13:42	And shall cast them into a **f** of fire:	2575
	13:50	And shall cast them into the **f** of fire:	2575
Rev	1:15	unto fine brass, as if they burned in a **f**;	2575
	9: 2	out of the pit, as the smoke of a great **f**;	2575

FURNACES (2) [FURNACE]
Ne	3:11	the other piece, and the tower of the **f**.	8574
	12:38	from beyond the tower of the **f** even unto	8574

FURNISH (4) [FURNISHED, FURNITURE]
Dt	15:14	Thou shalt **f** him **liberally** out of	6059+6059
Ps	78:19	Can God **f** a table in the wilderness?	6186
Isa	65:11	**f** the drink offering **unto** *that* number.	4390
Jer	46:19	**f** thyself to go into captivity:	3627+6213

FURNISHED (6) [FURNISH]
1Ki	9:11	(*Now* Hiram the king of Tyre had **f**	5375
Pr	9: 2	her wine; she hath also **f** her table.	6186
Mt	22:10	good: and the wedding was **f** with guests.	4130
Mk	14:15	he will shew you a large upper room **f**	4766
Lk	22:12	he shall shew you a large upper room **f**:	4766
2Ti	3:17	**throughly f** unto all good works.	1822

FURNISHINGS See FURNITURE

FURNITURE (8) [FURNISH]
Ge	31:34	put them in the camel's **f**, and sat upon	3733
Ex	31: 7	thereupon, and all the **f** of the tabernacle,	3627
	31: 8	table and his **f**, and the pure candlestick	3627
	31: 8	the pure candlestick with all his **f**,	3627
	31: 9	the altar of burnt offering with all his **f**,	3627
	35:14	his **f**, and his lamps, with the oil for	3627
	39:33	tent, and all his **f**, his taches, his boards,	3627
Na	2: 9	store *and* glory out of all the pleasant **f**.	3627

FURROW (1) [FURROWS]
Job	39:10	bind the unicorn *with* his band in the **f**?	8525

FURROWS (8) [FURROW]
Job	31:38	or that the **f** likewise thereof complain;	8525
Ps	65:10	*thou* settlest the **f** thereof: thou makest it	1418
	129: 3	upon my back: they made long their **f**.	4618
Eze	17: 7	that *he* might water it by the **f** of her	6170
	17:10	it shall wither in the **f** where it grew.	6170
Hos	10: 4	up as hemlock in the **f** of the field.	8525
	10:10	*they* shall bind themselves in their two **f**.	5772
	12:11	their altars *are* as heaps in the **f** of	8525

FURTHER (24) [FAR, FURTHERANCE, FURTHERED, FURTHERMORE]
Nu	22:26	the angel of the LORD went **f**,	3254
Dt	20: 8	the officers shall speak **f** unto the people,	3254
1Sa	10:22	Therefore they inquired of the LORD **f**,	5750
Est	9:12	or what *is* thy request **f**? and it shall be	5750
Job	38:11	Hitherto shalt thou come, but no **f**:	3254
	40: 5	yea, twice; but I will **proceed** no **f**.	3254
Ps	140: 8	**f** not his wicked device; *lest* they exalt	6329
Ecc	8:17	seek *it* out, yet he shall not find *it;* yea **f**,	1571
	12:12	**f**, by these, my son, be admonished:	3148
Mt	26:39	he **went** a little **f**, and fell on his face,	4281

Mt	26:65	what **f** need have we of witnesses?	2089
Mk	1:19	And when he had **gone** a little **f** thence,	4260
	5:35	why troublest thou the Master **any f**?	2089
	14:63	saith, What need we **any f** witnesses?	2089
Lk	22:71	they said, What need we **any f** witness?	2089
	24:28	he made as though *he* would have gone **f**.	4208
Ac	4:17	But that it spread no **f** among	1909+4183
	4:21	So when they had **f** threatened *them*,	4324
	12: 3	the Jews, he **proceeded f** to take Peter	4369
	21:28	and brought Greeks also into the temple,	2089
	24: 4	that I be not **f** tedious unto thee,	1909+4183
	27:28	and when they had **gone** a little **f**,	1339
2Ti	3: 9	But they shall proceed no **f**: for	1909+4183
Heb	7:11	what **f** need *was* there that another priest	2089

FURTHERANCE (2) [FURTHER]
Php	1:12	fallen out rather unto the **f** of the gospel;	4297
	1:25	continue with you all for your **f** and	4297

FURTHERED (1) [FURTHER]
Ezr	8:36	they **f** the people, and the house of God.	5375

FURTHERMORE (14) [FURTHER]
Ex	4: 6	the LORD said **f** unto him, Put now thine	5750
Dt	4:21	**F** the LORD was angry with me for	2050.1
	9:13	**F** the LORD spake unto me, saying,	2050.1
1Sa	24:10	David said **f**, *As* the LORD liveth,	2050.1
1Ch	17:10	**F** I tell thee that the LORD will build	2050.1
	27:16	**F** over the tribes of Israel: the ruler of	2050.1
	29: 1	**F** David the king said unto all	2050.1
2Ch	4: 9	**F** he made the court of the priests,	2050.1
Job	34: 1	**F** Elihu answered and said,	2050.1
Eze	8: 6	He said **f** unto me, Son of man, seest	2050.1
	23:40	**f**, that ye have sent for men to come from	637
2Co	2:12	**F**, when I came to Troas to **preach** Christ's	1161
1Th	4: 1	**F** then we beseech you, brethren,	3062
Heb	12: 9	**F** we have had fathers of our	1534+3303+3588

FURY (70) [FURIOUS, FURIOUSLY]
Ge	27:44	few days, until thy brother's **f** turn away;	2534
Lev	26:28	I will walk contrary unto you also in **f**;	2534
Job	20:23	shall cast the **f** of his wrath upon him,	2740
Isa	27: 4	**F** is not in me: who would set the briers	2534
	34: 2	nations, and *his* **f** upon all their armies:	2534
	42:25	Therefore he hath poured upon him the **f**	2534
	51:13	day because of the **f** of the oppressor,	2534
	51:13	and where *is* the **f** of the oppressor?	2534
	51:17	at the hand of the LORD the cup of his **f**;	2534
	51:20	*they are* full *of* the **f** of the LORD,	2534
	51:22	even the dregs of the cup of my **f**;	2534
	59:18	he will repay, **f** to his adversaries,	2534
	63: 3	in mine anger, and trample them in my **f**;	2534
	63: 5	unto me; and my **f**, it upheld me.	2534
	63: 6	them drunk in my **f**, and I will bring	2534
Jer	4: 4	lest my **f** come forth like fire, and burn	2534
	6:11	Therefore I am full *of* the **f** of the LORD;	2534
	7:20	my **f** *shall* be poured out upon this place,	2534
	10:25	Pour out thy **f** upon the heathen that	2534
	21: 5	in anger, and in **f**, and in great wrath.	2534
	21:12	lest my **f** go out like fire, and burn that	2534
	23:19	whirlwind of the LORD is gone forth in **f**,	2534
	25:15	Take the wine cup of this **f** at mine hand,	2534
	30:23	the LORD goeth forth with **f**,	2534
	32:31	of my **f** from the day that they built it	2534
	32:37	anger, and in my **f**, and in great wrath;	2534
	33: 5	I have slain in mine anger and in my **f**,	2534
	36: 7	the **f** that the LORD hath pronounced	2534
	42:18	my **f** hath been poured forth upon	2534
	42:18	so shall my **f** be poured forth upon you,	2534
	44: 6	Wherefore my **f** and mine anger was	2534
La	2: 4	of Zion: he poured out his **f** like fire.	2534
	4:11	The LORD hath accomplished his **f**;	2534
Eze	5:13	and I will cause my **f** to rest upon them,	2534
	5:13	when I have accomplished my **f** in them.	2534
	5:15	in anger and in **f** and in furious rebukes.	2534
	6:12	thus will I accomplish my **f** upon them.	2534
	7: 8	will I shortly pour out my **f** upon thee,	2534
	8:18	Therefore will I also deal in **f**: mine eye	2534
	9: 8	thy pouring out of thy **f** upon Jerusalem?	2534
	13:13	even rent *it with* a stormy wind in my **f**;	2534
	13:13	great hailstones in *my* **f** to consume *it*.	2534
	14:19	pour out my **f** upon it in blood, to cut off	2534
	16:38	I will give thee blood in **f** and jealousy.	2534
	16:42	So will I make my **f** towards thee to rest,	2534
	19:12	she was plucked up in **f**, she was cast	2534
	20: 8	I said, *I* will pour out my **f** upon them	2534
	20:13	*I* would pour out my **f** upon them in	2534
	20:21	I said, *I* would pour out my **f** upon them,	2534
	20:33	with **f** poured out, will I rule over you:	2534
	20:34	stretched out arm, and with **f** poured out.	2534
	21:17	and I will cause my **f** to rest:	2534
	22:20	I gather *you* in mine anger and in my **f**,	2534
	22:22	LORD have poured out my **f** upon you.	2534
	24: 8	That it might cause **f** to come up to take	2534
	24:13	till I have caused my **f** to rest upon thee.	2534
	25:14	to mine anger and according to my **f**;	2534
	30:15	I will pour my **f** upon Sin, the strength of	2534
	36: 6	I have spoken in my jealousy and in my **f**,	2534
	36:18	Wherefore I poured my **f** upon them for	2534
	38:18	*that* my **f** shall come up in my face.	2534
Da	3:13	and *I* commanded to bring Shadrach,	2528
	3:19	Nebuchadnezzar full *of* **f**, and the form	2528
	8: 6	and ran unto him in the **f** of his power.	2534
	9:16	thy **f** be turned away from thy city	2534

Da	11:44	he shall go forth with great **f** to destroy,	2534
Mic	5:15	in anger and **f** upon the heathen,	2534
Na	1: 6	his **f** is poured out like fire, and the rocks	2534
Zec	8: 2	and I was jealous for her *with* great **f**.	2534

FUTILE See VANITIES; VANITY

FUTILITY See VANITIES; VANITY

FUTURE See HEREAFTER

G

GAAL (9)
Jdg	9:26	**G** the son of Ebed came with his brethren,	1603
	9:28	**G** the son of Ebed said, Who *is* Abimelech,	1603
	9:30	city heard the words of **G** the son of Ebed,	1603
	9:31	**G** the son of Ebed and his brethren be	1603
	9:35	**G** the son of Ebed went out, and stood *in*	1603
	9:36	when **G** saw the people, he said to Zebul,	1603
	9:37	**G** spake again and said, See there come	1603
	9:39	**G** went out before the men of Shechem,	1603
	9:41	Zebul thrust out **G** and his brethren,	1603

GAASH (4)
Jos	24:30	on the north side of the hill of **G**.	1608
Jdg	2: 9	of Ephraim, on the north side of the hill **G**.	1608
2Sa	23:30	the Pirathonite, Hiddai of the brooks of **G**,	1608
1Ch	11:32	Hurai of the brooks of **G**, Abiel	1608

GABA (2)
Jos	18:24	and Ophni, and **G**;	1387
Ezr	2:26	children of Ramah and **G**, six hundred	1387

GABBAI (1)
Ne	11: 8	after him **G**, Sallai, nine hundred twenty	1373

GABBATHA (1)
Jn	19:13	the Pavement, but in the Hebrew, **G**.	1042

GABRIEL (4)
Da	8:16	called, and said, **G**, make this *man* to	1403
	9:21	I *was* speaking in prayer, even the man **G**,	1403
Lk	1:19	I am **G**, that stand in the presence of God;	1043
	1:26	And in the sixth month the angel **G** was	1043

GAD (72) [BAAL-GAD, DIBON-GAD, GADITE, GADITES]
Ge	30:11	troop cometh: and she called his name **G**.	1410
	35:26	of Zilpah, Leah's handmaid; **G**, and Asher:	1410
	46:16	the sons of **G**; Ziphion, and Haggi, Shuni,	1410
	49:19	**G**, a troop shall overcome him: but he	1410
Ex	1: 4	Dan, and Naphtali, **G**, and Asher.	1410
Nu	1:14	Of **G**; Eliasaph the son of Deuel.	1410
	1:24	Of the children of **G**, by their generations,	1410
	1:25	*even* of the tribe of **G**, *were* forty and	1410
	2:14	the tribe of **G**: and the captain of the sons	1410
	2:14	the captain of the sons of **G** *shall be*	1410
	7:42	prince of the children of **G**, offered:	1410
	10:20	**G** *was* Eliasaph the son of Deuel.	1410
	13:15	Of the tribe of **G**, Geuel the son of Machi.	1410
	26:15	The children of **G** after their families:	1410
	26:18	These *are* the families of the children of **G**	1410
	32: 1	the children of **G** had a very great	1410
	32: 2	The children of **G** and the children of	1410
	32: 6	Moses said unto the children of **G** and	1410
	32:25	the children of **G** and the children of	1410
	32:29	If the children of **G** and the children of	1410
	32:31	the children of **G** and the children of	1410
	32:33	*even* to the children of **G**, and to	1410
	32:34	children of **G** built Dibon, and Ataroth,	1410
	34:14	the tribe of the children of **G** according to	1425
Dt	27:13	**G**, and Asher, and Zebulun, Dan,	1410
	33:20	Of **G** he said, Blessed *be* he that enlargeth	1410
	33:20	he said, Blessed *be* he that enlargeth **G**:	1410
Jos	4:12	the children of **G**, and half the tribe of	1410
	13:24	gave *inheritance* unto the tribe of **G**,	1410
	13:24	*even* unto the children of **G** according to	1410
	13:28	*is* the inheritance of the children of **G**	1410
	18: 7	**G**, and Reuben, and half the tribe of	1410
	20: 8	Ramoth in Gilead out of the tribe of **G**,	1410
	21: 7	out of the tribe of **G**, and out of the tribe	1410
	21:38	out of the tribe of **G**, Ramoth in Gilead	1410
	22: 9	of Reuben and the children of **G** and	1410
	22:10	of Reuben and the children of **G** and	1410
	22:11	of Reuben and the children of **G** and	1410
	22:13	to the children of **G**, and to the half tribe	1410
	22:15	to the children of **G**, and to the half tribe	1410
	22:21	of Reuben and the children of **G** and	1410
	22:25	ye children of Reuben and children of **G**;	1410
	22:30	the children of **G** and the children of	1410
	22:31	to the children of **G**, and to the children	1410
	22:32	from the children of **G**, out of the land of	1410
	22:33	the children of Reuben and **G** dwelt.	1410
	22:34	the children of **G** called the altar *Ed:* for it	1410
1Sa	13: 7	went over Jordan *to* the land of **G**	1410

1Sa	22: 5 the prophet **G** said unto David, Abide not	1410
2Sa	24: 5 that *lieth* in the midst of the river of **G**,	1410
	24:11 of the LORD came unto the prophet **G**,	1410
	24:13 So **G** came to David, and told him,	1410
	24:14 David said unto **G**, I am in a great strait:	1410
	24:18 **G** came that day to David, and said unto	1410
	24:19 David, according to the saying of **G**.	1410
1Ch	2: 2 and Benjamin, Naphtali, **G**, and Asher.	1410
	5:11 the children of **G** dwelt over against them,	1410
	6:63 out of the tribe of **G**, and out of the tribe	1410
	6:80 out of the tribe of **G**; Ramoth in Gilead	1410
	12:14 These *were* of the sons of **G**, captains of	1410
	21: 9 the LORD spake unto **G**, David's seer,	1410
	21:11 So **G** came to David, and said unto him,	1410
	21:13 David said unto **G**, I am in a great strait:	1410
	21:18 the angel of the LORD commanded **G** to	1410
	21:19 David went up at the saying of **G**, which	1410
	29:29 prophet, and in the book of **G** the seer,	1410
2Ch	29:25 of **G** the king's seer, and Nathan	1410
Jer	49: 1 why *then* doth their king inherit **G**,	1410
Eze	48:27 east side unto the west side, **G** a *portion*.	1410
	48:28 by the border of **G**, at the south side	1410
	48:34 one gate of **G**, one gate of Asher, one gate	1410
Rev	7: 5 Of the tribe of **G** *were* sealed twelve	1045

GADARENES (3)

Mk	5: 1 side of the sea, into the country of the **G**.	1046
Lk	8:26 And they arrived at the country of the **G**,	1046
	8:37 **G** round about besought him to depart	1046

GADDEST (1)

Jer	2:36 Why **g** thou **about** *so* much to change thy	235

GADDI (1)

Nu	13:11 the tribe of Manasseh, **G** the son of Susi.	1426

GADDIEL (1)

Nu	13:10 Of the tribe of Zebulun, **G** the son of Sodi.	1427

GADI (2)

2Ki	15:14 For Menahem the son of **G** went up from	1424
	15:17 Menahem the son of **G** to reign over	1424

GADITE (1) [GAD]

2Sa	23:36 the son of Nathan of Zobah, Bani the **G**,	1425

GADITES (14) [GAD]

Dt	3:12 gave I unto the Reubenites and to the **G**.	1425
	3:16 unto the **G** I gave from Gilead even unto	1425
	4:43 Ramoth in Gilead, of the **G**; and Golan in	1425
	29: 8 the **G**, and to the half tribe of Manasseh.	1425
Jos	1:12 the **G**, and to half the tribe of Manasseh,	1425
	12: 6 and the **G**, and the half tribe of Manasseh.	1425
	13: 8 the **G** have received their inheritance,	1425
	22: 1 the **G**, and the half tribe of Manasseh,	1425
2Ki	10:33 the **G**, and the Reubenites,	1425
1Ch	5:18 the **G**, and half the tribe of Manasseh,	1425
	5:26 the **G**, and half the tribe of Manasseh,	1425
	12: 8 of the **G** there separated themselves unto	1425
	12:37 the **G**, and of the half tribe of Manasseh,	1425
	26:32 the **G**, and the half tribe of Manasseh,	1425

GAHAM (1)

Ge	22:24 and **G**, and Thahash, and Maachah.	1514

GAHAR (2)

Ezr	2:47 the children of **G**, the children of Reaiah,	1515
Ne	7:49 the children of Giddel, the children of **G**,	1515

GAIN (30) [GAINED, GAINS]

Jdg	5:19 of Megiddo; they took no **g** of money.	1215
Job	22: 3 *is it* **g** *to him*, that thou makest thy ways	1215
Pr	1:19 of every one that is **greedy of g**;	1214+1215
	3:14 of silver, and the **g** thereof than fine gold.	8393
	15:27 He that is **greedy of g** troubleth	1214+1215
	28: 8 and **unjust g** increaseth his substance,	8636
Isa	33:15 he that despiseth the **g** of oppressions,	1215
	56:11 every one for his gain, from his quarter.	1215
Eze	22:13 thy **dishonest g** which thou hast made,	1215
	22:27 destroy souls; to **get dishonest g**.	1214+1215
Da	2: 8 I know of certainty that ye would **g**	2084
	11:39 over many, and shall divide the land for **g**.	4242
Mic	4:13 I will consecrate their **g** unto the LORD,	1215
Mt	16:26 if he shall **g** the whole world, and lose his	2770
Mk	8:36 if he shall **g** the whole world, and lose his	2770
Lk	9:25 if he **g** the whole world, and lose himself,	2770
Ac	16:16 which brought her masters much **g** by	2039
	19:24 brought no small **g** unto the craftsmen;	2039
1Co	9:19 servant unto all, that I might **g** the more.	2770
	9:20 became as a Jew, that I might **g** the Jews;	2770
	9:20 I might **g** them that are under the law;	2770
	9:21 I might **g** them *that are* without law.	2770
	9:22 I as weak, that I might **g** the weak:	2770
2Co	12:17 Did I **make a g** of you by any of them	4122
	12:18 Did Titus **make a g** of you? walked we	4122
Php	1:21 For to me to live *is* Christ, and to die *is* **g**.	2771
	3: 7 But what *things* were **g** to me, those I	2771
1Ti	6: 5 of the truth, supposing that **g** is godliness:	4200
	6: 6 But godliness with contentment is great **g**.	4200
Jas	4:13 there a year, and buy and sell, and **get g**:	2770

GAINED (10) [GAIN]

Job	27: 8 though he hath **g**, when God taketh away	1214
Eze	22:12 thou hast **greedily g** of thy neighbours by	1214
Mt	18:15 shall hear thee, thou hast **g** thy brother.	2770
	25:17 *had received* two, he also **g** other two.	2770

Mt	25:20 I have **g** besides them five talents moe.	2770
	25:22 I have **g** two other talents besides them.	2770
Lk	19:15 how much every *man* had **g by trading**.	1281
	19:16 Lord, thy pound hath **g** ten pounds.	4333
	19:18 Lord, thy pound hath **g** five pounds.	4160
Ac	27:21 and to have **g** this harm and loss.	2770

GAINS (1) [GAIN]

Ac	16:19 saw that the hope of their **g** was gone,	2039

GAINSAY (1) [GAINSAYERS, GAINSAYING, SAY]

Lk	21:15 adversaries shall not be able to **g** nor resist.	471

GAINSAYERS (1) [GAINSAY]

Tit	1: 9 both to exhort and to convince the **g**.	483

GAINSAYING (3) [GAINSAY]

Ac	10:29 Therefore came I *unto you* **without g**,	369
Ro	10:21 my hands unto a disobedient and **g** people.	483
Jude	1:11 for reward, and perished in the **g** of Core.	485

GAIUS (5)

Ac	19:29 and having caught **G** and Aristarchus,	1050
	20: 4 and **G** of Derbe, and Timotheus;	1050
Ro	16:23 **G** mine host, and of the whole church,	1050
1Co	1:14 baptized none of you, but Crispus and **G**;	1050
3Jn	1: 1 The elder unto the wellbeloved **G**, whom	1050

GALAL (3)

1Ch	9:15 and **G**, and Mattaniah the son of Micah,	1559
	9:16 the son of **G**, the son of Jeduthun,	1559
Ne	11:17 the son of **G**, the son of Jeduthun.	1559

GALATIA (6) [GALATIANS]

Ac	16: 6 throughout Phrygia and the region **of G**,	1054
	18:23 and went over *all* the country of **G** and	1054
1Co	16: 1 I have given order to the churches of **G**;	1053
Gal	1: 2 are with me, unto the churches of **G**:	1053
2Ti	4:10 Crescens to **G**, Titus unto Dalmatia.	1053
1Pe	1: 1 **G**, Cappadocia, Asia, and Bithynia,	1053

GALATIANS (2) [GALATIA]

Gal	3: 1 O foolish **G**, who hath bewitched you,	1052
	6: S Unto the **G** written from Rome.	1052

GALBANUM (1)

Ex	30:34 sweet spices, stacte, and onycha, and **g**;	2464

GALEED (2)

Ge	31:47 it Jegar-sahadutha: but Jacob called it **G**.	1567
	31:48 Therefore was the name of it called **G**;	1567

GALILEAN (3) [GALILEE]

Mk	14:70 for thou *art* a **G**, and thy speech agreeth	1057
Lk	22:59 *fellow* also was with him: for he is a **G**.	1057
	23: 6 he asked whether the man were a **G**.	1057

GALILEANS (5) [GALILEE]

Lk	13: 1 that season some that told him of the **G**,	1057
	13: 2 Suppose ye that these **G** were sinners	1057
	13: 2 Galileans were sinners above all the **G**,	1057
Jn	4:45 come into Galilee, the **G** received him,	1057
Ac	2: 7 Behold, are not all these which speak **G**?	1057

GALILEE (72) [GALILEAN, GALILEANS]

Jos	20: 7 they appointed Kedesh in **G** in mount	1551
	21:32 Naphtali, Kedesh in **G** with her suburbs,	1551
1Ki	9:11 gave Hiram twenty cities in the land of **G**.	1551
2Ki	15:29 Kedesh, and Hazor, and Gilead, and **G**,	1551
1Ch	6:76 Kedesh in **G** with her suburbs,	1551
Isa	9: 1 sea, beyond Jordan, in **G** of the nations.	1551
Mt	2:22 he turned aside into the parts of **G**:	1056
	3:13 Then cometh Jesus from **G** to Jordan unto	1056
	4:12 was cast into prison, he departed into **G**;	1056
	4:15 the sea, beyond Jordan, **G** of the Gentiles;	1056
	4:18 And Jesus, walking by the sea of **G**,	1056
	4:23 And Jesus went about all **G**, teaching in	1056
	4:25 him great multitudes *of people* from **G**,	1056
	15:29 and came nigh unto the sea of **G**;	1056
	17:22 while they abode in **G**, Jesus said unto	1056
	19: 1 he departed from **G**, and came into	1056
	21:11 is Jesus the prophet of Nazareth of **G**.	1056
	26:32 risen *again*, I will go before you into **G**.	1056
	26:69 saying, Thou also wast with Jesus **of G**.	1057
	27:55 which followed Jesus from **G**,	1056
	28: 7 and behold, he goeth before you into **G**;	1056
	28:10 go tell my brethren that they go into **G**,	1056
	28:16 the eleven disciples went *away* into **G**,	1056
Mk	1: 9 *that* Jesus came from Nazareth of **G**,	1056
	1:14 John was put in prison, Jesus came into **G**,	1056
	1:16 Now as he walked by the sea of **G**, he saw	1056
	1:28 throughout all the region round about **G**.	1056
	1:39 in their synagogues throughout all **G**,	1056
	3: 7 a great multitude from **G** followed him,	1056
	6:21 high captains, and chief *estates* of **G**;	1056
	7:31 and Sidon, he came unto the sea of **G**,	1056
	9:30 departed thence, and passed through **G**;	1056
	14:28 I am risen, I will go before you into **G**.	1056
	15:41 (Who also, when he was in **G**,	1056
	16: 7 Peter that he goeth before you into **G**:	1056
Lk	1:26 was sent from God unto a city of **G**,	1056
	2: 4 And Joseph also went up from **G**, out of	1056
	2:39 they returned into **G**, to their own city	1056
	3: 1 and Herod being tetrarch of **G**,	1056
	4:14 returned in the power of the Spirit into **G**:	1056
	4:31 city of **G**, and taught them on the sabbath	1056

Lk	4:44 And he preached in the synagogues of **G**.	1056
	5:17 which were come out of every town of **G**,	1056
	8:26 the Gadarenes, which is over against **G**.	1056
	17:11 through the midst of Samaria and **G**.	1056
	23: 5 all Jewry, beginning from **G** to this place.	1056
	23: 6 Pilate heard of **G**, he asked whether	1056
	23:49 the women that followed him from **G**,	1056
	23:55 which came with him from **G**,	1056
	24: 6 he spake unto you when he was yet in **G**,	1056
Jn	1:43 following Jesus would go forth into **G**,	1056
	2: 1 day there was a marriage in Cana of **G**;	1056
	2:11 of miracles did Jesus in Cana of **G**,	1056
	4: 3 He left Judea, and departed again into **G**.	1056
	4:43 he departed thence, and went into **G**.	1056
	4:45 Then when he was come into **G**,	1056
	4:46 So Jesus came again into Cana of **G**,	1056
	4:47 that Jesus was come out of Judea into **G**,	1056
	4:54 when he was come out of Judea into **G**.	1056
	6: 1 these *things* Jesus went over the sea of **G**,	1056
	7: 1 After these *things* Jesus walked in **G**: for	1056
	7: 9 *words* unto them, he abode *still* in **G**.	1056
	7:41 some said, Shall Christ come out of **G**?	1056
	7:52 and said unto him, Art thou also of **G**?	1056
	7:52 and look: for out of **G** ariseth no prophet.	1056
	12:21 which was of Bethsaida of **G**,	1056
	21: 2 Nathanael of Cana in **G**, and the *sons*	1056
Ac	1:11 Which also said, Ye men of **G**, why stand	1057
	5:37 After this *man* rose up Judas of **G**	1057
	9:31 throughout all Judea and **G** and Samaria,	1056
	10:37 began from **G**, after the baptism which	1056
	13:31 came up with him from **G** to Jerusalem,	1056

GALL (14)

Dt	29:18 be among you a root that beareth **g**	7219
	32:32 their grapes *are* grapes of **g**, their clusters	7219
Job	16:13 he poureth out my **g** upon the ground.	4845
	20:14 is turned, *it is* the **g** of asps within him.	4846
	20:25 the glistering sword cometh out of his **g**:	4846
Ps	69:21 They gave me also **g** for my meat;	7219
Jer	8:14 given us water of **g** to drink, because	7219
	9:15 and give them water of **g** to drink.	7219
	23:15 and make them drink the water of **g**:	7219
La	3: 5 and compassed *me* with **g** and travail.	7219
	3:19 my misery, the wormwood and the **g**.	7219
Am	6:12 for ye have turned judgment into **g**,	7219
Mt	27:34 gave him vinegar to drink mingled with **g**:	5521
Ac	8:23 For I perceive that thou art in the **g** of	5521

GALLANT (1)

Isa	33:21 with oars, neither shall **g** ship pass thereby.	117

GALLERIES (4) [GALLERY]

SS	7: 5 head like purple; the king *is* held in the **g**.	7298
Eze	41:15 the **g** thereof on the one side and on the	862
	41:16 the **g** round about on their three *stories*,	862
	42: 5 for the **g** were higher than these, than	862

GALLERY (2) [GALLERIES]

Eze	42: 3 *was* **g** against gallery in three *stories*.	862
	42: 3 *was* gallery against **g** in three *stories*.	862

GALLEY (1)

Isa	33:21 wherein shall go no **g** with oars, neither	590

GALLIM (2)

1Sa	25:44 Phalti the son of Laish, which *was* of **G**.	1554
Isa	10:30 Lift up thy voice, O daughter of **G**: cause	1530

GALLIO (3)

Ac	18:12 And when **G** was the deputy of Achaia,	1058
	18:14 **G** said unto the Jews, If it were a matter	1058
	18:17 And **G** cared for none of those *things*.	1058

GALLONS See FIRKINS

GALLOWS (8)

Est	5:14 Let a **g** be made of fifty cubits high, and to	6086
	5:14 and he caused the **g** to be made.	6086
	6: 4 on the **g** that he had prepared for him.	6086
	7: 9 Behold also, the **g** fifty cubits high,	6086
	7:10 they hanged Haman on the **g** that he had	6086
	8: 7 they have hanged upon the **g**, because	6086
	9:13 Haman's ten sons be hanged upon the **g**.	6086
	9:25 and his sons should be hanged on the **g**.	6086

GAMALIEL (7)

Nu	1:10 of Manasseh; **G** the son of Pedahzur.	1583
	2:20 Manasseh *shall be* **G** the son of Pedahzur.	1583
	7:54 On the eighth day *offered* **G** the son of	1583
	7:59 this *was* the offering of **G** the son of	1583
	10:23 of Manasseh *was* **G** the son of Pedahzur.	1583
Ac	5:34 a Pharisee, named **G**, a doctor of law,	1059
	22: 3 yet brought up in this city at the feet of **G**,	1059

GAME See VENISON

GAMMAD See GAMMADIMS

GAMMADIMS (1)

Eze	27:11 about, and the **G** were in thy towers:	1575

GAMUL (1) [BETH-GAMUL]

1Ch	24:17 to Jachin, the two and twentieth to **G**,	1577

GANGRENE See CANKER

G

GAP (1) [GAPS]
Eze 22:30 stand in the **g** before me for the land, 6556

GAPED (2)
Job 16:10 They have **g** upon me with their mouth, 6473
Ps 22:13 They **g** upon me *with* their mouths, *as a* 6475

GAPS (1) [GAP]
Eze 13: 5 Ye have not gone up into the **g**, 6556

GARDEN (52) [GARDENER, GARDENS]
Ge 2: 8 the LORD God planted a **g** eastward in 1588
2: 9 the tree of life also in the midst of the **g**, 1588
2:10 a river went out of Eden to water the **g**; 1588
2:15 put him into the **g** of Eden to dress it and 1588
2:16 Of every tree of the **g** thou mayest freely 1588
3: 1 Ye shall not eat of every tree of the **g**? 1588
3: 2 may eat of the fruit of the trees of the **g**: 1588
3: 3 of the tree which *is* in the midst of the **g**, 1588
3: 8 God walking in the **g** in the cool of the 1588
3: 8 the LORD God amongst the trees of the **g**. 1588
3:10 heard thy voice in the **g**, and I was afraid, 1588
3:23 God sent him forth from the **g** of Eden, 1588
3:24 he placed at the east of the **g** of Eden 1588
13:10 *even* as the **g** of the LORD, 1588
Dt 11:10 wateredst *it* with thy foot, as a **g** of herbs: 1588
1Ki 21: 2 that I may have it for a **g** of herbs, 1588
2Ki 9:27 *this,* he fled *by* the way of the **g** house. 1588
21:18 was buried in the **g** of his own house, 1588
21:18 of his own house, in the **g** of Uzza: 1588
21:26 he was buried in his sepulchre in the **g** of 1588
25: 4 two walls, which *is* by the king's **g**: 1588
Ne 3:15 wall of the pool of Siloah by the king's **g**, 1588
Est 1: 5 in the court of the king's **g**; 1594
7: 7 wine in his wrath *went* into the palace **g**: 1594
7: 8 the king returned out of the palace **g** into 1594
Job 8:16 and his branch shooteth forth in his **g**, 1593
SS 4:12 A **g** inclosed *is* my sister, *my* spouse; 1588
4:16 blow upon my **g**, *that* the spices thereof 1588
4:16 Let my beloved come into his **g**, and eat 1588
5: 1 am come into my **g**, my sister, *my* spouse: 1588
6: 2 My beloved is gone down into his **g**, 1588
6:11 I went down into the **g** of nuts to see 1594
Isa 1: 8 as a lodge in a **g of cucumbers**, as a 4750
1:30 leaf fadeth, and as a **g** that hath no water. 1593
51: 3 and her desert like the **g** of the LORD; 1588
58:11 thou shalt be like a watered **g**, and like a 1588
61:11 as the **g** causeth the things that are sown 1593
Jer 31:12 their soul shall be as a watered **g**; 1588
39: 4 *by* the way of the king's **g**, by the gate 1588
52: 7 the two walls, which *was* by the king's **g**; 1588
La 2: 6 away his tabernacle, as *if it were of* a **g**: 1588
Eze 28:13 Thou hast been in Eden the **g** of God; 1588
31: 8 The cedars in the **g** of God could not hide 1588
31: 8 nor any tree in the **g** of God was like unto 1588
31: 9 that *were* in the **g** of God, envied him. 1588
36:35 was desolate is become like the **g** of Eden; 1588
Joel 2: 3 the land *is* as the **g** of Eden before them, 1588
Lk 13:19 which a man took, and cast into his **g**; 2779
Jn 18: 1 where was a **g**, into the which he entered, 2779
18:26 Did not I see thee in the **g** with him? 2779
19:41 where he was crucified there was a **g**; 2779
19:41 in the **g** a new sepulchre, wherein was 2779

GARDENER (1) [GARDEN]
Jn 20:15 She, supposing him to be the **g**, saith unto 2780

GARDENS (12) [GARDEN]
Nu 24: 6 they spread forth, as **g** by the river side, 1593
Ecc 2: 5 I made me **g** and orchards, and I planted 1593
SS 4:15 A fountain of **g**, a well of living waters, 1588
6: 2 to feed in the **g**, and to gather lilies. 1588
8:13 that dwellest in the **g**, the companions 1588
Isa 1:29 ye shall be confounded for the **g** that ye 1593
65: 3 that sacrificeth in **g**, and burneth incense 1593
66:17 purify themselves in the **g** behind one *tree* 1593
Jer 29: 5 *in them;* and plant **g**, and eat the fruit 1593
29:28 *in them;* and plant **g**, and eat the fruit 1593
Am 4: 9 when your **g** and your vineyards and 1593
9:14 they shall also make **g**, and eat the fruit of 1593

GAREB (3)
2Sa 23:38 Ira an Ithrite, **G** an Ithrite, 1619
1Ch 11:40 Ira the Ithrite, **G** the Ithrite, 1619
Jer 31:39 go forth over against it upon the hill **G**, 1619

GARLANDS (1)
Ac 14:13 brought oxen and **g** unto the gates, 4725

GARLICK (1)
Nu 11: 5 and the leeks, and the onions, and the **g**: 7762

GARMENT (86) [GARMENTS]
Ge 9:23 Shem and Japheth took a **g**, and laid *it* 8071
25:25 first came out red, all over like a hairy **g**; 155
39:12 she caught him by his **g**, saying, Lie with 899
39:12 he left his **g** in her hand, and fled, 899
39:13 when she saw that he had left his **g** in her 899
39:15 that he left his **g** with me, and fled, 899
39:16 laid up his **g** by her, until his lord came 899
39:18 that he left his **g** with me, and fled out. 899
Lev 6:10 the priest shall put on his linen **g**, 4055
6:27 sprinkled of the blood thereof upon *any* **g**, 899
13:47 The **g** also that the plague of leprosy is in, 899
13:47 *whether it be* a woollen **g**, or a linen 899

Lev 13:47 *it be* a woollen garment, or a linen **g**; 899
13:49 the plague be greenish or reddish in the **g**, 899
13:51 if the plague be spread in the **g**, either in 899
13:52 He shall therefore burn *that* **g**, whether 899
13:53 behold, the plague be not spread in the **g**, 899
13:56 he shall rend it out of the **g**, or out of 899
13:57 if it appear still in the **g**, either in the warp, 899
13:58 the **g**, either warp, or woof, 899
13:59 *is* the law of the plague of leprosy in a **g** 899
14:55 And for the leprosy of a **g**, and of a house, 899
15:17 every **g**, and every skin, whereon is the 899
19:19 neither shall a **g** mingled of linen and 899
Dt 22: 5 neither shall a man put on a woman's **g**: 8071
22:11 Thou shalt not wear a **g of divers sorts**, 8162
Jos 7:21 among the spoils a goodly Babylonish **g**, 155
7:24 the **g**, and the wedge of gold, and his sons, 155
Jdg 8:25 willingly **g** *them*. And they spread a **g**, 8071
2Sa 13:18 she had a **g** of divers colours upon her: 3801
13:19 rent her **g** of divers colours that *was* on 3801
20: 8 Joab's **g** that he had put on *was* girded 4055
1Ki 11:29 he had clad himself with a new **g**; 8008
11:30 Ahijah caught the new **g** that *was* on him, 8008
2Ki 9:13 took every man his **g**, and put *it* under him 899
Ezr 9: 3 I rent my **g** and my mantle, and pluckt off 899
9: 5 having rent my **g** and my mantle, I fell 899
Est 8:15 and *with* a **g** of fine linen and purple: 8509
Job 13:28 consumeth, as a **g** that is moth-eaten. 899
30:18 By the great force of *my disease* is my **g** 3830
38: 9 When I made the cloud the **g** thereof, 3830
38:14 as clay *to* the seal; and they stand as a **g**. 3830
41:13 Who can discover the face of his **g**? 3830
Ps 69:11 I made sackcloth also my **g**; and I became 3830
73: 6 as a chain; violence covereth them *as a* **g**. 7897
102:26 yea, all of them shall wax old like a **g**; *as a* 899
104: 2 coverest *thyself with* light as with a **g**: 8008
104: 6 coveredst it *with* the deep as with a **g**: 3830
109:18 himself with cursing like as with his **g**, 4055
109:19 Let it be unto him as the **g** *which* covereth 899
Pr 20:16 Take his **g** that is surety for a stranger, 899
25:20 he that taketh away a **g** in cold weather, 899
27:13 Take his **g** that is surety for a stranger, 899
30: 4 who hath bound the waters in a **g**? 8071
Isa 50: 9 lo, they all shall wax old as a **g**; the moth 899
51: 6 the earth shall wax old like a **g**, and they 899
51: 8 For the moth shall eat them up like a **g**, 899
61: 3 the **g** of praise for the spirit of heaviness; 4594
Jer 43:12 of Egypt, as a shepherd putteth on his **g**; 899
Eze 18: 7 and hath covered the naked with a **g**; 899
18:16 and hath covered the naked with a **g**, 899
Da 7: 9 whose **g** *was* white as snow, and the hair 3831
Mic 2: 8 ye pull off the robe with the **g** from them 8008
Hag 2:12 If one bear holy flesh in the skirt of his **g**, 899
Zec 13: 4 shall they wear a rough **g** to deceive: 155
Mal 2:16 for one covereth violence with his **g**, 3830
Mt 9:16 a piece of new cloth unto an old **g**; 2440
9:16 is put in to fill it up taketh from the **g**, 2440
9:20 *him,* and touched the hem of his **g**: 2440
9:21 If I may but touch his **g**, I shall be whole. 2440
14:36 they might only touch the hem of his **g**: 2440
22:11 a man which had not on a wedding **g**: 1742
22:12 thou in hither not having a wedding **g**? 1742
Mk 2:21 seweth a piece of new cloth on an old **g**: 2440
5:27 in the press behind, and touched his **g**. 2440
6:56 touch if it were but the border of his **g**: 2440
10:50 away his **g**, rose, and came to Jesus. 2440
13:16 not turn back again for to take up his **g**. 2440
16: 5 the right side, clothed in a **long** white **g**; 4749
Lk 5:36 No *man* putteth a piece of a new **g** upon 2440
8:44 and touched the border of his **g**: 2440
22:36 no sword, let him sell his **g**, and buy one. 2440
Ac 12: 8 Cast thy **g** about thee, and follow me. 2440
Heb 1:11 they all shall wax old as *doth* a **g**; 2440
Jude 1:23 hating even the **g** spotted by the flesh. 5509
Rev 1:13 **clothed with a g** down to the foot, 1746

GARMENTS (103) [GARMENT]
Ge 35: 2 and be clean, and change your **g**: 8071
38:14 And she put her widow's **g** off from her, 899
38:19 and put on the **g** of her widowhood. 899
49:11 he washed his **g** in wine, and his clothes 3830
Ex 28: 2 thou shalt make holy **g** for Aaron thy 899
28: 3 they may make Aaron's **g** to consecrate 899
28: 4 these *are* the **g** which they shall make; 899
28: 4 they shall make holy **g** for Aaron thy 899
29: 5 thou shalt take the **g**, and put upon Aaron 899
29:21 upon his **g**, and upon his sons, and upon 899
29:21 and upon the **g** of his sons with him: 899
29:21 his **g**, and his sons, and his sons' **garments** 899
29:21 his and his sons, and his sons' **g** with him. 899
29:29 the holy **g** of Aaron shall be his sons' *after* 899
31:10 the holy **g** for Aaron the priest, 899
31:10 the **g** of his sons, to minister in the priest's 899
35:19 do service in the holy *place,* the holy **g** for 899
35:19 the **g** of his sons, to minister in the priest's 899
35:21 and for all his service, and for the holy **g**. 899
39: 1 holy *place,* and made the holy **g** for Aaron; 899
39:41 and the holy **g** for Aaron the priest, 899
39:41 his sons' **g**, to minister in the priest's office. 899
40:13 thou shalt put upon Aaron the holy **g**, 899
Lev 6:11 he shall put off his **g**, and put on other 899
6:11 put on other **g**, and carry forth the ashes 899
8: 2 the **g**, and the anointing oil, and a bullock 899
8:30 *and* upon his **g**, and upon his sons, 899
8:30 his sons, and upon his sons' **g** with him; 899
8:30 *and* his **g**, and his sons, and his sons' 899

Lev 8:30 and his sons, and his sons' **g** with him. 899
16: 4 these *are* holy **g**; therefore shall he wash 899
16:23 shall put off the linen **g**, which he put on 899
16:24 put on his **g**, and come forth, and offer his 899
16:32 put on the linen clothes, *even* the holy **g**: 899
21:10 that is consecrated to put on the **g**, shall 899
Nu 15:38 of their **g** throughout their generations, 899
20:26 strip Aaron of his **g**, and put them upon 899
20:28 Moses stripped Aaron of his **g**, and put 899
Jos 9: 5 upon their feet, and old **g** upon them; 8008
9:13 these our **g** and our shoes are become old 8008
Jdg 14:12 you thirty sheets and thirty change of **g**: 899
14:13 me thirty sheets and thirty change of **g**. 899
14:19 gave change of **g** unto them which NIH
1Sa 18: 4 gave it to David, and his **g**, even to his 4055
2Sa 10: 4 cut off their **g** in the middle, *even* to their 4063
13:31 and tare his **g**, and lay on the earth; 899
1Ki 10:25 **g**, and armour, and spices, horses, 8008
2Ki 5:22 a talent of silver, and two changes of **g**. 899
5:23 with two changes of **g**, and laid *them* 899
5:26 to receive **g**, and oliveyards, and vineyards, 899
7:15 lo, all the way *was* full of **g** and vessels, 899
25:29 changed his prison **g**: and he did eat bread 899
1Ch 19: 4 cut off their **g** in the midst hard by *their* 4063
Ezr 2:69 of silver, and one hundred priests' **g**. 3801
Ne 7:70 five hundred and thirty priests' **g**. 3801
7:72 and threescore and seven priests' **g**. 3801
Job 37:17 How thy **g** are warm, when he quieteth 899
Ps 22:18 They part my **g** among them, and cast lots 899
45: 8 All thy **g** *smell* of myrrh, and aloes, 899
133: 2 that went down to the skirts of his **g**; 4060
Ecc 9: 8 Let thy **g** be always white; and let thy 899
SS 4:11 the smell of thy **g** *is* like the smell of 8008
Isa 9: 5 confused noise, and **g** rolled in blood; 8071
52: 1 put on thy beautiful **g**, O Jerusalem; 899
59: 6 Their webs shall not become **g**, neither 899
59:17 he put on the **g** of vengeance *for* clothing, 899
61:10 for he hath clothed me with the **g** of 899
63: 1 from Edom, with dyed **g** from Bozrah? 899
63: 2 thy **g** like him that treadeth in the winefat? 899
63: 3 their blood shall be sprinkled upon my **g**, 899
Jer 36:24 afraid, nor rent their **g**, *neither* the king, 899
52:33 changed his prison **g**: and he did 899
La 4:14 so that *men* could not touch their **g**. 3830
Eze 16:16 of thy **g** thou didst take, and deckedst thy 899
16:18 tookest thy broidered **g**, and coveredst 899
26:16 their robes, and put off their broidered **g**, 899
42:14 there they shall lay their **g** wherein they 899
42:14 shall put on other **g**, and shall approach to 899
44:17 they shall be clothed with linen **g**; 899
44:19 they shall put off their **g** wherein they 899
44:19 chambers, and they shall put on other **g**; 899
44:19 shall not sanctify the people with their **g**. 899
Da 3:21 their *other* **g**, and were cast into the midst 3831
Joel 2:13 not your **g**, and turn unto the LORD your 899
Zec 3: 3 Now Joshua was clothed with filthy **g**, 899
3: 4 Take away the filthy **g** from him. 899
3: 5 upon his head, and clothed him with **g**. 899
Mt 21: 8 a very great multitude spread their **g** 2440
23: 5 and enlarge the borders of their **g**, 2440
27:35 crucified him, and parted his **g**, casting 2440
27:35 They parted my **g** among them, 2440
Mk 11: 7 the colt to Jesus, and cast their **g** on him; 2440
11: 8 And many spread their **g** in the way: 2440
15:24 they parted his **g**, casting lots upon them, 2440
Lk 19:35 and they cast their **g** upon the colt, 2440
24: 4 two men stood by them in shining **g**: 2067
Jn 13: 4 riseth from supper, and laid aside his **g**; 2440
13:12 and had taken his **g**, and was set down 2440
19:23 took his **g**, and made four parts, to every 2440
Ac 9:39 the coats and **g** which Dorcas made, 2440
Jas 5: 2 are corrupted, and your **g** are motheaten. 2440
Rev 3: 4 in Sardis, which have not defiled their **g**; 2440
16:15 and keepeth his **g**, lest he walk naked, 2440

GARMITE (1)
1Ch 4:19 the father of Keilah the **G**, 1636

GARNER (2) [GARNERS]
Mt 3:12 his floor, and gather his wheat into the **g**; 596
Lk 3:17 and will gather the wheat into his **g**; 596

GARNERS (2) [GARNER]
Ps 144:13 *That* our **g** *may be* full, affording all 4200
Joel 1:17 the **g** are laid desolate, the barns are 214

GARNISH (1) [GARNISHED]
Mt 23:29 and the sepulchres of the righteous, 2885

GARNISHED (5) [GARNISH]
2Ch 3: 6 he **g** the house with precious stones for 6823
Job 26:13 By his spirit he hath **g** the heavens; 8235
Mt 12:44 come, he findeth *it* empty, swept, and **g**. 2885
Lk 11:25 he cometh, he findeth *it* swept and **g**. 2885
Rev 21:19 **g** with all *manner of* precious stones. 2885

GARRISON (13) [GARRISONS]
1Sa 10: 5 of God, where *is* the **g** of the Philistines: 5333
13: 3 Jonathan smote the **g** of the Philistines 5333
13: 4 Saul had smitten a **g** of the Philistines, 5333
13:23 the **g** of the Philistines went out to 4673
14: 1 and let us go over to the Philistines' **g**, 4673
14: 4 sought to go over unto the Philistines' **g**, 4673
14: 6 let us go over unto the **g** of these 4673
14:11 themselves unto the **g** of the Philistines: 4673

1Sa 14:12 the men of the **g** answered Jonathan and	4675
14:15 the **g**, and the spoilers, they also trembled	4673
2Sa 23:14 the **g** of the Philistines *was* then	4673
1Ch 11:16 the Philistines' **g** *was* then at Beth-lehem.	5333
2Co 11:32 with a **g**, desirous to apprehend me:	NIG

GARRISONS (7) [GARRISON]

2Sa 8: 6 David put **g** in Syria of Damascus:	5333
8:14 he put **g** in Edom; throughout all Edom	5333
8:14 throughout all Edom put he **g**, and all	5333
1Ch 18: 6 David put **g** in Syria-damascus;	NIH
18:13 he put **g** in Edom; and all the Edomites	5333
2Ch 17: 2 set **g** in the land of Judah, and in the cities	5333
Eze 26:11 thy strong **g** shall go down to the ground.	4676

GASHMU (1) [GESHEM]

Ne 6: 6 **G** saith *it, that* thou and the Jews think to	1654

GAT (20) [GET]

Ge 19:27 Abraham **g up early** in the morning to	7925
Ex 24:18 the cloud, and **g** him **up** into the mount:	5927
Nu 11:30 Moses **g** him into the camp, he and	622
14:40 **g** them **up** into the top of the mountain,	5927
16:27 they **g** up from the tabernacle of Korah,	5927
Jdg 9:48 Abimelech **g** him **up** *to* mount Zalmon,	5927
9:51 **g** them **up** to the top of the tower.	5927
19:28 man rose up, and **g** him unto his place.	1980
1Sa 13:15 **g** him up from Gilgal *unto* Gibeah of	5927
24:22 and his men **g** them **up** unto the hold.	5927
26:12 they **g** them **away**, and no man saw *it,*	1980
2Sa 4: 7 **g** them **away** through the plain all night.	1980
8:13 David **g** him a name when he returned	6213
13:29 every man **g** him **up** upon his mule,	7392
17:23 arose, and **g** him *home* to his house, to	1980
19: 3 the people **g** them by stealth that day *into*	935
1Ki 1: 1 him with clothes, but he **g** no **heat.**	3179
Ps 116: 3 and the pains of hell **g hold upon** me:	4672
Ecc 2: 8 I **g** me *men* singers and *women* singers,	6213
La 5: 9 We **g** our bread with *the peril of* our lives	935

GATAM (3)

Ge 36:11 Omar, Zepho, and **G**, and Kenaz.	1609
36:16 Duke Korah, duke **G**, *and* duke Amalek:	1609
1Ch 1:36 Omar, Zephi, and **G**, Kenaz, and Timna,	1609

GATE (275) [GATES]

Ge 19: 1 at even; and Lot sat in the **g** of Sodom:	8179
22:17 seed shall possess the **g** of his enemies;	8179
23:10 of all that went in *at* the **g** of his city,	8179
23:18 before all that went in *at* the **g** of his city.	8179
24:60 let thy seed possess the **g** of those which	8179
28:17 house of God, and this *is* the **g** of heaven.	8179
34:20 Shechem his son came unto the **g** of their	8179
34:24 all that went out of the **g** of his city;	8179
34:24 all that went out of the **g** of his city.	8179
Ex 27:14 The hangings of the **g** shall	NIH
27:16 for the **g** of the court *shall be* a hanging of	8179
32:26 Then Moses stood in the **g** of the camp,	8179
32:27 out from **g** to gate throughout the camp,	8179
32:27 out from gate to **g** throughout the camp,	8179
38:14 The hangings of the *one* side *of the* **g**	NIH
38:15 for the other side of the court **g**, on this	8179
38:18 the hanging for the **g** of the court *was*	8179
38:31 sockets of the court **g**, and all the pins	8179
39:40 the hanging for the court **g**, his cords,	8179
40: 8 and hang up the hanging at the court **g.**	8179
40:33 and set up the hanging of the court **g.**	8179
Nu 4:26 the hanging for the door of the **g** of	8179
Dt 21:19 of his city, and unto the **g** of his place;	8179
22:15 unto the elders of the city in the **g:**	8179
22:24 ye shall bring them both out unto the **g**	8179
25: 7 let his brother's wife go up to the **g** unto	8179
Jos 2: 5 pass *about the time* of shutting of the **g,**	8179
2: 7 when none went out, they shut the **g.**	8179
7: 5 for they chased them *from* before the **g**	8179
8:29 cast it at the entering of the **g** of the city,	8179
20: 4 stand *at* the entering of the **g** of the city,	8179
Jdg 9:35 stood *in* the entering of the **g** of the city:	8179
9:40 *even* unto the entering of the **g.**	8179
9:44 stood *in* the entering of the **g** of the city:	8179
16: 2 laid wait for him all night in the **g** of	8179
16: 3 took the doors of the **g** of the city,	8179
18:16 of Dan, stood *by* the entering of the **g.**	8179
18:17 the priest stood *in* the entering of the **g.**	8179
Ru 4: 1 went Boaz up *to* the **g**, and sat him down	8179
4:10 his brethren, and from the **g** of his place:	8179
4:11 all the people that *were* in the **g,**	8179
1Sa 4:18 the seat backward by the side of the **g,**	8179
9:18 Saul drew near to Samuel in the **g,**	8179
21:13 scrabled on the doors of the **g**, and let his	8179
2Sa 3:27 Joab took him aside in the **g** to speak with	8179
10: 8 battle in array *at* the entering in of the **g:**	8179
11:23 them *even* unto the entering of the **g:**	8179
15: 2 early, and stood beside the way of the **g:**	8179
18: 4 the king stood by the **g** side, and all	8179
18:24 *up* to the roof over the **g** unto the wall,	8179
18:33 went up to the chamber over the **g,**	8179
19: 8 the king rose, and sat in the **g.** And they	8179
19: 8 Behold, the king doth sit in the **g,**	8179
23:15 the well of Beth-lehem, which *is* by the **g.**	8179
23:16 that *was* by the **g**, and took *it,* and	8179
1Ki 17:10 when he came to the **g** of the city,	8179
22:10 in a void place *in* the entrance of the **g** of	6607
2Ki 7: 1 of barley for a shekel, in the **g** of Samaria.	8179
7: 3 leprous men *at* the entering in of the **g:**	8179

2Ki 7:17 he leaned to have the charge of the **g:**	8179
7:17 the people trode upon him in the **g,**	8179
7:18 be to morrow about *this* time in the **g,**	8179
7:20 for the people trode upon him in the **g,**	8179
9:31 as Jehu entered in at the **g**, she said,	8179
10: 8 the entering in of the **g** until the morning.	8179
11: 6 And a third *part shall be* at the **g** of Sur;	8179
11: 6 and a third *part* at the **g** behind the guard:	8179
11:19 came *by* the way of the **g** of the guard *to*	8179
14:13 of Ephraim unto the corner gate,	8179
14:13 the gate of Ephraim unto the corner **g,**	8179
15:35 He built the higher **g** of the house of	8179
23: 8 of Joshua the governor of the city,	8179
23: 8 *were* on a man's left hand at the **g** of	8179
25: 4 *by* the way of the **g** between two walls,	8179
1Ch 9:18 Who hitherto *waited* in the **g**	8179
11:17 of the well of Beth-lehem, that *is* at the **g.**	8179
11:18 that *was* by the **g**, and took *it,* and	8179
19: 9 put the battle in array *before* the **g** of	6607
26:13 their fathers, for *every* **g.** 8179+8179+2050.1	
26:16 with the Shallecheth, by the causeway	8179
2Ch 8:14 their courses at *every* **g:** 8179+8179+2050.1	
18: 9 *at* the entering in of the **g** of Samaria;	8179
23: 5 a third *part* at the **g** of the foundation:	8179
23:15 of the horse **g** *by* the king's house,	8179
23:20 they came through the high **g** *into*	8179
24: 8 set it without at the **g** of the house of	8179
25:23 from the **g** of Ephraim to the corner gate,	8179
25:23 from the gate of Ephraim to the corner **g,**	8179
26: 9 built towers in Jerusalem at the corner **g,**	8179
26: 9 at the valley **g**, and at the turning *of*	8179
27: 3 He built the high **g** of the house of	8179
32: 6 to him in the street of the **g** of the city,	8179
33:14 even to the entering in at the fish **g,**	8179
35:15 porters *waited* at *every* **g:** 8179+8179+2050.1	
Ne 2:13 I went out by night by the **g** of the valley,	8179
2:14 I went on to the **g** of the fountain,	8179
2:15 entered by the **g** of the valley, and *so*	8179
3: 1 the priests, and they built the sheep **g;**	8179
3: 3 the fish **g** did the sons of Hassenaah build,	8179
3: 6 Moreover the old **g** repaired Jehoiada	8179
3:13 The valley **g** repaired Hanun,	8179
3:13 cubits on the wall unto the dung **g.**	8179
3:14 the dung **g** repaired Malchiah the son of	8179
3:15 the **g** of the fountain repaired Shallum	8179
3:26 unto *the place* over against the water **g**	8179
3:28 above the horse **g** repaired the priests,	8179
3:29 of Shechaniah, the keeper of the east **g.**	8179
3:31 over against the **g** Miphkad, and to	8179
3:32 unto the sheep **g** repaired the goldsmiths	8179
8: 1 the street that *was* before the water **g;**	8179
8: 3 water **g** from the morning until midday,	8179
8:16 the street of the water **g**, and in the street	8179
8:16 and in the street of the **g** of Ephraim.	8179
12:31 hand upon the wall toward the dung **g:**	8179
12:37 at the fountain **g**, which *was* over against	8179
12:37 David, even unto the water **g** east*ward.*	8179
12:39 from above the **g** of Ephraim,	8179
12:39 above the old **g**, and above the fish gate,	8179
12:39 above the fish **g**, and the tower of	8179
12:39 tower of Meah, even unto the sheep **g:**	8179
12:39 and they stood still in the prison **g.**	8179
Est 2:19 then Mordecai sat in the king's **g.**	8179
2:21 while Mordecai sat in the king's **g,**	8179
3: 2 that *were* in the king's **g**, bowed,	8179
3: 3 which *were* in the king's **g**, said unto	8179
4: 2 came even before the king's **g:** for none	8179
4: 2 for none might enter into the king's **g**	8179
4: 6 the city, which *was* before the king's **g.**	8179
5: 1 over against the **g** of the house.	6607
5: 9 Haman saw Mordecai in the king's **g,**	8179
5:13 Mordecai the Jew sitting at the king's **g.**	8179
6:10 the Jew, that sitteth at the king's **g:**	8179
6:12 Mordecai came again to the king's **g.**	8179
Job 5: 4 safety, and they are crushed in the **g,**	8179
29: 7 I went out *to* the **g** through the city,	8179
31:21 fatherless, when I saw my help in the **g:**	8179
Ps 69:12 They that sit in the **g** speak against me;	8179
118:20 This **g** of the LORD, into which	8179
127: 5 shall speak with the enemies in the **g.**	8179
Pr 17:19 he that exalteth his **g** seeketh destruction.	6607
22:22 neither oppress the afflicted in the **g:**	8179
24: 7 fool: he openeth not his mouth in the **g.**	8179
SS 7: 4 in Heshbon, by the **g** of Bath-rabbim:	8179
Isa 14:31 Howl, O **g**; cry, O city; thou;	8179
22: 7 shall set themselves in array at the **g.**	8179
24:12 and the **g** is smitten *with* destruction.	8179
28: 6 to them that turn the battle to the **g.**	8179
29:21 a snare for him that reproveth in the **g,**	8179
Jer 7: 2 Stand in the **g** of the LORD's house,	8179
17:19 stand in the **g** of the children of the	8179
19: 2 which *is* by the entry of the east **g,**	8179
20: 2 him in the stocks that *were* in the high **g**	8179
26:10 sat down in the entry of the new **g** of	8179
31:38 of Hananeel unto the **g** of the corner.	8179
31:40 unto the corner of the horse **g** towards	8179
36:10 the higher court *at* the entry of the new **g**	8179
37:13 when he was in the **g** of Benjamin,	8179
38: 7 the king then sitting in the **g** of Benjamin;	8179
39: 3 sat in the middle **g**, *even* Nergal-sharezer,	8179
39: 4 by the **g** betwixt the two walls:	8179
39: 4 the way of the **g** between the two walls.	8179
La 5:14 The elders have ceased from the **g,**	8179
Eze 8: 3 to the door of the inner **g** that looketh	8179
8: 5 northward at the **g** of the altar this image	8179

Eze 8:14 he brought me to the door of the **g** of	8179
9: 2 men came from the way of the higher **g,**	8179
10:19 *one* stood *at* the door of the east **g** of	8179
11: 1 brought me unto the east **g** of the LORD's	8179
11: 1 behold at the door of the **g** five and	8179
40: 3 a measuring reed; and he stood in the **g.**	8179
40: 6 came he unto the **g** which looketh toward	8179
40: 6 and measured the threshold of the **g,**	8179
40: 6 the other threshold of the **g**, which *was*	NIH
40: 7 the threshold of the **g** by the porch of	8179
40: 7 the porch of the **g** within *was* one reed.	8179
40: 8 He measured also the porch of the **g,**	8179
40: 9 measured he the porch of the **g,**	8179
40: 9 and the porch of the **g** *was* inward.	8179
40:10 the little chambers of the **g** eastward	8179
40:11 the breadth of the entry of the **g,**	8179
40:11 *and* the length of the **g**, thirteen cubits.	8179
40:13 the **g** from the roof of *one* little chamber	8179
40:14 the post of the court round about the **g.**	8179
40:15 from the face of the **g** of the entrance	8179
40:15 the porch of the inner **g** were sixty cubits.	8179
40:16 to their posts within the **g** round about,	8179
40:19 **g** unto the forefront of the inner court	8179
40:20 the **g** of the outward court that looked	8179
40:21 were after the measure of the first **g:**	8179
40:22 after the measure of the **g** that looketh	8179
40:23 the **g** of the inner court *was* over against	8179
40:23 *was* over against the **g** toward the north,	8179
40:23 he measured from **g** to gate an hundred	8179
40:23 he measured from gate to **g** an hundred	8179
40:24 south, and behold a **g** toward the south:	8179
40:27 *there was* a **g** in the inner court toward	8179
40:27 he measured from **g** to gate toward	8179
40:27 he measured from gate to **g** toward	8179
40:28 me to the inner court by the south **g:**	8179
40:28 he measured the south **g** according to	8179
40:32 he measured the **g** according to these	8179
40:35 he brought me to the north **g,**	8179
40:39 In the porch of the **g** were two tables on	8179
40:40 one goeth up to the entry of the north **g,**	8179
40:40 which *was* at the porch of the **g**, were	8179
40:41 tables on that side, by the side of the **g,**	8179
40:44 without the inner **g** were the chambers	8179
40:44 which *was* at the side of the north **g;**	8179
40:44 one at the side of the east **g** *having*	8179
40:48 the breadth of the **g** *was* three cubits on	8179
42:15 he brought me forth toward the **g** whose	8179
43: 1 Afterward he brought me to the **g**, *even*	8179
43: 1 *even* the **g** that looketh toward the east:	8179
43: 4 the **g** whose prospect *is* toward the east.	8179
44: 1 he brought me back the way of the **g** of	8179
44: 2 **g** shall be shut, it shall not be opened,	8179
44: 3 enter by the way of the porch of that **g,**	8179
44: 4 brought he me the way of the north **g**	8179
45:19 upon the posts of the **g** of the inner court.	8179
46: 1 The **g** of the inner court that looketh	8179
46: 2 by the way of the porch of *that* **g** without,	8179
46: 2 shall stand by the post of the **g,**	8179
46: 2 he shall worship at the threshold of the **g:**	8179
46: 2 the **g** shall not be shut until the evening.	8179
46: 3 of this **g** before the LORD in the sabbaths	8179
46: 8 go in *by* the way of the porch of that **g,**	8179
46: 9 that entereth in *by* the way of the north **g**	8179
46: 9 shall go out *by* the way of the south **g;**	8179
46: 9 he that entereth *by* the way of the south **g**	8179
46: 9 shall go forth *by* the way of the north **g:**	8179
46: 9 he shall not return *by* the way of the **g**	8179
46:12 open him the **g** that looketh *toward* the	8179
46:12 after his going forth *one* shall shut the **g.**	8179
46:19 the entry, which *was* at the side of the **g,**	8179
47: 2 brought me out *of* the way of the **g**	8179
47: 2 utter *g* by the way that looketh east*ward;*	8179
48:31 one **g** of Reuben, one gate of Judah,	8179
48:31 one gate of Judah, one gate of Levi.	8179
48:31 one gate of Judah, one gate of Levi.	8179
48:32 one gate of Joseph, one gate of Benjamin,	8179
48:32 one gate of Benjamin, one gate of Dan.	8179
48:32 one gate of Benjamin, one **g** of Dan.	8179
48:33 one gate of Simeon, one gate of Issachar,	8179
48:33 one gate of Simeon, one **g** of Issachar,	8179
48:33 one gate of Issachar, one **g** of Zebulun.	8179
48:34 one gate of Gad, one gate of Asher, one gate	8179
48:34 one gate of Gad, one **g** of Asher, one gate	8179
48:34 one gate of Asher, one **g** of Naphtali.	8179
Da 2:49 but Daniel *sat* in the **g** of the king.	8651
Am 5:10 They hate him that rebuketh in the **g,**	8179
5:12 they turn aside the poor in the **g** *from*	8179
5:15 good, and establish judgment in the **g:**	8179
Ob 1:13 shouldest not have entered into the **g**	8179
Mic 1: 9 he is come unto the **g** of my people, *even*	8179
1:12 from the LORD unto the **g** of Jerusalem.	8179
2:13 passed through the **g**, and are gone out	8179
Zep 1:10 *shall be* the noise of a cry from the fish **g,**	8179
Zec 14:10 from Benjamin's **g** unto the place of	8179
14:10 gate unto the place of the first **g,**	8179
14:10 unto the corner **g**, and *from* the tower of	8179
Mt 7:13 Enter ye in at the strait **g:** for wide *is*	4439
7:13 for wide *is* the **g**, and broad *is* the way,	4439
7:14 Because strait *is* the **g**, and narrow *is*	4439
Lk 7:12 Now when he came nigh to the **g** of	4439
13:24 Strive to enter in at the strait **g:** for many,	4439
16:20 which was laid at his **g**, full of sores,	4440
Ac 3: 2 they laid daily at the **g** of the temple	2374
3:10 for alms at the Beautiful **g** of the temple:	4439
10:17 Simon's house, and stood before the **g,**	4440

Ac	12:10 they came unto the iron **g** that leadeth	4439
	12:13 as Peter knocked at the door of the **g**,	4440
	12:14 she opened not the **g** for gladness,	4440
	12:14 and told how Peter stood before the **g**.	4440
Heb	13:12 his own blood, suffered without the **g**.	4439
Rev	21:21 every several **g** was of one pearl:	4440

GATES (144) [GATE]

Ex	20:10 nor thy stranger that *is* within thy **g**:	8179
Dt	3: 5 fenced *with* high walls, **g**, and bars;	1817
	5:14 nor thy stranger that *is* within thy **g**,	8179
	6: 9 the posts of thy house, and on thy **g**.	8179
	11:20 posts of thine house, and upon thy **g**.	8179
	12:12 and the Levite that *is* within your **g**;	8179
	12:15 thou mayest kill and eat flesh in all thy **g**,	8179
	12:17 mayest not eat within thy **g** the tithe	8179
	12:18 and the Levite that *is* within thy **g**,	8179
	12:21 shalt eat in thy **g** whatsoever thy soul	8179
	14:21 give it unto the stranger that *is* in thy **g**,	8179
	14:27 the Levite that *is* within thy **g**; thou shalt	8179
	14:28 year, and shalt lay *it* up within thy **g**:	8179
	14:29 the widow, which *are* within thy **g**,	8179
	15: 7 **g** in thy land which the Lord thy God	8179
	15:22 Thou shalt eat it within thy **g**: the unclean	8179
	16: 5 sacrifice the passover within any of thy **g**,	8179
	16:11 the Levite that *is* within thy **g**,	8179
	16:14 and the widow, that *are* within thy **g**,	8179
	16:18 officers shalt thou make thee in all thy **g**,	8179
	17: 2 within any of thy **g** which the Lord thy	8179
	17: 5 unto thy **g**, *even that* man or *that* woman,	8179
	17: 8 matters of controversy within thy **g**:	8179
	18: 6 if a Levite come from any of thy **g** out of	8179
	23:16 which he shall choose in one of thy **g**,	8179
	24:14 that *are* in thy land within thy **g**:	8179
	26:12 that they may eat within thy **g**,	8179
	28:52 he shall besiege thee in all thy **g**, until thy	8179
	28:52 he shall besiege thee in all thy **g**:	8179
	28:55 enemies shall distress thee in all thy **g**.	8179
	28:57 thine enemy shall distress thee in thy **g**.	8179
	31:12 and thy stranger that *is* within thy **g**,	8179
Jos	6:26 in his youngest *son* shall he set up the **g**	1817
Jdg	5: 8 chose new gods; then *was* war in the **g**.	8179
	5:11 the people of the Lord go down to the **g**.	8179
1Sa	17:52 come *to* the valley, and to the **g** of Ekron.	8179
	23: 7 by entering into a town that hath **g** and	1817
2Sa	18:24 David sat between the two **g**:	8179
1Ki	16:34 set up the **g** thereof in his youngest *son*	1817
2Ki	23: 8 brake down the high places of the **g** that	8179
1Ch	9: 9 keepers of the **g** of the tabernacle:	5592
	9:22 to be porters in the **g** were two hundred	5592
	9:23 their children had the oversight of the **g**	8179
	22: 3 for the nails for the doors of the **g**,	8179
2Ch	8: 5 fenced cities, *with* walls, **g**, and bars;	1817
	14: 7 walls, and towers, **g**, and bars,	1817
	23:19 he set the porters at the **g** of the house of	8179
	31: 2 to praise in the **g** of the tents of	8179
Ne	1: 3 and the **g** thereof are burnt with fire.	8179
	2: 3 and the **g** thereof are consumed with fire?	8179
	2: 8 **g** of the palace which *appertained* to	8179
	2:13 the **g** thereof were consumed with fire.	8179
	2:17 and the **g** thereof are burnt with fire:	8179
	6: 1 I had not set up the doors upon the **g**;)	8179
	7: 3 Let not the **g** of Jerusalem be opened	8179
	11:19 and their brethren that kept the **g**,	8179
	12:25 the ward at the thresholds of the **g**.	8179
	12:30 purified the people, and the **g**, and the	8179
	13:19 that when the **g** of Jerusalem began to be	8179
	13:19 I commanded that the **g** should be shut,	1817
	13:19 *some* of my servants set I at the **g**,	8179
	13:22 *that* they should come *and* keep the **g**,	8179
Job	38:17 Have the **g** of death been opened unto	8179
Ps	9:13 that liftest me up from the **g** of death:	8179
	9:14 I may shew forth all thy praise in the **g**	8179
	24: 7 Lift up your heads, O ye **g**; and be ye lift	8179
	24: 9 Lift up your heads, O ye **g**; even lift *them*	8179
	87: 2 The Lord loveth the **g** of Zion more than	8179
	100: 4 Enter *into* his **g** with thanksgiving,	8179
	107:16 For he hath broken the **g** of brass,	1817
	107:18 and they draw near unto the **g** of death.	8179
	118:19 Open to me the **g** of righteousness: I will	8179
	122: 2 Our feet shall stand within thy **g**,	8179
	147:13 he hath strengthened the bars of thy **g**;	8179
Pr	1:21 of concourse, in the openings of the **g**:	8179
	8: 3 crieth at the **g**, at the entry of the city,	8179
	8:34 watching daily at my **g**, waiting at the	1817
	14:19 and the wicked at the **g** of the righteous.	8179
	31:23 Her husband is known in the **g**, when he	8179
	31:31 let her own works praise her in the **g**.	8179
SS	7:13 at our **g** are all *manner of* pleasant *fruits*,	6607
Isa	3:26 her **g** shall lament and mourn;	6607
	13: 2 that they may go *into* the **g** of the nobles.	6607
	26: 2 Open ye the **g**, that the righteous nation	8179
	38:10 my days, I shall go to the **g** of the grave:	8179
	45: 1 to open before him the **two leaved g**;	1817
	45: 1 leaved gates; and the **g** shall not be shut;	8179
	45: 2 I will break in pieces the **g** of brass,	1817
	54:12 thy of carbuncles, and all thy borders of	8179
	60:11 Therefore thy **g** shall be open continually;	8179
	60:18 call thy walls Salvation, and thy **g** Praise.	8179
	62:10 Go through, go through the **g**; prepare	8179
Jer	1:15 *at* the entering of the **g** of Jerusalem,	8179
	7: 2 that enter in at these **g** to worship	8179
	14: 2 mourneth, and the **g** thereof languish;	8179
	15: 7 I will fan them with a fan in the **g** of	8179
	17:19 they go out, and in all the **g** of Jerusalem;	8179

Jer	17:20 of Jerusalem, that enter in by these **g**:	8179
	17:21 nor bring *it* in by the **g** of Jerusalem;	8179
	17:24 bring in no burden through the **g** of this	8179
	17:25 there enter into the **g** of this city kings	8179
	17:27 even entering in at the **g** of Jerusalem on	8179
	17:27 will I kindle a fire in the **g** thereof,	8179
	22: 2 and thy people that enter in by these **g**:	8179
	22: 4 shall there enter in by the **g** of this house	8179
	22:19 and cast forth beyond the **g** of Jerusalem.	8179
	49:31 the Lord, which have neither **g** nor bars,	1817
	51:58 her high **g** shall be burnt with fire;	8179
La	1: 4 all her **g** are desolate: her priests sigh:	8179
	2: 9 Her **g** are sunk into the ground; he hath	8179
	4:12 enemy should have entered into the **g** of	8179
Eze	21:15 the point of the sword against all their **g**,	8179
	21:22 to appoint *battering* rams against the **g**,	8179
	26: 2 she is broken *that* was the **g** of the people:	1817
	26:10 chariots, when he shall enter into thy **g**,	8179
	38:11 and having neither bars nor **g**,	1817
	40:18 the pavement by the side of the **g** over	8179
	40:18 length of the **g** was the lower pavement.	8179
	40:38 entries thereof *were* by the posts of the **g**,	8179
	44:11 *having* charge at the **g** of the house,	8179
	44:17 when they enter in at the **g** of the inner	8179
	44:17 whiles they minister in the **g** of the inner	8179
	48:31 the **g** of the city *shall be* after the names	8179
	48:31 three **g** northward; one gate of Reuben,	8179
	48:32 three **g**; and one gate of Joseph, one gate	8179
	48:33 three **g**; one gate of Simeon, one gate of	8179
	48:34 and five hundred, *with* their three **g**;	8179
Ob	1:11 foreigners entered *into* his **g**, and cast lots	8179
Na	2: 6 The **g** of the rivers shall be opened,	8179
	3:13 the **g** of thy land shall be set wide open	8179
Zec	8:16 judgment of truth and peace in your **g**:	8179
Mt	16:18 the **g** of hell shall not prevail against it.	4439
Ac	9:24 And they watched the **g** day and to	4439
	14:13 brought oxen and garlands unto the **g**,	4440
Rev	21:12 and had twelve **g**, and at the gates twelve	4440
	21:12 and at the **g** twelve angels,	4440
	21:13 On the east three **g**; on the north three	4440
	21:13 the east three gates; on the north three **g**;	4440
	21:13 on the south three **g**; and on the west	4440
	21:13 three gates; and on the west three **g**.	4440
	21:15 and the **g** thereof, and the wall thereof.	4440
	21:21 And the twelve **g** were twelve pearls;	4440
	21:25 And the **g** of it shall not be shut at all by	4440
	22:14 may enter in through the **g** into the city.	4440

GATH (33) [GATH-HEPHER, GATH-RIMMON, GITTITE, GITTITES, MORESHETH-GATH]

Jos	11:22 only in Gaza, in **G**, and in Ashdod,	1661
1Sa	5: 8 the God of Israel be carried about *unto* **G**.	1661
	6:17 Askelon one, for **G** one, for Ekron one;	1661
	7:14 to Israel, from Ekron even unto **G**;	1661
	17: 4 Goliath, of **G**, whose height *was* six	1661
	17:23 the Philistine of **G**, Goliath by name,	1661
	17:52 Shaaraim, even unto **G**, and unto Ekron.	1661
	21:10 Saul, and went to Achish the king of **G**.	1661
	21:12 was sore afraid of Achish the king of **G**.	1661
	27: 2 Achish, the son of Maoch, king of **G**.	1661
	27: 3 David dwelt with Achish at **G**, he and	1661
	27: 4 was told Saul that David was fled *to* **G**:	1661
	27:11 to bring *tidings to* **G**, saying, Lest they	1661
2Sa	1:20 Tell *it* not in **G**, publish *it* not in the	1661
	15:18 men which came after him from **G**,	1661
	21:20 there was yet a battle in **G**, where was a	1661
	21:22 These four were born to the giant in **G**,	1661
1Ki	2:39 unto Achish son of Maachah king of **G**.	1661
	2:39 Behold, thy servants *be* in **G**.	1661
	2:40 went to **G** to Achish to seek his servants:	1661
	2:40 and brought his servants from **G**.	1661
	2:41 Shimei had gone from Jerusalem *to* **G**,	1661
2Ki	12:17 up, and fought against **G**, and took it:	1661
1Ch	7:21 whom the men of **G** that were born in	1661
	8:13 who drove away the inhabitants of **G**:	1661
	18: 1 took **G** and her towns out of the hand of	1661
	20: 6 yet again there was war at **G**, where was	1661
	20: 8 These were born unto the giant in **G**;	1661
2Ch	11: 8 And **G**, and Mareshah, and Ziph,	1661
	26: 6 brake down the wall of **G**, and the wall	1661
Ps	56: T when the Philistines took him in **G**.	1661
Am	6: 2 go down *to* **G** of the Philistines: *be they*	1661
Mic	1:10 Declare ye *it* not at **G**, weep ye not at all:	1661

GATHER (165) [GATHERED, GATHERER, GATHEREST, GATHERETH, GATHERING, GATHERINGS, GRAPEGATHERER, GRAPEGATHERERS, GRAPE-GATHERERS, INGATHERING]

Ge	6:21 that is eaten, and thou shalt **g** *it* to thee;	622
	31:46 Jacob said unto his brethren, **G** stones;	3950
	34:30 shall **g** themselves **together** against me,	6908
	41:35 let them **g** all the food of those good years	6908
	49: 1 his sons, and said, **G** yourselves **together**,	622
	49: 2 **G** yourselves **together**, and hear, ye sons	6908
Ex	3:16 **g** the elders of Israel **together**, and say	622
	5: 7 let them go and **g** straw for themselves.	7197
	5:12 Egypt to **g stubble** instead of straw.	7179+7197
	9:19 and **g** thy cattle, and all that thou hast in	5756
	16: 4 shall go out and **g** a certain rate every day,	3950
	16: 5 it shall be twice as much as they **g** daily.	3950
	16:16 **G** of it every man according to his eating,	3950
	16:26 Six days ye shall **g** it; but on the seventh	3950
	16:27 of the people on the seventh day for to **g**,	3950
	23:10 thy land, and shalt **g** in the fruits thereof:	622

Lev	8: 3 thou all the congregation **together** unto	6950
	19: 9 neither shalt thou **g** the gleanings of thy	3950
	19:10 neither shalt thou **g** *every* grape of thy	3950
	23:22 neither shalt thou **g** *any* gleaning of thy	3950
	25: 3 prune thy vineyard, and **g** in the fruit	622
	25: 5 neither **g** the grapes of thy vine undressed:	1219
	25:11 **g** the grapes in it of thy vine undressed.	1219
	25:20 we shall not sow, nor **g** in our increase:	622
Nu	8: 9 the whole assembly of the children of	6950
	Israel **together**:	
	10: 4 of Israel, shall **g** themselves unto thee.	3259
	11:16 **G** unto me seventy men of the elders of	622
	19: 9 a man *that is* clean shall **g** up the ashes of	622
	20: 8 thou the assembly **together**, thou,	6950
	21:16 **G** the people **together**, and I will give	622
Dt	4:10 **G** me the people **together**, and I will	6950
	11:14 thou mayest **g** in thy corn, and thy wine,	622
	13:16 shalt **g** all the spoil of it into the midst	6908
	28:30 and shalt not **g** the grapes thereof.	2490
	28:38 out *into* the field, and shalt **g** but little in;	622
	28:39 nor **g** the grapes; for the worms shall eat	103
	30: 3 return and **g** thee from all the nations,	6908
	30: 4 from thence will the Lord thy God **g**	6908
	31:12 **G** the people **together**, men, and women	6950
	31:28 **G** unto me all the elders of your tribes,	6950
Ru	2: 7 after the reapers amongst the sheaves:	622
1Sa	7: 5 **G** all Israel to Mizpeh, and I will pray for	6908
2Sa	3:21 and will **g** all Israel unto my lord the king,	6908
	12:28 therefore **g** the rest of the people **together**,	622
1Ki	18:19 and **g** to me all Israel unto mount Carmel,	6908
2Ki	4:39 one went out into the field to **g** herbs,	3950
	22:20 I will **g** thee unto thy fathers, and thou	622
1Ch	16:35 **g** us **together**, and deliver us from	6908
	22: 2 David commanded to **g together**	3664
2Ch	24: 5 of all Israel money to repair the house of	6908
	34:28 I will **g** thee to thy fathers, and thou shalt	622
Ezr	10: 7 that *they* should **g** themselves **together**	6908
Ne	1: 9 *yet* will I **g** them from thence,	6908
	7: 5 God put into mine heart to **g together**	6908
	12:44 **g** into them out of the fields of the cities	3664
Est	2: 3 they may **g together** all the fair young	6908
	4:16 **g together** all the Jews that are present	3664
	8:11 in every city to **g** themselves **together**,	6950
Job	11:10 or **g together**, then who can hinder him?	6950
	24: 6 and they **g** the vintage of the wicked.	3953
	34:14 If he set his heart upon *man*, *if* he **g** unto	622
	39:12 home thy seed, and **g** *it* into thy barn?	622
Ps	26: 9 **G** not my soul with sinners, nor my life	622
	39: 6 and knoweth not who shall **g** them.	622
	50: 5 **G** my saints together unto me; those that	622
	56: 6 They **g** themselves **together**, they hide	1481
	94:21 They **g** themselves **together** against	1413
	104:22 they **g** themselves **together**, and lay them	622
	104:28 thou givest them they **g**: thou openest	3950
	106:47 God, and **g** us from among the heathen,	6908
Pr	28: 8 shall **g** it for him that will pity the poor.	6908
Ecc	2:26 he giveth travail, to **g** and to heap up,	622
	3: 5 and a time to **g** stones **together**;	3664
SS	6: 2 to feed in the gardens, and to **g** lilies.	3950
Isa	10:31 inhabitants of Gebim **g** themselves **to flee**.	5756
	11:12 **g together** the dispersed of Judah from	6908
	34:15 lay, and hatch, and **g** under her shadow:	1716
	40:11 he shall **g** the lambs with his arm,	6908
	43: 5 from the east, and **g** thee from the west;	6908
	49:18 all these **g** themselves **together**,	6908
	54: 7 but with great mercies will I **g** thee.	6908
	54:15 they shall **surely g together**,	1481+1481
	54:15 whosoever shall **g together** against thee	1481
	56: 8 Yet will I **g** *others* to him, besides those	6908
	60: 4 all they **g** themselves **together**, they come	6908
	62:10 cast up the highway; **g** out the stones;	5619
	66:18 that *I* will **g** all nations and tongues;	6908
Jer	4: 5 cry, **g together**, and say,	4390
	6: 1 **g** yourselves **to flee** out of the midst of	5756
	7:18 The children **g** wood, and the fathers	3950
	9:22 the harvestman, and none shall **g** *them*.	622
	10:17 **G** up thy wares out of the land,	622
	23: 3 I will **g** the remnant of my flock out of all	6908
	29:14 I will **g** you from all the nations,	6908
	31: 8 and **g** them from the coasts of the earth,	6908
	31:10 He that scattered Israel will **g** him,	6908
	32:37 Behold, I *will* **g** them out of all countries,	6908
	40:10 ye, ye wine, and summer fruits, and oil,	622
	49: 5 none shall **g** up him that wandereth.	6908
	49:14 *saying*, **G** ye **together**, and come against	6908
	51:11 the shields: the Lord hath raised up	4390
Eze	11:17 I will even **g** you from the people,	6908
	16:37 Behold therefore, I will **g** all thy lovers,	6908
	16:37 I will even **g** them round about against	6908
	20:34 will **g** you out of the countries wherein ye	6908
	20:41 **g** you out of the countries wherein ye	6908
	22:19 I will **g** you into the midst of Jerusalem.	6908
	22:20 *As they* silver, and brass, and iron,	6910
	22:20 to melt *it*; so will I **g** *you* in mine anger	6908
	22:21 I will **g** you, and blow upon you in the fire	3664
	24: 4 **G** the pieces thereof into it, *even* every	622
	29:13 At the end of forty years will I **g**	6908
	34:13 **g** them from the countries, and will bring	6908
	36:24 **g** you out of all countries, and will bring	6908
	37:21 will **g** them on every side, and bring them	6908
	39:17 **g** yourselves on every side to my sacrifice	622
Da	3: 2 the king sent to **g together**	3673
Hos	8:10 now will I **g** them, and they shall sorrow	6908
	9: 6 Egypt shall **g** them **up**, Memphis shall	6908

G

Joel	1:14	**g** the elders *and* all the inhabitants of	622

Joel 1:14 **g** the elders *and* all the inhabitants of 622
2: 6 much pained: all faces shall **g** blackness. 6908
2:16 **G** the people, sanctify the congregation, 622
2:16 **g** the children, and those that suck 622
3: 2 I will also **g** all nations, and will bring 6908
3:11 and **g** yourselves **together** round about: 6908
Mic 2:12 will **surely g** the remnant of Israel; 6908+6908
4: 6 I will **g** her that is driven out, and *her* 622
4:12 for he shall **g** them as the sheaves into 6908
5: 1 Now **g** thyself **in troops,** O daughter of 1413
Na 2:10 and the faces of them all **g** blackness. 6908
Hab 1: 9 and they shall **g** the captivity as the sand. 622
1:15 in their net, and **g** them in their drag: 622
Zep 2: 1 **G** yourselves **together,** yea, 7197
2: 1 yea, **g together,** O nation not desired; 7197
3: 8 for my determination *is* to **g** the nations, 622
3:18 I will **g** them *that are* sorrowful for 622
3:19 halteth, and **g** her that was driven out; 6908
3:20 you *again,* even in the time that I **g** you: 6908
Zec 10: 8 I will hiss for them, and **g** them; for I 6908
10:10 land of Egypt, and **g** them out of Assyria; 6908
14: 2 For I will **g** all nations against Jerusalem to 622
Mt 3:12 his floor, and **g** his wheat into the garner; 4863
6:26 neither do they reap, nor **g** into barns; 4863
7: 16 Do men **g** grapes of thorns, or figs of 4816
13:28 thou then *that* we go and **g** them **up?** 4816
13:29 lest while ye **g up** the tares, ye root up 4816
13:30 **G** ye **together** first the tares, and bind 4816
13:30 burn them: but **g** the wheat into my barn. 4863
13:41 they shall **g** out of his kingdom all things 4816
24:31 they shall **g together** his elect from the 1996
25:26 not, and **g** where I have not strawed: 4863
Mk 13:27 shall **g together** his elect from the four 1996
Lk 3:17 and will **g** the wheat into his garner; 4863
6:44 For of thorns men do not **g** figs, nor of a 4816
6:44 nor of a bramble bush **g** they grapes. 5166
13:34 a hen *doth* **g** her brood under *her* wings, NIG
Jn 6:12 **G up** the fragments that remain, 4863
11:52 he should **g together** in one 4863
15: 6 *men* **g** them, and cast *them* into the fire, 4863
Eph 1:10 **g together in one** all *things* in Christ, 346
Rev 14:18 **g** the clusters of the vine of the earth; 5166
16:14 to **g** them to the battle of that great day of 4863
19:17 **g** yourselves unto the supper of 4863
20: 8 and Magog, to **g** them **together** to battle: 4863

GATHERED (267) [GATHER]

Ge 1: 9 the heaven be **g together** unto one place, 6960
12: 5 all their substance that they had **g,** 7408
25: 8 and full *of years;* and was **g** to his people. 622
25:17 died; and was **g** unto his people. 622
29: 3 were all the flocks **g:** and they rolled 622
29: 7 time that the cattle should be **g together:** 622
29: 8 until all the flocks be **g together,** 622
29:22 Laban **g together** all the men of the place, 622
35:29 died, and was **g** unto his people, *being* old 622
41:48 he **g up** all the food of the seven years, 6908
41:49 Joseph **g** corn as the sand of the sea, 6651
47:14 Joseph **g up** all the money that was found 3950
49:29 unto them, I *am to be* **g** unto my people: 622
49:33 he **g up** his feet into the bed, and yielded 622
49:33 up the ghost, and was **g** unto his people. 622
Ex 4:29 **g together** all the elders of the children of 622
8:14 they **g** them **together** upon heaps. 6651
15: 8 thy nostrils the waters were **g together,** 6192
16:17 did so, and **g,** some more, some less. 3950
16:18 he that **g much** had nothing over; 7235
16:18 and he that **g little** had no lack; 4591
16:18 they **g** every man according to his eating. 3950
16:21 they **g** it every morning, every man 3950
16:22 on the sixth day they **g** twice as much 3950
23:16 when thou hast **g in** thy labours out of 622
32: 1 the people **g** themselves **together** unto 6950
32:26 all the sons of Levi **g** themselves **together** 622
35: 1 all the congregation of the children of
Israel **together,** 6950
Lev 8: 4 assembly was **g together** unto the door 6950
23:39 when ye have **g in** the fruit of the land, 622
26:25 ye are **g together** within your cities, 622
Nu 10: 7 the congregation is to be **g together,** 6950
11: 8 **g** *it,* and ground *it* in mills, or beat *it* in a 3950
11:22 all the fish of the sea be **g together** for 622
11:24 the seventy men of the elders of 622
11:32 all the next day, and they **g** the quails: 622
11:32 he that **g least** gathered ten homers: 4591
11:32 he that gathered least **g** ten homers: 622
14:35 that are **g together** against me: 3259
15:32 they found a man that **g** sticks upon 7197
16: 3 they **g** themselves **together** against Moses 6950
16:11 all thy company *are* **g together** against 3259
16:19 Korah all the congregation against them 6950
16:42 when the congregation was **g** against 6950
20: 2 they **g** themselves **together** against Moses 6950
20:10 Aaron **g** the congregation **together** before 6950
20:24 Aaron shall be **g** unto his people: for he 622
20:26 Aaron shall be **g** *unto his people,* and 622
21:23 Sihon **g** all his people **together,** 622
27: 3 themselves **together** against the LORD 3259
27:13 thou also shalt be **g** unto thy people, 622
27:13 thy people, as Aaron thy brother was **g.** 622
31: afterward shalt thou be **g** unto thy people. 622
Dt 16:13 after that thou hast **g** in thy corn and thy 622
32:50 thou goest up, and be **g** unto thy people; 622
32:50 in mount Hor, and was **g** unto his people: 622
33: 5 *and* the tribes of Israel were **g together.** 622

Jos 9: 2 That they **g** themselves together, to fight 6908
10: 5 **g** themselves **together,** and went up, 6908
10: 6 the mountains are **g together** against us. 6908
22:12 of Israel **g** themselves **together** *at* Shiloh, 6950
24: 1 Joshua **g** all the tribes of Israel to Shechem, 622
Jdg 1: 7 toes cut off, **g** *their meat* under my table: 3950
2:10 also all that generation were **g** unto their 622
3:13 he **g** unto him the children of Ammon and 622
4:13 Sisera **g together** all his chariots, *even* 2199
6:33 the children of the east were **g** together, 622
6:34 a trumpet; and Abi-ezer was **g** after him. 2199
6:35 all Manasseh; who also was **g** after him: 2199
7:23 men of Israel **g** themselves **together** out 6817
7:24 men of Ephraim **g** themselves **together,** 6817
9: 6 And all the men of Shechem **g together,** 622
9:27 their vineyards, and trode *the grapes,* 1219
9:47 the tower of Shechem were **g together.** 6908
10:17 the children of Ammon were **g together** 6817
11: 3 there were **g** vain men to Jephthah, 3950
11:20 Sihon **g** all his people **together,** 622
12: 1 men of Ephraim **g themselves together,** 6817
12: 4 Jephthah **g together** all the men of Gilead 6908
16:23 lords of the Philistines **g** them **together** 622
18:22 near to Micah's house were **g together,** 2199
20: 1 the congregation was **g together** as one 6950
20:11 So all the men of Israel were **g** against 622
20:14 **g** themselves **together** out of the cities 622
1Sa 5: 8 **g** all the lords of the Philistines unto them, 622
5:11 **g together** all the lords of the Philistines, 622
7: 6 **g together** to Mizpeh, and drew water, 6908
7: 7 of Israel were **g together** to Mizpeh, 6908
8: 4 elders of Israel **g** themselves **together,** 6908
13: 5 Philistines **g** themselves **together** to fight 622
13:11 the Philistines **g** themselves **together** *at* 622
14:48 he **g** a host, and smote the Amalekites, 6213
15: 4 Saul **g** the people **together,** 8085
17: 1 the Philistines **g together** their armies 622
17: 1 were **g together** *at* Shochoh, 622
17: 2 and the men of Israel were **g together,** 622
20:38 Jonathan's lad **g up** the arrows, 3950
22: 2 discontented, **g** themselves unto him; 6908
25: 1 all the Israelites were **g together,** 6908
28: 1 the Philistines **g** their armies **together** 6908
28: 4 the Philistines **g** themselves **together,** 6908
28: 4 Saul **g** all Israel **together,** and they 6908
29: 1 Now the Philistines **g together** all their 6908
2Sa 2:25 **g** themselves **together** after Abner, 6908
2:30 when he had **g** all the people **together,** 6908
6: 1 David **g together** all the chosen *men* of 6908
10:15 before Israel, they **g** themselves **together.** 622
10:17 all Israel **together,** and passed over 622
12:29 David **g** all the people **together,** and went 622
14:14 which cannot be **g up** *again;* neither doth 622
17:11 all Israel be **generally g** unto thee, 622+622
20:14 they were **g together,** and went also after 6950
21:13 the bones of them that were hanged. 622
23: 9 *that* were there **g together** to battle, 622
23:11 Philistines were **g together** into a troop, 622
1Ki 10:26 Solomon **g together** chariots and 622
11:24 he **g** men unto him, and became captain 6908
18:20 the prophets **together** unto mount 6908
20: 1 the king of Syria **g** all his host **together** 6908
22: 6 king of Israel **g** the prophets **together,** 6908
2Ki 3:21 all that were able to put on armour, 6817
4:39 thereof wild gourds his lap full, 3950
6:24 that Ben-hadad king of Syria **g** all his host, 6908
10:18 Jehu **g** all the people **together,** 6908
22: 4 which the keepers of the door have **g** of 622
22: 9 Thy servants have **g** the money that was 5413
22:20 thou shalt be **g** into thy grave in peace; 622
23: 1 they **g** unto him all the elders of Judah 622
1Ch 11: 1 all Israel **g** themselves to David unto 6908
11:13 there the Philistines were **g together** to 622
13: 5 David **g** all Israel **together,** from Shihor 6950
15: 3 David **g** all Israel to Jerusalem, 6950
19: 7 **g** themselves **together** from their cities, 622
19:17 he **g** all Israel, and passed over Jordan, 622
23: 2 he **g together** all the princes of Israel, 622
2Ch 1:14 And Solomon **g** chariots and horsemen:
1:14 he **g** *of* the house of Judah and Benjamin 6950
11: 1 that were **g together** to Jerusalem because 622
13: 7 there are **g** unto him vain men, 6908
15: 9 he **g** all Judah and Benjamin, 622
15:10 they **g** themselves **together** *at* Jerusalem 6908
18: 5 Therefore the king of Israel **g together** of 6908
20: 4 Judah **g** themselves **together,** to ask *help* 6908
23: 2 the Levites out of all the cities of Judah, 6908
24: 5 he **g together** the priests and the Levites, 6908
24:11 day by day, and **g** money in abundance. 622
25: 5 Moreover Amaziah **g** Judah **together,** 6908
28:24 Ahaz **g together** the vessels of the house 622
29: 4 and **g** them **together** into the east street, 622
29:15 they **g** their brethren, 622
29:20 **g** the rulers of the city, and went up to 622
30: 3 **g** themselves **together** to Jerusalem. 622
32: 4 So there was **g** much people **together,** 6908
32: 6 **g** them **together** to him in the street of 6908
34: 9 the Levites that kept the doors had **g** 622
34:17 they have **g together** the money that was 5413
34:28 and thou shalt be **g** to thy grave in peace, 622
34:29 **g together** all the elders of Judah and 622
Ezr 3: 1 the people **g** themselves **together** as one 622
7:28 I **g together** out of Israel chief *men* to go 6908
8:15 I **g** them **together** to the river that 6908
10: 9 Benjamin **g** themselves **together** *unto* 6908

Ne 5:16 all my servants *were* **g** thither unto 6908
8: 1 the people **g** themselves **together** as one 622
8:13 on the second day were **g together** the 622
12:28 sons of the singers **g** themselves **together,** 622
13:11 I **g** them **together,** and set them in their 6908
Est 2: 8 when many maidens were **g together** 6908
2:19 when the virgins were **g together** 6908
9: 2 The Jews **g** themselves **together** in their 6950
9:15 themselves **together** on the fourteenth 6950
9:16 king's provinces **g** themselves **together,** 6950
Job 16:10 they have **g** themselves **together** against 4390
27:19 *man* shall lie down, but he shall not be **g:** 622
30: 7 under the nettles they were **g together.** 5596
Ps 35:15 they rejoiced, and **g** themselves **together:** 622
35:15 *yea,* the abjects **g** themselves **together** 622
47: 9 The princes of the people are **g together,** 622
59: 3 the mighty are **g** against me; not *for* my 1481
102:22 When the people are **g** together, 6908
107: 3 **g** them out of the lands, from the east, 6908
140: 2 continually are they **g together** *for* war. 1481
Pr 27:25 and herbs of the mountains are **g.** 622
30: 4 who hath **g** the wind in his fists? 622
Ecc 2: 8 I **g** me also silver and gold, and the 3664
SS 5: 1 I have **g** my myrrh with my spice; I have 717
Isa 5: 2 **g out** the **stones** thereof, and planted it 5619
10:14 eggs *that are* left, have I **g** all the earth; 622
13: 4 of the kingdoms of nations **g together:** 622
22: 9 **g together** the waters of the lower pool. 6908
24:22 they shall be **g together,** *as* prisoners 622+626
24:22 *as* prisoners are **g** in the pit, and shall be NIH
27:12 ye shall be **g** one by one, O ye children of 3950
34: 4 your spoil shall be **g** *like* the gathering of 622
34:15 there shall the vultures also be **g,** every 6908
34:16 and his spirit it hath **g** them. 6908
43: 9 Let all the nations be **g together,** and let 6908
44:11 let them all be **g together,** let them stand 6908
49: 5 again to him, Though Israel be not **g,** 622
56: 8 to him, besides those that are **g** unto him. 6908
60: 7 All the flocks of Kedar shall be **g together** 6908
62: 9 they that have **g** it shall eat it, and praise 622
Jer 3:17 all the nations shall be **g** unto it, 6960
8: 2 they shall not be **g,** nor be buried; they 622
25:33 not be lamented, neither **g,** nor buried; 622
26: 9 all the people were **g** against Jeremiah in 6950
40:12 and **g** wine and summer fruits very much. 622
40:15 that all the Jews which are **g** unto thee 6908
Eze 28:25 When I shall have **g** the house of Israel 6908
29: 5 thou shalt not be brought together, nor **g:** 6908
38: 8 *and is* **g** out of many people, against 6908
38:12 the people *that are* **g** out of the nations, 6908
38:13 hast thou **g** thy company to take a prey? 6950
39:27 **g** them out of their enemies' lands, 6908
39:28 I have **g** them unto their own land, 3664
Da 3: 3 were **g together** unto the dedication of 3673
3:27 being **g together,** saw these men, 3673
Hos 1:11 and the children of Israel be **g together,** 6908
10:10 the people shall be **g** against them, 622
Mic 1: 7 for she **g** it of the hire of a harlot, 6908
4:11 Now also many nations are **g** against thee, 622
7: 1 for I am as when they have **g** the summer 625
Zec 12: 3 of the earth be **g together** against it. 622
14:14 heathen round about shall be **g together,** 622
Mt 2: 4 all the chief priests and scribes of the
people **together,** 4863
13: 2 great multitudes were **g together** unto 4863
13:40 As therefore the tares are **g** and burnt in 4816
13:47 *was* cast into the sea, and **g** of every kind: 4863
13:48 **g** the good into vessels, but cast the bad 4816
18:20 or three are **g together** in my name, 4863
22:10 and **g together** all as many as they found, 4863
22:34 to silence, they were **g together.** 4863
22:41 While the Pharisees were **g together,** 4863
23:37 would I have **g** thy children **together,** 1996
24:28 there will the eagles be **g together.** 4863
25:32 And before him shall be **g** all nations: 4863
27:17 Therefore when they were **g together,** 4863
27:27 **g** unto him the whole band *of soldiers.* 4863
Mk 1:33 all the city was **g together** at the door. 1996
2: 2 And straightway many were **g together,** 4863
4: 1 there was **g** unto him a great multitude, 4863
5:21 the other side, much people **g** unto him: 4863
6:30 And the apostles **g** themselves **together** 4863
Lk 8: 4 And when much people were **g together,** 4896
11:29 when the people were **g thick together,** 1865
12: 1 when there were **g together** an 1996
13:34 would I have **g** thy children **together,** 1996
15:13 days after the younger son **g** all **together,** 4863
17:37 *is,* thither will the eagles be **g together.** 4863
24:33 and found the eleven **g together,** 4867
Jn 6:13 Therefore they **g** *them* **together,** 4863
11:47 Then **g** the chief priests and the Pharisees 4863
Ac 4: 6 high priest, were **g together** at Jerusalem. 4863
4:26 rulers were **g together** against the Lord, 4863
4:27 and the people of Israel, were **g together,** 4863
12:12 where many were **g together** praying. 4867
14:27 come, and had **g** the church **together,** 4863
15:30 when they had **g** the multitude **together,** 4863
17: 5 **g a company,** and set all the city on an 3792
20: 8 where they were **g together,** 4863
28: 3 And when Paul had **g** a bundle of sticks, 4962
1Co 5: 4 when ye are **g together,** and my spirit, 4863
2Co 8:15 He that *had* **g** much had nothing over; NIG
8:15 and he that *had* **g** little had no lack. NIG
Rev 14:19 and **g** the vine of the earth, and cast *it into* 5166
16:16 he **g** them **together** into a place called 4863

Rev 19:19 **g** together to make war against him that *4863*

GATHERER (1) [GATHER]
Am 7:14 *was* a herdman, and a **g** of sycomore fruit: 1103

GATHEREST (1) [GATHER]
Dt 24:21 When thou **g** the **grapes** of thy vineyard, 1219

GATHERETH (17) [GATHER]
Nu 19:10 he that **g** the ashes of the heifer shall wash 622
Ps 33: 7 He **g** the waters of the sea **together** as a 3664
 41: 6 his heart **g** iniquity to itself; *when* he 6908
 147: 2 he **g** together the outcasts of Israel. 3664
Pr 6: 8 the summer, *and* **g** her food in the harvest. 103
 10: 5 He that **g** in summer *is* a wise son: 103
 13:11 but he that **g** by labour shall increase. 6908
Isa 10:14 as *one* **g** eggs *that are* left, have I gathered 622
 17: 5 it shall be as when the harvestman **g** 622
 17: 5 it shall be as he that **g** ears in the valley of 3950
 56: 8 The Lord God which **g** the outcasts of 6908
Na 3:18 upon the mountains, and no man **g** *them*. 6908
Hab 2: 5 **g** unto him all nations, and heapeth unto 622
Mt 12:30 he that **g** not with me scattereth abroad. 4863
 23:37 even as a hen **g** her chickens under *her* 1996
Lk 11:23 and he that **g** not with me scattereth. 4863
Jn 4:36 and **g** fruit unto life eternal: 4863

GATHERING (11) [GATHER]
Ge 1:10 **g** together of the waters called he Seas: 4723
 49:10 and unto him *shall* the **g** of the people *be*. 3349
Nu 15:33 they that found him **g** sticks brought him 7197
1Ki 17:10 the widow woman *was* there **g** of sticks: 7197
 17:12 I *am* **g** two sticks, that I may go in 7197
2Ch 20:25 they were three days in **g** of the spoil, 962
Isa 32:10 the vintage shall fail, the **g** shall not come. 625
 33: 4 your spoil shall be gathered *like* the **g** of 625
Mt 25:24 and **g** where thou hast not strawed: 4863
Ac 16:10 assuredly **g** that the Lord had called us 4822
2Th 2: 1 and *by* our **g** together unto him, 1997

GATHERINGS (1) [GATHER]
1Co 16: 2 that there be no **g** when I come. 3048

GATH-HEPHER (1) [GATH, GITTAH-HEPHER, HEPHER]
2Ki 14:25 of Amittai, the prophet, which *was* of **G**. 1661

GATH-RIMMON (4) [GATH, RIMMON]
Jos 19:45 and Jehud, and Bene-berak, and **G**, 1667
 21:24 with her suburbs, **G** with her suburbs, 1667
 21:25 her suburbs, and **G** with her suburbs, 1667
1Ch 6:69 her suburbs, and **G** with her suburbs, 1667

GAVE (465) [GIVE]
Ge 2:20 Adam **g** names to all cattle, and to the 7121
 3: 6 and **g** also unto her husband with her; 5414
 3:12 she **g** me of the tree, and I did eat. 5414
 14:20 into thy hand. And he **g** him tithes of all. 5414
 16: 3 **g** her to her husband Abram to be his 5414
 18: 7 and good, and **g** *it* unto a young man; 5414
 20:14 **g** *them* unto Abraham, and restored him 5414
 21:14 and a bottle of water, and **g** *it* unto Hagar, 5414
 21:19 bottle *with* water, and **g** the lad **drink**. 8248
 21:27 and oxen, and **g** *them* to Abimelech; 5414
 21:18 pitcher upon her hand, and **g** him **drink**. 8248
 24:32 straw and provender for the camels, 5414
 24:53 and raiment, and **g** *them* to Rebekah: 5414
 24:53 also to her brother and to her mother 5414
 25: 5 Abraham **g** all that he had unto Isaac. 5414
 25: 6 Abraham **g** gifts, and sent them away 5414
 25: 8 Abraham **g** up the ghost, and died in a 1478
 25:17 he **g** up the ghost and died; 1478
 25:34 Jacob **g** Esau bread and pottage of lentiles; 5414
 27:17 she **g** the savoury meat and the bread, 5414
 28: 4 a stranger, which God **g** unto Abraham. 5414
 28: 6 that as he blessed him he **g** him a **charge**, 6680
 29:24 Laban **g** unto his daughter Leah Zilpah 5414
 29:28 he **g** him Rachel his daughter to wife *also*. 5414
 29:29 Laban **g** to Rachel his daughter Bilhah his 5414
 30: 4 she **g** him Bilhah her handmaid to wife: 5414
 30: 9 Zilpah her maid, and **g** her Jacob to wife. 5414
 30:35 and **g** *them* into the hand of his sons. 5414
 35: 4 they **g** unto Jacob all the strange gods 5414
 35:12 The land which I **g** Abraham and Isaac, 5414
 35:29 Isaac **g** up the ghost, and died, 1478
 38:18 he **g** *it* her, and came in unto her, 5414
 38:26 that I **g** her not to Shelah my son. 5414
 39:21 **g** him favour in the sight of the keeper of 5414
 40:11 and I **g** the cup into Pharaoh's hand. 5414
 40:21 and he **g** the cup into Pharaoh's hand: 5414
 41:45 he **g** him to wife Asenath the daughter of 5414
 43:24 **g** *them* water, and they washed their feet; 5414
 43:24 their feet; and he **g** their asses provender. 5414
 45:21 Joseph **g** them wagons, according to 5414
 45:21 and **g** them provision for the way. 5414
 45:22 To all of them he **g** each man changes of 5414
 45:22 but to Benjamin he **g** three hundred *pieces* of 5414
 46:18 whom Laban **g** to Leah his daughter, 5414
 46:25 which Laban **g** unto Rachel his daughter, 5414
 47:11 **g** them a possession in the land of Egypt, 5414
 47:17 Joseph **g** them bread *in exchange* for 5414
 47:22 eat their portion which Pharaoh **g** them: 5414
Ex 2:21 and he **g** Moses Zipporah his daughter. 5414
 6:13 gave them a **charge** unto the children of 6680
 11: 3 the Lord **g** the people favour in the sight 5414
 12:36 the Lord **g** the people favour in the sight 5414

Ex 14:20 but it **g** **light** by night *to these:* 215
 31:18 **g** unto Moses, when he had made an end 5414
 32:24 So they **g** *it* me: then I cast it into the fire, 5414
 34:32 he **g** them **in commandment** all that 6680
 36: 6 Moses **g** commandment, and they 6680
Nu 3:51 Moses **g** the money of them that were 5414
 7: 6 the oxen, and **g** them unto the Levites 5414
 7: 7 four oxen he **g** unto the sons of Gershon, 5414
 7: 8 eight oxen he **g** unto the sons of Merari, 5414
 7: 9 unto the sons of Kohath he **g** none: 5414
 11:25 him, and **g** *it* unto the seventy elders: 5414
 17: 6 every one of their princes **g** him a rod 5414
 27:23 hands upon him, and **g** him a **charge**, 6680
 31:41 Moses **g** the tribute, *which was* 5414
 31:47 of beast, and **g** them unto the Levites, 5414
 32:33 Moses **g** unto them, *even* to the children 5414
 32:38 other names unto the cities which they 7121
 32:40 Moses **g** Gilead unto Machir the son of 5414
Dt 2:12 which the Lord **g** unto them.) 5414
 3:12 **g** I unto the Reubenites and to the 5414
 3:13 of Og, **g** I unto the half tribe of Manasseh; 5414
 3:15 And I **g** Gilead unto Machir. 5414
 3:16 unto the Gadites I **g** from Gilead even 5414
 9:11 *that* the Lord **g** me the two tables of 5414
 10: 4 and the Lord **g** them unto me. 5414
 22:16 I **g** my daughter unto this man to wife, 5414
 29: 8 **g** *it* for an inheritance unto the Reubenites 5414
 31:23 he **g** Joshua the son of Nun **a charge**, 6680
Jos 1:14 remain in the land which Moses **g** you 5414
 1:15 which Moses the Lord's servant **g** you 5414
 11:23 Joshua **g** it for an inheritance unto Israel 5414
 12: 6 Moses the servant of the Lord **g** it *for* a 5414
 12: 7 which Joshua **g** unto the tribes of Israel 5414
 13: 8 with whom Moses **g**, beyond Jordan 5414
 13: 8 *even* as Moses the servant of the Lord **g** 5414
 13:14 Only unto the tribe of Levi he **g** none 5414
 13:15 Moses **g** unto the tribe of the children of 5414
 13:24 Moses **g** *inheritance* unto the tribe of Gad, 5414
 13:29 Moses **g** *inheritance* unto the half tribe of 5414
 13:33 unto the tribe of Levi Moses **g** not *any* 5414
 14: 3 unto the Levites he **g** none inheritance 5414
 14: 4 **g** no part unto the Levites in the land, 5414
 14:13 **g** unto Caleb the son of Jephunneh 5414
 15:13 Caleb the son of Jephunneh he **g** a part 5414
 15:17 he **g** him Achsah his daughter to wife. 5414
 15:19 he **g** her the upper springs, and the nether 5414
 17: 4 **g** them an inheritance among the brethren 5414
 18: 7 which Moses the servant of the Lord **g** 5414
 19:49 the children of Israel **g** an inheritance to 5414
 19:50 to the word of the Lord they **g** 5414
 21: 3 the children of Israel **g** unto the Levites 5414
 21: 8 the children of Israel **g** by lot unto 5414
 21: 9 they **g** out of the tribe of the children of 5414
 21:11 they **g** them the city of Arbah the father of 5414
 21:12 they **g** to Caleb the son of Jephunneh for 5414
 21:13 Thus they **g** to the children of Aaron 5414
 21:21 they **g** them Shechem with her suburbs 5414
 21:27 of the *other* half tribe of Manasseh they **g** NIH
 21:43 the Lord **g** unto Israel all the land which 5414
 21:44 the Lord **g** them **rest** round about, 5117
 22: 4 which Moses the servant of the Lord **g** 5414
 22: 7 unto the *other* half thereof **g** Joshua 5414
 24: 3 and multiplied his seed, and **g** him Isaac. 5414
 24: 4 I **g** unto Isaac Jacob and Esau: and I gave 5414
 24: 4 I **g** unto Esau mount Seir, to possess it; 5414
 24: 8 I **g** them into your hand, that ye might 5414
Jdg 1:13 he **g** him Achsah his daughter to wife. 5414
 1:15 Caleb **g** her the upper springs and 5414
 1:20 they **g** Hebron unto Caleb, as Moses said: 5414
 3: 6 their daughters to their sons, 5414
 4:19 milk, and **g** him **drink**, and covered him. 8248
 5:25 He asked water, *and* she **g** him milk; 5414
 6: 9 from before you, and **g** you their land; 5414
 9: 4 they **g** him threescore and ten *pieces* of 5414
 14: 9 and he **g** them, and they did eat: 5414
 14:19 **g** change *of garments* unto them which 5414
 15: 2 therefore I **g** her to thy companion: 5414
 17: 4 **g** them to the founder, who made thereof 5414
 19:21 house, and **g** **provender** unto the asses: 1101
 20:36 for the men of Israel **g** place to 5414
 21:14 they **g** them wives which they had saved 5414
Ru 2:18 **g** to her that she had reserved after she 5414
 3:17 These six *measures* of barley **g** he me; 5414
 4: 7 off his shoe, and **g** *it* to his neighbour: 5414
 4:13 the Lord **g** her conception, and she bare 5414
 4:17 the *women* her neighbours **g** it a name, 7121
1Sa 1: 4 he **g** to Peninnah his wife, and to all her 5414
 1: 5 unto Hannah he **g** a worthy portion; 5414
 1:23 her son **suck** until she weaned him. 3243
 9:23 Bring the portion which I **g** thee, of which 5414
 10: 9 from Samuel, God **g** him another heart: 2015
 18: 4 **g** it to David, and his garments, even to 5414
 18:27 and they **g** them **in full tale** to the king, 4390
 18:27 Saul **g** him Michal his daughter to wife. 5414
 20:40 Jonathan **g** his artillery unto his lad, 5414
 21: 6 So the priest **g** him hallowed *bread:* for 5414
 22:10 he **g** him victuals, and gave him the sword of 5414
 22:10 the sword of Goliath the Philistine. 5414
 27: 6 Achish **g** him Ziklag that day: wherefore 5414
 30:11 David, and **g** him bread, and he did eat; 5414
 30:12 they **g** him a piece of a cake *of figs,* and 5414
2Sa 12: 8 I **g** thee thy master's house, and thy 5414
 12: 8 **g** thee the house of Israel and of Judah; 5414
 18: 5 **g** all the captains **charge** concerning 6680
 24: 9 Joab **g** up the sum of the number of 5414

1Ki 4:29 God **g** Solomon wisdom and 5414
 5:10 So Hiram **g** Solomon cedar trees and 5414
 5:11 Solomon **g** Hiram twenty thousand 5414
 5:11 thus **g** Solomon to Hiram year by year. 5414
 5:12 the Lord **g** Solomon wisdom, as he 5414
 9:11 king Solomon **g** Hiram twenty cities in 5414
 10:10 she **g** the king an hundred and 5414
 10:10 the queen of Sheba **g** to king Solomon. 5414
 10:13 Solomon **g** unto the queen of Sheba all 5414
 10:13 besides *that* which Solomon **g** her of his 5414
 11:18 which **g** him a house, and appointed him 5414
 11:18 appointed him victuals, and **g** him land. 5414
 11:19 that he **g** him to wife the sister of his own 5414
 12:13 old men's **counsel** that they **g** him; 3289+6098
 13: 3 he **g** a sign the same day, saying, This *is* 5414
 14: 8 from the house of David, and **g** it thee: 5414
 14:15 he **g** to their fathers, and shall scatter 5414
 19:21 and **g** unto the people, and they did eat. 5414
2Ki 10:15 he **g** *him* his hand; and he took him up to 5414
 11:12 upon him, and **g** *him* the Testimony; NIH
 12:11 they **g** the money, being told, into the 5414
 12:14 they **g** that to the workmen, 5414
 13: 5 (And the Lord **g** Israel a saviour, 5414
 15:19 Menahem **g** Pul a thousand talents of 5414
 17: 3 became his servant, and **g** him presents. 7725
 18:15 Hezekiah **g** *him* all the silver that was 5414
 18:16 and **g** it to the king of Assyria. 5414
 21: 8 out of the land which I **g** their fathers; 5414
 22: 8 Hilkiah **g** the book to Shaphan, and he 5414
 23:35 Jehoiakim **g** the silver and the gold to 5414
 23: 5 to Riblah; and they **g** judgment upon him. 1696
1Ch 2:35 Sheshan **g** his daughter to Jarha his 5414
 6:55 they **g** them Hebron in the land of Judah, 5414
 6:56 they **g** to Caleb the son of Jephunneh. 5414
 6:57 to the sons of Aaron they **g** the cities of 5414
 6:64 the children of Israel **g** to the Levites 5414
 6:65 **g** by lot out of the tribe of the children 5414
 6:67 they **g** unto them, *of* the cities of refuge, 5414
 6:67 they **g** also Gezer with her suburbs, NIH
 14:12 David **g** a **commandment**, and they 559
 21: 5 Joab **g** the sum of the number of the 5414
 21:25 So David **g** to Ornan for the place six 5414
 25: 5 God **g** to Heman fourteen sons and 5414
 28:11 David **g** to Solomon his son the pattern of 5414
 28:14 He **g** of gold by weight for *things* of gold, NIH
 28:16 *by* weight he **g** gold for the tables of NIH
 28:17 for the golden basons he **g** gold by weight NIH
 29: 7 **g** for the service of the house of God *of* 5414
 29: 8 **g** *them* to the treasure of the house of 5414
2Ch 9: 9 she **g** the king an hundred and 5414
 9: 9 as the queen of Sheba **g** king Solomon. 5414
 9:12 king Solomon **g** to the queen of Sheba all 5414
 10: 8 **counsel** which the old men **g** him, 3289+6098
 11:23 he **g** victual in abundance. And he 5414
 13: 5 **g** the kingdom over Israel to David for 5414
 13:15 men of Judah **g** a **shout**: and as the men 7321
 15:15 and the Lord **g** them **rest** round about. 5117
 20:30 for his God **g** him **rest** round about. 5117
 21: 3 their father **g** them great gifts of silver, 5414
 21: 3 the kingdom **g** he to Jehoram; because 5414
 23:11 **g** *him* the Testimony, and made him king. NIH
 24:12 Jehoiada **g** it to such as did the work of 5414
 26: 8 the Ammonites **g** gifts to Uzziah: 5414
 27: 5 the children of Ammon **g** him the same 5414
 28:15 gave **to eat** and to drink, 398
 28:21 and **g** *it* unto the king of Assyria: 5414
 30: 7 *who* therefore **g** them **up** to desolation, 5414
 30:24 the princes **g** to the congregation a 7311
 32:24 he spake unto him, and he **g** him a sign. 5414
 34:10 they **g** it *to* the workmen that wrought in 5414
 34:11 and builders **g** they *it*, to buy hewn stone, 5414
 35: 7 Josiah **g** to the people, *of* the flock, lambs 7311
 35: 8 his princes **g** willingly unto the people, 7311
 35: 8 **g** unto the priests for the passover 7311
 35: 9 unto the Levites for passover *offerings* 7311
 36:17 for age: he **g** *them* all into his hand. 5414
Ezr 2:69 They **g** after their ability unto the treasure 5414
 3: 7 They **g** money also unto the masons, 5414
 5:12 **g** them into the hand of Nebuchadnezzar 3052
 7:11 king Artaxerxes **g** unto Ezra the priest, 5414
 10:19 they **g** their hands that *they* would put 5414
Ne 2: 1 I took up the wine, and **g** *it* unto the king. 5414
 2: 9 the river, and **g** them the king's letters. 5414
 7: 2 **g** my brother Hanani, and Hananiah
 the ruler of the palace, **charge** 6680
 7:70 some of the chief of the fathers **g** unto 5414
 7:70 The Tirshatha **g** to the treasure a thousand 5414
 7:71 *some* of the chief of the fathers **g** to 5414
 7:72 *that* which the rest of the people **g** *was* 5414
 8: 8 **g** the sense, and caused *them* to 7760
 12:31 great *companies* of them that **g** thanks, NIH
 12:38 the other *company* of them that **g** thanks NIH
 12:40 stood the two *companies* of them that **g** NIH
 12:47 the portions of the singers and the 5414
Est 1: 7 they **g** them **drink** in vessels of gold, 8248
 2: 9 he speedily **g** her her things for 5414
 2:18 **g** gifts, according to the state of the king. 5414
 3:10 **g** *it* unto Haman the son of Hammedatha 5414
 4: 5 **g** him a **commandment** to Mordecai, 6680
 4: 8 Also he **g** him the copy of the writing of 5414
 4:10 **g** him **commandment** unto Mordecai: 6680
 8: 2 from Haman, and **g** *it* unto Mordecai. 5414
Job 1:21 the Lord **g**, and the Lord hath taken 5414
 19:16 my servant, and he **g** *me* no **answer**; 6030
 29:11 the eye saw *me*, it **g** **witness** to me: 5749

G

G

Ref	Text	Strong's
Job 29:21	Unto me men **g** ear, and waited,	8085
32:11	I **g** ear to your reasons, whilst you	238
42:10	also the LORD **g** Job twice as much as he	3254
42:11	every man also **g** him a piece of money,	5414
42:15	their father **g** them inheritance among	5414
Ps 18:13	the heavens, and the Highest **g** his voice;	5414
68:11	The Lord **g** the word: great was	5414
69:21	They **g** me also gall for my meat; and	5414
69:21	in my thirst they **g** me vinegar **to drink**.	8248
77: 1	with my voice; and he **g** ear unto me.	238
78:15	**g** them drink as out of the great depths.	8248
78:29	well filled: for he **g** them their own desire;	935
78:46	**g** also their increase unto the caterpillar,	5414
78:48	He **g** up their cattle also to the hail,	5462
78:50	but **g** their life over to the pestilence;	5462
78:62	He **g** his people **over** also unto the sword;	5462
81:12	I **g** them **up** unto their own heart's lust:	7971
99: 7	and the ordinance that he **g** them.	5414
105:32	He **g** them hail for rain, and flaming fire	5414
105:44	**g** them the lands of the heathen:	5414
106:15	he **g** them their request; but sent leanness	5414
106:41	he **g** them into the hand of the heathen;	5414
135:12	**g** their land for an heritage, an heritage	5414
136:21	**g** their land for an heritage: for his mercy	5414
Pr 8:29	When he **g** to the sea his decree, that	7760
Ecc 1:13	I **g** my heart to seek and search out by	5414
1:17	I **g** my heart to know wisdom, and to	5414
12: 7	the spirit shall return unto God who **g** it.	5414
12: 9	he **g** **good heed**, and sought out, and set	239
SS 5: 6	I called him, but he **g** me no **answer**.	6030
Isa 41: 2	**g** the nations before him, and made him	5414
41: 2	he **g** them as the dust to his sword,	5414
42:24	Who **g** Jacob for a spoil, and Israel to	5414
43: 3	I **g** Egypt for thy ransom, Ethiopia and	5414
50: 6	I **g** my back to the smiters, and my cheeks	5414
Jer 7: 7	in the land that I **g** to your fathers, for ever	5414
7:14	unto the place which I **g** to you, and	5414
16:15	into their land that I **g** unto their fathers.	5414
17: 4	discontinue from thine heritage that I **g**	5414
23:39	the city that I **g** you and your fathers,	5414
24:10	from off the land that I **g** unto them	5414
30: 3	return to the land that I **g** to their fathers,	5414
32:12	**g** it to Baruch the scribe, the son of	5414
36:32	**g** it to Baruch the scribe, the son of	5414
39: 5	Hamath, where he **g** judgment upon him.	1696
39:10	**g** them vineyards and fields at the same	5414
39:11	**g** charge concerning Jeremiah to	6680
40: 5	So the captain of the guard **g** him victuals	5414
44:30	I **g** Zedekiah king of Judah into the hand	5414
52: 9	Hamath; where he **g** judgment upon him.	1696
La 1:19	mine elders **g up the ghost** in the city,	1478
Eze 16:19	My meat also which I **g** thee, fine flour,	5414
20:11	I **g** them my statutes, and shewed them	5414
20:12	Moreover also I **g** them my sabbaths,	5414
20:25	Wherefore I **g** them also statutes that	5414
36:28	ye shall dwell in the land that I **g** to your	5414
39:23	**g** them into the hand of their enemies.	5414
Da 1: 2	the Lord **g** Jehoiakim king of Judah into	5414
1: 7	Unto whom the prince of the eunuchs **g**	7760
1: 7	for he **g** unto Daniel the name of	7760
1:16	that they should drink; and **g** them pulse.	5414
1:17	God **g** them knowledge and skill in all	5414
2:48	**g** him many great gifts, and made him	3052
5:18	the most high God **g** Nebuchadnezzar thy	3052
5:19	for the majesty that he **g** him, all people,	3052
6:10	prayed, and **g** thanks before his God,	3029
Hos 2: 8	For she did not know that I **g** her corn,	5414
13:11	I **g** thee a king in mine anger, and took	8248
Am 2:12	ye **g** the Nazarites wine **to drink**;	8248
Mal 2: 5	I **g** him for the fear wherewith he	
Mt 8:18	he **g** **commandment** to depart unto	2753
10: 1	he **g** them power against unclean spirits,	1325
14:19	and **g** the loaves to his disciples,	1325
15:36	and **g** **thanks**, and brake them, and gave	2168
15:36	and brake them, and **g** to his disciples,	1325
21:23	and who **g** thee this authority?	1325
25:15	And unto one he **g** five talents, to another	1325
25:35	For I was a hungred, and ye **g** me meat:	1325
25:35	I was thirsty, and ye **g** me **drink**: I was a	4222
25:37	fed **thee**? or thirsty, and **g** **thee** drink?	4222
25:42	I was a hungred, and ye **g** me no meat:	1325
25:42	I was thirsty, and ye **g** me no **drink**:	4222
26:26	and brake it, and **g** it to the disciples,	1325
26:27	and **g** **thanks**, and gave it to them,	2168
26:27	and gave thanks, and **g** it to them, saying,	1325
26:48	Now he that betrayed him **g** them a sign,	1325
27:10	And **g** them for the potter's field,	1325
27:34	They **g** him vinegar to drink mingled with	1325
27:48	and put it on a reed, and **g** him **to drink**.	4222
28:12	they **g** large money unto the soldiers,	1325
Mk 2:26	and also to them which were with him?	1325
5:13	And forthwith Jesus **g** them **leave**.	2010
6: 7	**g** them power over unclean spirits;	1325
6:28	head in a charger, and **g** it to the damsel:	1325
6:28	and the damsel **g** it to her mother.	1325
6:41	them to his disciples to set before them;	1325
8: 6	and **g** **thanks**, and brake, and gave to his	2168
8: 6	to his disciples to set before them; and	1325
11:28	who **g** thee this authority to do these	1325
13:34	and **g** authority to his servants, and to	1325
14:22	and brake it, and **g** to them, and said,	1325
14:23	he had given thanks, he **g** it to them:	1325
15:23	they **g** him to drink wine mingled with	1325
15:36	and **g** him **to drink**, saying, Let alone;	4222
15:37	with a loud voice, and **g up the ghost**.	1606

Ref	Text	Strong's
Mk 15:39	so cried out, and **g up the ghost**, he said,	1606
15:45	of the centurion, he **g** the body to Joseph.	1433
Lk 2:38	instant **g** thanks likewise **unto** the Lord,	437
4:20	and he **g** it **again** to the minister,	591
6: 4	and **g** also to them that were with him;	1325
7:21	and unto many that were blind he **g**	5483
9: 1	and **g** them power and authority over all	1325
9:16	**g** to the disciples to set before	1325
10:35	**g** them to the host, and said unto him,	1325
15:16	swine did eat: and no man **g** unto him.	1325
18:43	when they saw it, **g** praise unto God.	1325
20: 2	or who is he that **g** thee this authority?	1325
22:17	and **g** **thanks**, and said, Take this,	2168
22:19	and **g** **thanks**, and brake it, and gave unto	2168
22:19	and brake it, and **g** unto them, saying,	1325
23:24	Pilate **g** **sentence** that it should be as	1948
23:29	and the paps which never **g** suck.	2337
23:46	and having said thus, he **g up the ghost**.	1606
24:30	and blessed it, and brake, and **g** to them.	1929
24:42	And they **g** him a piece of a broiled fish,	1929
Jn 1:12	them **g** he power to become the sons of	1325
3:16	world, that he **g** his only begotten Son,	1325
4: 5	near to the parcel of ground that Jacob **g**	1325
4:12	which **g** us the well, and drank thereof	1325
6:31	He **g** them bread from heaven to eat.	1325
6:32	Moses **g** you not that bread from heaven;	1325
7:22	Moses therefore **g** unto you circumcision;	1325
10:29	My Father, which **g** them me, is greater	1325
12:49	he **g** me a commandment, what I should	1325
13:26	he **g** it to Judas Iscariot, the son of Simon.	1325
14:31	and as the Father **g** me **commandment**,	1781
18:14	was he, which **g** **counsel** to the Jews,	4823
19: 9	art thou? But Jesus **g** him no answer.	1325
19:30	he bowed his head, and **g up the ghost**.	3860
19:38	Pilate **g** him **leave**. He came therefore,	2010
Ac 1:26	they **g** **forth** their lots; and the lot fell	1325
2: 4	as the Spirit **g** them utterance.	1325
3: 5	And he **g** heed unto them, expecting to	NIG
4:33	with great power **g** the apostles witness	591
5: 5	words fell down, and **g up the ghost**:	1634
7: 5	And he **g** him none inheritance in it, no,	1325
7: 8	he **g** him the covenant of circumcision:	1325
7:10	and **g** him favour and wisdom in the sight	1325
7:42	**g** them up to worship the host of heaven;	3860
8: 6	And the people with one accord **g heed**	4337
8:10	To whom they all **g heed**, from the least	4337
9:41	And he **g** her his hand, and lift her up,	1325
10: 2	which **g** much alms to the people,	4160
11:17	as God **g** them the like gift as he did unto	1325
12:22	And the people **g a shout**, saying, It is	2019
12:23	him, because he **g** not God the glory:	1325
12:23	was eaten of worms, and **g up the ghost**.	1634
13:20	after that he **g** unto them judges about	1325
13:21	and God **g** unto them Saul the son of Cis,	1325
13:22	to whom also he **g** **testimony**, and said,	3140
14: 3	which **g** **testimony** unto the word of his	3140
14:17	and **g** us rain from heaven,	1325
15:12	and **g** **audience** to Barnabas and Paul,	191
15:24	to whom we **g** no such **commandment**:	1291
22:22	they **g** him **audience** unto this word,	191
23:30	**g** **commandment** to his accusers also to	3853
26:10	put to death, I **g** my voice against them.	2702
27: 3	**g** him **liberty** to go unto his friends to	2010
27:35	**g** **thanks** to God in presence of them all:	2168
Ro 1:24	Wherefore God also **g** them **up** to	3860
1:26	For this cause God **g** them **up** unto vile	3860
1:28	God **g** them **over** to a reprobate mind,	3860
1Co 3: 5	even as the Lord **g** to every man?	1325
3: 6	Apollos watered; but God **g** the **increase**.	837
2Co 8: 5	but first **g** their own selves to the Lord,	1325
Gal 1: 4	Who **g** himself for our sins, that he might	1325
2: 5	To whom we **g** **place** by subjection,	1502
2: 9	they **g** to me and Barnabas the right hands	1325
2:20	who loved me, and **g** himself for me.	3860
3:18	but God **g** it to Abraham by promise.	5483
Eph 1:22	**g** him to be the head over all **things** to	1325
4: 8	captivity captive, and **g** gifts unto men.	1325
4:11	And he **g** some, apostles; and some,	1325
5:25	loved the church, and **g** himself for it;	3860
1Th 4: 2	For ye know what commandments we **g**	1325
1Ti 2: 6	Who **g** himself a ransom for all, to be	1325
Tit 2:14	**g** himself for us, that he might redeem	1325
Heb 7: 2	To whom also Abraham **g** a tenth **part** of	3307
7: 4	Abraham **g** the tenth of the spoils.	
7:13	which no man **g** **attendance** at the altar.	4337
11:22	**g** **commandment** concerning his bones.	1781
12: 9	corrected us, and we **g** them **reverence**:	1788
Jas 5:18	the heaven **g** rain, and the earth brought	1325
1Pe 1:21	him up from the dead, and **g** him glory;	1325
1Jn 3:23	one another, as he **g** us commandment.	1325
5:10	he believeth not the record that God **g** of	3140
Jude 1: 3	when I **g** all diligence to write unto you	4160
Rev 1: 1	of Jesus Christ, which God **g** unto him,	1325
2:21	And I **g** her space to repent of her	1325
11:13	and **g** glory to the God of heaven.	1325
13: 2	and the dragon **g** him his power,	1325
13: 4	And they worshipped the dragon which **g**	1325
15: 7	one of the four beasts **g** unto the seven	1325
20:13	the sea **g up** the dead which were in it;	1325

GAVEST (34) [GIVE]

Ref	Text	Strong's
Ge 3:12	The woman whom thou **g** to be with me,	5414
1Ki 8:34	the land which thou **g** unto their fathers.	5414
8:40	in the land which thou **g** unto our fathers.	5414
8:48	which thou **g** unto their fathers, the city	5414
2Ch 6:25	again unto the land which thou **g** to them	5414
6:31	long as they live in the land which thou **g**	5414
6:38	which thou **g** unto their fathers,	5414
20: 7	**g** it to the seed of Abraham thy friend for	5414
Ne 9: 7	and **g** him the name of Abraham;	7760
9:13	**g** them right judgments, and true laws,	5414
9:15	**g** them bread from heaven for	5414
9:20	Thou also thy good spirit to instruct	5414
9:20	and **g** them water for their thirst.	5414
9:22	Moreover thou **g** them kingdoms and	5414
9:24	Canaanites, and **g** them into their hands,	5414
9:27	according to thy manifold mercies thou **g**	5414
9:30	**g** thou them into the hand of the people	5414
9:35	in thy great goodness that thou **g** them,	5414
9:35	and fat land which thou **g** before them,	5414
9:36	for the land that thou **g** unto our fathers	5414
Job 39:13	**G** thou the goodly wings unto the	NIH
Ps 24: 7	He asked life of thee, and thou **g** it him,	5414
74:14	**g** him to be meat to the people inhabiting	5414
Lk 7:44	thou **g** me no water for my feet:	1325
7:45	thou **g** me no kiss: but this **woman** since	1325
15:29	yet thou never **g** me a kid, that I might	1325
19:23	then not thou my money into the bank,	1325
Jn 17: 4	I have finished the work which thou **g** me	1325
17: 6	men which thou **g** me out of the world:	1325
17: 6	thine they were, and thou **g** them me;	1325
17: 8	unto them the words which thou **g** me;	1325
17:12	those that thou **g** me I have kept,	1325
17:22	And the glory which thou **g** me I have	1325
18: 9	them which thou **g** me have I lost none.	1325

GAY (1)

Ref	Text	Strong's
Jas 2: 3	respect to him that weareth the **g** clothing,	2986

GAZA (19) [GAZATHITES, GAZITES]

Ref	Text	Strong's
Ge 10:19	as thou comest to Gerar, unto **G**;	5804
Jos 10:41	them from Kadesh-barnea even unto **G**,	5804
11:22	only in **G**, in Gath, and in Ashdod,	5804
15:47	**G** with her towns and her villages,	5804
Jdg 1:18	Also Judah took **G** with the coast thereof,	5804
6: 4	till thou come unto **G**, and left no	5804
16: 1	Samson to **G**, and saw there a harlot,	5804
16:21	brought him down to **G**, and bound him	5804
1Sa 6:17	for Ashdod one, for **G** one, for Askelon	5804
2Ki 18: 8	even unto **G**, and the borders thereof,	5804
1Ch 7:28	unto **G** and the towns thereof:	5804
Jer 47: 1	before that Pharaoh smote **G**.	5804
47: 5	Baldness is come upon **G**; Ashkelon is cut	5804
Am 1: 6	For three transgressions of **G**, and for four	5804
1: 7	I will send a fire on the wall of **G**,	5804
Zep 2: 4	For **G** shall be forsaken, and Ashkelon a	5804
Zec 9: 5	**G** also shall see it, and be very sorrowful,	5804
9: 5	the king shall perish from **G**,	5804
Ac 8:26	that goeth down from Jerusalem unto **G**,	1048

GAZATHITES (1) [GAZA]

Ref	Text	Strong's
Jos 13: 3	the **G**, and the Ashdothites,	5841

GAZE (1) [GAZING, GAZING-STOCK, GAZINGSTOCK, STARGAZERS]

Ref	Text	Strong's
Ex 19:21	they break through unto the LORD to **g**,	7200

GAZELLE See ROEBUCK; ROES

GAZER (2)

Ref	Text	Strong's
2Sa 5:25	from Geba until thou come to **G**.	1507
1Ch 14:16	of the Philistines from Gibeon even to **G**.	1507

GAZEZ (2)

Ref	Text	Strong's
1Ch 2:46	bare Haran, and Moza, and **G**:	1495
2:46	Moza, and Gazez: and Haran begat **G**.	1495

GAZING (1) [GAZE]

Ref	Text	Strong's
Ac 1:11	of Galilee, why stand ye **g** up into heaven?	1689

GAZINGSTOCK, GAZING-STOCK (2) [GAZE]

Ref	Text	Strong's
Na 3: 6	make thee vile, and will set thee as a **g**.	7210
Heb 10:33	whilst ye were made a **g** both by	2301

GAZITES (1) [GAZA]

Ref	Text	Strong's
Jdg 16: 2	And it was told the **G**, saying, Samson is	5841

GAZZAM (2)

Ref	Text	Strong's
Ezr 2:48	children of Nekoda, the children of **G**,	1502
Ne 7:51	The children of **G**, the children of Uzza,	1502

GE HARASHIM See CHARASHIM

GEBA (13)

Ref	Text	Strong's
Jos 21:17	with her suburbs, **G** with her suburbs,	1387
1Sa 13: 3	garrison of the Philistines that was in **G**,	1387
2Sa 5:25	smote the Philistines from **G** until thou	1387
1Ki 15:22	king Asa built with them **G** of Benjamin,	1387
2Ki 23: 8	from **G** to Beer-sheba, and brake down	1387
1Ch 6:60	**G** with her suburbs, and Alemeth with	1387
8: 6	of the fathers of the inhabitants of **G**,	1387
2Ch 16: 6	and he built therewith **G** and Mizpah.	1387
Ne 7:30	The men of Ramah and **G**, six hundred	1387
11:31	The children of Benjamin from **G**	1387
12:29	and out of the fields of **G** and Azmaveth:	1387
Isa 10:29	they have taken up their lodging at **G**;	1387
Zec 14:10	from **G** to Rimmon south of Jerusalem.	1387

GEBAL (2) [GIBLITES]

Ref	Text	Strong's
Ps 83: 7	**G**, and Ammon, and Amalek;	1381
Eze 27: 9	The ancients of **G** and the wise men	1380

GEBALITES See GIBLITES

GEBER (2)
1Ki	4:13 The son of **G**, in Ramoth-gilead; to him	1398
	4:19 **G** the son of Uri *was* in the country of	1398

GEBIM (1)
Isa	10:31 the inhabitants of **G** gather themselves to	1374

GEDALIAH (32)
2Ki	25:22 even over them he made **G** the son of	1436
	25:23 that the king of Babylon had made **G**	1436
	25:23 there came to **G** *to* Mizpah, even Ishmael	1436
	25:24 And **G** sware to them, and to their men,	1436
	25:25 smote **G**, that he died, and the Jews and	1436
1Ch	25: 3 **G**, and Zeri, and Jeshaiah, Hashabiah,	1436
	25: 9 the second *to* **G**, who with his brethren	1436
Ezr	10:18 Maaseiah, and Eliezer, and Jarib, and **G**.	1436
Jer	38: 1 the son of Pashur, and Jucal the son of	1436
	39:14 committed him unto **G** the son of Ahikam	1436
	40: 5 *he said*, Go back also to **G** the son of	1436
	40: 6 went Jeremiah unto **G** the son of Ahikam	1436
	40: 7 that the king of Babylon had made **G**	1436
	40: 8 they came to **G** to Mizpah, even Ishmael	1436
	40: 9 **G** the son of Ahikam the son of Shaphan	1436
	40:11 that he had set over them **G** the son of	1436
	40:12 to **G**, unto Mizpah, and gathered wine	1436
	40:13 *were* in the fields, came to **G** to Mizpah,	1436
	40:14 the son of Ahikam believed them not.	1436
	40:15 Johanan the son of Kareah spake to **G** in	1436
	40:16 **G** the son of Ahikam said unto Johanan	1436
	41: 1 unto **G** the son of Ahikam to Mizpah;	1436
	41: 2 smote **G** the son of Ahikam the son of	1436
	41: 3 with **G** at Mizpah, and the Chaldeans	1436
	41: 4 pass the second day after *he* had slain **G**,	1436
	41: 6 them, Come to **G** the son of Ahikam.	1436
	41: 9 men, whom he had slain because of **G**,	1436
	41:10 had committed to **G** the son of Ahikam:	1436
	41:16 *that* he had slain **G** the son of Ahikam,	1436
	41:18 Ishmael the son of Nethaniah had slain **G**	1436
	43: 6 **G** the son of Ahikam the son of Shaphan,	1436
Zep	1: 1 the son of **G**, the son of Amariah, the son	1436

GEDEON (1) [GIDEON]
Heb	11:32 for the time would fail me to tell of **G**,	*1066*

GEDER (1)
Jos	12:13 king of Debir, one; the king of **G**, one;	1445

GEDERAH (1)
Jos	15:36 and Adithaim, and **G**, and Gederothaim;	1449

GEDERATHITE (1)
1Ch	12: 4 Jahaziel, and Johanan, and Josabad the **G**,	1452

GEDERITE (1)
1Ch	27:28 in the low plains *was* Baal-hanan the **G**:	1451

GEDEROTH (2)
Jos	15:41 **G**, Beth-dagon, and Naamah,	1450
2Ch	28:18 **G**, and Shocho with the villages thereof,	1450

GEDEROTHAIM (1)
Jos	15:36 and Adithaim, and Gederah, and **G**;	1453

GEDOR (7)
Jos	15:58 Halhul, Beth-zur, and **G**,	1446
1Ch	4: 4 Penuel the father of **G**, and Ezer the	1446
	4:18 wife Jehudijah bare Jered the father of **G**,	1446
	4:39 they went to the entrance of **G**, *even* unto	1446
	8:31 And **G**, and Ahio, and Zacher.	1446
	9:37 **G**, and Ahio, and Zechariah, and Mikloth.	1446
	12: 7 and Zebadiah, the sons of Jeroham of **G**.	1446

GEHAZI (12)
2Ki	4:12 he said to **G** his servant, Call this	1522
	4:14 **G** answered, Verily she hath no child,	1522
	4:25 that he said to **G** his servant, Behold,	1522
	4:27 **G** came near to thrust her away.	1522
	4:29 he said to **G**, Gird up thy loins, and take	1522
	4:31 **G** passed on before them, and laid the	1522
	4:36 he called **G**, and said, Call this	1522
	5:20 **G**, the servant of Elisha the man of God,	1522
	5:21 So **G** followed after Naaman. And when	1522
	5:25 said unto him, Whence *comest thou*, **G**?	1522
	8: 4 the king talked with **G** the servant of	1522
	8: 5 said, My lord, O king, this *is* the	1522

GELILOTH (1)
Jos	18:17 *to* En-shemesh, and went forth toward **G**,	1553

GEMALLI (1)
Nu	13:12 Of the tribe of Dan, Ammiel the son of **G**.	1582

GEMARIAH (5)
Jer	29: 3 son of Shaphan, and the son of Hilkiah,	1587
	36:10 in the chamber of **G** the son of Shaphan	1587
	36:11 When Michaiah the son of **G**, the son of	1587
	36:12 the son of Shaphan, and Zedekiah	1587
	36:25 **G** had made intercession to the king that	1587

GENDER (2) [GENDERED, GENDERETH]
Lev	19:19 Thou shalt not let thy cattle **g with** a	7250
2Ti	2:23 knowing that they do **g** strifes.	*1080*

GENDERED (1) [GENDER]
Job	38:29 the hoary frost of heaven, who hath **g** it?	3205

GENDERETH (2) [GENDER]
Job	21:10 Their bull **g**, and faileth not; their cow	5674
Gal	4:24 which **g** to bondage, which is Agar.	*1080*

GENEALOGIES (8) [GENEALOGY]
1Ch	5:17 All these were **reckoned by g** in the days	3187
	7: 5 **reckoned** in all by their **g**, of	3187
	7: 7 were **reckoned by** their **g** twenty and	3187
	9: 1 So all Israel were **reckoned by g**;	3187
2Ch	12:15 and of Iddo the seer concerning **g**?	3187
	31:19 to all that were **reckoned by g** among	3187
1Ti	1: 4 Neither give heed to fables and endless **g**	*1076*
Tit	3: 9 and **g**, and contentions, and strivings	*1076*

GENEALOGY (15) [GENEALOGIES]
1Ch	4:33 These *were* their habitations, and their **g**.	3187
	5: 1 the **g** is not to be **reckoned** after	3187
	5: 7 the **g** of their generations was **reckoned**,	3187
	7: 9 the **number** of them, **after** their **g** by	3187
	7:40 the number **throughout** the **g** of them	3187
	9:22 These were **reckoned** by their **g** in their	3187
2Ch	31:16 Beside their **g** of males, from three years	3187
	31:17 Both *to* the **g** of the priests by the house	3187
	31:18 to the **g** of all their little ones, their wives,	3187
Ezr	2:62 *among* those that were **reckoned by g**,	3187
	8: 1 *this is* the **g** of them that went up with me	3187
	8: 3 him were **reckoned by g** of the males	3187
Ne	7: 5 that *they* might be **reckoned by g**.	3187
	7: 5 I found a register of the **g** of them which	3188
	7:64 *among* those that were **reckoned by g**,	3187

GENERAL (2) [GENERALLY]
1Ch	27:34 and the **g** of the king's army *was* Joab.	8269
Heb	12:23 To the **g assembly**, and church of	*3831*

GENERALLY (2) [GENERAL]
2Sa	17:11 all Israel be **g gathered** unto thee,	622+622
Jer	48:38 *There shall be* lamentation **g** upon all	3605

GENERATION (107) [GENERATIONS]
Ge	7: 1 have I seen righteous before me in this **g**.	1755
	15:16 the fourth **g** they shall come hither again:	1755
	50:23 **g**: the children also of Machir the son of	NIH
Ex	1: 6 and all his brethren, and all that **g**.	1755
	17:16 war with Amalek *from* **g** to generation.	1755
	17:16 war with Amalek from generation *to* **g**.	1755
	20: 5 third and fourth *g* of them that hate me;	NIH
	34: 7 unto the third and to the fourth **g**.	NIH
Nu	14:18 the children unto the third and fourth *g*.	NIH
	32:13 until all the **g**, that had done evil in	1755
Dt	1:35 men of this evil **g** see that good land,	1755
	2:14 until all the **g** of the men of war were	1755
	5: 9 third and fourth *g* of them that hate me,	NIH
	23: 2 even *to* his tenth **g** shall he not enter into	1755
	23: 3 even *to* their tenth **g** shall they not enter	1755
	23: 8 congregation of the Lᴏʀᴅ *in* their third **g**.	1755
	29:22 So that the **g** to come of your children	1755
	32: 5 *they are* a perverse and crooked **g**.	1755
	32:20 *shall be*: for they *are* a very froward **g**,	1755
Jdg	2:10 also all that **g** were gathered unto their	1755
	2:10 there arose another **g** after them,	1755
2Ki	10:30 thy children of the fourth **g** shall sit on	NIH
	15:12 the throne of Israel unto the fourth **g**.	NIH
Est	9:28 throughout **every g**, 1755+1755+3605+2050.1	
Ps	12: 7 thou shalt preserve them from this **g** for	1755
	14: 5 for God *is* in the **g** of the righteous.	1755
	22:30 it shall be accounted to the Lord for a **g**.	1755
	24: 6 This *is* the **g** of them that seek him,	1755
	48:13 that ye may tell *it* to the **g** following.	1755
	49:19 He shall go to the **g** of his fathers;	1755
	71:18 I have shewed thy strength unto *this* **g**,	1755
	73:15 I should offend *against* the **g** of thy	1755
	78: 4 shewing to the **g** to come the praises of	1755
	78: 6 That the **g** to come might know *them*,	1755
	78: 8 their fathers, a stubborn and rebellious **g**;	1755
	78: 8 a **g** *that* set not their heart aright,	1755
	95:10 Forty years long was I grieved with *this* **g**,	1755
	102:18 This shall be written for the **g** to come:	1755
	109:13 the **g** following let their name be blotted	1755
	112: 2 the **g** of the upright shall be blessed.	1755
	145: 4 One **g** shall praise thy works to another,	1755
Pr	27:24 crown *endure* to **every** *g*? 1755+1755+2050.1	
	30:11 *There is* a **g** *that* curseth their father,	1755
	30:12 *There is* a **g** *that are* pure in their own	1755
	30:13 *There is* a **g**, O how lofty are their eyes!	1755
	30:14 *There is* a **g**, whose teeth *are as* swords,	1755
Ecc	1: 4 *One g* passeth away,	1755
	1: 4 passeth away, and *another* **g** cometh:	1755
Isa	13:20 neither shall it be dwelt in from **g** to	1755
	13:20 shall it be dwelt in from generation to **g**:	1755
	34:10 from **g** to generation it shall lie waste;	1755
	34:10 from generation to **g** it shall lie waste;	1755
	34:17 from **g** to generation shall they dwell	1755
	34:17 from generation to **g** shall they dwell	1755
	51: 8 and my salvation from **g** to generation.	1755
	51: 8 and my salvation from generation to **g**.	1755
	53: 8 who shall declare his **g**? for he was cut off	1755
Jer	2:31 O **g**, see ye the word of the Lᴏʀᴅ. Have I	1755
	7:29 and forsaken the **g** of his wrath.	1755
	50:39 neither shall it be dwelt in from **g** to	1755
	50:39 from generation to **g** shall it be dwelt in	1755
La	5:19 for ever; thy throne from **g** to generation.	1755

GENERATIONS (118) [GENERATION]
	5:19 for ever; thy throne from generation to **g**.	1755
Da	4: 3 and his dominion *is* from **g** to generation.	1859
	4: 3 and his dominion *is* from generation to **g**.	1859
	4:34 and his kingdom *is* from **g** to generation:	1859
	4:34 and his kingdom *is* from generation to **g**.	1859
Joel	1: 3 children, and their children another **g**.	1755
	3:20 and Jerusalem from **g** to generation.	1755
	3:20 and Jerusalem from generation to **g**.	1755
Mt	1: 1 The book of the **g** of Jesus Christ, the son	*1078*
	3: 7 he said unto them, O **g** of vipers,	*1081*
	11:16 whereunto shall I liken this **g**? It is like	*1074*
	12:34 O **g** of vipers, how can ye, being evil,	*1081*
	12:39 and adulterous **g** seeketh after a sign;	*1074*
	12:41 shall rise in judgment with this **g**,	*1074*
	12:42 shall rise up in the judgment with this **g**,	*1074*
	12:45 so shall it be also unto this wicked **g**.	*1074*
	16: 4 and adulterous **g** seeketh after a sign;	*1074*
	17:17 and said, O faithless and perverse **g**,	*1074*
	23:33 Ye serpents, *ye* **g** of vipers, how can ye	*1081*
	23:36 All these *things* shall come upon this **g**.	*1074*
	24:34 I say unto you, This **g** shall not pass,	*1074*
Mk	8:12 saith, Why doth this **g** seek after a sign?	*1074*
	8:12 There shall no sign be given unto this **g**.	*1074*
	8:38 my words in this adulterous and sinful **g**;	*1074*
	9:19 answereth him, and saith, O faithless **g**,	*1074*
	13:30 I say unto you, that this **g** shall not pass,	*1074*
Lk	1:50 them that fear him from **g** to generation.	*1074*
	1:50 them that fear him from generation to **g**.	*1074*
	3: 7 of vipers, who hath warned you to flee	*1081*
	7:31 then shall I liken the men of this **g**?	*1074*
	9:41 saith, O faithless and perverse **g**,	*1074*
	11:29 he began to say, This is an evil **g**:	*1074*
	11:30 so shall also the Son of man be to this **g**.	*1074*
	11:31 in the judgment with the men of this **g**,	*1074*
	11:32 shall rise up in the judgment with this **g**,	*1074*
	11:50 of the world, may be required of this **g**;	*1074*
	11:51 say unto you, It shall be required of this **g**.	*1074*
	16: 8 the children of this world are in their **g**	*1074*
	17:25 many *things*, and be rejected of this **g**.	*1074*
	21:32 This **g** shall not pass away, till all be	*1074*
Ac	2:40 Save yourselves from this untoward **g**.	*1074*
	8:33 and who shall declare his **g**? for his life is	*1074*
	13:36 after he had served his own **g** by the will	*1074*
Heb	3:10 Wherefore I was grieved with that **g**,	*1074*
1Pe	2: 9 But ye *are* a chosen, a royal priesthood,	*1085*

GENERATIONS (118) [GENERATION]
Ge	2: 4 These *are* the **g** of the heavens and of	8435
	5: 1 This *is* the book of the **g** of Adam.	8435
	6: 9 These *are* the **g** of Noah: Noah was a just	8435
	6: 9 Noah was a just man *and* perfect in his **g**,	8435
	9:12 creature that *is* with you, for perpetual **g**:	1755
	10: 1 Now these *are* the **g** of the sons of Noah,	8435
	10:32 of Noah, after their **g**, in their nations:	8435
	11:10 These *are* the **g** of Shem: Shem *was* an	8435
	11:27 these *are* the **g** of Terah: Terah begat	8435
	17: 7 thy seed after thee in their **g** for an	1755
	17: 9 thou, and thy seed after thee in their **g**.	1755
	17:12 every man *child* in your **g**, he that is born	1755
	25:12 Now these *are* the **g** of Ishmael,	8435
	25:13 by their names, according to their **g**:	8435
	25:19 these *are* the **g** of Isaac, Abraham's son:	8435
	36: 1 these *are* the **g** of Esau, who *is* Edom.	8435
	36: 9 these *are* the **g** of Esau the father of	8435
	37: 2 These *are* the **g** of Jacob. Joseph,	8435
Ex	3:15 and this *is* my memorial unto **all g**. 1755+1755	
	6:16 of the sons of Levi according to their **g**;	8435
	6:19 the families of Levi according to their **g**.	8435
	12:14 it a feast to the Lᴏʀᴅ throughout your **g**;	1755
	12:17 shall ye observe this day in your **g** by an	1755
	12:42 of all the children of Israel in their **g**.	1755
	16:32 Fill an omer of it to be kept for your **g**;	1755
	16:33 before the Lᴏʀᴅ, to be kept for your **g**.	1755
	27:21 *shall be* a statute for ever unto their **g** on	1755
	29:42 *at* the door of the tabernacle of	1755
	30: 8 before the Lᴏʀᴅ throughout your **g**.	1755
	30:10 atonement upon it throughout your **g**:	1755
	30:21 him and to his seed throughout their **g**.	1755
	30:31 anointing oil unto me throughout your **g**.	1755
	31:13 between me and you throughout your **g**;	1755
	31:16 observe the sabbath throughout their **g**,	1755
	40:15 everlasting priesthood throughout their **g**.	1755
Lev	3:17 *It shall be* a perpetual statute for your **g**	1755
	6:18 *It shall be* a statute for ever in your **g**	1755
	7:36 by a statute for ever throughout their **g**.	1755
	10: 9 *be* a statute for ever throughout your **g**:	1755
	17: 7 for ever unto them throughout their **g**.	1755
	21:17 Whosoever *he be* of thy seed in their **g**	1755
	22: 3 *he be* of all your seed among your **g**,	1755
	23:14 throughout your **g** in all your dwellings.	1755
	23:21 in all your dwellings throughout your **g**.	1755
	23:31 throughout your **g** in all your dwellings.	1755
	23:41 *It shall be* a statute for ever in your **g**:	1755
	23:43 That your **g** may know that I made	1755
	24: 3 *it shall be* a statute for ever in your **g**.	1755
	25:30 to him that bought it throughout his **g**:	1755
Nu	1:20 Israel's eldest son, *by* their **g**, after their	8435
	1:22 of Simeon, *by* their **g**, after their families,	8435
	1:24 of Gad, *by* their **g**, after their families,	8435
	1:26 of Judah, *by* their **g**, after their families,	8435
	1:28 of Issachar, *by* their **g**, after their families,	8435
	1:30 of Zebulun, *by* their **g**, after their families,	8435
	1:32 their **g**, after their families, by the house	8435
	1:34 their **g**, after their families, by the house	8435
	1:36 their **g**, after their families, by the house	8435

G

G

Nu 1:38 of Dan, *by* their **g**, after their families, 8435
 1:40 of Asher, *by* their **g**, after their families, 8435
 1:42 *throughout* their **g**, after their families, 8435
 3: 1 These also *are* the **g** of Aaron and Moses 8435
 10: 8 an ordinance for ever throughout your **g**, 1755
 15:14 or whosoever *be* among you in your **g**, 1755
 15:15 *with you*, an ordinance for ever in your **g**: 1755
 15:21 unto the Lᴏʀᴅ a heave offering in your **g**. 1755
 15:23 and henceforward among your **g**; 1755
 15:38 of their garments throughout their **g**, 1755
 18:23 *be* a statute for ever throughout your **g**, 1755
 35:29 throughout your **g** in all your dwellings. 1755
Dt 7: 9 keep his commandments to a thousand **g**; 1755
 32: 7 the years of **many g**: 1755+1755+2050.1
Jos 22:27 between us, and you, and our **g** after us, 1755
 22:28 *so* say to us or to our **g** in time to come, 1755
Jdg 3: 2 Only that the **g** of the children of Israel 1755
Ru 4:18 Now these *are* the **g** of Pharez: 8435
1Ch 1:29 *are* their **g**: The firstborn of Ishmael, 8435
 5: 7 when the genealogy of their **g** was 8435
 7: 2 *were* valiant *men* of might in their **g**, 8435
 7: 4 with them, by their **g**, after the house of 8435
 7: 9 of them, after their genealogy by their **g**, 8435
 8:28 *were* heads of the fathers, by their **g**, 8435
 9: 9 according to their **g**, nine hundred and 8435
 9:34 the Levites *were* chief throughout their **g**; 8435
 16:15 *which* he commanded to a thousand **g**, 1755
 26:31 according to the **g** of his fathers. 8435
Job 42:16 his sons, and his sons' sons, *even* four **g**. 1755
Ps 33:11 of his heart to **all g**. 1755+1755+2050.1
 45:17 in **all g**. 1755+1755+3605+2050.1
 49: 1 dwelling places to **all g**, 1755+1755+2050.1
 61: 6 *and* his years as **many g**: 1755+1755+2050.1
 72: 5 moon endure, **throughout all g**, 1755+1755
 79:13 forth thy praise to **all g**. 1755+1755+2050.1
 85: 5 out thine anger to **all g**? 1755+1755+2050.1
 89: 1 thy faithfulness to **all g**. 1755+1755+2050.1
 89: 4 build up thy throne to **all g**. 1755+1755+2050.1
 90: 1 our dwelling place in **all g**. 1755+1755+2050.1
 100: 5 his truth *endureth* to **all g**. 1755+1755+2050.1
 102:12 remembrance unto **all g**. 1755+1755+2050.1
 102:24 thy years *are* throughout **all g**. 1755+1755
 105: 8 he commanded to a thousand **g**, 1755
 106:31 unto **all g** for evermore. 1755+1755+2050.1
 119:90 faithfulness *is* unto **all g**: 1755+1755+2050.1
 135:13 O Lᴏʀᴅ, throughout **all g**. 1755+1755+2050.1
 145:13 *endureth* throughout **all g**. 1755+1755+2050.1
 146:10 God, O Zion, unto **all g**. 1755+1755+2050.1
Isa 41: 4 done *it*, calling the **g** from the beginning? 1755
 51: 9 as *in* the ancient days, *in* the **g** of old. 1755
 58:12 foundations of **many g**; 1755+1755+2050.1
 60:15 a joy of **many g**. 1755+1755+2050.1
 61: 4 the desolations of **many g**. 1755+1755+2050.1
Joel 2: 2 to the years of **many g**. 1755+1755+2050.1
Mt 1:17 So all the **g** from Abraham to David *are* 1074
 1:17 from Abraham to David *are* fourteen **g**; 1074
 1:17 carrying away into Babylon *are* fourteen **g**; 1074
 1:17 into Babylon unto Christ *are* fourteen **g**. 1074
Lk 1:48 from henceforth all **g** shall call me blessed. 1074
Col 1:26 hath been hid from ages and from **g**, 1074

GENESARET (1) [GENNESARET]

Mk 6:53 they came into the land of **G**, and drew to 1082

GENNESARET (2) [GENNESARET]

Mt 14:34 gone over, they came into the land of **G**. 1082
Lk 5: 1 of God, he stood by the lake of **G**, 1082

GENTILE (2) [GENTILES]

Ro 2: 9 of the Jew first, and *also* of the **G**; 1672
 2:10 to the Jew first, and *also* of the **G**: 1672

GENTILES (129) [GENTILE]

Ge 10: 5 By these were the isles of the **G** divided 1471
Jdg 4: 2 which dwelt in Harosheth of the **G**. 1471
 4:13 from Harosheth of the **G** unto the river of 1471
 4:16 after the host, unto Harosheth of the **G**: 1471
Isa 11:10 of the people; to it shall the **G** seek: 1471
 42: 1 he shall bring forth judgment to the **G**. 1471
 42: 6 of the people, for a light of the **G**; 1471
 49: 6 I will also give thee for a light to the **G**, 1471
 49:22 I will lift up mine hand to the **G**, and set 1471
 54: 3 thy seed shall inherit the **G**, and make 1471
 60: 3 the **G** shall come to thy light, and kings to 1471
 60: 5 the forces of the **G** shall come unto thee. 1471
 60:11 may bring unto thee the forces of the **G**, 1471
 60:16 Thou shalt also suck the milk of the **G**, 1471
 61: 6 ye shall eat the riches of the **G**, and in 1471
 61: 9 their seed shall be known among the **G**, 1471
 62: 2 the **G** shall see thy righteousness, 1471
 66:12 the glory of the **G** like a flowing stream: 1471
 66:19 they shall declare my glory among the **G** 1471
Jer 4: 7 and the destroyer of the **G** is on his way; 1471
 14:22 Are there *any* among the vanities of the **G** 1471
 16:19 the **G** shall come unto thee from the ends 1471
 46: 1 to Jeremiah the prophet against the **G**; 1471
La 2: 9 king and her princes *are* among the **G**: 1471
Eze 4:13 Israel eat their defiled bread among the **G**, 1471
Hos 8: 8 now shall they be among the **G** as a vessel 1471
Joel 3: 9 Proclaim ye this among the **G**; Prepare 1471
Mic 5: 8 remnant of Jacob shall be among the **G** 1471
Zec 1:21 fray them, to cast out the horns of the **G**, 1471
Mal 1:11 my name *shall be* great among the **G**; 1471
Mt 4:15 the sea, beyond Jordan, Galilee of the **G**; 1484
 6:32 (For after all these *things* do the **G** seek): 1484

Mt 10: 5 Go not into the way of the **G**, and into 1484
 10:18 for a testimony against them and the **G**. 1484
 12:18 and he shall shew judgment to the **G**. 1484
 12:21 And in his name shall the **G** trust. 1484
 20:19 And shall deliver him to the **G** to mock, 1484
 20:25 know that the princes of the **G** exercise 1484
Mk 10:33 to death, and shall deliver him to the **G**: 1484
 10:42 over the **G** exercise lordship over them; 1484
Lk 2:32 A light to lighten the **G**, and the glory of 1484
 18:32 For he shall be delivered unto the **G**, 1484
 21:24 Jerusalem shall be trodden down of the **G**, 1484
 21:24 until the times of the **G** be fulfilled. 1484
 22:25 The kings of the **G** exercise lordship over 1484
Jn 7:35 he go unto the dispersed among the **G**, 1672
 7:35 among the Gentiles, and teach the **G**? 1672
Ac 4:27 with the, and the people of Israel, 1484
 7:45 in with Jesus into the possession of the **G**, 1484
 9:15 to bear my name before the **G**, and kings, 1484
 10:45 that on the **G** also was poured out the gift 1484
 11: 1 that were in Judea heard that the **G** 1484
 11:18 Then hath God also to the **G** granted 1484
 13:42 the **G** besought that these words might be 1484
 13:46 of everlasting life, lo, we turn to the **G**. 1484
 13:47 I have set thee to be a light of the **G**, 1484
 13:48 when the **G** heard *this*, they were glad, 1484
 14: 2 But the unbelieving Jews stirred up the **G**, 1484
 14: 5 there was an assault made both of the **G**, 1484
 14:27 had opened the door of faith unto the **G**. 1484
 15: 3 declaring the conversion of the **G**: 1484
 15: 7 that the **G** by my mouth should hear 1484
 15:12 wonders God had wrought among the **G** 1484
 15:14 how God at the first did visit the **G**, 1484
 15:17 and all the **G**, upon whom my name is 1484
 15:19 which from among the **G** are turned to 1484
 15:23 brethren which are of the **G** in Antioch 1484
 18: 6 from henceforth I will go unto the **G**. 1484
 21:11 shall deliver *him* into the hands of the **G**. 1484
 21:19 wrought among the **G** by his ministry. 1484
 21:21 which are among the **G** to forsake Moses, 1484
 21:25 As touching the **G** which believe, we 1484
 22:21 for I will send thee far hence unto the **G**. 1484
 26:17 and *from* the **G**, unto whom now I send 1484
 26:20 and *then* to the **G**, that *they* should repent 1484
 26:23 shew light unto the people, and to the **G**. 1484
 28:28 the salvation of God is sent unto the **G**, 1484
Ro 1:13 among you also, even as among other **G**. 1484
 2:14 For when the **G**, which have not the law, 1484
 2:24 is blasphemed among the **G** through you, 1484
 3: 9 we have before proved both Jews and **G**, 1672
 3:29 *he* not also of the **G**? Yes, of the Gentiles 1484
 3:29 not also of the Gentiles? Yes, of the **G** also: 1484
 9:24 not of the Jews only, but also of the **G**? 1484
 9:30 That the **G**, which followed not *after* 1484
 11:11 their fall salvation *is come* unto the **G**, 1484
 11:12 diminishing of them the riches of the **G**; 1484
 11:13 For I speak to you **G**, inasmuch as I am 1484
 11:13 inasmuch as I am the apostle of the **G**, 1484
 11:25 until the fulness of the **G** be come in. 1484
 15: 9 And that the **G** might glorify God for *his* 1484
 15: 9 cause I will confess to thee among the **G**, 1484
 15:10 he saith, Rejoice, ye **G**, with his people. 1484
 15:11 And again, Praise the Lord, all ye **G**; 1484
 15:12 and he that *shall* rise to reign over the **G**; 1484
 15:12 over the Gentiles; in him shall the **G** trust. 1484
 15:16 be the minister of Jesus Christ to the **G**, 1484
 15:16 that the offering up of the **G** might be 1484
 15:18 make the **G** obedient, by word and deed, 1484
 15:27 For if the **G** have been made partakers of 1484
 16: 4 but also all the churches of the **G**. 1484
1Co 5: 1 is not so much as named amongst the **G**, 1484
 10:20 But I *say*, that the *things* which the **G** 1484
 10:32 neither to the Jews, nor to the **G**, 1672
 12: 2 Ye know that ye were **G**, carried away 1484
 12:13 whether *we be* Jews or **G**, whether *we be* 1672
Gal 2: 2 *that* gospel which I preach among the **G**, 1484
 2: 8 *same* was mighty in me towards the **G**:) 1484
 2:12 came from James, he did eat with the **G**: 1484
 2:14 livest **after the manner of G**, and not as 1483
 2:14 why compellest thou the **G** to live as do 1484
 2:15 Jews by nature, and not sinners of the **G**, 1484
 3:14 come on the **G** through Jesus Christ; 1484
Eph 2:11 ye *being* in time passed **G** in the flesh, 1484
 3: 1 the prisoner of Jesus Christ for you **G**, 1484
 3: 6 That the **G** should be fellowheirs, 1484
 3: 8 that *I* should preach among the **G** 1484
 4:17 that ye henceforth walk not as other **G** 1484
Col 1:27 of the glory of this mystery among the **G**; 1484
1Th 2:16 Forbidding us to speak to the **G** that they 1484
 4: 5 even as the **G** which know not God: 1484
1Ti 2: 7 a teacher of the **G** in faith and verity. 1484
 3:16 seen of angels, preached unto the **G**, 1484
2Ti 1:11 and an apostle, and a teacher of the **G**. 1484
 4:17 known, and *that* all the **G** might hear: 1484
1Pe 2:12 your conversation honest among the **G**: 1484
 4: 3 us to have wrought the will of the **G**, 1484
3Jn 1: 7 they went forth, taking nothing of the **G**. 1484
Rev 11: 2 measure it not; for it is given unto the **G**: 1484

GENTLE (5) [GENTLENESS, GENTLY]

1Th 2: 7 we were **g** among you, *even* as a nurse 2261
2Ti 2:24 be **g** unto all *men*, apt to teach, patient, 2261
Tit 3: 2 *but* **g**, shewing all meekness unto all men. 1933
Jas 3:17 peaceable, **g**, *and* easy to be intreated, 1933
1Pe 2:18 not only to the good and **g**, but also to 1933

GENTLENESS (4) [GENTLE]

2Sa 22:36 and thy **g** hath made me great. 6031
Ps 18:35 me up, and thy **g** hath made me great. 6037
2Co 10: 1 you by the meekness and **g** of Christ, 1932
Gal 5:22 peace, longsuffering, **g**, goodness, faith, 5544

GENTLY (2) [GENTLE]

2Sa 18: 5 saying, *Deal* **g** for my sake with 328+3807.1
Isa 40:11 shall **g** lead those that are with young. 5095

GENUBATH (2)

1Ki 11:20 the sister of Tahpenes bare him **G** his son, 1592
 11:20 **G** was *in* Pharaoh's household among 1592

GERA (9)

Ge 46:21 Ashbel, **G**, and Naaman, Ehi, and Rosh, 1617
Jdg 3:15 Ehud the son of **G**, a Benjamite, a man 1617
2Sa 16: 5 whose name *was* Shimei, the son of **G**: 1617
 19:16 Shimei the son of **G**, a Benjamite, 1617
 19:18 Shimei the son of **G** fell down before 1617
1Ki 2: 8 *thou hast* with thee Shimei the son of **G**, 1617
1Ch 8: 3 of Bela were, Addar, and **G**, and Abihud, 1617
 8: 5 And **G**, and Shephuphan, and Huram. 1617
 8: 7 Naaman, and Ahiah, and **G**, he removed 1617

GERAHS (5)

Ex 30:13 (a shekel *is* twenty **g**:) a half shekel shall 1626
Lev 27:25 sanctuary: twenty **g** shall be the shekel. 1626
Nu 3:47 thou take *them*: (the shekel *is* twenty **g**:) 1626
 18:16 of the sanctuary, which *is* twenty **g**: 1626
Eze 45:12 the shekel *shall be* twenty **g**: 1626

GERAR (10)

Ge 10:19 as thou comest to **G**, unto Gaza; 1642
 20: 1 and Shur, and sojourned in **G**. 1642
 20: 2 Abimelech king of **G** sent, and took Sarah. 1642
 26: 1 Abimelech king of the Philistims unto **G**. 1642
 26: 6 And Isaac dwelt in **G**: 1642
 26:17 pitched his tent in the valley of **G**, 1642
 26:20 the herdmen of **G** did strive with Isaac's 1642
 26:26 Abimelech went to him from **G**, 1642
2Ch 14:13 *were* with him pursued them unto **G**: 1642
 14:14 they smote all the cities round about **G**; 1642

GERGESENES (1)

Mt 8:28 the other side into the country of the **G**, 1086

GERIZIM (3) [GERIZZIM]

Dt 11:29 shalt put the blessing upon mount **G**, 1630
Jos 8:33 half of them over against mount **G**, 1630
Jdg 9: 7 he went and stood in the top of mount **G**, 1630

GERIZZIM (1) [GERIZIM]

Dt 27:12 These shall stand upon mount **G** to bless 1630

GERSHOM (14)

Ex 2:22 bare *him* a son, and he called his name **G**: 1647
 18: 3 which the name of the one *was* **G**; for he 1647
Jdg 18:30 Jonathan, the son of **G**, the son of 1647
1Ch 6:16 The sons of Levi; **G**, Kohath, and Merari. 1647
 6:17 these *be* the names of the sons of **G**; 1647
 6:20 Of **G**; Libni his son, Jahath his son, 1647
 6:43 of Jahath, the son of **G**, the son of Levi. 1647
 6:62 to the sons of **G** throughout their families 1647
 6:71 Unto the sons of **G** *were* given out of 1647
 15: 7 Of the sons of **G**; Joel the chief, 1647
 23:15 The sons of Moses *were*, **G**, and Eliezer. 1647
 23:16 Of the sons of **G**, Shebuel *was* the chief. 1647
 26:24 Shebuel the son of **G**, the son of Moses, 1647
Ezr 8: 2 Of the sons of Phinehas; **G**: of the sons of 1647

GERSHON (18) [GERSHONITE, GERSHONITES]

Ge 46:11 the sons of Levi; **G**, Kohath, and Merari. 1648
Ex 6:16 **G**, and Kohath, and Merari: 1648
 6:17 The sons of **G**; Libni, and Shimi, 1648
Nu 3:17 their names; **G**, and Kohath, and Merari. 1648
 3:18 these *are* the names of the sons of **G** by 1648
 3:21 Of **G** *was* the family of the Libnites, 1648
 3:25 the charge of the sons of **G** in 1648
 4:22 Take also the sum of the sons of **G**, 1648
 4:28 **G** in the tabernacle of the congregation: 1649
 4:38 that were numbered of the sons of **G**, 1648
 4:41 numbered of the families of the sons of **G**, 1648
 7: 7 and four oxen he gave unto the sons of **G**, 1648
 10:17 the sons of **G** and the sons of Merari set 1648
 26:57 of the **G**, the family of the Gershonites: 1648
Jos 21: 6 the children of **G** *had* by lot out of 1648
 21:27 unto the children of **G**, of the families of 1648
1Ch 6: 1 the sons of Levi; **G**, Kohath, and Merari. 1648
 23: 6 of Levi, *namely*, **G**, Kohath, and Merari. 1648

GERSHONITE (3) [GERSHON]

1Ch 26:21 the sons of Laadan, chief fathers, 1649
 26:21 *even* of Laadan the **G**, *were* Jehieli. 1649
 29: 8 of the Lᴏʀᴅ, by the hand of Jehiel the **G**. 1649

GERSHONITES (9) [GERSHON]

Nu 3:21 these *are* the families of the **G**. 1649
 3:23 The families of the **G** shall pitch behind 1649
 3:24 chief of the house of the father of the **G** 1649
 4:24 This *is* the service of the families of the **G**, 1649
 4:27 be all the service of the sons of the **G**, 1649
 26:57 Gershon, the family of the **G**: of Kohath, 1649
Jos 21:33 All the cities of the **G** according to their 1649
1Ch 23: 7 Of the **G** *were*, Laadan, and Shimei. 1649
2Ch 29:12 of the **G**; Joah the son of Zimmah, 1649

GESHAN (1)
1Ch 2:47 **G**, and Pelet, and Ephah, and Shaaph. 1529

GESHEM (3) [GASHMU]
Ne 2:19 the Ammonite, and **G** the Arabian, 1654
 6: 1 **G** the Arabian, and the rest of our 1654
 6: 2 Sanballat and **G** sent unto me, saying, 1654

GESHUR (8) [GESHURI, GESHURITES]
2Sa 3: 3 Maacah the daughter of Talmai king of **G**; 1650
 13:37 to Talmai, the son of Ammihud, king of **G**. 1650
 13:38 and went to **G**, and was there three years. 1650
 14:23 So Joab arose and went to **G**, 1650
 14:32 to say, Wherefore am I come from **G**? 1650
 15: 8 vowed a vow while I abode at **G** in Syria, 1650
1Ch 2:23 he took **G**, and Aram, with the towns of 1650
 3: 2 the daughter of Talmai king of **G**: 1650

GESHURI (2) [GESHUR]
Dt 3:14 the country of Argob unto the coasts of **G** 1651
Jos 13: 2 the borders of the Philistines, and all **G**, 1651

GESHURITES (5) [GESHUR]
Jos 12: 5 unto the border of the **G** and 1651
 13:11 the border of the **G** and Maachathites, 1651
 13:13 the children of Israel expelled not the **G**, 1651
 13:13 the **G** and the Maachathites dwell among 1650
1Sa 27: 8 invaded the **G**, and the Gezrites, 1651

GET (118) [GAT, GETTETH, GETTING, GOT, GOTTEN]
Ge 12: 1 **g** thee out of thy country, and from thy 1980
 19:14 and said, Up, **g** ye **out** of this place; 3318
 22: 2 and **g** thee into the land of Moriah; 1980
 31:13 **g** thee **out** from this land, and return unto 3318
 34: 4 saying, **G** me this damsel to wife. 3947
 34:10 therein, and **g** you **possessions** therein. 270
 42: 2 **g** you **down** thither, and buy for us from 3381
 44:17 you, **g** you in peace unto your father. 5927
 45:17 and go, **g** you unto the land of Canaan: 935
Ex 1:10 and *so* **g** them **up** out of the land. 5927
 5: 4 their works? **g** you unto your burdens. 1980
 5:11 you straw where you can find *it*: yet not 3947
 7:15 **G** thee unto Pharaoh in the morning; 1980
 10:28 **g** thee from me, take heed to thyself, 1980
 11: 8 **G** thee **out**, and all the people that follow 3318
 12:31 *and* **g** you **forth** from amongst my people, 3318
 14:17 I will **g** me **honour** upon Pharaoh, 3513
 19:24 **g** thee **down**, and thou shalt come **up**, 3381
 32: 7 LORD said unto Moses, Go, **g** thee **down**; 3381
Lev 14:21 cannot *g so much*; then he shall 3027+5381
 14:22 such as he is **able to g**; 3027+5381
 14:30 young pigeons, such as he **can g**; 3027+5381
 14:31 such as he is **able to g**, the one 3027+5381
 14:32 whose **hand** is not **able to g** *that* 3027+5381
Nu 6:21 besides *that* that his hand shall **g**: 5381
 13:17 **G** you **up** this *way* southward, and go up 5927
 14:25 **g** you *into* the wilderness *by* the way of 5265
 16:24 **G** you **up** from about the tabernacle of 5927
 16:45 **G** you **up** from this congregation, 7426
 22:13 the princes of Balak, **G** you into your land: 1980
 22:34 it displease thee, I will **g** me **back again**. 7725
 27:12 **G** thee **up** into this mount Abarim, 5927
Dt 2:13 *said I*, and **g** you **over** the brook Zered. 5674
 3:27 **G** thee **up** *into* the top of Pisgah, and lift 5927
 5:30 say to them, **G** you into your tents **again**. 7725
 8:18 for *it is* he that giveth power to **g** 6213
 9:12 Arise, **g** thee **down** quickly from hence; 3381
 17: 8 **g** thee **up** into the place which the LORD 5927
 28:43 The stranger that *is* within thee shall **g up** 5927
 32:49 **G** thee **up** into this mountain Abarim, 5927
Jos 2:16 said unto them, **G** you to the mountain, 1980
 7:10 the LORD said unto Joshua, **G** thee **up**; 6965
 17:15 *then* **g** thee **up** to the wood *country*, and 5927
 22: 4 **g** ye unto your tents, *and* unto the land of 1980
Jdg 7: 9 him, Arise, **g** thee **down** unto the host; 3381
 14: 2 therefore **g** her for me to wife. 3947
 14: 3 Samson said unto his father, **G** her for me; 3947
 19: 9 to morrow **g** you **early** on your way, that 7925
Ru 3: 3 upon thee, and **g** thee **down** *to* the floor: 3381
1Sa 9: 3 therefore **g** you **up**; for about *this* time 5927
 15: 6 **g** you **down** from among the Amalekites, 3381
 20:29 let me **g away**, I pray thee, and see my 4422
 22: 5 depart, and **g** thee *into* the land of Judah. 935
 23:26 David made haste to **g away** for fear of 1980
 25: 5 **G** you **up** to Carmel, and go to Nabal, 5927
2Sa 20: 6 lest he **g** him fenced cities, and escape us. 4672
1Ki 1: 2 that my lord the king may **g heat**. 2552
 1:13 Go and **g** thee **in** unto king David, 935
 2:26 **G** thee to Anathoth, unto thine own 1980
 12:18 made speed to **g** *him* **up** to *his* chariot, 5927
 14: 2 he wife of Jeroboam; and **g** thee to Shiloh: 1980
 14:12 therefore, **g** thee to thine own house; 1980
 17: 3 **G** thee hence, and turn thee eastward, 1980
 17: 9 Arise, **g** thee to Zarephath, which 1980
 18:41 said unto Ahab, **G** thee **up**, eat and drink; 5927
 18:44 Prepare *thy chariot*, and **g** thee **down**, 3381
2Ki 3:13 **g** thee to the prophets of thy father, 1980
 7:12 shall catch them alive, and **g** into the city. 935
2Ch 10:18 Rehoboam made speed to **g** *him* **up** to 5927
Ne 9:10 So didst thou **g** thee a name, *as it is* this 6213
Ps 119:104 Through thy precepts I **g** understanding: NIH
Pr 4: 5 wisdom, get understanding: forget *it* 7069
 4: 5 wisdom, **g** understanding: forget *it* not; 7069
 4: 7 the principal thing; therefore **g** wisdom: 7069

Pr 4: 7 and with all thy getting **g** understanding. 7069
 6:33 A wound and dishonour shall he **g**; 4672
 16:16 How much better *is it* to **g** wisdom than 7069
 16:16 to **g** understanding rather to be chosen 7069
 17:16 a price in the hand of a fool to **g** wisdom, 7069
 22:25 learn his ways, and **g** a snare to thy soul. 3947
Ecc 3: 6 A time to **g**, and a time to lose; a time to 1245
SS 4: 6 I will **g** me to the mountain of myrrh, 1980
 7:12 Let us **g up early** to the vineyards; let us 7925
Isa 22:15 Go, **g** thee unto this treasurer, *even* unto 935
 30:11 **G** you **out** of the way, turn aside out of 5493
 30:22 thou shalt say unto it, **G** thee **hence**. 3318
 40: 9 **g** thee **up** into the high mountain; 5927
 47: 5 Sit thou silent, and **g** thee into darkness, 935
Jer 5: 5 I will **g** me unto the great men, 1980
 13: 1 Go and **g** thee a linen girdle, and put it 7069
 19: 1 Go and **g** a potter's earthen bottle, 7069
 46: 4 **g up**, ye horsemen, and stand forth with 5927
 48: 9 unto Moab, that it may flee and **g away** 3318
 49:30 Flee, **g** you far off, dwell deep, O ye 5110
 49:31 Arise, **g** you **up** unto the wealthy nation, 5927
La 3: 7 hedged me about, that I cannot **g out**: 3318
Eze 3: 4 go, **g** thee unto the house of Israel, 935
 3:11 go, **g** thee to them of the captivity, unto NIH
 11:15 have said, **G** ye far from the LORD: NIH
 22:27 destroy souls, to **g dishonest gain**. 1214+1215
Da 4:14 let the beasts **g away** from under it, 5111
Joel 3:13 come, **g** you **down**; for the press is full, 3381
Zep 3:19 I will **g** them praise and fame in every 7760
Zec 6: 7 **G** ye *hence*, walk to and fro through 1980
Mt 4:10 Jesus unto him, **G** thee **hence**, Satan: 5217
 14:22 constrained his disciples to **g** into a ship, 1684
 16:23 said unto Peter, **G** thee behind me, Satan: 5217
Mk 6:45 constrained his disciples to **g** into the ship, 1684
 8:33 saying, **G** thee behind me, Satan: 5217
Lk 4: 8 said unto him, **G** thee behind me, Satan: 5217
 9:12 round about, and lodge, and **g** victuals: 2147
 13:31 unto him, **G** *thee* **out**, and depart hence: 1831
Ac 7: 3 **G** thee **out** of thy country, 1831
 10:20 and **g** *thee* **down**, and go with them, 2597
 22:18 and **g** *thee* quickly **out** of Jerusalem: 1831
 27:43 first into *the sea*, and **g** to land: 1826
2Co 2:11 lest Satan should **g an advantage** of us: 4122
Jas 4:13 there a year, and buy and sell, and **g gain**: 2770

GETHER (2)
Ge 10:23 of Aram; Uz, and Hul, and **G**, and Mash. 1666
1Ch 1:17 and Uz, and Hul, and **G**, and Meshech. 1666

GETHSEMANE (2)
Mt 26:36 Jesus with them unto a place called **G**, 1068
Mk 14:32 they came to a place which was named **G**: 1068

GETTETH (9) [GET]
2Sa 5: 8 Whosoever **g up** to the gutter, 5060
Pr 3:13 and the man that **g** understanding. 6329
 9: 7 He that reproveth a scorner **g** to himself 3947
 9: 7 he that rebuketh a wicked *man* **g** himself NIH
 15:32 he that heareth reproof **g** understanding. 7069
 18:15 The heart of the prudent **g** knowledge; 7069
 19: 8 He that **g** wisdom loveth his own soul: 7069
Jer 17:11 *so* he that **g** riches, and not by right, 6213
 48:44 he that **g up** out of the pit shall be taken 5927

GETTING (3) [GET]
Ge 31:18 which he had gotten, the cattle of his **g**, 7075
Pr 4: 7 and with all thy **g** get understanding. 7075
 21: 6 The **g** of treasures by a lying tongue *is a* 6467

GEUEL (1)
Nu 13:15 Of the tribe of Gad, **G** the son of Machi. 1345

GEZER (13) [GEZRITES]
Jos 10:33 Horam king of **G** came up to help Lachish 1507
 12:12 king of Eglon, one; the king of **G**, one; 1507
 16: 3 coast of Beth-horon the nether, and to **G**: 1507
 16:10 not out the Canaanites that dwelt in **G**: 1507
 21:21 for the slayer; and **G** with her suburbs, 1507
Jdg 1:29 drive out the Canaanites that dwelt in **G**; 1507
 1:29 the Canaanites dwelt in **G** among them. 1507
1Ki 9:15 and Hazor, and Megiddo, and **G**. 1507
 9:16 taken **G**, and burnt it with fire, and slain 1507
 9:17 Solomon built **G**, and Beth-horon 1507
1Ch 6:67 *they gave* also **G** with her suburbs, 1507
 7:28 and eastward Naaran, and westward **G**, 1507
 20: 4 that there arose war at **G** with 1507

GEZRITES (1) [GEZER]
1Sa 27: 8 and the **G**, and the Amalekites: 1511

GHOST (109)
Ge 25: 8 Abraham **gave up the g**, and died in a 1478
 25:17 he **gave up the g** and died; 1478
 35:29 Isaac **gave up the g**, and died, 1478
 49:33 **yielded up the g**, and was gathered unto 1478
Job 3:11 *why* did I *not* **give up the g** when I came 1478
 10:18 *Oh that* I had **given up the g**, and no eye 1478
 11:20 *shall be* as the **giving up of the g**. 4646+5315
 13:19 if I hold my tongue, I shall **give up the g**. 1478
 14:10 man **giveth up the g**, and where *is he*? 1478
Jer 15: 9 she hath **given up the g**; her sun 5301+5315
La 1:19 mine elders **gave up the g** in the city, 1478
Mt 1:18 she was found with child of the Holy **G**. 4151
 1:20 is conceived in her is of the Holy **G**. 4151
 3:11 he shall baptize you with the Holy **G**, 4151
 12:31 blasphemy against the *Holy* **G** shall not 4151

Mt 12:32 whosoever speaketh against the Holy **G**, 4151
 27:50 again with a loud voice, yielded up the **g**. 4151
 28:19 and of the Son, and of the Holy **G**: 4151
Mk 1: 8 but he shall baptize you with the Holy **G**. 4151
 3:29 against the Holy **G** hath never forgiveness, 4151
 12:36 For David himself said by the Holy **G**, 4151
 13:11 for it is not ye that speak, but the Holy **G**. 4151
 15:37 with a loud voice, and **gave up the g**. 1606
 15:39 so cried out, and **gave up the g**, he said, 1606
Lk 1:15 and he shall be filled with the Holy **G**, 4151
 1:35 The Holy **G** shall come upon thee, 4151
 1:41 and Elisabeth was filled with the Holy **G**: 4151
 1:67 Zacharias was filled with the Holy **G**, 4151
 2:25 of Israel: and the Holy **G** was upon him. 4151
 2:26 it was revealed unto him by the Holy **G**, 4151
 3:16 he shall baptize you with the Holy **G** and 4151
 3:22 And the Holy **G** descended in a bodily 4151
 4: 1 And Jesus being full of the Holy **G** 4151
 12:10 against the Holy **G** it shall not be forgiven. 4151
 12:12 the Holy **G** shall teach you in the same 4151
 23:46 and having said thus, he **gave up the g**. 1606
Jn 1:33 is he which baptizeth with the Holy **G**. 4151
 7:39 for the Holy **G** was not yet *given;* because 4151
 14:26 But the Comforter, *which is* the Holy **G**, 4151
 19:30 he bowed *his* head, and gave up the **g**. 4151
 20:22 saith unto them, Receive ye the Holy **G**: 4151
Ac 1: 2 that he through the Holy **G** had given 4151
 1: 5 ye shall be baptized with the Holy **G** not 4151
 1: 8 after that the Holy **G** is come upon you: 4151
 1:16 which the Holy **G** by the mouth of David 4151
 2: 4 And they were all filled with the Holy **G**, 4151
 2:33 of the Father the promise of the Holy **G**, 4151
 2:38 ye shall receive the gift of the Holy **G**. 4151
 4: 8 Then Peter, filled with the Holy **G**, 4151
 4:31 and they were all filled with the Holy **G**, 4151
 5: 3 filled thine heart to lie to the Holy **G**, 4151
 5: 5 words fell down, and **gave up the g**: 1634
 5:10 at his feet, and **yielded up the g**: 1634
 5:32 *so is* also the Holy **G**, whom God hath 4151
 6: 3 full of the Holy **G** and wisdom, whom we 4151
 6: 5 a man full of faith and of the Holy **G**, 4151
 7:51 and ears, ye do always resist the Holy **G**: 4151
 7:55 he, being full of the Holy **G**, looked up 4151
 8:15 that they might receive the Holy **G**: 4151
 8:17 on them, and they received the Holy **G**. 4151
 8:18 the apostles' hands the Holy **G** was given, 4151
 8:19 I lay hands, he may receive the Holy **G**. 4151
 9:17 thy sight, and be filled with the Holy **G**. 4151
 9:31 and in the comfort of the Holy **G**, 4151
 10:38 Jesus of Nazareth with the Holy **G** 4151
 10:44 the Holy **G** fell on all them which heard 4151
 10:45 was poured out the gift of the Holy **G**. 4151
 10:47 which have received the Holy **G** as well 4151
 11:15 I began to speak, the Holy **G** fell on them, 4151
 11:16 but ye shall be baptized with the Holy **G**. 4151
 11:24 and full of the Holy **G** and of faith: 4151
 12:23 was eaten of worms, and **gave up the g**. 1634
 13: 2 and fasted, the Holy **G** said, Separate me 4151
 13: 4 So they, being sent forth by the Holy **G**, 4151
 13: 9 filled with the Holy **G**, set his eyes on 4151
 13:52 were filled with joy, and with the Holy **G**. 4151
 15: 8 them witness, giving them the Holy **G**, 4151
 15:28 For it seemed good to the Holy **G**, 4151
 16: 6 were forbidden of the Holy **G** to preach 4151
 19: 2 Have ye received the Holy **G** since ye 4151
 19: 2 as heard whether there be *any* Holy **G**. 4151
 19: 6 upon them, the Holy **G** came on them; 4151
 20:23 Save that the Holy **G** witnesseth in every 4151
 20:28 over the which the Holy **G** hath made 4151
 21:11 and feet, and said, Thus saith the Holy **G**, 4151
 28:25 Well spake the Holy **G** by Esaias 4151
Ro 5: 5 by the Holy **G** which is given unto us. 4151
 9: 1 I also bearing me witness in the Holy **G**, 4151
 14:17 and peace, and joy in the Holy **G**. 4151
 15:13 hope, through the power of the Holy **G**. 4151
 15:16 being sanctified by the Holy **G**. 4151
1Co 2:13 but which the Holy **G** teacheth; 4151
 6:19 the temple of the Holy **G** which is in you, 4151
 12: 3 that Jesus is the Lord, but by the Holy **G**. 4151
2Co 6: 6 by kindness, by the Holy **G**, 4151
 13:14 the communion of the Holy **G**, *be* with 4151
1Th 1: 5 in the Holy **G**, and in much assurance; 4151
 1: 6 much affliction, with joy of the Holy **G**: 4151
2Ti 1:14 keep by the Holy **G** which dwelleth in us. 4151
Tit 3: 5 and renewing of the Holy **G**; 4151
Heb 2: 4 divers miracles, and gifts of the Holy **G**, 4151
 3: 7 Wherefore, as the Holy **G** saith, To day if 4151
 6: 4 and were made partakers of the Holy **G**, 4151
 9: 8 The Holy **G** this signifying, that the way 4151
 10:15 the Holy **G** also is a witness to us: 4151
1Pe 1:12 with the Holy **G** sent *down* from heaven; 4151
2Pe 1:21 spake *as they were* moved by the Holy **G**. 4151
1Jn 5: 7 the Father, the Word, and the Holy **G**: 4151
Jude 1:20 most holy faith, praying in the Holy **G**, 4151

GIAH (1)
2Sa 2:24 that *lieth* before **G** *by* the way of 1520

GIANT (8) [GIANTS]
2Sa 21:16 which *was* of the sons of the **g**, 7497
 21:18 Saph, which *was* of the sons of the **g**. 7497
 21:20 number; and he also was born to the **g**. 7497
 21:22 These four were born to the **g** in Gath, 7497
1Ch 20: 4 *that was* of the children of the **g**, 7497
 20: 6 *foot;* and he also was the son of the **g**. 7497

G

1Ch 20: 8 These were born unto the **g** in Gath; 7497
Job 16:14 breach, he runneth upon me like a **g**. 1368

GIANTS (13) [GIANT]

Ge 6: 4 There were **g** in the earth in those days; 5303
Nu 13:33 there we saw the **g**, the sons of Anak, 5303
13:33 the sons of Anak, *which come* of the **g**: 5303
Dt 2:11 Which also were accounted **g**, 7497
2:20 (That also was accounted a land of **g**; 7497
2:20 **g** dwelt therein in old time; 7497
3:11 of Bashan remained of the remnant of **g**; 7497
3:13 Bashan, which was called the land of **g**: 7497
Jos 12: 4 *which was* of the remnant of the **g**, 7497
13:12 who remained of the remnant of the **g** 7497
15: 8 which *is* at the end of the valley of the **g** 7497
17:15 in the land of the Perizzites and of the **g**, 7497
18:16 *is* in the valley of the **g** on the north, 7497

GIBBAR (1)

Ezr 2:20 The children of **G**, ninety and five. 1402

GIBBETHON (6)

Jos 19:44 And Eltekeh, and **G**, and Baalath, 1405
21:23 with her suburbs, **G** with her suburbs, 1405
1Ki 15:27 Baasha smote him at **G**, which *belongeth* 1405
15:27 for Nadab and all Israel laid siege to **G**. 1405
16:15 the people *were* encamped against **G**, 1405
16:17 Omri went up from **G**, and all Israel with 1405

GIBEA

1Ch 2:49 father of Machbenah, and the father of **G**: 1388

GIBEAH (48) [GIBEATH, GIBEATHITE]

Jos 15:57 Cain, **G**, and Timnah; ten cities with their 1390
Jdg 19:12 children of Israel; we will pass over to **G**. 1390
19:13 to lodge all night, in **G**, or in Ramah. 1390
19:14 down upon them *when they were* by **G**, 1390
19:15 aside thither, to go in *and* to lodge in **G**: 1390
19:16 mount Ephraim; and he sojourned in **G**: 1390
20: 4 came into **G** that *belongeth* to Benjamin, 1390
20: 5 the men of **G** rose against me, and beset 1390
20: 9 *shall* be the thing which we will do to **G**; 1390
20:10 do, when they come to **G** of Benjamin, 1387
20:13 the children of Belial, which *are* in **G**, 1390
20:14 together out of the cities unto **G**, 1390
20:15 drew sword, beside the inhabitants of **G**, 1390
20:19 in the morning, and encamped against **G**. 1390
20:20 in array to fight against them at **G**. 1390
20:21 children of Benjamin came forth out of **G**, 1390
20:25 went forth against them out of **G** 1390
20:29 And Israel set liers in wait round about **G**. 1390
20:30 put *themselves* in array against **G**, as at 1390
20:31 other to **G** in the field, about thirty men 1390
20:33 places, *even* out of the meadows of **G**. 1387
20:34 there came against **G** ten thousand chosen 1390
20:36 liers in wait which they had set beside **G**. 1390
20:37 liers in wait hasted, and rushed upon **G**; 1390
20:43 them down with ease over against **G** 1390
1Sa 10:26 Saul also went home to **G**; and there went 1390
11: 4 came the messengers *to* **G** of Saul, 1390
13: 2 a thousand were with Jonathan in **G** of 1390
13:15 gat him up from Gilgal *unto* **G** of 1390
13:16 with them, abode in **G** of Benjamin: 1387
14: 2 Saul tarried in the uttermost part of **G** 1390
14: 5 and the other southward over against **G**. 1387
14:16 the watchmen of Saul in **G** of Benjamin 1390
15:34 Saul went up to his house *to* **G** of Saul. 1390
22: 6 (now Saul abode in **G** under a tree in 1390
23:19 came up the Ziphites to Saul to **G**, saying, 1390
26: 1 The Ziphites came unto Saul to **G**, saying, 1390
2Sa 6: 3 of the house of Abinadab that *was* in **G**: 1390
6: 4 of the house of Abinadab which *was* at **G**, 1390
21: 6 them up unto the LORD in **G** of Saul, 1390
23:29 Ittai the son of Ribai out of **G** of 1390
1Ch 11:31 Ithai the son of Ribai of **G**, that pertained 1390
2Ch 13: 2 *was* Michaiah the daughter of Uriel of **G**. 1390
Isa 10:29 at Geba; Ramah is afraid; **G** of Saul is fled. 1390
Hos 5: 8 Blow ye the cornet in **G**, *and* the trumpet 1390
9: 9 corrupted *themselves*, as *in* the days of **G**: 1390
10: 9 thou hast sinned from the days of **G**: 1390
10: 9 the battle in **G** against the children of 1390

GIBEATH (1) [GIBEAH]

Jos 18:28 which *is* Jerusalem, **G**, *and* Kirjath; 1390

GIBEATHITE (1) [GIBEAH]

1Ch 12: 3 then Joash, the sons of Shemaah the **G**; 1395

GIBEON (37) [GIBEONITE, GIBEONITES]

Jos 9: 3 when the inhabitants of **G** heard what 1391
9:17 Now their cities *were* **G**, and Chephirah, 1391
10: 1 how the inhabitants of **G** had made peace 1391
10: 2 feared greatly, because **G** *was* a great city, 1391
10: 4 and help me, that we may smite **G**: 1391
10: 5 encamped before **G**, and made war 1391
10: 6 men of **G** sent unto Joshua to the camp 1391
10:10 slew them *with* a great slaughter at **G**, 1391
10:12 of Israel, Sun, stand thou still upon **G**; 1391
10:41 all the country of Goshen, even unto **G**: 1391
11:19 save the Hivites the inhabitants of **G**: 1391
18:25 **G**, and Ramah, and Beeroth, 1391
21:17 **G** with her suburbs, Geba with her 1391
2Sa 2:12 of Saul, went out from Mahanaim to **G**. 1391
2:13 and met together by the pool of **G**: 1391
2:16 called Helkath-hazzurim, which *is* in **G**. 1391
2:24 Giah *by* the way of the wilderness of **G**. 1391

2Sa 3:30 he had slain their brother Asahel at **G** in 1391
20: 8 *were* at the great stone which *is* in **G**, 1391
1Ki 3: 4 the king went to **G** to sacrifice there; 1391
3: 5 In **G** the LORD appeared to Solomon in a 1391
9: 2 as he had appeared unto him at **G**. 1391
1Ch 8:29 at **G** dwelt the father of Gibeon; 1391
8:29 in Gibeon dwelt the father of **G**; 1391
9:35 In **G** dwelt the father of Gibeon, Jehiel, 1391
9:35 in Gibeon dwelt the father of **G**, Jehiel, 1391
14:16 of the Philistines from **G** even to Gazer. 1391
16:39 the LORD in the high place that *was* at **G**, 1391
21:29 at that season in the high place at **G**. 1391
2Ch 1: 3 went to the high place that *was* at **G**; 1391
1:13 the high place that *was* at **G** *to* Jerusalem, 1391
Ne 3: 7 the men of **G**, and of Mizpah, 1391
7:25 The children of **G**, ninety and five. 1391
Isa 28:21 he shall be wroth as *in* the valley of **G**, 1391
Jer 28: 1 son of Azur the prophet, which *was* of **G**, 1391
41:12 him by the great waters that *are* in **G**, 1391
41:16 whom he had brought again from **G**: 1391

GIBEONITE (2) [GIBEON]

1Ch 12: 4 Ismaiah the **G**, a mighty *man* among 1393
Ne 3: 7 next unto them repaired Melatiah the **G**, 1393

GIBEONITES (6) [GIBEON]

2Sa 21: 1 *his* bloody house, because he slew the **G**. 1393
21: 2 the king called the **G**, and said unto them; 1393
21: 2 (now the **G** *were* not of the children of 1393
21: 3 Wherefore David said unto the **G**, 1393
21: 4 **G** said unto him, We will have no silver 1393
21: 9 delivered them into the hands of the **G**, 1393

GIBLITES (1) [GEBAL]

Jos 13: 5 the land of the **G**, and all Lebanon, 1382

GIDDALTI (2)

1Ch 25: 4 Hanani, Eliathah, **G**, and Romamti-ezer, 1437
25:29 The two and twentieth to **G**, *he*, his sons, 1437

GIDDEL (4)

Ezr 2:47 The children of **G**, the children of Gahar, 1435
2:56 the children of Darkon, the children of **G**, 1435
Ne 7:49 The children of **G**, the children of Gahar, 1435
7:58 the children of Darkon, the children of **G**, 1435

GIDEON (39) [GEDEON, JERUBBAAL]

Jdg 6:11 son **G** threshed wheat by the winepress, 1439
6:13 **G** said unto him, O my lord, if the LORD 1439
6:19 **G** went in, and made ready a kid, 1439
6:22 when **G** perceived that he *was* an angel 1439
6:22 the LORD, **G** said, Alas, O Lord GOD! 1439
6:24 **G** built an altar there unto the LORD, 1439
6:27 **G** took ten men of his servants, and did as 1439
6:29 the son of Joash hath done this thing. 1439
6:34 the spirit of the LORD came upon **G**, 1439
6:36 **G** said unto God, If thou wilt save Israel 1439
6:39 **G** said unto God, Let not thine anger be 1439
7: 1 who *is* **G**, and all the people that *were* 1439
7: 2 the LORD said unto **G**, The people that 1439
7: 4 the LORD said unto **G**, The people *are* yet 1439
7: 5 the LORD said unto **G**, Every one that 1439
7: 7 the LORD said unto **G**, By the three 1439
7:13 when **G** was come, behold, *there was* a 1439
7:14 This *is* nothing else save the sword of **G** 1439
7:15 when **G** heard the telling of the dream, 1439
7:18 say, The sword of the LORD, and of **G**. 1439
7:19 So **G**, and the hundred men that *were* 1439
7:20 The sword of the LORD, and of **G**. 1439
7:24 **G** sent messengers throughout all mount 1439
7:25 and Zeeb to **G** on the *other* side Jordan. 1439
8: 4 **G** came to Jordan, *and* passed over, 1439
8: 7 **G** said, Therefore when the LORD hath 1439
8:11 **G** went up *by* the way of them that dwelt 1439
8:13 the son of Joash returned from battle 1439
8:21 **G** arose, and slew Zebah and Zalmunna, 1439
8:22 the men of Israel said unto **G**, Rule thou 1439
8:23 **G** said unto them, I will not rule over you, 1439
8:24 **G** said unto them, I would desire a 1439
8:27 **G** made an ephod thereof, and put it in 1439
8:27 which *thing* became a snare unto **G**, 1439
8:28 in quietness forty years in the days of **G**. 1439
8:30 **G** had threescore and ten sons of his body 1439
8:32 **G** the son of Joash died in a good old age, 1439
8:33 it came to pass, as soon as **G** was dead, 1439
8:35 it to the house of Jerubbaal, *namely*, **G**, 1439

GIDEONI (5)

Nu 1:11 Of Benjamin; Abidan the son of **G**. 1441
2:22 of Benjamin *shall be* Abidan the son of **G**. 1441
7:60 On the ninth day Abidan the son of **G**, 1441
7:65 *was* the offering of Abidan the son of **G**. 1441
10:24 of Benjamin *was* Abidan the son of **G**. 1441

GIDOM (1)

Jdg 20:45 pursued hard after them unto **G**, 1440

GIER (2)

Lev 11:18 swan, and the pelican, and the **g eagle**, 7360
Dt 14:17 and the **g eagle**, and the cormorant, 7360

GIFT (59) [GIVE]

Ge 34:12 Ask me never so much dowry and **g**, 4976
Ex 23: 8 thou shalt take no **g**: for the gift blindeth 7810
23: 8 for the **g** blindeth the wise, 7810
Nu 8:19 I have given the Levites *as* a **g** to Aaron 5414

Nu 18: 6 to you *they are* given *as* a **g** for the LORD, 4979
18: 7 priest's office *unto you as* a service of **g**: 4979
18:11 the heave offering of their **g**, with all 4976
Dt 16:19 not respect persons, neither take a **g**: 7810
16:19 for a **g** doth blind the eyes of the wise, 7810
2Sa 19:42 the king's *cost?* or hath he given us *any* **g**? 5375
Ps 45:12 daughter of Tyre *shall be* there with a **g**; 4503
Pr 17: 8 A **g** *is as* a precious stone in the eyes of 7810
17:23 A wicked *man* taketh a **g** out of the 7810
18:16 A man's **g** maketh room for him, 4976
21:14 A **g** in secret pacifieth anger: and a reward 4976
25:14 Whoso boasteth himself of a false **g** *is like* 4991
Ecc 3:13 good of all his labour, it *is* the **g** of God. 4991
5:19 riches in his labour; this *is* the **g** of God. 4991
7: 7 mad; and a **g** destroyeth the heart. 4979
Eze 46:16 If the prince give a **g** unto any of his sons, 4979
46:17 if he give a **g** of his inheritance to one of 4979
Mt 5: 23 Therefore if thou bring thy **g** to the altar, 1435
5:24 Leave there thy **g** before the altar, 1435
5:24 brother, and then come and offer thy **g**. 1435
8: 4 offer the **g** that Moses commanded for a 1435
15: 5 say to *his* father or *his* mother, It is a **g**, 1435
23:18 swearest by the **g** that is upon it, 1435
23:19 the **g**, or the altar that sanctifieth the gift? 1435
23:19 the gift, or the altar that sanctifieth the **g**? 1435
Mk 7:11 or mother, It *is* Corban, that is to say, a **g**, 1435
Jn 4:10 If thou knewest the **g** of God, and who it 1431
Ac 2:38 ye shall receive the **g** of the Holy Ghost. 1431
8:20 thou hast thought that the **g** of God may 1431
10:45 was poured out the **g** of the Holy Ghost. 1431
11:17 God gave them the like **g** as he *did* unto 1431
Ro 1:11 I may impart unto you some spiritual **g**, 5486
5:15 not as the offence, so also *is* the **free g**. 5486
5:15 and the **g** by grace, which is by one man, 1431
5:16 as *it was* by one that sinned, *so is* the **g**: 1434
5:16 the **free g** *is* of many offences unto 5486
5:17 of the **g** of righteousness shall reign in life 1431
5:18 by the righteousness of one *the free* **g** NIG
6:23 the **g** of God *is* eternal life through Jesus 5486
1Co 7: 7 So that ye come behind in no **g**; waiting 5486
7: 7 But every man hath his proper **g** of God, 5486
13: 2 And though I have the **g** *of* prophecy, NIG
2Co 1:11 that for the **g** *bestowed* upon us by 5486
8: 4 intreaty that we would receive the **g**, 5485
9:15 Thanks *be* unto God for his unspeakable **g**. 1431
Eph 2: 8 that not of yourselves: it *is* the **g** of God: 1435
3: 7 according to the **g** of the grace of God 1431
4: 7 to the measure of the **g** of Christ. 1431
Php 4:17 Not because I desire a **g**: but I desire fruit 1390
1Ti 4:14 Neglect not the **g** that is in thee, which 5486
2Ti 1: 6 that *thou* stir up the **g** of God, 5486
Heb 6: 4 and have tasted of the heavenly **g**, 1431
Jas 1:17 Every good **g** and every perfect gift is 1394
1:17 gift and every perfect **g** is from above, 1434
1Pe 4:10 As every man hath received *the* **g**, even 5486

GIFTS (53) [GIVE]

Ge 25: 6 Abraham gave **g**, and sent them away 4979
Ex 28:38 of Israel shall hallow in all their holy **g**; 4979
Lev 23:38 beside your **g**, and beside all your vows, 4979
Nu 18:29 Out of all your **g** ye shall offer every heave 4979
2Sa 8: 2 became David's servants, and brought **g**. 4503
8: 6 became servants to David, and brought **g**. 4503
1Ch 18: 2 became David's servants, and brought **g**. 4503
18: 6 became David's servants, and brought **g**. 4503
2Ch 19: 7 nor respect of persons, nor taking of **g**. 7810
21: 3 their father gave them great **g** of silver, 4503
26: 8 the Ammonites gave **g** to Uzziah: 4503
32:23 many brought **g** unto the LORD to 4503
Est 2:18 gave **g**, according to the state of the king. 4864
9:22 one to another, and **g** to the poor. 4979
Ps 68:18 thou hast received **g** for men; yea, 4979
72:10 the kings of Sheba and Seba shall offer **g**. 814
Pr 6:35 rest content, though thou givest many **g**. 7810
15:27 house; but he that hateth **g** shall live. 4979
19: 6 *man is* a friend to him that **giveth g**. 4976
29: 4 but he that receiveth **g** overthroweth it. 8641
Isa 1:23 every one loveth **g**, and followeth after 7810
Eze 16:33 They give **g** to all whores: but thou givest 5078
16:33 thou givest thy **g** to all thy lovers, 5083
20:26 I polluted them in their own **g**, in that 4979
20:31 For when *ye* offer your **g**, when ye make 4979
20:39 ye my holy name no more with your **g**, 4979
22:12 In thee have they taken *g* to shed blood; 7810
Da 2: 6 ye shall receive of me **g** and rewards and 4978
2:48 gave him many great **g**, and made him 4978
5:17 Let thy **g** be to thyself, and give thy 4978
Mt 2:11 their treasures, they presented unto him **g**; 1435
7:11 know how to give good **g** unto your 1390
Lk 11:13 know how to give good **g** unto your 1390
21: 1 saw the rich *men* casting their **g** into 1435
21: 5 it was adorned with goodly stones and **g**, 334
Ro 11:29 For the **g** and calling of God *are* without 5486
12: 6 **g** differing according to the grace that is 5486
1Co 12: 1 Now concerning spiritual **g**, brethren, NIG
12: 4 there are diversities of **g**, but the same 5486
12: 9 to another the **g** of healing by the same 5486
12:28 then **g** of healings, helps, governments, 5486
12:30 Have all the **g** of healing? do all speak with 5486
12:31 covet earnestly the best **g**: and yet shew 5486
14: 1 desire spiritual **g**, but rather that ye may NIG
14:12 forasmuch as ye are zealous of spiritual **g**, NIG
Eph 4: 8 captivity captive, and gave **g** unto men. 1390
Heb 2: 4 divers miracles, and **g** of the Holy Ghost, 3311
5: 1 that he may offer both **g** and sacrifices for 1435

Heb 8: 3 For every high priest is ordained to offer **g** 1435
8: 4 seeing that there are priests that offer **g** 1435
9: 9 which were offered both **g** and sacrifices, 1435
11: 4 he was righteous, God testifying of his **g**: 1435
Rev 11:10 and shall send **g** one to another; 1435

GIHON (6)
Ge 2:13 name of the second river is **G**: the same 1521
1Ki 1:33 own mule, and bring him down to **G**: 1521
1:38 king David's mule, and brought him to **G**. 1521
1:45 the prophet have anointed him king in **G**: 1521
2Ch 32:30 also stopped the upper watercourse of **G**, 1521
33:14 on the west side of **G**, in the valley, even 1521

GILALAI (1)
Ne 12:36 Shemaiah, and Azareel, Milalai, **G**, Maai, 1562

GILBOA (8)
1Sa 28: 4 all Israel together, and they pitched in **G**. 1533
31: 1 and fell down slain in mount **G**. 1533
31: 8 and his three sons fallen in mount **G**. 1533
2Sa 1: 6 As I happened by chance upon mount **G**, 1533
1:21 Ye mountains of **G**, let there be no dew, 1533
21:12 when the Philistines had slain Saul in **G**: 1533
1Ch 10: 1 and fell down slain in mount **G**. 1533
10: 8 Saul and his sons fallen in mount **G**. 1533

GILEAD (100) [GILEAD'S, GILEADITE, GILEADITES, JABESH-GILEAD, RAMOTH-GILEAD]
Ge 31:21 and set his face toward the mount **G**. 1568
31:23 and they overtook him in the mount **G**. 1568
31:25 his brethren pitched in the mount of **G**. 1568
37:25 a company of Ishmeelites came from **G** 1568
Nu 26:29 Machir begat **G**: of Gilead come the 1568
26:29 of **G** come the family of the Gileadites. 1568
26:30 These are the sons of **G**: of Jeezer, 1568
27: 1 Hepher, the son of **G**, the son of Machir, 1568
32: 1 the land of **G**, that behold, the place was 1568
32:26 cattle, shall be there in the cities of **G**: 1568
32:29 ye shall give them the land of **G** for a 1568
32:39 Machir the son of Manasseh went to **G**, 1568
32:40 Moses gave **G** unto Machir the son of 1568
36: 1 of the families of the children of **G**, 1568
Dt 2:36 the city that is by the river, even unto **G**, 1568
3:10 and all **G**, and all Bashan, unto Salchah 1568
3:12 mount **G**, and the cities thereof, gave I 1568
3:13 the rest of **G**, and all Bashan, being 1568
3:15 And I gave **G** unto Machir. 1568
3:16 unto the Gadites I gave from **G** even unto 1568
4:43 Ramoth in **G**, of the Gadites; and Golan 1568
34: 1 the LORD shewed him all the land of **G**, 1568
Jos 12: 2 from half **G**, even unto the river Jabbok, 1568
12: 5 and the Maachathites, and half **G**, 1568
13:11 **G**, and the border of the Geshurites and 1568
13:25 all the cities of **G**, and half the land of 1568
13:31 half **G**, and Ashtaroth, and Edrei, cities of 1568
17: 1 the firstborn of Manasseh, the father of **G**: 1568
17: 1 of war, therefore he had **G** and Bashan. 1568
17: 3 Hepher, the son of **G**, the son of Machir, 1568
17: 5 beside the land of **G** and Bashan, 1568
17: 6 rest of Manasseh's sons had the land of **G**. 1568
20: 8 Ramoth in **G** out of the tribe of Gad, 1568
21:38 of Gad, Ramoth in **G** with her suburbs, 1568
22: 9 to go unto the country of **G**, to the land 1568
22:13 half tribe of Manasseh, into the land of **G**, 1568
22:15 unto the land of **G**, and they spake with 1568
22:32 out of the land of **G**, unto the children of 1568
Jdg 5:17 **G** abode beyond Jordan: and why did Dan 1568
7: 3 return and depart early from mount **G**. 1568
10: 4 unto this day, which are in the land of **G**. 1568
10: 8 the land of the Amorites, which is in **G**. 1568
10:17 gathered together, and encamped in **G**. 1568
10:18 and princes of **G** said one to another, 1568
10:18 be head over all the inhabitants of **G**. 1568
11: 1 the son of a harlot: and **G** begat Jephthah. 1568
11: 5 the elders of **G** went to fetch Jephthah 1568
11: 7 Jephthah said unto the elders of **G**, Did 1568
11: 8 the elders of **G** said unto Jephthah, 1568
11: 8 be our head over all the inhabitants of **G**. 1568
11: 9 Jephthah said unto the elders of **G**, If ye 1568
11:10 the elders of **G** said unto Jephthah, 1568
11:11 Jephthah went with the elders of **G**, 1568
11:29 he passed over **G** and Manasseh, 1568
11:29 passed over Mizpeh of **G**, and from 1568
11:29 from Mizpeh of **G** he passed over unto 1568
12: 4 gathered together all the men of **G**, 1568
12: 4 the men of **G** smote Ephraim, because 1568
12: 5 that the men of **G** said unto him, Art thou 1568
12: 7 and was buried in one of the cities of **G**. 1568
20: 1 with the land of **G**, unto the LORD in 1568
1Sa 13: 7 over Jordan to the land of Gad and **G**. 1568
2Sa 2: 9 he made him king over **G**, and over 1568
17:26 and Absalom pitched in the land of **G**. 1568
24: 6 they came to **G**, and to the land of 1568
1Ki 4:13 Jair the son of Manasseh, which are in **G**; 1568
4:19 the son of Uri was in the country of **G**, 1568
17: 1 who was of the inhabitants of **G**, said 1568
22: 3 Know ye that Ramoth in **G** is ours, 1568
2Ki 10:33 all the land of **G**, the Gadites, 1568
10:33 by the river Arnon, even **G** and Bashan. 1568
15:29 and Hazor, and Gilead, and Galilee, 1568
1Ch 2:21 to the daughter of Machir the father of **G**, 1568
2:22 three and twenty cities in the land of **G**. 1568
2:23 to the sons of Machir the father of **G**. 1568
5: 9 cattle were multiplied in the land of **G**. 1568

1Ch 5:10 tents throughout all the east land of **G**. 1568
5:14 the son of Jaroah, the son of **G**, the son of 1568
5:16 they dwelt in **G** in Bashan, and in her 1568
6:80 Ramoth in **G** with her suburbs, 1568
7:14 Aramitess bare Machir the father of **G**: 1568
7:17 These were the sons of **G**, the son of 1568
26:31 them mighty men of valour at Jazer of **G**, 1568
27:21 Of the half tribe of Manasseh in **G**, 1568
Ps 60: 7 **G** is mine, and Manasseh is mine; 1568
108: 8 **G** is mine; Manasseh is mine; Ephraim 1568
SS 4: 1 flock of goats, that appear from mount **G**. 1568
6: 5 is as a flock of goats that appear from **G**. 1568
Jer 8:22 there no balm in **G**; is there no physician 1568
22: 6 Thou art **G** unto me, and the head of 1568
46:11 Go up into **G**, and take balm, O virgin, 1568
50:19 be satisfied upon mount Ephraim and **G**. 1568
Eze 47:18 from **G**, and from the land of Israel by 1568
Hos 6: 8 **G** is a city of them that work iniquity, 1568
12:11 Is there iniquity in **G**? surely they are 1568
Am 1: 3 they have threshed **G** with threshing 1568
1:13 have ript up the women with child at **G**, 1568
Ob 1:19 of Samaria: and Benjamin shall possess **G**. 1568
Mic 7:14 let them feed in Bashan and **G**, as in 1568
Zec 10:10 I will bring them into the land of **G** and 1568

GILEAD'S (1) [GILEAD]
Jdg 11: 2 **G** wife bare him sons; and his wife's sons 1568

GILEADITE (9) [GILEAD]
Jdg 10: 3 a **G**, and judged Israel twenty and 1569
11: 1 Now Jephthah the **G** was a mighty man of 1569
12: 7 died Jephthah the **G**, and was buried in 1569
2Sa 17:27 and Barzillai the **G** of Rogelim, 1569
19:31 Barzillai the **G** came down from Rogelim, 1569
1Ki 2: 7 kindness unto the sons of Barzillai the **G**, 1569
Ezr 2:61 a wife of the daughters of Barzillai the **G**, 1569
Ne 7:63 of the daughters of Barzillai the **G** to wife, 1569

GILEADITES (4) [GILEAD]
Nu 26:29 of Gilead come the family of the **G**. 1569
Jdg 12: 4 Ye **G** are fugitives of Ephraim among 1568
12: 5 the **G** took the passages of Jordan before 1568
2Ki 15:25 and with him fifty men of the **G**: 1121+1569

GILGAL (41)
Dt 11:30 dwell in the champaign over against **G**, 1537
Jos 4:19 encamped in **G**, in the east border of 1537
4:20 took out of Jordan, did Joshua pitch in **G**. 1537
5: 9 the name of the place is called **G** 1537
5:10 the children of Israel encamped in **G**, 1537
9: 6 they went to Joshua unto the camp at **G**, 1537
10: 6 sent unto Joshua to the camp to **G**, 1537
10: 7 So Joshua ascended from **G**, he, and all 1537
10: 9 and went up from **G** all night. 1537
10:15 all Israel with him, unto the camp to **G**. 1537
10:43 all Israel with him, unto the camp to **G**. 1537
12:23 one; the king of the nations of **G**, one; 1537
14: 6 children of Judah came unto Joshua in **G**: 1537
15: 7 so northward, looking toward **G**, that is 1537
Jdg 2: 1 an angel of the LORD came up from **G** to 1537
3:19 again from the quarries that were by **G**, 1537
1Sa 7:16 **G**, and Mizpeh, and judged Israel in all 1537
10: 8 thou shalt go down before me to **G**; 1537
11:14 let us go to **G**, and renew the kingdom 1537
11:15 all the people went to **G**; and there they 1537
11:15 made Saul king before the LORD in **G**; 1537
13: 4 were called together after Saul to **G**. 1537
13: 7 he was yet in **G**, and all the people 1537
13: 8 appointed: but Samuel came not to **G**; 1537
13:12 will come down now upon me to **G**, 1537
13:15 gat him up from **G** unto Gibeah of 1537
15:12 and passed on, and gone down to **G**. 1537
15:21 to sacrifice unto the LORD thy God in **G**. 1537
15:33 Agag in pieces before the LORD in **G**. 1537
2Sa 19:15 Judah came to **G**, to go to meet the king, 1537
19:40 the king went on to **G**, and Chimham 1537
2Ki 2: 1 that Elijah went with Elisha from **G**. 1537
4:38 Elisha came again to **G**: and there was a 1537
Ne 12:29 Also from the house of **G**, and out of 1537
Hos 4:15 come not ye unto **G**, neither go ye up to 1537
9:15 All their wickedness is in **G**, for there I 1537
12:11 they sacrifice bullocks in **G**; yea, 1537
Am 4: 4 at **G** multiply transgression; and bring 1537
5: 5 nor enter into **G**, and pass not to 1537
5: 5 for **G** shall surely go into captivity, 1537
Mic 6: 5 Beor answered him; from Shittim unto **G**; 1537

GILOH (2) [GILONITE]
Jos 15:51 Goshen, and Holon, and **G**; eleven cities 1542
2Sa 15:12 from his city, even from **G**, 1542

GILONITE (2) [GILOH]
2Sa 15:12 Absalom sent for Ahithophel the **G**, 1526
23:34 Eliam the son of Ahithophel the **G**, 1526

GIMZO (1)
2Ch 28:18 **G** also and the villages thereof: 1579

GIN (2) [see also GRIN, GRINS]
Isa 8:14 for a **g** and for a snare to the inhabitants 6341
Am 3: 5 upon the earth, where no **g** is for him? 4170

GINATH (2)
1Ki 16:21 of the people followed Tibni the son of **G**, 1527
16:22 people that followed Tibni the son of **G**: 1527

GINNETHO (1) [GINNETHON]
Ne 12: 4 Iddo, **G**, Abijah, 1599

GINNETHON (2) [GINNETHO]
Ne 10: 6 Daniel, **G**, Baruch, 1599
12:16 Of Iddo, Zechariah; of **G**, Meshullam; 1599

GIRD (27) [GIRDED, GIRDEDST, GIRDETH, GIRDING, GIRDLE, GIRDLES, GIRT, UNDERGIRDING, UNGIRDED]
Ex 29: 5 **g** him with the curious girdle of the ephod: 640
29: 9 thou shalt **g** them with girdles, Aaron and 2296
Jdg 3:16 he did **g** it under his raiment upon his 2296
1Sa 25:13 his men, **G** you on every man his sword. 2296
2Sa 3:31 **g** you with sackcloth, and mourn before 2296
2Ki 4:29 **G** up thy loins, and take my staff in thine 2296
9: 1 **G** up thy loins, and take this box of oil in 2296
Job 38: 3 **G** up now thy loins like a man; for I will 247
40: 7 **G** up thy loins now like a man: I will 247
Ps 45: 3 **G** thy sword upon thy thigh, O most 2296
Isa 8: 9 yourselves, and ye shall be broken in 247
8: 9 yourselves, and ye shall be broken in 247
15: 3 their streets they shall **g** themselves with 2296
32:11 ye bare, and **g** sackcloth upon your loins. 2290
Jer 1:17 Thou therefore **g** up thy loins, and arise, 247
4: 8 For this **g** you with sackcloth, lament 2296
6:26 **g** thee with sackcloth, and wallow 2296
49: 3 daughters of Rabbah, **g** you with sackcloth; 2296
Eze 7:18 They shall also **g** themselves with 2296
27:31 **g** them with sackcloth, and they shall 2296
44:18 shall not **g** themselves with any thing 2296
Joel 1:13 **g** yourselves, and lament, ye priests: 2296
Lk 12:37 that he shall **g** himself, and make them to 4024
17: 8 and **g** thyself, and serve me, till I have 4024
Jn 21:18 and another shall **g** thee, and carry thee 2224
Ac 12: 8 **g** thyself, and bind on thy sandals. 4024
1Pe 1:13 Wherefore **g** up the loins of your mind, 328

GIRDED (32) [GIRD]
Ex 12:11 with your loins **g**, your shoes on your feet, 2296
Lev 8: 7 **g** him with the girdle, and clothed him 2296
8: 7 he **g** him with the curious girdle of 2296
8:13 **g** them with girdles, and put bonnets 2296
16: 4 shall be **g** with a linen girdle, and with 2296
Dt 1:41 ye had **g** on every man his weapons 2296
1Sa 2:18 being a child, **g** with a linen ephod. 2296
17:39 David **g** his sword upon his armour, 2296
25:13 they **g** on every man his sword; 2296
25:13 sword; and David also **g** on his sword: 2296
2Sa 6:14 and David was **g** with a linen ephod. 2296
20: 8 Joab's garment that he had put on was **g** 2296
21:16 he being **g** with a new sword, thought to 2296
22:40 thou hast **g** me with strength to battle: 247
1Ki 18:46 he **g** up his loins, and ran before Ahab to 8151
20:32 So they **g** sackcloth on their loins, 2296
Ne 4:18 every one had his sword **g** by his side, 631
Ps 18:39 For thou hast **g** me with strength unto 247
30:11 off my sackcloth, and **g** me with gladness; 247
65: 6 fast the mountains; being **g** with power: 247
93: 1 strength, wherewith he hath **g** himself; 247
109:19 for a girdle wherewith he is **g** continually. 2296
Isa 45: 5 thee though thou hast not known me: 247
La 2:10 they have **g** themselves with sackcloth: 2296
Eze 16:10 thee about with fine linen, 2280
23:15 **G** with girdles upon their loins, 2289
Da 10: 5 whose loins were **g** with fine gold of 2296
Joel 1: 8 Lament like a virgin **g** with sackcloth for 2296
Lk 12:35 Let your loins be **g** about, and your lights 4024
Jn 13: 4 and took a towel, and **g** himself. 1241
13: 5 them with the towel wherewith he was **g**. 1241
Rev 15: 6 having their breasts **g** with golden girdles. 4024

GIRDEDST (1) [GIRD]
Jn 21:18 thou **g** thyself, and walkedst whither thou 2224

GIRDETH (4) [GIRD]
1Ki 20:11 Let not him that **g** on his harness 2296
Job 12:18 of kings, and **g** their loins with a girdle. 631
Ps 18:32 It is God that **g** me with strength, 247
Pr 31:17 She **g** her loins with strength, 2296

GIRDING (2) [GIRD]
Isa 3:24 instead of a stomacher a **g** of sackcloth; 4228
22:12 and to baldness, and to **g** with sackcloth: 2296

GIRDLE (38) [GIRD]
Ex 28: 4 a broidered coat, a mitre, and a **g**: 73
28: 8 the curious **g** of the ephod, which is 2805
28:27 above the curious **g** of the ephod. 2805
28:28 that it may be above the curious **g** of 2805
28:39 and thou shalt make the **g** of needlework. 73
29: 5 gird him with the curious **g** of the ephod: 2805
39: 5 the curious **g** of his ephod, that was upon 2805
39:20 above the curious **g** of the ephod. 2805
39:21 that it might be above the curious **g** of 73
39:29 a **g** of fine twined linen, and blue, 73
Lev 8: 7 girded him with the **g**, and clothed him 2805
8: 7 he girded him with the curious **g** of 2805
16: 4 and shall be girded with a linen **g**, 73
1Sa 18: 4 his sword, and to his bow, and to his **g**. 2289
2Sa 18:11 given thee ten shekels of silver, and a **g**. 2290
20: 8 upon it a **g** with a sword fastened upon 2290
1Ki 2: 5 put the blood of war upon his **g** that was 2290
2Ki 1: 8 girt with a **g** of leather about his loins. 232
Job 12:18 of kings, and girdeth their loins with a **g**. 232

G

Ps 109:19 for a **g** where *with* he is girded continually. 4206
Isa 3:24 instead of a **g** a rent; and instead of well 2290
 5:27 neither shall the **g** of their loins be loosed, 232
 11: 5 righteousness shall be the **g** of his loins, 232
 11: 5 his loins, and faithfulness the **g** of his reins. 232
 22:21 strengthen him *with* thy **g**, and I will 73
Jer 13: 1 Go and get thee a linen **g**, and put it upon 232
 13: 2 So I got a **g**, according to the word of 232
 13: 4 Take the **g** that thou hast got, which *is* 232
 13: 6 to Euphrates, and take the **g** from thence, 232
 13: 7 took the **g** from the place where I had hid 232
 13: 7 behold, the **g** was marred, it was profitable 232
 13:10 to worship them, shall even be as this **g**, 232
 13:11 For as the **g** cleaveth to the loins of a man, 232
Mt 3: 4 and a leathern **g** about his loins; 2223
Mk 1: 6 and with a **g** of a skin about his loins; 2223
Ac 21:11 took Paul's **g**, and bound *his own* hands 2223
 21:11 Jerusalem bind the man that oweth this **g**, 2223
Rev 1:13 and girt about the paps with a golden **g**. 2223

GIRDLES (6) [GIRD]

Ex 28:40 thou shalt make for them **g**, and bonnets 73
 29: 9 thou shalt gird them *with* **g**, Aaron and 73
Lev 8:13 girded them *with* **g**, and put bonnets upon 73
Pr 31:24 and delivereth **g** unto the merchant. 2289
Eze 23:15 Girded with **g** upon their loins, exceeding 232
Rev 15: 6 having their breasts girded with golden **g**. 2223

GIRGASHITE (2) [GIRGASHITES]

Ge 10:16 the Jebusite, and the Amorite, and the **G**, 1622
1Ch 1:14 Jebusite also, and the Amorite, and the **G**, 1622

GIRGASHITES (5) [GIRGASHITE]

Ge 15:21 and the **G**, and the Jebusites. 1622
Dt 7: 1 the **G**, and the Amorites, 1622
Jos 3:10 **G**, and the Amorites, and the Jebusites. 1622
 24:11 and the **G**, the Hivites, and the Jebusites; 1622
Ne 9: 8 Perizzites, and the Jebusites, and the **G**, 1622

GIRL (1) [GIRLS]

Joel 3: 3 sold a **g** for wine, that they might drink. 3207

GIRLS (1) [GIRL]

Zec 8: 5 boys and **g** playing in the streets thereof. 3207

GIRT (5) [GIRD]

1Sa 2: 4 they that stumbled are **g** with strength. 247
2Ki 1: 8 **g** with a girdle of leather about his loins. 247
Jn 21: 7 he **g** *his* fisher's coat *unto him*, (for he 1241
Eph 6:14 having your loins **g** about with truth, 4024
Rev 1:13 and **g** about the paps with a golden girdle. 4024

GIRZITES See GEZRITES

GISHPA See GISPA

GISPA (1)

Ne 11:21 and Ziha and **G** *were* over the Nethinims. 1658

GITTAH-HEPHER (1) [GATH-HEPHER]

Jos 19:13 thence passeth on along on the east to **G**, 1661

GITTAIM (2)

2Sa 4: 3 the Beerothites fled to **G**, 1664
Ne 11:33 Hazor, Ramah, **G**, 1664

GITTITE (8) [GATH]

2Sa 6:10 aside *into* the house of Obed-edom the **G**. 1663
 6:11 house of Obed-edom the **G** three months: 1663
 15:19 said the king to Ittai the **G**, Wherefore 1663
 15:22 Ittai the **G** passed over, and all his men, 1663
 18: 2 a third part under the hand of Ittai the **G**. 1663
 21:19 slew *the brother of* Goliath the **G**, 1663
1Ch 13:13 aside into the house of Obed-edom the **G**. 1663
 20: 5 slew Lahmi the brother of Goliath the **G**, 1663

GITTITES (2) [GATH]

Jos 13: 3 Eshkalonites, the **G**, and the Ekronites; 1663
2Sa 15:18 and all the Pelethites, and all the **G**, 1663

GITTITH (3)

Ps 8: T To the chief Musician upon **G**, A Psalm of 1665
 81: T To the chief Musician upon **G**, *A Psalm* of 1665
 84: T To the chief Musician upon **G**, A Psalm 1665

GIVE (880) [GAVE, GAVEST, GIFT, GIFTS, GIVEN, GIVER, GIVEST, GIVETH, GIVING, LAWGIVER, THANKSGIVING, THANKSGIVINGS]

Ge 1:15 of the heaven to **g** light upon the earth: 215
 1:17 of the heaven to **g** light upon the earth, 215
 12: 7 and said, Unto thy seed will I **g** this land: 5414
 13:15 thee will I **g** it, and to thy seed for ever. 5414
 13:17 the breadth of it; for I will **g** it unto thee. 5414
 14:21 **G** me the persons, and take the goods to 5414
 15: 2 Lord GOD, what wilt thou **g** me, 5414
 15: 7 to **g** thee this land to inherit it. 5414
 17: 8 I will **g** unto thee, and to thy seed after 5414
 17:16 bless her, and **g** thee a son also of her: 5414
 23: 4 **g** me a possession of a buryingplace with 5414
 23: 9 That he may **g** me the cave of Machpelah, 5414
 23: 9 as much money as it is worth he shall **g** 5414
 23:11 the field I **g** thee, and the cave that *is* 5414
 23:11 and the cave that *is* therein, I **g** it thee; 5414
 23:11 the presence of the sons of my people **g** I 5414
 23:13 saying, But if thou *wilt* **g** *it*, I pray thee, NIH
 23:13 I will **g** *thee* money for the field; take *it* 5414
 24: 7 saying, Unto thy seed will I **g** this land; 5414

Ge 24:14 Drink, and I will **g** thy camels **drink** also: 8248
 24:41 if they **g** not thee *one*, thou shalt be clear 5414
 24:43 **G** me, I pray thee, a little water of
 thy pitcher **to drink**; 8248
 24:46 Drink, and I will **g** thy camels **drink** also: 8248
 26: 3 I will **g** all these countries, and I will 5414
 26: 4 will **g** unto thy seed all these countries; 5414
 27:28 God **g** thee of the dew of heaven, 5414
 28: 4 **g** the blessing of Abraham, to thee, 5414
 28:13 to thee will I **g** it, and to thy seed; 5414
 28:20 will **g** me bread to eat, and raiment to put 5414
 28:22 all that thou shalt **g** me I will surely give 5414
 28:22 will **surely g the tenth** unto thee. 6237+6237
 29:19 Laban said, *It is* better that I **g** her to thee, 5414
 29:19 than that I should **g** her to another man: 5414
 29:21 **G** me my wife, for my days are fulfilled, 3051
 29:26 to **g** the younger before the firstborn. 5414
 29:27 we will **g** thee this also for the service 5414
 30: 1 unto Jacob, **G** me children, or else I die. 3051
 30:14 **G** me, I pray thee, of thy son's mandrakes. 5414
 30:26 **G** *me* my wives and my children, for 5414
 30:28 Appoint me thy wages, and I will **g** *it*. 5414
 30:31 he said, What shall I **g** thee? And Jacob 5414
 30:31 Jacob said, Thou shalt not **g** me any thing: 5414
 34: 8 I pray you **g** her to him to wife. 5414
 34: 9 your daughters unto us, and take our 5414
 34:11 and what ye shall say unto me I will **g**. 5414
 34:12 I will **g** according as ye shall say unto me: 5414
 34:12 say unto me: but **g** me the damsel to wife. 5414
 34:14 our sister to one that is uncircumcised; 5414
 34:16 will we **g** our daughters unto you, and we 5414
 34:21 wives, and let us **g** them our daughters. 5414
 35:12 thee I will **g** it, and to thy seed after thee 5414
 35:12 to thy seed after thee will I **g** the land. 5414
 38: 9 lest that he should **g** seed to his brother. 5414
 38:16 she said, What wilt thou **g** me, that thou 5414
 38:17 she said, Wilt thou **g** *me* a pledge, till 5414
 38:18 he said, What pledge shall I **g** thee? 5414
 41:16 God shall **g** Pharaoh **an answer** of peace. 6030
 42:25 and to **g** them provision for the way: 5414
 42:27 one *of them* opened his sack to **g** his ass 5414
 43:14 Almighty **g** you mercy before the man, 5414
 45:18 I will **g** you the good of the land of Egypt, 5414
 47:15 came unto Joseph, and said, **G** us bread: 3051
 47:16 Joseph said, **G** your cattle; and I will give 3051
 47:16 I will **g** you for your cattle, if money fail. 5414
 47:19 **g** us seed, that we may live, and not die, 5414
 47:24 you shall **g** the fifth *part* unto Pharaoh, 5414
 48: 4 will **g** this land to thy seed after thee *for* 5414
Ex 2: 9 it for me, and I will **g** *thee* thy wages. 5414
 3:21 I will **g** this people favour in the sight of 5414
 5: 7 Ye shall no more **g** the people straw to 5414
 5:10 saith Pharaoh, I will not **g** you straw. 5414
 6: 4 to **g** them the land of Canaan, the land of 5414
 6: 8 *concerning* the which I did swear to **g** it 5414
 6: 8 Jacob; and I will **g** it you *for* an heritage: 5414
 10:25 must **g** us also sacrifices 3027+5414+871.1
 12:25 to the land which the LORD will **g** you, 5414
 13: 5 he sware unto thy fathers to **g** thee, 5414
 13:11 and to thy fathers, and shall **g** it thee, 5414
 13:21 by night in a pillar of fire, to **g** them **light**; 215
 15:26 wilt **g** ear to his commandments, 238
 16: 8 *This shall be,* when the LORD shall **g** you 5414
 17: 2 and said, **G** us water that we may drink. 5414
 18:19 I will **g** thee **counsel**, and God shall be 3289
 21:23 then thou shalt **g** life for life, 5414
 21:30 he shall **g** *for* the ransom of his life 5414
 21:32 he shall **g** unto their master thirty shekels 5414
 21:34 *and* **g** money unto the owner of them; 7725
 22:17 If her father utterly refuse to **g** her unto 5414
 22:29 the firstborn of thy sons shalt thou **g** unto 5414
 22:30 on the eighth day thou shalt **g** it me. 5414
 24:12 I will **g** thee tables of stone, and a law, 5414
 25:16 ark the Testimony which I shall **g** thee. 5414
 25:21 shalt put the Testimony that I shall **g** thee. 5414
 25:22 **g** thee **in commandment** unto the 6680
 25:37 that they may **g** light over against it. 215
 30:12 shall they **g** every man a ransom for his 5414
 30:13 This they shall **g**, every one that passeth 5414
 30:14 above, shall **g** an offering unto the LORD. 5414
 30:15 The rich shall not **g more**, and the poor 7235
 30:15 poor shall not **g less** than half a shekel, 4591
 30:15 when *they* **g** an offering unto the LORD, 5414
 32:13 all this land that I have spoken of will I **g** 5414
 33: 1 to Jacob, saying, Unto thy seed will I **g** it: 5414
 33:14 shall go *with thee,* and I will **g** thee **rest**. 5117
Lev 5:16 fifth *part* thereto, and **g** it unto the priest: 5414
 6: 5 **g** it unto him to whom it appertaineth, 5414
 7:32 right shoulder shall ye **g** unto the priest 5414
 14:34 I **g** to you for a possession, and I put 5414
 15:14 and **g** them unto the priest: 5414
 20:24 and I will **g** it unto you to possess it, 5414
 22:14 shall **g** *it* unto the priest with the holy 5414
 23:10 When ye be come into the land which I **g** 5414
 23:38 which ye **g** unto the LORD. 5414
 25: 2 ye come into the land which I **g** you, 5414
 25:37 Thou shalt not **g** him thy money upon 5414
 25:38 to **g** you the land of Canaan, *and* to be 5414
 25:51 **g** again the price of his redemption out of 7725
 25:52 **g** *him* **again** the price of his redemption. 7725
 26: 4 I will **g** you rain in due season, and the 5414
 26: 6 I will **g** peace in the land, and ye shall lie 5414
 27:23 he shall **g** thine estimation in that day, *as* 5414
Nu 3: 9 thou shalt **g** the Levites unto Aaron and 5414
 3:48 and **g** the money, wherewith the 5414

Nu 5: 7 **g** *it* unto *him* against whom he hath 5414
 6:26 countenance upon thee, and **g** thee peace. 7760
 7: 5 thou shalt **g** them unto the Levites, to 5414
 8: 2 the seven lamps shall **g light** over against 215
 10:29 of which the LORD said, I will **g** it you: 5414
 11: 4 and said, Who shall **g** us flesh **to eat**? 398
 11:13 Whence should I have flesh to **g** unto all 5414
 11:13 saying, **G** us flesh, that we may eat. 5414
 11:18 saying, Who shall **g** us flesh to eat? 398
 11:18 therefore the LORD will **g** you flesh, 5414
 11:21 thou hast said, I will **g** them flesh, that 5414
 13: 2 which I **g** unto the children of Israel: 5414
 14: 8 he will bring us into this land, and **g** it us; 5414
 15: 2 of your habitations, which I **g** unto you, 5414
 15:21 Of the first of your dough ye shall **g** unto 5414
 18:28 ye shall **g** thereof the LORD's heave 5414
 19: 3 ye shall **g** her unto Eleazar the priest, 5414
 20: 8 it shall **g forth** his water, and thou shalt 5414
 20: 8 the congregation and their beasts **drink**. 8248
 20:21 Thus Edom refused to **g** Israel passage 5414
 21:16 people together, and I will **g** them water. 5414
 22:13 for the LORD refuseth to **g** me **leave** to go 5414
 22:18 Balak would **g** me his house full *of* silver 5414
 24:13 Balak would **g** me his house full *of* silver 5414
 25:12 I **g** unto him my covenant of peace: 5414
 26:54 many thou shalt **g** the **more** inheritance, 7235
 26:54 to few thou shalt **g** the **less** inheritance: 4591
 27: 4 Unto us *therefore* a possession among 5414
 27: 7 shalt **surely g** them a possession 5414+5414
 27: 9 shall **g** his inheritance unto his brethren. 5414
 27:10 ye shall **g** his inheritance unto his father's 5414
 27:11 shall **g** his inheritance unto his kinsman 5414
 27:19 and **g** him **a charge** in their sight. 6680
 31:29 their half, and **g** *it* unto Eleazar the priest, 5414
 31:30 *of* beasts, and **g** them unto the Levites, 5414
 32:29 ye shall **g** them the land of Gilead for a 5414
 33:54 the moe ye shall **g** the **more** inheritance, 7235
 33:54 the fewer ye shall **g** the **less** inheritance: 4591
 34:13 which the LORD commanded to **g** unto 5414
 35: 2 that they **g** unto the Levites of 5414
 35: 2 ye shall **g** *also* unto the Levites suburbs 5414
 35: 4 cities, which ye shall **g** unto the Levites, 5414
 35: 6 *among* the cities which ye shall **g** unto 5414
 35: 7 *So* all the cities which ye shall **g** to 5414
 35: 7 them *shall* ye **g** with their suburbs. NIH
 35: 8 the cities which ye shall **g** *shall be* of 5414
 35: 8 *them that have* many ye shall **g many**; 7235
 35: 8 from *them that have* few ye shall **g few**: 4591
 35: 8 every one shall **g** of his cities unto 5414
 35:13 *of these* cities which ye shall **g** six cities 5414
 35:14 Ye shall **g** three cities on *this* side Jordan, 5414
 35:14 cities shall ye **g** in the land of Canaan, 5414
 36: 2 The LORD commanded my lord to **g** 5414
 36: 2 **g** the inheritance of Zelophehad our 5414
Dt 1: 8 **g** unto them and to their seed after them. 5414
 1:20 which the LORD our God doth **g** unto us. 5414
 1:25 land which the LORD our God doth **g** us. 5414
 1:35 which I sware to **g** unto your fathers, 5414
 1:36 him will I **g** the land that he hath trodden 5414
 1:39 them will I **g** it, and they shall possess 5414
 1:45 to your voice, nor **g ear** unto you. 238
 2: 5 for I will not **g** you of their land, no, not 5414
 2: 9 for I will not **g** thee of their land *for* a 5414
 2:19 for I will not **g** thee of the land of 5414
 2:28 **g** me water for money, that I may drink: 5414
 2:31 I have begun to **g** Sihon and his land 5414
 4:38 to **g** thee their land *for* an inheritance, as 5414
 5:31 they may do *them* in the land which I **g** 5414
 6:10 to Jacob, to **g** thee great and goodly cities, 5414
 6:23 to **g** us the land which he sware unto our 5414
 7: 3 daughter thou shalt not **g** unto his son, 5414
 7:13 he sware unto thy fathers to **g** thee. 5414
 10:11 which I sware unto their fathers to **g** unto 5414
 11: 9 sware unto your fathers to **g** unto them 5414
 11:14 That I will **g** *you* the rain of your land in 5414
 11:21 LORD sware unto your fathers to **g** them, 5414
 14:21 thou shalt **g** it unto the stranger that *is* in 5414
 15:10 Thou shalt **surely g** him, 5414+5414
 15:14 hath blessed thee thou shalt **g** unto him. 5414
 16:10 which thou shalt **g** *unto the* LORD thy 5414
 16:17 Every man *shall* **g** as he is able, according NIH
 18: 3 they shall **g** unto the priest the shoulder, 5414
 18: 4 the fleece of thy sheep, shalt thou **g** him. 5414
 19: 8 **g** thee all the land which he promised to 5414
 19: 8 which he promised to **g** unto thy fathers; 5414
 20:16 which the LORD thy God doth **g** thee *for* 5414
 22:14 **g** occasions of speech against her, 7760
 22:19 **g** *them* unto the father of the damsel, 5414
 22:29 the man that lay with her shall **g** unto 5414
 23:14 and to **g up** thine enemies before thee; 5414
 24: 1 **g** it in her hand, and send her out of his 5414
 24:15 At his day thou shalt **g** *him* his hire, 5414
 25: 3 Forty **stripes** he may **g** him, 5221
 26: 3 LORD sware unto our fathers for to **g** us. 5414
 28:11 LORD sware unto thy fathers to **g** thee. 5414
 28:12 the heaven to **g** the rain unto thy land in 5414
 28:55 So that *he* will not **g** to any of them of 5414
 28:65 the LORD shall **g** thee there a trembling 5414
 30:20 to Isaac, and to Jacob, to **g** them. 5414
 31: 5 The LORD shall **g** them **up** before your 5414
 31: 7 hath sworn unto their fathers to **g** them; 5414
 31:14 that I may **g** him **a charge**. 6680
 32: 1 **G ear**, O ye heavens, and I will speak; 238
 32:49 which I **g** unto the children of Israel for a 5414
 32:52 the land which I **g** the children of Israel. 5414

Dt	34: 4 Jacob, saying, I will g it unto thy seed:	5414
Jos	1: 2 unto the land which I do g to them,	5414
	1: 6 I sware unto their fathers to **give**	5414
	2:12 my father's house, and g me a true token:	5414
	5: 6 unto their fathers that he would g us,	5414
	7:19 said unto Achan, My son, g, I pray thee,	7760
	8:18 toward Ai; for I will g it into thine hand.	5414
	9:24 his servant Moses to g you all the land,	5414
	14:12 Now therefore g me this mountain,	5414
	15:16 him will I g Achsah my daughter to wife.	5414
	15:19 Who answered, G me a blessing; for thou	5414
	15:19 a south land; g me also springs of water.	5414
	17: 4 The Lord commanded Moses to g us an	5414
	18: 4 G out from among you three men for	3051
	20: 4 g him a place, that he may dwell among	5414
	21: 2 hand of Moses to g us cities to dwell in,	5414
	21:43 which he sware to g unto their fathers;	5414
Jdg	1:12 him will I g Achsah my daughter to wife.	5414
	1:15 she said unto him, G me a blessing;	3051
	1:15 a south land; g me also springs of water.	5414
	4:19 G me, I pray thee, a little water **to drink**;	8248
	5: 3 g ear, O ye princes; I, *even* I, will sing	238
	7: 2 me to the g the Midianites into their hands,	5414
	8: 5 unto the men of Succoth, G, I pray you,	5414
	8: 6 that we should g bread unto thine army?	5414
	8:15 that we should g bread unto thy men *that*	5414
	8:24 that you would g me every man	5414
	8:25 We will **willingly** g them.	5414+5414
	14:12 I will g you thirty sheets and thirty	5414
	14:13 shall ye g me thirty sheets and	5414
	16: 5 we will g thee every one *of us* eleven	5414
	17:10 I will g thee ten *shekels* of silver by	5414
	20: 7 of Israel; g here your advice and counsel.	3051
	21: 1 There shall not any of us g his daughter	5414
	21: 7 not g them of our daughters to wives?	5414
	21:18 Howbeit we may not g them wives of our	5414
	21:22 for ye did not g unto them at *this* time,	5414
Ru	4:12 of the seed which the Lord shall g thee	5414
1Sa	1:11 wilt g unto thine handmaid a man child,	5414
	1:11 I will g him unto the Lord all the days of	5414
	2:10 he shall g strength unto his king,	5414
	2:15 G flesh to roast for the priest;	5414
	2:16 Nay; but thou shalt g it me now:	5414
	2:20 The Lord g thee seed of this woman for	7760
	2:28 did I g unto the house of thy father all	5414
	2:32 in all *the wealth* which *God* shall g Israel:	3190
	6: 5 ye shall g glory unto the God of Israel:	5414
	6: 8 when they said, G us a king to judge us.	5414
	8:14 best of *them*, and g *them* to his servants.	5414
	8:15 and g to his officers, and to his servants.	5414
	9: 8 *that* will I g to the man of God, to tell us	5414
	10: 4 thee, and g thee two *loaves* of bread,	5414
	11: 3 said unto him, G us seven days' **respite**,	7503
	14:41 G a perfect *lot*. And Saul and	3051
	17:10 g me a man, that we may fight together.	5414
	17:25 will g him his daughter, and make his	5414
	17:44 I will g thy flesh unto the fowls of the air,	5414
	17:46 I will g the carcases of the host of	5414
	17:47 and he will g you into our hands.	5414
	18:17 daughter Merab, her will I g thee to wife:	5414
	18:21 Saul said, I will g him her, that she may	5414
	21: 3 g me five *loaves* of bread in mine hand,	5414
	21: 9 said, *There is* none like that; g it me.	5414
	22: 7 will the son of Jesse g every one of you	5414
	25: 8 g, I pray thee, whatsoever cometh to	5414
	25:11 g it unto men, whom I know not whence	5414
	27: 5 let them g me a place in some town in	5414
	30:22 we will not g them *ought* of the spoil that	5414
2Sa	12:11 g *them* unto thy neighbour, and he shall	1262
	13: 5 g me meat, and dress the meat in my	1262
	14: 8 and I will g **charge** concerning thee.	6680
	16:20 G counsel among you what we shall do.	3051
	21: 6 And the king said, I will g *them*.	5414
	22:50 Therefore I will g **thanks** unto thee,	3034
	23:15 that one would g me **drink** *of* the water	8248
	24:23 did Araunah, *as* a king, g unto the king.	5414
1Ki	1:12 let me, I pray thee, g thee **counsel**,	3289+6098
	2:17 that he g me Abishag the Shunammite to	5414
	3: 5 and God said, Ask what I shall g thee.	5414
	3: 9 G therefore thy servant an understanding	5414
	3:21 I rose in the morning to g my child **suck**,	3243
	3:25 g half to the one, and half to the other.	5414
	3:26 g her the living child, and in no wise slay	5414
	3:27 G her the living child, and in no wise slay	5414
	5: 6 unto thee will I g hire for thy servants	5414
	8:32 to g him according to his righteousness.	5414
	8:36 g rain upon thy land, which thou hast	5414
	8:39 g and to every man according to his ways,	5414
	8:50 g them compassion before them who	5414
	11:11 from thee, and will g it to thy servant.	5414
	11:13 will g one tribe to thy son for David my	5414
	11:31 of Solomon, and will g ten tribes to thee:	5414
	11:35 and will g it thee, *even* ten tribes.	5414
	11:36 unto his son will I g one tribe, that David	5414
	11:38 for David, and will g Israel unto thee.	5414
	12: 9 What **counsel** give ye that we may answer	3289
	13: 7 refresh *thyself*, and I will g thee a reward.	5414
	13: 8 If thou wilt g me half thine house, I will	5414
	14:16 he shall g Israel **up** because of the sins of	5414
	15: 4 his God g him a lamp in Jerusalem,	5414
	17:19 he said unto her, G me thy son. And he	5414
	18:23 Let them therefore g us two bullocks;	5414
	21: 2 unto Naboth, saying, G me thy vineyard,	5414
	21: 2 will g thee for it a better vineyard than it;	5414
	21: 2 I will g thee the worth of it *in* money.	5414

1Ki	21: 3 I should g the inheritance of my fathers	5414
	21: 4 I will not g thee the inheritance of my	5414
	21: 6 unto him, G me thy vineyard for money;	5414
	21: 6 I will g thee *another* vineyard for it:	5414
	21: 7 I will g thee the vineyard of Naboth	5414
	21:15 which he refused to g thee for money.	5414
2Ki	4:42 he said, G unto the people, that they may	5414
	4:43 said again, G the people, that they may	5414
	5:22 g them, I pray thee, a talent of silver,	5414
	6:28 This woman said unto me, G thy son,	5414
	6:29 next day, G thy son, that we may eat him:	5414
	8:19 as he promised him to g to him alway a	5414
	10:15 If it be, g *me* thine hand. And he gave	5414
	11:10 captains over hundreds did the priest g	5414
	14: 9 g thy daughter to my son to wife;	5414
	15:20 *of* silver, to g to the king of Assyria.	5414
	18:23 g **pledges** to my lord the king of Assyria,	6148
	22: 5 let them g it to the doers of the work	5414
	23:35 he taxed the land to g the money	5414
	23:35 his taxation, to g *it* unto Pharaoh-nechoh.	5414
1Ch	11:17 that one would g me **drink** *of* the water	8248
	16: 8 G **thanks** unto the Lord, call upon his	3034
	16:18 Unto thee will I g the land of Canaan,	5414
	16:28 G unto the Lord, ye kindreds of	3051
	16:28 g unto the Lord glory and strength.	3051
	16:29 G unto the Lord the glory due unto his	3051
	16:34 O g **thanks** unto the Lord; for *he is*	3034
	16:35 that *we may* g **thanks** to thy holy name,	3034
	16:41 to g **thanks** to the Lord, because	3034
	21:23 I g *thee* the oxen *also* for burnt offerings,	5414
	21:23 the wheat for the meat offering; I g *it* all.	5414
	22: 9 I will g him **rest** from all his enemies	5117
	22: 9 I will g peace and quietness unto Israel in	5414
	22:12 Only the Lord g thee wisdom and	5414
	22:12 and g thee **charge** concerning Israel,	6680
	25: 3 to g **thanks** and to praise the Lord.	3034
	29:12 to make great, and to g **strength** unto all.	2388
	29:19 unto Solomon my son a perfect heart,	5414
2Ch	1: 7 said unto him, Ask what I shall g thee.	5414
	1:10 G me now wisdom and knowledge, that I	5414
	1:12 I will g thee riches, and wealth, and	5414
	2:10 I will g to thy servants, the hewers	5414
	10: 6 What **counsel** g ye *me* to return answer	3289
	10: 9 What **advice** g ye that we may return	3289
	21: 7 as he promised to g a light to him and to	5414
	24:19 against them: but they would not g **ear**.	238
	25: 9 The Lord is able to g thee much more	5414
	25:18 G thy daughter to my son to wife:	5414
	30:12 Also in Judah the hand of God was to g	5414
	30:24 For Hezekiah king of Judah did g to	7311
	31: 2 to g **thanks**, and to praise in the gates of	3034
	31: 4 Jerusalem to g the portion of the priests	5414
	31:15 office, to g to their brethren by courses,	5414
	31:19 to g portions to all the males among	5414
	32:11 not Hezekiah persuade you to g **over**	5414
	35:12 they might g according to the divisions	5414
Ezr	4:21 G ye now commandment to cause these	7761
	9: 8 and to g us a nail in his holy place,	5414
	9: 8 and g us a little reviving in our bondage.	5414
	9: 9 to g us a reviving, to set up the house of	5414
	9: 9 to g us a wall in Judah and in Jerusalem.	5414
	9:12 g not your daughters unto their sons,	5414
Ne	2: 8 that he may g me timber to make beams	5414
	4: 4 g them for a prey in the land of captivity:	5414
	9: 8 madest a covenant with him to g the land	5414
	9: 8 to g *it, I say,* to his seed,	5414
	9:12 to g them **light** in the way wherein they	215
	9:15 land which thou hadst sworn to g them.	5414
	9:30 yet would they not g **ear**: therefore	238
	10:30 that we would not g our daughters unto	5414
	12:24 against them, to praise *and* to g **thanks**,	3034
	13:25 Ye shall not g your daughters unto	5414
Est	1:19 the king her royal estate unto another	5414
	1:20 all the wives shall g to their husbands	5414
	8: 1 On that day did the king Ahasuerus g	5414
Job	2: 4 all that a man hath will he g for his life.	5414
	3:11 *why* did I *not* g **up the ghost** when I	1478
	6:22 or, G a reward for me of your substance?	7809
	13:19 I hold my tongue, I shall g **up the ghost.**	1478
	32:21 let me g **flattering titles** unto man.	3655
	32:22 For I know not to g **flattering titles;** *in*	3655
	34: 2 ye wise *men*; and g **ear** unto me,	238
Ps	2: 8 I shall g *thee* the heathen *for* thine	5414
	5: 1 G **ear** to my words, O Lord, consider my	238
	6: 5 in the grave who shall g thee **thanks?**	3034
	17: 1 attend unto my cry, g **ear** unto my prayer,	238
	18:49 Therefore will I g **thanks** unto thee,	3034
	28: 4 G them according to their deeds,	5414
	28: 4 g them after the work of their hands;	5414
	29: 1 G unto the Lord, O ye mighty, give unto	3051
	29: 1 g unto the Lord glory and strength.	3051
	29: 2 G unto the Lord the glory due unto his	3051
	29:11 The Lord will g **strength** unto his	5414
	30: 4 g **thanks** at the remembrance of his	3034
	30:12 God, I will g **thanks** unto thee for ever.	3034
	35:18 I will g thee **thanks** in the great	3034
	37: 4 he shall g thee the desires of thine heart.	5414
	39:12 O Lord, and g **ear** unto my cry;	238
	49: 1 g **ear**, all ye inhabitants of the world:	238
	49: 7 brother, nor g to God a ransom for him:	5414
	51:16 else would I g *it*: thou delightest not in	5414
	54: 2 O God; g **ear** to the words of my mouth.	238
	55: 1 G **ear** to my prayer, O God; and hide not	238
	57: 7 heart is fixed: I will sing and g **praise.**	2167

Ps	60:11 G us help from trouble: for vain *is* the	3051
	72: 1 G the king thy judgments, O God,	5414
	75: 1 Unto thee, O God, do we g **thanks**,	3034
	75: 1 give thanks, *unto thee* do we g **thanks**	3034
	78: 1 G **ear**, O my people, to my law: incline	238
	78:20 streams overflowed; can he g bread also?	5414
	79:13 sheep of thy pasture will g thee **thanks**	3034
	80: 1 G **ear**, O Shepherd of Israel, thou that	238
	84: 8 my prayer: g **ear**, O God of Jacob. Selah.	238
	84:11 the Lord will g grace and glory: no good	5414
	85:12 Yea, the Lord shall g *that which is* good;	5414
	86: 6 G **ear**, O Lord, unto my prayer;	238
	86:16 g thy strength unto thy servant,	5414
	91:11 he shall g his angels **charge** over thee,	6680
	92: 1 *It is* a good *thing* to g **thanks** unto	3034
	94:13 *thou* mayest g him **rest** from the days	8252
	96: 7 G unto the Lord, O ye kindreds of	3051
	96: 7 g unto the Lord glory and strength.	3051
	96: 8 G unto the Lord the glory due unto his	3051
	97:12 g **thanks** at the remembrance of his	3034
	104:11 They g **drink** to every beast of the field:	8248
	104:27 *thou* mayest g *them* their meat in due	5414
	105: 1 O g **thanks** unto the Lord; call upon his	3034
	105:11 Unto thee will I g the land of Canaan,	5414
	105:39 a covering; and fire to g **light** in the night.	215
	106: 1 O g **thanks** unto the Lord; for *he is*	3034
	106:47 to g **thanks** unto thy holy name,	3034
	107: 1 O g **thanks** unto the Lord, for *he is*	3034
	108: 1 I will sing and g **praise**, even with my	2167
	108:12 G us help from trouble: for vain *is* the	3051
	109: 4 my adversaries: but I g *myself unto* prayer.	NIH
	111: 6 that he may g them the heritage of	5414
	115: 1 not unto us, but unto thy name g glory,	5414
	118: 1 O g **thanks** unto the Lord; for *he is*	3034
	118:29 O g **thanks** unto the Lord; for *he is*	3034
	119:34 G me **understanding**, and I shall keep	995
	119:62 At midnight I will rise to g **thanks** unto	3034
	119:73 g me **understanding**, that I may learn thy	995
	119:125 g me **understanding**, that I may know	995
	119:144 g me **understanding**, and I shall live.	995
	119:169 g me **understanding** according to thy	995
	122: 4 to g **thanks** unto the name of the Lord.	3034
	132: 4 I will not g sleep to mine eyes,	5414
	136: 1 O g **thanks** unto the Lord; for *he is*	3034
	136: 2 O g **thanks** unto the God of gods: for his	3034
	136: 3 O g **thanks** to the Lord of lords: for his	3034
	136:26 O g **thanks** unto the God of heaven: for	3034
	140:13 Surely the righteous shall g **thanks** unto	3034
	141: 1 g **ear** unto my voice, when I cry unto	238
	143: 1 O Lord, g **ear** to my supplications;	238
Pr	1: 4 To g subtilty to the simple, to the young	5414
	3:28 and come again, and to morrow I will g;	5414
	4: 2 For I g you good doctrine, forsake you	5414
	4: 9 She shall g to thine head an ornament of	5414
	5: 9 Lest thou g thine honour unto others,	5414
	6: 4 G not sleep to thine eyes, nor slumber to	5414
	6:31 he shall g all the substance of his house.	5414
	9: 9 G **instruction** to a wise *man*, and he will	5414
	23:26 g me thine heart, and let thine eyes	5414
	25:21 enemy *be* hungry, g him bread **to eat**;	398
	25:21 if he be thirsty, g him water **to drink**:	8248
	29:15 The rod and reproof g wisdom: but a	5414
	29:17 Correct thy son, and he shall g thee **rest**;	5117
	29:17 yea, he shall g delight unto thy soul.	5414
	30: 8 g me neither poverty nor riches; feed me	5414
	30:15 hath two daughters, *crying*, G, give.	3051
	30:15 hath two daughters, *crying*, Give, g.	3051
	31: 3 G not thy strength unto women, nor thy	5414
	31: 6 G strong drink unto him that is ready to	5414
	31:31 G her of the fruit of her hands; and let her	5414
Ecc	2: 3 I sought in mine heart to g myself unto	4900
	2:26 that he may g to *him that is* good before	5414
	5: 1 to hear, than to g the sacrifice of fools:	5414
	11: 2 G a portion to seven, and also to eight;	5414
SS	2:13 the vines *with* the tender grape g a *good*	5414
	7:12 bud forth: there will I g thee my loves.	5414
	7:13 The mandrakes g a smell, and at our gates	5414
	8: 7 if a man would g all the substance of his	5414
Isa	1: 2 Hear, O heavens, and g **ear**, O earth:	238
	1:10 g **ear** unto the law of our God, ye people	238
	3: 4 I will g children *to be* their princes,	5414
	7:14 Therefore the Lord himself shall g you a	5414
	7:22 the abundance of milk *that* they shall g	6213
	8: 9 pieces; and g **ear**, all ye of far countries:	238
	10: 6 people of my wrath will I g him **a charge**,	6680
	13:10 the constellations thereof shall not g their	1984
	14: 3 Lord shall g thee **rest** from thy sorrow,	5117
	19: 4 the Egyptians will I g **over** into the hand	5534
	28:23 G ye **ear**, and hear my voice; hearken,	238
	30:20 *though* the Lord g you the bread of	5414
	30:23 shall he g the rain of thy seed, that thou	5414
	32: 9 careless daughters, g **ear** unto my speech.	238
	36: 8 Now therefore g **pledges**, I pray thee,	6148
	36: 8 and I will g thee two thousand horses,	5414
	41:27 I will g to Jerusalem one that bringeth	5414
	42: 6 and g thee for a covenant of the people,	5414
	42: 8 my glory will I not g to another, neither	5414
	42:12 Let them g glory unto the Lord,	7760
	42:23 Who among you will g **ear** to this? *who*	238
	43: 4 therefore will I g men for thee,	5414
	43: 6 G **up**; and to the south, Keep not back:	5414
	43:20 because I g waters in the wilderness,	6148
	43:20 to g **drink** to my people, my chosen.	8248
	45: 3 I will g thee the treasures of darkness,	5414
	48:11 and I will not g my glory unto another.	5414

G

G

Isa	49: 6	will also **g** thee for a light to the Gentiles,	5414
	49: 8	and **g** thee for a covenant of the people,	5414
	49:20	for me: **g** place to me that I may dwell.	5066
	51: 4	people; and **g** ear unto me, O my nation:	238
	55:10	that it may **g** seed to the sower,	5414
	56: 5	Even unto them will I **g** in mine house	5414
	56: 5	I will **g** them an everlasting name, that	5414
	60:19	for brightness shall the moon **g** light	215
	61: 3	to **g** unto them beauty for ashes, the oil of	5414
	62: 7	**g** him no rest, till he establish, and till he	5414
	62: 8	I will no more **g** thy corn *to be* meat	5414
Jer	3:15	I will **g** you pastors according to mine	5414
	3:19	the children, and **g** thee a pleasant land,	5414
	4:12	now also will I **g** sentence against them.	1696
	4:16	**g** out their voice against the cities of	5414
	6:10	and **g** warning, that they may hear?	5749
	8:10	Therefore will I **g** their wives unto others,	5414
	9:15	and **g** them water of gall **to drink**.	8248
	11: 5	to **g** them a land flowing with milk and	5414
	13:15	Hear ye, and **g** ear; be not proud.	238
	13:16	**G** glory to the Lord your God, before he	5414
	14:13	I will **g** you assured peace in this place.	5414
	14:22	can the heavens **g** showers? *art* not thou	5414
	15:13	thy treasures will I **g** to the spoil without	5414
	16: 7	**g** them the cup of consolation **to drink**	8248
	17: 3	will **g** thy substance *and* all thy treasures	5414
	17:10	to **g** every man according to his ways,	5414
	18:18	and let us not **g** heed to any of his words.	7181
	18:19	**G** heed to me, O Lord, and hearken to	7181
	19: 7	their carcases will I **g** to be meat for	5414
	20: 4	I will **g** all Judah into the hand of the king	5414
	20: 5	I will **g** into the hand of their enemies,	5414
	22:25	will **g** thee into the hand of them that seek	5414
	24: 7	I will **g** them a heart to know me, that I	5414
	24: 8	So will I **g** Zedekiah the king of Judah,	5414
	25:30	shall **g** a shout, as they tread	1959+6030
	25:31	**g** them that *are* wicked to the sword,	5414
	26:24	that *they* should not **g** him into the hand	5414
	29: 6	**g** your daughters to husbands, that they	5414
	29:11	and not of evil, to **g** you an expected end.	5414
	30:16	all that prey upon thee will I **g** for a prey.	5414
	32: 3	I *will* **g** this city into the hand of the king	5414
	32:19	to **g** every one according to his ways,	5414
	32:22	thou didst swear to their fathers to **g**	5414
	32:28	I *will* **g** this city into the hand of	5414
	32:39	I will **g** them one heart, and one way,	5414
	34: 2	I *will* **g** this city into the hand of the king	5414
	34:18	I will **g** the men that have transgressed my	5414
	34:20	I will even **g** them into the hand of their	5414
	34:21	his princes will I **g** into the hand of their	5414
	35: 2	the chambers, and **g** them wine **to drink**.	8248
	37:21	that *they* should **g** him daily a piece of	5414
	38:15	if I **g** thee **counsel**, wilt thou not hearken	3289
	38:16	neither will I **g** thee into the hand of these	5414
	44:30	I will **g** Pharaoh-hophra king of Egypt into	5414
	45: 5	thy life will I **g** unto thee for a prey in all	5414
	48: 9	**G** wings unto Moab, that it may flee and	5414
	50:34	that he may **g** **rest** to the land,	7280
La	2:18	**g** thyself no rest; let not the apple of thine	5414
	3:65	**G** them sorrow of heart, thy curse unto	5414
Eze	4: 3	breast, they **g** **suck** to their young ones:	3243
	2: 8	open thy mouth, and eat that I **g** thee.	5414
	3: 3	fill thy bowels with this roll that I **g** thee.	5414
	3:17	mouth, and **g** them **warning** from me.	2094
	7:21	I will **g** it into the hands of the strangers	5414
	11: 2	and a wicked **counsel** in this city:	3289+6098
	11:17	and I will **g** you the land of Israel.	5414
	11:19	I will **g** them one heart, and I will put a	5414
	11:19	flesh, and will **g** them a heart of flesh.	5414
	15: 6	so will I **g** the inhabitants of Jerusalem.	5414
	16:33	They **g** gifts to all whores: but thou givest	5414
	16:36	children, which thou didst **g** unto them;	5414
	16:38	I will **g** thee blood in fury and jealousy.	5414
	16:39	I will also **g** thee into their hand,	5414
	16:41	and thou also shalt **g** no hire any more.	5414
	16:61	I will **g** them unto thee for daughters,	5414
	17:15	that *they* might **g** him horses and	5414
	20:28	the which I lifted up mine hand to **g** it to	5414
	20:42	lifted up mine hand to **g** it to your fathers.	5414
	21:11	to **g** it into the hand of the slayer.	5414
	21:27	come whose right it is; and I will **g** it *him.*	5414
	23:31	therefore will I **g** her cup into thine hand.	5414
	23:46	*will* **g** them to be removed and spoiled.	5414
	25:10	and will **g** them in possession,	5414
	29:19	I *will* **g** the land of Egypt unto	5414
	29:21	I will **g** thee the opening of the mouth in	5414
	32: 7	and the moon shall not **g** her **light**.	215+216
	33:15	**g** again that he had robbed, walk in	7999
	33:27	him that *is* in the open field will I **g** to	5414
	36:26	A new heart also will I **g** you, and a new	5414
	36:26	flesh, and I will **g** you a heart of flesh.	5414
	39: 4	I will **g** thee unto the ravenous birds of	5414
	39:11	*that* I will **g** unto Gog a place there of	5414
	43:19	thou shalt **g** to the priests the Levites that	5414
	44:28	ye shall **g** them no possession in Israel:	5414
	44:30	ye shall also **g** unto the priest the first of	5414
	45: 8	*rest* of the land shall they **g** to the house	5414
	45:13	ye shall **g** the **sixth part** of an ephah of a	8341
	45:16	All the people of the land shall **g**	413+1961
	45:17	it shall be the prince's part *to g* burnt	NIH
	46: 5	for the lambs as he shall be able to **g**,	4991
	46:11	to the lambs as he is able to **g**, and a hin	4991
	46:16	If the prince **g** a gift unto any of his sons,	5414
	46:17	if he **g** a gift of his inheritance to one of	5414
	46:18	he shall **g** his sons **inheritance** out of his	5157

Eze	47:14	up mine hand to **g** it unto your fathers:	5414
	47:23	there shall ye **g** *him* his inheritance,	5414
Da	1:12	let them **g** us pulse to eat, and water to	5414
	2:16	desired of the king that he would **g** him	5415
	5:17	to thyself, and **g** thy rewards to another;	3052
	6: 2	that the princes might **g** accounts unto	3052
	8:13	to **g** both the sanctuary and the host to be	5414
	9:22	I am now come forth to **g** thee **skill** and	7919
	11:17	he shall **g** him the daughter of women,	5414
	11:21	to whom they shall not **g** the honour of	5414
Hos	2: 5	that **g** me my bread and my water,	5414
	2:15	I will **g** her her vineyards from thence,	5414
	4:18	her rulers *with* shame do love, **G** ye.	3051
	5: 1	Israel; and **g** ye **ear**, O house of the king;	238
	9:14	**G** them, O Lord: what wilt thou give?	5414
	9:14	wilt thou **g**? give them a miscarrying	5414
	9:14	**g** them a miscarrying womb and	5414
	11: 8	How shall I **g** thee **up**, Ephraim? *how*	5414
	13:10	thou saidst, **G** me a king and princes?	5414
Joel	1: 2	Hear this, ye old men, and **g** **ear**, all ye	238
	2:17	and **g** not thine heritage to reproach,	5414
Mic	1:14	Therefore shalt thou **g** presents to	5414
	5: 3	will he **g** them **up**, until the time	5414
	6: 7	shall I **g** my firstborn *for* my transgression,	5414
	6:14	*that* which thou deliverest will I **g** **up** to	5414
Hag	2: 9	in this place will I **g** peace, saith	5414
Zec	3: 7	I will **g** thee places to walk among these	5414
	8:12	the vine shall **g** her fruit, and the ground	5414
	8:12	the ground shall **g** her increase,	5414
	8:12	and the heavens shall **g** their dew;	5414
	10: 1	**g** them showers of rain, to every one grass	5414
	11:12	them, If ye think good, **g** me my price;	3051
Mal	2: 2	to **g** glory unto my name, saith the Lord	5414
Mt	4: 6	He shall **g** his angels **charge** concerning	1781
	4: 9	unto him, All these *things* will I **g** thee,	1325
	5:31	let him **g** her a writing of divorcement:	1325
	5:42	**G** to him that asketh thee, and from him	1325
	6:11	**G** us this day our daily bread.	1325
	7: 6	that which is holy unto the dogs,	1325
	7: 9	his son ask bread, will he **g** him a stone?	1929
	7:10	if he ask a fish, will he **g** him a serpent?	1929
	7:11	know how to **g** good gifts unto your	1325
	7:11	**g** good *things* to them that ask him?	1325
	9:24	said unto them, **G** place: for the maid is	402
	10: 8	devils: freely ye have received, freely **g**.	1325
	10:42	whosoever shall **g** **to drink** unto one	4222
	11:28	are heavy laden, and I will **g** you **rest**.	373
	12:36	they shall **g** account thereof in the day of	591
	14: 7	he promised with an oath to **g**	1325
	14: 8	**G** me here John Baptist's head in a	1325
	14:16	They need not depart; **g** ye them to eat.	1325
	16:19	And I will **g** unto thee the keys of	1325
	16:26	what shall a man **g** in exchange for his	1325
	17:27	take, and **g** unto them for me and thee.	1325
	19: 7	command to **g** a writing of divorcement,	1325
	19:21	and **g** to the poor, and thou shalt have	1325
	20: 4	and whatsoever is right I will **g** you.	1325
	20: 8	Call the labourers, and **g** them *their* hire,	591
	20:14	I will **g** unto this last, even as unto thee.	1325
	20:23	is not mine to **g**, but *it shall be given to*	1325
	20:28	and to **g** his life a ransom for many.	1325
	22:17	it lawful to **g** tribute unto Cesar, or not?	1325
	24:19	and to them that **g** **suck** in those days.	2337
	24:29	and the moon shall not **g** her light,	1325
	24:45	to **g** them meat in due season?	1325
	25: 8	said unto the wise, **G** us of your oil;	1325
	25:28	and **g** it unto him which hath ten talents.	1325
	26:15	And said *unto them,* What will ye **g** me,	1325
	26:53	he shall presently **g** me more than twelve	3936
Mk	6:22	whatsoever thou wilt, and I will **g** *it* thee.	1325
	6:23	I will **g** *it* thee, unto the half of my	1325
	6:25	that thou **g** me by and by in a charger	1325
	6:37	and said unto them, **G** ye them to eat.	1325
	6:37	pennyworth of bread, and **g** them to eat?	1325
	8:37	Or what shall a man **g** in exchange for his	1325
	9:41	**g** you a cup of water **to drink** in my name	4222
	10:21	and **g** to the poor, and thou shalt have	1325
	10:40	and on my left hand is not mine to **g**;	1325
	10:45	and to **g** his life a ransom for many.	1325
	12: 9	and will **g** the vineyard unto others.	1325
	12:14	Is it lawful to **g** tribute to Cesar, or not?	1325
	12:15	Shall we **g**, or shall we not give? But he,	1325
	12:15	Shall we **g**, or shall we not **g**? But he,	1325
	13:17	and to them that **g** **suck** in those days.	2337
	13:24	and the moon shall not **g** her light,	1325
	14:11	were glad, and promised to **g** him money.	1325
Lk	1:32	the Lord God shall **g** unto him the throne	1325
	1:77	To **g** knowledge of salvation unto his	1325
	1:79	To **g** **light** to them that sit in darkness and	2014
	4: 6	All this power will I **g** thee, and the glory	1325
	4: 6	unto me; and to whomsoever I will I **g** it.	1325
	4:10	he shall **g** his angels **charge** over thee,	1781
	6:30	**G** to every man that asketh of thee;	1325
	6:38	**G**, and it shall be given you;	1325
	6:38	over, shall men **g** into your bosom.	1325
	8:55	and he commanded to **g** her meat.	1325
	9:13	But he said unto them, **G** ye them to eat.	1325
	10: 7	drinking such *things* as they **g**:	3588+3844
	10:19	I **g** unto you power to tread on serpents	1325
	11: 3	**G** us day by day our daily bread.	1325
	11: 7	with me in bed; I cannot rise and **g** thee?	1325
	11: 8	Though he will not rise and **g** him,	1325
	11: 8	will rise and **g** him as many as he needeth.	1325
	11:11	you that is a father, will he **g** him a stone?	1929
	11:11	a fish, will he for a fish **g** him a serpent?	1929

Lk	11:13	know how to **g** good gifts unto your	1325
	11:13	the Holy Spirit to them that ask him?	1325
	11:36	shining of a candle doth **g** thee **light**.	5461
	11:41	But rather **g** alms of *such things as you*	1325
	12:32	for it is your Father's good pleasure to **g**	1325
	12:33	Sell that ye have, and **g** alms;	1325
	12:42	to **g** them their portion of meat in due	1325
	12:51	Suppose ye that I am come to **g** peace on	1325
	12:58	**g** diligence that *thou* mayest be delivered	1325
	14: 9	and say to thee, **G** this *man* place;	1325
	15:12	**g** me the portion of goods that falleth to	1325
	16: 2	**g** an account of thy stewardship; for thou	591
	16:12	who shall **g** you that which is your own?	1325
	17:18	are not found that returned to **g** glory	1325
	18:12	in the week, I **g** tithes of all that I possess.	586
	19: 8	Lord, the half of my goods I **g** to the poor;	1325
	19:24	and **g** it to him that hath ten pounds.	1325
	20:10	that they should **g** him of the fruit of	1325
	20:16	and shall **g** the vineyard to others.	1325
	20:22	Is it lawful for us to **g** tribute unto Cesar,	1325
	21:15	For I will **g** you a mouth and wisdom,	1325
	21:23	and to them that **g** **suck**, in those days,	2337
	22: 5	glad, and covenanted to **g** him money.	1325
	23: 2	forbidding to **g** tribute to Cesar, saying	1325
Jn	1:22	we may **g** an answer to them that sent	1325
	4: 7	Jesus saith unto her, **G** me to drink.	1325
	4:10	who it is that saith to thee, **G** me to drink;	1325
	4:14	water that I shall **g** him shall never thirst;	1325
	4:14	the water that I shall **g** him shall be in him	1325
	4:15	Sir, **g** me this water, that I thirst not,	1325
	6:27	which the Son of man shall **g** unto you:	1325
	6:34	unto him, Lord, evermore **g** us this bread.	1325
	6:51	and the bread that I will **g** is my flesh,	1325
	6:51	which I will **g** for the life of the world.	1325
	6:52	How can this man **g** us *his* flesh to eat?	1325
	7:19	Did not Moses **g** you the law, and *yet*	1325
	9:24	and said unto him, **G** God the praise:	1325
	10:28	And I **g** unto them eternal life;	1325
	11:22	thou wilt ask of God, God will **g** *it* thee.	1325
	13:26	He it is, to whom I shall **g** a sop,	1929
	13:29	or that he should **g** something to the poor.	1325
	13:34	A new commandment I **g** unto you, That	1325
	14:16	and he shall **g** you another Comforter,	1325
	14:27	I leave with you, my peace I **g** unto you:	1325
	14:27	not as the world giveth, **g** I unto you.	1325
	15:16	the Father in my name, he may **g** it you.	1325
	16:23	the Father in my name, he will **g** *it* you.	1325
	17: 2	that he should **g** eternal life to as many as	1325
Ac	3: 6	have I none; but such as I have **g** I thee:	1325
	5:31	for to **g** repentance to Israel,	1325
	6: 4	But we will **g** ourselves **continually** to	4342
	7: 5	yet he promised that *he* would **g** it to him	1325
	7:38	who received the lively oracles to **g** unto	1325
	8:19	Saying, **G** me also this power, that on	1325
	10:43	To him **g** all the prophets **witness**,	3140
	13:16	Israel, and *ye* that fear God, **g** **audience**.	191
	13:34	I will **g** you the sure mercies of David.	1325
	19:40	there being no cause whereby we may **g**	591
	20:32	to **g** you an inheritance among all them	1325
	20:35	It is more blessed to **g** than to receive.	1325
Ro	8:32	shall he not with him also **freely** **g** us	5483
	12:19	but *rather* **g** place unto wrath:	1325
	12:20	feed him; if he thirst, **g** him **drink**:	4222
	14:12	every one of us shall **g** account of himself	1325
	16: 4	unto whom not only I **g** **thanks**, but also	2168
1Co	7: 5	that ye may **g** yourselves to fasting and	4980
	7:25	yet I **g** *my* judgment, as one that hath	1325
	10:30	spoken of for *that for* which I **g** thanks?	2168
	10:32	**G** none offence, neither to the Jews, nor	1096
	12: 3	Wherefore I **g** you **to understand**, that	1107
	13: 3	and though I **g** my body to be burned,	3860
	14: 7	except they **g** a distinction in the sounds,	1325
	14: 8	For if the trumpet **g** an uncertain sound,	1325
2Co	4: 6	**g** the light of the knowledge of the glory	NIG
	5:12	but **g** you occasion to glory on our behalf,	1325
	8:10	And herein I **g** *my* advice: for this is	1325
	9: 7	in *his* heart, *so let him* **g**; not grudgingly,	NIG
Eph	1:16	Cease not to **g** **thanks** for you,	2168
	1:17	may **g** unto you the spirit of wisdom and	1325
	4:27	Neither **g** place to the devil.	1325
	4:28	he may have to **g** to him that needeth.	3330
	5:14	the dead, and Christ shall **g** thee **light**.	2017
Col	3:16	We **g** **thanks** to God and the Father of	2168
	4: 1	**g** unto *your* servants that which is just	3930
1Th	1: 2	We **g** **thanks** to God always for you all,	2168
	5:18	In every thing **g** **thanks**: for this *is* the	2168
2Th	2:13	But we are bound to **g** **thanks** alway to	2168
	3:16	the Lord of peace himself **g** you peace	1325
1Ti	1: 4	Neither **g** **heed** to fables and	4337
	4:13	Till I come, **g** **attendance** to reading,	4337
	4:15	Meditate upon these *things*; **g** thyself	1510
	5: 7	And these *things* **g** in charge, that they	3853
	5:14	**g** none occasion to the adversary to speak	1325
	6:13	I **g** thee **charge** in the sight of God,	3853
2Ti	1:16	The Lord **g** mercy unto the house of	1325
	2: 7	Lord **g** thee understanding in all *things.*	1325
	2:25	God peradventure will **g** them repentance	1325
	4: 8	the righteous judge, shall **g** me at that day:	591
Heb	2: 1	**g** the more earnest **heed** to the *things*	4337
	3:17	as they that must **g** account, that they may	1325
Jas	2:16	notwithstanding ye **g** them not those	1325
1Pe	3:15	be ready always to **g** an answer to every	NIG
	5: 5	Who **g** account to him that is ready	591
2Pe	1:10	**g** **diligence** to make your calling and	4704
1Jn	5:16	he shall **g** him life for them that sin not	1325

Rev	2: 7	To him that overcometh will I **g** to eat of	1325
	2:10	death, and I will **g** thee a crown of life.	1325
	2:17	To him that overcometh will I **g** to eat of	1325
	2:17	and will **g** him a white stone, and in	1325
	2:23	I will **g** unto every one of you according	1325
	2:26	to him will I **g** power over the nations:	1325
	2:28	And I will **g** him the morning star.	1325
	4: 9	when *those* beasts **g** glory and honour	1325
	10: 9	and said unto him, **G** me the little book.	1325
	11: 3	I will *power* unto my two witnesses,	1325
	11:17	Saying, We **g** thee **thanks**, O Lord God	2168
	11:18	that *thou* shouldest **g** reward unto thy	1325
	13:15	he had power to **g** life unto the image	1325
	14: 7	loud voice, Fear God, and **g** glory to him;	1325
	16: 9	and they repented not to **g** him glory.	1325
	16:19	to **g** unto her the cup of the wine of	1325
	17:13	and shall **g** their power and strength unto	1239
	17:17	and **g** their kingdom unto the beast,	1325
	18: 7	so much torment and sorrow **g** her:	1325
	19: 7	be glad and rejoice, and **g** honour to him:	1325
	21: 6	I will **g** unto him that is athirst of	1325
	22:12	to **g** every man according as his work shall	591

GIVE LIFE See QUICKEN

GIVE TO NEEDY See ALMS

GIVEN (498) [GIVE]

Ge	1:29	I have **g** you every herb bearing seed,	5414
	1:30	*is* life, *I have* **g** every green herb for meat:	NIH
	9: 3	even as the green herb have I **g** you all	5414
	15: 3	Behold, to me thou hast **g** no seed:	5414
	15:18	saying, Unto thy seed have I **g** this land,	5414
	16: 5	I have **g** my maid into thy bosom;	5414
	20:16	I have **g** thy brother a thousand *pieces of*	5414
	21: 7	that Sarah should have **g** children **suck**?	3243
	24:35	hath **g** him flocks, and herds, and silver,	5414
	24:36	and unto him hath he **g** all that he hath.	5414
	27:37	his brethren have I **g** to him for servants;	5414
	29:33	he hath therefore **g** me this *son* also:	5414
	30: 6	heard my voice, and hath **g** me a son:	5414
	30:18	God hath **g** me my hire, because I have	5414
	30:18	I have **g** my maiden to my husband:	5414
	31: 9	cattle of your father, and **g** *them* to me.	5414
	33: 5	children which God hath **graciously g**	2603
	38:14	and she was not **g** unto him to wife.	5414
	43:23	hath **g** you treasure in your sacks:	5414
	48: 9	whom God hath **g** me in this *place.*	5414
	48:22	Moreover I have **g** to thee one portion	5414
Ex	5:16	*There is* no straw **g** unto thy servants,	5414
	5:18	for there shall no straw be **g** you, yet shall	5414
	16:15	This *is* the bread which the Lord hath **g**	5414
	16:29	for that the Lord hath **g** you the sabbath,	5414
	21: 4	If his master have **g** him a wife,	5414
	31: 6	I, behold, I have **g** with him Aholiab,	5414
Lev	6:17	I have **g** it *unto them for* their portion of	5414
	7:34	have **g** them unto Aaron the priest and	5414
	7:36	Which the Lord commanded to be **g**	5414
	10:14	*which* are **g** out of the sacrifices of peace	5414
	10:17	*God* hath **g** it you to bear the iniquity of	5414
	17:11	I have **g** it to you upon the altar to make	5414
	19:20	not at all redeemed, nor freedom **g** her;	5414
	20: 3	he hath **g** of his seed unto Molech;	5414
Nu	3: 9	they are **wholly g** unto him out of	5414+5414
	8:16	they are **wholly g** unto me from	5414+5414
	8:19	I have **g** the Levites *as* a gift to Aaron and	5414
	16:14	or **g** us inheritance of fields and vineyards:	5414
	18: 6	to you *they are* **g** *as* a gift for the Lord,	5414
	18: 7	I have **g** your priest's office *unto you as* a	5414
	18: 8	also have **g** thee the charge of mine heave	5414
	18: 8	unto thee have I **g** them by reason of	5414
	18:11	I have **g** them unto thee, and to thy sons	5414
	18:12	offer unto the Lord, them have I **g** thee.	5414
	18:19	have I **g** thee, and thy sons and thy	5414
	18:21	I have **g** the children of Levi all the tenth	5414
	18:24	I have **g** to the Levites to inherit:	5414
	18:26	have **g** you from them for your inheritance	5414
	20:12	into the land which I have **g** them.	5414
	20:24	which I have **g** unto the children of Israel,	5414
	21:29	he hath **g** his sons that escaped,	5414
	26:54	to every one shall his inheritance be **g**	5414
	26:62	there was no inheritance **g** them among	5414
	27:12	see the land which I have **g** unto	5414
	32: 5	let this land be **g** unto thy servants for a	5414
	32: 7	the land which the Lord hath **g** them?	5414
	32: 9	into the land which the Lord hath **g** them.	5414
	33:53	for I have **g** you the land to possess it.	5414
Dt	1: 3	had **g** him **in commandment** unto them;	6680
	2: 5	I have **g** mount Seir unto Esau *for* a	5414
	2: 9	I have **g** Ar unto the children of Lot *for* a	5414
	2:19	I have **g** it unto the children of Lot *for* a	5414
	2:24	I have **g** into thine hand Sihon the Amorite,	5414
	3:18	The Lord your God hath **g** you this land	5414
	3:19	shall abide in your cities which I have **g**	5414
	3:20	Until the Lord have **g** rest unto your	5117
	3:20	your God hath **g** them beyond Jordan:	5414
	3:20	unto his possession, which I have **g** you.	5414
	8:10	for the good land which he hath **g** thee.	5414
	9:23	and possess the land which I have **g** you;	5414
	12:15	the Lord thy God which he hath **g** thee:	5414
	12:21	of thy flock, which the Lord hath **g** thee,	5414
	13:12	which the Lord thy God hath **g** thee to	5414
	16:17	The Lord thy God which he hath **g** thee.	5414
	20:14	which the Lord thy God hath **g** thee.	5414
	22:17	hath **g** occasions of speech *against* her,	7760

Dt	25:19	when the Lord thy God hath **g** thee **rest**	5117
	26: 9	hath **g** us this land, *even* a land that	5414
	26:10	the land, which thou, O Lord, hast **g** me.	5414
	26:11	the Lord thy God hath **g** thee,	5414
	26:12	hast **g** *it* unto the Levite, the stranger,	5414
	26:13	also have **g** them unto the Levite,	5414
	26:14	*use,* nor **g** *ought* thereof for the dead:	5414
	26:15	and the land which thou hast **g** us,	5414
	28:31	thy sheep *shall be* **g** unto thine enemies,	5414
	28:32	thy daughters *shall be* **g** unto another	5414
	28:52	which the Lord thy God hath **g** thee.	5414
	28:53	which the Lord thy God hath **g** thee,	5414
	29: 4	Yet the Lord hath not **g** you a heart to	5414
	29:26	and *whom* he had not **g** unto them:	2505
Jos	1: 3	that have I **g** unto you, as I said unto	5414
	1:13	The Lord your God hath **g** you **rest**,	5117
	1:13	given you rest, and hath **g** you this land.	5414
	1:15	the Lord have **g** your brethren **rest**,	5117
	1:15	as *he hath* **g** you, and they also have	NIH
	2: 9	I know that the Lord hath **g** you	5414
	2:14	when the Lord hath **g** us the land,	5414
	6: 2	I have **g** into thine hand Jericho,	5414
	6:16	Shout; for the Lord hath **g** you the city.	5414
	8: 1	I have **g** into thy hand the king of Ai,	5414
	14: 3	For Moses had **g** the inheritance of two	5414
	15:19	blessing; for thou hast **g** me a south land	5414
	17:14	Why hast thou **g** me *but* one lot and	5414
	18: 3	Lord God of your fathers hath **g** you?	5414
	22: 4	now the Lord your God hath **g** rest unto	5117
	22: 7	Moses had **g** *possession* in Bashan:	5414
	23: 1	**g** rest unto Israel from all their enemies	5117
	23:13	which the Lord your God hath **g** you.	5414
	23:15	which the Lord your God hath **g** you.	5414
	23:16	the good land which he hath **g** unto you.	5414
	24:13	I have **g** you a land for which ye did not	5414
	24:33	which was **g** him in mount Ephraim.	5414
Jdg	1:15	for thou hast **g** me a south land; give me	5414
	14:20	Samson's wife was **g** to his companion,	NIH
	15: 6	his wife, and **g** her to his companion.	5414
	15:18	Thou hast **g** this great deliverance into	5414
	18:10	for God hath **g** it into your hands; a place	5414
Ru	2:12	a full reward be **g** thee of the Lord	4480+5973
1Sa	1:27	the Lord hath **g** me my petition which I	5414
	1:28	hath **g** it to a neighbour of thine, *that is*	5414
	18:19	daughter should have been **g** to David,	5414
	18:19	she was **g** unto Adriel the Meholathite	5414
	22:13	that thou hast **g** him bread and a sword,	5414
	25:27	let it even be **g** unto the young men that	5414
	25:44	Saul had **g** Michal his daughter,	5414
	28:17	and **g** it to thy neighbour, *even* to David:	5414
	30:23	with *that* which the Lord hath **g** us,	5414
2Sa	4:10	who *thought* that I would have **g** him a	5414
	7: 1	the Lord had **g** him **rest** round about	5117
	9: 9	I have **g** unto thy master's son all that	5414
	12: 8	I would **moreover** have **g** unto thee such	3254
	12:14	**g** great occasion to the enemies	
		of the Lord **to blaspheme**,	5006+5006
	17: 7	**counsel** that Ahithophel hath **g**	3289+6098
	18:11	I would have **g** thee ten *shekels of* silver,	5414
	19:42	the king's *cost?* or hath he **g** us *any* gift?	5375
	22:36	Thou hast also **g** me the shield of thy	5414
	22:41	Thou hast also **g** me the necks of mine	5414
1Ki	1:48	which hath **g** *one* to sit on my throne *this*	5414
	2:21	Let Abishag the Shunammite be **g** to	5414
	3: 6	that thou hast **g** him a son to sit on his	5414
	3:12	have **g** thee a wise and an understanding	5414
	3:13	have also **g** thee *that* which thou hast not	5414
	5: 4	now the Lord my God hath **g** me **rest** on	5117
	5: 7	which hath **g** unto David a wise son over	5414
	8:36	which thou hast **g** to thy people for an	5414
	8:56	that hath **g** rest unto his people Israel,	5414
	9: 7	out of the land which I have **g** them;	5414
	9:12	see the cities which Solomon had **g** him;	5414
	9:13	cities *are* these which thou hast **g** me,	5414
	9:16	**g** it *for* a present unto his daughter,	5414
	12: 8	**counsel** of the old men,	
		which they had **g**	3289+6098
	13: 5	of God had **g** by the word of the Lord.	5414
		they took the bullock which was **g** them,	5414
2Ki	5: 1	by him the Lord had **g** deliverance unto	5414
	5:17	be **g** to thy servant two mules' burden of	5414
	8:29	which the Syrians had **g** him at Ramah,	5221
	9:15	the wounds which the Syrians had **g** him,	5221
	23:11	that the kings of Judah had **g** to the sun,	5414
	25:30	allowance was a continual allowance **g**	5414
1Ch	5: 1	birthright was **g** unto the sons of Joseph	5414
	6:61	*were* cities **g** out of the half tribe,	NIH
	6:63	Unto the sons of Merari *were* **g** by lot,	NIH
	6:71	Unto the sons of Gershom *were* **g** out of	NIH
	6:77	Merari *were* **g** out of the tribe of Zebulun,	NIH
	6:78	*were* **g** *them* out of the tribe of Reuben,	NIH
	22:18	hath he *not* **g** you **rest** on every side?	5117
	22:18	for he hath **g** the inhabitants of the land	5414
	23:25	The Lord God of Israel hath **g** rest unto	5117
	28: 5	(for the Lord hath **g** me many sons,)	5414
	29: 3	*which* I have **g** to the house of my God,	5414
	29:14	of thee, and of thine own have we **g** thee.	5414
2Ch	2:12	who hath **g** to David the king a wise son,	5414
	6:27	which thou hast **g** unto thy people for an	5414
	7:20	roots out of my land which I have **g** them;	5414
	14: 6	because the Lord had **g** him **rest**.	5117
	14: 7	and he hath **g** us **rest** on every side.	5117
	20:11	thou hast **g** us **to inherit**.	3423
	22: 6	the wounds which were **g** him at Ramah,	5221
	25: 9	which I have **g** to the army of Israel?	5414

2Ch	32:29	for God had **g** him substance very much.	5414
	34:14	book of the law of the Lord **g** by Moses.	NIH
	34:18	Hilkiah the priest hath **g** me a book.	5414
	36:23	earth hath the Lord God of heaven **g** me;	5414
Ezr	1: 2	The Lord God of heaven hath **g** me all	5414
	4:21	*another* commandment shall be **g** from	7761
	6: 4	let the expences be **g** out of the king's	3052
	6: 8	forthwith expences be **g** unto these men,	3052
	6: 9	let *it be* **g** them day by day without fail:	3052
	7: 6	which the Lord God of Israel had **g**:	5414
	7:19	The vessels also that *are* **g** thee for	3052
	9:13	and hast **g** us *such* deliverance as this;	5414
Ne	2: 7	let letters be **g** me to the governors	5414
	10:29	was **g** by Moses the servant of God,	5414
	13: 5	which was commanded *to be* **g** to	NIH
	13:10	had not been **g** *them:* for the Levites	5414
Est	2: 3	let their things for purification be **g** them:	5414
	2: 9	*which were* meet to be **g** her,	5414
	2:13	whatsoever she desired was **g** her to go	5414
	3:11	The silver *is* **g** to thee, the people also,	5414
	3:14	**g** in every province *was* published unto	5414
	3:15	the decree was **g** in Shushan the palace.	5414
	4: 8	that was **g** at Shushan to destroy them,	5414
	5: 3	it shall be even **g** thee to the half of	5414
	5: 6	let my life be **g** me at my petition,	5414
	7: 3	let my life be **g** me at my petition,	5414
	8: 7	I have **g** Esther the house of Haman,	5414
	8:13	**g** in every province *was* published unto	5414
	8:14	the decree was **g** at Shushan the palace.	5414
	9:14	the decree was **g** at Shushan; and they	5414
Job	3:20	Wherefore is light **g** to him that is in	5414
	3:23	*Why is* light **g** to a man whose way is hid,	NIH
	9:24	The earth is **g** into the hand of the wicked	5414
	10:18	*Oh that* I had **g up the ghost**, and no eye	1478
	15:19	Unto whom alone the earth was **g**,	5414
	22: 7	hast not **g** water to the weary **to drink**,	8248
	24:23	*Though* it be **g** him *to be* in safety,	5414
	33: 4	the breath of the Almighty hath **g** me **life**.	2421
	34:13	Who hath **g** him **a charge** over the earth?	6485
	37:10	By the breath of God frost is **g**:	5414
	38:36	or who hath **g** understanding to the heart?	5414
	39:19	Hast thou **g** the horse strength? hast thou	5414
Ps	16: 7	bless the Lord, who hath **g** me **counsel**	3289
	18:35	Thou hast also **g** me the shield of thy	5414
	18:40	Thou hast also **g** me the necks of mine	5414
	21: 2	Thou hast **g** him his heart's desire,	5414
	44:11	Thou hast **g** us like sheep appointed for	5414
	60: 4	Thou hast **g** a banner to them that fear	5414
	61: 5	thou hast **g** *me* the heritage of those that	5414
	71: 3	thou hast **g commandment** to save me;	6680
	72:15	and to him shall be **g** of the gold of Sheba;	5414
	78:24	and had **g** them *of* the corn of heaven.	5414
	78:63	their maidens were not **g to marriage**.	1984
	79: 2	dead bodies of thy servants have they **g**	5414
	111: 5	He hath **g** meat unto them that fear him:	5414
	112: 9	He hath dispersed, he hath **g** to the poor;	5414
	115:16	earth hath he **g** to the children of men.	5414
	118:18	but he hath not **g** me **over** unto death.	5414
	120: 3	What shall be **g** unto thee? or what shall	5414
	124: 6	who hath not **g** us *as* a prey to their teeth.	5414
Pr	19:17	which he hath **g** will he pay him again.	1576
	23: 2	throat, if thou *be* a man **g to appetite**.	5315
	24:21	not with them that are **g to change**:	8138
Ecc	1:13	this sore travail hath God **g** to the sons of	5414
	3:10	which God hath **g** to the sons of men to	5414
	5:19	man also to whom God hath **g** riches	5414
	5:19	hath **g** him **power** to eat thereof,	7980
	6: 2	man to whom God hath **g** riches, wealth,	5414
	6: 2	wickedness deliver **those that are g** to it.	1167
	9: 9	which he hath **g** thee under the sun,	5414
	12:11	*which* are **g** from one shepherd.	5414
Isa	3:11	the reward of his hands shall be **g** him.	6213
	8:18	the children whom the Lord hath **g** me	5414
	9: 6	unto us a child is born, unto us a Son is **g**:	5414
	23:11	the Lord hath **g a commandment**	6680
	33:16	bread *shall be* **g** him; his waters *shall be*	5414
	35: 2	the glory of Lebanon shall be **g** unto it,	5414
	37:10	Jerusalem shall not be **g** into the hand of	5414
	43:28	have **g** Jacob to the curse, and Israel to	5414
	47: 6	and **g** them into thine hand:	5414
	47: 8	*that art* **g to pleasures**, that dwellest	5719
	50: 4	The Lord God hath **g** me the tongue of	5414
	55: 4	I have **g** him *for* a witness to the people,	5414
Jer	3: 8	put her away, and **g** her a bill of divorce;	5414
	3:18	**g for an inheritance** unto your fathers.	5157
	6:13	every one *is* **g to covetousness**;	1214+1215
	8:10	unto the greatest is **g** to covetousness,	1214
	8:13	*the things that* I have **g** them shall pass	5414
	8:14	**g** us water of gall **to drink**, because	8248
	11:18	the Lord hath **g** me **knowledge** *of it,*	3045
	12: 7	I have **g** the dearly beloved of my soul	5414
	13:20	where *is* the flock *that* was **g** thee,	5414
	15: 9	she hath **g up the ghost**; her sun	5301+5315
	21:10	it shall be **g** into the hand of the king of	5414
	25: 5	dwell in the land that the Lord hath **g**	5414
	27: 5	have **g** it unto whom it seemed meet unto	5414
	27: 6	now have I **g** all these lands into the hand	5414
	27: 6	the beasts of the field have I **g** him also to	5414
	28:14	I have **g** him the beasts of the field also.	5414
	32:22	hast **g** them this land, which thou didst	5414
	32:24	city is **g** into the hand of the Chaldeans,	5414
	32:25	for the city is **g** into the hand of	5414
	32:43	it is **g** into the hand of the Chaldeans.	5414
	35:15	ye shall dwell in the land which I have **g**	5414
	38: 3	This city shall **surely** be **g** into	5414+5414
	38:18	shall this city be **g** into the hand of	5414

Jer	39:17 shalt not be **g** into the hand of the men	5414
	44:20 the people which had **g** him *that* **answer,**	6030
	47: 7 seeing the LORD hath **g** it **a charge**	6680
	50:15 she hath **g** her hand: her foundations are	5414
	52:34 was a continual diet **g** him of the king	5414
La	1:11 they have **g** their pleasant things for meat	5414
	2: 7 he hath **g up** into the hand of the enemy	5462
	5: 6 We have **g** the hand *to* the Egyptians,	5414
Eze	3:20 because thou hast not **g** him **warning,**	2094
	4:15 I have **g** thee cow's dung for man's dung,	5414
	11:15 unto us is this land **g** in possession.	5414
	15: 6 which I have **g** to the fire for fuel, so will I	5414
	16:17 which I had **g** thee, and madest to thyself	5414
	16:34 no reward is **g** unto thee, therefore thou	5414
	17:18 he had **g** his hand, and hath done all these	5414
	18: 7 hath **g** his bread to the hungry,	5414
	18: 8 He *that* hath not **g forth** upon usury,	5414
	18:13 Hath **g forth** upon usury, and hath taken	5414
	18:16 *but* hath **g** his bread to the hungry,	5414
	20:15 land which I had **g** *them,* flowing with	5414
	21:11 he hath **g** it to be furbished, that it may be	5414
	28:25 shall they dwell in their land that I have **g**	5414
	29: 5 I have **g** thee for meat to the beasts of	5414
	29:20 I have **g** him the land of Egypt *for* his	5414
	33:24 are many; the land is **g** us for inheritance.	5414
	35:12 laid desolate, they are **g** us to consume.	5414
	37:25 they shall dwell in the land that I have **g**	5414
	47:11 shall not be healed; they shall be **g** to salt.	5414
Da	2:23 who hast **g** me wisdom and might,	3052
	2:37 for the God of heaven hath **g** thee a	3052
	2:38 fowls of the heaven hath he **g** into thine	3052
	4:16 let a beast's heart be **g** unto him;	3052
	5:28 divided, and **g** to the Medes and Persians.	3052
	7: 4 as a man, and a man's heart was **g** to it.	3052
	7: 6 four heads; and dominion *was* **g** to it.	3052
	7:11 destroyed, and **g** to the burning flame.	3052
	7:14 there *was* **g** him dominion, and glory,	3052
	7:22 judgment *was* **g** to the saints of the most	3052
	7:25 they shall be **g** into his hand until a time	3052
	7:27 *shall be* **g** to the people of the saints of	3052
	8:12 host was **g** him against the daily *sacrifice*	5414
	11: 6 shall be **g up,** and they that brought her,	5414
	11:11 but the multitude shall be **g** into his hand.	5414
Hos	2: 9 and my flax **g** to cover her nakedness.	NIH
	2:12 *are* my rewards that my lovers have **g**	5414
Joel	2:23 for he hath **g** you the former rain	5414
	3: 3 have **g** a boy for a harlot, and sold a girl	5414
Am	4: 6 I also have **g** you cleanness of teeth in all	5414
	9:15 up out of their land which I have **g** them,	5414
Na	1:14 the LORD hath **g** a **commandment**	6680
Mt	7: 7 Ask, and it shall be **g** you; seek,	1325
	9: 8 which had **g** such power unto men.	1325
	10:19 it shall be **g** you in that *same* hour what	1325
	12:39 and there shall no sign be **g** to it,	1325
	13:11 Because it is **g** unto you to know	1325
	13:11 of heaven, but to them it is not **g.**	1325
	13:12 to him shall be **g,** and he shall have **more**	1325
	14: 9 at meat, he commanded *it* to be **g** her.	1325
	14:11 brought in a charger, and **g** to the damsel:	1325
	16: 4 and there shall no sign be **g** unto it,	1325
	19:11 this saying, save *they* to whom it is **g.**	1325
	20:23 *shall be* **g** to them for whom it is prepared	NIG
	21:43 **g** to a nation bringing forth the fruits	1325
	22:30 neither marry, nor are **g in marriage,**	1547
	25:29 For unto every one that hath be **g,**	1325
	26: 9 been sold for much, and **g** to the poor.	1325
	28:18 All power is **g** unto me in heaven and	1325
Mk	4:11 Unto you it is **g** to know the mystery of	1325
	4:24 and unto you that hear shall **more** be **g.**	4369
	4:25 For he that hath, to him shall be **g:**	1325
	5:43 that *something* should be **g** her	1325
	6: 2 what wisdom *is this* which is **g** unto him,	1325
	8:12 There shall no sign be **g** unto this	1325
	10:40 *shall be* **g** to them for whom it is prepared.	NIG
	12:25 neither marry, nor are **g in marriage;**	1061
	13:11 whatsoever shall be **g** you in that hour,	1325
	14: 5 and have been **g** to the poor.	1325
	14:23 and when he had **g thanks,** he gave *it* to	2168
	14:44 And he that betrayed him had **g** them a	1325
Lk	6:38 Give, and it shall be **g** unto you;	1325
	8:10 Unto you it is **g** to know the mysteries of	1325
	8:18 for whosoever hath, to him shall be **g;**	1325
	11: 9 I say unto you, Ask, and it shall be **g** you;	1325
	11:29 there shall no sign be **g** it, but the sign	1325
	12:48 *stripes.* For unto whomsoever much is **g,**	1325
	17:27 married *wives,* they were **g in marriage,**	1547
	19:15 unto him, to whom he had **g** the money,	1325
	19:26 unto every one which hath shall be **g;**	1325
	20:34 this world marry, and are **g in marriage:**	1548
	20:35 neither marry, nor are **g in marriage:**	1548
	22:19 This is my body which is **g** for you:	1325
Jn	1:17 For the law was **g** by Moses, *but* grace	1325
	3:27 except it be **g** him from heaven.	1325
	3:35 Son, and hath **g** all *things* into his hand.	1325
	4:10 and he would have **g** thee living water.	1325
	5:26 he **g** to the Son to have life in himself;	1325
	5:27 And hath **g** him authority to execute	1325
	5:36 the works which the Father hath **g** me to	1325
	6:11 when he had **g thanks,** he distributed	1325
	6:23 bread, after that the Lord had **g thanks:)**	2168
	6:39 of all which he hath **g** me I should lose	1325
	6:65 except it were **g** unto him of my Father.	1325
	7:39 for the Holy Ghost was not yet **g;** because	NIG
	11:57 and the Pharisees had **g** a commandment,	1325
	12: 5 three hundred pence, and **g** to the poor?	1325

Jn	13: 3 Jesus knowing that the Father had **g** all	1325
	13:15 For I have **g** you an example, that ye	1325
	17: 2 As thou hast **g** him power over all flesh,	1325
	17: 2 eternal life to as many as thou hast **g** him.	1325
	17: 7 whatsoever thou hast **g** me are of thee.	1325
	17: 8 For I have **g** unto them the words which	1325
	17: 9 but for *them* which thou hast **g** me;	1325
	17:11 own name those whom thou hast **g** me,	1325
	17:14 I have **g** them thy word; and the world	1325
	17:22 which thou gavest me I have **g** them;	1325
	17:24 will that they also, whom thou hast **g** me,	1325
	17:24 behold my glory, which thou hast **g** me:	1325
	18:11 the cup which my Father hath **g** me, shall	1325
	19:11 except it were **g** thee from above:	1325
Ac	1: 2 **g commandments** unto the Apostles	1781
	3:16 the faith which is by him hath **g** him this	1325
	4:12 other name under heaven **g** among men,	1325
	5:32 whom God hath **g** to them that obey him,	1325
	8:18 the apostles' hands the Holy Ghost was **g.**	1325
	17:16 saw the city **wholly g** to idolatry.	1510+2712
	17:31 he hath **g** assurance unto all *men,*	3930
	20: 2 had **g** them much **exhortation,**	3056+3870
	21:40 when he had **g** him **licence,** Paul stood	2010
	24:26 money should have been **g** him of Paul,	1325
	27:24 God hath **g** thee all them that sail with	5483
Ro	5: 5 by the Holy Ghost which is **g** unto us.	1325
	11: 8 God hath **g** them the spirit of slumber,	1325
	11:35 who hath **first g** to him, and it shall be	4272
	12: 3 For I say, through the grace **g** unto me,	1325
	12: 6 according to the grace that is **g** to us,	1325
	12:13 to the necessity of saints; **g** to hospitality.	1377
	15:15 of the grace that is **g** to me of God,	1325
1Co	1: 4 for the grace of God which is **g** you by	1325
	2:12 the *things* that are **freely g** to us of God.	5483
	3:10 According to the grace of God which is **g**	1325
	11:15 to her: for *her* hair is **g** her for a covering.	1325
	11:24 And when he had **g thanks,** he brake *it,*	2168
	12: 7 But the manifestation of the Spirit is **g** to	1325
	12: 8 For to one is **g** by the Spirit the word of	1325
	12:24 having **g** more abundant honour to that	1325
	16: 1 as I have **g order** to the churches of	1299
2Co	1:11 **thanks** may be **g** by many on our behalf.	2168
	1:22 **g** the earnest of the Spirit in our hearts.	1325
	5: 5 who also hath **g** unto us the earnest of	1325
	5:18 hath **g** to us the ministry of reconciliation;	1325
	9: 9 dispersed abroad; he hath **g** to the poor:	1325
	10: 8 which the Lord hath **g** us for edification,	1325
	12: 7 there was **g** to me a thorn in the flesh,	1325
	13:10 which the Lord hath **g** me to edification,	1325
Gal	2: 9 perceived the grace that was **g** unto me,	1325
	3:21 for if there had been a law **g** which could	1325
	3:21 a law given which could have **g life,**	2227
	3:22 Christ might be **g** to them that believe.	1325
	4:15 your own eyes, and have **g** *them* to me.	1325
Eph	3: 2 grace of God which is **g** me to you-ward:	1325
	3: 7 according to the gift of the grace of God **g**	1325
	3: 8 than the least of all saints, is this grace **g,**	1325
	4: 7 But unto every one of us is **g** grace	1325
	4:19 **g** themselves **over** unto lasciviousness,	3860
	5: 2 and hath **g** himself for us an offering and	3860
	6:19 for me, that utterance may be **g** unto me,	1325
Php	1:29 For unto you it is **g** in the behalf of Christ,	5483
	2: 9 **g** him a name which is above every name:	5483
Col	1:25 of God which is **g** to me for you,	1325
1Th	4: 8 who hath also **g** unto us his holy Spirit.	1325
2Th	2:16 and hath **g** *us* everlasting consolation and	1325
1Ti	2: 6 **g** to hospitality, apt to teach;	5382
	3: 3 Not **g to wine,** no striker, not greedy of	3943
	3: 8 not doubletongued, not **g** to much wine,	4337
	4:14 is in thee, which was **g** thee by prophecy,	1325
2Ti	1: 7 For God hath not **g** us the spirit of fear;	1325
	1: 9 which was **g** us in Christ Jesus before	1325
	3:16 All scripture *is* **g by inspiration of God,**	2315
Tit	1: 7 not soon angry, not **g to wine,** no striker,	3943
	1: 7 to wine, no striker, not **g to filthy lucre;**	146
	2: 3 not false accusers, not **g** to much wine,	1402
Phm	1:22 through your prayers I shall be **g** unto you.	5483
Heb	2:13 I, and the children which God hath **g** me.	1325
	4: 8 For if Jesus had **g** them **rest,** *then* would	2664
Jas	1: 5 and upbraideth not; and it shall be **g** him.	1325
2Pe	1: 3 According as his divine power hath **g** unto	1433
	1: 4 Whereby are **g** unto us exceeding great	1433
	3:15 wisdom **g** unto him hath written unto you	1325
1Jn	3:24 in us, by the Spirit which he hath **g** us.	1325
	4:13 in us, because he hath **g** us of his Spirit.	1325
	5:11 that God hath **g** to us eternal life,	1325
	5:20 and hath **g** us an understanding, that we	1325
Rev	6: 2 had a bow; and a crown was **g** unto him:	1325
	6: 4 *power* was **g** to him that sat thereon to	1325
	6: 4 and there was **g** unto him a great sword.	1325
	6: 8 power was **g** unto them over the fourth	1325
	6:11 And white robes were **g** unto every one	1325
	7: 2 to whom it was **g** to hurt the earth and	1325
	8: 2 and to them were **g** seven trumpets.	1325
	8: 3 and there was **g** unto him much incense,	1325
	9: 1 him was **g** the key of the bottomless pit.	1325
	9: 3 and unto them was **g** power,	1325
	9: 5 And to them it was **g** that they should not	1325
	11: 1 there was **g** me a reed like unto a rod:	1325
	11: 2 it not; for it is **g** unto the Gentiles:	1325
	12:14 And to the woman were **g** two wings of a	1325
	13: 5 And there was **g** unto him a mouth	1325
	13: 5 power to continue forty	1325
	13: 7 And it was **g** unto him to make war with	1325
	13: 7 and power was **g** him over all kindreds,	1325

Rev	16: 6 and thou hast **g** them blood to drink;	1325
	16: 8 *power* was **g** unto him to scorch men	1325
	20: 4 them, and judgment was **g** unto them:	1325

GIVER (2) [GIVE]

Isa	24: 2 of usury, so *with* the **g of usury** to him.	5383
2Co	9: 7 of necessity: for God loveth a cheerful **g.**	1395

GIVEST (12) [GIVE]

Dt	15: 9 thy poor brother, and thou **g** him nought;	5414
	15:10 heart shall not be grieved when thou **g**	5414
Job	35: 7 If thou be righteous, what **g** thou him?	5414
Ps	50:19 Thou **g** thy mouth to evil, and thy tongue	7971
	80: 5 **g** them tears **to drink** *in great* measure.	8248
	104:28 thou **g** them they gather: thou openest	5414
	145:15 thou **g** them their meat in due season.	5414
Pr	6:35 rest content, though thou **g many** gifts.	7235
Eze	3:18 thou **g** him not **warning,** nor speakest to	2094
	16:33 thou **g** thy gifts to all thy lovers,	5414
	16:34 in that thou **g** a reward, and no reward is	5414
1Co	14:17 thou verily **g thanks** well, but the other	2168

GIVETH (126) [GIVE]

Ge	49:21 *is* a hind let loose: he **g** goodly words.	5414
Ex	16:29 he **g** you on the sixth day the bread of two	5414
	20:12 the land which the LORD thy God **g** thee.	5414
	25: 2 of every man that **g** it **willingly** with his	5068
Lev	20: 2 that **g** *any* of his seed unto Molech;	5414
	20: 4 when he **g** of his seed unto Molech,	5414
	27: 9 all that *any man* **g** of such unto the LORD	5414
Nu	5:10 whatsoever any man **g** the priest, it shall	5414
Dt	2:29 the land which the LORD our God **g** us.	5414
	4: 1 the LORD God of your fathers **g** you.	5414
	4:21 which the LORD thy God **g** thee *for* an	5414
	4:40 which the LORD thy God **g** thee, for ever.	5414
	5:16 in the land which the LORD thy God	5414
	8:18 *it is* he that **g** thee power to get wealth,	5414
	9: 6 that the LORD thy God **g** thee not this	5414
	11:17 off the good land which the LORD **g** you.	5414
	11:31 land which the LORD your God **g** you,	5414
	12: 1 which the LORD God of thy fathers **g**	5414
	12: 9 which the LORD your God **g** you.	5414
	12:10 the LORD your God **g** you **to inherit.**	5157
	12:10 he **g** you **rest** from all your enemies	5117
	13: 1 of dreams, and **g** thee a sign or a wonder,	5414
	15: 4 God **g** thee *for* an inheritance to possess	5414
	15: 7 thy land which the LORD thy God **g** thee,	5414
	16: 5 which the LORD thy God **g** thee:	5414
	16:18 which the LORD thy God **g** thee.	5414
	16:20 the land which the LORD thy God **g** thee.	5414
	17: 2 gates which the LORD thy God **g** thee,	5414
	17:14 the land which the LORD thy God **g** thee,	5414
	18: 9 the land which the LORD thy God **g** thee,	5414
	19: 1 whose land the LORD thy God **g** thee,	5414
	19: 2 which the LORD thy God **g** thee to	5414
	19: 3 the LORD thy God **g** thee **to inherit,**	5157
	19:10 which the LORD thy God **g** thee *for* an	5414
	19:14 the land which the LORD thy God **g** thee to possess it.	5414
	21: 1 the LORD thy God **g** thee to possess it,	5414
	21:23 which the LORD thy God **g** thee *for* an	5414
	24: 3 **g** *it* in her hand, and sendeth her out of	5414
	24: 4 which the LORD thy God **g** thee *for* an	5414
	25:15 the land which the LORD thy God **g** thee.	5414
	25:19 in the land which the LORD thy God	5414
	26: 1 LORD thy God **g** thee *for* an inheritance,	5414
	26: 2 of thy land which the LORD thy God **g** thee,	5414
	27: 2 the land which the LORD thy God **g** thee,	5414
	27: 3 the land which the LORD thy God **g** thee,	5414
	28: 8 the land which the LORD thy God **g** thee.	5414
Jos	1:11 which the LORD your God **g** you to	5414
	1:15 land which the LORD your God **g** them:	5414
Jdg	11:24 Chemosh thy god **g** thee **to possess?**	3423
	21:18 Cursed *be* he that **g** a wife to Benjamin.	5414
Job	5:10 Who **g** rain upon the earth,	5414
	14:10 man **g up the ghost,** and where *is* he?	1478
	32: 8 of the Almighty **g** them **understanding.**	995
	33:13 he **g** not **account** of any of his matters.	6030
	34:29 When he **g quietness,** who then can	8252
	35:10 God my Maker, who **g** songs in the night;	5414
	35:12 none **g answer,** because of the pride of	6030
	36: 6 life of the wicked: but **g** right to the poor.	5414
	36:31 he the people; he **g** meat in abundance.	5414
Ps	18:50 **Great** deliverance **g** he to his king;	1431
	37:21 but the righteous sheweth mercy, and **g.**	5414
	68:35 the God of Israel *is* he that **g** strength and	5414
	119:130 The entrance of thy words **g light;** it giveth	215
	119:130 it **g understanding** unto the simple.	995
	127: 2 of sorrows: *for* so he **g** his beloved sleep.	5414
	136:25 Who **g** food to all flesh: for his mercy	5414
	144:10 *It is* he that **g** salvation unto kings:	5414
	146: 7 which **g** food to the hungry. The LORD	5414
	147: 9 He **g** to the beast his food, *and to* the	5414
	147:16 He **g** snow like wool: he scattereth	5414
Pr	2: 6 For the LORD **g** wisdom: out of his	5414
	3:34 scorners: but he **g** grace unto the lowly.	5414
	13:15 Good understanding **g** favour: but the way	5414
	17: 4 A wicked doer **g heed** to false lips;	7181
	17: 4 *and a* liar **g ear** to a naughty tongue.	238
	19: 6 every *man is* a friend to him that **g gifts.**	4976
	21:26 but the righteous **g** and spareth not.	5414
	22: 9 blessed; for he **g** of his bread to the poor.	5414
	22:16 his *riches, and* he that **g** to the rich,	5414
	23:31 when it **g** his colour in the cup, *when* it	5414
	24:26 *Every man* shall kiss *his* lips that **g** a right	7725
	26: 8 in a sling, so *is* he that **g** honour to a fool.	5414

Pr 28:27 He that **g** unto the poor *shall* not lack: 5414
31:15 **g** meat to her household, and a portion to 5414
Ecc 2:26 God **g** to a man that *is* good in his sight 5414
2:26 to the sinner he **g** travail, to gather and 5414
5:18 all the days of his life, which God **g** him: 5414
6: 2 yet God **g** him not **power** to eat thereof, 7980
7:12 *that* wisdom **g** life to them that have it. 2421
8:15 his life, which God **g** him under the sun. 5414
Isa 40:29 He **g** power to the faint; and to *them that* 5414
42: 5 he that **g** breath unto the people upon it, 5414
Jer 5:24 that **g** rain, both the former and the latter, 5414
22:13 wages, and **g** him not *for* his work; 5414
31:35 which **g** the sun for a light by day, 5414
La 3:30 He **g** *his* cheek to him that smiteth him: 5414
Da 2:21 he **g** wisdom unto the wise, 3052
4:17 **g** it to whomsoever he will, and setteth up 5415
4:25 of men, and **g** it to whomsoever he will. 5415
4:32 of men, and **g** it to whomsoever he will. 5415
Hab 2:15 unto him that **g** his neighbour **drink**, 8248
Mt 5:15 it **g** light unto all that are in the house. 2989
Jn 3:34 for God **g** not the Spirit by measure *unto* 1325
6:32 my Father **g** you the true bread from 1325
6:33 from heaven, and **g** life unto the world. 1325
6:37 All that the Father **g** me shall come to me; 1325
10:11 the good shepherd **g** his life for the sheep. 5087
14:27 not as the world **g**, give I unto you. 1325
21:13 bread, and **g** them, and fish likewise. 1325
Ac 17:25 though he needed any *thing*, seeing he **g** 1325
Ro 12: 8 he that **g**, *let him do it* with simplicity; 3330
14: 6 eateth to the Lord, for he **g** God **thanks**, 2168
14: 6 Lord he eateth not, and **g** God **thanks**. 2168
1Co 3: 7 watereth; but God that **g** the **increase**. 837
7:38 he that **g** *her* in marriage doeth well; 1547
7:38 that **g** *her* not in marriage doeth better. 1547
15:38 God **g** it a body as it hath pleased him, 1325
15:57 which **g** us the victory through our Lord 1325
2Co 3: 6 for the letter killeth, but the spirit **g** life. 2227
1Ti 6:17 who **g** us richly *all things* to enjoy; 3030
Jas 1: 5 that **g** to all *men* liberally, 1325
4: 6 But he **g** more grace. Wherefore *he* saith, 1325
4: 6 the proud, but **g** grace unto the humble. 1325
1Pe 4:11 *him do* it as of the ability which God **g**: 5524
5: 5 the proud, and **g** grace to the humble. 1325
Rev 22: 5 of the sun; for the Lord God **g** them **light**: 5461

GIVING (29) [GIVE]

Ge 24:19 she had done **g** him **drink**, she said, 8248
Dt 10:18 the stranger, in **g** him food and raiment. 5414
21:17 by **g** him a double portion of all that he 5414
Ru 1: 6 had visited his people in **g** them bread. 5414
1Ki 5: 9 my desire, in **g** food for my household. 5414
2Ch 6:23 by **g** him according to his righteousness. 5414
Ezr 3:11 in praising and **g thanks** unto the LORD, 3034
Job 11:20 *shall be as* the **g** up of the ghost. 4646+5315
Mt 24:38 **drinking, marrying and g in marriage**, 1547
Lk 17:16 on *his* face at his feet, **g** him **thanks**: 2168
Ac 8: 9 **g** out that himself was some great one: 3004
-15: 8 them witness, **g** them the Holy Ghost, 1325
Ro 4:20 but was strong in faith, **g** glory to God; 1325
9: 4 and the **g** of the law, and the service of 3548
1Co 14: 7 *And* even *things* without life **g** sound, 1325
14:16 unlearned say Amen at thy **g** of **thanks**, 2169
2Co 6: 3 **G** no offence in any *thing*, that the 1325
Eph 5: 4 not convenient: but rather **g** of **thanks**. 2169
5:20 **G thanks** always for all *things* unto God 2168
Php 4:15 communicated with me as concerning **g** 1394
Col 1:12 **G thanks** unto the Father, which hath 2168
3:17 **g thanks** to God and the Father by him. 2168
1Ti 2: 1 prayers, intercessions, *and* **g** of **thanks**, 2169
4: 1 **g heed** to seducing spirits, and doctrines 4337
Tit 1:14 Not **g heed** to Jewish fables, 4337
Heb 13:15 the fruit of *our* lips **g thanks** to his name. 3670
1Pe 3: 7 **g** honour unto the wife, as unto the weaker 632
2Pe 1: 5 beside this, **g** all diligence, add to your 3923
Jude 1: 7 **g** themselves **over to fornication**, 1608

GIZONITE (1)

1Ch 11:34 The sons of Hashem the **G**, Jonathan 1493

GLAD (89) [GLADLY, GLADNESS]

Ex 4:14 he seeth thee, he will be **g** in his heart. 8055
Jdg 18:20 the priest's heart was **g**, and he took 3190
1Sa 11: 9 *it* to the men of Jabesh; and they were **g**. 8055
1Ki 8:66 of heart for all the goodness that 2896
1Ch 16:31 Let the heavens be **g**, and let the earth 8055
2Ch 7:10 and merry in heart for the goodness that 8056
Est 5: 9 forth that day joyful and with a **g** heart: 2896
8:15 the city of Shushan rejoiced and was **g**. 8056
Job 3:22 Which rejoice exceedingly, *and* are **g**, 7797
22:19 The righteous see *it*, and are **g**: 8055
Ps 9: 2 I will be **g** and rejoice in thee: I will sing 8055
14: 7 Jacob shall rejoice, *and* Israel shall be **g**. 8055
16: 9 Therefore my heart is **g**, and my glory 8055
21: 6 thou hast made him exceeding **g** with thy 8057
31: 7 I will be **g** and rejoice in thy mercy: 1523
32:11 Be **g** in the LORD, and rejoice, 8055
34: 2 the humble shall hear *thereof*, and be **g**. 8055
35:27 Let them shout for joy, and be **g**, 8055
40:16 that seek thee rejoice and be **g** in thee: 8055
45: 8 *whereby* they have **made** thee **g**. 8055
46: 4 streams whereof shall **make g** the city 8055
48:11 let the daughters of Judah be **g**, because 1523
53: 6 Jacob shall rejoice, *and* Israel shall be **g**. 8055
64:10 The righteous shall be **g** in the LORD, 8055
67: 4 O let the nations be **g** and sing for joy: 8055

Ps 68: 3 let the righteous be **g**; let them rejoice 8055
69:32 The humble shall see *this*, *and* be **g**: 8055
70: 4 that seek thee rejoice and be **g** in thee: 8055
90:14 that we may rejoice and be **g** all our days. 8055
90:15 **Make** us **g** according to the days 8055
92: 4 hast **made** me **g** through thy work: 8055
96:11 heavens rejoice, and let the earth be **g**; 1523
97: 1 let the multitude of isles be **g** *thereof*. 8055
97: 8 **g**, and the daughters of Judah rejoiced, 8055
104:15 wine *that* **maketh g** the heart of man, 8055
104:34 shall be sweet: I will be **g** in the LORD. 8055
105:38 Egypt was **g** when they departed; 8055
107:30 are they **g** because they be quiet; 8055
118:24 hath made; we will rejoice and be **g** in it. 8055
119:74 that fear thee will be **g** when they see 8055
122: 1 I was **g** when they said unto me, Let us go 8055
126: 3 great things for us; *whereof* we are **g**. 8056
Pr 10: 1 wise son **maketh** a father: but a foolish 8055
12:25 it stoop: but a good word **maketh** it **g**. 8055
15:20 wise son **maketh** a father: but a foolish 8056
17: 5 he that is **g** at calamities shall not be 8056
23:25 Thy father and thy mother shall be **g**, 8055
24:17 not thine heart be **g** when he stumbleth: 1523
27:11 My son, be wise, and **make** my heart **g**, 8055
SS 1: 4 We will be **g** and rejoice in thee, we will 1523
Isa 25: 9 we will be **g** and rejoice in his salvation. 1523
35: 1 and the solitary place shall be **g** *for* them; 7797
39: 2 Hezekiah was **g** of them, and shewed 8055
65:18 be you **g** and rejoice for ever *in that* 7797
66:10 and be **g** with her, all ye that love her; 1523
Jer 20:15 unto thee; **making** him **very g**. 8055+8055
41:13 that were with him, then they were **g**. 8055
50:11 Because ye were **g**, because ye rejoiced, 8055
La 1:21 they are **g** that thou hast done *it*: thou 7797
4:21 Rejoice and be **g**, O daughter of Edom, 8055
Da 6:23 Then was the king exceeding **g** for him, 2868
Hos 7: 3 they **make** the king **g** with their 8055
Joel 2:21 Fear not, O land; be **g** and rejoice: 1523
2:23 Be **g** then, ye children of Zion, 1523
Jnh 4: 6 **exceeding g** of the gourd. 1419+8055+8057
Hab 1:15 drag: therefore they rejoice and are **g**. 1523
Zep 3:14 be **g** and rejoice with all the heart, 8055
Zec 10: 7 yea, their children shall see *it*, and be **g**; 8055
Mt 5:12 Rejoice, and be **exceeding g**: for great *is* 21
Mk 14:11 And when they heard *it*, they were **g**, 5463
Lk 1:19 thee, and to **shew** thee these **g** tidings. 2097
8: 1 shewing the **g** tidings of the kingdom of 2097
15:32 that we should make merry, and be **g**: 5463
22: 5 And they were **g**, and covenanted to give 5463
23: 8 Herod saw Jesus, he was exceeding **g**: 5463
Jn 8:56 to see my day: and he saw *it*, and was **g**. 5463
11:15 And I am **g** for your sakes that I was not 5463
20:20 Then were the disciples **g**, when they saw 5463
Ac 2:26 my heart rejoice, and my tongue was **g**; 21
11:23 grace of God, was **g**, and exhorted *them* 5463
13:32 And we **declare** unto you **g tidings**, 2097
13:48 the Gentiles heard *this*, they were **g**, 2097
Ro 10:15 and **bring g** tidings of good *things*! 2097
16:19 is come abroad unto all *men*. I am **g** 5463
1Co 16:17 I am **g** of the coming of Stephanas and 5463
2Co 2: 2 who is he then that **maketh** me **g**, 2165
13: 9 For we are **g**, when we are weak, and ye 5463
1Pe 4:13 ye may be **g** also with exceeding joy. 5463
Rev 19: 7 Let us be **g** and rejoice, and give honour 5463

GLADLY (8) [GLAD]

Mk 6:20 he did many *things*, and heard him **g**. 2234
12:37 And the common people heard him **g**. 2234
Lk 8:40 was returned, the people **g received** him: 588
Ac 2:41 Then they that **g** received his word were 780
21:17 to Jerusalem, the brethren received us **g**. 780
2Co 11:19 For ye suffer fools **g**, seeing ye *yourselves* 2234
12: 9 **Most g** therefore will I rather glory in my 2236
12:15 And I will **very g** spend and be spent for 2236

GLADNESS (47) [GLAD]

Nu 10:10 Also in the day of your **g**, and in your 8057
Dt 28:47 with **g** of heart, for the abundance of all 2898
2Sa 6:12 Obed-edom *into* the city of David with **g**. 8057
1Ch 16:27 strength and **g** *are* in his place. 2304
29:22 before the LORD on that day with great **g**. 8057
2Ch 29:30 they *sang* praises with **g**, and they bowed 8057
30:21 unleavened bread seven days with great **g**: 8057
30:23 and they kept *other* seven days *with* **g**. 8057
Ne 8:17 done so. And there was very great **g**. 8057
12:27 to keep the dedication with **g**, both with 8057
Est 8:16 had light, and **g**, and joy, and honour. 8057
8:17 Jews had joy and **g**, a feast and a good 8342
9:17 and made it a day of feasting and **g**. 8057
9:18 and made it a day of feasting and **g**. 8057
9:19 day of the month Adar *a day of* **g** 8057
Ps 4: 7 Thou hast put **g** in my heart, more than 8057
30:11 off my sackcloth, and girded me *with* **g**; 8342
45: 7 anointed thee *with* the oil of **g** above 8342
45:15 **g** and rejoicing shall they be brought: 8057
51: 8 Make me to hear joy and **g**; *that* the 8057
97:11 righteous, and **g** for the upright in heart. 8057
100: 2 Serve the LORD with **g**: come before his 8057
105:43 people with joy, *and* his chosen with **g**: 7440
106: 5 that *I* may rejoice in the **g** of thy nation, 8057
Pr 10:28 The hope of the righteous *shall be* **g**: 8057
SS 3:11 and in the day of the **g** of his heart. 8057
Isa 16:10 is taken away, and joy out of the 8057
22:13 behold joy and **g**, slaying oxen, 8057
30:29 **g** of heart, as when one goeth with a pipe 8057

Isa 35:10 they shall obtain joy and **g**, and sorrow 8057
51: 3 joy and **g** shall be found therein, 8057
51:11 they shall obtain **g** and joy; *and* sorrow 8342
Jer 7:34 the voice of mirth, and the voice of **g**, 8057
16: 9 the voice of mirth, and the voice of **g**, 8057
25:10 voice of **g**, the voice of the bridegroom, 8057
31: 7 Sing with **g** for Jacob, and shout among 8057
33:11 The voice of joy, and the voice of **g**, 8057
48:33 and **g** is taken from the plentiful field, 1524
Joel 1:16 joy and **g** from the house of our God? 1524
Zec 8:19 shall be to the house of Judah joy and **g**, 1524
Mk 4:16 the word, immediately receive it with **g**; 5479
Lk 1:14 thou shalt have joy and **g**; and many shall 20
Ac 2:46 did eat *their* meat with **g** and singleness of 20
12:14 she opened not the gate for **g**, but ran in, 5479
14:17 filling our hearts with food and **g**. 2167
Php 2:29 therefore in the Lord with all **g**; 5479
Heb 1: 9 hath anointed thee *with* the oil of **g** above 20

GLASS (9) [GLASSES, LOOKING-GLASSES]

Job 37:18 *is* strong, *and* as a molten **looking g**? 7209
1Co 13:12 For now we see through a **g**, darkly; 2072
2Co 3:18 with open face **beholding as in a g** 2072
Jas 1:23 a man beholding his natural face in a **g**: 2072
Rev 4: 6 before the throne *there was* a sea of **g** 5193
15: 2 And I saw as *it were* a sea of **g** mingled 5193
15: 2 stand on the sea of **g**, having the harps of 5193
21:18 the city *was* pure gold, like unto clear **g**. 5194
21:21 *was* pure gold, as *it were* transparent **g**. 5194

GLASSES (1) [GLASS]

Isa 3:23 The **g**, and the fine linen, and the hoods, 1549

GLEAN (10) [GLEANED, GLEANING, GLEANINGS, GRAPEGLEANINGS]

Lev 19:10 thou shalt not **g** thy vineyard, neither 5953
Dt 24:21 vineyard, thou shalt not **g** *it* afterward: 5953
Ru 2: 2 ears of corn after *him* in whose sight I 3950
2: 7 let me **g** and gather after the reapers 3950
2: 8 Go not to **g** in another field, neither go 3950
2:15 when she was risen up to **g**, Boaz 3950
2:15 Let her **g** even among the sheaves, 3950
2:16 leave *them*, that she may **g** *them*, and 3950
2:23 she kept fast by the maidens of Boaz to **g** 3950
Jer 6: 9 shall **throughly g** the remnant 5953+5953

GLEANED (6) [GLEAN]

Jdg 20:45 they **g** of them in the highways five 5953
Ru 2: 3 came, and **g** in the field after the reapers: 3950
2:17 she **g** in the field until even, and beat out 3950
2:17 until even, and beat out that she had **g**: 3950
2:18 her mother in law saw what she had **g**: 3950
2:19 said unto her, Where hast thou **g** to day? 3950

GLEANING (5) [GLEAN]

Lev 23:22 neither shalt thou gather *any* **g** of thy 3951
Jdg 8: 2 *Is* not the **g** of the grapes of Ephraim 5955
Isa 17: 6 Yet **g** grapes shall be left in it, 5955
24:13 as the **g** grapes when the vintage is done. 5955
Jer 49: 9 would they not leave *some* **g** grapes? 5955

GLEANINGS (1) [GLEAN]

Lev 19: 9 neither shalt thou gather the **g** of thy 3951

GLEDE (1)

Dt 14:13 the **g**, and the kite, and the vulture after 7201

GLISTERING (3)

1Ch 29: 2 **g** stones, and of divers colours, 6320
Job 20:25 yea, the **g** sword cometh out of his gall: 1300
Lk 9:29 and his raiment *was* white and **g**. 1823

GLITTER (1) [GLITTERING]

Eze 21:10 slaughter; *it is* furbished that it may **g**: 1300

GLITTERING (5) [GLITTER]

Dt 32:41 If I whet my **g** sword, and mine hand take 1300
Job 39:23 against him, the **g** spear and the shield. 3851
Eze 21:28 *is* furbished, to consume because of the **g**: 1300
Na 3: 3 up both the bright sword and the **g** spear: 1300
Hab 3:11 went, *and* at the shining of thy **g** spear. 1300

GLOOMINESS (2)

Joel 2: 2 A day of darkness and of **g**, a day of clouds 653
Zep 1:15 and desolation, a day of darkness and **g**, 653

GLORIEST (1) [GLORY]

Jer 49: 4 Wherefore **g** thou in the valleys, 1984

GLORIETH (3) [GLORY]

Jer 9:24 let him that **g** glory in this, that *he* 1984
1Co 1:31 That, according as it is written, He that **g**, 2744
2Co 10:17 But he that **g**, let him glory in the Lord. 2744

GLORIFIED (50) [GLORY]

Lev 10: 3 and before all the people I will be **g**. 3513
Isa 26:15 thou art **g**: thou hadst removed *it* far *unto* 3513
44:23 redeemed Jacob, and **g** himself in Israel. 6286
49: 3 my servant, O Israel, in whom I will be **g**. 6286
55: 5 the Holy One of Israel; for he hath **g** thee. 6286
60: 9 One of Israel, because he hath **g** thee. 6286
60:21 the work of my hands, that *I* may be **g**. 6286
61: 3 planting of the LORD, that *he* might be **g**. 6286
66: 5 my name's sake, said, Let the LORD be **g**: 3513
Eze 28:22 and I will be **g** in the midst of thee: 3513
39:13 them a renown the day that I shall be **g**, 3513

Da	5:23	whose *are* all thy ways, hast thou not **g**:	1922
Hag	1: 8	in it, and I will be **g**, saith the LORD.	3513
Mt	9: 8	and **g** God, which had given such power	1392
	15:31	blind to see: and they **g** the God of Israel.	1392
Mk	2:12	and **g** God, saying, We never saw it on	1392
Lk	4:15	taught in their synagogues, being **g** of all.	1392
	5:26	and they **g** God, and were filled with fear,	1392
	7:16	and they **g** God, saying, That a great	1392
	13:13	she was made straight, and **g** God.	1392
	17:15	turned back, and with a loud voice **g** God,	1392
	23:47	he **g** God, saying, Certainly this was a	1392
Jn	7:39	*given;* because that Jesus was not yet **g**.)	1392
	11: 4	that the Son of God might be **g** thereby.	1392
	12:16	but when Jesus was **g**, then	1392
	12:23	is come, that the Son of man should be **g**.	1392
	12:28	*saying,* I have both **g** *it*, and will glorify *it*	1392
	13:31	Now is the Son of man **g**, and God is	1392
	13:31	Son of man glorified, and God is **g** in him.	1392
	13:32	If God be **g** in him, God shall also glorify	1392
	14:13	I do, that the Father may be **g** in the Son.	1392
	15: 8	Herein is my Father **g**, that ye bear much	1392
	17: 4	I have **g** thee on the earth: I have finished	1392
	17:10	and thine are mine; and I am **g** in them.	1392
Ac	3:13	God of our fathers, hath **g** his Son Jesus;	1392
	4:21	all *men* **g** God for that which was done.	1392
	11:18	they held their peace, and **g** God, saying,	1392
	13:48	were glad, and **g** the word of the Lord:	1392
	21:20	And when they heard *it*, they **g** the Lord,	1392
Ro	1:21	they knew God, they **g** *him* not as God,	1392
	8:17	*him,* that we may be also **g together**,	4888
	8:30	and whom he justified, them he also **g**.	1392
Gal	1:24	And they **g** God in me.	1392
2Th	1:10	When he shall come to be **g** in his saints,	1740
	1:12	of our Lord Jesus Christ may be **g** in you,	1740
	1:12	course, and be **g**, even as *it is* with you:	1392
Heb	5: 5	So also Christ **g** not himself to be made a	1392
1Pe	4:11	that God in all *things* may be **g** through	1392
	4:14	is evil spoken of, but on your part he is **g**.	1392
Rev	18: 7	How much she hath **g** herself,	1392

GLORIFIETH (1) [GLORY]

Ps	50:23	Whoso offereth praise **g** me: and to him	3513

GLORIFY (25) [GLORY]

Ps	22:23	all ye the seed of Jacob, **g** him;	3513
	50:15	I will deliver thee, and thou shalt **g** me.	3513
	86: 9	thee, O Lord; and shall **g** thy name.	3513
	86:12	and I will **g** thy name for evermore.	3513
Isa	24:15	Wherefore **g** ye the LORD in the fires,	3513
	25: 3	Therefore shall the strong people **g** thee,	3513
	60: 7	and I will **g** the house of my glory.	6286
Jer	30:19	I will also **g** them, and they shall not be	3513
Mt	5:16	and **g** your Father which is in heaven.	1392
Jn	12:28	Father, **g** thy name. Then came there a	1392
	12:28	I have both glorified *it*, and will **g** *it* again.	1392
	13:32	in him, God shall also **g** him in himself,	1392
	13:32	in himself, and shall straightway **g** him.	1392
	16:14	shall **g** me: for he shall receive of mine,	1392
	17: 1	**g** thy Son, that thy Son also may glorify	1392
	17: 1	thy Son, that thy Son also may **g** thee:	1392
	17: 5	**g** thou me with thine own self with	1392
	21:19	signifying by what death he should **g** God.	1392
Ro	15: 6	with one mind *and* one mouth **g** God,	1392
	15: 9	And that the Gentiles might **g** God for *his*	1392
1Co	6:20	therefore **g** God in your body, and in your	1392
2Co	9:13	**g** God for your professed subjection unto	1392
1Pe	2:12	behold, **g** God in the day of visitation.	1392
	4:16	but let him **g** God on this behalf.	1392
Rev	15: 4	not fear thee, O Lord, and **g** thy name?	1392

GLORIFYING (3) [GLORY]

Lk	2:20	**g** and praising God for all *the things* that	1392
	5:25	and departed to his own house, **g** God.	1392
	18:43	his sight, and followed him, **g** God:	1392

GLORIOUS (45) [GLORY]

Ex	15: 6	O LORD, is **become g** in power:	142
	15:11	who *is* like thee, **g** in holiness, fearful *in*	142
Dt	28:58	that *thou* mayest fear this **g** and fearful	3513
2Sa	6:20	said, How **g** was the king of Israel to day,	3513
1Ch	29:13	we thank thee, and praise thy **g** name.	8597
Ne	9: 5	blessed be thy **g** name, which *is* exalted	3519
Est	1: 4	When he shewed the riches of his **g**	3519
Ps	45:13	The king's daughter *is* all **g** within:	3520
	66: 2	honour of his name: make his praise **g**.	3519
	72:19	blessed *be* his **g** name for ever: and let	3519
	76: 4	Thou *art* more **g** *and* excellent than	215
	87: 3	**G** *things* are spoken of thee, O city of	3513
	111: 3	His work *is* honourable and **g**:	1926
	145: 5	will speak of the **g** honour of thy majesty,	3519
	145:12	and the **g** majesty of his kingdom.	3519
Isa	4: 2	branch of the LORD be beautiful and **g**,	3519
	11:10	the Gentiles seek: and his rest shall be **g**.	3519
	22:23	he shall be for a **g** throne to his father's	3519
	28: 1	whose beauty *is* a fading flower,	6643
	28: 4	the **g** beauty, which *is* on the head of the	6643
	30:30	the LORD shall cause his **g** voice to be	1935
	33:21	there the **g** LORD *will be* unto us a place of	117
	49: 5	yet shall I be **g** in the eyes of the LORD,	3513
	60:13	and I will **make** the place of my feet **g**.	3513
	63: 1	this *that is* **g** in his apparel, travelling in	1921
	63:12	the right hand of Moses with his **g** arm,	8597
	63:14	thy people, to make thyself a **g** name.	8597
Jer	17:12	A **g** high throne from the beginning *is*	3519
Eze	27:25	and **made** very **g** in the midst of the seas.	3513

Da	11:16	he shall stand in the **g** land, which by his	6643
	11:41	shall enter also into the **g** land,	6643
	11:45	between the seas in the **g** holy mountain;	6643
Lk	13:17	all the people rejoiced for all the **g** *things*	1741
Ro	8:21	into the **g** liberty of the children of God.	1391
2Co	3: 7	*and* engraven in stones, was **g**,	1391+1722
	3: 8	of the spirit be rather **g**?	1391+1722
	3:10	For even that which was **made g** had no	1392
	3:11	if that which is done away *was* **g**,	1223+1391
	3:11	more that which remaineth *is* **g**.	1391+1722
	4: 4	lest the light of the **g** gospel of Christ,	1391
Eph	5:27	That he might present it to himself a **g**	1741
Php	3:21	that it may be fashioned like unto his **g**	1391
Col	1:11	according to his **g** power, unto all patience	1391
1Ti	1:11	According to the **g** gospel of the blessed	1391
Tit	2:13	and the appearing of the great God and	1391

GLORIOUSLY (3) [GLORY]

Ex	15: 1	for he hath **triumphed g**:	1342+1342
	15:21	for he hath **triumphed g**;	1342+1342
Isa	24:23	in Jerusalem, and before his ancients **g**.	3519

GLORY (402) [GLORIEST, GLORIETH, GLORIFIED, GLORIFIETH, GLORIFY, GLORIFYING, GLORIOUS, GLORIOUSLY, GLORYING, VAINGLORY]

Ge	31: 1	of our father's hath he gotten all this **g**.	3519
	45:13	you shall tell my father of all my **g** in	3519
Ex	8: 9	Moses said unto Pharaoh, **G** over me:	6286
	16: 7	then ye shall see the **g** of the LORD;	3519
	16:10	the **g** of the LORD appeared in the cloud.	3519
	24:16	the **g** of the LORD abode upon mount	3519
	24:17	the sight of the **g** of the LORD *was* like	3519
	28: 2	Aaron thy brother, for **g** and for beauty.	3519
	28:40	thou make for them, for **g** and for beauty.	3519
	29:43	*tabernacle* shall be sanctified by my **g**.	3519
	33:18	he said, I beseech thee, shew me thy **g**.	3519
	33:22	come to pass, while my **g** passeth by,	3519
	40:34	the **g** of the LORD filled the tabernacle.	3519
	40:35	the **g** of the LORD filled the tabernacle.	3519
Lev	9: 6	the **g** of the LORD shall appear unto you.	3519
	9:23	the **g** of the LORD appeared unto all	3519
Nu	14:10	the **g** of the LORD appeared in	3519
	14:21	all the earth shall be filled *with* the **g** of	3519
	14:22	all *those* men which have seen my **g**,	3519
	16:19	the **g** of the LORD appeared unto all	3519
	16:42	and the **g** of the LORD appeared.	3519
	20: 6	the **g** of the LORD appeared unto them.	3519
Dt	5:24	the LORD our God hath shewed us his **g**	3519
	33:17	His **g** *is like* the firstling of his bullock,	1926
Jos	7:19	**g** to the LORD God of Israel,	3519
1Sa	2: 8	and to make them inherit the throne of **g**:	3519
	4:21	The **g** is departed from Israel:	3519
	4:22	she said, The **g** is departed from Israel:	3519
	6: 5	and ye shall give **g** unto the God of Israel:	3519
1Ki	8:11	for the **g** of the LORD had filled the house	3519
2Ki	14:10	**g** *of this,* and tarry at home: for why	3513
1Ch	16:10	**G** ye in his holy name: let the heart of	1984
	16:24	Declare his **g** among the heathen,	3519
	16:27	**G** and honour *are* in his presence;	1935
	16:28	give unto the LORD **g** and strength.	3519
	16:29	Give unto the LORD the **g** due unto his	3519
	16:35	to thy holy name, *and* **g** in thy praise.	7623
	22: 5	of fame and of **g** throughout all countries:	8597
	29:11	the **g**, and the victory, and the majesty:	8597
2Ch	5:14	for the **g** of the LORD had filled the house	3519
	7: 1	and the **g** of the LORD filled the house.	3519
	7: 2	the **g** of the LORD had filled	3519
	7: 3	and the **g** of the LORD upon the house,	3519
Est	5:11	Haman told them of the **g** of his riches,	3519
Job	19: 9	He hath stript me of my **g**, and taken	3519
	29:20	My **g** *was* fresh in me, and my bow was	3519
	39:20	the **g** of his nostrils *is* terrible.	1935
	40:10	and array thyself with **g** and beauty.	1935
Ps	3: 3	my **g**, and the lifter up of mine head.	3519
	4: 2	how long *will ye turn* my **g** into shame?	3519
	8: 1	who hast set thy **g** above the heavens.	1935
	8: 5	hast crowned him *with* **g** and honour.	3519
	16: 9	my heart is glad, and my **g** rejoiceth:	3519
	19: 1	The heavens declare the **g** of God;	3519
	21: 5	His **g** *is* great in thy salvation: honour	3519
	24: 7	and the King of **g** shall come in.	3519
	24: 8	Who *is* this King of **g**? The LORD strong	3519
	24: 9	and the King of **g** shall come in.	3519
	24:10	Who is this King of **g**? The LORD of	3519
	24:10	The LORD of hosts, he *is* the King of **g**.	3519
	29: 1	give unto the LORD **g** and strength.	3519
	29: 2	Give unto the LORD the **g** due unto his	3519
	29: 3	the God of **g** thundereth: the LORD *is*	3519
	29: 9	his temple doth every one speak of *his* **g**.	3519
	30:12	To the end that my **g** may sing *praise* to	3519
	45: 3	*most* mighty, *with* thy **g** and thy majesty.	1935
	49:16	when the **g** of his house is increased;	3519
	49:17	his **g** shall not descend after him.	3519
	57: 5	heavens; *let* thy **g** *be* above all the earth.	3519
	57: 8	Awake up, my **g**; awake, psaltery and	3519
	57:11	heavens; *let* thy **g** *be* above all the earth.	3519
	62: 7	In God *is* my salvation and my **g**: the rock	3519
	63: 2	to see thy power and thy **g**, so *as* I have	3519
	63:11	every one that sweareth by him shall **g**:	1984
	64:10	him; and all the upright in heart shall **g**.	1984
	72:19	let the whole earth be filled *with* his **g**;	3519
	73:24	counsel, and afterward receive me *to* **g**.	3519
	78:61	and his **g** into the enemy's hand.	8597
	79: 9	of our salvation, for the **g** of thy name:	3519

Ps	84:11	the LORD will give grace and **g**: no good	3519
	85: 9	fear him; that **g** may dwell in our land.	3519
	89:17	For thou *art* the **g** of their strength:	8597
	89:44	Thou hast made his **g** to cease, and cast	2892
	90:16	servants, and thy **g** unto their children.	1926
	96: 3	Declare his **g** among the heathen,	3519
	96: 7	give unto the LORD **g** and strength.	3519
	96: 8	Give unto the LORD the **g** due unto his	3519
	97: 6	and all the people see his **g**.	3519
	102:15	and all the kings of the earth thy **g**.	3519
	102:16	build up Zion, he shall appear in his **g**.	3519
	104:31	of the LORD shall endure for ever:	3519
	105: 3	**G** ye in his holy name: let the heart of	1984
	106: 5	that *I may* **g** with thine inheritance.	1984
	106:20	Thus they changed their **g** into	3519
	108: 1	will sing and give praise, even *with* my **g**.	3519
	108: 5	heavens: and thy **g** above all the earth.	3519
	113: 4	all nations, *and* his **g** above the heavens.	3519
	115: 1	not unto us, but unto thy name give **g**,	3519
	138: 5	for great *is* the **g** of the LORD.	3519
	145:11	They shall speak of the **g** of thy kingdom,	3519
	148:13	his **g** *is* above the earth and heaven.	1935
	149: 5	Let the saints be joyful in **g**: let them sing	3519
Pr	3:35	The wise shall inherit **g**: but shame shall	3519
	4: 9	a crown of **g** shall she deliver *to* thee.	8597
	16:31	The hoary head *is* a crown of **g**, *if* it be	8597
	17: 6	and the **g** of children *are* their fathers.	8597
	19:11	and *it is* his **g** to pass over a transgression.	8597
	20:29	of young men *is* their strength:	8597
	25: 2	*It is* the **g** of God to conceal a thing:	3519
	25:27	*for men* to search their own **g** *is not* glory.	3519
	25:27	for men to search their own glory *is not* **g**.	3519
	28:12	righteous *men* do rejoice, *there* is great **g**:	8597
Isa	2:10	of the LORD, and for the **g** of his majesty.	1926
	2:19	of the LORD, and for the **g** of his majesty,	1926
	2:21	of the LORD, and for the **g** of his majesty,	1926
	3: 8	the LORD, to provoke the eyes of his **g**.	3519
	4: 5	for upon all the **g** *shall be* a defence.	3519
	5:14	their **g**, and their multitude, and their	1926
	6: 3	of hosts: the whole earth *is* full of his **g**.	3519
	8: 7	*even* the king of Assyria, and all his **g**:	3519
	10: 3	for help? and where will ye leave your **g**?	3519
	10:12	of Assyria, and the **g** of his high looks.	8597
	10:16	under his **g** he shall kindle a burning like	3519
	10:18	shall consume his **g** of his forest, and of	3519
	13:19	Babylon, the **g** of kingdoms, the beauty of	6643
	14:18	of the nations, *even* all of them, lie in **g**,	3519
	16:14	and the **g** of Moab shall be contemned,	3519
	17: 3	they shall be as the **g** of the children of	3519
	17: 4	*that* the **g** of Jacob shall be made thin,	3519
	20: 5	their expectation, and of Egypt their **g**.	8597
	21:16	a hireling, and all the **g** of Kedar shall fail:	3519
	22:18	there the chariots of thy **g** *shall be*	3519
	22:24	they shall hang upon him all the **g** of his	3519
	23: 9	stain the pride of all **g**, *and* to bring into	6643
	24:16	we heard songs, *even* **g** to the righteous.	6643
	28: 5	the LORD of hosts be for a crown of **g**,	6643
	35: 2	the **g** of Lebanon shall be given unto it,	3519
	35: 2	they shall see the **g** of the LORD,	3519
	40: 5	the **g** of the LORD shall be revealed,	3519
	41:16	and shalt **g** in the Holy One of Israel.	1984
	42: 8	my **g** will I not give to another, neither	3519
	42:12	Let them give **g** unto the LORD,	3519
	43: 7	for I have created him for my **g**, I have	3519
	44:25	the seed of Israel be justified, and shall **g**.	1984
	46:13	place salvation in Zion for Israel my **g**.	8597
	48:11	and I will not give my **g** unto another.	3519
	58: 8	the **g** of the LORD shall be thy rereward.	3519
	59:19	and his **g** from the rising of the sun.	3519
	60: 1	and the **g** of the LORD is risen upon thee.	3519
	60: 2	and his **g** shall be seen upon thee.	3519
	60: 7	and I will glorify the house of my **g**.	8597
	60:13	The **g** of Lebanon shall come unto thee,	3519
	60:19	an everlasting light, and thy God thy **g**.	8597
	61: 6	and in their **g** shall you boast yourselves.	3519
	62: 2	see thy righteousness, and all kings thy **g**:	3519
	62: 3	Thou shalt also be a crown of **g** in the	8597
	63:15	the habitation of thy holiness and of thy **g**:	8597
	66:11	be delighted with the abundance of her **g**.	3519
	66:12	the **g** of the Gentiles like a flowing stream:	3519
	66:18	and they shall come, and see my **g**.	3519
	66:19	heard my fame, neither have seen my **g**,	3519
	66:19	shall declare my **g** among the Gentiles.	3519
Jer	2:11	my people have changed their **g** for *that*	1984
	4: 2	in him, and in him shall they **g**.	1984
	9:23	Let not the wise *man* **g** in his wisdom,	1984
	9:23	neither let the mighty *man* **g** in his might,	1984
	9:23	let not the rich *man* **g** in his riches:	1984
	9:24	let him that glorieth **g** in this, that *he*	1984
	13:11	for a name, and for a praise, and for a **g**:	8597
	13:16	Give **g** to the LORD your God, before he	3519
	13:18	come down, *even* the crown of your **g**.	8597
	14:21	do not disgrace the throne of thy **g**:	3519
	22:18	for him, *saying,* Ah lord! or, Ah his **g**!	1935
	48:18	come down from *thy* **g**, and sit in thirst;	3519
Eze	1:28	of the likeness of the **g** of the LORD.	3519
	3:12	*saying,* Blessed *be* the **g** of the LORD	3519
	3:23	behold, the **g** of the LORD stood there,	3519
	3:23	as the **g** which I saw by the river of:	3519
	8: 4	the **g** of the God of Israel *was* there,	3519
	9: 3	the **g** of the God of Israel was gone up	3519
	10: 4	the **g** of the LORD went up from	3519
	10: 4	full of the brightness of the LORD's **g**.	3519
	10:18	the **g** of the LORD departed from off	3519
	10:19	the **g** of the God of Israel *was* over them	3519

Eze	11:22 the **g** of the God of Israel *was* over them	3519
	11:23 the **g** of the LORD went up from the midst	3519
	20: 6 and honey, which *is* the **g** of all lands;	6643
	20:15 and honey, which *is* the **g** of all lands;	6643
	24:25 the joy of their **g**, the desire of their eyes,	8597
	25: 9 the **g** of the country, Beth-jeshimoth,	6643
	26:20 and I shall set **g** in the land of the living;	6643
	31:18 To whom art thou thus like in **g** and	3519
	39:21 And I will set my **g** among the heathen,	3519
	43: 2 the **g** of the God of Israel came from	3519
	43: 2 and the earth shined with his **g**.	3519
	43: 4 the **g** of the LORD came into the house by	3519
	43: 5 the **g** of the LORD filled the house.	3519
	44: 4 the **g** of the LORD filled the house of	3519
Da	2:37 a kingdom, power, and strength, and **g**.	3367
	4:36 for the **g** of my kingdom, mine honour	3367
	5:18 and majesty, and **g**, and honour:	3367
	5:20 and they took *his* **g** from them;	3367
	7:14 **g**, and a kingdom, that all people, nations,	3367
	11:20 a raiser of taxes *in* the **g** of the kingdom:	1925
	11:39 he shall acknowledge *and* increase *with* **g**.	3519
Hos	4: 7 *therefore* will I change their **g** into shame.	3519
	9:11 their **g** shall fly away like a bird, from	3519
	10: 5 for the **g** thereof, because it is departed	3519
Mic	1:15 shall come unto Adullam the **g** of Israel.	3519
	2: 9 have ye taken *away* my **g** for ever.	1926
Na	2: 9 *and* **g** out of all the pleasant furniture.	3519
Hab	2:14 with the knowledge of the **g** of the LORD,	3519
	2:16 Thou art filled *with* shame for **g**: drink	3519
	2:16 and shameful spuing *shall be* on thy **g**.	3519
	3: 3 His **g** covered the heavens, and the earth	1935
Hag	2: 3 you that saw this house in her first **g**?	3519
	2: 7 I will fill this house *with* **g**, saith	3519
	2: 9 The **g** of this latter house shall be greater	3519
Zec	2: 5 and will be the **g** in the midst of her.	3519
	2: 8 After the **g** hath he sent me unto the	3519
	6:13 he shall bear the **g**, and shall sit and	1935
	11: 3 of the shepherds; for their **g** is spoiled:	155
	12: 7 that the **g** of the house of David and	8597
	12: 7 the **g** of the inhabitants of Jerusalem do	8597
Mal	2: 2 to give **g** unto my name, saith the LORD	3519
Mt	4: 8 kingdoms of the world, and the **g** of them;	*1391*
	6: 2 the streets, that they may **have g** of men.	*1392*
	6:13 and the power, and the **g**, for ever.	*1391*
	6:29 That even Solomon in all his **g** was not	*1391*
	16:27 For the Son of man shall come in the **g** of	*1391*
	19:28 Son of man shall sit in the throne of his **g**,	*1391*
	24:30 clouds of heaven with power and great **g**.	*1391*
	25:31 When the Son of man shall come in his **g**,	*1391*
	25:31 then shall he sit upon the throne of his **g**:	*1391*
Mk	8:38 when he cometh in the **g** of his Father	*1391*
	10:37 and the other on thy left hand, in thy **g**.	*1391*
	13:26 in *the* clouds with great power and **g**.	*1391*
Lk	2: 9 of the Lord shone round about them:	*1391*
	2:14 **G** to God in the highest, and on earth	*1391*
	2:32 the Gentiles, and the **g** of thy people Israel.	*1391*
	4: 6 power will I give thee, and the **g** of them:	*1391*
	9:26 when he shall come in his own **g**, and	*1391*
	9:31 Who appeared in **g**, and spake of his	*1391*
	9:32 saw his **g**, and the two men that stood	*1391*
	12:27 *that* Solomon in all his **g** was not arrayed	*1391*
	17:18 are not found that returned to give **g**	*1391*
	19:38 peace in heaven, and **g** in the highest.	*1391*
	21:27 coming in a cloud with power and great **g**.	*1391*
	24:26 these *things*, and to enter into his **g**?	*1391*
Jn	1:14 dwelt among us, (and we beheld his **g**,	*1391*
	1:14 the **g** as of the only begotten of the Father,	*1391*
	2:11 of Galilee, and manifested forth his **g**;	*1391*
	7:18 speaketh of himself seeketh his own **g**:	*1391*
	7:18 but he that seeketh his **g** that sent him,	*1391*
	8:50 And I seek not mine own **g**: there is *one*	*1391*
	11: 4 is not unto death, but for the **g** of God,	*1391*
	11:40 thou shouldest see the **g** of God?	*1391*
	12:41 when he saw his **g**, and spake of him.	*1391*
	17: 5 **g** which I had with thee before the world	*1391*
	17:22 And the **g** which thou gavest me I have	*1391*
	17:24 they may behold my **g**, which thou hast	*1391*
Ac	7: 2 The God of **g** appeared unto our father	*1391*
	7:55 and saw the **g** of God, and Jesus standing	*1391*
	12:23 him, because he gave not God the **g**:	*1391*
	22:11 And when I could not see for the **g** of that	*1391*
Ro	1:23 And changed the **g** of the uncorruptible	*1391*
	2: 7 continuance in well doing seek for **g**	*1391*
	2:10 **g**, honour, and peace, to every man that	*1391*
	3: 7 *more* abounded through my lie unto his **g**;	*1391*
	3:23 and come short of the **g** of God.	*1391*
	4: 2 justified by works, he hath whereof to **g**;	2745
	4:20 but was strong in faith, giving **g** to God;	*1391*
	5: 2 and rejoice in hope of the **g** of God.	*1391*
	5: 3 not only *so*, but we **g** in tribulations also:	2744
	6: 4 up from the dead by the **g** of the Father,	*1391*
	8:18 with the **g** which shall be revealed in us.	*1391*
	9: 4 the **g**, and the covenants, and the giving	*1391*
	9:23 the riches of his **g** on the vessels of mercy,	*1391*
	9:23 which he had afore prepared unto **g**,	*1391*
	11:36 are all *things*: to whom *be* **g** for ever.	*1391*
	15: 7 as Christ also received us, to the **g** of God.	*1391*
	15:17 whereof *I* may **g** through Jesus Christ in	2746
	16:27 *be* **g** through Jesus Christ for ever.	*1391*
1Co	1:29 That no flesh should **g** in his presence.	2744
	1:31 He that glorieth, let him **g** in the Lord.	2744
	2: 7 God ordained before the world unto our **g**:	*1391*
	2: 8 would not have crucified the Lord of **g**.	*1391*
	3:21 Therefore let no *man* **g** in men. For all	2744
	4: 7 if thou didst receive *it*, why dost thou **g**,	2744

1Co	9:16 I preach the gospel, I have nothing to **g** of:	2745
	10:31 whatsoever ye do, do all to the **g** of God.	*1391*
	11: 7 as he is the image and **g** of God:	*1391*
	11: 7 God: but the woman is the **g** of the man.	*1391*
	11:15 if a woman have long hair, it is a **g** to her:	*1391*
	15:40 but the **g** of the celestial *is* one,	*1391*
	15:40 one, and the **g** of the terrestrial *is* another.	NIG
	15:41 *is* one **g** of the sun, and another glory	*1391*
	15:41 and another **g** of the moon,	*1391*
	15:41 of the moon, and another **g** of the stars:	*1391*
	15:41 one star differeth from *another* star in **g**.	*1391*
	15:43 It is sown in dishonour; it is raised in **g**:	*1391*
2Co	1:20 in him Amen, unto the **g** of God by us.	*1391*
	3: 7 of Moses for the **g** of his countenance;	*1391*
	3: 7 which **g** was to be done away:	NIG
	3: 9 if the ministration of condemnation *be* **g**,	*1391*
	3: 9 ministration of righteousness exceed in **g**.	*1391*
	3:10 made glorious **had** no **g** in this respect,	*1392*
	3:10 by reason of the **g** that excelleth.	*1391*
	3:18 open face beholding as in a glass the **g**	*1391*
	3:18 are changed *into* the same image from **g** to	*1391*
	3:18 *into* the same image from glory to **g**,	*1391*
	4: 6 to give the light of the knowledge of the **g**	*1391*
	4:15 of many redound to the **g** of God.	*1391*
	4:17 more exceeding *and* eternal weight of **g**;	*1391*
	5:12 but give you occasion to **g** on our behalf,	2745
	5:12 to *answer* them which **g** in appearance,	2744
	8:19 which is administered by us to the **g** of	*1391*
	8:23 of the churches, *and* the **g** of Christ.	*1391*
	10:17 But he that glorieth, let him **g** in the Lord.	2744
	11:12 that wherein they **g**, they may be found	2744
	11:18 Seeing that many **g** after the flesh, I will	2744
	11:18 many glory after the flesh, I will **g** also.	2744
	11:30 If I must needs **g**, I will glory of the *things*	2744
	11:30 I will **g** of the *things* which concern mine	2744
	12: 1 It is not expedient for me doubtless to **g**.	2744
	12: 5 Of such a one will I **g**: yet of myself I will	2744
	12: 5 yet of myself I will not **g**, but in mine	2744
	12: 6 For though I would desire to **g**, I shall not	2744
	12: 9 therefore will I rather **g** in my infirmities,	2744
Gal	1: 5 To whom *be* **g** for ever and ever. Amen.	*1391*
	5:26 Let us not be desirous of **vain g**,	2755
	6:13 that they may **g** in your flesh.	2744
	6:14 But God forbid that I should **g**, save in	2744
Eph	1: 6 To the praise of the **g** of his grace,	*1391*
	1:12 That we should be to the praise of his **g**,	*1391*
	1:14 unto the praise of his **g**.	*1391*
	1:17 of our Lord Jesus Christ, the Father of **g**,	*1391*
	1:18 what the riches of the **g** of his inheritance	*1391*
	3:13 at my tribulations for you, which is your **g**.	*1391*
	3:16 grant you, according to the riches of his **g**,	*1391*
	3:21 Unto him *be* **g** in the church by Christ	*1391*
Php	1:11 which are by Jesus Christ unto the **g** and	*1391*
	2:11 Christ *is* Lord, to the **g** of God the Father.	*1391*
	3:19 *their* belly, and *whose* **g** *is* in their shame,	*1391*
	4:19 according to his riches in **g** by Christ Jesus.	*1391*
	4:20 and our Father *be* **g** for ever and ever.	*1391*
Col	1:27 the **g** of this mystery among the Gentiles;	*1391*
	1:27 which is Christ in you, the hope of **g**:	*1391*
	3: 4 then shall ye also appear with him in **g**.	*1391*
1Th	2: 6 Nor of men sought we **g**, neither of you,	*1391*
	2:12 hath called you unto his kingdom and **g**.	*1391*
	2:20 For ye are our **g** and joy.	*1391*
2Th	1: 4 So that we ourselves **g** in you in	2744
	1: 9 of the Lord, and from the **g** of his power;	*1391*
	2:14 to the obtaining of the **g** of our Lord Jesus	*1391*
1Ti	1:17 *be* honour and **g** for ever and ever.	*1391*
	3:16 on in the world, received up into **g**.	*1391*
2Ti	2:10 which is in Christ Jesus with eternal **g**.	*1391*
	4:18 to whom *be* **g** for ever and ever. Amen.	*1391*
Heb	1: 3 Who being the brightness of *his* **g**,	*1391*
	2: 7 thou crownedst him with **g** and honour,	*1391*
	2: 9 of death, crowned with **g** and honour;	*1391*
	2:10 all *things*, in bringing many sons unto **g**,	*1391*
	3: 3 this *man* was counted worthy of more **g**	*1391*
	9: 5 over it the cherubims of **g** shadowing	*1391*
	13:21 to whom *be* **g** for ever and ever.	*1391*
Jas	2: 1 *the* Lord of **g**, with respect of persons.	*1391*
	3:14 **g** not, and lie *not* against the truth.	2620
1Pe	1: 7 and **g** at the appearing of Jesus Christ:	*1391*
	1: 8 rejoice with joy unspeakable and **full of g**:	*1392*
	1:11 of Christ, and the **g** that should follow.	*1391*
	1:21 him up from the dead, and gave him **g**;	*1391*
	1:24 and all the **g** of man as the flower of grass.	*1391*
	2:20 what **g** *is it*, if, when ye be buffeted for	2811
	4:13 that, when his **g** shall be revealed, ye may	*1391*
	4:14 happy *are ye*; for the spirit of **g** and of God	*1391*
	5: 1 also a partaker of the **g** that shall be	*1391*
	5: 4 shall receive a crown of **g** that fadeth not	*1391*
	5:10 who hath called us into his eternal **g** by	*1391*
	5:11 To him *be* **g** and dominion for ever and	*1391*
2Pe	1: 3 knowledge of him that hath called us to **g**	*1391*
	1:17 from God the Father honour and **g**,	*1391*
	1:17 such a voice to him from the excellent **g**,	*1391*
	3:18 To him *be* **g** both now and for ever.	*1391*
Jude	1:24 the presence of his **g** with exceeding joy,	*1391*
	1:25 *be* **g** and majesty, dominion and power,	*1391*
Rev	1: 6 to him *be* **g** and dominion for ever and	*1391*
	4: 9 And when *those* beasts give **g** and honour	*1391*
	4:11 to receive **g** and honour and power:	*1391*
	5:12 strength, and honour, and **g**, and blessing.	*1391*
	5:13 Blessing, and honour, and **g**, and power,	*1391*
	7:12 and **g**, and wisdom, and thanksgiving,	*1391*
	11:13 and gave **g** to the God of heaven.	*1391*
	14: 7 a loud voice, Fear God, and give **g** to him;	*1391*

Rev	15: 8 was filled with smoke from the **g** of God,	*1391*
	16: 9 and they repented not to give him **g**.	*1391*
	18: 1 and the earth was lightened with his **g**.	*1391*
	19: 1 Alleluia; Salvation, and **g**, and honour,	*1391*
	21:11 Having the **g** of God: and her light *was*	*1391*
	21:23 for the **g** of God did lighten it,	*1391*
	21:24 the kings of the earth do bring their **g** and	*1391*
	21:26 And they shall bring the **g** and honour of	*1391*

GLORYING (4) [GLORY]

1Co	5: 6 Your **g** *is* not good. Know ye not that a	2745
	9:15 that any *man* should make my **g** void.	2745
2Co	7: 4 great toward you, great *is* my **g** of you:	2746
	12:11 am become a fool in **g**; ye have compelled	2744

GLOWING METAL See AMBER

GLUTTON (2) [GLUTTONOUS]

Dt	21:20 obey our voice; *he is* a **g**, and a drunkard.	2151
Pr	23:21 and the **g** shall come to poverty:	2151

GLUTTONOUS (2) [GLUTTON]

Mt	11:19 Behold a man **g**, and a winebibber,	*5314*
Lk	7:34 ye say, Behold a **g** man, and a winebibber,	*5314*

GNASH (2) [GNASHED, GNASHETH, GNASHING]

Ps	112:10 he shall **g** *with* his teeth, and melt away:	2786
La	2:16 they hiss and **g** the teeth: they say, We	2786

GNASHED (2) [GNASH]

Ps	35:16 in feasts, they **g** upon me *with* their teeth.	2786
Ac	7:54 and they **g** on him *with their* teeth.	*1031*

GNASHETH (3) [GNASH]

Job	16: 9 he **g** upon me with his teeth; mine enemy	2786
Ps	37:12 the just, and **g** upon him *with* his teeth.	2786
Mk	9:18 and **g** with his teeth, and pineth away:	*5149*

GNASHING (7) [GNASH]

Mt	8:12 there shall be weeping and **g** of teeth.	*1030*
	13:42 fire: there shall be wailing and **g** of teeth.	*1030*
	13:50 fire: there shall be wailing and **g** of teeth.	*1030*
	22:13 there shall be weeping and **g** of teeth.	*1030*
	24:51 there shall be weeping and **g** of teeth.	*1030*
	25:30 there shall be weeping and **g** of teeth.	*1030*
Lk	13:28 There shall be weeping and **g** of teeth,	*1030*

GNAT (1)

Mt	23:24 strain out a **g**, and swallow a camel.	*2971*

GNAW (1) [GNAWED]

Zep	3: 3 they **g** not the **bones** till the morrow.	1633

GNAWED (1) [GNAW]

Rev	16:10 and they **g** their tongues for pain,	*3145*

GO (1492) [GOEST, GOETH, GOING, GOINGS, GONE, OUTGOINGS, OUTWENT, WENT, WENTEST]

Ge	3:14 upon thy belly shalt thou **g**, and dust shalt	1980
	8:16 **G** forth of the ark, thou, and thy wife,	3318
	9:10 all that **g** *out* of the ark, to every beast	3318
	11: 3 **G** to, let us make brick, and burn *them*	3051
	11: 4 they said, **G to**, let us build us a city and	3051
	11: 7 **G to**, let us go down, and there confound	3051
	11: 7 let us go **down**, and there confound their	3381
	11:31 Chaldees, to **g** into the land of Canaan;	1980
	12: 5 they went forth to **g** into the land of	1980
	12:19 behold thy wife, take *her*, and **g** thy way.	1980
	13: 9 the left hand, then I will **g** to the **right**;	3231
	13: 9 the right hand, then I will **g** to the **left**.	8041
	15: 2 seeing I **g** childless, and the steward of	1980
	15:15 thou shalt **g** to thy fathers in peace;	935
	16: 2 I pray thee, **g in** unto my maid; it may be	935
	16: 8 whither wilt thou **g**? And she said, I flee	1980
	18:21 I will **g down** now, and see whether they	3381
	19: 2 ye shall rise up early, and **g** on your ways.	1980
	19:34 thou **in**, *and* lie with him, that we may	935
	22: 5 I and the lad will **g** yonder and worship,	1980
	24: 4 thou shalt **g** unto my country, and to my	1980
	24:11 *even* the time that *women* **g** *out* to draw	3318
	24:38 thou shalt **g** unto my father's house,	1980
	24:42 if now thou do prosper my way which I **g**:	1980
	24:51 *her*, and **g**, and let her be thy master's	1980
	24:55 at the least ten; after *that* she shall **g**.	1980
	24:56 send me away that I may **g** to my master.	1980
	24:58 said unto her, Wilt thou **g** with this man?	1980
	24:58 go with this man? And she said, I will **g**.	1980
	26: 2 him, and said, **G** not **down** into Egypt;	3381
	26:16 Abimelech said unto Isaac, **G** from us;	1980
	27: 3 **g** *out* to the field, and take me *some*	3318
	27: 9 **G** now to the flock, and fetch me from	1980
	27:13 only obey my voice, and **g** fetch me *them*.	1980
	28: 2 Arise, **g** to Padan-aram, to the house of	1980
	28:20 will keep me in this way that I **g**,	1980
	29: 7 water ye the sheep, and **g** *and* feed *them*.	1980
	29:21 days are fulfilled, that I may **g in** unto her.	935
	30: 3 Behold my maid Bilhah, **g in** unto her;	935
	30:25 that I may **g** unto mine own place,	1980
	30:26 whom I have served thee, and let me **g**:	1980
	31:18 for to **g** to Isaac his father in the land of	935
	32:26 he said, **Let** me **g**, for the day breaketh.	7971
	32:26 he said, I will not **let** thee **g**, except thou	7971
	33:12 and let us **g**, and I will go before thee.	1980
	33:12 and let us **go**, and I will before thee.	1980
	35: 1 Arise, **g up** to Beth-el, and dwell there:	5927

G

Ge 35: 3 let us arise, and **g up** to Beth-el; and I 5927
37:14 said to him, **G**, I pray thee, see whether 1980
37:17 for I heard *them* say, Let us **g** to Dothan. 1980
37:30 The child *is* not; and I, whither shall I **g**? 935
37:35 For I will **g down** into the grave unto my 3381
38: 8 **G in** unto thy brother's wife, and marry 935
38:16 **G to**, I pray thee, let me come in unto 3051
41:55 unto all the Egyptians, **G** unto Joseph; 1980
42:15 By the life of Pharaoh ye shall not **g forth** 3318
42:19 **g** ye, carry corn *for* the famine of your 1980
42:38 said, My son shall not **g down** with you; 3381
42:38 befall him by the way in the which ye **g**, 1980
43: 2 unto them, **G again**, buy us a little food. 7725
43: 4 we will **g down** and buy thee food; 3381
43: 5 wilt not send *him*, we will not **g down**: 3381
43: 8 the lad with me, and we will arise and **g**; 1980
43:13 and arise, **g again** unto the man: 7725
44:25 **G again**, *and* buy us a little food. 7725
44:26 we said, We cannot **g down**: if our 3381
44:26 brother be with us, then will we **g down**: 3381
44:33 and let the lad **g up** with his brethren. 5927
44:34 For how shall I **g up** to my father, 5927
45: 1 **Cause** every man to **g out** from me. 3318
45: 9 and **g up** to my father, and say unto him, 5927
45:17 lade your beasts, and **g**, get you unto 1980
45:28 yet alive: I will **g** and see him before I die. 1980
46: 3 fear not to **g down** into Egypt; for I will 3381
46: 4 I will **g down** with thee into Egypt; 3381
46:31 I will **g up**, and shew Pharaoh, and say 5927
50: 5 Now therefore let me **g up**, I pray thee, 5927
50: 6 Pharaoh said, **G up**, and bury thy father, 5927

Ex 2: 7 Shall I **g** and call to thee a nurse of 1980
2: 8 Pharaoh's daughter said to her, **G**. 1980
3:11 that I should **g** unto Pharaoh, and that I 1980
3:16 **G**, and gather the elders of Israel together, 1980
3:18 now let us **g**, we beseech thee, three days' 1980
3:19 that the king of Egypt will not let you **g**, 1980
3:20 and after that he will **let** you **g**. 7971
3:21 it shall come to pass, that, when ye **g**, 1980
3:21 that, when ye go, ye shall not **g** empty: 1980
4:12 Now therefore **g**, and I will be with thy 1980
4:18 Let me **g**, I pray thee, and return unto my 1980
4:18 And Jethro said to Moses, **G** in peace. 1980
4:19 Moses in Midian, **G**, return *into* Egypt: 1980
4:21 heart, that he shall not **let** the people **g**. 7971
4:23 I say unto thee, **Let** my son **g**, that he 7971
4:23 *if* thou refuse to **let** him **g**, behold, I will 7971
4:26 So he **let** him **g**: then she said, A bloody 7503
4:27 **G** into the wilderness to meet Moses. 1980
5: 1 LORD God of Israel, **Let** my people **g**, 7971
5: 2 that I should obey his voice to **let** Israel **g**? 7971
5: 2 not the LORD, neither will I **let** Israel **g**. 7971
5: 3 let us **g**, we pray thee, three days' journey 1980
5: 7 let them **g** and gather straw for 1980
5: 8 Let us **g** *and* sacrifice to our God. 1980
5:11 **G** ye, get you straw where you can find *it*: 1980
5:17 Let us **g** *and* do sacrifice to the LORD. 1980
5:18 **G** therefore now, *and* work; for there 1980
6: 1 for with a strong hand shall he **let** them **g**, 7971
6:11 **G in**, speak unto Pharaoh king of Egypt, 935
6:11 he **let** the children of Israel **g** out of his 7971
7:14 hardened, he refuseth to **let** the people **g**. 7971
7:16 saying, **Let** my people **g**, that they may 7971
8: 1 unto Pharaoh, and say unto him, 935
8: 1 Thus saith the LORD, **Let** my people **g**, 7971
8: 2 if thou refuse to **let** *them* **g**, behold, I will 7971
8: 3 which shall **g up** and come into thine 5927
8: 8 I will **let** the people **g**, that they may do 7971
8:20 Thus saith the LORD, **Let** my people **g**, 7971
8:21 Else, if thou wilt not **let** my people **g**, 7971
8:25 for Moses and for Aaron, and said, **G** ye, 1980
8:27 We will **g** three days' journey into 1980
8:28 Pharaoh said, I will **let** you **g**, that ye may 7971
8:28 only you shall not **g** very far away: 1980
8:29 I **g out** from thee, and I will intreat 3318
8:29 **letting** the people **g** to sacrifice to 7971
8:32 also, neither would he **let** the people **g**. 7971
9: 1 Moses, **G in** unto Pharaoh, and tell him, 935
9: 1 **Let** my people **g**, that they may serve me. 7971
9: 2 For if thou refuse to **let** *them* **g**, and wilt 7971
9: 7 and he did not **let** the people **g**. 7971
9:13 **Let** my people **g**, that they may serve me. 7971
9:17 my people, that *thou* wilt not **let** them **g**? 7971
9:28 I will **let** you **g**, and ye shall stay no 7971
9:35 would he **let** the children of Israel **g**; 7971
10: 1 said unto Moses, **G in** unto Pharaoh: 935
10: 3 **let** my people **g**, that they may serve me. 7971
10: 4 Else, if thou refuse to **let** my people **g**, 7971
10: 7 **let** the men **g**, that they may serve 7971
10: 8 he said unto them, **G**, serve the LORD 1980
10: 8 your God: *but* who *are* they that shall **g**? 1980
10: 9 We will **g** with our young and with our 1980
10: 9 our flocks and with our herds will we **g**; 1980
10:10 as I will **let** you **g**, and your little ones: 7971
10:11 **g** now ye *that are* men, and serve 1980
10:20 he would not **let** the children of Israel **g**. 7971
10:24 and said, **G** ye, serve the LORD: 1980
10:24 let your little ones also **g** with you. 1980
10:26 Our cattle also shall **g** with us; there shall 1980
10:27 and he would not **let** them **g**. 7971
11: 1 afterwards he will **let** you **g** hence: 7971
11: 1 when he shall **let** *you* **g**, he shall surely 7971
11: 4 About midnight will I **g out** into the midst 3318
11: 8 after that I will **g out**. And he went out 3318
11:10 he would not **let** the children of Israel **g** 7971

Ex 12:22 none of you shall **g out** at the door of his 3318
12:31 and **g**, serve the LORD, as ye have said. 1980
13:15 when Pharaoh would hardly **let** us **g**, 7971
13:17 pass, when Pharaoh had let the people **g**, 7971
13:21 to give them light; to **g** by day and by night: 1980
14: 5 that we have **let** Israel **g** from serving us? 7971
14:15 children of Israel, that they **g forward**: 5265
14:16 children of Israel shall **g** on dry *ground* 935
14:21 the LORD **caused** the sea to **g** *back* by a 1980
16: 4 the people shall **g out** and gather a certain 3318
16:29 let no man **g out** of his place on the 3318
17: 5 **G on** before the people, and take with 5674
17: 5 the river, take in thine hand, and **g**. 1980
17: 9 men, and **g out**, fight with Amalek: 3318
18:23 all this people shall also **g** to their place in 935
19:10 **G** unto the people, and sanctify them 1980
19:12 *that* ye **g** *not* **up** into the mount, 5927
19:21 unto Moses, **G** down, charge the people, 3381
20:26 Neither shalt thou **g up** by steps unto 5927
21: 2 in the seventh he shall **g out** free for 3318
21: 3 in by himself, he shall **g out** by himself: 3318
21: 3 then his wife shall **g out** with him. 3318
21: 4 master's, and he shall **g out** by himself. 3318
21: 5 and my children; I will not **g out** free: 3318
21: 7 shall not **g out** as the menservants do. 3318
21:11 then shall she **g out** free without money. 3318
21:26 he shall let him **g** free for his eye's sake. 7971
21:27 he shall let him **g** free for his tooth's sake. 7971
23:23 For mine Angel shall **g** before thee, 1980
24: 2 neither shall the people **g up** with him. 5927
30:20 When they **g** into the tabernacle of 935
32: 1 make us gods, which shall **g** before us; 1980
32: 1 said unto Moses, **G**, get thee down; 1980
32:23 Make us gods, which shall **g** before us: 1980
32:27 *and* **g in** and out from gate to gate 5674
32:30 now I will **g up** unto the LORD; 5927
32:34 Therefore now **g**, lead the people unto 1980
32:34 behold, mine Angel shall **g** before thee: 1980
33: 1 *and* **g up**, thou and the people 5927
33: 3 for I will not **g up** in the midst of thee; 5927
33:14 My presence shall **g** *with thee*, and I will 1980
33:15 If thy presence **g** not *with me*, carry us not 1980
34: 9 let my Lord, I pray thee, **g** amongst us; 1980
34:15 they **g a whoring** after their gods, 2181
34:16 their daughters **g a whoring** after their 2181
34:16 **make** thy sons **g a whoring** after their 2181
34:24 when thou shalt **g up** to appear before 5927

Lev 4:15 upon the altar; it shall never **g out**. 3518
8:33 ye shall not **g out** of the door of 3318
9: 7 **G** unto the altar, and offer thy sin offering 7126
10: 7 ye shall not **g out** from the door of 3318
10: 9 when ye **g** into the tabernacle of 935
11:27 among all *manner of* beasts that **g** on *all* 1980
14: 3 the priest shall **g forth** out of the camp; 3318
14:36 before the priest **g** *into it* to see the plague, 935
14:36 afterward the priest shall **g in** to see 935
14:38 the priest shall **g out** of the house to 3318
14:53 he shall **let g** the living bird out of the city 7971
15:16 if any man's seed of copulation **g out** from 3318
16:10 to **let** him **g** for a scapegoat into 7971
16:18 he shall **g out** unto the altar that *is* before 3318
16:22 he shall **let g** the goat in the wilderness. 7971
16:26 he that **let g** the goat for the scapegoat 7971
19:16 Thou shalt not **g up and down** *as a* 1980
20: 5 and all that **g a whoring** after him, 2181
20: 6 after wizards, to **g a whoring** after them, 2181
21:11 Neither shall he **g in** to any dead body, 935
21:12 Neither shall he **g out** of the sanctuary, 3318
21:23 Only he shall not **g** in unto the vail, 935
25:28 in the jubile it shall **g out**, and he shall 3318
25:30 it shall not **g out** in the jubile. 3318
25:31 they shall **g out** in the jubile. 3318
25:33 shall **g out** in the *year of* jubile: 3318
25:54 then he shall **g out** in the year of jubile, 3318
26: 6 shall the sword **g** through your land. 5674
26:13 of your yoke, and **made** you **g** upright. 5674

Nu 1: 3 *that are* able to **g forth** to war in Israel: 3318
1:20 all that *were* able to **g forth** *to* war; 3318
1:22 all that *were* able to **g forth** *to* war; 3318
1:24 all that *were* able to **g forth** *to* war; 3318
1:26 all that *were* able to **g forth** *to* war; 3318
1:28 all that *were* able to **g forth** *to* war; 3318
1:30 all that *were* able to **g forth** *to* war; 3318
1:32 all that *were* able to **g forth** *to* war; 3318
1:34 all that *were* able to **g forth** *to* war; 3318
1:36 all that *were* able to **g forth** *to* war; 3318
1:38 all that *were* able to **g forth** *to* war; 3318
1:40 all that *were* able to **g forth** *to* war; 3318
1:42 all that *were* able to **g forth** *to* war; 3318
1:45 all that *were* able to **g forth** *to* war in 3318
2:24 they shall **g forward** in the third rank. 5265
2:31 shall **g** hindmost with their standards. 5265
4:19 holy *things*: Aaron and his sons shall **g in**, 935
4:20 they shall not **g** in to see when the holy 935
5:12 If any man's wife **g aside**, and commit a 7847
5:22 water that causeth the curse shall **g** into 935
8:15 after that shall the Levites **g in** to do 935
8:24 upward they shall **g in** to wait upon 935
10: 5 that lie on the east parts shall **g forward**. 5265
10: 9 ye **g** *to* war in your land against the enemy 935
10:30 he said unto him, I will not **g**; but I will 1980
10:32 shall be, if thou **g** with us, yea, it shall be, 1980
13:17 and **g up** into the mountain: 5927
13:30 Let us **g up at once**, and possess it; 5927+5927
13:31 We be not able to **g up** against the people; 5927

Nu 14:40 will **g up** unto the place which the LORD 5927
14:42 **G** not up, for the LORD *is* not among 5927
14:44 they presumed to **g up** unto the hill top: 5927
15:39 after which ye use to **g a whoring**: 2181
16:30 and they **g down** quick into the pit; 3381
16:46 quickly unto the congregation, 1980
20:17 we will **g** *by* the king's *high* way, we will 1980
20:19 said unto him, We will **g** by the high way: 5927
20:19 *doing any* thing *else*, **g through** on 5674
20:20 he said, Thou shalt not **g through**. 5674
21:22 we will **g along** by the king's *high* way, 1980
22:12 Balaam, Thou shalt not **g** with them; 1980
22:13 refuseth to give me leave to **g** with you. 1980
22:18 I cannot **g beyond** the word of the LORD 5674
22:20 to call thee, rise up, *and* **g** with them; 1980
22:35 LORD said unto Balaam, **G** with the men: 1980
23: 3 Stand by thy burnt offering, and I will **g**: 1980
23:16 said, **G again** unto Balak, and say thus. 7725
24:13 I cannot **g beyond** the commandment of 5674
24:14 now behold, I **g** unto my people: come 1980
26: 2 all that *are* able to **g** *to* war in Israel. 3318
27:17 Which may **g out** before them, 3318
27:17 which may **g in** before them, and which 935
27:21 at his word shall they **g out**, and at his 3318
31: 3 let them **g** against the Midianites, 1961
31:23 ye shall **make** *it* **g** the fire, and it shall be 5674
31:23 that abideth not the fire ye shall **make g** 5674
32: 6 Shall your brethren **g** to war, and shall ye 935
32: 9 that *they* should not **g** into the land which 935
32:17 we ourselves will **g ready armed** before 2502
32:20 if ye will **g armed** before the LORD to 2502
32:21 will **g** all of you armed **over** Jordan before 5674
34: 4 shall **g on** *to* Hazar-addar, and pass on to 3318
34: 9 the border shall **g on** to Ziphron, 3318
34:11 the coast shall **g down** from Shepham *to* 3381
34:12 the border shall **g down** to Jordan, 3381

Dt 1: 7 **g** *to* the mount of the Amorites, and unto 935
1: 8 **g in** and possess the land which the LORD 935
1:21 **g up** and possess *it*, as the LORD God of 5927
1:22 word again by what way we must **g up**, 5927
1:26 Notwithstanding ye would not **g up**, 5927
1:28 Whither shall we **g up**? our brethren have 5927
1:33 to shew you by what way ye should **g**, 1980
1:37 Thou also shalt not **g in** thither. 935
1:38 standeth before thee, he shall **g in** thither: 935
1:39 they shall **g in** thither, and unto them will 935
1:41 against the LORD, we will **g up** and fight, 5927
1:41 war, ye were ready to **g up** into the hill. 5927
1:42 Say unto them, **G** not **up**, neither fight; 5927
2:27 I will **g along** by the high way, I will 1980
3:25 let me **g over**, and see the good land that 5674
3:27 for thou shalt not **g over** this Jordan. 5674
3:28 for he shall **g over** before this people, 5674
4: 1 **g in** and possess the land which the LORD 935
4: 5 so in the land whither ye **g** to possess it. 935
4:14 in the land whither ye **g over** to possess 5674
4:21 sware that I should not **g over** Jordan, 5674
4:21 that *I* should not **g in** unto *that* good land, 935
4:22 die in this land, I *must* not **g over** Jordan: 5674
4:22 *shall* **g over**, and possess that good land. 5674
4:26 whereunto ye **g over** Jordan to possess 5674
4:34 Or hath God assayed to **g** *and* take him a 935
4:40 that it may **g well** with thee, and with 3190
5:16 and that it may **g well** with thee, 3190
5:27 **G** thou **near**, and hear all that the LORD 7126
5:30 **G** say to them, Get you into your tents 1980
6: 1 in the land whither ye **g** to possess it: 5674
6:14 Ye shall not **g** after other gods, of the gods 1980
6:18 thou mayest **g in** and possess the good 935
8: 1 **g in** and possess the land which the LORD 935
9: 1 to **g in** to possess nations greater and 935
9: 5 heart, dost thou **g** to possess their land: 935
9:23 **G up** and possess the land which I have 5927
10:11 that they may **g in** and possess the land, 935
11: 8 be strong, and **g in** and possess the land, 935
11: 8 the land, whither ye **g** to possess it; 5674
11:11 the land, whither ye **g** to possess it, *is a* 5674
11:28 to **g** after other gods, which ye have not 1980
11:31 For ye shall pass over Jordan to **g in** to 935
12:10 *when* ye **g over** Jordan and dwell in 5674
12:25 that it may **g well** with thee, and with 3190
12:26 **g** unto the place which the LORD shall 935
12:28 that it may **g well** with thee, and with 3190
13: 2 saying, Let us **g** after other gods, 1980
13: 6 Let us **g** and serve other gods, 1980
13:13 saying, Let us **g** and serve other gods, 1980
14:25 shalt **g** unto the place which the LORD 1980
15:12 the seventh year thou shalt **let** him **g** free 7971
15:13 thou shalt not **let** him **g away** empty: 7971
15:16 unto thee, I will not **g away** from thee; 3318
16: 7 turn in the morning, and **g** unto thy tents. 1980
19:13 from Israel, that *it may* **g** well with thee. NIH
19:21 *but* life *shall* **g** for life, eye for eye, tooth NIH
20: 5 let him **g** and return to his house, lest he 1980
20: 6 let him *also* **g** and return unto his house, 1980
20: 7 let him **g** and return unto his house, lest 1980
20: 8 let him **g** and return unto his house, lest 1980
21:13 after that thou shalt **g in** unto her, and be 935
21:14 then thou shalt **let** her **g** whither she will; 7971
22: 1 see thy brother's ox or his sheep **g astray**, 5080
22: 7 shalt **in any wise let** the dam **g**, 7971+7971
22:13 a wife, and **g** in unto her, and hate her, 935
23:10 shall he **g abroad out** of the camp, 3318
23:12 whither thou shalt **g forth** abroad: 3318
24: 2 she may **g** and be another man's *wife*. 1980

Dt	24: 5 a new wife, he shall not **g out** to war,	3318
	24:10 thou shalt not **g** into his house to fetch his	935
	24:15 neither shall the sun **g down** upon it;	935
	24:19 field, thou shalt not **g again** to fetch it:	7725
	24:20 thou shalt not **g over the boughs** again:	6286
	25: 5 her husband's brother shall **g in** unto her,	935
	25: 7 let his brother's wife **g up** to the gate	5927
	26: 2 shalt **g** unto the place which the LORD	1980
	26: 3 thou shalt **g** unto the priest that shall be in	935
	27: 3 that thou mayest **g in** unto the land which	935
	28:14 thou shalt not **g aside** from any of	5493
	28:14 left, to **g** after other gods to serve them.	1980
	28:25 thou shalt **g out** one way against them,	3318
	28:41 enjoy them; for they shall **g** into captivity.	1980
	29:18 to **g** and serve the gods of these nations;	1980
	30:12 Who shall **g up** for us to heaven,	5927
	30:13 Who shall **g over** the sea for us, and bring	5674
	30:18 whither thou passest over Jordan to **g** to	935
	31: 2 day; I can no more **g out** and come in:	3318
	31: 2 me, Thou shalt not **g over** this Jordan.	5674
	31: 3 he will **g over** before thee, and he will	5674
	31: 3 *and* Joshua, he shall **g over** before thee,	5674
	31: 6 thy God, he *it is* that doth **g** with thee:	1980
	31: 7 for thou must **g** with this people unto	935
	31: 8 the LORD, he *it is* that doth **g** before thee;	1980
	31:13 land whither ye **g over** Jordan to possess	5674
	31:16 **g a whoring** after the gods of the	2181
	31:16 whither they **g** to be amongst them,	935
	31:21 their imagination which they **g about**,	6213
	32:47 whither ye **g over** Jordan to possess it.	5674
	32:52 thou shalt not **g** thither unto the land	935
	34: 4 eyes, but thou shalt not **g over** thither.	5674
Jos	1: 2 **g over** this Jordan, thou, and all this	5674
	1:11 this Jordan, to **g in** to possess the land,	935
	1:16 whithersoever thou sendest us, we will **g**.	1980
	2: 1 **G** view the land, even Jericho.	1980
	2:16 and afterward may ye **g** your way.	1980
	2:19 *that* whosoever shall **g out** of the doors of	3318
	3: 3 remove from your place, and **g** after it.	1980
	3: 4 may know the way by which ye must **g**:	1980
	6: 3 of war, *and* **g round about** the city once.	5362
	6:22 **G** *into* the harlot's house, and bring out	935
	7: 2 saying, **G up** and view the country.	5927
	7: 3 said unto him, Let not all the people **g up**;	5927
	7: 3 or three thousand men **g up** and smite Ai;	5927
	8: 1 of war with thee, and arise, **g up** to Ai:	5927
	8: 3 all the people of war, to **g up** *against* Ai:	5927
	8: 4 not very **far** from the city, but be ye all	7368
	9:11 **g** to meet them, and say unto them, We	1980
	9:12 on the day we came forth to **g** unto you;	1980
	10:13 hasted not to **g down** about a whole day.	935
	14:11 for war, both to **g out**, and to come in.	3318
	18: 3 How long *are* you slack to **g** to possess	935
	18: 4 through the land, and describe it	1980
	18: 8 **G** and walk through the Gilead,	1980
	22: 9 unto the country of Gilead, to the land	1980
	22:12 *at* Shiloh, to **g up** to war against them.	5927
	22:33 did not intend to **g up** against them in	5927
	23:12 Else if ye do **in any wise g back**,	7725+7725
	23:12 and **g in** unto them, and they to you:	935
Jdg	1: 1 Who shall **g up** for us against	5927
	1: 2 the LORD said, Judah shall **g up**: behold,	5927
	1: 3 likewise will **g** with thee into thy lot.	1980
	1:25 but they **let g** the man and all his family.	7971
	2: 1 **made** you to **g up** out of Egypt,	5927
	2: 6 when Joshua had **let** the people **g**,	7971
	4: 6 *saying,* **G** and draw toward mount Tabor,	1980
	4: 8 If thou wilt **g** with me, then I will go:	1980
	4: 8 If thou wilt go with me, then I will **g**:	1980
	4: 8 go with me, *then* I will not	1980
	4: 8 wilt not go with me, *then* I will not **g**.	1980
	4: 9 she said, I will **surely g** with thee:	1980+1980
	5:11 shall the people of the LORD **g down** to	3381
	6:14 **G** in this thy might, and thou shalt save	1980
	6:14 **G** in this thy might, and thou shalt save	1980
	7: 3 therefore **g to**, proclaim in the ears of	4994
	7: 4 This shall **g** with thee, the same shall go	1980
	7: 4 go with thee, the same shall **g** with thee;	1980
	7: 4 This shall not **g** with thee, the same shall	1980
	7: 4 not go with thee, the same shall not **g**.	1980
	7: 7 let all the *other* people **g** every man unto	1980
	7:10 if thou fear to **g down**, go thou with	3381
	7:10 **g** thou with Phurah thy servant **down** to	3381
	7:11 strengthened to **g down** unto the host.	3381
	9: 9 and **g** to be promoted over the trees?	1980
	9:11 and **g** to be promoted over the trees?	1980
	9:13 and **g** to be promoted over the trees?	1980
	9:38 **g out**, I pray now, and fight with them.	3318
	10:14 **G** and cry unto the gods which ye have	1980
	11: 8 that thou mayest **g** with us,	1980
	11:35 unto the LORD, and I cannot **g back**.	7725
	11:37 that I may **g up** and down upon	1980
	11:38 he said, **G**. And he sent her away *for* two	1980
	12: 1 and didst not call us to **g** with thee?	1980
	12: 5 which were escaped said, Let me **g over**;	5674
	15: 1 I will **g in** to my wife into the chamber.	935
	15: 1 her father would not suffer him to **g in**.	935
	15: 5 he **let** *them* into the standing corn of	7971
	16:17 my strength will **g** from me, and I shall	5493
	16:20 I will **g out** as at other times *before,* and	3318
	17: 9 I **g** to sojourn where I may find *a place.*	1980
	18: 2 they said unto them, **G**, search the land:	1980
	18: 5 our way which we shall be prosperous.	1980
	18: 6 the priest said unto them, **G** in peace:	1980
	18: 6 the LORD *is* your way wherein ye **g**.	1980
	18: 9 Arise, that we may **g up** against them:	5927

Jdg	18: 9 not slothful to **g**, *and* to enter to possess	1980
	18:10 When ye **g**, ye shall come unto a people	935
	18:19 **g** with us, and be to us a father and a	1980
	19: 5 of bread, and afterward **g** your way.	1980
	19: 9 on your way, that thou mayest **g** home.	1980
	19:15 thither, to **g in** *and* to lodge in Gibeah:	935
	19:25 the day began to spring, they **let** her **g**.	7971
	19:27 of the house, and went out to **g** his way:	1980
	20: 8 We will not any of *us* **g** to his tent,	1980
	20: 9 to Gibeah; *we will* **g up** by lot against it;	NIH
	20:14 to **g out** to battle against the children of	3318
	20:18 Which of us shall **g up** first to the battle	5927
	20:18 And the LORD said, Judah *shall* **g up** first.	5927
	20:23 Shall I **g up** again to battle against	5066
	20:23 And the LORD said, **G up** against him.)	5927
	20:28 Shall I yet again **g up** to battle against	3318
	20:28 the LORD said, **G up**; for to morrow	5927
	21:10 **G** and smite the inhabitants of	1980
	21:20 **G** and lie in wait in the vineyards;	1980
	21:21 of Shiloh, and **g** to the land of Benjamin.	1980
Ru	1: 8 **G**, return each to her mother's house:	1980
	1:11 why will you **g** with me? *are there* yet	1980
	1:12 **g** *your way;* for I am too old to have a	1980
	1:16 for whither thou goest, I will **g**;	1980
	1:18 she *was* stedfastly minded to **g** with her,	1980
	2: 2 Let me now **g** to the field, and glean ears	1980
	2: 2 And she said unto her, **G**, my daughter.	1980
	2: 8 **G** not to glean in another field, neither go	1980
	2: 8 neither **g** from hence, but abide here fast	5674
	2: 9 that they do reap, and **g** thou after them:	1980
	2: 9 **g** unto the vessels, and drink of *that*	1980
	2:22 that thou **g out** with his maidens,	3318
	3: 4 and thou shalt **g in**, and uncover his feet,	935
	3:17 me, **G** not empty unto thy mother in law.	935
1Sa	1:17 Eli answered and said, **G** in peace:	1980
	1:22 *I will not* **g up** until the child be weaned,	NIH
	3: 9 Eli said unto Samuel, **G**, lie down:	1980
	5:11 let it **g again** to his own place, that it slay	7725
	6: 6 did they not **let** the people **g**,	7971
	6: 8 and send it away, that it may **g**.	1980
	6:20 and to whom shall he **g up** from us?	5927
	8:20 and **g out** before us, and fight our battles.	3318
	8:22 of Israel, **G** ye every man unto his city.	1980
	9: 3 with thee, and arise, and seek the asses.	1980
	9: 6 now let us **g** thither; peradventure he can	1980
	9: 6 he can shew us our way that we should **g**.	1980
	9: 7 behold, if we **g**, what shall we bring	1980
	9: 9 he spake, Come, and let us **g** to the seer:	1980
	9:10 to his servant, Well said; come, let us **g**.	1980
	9:13 before he **g up** to the high place to eat:	5927
	9:14 them, for to **g up** to the high place.	5927
	9:19 **g up** before me *unto* the high place; for	5927
	9:19 to morrow I will **let** thee **g**, and will tell	7971
	10: 3 shalt thou **g on** forward from thence,	2498
	10: 8 thou shalt **g down** before me *to* Gilgal;	3381
	10: 9 when he had turned his back to **g** from	1980
	11:14 let us **g** to Gilgal, and renew the kingdom	1980
	12:21 *ye* **g** after vain *things,* which cannot	NIH
	14: 1 let us **g over** to the Philistines' garrison,	5674
	14: 4 *by* which Jonathan sought to **g over** unto	5674
	14: 6 let us **g over** unto the garrison of these	5674
	14: 9 in our place, and will not **g up** unto them.	5927
	14:10 Come up unto us; then we will **g up**:	5927
	14:36 Let us **g down** after the Philistines by	3381
	14:37 Shall I **g down** after the Philistines?	3381
	15: 3 Now **g** and smite Amalek,	1980
	15: 6 Saul said unto the Kenites, **G**, depart,	1980
	15:18 **G** and utterly destroy the sinners	1980
	15:27 Samuel turned about to **g away**, he laid	1980
	16: 1 fill thine horn *with* oil, and **g**, I will send	1980
	16: 2 Samuel said, How can I **g**? if Saul hear *it,*	1980
	17:32 thy servant will **g** and fight with this	1980
	17:33 art not able to **g** against this Philistine	1980
	17:37 **G**, and the LORD be with thee.	1980
	17:39 upon his armour, and he assayed to **g**;	1980
	17:39 David said unto Saul, I cannot **g** with	1980
	17:55 when Saul saw David **g forth** against	3318
	18: 2 would let him **g** no more **home** *to* his	7725
	19: 3 I will **g out** and stand beside my father in	3318
	19:17 Saul, He said unto me, **Let** me **g**;	7971
	20: 5 let me **g**, that I may hide myself in	7971
	20:11 Come, and let us **g out** *into* the field.	3318
	20:13 thee away, that thou mayest **g** in peace:	1980
	20:19 *then* thou shalt **g down** quickly,	3381
	20:21 behold, I will send a lad, *saying,* **G**,	1980
	20:22 **g** *thy way:* for the LORD hath sent thee	1980
	20:28 David earnestly asked *leave* of me *to* **g** to	NIH
	20:29 he said, **Let** me **g**, I pray thee; for our	7971
	20:40 said unto him, **G**, carry *them* to the city.	1980
	20:42 Jonathan said to David, **G** in peace,	1980
	23: 2 Shall I **g** and smite these Philistines?	1980
	23: 2 **G**, and smite the Philistines,	1980
	23: 4 and said, Arise, **g down** to Keilah:	3381
	23: 8 to **g down** to Keilah, to besiege David	3381
	23:13 and went whithersoever they could **g**.	1980
	23:13 from Keilah; and he forbare to **g forth**.	3318
	23:22 **G**, I pray you, prepare yet, and know and	1980
	23:23 with the certainty, and I will **g** with you:	1980
	24:19 his enemy, will he **let** him **g** well away?	7971
	25: 5 **g** to Nabal, and greet him in my name:	935
	25:19 said unto her servants, **G on** before me;	5674
	25:35 unto her, **G up** in peace to thine house;	5927
	26: 6 Who will **g down** with me to Saul to	3381
	26: 6 Abishai said, I will **g down** with thee.	3381
	26:11 and the cruse of water, and let us **g**.	1980

1Sa	26:19 of the LORD, saying, **G**, serve other gods.	1980
	28: 1 that thou shalt **g out** with me to battle,	3318
	28: 7 that I may **g** to her, and inquire of her.	1980
	29: 4 that he may **g again** to his place,	7725
	29: 4 let him not **g down** with us to battle,	3381
	29: 7 Wherefore now return, and **g** in peace,	1980
	29: 8 that I may not **g** fight against the enemies	935
	29: 9 He shall not **g up** with us to the battle.	5927
	30:10 faint that they could not **g over** the brook	5674
2Sa	1:15 and said, **G near**, *and* fall upon him.	5066
	2: 1 Shall I **g up** into any of the cities of Judah?	5927
	2: 1 the LORD said unto him, **G up**.	5927
	2: 1 David said, Whither shall I **g up**? And he	5927
	3:16 said Abner unto him, **G**, return. And he	1980
	3:21 I will arise and **g**, and will gather all Israel	1980
	5:19 Shall I **g up** to the Philistines?	5927
	5:19 the LORD said unto David, **G up**: for I	5927
	5:23 the LORD, he said, Thou shalt not **g up**;	5927
	5:24 for then shall the LORD **g out** before thee,	3318
	7: 3 the king, **G**, do all that *is* in thine heart;	1980
	7: 5 **G** and tell my servant David, Thus saith	1980
	11: 1 at the time when kings **g forth** *to battle,*	3318
	11: 8 **G down** to thy house, and wash thy feet.	3381
	11:10 didst thou not **g down** unto thine house?	3381
	11:11 shall I then **g** into mine house, to eat and	935
	12:23 I shall **g** to him, but he shall not return to	1980
	13: 7 **G** now to thy brother Amnon's house,	1980
	13:13 whither shall I **cause** my shame to **g**?	1980
	13:24 and his servants **g** with thy servant.	1980
	13:25 Nay, my son, let us not all now **g**,	1980
	13:25 howbeit he would not **g**, but blessed him.	1980
	13:26 thee, let my brother Amnon **g** with us.	1980
	13:26 unto him, Why should he **g** with thee?	1980
	13:27 he **let** Amnon and all the king's sons **g**	7971
	13:39 *the soul of* king David longed to **g forth**	3318
	14: 8 **G** to thine house, and I will give charge	1980
	14:21 therefore, bring the young man Absalom	1980
	14:30 he hath barley there; **g** and set it on fire.	1980
	15: 7 I pray thee, let me **g** and pay my vow,	1980
	15: 9 the king said unto him, **G** in peace. So he	1980
	15:20 I *this* day make thee **g up and down**	1980
	15:20 seeing I **g** whither I may, return thou,	1980
	15:22 David said to Ittai, **G** and pass over.	1980
	16: 9 let me **g over**, I pray thee, and take off his	5674
	16:21 **G in** unto thy father's concubines,	935
	17:11 *that* thou **g** to battle in thine own person.	1980
	18: 2 **surely g forth** with you myself	3318+3318
	18: 3 people answered, Thou shalt not **g forth**:	3318
	18:21 **G** tell the king what thou hast seen.	1980
	19: 7 **g forth**, and speak comfortably unto thy	3318
	19: 7 I swear by the LORD, if thou **g** not **forth**,	3318
	19:15 came to Gilgal, to **g** to meet the king,	1980
	19:20 to **g down** to meet my lord the king.	3381
	19:26 that I may ride thereon, and **g** to the king;	1980
	19:34 that I should **g up** with the king unto	5927
	19:36 Thy servant will **g** a little *way* **over** Jordan	5674
	19:37 let him **g over** with my lord the king;	5674
	19:38 Chimham shall **g over** with me, and I will	5674
	20:11 he that *is* for David, **let** him **g** after Joab.	NIH
	21:17 shalt **g** no more **out** with us to battle,	3318
	24: 1 them to say, **G**, number Israel and Judah.	1980
	24: 2 **G** now through all the tribes of Israel,	7751
	24:12 and say unto David, Thus saith	1980
	24:18 day to David, and said unto him, **G up**,	5927
1Ki	1:13 **G** and get thee in unto king David,	1980
	1:53 Solomon said unto him, **G** to thine house.	1980
	2: 2 I **g** the way of all the earth: be thou strong	1980
	2: 6 let not his hoar head **g down** *to* the grave	3381
	2:29 son of Jehoiada, saying, **G**, fall upon him.	1980
	2:36 and **g** not **forth** thence any whither.	3318
	3: 7 I know not *how* to **g out** or come in.	3318
	8:44 If thy people **g out** to battle against their	3318
	9: 6 **g** and serve other gods, and worship them	1980
	11: 2 Ye shall not **g** in to them, neither shall	935
	11:10 that *he* should not **g** after other gods:	1980
	11:17 father's servants with him, to **g** *into* Egypt;	935
	11:21 that I may **g** to mine own country.	1980
	11:22 thou seekest to **g** to thine own country?	1980
	11:22 howbeit let me **g in any wise**.	7971+7971
	12:24 Thus saith the LORD, Ye shall not **g up**,	5927
	12:27 If this people **g up** to do sacrifice in	5927
	12:27 and **g again** to Rehoboam king of Judah.	7725
	12:28 too much for you to **g up** *to* Jerusalem:	5927
	13: 8 half thine house, I will not **g in** with thee,	935
	13:16 not return with thee, nor **g in** with thee:	935
	13:17 nor turn again to **g** by the way that thou	1980
	14: 3 and a cruse of honey, and **g** to him:	935
	14: 7 **G**, tell Jeroboam, Thus saith the LORD	1980
	15:17 that *he* might not suffer *any* to **g out** or	3318
	17:12 that I may **g** in and dress it for me and my	935
	17:13 Fear not; **g** *and* do as thou hast said:	935
	18: 1 saying, **G**, shew thyself unto Ahab;	1980
	18: 5 **G** into the land, unto all fountains of	1980
	18: 8 I *am:* **g**, tell thy lord, Behold, Elijah *is*	1980
	18:11 **G**, tell thy lord, Behold, Elijah *is here.*	1980
	18:14 **G**, tell thy lord, Behold, Elijah *is here:* and	1980
	18:43 servant, **G up** now, look toward the sea.	5927
	18:43 And he said, **G again** seven times.	7725
	18:44 said, **G up**, say unto Ahab, Prepare *thy*	5927
	19:11 **G forth**, and stand upon the mount before	3318
	19:15 the LORD said unto him, **G**, return on thy	1980
	19:20 he said unto him, **G** back again: for what	1980
	20:22 said unto him, **G**, strengthen thyself,	1980
	20:31 our heads, and **g out** to the king of Israel:	3318
	20:33 he said, **G** ye, bring him. Then Ben-hadad	935

G

1Ki 20:42 Because thou hast **let g** out of *thy* hand a	7971
20:42 therefore thy life shall **g** for his life,	1961
21:16 that Ahab rose up to **g down** to	3381
21:18 **g** to meet Ahab king of Israel,	1980
22: 4 Wilt thou **g** with me to battle *to*	1980
22: 6 Shall I **g** against Ramoth-gilead to battle,	1980
22: 6 they said, **G** up; for the Lord shall deliver	5927
22:12 **G up** to Ramoth-gilead, and prosper:	5927
22:15 shall we **g** against Ramoth-gilead to battle,	1980
22:15 he answered him, **G**, and prosper:	5927
22:20 that he may **g up** and fall at	1980
22:22 I will **g forth**, and I will be a lying spirit in	3318
22:22 and prevail also: **g forth**, and do so.	3318
22:25 when thou shalt **g into** an inner chamber	935
22:48 Jehoshaphat made ships of Tharshish to **g**	1980
22:49 Let my servants **g** with thy servants in	1980
2Ki 1: 2 sent messengers, and said unto them, **G**,	1980
1: 3 **g up** to meet the messengers of the king	5927
1: 3 *that* ye **g** to inquire of Baal-zebub the god	1980
1: 6 a man up to meet us, and said unto us, **G**,	1980
1:15 said unto Elijah, **G down** with him:	3381
2:16 let them **g**, we pray thee, and seek thy	1980
2:18 unto him, Did I not say unto you, **G** not?	1980
2:23 mocked him, and said unto him, **G up**,	5927
2:23 thou bald head; **g up**, thou bald head.	5927
3: 7 thou **g** with me against Moab to battle?	1980
3: 7 he said, I will **g up**: I *am* as thou *art,* my	5927
3: 8 he said, Which way shall we **g up**?	5927
4: 3 he said, **G**, borrow thee vessels abroad of	1980
4: 7 **G**, sell the oil, and pay thy debt,	1980
4:23 Wherefore wilt thou **g** to him to day?	1980
4:24 **g** forward; *slack* not *thy* riding for me,	1980
4:29 **g** thy way: if thou meet any man,	1980
5: 5 **G** to, go, and I will send a letter unto	1980
5: 5 **g**, and I will send a letter unto the king of	935
5:10 **G** and wash in Jordan seven times,	1980
5:19 he said unto him, **G** in peace. So he	1980
5:24 and he **let** the men **g**, and they departed.	7971
6: 2 Let us **g**, we pray thee, unto Jordan,	1980
6: 2 we may dwell. And he answered, **G** ye.	1980
6: 3 I pray thee, and **g** with thy servants.	1980
6: 3 thy servants. And he answered, I will **g**.	1980
6:13 **G** and spy where he *is*, that I may send	1980
6:22 may eat and drink, and **g** to their master.	1980
7: 5 to **g** unto the camp of the Syrians:	935
7: 9 we may **g** and tell the king's household.	935
7:14 the host of the Syrians, saying, **G** and see.	1980
8: 1 thou and thine household,	1980
8: 8 **g**, meet the man of God, and inquire of	1980
8:10 Elisha said unto him, **G**, say unto him,	1980
9: 1 oil in thine hand, and **g** *to* Ramoth-gilead:	1980
9: 2 **g in**, and make him arise up from among	935
9:15 let none **g forth** *nor* escape out of the city	3318
9:15 out of the city to **g** to tell *it* in Jezreel.	1980
9:34 **G**, see now this cursed *woman*, and	6485
10:13 we **g down** to salute the children of	3381
10:24 *he that* letteth him **g**, his life *shall be* for	NIH
10:25 and to the captains, **G in**, *and* slay them;	935
11: 7 two parts of all you that **g forth** on	3318
11: 9 them that should **g** out on the sabbath,	3318
12:17 Hazael set his face to **g up** to Jerusalem.	5927
17:27 let them **g** and dwell there, and let him	1980
18:21 it will **g** into his hand, and pierce it:	935
18:25 **G up** against this land, and destroy it.	5927
19:31 For out of Jerusalem shall **g forth** a	3318
20: 5 on the third day thou shalt **g up** *unto*	5927
20: 8 *that* I shall **g up** *into* the house of	5927
20: 9 shall the shadow **g forward** ten degrees,	1980
20: 9 ten degrees, or **g back** ten degrees?	7725
20:10 is a light thing for the shadow to **g down**	5186
22: 4 **G up** to Hilkiah the high priest, that he	5927
22:13 **G** ye, inquire of the LORD for me,	1980
1Ch 7:11 two hundred *soldiers,* fit to **g** out *for* war	3318
14:10 Shall I **g up** against the Philistines?	5927
14:10 the LORD said unto him, **G up**; for I will	5927
14:14 God said unto him, **G** not **up** after them;	5927
14:15 *that* then thou shalt **g** out to battle:	3318
17: 4 **G** and tell David my servant, Thus saith	1980
17:11 thy days be expired that *thou* must **g**	3212
20: 1 at the time that kings **g** out to battle, Joab	3318
21: 2 to Joab and to the rulers of the people, **G**,	1980
21:10 **G** and tell David, saying, Thus saith	1980
21:18 David should **g up**, and set up an altar	5927
21:30 David could not **g** before it to inquire of	1980
2Ch 1:10 that I may **g** out and come in before this	3318
6:34 If thy people **g** out to war against their	3318
7:19 shall ye serve other gods,	1980
11: 4 Thus saith the LORD, Ye shall not **g up**,	5927
14:11 in thy name we **g** against this multitude.	935
16: 1 to the intent that *he* might let none **g** out	3318
16: 3 **g**, break thy league with Baasha king of	1980
18: 2 persuaded him to **g up** *with* him to	5927
18: 3 Wilt thou **g** with me to Ramoth-gilead?	1980
18: 5 Shall we **g** to Ramoth-gilead to battle,	1980
18: 5 they said, **G up**; for God will deliver *it*	5927
18:11 **G up** to Ramoth-gilead, and prosper:	5927
18:14 shall we **g** to Ramoth-gilead to battle,	1980
18:14 **G up**, and prosper, and they shall be	5927
18:19 that he may **g up** and fall at	5927
18:21 I will **g** out, and be a lying spirit in	3318
18:21 shalt also prevail: **g** out, and do *even* so.	3318
18:24 shalt **g into** an inner chamber to hide	935
18:29 disguise myself, and will **g** to the battle;	935
20:16 To morrow **g** ye **down** against them:	3381
20:17 to morrow **g out** against them:	3318

2Ch 20:27 them, to **g again** to Jerusalem with joy;	7725
20:36 with him to make ships to **g** to Tarshish.	1980
20:37 that they were not able to **g** to Tarshish.	1980
21:13 **made** Judah and the inhabitants of	
Jerusalem **to g a whoring**,	2181
23: 6 Levites; they shall **g in**, for they *are* holy:	935
23: 8 with them that were to **g out** on	3318
24: 5 **G out** unto the cities of Judah,	3318
25: 5 choice men, *able* to **g forth** to war,	3318
25: 7 king, let not the army of Israel **g** with thee;	935
25: 8 if thou *wilt* **g**, do *it,* be strong for the battle:	935
25:10 to **g** home *again:* wherefore their anger	1980
25:13 that *they* should not **g** with him to battle,	1980
26:18 **g** out of the sanctuary; for thou hast	3318
26:20 yea, himself hasted also to **g out**, because	3318
34:21 **G**, inquire of the LORD for me,	1980
36:23 his God *be* with him, and let him **g up**.	5927
Ezr 1: 3 let him **g up** to Jerusalem, which *is* in	5927
1: 5 to **g up** to build the house of the LORD	5927
5:15 said unto him, Take these vessels, **g**,	236
7: 9 month began he to **g up** from Babylon,	4609
7:13 *are* minded of their own freewill to **g**	1946
7:13 to go up to Jerusalem, **g** with thee.	1946
7:28 out of Israel chief *men* to **g up** with me.	5927
8:31 of the first month, to **g** *unto* Jerusalem:	1980
Ne 9:11 The land, *unto* which ye **g** to possess it,	935
3:15 unto the stairs that **g down** from the city	3381
4: 3 Even *that* which they build, if a fox **g** up,	5927
6:11 *being* as I *am,* would **g** into the temple to	935
6:11 the temple to save his life? I will not **g in**.	935
8:10 **G** your way, eat the fat, and drink	1980
8:15 **G forth** *unto* the mount, and fetch olive	3318
9:12 light in the way wherein they should **g**.	1980
9:15 promisedst them that *they* should **g in** to	935
9:19 and the way wherein they should **g**.	1980
9:23 that *they* should **g in** to possess *it.*	935
Est 1:19 let there **g** a royal commandment from	3318
2:12 turn was come to **g in** to king Ahasuerus,	935
2:13 whatsoever she desired was given her to **g**	935
2:15 was come to **g in** unto the king, she	935
4: 8 to charge her *that she* should **g in** unto	935
4:16 **G**, gather together all the Jews that are	1980
4:16 so will I **g in** unto the king, which *is* not	935
5:14 **g** thou **in** merrily with the king unto	935
Job 4:21 excellency *which is* in them **g away**?	5265
6:18 aside; they **g** to nothing, and perish.	5927
10:21 Before I **g** whence I shall not return,	1980
15:13 lettest *such* words **g** out of thy mouth?	1980
15:30 the breath of his mouth shall he **g away**.	5493
16:22 shall **g** the way *whence* I shall not return.	1980
17:16 They shall **g down** to the bars of the pit,	3381
20:26 it shall **g ill** with him that is left in his	3415
21:13 and in a moment **g down** to the grave.	2865
21:29 ye not asked them that **g by** the way?	5674
23: 8 I **g** forward, but he *is* not *there;* and	1980
24: 5 in the desert, they **g forth** to their work;	3318
24:10 They **cause** *him* to **g** naked without	1980
27: 6 I hold fast, and will not **let** it **g**:	7503
31:37 as a prince would I **g near** unto him.	7126
37: 8 the beasts **g** into dens, and remain in their	935
38:35 that they may **g**, and say unto thee,	1980
39: 4 they **g forth**, and return not unto thee.	3318
41:19 Out of his mouth **g** burning lamps,	1980
42: 8 to my servant Job, and offer up for	1980
Ps 22:29 all they that **g down** to the dust shall bow	3381
26: 4 neither will I **g** with dissemblers.	935
28: 1 I become like them that **g down** into	3381
30: 3 that I should not **g down** *to* the pit.	3381
30: 9 in my blood, when I **g down** to the pit?	3381
32: 8 teach thee in the way which thou shalt **g**:	1980
38: 6 I **g** mourning all the day long.	1980
39:13 before I **g** hence, and be no more.	1980
42: 9 why **g** I mourning because of	1980
43: 2 why **g** I mourning because of	1980
43: 4 will I **g** unto the altar of God, unto God	935
48:12 Walk about Zion, and **g round about** her:	5362
49:19 He shall **g** to the generation of his fathers;	935
55:10 night they **g about** it upon the walls	5437
55:15 *and* let them **g down** quick *into* hell:	3381
58: 3 they **g astray** as soon as they be born,	8582
59: 6 like a dog, and **g round about** the city.	5437
59:14 like a dog, and **g round about** the city.	5437
60:10 *which* didst not **g** out with our armies?	3318
63: 9 to destroy *it,* shall **g** into the lower parts of	935
66:13 I will **g** *into* thy house with burnt offerings:	935
71:16 I will **g in** the strength of the Lord GOD:	935
73:27 all them that **g a whoring** from thee.	2181
78:52 **made** his own people **to g forth** like	5265
80:18 So will not we **g** *back* from thee:	5472
84: 7 They **g** from strength to strength, *every*	1980
85:13 Righteousness shall **g** before him;	1980
88: 4 I am counted with them that **g down** into	3381
89:14 mercy and truth shall **g before** thy face.	6923
104: 8 They **g up** by the mountains; they **g**	1980
104: 8 they **g down** by the valleys unto the place	3381
104:26 There **g** the ships: *there is* that leviathan,	1980
105:20 ruler of the people, and let him **g free**.	6605
107: 7 *that they* might **g** to a city of habitation.	1980
107:23 They that **g down** to the sea in ships,	3381
107:26 they **g down** *again* to the depths;	3381
108:11 not thou, O God, **g forth** with our hosts?	3318
115:17 neither any that **g down** into silence.	3381
118:19 I will **g** into them, *and* I will praise	935
119:35 **Make** me to **g** in the path of thy	1869
122: 1 Let us **g** *into* the house of the LORD.	1980

Ps 122: 4 Whither the tribes **g up**, the tribes of	5927
129: 8 Neither do they which **g by** say,	5674
132: 3 of my house, nor **g up** into my bed;	5927
132: 7 We will **g** into his tabernacles: we will	935
139: 7 Whither shall I **g** from thy spirit?	1980
143: 7 lest I be like unto them that **g down** into	3381
Pr 1:12 whole, as those that **g down** into the pit:	3381
2:19 None that **g** *unto* her return *again,* neither	935
3:28 **G**, and come again, and to morrow I will	1980
4:13 Take fast hold of instruction; let *her* not **g**:	7503
4:14 and **g** not in the way of evil *men.*	833
5: 5 Her feet **g down** to death; her steps take	3381
5:23 the greatness of his folly he shall **g astray**.	7686
6: 3 **g**, humble thyself, and make sure thy	1980
6: 6 **G** to the ant, thou sluggard; consider her	1980
6:28 Can one **g** upon hot coals, and his feet not	1980
7:25 to her ways, **g** not **astray** in her paths.	8582
9: 6 live; and **g** in the way of understanding.	833
9:15 To call passengers who **g right** *on* their	3474
14: 7 **G** from the presence of a foolish man,	1980
15:12 neither will he **g** unto the wise.	1980
18: 8 they **g down** *into* the innermost parts of	3381
19: 7 how much more do his friends **g far** from	7368
22: 6 **in the way** he should **g**:	1870+5921+6310
22:10 the scorner, and contention shall **g** out;	3318
22:24 and with a furious man thou shalt not **g**:	935
23:30 at the wine; they that **g** to seek mixt wine.	1980
25: 8 **G** not **forth** hastily to strive, lest *thou*	3318
26:22 they **g down** into the innermost parts of	3381
27:10 neither **g** *into* thy brother's house in the	935
28:10 Whoso **causeth** the righteous to **g astray**	7686
30:27 yet **g** they **forth** all of them by bands;	3318
30:29 There be three *things* which **g** well, yea,	6806
Ecc 2: 1 said in mine heart, **G** to now, I will prove	1980
3:20 All **g** unto one place; all are of the dust,	1980
5:15 naked shall he return to **g** as he came,	1980
5:16 *that* in all points as he came, so shall he **g**:	1980
6: 6 he seen no good: do not all **g** to one place?	1980
7: 2 *It is* better to **g** to the house of mourning,	1980
7: 2 than to **g** to the house of feasting:	1980
8: 3 Be not hasty to **g** out of his sight: stand	1980
9: 3 live, and after that *they* **g** to the dead.	NIH
9: 7 **G** *thy way,* eat thy bread with joy,	1980
10:15 he knoweth not how to **g** to the city.	1980
12: 5 and the mourners **g about** the streets:	5437
SS 1: 8 **g** thy **way forth** by the footsteps of	3318
3: 2 **g about** the city in the streets and in	5437
3: 3 The watchmen that **g about** the city	5437
3: 4 I held him, and would not **let** him **g**,	7503
3:11 **G forth**, O ye daughters of Zion,	3318
6: 6 of sheep which **g up** from the washing,	5927
7: 8 I said, I will **g up** to the palm tree, I will	5927
7:11 my beloved, let us **g forth** *into* the field;	3318
Isa 2: 3 many people shall **g** and say, Come ye,	1980
2: 3 let us **g up** to the mountain of the LORD,	5927
2: 3 for out of Zion shall **g forth** the law,	3318
2:19 they shall **g** into the holes of the rocks,	935
2:21 To **g** into the clifts of the rocks, and into	935
3:16 walking and mincing *as* they **g**,	1980
5: 5 now **g to**, I will tell you what *I will* do to	4994
5:24 and their blossom shall **g up** as dust:	5927
6: 8 Whom shall I send, and who will **g** for us?	1980
6: 9 he said, **G**, and tell this people, Hear ye	1980
7: 3 **G forth** now to meet Ahaz, thou,	3318
7: 6 Let us **g up** against Judah, and vex it,	5927
8: 6 the waters of Shiloah that **g** softly,	1980
8: 7 all his channels, and **g** over all his banks:	1980
8: 8 he shall overflow and **g over**, he shall	5674
11:15 and **make** men **g over** dryshod.	1869
13: 2 they may **g** *into* the gates of the nobles.	935
14:19 that **g down** to the stones of the pit;	3381
15: 5 Luhith with weeping shall they **g** it **up**;	5927
18: 2 **G**, ye swift messengers, to a nation	1980
20: 2 **G** and loose the sackcloth from off thy	1980
21: 2 **G up**, O Elam: besiege, O Media;	5927
21: 6 **G**, set a watchman, let him declare what	1980
22:15 **G**, get thee unto this treasurer, *even* unto	1980
23:16 Take a harp, **g about** the city, thou harlot	5437
27: 4 I would **g** through them, I would burn	6585
28:13 that they might **g**, and fall backward,	1980
30: 2 That walk to **g down** *into* Egypt,	3381
30: 8 Now **g**, write it before them in a table,	935
31: 1 to them that **g down** *to* Egypt for help;	3381
33:21 wherein shall **g** no galley with oars,	1980
34:10 the smoke thereof shall **g up** for ever:	5927
35: 9 *any* ravenous beast shall **g up** thereon,	5927
36: 6 it will **g** into his hand, and pierce it:	935
36:10 **G up** against this land, and destroy it.	5927
37:32 For out of Jerusalem shall **g forth** a	3318
38: 5 **G** and say to Hezekiah, Thus saith	1980
38:10 days, I shall **g** to the gates of the grave:	1980
38:15 hath done *it:* I shall **g softly** all my	1718
38:18 they that **g down** into the pit cannot hope	3381
38:22 What *is* the sign that I shall **g up** to	5927
42:10 ye that **g down** to the sea, and all that is	3381
42:13 The LORD shall **g forth** as a mighty *man,*	3318
45: 2 I will **g** before thee, and make the crooked	1980
45:13 my city, and he shall **let g** my captives,	7971
45:16 they shall **g** to confusion together *that are*	1980
48:17 thee by the way *that* thou shouldest **g**.	1980
48:20 **G** ye forth of Babylon, flee ye from	3318
49: 9 *thou* mayest say to the prisoners, **G forth**;	3318
49:17 they that made thee waste shall **g forth** of	3318
51:23 thy soul, Bow down, that we may **g over**:	5674
52:11 depart ye, **g** ye **out** from thence,	3318

Isa 52:11 touch no unclean *thing;* **g** ye **out** of 3318
52:12 For ye shall not **g out** with haste, nor go 3318
52:12 shall not go out with haste, nor **g** by flight: 1980
52:12 for the LORD will **g** before you; 1980
54: 9 of Noah should no more **g** over the earth; 5674
55:12 ye shall **g out** with joy, and be led forth 3318
58: 6 to **let** the oppressed **g** free, and *that* ye 7971
58: 8 thy righteousness shall **g** before thee; 1980
60:20 Thy sun shall no more **g down**; neither 935
62: 1 until the righteousness thereof **g forth** as 3318
62:10 **G through**, go through the gates; 5674
62:10 Go through, **g through** the gates; 5674
66:24 they shall **g forth**, and look upon 3318

Jer 1: 7 for thou shalt **g** to all that I shall send 1980
2: 2 **G** and cry in the ears of Jerusalem, saying, 1980
2:25 loved strangers, and after them will I **g**. 1980
2:37 thou shalt **g forth** from him, 3318
3: 1 she **g** from him, and become another 1980
3:12 **G** and proclaim these words toward 1980
4: 5 and let us **g** into the defenced cities. 935
4:29 they shall **g** into thickets, and climb up 935
5:10 **G** ye **up** upon her walls, and destroy; 5927
6: 4 her; arise, and let us **g up** at noon. 5927
6: 5 let us **g** by night, and let us destroy her 5927
6:25 **G** not **forth** *into* the field, nor walk by 3318
7:12 **g** ye now unto my place which *was* in 1980
9: 2 might leave my people, and **g** from them! 1980
10: 5 needs be borne, because they cannot **g**. 6805
11:12 of Judah and inhabitants of Jerusalem **g**, 1980
13: 1 **G** and get thee a linen girdle, and put it 1980
13: 4 **g** to Euphrates, and hide it there in a hole 1980
13: 6 **g** to Euphrates, and take the girdle from 1980
14:18 If I **g forth** *into* the field, then behold 3318
14:18 the priest **g** about into a land that they 5503
15: 1 out of my sight, and let them **g forth**. 3318
15: 2 say unto thee, Whither shall we **g forth**? 3318
15: 5 who shall **g aside** to ask how thou doest? 5493
16: 5 neither **g** to lament nor bemoan them: 1980
16: 8 Thou shalt not also **g** *into* the house of 935
17:19 **G** and stand in the gate of the children of 1980
17:19 the which they **g out**, and in all the gates 3318
18: 2 **g down** *to* the potter's house, and there I 3381
18:11 Now therefore **g to**, speak to the men of 4994
19: 1 **G** and get a potter's earthen bottle, 1980
19: 2 **g forth** unto the valley of the son of 3318
19:10 in the sight of the men that **g** with thee. 1980
20: 6 all that dwell in thine house shall **g** into 1980
21: 2 works, that he may **g up** from us. 5927
21:12 lest my fury **g out** like fire, and burn that 3318
22: 1 **G down** *to* the house of the king of Judah 3381
22:20 **G up** *to* Lebanon, and cry; and lift up thy 5927
22:22 and thy lovers shall **g** into captivity: 1980
25: 6 **g** not after other gods to serve them, 1980
25:32 evil *shall* **g forth** from nation to nation, 3318
27:18 and at Jerusalem, **g** not to Babylon. 935
28:13 **G** and tell Hananiah, saying, Thus saith 1980
29:12 ye shall **g** and pray unto me, and I will 1980
30:16 every one of them, shall **g** into captivity; 1980
31: 4 shalt **g forth** in the dances of them that 3318
31: 6 let us **g up** *to* Zion unto the LORD our 5927
31:22 How long wilt thou **g about**, O thou 2559
31:24 and they that **g forth** with flocks. 5265
31:39 the measuring line shall yet **g forth** over 3318
34: 2 **G** and speak to Zedekiah king of Judah, 1980
34: 3 to mouth, and thou shalt **g** *to* Babylon. 935
34: 9 *being* a Hebrew or a Hebrewess, **g** free; 7971
34:10 and every one his maidservant, **g** free, 7971
34:10 then they obeyed, and **let** them **g**. 7971
34:11 whom they had **let g** free, to return, 7971
34:14 At the end of seven years **let** ye **g** every 7971
34:14 thou shalt **let** him **g** free from thee: 7971
35: 2 **G** unto the house of the Rechabites, 1980
35:11 let us **g** *to* Jerusalem for fear of the army of 935
35:13 **G** and tell the men of Judah and 1980
35:15 **g** not after other gods to serve them, 1980
36: 5 I cannot **g** *into* the house of the LORD: 935
36: 6 Therefore **g** thou, and read in the roll, 935
36:19 **G**, hide thee, thou and Jeremiah; 1980
37:12 Jeremiah went forth out of Jerusalem to **g** 1980
38:17 If thou wilt **assuredly g forth** unto 3318+3318
38:18 if thou wilt not **g forth** to the king of 3318
38:21 if thou refuse to **g forth**, this *is* the word 3318
39:16 **g** and speak to Ebed-melech the 1980
40: 1 of the guard had **let** him **g** from Ramah, 7971
40: 4 good and convenient for thee to **g**, 1980
40: 4 and convenient for thee to go, thither **g**. 1980
40: 5 *said*, **G back** also to Gedaliah the son of 7725
40: 5 **g** wheresoever it seemeth convenient unto 1980
40: 5 it seemeth convenient unto thee to **g**. 1980
40: 5 him victuals and a reward, and **let** him **g**. 7971
40:15 saying, **Let** me **g**, I pray thee, and I will 1980
41:10 and departed to **g over** to the Ammonites 5674
41:17 *is* by Beth-lehem, to **g** to enter *into* Egypt, 1980
42: 3 we will **g** *into* the land of Egypt, where we 935
42:15 to enter *into* Egypt, and **g** to sojourn there; 935
42:17 that **g** *into* Egypt to sojourn there; 935
42:19 ye remnant of Judah; **G** ye not *into* Egypt: 935
42:22 in the place whither ye desire to **g** *and* 935
43: 2 to say, **G** not *into* Egypt to sojourn there: 935
43:12 and he shall **g forth** from thence in peace. 3318
44:12 that have set their faces to **g** *into* the land 935
46: 8 I will **g up**, *and* will cover the earth; 5927
46:11 **G up** *into* Gilead, and take balm, O virgin, 5927
46:16 let us **g again** to our own people, and to 7725
46:19 furnish thyself to **g into captivity**: 1473

Jer 46:22 The voice thereof shall **g** like a serpent; 1980
48: 5 of Luhith continual weeping shall **g up**; 5927
48: 7 Chemosh shall **g forth** into captivity *with* 3318
49: 3 for their king shall **g** into captivity, 1980
49:12 shall **altogether g unpunished?** 5352+5352
49:12 thou shalt not **g unpunished**, 5352
49:28 **g up** to Kedar, and spoil the men of 5927
50: 3 they shall **g**, and seek the LORD their 1980
50: 6 shepherds have **caused** them to **g astray**, 8582
50: 8 **g forth** out of the land of the Chaldeans, 3318
50:21 **G up** against the land of Merethaim, 5927
50:27 let them **g down** to the slaughter: 3381
50:33 held them fast; they refused to **let** them **g**. 7971
51: 9 let us every one into his own country: 1980
51:45 **g** ye **out** of the midst of her, and deliver 3318
51:50 escaped the sword, **g** *away*, stand not still: 1980
La 4:18 our steps, that *we* cannot **g** in our streets: 1980
Eze 1:12 whither the spirit was to **g**, they went; 1980
1:20 Whithersoever the spirit was to **g**, 1980
1:20 they went, thither *was their* spirit to **g**; 1980
3: 1 and **g** speak unto the house of Israel. 1980
3: 4 he said unto me, Son of man, **g**, get thee 1980
3:11 **g**, get thee to them of the captivity, unto 1980
3:22 **g forth** into the plain, and I will there talk 3318
3:24 spake with me, and said unto me, **G**, 935
3:25 and thou shalt not **g out** among them: 3318
6: 9 which **g** a whoring after their idols: 2181
8: 6 that *I* should **g far off** from my sanctuary? 7368
8: 9 **G in**, and behold the wicked abominations 935
9: 4 **G through** the midst of the city through 5674
9: 5 **G** ye after him through the city, and smite 5674
9: 7 **g** ye forth. And they went forth, 3318
10: 2 **G in** between the wheels, *even* under 935
12: 4 thou shalt **g forth** at even in their sight, 3318
12: 4 as they that **g forth** into captivity. 4161
12:11 they shall remove *and* **g** into captivity. 1980
12:12 shoulder in the twilight, and shall **g forth**: 3318
13:20 from your arms, and will let the souls **g**, 7971
14:11 of Israel may **g** no more **astray** from me, 8582
14:17 and say, Sword, **g** through the land; 5674
15: 7 they shall **g out** from *one* fire, and 3318
20:10 Wherefore I **caused** them to **g forth** out 3318
20:29 What *is* the high place whereunto ye **g**? 935
20:39 **G** ye, serve ye every one his idols, 1980
21: 4 shall my sword **g forth** out of his sheath 3318
21:16 Go thee **one way or other**, *either* on the 258
23:44 as *they* **g in** unto a woman that playeth 935
24:14 I will do *it;* I will not **g back**, neither will 6544
26:11 thy strong garrisons shall **g down** to 3381
26:20 of old, with them that **g down** to the pit, 3381
30: 9 In that day shall messengers **g forth** from 3318
30:17 and these *cities* shall **g** into captivity. 1980
30:18 and her daughters shall **g** into captivity. 1980
31:14 men, with them that **g down** into the pit. 3381
32:18 with them that **g down** into the pit. 3381
32:19 **g down**, and be thou laid with 3381
32:24 shame with them that **g down** to the pit. 3381
32:25 shame with them that **g down** to the pit: 3381
32:29 and with them that **g down** to the pit. 3381
32:30 bear their shame with them that **g down** 3381
38:11 will **g up** to the land of unwalled villages; 5927
38:11 I will **g** to them that are at rest, that dwell 935
39: 9 dwell in the cities of Israel shall **g forth**, 3318
40:26 *there* were seven steps to **g up** to it, 5930
42:14 shall they not **g out** of the holy *place* into 3318
44: 3 and shall **g out** by the way of the same. 3318
44:19 when they **g forth** into the utter court, 3318
46: 2 he shall **g forth**; but the gate shall not be 3318
46: 8 he shall **g in** *by* the way of the porch of 935
46: 8 and he shall **g forth** by the way thereof. 3318
46: 9 shall **g out** *by* the way of the south gate; 3318
46: 9 shall **g forth** *by* the way of the north gate; 3318
46: 9 came in, but shall **g forth** over against it. 3318
46:10 of them, when they **g in**, shall go in; 935
46:10 of them, when they go in, shall **g** in; 935
46:10 and when they **g forth**, shall go forth. 3318
46:10 and when they go forth, shall **g** forth. 3318
46:12 he shall **g forth**; and after his going forth 3318
47: 8 **g down** into the desert, and go into the 3381
47: 8 down into the desert, and **g** into the sea: 935
47:15 the way of Hethlon, as *men* **g** to Zedad; 935
Da 11:44 he shall **g forth** with great fury to destroy, 1980
12: 9 he said, **G** thy way, Daniel: for the words 1980
12:13 thou thy way till the end *be:* for thou 1980
Hos 1: 2 the LORD said to Hosea, **G**, take unto 1980
2: 5 for she said, I will **g** after my lovers, 1980
2: 7 I will **g** and return to my first husband; 1980
3: 1 said the LORD unto me, **G** yet, love a 1980
4:15 neither ye **g up** *to* Beth-aven, nor swear, 5927
5: 6 They shall **g** with their flocks and with 1980
5:14 I, *even* I, will tear and **g away**; I will take 1980
5:15 I will **g** *and* return to my place, till they 1980
7:11 they call *to* Egypt, they **g** *to* Assyria. 1980
7:12 When they shall **g**, I will spread my net 1980
11: 3 I **taught** Ephraim also to **g**, taking them 7270
Joel 2:16 let the bridegroom **g forth** of his chamber, 3318
Am 1: 5 the people of Syria shall **g into captivity** 1540
1:15 their king shall **g** into captivity, he and 1980
2: 7 his father will **g in** unto the *same* maid, 1980
4: 3 ye shall **g out** at the breaches, every *cow* 3318
5: 5 Gilgal shall **surely g into captivity**, 1540+1540
5:27 **cause** you to **g** into captivity beyond 1540
6: 2 from thence ye *to* Hamath the great: 1980
6: 2 **g down** *to* Gath of the Philistines: *be they* 3381
6: 7 Therefore now shall they **g captive** with 1540

Am 6: 7 go captive with the first that **g captive**, 1540
7:12 Amaziah said unto Amos, O thou seer, **g**, 1980
7:15 the LORD said unto me, **G**, prophesy unto 1980
7:17 Israel shall **surely g** into captivity 1540+1540
8: 9 I will **cause** the sun to **g down** at noon, 935
9: 4 though they **g** into captivity before their 1980
Jnh 1: 2 Arise, **g** to Nineveh, *that* great city, 1980
1: 3 to **g** with them unto Tarshish from 935
1: 2 Arise, **g** unto Nineveh, *that* great city, 1980
Mic 1: 8 and howl, I will **g** stript and naked: 1980
2: 3 your necks; neither shall ye **g** haughtily; 1980
3: 6 the sun shall **g down** over the prophets, 935
4: 2 let us **g up** to the mountain of the LORD, 5927
4: 2 for the law shall **g forth** of Zion, 3318
4:10 for now shalt thou **g forth** out of the city, 3318
4:10 field, and thou shalt **g** *even* to Babylon; 935
5: 8 if he **g through**, both treadeth down, 5674
Na 3:14 go into clay, and tread the morter, 935
Hab 1: 4 and judgment doth never **g forth**: 3318
Hag 1: 8 **G up** *to* the mountain, and bring wood, 5927
Zec 6: 5 *which* **g forth** from standing before 3318
6: 6 black horses which *are* therein **g forth** 3318
6: 6 the white **g forth** after them; 3318
6: 6 the grisled **g forth** toward the south 3318
6: 7 sought to **g** that *they* might walk to and 1980
6: 8 these that **g** toward the north country 3318
6:10 **g** *into* the house of Josiah the son of 935
8:21 the inhabitants of one *city* shall **g** to 1980
8:21 Let us **speedily g** before 1980+1980
8:21 to seek the LORD of hosts: I will **g** also. 1980
8:23 that is a Jew, saying, We will **g** with you: 1980
9:14 his arrow shall **g forth** as the lightning: 3318
9:14 and shall **g** with whirlwinds of the south. 1980
14: 2 half of the city shall **g forth** into captivity, 3318
14: 3 shall the LORD **g forth**, and fight against 3318
14: 8 *that* living waters shall **g out** from 3318
14:16 **g up** from year to year to worship the 5927
14:18 if the family of Egypt **g** not **up**, 5927
Mal 4: 2 ye shall **g forth**, and grow up as calves of 3318
Mt 2: 8 **G** and search diligently for the young 4198
2:20 his mother, and **g** into the land of Israel: 4198
2:22 father Herod, he was afraid to **g** thither: 565
5:24 thy gift before the altar, and **g** thy way; 5217
5:41 whosoever shall **compel** thee to **g** a mile, 29
5:41 thee to go a mile, **g** with him twain. 5217
7:13 and many there be which **g in** thereat: 1525
8: 4 See thou tell no *man;* but **g** thy way, 5217
8: 9 and I say to this *man*, **G**, and he goeth; 4198
8:13 Jesus said unto the centurion, **G** thy way; 5217
8:21 suffer me first to **g** and bury my father. 565
8:31 suffer us to **g away** into the herd of swine. 565
8:32 he said unto them, **G**. And when they 5217
9: 6 take up thy bed, and **g** unto thine house. 5217
9:13 But **g** ye and learn what *that* meaneth, 4198
10: 5 **G** not into the way of the Gentiles, 565
10: 6 But **g** rather to the lost sheep of the house 4198
10: 7 And as ye **g**, preach, saying, The kingdom 4198
10:11 worthy; and there abide till ye **g thence**. 1831
11: 4 **G** and shew John again *those things* 4198
13:28 thou then *that* we **g** and gather them up? 565
14:15 that they may **g** into the villages, 565
14:22 and to **g before** him unto the other side, 4254
14:29 he walked on the water, to **g** to Jesus. 2064
16:21 how that he must **g** unto Jerusalem, 565
17:27 **g** thou to the sea, and cast a hook, 4198
18:15 **g** and tell him his fault between thee and 5217
19:21 **g** *and* sell that thou hast, and give to 5217
19:24 It is easier for a camel to **g through** 1330
20: 4 **G** ye also into the vineyard, 5217
20: 7 unto them, **G** ye also into the vineyard; 5217
20:14 Take *that* thine is, and **g** thy way: I will 5217
20:18 Behold, we **g up** to Jerusalem; and the 305
21: 2 **G** into the village over against you, 4198
21:28 said, Son, **g** work to day in my vineyard. 5217
21:30 he answered and said, I **g**, sir: NIG
21:31 **g** into the kingdom of God **before** you. 4254
22: 9 **G** ye therefore into the highways, 4198
23:13 for ye neither **g in** yourselves, 1525
23:13 suffer ye them that are entering to **g in**. 1525
24:26 Behold, he is in the desert; **g** not **forth**: 1831
25: 6 bridegroom cometh; **g** ye **out** to meet 1831
25: 9 but **g** ye rather to them that sell, and buy 4198
25:46 And these shall **g away** into everlasting 565
26:18 **G** into the city to such a man, and say 5217
26:32 But after I am risen *again*, I will **g before** 4254
26:36 Sit ye here, while I **g** and pray yonder. 565
27:65 **g** your way, make *it* as sure as you can. 5217
28: 7 And quickly, and tell his disciples that 4198
28:10 **g** tell my brethren that they go into 5217
28:10 tell my brethren that they **g** into Galilee, 565
28:19 **G** ye therefore, and teach all nations, 4198
Mk 1:38 unto them, Let us **g** into the next towns, 71
1:44 say nothing to any *man:* but **g** thy way, 5217
2:11 thy bed, and **g** thy way into thine house. 5217
5:19 **G** home to thy *friends*, and tell them how 5217
5:34 **g** in peace, and be whole of thy plague. 5217
6:36 they may **g** into the country round about, 565
6:37 we **g** and buy two hundred pennyworth 565
6:38 **g** and see. And when they knew, they say, 5217
6:45 to **g** to the other side **before** unto 4254
7:29 said unto her, For this saying **g** thy way; 5217
8:26 Neither **g into** the town, nor tell *it* 1525
9:43 than having two hands to **g into** hell, into 565
10:21 **g** thy way, sell whatsoever thou hast, 5217
10:25 easier for a camel to **g through** the eye 1330

G

G

Mk 10:33 *Saying,* Behold, we **g up** to Jerusalem; 305
10:52 And Jesus said unto him, **G** thy way; 5217
11: 2 **G** your way into the village over against 5217
11: 6 had commanded: and they **let** them **g**. 863
12:38 which love to **g** in long clothing, 4043
13:15 the housetop not **g down** into the house, 2597
14:12 Where wilt thou *that* we **g** and prepare 565
14:13 **G** ye into the city, and there shall meet 5217
14:14 And wheresoever he shall **g** in, say ye to 1525
14:28 am risen, I will **g before** you into Galilee. 4254
14:42 Rise up, let us **g**; lo, he that betrayeth me 71
16: 7 **g** your way, tell his disciples and Peter 5217
16:15 **G** ye into all the world, and preach 4198
Lk 1:17 And he shall **g before** him in the spirit and 4281
1:76 for thou shalt **g before** the face of the Lord 4313
2:15 Let us now **g** *even* unto Bethlehem, 1330
5:14 And he charged him to tell no *man*: but **g**, 565
5:24 take up thy couch, and **g** into thine house. 4198
7: 8 and I say unto one, **G**, and he goeth; 4198
7:22 **G** your way, and tell John what *things* ye 4198
7:50 Thy faith hath saved thee; **g** in peace. 4198
8:14 **g forth**, and are choked with cares and 4198
8:22 Let us **g over** unto the other side of 1330
8:31 not command them to **g out** into the deep. 565
8:48 faith hath made thee whole; **g** in peace.) 4198
8:51 he suffered no *man* to **g** in, save Peter, 1525
9: 5 receive you, when ye **g out** of that city, 1831
9:12 that they may **g** into the towns and 565
9:13 except we should **g** and buy meat for all 4198
9:51 he stedfastly set his face to **g** to Jerusalem, 4198
9:53 his face was *as though* he would **g** to 4198
9:59 suffer me first to **g** and bury my father. 565
9:60 **g** thou and preach the kingdom of God. 565
9:61 but let me first **g** bid them farewell, NIG
10: 3 **G** your ways: behold, I send you forth as 5217
10: 7 of his hire. **G** not from house to house. 3327
10:10 *g your ways* **out** into the streets of 1831
10:37 Jesus unto him, **G**, and do thou likewise. 4198
11: 5 and shall **g** unto him at midnight, 4198
13:32 **G** ye, and tell that fox, Behold, I cast out 4198
14: 4 took *him*, and healed him, and **let** *him* **g**; 630
14:10 **g** and sit down in the lowest room; 4198
14:10 may say unto thee, Friend, **g up** higher: 4320
14:18 of ground, and I must needs **g** and see it: 1831
14:19 five yoke of oxen, and I **g** to prove them: 4198
14:21 **G out** quickly into the streets and lanes of 1831
14:23 **G out** into the highways and hedges, 1831
15: 4 **g** after that which is lost, until he find 4198
15:18 I will arise and **g** to my father, and will 4198
15:28 And he was angry, and would not **g** in: 1525
17: 7 from the field, **G**, and sit down to meat? 3928
17:14 **G** shew yourselves unto the priests. 4198
17:19 *g thy way*: thy faith hath made thee whole 4198
17:23 see there: **g** not **after** them, nor follow 565
18:25 For it is easier for a camel to **g** through a 1525
18:31 we **g up** to Jerusalem, and all *things* that 305
19:30 ye into the village over against *you*; in 5217
21: 8 near: **g** ye not therefore after them. 4198
22: 8 saying, **G** and prepare us the passover, 4198
22:33 Lord, I am ready to **g** with thee, both into 4198
22:68 *you*, you will not answer me, nor **let** *me* **g**. 630
23:22 I will therefore chastise him, and **let** *him* **g**. 630
Jn 1:43 The day following Jesus would **g forth** into 1831
4: 4 And he must needs **g through** 1330
4:16 **G**, call thy husband, and come hither. 5217
4:50 saith unto him, **G** *thy way*; thy son liveth. 4198
6:67 unto the twelve, Will ye also **g away**? 5217
6:68 answered him, Lord, to whom shall we **g**? 565
7: 3 unto him, Depart hence, and **g** into Judea, 5217
7: 8 **G** ye **up** unto this feast: I go not up yet 305
7: 8 I **g** not up yet unto this feast; for my time 305
7:19 the law? Why **g** ye **about** to kill me? 2212
7:33 and *then* I **g** unto him that sent me. 5217
7:35 Whither will he **g**, that we shall not find 4198
7:35 will he **g** unto the dispersed among 4198
8:11 unto her, Neither do I condemn thee: **g**, 4198
8:14 I know whence I came, and whither I **g**; 5217
8:14 tell whence I come, and whither I **g**. 5217
8:21 I **g** my way, and ye shall seek me, 5217
8:21 in your sins: whither I **g**, ye cannot come. 5217
8:22 because he saith, Whither I **g**, ye cannot 5217
9: 7 And said unto him, **G**, wash in the pool of 5217
9:11 **G** to the pool of Siloam, and wash: 5217
10: 9 and shall **g in** and out, and find pasture. 1525
11: 7 to *his* disciples, Let us **g** into Judea again. 71
11:11 but I **g**, that I may awake him out of sleep. 4198
11:15 believe; nevertheless let us **g** unto him. 71
11:16 unto *his* fellow-disciples, Let us also **g**, 71
11:44 unto him, Loose him, and let *him* **g**. 5217
13:33 the Jews, Whither I **g**, ye cannot come; 5217
13:36 Jesus answered him, Whither I **g**, 5217
14: 2 told you. I **g** to prepare a place for you. 4198
14: 3 And if I **g** and prepare a place for you, 4198
14: 4 whither I **g** ye know, and the way ye 5217
14:12 shall he do; because I **g** unto my Father. 4198
14:28 I **g away**, and come *again* unto you. 5217
14:28 because I said, I **g** unto the Father: 4198
14:31 even so I do. Arise, let us **g** hence. 71
15:16 that you should **g** and bring forth fruit, 5217
16: 5 But now I **g** my way to him that sent me; 5217
16: 7 It is expedient for you that I **g away**: 565
16: 7 for if I **g** not **away**, the Comforter will not 565
16:10 I **g** to my Father, and ye see me no 5217
16:16 ye shall see me, because I **g** to the Father. 5217
16:17 see me: and, Because I **g** to the Father? 5217

Jn 16:28 I leave the world, and **g** to the Father. 4198
18: 8 ye seek me, let these **g** their way: 5217
19:12 cried out, saying, If thou **let** this *man* **g**, 630
20:17 but **g** to my brethren, and say unto them, 4198
21: 3 Simon Peter saith unto them, I **g** a fishing. 5217
21: 3 They say unto him, We also **g** with thee. 2064
Ac 1:11 *in* like manner as ye have seen him **g** 4198
1:25 that *he* might **g** to his own place. 4198
3: 3 and John about to **g** into the temple, 1524
3:13 when he was determined to **let** *him* **g**. 630
4:15 them to **g aside** out of the council, 565
4:21 further threatened *them*, they **let** them **g**, 630
4:23 And being **let g**, they went to their own 630
5:20 **G**, stand and speak in the temple to 630
5:41 in the name of Jesus, and **let** them **g**. 630
7:40 Aaron, Make us gods to **g before** us: 4313
8:26 **g** toward the south unto the way that 4198
8:29 **G near**, and join thyself to this chariot. 4334
9: 6 and **g into** the city, and it shall be 1525
9:11 **g** into the street which is called Straight, 4198
9:15 **G** *thy way*: for he is a chosen vessel unto 4198
10:20 and get *thee* down, and **g** with them, 4198
11:12 And the Spirit bade me **g** with them, 4905
11:22 that *he* should **g** as far as Antioch. 1330
12:17 **G** shew these *things* unto James, and to NIG
15: 2 should **g up** to Jerusalem unto the apostles 305
15:33 they were **let g** in peace from the brethren 630
15:36 Let us **g again** and visit our brethren in 1994
16: 3 Him would Paul have to **g forth** with him; 1831
16: 7 to Mysia, they assayed to **g** into Bithynia: 4198
16:10 immediately we endeavoured to **g** into 1831
16:35 the sergeants, saying, **Let** those men **g**. 630
16:36 The magistrates have sent to **let** you **g**: 630
16:36 now therefore depart, and **g** in peace. 4198
17: 9 Jason, and *of* the other, they **let** them **g**. 630
17:14 sent away Paul to **g** as *it were* to the sea: 4198
18: 6 henceforth I will **g** unto the Gentiles. 4198
19:21 and Achaia, to **g** to Jerusalem, saying, 4198
20: 1 and departed for to **g** into Macedonia. 4198
20:13 he appointed, minding himself to **g afoot**. 3978
20:22 I **g** bound in the spirit unto Jerusalem, 4198
21: 4 that *he* should not **g up** to Jerusalem. 305
21:12 besought him not to **g up** to Jerusalem. 305
22:10 unto me, Arise, and **g into** Damascus; 4198
23:10 commanded the soldiers to **g down**, 2597
23:23 Make ready two hundred soldiers to **g** to 4198
23:32 the morrow they left the horsemen to **g** 4198
24:25 and answered, **G** *thy way* for this *time*; 4198
25: 5 **g down with** *me*, and accuse this man, 4782
25: 9 Wilt thou **g up** to Jerusalem, and there be 305
25:12 unto Cesar? unto Cesar shalt thou **g**. 4198
25:20 I asked *him* whether he would **g** to 4198
27: 3 gave *him* liberty to **g** unto *his* friends to 4198
28:18 would have **let** *me* **g**, because there was 630
28:26 Saying, **G** unto this people, and say, 4198
Ro 15:25 But now I **g** unto Jerusalem to minister 4198
1Co 5:10 for then must ye needs **g out** of the world. 1831
6: 1 **g to law** before the unjust, and not before 2919
6: 7 ye **g to law** one with another. 2192+2917
10:27 you *to a feast*, and ye be disposed to **g**; 4198
16: 4 if it be meet that I **g** also, they shall go 4198
16: 4 meet that I **g** also, they shall with me. 4198
16: 6 me on my journey whithersoever I **g**. 4198
2Co 9: 5 that they would **g before** unto you, 4281
Gal 2: 9 that we *should* **g** unto the heathen, NIG
Eph 4:26 let not the sun **g down** upon your wrath: 1931
Php 2:23 I shall see **how it will g** with me. 3588+4012
1Th 4: 6 That no *man* **g beyond** and defraud his 5233
Heb 6: 1 of Christ, let us **g** on unto perfection: 5342
6:13 Let us **g forth** therefore unto him without 1831
Jas 4:13 **G** to now, ye that say, To day or 71
4:13 or to morrow we will **g** into such a city, 4198
5: 1 **G** to now, ye rich *men*, weep and howl 71
Rev 3:12 of my God, and he shall **g** no more out: 1831
10: 8 **G** *and* take the little book which is open 5217
13:10 He that leadeth into captivity *shall* **g** into 5217
16: 1 **G** your ways, and pour out the vials of 5217
16:14 which **g forth** unto the kings of the earth 1607
17: 8 the bottomless *pit*, and **g** into perdition: 5217
20: 8 And shall **g out** to deceive the nations 1831

GOAD (1) [GOADS]
Jdg 3:31 Philistines six hundred men with an ox **g**: 4451

GOADS (2) [GOAD]
1Sa 13:21 for the axes, and to sharpen the **g**. 1861
Ecc 12:11 words of the wise *are* as **g**, and as nails 1861

GOAH See GOATH

GOAT (35) [GOATS, GOATS', GOATSKINS, SCAPEGOAT]
Ge 15: 9 a **she g** of three years old, and a ram of 5795
Lev 3:12 if his offering *be* a **g**, then he shall offer it 5795
4:24 shall lay his hand upon the head of the **g**, 8163
7:23 no *manner* fat, of ox, or of sheep, or of **g**. 5795
9:15 the people's offering, and took the **g**, 8163
10:16 Moses diligently sought the **g** of the sin 8163
16: 9 Aaron shall bring the **g** upon which 8163
16:10 the **g**, on which the lot fell to be 8163
16:15 shall he kill the **g** of the sin offering, that 8163
16:18 of the blood of the **g**, and put *it* upon 8163
16:20 and the altar, he shall bring the live **g**: 8163
16:21 his hands upon the head of the live **g**, 8163

Lev 16:21 putting them upon the head of the **g**, 8163
16:22 **g** bear upon him all their iniquities 8163
16:22 he shall let go the **g** in the wilderness. 8163
16:26 he that let go the **g** for the scapegoat shall 8163
16:27 sin offering, and the **g** for the sin offering, 8163
17: 3 lamb, or **g**, in the camp, or that killeth *it* 5795
22:27 or a sheep, or a **g**, is brought forth, then 5795
Nu 15:27 he shall bring a **she g** of the first year for 5795
18:17 or the firstling of a **g**, thou shalt not 5795
28:22 one **g** for a sin offering; beside 8163
29:22 one **g** for a sin offering; beside 8163
29:28 one **g** for a sin offering; beside 8163
29:31 one **g** for a sin offering; beside 8163
29:34 one **g** for a sin offering; beside 8163
29:38 one **g** for a sin offering; beside 8163
Dt 14: 4 eat: the ox, the sheep, and the **g**, 5795+7716
14: 5 **wild g**, and the pygarg, and the wild ox, 689
Pr 30:31 a **he g** also; and a king, against whom 8495
Eze 43:25 days shalt thou prepare every day a **g** 8163
Da 8: 5 **g** came from the west on 5795+6842
8: 5 **g** *had* a notable horn between his eyes. 6842
8: 8 the **he g** waxed very great: 5795+6842
8:21 the rough **g** *is* the king of Grecia: 6842

GOAT IDOLS See DEVILS

GOATH
Jer 31:39 hill Gareb, and shall compass about to **G**. 1601

GOATS (87) [GOAT]
Ge 27: 9 me from thence two good kids of the **g**; 5795
27:16 she put the skins of the kids of the **g** upon 5795
30:32 the spotted and speckled among the **g**, 5795
30:33 not speckled and spotted amongst the **g**, 5795
30:35 he removed that day the **he g** that were 8495
30:35 all the **she g** that were speckled and 5795
31:38 and thy **she g** have not cast their young, 5795
32:14 Two hundred **she g**, and twenty he goats, 5795
32:14 twenty **he g**, two hundred ewes, 8495
37:31 killed a kid of the **g**, and dipped the coat 5795
Ex 12: 5 take *it* out from the sheep, or from the **g**: 5795
Lev 1:10 sheep, or of the **g**, for a burnt sacrifice; 5795
4:23 a kid of the **g**, a male without blemish; 5795
4:28 a kid of the **g**, a female without blemish; 5795
5: 6 a lamb or a kid of the **g**, for a sin offering; 5795
9: 3 Take ye a kid of the **g**, for a sin offering; 5795
16: 5 Israel two kids of the **g** for a sin offering, 5795
16: 7 he shall take the two **g**, and present them 8163
16: 8 Aaron shall cast lots upon the two **g**; 8163
22:19 of the beeves, of the sheep, or of the **g**. 5795
23:19 ye shall sacrifice one kid of the **g** for a sin 5795
Nu 7:16 One kid of the **g** for a sin offering: 5795
7:17 two oxen, five rams, five he **g**, five lambs 6260
7:22 One kid of the **g** for a sin offering: 5795
7:23 two oxen, five rams, five he **g**, five lambs 6260
7:28 One kid of the **g** for a sin offering: 5795
7:29 two oxen, five rams, five he **g**, five lambs 6260
7:34 One kid of the **g** for a sin offering: 5795
7:35 two oxen, five rams, five he **g**, five lambs 6260
7:40 One kid of the **g** for a sin offering: 5795
7:41 two oxen, five rams, five **he g**, five lambs 6260
7:46 One kid of the **g** for a sin offering: 5795
7:47 two oxen, five rams, five **he g**, five lambs 6260
7:52 One kid of the **g** for a sin offering: 5795
7:53 two oxen, five rams, five **he g**, five lambs 6260
7:58 One kid of the **g** for a sin offering: 5795
7:59 two oxen, five rams, five **he g**, five lambs 6260
7:64 One kid of the **g** for a sin offering: 5795
7:65 two oxen, five rams, five **he g**, five lambs 6260
7:70 One kid of the **g** for a sin offering: 5795
7:71 two oxen, five rams, five **he g**, five lambs 6260
7:76 One kid of the **g** for a sin offering: 5795
7:77 two oxen, five rams, five **he g**, five lambs 6260
7:82 One kid of the **g** for a sin offering: 5795
7:83 two oxen, five rams, five **he g**, five lambs 6260
7:87 the kids of the **g** for sin offering twelve. 6260
7:88 bullocks, the rams sixty, the **he g** sixty, 6260
15:24 and one kid of the **g** for a sin offering. 5795
28:15 one kid of the **g** for a sin offering unto 5795
28:30 one kid of the **g**, to make an atonement 5795
29: 5 one kid of the **g** for a sin offering, to make 5795
29:11 One kid of the **g** *for* a sin offering; beside 5795
29:16 one kid of the **g** *for* a sin offering; beside 5795
29:19 one kid of the **g** *for* a sin offering; beside 5795
29:25 one kid of the **g** *for* a sin offering; beside 5795
Dt 32:14 and rams of the breed of Bashan, and **g**, 6260
1Sa 24: 2 his men upon the rocks of the **wild g**. 3277
25: 2 three thousand sheep, and a thousand **g**: 5795
2Ch 17:11 seven thousand and seven hundred **he g**. 8495
29:21 seven lambs, and seven **he g**, 5795+6842
29:23 they brought forth the **he g** for the sin 8163
Ezr 6:17 offering for all Israel, twelve **he g**, 5796+6841
8:35 lambs, twelve **he g** *for* a sin offering: 6842
Job 39: 1 Knowest thou the time when the **wild g** 3277
Ps 50: 9 of thy house, *nor* **he g** out of thy folds. 6260
50:13 the flesh of bulls, or drink the blood of **g**? 6260
66:15 of rams; I will offer bullocks with **g**. 6260
104:18 The high hills *are* a refuge for the **wild g**; 3277
Pr 27:26 and the **g** *are* the price of the field. 6260
SS 4: 1 thy hair *is* as a flock of **g**, that appear from 5795
6: 5 thy hair *is* as a flock of **g** that appear from 5795
Isa 1:11 blood of bullocks, or of lambs, or of **he g**. 6260
34: 6 *and* with the blood of lambs and **g**, 6260
Jer 50: 8 and be as the **he g** before the flocks. 6260
51:40 to the slaughter, like rams with **he g**. 6260

Eze 27:21 with thee in lambs, and rams, and **g:** 6260
 34:17 cattle, between the rams and the **he g.** 6260
 39:18 of rams, of lambs, and of **g,** of bullocks, 6260
 43:22 the **g** without blemish for a sin offering; 5795
 45:23 and a kid of the **g** daily *for* a sin offering. 5795
Zec 10: 3 the shepherds, and I punished the **g:** 6260
Mt 25:32 a shepherd divideth *his* sheep from the **g:** 2056
 25:33 on his right hand, but the **g** on the left. 2055
Heb 9:12 Neither by the blood of **g** and calves, 5131
 9:13 For if the blood of bulls and of **g,** 5131
 9:19 he took the blood of calves and of **g,** 5131
 10: 4 of bulls and of **g** should take away sins. 5131

GOATS' (10) [GOAT]

Ex 25: 4 and scarlet, and fine linen, and **g** *hair,* 5795
 26: 7 thou shalt make curtains *of* **g** *hair* to be a 5795
 35: 6 and scarlet, and fine linen, and **g** *hair,* 5795
 35:23 **g** *hair,* and red skins of rams, 5795
 35:26 stirred them up in wisdom spun **g** *hair.* 5795
 36:14 he made curtains *of* **g** *hair* for the tent 5795
Nu 31:20 all work of **g** *hair,* and all things made of 5795
1Sa 19:13 put a pillow of **g** *hair* for his bolster, 5795
 19:16 with a pillow of **g** *hair* for his bolster, 5795
Pr 27:27 shalt have **g** milk enough for thy food, 5795

GOATSKINS (1) [GOAT, SKIN]

Heb 11:37 wandered about in sheepskins and **g;** 122+1192

GOB (2)

2Sa 21:18 again a battle with the Philistines at **G:** 1359
 21:19 there was again a battle in **G** with 1359

GOBLET (1)

SS 7: 2 Thy navel *is* like a round **g,** *which* wanteth 101

GOD (4135) [BETH-EL, GOD'S, GOD-WARD, GODDESS, GODHEAD, GODLINESS, GODLY, GODS, UNGODLINESS; See also GOD*]

Ge 1: 1 In the beginning **G** created the heaven and 430
 1: 2 the Spirit of **G** moved upon the face of 430
 1: 3 **G** said, Let there be light: and there was 430
 1: 4 **G** saw the light, that *it was* good: 430
 1: 4 and **G** divided the light from the darkness. 430
 1: 5 **G** called the light Day, and the darkness he 430
 1: 6 **G** said, Let there be a firmament in the 430
 1: 7 **G** made the firmament, and divided 430
 1: 8 **G** called the firmament Heaven. 430
 1: 9 **G** said, Let the waters under the heaven be 430
 1:10 called the dry *land* Earth; 430
 1:10 called he Seas: and **G** saw that *it was* good. 430
 1:11 **G** said, Let the earth bring forth grass, 430
 1:12 after his kind: and **G** saw that *it was* good. 430
 1:14 **G** said, Let there be lights in the firmament 430
 1:16 made two great lights; the greater light 430
 1:17 **G** set them in the firmament of the heaven 430
 1:18 the darkness: and **G** saw that *it was* good. 430
 1:20 **G** said, Let the waters bring forth 430
 1:21 **G** created great whales, and every living 430
 1:21 after his kind: and **G** saw that *it was* good. 430
 1:22 And **G** blessed them, saying, Be fruitful, 430
 1:24 **G** said, Let the earth bring forth the living 430
 1:25 **G** made the beast of the earth after his kind 430
 1:25 after his kind: and **G** saw that *it was* good. 430
 1:26 **G** said, Let us make man in our image, 430
 1:27 So **G** created man in his own image, 430
 1:27 in the image of **G** created he him; 430
 1:28 **G** blessed them, and God said unto them, 430
 1:28 **G** said unto them, Be fruitful, and multiply 430
 1:29 **G** said, Behold, I have given you every 430
 1:31 **G** saw every thing that he had made, 430
 2: 2 on the seventh day **G** ended his work 430
 2: 3 **G** blessed the seventh day, and sanctified 430
 2: 3 rested from all his work which **G** created 430
 2: 4 in the day that the Lord **G** made the earth 430
 2: 5 for the Lord **G** had not caused it to rain 430
 2: 7 the Lord **G** formed man *of* the dust of 430
 2: 8 the Lord **G** planted a garden eastward in 430
 2: 9 out of the ground made the Lord **G** to 430
 2:15 the Lord **G** took the man, and put him 430
 2:16 the Lord **G** commanded the man, saying, 430
 2:18 the Lord **G** said, *It is* not good that 430
 2:19 out of the ground the Lord **G** formed 430
 2:21 the Lord **G** caused a deep sleep to fall 430
 2:22 which the Lord **G** had taken from man, 430
 3: 1 of the field which the Lord **G** had made. 430
 3: 1 said unto the woman, Yea, hath **G** said, 430
 3: 3 **G** hath said, Ye shall not eat of it, 430
 3: 5 For **G** doth know that in the day ye eat 430
 3: 8 they heard the voice of the Lord **G** 430
 3: 8 Lord **G** amongst the trees of the garden. 430
 3: 9 the Lord **G** called unto Adam, 430
 3:13 the Lord **G** said unto the woman, What *is* 430
 3:14 the Lord **G** said unto the serpent, 430
 3:21 to his wife did the Lord **G** make coats of 430
 3:22 the Lord **G** said, Behold, the man is 430
 3:23 Therefore the Lord **G** sent him forth from 430
 4:25 **G,** *said she,* hath appointed me another 430
 5: 1 the day that **G** created man, 430
 5: 1 in the likeness of **G** made he him; 430
 5:22 Enoch walked with **G** after he begat 430
 5:24 Enoch walked with **G:** and he *was* not; 430
 5:24 with God: and he *was* not; for **G** took him. 430
 6: 2 the sons of **G** saw the daughters of men 430
 6: 4 when the sons of **G** came in unto 430
 6: 9 his generations, *and* Noah walked with **G.** 430

Ge 6:11 The earth also was corrupt before **G,** 430
 6:12 **G** looked upon the earth, and, behold, 430
 6:13 **G** said unto Noah, The end of all flesh is 430
 6:22 according to all that **G** commanded him, 430
 7: 9 the female, as **G** had commanded Noah. 430
 7:16 of all flesh, as **G** had commanded him: 430
 8: 1 **G** remembered Noah, and every living 430
 8: 1 **G** made a wind to pass over the earth, 430
 8:15 And **G** spake unto Noah, saying, 430
 9: 1 **G** blessed Noah and his sons, and said unto 430
 9: 6 shed: for in the image of **G** made he man. 430
 9: 8 **G** spake unto Noah, and to his sons with 430
 9:12 **G** said, This *is* the token of the covenant 430
 9:16 the everlasting covenant between **G** 430
 9:17 **G** said unto Noah, This *is* the token of 430
 9:26 he said, Blessed *be* the Lord **G** of Shem; 430
 9:27 **G** shall enlarge Japheth, and he shall dwell 430
 14:18 and he *was* the priest of the most high **G.** 410
 14:19 said, Blessed *be* Abram of the most high **G,** 410
 14:20 blessed *be* the most high **G,** which hath 410
 14:22 the most high **G,** the possessor of heaven 410
 16:13 that spake unto her, Thou **G** seest me: 410
 17: 1 and said unto him, I *am* the Almighty **G;** 410
 17: 3 on his face: and **G** talked with him, saying, 430
 17: 7 to be a **G** unto thee, and to thy seed after 430
 17: 8 possession; and I will be their **G.** 430
 17: 9 **G** said unto Abraham, Thou shalt keep my 430
 17:15 **G** said unto Abraham, *As for* Sarai thy wife, 430
 17:18 Abraham said unto **G,** O that Ishmael 430
 17:19 **G** said, Sarah thy wife shall bear thee a son 430
 17:22 with him, and **G** went up from Abraham. 430
 17:23 the selfsame day, as **G** had said unto him. 430
 19:29 when **G** destroyed the cities of the plain, 430
 19:29 **G** remembered Abraham, and sent Lot 430
 20: 3 **G** came to Abimelech in a dream by night, 430
 20: 6 **G** said unto him in a dream, Yea, I know 430
 20:11 Surely the fear of **G** *is* not in this place; 430
 20:13 when **G** caused me to wander from my 430
 20:17 Abraham prayed unto **G:** and God healed 430
 20:17 **G** healed Abimelech, and his wife, 430
 21: 2 at the set time of which **G** had spoken to 430
 21: 4 eight days old, as **G** had commanded him. 430
 21: 6 **G** hath made me to laugh, *so that* all that 430
 21:12 **G** said unto Abraham, Let it not be 430
 21:17 **G** heard the voice of the lad; and the angel 430
 21:17 angel of **G** called to Hagar out of heaven, 430
 21:17 **G** hath heard the voice of the lad where 430
 21:19 **G** opened her eyes, and she saw a well of 430
 21:20 **G** was with the lad; and he grew, 430
 21:22 **G** *is* with thee in all that thou doest: 430
 21:23 swear unto me here by **G** that thou wilt 430
 21:33 the name of the Lord, the everlasting **G.** 410
 22: 1 that **G** did tempt Abraham, and said unto 430
 22: 3 went unto the place of which **G** had told 430
 22: 8 **G** will provide himself a lamb for a burnt 430
 22: 9 came to the place which **G** had told him 430
 22:12 for now I know that thou fearest **G,** 430
 24: 3 the **G** of heaven, and the God of the earth, 430
 24: 3 the God of heaven, and the **G** of the earth, 430
 24: 7 The Lord **G** of heaven, which took me 430
 24:12 O Lord **G** of my master Abraham, I pray 430
 24:27 Blessed *be* the Lord **G** of my master 430
 24:42 said, O Lord **G** of my master Abraham, 430
 24:48 blessed the Lord **G** of my master 430
 25:11 of Abraham, that **G** blessed his son Isaac; 430
 26:24 said, I *am* the **G** of Abraham thy father: 430
 27:20 Because the Lord thy **G** brought *it* to me. 430
 27:28 **G** give thee of the dew of heaven, 430
 28: 3 **G** Almighty bless thee, and make thee 410
 28: 4 a stranger, which **G** gave unto Abraham. 430
 28:12 behold the angels of **G** ascending and 430
 28:13 I *am* the Lord **G** of Abraham thy father, 430
 28:13 of Abraham thy father, and the **G** of Isaac: 430
 28:17 this *is* none other but the house of **G,** 430
 28:20 If **G** will be with me, and will keep me in 430
 28:21 in peace; then shall the Lord be my **G:** 430
 30: 6 **G** hath judged me, and hath also heard my 430
 30:17 **G** hearkened unto Leah, and she conceived 430
 30:18 **G** hath given *me* my hire, because I have 430
 30:20 **G** hath endued me with a good dowry; 430
 30:22 **G** remembered Rachel, and God hearkened 430
 30:22 hearkened to her, and opened her womb 430
 30:23 and said, **G** hath taken away my reproach: 430
 31: 5 the **G** of my father hath been with me. 430
 31: 7 but **G** suffered him not to hurt me. 430
 31: 9 Thus **G** hath taken away the cattle of your 430
 31:11 the angel of **G** spake unto me in a dream, 430
 31:13 the **G** of Beth-el, where thou anointedst 410
 31:16 For all the riches which **G** hath taken from 430
 31:16 whatsoever **G** hath said unto thee, 430
 31:24 came to Laban the Syrian in a dream by 430
 31:29 the **G** of your father spake unto me 430
 31:42 Except the **G** of my father, the God of 430
 31:42 the **G** of Abraham, and the fear of Isaac, 430
 31:42 **G** hath seen mine affliction and the labour 430
 31:50 see, **G** is witness betwixt me and thee. 430
 31:53 the **G** of Abraham, and the God of Nahor, 430
 31:53 The God of Abraham, and the **G** of Nahor, 430
 31:53 of their father, judge betwixt us. 430
 32: 1 on his way, and the angels of **G** met him. 430
 32: 9 of my father Abraham, and God of my 430
 32: 9 father Abraham, and **G** of my father Isaac, 430
 32:28 for as a prince hast thou power with **G** and 430
 32:30 for I have seen **G** face to face, and my life 430
 33: 5 children which **G** hath graciously given

Ge 33:10 as though I had seen the face of **G,** 430
 33:11 because **G** hath dealt graciously with me, 430
 35: 1 **G** said unto Jacob, Arise, go up to Beth-el, 430
 35: 1 make there an altar unto **G,** that appeared 410
 35: 3 I will make there an altar unto **G,** 410
 35: 5 the terror of **G** was upon the cities that 430
 35: 7 because there **G** appeared unto him, when 430
 35: 9 **G** appeared unto Jacob again, when he 430
 35:10 **G** said unto him, Thy name *is* Jacob: 430
 35:11 **G** said unto him, I *am* God Almighty: 410
 35:11 God said unto him, I *am* **G** Almighty: 410
 35:13 **G** went up from him in the place where he 430
 35:15 called the name of the place where **G** 430
 39: 9 this great wickedness, and sin against **G?** 430
 40: 8 *Do not* interpretations *belong* to **G?** 430
 41:16 **G** shall give Pharaoh an answer of peace. 430
 41:25 hath shewed Pharaoh what he *is* about 430
 41:28 What **G** *is* about to do he sheweth unto 430
 41:32 *it is* because the thing *is* established by **G,** 430
 41:32 by God, and **G** will shortly bring it to pass. 430
 41:38 this *is,* a man in whom the spirit of **G** *is?* 430
 41:39 Forasmuch as **G** hath shewed thee all this, 430
 41:51 For **G,** *said he,* hath made me forget all my 430
 41:52 For **G** hath caused me to be fruitful in 430
 42:18 third day, This do, and live; for I fear **G:** 430
 42:28 What *is* this *that* **G** hath done unto us? 430
 43:14 **G** Almighty give you mercy before the man 410
 43:23 your **G,** and the God of your father, 430
 43:23 your God, and the **G** of your father, 430
 43:29 he said, **G** be gracious unto thee, my son. 430
 44: 7 **G** forbid that thy servants should do 2486
 44:16 **G** hath found out the iniquity of thy 430
 44:17 he said, **G** forbid that I should do so: 2486
 45: 5 for **G** did send me before you to preserve 430
 45: 7 **G** sent me before you to preserve you a 430
 45: 8 *it was* not you *that* sent me hither, but **G:** 430
 45: 9 **G** hath made me lord of all Egypt: 430
 46: 1 offered sacrifices unto the **G** of his father 430
 46: 2 **G** spake unto Israel in the visions of 430
 46: 3 he said, I *am* **G,** the God of thy father: 410
 46: 3 he said, I *am* God, the **G** of thy father: 430
 48: 3 **G** Almighty appeared unto me at Luz in 410
 48: 9 whom **G** hath given me in this *place.* 430
 48:11 and lo, **G** hath shewed me also thy seed. 430
 48:15 he blessed Joseph, and said, **G,** before 430
 48:15 Which fed me all my life long unto this 430
 48:20 **G** make thee as Ephraim and as Manasseh: 430
 48:21 **G** shall be with you, and bring you again 430
 49:24 by the hands of the mighty **G** of Jacob; NIH
 49:25 by the **G** of thy father, who shall help 410
 50:17 the trespass of the servants of the **G** 430
 50:19 Fear not: for *am* I in the place of **G?** 430
 50:20 Meant it unto good, to bring to pass, 430
 50:24 **G** will surely visit you, and bring you out 430
 50:25 **G** will surely visit you, and ye shall carry 430
Ex 1:17 the midwives feared **G,** and did not as 430
 1:20 Therefore **G** dealt well with the midwives: 430
 1:21 to pass, because the midwives feared **G,** 430
 2:23 their cry came up unto **G** by reason of 430
 2:24 **G** heard their groaning, 430
 2:24 remembered his covenant with Abraham 430
 2:25 **G** looked upon the children of Israel, 430
 2:25 of Israel, and **G** had respect unto *them.* 430
 3: 1 came to the mountain of **G,** *even* to Horeb. 430
 3: 4 called unto him out of the midst of 430
 3: 6 he said, I *am* the **G** of thy father, 430
 3: 6 the **G** of Abraham, the God of Isaac, 430
 3: 6 the God of Isaac, and the **G** of Jacob. 430
 3: 6 the God of Isaac, and the **G** of Jacob. 430
 3: 6 his face; for he was afraid to look upon **G.** 430
 3:11 Moses said unto **G,** Who *am* I, that I 430
 3:12 ye shall serve **G** upon this mountain. 430
 3:13 Moses said unto **G,** Behold, *when* I come 430
 3:13 The **G** of your fathers hath sent me unto 430
 3:14 And **G** said unto Moses, I AM THAT I AM: 430
 3:15 **G** said moreover unto Moses, Thus shalt 430
 3:15 The Lord **G** of your fathers, the God of 430
 3:15 the **G** of Abraham, the God of Isaac, 430
 3:15 the God of Isaac, and the God of Jacob, 430
 3:15 the God of Isaac, and the **G** of Jacob, 430
 3:16 unto them, The Lord **G** of your fathers, 430
 3:16 of Abraham, of Isaac, and of Jacob, 430
 3:18 The Lord **G** of the Hebrews hath met 430
 3:18 that we may sacrifice to the Lord our **G.** 430
 4: 1 That they may believe that the Lord **G** of 430
 4: 5 the **G** of Abraham, the God of Isaac, 430
 4: 5 the God of Isaac, and the God of Jacob, 430
 4: 5 the God of Isaac, and the **G** of Jacob, 430
 4:16 and thou shalt be to him instead of **G.** 430
 4:20 and Moses took the rod of **G** in his hand. 430
 4:27 him in the mount of **G,** and kissed him. 430
 5: 1 Thus saith the Lord **G** of Israel, 430
 5: 3 The **G** of the Hebrews hath met with us: 430
 5: 3 and sacrifice unto the Lord our **G;** 430
 5: 8 saying, Let us go *and* sacrifice to our **G.** 430
 6: 2 **G** spake unto Moses, and said unto him, 430
 6: 3 *the name* of **G** Almighty, but *by* my name 410
 6: 7 for a people, and I will be to you a **G:** 430
 6: 7 ye shall know that I *am* the Lord your **G,** 430
 7: 1 See, I have made thee a **G** to Pharaoh: 430
 7:16 The Lord **G** of the Hebrews hath sent me 430
 8:10 *there is* none like unto the Lord our **G.** 430
 8:19 said unto Pharaoh, This *is* the finger of **G:** 430
 8:25 said, Go ye, sacrifice to your **G** in the land. 430
 8:26 of the Egyptians to the Lord our **G:** 430

G

Ex	8:27 sacrifice to the Lord our **G**, as he shall	430
	8:28 that ye may sacrifice to the Lord your **G**	430
	9: 1 Thus saith the Lord **G** of the Hebrews,	430
	9:13 Thus saith the Lord **G** of the Hebrews,	430
	9:30 know that ye will not yet fear the Lord **G**.	430
	10: 3 Thus saith the Lord **G** of the Hebrews,	430
	10: 7 that they may serve the Lord their **G**:	430
	10: 8 unto them, Go, serve the Lord your **G**:	430
	10:16 I have sinned against the Lord your **G**,	430
	10:17 *this* once, and intreat the Lord your **G**,	430
	10:25 we may sacrifice unto the Lord our **G**.	430
	10:26 must we take to serve the Lord our **G**;	430
	13:17 that **G** led them not *through* the way of	430
	13:17 for **G** said, Lest peradventure the people	430
	13:18 **G** led the people about, *through* the way	430
	13:19 of Israel, saying, **G** will surely visit you;	430
	14:19 angel of **G**, which went before the camp	430
	15: 2 he *is* my **G**, and I will prepare him a	410
	15: 2 my father's **G**, and I will exalt him.	430
	15:26 hearken to the voice of the Lord thy **G**,	430
	16: 3 **Would to G** we had died by the	4310+5414
	16:12 ye shall know that I *am* the Lord your **G**.	430
	17: 9 of the hill with the rod of **G** in mine hand.	430
	18: 1 I heard of all that **G** had done for Moses,	430
	18: 4 for the **G** of my father, *said he, was* mine	430
	18: 5 where he encamped *at* the mount of **G**:	430
	18:12 took a burnt offering and sacrifices for **G**:	430
	18:12 bread with Moses' father in law before **G**.	430
	18:15 the people come unto me to inquire of **G**:	430
	18:16 I do make *them* know the statutes of **G**,	430
	18:19 thee counsel, and **G** shall be with thee:	430
	18:19 that thou mayest bring the causes unto **G**:	430
	18:21 such as fear **G**, men of truth,	430
	18:23 **G** command thee *so*, then thou shalt be	430
	19: 3 Moses went up unto **G**, and the Lord	430
	19:17 people out of the camp to meet with **G**;	430
	19:19 and **G** answered him by a voice.	430
	20: 1 And **G** spake all these words, saying,	430
	20: 2 I *am* the Lord thy **G**, which have brought	430
	20: 5 for I the Lord thy **G** *am* a jealous God,	430
	20: 5 for I the Lord thy God *am* a jealous **G**,	410
	20: 7 take the name of the Lord thy **G** in vain;	430
	20:10 day *is* the sabbath of the Lord thy **G**:	430
	20:12 land which the Lord thy **G** giveth thee.	430
	20:19 but let not **G** speak with us, lest we die.	430
	20:20 **G** is come to prove you, and that his fear	430
	20:21 unto the thick darkness where **G** *was*.	430
	21:13 in wait, but **G** deliver *him* into his hand;	430
	22:20 He that sacrificeth unto *any* **g**, save unto	430
	23:19 bring *into* the house of the Lord thy **G**.	430
	23:25 ye shall serve the Lord your **G**,	430
	24:10 they saw the **G** of Israel: and *there was*	430
	24:11 also they saw **G**, and did eat and drink.	430
	24:13 and Moses went up into the mount of **G**.	430
	29:45 the children of Israel, and will be their **G**.	430
	29:46 shall know that I *am* the Lord their **G**,	430
	29:46 amongst them: I *am* the Lord their **G**.	430
	31: 3 I have filled him *with* the spirit of **G**,	430
	31:18 of stone, written with the finger of **G**.	430
	32:11 And Moses besought the Lord his **G**,	430
	32:16 the tables *were* the work of **G**,	430
	32:16 the writing *was* the writing of **G**, graven	430
	32:27 Thus saith the Lord **G** of Israel,	430
	34: 6 The Lord **G**, merciful and gracious,	410
	34:14 For thou shalt worship no other **g**:	410
	34:14 whose name *is* Jealous, *is* a jealous **G**:	410
	34:23 before the Lord God, the **G** of Israel.	430
	34:24 before the Lord thy **G** thrice in the year.	430
	34:26 bring *unto* the house of the Lord thy **G**.	430
	35:31 he hath filled him with the spirit of **G**,	430
Lev	2:13 thy **G** to be lacking from thy meat offering:	430
	4:22 **G** *concerning things* which should not be	430
	10:17 **G** hath given it you to bear the iniquity of	NIH
	11:44 For I *am* the Lord your **G**: ye shall	430
	11:45 up out of the land of Egypt, to be your **G**:	430
	18: 2 and say unto them, I *am* the Lord your **G**.	430
	18: 4 to walk therein: I *am* the Lord your **G**.	430
	18:21 shalt thou profane the name of thy **G**:	430
	18:30 yourselves therein: I *am* the Lord your **G**.	430
	19: 2 be holy: for I the Lord your **G** *am* holy.	430
	19: 3 keep my sabbaths: I *am* the Lord your **G**.	430
	19: 4 molten gods: I *am* the Lord your **G**.	430
	19:10 and stranger: I *am* the Lord your **G**.	430
	19:12 shalt thou profane the name of thy **G**:	430
	19:14 before the blind, but shalt fear thy **G**:	430
	19:25 increase thereof: I *am* the Lord your **G**.	430
	19:31 defiled by them: I *am* the Lord your **G**.	430
	19:32 the face of the old man, and fear thy **G**:	430
	19:34 the land of Egypt: I *am* the Lord your **G**.	430
	19:36 I *am* the Lord your **G**, which brought you	430
	20: 7 and be ye holy: for I *am* the Lord your **G**.	430
	20:24 I *am* the Lord your **G**, which have	430
	21: 6 They shall be holy unto their **G**,	430
	21: 6 and not profane the name of their **G**:	430
	21: 6 and the bread of their **G**, they do offer:	430
	21: 7 her husband: for he *is* holy unto his **G**.	430
	21: 8 for he offereth the bread of thy **G**:	430
	21:12 nor profane the sanctuary of his **G**;	430
	21:12 for the crown of the anointing oil of his **G**	430
	21:17 not approach to offer the bread of his **G**.	430
	21:21 not come nigh to offer the bread of his **G**.	430
	21:22 He shall eat the bread of his **G**, *both* of	430
	22:25 offer the bread of your **G** of any of these;	430
	22:33 you out of the land of Egypt, to be your **G**:	430
	23:14 ye have brought an offering unto your **G**:	430

Lev	23:22 and to the stranger: I *am* the Lord your **G**.	430
	23:28 for you before the Lord your **G**.	430
	23:40 ye shall rejoice before the Lord your **G**	430
	23:43 the land of Egypt: I *am* the Lord your **G**.	430
	24:15 Whosoever curseth his **G** shall bear his sin.	430
	24:22 own country: for I *am* the Lord your **G**:	430
	25:17 one another; but thou shalt fear thy **G**:	430
	25:17 fear thy **G**: for I *am* the Lord your **G**.	430
	25:36 fear thy **G**; that thy brother may live with	430
	25:38 I *am* the Lord your **G**, which brought you	430
	25:38 you the land of Canaan, *and* to be your **G**.	430
	25:43 over him with rigour; but shalt fear thy **G**.	430
	25:55 the land of Egypt: I *am* the Lord your **G**.	430
	26: 1 down unto it: for I *am* the Lord your **G**.	430
	26:12 will be your **G**, and ye shall be my people.	430
	26:13 I *am* the Lord your **G**, which brought you	430
	26:44 with them: for I *am* the Lord their **G**.	430
	26:45 of the heathen, that *I* might be their **G**:	430
Nu	6: 7 the consecration of his **G** *is* upon his head.	430
	10: 9 be remembered before the Lord your **G**,	430
	10:10 be to you for a memorial before your **G**:	430
	10:10 before your God: I *am* the Lord your **G**.	430
	11:29 **would G** that all the Lord's	4310+5414
	12:13 Heal her now, O **G**, I beseech thee.	410
	14: 2 **Would G that** we had died in the land of	3863
	14: 2 **would G** we had died in this wilderness!	3863
	15:40 and be holy unto your **G**.	430
	15:41 I *am* the Lord your **G**, which brought you	430
	15:41 you out of the land of Egypt, to be your **G**:	430
	15:41 to be your God: I *am* the Lord your **G**.	430
	16: 9 that the **G** of Israel hath separated you	430
	16:22 they fell upon their faces, and said, O **G**,	410
	16:22 O God, the **G** of the spirits of all flesh,	430
	20: 3 **Would G** that we had died when our	3863
	21: 5 the people spake against **G**,	430
	22: 9 came unto Balaam, and said, What men	430
	22:10 Balaam said unto **G**, Balak the son of	430
	22:12 **G** said unto Balaam, Thou shalt not go	430
	22:18 go beyond the word of the Lord my **G**,	430
	22:20 **G** came unto Balaam at night, and said	430
	22:38 the word that **G** putteth in my mouth, that	430
	23: 4 **G** met Balaam: and he said unto him,	430
	23: 8 shall I curse, whom **G** hath not cursed?	410
	23:19 **G** *is* not a man, that he should lie; neither	410
	23:21 the Lord his **G** *is* with him, and the shout	410
	23:22 **G** brought them out of Egypt; he hath as it	410
	23:23 and of Israel, What hath **G** wrought!	410
	23:27 peradventure it will please **G** that thou	430
	24: 2 and the spirit of **G** came upon him.	430
	24: 4 He hath said, which heard the words of **G**,	410
	24: 8 **G** brought him forth out of Egypt; he hath	410
	24:16 which heard the words of **G**, and knew	410
	24:23 Alas, who shall live when **G** doeth this!	410
	25:13 because he was zealous for his **G**,	430
	27:16 the Lord, the **G** of the spirits of all flesh,	430
Dt	1: 6 The Lord our **G** spake unto us in Horeb,	430
	1:10 The Lord your **G** hath multiplied you,	430
	1:11 (The Lord **G** of your fathers make you a	430
	1:19 as the Lord our **G** commanded us;	430
	1:20 which the Lord our **G** doth give unto us.	430
	1:21 the Lord thy **G** hath set the land before	430
	1:21 possess *it*, as the Lord **G** of thy fathers	430
	1:25 *It is* a good land which the Lord our **G**	430
	1:26 the commandment of the Lord your **G**:	430
	1:30 The Lord your **G** which goeth before	430
	1:31 seen how that the Lord thy **G** bare thee,	430
	1:32 thing ye did not believe the Lord your **G**,	430
	1:41 according to all that the Lord our **G**	430
	2: 7 For the Lord thy **G** hath blessed thee in	430
	2: 7 these forty years the Lord thy **G** hath	430
	2:29 the land which the Lord our **G** giveth us.	430
	2:30 for the Lord thy **G** hardened his spirit,	430
	2:33 the Lord our **G** delivered him before us;	430
	2:36 the Lord our **G** delivered all unto us:	430
	2:37 nor *unto* whatsoever the Lord our **G**	430
	3: 3 So the Lord our **G** delivered into our	430
	3:18 The Lord your **G** hath given you this land	430
	3:20 your **G** hath given them beyond Jordan:	430
	3:21 your **G** hath done unto these two kings:	430
	3:22 for the Lord your **G** he shall fight for	430
	3:24 for what **G** *is there* in heaven or in earth,	410
	4: 1 possess the land which the Lord **G** of	430
	4: 2 the Lord your **G** which I command you.	430
	4: 3 the Lord thy **G** hath destroyed them from	430
	4: 4 ye that did cleave unto the Lord your **G**	430
	4: 5 even as the Lord my **G** commanded me,	430
	4: 7 *so* great, who hath **G** *so* nigh unto them,	430
	4: 7 as the Lord our **G** *is* in all *things that* we	430
	4:10 stoodest before the Lord thy **G** in Horeb,	430
	4:19 which the Lord thy **G** hath divided unto	430
	4:21 which the Lord thy **G** giveth thee *for* an	430
	4:23 forget the covenant of the Lord your **G**,	430
	4:23 the Lord thy **G** hath forbidden thee.	430
	4:24 For the Lord thy **G** *is* a consuming fire,	430
	4:24 God *is* a consuming fire, *even* a jealous **G**.	410
	4:25 do evil in the sight of the Lord thy **G**,	430
	4:29 thence thou shalt seek the Lord thy **G**,	430
	4:30 if thou turn to the Lord thy **G**,	430
	4:31 (For the Lord thy **G** *is* a merciful God;)	430
	4:31 (For the Lord thy God *is* a merciful **G**;)	410
	4:32 since the day that **G** created man upon	430
	4:33 Did *ever* people hear the voice of **G**	430
	4:34 Or hath **G** assayed to go *and* take him a	430
	4:34 according to all that the Lord your **G** did	430
	4:35 thou mightest know that the Lord he *is* **G**;	430

Dt	4:39 that the Lord he *is* **G** in heaven above,	430
	4:40 which the Lord thy **G** giveth thee,	430
	5: 2 The Lord our **G** made a covenant with us	430
	5: 6 I *am* the Lord thy **G**, which brought thee	430
	5: 9 for I the Lord thy **G** *am* a jealous God,	430
	5: 9 for I the Lord thy God *am* a jealous **G**,	410
	5:11 take the name of the Lord thy **G** in vain:	430
	5:12 as the Lord thy **G** hath commanded thee.	430
	5:14 day *is* the sabbath of the Lord thy **G**:	430
	5:15 *that* the Lord thy **G** brought thee out	430
	5:15 the Lord thy **G** commanded thee to keep	430
	5:16 as the Lord thy **G** hath commanded thee;	430
	5:16 in the land which the Lord thy **G** giveth	430
	5:24 the Lord our **G** hath shewed us his glory	430
	5:24 we have seen this day that **G** doth talk	430
	5:25 if we hear the voice of the Lord our **G**	430
	5:26 that hath heard the voice of the living **G**	430
	5:27 and hear all that the Lord our **G** shall say:	430
	5:27 speak thou unto us all that the Lord our **G**	430
	5:32 as the Lord your **G** hath commanded you:	430
	5:33 the Lord your **G** hath commanded you,	430
	6: 1 which the Lord your **G** commanded to	430
	6: 2 That thou mightest fear the Lord thy **G**,	430
	6: 3 as the Lord **G** of thy fathers hath	430
	6: 4 O Israel: The Lord our **G** *is* one Lord:	430
	6: 5 thou shalt love the Lord thy **G** with all	430
	6:10 when the Lord thy **G** shall have brought	430
	6:13 Thou shalt fear the Lord thy **G**,	430
	6:15 (For the Lord thy **G** *is* a jealous God	430
	6:15 (For the Lord thy God *is* a jealous **G**	410
	6:15 lest the anger of the Lord thy **G** be	430
	6:16 Ye shall not tempt the Lord your **G**, as ye	430
	6:17 the commandments of the Lord your **G**,	430
	6:20 which the Lord our **G** hath commanded	430
	6:24 to fear the Lord our **G**, for our good	430
	6:25 commandments before the Lord our **G**,	430
	7: 1 When the Lord thy **G** shall bring thee	430
	7: 2 when the Lord thy **G** shall deliver them	430
	7: 6 *art* a holy people unto the Lord thy **G**:	430
	7: 6 the Lord thy **G** hath chosen thee to be a	430
	7: 9 Know therefore that the Lord thy **G**, he *is*	430
	7: 9 he *is* **G**, the faithful God, which keepeth	430
	7: 9 he *is* God, the faithful **G**, which keepeth	410
	7:12 that the Lord thy **G** shall keep unto thee	430
	7:16 which the Lord thy **G** shall deliver thee;	430
	7:18 shalt well remember what the Lord thy **G**	430
	7:19 where*by* the Lord thy **G** brought thee out:	430
	7:19 shall the Lord thy **G** do unto all	430
	7:20 Moreover the Lord thy **G** will send	430
	7:21 for the Lord thy **G** *is* among you,	430
	7:21 God *is* among you, a mighty **G** and terrible.	410
	7:22 the Lord thy **G** will put out those nations	430
	7:23 the Lord thy **G** shall deliver them unto	430
	7:25 it *is* an abomination to the Lord thy **G**.	430
	8: 2 **G** led thee these forty years in	430
	8: 5 *so* the Lord thy **G** chasteneth thee.	430
	8: 6 the commandments of the Lord thy **G**,	430
	8: 7 For the Lord thy **G** bringeth thee into a	430
	8:10 thou shalt bless the Lord thy **G** for	430
	8:11 that thou forget not the Lord thy **G**,	430
	8:14 lifted up, and thou forget the Lord thy **G**,	430
	8:18 But thou shalt remember the Lord thy **G**:	430
	8:19 if thou do at all forget the Lord thy **G**,	430
	8:20 unto the voice of the Lord your **G**.	430
	9: 3 that the Lord thy **G** *is* he which goeth	430
	9: 4 after that the Lord thy **G** hath cast them	430
	9: 5 doth drive them out from before thee,	430
	9: 6 that the Lord thy **G** giveth thee not this	430
	9: 7 how thou provokedst the Lord thy **G** to	430
	9:10 of stone written with the finger of **G**;	430
	9:16 ye had sinned against the Lord your **G**,	430
	9:23 the commandment of the Lord your **G**,	430
	10: 9 according as the Lord thy **G** promised	430
	10:12 what doth the Lord thy **G** require of thee,	430
	10:12 to fear the Lord thy **G**, to walk in all his	430
	10:12 to serve the Lord thy **G** with all thy heart	430
	10:14 heaven of heavens *is* the Lord's thy **G**,	430
	10:17 For the Lord your **G** *is* God of gods,	430
	10:17 For the Lord your God *is* **G** of gods,	430
	10:17 lords, a great **G**, a mighty, and a terrible,	430
	10:20 Thou shalt fear the Lord thy **G**; him shalt	430
	10:21 He *is* thy praise, and he *is* thy **G**, that hath	430
	10:22 now the Lord thy **G** hath made thee as	430
	11: 1 Therefore thou shalt love the Lord thy **G**,	430
	11: 2 seen the chastisement of the Lord your **G**,	430
	11:12 A land which the Lord thy **G** careth for:	430
	11:12 the eyes of the Lord thy **G** *are* always	430
	11:13 to love the Lord your **G**, and to serve him	430
	11:22 to do them, to love the Lord your **G**,	430
	11:25 *for* the Lord your **G** shall lay the fear of	430
	11:27 the commandments of the Lord your **G**,	430
	11:28 the commandments of the Lord your **G**,	430
	11:29 when the Lord thy **G** hath brought thee in	430
	11:31 land which the Lord your **G** giveth you,	430
	12: 1 which the Lord **G** of thy fathers giveth	430
	12: 4 Ye shall not do so unto the Lord your **G**	430
	12: 5 unto the place which the Lord your **G**	430
	12: 7 there ye shall eat before the Lord your **G**,	430
	12: 7 where*in* the Lord thy **G** hath blessed thee.	430
	12: 9 which the Lord your **G** giveth you.	430
	12:10 dwell in the land which the Lord your **G**	430
	12:11 **G** shall choose to cause his name to dwell	430
	12:12 ye shall rejoice before the Lord your **G**,	430
	12:15 the Lord thy **G** which he hath given thee:	430
	12:18 thou must eat them before the Lord thy **G**	430

G

Dt 12:18 place which the LORD thy **G** shall choose, 430
12:18 thou shalt rejoice before the LORD thy **G** 430
12:20 When the LORD thy **G** shall enlarge thy 430
12:21 If the place which the LORD thy **G** hath 430
12:27 upon the altar of the LORD thy **G**: 430
12:27 out upon the altar of the LORD thy **G**, 430
12:28 and right in the sight of the LORD thy **G**. 430
12:29 When the LORD thy **G** shall cut off 430
12:31 Thou shalt not do so unto the LORD thy **G**: 430
13: 3 for the LORD your **G** proveth you, to know 430
13: 3 love the LORD your **G** with all your heart 430
13: 4 Ye shall walk after the LORD your **G**, 430
13: 5 to turn you away from the LORD your **G**, 430
13: 5 LORD thy **G** commanded thee to walk in. 430
13:10 to thrust thee away from the LORD thy **G**, 430
13:12 which the LORD thy **G** hath given thee to 430
13:16 thereof every whit, for the LORD thy **G**: 430
13:18 hearken to the voice of the LORD thy **G**, 430
13:18 is right in the eyes of the LORD thy **G**. 430
14: 1 Ye are the children of the LORD your **G**: 430
14: 2 art a holy people unto the LORD thy **G**, 430
14:21 art a holy people unto the LORD thy **G**, 430
14:23 And thou shalt eat before the LORD thy **G**, 430
14:23 learn to fear the LORD thy **G** always. 430
14:24 which the LORD thy **G** shall choose to set 430
14:24 when the LORD thy **G** hath blessed thee: 430
14:25 place which the LORD thy **G** shall choose: 430
14:26 shalt eat there before the LORD thy **G**, 430
14:29 that the LORD thy **G** may bless thee in all 430
15: 4 giveth thee for an inheritance to possess 430
15: 5 hearken unto the voice of the LORD thy **G**, 430
15: 6 For the LORD thy **G** blesseth thee, as he 430
15: 7 land which the LORD thy **G** giveth thee, 430
15:10 that for this thing the LORD thy **G** shall 430
15:14 of that wherewith the LORD thy **G** hath 430
15:15 and the LORD thy **G** redeemed thee: 430
15:18 the LORD thy **G** shall bless thee in all that 430
15:19 thou shalt sanctify unto the LORD thy **G**: 430
15:20 Thou shalt eat it before the LORD thy **G** 430
15:21 shalt not sacrifice it unto the LORD thy **G**: 430
16: 1 keep the passover unto the LORD thy **G**: 430
16: 1 for in the month of Abib the LORD thy **G** 430
16: 2 the passover unto the LORD thy **G**, 430
16: 5 which the LORD thy **G** giveth thee: 430
16: 6 at the place which the LORD thy **G** shall 430
16: 7 eat it in the place which the LORD thy **G** 430
16: 8 be a solemn assembly to the LORD thy **G**: 430
16:10 with a tribute of a freewill offering of 430
16:10 **G**, according as the LORD thy God hath NIH
16:10 as the LORD thy **G** hath blessed thee: 430
16:11 thou shalt rejoice before the LORD thy **G**, 430
16:11 in the place which the LORD thy **G** hath 430
16:15 **G** in the place which the LORD shall 430
16:15 the LORD thy **G** shall bless thee in all thy 430
16:16 thy **G** in the place which he shall choose; 430
16:17 the LORD thy **G** which he hath given thee. 430
16:18 which the LORD thy **G** giveth thee, 430
16:20 inherit the land which the LORD thy **G** 430
16:21 near unto the altar of the LORD thy **G**, 430
16:22 any image; which the LORD thy **G** hateth. 430
17: 1 unto the LORD thy **G** any bullock, 430
17: 1 is an abomination unto the LORD thy **G**. 430
17: 2 gates which the LORD thy **G** giveth thee, 430
17: 2 in the sight of the LORD thy **G**, 430
17: 8 place which the LORD thy **G** shall choose; 430
17:12 to minister there before the LORD thy **G**, 430
17:14 land which the LORD thy **G** giveth thee, 430
17:15 whom the LORD thy **G** shall choose: 430
17:19 that he may learn to fear the LORD his **G**, 430
18: 5 For the LORD thy **G** hath chosen him out 430
18: 7 minister in the name of the LORD his **G**, 430
18: 9 land which the LORD thy **G** giveth thee, 430
18:12 of these abominations the LORD thy **G** 430
18:13 shalt be perfect with the LORD thy **G**. 430
18:14 For the LORD thy **G** hath not suffered thee so 430
18:15 The LORD thy **G** will raise up unto thee a 430
18:16 thy **G** in Horeb in the day of the assembly, 430
18:16 hear again the voice of the LORD my **G**, 430
19: 1 When the LORD thy **G** hath cut off 430
19: 1 whose land the LORD thy **G** giveth thee, 430
19: 2 which the LORD thy **G** giveth thee to 430
19: 3 which the LORD thy **G** giveth thee to 430
19: 8 if the LORD thy **G** enlarge thy coast, as he 430
19: 9 to love the LORD thy **G**, and to walk ever 430
19:10 which the LORD thy **G** giveth thee for an 430
19:14 the LORD thy **G** giveth thee to possess it. 430
20: 1 for the LORD thy **G** is with thee, 430
20: 4 For the LORD your **G** is he that goeth with 430
20:13 when the LORD thy **G** hath delivered it 430
20:14 which the LORD thy **G** hath given thee. 430
20:16 which the LORD thy **G** doth give thee for 430
20:17 as the LORD thy **G** hath commanded thee: 430
20:18 so should ye sin against the LORD your **G**. 430
21: 1 the LORD thy **G** giveth thee to possess it, 430
21: 5 for them the LORD thy **G** hath chosen to 430
21:10 the LORD thy **G** hath delivered them into 430
21:23 (for he that is hanged is accursed of **G**;) 430
21:23 which the LORD thy **G** giveth thee for an 430
22: 5 so are abomination unto the LORD thy **G**. 430
23: 5 Nevertheless the LORD thy **G** would not 430
23: 5 the LORD thy **G** turned the curse into a 430
23: 5 because the LORD thy **G** loved thee. 430
23:14 For the LORD thy **G** walketh in the midst 430
23:18 into the house of the LORD thy **G** for any 430
23:18 are abomination unto the LORD thy **G**. 430

Dt 23:20 that the LORD thy **G** may bless thee in all 430
23:21 shalt vow a vow unto the LORD thy **G**, 430
23:21 for the LORD thy **G** will surely require it 430
23:23 as thou hast vowed unto the LORD thy **G**, 430
24: 4 which the LORD thy **G** giveth thee for an 430
24: 9 Remember what the LORD thy **G** did unto 430
24:13 unto thee before the LORD thy **G**. 430
24:18 the LORD thy **G** redeemed thee thence: 430
24:19 that the LORD thy **G** may bless thee in all 430
25:15 land which the LORD thy **G** giveth thee. 430
25:16 are an abomination unto the LORD thy **G**. 430
25:18 wast faint and weary; and he feared not **G**. 430
25:19 when the LORD thy **G** hath given thee rest 430
25:19 in the land which the LORD thy **G** giveth 430
26: 1 LORD thy **G** giveth thee for an inheritance, 430
26: 2 thy land that the LORD thy **G** giveth thee, 430
26: 2 thy **G** shall choose to place his name there. 430
26: 3 I profess this day unto the LORD thy **G**, 430
26: 4 down before the altar of the LORD thy **G**. 430
26: 5 and say before the LORD thy **G**, 430
26: 7 when we cried unto the LORD **G** of our 430
26:10 thou shalt set it before the LORD thy **G**, 430
26:10 and worship before the LORD thy **G**: 430
26:11 the LORD thy **G** hath given unto thee, 430
26:13 thou shalt say before the LORD thy **G**, 430
26:14 hearkened to the voice of the LORD my **G**, 430
26:16 This day the LORD thy **G** hath commanded 430
26:17 avouched the LORD this day to be thy **G**, 430
26:19 be a holy people unto the LORD thy **G**, 430
27: 2 land which the LORD thy **G** giveth thee, 430
27: 3 land which the LORD thy **G** giveth thee, 430
27: 3 as the LORD **G** of thy fathers hath 430
27: 5 thou build an altar unto the LORD thy **G**, 430
27: 6 altar of the LORD thy **G** of whole stones: 430
27: 6 offerings thereon unto the LORD thy **G**: 430
27: 7 and rejoice before the LORD thy **G**. 430
27: 9 art become the people of the LORD thy **G**. 430
27:10 obey the voice of the LORD thy **G**, 430
28: 1 unto the voice of the LORD thy **G**, 430
28: 1 that the LORD thy **G** will set thee on high 430
28: 2 hearken unto the voice of the LORD thy **G**. 430
28: 8 land which the LORD thy **G** giveth thee. 430
28: 9 the commandments of the LORD thy **G**, 430
28:13 the commandments of the LORD thy **G**, 430
28:15 hearken unto the voice of the LORD thy **G**, 430
28:45 not unto the voice of the LORD thy **G**, 430
28:47 Because thou servedst not the LORD thy **G** 430
28:52 which the LORD thy **G** hath given thee. 430
28:53 which the LORD thy **G** hath given thee, 430
28:58 and fearful name, THE LORD THY **G**; 430
28:62 not obey the voice of the LORD thy **G**, 430
28:67 shalt say, **Would G** it were even! 4310+5414
28:67 say, **Would G** it were morning! 4310+5414
29: 6 might know that I am the LORD your **G**. 430
29:10 day all of you before the LORD your **G**; 430
29:12 enter into covenant with the LORD thy **G**, 430
29:12 which the LORD thy **G** maketh with thee 430
29:13 he may be unto thee a **G**, as he hath said 430
29:15 with us this day before the LORD our **G**, 430
29:18 away this day from the LORD our **G**, 430
29:25 covenant of the LORD **G** of their fathers, 430
29:29 secret things belong unto the LORD our **G**: 430
30: 1 whither the LORD thy **G** hath driven thee, 430
30: 2 And shalt return unto the LORD thy **G**, 430
30: 3 the LORD thy **G** will turn thy captivity, 430
30: 3 whither the LORD thy **G** hath scattered 430
30: 4 from thence will the LORD thy **G** gather 430
30: 5 the LORD thy **G** will bring thee into 430
30: 6 the LORD thy **G** will circumcise thine 430
30: 6 to love the LORD thy **G** with all thine 430
30: 7 the LORD thy **G** will put all these curses 430
30: 9 the LORD thy **G** will make thee plenteous 430
30:10 hearken unto the voice of the LORD thy **G**, 430
30:10 if thou turn unto the LORD thy **G** with all 430
30:16 thee this day to love the LORD thy **G**, 430
30:16 the LORD thy **G** shall bless thee in the land 430
30:20 That thou mayest love the LORD thy **G**, 430
31: 3 The LORD thy **G**, he will go over before 430
31: 6 for the LORD thy **G**, it is that doth go 430
31:11 thy **G** in the place which he shall choose, 430
31:12 fear the LORD your **G**, and observe to do 430
31:13 and learn to fear the LORD your **G**, 430
31:17 upon us, because our **G** is not amongst us? 430
32: 3 ascribe ye greatness unto our **G**. 430
32: 4 a **G** of truth and without iniquity, just and 410
32:12 and there was no strange **g** with him. 430
32:15 then he forsook **G** which made him, 433
32:17 They sacrificed unto devils, not to **G**; 433
32:18 and hast forgotten **G** that formed thee. 410
32:21 me to jealousy with that which is not **G**; 410
32:39 even I, am he, and there is no **g** with me: 410
33: 1 wherewith Moses the man of **G** blessed 410
33:26 There is none like unto the **G** of Jeshurun, 410
33:27 The eternal **G** is thy refuge, and 410
Jos 1: 9 for the LORD thy **G** is with thee 430
1:11 which the LORD your **G** giveth you to 430
1:13 The LORD your **G** hath given you rest, 430
1:15 land which the LORD your **G** giveth them: 430
1:17 only the LORD thy **G** be with thee, as he 430
2:11 for the LORD your **G**, he is God in heaven 430
2:11 he is **G** in heaven above, and in earth 430
3: 3 ark of the covenant of the LORD your **G**, 430
3: 9 and hear the words of the LORD your **G**. 430
3:10 Hereby ye shall know that the living **G** is 410

Jos 4: 5 the LORD your **G** into the midst of Jordan, 430
4:23 For the LORD your **G** dried up the waters 430
4:23 as the LORD your **G** did to the Red sea, 430
4:24 that ye might fear the LORD your **G** for 430
7: 7 **would to G** we had been content 3863+2050.1
7:13 for thus saith the LORD **G** of Israel, 430
7:19 glory to the LORD **G** of Israel, 430
7:20 Indeed I have sinned against the LORD **G** 430
8: 7 for the LORD your **G** will deliver it into 430
8:30 Joshua built an altar unto the LORD **G** of 430
9: 9 because of the name of the LORD thy **G**: 430
9:18 sworn unto them by the LORD **G** of Israel. 430
9:19 We have sworn unto them by the LORD **G** 430
9:23 drawers of water for the house of my **G**. 430
9:24 how that the LORD thy **G** commanded his 430
10:19 for the LORD your **G** hath delivered them 430
10:40 as the LORD **G** of Israel commanded. 430
10:42 the LORD **G** of Israel fought for Israel. 430
13:14 the sacrifices of the LORD **G** of Israel 430
13:33 the LORD **G** of Israel was their 430
14: 6 unto Moses the man of **G** concerning me 430
14: 8 I wholly followed the LORD my **G**. 430
14: 9 hast wholly followed the LORD my **G**. 430
14:14 that he wholly followed the LORD **G** of 430
18: 3 which the LORD **G** of your fathers hath 430
18: 6 lots for you here before the LORD our **G**. 430
22: 3 of the commandment of the LORD your **G**. 430
22: 4 now the LORD your **G** hath given rest unto 430
22: 5 to love the LORD your **G**, and to walk in 430
22:16 ye have committed against the LORD **G** of Israel, 430
22:19 altar beside the altar of the LORD our **G**. 430
22:22 The LORD **G** of gods, the LORD God of 410
22:22 the LORD **G** of gods, he knoweth, 410
22:24 What have you to do with the LORD **G** of 430
22:29 **G** forbid that we should rebel against 2486
22:29 besides the altar of the LORD our **G** that is 430
22:33 the children of Israel blessed **G**, and did not 430
22:34 a witness between us that the LORD is **G**. 430
23: 3 ye have seen all that the LORD your **G** 430
23: 3 for the LORD your **G** is he that hath fought 430
23: 5 the LORD your **G**, he shall expel them 430
23: 5 as the LORD your **G** hath promised unto 430
23: 8 cleave unto the LORD your **G**, as ye have 430
23:10 for the LORD your **G**, he it is that fighteth 430
23:11 that ye love the LORD your **G**. 430
23:13 for a certainty that the LORD your **G** 430
23:13 which the LORD your **G** hath given you. 430
23:14 the LORD your **G** spake concerning you; 430
23:15 which the LORD your **G** promised you; 430
23:15 which the LORD your **G** hath given you. 430
23:16 the covenant of the LORD your **G**, 430
24: 1 and they presented themselves before **G**. 430
24: 2 Thus saith the LORD **G** of Israel, 430
24:16 **G** forbid that we should forsake 2486
24:17 For the LORD our **G**, he it is that brought 430
24:18 we also serve the LORD; for he is our **G**. 430
24:19 for he is a holy **G**; he is a jealous God; 430
24:19 for he is a holy God; he is a jealous **G**, 410
24:23 incline your heart unto the LORD **G** of 430
24:24 The LORD our **G** will we serve, and his 430
24:26 these words in the book of the law of **G**, 430
24:27 a witness unto you, lest ye deny your **G**. 430
Jdg 1: 7 as I have done, so **G** hath requited me. 430
2:12 they forsook the LORD **G** of their fathers, 430
3: 7 forgat the LORD their **G**, 430
3:20 I have a message from **G** unto thee. 430
4: 6 Hath not the LORD **G** of Israel 430
4:23 So **G** subdued on that day Jabin the king of 430
5: 3 I will sing praise to the LORD **G** of Israel. 430
5: 5 even that Sinai from before the LORD **G** of 430
6: 8 Thus saith the LORD **G** of Israel, 430
6:10 I said unto you, I am the LORD your **G**; 430
6:20 the angel of **G** said unto him, Take the 430
6:26 build an altar unto the LORD thy **G** upon 430
6:31 if he be a **g**, let him plead for himself, 430
6:36 Gideon said unto **G**, If thou wilt save Israel 430
6:39 Gideon said unto **G**, Let not thine anger be 430
6:40 **G** did so that night: for it was dry upon 430
7:14 for into his hand hath **G** delivered Midian, 430
8: 3 **G** hath delivered into your hands the 430
8:33 after Baalim, and made Baal-berith their **g**. 430
8:34 Israel remembered not the LORD their **G**, 430
9: 7 of Shechem, that **G** may hearken unto you. 430
9: 9 wherewith by me they honour **G** and man, 430
9:13 which cheereth **G** and man, and go to be 430
9:23 sent an evil spirit between Abimelech 430
9:27 went into the house of their **g**, and did eat 430
9:29 **would to G** this people were 4310+5414
9:46 into a hold of the house of the **g** Berith. 410
9:56 Thus **G** rendered the wickedness of 430
9:57 all the evil of the men of Shechem did **G** 430
10:10 both because we have forsaken our **G**, 430
11:21 And the LORD **G** of Israel delivered Sihon 430
11:23 So now the LORD **G** of Israel hath 430
11:24 Chemosh thy **g** giveth thee to possess? 430
11:24 So whomsoever the LORD our **G** shall 430
13: 5 the child shall be a Nazarite unto **G** from 430
13: 6 A man of **G** came unto me, 430
13: 6 was like the countenance of an angel of **G**, 430
13: 7 to **G** from the womb to the day of his 430
13: 8 the man of **G** which thou didst send come 430
13: 9 **G** hearkened to the voice of Manoah; 430
13: 9 the angel of **G** came again unto the woman 430
13:22 shall surely die, because we have seen **G**. 430
15:19 **G** clave a hollow place that was in the jaw, 430

G

Jdg 16:17 for I *have been* a Nazarite unto **G** from my 430
16:23 to offer a great sacrifice unto Dagon their **g**, 430
16:23 Our **g** hath delivered Samson our enemy 430
16:24 the people saw him, they praised their **g**: 430
16:24 Our **g** hath delivered into our hands our 430
16:28 I pray thee, only this once, O **G**, 430
18: 5 unto him, Ask *counsel*, we pray thee, of **G**, 430
18:10 for **G** hath given it into your hands; a place 430
18:31 all the time that the house of **G** was in 430
20: 2 in the assembly of the people of **G**, 430
20:18 went up *to* the house of **G**, 410
20:18 of God, and asked *counsel* of **G**, and said, 430
20:26 and came *unto* the house of **G**, and wept, 410
20:27 (for the ark of the covenant of **G** *was* there 410
20:31 *of* which one goeth up *to* the house of **G**, 410
21: 2 And the people came *to* the house of **G**, 430
21: 2 abode there till even before **G**, and lift up 430
21: 3 said, O Lord **G** of Israel, why is this 430
Ru 1:16 *shall be* my people, and thy **G** my God: 430
1:16 *shall be* my people, and thy God my **G**: 430
2:12 a full reward be given thee of the Lord **G** 430
1Sa 1:17 the **G** of Israel grant *thee* thy petition that 430
2: 2 neither *is there* any rock like our **G**. 430
2: 3 for the Lord *is* a **G** of knowledge, 410
2:27 there came a man of **G** unto Eli, 430
2:30 Wherefore the Lord **G** of Israel saith, 430
2:32 all *the wealth* which *G* shall give Israel: NIH
3: 3 ere the lamp of **G** went out in the temple 430
3: 3 where the ark of **G** *was*, and Samuel was 430
3:17 **G** do so to thee, and more also, if thou hide 430
4: 4 there with the ark of the covenant of **G**. 430
4: 7 for they said, **G** is come into the camp. 430
4:11 the ark of **G** was taken; and the two sons 430
4:13 for his heart trembled for the ark of **G**. 430
4:17 are dead, and the ark of **G** is taken. 430
4:18 when he made mention of the ark of **G**, 430
4:19 she heard the tidings that the ark of **G** 430
4:21 because the ark of **G** was taken, and 430
4:22 from Israel: for the ark of **G** is taken. 430
5: 1 The Philistines took the ark of **G**, 430
5: 2 When the Philistines took the ark of **G**, 430
5: 7 The ark of the **G** of Israel shall not abide 430
5: 7 is sore upon us, and upon Dagon our **g**. 430
5: 8 What shall we do with the ark of the **G** of 430
5: 8 Let the ark of the **G** of Israel be carried 430
5: 8 they carried the ark of the **G** of Israel about 430
5:10 Therefore they sent the ark of **G** *to* Ekron. 430
5:10 to pass, as the ark of **G** came *to* Ekron, 430
5:10 They have brought about the ark of the **G** of 430
5:11 Send away the ark of the **G** of Israel, 430
5:11 city; the hand of **G** was very heavy there. 430
6: 3 If ye send away the ark of the **G** of Israel, 430
6: 5 and ye shall give glory unto the **G** of Israel: 430
6:20 is able to stand before this holy Lord **G**? 430
7: 8 Cease not to cry unto the Lord our **G** for 430
9: 6 *there is* in this city a man of **G**, and *he is* 430
9: 7 *is* not a present to bring to the man of **G**: 430
9: 8 will I give to the man of **G**, to tell us our 430
9: 9 when a man went to inquire of **G**, thus he 430
9:10 unto the city where the man of **G** *was*. 430
9:27 that I may shew thee the word of **G**. 430
10: 3 three men going up to **G** to Beth-el, 430
10: 5 After that thou shalt come to the hill of **G**, 430
10: 7 as occasion serve thee; for **G** *is* with thee. 430
10: 9 from Samuel, **G** gave him another heart: 430
10:10 the spirit of **G** came upon him, 430
10:18 Thus saith the Lord **G** of Israel, I brought 430
10:19 ye have *this* day rejected your **G**, 430
10:24 shouted, and said, **G save** the king. 2421
10:26 of men, whose hearts **G** had touched. 430
11: 6 the spirit of **G** came upon Saul when he 430
12: 9 when they forgat the Lord **G**, 430
12:12 when the Lord your **G** *was* your king. 430
12:14 you continue following the Lord your **G**: 430
12:19 Pray for thy servants unto the Lord thy **G**, 430
12:23 **G forbid** that I should sin against 2486
13:13 the commandment of the Lord thy **G**, 430
14:18 said unto Ahiah, Bring hither the ark of **G**. 430
14:18 For the ark of **G** was at that time with 430
14:36 the priest, Let us draw near hither unto **G**. 430
14:37 Saul asked *counsel* of **G**, Shall I go down 430
14:41 Therefore Saul said unto the Lord **G** of 430
14:44 Saul answered, **G** do so and more also: 430
14:45 **G forbid**: *as* the Lord liveth, there shall 2486
14:45 for he hath wrought with **G** this day. 430
15:15 to sacrifice unto the Lord thy **G**; 430
15:21 to sacrifice unto the Lord thy **G** in Gilgal. 430
15:30 that I may worship the Lord thy **G**. 430
16:15 an evil spirit from **G** troubleth thee. 430
16:16 when the evil spirit from **G** is upon thee, 430
16:23 the *evil* spirit from **G** was upon Saul, 430
17:26 he should defy the armies of the living **G**? 430
17:36 he hath defied the armies of the living **G**. 430
17:45 the **G** of the armies of Israel, whom thou 430
17:46 all the earth may know that there is a **G** 430
18:10 that the evil spirit from **G** came upon Saul, 430
19:20 the spirit of **G** was upon the messengers of 430
19:23 the spirit of **G** was upon him also, 430
20: 2 said unto him, **G forbid**; thou shalt not 2486
20:12 said unto David, O Lord **G** of Israel, 430
22: 3 you, till I know what **G** will do for me. 430
22:13 a sword, and *hast* inquired of **G** for him, 430
22:15 Did I then begin to inquire of **G** for him? 430
23: 7 **G** hath delivered him into mine hand; 430
23:10 said David, O Lord **G** of Israel, 430

1Sa 23:11 O Lord **G** of Israel, I beseech thee, 430
23:14 but **G** delivered him not into his hand. 430
23:16 the wood, and strengthened his hand in **G**. 430
25:22 more also do **G** unto the enemies of David, 430
25:29 in the bundle of life with the Lord thy **G**; 430
25:32 Blessed *be* the Lord **G** of Israel, 430
25:34 very deed, *as the* Lord **G** of Israel liveth, 430
26: 8 **G** hath delivered thine enemy into thine 430
28:15 is departed from me, and answereth me 430
29: 9 thou *art* good in my sight, as an angel of **G**: 430
30: 6 encouraged himself in the Lord his **G**. 430
30:15 he said, Swear unto me by **G**, that thou 430
2Sa 2:27 Joab said, As **G** liveth, unless thou hadst 430
3: 9 So do **G** to Abner, and more also, except, 430
3:35 So do **G** to me, and more also, 430
5:10 and the Lord **G** of hosts *was* with him. 430
6: 2 to bring up from thence the ark of **G**, 430
6: 3 they set the ark of **G** upon a new cart, 430
6: 4 *was* at Gibeah, accompanying the ark of **G**: 430
6: 6 Uzzah put forth *his hand* to the ark of **G**, 430
6: 7 **G** smote him *there* for his error; and there 430
6: 7 *his* error; and there he died by the ark of **G**. 430
6:12 unto him, because of the ark of **G**. 430
6:12 brought up the ark of **G** from the house of 430
7: 2 but the ark of **G** dwelleth within curtains. 430
7:22 Wherefore thou art great, O Lord **G**: 136
7:22 neither *is there any* **G** beside thee, 430
7:23 whom **G** went to redeem for a people to 430
7:24 and thou, Lord, art become their **G**. 430
7:25 now, O Lord **G**, the word that thou hast 430
7:26 The Lord of hosts *is* the **G** over Israel: 430
7:27 For thou, O Lord of hosts, **G** of Israel, 430
7:28 thou *art* that **G**, and thy words be true, 430
9: 3 I may shew the kindness of **G** unto him? 430
10:12 for our people, and for the cities of our **G**: 430
12: 7 Thus saith the Lord **G** of Israel, 430
12:16 David therefore besought **G** for the child; 430
14:11 let the king remember the Lord thy **G**, 430
14:13 such a thing against the people of **G**? 430
14:14 neither doth **G** respect *any* person: 430
14:16 son together out of the inheritance of **G**. 430
14:17 for as an angel of **G**, so *is* my lord the king 430
14:17 the Lord thy **G** will be with thee. 430
14:20 according to the wisdom of an angel of **G**, 430
15:24 bearing the ark of the covenant of **G**: 430
15:24 they set down the ark of **G**; 430
15:25 Carry back the ark of **G** *into* the city: 430
15:29 Abiathar carried the ark of **G** again *to* 430
15:32 *of the* mount, where he worshipped **G**, 430
16:16 **G save** the king, God save the king. 2421
16:16 God save the king, **G save** the king. 2421
16:23 if a man had inquired at the oracle of **G**: 430
18:28 and said, Blessed *be* the Lord thy **G**, 430
18:33 would **G** I had died for thee, O Absalom, 5414
19:13 do so to me, and more also, if thou be 430
19:27 but my lord the king *is* as an angel of **G**: 430
21:14 And after that **G** was intreated for the land. 430
22: 3 The **G** of my rock; in him will I trust: *he is* 430
22: 7 called upon the Lord, and cried to my **G**: 430
22:22 have not wickedly departed from my **G**. 430
22:30 troop: by my **G** have I leaped over a wall. 430
22:31 *As for* **G**, his way *is* perfect; the word of 410
22:32 For who *is* **G**, save the Lord? and who *is* 410
22:32 the Lord? and who *is* a rock, save our **G**? 410
22:33 **G** *is* my strength *and* power: and he 410
22:47 be the **G** of the rock of my salvation. 430
22:48 *It is* **G** that avengeth me, and that bringeth 410
23: 1 anointed of the **G** of Jacob, and the sweet 430
23: 3 The **G** of Israel said, the Rock of Israel 430
23: 3 men *must be* just, ruling in the fear of **G**. 430
23: 5 Although my house *be* not so with **G**; 410
24: 3 Now the Lord thy **G** add unto the people, 430
24:23 the king, The Lord thy **G** accept thee. 430
24:24 my **G** of that which doth cost me nothing. 430
1Ki 1:17 thou swarest by the Lord thy **G** unto thine 430
1:25 him, and say, **G save** king Adonijah. 2421
1:30 Even as I sware unto thee by the Lord **G** 430
1:34 and say, **G save** king Solomon. 2421
1:36 the Lord **G** of my lord the king say so 430
1:39 all the people said, **G save** king Solomon. 2421
1:47 to make the name of Solomon better than 430
1:48 the king, Blessed *be* the Lord **G** of Israel, 430
2: 3 keep the charge of the Lord thy **G**, 430
2:23 do so to me, and more also, 430
3: 5 and **G** said, Ask what I shall give thee. 430
3: 7 now, O Lord my **G**, thou hast made thy 430
3:11 **G** said unto him, Because thou hast asked 430
3:28 for they saw that the wisdom of **G** *was* in 430
4:29 **G** gave Solomon wisdom and 430
5: 3 for the wars which were about him 430
5: 4 now the Lord my **G** hath given me rest on 430
5: 5 a house unto the name of the Lord my **G**, 430
8:15 he said, Blessed *be* the Lord **G** of Israel, 430
8:17 for the name of the Lord **G** of Israel. 430
8:20 for the name of the Lord **G** of Israel. 430
8:23 he said, Lord **G** of Israel, *there is* no God 430
8:23 *there is* no **G** like thee, in heaven above, 430
8:25 Therefore now, Lord **G** of Israel, 430
8:26 O **G** of Israel, let thy word, I pray thee, 430
8:27 will **G** indeed dwell on the earth? behold, 430
8:28 to his supplication, O Lord my **G**, 430
8:57 The Lord our **G** be with us, as he was 430
8:59 be nigh unto the Lord our **G** day and 430
8:60 of the earth may know that the Lord *is* **G**, 430
8:61 therefore be perfect with the Lord our **G**, 430

1Ki 8:65 before the Lord our **G**, seven days and 430
9: 9 Because they forsook the Lord their **G**, 430
10: 9 Blessed be the Lord thy **G**, 430
10:24 his wisdom, which **G** had put in his heart. 430
11: 4 heart was not perfect with the Lord his **G**, 430
11: 9 his heart was turned from the Lord **G** of 430
11:23 **G** stirred him up *another* adversary, Rezon 430
11:31 saith the Lord, the **G** of Israel, Behold, 430
11:33 Chemosh the **g** of the Moabites, and 430
11:33 Milcom the **g** of the children of Ammon, 430
12:22 the word of **G** came unto Shemaiah the 430
12:22 of God came unto Shemaiah the man of **G**, 430
13: 1 there came a man of **G** out of Judah by 430
13: 5 Jeroboam heard the saying of the man of **G**, 430
13: 5 according to the sign which the man of **G** 430
13: 6 king answered and said unto the man of **G**, 430
13: 6 Intreat now the face of the Lord thy **G**, 430
13: 6 And the man of **G** besought the Lord, 430
13: 7 the king said unto the man of **G**, Come 430
13: 8 the man of **G** said unto the king, If thou 430
13:11 all the works that the man of **G** had 430
13:12 had seen what way the man of **G** went, 430
13:14 went after the man of **G**, and found him 430
13:14 *Art* thou the man of **G** that camest from 430
13:21 cried unto the man of **G** that came from 430
13:21 which the Lord thy **G** commanded thee, 430
13:26 It *is* the man of **G**, who was disobedient 430
13:29 took up the carcase of the man of **G**, 430
13:31 sepulchre wherein the man of **G** *is* buried; 430
14: 7 Thus saith the Lord **G** of Israel, 430
14:13 of Israel in the house of Jeroboam. 430
15: 3 heart was not perfect with the Lord his **G**, 430
15: 4 did his **G** give him a lamp in Jerusalem, 430
15:30 provoked the Lord **G** of Israel to anger. 430
16:13 in provoking the Lord **G** of Israel to 430
16:26 to provoke the Lord **G** of Israel to anger 430
16:33 Ahab did more to provoke the Lord **G** of 430
17: 1 *As* the Lord **G** of Israel liveth, 430
17:12 she said, *As* the Lord thy **G** liveth, I have 430
17:14 For thus saith the Lord **G** of Israel, 430
17:18 have I to do with thee, O thou man of **G**? 430
17:20 unto the Lord, and said, O Lord my **G**, 430
17:21 and said, O Lord my **G**, I pray thee, 430
17:24 *by* this I know that thou *art* a man of **G**, 430
18:10 *As* the Lord thy **G** liveth, there is no 430
18:21 if the Lord *be* **G**, follow him: but if Baal, 430
18:24 **G** that answereth by fire, let him be God. 430
18:24 God that answereth by fire, let him be **G**. 430
18:27 for he *is* a **g**; either he is talking, or he is 430
18:36 and said, Lord **G** of Abraham, Isaac, 430
18:36 let it be known *this* day that thou *art* **G** in 430
18:37 may know that thou *art* the Lord **G**, 430
18:39 they said, The Lord, he *is* the **G**; 430
18:39 he *is* the God; the Lord, he *is* the **G**. 430
19: 8 forty nights unto Horeb the mount of **G**. 430
19:10 I have been very jealous for the Lord **G** 430
19:14 I have been very jealous for the Lord **G** 430
20:28 there came a man of **G**, and spake unto 430
20:28 The Lord *is* **G** of the hills, but he *is* not 430
20:28 he *is* not **G** of the valleys, therefore will I 430
21:10 Thou didst blaspheme **G** and the king. 430
21:13 Naboth did blaspheme **G** and the king. 430
22:53 provoked to anger the Lord **G** of Israel, 430
2Ki 1: 2 inquire of Baal-zebub the **g** of Ekron 430
1: 3 *Is it* not because *there is* not a **G** in Israel, 430
1: 3 *that* ye go to inquire of Baal-zebub the **g** of 430
1: 6 *Is it* not because *there is* not a **G** in Israel, 430
1: 6 to inquire of Baal-zebub the **g** of Ekron? 430
1: 9 Thou man of **G**, the king hath said, 430
1:10 If I *be* a man of **G**, then let fire come down 430
1:11 answered and said unto him, O man of **G**, 430
1:12 and said unto them, If I *be* a man of **G**, 430
1:12 the fire of **G** came down from heaven, 430
1:13 O man of **G**, I pray thee, let my life, 430
1:16 to inquire of Baal-zebub the **g** of Ekron, 430
1:16 *is* no **G** in Israel to inquire of his word? 430
2:14 and said, Where *is* the Lord **G** of Elijah? 430
4: 7 she came and told the man of **G**. And he 430
4: 9 I perceive that this *is* a holy man of **G**, 430
4:16 she said, Nay, my lord, thou man of **G**, 430
4:21 and laid him on the bed of the man of **G**, 430
4:22 that I may run to the man of **G**, 430
4:25 came unto the man of **G** to mount Carmel. 430
4:25 pass, when the man of **G** saw her afar off, 430
4:27 when she came to the man of **G** to the hill, 430
4:27 the man of **G** said, Let her alone; for her 430
4:40 they cried out, and said, O thou man of **G**, 430
4:42 brought the man of **G** bread of the 430
5: 3 Would **G** my lord *were* with the prophet 305
5: 7 and said, *Am* I **G**, to kill and to make alive, 430
5: 8 when Elisha the man of **G** had heard that 430
5:11 call on the name of the Lord his **G**, 430
5:14 according to the saying of the man of **G**: 430
5:15 he returned to the man of **G**, he and all his 430
5:15 now I know that *there is* no **G** in all the 430
5:20 the servant of Elisha the man of **G**, said, 430
6: 6 the man of **G** said, Where fell it? And he 430
6: 9 the man of **G** sent unto the king of Israel, 430
6:10 to the place which the man of **G** told him 430
6:15 the servant of the man of **G** was risen 430
6:31 he said, **G** do so and more also to me, 430
7: 2 the king leaned answered the man of **G**, 430
7:17 and he died, as the man of **G** had said, 430
7:18 came to pass as the man of **G** had spoken 430
7:19 *that* lord answered the man of **G**, and said, 430

2Ki	
8: 2 and did after the saying of the man of **G**:	430
8: 4 with Gehazi the servant of the man of **G**,	430
8: 7 saying, The man of **G** is come hither.	430
8: 8 go, meet the man of **G**, and inquire of	430
8:11 *he* was ashamed: and the man of **G** wept.	430
9: 6 unto him, Thus saith the Lord **G** of Israel,	430
10:31 of the Lord **G** of Israel with all his heart:	430
11:12 their hands, and said, **G** save the king.	2421
13:19 the man of **G** was wroth with him,	430
14:25 according to the word of the Lord **G** of	430
16: 2 *was* right in the sight of the Lord his **G**,	430
17: 7 had sinned against the Lord their **G**,	430
17: 9 *were* not right against the Lord their **G**.	430
17:14 that did not believe in the Lord their **G**.	430
17:16 the commandments of the Lord their **G**,	430
17:19 the commandments of the Lord their **G**,	430
17:26 know not the manner of the **G** of the land:	430
17:26 they know not the manner of the **G** of	430
17:27 let him teach them the manner of the **G** of	430
17:39 the Lord your **G** ye shall fear;	430
18: 5 He trusted in the Lord **G** of Israel;	430
18:12 obeyed not the voice of the Lord their **G**,	430
18:22 say unto me, We trust in the Lord our **G**:	430
19: 4 It may be the Lord thy **G** will hear all	430
19: 4 master hath sent to reproach the living **G**;	430
19: 4 words which the Lord thy **G** hath heard:	430
19:10 Let not thy **G** in whom thou trustest	430
19:15 said, O Lord **G** of Israel, which dwellest	430
19:15 thou *art* the **G**, *even* thou alone, of all	430
19:16 hath sent him to reproach the living **G**.	430
19:19 O Lord our **G**, I beseech thee,	430
19:19 earth may know that thou *art* the Lord **G**,	430
19:20 Thus saith the Lord **G** of Israel,	430
19:37 worshipping *in* the house of Nisroch his **g**,	430
20: 5 saith the Lord, the **G** of David thy father,	430
21:12 Therefore thus saith the Lord **G** of Israel,	430
21:22 And he forsook the Lord **G** of his fathers,	430
22:15 Thus saith the Lord **G** of Israel,	430
22:18 to him, Thus saith the Lord **G** of Israel,	430
23:16 the Lord which the man of **G** proclaimed,	430
23:17 *It is* the sepulchre of the man of **G**,	430
23:21 Keep the passover unto the Lord your **G**,	430
1Ch	
4:10 And Jabez called on the **G** of Israel, saying,	430
4:10 **G** granted *him* that which he requested.	430
5:20 for they cried to **G** in the battle, and he	430
5:22 many slain, because the war *was* of **G**.	430
5:25 they transgressed against the **G** of their	430
5:25 the land, whom **G** destroyed before them.	430
5:26 the **G** of Israel stirred up the spirit of Pul	430
6:48 service of the tabernacle of the house of **G**.	430
6:49 to all that Moses the servant of **G**	430
9:11 son of Ahitub, the ruler of the house of **G**;	430
9:13 the work of the service of the house of **G**.	430
9:26 and treasuries of the house of **G**.	430
9:27 they lodged round about the house of **G**,	430
11: 2 the Lord thy **G** said unto thee, Thou shalt	430
11:19 My **G** forbid it me, that *I* should do this	430
12:17 the **G** of our fathers look *thereon*, and	430
12:18 *be* to thine helpers; for thy **G** helpeth thee.	430
12:22 until it was a great host, like the host of **G**.	430
13: 2 and *that it be* of the Lord our **G**,	430
13: 3 let us bring again the ark of our **G** to us:	430
13: 5 to bring the ark of **G** from Kirjath-jearim.	430
13: 6 to bring up thence the ark of **G** the Lord,	430
13: 7 they carried the ark of **G** in a new cart out	430
13: 8 all Israel played before **G** with all *their*	430
13:10 to the ark: and there he died before **G**.	430
13:12 David was afraid of **G** that day, saying,	430
13:12 shall I bring the ark of **G** *home* to me?	430
13:14 the ark of **G** remained with the family of	430
14:10 David inquired of **G**, saying, Shall I go up	430
14:11 **G** hath broken in upon mine enemies by	430
14:14 Therefore David inquired again of **G**;	430
14:14 **G** said unto him, Go not up after them;	430
14:15 for **G** is gone forth before thee to smite	430
14:16 David therefore did as **G** commanded him:	430
15: 1 prepared a place for the ark of **G**,	430
15: 2 None ought to carry the ark of **G** but	430
15: 2 the Lord chosen to carry the ark of **G**,	430
15:12 **G** of Israel unto *the place that* I have	430
15:13 the Lord our **G** made a breach upon us,	430
15:14 bring up the ark of the Lord **G** of Israel.	430
15:15 children of the Levites bare the ark of **G**	430
15:24 with the trumpets before the ark of **G**:	430
15:26 **G** helped the Levites that bare the ark	430
16: 1 So they brought the ark of **G**, and set it in	430
16: 1 and peace offerings before **G**.	430
16: 4 to thank and praise the Lord **G** of Israel:	430
16: 6 before the ark of the covenant of **G**.	430
16:14 He *is* the Lord our **G**; his judgments *are*	430
16:35 of our salvation, and gather us together,	430
16:36 Blessed *be* the Lord **G** of Israel for ever	430
16:42 sound, and with musical instruments of **G**.	430
17: 2 all that *is* in thine heart; for **G** is with thee.	430
17: 3 that the word of **G** came to Nathan, saying,	430
17:16 *am* I, O Lord **G**, and what *is* mine house,	430
17:17 this was a small thing in thine eyes, O **G**;	430
17:17 estate of a high degree, O Lord **G**.	430
17:20 neither *is there any* **G** besides thee,	430
17:21 whom **G** went to redeem *to be* his own	430
17:22 and thou, Lord, becamest their **G**.	430
17:24 The Lord of hosts *is* the **G** of Israel,	430
17:24 *is* the God of Israel, *even* a **G** to Israel:	430
17:25 thou, O my **G**, hast told thy servant that	430
17:26 *art* **G**, and hast promised this goodness	430

1Ch	
19:13 for our people, and for the cities of our **G**:	430
21: 7 God was displeased with this thing; therefore	430
21: 8 David said unto **G**, I have sinned greatly,	430
21:15 sent an angel unto Jerusalem to destroy	430
21:17 David said unto **G**, *Is it* not I that	430
21:17 O Lord my **G**, be on me, and on my	430
21:30 could not go before it to inquire of **G**:	430
22: 1 This *is* the house of the Lord **G**,	430
22: 2 wrought stones to build the house of **G**.	430
22: 6 to build a house for the Lord **G** of Israel.	430
22: 7 a house unto the name of the Lord my **G**:	430
22:11 and build the house of the Lord thy **G**.	430
22:12 mayest keep the law of the Lord thy **G**.	430
22:18 *Is* not the Lord your **G** with you?	430
22:19 and your soul to seek the Lord your **G**;	430
22:19 and build ye the sanctuary of the Lord **G**,	430
22:19 of the Lord, and the holy vessels of **G**,	430
23:14 Now *concerning* Moses the man of **G**	430
23:25 The Lord **G** of Israel hath given rest unto	430
23:28 the work of the service of the house of **G**;	430
24: 5 governors *of the house of* **G**, were of	430
24:19 as the Lord **G** of Israel had commanded	430
25: 5 Heman the king's seer in the words of **G**,	430
25: 5 **G** gave to Heman fourteen sons and	430
25: 6 harps, for the service of the house of **G**,	430
26: 5 Peulthai the eighth: for **G** blessed him.	430
26:20 *was* over the treasures of the house of **G**,	430
26:32 for every matter pertaining to **G**,	430
28: 2 for the footstool of our **G**, and had made	430
28: 3 **G** said unto me, Thou shalt not build a	430
28: 4 Howbeit the Lord **G** of Israel chose me	430
28: 8 in the audience of our **G**, keep and seek for	430
28: 8 the commandments of the Lord your **G**:	430
28: 9 know thou the **G** of thy father, and serve	430
28:12 of the treasuries of the house of **G**,	430
28:20 for the Lord **G**, *even* my **G**, *will be*	430
28:20 Lord God, *even* my **G**, *will be* with thee;	430
28:21 *thee* for all the service of the house of **G**:	430
29: 1 whom alone **G** hath chosen, *is yet* young	430
29: 1 palace *is* not for man, but for the Lord **G**.	430
29: 2 the gold for *things to be made of* gold,	430
29: 3 set my affection to the house of my **G**,	430
29: 3 which I have given to the house of my **G**,	430
29: 7 gave for the service of the house of **G** *of*	430
29:10 Lord **G** of Israel our father, for ever and	430
29:13 **G**, we thank thee, and praise thy glorious	430
29:16 O Lord our **G**, all this store that we have	430
29:17 know also, my **G**, that thou triest the heart,	430
29:18 O Lord **G** of Abraham, Isaac,	430
29:20 Now bless the Lord your **G**.	430
29:20 all the congregation blessed the Lord **G**	430
2Ch	
1: 1 the Lord his **G** *was* with him,	430
1: 3 the tabernacle of the congregation of **G**,	430
1: 4 the ark that David brought up from	430
1: 7 In that night did **G** appear unto Solomon,	430
1: 8 Solomon said unto **G**, Thou hast shewed	430
1: 9 Now, O Lord **G**, let thy promise unto	430
1:11 **G** said to Solomon, Because this was in	430
2: 4 a house to the name of the Lord my **G**,	430
2: 4 on the solemn feasts of the Lord our **G**.	430
2: 5 is great: for great *is* our **G** above all gods.	430
2:12 Blessed *be* the Lord **G** of Israel,	430
3: 3 for the building of the house of **G**.	430
4:11 make for king Solomon for the house of **G**;	430
4:19 all the vessels that *were for* the house of **G**,	430
5: 1 he among the treasures of the house of **G**.	430
5:14 of the Lord had filled the house of **G**.	430
6: 4 he said, Blessed *be* the Lord **G** of Israel,	430
6: 7 for the name of the Lord **G** of Israel.	430
6:10 for the name of the Lord **G** of Israel.	430
6:14 said, O Lord **G** of Israel, *there is* no God	430
6:14 *there is* no **G** like thee in the heaven, nor	430
6:16 Now therefore, O Lord **G** of Israel,	430
6:17 Now then, O Lord **G** of Israel, let thy	430
6:18 will **G** in very deed dwell with men on	430
6:19 to his supplication, O Lord my **G**,	430
6:40 Now, my **G**, let, I beseech thee, thine eyes	430
6:41 Now therefore arise, O Lord **G**, into thy	430
6:41 let thy priests, O Lord **G**, be clothed *with*	430
6:42 O Lord **G**, turn not away the face of thine	430
7: 5 all the people dedicated the house of **G**.	430
7:22 Because they forsook the Lord **G** of their	430
8:14 so had David the man of **G** commanded.	430
9: 8 Blessed be the Lord thy **G**,	430
9: 8 his throne, to be king for the Lord thy **G**:	430
9: 8 because thy **G** loved Israel, to establish	430
9:23 his wisdom, that **G** had put in his heart.	430
10:15 for the cause was of **G**, that the Lord	430
11: 2 the **G** came to Shemaiah the man of **G**,	430
11:16 the Lord **G** of Israel came *to* Jerusalem,	430
11:16 to sacrifice unto the Lord **G** of their	430
13: 5 Ought you not to know that the Lord **G** of	430
13:10 the Lord *is* our **G**, and we have not	430
13:11 for we keep the charge of the Lord our **G**;	430
13:12 **G** himself *is* with us for *our* captain,	430
13:12 fight ye not against the Lord **G** of your	430
13:15 that **G** smote Jeroboam and all Israel before	430
13:16 and **G** delivered them into their hand.	430
13:18 they relied upon the Lord **G** of their	430
14: 2 and right in the eyes of the Lord his **G**:	430
14: 4 commanded Judah to seek the Lord **G** of	430
14: 7 because we have sought the Lord **G** of	430
14:11 Asa cried unto the Lord his **G**, and said,	430
14:11 help us, O Lord our **G**; for we rest on	430
14:11 O Lord, thou *art* our **G**; let not man	430

2Ch	
15: 1 the spirit of **G** came upon Azariah the son	430
15: 3 season Israel *hath been* without the true **G**,	430
15: 4 trouble did turn unto the Lord **G** of Israel,	430
15: 6 for **G** did vex them with all adversity.	430
15: 9 when they saw that the Lord his **G** *was*	430
15:12 Lord **G** of their fathers with all their heart	430
15:13 Lord **G** of Israel should be put to death,	430
15:18 he brought *into* the house of **G** the things	430
16: 7 not relied on the Lord thy **G**, therefore	430
17: 4 sought to the Lord **G** of his father,	430
18: 5 for **G** will deliver *it* into the king's hand.	430
18:13 even what my **G** saith, that will I speak.	430
18:31 and **G** moved them *to depart* from him.	430
19: 3 and hast prepared thine heart to seek **G**.	430
19: 4 brought them back unto the Lord **G** of	430
19: 7 *there* is no iniquity with the Lord our **G**,	430
20: 6 said, O Lord **G** of our fathers, *art* not thou	430
20: 6 of our fathers, *art* not thou **G** in heaven?	430
20: 7 *Art* not thou our **G**, who didst drive out	430
20:12 O our **G**, wilt thou not judge them? for we	430
20:19 stood up to praise the Lord **G** of Israel	430
20:20 Believe in the Lord your **G**, so shall you	430
20:29 the fear of **G** was on all the kingdoms of	430
20:30 for his **G** gave him rest round about.	430
20:33 their hearts unto the **G** of their fathers.	430
21:10 he had forsaken the Lord **G** of his fathers.	430
21:12 Thus saith the Lord **G** of David thy	430
22: 7 the destruction of Ahaziah was of **G** by	430
22:12 he was with them hid in the house of **G**	430
23: 3 covenant with the king in the house of **G**.	430
23: 9 David's, which *were in* the house of **G**.	430
23:11 anointed him, and said, **G** save the king.	2421
24: 5 repair the house of your **G** from year to	430
24: 7 had broken up the house of **G**;	430
24: 9 of **G** laid upon Israel in the wilderness.	430
24:13 they set the house of **G** in his state,	430
24:16 both towards **G**, and *towards* his house.	430
24:18 they left the house of the Lord **G** of their	430
24:20 the spirit of **G** came upon Zechariah the	430
24:20 and said unto them, Thus saith **G**,	430
24:24 they had forsaken the Lord **G** of their	430
24:27 and the repairing of the house of **G**,	430
25: 7 there came a man of **G** to him, saying,	430
25: 8 **G** shall make thee fall before the enemy:	430
25: 8 **G** hath power to help, and to cast down.	430
25: 9 Amaziah said to the man of **G**, But what	430
25: 9 the man of **G** answered, The Lord is able	430
25:16 I know that **G** hath determined to destroy	430
25:20 it *came* of **G**, that *he* might deliver them	430
25:24 found in the house of **G** with Obed-edom,	430
26: 5 he sought **G** in the days of Zechariah,	430
26: 5 had understanding in the visions of **G**:	430
26: 5 sought the Lord, **G** made him to prosper.	430
26: 7 **G** helped him against the Philistines,	430
26:16 he transgressed against the Lord his **G**,	430
26:18 *it be* for thine honour from the Lord his **G**.	430
27: 6 prepared his ways before the Lord his **G**.	430
28: 5 Wherefore the Lord his **G** delivered him	430
28: 6 they had forsaken the Lord **G** of their	430
28: 9 the Lord **G** of your fathers was wroth	430
28:10 with you, sins against the Lord your **G**?	430
28:24 together the vessels of the house of **G**,	430
28:24 cut in pieces the vessels of the house of **G**,	430
28:25 provoked to anger the Lord **G** of his	430
29: 5 sanctify the house of the Lord **G** of your	430
29: 6 was evil in the eyes of the Lord our **G**,	430
29: 7 in the holy *place* unto the **G** of Israel.	430
29:10 a covenant with the Lord **G** of Israel,	430
29:36 people, that **G** had prepared the people:	430
30: 1 to keep the passover unto the Lord **G** of	430
30: 5 unto the Lord **G** of Israel at Jerusalem:	430
30: 6 turn again unto the Lord **G** of Abraham,	430
30: 7 which trespassed against the Lord **G** of	430
30: 8 serve the Lord your **G**, that the fierceness	430
30: 9 for the Lord your **G** *is* gracious and	430
30:12 Also in Judah the hand of **G** was to give	430
30:16 to the law of Moses the man of **G**:	430
30:19 *That* prepareth his heart to seek **G**,	430
30:19 to seek God, the Lord **G** of his fathers,	430
30:22 making confession to the Lord **G** of their	430
31: 6 were consecrated unto the Lord their **G**,	430
31:13 and Azariah the ruler of the house of **G**.	430
31:14 *was* over the freewill offerings of **G**,	430
31:20 and right and truth before the Lord his **G**.	430
31:21 he began in the service of the house of **G**,	430
31:21 and in the commandments, to seek his **G**,	430
32: 8 with us *is* the Lord our **G** to help us,	430
32:11 The Lord our **G** shall deliver us out of	430
32:14 your **G** should be able to deliver you out	430
32:15 for no **g** of any nation or kingdom was able	433
32:15 how much less shall your **G** deliver you	430
32:16 spake yet *more* against the Lord **G**,	430
32:17 He wrote also letters to rail on the Lord **G**	430
32:17 shall not the **G** of Hezekiah deliver his	430
32:19 they spake against the **G** of Jerusalem,	430
32:21 when he was come *into* the house of his **g**,	430
32:29 for **G** had given him substance very much.	430
32:31 **G** left him, to try him, that *he* might know	430
33: 7 which he had made, in the house of **G**,	430
33: 7 of which **G** had said to David and	430
33:12 he besought the Lord his **G**,	430
33:12 humbled himself greatly before the **G** of	430
33:13 Manasseh knew that the Lord he *was* **G**.	430
33:16 commanded Judah to serve the Lord **G** of	430
33:17 *yet* unto the Lord their **G** only.	430

G

2Ch 33:18	his prayer unto his **G**, and the words of	430
33:18	him in the name of the Lord **G** of Israel,	430
33:19	**G** was intreated of him, and all his sin,	NIH
34: 3	he began to seek after the **G** of David his	430
34: 8	to repair the house of the Lord his **G**.	430
34: 9	that was brought *into* the house of **G**,	430
34:23	Thus saith the Lord **G** of Israel,	430
34:26	Thus saith the Lord **G** of Israel	430
34:27	and thou didst humble thyself before **G**,	430
34:32	did according to the covenant of **G**,	430
34:32	covenant of God, the **G** of their fathers.	430
34:33	to serve, *even* to serve the Lord their **G**.	430
34:33	following the Lord, the **G** of their fathers.	430
35: 3	serve now the Lord your **G**, and his	430
35: 8	and Jehiel, rulers of the house of **G**,	430
35:21	for **G** commanded me to make haste:	430
35:21	forbear thee from meddling with **G**, who	430
35:22	the words of Necho from the mouth of **G**.	430
36: 5	*was* evil in the sight of the Lord his **G**.	430
36:12	*was* evil in the sight of the Lord his **G**.	430
36:13	who had made him swear by **G**:	430
36:13	from turning unto the Lord **G** of Israel.	430
36:15	the Lord **G** of their fathers sent to them	430
36:16	they mocked the messengers of **G**,	430
36:18	all the vessels of the house of **G**, great and	430
36:19	they burnt the house of **G**, and brake	430
36:23	hath the Lord **G** of heaven given me;	430
36:23	The Lord his **G** *be* with him, and let him	430
Ezr 1: 2	The Lord **G** of heaven hath given me all	430
1: 3	his **G** be with him, and let him go up to	430
1: 3	build the house of the Lord **G** of Israel,	430
1: 3	of the Lord God of Israel, (he *is* the **G**,)	430
1: 4	for the house of **G** that *is* in Jerusalem.	430
1: 5	with all *them* whose spirit **G** had raised,	430
2:68	offered freely for the house of **G** to set it	430
3: 2	and builded the altar of the **G** of Israel,	430
3: 2	written in the law of Moses the man of **G**.	430
3: 8	coming unto the house of **G** at Jerusalem,	430
3: 9	forward the workmen in the house of **G**:	430
4: 1	the temple unto the Lord **G** of Israel;	430
4: 2	for we seek your **G**, as ye *do;* and we do	430
4: 3	do with us to build a house unto our **G**;	430
4: 3	will build unto the Lord **G** of Israel,	430
4:24	ceased the work of the house of the **G**	426
5: 1	Jerusalem in the name of the **G** of Israel,	426
5: 2	began to build the house of **G** which *is* at	426
5: 2	with them *were* the prophets of **G** helping	426
5: 5	the eye of their **G** was upon the elders of	426
5: 8	the house of the great **G**, which *is* builded	426
5:11	We are the servants of the **G** of heaven	426
5:12	that our fathers had provoked the **G** of	426
5:13	made a decree to build this house of **G**.	426
5:14	also of gold and silver of the house of **G**,	426
5:15	let the house of **G** be builded in his place.	426
5:16	laid the foundation of the house of **G**	426
5:17	king to build this house of **G** at Jerusalem,	426
6: 3	*concerning* the house of **G** at Jerusalem,	426
6: 5	and silver vessels of the house of **G**,	426
6: 5	place, and place *them* in the house of **G**.	426
6: 7	Let the work of this house of **G** alone;	426
6: 7	elders of the Jews build this house of **G**	426
6: 8	Jews for the building of this house of **G**:	426
6: 9	for the burnt offerings of the **G** of heaven,	426
6:10	of sweet savours unto the **G** of heaven,	426
6:12	the **G** that hath caused his name to dwell	426
6:12	to destroy this house of **G** which *is* at	426
6:14	to the commandment of the **G** of Israel,	426
6:16	kept the dedication of this house of **G** with	426
6:17	offered at the dedication of this house of **G**	426
6:18	for the service of **G**, which *is* at Jerusalem;	426
6:21	to seek the **G** of Israel, did eat,	430
6:22	their hands in the work of the house of **G**,	430
6:22	work of the house of God, the **G** of Israel.	430
7: 6	which the Lord **G** of Israel had given:	430
7: 6	according to the hand of the Lord his **G**	430
7: 9	according to the good hand of his **G** upon	426
7:12	a scribe of the law of the **G** of heaven,	426
7:14	according to the law of thy **G** which *is* in	426
7:15	have freely offered unto the **G** of Israel,	426
7:16	offering willingly for the house of their **G**	426
7:17	the house of your **G** which *is* in Jerusalem.	426
7:18	and gold, that do after the will of your **G**.	426
7:19	thee for the service of the house of thy **G**,	426
7:19	deliver thou before the **G** of Jerusalem.	426
7:20	*shall* be needful for the house of thy **G**,	426
7:21	the scribe of the law of the **G** of heaven,	426
7:23	Whatsoever *is* commanded by the **G** of	426
7:23	it be diligently done for the house of the **G**	426
7:24	or ministers of this house of **G**,	426
7:25	Ezra, after the wisdom of thy **G**, that *is*	426
7:25	river, all such as know the laws of thy **G**;	426
7:26	whosoever will not do the law of thy **G**,	426
7:27	Blessed *be* the Lord **G** of our fathers,	430
7:28	the hand of the Lord my **G** *was* upon me,	430
8:17	unto us ministers for the house of our **G**.	430
8:18	by the good hand of our **G** upon us they	430
8:21	*we* might afflict ourselves before our **G**,	430
8:22	hand of our **G** *is* upon all them for good	430
8:23	So we fasted and besought our **G** for this:	430
8:25	*even* the offering of the house of our **G**,	430
8:28	offering unto the Lord **G** of your fathers.	430
8:30	to Jerusalem unto the house of our **G**.	430
8:31	the hand of our **G** was upon us,	430
8:33	the vessels weighed in the house of our **G**	430
8:35	offered burnt offerings unto the **G** of Israel,	430

Ezr 8:36	furthered the people, and the house of **G**.	430
9: 4	trembled at the words of the **G** of Israel,	430
9: 5	spread out my hands unto the Lord my **G**,	430
9: 6	O my **G**, I am ashamed and blush to lift	430
9: 6	and blush to lift up my face to thee, my **G**:	430
9: 8	hath been *shewed* from the Lord our **G**,	430
9: 8	our **G** may lighten our eyes, and give us	430
9: 9	yet our **G** hath not forsaken us in our	430
9: 9	to set up the house of our **G**, and to repair	430
9:10	now, O our **G**, what shall we say after this?	430
9:13	that thou our **G** hast punished us less	430
9:15	O Lord **G** of Israel, thou *art* righteous:	430
10: 1	himself down before the house of **G**,	430
10: 2	We have trespassed against our **G**,	430
10: 3	let us make a covenant with our **G** to put	430
10: 3	tremble at the commandment of our **G**;	430
10: 6	Ezra rose up from before the house of **G**,	430
10: 9	people sat in the street of the house of **G**,	430
10:11	make confession unto the Lord **G** of your	430
10:14	the fierce wrath of our **G** for this matter	430
Ne 1: 4	and prayed before the **G** of heaven,	430
1: 5	O Lord **G** of heaven, the great and	430
1: 5	the great and terrible **G**, that keepeth	410
2: 4	So I prayed to the **G** of heaven.	430
2: 8	according to the good hand of my **G** upon	430
2:12	neither told I *any* man what my **G** had put	430
2:18	I told them of the hand of my **G** which	430
2:20	said unto them, The **G** of heaven, he will	430
4: 4	Hear, O our **G**; for we are despised:	430
4: 9	we made our prayer unto our **G**,	430
4:15	had brought their counsel to nought,	430
4:20	ye thither unto us: our **G** shall fight for us.	430
5: 9	ought we not to walk in the fear of our **G**	430
5:13	So **G** shake out every man from his house,	430
5:15	but so did not I, because of the fear of **G**.	430
5:19	Think upon me, my **G**, for good,	430
6: 9	therefore, O **G**, strengthen my hands.	NIH
6:10	Let us meet together in the house of **G**,	430
6:12	lo, I perceived that **G** had not sent him;	430
6:14	**G**, think thou upon Tobiah and Sanballat	430
6:16	that this work was wrought of our **G**.	430
7: 2	a faithful man, and feared **G** above many.	430
7: 5	my **G** put into mine heart to gather	430
8: 6	Ezra blessed the Lord, the great **G**.	430
8: 8	So they read in the book in the law of **G**	430
8: 9	*This* day *is* holy unto the Lord your **G**;	430
8:16	in the courts of the house of **G**, and in	430
8:18	he read in the book of the law of **G**.	430
9: 3	Lord their **G** *one* fourth *part* of the day;	430
9: 3	and worshipped the Lord their **G**.	430
9: 4	with a loud voice unto the Lord their **G**.	430
9: 5	and bless the Lord your **G** for ever and	430
9: 7	Thou *art* the Lord the **G**, who didst	430
9:17	thou *art* a **G** ready to pardon, gracious and	433
9:18	This *is* thy **G** that brought thee up out of	430
9:31	for thou *art* a gracious and merciful **G**.	410
9:32	**G**, the great, the mighty, and the terrible	430
9:32	the great, the mighty, and the terrible **G**,	410
10:28	the people of the lands unto the law of **G**,	430
10:29	was given by Moses the servant of **G**,	430
10:32	for the service of the house of our **G**;	430
10:33	and *for* all the work of the house of our **G**.	430
10:34	to bring *it* into the house of our **G**,	430
10:34	to burn upon the altar of the Lord our **G**,	430
10:36	our flocks, to bring to the house of our **G**,	430
10:36	priests that minister in the house of our **G**:	430
10:37	to the chambers of the house of our **G**;	430
10:38	tithe of the tithes unto the house of our **G**,	430
10:39	we will not forsake the house of our **G**.	430
11:11	of Ahitub, *was* the ruler of the house of **G**.	430
11:16	of the outward business of the house of **G**.	430
11:22	*were* over the business of the house of **G**,	430
11:24	the commandment of David the man of **G**,	430
12:36	instruments of David the man of **G**,	430
12:40	*them that gave* thanks in the house of **G**,	430
12:43	**G** had made them rejoice *with* great joy:	430
12:45	and the porters kept the ward of their **G**,	430
12:46	songs of praise and thanksgiving unto **G**.	430
13: 1	come into the congregation of **G** for ever;	430
13: 2	howbeit our **G** turned the curse into a	430
13: 4	of the chamber of the house of our **G**,	430
13: 7	a chamber in the courts of the house of **G**.	430
13: 9	I again the vessels of the house of **G**,	430
13:11	and said, Why is the house of **G** forsaken?	430
13:14	Remember me, O my **G**, concerning this,	430
13:14	that I have done for the house of my **G**,	430
13:18	*did not* our **G** bring all this evil upon us,	430
13:22	Remember me, O my **G**, *concerning* this	430
13:25	off their hair, and made them swear by **G**,	430
13:26	who was beloved of his **G**, and God made	430
13:26	and **G** made him king over all Israel:	430
13:27	to transgress against our **G** in marrying	430
13:29	O my **G**, because they have defiled	430
13:31	Remember me, O my **G**, for good.	430
Job 1: 1	and one that feared **G**, and eschewed evil.	430
1: 5	have sinned, and cursed **G** in their hearts.	430
1: 6	Now there was a day when the sons of **G**	430
1: 8	one that feareth **G**, and escheweth evil?	430
1: 9	and said, Doth Job fear **G** for nought?	430
1:16	The fire of **G** is fallen from heaven,	430
1:22	Job sinned not, nor charged **G** foolishly.	430
2: 1	Again there was a day when the sons of **G**	430
2: 3	one that feareth **G**, and escheweth evil?	430
2: 9	retain thine integrity? curse **G**, and die.	430
2:10	shall we receive good at the hand of **G**,	430

Job 3: 4	let not **G** regard it from above, neither let	433
3:23	way is hid, and whom **G** hath hedged in?	433
4: 9	By the blast of **G** they perish, and by the	433
4:17	Shall mortal man be more just than **G**?	433
5: 8	I would seek unto **G**, and unto God would	433
5: 8	and unto **G** would I commit my cause:	430
5:17	happy *is* the man whom **G** correcteth:	433
6: 4	the terrors of **G** do set *themselves* in array	433
6: 8	**G** would grant *me* the thing that I long	433
6: 9	*that* it would please **G** to destroy me:	433
8: 3	Doth **G** pervert judgment? or doth	410
8: 5	If thou wouldest seek unto **G** betimes,	410
8:13	So *are* the paths of all that forget **G**;	410
8:20	**G** will not cast away a perfect *man*,	410
9: 2	truth: but how should man be just with **G**?	410
9:13	*If* **G** will not withdraw his anger, the proud	433
10: 2	I will say unto **G**, Do not condemn me;	433
11: 5	O that **G** would speak, and open his lips	433
11: 6	that **G** exacteth of thee *less* than thine	433
11: 7	Canst thou *by* searching find out **G**?	433
12: 4	calleth upon **G**, and he answereth him:	433
12: 6	and they that provoke **G** are secure;	410
12: 6	into whose hand **G** bringeth *abundantly*.	433
13: 3	Almighty, and I desire to reason with **G**.	410
13: 7	Will you speak wickedly for **G**?	410
13: 8	accept his person? will ye contend for **G**?	410
15: 4	off fear, and restrainest prayer before **G**.	410
15: 8	Hast thou heard the secret of **G**?	433
15:11	*Are* the consolations of **G** small with thee?	410
15:13	That thou turnest thy spirit against **G**,	410
15:25	For he stretcheth out his hand against **G**,	410
16:11	**G** hath delivered me to the ungodly,	410
16:20	*but* mine eye poureth out *tears* unto **G**.	433
16:21	O that *one* might plead for a man with **G**,	433
18:21	is the place *of him that* knoweth not **G**.	410
19: 6	Know now that **G** hath overthrown me,	433
19:21	for the hand of **G** hath touched me.	433
19:22	Why do ye persecute me as **G**, and are not	410
19:26	this *body*, yet in my flesh shall I see **G**:	433
20:15	again: **G** shall cast them out of his belly.	410
20:23	**G** shall cast the fury of his wrath upon	NIH
20:29	*is* the portion of a wicked man from **G**,	430
20:29	the heritage appointed unto him by **G**.	410
21: 9	fear, neither *is* the rod of **G** upon them.	433
21:14	they say unto **G**, Depart from us;	410
21:17	**G** distributeth sorrows in his anger.	NIH
21:19	**G** layeth up his iniquity for his children:	433
21:22	Shall *any* teach **G** knowledge? seeing he	410
22: 2	Can a man be profitable unto **G**, as he	410
22:12	*Is* not **G** *in* the height of heaven?	433
22:13	thou sayest, How doth **G** know? can he	410
22:17	Which said unto **G**, Depart from us:	410
22:26	and shalt lift up thy face unto **G**.	433
23:16	For **G** maketh my heart soft,	410
24:12	crieth out: yet **G** layeth not folly *to them*.	433
25: 4	How then can man be justified with **G**?	410
27: 2	*As* **G** liveth, *who* hath taken away my	410
27: 3	in me, and the spirit of **G** *is* in my nostrils;	433
27: 5	**G** forbid that I should justify you: till I die	2486
27: 8	gained, when **G** taketh away his soul?	410
27: 9	Will **G** hear his cry when trouble cometh	410
27:10	the Almighty? will he always call upon **G**?	433
27:11	I will teach you by the hand of **G**: *that*	410
27:13	*is* the portion of a wicked man with **G**,	410
27:22	For **G** shall cast upon him, and not spare:	NIH
28:23	**G** understandeth the way thereof,	430
29: 2	as *in* the days *when* **G** preserved me;	433
29: 4	when the secret of **G** *was* upon my	433
31: 2	For what portion of **G** *is there* from above?	433
31: 6	that **G** may know mine integrity.	433
31:14	What then shall I do when **G** riseth up?	410
31:23	For destruction from **G** *was* a terror to me,	410
31:28	I should have denied the **G** *that is* above.	410
32: 2	because he justified himself rather than **G**.	430
32:13	wisdom: **G** thrusteth him down, not man.	410
33: 4	The Spirit of **G** hath made me,	410
33:12	answer thee, that **G** is greater than man.	433
33:14	For **G** speaketh once, yea twice, *yet man*	410
33:26	He shall pray unto **G**, and he will be	433
33:29	all these *things* worketh **G** oftentimes with	410
34: 5	and **G** hath taken away my judgment.	410
34: 9	that he should delight himself with **G**.	430
34:10	far be it from **G**, *that he should do*	410
34:12	Yea, surely **G** will not do wickedly,	410
34:23	*he* should enter into judgment with **G**.	410
34:31	Surely it is *meet to be* said unto **G**, I have	410
34:37	and multiplieth his words against **G**.	410
35:10	none saith, Where *is* **G** my Maker,	433
35:13	Surely **G** will not hear vanity, neither will	410
36: 5	**G** is mighty, and despiseth not *any: he is*	410
36:22	Behold, **G** exalteth by his power:	410
36:26	Behold, **G** is great, and we know *him* not,	410
37: 5	**G** thundereth marvellously with his voice;	410
37:10	By the breath of **G** frost is given:	410
37:14	and consider the wondrous works of **G**.	410
37:15	Dost thou know when **G** disposed them,	433
37:22	out of the north: with **G** *is* terrible majesty.	433
38: 7	and all the sons of **G** shouted for joy?	430
38:41	when his young ones cry unto **G**,	410
39:17	Because **G** hath deprived her of wisdom,	433
40: 2	instruct *him*? he that reproveth **G**,	433
40: 9	Hast thou an arm like **G**? or, canst thou	410
40:19	He *is* the chief of the ways of **G**: he that	410
Ps 3: 2	of my soul, *There is* no help for him in **G**.	430
3: 7	Arise, O Lord; save me, O my **G**:	430

Ps		
4: 1 me when I call, O **G** of my righteousness:	430	
5: 2 the voice of my cry, my King, and my **G**:	430	
5: 4 For **G** art not a **G** that hath pleasure in	410	
5:10 Destroy thou them, O **G**; let them fall by	430	
7: 1 O Lord my **G**, in thee do I put my trust:	430	
7: 3 O Lord my **G**, if I have done this; if there	430	
7: 9 for the righteous **G** trieth the hearts and	430	
7:10 My defence is of **G**, which saveth	430	
7:11 **G** judgeth the righteous, and God is angry	430	
7:11 and **G** is angry with the wicked every day.	430	
9:17 into hell, and all the nations that forget **G**.	430	
10: 4 will not seek after **G**: God is not in all his	NIH	
10: 4 will not seek after God: **G** is not in all his	410	
10:11 He hath said in his heart, **G** hath forgotten:	410	
10:12 Arise, O Lord; O **G**, lift up thine hand:	410	
10:13 Wherefore doth the wicked contemn **G**?	430	
13: 3 Consider and hear me, O Lord my **G**:	430	
14: 1 fool hath said in his heart, There is no **G**.	430	
14: 2 were any that did understand, and seek **G**.	430	
14: 5 for **G** is in the generation of the righteous.	430	
16: 1 Preserve me, O **G**: for in thee do I put my	410	
16: 4 g: their drink offerings of blood will I not	NIH	
17: 6 upon thee, for thou wilt hear me, O **G**:	410	
18: 2 my **G**, my strength, in whom I will trust;	410	
18: 6 upon the Lord, and cried unto my **G**:	430	
18:21 have not wickedly departed from my **G**.	430	
18:28 the Lord my **G** will enlighten my	430	
18:29 and by my **G** have I leaped over a wall.	430	
18:30 As for **G**, his way is perfect: the word of	410	
18:31 For who is **G** save the Lord? or who is a	433	
18:31 the Lord? or who is a rock save our **G**?	430	
18:32 It is **G** that girdeth me with strength,	410	
18:46 and let the **G** of my salvation be exalted.	410	
18:47 It is **G** that avengeth me, and subdueth	410	
19: 1 The heavens declare the glory of **G**;	410	
20: 1 the name of the **G** of Jacob defend thee;	430	
20: 5 in the name of our **G** we will set up our	430	
20: 7 remember the name of the Lord our **G**.	430	
22: 1 My **G**, my God, why hast thou forsaken	410	
22: 1 My God, my God, why hast thou forsaken	430	
22: 2 O my **G**, I cry in the daytime,	430	
22:10 thou art my **G** from my mother's belly.	410	
24: 5 righteousness from the **G** of his salvation.	430	
25: 2 O my **G**, I trust in thee: let me not be	430	
25: 5 for thou art the **G** of my salvation; on thee	430	
25:22 Redeem Israel, O **G**, out of all his troubles.	430	
27: 9 neither forsake me, O **G** of my salvation.	430	
29: 3 the **G** of glory thundereth: the Lord is	410	
30: 2 O Lord my **G**, I cried unto thee,	430	
30:12 O Lord my **G**, I will give thanks unto	430	
31: 5 hast redeemed me, O Lord **G** of truth.	430	
31:14 in thee, O Lord: I said, Thou art my **G**.	430	
33:12 Blessed is the nation whose **G** is	430	
35:23 even unto my cause, my **G** and my Lord.	430	
35:24 Judge me, O Lord my **G**, according to thy	430	
36: 1 that there is no fear of **G** before his eyes.	430	
36: 7 How excellent is thy lovingkindness, O **G**!	430	
37:31 The law of his **G** is in his heart; none of	430	
38:15 do I hope: thou wilt hear, O Lord my **G**.	430	
38:21 O Lord: O my **G**, be not far from me.	430	
40: 3 in my mouth, even praise unto our **G**:	430	
40: 5 Many, O Lord my **G**, are thy wonderful	430	
40: 8 I delight to do thy will, O my **G**: yea,	430	
40:17 my deliverer; make no tarrying, O my **G**.	430	
41:13 Blessed be the Lord **G** of Israel from	430	
42: 1 so panteth my soul after thee, O **G**.	430	
42: 2 My soul thirsteth for **G**, for the living God:	430	
42: 2 My soul thirsteth for God, for the living **G**:	410	
42: 2 when shall I come and appear before **G**?	430	
42: 3 continually say unto me, Where is thy **G**?	430	
42: 4 I went with them to the house of **G**, with	430	
42: 5 hope thou in **G**: for I shall yet praise him	430	
42: 6 O my **G**, my soul is cast down within me:	430	
42: 8 and my prayer unto the **G** of my life.	410	
42: 9 I will say unto **G** my rock, Why hast thou	410	
42:10 they say daily unto me, Where is thy **G**?	430	
42:11 hope thou in **G**: for I shall yet praise him,	430	
42:11 the health of my countenance, and my **G**.	430	
43: 1 **G**, and plead my cause against an ungodly	430	
43: 2 For thou art the **G** of my strength: why	430	
43: 4 will I go unto the altar of **G**, unto God my	430	
43: 4 altar of God, unto **G** my exceeding joy:	410	
43: 4 the harp will I praise thee, O my God.	430	
43: 4 the harp will I praise thee, O God my **G**.	430	
43: 5 hope in **G**: for I shall yet praise him,	430	
43: 5 the health of my countenance, and my **G**.	430	
44: 1 our ears, O **G**, our fathers have told us,	430	
44: 4 Thou art my King, O **G**:	430	
44: 8 In **G** we boast all the day long,	430	
44:20 If we have forgotten the name of our **G**,	430	
44:20 or stretched out our hands to a strange **g**;	410	
44:21 Shall not **G** search this out? for he	430	
45: 2 therefore **G** hath blessed thee for ever.	430	
45: 6 Thy throne, O **G**, is for ever and ever:	430	
45: 7 therefore **G**, thy God, hath anointed thee	430	
45: 7 therefore God, thy **G**, hath anointed thee	430	
46: 1 **G** is our refuge and strength, a very	430	
46: 4 whereof shall make glad the city of **G**,	430	
46: 5 **G** is in the midst of her; she shall not be	430	
46: 5 **G** shall help her, and that right early.	430	
46: 7 is with us; the **G** of Jacob is our refuge.	430	
46:10 Be still, and know that I am **G**: I will be	430	
46:11 is with us; the **G** of Jacob is our refuge.	430	
47: 1 shout unto **G** with the voice of triumph.	430	
47: 5 **G** is gone up with a shout, the Lord with	430	

Ps		
47: 6 Sing praises to **G**, sing praises: sing	430	
47: 7 For **G** is the King of all the earth: sing ye	430	
47: 8 **G** reigneth over the heathen: God sitteth	430	
47: 8 **G** sitteth upon the throne of his holiness.	430	
47: 9 even the people of the **G** of Abraham:	430	
47: 9 for the shields of the earth belong unto **G**:	430	
48: 1 greatly to be praised in the city of our **G**,	430	
48: 3 **G** is known in her palaces for a refuge.	430	
48: 8 of the Lord of hosts, in the city of our **G**:	430	
48: 8 our God: **G** will establish it for ever. Selah.	430	
48: 9 O **G**, in the midst of thy temple.	430	
48:10 O **G**, so is thy praise unto the ends of	430	
48:14 For this **G** is our God for ever and ever:	430	
48:14 For this God is our **G** for ever and ever:	430	
49: 7 brother, nor give to **G** a ransom for him:	430	
49:15 **G** will redeem my soul from the power of	430	
50: 1 The mighty **G**, even the Lord,	430	
50: 2 the perfection of beauty, **G** hath shined.	430	
50: 3 Our **G** shall come, and shall not keep	430	
50: 6 for **G** is judge himself. Selah.	430	
50: 7 testify against thee: I am **G**, even thy God.	430	
50: 7 testify against thee: I am God, even thy **g**.	430	
50:14 Offer unto **G** thanksgiving; and pay thy	430	
50:16 unto the wicked **G** saith, What hast thou	430	
50:22 Now consider this, ye that forget **G**, lest I	433	
50:23 aright will I shew the salvation of **G**.	430	
51: 1 Have mercy upon me, O **G**, according to	430	
51:10 Create in me a clean heart, O **G**;	430	
51:14 O **G**, thou God of my salvation:	430	
51:14 O God, thou **G** of my salvation:	430	
51:17 The sacrifices of **G** are a broken spirit:	430	
51:17 a broken and a contrite heart, O **G**, thou	430	
52: 1 mighty man? the goodness of **G** endureth	410	
52: 5 **G** shall likewise destroy thee for ever,	410	
52: 7 the man that made not **G** his strength;	430	
52: 8 like a green olive tree in the house of **G**:	430	
52: 8 trust in the mercy of **G** for ever and ever.	430	
53: 1 fool hath said in his heart, There is no **G**.	430	
53: 2 **G** looked down from heaven upon	430	
53: 2 any that did understand, that did seek **G**.	430	
53: 4 eat bread: they have not called upon **G**.	430	
53: 5 for **G** hath scattered the bones of him that	430	
53: 5 to shame, because **G** hath despised them.	430	
53: 6 When **G** bringeth back the captivity of his	430	
54: 1 Save me, O **G**, by thy name, and judge me	430	
54: 2 Hear my prayer, O **G**; give ear to the	430	
54: 3 they have not set **G** before them. Selah.	430	
54: 4 Behold, **G** is mine helper: the Lord is with	430	
55: 1 Give ear to my prayer, O **G**; and hide not	430	
55:14 walked unto the house of **G** in company.	430	
55:16 As for me, I will call upon **G**;	430	
55:19 **G** shall hear, and afflict them, even he that	410	
55:19 have no changes, therefore they fear not **G**.	430	
55:23 O **G**, shalt bring them down into the pit	430	
56: 1 Be merciful unto me, O **G**: for man would	430	
56: 4 In **G** I will praise his word, in God I have	430	
56: 4 praise his word, in **G** I have put my trust;	430	
56: 7 in thine anger cast down the people, O **G**.	430	
56: 9 turn back: this I know; for **G** is for me.	430	
56:10 In **G** will I praise his word: in the Lord	430	
56:11 In **G** have I put my trust: I will not be	430	
56:12 Thy vows are upon me, O **G**: I will render	430	
56:13 that I may walk before **G** in the light of	430	
57: 1 unto me, O **G**, be merciful unto me:	430	
57: 2 I will cry unto **G** most High; unto God	430	
57: 2 unto **G** that performeth all things for me.	410	
57: 3 **G** shall send forth his mercy and his truth.	430	
57: 5 Be thou exalted, O **G**, above the heavens;	430	
57: 7 My heart is fixed, O **G**, my heart is fixed:	430	
57:11 Be thou exalted, O **G**, above the heavens:	430	
58: 6 Break their teeth, O **G**, in their mouth:	430	
58:11 verily he is a **G** that judgeth in the earth.	430	
59: 1 Deliver me from mine enemies, O my **G**:	430	
59: 5 Thou therefore, O Lord **G** of hosts,	430	
59: 5 O Lord God of hosts, the **G** of Israel,	430	
59: 9 will I wait upon thee: for **G** is my defence.	430	
59:10 The **G** of my mercy shall prevent me:	430	
59:10 **G** shall let me see my desire upon mine	430	
59:13 let them know that **G** ruleth in Jacob unto	430	
59:17 for **G** is my defence, and the God of my	430	
59:17 is my defence, and the **G** of my mercy.	430	
60: 1 O **G**, thou hast cast us off, thou hast	430	
60: 6 **G** hath spoken in his holiness; I will rejoice	430	
60:10 not thou, O **G**, which hadst cast us off?	430	
60:10 O **G**, which didst not go out with our	430	
60:12 Through **G** we shall do valiantly: for he	430	
61: 1 Hear my cry, O **G**; attend unto my prayer.	430	
61: 5 For thou, O **G**, hast heard my vows:	430	
61: 7 He shall abide before **G** for ever: O prepare	430	
62: 1 Truly my soul waiteth upon **G**: from him	430	
62: 5 My soul, wait thou only upon **G**; for my	430	
62: 7 In **G** is my salvation and my glory:	430	
62: 7 of my strength, and my refuge, is in **G**.	430	
62: 8 heart before him: **G** is a refuge for us.	430	
62:11 **G** hath spoken once; twice have I heard	430	
62:11 heard this; that power belongeth unto **G**.	430	
63: 1 **G**, thou art my God; early will I seek thee:	430	
63: 1 God, thou art my **G**; early will I seek thee:	410	
63:11 the king shall rejoice in **G**; every one that	430	
64: 1 Hear my voice, O **G**, in my prayer:	430	
64: 7 **G** shall shoot at them with an arrow;	430	
64: 9 shall fear, and shall declare the work of **G**;	430	
65: 1 Praise waiteth for thee, O **G**, in Zion:	430	
65: 5 wilt thou answer us, O **G** of our salvation;	430	
65: 9 thou greatly enrichest it with the river of **G**,	430	

Ps		
66: 1 Make a joyful noise unto **G**, all ye lands:	430	
66: 3 Say unto **G**, How terrible art thou in thy	430	
66: 5 Come and see the works of **G**: he is terrible	430	
66: 8 O bless our **G**, ye people, and make	430	
66:10 For thou, O **G**, hast proved us: thou hast	430	
66:16 all ye that fear **G**, and I will declare what	430	
66:19 verily **G** hath heard me; he hath attended	430	
66:20 Blessed be **G**, which hath not turned away	430	
67: 1 **G** be merciful unto us, and bless us;	430	
67: 3 Let the people praise thee, O **G**; let all	430	
67: 5 Let the people praise thee, O **G**; let all	430	
67: 6 and **G**, even our own God, shall bless us.	430	
67: 6 and God, even our own **G**, shall bless us.	430	
67: 7 **G** shall bless us; and all the ends of the	430	
68: 1 Let **G** arise, let his enemies be scattered:	430	
68: 2 let the wicked perish at the presence of **G**.	430	
68: 3 be glad; let them rejoice before **G**.	430	
68: 4 Sing unto **G**, sing praises to his name:	430	
68: 5 of the widows, is **G** in his holy habitation.	430	
68: 6 **G** setteth the solitary in families: he	430	
68: 7 O **G**, when thou wentest forth before thy	430	
68: 8 heavens also dropped at the presence of **G**;	430	
68: 8 itself was moved at the presence of **G**,	430	
68: 8 at the presence of God, the **G** of Israel.	430	
68: 9 Thou, O **G**, didst send a plentiful rain,	430	
68:10 thou, O **G**, hast prepared of thy goodness	430	
68:15 The hill of **G** is as the hill of Bashan; a high	430	
68:16 the hill which **G** desireth to dwell in;	430	
68:17 The chariots of **G** are twenty thousand,	430	
68:18 that the Lord **G** might dwell among	430	
68:19 with benefits, even the **G** of our salvation.	430	
68:20 He that is our **G** is the God of salvation;	410	
68:20 He that is our God is the **G** of salvation;	430	
68:21 **G** shall wound the head of his enemies,	430	
68:24 They have seen thy goings, O **G**; even	430	
68:24 even the goings of my **G**, my King,	410	
68:26 Bless ye **G** in the congregations, even	430	
68:28 Thy **G** hath commanded thy strength:	430	
68:28 strengthen, O **G**, that which thou hast	430	
68:31 shall soon stretch out her hands unto **G**.	430	
68:32 Sing unto **G**, ye kingdoms of the earth;	430	
68:34 Ascribe ye strength unto **G**: his excellency	430	
68:35 **G**, thou art terrible out of thy holy places:	430	
68:35 the **G** of Israel is he that giveth strength	410	
68:35 and power unto his people. Blessed be **G**.	430	
69: 1 Save me, O **G**; for the waters are come in	430	
69: 3 mine eyes fail while I wait for my **G**.	430	
69: 5 O **G**, thou knowest my foolishness;	430	
69: 6 be confounded for my sake, O **G** of Israel.	430	
69:13 O, in the multitude of thy mercy hear me,	430	
69:29 let thy salvation, O **G**, set me up on high.	430	
69:30 I will praise the name of **G** with a song,	430	
69:32 and your heart shall live that seek **G**.	430	
69:35 For **G** will save Zion, and will build	430	
70: 1 Make haste, O **G**, to deliver me;	430	
70: 4 say continually, Let **G** be magnified.	430	
70: 5 haste unto me, O **G**: thou art my help	430	
71: 4 Deliver me, O my **G**, out of the hand of	430	
71:11 Saying, **G** hath forsaken him: persecute	430	
71:12 O **G**, be not far from me: O my God,	430	
71:12 from me: O my **G**, make haste for my help.	430	
71:17 O **G**, thou hast taught me from my youth:	430	
71:18 also when I am old and grayheaded, O **G**,	430	
71:19 Thy righteousness also, O **G**, is very high,	430	
71:19 high, who hast done great things: O **G**,	430	
71:22 with the psaltery, even thy truth, O my **G**:	430	
72: 1 O **G**, and thy righteousness unto the king's	430	
72:18 Blessed be the Lord **G**, the God of Israel,	430	
72:18 Blessed be the Lord God, the **G** of Israel,	430	
73: 1 Truly **G** is good to Israel, even to such as	430	
73:11 they say, How doth **G** know? and is there	410	
73:17 Until I went into the sanctuary of **G**; then	430	
73:26 but **G** is the strength of my heart,	430	
73:28 it is good for me to draw near to **G**: I have	430	
74: 1 O **G**, why hast thou cast us off for ever?	430	
74: 8 have burnt up all the synagogues of **G**	410	
74:10 **G**, how long shall the adversary reproach?	430	
74:12 For **G** is my King of old, working salvation	430	
74:22 Arise, O **G**, plead thine own cause:	430	
75: 1 Unto thee, O **G**, do we give thanks,	430	
75: 7 But **G** is the judge: he putteth down one,	430	
75: 9 I will sing praises to the **G** of Jacob.	430	
76: 1 In Judah is **G** known: his name is great in	430	
76: 6 At thy rebuke, O **G** of Jacob, both	430	
76: 9 When **G** arose to judgment, to save all	430	
76:11 Vow, and pay unto the Lord your **G**:	430	
77: 1 I cried unto **G** with my voice, even unto God	430	
77: 1 with my voice, even unto **G** with my voice;	430	
77: 3 I remembered **G**, and was troubled:	430	
77: 9 Hath **G** forgotten to be gracious? hath he	410	
77:13 Thy way, O **G**, is in the sanctuary: who	430	
77:13 who is so great a **G** as our God?	410	
77:13 who is so great a God as our **G**?	410	
77:14 Thou art the **G** that doest wonders: thou	410	
77:16 saw thee, O **G**, the waters saw thee,	430	
78: 7 That they might set their hope in **G**,	430	
78: 7 not forget the works of **G**, but keep his	410	
78: 8 and whose spirit was not stedfast with **G**.	430	
78:10 They kept not the covenant of **G**,	410	
78:18 tempted **G** in their heart by asking meat	430	
78:19 Yea, they spake against **G**; they said,	430	
78:19 Can **G** furnish a table in the wilderness?	430	
78:22 Because they believed not in **G**,	430	
78:31 The wrath of **G** came upon them,	430	
78:34 they returned and inquired early after **G**.	410	

G

Ps	78:35 they remembered that **G** *was* their rock,	430
	78:35 their rock, and the high **G** their redeemer.	410
	78:41 they turned *back* and tempted **G**,	430
	78:56 tempted and provoked the most high **G**,	430
	78:59 When **G** heard *this*, he was wroth,	430
	79: 1 O **G**, the heathen are come into thine	430
	79: 9 Help us, O **G** of our salvation, for the glory	430
	79:10 should the heathen say, Where *is* their **G**?	430
	80: 3 us again, O **G**, and cause thy face to shine;	430
	80: 4 O Lord **G** *of* hosts, how long wilt thou be	430
	80: 7 O **G** *of* hosts, and cause thy face to shine;	430
	80:14 Return, we beseech thee, O **G** *of* hosts:	430
	80:19 Turn us again, O Lord **G** *of* hosts,	430
	81: 1 Sing aloud unto **G** our strength: make a	430
	81: 1 make a joyful noise unto the **G** of Jacob.	430
	81: 4 for Israel, *and* a law of the **G** of Jacob.	430
	81: 9 There shall no strange **g** be in thee;	410
	81: 9 neither shalt thou worship *any* strange **g**.	410
	81:10 I *am* the Lord thy **G**, which brought thee	430
	82: 1 **G** standeth in the congregation of	430
	82: 8 Arise, O **G**, judge the earth: for thou shalt	430
	83: 1 Keep not thou silence, O **G**: hold not thy	430
	83: 1 hold not thy peace, and be not still, O **G**.	410
	83:12 Let us take to ourselves the houses of **G** in	430
	83:13 O my **G**, make them like a wheel;	430
	84: 2 my flesh crieth out for the living **G**.	410
	84: 3 O Lord of hosts, my King, and my **G**.	430
	84: 7 *one of them* in Zion appeareth before **G**.	430
	84: 8 O **G** *of* hosts, hear my prayer:	430
	84: 8 my prayer: give ear, O **G** of Jacob. Selah.	430
	84: 9 O **G** our shield, and look upon the face of	410
	84:10 be a doorkeeper in the house of my **G**,	430
	84:11 For the Lord **G** *is* a sun and shield:	430
	85: 4 **G** of our salvation, and cause thine anger	430
	85: 8 I will hear what **G** the Lord will speak:	410
	86: 2 thou my **G**, save thy servant that trusteth	430
	86:10 doest wondrous *things:* thou *art* **G** alone.	430
	86:12 I will praise thee, O Lord my **G**, with all	430
	86:14 O **G**, the proud are risen against me,	430
	86:15 *art* a **G** full of compassion, and gracious,	410
	87: 3 *things* are spoken of thee, O city of **G**.	430
	88: 1 O Lord **G** of my salvation, I have cried	430
	89: 7 **G** *is* greatly to be feared in the assembly of	410
	89: 8 O Lord **G** of hosts, who *is* a strong	430
	89:26 my **G**, and the rock of my salvation.	410
	90: 1 A Prayer of Moses the man of **G**.	430
	90: 2 from everlasting to everlasting, thou *art* **G**.	410
	90:17 let the beauty of the Lord our **G** be upon	430
	91: 2 and my fortress: my **G**; in him will I trust.	430
	92:13 Lord shall flourish in the courts of our **G**.	430
	94: 1 O Lord **G**, to whom vengeance	410
	94: 1 O **G**, to whom vengeance belongeth,	430
	94: 7 neither shall the **G** of Jacob regard *it*.	430
	94:22 and my **G** *is* the rock of my refuge.	430
	94:23 *yea,* the Lord our **G** shall cut them off.	430
	95: 3 For the Lord *is* a great **G**, and a great	410
	95: 7 For he *is* our **G**; and we *are* the people of	430
	98: 3 the earth have seen the salvation of our **G**.	430
	99: 5 Exalt ye the Lord our **G**, and worship at	430
	99: 8 Thou answeredst them, O Lord our **G**:	430
	99: 8 thou wast a **G** that forgavest them,	410
	99: 9 Exalt the Lord our **G**, and worship at his	430
	99: 9 his holy hill; for the Lord our **G** *is* holy.	430
	100: 3 Know ye that the Lord he *is* **G**: *it is* he	430
	102:24 I said, O my **G**, take me not away in	410
	104: 1 O Lord my **G**, thou art very great;	430
	104:21 *their* prey, and seek their meat from **G**.	410
	104:33 I will sing *praise* to my **G** while I have my	430
	105: 7 He *is* the Lord our **G**: his judgments *are*	430
	106:14 wilderness, and tempted **G** in the desert.	410
	106:21 They forgat **G** their saviour, which had	410
	106:47 O Lord our **G**, and gather us from among	430
	106:48 Blessed *be* the Lord **G** of Israel from	430
	107:11 they rebelled against the words of **G**,	410
	108: 1 O **G**, my heart is fixed; I will sing and	430
	108: 5 Be thou exalted, O **G**, above the heavens:	430
	108: 7 **G** hath spoken in his holiness; I will rejoice	430
	108:11 *Wilt* not thou, O **G**, who hast cast us off?	430
	108:11 not thou, O **G**, go forth with our hosts?	430
	108:13 Through **G** we shall do valiantly: for he	430
	109: 1 Hold not thy peace, O **G** of my praise;	430
	109:26 Help me, O Lord my **G**: O save me	430
	113: 5 Who *is* like unto the Lord our **G**,	430
	114: 7 the Lord, at the presence of the **G** of Jacob;	433
	115: 2 the heathen say, Where *is* now their **G**?	430
	115: 3 our **G** *is* in the heavens: he hath done	430
	116: 5 and righteous; yea, our **G** *is* merciful.	430
	118:27 **G** *is* the Lord, which hath shewed us	410
	118:28 Thou *art* my **G**, and I will praise thee:	430
	118:28 thee: *thou art* my **G**, I will exalt thee.	430
	119:115 I will keep the commandments of my **G**.	430
	122: 9 Because of the house of the Lord our **G** I	430
	123: 2 so our eyes *wait* upon the Lord our **G**,	430
	132: 2 and vowed unto the mighty *G* of Jacob;	NIH
	132: 5 a habitation for the mighty *G* of Jacob.	NIH
	135: 2 in the courts of the house of our **G**,	430
	136: 2 O give thanks unto the **G** of gods: for his	430
	136:26 O give thanks unto the **G** of heaven: for	410
	139:17 also are thy thoughts unto me, O **G**!	410
	139:19 Surely thou wilt slay the wicked, O **G**:	433
	139:23 Search me, O **G**, and know my heart:	410
	140: 6 I said unto the Lord, Thou *art* my **G**:	410
	143:10 Teach me to do thy will; for thou *art* my **G**:	430
	144: 9 I will sing a new song unto thee, O **G**:	430
	144:15 *is that* people, whose **G** *is* the Lord.	430

Ps	145: 1 I will extol thee, my **G**, O king; and I will	430
	146: 2 I will sing *praises* unto my **G** while I have	430
	146: 5 Happy *is* he that *hath* the **G** of Jacob for his	410
	146: 5 his help, whose hope *is* in the Lord his **G**:	430
	146:10 *even* thy **G**, O Zion, unto all generations.	430
	147: 1 for *it is* good to sing *praises* unto our **G**;	430
	147: 7 sing *praise* upon the harp unto our **G**:	430
	147:12 O Jerusalem; praise thy **G**, O Zion.	430
	149: 6 the high *praises* of **G** *be* in their mouth,	410
	150: 1 Praise **G** in his sanctuary: praise him in	410
Pr	2: 5 of the Lord, and find the knowledge of **G**.	430
	2:17 and forgetteth the covenant of her **G**.	430
	3: 4 good understanding in the sight of **G** and	430
	21:12 **G** overthroweth the wicked for *their*	NIH
	25: 2 *It is* the glory of **G** to conceal a thing:	430
	26:10 The great **G** that formed all *things* both	NIH
	30: 5 Every word of **G** *is* pure: he *is* a shield	433
	30: 9 steal, and take the name of my **G** *in vain.*	430
Ecc	1:13 this sore travail hath **G** given to the sons of	430
	2:24 also I saw, that it *was* from the hand of **G**.	430
	2:26 For **G** giveth to a man that *is* good in his	NIH
	2:26 he may give to *him* that is good before **G**.	430
	3:10 which **G** hath given to the sons of men to	430
	3:11 that no man can find out the work that **G**	430
	3:13 the good of all his labour, it *is* the gift of **G**.	430
	3:14 I know that, whatsoever **G** doeth, it shall	430
	3:14 **G** doeth *it,* that *men* should fear before	430
	3:15 and **G** requireth that which is past.	430
	3:17 **G** shall judge the righteous and the wicked:	430
	3:18 that **G** might manifest them, and that *they*	430
	5: 1 foot when thou goest to the house of **G**,	430
	5: 2 heart be hasty to utter *any* thing before **G**:	430
	5: 2 for **G** *is* in heaven, and thou upon earth:	430
	5: 4 When thou vowest a vow unto **G**, defer	430
	5: 6 wherefore should **G** be angry at thy voice,	430
	5: 7 *are* also *divers* vanities: but fear thou **G**.	430
	5:18 all the days of his life, which **G** giveth him:	430
	5:19 Every man also to whom **G** hath given	430
	5:19 to rejoice in his labour; this *is* the gift of **G**.	430
	5:20 answereth *him* in the joy of his heart.	430
	6: 2 A man to whom **G** hath given riches,	430
	6: 2 yet **G** giveth him not power to eat thereof,	430
	7:13 Consider the work of **G**: for who can make	430
	7:14 **G** also hath set the one over against	430
	7:18 for he that feareth **G** shall come forth of	430
	7:26 whoso pleaseth **G** shall escape from her;	430
	7:29 I found, that **G** hath made man upright;	430
	8: 2 and that in regard of the oath of **G**.	430
	8:12 that it shall be well with them that fear **G**,	430
	8:13 shadow; because he feareth not before **G**.	430
	8:15 his life, which **G** giveth him under the sun.	430
	8:17 I beheld all the work of **G**, that a man	430
	9: 1 and their works, *are* in the hand of **G**:	430
	9: 7 heart; for **G** now accepteth thy works.	430
	11: 5 thou knowest not the works of **G** who	430
	11: 9 that for all these *things* **G** will bring thee	430
	12: 7 the spirit shall return unto **G** who gave it.	430
	12:13 Fear **G**, and keep his commandments:	430
	12:14 **G** shall bring every work into judgment,	430
Isa	1:10 give ear unto the law of our **G**, ye people	430
	2: 3 the Lord, to the house of the **G** of Jacob;	430
	5:16 **G** that is holy shall be sanctified in	410
	7:11 Ask thee a sign of the Lord thy **G**; ask it	430
	7:13 weary men, but will ye weary my **G** also?	430
	8:10 and it shall not stand: for **G** *is* with us.	410
	8:19 should not a people seek unto their **G**?	430
	8:21 curse their king and their **G**,	430
	9: 6 Counseller, The mighty **G**, The everlasting	410
	10:21 the remnant of Jacob, unto the mighty **G**.	410
	12: 2 Behold, **G** *is* my salvation; I will trust,	410
	13:19 shall be as when **G** overthrew Sodom and	430
	14:13 I will exalt my throne above the stars of **G**:	410
	17: 6 saith the Lord **G** of Israel.	430
	17:10 Because thou hast forgotten the **G** of thy	430
	17:13 *G* shall rebuke them, and they shall flee far	NIH
	21:10 the **G** of Israel, have I declared unto you.	430
	21:17 for the Lord **G** of Israel hath spoken *it.*	430
	24:15 *even* the name of the Lord **G** of Israel in	430
	25: 1 O Lord, thou *art* my **G**, I will exalt thee,	430
	25: 9 shall be said in that day, Lo, this *is* our **G**;	430
	26: 1 salvation will **G** appoint *for* walls and	NIH
	26:13 O Lord our **G**, *other* lords besides thee	430
	28:26 For his **G** doth instruct him to discretion,	430
	29:23 One of Jacob, and shall fear the **G** of Israel.	430
	30:18 for the Lord *is* a **G** of judgment:	430
	31: 3 Now the Egyptians *are* men, and not **G**;	410
	35: 2 of the Lord, *and* the excellency of our **G**.	430
	35: 4 behold, your **G** will come *with* vengeance,	430
	35: 4 vengeance, *even* **G** *with* a recompence;	430
	36: 7 say to me, We trust in the Lord our **G**:	430
	37: 4 It may be the Lord thy **G** will hear	430
	37: 4 master hath sent to reproach the living **G**,	430
	37: 4 words which the Lord thy **G** hath heard:	430
	37:10 Let not thy **G**, in whom thou trustest,	430
	37:16 O Lord of hosts, **G** of Israel, that dwellest	430
	37:16 thou *art* the **G**, *even* thou alone, of all	430
	37:17 which hast sent to reproach the living **G**.	430
	37:20 Now therefore, O Lord our **G**, save us	430
	37:21 Thus saith the Lord **G** of Israel,	430
	37:38 worshipping *in* the house of Nisroch his **g**,	430
	38: 5 saith the Lord, the **G** of David thy father,	430
	40: 1 comfort ye my people, saith your **G**.	430
	40: 3 straight in the desert a highway for our **G**.	430
	40: 8 but the word of our **G** shall stand for ever.	430
	40: 9 unto the cities of Judah, Behold your **G**.	430

Isa	40:18 To whom then will ye liken **G**?	410
	40:27 my judgment is passed over from my **G**?	430
	40:28 *that* the everlasting **G**, the Lord,	430
	41:10 be not dismayed; for I *am* thy **G**: I will	430
	41:13 For I the Lord thy **G** will hold thy right	430
	41:17 *I* the **G** of Israel will not forsake them.	430
	42: 5 Thus saith the Lord, he that created	410
	43: 3 For I *am* the Lord thy **G**, the Holy One of	430
	43:10 before me there was no **G** formed,	410
	43:12 when *there was* no strange **g** among you:	NIH
	43:12 my witnesses, saith the Lord, that I *am* **G**.	410
	44: 6 *am* the last; and besides me *there is* no **G**.	430
	44: 8 Is there a **G** besides me? yea, *there is* no	433
	44: 8 yea, *there is* no **G**; I know not *any.*	6697
	44:10 Who hath formed a **g**, or molten a graven	410
	44:15 he maketh a **g**, and worshippeth *it; he*	430
	44:17 the residue thereof he maketh a **g**, *even* his	410
	44:17 and saith, Deliver me; for thou *art* my **g**.	410
	45: 3 call *thee* by thy name, *am* the **G** of Israel.	430
	45: 5 *is* none else, *there is* no **G** besides me:	430
	45:14 unto thee, *saying,* Surely **G** *is* in thee;	410
	45:14 and *there is* none else, *there is* no **G**.	430
	45:15 Verily thou *art* a **G** that hidest thyself,	410
	45:15 hidest thyself, O **G** of Israel, the saviour.	430
	45:18 **G** himself that formed the earth and made	430
	45:20 and pray unto a **g** *that* cannot save.	410
	45:21 *there is* no **G** else beside me; a just **G**	430
	45:21 a just **G** and a saviour; *there is* none beside	410
	45:22 for I *am* **G**, and *there is* none else.	410
	46: 6 hire a goldsmith; and he maketh it a **g**:	410
	46: 9 I *am* **G**, and *there is* none else; *I am* God,	410
	46: 9 I *am* **G**, and *there is* none like me.	430
	48: 1 make mention of the **G** of Israel, *but* not in	430
	48: 2 and stay themselves upon the **G** of Israel;	430
	48:17 I *am* the Lord thy **G** which teacheth thee	430
	49: 4 with the Lord, and my work with my **G**.	430
	49: 5 the Lord, and my **G** shall be my strength.	430
	50:10 name of the Lord, and stay upon his **G**.	430
	51:15 I *am* the Lord thy **G**, that divided the sea,	430
	51:20 the fury of the Lord, the rebuke of thy **G**.	430
	51:22 thy **G** *that* pleadeth the cause of his people,	430
	52: 7 that saith unto Zion, Thy **G** reigneth!	430
	52:10 the earth shall see the salvation of our **G**.	430
	52:12 and the **G** of Israel *will be* your rereward.	430
	53: 4 him stricken, smitten of **G**, and afflicted.	430
	54: 5 **G** of the whole earth shall he be called.	430
	54: 6 when thou wast refused, saith thy **G**.	430
	55: 5 run unto thee because of the Lord thy **G**,	430
	55: 7 to our **G**, for he will abundantly pardon;	430
	57:21 *is* no peace, saith my **G**, to the wicked.	430
	58: 2 and forsook not the ordinance of their **G**:	430
	58: 2 they take delight in approaching to **G**.	430
	59: 2 have separated between you and your **G**,	430
	59:13 departing away from our **G**,	430
	60: 9 unto the name of the Lord thy **G**,	430
	60:19 an everlasting light, and thy **G** thy glory.	430
	61: 2 and the day of vengeance of our **G**;	430
	61: 6 *men* shall call you the Ministers of our **G**:	430
	61:10 my soul shall be joyful in my **G**;	430
	62: 3 and a royal diadem in the hand of thy **G**.	430
	62: 5 the bride, *so* shall thy **G** rejoice over thee.	430
	64: 4 neither hath the eye seen, O **G**, besides	430
	65:16 earth shall bless himself in the **G** of truth;	430
	65:16 in the earth shall swear by the **G** of truth;	430
	66: 9 forth, and shut *the womb?* saith thy **G**.	430
Jer	2:17 in that thou hast forsaken the Lord thy **G**,	430
	2:19 that thou hast forsaken the Lord thy **G**,	430
	3:13 hast transgressed against the Lord thy **G**,	430
	3:21 *and* they have forgotten the Lord their **G**.	430
	3:22 unto thee; for thou *art* the Lord our **G**.	430
	3:23 truly in the Lord our **G** *is* the salvation of	430
	3:25 we have sinned against the Lord our **G**,	430
	3:25 not obeyed the voice of the Lord our **G**.	430
	5: 4 of the Lord, *nor* the judgment of their **G**.	430
	5: 5 of the Lord, *and* the judgment of their **G**:	430
	5:14 Wherefore thus saith the Lord **G** of hosts,	430
	5:19 Wherefore doth the Lord our **G** all these	430
	5:24 Let us now fear the Lord our **G**,	430
	7: 3 the **G** of Israel, Amend your ways and	430
	7:21 saith the Lord of hosts, the **G** of Israel;	430
	7:23 I will be your **G**, and ye shall be my people:	430
	7:28 obeyeth not the voice of the Lord their **G**,	430
	8:14 for the Lord our **G** hath put us to silence,	430
	9:15 saith the Lord of hosts, the **G** of Israel;	430
	10:10 the Lord *is* the true **G**, he *is* the living	430
	10:10 he *is* the living **G**, and an everlasting king:	430
	11: 3 Thus saith the Lord **G** of Israel,	430
	11: 4 ye be my people, and I will be your **G**:	430
	13:12 Thus saith the Lord **G** of Israel,	430
	13:16 Give glory to the Lord your **G**, before he	430
	14:22 *art* not thou he, O Lord our **G**? therefore	430
	15:16 called by thy name, O Lord **G** of hosts.	430
	16: 9 saith the Lord of hosts, the **G** of Israel;	430
	16:10 have committed against the Lord our **G**?	430
	19: 3 saith the Lord of hosts, the **G** of Israel;	430
	19:15 saith the Lord of hosts, the **G** of Israel;	430
	21: 4 Thus saith the Lord **G** of Israel; Behold,	430
	22: 9 the covenant of the Lord their **G**,	430
	23: 2 Therefore thus saith the Lord **G** of Israel	430
	23:23 *Am* I a **G** at hand, saith the Lord,	430
	23:23 saith the Lord, and not a **G** afar off?	430
	23:36 have perverted the words of the living **G**,	430
	23:36 living God, of the Lord of hosts our **G**.	430
	24: 5 Thus saith the Lord, the **G** of Israel;	430
	24: 7 shall be my people, and I will be their **G**:	430

Jer 25:15 For thus saith the LORD **G** of Israel unto 430
25:27 saith the LORD of hosts, the **G** of Israel; 430
26:13 and obey the voice of the LORD your **G**; 430
26:16 to us in the name of the LORD our **G**. 430
27: 4 saith the LORD of hosts, the **G** of Israel; 430
27:21 saith the LORD of hosts, the **G** of Israel, 430
28: 2 the LORD of hosts, the **G** of Israel, saying, 430
28:14 saith the LORD of hosts, the **G** of Israel; 430
29: 4 saith the LORD of hosts, the **G** of Israel; 430
29: 8 saith the LORD of hosts, the **G** of Israel; 430
29:21 the **G** of Israel, of Ahab the son of Kolaiah, 430
29:25 the LORD of hosts, the **G** of Israel, saying, 430
30: 2 Thus speaketh the LORD **G** of Israel, 430
30: 9 But they shall serve the LORD their **G**, 430
30:22 shall be my people, and I will be your **G**. 430
31: 1 will I be the **G** of all the families of Israel, 430
31: 6 let us go up to Zion unto the LORD our **G**. 430
31:18 be turned; for thou art the LORD my **G**. 430
31:23 saith the LORD of hosts, the **G** of Israel; 430
31:33 be their **G**, and they shall be my people. 430
32:14 saith the LORD of hosts, the **G** of Israel; 430
32:15 saith the LORD of hosts, the **G** of Israel; 430
32:18 the Great, the Mighty **G**, the LORD of 410
32:27 Behold, I am the LORD, the **G** of all flesh: 430
32:36 the **G** of Israel, concerning this city, 430
32:38 shall be my people, and I will be their **G**: 430
33: 4 For thus saith the LORD, the **G** of Israel, 430
34: 2 Thus saith the LORD, the **G** of Israel; 430
34:13 Thus saith the LORD, the **G** of Israel, 430
35: 4 Hanan, the son of Igdaliah, a man of **G**, 430
35:13 saith the LORD of hosts, the **G** of Israel; 430
35:17 Therefore thus saith the LORD **G** of hosts, 430
35:17 the LORD God of Israel, the **G** of Israel; 430
35:18 saith the LORD of hosts, the **G** of Israel; 430
35:19 saith the LORD of hosts, the **G** of Israel; 430
37: 3 Pray now unto the LORD our **G** for us. 430
37: 7 Thus saith the LORD, the **G** of Israel; 430
38:17 the **G** of hosts, the God of Israel; 430
38:17 the God of hosts, the God of Israel; 430
39:16 saith the LORD of hosts, the **G** of Israel; 430
40: 2 The LORD thy **G** hath pronounced this evil 430
42: 2 pray for us unto the LORD thy **G**, even for 430
42: 3 That the LORD thy **G** may shew us 430
42: 4 I will pray unto the LORD your **G** 430
42: 5 the LORD thy **G** shall send thee to us. 430
42: 6 we will obey the voice of the LORD our **G**, 430
42: 6 we obey the voice of the LORD our **G**. 430
42: 9 Thus saith the LORD, the **G** of Israel, 430
42:13 obey the voice of the LORD your **G**, 430
42:15 saith the LORD of hosts, the **G** of Israel; 430
42:18 saith the LORD of hosts, the **G** of Israel; 430
42:20 when ye sent me unto the LORD your **G**, 430
42:20 Pray for us unto the LORD our **G**; 430
42:20 according unto all that the LORD our **G** 430
42:21 not obeyed the voice of the LORD their **G**, 430
43: 1 people all the words of the LORD their **G**, 430
43: 1 for which the LORD their **G** had sent him 430
43: 2 the LORD our **G** hath not sent thee to say, 430
43:10 saith the LORD of hosts, the **G** of Israel; 430
44: 2 saith the LORD of hosts, the **G** of Israel; 430
44: 7 the **G** of hosts, the God of Israel; 430
44: 7 the God of hosts, the **G** of Israel; 430
44:11 saith the LORD of hosts, the **G** of Israel, saying; 430
44:25 the LORD of hosts, the **G** of Israel, saith; 430
45: 2 the **G** of Israel, unto thee, O Baruch; 430
46:25 The LORD of hosts, the **G** of Israel, saith; 430
48: 1 saith the LORD of hosts, the **G** of Israel; 430
50: 4 they shall go, and seek the LORD their **G**. 430
50:18 saith the LORD of hosts, the **G** of Israel; 430
50:28 in Zion the vengeance of the LORD our **G**, 430
50:40 As **G** overthrew Sodom and Gomorrah 430
51: 5 nor Judah of his **G**, of the LORD of hosts; 430
51:10 in Zion the work of the LORD our **G**. 430
51:33 saith the LORD of hosts, the **G** of Israel; 410
51:56 for the LORD **G** of recompences shall 410
La 3:41 with our hands unto **G** in the heavens. 410
Eze 1: 1 were opened, and I saw visions of **G**. 430
1: 3 me in the visions of the **G** to Jerusalem, 430
8: 4 the glory of the **G** of Israel was there, 430
9: 3 the glory of the **G** of Israel was gone up 430
10: 5 as the voice of the Almighty **G** when he 410
10:19 the glory of the **G** of Israel was over them 430
10:20 the **G** of Israel by the river of Chebar, 430
11:20 shall be my people, and I will be their **G**. 430
11:22 the glory of the **G** of Israel was over them 430
11:24 brought me in vision by the Spirit of **G** 430
14:11 and I may be their **G**, saith the Lord GOD. 430
20: 5 unto them, saying, I am the LORD your **G**; 430
20: 7 the idols of Egypt: I am the LORD your **G**. 430
20:19 I am the LORD your **G**; walk in my 430
20:20 ye may know that I am the LORD your **G**. 430
28: 2 thou hast said, I am a **G**, I sit in the seat of 410
28: 2 hast said, I am a God, I sit in the seat of **G**, 430
28: 2 yet thou art a man, and not **G**, though thou 410
28: 2 thou set thine heart as the heart of **G**: 430
28: 6 thou hast set thine heart as the heart of **G**; 430
28: 9 say before him that slayeth thee, I am **G**? 430
28: 9 thou shalt be a man, and no **G**, in the hand 410
28:13 Thou hast been in Eden the garden of **G**; 430
28:14 thou wast upon the holy mountain of **G**; 430
28:16 thee as profane out of the mountain of **G**: 430
28:26 shall know that I am the LORD their **G**. 430
31: 8 cedars in the garden of **G** could not hide 430
31: 8 nor any tree in the garden of **G** was like 430
31: 9 that were in the garden of **G**, envied him. 430

Eze 34:24 I the LORD will be their **G**, and my servant 430
34:30 that I the LORD their **G** am with them, 430
34:31 are men, and I am your **G**, saith the Lord 430
36:28 shall be my people, and I will be your **G**. 430
37:23 they be my people, and I will be their **G**. 430
37:27 I will be their **G**, and they shall be my 430
39:22 that I am the LORD their **G** from that day 430
39:28 they know that I am the LORD their **G**, 430
40: 2 In the visions of **G** brought he me into 430
43: 2 the glory of the **G** of Israel came from 430
44: 2 because the LORD, the **G** of Israel, 430
Da 1: 2 with part of the vessels of the house of **G**: 430
1: 2 the land of Shinar to the house of his **g**; 430
1: 2 the vessels into the treasure house of his **g**. 430
1: 9 Now **G** had brought Daniel into favour and 430
1:17 gave them knowledge and skill in all 430
2:18 That they would desire mercies of the **G** of 430
2:19 Then Daniel blessed the **G** of heaven. 426
2:20 Blessed be the name of **G** for ever and ever: 426
2:23 and praise thee, O thou **G** of my fathers, 426
2:28 is a **G** in heaven that revealeth secrets, 426
2:37 for the **G** of heaven hath given thee a 426
2:44 in the days of these kings shall the **G** of 426
2:45 the great **G** hath made known to the king 426
2:47 a truth it is, that your **G** is a God of gods, 426
2:47 a truth it is, that your God is a God of gods, 426
3:15 who is that **G** that shall deliver you out of 426
3:17 our **G** whom we serve is able to deliver us 426
3:25 the form of the fourth is like the Son of **G**. 426
3:26 servants of the most high **G**, come forth, 426
3:28 said, Blessed be the **G** of Shadrach, 426
3:28 they might not serve nor worship any **g**, 426
3:28 nor worship any god, except their own **G**: 426
3:29 which speak any thing amiss against the **G** 426
3:29 there is no other **G** that can deliver after 426
4: 2 wonders that the high **G** hath wrought 426
4: 8 according to the name of my **g**, and in 426
5: 3 of the house of **G** which was at Jerusalem; 426
5:18 the most high **G** gave Nebuchadnezzar thy 426
5:21 till he knew that the most high **G** ruled in 426
5:23 the **G** in whose hand thy breath is, and 426
5:26 **G** hath numbered thy kingdom, 426
6: 5 it against him concerning the law of his **G**. 426
6: 7 whosoever shall ask a petition of any **G** 426
6:10 prayed, and gave thanks before his **G**, as 426
6:11 and making supplication before his **G**. 426
6:12 man that shall ask a petition of any **G** 426
6:16 Thy **G** whom thou servest continually, 426
6:20 O Daniel, servant of the living **G**, is thy 426
6:20 servant of the living God, is thy **G**, 426
6:22 My **G** hath sent his angel, and hath shut 426
6:23 upon him, because he believed in his **G**. 426
6:26 and fear before the **G** of Daniel: 426
6:26 for he is the living **G**, and stedfast for ever, 426
9: 3 I set my face unto the Lord **G**, to seek by 430
9: 4 I prayed unto the LORD my **G**, 430
9: 4 and said, O Lord, the great and dreadful **G**, 410
9: 9 To the Lord our **G** belong mercies and 430
9:10 we obeyed the voice of the LORD our **G**, 430
9:11 in the law of Moses the servant of **G**, 430
9:13 we not our prayer before the LORD our **G**, 430
9:14 for the LORD our **G** is righteous in all his 430
9:15 now, O Lord our **G**, that hast brought thy 430
9:17 Now therefore, O our **G**, hear the prayer 430
9:18 O my **G**, incline thine ear, and hear; 430
9:19 do; defer not, for thine own sake, O my **G**: 430
9:20 my **G** for the holy mountain of my God; 430
9:20 my God for the holy mountain of my **G**; 430
10:12 to chasten thyself before thy **G**, thy words 430
11:32 the people that do know their **G** shall be 430
11:36 magnify himself above every **g**, 410
11:36 speak marvellous things against the **G** 410
11:37 Neither shall he regard the **G** of his fathers, 430
11:37 nor the desire of women, nor regard any **g**: 433
11:38 his estate shall he honour the **G** of forces: 433
11:38 a **g** whom his fathers knew not shall he 433
11:39 in the most strong holds with a strange **g**, 433
Hos 1: 6 **G** said unto him, Call her name NIH
1: 7 will save them by the LORD their **G**, 430
1: 9 said **G**, Call his name Lo-ammi: for ye are NIH
1: 9 not my people, and I will not be your **G**. NIH
1:10 unto them, Ye are the sons of the living **G**. 410
2:23 and they shall say, Thou art my **G**. 430
3: 5 seek the LORD their **G**, and David their 430
4: 1 mercy, nor knowledge of **G** in the land. 430
4: 6 thou hast forgotten the law of thy **G**, 430
4:12 have gone a whoring from under their **G**: 430
5: 4 not frame their doings to turn unto their **G**: 430
5: 6 the knowledge of **G** more than burnt 430
7:10 they do not return to the LORD their **G**, 430
8: 2 shall cry unto me, My **G**, we know thee. 430
8: 6 workman made it; therefore it is not **G**: 430
9: 1 for thou hast gone a whoring from thy **G**, 430
9: 8 watchman of Ephraim was with my **G**; 430
9: 8 his ways, and hatred in the house of his **G**. 430
9:17 My **G** will cast them away, because they 430
11: 9 for I am **G**, and not man; the Holy One is 410
11:12 Judah yet ruleth with **G**, and is faithful 430
12: 3 and by his strength he had power with **G**: 430
12: 5 Even the LORD **G** of hosts; the LORD is 430
12: 6 Therefore turn thou to thy **G**: keep mercy 430
12: 6 judgment, and wait on thy **G** continually. 430
12: 9 I that am the LORD thy **G** from the land of 430
13: 4 Yet I am the LORD thy **G** from the land of 430
13: 4 Egypt, and thou shalt know no **g** but me: 430

Hos 13:16 for she hath rebelled against her **G**: 430
14: 1 O Israel, return unto the LORD thy **G**; 430
Joel 1:13 night in sackcloth, ye ministers of my **G**; 430
1:13 is withholden from the house of your **G**. 430
1:14 land into the house of the LORD your **G**, 430
1:16 and gladness from the house of our **G**? 430
2:13 and turn unto the LORD your **G**: 430
2:14 a drink offering unto the LORD your **G**? 430
2:17 say among the people, Where is their **G**? 430
2:23 of Zion, and rejoice in the LORD your **G**: 430
2:26 and praise the name of the LORD your **G**, 430
2:27 that I am the LORD your **G**, and none else: 430
3:17 I am the LORD your **G** dwelling in Zion, 430
Am 2: 8 of the condemned in the house of their **g**. 430
3:13 saith the Lord GOD, the **G** of hosts, 430
4:11 as **G** overthrew Sodom and Gomorrah, 430
4:12 unto thee, prepare to meet thy **G**, O Israel. 430
4:13 The LORD, The **G** of hosts, is his name. 430
5:14 so the LORD, the **G** of hosts, shall be with 430
5:15 it may be that the LORD **G** of hosts will be 430
5:16 the **G** of hosts, the Lord, saith thus; 430
5:26 and Chiun your images, the star of your **g**, 430
5:27 the LORD, whose name is The **G** of hosts. 430
6: 8 saith the LORD the **G** of hosts, I abhor 430
6:14 of Israel, saith the LORD the **G** of hosts; 430
8:14 of Samaria, and say, Thy **g**, O Dan, liveth; 430
9:15 I have given them, saith the LORD thy **G**. 430
Jnh 1: 5 cried every man unto his **G**, and cast forth 430
1: 6 call upon thy **G**, if so be that God will 430
1: 6 if so be that **G** will think upon us, that we 430
1: 9 I fear the LORD, the **G** of heaven, 430
2: 1 Jonah prayed unto the LORD his **G** out of 430
2: 6 my life from corruption, O LORD my **G**. 430
3: 5 So the people of Nineveh believed **G**, 430
3: 8 with sackcloth, and cry mightily unto **G**: 430
3: 9 Who can tell if **G** will turn and repent, 430
3:10 saw their works, that they turned from 430
3:10 **G** repented of the evil, that he had said 430
4: 2 for I knew that thou art a gracious **G**, 410
4: 6 the LORD **G** prepared a gourd, and made it 430
4: 7 **G** prepared a worm when the morning 430
4: 8 that **G** prepared a vehement east wind; 430
4: 9 **G** said to Jonah, Doest thou well to be 430
Mic 3: 7 their lips; for there is no answer of **G**. 430
3: 2 and to the house of the **G** of Jacob; 430
4: 5 will walk every one in the name of his **g**, 430
4: 5 in the name of the LORD our **G** for ever 430
5: 4 majesty of the name of the LORD his **G**; 430
6: 6 and bow myself before the high **G**? 430
6: 8 mercy, and to walk humbly with thy **G**? 430
7: 7 I will wait for the **G** of my salvation: 430
7: 7 God of my salvation: my **G** will hear me. 430
7:10 said unto me, Where is the LORD thy **G**? 430
7:17 they shall be afraid of the LORD our **G**, 430
7:18 Who is a **G** like unto thee, that pardoneth 410
Na 1: 2 **G** is jealous, and the LORD revengeth; 410
Hab 1:11 offend, imputing this his power unto his **g**. 433
1:12 O LORD my **G**, mine Holy One? 430
1:12 and, O **mighty G**, thou hast established 6697
3: 3 **G** came from Teman, and the Holy One 433
3:18 I will joy in the **G** of my salvation. 430
Zep 2: 7 for the LORD their **G** shall visit them, 430
2: 9 saith the LORD of hosts, the **G** of Israel, 430
3: 2 in the LORD; she drew not near to her **G**. 430
3:17 The LORD thy **G** in the midst of thee is 430
Hag 1:12 obeyed the voice of the LORD their **G**, 430
1:12 as the LORD their **G** had sent him, 430
1:14 in the house of the LORD of hosts, their **G**, 430
Zec 6:15 obey the voice of the LORD your **G**. 410
7: 2 When they had sent unto the house of **G** 410
8: 8 I will be their **G**, in truth and 430
8:23 for we have heard that **G** is with you. 430
9: 7 shall be for our **G**, and he shall be as a 430
9:16 the LORD their **G** shall save them in that 430
10: 6 for I am the LORD their **G**, and will hear 430
11: 4 Thus saith the LORD my **G**; Feed the flock 430
12: 5 my strength in the LORD of hosts their **G**. 430
12: 8 the house of David shall be as **G**, 430
13: 9 and they shall say, The LORD is my **G**. 430
Mal 1: 9 **G** that he will be gracious unto us: 410
2:10 hath not one **G** created us? why do we 410
2:11 hath married the daughter of a strange **g**. 410
2:16 For the LORD, the **G** of Israel, saith that he 430
2:17 in them; or, Where is the **G** of judgment? 430
3: 8 Will a man rob **G**? Yet ye have robbed me. 430
3:14 Ye have said, It is vain to serve **G**: 430
3:15 yea, they that tempt **G** are even delivered. 430
3:18 between him that serveth **G** and him that 430
Mt 1:23 which being interpreted is, **G** with us. 2316
2:12 And being **warned** of **G** in a dream that 5537
2:22 being **warned** of **G** in a dream, 5537
3: 9 that **G** is able of these stones to raise up 2316
3:16 he saw the Spirit of **G** descending like a 2316
4: 3 to him, he said, If thou be the Son of **G**, 2316
4: 4 that proceedeth out of the mouth of **G**. 2316
4: 6 thou be the Son of **G**, cast thyself down: 2316
4: 7 Thou shalt not tempt the Lord thy **G**. 2316
4:10 shalt worship the Lord thy **G**. 2316
5: 8 are the pure in heart: for they shall see **G**. 2316
5: 9 for they shall be called the children of **G**. 2316
6:24 Ye cannot serve **G** and mammon. 2316
6:30 if **G** so clothe the grass of the field, 2316
6:33 But seek ye first the kingdom of **G**, 2316
8:29 to do with thee, Jesus, thou Son of **G**? 2316

G

G

Mt	9: 8 and glorified **G**, which had given such	2316
	12: 4 How he entered into the house of **G**,	2316
	12:28 But if I cast out devils by the Spirit of **G**,	2316
	12:28 then the kingdom of **G** is come unto you.	2316
	14:33 saying, Of a truth thou art the Son of **G**.	2316
	15: 3 commandment of **G** by your tradition?	2316
	15: 4 For **G** commanded, saying, Honour thy	2316
	15: 6 of **G** of none effect by your tradition.	2316
	15:31 to see: and they glorified the **G** of Israel.	2316
	16:16 art the Christ, the Son of the living **G**.	2316
	16:23 savourest not the *things* that be of **G**,	2316
	19: 6 What therefore **G** hath joined together,	2316
	19:17 *there is* none good but one, *that is,* **G**:	2316
	19:24 rich *man* to enter into the kingdom of **G**.	2316
	19:26 but with **G** all *things* are possible.	2316
	21:12 And Jesus went into the temple of **G**,	2316
	21:31 the harlots go into the kingdom of **G**	2316
	21:43 The kingdom of **G** shall be taken from	2316
	22:16 true, and teachest the way of **G** in truth,	2316
	22:21 and unto **G** the *things* that are God's.	2316
	22:29 the scriptures, nor the power of **G**.	2316
	22:30 but are as *the* angels of **G** in heaven.	2316
	22:31 that which was spoken unto you by **G**,	2316
	22:32 I am the **G** of Abraham, and the God of	2316
	22:32 and the **G** of Isaac, and the God of Jacob?	2316
	22:32 and the God of Isaac, and the God of Jacob?	2316
	22:32 **G** is not the God of the dead, but of	2316
	22:32 God is not the **G** of the dead, but of	2316
	22:37 Thou shalt love the Lord thy **G** with all	2316
	23:22 sweareth by the throne of **G**, and by him	2316
	26:61 I am able to destroy the temple of **G**,	2316
	26:63 unto him, I adjure thee by the living **G**,	2316
	26:63 whether thou be the Christ, the Son of **G**.	2316
	27:40 If thou be the Son of **G**, come down from	2316
	27:43 He trusted in **G**; let him deliver him now,	2316
	27:43 have him: for he said, I am the Son of **G**.	2316
	27:46 that is to say, My **G**, my God, why hast	2316
	27:46 that is to say, My God, my **G**, why hast	2316
	27:54 saying, Truly this was the Son of **G**.	2316
Mk	1: 1 the gospel of Jesus Christ, the Son of **G**;	2316
	1:14 preaching the gospel of the kingdom of **G**,	2316
	1:15 and the kingdom of **G** is at hand:	2316
	1:24 thee who thou art, the Holy One of **G**.	2316
	2: 7 who can forgive sins but **G** only?	2316
	2:12 glorified **G**, saying, We never saw *it* on	2316
	2:26 How he went into the house of **G** in	2316
	3:11 and cried, saying, Thou art the Son of **G**.	2316
	3:35 For whosoever shall do the will of **G**,	2316
	4:11 know the mystery of the kingdom of **G**:	2316
	4:26 And he said, So is the kingdom of **G**, as if	2316
	4:30 shall we liken the kingdom of **G**?	2316
	5: 7 Jesus, *thou* Son of the most high **G**?	2316
	5: 7 I adjure thee by **G**, that thou torment me	2316
	7: 8 For laying aside the commandment of **G**,	2316
	7: 9 well ye reject the commandment of **G**,	2316
	7:13 Making the word of **G** of none effect	2316
	8:33 savourest not the *things* that be of **G**,	2316
	9: 1 they have seen the kingdom of **G** come	2316
	9:47 into the kingdom of **G** with one eye,	2316
	10: 6 But from the beginning of the creation **G**	2316
	10: 9 What therefore **G** hath joined together,	2316
	10:14 not: for of such is the kingdom of **G**.	2316
	10:15 receive the kingdom of **G** as a little child,	2316
	10:18 *there is* none good but one, *that is,* **G**.	2316
	10:23 have riches enter into the kingdom of **G**!	2316
	10:24 in riches to enter into the kingdom of **G**!	2316
	10:25 rich *man* to enter into the kingdom of **G**.	2316
	10:27 men *it is* impossible, but not with **G**:	2316
	10:27 for with **G** all *things* are possible.	2316
	11:22 saith unto them, Have faith in **G**.	2316
	12:14 men, but teachest the way of **G** in truth:	2316
	12:17 and to **G** the *things* that are God's.	2316
	12:24 the scriptures, neither the power of **G**?	2316
	12:26 in the bush **G** spake unto him, saying,	2316
	12:26 I *am* the **G** of Abraham, and the God of	2316
	12:26 and the **G** of Isaac, and the God of Jacob?	2316
	12:26 and the God of Isaac, and the God of Jacob?	2316
	12:27 He is not the **G** of the dead, but the God	2316
	12:27 God of the dead, but the **G** of the living:	2316
	12:29 O Israel; The Lord our **G** is one Lord:	2316
	12:30 thou shalt love the Lord thy **G** with all	2316
	12:32 there is one **G**; and there is none other	2316
	12:34 Thou art not far from the kingdom of **G**.	2316
	13:19 creation which **G** created unto this time,	2316
	14:25 that I drink it new in the kingdom of **G**.	2316
	15:34 being interpreted, My **G**, my God,	2316
	15:34 being interpreted, My God, my **G**,	2316
	15:39 he said, Truly this man was the Son of **G**.	2316
	15:43 which also waited for the kingdom of **G**,	2316
	16:19 heaven, and sat on the right hand of **G**.	2316
Lk	1: 6 And they were both righteous before **G**,	2316
	1: 8 office before **G** in the order of his course,	2316
	1:16 of Israel shall he turn to the Lord their **G**.	2316
	1:19 Gabriel, that stand in the presence of **G**;	2316
	1:26 was sent from **G** unto a city of Galilee,	2316
	1:30 Mary: for thou hast found favour with **G**.	2316
	1:32 the Lord **G** shall give unto him the throne	2316
	1:35 born of thee shall be called the Son of **G**.	2316
	1:37 For with **G** nothing shall be unpossible.	2316
	1:47 And my spirit hath rejoiced in **G** my	2316
	1:64 and he spake, and praised **G**.	2316
	1:68 Blessed *be* the Lord **G** of Israel; for he	2316
	1:78 Through the tender mercy of our **G**,	2316
	2:13 of the heavenly host praising **G**,	2316
	2:14 Glory to **G** in the highest, and on earth	2316

Lk	2:20 praising **G** for all *the things* that they had	2316
	2:28 *up* in his arms, and blessed **G**, and said,	2316
	2:37 served **G** with fastings and prayers night	NIG
	2:40 and the grace of **G** was upon him.	2316
	2:52 stature, and in favour with **G** and man.	2316
	3: 2 the word of **G** came unto John the son of	2316
	3: 6 And all flesh shall see the salvation of **G**.	2316
	3: 8 That **G** is able of these stones to raise up	2316
	3:38 *son* of Adam, which was *the son* of **G**.	2316
	4: 3 said unto him, If thou be the Son of **G**,	2316
	4: 4 by bread alone, but by every word of **G**.	2316
	4: 8 Thou shalt worship the Lord thy **G**,	2316
	4: 9 said unto him, If thou be the Son of **G**,	2316
	4:12 Thou shalt not tempt the Lord thy **G**.	2316
	4:34 thee who thou art, the Holy One of **G**.	2316
	4:41 and saying, Thou art Christ the Son of **G**.	2316
	4:43 I must preach the kingdom of **G** to other	2316
	5: 1 pressed upon him to hear the word of **G**,	2316
	5:21 Who can forgive sins, but **G** alone?	2316
	5:25 departed to his own house, glorifying **G**.	2316
	5:26 and they glorified **G**, and were filled with	2316
	6: 4 How he went into the house of **G**,	2316
	6:12 and continued all night in prayer to **G**.	2316
	6:20 ye poor: for yours is the kingdom of **G**.	2316
	7:16 and they glorified **G**, saying, That a great	2316
	7:16 and, That **G** hath visited his people.	2316
	7:28 he that is least in the kingdom of **G** is	2316
	7:29 heard *him,* and the publicans, justified **G**,	2316
	7:30 lawyers rejected the counsel of **G** against	2316
	8: 1 the glad tidings of the kingdom of **G**:	2316
	8:10 know the mysteries of the kingdom of **G**:	2316
	8:11 parable is this: The seed is the word of **G**.	2316
	8:21 are these which hear the word of **G**,	2316
	8:28 thee, Jesus, *thou* Son of **G** most high?	2316
	8:39 shew how great *things* **G** hath done unto	2316
	9: 2 sent them to preach the kingdom of **G**,	2316
	9:11 spake unto them of the kingdom of **G**,	2316
	9:20 Peter answering said, The Christ of **G**.	2316
	9:27 of death, till they see the kingdom of **G**.	2316
	9:43 all amazed at the mighty power of **G**.	2316
	9:60 go thou and preach the kingdom of **G**.	2316
	9:62 looking back, is fit for the kingdom of **G**.	2316
	10: 9 The kingdom of **G** is come nigh unto you.	2316
	10:11 that the kingdom of **G** is come nigh unto	2316
	10:27 Thou shalt love the Lord thy **G** with all	2316
	11:20 if I with the finger of **G** cast out devils,	2316
	11:20 no doubt the kingdom of **G** is come upon	2316
	11:28 blessed *are* they that hear the word of **G**,	2316
	11:42 pass over judgment and the love of **G**:	2316
	11:49 Therefore also said the wisdom of **G**, I	2316
	12: 6 not one of them is forgotten before **G**?	2316
	12: 8 also confess before the angels of **G**:	2316
	12: 9 shall be denied before the angels of **G**:	2316
	12:20 **G** said unto him, *Thou* fool, this night	2316
	12:21 for himself, and is not rich towards **G**.	2316
	12:24 storehouse nor barn; and **G** feedeth them:	2316
	12:28 If then **G** so clothe the grass, which is to	2316
	12:31 But rather seek ye the kingdom of **G**;	2316
	13:13 she was made straight, and glorified **G**.	2316
	13:18 Unto what is the kingdom of **G** like?	2316
	13:20 shall I liken the kingdom of **G**?	2316
	13:28 in the kingdom of **G**, and you yourselves	2316
	13:29 and shall sit down in the kingdom of **G**.	2316
	14:15 that shall eat bread in the kingdom of **G**.	2316
	15:10 of **G** over one sinner that repenteth.	2316
	16:13 Ye cannot serve **G** and mammon.	2316
	16:15 before men; but **G** knoweth your hearts:	2316
	16:15 men is abomination in the sight of **G**.	2316
	16:16 since that time the kingdom of **G** is	2316
	17:15 and with a loud voice glorified **G**,	2316
	17:18 found that returned to give glory to **G**,	2316
	17:20 when the kingdom of **G** should come,	2316
	17:20 The kingdom of **G** cometh not with	2316
	17:21 behold, the kingdom of **G** is within you.	2316
	18: 2 feared not **G**, neither regarded man:	2316
	18: 4 Though I fear not **G**, nor regard man;	2316
	18: 7 And shall not **G** avenge his own elect,	2316
	18:11 prayed thus with himself, **G**, I thank thee,	2316
	18:13 saying, **G** be merciful to me a sinner.	2316
	18:16 not: for of such is the kingdom of **G**.	2316
	18:17 **G** as a little child shall in no wise enter	2316
	18:19 none *is* good, save one, *that is,* **G**.	2316
	18:24 have riches enter into the kingdom of **G**!	2316
	18:25 rich *man* to enter into the kingdom of **G**.	2316
	18:27 unpossible with men are possible with **G**.	2316
	18:43 his sight, and followed him, glorifying **G**:	2316
	18:43 when they saw *it,* gave praise unto **G**.	2316
	19:11 thought that the kingdom of **G** should	2316
	19:37 praise **G** with a loud voice for all	2316
	20:16 they heard *it,* they said, **G** forbid.	1096+3361
	20:21 *of any,* but teachest the way of **G** truly:	2316
	20:25 and unto **G** the *things* which be God's.	2316
	20:36 and are the children of **G**, being	2316
	20:37 when he calleth the Lord the **G** of	2316
	20:37 and the **G** of Isaac, and the God of Jacob.	2316
	20:37 and the God of Isaac, and the **G** of Jacob.	2316
	20:38 For he is not a **G** of the dead, but of	2316
	21: 4 abundance cast in unto the offerings of **G**:	2316
	21:31 know ye that the kingdom of **G** is nigh at	2316
	22:16 until it be fulfilled in the kingdom of **G**.	2316
	22:18 until the kingdom of **G** shall come.	2316
	22:69 sit on the right hand of the power of **G**.	2316
	22:70 said they, Art thou then the Son of **G**?	2316
	23:35 if he be Christ, the chosen of **G**.	2316
	23:40 him, saying, Dost thou not fear **G**,	2316

Lk	23:47 he glorified **G**, saying, Certainly this was	2316
	23:51 also himself waited for the kingdom of **G**.	2316
	24:19 and word before **G** and all the people:	2316
	24:53 in the temple, praising and blessing **G**.	2316
Jn	1: 1 and the Word was with **G**, and the Word	2316
	1: 1 was with God, and the Word was **G**.	2316
	1: 2 The same was in the beginning with **G**.	2316
	1: 6 was a man sent from **G**, whose name	2316
	1:12 gave he power to become the sons of **G**,	2316
	1:13 the flesh, nor of the will of man, but of **G**.	2316
	1:18 No *man* hath seen **G** at any time; the only	2316
	1:29 and saith, Behold the Lamb of **G**,	2316
	1:34 and bare record that this is the Son of **G**.	2316
	1:36 walked, he saith, Behold the Lamb of **G**.	2316
	1:49 unto him, Rabbi, thou art the Son of **G**;	2316
	1:51 and the angels of **G** ascending and	2316
	3: 2 that thou art a teacher come from **G**:	2316
	3: 2 that thou doest, except **G** be with him.	2316
	3: 3 he cannot see the kingdom of **G**.	2316
	3: 5 he cannot enter into the kingdom of **G**.	2316
	3:16 For **G** so loved the world, that he gave	2316
	3:17 For **G** sent not his Son into the world to	2316
	3:18 the name of the only begotten Son of **G**.	2316
	3:21 manifest, that they are wrought in **G**.	2316
	3:33 hath set to *his* seal that **G** is true.	2316
	3:34 For he whom **G** hath sent speaketh	2316
	3:34 God hath sent speaketh the words of **G**:	2316
	3:34 for **G** giveth not the Spirit by measure	2316
	3:36 life; but the wrath of **G** abideth on him.	2316
	4:10 If thou knewest the gift of **G**, and who it	2316
	4:24 **G** *is* a Spirit: and they that worship him	2316
	5:18 but said also that **G** was his Father,	2316
	5:18 his Father, making himself equal with **G**.	2316
	5:25 dead shall hear the voice of the Son of **G**:	2316
	5:42 that ye have not the love of **G** in you.	2316
	5:44 seek not the honour that *cometh* from **G**	2316
	6:27 you: for him hath **G** the Father sealed.	2316
	6:28 do, that we might work the works of **G**?	2316
	6:29 said unto them, This is the work of **G**,	2316
	6:33 For the bread of **G** is he which cometh	2316
	6:45 And they shall be all taught of **G**.	2316
	6:46 save he which is of **G**, he hath seen	2316
	6:69 art *that* Christ, the Son of the living **G**.	2316
	7:17 whether it be of **G**, or *whether* I speak of	2316
	8:40 you the truth, which I have heard of **G**:	2316
	8:41 fornication; we have one Father, *even* **G**.	2316
	8:42 If **G** were your Father, ye would love me:	2316
	8:42 for I proceeded forth and came from **G**;	2316
	8:47 He that is of **G** heareth God's words:	2316
	8:47 hear *them* not, because ye are not of **G**.	2316
	8:54 of whom ye say, that he is your **G**:	2316
	9: 3 that the works of **G** should be made	2316
	9:16 This man is not of **G**, because he keepeth	2316
	9:24 and said unto him, Give **G** the praise:	2316
	9:29 We know that **G** spake unto Moses: *as*	2316
	9:31 we know that **G** heareth not sinners:	2316
	9:31 but if any *man* be a **worshipper of G**,	2318
	9:33 If this *man* were not of **G**, he could do	2316
	9:35 Dost thou believe on the Son of **G**?	2316
	10:33 that thou, being a man, makest thyself **G**.	2316
	10:35 unto whom the word of **G** came,	2316
	10:36 because I said, I am the Son of **G**?	2316
	11: 4 is not unto death, but for the glory of **G**,	2316
	11: 4 that the Son of **G** might be glorified	2316
	11:22 now, whatsoever thou wilt ask of **G**,	2316
	11:22 thou wilt ask of God, **G** will give *it* thee.	2316
	11:27 that thou art the Christ, the Son of **G**,	2316
	11:40 thou shouldest see the glory of **G**?	2316
	11:52 children of **G** that were scattered abroad.	2316
	12:43 praise of men more than the praise of **G**.	2316
	13: 3 that he was come from **G**, and went to	2316
	13: 3 he was come from God, and went to **G**;	2316
	13:31 man glorified, and **G** is glorified in him.	2316
	13:32 If **G** be glorified in him, God shall also	2316
	13:32 him, **G** shall also glorify him in himself,	2316
	14: 1 ye believe in **G**, believe also in me.	2316
	16: 2 you will think that he doeth **G** service.	2316
	16:27 have believed that I came out from **G**.	2316
	16:30 believe that thou camest forth from **G**.	2316
	17: 3 they might know thee the only true **G**,	2316
	19: 7 because he made himself the Son of **G**.	2316
	20:17 your Father; and *to* my **G**, and your God.	2316
	20:17 your Father; and *to* my God, and your **G**.	2316
	20:28 and said unto him, My Lord and my **G**.	2316
	20:31 that Jesus is the Christ, the Son of **G**;	2316
	21:19 by what death he should glorify **G**.	2316
Ac	1: 3 *things* pertaining to the kingdom of **G**:	2316
	2:11 in our tongues the wonderful works of **G**.	2316
	2:17 come to pass in the last days, saith **G**,	2316
	2:22 a man approved of **G** among you by	2316
	2:22 which **G** did by him in the midst of you,	2316
	2:23 and foreknowledge of **G**,	2316
	2:24 Whom **G** hath raised up, having loosed	2316
	2:30 knowing that **G** had sworn with an oath	2316
	2:32 This Jesus hath **G** raised up, whereof we	2316
	2:33 Therefore being by the right hand of **G**	2316
	2:36 that **G** hath made that same Jesus, whom	2316
	2:39 *even* as many as the Lord our **G** shall call.	2316
	2:47 Praising **G**, and having favour with all	2316
	3: 8 walking, and leaping, and praising **G**.	2316
	3: 9 people saw him walking and praising **G**:	2316
	3:13 The **G** of Abraham, and of Isaac,	2316
	3:13 Isaac, and of Jacob, the **G** of our fathers,	2316
	3:15 life, whom **G** hath raised from the dead;	2316
	3:18 But *those things,* which **G** before had	2316

Ac	3:21 **G** hath spoken by the mouth of all his	2316
	3:22 A prophet shall the Lord your **G** raise up	2316
	3:25 of the covenant which **G** made with our	2316
	3:26 Unto you first **G**, having raised up his Son	2316
	4:10 crucified, whom **G** raised from the dead,	2316
	4:19 Whether it be right in the sight of **G** to	2316
	4:19 to hearken unto you more than unto **G**,	2316
	4:21 for all *men* glorified **G** for that which was	2316
	4:24 lift up their voice to **G** with one accord,	2316
	4:24 said, Lord, thou *art* **G**, which hast made	2316
	4:31 they spake the word of **G** with boldness.	2316
	5: 4 thou hast not lied unto men, but unto **G**.	2316
	5:29 We ought to obey **G** rather than men.	2316
	5:30 The **G** of our fathers raised up Jesus,	2316
	5:31 Him hath **G** exalted with his right hand	2316
	5:32 **G** hath given to them that obey him.	2316
	5:39 But if it be of **G**, ye cannot overthrow it;	2316
	5:39 ye be found even to **fight against G.**	2314
	6: 2 that we should leave the word of **G**,	2316
	6: 7 And the word of **G** increased;	2316
	6:11 words against Moses, and *against* **G**.	2316
	7: 2 The **G** of glory appeared unto our father	2316
	7: 6 And **G** spake on this wise, That his seed	2316
	7: 7 shall be in bondage will I judge, said **G**:	2316
	7: 9 Joseph into Egypt: but **G** was with him,	2316
	7:17 **G** had sworn to Abraham, the people	2316
	7:25 that by his hand would **G** deliver them:	2316
	7:32 *Saying,* I *am* the **G** of thy fathers, the God	2316
	7:32 the **G** of Abraham, and the God of Isaac,	2316
	7:32 the **G** of Isaac, and the God of Jacob.	2316
	7:32 and the God of Isaac, and the **G** of Jacob.	2316
	7:35 the same did **G** send *to be* a ruler and	2316
	7:37 A prophet shall the Lord your **G** raise up	2316
	7:42 Then **G** turned, and gave them up to	2316
	7:43 Moloch, and the star of your **g** Remphan,	2316
	7:45 whom **G** drave out before the face of our	2316
	7:46 Who found favour before **G**, and desired	2316
	7:46 desired to find a tabernacle for the **G** of	2316
	7:55 saw the glory of **G**, and Jesus standing	2316
	7:55 Jesus standing on the right hand of **G**,	2316
	7:56 of man standing on the right hand of **G**,	2316
	7:59 calling upon **G**, and saying, Lord Jesus,	NIG
	8:10 saying, This *man* is the great power of **G**.	2316
	8:12 the *things* concerning the kingdom of **G**,	2316
	8:14 that Samaria had received the word of **G**,	2316
	8:20 thou hast thought that the gift of **G** may	2316
	8:21 for thy heart is not right in the sight of **G**.	2316
	8:22 of this thy wickedness, and pray **G**,	2316
	8:37 I believe that Jesus Christ is the Son of **G**.	2316
	9:20 the synagogues, that he is the Son of **G**.	2316
	10: 2 and one that feared **G** with all his house,	2316
	10: 2 to the people, and prayed to **G** alway.	2316
	10: 3 an angel of **G** coming in to him,	2316
	10: 4 are come up for a memorial before **G**.	2316
	10:15 What **G** hath cleansed, *that* call not thou	2316
	10:22 one that feareth **G**, and of good report	2316
	10:22 was **warned from G** by a holy angel to	5537
	10:28 **G** hath shewed me that *I* should not call	2316
	10:31 are had in remembrance in the sight of **G**,	2316
	10:33 are we all here present before **G**,	2316
	10:33 all *things* that are commanded thee of **G**.	2316
	10:34 a truth I perceive that **G** is no respecter	2316
	10:36 word which **G** sent unto the children of	NIG
	10:38 How **G** anointed Jesus of Nazareth with	2316
	10:38 of the devil; for **G** was with him.	2316
	10:40 Him **G** raised up the third day,	2316
	10:41 but unto witnesses chosen before of **G**,	2316
	10:42 ordained of **G** *to be* the Judge of quick	2316
	10:46 speak with tongues, and magnify **G**.	2316
	11: 1 Gentiles had also received the word of **G**.	2316
	11: 9 What **G** hath cleansed, *that* call not thou	2316
	11:17 **G** gave them the like gift as *he did* unto	2316
	11:17 what was I, that I could withstand **G**?	2316
	11:18 held their peace, and glorified **G**, saying,	2316
	11:18 Then hath **G** also to the Gentiles granted	2316
	11:23 and had seen the grace of **G**, was glad,	2316
	12: 5 ceasing of the church unto **G** for him.	2316
	12:22 *saying, It is* the voice of a **g**, and not of a	2316
	12:23 because he gave not **G** the glory:	2316
	12:24 But the word of **G** grew and multiplied.	2316
	13: 5 they preached the word of **G** in	2316
	13: 7 Saul, and desired to hear the word of **G**.	2316
	13:16 Men of Israel, and *ye* that fear **G**,	2316
	13:17 The **G** of this people of Israel chose our	2316
	13:21 and **G** gave unto them Saul the son of Cis,	2316
	13:23 Of this *man's* seed hath **G** according to	2316
	13:26 and whosoever among you feareth **G**,	2316
	13:30 But **G** raised him from the dead:	2316
	13:33 **G** hath fulfilled the same unto us their	2316
	13:36 his own generation by the will of **G**,	2316
	13:37 whom **G** raised *again*, saw no corruption.	2316
	13:43 them to continue in the grace of **G**.	2316
	13:44 city together to hear the word of **G**.	2316
	13:46 It was necessary that the word of **G**	2316
	14:15 turn from these vanities unto the living **G**,	2316
	14:22 tribulation enter into the kingdom of **G**.	2316
	14:26 of **G** for the work which they fulfilled.	2316
	14:27 they rehearsed all that **G** had done with	2316
	15: 4 they declared all *things* that **G** had done	2316
	15: 7 ye know how that a good while ago **G**	2316
	15: 8 And **G**, which knoweth the hearts,	2316
	15:10 Now therefore why tempt ye **G**, to put a	2316
	15:12 wonders **G** had wrought among	2316
	15:14 Simeon hath declared how **G** at the first	2316
	15:18 Known unto **G** are all his works from	2316

Ac	15:19 from among the Gentiles are turned to **G**:	2316
	15:40 by the brethren unto the grace of **G**.	2316
	16:14 the city of Thyatira, which worshipped **G**,	2316
	16:17 men are the servants of the most high **G**,	2316
	16:25 and Silas prayed, and sang praises unto **G**:	2316
	16:34 rejoiced, believing in **G** with all his house.	2316
	17:13 word of **G** was preached of Paul at Berea,	2316
	17:23 this inscription, TO *THE* UNKNOWN **G**.	2316
	17:24 that made the world and all *things*,	2316
	17:29 then as we are the offspring of **G**,	2316
	17:30 And the times of *this* ignorance **G** winked	2316
	18: 7 named Justus, one that worshipped **G**,	2316
	18:11 teaching the word of **G** among them.	2316
	18:13 This *fellow* persuadeth men to worship **G**	2316
	18:21 but I will return again unto you, if **G** will.	2316
	18:26 expounded unto him the way of **G** more	2316
	19: 8 the *things* concerning the kingdom of **G**.	2316
	19:11 And **G** wrought special miracles by	2316
	19:20 So mightily grew the word of **G** and	2962
	20:21 repentance toward **G**, and faith toward	2316
	20:24 to testify the gospel of the grace of **G**.	2316
	20:25 I have gone preaching the kingdom of **G**,	2316
	20:27 to declare unto you all the counsel of **G**.	2316
	20:28 to feed the church of **G**, which he hath	2316
	20:32 I commend you to **G**, and to the word of	2316
	21:19 declared particularly what *things* **G** had	2316
	22: 3 and was zealous towards **G**, as ye all are	2316
	22:14 The **G** of our fathers hath chosen thee,	2316
	23: 1 lived in all good conscience before **G**	2316
	23: 3 **G** shall smite thee, *thou* whited wall:	2316
	23: 9 spoken to him, let us not **fight against G.**	2313
	24:14 so worship I the **G** of my fathers,	2316
	24:15 And have hope towards **G**, which they	2316
	24:16 a conscience void of offence toward **G**,	2316
	26: 6 the promise made of **G** unto *our* fathers:	2316
	26: 7 instantly serving *G* day and night, hope to	NIG
	26: 8 with you, that **G** should raise the dead?	2316
	26:18 and *from* the power of Satan unto **G**,	2316
	26:20 that *they* should repent and turn to **G**,	2316
	26:22 Having therefore obtained help of **G**,	2316
	26:29 Paul said, I would to **G**, that not only	2316
	27:23 stood by me this night *the* angel of **G**,	2316
	27:24 **G** hath given thee all them that sail with	2316
	27:25 for I believe **G**, that it shall be even as it	2316
	27:35 gave thanks to **G** in presence of *them* all:	2316
	28: 6 *their minds*, and said that he was a **g**.	2316
	28:15 saw, he thanked **G**, and took courage.	2316
	28:23 and testified the kingdom of **G**,	2316
	28:28 that the salvation of **G** is sent unto	2316
	28:31 Preaching the kingdom of **G**,	2316
Ro	1: 1 apostle, separated unto the gospel of **G**,	2316
	1: 4 *And* declared *to be* the Son of **G** with	2316
	1: 7 Rome, beloved of **G**, called *to be* saints:	2316
	1: 7 to you and peace from **G** our Father,	2316
	1: 8 thank my **G** through Jesus Christ for you	2316
	1: 9 For **G** is my witness, whom I serve with	2316
	1:10 by the will of **G** to come unto you.	2316
	1:16 for it is the power of **G** unto salvation to	2316
	1:17 For therein is the righteousness of **G**	2316
	1:18 the wrath of **G** is revealed from heaven	2316
	1:19 Because that which may be known of **G** is	2316
	1:19 in them; for **G** hath shewed *it* unto them.	2316
	1:21 Because that, when they knew **G**,	2316
	1:21 knew God, they glorified *him* not as **G**,	2316
	1:23 **G** into an image made like to corruptible	2316
	1:24 Wherefore **G** also gave them up to	2316
	1:25 Who changed the truth of **G** into a lie,	2316
	1:26 For this cause **G** gave them up unto vile	2316
	1:28 even as they did not like to retain **G** in	2316
	1:28 **G** gave them over to a reprobate mind,	2316
	1:30 **haters of G**, despiteful, proud, boasters,	2319
	1:32 knowing the judgment of **G**, that they	2316
	2: 2 But we are sure that the judgment of **G** is	2316
	2: 3 that thou shalt escape the judgment of **G**?	2316
	2: 4 knowing that the goodness of **G** leadeth	2316
	2: 5 revelation of the righteous judgment of **G**;	2316
	2:11 For there is no respect of persons with **G**.	2316
	2:13 the hearers of the law *are* just before **G**,	2316
	2:16 In the day when **G** shall judge the secrets	2316
	2:17 in the law, and makest thy boast of **G**,	2316
	2:23 breaking the law dishonourest thou **G**?	2316
	2:24 For the name of **G** is blasphemed among	2316
	2:29 whose praise *is* not of men, but of **G**.	2316
	3: 2 them were committed the oracles of **G**.	2316
	3: 3 shall their unbelief make the faith of **G**	2316
	3: 4 **G forbid**: yea, let God be true,	1096+3361
	3: 4 let **G** be true, but every man a liar; as it	2316
	3: 5 commend the righteousness of **G**,	2316
	3: 5 *Is* **G** unrighteous who taketh vengeance?	2316
	3: 6 **G forbid**: for then how shall **G**	1096+3361
	3: 6 then how shall **G** judge the world?	2316
	3: 7 For if the truth of **G** hath *more* abounded	2316
	3:11 there is none that seeketh after **G**.	2316
	3:18 There is no fear of **G** before their eyes.	2316
	3:19 the world may become guilty before **G**.	2316
	3:21 But now the righteousness of **G** without	2316
	3:22 Even the righteousness of **G** *which* is by	2316
	3:23 and come short of the glory of **G**;	2316
	3:25 **G** hath set forth *to be* a propitiation	2316
	3:25 are past, through the forbearance of **G**;	2316
	3:29 *Is he* the **G** of the Jews only? *is he* not	2316
	3:30 Seeing *it is* one **G**, which shall justify	2316
	3:31 **G forbid**: yea, we establish the law.	1096+3361
	4: 2 hath whereof to glory; but not before **G**.	2316
	4: 3 Abraham believed **G**, and it was counted	2316

Ro	4: 6 unto whom **G** imputeth righteousness	2316
	4:17 *even* **G**, who quickeneth the dead,	2316
	4:20 He staggered not at the promise of **G**	2316
	4:20 but was strong in faith, giving glory to **G**;	2316
	5: 1 we have peace with **G** through our Lord	2316
	5: 2 and rejoice in hope of the glory of **G**.	2316
	5: 5 the love of **G** is shed abroad in our hearts	2316
	5: 8 But **G** commendeth his love toward us,	2316
	5:10 were reconciled to **G** by the death of his	2316
	5:11 we also joy in **G** through our Lord Jesus	2316
	5:15 much more the grace of **G**, and the gift by	2316
	6: 2 **G forbid**. How shall we, that are	1096+3361
	6:10 but in that he liveth, he liveth unto **G**.	2316
	6:11 alive unto **G** through Jesus Christ our	2316
	6:13 but yield yourselves unto **G**, as *those that*	2316
	6:13 *as* instruments of righteousness unto **G**.	2316
	6:15 the law, but under grace? **G forbid**.	1096+3361
	6:17 **G** be thanked, that ye were the servants	2316
	6:22 and become servants to **G**, ye have your	2316
	6:23 the gift of **G** *is* eternal life through Jesus	2316
	7: 4 that we should bring forth fruit unto **G**.	2316
	7: 7 **G forbid**. Nay, I had not known	1096+3361
	7:13 **G forbid**. But sin, that it might	1096+3361
	7:22 For I delight in the law of **G** after	2316
	7:25 I thank **G** through Jesus Christ our Lord.	2316
	7:25 the mind I myself serve the law of **G**;	2316
	8: 3 **G** sending his own Son in the likeness of	2316
	8: 7 the carnal mind *is* enmity against **G**:	2316
	8: 7 for it is not subject to the law of **G**,	2316
	8: 8 they that are in the flesh cannot please **G**.	2316
	8: 9 if so be that the Spirit of **G** dwell in you.	2316
	8:14 For as many as are led by the Spirit of **G**,	2316
	8:14 the Spirit of God, they are the sons of **G**.	2316
	8:16 our spirit, that we are the children of **G**:	2316
	8:17 heirs of **G**, and joint-heirs with Christ;	2316
	8:19 for the manifestation of the sons of **G**.	2316
	8:21 the glorious liberty of the children of **G**.	2316
	8:27 for the saints according to *the will of* **G**.	2316
	8:28 together for good to them that love **G**,	2316
	8:31 then say to these *things*? If **G** *be* for us,	2316
	8:33 of God's elect? *It is* **G** that justifieth:	2316
	8:34 *again*, who is even at the right hand of **G**,	2316
	8:39 be able to separate us from the love of **G**,	2316
	9: 4 and the service of **G**, and the promises;	NIG
	9: 5 *came*, who is over all, **G** blessed for ever.	2316
	9: 6 Not as though the word of **G** hath taken	2316
	9: 8 the flesh, these *are* not the children of **G**:	2316
	9:11 the purpose of **G** according to election	2316
	9:14 *Is there* unrighteousness with **G**?	2316
	9:14 with God? **G forbid**.	1096+3361
	9:16 runneth, but of **G** that sheweth mercy.	2316
	9:20 who art thou that repliest against **G**?	2316
	9:22 What if **G**, willing to shew *his* wrath,	2316
	9:26 they be called the children of the living **G**.	2316
	10: 1 heart's desire and prayer to **G** for Israel is,	2316
	10: 2 them record that they have a zeal of **G**,	2316
	10: 3 themselves unto the righteousness of **G**,	2316
	10: 9 shalt believe in thine heart that **G** hath	2316
	10:17 by hearing, and hearing by the word of **G**.	2316
	11: 1 I say then, Hath **G** cast away his people?	2316
	11: 1 **G forbid**. For I also am an Israelite,	1096+3361
	11: 2 **G** hath not cast away his people which he	2316
	11: 2 how he maketh intercession to **G** against	2316
	11: 4 what saith the **answer of G** unto him?	5538
	11: 8 **G** hath given them the spirit of slumber,	2316
	11:11 that they should fall? **G forbid**:	1096+3361
	11:21 For if **G** spared not the natural branches,	2316
	11:22 therefore the goodness and severity of **G**:	2316
	11:23 for **G** is able to graff them in again.	2316
	11:29 and calling of **G** *are* without repentance.	2316
	11:30 as ye in times past have not believed **G**,	2316
	11:32 **G** hath concluded *them* all in unbelief,	2316
	11:33 of the wisdom and knowledge of **G**!	2316
	12: 1 brethren, by the mercies of **G**,	2316
	12: 1 holy, acceptable unto **G**, *which is* your	2316
	12: 2 and acceptable, and perfect, will of **G**.	2316
	12: 3 according as **G** hath dealt to every man	2316
	13: 1 there is no power but of **G**: the powers	2316
	13: 1 the powers that be are ordained of **G**.	2316
	13: 2 the power, resisteth the ordinance of **G**:	2316
	13: 4 for he is the minister of **G** to thee for good.	2316
	13: 4 for he is the minister of **G**, a revenger to	2316
	14: 3 him that eateth: for **G** hath received him.	2316
	14: 4 up: for **G** is able to make him stand.	2316
	14: 6 to the Lord, for he giveth **G** thanks;	2316
	14: 6 Lord he eateth not, and giveth **G** thanks.	2316
	14:11 me, and every tongue shall confess to **G**.	2316
	14:12 of us shall give account of himself to **G**.	2316
	14:17 For the kingdom of **G** is not meat and	2316
	14:18 *things* serveth Christ *is* acceptable to **G**,	2316
	14:20 For meat destroy not the work of **G**.	2316
	14:22 have *it* to thyself before **G**. Happy *is* he	2316
	15: 5 Now the **G** of patience and consolation	2316
	15: 6 with one mind *and* one mouth glorify **G**,	2316
	15: 7 Christ also received us, to the glory of **G**.	2316
	15: 8 of the circumcision for the truth of **G**,	2316
	15: 9 And that the Gentiles might glorify **G** for	2316
	15:13 Now the **G** of hope fill you with all joy	2316
	15:15 of the grace that is given to me of **G**,	2316
	15:16 ministering the gospel of **G**, that	2316
	15:17 Christ *in those things* which pertain to **G**.	2316
	15:19 wonders, by the power of the Spirit of **G**;	2316
	15:30 with me in *your* prayers to **G** for me;	2316
	15:32 come unto you with joy by the will of **G**,	2316
	15:33 Now the **G** of peace *be* with you all.	2316

G

G

Ro 16:20 And the **G** of peace shall bruise Satan — 2316
16:26 to the commandment of the everlasting **G**, — 2316
16:27 To **G** only wise, *be* glory through Jesus — 2316
1Co 1: 1 of Jesus Christ through the will of **G**, — 2316
1: 2 Unto the church of **G** which is at Corinth, — 2316
1: 3 from **G** our Father, and *from* the Lord — 2316
1: 4 I thank my **G** always on your behalf, — 2316
1: 4 for the grace of **G** which is given you by — 2316
1: 9 **G** *is* faithful, by whom ye were called — 2316
1:14 I thank **G** that I baptized none of you, — 2316
1:18 us which are saved it is the power of **G**. — 2316
1:20 hath not **G** made foolish the wisdom of — 2316
1:21 after that in the wisdom of **G** the world — 2316
1:21 of God the world by wisdom knew not **G**, — 2316
1:21 pleased **G** by the foolishness of preaching — 2316
1:24 Christ the power of **G**, and the wisdom of — 2316
1:24 the power of God, and the wisdom of **G**. — 2316
1:25 Because the foolishness of **G** is wiser than — 2316
1:25 the weakness of **G** is stronger than men. — 2316
1:27 But **G** hath chosen the foolish *things* of — 2316
1:27 **G** hath chosen the weak *things* of the — 2316
1:28 hath **G** chosen, *yea*, and *things* which are — 2316
1:30 who of **G** is made unto us wisdom, — 2316
2: 1 declaring unto you the testimony of **G**. — 2316
2: 5 wisdom of men, but in the power of **G**. — 2316
2: 7 But we speak the wisdom of **G** in a — 2316
2: 7 the hidden *wisdom*, which **G** ordained — 2316
2: 9 *things* which **G** hath prepared for them — 2316
2:10 But **G** hath revealed *them* unto us by his — 2316
2:10 all *things*, yea, the deep things of **G**. — 2316
2:11 so the *things* of **G** knoweth no *man*, but — 2316
2:11 God knoweth no *man*, but the Spirit of **G**. — 2316
2:12 of the world, but the Spirit which is of **G**; — 2316
2:12 the *things* that are freely given to us of **G**. — 2316
2:14 receiveth not the *things* of the Spirit of **G**: — 2316
3: 6 Apollos watered; but **G** gave the increase. — 2316
3: 7 but **G** that giveth the increase. — 2316
3: 9 For we are labourers together with **G**: — 2316
3:10 According to the grace of **G** which is — 2316
3:16 Know ye not that ye are the temple of **G**, — 2316
3:16 and *that* the Spirit of **G** dwelleth in you? — 2316
3:17 If any *man* defile the temple of **G**, — 2316
3:17 the temple of God, him shall **G** destroy; — 2316
3:17 for the temple of **G** is holy, which *temple* — 2316
3:19 of this world is foolishness with **G**. — 2316
4: 1 and stewards of the mysteries of **G**. — 2316
4: 5 then shall every man have praise of **G**. — 2316
4: 8 I would to **G** ye did reign, that we also — NIG
4: 9 For I think that **G** hath set forth us — 2316
4:20 For the kingdom of **G** *is* not in word, — 2316
5:13 But them that are without **G** judgeth. — 2316
6: 9 shall not inherit the kingdom of **G**? — 2316
6:10 shall inherit the kingdom of **G**. — 2316
6:11 the Lord Jesus, and by the Spirit of our **G**. — 2316
6:13 but **G** shall destroy both it and them. — 2316
6:14 And **G** hath both raised up the Lord, — 2316
6:15 the members of a harlot? **G forbid**. — 1096+3361
6:19 which ye have of **G**, and ye are not your — 2316
6:20 therefore glorify **G** in your body, — 2316
7: 7 But every man hath his proper gift of **G**, — 2316
7:15 cases: but **G** hath called us to peace. — 2316
7:17 But as **G** hath distributed to every man, — 2316
7:19 the keeping of the commandments of **G**. — 2316
7:24 he is called, therein abide with **G**. — 2316
7:40 I think also that *I* have the Spirit of **G**. — 2316
8: 3 But if any *man* love **G**, the same is known — 2316
8: 4 and that *there is* none other **G** but one. — 2316
8: 6 But to us *there is but* one **G**, the Father, — 2316
8: 8 But meat commendeth us not to **G**: — 2316
9: 9 out the corn. Doth **G** take care for oxen? — 2316
9:21 (being not without law to **G**, but under — 2316
10: 5 But with many of them **G** was not well — 2316
10:13 but **G** *is* faithful, who will not suffer you — 2316
10:20 they sacrifice to devils, and not to **G**: — 2316
10:31 whatsoever ye do, do all to the glory of **G**. — 2316
10:32 to the Gentiles, nor to the church of **G**: — 2316
11: 3 *is* the man; and the head of Christ *is* **G**. — 2316
11: 7 as he is the image and glory of **G**: — 2316
11:12 also by the woman; but all *things* of **G**. — 2316
11:13 is it comely that a woman pray unto **G** — 2316
11:16 such custom, neither the churches of **G**. — 2316
11:22 to drink *in?* or despise ye the church of **G**, — 2316
12: 3 that no *man* speaking by the Spirit of **G** — 2316
12: 6 it is the same **G** which worketh all in all. — 2316
12:18 But now hath **G** set the members every — 2316
12:24 but **G** hath tempered the body together, — 2316
12:28 And **G** hath set some in the church, — 2316
14: 2 speaketh not unto men, but unto **G**: — 2316
14:18 I thank my **G**, I speak with tongues more — 2316
14:25 down on *his* face he will worship **G**, — 2316
14:25 and report that **G** is in you of a truth. — 2316
14:28 and let him speak to himself, and to **G**. — 2316
14:33 For **G** is not *the* author of confusion, — 2316
14:36 came the word of **G** out from you? — 2316
15: 9 because I persecuted the church of **G**. — 2316
15:10 But by the grace of **G** I am what I am: — 2316
15:10 but the grace of **G** which was with me. — 2316
15:15 and are found false witnesses of **G**; — 2316
15:15 we have testified of **G** that he raised up — 2316
15:24 have delivered up the kingdom to **G**, — 2316
15:28 *things* under him, that **G** may be all in all. — 2316
15:34 for some have not the knowledge of **G**: — 2316
15:38 But **G** giveth it a body as it hath pleased — 2316
15:50 blood cannot inherit the kingdom of **G**; — 2316
15:57 But thanks be to **G**, which giveth us — 2316

1Co 16: 2 as **G** hath prospered him, that there be no — NIG
2Co 1: 1 an apostle of Jesus Christ by the will of **G**, — 2316
1: 1 unto the church of **G** which is at Corinth, — 2316
1: 2 be to you and peace from **G** our Father, — 2316
1: 3 Blessed *be* **G**, even the Father of our Lord — 2316
1: 3 of mercies, and the **G** of all comfort; — 2316
1: 4 we ourselves are comforted of **G**. — 2316
1: 9 but in **G** which raiseth the dead: — 2316
1:12 fleshly wisdom, but by the grace of **G**, — 2316
1:18 But as **G** *is* true, our word toward you — 2316
1:19 For the Son of **G**, Jesus Christ, who was — 2316
1:20 For all the promises of **G** in him *are* yea, — 2316
1:20 in him Amen, unto the glory of **G** by us. — 2316
1:21 you in Christ, and hath anointed us, *is* **G**; — 2316
1:23 Moreover I call **G** for a record upon my — 2316
2:14 Now thanks *be* unto **G**, which always — 2316
2:15 we are unto **G** a sweet savour of Christ, — 2316
2:17 as many, which corrupt the word of **G**: — 2316
2:17 as of sincerity, but as of **G**, in the sight — 2316
2:17 in the sight of **G** speak we in Christ. — 2316
3: 3 ink, but with the Spirit of the living **G**; — 2316
3: 5 of ourselves; but our sufficiency *is* of **G**; — 2316
4: 2 nor handling the word of **G** deceitfully; — 2316
4: 2 every man's conscience in the sight of **G**. — 2316
4: 4 In whom the **G** of this world hath blinded — 2316
4: 4 who is the image of **G**, should shine unto — 2316
4: 6 For **G**, who commanded the light to shine — 2316
4: 6 the glory of **G** in the face of Jesus Christ. — 2316
4: 7 the excellency of the power may be of **G**, — 2316
4:15 of many redound to the glory of **G**. — 2316
5: 1 have a building of **G**, a house not made — 2316
5: 5 wrought us for the selfsame thing *is* **G**, — 2316
5:11 but we are made manifest unto **G**; — 2316
5:13 we be besides ourselves, *it is* to **G**: — 2316
5:18 And all *things are* of **G**, who hath — 2316
5:19 that **G** was in Christ reconciling the world — 2316
5:20 as though **G** did beseech *you* by us: — 2316
5:20 in Christ's stead, be ye reconciled to **G**. — 2316
5:21 be made the righteousness of **G** in him. — 2316
6: 1 that ye receive not the grace of **G** in vain. — 2316
6: 4 approving ourselves as the ministers of **G**, — 2316
6: 7 By the word of truth, by the power of **G**, — 2316
6:16 what agreement hath the temple of **G** — 2316
6:16 for ye are the temple of the living **G**; — 2316
6:16 as **G** hath said, I will dwell in them, — 2316
6:16 and walk in *them*; and I will be their **G**, — 2316
7: 1 spirit, perfecting holiness in the fear of **G**. — 2316
7: 6 Nevertheless **G**, that comforteth *those* — 2316
7:12 our care for you in the sight of **G** might — 2316
8: 1 we do you to wit of the grace of **G** — 2316
8: 5 to the Lord, and unto us by the will of **G**. — 2316
8:16 But thanks *be* to **G**, which put the same — 2316
9: 7 of necessity: for **G** loveth a cheerful giver. — 2316
9: 8 And **G** *is* able to make all grace abound — 2316
9:11 causeth through us thanksgiving to **G**. — 2316
9:12 also by many thanksgivings unto **G**; — 2316
9:13 for your professed subjection unto **G** — 2316
9:14 you for the exceeding grace of **G** in you. — 2316
9:15 Thanks *be* unto **G** for his unspeakable gift. — 2316
10: 4 mighty through **G** to the pulling down of — 2316
10: 5 exalteth itself against the knowledge of **G**, — 2316
10:13 of the rule which **G** hath distributed to us, — 2316
11: 1 Would *to* **G** you could bear with me a — NIG
11: 7 I have preached to you the gospel of **G** — 2316
11:11 because I love you not? **G** knoweth. — 2316
11:31 **G** and Father of our Lord Jesus Christ, — 2316
12: 2 knoweth;) such a one caught up to **G** — 2316
12: 3 out of the body, I cannot tell: **G** knoweth;) — 2316
12:19 we speak before **G** in Christ: but *we do* all — 2316
12:21 my **G** will humble *me* among you, — 2316
13: 4 yet he liveth by the power of **G**. — 2316
13: 4 we shall live with him by the power of **G** — 2316
13: 7 I pray to **G** that ye do no evil; not that — 2316
13:11 and the **G** of love and peace shall be with — 2316
13:14 and the love of **G**, and the communion of — 2316
Gal 1: 1 by Jesus Christ, and **G** the Father, — 2316
1: 3 *be* to you and peace from **G** the Father, — 2316
1: 4 according to the will of **G** and our Father, — 2316
1:10 For do I now persuade men, or **G**? or do I — 2316
1:13 measure I persecuted the church of **G**, — 2316
1:15 But when it pleased **G**, who separated me — 2316
1:20 unto you, behold, before **G**, I lie not. — 2316
1:24 And they glorified **G** in me. — 2316
2: 6 **G** accepteth no man's person:) for they — 2316
2:17 the minister of sin? **G forbid**. — 1096+3361
2:19 dead to the law, that I might live unto **G**. — 2316
2:20 flesh I live by the faith of the Son of **G**, — 2316
2:21 I do not frustrate the grace of **G**: for if — 2316
3: 6 Even as Abraham believed **G**, and it was — 2316
3: 8 that **G** would justify the heathen — 2316
3:11 is justified by the law in the sight of **G**, — 2316
3:17 that was confirmed before of **G** in Christ, — 2316
3:18 but **G** gave *it* to Abraham by promise. — 2316
3:20 is not *a mediator* of one, but **G** is one. — 2316
3:21 *Is* the law then against the promises of **G**? — 2316
3:21 **G forbid**: for if there had been a — 1096+3361
3:26 For ye are all the children of **G** by faith in — 2316
4: 4 **G** sent forth his Son, made of a woman, — 2316
4: 6 **G** hath sent forth the Spirit of his Son into — 2316
4: 7 if a son, then an heir of **G** through Christ. — 2316
4: 8 then, when ye knew not **G**, ye did — 2316
4: 9 after that ye have known **G**, or rather are — 2316
4: 9 or rather are known of **G**, how turn ye — 2316
4:14 but received me as an angel of **G**, *even* as — 2316
5:21 *things* shall not inherit the kingdom of **G**. — 2316

Gal 6: 7 Be not deceived; **G** is not mocked: — 2316
6:14 But **G forbid** that I should glory, — 1096+3361
6:16 and mercy, and upon the Israel of **G**. — 2316
Eph 1: 1 an apostle of Jesus Christ by the will of **G**, — 2316
1: 2 **G** our Father, and *from* the Lord Jesus — 2316
1: 3 Blessed *be* the **G** and Father of our Lord — 2316
1:17 That the **G** of our Lord Jesus Christ, — 2316
2: 4 But **G**, who is rich in mercy, for his great — 2316
2: 8 that not of yourselves: *it is* the gift of **G**: — 2316
2:10 which **G** hath before ordained that we — 2316
2:12 no hope, and **without** **G** in the world: — 112
2:16 And *that* he might reconcile both unto **G** — 2316
2:19 the saints, and of the household of **G**; — 2316
2:22 for a habitation of **G** through the Spirit. — 2316
3: 2 grace of **G** which is given me to — 2316
3: 7 according to the gift of the grace of **G** — 2316
3: 9 of the world hath been hid in **G**, — 2316
3:10 by the church the manifold wisdom of **G**, — 2316
3:19 might be filled with all the fulness of **G**. — 2316
4: 6 One **G** and Father of all, who *is* above all, — 2316
4:13 and of the knowledge of the Son of **G**, — 2316
4:18 being alienated from the life of **G** through — 2316
4:24 which after **G** is created in righteousness — 2316
4:30 And grieve not the holy Spirit of **G**, — 2316
4:32 even as **G** for Christ's sake hath forgiven — 2316
5: 1 Be ye therefore followers of **G**, as dear — 2316
5: 2 sacrifice to **G** for a sweetsmelling savour. — 2316
5: 5 in the kingdom of Christ and of **G**. — 2316
5:20 Giving thanks always for all *things* unto **G** — 2316
5:21 yourselves one to another in the fear of **G**. — 2316
6: 6 doing the will of **G** from the heart; — 2316
6:11 Put on the whole armour of **G**, that ye — 2316
6:13 take unto *you* the whole armour of **G**, — 2316
6:17 of the Spirit, which is the word of **G**: — 2316
6:23 from **G** the Father and the Lord Jesus — 2316
Php 1: 2 **G** our Father, and *from* the Lord Jesus — 2316
1: 3 I thank my **G** upon every remembrance — 2316
1: 8 For **G** is my record, how *greatly* I long — 2316
1:11 Christ unto the glory and praise of **G**. — 2316
1:28 but to you of salvation, and that of **G**. — 2316
2: 6 being in the form of **G**, thought it not — 2316
2: 6 thought it not robbery to be equal with **G**: — 2316
2: 9 Wherefore **G** also hath highly exalted him, — 2316
2:11 *is* Lord, to the glory of **G** the Father. — 2316
2:13 For it is **G** which worketh in you both to — 2316
2:15 harmless, the sons of **G** without rebuke, — 2316
2:27 but **G** had mercy on him; and not on him — 2316
3: 3 which worship **G** in the spirit, — 2316
3: 9 the righteousness which is of **G** by faith: — 2316
3:14 of the high calling of **G** in Christ Jesus. — 2316
3:15 **G** shall reveal even this unto you. — 2316
3:19 whose **G** is *their* belly, and *whose* glory *is* — 2316
4: 6 let your requests be made known unto **G**. — 2316
4: 7 And the peace of **G**, which passeth all — 2316
4: 9 do: and the **G** of peace shall be with you. — 2316
4:18 a sacrifice acceptable, well pleasing to **G**. — 2316
4:19 But my **G** shall supply all your need — 2316
4:20 Now unto **G** and our Father *be* glory for — 2316
Col 1: 1 an apostle of Jesus Christ by the will of **G**, — 2316
1: 2 from **G** our Father and the Lord Jesus — 2316
1: 3 We give thanks to **G** and the Father of our — 2316
1: 6 of *it*, and knew the grace of **G** in truth: — 2316
1:10 and increasing in the knowledge of **G**; — 2316
1:15 Who is the image of the invisible **G**, — 2316
1:25 according to the dispensation of **G** which — 2316
1:25 to me for you, to fulfil the word of **G**; — 2316
1:27 To whom **G** would make known what *is* — 2316
2: 2 acknowledgement of the mystery of **G**, — 2316
2:12 through the faith of the operation of **G**, — 2316
2:19 increaseth *with* the increase of **G**. — 2316
3: 1 Christ sitteth on the right hand of **G**. — 2316
3: 3 and your life is hid with Christ in **G**. — 2316
3: 6 For which *things'* sake the wrath of **G** — 2316
3:12 as the elect of **G**, holy and beloved, — 2316
3:15 And let the peace of **G** rule in your hearts, — 2316
3:17 giving thanks to **G** and the Father by him. — 2316
3:22 but in singleness of heart, fearing **G**: — 2316
4: 3 that **G** would open unto us a door of — 2316
4:11 *my* fellowworkers unto the kingdom of **G**, — 2316
4:12 and complete in all the will of **G**. — 2316
1Th 1: 1 Thessalonians which *is* in **G** the Father — 2316
1: 1 from **G** our Father, and the Lord Jesus — 2316
1: 2 We give thanks to **G** always for you all, — 2316
1: 3 in the sight of **G** and our Father; — 2316
1: 4 brethren beloved, your election of **G**. — 2316
1: 9 how ye turned to **G** from idols to serve — 2316
1: 9 from idols to serve the living and true **G**, — 2316
2: 2 we were bold in our **G** to speak unto you — 2316
2: 2 the gospel of **G** with much contention. — 2316
2: 4 But as we were allowed of **G** to be put in — 2316
2: 4 not as pleasing men, but **G**, which trieth — 2316
2: 5 nor a cloke of covetousness; **G** is witness: — 2316
2: 8 not the gospel of **G** only, but also our — 2316
2: 9 we preached unto you the gospel of **G**. — 2316
2:10 and **G** *also*, how holily and justly and — 2316
2:12 That ye would walk worthy of **G**, who — 2316
2:13 For this cause also thank we **G** without — 2316
2:13 when ye received the word of **G** which — 2316
2:13 men, but as it is in truth, the word of **G**, — 2316
2:14 became followers of the churches of **G** — 2316
2:15 and they please not **G**, and are contrary — 2316
3: 2 and minister of **G**, and our fellowlabourer — 2316
3: 9 For what thanks can we render to **G** again — 2316
3: 9 we joy for your sakes before our **G**; — 2316

1Th	3:11 Now **G** himself and our Father,	2316
	3:13 hearts unblameable in holiness before **G**,	2316
	4: 1 how ye ought to walk and to please **G**,	2316
	4: 3 For this is the will of **G**, *even* your	2316
	4: 5 even as the Gentiles which know not **G**:	2316
	4: 7 **G** hath not called us unto uncleanness,	2316
	4: 8 that despiseth, despiseth not man, but **G**,	2316
	4: 9 for ye yourselves are **taught of G** to love	2312
	4:14 also which sleep in Jesus will **G** bring	2316
	4:16 the archangel, and with the trump of **G**:	2316
	5: 9 For **G** hath not appointed us to wrath,	2316
	5:18 for this *is* the will of **G** in Christ Jesus	2316
	5:23 And the very **G** of peace sanctify you	2316
	5:23 *I pray* **G** your whole spirit and soul and	NIG
2Th	1: 1 the church of the Thessalonians in **G**	2316
	1: 2 from **G** our Father and the Lord Jesus	2316
	1: 3 We are bound to thank **G** always for you,	2316
	1: 4 in the churches of **G** for your patience	2316
	1: 5 token of the righteous judgment of **G**,	2316
	1: 5 be counted worthy of the kingdom of **G**,	2316
	1: 6 Seeing *it is* a righteous *thing* with **G** to	2316
	1: 8 vengeance on them that know not **G**,	2316
	1:11 that our **G** would count you worthy of	2316
	1:12 according to the grace of our **G** and	2316
	2: 4 exalteth himself above all that is called **G**,	2316
	2: 4 that he as God sitteth in the temple of God,	NIG
	2: 4 that he as God sitteth in the temple of **G**,	2316
	2: 4 of God, shewing himself that he is **G**.	2316
	2:11 for this cause **G** shall send them strong	2316
	2:13 bound to give thanks alway to **G** for you,	2316
	2:13 **G** hath from the beginning chosen you to	2316
	2:16 **G**, even our Father, which hath loved	2316
	3: 5 direct your hearts into the love of **G**,	2316
1Ti	1: 1 by the commandment of **G** our Saviour,	2316
	1: 2 from **G** our Father and Jesus Christ our	2316
	1:11 to the glorious gospel of the blessed **G**,	2316
	1:17 immortal, invisible, the only wise **G**,	2316
	2: 3 acceptable in the sight of **G** our Saviour;	2316
	2: 5 For *there is* one **G**, and one mediator	2316
	2: 5 and one mediator between **G** and men,	2316
	3: 5 shall he take care of the church of **G**?)	2316
	3:15 to behave thyself in the house of **G**,	2316
	3:15 which is the church of the living **G**,	2316
	3:16 **G** was manifest in the flesh, justified in	2316
	4: 3 which **G** hath created to be received with	2316
	4: 4 For every creature of **G** *is* good,	2316
	4: 5 For it is sanctified by the word of **G** and	2316
	4:10 because we trust in the living **G**,	2316
	5: 4 for that is good and acceptable before **G**.	2316
	5: 5 trusteth in **G**, and continueth in	2316
	5:21 I charge *thee* before **G**, and the Lord Jesus	2316
	6: 1 the name of **G** and *his* doctrine be not	2316
	6:11 But thou, O man of **G**, flee these *things*;	2316
	6:13 I give thee charge in the sight of **G**,	2316
	6:17 in uncertain riches, but in the living **G**,	2316
2Ti	1: 1 apostle of Jesus Christ by the will of **G**,	2316
	1: 2 from **G** the Father and Christ Jesus our	2316
	1: 3 I thank **G**, whom I serve from *my*	2316
	1: 6 that *thou* stir up the gift of **G**,	2316
	1: 7 For **G** hath not given us the spirit of fear;	2316
	1: 8 the gospel according to the power of **G**;	2316
	2: 9 bonds; but the word of **G** is not bound.	2316
	2:15 Study to shew thyself approved unto **G**,	2316
	2:19 the foundation of **G** standeth	2316
	2:25 if **G** peradventure will give them	2316
	3: 4 of pleasures more than **lovers of G**;	5377
	3:16 scripture *is* **given by inspiration** of **G**,	2315
	3:17 That the man of **G** may be perfect,	2316
	4: 1 I charge *thee* therefore before **G**,	2316
	4:16 *I pray* **G** that it may not be laid to their	NIG
Tit	1: 1 a servant of **G**, and an apostle of Jesus	2316
	1: 2 of eternal life, which **G**, that cannot lie,	2316
	1: 3 to the commandment of **G** our Saviour;	2316
	1: 4 from **G** the Father and the Lord Jesus	2316
	1: 7 must be blameless, as the steward of **G**;	2316
	1:16 They profess that *they* know **G**;	2316
	2: 5 that the word of **G** be not blasphemed.	2316
	2:10 that they may adorn the doctrine of **G**	2316
	2:11 For the grace of **G** that bringeth salvation	2316
	2:13 the glorious appearing of the great **G** and	2316
	3: 4 love of **G** our Saviour toward man	2316
	3: 8 that they which have believed in **G** might	2316
Phm	1: 3 from **G** our Father and the Lord Jesus	2316
	1: 4 I thank my **G**, making mention of thee	2316
Heb	1: 1 **G**, who at sundry times and in divers	2316
	1: 6 And let all the angels of **G** worship him.	2316
	1: 8 Thy throne, O **G**, *is* for ever and ever:	2316
	1: 9 therefore, *even* thy God, hath anointed	2316
	1: 9 therefore God, *even* thy **G**, hath anointed	2316
	2: 4 **G** also bearing *them* witness, both with	2316
	2: 9 that he by the grace of **G** should taste	2316
	2:13 and the children which **G** hath given me.	2316
	2:17 high priest *in things* pertaining to **G**,	2316
	3: 4 *man;* but he that built all *things* is **G**.	2316
	3:12 unbelief, in departing from the living **G**.	2316
	4: 4 did rest the seventh day from all his	2316
	4: 9 therefore a rest to the people of **G**.	2316
	4:10 from his own works, as **G** *did* from his.	2316
	4:12 For the word of **G** *is* quick, and powerful,	2316
	4:14 Jesus the Son of **G**, let us hold fast *our*	2316
	5: 1 for men *in things* pertaining to **G**,	2316
	5: 4 but he that is called of **G**, as *was* Aaron.	2316
	5:10 Called of **G** a high priest after the order of	2316
	5:12 *be* the first principles of the oracles of **G**;	2316
	6: 1 from dead works, and of faith towards **G**,	2316

Heb	6: 3 And this will we do, if **G** permit.	2316
	6: 5 And have tasted the good word of **G**,	2316
	6: 6 crucify to themselves the Son of **G** afresh,	2316
	6: 7 it is dressed, receiveth blessing from **G**:	2316
	6:10 For **G** *is* not unrighteous to forget your	2316
	6:13 For when **G** made promise to Abraham,	2316
	6:17 Wherein **G**, willing more abundantly to	2316
	6:18 in which *it was* impossible for **G** to lie,	2316
	7: 1 king of Salem, priest of the most high **G**,	2316
	7: 3 of life; but made like unto the Son of **G**;	2316
	7:19 *did;* by the which we draw nigh unto **G**.	2316
	7:25 the uttermost that come unto **G** by him,	2316
	8: 5 **admonished of G** when he was about to	5537
	8:10 I will be to them a **G**, and they shall be	2316
	9: 6 accomplishing the service of **G**.	NIG
	9:14 Spirit offered himself without spot to **G**,	2316
	9:14 from dead works to serve the living **G**?	2316
	9:20 *is* the blood of the testament which **G**	2316
	9:24 to appear in the presence of **G** for us:	2316
	10: 7 it is written of me,) to do thy will, O **G**.	2316
	10: 9 said he, Lo, I come to do thy will, O **G**.	2316
	10:12 sat down on the right hand of **G**;	2316
	10:21 *having* a high priest over the house of **G**;	2316
	10:29 hath trodden under foot the Son of **G**,	2316
	10:31 to fall into the hands of the living **G**.	2316
	10:36 that, after ye have done the will of **G**,	2316
	11: 3 worlds were framed by the word of **G**,	2316
	11: 4 By faith Abel offered unto **G** a more	2316
	11: 4 he was righteous, **G** testifying of his gifts:	2316
	11: 5 not found, because **G** had translated him:	2316
	11: 5 he had this testimony, that *he* pleased **G**.	2316
	11: 6 that cometh to **G** must believe that he is,	2316
	11: 7 being **warned of G** of *things* not seen as	5537
	11:10 whose builder and maker *is* **G**.	2316
	11:16 wherefore **G** is not ashamed to be called	2316
	11:16 God is not ashamed to be called their **G**:	2316
	11:19 Accounting that **G** *was* able to raise *him*	2316
	11:25 to suffer affliction with the people of **G**,	2316
	11:40 **G** having provided some better *thing* for	2316
	12: 2 down at the right hand of the throne of **G**.	2316
	12: 7 **G** dealeth with you as with sons;	2316
	12:15 lest any *man* fail of the grace of **G**;	2316
	12:22 and unto the city of the living **G**,	2316
	12:23 to **G** the Judge of all, and to the spirits	2316
	12:28 whereby we may serve **G** acceptably with	2316
	12:29 For our **G** *is* a consuming fire.	2316
	13: 4 and adulterers **G** will judge.	2316
	13: 7 have spoken unto you the word of **G**:	2316
	13:15 let us offer the sacrifice of praise to **G**	2316
	13:16 for with such sacrifices **G** is well pleased.	2316
	13:20 Now the **G** of peace, that brought again	2316
Jas	1: 1 servant of **G** and of the Lord Jesus Christ,	2316
	1: 5 any of you lack wisdom, let him ask of **G**,	2316
	1:13 when he is tempted, I am tempted of **G**:	2316
	1:13 for **G** cannot be tempted with evil,	2316
	1:20 man worketh not the righteousness of **G**.	2316
	1:27 Pure religion and undefiled before **G** and	2316
	2: 5 Hath not **G** chosen the poor of this world	2316
	2:19 Thou believest that there is one **G**;	2316
	2:23 Abraham believed **G**, and it was imputed	2316
	2:23 and he was called the Friend of **G**.	2316
	3: 9 Therewith bless we **G**, even the Father;	2316
	3: 9 which are made after the similitude of **G**.	2316
	4: 4 friendship of the world is enmity with **G**?	2316
	4: 4 be a friend of the world is the enemy of **G**.	2316
	4: 6 resisteth the proud, but giveth grace	2316
	4: 7 Submit yourselves therefore to **G**. Resist	2316
	4: 8 Draw nigh to **G**, and he will draw nigh to	2316
1Pe	1: 2 according to the foreknowledge of **G**	2316
	1: 3 Blessed *be* the **G** and Father of our Lord	2316
	1: 5 Who are kept by the power of **G** through	2316
	1:21 Who by him do believe in **G**, that raised	2316
	1:21 that your faith and hope might be in **G**.	2316
	1:23 by the word of **G**, which liveth and	2316
	2: 4 of men, but chosen of **G**, *and* precious,	2316
	2: 5 acceptable to **G** by Jesus Christ.	2316
	2:10 a people, that *are* now the people of **G**:	2316
	2:12 glorify **G** in the day of visitation.	2316
	2:15 so is the will of **G**, that with well doing	2316
	2:16 of maliciousness, but as the servants of **G**.	2316
	2:17 brotherhood. Fear **G**. Honour the king.	2316
	2:19 if a man for conscience toward **G** endure	2316
	2:20 take it patiently, this *is* acceptable with **G**.	2316
	3: 4 which is in the sight of **G** of great price.	2316
	3: 5 who trusted in **G**, adorned themselves,	2316
	3:15 But sanctify the Lord **G** in your hearts:	2316
	3:17 For *it is* better, if the will of **G** be so,	2316
	3:18 the unjust, that he might bring us to **G**,	2316
	3:20 once the longsuffering of **G** waited in	2316
	3:21 answer of a good conscience toward **G**,)	2316
	3:22 heaven, and is on the right hand of **G**;	2316
	4: 2 to the lusts of men, but to the will of **G**.	2316
	4: 6 but live according to **G** in the spirit.	2316
	4:10 good stewards of the manifold grace of **G**.	2316
	4:11 *let him* speak as the oracles of **G**;	2316
	4:11 *let him do it* as of the ability which **G**	2316
	4:11 that **G** in all *things* may be glorified	2316
	4:14 spirit of glory and of **G** resteth upon you:	2316
	4:16 but let him glorify **G** on this behalf.	2316
	4:17 judgment must begin at the house of **G**:	2316
	4:17 *be* of them that obey not the gospel of **G**?	2316
	4:19 commit the keeping of their souls	2316
	5: 2 Feed the flock of **G** which is among you,	2316
	5: 5 for **G** resisteth the proud, and giveth grace	2316
	5: 6 therefore under the mighty hand of **G**,	2316

1Pe	5:10 But the **G** of all grace, who hath called us	2316
	5:12 testifying that this is the true grace of **G**	2316
2Pe	1: 1 with us through the righteousness of **G**	2316
	1: 2 unto you through the knowledge of **G**,	2316
	1:17 For he received from **G** the Father honour	2316
	1:21 holy men of **G** spake *as they were* moved	2316
	2: 4 For if **G** spared not the angels that sinned,	2316
	3: 5 that by the word of **G** the heavens were	2316
	3:12 hasting *unto* the coming of the day of **G**,	2316
1Jn	1: 5 that **G** is light, and in him is no darkness	2316
	2: 5 in him verily is the love of **G** perfected:	2316
	2:14 and the word of **G** abideth in you,	2316
	2:17 that doeth the will of **G** abideth for ever.	2316
	3: 1 that we should be called the sons of **G**:	2316
	3: 2 are we the sons of **G**, and it doth not	2316
	3: 8 For this purpose the Son of **G** was	2316
	3: 8 Whosoever is born of **G** doth not commit	2316
	3: 9 he cannot sin, because he is born of **G**.	2316
	3:10 In this the children of **G** are manifest,	2316
	3:10 doeth not righteousness is not of **G**,	2316
	3:16 Hereby perceive we the love of **G**, because	NIG
	3:17 how dwelleth the love of **G** in him?	2316
	3:20 **G** is greater than our heart,	2316
	3:21 *then* have we confidence towards **G**.	2316
	4: 1 but try the spirits whether they are of **G**:	2316
	4: 2 Hereby know ye the Spirit of **G**:	2316
	4: 2 Jesus Christ is come in the flesh is of **G**:	2316
	4: 3 Christ is come in the flesh is not of **G**:	2316
	4: 4 Ye are of **G**, little children,	2316
	4: 6 We are of **G**: he that knoweth God	2316
	4: 6 he that knoweth **G** heareth us; *he* that is	2316
	4: 6 he that is not of **G** heareth not us.	2316
	4: 7 for love is of **G**; and every one that loveth	2316
	4: 7 and every one that loveth is born of **G**,	2316
	4: 7 loveth is born of God, and knoweth **G**.	2316
	4: 8 that loveth not, knoweth not **G**; for God	2316
	4: 8 knoweth not God; for **G** is love.	2316
	4: 9 In this was manifested the love of **G**	2316
	4: 9 that **G** sent his only begotten Son into	2316
	4:10 that we loved **G**, but that he loved us,	2316
	4:11 Beloved, if **G** so loved us, we ought also	2316
	4:12 No *man* hath seen **G** at any time.	2316
	4:12 **G** dwelleth in us, and his love is perfected	2316
	4:15 shall confess that Jesus is the Son of **G**,	2316
	4:15 **G** dwelleth in him, and he in God.	2316
	4:15 God dwelleth in him, and he in **G**.	2316
	4:16 and believed the love that **G** hath to us.	2316
	4:16 **G** is love; and he that dwelleth in love	2316
	4:16 he that dwelleth in love dwelleth in **G**,	2316
	4:16 in love dwelleth in God, and **G** in him.	2316
	4:20 I love **G**, and hateth his brother, he is a	2316
	4:20 can he love **G** whom he hath not seen?	2316
	4:21 he who loveth **G** love his brother also.	2316
	5: 1 that Jesus is the Christ is born of **G**:	2316
	5: 2 we know that we love the children of **G**,	2316
	5: 2 when we love **G**, and keep his	2316
	5: 3 For this is the love of **G**, that we keep his	2316
	5: 4 For whatsoever is born of **G** overcometh	2316
	5: 5 that believeth that Jesus is the Son of **G**?	2316
	5: 9 of men, the witness of **G** is greater:	2316
	5: 9 for this is the witness of **G** which he hath	2316
	5:10 He that believeth on the Son of **G** hath	2316
	5:10 that believeth not **G** hath made him a	2316
	5:10 he believeth not the record that **G** gave of	2316
	5:11 that **G** hath given to us eternal life,	2316
	5:12 that hath not the Son of **G** hath not life.	2316
	5:13 that believe on the name of the Son of **G**;	2316
	5:13 may believe on the name of the Son of **G**.	2316
	5:18 We know that whosoever is born of **G**	2316
	5:18 he that is begotten of **G** keepeth himself,	2316
	5:19 *And* we know that we are of **G**,	2316
	5:20 And we know that the Son of **G** is come,	2316
	5:20 This is the true **G**, and eternal life.	2316
2Jn	1: 3 **G** the Father, and from the Lord Jesus	2316
	1: 9 not in the doctrine of Christ, hath not **G**.	2316
	1:10 *your* house, neither bid him **G speed**:	5463
	1:11 he that biddeth him **G speed** is partaker	5463
3Jn	1:11 He that doeth good is of **G**: but he that	2316
	1:11 but he that doeth evil hath not seen **G**.	2316
Jude	1: 1 them that are sanctified by **G** the Father,	2316
	1: 4 ungodly *men*, turning the grace of our **G**	2316
	1: 4 denying the only Lord **G**, and our Lord	2316
	1:21 Keep yourselves in the love of **G**,	2316
	1:25 To the only wise **G** our Saviour, *be* glory	2316
Rev	1: 1 of Jesus Christ, which **G** gave unto him,	2316
	1: 2 Who bare record of the word of **G**,	2316
	1: 6 kings and priests unto **G** and his Father;	2316
	1: 9 for the word of **G**, and for the testimony	2316
	2: 7 which is in the midst of the paradise of **G**.	2316
	2:18 These *things* saith the Son of **G**, who hath	2316
	3: 1 saith he that hath the seven spirits of **G**,	2316
	3: 2 not found thy works perfect before **G**.	2316
	3:12 I make a pillar in the temple of my **G**,	2316
	3:12 I will write upon him the name of my **G**,	2316
	3:12 the name of the city of my **G**, *which is*	2316
	3:12 cometh down out of heaven from my **G**:	2316
	3:14 the beginning of the creation of **G**;	2316
	4: 5 throne, which are the seven spirits of **G**.	2316
	4: 8 Holy, holy, holy, Lord **G** Almighty,	2316
	5: 6 which are the seven spirits of **G** sent forth	2316
	5: 9 hast redeemed us to **G** by thy blood out of	2316
	5:10 And hast made us unto our **G** kings and	2316
	6: 9 of them that were slain for the word of **G**,	2316
	7: 2 the east, having the seal of the living **G**:	2316
	7: 3 till we have sealed the servants of our **G**	2316

G

Rev		
7:10	Salvation to our **G** which sitteth upon	2316
7:11	throne on their faces, and worshipped **G**,	2316
7:12	might, *be* unto our **G** for ever and ever.	2316
7:15	Therefore are they before the throne of **G**,	2316
7:17	**G** shall wipe away all tears from their	2316
8: 2	the seven angels which stood before **G**;	2316
8: 4	ascended up before **G** out of the angel's	2316
9: 4	have not the seal of **G** in their foreheads.	2316
9:13	of the golden altar which is before **G**,	2316
10: 7	the mystery of **G** should be finished,	2316
11: 1	measure the temple of **G**, and the altar,	2316
11: 4	two candlesticks standing before the **G**	2316
11:11	a half the spirit of life from **G** entered into	2316
11:13	and gave glory to the **G** of heaven.	2316
11:16	which sat before **G** on their seats,	2316
11:16	fell upon their faces, and worshipped **G**,	2316
11:17	O Lord **G** Almighty, which art, and wast,	2316
11:19	the temple of **G** was opened in heaven,	2316
12: 5	and her child was caught up unto **G**,	2316
12: 6	where she hath a place prepared of **G**,	2316
12:10	and the kingdom of our **G**, and the power	2316
12:10	which accused them before our **G** day	2316
12:17	which keep the commandments of **G**,	2316
13: 6	his mouth in blasphemy against **G**,	2316
14: 4	*being* the firstfruits unto **G** and to	2316
14: 5	are without fault before the throne of **G**,	2316
14: 7	loud voice, Fear, and give glory to him;	2316
14:10	shall drink of the wine of the wrath of **G**,	2316
14:12	they that keep the commandments of **G**.	2316
14:19	the great winepress of the wrath of **G**.	2316
15: 1	for in them is filled up the wrath of **G**.	2316
15: 2	the sea of glass, having *the* harps of **G**.	2316
15: 3	sing the song of Moses the servant of **G**,	2316
15: 3	*are* thy works, Lord **G** Almighty;	2316
15: 7	seven golden vials full of the wrath of **G**,	2316
15: 8	filled with smoke from the glory of **G**,	2316
16: 1	pour out the vials of the wrath of **G** upon	2316
16: 7	Lord **G** Almighty, true and righteous *are*	2316
16: 9	blasphemed the name of **G**, which hath	2316
16:11	And blasphemed the **G** of heaven because	2316
16:14	the battle of that great day of **G** Almighty.	2316
16:19	Babylon came in remembrance before **G**,	2316
16:21	and men blasphemed **G** because of	2316
17:17	For **G** hath put in their hearts to fulfil his	2316
17:17	until the words of **G** shall be fulfilled.	2316
18: 5	and **G** hath remembered her iniquities.	2316
18: 8	strong *is* the Lord **G** who judgeth her.	2316
18:20	for **G** hath avenged you on her.	2316
19: 1	honour, and power, unto the Lord our **G**:	2316
19: 4	and worshipped **G** that sat on the throne,	2316
19: 5	saying, Praise our **G**, all ye his servants,	2316
19: 6	for the Lord **G** Omnipotent reigneth.	2316
19: 9	unto me, These are the true sayings of **G**.	2316
19:10	worship **G**: for the testimony of Jesus is	2316
19:13	and his name is called The Word of **G**.	2316
19:15	the fierceness and wrath of Almighty **G**.	2316
19:17	together unto the supper of the great **G**;	2316
20: 4	for the word of **G**, and which had not	2316
20: 6	they shall be priests of **G** and of Christ,	2316
20: 9	fire came down from **G** out of heaven,	2316
20:12	the dead, small and great, stand before **G**;	2316
21: 2	coming down from **G** out of heaven,	2316
21: 3	the tabernacle of **G** *is* with men, and he	2316
21: 3	and **G** himself shall be with them,	2316
21: 3	shall be with them, *and be* their **G**.	2316
21: 4	**G** shall wipe away all tears from their	2316
21: 7	shall inherit all *things;* and I will be his **G**,	2316
21:10	descending out of heaven from **G**,	2316
21:11	Having the glory of **G**: and her light *was*	2316
21:22	for the Lord **G** Almighty and the Lamb are	2316
21:23	for the glory of **G** did lighten it,	2316
22: 1	proceeding out of the throne of **G** and	2316
22: 3	but the throne of **G** and of the Lamb shall	2316
22: 5	the sun; for the Lord **G** giveth them light:	2316
22: 6	the Lord **G** of the holy prophets sent his	2316
22: 9	keep the sayings of this book: worship **G**.	2316
22:18	If any *man* shall add unto these *things,*	2316
22:19	**G** shall take away his part out of the book	2316

GOD* (309) [LORD*; this is the proper name of God, *Yahweh* or *Jehovah,* often used in the phrase Lord GOD]

Ge		
6: 5	**G** saw that the wickedness of man *was*	3068
15: 2	Abram said, Lord **G**, what wilt thou give	3068
15: 8	he said, Lord **G**, whereby shall I know	3068
Ex 23:17	thy males shall appear before the Lord **G**,	3068
34:23	men children appear before the Lord **G**,	3068
Dt 3:24	O Lord **G**, thou hast begun to shew thy	3068
9:26	unto the Lᴏʀᴅ, and said, O Lord **G**,	3068
Jos 7: 7	Joshua said, Alas, O Lord **G**,	3068
Jdg 6:22	the Lᴏʀᴅ, Gideon said, Alas, O Lord **G**!	3068
16:28	O Lord **G**, remember me, I pray thee,	3068
2Sa 7:18	and he said, Who am I, O Lord **G**?	3068
7:19	yet a small thing in thy sight, O Lord **G**;	3068
7:19	*is* this the manner of man, O Lord **G**?	3068
7:20	for thou, Lord **G**, knowest thy servant.	3068
7:28	now, O Lord **G**, thou *art* that God,	3068
7:29	for thou, O Lord **G**, hast spoken *it:* and	3068
22:12	Who can tell *whether* **G** will be gracious	3068
1Ki 2:26	thou barest the ark of the Lord **G** before	3068
8:53	our fathers out of Egypt, O Lord **G**.	3068
Ps 68:20	**G** the Lord *belong* the issues from	3068
69: 6	O **G** of hosts, be ashamed for my	3068
71: 5	For thou *art* my hope, O Lord **G**: thou *art*	3068
71:16	I will go in the strength of the Lord **G**,	3068

Ps		
73:28	I have put my trust in the Lord **G**, that *I*	3068
109:21	do thou for me, O **G** the Lord, for thy	3068
140: 7	**G** the Lord, the strength of my salvation,	3068
141: 8	mine eyes *are* unto thee, O **G** the Lord:	3068
Isa 3:15	of the poor? saith the Lord **G** of hosts.	3068
7: 7	Thus saith the Lord **G**, It shall not stand,	3068
10:23	For the Lord **G** of hosts shall make a	3068
10:24	Therefore thus saith the Lord **G** of hosts,	3068
22: 5	of perplexity by the Lord **G** of hosts in	3068
22:12	in that day did the Lord **G** of hosts call to	3068
22:14	you till ye die, saith the Lord **G** of hosts.	3068
22:15	Thus saith the Lord **G** of hosts, Go, get	3068
25: 8	the Lord **G** will wipe away tears from off	3068
28:16	Therefore thus saith the Lord **G**, Behold,	3068
28:22	for I have heard from the Lord **G** of hosts	3068
30:15	For thus saith the Lord **G**, the Holy One	3068
40:10	the Lord **G** will come with strong *hand,*	3068
48:16	now the Lord **G**, and his Spirit, hath sent	3068
49:22	Thus saith the Lord **G**, Behold, I will lift	3068
50: 4	The Lord **G** hath given me the tongue of	3068
50: 5	The Lord **G** hath opened mine ear,	3068
50: 7	For the Lord **G** will help me;	3068
50: 9	the Lord **G** will help me; who *is* he	3068
52: 4	thus saith the Lord **G**, My people went	3068
56: 8	The Lord **G** which gathereth the outcasts	3068
61: 1	The Spirit of the Lord **G** *is* upon me;	3068
61:11	so the Lord **G** will cause righteousness	3068
65:13	Therefore thus saith the Lord **G**, Behold,	3068
65:15	for the Lord **G** shall slay thee, and call his	3068
Jer 1: 6	Ah, Lord **G**, behold, I cannot speak:	3068
2:19	*is* not in thee, saith the Lord **G** of hosts.	3068
2:22	*is* marked before me, saith the Lord **G**.	3068
4:10	(Then said I, Ah, Lord **G**! surely thou hast	3068
7:20	Therefore thus saith the Lord **G**, Behold,	3068
14:13	Ah Lord **G**! behold, the prophets say	3068
32:17	Ah Lord **G**! behold, thou hast made	3068
32:25	hast said unto me, O Lord **G**, Buy thee	3068
44:26	land of Egypt, saying, The Lord **G** liveth.	3068
46:10	For this *is* the day of the Lord **G** of hosts,	3068
46:10	for the Lord **G** of hosts hath a sacrifice in	3068
49: 5	a fear upon thee, saith the Lord **G** of hosts,	3068
50:25	for this *is* the work of the Lord **G** of hosts	3068
50:31	most proud, saith the Lord **G** of hosts:	3068
Eze 2: 4	say unto them, Thus saith the Lord **G**.	3068
3:11	and tell them, Thus saith the Lord **G**;	3068
3:27	say unto them, Thus saith the Lord **G**;	3068
4:14	Ah Lord **G**, behold, my soul *hath* not	3068
5: 5	Thus saith the Lord **G**; This *is* Jerusalem:	3068
5: 7	Therefore thus saith the Lord **G**;	3068
5: 8	Therefore thus saith the Lord **G**; Behold,	3068
5:11	Wherefore, as I live, saith the Lord **G**;	3068
6: 3	of Israel, hear the word of the Lord **G**;	3068
6: 3	Thus saith the Lord **G** to the mountains,	3068
6:11	Thus saith the Lord **G**; Smite with thine	3068
7: 2	thus saith the Lord **G** unto the land of	3068
7: 5	Thus saith the Lord **G**; An evil, an only	3068
8: 1	that the hand of the Lord **G** fell there	3068
9: 8	my face, and cried, and said, Ah Lord **G**,	3068
11: 7	Therefore thus saith the Lord **G**; Your	3068
11: 8	bring a sword upon you, saith the Lord **G**.	3068
11:13	*with* a loud voice, and said, Ah Lord **G**!	3068
11:16	Therefore say, Thus saith the Lord **G**;	3068
11:17	Therefore say, Thus saith the Lord **G**;	3068
11:21	upon their own heads, saith the Lord **G**.	3068
12:10	thou unto them, Thus saith the Lord **G**;	3068
12:19	the Lord **G**, of the inhabitants	3068
12:23	them therefore, Thus saith the Lord **G**;	3068
12:25	and will perform it, saith the Lord **G**.	3068
12:28	say unto them, Thus saith the Lord **G**;	3068
12:28	spoken shall be done, saith the Lord **G**.	3068
13: 3	Thus saith the Lord **G**; Woe unto	3068
13: 8	Therefore thus saith the Lord **G**;	3068
13: 8	I *am* against you, saith the Lord **G**.	3068
13: 9	and ye shall know that I *am* the Lord **G**.	3068
13:13	Therefore thus saith the Lord **G**; I will	3068
13:16	and *there* is no peace, saith the Lord **G**.	3068
13:18	say, Thus saith the Lord **G**; Woe to	3068
13:20	Wherefore thus saith the Lord **G**; Behold,	3068
14: 4	say unto them, Thus saith the Lord **G**;	3068
14: 6	house of Israel, Thus saith the Lord **G**;	3068
14:11	may be their God, saith the Lord **G**.	3068
14:14	by their righteousness, saith the Lord **G**.	3068
14:16	men *were* in it, *as* I live, saith the Lord **G**,	3068
14:18	men *were* in it, *as* I live, saith the Lord **G**,	3068
14:20	Job, *were* in it, *as* I live, saith the Lord **G**,	3068
14:21	thus saith the Lord **G**; How much more	3068
14:23	all that I have done in it, saith the Lord **G**.	3068
15: 6	Therefore thus saith the Lord **G**;	3068
15: 8	committed a trespass, saith the Lord **G**.	3068
16: 3	Thus saith the Lord **G** unto Jerusalem;	3068
16: 8	the Lord **G**, and thou becamest mine.	3068
16:14	I had put upon thee, saith the Lord **G**.	3068
16:19	and *thus* it was, saith the Lord **G**.	3068
16:23	(woe, woe unto thee! saith the Lord **G**;)	3068
16:30	weak *is* thine heart, saith the Lord **G**,	3068
16:36	Thus saith the Lord **G**; Because thy	3068
16:43	way upon *thine* head, saith the Lord **G**:	3068
16:48	*As* I live, saith the Lord **G**, Sodom thy	3068
16:59	For thus saith the Lord **G**; I will even deal	3068
16:63	all that thou hast done, saith the Lord **G**.	3068
17: 3	say, Thus saith the Lord **G**; A great eagle	3068
17: 9	Say thou, Thus saith the Lord **G**; Shall it	3068
17:16	*As* I live, saith the Lord **G**, surely in	3068
17:19	Therefore thus saith the Lord **G**; *As* I live,	3068
17:22	Thus saith the Lord **G**; I will also take of	3068

Eze		
18: 3	*As* I live, saith the Lord **G**, ye shall not	3068
18: 9	he shall surely live, saith the Lord **G**.	3068
18:23	saith the Lord **G**: *and* not that he should	3068
18:30	according to his ways, saith the Lord **G**.	3068
18:32	death of him that dieth, saith the Lord **G**:	3068
20: 3	say unto them, Thus saith the Lord **G**;	3068
20: 3	*As* I live, saith the Lord **G**, I will not be	3068
20: 5	say unto them, Thus saith the Lord **G**;	3068
20:27	say unto them, Thus saith the Lord **G**;	3068
20:30	house of Israel, Thus saith the Lord **G**;	3068
20:31	*As* I live, saith the Lord **G**, I will not be	3068
20:33	*As* I live, saith the Lord **G**, surely with a	3068
20:36	so will I plead with you, saith the Lord **G**.	3068
20:39	O house of Israel, thus saith the Lord **G**;	3068
20:40	saith the Lord **G**, there shall all the house	3068
20:44	O ye house of Israel, saith the Lord **G**.	3068
20:47	Thus saith the Lord **G**; Behold, I *will*	3068
21: 7	shall be brought to pass, saith the Lord **G**.	3068
21:13	it shall be no *more,* saith the Lord **G**.	3068
21:24	Therefore thus saith the Lord **G**;	3068
21:26	Thus saith the Lord **G**; Remove	3068
21:28	Thus saith the Lord **G** concerning	3068
22: 3	say thou, Thus saith the Lord **G**, The city	3068
22:12	and hast forgotten me, saith the Lord **G**.	3068
22:19	Therefore thus saith the Lord **G**;	3068
22:28	unto them, saying, Thus saith the Lord **G**,	3068
22:31	upon their heads, saith the Lord **G**.	3068
23:22	O Aholibah, Thus saith the Lord **G**;	3068
23:28	For thus saith the Lord **G**; Behold, I *will*	3068
23:32	Thus saith the Lord **G**; Thou shalt drink	3068
23:34	for I have spoken *it,* saith the Lord **G**.	3068
23:35	Therefore thus saith the Lord **G**;	3068
23:46	For thus saith the Lord **G**; *I will* bring up	3068
23:49	and ye shall know that I *am* the Lord **G**.	3068
24: 3	and say unto them, Thus saith the Lord **G**;	3068
24: 6	Wherefore thus saith the Lord **G**; Woe to	3068
24: 9	Therefore thus saith the Lord **G**; Woe to	3068
24:14	shall they judge thee, saith the Lord **G**.	3068
24:21	the house of Israel, Thus saith the Lord **G**;	3068
24:24	ye shall know that I *am* the Lord **G**.	3068
25: 3	Hear the word of the Lord **G**;	3068
25: 3	Thus saith the Lord **G**; Because thou	3068
25: 6	For thus saith the Lord **G**; Because thou	3068
25: 8	Thus saith the Lord **G**; Because that Moab	3068
25:12	Thus saith the Lord **G**; Because that Edom	3068
25:13	Therefore thus saith the Lord **G**; I will	3068
25:14	know my vengeance, saith the Lord **G**.	3068
25:15	Thus saith the Lord **G**; Because	3068
25:16	Therefore thus saith the Lord **G**; Behold,	3068
26: 3	for I have spoken *it,* saith the Lord **G**.	3068
26: 7	For thus saith the Lord **G**; Behold, I *will*	3068
26:14	Lᴏʀᴅ have spoken *it,* saith the Lord **G**.	3068
26:15	Thus saith the Lord **G** to Tyrus; Shall not	3068
26:19	For thus saith the Lord **G**; When I shall	3068
26:21	never be found again, saith the Lord **G**.	3068
27: 3	for many isles, Thus saith the Lord **G**;	3068
28: 2	prince of Tyrus, Thus saith the Lord **G**;	3068
28: 6	Therefore thus saith the Lord **G**;	3068
28:10	for I have spoken *it,* saith the Lord **G**.	3068
28:12	and say unto him, Thus saith the Lord **G**;	3068
28:22	say, Thus saith the Lord **G**; Behold, I *am*	3068
28:24	they shall know that I *am* the Lord **G**.	3068
28:25	Thus saith the Lord **G**; When I shall have	3068
29: 3	Speak, and say, Thus saith the Lord **G**;	3068
29: 8	Therefore thus saith the Lord **G**; Behold,	3068
29:13	Yet thus saith the Lord **G**; At the end of	3068
29:16	they shall know that I *am* the Lord **G**.	3068
29:19	Therefore thus saith the Lord **G**; Behold,	3068
29:20	they wrought for me, saith the Lord **G**.	3068
30: 2	prophesy and say, Thus saith the Lord **G**;	3068
30: 6	fall in it by the sword, saith the Lord **G**.	3068
30:10	Thus saith the Lord **G**; I will also make	3068
30:13	Thus saith the Lord **G**; I will also destroy	3068
30:22	Therefore thus saith the Lord **G**; Behold,	3068
31:10	Therefore thus saith the Lord **G**;	3068
31:15	Thus saith the Lord **G**; In the day when	3068
31:18	and all his multitude, saith the Lord **G**.	3068
32: 3	Thus saith the Lord **G**; I will therefore	3068
32: 8	darkness upon thy land, saith the Lord **G**.	3068
32:11	For thus saith the Lord **G**; The sword of	3068
32:14	rivers to run like oil, saith the Lord **G**.	3068
32:16	for all her multitude, saith the Lord **G**.	3068
32:31	army slain by the sword, saith the Lord **G**.	3068
32:32	and all his multitude, saith the Lord **G**.	3068
33:11	Say unto them, *As* I live, saith the Lord **G**,	3068
33:25	say unto them, Thus saith the Lord **G**;	3068
33:27	thus unto them, Thus saith the Lord **G**;	3068
34: 2	Thus saith the Lord **G** unto the shepherds	3068
34: 8	saith the Lord **G**, surely because my flock	3068
34:10	Thus saith the Lord **G**; Behold, I *am*	3068
34:11	For thus saith the Lord **G**; Behold,	3068
34:15	cause them to lie down, saith the Lord **G**.	3068
34:17	you, O my flock, saith the Lord **G**; Behold,	3068
34:20	Therefore thus saith the Lord **G** unto	3068
34:30	of Israel, *are* my people, saith the Lord **G**.	3068
34:31	*and* I *am* your God, saith the Lord **G**.	3068
35: 3	say unto it, Thus saith the Lord **G**; Behold,	3068
35: 6	Therefore, *as* I live, saith the Lord **G**,	3068
35:11	Therefore, *as* I live, saith the Lord **G**,	3068
35:14	Thus saith the Lord **G**; When the whole	3068
36: 2	Thus saith the Lord **G**; Because the enemy	3068
36: 3	and say, Thus saith the Lord **G**;	3068
36: 4	of Israel, hear the word of the Lord **G**;	3068

Eze	36: 4	Thus saith the Lord **G** to the mountains,	3068
	36: 5	Therefore thus saith the Lord **G**; Surely in	3068
	36: 6	and to the valleys, Thus saith the Lord **G**;	3068
	36: 7	Therefore thus saith the Lord **G**; I have	3068
	36:13	thy nations any more, saith the Lord **G**.	3068
	36:14	nations to fall any more, saith the Lord **G**.	3068
	36:15	nations to fall any more, saith the Lord **G**.	3068
	36:22	house of Israel, Thus saith the Lord **G**;	3068
	36:23	that I *am* the Lord, saith the Lord **G**,	3068
	36:32	for your sakes do I *this*, saith the Lord **G**,	3068
	36:33	Thus saith the Lord **G**; In the day that I	3068
	36:37	Thus saith the Lord **G**; I will yet *for* this	3068
	37: 3	And I answered, O Lord **G**, thou knowest.	3068
	37: 5	say to the wind, Thus saith the Lord **G**;	3068
	37: 9	say to the wind, Thus saith the Lord **G**;	3068
	37:12	say unto them, Thus saith the Lord **G**,	3068
	37:19	Say unto them, Thus saith the Lord **G**;	3068
	37:21	say unto them, Thus saith the Lord **G**;	3068
	38: 3	say, Thus saith the Lord **G**; Behold, I *am*	3068
	38:10	Thus saith the Lord **G**; It shall also come	3068
	38:14	and say unto Gog, Thus saith the Lord **G**;	3068
	38:17	Thus saith the Lord **G**; *Art* thou he of	3068
	38:18	saith the Lord **G**, *that* my fury shall come	3068
	38:21	all my mountains, saith the Lord **G**:	3068
	39: 1	and say, Thus saith the Lord **G**;	3068
	39: 5	for I have spoken *it*, saith the Lord **G**.	3068
	39: 8	is come, and it is done, saith the Lord **G**.	3068
	39:10	those that robbed them, saith the Lord **G**.	3068
	39:13	that I shall be glorified, saith the Lord **G**;	3068
	39:17	son of man, thus saith the Lord **G**;	3068
	39:20	*with* all men of war, saith the Lord **G**.	3068
	39:25	Therefore thus saith the Lord **G**; Now will	3068
	39:29	upon the house of Israel, saith the Lord **G**.	3068
	43:18	Son of man, thus saith the Lord **G**;	3068
	43:19	to minister unto me, saith the Lord **G**,	3068
	43:27	and I will accept you, saith the Lord **G**.	3068
	44: 6	house of Israel, Thus saith the Lord **G**;	3068
	44: 9	Thus saith the Lord **G**; No stranger,	3068
	44:12	saith the Lord **G**, and they shall bear their	3068
	44:15	the fat and the blood, saith the Lord **G**:	3068
	44:27	offer his sin offering, saith the Lord **G**.	3068
	45: 9	Thus saith the Lord **G**; Let it suffice you,	3068
	45: 9	from my people, saith the Lord **G**.	3068
	45:15	reconciliation for them, saith the Lord **G**.	3068
	45:18	Thus saith the Lord **G**; In the first *month*,	3068
	46: 1	Thus saith the Lord **G**; The gate of	3068
	46:16	Thus saith the Lord **G**; If the prince give a	3068
	47:13	Thus saith the Lord **G**; This *shall be*	3068
	47:23	*him* his inheritance, saith the Lord **G**.	3068
	48:29	these *are* their portions, saith the Lord **G**.	3068
Am	1: 8	Philistines shall perish, saith the Lord **G**.	3068
	3: 7	Surely the Lord **G** will do nothing, but he	3068
	3: 8	the Lord **G** hath spoken, who can but	3068
	3:11	Therefore thus saith the Lord **G**;	3068
	3:13	saith the Lord **G**, the God of hosts,	3068
	4: 2	The Lord **G** hath sworn by his holiness,	3068
	4: 5	O ye children of Israel, saith the Lord **G**.	3068
	5: 3	For thus saith the Lord **G**; The city that	3068
	6: 8	The Lord **G** hath sworn by himself, saith	3068
	7: 1	Thus hath the Lord **G** shewed unto me;	3068
	7: 2	I said, O Lord **G**, forgive, I beseech thee:	3068
	7: 4	Thus hath the Lord **G** shewed unto me:	3068
	7: 4	the Lord **G** called to contend by fire,	3068
	7: 5	said I, O Lord **G**, cease, I beseech thee:	3068
	7: 6	This also shall not be, saith the Lord **G**.	3068
	8: 1	Thus hath the Lord **G** shewed unto me:	3068
	8: 3	be howlings in that day, saith the Lord **G**:	3068
	8: 9	to pass in that day, saith the Lord **G**,	3068
	8:11	Behold, the days come, saith the Lord **G**,	3068
	9: 5	the Lord **G** of hosts *is* he that toucheth	3068
	9: 8	the eyes of the Lord **G** *are* upon the sinful	3068
Ob	1: 1	Thus saith the Lord **G** concerning Edom,	3068
Mic	1: 2	let the Lord **G** be witness against you,	3068
Hab	3:19	The Lord **G** *is* my strength, and he will	3068
Zep	1: 7	thy peace at the presence of the Lord **G**:	3068
Zec	9:14	the Lord **G** shall blow the trumpet,	3068

GOD'S (26) [GOD]

Ge	28:22	I have set *for* a pillar, shall be **G** house.	430
	30: 2	said, *Am* I in **G** stead, who hath withheld	430
	32: 2	Jacob saw them, he said, This *is* **G** host:	430
Nu	22:22	**G** anger was kindled because he went:	430
Dt	1:17	of the face of man; for the judgment *is* **G**:	430
2Ch	20:15	for the battle *is* not yours, but **G**.	430+3807.1
Ne	10:29	a curse, and into an oath, to walk in **G** law,	430
Job	33: 6	I *am* according to thy wish in **G** stead:	410
	35: 2	My righteousness *is* more than **G**?	410
	36: 2	thee that *I* have yet to speak on **G** behalf.	433
Mt	5:34	neither by heaven; for it is **G** throne:	2316
	22:21	and unto God the *things* that are **G**.	2316
Mk	12:17	and to God the *things* that are **G**.	2316
Lk	18:29	or children, for the kingdom of **G** sake,	2316
	20:25	and unto God the *things* which be **G**.	2316
Jn	8:47	He that is of God heareth **G** words:	2316
Ac	23: 4	stood by said, Revilest thou **G** high priest?	2316
Ro	8:33	Who shall lay any thing to the charge of **G**	2316
	10: 3	they being ignorant of **G** righteousness,	2316
	13: 6	for they are **G** ministers,	2316
1Co	3: 9	are **G** husbandry, *ye are* God's building.	2316
	3: 9	are God's husbandry, *ye are* **G** building.	2316
	3:23	And ye *are* Christ's; and Christ *is* **G**.	2316
	6:20	body, and in your spirit, which are **G**.	2316
Tit	1: 1	according to the faith of **G** elect,	2316
1Pe	5: 3	Neither as being lords over **G** heritage,	NIG

GODDESS (5) [GOD]

1Ki	11: 5	For Solomon went after Ashtoreth the **g** of	430
	11:33	have worshipped Ashtoreth the **g** of	430
Ac	19:27	also that the temple of the great **g** Diana	2299
	19:35	is a worshipper of the great **g** Diana,	2299
	19:37	churches, nor yet blasphemers of your **g**.	2299

GODHEAD (3) [GOD]

Ac	17:29	we ought not to think that the **G** is like	2304
Ro	1:20	are made, *even* his eternal power and **G**;	2305
Col	2: 9	in him dwelleth all the fulness of the **G**	2320

GODLINESS (15) [GOD]

1Ti	2: 2	and peaceable life in all **g** and honesty.	2150
	2:10	(which becometh women professing **g**)	2317
	3:16	controversy great is the mystery of **g**:	2150
	4: 7	and exercise thyself *rather* unto **g**.	2150
	4: 8	**g** is profitable unto all *things*, having	2150
	6: 3	to the doctrine which is according to **g**;	2150
	6: 5	of the truth, supposing that gain is **g**:	2150
	6: 6	But **g** with contentment is great gain.	2150
	6:11	**g**, faith, love, patience, meekness.	2150
2Ti	3: 5	Having a form of **g**, but denying the power	2150
Tit	1: 1	of the truth which is after **g**,	2150
2Pe	1: 3	all *things* that *pertain* unto life and **g**,	2150
	1: 6	to temperance patience; and to patience **g**;	2150
	1: 7	And to **g** brotherly kindness;	2150
	3:11	ye to be in all holy conversation and **g**,	2150

GODLY (15) [GOD]

Ps	4: 3	hath set apart *him* that is **g** for himself:	2623
	12: 1	Help, Lord; for the **g** man ceaseth;	2623
	32: 6	For this shall every one *that is* **g** pray unto	2623
Mal	2:15	That he might seek a **g** seed. Therefore	2316
2Co	1:12	that in simplicity and **g** sincerity, not with	2316
	7: 9	for ye were made sorry after a **g** manner,	2316
	7:10	For **g** sorrow worketh repentance	2316+2596
	7:11	thing, that ye sorrowed after a **g** sort,	2316
	11: 2	For I am jealous over you with **g** jealousy:	2316
1Ti	1: 4	rather than **g** edifying which is in faith:	2316
2Ti	3:12	all that will live **g** in Christ Jesus shall	2153
Tit	2:12	and **g**, in *this* present world;	2153
Heb	12:28	God acceptably with reverence and **g** fear:	2124
2Pe	2: 9	The Lord knoweth *how* to deliver the **g**	2152
3Jn	1: 6	forward on their journey after a **g** sort,	2316

GODS (244) [GOD]

Ge	3: 5	ye shall be as **g**, knowing good and evil.	430
	31:30	*yet* wherefore hast thou stolen my **g**?	430
	31:32	With whomsoever thou findest thy **g**,	430
	35: 2	Put away the strange *gods* that *are* among you,	430
	35: 4	they gave unto Jacob all the strange **g**	430
Ex	12:12	against all the **g** of Egypt I will execute	430
	15:11	*is* like unto thee, O Lord, among the **g**?	410
	18:11	I know that the Lord *is* greater than all **g**:	430
	20: 3	Thou shalt have no other **g** before me.	430
	20:23	Ye shall not make with me **g** of silver,	430
	20:23	neither shall ye make unto you **g** of gold.	430
	22:28	Thou shalt not revile the **g**, nor curse	430
	23:13	make no mention of the name of other **g**,	430
	23:24	Thou shalt not bow down to their **g**,	430
	23:32	no covenant with them, nor with their **g**.	430
	23:33	for if thou serve their **g**, it will surely be a	430
	32: 1	unto him, Up, make us **g**, which shall go	430
	32: 4	they said, These *be* thy **g**, O Israel,	430
	32: 8	and said, These *be* thy **g**, O Israel,	430
	32:23	For they said unto me, Make us **g**,	430
	32:31	a great sin, and have made them **g** of gold.	430
	34:15	they go a whoring after their **g**,	430
	34:15	do sacrifice unto their **g**, and *one* call thee,	430
	34:16	their daughters go a whoring after their **g**,	430
	34:16	make thy sons go a whoring after their **g**.	430
	34:17	Thou shalt make thee no molten **g**.	430
Lev	19: 4	idols, nor make to yourselves molten **g**:	430
Nu	25: 2	the people unto the sacrifices of their **g**:	430
	25: 2	people did eat, and bowed down to their **g**.	430
	33: 4	upon their **g** also the Lord executed	430
Dt	4:28	there ye shall serve **g**, the work of men's	430
	5: 7	Thou shalt have none other **g** before me.	430
	6:14	Ye shall not go after other **g**, of the gods of	430
	6:14	of the **g** of the people which *are* round	430
	7: 4	following me, that they may serve other **g**;	430
	7:16	neither shalt thou serve their **g**; for that	430
	7:25	The graven images of their **g** shall ye burn	430
	8:19	walk after other **g**, and serve them,	430
	10:17	For the Lord your God *is* God of **g**,	430
	11:16	and serve other **g**, and worship them;	430
	11:28	to go after other **g**, which ye have not	430
	12: 2	which ye shall possess served their **g**,	430
	12: 3	hew down the graven images of their **g**,	430
	12:30	that thou inquire not after their **g**, saying,	430
	12:30	How did these nations serve their **g**?	430
	12:31	he hateth, have they done unto their **g**;	430
	12:31	they have burnt in the fire to their **g**.	430
	13: 2	saying, Let us go after other **g**, which thou	430
	13: 6	saying, Let us go and serve other **g**,	430
	13: 7	*Namely*, of the **g** of the people which *are*	430
	13:13	saying, Let us go and serve other **g**, which	430
	17: 3	hath gone and served other **g**,	430
	18:20	or that shall speak in the name of other **g**,	430
	20:18	which they have done unto their **g**;	430
	28:14	the left, to go after other **g** to serve them.	430
	28:36	there shalt thou serve other **g**, wood and	430
	28:64	there thou shalt serve other **g**, which	430
	29:18	to go *and* serve the **g** of these nations;	430

Dt	29:26	For they went and served other **g**,	430
	29:26	**g** whom they knew not, and *whom* he had	430
	30:17	and worship other **g**, and serve them;	430
	31:16	go a whoring after the **g** of the strangers of	430
	31:18	in that they are turned unto other **g**.	430
	31:20	they turn unto other **g**, and serve them,	430
	32:16	**g**, with abominations provoked him to	NIH
	32:17	*to* **g** whom they knew not, *to* new *gods*	NIH
	32:17	knew not, *to* new **g** *that* came newly up,	NIH
	32:37	shall say, Where *are* their **g**, *their* rock in	430
Jos	22:22	The Lord God of **g**, the Lord God of	430
	22:22	the Lord God of **g**, he knoweth,	430
	23: 7	make mention of the name of their **g**,	430
	23:16	have gone and served other **g**,	430
	24: 2	father of Nachor: and they served other **g**.	430
	24:14	put away the **g** which your fathers served	430
	24:15	whether the **g** which your fathers served	430
	24:15	or the **g** of the Amorites, in whose land ye	430
	24:16	should forsake the Lord, to serve other **g**;	430
	24:20	serve strange **g**, then he will turn and do	430
	24:23	the strange **g** which *are* among you,	430
Jdg	2: 3	and their **g** shall be a snare unto you.	430
	2:12	of the land of Egypt, and followed other **g**,	430
	2:12	of the **g** of the people that *were* round	430
	2:17	they went a whoring after other **g**,	430
	2:19	in following other **g** to serve them,	430
	3: 6	daughters to their sons, and served their **g**.	430
	5: 8	They chose new **g**; then *was* war in	430
	6:10	fear not the **g** of the Amorites, in whose	430
	10: 6	the **g** of Syria, and the gods of Zidon,	430
	10: 6	the **g** of Zidon, and the gods of Moab,	430
	10: 6	the **g** of Moab, and the gods of the children	430
	10: 6	the **g** of the children of Ammon,	430
	10: 6	the **g** of the Philistines, and forsook	430
	10:13	ye have forsaken me, and served other **g**:	430
	10:14	and cry unto the **g** which ye have chosen;	430
	10:16	they put away the strange **g** from among	430
	17: 5	the man Micah had a house of **g**,	430
	18:24	Ye have taken away my **g** which I made,	430
	18:24	gone back unto her people, and unto her **g**:	430
Ru	1:15	gone back unto her people, and unto her **g**:	430
1Sa	4: 8	these *are* the **G** that smote the Egyptians	430
	6: 5	from off your **g**, and from off your land.	430
	7: 3	*then* put away the strange **g** and Ashtaroth	430
	8: 8	served other **g**, so do they also unto thee.	430
	17:43	And the Philistine cursed David by his **g**.	430
	26:19	of the Lord, saying, Go, serve other **g**.	430
	28:13	Saul, I saw **g** ascending out of the earth.	430
2Sa	7:23	from Egypt, *from* the nations and their **g**?	430
1Ki	9: 6	go and serve other **g**, and worship them:	430
	9: 9	have taken hold upon other **g**,	430
	11: 2	will turn away your heart after their **g**:	430
	11: 4	wives turned away his heart after other **g**:	430
	11: 8	burnt incense and sacrificed unto their **g**.	430
	11:10	thing, that *he* should not go after other **g**:	430
	12:28	behold thy **g**, O Israel, which brought thee	430
	14: 9	for thou hast gone and made thee other **g**,	430
	18:24	call ye on the name of your **g**, and I will	430
	18:25	call on the name of your **g**, but put no fire	430
	19: 2	So let the **g** do *to* me, and more also,	430
	20:10	said, The **g** do so unto me, and more also,	430
	20:23	said unto him, Their **g** *are* gods of the hills;	430
	20:23	said unto him, Their **g** *are* gods of the hills;	430
2Ki	5:17	burnt offering nor sacrifice unto other **g**,	430
	17: 7	king of Egypt, and had feared other **g**,	430
	17:29	Howbeit every nation made **g** of their own,	430
	17:31	and Anammelech, the **g** of Sepharvaim.	430
	17:33	feared the Lord, and served their own **g**,	430
	17:35	saying, Ye shall not fear other **g**,	430
	17:37	for evermore; and ye shall not fear other **g**,	430
	17:38	not forget; neither shall ye fear other **g**.	430
	18:33	Hath any of the **g** of the nations delivered	430
	18:34	Where *are* the **g** of Hamath, and of Arpad?	430
	18:34	where *are* the **g** of Sepharvaim, Hena,	430
	18:35	Who *are* they among all the **g** of	430
	19:12	Have the **g** of the nations delivered them	430
	19:18	have cast their **g** into the fire: for they	430
	19:18	for they *were* no **g**, but the work of men's	430
	22:17	and have burnt incense unto other **g**,	430
1Ch	5:25	went a whoring after the **g** of the people	430
	10:10	they put his armour *in* the house of their **g**,	430
	14:12	when they had left their **g** there, David	430
	16:25	he also *is* to be feared above all **g**.	430
	16:26	For all the **g** of the people *are* idols:	430
2Ch	2: 5	is great: for great *is* our God above all **g**.	430
	7:19	shall go and serve other **g**,	430
	7:22	laid hold on other **g**, and worshipped them,	430
	13: 8	which Jeroboam made you for **g**.	430
	13: 9	may be a priest of *them that are* no **g**.	430
	14: 3	he took away the altars of the strange *g*,	NIH
	25:14	he brought the **g** of the children of Seir,	430
	25:14	set them up to be his **g**, and bowed down	430
	25:15	Why hast thou sought after the **g** of	430
	25:20	because they sought after the **g** of Edom.	430
	28:23	For he sacrificed unto the **g** of Damascus,	430
	28:23	Because the **g** of the kings of Syria help	430
	28:25	high places to burn incense unto other **g**,	430
	32:13	were the **g** of the nations of *those* lands	430
	32:14	Who *was* there among all the **g** of those	430
	32:17	As the **g** of the nations of *other* lands have	430
	32:19	as against the **g** of the people of the earth,	430
	33:15	took away the strange **g**, and the idol out	430
	34:25	and have burned incense unto other **g**,	430
Ezr	1: 7	and had put them in the house of his **g**;	430
Ps	82: 1	of the mighty; he judgeth among the **g**.	430

G (sidebar tab)

G

Ps
82: 6 I have said, Ye are **g**; and all of you are 430
86: 8 Among the **g** there is none like unto thee, 430
95: 3 is a great God, and a great King above all **g**. 430
96: 4 to be praised: he is to be feared above all **g**. 430
96: 5 For all the **g** of the nations are idols: 430
97: 7 themselves of idols: worship him, all ye **g**. 430
97: 9 the earth: thou art exalted far above all **g**. 430
135: 5 is great, and that our Lord is above all **g**. 430
136: 2 O give thanks unto the God of **g**: for his 430
138: 1 before the **g** will I sing praise unto thee. 430
Isa 21: 9 the graven images of her **g** he hath broken 430
36:18 Hath any of the **g** of the nations delivered 430
36:19 Where are the **g** of Hamath and Arphad? 430
36:19 where are the **g** of Sepharvaim? and have 430
36:20 Who are they amongst all the **g** of these 430
37:12 Have the **g** of the nations delivered them 430
37:19 have cast their **g** into the fire: for they 430
37:19 for they were no **g**, but the work of men's 430
41:23 that we may know that ye are **g**. 430
42:17 say to the molten images, Ye are our **g**. 430
Jer 1:16 have burnt incense unto other **g**, 430
2:11 Hath a nation changed their **g**, which are 430
2:11 changed their gods, which are yet no **g**? 430
2:28 where are thy **g** that thou hast made thee? 430
2:28 to the number of thy cities are thy **g**, 430
5: 7 and sworn by them that are no **g**: 430
5:19 served strange **g** in your land, so shall ye 430
7: 6 neither walk after other **g** to your hurt: 430
7: 9 and walk after other **g** whom ye know not; 430
7:18 to pour out drink offerings unto other **g**, 430
10:11 The **g** that have not made the heavens and 426
11:10 and they went after other **g** to serve them: 430
11:12 unto the **g** unto whom they offer incense: 430
11:13 to the number of thy cities were thy **g**, 430
13:10 walk after other **g**, to serve them, 430
16:11 have walked after other **g**, and have served 430
16:13 there shall ye serve other **g** day and night; 430
16:20 Shall a man make gods unto himself, 430
16:20 gods unto himself, and they are no **g**? 430
19: 4 and have burnt incense in it unto other **g**, 430
19:13 poured out drink offerings unto other **g**. 430
22: 9 and worshipped other **g**, and served them. 430
25: 6 go not after other **g** to serve them, 430
32:29 poured out drink offerings unto other **g**, 430
35:15 go not after other **g** to serve them, 430
43:12 I will kindle a fire in the houses of the **g** of 430
43:13 the houses of the **g** of the Egyptians shall 430
44: 3 to serve other **g**, whom they knew not, 430
44: 5 to burn no incense unto other **g**, 430
44: 8 burning incense unto other **g** in the land 430
44:15 wives had burnt incense unto other **g**, 430
46:25 and Egypt, with their **g**, and their kings; 430
48:35 and him that burneth incense to his **g**. 430
Da 2:11 except the **g**, whose dwelling is not with 426
2:47 a truth it is, that your God is a God of **g**, 426
3:12 serve not thy **g**, nor worship the golden 426
3:14 and Abed-nego, do not ye serve my **g**, 426
3:18 O king, that we will not serve thy **g**, 426
4: 8 and in whom is the spirit of the holy **g**: 426
4: 9 know that the spirit of the holy **g** is in thee, 426
4:18 able; for the spirit of the holy **g** is in thee. 426
5: 4 praised the **g** of gold, and of silver, of brass, 426
5:11 in whom is the spirit of the holy **g**; 426
5:11 and wisdom, like the wisdom of the **g**, 426
5:14 that the spirit of the **g** is in thee, 426
5:23 thou hast praised the **g** of silver, and gold, 426
11: 8 shall also carry captives into Egypt their **g**, 430
11:36 marvellous things against the God of **g**, 410
Hos 3: 1 who look to other **g**, and love flagons of 430
14: 3 to the work of our hands, Ye are our **g**: 430
Na 1:14 out of the house of thy **g** will I cut off 430
Zep 2:11 for he will famish all the **g** of the earth: 430
Jn 10:34 it not written in your law, I said, Ye are **g**? 2316
10:35 If he called them **g**, unto whom the word 2316
Ac 7:40 unto Aaron, Make us **g** to go before us: 2316
14:11 The **g** are come down to us in the likeness 2316
17:18 seemeth to be a setter forth of strange **g**: 1140
19:26 much people, saying that they be no **g**, 2316
1Co 8: 5 For though there be that are called **g**, 2316
8: 5 (as there be **g** many, and lords many,) 2316
Gal 4: 8 unto them which by nature are no **g**. 2316

GOD-WARD (3) [GOD]
Ex 18:19 be thou for the people to **G**, 430+4136+1886.1
2Co 3: 4 such trust have we through Christ to **G**: 2316
1Th 1: 8 in every place your faith to **G** is spread 2316

GOEST (46) [GO]
Ge 10:19 as thou **g** unto Sodom, and Gomorrah, 935
10:30 as thou **g** unto Sephar, a mount of the east. 935
25:18 is before Egypt, as thou **g** towards Assyria. 935
28:15 keep thee in all places whither thou **g**, 1980
32:17 whither thou? and whose are these 1980
Ex 4:21 When thou **g** to return into Egypt, 935
33:16 is it not in that thou **g** with us? so shall 1980
34:12 the inhabitants of the land whither thou **g**, 935
Nu 14:14 that thou **g** before them, by day time in a 1980
Dt 7: 1 into the land whither thou **g** to possess it, 935
11:10 the land, whither thou **g** in to possess it, 935
11:29 unto the land whither thou **g** to possess it, 935
12:29 whither thou **g** to possess them, 935
20: 1 When thou **g** out to battle against thine 3318
21:10 When thou **g** forth to war against thine 3318
23:20 to in the land whither thou **g**. 935
28: 6 blessed shalt thou be when thou **g** out. 3318

Dt 28:19 cursed shalt thou be when thou **g** out. 3318
28:21 off the land, whither thou **g** to possess it. 935
28:63 off the land whither thou **g** to possess it. 935
30:16 in the land whither thou **g** to possess it. 935
32:50 die in the mount whither thou **g** up, 5927
Jos 1: 7 mayest prosper whithersoever thou **g**. 1980
1: 9 God is with thee whithersoever thou **g**. 1980
Jdg 14: 3 that thou **g** to take a wife 1980
19:17 the old man said, Whither **g** thou? 1980
Ru 1:16 for whither thou **g**, I will go; 1980
1Sa 27: 8 inhabitants of the land as thou **g** to Shur, 935
28:22 have strength, when thou **g** on thy way. 1980
2Sa 15:19 Gittite, Wherefore **g** thou also with us? 1980
1Ki 2:37 on the day thou **g** out, and passest over 3318
2:42 on the day thou **g** out, and walkest 3318
Ps 44: 9 shame; and **g** not forth with our armies. 3318
Pr 4:12 When thou **g** thy steps shall not be 1980
6:22 When thou **g**, it shall lead thee; when 1980
Ecc 5: 1 Keep thy foot when thou **g** to the house 1980
9:10 wisdom, in the grave, whither thou **g**. 1980
Jer 45: 5 for a prey in all places whither thou **g**. 1980
Zec 2: 2 said I, Whither **g** thou? And he said unto 1980
Mt 8:19 I will follow thee whithersoever thou **g**. 565
Lk 9:57 I will follow thee whithersoever thou **g**. 565
12:58 When thou **g** with thine adversary to 5217
Jn 11: 8 to stone thee; and **g** thou thither again? 5217
13:36 said unto him, Lord, whither **g** thou? 5217
14: 5 Lord, we know not whither thou **g**; 5217
16: 5 none of you asketh me, Whither **g** thou? 5217

GOETH (135) [GO]
Ge 2:14 that is it which **g** toward the east of 1980
32:20 I will appease him with the present that **g** 1980
33:14 according as the cattle that **g** before me 7272
38:13 Behold thy father in law **g** up to Timnah 5927
Ex 7:15 go out unto the water; and thou shalt 3318
22:26 it unto him by that the sun **g** down: 935
28:29 when he **g** in unto the holy place, for a 935
28:30 when he **g** in before the LORD: 935
28:35 sound shall be heard when he **g** in unto 935
Lev 11:21 flying creeping thing that **g** upon all four, 1980
11:27 whatsoever **g** upon his paws, among all 1980
11:42 Whatsoever **g** upon the belly, 1980
11:42 whatsoever **g** upon all four, 1980
14:46 Moreover he that **g** into the house all 935
15:32 of him whose seed **g** from him, and is 3318
16:17 **g** in to make an atonement in the holy 935
22: 3 that **g** unto the holy things which 7126
22: 4 dead, or a man whose seed **g** from him; 3318
27:21 the field, when it **g** out in the jubile, 3318
Nu 5:29 when a wife **g** aside to another instead 7847
21:15 the stream of the brooks that **g** down to 5186
Dt 1:30 The LORD your God which **g** before you, 1980
9: 3 the LORD thy God is he which **g** over 5674
11:30 by the way where the sun **g** down, 3996
19: 5 As when a man **g** into the wood with his 935
20: 4 For the LORD your God is he that **g** with 1980
23: 9 When the host **g** forth against thine 3318
24:13 the pledge again when the sun **g** down, 935
Jos 10:10 chased them along the way that **g** up to 4608
11:17 from the mount Halak, that **g** up to Seir, 5927
12: 7 unto the mount Halak, that **g** up to Seir; 5927
16: 1 to the wilderness that **g** up from Jericho 5927
16: 2 **g** out from Beth-el to Luz, 3318
16: 3 **g** down westward to the coast of Japhleti, 3318
19:12 then **g** up to Daberath, and goeth up to 3318
19:12 goeth out to Daberath, and **g** up to Japhia, 5927
19:13 and **g** out to Remmon-methoar to Neah; 3318
19:27 and **g** out to Cabul on the left hand, 3318
19:34 **g** out from thence to Hukkok, 3318
Jdg 5:31 as the sun when he **g** forth in his might. 3318
20:31 which one **g** up to the house of God, 5927
21:19 on the east side of the highway that **g** up 5927
1Sa 5:18 that when my master **g** into the house of 935
11: 8 be ye with the king as he **g** out and as he 3318
12:20 house of Millo, which **g** down to Silla. 3381
2Ki 23: 7 when he cometh, and when he **g** out. 3318
Ezr 7: 8 this work **g** fast on, and prospereth in 5648
Job 7: 9 that **g** down to the grave shall come up 3381
9:11 Lo, he **g** by me, and I see him not: 5674
34: 8 Which **g** in company with the workers of 732
37: 2 and the sound that **g** out of his mouth. 3318
39:21 He **g** on to meet the armed men. 3318
41:20 Out of his nostrils **g** smoke, as out of a 3318
41:21 and a flame **g** out of his mouth. 3318
Ps 17: 1 my prayer, that **g** not out of feigned lips. NIH
41: 6 to itself; when he **g** abroad, he telleth it. 1980
68:21 hairy scalp of such a one as **g** on still in 1980
88:16 Thy fierce wrath **g** over me; thy terrors 5674
97: 3 A fire **g** before him, and burneth up his 1980
104:23 Man **g** forth unto his work and to his 3318
126: 6 He that **g** forth and weepeth, 1980+3318
146: 4 breath **g** forth, he returneth to his earth; 3318
Pr 6:29 So he that **g** in to his neighbour's wife; 935
7:22 He **g** after her straightway, as an ox goeth 1980
7:22 as an ox **g** to the slaughter, or as a fool to 935
11:10 When it **g** well with the righteous, 2898
16:18 Pride **g** before destruction, and a haughty NIH
16:19 he that **g** about as a talebearer revealeth 1980
26: 9 As a thorn **g** up into the hand of a 5927
26:20 Where no wood is, there the fire **g** out: 3518
31:18 is good: her candle **g** not out by night. 3518

Ecc
1: 5 the sun **g** down, and hasteth to his place 935
1: 6 The wind **g** toward the south, 1980
3:21 Who knoweth the spirit of man that **g** 5927
3:21 the spirit of the beast that **g** downward to 3381
12: 5 because man **g** to his long home, 1980
SS 7: for my beloved, that **g** down sweetly, 1980
Isa 28:19 From the time that it **g** forth it shall take 5674
30:29 as when one **g** with a pipe to come into 1980
55:11 So shall my word be that **g** forth out of 3318
59: 8 therein shall not know peace. 1869
63:14 As a beast **g** down into the valley, 3381
Jer 5: 6 every one that **g** out thence shall be torn 3318
6: 4 for the day **g** away, for the shadows of 6437
21: 9 that **g** out, and falleth to the Chaldeans 3318
22:10 weep sore for him that **g** away: for he 1980
30:23 the whirlwind of the LORD **g** forth with 3318
38: 2 that **g** forth to the Chaldeans shall live; 3318
44:17 thing **g** forth out of our own mouth, 3318
49:17 every one that **g** by it shall be astonished, 5674
50:13 every one that **g** by Babylon shall be 5674
Eze 7:14 make all ready; but none **g** to the battle: 1980
33:31 but their heart **g** after their covetousness. 1980
40:40 as one **g** up to the entry of the north gate, 5927
42: 9 as one **g** into them from the utter court. 935
44:27 in the day that he **g** into the sanctuary, 935
48: 1 as one **g** to Hamath, Hazar-enan, 935
Hos 6: 4 and as the early dew it **g** away. 1980
6: 5 judgments are as the light that **g** forth. 3318
Zec 5: 3 This is the curse that **g** forth over the 3318
5: 5 eyes, and see what is this that **g** forth. 3318
5: 6 he said, This is an ephah that **g** forth. 3318
Mt 8: 9 and I say to this man, Go, and he **g**; 4198
12:45 Then **g** he, and taketh with himself seven 4198
13:44 for joy thereof **g** and selleth all that he 5217
15:11 Not that which **g** into the mouth 1525
15:17 whatsoever entereth in at the mouth **g** 5562
17:21 this kind **g** not out but by prayer 1607
18:12 and **g** into the mountains, and seeketh 4198
26:24 The Son of man **g** as it is written of him: 5217
28: 7 behold, he **g** before you into Galilee; 4254
Mk 3:13 And he **g** up into a mountain, 305
7:19 into the belly, and **g** out into the draught, 1607
14:21 The Son of man indeed **g**, as it is written 5217
14:45 straightway to him, and saith, Master, 4334
16: 7 Peter that he **g** before you into Galilee; 4254
Lk 7: 8 and I say unto one, Go, and he **g**; 4198
11:26 Then **g** he, and taketh to him seven other 4198
22:22 And truly the Son of man **g**, as it was 4198
Jn 3: 8 tell whence it cometh, and whither it **g**: 5217
7:20 hast a devil: who **g** about to kill thee? 2212
10: 4 he **g** before them, and the sheep follow 4198
11:31 She **g** unto the grave to weep there. 5217
12:35 in darkness knoweth not whither he **g**. 5217
Ac 8:26 that **g** down from Jerusalem unto Gaza, 2597
1Co 6: 6 But brother **g** to law with brother, 2919
9: 7 Who **g** a warfare any time at his own 4754
Jas 1:24 and **g** his way, and straightway forgetteth 565
1Jn 2:11 and knoweth not whither he **g**, because 5217
Rev 14: 4 follow the Lamb whithersoever he **g**. 5217
17:11 and is of the seven, and **g** into perdition, 5217
19:15 And out of his mouth **g** a sharp sword, 1607

GOG (11) [HAMON-GOG]
1Ch 5: 4 his son, **G** his son, Shimei his son, 1463
Eze 38: 2 Son of man, set thy face against **G**, 1463
38: 3 Behold, I am against thee, O **G**, the chief 1463
38:14 son of man, prophesy and say unto **G**, 1463
38:16 sanctified in thee, O **G**, before their eyes. 1463
38:18 **G** shall come against the land of Israel, 1463
39: 1 son of man, prophesy against **G**, and say, 1463
39: 1 Behold, I am against thee, O **G**, the chief 1463
39:11 that I will give unto **G** a place there of 1463
39:11 there shall they bury **G** and all his 1463
Rev 20: 8 **G** and Magog, to gather them together to 1136

GOING (92) [GO]
Ge 15: 9 on still toward the south. 1980
15:12 when the sun was **g** down, a deep sleep 935
37:25 and myrrh, **g** to carry it down to Egypt. 1980
Ex 17:12 his hands were steady until the **g** down of 935
23: 4 meet thine enemy's ox or his ass **g** astray, 8582
37:18 six branches **g** out of the sides thereof; 3318
37:19 throughout the six branches **g** out of 3318
37:21 according to the six branches **g** out of it. 3318
Lev 11:20 All fowls that creep, **g** upon all four, 1980
Nu 32: 7 **g** over into the land which the LORD hath 5674
34: 4 the **g** forth thereof shall be from the 8444
Dt 16: 6 at the **g** down of the sun, at the season 935
33:18 he said, Rejoice, Zebulun, in thy **g** out; 3318
Jos 1: 4 unto the great sea toward the **g** down of 3996
6: 9 the priests **g** on, and blowing with 1980
6:11 compassed the city, **g** about it once: 5362
6:13 the priests **g** on, and blowing with 1980
7: 5 and smote them in the **g** down: 4174
10:11 and were in the **g** down to Beth-horon, 4174
10:27 came to pass at the time of the **g** down of 935
15: 7 that is before the **g** up to Adummim, 4608
18:17 which is over against the **g** up of 4608
23:14 this day I am **g** the way of all the earth: 1980
Jdg 1:36 Amorites was from the **g** up to Akrabbim, 4608
19:18 I am now **g** to the house of the LORD; 1980
19:28 he said unto her, Up, and let us be **g**. 1980
1Sa 9:11 they found young maidens **g** out to draw 3318
9:27 And as they were **g** down to the end of 3381
10: 3 shall meet thee three men **g** up to God 5927

1Sa	17:20 as the host was **g** forth to the fight,	3318
	29: 6 thy **g out** and thy coming in with me	3318
2Sa	2:19 in **g** he turned not to the right hand nor	1980
	3:25 to know thy **g out** and thy coming in,	4161
	5:24 when thou hearest the sound of a **g** in	6807
1Ki	17:11 as she was **g** to fetch *it*, he called to her,	1980
	22:36 the host about the **g down** of the sun,	935
2Ki	2:23 as he was **g up** by the way, there came	5927
	9:27 *And they did so* at the **g up** to Gur,	4608
	19:27 thy **g out**, and thy coming in, and thy rage	3318
1Ch	14:15 when thou shalt hear a sound of **g** in	6807
	26:16 by the causeway of the **g up**, ward against	5927
2Ch	11: 4 and returned from **g** against Jeroboam.	1980
	18:34 about the time of the sun **g down** he died.	935
Ne	3:19 another piece over against the **g up** to	5927
	3:31 and to the **g up** of the corner.	5944
	3:32 between the **g up** of the corner unto	5944
	12:37 at the **g up** of the wall, above the house	4608
Job	1: 7 From **g to** and **fro** in the earth,	7751
	2: 2 From **g to** and **fro** in the earth,	7751
	33:24 Deliver him from **g down** *to* the pit:	3381
	33:28 will deliver his soul from **g** into the pit,	5674
Ps	19: 6 His **g forth** *is* from the end of the heaven,	4161
	50: 1 of the sun unto the **g down** thereof.	3996
	104:19 seasons: the sun knoweth his **g down**.	3996
	113: 3 the rising of the sun unto the **g down**	3996
	121: 8 The LORD shall preserve thy **g out** and	3318
	144:14 *that there be* no breaking in, nor **g out**;	3318
Pr	7:27 to hell, **g down** to the chambers of death.	3381
	14:15 the prudent *man* looketh well to his **g**.	838
	30:29 which go well, yea, four are comely in **g**:	1980
Isa	13:10 the sun shall be darkened in his **g forth**,	3318
	37:28 thy **g out**, and thy coming in, and thy rage	3318
Jer	48: 5 For *in* the **g up** of Luhith continual	4608
	48: 5 in the **g down** of Horonaim the enemies	4174
	50: 4 of Judah together, and weeping:	1980
Eze	27:19 **g to** and **fro** occupied in thy fairs:	235+4480
	40:31 and the **g up** to it *had* eight steps.	4608
	40:34 side: and the **g up** to it *had* eight steps.	4608
	40:37 side: and the **g up** to it *had* eight steps.	4608
	44: 5 with every **g forth** of the sanctuary.	4161
	46:12 after his **g forth** *one* shall shut the gate.	3318
Da	6:14 he laboured till the **g down** of the sun to	4606
	9:25 from the **g forth** of the commandment	4161
Hos	6: 3 his **g forth** *is* prepared as the morning;	4161
Jnh	1: 3 Joppa; and he found a ship **g** to Tarshish:	935
Mal	1:11 **g down** of the same my name *shall be*	3996
Mt	4:21 And **g on** from thence, he saw other two	4260
	20:17 Jesus **g up** to Jerusalem took the twelve	305
	26:46 Rise, let us be **g**: behold, he is at hand that	71
	28:11 Now when they were **g**, behold, some of	4198
Mk	6:31 for there were many coming and **g**,	5217
	10:32 they were in the way **g up** to Jerusalem,	305
Lk	14:31 to make war against another king,	4198
Jn	4:51 And as he was now **g down**, his servants	2597
	8:59 **g** through the midst of them, and so	1330
Ac	9:28 them coming in and **g out** at Jerusalem.	1607
	20: 5 These **g before** tarried for us at Troas.	4281
Ro	10: 3 **g about** to establish their own	2212
1Ti	5:24 open beforehand, **g before** to judgment;	4254
Heb	7:18 commandment **g before** for the weakness	4254
1Pe	2:25 ye were as sheep **g astray**; but are now	4105
Jude	1: 7 and **g** after strange flesh, are set forth for	565

GOINGS (26) [GO]

Nu	33: 2 Moses wrote their **g out** according to	4161
	33: 2 their journeys according to their **g out**.	4161
	34: 5 and the **g out** of it shall be at the sea.	8444
	34: 8 **g forth** of the border shall be to Zedad:	8444
	34: 9 and the **g out** of it shall be at Hazar-enan:	8444
	34:12 and the **g out** of it shall be *at* the salt sea:	8444
Jos	15: 4 the **g out** of that coast were at the sea:	8444
	15: 7 and the **g out** thereof were at En-rogel:	8444
	15:11 the **g out** of the border were at the sea.	8444
	16: 3 and the **g out** thereof are at the sea.	8444
	16: 8 and the **g out** thereof were at the sea.	8444
	18:12 the **g out** thereof were at the wilderness	8444
	18:14 the **g out** thereof were at Kirjath-baal,	8444
Job	34:21 the ways of man, and he seeth all his **g**.	6806
Ps	17: 5 Hold up my **g** in thy paths, *that* my	838
	40: 2 feet upon a rock, *and* established my **g**.	838
	68:24 They have seen thy **g**, O God; *even*	1979
	68:24 *even* the **g** of my God, my King,	1979
	140: 4 who have purposed to overthrow my **g**.	6471
Pr	5:21 of the LORD, and he pondereth all his **g**.	4570
	20:24 Man's **g** *are* of the LORD; how can a man	4703
Isa	59: 8 and *there is* no judgment in their **g**:	4570
Eze	42:11 all their **g out** were both according to	4161
	43:11 the **g out** thereof, and the comings in	4161
	48:30 *are* the **g out** of the city: on the north	8444
Mic	5: 2 whose **g forth** *have* been from of old,	4163

GOLAN (4)

Dt	4:43 and **G** in Bashan, of the Manassites.	1474
Jos	20: 8 **G** in Bashan out of the tribe of Manasseh.	1474
	21:27 *they gave* **G** in Bashan with her suburbs,	1474
1Ch	6:71 **G** in Bashan with her suburbs.	1474

GOLD (417) [GOLDEN, GOLDSMITH, GOLDSMITH'S, GOLDSMITHS]

Ge	2:11 whole land of Havilah, where *there is* **g**;	2091
	2:12 **g** of that land *is* good: there *is* bdellium	2091
	13: 2 *was* very rich in cattle, in silver, and in **g**.	2091
	24:22 for her hands of ten *shekels* weight of **g**;	2091
	24:35 **g**, and menservants, and maidservants,	2091

Ge	24:53 jewels of **g**, and raiment, and gave *them*	2091
	41:42 linen, and put a **g** chain about his neck;	2091
	44: 8 steal out of thy lord's house silver or **g**?	2091
Ex	3:22 of silver, and jewels of **g**, and raiment:	2091
	11: 2 jewels of silver, and jewels of **g**.	2091
	12:35 of silver, and jewels of **g**, and raiment:	2091
	20:23 neither shall ye make unto you gods of **g**.	2091
	25: 3 take of them; **g**, and silver, and brass,	2091
	25:11 thou shalt overlay it with pure **g**, within	2091
	25:11 shalt make upon it a crown of **g** round	2091
	25:12 thou shalt cast four rings of **g** for it,	2091
	25:13 of shittim wood, and overlay them with **g**.	2091
	25:17 thou shalt make a mercy seat *of* pure **g**:	2091
	25:18 thou shalt make two cherubims of **g**,	2091
	25:24 thou shalt overlay it with pure **g**,	2091
	25:24 make thereto a crown *of* **g** round about.	2091
	25:26 thou shalt make for it four rings of **g**,	2091
	25:28 overlay them with **g**, that the table may	2091
	25:29 of pure **g** shalt thou make them.	2091
	25:31 thou shalt make a candlestick of pure **g**:	2091
	25:36 all it *shall be* one beaten work *of* pure **g**.	2091
	25:38 the snuffdishes thereof, *shall be of* pure **g**.	2091
	25:39 *Of* a talent of pure **g** shall he make it,	2091
	26: 6 thou shalt make fifty taches of **g**,	2091
	26:29 thou shalt overlay the boards with **g**,	2091
	26:29 make rings of **g** for places for the bars:	2091
	26:29 and thou shalt overlay the bars with **g**.	2091
	26:32 pillars of shittim *wood* overlaid with **g**:	2091
	26:32 their hooks *shall be* of **g**, upon the four	2091
	26:37 shittim *wood*, and overlay them with **g**,	2091
	26:37 with gold, *and* their hooks *shall be of* **g**;	2091
	28: 5 they shall take **g**, and blue, and purple,	2091
	28: 6 they shall make the ephod of **g**, of blue,	2091
	28: 8 of **g**, of blue, and purple, and scarlet,	2091
	28:11 shalt make them to be set in *ouches of* **g**.	2091
	28:13 And thou shalt make ouches *of* **g**;	2091
	28:14 two chains *of* pure **g** at the ends;	2091
	28:15 of **g**, of blue, and of purple, and of scarlet,	2091
	28:20 they shall be set in **g** in their inclosings.	2091
	28:22 at the ends of wreathen work *of* pure **g**.	2091
	28:23 make upon the breastplate two rings of **g**,	2091
	28:24 shalt put the two wreathen *chains* of **g**	2091
	28:26 thou shalt make two rings of **g**,	2091
	28:27 two *other* rings of **g** thou shalt make,	2091
	28:33 and bells of **g** between them round about:	2091
	28:36 thou shalt make a plate *of* pure **g**,	2091
	30: 3 thou shalt overlay it with pure **g**, the top	2091
	30: 3 thou shalt make unto it a crown *of* **g**	2091
	30: 5 shittim *wood*, and overlay them with **g**.	2091
	31: 4 to work in **g**, and in silver, and in brass,	2091
	32:24 Whosoever hath any **g**, let them break *it*	2091
	32:31 great sin, and have made them gods of **g**.	2091
	35: 5 of the LORD; **g**, and silver, and brass,	2091
	35:22 and rings, and tablets, all jewels of **g**:	2091
	35:22 *offered* an offering of **g** unto the LORD.	2091
	35:32 to work in **g**, and in silver, and in brass,	2091
	36:13 he made fifty taches of **g**, and coupled	2091
	36:34 he overlaid the boards with **g**, and made	2091
	36:34 made their rings of **g** *to be* places for	2091
	36:34 for the bars, and overlaid the bars with **g**.	2091
	36:36 shittim *wood*, and overlaid them with **g**:	2091
	36:36 hooks *were* of **g**; and he cast for them	2091
	36:38 their chapiters and their fillets with **g**:	2091
	37: 2 he overlaid it with pure **g** within	2091
	37: 2 and made a crown *of* **g** to it round about.	2091
	37: 3 he cast for it four rings of **g**, *to be set* by	2091
	37: 4 shittim *wood*, and overlaid them with **g**.	2091
	37: 6 he made the mercy seat *of* pure **g**:	2091
	37: 7 he made two cherubims *of* **g**, beaten out	2091
	37:11 he overlaid it with pure **g**, and made	2091
	37:11 thereunto a crown *of* **g** round about.	2091
	37:12 made a crown *of* **g** for the border thereof	2091
	37:13 he cast for it four rings of **g**, and put	2091
	37:15 overlaid them with **g**, to bear the table.	2091
	37:16 and *his* covers to cover withal, *of* pure **g**.	2091
	37:17 he made the candlestick *of* pure **g**:	2091
	37:22 all of it *was* one beaten work *of* pure **g**.	2091
	37:23 snuffers, and his snuffdishes, *of* pure **g**.	2091
	37:24 *Of* a talent *of* pure **g** made he it, and all	2091
	37:26 overlaid it with pure **g**, *both* the top of it,	2091
	37:26 also he made unto it a crown *of* **g** round	2091
	37:27 he made two rings of **g** for it under	2091
	37:28 shittim *wood*, and overlaid them with **g**.	2091
	38:24 All the **g** that was occupied for the work	2091
	38:24 the holy *place*, even the **g** of the offering,	2091
	39: 2 he made the ephod of **g**, blue, and purple,	2091
	39: 3 And they did beat the **g** into thin plates,	2091
	39: 5 of **g**, blue, and purple, and scarlet,	2091
	39: 6 onyx stones inclosed in ouches of **g**,	2091
	39: 8 of **g**, blue, and purple, and scarlet,	2091
	39:13 *they were* inclosed in ouches *of* **g** in their	2091
	39:15 at the ends, of wreathen work *of* pure **g**.	2091
	39:16 they made two ouches of **g**, and two gold	2091
	39:16 two ouches of gold, and two **g** rings;	2091
	39:17 they put the two wreathen *chains* of **g** in	2091
	39:19 they made two rings of **g**, and put *them*	2091
	39:25 made bells of pure **g**, and put the bells	2091
	39:30 the plate of the holy crown *of* pure **g**,	2091
	40: 5 thou shalt set the altar of **g** for the incense	2091
Nu	7:14 One spoon of ten *shekels* of **g**, full of	2091
	7:20 One spoon of **g** of ten *shekels*, full of	2091
	7:84 twelve silver bowls, twelve spoons of **g**:	2091
	7:86 all the **g** of the spoons *was* an hundred	2091
	8: 4 work of the candlestick *was* of beaten **g**,	2091
	22:18 give me his house full *of* silver and **g**,	2091

Nu	24:13 give me his house full *of* silver and **g**,	2091
	31:22 Only the **g**, and the silver, the brass,	2091
	31:50 jewels of **g**, chains, and bracelets, rings,	2091
	31:51 and Eleazar the priest took the **g** of them,	2091
	31:52 all the **g** of the offering that they offered	2091
	31:54 the priest took the **g** of the captains	2091
Dt	7:25 not desire the silver or **g** *that is* on them,	2091
	8:13 thy silver and thy **g** is multiplied,	2091
	17:17 he greatly multiply to himself silver and **g**.	2091
	29:17 their idols, wood and stone, silver and **g**,	2091
Jos	6:19 and **g**, and vessels of brass and iron,	2091
	6:24 the **g**, and the vessels of brass and of iron,	2091
	7:21 a wedge of **g** of fifty shekels weight, then	2091
	7:24 the wedge of **g**, and his sons, and his	2091
	22: 8 with **g**, and with brass, and with iron,	2091
Jdg	8:26 thousand and seven hundred *shekels* of **g**;	2091
1Sa	6: 8 put the jewels of **g**, which ye return him	2091
	6:11 the coffer with the mice of **g** and	2091
	6:15 wherein the jewels of **g** *were*, and put	2091
2Sa	1:24 who put on ornaments of **g** upon your	2091
	8: 7 David took the shields of **g** that were on	2091
	8:10 and vessels of **g**, and vessels of brass:	2091
	8:11 that he had dedicated of all nations	2091
	12:30 the weight whereof *was* a talent of **g** with	2091
	21: 4 We will have no silver nor **g** of Saul, nor	2091
1Ki	6:20 he overlaid it with pure **g**; and *so*	2091
	6:21 overlaid the house within with pure **g**:	2091
	6:21 he made a partition by the chains of **g**	2091
	6:21 the oracle; and he overlaid it with **g**.	2091
	6:22 the whole house he overlaid with **g**, until	2091
	6:22 that *was* by the oracle he overlaid with **g**.	2091
	6:28 And he overlaid the cherubims with **g**.	2091
	6:30 the floor of the house he overlaid with **g**,	2091
	6:32 overlaid *them* with **g**, and spread gold	2091
	6:32 spread **g** upon the cherubims, and upon	2091
	6:35 covered *them* with **g** fitted upon the	2091
	7:48 the altar of **g**, and the table of gold,	2091
	7:48 the altar of gold, and the table *of* **g**,	2091
	7:49 candlesticks of pure **g**, five on the right	2091
	7:49 and the lamps, and the tongs *of* **g**,	2091
	7:50 the spoons, and the censers *of* pure **g**;	2091
	7:50 the hinges of **g**, *both* for the doors of	2091
	7:51 *even* the silver, and the **g**, and the vessels,	2091
	9:11 with cedar trees and fir trees, and with **g**,	2091
	9:14 sent to the king sixscore talents of **g**.	2091
	9:28 fet from thence, four hundred and	2091
	10: 2 and very much **g**, and precious stones:	2091
	10:10 king an hundred and twenty talents of **g**,	2091
	10:11 also of Hiram, that brought **g** from Ophir,	2091
	10:14 the weight of **g** that came to Solomon	2091
	10:14 hundred threescore and six talents of **g**,	2091
	10:16 made two hundred targets of beaten **g**:	2091
	10:16 six hundred *shekels* of **g** went to one	2091
	10:17 *made* three hundred shields of beaten **g**;	2091
	10:17 three pound of **g** went to one shield:	2091
	10:18 of ivory, and overlaid it with the best **g**.	2091
	10:21 Solomon's drinking vessels *were* of **g**,	2091
	10:21 of the forest of Lebanon *were of* pure **g**;	2091
	10:22 bringing **g**, and silver, ivory, and apes,	2091
	10:25 vessels of **g**, and garments, and armour,	2091
	12:28 two calves of **g**, and said unto them,	2091
	14:26 he took away all the shields of **g** which	2091
	15:15 of the LORD, silver, and **g**, and vessels.	2091
	15:18 the **g** that were left in the treasures of	2091
	15:19 sent unto thee a present of silver and **g**;	2091
	20: 3 Thy silver and thy **g** *is* mine; thy wives	2091
	20: 5 thy **g**, and thy wives, and thy children;	2091
	20: 7 and for my silver, and for my **g**;	2091
	22:48 ships of Tharshish to go to Ophir for **g**:	2091
2Ki	5: 5 six thousand *pieces* of **g**, and ten changes	2091
	7: 8 and **g**, and raiment, and went and hid *it*;	2091
	12:13 any vessels of **g**, or vessels of silver,	2091
	12:18 all the **g** that was found in the treasures	2091
	14:14 he took all the **g** and silver, and all	2091
	16: 8 **g** that was found *in* the house of	2091
	18:14 talents of silver and thirty talents of **g**.	2091
	18:16 that time did Hezekiah cut off the **g** from	NIH
	20:13 the **g**, and the spices, and the precious	2091
	23:33 talents of silver, and a talent of **g**.	2091
	23:35 gave the silver and the **g** to Pharaoh;	2091
	23:35 of the people of the land,	2091
	24:13 cut in pieces all the vessels of **g** which	2091
	25:15 *and such* things as *were of* **g**, in gold,	2091
	25:15 *were of* gold, in **g**, and *of* silver, in silver,	2091
1Ch	18: 7 David took the shields of **g** that were on	2091
	18:10 *with him* all *manner of* vessels of **g** and	2091
	18:11 the **g** that he brought from all *these*	2091
	20: 2 found it to weigh a talent of **g**,	2091
	21:25 place six hundred shekels of **g** by weight.	2091
	22:14 LORD an hundred thousand talents *of* **g**,	2091
	22:16 Of the **g**, the silver, and the brass,	2091
	28:14 *He gave* of **g** by weight for *things* of gold,	2091
	28:14 *He gave* of gold by weight for *things* of **g**,	2091
	28:15 Even the weight for the candlesticks of **g**,	2091
	28:15 *for* their lamps of **g**, by weight for every	2091
	28:16 *by* weight he gave **g** for the tables of	2091
	28:17 Also pure **g** for the fleshhooks,	2091
	28:17 the golden basons he gave **g** by weight	NIH
	28:18 the altar of incense refined **g** by weight;	2091
	28:18 **g** for the pattern of the chariot of	2091
	29: 2 God the **g** for *things* to be made of gold,	2091
	29: 2 God the gold for *things* to be made of **g**,	2091
	29: 3 of mine own proper good, *of* **g** and silver,	2091
	29: 4 *Even* three thousand talents of **g**,	2091
	29: 4 of the **g** of Ophir, and seven thousand	2091

G

1Ch 29: 5 The **g** for *things of* gold, and the silver for 2091
29: 5 The gold for *things of* **g**, and the silver for 2091
29: 7 house of God *of* **g** five thousand talents 2091
2Ch 1:15 and **g** at Jerusalem *as* plenteous as stones, 2091
2: 7 therefore a man cunning to work in **g**, 2091
2:14 skilful to work in **g**, and in silver, in brass, 2091
3: 4 and he overlaid it within with pure **g**. 2091
3: 5 which he overlaid with fine **g**, 2091
3: 6 for beauty: and the gold *was* gold of Parvaim. 2091
3: 6 for beauty: and the gold *was* **g** of Parvaim. 2091
3: 7 thereof, and the doors thereof, with **g**; 2091
3: 8 he overlaid it with fine **g**, *amounting* to 2091
3: 9 weight of the nails *was* fifty shekels of **g**. 2091
3: 9 he overlaid the upper chambers with **g**. 2091
3:10 of image work, and overlaid them with **g**. 2091
4: 7 he made ten candlesticks of **g** according to 2091
4: 8 And he made an hundred basons of **g**. 2091
4:20 the manner before the oracle, *of* pure **g**; 2091
4:21 *made* he of **g**, *and* that perfect gold; 2091
4:21 *made* he of gold, and that perfect **g**; 2091
4:22 the spoons, and the censers, of pure **g**: 2091
4:22 of the house of the temple, *were* of **g**. 2091
5: 1 and the **g**, and all the instruments, 2091
8:18 thence four hundred and fifty talents of **g**, 2091
9: 1 and **g** in abundance, and precious stones; 2091
9: 9 king an hundred and twenty talents of **g**, 2091
9:10 which brought **g** from Ophir, 2091
9:13 the weight of **g** that came to Solomon 2091
9:13 and threescore and six talents of **g**; 2091
9:14 governors of the country brought **g** and 2091
9:15 made two hundred targets *of* beaten **g**: 2091
9:15 six hundred *shekels* of beaten **g** went to 2091
9:16 hundred shields *made he of* beaten **g**: 2091
9:16 three hundred *shekels* of **g** went to one 2091
9:17 of ivory, and overlaid it with pure **g**. 2091
9:18 a footstool of **g**, *which were* fastened 2091
9:20 vessels of king Solomon *were* of **g**, 2091
9:20 of the forest of Lebanon *were of* pure **g**: 2091
9:21 came the ships of Tarshish bringing **g**, 2091
9:24 vessels of **g**, and raiment, harness, 2091
12: 9 he carried away also the shields of **g** 2091
13:11 candlestick of **g** with the lamps thereof, 2091
15:18 had dedicated, silver, and **g**, and vessels. 2091
16: 2 **g** out of the treasures of the house of 2091
16: 3 behold, I have sent thee silver and **g**; 2091
21: 3 of **g**, and of precious things, with fenced 2091
24:14 and spoons, and vessels of **g** and silver. 2091
25:24 *he took* all the **g** and the silver, and all 2091
32:27 for **g**, and for precious stones, 2091
36: 3 hundred talents of silver and a talent of **g**. 2091
Ezr 1: 4 with **g**, and with goods, and with beasts, 2091
1: 6 with **g**, with goods, and with beasts, 2091
1: 9 thirty chargers of **g**, a thousand chargers 2091
1:10 Thirty basons of **g**, silver basons of a 2091
1:11 All the vessels of **g** and of silver *were* five 2091
2:69 and one thousand drams *of* **g**, 2091
5:14 vessels also of **g** and of silver of the house 1722
7:15 to carry the silver and **g**, which the king 1722
7:16 **g** that thou canst find in all the province 1722
7:18 to do with the rest of the silver and **g**, 1722
8:25 the silver, and the **g**, and the vessels, 2091
8:26 *and of* **g** an hundred talents; 2091
8:27 Also twenty basons of **g**, of a thousand 2091
8:27 two vessels of fine copper, precious as **g**. 2091
8:28 the **g** *are* a freewill offering unto 2091
8:30 of the silver, and the **g**, and the vessels, 2091
8:33 fourth day was the silver and the **g** and 2091
Ne 7:70 to the treasure a thousand drams *of* **g**, 2091
7:71 of the work twenty thousand drams *of* **g**, 2091
7:72 gave *was* twenty thousand drams *of* **g**, 2091
Est 1: 6 the beds *were* of **g** and silver, upon a 2091
1: 7 *they* gave *them* drink in vessels of **g**, 2091
8:15 a great crown of **g**, and with a garment 2091
Job 3:15 with princes that had **g**, who filled their 2091
22:24 shalt thou lay up **g** as dust, and *the gold* 1220
22:24 *the g of* Ophir as the stones of the brooks. NIH
23:10 he hath tried me, I shall come forth as **g**. 2091
28: 1 and a place for **g** where they fine it. 2091
28: 6 place of sapphires: and it hath dust of **g**. 2091
28:15 cannot be gotten for **g**, neither shall silver 5458
28:16 It cannot be valued with the **g** of Ophir, 3800
28:17 The **g** and the crystal cannot equal it: 2091
28:17 of it *shall not be for* jewels of fine **g**. 6337
28:19 neither shall it be valued with pure **g**. 3800
31:24 If I have made **g** my hope, or have said to 2091
31:24 or have said to the fine **g**, *Thou art* my 3800
36:19 no, not **g**, nor all the forces of strength. 1222
42:11 of money, and every one an earring of **g**. 2091
Ps 19:10 More to be desired *are they* than **g**, yea, 2091
19:10 *are they* than gold, yea, than much fine **g**: 6337
21: 3 settest a crown of pure **g** on his head. 6337
45: 9 hand did stand the queen in **g** of Ophir. 3800
45:13 her clothing *is* of wrought **g**. 2091
68:13 silver, and her feathers with yellow **g**. 2742
72:15 to him shall be given of the **g** of Sheba: 2091
105:37 brought them forth also with silver and **g**: 2091
115: 4 Their idols *are* silver and **g**, the work of 2091
119:72 is better unto me than thousands of **g** 2091
119:127 I love thy commandments above **g**; 2091
119:127 above gold; yea, above fine **g**. 6337
135:15 The idols of the heathen *are* silver and **g**, 2091
Pr 3:14 of silver, and the gain thereof than fine **g**. 2742
8:10 and knowledge rather than choice **g**. 2742
8:19 My fruit *is* better than **g**, yea, than fine 2742
8:19 fruit *is* better than gold, yea, than fine **g**; 6337

Pr 11:22 *As* a jewel of **g** in a swine's snout, *so is a* 2091
16:16 much better *is it* to get wisdom than **g**! 2742
17: 3 pot *is* for silver, and the furnace for **g**: 2091
20:15 There is **g**, and a multitude of rubies: 2091
22: 1 loving favour rather than silver and **g**. 2091
25:11 A word fitly spoken *is like* apples of **g** in 2091
25:12 As an earring of **g**, and an ornament of 2091
25:12 ornament of **fine g**, *so is* a wise reprover 3800
27:21 fining pot for silver, and the furnace for **g**; 2091
Ecc 2: 8 I gathered me also silver and **g**, 2091
SS 1:10 rows *of jewels*, thy neck with chains of **g**. NIH
1:11 will make thee borders of **g** with studs 2091
3:10 the bottom thereof *of* **g**, the covering of it 2091
5:11 His head *is* as the most **fine g**, his locks 6337
5:14 hands *are* as **g** rings set with the beryl. 2091
5:15 of marble, set upon sockets of **fine g**. 6337
Isa 2: 7 Their land also is full *of* silver and **g**, 2091
2:20 cast his idols of silver, and his idols of **g**, 2091
13:12 make a man more precious than **fine g**; 6337
13:17 and *as for* **g**, they shall not delight in it. 2091
30:22 the ornament of thy molten images of **g**: 2091
31: 7 his idols of **g**, which your own hands 2091
39: 2 the **g**, and the spices, and the precious 2091
40:19 the goldsmith spreadeth it over with **g**, 2091
46: 6 They lavish **g** out of the bag, 2091
60: 6 they shall bring **g** and incense; 2091
60: 9 their silver and their **g** with them, 2091
60:17 For brass I will bring **g**, and for iron I will 2091
Jer 4:30 thou deckest thee with ornaments of **g**, 2091
4: 4 They deck it with silver and with **g**; 2091
10: 9 **g** from Uphaz, the work of the workman, 2091
52:19 *that* which *was* of **g** in gold, and *that* 2091
52:19 *that* which *was* of gold in **g**, and *that* 2091
La 4: 1 How is the **g** become dim! *how* is the 2091
4: 1 *how* is the most **fine g** changed! 3800
4: 2 sons of Zion, comparable to **fine g**, 6337
Eze 7:19 the streets, and their **g** shall be removed: 2091
7:19 their **g** shall not be able to deliver them 2091
16:13 Thus wast thou decked *with* **g** and silver; 2091
16:17 hast also taken thy fair jewels of my **g** 2091
27:22 and with all precious stones, and **g**. 2091
28: 4 hast gotten **g** and silver into thy treasures: 2091
28:13 the emerald, and the carbuncle, and **g**: 2091
38:13 to carry away silver and **g**, to take *away* 2091
Da 2:32 This image's head *was* of fine **g**, his breast 1722
2:35 the clay, the brass, the silver, and the **g**, 1722
2:38 over them all. Thou *art* this head of **g**. 1722
2:45 the brass, the clay, the silver, and the **g**; 1722
3: 1 the king made an image of **g**, 1722
5: 4 praised the gods of **g**, and of silver, 1722
5: 7 *have* a chain of **g** about his neck, 1722
5:16 *have* a chain of **g** about thy neck, 1722
5:23 **g**, of brass, iron, wood, and stone, which 1722
5:29 *put* a chain of **g** about his neck, and made 1722
10: 5 whose loins *were* girded with **fine g** of 3800
11: 8 their precious vessels *of* silver and *of* **g**; 2091
11:38 fathers knew not shall he honour with **g**, 2091
11:43 shall have power over the treasures of **g** 2091
Hos 2: 8 and oil, and multiplied her silver and **g**, 2091
8: 4 and their **g** have they made them idols, 2091
Joel 3: 5 ye have taken my silver and my **g**, 2091
Na 2: 9 ye the spoil of silver, take the spoil of **g**: 2091
Hab 2:19 it *is* laid over *with* **g** and silver, and *there* 2091
Zep 1:18 Neither their silver nor their **g** shall be 2091
Hag 2: 8 The silver *is* mine, and the **g** *is* mine, 2091
Zec 4: 2 and behold, a candlestick all of **g**, 2091
6:11 take silver and **g**, and make crowns, 2091
9: 3 and **fine g** as the mire of the streets. 2742
13: 9 is refined, and will try them as **g** is tried: 2091
14:14 and silver, and apparel, in great 2091
Mal 3: 3 of Levi, and purge them as **g** and silver, 2091
Mt 2:11 gifts; **g**, and frankincense, and myrrh. 5557
10: 9 Provide neither **g**, nor silver, nor brass in 5557
23:16 whosoever shall swear by the **g** of 5557
23:17 the **g**, or the temple that sanctifieth 5557
23:17 the **g**, or the temple that sanctifieth the **g**? 5557
Ac 3: 6 Then Peter said, Silver and **g** have I none; 5553
17:29 to think that the Godhead is like unto **g**, 5557
20:33 coveted no *man's* silver, or **g**, or apparel. 5553
1Co 3:12 if any *man* build upon this foundation **g**, 5557
1Ti 2: 9 or **g**, or pearls, or costly array; 5557
2Ti 2:20 great house there are not only vessels of **g** 5552
Heb 9: 4 the covenant overlaid round about with **g**, 5553
Jas 2: 2 unto your assembly a man **with a g** ring, 5554
5: 3 Your **g** and silver is cankered; and the rust 5557
1Pe 1: 7 *being* much more precious than of **g** that 5553
1:18 with corruptible *things*, *as* silver and **g**, 5553
3: 3 and of wearing of **g**, or of putting on of 5553
Rev 3:18 I counsel thee to buy of me **g** tried in 5553
4: 4 and they had on their heads crowns of **g**. 5552
9: 7 their heads *were* as *it were* crowns like **g**, 5557
9:20 should not worship devils, and idols of **g**, 5557
17: 4 and **decked with g** and 5557+5558
18:12 The merchandise of **g**, and silver, 5557
18:16 and decked with **g**, and precious stones, 5557
21:18 and the city *was* pure **g**, like unto clear 5557
21:21 and the street of the city *was* pure **g**, as *it* 5553

GOLDEN (66) [GOLD]

Ge 24:22 that the man took a **g** earring of half a 2091
Ex 25:25 thou shalt make a **g** crown to the border 2091
28:34 A **g** bell and a pomegranate, a golden bell 2091
28:34 pomegranate, a golden bell and a pomegranate, 2091
30: 4 two **g** rings shalt thou make to it under 2091
32: 2 said unto them, Break off the **g** earrings, 2091

Ex 32: 3 all the people brake off the **g** earrings 2091
39:20 they made two *other* **g** rings, and put 2091
39:38 the altar, and the anointing oil, 2091
40:26 he put the **g** altar in the tent of 2091
Lev 8: 9 did he put the **g** plate, to wit, the holy crown; 2091
Nu 4:11 upon the **g** altar they shall spread a cloth 2091
7:26 spoon of ten *shekels*, full *of* incense: 2091
7:32 spoon *of* ten *shekels*, full *of* incense: 2091
7:38 spoon of ten *shekels*, full *of* incense: 2091
7:44 spoon of ten *shekels*, full *of* incense: 2091
7:50 spoon of ten *shekels*, full *of* incense: 2091
7:56 spoon of ten *shekels*, full *of* incense: 2091
7:62 spoon of ten *shekels*, full *of* incense: 2091
7:68 spoon of ten *shekels*, full *of* incense: 2091
7:74 spoon of ten *shekels*, full *of* incense: 2091
7:80 spoon of ten *shekels*, full *of* incense: 2091
7:86 spoons *were* twelve, full *of* incense. 2091
Jdg 8:24 [For they had **g** earrings, because they 2091
8:26 the weight of the **g** earrings that he 2091
1Sa 6: 4 Five **g** emerods, and five golden mice, 2091
6: 4 Five golden emerods, and five **g** mice, 2091
6:17 these *are* the **g** emerods which 2091
6:18 the **g** mice, *according to* the number of 2091
2Ki 10:29 *to wit*, the **g** calves that *were* in Beth-el, 2091
1Ch 28:17 for the **g** basons he gave gold by weight 2091
2Ch 4:19 the **g** altar also, and the tables whereon 2091
13: 8 and *there are* with you **g** calves, 2091
Ezr 6: 5 let the **g** and silver vessels of the house 1722
Est 4:11 the king shall hold out the **g** sceptre, 2091
5: 2 the king held out to Esther the **g** sceptre 2091
8: 4 the king held out the **g** sceptre toward 2091
Ecc 12: 6 or the **g** bowl be broken, or the pitcher 2091
Isa 13:12 even a man than the **g** wedge of Ophir. 3800
14: 4 the oppressor ceased! the **g** city ceased! 4062
Jer 51: 7 Babylon *hath been* a **g** cup in the LORD'S 2091
Da 3: 5 worship the **g** image that Nebuchadnezzar 1722
3: 7 worshipped the **g** image that 1722
3:10 shall fall down and worship the **g** image: 1722
3:12 nor worship the **g** image which thou hast 1722
3:14 nor worship the **g** image which I have set 1722
3:18 nor worship the **g** image which thou hast 1722
5: 2 commanded to bring the **g** and 1722
5: 3 they brought the **g** vessels that were taken 1722
Zec 4:12 **g** pipes empty the golden *oil* out of 2091
4:12 pipes empty the **g** *oil* out of themselves? 2091
Heb 9: 4 Which had the **g** censer, and the ark of 5552
9: 4 wherein *was* the **g** pot that had manna, 5552
Rev 1:12 being turned, I saw seven **g** candlesticks; 5552
1:13 and girt about the paps with a **g** girdle. 5552
1:20 right hand, and the seven **g** candlesticks. 5552
2: 1 who walketh in the midst of the seven **g** 5552
5: 8 and **g** vials full of odours, which are 5552
8: 3 and stood at the altar, having a **g** censer; 5552
8: 3 the **g** altar which was before the throne. 5552
9:13 heard a voice from the four horns of the **g** 5552
14:14 having on his head a **g** crown, and in his 5552
15: 6 having their breasts girded with **g** girdles. 5552
15: 7 seven **g** vials full of the wrath of God, 5552
17: 4 having a **g** cup in her hand full of 5552
21:15 he that talked with me had a **g** reed to 5552

GOLDSMITH (3) [GOLD]

Isa 40:19 the **g** spreadeth it over with gold, 6884
41: 7 So the carpenter encouraged the **g**, 6884
46: 6 weigh silver in the balance, *and* hire a **g**; 6884

GOLDSMITH'S (1) [GOLD]

Ne 3:31 After him repaired Malchiah the **g** son 6885

GOLDSMITHS (2) [GOLD]

Ne 3: 8 Uzziel the son of Harhaiah, *of* the **g**. 6884
3:32 corner unto the sheep gate repaired the **g** 6884

GOLGOTHA (3) [CALVARY]

Mt 27:33 they were come unto a place called **G**, 1115
Mk 15:22 And they bring him unto the place **G**, 1115
Jn 19:17 a skull, which is called in the Hebrew **G**: 1115

GOLIATH (6)

1Sa 17: 4 named **G**, of Gath, whose height *was* six 1555
17:23 the Philistine of Gath, **G** by name, 1555
21: 9 priest said, The sword of **G** the Philistine. 1555
22:10 gave him the sword of **G** the Philistine. 1555
2Sa 21:19 slew *the brother of* **G** the Gittite, 1555
1Ch 20: 5 slew Lahmi the brother of **G** the Gittite, 1555

GOMER (6)

Ge 10: 2 **G**, and Magog, and Madai, and Javan, 1586
10: 3 the sons of **G**; Ashkenaz, and Riphath, 1586
1Ch 1: 5 **G**, and Magog, and Madai, and Javan, 1586
1: 6 the sons of **G**; Ashkenaz, and Riphath, 1586
Eze 38: 6 **G**, and all his bands; the house of 1586
Hos 1: 3 and took **G** the daughter of Diblaim; 1586

GOMORRAH (19) [GOMORRHA]

Ge 10:19 **G**, and Admah, and Zeboim, even unto 6017
13:10 destroyed Sodom and **G**, 6017
14: 2 with Birsha king of **G**, Shinab king of 6017
14: 8 the king of **G**, and the king of Admah, 6017
14:10 the kings of Sodom and **G** fled, 6017
14:11 they took all the goods of Sodom and **G**, 6017
18:20 Because the cry of Sodom and **G** is great, 6017
19:24 upon **G** brimstone and fire from 6017
19:28 he looked toward Sodom and **G**, 6017
Dt 29:23 of Sodom, and **G**, Admah, and Zeboim, 6017

Dt	32:32 the vine of Sodom, and of the fields of **G**:	6017	
Isa	1: 9 and we should have been like unto **G**.	6017	
	1:10 unto the law of our God, ye people of **G**.	6017	
	13:19 as when God overthrew Sodom and **G**.	6017	
Jer	23:14 Sodom, and the inhabitants thereof as **G**.	6017	
	49:18 and **G** and the neighbour *cities* thereof,	6017	
	50:40 As God overthrew Sodom and **G** and	6017	
Am	4:11 as God overthrew Sodom and **G**,	6017	
Zep	2: 9 the children of Ammon as **G**, *even*	6017	

GOMORRHA (5) [GOMORRAH]

Mt	10:15 of Sodom and **G** in the day of judgment,	1116
Mk	6:11 for Sodom and **G** in the day of judgment,	1116
Ro	9:29 as Sodoma, and been made like unto **G**.	1116
2Pe	2: 6 **G** into ashes condemned *them* with an	1116
Jude	1: 7 *Even* as Sodom and **G**, and the cities	1116

GONE (214) [GO]

Ge	27:30 Jacob was yet **scarce g** out from 3318+3318	
	28: 7 and his mother, and was **g** to Padan-aram;	1980
	31:30 *though* thou wouldest **needs be g**,	1980+1980
	34:17 we take our daughter, and we will be **g**.	1980
	42:33 the famine of your households, and be **g**:	1980
	44: 4 *And* when they were **g** out of the city,	3318
	49: 9 from the prey, my son, thou art **g up**:	5927
Ex	9:29 him, As soon as I am **g** out of the city,	3318
	12:32 and your herds, as ye have said, and be **g**;	1980
	16:14 when the dew that lay was **g up**, behold,	5927
	19: 1 when the children of Israel were **g forth**	3318
	33: 8 until he was **g** into the tabernacle.	935
Lev	17: 7 after whom they have **g a whoring**.	2181
Nu	5:19 if thou hast not **g aside** *to* uncleanness	7847
	5:20 if thou hast **g aside** *to another* instead of	7847
	7:89 when Moses was **g** into the tabernacle of	935
	13:32 through which we have **g** to search it,	5674
	16:46 for there is wrath **g** out from the LORD;	3318
	21:28 For there is a fire **g** out of Heshbon,	3318
Dt	9: 1 I was **g up** into the mount to receive	5927
	13:13 are **g** out from among you,	3318
	17: 3 hath **g** and served other gods,	1980
	23:23 That which is **g** out of thy lips thou	4161
	27: 4 Therefore it shall be when ye be **g over**	5674
	32:36 when he seeth that *their* power is **g**,	235
Jos	2: 7 which pursued after them were **g** out,	3318
	4:23 up from before us, until we were **g over**:	5674
	23:16 have **g** and served other gods,	1980
Jdg	3:24 When he was **g** out, his servants came;	3318
	4:12 of Abinoam was **g up** to mount Tabor.	5927
	4:14 is not the LORD **g** out before thee?	3318
	18:24 made, and the priest, and ye are **g away**:	1980
	20: 3 children of Israel were **g up** to Mizpeh.	5927
Ru	1:13 the hand of the LORD is **g** out against me.	3318
	1:15 sister in law is **g back** unto her people,	7725
1Sa	14: 3 people knew not that Jonathan was **g**.	1980
	14:17 Number now, and see who is **g** from us.	1980
	15:12 is **g about**, and passed on, and gone down	5437
	15:12 and passed on, and **g down** to Gilgal.	3381
	15:20 have **g** the way which the LORD sent me,	1980
	20:41 *And* as soon as the lad was **g**, David arose	935
	25:37 when the wine was **g** out of Nabal,	3318
2Sa	2:27 in the morning the people had **g up** every	5927
	3: 7 Wherefore hast thou **g in** unto my father's	935
	3:22 sent him away, and he was **g** in peace.	1980
	3:23 hath sent him away, and he is **g** in peace.	1980
	3:24 sent him away, and he is **quite g**?	1980+1980
	6:13 ark of the LORD had **g six paces**,	6805+6806
	13:15 And Amnon said unto her, Arise, be **g**.	1980
	17:20 They be **g over** the brook of water.	5674
	17:22 one *of them* that was not **g over** Jordan.	5674
	23: 9 and the men of Israel were **g away**:	5927
	24: 8 So when they had **g** through all the land,	7751
1Ki	1:25 For he is **g down** *this* day, and hath slain	3381
	2:41 was told Solomon that Shimei had **g** from	1980
	9:16 *For* Pharaoh king of Egypt had **g up**,	5927
	11:15 Joab the captain of the host was **g up** to	5927
	13:24 he was **g**, a lion met him by the way,	1980
	14: 9 for thou hast **g** and made thee other gods,	1980
	14:10 *a man* taketh away dung, till it be **all g**.	8552
	18:12 to pass, *as soon as* I am **g** from thee,	1980
	20:40 was busy here and there, he was **g**.	369
	21:18 whither he is **g down** to possess it.	3381
	22:13 the messenger that was **g** to call Micaiah	1980
2Ki	1: 4 from *that* bed on which thou art **g up**,	5927
	1: 6 from *that* bed on which thou art **g up**,	5927
	1:16 off *that* bed on which thou art **g up**,	5927
	2: 9 it came to pass, when they were **g over**,	5674
	5: 2 the Syrians had **g** out *by* companies,	3318
	6:15 **g forth**, behold, a host compassed the city	3318
	7:12 are they **g** out of the camp to hide	3318
	20: 4 afore Isaiah was **g** out into the middle	3318
	20:11 which it had **g down** in the dial of Ahaz.	3381
1Ch	14:15 for God is **g forth** before thee to smite	3318
	17: 5 have **g** from tent to tent, and from *one*	1961
Job	1: 5 the days of *their* feasting were **g about**,	5362
	7: 4 When shall I arise, and the night be **g**?	4059
	19:10 destroyed me on every side, and I am **g**:	1980
	23:12 Neither have I **g back from**	4185
	24:24 a little while, but are **g** and brought low,	369
	28: 4 are dried up, they are **g away** from men.	5128
Ps	14: 3 They are all **g aside**, they are *all* together	5493
	19: 4 Their line is **g** out through all the earth,	3318
	38: 4 For mine iniquities are **g over** mine head:	5674
	38:10 light of mine eyes, it also is **g** from me.	369
	42: 4 for I had **g** with the multitude, I went	5674
	42: 7 thy waves and thy billows are **g** over me.	5674

Ps	47: 5 God is **g up** with a shout, the LORD with	5927	
	51: 1 unto him, after he had **g in** to Bath-sheba.	935	
	53: 3 Every one of them is **g back**, they are	5472	
	73: 2 *for* me, my feet were almost **g**; my steps	5186	
	77: 8 Is his mercy **clean g** for ever? doth *his*	656	
	89:34 alter the **thing that is g** out of my lips.	4161	
	103:16 For the wind passeth over it, and it is **g**;	369	
	109:23 I am **g** like the shadow when it declineth:	1980	
	119:176 I have **g astray** like a lost sheep; seek thy	8582	
	124: 4 the stream had **g over** our soul:	5674	
	124: 5 the proud waters had **g over** our soul.	5674	
Pr	7:19 *is* not at home, he is **g** a long journey:	1980	
	20:14 when he is **g** his **way**, then he boasteth.	235	
Ecc	8:10 come and **g** from the place of the holy,	1980	
SS	2:11 the winter is past, the rain is over and **g**;	1980	
	5: 6 had withdrawn himself, *and* was **g**:	5674	
	6: 1 Whither is thy beloved **g**, O thou fairest	1980	
	6: 2 My beloved is **g down** into his garden,	3381	
Isa	1: 4 unto anger, they are **g away** backward.	2114	
	5:13 Therefore my people are **g into captivity**,	1540	
	10:29 They are **g over** the passage: they have	5674	
	15: 2 He is **g up** to Bajith, and to Dibon,	5927	
	15: 8 For the cry is **g round about** the borders	5362	
	16: 8 are stretched out, they are **g over** the sea.	5674	
	22: 1 thou art wholly **g up** to the housetops?	5927	
	24:11 joy is darkened, the mirth of the land is **g**.	1540	
	38: 8 which is **g down** in the sun dial of Ahaz,	3381	
	38: 8 by which degrees it was **g down**.	3381	
	41: 3 *even* by the way that he had not **g** with	935	
	45:23 the word is **g** out of my mouth *in*	3318	
	46: 2 but themselves are **g** into captivity.	1980	
	51: 5 my salvation is **g forth**, and mine arms	3318	
	53: 6 All we like sheep have **g astray**; we have	8582	
	57: 8 *thyself to another* than me, and art **g up**;	5927	
Jer	2: 5 that they are **g far** from me,	7368	
	2:23 not polluted, I have not **g** after Baalim?	1980	
	3: 6 she is **g up** upon every high mountain	1980	
	4: 7 he is **g forth** from his place to make thy	3318	
	5:23 a rebellious heart; they are revolted and **g**.	1980	
	9:10 and the beast are fled; they are **g**.	1980	
	10:20 my children are **g forth** *of* me, and they	3318	
	14: 2 and the cry of Jerusalem is **g up**.	5927	
	15: 6 saith the LORD, thou art **g backward**:	1980	
	15: 9 her sun is **g down** while *it was* yet day:	935	
	23:15 is profaneness **g forth** into all the land.	3318	
	23:19 a whirlwind of the LORD is **g forth** in	3318	
	29:16 *of* your brethren that are not **g forth** with	3318	
	34:21 Babylon's army, which are **g up** from you.	5927	
	40: 5 while he was **g**, he said, he said,	7725	
	44: 8 ye be **g** to dwell, that ye might cut	935	
	44:14 are **g** into the land of Egypt to sojourn	935	
	44:28 that are **g** into the land of Egypt to sojourn	935	
	48:11 to vessel, neither hath he **g** into captivity:	1980	
	48:15 **g up** *out* of her cities, and his chosen	5927	
	48:15 his chosen young men are **g down** to	3381	
	48:32 thy plants are **g over** the sea, they reach	5674	
	50: 6 they have **g** from mountain to hill,	1980	
La	1: 3 Judah is **g into captivity** because	1540	
	1: 5 her children are **g** *into* captivity before	1980	
	1: 6 they are **g** without strength before	1980	
	1:18 and my young men are **g** into captivity.	1980	
Eze	7:10 the morning is **g forth**; the rod hath	3318	
	9: 3 the glory of the God of Israel was **g up**	5927	
	13: 5 Ye have not **g up** into the gaps,	5927	
	19:14 fire is **g** out of a rod of her branches,	3318	
	23:30 thou hast **g a whoring** after the heathen,	2181	
	24: 6 and whose scum is not **g** out of it!	3318	
	31:12 the people of the earth are **g down** from	3381	
	32:21 they are **g down**, they lie uncircumcised,	3381	
	32:24 which are **g down** uncircumcised into	3381	
	32:27 which are **g down** to hell with their	3381	
	32:30 which are **g down** with the slain;	3381	
	36:20 the LORD, and are **g forth** out of his land.	3318	
	37:21 whither they be **g**, and will gather them	1980	
	44:10 the Levites that are **g away far** from me,	7368	
Da	2: 5 to the Chaldeans, The thing is **g** from me:	230	
	2: 8 because ye see the thing is **g** from me.	230	
	2:14 which was **g forth** to slay the wise *men*	5312	
	10:20 I am **g forth**, lo, the prince of Grecia	3318	
Hos	4:12 they have **g a whoring** from under their	2181	
	8: 9 For they are **g up** to Assyria, a wild ass	5927	
	9: 1 for thou hast **g a whoring** from thy God,	2181	
	9: 6 For lo, they are **g** because of destruction:	1980	
Am	8: 5 Saying, When will the new moon be **g**,	5674	
Jnh	1: 5 Jonah was **g down** into the sides of	3381	
Mic	1:16 for they are **g into captivity** from thee.	1540	
	2:13 through the gate, and are **g** out by it:	3318	
Mal	3: 7 ye are **g away** from mine ordinances,	5493	
Mt	10:23 shall not have **g over** the cities of Israel,	5055	
	12:43 When the unclean spirit is **g out** of a man,	1831	
	14:34 when they were **g over**, they came into	1276	
	18:12 and one of them be **g astray**, doth he not	4105	
	18:12 and seeketh that which is **g astray**?	4105	
	25: 8 us of your oil; for our lamps are **g** out.	4570	
	26:71 And when he was **g** out into the porch,	1831	
Mk	1:19 when he had **g** a little **further** thence,	4260	
	5:30 in himself that virtue had **g** out of him,	1831	
	7:29 way; the devil is **g** out of thy daughter.	1831	
	7:30 found the devil **g** out, and *her* daughter	1831	
	10:17 And when he was **g forth** into the way,	1607	
Lk	2:15 as the angels were **g away** from them into	565	
	5: 2 but the fishermen were **g** out of them,	576	
	8:46 for I perceive that virtue is **g** out of me.	1831	
	11:14 the devil was **g** out, the dumb spake;	1831	
	11:24 When the unclean spirit is **g** out of a man,	1831	

Lk	19: 7 That he was **g** to be guest with a man	1525	
	24:28 made as though *he* would have **g** further.	4198	
Jn	4: 8 his disciples were **g away** unto the city	565	
	6:22 but *that* his disciples were **g away** alone;	565	
	7:10 But when his brethren were **g up**, then	305	
	12:19 behold, the world is **g** after him.	565	
	13:31 Therefore, when he was **g out**, Jesus said,	1831	
Ac	13: 6 when they had **g through** the isle unto	1330	
	13:42 And when the Jews were **g out** of	1826	
	16: 6 when they had **g throughout** Phrygia	1330	
	16:19 saw that the hope of their gains was **g**,	1831	
	18:22 and **g up**, and saluted the church,	305	
	20: 2 And when he had **g over** those parts,	1330	
	20:25 among whom I have **g** preaching	1330	
	24: 6 Who also hath **g about** to profane	3985	
	26:31 when they were **g aside**, they talked	402	
	27:28 and when they had **g** a little **further**,	1339	
Ro	3:12 They are all **g out of the way**, they are	1578	
1Pe	3:22 Who is **g** into heaven, and is on the right	4198	
2Pe	2:15 forsaken the right way, and are **g astray**,	4105	
1Jn	4: 1 many false prophets are **g out** into	1831	
Jude	1:11 for they have **g** in the way of Cain,	4198	

GOOD (720) [BEST, BETTER, BETTERED, GOODLIER, GOODLIEST, GOODLINESS, GOODLY, GOODMAN, GOODNESS, GOODNESS', GOODS]

Ge	1: 4 God saw the light, that *it was* **g**:	2896	
	1:10 called he Seas: and God saw that *it was* **g**.	2896	
	1:12 after his kind: and God saw that *it was* **g**.	2896	
	1:18 the darkness: and God saw that *it was* **g**.	2896	
	1:21 after his kind: and God saw that *it was* **g**.	2896	
	1:25 after his kind: and God saw that *it was* **g**.	2896	
	1:31 he had made, and, behold, *it was* very **g**.	2896	
	2: 9 is pleasant to the sight, and **g** for food;	2896	
	2: 9 and the tree of knowledge of **g** and evil.	2896	
	2:12 gold of that land *is* **g**: there *is* bdellium	2896	
	2:17 the tree of the knowledge of **g** and evil,	2896	
	2:18 *It is* not **g** that the man should be alone;	2896	
	3: 5 ye shall be as gods, knowing **g** and evil.	2896	
	3: 6 the woman saw that the tree *was* **g** for	2896	
	3:22 become as one of us, to know **g** and evil:	2896	
	15:15 thou shalt be buried in a **g** old age.	2896	
	18: 7 fetch a calf tender and **g**, and gave *it* unto	2896	
	19: 8 and do to them as *is* **g** in your eyes:	2896	
	21:16 her down over against *him* a **g way off**,	7368	
	24:12 **send me g speed** this day, 6440+7136+3807.1		
	24:50 we cannot speak unto thee bad or **g**.	2896	
	25: 8 died in a **g** old age, an old man, and full	2896	
	26:29 as we have done unto thee nothing but **g**,	2896	
	27: 9 fetch me from thence two **g** kids of	2896	
	27:46 the daughters of the land, **what g** 4100+3807.1		
	30:20 God hath endued me with a **g** dowry;	2896	
	31:24 that thou speak not to Jacob either **g**	2896	
	31:29 that thou speak not to Jacob either **g**	2896	
	32:12 I will **surely do** thee **g**, and make 3190+3190		
	40:16 baker saw that the interpretation was **g**,	2896	
	41: 5 corn came up upon one stalk, rank and **g**.	2896	
	41:22 ears came up in one stalk, full and **g**:	2896	
	41:24 the thin ears devoured the seven **g** ears:	2896	
	41:26 The seven **g** kine *are* seven years;	2896	
	41:26 the seven **g** ears *are* seven years:	2896	
	41:35 them gather all the food of those **g** years	2896	
	41:37 the thing was **g** in the eyes of Pharaoh,	3190	
	43:28 Thy servant our father *is* **in g health**,	7965	
	44: 4 Wherefore have ye rewarded evil for **g**?	2896	
	45:18 I will give you the **g** of the land of Egypt,	2898	
	45:20 for the **g** of all the land of Egypt *is* yours.	2898	
	45:23 asses laden with the **g things** of Egypt,	2898	
	46:29 neck, and wept on his neck a **g while**.	5750	
	49:15 he saw that rest *was* **g**, and the land that	2896	
	50:20 *but* God meant it unto **g**, to bring to pass,	2896	
Ex	3: 8 bring them up out of that land unto a **g**	2896	
	18:17 him, The thing that thou doest *is* not **g**.	2896	
	21:34 The owner of the pit shall **make** *it* **g**,	7999	
	22:11 *thereof*, and he shall not **make** *it* **g**.	7999	
	22:13 he shall not **make** *g* that which was torn.	7999	
	22:14 with it, he shall **surely make** *it* **g**. 7999+7999		
	22:15 *thereof* *be* with it, he shall not **make** *it* **g**	7999	
Lev	5: 4 with *his* lips to do evil, or to **do g**,	3190	
	24:18 he that killeth a beast shall **make** it **g**;	7999	
	27:10 a **g** for a bad, or a bad for a **good**:	2896	
	27:10 a **good** for a bad, or a bad for a **g**:	2896	
	27:12 shall value it, whether it be **g** or bad:	2896	
	27:14 shall estimate it, whether it be **g** or bad:	2896	
	27:33 shall not search whether it be **g** or bad,	2896	
Nu	10:29 thou with us, and we will **do** thee **g**:	2895	
	10:29 for the LORD hath spoken **g** concerning	2896	
	13:19 that they dwell in, whether it *be* **g** or bad;	2896	
	13:20 be ye **of g courage**, and bring of the fruit	2388	
	14: 7 to search it, *is* an exceeding **g** land.	2896	
	23:19 he spoken, and shall he not **make** it **g**?	6965	
	24:13 to do *either* **g** or bad of mine own mind;	2896	
Dt	1:14 The thing which thou hast spoken *is* **g**	2896	
	1:25 *It is* a **g** land which the LORD our God	2896	
	1:35 of this evil generation see that **g** land,	2896	
	1:39 *in that* day had no knowledge between **g**	2896	
	2: 4 take ye **g** heed unto yourselves therefore:	3966	
	3:25 and see that **g** land that *is* beyond Jordan,	2896	
	4:15 Take ye therefore **g** heed unto yourselves,	3966	
	4:21 that *I* should not go in unto that **g** land,	2896	
	4:22 ye shall go over, and possess that **g** land,	2896	
	6:11 houses full *of* all **g** *things*, which thou	2898	
	6:18 is right and **g** in the sight of the LORD:	2896	
	6:18 possess the **g** land which the LORD sware	2896	

G

Dt	6:24 fear the LORD our God, for our **g** always,	2896
	8: 7 thy God bringeth thee into a **g** land,	2896
	8:10 for the **g** land which he hath given thee.	2896
	8:16 prove thee, to **do** thee **g** at thy latter end;	3190
	9: 6 **g** land to possess it for thy righteousness;	2896
	10:13 which I command thee *this* day for thy **g**?	2896
	11:17 *lest* ye perish quickly from off the **g** land	2896
	12:28 when thou doest *that which is* **g** and right	2896
	26:11 thou shalt rejoice in every **g** *thing* which	2896
	28:12 The LORD shall open unto thee his **g**	2896
	28:63 the LORD rejoiced over you to **do** you **g**,	3190
	30: 5 will **do** thee **g**, and multiply thee above	3190
	30: 9 cattle, and in the fruit of thy land, for **g**;	2896
	30: 9 LORD will again rejoice over thee for **g**,	2896
	30:15 I have set before thee *this* day life and **g**,	2896
	31: 6 Be strong and **of a g courage**, fear not,	553
	31: 7 of all Israel, Be strong and **of a g courage**:	553
	31:23 said, Be strong and **of a g courage**:	553
	33:16 the **g** will of him that dwelt in the bush:	7522
Jos	1: 6 Be strong and **of a g courage**: for unto	553
	1: 8 and then thou shalt **have g success**.	7919
	1: 9 strong and **of a g courage**; be not afraid,	553
	1:18 death: only be strong and **of a g courage**.	553
	9:25 as it seemeth **g** and right unto thee to do	2896
	10:25 be dismayed, be strong and **of a g courage**:	553
	21:45 There failed not ought of any **g** thing	2896
	23:11 Take **g** heed therefore unto yourselves,	3966
	23:13 until ye perish from off this **g** land which	2896
	23:14 that not one thing hath failed of all the **g**	2896
	23:15 *that* as all **g** things are come upon you,	2896
	23:15 he have destroyed you from off this **g**	2896
	23:16 ye shall perish from off the **g** land	2896
	24:20 after that he hath **done** you **g**.	3190
Jdg	8:32 the son of Joash died in a **g** old age,	2896
	9:11 my **g** fruit, and go to be promoted over	2896
	10:15 do thou unto us whatsoever seemeth **g**	2896
	17:13 Now know I that the LORD will **do** me **g**,	3190
	18: 9 seen the land, and behold, it is very **g**:	2896
	18:22 *And* when they were a **g** way	7368
	19:24 do with them what seemeth **g** unto you:	2896
Ru	2:22 It is **g**, my daughter, that thou go out with	2896
1Sa	1:23 said unto her, Do what seemeth thee **g**;	2896
	2:24 my sons; for *it is* no **g** report that I hear:	2896
	3:18 let him do what seemeth him **g**.	2896
	11:10 ye shall do with us all that seemeth **g** unto	2896
	12:23 I will teach you the **g** and the right way:	2896
	14:36 Do whatsoever seemeth **g** unto thee.	2896
	14:40 unto Saul, Do what seemeth **g** unto thee.	2896
	15: 9 *that was* **g**, and would not utterly destroy	2896
	19: 4 Jonathan spake **g** of David unto Saul his	2896
	19: 4 his works *have been* to thee-ward very **g**:	2896
	20:12 *if there be* **g** toward David, and I then	2895
	24: 4 do to him as it shall seem **g** unto thee.	3190
	24:17 for thou hast rewarded me **g**, whereas I	2896
	24:19 wherefore the LORD reward thee **g** for	2896
	25: 3 *she was* a woman of **g** understanding,	2896
	25: 8 for we come in a **g** day: give, I pray thee,	2896
	25:15 the men *were* very **g** unto us, and we	2896
	25:21 and he hath requited me evil for **g**.	2896
	25:30 the **g** that he hath spoken concerning	2896
	26:16 This *thing is* not **g** that thou hast done.	2896
	29: 6 thy coming in with me in the host *is* **g** in	2896
	29: 9 I know that thou *art* **g** in my sight,	2896
2Sa	3:19 in Hebron all that seemed **g** to Israel,	2896
	3:19 that seemed **g** to the whole house of	NIH
	4:10 thinking to have **brought g tidings**,	1319
	6:19 a **g** piece *of flesh*, and a flagon of wine.	829
	10:12 Be **of g courage**, and let us play the men	2388
	10:12 the LORD do that which seemeth him **g**.	2896
	13:22 his brother Amnon neither **g** nor bad:	2896
	14:17 *is* my lord the king to discern **g** and bad:	2896
	14:32 *it had been* **g** for me *to have been* there	2896
	15: 3 him, See, thy matters *are* **g** and right;	2896
	15:26 let him do to me as seemeth **g** unto him.	2896
	16:12 that the LORD will requite me **g** for his	2896
	17: 7 hath given *is* not **g** at this time.	2896
	17:14 to defeat the **g** counsel of Ahithophel,	2896
	18:27 He *is* a **g** man, and cometh with good	2896
	18:27 a good man, and cometh with **g** tidings.	2896
	19:18 and to do what he thought **g**.	2896
	19:27 do therefore what *is* **g** in thine eyes.	2896
	19:35 *and* can I discern between **g** and evil?	2896
	19:37 do to him what shall seem **g** unto thee.	2896
	19:38 I will do to him *that* which shall seem **g**	2896
	24:22 and offer up what seemeth **g** unto him:	2896
1Ki	1:42 *art* a valiant man, and bringest **g** tidings.	2896
	2:38 said unto the king, The saying *is* **g**.	2896
	2:42 unto me, The word *that* I have heard *is* **g**.	2896
	3: 9 that *I* may discern between **g** and bad:	2896
	8:36 that thou teach them the **g** way wherein	2896
	8:56 hath not failed one word of all his **g**	2896
	12: 7 speak **g** words to them, then they will be	2896
	14:13 in him there is found *some* **g** thing	2896
	14:15 he shall root up Israel out of this **g** land,	2896
	21: 2 *or*, if it seem **g** to thee, I will give thee	2896
	22: 8 he doth not prophesy **g** concerning me,	2896
	22:13 the words of the prophets *declare* **g** unto	2896
	22:13 one of them, and speak *that which is* **g**.	2896
	22:18 he would prophesy no **g** concerning me,	2896
2Ki	3:19 shall fell every **g** tree, and stop all wells	2896
	3:19 mar every **g** piece of land with stones.	2896
	3:25 on every **g** piece of land cast every man	2896
	3:25 wells of water, and felled all the **g** trees:	2896
	7: 9 this day *is* a day of **g tidings**, and we	1309
	8: 9 even *of* every **g** thing of Damascus,	2898

2Ki	10: 5 do thou *that* which *is* **g** in thine eyes.	2896
	20: 3 have done *that* which *is* **g** in thy sight.	2896
	20:19 **G** *is* the word of the LORD which thou	2896
	20:19 *Is* it not **g**, if peace and truth be in my	NIH
1Ch	4:40 they found fat pasture and **g**, and the land	2896
	13: 2 If *it seem* **g** unto you, and *that it be* of	2895
	16: 3 a **g** piece *of flesh*, and a flagon *of wine*.	829
	16:34 for **g**; for his mercy *endureth* for ever.	2896
	19:13 Be **of g courage**, and let us behave	2388
	19:13 let the LORD do *that* which *is* **g** in his	2896
	21:23 let my lord the king do *that which is* **g** in	2896
	22:13 be strong, and **of g courage**; dread not,	553
	28: 8 ye may possess *this* **g** land, and leave *it*	2896
	28:20 Be strong and **of g courage**, and do *it*:	553
	29: 3 I have of mine own **proper g**, *of* gold and	5459
	29:28 he died in a **g** old age, full of days, riches,	2896
2Ch	5:13 praised the LORD, *saying*, For he *is* **g**;	2896
	6:27 when thou hast taught them the **g** way,	2896
	7: 3 praised the LORD, *saying*, For he *is* **g**;	2896
	10: 7 please them, and speak **g** words to them,	2896
	14: 2 Asa did *that* which *was* **g** and right in	2896
	18: 7 for he never prophesied **g** unto me,	2896
	18:12 the words of the prophets *declare* **g** to	2896
	18:12 be like one of theirs, and speak thou **g**.	2896
	18:17 *that* he would not prophesy **g** unto me,	2896
	19: 3 Nevertheless there *are* **g** things found in	2896
	19:11 and the LORD shall be with the **g**.	2896
	24:16 because he had done **g** in Israel,	2896
	30:18 The **g** LORD pardon every one	2896
	30:22 that taught the **g** knowledge of the LORD:	2896
	31:20 wrought *that which was* **g** and right and	2896
Ezr	3:11 because *he is* **g**, for his mercy *endureth*	2896
	5:17 Now therefore, if *it seem* **g** to the king,	2869
	7: 9 according to the **g** hand of his God upon	2896
	7:18 whatsoever shall **seem g** to thee, and to	3191
	8:18 by the **g** hand of our God upon us they	2896
	8:22 hand of our God *is* upon all them for **g**;	2896
	9:12 eat the **g** of the land, and leave *it* for an	2898
Ne	2: 8 according to the **g** hand of my God upon	2896
	2:18 hand of my God which was **g** upon me;	2896
	2:18 they strengthened their hands for *this* **g**	2896
	5: 9 Also I said, It *is* not **g** that ye do: ought ye	2896
	5:19 Think upon me, my God, for **g**,	2896
	6:19 Also they reported his **g deeds** before me,	2896
	9:13 true laws, **g** statutes and commandments:	2896
	9:20 Thou gavest also thy **g** spirit to instruct	2896
	9:36 to eat the fruit thereof and the **g** thereof,	2898
	13:14 wipe not out my **g deeds** that I have	2617
	13:31 Remember me, O my God, for **g**.	2896
Est	3:11 to do with them as it seemeth **g** to thee.	2896
	5: 4 If *it seem* **g** unto the king, let the king	2895
	7: 9 who had spoken **g** for the king, standeth	2896
	8:17 had joy and gladness, a feast and a **g** day.	2896
	9:19 a **g** day, and *of* sending portions one to	2896
	9:22 to joy, and from mourning into a **g** day:	2896
Job	2:10 shall we receive **g** at the hand of God,	2896
	5:27 it *is*; hear it, and know thou *it* for thy **g**.	3807.1
	7: 7 life *is* wind: mine eye shall no more see **g**.	2896
	9:25 than a post: they flee away, they see no **g**.	2896
	10: 3 *Is it* **g** unto thee that thou shouldest	2895
	13: 9 *Is it* **g** that he should search you out?	2895
	15: 3 speeches wherewith he can **do** no **g**?	3276
	21:16 their **g** *is* not in their hand: the counsel	2898
	22:18 Yet he filled their houses with **g things**:	2896
	22:21 at peace: thereby **g** shall come *unto* thee.	2896
	24:21 and **doeth** not **g** to the widow.	3190
	30:26 When I looked for **g**, then evil came *unto*	2896
	34: 4 let us know among ourselves what *is* **g**.	2896
	39: 4 young ones are **in g liking**, they grow	2492
Ps	4: 6 may that say, Who will shew us *any* **g**?	2896
	14: 1 *there is* none that doeth **g**.	2896
	14: 3 *there is* none that doeth **g**, no, not one.	2896
	25: 8 **G** and upright *is* the LORD: therefore	2896
	27:14 be **of g courage**, and he shall strengthen	2388
	31:24 Be **of g courage**, and he shall strengthen	2388
	34: 8 O taste and see that the LORD *is* **g**:	2896
	34:10 the LORD shall not want any **g** thing.	2896
	34:12 *and* loveth *many* days, that *he* may see **g**?	2896
	34:14 Depart from evil, and do **g**; seek peace,	2896
	35:12 rewarded me evil for **g** *to* the spoiling	2896
	36: 3 he hath left off to be wise, *and* to **do g**.	3190
	36: 4 he setteth himself in a way *that is* not **g**;	2896
	37: 3 Trust in the LORD, and do **g**;	2896
	37:23 The steps of a **g** man are ordered by	NIH
	37:27 Depart from evil, and do **g**; and dwell for	2896
	38:20 They also that render evil for **g** are mine	2896
	38:20 because I follow *the thing that* **g** is.	2896
	39: 2 silence, I held my peace, *even* from **g**;	2896
	45: 1 My heart is inditing a **g** matter: I speak of	2896
	51:18 **Do g** in thy good pleasure unto Zion:	3190
	51:18 Do good in thy **g** pleasure unto Zion:	7522
	52: 3 Thou lovest evil more than **g**;	2896
	52: 9 on thy name; for *it is* **g** before thy saints.	2896
	53: 1 *there is* none that doeth **g**.	2896
	53: 3 *there is* none that doeth **g**, no, not one.	2896
	54: 6 will praise thy name, O LORD; for *it is* **g**.	2896
	69:16 O LORD; for thy lovingkindness *is* **g**:	2896
	73: 1 Truly God *is* **g** to Israel, *even* to such as	2896
	73:28 *it is* **g** for me to draw near to God: I have	2896
	84:11 no **g** *thing* will he withhold from them	2896
	85:12 Yea, the LORD shall give *that which is* **g**;	2896
	86: 5 thou, Lord, *art* **g**, and ready to forgive;	2896
	86:17 Shew me a token for **g**; that they which	2896
	92: 1 *It is* a **g** *thing* to give thanks unto	2896

Ps	100: 5 For the LORD *is* **g**; his mercy *is*	2896
	103: 5 Who satisfieth thy mouth with **g** *things*;	2896
	104:28 openest thine hand, they are filled *with* **g**.	2896
	106: 1 O give thanks unto the LORD; for *he is* **g**:	2896
	106: 5 That *I* may see the **g** of thy chosen, that *I*	2896
	107: 1 O give thanks unto the LORD, for *he is* **g**:	2896
	109: 5 they have rewarded me evil for **g**, and	2896
	109:21 because thy mercy *is* **g**, deliver thou me.	2896
	111:10 a understanding have all they that do	2896
	112: 5 A **g** man sheweth favour, and lendeth:	2896
	118: 1 O give thanks unto the LORD; for *he is* **g**:	2896
	118:29 O give thanks unto the LORD; for *he is* **g**:	2896
	119:39 which I fear: for thy judgments *are* **g**.	2896
	119:66 Teach me **g** judgment and knowledge:	2898
	119:68 Thou *art* **g**, and doest good; teach me thy	2896
	119:68 Thou *art* good, and **doest g**; teach me thy	2895
	119:71 *It is* **g** for me that I have been afflicted;	2896
	119:122 Be surety for thy servant for **g**: let not	2896
	122: 9 of the LORD our God I will seek thy **g**.	2896
	125: 4 **Do g**, O LORD, unto *those that be* **g**, and	2895
	125: 4 unto *those that be* **g**, and to *them that*	2896
	128: 5 thou shalt see the **g** of Jerusalem all	2898
	133: 1 how **g** and how pleasant *it is* for brethren	2896
	135: 3 Praise the LORD; for the LORD *is* **g**:	2896
	136: 1 O give thanks unto the LORD; for *he is* **g**:	2896
	143:10 thy spirit *is* **g**; lead me into the land of	2896
	145: 9 The LORD *is* **g** to all: and his tender	2896
	147: 1 for *it is* **g** to sing *praises* unto our God;	2896
Pr	2: 9 judgment, and equity; *yea*, every **g** path.	2896
	2:20 That thou mayest walk in the way of **g**	2896
	3: 4 and **g** understanding in the sight of God	2896
	3:27 Withhold not **g** from them to whom it is	2896
	4: 2 For I give you **g** doctrine, forsake you not	2896
	11:17 merciful man **doeth g** to his own soul:	1580
	11:23 The desire of the righteous *is* only **g**:	2896
	11:27 He that diligently seeketh **g** procureth	2896
	12: 2 A **g** man obtaineth favour of the LORD:	2896
	12:14 man shall be satisfied *with* **g** by the fruit	2896
	12:25 it stoop: but a **g** word maketh it glad.	2896
	13: 2 man shall eat **g** by the fruit of *his* mouth:	2896
	13:15 **G** understanding giveth favour: but the	2896
	13:21 but to the righteous **g** shall be repayed.	2896
	13:22 A **g** *man* leaveth an inheritance to *his*	2896
	14:14 a **g** *man shall be satisfied* from himself.	2896
	14:19 The evil bow before the **g**; and the	2896
	14:22 and truth *shall be* to them that devise **g**.	2896
	15: 3 every place, beholding the evil and the **g**.	2896
	15:23 word *spoken* in due season, how **g** *is it!*	2896
	15:30 *and* a **g** report maketh the bones fat.	2896
	16:20 that handleth a matter wisely shall find **g**:	2896
	16:29 leadeth him into the way *that is* not **g**.	2896
	17:13 Whoso rewardeth evil for **g**, evil shall not	2896
	17:20 He that hath a froward heart findeth no **g**:	2896
	17:22 A merry heart **doeth g** *like* a medicine:	3190
	17:26 to punish the just *is* not **g**, *nor* to strike	2896
	18: 5 *It is* not **g** to accept the person of	2896
	18:22 *Whoso* findeth a wife findeth a **g** *thing*,	2896
	19: 2 soul *be* without knowledge, *it is* not **g**;	2896
	19: 8 that keepeth understanding shall find **g**.	2896
	20:18 by counsel: and with **g advice** make war.	8458
	20:23 the LORD; and a false balance *is* not **g**.	2896
	22: 1 A **g** *name is* rather to be chosen than great	NIH
	24:13 My son, eat thou honey, because *it is* **g**;	2896
	24:23 *It is* not **g** to have respect of persons in	2896
	24:25 and a **g** blessing shall come upon them.	2896
	25:25 so *is* **g** news from a far country.	2896
	25:27 *It is* not **g** to eat much honey: so *for men*	2896
	28:10 the upright shall have **g** *things* in	2896
	28:21 To have respect of persons *is* not **g**: for	2896
	31:12 She will do him **g** and not evil all the days	2896
	31:18 She perceiveth that her merchandise *is* **g**:	2896
Ecc	2: 3 I might see what *was that* **g** for the sons	2896
	2:24 he should make his soul enjoy **g** in his	2896
	2:26 For God giveth to a man *that is* **g** in his	2896
	2:26 that *he* may give to *him that is* **g** before	2896
	3:12 I know that *there is* no **g** in them, but for	2896
	3:12 *a man* to rejoice, and to do **g** in his life.	2896
	3:13 drink, and enjoy the **g** of all his labour,	2896
	4: 8 do I labour, and bereave my soul of **g**?	2896
	4: 9 they have a **g** reward for their labour.	2896
	5:11 what **g** *is* there to the owners thereof,	3788
	5:18 *it is* **g** and comely *for one* to eat and	2896
	5:18 to enjoy the **g** of all his labour that he	2896
	6: 3 his soul be not filled with **g**, and also *that*	2896
	6: 6 years twice *told*, yet hath he seen no **g**:	2896
	6:12 who knoweth what *is* **g** for man in *this*	2896
	7: 1 A **g** *name is* better than precious ointment;	NIH
	7:11 Wisdom *is* **g** with an inheritance: and *by*	2896
	7:18 *It is* **g** that thou shouldest take hold of	2896
	7:20 earth, that doeth **g**, and sinneth not.	2896
	9: 2 to the **g** and to the clean, and to	2896
	9: 2 as *is* the **g**, so *is* the sinner: *and* he that	2896
	9:18 war: but one sinner destroyeth much **g**.	2896
	11: 6 or whether they both *shall be* alike **g**.	2896
	12: 9 he **gave g** heed, and sought out, *and* set	239
	12:14 with every secret *thing*, whether *it be* **g**,	2896
SS	1: 3 Because of the savour of thy **g** ointments	2896
	2:13 the vines with the tender grape give a **g**	NIH
Isa	1:19 obedient, ye shall eat the **g** of the land:	2898
	5:20 Woe unto them that call evil **g**, and good	2896
	5:20 unto them that call evil good, and **g** evil;	2896
	7:15 know to refuse the evil, and choose the **g**.	2896
	7:16 know to refuse the evil, and choose the **g**,	2896
	38: 3 have done *that* which *is* **g** in thy sight.	2896
	39: 8 **G** *is* the word of the LORD which thou	2896

Isa	40: 9 Zion, that **bringest g tidings**, get thee up	1319
	40: 9 Jerusalem, that **bringest g tidings**, lift up	1319
	41: 6 one said to his brother, Be of **g courage**.	2388
	41:23 yea, do **g**, or do evil, that we may be	3190
	41:27 to Jerusalem one that **bringest g tidings**.	1319
	52: 7 the feet of him that **bringeth g tidings**,	1319
	52: 7 that **bringeth g tidings** of good,	1319
	52: 7 that bringeth good tidings of **g**,	2896
	55: 2 eat ye that which is **g**, and let your soul	2896
	61: 1 me to **preach g tidings unto** the meek;	1319
	65: 2 which walketh in a way that was not **g**,	2896
Jer	4:22 but to do **g** they have no knowledge.	3190
	5:25 your sins have withholden **g** things from	2896
	6:16 where is the **g** way, and walk therein,	2896
	8:15 no **g** came; and for a time of health,	2896
	10: 5 do evil, neither also is it in them to do **g**.	3190
	13:10 be as this girdle, which is **g** for nothing.	6743
	13:23 may ye also do **g**, that are accustomed	3190
	14:11 Pray not for this people for their **g**.	2896
	14:19 we looked for peace, and there is no **g**;	2896
	17: 6 and shall not see when **g** cometh;	2896
	18: 4 as seemed to the potter to make it.	3474
	18:10 not my voice, then I will repent of the **g**,	2896
	18:11 and **make** your ways and your doings **g**.	3190
	18:20 Shall evil be recompensed for **g**? for they	2896
	18:20 I stood before thee to speak **g** for them,	2896
	21:10 for evil, and not for **g**, saith the LORD:	2896
	24: 2 One basket had very **g** figs, even like	2896
	24: 3 the figs, very good; and the evil,	2896
	24: 3 the good figs, very **g**; and the evil,	2896
	24: 5 Like these **g** figs, so will I acknowledge	2896
	24: 5 into the land of the Chaldeans for their **g**.	2896
	24: 6 For I will set mine eyes upon them for **g**,	2896
	26:14 do with me as seemeth **g** and meet unto	2896
	29:10 perform my **g** word towards you,	2896
	29:32 neither shall he behold the **g** that I will do	2896
	32:39 for the **g** of them, and of their children	2896
	32:40 not turn away from them, to do them **g**;	3190
	32:41 I will rejoice over them to do them **g**,	2895
	32:42 I bring upon them all the **g** that I have	2896
	33: 9 which shall hear all the **g** that I do unto	2896
	33:11 for the LORD is **g**; for his mercy endureth	2896
	33:14 I will perform that **g** thing which I have	2896
	39:16 upon this city for evil, and not for **g**;	2896
	40: 4 If it seem **g** unto thee to come with me	2896
	40: 4 whither it seemeth **g** and convenient for	2896
	42: 6 Whether it be **g**, or whether it be evil,	2896
	44:27 watch over them for evil, and not for **g**:	2896
La	3:25 The LORD is **g** unto them that wait for	2896
	3:26 It is **g** that a man should both hope and	2896
	3:27 It is **g** for a man that he bear the yoke in	2896
	3:38 the most High proceedeth not evil and **g**.	2896
Eze	16:50 therefore I took them away as I saw **g**.	NIH
	17: 8 It was planted in a **g** soil by great waters,	2896
	18:18 did that which is not **g** among his people,	2896
	20:25 I gave them also statutes that were not **g**,	2896
	24: 4 even every **g** piece, the thigh,	2896
	34:14 I will feed them in a **g** pasture,	2896
	34:14 there shall they lie in a **g** fold, and in a fat	2896
	34:18 unto you to have eaten up the **g** pasture,	2896
	36:31 doings that were not **g**, and shall lothe	2896
Da	4: 2 I thought it **g** to shew the signs and	8232
Hos	4:13 elms, because the shadow thereof is **g**:	2896
	8: 3 Israel hath cast off the thing that is **g**:	2896
Am	5:14 Seek **g**, and not evil, that ye may live:	2896
	5:15 love the **g**, and establish judgment in	2896
	9: 4 eyes upon them for evil, and not for **g**.	2896
Mic	1: 2 of Maroth waited carefully for **g**:	2896
	2: 7 do not my words do **g** to him that	3190
	3: 2 Who hate the **g**, and love the evil;	2896
	6: 8 He hath shewed thee, O man, what is **g**;	2896
	7: 2 The **g** man is perished out of the earth:	2623
Na	1: 7 The LORD is **g**, a strong hold in the day	2896
	1:15 the feet of him that **bringeth g tidings**,	1319
Zep	1:12 in their heart, The LORD will not do **g**,	3190
Zec	1:13 angel that talked with me with **g** words	2896
	11:12 them, If ye think **g**, give me my price;	2896
Mal	2:13 or receiveth it with **g will** at your hand.	7522
	2:17 Every one that doeth evil is **g** in the sight	2896
Mt	3:10 every tree which bringeth not forth **g** fruit	2570
	5:13 thenceforth for nothing, but to be cast	2480
	5:16 that they may see your **g** works,	2570
	5:44 do **g** to them that hate you, and pray for	2573
	5:45 his sun to rise on the evil and on the **g**,	18
	7:11 how to give **g** gifts unto your children,	18
	7:11 give **g** things to them that ask him?	18
	7:17 so every **g** tree bringeth forth good fruit;	18
	7:17 so every good tree bringeth forth **g** fruit;	2570
	7:18 A **g** tree cannot bring forth evil fruit,	18
	7:18 can a corrupt tree bring forth **g** fruit.	2570
	7:19 Every tree that bringeth not forth **g** fruit is	2570
	8:30 And there was a **g way off** from them a	3112
	9: 2 Son, **be of g cheer**; thy sins be forgiven	2293
	9:22 he said, Daughter, **be of g comfort**;	2293
	11:26 Father; for so it seemed **g** in thy sight.	2107
	12:33 Either make the tree **g**, and his fruit good;	2570
	12:33 Either make the tree good, and his fruit **g**;	2570
	12:34 speak **g** things? for out of the abundance of	18
	12:35 **g** man out of the good treasure of the heart	18
	12:35 good man out of the **g** treasure of the heart	18
	12:35 of the heart bringeth forth **g** things:	18
	13: 8 But other fell into **g** ground,	2570
	13:23 he that received seed into the **g** ground	2570
	13:24 a man which sowed **g** seed in his field?	2570
	13:27 didst not thou sow **g** seed in thy field?	2570

Mt	13:37 He that soweth the **g** seed is the Son of	2570
	13:38 **g** seed are the children of the kingdom;	2570
	13:48 and gathered the **g** into vessels, but cast	2570
	14:27 spake unto them, saying, **Be of g cheer**;	2293
	17: 4 unto Jesus, Lord, it is **g** for us to be here:	2570
	19:10 so with his wife, it is not **g** to marry.	4851
	19:16 one came and said unto him, **G** Master,	18
	19:16 Good Master, what **g** thing shall I do,	18
	19:16 he said unto him, Why callest thou me **g**?	18
	19:17 there is none **g** but one, that is, God:	18
	20:15 Is thine eye evil, because I am **g**?	18
	22:10 all as many as they found, both bad and **g**:	18
	25:21 Well done, thou **g** and faithful servant:	18
	25:23 him, Well done, **g** and faithful servant;	18
	26:10 for she hath wrought a **g** work upon me.	2570
	26:24 it had been **g** for that man if he had not	2570
Mk	3: 4 Is it lawful to do **g** on the sabbath days,	15
	4: 8 And other fell on **g** ground, and did yield	2570
	4:20 And these are they which are sown on **g**	2570
	6:50 and saith unto them, **Be of g cheer**:	2293
	9: 5 to Jesus, Master, it is **g** for us to be here:	2570
	9:50 Salt is **g**: but if the salt have lost his	2570
	10:17 kneeled to him, and asked him, **G** Master,	18
	10:18 Jesus said unto him, Why callest thou me **g**?	18
	10:18 there is none **g** but one, that is, God.	18
	10:49 saying unto him, **Be of g comfort**, rise;	2293
	14: 6 she hath wrought a **g** work on me.	2570
	14: 7 whensoever ye will ye may do them **g**:	2095
	14:21 **g** were it for that man if he had never	2570
Lk	1: 3 It **seemed g** to me also, having had	1380
	1:53 He hath filled the hungry with **g** things;	18
	2:10 I **bring** you **g** tidings of great joy,	2097
	2:14 and on earth peace, **g will** towards men.	2107
	3: 9 which bringeth not forth **g** fruit is hewn	2570
	6:27 enemies, do **g** to them which hate you,	2573
	6:33 if ye do **g** to them which do good to you,	15
	6:33 if ye do good to them which **do g** to you,	15
	6:35 do **g**, and lend, hoping for nothing again;	15
	6:38 **g** measure, pressed down,	2570
	6:43 a **g** tree bringeth not forth corrupt fruit;	2570
	6:43 neither doth a corrupt tree bring forth **g**	2570
	6:45 A **g** man out of the good treasure of his heart	18
	6:45 A good man out of the **g** treasure of his heart	18
	6:45 of his heart bringeth forth that which is **g**;	18
	8: 8 And other fell on **g** ground, and sprang up,	18
	8:15 that on the **g** ground are they, which in	2570
	8:15 in an honest and **g** heart, having heard	18
	8:48 unto her, Daughter, **be of g comfort**:	2293
	9:33 Jesus, Master, it is **g** for us to be here:	2570
	10:21 Father; for so it seemed **g** in thy sight.	2107
	10:42 and Mary hath chosen that **g** part, which	18
	11:13 how to give **g** gifts unto your children:	18
	12:32 for it is your Father's **g pleasure** to give	2106
	14:34 Salt is **g**: but if the salt have lost his	2570
	16:25 in thy lifetime receivedst thy **g** things,	18
	18:18 a certain ruler asked him, saying, **G** Master,	18
	18:19 Jesus said unto him, Why callest thou me **g**?	18
	18:19 me good? none is **g**, save one, that is, God.	18
	19:17 And he said unto him, Well, thou **g** servant:	18
	23:50 counseller; and he was a **g** man, and a just:	18
Jn	1:46 there any **g** thing come out of Nazareth?	18
	2:10 man at the beginning doth set forth **g**	2570
	2:10 but thou hast kept the **g** wine until now.	2570
	5:29 that have done **g**, unto the resurrection	18
	7:12 some said, He is a **g** man: others said, Nay;	18
	10:11 I am the **g** shepherd: the **g** shepherd	2570
	10:11 **g** shepherd giveth his life for the sheep.	2570
	10:14 I am the **g** shepherd, and know my	2570
	10:32 Many **g** works have I shewed you from	2570
	10:33 saying, For a **g** work we stone thee not;	2570
	16:33 but **be of g cheer**; I have overcome	2293
Ac	4: 9 If we this day be examined of the **g** deed	2108
	9:36 this woman was full of **g** works and	18
	10:22 of **g report** among all the nation of	3140
	10:38 who went about **doing g**, and healing all	2109
	11:24 For he was a **g** man, and full of the Holy	18
	14:17 himself without witness, in that he did **g**,	15
	15: 7 know how that a **g while ago**	575+744+2250
	15:25 It **seemed g** unto us, being assembled	1380
	15:28 For it **seemed g** to the Holy Ghost,	1380
	15:38 But Paul **thought** not **g** to take him with	515
	18: 3 this tarried there yet a **g while**,	2250+2425
	22:12 **having a g report** of all the Jews which	3140
	23: 1 I have lived in all **g** conscience before God	18
	23:11 by him, and said, **Be of g cheer**, Paul:	2293
	27:22 And now I exhort you to **be of g cheer**:	2114
	27:25 sirs, **be of g cheer**: for I believe	2114
	27:36 Then were they all **of g cheer**,	2115
Ro	2:10 and peace, to every man that worketh **g**,	18
	3: 8 we say,) Let us do evil, that **g** may come?	18
	3:12 there is none that doeth **g**, no, not one.	5544
	5: 7 yet peradventure for a **g** man some would	18
	7:12 the commandment holy, and just, and **g**.	18
	7:13 then that which is **g** made death unto me?	18
	7:13 working death in me by that which is **g**;	18
	7:16 I consent unto the law that it is **g**.	2570
	7:18 dwelleth no **g** thing: for to will is present	18
	7:18 how to perform that which is **g** I find not.	2570
	7:19 For the **g** that I would I do not: but the evil	18
	7:21 find then a law, that, when I would do **g**,	2570
	8:28 work together for **g** to them that love God,	18
	9:11 yet born, having neither done any **g** or evil,	18
	10:15 of peace, and bring glad tidings of **g** things!	18
	11:24 contrary to nature into a **g** olive tree:	2565

Ro	12: 2 that ye may prove what is that **g**,	18
	12: 9 that which is evil; cleave to that which is **g**.	18
	12:21 overcome of evil, but overcome evil with **g**.	18
	13: 3 For rulers are not a terror to **g** works,	18
	13: 3 that which is **g**, and thou shalt have praise	18
	13: 4 For he is the minister of God to thee for **g**.	18
	14:16 Let not then your **g** be evil spoken of:	18
	14:21 It is **g** neither to eat flesh, nor to drink	2570
	15: 2 his neighbour for his **g** to edification.	18
	16:18 and by **g words** and fair speeches deceive	5542
	16:19 would have you wise unto that which is **g**,	18
1Co	5: 6 Your glorying is not **g**. Know ye not that a	2570
	7: 1 It is **g** for a man not to touch a woman.	2570
	7: 8 It is **g** for them if they abide even as I.	2570
	7:26 that this is **g** for the present distress,	2570
	7:26 I say, that it is **g** for a man so to be.	2570
	15:33 evil communications corrupt **g** manners.	5543
2Co	5:10 that he hath done, whether it be **g** or bad.	18
	6: 8 dishonour, by evil report and **g report**:	2162
	9: 8 in all things, may abound to every **g** work:	18
	13:11 **Be of g comfort**, be of one	3870
Gal	4:18 But it is **g** to be zealously affected always	2570
	4:18 be zealously affected always in a **g** thing,	2570
	6: 6 unto him that teacheth in all **g** things.	18
	6:10 let us do **g** unto all men, especially unto	18
Eph	1: 5 according to the **g pleasure** of his will,	2107
	1: 9 according to his **g pleasure** which he had	2107
	2:10 created in Christ Jesus unto **g** works,	18
	4:28 with his hands the thing which is **g**,	18
	4:29 but that which is **g** to the use of edifying,	18
	6: 7 With **g will** doing service, as to the Lord,	2133
	6: 8 Knowing that whatsoever **g** thing any man	18
Php	1: 6 work in you will perform it until the day	18
	1:15 envy and strife; and some also of **g will**:	2107
	2:13 both to will and to do of his **g pleasure**.	2107
	2:19 that I also may be **of g comfort**, when I	2174
	4: 8 whatsoever things are of **g report**;	2163
Col	1:10 being fruitful in every **g** work,	18
1Th	3: 1 **thought** it **g** to be left at Athens alone;	2106
	3: 6 and **brought** us **g tidings** of your faith	2097
	3: 6 that ye have **g** remembrance of us always,	18
	5:15 any man; but ever follow that which is **g**,	18
	5:21 Prove all things; hold fast that which is **g**.	2570
2Th	1:11 fulfil all the **g pleasure** of his goodness,	2107
	2:16 and hope through grace,	18
	2:17 and stablish you in every **g** word and work.	18
1Ti	1: 5 of a **g** conscience, and of faith unfeigned:	18
	1: 8 we know that the law is **g**, if a man use	2570
	1:18 thou by them mightest war a **g** warfare;	2570
	1:19 Holding faith, and a **g** conscience;	18
	2: 3 For this is **g** and acceptable in the sight of	2570
	2:10 women professing godliness) with **g** works.	18
	3: 1 office of a bishop, he desireth a **g** work.	2570
	3: 2 vigilant, sober, of **g behaviour**, given to	2887
	3: 7 Moreover he must have a **g** report of	2570
	3:13 well purchase to themselves a **g** degree,	2570
	4: 4 For every creature of God is **g**,	2570
	4: 6 thou shalt be a **g** minister of Jesus Christ,	2570
	4: 6 up in the words of faith and of **g** doctrine,	2570
	5: 4 for that is **g** and acceptable before God.	2570
	5:10 Well reported of for **g** works; if she have	2570
	5:10 she have diligently followed every **g** work.	18
	5:25 Likewise also the **g** works of some are	2570
	6:12 Fight the **g** fight of faith, lay hold on	2570
	6:12 hast professed a **g** profession before many	2570
	6:13 who before Pontius Pilate witnessed a **g**	2570
	6:18 That they **do g**, that they be rich in good	14
	6:18 that they be rich in **g** works, ready to	2570
	6:19 Laying up in store for themselves a **g**	2570
2Ti	1:14 That **g** thing which was committed unto	2570
	2: 3 as a **g** soldier of Jesus Christ.	2570
	2:21 use, and prepared unto every **g** work.	18
	3: 3 fierce, **despisers of** those that are **g**,	865
	3:17 throughly furnished unto all **g** works.	18
	4: 7 I have fought a **g** fight, I have finished my	2570
Tit	1: 8 a **lover of g men**, sober, just, holy,	5358
	1:16 and unto every **g** work reprobate.	18
	2: 3 to much wine, **teachers of g things**;	2567
	2: 5 be discreet, chaste, keepers at home, **g**,	18
	2: 7 In all things shewing thyself a pattern of **g**	2570
	2:10 Not purloining, but shewing all **g** fidelity;	18
	2:14 a peculiar people, zealous of **g** works.	2570
	3: 1 magistrates, to be ready to every **g** work,	18
	3: 8 might be careful to maintain **g** works.	2570
	3: 8 things are **g** and profitable unto men.	2570
	3:14 let ours also learn to maintain **g** works	2570
Phm	1: 6 every **g** thing which is in you in Christ	18
Heb	5:14 their senses exercised to discern both **g**	2570
	6: 5 And have tasted the **g** word of God,	2570
	9:11 But Christ being come a high priest of **g**	18
	10: 1 For the law having a shadow of **g** things to	18
	10:24 to provoke unto love and to **g** works:	2570
	11: 2 For by it the elders obtained a **g** report.	3140
	11:12 him **as g as dead**, so many as the stars	3499
	11:39 having **obtained a g report** through faith,	3140
	13: 9 For it is a **g** thing that the heart be	2570
	13:16 to do **g** and to communicate forget not:	2140
	13:18 for we trust we have a **g** conscience, in all	2570
	13:21 Make you perfect in every **g** work to do his	18
Jas	1:17 Every **g** gift and every perfect gift is from	18
	2: 3 say unto him, Sit thou here in a **g** place;	2573
	3:13 let him shew out of a **g** conversation his	2570
	3:17 full of mercy and **g** fruits, without partiality,	18
	4:17 Therefore to him that knoweth to do **g**,	2570
1Pe	2:12 they may by your **g** works, which they	2570

G

1Pe 2:18 not only to the **g** and gentle, but also to *18*
 3:10 For he that will love life, and see **g** days, *18*
 3:11 let him eschew evil, and do **g**; let him seek *18*
 3:13 if ye be followers of *that which is* **g**? *18*
 3:16 Having a **g** conscience; that, whereas they *18*
 3:16 falsely accuse your conversation in Christ. *18*
 3:21 the answer of a **g** conscience toward God,) *18*
 4:10 **g** stewards of the manifold grace of God. *2570*
1Jn 3:17 whoso hath *this* world's **g**, and seeth his *979*
3Jn 1:11 not *that which is* evil, but *that which is* **g**. *18*
 1:11 He that *doeth* **g** is of God: but he that *15*
 1:12 Demetrius **hath g report** of all *men,* and *3140*

GOODLIER (1) [GOOD]
1Sa 9: 2 the children of Israel a **g** person than he: 2896

GOODLIEST (1) [GOOD]
1Sa 8:16 your **g** young men, and your asses, 2896
1Ki 20: 3 and thy children, *even* the **g**, *are* mine. 2896

GOODLINESS (1) [GOOD]
Isa 40: 6 the **g** thereof *is* as the flower of the field: 2617

GOODLY (33) [GOOD]
Ge 27:15 Rebekah took **g** raiment of her eldest son 2532
 39: 6 Joseph was a **g** *person,* and 3303+8389
 49:21 *is* a hind let loose: he giveth **g** words. 8233
Ex 2: 2 when she saw him that he *was a* **g** *child,* 2896
 39:28 **g** bonnets *of* fine linen, and linen 6287
Lev 23:40 you on the first day the boughs of **g** trees, 1926
Nu 24: 5 How **g** are thy tents, O Jacob, 2895
 31:10 dwelt, and all their **g** castles, with fire. 2918
Dt 3:25 that **g** mountain, and Lebanon. 2896
 6:10 to Jacob, to give thee great and **g** cities, 2896
 8:12 hast built **g** houses, and dwelt *therein;* 2896
Jos 7:21 When I saw among the spoils a **g** 2896
1Sa 9: 2 was Saul, a choice young *man,* and a **g**: 2896
 16:12 a beautiful countenance, and **g** to look to. 2896
2Sa 23:21 he slew an Egyptian, a **g** man: 4758
1Ki 1: 6 he also *was* a very **g** *man;* and 2896+8389
2Ch 36:10 with the **g** vessels of the house of 2532
 36:19 and destroyed all the **g** vessels thereof. 4261
Job 39:13 *thou* **g** wings unto the peacocks? 7443
Ps 16: 6 pleasant *places;* yea, I have a **g** heritage. 8231
 80:10 the boughs thereof *were* like the **g** cedars. 410
Jer 3:19 a **g** heritage of the hosts of nations? 6643
 11:16 A green olive tree, fair, *and* of **g** fruit: 8389
Eze 17: 8 might bear fruit, that *it* might be a **g** vine. 155
 17:23 and bear fruit, and be a **g** cedar: 117
Hos 10: 1 of his land they have **made g** images. 2895
Joel 3: 5 have carried into your temples my **g** 2896
Zec 10: 3 made them as his **g** horse in the battle. 1935
 11:13 a **g** price that I was prised at of them. 145
Mt 13:45 unto a merchant man, seeking **g** pearls: 2570
Lk 21: 5 it was adorned with **g** stones and gifts, 2570
Jas 2: 2 in **g** apparel, and there come in also a 2986
Rev 18:14 *were* dainty and **g** are departed from thee, 2986

GOODMAN (6) [GOOD, MAN]
Pr 7:19 For the **g** *is* not at home, he is gone a long 376
Mt 20:11 murmured against the **g of the house,** 3617
 24:43 that if the **g of the house** had known in 3617
Mk 14:14 say ye to the **g of the house,** The Master 3617
Lk 12:39 if the **g of the house** had known what 3617
 22:11 And ye shall say unto the **g of the house,** 3617

GOODNESS (50) [GOOD]
Ex 18: 9 Jethro rejoiced for all the **g** which 2896
 33:19 I will make all my **g** pass before thee, 2898
 34: 6 and abundant in **g** and truth, 2617
Nu 10:32 *that* what **g** the Lord shall do unto us, 2896
Jdg 8:35 according to all the **g** which he had 2896
2Sa 7:28 hast promised this **g** unto thy servant: 2896
1Ki 8:66 glad of heart for all the **g** that the Lord 2896
1Ch 17:26 hast promised this **g** unto thy servant: 2896
2Ch 6:41 and let thy saints rejoice in **g**. 2896
 7:10 merry in heart for the **g** that the Lord 2896
 32:32 the acts of Hezekiah, and his **g**, behold, 2617
 35:26 the rest of the acts of Josiah, and his **g**, 2617
Ne 9:25 and delighted themselves in thy great **g**. 2898
 9:35 in thy great **g** that thou gavest them, 2898
Ps 16: 2 *art* my Lord: my **g** *extendeth* not to thee; 2896
 21: 3 preventest him *with* the blessings of **g**: 2896
 23: 6 Surely **g** and mercy shall follow me all 2896
 27:13 **g** of the Lord in the land of the living. 2898
 31:19 how great *is* thy **g**, which thou hast laid 2898
 33: 5 the earth is full *of* the **g** of the Lord. 2617
 52: 1 O mighty *man?* the **g** of God *endureth* 2617
 65: 4 we shall be satisfied with the **g** of thy 2898
 65:11 Thou crownest the year with thy **g**; 2896
 68:10 God, hast prepared of thy **g** for the poor. 2896
 107: 8 *men* would praise the Lord *for* his **g**, 2617
 107: 9 and filleth the hungry soul *with* **g**. 2896
 107:15 *men* would praise the Lord *for* his **g**, 2617
 107:21 *men* would praise the Lord *for* his **g**, 2617
 107:31 *men* would praise the Lord *for* his **g**, 2617
 144: 2 My **g**, and my fortress; my high tower, 2617
 145: 7 utter the memory of thy great **g**, 2898
Pr 20: 6 men will proclaim every one his own **g**: 2617
Isa 63: 7 the great **g** towards the house of Israel, 2898
Jer 2: 7 to eat the fruit thereof and the **g** thereof; 2898
 31:12 shall flow *together* to the **g** of the Lord, 2898
 31:14 my people shall be satisfied with my **g**, 2898
 33: 9 they shall fear and tremble for all the **g** 2896
Hos 3: 5 fear the Lord and his **g** in the latter days. 2898

Hos 6: 4 for your **g** *is* as a morning cloud, and as 2617
 10: 1 according to the **g** of his land they have 2896
Zec 9:17 For how great *is* his **g**, and how great *is* 2898
Ro 2: 4 Or despisest thou the riches of his **g** and 5544
 2: 4 not knowing that the **g** of God leadeth 5543
 11:22 therefore the **g** and severity of God: 5544
 11:22 but toward thee, **g**, if thou continue in *his* 5544
 11:22 **g**, if thou continue in *his* **g**: 5544
 15:14 my brethren, that ye are also full of **g**, 19
Gal 5:22 peace, longsuffering, gentleness, **g**, faith, 19
Eph 5: 9 [For the fruit of the Spirit *is* in all **g** and 19
2Th 1:11 and fulfil all the good pleasure of *his* **g**, 19

GOODNESS' (1) [GOOD]
Ps 25: 7 mercy remember thou me for thy **g** sake, 2898

GOODS (42) [GOOD]
Ge 14:11 they took all the **g** of Sodom and 7399
 14:12 dwelt in Sodom, and his **g**, and departed. 7399
 14:16 brought back all the **g**, and also brought 7399
 14:16 **g**, and the women also, and the people. 7399
 14:21 me the persons, and take the **g** to thyself. 7399
 24:10 all the **g** of his master *were* in his hand: 2898
 31:18 all his **g** which he had gotten, the cattle 7399
 46: 6 they took their cattle, and their **g**, 7399
Ex 22: 8 have put his hand unto his neighbour's **g**. 4399
 22:11 not put his hand unto his neighbour's **g**; 4399
Nu 16:32 appertained unto Korah, and all *their* **g**. 7399
 31: 9 and all their flocks, and all their **g**. 2428
 35: 3 and for their **g**, and for all their beasts. 7399
Dt 28:11 the Lord shall make thee plenteous in **g**, 2896
2Ch 21: 4 thy children, and thy wives, and all thy **g**: 7399
Ezr 1: 4 with gold, and with **g**, and with beasts, 7399
 1: 6 with **g**, and with beasts, and with precious 7399
 6: 8 that of the king's **g**, *even* of the tribute 5232
 7:26 to confiscation of **g**, or to imprisonment. 5232
Ne 9:25 land, and possessed houses full *of* all **g**, 2898
Job 20:10 poor, and his hands shall restore their **g**. 202
 20:21 there shall no *man* look for his **g**. 2898
 20:28 *his* **g** shall flow away in the day of his NIH
Ecc 5:11 When **g** increase, they are increased that 2896
Eze 38:12 which have gotten cattle and **g**, that dwell 7075
 38:13 and gold, to take *away* cattle and **g**, 7075
Zep 1:13 Therefore their **g** shall become a booty, 2428
Mt 12:29 and spoil his **g**, except he first bind 4632
 24:47 he shall make him ruler over all his **g**. 5225
 25:14 and delivered unto them his **g**. 5225
Mk 3:27 and spoil his **g**, except he will first bind 4632
Lk 6:30 him that taketh away thy **g** ask *them* not NIG
 11:21 keepeth his palace, his **g** are in peace: 5225
 12:18 there will I bestow all my fruits and my **g**. 18
 12:19 thou hast much **g** laid up for many years; 18
 15:12 give me the portion of **g** that falleth to *me.* 3776
 16: 1 unto him that he had wasted his **g**. 5225
 19: 8 Lord, the half of my **g** I give to the poor; 5225
Ac 2:45 And sold their possessions and **g**, 5223
1Co 13: 3 And though I bestow all my **g** to feed 5225
Heb 10:34 and took joyfully the spoiling of your **g**, 5225
Rev 3:17 and **increased with g**, and have need of 4147

GOPHER (1)
Ge 6:14 Make thee an ark of **g** wood; rooms shalt 1613

GORE (1) [GORED]
Ex 21:28 an ox **g** a man or a woman, that they die: 5055

GORED (2) [GORE]
Ex 21:31 Whether he have **g** a son, or have gored a 5055
 21:31 he have gored a son, or have **g** a daughter, 5055

GORGEOUS (1) [GORGEOUSLY]
Lk 23:11 mocked *him,* and arrayed him in a **g** robe, 2986

GORGEOUSLY (2) [GORGEOUS]
Eze 23:12 captains and rulers clothed **most g**, 4358
Lk 7:25 they which are **g** apparelled, 1722+1741

GOSHEN (15)
Ge 45:10 thou shalt dwell in the land of **G**, 1657
 46:28 unto Joseph, to direct his face unto **G**; 1657
 46:28 and they came into the land of **G**. 1657
 46:29 to **G**, and presented himself unto him; 1657
 46:34 that ye may dwell in the land of **G**; 1657
 47: 1 and behold, they *are* in the land of **G**. 1657
 47: 4 let thy servants dwell in the land of **G**. 1657
 47: 6 to dwell; in the land of **G** let them dwell: 1657
 47:27 in the land of Egypt, in the country of **G**; 1657
 50: 8 their herds, they left in the land of **G**. 1657
Ex 8:22 I will sever in that day the land of **G**, 1657
 9:26 Only in the land of **G**, where the children 1657
Jos 10:41 all the country of **G**, even unto Gibeon. 1657
 11:16 the south *country,* and all the land of **G**, 1657
 15:51 **G**, and Holon, and Giloh; eleven cities 1657

GOSPEL (101) [GOSPEL'S]
Mt 4:23 and preaching the **g** of the kingdom, 2098
 9:35 and preaching the **g** of the kingdom, 2098
 11: 5 the poor have **the g preached** to them. 2097
 24:14 And this **g** of the kingdom shall be 2098
 26:13 Wheresoever this **g** shall be preached in 2098
Mk 1: 1 The beginning of the **g** of Jesus Christ, 2098
 1:14 preaching the **g** of the kingdom of God, 2098
 1:15 is at hand: repent ye, and believe the **g**. 2098
 13:10 the **g** must first be published among all 2098
 14: 9 Wheresoever this **g** shall be preached 2098
 16:15 and preach the **g** to every creature. 2098

Lk 4:18 he hath anointed me to **preach the g** to 2097
 7:22 are raised, to the poor **the g** is **preached**. 2097
 9: 6 **preaching** the **g**, and healing every 2097
 20: 1 and **preached the g**, the chief priests and 2097
Ac 8:25 **preached the g** in many villages of 2097
 14: 7 And there they **preached the g**. 2097
 14:21 when they had **preached the g** to that 2097
 15: 7 my mouth should hear the word of the **g**, 2098
 16:10 called us for to **preach the g** unto them. 2097
 20:24 to testify the **g** of the grace of God. 2098
Ro 1: 1 an apostle, separated unto the **g** of God, 2098
 1: 9 whom I serve with my spirit in the **g** of 2098
 1:15 I am ready to **preach the g** to you that 2097
 1:16 For I am not ashamed of the **g** of Christ: 2098
 2:16 of men by Jesus Christ according to my **g**. 2098
 10:15 feet of them that **preach the g** of peace, 2097
 10:16 But they have not all obeyed the **g**. 2098
 11:28 As concerning the **g**, *they are* enemies for 2098
 15:16 ministering the **g** of God, that the offering 2098
 15:19 I have fully preached the **g** of Christ. 2098
 15:20 Yea, so have I strived to **preach the g**, 2097
 15:29 fulness of the blessing of the **g** of Christ. 2098
 16:25 power to stablish you according to my **g**, 2098
1Co 1:17 me not to baptize, but to **preach the g**: 2097
 4:15 Jesus I have begotten you through the **g**. 2098
 9:12 all *things,* lest we should hinder the **g** 2098
 9:14 preach the **g** should live of the gospel. 2098
 9:14 preach the gospel should live of the **g**. 2098
 9:16 though I **preach** the **g**, I have nothing 2097
 9:16 woe is unto me, if I **preach** not the **g**! 2097
 9:17 a dispensation *of the* **g** is committed unto NIG
 9:18 *Verily* that, when I **preach the g**, I may 2097
 9:18 may make the **g** of Christ without charge, 2098
 9:18 that *I* abuse not my power in the **g**. 2098
 15: 1 I declare unto you the **g** which I preached 2098
2Co 2:12 I came to Troas to *preach* Christ's **g**, 2098
 4: 3 But if our **g** be hid, it is hid to them that 2098
 4: 4 lest the light of the glorious **g** of Christ, 2098
 8:18 whose praise *is* in the **g** throughout all 2098
 9:13 professed subjection unto the **g** of Christ, 2098
 10:14 to you also in *preaching* the **g** of Christ: 2098
 10:16 To **preach the g** in the *regions* beyond 2097
 11: 4 which ye have not received, or another **g**, 2098
 11: 7 have preached to you the **g** of God freely? 2098
Gal 1: 6 into the grace of Christ unto another **g**: 2098
 1: 7 and would pervert the **g** of Christ. 2098
 1: 8 **preach** any other **g** unto you than *that* 2097
 1: 9 If any *man* **preach** any other **g** unto you 2097
 1:11 the **g** which was preached of me is not 2098
 2: 2 communicated unto them *that* **g** which I 2098
 2: 5 that the truth of the **g** might continue 2098
 2: 7 when they saw that the **g** of 2098
 2: 7 the **g** of the circumcision *was* unto Peter; NIG
 2:14 uprightly according to the truth of the **g**, 2098
 3: 8 **preached before the g** unto Abraham, 4283
 4:13 I **preached the g** unto you at the first. 2097
Eph 1:13 the word of truth, the **g** of your salvation: 2098
 3: 6 partakers of his promise in Christ by the **g**: 2098
 6:15 with the preparation of the **g** of peace; 2098
 6:19 to make known the mystery of the **g**, 2098
Php 1: 5 For your fellowship in the **g** from the first 2098
 1: 7 *in* the defence and confirmation of the **g**, 2098
 1:12 out rather unto the furtherance of the **g**; 2098
 1:17 that I am set for the defence of the **g**. 2098
 1:27 be as it becometh the **g** of Christ: 2098
 1:27 striving together for the faith of the **g**; 2098
 2:22 father, he hath served with me in the **g**. 2098
 4: 3 *women* which laboured with me in the **g**, 2098
 4:15 know also, that in the beginning of the **g**, 2098
Col 1: 5 before in the word of the truth of the **g**; 2098
 1:23 not moved away from the hope of the **g**, 2098
1Th 1: 5 our **g** came not unto you in word only, 2098
 2: 2 you the **g** of God with much contention. 2098
 2: 4 of God to be put in trust with the **g**, 2098
 2: 8 not the **g** of God only, but also our own 2098
 2: 9 we preached unto you the **g** of God. 2098
 3: 2 and our fellowlabourer in the **g** of Christ, 2098
2Th 1: 8 that obey not the **g** of our Lord Jesus 2098
 2:14 Whereunto he called you by our **g**, 2098
1Ti 1:11 According to the glorious **g** of the blessed 2098
2Ti 1: 8 be thou partaker of the afflictions of the **g** 2098
 1:10 and immortality to light through the **g**: 2098
 2: 8 raised from the dead according to my **g**: 2098
Phm 1:13 ministered unto me in the bonds of the **g**: 2098
Heb 4: 2 For unto us was **the g preached**, as well 2097
1Pe 1:12 **preached the g** unto you with the Holy 2097
 1:25 which by the **g** is **preached** unto you. 2097
 4: 6 for this cause was the **g** preached also 2097
 4:17 of them that obey not the **g** of God? 2098
Rev 14: 6 having the everlasting **g** to preach unto 2098

GOSPEL'S (3) [GOSPEL]
Mk 8:35 shall lose his life for my sake and the **g**, 2098
 10:29 children, or lands, for my sake, and the **g**, 2098
1Co 9:23 this I do for the **g** sake, that I might be 2098

GOSSIP See TALEBEARER

GOSSIPS See TATTLERS

GOT (7) [GET]
Ge 36: 6 which he had **g** in the land of Canaan; 7408
 39:12 in her hand, and fled, and **g** him out. 3318
 39:15 with me, and fled, and **g** him out. 3318
Ps 44: 3 For they **g** not the land **in possession** by 3423
Ecc 2: 7 I **g** me servants and maidens, 7069

Jer 13: 2 So I *g* a girdle, according to the word of | 7069
13: 4 Take the girdle that thou hast *g*, which *is* | 7069

GOTTEN (25) [GET]

Ge 4: 1 and said, I have *g* a man from the LORD. | 7069
12: 5 and the souls that they had *g* in Haran; | 6213
31: 1 *that* which *was* of our father's hath he *g* | 6213
31:18 all his goods which he had *g*, the cattle of | 7408
31:18 getting, which he had *g*, in Padan-aram, | 7408
46: 6 which they had *g* in the land of Canaan, | 7408
Ex 14:18 when I have *g* me **honour** upon Pharaoh, | 3513
Lev 6: 4 thing which he hath **deceitfully** *g*, | 6231+6233
Nu 31:50 what every man hath *g*, *of* jewels of gold, | 4672
Dt 8:17 the might of mine hand hath *g* me this | 6213
2Sa 17:13 if he be into a city, then shall all Israel | 622
Job 28:15 It cannot be *g* for gold, neither shall silver | 5414
31:25 and because mine hand had *g* much; | 4672
Ps 98: 1 and his holy arm, hath *g* him the **victory**. | 3467
Pr 13:11 Wealth *g* by vanity shall be diminished: | NIH
20:21 An inheritance *may be* *g* **hastily** at | 926
Ecc 1:16 have *g* **more** wisdom than all *they* that | 3254
Isa 15: 7 Therefore the abundance they have *g* | 6213
Jer 48:36 the riches *that* he hath *g* are perished. | 6213
Eze 28: 4 with thine understanding thou hast *g* thee | 6213
28: 4 hast *g* gold and silver into thy treasures: | 6213
38:12 have *g* cattle and goods, that dwell in | 6213
Da 9:15 and hast *g* thee renown, as *at* this day; | 6213
Ac 21: 1 that after we were *g* **from** them, | 645
Rev 15: 2 that had **the victory** over the beast, | 3528

GOURD (5) [GOURDS]

Jnh 4: 6 the LORD God prepared a *g*, and made *it* | 7021
4: 6 So Jonah was exceeding glad of the *g*. | 7021
4: 7 and it smote the *g*, that it withered. | 7021
4: 9 Doest thou well to be angry for the *g*? | 7021
4:10 the LORD, Thou hast had pity on the *g*, | 7021

GOURDS (1) [GOURD]

2Ki 4:39 gathered thereof wild *g* his lap full, | 6498

GOVERN (3) [GOVERNMENT, GOVERNMENTS, GOVERNOR, GOVERNOR'S, GOVERNORS]

1Ki 21: 7 Dost thou now *g* the kingdom of Israel? | 6213
Job 34:17 Shall even he that hateth right *g*? | 2280
Ps 67: 4 and *g* the nations upon earth. | 5148

GOVERNMENT (4) [GOVERN]

Isa 9: 6 the *g* shall be upon his shoulder: | 4951
9: 7 Of the increase of *his* *g* and peace *there* | 4951
22:21 and I will commit thy *g* into his hand: | 4475
2Pe 2:10 in the lust of uncleanness, and despise *g*. | 2963

GOVERNMENTS (1) [GOVERN]

1Co 12:28 then gifts of healings, helps, *g*, | 2941

GOVERNOR (59) [GOVERN]

Ge 42: 6 Joseph *was* the *g* over the land, *and* he *it* | 7989
45:26 he *is* *g* over all the land of Egypt. | 4910
1Ki 18: 3 which *was* the *g*[6] of *his* house. | 5921
22:26 him back unto Amon the *g* of the city, | 8269
2Ki 23: 8 in of the gate of Joshua the *g* of the city, | 8269
25:23 king of Babylon had **made** Gedaliah *g*, | 6485
1Ch 29:22 *him* unto the LORD to be the **chief** *g*, | 5057
2Ch 1: 2 to the judges, and to every *g* in all Israel, | 5387
18:25 carry him back to Amon the *g* of the city, | 8269
28: 7 Azrikam the *g* of the house, and Elkanah | 5057
34: 8 Maaseiah the *g* of the city, and Joah the | 8269
Ezr 5: 3 *g* on *this* side the river, | 6347
5: 6 *g* on *this* side the river, | 6347
5:14 *was* Sheshbazzar, whom he had made *g*; | 6347
6: 6 *therefore,* Tatnai, *g* beyond the river, | 6347
6: 7 let the *g* of the Jews and the elders of | 6347
6:13 Tatnai, *g* on *this* side the river, | 6347
Ne 3: 7 unto the throne of the *g* on *this* side | 6346
5:14 to be their *g* in the land of Judah, | 6346
5:14 have not eaten the bread of the *g*. | 6346
5:18 *all* this required not I the bread of the *g*, | 6346
12:26 the days of Nehemiah the *g*, and of Ezra | 6346
Ps 22:28 and *he* is the *g* among the nations. | 4910
Jer 20: 1 who *was* also chief *g* in the house of | 6496
30:21 their *g* shall proceed from the midst of | 4910
40: 5 whom the king of Babylon hath **made** *g* | 6485
40: 7 **made** Gedaliah the son of Ahikam *g* in | 6485
41: 2 whom the king of Babylon had **made** *g* | 6485
41:18 whom the king of Babylon had **made** *g* in | 6485
Hag 1: 1 of Judah, and to Joshua the son of | 6346
1:14 *g* of Judah, and the spirit of Joshua the | 6346
2: 2 *g* of Judah, and to Joshua the son of | 6346
2:21 Speak to Zerubbabel, *g* of Judah, saying, | 6346
Zec 9: 7 he shall be as a *g* in Judah, and Ekron as | 441
Mal 1: 8 offer it now unto thy *g*; will he be pleased | 6346
Mt 2: 6 for out of thee shall come a *G*, that shall | 2233
27: 2 and delivered him to Pontius Pilate the *g*. | 2232
27:11 And Jesus stood before the *g*: | 2232
27:11 And the *g* asked him, saying, Art thou | 2232
27:14 insomuch that the *g* marvelled greatly. | 2232
27:15 at *that* feast the *g* was wont to release | 2232
27:21 The *g* answered and said unto them, | 2232
27:23 And the *g* said, Why, what evil hath he | 2232
27:27 Then the soldiers of the *g* took Jesus into | 2232
Lk 2: 2 first made when Cyrenius was *g* of Syria.) | 2230
3: 1 Pontius Pilate being *g* of Judea, | 2230
20:20 unto the power and authority of the *g*. | 2232
Jn 2: 8 and bear unto the *g* of the feast. | 755
2: 9 the *g* of the feast called the bridegroom, | 755

Ac 7:10 and he made him *g* over Egypt and all his | 2233
23:24 and bring *him* safe unto Felix the *g*. | 2232
23:26 Claudius Lysias unto the most excellent *g* | 2232
23:33 and delivered the epistle to the *g*, | 2232
23:34 And when the *g* had read *the letter,* he | 2232
24: 1 who informed the *g* against Paul. | 2232
24:10 after that the *g* had beckoned unto him to | 2232
26:30 thus spoken, the king rose up, and the *g*, | 2232
2Co 11:32 In Damascus the *g* under Aretas the king | 1481
Jas 3: 4 small helm, whithersoever the *g* listeth. | 3730

GOVERNOR'S (1) [GOVERN]

Mt 28:14 And if this come to the *g* ears, we will | 2232

GOVERNORS (22) [GOVERN]

Jdg 5: 9 My heart *is* toward the *g* of Israel, | 2710
5:14 out of Machir came down a *g*, and out of | 2710
1Ki 10:15 of Arabia, and *of* the *g* of the country. | 6346
1Ch 24: 5 the *g* of the sanctuary, and governors *of* | 8269
24: 5 *of the house* of God, were of the sons | 8269
2Ch 9:14 *g* of the country brought gold and silver | 6346
23:20 the *g* of the people, and all the people of | 4910
Ezr 8:36 and for the *g* on *this* side the river: | 6346
Ne 2: 7 let letters be given me to the *g* beyond | 6346
2: 9 I came to the *g* beyond the river, | 6346
5:15 the former *g* that had been before me | 6346
Est 3:12 to the *g* that *were* over every province, | 6346
Da 2:48 chief of the *g* over all the wise *men* of | 5460
3: 2 the *g*, and the captains, the judges, | 5460
3: 3 the *g* and captains, the judges, | 5460
3:27 *g*, and captains, and the king's counsellers | 5460
6: 7 the *g*, and the princes, the counsellers | 5460
Zec 12: 5 the *g* of Judah shall say in their heart, | 441
12: 6 In that day will I make the *g* of Judah like | 441
Mt 10:18 ye shall be brought before *g* and kings | 2232
Gal 4: 2 *g* until the time appointed of the father. | 3623
1Pe 2:14 unto *g*, as unto them that are sent by him | 2232

GOZAN (5)

2Ki 17: 6 in Halah and in Habor *by* the river of *G*, | 1470
18:11 in Halah and in Habor *by* the river of *G*, | 1470
19:12 as *G*, and Haran, and Rezeph, | 1470
1Ch 5:26 Habor, and Hara, and to the river *G*, | 1470
Isa 37:12 as *G*, and Haran, and Rezeph, | 1470

GRACE (170) [GRACIOUS, GRACIOUSLY]

Ge 6: 8 Noah found *g* in the eyes of the LORD. | 2580
19:19 thy servant hath found *g* in thy sight, | 2580
32: 5 tell my lord, that I may find *g* in thy sight. | 2580
33: 8 *are* to find *g* in the sight of my lord. | 2580
33:10 if now I have found *g* in thy sight, then | 2580
33:15 let me find *g* in the sight of my lord. | 2580
34:11 Let me find *g* in your eyes, and what ye | 2580
39: 4 Joseph found *g* in his sight, and he served | 2580
47:25 let us find *g* in the sight of my lord, | 2580
47:29 If now I have found *g* in thy sight, put, | 2580
50: 4 If now I have found *g* in your eyes, speak, | 2580
Ex 33:12 and thou hast also found *g* in my sight. | 2580
33:13 I pray thee, if I have found *g* in thy sight, | 2580
33:13 know thee, that I may find *g* in thy sight: | 2580
33:16 and thy people have found *g* in thy sight? | 2580
33:17 for thou hast found *g* in my sight, | 2580
34: 9 If now I have found *g* in thy sight, O Lord, | 2580
Nu 32: 5 said they, if we have found *g* in thy sight, | 2580
Jdg 6:17 If now I have found *g* in thy sight, then | 2580
Ru 2: 2 after *him* in whose sight I shall find *g*. | 2580
2:10 Why have I found *g* in thine eyes, | 2580
1Sa 1:18 Let thine handmaid find *g* in thy sight. | 2580
20: 3 that I have found *g* in thine eyes; | 2580
27: 5 If I have now found *g* in thine eyes, | 2580
2Sa 14:22 knoweth that I have found *g* in thy sight, | 2580
16: 4 I humbly beseech thee *that* I may find *g* | 2580
Ezr 9: 8 now for a little space *g* hath been *shewed* | 8467
Est 2:17 she obtained *g* and favour in his sight | 2580
Ps 45: 2 *g* is poured into thy lips: therefore God | 2580
84:11 the LORD will give *g* and glory: no good | 2580
Pr 1: 9 For they *shall be* an ornament of *g* unto | 2580
3:22 be life unto thy soul, and *g* to thy neck. | 2580
3:34 scorners: but he giveth *g* unto the lowly. | 2580
4: 9 shall give to thine head an ornament of *g*: | 2580
22:11 *for* the *g* of his lips the king *shall be* his | 2580
Jer 31: 2 of the sword found *g* in the wilderness; | 2580
Zec 4: 7 *with* shoutings, *crying,* *G*, grace unto it. | 2580
4: 7 *with* shoutings, *crying,* Grace, *g* unto it. | 2580
12:10 the spirit of *g* and of supplications; | 2580
Lk 2:40 and the *g* of God was upon him. | 5485
Jn 1:14 begotten of the Father,) full of *g* and truth. | 5485
1:16 have all we received, and *g* for grace. | 5485
1:16 have all we received, and grace for *g*. | 5485
1:17 *but* *g* and truth came by Jesus Christ. | 5485
Ac 4:33 Lord Jesus: and great *g* was upon them all. | 5485
11:23 and had seen the *g* of God, was glad, | 5485
13:43 them to continue in the *g* of God. | 5485
14: 3 gave testimony unto the word of his *g*, | 5485
14:26 of God for the work which they fulfilled. | 5485
15:11 But we believe that through the *g* of | 5485
15:40 by the brethren unto the *g* of God. | 5485
18:27 much which had believed through *g*: | 5485
20:24 to testify the gospel of the *g* of God. | 5485
20:32 you to God, and to the word of his *g*, | 5485
Ro 1: 5 By whom we have received *g* and | 5485
1: 7 *G* to you and peace from God our Father, | 5485
3:24 Being justified freely by his *g* through | 5485
4: 4 worketh is the reward not reckoned of *g*, | 5485
4:16 *it is* of faith, that *it might be* by *g*; | 5485

Ro 5: 2 by faith into this *g* wherein we stand, | 5485
5:15 much more the *g* of God, and the gift by | 5485
5:15 and the gift by *g*, which is by one man, | 5485
5:17 more they which receive abundance of *g* | 5485
5:20 sin abounded, *g* did much more abound: | 5485
5:21 might *g* reign through righteousness unto | 5485
6: 1 we continue in sin, that *g* may abound? | 5485
6:14 for ye are not under the law, but under *g*. | 5485
6:15 we are not under the law, but under *g*? | 5485
11: 5 a remnant according to the election of *g*. | 5485
11: 6 And if by *g*, *then* is it no more of works: | 5485
11: 6 otherwise *g* is no more grace. | 5485
11: 6 otherwise grace is no more *g*. | 5485
11: 6 But if *it be* of works, *then* is it no more *g*: | 5485
12: 3 For I say, through the *g* given unto me, | 5485
12: 6 gifts differing according to the *g* that is | 5485
15:15 of the *g* that is given to me of God, | 5485
16:20 The *g* of our Lord Jesus Christ *be* with | 5485
16:24 The *g* of our Lord Jesus Christ *be* with | 5485
1Co 1: 3 *G* be unto you, and peace, from God our | 5485
1: 4 for the *g* of God which is given you by | 5485
3:10 According to the *g* of God which is given | 5485
10:30 For if I by *g* be a partaker, why am I evil | 5485
15:10 But by the *g* of God I am what I am: | 5485
15:10 his *g* which was *bestowed* upon me was | 5485
15:10 but the *g* of God which was with me. | 5485
16:23 The *g* of *our* Lord Jesus Christ *be* with | 5485
2Co 1: 2 *G* be to you and peace from God our | 5485
1:12 with fleshly wisdom, but by the *g* of God, | 5485
4:15 that the abundant *g* might through | 5485
6: 1 that ye receive not the *g* of God in vain. | 5485
8: 1 do you to wit of the *g* of God bestowed | 5485
8: 6 would also finish in you the same *g* also. | 5485
8: 7 to us, *see* that ye abound in this *g* also. | 5485
8: 9 ye know the *g* of our Lord Jesus Christ, | 5485
8:19 the churches to travel with us with this *g*, | 5485
9: 8 And God *is* able to make all *g* abound | 5485
9:14 which long after you for the exceeding *g* | 5485
12: 9 said unto me, My *g* is sufficient for thee: | 5485
13:14 The *g* of the Lord Jesus Christ, and the | 5485
Gal 1: 3 *G* be to you and peace from God | 5485
1: 6 into the *g* of Christ unto another gospel: | 5485
1:15 mother's womb, and called *me* by his *g*, | 5485
2: 9 perceived the *g* that was given unto me, | 5485
2:21 I do not frustrate the *g* of God: for if | 5485
5: 4 justified by the law; ye are fallen from *g*. | 5485
6:18 the *g* of our Lord Jesus Christ *be* with | 5485
Eph 1: 2 *G* be to you, and peace, from God our | 5485
1: 6 To the praise of the glory of his *g*, | 5485
1: 7 of sins, according to the riches of his *g*; | 5485
2: 5 together with Christ, (by *g* ye are saved;) | 5485
2: 7 *g* in *his* kindness towards us through | 5485
2: 8 For by *g* are ye saved through faith; | 5485
3: 2 ye have heard of the dispensation of the *g* | 5485
3: 7 according to the gift of the *g* of God given | 5485
3: 8 than the least of all saints, is this *g* given, | 5485
4: 7 But unto every one of us is given *g* | 5485
4:29 that it may minister *g* unto the hearers. | 5485
6:24 *G* be with all them that love our Lord | 5485
Php 1: 2 *G* be unto you, and peace, from God our | 5485
1: 7 of the gospel, ye all are partakers of my *g*. | 5485
4:23 The *g* of our Lord Jesus Christ *be* with you | 5485
Col 1: 2 *G* be unto you, and peace, from God | 5485
1: 6 of *it*, and knew the *g* of God in truth: | 5485
3:16 singing with *g* in your hearts to the Lord. | 5485
4: 6 Let your speech *be* alway with *g*, | 5485
4:18 my bonds. *G* be with you. Amen. | 5485
1Th 1: 1 *G* be unto you, and peace, from God our | 5485
5:28 The *g* of our Lord Jesus Christ *be* with | 5485
2Th 1: 2 *G* unto you, and peace, from God our | 5485
1:12 according to the *g* of our God and the | 5485
2:16 and good hope through *g*, | 5485
3:18 The *g* of our Lord Jesus Christ *be* with | 5485
1Ti 1: 2 *G*, mercy, *and* peace, from God our | 5485
1:14 And the *g* of our Lord was exceeding | 5485
6:21 the faith. *G* be with thee. Amen. | 5485
2Ti 1: 2 *G*, mercy, *and* peace, from God our | 5485
1: 9 but according to his own purpose and *g*, | 5485
2: 1 be strong in the *g* that is in Christ Jesus. | 5485
4:22 be with thy spirit. *G* be with you. Amen. | 5485
Tit 1: 4 *G*, mercy, *and* peace, from God the | 5485
2:11 For the *g* of God that bringeth salvation | 5485
3: 7 That being justified by his *g*, we should be | 5485
3:15 us in the faith. *G* be with you all. Amen. | 5485
Phm 1: 3 *G* to you, and peace, from God our Father | 5485
1:25 The *g* of our Lord Jesus Christ *be* with | 5485
Heb 2: 9 that he by the *g* of God should taste death | 5485
4:16 come boldly unto the throne of *g*, | 5485
4:16 and find *g* to help in time of need. | 5485
10:29 hath done despite unto the Spirit of *g*? | 5485
12:15 diligently lest any *man* fail of the *g* | 5485
12:28 let us have *g*, whereby we may serve God | 5485
13: 9 *thing* that the heart be established with *g*; | 5485
13:25 *G* be with you all. Amen. | 5485
Jas 1:11 and the *g* of the fashion of it perisheth: | 2143
4: 6 But he giveth more *g*. Wherefore *he* saith, | 5485
4: 6 the proud, but giveth *g* unto the humble. | 5485
1Pe 1: 2 *G* unto you, and peace, be multiplied. | 5485
1:10 who prophesied of the *g* *that should come* | 5485
1:13 hope to the end for the *g* that is *to be* | 5485
3: 7 as *being* heirs together of the *g* of life; | 5485
4:10 good stewards of the manifold *g* of God. | 5485
5: 5 the proud, and giveth *g* to the humble. | 5485
5:10 But the God of all *g*, who hath called us | 5485
5:12 testifying that this is the true *g* of God | 5485

2Pe 1: 2 **G** and peace be multiplied unto you 5485
3:18 grow in g, and in the knowledge of our 5485
2Jn 1: 3 **G** be with you, mercy, and peace, 5485
Jude 1: 4 ungodly men, turning the g of our God 5485
Rev 1: 4 **G** be unto you, and peace, from him 5485
22:21 The g of our Lord Jesus Christ be with 5485

GRACIOUS (31) [GRACE]
Ge 43:29 And he said, God be g unto thee, my son. 2603
Ex 22:27 unto me, that I will hear; for I am g. 2587
33:19 will be g to whom I will be gracious, 2603
33:19 will be gracious to whom I will be g, 2603
34: 6 merciful and g, longsuffering, 2587
Nu 6:25 face shine upon thee, and be g unto thee: 2603
2Sa 12:22 Who can tell whether GOD will be g to 2603
2Ki 13:23 the LORD was g unto them, 2603
2Ch 30: 9 for the LORD your God is g and merciful, 2587
Ne 9:17 g and merciful, slow to anger, and of 2587
9:31 for thou art a g and merciful God. 2587
Job 33:24 he is g unto him, and saith, Deliver him 2603
Ps 77: 9 Hath God forgotten to be g? hath he in 2589
86:15 g, longsuffering, and plenteous in mercy 2587
103: 8 The LORD is merciful and g, slow to 2587
111: 4 the LORD is g and full of compassion. 2587
112: 4 he is g, and full of compassion, 2587
116: 5 **G** is the LORD, and righteous; yea, 2587
145: 8 The LORD is g, and full of compassion; 2587
Pr 11:16 A g woman retaineth honour. 2580
Ecc 10:12 The words of a wise man's mouth are g; 2580
Isa 30:18 that he may be g unto you, and therefore 2603
30:19 he will be very g unto thee at 2603+2603
33: 2 O LORD, be g unto us; we have waited 2603
Jer 22:23 how g shalt thou be when pangs come 2603
Joel 2:13 for he is g and merciful, slow to anger, 2587
Am 5:15 will be g unto the remnant of Joseph. 2603
Jnh 4: 2 for I knew that thou art a g God, 2587
Mal 1: 9 beseech God that he will be g unto us: 2603
Lk 4:22 wondered at the g words which 5485
1Pe 2: 3 If so be ye have tasted that the Lord is g. 5543

GRACIOUSLY (4) [GRACE]
Ge 33: 5 The children which God hath g given thy 2603
33:11 because God hath dealt g with me, 2603
Ps 119:29 the way of lying: and grant me thy law g. 2603
Hos 14: 2 Take away all iniquity, and receive us g: 2896

GRAFF (1) [GRAFFED]
Ro 11:23 for God is able to g them in again. 1461

GRAFFED (5) [GRAFF]
Ro 11:17 wert g in amongst them, and with them 1461
11:19 were broken off, that I might be g in. 1461
11:23 bide not still in unbelief, shall be g in: 1461
11:24 wert g contrary to nature into a good olive 1461
11:24 which be the natural branches, be g into 1461

GRAFT; GRAFTED See GRAFF; GRAFFED

GRAIN (8)
Am 9: 9 shall not the least g fall upon the earth. 6872
Mt 13:31 heaven is like unto a g of mustard seed, 2848
17:20 If ye have faith as a g of mustard seed, 2848
Mk 4:31 It is like a g of mustard seed, which, 2848
Lk 13:19 It is like a g of mustard seed, which a 2848
17: 6 If ye had faith as a g of mustard seed, 2848
1Co 15:37 but bare g, it may chance of wheat, 2848
15:37 may chance of wheat, or of some other g. NIG

GRANDMOTHER (1) [MOTHER]
2Ti 1: 5 which dwelt first in thy g Lois, 3125

GRANT (22) [GRANTED]
Lev 25:24 all the land of your possession ye shall g 5414
Ru 1: 9 The LORD g you that you may find rest, 5414
1Sa 1:17 the God of Israel g thee thy petition that 5414
1Ch 21:22 **G** me the place of this threshingfloor, 5414
21:22 thou shalt g it me for the full price: that 5414
2Ch 12: 7 but I will g them some deliverance, 5414
Ezr 3: 7 according to the g that they had of Cyrus 7558
Ne 1:11 and g him mercy in the sight of this man. 5414
Est 5: 8 if it please the king to g my petition, 5414
Job 6: 8 God would g me the thing that I long 5414
Ps 20: 4 **G** thee according to thine own heart, 5414
85: 7 O LORD, and g us thy salvation. 5414
119:29 of lying: and g me thy law graciously. 2603
140: 8 **G** not, O LORD, the desires of 5414
Mt 20:21 **G** that these my two sons may sit, 3004
Mk 10:37 said unto him, **G** unto us that we may sit, 1325
Lk 1:74 That he would g unto us, that we being 1325
Ac 4:29 and g unto thy servants, that with all 1325
Ro 15: 5 consolation g you to be likeminded one 1325
Eph 3:16 That he would g you, according to 1325
2Ti 1:18 The Lord g unto him that he may find 1325
Rev 3:21 To him that overcometh will I g to sit 1325

GRANTED (15) [GRANT]
1Ch 4:10 And God g him that which he requested. 935
2Ch 1:12 Wisdom and knowledge is g unto thee; 5414
Ezr 7: 6 the king g him all his request, according 5414
Ne 2: 8 king g me, according to the good hand 5414
Est 5: 6 it shall be g thee: and what is thy request? 5414
7: 2 it shall be g thee: and what is thy request? 5414
8:11 Wherein the king g the Jews which were 5414
9:12 it shall be g thee: or what is thy request 5414
9:13 let it be g to the Jews which are in 5414
Job 10:12 Thou hast g me life and favour, 6213

Pr 10:24 but the desire of the righteous shall be g. 5414
Ac 3:14 desired a murderer to be g unto you; 5483
11:18 Then hath God also to the Gentiles g 1325
14: 3 g signs and wonders to be done by their 1325
Rev 19: 8 to her was g that she should be arrayed 1325

GRAPE (8) [GRAPEGATHERER, GRAPEGATHERERS, GRAPE-GATHERERS, GRAPEGLEANINGS, GRAPES]
Lev 19:10 neither shalt thou gather every g of thy 6528
Dt 32:14 didst drink the pure blood of the g. 6025
Job 15:33 shall shake off his unripe g as the vine, 1154
SS 2:13 the vines with the tender g give a good 5563
7:12 whether the tender g appear, 5563
Isa 18: 5 and the sour g is ripening in the flower, 1155
Jer 31:29 The fathers have eaten a sour g, 1155
31:30 man that eateth the sour g, his teeth 1155

GRAPEGATHERER (1) [GRAPE, GATHER]
Jer 6: 9 back thine hand as a g into the baskets. 1219

GRAPEGATHERERS, GRAPE-GATHERERS (2) [GRAPE, GATHER]
Jer 49: 9 If g come to thee, would they not leave 1219
Ob 1: 5 the g came to thee, would they not leave 1219

GRAPEGLEANINGS (1) [GRAPE, GLEAN]
Mic 7: 1 the summer fruits, as the g of the vintage: 5955

GRAPES (37) [GRAPE]
Ge 40:10 the clusters thereof brought forth ripe g: 6025
40:11 I took the g, and pressed them into 6025
49:11 in wine, and his clothes in the blood of g: 6025
Lev 25: 5 neither gather the g of thy vine undressed: 6025
25:11 gather the g in it of thy vine undressed. NIH
Nu 6: 3 neither shall he drink any liquor of g, 6025
6: 3 liquor of grapes, nor eat moist g, or dried. 6025
13:20 the time was the time of the first ripe g. 6025
13:23 thence a branch with one cluster of g, 6025
13:24 of the cluster of g which the children of 811
Dt 23:24 thou mayest eat g thy fill at thine own 6025
24:21 thou gatherest the g of thy vineyard, 1219
28:30 and shalt not gather the g thereof. 2490
28:39 nor gather the g, for the worms shall eat NIH
32:32 their g are grapes of gall, their clusters are 6025
32:32 their grapes are g of gall, their clusters are 6025
Jdg 8: 2 Is not the gleaning of the g of Ephraim 5955
9:27 trode the g, and made merry, and went NIH
Ne 13:15 g, and figs, and all manner of burdens, 6025
SS 2:15 the vines: for our vines have tender g. 5563
7: 7 palm tree, and thy breasts to clusters of g. 6025
Isa 5: 2 he looked that it should bring forth g, 6025
5: 2 forth grapes, and it brought forth wild g. 891
5: 4 when I looked that it should bring forth g, 6025
5: 4 bring forth grapes, brought it forth wild g? 891
17: 6 Yet gleaning g shall be left in it, 5955
24:13 the gleaning g when the vintage is done. 5955
Jer 8:13 there shall be no g on the vine, nor figs 6025
25:30 as they that tread the g, against all NIH
49: 9 would they not leave some gleaning g? 5955
Hos 9:10 I found Israel like g in the wilderness; 6025
Am 9:13 the treader of g him that soweth seed; 6025
Ob 1: 5 to thee, would they not leave some g? 5955
Mt 7:16 Do men gather g of thorns, or figs of 4718
Lk 6:44 nor of a bramble bush gather they g. 4718
Rev 14:18 vine of the earth; for her g are fully ripe. 4718

GRASS (62)
Ge 1:11 God said, Let the earth bring forth g, 1877
1:12 the earth brought forth g, and herb 1877
Nu 22: 4 as the ox licketh up the g of the field. 3418
Dt 11:15 I will send g in thy fields for thy cattle, 6212
29:23 nor beareth, nor any g groweth therein, 6212
32: 2 herb, and as the showers upon the g: 6212
2Sa 23: 4 as the tender g springing out of the earth 1877
1Ki 18: 5 peradventure we may find g to save 2682
2Ki 19:26 they were as the g of the field, and as 6212
19:26 as the g on the housetops, and as corn 2682
Job 5:25 and thine offspring as the g of the earth. 6212
6: 5 Doth the wild ass bray when he hath g? 1877
40:15 I made with thee; he eateth g as an ox. 2682
Ps 37: 2 they shall soon be cut down like the g, 2682
72: 6 come down like rain upon the mown g, 1488
72:16 they of the city shall flourish like g of 6212
90: 5 in the morning they are like g which 2682
92: 7 When the wicked spring as the g, 6212
102: 4 My heart is smitten, and withered like g; 6212
102:11 that declineth; and I am withered like g. 6212
103:15 As for man, his days are as g: as a flower 2682
104:14 He causeth the g to grow for the cattle, 2682
106:20 into the similitude of an ox that eateth g. 6212
129: 6 Let them be as the g upon the housetops, 2682
147: 8 maketh g to grow upon the mountains. 2682
Pr 19:12 lion; but his favour is as dew upon the g. 6212
27:25 the tender g sheweth itself, and herbs of 1877
Isa 15: 6 the g faileth, there is no green thing. 1877
35: 7 shall be g with reeds and rushes. 2682
37:27 they were as the g of the field, and as 6212
37:27 as the g on the housetops, and as corn 2682
40: 6 All flesh is g, and all the goodliness 2682
40: 7 The g withereth, the flower fadeth: 2682
40: 7 bloweth upon it: surely the people is g. 2682
40: 8 The g withereth, the flower fadeth: 2682
44: 4 they shall spring up as among the g, 2682

Isa 51:12 the son of man which shall be made as g; 2682
Jer 14: 5 and forsook it, because there was no g. 1877
14: 6 eyes did fail, because there was no g. 6212
50:11 ye are grown fat as the heifer at g, 1877
Da 4:15 and brass, in the tender g of the field, 1883
4:15 his portion be with the beasts in the g of 6211'
4:23 and brass, in the tender g of the field; 1883
4:25 they shall make thee to eat g as oxen, 6211'
4:32 they shall make thee to eat g as oxen, 6211'
4:33 did eat g as oxen, and his body was wet 6211'
5:21 they fed him with g like oxen, and his 6211'
Am 7: 2 made an end of eating the g of the land, 6212
Mic 5: 7 as the showers upon the g, that tarrieth 6212
Zec 10: 1 of rain, to every one g in the field. 6212
Mt 6:30 if God so clothe the g of the field, 5528
14:19 the multitude to sit down on the g, 5528
Mk 6:39 sit down by companies upon the green g. 5528
Lk 12:28 If then God so clothe the g, which is 5528
Jn 6:10 Now there was much g in the place. 5528
Jas 1:10 as the flower of the g he shall pass away. 5528
1:11 but it withereth the g, and the flower 5528
1Pe 1:24 For all flesh is as g, and all the glory of 5528
1:24 all the glory of man as the flower of g. 5528
1:24 The g withereth, and the flower thereof 5528
Rev 8: 7 burnt up, and all green g was burnt up. 5528
9: 4 they should not hurt the g of the earth, 5528

GRASSHOPPER (3) [GRASSHOPPERS]
Lev 11:22 after his kind, and the g after his kind. 2284
Job 39:20 Canst thou make him afraid as a g? 697
Ecc 12: 5 the g shall be a burden, and desire shall 2284

GRASSHOPPERS (7) [GRASSHOPPER]
Nu 13:33 we were in our own sight as g, and so 2284
Jdg 6: 5 tents, and they came as g for multitude; 697
7:12 lay along in the valley like g for multitude; 697
Isa 40:22 and the inhabitants thereof are as g; 2284
Jer 46:23 because they are more than the g, 697
Am 7: 1 he formed g in the beginning of 1462
Na 3:17 and thy captains as the great g, 1462+1462

GRATE (6) [GRAVE, GRAVE'S, GRAVECLOTHES, GRAVED, GRAVEN, GRAVES, GRAVETH, GRAVING, GRAVINGS]
Ex 27: 4 thou shalt make for it a g of network of 4345
35:16 altar of burnt offering with his brasen g, 4345
38: 4 made for the altar a brasen g of network 4345
38: 5 cast four rings for the four ends of the g 4345
38:30 the brasen g for it, and all the vessels of 4345
39:39 his g of brass, his staves, and all his 4345

GRATING See NETWORKS

GRAVE (67) [GRATE]
Ge 35:20 Jacob set a pillar upon her g: that is 6900
35:20 is the pillar of Rachel's g unto this day. 6900
37:35 I will go down into the g unto my son 7585
42:38 my gray hairs with sorrow to the g. 7585
44:29 my gray hairs with sorrow to the g. 7585
44:31 servant our father with sorrow to the g. 7585
50: 5 in my g which I have digged for me in 6913
Ex 28: 9 g on them the names of the children of 6605
28:36 upon it, like the engravings of a signet, 6605
Nu 19:16 a dead body, or a bone of a man, or a g, 6913
19:18 a bone, or one slain, or one dead, or a g: 6913
1Sa 2: 6 bringeth down to the g, and bringeth up. 7585
2Sa 3:32 up his voice, and wept at the g of Abner; 6913
19:37 and be buried by the g of my father and 6913
1Ki 2: 6 let not his hoar head go down to the g in 7585
2: 9 hoar head bring thou down to the g with 7585
13:30 he laid his carcase in his own g; 6913
14:13 he only of Jeroboam shall come to the g, 6913
2Ki 22:20 shalt be gathered into thy g in peace; 6913
2Ch 2: 7 skill to g with the cunning 6603+6605+3807.1
2:14 to g any manner of graving, and to find 6605
34:28 thou shalt be gathered to thy g in peace, 6913
Job 3:22 are glad, when they can find the g? 6913
5:26 Thou shalt come to thy g in a full age, 6913
7: 9 that goeth down to the g shall come up 7585
10:19 been carried from the womb to the g. 6913
14:13 O that thou wouldest hide me in the g, 7585
17:13 If I wait, the g is mine house: I have 7585
21:13 and in a moment go down to the g. 7585
21:32 Yet shall he be brought to the g, 6913
24:19 so doth the g those which have sinned. 7585
30:24 he will not stretch out his hand to the g, 5856
33:22 his soul draweth near unto the g, 7845
Ps 6: 5 in the g who shall give thee thanks? 7585
30: 3 thou hast brought up my soul from the g: 7585
31:17 ashamed, and let them be silent in the g. 7585
49:14 Like sheep they are laid in the g; 7585
49:14 their beauty shall consume in the g from 7585
49:15 redeem my soul from the power of the g: 7585
88: 3 and my life draweth nigh unto the g. 7585
88: 5 the dead, as the slain that lie in the g, 6913
88:11 thy lovingkindness be declared in the g? 6913
89:48 deliver his soul from the hand of the g? 7585
Pr 1:12 Let us swallow them up alive as the g; 7585
30:16 The g; and the barren womb; the earth 7585
Ecc 9:10 nor knowledge, nor wisdom, in the g, 7585
SS 8: 6 strong as death; jealousy is cruel as the g: 7585
Isa 14:11 Thy pomp is brought down to the g, 7585
14:19 thou art cast out of thy g like an 6913
38:10 my days, I shall go to the gates of the g: 7585
38:18 For the g cannot praise thee, death can 7585

Isa	53: 9 he made his **g** with the wicked,	6913
Jer	20:17 or that my mother might have been my **g**,	6913
Eze	31:15 In the day when he went down to the **g**	7585
	32:23 and her company is round about her **g**:	6900
	32:24 and all her multitude round about her **g**,	6900
Hos	13:14 ransom them from the power of the **g**;	7585
	13:14 plagues; O **g**, I will be thy destruction:	7585
Na	1:14 I will make thy **g**; for thou art vile.	6913
Jn	11:17 found that he had lien in the **g** four days	3419
	11:31 She goeth unto the **g** to weep there.	3419
	11:38 again groaning in himself cometh to the **g**.	3419
	12:17 him when he called Lazarus out of his **g**,	3419
1Co	15:55 is thy sting? O **g**, where is thy victory?	86
1Ti	3: 8 Likewise must the deacons be **g**,	4586
	3:11 Even so must their wives be **g**,	4586
Tit	2: 2 temperate, sound in faith, in charity,	4586

GRAVE'S (1) [GRATE]

Ps	141: 7 Our bones are scattered at the **g** mouth,	7585

GRAVECLOTHES (1) [CLOTHE, GRATE]

Jn	11:44 came forth, bound hand and foot with **g**:	2750

GRAVED (2) [GRATE]

1Ki	7:36 he **g** cherubims, lions, and palm trees,	6605
2Ch	3: 7 with gold; and **g** cherubims on the walls.	6605

GRAVEL (3)

Pr	20:17 his mouth shall be filled with **g**.	2687
Isa	48:19 the offspring of thy bowels like the **g**	4579
La	3:16 hath also broken my teeth with **g** stones,	2687

GRAVEN (55) [GRATE]

Ex	20: 4 shalt not make unto thee any **g image**,	6459
	32:16 was the writing of God, **g** upon the tables.	2801
	39: 6 **g** as signets are graven, with the names of	6603
	39: 6 graven as signets are, with the names of	6605
Lev	26: 1 Ye shall make you no idols nor **g image**,	6459
Dt	4:16 and make you a **g image**,	6459
	4:23 make you a **g image**, or the likeness of	6459
	4:25 corrupt yourselves, and make a **g image**,	6459
	5: 8 Thou shalt not make thee any **g image**,	6459
	7: 5 and burn their **g images** with fire.	6456
	7:25 The **g images** of their gods shall ye burn	6456
	12: 3 you shall hew down the **g images** of	6456
	27:15 Cursed be the man that maketh any **g** or	6459
Jdg	17: 3 to make a **g image** and a molten image:	6459
	17: 4 made thereof a **g image** and a molten	6459
	18:14 and a **g image**, and a molten image?	6459
	18:17 and took the **g image**, and the ephod,	6459
	18:20 the **g image**, and went in the midst of	6459
	18:30 the children of Dan set up the **g image**:	6459
	18:31 they set them up Micah's **g image**,	6459
2Ki	17:41 their **g images**, both their children,	6456
	21: 7 he set a **g image** of the grove that he	6459
2Ch	33:19 set up groves and **g images**, before he	6456
	34: 7 had beaten the **g images** into powder,	6456
Job	19:24 That they were **g** with an iron pen and	2672
Ps	78:58 him to jealousy with their **g images**.	6456
	97: 7 be all they that serve **g images**,	6459
Isa	10:10 whose **g images** did excel them of	6456
	21: 9 the **g images** of her gods he hath broken	6456
	30:22 the covering of thy **g images** of silver,	6456
	40:19 The workman melteth a **g image**,	6459
	40:20 cunning workman to prepare a **g image**,	6459
	42: 8 another, neither my praise to **g images**.	6456
	42:17 that trust in **g images**, that say to	6459
	44: 9 They that make a **g image** are all of them	6459
	44:10 molten a **g image** that is profitable for	6459
	44:15 worshippeth it; he maketh it a **g image**,	6459
	44:17 he maketh a god, even his **g image**:	6459
	45:20 that set up the wood of their **g image**,	6459
	48: 5 my **g image**, and my molten image,	6459
	49:16 have **g** thee upon the palms of my hands;	2710
Jer	8:19 me to anger with their **g images**,	6456
	10:14 founder is confounded by the **g image**:	6459
	17: 1 it is upon the table of their heart,	2790
	50:38 for it is the land of **g images**, and they	6456
	51:17 founder is confounded by the **g image**:	6459
	51:47 will do judgment upon the **g images**	6456
	51:52 I will do judgment upon her **g images**:	6456
Hos	11: 2 and burned incense to **g images**.	6456
Mic	1: 7 all the **g images** thereof shall be beaten	6456
	5:13 Thy **g images** also will I cut off,	6456
Na	1:14 of thy gods will I cut off the **g image**	6459
Hab	2:18 What profiteth the **g image** that the	6459
	2:18 image that the maker thereof hath **g** it;	6458
Ac	17:29 or stone, **g** by art and man's device.	5480

GRAVES (21) [GRATE]

Ex	14:11 Because there were no **g** in Egypt,	6913
2Ki	23: 6 cast the powder thereof upon the **g** of	6913
2Ch	34: 4 strowed it upon the **g** of them that had	6913
Job	17: 1 days are extinct, the **g** are ready for me.	6913
Isa	65: 4 Which remain among the **g**, and lodge in	6913
Jer	8: 1 inhabitants of Jerusalem, out of their **g**:	6913
	26:23 cast his dead body into the **g** of	6913
Eze	32:22 his **g** are about him: all of them slain,	6913
	32:23 Whose **g** are set in the sides of the pit,	6913
	32:25 her **g** are round about him: all of them	6913
	32:26 her **g** are round about him: all of them	6913
	37:12 I will open your **g**, and cause you to come	6913
	37:12 cause you to come up out of your **g**,	6913
	37:13 when I have opened your **g**, O my people,	6913
	37:13 and brought you up out of your **g**,	6913

Eze	39:11 I will give unto Gog a place there of **g**	6913
Mt	27:52 the **g** were opened; and many bodies	3419
	27:53 And came out of the **g** after his	3419
Lk	11:44 for ye are as **g** which appear not,	3419
Jn	5:28 the which all that are in the **g** shall hear	3419
Rev	11: 9 not suffer their dead bodies to be put in **g**.	3418

GRAVETH (1) [GRATE]

Isa	22:16 that **g** a habitation for himself in a rock?	2710

GRAVING (3) [GRATE]

Ex	32: 4 fashioned it with a **g tool**, after he had	2747
2Ch	2:14 to grave any manner of **g**, and to find	6603
Zec	3: 9 behold, I will engrave the **g** thereof,	6603

GRAVINGS (1) [GRATE]

1Ki	7:31 upon the mouth of it were **g** with their	4734

GRAVITY (2)

1Ti	3: 4 his children in subjection with all **g**;	4587
Tit	2: 7 shewing uncorruptness, **g**, sincerity,	4587

GRAY (6) [GRAYHEADED]

Ge	42:38 shall ye bring down my **g hairs** with	7872
	44:29 ye shall bring down my **g hairs** with	7872
	44:31 thy servants shall bring down the **g hairs**	7872
Dt	32:25 the suckling also with the man of **g hairs**.	7872
Pr	20:29 and the beauty of old men is the **g head**.	7872
Hos	7: 9 yea, **g hairs** are here and there upon him,	7872

GRAYHEADED (3) [GRAY, HEAD]

1Sa	12: 2 I am old and **g**; and behold, my sons are	7867
Job	15:10 are both the **g** and very aged men,	7867
Ps	71:18 Now also when I am old and **g**, O God,	7872

GREASE (1)

Ps	119:70 Their heart is as fat as **g**; but I delight in	2459

GREAT (962) [GREATER, GREATEST, GREATLY, GREATNESS]

Ge	1:16 God made two **g** lights; the greater light	1419
	1:21 God created **g** whales, and every living	1419
	6: 5 wickedness of man was **g** in the earth,	7227
	7:11 same day were all the fountains of the **g**	7227
	10:12 and Calah: the same is a **g** city.	1419
	12: 2 I will make of thee a **g** nation, and I will	1419
	12: 2 I will bless thee, and **make** thy name **g**;	1431
	12:17 his house with **g** plagues because of Sarai	7227
	13: 6 for their substance was **g**, so that they	7227
	15: 1 thy shield, and thy exceeding **g** reward.	7235
	15:12 lo, a horror of **g** darkness fell upon him.	1419
	15:14 afterward shall they come out with **g**	1419
	15:18 from the river of Egypt unto the **g** river,	1419
	17:20 he beget, and I will make him a **g** nation.	1419
	18:18 that Abraham shall surely become a **g**	1419
	18:20 the cry of Sodom and Gomorrah is **g**,	7227
	19:11 house with blindness, both small and **g**;	1419
	19:13 the cry of them is **waxen g** before the	1431
	20: 9 on me and on my kingdom a **g** sin?	1419
	21: 8 Abraham made a **g** feast the same day	1419
	21:18 hand; for I will make him a **g** nation.	1419
	24:35 my master greatly; and he is become **g**:	1431
	26:13 the man **waxed g**, and went forward,	1431
	26:13 and grew until he **became** very **g**:	1431
	26:14 of herds, and **g store** of servants:	7227
	27:34 cried with a **g** and exceeding bitter cry,	1419
	29: 2 a **g** stone was upon the well's mouth.	1419
	30: 8 With **g** wrestlings have I wrestled with	430
	39: 9 how then can I do this **g** wickedness,	1419
	41:29 there come seven years of **g** plenty	1419
	45: 7 and to save your lives by a **g** deliverance.	1419
	46: 3 for I will there make of thee a **g** nation.	1419
	48:19 become a people, and he also shall be **g**:	1431
	50: 9 horsemen: and it was a very **g** company.	3515
	50:10 they mourned with a **g** and very sore	1419
Ex	3: 3 I will now turn aside, and see this **g** sight,	1419
	6: 6 stretched out arm, and with **g** judgments:	1419
	7: 4 out of the land of Egypt by **g** judgments.	1419
	11: 3 Moreover the man Moses was very **g** in	1419
	11: 6 there shall be a **g** cry throughout all	1419
	11: 8 he went out from Pharaoh in a **g** anger.	2750
	12:30 and there was a **g** cry in Egypt;	1419
	14:31 Israel saw that **g** work which the LORD	1419
	18:22 that every **g** matter they shall bring unto	1419
	19:20 upon the **g toe** of their right foot,	931
	32:10 and I will make of thee a **g** nation.	1419
	32:11 out of the land of Egypt with **g** power,	1419
	32:21 thou hast brought so **g** a sin upon them?	1419
	32:30 unto the people, Ye have sinned a **g** sin:	1419
	32:31 this people have sinned a **g** sin,	1419
Lev	8:23 and upon the **g toe** of his right foot.	931
	8:24 and upon the **g toe** of their right feet:	931
	11:17 owl, and the cormorant, and the **g owl**,	3244
	14:14 and upon the **g toe** of his right foot:	931
	14:17 and upon the **g toe** of his right foot:	931
	14:25 and upon the **g toe** of his right foot,	931
	14:28 and upon the **g toe** of his right foot,	931
Nu	11:33 the LORD smote the people with a very **g**	7227
	13:28 and the cities are walled, and very **g**:	1419
	13:32 that we saw in it are men of a **g** stature.	4060
	14:17 let the power of my Lord be **g**,	1431
	14:18 of **g** mercy, forgiving iniquity and	7227
	22:17 I will promote thee unto **very g** honour,	3966
	23:24 the people shall rise up as a **g lion**,	3833
	24: 9 he lay down as a lion, and as a **g lion**:	3833
	24:11 to **promote** thee **unto g** honour;	3513+3513

Nu	32: 1 children of Gad had a very **g** multitude	6099
	34: 6 shall even have the **g** sea for a border:	1419
	34: 7 from the **g** sea ye shall point out for you	1419
Dt	1: 7 unto Lebanon, unto the **g** river, the river	1419
	1:17 ye shall hear the small as well as the **g**;	1419
	1:19 we went **through** all that **g** and terrible	1419
	1:28 the cities are **g** and walled up to heaven;	1419
	2: 7 he knoweth thy walking **through** this **g**	1419
	2:10 a people **g**, and many, and tall,	1419
	2:21 A people **g**, and many, and tall,	1419
	3: 5 bars; beside unwalled towns a **g** many.	3966
	4: 6 Surely this **g** nation is a wise and	1419
	4: 7 what nation is there so **g**, who hath God	1419
	4: 8 what nation is there so **g**, that hath	1419
	4:32 hath been any such thing as this **g** thing	1419
	4:34 by a stretched out arm, and by **g** terrors,	1419
	4:36 upon earth he shewed thee his **g** fire;	1419
	5:22 and of the thick darkness, with a **g** voice:	1419
	5:25 for this **g** fire will consume us: if we hear	1419
	6:10 to Jacob, to give thee **g** and goodly cities,	1419
	6:22 shewed signs and wonders, and **g** and sore,	1419
	7:19 The **g** temptations which thine eyes saw,	1419
	8:15 Who led thee through that **g** and terrible	1419
	9: 1 cities **g** and fenced up to heaven,	1419
	9: 2 A people and tall, the children of	1419
	10:17 of lords, a **g** God, a mighty, and a terrible,	1419
	10:21 hath done for thee these **g** and terrible	1419
	11: 7 your eyes have seen all the **g** acts of	1419
	14:16 little owl, and the **g owl**, and the swan,	3244
	18:16 neither let me see this **g** fire any more,	1419
	25:13 in thy bag divers weights, a **g** and a small.	1419
	25:14 house divers measures, a **g** and a small.	1419
	26: 5 there a nation, **g**, mighty, and populous:	1419
	26: 8 with **g** terribleness, and with signs,	1419
	27: 2 that thou shalt set thee up **g** stones,	1419
	28:59 even **g** plagues, and of long continuance,	1419
	29: 3 The **g** temptations which thine eyes have	1419
	29: 3 seen, the signs, and those **g** miracles:	1419
	29:24 what meaneth the heat of this **g** anger?	1419
	29:28 in **g** indignation, and cast them into	1419
	34:12 in all the **g** terror which Moses shewed in	1419
Jos	1: 4 and this Lebanon even unto the **g** river,	1419
	1: 4 unto the **g** sea toward the going down of	1419
	6: 5 all the people shall shout **with** a **g** shout;	1419
	6:20 the people shouted **with** a **g** shout, that	1419
	7: 9 and what wilt thou do unto thy **g** name?	1419
	7:26 they raised over him a **g** heap of stones	1419
	8:29 raise thereon a **g** heap of stones,	1419
	9: 1 in all the coasts of the **g** sea over against	1419
	10: 2 because Gibeon was a **g** city,	1419
	10:10 slew them with a **g** slaughter at Gibeon,	1419
	10:11 the LORD cast down **g** stones from	1419
	10:18 Roll **g** stones upon the mouth of the cave,	1419
	10:20 of slaying them with a very **g** slaughter,	1419
	10:27 laid **g** stones in the cave's mouth,	1419
	11: 8 chased them unto **g** Zidon,	7227
	14:12 and that the cities were **g** and fenced:	1419
	14:15 which Arba was a **g** man among	1419
	15:12 the west border was to the **g** sea,	1419
	15:47 and the sea, and the border thereof.	1419
	17:14 portion to inherit, seeing I am a **g** people,	7227
	17:15 If thou be a **g** people, then get thee up to	7227
	17:17 art a **g** people, and hast **g** great power:	7227
	17:17 art a great people, and hast **g** power:	1419
	19:28 Hammon, and Kanah, even unto **g** Zidon;	7227
	22:10 there an altar by Jordan, a **g** altar to see to.	1419
	23: 4 cut off, even unto the **g** sea westward.	1419
	23: 9 hath driven out from before you **g** nations	1419
	24:17 which did those **g** signs in our sight,	1419
	24:26 took a **g** stone, and set it up there under	1419
Jdg	1: 6 and cut off his thumbs and his **g toes**.	7272
	1: 7 their thumbs and their **g toes** cut off,	7272
	2: 7 who had seen all the **g** works of	1419
	5:15 For the divisions of Reuben there were **g**	1419
	5:16 For the divisions of Reuben there were **g**	1419
	11:33 of the vineyards, with a very **g** slaughter.	1419
	12: 2 people were at **g** strife with the children	3966
	15: 8 them hip and thigh with a **g** slaughter:	1419
	15:18 Thou hast given this **g** deliverance into	1419
	16: 5 see wherein his **g** strength lieth, and	1419
	16: 6 wherein thy **g** strength lieth, and	1419
	16:15 hast not told me wherein thy **g** strength	1419
	16:23 offer a **g** sacrifice unto Dagon their god,	1419
	20:38 that they should make a **g** flame with	7235
	21: 5 For they had made a **g** oath concerning	1419
1Sa	2:17 young men was very **g** before the LORD:	1419
	4: 5 all Israel shouted with a **g** shout, so that	1419
	4: 6 What meaneth the noise of this **g** shout in	1419
	4:10 there was a very **g** slaughter; for there fell	1419
	4:17 there hath been also a **g** slaughter among	1419
	5: 9 against the city with a very **g** destruction:	1419
	5: 9 both small and **g**, and they had emerods	1419
	6: 9 then he hath done us this **g** evil:	1419
	6:14 stood there, where there was a **g** stone:	1419
	6:15 gold were, and put them on the **g** stone:	1419
	6:18 even unto the **g stone** of Abel,	1419
	6:19 many of the people with a **g** slaughter.	1419
	7:10 the LORD thundered with a **g** thunder on	1419
	12:16 Now therefore stand and see this **g** thing,	1419
	12:17 and see that your wickedness is **g**,	7227
	12:22 forsake his people for his **g** name's sake:	1419
	12:24 consider how **g things** he hath **done** for	1431
	14:15 quaked: so it was a **very g** trembling.	430
	14:20 and there was a very **g** discomfiture.	1419
	14:33 roll a **g** stone unto me this day.	1419

G

1Sa 14:45 hath wrought this **g** salvation in Israel? — 1419
15:22 Hath the LORD *as g* delight in burnt — NIH
17:25 the king will enrich him *with* **g** riches, — 1419
19: 5 the LORD wrought a **g** salvation for all — 1419
19: 8 and slew them *with* a **g** slaughter; — 1419
19:22 and came to a **g** well that *is* in Sechu: — 1419
20: 2 father will do nothing *either* **g** or small, — 1419
23: 5 and smote them *with* a **g** slaughter. — 1419
25: 2 the man *was* very **g**, and he had three — 1419
26:13 afar off; a **g** space *being* between them: — 7227
26:25 thou shalt both **do g** things, — 6213+6213
30: 2 either **g** or small, but carried *them* away, — 1419
30:16 of all the **g** spoil that they had taken out — 1419
30:19 neither small nor **g**, neither sons nor — 1419

2Sa 3:22 troop, and brought in a **g** spoil with them: — 7227
3:38 and a **g** man fallen this day in Israel? — 1419
5:10 grew **g**, and the LORD God of hosts *was* — 1419
7: 9 thy sight, and have made thee a **g** name, — 1419
7: 9 like unto the name of the **g** men that *are* — 1419
7:19 house for a **g** *while* to come. — 4480+7350
7:21 hast thou done all these **g** things, — 1420
7:22 Wherefore thou art **g**, O LORD God: — 1431
7:23 to do for you **g** things and terrible, — 1420
12:14 *given* **g** occasion to the enemies — 5006+5006
of the LORD **to blaspheme**,
12:30 he brought forth the spoil of the city in **g** — 3966
18: 7 there was there a **g** slaughter that day *of* — 1419
18: 9 mule went under the thick boughs of a **g** — 1419
18:17 cast him into a **g** pit in the wood, and laid — 1419
18:17 laid a very **g** heap of stones upon him: — 1419
18:29 I saw a **g** tumult, but I knew not what *it* — 1419
19:32 at Mahanaim; for he *was* a very **g** man. — 1419
20: 8 When they *were* at the **g** stone which *is* — 1419
21:20 where was a man of **g** stature, that had — NIH
22:36 and thy gentleness hath **made** me **g**. — 7235
23:10 the LORD wrought a **g** victory that day; — 1419
23:12 and the LORD wrought a **g** victory. — 1419
24:14 David said unto Gad, I am in a **g** strait: — 3966
24:14 hand of the LORD; for his mercies *are* **g**: — 7227

1Ki 1:40 rejoiced *with* **g** joy, so that the earth rent — 1419
3: 4 for that *was* the **g** high place: — 1419
3: 6 thy servant David my father *a* mercy, — 1419
3: 6 thou hast kept for him this **g** kindness, — 1419
3: 8 a **g** people, that cannot be numbered nor — 7227
3: 9 is able to judge this thy *so* a people? — 3515
4:13 threescore **g** cities *with* walls and — 1419
5: 7 unto David a wise son over this **g** people. — 7227
5:17 they brought **g** stones, costly stones, — 1419
7: 9 and *so* on the outside toward the **g** court. — 1419
7:10 *even* **g** stones, stones of ten cubits, — 1419
7:12 the **g** court round about *was with* three — 1419
8:42 (For they shall hear of thy **g** name, and of — 1419
8:65 and all Israel with him, a **g** congregation, — 1419
10: 2 she came to Jerusalem with a very **g** train, — 3515
10:10 spices very **g** store, and precious stones: — 7235
10:11 brought in from Ophir **g** plenty of almug — 3966
10:18 Moreover the king made a **g** throne of — 1419
11:19 Hadad found **g** favour in the sight of — 3966
18:32 *as* **g** as would contain two measures of — 3509.1
18:45 and wind, and there was a **g** rain. — 1419
19: 7 eat; because the journey *is* too **g** for thee. — 7227
19:11 a **g** and strong wind rent the mountains, — 1419
20:13 Hast thou seen all this **g** multitude? — 1419
20:21 and slew the Syrians with a **g** slaughter. — 1419
20:28 will I deliver all this **g** multitude into — 1419
22:31 saying, Fight neither with small nor **g**, — 1419

2Ki 3:27 there was **g** indignation against Israel: — 1419
4: 8 to Shunem, where *was* a **g** woman; — 1419
4:38 Set on the **g** pot, and seethe pottage for — 1419
5: 1 was a **g** man with his master, — 1419
5:13 the prophet had bid thee *do some* **g** thing, — 1419
6:14 horses, and chariots, and a **g** host: — 3515
6:23 he prepared **g** provision for them: — 1419
6:25 there was a **g** famine in Samaria: — 1419
7: 6 of horses, *even* the noise of a **g** host: — 1419
8: 4 all the **g** things that Elisha hath done. — 1419
8:13 a dog, that he should do this **g** thing? — 1419
10: 6 were with the **g** men of the city, — 1419
10:11 all his **g** men, and his kinsfolks, — 1419
10:19 for I have a **g** sacrifice to *do* to Baal; — 1419
16:15 Upon the **g** altar burn the morning burnt — 1419
17:21 the LORD, and made them sin a **g** sin. — 1419
17:36 up out of the land of Egypt with **g** power — 3515
18:17 Hezekiah with a **g** host *against* Jerusalem. — 3515
18:19 Thus saith the **g** king, the king of Assyria, — 1419
18:28 saying, Hear the word of the **g** king, — 1419
22:13 for **g** *is* the wrath of the LORD that *is* — 1419
23: 2 and all the people, both small and **g**: — 1419
23:26 not from the fierceness of his **g** wrath, — 1419
25: 9 every **g** *man's* house burnt he with fire. — 1419
25:26 both small and **g**, and the captains of — 1419

1Ch 11:14 the LORD saved *them by* a **g** deliverance. — 1419
11:23 a man of **g** stature, five cubits *high*; and — NIH
12:22 until it was a **g** host, like the host of God. — 1419
16:25 For **g** *is* the LORD, and greatly to be — 1419
17: 8 name of the **g** men that *are* in the earth. — 1419
17:17 house for a **g** *while* to come. — 4480+7350
17:19 in making known all *these* **g** things. — 1420
20: 6 was a man of **g** stature, whose fingers — NIH
21:13 David said unto Gad, I am in a **g** strait: — 3966
21:13 of the LORD; for very **g** *are* his mercies: — 7227
22: 8 blood abundantly, and hast made **g** wars: — 1419
25: 8 against *ward*, as well the small as the **g**, — 1419
26:13 they cast lots, as well the small as the **g**, — 1419
29: 1 *yet* young and tender, and the work *is* **g**: — 1419

1Ch 29: 9 David the king also rejoiced *with* **g** joy. — 1419
29:12 in thine hand *it is* to **make g**, and to give — 1431
29:22 drink before the LORD on that day with **g** — 1419

2Ch 1: 8 Thou hast shewed **g** mercy unto David — 1419
1:10 can judge this thy people, *that is so* **g**? — 1419
2: 5 the house which I build *is* **g**: for great *is* — 1419
2: 5 is great: for **g** *is* our God above all gods. — 1419
2: 9 I am about to build *shall be* wonderful **g**. — 1419
4: 9 and the court, and doors for the court, — 1419
4:18 Thus Solomon made all these vessels in **g** — 3966
6:32 come from a far country for thy **g** name's — 1419
7: 8 all Israel with him, a very **g** congregation, — 1419
9: 1 with a very **g** company, and camels that — 3515
9: 9 spices **g** abundance, and precious stones: — 3966
9:17 Moreover the king made a **g** throne of — 1419
13: 8 ye *be* a **g** multitude, and *there are* with — 7227
13:17 his people slew them *with* a **g** slaughter: — 7227
15: 5 **g** vexations *were* upon all the inhabitants — 7227
15:13 whether small or **g**, whether man or — 1419
16:12 until his disease *was* exceeding **g**: yet in — NIH
16:14 and they made a very **g** burning for him. — 1419
17:12 And Jehoshaphat waxed **g** exceedingly; — 1432
18:30 saying, Fight ye not with small or **g**, — 1419
20: 2 There cometh a **g** multitude against thee — 7227
20:12 for we have no might against this **g** — 7227
20:15 dismayed by reason of this **g** multitude; — 7227
21: 3 their father gave them **g** gifts of silver, — 7227
21:14 *with* a **g** plague will the LORD smite thy — 7227
21:15 thou *shalt* have **g** sickness by disease of — 7227
24:24 the LORD delivered a very **g** host into — 1419
24:25 from him, (for they left him in **g** diseases,) — 7227
26:15 and they returned home in **g** anger. — 2750
26:15 to shoot arrows and **g** stones withal. — 1419
28: 5 carried away a **multitude** of them — 1419
28: 5 who smote him *with* a **g** slaughter. — 1419
28:13 for our trespass is **g**, and *there is* fierce — 7227
30:13 the second month, a very **g** congregation. — 7230
30:21 bread seven days with **g** gladness: — 1419
30:24 a **g number** of priests sanctified — 7230+3807.1
30:26 So there was **g** joy in Jerusalem: for since — 1419
31:10 and that which is left *is* this **g** store. — 1995
31:15 courses, as well to the **g** as to the small: — 1419
33:14 **raised** it up a very **g** height, — 1361
34:21 for **g** *is* the wrath of the LORD that is — 1419
34:30 Levites, and all the people, **g** and small: — 1419
36:18 **g** and small, and the treasures of — 1419

Ezr 3:11 all the people shouted *with* a **g** shout, — 1419
4:10 the rest of the nations whom the **g** and — 7229
5: 8 the house of the **g** God, which *is* builded — 7229
5: 8 which *is* builded *with* **g** stones, — 1560
5:11 a **g** king of Israel builded and set up. — 7229
6: 4 three rows of **g** stones, and a row of — 1560
9: 7 we *been* in a **g** trespass unto this day; — 1419
9:13 for our evil deeds, and for our **g** trespass, — 1419
10: 1 out of Israel a very **g** congregation *of men* — 7227
10: 9 because of *this* matter, and for the **g** rain. — 1653

Ne 1: 3 there in the province *are* in **g** affliction — 1419
1: 5 the **g** and terrible God, that keepeth — 1419
1:10 thou hast redeemed by thy **g** power, — 1419
3:27 over against the **g** tower that lieth out, — 1419
4: 1 took **g** indignation, and mocked the Jews, — 7235
4:14 *which is* **g** and terrible, and fight for your — 1419
4:19 The work *is* **g** and large, and we *are* — 7235
5: 1 was a **g** cry of the people and of their — 1419
5: 7 And I set a **g** assembly against them. — 1419
6: 3 I *am* doing a **g** work, so that I cannot — 1419
7: 4 Now the city *was* large and **g**: — 1419
8: 6 Ezra blessed the LORD, the **g** God. — 1419
8:12 to make **g** mirth, because they had — 1419
8:17 done so. And there was very **g** gladness. — 1419
9:17 of **g** kindness, and forsookest them not. — 7227
9:18 Egypt, and had wrought **g** provocations; — 1419
9:25 delighted themselves in thy **g** goodness. — 1419
9:26 to thee, and they wrought **g** provocations. — 1419
9:31 Nevertheless for thy **g** mercies' sake thou — 7227
9:32 God, the **g**, the mighty, and the terrible — 7227
9:35 in thy **g** goodness that thou gavest them, — 7227
9:37 at their pleasure, and we *are* in **g** distress. — 1419
11:14 was Zabdiel, the son of *one of* the **g** men. — 1419
12:31 appointed two **g** companies of them that — 1419
12:43 Also that day they offered **g** sacrifices, — 1419
12:43 God had made them rejoice *with* **g** joy: — 1419
13: 5 he had prepared for him a **g** chamber, — 1419
13:27 hearken unto you to do all this **g** evil, — 1419

Est 1: 5 both unto **g** and small, seven days, — 1419
1:20 throughout all his empire, (for it *is* **g**,) — 7227
1:20 husbands honour, both to **g** and small. — 1419
2:18 king made a **g** feast unto all his princes — 1419
4: 3 *there was* **g** mourning among the Jews, — 1419
8:15 a **g** crown of gold, and *with* a garment — 1419
9: 4 For Mordecai *was* **g** in the king's house, — 1419
10: 3 **g** among the Jews, and accepted of — 1419

Job 1: 3 she asses, and a very **g** household; — 7227
1:19 there came a **g** wind from the wilderness, — 1419
2:13 for they saw that *his* grief was very **g**. — 1419
3:19 The small and **g** are there; and the servant — 1419
5: 9 Which doeth **g** things and unsearchable; — 1419
5:25 shalt know also that thy seed *shall be* **g**, — 7227
9:10 Which doeth **g** things past finding out; — 1419
22: 5 *Is* not thy wickedness **g**? — 7227
23: 6 he plead against me with *his* **g** power? — 7230
30:18 By the **g** force of *my* disease is my — 7230
31:25 If I rejoiced because my wealth *was* **g**, — 7227
31:34 Did I fear a **g** multitude, or did — 7227
32: 9 **G** men are not *always* wise: neither do — 7227

Job 35:15 yet he knoweth *it* not in **g** extremity: — 3966
36:18 then a **g** ransom cannot deliver thee. — 7230
36:26 Behold, God *is* **g**, and we know *him* not, — 7689
37: 5 **g** things doeth he, which we cannot — 1419
37: 6 rain, and *to* the **g** rain of his strength. — 4306
38:21 or *because* the number of thy days *is* **g**? — 7227
39:11 thou trust him, because his strength *is* **g**? — 1419

Ps 14: 5 There were they **in g** fear: for God — 6342+6343
18:35 and thy gentleness hath **made** me **g**. — 7235
18:50 **G** deliverance *giveth* he to his king; — 1431
19:11 *and* in keeping of them *there is* **g** reward. — 7227
19:13 be innocent from the **g** transgression. — 7227
21: 5 His glory *is* **g** in thy salvation: honour and — 1419
22:25 My praise *shall be* of thee in the **g** — 7227
25:11 O LORD, pardon mine iniquity; for it *is* **g**. — 7227
31:19 how **g** *is* thy goodness, which thou hast — 7227
32: 6 surely in the floods of **g** waters they shall — 7227
33:17 neither shall he deliver *any* by his **g** — 7230
35:18 I will give thee thanks in the **g** — 7227
36: 6 Thy righteousness *is* like the **g** mountains; — 410
36: 6 thy judgments *are* a **g** deep: — 7227
37:35 I have seen the wicked in **g** power, — 6184
40: 9 I have preached righteousness in the **g** — 7227
40:10 and thy truth from the **g** congregation. — 7227
47: 2 terrible; *he is* a **g** King over all the earth. — 1419
48: 1 **G** *is* the LORD, and greatly to be praised — 1419
48: 2 sides of the north, the city of the **g** King. — 7227
53: 5 There were they **in g** fear, *where* — 6342+6343
57:10 For thy mercy *is* **g** unto the heavens, — 1419
58: 6 break out the **g** teeth of the young lions, — 4459
68:11 *g* *was* the company of those that published — 1419
71:19 high, who hast done **g** things: O God, — 1419
71:20 which, hast shewed me **g** and — 7227
76: 1 *is* God known: his name *is* **g** in Israel. — 1419
77:13 who *is* so **g** a God as *our* God? — 1419
77:19 path in the **g** waters, and thy footsteps — 7227
78:15 gave *them* drink as *out of* the **g** depths. — 7227
78:71 From following the *ewes* **g** with young — 5763
80: 5 givest them tears to drink in **g** measure. — NIH
86:10 For thou *art* **g**, and doest wondrous — 1419
86:13 For **g** *is* thy mercy toward me: — 1419
92: 5 O LORD, how **g** are thy works! *and* — 1431
95: 3 For the LORD *is* a **g** God, and a great — 1419
95: 3 a great God, and a **g** King above all gods. — 1419
96: 4 For the LORD *is* **g**, and greatly to be — 1419
99: 2 The LORD *is* **g** in Zion; and he *is* high — 1419
99: 3 Let them praise thy **g** and terrible name; — 1419
103:11 **g** is his mercy toward them that fear him. — 1396
104: 1 O LORD my God, thou art very **g**; — 1431
104:25 *So is* this **g** and wide sea, wherein *are* — 1419
104:25 both small and **g** beasts. — 1419
106:21 which had done **g** things in Egypt; — 1419
107:23 sea in ships, that do business in **g** waters; — 7227
108: 4 For thy mercy *is* **g** above the heavens: — 1419
111: 2 The works of the LORD *are* **g**, sought out — 1419
115:13 fear the LORD, *both* small and **g**. — 1419
117: 2 For his merciful kindness is **g** toward us: — 1396
119:156 thy tender mercies, O LORD: — 7227
119:162 at thy word, as one that findeth **g** spoil. — 7227
119:165 **G** peace have they which love thy law: — 7227
126: 2 The LORD hath done **g** things for them. — 1431
126: 3 The LORD hath done **g** things for us; — 1431
131: 1 neither do I exercise myself in **g** *matters*, — 1419
135: 5 For I know that the LORD *is* **g**, — 1419
135:10 Who smote **g** nations, and slew mighty — 7227
136: 4 To him who alone doeth **g** wonders: for — 1419
136: 7 To him that made **g** lights: for his mercy — 1419
136:17 To him which smote **g** kings: for his — 1419
138: 5 for **g** *is* the glory of the LORD. — 1419
139:17 O God! how **g** is the sum of them! — 6105
144: 7 rid me, and deliver me out of **g** waters, — 7227
145: 3 **G** *is* the LORD, and greatly to be praised; — 1419
145: 7 utter the memory of thy **g** goodness, — 7227
145: 8 slow to anger, and of **g** mercy. — 1419
147: 5 **G** *is* our Lord, and of great power: — 1419
147: 5 Great *is* our Lord, and of **g** power: — 7227

Pr 13: 7 maketh himself poor, yet *hath* **g** riches. — 7227
14:29 *He that is* slow to wrath *is* of **g** — 7227
15:16 with the fear of the LORD than **g** treasure — 7227
16: 8 Better *is* a little with righteousness than **g** — 7230
18: 9 work is brother to **him that is** a **g** waster. — 1167
18:16 for him, and bringeth him before **g** men. — 1419
19:19 *A man* of **g** wrath *shall* suffer punishment: — 1419
22: 1 *good* name *is* rather to be chosen than **g** — 7227
25: 6 and stand not in the place of **g** *men*: — 1419
26:10 The **g** *God* formed all *things* both — 7227
28:12 righteous *men* do rejoice, *there is* **g** glory: — 7227
28:16 understanding *is* also a **g** oppressor: — 7227

Ecc 1:16 I am **come to g** estate, and have gotten — 1431
1:16 my heart had **g** experience of wisdom and — 7235
2: 4 I **made g** works; I builded me houses; — 1431
2: 7 also I had **g** possessions of great and — 7235
2: 7 had **g**reat possessions of **g** and small **cattle** — 1241
2: 9 I was **g**, and increased more than all that — 1431
2:21 This also *is* vanity and a **g** evil. — 7227
8: 6 the misery of man *is* **g** upon him. — 7227
9:13 under the sun, and it *seemed* **g** unto me: — 1419
9:14 there came a **g** king against it, — 1419
9:14 and built **g** bulwarks against it: — 1419
10: 4 thy place; for yielding pacifieth **g** offences. — 1419
10: 6 Folly is set in **g** dignity, and the rich sit in — 7227

SS 2: 3 down under his shadow **with g** delight, — 2530

Isa 5: 9 and the **g** man humbleth himself: — NIH
5: 9 *even* **g** and fair, without inhabitant. — 1419
6:12 *there* be a **g** forsaking in the midst of — 7227

Isa		
8: 1	Take thee a **g** roll, and write in it with a	1419
9: 2	walked in darkness have seen a **g** light;	1419
12: 6	for **g** *is* the Holy One of Israel in the midst	1419
13: 4	in the mountains, like as of a **g** people;	7227
16:14	be contemned, with all *that* **g** multitude;	7227
19:20	and a **g** one, and he shall deliver them.	1419
23: 3	by **g** waters the seed of Sihor, the harvest	7227
27: 1	day the LORD with his sore and **g** and	1419
27:13	*that* the trumpet shall be blown,	1419
29: 6	noise, *with* storm and tempest,	1419
30:25	streams of waters in the day of the **g**	7227
32: 2	as the shadow of a **g** rock in a weary land.	3515
33:23	is the prey of a **g** spoil divided; the lame	4766
34: 6	and a **g** slaughter in the land of Idumea.	1419
34:15	There shall the **g** owl make her nest,	7091
36: 2	unto king Hezekiah with a **g** army.	3515
36: 4	Thus saith the **g** king, the king of Assyria,	1419
36:13	said, Hear ye the words of the **g** king,	1419
38:17	for peace I had **g** bitterness:	4751+4843
47: 9	**g** abundance of thine enchantments.	3966
51:10	dried the sea, the waters of the **g** deep;	7227
53:12	will I divide him a *portion* with the **g**,	1419
54: 7	but with **g** mercies will I gather thee.	1419
54:13	and **g** *shall be* the peace of thy children.	7227
63: 7	**g** goodness towards the house of Israel,	7227
Jer		
4: 6	evil from the north, and a **g** destruction.	1419
5: 5	I will get me unto the **g men**,	1419
5:27	therefore they are become **g**,	1431
6: 1	out of the north, and **g** destruction.	1419
6:22	a **g** nation shall be raised from the sides of	1419
10: 6	thou *art* **g**, and thy name *is* great in might.	1419
10: 6	thou *art* great, and thy name *is* **g** in might.	1419
10:22	a commotion out of the north country,	1419
11:16	the noise of a **g** tumult he hath kindled	1419
13: 9	of Judah, and the **g** pride of Jerusalem.	7227
14:17	of my people is broken *with* a **g** breach,	1419
16:10	Both the **g** and the small shall die in this	1419
16:10	pronounced all this **g** evil against us?	1419
20:17	and her womb *to be* always **g** *with* me.	2030
21: 5	in anger, and in fury, and in **g** wrath.	1419
21: 6	and beast: they shall die of a **g** pestilence.	1419
22: 8	hath the LORD done thus unto this **g** city?	1419
25:14	kings shall serve themselves of them	1419
25:32	a whirlwind shall be raised up from	1419
26:19	Thus *might* we procure **g** evil against our	1419
27: 5	by my **g** power and by my outstretched	1419
27: 7	and **g** kings shall serve themselves of him.	1419
28: 8	against **g** kingdoms, of war, and of evil,	1419
30: 7	for that day *is* **g**, so that none *is* like it:	1419
31: 8	a **g** company shall return thither.	1419
32:17	the earth by thy **g** power and stretched	1419
32:18	the **G**, the Mighty God, the LORD of	1419
32:19	**G** in counsel, and mighty in work:	1419
32:21	a stretched out arm, and with **g** terror;	1419
32:37	anger, and in my fury, and in **g** wrath;	1419
32:42	Like as I have brought all this **g** evil upon	1419
33: 3	shew thee **g** and mighty *things*, which	1419
36: 7	for **g** *is* the anger and the fury that	1419
41:12	found him by the **g** waters that *are* in	7227
43: 9	Take *g* stones in thine hand, and hide	1419
44: 7	Wherefore commit ye *this* **g** evil against	1419
44:15	the women that stood by, a **g** multitude,	1419
44:26	Behold, I have sworn by my **g** name,	1419
45: 5	seekest thou **g** *things* for thyself? seek	1419
48: 3	Horonaim, spoiling and **g** destruction.	1419
50: 9	of **g** nations from the north country:	1419
50:22	battle *is* in the land, and of **g** destruction.	1419
50:41	a **g** nation, and many kings shall be raised	1419
51:54	**g** destruction from the land of	1419
51:55	and destroyed out of her the **g** voice;	1419
51:55	when her waves do roar like **g** waters,	7227
52:13	all the houses of the **g men**, burnt he	1419
La		
1: 1	she *that was* **g** among the nations,	7227
1: 3	of affliction, and because of **g** servitude:	7230
2:13	for thy breach *is* like the sea: who can	1419
3:23	new every morning: **g** *is* thy faithfulness.	7227
Eze		
1: 4	a **g** cloud, and a fire infolding itself,	1419
1:24	like the noise of **g** waters, as the voice of	7227
3:12	I heard behind me a voice of a **g** rushing,	1419
3:13	against them, and a noise of a **g** rushing.	1419
8: 6	the abominations that the house of	1419
9: 9	house of Israel and Judah *is* exceeding **g**,	1419
13:11	ye, O **g hailstones**, shall fall;	68+417
13:13	**g hailstones** in *my* fury to consume *it*.	68+417
16: 7	thou hast increased and **waxen g**,	1431
16:26	the Egyptians thy neighbours, **g** of flesh;	1432
17: 3	A **g** eagle with great wings, longwinged,	1419
17: 3	A great eagle with **g** wings, longwinged,	1419
17: 5	he placed *it* by **g** waters, *and* set it *as* a	7227
17: 7	There was also another **g** eagle with great	1419
17: 7	There was also another great eagle with **g**	1419
17: 8	It *was* planted in a good soil by **g** waters,	7227
17: 9	even without **g** power or many people to	1419
17:17	and **g** company make for him in the war,	7227
21:14	it *is* the sword of the **g** men *that are* slain,	1419
23:23	and rulers, **g lords** and renowned,	7991
24: 9	I will even **make** the pile for fire **g**.	1431
24:12	and her **g** scum went not forth out of her:	7227
25:17	I will execute **g** vengeance upon them	7227
26:19	upon thee, and **g** waters shall cover thee;	1419
27:26	Thy rowers have brought thee into **g**	7227
28: 5	By thy **g** wisdom *and* by thy traffick hast	7230
29: 3	the **g** dragon that lieth in the midst of his	1419
29:18	army to serve a **g** service against Tyrus:	1419
30: 4	and **g pain** shall be in Ethiopia, when the slain	2479

Eze		
30: 9	**g pain** shall come upon them, as *in* the	2479
30:16	Sin shall **have g pain**, and No shall	2342+2342
31: 4	The waters **made** him **g**, the deep set him	1431
31: 6	and under his shadow dwelt all **g** nations.	7227
31: 7	his branches: for his root was by **g** waters.	7227
31:15	and the waters were stayed:	7227
32:13	beasts thereof from besides the **g** waters;	7227
36:23	I will sanctify my **g** name, which was	1419
37:10	up upon their feet, an exceeding **g** army.	1419
38: 4	armour, *even* a **g** company *with* bucklers	7227
38:13	*away* cattle and goods, to take a **g** spoil?	1419
38:15	a **g** company, and a mighty army:	1419
38:19	in that day there shall be a **g** shaking	1419
38:22	and **g hailstones**, fire, and brimstone.	68+417
39:17	*even* a **g** sacrifice upon the mountains of	1419
41: 8	chambers *were* a full reed of six cubits.	679
47: 9	there shall be a very **g multitude** of fish,	7227
47:10	as the fish of the **g** sea, exceeding many.	1419
47:15	from the **g** sea, the way of Hethlon,	1419
47:19	of strife *in* Kadesh, *the* river to the **g** sea.	1419
47:20	The west side also *shall be* the **g** sea from	1419
48:28	and *to* the river toward the **g** sea.	1419
Da		
2: 6	of me gifts and rewards and **g** honour:	7690
2:31	O king, sawest, and behold a **g** image.	7690
2:31	This **g** image, whose brightness *was*	7229
2:35	stone that smote the image became a **g**	7229
2:45	the **g** God hath made known to the king	7229
2:48	the king **made** Daniel a **g** man,	7236
2:48	gave him many **g** gifts, and made him	7260
4: 3	How **g** *are* his signs! and how mighty *are*	7260
4:10	of the earth, and the height thereof *was* **g**.	7690
4:30	spake, and said, *Is* not this **g** Babylon,	7229
5: 1	Belshazzar the king made a **g** feast to a	7229
7: 2	of the heaven strove upon the **g** sea.	7229
7: 3	four **g** beasts came up from the sea,	7260
7: 7	exceedingly; and it had **g** iron teeth:	7260
7: 8	of man, and a mouth speaking **g** *things*.	7260
7:11	the voice of the **g** words which the horn	7260
7:17	These **g** beasts, which *are* four, *are* four	7260
7:20	a mouth that spake **very g** *things*, whose	7229
7:25	he shall speak **g** words against the most	NIH
8: 4	did according to his will, and became **g**.	1431
8: 8	Therefore the he goat **waxed** very **g**:	1431
8: 8	he was strong, the **g** horn was broken;	1419
8: 9	which waxed exceeding **g**, toward	1431
8:10	it **waxed g**, *even* to the host of heaven;	1431
8:21	the **g** horn that *is* between his eyes *is*	1419
9: 4	and said, O Lord, the **g** and dreadful God,	1419
9:12	judged us, by bringing upon us a **g** evil:	1419
9:18	righteousnesses, but for thy **g** mercies.	7227
10: 1	I was by the side of the **g** river, which *is*	1419
10: 7	a **g** quaking fell upon them, so that they	1419
10: 8	saw this **g** vision, and there remained no	1419
11: 3	that shall rule *with* **g** dominion,	7227
11: 5	his dominion *shall be* a **g** dominion.	7227
11:10	and shall assemble a multitude of **g** forces:	7227
11:11	he shall set forth a **g** multitude;	7227
11:13	come after certain years with a **g** army	1419
11:25	the king of the south with a **g** army;	1419
11:25	shall be stirred up to battle with a very **g**	1419
11:28	shall he return *into* his land with **g** riches;	1419
11:44	he shall go forth with **g** fury to destroy,	1419
12: 1	**g** prince which standeth for the children	1419
Hos		
1: 2	hath **committed g whoredom**,	2181+2181
1:11	the land: for **g** *shall be* the day of Jezreel.	1419
8:12	I have written to him the **g things** of my	7230
9: 7	of thine iniquity, and the **g** hatred.	7230
10:15	because of your **wickedness**;	7451+7465
13: 5	the wilderness, in the land of **g drought**.	8514
Joel		
1: 6	and he hath the cheek-teeth of a **g lion**.	3833
2: 2	a **g** people and a strong; there hath not	7227
2:11	for his camp *is* very **g**: for *he is* strong that	7227
2:11	for the day of the LORD *is* **g** and	1419
2:13	of **g** kindness, and repenteth him of	7227
2:20	because he hath done **g things**.	1431
2:21	rejoice: for the LORD will do **g things**.	1431
2:25	my **g** army which I sent among you.	1419
2:31	before the **g** and the terrible day of	1419
3:13	fats overflow; for their wickedness *is* **g**.	7227
Am		
3: 9	behold the **g** tumults in the midst thereof,	7227
3:15	the **g** houses shall have an end, saith	7227
6: 2	and from thence go ye *to* Hamath the **g**:	7227
6:11	he will smite the **g** house *with* breaches,	1419
7: 4	it devoured the **g** deep, and did eat up a	7227
8: 5	the shekel **g**, and falsifying the balances	1431
Jnh		
1: 2	to Nineveh, *that* **g** city, and cry against it;	1419
1: 4	the LORD sent out a **g** wind into the sea,	1419
1:12	for I know that for my sake this **g** tempest	1419
1:17	Now the LORD had prepared a **g** fish to	1419
3: 2	**g** city, and preach unto it the preaching	1419
3: 3	Now Nineveh was an exceeding **g** city of	1419
4: 2	of **g** kindness, and repentest thee of	7227
4:11	should not I spare Nineveh, *that* **g** city,	1419
Mic		
2:12	they shall **make g noise** by reason of	1949
5: 4	for now shall he be **g** unto the ends of	1431
7: 3	the **g** *man*, he uttereth his mischievous	1419
Na		
1: 3	**g** in power, and will not at all acquit	1419
3: 3	of slain, and a **g** number of carcases;	3514
3:10	and all her **g** *men* were bound in chains.	1419
3:17	thy captains *are* as the **g grasshoppers**,	1462+1462
Hab		
3:15	horses, *through* the heap of **g** waters.	7227
Zep		
1:10	second, and a **g** crashing from the hills.	1419
1:14	The **g** day of the LORD *is* near, *it is* near,	1419
Zec		
1:14	and for Zion with a **g** jealousy.	1419
4: 7	Who *art* thou, O **g** mountain?	1419

Zec		
7:12	came a **g** wrath from the LORD of hosts.	1419
8: 2	I was jealous for Zion *with* **g** jealousy,	1419
8: 2	and I was jealous for her *with* **g** fury.	1419
9:17	For **how g** *is* his goodness, and how great	4100
9:17	*is* his goodness, and **how g** is his beauty!	4100
12:11	In that day shall there be a **g** mourning in	1431
14: 4	west, *and there shall be* a very **g** valley;	1419
14:13	*that* a **g** tumult from the LORD shall be	7227
14:14	and silver, and apparel, in **g** abundance.	3966
Mal		
1:11	my name *shall be* **g** among the Gentiles;	1419
1:11	my name *shall be* **g** among the heathen,	1419
1:14	Lord a corrupt *thing*: for I *am* a **g** King,	1419
4: 5	the prophet before the coming of the **g**	1419
Mt		
2:10	star, they rejoiced *with* exceeding **g** joy.	3173
2:18	and weeping, and **g** mourning,	4183
4:16	The people which sat in darkness saw **g**	3173
4:25	And there followed him **g** multitudes *of*	4183
5:12	for **g** *is* your reward in heaven: for so	4183
5:19	teach *them*, the same shall be called the **g**	3173
5:35	for it is the city of the **g** King.	3173
6:23	be darkness, **how g** *is* that darkness?	4214
7:27	and it fell: and **g** was the fall of it.	3173
8: 1	the mountain, **g** multitudes followed him.	4183
8:10	have not found so **g** faith, no not in Israel.	5118
8:18	Now when Jesus saw **g** multitudes about	4183
8:24	there arose a **g** tempest in the sea,	3173
8:26	and the sea; and there was a **g** calm.	3173
12:15	and **g** multitudes followed him,	4183
13: 2	And **g** multitudes were gathered together	4183
13:46	when he had found one pearl of **g** price,	4186
14:14	saw a **g** multitude, and was moved with	4183
15:28	said unto her, O woman, **g** *is* thy faith:	3173
15:30	And **g** multitudes came unto him,	4183
15:33	the wilderness, as to fill so **g** a multitude?	5118
19: 2	And **g** multitudes followed him;	4183
19:22	away sorrowful: for he had **g** possessions.	4183
20:25	they *that are* exercise authority upon	3173
20:26	but whosoever will be **g** among you,	3173
20:29	from Jericho, a **g** multitude followed him.	4183
21: 8	And a **very g** multitude spread their	4183
22:36	which is the **g** commandment in the law?	3173
22:38	This is the first and **g** commandment.	3173
24:21	For then shall be **g** tribulation, such as	3173
24:24	and shall shew **g** signs and wonders;	3173
24:30	clouds of heaven with power and **g** glory.	4183
24:31	he shall send his angels with a **g** sound	3173
26:47	with him a **g** multitude with swords and	4183
27:60	he rolled a **g** stone to the door of	3173
28: 2	And behold, there was a **g** earthquake:	3173
28: 8	from the sepulchre with fear and **g** joy;	3173
Mk		
1:35	rising up a **g while** before day, he went	3029
3: 7	a **g** multitude from Galilee followed him,	4183
3: 8	about Tyre and Sidon, a **g** multitude,	4183
3: 8	they had heard **what g** *things* he did,	3745
4: 1	was gathered unto him a **g** multitude,	4183
4:32	all herbs, and shooteth out **g** branches;	3173
4:37	And there arose a **g** storm of wind,	3173
4:39	the wind ceased, and there was a **g** calm.	3173
5:11	the mountains a **g** herd of swine feeding.	4183
5:19	tell them **how g** *things* the Lord hath	3745
5:20	to publish in Decapolis **how g** *things*	3745
5:42	And they were astonished with a **g**	3173
7:36	the more a **g deal** they published *it*;	4054
8: 1	In those days the multitude being **very g**,	3827
9:14	he saw a **g** multitude about them,	4183
10:22	away grieved: for he had **g** possessions.	4183
10:42	**g** ones exercise authority upon them.	3173
10:43	but whosoever will be **g** among you,	3173
10:46	his disciples and a **g number** of people,	2425
10:48	he cried the more a **g deal**, Thou Son of	4183
13: 2	unto him, Seest thou these **g buildings**?	3173
13:26	man coming in the clouds with **g** power	4183
14:43	with him a **g** multitude with swords and	4183
16: 4	stone was rolled away: for it was very **g**.	3173
Lk		
1:15	For he shall be **g** in the sight of the Lord,	3173
1:32	He shall be **g**, and shall be called the Son	3173
1:49	*that is* mighty hath done to me **g things**;	3167
1:58	the Lord had **shewed g** mercy upon her;	3170
2: 5	his espoused wife, being **g with child**;	1471
2:10	I bring you good tidings of **g** joy,	3173
2:36	of the tribe of Aser: she was of a **g** age,	4183
4:25	**g** famine was throughout all the land;	3173
4:38	wife's mother was taken with a **g** fever;	3173
5: 6	they inclosed a **g** multitude of fishes:	4183
5:15	and **g** multitudes came together to hear,	4183
5:29	And Levi made him a **g** feast in his own	3173
5:29	there was a **g** company of publicans and	4183
6:17	a **g** multitude of people out of all Judea	4183
6:23	for behold, your reward *is* **g** in heaven:	4183
6:35	your reward shall be **g**, and ye shall be	4183
6:49	it fell; and the ruin of that house was **g**.	4183
7: 9	not found so **g** faith, no, not in Israel.	5118
7:16	That a **g** prophet is risen up among us;	3173
8:37	them; for they were taken with **g** fear:	3173
8:39	shew **how g things** God hath done unto	3745
8:39	throughout the whole city **how g**	3745
9:48	least among you all, the same shall be **g**.	3173
10: 2	The harvest truly *is* **g**, but the labourers	3173
10:13	they had a **g while ago** repented, sitting	3819
13:19	and it grew, and waxed a **g** tree;	3173
14:16	A certain man made a **g** supper,	3173
14:25	And there went **g** multitudes with him:	4183
14:32	else, while the other is yet a **g way off**,	4206
15:20	when he was yet a **g way** off, his father	3112
16:26	between us and you there is a **g** gulf fixed:	3173

G

G

Lk	21:11 g earthquakes shall be in divers places,	3173
	21:11 and g signs shall there be from heaven.	3173
	21:23 for there shall be g distress in the land,	3173
	21:27 in a cloud with power and g glory.	4183
	22:44 his sweat was as it were g drops of blood	NIG
	23:27 And there followed him a g company of	4183
	24:52 and returned to Jerusalem with g joy:	3173
Jn	5: 3 In these lay a g multitude of impotent	4183
	6: 2 And a g multitude followed him, because	4183
	6: 5 and saw a g company come unto him,	4183
	6:18 And the sea arose by reason of a g wind	3173
	7:37 that g day of the feast, Jesus stood and	3173
	21:11 and drew the net to land full of g fishes,	3173
Ac	2:20 before that g and notable day of the Lord	3173
	4:33 with g power gave the apostles witness	3173
	4:33 Jesus: and g grace was upon them all.	3173
	5: 5 fear came on all them that heard these	3173
	5:11 And g fear came upon all the church,	3173
	6: 7 a g company of the priests were obedient	4183
	6: 8 did g wonders and miracles among	3173
	7:11 land of Egypt and Canaan, and g affliction:	3173
	8: 1 At that time there was a g persecution	3173
	8: 2 and made g lamentation over him.	3173
	8: 8 And there was g joy in that city.	3173
	8: 9 giving out that himself was some g one:	3173
	8:10 saying, This man is the g power of God.	3173
	8:27 an eunuch of g authority under Candace	1413
	9:16 For I will shew him how g things he	3745
	10:11 as it had been a g sheet knit at the four	
	11: 5 vessel descend, as it had been a g sheet,	3173
	11:21 and a g number believed, and turned unto	4183
	11:28 by the Spirit that there should be g	3173
	14: 1 that a g multitude both of the Jews and	4183
	15: 3 they caused g joy unto all the brethren.	3173
	16:26 And suddenly there was a g earthquake,	3173
	17: 4 and of the devout Greeks a g multitude,	4183
	19:27 that the temple of the g goddess Diana	3173
	19:28 saying, G is Diana of the Ephesians.	3173
	19:34 cried out, G is Diana of the Ephesians.	3173
	19:35 is a worshipper of the g goddess Diana,	3173
	21:40 And when there was made a g silence,	4183
	22: 6 there shone from heaven a g light	2425
	22:28 With a g sum obtained I this freedom.	4183
	23: 9 there arose a g cry: and the scribes that	3173
	23:10 And when there arose a g dissension,	4183
	23:14 bound ourselves under a g curse,	331+332
	24: 2 Seeing that by thee we enjoy g quietness,	4183
	24: 7 with g violence took him away out of our	4183
	25:23 with g pomp, and were entered into	4183
	26:22 this day, witnessing both to small and g,	3173
	28: 6 but after they had looked a g while,	1909+4183
	28:29 and had g reasoning among themselves.	
Ro	9: 2 That I have g heaviness and	3173
	15:23 a g desire these many years to come	1974
1Co	9:11 g thing if we shall reap your carnal	3173
	16: 9 For a g door and effectual is opened unto	3173
2Co	1:10 Who delivered us from so g a death,	5082
	3:12 such hope, we use g plainness of speech:	4183
	7: 4 G is my boldness of speech toward you,	4183
	7: 4 toward you, g is my glorying of you:	4183
	8: 2 How that in a g trial of affliction	4183
	8:22 the g confidence which I have in you.	4183
	11:15 Therefore it is no g thing if his ministers	3173
Eph	2: 4 for his g love wherewith he loved us,	4183
	5:32 This is a g mystery: but I speak	3173
Col	2: 1 For I would that ye knew what g conflict	2245
	4:13 he hath a g zeal for you, and them that	4183
1Th	2:17 abundantly to see your face with g desire.	
1Ti	3:13 g boldness in the faith which is in Christ	4183
	3:16 And without controversy g is the mystery	3173
	6: 6 But godliness with contentment is g gain.	3173
2Ti	2:20 But in a g house there are not only vessels	3173
Tit	2:13 the glorious appearing of the g God and	3173
Phm	1: 7 For we have g joy and consolation in thy	
Heb	2: 3 we escape, if we neglect so g salvation;	5082
	4:14 Seeing then that we have a g high priest,	3173
	7: 4 Now consider how g this man was, unto	4080
	10:32 ye endured a g fight of afflictions;	4183
	10:35 which hath g recompence of reward.	3173
	12: 1 about with so g a cloud of witnesses,	5118
	13:20 that g shepherd of the sheep, through	3173
Jas	3: 4 which though they be so g, and are driven	5082
	3: 5 is a little matter, and boasteth g things.	3173
	3: 5 how g a matter a little fire kindleth.	2245
1Pe	3: 4 which is in the sight of God of g price.	4185
2Pe	1: 4 Whereby are given unto us exceeding g	3176
	2:18 For when they speak g swelling words of	5246
	3:10 heavens shall pass away with a g noise,	4500
Jude	1: 6 darkness unto the judgment of the g day.	3173
	1:16 their mouth speaketh g swelling words,	5246
Rev	1:10 and heard behind me a g voice, as of a	3173
	2:22 that commit adultery with her into g	3173
	6: 4 and there was given unto him a g sword.	3173
	6:12 seal, and, lo, there was a g earthquake;	3173
	6:15 and the g men, and the rich men, and	3175
	6:17 For the g day of his wrath is come;	
	7: 9 After this I beheld, and, lo, a g multitude,	4183
	7:14 These are they which came out of g	3173
	8: 8 as it were a g mountain burning with fire	3173
	8:10 and there fell a g star from heaven,	3173
	9: 2 of the pit, as the smoke of a g furnace;	3173
	9:14 are bound in the g river Euphrates.	3173
	11: 8 bodies shall lie in the street of the g city,	3173
	11:11 g fear fell upon them which saw them.	3173
	11:12 And they heard a g voice from heaven	3173

Rev	11:13 And the same hour was there a g	3173
	11:15 and there were g voices in heaven,	3173
	11:17 thou hast taken to thee thy g power,	3173
	11:18 and them that fear thy name, small and g;	3173
	11:19 and an earthquake, and g hail.	3173
	12: 1 And there appeared a g wonder in heaven;	3173
	12: 3 and behold a g red dragon, having seven	3173
	12: 9 And the g dragon was cast out, that old	3173
	12:12 having g wrath, because he knoweth that	3173
	12:14 were given two wings of a g eagle,	3173
	13: 2 his power, and his seat, and g authority.	3173
	13: 5 unto him a mouth speaking g things	3173
	13:13 he doeth g wonders, so that he maketh	3173
	13:16 both small and g, rich and poor, free and	3173
	14: 2 and as the voice of a g thunder:	3173
	14: 8 Babylon is fallen, is fallen, that g city,	3173
	14:19 cast it into the g winepress of the wrath	3173
	15: 1 another sign in heaven, g and marvellous,	3173
	15: 3 saying, G and marvellous are thy works,	3173
	16: 1 And I heard a g voice out of the temple	3173
	16: 9 And men were scorched with g heat,	3173
	16:12 out his vial upon the g river Euphrates;	3173
	16:14 gather them to the battle of that g day of	3173
	16:17 there came a g voice out of the temple of	3173
	16:18 there was a g earthquake, such as was	3173
	16:18 so mighty an earthquake, and so g.	3173
	16:19 the g city was divided into three parts,	3173
	16:19 and g Babylon came in remembrance before	3173
	16:21 And there fell upon men a g hail out of	3173
	16:21 for the plague thereof was exceeding g.	3173
	17: 1 will shew unto thee the judgment of the g	3173
	17: 5 MYSTERY, BABYLON THE G,	3173
	17: 6 I saw her, I wondered with g admiration.	3173
	17:18 the woman which thou sawest is that g	3173
	18: 1 come down from heaven, having g power;	3173
	18: 2 saying, Babylon the g is fallen, is fallen,	3173
	18:10 saying, Alas, alas, that g city Babylon,	3173
	18:16 And saying, Alas, alas, that g city, that was	3173
	18:17 in one hour so g riches is come to nought.	5118
	18:18 saying, What city is like unto this g city?	3173
	18:19 and wailing, saying, Alas, alas, that g city,	3173
	18:21 a mighty angel took up a stone like a g	3173
	18:21 Thus with violence shall that g city	3173
	18:23 for thy merchants were the g men of	3175
	19: 1 And after these things I heard a g voice of	3173
	19: 2 for he hath judged the g whore, which did	3173
	19: 5 and ye that fear him, both small and g.	3173
	19: 6 And I heard as it were the voice of a g	4183
	19:17 together unto the supper of the g God;	3173
	19:18 both free and bond, both small and g.	3173
	20: 1 bottomless pit and a g chain in his hand.	3173
	20:11 And I saw a g white throne, and him that	3173
	20:12 the dead, small and g, stand before God;	3173
	21: 3 I heard a g voice out of heaven saying,	3173
	21:10 he carried me away in the spirit to a g	3173
	21:10 mountain, and shewed me that g city,	3173
	21:12 had a wall g and high, and had twelve	3173

GREATER (77) [GREAT]

Ge	1:16 g light to rule the day, and the lesser	1419
	4:13 My punishment is g than I can bear.	1419
	39: 9 There is none g in this house than I;	1419
	41:40 only in the throne will I be g than thou.	1431
	48:19 his younger brother shall be g than he,	1431
Ex	18:11 Now I know that the Lord is g than all	1419
Nu	14:12 will make of thee a g nation and	1419
Dt	1:28 The people is g and taller than we;	1419
	4:38 To drive out nations from before thee g	1419
	7: 1 seven nations g and mightier than thou;	7227
	9: 1 to go in to possess nations g and	1419
	9:14 of thee a nation mightier and g than they.	7227
	11:23 ye shall possess g nations and mightier	1419
Jos	10: 2 because it was g than Ai, and all the men	1419
1Sa	14:30 for had there not been now a much g	7235
2Sa	13:15 g than the love wherewith he had loved	1419
	13:16 this evil in sending me away is g than	1419
1Ki	1:37 make his throne g than the throne of my	1431
	1:47 and make his throne g than thy throne.	1431
1Ch	11: 9 So David waxed g and greater:	1980+1980
	11: 9 So David waxed greater and g:	1419
2Ch	3: 5 the house he cieled with fir tree, which	1419
Est	9: 4 for this man Mordecai waxed g and	1980
	9: 4 this man Mordecai waxed greater and g,	1419
Job	33:12 will answer thee, that God is g than man.	7235
La	4: 6 g than the punishment of the sin of	1431
Eze	8: 6 and thou shalt see g abominations.	1419
	8:13 thou shalt see g abominations that they	1419
	8:15 thou shalt see g abominations than these.	1419
	43:14 from the lesser settle even to the g settle	1419
Da	11:13 shall set forth a multitude g than	7227
Am	6: 2 or their border g than your border?	7227
Hag	2: 9 The glory of this latter house shall be g	1419
Mt	11:11 hath not risen a g than John the Baptist:	
	11:11 in the kingdom of heaven is g than he.	3187
	12: 6 in this place is one g than the temple.	3187
	12:41 and behold, a g than Jonas is here.	4183
	12:42 and behold, a g than Solomon is here.	4183
	23:14 ye shall receive the g damnation.	4053
	23:17 whether is g, the gold, or the temple that	3187
	23:19 whether is g, the gift, or the altar that	3187
Mk	4:32 and becometh g than all herbs,	3187
	12:31 is none other commandment g than	
	12:40 these shall receive g damnation.	4053
Lk	7:28 is not a g prophet than John the Baptist:	3187
	7:28 least in the kingdom of God is g than he.	3187

Lk	11:31 and behold, a g than Solomon is here.	4183
	11:32 and a g than Jonas is here.	4183
	12:18 I will pull down my barns, and build g;	3187
	20:47 the same shall receive g damnation.	4054
	22:27 For whether is g, he that sitteth at meat,	3187
Jn	1:50 thou shalt see g things than these.	3187
	4:12 Art thou g than our father Jacob,	3187
	5:20 he will shew him g works than these,	3187
	5:36 But I have g witness than that of John:	3187
	8:53 Art thou g than our father Abraham,	3187
	10:29 which gave them me, is g than all;	3187
	13:16 The servant is not g than his lord;	3187
	13:16 neither he that is sent g than he that sent	3187
	14:12 and g works than these shall he do;	3187
	14:28 unto the Father: for my Father is g than I.	3187
	15:13 G love hath no man than this, that a man	3187
	15:20 The servant is not g than his lord.	3187
	19:11 he that delivered me unto thee hath the g	3187
Ac	15:28 to lay upon you no g burden than these	4183
1Co	14: 5 for g is he that prophesieth than he that	3187
	15: 6 of whom the g part remain unto this	4183
Heb	6:13 he could swear by no g, he sware	3187
	6:16 men verily swear by the g: and an oath	3187
	9:11 by a g and more perfect tabernacle,	3187
	11:26 g riches than the treasures in Egypt:	3187
Jas	3: 1 knowing that we shall receive the g	3187
2Pe	2:11 which are g in power and might,	3187
1Jn	3:20 God is g than our heart, and knoweth all	3187
	4: 4 because g is he that is in you, than he that	3187
	5: 9 witness of men, the witness of God is g:	
3Jn	1: 4 I have no g joy than to hear that my	3186

GREATEST (21) [GREAT]

1Ch	12:14 an hundred, and the g over a thousand.	1419
	12:29 for hitherto the g part of them had kept	4768
Job	1: 3 that this man was the g of all the men of	1419
Jer	6:13 from the least of them even unto the g	1419
	8:10 even unto the g is given to covetousness,	1419
	31:34 from the least of them unto the g of them,	1419
	42: 1 the people from the least even unto the g,	1419
	42: 8 all the people from the least even to the g,	1419
	44:12 from the least even unto the g, by the	1419
Jnh	3: 5 from the g of them even to the least of	1419
Mt	13:32 it is the g among herbs, and becometh a	3187
	18: 1 Who is the g in the kingdom of heaven?	3187
	18: 4 the same is g in the kingdom of heaven.	3187
	23:11 But he that is g among you shall be your	3187
Mk	9:34 among themselves, who should be the g.	3187
Lk	9:46 among them, which of them should be g.	3187
	22:24 of them should be accounted the g.	3187
	22:26 but he that is g among you, let him be as	3187
Ac	8:10 gave heed, from the least to the g, saying,	3173
1Co	13:13 these three; but the g of these is charity.	3187
Heb	8:11 all shall know me, from the least to the g.	3173

GREATLY (87) [GREAT]

Ge	3:16 I will g multiply thy sorrow and	7235+7235
	7:18 and were increased g upon the earth;	3966
	19: 3 he pressed upon them g; and they turned	3966
	24:35 the Lord hath blessed my master g;	3966
	32: 7 Then Jacob was g afraid and distressed:	3966
Ex	19:18 furnace, and the whole mount quaked g.	3966
Nu	11:10 and the anger of the Lord was kindled g;	3966
	14:39 of Israel: and the people mourned g.	3966
Dt	15: 4 for the Lord shall g bless thee in	1288+1288
	17:17 shall he g multiply to himself silver	3966
Jos	10: 2 That they feared g, because Gibeon was a	3966
Jdg	2:15 unto them: and they were g distressed.	3966
	6: 6 Israel was g impoverished because of	3966
1Sa	11: 6 tidings, and his anger was kindled g.	3966
	11:15 and all the men of Israel rejoiced g.	3966
	12:18 all the people g feared the Lord and	3966
	16:21 he loved him g; and he became his	3966
	17:11 they were dismayed, and g afraid.	3966
	28: 5 he was afraid, and his heart g trembled.	3966
	30: 6 David was g distressed; for the people	3966
2Sa	10: 5 because the men were g ashamed.	3966
	12: 5 David's anger was g kindled against	3966
	24:10 I have sinned g in that I have done:	3966
1Ki	2:12 and his kingdom was established g.	3966
	5: 7 that he rejoiced g, and said, Blessed be	3966
	18: 3 (Now Obadiah feared the Lord g:	3966
1Ch	4:38 house of their fathers increased g.	7230+3807.1
	16:25 great is the Lord, and g to be praised:	3966
	19: 5 for the men were g ashamed.	3966
	21: 8 I have sinned g, because I have done this	3966
2Ch	25:10 their anger was g kindled against Judah,	3966
	33:12 humbled himself g before the God of his	3966
Job	3:25 the thing which I g feared is come	6342+6343
	8: 7 yet thy latter end should g increase.	3966
Ps	21: 1 in thy salvation how g shall he rejoice!	3966
	28: 7 therefore my heart g rejoiceth;	5937
	38: 6 am troubled; I am bowed down g;	3966+5704
	45:11 So shall the king g desire thy beauty:	183
	47: 9 earth belong unto God: he is g exalted.	3966
	48: 1 and g to be praised in the city of our God,	3966
	62: 2 he is my defence; I shall not be g moved.	7227
	65: 9 thou g enrichest it with the river of God,	7227
	71:23 My lips shall g rejoice when I sing unto	7442
	78:59 he was wroth, and g abhorred Israel:	3966
	89: 7 God is g to be feared in the assembly of	7227
	96: 4 the Lord is great, and g to be praised:	3966
	105:24 he increased his people g; and made them	3966
	107:38 them also, so that they are multiplied g;	3966
	109:30 I will g praise the Lord with my mouth;	3966

Ps	112: 1	*that* delighteth **g** in his commandments.	3966
	116:10	therefore have I spoken: I was **g** afflicted:	3966
	119:51	proud have had me **g** in derision:	3966+5704
	145: 3	Great *is* the Lord, and **g** to be praised;	3966
Pr	23:24	of the righteous shall **g rejoice**:	1523+1524
Isa	42:17	back, they shall be **g ashamed**,	954+1322
	61:10	I will **g rejoice** in the Lord,	7797+7797
Jer	3: 1	shall not that land be **g polluted**?	2610+2610
	4:10	surely thou hast **g deceived** this	5377+5377
	9:19	we are **g** confounded, because we have	3966
	20:11	they shall be **g** ashamed: for they shall not	3966
Eze	20:13	in them; and my sabbaths they **g** polluted:	3966
	25:12	hath **g offended**, and revenged	816+816
Da	5: 9	*was* king Belshazzar **g** troubled,	7690
	9:23	to shew *thee*; for thou *art* **g beloved**:	2532
	10:11	unto me, O Daniel, a man **g beloved**,	2532
	10:19	O man **g beloved**, fear not: peace *be*	2532
Ob	1: 2	among the heathen: thou *art* **g** despised.	3966
Zep	1:14	the Lord *is* near, *it is* near, and hasteth **g**,	3966
Zec	9: 9	Rejoice **g**, O daughter of Zion; shout,	3966
Mt	27:14	insomuch that the governor marvelled **g**.	3029
	27:54	that were done, they feared **g**, saying,	4970
Mk	5:23	And besought him **g**, saying, My little	4183
	5:38	and them that wept and wailed **g**,	4183
	9:15	**g amazed**, and running to *him* saluted	1568
	12:27	God of the living: ye therefore do **g** err.	4183
Jn	3:29	**rejoiceth g** because of	5463+5479
Ac	3:11	that is called Solomon's, **g wondering**.	1569
	6: 7	of the disciples multiplied in Jerusalem **g**;	4970
1Co	16:12	I **g** desired him to come unto you with	4183
Php	1: 8	how **g** I long after you all in the bowels of	NIG
	4:10	But I rejoiced in the Lord **g**, that now at	3171
1Th	3: 6	**desiring g** to see us, as we also *to see*	1971
2Ti	1: 4	**g desiring** to see thee, being mindful of	1971
	4:15	for he hath **g** withstood our words.	3029
1Pe	1: 6	Wherein ye **g** rejoice, though now for a	21
2Jn	1: 4	I rejoiced **g** that I found of thy children	3029
3Jn	1: 3	For I rejoiced **g**, when *the* brethren came	3029

GREATNESS (32) [GREAT]

Ex	15: 7	in the **g** of thine excellency thou hast	7230
	15:16	by the **g** of thine arm they shall be *as* still	1419
Nu	14:19	people according unto the **g** of thy mercy,	1433
Dt	3:24	thou hast begun to shew thy servant thy **g**,	1433
	5:24	God hath shewed us his glory and his **g**,	1433
	9:26	which thou hast redeemed through thy **g**,	1433
	11: 2	his **g**, his mighty hand, and his stretched	1433
	32: 3	of the Lord: ascribe ye **g** unto our God.	1433
1Ch	17:19	thine own heart, hast thou done all this **g**,	1420
	17:21	make thee a name of **g** and terribleness,	1420
	29:11	*is* the **g**, and the power, and the glory,	1420
2Ch	9: 6	the *one* half of the **g** of thy wisdom was	4768
	24:27	of the burdens *laid* upon him,	7230
Ne	13:22	spare me according to the **g** of thy mercy.	7230
Est	10: 2	and the declaration of the **g** of Mordecai,	1420
Ps	66: 3	through the **g** of thy power shall thine	7230
	71:21	Thou shalt increase my **g**, and comfort	1420
	79:11	according to the **g** of thy power:	1433
	145: 3	to be praised; and his **g** is unsearchable.	1420
	145: 6	thy terrible acts: and I will declare thy **g**.	1420
	150: 2	praise him according to his excellent **g**.	1433
Pr	5:23	and in the **g** of his folly he shall go astray.	7230
Isa	40:26	he calleth them all by names by the **g** of	7230
	57:10	Thou art wearied in the **g** of thy way;	7230
	63: 1	travelling in the **g** of his strength?	7230
Jer	13:22	For the **g** of thine iniquity are thy skirts	7230
Eze	31: 2	multitude; Whom art thou like in thy **g**?	1433
	31: 7	Thus was he fair in his **g**, in the length of	1433
	31:18	in glory and in **g** among the trees of Eden?	1433
Da	4:22	for thy **g** is grown, and reacheth unto	7238
	7:27	the **g** of the kingdom under the whole	7238
Eph	1:19	And what *is* the exceeding **g** of his power	3174

GREAVES (1)

| 1Sa | 17: 6 | *had* **g** of brass upon his legs, and a target | 4697 |

GRECIA (3) [GREECE]

Da	8:21	the rough goat *is* the king of **G**:	3120
	10:20	gone forth, lo, the prince of **G** shall come.	3120
	11: 2	he shall stir up all against the realm of **G**.	3120

GRECIANS (4) [GREECE]

Joel	3: 6	Jerusalem have ye sold unto the **G**,	1121+3125
Ac	6: 1	there arose a murmuring of the **G** against	1675
	9:29	Lord Jesus, and disputed against the **G**:	1675
	11:20	unto the **G**, preaching the Lord Jesus.	1675

GREECE (2) [GRECIA, GRECIANS, GREEK, GREEKS]

Zec	9:13	O **G**, and made thee as the sword of a	3120
Ac	20: 2	them much exhortation, he came into **G**,	1671

GREEDILY (3) [GREEDINESS]

Pr	21:26	He **coveteth g** all the day long:	183+8378
Eze	22:12	thou hast **g gained** of thy neighbours by	1214
Jude	1:11	**ran g** after the error of Balaam for reward	1632

GREEDINESS (1) [GREEDILY, GREEDY]

| Eph | 4:19 | to work all uncleanness with **g**. | 4124 |

GREEDY (6) [GREEDINESS]

Ps	17:12	Like as a lion *is* **g** of his prey, and as	3700
Pr	1:19	ways of every one that is **g of gain**;	1214+1215
	15:27	He that is **g of gain** troubleth his	1214+1215
Isa	56:11	they *are* **g** dogs *which* can never	5315+5794
1Ti	3: 3	to wine, no striker, not **g of filthy lucre**;	146
	3: 8	given to much wine, not **g of filthy lucre**;	146

GREEK (12) [GREECE]

Mk	7:26	The woman was a **G**, a Syrophenician by	1674
Lk	23:38	also was written over him in letters of **G**,	1673
Jn	19:20	was written in Hebrew, *and* **G**, *and* Latin.	1676
Ac	16: 1	and believed; but his father *was* a **G**:	1672
	16: 3	for they knew all that his father was a **G**.	1672
	21:37	Who said, Canst thou speak **G**?	1676
Ro	1:16	to the Jew first, and *also* to the **G**.	1672
	10:12	no difference between the Jew and the **G**:	1672
Gal	2: 3	Titus, who was with me, being a **G**,	1672
	3:28	There is neither Jew nor **G**, there is	1672
Col	3:11	Where there is neither **G** nor Jew,	1672
Rev	9:11	in the **G** tongue hath *his* name Apollyon.	1673

GREEKS (14) [GREECE]

Jn	12:20	there were certain **G** among them that	1672
Ac	14: 1	of the Jews and *also* of the **G** believed.	1672
	17: 4	and of the devout **G** a great multitude,	1672
	17:12	of honourable women which were **G**,	1674
	18: 4	and persuaded the Jews and the **G**.	1672
	18:17	Then all the **G** took Sosthenes, the *chief*	1672
	19:10	word of the Lord Jesus, both Jews and **G**.	1672
	19:17	the Jews and **G** also dwelling at Ephesus;	1672
	20:21	*also* to the **G**, repentance toward God,	1672
	21:28	further brought **G** also into the temple,	1672
Ro	1:14	I am debtor both to the **G**, and to	1672
1Co	1:22	a sign, and the **G** seek after wisdom:	1672
	1:23	and unto the **G** foolishness;	1672
	1:24	Jews and **G**, Christ the power of God,	1672

GREEN (41) [GREENISH, GREENNESS]

Ge	1:30	*is* life, *I have* given every **g** herb for meat:	3418
	9: 3	even as the **g** herb have I given you all	3418
	30:37	Jacob took him rods of **g** poplar, and of	3892
Ex	10:15	remained not any **g thing** in the trees,	3418
Lev	2:14	*even* **g** ears of corn dried by the fire,	24
	23:14	bread, nor parched *corn*, nor **g** ears,	3759
Dt	12: 2	upon the hills, and under every **g** tree:	7488
Jdg	16: 7	If they bind me with seven **g** withs that	3892
	16: 8	seven **g** withs which had not been dried,	3892
1Ki	14:23	on every high hill, and under every **g** tree.	7488
2Ki	16: 4	and on the hills, and under every **g** tree.	7488
	17:10	in every high hill, and under every **g** tree:	7488
	19:26	the herb, *as* the grass on the housetops,	3419
2Ch	28: 4	and on the hills, and under every **g** tree.	7488
Est	1: 6	*were* **g**, and blue *hangings*, fastened with cords	3768
Job	8:16	He *is* **g** before the sun, and his branch	7373
	15:32	his time, and his branch shall not be **g**.	7488
	39: 8	and he searcheth after every **g thing**.	3387
Ps	23: 2	He maketh me to lie down in **g** pastures:	1877
	37: 2	like the grass, and wither as the **g** herb.	3418
	37:35	and spreading himself like a **g** bay tree.	7488
	52: 8	*am* like a **g** olive tree in the house of God:	7488
SS	1:16	yea, pleasant: also our bed *is* **g**.	7488
	2:13	The fig tree putteth forth her **g** figs,	6291
Isa	15: 6	the grass faileth, there is no **g thing**.	3418
	37:27	the herb, *as* the grass on the housetops,	3419
	57: 5	yourselves with idols under every **g** tree,	7488
Jer	2:20	and under every **g** tree thou wanderest,	7488
	3: 6	high mountain and under every **g** tree,	7488
	3:13	ways to the strangers under every **g** tree,	7488
	11:16	A **g** olive tree, fair, *and* of goodly fruit:	7488
	17: 2	their groves by the **g** trees upon the high	7488
	17: 8	when heat cometh, but her leaf shall be **g**;	7488
Eze	6:13	under every **g** tree, and under every thick	7488
	17:24	have dried up the **g** tree, and have made	3892
	20:47	it shall devour every **g** tree in thee,	3892
Hos	14: 8	I *am* like a **g** fir tree. From me is thy fruit	7488
Mk	6:39	sit down by companies upon the **g** grass.	5515
Lk	23:31	For if they do these *things* in a **g** tree,	5200
Rev	8: 7	burnt up, and all **g** grass was burnt up.	5515
	9: 4	neither any **g thing**, neither any tree;	5515

GREENISH (2) [GREEN]

Lev	13:49	the plague be **g** or reddish in the garment,	3422
	14:37	**g** or reddish, which in sight *are* lower	3422

GREENNESS (1) [GREEN]

| Job | 8:12 | Whilst it *is* yet in his **g**, *and* not cut down, | 3 |

GREET (16) [GREETETH, GREETING, GREETINGS]

1Sa	25: 5	and **g** him in my name:	7592+7965+3807.1
Ro	16: 3	**G** Priscilla and Aquila my helpers in Christ	782
	16: 5	**g** the church that is in their house.	NIG
	16: 6	**G** Mary, who bestowed much labour on	782
	16: 8	**G** Amplias my beloved in the Lord.	782
	16:11	**G** them that be of the *household* of	782
1Co	16:20	All the brethren **g** you. Greet ye one	782
	16:20	ye one another with an holy kiss.	782
2Co	13:12	**G** one another with a holy kiss.	782
Php	4:21	The brethren which are with me **g** you.	782
Col	4:14	the beloved physician, and Demas, **g** you.	782
1Th	5:26	**G** all the brethren with a holy kiss.	782
Tit	3:15	**G** them that love us in the faith. Grace *be*	782
1Pe	5:14	**G** ye one another with a kiss of charity.	782
2Jn	1:13	The children of thy elect sister **g** thee.	782
3Jn	1:14	friends salute thee. **G** the friends by name.	782

GREETETH (1) [GREET]

| 2Ti | 4:21 | Eubulus **g** thee, and Pudens, and Linus, | 782 |

GREETING (3) [GREET]

Ac	15:23	brethren send **g** unto the brethren which	5463
	23:26	most excellent governor Felix *sendeth* **g**.	5463
Jas	1: 1	tribes which are scattered abroad, **g**.	5463

GREETINGS (3) [GREET]

Mt	23: 7	And **g** in the markets, and to be called of	783
Lk	11:43	in the synagogues, and **g** in the markets.	783
	20:46	and love **g** in the markets, and the highest	783

GREW (28) [GROW]

Ge	2: 5	and every herb of the field before it **g**:	6779
	19:25	**that which g** upon the ground.	6780
	21: 8	the child **g**, and was weaned:	1431
	21:20	he **g**, and dwelt in the wilderness,	1431
	25:27	boys **g**: and Esau was a cunning hunter,	1431
	26:13	and **g** until he became very great:	1432
	47:27	and **g**, and multiplied exceedingly.	6509
Ex	1:12	the more they multiplied and **g**.	6555
	2:10	the child **g**, and she brought him unto	1431
Jdg	11: 2	his wife's sons **g up**, and they thrust out	1431
	13:24	the child **g**, and the Lord blessed him.	1431
1Sa	2:21	And the child Samuel **g** before the Lord.	1431
	2:26	the child Samuel **g** on, and was in favour	1432
	3:19	Samuel **g**, and the Lord was with him,	1431
2Sa	5:10	**g great**, and the Lord God of hosts *was*	1419
	12: 3	it **g up** together with him, and with his	1431
Eze	17: 6	it **g**, and became a spreading vine of low	6779
	17:10	it shall wither in the furrows where it **g**.	6780
Da	4:11	The tree **g**, and was strong, and the height	7236
	4:20	thou sawest, which **g**, and was strong,	7236
Mk	4: 7	and the thorns **g up**, and choked it,	305
	5:26	bettered, but rather **g** worse,	1519+2064
Lk	1:80	the child **g**, and waxed strong in spirit,	837
	2:40	the child **g**, and waxed strong in spirit,	837
	13:19	and it **g**, and waxed a great tree;	837
Ac	7:17	the people **g** and multiplied in Egypt,	837
	12:24	But the word of God **g** and multiplied.	837
	19:20	So mightily **g** the word of God and	837

GREYHOUND (1)

| Pr | 30:31 | A **g**; a he goat also; and a king, | 2223+4975 |

GRIEF (26) [GRIEFS, GRIEVANCE, GRIEVE, GRIEVED, GRIEVETH, GRIEVING, GRIEVOUS, GRIEVOUSLY, GRIEVOUSNESS]

Ge	26:35	Which were a **g** of mind unto Isaac and	4786
1Sa	1:16	complaint and **g** have I spoken hitherto.	3708
	25:31	That this shall be no **g** unto thee,	6330
2Ch	6:29	shall know his own sore and his own **g**,	4341
Job	2:13	for they saw that *his* **g** was very great.	3511
	6: 2	Oh that my **g** were throughly weighed,	3708
	16: 5	moving of my lips should assuage *your* **g**.	NIH
	16: 6	Though I speak, my **g** is not assuaged:	3511
Ps	6: 7	Mine eye is consumed because of **g**;	3708
	31: 9	eye is consumed with **g**, *yea*, my soul	3708
	31:10	For my life is spent with **g**, and my years	3015
	69:26	they talk to the **g** of those whom thou	4341
Pr	17:25	A foolish son *is* a **g** to his father,	3708
Ecc	1:18	For in much wisdom *is* much **g**: and he	3708
	2:23	all his days *are* sorrows, and his travail **g**:	3708
Isa	17:11	harvest *shall be* a heap in the day of **g**	2470
	53: 3	a man of sorrows, and acquainted with **g**:	2483
	53:10	to bruise him; he hath **put** *him* **to g**:	2470
Jer	6: 7	before me continually *is* **g** and wounds.	2483
	10:19	I said, Truly this *is* a **g**, and I must bear it.	2483
	45: 3	for the Lord hath added **g** to my sorrow;	3015
La	3:32	though he **cause g**, yet will he have	3013
Jnh	4: 6	over his head, to deliver him from his **g**.	7451
2Co	2: 5	But if any have **caused g**, he hath not	3076
Heb	13:17	they may do it with joy, and not with **g**:	4727
1Pe	2:19	for conscience toward God endure **g**,	3077

GRIEFS (2)

| Isa | 53: 4 | Surely he hath borne our **g**, and carried | 2483 |

GRIEVANCE (1) [GRIEF]

| Hab | 1: 3 | me iniquity, and cause *me* to behold **g**? | 5999 |

GRIEVE (5) [GRIEF]

1Sa	2:33	consume thine eyes, and to **g** thine heart:	109
1Ch	4:10	keep *me* from evil, that it may not **g** me.	6087
Ps	78:40	the wilderness, *and* **g** him in the desert!	6087
La	3:33	For he doth not afflict willingly nor **g**	3013
Eph	4:30	And **g** not the holy Spirit of God,	3076

GRIEVED (40) [GRIEF]

Ge	6: 6	on the earth, and it **g** him at his heart.	6087
	34: 7	when they heard *it:* and the men were **g**,	6087
	45: 5	Now therefore be not **g**, nor angry with	6087
	49:23	The archers have **sorely** **g** him, and shot	4843
Ex	1:12	they were **g** because of the children of	6973
Dt	15:10	heart shall not be **g** when thou givest	3415
Jdg	10:16	and his soul was **g** for the misery of Israel.	7114
1Sa	1: 8	why is thy heart **g**? *am* not I better to	3415
	15:11	it **g** Samuel; and he cried unto the Lord	2734
	20: 3	lest Jonathan know this, lest he be **g**:	6087
	20:34	for he was **g** for David, because his father	6087
	30: 6	because the soul of all the people was **g**,	4843
2Sa	19: 2	that day how the king was **g** for his son.	6087
Ne	2:10	**g** them **exceedingly** that	1419+7451+7489
	5: 6	for the day *is* holy; neither be ye **g**.	
	13: 8	it **g** me sore: therefore I cast forth all	3415
Est	4: 4	the queen exceedingly **g**; and she sent	2342
Job	4: 2	to commune with thee, wilt thou be **g**?	3811
	30:25	trouble? was *not* my soul **g** for the poor?	5701
Ps	73:21	Thus my heart was **g**, and I was pricked	2556
	95:10	Forty years long was I **g** with *this*	6962
	112:10	The wicked shall see *it*, and be **g**; he shall	3707
	119:158	I beheld the transgressors, and was **g**;	6962

Ps 139:21 am not I **g** with those that rise up against 6962
Isa 54: 6 thee as a woman forsaken and **g** in spirit, 6087
 57:10 of thine hand; therefore thou wast not **g**. 2470
Jer 5: 3 hast stricken them, but they have not **g**; 2342
Da 7:15 I Daniel was **g** in my spirit in the midst of 3735
 11:30 therefore he shall be **g**, and return, 3512
Am 6: 6 they are not **g** for the affliction of Joseph. 2470
Mk 3: 5 being **g** for the hardness of their hearts, 4818
 10:22 was sad at *that* saying, and went away **g**: 3076
Jn 21:17 Peter was **g** because he said unto him 3076
Ac 4: 2 Being **g** that they taught the people, 1278
 16:18 being **g**, turned and said to the spirit, 1278
Ro 14:15 But if thy brother be **g** with *thy* meat, 3076
2Co 2: 4 not that you should be **g**, but that ye 3076
 2: 5 grief, he hath not **g** me, but in part: 3076
Heb 3:10 Wherefore I was **g** with that generation, 4360
 3:17 But with whom was he **g** forty years? 4360

GRIEVETH (2) [GRIEF]
Ru 1:13 for it **g** me much for your sakes that 4843
Pr 26:15 it **g** him to bring it again to his mouth. 3811

GRIEVING (1) [GRIEF]
Eze 28:24 nor *any* **g** thorn of all *that are* round 3510

GRIEVOUS (38) [GRIEF]
Ge 12:10 for the famine *was* **g** in the land. 3515
 18:20 is great, and because their sin is very **g**; 3513
 21:11 the thing was very **g** in Abraham's sight 3415
 21:12 Let it not be **g** in thy sight because of 3415
 41:31 famine following; for it *shall be* very **g**. 3515
 50:11 This *is* a mourning to the Egyptians: 3515
Ex 8:24 there came a **g** swarm *of flies* into 3515
 9: 3 sheep: *there shall be* a very **g** murrain. 3515
 9:18 time I will cause it to rain a very **g** hail, 3515
 9:24 and fire mingled with the hail, very **g**, 3515
 10:14 very **g** *were they;* before them there were 3515
1Ki 2: 8 cursed me with a **g** curse in the day 4834
 12: 4 Thy father **made** our yoke **g**: now 7185
 12: 4 make thou the **g** service of thy father, 7186
2Ch 10: 4 Thy father **made** our yoke **g**: now 7185
 10: 4 ease thou somewhat the **g** servitude of 7186
Ps 10: 5 His ways are always **g**; thy judgments *are* 2342
 31:18 which speak **g things** proudly and 6277
Pr 15: 1 away wrath: but **g** words stir up anger. 6089
 15:10 Correction *is* **g** unto him that forsaketh 7451
Ecc 2:17 work that is wrought under the sun *is* **g** 7451
Isa 15: 4 shall cry out; his life shall be **g** unto him. 3415
 21: 2 A **g** vision is declared unto me; 7186
Jer 6:28 They are all **g** revolters, walking with 5493
 10:19 my wound *is* **g**: but I said, Truly this *is* a 2470
 14:17 *with* a great breach, *with* a very **g** blow. 2470
 16: 4 They shall die of **g** deaths; they shall not 8463
 23:19 is gone forth *in* fury, even a **g** whirlwind; 2342
 30:12 bruise *is* incurable, *and* thy wound *is* **g**. 2470
Na 3:19 no healing of thy bruise; thy wound *is* **g**: 2470
Mt 23: 4 bind **heavy burdens and g to be borne**, 1419
Lk 11:46 **lade men *with* burdens g to be borne**, 1419
Ac 20:29 that after my departing shall **g** wolves enter 926
 25: 7 laid many and **g** complaints against Paul, 926
Php 3: 1 me indeed *is not* **g**, but for you *it is* safe. 3636
Heb 12:11 the present seemeth to be joyous, but **g**: 3077
1Jn 5: 3 and his commandments are not **g**. 926
Rev 16: 2 **g** sore upon the men which had the mark 4190

GRIEVOUSLY (7) [GRIEF]
Isa 9: 1 did **more g afflict** *her by* the way 3513
Jer 23:19 shall **fall g** upon the head of the wicked. 2342
La 1: 8 Jerusalem hath **g sinned**; therefore 2398+2399
 1:20 within me; for I have **g rebelled**; 4784+4784
Eze 14:13 against me by **trespassing g**, 4603+4604
Mt 8: 6 at home sick of the palsy, **g** tormented. 1171
 15:22 my daughter is **g** vexed with a devil. 2560

GRIEVOUSNESS (2) [GRIEF]
Isa 10: 1 that write **g** which they have prescribed; 5999
 21:15 the bent bow, and from the **g** of war. 3514

GRIN (1) [GRINS; see also GIN]
Job 18: 9 The **g** shall take *him* by the heel, 6341

GRIND (7) [GRINDERS, GRINDING]
Jdg 16:21 brass; and he did **g** in the prison house. 2912
Job 31:10 *Then* let my wife **g** unto another, 2912
Isa 3:15 to pieces, and **g** the faces of the poor? 2912
 47: 2 Take the millstones, and **g** meal: 2912
La 5:13 They took the young men to **g**, 2911
Mt 21:44 it shall fall, it will **g him to powder**. 3039
Lk 20:18 it shall fall, it will **g him to powder**. 3039

GRINDERS (1) [GRIND]
Ecc 12: 3 the **g** cease because they are few, 2912

GRINDING (3) [GRIND]
Ecc 12: 4 the sound of the **g** is low, and he shall 2913
Mt 24:41 Two **women shall be g at the mill;** *the* one 229
Lk 17:35 Two **women shall be g together;** *the* one 229

GRINS (2) [GRIN; see also GIN]
Ps 140: 5 by the way side; they have set **g** for me. 4170
 141: 9 and the **g** of the workers of iniquity. 4170

GRISLED (3)
Ge 31:10 cattle *were* ringstraked, speckled, and **g**. 1261
 31:12 the cattle *are* ringstraked, speckled, and **g**: 1261
Zec 6: 3 and in the fourth chariot **g** *and* bay horses. 1261

Zec 6: 6 the **g** go forth toward the south country. 1261

GROAN (7) [GROANED, GROANETH, GROANING, GROANINGS]
Job 24:12 Men **g** from out of the city, and the soul 5008
Jer 51:52 through all her land the wounded shall **g**. 602
Eze 30:24 he shall **g** before him *with* the groanings 5008
Joel 1:18 How do the beasts **g**! the herds of cattle 584
Ro 8:23 even we ourselves **g** within ourselves, 4727
2Co 5: 2 For in this we **g**, earnestly desiring to be 4727
 5: 4 For we that are in *this* tabernacle do **g**, 4727

GROANED (1) [GROAN]
Jn 11:33 he **g** in the spirit, and was troubled, 1690

GROANETH (1) [GROAN]
Ro 8:22 For we know that the whole creation **g** 4959

GROANING (9) [GROAN]
Ex 2:24 God heard their **g**, and God remembered 5009
 6: 5 I have also heard the **g** of the children of 5009
Job 23: 2 my stroke is heavier than my **g**. 585
Ps 6: 6 I am weary with my **g**; all the night make 585
 38: 9 before thee; and my **g** is not hid from thee. 585
 102: 5 By reason of the voice of my **g** my bones 585
 102:20 To hear the **g** of the prisoner; to loose 603
Jn 11:38 again **g** in himself cometh to the grave. 1690
Ac 7:34 and I have heard their **g**, and am come 4726

GROANINGS (3) [GROAN]
Jdg 2:18 their **g** by reason of them that oppressed 5009
Eze 30:24 he shall groan before him *with* the **g** of a 5009
Ro 8:26 for us with **g** which cannot be uttered. 4726

GROPE (5) [GROPETH]
Dt 28:29 thou shalt **g** at noondays, as the blind 4959
Job 5:14 and **g** in the noonday as in the night. 4959
 12:25 They **g** in the dark without light, 4959
Isa 59:10 We **g** for the wall like the blind, 1659
 59:10 the blind, and we **g** as if *we had* no eyes: 1659

GROPETH (1) [GROPE]
Dt 28:29 as the blind **g** in darkness, and thou shalt 4959

GROSS (4)
Isa 60: 2 the earth, and **g darkness** the people: 6205
Jer 13:16 of death, *and* make *it* **g darkness**. 6205
Mt 13:15 For this people's heart is **waxed g**, 3975
Ac 28:27 For the heart of this people is **waxed g**, 3975

GROUND (192) [AGROUND, GROUNDED]
Ge 2: 5 and *there was* not a man to till the **g**. 127
 2: 6 and watered the whole face of the **g**. 127
 2: 7 God formed man *of* the dust of the **g**, 127
 2: 9 out of the **g** made the Lord God to grow 127
 2:19 out of the **g** God formed every 127
 3:17 cursed *is* the **g** for thy sake; in sorrow shalt 127
 3:19 thou eat bread, till thou return to the **g**; 127
 3:23 to till the **g** from whence he was taken. 127
 4: 2 of sheep, but Cain was a tiller of the **g**. 127
 4: 3 that Cain brought of the fruit of the **g** an 127
 4:10 brother's blood crieth unto me from the **g**. 127
 4:12 When thou tillest the **g**, it shall not 127
 5:29 of the **g** which the Lord hath cursed. 127
 7:23 which *was* upon the face of the **g**, 127
 8: 8 were abated from off the face of the **g**; 127
 8:13 and behold, the face of the **g** was dry. 127
 8:21 I will not again curse the **g** any more for 127
 18: 2 door, and bowed himself toward the **g**, 776
 19: 1 bowed himself with his face toward the **g**; 776
 19:25 cities, and that which grew upon the **g**. 127
 33: 3 and bowed himself to the **g** seven times, 776
 38: 9 brother's wife, that he spilled *it* on the **g**, 776
 44:11 took down every man his sack to the **g**, 776
 44:14 there: and they fell before him on the **g**. 776
Ex 3: 5 the place whereon thou standest *is* holy **g**. 127
 4: 3 he said, Cast it on the **g**. And he cast it on 776
 4: 3 cast it on the **g**, and it became a serpent; 776
 8:21 *of flies,* and also the **g** whereon they *are.* 127
 9:23 hail, and the fire ran along upon the **g**; 776
 14:16 the children of Israel shall go on dry **g** NIH
 14:22 into the midst of the sea upon the dry **g**: NIH
 16:14 *as* small as the hoar frost on the **g**. 776
 32:20 **g** it to powder, and strawed *it* upon 2912
Lev 20:25 *of living thing* that creepeth on the **g**, 127
Nu 11: 8 gathered *it,* and **g** *it* in mills, or beat *it* in 2912
 16:31 the **g** clave asunder that *was* under them: 127
Dt 4:18 of any *thing* that creepeth on the **g**, 127
 9:21 stamped it, and **g** *it* **very small**, 2912+3190
 15:23 thou shalt pour it upon the **g** as water. 776
 22: 6 or on the **g**, *whether they be* young ones, 776
 28: 4 fruit of thy **g**, and the fruit of thy cattle, 127
 28:11 fruit of thy cattle, and in the fruit of thy **g**, 127
 28:56 sole of her foot upon the **g** for delicateness 776
Jos 3:17 stood firm on dry **g** in the midst of Jordan, NIH
 3:17 all the Israelites passed over on dry **g**, NIH
 24:32 in a parcel of **g** which Jacob bought of 7704
Jdg 4:21 into his temples, and fastened *it* into the **g**: 776
 6:39 and upon all the **g** let there be dew. 776
 6:40 fleece only, and there was dew on all the **g**. 776
 13:20 looked on *it,* and fell on their faces to the **g**. 776
 20:21 destroyed *down* to the **g** of the Israelites 776
 20:25 destroyed *down* to the **g** of the children of 776
Ru 2:10 bowed herself to the **g**, and said unto him, 776
1Sa 3:19 and did let none of his words fall to the **g**. 776
 5: 4 Dagon *was* fallen upon his face to the **g** 776

1Sa 8:12 **will set them** to ear his **g**, and to reap his 2758
 14:25 a wood; and there was honey upon the **g**. 7704
 14:32 oxen, and calves, and slew *them* on the **g**: 776
 14:45 shall not one hair of his head fall to the **g**; 776
 20:31 long as the son of Jesse liveth upon the **g**, 127
 20:41 fell on his face to the **g**, and bowed himself 776
 25:23 on her face, and bowed herself *to* the **g**, 776
 26: 7 and his spear stuck in the **g** at his bolster: 776
 28:14 he stooped *with his* face to the **g**, 776
2Sa 2:22 wherefore should I smite thee to the **g**? 776
 8: 2 with a line, casting them down to the **g**; 776
 14: 4 she fell on her face to the **g**, 776
 14:14 needs die, and *are* as water spilt on the **g**, 776
 14:22 Joab fell to the **g** on his face, 776
 14:33 bowed himself on his face to the **g** before 776
 17:12 *light* upon him as the dew falleth on the **g**: 127
 17:19 well's mouth, and spread **g corn** thereon; 7383
 18:11 didst thou not smite him there to the **g**? 776
 20:10 fifth *rib,* and shed out his bowels to the **g**, 776
 23:11 where was a piece of **g** full *of* lentiles: 7704
 23:12 he stood in the midst of the **g**, 2513
 24:20 before the king *on* his face upon the **g**. 776
1Ki 1:23 before the king with his face to the **g**. 776
 7:46 the clay **g** between Succoth and Zarthan. 127
2Ki 2: 8 so that they two went over on dry **g**. NIH
 2:15 bowed themselves to the **g** before him. 776
 2:19 but the water *is* naught, and the **g** barren. 776
 4:37 bowed herself to the **g**, and took up her 776
 9:26 cast him into the plat of **g**, according to NIH
 13:18 unto the king of Israel, Smite upon the **g**. 776
1Ch 11:13 where was a parcel of **g** full *of* barley; 7704
 21:21 himself to David *with his* face to the **g**. 776
 27:26 tillage of the **g** was Ezri the son of Chelub: 127
2Ch 4:17 in the clay **g** between Succoth and 127
 7: 3 *their* faces to the **g** upon the pavement, 776
 20:18 bowed his head *with his* face to the **g**: 776
Ne 8: 6 the Lord *with their* faces to the **g**. 776
 10:35 to bring the firstfruits of our **g**, 127
 10:37 the tithes of our **g** unto the Levites, that 127
Job 1:20 fell down upon the **g**, and worshipped, 776
 2:13 they sat down with him upon the **g** seven 776
 5: 6 neither doth trouble spring out of the **g**; 127
 14: 8 earth, and the stock thereof die in the **g**; 6083
 16:13 he poureth out my gall upon the **g**. 776
 18:10 snare *is* laid for him in the **g**, and a trap 776
 38:27 To satisfy the desolate and waste **g**, NIH
 39:24 He swalloweth the **g** with fierceness and 776
Ps 74: 7 the dwelling place of thy name to the **g**. 776
 89:39 profaned his crown *by* casting *it* to the **g**. 776
 89:44 cease, and cast his throne down to the **g**. 776
 105:35 land, and devoured the fruit of their **g**. 127
 107:33 and the watersprings into **dry g**; 6774
 107:35 water, and dry **g** into watersprings; 776
 143: 3 he hath smitten my life down to the **g**; 776
 147: 6 he casteth the wicked down to the **g**. 776
Isa 3:26 and she *being* desolate shall sit upon the **g**. 776
 14:12 art thou cut down to the **g**, which didst 776
 21: 9 of her gods he hath broken unto the **g**. 776
 25:12 low, *and* bring to the **g**, *even* to the dust. 776
 26: 5 it low; he layeth it low, *even* to the **g**; 776
 28:24 doth he open and break the clods of his **g**? 127
 29: 4 shalt speak out of the **g**, and thy speech 776
 29: 4 out of the **g**, and thy speech shall whisper 776
 30:23 thy seed, that thou shalt sow the **g** withal; 127
 30:24 the young asses that ear the **g** shall eat 127
 35: 7 the **parched g** shall become a pool, 8273
 44: 3 floods upon the dry **g**: I will pour my spirit NIH
 47: 1 O virgin daughter of Babylon, sit on the **g**: 776
 51:23 thou hast laid thy body as the **g**, and as 776
 53: 2 tender plant, and as a root out of a dry **g**: 776
Jer 4: 3 **Break up your fallow g**, and sow not 5215
 7:20 of the field, and upon the fruit of the **g**; 127
 14: 2 they are black unto the **g**; and the cry of 776
 14: 4 the **g** is chapt, for there was no rain 127
 25:33 nor buried; they shall be dung upon the **g**. 127
 27: 5 the man and the beast that *are* upon the **g**, 776
La 2: 2 he hath brought *them* down to the **g**: 776
 2: 9 Her gates are sunk into the **g**; he hath 776
 2:10 of the daughter of Zion sit upon the **g**, 776
 2:10 Jerusalem hang down their heads to the **g**. 776
 2:21 and the old lie on the **g** in the streets: 776
Eze 12: 6 cover thy face, that thou see not the **g**. 776
 12:12 face, that he see not the **g** with *his* eyes. 776
 13:14 and bring it down to the **g**, 776
 19:12 she was cast down to the **g**, and the east 776
 19:13 in the wilderness, in a dry and thirsty **g**. 776
 24: 7 she poured it not upon the **g**, to cover it 776
 26:11 thy strong garrisons shall go down to the **g**. 776
 26:16 they shall sit upon the **g**, and shall tremble 776
 28:17 I will cast thee to the **g**, I will lay thee 776
 38:20 shall fall, and every wall shall fall to the **g**. 776
 41:16 *from* the **g** up to the windows, 776
 41:20 From the **g** unto above the door *were* 776
 42: 6 the lowest and the middlemost from the **g**. 776
 43:14 from the bottom *upon* the **g** *even* to 776
Da 8: 5 of the whole earth, and touched not the **g**: 776
 8: 7 he cast him down to the **g**, and stamped 776
 8:10 *some* of the host and of the stars to the **g**, 776
 8:12 and it cast down the truth to the **g**; 776
 8:18 in a deep sleep on my face toward the **g**: 776
 10: 9 on my face, and my face toward the **g**. 776
 10:15 I set my face toward the **g**, and I became 776
Hos 2:18 and *with* the creeping things of the **g**: 127
 10:12 reap in mercy; break up your **fallow g**: 5215
Am 3:14 the altar shall be cut off, and fall to the **g**. 776

G

Ob	1: 3 heart, Who shall bring me down *to* the **g**	776
Hag	1:11 and upon *that* which the **g** bringeth forth,	127
Zec	8:12 shall give her increase, and the heavens	776
Mal	3:11 he shall not destroy the fruits of your **g**;	127
Mt	10:29 of them shall not fall on the **g** without	1093
	13: 8 But other fell into good **g**,	1093
	13:23 he that received seed into the good **g** is	1093
	15:35 the multitude to sit down on the **g**.	1093
Mk	4: 5 some fell on **stony g**, where it had not	4075
	4: 8 other fell on good **g**, and did yield fruit	1093
	4:16 likewise which are sown on **stony g**;	4075
	4:20 are they which are sown on good **g**;	1093
	4:26 as if a man should cast seed into the **g**,	1093
	8: 6 the people to sit down on the **g**:	1093
	9:20 and he fell on the **g**,	1093
	14:35 fell on the **g**, and prayed that, if it were	1093
Lk	8: 8 And other fell on good **g**, and sprang up,	1093
	8:15 that on the good **g** are they, which in an	1093
	12:16 The **g** of a certain rich man brought forth	5561
	13: 7 cut it down; why cumbereth it the **g**?	1093
	14:18 I have bought a **piece of g**, and I must	68
	19:44 shall **lay** thee **even with the g**, and thy	1474
	22:44 great drops of blood falling down to the **g**	1093
Jn	4: 5 near to the **parcel of g** that Jacob gave to	5564
	8: 6 and with *his* finger wrote on the **g**,	1093
	8: 8 he stooped down, and wrote on the **g**.	1093
	9: 6 he spat **on the g**, and made clay of	5476
	12:24 Except a corn of wheat fall into the **g** and	1093
	18: 6 they went backward, and fell **to the g**.	5476
Ac	7:33 the place where thou standest is holy **g**.	1093
	22: 7 And I fell unto the **g**, and heard a voice	1475
1Ti	3:15 living God, the pillar and **g** of the truth.	1477

GROUNDED (3) [GROUND]

Isa	30:32 in every *place* where the **g** staff shall pass,	4145
Eph	3:17 faith; that ye, being rooted and **g** in love,	2311
Col	1:23 If ye continue in the faith **g** and settled,	2311

GROVE (17) [GROVES]

Ge	21:33 And *Abraham* planted a **g** in Beer-sheba,	815
Dt	16:21 Thou shalt not plant thee a **g** *of* any trees	842
Jdg	6:25 hath, and cut down the **g** that *is* by it:	842
	6:26 a burnt sacrifice with the wood of the **g**	842
	6:28 the **g** was cut down that *was* by it,	842
	6:30 he hath cut down the **g** that *was* by it.	842
1Ki	15:13 because she had made an idol in a **g**;	842
	16:33 Ahab made a **g**; and Ahab did more to	842
2Ki	13: 6 there remained the **g** also in Samaria.)	842
	17:16 made a **g**, and worshipped all the host of	842
	21: 3 and made a **g**, as did Ahab king of Israel;	842
	21: 7 he set a graven image of the **g** that he had	842
	23: 4 for the **g**, and for all the host of heaven:	842
	23: 6 he brought out the **g** from the house of	842
	23: 7 the women wove hangings for the **g**.	842
	23:15 *it* small to powder, and burnt the **g**.	842
2Ch	15:16 because she had made an idol in a **g**:	842

GROVES (24) [GROVE]

Ex	34:13 break their images, and cut down their **g**:	842
Dt	7: 5 cut down their **g**, and burn their graven	842
	12: 3 their pillars, and burn their **g** with fire;	842
Jdg	3: 7 their God, and served Baalim and the **g**.	842
1Ki	14:15 because they have made their **g**,	842
	14:23 images, and **g**, on every high hill,	842
	18:19 and the prophets of the **g** four hundred,	842
2Ki	17:10 them up images and **g** in every high hill,	842
	18: 4 cut down the **g**, and brake in pieces	842
	23:14 cut down the **g**, and filled their places *with*	842
2Ch	14: 3 down the images, and cut down the **g**:	842
	17: 6 away the high places and **g** out of Judah.	842
	19: 3 in that thou hast taken away the **g** out of	842
	24:18 of their fathers, and served **g** and idols:	842
	31: 1 the images *in* pieces, and cut down the **g**,	842
	33: 3 made **g**, and worshipped all the host of	842
	33:19 set up and graven images, before he was	842
	34: 3 he, and the carved images, and the	842
	34: 4 the **g**, and the carved images, and the	842
	34: 7 he had broken down the altars and the **g**,	842
Isa	17: 8 have made, either the **g**, or the images.	842
	27: 9 the **g** and images shall not stand up.	842
Jer	17: 2 their **g** by the green trees upon the high	842
Mic	5:14 pluck up thy **g** out of the midst of thee,	842

GROW (38) [GREW, GROWETH, GROWN, GROWTH]

Ge	2: 9 **made** the LORD God **to g** every tree that	6779
	48:16 let them **g** into a multitude in the midst of	1711
Nu	6: 5 shall let the locks of the hair of his head **g**	1431
Jdg	16:22 Howbeit the hair of his head began to **g**	6779
2Sa	23: 5 *my* desire, although he **make** *it* not to **g**.	6779
2Ki	19:29 year **such things as g of** themselves,	5599
Ezr	4:22 why should damage **g** to the hurt of	7680
Job	8:11 Can the rush **g up** without mire?	1342
	8:11 can the flag **g** without water?	7685
	8:19 way, and out of the earth shall others **g**.	6779
	14:19 washest away the **things which g** out	5599
	31:40 Let thistles **g** instead of wheat,	3318
	39: 4 are in good liking, they **g up** with corn;	7235
Ps	92:12 he shall **g** like a cedar in Lebanon.	7685
	104:14 He **causeth** the grass **to g** for the cattle,	6779
	147: 8 who **maketh** grass **to g** *upon*	6779
Ecc	11: 5 how the bones *do* **g** in the womb of her	NIH
Isa	11: 1 and a Branch shall **g** out of his roots:	6509
	17:11 the day shalt thou **make** thy plant to **g**,	7735
	53: 2 For he shall **g up** before him as a tender	5927

Jer	12: 2 they **g**, yea, they bring forth fruit: thou *art*	1980
	33:15 cause the Branch of righteousness **to g up**	6779
Eze	44:20 heads, nor **suffer** *their* locks **to g** long;	7971
	47:12 and on that side, shall **g** all trees for meat,	5927
Hos	14: 5 he shall **g** as the lily, and cast forth his	6524
	14: 7 shall revive *as* the corn, and **g** as the vine:	6524
Jnh	4:10 hast not laboured, neither **madest** it **g**;	1431
Zec	6:12 he shall **g up** out of his place, and he shall	6779
Mal	4: 2 go forth, and **g up** as calves of the stall.	6335
Mt	6:28 Consider the lilies of the field, how they **g**;	837
	13:30 Let both **g together** until the harvest:	4885
	21:19 Let no fruit **g** on thee henceforward for	1096
Mk	4:27 day, and the seed should spring and **g up**,	3373
Lk	12:27 Consider the lilies how they **g**: they toil	837
Ac	5:24 doubted of them whereunto this would **g**.	1096
Eph	4:15 may **g** *up* into him *in* all *things*, which is	837
1Pe	2: 2 milk of the word, that ye may **g** thereby:	837
2Pe	3:18 But **g** in grace, and *in* the knowledge of	837

GROWETH (14) [GROW]

Ex	10: 5 shall eat every tree which **g** for you out of	6779
Lev	13:39 it *is* a freckled spot *that* **g** in the skin:	6524
	25: 5 **That which g** of it own accord of thy	5599
	25:11 neither reap **that which g** of itself in it,	5599
Dt	29:23 nor beareth, nor any grass **g** therein,	5927
Jdg	19: 9 behold, the day **g to an end**, lodge here,	2583
Job	38:38 When the dust **g** into hardness,	3332
Ps	90: 5 morning *they are* like grass *which* **g** up.	2498
	90: 6 In the morning it flourisheth, and **g up**;	2498
	129: 6 which withereth afore it **g up**:	8025
Isa	37:30 Ye shall eat *this* year **such as g** of itself;	5599
Mk	4:32 **g up**, and becometh greater than all herbs,	305
Eph	2:21 together **g** unto a holy temple in the Lord:	837
2Th	1: 3 because that your faith **g exceedingly**,	5232

GROWN (23) [GROW]

Ge	38:11 father's house, till Shelah my son be **g**:	1431
	38:14 she saw that Shelah was **g**, and she was	1431
Ex	2:11 to pass in those days, when Moses was **g**,	1431
	9:32 were not smitten: for they *were* **not g** up.	648
Lev	13:37 and *that* there is black hair **g** therein;	6779
Dt	32:15 thou art waxed fat, thou art **g thick**, thou	5666
Ru	1:13 Would ye tarry for them till they were **g**?	1431
2Sa	10: 5 Tarry at Jericho until your beards be **g**,	6779
1Ki	12: 8 the young men that were **g** up with him,	1431
	12:10 the young men that were **g** up with him	1431
2Ki	4:18 when the child was **g**, it fell on a day,	1431
	19:26 and *as* corn blasted before it be **g up**.	7054
1Ch	19: 5 Tarry at Jericho until your beards be **g**,	6779
Ezr	9: 6 and our trespass is **g** up unto the heavens.	1431
Ps	144:12 That our sons *may be* as plants **g** up in	1431
Pr	24:31 it was all **g over** *with* thorns,	5927
Isa	37:27 and *as* corn blasted before it be **g up**.	7054
Jer	50:11 because ye are **g fat** as the heifer at grass,	6335
Eze	16: 7 thine hair is **g**, whereas thou *wast* naked	6779
Da	4:22 O king, that art **g** and become strong;	7236
	4:22 for thy greatness is **g**, and reacheth unto	7236
	4:33 till his hairs were **g** like eagles' *feathers*,	7236
Mt	13:32 but when it is **g**, it is the greatest among	837

GROWTH (2) [GROW]

Am	7: 1 of the shooting up of the **latter g**;	3954
	7: 1 *it was* the **latter g** after the king's	3954

GRUDGE (3) [GRUDGING, GRUDGINGLY]

Lev	19:18 nor **bear any g against** the children of	5201
Ps	59:15 for meat, and **g** if they be not satisfied.	3885
Jas	5: 9 **G** not one against another, brethren, lest	4727

GRUDGING (1) [GRUDGE]

1Pe	4: 9 Use hospitality one to another without **g**.	1112

GRUDGINGLY (1) [GRUDGE]

2Co	9: 7 in *his* heart, *so let him give*; not **g**,	1537+3077

GRUMBLE; GRUMBLED; GRUMBLERS; GRUMBLING See MURMUR MURMURED; MURMURERS; MURMURING; MURMURINGS

GUARANTEE; GUARANTEED See SURETY

GUARD (50) [GUARD'S, SAFEGUARD]

Ge	37:36 officer of Pharaoh's, *and* captain of the **g**.	2876
	39: 1 of Pharaoh, captain of the **g**, an Egyptian,	2876
	40: 3 *in* the house of the captain of the **g**,	2876
	40: 4 the captain of the **g** charged Joseph with	2876
	41:12 a Hebrew, servant to the captain of the **g**;	2876
2Sa	23:23 *first* three. And David set him over his **g**.	4928
1Ki	14:27 *them* unto the hands of the chief of the **g**,	7323
	14:28 *that* the **g** bare them, and brought them	7323
	14:28 brought them back into the **g** chamber.	7323
2Ki	10:25 Jehu said to the **g** and to the captains,	7323
	10:25 the **g** and the captains cast *them* out,	7323
	11: 4 with the captains and the **g**,	7323
	11: 6 and a third *part* at the gate behind the **g**:	7323
	11:11 the **g** stood, every man with his weapons	7323
	11:13 when Athaliah heard the noise of the **g**	7323
	11:19 and the **g**, and all the people of the land;	7323
	11:19 came *by* the way of the gate of the **g to**	7323
	25: 8 came Nebuzar-adan, captain of the **g**,	2876
	25:10 that *were with* the captain of the **g**,	2876
	25:11 Nebuzar-adan the captain of the **g** carry	2876
	25:12 the captain of the **g** left of the poor of	2876
	25:15 *in* silver, the captain of the **g** took *away*.	2876
	25:18 captain of the **g** took Seraiah the chief	2876
	25:20 Nebuzar-adan captain of the **g** took these,	2876

1Ch	11:25 *first* three: and David set him over his **g**.	4928
2Ch	12:10 *them* to the hands of the chief of the **g**,	7323
	12:11 the **g** came and fet them, and brought	7323
	12:11 brought them again into the **g** chamber.	7323
Ne	4:22 that in the night they may be a **g** to us,	4929
	4:23 nor the men of the **g** which followed me,	4929
Jer	39: 9 Nebuzar-adan the captain of the **g** carried	2876
	39:10 Nebuzar-adan the captain of the **g** left of	2876
	39:11 to Nebuzar-adan the captain of the **g**,	2876
	39:13 Nebuzar-adan the captain of the **g** sent,	2876
	40: 1 that Nebuzar-adan the captain of the **g**	2876
	40: 2 the captain of the **g** took Jeremiah,	2876
	40: 5 So the captain of the **g** gave him victuals	2876
	41:10 whom Nebuzar-adan the captain of the **g**	2876
	43: 6 had left with Gedaliah the son of	2876
	52:12 came Nebuzar-adan, captain of the **g**,	2876
	52:14 that *were* with the captain of the **g**,	2876
	52:15 Nebuzar-adan the captain of the **g** carried	2876
	52:16 Nebuzar-adan the captain of the **g** left	2876
	52:19 *in* silver, took the captain of the **g** *away*.	2876
	52:24 the captain of the **g** took Seraiah the chief	2876
	52:26 So Nebuzar-adan the captain of the **g** took	2876
	52:30 **g** carried away captive *of* the Jews seven	2876
Eze	38: 7 unto thee, and be thou a **g** unto them.	4929
Da	2:14 to Arioch the captain of the king's **g**,	2877
Ac	28:16 the prisoners to the **captain of the g**:	4759

GUARD'S (1) [GUARD]

Ge	41:10 put me in ward *in* the captain of the **g**	2876

GUARDIANS See TUTORS

GUDGODAH (2)

Dt	10: 7 From thence they journeyed *unto* G;	1412
	10: 7 from G to Jotbath, a land of rivers of	1412

GUEST (1) [GUESTCHAMBER, GUESTS]

Lk	19: 7 That he was gone to be **g** with a man	2647

GUEST ROOM See GUESTCHAMBER

GUESTCHAMBER (2) [CHAMBER, GUEST]

Mk	14:14 house, The Master saith, Where is the **g**,	2646
Lk	22:11 Master saith unto thee, Where is the **g**,	2646

GUESTS (6) [GUEST]

1Ki	1:41 all the **g** that *were* with him heard *it* as	7121
	1:49 all the **g** that *were* with Adonijah were	7121
	9:18 *and that* her **g** *are* in the depths of hell.	7121
Zep	1: 7 prepared a sacrifice, he hath bid his **g**.	7121
Mt	22:10 and the wedding was furnished with **g**.	345
	22:11 And when the king came in to see the **g**,	345

GUIDE (23) [GUIDED, GUIDES, GUIDING]

Job	38:32 or canst thou **g** Arcturus with his sons?	5148
Ps	25: 9 The meek will he **g** in judgment:	1869
	31: 3 for thy name's sake lead me, and **g** me.	5095
	32: 8 thou shalt go: I will **g** thee with mine eye.	3289
	48:14 ever: he will be our **g** *even* unto death.	5090
	55:13 equal, my **g**, and mine acquaintance.	441
	73:24 Thou shalt **g** me with thy counsel,	5148
	112: 5 he will **g** his affairs with discretion.	3557
Pr	2:17 Which forsaketh the **g** of her youth,	441
	6: 7 Which having no **g**, overseer, or ruler,	7101
	11: 3 The integrity of the upright shall **g** them:	5148
	23:19 be wise, and **g** thine heart in the way.	833
Isa	49:10 even by the springs of water shall he **g**	5095
	51:18 *There is* none to **g** her among all the sons	5095
	58:11 the LORD shall **g** thee continually,	5148
Jer	3: 4 My father, thou *art* the **g** of my youth?	441
Mic	7: 5 in a friend, put ye not confidence in a **g**:	441
Lk	1:79 to **g** our feet into the way of peace.	2720
Jn	16:13 is come, he will **g** you into all truth:	3594
Ac	1:16 which was **g** to them that took Jesus.	3595
	8:31 can I, except some *man* should **g** me?	3594
Ro	2:19 art confident that thou thyself art a **g**	3595
1Ti	5:14 marry, bear children, **g the house**,	3616

GUIDED (5) [GUIDE]

Ex	15:13 thou hast **g** *them* in thy strength unto thy	5095
2Ch	32:22 of all *other*, and **g** them on every side.	5095
Job	31:18 I have **g** her from my mother's womb;)	5148
Ps	78:52 and **g** them in the wilderness like a flock.	5090
	78:72 **g** them by the skilfulness of his hands.	5148

GUIDES (2) [GUIDE]

Mt	23:16 Woe unto you, *ye* blind **g**, which say,	3595
	23:24 Ye blind **g**, which strain out a gnat,	3595

GUIDING (1) [GUIDE]

Ge	48:14 Manasseh's head, **g** his hands **wittingly**;	7919

GUILE (11)

Ex	21:14 upon his neighbour, to slay him with **g**;	6195
Ps	32: 2 and in whose spirit *there is* no **g**.	7423
	34:13 from evil, and thy lips from speaking **g**.	4820
	55:11 and **g** depart not from her streets.	4820
Jn	1:47 an Israelite indeed, in whom is no **g**.	1388
2Co	12:16 being crafty, I caught you with **g**.	1388
1Th	2: 3 of deceit, nor of uncleanness, nor in **g**:	1388
1Pe	2: 1 and all **g**, and hypocrisies, and envies,	1388
	2:22 no sin, neither was found in his mouth:	1388
	3:10 evil, and his lips that *they* speak no **g**:	1388
Rev	14: 5 And in their mouth was found no **g**:	1388

G

GUILT (2) [BLOODGUILTINESS, GUILTINESS, GUILTLESS, GUILTY]
Dt 19:13 shalt put away *the* **g** *of* innocent blood NIH
 21: 9 So shalt thou put away *the* **g** *of* innocent NIH

GUILTINESS (1) [GUILT]
Ge 26:10 thou shouldest have brought **g** upon us. 817

GUILTLESS (10) [GUILT]
Ex 20: 7 for the Lord will not **hold** him **g** that 5352
Nu 5:31 shall the man be **g** from iniquity, and this 5352
 32:22 be **g** before the Lord, and before Israel; 5355
Dt 5:11 for the Lord will not **hold** *him* **g** that 5352
Jos 2:19 *shall* be upon his head, and we *will be* **g**: 5355
1Sa 26: 9 against the Lord's anointed, and be **g**? 5355
2Sa 3:28 my kingdom *are* **g** before the Lord for 5355
 14: 9 and the king and his throne *be* **g**. 5355
1Ki 2: 9 Now therefore **hold** him not **g**: for thou 5352
Mt 12: 7 ye would not have condemned the **g**. 338

GUILTY (26) [GUILT]
Ge 42:21 We *are* verily **g** concerning our brother, 818
Ex 34: 7 *that* will by no means clear *the* **g**, visiting NIH
Lev 4:13 which should not be done, and are **g**; 816
 4:22 which should not be done, and is **g**; 816
 4:27 which ought not to be done, and be **g**; 816
 5: 2 from him; he also shall be unclean, and **g**. 816
 5: 3 when he knoweth *of it*, then he shall be **g**. 816
 5: 4 *of it*, then he shall be **g** in one of these. 816
 5: 5 when he shall be **g** in one of these *things*, 816
 5:17 not, yet is he **g**, and shall bear his iniquity. 816
 6: 4 shall be, because he hath sinned, and is **g**, 816
Nu 5: 6 against the Lord, and that person be **g**, 816
 14:18 by no means clearing *the* **g**, visiting NIH
 35:27 the slayer; he shall not be **g** of blood: 3807.1
 35:31 life of a murderer, which *is* **g** of death: 7563
Jdg 21:22 them at *this* time, *that* you should be **g**. 816
Ezr 10:19 being **g**, they *offered* a ram of the flock for 818
Pr 30:10 lest he curse thee, and thou be **found g**. 816
Eze 22: 4 Thou art become **g** in thy blood that thou 816
Zec 11: 5 slay them, and **hold** themselves not **g**: 816
Mt 23:18 by the gift that is upon it, he is **g**. 3784
 26:66 They answered and said, He is **g** of death. 1777
Mk 14:64 And they all condemned him to be **g** of 1777
Ro 3:19 all the world may become **g before** God. 5267
1Co 11:27 shall be **g** of the body and blood of 1777
Jas 2:10 and *yet* offend in one *point*, he is **g** of all. 1777

GULF (1)
Lk 16:26 between us and you there is a great **g** 5490

GULL See CUCKOW

GUM RESIN See STACTE

GUNI (4) [GUNITES]
Ge 46:24 Jahzeel, and **G**, and Jezer, and Shillem. 1476
Nu 26:48 of **G**, the family of the Gunites: 1476
1Ch 5:15 Ahi the son of Abdiel, the son of **G**, 1476
 7:13 Jahziel, and **G**, and Jezer, and Shallum, 1476

GUNITES (1) [GUNI]
Nu 26:48 of Guni, the family of the **G**: 1477

GUR (1)
2Ki 9:27 *And they did so* at the going up to **G**, 1483

GUR-BAAL (1) [BAAL]
2Ch 26: 7 against the Arabians that dwelt in **G**, 1485

GUSH (1) [GUSHED]
Jer 9:18 and our eyelids **g out** with waters. 5140

GUSHED (5) [GUSH]
1Ki 18:28 lancets, till the blood **g out** upon them. 8210
Ps 78:20 that the waters **g out**, and the streams 2100
 105:41 opened the rock, and the waters **g out**; 2100
Isa 48:21 clave the rock also, and the waters **g out**. 2100
Ac 1:18 in the midst, and all his bowels **g out**. 1632

GUTTER (1) [GUTTERS]
2Sa 5: 8 Whosoever getteth up to the **g**, 6794

GUTTERS (2) [GUTTER]
Ge 30:38 **g** in the watering troughs when the flocks 7298
 30:41 rods before the eyes of the cattle in the **g**, 7298

H

HA (2) [AHA]
Job 39:25 He saith among the trumpets, **H, ha**; 1889
 39:25 He saith among the trumpets, **Ha, h**; 1889

HAAHASHTARI (1)
1Ch 4: 6 and Hepher, and Temeni, and **H**. 326

HABAIAH (2)
Ezr 2:61 the children of **H**, the children of Koz, 2252
Ne 7:63 the children of **H**, the children of Koz, 2252

HABAKKUK (2)
Hab 1: 1 The burden which **H** the prophet did see. 2265
 3: 1 prayer of **H** the prophet upon Shigionoth. 2265

HABAZINIAH (1)
Jer 35: 3 the son of **H**, and his brethren, and all his 2262

HABAZZINIAH See HABAZINIAH

HABERGEON (3) [HABERGEONS]
Ex 28:32 as it were the hole of an **h**, *that* it be not 8473
 39:23 as the hole of an **h**, *with* a band round 8473
Job 41:26 cannot hold: the spear, the dart, nor the **h**. 8302

HABERGEONS (2) [HABERGEON]
2Ch 26:14 **h**, and bows, and slings to cast stones. 8302
Ne 4:16 the shields, and the bows, and the **h**; 8302

HABIT See WONT

HABITABLE (1) [INHABIT]
Pr 8:31 Rejoicing in the **h** part of his earth; 8398

HABITATION (58) [INHABIT]
Ex 15: 2 *is* my God, and I will **prepare** him a **h**; 5115
 15:13 *them* in thy strength unto thy holy **h**. 5116
Lev 13:46 without the camp *shall* his **h** be. 4186
Dt 12: 5 *even* unto his **h** shall ye seek, 7931
 26:15 Look down from thy holy **h**, from heaven, 4583
1Sa 2:29 which I have commanded *in my* **h**; 5116
 2:32 thou shalt see an enemy *in my* **h**, in all 4583
2Sa 15:25 me again, and shew me *both* it, and his **h**: 5116
2Ch 6: 2 I have built a house of **h** for thee, 2073
 29: 6 turned away their faces from the **h** of 4908
Ezr 7:15 the God of Israel, whose **h** *is* in Jerusalem, 4907
Job 5: 3 taking root: but suddenly I cursed his **h**. 5116
 5:24 thou shalt visit thy **h**, and shalt not sin. 5116
 8: 6 make the **h** of thy righteousness 5116
 18:15 brimstone shall be scattered upon his **h**. 5116
Ps 26: 8 I have loved the **h** of thy house, 4583
 33:14 From the place of his **h** he looketh upon 3427
 68: 5 judge of the widows, *is* God in his holy **h**. 4583
 69:25 Let their **h** be desolate; *and* let none dwell 2918
 71: 3 Be thou my strong **h**, whereunto *I* may 4583
 89:14 and judgment *are* the **h** of thy throne: 4349
 91: 9 *is* my refuge, *even* the most High, thy **h**; 4583
 97: 2 and judgment *are* the **h** of his throne. 4349
 104:12 shall the fowls of the heaven have their **h**, 7931
 107: 7 way, that *they* might go to a city of **h**. 4186
 107:36 dwell, that they may prepare a city for **h**; 4186
 132: 5 a **h** for the mighty *God* of Jacob. 4908
 132:13 chosen Zion; he hath desired *it* for his **h**. 4186
Pr 3:33 but he blesseth the **h** of the just. 5116
Isa 22:16 *and* that graveth a **h** for himself in a rock? 4908
 27:10 and the **h** forsaken, and left like a 5116
 32:18 my people shall dwell in a peaceable **h**, 5116
 33:20 thine eyes shall see Jerusalem a quiet **h**, 5116
 34:13 it shall be a **h** of dragons, *and* a court for 5116
 35: 7 in the **h** of dragons, where each lay, 5116
 63:15 behold from the **h** of thy holiness and 2073
Jer 9: 6 Thine **h** *is* in the midst of deceit; 3427
 10:25 and have made his **h** desolate. 5116
 25:30 and utter his voice from his holy **h**; 4583
 25:30 he shall mightily roar upon his **h**; he shall 5116
 31:23 O **h** of justice, *and* mountain of holiness 5116
 33:12 shall be a **h** of shepherds causing *their* 5116
 41:17 and dwelt in the **h** of Chimham, 1628
 49:19 of Jordan against the **h** of the strong; 5116
 50: 7 the **h** of justice, even the Lord, the hope 5116
 50:19 I will bring Israel again to his **h**, 5116
 50:44 of Jordan unto the **h** of the strong: 5116
 50:45 surely he shall make *their* **h** desolate with 5116
Eze 29:14 land of Pathros, into the land of their **h**; 4351
Da 4:21 the fowls of the heaven had their **h**: 7932
Ob 1: 3 in the clefts of the rock, whose **h** *is* high; 7675
Hab 3:11 The sun *and* moon stood still in *their* **h**: 2073
Zec 2:13 for he is raised up out of his holy **h**. 4583
Ac 1:20 Let his **h** be desolate, and let no man dwell 1886
 17:26 appointed, and the bounds of their **h**; 2733
Eph 2:22 together for a **h** of God through the Spirit. 2732
Jude 1: 6 not their first estate, but left their own **h**, 3613
Rev 18: 2 is fallen, and is become the **h** of devils, 2732

HABITATIONS (20) [INHABIT]
Ge 36:43 according to their **h** in the land of their 4186
 49: 5 instruments of cruelty *are in* their **h**. 4380
Ex 12:20 all your **h** shall ye eat unleavened bread. 4186
 35: 3 Ye shall kindle no fire throughout your **h** 4186
Lev 23:17 Ye shall bring out of your **h** two wave 4186
Nu 15: 2 When ye be come into the land of your **h**, 4186
1Ch 4:33 These *were* their **h**, and their genealogy. 4186
 4:41 the **h** that were found there, 4583
 7:28 **h** *were*, Beth-el and the towns thereof, 4186
Ps 74:20 of the earth are full of the **h** of cruelty. 4999
 78:28 midst of their camp, round about their **h**. 4908
Isa 54: 2 them stretch forth the curtains of thine **h**: 4908
Jer 9:10 for the **h** of the wilderness a lamentation, 4999
 21:13 against us? or who shall enter into our **h**? 4585
 25:37 the peaceable **h** are cut down because of 4999
 49:20 surely he shall make their **h** desolate with 5116
La 2: 2 The Lord hath swallowed up all the **h** of 4999
Eze 6:14 wilderness toward Diblath, in all their **h**: 4186

HABAIAH (2)
Am 1: 2 the **h** of the shepherds shall mourn, 4999
Lk 16: 9 they may receive you into everlasting **h**. 4633

HABOR (3)
2Ki 17: 6 in Halah and in **H** *by* the river of Gozan, 2249
 18:11 in Halah and in **H** *by* the river of Gozan, 2249
1Ch 5:26 **H**, and Hara, and to the river Gozan, 2249

HACALIAH See HACHALIAH

HACHALIAH (2)
Ne 1: 1 The words of Nehemiah the son of **H**. 2446
 10: 1 the Tirshatha, the son of **H**, and Zidkijah, 2446

HACHILAH (3)
1Sa 23:19 in the hill of **H**, which *is* on the south of 2444
 26: 1 not David hide himself in the hill of **H**, 2444
 26: 3 Saul pitched in the hill of **H**, which *is* 2444

HACHMONI (1) [HACHMONITE]
1Ch 27:32 Jehiel the son of **H** *was* with the king's 2453

HACHMONITE (1) [HACHMONI]
1Ch 11:11 a **H**, the chief of the captains: 1121+2453

HACMONI See HACHMONI

HACMONITE See HACHMONITE

HAD (2030) [HAVE]
Ge 1:31 God saw every thing that he **h** made, NIH
 2: 2 God ended his work which he **h** made; NIH
 2: 2 day from all his work which he **h** made. NIH
 2: 3 that in it he **h** rested from all his work NIH
 2: 5 for the Lord God **h** not caused it to rain NIH
 2: 8 there he put the man whom he **h** formed. NIH
 2:22 which the Lord God **h** taken from man, NIH
 3: 1 of the field which the Lord God **h** made. NIH
 4: 4 the Lord **h** respect unto Abel and to his NIH
 4: 5 and to his offering he **h** not respect. NIH
 5: 4 the days of Adam after he **h** begotten Seth NIH
 6: 6 it repented the Lord that he **h** made man NIH
 6:12 for all flesh **h** corrupted his way upon NIH
 7: 9 the female, as God **h** commanded Noah. NIH
 7:16 of all flesh, as God **h** commanded him: NIH
 8: 6 the window of the ark which he **h** made NIH
 9:24 knew what his younger son **h** done unto NIH
 11: 3 they **h** brick for stone, and slime 1961+3807.1
 11: 3 and slime **h** they for morter. 1961+3807.1
 11:30 But Sarai was barren; she **h** no child. 3807.1
 12: 1 Now the Lord **h** said unto Abram, NIH
 12: 4 as the Lord **h** spoken unto him; NIH
 12: 5 all their substance that they **h** gathered, NIH
 12: 5 and the souls that they **h** gotten in Haran; NIH
 12:16 **h** sheep, and oxen, and he asses, 1961+3807.1
 12:20 away, and his wife, and all that he **h**. 3807.1
 13: 1 and all that he **h**, and Lot with him, 3807.1
 13: 3 unto the place where his tent **h** been at NIH
 13: 4 altar, which he **h** made there at the first: NIH
 13: 5 flocks, and herds, and tents. 1961+3807.1
 14:13 there came one that **h** escaped, NIH
 16: 1 him no *children:* and she **h** a handmaid, NIH
 16: 3 Abram **h** dwelt ten years in the land 3807.1
 16: 4 when she saw that she **h** conceived, NIH
 16: 5 when she saw that she **h** conceived, I was NIH
 17:23 the selfsame day, as God **h** said unto him. NIH
 18: 8 the calf which he **h** dressed, and set *it* NIH
 18:33 as soon as he **h** left communing with NIH
 19:17 when they **h** brought them forth abroad, NIH
 20: 4 Abimelech **h** not come near her: NIH
 20:18 For the Lord **h** fast closed up all NIH
 21: 1 the Lord visited Sarah as he **h** said, NIH
 21: 1 the Lord did unto Sarah as he **h** spoken. NIH
 21: 2 at the set time of which God **h** spoken to NIH
 21: 4 eight days old, as God **h** commanded him. NIH
 21: 9 she **h** born unto Abraham, mocking. NIH
 21:25 which Abimelech's servants **h** violently NIH
 22: 3 went unto the place of which God **h** told NIH
 22: 9 they came to the place which God **h** told NIH
 23:16 which he **h** named in the audience of NIH
 24: 1 the Lord **h** blessed Abraham in all NIH
 24: 2 his house that ruled over all that he **h**, 3807.1
 24:15 before he **h** done speaking, that behold, NIH
 24:16 a virgin, neither **h** any man known her: NIH
 24:19 she **h** done giving him drink, she said, NIH
 24:21 to wit whether the Lord **h** made his NIH
 24:22 to pass, as the camels **h** done drinking, NIH
 24:29 Rebekah **h** a brother, and his name *was* 3807.1
 24:45 before I **h** done speaking in mine heart, NIH
 24:48 which **h** led me in the right way to take NIH
 24:65 For she **h** said unto the servant, What man NIH
 24:65 servant **h** said, It *is* my master: therefore NIH
 24:66 the servant told Isaac all things that he **h** NIH
 25: 5 Abraham gave all that he **h** unto Isaac. 3807.1
 25: 6 which Abraham **h**, Abraham gave gifts, 3807.1
 26: 8 pass, when he **h** been there a long time, NIH
 26:14 For he **h** possession of flocks, 1961+3807.1
 26:15 **h** digged in the days of Abraham his father, NIH
 26:15 the Philistims **h** stopped them, NIH
 26:18 which they **h** digged in the days of NIH
 26:18 for the Philistims **h** stopped them after NIH
 26:18 names by which his father **h** called them. NIH
 26:32 told him concerning the well which they **h** NIH
 27:17 and the bread, which she **h** prepared, NIH
 27:30 as soon as Isaac **h** made an end of blessing NIH
 27:31 he also **h** made savoury meat, and brought NIH

Ge 28: 6 When Esau saw that Isaac **h** blessed Jacob,	NIH
28: 9 unto the wives which he **h** Mahalath	3807.1
28:18 the stone that he **h** put *for* his pillows,	NIH
29:16 Laban **h** two daughters: the name of	3807.1
29:20 *but* a few days, for the love he **h** to her.	NIH
30: 9 When Leah saw that she **h** left bearing,	NIH
30:25 came to pass, when Rachel **h** born Joseph,	NIH
30:35 *and* every one that **h** *some* white in it,	NIH
30:38 he set the rods which he **h** pilled before	NIH
30:43 **h** much cattle, and maidservants,	1961+3807.1
31:18 all his goods which he **h** gotten, the cattle	NIH
31:18 which he **h** gotten in Padan-aram,	NIH
31:19 Rachel **h** stolen the images that *were* her	NIH
31:21 he fled with all that he **h**; and he rose	3807.1
31:25 Jacob **h** pitched his tent in the mount:	NIH
31:32 For Jacob knew not that Rachel **h** stolen	NIH
31:34 Now Rachel **h** taken the images,	NIH
31:42 and the fear of Isaac, **h** been with me,	NIH
32:23 over the brook, and sent over that he **h**.	3807.1
33:10 as though I **h** seen the face of God,	NIH
33:19 of a field, where he **h** spread his tent,	NIH
34: 5 Jacob heard that he **h** defiled Dinah his	NIH
34: 7 he **h** wrought folly in Israel in lying with	NIH
34:13 because he **h** defiled Dinah their sister:	NIH
34:19 because he **h** delight in Jacob's daughter:	NIH
34:27 the city, because they **h** defiled their sister.	NIH
35:16 Rachel travailed, and she **h** hard labour.	NIH
36: 6 which he **h** got in the land of Canaan.	NIH
38:15 a harlot; because she **h** covered her face.	NIH
38:30 that he **h** the scarlet thread upon his hand:	NIH
39: 1 which **h** brought him down thither.	NIH
39: 4 all *that* he **h** he put into his hand.	3426+3807.1
39: 5 came to pass from the time *that* he **h** made	3807.1
39: 5 over all that he **h**, that the Lord	3426+3807.1
39: 5 was upon all that he **h** in the house	3426+3807.1
39: 6 he left all that he **h** in Joseph's hand;	3807.1
39: 6 he knew not ought he **h**, save the bread	854
39:13 when she saw that he **h** left his garment in	NIH
40: 1 *his* baker **h** offended their lord the king of	NIH
40:16 I **h** three white baskets on my head:	NIH
40:22 baker: as Joseph **h** interpreted to them.	NIH
41:21 when they **h** eaten them up, it could not	NIH
41:21 it could not be known that they **h** eaten	NIH
41:43 ride in the second chariot which he **h**;	3807.1
41:54 began to come, according as Joseph **h** said:	NIH
43: 2 when they **h** eaten up the corn which	NIH
43: 2 corn which they **h** brought out of Egypt,	NIH
43: 6 *as* to tell the man whether ye **h** yet a	3807.1
43:10 For except we **h** lingered, surely now we	NIH
43:10 now we **h** returned this second time.	NIH
43:23 I **h** your money. And he brought	413+935
44: 2 did according to the word that Joseph **h**	NIH
45:27 of Joseph, which he **h** said unto them:	NIH
45:27 when he saw the wagons which Joseph **h**	NIH
46: 1 his journey with all that he **h**,	2050.2+3807.1
46: 5 in the wagons which Pharaoh **h** sent to	NIH
46: 6 which they **h** gotten in the land of Canaan,	NIH
47:11 of Rameses, as Pharaoh **h** commanded.	NIH
47:18 is spent; my lord also **h** our herds of cattle;	413
47:22 for the priests **h** a portion assigned them of	NIH
47:27 and they **h** possession therein, and grew,	270
48:11 Joseph, I **h** not thought to see thy face:	NIH
49:33 Jacob **h** made an end of commanding	NIH
50:14 his father, after he **h** buried his father.	NIH
Ex 2: 6 when she **h** opened *it*, she saw the child:	NIH
2: 6 she **h** compassion on him, and said,	2550
2:16 Now the priest of Midian **h** seven	3807.1
2:25 of Israel, and God **h** respect unto *them*.	3045
4:28 the words of the Lord who **h** sent him,	NIH
4:28 all the signs which he **h** commanded him.	NIH
4:30 which the Lord **h** spoken unto Moses,	NIH
4:31 when they heard that the Lord **h** visited	NIH
4:31 that he **h** looked upon their affliction,	NIH
5:14 which Pharaoh's taskmasters **h** set over	NIH
7:10 they did so as the Lord **h** commanded:	NIH
7:13 not unto them; as the Lord **h** said.	NIH
7:22 hearken unto them; as the Lord **h** said.	NIH
7:25 after *that* the Lord **h** smitten the river.	NIH
8:12 of the frogs which he **h** brought against	NIH
8:15 not unto them; as the Lord **h** said.	NIH
8:19 not unto them; as the Lord **h** said.	NIH
9:12 as the Lord **h** spoken unto Moses.	NIH
9:35 as the Lord **h** spoken by Moses.	NIH
10:15 the fruit of the trees which the hail **h** left:	NIH
10:23 all the children of Israel **h** light in	1961+3807.1
12:28 did as the Lord **h** commanded Moses and	NIH
12:39 neither **h** they prepared for themselves	NIH
13:17 pass, when Pharaoh **h** let the people go,	NIH
13:19 he **h** straitly sworn the children of Israel,	NIH
14:12 For *it* **h** been better for us to serve	NIH
15:25 *which* when he **h** cast into the waters,	NIH
16: 3 Would to God we **h** died by the hand of	NIH
16:18 he that gathered much **h** nothing over,	5736
16:18 and he that gathered little **h** no *lack*;	2637
17:10 So Joshua did as Moses **h** said to him,	NIH
18: 1 heard of all that God **h** done for Moses,	NIH
18: 1 that the Lord **h** brought Israel out of	NIH
18: 2 Moses' wife, after he **h** sent her *back*,	NIH
18: 8 all that the Lord **h** done unto Pharaoh	NIH
18: 8 all the travail that **h** come upon them by	NIH
18: 9 which the Lord **h** done to Israel,	NIH
18: 9 whom he **h** delivered out of the hand of	NIH
18:24 his father in law, and did all that he **h** said.	NIH
19: 2 of Sinai, and **h** pitched in the wilderness;	NIH
31:18 when he **h** made an end of communing	NIH

Ex 32: 4 after he **h** made it a molten calf:	NIH
32:20 he took the calf which they **h** made,	NIH
32:25 (for Aaron **h** made them naked unto *their*	NIH
32:29 For Moses **h** said, Consecrate yourselves to	NIH
33: 5 For the Lord **h** said unto Moses,	NIH
34: 4 as the Lord **h** commanded him,	NIH
34:32 Lord **h** spoken with him in mount Sinai.	NIH
34:33 till Moses **h** done speaking with them,	NIH
35:25 brought that which they **h** spun, *both* of	NIH
35:29 which the Lord **h** commanded to be	NIH
36: 1 according to all that the Lord **h**	NIH
36: 2 in whose heart the Lord **h** put wisdom,	NIH
36: 3 which the children of Israel **h** brought for	NIH
36: 7 For the stuff *they* **h** was sufficient for all	NIH
36:22 One board **h** two tenons, equally distant	3807.1
39:43 they **h** done it as the Lord had	NIH
39:43 they had done it as the Lord **h**	NIH
39:43 had commanded, *even* so **h** they done it:	NIH
40:23 as the Lord **h** commanded Moses.	NIH
Lev 5:10 for him for his sin which he **h** sinned,	NIH
10: 5 coats out of the camp; as Moses **h** said.	NIH
10:19 *if* I **h** eaten the sin offering to day, should it	NIH
21: 3 which hath **h** no husband;	1961+3807.1
24:23 that they should bring forth him that **h**	NIH
Nu 1:48 For the Lord **h** spoken unto Moses,	NIH
3: 4 of Sinai, and they **h** no children:	1961+3807.1
7: 1 came to pass on the day that Moses **h**	3807.1
7: 1 **h** anointed it, and sanctified it, and all	NIH
7: 1 and **h** anointed them, and sanctified them;	NIH
8: 4 pattern which the Lord **h** shewed Moses,	NIH
8:22 as the Lord **h** commanded Moses	NIH
12: 1 of the Ethiopian woman whom he **h**	NIH
12: 1 for he **h** married an Ethiopian woman.	NIH
12:14 If her father **h** but spit in her face,	NIH
13:32 they **h** searched unto the children of Israel,	NIH
14: 2 Would God that we **h** died in Egypt!	NIH
14: 2 would God we **h** died in this wilderness!	NIH
14:24 because he **h** another spirit with him,	1961
16:31 as he **h** made an end of speaking all these	NIH
16:39 wherewith they that were burnt **h** offered;	NIH
20: 3 Would God that we **h** died when our	NIH
21: 9 to pass, that if a serpent **h** bitten *any* man,	NIH
21:26 who **h** fought against the former king of	NIH
22: 2 the son of Zippor saw all that Israel **h**	NIH
22:33 unless she **h** turned from me, surely now	NIH
22:33 surely now also I **h** slain thee, and saved	NIH
23: 2 Balak did as Balaam **h** spoken; and Balak	NIH
23:30 Balak did as Balaam **h** said, and offered a	NIH
26:33 Zelophehad the son of Hepher **h**	1961+3807.1
26:65 For the Lord **h** said of them, They shall	NIH
27: 3 in his own sin, and **h** no sons.	1961+3807.1
30: 6 if she **h** at all a husband,	1961+1961+3807.1
31:32 the prey which the men of war **h** caught,	NIH
31:35 of women that **h** not known man by lying	NIH
31:53 (For the men of war **h** taken spoil,	NIH
32: 1 children of Gad **h** a very great	1961+3807.1
32: 9 the land which the Lord **h** given them.	NIH
32:13 that **h** done evil in the sight of the Lord,	NIH
33: 4 which the Lord **h** smitten among them:	NIH
Dt 1: 3 according unto all that the Lord **h** given	NIH
1: 4 After he **h** slain Sihon the king of	NIH
1:39 *in that* day **h** no **knowledge** between	3045
1:41 when ye **h** girded on every man his	NIH
2:12 when they **h** destroyed them from before	NIH
7: 8 he would keep the oath which he **h** sworn	NIH
9:16 ye **h** sinned against the Lord your God,	NIH
9:16 your God, *and* **h** made you a molten calf:	NIH
9:16 ye **h** turned aside quickly out of the way	NIH
9:16 way which the Lord **h** commanded you.	NIH
9:21 the calf which ye **h** made, and burnt it	NIH
9:25 the Lord **h** said he would destroy you.	NIH
10: 5 put the tables in the ark which I **h** made;	NIH
10:15 Only the Lord **h** a **delight** in thy fathers	2836
19:19 as he **h** thought to have done unto his	NIH
29:26 and *whom* he **h** not given unto them:	NIH
31:24 when Moses **h** made an end of writing	NIH
32:30 except their Rock **h** sold them,	NIH
32:30 sold them, and the Lord **h** shut them up?	NIH
34: 9 for Moses **h** laid his hands upon him:	NIH
Jos 2: 6 she **h** brought them up to the roof of	NIH
2: 6 which she **h** laid in order upon the roof.	NIH
2:11 as soon as we **h** heard *these things,* our	NIH
4: 4 whom he **h** prepared of the children of	NIH
5: 1 heard that the Lord **h** dried up the waters	NIH
5: 5 out of Egypt, *them* they **h** not circumcised.	NIH
5: 7 they **h** not circumcised them by the way.	NIH
5: 8 when they **h** done circumcising all	NIH
5:12 they **h** eaten of the old corn of the land;	NIH
5:12 neither **h** the children of Israel manna any	1961
6: 8 when Joshua **h** spoken unto the people,	NIH
6:10 Joshua **h** commanded the people, saying,	NIH
6:22 Joshua **h** said unto the two men that had	NIH
6:22 Joshua had said unto the two men that **h**	NIH
6:23 and her brethren, and all that she **h**;	3807.1
6:25 father's household, and all that she **h**;	3807.1
7: 7 would to God we **h** been content,	NIH
7:24 sheep, and his tent, and all that he **h**:	3807.1
7:25 after they **h** stoned them with stones.	NIH
8:13 when they **h** set the people, *even* all the	NIH
8:18 Joshua stretched out the spear that *he* **h** in	NIH
8:19 they ran as soon as *he* **h** stretched out his	NIH
8:20 they **h** no power to flee this way or	1961
8:21 all Israel saw that the ambush **h** taken	NIH
8:24 when Israel **h** made an end of slaying all	NIH
8:26 until *he* **h** utterly destroyed all	NIH

Jos 8:33 as Moses the servant of the Lord **h**	NIH
9: 3 heard what Joshua **h** done unto Jericho	NIH
9: 4 and made as if they **h** been ambassadors,	NIH
9:16 after they **h** made a league with them,	NIH
9:18 the princes of the congregation **h** sworn	NIH
9:21 as the princes **h** promised them.	NIH
10: 1 when Adoni-zedek king of Jerusalem **h**	NIH
10: 1 had heard how Joshua **h** taken Ai,	NIH
10: 1 had taken Ai, and utterly destroyed it;	NIH
10: 1 as he **h** done to Jericho and her king,	NIH
10: 1 her king, so he **h** done to Ai and her king;	NIH
10: 1 how the inhabitants of Gibeon **h** made	NIH
10:13 until the people **h** avenged themselves	NIH
10:20 the children of Israel **h** made an end of	NIH
10:27 them into the cave wherein they **h** hidden	NIH
10:32 according to all that he **h** done to Libnah.	NIH
10:33 until he **h** left him none remaining.	NIH
10:35 according to all that he **h** done to Lachish.	NIH
10:37 according to all that he **h** done to Eglon;	NIH
10:39 as he **h** done to Hebron, so he did to Debir,	NIH
10:39 he **h** done also to Libnah, and to her king.	NIH
11: 1 when Jabin king of Hazor **h** heard *those*	NIH
11:14 until they **h** destroyed them, neither left	NIH
14: 3 For Moses **h** given the inheritance of two	NIH
14:15 And the land **h** rest from war.	8252
17: 1 therefore he **h** Gilead and Bashan.	1961+3807.1
17: 3 **h** no sons, but daughters:	NIH
17: 6 Because the daughters of Manasseh **h** an	5157
17: 6 the rest of Manasseh's sons **h**	1961+3807.1
17: 8 *Now* Manasseh **h** the land of	1961+3807.1
17:11 Manasseh **h** in Issachar and	1961+3807.1
18: 2 which **h** not *yet* received their inheritance.	NIH
19: 2 they **h** in their inheritance	1961+3807.1
19: 9 the children of Simeon **h** their inheritance	NIH
19:49 When they **h** made an end of dividing	NIH
21: 4 **h** by lot out of the tribe of Judah,	1961+3807.1
21: 5 the rest of the children of Kohath **h** by lot	NIH
21: 6 the children of Gershon **h** by lot out of	NIH
21: 7 The children of Merari by their families **h**	NIH
21:10 *were* of the children of Levi, **h**.	1961+3807.1
21:20 even they **h** the cities of their lot out of	1961
21:45 Lord **h** spoken unto the house of Israel;	NIH
22: 7 Moses **h** given possession in Bashan:	NIH
23: 1 **h** given rest unto Israel from all their	NIH
24:31 which **h** known all the works of	NIH
24:31 of the Lord, that he **h** done for Israel.	NIH
Jdg 1: 8 the children of Judah **h** fought against	NIH
1: 8 **h** taken it, and smitten it with the edge of	NIH
1:19 because they **h** chariots of iron.	3807.1
2: 6 when Joshua **h** let the people go,	NIH
2: 7 who **h** seen all the great works of	NIH
2:10 nor yet the works which he **h** done for	NIH
2:15 as the Lord **h** said, and as the Lord	NIH
2:15 and as the Lord **h** sworn unto them:	NIH
3: 1 *even* as many of *Israel* as **h** not known all	NIH
3:11 the land **h** rest forty years. And Othniel	8252
3:12 they **h** done evil in the sight of the Lord.	NIH
3:16 Ehud made him a dagger which **h** two	3807.1
3:18 he **h** made an end to offer the present,	NIH
3:20 which he **h** for himself alone.	NIH
3:30 And the land **h** rest fourscore years.	NIH
4: 3 for he **h** nine hundred chariots of iron;	3807.1
4:11 **h** severed himself from the Kenites,	NIH
4:18 he **h** turned in unto her into the tent,	NIH
4:24 they **h** destroyed Jabin king of Canaan.	NIH
5:26 when she **h** pierced and stricken through	NIH
5:31 And the land **h** rest forty years.	8252
6: 3 *so* it was, when Israel **h** sown, that	NIH
6:27 and did as the Lord **h** said unto him:	NIH
7:19 and *they* **h** but newly set the watch:	NIH
8: 3 abated toward him, when he **h** said that.	NIH
8: 8 as the men of Succoth **h** answered *him.*	NIH
8:19 if ye **h** saved them alive, I would not slay	NIH
8:24 [For they **h** golden earrings, because	3807.1
8:30 Gideon **h** threescore and ten sons	1961+3807.1
8:30 for he **h** many wives.	1961+3807.1
8:34 who **h** delivered them out of the hands of	NIH
8:35 according to all the goodness which he **h**	NIH
9:22 When Abimelech **h** reigned three years	NIH
10: 4 he **h** thirty sons that rode on	1961+3807.1
10: 4 they **h** thirty cities, which are called	3807.1
11:34 he **h** neither son nor daughter.	NIH
11:39 *according to* his vow which he **h** vowed:	1961+3807.1
12: 9 he **h** thirty sons,	NIH
12:14 **h** forty sons and thirty nephews,	1961+3807.1
14: 4 at that time the Philistines **h** dominion	4910
14: 6 rent a kid, and *he* **h** nothing in his hand:	NIH
14: 6 his father or his mother what he **h** done.	NIH
14: 9 told not them that he **h** taken the honey	NIH
14:18 If ye **h** not plowed with my heifer,	NIH
14:18 my heifer, ye **h** not found out my riddle.	NIH
14:20 whom he **h** used as his friend.	NIH
15: 5 he **h** set the brands on fire, he let *them*	NIH
15: 6 because he **h** taken his wife, and given her	NIH
15:17 when he **h** made an end of speaking,	NIH
15:19 when he **h** drunk, his spirit came again,	NIH
16: 8 seven green withs which **h** not been dried,	NIH
16:18 when Delilah saw that he **h** told her all his	NIH
17: 3 when he **h** restored the eleven hundred	NIH
17: 3 I **h** wholly dedicated the silver unto	NIH
17: 5 the man Micah **h** a house of gods,	3807.1
18: 1 **h** not fallen unto them among the tribes of	NIH
18: 7 and **h** no business with *any* man.	3807.1
18:27 they took *the things* which Micah **h** made,	NIH
18:27 the priest which he **h**,	1961+3807.1

Jdg 18:28 and they **h** no business with *any* man; 3807.1
19: 6 the damsel's father **h** said unto the man, NIH
19:17 when he **h** lift up his eyes, he saw a NIH
20:36 in wait which they **h** set beside Gibeah. NIH
21: 1 the men of Israel **h** sworn in Mizpeh, NIH
21: 5 For *they* **h** made a great oath concerning NIH
21:12 that **h** known no man by lying with *any* NIH
21:14 they gave them wives which they **h** saved NIH
21:15 that the LORD **h** made a breach in NIH

Ru 1: 6 she **h** heard in the country of Moab how NIH
1: 6 visited his people in giving them bread. NIH
2: 1 Naomi **h** a kinsman of her husband's, 3807.1
2:17 and beat out that she **h** gleaned: NIH
2:18 mother in law saw what she **h** gleaned: NIH
2:18 gave to her that she **h reserved** after she 3498
2:19 mother in law with whom she **h** wrought, NIH
3: 7 Boaz **h** eaten and drunk, and his heart NIH
3:18 told her all that the man **h** done to her. NIH

1Sa 1: 2 he **h** two wives; the name of the one 3807.1
1: 2 Peninnah **h** children, 1961+3807.1
1: 2 children, but Hannah **h** no children. 3807.1
1: 5 but the LORD **h** shut up her womb. NIH
1: 6 because the LORD **h** shut up her womb. NIH
1: 9 So Hannah rose up after *they* **h** eaten in NIH
1: 9 eaten in Shiloh, and after *they* **h** drunk. NIH
1:13 therefore Eli thought she **h** been drunken. NIH
1:20 come about after Hannah **h** conceived, NIH
1:24 when she **h** weaned him, she took him NIH
3: 8 Eli perceived that the LORD **h** called NIH
4:18 heavy. And he **h** judged Israel forty years. NIH
5: 9 it was *so*, that after they **h** carried it about, NIH
5: 9 and they **h** emerods in their secret parts. NIH
6: 6 when they **h** wrought wonderfully among NIH
6:16 the five lords of the Philistines **h** seen NIH
6:19 they **h** looked into the ark of the LORD, NIH
6:19 smitten *many* of the people NIH
7:14 the cities which the Philistines **h** taken NIH
9: 2 he **h** a son, whose name *was* Saul, 1961+3807.1
9:15 Now the LORD **h** told Samuel in his ear a NIH
10: 9 when he **h** turned his back to go from NIH
10:13 when he **h** made an end of prophesying, NIH
10:20 when Samuel **h** caused all the tribes of NIH
10:21 When he **h** caused the tribe of Benjamin NIH
10:26 of men, whose hearts God **h** touched. NIH
13: 1 when he **h** reigned two years over Israel, NIH
13: 4 all Israel heard say *that* Saul **h** smitten a NIH
13: 4 Israel also was **h** in **abomination** with 887
13: 8 according to the set time that Samuel **h** NIH
13:10 that as soon as he **h** made an end of 3807.1
13:21 Yet they **h** a file for the mattocks, 1961
14:11 of the holes where they **h** hid themselves. NIH
14:17 when they **h** numbered, behold Jonathan NIH
14:22 Likewise all the men of Israel which **h** hid NIH
14:24 for Saul **h** adjured the people, saying, NIH
14:30 if haply the people **h** eaten freely to day of NIH
14:30 for **h** there not been now a much greater NIH
15:35 the LORD repented that he **h** made Saul NIH
17: 5 *he* **h** a helmet of brass upon his head, NIH
17: 6 *he* **h** greaves of brass upon his legs, NIH
17:12 name *was* Jesse; and he **h** eight sons: 3807.1
17:20 and went, as Jesse **h** commanded him; NIH
17:21 the Philistines **h** put *the battle* in array, NIH
17:39 for he **h** not proved *it*. NIH
17:40 them in a shepherd's bag which he **h**, 3807.1
19:18 and told him all that Saul **h** done to him. NIH
20:34 because his father **h** done him shame. NIH
20:37 place of the arrow which Jonathan **h** shot, NIH
22:21 Abiathar shewed David that Saul **h** slain NIH
24: 5 him, because he **h** cut off Saul's skirt. NIH
24:10 **h** delivered thee to day into mine hand in NIH
24:16 when David **h** made an end of speaking NIH
24:18 forasmuch as when the LORD **h** delivered NIH
25: 2 he **h** three thousand sheep, 3807.1
25:21 Now David **h** said, Surely in vain have I NIH
25:34 surely there **h** not been left unto Nabal by NIH
25:35 her hand *that* which she **h** brought him, NIH
25:37 his wife **h** told him these things, that his NIH
25:44 Saul **h** given Michal his daughter, NIH
26: 5 came to the place where Saul **h** pitched: NIH
28: 3 all Israel **h** lamented him, and buried him NIH
28: 3 Saul **h** put away those that had familiar NIH
28: 3 Saul had put away those that **h** familiar NIH
28:20 for he **h** eaten no bread all the day, nor all NIH
28:24 the woman **h** a fat calf in the house; 3807.1
30: 1 that the Amalekites **h** invaded the south, NIH
30: 2 **h** taken the women captives, that *were* NIH
30: 4 until they **h** no more power to weep. 871.1
30:12 when he **h** eaten, his spirit came again to NIH
30:12 for he **h** eaten no bread, nor drunk *any* NIH
30:16 when he **h** brought him down, behold NIH
30:16 of all the great spoil that they **h** taken out NIH
30:18 David recovered all that the Amalekites **h** NIH
30:19 nor any *thing* that they **h** taken to them: NIH
30:21 whom they **h** made also to abide at NIH
31:11 that which the Philistines **h** done to Saul, NIH

2Sa 1: 1 and David **h** abode two days in Ziklag; NIH
1:21 *though he* **h** not *been* anointed with oil. NIH
2:27 in the morning the people **h** gone up NIH
2:30 he **h** gathered all the people together, NIH
2:31 the servants of David **h** smitten of NIH
3: 7 Saul **h** a concubine, whose name *was* 3807.1
3:17 Abner **h** communication with the elders 1961
3:22 for he **h** sent him away, and he was gone NIH
3:30 he **h** slain their brother Asahel at Gibeon NIH
4: 2 Saul's son **h** two men *that were* captains 1961

2Sa 4: 4 **h** a son *that was* lame of *his* feet, 3807.1
5:12 David perceived that the LORD **h** NIH
5:12 he **h** exalted his kingdom for his people NIH
5:17 when the Philistines heard that they **h** NIH
5:25 did so, as the LORD **h** commanded him; NIH
6: 8 the LORD **h** made a breach upon Uzzah: NIH
6:13 the ark of the LORD **h** gone six paces, NIH
6:17 the midst of the tabernacle that David **h** NIH
6:18 soon as David **h** made an end of offering NIH
6:22 of them shall I be **h** in honour. 3513
6:23 **h** no child unto the day of her 1961+3807.1
7: 1 the LORD **h** given him rest round about NIH
8: 9 David **h** smitten all the host of Hadadezer, NIH
8:10 because he **h** fought against Hadadezer, NIH
8:10 Hadadezer **h** wars with Toi. 376+1961+4421
8:11 gold that he **h** dedicated of all nations NIH
9: 2 when they **h** called him unto David, NIH
9:10 Now Ziba **h** fifteen sons and 3807.1
9:12 Mephibosheth **h** a young son, 3807.1
11:10 when they **h** told David, saying, Uriah NIH
11:13 when David **h** called him, he did eat and NIH
11:22 shewed David all that Joab **h** sent him for. NIH
11:27 the thing that David **h** done displeased NIH
12: 2 The rich *man* **h** exceeding many 1961+3807.1
12: 3 the poor *man* **h** nothing, save one little 3807.1
12: 3 which he **h** bought and nourished up: NIH
12: 6 did this thing, and because he **h** no **pity.** 2550
12: 8 if *that* **h** been too little, I would moreover NIH
13: 1 that Absalom the son of David **h** a fair 3807.1
13: 3 Amnon a friend, whose name *was* 3807.1
13:10 Tamar took the cakes which she **h** made, NIH
13:11 she **h** brought *them* unto him to eat, NIH
13:15 than the love wherewith he **h** loved her. NIH
13:18 *h* a garment of divers colours upon her: NIH
13:22 because he **h** forced his sister Tamar. NIH
13:23 that Absalom **h** sheepshearers in 1961
13:28 Absalom **h** commanded his servants, NIH
13:29 unto Amnon as Absalom **h** commanded. NIH
13:36 soon as he **h** made an end of speaking, 3807.1
14: 2 as a woman that **h** a long time mourned NIH
14: 6 thy handmaid **h** two sons, and they two 3807.1
14:32 it **h** been good for me *to have been* there NIH
14:33 when he **h** called for Absalom, he came to NIH
15: 2 *that* when any man that **h** a 1961+3807.1
15:24 until all the people **h** done passing out of NIH
15:30 his head covered, and he went 3807.1
16:23 *was* as if a man **h** inquired at the oracle of NIH
17:14 For the LORD **h** appointed to defeat NIH
17:18 in Bahurim, which **h** a well in his court; 3807.1
17:20 when they **h** sought and could not find NIH
18:18 Now Absalom in his lifetime **h** taken and NIH
18:33 would God I **h** died for thee, O Absalom, NIH
19: 6 if Absalom **h** lived, and all we had died NIH
19: 6 all we **h** died *this* day, then it had pleased NIH
19: 6 died *this* day, then it **h** pleased thee well. NIH
19: 8 for Israel **h** fled every man to his tent. NIH
19:24 **h** neither dressed his feet, nor trimmed his NIH
19:32 he **h** provided the king of sustenance while NIH
19:43 that our advice should not be first **h** in 3807.1
20: 3 whom he **h** left to keep the house, NIH
20: 5 the set time which he **h** appointed him. NIH
20: 8 Joab's garment that he **h** put on *was* girded NIH
21: 2 the children of Israel **h** sworn unto them: NIH
21:11 of Aiah, the concubine of Saul, **h** done. NIH
21:12 which **h** stolen them from the street of NIH
21:12 where the Philistines **h** hanged them, NIH
21:12 when the Philistines **h** slain Saul in Gilboa: NIH
21:15 the Philistines **h** yet war 1961+3807.1
21:20 that **h** on every hand six fingers, NIH
22: 1 **h** delivered him out of the hand of all his NIH
22:38 turned not again until I **h** consumed them. NIH
23: 8 of the mighty *men* whom David **h:** 3807.1
23:18 and **h** the name among three. 3807.1
23:20 of Kabzeel, who **h** done many acts, NIH
23:21 the Egyptian **h** a spear in his hand; NIH
23:22 **h** the name among three mighty *men.* 3807.1
24: 8 when they **h** gone through all the land, NIH
24:10 David's heart smote him after that he **h** NIH

1Ki 1: 6 his father **h** not displeased him at any time NIH
1:41 heard *it* as they **h** made an end of eating. NIH
2:28 for Joab **h** turned after Adonijah, though NIH
2:41 it was told Solomon that Shimei **h** gone NIH
3: 1 he **h** made an end of building his own NIH
3:10 the Lord, that Solomon **h** asked this thing. NIH
3:21 when I **h** considered it in the morning, NIH
3:28 of the judgment which the king **h** judged; NIH
4: 2 these *were* the princes which he **h;** 3807.1
4: 7 Solomon **h** twelve officers over all Israel, 3807.1
4:11 which **h** Taphath the daughter of 1961+3807.1
4:14 Ahinadab the son of Iddo **h** Mahanaim: NIH
4:24 For he **h** dominion over all *the region* on NIH
4:24 **h** peace on all sides round about 1961+3807.1
4:26 Solomon **h** forty thousand stalls 1961+3807.1
4:34 of the earth, which **h** heard of his wisdom. NIH
5: 1 for he **h** heard that they **h** anointed him NIH
5: 1 for he **h** heard that they **h** anointed him NIH
5: 7 Solomon **h** threescore and 1961+3807.1
6:22 gold, until *he* **h** finished all the house: NIH
7: 8 his house where he dwelt **h** another court NIH
7: 8 whom he **h** taken *to wife*, like unto this NIH
7:20 the chapiters upon the two pillars **h** NIH
7:28 *was on* this *manner:* they **h** borders, 3807.1
7:30 every base **h** four brasen wheels, NIH
7:30 the four corners thereof **h** undersetters: 3807.1
7:37 all of them **h** one casting, one measure, NIH

1Ki 7:51 things which David his father **h** dedicated; NIH
8:11 for the glory of the LORD **h** filled NIH
8:54 *that* when Solomon **h** made an end of NIH
8:66 the good **h** done for David his servant, NIH
9: 1 when Solomon **h** finished the building of NIH
9: 2 as he **h** appeared unto him at Gibeon. NIH
9:10 when Solomon **h** built the two houses, NIH
9:11 (Now Hiram the king of Tyre **h** furnished NIH
9:12 the cities which Solomon **h** given him; NIH
9:16 For Pharaoh king of Egypt **h** gone up, NIH
9:19 the cities of store that Solomon **h,** 1961+3807.1
9:24 her house which *Solomon* **h** built for her: NIH
9:27 shipmen that **h** knowledge of the sea, NIH
10: 4 when the queen of Sheba **h** seen all NIH
10: 4 and the house that he **h** built, NIH
10: 7 I came, and mine eyes **h** seen *it:* NIH
10:15 Besides *that* he **h** of the merchantmen, NIH
10:19 The throne **h** six steps, and the top of 3807.1
10:22 For the king **h** at sea a navy of Tharshish 3807.1
10:24 wisdom, which God **h** put in his heart. NIH
10:26 **h** a thousand and four hundred NIH
10:28 Solomon **h** horses brought out of Egypt, 3807.1
11: 3 he **h** seven hundred wives, 1961+3807.1
11: 9 Israel, which **h** appeared unto him twice, NIH
11:10 **h** commanded him concerning this thing, NIH
11:15 after he **h** smitten every male in Edom; NIH
11:16 until he **h** cut off every male in Edom:) NIH
11:29 he **h** clad himself with a new garment; NIH
12: 8 which they **h** given him, and consulted NIH
12:12 as the king **h** appointed, saying, Come to NIH
12:32 sacrificing unto the calves that he **h** made: NIH
12:32 of the high places which he **h** made. NIH
12:33 So he offered upon the altar which he **h** NIH
12:33 in the month which he **h** devised of his NIH
13: 4 which **h** cried against the altar in Beth-el, NIH
13: 5 of God **h** given by the word of the LORD. NIH
13:11 him all the works which the man of God **h** NIH
13:11 words which he **h** spoken unto the king, NIH
13:12 For his sons **h** seen what way the man of NIH
13:23 after he **h** eaten bread, and after he had NIH
13:23 he had eaten bread, and after he **h** drunk, NIH
13:23 for the prophet whom he **h** brought NIH
13:28 the lion **h** not eaten the carcase, nor torn NIH
13:31 came to pass, after he **h** buried him, that NIH
14:22 with their sins which they **h** committed, NIH
14:22 above all that their fathers **h** done. NIH
14:26 shields of gold which Solomon **h** made. NIH
15: 3 of his father, which he **h** done before him: NIH
15:12 removed all the idols that his fathers **h** NIH
15:13 because she **h** made an idol in a grove; NIH
15:15 brought in *the things* which his father **h** NIH
15:15 the *things* which himself **h** dedicated, NIH
15:20 the captains of the hosts which he **h** 3807.1
15:22 where*with* Baasha **h** builded. NIH
15:29 until *he* **h** destroyed him, according unto NIH
16:31 as if it **h** been a light thing for him to walk NIH
16:32 house of Baal, which he **h** built in Samaria. NIH
17: 7 because there **h** been no rain in the land. NIH
19: 1 Ahab told Jezebel all that Elijah **h** done, NIH
19: 1 withal how he **h** slain all the prophets with NIH
21: 1 *that* Naboth the Jezreelite **h** a 1961+3807.1
21: 4 of the word which Naboth the Jezreelite **h** NIH
21: 4 for he **h** said, I will not give thee NIH
21:11 did as Jezebel **h** sent unto them, *and as it* NIH
21:11 as *it was* written in the letters which she **h** NIH
22:31 two captains that **h** rule over *his* chariots, NIH
22:53 according unto all that his father **h** done. NIH

2Ki 1:17 word of the LORD which Elijah **h** spoken. NIH
1:17 of Judah; because he **h** no son. 1961+3807.1
2:14 when he also **h** smitten the waters, they NIH
3: 2 the image of Baal that his father **h** made. NIH
4:12 he **h** called her, she stood before him. NIH
4:15 he **h** called her, she stood in the door. NIH
4:17 bare a son at that season that Elisha **h** said NIH
4:20 when he **h** taken him, and brought him to NIH
5: 1 by him the LORD **h** given deliverance NIH
5: 2 the Syrians **h** gone out *by* companies, NIH
5: 2 **h** brought away captive out of the land of NIH
5: 7 when the king of Israel **h** read the letter, NIH
5: 8 when Elisha the man of God **h** heard that NIH
5: 8 that the king of Israel **h** rent his clothes, NIH
5:13 *if* the prophet **h** bid thee *do some* great NIH
6:23 they **h** eaten and drunk, he sent them NIH
6:30 he **h** sackcloth within upon his flesh. NIH
7: 6 the Lord **h** made the host of the Syrians NIH
7:15 the Syrians **h** cast away in their haste. NIH
7:17 and he died, as the man of God **h** said, NIH
7:18 came to pass as the man of God **h** spoken NIH
8: 1 whose son he **h** restored to life, saying, NIH
8: 5 he was telling the king how he **h** restored NIH
8: 5 woman, whose son he **h** restored to life, NIH
8:29 which the Syrians **h** given him at Ramah, NIH
9:14 Now Joram **h** kept Ramoth-gilead, 1961
9:15 wounds which the Syrians **h** given him, NIH
9:31 she said, *H* Zimri peace, who slew his NIH
10: 1 Ahab **h** seventy sons in Samaria. 3807.1
10:17 till he **h** destroyed him, according to NIH
10:25 as soon as he **h** made an end of offering NIH
11:15 For the priest **h** said, Let her not be slain NIH
12: 6 year of king Jehoash the priests **h** NIH
12:11 that **h** the **oversight** *of* the house of 6485
12:18 **h** dedicate, and his own hallowed *things*, NIH
13: 7 for the king of Syria **h** destroyed them, NIH
13: 7 **h** made them like the dust by threshing. NIH
13:23 **h compassion** on them, and had respect 7355

2Ki 13:23 **h** respect unto them, because of his	NIH	
13:25 which **h** taken out of the hand of	NIH	
14: 5 that he slew his servants which **h** slain	NIH	
15: 3 according to all that his father Amaziah **h** done.	NIH	
15: 9 sight of the LORD, as his fathers **h** done.	NIH	
15:34 to all that his father Uzziah **h** done.	NIH	
16:11 all that king Ahaz **h** sent from Damascus:	NIH	
16:18 covert for the sabbath that they **h** built in	NIH	
17: 4 for he **h** sent messengers to So king of	NIH	
17: 4 king of Assyria, as he **h** done year by year:	NIH	
17: 7 that the children of Israel **h** sinned against	NIH	
17: 7 which **h** brought them up out of the land	NIH	
17: 7 king of Egypt, and **h** feared other gods,	NIH	
17: 8 of the kings of Israel, which they **h** made.	NIH	
17:12 whereof the LORD **h** said unto them,	NIH	
17:15 *concerning* whom the LORD **h** charged	NIH	
17:20 until he **h** cast them out of his sight.	NIH	
17:23 he **h** said by all his servants the prophets.	NIH	
17:28 of the priests whom they **h** carried away	NIH	
17:29 high places which the Samaritans **h** made,	NIH	
17:35 With whom the LORD **h** made a covenant,	NIH	
18: 4 the brasen serpent that Moses **h** made:	NIH	
18:16 which Hezekiah king of Judah **h** overlaid,	NIH	
18:18 they **h** called to the king, there came	NIH	
19: 8 for he **h** heard that he was departed from	NIH	
20:11 by which it **h** gone down in the dial of	NIH	
20:12 he **h** heard that Hezekiah had been sick.	NIH	
20:12 he had heard that Hezekiah had been sick.	NIH	
21: 3 which Hezekiah his father **h** destroyed;	NIH	
21: 7 set a graven image of the grove that he **h**	NIH	
21:16 till he **h** filled Jerusalem from one end to	NIH	
21:24 people of the land slew all them that **h**	NIH	
22:11 when the king **h** heard the words of	NIH	
23: 5 the kings of Judah **h** ordained to burn	NIH	
23: 8 defiled the high places where the priests **h**	NIH	
23:11 that the kings of Judah **h** given to the sun,	NIH	
23:12 which the kings of Judah **h** made,	NIH	
23:12 the altars which Manasseh **h** made in	NIH	
23:13 Solomon the king of Israel **h** builded	NIH	
23:15 **h** made, both that altar and the high place	NIH	
23:19 the kings of Israel **h** made to provoke	NIH	
23:19 to all the acts that he **h** done in Beth-el.	NIH	
23:26 of all the provocations that Manasseh **h**	NIH	
23:29 him at Megiddo, when he **h** seen him.	NIH	
23:32 according to all that his fathers **h** done.	NIH	
23:37 according to all that his fathers **h** done.	NIH	
24: 7 for the king of Babylon **h** taken from	NIH	
24: 9 according to all that his father **h** done.	NIH	
24:13 Israel **h** made in the temple of the LORD,	NIH	
24:13 of the LORD, as the LORD **h** said.	NIH	
24:19 according to all that Jehoiakim **h** done.	NIH	
24:20 until he **h** cast them out from his presence,	NIH	
25:16 the bases which Solomon **h** made for	NIH	
25:17 like unto these **h** the second pillar with	3807.1	
25:22 whom Nebuchadnezzar king of Babylon **h**	NIH	
25:23 heard that the king of Babylon **h** made	NIH	
1Ch 2:22 who **h** three and twenty cities in	1961+3807.1	
2:26 Jerahmeel also another wife,	1961+3807.1	
2:34 Now Sheshan **h** no sons,	1961+3807.1	
2:34 Sheshan **h** a servant, an Egyptian,	3807.1	
2:52 the father of Kirjath-jearim **h** sons;	1961+3807.1	
4: 5 Ashur the father of Tekoa **h** two	1961+3807.1	
4:22 who **h** the dominion in Moab,	NIH	
4:27 Shimei **h** sixteen sons and six daughters	3807.1	
4:27 his brethren **h** not many children,	NIH	
4:40 for *they* of Ham **h** dwelt there of old.	NIH	
6:31 of the LORD, after that the ark **h** rest.	NIH	
6:32 until Solomon **h** built the house of	NIH	
6:49 Moses the servant of God **h** commanded.	NIH	
6:66 **h** cities of their coasts out of the tribe of	1961	
7: 4 thousand *men*: for they **h** many wives	NIH	
7:15 and Zelophehad **h** daughters.	1961+3807.1	
8: 8 of Moab, after he **h** sent them away;	NIH	
8:38 Azel **h** six sons, whose names *are* these,	3807.1	
8:40 and **h** many sons, and sons' sons,	7235	
9:23 their children the oversight of the gates	NIH	
9:28 *certain* of them **h** the charge of	NIH	
9:31 he **h** the set office over the things that were	871.1	
9:44 Azel **h** six sons, whose names *are* these,	3807.1	
10: 9 when they **h** stripped him, they took his	NIH	
10:11 all that the Philistines **h** done to Saul,	NIH	
10:13 also for asking *counsel* of *one that* **h** a	NIH	
11:10 of the mighty *men* whom David **h**,	3807.1	
11:11 of the mighty *men* whom David **h**;	3807.1	
11:20 and **h** a name among the three.	3807.1	
11:22 man of Kabzeel, who **h** done many acts;	NIH	
11:24 the name among the three mighties.	3807.1	
12:15 when it **h** overflown all his banks;	NIH	
12:29 hitherto the greatest part of them **h** kept	NIH	
12:32 that **h understanding** of the times,	998+3045	
12:39 for their brethren **h** prepared for them.	NIH	
13:11 the LORD **h** made a breach upon Uzza:	NIH	
13:14 house of Obed-edom, and all that he **h**.	3807.1	
14: 2 David perceived that the LORD **h**	NIH	
14: 4 children which he **h** in Jerusalem	1961+3807.1	
14:12 when they **h** left their gods there, David	NIH	
15: 3 unto his place, which he **h** prepared for it.	NIH	
15:27 David also **h** upon him an ephod of linen.	NIH	
16: 1 set it in the midst of the tent that David **h**	NIH	
16: 2 when David **h** made an end of offering	NIH	
18: 9 **h** smitten the whole host of Hadarezer king of	NIH	
18:10 because he **h** fought against Hadarezer,	NIH	
18:10 (for Hadarezer **h** war **with** Tou;)	376+1961+4421	
19: 6 they **h** made themselves odious to David,	NIH	
19:17 So when David **h** put the battle in array	NIH	

1Ch 21:28 **h** answered him in the threshingfloor of	NIH	
23:11 Jeush and Beriah **h** not many sons;	NIH	
23:17 Eliezer **h** none other sons;	1961+3807.1	
23:22 and **h** no sons, but daughters:	1961+3807.1	
24: 2 their father, and **h** no children:	1961+3807.1	
24:19 as the LORD God of Israel **h** commanded	NIH	
24:28 came Eleazar, who **h** no sons.	1961+3807.1	
26: 9 Meshelemiah **h** sons and brethren,	3807.1	
26:10 of the children of Merari, **h** sons;	3807.1	
26:26 and the captains of the host, **h** dedicated.	NIH	
26:28 and Joab the son of Zeruiah, **h** dedicated;	NIH	
26:28 whosoever **h** dedicated *anything, it was*	NIH	
27:23 the LORD **h** said *he* would increase Israel	NIH	
28: 2 for me, I **h** in mine heart to build a house	NIH	
28: 2 God, and **h** made ready for the building:	NIH	
28:12 the pattern of all that he **h** by	1961+5973	
29:25 upon him *such* royal majesty as **h**	NIH	
2Ch 1: 3 which Moses the servant of the LORD **h**	NIH	
1: 4 the ark of God **h** David brought up from	NIH	
1: 4 to *the place which* David **h** prepared for it:	NIH	
1: 4 for he **h** pitched a tent for it at Jerusalem.	NIH	
1: 5 the son of Uri, the son of Hur, **h** made,	NIH	
1:12 as none of the kings have **h** that *have*	1961	
1:14 he **h** a thousand and four hundred	1961+3807.1	
1:16 Solomon **h** horses brought out of Egypt,	3807.1	
2:17 David his father **h** numbered them;	NIH	
3: 1 in the place that David **h** prepared in	NIH	
5: 1 *things* that David his father **h** dedicated;	NIH	
5:14 for the glory of the LORD **h** filled	NIH	
6:13 For Solomon **h** made a brasen scaffold,	NIH	
6:13 and set it in the midst of the court:	NIH	
7: 1 Now when Solomon **h** made an end of	NIH	
7: 2 the glory of the LORD **h** filled	NIH	
7: 6 which David the king **h** made to praise	NIH	
7: 7 the brasen altar which Solomon **h** made	NIH	
7:10 that the LORD **h** shewed unto David,	NIH	
8: 1 wherein Solomon **h** built the house of	NIH	
8: 2 That the cities which Huram **h** restored to	NIH	
8: 6 the store cities that Solomon **h**,	1961+3807.1	
8:11 unto the house that he **h** built for her:	NIH	
8:12 which he **h** built before the porch,	NIH	
8:14 so **h** David the man of God commanded.	NIH	
8:18 and servants that **h** knowledge of the sea;	NIH	
9: 3 the queen of Sheba **h** seen the wisdom	NIH	
9: 3 of Solomon, and the house that he **h** built,	NIH	
9: 6 I came, and mine eyes **h** seen *it*:	NIH	
9:12 besides *that* which she **h** brought unto	NIH	
9:23 his wisdom, that God **h** put in his heart.	NIH	
9:25 Solomon **h** four thousand stalls	1961+3807.1	
10: 2 whither he **h** fled from the presence of	NIH	
10: 6 **h** stood before Solomon his father while	1961	
11:14 his sons **h** cast them off from executing	NIH	
11:15 and for the calves which he **h** made.	NIH	
12: 1 Rehoboam **h** established the kingdom,	NIH	
12: 1 he strengthened himself, he forsook the law	NIH	
12: 2 they **h** transgressed against the LORD,	NIH	
12: 9 shields of gold which Solomon **h** made.	NIH	
12:13 the city which the LORD **h** chosen out of	NIH	
14: 6 for the land **h** rest, and he had no war in	NIH	
14: 6 had rest, and he **h** no war in those years;	5973	
14: 6 because the LORD **h** given him rest.	NIH	
14: 8 Asa **h** an army of *men* that bare	1961+3807.1	
15: 8 out of the cities which he **h** taken from	NIH	
15:11 of the spoil *which* they **h** brought,	NIH	
15:15 for they **h** sworn with all their heart,	NIH	
15:16 because she **h** made an idol in a grove:	NIH	
15:18 God *the things* that his father **h** dedicated,	NIH	
15:18 he himself **h** dedicated, silver, and gold,	NIH	
16:14 which he **h** made for himself in the city of	NIH	
17: 2 of Ephraim, which Asa his father **h** taken.	NIH	
17: 5 **h** riches and honour in	1961+3807.1	
17: 9 **h** the book of the law of the LORD with	NIH	
17:13 he **h** much business in the cities of	1961+3807.1	
18: 1 Now Jehoshaphat **h** riches and	1961+3807.1	
18: 2 for the people that he **h** with him,	NIH	
18:10 Zedekiah the son of Chenaanah **h** made	NIH	
18:30 Now the king of Syria **h** commanded	NIH	
20:21 when he **h** consulted with the people,	NIH	
20:23 they **h** made an end of the inhabitants	NIH	
20:27 for the LORD **h** made them to rejoice over	NIH	
20:29 when they **h** heard that the LORD fought	NIH	
20:33 for as yet the people **h** not prepared their	NIH	
21: 2 he **h** brethren the sons of Jehoshaphat,	3807.1	
21: 6 for he **h** the daughter of Ahab	1961+3807.1	
21: 7 the covenant that he **h** made with David,	NIH	
21:10 he **h** forsaken the LORD God of his	NIH	
22: 1 Arabians to the camp **h** slain all the eldest.	NIH	
22: 7 whom the LORD **h** anointed to cut off	NIH	
22: 9 when they **h** slain him, they buried him:	NIH	
22: 9 the house of Ahaziah **h** no power to keep	NIH	
23: 8 that Jehoiada the priest **h** commanded,	NIH	
23: 9 and shields, that *h been* king David's,	NIH	
23:18 whom David **h** distributed in the house of	NIH	
23:21 after that they **h** slain Athaliah with	NIH	
24: 7 **h** broken up the house of God	NIH	
24:10 into the chest, until *they* **h** made an end.	NIH	
24:14 when they **h** finished *it,* they brought	NIH	
24:16 because he **h** done good in Israel,	NIH	
24:22 which Jehoiada his father **h** done to him,	NIH	
24:24 they **h** forsaken the LORD God of their	NIH	
25: 3 that he slew his servants that **h** killed	NIH	
26: 5 **h understanding** in the visions of	995	
26:10 for he **h** much cattle, both in	1961+3807.1	
26:11 Moreover Uzziah **h** a host of	1961+3807.1	
26:19 *h* a censer in his hand to burn incense:	NIH	

2Ch 26:20 go out, because the LORD **h** smitten him.	NIH	
28: 3 **h** cast out before the children of Israel.	NIH	
28: 6 they **h** forsaken the LORD God of their	NIH	
28:17 For again the Edomites **h** come and	NIH	
28:18 The Philistines also **h** invaded the cities of	NIH	
28:18 taken Beth-shemesh, and Ajalon,	NIH	
29: 2 according to all that David his father **h**	NIH	
29:22 likewise, when they **h** killed the rams,	NIH	
29:29 when *they* **h** made an end of offering,	NIH	
29:34 until the *other* priests **h** sanctified	NIH	
29:36 people, that God **h** prepared the people:	NIH	
30: 2 For the king **h** taken counsel,	NIH	
30: 3 the priests **h** not sanctified themselves	NIH	
30: 3 neither **h** the people gathered themselves	NIH	
30: 5 they **h** not done *it* of a long *time* in such	NIH	
30:17 the Levites **h** the charge of the killing of	5921	
30:18 and Zebulun, **h** not cleansed themselves,	NIH	
31: 1 until *they* **h** utterly destroyed *them all.*	NIH	
31:10 we have **h** enough to eat, and have left	7646	
32:27 **h** exceeding much riches	1961+3807.1	
32:29 for God **h** given him substance very much.	NIH	
33: 2 whom the LORD **h** cast out before	NIH	
33: 3 which Hezekiah his father **h** broken down,	NIH	
33: 4 whereof the LORD **h** said, In Jerusalem	NIH	
33: 7 the idol which he **h** made, in the house of	NIH	
33: 7 of which God **h** said to David and	NIH	
33: 9 whom the LORD **h** destroyed before	NIH	
33:15 all the altars that he **h** built in the mount	NIH	
33:22 images which Manasseh his father **h** made,	NIH	
33:23 as Manasseh his father **h** humbled himself;	NIH	
33:25 the people of the land slew all them that **h**	NIH	
34: 4 strowed *it* upon the graves of them that **h**	NIH	
34: 7 when he **h** broken down the altars and	NIH	
34: 7 **h** beaten the graven images into powder,	NIH	
34: 8 he **h** purged the land, and the house,	NIH	
34: 9 which the Levites that kept the doors **h**	NIH	
34:10 the oversight of the house of the LORD,	NIH	
34:11 which the kings of Judah **h** destroyed.	NIH	
34:19 the king **h** heard the words of the law,	NIH	
34:22 *they* that the king **h** appointed, went to	NIH	
35:20 this, when Josiah **h** prepared the temple,	NIH	
35:24 put him in the second chariot that he **h**;	3807.1	
36:13 who **h** made him swear by God:	NIH	
36:14 LORD which he **h** hallowed in Jerusalem.	NIH	
36:15 because he **h compassion** on his people,	2550	
36:17 he **h** no **compassion** upon young man or	2550	
36:20 that **h** escaped from the sword carried	NIH	
36:21 until the land **h** enjoyed her sabbaths:	NIH	
Ezr 1: 5 with all *them* whose spirit God **h** raised,	NIH	
1: 7 which Nebuchadnezzar **h** brought forth	NIH	
1: 7 and **h** put them in the house of his gods;	NIH	
2: 1 *of* those which **h** been carried away,	NIH	
2: 1 of Babylon **h** carried away unto Babylon,	NIH	
3: 7 to the grant that they **h** of Cyrus	5921	
3:12 *were* ancient men that **h** seen the first	NIH	
5:12 after that our fathers **h** provoked the God	NIH	
5:14 whom he **h** made governor;	NIH	
6:13 according to that which Darius the king **h**	NIH	
6:21 all such as **h** separated themselves unto	NIH	
6:22 for the LORD **h** made them joyful,	NIH	
7: 6 which the LORD God of Israel **h** given:	NIH	
7:10 For Ezra **h** prepared his heart to seek	NIH	
8:20 the princes **h** appointed for the service	3807.1	
8:22 because we **h** spoken unto the king,	NIH	
8:25 and all Israel *there* present, **h** offered:	NIH	
8:35 *Also* the children of those that **h** been	NIH	
9: 4 of the transgression of those that **h** been	NIH	
10: 1 when Ezra **h** prayed, and when he had	NIH	
10: 1 when he **h** confessed, weeping and	NIH	
10: 6 of the transgression of them that **h** been	NIH	
10: 8 of those that **h** been carried away.	NIH	
10:17 they made an end with all the men that **h**	NIH	
10:18 were found that **h** taken strange wives:	NIH	
10:44 All these **h** taken strange wives:	NIH	
10:44 *some* of them **h** wives by *whom* they had	3426	
10:44 had wives and had wives by *whom* they **h**	7760	
Ne 1: 2 I asked them concerning the Jews that **h**	NIH	
2: 1 Now I **h** not been *beforetime* sad in his	NIH	
2: 9 Now the king **h** sent captains of the army	NIH	
2:12 told I *any* man what my God **h** put	NIH	
2:16 neither **h** I as yet told *it* to the Jews, nor	NIH	
2:18 as also the king's words that he **h** spoken	NIH	
4: 6 for the people **h** a mind to work.	1961+3807.1	
4:15 God **h** brought their counsel to nought,	NIH	
4:18 every one **h** his sword girded by his side,	NIH	
5:15 former governors that *h been* before me	NIH	
5:15 taken of them bread and wine,	NIH	
6: 1 heard that I **h** builded the wall,	NIH	
6: 1 at that time I **h** not set up the doors	NIH	
6:12 lo, I perceived that God **h** not sent him;	NIH	
6:12 for Tobiah and Sanballat **h** hired him.	NIH	
6:18 his son Johanan **h** taken the daughter of	NIH	
7: 1 I **h** set up the doors, and the porters and	NIH	
7: 6 *of* those that **h** been carried away,	NIH	
7: 6 the king of Babylon **h** carried away,	NIH	
7:67 they **h** two hundred forty and five	3807.1	
8: 1 which the LORD **h** commanded to Israel.	NIH	
8: 4 which they **h** made for the purpose;	NIH	
8:12 they **h** understood the words that were	NIH	
8:14 which the LORD **h** commanded by Moses,	NIH	
8:17 day **h** not the children of Israel done so.	NIH	
9:18 when they **h** made them a molten calf,	NIH	
9:18 Egypt, and **h** wrought great provocations;	NIH	
9:28 after they **h** rest, they did evil again	3807.1	
9:28 so that they **h** the dominion over them:	NIH	

H

H

Ne 10:28 all they that **h** separated themselves from NIH
11:16 **h the oversight** of the outward business 5921
12:29 for the singers **h** builded them villages NIH
12:43 God **h** made them rejoice *with* great joy: NIH
13: 3 came to pass, when they **h** heard the law, NIH
13: 5 he **h** prepared for him a great chamber, NIH
13:10 perceived that the portions of the Levites **h** NIH
13:23 those days also saw I Jews *that* **h** married NIH
Est 1: 8 the king **h** appointed to all the officers of NIH
1: 1 what she **h** done, and what was decreed NIH
2: 6 Who **h** been carried away from Jerusalem NIH
2: 6 **h** been carried away with Jeconiah king of NIH
2: 6 the king of Babylon **h** carried away. NIH
2: 7 for she **h** neither father nor mother, 3807.1
2:10 Esther **h** not shewed her people nor her NIH
2:10 Mordecai **h** charged her that she should NIH
2:12 after that she **h** been twelve months, NIH
2:15 who **h** taken *her* for his daughter, NIH
2:20 Esther **h** not *yet* shewed her kindred nor NIH
2:20 her people; as Mordecai **h** charged her: NIH
3: 2 for the king **h** so commanded concerning NIH
3: 4 for he **h** told them that he *was* a Jew. NIH
3: 6 for they **h** shewed him the people of NIH
3:12 **h** commanded unto the king's lieutenants, NIH
4: 5 whom he **h** appointed to attend upon her, NIH
4: 7 Mordecai told him of all that **h** happened NIH
4: 7 of the sum of the money that Haman **h** NIH
4:17 did according to all that Esther **h** NIH
5: 5 Haman came to the banquet that Esther **h** NIH
5:11 *the things* where*in* the king **h** promoted NIH
5:11 how he **h** advanced him above the princes NIH
5:12 king unto the banquet that she **h** prepared NIH
6: 2 that Mordecai **h** told of Bigthana and NIH
6: 4 on the gallows that he **h** prepared for him. NIH
6:13 all his friends every *thing* that **h** befallen NIH
6:14 unto the banquet that Esther **h** prepared. NIH
7: 4 if we **h** been sold for bondmen and NIH
7: 4 and bondwomen, I **h** held my tongue, NIH
7: 9 which Haman **h** made for Mordecai, NIH
7: 9 who **h** spoken good for the king, standeth NIH
7:10 gallows that he **h** prepared for Mordecai. NIH
8: 1 for Esther **h** told what he *was* unto her. NIH
8: 2 which he **h** taken from Haman, and gave NIH
8: 3 his device that he **h** devised against NIH
8:16 The Jews **h** light, and gladness, 1961+3807.1
8:17 the Jews **h** joy and gladness, a feast and 3807.1
9: 1 Jews **h** rule over them that hated them;) NIH
9:16 rest from their enemies, and slew of NIH
9:23 the Jews undertook to do as they **h** begun, NIH
9:23 and as Mordecai **h** written unto them; NIH
9:24 devised against the Jews to destroy NIH
9:24 **h** cast Pur, that *is*, the lot, to consume NIH
9:26 *of that* which they **h** seen concerning this NIH
9:26 this *matter*, and which **h** come unto them, NIH
9:31 and Esther the queen **h** enjoined them, NIH
9:31 as they **h** decreed for themselves and NIH
Job 2:11 they **h** made an appointment together to NIH
3:13 should have slept: then **h** I been at rest, 3807.1
3:15 Or with princes that **h** gold, who filled 3807.1
3:16 as a hidden untimely birth I **h** not been; NIH
3:26 I was not in safety, neither **h** I rest, NIH
6:20 were confounded because they **h** hoped; NIH
9:16 If I **h** called, and he had answered me; NIH
9:16 If I had called, and he **h** answered me, NIH
9:16 would I not believe that he **h** hearkened NIH
10:18 *that* I **h** given up the ghost, and no eye NIH
10:18 given up the ghost, and no eye **h** seen me! NIH
10:19 I should have been as though I **h** not been; NIH
22: 8 *as for* the mighty man, he **h** the earth; 3807.1
24:16 *which* they **h** marked for themselves in NIH
29:12 and *him that* **h** none to help him. NIH
31:25 and because mine hand **h** gotten much; NIH
31:31 said not, O that we **h** of his flesh! NIH
31:35 and *that* mine adversary **h** written a book. NIH
32: 3 because they **h** found no answer, NIH
32: 3 no answer, and *yet* **h** condemned Job. NIH
32: 4 Now Elihu **h** waited till Job had spoken, NIH
32: 4 Now Elihu had waited till Job **h** spoken, NIH
32:16 When I **h** waited, (for they spake not, NIH
38: 8 *as if* it **h** issued out of the womb? NIH
42: 7 after the LORD **h** spoken these words NIH
42:10 gave Job twice as much as he **h** before. 3807.1
42:11 all *they that* **h** been *of* his acquaintance NIH
42:11 evil that the LORD **h** brought upon him: NIH
42:12 for he **h** fourteen thousand sheep, 1961+3807.1
42:13 He **h** also seven sons and 1961+3807.1
Ps 27:13 I **h** *fainted*, unless I had believed to see NIH
27:13 I *had fainted*, unless I believed to see NIH
35:14 I behaved myself as though *he* **h** *been* my NIH
42: 4 for I **h** gone with the multitude, I went NIH
51: T after he **h** gone in to Bath-sheba. NIH
55: 6 O that I **h** wings like a dove, *for then* 3807.1
73: 2 almost gone; my steps **h** well nigh slipt. NIH
74: 5 *man* was famous according as he **h** lifted NIH
78:11 and his wonders that he **h** shewed them. NIH
78:23 Though he **h** commanded the clouds from NIH
78:24 **h** rained down manna upon them to eat, NIH
78:24 and **h** given them of the corn of heaven. NIH
78:43 How he **h** wrought his signs in Egypt, NIH
78:44 **h** turned their rivers into blood; NIH
78:54 *which* his right hand **h** purchased. NIH
81:13 O that my people **h** hearkened unto me, NIH
81:13 unto me, *and* Israel **h** walked in my ways! NIH
84:10 I **h** rather be a doorkeeper in the house of NIH
89: 7 to be **h** in reverence of all them that are 3372

Ps 94:17 Unless the LORD *h* **been** my help, my soul NIH
94:17 my soul **h** almost dwelt *in* silence. NIH
105:26 servant; *and* Aaron whom he **h** chosen. NIH
106:21 which **h** done great *things* in Egypt; NIH
106:23 **h** not Moses his chosen stood before him NIH
119:51 The proud have **h** me greatly **in derision:** 3887
119:56 This I **h**, because I kept thy 1961+3807.1
119:87 They **h** almost consumed me upon earth; NIH
119:92 Unless thy law **h** *been* my delights, NIH
124: 1 If *it* **h** not *been* the LORD who was on our NIH
124: 2 If *it* **h** not *been* the LORD who was on our NIH
124: 3 they **h** swallowed us up quick, when their NIH
124: 4 the waters **h** overwhelmed us, the stream NIH
124: 4 the stream **h** gone over our soul: NIH
124: 5 the proud waters **h** gone over our soul. NIH
Pr 8:26 While as yet he **h** not made the earth, NIH
24:31 *and* nettles **h** covered the face thereof, NIH
Ecc 1:16 my heart **h** great **experience** of wisdom 7200
2: 7 and **h** servants born in *my* house; 1961
2: 7 also I **h** great possessions of great and 1961
2:11 I looked on all the works that my hands **h** NIH
2:11 and on the labour that I **h** laboured to do: NIH
2:18 I hated all my labour which I *h* taken NIH
4: 1 oppressed, and they **h** no comforter; 3807.1
4: 1 *was* power; but they **h** no comforter. 3807.1
8:10 who **h** come and gone from the place of NIH
8:10 were forgotten in the city where they **h** NIH
SS 3: 4 until I **h** brought him into my mother's NIH
5: 6 my beloved **h** withdrawn himself, NIH
8:11 Solomon **h** a vineyard at 1961+3807.1
Isa 1: 9 Except the LORD of hosts **h** left unto us a 3807.1
6: 2 each one **h** six wings; with twain he 3807.1
6: 6 *which* he **h** taken with the tongs from off NIH
22:11 neither **h** respect unto him that fashioned NIH
26:13 besides thee have **h** **dominion over** us: 1166
29:16 that framed it, He **h** no understanding? NIH
37: 8 for he **h** heard that he was departed from NIH
38: 9 when he **h** been sick, and was recovered NIH
38:17 Behold, for peace I **h** great bitterness: 3807.1
38:21 For Isaiah **h** said, Let them take a lump of NIH
38:22 Hezekiah also **h** said, What *is* the sign NIH
39: 1 for he **h** heard that he had been sick, NIH
39: 1 for he had heard that he **h** been sick, NIH
41: 3 *by* the way *that* he **h** not gone with his NIH
48:18 **h** thy peace been as a river, NIH
48:19 Thy seed also **h** been as the sand, NIH
49:21 was left alone; these, where *h* they *been*? NIH
52:15 for *that* which **h** not been told them shall NIH
52:15 *that* which they **h** not heard shall they NIH
53: 9 because he **h** done no violence, neither NIH
59:10 blind, and we grope as *if we h* no eyes: NIH
60:10 but in my favour have I **h mercy** on thee. 7355
Jer 2:21 Yet I **h** planted thee a noble vine, wholly NIH
3: 7 I said after she **h** done all these *things*, NIH
3: 8 committed adultery I **h** put her away, NIH
4:23 and the heavens, and they *h* no light. NIH
5: 7 when I **h** fed them to the full, they then NIH
6:15 they ashamed when they **h** committed NIH
8:12 they ashamed when they **h** committed NIH
9: 2 that I **h** in the wilderness a lodging place NIH
11:19 I knew not that they **h** devised devices NIH
13: 7 the girdle from the place where I **h** hid NIH
16:15 all the lands whither he **h** driven them: NIH
19:14 whither the LORD **h** sent him to prophesy; NIH
23: 8 all countries whither I **h** driven them; NIH
23:22 if they **h** stood in my counsel, NIH
23:22 **h** caused my people to hear my words, NIH
24: 1 carried away captive Jeconiah the son of NIH
24: 1 and **h** brought *them to* Babylon. NIH
24: 2 One basket *h* very good figs, *even* like NIH
24: 2 the other basket *h* very naughty figs, NIH
25:17 to drink, unto whom the LORD **h** sent me: NIH
26: 8 Jeremiah **h** made an end of speaking NIH
26: 8 commanded *him* to speak unto all NIH
26:19 evil which he **h** pronounced against them? NIH
28:12 broken the yoke from off the neck of NIH
29: 1 all the people whom Nebuchadnezzar **h** NIH
32: 3 Zedekiah king of Judah **h** shut him up, NIH
32:16 Now when I **h** delivered the evidence of NIH
34: 8 after that the king Zedekiah **h** made a NIH
34:10 which **h** entered into the covenant, NIH
34:11 whom they **h** let go free, to return, NIH
34:15 turned, and **h** done right in my sight, NIH
34:15 ye **h** made a covenant before me in NIH
34:16 whom ye **h** set at liberty at their pleasure, NIH
34:18 covenant which they **h** made before me, NIH
36: 4 which he **h** spoken unto him, upon a roll NIH
36:11 **h** heard out of the book all the words of NIH
36:13 unto them all the words that he **h** heard, NIH
36:16 it came to pass when they **h** heard all NIH
36:23 when Jehudi **h** read three or four leaves, NIH
36:25 Gemariah **h** made intercession to the king NIH
36:27 after that the king **h** burnt the roll, NIH
36:32 Jehoiakim king of Judah **h** burnt in the fire: NIH
37: 4 for they **h** not put him *into* prison. NIH
37:10 For though ye **h** smitten the whole army NIH
37:15 the scribe: for they **h** made that the prison. NIH
37:16 Jeremiah remained there many days; NIH
38: 1 heard the words that Jeremiah **h** spoken NIH
38: 7 heard that they **h** put Jeremiah in NIH
38:27 these words that the king **h** commanded. NIH
39: 5 when they **h** taken him, they brought him NIH
39:10 which **h** nothing, in the land of Judah, 3807.1
40: 1 of the guard **h** let him go from Ramah, NIH
40: 1 he **h** taken him being bound in chains NIH

Jer 40: 7 heard that the king of Babylon **h** made NIH
40: 7 **h** committed unto him men, and women, NIH
40:11 heard that the king of Babylon **h** left a NIH
40:11 he **h** set over them Gedaliah the son of NIH
41: 2 the king of Babylon **h** made governor NIH
41: 4 it came to pass the second day after **h** NIH
41: 9 Now the pit wherein Ishmael **h** cast all NIH
41: 9 whom he **h** slain because of Gedaliah, NIH
41: 9 *was* it which Asa the king **h** made for fear NIH
41:10 committed to Gedaliah the son of NIH
41:11 that Ishmael the son of Nethaniah **h** done, NIH
41:14 So all the people that Ishmael **h** carried NIH
41:16 all the remnant of the people whom he **h** NIH
41:16 after *that* he **h** slain Gedaliah the son of NIH
41:16 whom he **h** brought again from Gibeon: NIH
41:18 Ishmael the son of Nethaniah **h** slain NIH
43: 1 *that* when Jeremiah **h** made an end of NIH
43: 1 *for* which the LORD their God **h** sent him NIH
43: 5 whither they **h** been driven, to dwell in NIH
43: 6 left with Gedaliah the son of Ahikam NIH
44:15 the men which knew that their wives **h** NIH
44:17 for *then* **h** we **plenty** of victuals, 7646
44:20 to all the people which **h** given him *that* NIH
45: 1 when he **h** written these words in a book NIH
52: 2 according to all that Jehoiakim **h** done. NIH
52: 3 till he **h** cast them out from his presence, NIH
52:20 which king Solomon **h** made in the house NIH
52:25 which **h** the charge of the men of war; 1961
La 1: 7 things that she **h** in the days of old, 1961
1: 9 she **h** no comforter. O LORD, behold 3807.1
2:17 The LORD hath done *that* which he **h** NIH
2:17 he hath fulfilled his word that he **h** NIH
Eze 1: 5 they **h** the likeness of a man. NIH
1: 6 one **h** four faces, and every one **h**ad 3807.1
1: 6 four faces, and every one **h** four wings. 3807.1
1: 8 *they h* the hands of a man under their NIH
1: 8 they four **h** faces and their wings. 3807.1
1:10 they four **h** the face of a man, 3807.1
1:10 they four also **h** the face of an ox on the left 3807.1
1:10 they four also **h** the face of an eagle. 3807.1
1:16 they four **h** one likeness: NIH
1:23 every one **h** two, which covered on this 3807.1
1:23 on this *side*, and every one **h** two, 3807.1
1:25 they stood, *and* **h** let down their wings. NIH
1:27 of fire, and it **h** brightness round about. 3807.1
3: 6 Surely, **h** I sent thee to them, they would NIH
8: 8 I **h** digged in the wall, behold a door. NIH
9: 3 which *h* the writer's inkhorn by his side; NIH
9:11 which **h** the inkhorn by his side, NIH
10: 6 when he **h** commanded the man clothed NIH
10:10 appearances, they four **h** one likeness, NIH
10:10 if a wheel **h** been in the midst of a wheel. NIH
10:12 *even* the wheels that they four **h**. 3807.1
10:14 *every* one **h** four faces: the first face *was* 3807.1
10:21 Every one **h** four faces apiece, and every 3807.1
11:24 So the vision that I **h** seen went up from NIH
11:25 all the things that the LORD **h** shewed me. NIH
16:14 which I **h** put upon thee, saith the Lord NIH
16:17 I **h** given thee, and madest to thyself NIH
17: 3 full *of* feathers, which **h** divers colours, 3807.1
17:18 he **h** given his hand, and hath done all NIH
19: 5 Now when she saw that she **h** waited, NIH
19:11 she **h** strong rods for the sceptres of them 1961
20: 6 Egypt into a land that I **h** espied for them, NIH
20:15 which I **h** given *them*, flowing with milk NIH
20:24 they **h** not executed my judgments, NIH
20:24 despised my statutes, and had polluted NIH
20:24 **h** polluted my sabbaths, and their eyes NIH
20:28 *For* when I **h** brought them into the land, NIH
23:10 for they **h** executed judgment upon her. NIH
23:19 she **h** played the harlot in the land NIH
23:32 be laughed to scorn and **h** in derision; 3807.1
23:39 when they **h** slain their children to their NIH
29:18 yet **h** he no wages, nor his army, 1961+3807.1
29:18 for the service that he **h** served against it: NIH
33:15 give again that he **h** robbed, walk in NIH
33:21 *that* one that I **h** escaped out of Jerusalem NIH
33:22 **h** opened my mouth, until *he* came to me NIH
35: 5 Because thou hast **h** a perpetual 1961+3807.1
35: 5 in the time *that their* iniquity *h* an end: NIH
36:18 the blood that they **h** shed upon the land, NIH
36:18 their idols *wherewith* they **h** polluted it: NIH
36:21 I **h** pity for mine holy name, which 2550
36:21 the house of Israel **h** profaned among NIH
40:10 the posts **h** one measure on this side 3807.1
40:26 it **h** palm trees, one on this side, 3807.1
40:31 and the going up to it *h* eight steps. NIH
40:34 and the going up to it *h* eight steps. NIH
40:37 and the going up to it *h* eight steps. NIH
41: 6 they **h** not hold in the wall of the house. 1961
41:18 a cherub; and *every* cherub **h** two faces; 3807.1
41:23 temple and the sanctuary **h** two doors. 3807.1
41:24 the doors **h** two leaves *apiece*, two 3807.1
42: 6 **h** not pillars as the pillars of the courts: 3807.1
42:15 when he **h** made an end of measuring NIH
42:20 it **h** a wall round about, five hundred 3807.1
44:22 or a widow *that* **h** a priest **before**. 1961+4480
44:25 for sister that hath **h** no husband, 1961+3807.1
47: 3 when the man that the line in his hand NIH
47: 7 when I **h** returned, behold, at the bank NIH
Da 1: 4 such as *h* ability in them to stand in NIH
1: 9 God **h** brought Daniel into favour and NIH
1:11 the prince of the eunuchs **h** set over NIH
1:17 Daniel **h** understanding in all visions and NIH
1:18 at the end of the days that the king **h** 3807.1

Da	2:24 whom the king **h** ordained to destroy	NIH
	3: 2 which Nebuchadnezzar the king **h** set up.	NIH
	3: 3 that Nebuchadnezzar the king **h** set up;	NIH
	3: 3 the image that Nebuchadnezzar **h** set up.	NIH
	3: 7 that Nebuchadnezzar the king **h** set up.	NIH
	3:27 upon whose bodies the fire **h** no power,	NIH
	3:27 nor the smell of fire **h** passed on them.	NIH
	4:12 the beasts of the field **h** shadow under it,	NIH
	4:21 the fowls of the heaven **h** their habitation:	NIH
	5: 2 taken out of the temple which *was* in	NIH
	6:24 they brought those men which **h** accused	NIH
	6:24 the lions the mastery of them,	NIH
	7: 1 king of Babylon Daniel **h**ˢ a dream	2370
	7: 4 *was* like a lion, and **h** eagle's wings:	3807.2
	7: 5 it **h** three ribs in the mouth of it between	NIH
	7: 6 which **h** upon the back of it four wings	3807.2
	7: 6 the beast **h** also four heads;	3807.2
	7: 7 and it **h** great iron teeth:	3807.2
	7: 7 that *were* before it; and it **h** ten horns.	3807.2
	7:12 they their dominion taken away:	NIH
	7:20 *of* that horn that **h** eyes, and a mouth	3807.2
	8: 3 stood before the river a ram which **h**	3807.1
	8: 6 goat **h** a notable horn between his eyes.	NIH
	8: 6 he came to the ram that **h** two horns,	1167
	8: 6 which I **h** seen standing before the river,	NIH
	8:15 seen the vision, and sought for	NIH
	9:21 whom I **h** seen in the vision at	NIH
	10: 1 and **h** understanding of the vision.	3807.1
	10:11 when he **h** spoken this word unto me,	NIH
	10:15 when he **h** spoken such words unto me,	NIH
	10:19 when he **h** spoken unto me, I was	NIH
Hos	1: 8 Now when she **h** weaned Lo-ruhamah,	NIH
	2:23 I will have mercy upon her that **h** not	NIH
	12: 3 by his strength he **h** power with God:	8280
	12: 4 **h power** over *the* angel, and prevailed;	7786
Am	7: 2 *that* when they **h** made an end of eating	NIH
Ob	1: 5 would they not have stolen till they **h**	NIH
	1:16 they shall be as though they **h** not been.	NIH
Jnh	1:10 of the Lᴏʀᴅ, because he **h** told them.	NIH
	1:17 Now the Lᴏʀᴅ **h** prepared a great fish to	NIH
	3:10 he **h** said that he would do unto them:	NIH
	4:10 the Lᴏʀᴅ, Thou hast **h pity** on the gourd,	2347
Na	3: 8 *that* **h** the waters round about it,	NIH
Hab	3: 4 light; he **h** horns *coming* out of his hand:	NIH
Hag	1:12 as the Lᴏʀᴅ their God **h** sent him,	NIH
Zec	1:12 which thou hast **h** indignation these	NIH
	5: 9 they **h** wings like the wings of a stork:	3807.1
	7: 2 When they **h** sent *unto* the house of God	NIH
	10: 6 they shall be as though I **h** not cast them	NIH
	11:10 *I* might break my covenant which I **h**	NIH
Mal	2:15 Yet **h** he the residue of the spirit.	NIH
Mt	1: 6 the king begat Solomon of *her that* **h**,	NIG
	1:24 did as the angel of the Lord **h** bidden him,	NIG
	1:25 And knew her not till she **h** brought forth	NIG
	2: 3 Herod the king **h** heard *these things*,	NIG
	2: 4 when he **h** gathered all the chief priests	NIG
	2: 7 when he **h** privily called the wise men,	NIG
	2: 9 they **h** heard the king, they departed;	NIG
	2:11 and when they **h** opened their treasures,	NIG
	2:16 according to the time which he **h** diligently	NIG
	3: 4 And the same John **h** his raiment of	2192
	4: 2 And when he **h** fasted forty days and	NIG
	4:12 when Jesus **h** heard that John was cast	NIG
	4:24 lunatick, and those that **h the palsy**;	3885
	7:28 pass, when Jesus **h** ended these sayings,	NIG
	9: 8 which **h** given such power unto men.	NIG
	10: 1 when he **h** called unto *him* his twelve	NIG
	11: 1 Jesus **h** made an end of commanding	NIG
	11: 2 Now when John **h** heard in the prison	NIG
	11:21 **h** been done in Tyre and Sidon they would	NIG
	11:21 been done in thee, **h** been done in Sodom,	NIG
	12: 7 if ye **h** known what *this* meaneth, I will	NIG
	12:10 was a man which **h** *his* hand withered.	2192
	13: 5 fell upon stony *places*, where they **h**	2192
	13: 5 because *they* **h** no deepness of earth:	2192
	13: 6 because *they* **h** not root, they withered	2192
	13:46 when he **h** found one pearl of great price,	NIG
	13:46 went and sold all that he **h**, and bought it.	2192
	13:53 *that* when Jesus **h** finished these parables,	NIG
	14: 3 For Herod **h** laid hold on John,	NIG
	14:13 when the people **h** heard *thereof*, they	NIG
	14:21 And they that **h** eaten were about five	NIG
	14:23 And when he **h** sent the multitudes away,	NIG
	14:35 men of that place **h knowledge** of him,	1921
	16: 5 other side, they **h** forgotten to take bread.	NIG
	17: 8 When they lift up their eyes, they saw	NIG
	18:24 And when he **h** begun to reckon, one was	NIG
	18:25 But forasmuch as he **h** not to pay, his lord	2192
	18:25 all that he **h**, and payment to be made.	2192
	18:32 Then his lord, after that he **h** called him,	NIG
	18:33 not thou also have **h compassion**	1653
	18:33 fellowservant, even as I **h pity** on thee?	1653
	19: 1 *that* when Jesus **h** finished these sayings,	NIG
	19:22 sorrowful: for he **h** great possessions.	2192
	20: 2 And when he **h** agreed with the labourers	NIG
	20:11 when they **h** received *it*, they	NIG
	20:34 So Jesus **h compassion** *on them*, and	4697
	21:28 A *certain* man **h** two sons; and he came	2192
	21:32 when ye **h** seen *it*, repented not afterward,	NIG
	21:45 and Pharisees **h** heard his parables,	NIG
	22:11 he saw there a man which **h** not on a	1746
	22:22 When they **h** heard *these words*, they	NIG
	22:25 when he **h** married *a wife*, deceased, and,	NIG
	22:28 she be of the seven? for they all **h** her.	2192
	22:34 when the Pharisees **h** heard that he had	NIG

Mt	22:34 when the Pharisees had heard that he **h**	NIG
	23:30 If we **h** been in the days of our fathers,	NIG
	24:43 that if the goodman of the house **h** known	NIG
	25:16 Then he that **h** received the five talents	NIG
	25:17 And likewise he that **h** *received* two,	NIG
	25:18 But he that **h** received the one went and	NIG
	25:20 *so* he that **h** received five talents came	NIG
	25:22 He also that **h** received two talents came	NIG
	25:24 Then he which **h** received the one talent	NIG
	26: 1 when Jesus **h** finished all these sayings,	NIG
	26: 8 his disciples saw *it*, they **h indignation**,	23
	26:19 And the disciples did as Jesus **h** appointed	NIG
	26:24 it **h** been good for that man if he had not	NIG
	26:24 it had been good for that man if he **h** not	NIG
	26:30 when they **h** sung a hymn, they went	NIG
	26:57 And they that **h** laid hold on Jesus led *him*	NIG
	27: 2 when they **h** bound him, they led *him*	NIG
	27: 3 Judas, which **h** betrayed him, when he	NIG
	27:16 they **h** then a notable prisoner,	2192
	27:18 he knew that for envy they **h** delivered	NIG
	27:26 when he **h** scourged Jesus, he delivered	NIG
	27:29 when they **h** platted a crown of thorns,	NIG
	27:31 after that they **h** mocked him, they took	NIG
	27:34 when he **h** tasted *thereof*, he would not	NIG
	27:50 when he **h** cried again with a loud voice,	NIG
	27:59 And when Joseph **h** taken the body,	NIG
	28:12 **h** taken counsel, they gave large money	NIG
	28:16 into a mountain where Jesus **h** appointed	NIG
Mk	1:19 when he **h** gone a little further thence,	NIG
	1:22 he taught them as *one* that **h** authority,	2192
	1:26 And when the unclean spirit **h** torn him,	NIG
	1:37 when they **h** found him, they said unto	NIG
	1:42 And as soon as he **h** spoken,	NIG
	2: 4 when they **h** broken *it* up, they let down	2192
	2:25 when he **h** need, and was a hungred,	2192
	3: 1 was a man there which **h** a withered	2192
	3: 3 And he saith unto the man which **h**	2192
	3: 5 when he **h** looked round about on them	NIG
	3: 8 they **h** heard what great *things* he did,	NIG
	3:10 For he **h** healed many; insomuch that *they*	NIG
	3:10 for to touch him, as many as **h** plagues.	2192
	4: 5 stony ground, where it **h** not much earth;	2192
	4: 5 sprang up, because *it* **h** no depth of earth:	2192
	4: 6 because it **h** no root, it withered away.	2192
	4:36 And when they **h** sent away the multitude,	NIG
	5: 3 Who **h** *his* dwelling among the tombs;	2192
	5: 4 Because that he **h** been often bound with	NIG
	5: 4 chains **h** been plucked asunder by him,	NIG
	5:15 and **h** the legion, sitting, and clothed,	2192
	5:18 he that **h** been possessed with the devil	NIG
	5:19 and hath **h compassion** on thee.	1653
	5:20 how great *things* Jesus **h** done for him:	NIG
	5:25 which **h** an issue of blood twelve years,	1510
	5:26 And **h** suffered many *things* of many	NIG
	5:26 and **h** spent all that she had,	NIG
	5:26 and **h**ad spent all that she **h**,	3588+3844
	5:27 When she **h** heard of Jesus, came in	NIG
	5:30 in himself that virtue **h** gone out of him,	NIG
	5:32 about to see her that **h** done this *thing*.	NIG
	5:40 But when he **h** put *them* all out, he taketh	NIG
	6:17 Herod himself **h** sent forth and laid hold	NIG
	6:17 brother Philip's wife: for he **h** married her.	NIG
	6:18 John **h** said unto Herod, It is not lawful	NIG
	6:19 Therefore Herodias **h** a **quarrel against**	1758
	6:30 him all *things*, both what they **h** done,	NIG
	6:30 they had done, and what they **h** taught.	NIG
	6:31 And he **h** no **leisure** so much as to eat.	2119
	6:41 And when he **h** taken the five loaves and	NIG
	6:46 when he **h** sent them away, he departed	NIG
	6:49 they supposed *it* **h** been a spirit,	NIG
	6:53 And when they **h** passed over, they came	NIG
	7:14 And when he **h** called all the people unto	NIG
	7:25 young daughter **h** an unclean spirit,	2192
	7:32 and **h** an impediment in his speech;	NIG
	8: 7 And they **h** a few small fishes:	2192
	8: 9 And they that **h** eaten were about four	NIG
	8:14 *the disciples* **h** forgotten to take bread,	NIG
	8:14 neither **h** they in the ship with them more	2192
	8:23 when he **h** spit on his eyes, and put *his*	NIG
	8:33 when he **h** turned about and looked on	NIG
	8:34 when he **h** called the people unto *him*	NIG
	9: 8 when they **h** looked round about,	NIG
	9: 9 tell no *man* what *things* they **h** seen,	NIG
	9:34 for by the way they **h** disputed among	NIG
	9:36 and when he **h** taken him in his arms,	NIG
	10:22 away grieved: for he **h** great possessions.	2192
	11: 6 And they said unto them even as Jesus **h**	NIG
	11:11 when he **h** looked round about upon all	NIG
	12:12 for they knew that he **h** spoken the parable	NIG
	12:22 And the seven **h** her, and left no seed:	2083
	12:23 be of them? for the seven **h** her to wife.	2192
	12:28 perceiving that he **h** answered them well,	NIG
	12:44 she of her want did cast in all that she **h**,	2192
	13:20 except that the Lord **h** shortened *those*	NIG
	14: 4 And there were some that **h indignation**	23
	14:16 city, and found as he **h** said unto them:	NIG
	14:21 were it for that man if he **h** never been	NIG
	14:23 and when he **h** given thanks, he gave *it* to	NIG
	14:26 And when they **h** sung a hymn, they went	NIG
	14:44 And he that betrayed him **h** given them a	NIG
	15: 7 *which lay* bound with them that **h** made	NIG
	15: 7 committed murder in the insurrection.	NIG
	15: 8 *him* to do as he **h** ever done unto them.	NIG
	15:10 For he knew that the chief priests **h**	NIG

Mk	15:15 when he **h** scourged *him*, to be crucified.	NIG
	15:20 when they **h** mocked him, they took off	NIG
	15:24 when they **h** crucified him, they parted	NIG
	15:44 asked him whether he **h** been any while	NIG
	16: 1 and Salome, **h** bought *sweet* spices,	NIG
	16: 9 out of whom he **h** cast seven devils.	NIG
	16:10 and told them that **h** been with him,	NIG
	16:11 when they **h** heard that he was alive,	NIG
	16:11 and **h** been seen of her, believed not.	NIG
	16:14 they believed not them which **h** seen him	NIG
	16:19 after then the Lord **h** spoken unto them,	NIG
Lk	1: 3 having **h** perfect understanding of all	NIG
	1: 7 they **h** no child, because that Elisabeth	1510
	1:22 they perceived that he **h** seen a vision in	NIG
	1:58 her cousins heard how the Lord **h** shewed	NIG
	2:17 when they **h** seen *it*, they made known	NIG
	2:20 praising God for all *the* things that they **h**	NIG
	2:26 before he **h** seen the Lord's Christ.	NIG
	2:36 **h** lived with a husband seven years from	NIG
	2:39 And when they **h** performed all *things*	NIG
	2:43 when they **h** fulfilled the days, as they	NIG
	3:19 and for all the evils which Herod **h** done,	NIG
	4:13 And when the devil **h** ended all	NIG
	4:16 to Nazareth, where he **h** been brought up:	NIG
	4:17 when he **h** opened the book, he found	NIG
	4:33 which **h** a spirit of an unclean devil,	2192
	4:35 And when the devil **h** thrown him in	NIG
	4:40 they that **h** *any* sick with divers diseases	2192
	5: 4 when he **h** left speaking, he said unto	NIG
	5: 6 when they **h** this done, they inclosed a	NIG
	5: 9 at the draught of the fishes which they **h**	NIG
	5:11 And when they **h** brought *their* ships to	NIG
	6: 8 to the man which **h** the withered hand,	2192
	7: 1 Now when he **h** ended all his sayings in	NIG
	7:10 found the servant whole that **h** been sick.	NIG
	7:13 he **h compassion** on her, and said unto	4697
	7:39 when the Pharisee which **h** bidden him	NIG
	7:41 There was a certain creditor which **h** two	1510
	7:42 when they **h** nothing to pay, he frankly	2192
	8: 2 which **h** been healed of evil spirits and	NIG
	8:27 which **h** devils long time, and ware no	2192
	8:29 he **h** commanded the unclean spirit to	NIG
	8:29 oftentimes it **h** caught him: and he was	NIG
	8:42 For he **h** one only daughter, about twelve	1510
	8:43 which **h** spent all *her* living upon	NIG
	8:47 people for what cause she **h** touched him,	NIG
	9: 8 And of some, that Elias **h** appeared;	NIG
	9:10 returned, told him all that they **h** done.	NIG
	9:11 and healed them that **h** need of healing.	2192
	9:36 any of *those* things which they **h** seen.	NIG
	10:13 if the mighty works **h** been done in Tyre	NIG
	10:13 they **h** a great while ago repented, sitting	302
	10:33 he saw him, he **h compassion** *on him*,	4697
	10:39 she **h** a sister called Mary, which also	1510
	11:38 that he **h** not first washed before dinner.	NIG
	12:39 if the goodman of the house **h** known	NIG
	13: 1 whose blood Pilate **h** mingled with their	NIG
	13: 6 A certain *man* **h** a fig tree planted in his	2192
	13:11 there was a woman which **h** a spirit of	2192
	13:14 that Jesus **h** healed on the sabbath day,	NIG
	13:17 And when he **h** said these *things*, all his	NIG
	14: 2 man before him, which **h the dropsy**.	5203
	15: 9 for I have found the piece which I **h** lost.	NIG
	15:11 And he said, A certain man **h** two sons:	2192
	15:14 And when he **h** spent all, there arose a	NIG
	15:20 **h compassion**, and ran, and fell on his	4697
	16: 1 a certain rich man, which **h** a steward;	2192
	16: 1 the same was accused unto him that he **h**	NIG
	16: 8 unjust steward, because he **h** done wisely:	NIG
	17: 6 If ye **h** faith as a grain of mustard seed,	2192
	19:15 him, to whom he **h** given the money,	NIG
	19:15 he might know how much every *man* **h**	NIG
	19:28 And when he **h** thus spoken, he went	NIG
	19:32 and found even as he **h** said unto them.	NIG
	19:37 for all the mighty works that they **h** seen;	NIG
	20:19 for they perceived that he **h** spoken this	NIG
	20:33 of them is she? for seven **h** her to wife.	2192
	21: 4 **h** cast in all the living that she **h**.	2192
	22:13 and found as he **h** said unto them:	NIG
	22:55 when they **h** kindled a fire in the midst	NIG
	22:61 how he **h** said unto him, Before the cock	NIG
	22:64 And when they **h** blindfolded him,	NIG
	23: 8 because *he* **h** heard many *things* of him;	NIG
	23:13 he **h** called together the chief priests	NIG
	23:25 cast into prison, whom they **h** desired;	NIG
	23:46 when Jesus **h** cried with a loud voice,	NIG
	23:51 (The same **h** not consented to the counsel	1510
	24: 1 bringing the spices which they **h** prepared,	NIG
	24:14 of all these *things* which **h** happened.	NIG
	24:21 But we trusted that it **h** been he which	NIG
	24:23 that *they* **h** also seen a vision of angels,	NIG
	24:24 found *it* even so as the women **h** said:	NIG
	24:37 and supposed that *they* **h** seen a spirit.	NIG
	24:40 And when he **h** thus spoken, he shewed	NIG
Jn	2: 9 When the ruler of the feast **h** tasted	NIG
	2:15 And when he **h** made a scourge of small	NIG
	2:22 disciples remembered that he **h** said this	NIG
	2:22 and the word which Jesus **h** said.	NIG
	4: 1 Lord knew how the Pharisees **h** heard	NIG
	4:18 For thou hast **h** five husbands;	2192
	4:50 the man believed the word that Jesus **h**	NIG
	5: 4 made whole of whatsoever disease he **h**.	2722
	5: 5 **h** an infirmity thirty *and* eight years.	2192
	5: 6 knew that he **h** been now a long time	NIG

H

Jn	5:13 for Jesus **h** conveyed himself away,	NIG
	5:15 it was Jesus, which **h** made him whole.	NIG
	5:16 he **h** done these *things* on the sabbath	NIG
	5:16 because he not only **h** broken the sabbath,	NIG
	5:46 For **h** ye believed Moses, ye would have	NIG
	6:11 when he **h** given thanks, he distributed	NIG
	6:13 and above unto them that **h** eaten.	NIG
	6:14 they **h** seen the miracle that Jesus did,	NIG
	6:19 So when they **h** rowed about five and	NIG
	6:23 after that the Lord **h** given thanks:)	NIG
	6:25 And when they **h** found him on the other	NIG
	6:60 his disciples, when they heard *this*, said,	NIG
	7: 9 When he **h** said these *words* unto them,	NIG
	8: 3 and when they **h** set her in the midst,	NIG
	8:10 When Jesus **h** lift up *himself*, and saw	NIG
	8:19 if ye **h** known me, ye should have known	NIG
	9: 6 When he **h** thus spoken, he spat on	NIG
	9: 8 they which before **h** seen him that he was	NIG
	9:15 asked him how he **h** received his sight.	NIG
	9:18 he **h** been blind, and received his sight,	NIG
	9:18 until they called the parents of him that **h**	NIG
	9:22 for the Jews **h** agreed already, that if any	NIG
	9:35 Jesus heard that they **h** cast him out;	NIG
	9:35 and when he **h** found him, he said unto	NIG
	11: 6 he **h** heard therefore that he was sick,	NIG
	11:13 they thought that he **h** spoken of taking of	NIG
	11:17 he found that he **h** lien in the grave four	2192
	11:21 hadst been here, my brother **h** not died.	302
	11:28 when she **h** so said, she went her way,	NIG
	11:32 hadst been here, my brother **h** not died.	302
	11:43 when he thus spoken, he cried with a	NIG
	11:45 and **h** seen *the things* which Jesus did,	NIG
	11:46 and told them what *things* Jesus **h** done.	NIG
	11:57 the Pharisees **h** given a commandment,	NIG
	12: 1 where Lazarus was which **h** been dead,	NIG
	12: 6 and **h** the bag, and bare what was put	2192
	12: 9 whom he **h** raised from the dead.	NIG
	12:14 And Jesus, when he **h** found a young ass,	NIG
	12:16 *that* they **h** done these *things* unto him.	NIG
	12:18 for that they heard that he **h** done this	NIG
	12:37 But though he **h** done so many miracles	NIG
	13: 3 Jesus knowing that the Father **h** given all	NIG
	13:12 So after he **h** washed their feet,	NIG
	13:12 **h** taken his garments, and was set down	NIG
	13:21 When Jesus **h** thus said, he was troubled	NIG
	13:26 when I have dipped *it*. And when he **h**	NIG
	13:29 *of them* thought, because Judas **h** the bag,	2192
	13:29 had the bag, that Jesus **h** said unto him,	2192
	14: 7 If ye **h** known me, ye should have known	NIG
	15:22 If I **h** not come and spoken unto them,	NIG
	15:22 spoken unto them, they **h** not had sin:	2192
	15:22 spoken unto them, they had not **h** sin:	NIG
	15:24 If I **h** not done among them the works	NIG
	15:24 none other *man* did, they **h** not had sin:	2192
	15:24 none other *man* did, they had not **h** sin:	NIG
	17: 5 which I **h** with thee before the world was.	2192
	18: 1 When Jesus **h** spoken these *words*,	NIG
	18: 6 As soon then as he **h** said unto them, I am	NIG
	18:18 officers stood *there*, who **h** made a fire of	NIG
	18:22 And when he **h** thus spoken, one of	NIG
	18:24 Now Annas **h** sent him bound unto	NIG
	18:38 when he **h** said this, he went out again	NIG
	19:23 the soldiers, when they **h** crucified Jesus,	NIG
	19:30 therefore **h** received the vinegar,	NIG
	20:12 the feet, where the body of Jesus **h** lain.	NIG
	20:14 And when she **h** thus said, she turned	NIG
	20:18 told the disciples that she **h** seen the Lord,	NIG
	20:18 *that* he **h** spoken these *things* unto her.	NIG
	20:20 And when he **h** so said, he shewed unto	NIG
	20:22 And when he **h** said this, he breathed on	NIG
	21:15 when they **h** dined, Jesus saith to Simon	NIG
	21:19 when he **h** spoken this, he saith unto	NIG
Ac	1: 2 that he through the Holy Ghost **h** given	NIG
	1: 2 unto the Apostles whom he **h** chosen:	NIG
	1: 9 when he **h** spoken these *things*, while	NIG
	1:17 and **h** obtained part of this ministry.	NIG
	2:30 knowing that God **h** sworn with an oath	NIG
	2:44 were together, and **h** all *things* common;	2192
	2:45 parted them to all *men*, as every man **h**	2192
	3:10 amazement at that which **h** happened	NIG
	3:12 or holiness we **h** made this *man* to walk?	NIG
	3:18 But *those things*, which God before **h**	NIG
	4: 7 And when they **h** set them in the midst,	NIG
	4:13 of them, that they **h** been with Jesus.	NIG
	4:15 But when they **h** commanded them to go	NIG
	4:21 So when they **h** further threatened *them*,	NIG
	4:23 chief priests and elders **h** said unto them.	NIG
	4:31 And when they **h** prayed, the place was	NIG
	4:32 his own; but they **h** all *things* common.	1510
	4:35 unto every man according as he **h** need.	2192
	5:23 when we **h** opened, we found no *man*	NIG
	5:27 And when they **h** brought them, they set	NIG
	5:34 **h** in reputation among all the people,	NIG
	5:40 when they **h** called the apostles,	NIG
	6: 6 and when they **h** prayed, they laid *their*	NIG
	6:15 saw his face as it **h** been the face of an	NIG
	7: 5 seed after him, when *as yet* he **h** no child.	1510
	7:17 God **h** sworn to Abraham, the people	NIG
	7:36 after that he **h** shewed wonders and signs	NIG
	7:44 Our fathers **h** the tabernacle of Witness in	1510
	7:44 as he **h** appointed, speaking unto Moses,	NIG
	7:44 it according to the fashion that he **h** seen.	NIG
	7:60 And when he **h** said this, he fell asleep.	NIG
	8:11 to him they **h** regard, because that of	4337
	8:11 of long time he **h** bewitched them with	NIG

Ac	8:14 that Samaria **h** received the word of God,	NIG
	8:25 they **h** testified and preached the word	NIG
	8:27 who **h** the charge of all her treasure,	1510
	8:27 and **h** come to Jerusalem for to worship,	NIG
	9:18 fell from his eyes **as it h** been: scales;	5616
	9:19 And when he **h** received meat, he was	NIG
	9:27 unto them how he **h** seen the Lord	NIG
	9:27 and that he **h** spoken to him, and how he	NIG
	9:27 how he **h** preached boldly at Damascus in	NIG
	9:31 Then **h** the churches rest throughout all	2192
	9:33 which **h** kept his bed eight years, and was	NIG
	9:37 when they **h** washed, they laid *her* in	NIG
	9:38 the disciples **h** heard that Peter was there,	NIG
	9:41 when he **h** called the saints and widows,	NIG
	10: 8 And when he **h** declared all *these things*	NIG
	10:11 as *it h* been a great sheet knit at the four	NIG
	10:17 *this* vision which he **h** seen should mean,	NIG
	10:17 men which were sent from Cornelius **h**	NIG
	10:24 and **h** called together his kinsmen and	NIG
	10:31 thine alms are **h** in remembrance in	NIG
	11: 1 Gentiles **h** also received the word of God.	NIG
	11: 5 vessel descend, as *it h* been a great sheet,	NIG
	11: 6 Upon the which when I **h** fastened mine	NIG
	11:13 he shewed us how he **h** seen an angel	NIG
	11:23 and **h** seen the grace of God, was glad,	NIG
	11:26 when he **h** found him, he brought him	NIG
	12: 4 And when he **h** apprehended him, he put	NIG
	12:12 And when he **h** considered *the thing*, he	NIG
	12:16 and when they **h** opened *the door*, and	NIG
	12:17 unto them how the Lord **h** brought	NIG
	12:19 when Herod **h** sought for him,	NIG
	12:25 when they **h** fulfilled *their* ministry,	NIG
	13: 1 which **h** been brought up with Herod	NIG
	13: 3 And when they **h** fasted and prayed,	NIG
	13: 5 and they **h** also John to *their* minister.	2192
	13: 6 when they **h** gone through the isle unto	NIG
	13:19 when he **h** destroyed seven nations in	NIG
	13:22 when he **h** removed him, he raised up	NIG
	13:24 When John **h** first preached before his	NIG
	13:29 And when they **h** fulfilled all that was	NIG
	13:36 after he **h** served his own generation by	NIG
	14: 8 his mother's womb, who never **h** walked:	NIG
	14: 9 perceiving that he **h** faith to be healed,	2192
	14:11 when the people saw what Paul **h** done,	NIG
	14:18 that *they* **h** not done sacrifice unto them.	NIG
	14:19 out of the city, supposing he **h** been dead.	NIG
	14:21 And when they **h** preached the gospel to	NIG
	14:21 and **h** taught many, they returned *again* to	NIG
	14:23 And when they **h** ordained them elders in	NIG
	14:23 and **h** prayed with fasting,	NIG
	14:24 after they **h** passed throughout Pisidia,	NIG
	14:25 And when they **h** preached the word in	NIG
	14:26 whence they **h** been recommended to	NIG
	14:27 and **h** gathered the church together,	NIG
	14:27 they rehearsed all that God **h** done with	NIG
	14:27 how he **h** opened the door of faith unto	NIG
	15: 2 and Barnabas **h** no small dissension and	1096
	15: 4 they declared all *things* that God **h** done	NIG
	15: 7 And when there **h** been much disputing,	NIG
	15:12 God **h** wrought among the Gentiles	NIG
	15:13 And after they **h** held their peace,	NIG
	15:30 when they **h** gathered the multitude	NIG
	15:31 *Which* when they **h** read, they rejoiced for	NIG
	15:33 And after they **h** tarried *there* a space,	NIG
	16: 6 when they **h** gone throughout Phrygia	NIG
	16:10 And after he **h** seen the vision,	NIG
	16:10 gathering that the Lord **h** called us	NIG
	16:23 And when they **h** laid many stripes upon	NIG
	16:27 supposing that the prisoners **h** been fled.	NIG
	16:34 when he **h** brought them into his house,	NIG
	16:40 and when they **h** seen the brethren,	NIG
	17: 1 Now when they **h** passed through	NIG
	17: 9 And when they **h** taken security of Jason,	NIG
	17:13 But when the Jews of Thessalonica **h**	NIG
	18: 2 that Claudius **h** commanded all Jews to	NIG
	18:18 *his* head in Cenchrea: for he **h** a vow.	2192
	18:22 And when he **h** landed at Cesarea,	NIG
	18:23 And after he **h** spent some time *there*, he	NIG
	18:26 whom when Aquila and Priscilla **h** heard,	NIG
	18:27 helped them much which **h** believed	NIG
	19: 6 when Paul **h** laid *his* hands upon them,	NIG
	19:13 upon them to call over them which **h**	2192
	19:21 when he **h** passed through Macedonia and	NIG
	19:35 And when the townclerk **h** appeased	NIG
	19:41 And when he **h** thus spoken, he dismissed	NIG
	20: 2 And when he **h** gone over those parts,	NIG
	20: 2 and **h** given them much exhortation,	NIG
	20:11 was come up *again*, and **h** broken bread,	NIG
	20:13 for so he **h** appointed, minding himself to	1510
	20:16 For Paul **h** determined to sail by Ephesus,	NIG
	20:36 And when he **h** thus spoken, he kneeled	NIG
	21: 1 were gotten from them, and **h** launched,	NIG
	21: 3 when we **h** discovered Cyprus, we left	NIG
	21: 5 when we **h** accomplished *those* days,	1096
	21: 6 And when we **h** taken our leave one of	NIG
	21: 7 And when we **h** finished *our* course from	NIG
	21: 9 And the same *man* **h** four daughters,	1510
	21:19 And when he **h** saluted them, he declared	NIG
	21:19 declared particularly what *things* God **h**	NIG
	21:29 they **h** seen before with him in the city	1510
	21:29 whom they supposed that Paul **h** brought	NIG
	21:33 who he was, and what he **h** done.	1510
	21:40 And when he **h** given *him* licence,	NIG
	22:29 a Roman, and because he **h** bound him.	1510
	23: 7 And when he **h** so said, there arose a	NIG

Ac	23:12 eat nor drink till they **h** killed Paul.	NIG
	23:13 they were more *than* forty which **h**	NIG
	23:30 say before thee what *they* **h** against him.	NIG
	23:34 And when the governor **h** read *the letter*,	NIG
	24:10 that the governor **h** beckoned unto him	NIG
	24:19 and object, if they **h** ought against me.	2192
	25:12 when he **h** conferred with the council,	NIG
	25:14 And when they **h** been there many days,	NIG
	25:19 But **h** certain questions against him of	2192
	25:21 But when Paul **h** appealed to be reserved	NIG
	25:25 But when I found that he **h** committed	NIG
	25:26 king Agrippa, that, after examination **h**,	1096
	26:30 when he **h** thus spoken, the king rose	NIG
	26:32 at liberty, if he **h** not appealed unto Cesar.	NIG
	27: 4 And when we **h** launched from thence,	NIG
	27: 5 And when we **h** sailed over the sea of	NIG
	27: 7 And when we **h** sailed slowly many days,	NIG
	27:13 supposing that *they* **h** obtained *their*	NIG
	27:16 **h** much work to come by the boat: 2480+3433	
	27:17 Which when they **h** taken up, they used	NIG
	27:28 and when they **h** gone a little further,	NIG
	27:30 they **h** let down the boat into the sea,	NIG
	27:35 when he **h** thus spoken, he took bread,	NIG
	27:35 And when he **h** broken *it*, he began to eat.	NIG
	27:38 And when they **h** eaten enough,	NIG
	27:40 And when they **h** taken up the anchors,	NIG
	28: 3 And when Paul **h** gathered a bundle of	NIG
	28: 6 but after they **h** looked a great while,	NIG
	28: 9 which **h** diseases in the island, came,	2192
	28:11 which **h** wintered in the isle, *whose* sign	NIG
	28:18 Who, when they **h** examined me,	NIG
	28:19 not that I **h** ought to accuse my nation of.	2192
	28:23 And when they **h** appointed him a day,	NIG
	28:25 after that Paul **h** spoken one word,	NIG
	28:29 when he **h** said these *words*, the Jews	NIG
	28:29 and **h** great reasoning among themselves.	2192
Ro	1: 2 he **h** promised afore by his prophets	NIG
	4:11 faith which he **h** *yet* being uncircumcised:	NIG
	4:12 which he **h** being *yet* uncircumcised.	NIG
	4:21 what he **h** promised, he was able also to	NIG
	5:14 even over them that **h** not sinned after	NIG
	6:21 What fruit **h** ye then *in those things*	2192
	7: 7 I **h** not known sin, but by the law: for I	NIG
	7: 7 for I **h** not known lust, except the law had	NIG
	7: 7 the law **h** said, Thou shalt not covet.	NIG
	9:10 when Rebecca also **h** conceived by one,	2192
	9:23 which he **h** afore prepared unto glory,	NIG
	9:29 Except the Lord of sabaoth **h** left us a seed,	NIG
	9:29 we **h** been as Sodoma, and been made like	302
1Co	1:15 Lest any should say that I **h** baptized in	NIG
	2: 8 for **h** they known *it*, they would not have	1487
	7:29 have wives be as though they **h** none;	2192
	11:24 And when he **h** given thanks, he brake *it*,	NIG
	11:25 when *he* **h** supped, saying, This cup is	NIG
	14:19 Yet in the church I **h** rather speak five	2309
2Co	1: 9 But we **h** the sentence of death in	2192
	1:12 have **h** our conversation in the world,	390
	2:13 I **h** no rest in my spirit, because I found	2192
	3:10 made glorious **h** no glory in this respect,	1392
	7: 5 our flesh **h** no rest, but *we were* troubled	2192
	7:12 *I did it* not for his cause that **h** done	NIG
	8: 6 that as he **h** begun, so he would also finish	NIG
	8:15 that *h gathered* much had nothing over;	NIG
	8:15 that *had gathered* much **h** nothing **over**;	4121
	8:15 and he that *h gathered* little had no lack;	NIG
	8:15 and he that *had gathered* little **h** no lack.	1641
	9: 5 whereof ye **h** notice before, that the	4293
	11:21 as though we **h** been weak.	NIG
Gal	1:23 But they heard only, That he which	1510
	2: 2 any means I should run, or **h** run, in vain.	NIG
	3:21 if there **h** been a law given which could	NIG
	4:15 bear you record, that if *it h* been possible,	NIG
	4:22 For it is written, that Abraham **h** two sons,	2192
Eph	1: 9 according to his good pleasure which he **h**	NIG
	2: 3 **h** our conversation in times past in the	390
Php	2:26 that ye **h** heard that he had been sick.	NIG
	2:26 that ye had heard that he **h** been sick.	NIG
	2:27 God **h** mercy on him; and not on him	1653
	3:12 Not as though I **h** already attained,	NIG
1Th	1: 9 manner of entering in we **h** unto you,	2192
	2: 2 But even after that we **h** suffered before,	NIG
2Th	2:12 truth, but **h** pleasure in unrighteousness.	NIG
Tit	1: 5 elders in every city, as I **h** appointed thee:	NIG
Heb	1: 3 by himself purged our sins,	NIG
	2:14 destroy him that **h** the power of death,	2192
	3:16 some, when they **h** heard, did provoke:	NIG
	3:17 *was it* not with them that **h** sinned,	NIG
	4: 8 For if Jesus **h** given them rest, *then*	NIG
	5: 7 when he **h** offered up prayers and	NIG
	6:15 And so, after he **h** patiently endured,	NIG
	6:15 and blessed him that **h** the promises.	2192
	8: 7 For if that first *covenant* **h** been faultless,	NIG
	9: 1 Then verily the first *covenant* **h** also	2192
	9: 4 Which **h** the golden censer, and the ark	2192
	9: 4 *was* the golden pot that **h** manna,	2192
	9:19 For when Moses **h** spoken every precept	NIG
	10: 2 should have **h** no more conscience of sins.	2192
	10: 6 sacrifices for sin thou hast **h** no **pleasure**.	2106
	10:12 But this *man*, after he **h** offered one	NIG
	10:15 to us: for after that he **h** said before,	NIG
	10:34 For ye **h** compassion *of me* in my bonds,	4834
	11: 5 not found, because God **h** translated him:	NIG
	11: 5 for before his translation he **h** this	NIG
	11:11 she judged him faithful who **h** promised.	NIG

Heb 11:15	if they **h** been mindful of that *country*	NIG
11:15	they might have **h** opportunity to have	2192
11:17	he that **h** received the promises offered	NIG
11:26	for he **h** respect unto the recompence of	NIG
11:31	when she **h** received the spies with peace.	NIG
11:36	And others **h** trial of *cruel* mockings with	2983
12: 9	we have **h** fathers of our flesh	2192
Jas 2:21	when he **h** offered Isaac his son upon	NIG
2:25	when she **h** received the messengers,	NIG
2:25	and **h** sent *them* out another way?	NIG
1Pe 2:10	**h** not obtained mercy, but now have	NIG
2Pe 2:21	For it **h** been better for them not to have	NIG
1Jn 2: 7	an old commandment which ye **h** from	2192
2:19	for if they **h** been of us, they would *no*	NIG
2Jn 1: 5	but *that* which we **h** from the beginning,	2192
3Jn 1:13	I **h** many *things* to write,	2192
Rev 1:16	And he **h** in his right hand seven stars;	2192
4: 4	and they **h** on their heads crowns of gold.	2192
4: 7	and the third beast **h** a face as a man,	2192
4: 8	And the four beasts each of them six	2192
5: 6	stood a Lamb as *it* **h** been slain,	NIG
5: 8	And when he **h** taken the book, the four	NIG
6: 2	and he that sat on him **h** a bow;	2192
6: 3	And when he **h** opened the second seal,	NIG
6: 5	And when he **h** opened the third seal,	NIG
6: 5	he that sat on him **h** a pair of balances in	2192
6: 7	And when he **h** opened the fourth seal,	NIG
6: 9	when he **h** opened the fifth seal, I saw	NIG
6:12	And I beheld when he **h** opened the sixth	NIG
8: 1	And when he **h** opened the seventh seal,	NIG
8: 6	And the seven angels which **h** the seven	2192
8: 9	which were in the sea, and **h** life, died;	2192
9: 8	And they **h** hair as the hair of women,	2192
9: 9	And they **h** breastplates, as *it were*	2192
9:10	And they **h** tails like unto scorpions,	2192
9:11	And they **h** a king over them, *which is*	2192
9:14	Saying to the sixth angel which **h**	2192
9:19	and **h** heads, and with them they do hurt.	2192
10: 2	And he **h** in his hand a little book open:	2192
10: 3	when he **h** cried, seven thunders uttered	NIG
10: 4	when the seven thunders **h** uttered their	NIG
10:10	and as soon as I **h** eaten it, my belly was	NIG
13:11	and he **h** two horns like a lamb,	2192
13:14	he **h** power to do in the sight of the beast;	1325
13:14	which **h** the wound by a sword,	2192
13:15	he **h** power to give life unto the image	1325
13:17	save he that **h** the mark, or the name of	2192
14:18	from the altar, which **h** power over fire;	2192
14:18	with a loud cry to him that **h** the sharp	2192
15: 2	them that **h** gotten the victory over	NIG
16: 2	grievous sore upon the men which **h**	2192
17: 1	the seven angels which **h** the seven vials,	2192
18:19	wherein were made rich all that **h** ships in	2192
19:12	he **h** a name written, that no *man* knew,	2192
19:20	with which he deceived them that **h**	NIG
20: 4	and which **h** not worshipped the beast,	NIG
20: 4	neither **h** received *his* mark upon their	NIG
21: 9	**h** the seven vials full of the seven last	2192
21:12	And **h** a wall great and high,	2192
21:12	**h** twelve gates, and at the gates twelve	2192
21:14	And the wall of the city **h** twelve	2192
21:15	he that talked with me **h** a golden reed	2192
21:23	And the city **h** no need of the sun,	2192
22: 8	heard *them*. And when I **h** heard and	NIG

HADAD (14) [HADADEZER, HADADRIMMON]

Ge 36:35	Husham died, and **H** the son of Bedad,	1908
36:36	**H** died, and Samlah of Masrekah reigned	1908
1Ki 11:14	adversary unto Solomon, **H** the Edomite:	1908
11:17	That **H** fled, he and certain Edomites of	111
11:17	to go *into* Egypt; **H** *being yet* a little child.	1908
11:19	**H** found great favour in the sight of	1908
11:21	when **H** heard in Egypt that David slept	1908
11:21	**H** said to Pharaoh, Let me depart, that I	1908
11:25	beside the mischief that **H** *did:* and	1908
1Ch 1:30	and Dumah, Massa, **H**, and Tema,	2301
1:46	Husham was dead, **H** the son of Bedad,	1908
1:47	when **H** was dead, Samlah of Masrekah	1908
1:50	was dead, **H** reigned in his stead:	1908
1:51	**H** died also. And the dukes of Edom were;	1908

HADADEZER (9) [HADAD, HADAREZER]

2Sa 8: 3	David smote also **H**, the son of Rehob,	1909
8: 5	came to succour **H** king of Zobah,	1909
8: 7	of gold that were on the servants of **H**,	1909
8: 8	Betah, and from Berothai, cities of **H**,	1909
8: 9	that David had smitten all the host of **H**,	1909
8:10	because he had fought against **H**,	1909
8:10	for **H** had wars with Toi. And *Joram*	1909
8:12	of Amalek, and of the spoil of **H**, son of	1909
1Ki 11:23	fled from his lord **H** king of Zobah:	1909

HADADRIMMON (1) [HADAD, RIMMON]

Zec 12:11	as the mourning of **H** in the valley of	1910

HADAR (2) [HADAREZER]

Ge 25:15	**H**, and Tema, Jetur, Naphish,	2316
36:39	Achbor died, and **H** reigned in his stead:	1924

HADAREZER (12) [HADADEZER, HADAR]

2Sa 10:16	**H** sent, and brought out the Syrians that	1928
10:16	Shobach the captain of the host of **H**	1928
10:19	all the kings *that were* servants to **H**	1928
1Ch 18: 3	David smote **H** king of Zobah unto	1928
18: 5	Damascus came to help **H** king of Zobah,	1928

1Ch 18: 7	of gold that were on the servants of **H**,	1928
18: 8	from Tibhath, and from Chun, cities of **H**,	1928
18: 9	smitten all the host of **H** king of Zobah;	1928
18:10	because he had fought against **H**,	1928
18:10	for **H** had war with Tou;) and *with him*	1928
19:16	Shophach the captain of the host of **H**	1928
19:19	when the servants of **H** saw that they	1928

HADASHAH (1)

Jos 15:37	Zenan, and **H**, and Migdal-gad,	2322

HADASSAH (1) [ESTHER]

Est 2: 7	he brought up **H**, that *is*, Esther,	1919

HADATTAH See HAZOR HADATTAH

HADID (3)

Ezr 2:33	The children of Lod, **H**, and Ono,	2307
Ne 7:37	The children of Lod, **H**, and Ono,	2307
11:34	**H**, Zeboim, Neballat,	2307

HADLAI (1)

2Ch 28:12	son of Shallum, and Amasa the son of **H**,	2311

HADORAM (4)

Ge 10:27	And **H**, and Uzal, and Diklah,	1913
1Ch 1:21	**H** also, and Uzal, and Diklah,	1913
18:10	sent **H** his son to king David, to inquire	1913
2Ch 10:18	king Rehoboam sent **H** that *was* over	1913

HADRACH (1)

Zec 9: 1	of the word of the LORD in the land of **H**,	2317

HADST (22) [HAVE]

Ge 30:30	For *it was* little which thou **h**	1961+3807.1
31:42	surely thou **h** sent me away now empty.	NIH
Jdg 15: 2	I verily thought that thou **h** utterly hated	NIH
1Sa 24:18	thou **h** hasted and come to meet me,	NIH
2Sa 2:27	unless thou **h** spoken, surely then in	NIH
2Ki 13:19	thou smitten Syria till *thou* **h**	NIH
13:19	hadst thou smitten Syria till *thou* **h**	NIH
Ezr 9:14	be angry with us till *thou* **h** consumed *us,*	NIH
Ne 9:15	land which thou **h** sworn to give them.	5375
9:23	*concerning* which thou **h** promised to	NIH
Ps 44: 3	because thou **h** a *favour* unto them.	7521
60:10	not thou, O God, *which* **h** cast us off?	NIH
90: 2	or ever thou **h** formed the earth and	NIH
Isa 26:15	thou **h** removed *it* far *unto* all the ends of	NIH
48:18	O that thou **h** hearkened to my	NIH
Jer 3: 3	thou **h** a whore's forehead,	1961+3807.1
Jnh 2: 3	For thou **h** cast me *into* the deep,	NIH
Lk 19:42	*If thou* **h** *known, even thou, at least*	NIG
Jn 11:21	Lord, if thou **h** been here, my brother had	NIG
11:32	unto him, Lord, if thou **h** been here,	NIG
1Co 4: 7	thou glory, as if thou **h** not received *it?*	NIG
Heb 10: 8	neither **h** pleasure *therein:* which are	NIG

HAELEPH See ELEPH

HAFT (1)

Jdg 3:22	the **h** also went in after the blade;	5325

HAGABA (1) [HAGABA, HAGABAH]

Ezr 2:46	children of **H**, the children of Shalmai,	2285

HAGABA (1) [HAGAB]

Ne 7:48	children of Lebana, the children of **H**,	2286

HAGABAH (1) [HAGAB]

Ezr 2:45	the children of **H**, the children of Akkub,	2286

HAGAR (12) [AGAR]

Ge 16: 1	an Egyptian, whose name *was* **H**.	1904
16: 3	Sarai Abram's wife took **H** her maid	1904
16: 4	he went in unto **H**, and she conceived:	1904
16: 8	he said, **H**, Sarai's maid, whence camest	1904
16:15	**H** bare Abram a son: and Abram called	1904
16:15	his son's name, which **H** bare, Ishmael.	1904
16:16	when **H** bare Ishmael to Abram.	1904
21: 9	Sarah saw the son of **H** the Egyptian,	1904
21:14	and a bottle of water, and gave *it* unto **H**,	1904
21:17	angel of God called to **H** out of heaven,	1904
21:17	and said unto her, What aileth thee, **H**?	1904
25:12	Abraham's son, whom **H** the Egyptian,	1904

HAGARENES (1) [HAGARITES]

Ps 83: 6	the Ishmaelites; of Moab, and the **H**;	1905

HAGARITES (3) [HAGARENES, HAGERITE]

1Ch 5:10	days of Saul they made war with the **H**,	1905
5:19	they made war with the **H**, with Jetur,	1905
5:20	the **H** were delivered into their hand,	1905

HAGERITE (1) [HAGARITES]

1Ch 27:31	over the flocks *was* Jaziz the **H**. All these	1905

HAGGAI (11)

Ezr 5: 1	**H** the prophet, and Zechariah the son of	2292
6:14	the prophesying of **H** the prophet	2292
Hag 1: 1	came the word of the LORD by **H**	2292
1: 3	came the words of **H** the prophet, as the LORD	2292
1:12	by the hand of **H** the prophet, and	2292
1:13	spake **H** the LORD's messenger in	2292
2: 1	came the word of the LORD by the prophet **H**	2292
2:10	came the word of the LORD by **H**	2292
2:13	said **H**, If *one that is* unclean *by* a dead	2292
2:14	answered **H**, and said, So *is* this people,	2292

Hag 2:20	again the word of the LORD came unto **H**	2292

HAGGERI (1)

1Ch 11:38	brother of Nathan, Mibhar the son of **H**,	1905

HAGGI (2) [HAGGITES]

Ge 46:16	and Ezbon, Eri, and Arodi,	2291
Nu 26:15	of **H**, the family of the Haggites: of Shuni,	2291

HAGGIAH (1)

1Ch 6:30	Shimea his son, **H** his son, Asaiah his son.	2293

HAGGITES (1) [HAGGI]

Nu 26:15	of Haggi, the family of the **H**: of Shuni,	2291

HAGGITH (5)

2Sa 3: 4	the fourth, Adonijah the son of **H**;	2294
1Ki 1: 5	Adonijah the son of **H** exalted himself,	2294
1:11	that Adonijah the son of **H** doth reign,	2294
2:13	Adonijah the son of **H** came to Bath-sheba	2294
1Ch 3: 2	the fourth, Adonijah the son of **H**:	2294

HAGRI See HAGGERI

HAGRITE See HAGARITES; HAGERITE

HAI (2) [AI]

Ge 12: 8	Beth-el on the west, and **H** on the east:	5857
13: 3	at the beginning, between Beth-el and **H**;	5857

HAIL (36) [HAILSTONES, HAIL-STONES]

Ex 9:18	I will cause it to rain a very grievous **h**,	1259
9:19	the **h** shall come down upon them,	1259
9:22	there may be **h** in all the land of Egypt,	1259
9:23	the LORD sent thunder and **h**, and the fire	1259
9:23	the LORD rained **h** upon the land of	1259
9:24	So there was **h**, and fire mingled with	1259
9:24	fire mingled with the **h**, very grievous,	1259
9:25	the **h** smote throughout all the land of	1259
9:25	the **h** smote every herb of the field,	1259
9:26	children of Israel *were*, was there no **h**.	1259
9:28	be no *more* mighty thunderings and **h**;	1259
9:29	neither shall there be any more **h**;	1259
9:33	the thunders and **h** ceased, and the rain	1259
9:34	and the **h** and the thunders were ceased,	1259
10: 5	which remaineth unto you from the **h**,	1259
10:12	of the land, *even* all that the **h** hath left.	1259
10:15	all the fruit of the trees which the **h** had	1259
Job 38:22	or hast thou seen the treasures of the **h**,	1259
Ps 78:47	He destroyed their vines with **h**,	1259
78:48	He gave up their cattle also to the **h**,	1259
105:32	He gave them **h** for rain, *and* flaming fire	1259
148: 8	Fire, and **h**; snow, and vapour; stormy	1259
Isa 28: 2	*which* as a tempest of **h** *and* a destroying	1259
28:17	the **h** shall sweep away the refuge of lies,	1259
32:19	When it shall **h**, coming down *on*	1258
Hag 2:17	with **h** *in* all the labours of your hands;	1259
Mt 26:49	he came to Jesus, and said, **H**, master;	5463
27:29	and mocked him, saying, **H**, King of	5463
28: 9	behold, Jesus met them, saying, *All* **h**.	5463
Mk 15:18	began to salute him, **H**, King of the Jews.	5463
Lk 1:28	said, **H**, *thou that art* highly favoured,	5463
Jn 19: 3	And said, **H**, King of the Jews:	5463
Rev 8: 7	there followed **h** and fire mingled with	5464
11:19	and an earthquake, and great **h**.	5464
16:21	And there fell upon men a great **h** out of	5464
16:21	because of the plague of the **h**;	5464

HAILSTONES, HAIL-STONES (7) [HAIL, STONE]

Jos 10:11	which died with **h** than *they*	68+1259+1886.1
Ps 18:12	clouds passed, and coals of fire.	1259
18:13	gave his voice; **h** and coals of fire.	1259
Isa 30:30	*with* scattering, and tempest, and **h**,	68+1259
Eze 13:11	ye, O *great* **h**, shall fall; and a stormy	68+417
13:13	and *great* **h** in *my* fury to consume *it.*	68+417
38:22	and *great* **h**, fire, and brimstone.	68+417

HAIR (64) [HAIRS, HAIRY]

Ex 25: 4	and scarlet, and fine linen, and goats' **h**,	NIH
26: 7	thou shalt make curtains of goats' **h** to be	NIH
35: 6	and scarlet, and fine linen, and goats' **h**,	NIH
35:23	goats' **h**, and red skins of rams,	NIH
35:26	stirred them up in wisdom spun goats' **h**.	NIH
36:14	he made curtains of goats' **h** for the tent	NIH
Lev 13: 3	when the **h** in the plague is turned white,	8181
13: 4	and the **h** thereof be not turned white;	8181
13:10	it have turned the **h** white, and *there be*	8181
13:20	skin, and the **h** thereof be turned white;	8181
13:25	*if* the **h** in the bright spot be turned white,	8181
13:26	there be no white **h** in the bright spot,	8181
13:30	*be* in it a yellow thin **h**; then the priest	8181
13:31	skin, and *that there is* no black **h** in it;	8181
13:32	there be in it no yellow **h**, and the scall	8181
13:36	the priest shall not seek for yellow **h**:	8181
13:37	*that* there is black **h** grown up therein,	8181
13:40	the man whose **h** is *fallen off* his head,	4803
13:41	he that hath all his **h** *fallen off* from the part	4803
14: 8	shave off all his **h**, and wash *himself* in	8181
14: 9	*that* he shall shave all his **h** off his head	8181
14: 9	even all his **h** he shall shave off:	8181
Nu 6: 5	let the locks of the **h** of his head grow.	8181
6:18	shall take the **h** of the head of his	8181
6:19	after the **h** of his separation is shaven:	NIH
31:20	all work of goats' **h**, and all things made	NIH
Jdg 16:22	Howbeit the **h** of his head began to grow	8181
20:16	one could sling stones at a **h** breadth,	8185

H

1Sa	14:45 there shall not one **h** of his head fall to	8185
	19:13 put a pillow of goats' **h** for his bolster,	NIH
	19:16 with a pillow of goats' **h** for his bolster.	NIH
2Sa	14:11 there shall not one **h** of thy son fall to	8185
	14:26 because the **h** was heavy on him,	NIH
	14:26 he weighed the **h** of his head at two	8181
1Ki	1:52 there shall not a **h** of him fall to the earth:	8185
Ezr	9: 3 pluckt off the **h** of my head and of my	8181
Ne	13:25 pluckt off their **h**, and made them swear	4803
Job	4:15 my face; the **h** of my flesh stood up:	8185
SS	4: 1 thy **h** is as a flock of goats, that appear	8181
	6: 5 thy **h** is as a flock of goats that appear	8181
	7: 5 and the **h** of thine head like purple;	1803
Isa	3:24 instead of **well set h** baldness;	4639+4748
	7:20 Assyria, the head, and the **h** of the feet:	8181
	50: 6 cheeks to them that **plucked off** the **h**.	4803
Jer	7:29 Cut off thine **h**, O Jerusalem, and cast it	5145
Eze	5: 1 thee balances to weigh, and divide the **h**.	NIH
	16: 7 **h** is grown, whereas thou wast naked	8181
Da	3:27 nor was a **h** of their head singed,	8177
	7: 9 and the **h** of his head like the pure wool;	8177
Mt	3: 4 same John had his raiment of camel's **h**,	2359
	5:36 canst not make one **h** white or black.	2359
Mk	1: 6 And John was clothed with camel's **h**,	2359
Lk	21:18 there shall not a **h** of your head perish.	2359
Jn	11: 2 and wiped his feet with her **h**,	2359
	12: 3 of Jesus, and wiped his feet with her **h**:	2359
Ac	27:34 for there shall not a **h** fall from the head	2359
1Co	11:14 that, if a man **have long h**, it is a shame	2863
	11:15 But if a woman **have long h**, it is a glory	2863
	11:15 for her **h** is given her for a covering.	2864
1Ti	2: 9 and sobriety; not with **broided h**,	4117
1Pe	3: 3 that outward adorning of plaiting the **h**,	2359
Rev	6:12 the sun became black as sackcloth of **h**,	5155
	9: 8 And they had **h** as the hair of women,	2359
	9: 8 And they had hair as the **h** of women,	2359

HAIRS (15) [HAIR]

Ge	42:38 ye bring down my **gray h** with sorrow	7872
	44:29 shall bring down my **gray h** with sorrow	7872
	44:31 servants shall bring down the **gray h** of	7872
Lev	13:21 there be no white **h** therein, and if it be	8181
Dt	32:25 the suckling also with the man of **gray h**.	7872
Ps	40:12 they are moe than the **h** of mine head:	8185
	69: 4 a cause are moe than the **h** of mine head:	8185
Isa	46: 4 even to **hoar h** will I carry you: I have	7872
Da	4:33 till his **h** were grown like eagles' feathers,	8177
Hos	7: 9 yea, **gray h** are here and there upon him,	7872
Mt	10:30 But the very **h** of your head are all	2359
Lk	7:38 did wipe them with the **h** of her head,	2359
	7:44 and wiped them with the **h** of her head.	2359
	12: 7 But even the very **h** of your head are all	2359
Rev	1:14 His head and his **h** were white like wool,	2359

HAIRY (5) [HAIR]

Ge	25:25 came out red, all over like a **h** garment;	8181
	27:11 Esau my brother is a **h** man, and I am a	8163
	27:23 him not, because his hands were **h**,	8163
2Ki	1: 8 He was a **h** man, and girt with a girdle of	8181
Ps	68:21 the **h** scalp of such a one as goeth on still	8181

HAKILAH See HACHILAH

HAKKATAN (1)

Ezr	8:12 Johanan the son of **H**, and with him an	6997

HAKKOZ (1)

1Ch	24:10 The seventh to **H**, the eighth to Abijah,	6976

HAKUPHA (2)

Ezr	2:51 the children of **H**, the children of Harhur,	2709
Ne	7:53 the children of **H**, the children of Harhur,	2709

HALAH (3)

2Ki	17: 6 them in **H** and in Habor by the river	2477
	18:11 put them in **H** and in Habor by the river	2477
1Ch	5:26 brought them unto **H**, and Habor,	2477

HALAK (2)

Jos	11:17 Even from the mount **H**, that goeth up to	2510
	12: 7 of Lebanon even unto the mount **H**,	2510

HALE (1) [HALING]

Lk	12:58 lest he **h** thee to the judge, and the judge	2694

HALF (136)

Ge	24:22 a golden earring of **h a shekel** weight,	1235
Ex	24: 6 Moses took **h** of the blood, and put it in	2677
	24: 6 of the blood he sprinkled on the altar.	2677
	25:10 and a **h** shall be the length thereof,	2677
	25:10 a cubit and a **h** the breadth thereof,	2677
	25:10 and a cubit and a **h** the height thereof,	2677
	25:17 and a **h** shall be the length thereof,	2677
	25:17 and a cubit and a **h** the breadth thereof,	2677
	25:23 and a cubit and a **h** the height thereof,	2677
	26:12 the **h** curtain that remaineth, shall hang	2677
	26:16 and a **h** the breadth of one board.	2677
	30:13 **h** a shekel after the shekel of the	4276
	30:13 a **h** shekel shall be the offering of	4276
	30:15 poor shall give less than **h a shekel**,	4276
	30:23 and of sweet cinnamon **h so much**,	4276
	36:21 the breadth of a board one cubit and a **h**.	2677
	37: 1 two cubits and a **h** was the length of it,	2677
	37: 1 a cubit and a **h** the breadth of it,	2677
	37: 1 of it, and a cubit and a **h** the height of it:	2677
	37: 6 cubits and a **h** was the length thereof,	2677

Ex	37: 6 one cubit and a **h** the breadth thereof.	2677
	37:10 and a cubit and a **h** the height thereof:	2677
	38:26 bekah for every man, that is, **h** a shekel,	4276
Lev	6:20 **h** of it in the morning, and half thereof at	4276
	6:20 in the morning, and **h** thereof at night.	4276
Nu	12:12 whom the flesh is **h** consumed when he	2677
	15: 9 deals of flour mingled with **h** a hin of oil.	2677
	15:10 shalt bring for a drink offering **h** a hin	2677
	28:14 their drink offerings shall be **h** a hin of	2677
	31:29 Take it of their **h**, and give it unto Eleazar	4276
	31:30 the children of Israel's **h**, thou shalt take	4276
	31:36 the **h**, which was the portion of them	4275
	31:42 of the children of Israel's **h**, which Moses	4276
	31:43 (Now the **h** that pertained unto	4275
	31:47 Even of the children of Israel's **h**,	4276
	32:33 unto the tribe of Manasseh the son of	2677
	34:13 unto the nine tribes, and to the **h** tribe:	2677
	34:14 the tribe of Manasseh have received	2677
	34:15 tribe have received their inheritance	2677
Dt	3:12 **h** mount Gilead, and the cities thereof,	2677
	3:13 Og, gave I unto the **h** tribe of Manasseh;	2677
	3:16 the valley, and the border, even unto	8432
Jos	1:12 to **h** the tribe of Manasseh, spake Joshua,	2677
	4:12 of Gad, and the **h** tribe of Manasseh,	2677
	8:33 them over against mount Gerizim,	2677
	8:33 and **h** of them over against mount Ebal;	2677
	12: 2 h Gilead, even unto the river Jabbok,	2677
	12: 5 and the Maachathites, and **h** Gilead,	2677
	12: 6 the Gadites, and the **h** tribe of Manasseh.	2677
	13: 7 nine tribes, and the **h** tribe of Manasseh,	2677
	13:25 the land of the children of Ammon,	2677
	13:29 Moses gave inheritance unto the **h** tribe	2677
	13:29 this was the possession of the **h** tribe of	2677
	13:31 **h** Gilead, and Ashtaroth, and Edrei,	2677
	13:31 to the **one h** of the children of Machir	2677
	14: 2 for the nine tribes, and for the	2677
	14: 3 and a tribe on the other side Jordan:	2677
	18: 7 Reuben, and **h** the tribe of Manasseh,	2677
	21: 5 out of the **h** tribe of Manasseh, ten cities.	2677
	21: 6 out of the **h** tribe of Manasseh in Bashan,	2677
	21:25 out of the **h** tribe of Manasseh, Tanach	4276
	21:27 out of the other **h** tribe of Manasseh they	2677
	22: 1 the Gadites, and the **h** tribe of Manasseh,	2677
	22: 7 to the **one h** of the tribe of Manasseh	2677
	22: 7 unto the other **h** thereof gave Joshua	2677
	22: 9 and the **h** tribe of Manasseh returned,	2677
	22:10 **h** tribe of Manasseh built there an altar	2677
	22:11 h tribe of Manasseh have built an altar	2677
	22:13 of Gad, and to the **h** tribe of Manasseh,	2677
	22:15 of Gad, and to the **h** tribe of Manasseh,	2677
	22:21 and the **h** tribe of Manasseh answered,	2677
1Sa	14:14 within as it were a **h** acre of land,	2677
2Sa	10: 4 shaved off the **one h** of their beards,	2677
	18: 3 if **h** of us die, will they care for us:	2677
	19:40 the king, and also **h** the people of Israel.	2677
1Ki	3:25 give **h** to the one, and half to the other.	2677
	3:25 give half to the one, and **h** to the other.	2677
	7:31 the work of the base, a cubit and a **h**:	2677
	7:32 of a wheel was a cubit and a cubit.	2677
	7:35 a round compass of a **h** cubit high:	2677
	10: 7 and behold, the **h** was not told me:	2677
	13: 8 If thou wilt give me **h** thine house, I will	2677
	16: 9 captain of **h** his chariots, conspired	4276
	16:21 **h** of the people followed Tibni the son of	2677
	16:21 to make him king; and **h** followed Omri.	2677
1Ch	2:52 Haroeh, and **h** of the Manahethites.	2677
	2:54 and **h** of the Manahethites, the Zorites.	2677
	5:18 the Gadites, and the **h** tribe of Manasseh	2677
	5:23 the children of the **h** tribe of Manasseh	2677
	5:26 **h** tribe of Manasseh, and brought them	2677
	6:61 were cities given out of the **h** tribe,	2677
	6:61 namely, out of the **h** tribe of Manasseh,	4276
	6:70 out of the **h** tribe of Manasseh; Aner with	4276
	6:71 of the family of the **h** tribe of Manasseh,	2677
	12:31 of the **h** tribe of Manasseh eighteen	2677
	12:37 Gadites, and the **h** tribe of Manasseh,	2677
	26:32 the Gadites, and the **h** tribe of Manasseh,	2677
	27:20 the **h** tribe of Manasseh, Joel the son of	2677
	27:21 Of the **h** tribe of Manasseh in Gilead,	2677
2Ch	9: 6 the one **h** of the greatness of thy wisdom	2677
Ne	3: 9 Hur, the ruler of the **h** part of Jerusalem.	2677
	3:12 the ruler of the **h** part of Jerusalem,	2677
	3:16 the ruler of the **h** part of Beth-zur,	2677
	3:17 ruler of the **h** part of Keilah, in his part.	2677
	3:18 the ruler of the **h** part of Keilah.	2677
	4: 6 the wall was joined together unto the **h**	2677
	4:16 that the **h** of my servants wrought in	2677
	4:16 the other **h** of them held both the spears,	2677
	4:21 **h** of them held the spears from the rising	2677
	12:32 and **h** of the princes of Judah,	2677
	12:38 and the **h** of the people upon the wall,	2677
	12:40 and I, and the **h** of the rulers with me:	2677
	13:24 their children spake in the speech of	2677
Est	5: 3 it shall be even given thee to the **h** of	2677
	5: 6 even to the **h** of the kingdom it shall be	2677
	7: 2 even to the **h** of the kingdom.	2677
Ps	55:23 deceitful men shall not **live out h** their	2673
Eze	16:51 Neither hath Samaria committed **h** of thy	2677
	40:42 of a cubit and a **h** long, and a cubit and	2677
	40:42 a cubit and a **h** broad, and one cubit high:	2677
	43:17 the border about it shall be a **h** cubit;	2677
Da	12: 7 that it shall be for a time, times, and a **h**;	2677
Hos	3: 2 of barley, and a **homer** of barley:	3963
Zec	14: 2 **h** of the city shall go forth into captivity,	2677

Zec	14: 4 **h** of the mountain shall remove toward	2677
	14: 4 the north, and **h** of it toward the south.	2677
	14: 8 **h** of them toward the former sea,	2677
	14: 8 and **h** of them toward the hinder sea:	2677
Mk	6:23 give it thee, unto the **h** of my kingdom.	2255
Lk	10:30 and departed, leaving him **h** dead.	2253
	19: 8 the **h** of my goods I give to the poor;	2255
Rev	8: 1 in heaven about the space of **h** an hour.	2256
	11: 9 see their dead bodies three days and a **h**,	2255
	11:11 the spirit of life from God entered into	2255
	12:14 and times, and **h** a time, from the face of	2255

HALHUL (1)

Jos	15:58 **H**, Beth-zur, and Gedor,	2478

HALI (1)

Jos	19:25 and **H**, and Beten, and Achshaph,	2482

HALING (1) [HALE]

Ac	8: 3 and **h** men and women committed them	4951

HALL (8)

Mt	27:27 governor took Jesus into the **common h**,	4232
Mk	15:16 And the soldiers led him away into the **h**,	833
Lk	22:55 had kindled a fire in the midst of the **h**,	833
Jn	18:28 from Caiaphas unto the **h** of judgment:	4232
	18:28 went not into the **judgment h**,	4232
	18:33 Then Pilate entered into the **judgment h**	4232
	19: 9 And went again into the **judgment h**,	4232
Ac	23:35 him to be kept in Herod's **judgment h**.	4232

HALLELUIA See ALLELUIA

HALLOHESH (2)

Ne	3:12 unto him repaired Shallum the son of **H**,	3873
	10:24 **H**, Pileha, Shobek,	3873

HALLOW (15) [HALLOWED]

Ex	28:38 of Israel shall **h** in all their holy gifts;	6942
	29: 1 that thou shalt do unto them to **h** them,	6942
	40: 9 shalt **h** it, and all the vessels thereof:	6942
Lev	16:19 **h** it from the uncleanness of the children	6942
	22: 2 in those things which they **h** unto me:	6942
	22: 3 the children of Israel **h** unto the LORD,	6942
	22:32 of Israel: I am the LORD which **h** you,	6942
	25:10 ye shall **h** the fiftieth year,	6942
Nu	6:11 and shall **h** his head that same day.	6942
1Ki	8:64 The same day did the king **h** the middle	6942
Jer	17:22 do ye any work, but **h** ye the sabbath day,	6942
	17:24 the sabbath day, to do no work therein;	6942
	17:27 if you will not hearken unto me to **h**	6942
Eze	20:20 **h** my sabbaths; and they shall be a sign	6942
	44:24 and they shall **h** my sabbaths.	6942

HALLOWED (22) [HALLOW]

Ex	20:11 LORD blessed the sabbath day, and **h** it.	6942
	29:21 he shall be **h**, and his garments,	6942
Lev	12: 4 she shall touch no **h** thing, nor come into	6944
	19: 8 he hath profaned the **h** thing of	6944
	22:32 I will be **h** among the children of Israel:	6942
Nu	3:13 **h** unto me all the firstborn in Israel,	6942
	5:10 every man's **h** things shall be his:	6944
	16:37 thou the fire yonder; and scatter	6942
	16:38 before the LORD, therefore they are **h**:	6942
	18: 8 all the **h** things of the children of Israel;	6944
	18:29 even the **h** part thereof out of it.	4720
Dt	26:13 I have brought away the **h** things out of	6944
1Sa	21: 4 under mine hand, but there is **h** bread;	6944
	21: 6 So the priest gave him **h** bread: for there	6944
1Ki	9: 3 have **h** this house, which thou hast built,	6942
	9: 7 this house, which I have **h** for my name,	6942
2Ki	12:18 king of Judah took all the **h** things	6944
	12:18 his own **h** things, and all the gold that	6944
2Ch	7: 7 Moreover Solomon **h** the middle of	6942
	36:14 the LORD which he had **h** in Jerusalem.	6942
Mt	6: 9 Father which art in heaven, **H** be thy name.	37
Lk	11: 2 Father which art in heaven, **H** be thy name.	37

HALT (6) [HALTED, HALTETH, HALTING]

1Ki	18:21 How long **h** ye between two opinions?	6452
Ps	38:17 For I am ready to **h**, and my sorrow is	6761
Mt	18: 8 it is better for thee to enter into life **h** or	5560
Mk	9:45 it is better for thee to enter **h** into life,	5560
Lk	14:21 the maimed, and the **h**, and the blind.	5560
Jn	5: 3 **h**, withered, waiting for the moving of	5560

HALTED (2) [HALT]

Ge	32:31 rose upon him, and he **h** upon his thigh.	6760
Mic	4: 7 I will make her that **h** a remnant,	6760

HALTETH (2) [HALT]

Mic	4: 6 I assemble her that **h**, and I will gather	6760
Zep	3:19 I will save her that **h**, and gather her that	6760

HALTING (1) [HALT]

Jer	20:10 All my familiars watched for my **h**,	6763

HAM (17)

Ge	5:32 and Noah begat Shem, **H**, and Japheth.	2526
	6:10 begat three sons, Shem, **H**, and Japheth.	2526
	7:13 Shem, and **H**, and Japheth, the sons of	2526
	9:18 the ark, were Shem, and **H**, and Japheth:	2526
	9:18 Japheth: and **H** is the father of Canaan.	2526
	9:22 **H**, the father of Canaan, saw the	2526
	10: 1 the sons of Noah, Shem, **H**, and Japheth:	2526
	10: 6 And the sons of **H**; Cush, and Mizraim,	2526

Ge	10:20 These *are* the sons of **H**, after their	2526
	14: 5 Zuzims in **H**, and the Emims in Shaveh	1990
1Ch	1: 4 Noah, Shem, **H**, and Japheth.	2526
	1: 8 The sons of **H**; Cush, and Mizraim, Put,	2526
	4:40 for *they* of **H** had dwelt there of old.	2526
Ps	78:51 of *their* strength in the tabernacles of **H**:	2526
	105:23 and Jacob sojourned in the land of **H**.	2526
	105:27 and wonders in the land of **H**.	2526
	106:22 Wondrous works in the land of **H**,	2526

HAMAN (50) [HAMAN'S]

Est	3: 1 **H** the son of Hammedatha the Agagite,	2001
	3: 2 king's gate, bowed, and reverenced **H**:	2001
	3: 4 not unto them, that they told **H**,	2001
	3: 5 when **H** saw that Mordecai bowed not,	2001
	3: 5 him reverence, *then* was **H** full *of* wrath.	2001
	3: 6 sought to destroy all the Jews	2001
	3: 7 before **H** from day to day, and from	2001
	3: 8 **H** said unto king Ahasuerus, There is a	2001
	3:10 gave it unto **H** the son of Hammedatha	2001
	3:11 the king said unto **H**, The silver *is* given	2001
	3:12 there was written according to all that **H**	2001
	3:15 the king and **H** sat down to drink;	2001
	4: 7 of the sum of the money that **H** had	2001
	5: 4 **H** come *this* day unto the banquet that I	2001
	5: 5 the king said, Cause **H** to make haste,	2001
	5: 5 **H** came to the banquet that Esther had	2001
	5: 8 come to the banquet that I shall prepare	2001
	5: 9 went **H** forth that day joyful and with a	2001
	5: 9 when **H** saw Mordecai in the king's gate,	2001
	5:10 Nevertheless **H** refrained himself:	2001
	5:11 **H** told them of the glory of his riches,	2001
	5:12 **H** said moreover, Yea, Esther the queen	2001
	5:14 the thing pleased **H**; and he caused	2001
	6: 4 Now **H** was come into the outward court	2001
	6: 5 Behold, **H** standeth in the court.	2001
	6: 6 came in. And the king said unto him,	2001
	6: 6 Now **H** thought in his heart, To whom	2001
	6: 7 **H** answered the king, For the man whom	2001
	6:10 the king said to **H**, Make haste, *and* take	2001
	6:11 took **H** the apparel and the horse,	2001
	6:12 **H** hasted to his house mourning,	2001
	6:13 **H** told Zeresh his wife and all his friends	2001
	6:14 hasted to bring **H** unto the banquet that	2001
	7: 1 **H** came to banquet with Esther the queen.	2001
	7: 6 adversary and enemy *is* this wicked **H**.	2001
	7: 6 **H** was afraid before the king and the	2001
	7: 7 stood *up* to make request for his life to	2001
	7: 8 was fallen upon the bed whereon	2001
	7: 9 which **H** had made for Mordecai,	2001
	7: 9 for the king, standeth in the house of **H**.	2001
	7:10 So they hanged **H** on the gallows that he	2001
	8: 1 the Jews' enemy unto Esther the	2001
	8: 2 which he had taken from **H**, and gave it	2001
	8: 2 Esther set Mordecai over the house of **H**.	2001
	8: 3 put away the mischief of **H** the Agagite,	2001
	8: 5 **H** the son of Hammedatha the Agagite,	2001
	8: 7 I have given Esther the house of **H**,	2001
	9:10 ten sons of **H** the son of Hammedatha,	2001
	9:12 the palace, and the ten sons of **H**;	2001
	9:24 Because the son of Hammedatha,	2001

HAMAN'S (3) [HAMAN]

Est	7: 8 of the king's mouth, they covered **H** face.	2001
	9:13 **H** ten sons be hanged upon the gallows.	2001
	9:14 at Shushan; and they hanged **H** ten sons.	2001

HAMATH (34) [HAMATH-ZOBAH, HAMATHITE]

Nu	13:21 of Zin unto Rehob, as *men* come to **H**.	2574
	34: 8 out *your border* unto the entrance of **H**;	2574
Jos	13: 5 mount Hermon unto the entering into **H**.	2574
Jdg	3: 3 Baal-hermon unto the entering in of **H**.	2574
2Sa	8: 9 When Toi king of **H** heard that David	2574
1Ki	8:65 from the entering in of **H** unto the river	2574
2Ki	14:25 entering of **H** unto the sea of the plain,	2574
	14:28 **H**, *which belonged* to Judah, for Israel,	2574
	17:24 from **H**, and from Sepharvaim,	2574
	17:30 and the men of **H** made Ashima,	2574
	18:34 Where *are* the gods of **H**, and of Arpad?	2574
	19:13 Where *is* the king of **H**, and the king of	2574
	23:33 him in bands at Riblah in the land of **H**,	2574
	25:21 slew them at Riblah in the land of **H**.	2574
1Ch	18: 3 smote Hadarezer king of Zobah unto **H**,	2574
	18: 9 when Tou king of **H** heard how David	2574
2Ch	7: 8 from the entering in of **H** unto the river	2574
	8: 4 all the store cities, which he built in **H**.	2574
Isa	9: 9 *is* not **H** as Arpad? *is* not Samaria as	2574
	11:11 from **H**, and from the islands of the sea.	2574
	36:19 Where *are* the gods of **H** and of Arphad?	2574
	37:13 Where *is* the king of **H**, and the king of	2574
Jer	39: 5 of Babylon to Riblah in the land of **H**,	2574
	49:23 **H** is confounded, and Arpad: for they	2574
	52: 9 of Babylon to Riblah in the land of **H**,	2574
	52:27 them to death in Riblah in the land of **H**.	2574
Eze	47:16 **H**, Berothah, Sibraim, which *is* between	2574
	47:16 border of Damascus and the border of **H**;	2574
	47:17 north northward, and the border of **H**.	2574
	47:20 border, till *a man* come over against **H**.	2574
	48: 1 as *one* goeth to **H**, Hazar-enan, the border	2574
	48: 1 Damascus northward, to the coast of **H**;	2574
Am	6: 2 and from thence go ye to **H** the great?	2574
Zec	9: 2 **H** also shall border thereby; Tyrus,	2574

HAMATHITE (2) [HAMATH]

Ge	10:18 Arvadite, and the Zemarite, and the **H**:	2577

1Ch	1:16 Arvadite, and the Zemarite, and the **H**.	2577

HAMATH-ZOBAH (1) [HAMATH, ZOBAH]

2Ch	8: 3 Solomon went *to* **H**, and prevailed against	2574

HAMMATH (1)

Jos	19:35 Zer, and **H**, Rakkath, and Chinnereth,	2575

HAMMEDATHA (5)

Est	3: 1 Haman the son of **H** the Agagite,	4099
	3:10 gave it unto Haman the son of **H**	4099
	8: 5 by Haman the son of **H** the Agagite.	4099
	9:10 The ten sons of Haman the son of **H**,	4099
	9:24 Haman the son of **H**, the Agagite,	4099

HAMMELECH (2)

Jer	36:26 king commanded Jerahmeel the son of **H**,	4429
	38: 6 the dungeon of Malchiah the son of **H**,	4429

HAMMER (7) [HAMMERS]

Jdg	4:21 took a **h** in her hand, and went softly	4717
	5:26 and her right hand to the workmen's **h**;	1989
	5:26 with the **h** she smote Sisera, she smote off	NIH
1Ki	6: 7 that there was neither **h** nor axe *nor* any	4717
Isa	41: 7 he that smootheth *with* the **h** him that	6360
Jer	23:29 like a **h** *that* breaketh the rock in pieces?	6360
	50:23 How is the **h** of the whole earth cut	6360

HAMMERS (3) [HAMMER]

Ps	74: 6 work thereof at once with axes and **h**.	3597
Isa	44:12 fashioneth it with **h**, and worketh it with	4717
Jer	10: 4 they fasten it with nails and with **h**, that	4717

HAMMOLEKETH (1)

1Ch	7:18 his sister **H** bare Ishod, and Abiezer,	4447

HAMMON (2)

Jos	19:28 and Rehob, and, **H**, and Kanah,	2540
1Ch	6:76 with her suburbs, and Kirjathaim with	2540

HAMMOTH-DOR (1) [DOR]

Jos	21:32 **H** with her suburbs, and Kartan with her	2576

HAMMUEL See HAMUEL

HAMONAH (1)

Eze	39:16 also the name of the city *shall be* **H**.	1997

HAMON-GOG (2) [GOG]

Eze	39:11 and they shall call *it* The valley of **H**.	1995
	39:15 buriers have buried it in the valley of **H**.	1995

HAMOR (12) [EMMOR, HAMOR'S]

Ge	33:19 at the hand of the children of **H**,	2544
	34: 2 when Shechem the son of **H** the Hivite,	2544
	34: 4 Shechem spake unto his father **H**, saying,	2544
	34: 6 the father of Shechem went out unto	2544
	34: 8 **H** communed with them, saying, The	2544
	34:13 and **H** his father deceitfully,	2544
	34:18 their words pleased **H**, and Shechem	2544
	34:20 **H** and Shechem his son came unto the	2544
	34:24 unto **H** and unto Shechem his son	2544
	34:26 they slew **H** and Shechem his son with	2544
Jos	24:32 the father of Shechem for an hundred	2544
Jdg	9:28 the men of **H** the father of Shechem:	2544

HAMOR'S (1) [HAMOR]

Ge	34:18 pleased Hamor, and Shechem **H** son.	2544

HAMSTRING See HOUGH

HAMUEL (1)

1Ch	4:26 his son, Zacchur his son, Shimei his	2536

HAMUL (3) [HAMULITES]

Ge	46:12 the sons of Pharez were Hezron and **H**.	2538
Nu	26:21 of **H**, the family of the Hamulites.	2538
1Ch	2: 5 The sons of Pharez; Hezron, and **H**.	2538

HAMULITES (1) [HAMUL]

Nu	26:21 of Hamul, the family of the **H**.	2539

HAMUTAL (3)

2Ki	23:31 his mother's name *was* **H**, the daughter	2537
	24:18 his mother's name *was* **H**, the daughter	2537
Jer	52: 1 his mother's name *was* **H** the daughter	2537

HANAMEEL (4)

Jer	32: 7 **H** the son of Shallum thine uncle *shall*	2601
	32: 8 So **H** mine uncle's son came to me in	2601
	32: 9 I bought the field of **H** my uncle's son,	2601
	32:12 in the sight of **H** mine uncle's *son,* and	2601

HANAMEL See HANAMEEL

HANAN (12) [BAAL-HANAN, ELON-BETH-HANAN]

1Ch	8:23 And Abdon, and Zichri, and **H**,	2605
	8:38 and Sheariah, and Obadiah, and **H**:	2605
	9:44 and Sheariah, and Obadiah, and **H**:	2605
	11:43 **H** the son of Maachah, and Joshaphat	2605
Ezr	2:46 children of Shalmai, the children of **H**,	2605
Ne	7:49 The children of **H**, the children of Giddel,	2605
	8: 7 Jozabad, **H**, Pelaiah, and the Levites,	2605
	10:10 Shebaniah, Hodijah, Kelita, Pelaiah, **H**,	2605
	10:22 Pelatiah, **H**, Anaiah,	2605
	10:26 And Ahijah, **H**, Anan,	2605
	13:13 next to them *was* **H** the son of Zaccur,	2605

Jer	35: 4 into the chamber of the sons of **H**,	2605

HANANEEL (4)

Ne	3: 1 they sanctified it, unto the tower of **H**.	2606
	12:39 the tower of **H**, and the tower of Meah,	2606
Jer	31:38 tower of **H** unto the gate of the corner.	2606
Zec	14:10 *from* the tower of **H** unto the king's	2606

HANANEL See HANANEEL

HANANI (11)

1Ki	16: 1 came to Jehu the son of **H** against Baasha,	2607
	16: 7 **H** came the word of the Lord against	2607
1Ch	25: 4 **H**, Eliathah, Giddalti, and Romamti-ezer,	2607
	25:25 The eighteenth to **H**, *he*, his sons,	2607
2Ch	16: 7 at that time **H** the seer came to Asa king	2607
	19: 2 Jehu the son of **H** the seer went out to	2607
	20:34 written in the book of Jehu the son of **H**,	2607
Ezr	10:20 of the sons of Immer; **H**, and Zebadiah.	2607
Ne	1: 2 That **H**, one of my brethren, came,	2607
	7: 2 That I gave my brother **H**, and Hananiah	2607
	12:36 Gilalai, Maai, Nethaneel, and Judah, **H**,	2607

HANANIAH (29)

1Ch	3:19 and **H**, and Shelomith their sister:	2608
	3:21 the sons of **H**; Pelatiah, and Jesaiah:	2608
	8:24 And **H**, and Elam, and Antothijah,	2608
	25: 4 **H**, Hanani, Eliathah, Giddalti,	2608
	25:23 The sixteenth to **H**, *he*, his sons,	2608
2Ch	26:11 Maaseiah the ruler, under the hand of **H**,	2608
Ezr	10:28 Jehohanan, **H**, Zabbai, *and* Athlai.	2608
Ne	3: 8 Next unto him also repaired **H** the son of	2608
	3:30 repaired **H** the son of Shelemiah,	2608
	7: 2 **H** the ruler of the palace, charge over	2608
	10:23 Hoshea, **H**, Hashub,	2608
	12:12 of Seraiah, Meraiah; of Jeremiah, **H**,	2608
	12:41 Michaiah, Elioenai, Zechariah, *and* **H**,	2608
Jer	28: 1 *that* **H** the son of Azur the prophet,	2608
	28: 5 prophet **H** in the presence of the priests,	2608
	28:10 **H** the prophet took the yoke from off	2608
	28:11 **H** spake in the presence of all the people,	2608
	28:12 **H** the prophet had broken the yoke from	2608
	28:13 Go and tell **H**, saying, Thus saith	2608
	28:15 said the prophet Jeremiah unto **H**,	2608
	28:15 unto Hananiah the prophet, Hear now, **H**;	2608
	28:17 So **H** the prophet died the same year in	2608
	36:12 Zedekiah the son of **H**, and all the princes.	2608
	37:13 the son of Shelemiah, the son of **H**,	2608
Da	1: 6 Judah, Daniel, **H**, Mishael, and Azariah:	2608
	1: 7 to **H**, of Shadrach; and to Mishael,	2608
	1:11 set over Daniel, **H**, Mishael, and Azariah,	2608
	1:19 like Daniel, **H**, Mishael, and Azariah:	2608
	2:17 made the thing known to **H**, Mishael,	2608

HAND (1470) [BROKENHANDED, HANDBREADTH, HANDED, HANDFUL, HANDFULS, HANDS, HANDSTAVES, HANDWRITING, HANDYWORK, LEFTHANDED]

Ge	3:22 lest he put forth his **h**, and take also of	3027
	4:11 receive thy brother's blood from thy **h**.	3027
	8: 9 he put forth his **h**, and took her,	3027
	9: 2 of the sea; into your **h** are they delivered.	3027
	9: 5 at the **h** of every beast will I require it,	3027
	9: 5 will I require it, and at the **h** of man;	3027
	9: 5 at the **h** of every man's brother will I	3027
	13: 9 if *thou wilt take* the **left h**, then I will go	8040
	13: 9 if *thou depart to* the **right h**, then I will	3225
	14:15 which *is* on the **left h** of Damascus.	8040
	14:20 hath delivered thine enemies into thy **h**.	3027
	14:22 I have lift up mine **h** unto the Lord,	3027
	16: 6 unto Sarai, Behold, thy maid *is* in thy **h**;	3027
	16:12 his **h** *will be* against every man,	3027
	16:12 man, and every man's **h** against him;	3027
	19:10 the men put forth their **h**, and pulled Lot	3027
	19:16 the men laid hold upon his **h**, and upon	3027
	19:16 upon the **h** of his wife, and upon the hand	3027
	19:16 and upon the **h** of his two daughters;	3027
	21:18 lift up the lad, and hold him in thine **h**;	3027
	21:30 seven ewe lambs shalt thou take of my **h**,	3027
	22: 6 he took the fire in his **h**, and a knife;	3027
	22:10 Abraham stretched forth his **h**, and took	3027
	22:12 he said, Lay not thine **h** upon the lad,	3027
	24: 2 Put, I pray thee, thy **h** under my thigh:	3027
	24: 9 the servant put his **h** under the thigh of	3027
	24:10 all the goods of his master *were* in his **h**:	3027
	24:18 let down her pitcher upon her **h**,	3027
	24:49 I may turn to the **right h**, or to the left.	3225
	25:26 and his **h** took hold on Esau's heel;	3027
	27:17 had prepared, into the **h** of her son Jacob.	3027
	27:41 days of mourning for my father are at **h**;	7126
	30:35 and gave *them* into the **h** of his sons.	3027
	31:29 It is in the power of my **h** to do you hurt:	3027
	31:39 of my **h** didst thou require it,	3027
	32:11 I pray thee, from the **h** of my brother,	3027
	32:11 hand of my brother, from the **h** of Esau:	3027
	32:13 took of that which came to his **h** a present	3027
	32:16 delivered *them* into the **h** of his servants,	3027
	33:10 sight, then receive my present at my **h**:	3027
	33:19 at the **h** of the children of Hamor,	3027
	35: 4 all the strange gods which *were* in their **h**,	3027
	37:22 lay no **h** upon him, that he might rid him	3027
	37:27 and let not our **h** be upon him:	3027
	38:18 bracelets, and thy staff that *is* in thine **h**.	3027
	38:20 Judah sent the kid by the **h** of his friend	3027
	38:20 to receive *his* pledge from the woman's **h**:	3027

H

Ge 38:28 she travailed, that *the one* put out *his* **h**:	3027
38:28 and bound upon his **h** a scarlet thread,	3027
38:29 as he drew back his **h**, that, behold,	3027
38:30 that had the scarlet thread upon his **h**.	3027
39: 1 bought him of the **h** of the Ishmeelites,	3027
39: 3 made all that he did to prosper in his **h**.	3027
39: 4 and all *that* he had he put into his **h**.	3027
39: 6 he left all that he had in Joseph's **h**;	3027
39: 8 hath committed all that he hath to my **h**;	3027
39:12 he left his garment in her **h**, and fled,	3027
39:13 saw that he had left his garment in her **h**,	3027
39:22 **h** all the prisoners that *were* in the prison;	3027
39:23 not to any thing *that was* under his **h**;	3027
40:11 Pharaoh's cup *was* in my **h**: and I took	3027
40:11 and I gave the cup into Pharaoh's **h**.	3709
40:13 shalt deliver Pharaoh's cup into his **h**,	3027
40:21 and he gave the cup into Pharaoh's **h**:	3709
41:35 and lay up corn under the **h** of Pharaoh,	3027
41:42 Pharaoh took off his ring from his **h**,	3027
41:42 put it upon Joseph's **h**, and arrayed him	3027
41:44 without thee shall no man lift up his **h** or	3027
42:37 deliver him into my **h**, and I will bring	3027
43: 9 for him; of my **h** shalt thou require him:	3027
43:12 take double money in your **h**;	3027
43:12 of your sacks, carry *it* again in your **h**;	3027
43:15 they took double money in their **h**,	3027
43:21 we have brought it again in our **h**.	3027
43:26 present which *was* in their **h** into the	3027
44:17 *but* the man in whose **h** the cup is found,	3027
46: 4 Joseph shall put his **h** upon thine eyes.	3027
47:29 thy **h** under my thigh, and deal kindly	3027
48:13 Ephraim in his **right h** toward Israel's **left**	3225
48:13 in his right hand toward Israel's **left h**,	8040
48:13 Manasseh in his **left h** towards Israel's	8040
48:13 in his left hand towards Israel's **right h**,	3225
48:14 Israel stretched out his **right h**, and laid	3225
48:14 and his **left h** upon Manasseh's head,	8040
48:17 laid his right **h** upon the head of Ephraim,	3027
48:17 he held up his father's **h**, to remove it	3027
48:18 firstborn; put thy **right h** upon his head.	3225
48:22 which I took out of the **h** of the Amorite	3027
49: 8 shall *be* in the neck of thine enemies;	3027
Ex 2:19 An Egyptian delivered us out of the **h** of	3027
3: 8 deliver them out of the **h** of the Egyptians,	3027
3:19 will not let you go, no, not by a mighty **h**.	3027
3:20 I will stretch out my **h**, and smite Egypt	3027
4: 2 said unto him, What *is* that in thine **h**?	3027
4: 4 Put forth thine **h**, and take it by the tail.	3027
4: 4 he put forth his **h**, and caught it,	3027
4: 4 caught it, and it became a rod in his **h**:	3709
4: 6 him, Put now thine **h** into thy bosom.	3027
4: 6 he put his **h** into his bosom: and when	3027
4: 6 out, behold, his **h** *was* leprous as snow.	3027
4: 7 said, Put thine **h** into thy bosom again.	3027
4: 7 he put his **h** into his bosom again;	3027
4:13 by the **h** of *him whom* thou wilt send.	3027
4:17 thou shalt take this rod in thine **h**,	3027
4:20 and Moses took the rod of God in his **h**.	3027
4:21 which I have put in thine **h**:	3027
5:21 to put a sword in their **h** to slay us.	3027
6: 1 for with a strong **h** shall he let them go,	3027
6: 1 with a strong **h** shall he drive them out	3027
7: 4 that I may lay my **h** upon Egypt,	3027
7: 5 when I stretch forth mine **h** upon Egypt,	3027
7:15 to a serpent shalt thou take in thine **h**.	3027
7:17 I will smite with the rod that *is* in mine **h**	3027
7:19 stretch out thine **h** upon the waters of	3027
8: 5 Stretch forth thine **h** with thy rod over	3027
8: 6 Aaron stretched out his **h** over the waters	3027
8:17 Aaron stretched out his **h** with his rod,	3027
9: 3 the **h** of the Lᴏʀᴅ is upon thy cattle	3027
9:15 now I will stretch out my **h**, that I may	3027
9:22 Stretch forth thine **h** toward heaven,	3027
10:12 Stretch out thine **h** over the land of Egypt	3027
10:21 Stretch out thine **h** toward heaven,	3027
10:22 stretched forth his **h** toward heaven;	3027
12:11 on your feet, and your staff in your **h**;	3027
13: 3 for by strength of **h** the Lᴏʀᴅ brought	3027
13: 9 shall be for a sign unto thee upon thine **h**,	3027
13: 9 for with a strong **h** hath the Lᴏʀᴅ	3027
13:14 By strength of **h** the Lᴏʀᴅ brought us out	3027
13:16 it shall be for a token upon thine **h**,	3027
13:16 for by strength of **h** the Lᴏʀᴅ brought us	3027
14: 8 children of Israel went out with a high **h**.	3027
14:16 stretch out thine **h** over the sea,	3027
14:21 Moses stretched out his **h** over the sea;	3027
14:22 *were* a wall unto them on their **right h**,	3225
14:26 Stretch out thine **h** over the sea,	3027
14:27 Moses stretched forth his **h** over the sea,	3027
14:29 *were* a wall unto them on their **right h**,	3225
14:30 that day out of the **h** of the Egyptians;	3027
15: 6 Thy **right h**, O Lᴏʀᴅ, is become glorious	3225
15: 6 thy **right h**, O Lᴏʀᴅ, hath dashed in	3225
15: 9 draw my sword, my **h** shall destroy them.	3027
15:12 stretchedst out thy **right h**, the earth	3225
15:20 sister of Aaron, took a timbrel in her **h**;	3027
16: 3 Would to God we had died by the **h** of	3027
17: 5 smotest the river, take in thine **h**, and go.	3027
17: 9 of the hill with the rod of God in mine **h**.	3027
17:11 came to pass, when Moses held up his **h**,	3027
17:11 he let down his **h**, Amalek prevailed.	3027
18: 9 whom he had delivered out of the **h** of	3027
18:10 who hath delivered you out of the **h** of	3027
18:10 Egyptians, and out of the **h** of Pharaoh,	3027
18:10 people from under the **h** of the Egyptians.	3027

Ex 19:13 There shall not a **h** touch it, but he shall	3027
21:13 in wait, but God deliver *him* into his **h**;	3027
21:16 selleth him, or if he be found in his **h**,	3027
21:20 with a rod, and he die under his **h**;	3027
21:24 tooth for tooth, **h** for hand, foot for foot,	3027
21:24 tooth for tooth, hand for **h**, foot for foot,	3027
22: 4 If the theft be certainly found in his **h**	3027
22: 8 *to see* whether he have put his **h** unto his	3027
22:11 that he hath not put his **h** unto his	3027
23: 1 put not thine **h** with the wicked to be an	3027
23:31 the inhabitants of the land into your **h**;	3027
24:11 of the children of Israel he laid not his **h**:	3027
29:20 upon the thumb of their right **h**,	3027
32: 4 received *them* at their **h**, and fashioned it	3027
32:11 with great power, and with a mighty **h**?	3027
32:15 tables of the Testimony *were* in his **h**,	3027
33:22 cover thee with my **h** while I pass by:	3709
33:23 will take away mine **h**, and thou shalt see	3709
34: 4 and took in his **h** the two tables of stone.	3027
34:29 the two tables of Testimony in Moses' **h**,	3027
35:29 to be made by the **h** of Moses.	3027
38:15 on **this h** and that hand, *were* hangings	2088
38:15 on this hand and **that h**, *were* hangings	2088
38:21 by the **h** of Ithamar, son to Aaron the	3027
Lev 1: 4 he shall put his **h** upon the head of	3027
3: 2 he shall lay his **h** upon the head of his	3027
3: 8 he shall lay his **h** upon the head of his	3027
3:13 he shall lay his **h** upon the head of it,	3027
4: 4 shall lay his **h** upon the bullock's head,	3027
4:24 shall lay his **h** upon the head of the goat,	3027
4:29 shall lay his **h** upon the head of the sin	3027
4:33 shall lay his **h** upon the head of the sin	3027
8:23 upon the thumb of his right **h**, and upon	3027
8:36 the Lᴏʀᴅ commanded by the **h** of Moses.	3027
9:22 Aaron lift up his **h** towards the people,	3027
10:11 spoken unto them by the **h** of Moses.	3027
14:14 upon the thumb of his right **h**, and upon	3027
14:15 pour *it* into the **palm of** his own left **h**,	3709
14:16 right finger in the oil that *is* in his left **h**,	3709
14:17 of the rest of the oil that *is* in his **h** shall	3709
14:17 upon the thumb of his right **h**, and upon	3027
14:18 **h** he shall pour upon the head of him that	3709
14:25 upon the thumb of his right **h**, and upon	3027
14:26 of the oil into the **palm of** his own left **h**:	3709
14:27 in his left **h** seven times before the Lᴏʀᴅ:	3709
14:28 priest shall put of the oil that *is* in his **h**	3709
14:28 upon the thumb of his right **h**, and upon	3027
14:29 the rest of the oil that *is* in the priest's **h**	3709
14:32 whose **h** is not **able to get** *that*	3027+5381
16:21 shall send *him* away by the **h** of a fit man	3027
22:25 Neither from a stranger's **h** shall ye offer	3027
25:14 or buyest *ought* of thy neighbour's **h**,	3027
25:28 that which is sold shall remain in the **h** of	3027
26:25 ye shall be delivered into the **h** of	3027
26:46 Israel in mount Sinai by the **h** of Moses.	3027
Nu 4:28 charge *shall be* under the **h** of Ithamar	3027
4:33 under the **h** of Ithamar the son of Aaron	3027
4:37 of the Lᴏʀᴅ by the **h** of Moses.	3027
4:45 the word of the Lᴏʀᴅ by the **h** of Moses.	3027
4:49 they were numbered by the **h** of Moses,	3027
5:18 priest shall have in his **h** the bitter water	3027
5:25 jealousy offering out of the woman's **h**,	3027
6:21 besides *that* that his **h** shall get:	3027
7: 8 under the **h** of Ithamar the son of Aaron	3027
9:23 of the Lᴏʀᴅ by the **h** of Moses.	3027
10:13 of the Lᴏʀᴅ by the **h** of Moses.	3027
11:15 **kill** me, I pray thee, **out of h**,	2026+2026
11:23 Is the Lᴏʀᴅ's **h** waxed short?	3027
15:23 hath commanded you by the **h** of Moses,	3027
16:40 as the Lᴏʀᴅ said to him by the **h** of	3027
20:11 Moses lift up his **h**, and with his rod he	3027
20:17 we will not turn *to* the **right h** nor *to*	3225
20:20 with much people, and with a strong **h**.	3027
21: 2 wilt indeed deliver this people into my **h**,	3027
21:26 taken all his land out of his **h**, *even* unto	3027
21:34 for I have delivered him into thy **h**,	3027
22: 7 with the rewards of divination in their **h**;	3027
22:23 the way, and his sword drawn in his **h**:	3027
22:26 *was* no way to turn *either* to the **right h**	3225
22:29 I would there were a sword in mine **h**,	3027
22:31 in the way, and his sword drawn in his **h**:	3027
25: 7 and took a javelin in his **h**;	3027
27:18 *is* the spirit, and lay thine **h** upon him;	3027
27:23 as the Lᴏʀᴅ commanded by the **h** of	3027
31: 6 and the trumpets to blow in his **h**.	3027
33: 1 with their armies under the **h** of Moses	3027
33: 3 a high **h** in the sight of all the Egyptians.	3027
35:18 Or *if* he smite him with a **h** weapon of	3027
35:21 in enmity smite him with his **h**, that he	3027
35:25 out of the **h** of the revenger of blood,	3027
36:13 which the Lᴏʀᴅ commanded by the **h** of	3027
Dt 1:27 to deliver us into the **h** of the Amorites,	3027
2: 7 blessed thee in all the works of thy **h**:	3027
2:15 For indeed the **h** of the Lᴏʀᴅ was against	3027
2:24 have given into thy **h** Sihon the Amorite,	3027
2:27 I will neither turn *unto* the **right h** nor	3225
2:30 that he might deliver him into thy **h**,	3027
3: 2 all his people, and his land, into thy **h**;	3027
3: 8 we took at that time out of the **h** of the	3027
3:24 servant thy greatness, and thy mighty **h**:	3027
4:34 a mighty **h**, and by a stretched out arm,	3027
5:15 thee out thence through a mighty **h**	3027
5:32 ye shall not turn *to* the **right h** or	3225
6: 8 shalt bind them for a sign upon thine **h**,	3027
6:21 brought us out of Egypt with a mighty **h**:	3027

Dt 7: 8 Lᴏʀᴅ brought you out with a mighty **h**,	3027
7: 8 from the **h** of Pharaoh king of Egypt.	3027
7:19 the mighty **h**, and the stretched out arm,	3027
7:24 he shall deliver their kings into thine **h**:	3027
8:17 the might of mine **h** hath gotten me this	3027
9:26 forth out of Egypt with a mighty **h**.	3027
10: 3 mount, having the two tables in mine **h**.	3027
11: 2 his mighty **h**, and his stretched out arm,	3027
11:18 and bind them for a sign upon your **h**,	3027
12: 6 heave offerings of your **h**, and your vows,	3027
12: 7 ye shall rejoice in all that you put your **h**	3027
12:11 the heave offering of your **h**, and all your	3027
12:17 or heave offering of thine **h**:	3027
13: 9 thine **h** shall be first upon him to put him	3027
13: 9 and afterwards the **h** of all the people.	3027
13:17 nought of the cursed thing to thine **h**:	3027
14:25 bind up the money in thine **h**, and shalt	3027
14:29 all the work of thine **h** which thou doest.	3027
15: 3 which is thine with thy brother thine **h**	3027
15: 7 nor shut thine **h** from thy poor brother:	3027
15: 8 thou shalt open thine **h** wide unto him,	3027
15: 9 seventh year, the year of release, is **at h**;	7126
15:10 and in all that thou puttest thine **h** unto.	3027
15:11 Thou shalt open thine **h** wide unto thy	3027
16:10 a tribute of a freewill offering of thine **h**,	3027
17:11 shew thee, *to* the **right h**, nor *to* the left.	3225
17:20 *to* the **right h**, or *to* the left:	3225
19: 5 his **h** fetcheth a stroke with the axe to cut	3027
19:12 deliver him into the **h** of the avenger of	3027
19:21 tooth for tooth, **h** for hand, foot for foot.	3027
19:21 tooth for tooth, hand for **h**, foot for foot.	3027
23:20 **h** to in the land whither thou goest to	3027
23:25 thou mayest pluck the ears with thine **h**;	3027
24: 1 give *it* in her **h**, and send her out of his	3027
24: 3 giveth *it* in her **h**, and sendeth her out of	3027
25:11 out of the **h** of him that smiteth him,	3027
25:11 putteth forth her **h**, and taketh him by	3027
25:12 thou shalt cut off her **h**, thine eye shall	3709
26: 4 priest shall take the basket out of thine **h**,	3027
26: 8 us forth out of Egypt with a mighty **h**,	3027
28: 8 and in all that thou settest thine **h** unto;	3027
28:12 and to bless all the work of thine **h**:	3027
28:14 *to* the **right h**, or *to* the left, to go after	3225
28:20 that thou settest thine **h** unto for to do,	3027
28:32 and *there shall be* no might in thine **h**.	3027
30: 9 thee plenteous in every work of thine **h**,	3027
32:27 Our **h** is high, and the Lᴏʀᴅ hath not	3027
32:35 for the day of their calamity *is* **at h**,	7138
32:39 *is there any* that can deliver out of my **h**.	3027
32:40 For I lift up my **h** to heaven, and say,	3027
32:41 and mine **h** take hold on judgment;	3027
33: 2 from his **right h** *went* a fiery law for them.	3225
33: 3 the people; all his saints *are* in thy **h**:	3027
34:12 in all *that* mighty **h**, and in all the great	3027
Jos 1: 7 turn not from *it* to the **right h** or *to* the	3225
2:19 be on our head, if *any* **h** be upon him.	3027
4:24 the earth might know the **h** of the Lᴏʀᴅ,	3027
5:13 him with his sword drawn in his **h**:	3027
6: 2 I have given into thine **h** Jericho,	3027
7: 7 to deliver us into the **h** of the Amorites,	3027
8: 1 I have given into thy **h** the king of Ai,	3027
8: 7 your God will deliver it into your **h**.	3027
8:18 Stretch out the spear that *is* in thy **h**	3027
8:18 toward Ai; for I will give it into thine **h**.	3027
8:18 that *he had* in his **h** toward the city.	3027
8:19 as soon as *he* had stretched out his **h**:	3027
8:26 For Joshua drew not his **h** back,	3027
9:25 now, behold, we *are* in thine **h**: as it	3027
9:26 delivered them out of the **h** of the	3027
10: 6 Slack not thy **h** from thy servants;	3027
10: 8 for I have delivered them into thine **h**;	3027
10:19 God hath delivered them into your **h**.	3027
10:30 the king thereof, into the **h** of Israel;	3027
10:32 the Lᴏʀᴅ delivered Lachish into the **h** of	3027
11: 8 the Lᴏʀᴅ delivered them into the **h** of	3027
14: 2 as the Lᴏʀᴅ commanded by the **h** of	3027
17: 7 border went *along* on the **right h** unto	3225
19:27 and goeth out to Cabul on the **left h**,	8040
20: 2 whereof I spake unto you by the **h** of	3027
20: 5 shall not deliver the slayer up into his **h**;	3027
20: 9 not die by the **h** of the avenger of blood,	3027
21: 2 The Lᴏʀᴅ commanded by the **h** of	3027
21: 8 as the Lᴏʀᴅ commanded by the **h** of	3027
21:44 delivered all their enemies into their **h**.	3027
22: 9 the word of the Lᴏʀᴅ by the **h** of Moses.	3027
22:31 of Israel out of the **h** of the Lᴏʀᴅ.	3027
23: 6 turn not aside therefrom *to* the **right h**	3225
24: 8 I gave them into your **h**, that ye might	3027
24:10 you still: so I delivered you out of his **h**.	3027
24:11 and I delivered them into your **h**.	3027
Jdg 1: 2 I have delivered the land into his **h**.	3027
1: 4 and the Perizzites into their **h**:	3027
1:35 yet the **h** of the house of Joseph prevailed,	3027
2:15 the **h** of the Lᴏʀᴅ was against them for	3027
2:16 delivered them out of the **h** of those	3027
2:18 them out of the **h** of their enemies	3027
2:23 neither delivered he them into the **h** of	3027
3: 4 he commanded their fathers by the **h** of	3027
3: 8 he sold them into the **h** of	3027
3:10 king of Mesopotamia into his **h**;	3027
3:10 prevailed against Chushan-rishathaim.	3027
3:21 Ehud put forth his left **h**, and took	3027
3:28 your enemies the Moabites into your **h**.	3027
3:30 Moab was subdued that day under the **h**	3027
4: 2 the Lᴏʀᴅ sold them into the **h** of Jabin	3027

Jdg 4: 7 and I will deliver him into thine **h**. 3027
4: 9 for the LORD shall sell Sisera into the **h** 3027
4:14 LORD hath delivered Sisera into thine **h**: 3027
4:21 took a hammer in her **h**, and went softly 3027
4:24 the **h** of the children of Israel prospered, 3027
5:26 She put her **h** to the nail, and her right 3027
5:26 her **right h** to the workmen's hammer; 3225
6: 1 the LORD delivered them into the **h** of 3027
6: 2 the **h** of Midian prevailed against Israel: 3027
6: 9 I delivered you out of the **h** of 3027
6: 9 out of the **h** of all that oppressed you, 3027
6:14 thou shalt save Israel from the **h** of 3709
6:21 forth the end of the staff that *was* in his **h**, 3027
6:36 If thou wilt save Israel by mine **h**, as thou 3027
6:37 know that thou wilt save Israel by mine **h**, 3027
7: 2 saying, Mine own **h** hath saved me. 3027
7: 6 putting **h** to their mouth, were three 3027
7: 7 and deliver the Midianites into thine **h**: 3027
7: 8 So the people took victuals in their **h**, 3027
7: 9 for I have delivered it into thine **h**. 3027
7:14 *for* into his **h** hath God delivered Midian, 3027
7:15 for the LORD hath delivered into your **h** 3027
7:16 he put a trumpet in every man's **h**, 3027
8: 6 of Zebah and Zalmunna now in thine **h**, 3027
8: 7 Zebah and Zalmunna into mine **h**, 3027
8:15 of Zebah and Zalmunna now in thine **h**, 3027
8:22 for thou hast delivered us from the **h** of 3027
9:17 and delivered you out of the **h** of Midian: 3027
9:29 to God this people were under my **h**, 3027
9:48 Abimelech took an axe in his **h**, 3027
10:12 to me, and I delivered you out of their **h**. 3027
11:21 and all his people into the **h** of Israel, 3027
12: 3 and the LORD delivered them into my **h**: 3027
13: 1 the LORD delivered them into the **h** of 3027
13: 5 shall begin to deliver Israel out of the **h** 3027
14: 6 rent a kid, and *he had* nothing in his **h**: 3027
15:12 that we may deliver thee into the **h** of 3027
15:13 thee fast, and deliver thee into their **h**: 3027
15:15 put forth his **h**, and took it, and slew a 3027
15:17 he cast away the jawbone out of his **h**, 3027
15:18 deliverance into the **h** of thy servant: 3027
15:18 and fall into the **h** of the uncircumcised? 3027
16:18 unto her, and brought money in their **h**. 3027
16:23 delivered Samson our enemy into our **h**. 3027
16:26 said unto the lad that held him by the **h**, 3027
16:29 the one with his **right h**, and of the other 3225
17: 3 unto the LORD from my **h** for my son, 3027
18:19 lay thine **h** upon thy mouth, and go with 3027
20:28 morrow I will deliver them into thy **h**. 3027
20:48 as the beast, and all that **came to h**: 4672
Ru 1:13 the **h** of the Lord is gone out against me. 3027
4: 5 What day thou buyest the field of the **h** 3027
4: 9 and Mahlon's, of the **h** of Naomi. 3027
1Sa 2:13 with a fleshhook of three teeth in his **h**; 3027
4: 3 may save us out of the **h** of our enemies. 3709
4: 8 who shall deliver us out of the **h** of these 3027
5: 6 the **h** of the LORD was heavy upon them 3027
5: 7 for his **h** is sore upon us, and upon Dagon 3027
5: 9 the **h** of the LORD was against the city 3027
5:11 the **h** of God was very heavy upon them, 3027
6: 3 it shall be known to you why his **h** is not 3027
6: 5 peradventure he will lighten his **h** from 3027
6: 9 shall know that *it* is not his **h** that smote 3027
6:12 not aside *to* the **right h** or *to* the left; 3225
7: 3 he will deliver you out of the **h** of 3027
7: 8 that he will save us out of the **h** of 3027
7:13 the **h** of the LORD was against 3027
9: 8 have here at **h** the fourth part of a shekel 3027
9:16 *he* may save my people out of the **h** of 3027
10:18 you out of the **h** of the Egyptians, 3027
10:18 out of the **h** of all kingdoms, *and* of them 3027
12: 3 of whose **h** have I received *any* bribe to 3027
12: 4 hast thou taken ought of any man's **h**. 3027
12: 5 that ye have not found ought in my **h**. 3027
12: 9 sold them into the **h** of Sisera, captain of 3027
12: 9 into the **h** of the Philistines, and into 3027
12: 9 into the **h** of the king of Moab, 3027
12:10 deliver us out of the **h** of our enemies, 3027
12:11 you out of the **h** of your enemies, 3027
12:15 shall the **h** of the LORD be against you, 3027
13:22 **h** of any of the people that *were* with Saul 3027
14:10 the LORD hath delivered them into our **h**: 3027
14:12 hath delivered them into the **h** of Israel. 3027
14:19 said unto the priest, Withdraw thine **h**. 3027
14:26 but no man put his **h** to his mouth: 3027
14:27 forth the end of the rod that *was* in his **h**, 3027
14:27 honeycomb, and put his **h** to his mouth; 3027
14:37 thou deliver them into the **h** of Israel? 3027
14:43 the end of the rod that *was* in mine **h**, 3027
16:16 that he shall play with his **h**, and thou 3027
16:23 David took a harp, and played with his **h**: 3027
17:22 David left his carriage in the **h** of 3027
17:37 he will deliver me out of the **h** of this 3027
17:40 he took his staff in his **h**, and chose him 3027
17:40 even in a scrip; and his sling *was* in his **h**: 3027
17:46 will the LORD deliver thee into mine **h**; 3027
17:49 David put his **h** in *his* bag, and took 3027
17:50 *there* was no sword in the **h** of David. 3027
17:57 with the head of the Philistine in his **h**. 3027
18:10 David played with his **h**, as at other times: 3027
18:10 and *there* was a javelin in Saul's **h**. 3027
18:17 Let not mine **h** be upon him, but let 3027
18:17 let the **h** of the Philistines be upon him. 3027
18:21 the **h** of the Philistines may be against 3027
18:25 Saul thought to make David fall by the **h** 3027

1Sa 19: 5 For he did put his life in his **h**, and slew 3709
19: 9 sat in his house with his javelin in his **h**: 3027
19: 9 in his hand: and David played with *his* **h**. 3027
20:16 require *it* at the **h** of David's enemies. 3027
20:19 hide thyself when the business was *in h*, NIH
21: 3 Now therefore what is under thine **h**? 3027
21: 3 give *me* five *loaves of* bread in mine **h**, 3027
21: 4 *There is* no common bread under mine **h**, 3027
21: 8 is there not here under thine **h** spear or 3027
22: 6 having his spear in his **h**, and all his 3027
22:17 because their **h** also *is* with David, 3027
22:17 **h** to fall upon the priests of the LORD. 3027
23: 4 I will deliver the Philistines into thine **h**. 3027
23: 6 he came down *with* an ephod in his **h**. 3027
23: 7 God hath delivered him into mine **h**; 3027
23:11 men of Keilah deliver me up into his **h**? 3027
23:12 me and my men into the **h** of Saul? 3027
23:14 but God delivered him not into his **h**. 3027
23:16 wood, and strengthened his **h** in God. 3027
23:17 for the **h** of Saul my father shall not find 3027
23:20 *shall be* to deliver him into the king's **h**. 3027
24: 4 I will deliver thine enemy into thine **h**, 3027
24: 6 to stretch forth mine **h** against him, 3027
24:10 thee to day into mine **h** in the cave: 3027
24:10 will not put forth mine **h** against my lord; 3027
24:11 see, yea see the skirt of thy robe in my **h**: 3027
24:11 neither evil nor transgression in mine **h**, 3027
24:12 but mine **h** shall not be upon thee. 3027
24:13 but mine **h** shall not be upon thee. 3027
24:15 my cause, and deliver me out of thine **h**. 3027
24:18 the LORD had delivered me into thine **h**, 3027
24:20 of Israel shall be established in thine **h**. 3027
25: 8 whatsoever cometh to thine **h** unto thy 3027
25:26 *from* avenging thyself with thine own **h**, 3027
25:33 *from* avenging myself with mine own **h**. 3027
25:35 David received of her **h** *that* which she 3027
25:39 of my reproach from the **h** of Nabal, 3027
26: 8 hath delivered thine enemy into thine **h** 3027
26: 9 for who can stretch forth his **h** against 3027
26:11 mine **h** against the LORD'S anointed: 3027
26:18 have I done? or what evil *is* in mine **h**? 3027
26:23 for the LORD delivered thee into my **h** to 3027
26:23 I would not stretch forth mine **h** against 3027
27: 1 shall now perish one day by the **h** of Saul: 3027
27: 1 of Israel: so shall I escape out of his **h**. 3027
28:17 hath rent the kingdom out of thine **h**, 3027
28:19 with thee into the **h** of the Philistines: 3027
28:19 host of Israel into the **h** of the Philistines. 3027
28:21 I have put my life in my **h**, 3709
30:23 company that came against us into our **h**. 3027
2Sa 1:14 thine **h** to destroy the LORD'S anointed? 3027
2:19 going he turned not to the **right h** nor to 3225
2:21 thee aside to thy **right h** or to thy left, 3225
3: 8 not delivered thee into the **h** of David, 3027
3:12 behold, my **h** *shall be* with thee, to bring 3027
3:18 By the **h** of my servant David I will save 3027
3:18 Israel out of the **h** of the Philistines, 3027
3:18 and out of the **h** of all their enemies. 3027
4:11 therefore now require his blood of your **h**, 3027
5:19 wilt thou deliver them into mine **h**? 3027
5:19 deliver the Philistines into thine **h**. 3027
6: 6 Uzzah put forth *his* **h** to the ark of God, NIH
8: 1 David took Metheg-ammah out of the **h** 3027
10: 2 David sent to comfort him by the **h** of his 3027
10:10 delivered into the **h** of Abishai his brother 3027
11:14 to Joab, and sent *it* by the **h** of Uriah. 3027
12: 7 and I delivered thee out of the **h** of Saul; 3027
12:25 he sent by the **h** of Nathan the prophet, 3027
13: 5 that I may see *it*, and eat *it* at her **h**. 3027
13: 6 cakes in my sight, that I may eat at her **h**. 3027
13:10 the chamber, that I may eat of thine **h**. 3027
13:19 laid her **h** on her head, and went on 3027
14:16 to deliver his handmaid out of the **h** of 3709
14:19 *Is not* the **h** of Joab with thee in all this? 3027
14:19 can **turn to the right h** or to the left 3231
15: 5 he put forth his **h**, and took him, 3027
16: 6 all the mighty *men* were on his **right h** 3225
16: 8 kingdom into the **h** of Absalom thy son: 3027
18: 2 part of the people under the **h** of Joab, 3027
18: 2 third part under the **h** of Abishai the son 3027
18: 2 third part under the **h** of Ittai the Gittite. 3027
18:12 a thousand *shekels* of silver in mine **h**, 3709
18:12 *yet* would I not put forth mine **h** against 3027
18:14 he took three darts in his **h**, and thrust 3709
18:28 lift up their **h** against my lord the king. 3027
19: 9 The king saved us out of the **h** of our 3709
19: 9 he delivered us out of the **h** of 3027
20: 9 by the beard with the right **h** to kiss him. 3027
20:10 heed to the sword that *was* in Joab's **h**: 3027
20:21 hath lift up his **h** against the king, 3027
21:20 that had on every **h** six fingers, 3027
21:22 fell by the **h** of David, and by the hand of 3027
21:22 of David, and by the **h** of his servants. 3027
22: 1 him out of the **h** of all his enemies, 3709
22: 1 all his enemies, and out of the **h** of Saul: 3709
23:10 the Philistines until his was weary, 3027
23:10 weary, and his **h** clave unto the sword: 3027
23:21 the Egyptian had a spear in his **h**; 3027
23:21 plucked the spear out of the Egyptian's **h**, 3027
24:14 let us fall now into the **h** of the LORD; 3027
24:14 and let me not fall into the **h** of man. 3027
24:16 when the angel stretched out his **h** *upon* 3027
24:16 stay now thine **h**. And the angel of 3027
24:17 let thine **h**, I pray thee, be against me, 3027
1Ki 2:19 king's mother; and she sat on his **right h**. 3225

1Ki 2:25 king Solomon sent by the **h** of Benaiah 3027
2:46 the kingdom was established in the **h** of 3027
8:15 and hath with his **h** fulfilled *it*, saying, 3027
8:24 hast fulfilled *it* with thine **h**, as *it is* this 3027
8:42 of thy strong, and of thy stretched out 3027
8:53 as thou spakest by the **h** of Moses thy 3027
8:56 which he promised by the **h** of Moses his 3027
11:12 *but* I will rend it out of the **h** of thy son. 3027
11:26 even he lift up *his* **h** against the king. 3027
11:27 this *was* the cause that he lift up *his* **h** 3027
11:31 I will rent the kingdom out of the **h** of 3027
11:34 not take the whole kingdom out of his **h**: 3027
11:35 I will take the kingdom out of his son's **h**, 3027
13: 4 that he put forth his **h** from the altar, 3027
13: 4 his **h**, which he put forth against him, 3027
13: 6 that thy **h** may be restored me again. 3027
13: 6 the king's **h** was restored him again, 3027
14:18 which he spake by the **h** of his servant 3027
15:18 delivered them into the **h** of his servants: 3027
16: 7 by the **h** of the prophet Jehu the son of 3027
17:11 I pray thee, a morsel of bread in thine **h**. 3027
18: 9 deliver thy servant into the **h** of Ahab, 3027
18:44 little cloud out of the sea, like a man's **h**. 3709
18:46 the **h** of the LORD was on Elijah; 3027
20: 6 shall put *it* in their **h**, and take *it* away. 3027
20:13 I will deliver it into thine **h** *this* day; 3027
20:28 all this great multitude into thine **h**, 3027
20:42 thou hast let go out of *thy* **h** a man 3027
22: 3 it not out of the **h** of the king of Syria? 3027
22: 6 for the Lord shall deliver *it* into the **h** of 3027
22:12 LORD shall deliver *it* into the king's **h**. 3027
22:15 for the LORD shall deliver *it* into the **h** of 3027
22:19 of heaven standing by him on his **right h** 3225
22:34 Turn thine **h**, and carry me out of the 3027
2Ki 3:10 to deliver them into the **h** of Moab. 3027
3:13 to deliver them into the **h** of Moab. 3027
3:15 that the **h** of the LORD came upon him. 3027
3:18 will deliver the Moabites also into your **h**. 3027
4:29 take my staff in thine **h**, and go *thy way*: 3027
5:11 strike his **h** over the place, and recover 3027
5:18 he leaneth on my **h**, and I bow myself *in* 3027
5:24 he took *them* from their **h**, 3027
6: 7 to thee. And he put out his **h**, and took it. 3027
7: 2 on whose **h** the king leaned answered 3027
7:17 king appointed the lord on whose **h** he 3027
8: 8 Take a present in thine **h**, and go, meet 3027
8:20 his days Edom revolted from under the **h** 3027
8:22 Yet Edom revolted from under the **h** of 3027
9: 1 take this box of oil in thine **h**, and go *to* 3027
9: 7 servants of the LORD, at the **h** of Jezebel. 3027
10:15 If *it* be, give *me* thine **h**. And he gave *him* 3027
10:15 he gave *him* his **h**; and he took him up to 3027
11: 8 every man with his weapons in his **h**: 3027
11:11 every man with his weapons in his **h**, 3027
12:15 into whose **h** they delivered the money 3027
13: 3 delivered them into the **h** of Hazael king 3027
13: 3 into the **h** of Ben-hadad the son of Hazael, 3027
13: 5 that they went out from under the **h** of 3027
13:16 king of Israel, Put thine **h** upon the bow. 3027
13:16 he put his **h** *upon it*: and Elisha put his 3027
13:25 of Ben-hadad the son of Hazael the **h** 3027
13:25 which he had taken out of the **h** of 3027
14: 5 as the kingdom was confirmed in his **h**, 3027
14:25 which he spake by the **h** of his servant 3027
14:27 saved them by the **h** of Jeroboam the son 3027
15:19 that his **h** might be with him to confirm 3027
15:19 him to confirm the kingdom in his **h**. 3027
16: 7 save me out of the **h** of the king of Syria, 3709
16: 7 out of the **h** of the king of Israel, 3709
17: 7 under the **h** of Pharaoh king of Egypt, 3027
17:20 and delivered them into the **h** of spoilers, 3027
17:39 shall deliver you out of the **h** of all your 3027
18:21 it will go into his **h**, and pierce it: 3709
18:29 not be able to deliver you out of his **h**: 3027
18:30 this city shall not be delivered into the **h** 3027
18:33 land out of the **h** of the king of Assyria? 3027
18:34 they delivered Samaria out of mine **h**? 3027
18:35 delivered their country out of mine **h**, 3027
18:35 should deliver Jerusalem out of mine **h**? 3027
19:10 shall not be delivered into the **h** 3027
19:14 Hezekiah received the letter of the **h** of 3027
19:19 I beseech thee, save *thou* us out of his **h**, 3027
20: 6 city out of the **h** of the king of Assyria; 3709
21:14 deliver them into the **h** of their enemies; 3027
22: 2 not aside *to* the **right h** or *to* the left. 3225
22: 5 let them deliver it into the **h** of the doers 3027
22: 7 the money that was delivered into their **h**, 3027
22: 9 delivered it into the **h** of them that do 3027
23: 8 which *were* on a man's **left h** at the gate 8040
23:13 which *were* on the **right h** of the mount 3225
1Ch 4:10 thine **h** might be with me, and that thou 3027
5:10 with the Hagarites, who fell by their **h**: 3027
5:20 the Hagarites were delivered into their **h**, 3027
6:15 Jerusalem by the **h** of Nebuchadnezzar. 3027
6:39 brother Asaph, who stood on his **right h**, 3225
6:44 the sons of Merari *stood* on the **left h**: 8040
11:23 in the Egyptian's **h** *was* a spear like a 3027
11:23 pluckt the spear out of the Egyptian's **h**, 3027
12: 2 could **use** both **the right h** and the left in 3231
13: 9 Uzza put forth his **h** to hold the ark; 3027
13:10 him, because he put his **h** to the ark: 3027
14:10 wilt thou deliver them into mine **h**? 3027
14:10 up; for I will deliver them into thine **h**. 3027
14:11 mine **h** like the breaking forth of waters: 3027
16: 7 to thank the LORD into the **h** of Asaph 3027

1Ch 18: 1 her towns out of the **h** of the Philistines.	3027
19:11 unto the **h** of Abishai his brother,	3027
20: 6 six *on each* **h**, and six *on each* foot: and	NIH
20: 8 they fell by the **h** of David, and by the	3027
20: 8 of David, and by the **h** of his servants.	3027
21:13 let me fall now into the **h** of the LORD;	3027
21:13 but let me not fall into the **h** of man.	3027
21:15 *It is* enough, stay now thine **h**.	3027
21:16 a drawn sword in his **h** stretched out	3027
21:17 let thine **h**, I pray thee, O LORD my God,	3027
22:18 the inhabitants of the land into mine **h**;	3027
26:28 *it was* under the **h** of Shelomith,	3027
28:19 understand in writing by *his* **h** upon me,	3027
29: 8 by the **h** of Jehiel the Gershonite.	3027
29:12 in thine **h** *is* power and might;	3027
29:12 in thine **h** *it is* to make great, and to give	3027
29:16 for thine holy name *cometh* of thine **h**,	3027
2Ch 3:17 one on the **right h**, and the other on	3225
3:17 called the name of *that on* the **right h**	3233
4: 6 five on the **right h**, and five on the left,	3225
4: 7 five on the **right h**, and five on the left,	3225
6:15 hast fulfilled *it* with thine **h**, as *it is* this	3027
6:32 thy mighty **h**, and thy stretched out arm;	3027
10:15 which he spake by the **h** of Ahijah	3027
12: 5 have I also left you in the **h** of Shishak.	3027
12: 7 out upon Jerusalem by the **h** of Shishak.	3027
13: 8 the LORD in the **h** of the sons of David;	3027
13:16 and God delivered them into their **h**.	3027
16: 7 the king of Syria escaped out of thine **h**.	3027
16: 8 the LORD, he delivered them into thine **h**.	3027
17: 5 LORD stablished the kingdom in his **h**;	3027
18: 5 for God will deliver *it* into the king's **h**.	3027
18:11 for the LORD shall deliver *it* into the **h** of	3027
18:14 and they shall be delivered into your **h**.	3027
18:18 host of heaven standing on his **right h**	3225
18:33 he said to *his* chariot man, Turn thine **h**,	3027
20: 6 in thine **h** *is there not* power and might,	3027
21:10 the Edomites revolted from under the **h**	3027
21:10 also did Libnah revolt from under his **h**;	3027
23: 7 every man with his weapons in his **h**;	3027
23:10 every man having his weapon in his **h**,	3027
23:18 LORD by the **h** of the priests the Levites,	3027
24:11 the king's office by the **h** of the Levites,	3027
24:24 delivered a very great host into their **h**,	3027
25:15 deliver their own people out of thine **h**?	3027
25:20 that *he might* deliver them into the **h** *of*	3027
26:11 their account by the **h** of Jeiel the scribe	3027
26:11 the ruler, under the **h** of Hananiah,	3027
26:13 under their **h** *was* an army, three hundred	3027
26:19 and *had* a censer in his **h** to burn incense:	3027
28: 5 him into the **h** of the king of Syria;	3027
28: 5 was also delivered into the **h** of the king	3027
28: 9 he hath delivered them into your **h**,	3027
30: 6 that are escaped out of the **h** of the kings	3709
30:12 Also in Judah the **h** of God was to give	3027
30:16 *they received* of the **h** of the Levites.	3027
31:13 *were* overseers under the **h** of Cononiah	3027
32:11 us out of the **h** of the king of Assyria?	3709
32:13 able to deliver their lands out of mine **h**?	3027
32:14 could deliver his people out of mine **h**,	3027
32:14 be able to deliver you out of mine **h**?	3027
32:15 able to deliver his people out of mine **h**,	3027
32:15 mine hand, and out of the **h** of my fathers:	3027
32:15 shall your God deliver you out of mine **h**?	3027
32:17 not delivered their people out of mine **h**,	3027
32:17 Hezekiah deliver his people out of mine **h**.	3027
32:22 the inhabitants of Jerusalem from the **h** of	3027
32:22 from the **h** of all *other*, and guided them	3027
33: 8 and the ordinances by the **h** of Moses.	3027
34: 2 declined neither *to* the **right h**, nor *to*	3225
34: 9 doors had gathered of the **h** of Manasseh	3027
34:10 they put *it* in the **h** of the workmen that	3027
34:17 delivered it into the **h** of the overseers,	3027
34:17 overseers, and to the **h** of the workmen.	3027
35: 6 the word of the LORD by the **h** of Moses.	3027
36:17 for age: he gave *them* all into his **h**.	3027
Ezr 1: 8 forth by the **h** of Mithredath the treasurer,	3027
5:12 gave them into the **h** of Nebuchadnezzar	3028
6:12 that shall put to their **h** to alter *and*	3028
7: 6 according to the **h** of the LORD his God	3027
7: 9 according to the good **h** of his God upon	3027
7:14 to the law of thy God which *is* in thine **h**;	3028
7:25 that *is* in thine **h**, set magistrates and	3028
7:28 I was strengthened as the **h** of the LORD	3027
8:18 by the good **h** of our God upon us they	3027
8:22 by the **h** of our God *is* upon all them for good	3027
8:26 I even weighed unto their **h** six hundred	3027
8:31 the **h** of our God was upon us,	3027
8:31 he delivered us from the **h** of the enemy,	3709
8:33 by of Meremoth the son of Uriah the priest	3027
9: 2 the **h** of the princes and rulers hath been	3027
9: 7 been delivered into the **h** of the kings of	3027
Ne 1:10 by thy great power, and by thy strong **h**.	3027
2: 8 according to the good **h** of my God upon	3027
2:18 I told them of the **h** of my God which	3027
4:17 and with the other **h** held a weapon.	NIH
6: 5 the fifth time with an open letter in his **h**;	3027
8: 4 Hilkiah, and Maaseiah, on his **right h**;	3225
8: 4 and on his **left h**, Pedaiah, and Mishael,	8040
9:14 and laws, by the **h** of Moses thy servant:	3027
9:27 thou deliveredst them into the **h**	3027
9:27 who saved them out of the **h** of their	3027
9:28 thou them in the **h** of their enemies,	3027
9:30 gavest thou them into the **h** of the people	3027
11:24 *was* at the king's **h** in all matters	3027

Ne 12:31 whereof *one* went on the **right h** upon	3225
Est 2:21 sought to lay **h** on the king Ahasuerus.	3027
3:10 the king took his ring from his **h**,	3027
5: 2 the golden sceptre that *was* in his **h**.	3027
6: 2 sought to lay **h** on the king Ahasuerus.	3027
6: 9 horse be delivered to the **h** of one of	3027
8: 7 because he laid his **h** upon the Jews.	3027
9: 2 to lay **h** on such as sought their hurt:	3027
9:10 but on the spoil laid they not their **h**.	3027
9:15 but on the prey they laid not their **h**.	3027
Job 1:11 put forth thine **h** now, and touch all that	3027
1:12 only upon himself put not forth thine **h**.	3027
2: 5 put forth thine **h** now, and touch his bone	3027
2: 6 said unto Satan, Behold, he *is* in thine **h**;	3027
2:10 we receive good **at the h** of God,	854+4480
5:15 mouth, and from the **h** of the mighty.	3027
6: 9 *that* he would let loose his **h**, and cut me	3027
6:23 Or, Deliver me from the enemy's **h**?	3027
6:23 or, Redeem me from the **h** of the mighty?	3027
9:24 earth is given into the **h** of the wicked:	3027
9:33 *that* might lay his **h** upon us both.	3027
10: 7 *is* none that can deliver out of thine **h**.	3027
11:14 If iniquity *be* in thine **h**, put it far away,	3027
12: 6 into whose **h** God bringeth *abundantly*.	3027
12: 9 Who knoweth not in all these that the **h**	3027
12:10 In whose **h** *is* the soul of every living	3027
13:14 in my teeth, and put my life in mine **h**?	3709
13:21 Withdraw thine **h** far from me: and let not	3709
15:23 that the day of darkness is ready at his **h**.	3027
15:25 For he stretcheth out his **h** against God,	3027
19:21 for the **h** of God hath touched me.	3027
20:22 **h** of the wicked shall come *upon* him.	3027
21: 5 and lay *your* **h** upon *your* mouth.	3027
21:16 their good *is* not in their **h**: the counsel	3027
23: 9 On the **left h**, where he doth work,	8040
23: 9 *him*: he hideth *himself on* the **right h**,	3225
26:13 his **h** hath formed the crooked serpent.	3027
27:11 I will teach you by the **h** of God: *that*	3027
27:22 not spare: he would fain flee out of his **h**.	3027
28: 9 He putteth forth his **h** upon the rock;	3027
29: 9 and laid *their* **h** on their mouth.	3709
29:20 me, and my bow was renewed in my **h**.	3027
30:12 Upon *my* **right h** rise the youth;	3225
30:21 with thy strong **h** thou opposest thyself	3027
30:24 Howbeit *he* will not stretch out *his* **h** to	3027
31:21 have lift up my **h** against the fatherless,	3027
31:25 and because mine **h** had gotten much;	3027
31:27 or my mouth hath kissed my **h**:	3027
33: 7 neither shall my **h** be heavy upon thee.	405
34:20 mighty shall be taken away without **h**.	3027
35: 7 or what receiveth he of thine **h**?	3027
37: 7 He sealeth up the **h** of every man; that all	3027
40: 4 I will lay my **h** upon my mouth.	3027
40:14 thee that thine own **right h** can save thee.	3225
41: 8 Lay thine **h** upon him, remember the	3709
Ps 10:12 Arise, O LORD; O God, lift up thine **h**:	3027
10:14 and spite, to requite *it* with thy **h**:	3027
16: 8 because *he is* at my **right h**, I shall not be	3225
16:11 at thy **right h** *there are* pleasures for	3225
17: 7 O thou that savest by thy **right h** them	3225
17:14 From men *which are* thy **h**, O LORD,	3027
18: 1 him from the **h** of all his enemies,	3709
18: T of all his enemies, and from the **h** of Saul:	3027
18:35 thy **right h** hath holden me up,	3225
20: 6 with the saving strength of his **right h**.	3225
21: 8 Thine **h** shall find out all thine enemies:	3027
21: 8 thy **right h** shall find out those that hate	3225
26:10 and their **right h** is full *of* bribes.	3225
31: 5 Into thine **h** I commit my spirit: thou hast	3027
31: 8 hast not shut me up into the **h** of	3027
31:15 My times *are* in thy **h**: deliver me from	3027
31:15 deliver me from the **h** of mine enemies,	3027
32: 4 and night thy **h** was heavy upon me:	3027
36:11 let not the **h** of the wicked remove me.	3027
37:24 for the LORD upholdeth *him* with his **h**.	3027
37:33 The LORD will not leave him in his **h**,	3027
38: 2 in me, and thy **h** presseth me sore.	3027
39:10 I am consumed by the blow of thine **h**.	3027
44: 2 didst drive out the heathen *with* thy **h**,	3027
44: 3 thy **right h**, and thine arm, and the light	3225
45: 4 thy **right h** shall teach thee terrible *things*.	3225
45: 9 **right h** did stand the queen in gold of	3225
48:10 thy **right h** is full *of* righteousness.	3225
60: 5 save *with* thy **right h**, and hear me.	3225
63: 8 hard after thee: thy **right h** upholdeth me.	3225
71: 4 O my God, out of the **h** of the wicked,	3027
71: 4 out of the **h** of the unrighteous and	3709
73:23 thou hast holden *me* by my **right h**.	3225
74:11 Why withdrawest thou thy **h**, even thy	3027
74:11 thou thy hand, even thy **right h**?	3225
75: 8 For in the **h** of the LORD *there is* a cup,	3027
77:10 *I will remember* the years of the **right h**	3225
77:20 thy people like a flock by the **h** of Moses	3027
78:42 They remembered not his **h**: *nor* the day	3027
78:54 *which* his **right h** had purchased.	3225
78:61 and his glory into the enemy's **h**.	3027
80:15 the vineyard which thy **right h** hath	3225
80:17 Let thy **h** be upon the man of thy right	3027
80:17 thy hand be upon the man of thy **right h**,	3225
81:14 and turned my **h** against their adversaries.	3027
82: 4 rid *them* out of the **h** of the wicked.	3027
88: 5 no more: and they are cut off from thy **h**.	3027
89:13 strong is thy **h**, *and* high is thy right hand.	3027
89:13 strong is thy hand, *and* high is thy **right h**.	3225
89:21 With whom my **h** shall be established:	3027

Ps 89:25 I will set his **h** also in the sea, and his	3027
89:25 in the sea, and his **right h** in the rivers.	3225
89:42 Thou hast set up the **right h** of his	3225
89:48 shall he deliver his soul from the **h** of	3027
91: 7 thy side, and ten thousand at thy **right h**;	3225
95: 4 In his **h** *are* the deep places of the earth:	3027
95: 7 of his pasture, and the sheep of his **h**.	3027
97:10 he delivereth them out of the **h** of	3027
98: 1 hath done marvellous *things*: his **right h**,	3225
104:28 thou openest thine **h**, they are filled *with*	3027
106:10 saved them from the **h** of him that hated	3027
106:10 redeemed them from the **h** of the enemy.	3027
106:26 Therefore he lifted up his **h** against them,	3027
106:41 he gave them into the **h** of the heathen;	3027
106:42 brought into subjection under their **h**.	3027
107: 2 whom he hath redeemed from the **h** of	3027
108: 6 save *with* thy **right h**, and answer me.	3225
109: 6 and let Satan stand at his **right h**.	3225
109:27 That they may know that *this is* thy **h**;	3027
109:31 he shall stand at the **right h** of the poor,	3225
110: 1 unto my Lord, Sit thou at my **right h**,	3225
110: 5 The Lord at thy **right h** shall strike	3225
118:15 the **right h** of the LORD doeth valiantly.	3225
118:16 The **right h** of the LORD is exalted:	3225
118:16 the **right h** of the LORD doeth valiantly.	3225
119:109 My soul *is* continually in my **h**: yet do I	3709
119:173 Let thine **h** help me; for I have chosen	3027
121: 5 The LORD *is* thy shade upon thy **right h**.	3225
123: 2 as the eyes of servants *look* unto the **h** of	3027
123: 2 as the eyes of a maiden unto the **h** of her	3027
127: 4 As arrows *are* in the **h** of a mighty *man*;	3027
129: 7 Wherewith the mower filleth not his **h**,	3709
136:12 With a strong **h**, and with a stretched out	3027
137: 5 let my **right h** forget *her* cunning.	3225
138: 7 thou shalt stretch forth thine **h** against	3027
138: 7 and thy **right h** shall save me.	3225
139: 5 and before, and laid thine **h** upon me.	3709
139:10 Even there shall thy **h** lead me,	3027
139:10 lead me, and thy **right h** shall hold me.	3225
142: 4 I looked *on my* **right h**, and beheld,	3225
144: 7 Send thine **h** from above; rid me,	3027
144: 7 from the **h** of strange children;	3027
144: 8 their **right h** *is* a right hand of falsehood.	3225
144: 8 their right hand *is* a **right h** of falsehood.	3225
144:11 deliver me from the **h** of strange children,	3027
144:11 their **right h** *is* a right hand of falsehood.	3225
144:11 their right hand *is* a **right h** of falsehood.	3225
145:16 Thou openest thine **h**, and satisfiest	3027
149: 6 and a twoedged sword in their **h**;	3027
Pr 1:24 I have stretched out my **h**, and no man	3027
3:16 Length of days *is* in her **right h**; and in	3225
3:16 and in her **left h** riches and honour.	8040
3:27 when it is in the power of thine **h** to do *it*.	3027
4:27 Turn not *to* the **right h** nor *to* the left:	3225
6: 1 *if* thou hast stricken thy **h** with a stranger,	3709
6: 3 thou art come into the **h** of thy friend;	3709
6: 5 Deliver thyself as a roe from the **h** *of*	3027
6: 5 and as a bird from the **h** of the fowler.	3027
10: 4 poor that dealeth *with* a slack **h**:	3709
10: 4 but the **h** of the diligent maketh rich.	3027
11:21 *Though* **h** *join* in hand, the wicked shall	3027
11:21 *Though* hand *join* in **h**, the wicked shall	3027
12:24 The **h** of the diligent shall bear rule:	3027
16: 5 *though* **h** *join* in hand, he shall not be	3027
16: 5 *though* hand *join* in **h**, he shall not be	3027
17:16 *is there* a price in the **h** of a fool	3027
19:24 A slothful *man* hideth his **h** in *his* bosom,	3027
21: 1 The king's heart *is* in the **h** of the LORD,	3027
26: 6 He that sendeth a message by the **h** of a	3027
26: 9 *As* a thorn goeth up into the **h** of a	3027
26:15 The slothful hideth his **h** in *his* bosom;	3027
27:16 wind, and the ointment of his **right h**,	3225
30:32 thought evil, *lay thine* **h** upon thy mouth.	3027
31:20 She stretcheth out her **h** to the poor; yea,	3709
Ecc 2:24 also I saw, that it *was* from the **h** of God.	3027
5:14 a son, and *there is* nothing in his **h**.	3027
5:15 which he may carry away in his **h**.	3027
7:18 yea, also from this withdraw not thine **h**:	3027
9: 1 and their works, *are* in the **h** of God.	3027
9:10 Whatsoever thy **h** findeth to do, do *it* with	3027
10: 2 A wise *man's* heart *is* at his **right h**;	3225
11: 6 and in the evening withhold not thine **h**:	3027
SS 2: 6 His **left h** *is* under my head, and his right	8040
2: 6 head, and his **right h** doth embrace me.	3225
5: 4 My beloved put in his **h** by the hole *of*	3027
5: 4 his **left h** *should be* under my head,	8040
8: 3 and his **right h** should embrace me.	3225
Isa 1:12 who hath required this at your **h**, to tread	3027
1:25 I will turn my **h** upon thee, and purely	3027
3: 6 our ruler, and *let* this ruin *be* under thy **h**:	3027
5:25 he hath stretched forth his **h** against them,	3027
5:25 away, but his **h** *is* stretched out still.	3027
6: 6 unto me, having a live coal in his **h**,	3027
8:11 LORD spake thus to me with a strong **h**,	3027
9:12 away, but his **h** *is* stretched out still.	3027
9:17 away, but his **h** *is* stretched out still.	3027
9:20 he shall snatch on the **right h**,	3225
9:20 he shall eat on the **left h**, and they shall	8040
9:21 away, but his **h** *is* stretched out still.	3027
10: 4 away, but his **h** *is* stretched out still.	3027
10: 5 the staff in their **h** *is* mine indignation.	3027
10:10 As my **h** hath found the kingdoms of	3027
10:13 By the strength of my **h** I have done *it*,	3027
10:14 my **h** hath found as a nest the riches of	3027
10:32 he shall shake his **h** *against* the mount of	3027

H

Isa
11: 8	the weaned child shall put his **h** on	3027
11:11	*that* the Lord shall set his **h** again	3027
11:14	they shall lay their **h** upon Edom and	3027
11:15	with his mighty wind shall he shake his **h**	3027
13: 2	exalt the voice unto them, shake the **h**,	3027
13: 6	Howl ye; for the day of the Lord *is* **at h**;	7138
14:26	this *is* the **h** that is stretched out upon all	3027
14:27	disannul *it?* and his **h** *is* stretched out,	3027
19: 4	the Egyptians will I give over into the **h** of	3027
19:16	of the shaking of the **h** of the Lord of	3027
22:21	I will commit thy government into his **h**:	3027
23:11	He stretched out his **h** over the sea,	3027
25:10	For in this mountain shall the **h** of the	3027
26:11	Lord, *when* thy **h** is lifted up, they will	3027
28: 2	shall cast down to the earth with the **h**.	3027
28: 4	while it is yet in his **h** he eateth it up.	3709
30:21	when ye **turn to the right h**, and when	541
31: 3	When the Lord shall stretch out his **h**,	3027
34:17	his **h** hath divided it unto them by line:	3027
36: 6	lean, it will go into his **h**, and pierce it:	3709
36:15	city shall not be delivered into the **h** of	3027
36:18	land out of the **h** of the king of Assyria?	3027
36:19	have they delivered Samaria out of my **h**?	3027
36:20	have delivered their land out of my **h**,	3027
36:20	should deliver Jerusalem out of my **h**?	3027
37:10	Jerusalem shall not be given into the **h** of	3027
37:14	Hezekiah received the letter from the **h** of	3027
37:20	O Lord our God, save us from his **h**,	3027
38: 6	this city out of the **h** of the king of Assyria:	3709
40: 2	for she hath received of the Lord's **h**	3027
40:10	the Lord God will come with strong *h*,	NIH
40:12	the waters in the **hollow** of his **h**,	8168
41:10	I will uphold thee with the **right h** of my	3225
41:13	I the Lord thy God will hold thy **right h**,	3225
41:20	that the **h** of the Lord hath done this,	3027
42: 6	will hold thine **h**, and will keep thee,	3027
43:13	*is* none that can deliver out of my **h**:	3027
44: 5	another shall subscribe *with* his **h** unto	3027
44:20	nor say, *Is there* not a lie in my **right h**?	3225
45: 1	to Cyrus, whose **right h** I have holden,	3225
47: 6	and given them into thine **h**:	3027
48:13	Mine **h** also hath laid the foundation of	3027
48:13	my **right h** hath spanned the heavens;	3225
49: 2	in the shadow of his **h** hath he hid me,	3027
49:22	I will lift up mine **h** to the Gentiles,	3027
50: 2	Is my **h** shortened at all, that *it* cannot	3027
50:11	This shall ye have of mine **h**; ye shall lie	3027
51:16	covered thee in the shadow of mine **h**,	3027
51:17	which hast drunk at the **h** of the Lord	3027
51:18	*is there any* that taketh her by the **h**	3027
51:22	I have taken out of thine **h** the cup of	3027
51:23	I will put it into the **h** of them that afflict	3027
53:10	of the Lord shall prosper in his **h**.	3027
54: 3	For thou shalt break forth *on* the **right h**	3225
56: 2	and keepeth his **h** from doing any evil.	3027
57:10	thou hast found the life of thine **h**;	3027
59: 1	Behold, the Lord's **h** is not shortened,	3027
62: 3	shalt also be a crown of glory in the **h**	3027
62: 3	and a royal diadem in the **h** of thy God.	3709
62: 8	The Lord hath sworn by his **right h**,	3225
63:12	That led *them* by the **right h** of Moses	3225
64: 8	and we all *are* the work of thine **h**.	3027
66: 2	For all those *things* hath mine **h** made,	3027
66:14	the **h** of the Lord shall be known	3027

Jer
1: 9	the Lord put forth his **h**, and touched my	3027
6: 9	turn back thine **h** as a grapegatherer into	3027
6:12	for I will stretch out my **h** upon	3027
11:21	of the Lord, that thou die not by our **h**:	3027
12: 7	of my soul into the **h** of her enemies.	3709
15: 6	will I stretch out my **h** against thee,	3027
15:17	nor rejoiced; I sat alone because of thy **h**:	3027
15:21	I will deliver thee out of the **h** of	3027
15:21	I will redeem thee out of the **h** of	3709
16:21	I will cause them to know mine **h** and my	3027
18: 4	of clay was marred in the **h** of the potter:	3027
18: 6	as the clay *is* in the potter's **h**, so *are* ye in	3027
18: 6	so *are* ye in mine **h**, O house of Israel.	3027
20: 4	I will give all Judah into the **h** of the king	3027
20: 5	will I give into the **h** of their enemies,	3027
20:13	soul of the poor from the **h** of evildoers.	3027
21: 5	fight against you with an outstretched **h**	3027
21: 7	into the **h** of Nebuchadrezzar king of	3027
21: 7	into the **h** of their enemies, and into	3027
21: 7	and into the **h** of those that seek their life:	3027
21:10	it shall be given into the **h** of the king of	3027
21:12	deliver *him that is* spoiled out of the **h** of	3027
22: 3	deliver the spoiled out of the **h** of	3027
22:24	of Judah were the signet upon my right **h**,	3027
22:25	I will give thee into the **h** of them that	3027
22:25	I will give thee into the **h** of them that	3027
22:25	even into the **h** of Nebuchadrezzar king	3027
22:25	and into the **h** of the Chaldeans,	3027
23:23	*Am* I a God at **h**, saith the Lord,	7138
25:15	Take the wine cup of this fury at mine **h**,	3027
25:17	took I the cup at the Lord's **h**,	3027
25:28	if they refuse to take the cup at thine **h**	3027
26:14	As for me, behold, I *am* in your **h**: do	3027
26:24	Nevertheless the **h** of Ahikam the son of	3027
26:24	*they* should not give him into the **h** of	3027
27: 3	by the **h** of the messengers which come	3027
27: 6	have I given all these lands into the **h**	3027
27: 8	until I have consumed them by his **h**.	3027
29: 3	By the **h** of Elasah the son of Shaphan,	3027
29:21	I will deliver them into the **h** of	3027
31:11	ransomed him from the **h** of *him that was*	3027

Jer
31:32	in the day *that* I took them by the **h**,	3027
32: 3	I *will* give this city into the **h** of the king	3027
32: 4	not escape out of the **h** of the Chaldeans,	3027
32: 4	shall surely be delivered into the **h** of	3027
32:21	with a strong **h**, and with a stretched out	3027
32:24	the city is given into the **h** of	3027
32:25	for the city is given into the **h** of	3027
32:28	I *will* give this city into the **h** of	3027
32:28	into the **h** of Nebuchadrezzar king of	3027
32:36	It shall be delivered into the **h** of the king	3027
32:43	it is given into the **h** of the Chaldeans.	3027
34: 2	I *will* give this city into the **h** of the king	3027
34: 3	thou shalt not escape out of his **h**,	3027
34: 3	surely be taken, and delivered into his **h**;	3027
34:20	I will even give them into the **h** of their	3027
34:20	and into the **h** of them that seek their life:	3027
34:21	his princes will I give into the **h** of their	3027
34:21	into the **h** of them that seek their life,	3027
34:21	into the **h** of the king of Babylon's army,	3027
36:14	Take in thine **h** the roll wherein thou hast	3027
36:14	the son of Neriah took the roll in his **h**,	3027
37:17	thou shalt be delivered into the **h** of	3027
38: 3	This city shall surely be given into the **h**	3027
38: 5	the king said, Behold, he *is* in your **h**:	3027
38:16	neither will I give thee into the **h** of these	3027
38:18	shall this city be given into the **h** of	3027
38:18	and thou shalt not escape out of their **h**.	3027
38:19	lest they deliver me into their **h**,	3027
38:23	thou shalt not escape out of their **h**,	3027
38:23	shalt be taken by the **h** of the king of	3027
39:17	thou shalt not be given into the **h** of	3027
40: 4	the chains which *were* upon thine **h**.	3027
41: 5	with offerings and incense in their **h**,	3027
42:11	save you, and to deliver you from his **h**.	3027
43: 3	for to deliver us into the **h** of	3027
43: 9	Take great stones in thine **h**, and hide	3027
44:25	and fulfilled with your **h**, saying,	3027
44:30	king of Egypt into the **h** of his enemies,	3027
44:30	and into the **h** of them that seek his life;	3027
44:30	I gave Zedekiah king of Judah into the **h**	3027
46:24	she shall be delivered into the **h** of	3027
46:26	I will deliver them into the **h** of those	3027
46:26	into the **h** of Nebuchadrezzar king of	3027
46:26	of Babylon, and into the **h** of his servants:	3027
50:15	she hath given her **h**: her foundations are	3027
51: 7	*hath been* a golden cup in the Lord's **h**,	3027
51:25	I will stretch out mine **h** upon thee,	3027

La
1: 7	when her people fell into the **h** of	3027
1:10	The adversary hath spread out his **h** upon	3027
1:14	of my transgressions is bound by his **h**:	3027
2: 3	he hath drawn back his **right h** from	3225
2: 4	*he* stood *with* his **right h** as an adversary,	3225
2: 7	he hath given up into the **h** of the enemy	3027
2: 8	he hath not withdrawn his **h** from	3027
3: 3	he turneth his **h** *against me* all the day.	3027
5: 6	We have given the **h** *to* the Egyptians,	3027
5: 8	*is* none that doth deliver *us* out of their **h**.	3027
5:12	Princes are hanged up by their **h**:	3027

Eze
1: 3	the **h** of the Lord was there upon him.	3027
2: 9	I looked, behold, a **h** *was* sent unto me;	3027
3:14	the **h** of the Lord was strong upon me.	3027
3:18	but his blood will I require at thine **h**.	3027
3:20	but his blood will I require at thine **h**.	3027
3:22	the **h** of the Lord was there upon me;	3027
6:11	Smite with thine **h**, and stamp with thy	3709
6:14	So will I stretch out mine **h** upon them,	3027
8: 1	that the **h** of the Lord God fell there upon	3027
8: 3	he put forth the form of a **h**, and took me	3027
8:11	with every man his censer in his **h**;	3027
9: 1	man *with* his destroying weapon in his **h**.	3027
9: 2	every man a slaughter weapon in his **h**;	3027
10: 2	fill thine **h** *with* coals of fire from	2651
10: 7	*one* cherub stretched forth his **h** from	3027
10: 8	the form of a man's **h** under their wings.	3027
12: 7	I digged through the wall with mine **h**;	3027
12:23	The days are at **h**, and the effect of every	7126
13: 9	mine **h** shall be upon the prophets that	3027
13:21	deliver my people out of your **h**,	3027
13:21	they shall be no more in your **h** to be	3027
13:23	for I will deliver my people out of your **h**:	3027
14: 9	I will stretch out my **h** upon him,	3027
14:13	will I stretch out mine **h** upon it,	3027
16:27	I have stretched out my **h** over thee,	3027
16:39	I will also give thee into their **h**,	3027
16:46	her daughters that dwell at thy **left h**:	8040
16:46	that dwelleth at thy **right h**, *is* Sodom	3225
16:49	did she strengthen the **h** of the poor	3027
17:18	he had given his **h**, and hath done all	3027
18: 8	*that* hath withdrawn his **h** from iniquity,	3027
18:17	*That* hath taken off his **h** from the poor,	3027
20: 5	up mine **h** unto the seed of the house	3027
20: 5	when I lifted up mine **h** unto them,	3027
20: 6	In the day *that* I lifted up mine **h** unto	3027
20:15	Yet also I lifted up my **h** unto them in	3027
20:22	Nevertheless I withdrew mine **h**,	3027
20:23	I lifted up mine **h** unto them in the	3027
20:28	the which I lifted up mine **h** to give it to	3027
20:33	with a mighty **h**, and with a stretched out	3027
20:34	with a mighty **h**, and with a stretched out	3027
20:42	I lifted up mine **h** to give it to your fathers.	3027
21:11	to give it into the **h** of the slayer.	3027
21:16	*either* **on the right h**, *or* on the left,	3231
21:22	At his **right h** was the divination for	3225
21:24	ye shall be taken with the **h**.	3709
21:31	deliver thee into the **h** of brutish men,	3027

Eze
22:13	have smitten mine **h** at thy dishonest gain	3709
23: 9	Wherefore I have delivered her into the **h**	3027
23: 9	into the **h** of the Assyrians, upon whom	3027
23:28	I *will* deliver thee into the **h** *of them*	3027
23:28	into the **h** *of them* from whom thy mind	3027
23:31	therefore will I give her cup into thine **h**.	3027
25: 7	I will stretch out mine **h** upon thee,	3027
25:13	will also stretch out mine **h** upon Edom,	3027
25:14	upon Edom by the **h** of my people Israel:	3027
25:16	I will stretch out mine **h** upon	3027
27:15	isles *were* the merchandise of thine **h**:	3027
28: 9	no God, in the **h** of him that slayeth thee.	3027
28:10	the uncircumcised by the **h** of strangers:	3027
29: 7	When they took hold of thee by thy **h**,	3709
30:10	the **h** of Nebuchadrezzar king of Babylon.	3027
30:12	and sell the land into the **h** of the wicked:	3027
30:12	all that is therein, by the **h** of strangers:	3027
30:22	I will cause the sword to fall out of his **h**.	3027
30:24	of Babylon, and put my sword in his **h**:	3027
30:25	when I shall put my sword into the **h** of	3027
31:11	delivered him into the **h** of the mighty	3027
33: 6	blood will I require at the watchman's **h**.	3027
33: 8	but his blood will I require at thine **h**.	3027
33:22	Now the **h** of the Lord was upon me in	3027
34:10	I will require my flock at their **h**,	3027
34:27	delivered them out of the **h** of those that	3027
35: 3	I will stretch out mine **h** against thee,	3027
36: 7	have lifted up mine **h**, Surely the heathen	3027
36: 8	people of Israel; for they are **at h** to come.	7126
37: 1	The **h** of the Lord was upon me,	3027
37:17	and they shall become one in thine **h**.	3027
37:19	*is* in the **h** of Ephraim, and the tribes	3027
37:19	one stick, and they shall be one in mine **h**.	3027
37:20	shall be in thine **h** before their eyes.	3027
38:12	to turn thine **h** upon the desolate places	3027
39: 3	I will smite thy bow out of thy left **h**,	3027
39: 3	thine arrows to fall out of thy right **h**.	3027
39:21	and my **h** that I have laid upon them.	3027
39:23	gave them into the **h** of their enemies:	3027
40: 1	in the selfsame day the **h** of the Lord	3027
40: 3	a line of flax in his **h**, and a measuring	3027
40: 5	in the man's **h** a measuring reed of six	3027
40: 5	cubits *long* by the cubit and a **h breadth**:	2948
40:43	a **h broad**, fastened round about:	2948
43:13	The cubit *is* a cubit and a **h breadth**;	2948
44:12	have I lift up mine **h** against them,	3027
46: 7	the lambs according as his **h** shall attain	3027
47: 3	when the man that had the line in his **h**	3027
47:14	*concerning* the which I lifted up mine **h**	3027

Da
1: 2	gave Jehoiakim king of Judah into his **h**,	3027
2:38	of the heaven hath he given into thine **h**,	3028
3:17	he will deliver *us* out of thine **h**, O king.	3028
4:35	none can stay his **h**, or say unto him,	3028
5: 5	hour came forth fingers of a man's **h**,	3028
5: 5	the king saw the part of the **h** that wrote.	3028
5:23	the God in whose **h** thy breath *is*, and	3028
5:24	*was* the part of the **h** sent from him;	3028
7:25	they shall be given into his **h** until a time	3028
8: 4	*there any* that could deliver out of his **h**;	3027
8: 7	that could deliver the ram out of his **h**.	3027
8:25	he shall cause craft to prosper in his **h**;	3027
8:25	but he shall be broken without **h**.	3027
9:15	out of the land of Egypt with a mighty **h**,	3027
10:10	a **h** touched me, which set me upon	3027
11:11	the multitude shall be given into his **h**.	3027
11:16	which by his **h** shall be consumed.	3027
11:41	shall escape out of his **h**, *even* Edom,	3027
11:42	He shall stretch forth his **h** also upon	3027
12: 7	when he held up his **right h** and his left	3225
12: 7	his right hand and his **left h** unto heaven,	8040

Hos
2:10	and none shall deliver her out of mine **h**,	3027
7: 5	he stretched out his **h** with scorners.	3027
12: 7	the balances of deceit *are* in his **h**.	3027

Joel
1:15	for the day of the Lord *is* **at h**, and as a	7138
2: 1	of the Lord cometh, for *it is* **nigh at h**;	7138
3: 8	your daughters into the **h** of the children	3027

Am
1: 8	and I will turn mine **h** against Ekron:	3027
5:19	leaned his **h** on the wall, and a serpent bit	3027
7: 7	by a plumbline, with a plumbline in his **h**.	3027
9: 2	into hell, thence shall mine **h** take them;	3027

Jnh
4:11	that cannot discern between their **right h**	3225
4:11	between their right hand and their **left h**;	8040

Mic
2: 1	because it is in the power of their **h**.	3027
4:10	redeem thee from the **h** of thine enemies.	3709
5: 9	Thine **h** shall be lift up upon thine	3027
5:12	I will cut off witchcrafts out of thine **h**;	3027
7:16	they shall lay *their* **h** upon *their* mouth,	3027

Hab
2:16	the cup of the Lord's **right h** shall be	3225
3: 4	he had horns *coming* out of his **h**:	3027

Zep
1: 4	I will also stretch out mine **h** upon Judah,	3027
1: 7	for the day of the Lord *is* **at h**:	7138
2:13	he will stretch out his **h** against the north,	3027
2:15	passeth by her shall hiss, *and* wag his **h**.	3027

Zec
2: 1	a man with a measuring line in his **h**.	3027
2: 9	I *will* shake mine **h** upon them,	3027
3: 1	Satan standing at his **right h** to resist him.	3225
4:10	shall see the plummet in the **h** of	3027
8: 4	every man with his staff in his **h** for very	3027
11: 6	the men every one into his neighbour's **h**,	3027
11: 6	and into the **h** of his king:	3027
11: 6	and out of their **h** I will not deliver *them*.	3027
12: 6	about, on the **right h** and on the left:	3225
13: 7	I will turn mine **h** upon the little ones.	3027
14:13	they shall lay hold every one on the **h** of	3027
14:13	his **h** shall rise up against the hand of his	3027

H

H

Zec 14:13 his hand shall rise up against the **h** of his 3027
Mal 1:10 neither will I accept an offering at your **h**. 3027
 1:13 should I accept this of your **h**? saith 3027
 2:13 or receiveth *it with* good will at your **h**. 3027
Mt 3: 2 for the kingdom of heaven is at **h**. 1448
 3:12 Whose fan *is* in his **h**, and he will 5495
 4:17 Repent: for the kingdom of heaven is at **h** 1448
 5:30 And if thy right **h** offend thee, cut it off, 5495
 6: 3 let not thy left **h** know what thy right 710
 6: 3 not thy left hand know what thy right **h** 1188
 8: 3 Jesus put forth *his* **h**, and touched him, 5495
 8:15 And he touched her **h**, and the fever left 5495
 9:18 but come and lay thy **h** upon her, 5495
 9:25 took her by the **h**, and the maid arose. 5495
 10: 7 saying, The kingdom of heaven is at **h**. 1448
 12:10 was a man which had *his* **h** withered. 5495
 12:13 saith he to the man, Stretch forth thine **h**. 5495
 12:49 And he stretched forth his **h** toward his 5495
 14:31 immediately Jesus stretched forth his **h**. 5495
 18: 8 Wherefore if thy **h** or thy foot offend thee, 5495
 20:21 the one on thy **right h**, and the other on 1188
 20:23 baptized *with:* but to sit on my **right h**, 1188
 22:13 Bind him **h** and foot, and take him away, 5495
 22:44 unto my Lord, Sit thou on my **right h**, 1188
 25:33 he shall set the sheep on his **right h**, 1188
 25:34 the King say unto them on his **right h**, 1188
 25:41 shall he say also unto them on the **left h**, 2176
 26:18 The Master saith, My time is at **h**. 1451
 26:23 He that dippeth *his* **h** with me in the dish, 5495
 26:45 the hour is at **h**, and the Son of man is 1448
 26:46 behold, he is at **h** that doth betray me. 1448
 26:51 were with Jesus stretched out *his* **h**, 5495
 26:64 Son of man sitting on the **right h** of power 1188
 27:29 *it* upon his head, and a reed in his **right h**: 1188
 27:38 on the **right h**, and another on the left. 1188
Mk 1:15 and the kingdom of God is at **h**: 1448
 1:31 And he came and took her by the **h**, 5495
 1:41 put forth *his* **h**, and touched him, 5495
 3: 1 was a man there which had a withered **h**. 5495
 3: 3 unto the man which had the withered **h**, 5495
 3: 5 saith unto the man, Stretch forth thine **h**. 5495
 3: 5 his **h** was restored whole as the other. 5495
 5:41 he took the damsel by the **h**, 5495
 7:32 they beseech him to put *his* **h** upon him. 5495
 8:23 And he took the blind man by the **h**, 5495
 9:27 Jesus took him by the **h**, and lifted up 5495
 9:43 And if thy **h** offend thee, cut it off: it is 5495
 10:37 on thy **right h**, and the other on thy left 1188
 10:37 and the other on thy **left h**, in thy glory. 2176
 10:40 But to sit on my **right h** and on my left 1188
 10:40 and on my **left h** is not mine to give; 2176
 12:36 said to my Lord, Sit thou on my **right h**, 1188
 14:42 let us go; lo, he that betrayeth me is at **h**. 1448
 14:62 Son of man sitting on the **right h** of power 1188
 15:27 one on his **right h**, and the other on his 1188
 16:19 heaven, and sat on the **right h** of God. 1188
Lk 1: 1 Forasmuch as many have **taken in h** to 2021
 1:66 And the **h** of the Lord was with him. 5495
 1:71 and from the **h** of all that hate us; 5495
 1:74 *we* being delivered out of the **h** of our 5495
 3:17 Whose fan *is* in his **h**, and he will 5495
 5:13 And he put forth *his* **h**, and touched him, 5495
 6: 6 there was a man whose right **h** was 5495
 6: 8 to the man which had the withered **h**, 5495
 6:10 he said unto the man, Stretch forth thy **h**. 5495
 6:10 his **h** was restored whole as the other. 5495
 8:54 and took her by the **h**, and called, saying, 5495
 9:62 No *man* having put his **h** to the plough, 5495
 15:22 put *it* on him; and put a ring on his **h**, 5495
 20:42 said to my Lord, Sit thou on my **right h**, 1188
 21:30 selves that summer is now **nigh at h**. 1451
 21:31 ye that the kingdom of God is **nigh at h**. 1451
 22:21 the **h** of him that betrayeth me *is* with me 5495
 22:69 sit on the **right h** of the power of God. 1188
 23:33 one on the **right h**, and the other on 1188
Jn 2:13 And the Jews' passover was at **h**, 1451
 3:35 and hath given all *things* into his **h**. 5495
 7: 2 the Jews' feast of tabernacles was at **h**. 1451
 10:28 shall any *man* pluck them out of my **h**. 5495
 10:29 able to pluck *them* out of my Father's **h**. 5495
 10:39 take him: but he escaped out of their **h**, 5495
 11:44 bound **h** and foot with graveclothes; 5495
 11:55 And the Jews' passover was **nigh at h**: 1451
 18:22 **stroke** Jesus **with the palm of**
 his **h**, 1325+4475
 19:42 *day;* for the sepulchre was **nigh at h**. 1451
 20:25 and thrust my **h** into his side, I will not 5495
 20:27 reach hither thy **h**, and thrust *it* into my 5495
Ac 2:25 for he is on my **right h**, that I should not 1188
 2:33 Therefore being by the **right h** of God 1188
 2:34 unto my Lord, Sit thou on my **right h**, 1188
 3: 7 he took him by the right **h**, and lift *him* 5495
 4:28 to do whatsoever thy **h** and thy counsel 5495
 4:30 By stretching forth thine **h** to heal; 5495
 5:31 Him hath God exalted with his **right h** *to* 1188
 7:25 that God by his **h** would deliver them: 5495
 7:35 a deliverer by the **h** of the angel which 5495
 7:50 Hath not my **h** made all these *things*? 5495
 7:55 and Jesus standing on the **right h** of God, 1188
 7:56 the Son of man standing on the **right h** 1188
 9: 8 saw no *man:* but they **led** him **by the h**, 5496
 9:12 and putting *his* **h** on him, that he might 5495
 9:41 And he gave her *his* **h**, and lift her up, 5495
 11:21 And the **h** of the Lord was with them: 5495
 12:11 hath delivered me out of the **h** of Herod, 5495

Ac 12:17 beckoning unto them with the **h** to hold 5495
 13:11 the **h** of the Lord *is* upon thee, 5495
 13:11 seeking *some* to **lead** him **by the h**. 5497
 13:16 and beckoning with *his* **h** said, Men of 5495
 19:33 And Alexander beckoned with the **h**, 2176
 21: 3 we left it on the **left h**, and sailed into 2176
 21:40 beckoned with the **h** unto the people. 5495
 22:11 being **led by the h** of them that were 5496
 23:19 Then the chief captain took him by the **h**, 5495
 26: 1 Then Paul stretched forth the **h**, 5495
 28: 3 out of the heat, and fastened on his **h**. 5495
 28: 4 saw the venomous beast hang on his **h**, 5495
Ro 8:34 *again*, who is even at the **right h** of God, 1188
 13:12 The night is far spent, the day is at **h**: 1448
1Co 12:15 the foot shall say, Because I am not the **h**, 5495
 12:21 And the eye cannot say unto the **h**, I have 5495
 16:21 salutation of *me* Paul with mine own **h**. 5495
2Co 5: 1 a house **not made with h**, eternal in 886
 6: 7 armour of righteousness on the **right h** 1188
 10:16 of *things* **made ready** to our **h**. 1519+2092
Gal 3:19 *it was* ordained by angels in the **h** of a 5495
 6:11 have written unto you with mine own **h**. 5495
Eph 1:20 set *him* at his own **right h** in the heavenly 1188
Php 5: 8 be known unto all men. The Lord *is* at **h**. 1451
Col 3: 1 Christ sitteth on the **right h** of God. 1188
 4:18 The salutation by the **h** of me Paul. 5495
2Th 2: 2 from us, as that the day of Christ is at **h**. 1764
 3:17 The salutation of Paul with mine own **h**, 5495
2Ti 4: 6 and the time of my departure is at **h**. 2186
Phm 1:19 I Paul have written *it* with mine own **h**, 5495
Heb 1: 3 sat down on the **right h** of the Majesty 1188
 1:13 Sit on my **right h**, until I make thine 1188
 8: 1 who is set on the **right h** of the throne of 1188
 8: 9 to lead them out of the land of Egypt; 5495
 10:12 for ever, sat down on the **right h** of God; 1188
 12: 2 is set down at the **right h** of the throne of 1188
1Pe 3:22 into heaven, and is on the **right h** of God; 1188
 4: 7 But the end of all *things* is at **h**: be ye 1448
 5: 6 therefore under the mighty **h** of God, 5495
Rev 1: 3 are written therein: for the time *is* at **h**. 1451
 1:16 And he had in his right **h** seven stars: 5495
 1:17 And he laid his right **h** upon me, 5495
 1:20 stars which thou sawest in my **right h**, 1188
 2: 1 holdeth the seven stars in his **right h**, 1188
 5: 1 I saw in the **right h** of him that sat on 1188
 5: 7 took the book out of the **right h** of him 1188
 6: 5 on him had a pair of balances in his **h**. 5495
 8: 4 up before God out of the angel's **h**. 5495
 10: 2 And he had in his **h** a little book open: 5495
 10: 5 upon the earth lifted up his **h** to heaven, 5495
 10: 8 take the little book which is open in the **h** 5495
 10:10 I took the little book out of the angel's **h**, 5495
 13:16 receive a mark in their right **h**, or in their 5495
 14: 9 *his* mark in his forehead, or in his **h**, 5495
 14:14 golden crown, and in his **h** a sharp sickle. 5495
 17: 4 having a golden cup in her **h** full of 5495
 19: 2 avenged the blood of his servants at her **h**. 5495
 20: 1 bottomless *pit* and a great chain in his **h**. 5495
 22:10 prophecy of this book: for the time is at **h**. 1451

HANDBREADTH (5) [BREADTH, HAND]
Ex 25:25 thou shalt make unto it a border of a **h** 2948
 37:12 Also he made thereunto a border of a **h** 2948
1Ki 7:26 it *was* a **h** thick, and the brim thereof was 2947
2Ch 4: 5 the thickness of it *was* a **h**, and the brim 2947
Ps 39: 5 Behold, thou hast made my days *as* a **h**; 2947

HANDED (1) [HAND]
2Sa 17: 2 upon him while he *is* weary and weak **h**, 3027

HANDFUL (9) [HAND]
Lev 2: 2 shall **take** thereout his **h** of 4393+7061+7062
 5:12 priest shall **take** his **h** of it, 4393+7061+7062
 6:15 he shall take of it his **h**, of the flour of 7062
 9:17 took a **h** thereof, and burnt *it* upon 3709+4390
Nu 5:26 the priest shall **take a h** of the offering, 7061
1Ki 17:12 **h** of meal in a barrel, and a little oil 3709+4393
Ps 72:16 There shall be a **h** of corn in the earth 6451
Ecc 4: 6 Better *is* a **h** with quietness, 3709+4393
Jer 9:22 as the **h** after the harvestman, 5995

HANDFULS (5) [HAND]
Ge 41:47 years the earth brought forth by **h**. 7062
Ex 9: 8 Take to you **h** of ashes of 2651+4393
Ru 2:16 let fall also *some* of the **h** of purpose for 6653
1Ki 20:10 if the dust of Samaria shall suffice for **h** for 8168
Eze 13:19 will ye pollute me among my people for **h** 8168

HANDKERCHIEFS (1) [KERCHIEFS]
Ac 19:12 were brought unto the sick **h** or aprons, 4676

HANDLE (11) [HANDLED, HANDLES, HANDLETH, HANDLING]
Ge 4:21 was the father of all such as **h** the harp 8610
Jdg 5:14 out of Zebulun they that **h** the pen of 4900
1Ch 12: 8 battle, that could **h** shield and buckler, 6186
2Ch 25: 5 to war, that could **h** spear and shield. 270
Ps 115: 7 They *have* hands, but they **h** not: feet 4184
Jer 46: 9 and the Libyans, that **h** the shield; 8610
 46: 9 the Lydians, that **h** *and* bend the bow. 8610
Eze 27:29 all that **h** the oar, the mariners, *and* all 8610
Lk 24:39 **h** me, and see; for a spirit hath not flesh 5584
Col 2:21 (Touch not; taste not; **h** not; 2345

HANDLED (3) [HANDLE]
Eze 21:11 that it may be **h**: 3709+8610+871.1+1886.1
Mk 12: 4 head, and sent *him* away shamefully **h**. 821
1Jn 1: 1 and our hands have **h**, of the Word of life; 5584

HANDLES (1) [HANDLE]
SS 5: 5 smelling myrrh, upon the **h** of the lock. 3709

HANDLETH (3) [HANDLE]
Pr 16:20 that **h** a matter **wisely** shall find good: 7919
Jer 50:16 that **h** the sickle in the time of harvest; 8610
Am 2:15 Neither shall he stand that **h** the bow; 8610

HANDLING (2) [HANDLE]
Eze 38: 4 and shields, all of them **h** swords; 8610
2Co 4: 2 nor **h** the word of God **deceitfully**; 1389

HANDMAID (45) [MAID]
Ge 16: 1 no *children:* and she had a **h**, 8198
 25:12 Sarah's **h**, bare unto Abraham; 8198
 29:24 his daughter Leah Zilpah his maid *for* a **h**. 8198
 29:29 his daughter Bilhah his **h** to be her maid. 8198
 30: 4 And she gave him Bilhah her **h** to wife: 8198
 35:25 the sons of Bilhah, Rachel's; Dan, 8198
 35:26 the sons of Zilpah, Leah's **h**; Gad, 8198
Ex 23:12 the son of thy **h**, and the stranger, may be 519
Jdg 19:19 for thy **h**, and for the young man *which is* 519
Ru 2:13 thou hast spoken friendly unto thine **h**, 8198
 3: 9 And she answered, I *am* Ruth thine **h**: 519
 3: 9 spread therefore thy skirt over thine **h**; 519
1Sa 1:11 indeed look on the affliction of thine **h**, 519
 1:11 not forget thine **h**, but wilt give unto thine 519
 1:11 wilt give unto thine **h** a man child, then 519
 1:16 Count not thine **h** for a daughter of Belial: 519
 1:18 said, Let thine **h** find grace in thy sight. 8198
 25:24 me *let this* iniquity *be:* and let thine **h**, 519
 25:24 and hear the words of thine **h**. 519
 25:25 thine **h** saw not the young men of my lord, 519
 25:27 now this blessing which thine **h** hath 8198
 25:28 I pray thee, forgive the trespass of thine **h**: 519
 25:31 well with my lord, then remember thine **h**. 519
 25:41 *let* thine **h** *be* a servant to wash the feet of 519
 28:21 thine **h** hath obeyed thy voice, and I have 8198
 28:22 thou also unto the voice of thine **h**, 8198
2Sa 14: 6 thy **h** had two sons, and they two strove 8198
 14: 7 the whole family is risen against thine **h**, 8198
 14:12 the woman said, Let thine **h**, I pray thee, 8198
 14:15 **h** said, I will now speak unto the king; 8198
 14:15 the king will perform the request of his **h**. 519
 14:16 to deliver his **h** out of the hand of the man 519
 14:17 **h** said, The word of my lord the king 8198
 14:19 all these words in the mouth of thine **h**: 8198
 20:17 said unto him, Hear the words of thine **h**. 519
1Ki 1:13 O king, saidst unto thine **h**, saying, 519
 1:17 swarest by the Lᴏʀᴅ thy God unto thine **h**, 519
 3:20 thine **h** slept, and laid it in her bosom, 519
2Ki 4: 2 Thine **h** hath not any thing in the house, 8198
 4:16 thou man of God, do not lie unto thine **h**. 8198
Ps 86:16 thy servant, and save the son of thine **h**. 519
 116:16 I *am* thy servant, *and* the son of thy **h**: 519
Pr 30:23 and a **h** that is heir to her mistress. 8198
Jer 34:16 man his servant, and every man his **h**, 8198
Lk 1:38 And Mary said, Behold the **h** of the Lord; 1399

HANDMAIDEN (1) [MAID]
Lk 1:48 He hath regarded the low estate of his **h**: 1399

HANDMAIDENS (3) [MAID]
Ge 33: 6 the **h** came near, they and their children, 8198
Ru 2:13 though I be not like unto one of thy **h**. 8198
Ac 2:18 and on my **h** I will pour out in those days of 1399

HANDMAIDS (8) [MAID]
Ge 33: 1 and unto Rachel, and unto the two **h**. 8198
 33: 2 he put the **h** and their children foremost, 8198
2Sa 6:20 to day in the eyes of the **h** of his servants, 519
Isa 14: 2 the land of the Lᴏʀᴅ for servants and **h**: 8198
Jer 34:11 caused the servants and the **h**, whom 8198
 34:11 into subjection for servants and for **h**, 8198
 34:16 to be unto you for servants and for **h**, 8198
Joel 2:29 upon the **h** in those days will I pour out 8198

HANDS (459) [HAND]
Ge 5:29 us concerning our work and toil of our **h**, 3027
 16: 9 and submit thyself under her **h**. 3027
 20: 5 and innocency of my **h** have I done this. 3709
 24:22 two bracelets for her **h** of ten *shekels* 3027
 24:30 and bracelets upon his sister's **h**, 3027
 24:47 her face, and the bracelets upon her **h**, 3027
 27:16 skins of the kids of the goats upon his **h**, 3027
 27:22 but the **h** *are* the hands of Esau. 3027
 27:22 hands *are* the **h** of Esau. 3027
 27:23 him not, because his **h** were hairy, 3027
 27:23 hands were hairy, as his brother Esau's **h**: 3027
 31:42 mine affliction and the labour of my **h**, 3709
 37:21 and he delivered him out of their **h**; 3027
 37:22 that he might rid him out of their **h**, 3027
 43:22 we brought down in our **h** to buy food: 3709
 48:14 Manasseh's head, guiding his **h** wittingly; 3027
 49:24 the arms of his **h** were made strong by 3027
 49:24 by the **h** of the mighty *God* of Jacob; 3027
Ex 9:29 I will spread abroad my **h** unto the Lᴏʀᴅ; 3709
 9:33 spread abroad his **h** unto the Lᴏʀᴅ: 3709
 15:17 O Lord, *which* thy **h** have established. 3027
 17:12 Moses' **h** *were* heavy; and they took a

Ex
17:12 Aaron and Hur stayed up his **h**, the one — 3027
17:12 his **h** were steady until the going down of — 3027
29:10 his sons shall put their **h** upon the head of — 3027
29:15 his sons shall put their **h** upon the head of — 3027
29:19 his sons shall put their **h** upon the head of — 3027
29:24 thou shalt put all in the **h** of Aaron, — 3709
29:24 hands of Aaron, and in the **h** of his sons; — 3709
29:25 thou shalt receive them of their **h**, — 3027
30:19 and his sons shall wash their **h** and — 3027
30:21 So they shall wash their **h** and their feet, — 3027
32:19 he cast the tables out of his **h**, — 3027
35:25 were wise hearted did spin with their **h**, — 3027
40:31 Aaron and his sons washed their **h** and — 3027

Lev
4:15 **h** upon the head of the bullock before — 3027
7:30 His own **h** shall bring the offerings of — 3027
8:14 his sons laid their **h** upon the head of — 3027
8:18 his sons laid their **h** upon the head of — 3027
8:22 his sons laid their **h** upon the head of — 3027
8:24 upon the thumbs of their right **h**, — 3027
8:27 he put all upon Aaron's **h**, and upon his — 3709
8:27 upon his sons' **h**, and waved them *for* a — 3709
8:28 Moses took them from off their **h**, — 3709
15:11 not rinsed his **h** in water, he shall wash — 3027
16:12 his **h** full of sweet incense beaten small, — 2651
16:21 Aaron shall lay both his **h** upon the head — 3027
24:14 let all that heard *him* lay their **h** upon his — 3027

Nu
5:18 and put the offering of memorial in her **h**, — 3709
6:19 shall put *them* upon the **h** of the Nazarite, — 3027
8:10 children of Israel shall put their **h** upon — 3027
8:12 Levites shall lay their **h** upon the heads — 3027
24:10 and he smote his **h** together: — 3709
27:23 he laid his **h** upon him, and gave him a — 3027

Dt
1:25 took of the fruit of the land in their **h**, — 3027
3: 3 our God delivered into our **h** Og also, — 3027
4:28 the work of men's **h**, wood and stone, — 3027
9:15 tables of the covenant *were* in my two **h**. — 3027
9:17 cast them out of my two **h**, and brake — 3027
12:18 God in all that thou puttest thine **h** unto. — 3027
16:15 in all the works of thine **h**, therefore — 3027
17: 7 The **h** of the witnesses shall be first upon — 3027
17: 7 and afterward the **h** of all the people. — 3027
20:13 thy God hath delivered it into thine **h**, — 3027
21: 6 **h** over the heifer that is beheaded in — 3027
21: 7 and say, Our **h** have not shed this blood, — 3027
21:10 God hath delivered them into thine **h**, — 3027
24:19 may bless thee in all the work of thine **h**. — 3027
27:15 the work of the **h** of the craftsman, — 3027
31:29 him to anger through the work of your **h**. — 3027
33: 7 let his **h** *be* sufficient for him; and be thou — 3027
33:11 substance, and accept the work of his **h**: — 3027
34: 9 for Moses had laid his **h** upon him: — 3027

Jos
2:24 Truly the Lord hath delivered into our **h** — 3027

Jdg
2:14 he delivered them into the **h** of spoilers — 3027
2:14 he sold them into the **h** of their enemies — 3027
6:13 delivered us into the **h** of the Midianites. — 3709
7: 2 for me to give the Midianites into their **h**, — 3027
7:11 afterward shall thine **h** be strengthened to — 3027
7:19 brake the pitchers that *were* in their **h**. — 3027
7:20 held the lamps in their left **h**, — 3027
7:20 trumpets in their right **h** to blow *withal*: — 3027
8: 3 God hath delivered into your **h** the — 3027
8: 6 *Are* the **h** of Zebah and Zalmunna now in — 3709
8:15 *Are* the **h** of Zebah and Zalmunna now in — 3709
8:34 had delivered them out of the **h** of all — 3027
9:16 him according to the deserving of his **h**; — 3027
10: 7 he sold them into the **h** of the Philistines, — 3027
10: 7 and into the **h** of the children of Ammon. — 3027
11:30 the children of Ammon into mine **h**, — 3027
11:32 and the Lord delivered them into his **h**. — 3027
12: 2 ye delivered me not out of their **h**. — 3027
12: 3 I put my life in my **h**, and passed over — 3709
13:23 offering and a meat offering at our **h**, — 3027
14: 9 he took thereof in his **h**, and went on — 3709
15:14 and his bands loosed from off his **h**. — 3027
16:24 Our god hath delivered into our **h** our — 3027
18:10 for God hath given it into your **h**; a place — 3027
19:27 and her **h** *were* upon the threshold. — 3027

1Sa
5: 4 both the palms of his **h** *were* cut off upon — 3027
7:14 deliver out of the **h** of the Philistines. — 3027
10: 4 which thou shalt receive of their **h**. — 3027
11: 7 coasts of Israel by the **h** of messengers, — 3027
14:13 Jonathan climbed up upon his **h** and — 3027
14:48 delivered Israel out of the **h** of them that — 3027
17:47 and he will give you into our **h**. — 3027
21:13 feigned himself mad in their **h**, — 3027
30:15 nor deliver me into the **h** of my master, — 3027

2Sa
2: 7 now let your **h** be strengthened, — 3027
3:34 Thy **h** *were* not bound, nor thy feet put — 3027
4: 1 his **h** were feeble, and all the Israelites — 3027
4:12 cut off their **h** and their feet, — 3027
16:21 shall the **h** of all that *are* with thee be — 3027
21: 9 he delivered them into the **h** of — 3027
22:21 according to the cleanness of my **h** hath — 3027
22:35 He teacheth my **h** to war; so that a bow — 3027
23: 6 because they cannot be taken with **h**: — 3709

1Ki
8:22 and spread forth his **h** *toward* heaven. — 3709
8:38 and spread forth his **h** towards this house: — 3709
8:54 from kneeling on his knees with his **h** — 3709
14:27 committed *them* unto the **h** of the chief — 3027
16: 7 him to anger with the work of his **h**, — 3027

2Ki
3:11 which poured water on the **h** of Elijah. — 3027
4:34 upon his eyes, and his **h** upon his hands: — 3709
4:34 upon his eyes, and his hands upon his **h**: — 3027
5:20 in not receiving at his **h** *that* which — 3027
9:23 Joram turned his **h**, and fled, and said to

2Ki
9:35 and the feet, and the palms of *her* **h**. — 3027
10:24 whom I *have* brought into your **h** escape, — 3027
11:12 they clapt their **h**, and said, God save — 3709
11:16 laid **h** on her; and she went *by* the way — 3027
12:11 into the **h** of *them* that did the work, — 3027
13:16 Elisha put his **h** upon the king's hands. — 3027
13:16 Elisha put his hands upon the king's **h**. — 3027
19:18 the work of men's **h**, wood and stone: — 3027
22:17 me to anger with all the works of their **h**; — 3027

1Ch
12:17 *there is* no wrong in mine **h**, the God — 3709
25: 2 the sons of Asaph under the **h** of Asaph, — 3027
25: 3 six, under the **h** of their father Jeduthun, — 3027
25: 6 All these *were* under the **h** of their father — 3027
29: 5 all *manner of* work *to be made* by the **h** — 3027

2Ch
6: 4 who hath with his **h** fulfilled *that* which — 3027
6:12 of Israel, and spread forth his **h**: — 3709
6:13 and spread forth his **h** towards heaven, — 3027
6:29 and shall spread forth his **h** in this house: — 3709
8:18 Huram sent him by the **h** of his servants — 3027
12:10 committed *them* to the **h** of the chief of — 3027
15: 7 and let not your **h** be weak: — 3027
23:15 So they laid **h** on her; and when she was — 3027
29:23 and laid his **h** upon them: — 3027
32:19 *which were* the work of the **h** of man. — 3027
34:25 me to anger with all the works of their **h**; — 3027
35:11 priests sprinkled *the blood* from their **h**, — 3027

Ezr
1: 6 strengthened their **h** with vessels of silver, — 3027
4: 4 the people of the land weakened the **h** of — 3027
5: 8 goeth fast on, and prospereth in their **h**. — 3028
6:22 to strengthen their **h** in the work of — 3027
9: 5 spread out my **h** unto the Lord my God, — 3709
10:19 gave their **h** that *they* would put away — 3027

Ne
2:18 So they strengthened their **h** for *this* good — 3027
4:17 *every* one with one of his **h** wrought in — 3027
6: 9 Their **h** shall be weakened from the work, — 3027
6: 9 Now therefore, *O God,* strengthen my **h**. — 3027
8: 6 Amen, Amen, with lifting up their **h**: — 3027
9:24 and gavest them into their **h**, — 3027
13:21 if ye do *so* again, I will lay **h** on you. — 3027

Est
3: 6 he thought scorn to lay **h** on Mordecai — 3027
3: 9 **h** of those that have the charge of — 3027
9:16 but they laid not their **h** on the prey, — 3027

Job
1:10 thou hast blessed the work of his **h**, — 3027
4: 3 and thou hast strengthened the weak **h**. — 3027
5:12 their **h** cannot perform *their* enterprise. — 3027
5:18 he woundeth, and his **h** make whole. — 3027
9:30 water, and make my **h** never so clean; — 3709
10: 3 shouldest despise the work of thine **h**, — 3709
10: 8 Thine **h** have made me and fashioned me — 3027
11:13 and stretch out thine **h** toward him; — 3027
14:15 wilt have a desire to the work of thine **h**. — 3027
16:11 turned me over into the **h** of the wicked. — 3027
16:17 Not for *any* injustice in mine **h**: also my — 3709
17: 3 who *is he that* will strike **h** with me? — 3027
17: 9 he that hath clean **h** shall be stronger and — 3027
20:10 poor, and his **h** shall restore their goods. — 3027
22:30 it is delivered by the pureness of thine **h**. — 3709
27:23 shall clap their **h** at him, and shall hiss — 3027
30: 2 *might* the strength of their **h** profit — 3027
31: 7 and *if any* blot hath cleaved to my **h**; — 3709
34:19 poor? for they all *are* the work of his **h**. — 3027
34:37 he clappeth *his* **h** amongst us, — NIH

Ps
7: 3 done this; if there be iniquity in my **h**; — 3709
8: 6 have dominion over the works of thy **h**; — 3027
9:16 wicked is snared in the work of his own **h**. — 3709
18:20 according to the cleanness of my **h** hath — 3027
18:24 according to the cleanness of my **h** in his — 3027
18:34 He teacheth my **h** to war, so that a bow — 3027
22:16 they pierced my **h** and my feet. — 3027
24: 4 He that hath clean **h**, and a pure heart; — 3709
26:10 I will wash mine **h** in innocency: so will I — 3709
26:10 In whose **h** *is* mischief, and their right — 3027
28: 1 I lift up my **h** toward thy holy oracle. — 3027
28: 4 give them after the work of their **h**; — 3027
28: 5 the operation of his **h**, he shall destroy — 3027
44:20 or stretched out our **h** to a strange god; — 3709
47: 1 O clap *your* **h**, all ye people; shout unto — 3709
55:20 He hath put forth his **h** against such as be — 3027
58: 2 you weigh the violence of your **h** in — 3027
63: 4 I live: I will lift up my **h** in thy name. — 3709
68:31 Ethiopia shall soon stretch out her **h** unto — 3027
73:13 in vain, and washed my **h** in innocency. — 3709
76: 5 of the men of might have found their **h**. — 3709
78:72 guided them by the skilfulness of his **h**. — 3709
81: 6 his **h** were delivered from the pots. — 3027
88: 9 I have stretched out my **h** unto thee. — 3027
90:17 establish thou the work of our **h** upon us; — 3027
90:17 yea, the work of our **h** establish thou it. — 3027
91:12 They shall bear thee up in *their* **h**, lest — 3709
92: 4 I will triumph in the works of thy **h**. — 3027
95: 5 made it: and his **h** formed the dry *land*. — 3027
98: 8 Let the floods clap *their* **h**: let the hills be — 3709
102:25 and the heavens *are* the work of thy **h**. — 3027
111: 7 The works of his **h** *are* verity and — 3027
115: 4 *are* silver and gold, the work of men's **h**. — 3027
115: 7 They *have* **h**, but they handle not: feet — 3027
119:48 My **h** also will I lift up unto thy — 3709
119:73 Thy **h** have made me and fashioned me: — 3027
125: 3 lest the righteous put forth their **h** unto — 3027
128: 2 For thou shalt eat the labour of thine **h**: — 3027
134: 2 Lift up your **h** *in* the sanctuary, — 3027
135:15 *are* silver and gold, the work of men's **h**. — 3027
138: 8 forsake not the works of thine own **h**. — 3027
140: 4 O Lord, from the **h** of the wicked; — 3027
141: 2 the lifting up of my **h** *as* the evening — 3709

Ps
143: 5 thy works; I muse on the work of thy **h**. — 3027
143: 6 I stretch forth my **h** unto thee: my soul — 3027
144: 1 which teacheth my **h** to war, — 3027

Pr
6:10 a little folding of the **h** to sleep: — 3027
6:17 a **h** that shed innocent blood, — 3027
12:14 the recompence of a man's **h** shall be — 3027
14: 1 the foolish plucketh it down with her **h**. — 3027
17:18 A man void of understanding striketh **h**, — 3709
21:25 killeth him; for his **h** refuse to labour. — 3027
22:26 Be not thou *one* of them that strike **h**, — 3709
24:33 a little folding of the **h** to sleep: — 3027
30:28 The spider taketh hold with her **h**, — 3027
31:13 flax, and worketh willingly with her **h**. — 3027
31:16 with the fruit of her **h** she planteth a — 3709
31:19 She layeth her **h** to the spindle, — 3027
31:19 to the spindle, and her **h** hold the distaff. — 3709
31:20 she reacheth forth her **h** to the needy. — 3027
31:31 Give her of the fruit of her **h**; and let her — 3027

Ecc
2:11 I looked on all the works that my **h** had — 3027
4: 5 The fool foldeth his **h** together, — 3027
4: 6 than *both* the **h** full *with* travail and — 2651
5: 6 voice, and destroy the work of thine **h**? — 3027
7:26 *is* snares and nets, *and* her **h** *as* bands: — 3027
10:18 through idleness of the **h** the house — 3027

SS
5: 5 my **h** dropped *with* myrrh, and my fingers — 3027
5:14 His **h** *are as* gold rings set with the beryl: — 3027
7: 1 the work of the **h** of a cunning workman. — 3027

Isa
1:15 when ye spread forth your **h**, I will hide — 3709
1:15 will not hear: your **h** are full *of* blood. — 3027
2: 8 they worship the work of their own **h**, — 3027
3:11 for the reward of his **h** shall be given him. — 3027
5:12 neither consider the operation of his **h**. — 3027
13: 7 Therefore shall all **h** be faint, — 3027
17: 8 not look to the altars, the work of his **h**, — 3027
19:25 Assyria the work of my **h**, and Israel mine — 3027
25:11 he shall spread forth his **h** in the midst of — 3027
25:11 he that swimmeth spreadeth forth *his* **h** — NIH
25:11 pride together with the spoils of their **h**. — 3027
29:23 the work of mine **h**, in the midst of him, — 3027
31: 7 which your own **h** have made unto you — 3027
33:15 that shaketh his **h** from holding of bribes, — 3709
35: 3 Strengthen ye the weak **h**, and confirm — 3027
37:19 but the work of men's **h**, wood and stone: — 3027
45: 9 makest thou? or thy work, He hath no **h**? — 3027
45:11 concerning the work of my **h** command — 3027
45:12 I, *even* my **h**, have stretched out — 3027
49:16 graven thee upon the **palms** of *my* **h**; — 3709
55:12 all the trees of the field shall clap *their* **h**. — 3709
59: 3 For your **h** are defiled with blood, — 3709
59: 6 and the act of violence *is* in their **h**. — 3027
60:21 the work of my **h**, that *I* may be glorified. — 3027
65: 2 I have spread out mine **h** all the day unto — 3027
65:22 elect shall long enjoy the work of their **h**. — 3027

Jer
1:16 worshipped the works of their own **h**. — 3027
2:37 from him, and thine **h** upon thine head: — 3027
4:31 bewaileth herself, *that* spreadeth her **h**, — 3027
6:24 our **h** wax feeble: anguish hath taken hold — 3027
10: 3 the work of the **h** of the workman, with — 3027
10: 9 workman, and of the **h** of the founder: — 3027
19: 7 and by the **h** of them that seek their lives: — 3027
21: 4 the weapons of war that *are* in your **h**, — 3027
23:14 they strengthen also the **h** of evildoers, — 3027
25: 6 me not to anger with the works of your **h**; — 3027
25: 7 The works of your **h** to your own hurt. — 3027
25:14 according to the works of their own **h**: — 3027
30: 6 wherefore do I see every man *with* his **h** — 3027
32:30 me to anger with the work of their **h**, — 3027
33:13 shall the flocks pass again under the **h** of — 3027
38: 4 for thus he weakeneth the **h** of the men — 3027
38: 4 the **h** of all the people, in speaking such — 3027
44: 8 me unto wrath with the works of your **h**, — 3027
47: 3 back their children for feebleness of **h**; — 3027
48:37 upon all the **h** *shall be* cuttings, — 3027
50:43 report of them, and his **h** waxed feeble: — 3027

La
1:14 the Lord hath delivered me into *their* **h**, — 3027
1:17 Zion spreadeth forth her **h**, *and there is* — 3709
2:15 All that pass by clap *their* **h** at thee; — 3709
2:19 lift up thy **h** toward him for the life of thy — 3709
3:41 us lift up our heart with *our* **h** unto God — 3709
3:64 according to the work of their **h**. — 3027
4: 2 the work of the **h** of the potter! — 3027
4: 6 as in a moment, and no **h** stayed on her. — 3027
4:10 The **h** of the pitiful women have sodden — 3027

Eze
1: 8 *had* the **h** of a man under their wings — 3027
7:17 All **h** shall be feeble, and all knees shall be — 3027
7:21 I will give it into the **h** of the strangers for — 3027
7:27 the **h** of the people of the land shall be — 3027
10: 7 put *it* into the **h** of *him that was* clothed — 2651
10:12 their **h**, and their wings, and the wheels, — 3027
10:21 the likeness of the **h** of a man *was* under — 3027
11: 9 deliver you into the **h** of strangers, — 3027
13:22 strengthened the **h** of the wicked, that *he* — 3027
16:11 put bracelets upon thine **h**, and a chain — 3027
21: 7 all **h** shall be feeble, and every spirit shall — 3027
21:14 smite thine **h** **together**, — 413+3709+3709
21:17 also smite mine **h** **together**, — 413+3709+3709
22:14 heart endure, or can thine **h** be strong, — 3027
23:37 blood *is* in their **h**, and with their idols — 3027
23:42 which put bracelets upon their **h**, — 3027
23:45 *are* adulteresses, and blood *is* in their **h**. — 3027
25: 6 Because thou hast clapped *thine* **h**, — 3027

Da
2:34 till that a stone was cut out without **h**, — 3027
2:45 was cut out of the mountain without **h**, — 3028
3:15 God that shall deliver you out of my **h**? — 3028
10:10 my knees and *upon* the palms of my **h**. — 3027

Hos 14: 3 we say any more to the work of our **h**, 3027
Ob 1:13 have laid **h** on their substance in the day NIH
Jnh 3: 8 and from the violence *that is* in their **h**. 3709
Mic 5:13 no more worship the work of thine **h**. 3027
 7: 3 That *they* may do evil with both **h** 3709
Na 3:19 bruit of thee shall clap the **h** over thee: 3709
Hab 3:10 his voice, *and* lift up his **h** on high. 3027
Zep 3:16 *and* to Zion, Let not thine **h** be slack. 3027
Hag 1:11 *and* upon all the labour of the **h**. 3027
 2:14 *is* every work of their **h**; and *that* which 3027
 2:17 and with hail *in* all the labours of your **h**; 3027
Zec 4: 9 The **h** of Zerubbabel have laid 3027
 4: 9 his **h** shall also finish *it*; and thou shalt 3027
 8: 9 Let your **h** be strong, ye that hear in these 3027
 8:13 fear not, *but* let your **h** be strong. 3027
 13: 6 What *are* these wounds in thine **h**? 3027
Mt 4: 6 in *their* **h** they shall bear thee up, lest at 5495
 15: 2 for they wash not their **h** when they eat 5495
 15:20 eat with unwashen **h** defileth not a man. 5495
 17:22 Son of man shall be betrayed into the **h** 5495
 18: 8 rather than having two **h** or two feet to be 5495
 18:28 and he laid **h** on him, and took *him* by 2902
 19:13 he should put *his* **h** on them, and pray: 5495
 19:15 And he laid *his* **h** on them, 5495
 21:46 But when they sought to lay **h** on him, 2902
 26:45 the Son of man is betrayed into the **h** of 5495
 26:50 and laid **h** on Jesus, and took him. 5495
 26:67 smote *him* with the palms of their **h**, 4474
 27:24 and washed *his* **h** before the multitude, 5495
Mk 5:23 *I pray thee*, come and lay thy **h** on her: 5495
 6: 2 such mighty works are wrought by his **h**? 5495
 6: 5 that he laid *his* **h** upon a few sick *folk*, 5495
 7: 2 is to say, with unwashen, **h**, they found 5495
 7: 3 except they wash *their* **h** oft, eat not, 5495
 7: 5 elders, but eat bread with unwashen **h**? 5495
 8:23 spit on his eyes, and put *his* **h** upon him, 5495
 8:25 that he put *his* **h** again upon his eyes, 5495
 9:31 The Son of man is delivered into the **h** of 5495
 9:43 than having two **h** to go into hell, into 5495
 10:16 put *his* **h** upon them, and blessed them. 5495
 14:41 the Son of man is betrayed into the **h** of 5495
 14:46 they laid their **h** on him, and took him. 5495
 14:58 destroy this temple that is made with **h**, 5499
 14:58 I will build another made without **h**. 886
 14:65 strike him with the palms of
 their **h**. 906+4475
 16:18 they shall lay **h** on the sick, and they shall 5495
Lk 4:11 And in *their* **h** they shall bear thee up, 5495
 4:40 and he laid *his* **h** on every one of them, 5495
 6: 1 and did eat, rubbing *them* in *their* **h**. 5495
 9:44 shall be delivered into the **h** of men. 5495
 13:13 And he laid *his* **h** on her: 5495
 20:19 scribes the same hour sought to lay **h** on 5495
 21:12 they shall lay their **h** on you, 5495
 22:53 ye stretched forth no **h** against me: 5495
 23:46 Father, into thy **h** I commend my spirit: 5495
 24: 7 be delivered into the **h** of sinful men, 5495
 24:39 Behold my **h** and my feet, that it is I 5495
 24:40 he shewed them *his* **h** and *his* feet. 5495
 24:50 and he lift up his **h**, and blessed them. 5495
Jn 7:30 no *man* laid on him, because his hour 5495
 7:44 taken him; but no *man* laid **h** on him. 5495
 8:20 no *man* laid **h** on him; for his hour was 4084
 13: 3 the Father had given all *things* into his **h**, 5495
 13: 9 my feet only, but also *my* **h** and *my* head. 5495
 19: 3 and they smote him with their **h**. 1325+4475
 20:20 he shewed unto them *his* **h** and his side. 5495
 20:25 Except I shall see in his **h** the print of 5495
 20:27 Reach hither thy finger, and behold my **h**; 5495
 21:18 thou shalt stretch forth thy **h**, 5495
Ac 2:23 and by wicked **h** have crucified and slain: 5495
 4: 3 And they laid **h** on them, and put *them* in 5495
 5:12 And by the **h** of the apostles were many 5495
 5:18 And laid their **h** on the apostles, 5495
 6: 6 had prayed, they laid *their* **h** on them. 5495
 7:41 and rejoiced in the works of their own **h**. 5495
 7:48 dwelleth not in temples made with **h**; 5499
 8:17 Then laid they *their* **h** on them, 5495
 8:18 the apostles' **h** the Holy Ghost was given, 5495
 8:19 this power, that on whomsoever I lay **h**, 5495
 9:17 putting his **h** on him said, Brother Saul, 5495
 11:30 sent it to the elders by the **h** of Barnabas 5495
 12: 1 forth *his* **h** to vex certain of the church. 5495
 12: 7 And his chains fell off from his **h**. 5495
 13: 3 and prayed, and laid *their* **h** on them, 5495
 14: 3 and wonders to be done by their **h**. 5495
 17:24 dwelleth not in temples made with **h**; 5499
 17:25 Neither is worshipped with men's **h**, 5495
 19: 6 when Paul had laid *his* **h** upon them, 5495
 19:11 God wrought special miracles by the **h** 5495
 19:26 they be no gods, which are made with **h**: 5495
 20:34 that these **h** have ministered unto my 5495
 21:11 and bound his *own* **h** and feet, and said, 5495
 21:11 deliver *him* into the **h** of the Gentiles. 5495
 21:27 all the people, and laid **h** on him, 5495
 24: 7 violence took *him* away out of our **h**, 5495
 27:19 with our own **h** the tackling of the ship. 849
 28: 8 and laid *his* **h** on him, and healed him. 5495
 28:17 from Jerusalem into the **h** of the Romans. 5495
Ro 10:21 All day long have I stretched forth my **h** 5495
1Co 4:12 And labour, working with our own **h**: 5495
2Co 11:33 I let down by the wall, and escaped his **h**. 5495
Gal 2: 9 and Barnabas the right **h** of fellowship; 1188
Eph 2:11 the Circumcision in the flesh made by **h**; 5499
 4:28 with *his* **h** the *thing* which is good, 5495

Col 2:11 with the circumcision made without **h**, 886
1Th 4:11 and to work with your own **h**, 5495
1Ti 2: 8 lifting up holy **h**, without wrath and 5495
 4:14 with the laying on of the **h** of 5495
 5:22 Lay **h** suddenly on no *man*, neither be 5495
2Ti 1: 6 is in thee by the putting on of my **h**. 5495
Heb 1:10 and the heavens are the works of thine **h**: 5495
 2: 7 and didst set him over the works of thy **h**: 5495
 6: 2 of laying on of **h**, and of resurrection of 5495
 9:11 not made with **h**, that is to say, not of 5499
 9:24 into the holy *places* made with **h**, 5499
 10:31 *It is* a fearful *thing* to fall into the **h** of 5495
 12:12 Wherefore lift up the **h** which hang down, 5495
Jas 4: 8 Cleanse *your* **h**, *ye* sinners; and purify 5495
1Jn 1: 1 and our **h** have handled, of the Word of 5495
Rev 7: 9 with white robes, and palms in their **h**; 5495
 9:20 yet repented not of the works of their **h**, 5495
 20: 4 mark upon their foreheads, or in their **h**; 5495

HANDSOME See GOODLIER; GOODLIEST; GOODLY

HANDSTAVES (1) [HAND, STAFF]

Eze 39: 9 the **h**, and the spears, and they 3027+4731

HANDWRITING (1) [HAND, WRITE]

Col 2:14 Blotting out the **h** of ordinances that was 5498

HANDYWORK (1) [HAND, WORK]

Ps 19: 1 and the firmament sheweth his **h**. 3027+4639

HANES (1)

Isa 30: 4 at Zoan, and his ambassadors came to **H**. 2609

HANG (19) [HANGED, HANGETH, HANGING, HANGINGS]

Ge 40:19 from off thee, and shall **h** thee on a tree; 8518
Ex 26:12 over the backside of the tabernacle, 5628
 26:13 it shall **h** over the sides of the tabernacle 5628
 26:32 thou shalt **h** it upon four pillars of shittim 5414
 26:33 thou shalt **h up** the vail under the taches, 5414
 40: 8 and **h up** the hanging at the court gate. 5414
Nu 25: 4 h them **up** before the LORD against 3363
Dt 21:22 *be* put to death, and thou **h** him on a tree: 8518
 28:66 thy life shall **h** in doubt before thee; 8511
2Sa 21: 6 we will **h** them **up** unto the LORD in 3363
Est 6: 4 to speak unto the king to **h** Mordecai on 8518
 7: 9 Then the king said, **H** him thereon. 8518
SS 4: 4 whereon there **h** a thousand bucklers, 8518
Isa 22:24 they shall **h** upon him all the glory of his 8518
La 2:10 virgins of Jerusalem **h down** their heads 3381
Eze 15: 3 will *men* take a pin of it to **h** any vessel 8518
Mt 22:40 these two commandments **h** all the law 2910
Ac 28: 4 saw the *venomous* beast **h** on his hand, 2910
Heb 12:12 lift up the hands which **h down**, 3935

HANGED (30) [HANG]

Ge 40:22 he **h** the chief baker: as Joseph had 8518
 41:13 restored unto mine office, and him he **h**. 8518
Dt 21:23 (for he that is **h** *is* accursed of God;) 8518
Jos 8:29 king of Ai he **h** on a tree until eventide: 8518
 10:26 and slew then, and **h** them on five trees: 8518
2Sa 4:12 and **h** *them* **up** over the pool in Hebron. 8518
 17:23 **h** himself, and died, and was buried in 2614
 18:10 said, Behold, I saw Absalom **h** in an oak. 8518
 21: 9 they **h** them in the hill before the LORD: 3363
 21:12 where the Philistines had **h** them, when 8511
 21:13 gathered the bones of them that were **h**, 3363
Ezr 6:11 and being set up, let him be **h** thereon: 4223
Est 2:23 therefore they were both **h** on a tree: 8518
 5:14 king that Mordecai may be **h** thereon: 8518
 7:10 So they **h** Haman on the gallows that he 8518
 8: 7 him they have **h** upon the gallows, 8518
 9:13 let Haman's ten sons be **h** upon 8518
 9:14 Shushan; and they **h** Haman's ten sons. 8518
 9:25 and his sons should be **h** on the gallows. 8518
Ps 137: 2 We **h** our harps upon the willows in 8518
La 5:12 Princes are **h up** by their hand: the faces 8518
Eze 27:10 they **h** the shield and helmet in thee; 8518
 27:11 they **h** their shields upon thy walls round 8518
Mt 18: 6 better for him that a millstone were **h** 2910
 27: 5 and departed, and went and **h** himself. 519
Mk 9:42 is better for him that a millstone were **h** 4029
Lk 17: 2 a millstone were **h** about his neck, 4029
 23:39 one of the malefactors which were **h** 2910
Ac 5:30 up Jesus, whom ye slew and **h** on a tree: 2910
 10:39 whom they slew and **h** on a 2910

HANGETH (2) [HANG]

Job 26: 7 place, *and* **h** the earth upon nothing. 8518
Gal 3:13 Cursed *is* every one that **h** on a tree: 2910

HANGING (18) [HANG]

Ex 26:36 shalt make a **h** for the door of the tent, 4539
 26:37 thou shalt make for the **h** five pillars of 4539
 27:16 for the gate of the court *shall be* a **h** of 4539
 35:15 the **h** for the door at the entering in of 4539
 35:17 and the **h** for the door of the court, 4539
 36:37 made a **h** for the tabernacle door *of* blue, 4539
 38:18 the **h** for the gate of the court *was* 4539
 39:38 and the **h** for the tabernacle door, 4539
 39:40 the **h** for the court gate, his cords, 4539
 40: 5 put the **h** of the door to the tabernacle. 4539
 40: 8 and hang up the **h** at the court gate. 4539
 40:28 set up the **h** at the door of the tabernacle. 4539
 40:33 altar, and set up the **h** of the court gate. 4539

Nu 3:25 the **h** for the door of the tabernacle of 4539
 3:31 and the **h**, and all the service thereof. 4539
 4:25 the **h** for the door of the tabernacle of 4539
 4:26 the **h** for the door of the gate of the court, 4539
Jos 10:26 they were **h** upon the trees until 8518

HANGINGS (18) [HANG]

Ex 27: 9 south side southward *there shall be* **h** 7050
 27:11 *shall be* **h** of an hundred *cubits* long, 7050
 27:12 on the west side *shall be* **h** of fifty cubits: 7050
 27:14 The **h** of *one* side *of the gate shall be* 7050
 27:15 the other side *shall be* **h**, fifteen *cubits*: 7050
 35:17 The **h** of the court, his pillars, 7050
 38: 9 on the south side southward the **h** of 7050
 38:11 for the north side the **h** were an hundred NIH
 38:12 for the west side *were* **h** of fifty cubits, 7050
 38:14 The **h** of the *one* side of the gate were 7050
 38:15 and that hand, *were* **h** of fifteen cubits: 7050
 38:16 All the **h** of the court round about *were* 7050
 38:18 answerable to the **h** of the court. 7050
 39:40 The **h** of the court, his pillars, and his 7050
Nu 3:26 the **h** of the court, and the curtain for 7050
 4:26 the **h** of the court, and the hanging for 7050
2Ki 23: 7 where the women wove **h** for the grove. 1004
Est 1: 6 *were* blue, **h**, fastened with cords of fine linen NIH

HANIEL (1)

1Ch 7:39 the sons of Ulla; Arah, and **H**, and Rezia. 2592

HANNAH (13)

1Sa 1: 2 the name of the one *was* **H**, and the name 2584
 1: 2 had children, but **H** had no children. 2584
 1: 5 unto **H** he gave a worthy portion; for he 2584
 1: 5 he gave a worthy portion; for he loved **H**: 2584
 1: 8 husband to her, **H**, why weepest thou? 2584
 1: 9 **H** rose up after *they* had eaten in Shiloh, 2584
 1:13 Now **H**, she spake in her heart; only her 2584
 1:15 **H** answered and said, No, my lord, *I am* a 2584
 1:19 Elkanah knew **H** his wife; and the LORD 2584
 1:20 when the time was come about after **H** 2584
 1:22 **H** went not up; for she said unto her 2584
 2: 1 **H** prayed, and said, My heart rejoiceth in 2584
 2:21 the LORD visited **H**, so that she 2584

HANNATHON (1)

Jos 19:14 compasseth it on the north side *to* **H**: 2615

HANNIEL (1)

Nu 34:23 of Manasseh, **H** the son of Ephod. 2592

HANOCH (5) [HANOCHITES]

Ge 25: 4 Epher, and **H**, and Abidah, and Eldaah. 2585
 46: 9 **H**, and Phallu, and Hezron, and Carmi. 2585
Ex 6:14 Israel; **H**, and Pallu, Hezron, and Carmi: 2585
Nu 26: 5 *of whom cometh* the family of 2585
1Ch 5: 3 of Reuben the firstborn of Israel *were*, **H**, 2585

HANOCHITES (1) [HANOCH]

Nu 26: 5 *of whom cometh* the family of the **H**: 2599

HANUN (11)

2Sa 10: 1 and **H** his son reigned in his stead. 2586
 10: 2 I will shew kindness unto **H** the son of 2586
 10: 3 of Ammon said unto their lord, 2586
 10: 4 Wherefore **H** took David's servants, 2586
1Ch 19: 2 I will shew kindness unto **H** the son of 2586
 19: 2 the land of the children of Ammon to **H**, 2586
 19: 3 of the children of Ammon said to **H**, 2586
 19: 4 Wherefore **H** took David's servants, 2586
 19: 6 **H** and the children of Ammon sent a 2586
Ne 3:13 The valley gate repaired **H**, 2586
 3:30 **H** the sixth son of Zalaph, another piece. 2586

HAP (1) [HAPPEN]

Ru 2: 3 her **h** was to light on a part of the field 4745

HAPHARAIM (1)

Jos 19:19 And **H**, and Shion, and Anaharath, 2663

HAPLY (6) [HAPPEN]

1Sa 14:30 if **h** the people had eaten freely to day of 3863
Mk 11:13 if he might find any *thing* thereon: 686
Lk 14:29 Lest **h**, after he hath laid the foundation, 3379
Ac 5:39 lest **h** ye be found even to fight against 3379
 17:27 if **h** they might feel after him, 686+1065
2Co 9: 4 Lest **h** if they of Macedonia come with 3381

HAPPEN (4) [HAP, HAPLY, HAPPENED, HAPPENETH]

1Sa 28:10 there shall no punishment **h** to thee for 7136
Pr 12:21 There shall no evil **h** to the just: 579
Isa 41:22 *them* forth, and shew us what shall **h**: 7136
Mk 10:32 began to tell them what *things* should **h** 4819

HAPPENED (12) [HAPPEN]

1Sa 6: 9 smote us; it *was* a chance *that* **h** to us. 1961
2Sa 1: 6 I **h** by chance upon mount Gilboa, 7122+7136
 20: 1 there **h to be** there a man of Belial, 7122
Est 4: 7 Mordecai told him of all that had **h** unto 7122
Jer 44:23 therefore this evil is **h** unto you, as *at* this 7122
Lk 24:14 together of all these *things* which had **h** 4819
Ac 3:10 amazement at that which had **h** unto him. 4819
Ro 11:25 that blindness in part is **h** to Israel, until 1096
1Co 10:11 Now all these *things* **h** unto them for 4819
Php 1:12 the *things* which **h** unto me have fallen NIG
1Pe 4:12 as though *some* strange *thing* **h** unto you: 4819

2Pe 2:22 it is **h** unto them according to the true *4819*

HAPPENETH (6) [HAPPEN]

Ecc 2:14 I myself perceived also that one event **h** to 7136
2:15 As it **h** to the fool, so it happeneth even to 4745
2:15 happeneth to the fool, so it **h** even to me; 7136
8:14 that there be just *men*, unto whom it **h** 5060
8:14 there be wicked *men*, to whom it **h** 5060
9:11 skill; but time and chance **h** to them all. 7136

HAPPIER (1) [HAPPY]

1Co 7:40 But she is **h** if she so abide, after my *3107*

HAPPIZZEZ See APHSES

HAPPY (28) [HAPPIER]

Ge 30:13 Leah said, **H** am I, for the daughters will 837
Dt 33:29 **H** *art* thou, O Israel: who *is* like unto thee, 835
1Ki 10: 8 **H** *are* thy men, happy *are* these thy 835
10: 8 *are* thy men, **h** *are* these thy servants, 835
2Ch 9: 7 **H** *are* thy men, and happy *are* these thy 835
9: 7 *are* thy men, and **h** *are* these thy servants, 835
Job 5:17 **H** *is* the man whom God correcteth: 835
Ps 127: 5 **H** *is* the man that hath his quiver full of 835
128: 2 **h** *shalt* thou *be*, and *it shall be* well with 835
137: 8 **h** *shall* he *be*, that rewardeth thee as thou 835
137: 9 **H** *shall* he *be* that taketh and dasheth thy 835
144:15 **H** *is* that people, that is in such a case: *yea*, 835
144:15 yea, **h** *is* that people, whose God *is* 835
146: 5 **H** *is* he that *hath* the God of Jacob for his 835
Pr 3:13 **H** *is* the man *that* findeth wisdom, 835
3:18 and **h** *is* every one that retaineth her. 833
14:21 he that hath mercy on the poor, **h** *is* he. 835
16:20 and whoso trusteth in the LORD, **h** *is* he. 835
28:14 **H** *is* the man that feareth alway: but he 835
29:18 but he that keepeth the law, **h** *is* he. 835
Jer 12: 1 *wherefore* are all they **h** that deal very 7951
Mal 3:15 we **call** the proud **h**; yea, they that work 833
Jn 13:17 If ye know these *things*, **h** are ye if ye do *3107*
Ac 26: 2 I think myself **h**, king Agrippa, because *3107*
Ro 14:22 **H** *is* he that condemneth not himself in *3107*
Jas 5:11 Behold, we **count** them **h** which endure. *3106*
1Pe 3:14 **h** *are ye*: and be not afraid of their terror, *3107*
4:14 **h** *are ye*; for the spirit of glory and of God *3107*

HARA (1)

1Ch 5:26 Habor, and **H**, and to the river Gozan, 2024

HARADAH (2)

Nu 33:24 mount Shapher, and encamped in **H**. 2732
33:25 they removed from **H**, and pitched in 2732

HARAN (19) [BETH-HARAN, CHARRAN]

Ge 11:26 and begat Abram, Nahor, and **H**; 2039
11:27 Terah begat Abram, Nahor, and **H**; 2039
11:27 and Haran; and **H** begat Lot. 2039
11:28 **H** died before his father Terah in the land 2039
11:29 Milcah, the daughter of **H**, the father of 2039
11:31 Lot the son of **H** his son's son, and Sarai 2039
11:31 and they came unto **H**, and dwelt there. 2771
11:32 five years: and Terah died in **H**. 2771
12: 4 five years old when he departed out of **H**. 2771
12: 5 and the souls that they had gotten in **H**; 2771
27:43 arise, flee thou to Laban my brother in **H**; 2771
28:10 out from Beer-sheba, and went toward **H**. 2771
29: 4 *be* ye? And they said, Of **H** *are* we. 2771
2Ki 19:12 **H**, and Rezeph, and the children of Eden 2771
1Ch 2:46 bare **H**, and Moza, and Gazez: 2771
2:46 Moza, and Gazez: and **H** begat Gazez. 2771
23: 9 Shelomith, and Haziel, and **H**, three. 2039
Isa 37:12 **H**, and Rezeph, and the children of Eden 2771
Eze 27:23 **H**, and Canneh, and Eden, the merchants 2771

HARARITE (5)

2Sa 23:11 him *was* Shammah the son of Agee the **H**. 2043
23:33 Shammah the **H**, Ahiam the son of Sharar 2043
23:33 Ahiam the son of Sharar the **H**, 2043
1Ch 11:34 Jonathan the son of Shage the **H**, 2043
11:35 Ahiam the son of Sacar the **H**, Eliphal 2043

HARBONA (1) [HARBONAH]

Est 1:10 Biztha, **H**, Bigtha, and Abagtha, Zethar, 2726

HARBONAH (1) [HARBONA]

Est 7: 9 **H**, one of the chamberlains, said before 2726

HARD (45) [HARDEN, HARDENED, HARDENETH, HARDER, HARDHEARTED, HARDLY, HARDNESS]

Ge 18:14 is any thing too **h** for the LORD? 6381
35:16 Rachel travailed, and she had **h** labour. 7185
35:17 came to pass, when she was in **h** labour, 7185
Ex 1:14 made their lives bitter with **h** bondage, 7186
18:26 the **h** causes they brought unto Moses, 7186
Lev 3: 9 he take off **h** by the back bone; 5980+3807.1
Dt 1:17 cause that is too **h** for you, bring *it* unto 7185
15:18 it shall not seem **h** unto thee, when thou 7185
17: 8 If there arise a matter too **h** for thee in 6381
26: 6 afflicted us, and laid upon us **h** bondage: 7186
Jdg 9:52 **went h** unto the door of the tower to 5066
20:45 **pursued h** after them unto Gidom, 1692
1Sa 14:22 even they also **followed h** after them in 1692
31: 2 the Philistines **followed h** upon Saul and 1692
2Sa 1: 6 and horsemen **followed h** after him. 1692
3:39 these men the sons of Zeruiah *be* too **h** for 7186
13: 2 Amnon thought it **h** for him to do any 6381
1Ki 10: 1 she came to prove him with **h questions**. 2420

1Ki 21: 1 **h by** the palace of Ahab king of Samaria. 681
2Ki 2:10 he said, Thou hast asked a **h thing**: 7185
1Ch 10: 2 the Philistines **followed h** after Saul, 1692
19: 4 cut off their garments in the midst **h by** 5704
2Ch 9: 1 Solomon with **h questions** at Jerusalem, 2420
Job 41:24 as **h** as a piece of the nether *millstone*. 3332
Ps 60: 3 Thou hast shewed thy people **h** *things*: 7186
63: 8 My soul **followeth h** after thee: thy right 1692
88: 7 Thy wrath **lieth h** upon me, and thou 5564
94: 4 shall they utter *and* speak **h** *things? and* 6277
Pr 13:15 but the way of transgressors *is* **h**. 386
Isa 14: 3 from the **h** bondage wherein thou wast 7186
Jer 32:17 *and* there is nothing too **h** for thee: 6381
32:27 all flesh: is there any thing too **h** for me? 6381
Eze 3: 5 of a strange speech and of a **h** language, 3515
3: 6 of a strange speech and of a **h** language, 3515
Da 5:12 shewing of **h sentences**, and dissolving 280
Jnh 1:13 Nevertheless the men **rowed h** to bring 2864
Mt 25:24 Lord, I knew thee that thou art a **h man**, 4642
Mk 10:24 how **h** is it for them that trust in riches to 1422
Jn 6:60 had heard *this*, said, This is a **h** saying; 4642
Ac 9: 5 *it is* **h** for thee to kick against the pricks. 4642
18: 7 whose house **joined h** to the synagogue, 4927
26:14 *it is* **h** for thee to kick against the pricks. 4642
Heb 5:11 and **h** to be uttered, seeing ye are dull of 1421
2Pe 3:16 are some *things* **h** to be **understood**, 1425
Jude 1:15 of all *their* **h** *speeches* which ungodly 4642

HARDEN (12) [HARD]

Ex 4:21 I will **h** his heart, that he shall not let 2388
7: 3 I will **h** Pharaoh's heart, and multiply my 7185
14: 4 I will **h** Pharaoh's heart, that he shall 2388
14:17 I will **h** the hearts of the Egyptians, 2388
Dt 15: 7 thou shalt not **h** thy heart, nor shut thine 553
Jos 11:20 For it was of the LORD to **h** their hearts, 2388
1Sa 6: 6 Wherefore then do ye **h** your hearts, 3513
Job 6:10 yea, I would **h** myself in sorrow; let him 5539
Ps 95: 8 **H** not your heart, as *in* the provocation, 7185
Heb 3: 8 **H** not your hearts, as in the provocation, 4645
3:15 **h** not your hearts, as in the provocation. 4645
4: 7 ye will hear his voice, **h** not your hearts. 4645

HARDENED (33) [HARD]

Ex 7:13 he **h** Pharaoh's heart, that he hearkened 2388
7:14 Pharaoh's heart *is* **h**, he refuseth to let 2388
7:22 Pharaoh's heart was **h**, neither did he 2388
8:15 he **h** his heart, and hearkened not unto 3513
8:19 Pharaoh's heart was **h**, and he hearkened 2388
8:32 Pharaoh **h** his heart at this time also, 3513
9: 7 heart of Pharaoh was **h**, and he did not 3513
9:12 the LORD **h** the heart of Pharaoh, 2388
9:34 and **h** his heart, he and his servants. 3513
9:35 heart of Pharaoh was **h**, neither would 2388
10: 1 for I have **h** his heart, and the heart of his 3513
10:20 the LORD **h** Pharaoh's heart, so that he 2388
10:27 the LORD **h** Pharaoh's heart, 2388
11:10 the LORD **h** Pharaoh's heart, so that he 2388
14: 8 the LORD **h** the heart of Pharaoh king of 2388
Dt 2:30 for the LORD thy God **h** his spirit, 553
1Sa 6: 6 the Egyptians and Pharaoh **h** their hearts? 3513
2Ki 17:14 their necks, like to the neck of their 7185
2Ch 36:13 his heart from turning unto the LORD 553
Ne 9:16 **h** their necks, and hearkened not to thy 7185
9:17 **h** their necks, and in their rebellion 7185
9:29 and **h** their neck, and would not hear. 7185
Job 9: 4 who hath **h** *himself* against him, 7185
39:16 She is **h** against her young ones, as 7188
Isa 63:17 thy ways, *and* **h** our heart from thy fear? 7188
Jer 7:26 nor inclined their ear, but **h** their neck: 7185
19:15 because they have **h** their necks, that *they* 7185
Da 5:20 was lifted up, and his mind **h** in pride, 8631
Mk 6:52 of the loaves: for their heart was **h**. 4456
8:17 have ye your heart yet **h**? 4456
Jn 12:40 hath blinded their eyes, and **h** their heart; 4456
Ac 19: 9 when divers were **h**, and believed not, 4645
Heb 3:13 lest any of you be **h** through 4645

HARDENETH (4) [HARD]

Pr 21:29 A wicked man **h** his face: but *as for* 5810
28:14 he that **h** his heart shall fall into mischief. 7185
29: 1 He, that being often reproved **h** his neck, 7185
Ro 9:18 will *have* mercy, and whom he will he **h**. 4645

HARDER (3) [HARD]

Pr 18:19 A brother offended *is* **h** *to be won* than a NIH
Jer 5: 3 they have **made** their faces **h** than a rock; 2388
Eze 3: 9 As an adamant **h** than flint have I made 2389

HARDHEARTED (1) [HARD, HEART]

Eze 3: 7 house of Israel *are* impudent and **h**. 3820+7186

HARDLY (8) [HARD]

Ge 16: 6 when Sarai **dealt h** with her, she fled 6031
Ex 13:15 to pass, when Pharaoh would **h** let us go, 7185
Isa 8:21 pass through it, **h bestead** and hungry: 7185
Mt 19:23 That a rich *man* shall **h** enter into 1423
Mk 10:23 How **h** shall they that have riches enter 1423
Lk 9:39 and bruising him **h** departeth from him. 3425
18:24 How **h** shall they that have riches enter 1423
Ac 27: 8 passing it, came unto a place *which* 3433

HARDNESS (7) [HARD]

Job 38:38 When the dust groweth into **h**, 4165
Mt 19: 8 the **h** of your **hearts** suffered you to put 4641
Mk 3: 5 being grieved for the **h** of their hearts, 4457

Mk 10: 5 For the **h** of your **heart** he wrote you this 4641
16:14 them with their unbelief and **h** of **heart**, 4641
Ro 2: 5 But after thy **h** and impenitent heart 4643
2Ti 2: 3 therefore **endure h**, as a good soldier 2553

HARDSHIP; HARDSHIPS See TRAVAIL; TRAVAILED; TRAVAILEST; TRAVAILETH

HARE (2)

Lev 11: 6 the **h**, because he cheweth the cud, 768
Dt 14: 7 *as* the camel, and the **h**, and the coney: 768

HAREPH (1)

1Ch 2:51 of Beth-lehem, **H** the father of Beth-gader. 2780

HARETH (1)

1Sa 22: 5 and came *into* the forest of **H**. 2802

HARHAIAH (1)

Ne 3: 8 unto him repaired Uzziel the son of **H**, 2736

HARHAS (1)

2Ki 22:14 the son of **H**, keeper of the wardrobe; 2745

HARHUR (2)

Ezr 2:51 children of Hakupha, the children of **H**, 2744
Ne 7:53 children of Hakupha, the children of **H**, 2744

HARIM (11)

1Ch 24: 8 The third to **H**, the fourth to Seorim, 2766
Ezr 2:32 The children of **H**, three hundred and 2766
2:39 The children of **H**, a thousand and 2766
10:21 of the sons of **H**; Maaseiah, and Elijah, 2766
10:31 the sons of **H**; Eliezer, Ishijah, Malchiah, 2766
Ne 3:11 Malchijah the son of **H**, and Hashub 2766
7:35 The children of **H**, three hundred and 2766
7:42 The children of **H**, a thousand *and* 2766
10: 5 **H**, Meremoth, Obadiah, 2766
10:27 Malluch, **H**, Baanah. 2766
12:15 Of **H**, Adna; of Meraioth, Helkai; 2766

HARIPH (2)

Ne 7:24 children of **H**, an hundred *and* twelve. 2756
10:19 **H**, Anathoth, Nebai, 2756

HARLOT (40) [HARLOT'S, HARLOTS, HARLOTS']

Ge 34:31 he deal with our sister as with a **h**? 2181
38:15 Judah saw her, he thought her to be a **h**; 2181
38:21 Where is the **h**, that *was* openly by 6948
38:21 they said, There was no **h** in this *place*. 6948
38:22 *that* there was no **h** in this *place*. 6948
38:24 thy daughter in law hath **played the h**; 2181
Lev 21:14 or a divorced *woman*, or profane, *or* a **h**, 2181
Jos 6:17 only Rahab the **h** shall live, she and all 2181
6:25 Joshua saved Rahab the **h** alive, and her 2181
Jdg 11: 1 *man* of valour, and he *was* the son of a **h**: 2181
16: 1 and saw there a **h**, and went in unto her. 2181
Pr 7:10 met him a woman *with* the attire of a **h**, 2181
Isa 1:21 How is the faithful city become a **h**! 2181
23:15 of seventy years shall Tyre sing as a **h**. 2181
23:16 the city, thou **h** that hast been forgotten; 2181
Jer 2:20 tree thou wanderest, **playing the h**. 2181
3: 1 hast **played the h** with many lovers; 2181
3: 6 green tree, and there hath **played the h**. 2181
3: 8 feared not, but went and **played the h** 2181
Eze 16:15 **playedst** the **h** because of thy renown, 2181
16:16 and **playedst** the **h** thereupon: 2181
16:28 thou hast **played the h** with them, 2181
16:31 not been as a **h**, in that *thou* scornest 2181
16:35 Wherefore, O **h**, hear the word of 2181
16:41 cause thee to cease from **playing the h**, 2181
23: 5 Aholah **played the h** when she was mine; 2181
23:19 wherein she had **played the h** in the land 2181
23:44 go in unto a woman that **playeth the h**: 2181
Hos 2: 5 For their mother hath **played the h**: 2181
3: 3 shalt not **play the h**, and thou shalt not 2181
4:15 thou, Israel, **play the h**, yet let not 2181
Joel 3: 3 have given a boy for a **h**, and sold a girl 2181
Am 7:17 Thy wife shall be a **h** in the city, 2181
Mic 1: 7 for she gathered *it* of the hire of a **h**, 2181
1: 7 and they shall return to the hire of a **h**. 2181
Na 3: 4 of the whoredoms of the wellfavoured **h**, 2181
1Co 6:15 and make *them* the members of a **h**? 4204
6:16 ye not that he which is joined to a **h** 4204
Heb 11:31 By faith the **h** Rahab perished not with 4204
Jas 2:25 also was not Rahab the **h** justified 4204

HARLOT'S (2) [HARLOT]

Jos 2: 1 came *into* a **h** house, named Rahab, 2181
6:22 Go *into* the **h** house, and bring out 2181

HARLOTS (7) [HARLOT]

1Ki 3:16 were **h**, unto the king, and stood before 2181
Pr 29: 3 that keepeth company with **h** spendeth 2181
Hos 4:14 with whores, and they sacrifice with **h**: 6948
Mt 21:31 the **h** go into the kingdom of God before 4204
21:32 the publicans and the **h** believed him: 4204
Lk 15:30 which hath devoured thy living with **h**, 4204
Rev 17: 5 THE MOTHER OF **H** AND 4204

HARLOTS' (1) [HARLOT]

Jer 5: 7 assembled themselves by troops *in* the **h** 2181

HARM (16) [HARMLESS]

Ge 31:52 this heap and this pillar unto me, for **h**. 7451
Lev 5:16 **h** that he hath **done** in the holy *thing*, 2398

Nu	35:23 *was* not his enemy, neither sought his **h**:	7451
1Sa	26:21 for I will no more **do** thee **h**, because my	7489
2Sa	20: 6 of Bichri **do** us more **h** than *did* Absalom:	3415
2Ki	4:41 may eat. And there was no **h** in the pot.	7451
1Ch	16:22 mine anointed, and **do** my prophets no **h**.	7489
Ps	105:15 mine anointed, and **do** my prophets no **h**.	7489
Pr	3:30 without cause, if he have done thee no **h**.	7451
Jer	39:12 and look well to him, and do him no **h**;	7451
Ac	16:28 with a loud voice, saying, Do thyself no **h**:	2556
	27:21 and to have gained this **h** and loss.	5196
	28: 5 off the beast into the fire, and felt no **h**.	2556
	28: 6 and saw no **h** come to him, they changed	824
	28:21 that came shewed or spake any **h** of thee.	4190
1Pe	3:13 And who *is* he that will **h** you, if ye be	2559

HARMLESS (3) [HARM]

Mt	10:16 therefore wise as serpents, and **h** as doves.	185
Php	2:15 That ye may be blameless and **h**, the sons	185
Heb	7:26 *who is* holy, **h**, undefiled, separate from	172

HARMONY See CONCORD

HARNEPHER (1)

1Ch	7:36 and **H**, and Shual, and Beri, and Imrah,	2774

HARNESS (5) [HARNESSED]

1Ki	20:11 Let not him that girdeth on *his* **h**	NIH
	22:34 king of Israel between the joints of the **h**:	8302
2Ch	9:24 raiment, **h**, and spices, horses, and mules,	5402
	18:33 king of Israel between the joints of the **h**:	8302
Jer	46: 4 **H** the horses; and get up, ye horsemen.	631

H

HARNESSED (1) [HARNESS]

Ex	13:18 the children of Israel went up **h** out of	2571

HAROD (1) [HARODITE]

Jdg	7: 1 early, and pitched beside the well of **H**:	5878

HARODITE (2) [HAROD]

2Sa	23:25 Shammah the **H**, Elika the Harodite,	2733
	23:25 Shammah the Harodite, Elika the **H**,	2733

HAROEH (1)

1Ch	2:52 sons; **H**, *and* half of the Manahethites.	7204

HARORITE (1)

1Ch	11:27 Shammoth the **H**, Helez the Pelonite,	2033

HAROSHETH (3)

Jdg	4: 2 which dwelt in **H** of the Gentiles.	2800
	4:13 from **H** of the Gentiles unto the river of	2800
	4:16 after the host, unto **H** of the Gentiles:	2800

HARP (30) [HARPED, HARPERS, HARPING, HARPS]

Ge	4:21 was the father of all such as handle the **h**	3658
	31:27 and with songs, with tabret, and with **h**?	3658
1Sa	10: 5 a tabret, and a pipe, and a **h**, before them;	3658
	16:16 a man, *who is* a cunning player on a **h**:	3658
	16:23 that David took a **h**, and played with his	3658
1Ch	25: 3 who prophesied with a **h**, to give thanks	3658
Job	21:12 They take the timbrel and **h**, and rejoice	3658
	30:31 My **h** also is *turned* to mourning,	3658
Ps	33: 2 Praise the LORD with **h**: sing unto him	3658
	43: 4 yea, will I praise thee, O God	3658
	49: 4 I will open my dark saying upon the **h**.	3658
	57: 8 my glory; awake, psaltery and **h**:	3658
	71:22 unto thee will I sing with the **h**, O thou	3658
	81: 2 timbrel, the pleasant **h** with the psaltery.	3658
	92: 3 upon the **h** with a solemn sound.	3658
	98: 5 Sing unto the LORD with the **h**; with	3658
	98: 5 with the **h**, and the voice of a psalm.	3658
	108: 2 Awake, psaltery and **h**: I *myself* will	3658
	147: 7 sing *praise* upon the **h** unto our God:	3658
	149: 3 *praises* unto him with the timbrel and **h**.	3658
	150: 3 praise him with the psaltery and **h**.	3658
Isa	5:12 the **h**, and the viol, the tabret, and pipe,	3658
	16:11 Wherefore my bowels shall sound like a **h**	3658
	23:16 Take a **h**, go about the city, thou harlot	3658
	24: 8 rejoice endeth, the joy of the **h** ceaseth.	3658
Da	3: 5 flute, **h**, sackbut, psaltery, dulcimer,	7030
	3: 7 flute, **h**, sackbut, psaltery, and all kinds	7030
	3:10 flute, **h**, sackbut, psaltery, dulcimer,	7030
	3:15 flute, **h**, sackbut, psaltery, and dulcimer,	7030
1Co	14: 7 life giving sound, whether pipe or **h**,	2788

HARPED (1) [HARP]

1Co	14: 7 how shall it be known what is piped or **h**?	2789

HARPERS (2) [HARP]

Rev	14: 2 I heard the voice of **h** harping with their	2790
	18:22 And the voice of **h**, and musicians,	2790

HARPING (1) [HARP]

Rev	14: 2 I heard the voice of harpers **h** with their	2789

HARPIST See MINSTREL

HARPS (20) [HARP]

2Sa	6: 5 even on **h**, and on psalteries,	3658
1Ki	10:12 **h** also and psalteries for singers:	3658
1Ch	13: 8 with **h**, and with psalteries,	3658
	15:16 psalteries and **h** and cymbals, sounding,	3658
	15:21 with **h** on the Sheminith to excel.	3658
	15:28 making a noise with psalteries and **h**.	3658
	16: 5 Jeiel with psalteries and with **h**;	3658
	25: 1 Jeduthun, who should prophesy with **h**,	3658
	25: 6 with cymbals, psalteries, and **h**,	3658

2Ch	5:12 having cymbals and psalteries and **h**,	3658
	9:11 and **h** and psalteries for singers:	3658
	20:28 **h** and trumpets unto the house of	3658
	29:25 with psalteries, and with **h**, according to	3658
Ne	12:27 with cymbals, psalteries, and with **h**.	3658
Ps	137: 2 We hanged our **h** upon the willows in	3658
Isa	30:32 upon him, *it* shall be with tabrets and **h**:	3658
Eze	26:13 sound of thy **h** shall be no more heard.	3658
Rev	5: 8 having every one *of them* **h**,	2788
	14: 2 the voice of harpers harping with their **h**:	2788
	15: 2 on the sea of glass, having *the* **h** of God.	2788

HARROW (1) [HARROWS]

Job	39:10 or will he **h** the valleys after thee?	7702

HARROWS (2) [HARROW]

2Sa	12:31 under **h** of iron, and under axes of iron,	2757
1Ch	20: 3 and with **h** of iron, and with axes.	2757

HARSH See FROWARD; SHARPNESS; STOUT

HARSHA (2)

Ezr	2:52 the children of Mehida, the children of **H**,	2797
Ne	7:54 the children of Mehida, the children of **H**,	2797

HART (9) [HARTS]

Dt	12:15 as of the roebuck, and as of the **h**.	354
	12:22 Even as the roebuck and the **h** is eaten,	354
	14: 5 The **h**, and the roebuck, and the fallow	354
	15:22 *eat it* alike, as the roebuck, and as the **h**.	354
Ps	42: 1 As the **h** panteth after the water brooks,	354
SS	2: 9 My beloved *is* like a roe or a young **h**:	354
	2:17 a young **h** upon the mountains of Bether.	354
	8:14 a young **h** upon the mountains of spices.	354
Isa	35: 6 shall the lame *man* leap as a **h**,	354

HARTS (2) [HART]

1Ki	4:23 beside **h**, and roebucks, and fallowdeer,	354
La	1: 6 her princes are become like **h** *that* find no	354

HARUM (1)

1Ch	4: 8 and the families of Aharhel the son of **H**.	2037

HARUMAPH (1)

Ne	3:10 unto them repaired Jedaiah the son of **H**,	2739

HARUPHITE (1)

1Ch	12: 5 and Shemariah, and Shephatiah the **H**,	2741

HARUZ (1)

2Ki	21:19 the daughter of **H** of Jotbah.	2743

HARVEST (61) [HARVESTMAN]

Ge	8:22 seedtime and **h**, and cold and heat,	7105
	30:14 Reuben went in the days of wheat **h**,	7105
	45: 6 *there shall* neither *be* earing nor **h**.	7105
Ex	23:16 feast of **h**, the firstfruits of thy labours,	7105
	34:21 in earing time and in **h** thou shalt rest.	7105
	34:22 the firstfruits of wheat **h**, and the feast of	7105
Lev	19: 9 when ye reap the **h** of your land, thou	7105
	19: 9 shalt thou gather the gleanings of thy **h**.	7105
	23:10 reap the **h** thereof, then ye shall bring	7105
	23:10 of the firstfruits of your **h** unto the priest:	7105
	23:22 ye reap the **h** of your land, thou shalt	7105
	23:22 shalt thou gather *any* gleaning of thy **h**:	7105
	25: 5 it own accord of thy **h** thou shalt not reap,	7105
Dt	24:19 When thou **cuttest down** thine **h**	7105+7114
Jos	3:15 overfloweth all his banks all the time of **h**,	7105
Jdg	15: 1 the time of wheat **h**, that Samson visited	7105
Ru	1:22 Beth-lehem in the beginning of barley **h**.	7105
	2:21 men, until they have ended all my **h**.	7105
	2:23 of Boaz to glean unto the end of barley **h**	7105
	2:23 the end of barley harvest and of wheat **h**;	7105
1Sa	6:13 *were* reaping *their* wheat **h** in the valley:	7105
	8:12 to reap his **h**, and to make his instruments	7105
	12:17 *Is it* not wheat **h** to day? I will call unto	7105
2Sa	21: 9 and were put to death in the days of **h**,	7105
	21: 9 the first *days*, in the beginning of barley **h**.	7105
	21:10 from the beginning of **h** until water	7105
	23:13 came to David in the **h time** unto the	7105
Job	5: 5 Whose **h** the hungry eateth up, and taketh	7105
Pr	6: 8 *and* gathereth her food in the **h**.	7105
	10: 5 he that sleepeth in **h** *is* a son that causeth	7105
	20: 4 therefore shall he beg in **h**,	7105
	25:13 As the cold of snow in the time of **h**, *so is*	7105
	26: 1 as rain in **h**, so honour *is* not seemly for a	7105
Isa	9: 3 joy before thee according to the joy in **h**,	7105
	16: 9 thy summer fruits and for thy **h** is fallen.	7105
	17:11 the **h** *shall be* a heap in the day of grief	7105
	18: 4 *and* like a cloud of dew in the heat of **h**.	7105
	18: 5 For afore the **h**, when the bud is perfect,	7105
	23: Sihor, the **h** of the river, *is* her revenue;	7105
Jer	5:17 they shall eat up thine **h**, and thy bread,	7105
	5:24 unto us the appointed weeks of the **h**.	7105
	8:20 The **h** is past, the summer is ended,	7105
	50:16 that handleth the sickle in the time of **h**;	7105
	51:33 and the time of her **h** shall come.	7105
Hos	6:11 Also, O Judah, he hath set a **h** for thee,	7105
Joel	1:11 because the **h** of the field is perished.	7105
	3:13 Put ye in the sickle, for the **h** is ripe:	7105
Am	4: 7 *there were* yet three months to the **h**:	7105
Mt	9:37 The **h** truly *is* plenteous, but the labourers	2326
	9:38 Pray ye therefore the Lord of the **h**, that	2326
	9:38 he will send forth labourers into his **h**.	2326
	13:30 Let both grow together until the **h**:	2326
	13:30 in the time of **h** I will say to the reapers,	2326

Mt	13:39 the **h** is the end of the world;	2326
Mk	4:29 in the sickle, because the **h** is come.	2326
Lk	10: 2 The **h** truly *is* great, but the labourers *are*	2326
	10: 2 pray ye therefore the Lord of the **h**, that	2326
	10: 2 he would send forth labourers into his **h**.	2326
Jn	4:35 are yet four months, and *then* cometh **h**?	2326
	4:35 the fields; for they are white already to **h**.	2326
Rev	14:15 thee to reap; for the **h** of the earth is ripe.	2326

HARVESTMAN (2) [HARVEST, MAN]

Isa	17: 5 shall be as when the **h** gathereth the corn,	7105
Jer	9:22 as the handful after the **h**, and none shall	7114

HASADIAH (1)

1Ch	3:20 Ohel, and Berechiah, and **H**, Jushabhesed,	2619

HASENUAH (1)

1Ch	9: 7 the son of Hodaviah, the son of **H**,	5574

HASHABIAH (15)

1Ch	6:45 The son of **H**, the son of Amaziah,	2811
	9:14 the son of Azrikam, the son of **H**,	2811
	25: 3 Zeri, and Jeshaiah, **H**, and Mattithiah, six,	2811
	25:19 The twelfth to **H**, *he*, his sons,	2811
	26:30 **H** and his brethren, men of valour,	2811
	27:17 Of the Levites, **H** the son of Kemuel:	2811
2Ch	35: 9 his brethren, and **H** and Jeiel and Jozabad,	2811
Ezr	8:19 **H**, and with him Jeshaiah of the sons of	2811
	8:24 **H**, and ten of their brethren with them,	2811
Ne	3:17 Next unto him repaired **H**, the ruler of	2811
	10:11 Micha, Rehob, **H**,	2811
	11:15 Azrikam, the son of **H**, the son of Bunni;	2811
	11:22 the son of **H**, the son of Mattaniah,	2811
	12:21 Of Hilkiah, **H**; of Jedaiah, Nethaneel.	2811
	12:24 **H**, Sherebiah, and Jeshua the son of	2811

HASHABNAH (1)

Ne	10:25 Rehum, **H**, Maaseiah,	2812

HASHABNEIAH See HASHABNIAH

HASHABNIAH (2)

Ne	3:10 unto him repaired Hattush the son of **H**.	2813
	9: 5 Jeshua and Kadmiel, Bani, **H**, Sherebiah,	2813

HASHBADANA (1)

Ne	8: 4 and Malchiah, and Hashum, and **H**,	2806

HASHBADDANA See HASHBADANA

HASHEM (1)

1Ch	11:34 The sons of **H** the Gizonite, Jonathan	2044

HASHMONAH (2)

Nu	33:29 went from Mithcah, and pitched in **H**.	2832
	33:30 they departed from **H**, and encamped at	2832

HASHUB (4)

Ne	3:11 **H** the son of Pahath-moab, repaired	2815
	3:23 **H** over against their house.	2815
	10:23 Hoshea, Hananiah, **H**,	2815
	11:15 Shemaiah the son of **H**, the son of	2815

HASHUBAH (1)

1Ch	3:20 **H**, and Ohel, and Berechiah,	2807

HASHUM (5)

Ezr	2:19 The children of **H**, two hundred twenty	2828
	10:33 Of the sons of **H**; Mattenai, Mattathah,	2828
Ne	7:22 The children of **H**, three hundred twenty	2828
	8: 4 and Malchiah, and **H**, and Hashbadana	2828
	10:18 Hodijah, **H**, Bezai,	2828

HASHUPHA (1) [HASUPHA]

Ne	7:46 the children of Ziha, the children of **H**,	2817

HASRAH (1)

2Ch	34:22 the son of **H**, keeper of the wardrobe;	2641

HASSENAAH (1)

Ne	3: 3 the fish gate did the sons of **H** build,	5570

HASSENUAH See HASENUAH; SENUAH

HASSHUB (1)

1Ch	9:14 Shemaiah the son of **H**, the son of	2815

HAST (1071) [HAVE]

Ge	3:11 **h** thou eaten of the tree, whereof I	NIH
	3:13 woman, What *is* this *that* thou **h** done?	NIH
	3:14 Because thou **h** done this, thou *art* cursed	NIH
	3:17 Because thou **h** hearkened unto the voice	NIH
	3:17 **h** eaten of the tree, of which I commanded	NIH
	4:10 he said, What **h** thou done? the voice of	NIH
	4:14 thou **h** driven me out *this* day from the	NIH
	12:18 What *is* this *that* thou **h** done unto me?	NIH
	15: 3 Behold, to me thou **h** given no seed:	NIH
	18: 5 And they said, So do, as thou **h** said.	NIH
	19:12 said unto Lot, **H** thou here any besides?	3807.1
	19:12 and whatsoever thou **h** in the city,	3807.1
	19:19 thy sight, and thou **h** magnified thy mercy,	NIH
	19:19 thou **h** shewed unto me in saving my	NIH
	19:21 *this* city, for the which thou **h** spoken.	NIH
	20: 3 for the woman which thou **h** taken;	NIH
	20: 9 said unto him, What **h** thou done unto us?	NIH
	20: 9 that thou **h** brought on me and on my	NIH
	20: 9 thou **h** done deeds unto me that ought not	NIH

Ge	20:10 sawest thou, that thou **h** done this thing?	NIH	
	21:23 to the land wherein thou **h** sojourned.	NIH	
	21:29 lambs which thou **h** set by themselves?	NIH	
	22:12 seeing thou **h** not withheld thy son, thine	NIH	
	22:16 for because thou **h** done this thing,	NIH	
	22:16 **h** not withheld thy son, thine only *son:*	NIH	
	22:18 because thou **h** obeyed my voice.	NIH	
	24:14 *let the same be* she *that* thou **h** appointed	NIH	
	24:14 thereby shall I know that thou **h** shewed	NIH	
	26:10 What *is* this thou **h** done unto us?	NIH	
	27:20 How *is it that* thou **h** found *it so* quickly,	NIH	
	27:36 **h** thou not reserved a blessing for me?	NIH	
	27:38 Hast thou but one blessing, my father?	3807.1	
	27:45 he forget *that* which thou **h** done to him:	NIH	
	29:25 Laban, What *is* this thou **h** done unto me?	NIH	
	29:25 then **h** thou beguiled me?	NIH	
	30:15 *Is it* a small matter that thou **h** taken my	NIH	
	31:26 Laban said to Jacob, What **h** thou done,	NIH	
	31:26 that thou **h** stolen away unawares to me,	NIH	
	31:28 **h** not suffered me to kiss my sons and my	NIH	
	31:28 thou **h** now done foolishly in *so* doing.	NIH	
	31:30 *yet* wherefore **h** thou stolen my gods?	NIH	
	31:36 that thou **h** *so* hotly pursued after me?	NIH	
	31:37 Whereas thou **h** searched all my stuff,	NIH	
	31:37 what **h** thou found of all thy household	NIH	
	31:41 and thou **h** changed my wages ten times.	NIH	
	32:10 which thou **h** shewed unto thy servant;	NIH	
	32:28 for **as a prince h** thou **power** with God	8280	
	32:28 with God and with men, and **h** prevailed.	NIH	
	33: 9 brother; keep that thou **h** unto thyself.	3807.1	
	37:10 What *is* this dream that thou **h** dreamed?	NIH	
	38:23 I sent this kid, and thou **h** not found her.	NIH	
	38:29 she said, How **h** thou broken forth?	NIH	
	39:17 which thou **h** brought unto us,	NIH	
	45:10 and thy herds, and all that thou **h:**	3807.1	
	45:11 and thy household, and all that thou **h,**	3807.1	
	47:25 said, Thou **h** saved our lives: let us find	NIH	
	47:30 And he said, I will do as thou **h** said.	NIH	
Ex	3:12 When thou **h** brought forth the people out	NIH	
	4:10 nor since thou **h** spoken unto thy servant:	NIH	
	5:22 wherefore **h** thou *so* evil entreated this	NIH	
	5:22 people? why *is* it *that* thou **h** sent me?	NIH	
	5:23 neither **h** thou delivered thy people at all.	NIH	
	9:19 cattle, and all that thou **h** in the field;	3807.1	
	10:29 Moses said, Thou **h** spoken well, I will see	NIH	
	12:44 when thou **h** circumcised him, then shall	NIH	
	13:12 cometh of a beast which thou **h;**	1961+3807.1	
	14:11 **h** thou taken us away to die in	NIH	
	14:11 wherefore **h** thou dealt thus with us,	NIH	
	15: 7 in the greatness of thine excellency thou **h**	NIH	
	15:13 Thou in thy mercy **h** led forth the people	NIH	
	15:13 forth the people *which* thou **h** redeemed:	NIH	
	15:13 thou **h** guided *them* in thy strength unto	NIH	
	15:16 people pass over, *which* thou **h** purchased.	NIH	
	15:17 *which* thou **h** made for thee to dwell in,	NIH	
	17: 3 Wherefore *is* this *that* thou **h** brought us	NIH	
	20:25 lift up thy tool upon it, thou **h** polluted it.	NIH	
	23:16 labours, which thou **h** sown in the field:	NIH	
	23:16 when thou **h** gathered in thy labours out	NIH	
	29:36 when thou **h** made an atonement for it,	NIH	
	32:11 which thou **h** brought forth out of the land	NIH	
	32:21 that thou **h** brought *so* great a sin upon	NIH	
	32:32 out of thy book which thou **h** written.	NIH	
	33: 1 the people which thou **h** brought up out	NIH	
	33:12 thou **h** not let me know whom thou wilt	NIH	
	33:12 Yet thou **h** said, I know thee by name,	NIH	
	33:12 and thou **h** also found grace in my sight.	NIH	
	33:17 will do this thing also that thou **h** spoken:	NIH	
	33:17 for thou **h** found grace in my sight,	NIH	
Nu	5:19 if thou **h** not gone aside *to* uncleanness	NIH	
	5:20 if thou **h** gone aside *to another* instead of	NIH	
	11:11 Wherefore **h** thou afflicted thy servant?	NIH	
	11:21 thou **h** said, I will give them flesh,	NIH	
	14:17 according as thou **h** spoken, saying,	NIH	
	14:19 as thou **h** forgiven this people, from Egypt	NIH	
	16:13 *Is it* a small thing that thou **h** brought us	NIH	
	16:14 thou **h** not brought us into a land	NIH	
	22:28 that thou **h** smitten me these three times?	NIH	
	22:29 unto the ass, Because thou **h** mocked me:	NIH	
	22:30 which thou **h** ridden ever since *I was*	NIH	
	22:32 Wherefore **h** thou smitten thine ass these	NIH	
	23:11 unto Balaam, What **h** thou done unto me?	NIH	
	23:11 behold, thou **h** blessed *them* altogether.	NIH	
	24:10 thou **h** altogether blessed *them* these three	NIH	
	27:13 when thou **h** seen it, thou also shalt be	NIH	
Dt	1:14 The thing which thou **h** spoken *is* good *for*	NIH	
	1:31 where thou **h** seen how that the LORD thy	NIH	
	2: 7 *been* with thee; thou **h** lacked nothing.	NIH	
	3:24 **h** begun to shew thy servant thy	NIH	
	4:33 midst of the fire, as thou **h** heard, and live?	NIH	
	8:10 When thou **h** eaten and art full, then	NIH	
	8:12 Lest *when* thou **h** eaten and art full,	NIH	
	8:12 **h** built goodly houses, and dwelt *therein;*	NIH	
	8:13 and all that thou **h** is multiplied;	3807.1	
	9: 2 *of whom* thou **h** heard *say,* Who can stand	NIH	
	9:12 for thy people which thou **h** brought forth	NIH	
	9:26 which thou **h** redeemed through thy	NIH	
	9:26 which thou **h** brought forth out of Egypt	NIH	
	12:26 thy holy *things* which thou **h,**	1961+3807.1	
	13: 2 which thou **h** not known, and let us serve	NIH	
	13: 6 which thou **h** not known, thou, nor thy	NIH	
	16:13 after that thou **h** gathered in thy corn and	NIH	
	17: 4 thou **h** heard *of it,* and inquired diligently,	NIH	
	21: 8 whom thou **h** redeemed, and lay not	NIH	
	21:10 hands, and thou **h** taken them captive,	NIH	

Dt	21:11 **h a** desire unto her, that thou wouldest	2836	
	21:14 of her, because thou **h** humbled her.	NIH	
	22: 3 which he hath lost, and thou **h** found,	NIH	
	22: 9 the fruit of *thy* seed which thou **h** sown,	NIH	
	23:23 according as thou **h** vowed unto the LORD	NIH	
	23:23 which thou **h** promised with thy mouth.	NIH	
	24:19 **h** forgot a sheaf in the field, thou shalt not	NIH	
	26:10 which thou, O LORD, **h** given me.	NIH	
	26:12 When thou **h** made an end of tithing all	NIH	
	26:12 **h** given *it* unto the Levite, the stranger,	NIH	
	26:13 which thou **h** commanded me:	NIH	
	26:14 have done according to all that thou **h**	NIH	
	26:15 and the land which thou **h** given us,	NIH	
	26:17 Thou **h** avouched the LORD *this* day to be	NIH	
	28:20 thy doings, where*by* thou **h** forsaken me.	NIH	
	32:18 and **h** forgotten God that formed thee.	NIH	
Jos	2:17 thine oath which thou **h** made us swear.	NIH	
	2:20 will be quit of this oath which thou **h**	NIH	
	7: 7 wherefore **h** thou at all brought this people	NIH	
	7:19 tell me now what thou **h** done; hide *it* not	NIH	
	7:25 Joshua said, Why **h** thou troubled us?	NIH	
	14: 9 thou **h** wholly followed the LORD my	NIH	
	15:19 blessing; for thou **h** given me a south land;	NIH	
	17:14 Why **h** thou given me *but* one lot and	NIH	
	17:17 *art* a great people, and **h** great power:	NIH	
Jdg	1:15 for thou **h** given me a south land; give me	NIH	
	5:21 O my soul, thou **h** trodden down strength.	NIH	
	6:36 save Israel by mine hand, as thou **h** said,	NIH	
	6:37 save Israel by mine hand, as thou **h** said.	NIH	
	8: 1 Why **h** thou served us thus, that *thou*	NIH	
	8:22 for thou **h** delivered us from the hand of	NIH	
	9:38 not this the people that thou **h** despised?	NIH	
	11:12 saying, What **h** thou to do with me,	3807.1	
	11:35 thou **h** brought me very low, and thou art	NIH	
	11:36 *if* thou **h** opened thy mouth unto	NIH	
	14:16 thou **h** put forth a riddle unto the children	NIH	
	14:16 of my people, and **h** not told *it* me.	3807.1	
	15:11 what *is* this *that* thou **h** done unto us?	NIH	
	15:18 Thou **h** given this great deliverance into	NIH	
	16:10 thou **h** mocked me, and told me lies:	NIH	
	16:13 Hitherto thou **h** mocked me, and told me	NIH	
	16:15 thou **h** mocked me these three times,	NIH	
	16:15 **h** not told me wherein thy great strength	NIH	
	18: 3 in this *place?* and what **h** thou here?	3807.1	
Ru	2:11 that thou **h** done unto thy mother in law	NIH	
	2:11 *how* thou **h** left thy father and thy mother,	NIH	
	2:13 for that thou **h** comforted me, and for that	NIH	
	2:13 for that thou **h** spoken friendly unto thine	NIH	
	2:19 unto her, Where **h** thou gleaned to day?	NIH	
	3:10 *for* thou **h** shewed more kindness in	NIH	
	3:15 Bring the vail that *thou **h*** upon thee,	NIH	
1Sa	1:17 *thee* thy petition that thou **h** asked of him.	NIH	
	4:20 *unto her,* Fear not; for thou **h** born a son.	NIH	
	12: 4 they said, Thou **h** not defrauded us,	NIH	
	12: 4 neither **h** thou taken ought of any man's	NIH	
	13:11 Samuel said, What **h** thou done? And Saul	NIH	
	13:13 said to Saul, Thou **h** done foolishly:	NIH	
	13:13 thou **h** not kept the commandment of	NIH	
	13:14 thou **h** not kept *that* which the LORD	NIH	
	14:43 to Jonathan, Tell me what thou **h** done.	NIH	
	15:23 Because thou **h** rejected the word of	NIH	
	15:26 for thou **h** rejected the word of the LORD,	NIH	
	17:28 with whom **h** thou left those few sheep in	NIH	
	17:45 the armies of Israel, whom thou **h** defied.	NIH	
	19:17 Why **h** thou deceived me so, and sent	NIH	
	20: 8 for thou **h** brought thy servant into a	NIH	
	20:19 *when* thou **h** stayed three days, *then*	NIH	
	20:30 **h** chosen the son of Jesse to thine own	NIH	
	22:13 that thou **h** given him bread and a sword,	NIH	
	22:13 a sword, and **h** inquired of God for him,	NIH	
	24:17 for thou **h** rewarded me good, whereas I	NIH	
	24:18 thou **h** shewed *this* day how that thou	NIH	
	24:18 hast shewed *this* day how that thou **h**	NIH	
	24:19 for that thou **h** done unto me this day.	NIH	
	25: 6 and peace *be* unto all that thou **h.**	3807.1	
	25: 7 now I have heard that thou **h** shearers:	3807.1	
	25:31 either that thou **h** shed blood causeless,	NIH	
	25:33 which **h** kept me this day from coming to	NIH	
	26:15 then **h** thou not kept thy lord the king?	NIH	
	26:16 This thing *is* not good that thou **h** done.	NIH	
	28:12 to Saul, saying, Why **h** thou deceived me?	NIH	
	28:15 **h** thou disquieted me, to bring me up?	NIH	
	29: 4 thou **h** appointed him, and let him not	NIH	
	29: 6 thou **h** *been* upright, and thy going out	NIH	
	29: 8 what **h** thou found in thy servant so long	NIH	
2Sa	1:26 pleasant **h** thou been unto me: thy love	NIH	
	3: 7 Wherefore **h** thou gone in unto my father's	NIH	
	3:24 to the king, and said, What **h** thou done?	NIH	
	3:24 why *is* it *that* thou **h** sent him away,	NIH	
	6:22 the maidservants which thou **h** spoken of,	NIH	
	7:18 house, that thou **h** brought me hitherto?	NIH	
	7:19 thou **h** spoken also of thy servant's house	NIH	
	7:21 thou **h** done all these great things,	NIH	
	7:24 For thou **h** confirmed to thyself thy people	NIH	
	7:25 word that thou **h** spoken concerning this	NIH	
	7:25 establish *it* for ever, and do as thou **h** said.	NIH	
	7:27 of Israel, **h** revealed to thy servant, saying,	NIH	
	7:28 thou **h** promised this goodness unto thy	NIH	
	7:29 **h** spoken *it:* and with thy blessing let	NIH	
	11:19 When thou **h** made an end of telling	NIH	
	12: 9 Wherefore **h** thou despised	NIH	
	12: 9 **h** killed Uriah the Hittite with	NIH	
	12: 9 **h** taken his wife to be thy wife, and hast	NIH	
	12: 9 **h** slain him with the sword of the children	NIH	
	12:10 because thou **h** despised me, and hast	NIH	

2Sa	12:10 **h** taken the wife of Uriah the Hittite to be	NIH	
	12:14 by this deed thou **h** given great occasion	NIH	
	12:21 What thing *is* this that thou **h** done?	NIH	
	14:13 to thou thought such a thing against	NIH	
	15:35 *h* thou not there with thee Zadok and	NIH	
	16: 8 of Saul, in whose stead thou **h** reigned;	NIH	
	16:10 then say, Wherefore **h** thou done so?	NIH	
	18:21 Cushi, Go tell the king what thou **h** seen.	NIH	
	18:22 son, seeing that thou **h** no tidings ready?	NIH	
	19: 5 Thou **h** shamed *this* day the faces of all	NIH	
	19: 6 for thou **h** declared *this* day, that thou	NIH	
	22:36 Thou **h** also given me the shield of thy	NIH	
	22:37 Thou **h** enlarged my steps under me;	NIH	
	22:40 thou **h** girded me with strength to battle:	NIH	
	22:40 them that rose up against me **h** thou	NIH	
	22:41 Thou **h** also given me the necks of mine	NIH	
	22:44 also **h** delivered me from the strivings	NIH	
	22:44 thou **h** kept me to be head of the heathen:	NIH	
	22:49 thou also **h** lifted me up on high above	NIH	
	22:49 thou **h** delivered me from the violent man.	NIH	
1Ki	1: 6 any time in saying, Why **h** thou done so?	NIH	
	1:11 **H** thou not heard that Adonijah the son of	NIH	
	1:24 Nathan said, My lord O king, **h** thou said,	NIH	
	1:27 thou **h** not shewed *it* unto thy servant,	NIH	
	2: 8 *thou **h*** with thee Shimei the son of Gera,	NIH	
	2:26 thou **h** been afflicted in all where*in* my	NIH	
	2:43 then **h** thou not kept the oath of the LORD,	NIH	
	3: 6 Thou **h** shewed unto thy servant David my	NIH	
	3: 6 thou **h** kept for him this great kindness,	NIH	
	3: 6 that thou **h** given him a son to sit on his	NIH	
	3: 7 thou **h** made thy servant king instead of	NIH	
	3: 8 midst of thy people which thou **h** chosen,	NIH	
	3:11 Because thou **h** asked this thing,	NIH	
	3:11 and **h** not asked for thyself long life;	NIH	
	3:11 neither **h** asked riches for thyself, nor hast	NIH	
	3:11 nor **h** asked the life of thine enemies;	NIH	
	3:11 **h** asked for thyself understanding to	NIH	
	3:13 I have also given thee *that* which thou **h**	NIH	
	8:24 Who **h** kept with thy servant David my	NIH	
	8:24 **h** fulfilled *it* with thine hand, as *it is* this	NIH	
	8:25 they walk before me as thou **h** walked	NIH	
	8:29 toward the place of which thou **h** said,	NIH	
	8:36 which thou **h** given to thy people for an	NIH	
	8:44 toward the city which thou **h** chosen,	NIH	
	8:48 city which thou **h** chosen, and the house	NIH	
	9: 3 that thou **h** made before me:	NIH	
	9: 3 hallowed this house, which thou **h** built,	NIH	
	9:13 What cities *are* these which thou **h** given	NIH	
	11:11 thou **h** not kept my covenant and	NIH	
	11:22 what **h** thou lacked with me, that behold,	NIH	
	13:21 Forasmuch as thou **h** disobeyed the mouth	NIH	
	13:21 **h** not kept the commandment which	NIH	
	13:22 **h** eaten bread and drunk water in the	NIH	
	14: 8 *yet* thou **h** not been as my servant David,	NIH	
	14: 9 **h** done evil above all that were before	NIH	
	14: 9 for thou **h** gone and made thee other gods,	NIH	
	14: 9 to anger, and **h** cast me behind thy back:	NIH	
	16: 2 thou **h** walked in the way of Jeroboam,	NIH	
	16: 2 **h** made my people Israel to sin, to provoke	NIH	
	17:13 Fear not; go *and* do as thou **h** said:	NIH	
	17:20 thou also brought evil upon the widow	NIH	
	18:18 of the LORD, and thou **h** followed Baalim.	NIH	
	18:37 *that* thou **h** turned their heart back again.	NIH	
	20:13 **H** thou seen all this great multitude?	NIH	
	20:25 like the army that thou **h** lost, horse for	NIH	
	20:36 Because thou **h** not obeyed the voice of	NIH	
	20:40 *shall* thy judgment *be;* thyself **h** decided	NIH	
	20:42 thou **h** let go out of *thy* hand a man	NIH	
	21:19 Hast thou killed, and also taken possession?	NIH	
	21:20 Elijah, **H** thou found me, O mine enemy?	NIH	
	21:20 thou **h** sold thyself to work evil in the sight	NIH	
	21:22 for the provocation wherewith thou **h**	NIH	
2Ki	1:16 Forasmuch as thou **h** sent messengers to	NIH	
	2:10 he said, Thou **h** asked a hard thing:	NIH	
	4: 2 what **h** thou in the house?	3426+3807.1	
	4:13 **h** been careful to us with all this care;	NIH	
	5: 8 Wherefore **h** thou rent thy clothes?	NIH	
	6:22 thou **h** taken captive with thy sword	NIH	
	9:18 said, What **h** thou to do with peace?	3807.1	
	9:19 What **h** thou to do with peace?	3807.1	
	10:30 Because thou **h** done well in executing	NIH	
	10:30 **h** done unto the house of Ahab according	NIH	
	14:10 Thou **h** indeed smitten Edom,	NIH	
	17:26 The nations which thou **h** removed,	NIH	
	19: 6 Be not afraid of the words which thou **h**	NIH	
	19:11 thou **h** heard what the kings of Assyria	NIH	
	19:15 the earth; thou **h** made heaven and earth.	NIH	
	19:20 *That* which thou **h** prayed to me against	NIH	
	19:22 **h** thou reproached and blasphemed?	NIH	
	19:22 against whom **h** thou exalted *thy* voice,	NIH	
	19:23 By thy messengers thou **h** reproached	NIH	
	19:23 thou hast reproached the Lord, and **h** said,	NIH	
	19:25 **H** thou not heard long ago *how* I have	NIH	
	20:19 word of the LORD which thou **h** spoken.	NIH	
	22:18 *touching* the words which thou **h** heard;	NIH	
	22:19 thou **h** humbled thyself before the LORD,	NIH	
	22:19 **h** rent thy clothes, and wept before me;	NIH	
	23:17 proclaimed these things that thou **h** done	NIH	
1Ch	17: 8 have been with thee whithersoever thou **h**	NIH	
	17:16 that thou **h** brought me hitherto?	NIH	
	17:17 for thou **h** *also* spoken of thy servant's	NIH	
	17:17 **h** regarded me according to the estate of a	NIH	
	17:19 own heart, **h** thou done all this greatness,	NIH	
	17:21 whom thou **h** redeemed out of Egypt?	NIH	
	17:23 the thing that thou **h** spoken concerning	NIH	

H

H

1Ch 17:23 established for ever, and do as thou **h** said.	NIH
17:25 told thy servant that *thou* wilt build him	NIH
17:26 **h** promised this goodness unto thy servant;	NIH
22: 8 Thou **h** shed blood abundantly,	NIH
22: 8 blood abundantly, and **h** made great wars:	NIH
22: 8 thou **h** shed much blood upon the earth in	NIH
28: 3 because thou *h been* a man of war,	NIH
28: 3 *hast been* a man of war, and **h** shed blood.	NIH
28:20 until *thou* **h** finished all the work for	NIH
29:17 the heart, and **h** pleasure in uprightness.	7521
2Ch 1: 8 Thou **h** shewed great mercy unto David	NIH
1: 8 and **h** made me to reign in his stead.	NIH
1: 9 thou **h** made me king over a people like	NIH
1:11 **h** not asked riches, wealth, or honour,	NIH
1:11 enemies, neither yet **h** asked long life;	NIH
1:11 **h** asked wisdom and knowledge for	NIH
6:15 which **h** kept with thy servant David	NIH
6:15 father *that* which thou **h** promised him;	NIH
6:15 fulfilled *it* with thine hand, as *it is* this	NIH
6:16 father *that* which thou **h** promised him,	NIH
6:16 in my law, as thou **h** walked before me.	NIH
6:17 which **h** spoken unto thy servant	NIH
6:20 upon the place whereof thou **h** said that	NIH
6:27 when thou **h** taught them the good way,	NIH
6:27 which thou **h** given unto thy people for an	NIH
6:34 toward this city which thou **h** chosen,	NIH
6:38 *toward* the city which thou **h** chosen,	NIH
16: 7 Because thou **h** relied on the king of Syria,	NIH
16: 9 Herein thou **h** done foolishly: therefore	NIH
19: 3 that thou **h** taken away the groves out of	NIH
19: 3 and **h** prepared thine heart to seek God.	NIH
20:11 which thou **h** given us to inherit.	NIH
20:37 thou **h** joined thyself with Ahaziah,	NIH
21:12 Because thou **h** not walked in the ways of	NIH
21:13 walked in the way of the kings of Israel,	NIH
21:13 **h** made Judah and the inhabitants of	NIH
21:13 also **h** slain thy brethren of thy father's	NIH
24: 6 Why thou **h** not required of the Levites to	NIH
25:15 Why **h** thou sought after the gods of	NIH
25:16 because thou **h** done this, and hast not	NIH
25:16 and **h** not hearkened unto my counsel.	NIH
25:19 Lo, thou **h** smitten the Edomites;	NIH
26:18 of the sanctuary; for thou **h** trespassed;	NIH
34:26 the words which thou **h** heard;	NIH
Ezr 9:11 Which thou **h** commanded by thy servants	NIH
9:13 that thou our God **h** punished us less	NIH
9:13 and **h** given us *such* deliverance as this;	NIH
10:12 loud voice, As thou **h** said, so must we do.	NIH
Ne 1:10 thou **h** redeemed by thy great power,	NIH
6: 7 thou **h** also appointed prophets to preach	NIH
9: 6 **h** made heaven, the heaven of heavens,	NIH
9: 8 to his seed, and **h** performed thy words;	NIH
9:33 for thou **h** done right, but we have done	NIH
9:37 unto the kings whom thou **h** set over us	NIH
Est 6:10 thou **h** said, and do *even* so to Mordecai	NIH
6:10 let nothing fail of all that thou **h** spoken.	NIH
6:13 before whom thou **h** begun to fall,	NIH
Job 1: 8 **H** thou considered my servant Job,	NIH
1:10 **H** not thou made a hedge about him,	NIH
1:10 thou **h** blessed the work of his hands,	NIH
2: 3 **H** thou considered my servant Job,	NIH
4: 3 thou **h** instructed many, and thou hast	NIH
4: 3 and thou **h** strengthened the weak hands.	NIH
4: 4 and thou **h** strengthened the feeble knees.	NIH
7:20 why **h** thou set me as a mark against thee,	NIH
10: 4 **H** thou eyes of flesh? or seest thou as	3807.1
10: 9 that thou **h** made me as the clay;	NIH
10:10 **H** thou not poured me out as milk,	NIH
10:11 Thou **h** clothed me with skin and flesh,	NIH
10:11 and **h** fenced me with bones and sinews.	NIH
10:12 Thou **h** granted me life and favour,	NIH
10:13 these *things* **h** thou hid in thine heart:	NIH
10:18 **h** thou brought me forth out of the womb?	NIH
11: 4 For thou **h** said, My doctrine *is* pure,	NIH
14: 5 **h** appointed his bounds that he cannot	NIH
15: 8 **H** thou heard the secret of God?	NIH
16: 7 thou **h** made desolate all my company.	NIH
16: 8 thou **h** filled me with wrinkles, *which* is	3807.1
17: 4 For thou **h** hid their heart from	NIH
22: 6 For thou **h** taken a pledge from thy brother	NIH
22: 7 Thou **h** not given water to the weary to	NIH
22: 7 thou **h** withholden bread from the hungry.	NIH
22: 9 Thou **h** sent widows away empty,	NIH
22:15 **H** thou marked the old way which wicked	NIH
26: 2 How **h** thou helped *him that is* without	NIH
26: 3 How **h** thou counselled *him that hath* no	NIH
26: 3 *how* **h** thou plentifully declared the thing	NIH
26: 4 To whom **h** thou uttered words?	NIH
33: 8 Surely thou **h** spoken in mine hearing,	NIH
33:32 If *thou* **h** any thing to say, answer me:	3426
34:16 If now *thou* **h** understanding, hear this:	NIH
36:17 fulfilled the judgment of the wicked:	NIH
36:21 this **h** thou chosen rather than affliction.	NIH
36:23 or who can say, Thou **h** wrought iniquity?	NIH
37:18 **H** thou with him spread out the sky,	NIH
38: 4 declare, if thou **h** understanding.	3045
38:12 **H** thou commanded the morning since thy	NIH
38:16 **H** thou entered into the springs of the sea?	NIH
38:16 thou **h** walked in the search of the depth?	NIH
38:17 **h** thou seen the doors of the shadow of	NIH
38:18 **H** thou perceived the breadth of the earth?	NIH
38:22 **H** thou entered into the treasures of the	NIH
38:22 or **h** thou seen the treasures of the hail,	NIH
39:19 **H** thou given the horse strength? hast	NIH
39:19 **h** thou clothed his neck with thunder?	NIH

Job 40: 9 **H** thou an arm like God? or, canst thou	NIH
Ps 3: 7 for thou **h** smitten all mine enemies *upon*	NIH
3: 7 thou **h** broken the teeth of the ungodly.	NIH
4: 1 enlarged me *when I was* in distress;	NIH
4: 7 Thou **h** put gladness in my heart, more	NIH
7: 6 awake for me *to* the judgment *that* thou **h**	NIH
8: 1 who **h** set thy glory above the heavens.	NIH
8: 2 sucklings **h** thou ordained strength	NIH
8: 3 and the stars, which thou **h** ordained;	NIH
8: 5 For thou **h** made him a little lower than	NIH
8: 5 crowned him *with* glory and honour.	NIH
8: 6 thou **h** put all *things* under his feet:	NIH
9: 4 For thou **h** maintained my right and	NIH
9: 5 Thou **h** rebuked the heathen, thou hast	NIH
9: 5 the heathen, thou **h** destroyed the wicked,	NIH
9: 5 **h** put out their name for ever and ever.	NIH
9: 6 thou **h** destroyed cities; their memorial is	NIH
9:10 LORD, **h** not forsaken them that seek thee.	NIH
10:14 Thou **h** seen *it*; for thou beholdest	NIH
10:17 thou **h** heard the desire of the humble:	NIH
16: 2 *O my soul,* thou **h** said unto the LORD,	NIH
17: 3 Thou **h** proved mine heart; thou hast	NIH
17: 3 thou **h** visited *me* in the night; thou hast	NIH
17: 3 thou **h** tried me, *and* shalt find nothing;	NIH
18:35 Thou **h** also given me the shield of thy	NIH
18:36 Thou **h** enlarged my steps under me,	NIH
18:39 For thou **h** girded me *with* strength unto	NIH
18:39 thou **h** subdued under me those that rose	NIH
18:40 Thou **h** also given me the necks of mine	NIH
18:43 Thou **h** delivered me from the strivings of	NIH
18:43 **h** made me the head of the heathen:	NIH
18:48 thou **h** delivered me from the violent man.	NIH
21: 2 Thou **h** given him his heart's desire,	NIH
21: 2 **h** not withholden the request of his lips.	NIH
21: 5 honour and majesty **h** thou laid upon him.	NIH
21: 6 thou **h** made him most blessed for ever:	NIH
21: 6 thou **h** made him exceeding glad with thy	NIH
22: 1 God, my God, why **h** thou forsaken me?	NIH
22:15 thou **h** brought me into the dust of death.	NIH
22:21 for thou **h** heard me from the horns of	NIH
27: 9 thou **h** been my help; leave me not,	NIH
30: 1 for thou **h** lifted me up, and hast not made	NIH
30: 1 **h** not made my foes to rejoice over me.	NIH
30: 2 I cried unto thee, and thou **h** healed me.	NIH
30: 3 thou **h** brought up my soul from the grave:	NIH
30: 3 thou **h** kept me alive, that I should not go	NIH
30: 7 by thy favour thou **h** made my mountain	NIH
30:11 Thou **h** turned for me my mourning into	NIH
30:11 thou **h** put off my sackcloth, and girded	NIH
31: 5 thou **h** redeemed me, O LORD God of	NIH
31: 7 thou **h** considered my trouble; thou hast	NIH
31: 7 thou **h** known my soul in adversities;	NIH
31: 8 **h** not shut me up into the hand of	NIH
31: 8 **h** set my feet in a large room.	NIH
31:19 thou **h** laid up for them that fear thee;	NIH
31:19 thou **h** wrought for them that trust in	NIH
35:22 *This* thou **h** seen, O LORD: keep not	NIH
39: 5 thou **h** made my days *as* a handbreadth;	NIH
40: 5 thy wonderful works *which* thou **h** done,	NIH
40: 6 didst not desire; mine ears **h** thou opened:	NIH
40: 6 and sin offering **h** thou not required.	NIH
42: 9 God my rock, Why **h** thou forgotten me?	NIH
44: 7 thou **h** saved us from our enemies,	NIH
44: 7 and **h** put them to shame that hated us.	NIH
44: 9 thou **h** cast off, and put us to shame;	NIH
44:11 Thou **h** given us like sheep appointed for	NIH
44:11 and **h** scattered us among the heathen.	NIH
44:19 Though thou **h** sore broken us in the place	NIH
50:16 What **h** thou to do to declare my statutes,	NIH
50:18 and **h** been partaker with adulterers.	NIH
50:21 These *things* **h** thou done, and I kept	NIH
51: 8 *that* the bones which thou **h** broken may	NIH
52: 9 because thou **h** done *it*: and I will wait on	NIH
53: 5 thou **h** put *them* to shame, because God	NIH
56:13 For thou **h** delivered my soul from death:	NIH
59:16 for thou **h** been my defence and refuge in	NIH
60: 1 O God, thou **h** cast us off, thou hast	NIH
60: 1 thou hast cast us off, thou **h** scattered us,	NIH
60: 1 hast scattered us, thou **h** been displeased;	NIH
60: 2 Thou **h** made the earth to tremble; thou	NIH
60: 2 the earth to tremble; thou **h** broken it:	NIH
60: 3 Thou **h** shewed thy people hard *things*:	NIH
60: 3 **h** made us to drink the wine *of*	NIH
60: 4 Thou **h** given a banner to them that fear	NIH
61: 3 For thou **h** been a shelter for me,	NIH
61: 5 For thou, O God, **h** heard my vows:	NIH
61: 5 thou **h** given *me* the heritage of those that	NIH
63: 7 Because thou **h** been my help, therefore	NIH
65: 9 corn, when thou **h** so provided for it.	NIH
66:10 For thou, O God, **h** proved us: thou hast	NIH
66:10 thou **h** tried us, as silver is tried.	NIH
66:12 Thou **h** caused men to ride over our heads;	NIH
68:10 **h** prepared of thy goodness for the poor.	NIH
68:18 Thou **h** ascended on high, thou hast led	NIH
68:18 on high, thou **h** led captivity captive:	NIH
68:18 **h** received gifts for men; yea,	NIH
68:28 O God, that which thou **h** wrought for us.	NIH
69:19 Thou **h** known my reproach, and my	NIH
69:26 For they persecute *him* whom thou **h**	NIH
69:26 talk to the grief of those whom thou **h**	NIH
71: 3 thou **h** given commandment to save me;	NIH
71:17 O God, thou **h** taught me from my youth:	NIH
71:19 high, who **h** done great *things*: O God,	NIH
71:20 *Thou,* which **h** shewed me great and	NIH
71:23 and my soul, which thou **h** redeemed.	NIH

Ps 73:23 thou **h** holden *me* by my right hand.	NIH
73:27 destroyed all them that go a whoring	NIH
74: 1 O God, why **h** thou cast *us* off for ever?	NIH
74: 2 *which* thou **h** purchased of old;	NIH
74: 2 thine inheritance, *which* thou **h** redeemed;	NIH
74: 2 this mount Zion, wherein thou **h** dwelt.	NIH
74:16 thou **h** prepared the light and the sun.	NIH
74:17 Thou **h** set all the borders of the earth:	NIH
74:17 thou **h** made summer and winter.	NIH
77:14 thou **h** declared thy strength among	NIH
77:15 Thou **h** with *thine* arm redeemed thy	NIH
80: 8 Thou **h** brought a vine out of Egypt:	NIH
80: 8 **h** cast out the heathen, and planted it.	NIH
80:12 **h** thou *then* broken down her hedges,	NIH
85: 1 thou **h** been favourable unto thy land:	NIH
85: 1 thou **h** brought back the captivity of Jacob.	NIH
85: 2 Thou **h** forgiven the iniquity of thy people,	NIH
85: 2 of thy people, thou **h** covered all their sin.	NIH
85: 3 Thou **h** taken away all thy wrath: thou	NIH
85: 3 thou **h** turned *thyself* from the fierceness	NIH
86: 9 All nations whom thou **h** made shall come	NIH
86:13 thou **h** delivered my soul from the lowest	NIH
86:17 LORD, **h** holpen me, and comforted me.	NIH
88: 6 Thou **h** laid me in the lowest pit,	NIH
88: 7 and thou **h** afflicted *me* with all thy waves.	NIH
88: 8 Thou **h** put away mine acquaintance far	NIH
88: 8 thou **h** made me an abomination unto	NIH
88:18 Lover and friend **h** thou put far from me,	NIH
89:10 Thou **h** broken Rahab in pieces, as one	NIH
89:10 thou **h** scattered thine enemies with thy	NIH
89:11 the fulness thereof, thou **h** founded them.	NIH
89:12 and the south thou **h** created them:	NIH
89:13 Thou **h** a mighty arm: strong is thy hand	3807.1
89:38 thou **h** cast off and abhorred, thou hast	NIH
89:38 thou **h** been wroth with thine anointed.	NIH
89:39 Thou **h** made void the covenant of thy	NIH
89:39 thou **h** profaned his crown *by casting it* to	NIH
89:40 Thou **h** broken down all his hedges;	NIH
89:40 thou **h** brought his strong holds to ruin.	NIH
89:42 Thou **h** set up the right hand of his	NIH
89:42 thou **h** made all his enemies to rejoice.	NIH
89:43 Thou **h** also turned the edge of his sword,	NIH
89:43 and **h** not made him to stand in the battle.	NIH
89:44 Thou **h** made his glory to cease, and cast	NIH
89:45 The days of his youth **h** thou shortened;	NIH
89:45 thou **h** covered him with shame. Selah.	NIH
89:47 wherefore **h** thou made all men in vain?	NIH
90: 1 thou **h** been our dwelling place in all	NIH
90: 8 Thou **h** set our iniquities before thee,	NIH
90:15 to the days *wherein* thou **h** afflicted us,	NIH
91: 9 Because thou **h** made the LORD, *which is*	NIH
92: 4 LORD, **h** made me glad through thy work:	NIH
102:10 Thou **h** lifted me up, and cast me down.	NIH
102:25 Of old **h** thou laid the foundation of	NIH
104: 8 the place which thou **h** founded for them.	NIH
104: 9 Thou **h** set a bound *that* they may not	NIH
104:24 in wisdom **h** thou made them all:	NIH
104:26 *whom* thou **h** made to play therein.	NIH
108:11 *Wilt* not *thou,* O God, *who* **h** cast us off?	NIH
109:27 *is* thy hand; *that* thou, LORD, **h** done it.	NIH
110: 3 morning: thou **h** the dew of thy youth.	3807.1
116: 8 For thou **h** delivered my soul from death,	NIH
116:16 of thy handmaid: thou **h** loosed my bonds.	NIH
118:13 Thou **h** thrust sore at me that *I* might fall:	NIH
118:21 for thou **h** heard me, and art become my	NIH
119: 4 **h** commanded *us* to keep thy precepts	NIH
119:21 rebuked the proud *that are* cursed,	NIH
119:49 upon which thou **h** caused me to hope.	NIH
119:65 Thou **h** dealt well with thy servant,	NIH
119:75 *that* thou *in* faithfulness **h** afflicted me.	NIH
119:90 established the earth, and it abideth.	NIH
119:93 for with them thou **h** quickened me.	NIH
119:98 Thou *through* thy commandments **h** made	NIH
119:102 from thy judgments: for thou **h** taught me.	NIH
119:118 Thou **h** trodden down all them that err	NIH
119:138 Thy testimonies *that* thou **h** commanded	NIH
119:152 I have known of old that thou **h** founded	NIH
119:171 when thou **h** taught me thy statutes.	NIH
137: 8 that rewardeth thee as thou **h** served us.	NIH
138: 2 for thou **h** magnified thy word above all	NIH
139: 1 thou **h** searched me, and known *me.*	NIH
139: 5 Thou **h** beset me behind and before,	NIH
139:13 For thou **h** possessed my reins: thou hast	NIH
139:13 thou **h** covered me in my mother's womb.	NIH
140: 7 **h** covered my head in the day of battle.	NIH
Pr 3:28 I will give; when thou **h** it by thee.	3426
6: 1 thou **h** stricken thy hand with a stranger,	NIH
22:27 If thou **h** nothing to pay, why should he	3807.1
23: 8 The morsel *which* thou **h** eaten shalt thou	NIH
24:14 when thou **h** found *it,* then there shall be	NIH
25:16 **H** thou found honey? eat so much as is	NIH
30:32 thou **h** done foolishly in lifting up thyself,	NIH
30:32 or if thou **h** thought evil, *lay thine* hand	NIH
Ecc 5: 4 in fools: pay that which thou **h** vowed.	NIH
7:22 that thyself likewise **h** cursed others.	NIH
SS 1:15 behold, thou *art* fair; thou *h* doves' eyes.	NIH
4: 1 fair; thou *h* doves' eyes within thy locks:	NIH
4: 9 Thou **h** ravished my heart, my sister,	NIH
4: 9 thou **h** ravished my heart with one of	NIH
Isa 2: 6 Therefore thou **h** forsaken thy people	NIH
3: 6 *saying,* Thou **h** clothing, be thou our	3807.1
9: 3 Thou **h** multiplied the nation,	NIH
9: 4 For thou **h** broken the yoke of his burden,	NIH
14:13 thou **h** said in thine heart, I will ascend	NIH
14:20 because thou **h** destroyed thy land,	NIH

Isa 17:10 Because thou **h** forgotten the God of thy NIH
17:10 **h** not been mindful of the rock of thy NIH
22:16 What **h** thou here? and whom hast thou 3807.1
22:16 whom **h** thou here, that thou hast 3807.1
22:16 that thou **h** hewed thee out a sepulchre NIH
23:16 the city, thou harlot that **h** been forgotten; NIH
25: 1 name; for thou **h** done wonderful things; NIH
25: 2 For thou **h** made of a city a heap; *of a* NIH
25: 4 For thou **h** been a strength to the poor, NIH
26:12 thou also **h** wrought all our works in us. NIH
26:14 thou visited and destroyed them, NIH
26:15 Thou **h** increased the nation, O Lord, NIH
26:15 O Lord, thou **h** increased the nation: NIH
37: 6 not afraid of the words that thou **h** heard, NIH
37:11 thou **h** heard what the kings of Assyria NIH
37:16 the earth: thou **h** made heaven and earth. NIH
37:21 Whereas thou **h** prayed to me against NIH
37:23 **h** thou reproached and blasphemed? NIH
37:23 against whom **h** thou exalted *thy* voice, NIH
37:24 thy servants **h** thou reproached the Lord, NIH
37:24 hast thou reproached the Lord, and **h** said, NIH
37:26 **H** thou not heard long ago, *how* I have NIH
38:17 thou **h** in love to my soul *delivered it* from NIH
38:17 thou **h** cast all my sins behind thy back. NIH
39: 8 word of the Lord which thou **h** spoken. NIH
40:28 **H** thou not known? hast thou not heard, NIH
40:28 **h** thou not heard, *that* the everlasting God, NIH
43: 4 thou **h** been honourable, and I have loved NIH
43:22 But thou **h** not called upon me, O Jacob; NIH
43:22 but thou **h** been weary of me, O Israel. NIH
43:23 Thou **h** not brought me the small cattle of NIH
43:23 neither **h** thou honoured me *with* thy NIH
43:24 Thou **h** bought me no sweet cane with NIH
43:24 neither **h** thou filled me *with* the fat of thy NIH
43:24 thou **h** made me to serve with thy sins, NIH
43:24 thou **h** wearied me with thine iniquities. NIH
45: 4 though thou **h** not known me. NIH
45: 5 girded thee though thou **h** not known me: NIH
45:10 to the woman, What **h** thou brought forth? NIH
47: 6 upon the ancient **h** thou very heavily laid NIH
47:10 For thou **h** trusted in thy wickedness: NIH
47:10 thou **h** said, None seeth me. Thy wisdom NIH
47:10 thou **h** said in thine heart, I *am,* and NIH
47:12 wherein thou **h** laboured from thy youth; NIH
47:15 be unto thee *with* whom thou **h** laboured, NIH
48: 6 Thou **h** heard, see all this; and will not ye NIH
49:20 after thou **h** lost the other, shall say again NIH
51:13 **h** feared continually every day because of NIH
51:17 which **h** drunk at the hand of the Lord NIH
51:17 thou **h** drunken the dregs of the cup of NIH
51:23 thou **h** laid thy body as the ground, NIH
57: 6 to them **h** thou poured a drink offering, NIH
57: 6 thou **h** offered a meat offering. NIH
57: 7 and high mountain thou **h** set thy bed: NIH
57: 8 the posts **h** thou set up thy remembrance: NIH
57: 8 for thou **h** discovered *thyself* to another NIH
57: 8 thou **h** enlarged thy bed, and made thee *a* NIH
57:10 thou **h** found the life of thine hand; NIH
57:11 of whom **h** thou been afraid or feared, NIH
57:11 that thou **h** lied, and hast not remembered NIH
57:11 thou hast lied, and **h** not remembered me, NIH
60:15 Whereas thou **h** been forsaken and hated, NIH
62: 8 thy wine, for the which thou **h** laboured: NIH
63:17 why **h** thou made us to err from thy ways, NIH
64: 7 for thou **h** hid thy face from us, NIH
64: 7 consumed us, because of our iniquities. NIH
Jer 1:12 said the Lord unto me, Thou **h** well seen: NIH
2:17 **H** thou not procured this unto thyself, NIH
2:17 in that thou **h** forsaken the Lord thy God, NIH
2:18 now what **h** thou to do in the way of 3807.1
2:18 or what **h** thou to do in the way of 3807.1
2:19 that thou **h** forsaken the Lord thy God, NIH
2:23 in the valley, know what thou **h** done: NIH
2:27 and to a stone, Thou **h** brought me forth: NIH
2:28 *are* thy gods that thou **h** made thee? NIH
2:33 **h** thou also taught the wicked ones thy NIH
3: 1 thou **h** played the harlot with many lovers; NIH
3: 2 and see where thou **h** not been lien with. NIH
3: 2 In the ways **h** thou sat for them, NIH
3: 2 thou **h** polluted the land with thy NIH
3: 5 thou **h** spoken and done evil *things* as NIH
3: 6 **H** thou seen *that* which backsliding Israel NIH
3:13 that thou **h** transgressed against the Lord NIH
3:13 scattered thy ways to the strangers under NIH
4:10 surely thou **h** greatly deceived this people NIH
4:19 peace, because thou **h** heard, O my soul, NIH
5: 3 thou **h** stricken them, but they have not NIH
5: 3 thou **h** consumed them, *but* they have NIH
12: 2 Thou **h** planted them, yea, they have NIH
12: 3 thou **h** seen me, and tried mine heart NIH
12: 5 If thou **h** run with the footmen, NIH
13: 4 Take the girdle that thou **h** got, which *is* NIH
13:21 for thou **h** taught them *to be* captains, NIH
13:25 because thou **h** forgotten me, and trusted NIH
14:19 **H** thou utterly rejected Judah? hath thy NIH
14:19 why **h** thou smitten us, and *there* is no NIH
14:22 thee: for thou **h** made all these *things.* NIH
15: 6 Thou **h** forsaken me, saith the Lord, NIH
15:10 that thou **h** borne me a man of strife and NIH
15:17 for thou **h** filled me *with* indignation. NIH
20: 6 friends, to whom thou **h** prophesied lies. NIH
20: 7 thou **h** deceived me, and I was deceived: NIH
20: 7 thou art stronger than I, and **h** prevailed. NIH
26: 9 Why **h** thou prophesied in the name of NIH
28: 6 thy words which thou **h** prophesied, NIH

Jer 28:13 Thou **h** broken the yokes of wood; NIH
28:16 thou **h** taught rebellion against the Lord. NIH
29:25 Because thou **h** sent letters in thy name NIH
29:27 why **h** thou not reproved Jeremiah of NIH
30:13 bound up: thou **h** no healing medicines. 3807.1
31:18 himself *thus;* Thou **h** chastised me, NIH
32:17 thou **h** made the heaven and the earth by NIH
32:20 Which **h** set signs and wonders in the land NIH
32:20 and **h** made thee a name, as *at* this day; NIH
32:21 **h** brought forth thy people Israel out of NIH
32:22 **h** given them this land, which thou didst NIH
32:23 thou **h** caused all this evil to come upon NIH
32:24 what thou **h** spoken is come to pass; NIH
32:25 thou **h** said unto me, O Lord God, NIH
36: 6 which thou **h** written from my mouth, NIH
36:14 in thine hand the roll wherein thou **h** NIH
36:29 Thou **h** burnt this roll, saying, Why hast NIH
36:29 Why **h** thou written therein, saying, NIH
38:25 Declare unto us now what thou **h** said NIH
39:18 because thou **h** put thy trust in me, saith NIH
44:16 *As for* the word that thou **h** spoken unto NIH
48: 7 For because thou **h** trusted in thy works NIH
50:24 because thou **h** striven against the Lord. NIH
51:62 O Lord, thou **h** spoken against this place, NIH
51:63 when thou **h** made an end of reading this NIH
La 1:21 they are glad that thou **h** done *it:* thou wilt NIH
1:21 thou wilt bring the day *that* thou **h** called, NIH
1:22 as thou **h** done unto me for all my NIH
2:20 and consider to whom thou **h** done this. NIH
2:21 **h** slain *them* in the day of thine anger; NIH
2:21 thine anger; thou **h** killed, and *not* pitied. NIH
2:22 **h** called as *in* a solemn day my terrors NIH
3:17 **h** removed my soul far off from peace: NIH
3:42 and have rebelled: thou **h** not pardoned. NIH
3:43 Thou **h** covered with anger, NIH
3:43 thou **h** slain, thou hast not pitied. NIH
3:43 thou hast slain, thou **h** not pitied. NIH
3:44 Thou **h** covered thyself with a cloud, NIH
3:45 Thou **h** made us *as* the offscouring and NIH
3:56 Thou **h** heard my voice: hide not thine ear NIH
3:58 thou **h** pleaded the causes of my soul; NIH
3:58 of my soul; thou **h** redeemed my life. NIH
3:59 O Lord, thou **h** seen my wrong: NIH
3:60 Thou **h** seen all their vengeance *and* all NIH
3:61 Thou **h** heard their reproach, O Lord, NIH
5:22 thou **h** utterly rejected us; thou art very NIH
Eze 3:19 his iniquity; but thou **h** delivered thy soul. NIH
3:20 because thou **h** not given him warning, NIH
3:21 is warned; also thou **h** delivered thy soul. NIH
4: 6 thou **h** accomplished them, lie again NIH
4: 8 till thou **h** ended the days of thy siege. NIH
5:11 thou **h** defiled my sanctuary with all thy NIH
8:12 **h** thou seen what the ancients of the house NIH
8:15 unto me, **H** thou seen *this,* O son of man? NIH
8:17 unto me, **H** thou seen *this,* O son of man? NIH
9:11 I have done as thou **h** commanded me. NIH
16: 7 thou **h** increased and waxen great, NIH
16:17 Thou **h** also taken thy fair jewels of my NIH
16:18 thou **h** set mine oil and mine incense NIH
16:19 thou **h** even set it before them for a sweet NIH
16:20 Moreover thou **h** taken thy sons and thy NIH
16:20 thou **h** borne unto me, and these hast NIH
16:20 these **h** thou sacrificed unto them to be NIH
16:21 That thou **h** slain my children, NIH
16:22 thy whoredoms thou **h** not remembered NIH
16:24 thou **h** also built unto thee an eminent NIH
16:24 **h** made thee a high place in every street. NIH
16:25 Thou **h** built thy high place at every head NIH
16:25 **h** made thy beauty to be abhorred, NIH
16:25 **h** opened thy feet to every one that passed NIH
16:26 Thou **h** also committed fornication with NIH
16:26 **h** increased thy whoredoms, to provoke NIH
16:28 Thou **h** played the whore also with NIH
16:28 thou **h** played the harlot with them, NIH
16:29 **h** moreover multiplied thy fornication NIH
16:31 **h** not been as a harlot, in that *thou* NIH
16:37 with whom thou **h** taken pleasure, and all NIH
16:37 all *them* that thou **h** loved, with all *them* NIH
16:37 loved, with all *them* that thou **h** hated; NIH
16:43 Because thou **h** not remembered the days NIH
16:43 **h** fretted me in all these *things;* behold NIH
16:47 Yet **h** thou not walked after their ways, NIH
16:48 as thou **h** done, thou and thy daughters. NIH
16:51 thou **h** multiplied thine abominations more NIH
16:51 **h** justified thy sisters in all thine NIH
16:51 all thine abominations which thou **h** done. NIH
16:52 Thou also, which **h** judged thy sisters, NIH
16:52 **h** committed more abominable than they: NIH
16:52 in that thou **h** justified thy sisters. NIH
16:54 mayest be confounded in all that thou **h** NIH
16:58 Thou **h** borne thy lewdness and thine NIH
16:59 I will even deal with thee as thou **h** done, NIH
16:59 which **h** despised the oath in breaking NIH
16:63 toward thee for all that thou **h** done, NIH
22: 4 guilty in thy blood that thou **h** shed; NIH
22: 4 **h** defiled *thyself* in thine idols which thou NIH
22: 4 *thyself* in thine idols which thou **h** made; NIH
22: 4 thou **h** caused thy days to draw near, NIH
22: 8 Thou **h** despised mine holy *things,* NIH
22: 8 holy *things,* and **h** profaned my sabbaths. NIH
22:12 thou **h** taken usury and increase, NIH
22:12 thou **h** greedily gained of thy neighbours NIH
22:12 and **h** forgotten me, saith the Lord God. NIH
22:13 at thy dishonest gain which thou **h** made, NIH
23:30 thou **h** gone a whoring after the heathen, NIH

Eze 23:31 Thou **h** walked in the way of thy sister; NIH
23:35 Because thou **h** forgotten me, and cast me NIH
23:41 whereupon thou **h** set mine incense and NIH
25: 6 Because thou **h** clapped *thine* hands, NIH
27: 3 O Tyrus, thou **h** said, *I am* of perfect NIH
28: 2 thou **h** said, I *am* a God, I sit *in* the seat of NIH
28: 4 thine understanding thou **h** gotten thee NIH
28: 4 **h** gotten gold and silver into thy treasures: NIH
28: 5 by thy traffick **h** thou increased thy riches, NIH
28: 6 Because thou **h** set thine heart as the heart NIH
28:13 Thou **h** been in Eden the garden of God; NIH
28:14 thou **h** walked up and down in the midst NIH
28:16 of thee *with* violence, and thou **h** sinned: NIH
28:17 thou **h** corrupted thy wisdom by reason of NIH
28:18 Thou **h** defiled thy sanctuaries by NIH
31:10 Because thou **h** lifted up thyself in height, NIH
32: 9 the countries which thou **h** not known. NIH
33: 9 his iniquity; but thou **h** delivered thy soul. NIH
35: 5 Because thou **h** had a perpetual hatred, NIH
35: 5 **h** shed *the blood of* the children of Israel NIH
35: 6 sith thou **h** not hated blood, even blood NIH
35:10 Because thou **h** said, These two nations NIH
35:11 to thine envy which thou **h** used NIH
35:12 **h** spoken against the mountains of Israel, NIH
36:13 up men, and **h** bereaved thy nations; 1961
38:13 **h** thou gathered thy company to take a NIH
43:23 When thou **h** made an end of cleansing *it,* NIH
47: 6 **h** thou seen *this?* Then he brought me, NIH
Da 2:23 who **h** given me wisdom and might, NIH
2:23 **h** made known unto me now what we NIH
2:23 for thou **h** *now* made known unto us NIH
3:10 Thou, O king, **h** made a decree, that every NIH
3:12 There are certain Jews whom thou **h** set NIH
3:12 worship the golden image which thou **h** NIH
3:18 worship the golden image which thou **h** NIH
5:22 O Belshazzar, **h** not humbled thine heart, NIH
5:23 **h** lifted up thyself against the Lord of NIH
5:23 thou **h** praised the gods of silver, and gold, NIH
5:23 *are* all thy ways, **h** thou not glorified: 3807.2
6:12 **H** thou not signed a decree, that every NIH
6:13 nor the decree that thou **h** signed, NIH
9: 7 through all the countries whither thou **h** NIH
9:15 that **h** brought thy people forth out of NIH
9:15 and **h** gotten thee renown, as *at* this day, NIH
10:19 lord speak; for thou **h** strengthened me. NIH
Hos 4: 6 because thou **h** rejected knowledge, I will NIH
4: 6 thou **h** forgotten the law of thy God, NIH
9: 1 for thou **h** gone a whoring from thy God, NIH
9: 1 **h** loved a reward upon every cornfloor. NIH
10: 9 thou **h** sinned from the days of Gibeah: NIH
13: 9 Israel, *thou* **h** destroyed thyself; but in me NIH
14: 1 God; for thou **h** fallen by thine iniquity. NIH
Ob 1:15 as thou **h** done, it shall be done unto thee; NIH
Jnh 1:10 said unto him, Why **h** thou done this? NIH
1:14 O Lord, **h** done as it pleased thee. NIH
2: 6 yet **h** thou brought up my life from NIH
4:10 the Lord, Thou **h** had pity on the gourd, NIH
4:10 for the which thou **h** not laboured, neither NIH
Mic 7:20 which thou **h** sworn unto our fathers from NIH
Na 3:16 Thou **h** multiplied thy merchants above NIH
Hab 1:12 thou **h** ordained them for judgment; NIH
1:12 thou **h** established them for correction. NIH
2: 8 Because thou **h** spoiled many nations, NIH
2:10 Thou **h** consulted shame to thy house by NIH
2:10 people, and **h** sinned *against* thy soul. NIH
Zep 3:11 wherein thou **h** transgressed against me: NIH
Zec 1:12 which thou **h** had indignation these NIH
Mal 1: 2 Yet ye say, Wherein **h** thou loved us? NIH
2:14 against whom thou **h** dealt treacherously: NIH
Mt 5:26 till thou **h** paid the uttermost farthing. NIG
6: 6 closet, and when thou **h** shut thy door, NIG
8:13 as thou **h** believed, *so* be it done unto NIG
11:25 thou **h** hid these *things* from the wise and NIG
11:25 prudent, and **h** revealed them unto babes. NIG
17:27 and when thou **h** opened his mouth, NIG
18:15 shall hear thee, thou **h** gained thy brother. NIG
19:21 go *and* sell that thou **h**, and give to 5225
20:12 and thou **h** made them equal unto us, NIG
21:16 and sucklings thou **h** perfected praise? NIG
25:21 thou **h** been faithful over a few *things,* NIG
25:23 thou **h** been faithful over a few *things,* NIG
25:24 reaping where thou **h** not sown, NIG
25:24 and gathering where thou **h** not strawed: NIG
25:25 in the earth: lo, *there* thou **h** *that is* thine. 2192
26:25 is it I? He said unto him, Thou **h** said. NIG
26:64 Jesus saith unto him, Thou **h** said: NIG
27:46 God, my God, why **h** thou forsaken me? NIG
Mk 10:21 sell whatsoever thou **h**, and give to 2192
12:32 Well, Master, thou **h** said the truth: NIG
15:34 God, my God, why **h** thou forsaken me? NIG
Lk 1: 4 wherein thou **h** been instructed. NIG
1:30 Mary: for thou **h** found favour with God. NIG
2:31 Which thou **h** prepared before the face of NIG
2:48 Son, why **h** thou thus dealt with us? NIG
7:43 he said unto him, Thou **h** rightly judged. NIG
10:21 thou **h** hid these *things* from the wise NIG
10:21 prudent, and **h** revealed them unto babes: NIG
10:28 he said unto him, Thou **h** answered right: NIG
11:27 and the paps which thou **h** sucked. NIG
12:19 **h** much goods laid up for many years; 2192
12:20 *those things* be, which thou **h** provided? NIG
12:59 till thou **h** paid the very last mite. NIG
13:26 and thou **h** taught in our streets. NIG
14:22 it is done as thou **h** commanded, NIG
15:30 thou **h** killed for him the fatted calf. NIG

H

H

Lk 18:22 thou one *thing:* sell all that thou **h**, 2192
 19:17 thou **h** been faithful in a very little, NIG
 20:39 answering said, Master, thou **h** well said. NIG
 24:18 **h** not known the *things* which are come NIG
Jn 2:10 *but* thou **h** kept the good wine until now. NIG
 4:11 Sir, thou **h** nothing to draw with, 2192
 4:11 whence then **h** thou *that* living water? 2192
 4:17 Thou **h** well said, I have no husband. NIG
 4:18 For thou **h** had five husbands; and **h** NIG
 4:18 he whom thou now **h** is not thy husband: 2192
 6:68 we go? thou **h** the words of eternal life. 2192
 7:20 people answered and said, Thou **h** a devil: 2192
 8:48 that thou art a Samaritan, and **h** a devil? 2192
 8:52 Now we know that thou **h** a devil. 2192
 8:57 fifty years old, and **h** thou seen Abraham? NIG
 9:37 Thou **h** both seen him, and it is he that NIG
 11:41 Father, I thank thee that thou **h** heard me. NIG
 11:42 that they may believe that thou **h** sent me. NIG
 13: 8 If I wash thee not, thou **h** no part with 2192
 13:38 not crow, till thou **h** denied me thrice. NIG
 14: 9 and *yet* **h** thou not known me, Philip? NIG
 17: 2 As thou **h** given him power over all flesh, NIG
 17: 2 life to as many as thou **h** given him. NIG
 17: 3 and Jesus Christ, whom thou **h** sent. NIG
 17: 7 whatsoever thou **h** given me are of thee. NIG
 17: 9 but for *them* which thou **h** given me; NIG
 17:11 own name those whom thou **h** given me, NIG
 17:18 As thou **h** sent me into the world, even NIG
 17:21 the world may believe that thou **h** sent NIG
 17:23 that the world may know that thou **h** sent NIG
 17:23 and **h** loved them, as thou hast loved me. NIG
 17:23 hast loved them, as thou **h** loved me. NIG
 17:24 that they also, whom thou **h** given me, NIG
 17:24 behold my glory, which thou **h** given me: NIG
 17:25 these have known that thou **h** sent me. NIG
 17:26 thou **h** loved me may be in them, NIG
 18:35 thee unto me: what **h** thou done? NIG
 20:15 him *hence,* tell me where thou **h** laid him, NIG
 20:29 Thomas, because thou **h** seen me, thou NIG
 20:29 thou hast seen me, thou **h** believed: NIG
Ac 1:24 shew whether of these two thou **h** chosen, NIG
 2:28 **h** made known to me the ways of life; NIG
 4:24 which thou **h** made heaven, and earth, NIG
 4:25 Who by the mouth of thy servant David **h** NIG
 4:27 whom thou **h** anointed, both Herod, NIG
 5: 4 why **h** thou conceived this thing in thine NIG
 5: 4 thou **h** not lied unto men, but unto God. NIG
 8:20 thou **h** thought that the gift of God may be NIG
 8:21 Thou **h** neither part nor lot in this matter: 1510
 10:33 and thou **h** well done that thou art come. NIG
 22:15 witness unto all men of what thou **h** seen NIG
 23:11 for as thou **h** testified of me in Jerusalem, NIG
 23:19 asked *him,* What is it that thou **h** to tell me? 2192
 23:22 that thou **h** shewed these *things* to me. NIG
 24:10 Forasmuch as I know that thou **h** been of NIG
 25:12 answered, **H** thou appealed unto Cesar? NIG
 26:16 witness both of *these things* which thou **h** NIG
Ro 2:20 which **h** the form of knowledge and of 2192
 9:20 that formed *it,* Why **h** thou made me thus? NIG
 14:22 **H** thou faith? have *it* to thyself before God. 2192
1Co 4: 7 what **h** thou that thou didst not receive? 2192
 7:28 But and if thou marry, thou **h** not sinned; NIG
 8:10 if any *man* see thee which **h** knowledge 2192
Col 4: 6 good doctrine, whereunto thou **h** attained. NIG
1Ti 6:12 **h** professed a good profession before many NIG
2Ti 1:13 which thou **h** heard of me, in faith and NIG
 2: 2 And *the things* that thou **h** heard of me NIG
 3:10 But thou **h** fully known my doctrine, NIG
 3:14 thou in *the things* which thou **h** learned NIG
 3:14 thou hast learned and **h** been assured of, NIG
 3:14 knowing of whom thou **h** learned *them;* NIG
 3:15 And that from a child thou **h** known NIG
Phm 1: 5 which thou **h** toward the Lord Jesus, 2192
Heb 1: 9 Thou **h** loved righteousness, NIG
 1:10 in the beginning **h** laid the foundation of NIG
 2: 8 Thou **h** put all *things* in subjection under NIG
 10: 5 but a body **h** thou prepared me: NIG
 10: 6 *sacrifices* for sin thou **h** had no pleasure. NIG
Jas 2:18 may say, Thou **h** faith, and I have works: 2192
Rev 1:19 Write *the things* which thou **h** seen, NIG
 2: 2 thou **h** tried them which say *they* are NIG
 2: 2 and art not, and **h** found them liars: NIG
 2: 3 And **h** borne, and hast patience, and for NIG
 2: 3 patience, and for my name's sake 2192
 2: 3 and for my name's sake **h** laboured, NIG
 2: 3 sake hast laboured, and **h** not fainted. NIG
 2: 4 because thou **h** left thy first love. NIG
 2: 6 But this thou **h**, that thou hatest the deeds 2192
 2:13 fast my name, and **h** not denied my faith, NIG
 2:14 thou **h** there them that hold the doctrine 2192
 2:15 So thou also **h** them that hold the doctrine 2192
 3: 1 that thou **h** a name that thou livest, 2192
 3: 3 therefore how thou **h** received and heard, NIG
 3: 4 Thou **h** a few names even in Sardis, 2192
 3: 8 thou **h** a little strength, and hast kept my 2192
 3: 8 and **h** kept my word, and hast not denied NIG
 3: 8 my word, and **h** not denied my name. NIG
 3:10 Because thou **h** kept the word of my NIG
 3:11 hold *that* fast which thou **h**, that no *man* 2192
 4:11 for thou **h** created all *things,* and for thy NIG
 5: 9 **h** redeemed us to God by thy blood out of NIG
 5:10 And **h** made us unto our God kings and NIG
 11:17 thou **h** taken *to thee* thy great power, NIG
 11:17 *to thee* thy great power, and **h** reigned. NIG

Rev 16: 5 and shalt be, because thou **h** judged thus. NIG
 16: 6 and thou **h** given them blood to drink; NIG

HASTE (56) [HASTED, HASTEN, HASTENED, HASTENETH, HASTETH, HASTILY, HASTING, HASTY]

Ge 19:22 **H** thee, escape thither; for I cannot do 4116
 24:46 she made **h**, and let down her pitcher 4116
 43:30 Joseph made **h**; for his bowels did yern 4116
 45: 9 **H** you, and go up to my father, 4116
 45:13 shall **h** and bring down my father hither. 4116
Ex 10:16 Pharaoh called for Moses and Aaron in **h**; 4116
 12:11 staff in your hand; and ye shall eat it in **h**: 2649
 12:33 might send them out of the land in **h**; 4116
 34: 8 Moses made **h**, and bowed his head 4116
Dt 16: 3 camest forth out of the land of Egypt in **h**: 2649
 32:35 that shall come upon them make **h**. 2363
Jdg 9:48 me do, make **h**, *and* do as I *have* done. 4116
 9:54 the woman made **h**, and ran, 4116
1Sa 9:12 make **h** now, for he came to day to the 4116
 20:38 after the lad, Make speed, **h**, stay not. 2363
 21: 8 because the king's business required **h**. 5169
 23:26 David made **h** to get away for fear of 2648
 23:27 unto Saul, saying, **H** thee, and come; 4116
 25:18 Abigail made **h**, and took two hundred 4116
2Sa 4: 4 as she made **h** to flee, that he fell, 2648
2Ki 7:15 the Syrians had cast away in their **h**. 2648
2Ch 24: 5 to year, and *see that* ye **h** the matter. 4116
 35:21 for God commanded me to make **h**: 926
Ezr 4:23 they went up in **h** to Jerusalem unto 924
Est 6:10 Make **h**, *and* take the apparel and 4116
Job 20: 2 me to answer, and for *this* I make **h**. 2363
Ps 22:19 O my strength, **h** thee to help me. 2363
 31:22 For I said in my **h**, I am cut off from 2648
 38:22 Make **h** to help me, O Lord my salvation. 2363
 40:13 deliver me: O Lord, make **h** to help me. 2363
 70: 1 *Make* **h**, O God, to deliver me; make haste NIH
 70: 1 deliver me; make **h** to help me, O Lord. 2363
 70: 5 make **h** unto me, O God: thou *art* my 2363
 71:12 O my God, make **h** for my help. 2363
 116:11 I said in my **h**, All men *are* liars. 2648
 119:60 I made **h**, and delayed not to keep thy 2363
 141: 1 make **h** unto me; give ear unto my voice, 2363
Pr 1:16 run to evil, and make **h** to shed blood. 4116
 28:20 he that maketh **h** to be rich shall not be 213
SS 8:14 Make **h**, my beloved, and be thou like to 1272
Isa 28:16 he that believeth shall not make **h**. 2363
 49:17 Thy children shall make **h**; thy destroyers 4116
 52:12 For ye shall not go out with **h**, nor go by 2649
 59: 7 and they make **h** to shed innocent blood: 4116
Jer 9:18 let them make **h**, and take up a wailing 4116
Da 2:25 brought in Daniel before the king in **h**, 927
 3:24 rose up in **h**, *and* spake, and said unto his 927
 6:19 and went in **h** unto the den of lions. 927
Na 2: 5 they shall make **h** to the wall thereof, 4116
Mk 6:25 And she came in straightway with **h** unto 4710
Lk 1:39 and went into the hill country with **h**, into 4710
 2:16 And they came with **h**, and found Mary, 4692
 19: 5 Zaccheus, make **h**, and come down; 4692
 19: 6 And he made **h**, and came down, 4692
Ac 22:18 Make **h**, and get *thee* quickly out of 4692

HASTED (24) [HASTE]

Ge 18: 7 *it* unto a young man; and he **h** to dress it. 4116
 24:18 she **h**, and let down her pitcher upon her 4116
 24:20 she **h**, and emptied her pitcher into 4116
Ex 5:13 the taskmasters **h** *them*, saying, Fulfil your 213
Jos 4:10 and the people **h** and passed over. 4116
 8:14 when the king of Ai saw *it*, that they **h** 4116
 8:19 and took it, and **h** and set the city on fire. 4116
 10:13 and **h** not to go down about a whole day. 213
Jdg 20:37 liers in wait **h**, and rushed upon Gibeah; 2363
1Sa 17:48 that David **h**, and ran *toward* the army to 4116
 25:23 she **h**, and lighted off the ass, 4116
 25:34 except thou hadst **h** and come to meet 4116
 25:42 Abigail **h**, and rose, and rode upon an ass, 4116
 28:24 she **h**, and killed it, and took flour, 4116
2Sa 19:16 **h** and came down with the men of Judah 4116
1Ki 20:41 he **h**, and took the ashes away from his 4116
2Ki 9:13 they **h**, and took every man his garment, 4116
2Ch 26:20 yea, himself **h** also to go out, because 1765
Est 6:12 Haman **h** to his house mourning, 1765
 6:14 to bring Haman to the banquet that 926
Job 31: 5 with vanity, *or if* my foot hath **h** to deceit; 2363
Ps 48: 5 they were troubled, *and* **h** away. 2648
 104: 7 at the voice of thy thunder they **h** away. 2648
Ac 20:16 for he **h**, if it were possible for him, to be 4692

HASTEN (7) [HASTE]

1Ki 22: 9 said, **H** hither Micaiah the son of Imlah. 4116
Ps 16: 4 Their sorrows shall be multiplied *that* **h** 4116
 55: 8 I would **h** my escape from the windy 2363
Ecc 2:25 or who else can **h** *hereunto*, more than I? 2363
Isa 5:19 and **h** his work, that we may see *it:* and 2363
 60:22 I the Lord will **h** it in his time. 2363
Jer 1:12 for I will **h** my word to perform it. 8245

HASTENED (6) [HASTE]

Ge 18: 6 Abraham **h** into the tent unto Sarah, 4116
 19:15 the angels **h** Lot, saying, Arise, take thy 213
2Ch 24: 5 the matter. The Levites **h** *it* not. 4116
Est 3:15 being **h** by the king's commandment, 1765
 8:14 being **h** and pressed on by the king's 926
Jer 17:16 I have not **h** from *being* a pastor to follow 213

HASTENETH (1) [HASTE]

Isa 51:14 captive exile **h** that *he* may be loosed, 4116

HASTETH (9) [HASTE]

Job 9:26 swift ships: as the eagle *that* **h** to the prey. 2907
 40:23 Behold, he drinketh up a river, *and* **h** not: 2648
Pr 7:23 as a bird **h** to the snare, and knoweth not 4116
 19: 2 good; and he that **h** with *his* feet, sinneth. 213
 28:22 He that **h** to be rich *hath* an evil eye, 926
Ecc 1: 5 and to his place where he arose. 7602
Jer 48:16 *is* near to come, and his affliction **h** fast. 4116
Hab 1: 8 they shall fly as the eagle *that* **h** to eat. 2363
Zep 1:14 the Lord *is* near, *it is* near, and **h** greatly, 4118

HASTILY (8) [HASTE]

Ge 41:14 they **brought** him **h** out of the dungeon: 7323
Jdg 2:23 nations, without driving them out **h**; 4118
 9:54 he called unto the young man his 4120
1Sa 4:14 And the man came in **h**, and told Eli. 4116
1Ki 20:33 did **h** catch *it:* and they said, Thy brother 4116
Pr 20:21 An inheritance *may be* **gotten h** at 926
 25: 8 Go not forth **h** to strive, lest *thou know* 4118
Jn 11:31 that she rose up **h** and went out, 5030

HASTING (2) [HASTE]

Isa 16: 5 seeking judgment, and **h** righteousness. 4106
2Pe 3:12 and **h** *unto* the coming of the day of God, 4692

HASTY (9) [HASTE]

Pr 14:29 he that *is* **h** of spirit exalteth folly. 7116
 21: 5 but *of* every one that is **h** only to want. 213
 29:20 Seest thou a man that is **h** in his words? 213
Ecc 5: 2 let not thine heart be **h** to utter *any* thing 4116
 7: 9 Be not **h** in thy spirit to be angry: for anger 926
 8: 3 Be not **h** to go out of his sight: stand not 926
Isa 28: 4 *and* as the **h** fruit before the summer; 1061
Da 2:15 Why *is* the decree *so* **h** from the king? 2685
Hab 1: 6 the Chaldeans, *that* bitter **h** nation, 4116

HASUPHA (1) [HASHUPHA]

Ezr 2:43 the children of Ziha, the children of **H**, 2817

HATACH (4)

Est 4: 5 called Esther for **H**, *one* of the king's 2047
 4: 6 **H** went forth to Mordecai unto the street 2047
 4: 9 **H** came and told Esther the words of 2047
 4:10 Again Esther spake unto **H**, and gave him 2047

HATCH (2) [HATCHETH]

Isa 34:15 lay, and **h**, and gather under her shadow: 1234
 59: 5 They **h** cockatrice' eggs, and weave 1234

HATCHETH (1) [HATCH]

Jer 17:11 partridge sitteth *on* eggs, and **h** *them* not; 3205

HATE (87) [HATED, HATEFUL, HATEFULLY, HATERS, HATEST, HATETH, HATING, HATRED]

Ge 24:60 possess the gate of those which **h** them. 8130
 26:27 seeing ye me, and have sent me away 8130
 50:15 Joseph will peradventure **h** us, 7852
Ex 20: 5 and fourth *generation* of them that **h** me; 8130
Lev 19:17 shalt not **h** thy brother in thine heart: 8130
 26:17 they that **h** you shall reign over you; 8130
Nu 10:35 and let them that **h** thee flee before thee; 8130
Dt 5: 9 and fourth *generation* of them that **h** me, 8130
 7:10 repayeth them that **h** him to their face, 8130
 7:15 will lay them upon all *them* that **h** thee. 8130
 19:11 any man **h** his neighbour, and lie in wait 8130
 22:13 a wife, and go in unto her, and **h** her, 8130
 24: 3 the latter husband **h** her, and write her a 8130
 30: 7 them that **h** thee, which persecuted thee. 8130
 32:41 and will reward them that **h** me. 8130
 33:11 them that **h** him, that they rise not again. 8130
Jdg 1: 7 Did not ye **h** me, and expel me out of my 8130
 14:16 Thou dost but **h** me, and lovest me not: 8130
2Sa 22:41 that I might destroy them that **h** me. 8130
1Ki 22: 8 I **h** him; for he doth not prophesy good 8130
2Ch 18: 7 I **h** him; for he never prophesied good 8130
 19: 2 and love them that **h** the Lord? 8130
Job 8:22 They that **h** thee shall be clothed with 8130
Ps 9:13 trouble *which I suffer* of them that **h** me, 8130
 18:40 that I might destroy them that **h** me. 8130
 21: 8 thy right hand shall find out those that **h** 8130
 25:19 many; and they **h** me *with* cruel hatred. 8130
 34:21 that **h** the righteous shall be desolate. 8130
 35:19 let them wink *with* the eye that **h** 8130
 38:19 they that **h** me wrongfully are multiplied. 8130
 41: 7 All that **h** me whisper together against 8130
 44:10 and they which **h** us spoil for themselves. 8130
 55: 3 upon me, and in wrath they **h** me. 7852
 68: 1 let them also that **h** him flee before him. 8130
 69: 4 They that **h** me without a cause are moe 8130
 69:14 let me be delivered from them that **h** me, 8130
 83: 2 they that **h** thee have lift up the head. 8130
 86:17 that they which **h** me may see *it*, and 8130
 89:23 his face, and plague them that **h** him. 8130
 97:10 Ye that love the Lord, **h** evil: 8130
 101: 3 I **h** the work of them that turn aside; 8130
 105:25 He turned their heart to **h** his people, 8130
 118: 7 I see *my desire* upon them that **h** me. 8130
 119:104 I **h** every false way. 8130
 119:113 I **h** *vain* thoughts: but thy law do I love. 8130
 119:128 to be right; *and* I **h** every false way. 8130
 119:163 I **h** and abhor lying: *but* thy law do I love. 8130
 129: 5 confounded and turned back that **h** Zion. 8130

Ps	139:21 Do not I **h** them, O Lord, that hate thee?	8130
	139:21 I hate not, O Lord, that **h** thee?	8130
	139:22 I **h** them *with* perfect hatred: I count	8130
Pr	1:22 in their scorning, and fools **h** knowledge?	8130
	6:16 These six *things* doth the Lord **h**: yea,	8130
	8:13 The fear of the Lord *is* to **h** evil: pride,	8130
	8:13 evil way, and the froward mouth, do I **h**.	8130
	8:36 own soul: all they that **h** me love death.	8130
	9: 8 Reprove not a scorner, lest he **h** thee:	8130
	19: 7 All the brethren of the poor do **h** him:	8130
	25:17 lest he be weary of thee, and *so* **h** thee.	8130
	29:10 The bloodthirsty **h** the upright: but the	8130
Ecc	3: 8 A time to love, and a time to **h**; a time of	8130
Isa	61:8 for I the Lord love judgment, I **h** robbery	8130
Jer	44: 4 Oh, do not this abominable thing that I **h**.	8130
Eze	16:27 thee unto the will of them that **h**	8130
Da	4:19 the dream *be* to them that **h** thee,	8131
Am	5:10 They **h** him that rebuketh in the gate,	8130
	5:15 **H** the evil, and love the good,	8130
	5:21 I **h**, I despise your feast *days,* and I will	8130
Mic	3: 2 Who **h** the good, and love the evil;	8130
Zec	8:17 for all these *are things* that I **h**, saith	8130
Mt	5:43 love thy neighbour, and **h** thine enemy.	3404
	5:44 do good to them that **h** you, and pray for	3404
	6:24 for either he will **h** the one, and love	3404
	24:10 another, and shall **h** one another.	3404
Lk	1:71 and from the hand of all that **h** us;	3404
	6:22 men shall **h** you, and when they shall	3404
	6:27 do good to them which **h** you,	3404
	14:26 **h** not his father, and mother, and wife,	3404
	16:13 for either he will **h** the one, and love	3404
Jn	7: 7 The world cannot **h** you; but me it hateth,	3404
	15:18 If the world **h** you, ye know that it hated	3404
Ro	7:15 that do I not; but what I **h**, that do I.	3404
1Jn	3:13 my brethren, if the world **h** you.	3404
Rev	2: 6 deeds of the Nicolaitans, which I also **h**.	3404
	2:15 of the Nicolaitans, which *thing* I **h**.	3404
	17:16 these shall **h** the whore, and shall make	3404

HATED (60) [HATE]

Ge	27:41 Esau **h** Jacob because of the blessing	7852
	29:31 when the Lord saw that Leah *was* **h**,	8130
	29:33 the Lord hath heard that I *was* **h**,	8130
	37: 4 **h** him, and could not speak peaceably	8130
	37: 5 brethren: and they **h** him yet the more.	8130
	37: 8 they **h** him yet the more for his dreams,	8130
	49:23 grieved him, and shot *at him,* and **h** him:	7852
Dt	1:27 and said, Because the Lord **h** us,	8135
	4:42 and **h** him not in times past;	8130
	9:28 because he **h** them, he hath brought them	8135
	19: 4 whom he **h** not in time past;	8130
	19: 6 inasmuch as he **h** him not in time past.	8130
	21:15 **h**, and they have born him children,	8130
	21:15 children, *both* the beloved and the **h**,	8130
	21:15 *if* the firstborn son be hers that was **h**:	8146
	21:16 beloved firstborn before the son of the **h**,	8130
	21:17 he shall acknowledge the son of the **h** *for*	8130
Jos	20: 5 and **h** him not beforetime.	8130
Jdg	15: 2 that thou hadst **utterly h** her;	8130+8130
2Sa	5: 8 and the blind, *that are* **h** of David's soul,	8130
	13:15 her **exceedingly;**	1419+3966+8130+8135
	13:15 that the hatred wherewith he **h** her *was*	8130
	13:22 for Absalom **h** Amnon, because he had	8130
	22:18 strong enemy, *and* from them that **h** me:	8130
Est	9: 1 the Jews had rule over them that **h** them;)	8130
	9: 5 did what they would unto those that **h**	8130
Job	31:29 I rejoiced at the destruction of him that **h**	8130
Ps	18:17 enemy, and from them which **h** me:	8130
	26: 5 I have **h** the congregation of evildoers;	8130
	31: 6 I have **h** them that regard lying vanities:	8130
	44: 7 and hast put them to shame that **h** us.	8130
	55:12 **h** me *that* did magnify *himself* against me;	8130
	106:10 saved them from the hand of him that **h**	8130
	106:41 and they that **h** them ruled over them.	8130
Pr	1:29 For that they **h** knowledge, and did not	8130
	5:12 How have I **h** instruction, and my heart	8130
	14:17 and a man of wicked devices is **h**.	8130
	14:20 The poor is **h** even of his own neighbour:	8130
Ecc	2:17 Therefore I **h** life; because the work that	8130
	2:18 I **h** all my labour which I *had* taken under	8130
Isa	60:15 Whereas thou hast been forsaken and **h**,	8130
	66: 5 Your brethren that **h** you, that cast you	8130
Jer	12: 8 out against me: therefore have I **h** it.	8130
Eze	16:37 loved, with all *them* that thou hast **h**;	8130
	35: 6 sith thou hast not **h** blood, even blood	8130
Hos	9:15 *is* in Gilgal, for there I **h** them:	8130
Mal	1: 3 I **h** Esau, and laid his mountains and his	8130
Mt	10:22 ye shall be **h** of all *men* for my name's	3404
	24: 9 ye shall be **h** of all nations for my name's	3404
Mk	13:13 ye shall be **h** of all *men* for my name's	3404
Lk	19:14 his citizens **h** him, and sent a message	3404
	21:17 ye shall be **h** of all *men* for my name's	3404
Jn	15:18 ye know that it **h** me before it *hated* you.	3404
	15:18 ye know that it hated me before *it* **h** you.	NIG
	15:24 both seen and **h** both me and my Father.	3404
	15:25 in their law, They **h** me without a cause.	3404
	17:14 and the world hath **h** them, because	3404
Ro	9:13 Jacob have I loved, but Esau have I **h**.	3404
Eph	5:29 For no *man* ever yet **h** his own flesh;	3404
Heb	1: 9 hast loved righteousness, and **h** iniquity;	3404

HATEFUL (3) [HATE]

Ps	36: 2 until his iniquity be found to be **h**.	8130
Tit	3: 3 and envy, **h**, *and* hating one another.	4767

Rev	18: 2 and a cage of every unclean and **h** bird.	3404

HATEFULLY (1) [HATE]

Eze	23:29 they shall deal with thee **h**,	8135+871.1

HATERS (2) [HATE]

Ps	81:15 The **h** of the Lord should have	8130
Ro	1:30 **h** of God, despiteful, proud, boasters,	2319

HATEST (6) [HATE]

2Sa	19: 6 lovest thine enemies, and **h** thy friends:	8130
Ps	5: 5 thy sight: thou **h** all workers of iniquity:	8130
	45: 7 lovest righteousness, and **h** wickedness:	8130
	50:17 Seeing thou **h** instruction, and castest my	8130
Eze	23:28 into the hand *of them* whom thou **h**,	8130
Rev	2: 6 that thou **h** the deeds of the Nicolaitans,	3404

HATETH (31) [HATE]

Ex	23: 5 If thou see the ass of him that **h** thee	8130
Dt	7:10 he will not be slack to him that **h** him,	8130
	12:31 he, **h**, have they done unto their gods;	8130
	16:22 *any* image; which the Lord thy God **h**.	8130
	22:16 unto this man to wife, and he **h** her;	8130
Job	16: 9 He teareth *me in* his wrath, who **h** me:	7852
	34:17 Shall even he that **h** right govern?	8130
Ps	11: 5 and him that loveth violence his soul **h**.	8130
	120: 6 My soul hath long dwelt with him that **h**	8130
Pr	11:15 *for it:* and he that **h** suretiship *is* sure.	8130
	12: 1 but he that **h** reproof *is* brutish.	8130
	13: 5 A righteous *man* **h** lying: but a wicked	8130
	13:24 He that spareth his rod **h** his son:	8130
	15:10 the way: *and* he that **h** reproof shall die.	8130
	15:27 own house; but he that **h** gifts shall live.	8130
	26:24 He that **h** dissembleth with his lips,	8130
	26:28 A lying tongue **h** *those that are* afflicted	8130
	28:16 he that **h** covetousness shall prolong *his*	8130
	29:24 Whoso is partner with a thief **h** his own	8130
Isa	1:14 and your appointed feasts my soul **h**:	8130
Mal	2:16 of Israel, saith that he **h** putting away:	8130
Jn	3:20 For every one that doeth evil **h** the light,	3404
	7: 7 but me it **h**, because I testify of it, that	3404
	12:25 he that **h** his life in this world shall keep it	3404
	15:19 of the world, therefore the world **h** you.	3404
	15:23 He that **h** me hateth my Father also.	3404
	15:23 He that hateth me **h** my Father also.	3404
1Jn	2: 9 his brother, is in darkness *even* until	3404
	2:11 But he that **h** his brother is in darkness,	3404
	3:15 Whosoever **h** his brother is a murderer:	3404
	4:20 I love God, and **h** his brother, is a liar:	3404

HATH (2262) [HAVE]

Ge	1:20 the moving creature that **h** life,	NIH
	3: 1 he said unto the woman, Yea, **h** God said,	NIH
	3: 3 God said, Ye shall not eat of it,	NIH
	4:11 which **h** opened her mouth to receive thy	NIH
	4:25 *said she,* **h** appointed me another seed	NIH
	5:29 of the ground which the Lord **h** cursed.	NIH
	14:20 which **h** delivered thine enemies into thy	NIH
	16: 2 the Lord **h** restrained me from bearing:	NIH
	16:11 because the Lord **h** heard thy affliction.	NIH
	17:14 his people; he **h** broken my covenant.	NIH
	18:19 Abraham that which he **h** spoken of him.	NIH
	19:13 and the Lord **h** sent us to destroy it.	NIH
	19:19 thy servant **h** found grace in thy sight,	NIH
	21: 6 God **h** made me to laugh, *so that* all that	NIH
	21:12 in all that Sarah **h** said unto thee,	NIH
	21:17 for God **h** heard the voice of the lad where	NIH
	21:26 I wot not who **h** done this thing:	NIH
	22:20 she **h** also born children unto thy brother	NIH
	23: 9 the **h**, which *is* in the end of his field;	3807.1
	24:27 who **h** not left destitute my master of his	NIH
	24:35 the Lord **h** blessed my master greatly;	NIH
	24:35 **h** given him flocks, and herds, and silver,	NIH
	24:36 unto him he given all that he hath.	NIH
	24:36 unto him hath he given all that he **h**.	3807.1
	24:44 **h** appointed out for my master's son.	NIH
	24:51 son's wife, as the Lord **h** spoken.	NIH
	24:56 seeing the Lord **h** prospered my way;	NIH
	26:22 For now the Lord **h** made room for us,	NIH
	27:27 of a field which the Lord **h** blessed:	NIH
	27:33 where *is* he that **h** taken venison,	NIH
	27:35 and **h** taken away thy blessing.	NIH
	27:36 for he **h** supplanted me these two times:	NIH
	27:36 now he **h** taken away my blessing.	NIH
	29:32 Surely the Lord **h** looked upon my	NIH
	29:33 Because the Lord **h** heard that I *was*	NIH
	29:33 he **h** therefore given me this *son* also:	NIH
	30: 2 who **h** withheld from thee the fruit of	NIH
	30: 6 God **h** judged me, and hath also heard my	NIH
	30: 6 also heard my voice, and hath given me	NIH
	30: 6 heard my voice, and **h** given me a son:	NIH
	30:18 God **h** given *me* my hire, because I have	NIH
	30:20 God **h** endued me with a good dowry;	NIH
	30:23 and said, God **h** taken away my reproach:	NIH
	30:27 that the Lord **h** blessed me for thy sake.	NIH
	30:30 the Lord **h** blessed thee since my	NIH
	31: 1 Jacob **h** taken away all that *was* our	NIH
	31: 1 *that* which *was* of our father's **h** he gotten	NIH
	31: 5 the God of my father **h** been with me.	NIH
	31: 7 your father **h** deceived me, and changed	NIH
	31: 9 Thus God **h** taken away the cattle of your	NIH
	31:15 for he **h** sold us, and hath quite devoured	NIH
	31:15 and **h** quite devoured also our money.	NIH
	31:16 For all the riches which God **h** taken from	NIH
	31:16 whatsoever God **h** said unto thee,	NIH

Ge	31:42 God **h** seen mine affliction and the labour	NIH
	33: 5 The children which God **h** graciously given	NIH
	33:11 because God **h** dealt graciously with me,	NIH
	37:20 will say, *Some* evil beast **h** devoured him:	NIH
	37:33 son's coat; an evil beast **h** devoured him;	NIH
	38:24 Tamar thy daughter in law **h** played	NIH
	38:26 said, She **h** been more righteous than I;	NIH
	39: 8 committed all that he hath to my hand;	NIH
	39: 8 all that he **h** to my hand;	3426+3807.1
	39: 9 neither **h** he kept back any thing from me	NIH
	39:14 he **h** brought in a Hebrew unto us to	NIH
	41:25 God **h** shewed Pharaoh what he *is* about	NIH
	41:39 Forasmuch as God **h** shewed thee all this,	NIH
	41:51 *said he,* **h** made me forget all my toil,	NIH
	41:52 For God **h** caused me to be fruitful in	NIH
	42:28 What *is this that* God **h** done unto us?	NIH
	43:23 **h** given you treasure in your sacks:	NIH
	44:16 God **h** found out the iniquity of thy	NIH
	45: 6 For these two years *h* the famine *been* in	NIH
	45: 8 he **h** made me a father to Pharaoh,	NIH
	45: 9 God **h** made me lord of all Egypt:	NIH
	46:32 for their trade **h** been to feed cattle;	NIH
	46:34 Thy servants' trade **h** been about cattle	NIH
	48: 9 whom God **h** given me in this *place.*	NIH
	48:11 and lo, God **h** shewed me also thy seed.	NIH
Ex	3:13 The God of your fathers **h** sent me unto	NIH
	3:14 of Israel, I AM **h** sent me unto you.	NIH
	3:15 the God of Jacob, **h** sent me unto you:	NIH
	3:18 The Lord God of the Hebrews **h** met	NIH
	4: 1 The Lord **h** not appeared unto thee.	NIH
	4: 5 the God of Jacob, **h** appeared unto thee.	NIH
	4:11 unto him, Who **h** made man's mouth?	NIH
	5: 3 The God of the Hebrews **h** met with us:	NIH
	5:23 thy name, he **h** done evil to this people;	NIH
	7:16 The Lord God of the Hebrews **h** sent me	NIH
	9:18 such as **h** not been in Egypt since	NIH
	10:12 of the land, *even* all that the hail **h** left.	NIH
	12:25 according as he **h** promised, that ye shall	NIH
	13: 9 for with a strong hand **h** the Lord	NIH
	14: 3 the land, the wilderness **h** shut them in.	NIH
	15: 1 the Lord, for he **h** triumphed gloriously:	NIH
	15: 1 and his rider he **h** thrown into the sea.	NIH
	15: 4 and his host he **h** cast into the sea:	NIH
	15: 6 O Lord, **h** dashed in pieces the enemy.	NIH
	15:21 the Lord, for he **h** triumphed gloriously;	NIH
	15:21 and his rider he **h** thrown into the sea.	NIH
	16: 6 ye shall know that the Lord **h** brought	NIH
	16: 9 for he **h** heard your murmurings.	NIH
	16:15 This *is* the bread which the Lord **h** given	NIH
	16:16 This *is* the thing which the Lord **h**	NIH
	16:23 This *is that* which the Lord **h** said,	NIH
	16:29 for that the Lord **h** given you	NIH
	17:16 Because the Lord **h** sworn *that*	NIH
	18:10 who **h** delivered you out of the hand of	NIH
	18:10 who **h** delivered the people from under	NIH
	19: 8 All that the Lord **h** spoken we will do.	NIH
	21: 8 who **h** betrothed her to himself, then	3807.1
	21: 9 seeing he **h** dealt deceitfully with her.	NIH
	21:29 it **h** been testified to his owner, and he	NIH
	21:29 **h** not kept him in, but that he hath killed	NIH
	21:29 but that he **h** killed a man or a woman;	NIH
	21:36 *if* it be known that the ox **h** used to push	NIH
	21:36 past, and his owner **h** not kept him in;	NIH
	22:11 that he **h** not put his hand unto his	NIH
	24: 3 All the words which the Lord **h** said will	NIH
	24: 7 All that the Lord **h** said we will do,	NIH
	24: 7 which the Lord **h** made with you	NIH
	32:24 Whosoever **h** *any* gold, let them break	3807.1
	32:33 Whosoever **h** sinned against me, him will	NIH
	35: 1 These *are* the words which the Lord **h**	NIH
	35:10 make all that the Lord **h** commanded;	NIH
	35:30 the Lord **h** called by name Bezaleel	NIH
	35:31 he **h** filled him *with* the spirit of God,	NIH
	35:34 he **h** put in his heart that *he* may teach,	3807.1
	35:35 Them **h** he filled with wisdom of heart,	NIH
Lev	4: 3 him bring for his sin, which he **h** sinned,	NIH
	4:22 a ruler **h** sinned, and done somewhat	NIH
	4:23 Or if his sin, wherein he **h** sinned, come to	NIH
	4:28 Or if his sin, which he **h** sinned, come to	NIH
	4:28 for his sin which he **h** sinned.	NIH
	4:35 atonement for his sin that he **h** committed,	NIH
	5: 1 whether he **h** seen or known *of it;* if he do	NIH
	5: 5 confess that he **h** sinned in that *thing:*	NIH
	5: 6 the Lord for his sin which he **h** sinned,	NIH
	5: 7 which he **h** committed, two turtledoves,	NIH
	5:13 his sin that he **h** sinned in one of these,	NIH
	5:16 shall make amends for the harm that he **h**	NIH
	5:19 he **h** certainly trespassed against	NIH
	6: 2 by violence, or **h** deceived his neighbour;	NIH
	6: 4 shall be, because he **h** sinned, and is guilty,	NIH
	6: 4 or the thing which he **h** deceitfully gotten,	NIH
	6: 5 Or all *that* about which he **h** sworn falsely;	NIH
	6: 7 of all that he **h** done in trespassing therein.	NIH
	6:10 the ashes which the fire **h** consumed	NIH
	7: 8 of the burnt offering which he **h** offered.	NIH
	8:34 As he **h** done this day, *so* the Lord **h**	NIH
	8:34 *so* the Lord **h** commanded to do,	NIH
	10: 6 bewail the burning which the Lord **h**	NIH
	10:11 **h** spoken unto them by the hand of Moses.	NIH
	10:15 for ever; as the Lord **h** commanded.	NIH
	10:17 *God* **h** given it you to bear the iniquity of	NIH
	11: 9 whatsoever **h** fins and scales in	3807.1
	11:12 Whatsoever **h** no fins nor scales in	3807.1
	11:42 whatsoever **h** more feet among all	NIH
	12: 7 This *is* the law for her that **h** born a male	NIH

H

H

Lev 13: 4 priest shall shut up *him that* **h** the plague — NIH
13: 7 after that he **h** been seen of the priest for — NIH
13:12 leprosy cover all the skin of *him that* **h** — NIH
13:13 he shall pronounce *him* clean *that* **h** — NIH
13:17 priest shall pronounce *him* clean *that* **h** — NIH
13:29 woman **h** a plague upon the head — 1961+871.1
13:31 priest shall shut up *him that* **h** the plague — NIH
13:33 priest shall shut up *him that* **h** the scall — NIH
13:41 he that **h** his hair fallen off from the part of — NIH
13:50 shut up *it that* **h** the plague seven days: — NIH
14:43 after *that* he **h** taken away the stones, — NIH
14:43 after he **h** scraped the house, and after it — NIH
14:48 the plague **h** not spread in the house, — NIH
15: 2 When any man **h** a running issue out of — 1961
15: 4 he lieth that **h** the issue, is unclean: — NIH
15: 6 sat that **h** the issue shall wash his clothes, — NIH
15: 7 he that toucheth the flesh of him that **h** — NIH
15: 8 if he that **h** the issue spit upon him that is — NIH
15: 9 what saddle soever he rideth upon that **h** — NIH
15:11 whomsoever he toucheth that **h** the issue, — NIH
15:11 **h** not rinsed his hands in water, he shall — NIH
15:12 he toucheth which **h** the issue, shall be — NIH
15:13 when he that **h** an issue is cleansed of his — NIH
15:32 This *is* the law of him that **h** an issue, — NIH
15:33 of him that **h** an issue, of the man, — 2100
16:20 when he **h** made an end of reconciling — NIH
17: 2 This *is* the thing which the LORD **h** — 3807.1
17: 4 he **h** shed blood; and that man shall be cut — NIH
19: 8 he **h** profaned the hallowed *thing* of — NIH
19:22 the LORD for his sin which he **h** done: — NIH
19:22 the sin which he **h** done shall be forgiven — NIH
20: 3 he **h** given of his seed unto Molech, — NIH
20: 9 he **h** cursed his father or his mother; — NIH
20:11 the man that lieth with his father's wife **h** — NIH
20:17 he uncovered his sister's nakedness; — NIH
20:18 he discovered her fountain, and she — NIH
20:18 she uncovered the fountain of her blood: — NIH
20:20 he **h** uncovered his uncle's nakedness: — NIH
20:21 he **h** uncovered his brother's nakedness; — NIH
20:27 or woman that **h** a familiar spirit, — 1961+871.1
21: 3 nigh unto him, which **h** had no husband; — NIH
21:17 generations that **h** *any* blemish, — 1961+871.1
21:18 For whatsoever man *he be* that **h** a — 871.1
21:18 or he that **h** a flat nose, or any thing — NIH
21:20 that **h** a blemish in his eye, or be scurvy, — NIH
21:20 or scabbed, or **h** his stones broken; — NIH
21:21 No man that **h** a blemish, of the seed of — 871.1
21:21 he a blemish; he shall not come nigh to — 871.1
21:23 unto the altar, because he **h** a blemish; — 871.1
22: 4 of Aaron *is* a leper, or **h** a running issue; — NIH
22: 5 whatsoever uncleanness he **h**; — 3807.1
22: 6 The soul which **h** touched *any* such shall — NIH
22:20 *But* whatsoever **h** a blemish, *that* shall ye — 871.1
22:23 a lamb that **h** any thing **superfluous** or — 8311
24:14 Bring forth him that **h** cursed without — NIH
24:19 as he **h** done, so shall it be done to him; — NIH
24:20 as he **h** caused a blemish in a man, — NIH
25:25 **h** sold away *some* of his possession, — NIH
25:28 that **h** bought it until the year of jubile: — NIH
27:22 unto the LORD a field which he **h** bought, — NIH
27:28 devote unto the LORD of all that he **h**, — 3807.1

Nu 5: 2 every one that **h** an issue, and whosoever — NIH
5: 7 unto *him* against whom he **h** trespassed. — 816
5:20 *some* man **h** lain with thee beside thine — 5414
5:27 when he **h** made her to drink the water, — NIH
6: 9 he **h** defiled the head of his consecration; — NIH
6:21 This *is* the law of the Nazarite who **h** — NIH
10:29 for the LORD **h** spoken good concerning — NIH
12: 2 **H** the LORD indeed spoken only by — NIH
12: 2 he **h** not spoken also by us? — NIH
14: 3 wherefore **h** the LORD brought us unto — NIH
14:16 he **h** slain them in the wilderness. — NIH
14:24 spirit with him, and **h** followed me fully, — NIH
14:40 the place which the LORD **h** promised: — NIH
15:22 which the LORD **h** spoken unto Moses, — NIH
15:23 *Even* all that the LORD **h** commanded you — NIH
15:31 Because he **h** despised the word of — NIH
15:31 **h** broken his commandment, that soul — NIH
16: 5 *him* whom he **h** chosen will he cause — NIH
16: 9 that the God of Israel **h** separated you from — NIH
16:10 he brought thee near *to him*, and all thy — NIH
16:28 Hereby ye shall know that the LORD **h** — NIH
16:29 of all men; *then* the LORD **h** not sent me. — NIH
19: 2 the law which the LORD **h** commanded, — NIH
19:15 which **h** no covering bound upon it, — NIH
19:20 he **h** defiled the sanctuary of the LORD: — NIH
19:20 water of separation **h** not been sprinkled — NIH
20:14 knowest all the travail that **h** befallen — NIH
20:16 and **h** brought us forth out of Egypt; — NIH
21:28 it **h** consumed Ar of Moab, *and* the lords — NIH
21:29 he **h** given his sons that escaped, — NIH
22:10 king of Moab, **h** sent unto me, *saying*, — NIH
23: 7 Balak the king of Moab **h** brought me — NIH
23: 8 shall I curse, whom God **h** not cursed? — NIH
23: 8 I defy, *whom* the LORD **h** not defied? — NIH
23:12 that which the LORD **h** put in my mouth? — NIH
23:17 said unto him, What **h** the LORD spoken? — NIH
23:19 he said, and shall he not do *it?* or hath — NIH
23:19 shall he not do *it?* or **h** he spoken, — NIH
23:20 and he **h** blessed; and I cannot reverse it. — NIH
23:21 He **h** not beheld iniquity in Jacob, — NIH
23:21 neither **h** he seen perverseness in Israel: — NIH
23:22 he **h** as it were the strength of an unicorn. — NIH
23:23 and of Israel, What **h** God wrought! — NIH
24: 3 Balaam the son of Beor **h** said, and the — NIH

Nu 24: 3 and the man whose eyes are open **h** said: — NIH
24: 4 He **h** said, which heard the words of God, — NIH
24: 6 of lign aloes *which* the LORD **h** planted, — NIH
24: 8 he **h** as it were the strength of an unicorn: — NIH
24:11 the LORD **h** kept thee back from honour. — NIH
24:15 Balaam the son of Beor **h** said, and the — NIH
24:15 and the man whose eyes are open **h** said: — NIH
24:16 He **h** said, which heard the words of God, — NIH
25:11 **h** turned my wrath away from the children — NIH
27: 3 among his family, because he **h** no son? — NIH
30: 1 This *is* the thing which the LORD **h** — NIH
30: 4 her bond wherewith she **h** bound her soul, — NIH
30: 4 bond wherewith she **h** bound her soul — NIH
30: 5 of her bonds wherewith she **h** bound her — NIH
30:12 if her husband **h** utterly made them void, — NIH
30:12 her husband **h** made them void; — NIH
30:15 make them void after *that* he **h** heard — NIH
31:17 kill every woman that **h** known man by — NIH
31:19 whosoever **h** killed *any* person, — NIH
31:19 whosoever **h** touched *any* slain, purify — NIH
31:50 every man **h** gotten, *of* jewels of gold, — NIH
32: 7 the land which the LORD **h** given them? — NIH
32:21 until he **h** driven out his enemies from — NIH
32:24 do that which **h** proceeded out of your — NIH
32:31 As the LORD **h** said unto thy servants, — NIH
36: 5 The tribe of the sons of Joseph **h** said well. — NIH

Dt 1:10 The LORD your God **h** multiplied you, — NIH
1:11 and bless you, as he **h** promised you!) — NIH
1:21 the LORD thy God **h** set the land before — NIH
1:21 LORD God of thy fathers **h** said unto thee; — NIH
1:27 he **h** brought us forth out of the land of — NIH
1:36 him will I give the land that he **h** trodden — NIH
1:36 because he **h** wholly followed the LORD. — NIH
2: 7 For the LORD thy God **h** blessed thee in — NIH
2: 7 these forty years the LORD thy God *h* — NIH
3:18 The LORD your God **h** given you this land — NIH
3:20 your God **h** given them beyond Jordan: — NIH
3:21 your God **h** done unto these two kings: — NIH
4: 3 the LORD thy God **h** destroyed them from — NIH
4: 7 *so* great, who **h** God *so* nigh unto them, — NIH
4: 8 that **h** statutes and judgments *so* — 3807.1
4:19 which the LORD thy God **h** divided unto — NIH
4:20 the LORD **h** taken you, and brought you — NIH
4:23 the LORD thy God **h** forbidden thee. — NIH
4:32 whether there **h** been *any such thing* as — NIH
4:32 this great thing *is*, or **h** been heard like it? — NIH
4:34 Or **h** God assayed to go *and* take him a — NIH
5:12 as the LORD thy God **h** commanded thee. — NIH
5:16 as the LORD thy God **h** commanded thee; — NIH
5:24 the LORD our God **h** shewed us his glory — NIH
5:26 that **h** heard the voice of the living God — NIH
5:32 as the LORD your God **h** commanded you: — NIH
5:33 the LORD your God **h** commanded you, — NIH
6: 3 as the LORD God of thy fathers **h** — 3807.1
6:17 his statutes, which he **h** commanded thee. — NIH
6:19 from before thee, as the LORD **h** spoken. — NIH
6:20 which the LORD our God **h** commanded — NIH
6:25 LORD our God, as he **h** commanded us. — NIH
7: 1 cast out many nations before thee, — NIH
7: 6 the LORD thy God **h** chosen thee to be a — NIH
7: 8 **h** the LORD brought you out with a — NIH
8:10 for the good land which he **h** given thee. — NIH
8:17 the might of mine hand **h** gotten me this — NIH
9: 3 as the LORD **h** said unto thee. — NIH
9: 4 after that the LORD thy God **h** cast them — NIH
9: 4 For my righteousness the LORD **h** brought — NIH
9:28 he **h** brought them out to slay them in — NIH
10: 9 Wherefore Levi **h** no part nor — 1961+3807.1
10:21 that **h** done for thee these great and — NIH
10:22 now the LORD thy God **h** made thee as — NIH
11: 4 *how* the LORD **h** destroyed them unto this — NIH
11:25 ye shall tread upon, as he **h** said unto you. — NIH
11:29 when the LORD thy God **h** brought thee in — NIH
12: 7 where*in* the LORD thy God **h** blessed — NIH
12:12 as he **h** no part nor inheritance — 3807.1
12:15 the LORD thy God which he **h** given thee: — NIH
12:20 as he **h** promised thee, and thou shalt say, — NIH
12:21 If the place which the LORD thy God **h** — NIH
12:21 thy flock, which the LORD **h** given thee, — NIH
13: 5 he **h** spoken to turn *you* away from — NIH
13:10 he **h** sought to thrust thee away from — NIH
13:12 which the LORD thy God **h** given thee to — NIH
13:17 as he **h** sworn unto thy fathers; — NIH
14: 2 the LORD **h** chosen thee to be a peculiar — NIH
14:10 whatsoever **h** not fins and scales ye may — 3807.1
14:24 when the LORD thy God **h** blessed thee: — NIH
14:27 he **h** no part nor inheritance with thee. — 3807.1
14:29 he **h** no part nor inheritance with thee,) — 3807.1
15:14 *of that* wherewith the LORD thy God **h** — NIH
15:18 he **h** been worth a double hired servant — NIH
16:10 as the LORD thy God **h** blessed thee: — NIH
16:11 in the place which the LORD thy God **h** — NIH
16:17 the LORD thy God which he **h** given thee. — NIH
17: 2 that **h** wrought wickedness in the sight of — NIH
17: 3 **h** gone and served other gods, — NIH
17:16 forasmuch as the LORD **h** said unto you, — NIH
18: 2 their inheritance, as he **h** said unto them. — NIH
18: 5 For the LORD thy God **h** chosen him out — NIH
18:14 the LORD thy God **h** not suffered thee so — NIH
18:21 the word which the LORD **h** not spoken? — NIH
18:22 that *is* the thing which the LORD **h** not — NIH
18:22 the prophet **h** spoken it presumptuously: — NIH
19: 1 When the LORD thy God **h** cut off — NIH
19: 8 as he **h** sworn unto thy fathers, — NIH
19:18 *and* **h** testified falsely against his brother; — NIH

Dt 20: 5 man *is there* that **h** built a new house, — NIH
20: 5 built a new house, and **h** not dedicated it? — NIH
20: 6 what man *is he* that **h** planted a vineyard, — NIH
20: 6 a vineyard, and **h** not *yet* eaten of it? — NIH
20: 7 what man *is there* that **h** betrothed a wife, — NIH
20: 7 betrothed a wife, and **h** not taken her? — NIH
20:13 when the LORD thy God **h** delivered it — NIH
20:14 which the LORD thy God **h** given thee. — 3807.1
20:17 as the LORD thy God **h** commanded thee: — NIH
21: 1 *and* it be not known who **h** slain him: — NIH
21: 3 which **h** not been wrought with, — NIH
21: 3 *and* which **h** not drawn in the yoke; — NIH
21: 5 for them the LORD thy God **h** chosen to — NIH
21:10 the LORD thy God **h** delivered them into — NIH
21:16 sons to inherit *that* which he **h**, — 1961+3807.1
21:17 a double portion of all that he **h**: — 4672+3807.1
22: 3 which he **h** lost, and thou hast found, — NIH
22:17 he **h** given occasions of speech *against* — NIH
22:19 **h** brought up an evil name upon a virgin — NIH
22:21 because she **h** wrought folly in Israel, — NIH
22:24 he **h** humbled his neighbour's wife: — NIH
22:29 he **h** humbled her, he may not put — NIH
23: 1 the stones, or *his* privy member cut off, — NIH
24: 1 When a man **h** taken a wife, — NIH
24: 1 he **h** found some uncleanness in her: — NIH
24: 5 When a man **h** taken a new wife, he shall — NIH
24: 5 shall cheer up his wife which he **h** taken. — NIH
25:10 The house of him that **h** his shoe loosed. — NIH
25:19 when the LORD thy God **h** given thee — 3807.1
26: 9 he **h** brought us into this place, — NIH
26: 9 **h** given us this land, *even* a land that — NIH
26:11 the LORD thy God **h** given unto thee, — NIH
26:16 This day the LORD thy God **h** — NIH
26:18 the LORD **h** avouched thee *this* day to be — NIH
26:18 as he **h** promised thee, and that *thou* — NIH
26:19 high above all nations which he **h** made, — NIH
26:19 unto the LORD thy God, as he **h** spoken. — NIH
27: 3 as the LORD God of thy fathers **h** — NIH
28: 9 unto himself, as he **h** sworn unto thee, — NIH
28:52 which the LORD thy God **h** given thee. — NIH
28:53 which the LORD thy God **h** given thee. — NIH
28:55 because he **h** nothing left him in the siege, — NIH
29: 4 Yet the LORD **h** not given you a heart to — NIH
29:13 as he **h** said unto thee, and as he hath — NIH
29:13 he **h** sworn unto thy fathers, to Abraham, — NIH
29:22 the sicknesses which the LORD **h** laid — NIH
29:24 Wherefore **h** the LORD done thus unto — NIH
30: 1 whither the LORD thy God **h** driven thee, — NIH
30: 3 whither the LORD thy God **h** scattered — NIH
31: 2 also the LORD **h** said unto me, Thou shalt — NIH
31: 3 go over before thee, as the LORD **h** said. — NIH
31: 7 **h** sworn unto their fathers to give them; — NIH
32: 6 *is* not he thy father *that* **h** bought thee? — NIH
32: 6 he *not* made thee, and established thee? — NIH
32:27 is high, and the LORD **h** not done all this. — NIH

Jos 1:13 The LORD your God **h** given you rest, — 3807.1
1:13 you rest, and **h** given you this land. — 3807.1
1:15 as *he* **h** *given* you, and they also have — NIH
2: 9 I know that the LORD **h** given you — NIH
2:14 when the LORD **h** given us the land, — NIH
2:24 Truly the LORD **h** delivered into our — NIH
6:16 Shout; for the LORD **h** given you the city. — NIH
6:22 and all that she **h**, as ye sware unto her. — 3807.1
7:11 Israel **h** sinned, and they have also — NIH
7:15 be burnt with fire, he and all that he **h**: — NIH
7:15 he **h** transgressed the covenant of — NIH
7:15 and because he **h** wrought folly in Israel. — NIH
8:31 over which no man **h** lift up *any* iron: — NIH
10: 4 for it **h** made peace with Joshua and — NIH
10:19 for the LORD your God **h** delivered them — NIH
14:10 the LORD **h** kept me alive, as he said, — NIH
17:14 forasmuch as the LORD **h** blessed me — NIH
18: 3 which the LORD God of your fathers **h** — NIH
22: 4 now the LORD your God **h** given rest unto — NIH
22:25 For the LORD **h** made Jordan a border — NIH
23: 3 have seen all that the LORD your God **h** — NIH
23: 3 for the LORD your God *is* he that **h** fought — NIH
23: 5 as the LORD your God **h** promised unto — NIH
23: 9 For the LORD **h** driven out from before — NIH
23: 9 no man **h** *been able to* stand before you — NIH
23:10 that fighteth for you, as he **h** promised you. — NIH
23:13 which the LORD your God **h** given you. — NIH
23:14 that not one thing **h** failed of all the good — NIH
23:14 you, *and* not one thing **h** failed thereof. — NIH
23:15 which the LORD your God **h** given you. — NIH
23:16 the good land which he **h** given unto you. — NIH
24:20 after that he **h** done you good. — NIH
24:27 for it **h** heard all the words of the LORD — NIH

Jdg 1: 7 as I have done, so God **h** requited me. — NIH
2:20 Because that this people **h** transgressed my — NIH
3:28 for the LORD **h** delivered your enemies — NIH
4: 6 **H** not the LORD God of Israel — NIH
4:14 for this *is* the day in which the LORD **h** — NIH
6:13 now the LORD **h** forsaken us, — NIH
6:25 down the altar of Baal that thy father **h**, — NIH
6:29 one to another, Who **h** done this thing? — NIH
6:29 Gideon the son of Joash **h** done this thing. — NIH
6:30 because he **h** cast down the altar of Baal, — NIH
6:30 he **h** cut down the grove that *was* by it. — NIH
6:31 because *one* **h** cast down his altar. — NIH
6:32 because he **h** thrown down his altar. — NIH
7: 2 saying, Mine own hand **h** saved me. — NIH
7:14 *for* into his hand **h** God delivered Midian, — NIH
7:15 for the LORD **h** delivered into your hand — NIH
8: 3 God **h** delivered into your hands the — NIH

Jdg	8: 7 Therefore when the Lord **h** delivered	NIH
	11:23 So now the Lord God of Israel **h**	NIH
	11:36 do to me according to that which **h**	NIH
	11:36 forasmuch as the Lord **h** taken	NIH
	13:10 Behold, the man **h** appeared unto me,	NIH
	15: 6 the Philistines said, Who **h** done this?	NIH
	15:10 come up, to do to him as he **h** done to us.	NIH
	16:17 There **h** not come a rasor upon mine head;	NIH
	16:18 once, for he **h** shewed me all his heart.	NIH
	16:23 Our god **h** delivered Samson our enemy	NIH
	16:24 Our god **h** delivered into our hands our	NIH
	18: 4 and **h** hired me, and I am his priest.	NIH
	18:10 for God **h** given it into your hands; a place	3045
	21:11 and every woman that **h** lien by man.	3045
Ru	1:20 for the Almighty **h** dealt very bitterly with	NIH
	1:21 the Lord **h** brought me *home* again	NIH
	1:21 seeing the Lord **h** testified against me,	NIH
	1:21 and the Almighty **h** afflicted me?	NIH
	2: 7 **h** continued even from the morning until	NIH
	2:11 said unto her, It **h** fully been shewed me,	NIH
	2:20 who **h** not left off his kindness to the living	NIH
	4:14 which **h** not left thee *this* day without a	NIH
	4:15 to thee than seven sons, **h** born him.	NIH
1Sa	1:27 the Lord **h** given me my petition which I	I
	2: 5 that the barren **h** born seven; and she that	NIH
	2: 5 she that **h** many children is waxed feeble.	NIH
	2: 8 and he **h** set the world upon them.	NIH
	3:17 What *is* the thing that *the* Lord **h** said	NIH
	4: 3 Wherefore **h** the Lord smitten us to day	NIH
	4: 7 there **h** not been such *a thing* heretofore.	NIH
	4:17 there **h** been also a great slaughter among	NIH
	6: 7 on which there **h** come no yoke, and tie	NIH
	6: 9 *then* he **h** done us this great evil:	NIH
	7:12 Hitherto the Lord helped us.	NIH
	9:24 for unto *this* time **h** it been kept for thee	NIH
	10: 1 the Lord **h** anointed thee to be captain	NIH
	10: 2 lo, thy father **h** left the care of the asses,	NIH
	10:22 Behold, he **h** hid himself among the stuff.	NIH
	10:24 See ye him whom the Lord **h** chosen,	NIH
	11:13 for to day the Lord **h** wrought salvation	NIH
	12:13 behold, the Lord **h** set a king over you.	NIH
	12:22 it **h** pleased the Lord to make you his	NIH
	12:24 consider how great things he **h** done for	NIH
	13:14 the Lord **h** sought him a man after his	NIH
	13:14 commanded him to be captain	NIH
	14:10 for the Lord **h** delivered them into our	NIH
	14:12 for the Lord **h** delivered them into	NIH
	14:29 My father **h** troubled the land:	NIH
	14:38 and see wherein this sin **h** been *this* day.	NIH
	14:45 who **h** wrought this great salvation in	NIH
	14:45 for he **h** wrought with God this day.	NIH
	15:11 and **h** not performed my commandments.	NIH
	15:16 I will tell thee what the Lord **h** said to	NIH
	15:22 **H** the Lord *as great* delight in burnt	3807.1
	15:23 he **h** also rejected thee from *being* king.	NIH
	15:26 the Lord **h** rejected thee from being king	NIH
	15:28 The Lord **h** rent the kingdom of Israel	NIH
	15:28 **h** given it to a neighbour of thine, *that is*	NIH
	15:33 As thy sword **h** made women childless,	NIH
	16: 8 he said, Neither **h** the Lord chosen this.	NIH
	16: 9 he said, Neither **h** the Lord chosen this.	NIH
	16:10 unto Jesse, The Lord **h** not chosen these.	NIH
	16:22 for he **h** found favour in my sight.	NIH
	17:36 seeing he **h** defied the armies of the living	NIH
	18: 7 Saul **h** slain his thousands, and David his	NIH
	18:22 the king **h** delight in thee, and all his	NIH
	19: 4 because he **h** not sinned against thee,	NIH
	20:13 be with thee, as he **h** been with my father.	NIH
	20:15 not when the Lord **h** cut off the enemies	NIH
	20:22 go *thy way:* for the Lord **h** sent thee	NIH
	20:26 for he thought, Something **h** befallen him,	NIH
	20:29 for our family **h** a sacrifice in the city;	NIH
	20:29 he **h** commanded me *to be there:*	NIH
	20:32 shall he be slain? what **h** he done?	NIH
	21: 2 The king **h** commanded me a business,	NIH
	21: 2 me a business, and **h** said unto me,	NIH
	21:11 Saul **h** slain his thousands, and David his	NIH
	22: 8 is none that **h** shewed me that my son **h**	NIH
	22: 8 sheweth unto me that my son **h** stirred up	NIH
	23: 7 God **h** delivered him into mine hand;	NIH
	23: 7 by entering into a town that **h** gates and	NIH
	23:10 thy servant **h** certainly heard that Saul	NIH
	23:11 Saul come down, as thy servant **h** heard?	NIH
	23:22 his haunt is, *and* who **h** seen him there:	NIH
	25:21 all that this *fellow* **h** in the wilderness,	3807.1
	25:21 and he **h** requited me evil for good.	NIH
	25:26 seeing the Lord **h** withholden thee from	NIH
	25:27 this blessing which thine handmaid **h**	NIH
	25:28 evil **h** not been found in thee *all* thy days.	NIH
	25:30 good that he **h** spoken concerning thee,	NIH
	25:31 or that my lord **h** avenged himself:	NIH
	25:34 which **h** kept me back from hurting thee,	NIH
	25:39 that **h** pleaded the cause of my reproach	NIH
	25:39 of Nabal, and **h** kept his servant from evil:	NIH
	25:39 for the Lord **h** returned the wickedness	NIH
	26: 8 God **h** delivered thine enemy into thine	NIH
	27:12 He **h** made his people Israel utterly to	871.1
	28: 7 Seek me a woman that **h** a familiar spirit,	1172
	28: 7 *there is* a woman that **h** a familiar spirit at	1172
	28: 9 Behold, thou knowest what Saul **h** done,	NIH
	28: 9 how he **h** cut off those that have familiar	NIH
	28:17 the Lord **h** done to him, as he spake by	NIH
	28:17 for the Lord **h** rent the kingdom out of	NIH
	28:18 the Lord **h** done this thing unto thee this	NIH
	28:21 thine handmaid **h** obeyed thy voice,	NIH

1Sa	29: 3 which **h** been with me these days,	NIH
	30:23 with *that* which the Lord **h** given us,	NIH
	30:23 who **h** preserved us, and delivered	NIH
2Sa	1:16 for thy mouth **h** testified against thee,	NIH
	3: 9 as the Lord **h** sworn to David, even so	NIH
	3:18 do *it:* for the Lord **h** spoken of David,	NIH
	3:23 he **h** sent him away, and he is gone in	NIH
	3:29 the house of Joab one that **h** an issue,	2100
	4: 8 the Lord **h** avenged my lord the king this	NIH
	4: 9 who **h** redeemed my soul out of all	NIH
	5:20 The Lord **h** broken forth upon mine	NIH
	6:12 The Lord **h** blessed the house of	NIH
	7:27 thy servant found in his heart to pray	NIH
	9: 3 Jonathan **h** yet a son, *which is* lame on	3807.1
	9:11 According to all that my lord the king **h**	NIH
	10: 3 that he **h** sent comforters unto thee?	NIH
	10: 3 **h** not David *rather* sent his servants unto	NIH
	12: 5 the man that **h** done this *thing* shall surely	NIH
	12:13 The Lord also **h** put away thy sin;	NIH
	13:20 Amnon thy brother been with thee?	NIH
	13:24 Behold now, thy servant **h** sheepshearers;	NIH
	13:30 Absalom **h** slain all the king's sons,	NIH
	13:32 for by the appointment of Absalom *this* **h**	NIH
	14:19 from ought that my lord the king **h** spoken:	NIH
	14:20 To fetch about *this* form of speech **h** thy	NIH
	14:22 that the king **h** fulfilled the request of his	NIH
	14:30 field is near mine, and he **h** barley there;	3807.1
	15: 4 every man which **h** *any* suit or	1961+3807.1
	16: 8 The Lord **h** returned upon thee all	NIH
	16: 8 the Lord **h** delivered the kingdom into	NIH
	16:10 because the Lord **h** said unto him,	NIH
	16:11 let him curse; for the Lord **h** bidden him.	NIH
	16:21 which he **h** left to keep the house;	NIH
	17: 6 Ahithophel **h** spoken after this manner:	NIH
	17: 7 The counsel that Ahithophel **h** given *is not*	NIH
	17:21 for thus **h** Ahithophel counselled against	NIH
	18:19 how that the Lord **h** avenged him of his	NIH
	18:28 which **h** delivered up the men that lift up	NIH
	18:31 for the Lord **h** avenged thee *this* day of	NIH
	19:27 he **h** slandered thy servant unto my lord	NIH
	19:42 king's *cost?* or **h** he given us *any* gift?	3807.1
	20:21 he **h** lift up his hand against the king,	NIH
	22:21 according to the cleanness of my hands **h**	NIH
	22:25 Therefore the Lord **h** recompensed me	NIH
	22:36 and thy gentleness **h** made me great.	NIH
	23: 5 yet he **h** made with me an everlasting	NIH
1Ki	1:19 **h** slain oxen and fat cattle and sheep in	NIH
	1:19 **h** called all the sons of the king,	NIH
	1:19 but Solomon thy servant **h** he not called.	NIH
	1:25 **h** slain oxen and fat cattle and sheep in	NIH
	1:25 **h** called all the king's sons, and the	NIH
	1:26 and thy servant Solomon, **h** he not called.	NIH
	1:29 **h** redeemed my soul out of all distress,	NIH
	1:37 As the Lord **h** been with my lord	NIH
	1:43 our lord king David **h** made Solomon	NIH
	1:44 the king **h** sent with him Zadok the priest,	NIH
	1:48 which **h** given *one* to sit on my throne *this*	NIH
	1:51 he **h** caught hold on the horns of the altar,	NIH
	2:24 which **h** established me, and set me on	NIH
	2:24 who **h** made me a house, as he promised,	NIH
	2:31 Do as he **h** said, and fall upon him,	NIH
	2:38 as my lord the king **h** said, so will thy	NIH
	5: 4 now the Lord my God **h** given me rest	3807.1
	5: 7 which **h** given unto David a wise son over	NIH
	8:15 and **h** with his hand fulfilled *it,* saying,	NIH
	8:20 the Lord **h** performed his word that he	NIH
	8:56 that **h** given rest unto his people Israel,	NIH
	8:56 there **h** not failed one word of all his good	NIH
	8: 9 Why **h** the Lord done thus unto this land,	NIH
	9: 9 **h** the Lord brought upon them all this	NIH
	12:11 my father **h** chastised you with whips,	NIH
	13: 3 This *is* the sign which the Lord **h**	NIH
	13:26 the Lord **h** delivered him unto the lion,	NIH
	13:26 which **h** torn him, and slain him,	NIH
	14:11 of the air eat: for the Lord **h** spoken *it.*	NIH
	16:16 Zimri **h** conspired, and hath also slain	NIH
	16:16 hath conspired, and **h** also slain the king:	NIH
	18:10 whither my lord **h** not sent to seek thee:	NIH
	19:18 and every mouth which **h** not kissed him.	NIH
	22:23 the Lord **h** put a lying spirit in the mouth	NIH
	22:23 the Lord **h** spoken evil concerning thee.	NIH
	22:28 in peace, the Lord **h** not spoken by me.	NIH
2Ki	1: 9 man of God, the king **h** said, Come down.	NIH
	1:11 O man of God, thus **h** the king said,	NIH
	2: 2 for the Lord **h** sent me to Beth-el.	NIH
	2: 4 for the Lord **h** sent me *to* Jericho.	NIH
	2: 6 here; for the Lord **h** sent me to Jordan.	NIH
	2:16 lest peradventure the spirit of the Lord **h**	NIH
	3: 7 The king of Moab **h** rebelled against me:	NIH
	3:10 that the Lord **h** called these three kings	NIH
	3:13 for the Lord **h** called these three kings	NIH
	4: 2 Thine handmaid **h** not any thing in	3807.1
	4:14 she **h** no child, and her husband is	NIH
	4:27 the Lord **h** hid *it* from me, and hath not	NIH
	4:27 hath hid *it* from me, and **h** not told me.	NIH
	5:20 my master **h** spared Naaman this Syrian,	NIH
	5:22 My master **h** sent me, saying, Behold,	NIH
	6:29 we may eat him: and she **h** hid her son.	NIH
	6:32 See ye how this son of a murderer **h** sent	NIH
	7: 6 the king of Israel **h** hired against us	NIH
	8: 1 for the Lord **h** called for a famine;	NIH
	8: 4 all the great *things* that Elisha **h** done.	NIH
	8: 9 Thy son Ben-hadad king of Syria **h** sent me	NIH
	8:10 howbeit the Lord **h** shewed me that he	NIH
	8:13 The Lord **h** shewed me *that* thou *shalt* be	NIH

2Ki	10:10 for the Lord **h** done *that* which he spake	NIH
	14:10 and thine heart **h** lifted thee up:	NIH
	17:26 therefore he **h** sent lions among them,	NIH
	18:22 and whose altars Hezekiah **h** taken away,	NIH
	18:22 and **h** said to Judah and Jerusalem,	NIH
	18:27 **H** my master sent me to thy master,	NIH
	18:27 **h** he not *sent me* to the men which sit on	NIH
	18:33 **H** any of the gods of the nations delivered	NIH
	19: 4 whom the king of Assyria his master **h** sent	NIH
	19: 4 words which the Lord thy God **h** heard:	NIH
	19:16 which **h** sent him to reproach the living	NIH
	19:21 This *is* the word that the Lord **h** spoken	NIH
	19:21 The virgin the daughter of Zion **h** despised	NIH
	19:21 daughter of Jerusalem **h** shaken her head	NIH
	20: 9 that the Lord **h** will do the thing that he **h**	NIH
	21:11 Because Manasseh king of Judah **h** done	NIH
	21:11 **h** done wickedly above all that the	NIH
	21:11 **h** made Judah also to sin with his idols:	NIH
	22:10 Hilkiah the priest **h** delivered me a book.	NIH
	22:16 the book which the king of Judah **h** read:	NIH
1Ch	14:11 God **h** broken in upon mine enemies by	God
	15: 2 for them **h** the Lord chosen to carry	NIH
	16:12 Remember his marvellous works that he **h**	NIH
	16:17 confirmed the same to Jacob for a law,	NIH
	17:25 thy servant **h** found in *his heart* to pray	NIH
	19: 3 that he **h** sent comforters unto thee?	NIH
	22:11 of the Lord thy God, as he **h** said of thee.	NIH
	22:18 he **h** not given you rest on every side?	NIH
	22:18 for he **h** given the inhabitants of the land	NIH
	23:25 The Lord God of Israel **h** given rest unto	NIH
	28: 4 for he **h** chosen Judah to be the ruler;	NIH
	28: 5 (for the Lord **h** given me many sons,)	NIH
	28: 5 he **h** chosen Solomon my son to sit upon	NIH
	28:10 for the Lord **h** chosen thee to build a	NIH
	29: 1 whom alone God **h**, *is yet* young	NIH
2Ch	2:11 Because the Lord **h** loved his people,	NIH
	2:11 people, he **h** made thee king over them.	NIH
	2:12 who **h** given to David the king a wise son,	NIH
	2:15 and the wine, which my lord **h** spoken of,	NIH
	6: 1 The Lord **h** said that *he* would dwell in	NIH
	6: 4 who **h** with his hands fulfilled *that* which	NIH
	6:10 performed his word that he hath spoken:	NIH
	6:10 hath performed his word that he **h** spoken:	NIH
	7:21 Why **h** the Lord done thus unto this land,	NIH
	7:22 he **h** brought all this evil upon them.	NIH
	8: 6 whereunto the ark of the Lord **h** come.	NIH
	13: 6 is risen up, and **h** rebelled against his lord.	NIH
	14: 7 and he **h** given us rest on every side.	NIH
	15: 3 for a long season Israel *h* been without	NIH
	18:22 the Lord **h** put a lying spirit in the mouth	NIH
	18:22 and the Lord **h** spoken evil against thee.	NIH
	18:27 *then* **h** not the Lord spoken by me.	NIH
	20:37 the Lord **h** broken thy works.	NIH
	23: 3 as the Lord **h** said of the sons of David.	NIH
	24:20 the Lord, he **h** also forsaken you.	NIH
	25: 8 **h** power to help, and to cast down.	3426+871.1
	25:16 I know that God **h** determined to destroy	NIH
	28: 9 he **h** delivered them into your hand,	NIH
	29: 8 and he **h** delivered them to trouble,	NIH
	29:11 for the Lord **h** chosen you to stand	NIH
	30: 8 which he **h** sanctified for ever:	NIH
	31:10 for the Lord **h** blessed his people;	NIH
	32:12 **H** not the same Hezekiah taken away his	NIH
	34:18 Hilkiah the priest **h** given me a book.	NIH
	36:23 All the kingdoms of the earth **h** the Lord	NIH
	36:23 he **h** charged me to build him a house in	NIH
Ezr	1: 2 The Lord God of heaven **h** given me all	NIH
	1: 2 he **h** charged me to build him a house at	NIH
	4: 3 as king Cyrus the king of Persia **h**	NIH
	4:18 The letter which ye sent unto us *h* been	NIH
	4:19 search **h** been made, and it is found that	NIH
	4:19 it is found that this city of old time *h* made	NIH
	5: 3 Who **h** commanded you to build this	NIH
	5:16 since that time even until now *h* *it* been in	NIH
	6:12 the God that **h** caused his name to dwell	NIH
	7:27 which **h** put *such a thing* as this in	NIH
	7:28 extended mercy unto me before the	NIH
	9: 2 and rulers **h** been chief in this trespass.	NIH
	9: 8 now for a little space grace **h** been *shewed*	NIH
	9: 9 yet our God **h** not forsaken us in our	NIH
	9: 9 **h** extended mercy unto us in the sight of	NIH
Ne	9:32 that **h** come upon us, on our kings, on our	NIH
Est	1:15 that **h** not performed the commandment of	NIH
	1:16 Vashti the queen **h** not done wrong to	NIH
	5: 5 haste, that *he* may do as Esther **h** said.	NIH
	5: 8 and I will do to morrow as the king **h** said.	NIH
	6: 3 dignity **h** been done to Mordecai for	3807.1
Job	1:10 and about all that he **h** on every side?	3807.1
	1:11 touch all that he **h**, and he will curse	3807.1
	1:12 Behold, all that he **h** *is* in thy power;	3807.1
	1:16 **h** burnt up the sheep, and the servants,	NIH
	1:21 the Lord **h** taken *away;* blessed be	NIH
	2: 4 all that a man **h** will he give for his life.	NIH
	3:23 way is hid, and whom God **h** hedged in?	NIH
	5:16 So the poor **h** hope,	1961+3807.1
	6: 5 Doth the wild ass bray when he **h** grass?	NIH
	7: 8 The eye of him that **h** seen me shall see me	NIH
	9: 4 who **h** hardened *himself* against him,	NIH
	9: 4 *himself* against him, and **h** prospered?	NIH
	10:12 and thy visitation **h** preserved my spirit.	NIH
	12: 9 that the hand of the Lord **h** wrought this?	NIH
	12:13 he **h** counsel and understanding.	3807.1
	13: 1 mine eye **h** seen all *this,* mine ear hath	NIH
	13: 1 mine eye hath seen all *this,* mine ear **h**	NIH
	16: 7 he **h** made me weary: thou hast made	NIH

H

Job 16:11 God **h** delivered me to the ungodly, NIH
16:12 I was at ease, but he **h** broken me asunder: NIH
16:12 he **h** also taken *me* by my neck, NIH
17: 6 he hath made me also a byword of the people; NIH
17: 9 he that **h** clean hands shall be stronger NIH
19: 6 Know now that God **h** overthrown me, NIH
19: 6 and **h** compassed me with his net. NIH
19: 8 He **h** fenced up my way that I cannot pass, NIH
19: 8 and he **h** set darkness in my paths. NIH
19: 9 He **h** stript me of my glory, and taken NIH
19:10 He **h** destroyed me on every side, and I NIH
19:10 and mine hope he **h** removed like a tree. NIH
19:11 He **h** also kindled his wrath against me, NIH
19:13 He **h** put my brethren far from me, NIH
19:21 for the hand of God **h** touched me. NIH
20:15 He **h** swallowed down riches, and he shall NIH
20:19 Because he **h** oppressed *and hath* forsaken NIH
20:19 hath oppressed *and* **h** forsaken the poor; NIH
20:19 he **h** violently taken away a house which NIH
21:21 For what pleasure **h** he in his house after NIH
21:31 and who shall repay him *what* he **h** done? NIH
23:10 *when* he **h** tried me, I shall come forth as NIH
23:11 My foot **h** held his steps, his way have I NIH
23:17 *neither* **h** he covered the darkness from NIH
26: 2 savest thou the arm *that* **h** no strength? NIH
26: 3 How hast thou counselled *him that* **h** no NIH
26: 6 him, and destruction **h** no covering. NIH
26:10 He **h** compassed the waters with bounds, NIH
26:13 By his spirit he **h** garnished the heavens; NIH
26:13 his hand **h** formed the crooked serpent. NIH
27: 2 *who* **h** taken away my judgment; NIH
27: 2 and the Almighty, *who* **h** vexed my soul; NIH
27: 8 though he **h** gained, when God taketh NIH
28: 6 place of sapphires: and it **h** dust of gold. 3807.1
28: 7 and which the vulture's eye **h** not seen: NIH
30:11 Because he **h** loosed my cord, NIH
30:19 He **h** cast me into the mire, and I am NIH
31: 5 vanity, or *if* my foot **h** hasted to deceit; NIH
31: 7 If my step **h** turned out of the way, NIH
31: 7 and *if any* blot **h** cleaved to my hands; NIH
31:17 and the fatherless **h** not eaten thereof; NIH
31:27 my heart **h** been secretly enticed, NIH
31:27 or my mouth **h** kissed my hand: NIH
32:14 Now he **h** not directed *his* words against NIH
32:19 my belly *is* as wine *which* **h** no vent; NIH
33: 2 my tongue **h** spoken in my mouth. NIH
33: 4 The Spirit of God **h** made me, NIH
33: 4 the breath of the Almighty **h** given me life. NIH
34: 5 For Job **h** said, I am righteous: NIH
34: 5 and God **h** taken away my judgment. NIH
34: 9 he **h** said, It profiteth a man nothing that NIH
34:13 Who **h** given him a charge over the earth? NIH
34:13 or who **h** disposed the whole world? NIH
34:35 Job **h** spoken without knowledge, NIH
35:15 *it is* not *so*, he **h** visited in his anger; NIH
36:23 Who **h** enjoined him his way? or who can NIH
38: 5 Who **h** laid the measures thereof, if thou NIH
38: 5 or who **h** stretched the line upon it? NIH
38:25 Who **h** divided a watercourse for NIH
38:28 **H** the rain a father? or who hath 3426+3807.1
38:28 or who **h** begotten the drops of dew? NIH
38:29 hoary frost of heaven, who **h** gendered it? NIH
38:36 Who **h** put wisdom in the inward parts? NIH
38:36 who **h** given understanding to the heart? NIH
39: 5 Who **h** sent out the wild ass free? NIH
39: 5 who **h** loosed the bands of the wild ass? NIH
39:17 Because God **h** deprived her of wisdom, NIH
39:17 **h** he imparted to her understanding. NIH
41:11 Who **h** prevented me, that I should repay NIH
42: 7 *thing that is* right, as my servant Job **h**. NIH
Ps 2: 7 the LORD **h** said unto me, Thou *art* my NIH
4: 3 know that the LORD **h** set apart *him that is* NIH
5: 4 For thou *art* not a God that **h** pleasure in NIH
6: 8 for the LORD **h** heard the voice of my NIH
6: 9 The LORD **h** heard my supplication; NIH
7:12 he **h** bent his bow, and made it ready. NIH
7:13 **h** also prepared for him the instruments NIH
7:14 conceived mischief, and brought forth NIH
9: 7 he **h** prepared his throne for judgment. NIH
10: 6 He **h** said in his heart, I shall not be NIH
10:11 He **h** said in his heart, God hath forgotten: NIH
10:11 He hath said in his heart, God **h** forgotten: NIH
10:13 he **h** said in his heart, Thou wilt not NIH
13: 6 because he **h** dealt bountifully with me. NIH
14: 1 The fool **h** said in his heart, *There* is no NIH
16: 7 bless the LORD, who **h** given me counsel: NIH
18:20 to the cleanness of my hands **h** he NIH
18:24 Therefore **h** the LORD recompensed me NIH
18:35 thy right hand **h** holden me up, NIH
18:35 and thy gentleness **h** made me great. NIH
19: 4 In them **h** he set a tabernacle for the sun, NIH
22:24 For he **h** not despised nor abhorred NIH
22:24 neither **h** he hid his face from him; NIH
22:31 that *shall be* born, that he **h** done *this*. NIH
24: 2 For he **h** founded it upon the seas, NIH
24: 4 He that **h** clean hands, and a pure heart; NIH
24: 4 who **h** not lift up his soul unto vanity, NIH
28: 6 he **h** heard the voice of my supplications. NIH
31:21 he **h** shewed me his marvellous kindness NIH
33:12 the people *whom* he **h** chosen for his own NIH
35: 8 and let his net that he **h** hid catch himself: NIH
35:21 *and* said, Aha, aha, our eye **h** seen *it*. NIH
35:27 which **h** pleasure in the prosperity of his NIH
36: 3 he **h** left off to be wise, *and* to do good. NIH
37:16 A little that a righteous *man* **h** is better NIH

Ps 40: 3 he **h** put a new song in my mouth, NIH
41: 9 *of* my bread, **h** lift up *his* heel against me. NIH
44:15 and the shame of my face **h** covered me, NIH
45: 2 therefore God **h** blessed thee for ever. NIH
45: 7 **h** anointed thee *with* the oil of gladness NIH
46: 8 what desolations he **h** made in the earth. NIH
50: 1 **h** spoken, and called the earth from NIH
50: 2 the perfection of beauty, God **h** shined. NIH
53: 1 The fool **h** said in his heart, *There* is no NIH
53: 5 for God **h** scattered the bones of him that NIH
53: 5 to shame, because God **h** despised them. NIH
54: 7 For he **h** delivered me out of all trouble: NIH
54: 7 mine eye **h** seen *his desire* upon mine NIH
55: 5 upon me, and horror **h** overwhelmed me. NIH
55:18 He **h** delivered my soul in peace from NIH
55:20 He **h** put forth his hands against such as be NIH
55:20 peace with him: he **h** broken his covenant. NIH
60: 6 God **h** spoken in his holiness; I will NIH
62:11 God **h** spoken once; twice have I heard NIH
66:14 mouth **h** spoken, when I was in trouble. NIH
66:16 I will declare what he **h** done for my soul. NIH
66:19 *But* verily God **h** heard *me;* he hath NIH
66:19 *But* verily God hath heard *me;* he **h** NIH
66:20 which **h** not turned away my prayer, NIH
68:10 Thy congregation **h** dwelt therein: thou, NIH
68:28 Thy God **h** commanded thy strength: NIH
69: 7 borne reproach; shame **h** covered my face. NIH
69: 9 For the zeal of thine house **h** eaten me up; NIH
69:20 Reproach **h** broken my heart; and I am NIH
69:31 an ox *or* bullock that **h** horns and hoofs. NIH
71:11 Saying, God **h** forsaken him: persecute NIH
72:12 the poor also, and *him* that **h** no helper. 3807.1
74: 3 *even* all *that* the enemy **h** done wickedly NIH
74:18 *that* the enemy **h** reproached, O LORD, NIH
77: 9 **H** God forgotten to be gracious? hath he in NIH
77: 9 **h** he in anger shut up his tender mercies? NIH
78: 4 and his wonderful works that he **h** done. NIH
78:69 the earth which he **h** established for ever. NIH
80:15 vineyard which thy right hand **h** planted, NIH
84: 3 the sparrow **h** found a house, NIH
88: 4 the pit: I am as a man *that* **h** no strength: NIH
91:14 Because he **h** set his love upon me, NIH
91:14 on high, because he **h** known my name. NIH
93: 1 wherewith he **h** girded himself: NIH
98: 1 for he **h** done marvellous *things*: his right NIH
98: 1 his holy arm, **h** gotten him the victory. NIH
98: 2 The LORD **h** made known his salvation: NIH
98: 2 his righteousness **h** he openly shewed in NIH
98: 3 He **h** remembered his mercy and his truth NIH
100: 3 *it is* he *that* **h** made us, and not we NIH
101: 5 him that **h** a high look and a proud heart NIH
102:19 For he **h** looked down from the height of NIH
103:10 He **h** not dealt with us after our sins. NIH
103:12 far he **h** removed our transgressions from NIH
103:19 The LORD **h** prepared his throne in NIH
104:16 cedars of Lebanon, which he **h** planted; NIH
105: 5 Remember his marvellous works that he **h** NIH
105: 8 He **h** remembered his covenant for ever, NIH
107: 2 whom he **h** redeemed from the hand of NIH
107:16 For he **h** broken the gates of brass, NIH
108: 7 God **h** spoken in his holiness; I will rejoice, NIH
109:11 Let the extortioner catch all that he **h**; 3807.1
110: 4 The LORD **h** sworn, and will not repent, NIH
111: 4 He **h** made his wonderful works to be NIH
111: 5 He **h** given meat unto them that fear him: NIH
111: 6 He **h** shewed his people the power of his NIH
111: 9 He **h** commanded his covenant for ever: NIH
112: 9 He **h** dispersed, he hath given to the poor; NIH
112: 9 He hath dispersed, he **h** given to the poor; NIH
115: 3 he **h** done whatsoever he pleased. NIH
115:12 The LORD **h** been mindful of us: he will NIH
115:16 earth **h** he given to the children of men. NIH
116: 1 because he **h** heard my voice *and* NIH
116: 2 Because he **h** inclined his ear unto me, NIH
116: 7 for the LORD **h** dealt bountifully with NIH
118:18 The LORD **h** chastened me sore: NIH
118:18 but he **h** not given me over unto death. NIH
118:24 This *is* the day *which* the LORD **h** made; NIH
118:27 *is* the LORD, which **h** shewed us light: NIH
119:20 My soul breaketh for the longing *that it* **h** NIH
119:50 affliction: for thy word **h** quickened me. NIH
119:53 Horror **h** taken hold upon me because of NIH
119:139 My zeal **h** consumed me, because NIH
119:167 My soul **h** kept thy testimonies; and *I* love NIH
120: 6 My soul **h** long dwelt with him that hateth NIH
124: 6 **h** not given us *as* a prey to their teeth. NIH
126: 2 LORD **h** done great things for them. 3807.1
126: 3 The LORD **h** done great things for us; 3807.1
127: 5 Happy *is* the man that **h** his quiver full of NIH
129: 4 he **h** cut asunder the cords of the wicked. NIH
132:11 The LORD **h** sworn *in* truth unto David; NIH
132:13 For the LORD **h** chosen Zion; he hath NIH
132:13 he **h** desired *it* for his habitation. NIH
135: 4 For the LORD **h** chosen Jacob unto NIH
136:24 redeemed us from our enemies: for his NIH
138: 6 *be* high, yet he **h** **respect** unto the lowly: 7200
143: 3 For the enemy **h** persecuted my soul; NIH
143: 3 he **h** smitten my life down to the ground; NIH
143: 3 he **h** made me to dwell in darkness, as NIH
146: 5 Happy *is he* that **h** the God of Jacob for NIH
147:13 he **h** strengthened the bars of thy gates; NIH
147:13 he **h** blessed thy children within thee. NIH
147:20 He **h** not dealt so with any nation: and *as* NIH
148: 6 He **h** also stablished them for ever and NIH
148: 6 he **h** made a decree which shall not pass. NIH

Ps 150: 6 Let every *thing* that **h** breath praise NIH
Pr 3:19 The LORD by wisdom **h** founded NIH
3:19 by understanding **h** he established NIH
7:20 He **h** taken a bag of money with him, NIH
7:26 For she **h** cast down many wounded: yea, NIH
9: 1 Wisdom **h** builded her house, she hath NIH
9: 1 house, she **h** hewn out her seven pillars: NIH
9: 2 She **h** killed her beasts; she hath mingled NIH
9: 2 killed her beasts; she **h** mingled her wine; NIH
9: 2 her wine; she **h** also furnished her table. NIH
9: 3 She **h** sent forth her maidens: she crieth NIH
10:13 In the lips of him that **h understanding**: 995
10:23 but a man of understanding **h** wisdom. NIH
12: 9 *that is* despised, and **h** a servant, *is* better NIH
13: 4 of the sluggard desireth, and **h** nothing: NIH
13: 7 is that maketh himself rich, yet **h** nothing: NIH
13: 7 maketh himself poor, yet **h** great riches. NIH
14:20 neighbour: but the rich **h** many friends. NIH
14:21 he that **h mercy** on the poor, happy *is* he. 2603
14:31 that honoureth him **h mercy** on the poor. 2603
14:32 but the righteous **h** hope in his death. NIH
14:33 in the heart of him that **h understanding**: 995
15:14 The heart of him that **h understanding** 995
15:15 *he that is* of a merry heart **h** a continual NIH
15:23 man **h** joy by the answer of his mouth: 3807.1
16: 4 The LORD **h** made all *things* for himself: NIH
16:22 *is* a wellspring of life unto **him that h** it: 1167
17: 8 stone in the eyes of **him that h** it: 1167
17:16 to get wisdom, seeing *he* **h** no heart *to it?* NIH
17:20 He that **h** a froward heart findeth no good: NIH
17:20 he that **h** a perverse tongue falleth into NIH
17:21 and the father of a fool **h** no **joy**. 8055
17:24 *is* before him that **h understanding**: 995
17:27 He that **h knowledge** spareth his 1847+3045
18: 2 A fool **h** no delight in understanding, NIH
18:24 A man that **h** friends must shew himself NIH
19:17 He that **h pity** upon the poor lendeth 2603
19:17 that which he **h** given will he pay him NIH
19:23 *that* **h** *it* shall abide satisfied; he shall not NIH
19:25 reprove one that **h understanding**, 995
20:12 the LORD **h** made even both of them. NIH
22: 9 He that **h** a bountiful eye shall be blessed; NIH
23: 6 Eat thou not the bread of *him that* **h** an NIH
23:29 Who **h** woe? who hath sorrow? NIH
23:29 who **h** sorrow? who hath contentions? 3807.1
23:29 who **h** contentions? who hath babbling? 3807.1
23:29 who **h** babbling? who hath wounds 3807.1
23:29 who **h** wounds without cause? who 3807.1
23:29 without cause? who **h** redness of eyes? 3807.1
24:29 I will do so to him as he **h** done to me: NIH
25: 8 when thy neighbour **h** put thee to shame. NIH
25:28 He that **h** no rule over his own spirit *is like* NIH
28:11 the poor that **h** understanding searcheth NIH
28:22 He that hasteth to be rich **h** an evil eye, NIH
30: 4 Who **h** ascended up *into* heaven, NIH
30: 4 who **h** gathered the wind in his fists? NIH
30: 4 who **h** bound the waters in a garment? NIH
30: 4 established all the ends of the earth? NIH
30:15 The horseleach **h** two daughters, 3807.1

Ecc 1: 3 What profit **h** a man of all his labour which NIH
1: 9 The thing that **h** been, *it is* that which shall NIH
1:10 it **h** been already of old time, which was NIH
1:13 this sore travail **h** God given to the sons of NIH
2:12 *even* that which **h** been already done. NIH
2:21 yet to a man that **h** not laboured therein NIH
2:22 For what **h** man of all his labour, 1933+3807.1
2:22 wherein he **h** laboured under the sun? NIH
3: 9 What profit **h** he that worketh in *that* NIH
3:10 God **h** given to the sons of men to be NIH
3:11 **h** made every *thing* beautiful in his time: NIH
3:11 he **h** set the world in their heart, so that NIH
3:15 That which **h** been, *is* now; and *that* NIH
3:15 which *is* to be **h** already been; and God NIH
3:19 that a man **h** no **preeminence** above a 4195
4: 3 *he* than both they, which **h** not yet been, NIH
4: 3 who **h** not seen the evil work that is done NIH
4: 8 yea, he **h** neither child nor brother: 3807.1
4:10 for *he* **h** not another to help him up. NIH
5: 4 not to pay it; for *he* **h** no pleasure in fools: NIH
5:16 what profit **h** he that hath laboured for 3807.1
5:16 what profit hath he that **h** laboured for NIH
5:17 *he* **h** much sorrow and wrath with his NIH
5:19 Every man also to whom God **h** given NIH
5:19 **h** given him power to eat thereof, NIH
6: 2 A man to whom God **h** given riches, NIH
6: 5 he **h** not seen the sun, nor known NIH
6: 5 nor known *any thing*: this **h** more rest 3807.1
6: 6 years twice *told*, yet **h** he seen no good: NIH
6: 8 For what **h** the wise more than the fool? 3807.1
6: 8 what **h** the poor, that knoweth to walk 3807.1
6:10 That which **h** been is named already, NIH
7:13 *that* straight, which he **h** made crooked? NIH
7:14 God also **h** set the one over against NIH
7:29 I found, that God **h** made man upright; NIH
8: 8 *is* no man that **h** power over the spirit NIH
8: 8 neither *h* *he* power in the day of death: NIH
8:15 a man **h** no better *thing* under the sun, NIH
9: 9 which he **h** given thee under the sun, NIH
10:20 **that which h** wings shall tell the matter. 1167

SS 1: 4 the king **h** brought me *into* his chambers: NIH
1: 6 because the sun **h** looked upon me: NIH
3: 8 every man **h** his sword upon his thigh NIH
8: 6 of fire, *which* **h** a most vehement flame. NIH
8: 8 have a little sister, and she **h** no breasts: 3807.1

Isa 1: 2 for the LORD **h** spoken, I have nourished

Isa	1:12 who **h** required this at your hand, to tread	NIH
	1:20 for the mouth of the LORD **h** spoken *it*.	NIH
	1:30 fadeth, and as a garden that **h** no water.	NIH
	5: 1 My wellbeloved **h** a vineyard in a	1961+3807.1
	5:14 Therefore hell **h** enlarged herself,	NIH
	5:25 he **h** stretched forth his hand against them,	NIH
	5:25 hand against them, and **h** smitten them:	NIH
	6: 7 and said, Lo, this **h** touched thy lips;	NIH
	8:18 the children whom the LORD **h** given me	NIH
	9: 2 of death, upon them **h** the light shined.	NIH
	9: 8 into Jacob, and it **h** lighted upon Israel.	NIH
	10:10 As my hand **h** found the kingdoms of	NIH
	10:12 when the Lord **h** performed his whole	NIH
	10:14 my hand **h** found as a nest the riches of	NIH
	10:28 at Michmash he **h** laid up his carriages:	NIH
	12: 5 the LORD; for he **h** done excellent things:	NIH
	14: 4 and say, How **h** the oppressor ceased!	NIH
	14: 5 The LORD **h** broken the staff of	NIH
	14: 9 it **h** raised up from their thrones all	NIH
	14:24 The LORD of hosts **h** sworn, saying,	NIH
	14:27 For the LORD of hosts **h** purposed,	NIH
	14:32 That the LORD **h** founded Zion,	NIH
	16:13 This *is* the word that the LORD **h** spoken	NIH
	16:14 now the LORD **h** spoken, saying,	NIH
	19:12 let them know what the LORD of hosts **h**	NIH
	19:14 The LORD **h** mingled a perverse spirit in	NIH
	19:17 hosts, which he **h** determined against it.	NIH
	20: 3 Like as my servant Isaiah **h** walked naked	NIH
	21: 4 the night of my pleasure **h** he turned into	NIH
	21: 6 For thus **h** the Lord said unto me, Go, set	NIH
	21: 9 all the graven images of her gods he **h**	NIH
	21:16 For thus **h** the Lord said unto me, Within	NIH
	21:17 for the LORD God of Israel **h** spoken *it*.	NIH
	22:25 shall be cut off: for the LORD **h** spoken *it*.	NIH
	23: 4 for the sea **h** spoken, *even* the strength of	NIH
	23: 8 Who **h** taken this counsel against Tyre,	NIH
	23: 9 The LORD of hosts **h** purposed it, to stain	NIH
	23:11 the LORD **h** given a commandment	NIH
	24: 3 for the LORD **h** spoken this word.	NIH
	24: 6 Therefore the curse devoured the earth,	NIH
	25: 8 all the earth: for the LORD **h** spoken *it*.	NIH
	27: 7 **H** he smitten him, as he smote those that	NIH
	28: 2 The LORD **h** a mighty and strong one,	3807.1
	28:25 When he **h** made plain the face thereof,	NIH
	29: 4 as of one that **h** a familiar spirit, out of	NIH
	29: 8 behold, *he is* faint, and his soul **h** appetite:	NIH
	29:10 For the LORD **h** poured out upon you	NIH
	29:10 of deep sleep, and **h** closed your eyes:	NIH
	29:10 and your rulers, the seers he **h** covered.	NIH
	30:24 which **h** been winnowed with the shovel	NIH
	30:33 is prepared; he **h** made *it* deep *and* large:	NIH
	31: 4 For thus **h** the LORD spoken unto me,	NIH
	33: 5 he **h** filled Zion *with* judgment and	NIH
	33: 8 he **h** broken the covenant, he hath	NIH
	33: 8 he **h** despised the cities, he regardeth no	NIH
	33:14 fearfulness **h** surprised the hypocrites.	NIH
	34: 2 he **h** utterly destroyed them, he hath	NIH
	34: 2 he **h** delivered them to the slaughter.	NIH
	34: 6 for the LORD **h** a sacrifice in Bozrah,	3807.1
	34:16 for my mouth it **h** commanded,	NIH
	34:16 and his spirit it **h** gathered them.	NIH
	34:17 he **h** cast the lot for them, and his hand	NIH
	34:17 his hand **h** divided it unto them by line:	NIH
	36: 7 and whose altars Hezekiah **h** taken away,	NIH
	36:12 **H** my master sent me to thy master and	NIH
	36:12 *h he* not *sent me* to the men that sit upon	NIH
	36:18 **H** any of the gods of the nations delivered	NIH
	37: 4 the king of Assyria his master **h** sent	NIH
	37: 4 words which the LORD thy God **h** heard:	NIH
	37:17 which **h** sent to reproach the living God.	NIH
	37:22 This *is* the word which the LORD **h**	NIH
	37:22 **h** despised thee, *and* laughed thee to	NIH
	37:22 daughter of Jerusalem **h** shaken her head	NIH
	38: 7 that the LORD will do this thing that he **h**	NIH
	38:15 he **h** both spoken unto me, and himself	NIH
	38:15 himself **h** done *it*: I shall go softly all my	NIH
	40: 2 for she **h** received of the LORD'S hand	NIH
	40: 5 for the mouth of the LORD **h** spoken *it*.	NIH
	40:12 Who **h** measured the waters in the hollow	NIH
	40:13 Who **h** directed the spirit of the LORD,	NIH
	40:13 or *being* his counseller **h** taught him?	NIH
	40:20 that he **h** no oblation chooseth	NIH
	40:21 **h** it not been told you from the beginning?	NIH
	40:26 behold who **h** created these *things*, that	NIH
	41: 4 Who **h** wrought and done *it*, calling	NIH
	41:20 that the hand of the LORD **h** done this,	NIH
	41:20 and the Holy One of Israel **h** created it.	NIH
	41:26 Who **h** declared from the beginning, that	NIH
	42:25 Therefore he **h** poured upon him the fury	NIH
	42:25 it **h** set him on fire round about, yet he	NIH
	43:27 Thy first father **h** sinned, and thy teachers	NIH
	44:10 Who **h** formed a god, or molten a graven	NIH
	44:18 for he **h** shut their eyes, that *they* cannot	NIH
	44:20 a deceived heart **h** turned him aside, that	NIH
	44:23 for the LORD **h** done *it*: shout, ye lower	NIH
	44:23 for the LORD **h** redeemed Jacob,	NIH
	45: 9 thy work, He **h** no hands?	3807.1
	45:18 **h** established it, he created it not in vain,	NIH
	45:21 who **h** declared this from ancient time?	NIH
	45:21 *who* **h** told it from that time? *have* not I	NIH
	47:10 and thy knowledge, it **h** perverted thee;	NIH
	48: 5 Mine idol **h** done them, and my graven	NIH
	48: 5 my molten image, **h** commanded them.	NIH
	48:13 Mine hand also **h** laid the foundation of	NIH
	48:13 and my right hand **h** spanned the heavens:	NIH

Isa	48:14 among them **h** declared these *things*?	NIH
	48:14 these *things*? The LORD **h** loved him:	NIH
	48:16 the Lord GOD, and his Spirit, **h** sent me.	NIH
	48:20 The LORD **h** redeemed his servant Jacob.	NIH
	49: 1 The LORD **h** called me from the womb;	NIH
	49: 1 from the bowels of my mother he **h** made	NIH
	49: 2 he **h** made my mouth like a sharp sword;	NIH
	49: 2 in the shadow of his hand **h** he hid me,	NIH
	49: 2 a polished shaft; in his quiver **h** he hid me;	NIH
	49:10 for he that **h** mercy on them shall lead	7355
	49:13 for the LORD **h** comforted his people,	NIH
	49:14 The LORD **h** forsaken me, and my Lord	NIH
	49:14 forsaken me, and my Lord **h** forgotten me.	NIH
	49:21 Who **h** begotten me these, seeing I have	NIH
	49:21 who **h** brought up these? Behold, I was	NIH
	50: 4 The Lord GOD **h** given me the tongue of	NIH
	50: 5 The Lord GOD **h** opened mine ear,	NIH
	50:10 that walketh *in* darkness, and **h** no light?	NIH
	51: 9 *Art* thou not it that **h** cut Rahab,	NIH
	51:10 *Art* thou not it which **h** dried the sea,	NIH
	51:10 that **h** made the depths of the sea a way	NIH
	51:13 that **h** stretched forth the heavens,	NIH
	51:18 all the sons *whom* she **h** brought forth;	NIH
	51:18 hand of all the sons *that* she **h** brought up.	NIH
	52: 9 for the LORD **h** comforted his people,	NIH
	52: 9 his people, he **h** redeemed Jerusalem.	NIH
	52:10 The LORD **h** made bare his holy arm in	NIH
	53: 1 Who **h** believed our report? and to whom	NIH
	53: 2 he **h** no form nor comeliness; and when	NIH
	53: 4 Surely he **h** borne our griefs, and carried	NIH
	53: 6 the LORD **h** laid on him the iniquity of us	NIH
	53:10 to bruise him; he **h** put *him* to grief:	NIH
	53:12 because he **h** poured out his soul unto	NIH
	54: 6 For the LORD **h** called thee as a woman	NIH
	54:10 saith the LORD that **h** mercy on thee.	7355
	55: 1 ye to the waters, and he that **h** no money;	NIH
	55: 5 Holy One of Israel; for he **h** glorified thee.	NIH
	56: 3 that **h** joined himself to the LORD, speak,	NIH
	56: 3 The LORD **h** utterly separated me from his	NIH
	58:14 for the mouth of the LORD **h** spoken *it*.	NIH
	59: 3 your tongue **h** muttered perverseness.	NIH
	60: 9 One of Israel, because he **h** glorified thee.	NIH
	61: 1 the LORD **h** anointed me to preach good	NIH
	61: 1 **h** sent me to bind up the broken-hearted,	NIH
	61: 9 that they *are* the seed *which* the LORD **h**	NIH
	61:10 for he **h** clothed me with the garments of	NIH
	61:10 he **h** covered me with the robe of	NIH
	62: 8 The LORD **h** sworn by his right hand,	NIH
	62:11 the LORD **h** proclaimed unto the end of	NIH
	63: 7 according to all that the LORD **h** bestowed	NIH
	63: 7 which he **h** bestowed on them according	NIH
	64: 4 neither **h** the eye seen, O God, besides	NIH
	64: 4 *what* he **h** prepared for him that waiteth	NIH
	65:20 nor an old man that **h** not filled his days:	NIH
	66: 2 For all those *things* **h** mine hand made,	NIH
	66: 8 Who **h** heard such *a thing*? who hath seen	NIH
	66: 8 Who hath heard such *a thing*? who **h** seen	NIH
Jer	2:11 **H** a nation changed *their* gods, which *are*	NIH
	2:30 own sword **h** devoured your prophets,	NIH
	2:37 for the LORD **h** rejected thy confidences,	NIH
	3: 3 and there **h** been no latter rain;	NIH
	3: 6 seen *that* which backsliding Israel **h** done?	NIH
	3: 6 green tree, and there **h** played the harlot.	NIH
	3:10 for all this her treacherous sister Judah **h**	NIH
	3:11 The backsliding Israel **h** justified herself	NIH
	3:24 For shame **h** devoured the labour of our	NIH
	4:17 because she **h** been rebellious against me,	NIH
	4:27 For thus **h** the LORD said, The whole land	NIH
	5:23 this people **h** a revolting and	1961+3807.1
	6: 6 For thus **h** the LORD of hosts said,	NIH
	6:24 anguish **h** taken hold of us, *and* pain, as	NIH
	6:30 because the LORD **h** rejected them.	NIH
	7:29 for the LORD **h** rejected and forsaken	NIH
	8:14 for the LORD our God **h** put us to silence,	NIH
	8:21 black; astonishment **h** taken hold on me.	NIH
	9:12 whom the mouth of the LORD **h** spoken,	NIH
	10:12 He **h** made the earth by his power, he hath	NIH
	10:12 he **h** established the world by his wisdom,	NIH
	10:12 he **h** stretched out the heavens by his	NIH
	11:15 What **h** my beloved **to do** in mine	3807.1
	11:15 she **h** wrought lewdness *with* many,	NIH
	11:16 the noise of a great tumult he **h** kindled	NIH
	11:17 **h** pronounced evil against thee,	NIH
	11:18 the LORD **h** given me knowledge *of it*,	NIH
	13:15 be not proud: for the LORD **h** spoken.	NIH
	14:19 **h** thy soul lothed Zion? why hast thou	NIH
	15: 9 She that **h** borne seven languisheth:	NIH
	15: 9 she **h** given up the ghost; her sun is gone	NIH
	15: 9 she **h** been ashamed and confounded:	NIH
	16:10 Wherefore **h** the LORD pronounced all	NIH
	18:13 who **h** heard such *things*: the virgin of	NIH
	18:13 virgin of Israel **h** done a very horrible	NIH
	18:15 Because my people **h** forgotten me,	NIH
	20: 3 The LORD **h** not called thy name Pashur,	NIH
	20:13 he **h** delivered the soul of the poor from	NIH
	22: 8 Wherefore **h** the LORD done thus unto	NIH
	22:21 This *h been* thy manner from thy youth,	NIH
	23: 9 like a man whom wine **h** overcome,	NIH
	23:17 The LORD **h** said, Ye shall have peace;	NIH
	23:18 For who **h** stood in the counsel of	NIH
	23:18 and **h** perceived and heard his word?	NIH
	23:18 who **h** marked his word, and heard *it*?	NIH
	23:28 The prophet that **h** a dream, let him tell a	854
	23:28 he that **h** my word, let him speak my	854
	23:35 his brother, What **h** the LORD answered?	NIH

Jer	23:35 and, What **h** the LORD spoken?	NIH
	23:37 What **h** the LORD answered thee?	NIH
	23:37 and, What **h** the LORD spoken?	NIH
	25: 3 the word of the LORD **h** come unto me,	NIH
	25: 4 the LORD **h** sent unto you all his servants	NIH
	25:13 which Jeremiah **h** prophesied against all	NIH
	25:31 for the LORD **h** a controversy with	NIH
	25:36 *shall be heard*: for the LORD **h** spoiled	NIH
	25:38 He **h** forsaken his covert, as the lion:	NIH
	26:11 for he **h** prophesied against this city, as ye	NIH
	26:13 the evil that he **h** pronounced against you.	NIH
	26:15 for of a truth the LORD **h** sent me unto	NIH
	26:16 for he **h** spoken to us in the name of	NIH
	27:13 as the LORD **h** spoken against the nation	NIH
	28: 9 be known, that the LORD **h** truly sent him.	NIH
	28:15 The LORD **h** not sent thee;	NIH
	29:15 The LORD **h** raised us up prophets in	NIH
	29:26 The LORD **h** made thee priest in the stead	NIH
	29:31 Because that Shemaiah **h** prophesied unto	NIH
	29:32 he **h** taught rebellion against the LORD.	NIH
	31: 3 The LORD **h** appeared of old unto me,	NIH
	31:11 For the LORD **h** redeemed Jacob,	NIH
	31:22 for the LORD **h** created a new *thing* in	NIH
	32:31 this city **h** been to me *as* a provocation	NIH
	33:24 The two families which the LORD **h**	NIH
	33:24 hath chosen, he **h** even cast them off?	NIH
	34:14 a Hebrew, which **h** been sold unto thee;	NIH
	34:14 when he **h** served thee six years, thou	NIH
	35: 8 our father in all that he **h** charged us,	NIH
	35:16 but this people **h** not hearkened unto me:	NIH
	35:18 done according unto all that he **h**	NIH
	36: 7 the fury that the LORD **h** pronounced	NIH
	36:28 Jehoiakim the king of Judah **h** burnt.	NIH
	38:21 this *is* the word that the LORD **h** shewed	NIH
	40: 2 The LORD thy God **h** pronounced this evil	NIH
	40: 3 Now the LORD **h** brought *it*, and	NIH
	40: 3 and done according as he **h** said:	NIH
	40: 5 the king of Babylon **h** made governor	NIH
	40:14 hath sent Ishmael the son of Nethaniah to	NIH
	42:18 my fury **h** been poured forth upon	NIH
	42:19 The LORD **h** said concerning you, O ye	NIH
	42:21 nor any *thing* for the which he **h** sent me	NIH
	43: 2 The LORD our God **h** not sent thee to say,	NIH
	45: 3 for the LORD **h** added grief to my sorrow;	NIH
	46:10 for the Lord GOD of hosts **h** a sacrifice in	NIH
	46:12 thy shame, and thy cry **h** filled the land:	NIH
	46:12 for the mighty *man* **h** stumbled against	NIH
	46:17 a noise; he **h** passed the time appointed.	NIH
	47: 7 seeing the LORD **h** given it a charge	NIH
	47: 7 the sea shore? there **h** he appointed it.	NIH
	48: 8 shall be destroyed, as the LORD **h** spoken.	NIH
	48:11 Moab **h** been at ease from his youth,	NIH
	48:11 **h** settled on his lees, and hath not been	NIH
	48:11 **h** not been emptied from vessel to vessel,	NIH
	48:11 to vessel, neither **h** he gone into captivity:	NIH
	48:36 the riches *that* he **h** gotten are perished.	NIH
	48:39 how **h** Moab turned the back with shame!	NIH
	48:42 he **h** magnified *himself* against the LORD.	NIH
	49: 1 thus saith the LORD, **H** Israel no sons?	3807.1
	49: 1 **H** he no heir? why *then* doth their king	3807.1
	49:16 Thy terribleness **h** deceived thee,	NIH
	49:20 the LORD, that he **h** taken against Edom;	NIH
	49:20 he **h** purposed against the inhabitants of	NIH
	49:24 fear **h** seized on *her*: anguish and	NIH
	49:30 for Nebuchadrezzar king of Babylon **h**	NIH
	49:30 and **h** conceived a purpose against you.	NIH
	50: 6 My people **h** been lost sheep:	NIH
	50:14 for she **h** sinned against the LORD.	NIH
	50:15 she **h** given her hand: her foundations are	NIH
	50:15 upon her; as she **h** done, do unto her.	NIH
	50:17 first the king of Assyria **h** devoured him;	NIH
	50:17 this Nebuchadrezzar king of Babylon **h**	NIH
	50:25 The LORD **h** opened his armoury,	NIH
	50:25 **h** brought forth the weapons of his	NIH
	50:29 according to all that she **h** done, do unto	NIH
	50:29 for she **h** been proud against the LORD,	NIH
	50:43 The king of Babylon **h** heard the report of	NIH
	50:45 that he **h** taken against Babylon;	NIH
	50:45 and that he **h** purposed against the land of	NIH
	51: 5 For Israel *h* not *been* forsaken, nor Judah	NIH
	51: 7 Babylon *h been* a golden cup in	NIH
	51:10 The LORD **h** brought forth our	NIH
	51:11 the LORD **h** raised up the spirit of	NIH
	51:12 for the LORD **h** both devised and	NIH
	51:14 The LORD of hosts **h** sworn by himself,	NIH
	51:15 He **h** made the earth by his power, he	NIH
	51:15 he **h** established the world by his wisdom,	NIH
	51:15 **h** stretched out the heaven by his	NIH
	51:30 their might **h** failed; they became as	NIH
	51:34 Nebuchadrezzar the king of Babylon **h**	NIH
	51:34 he **h** crushed me, he hath made me an	NIH
	51:34 he **h** made me an empty vessel,	NIH
	51:34 he **h** swallowed me up like a dragon,	NIH
	51:34 he **h** filled his belly with my delicates,	NIH
	51:34 belly with my delicates, he **h** cast me out.	NIH
	51:44 his mouth that which he **h** swallowed up:	NIH
	51:49 As Babylon *h* caused the slain of Israel to	NIH
	51:51 shame **h** covered our faces: for strangers	NIH
	51:55 Because the LORD *h* spoiled Babylon,	NIH
La	1: 2 among all her lovers she **h** none to	3807.1
	1: 5 for the LORD **h** afflicted her for	NIH
	1: 8 Jerusalem **h** grievously sinned; therefore	NIH
	1: 9 for the enemy **h** magnified *himself*.	NIH
	1:10 The adversary **h** spread out his hand upon	NIH

H

La	1:10 for she **h** seen *that* the heathen entered into	NIH
	1:12 wherewith the Lord **h** afflicted *me* in	NIH
	1:13 From above **h** he sent fire into my bones,	NIH
	1:13 he **h** spread a net for my feet, he hath	NIH
	1:13 a net for my feet, he **h** turned me back;	NIH
	1:13 he **h** made me desolate *and* faint all the	NIH
	1:14 he **h** made my strength to fall, the Lord	NIH
	1:14 the Lord **h** delivered me into *their* hands,	NIH
	1:15 The Lord **h** trodden under foot all my	NIH
	1:15 he **h** called an assembly against me to	NIH
	1:15 the Lord **h** trodden the virgin,	NIH
	1:17 the Lord **h** commanded concerning	NIH
	2: 1 How **h** the Lord covered the daughter of	NIH
	2: 2 The Lord **h** swallowed up all the	NIH
	2: 2 the habitations of Jacob, and **h** not pitied:	NIH
	2: 2 he **h** thrown down in his wrath the strong	NIH
	2: 2 he **h** brought *them* down to the ground:	NIH
	2: 2 he **h** polluted the kingdom and the princes	NIH
	2: 3 He **h** cut off in *his* fierce anger all the horn	NIH
	2: 3 he **h** drawn back his right hand from	NIH
	2: 4 he **h** bent his bow like an enemy: he stood	NIH
	2: 5 he **h** swallowed up Israel, he hath	NIH
	2: 5 he **h** swallowed up all her palaces:	NIH
	2: 5 he **h** destroyed his strong holds,	NIH
	2: 5 **h** increased in the daughter of Judah	NIH
	2: 6 he **h** violently taken away his tabernacle,	NIH
	2: 6 he **h** destroyed his places of the assembly:	NIH
	2: 6 the Lord **h** caused the solemn feasts and	NIH
	2: 6 **h** despised in the indignation of his anger	NIH
	2: 7 The Lord **h** cast off his altar, he hath	NIH
	2: 7 off his altar, he **h** abhorred his sanctuary,	NIH
	2: 7 he **h** given up into the hand of the enemy	NIH
	2: 8 The Lord **h** purposed to destroy the wall	NIH
	2: 8 he **h** stretched out a line, he hath not	NIH
	2: 8 he **h** not withdrawn his hand from	NIH
	2: 9 he **h** destroyed and broken her bars:	NIH
	2:17 The Lord **h** done *that* which he had	NIH
	2:17 he **h** fulfilled his word that he had	NIH
	2:17 he **h** thrown down, and hath not pitied:	NIH
	2:17 he hath thrown down, and **h** not pitied:	NIH
	2:17 he **h** caused *thine* enemy to rejoice over	NIH
	2:17 he **h** set up the horn of thine adversaries,	NIH
	2:22 and brought up **h** mine enemy consumed.	NIH
	3: 1 I *am* the man that **h** seen affliction by	NIH
	3: 2 he **h** led me, and brought *me into*	NIH
	3: 4 My flesh and my skin **h** he made old;	NIH
	3: 4 hath he made old; he **h** broken my bones.	NIH
	3: 5 He **h** builded against me,	NIH
	3: 6 He **h** set me in dark places, as they that be	NIH
	3: 7 He **h** hedged me about, that I cannot get	NIH
	3: 7 get out: he **h** made my chain heavy.	NIH
	3: 9 He **h** inclosed my ways with hewn stone,	NIH
	3: 9 hewn stone, he **h** made my paths crooked.	NIH
	3:11 He **h** turned aside my ways, and pulled	NIH
	3:11 me in pieces: he **h** made me desolate.	NIH
	3:12 He **h** bent his bow, and set me as a mark	NIH
	3:13 He **h** caused the arrows of his quiver to	NIH
	3:15 He **h** filled me with bitterness, he hath	NIH
	3:15 he **h** made me drunken *with* wormwood.	NIH
	3:16 He **h** also broken my teeth with gravel	NIH
	3:16 stones, he **h** covered me with ashes.	NIH
	3:20 My soul **h** *them* still in remembrance,	NIH
	3:28 because he **h** borne *it* upon him.	NIH
	4:11 The Lord **h** accomplished his fury;	NIH
	4:11 he **h** poured out his fierce anger,	NIH
	4:11 **h** kindled a fire in Zion, and it hath	NIH
	4:11 it **h** devoured the foundations thereof.	NIH
	4:16 The anger of the Lord **h** divided them;	NIH
Eze	2: 3 a rebellious nation that **h** rebelled against	NIH
	2: 5 shall know that there **h** been a prophet	NIH
	3:20 righteousness which he **h** done shall not	NIH
	4:14 behold, my soul **h** not *been* polluted:	NIH
	5: 6 she **h** changed my judgments into	NIH
	6: 9 which **h** departed from me, and with their	NIH
	7:10 the rod **h** blossomed, pride hath budded.	NIH
	7:10 the rod hath blossomed, pride **h** budded.	NIH
	12: us not; the Lord **h** forsaken the earth.	NIH
	9: 9 The Lord **h** forsaken the earth,	NIH
	12: 9 Son of man, **h** not the house of Israel,	NIH
	13: 6 the Lord **h** not sent them: and they have	NIH
	14: 9 if the prophet be deceived when he **h**	NIH
	15: when the fire **h** devoured it, and it is	NIH
	16:48 Lord God, Sodom thy sister **h** not done,	NIH
	16:51 Neither **h** Samaria committed half of thy	NIH
	17:12 **h** taken the king thereof, and the princes	NIH
	17:13 **h** taken of the king's seed, and made a	NIH
	17:13 with him, and **h** taken an oath of him:	NIH
	17:13 he **h** also taken the mighty of the land:	NIH
	17:18 he **h** done all these *things*, he shall not	NIH
	17:19 surely mine oath that he **h** despised,	NIH
	17:19 and my covenant that he **h** broken,	NIH
	17:20 trespass that he **h** trespassed against me.	NIH
	18: 6 *And* **h** not eaten upon the mountains,	NIH
	18: 6 neither **h** lift up his eyes to the idols of	NIH
	18: 6 neither **h** defiled his neighbour's wife,	NIH
	18: 6 neither **h** come near to a menstruous	NIH
	18: 7 **h** not oppressed any, *but* hath restored *to*	NIH
	18: 7 *but* **h** restored to the debtor his pledge,	NIH
	18: 7 **h** spoiled none by violence, hath given his	NIH
	18: 7 **h** given his bread to the hungry,	NIH
	18: 7 and **h** covered the naked with a garment;	NIH
	18: 8 He *that* **h** not given forth upon usury,	NIH
	18: 8 upon usury, neither **h** taken any increase,	NIH
	18: 8 *that* **h** withdrawn his hand from iniquity,	NIH
	18: 8 **h** executed true judgment between man	NIH

Eze	18: 9 **H** walked in my statutes, and hath kept	NIH
	18: 9 and **h** kept my judgments, to deal truly;	NIH
	18:11 but even **h** eaten upon the mountains,	NIH
	18:12 **H** oppressed the poor and needy,	NIH
	18:12 the poor and needy, **h** spoiled by violence,	NIH
	18:12 **h** not restored the pledge, and hath lift up	NIH
	18:12 and **h** lift up his eyes to the idols,	NIH
	18:12 to the idols, **h** committed abomination,	NIH
	18:13 **H** given forth upon usury, and hath taken	NIH
	18:13 forth upon usury, and **h** taken increase:	NIH
	18:13 he **h** done all these abominations; he shall	NIH
	18:14 that seeth all his father's sins which he **h**	NIH
	18:15 *That* **h** not eaten upon the mountains,	NIH
	18:15 neither **h** lift up his eyes to the idols of	NIH
	18:15 Israel, **h** not defiled his neighbour's wife,	NIH
	18:16 Neither **h** oppressed any, hath not	NIH
	18:16 any, **h** not withholden the pledge,	NIH
	18:16 neither **h** spoiled by violence,	NIH
	18:16 *but* **h** given his bread to the hungry,	NIH
	18:16 and **h** covered the naked with a garment,	NIH
	18:17 *That* **h** taken off his hand from the poor,	NIH
	18:17 *that* **h** not received usury nor increase,	NIH
	18:17 **h** executed my judgments, hath walked in	NIH
	18:17 my judgments, **h** walked in my statutes;	NIH
	18:19 When the son **h** done that which is lawful	NIH
	18:19 *and* **h** kept all my statutes, and hath done	NIH
	18:19 and **h** done them, he shall surely live.	NIH
	18:21 turn from all his sins that he **h** committed,	NIH
	18:22 All his transgressions that he **h** committed,	NIH
	18:22 in his righteousness that he **h** done he	NIH
	18:24 All his righteousness that he **h** done shall	NIH
	18:24 in his trespass that he **h** trespassed,	NIH
	18:24 in his sin that he **h** sinned, in them shall	NIH
	18:26 for his iniquity that he **h** done shall he die.	NIH
	18:27 from his wickedness that he **h** committed,	NIH
	18:28 all his transgressions that he **h** committed,	NIH
	19:14 **h** devoured her fruit, so that she hath	NIH
	19:14 that she **h** no strong rod *to be* a 1961+871.1	
	21:11 he **h** given it to be furbished, that *it* may	NIH
	22:11 one **h** committed abomination with his	NIH
	22:11 another **h** lewdly defiled his daughter in	NIH
	22:11 another in thee **h** humbled his sister,	NIH
	22:13 at thy blood which **h** been in the midst of	NIH
	22:28 when the Lord **h** not spoken.	NIH
	24:12 She **h** wearied *herself with* lies,	NIH
	24:24 according to all that he **h** done shall ye do:	NIH
	25:12 Because that Edom **h** dealt against	NIH
	25:12 **h** greatly offended, and revenged himself	NIH
	26: 2 that Tyrus **h** said against Jerusalem,	NIH
	27:26 the east wind **h** broken thee in the midst	NIH
	29: 3 which he said, My river *is* mine own,	NIH
	29: 9 because he **h** said, The river *is* mine,	NIH
	31:10 he **h** shot up his top among the thick	NIH
	33:13 for his iniquity that he **h** committed, he	NIH
	33:16 None of his sins that he **h** committed shall	NIH
	33:16 he **h** done that which is lawful and right;	NIH
	33:32 lovely song *of* one that **h** a pleasant voice,	NIH
	33:33 shall they know that a prophet **h** been	NIH
	36: 2 Because the enemy **h** said against you,	NIH
	44: 2 **h** entered in by it, therefore it shall be	NIH
	44:25 or for sister that **h** had no husband,	NIH
Da	1:10 who **h** appointed your meat and your	NIH
	2:27 The secret which the king **h** demanded	NIH
	2:37 for the God of heaven **h** given thee a	NIH
	2:38 the fowls of the heaven **h** he given into	NIH
	2:38 and **h** made thee ruler over them all.	NIH
	2:45 the great God **h** made known to the king	NIH
	3: 5 that Nebuchadnezzar the king **h** set up:	NIH
	3:28 who **h** sent his angel, and delivered his	NIH
	4: 2 wonders that the high God **h** wrought	NIH
	5:26 God **h** numbered thy kingdom,	NIH
	6:22 My God **h** sent his angel, and hath shut	NIH
	6:22 **h** shut the lions' mouths, that they have	NIH
	6:27 who **h** delivered Daniel from the power of	NIH
	9:12 he **h** confirmed his words, which he spake	NIH
	9:12 under the whole heaven **h** not been done	NIH
	9:12 done as **h** been done upon Jerusalem.	NIH
	9:14 Therefore **h** the Lord watched upon	NIH
	11:12 when he **h** taken away the multitude,	NIH
Hos	1: 2 the land **h** committed great whoredom,	NIH
	2: 5 For their mother **h** played the harlot:	NIH
	2: 5 that conceived them **h** done shamefully:	NIH
	2:12 and her fig trees, whereof she **h** said,	NIH
	4: 1 for the Lord **h** a controversy with 3807.1	
	4:12 the spirit of whoredoms **h** caused *them*	NIH
	4:19 The wind **h** bound her up in her wings,	NIH
	5: 6 they shall not find *him;* he **h** withdrawn	NIH
	6: 1 for he **h** torn, and he will heal us; he hath	NIH
	6: 1 he **h** smitten, and he will bind us up.	NIH
	6:11 Also, O Judah, he **h** set a harvest for thee,	NIH
	7: 4 ceaseth from raising after he **h** kneaded	NIH
	7: 8 he **h** mixed himself among the people;	NIH
	7:12 as their congregation **h** heard.	NIH
	8: 3 Israel **h** cast off *the thing that is* good:	NIH
	8: 5 Thy calf, O Samaria, **h** cast *thee* off;	NIH
	8: 7 **h** no stalk: the bud shall yield no meal: 3807.1	
	8: 9 alone by himself: Ephraim **h** hired lovers.	NIH
	8:11 Because Ephraim **h** made many altars to	NIH
	8:14 For Israel **h** forgotten his Maker,	NIH
	8:14 and Judah **h** multiplied fenced cities:	NIH
	10: 1 to the multitude of his fruit he **h**	NIH
	12: 2 The Lord **h** also a controversy with 3807.1	
	12: 3 he **h** rebelled against her God:	NIH
Joel	1: 2 **H** this been in your days, or even in	NIH
	1: 4 That which the palmerworm **h** left hath	NIH

Joel	1: 4 That which the palmerworm **h** left **h**	NIH
	1: 4 that which the locust **h** left hath	NIH
	1: 4 that which the locust hath left **h**	NIH
	1: 4 that which the cankerworm **h** left hath	NIH
	1: 4 that which the cankerworm **h** left **h**	NIH
	1: 6 and he **h** the cheek-teeth of a great lion.	NIH
	1: 7 He **h** laid my vine waste, and barked my	NIH
	1: 7 he **h** made it clean bare, and cast *it* away;	NIH
	1:19 for the fire **h** devoured the pastures of	NIH
	1:19 the flame **h** burnt all the trees of the field.	NIH
	1:20 the fire **h** devoured the pastures of	NIH
	2: 2 there **h** not been ever the like, neither	NIH
	2:20 come up, because he **h** done great things.	NIH
	2:23 for he **h** given you the former rain	NIH
	2:25 to you the years that the locust **h** eaten,	NIH
	2:26 that he **h** dealt wondrously with you:	NIH
	2:32 as the Lord **h** said, and in the remnant	NIH
	3: 8 people far off: for the Lord **h** spoken *it.*	NIH
Am	3: 1 Hear this word that the Lord **h** spoken 3807.1	
	3: 4 roar in the forest, when he **h** no prey?	NIH
	3: 6 in a city, and the Lord **h** not done *it?*	NIH
	3: 8 The lion **h** roared, who will not fear?	NIH
	3: 8 the Lord God **h** spoken, who can but	NIH
	4: 2 The Lord God **h** sworn by his holiness,	NIH
	6: 8 The Lord God **h** sworn by himself, saith	NIH
	7: 1 Thus **h** the Lord God shewed unto me;	NIH
	7: 4 Thus **h** the Lord God shewed unto me:	NIH
	7:10 Amos **h** conspired against thee in the	NIH
	8: 1 Thus **h** the Lord God shewed unto me:	NIH
	8: 7 The Lord **h** sworn by the excellency of	NIH
	9: 6 and **h** founded his troop in the earth;	NIH
Ob	1: 3 The pride of thine heart **h** deceived thee,	NIH
	1:18 house of Esau; for the Lord **h** spoken *it.*	NIH
Jnh	1: 9 which **h** made the sea and the dry *land.*	NIH
Mic	2: 4 he **h** changed the portion of my people:	NIH
	2: 4 how **h** he removed *it* from me! turning	NIH
	2: 4 turning away he **h** divided our fields.	NIH
	4: 4 for the mouth of the Lord of hosts **h**	NIH
	5: 1 he **h** laid siege against us: they shall smite	NIH
	5: 3 until the time *that* she which travaileth **h**	NIH
	6: 2 for the Lord **h** a controversy with his 3807.1	
	6: 8 He **h** shewed thee, O man, what *is* good;	NIH
	6: 9 hear ye the rod, and who **h** appointed it.	NIH
Na	1: 3 the Lord **h** his way in the whirlwind	NIH
	1:14 the Lord **h** given a commandment	NIH
	2: 2 For the Lord **h** turned *away*	NIH
	3:19 upon whom **h** not thy wickedness passed	NIH
Hab	2:18 image that the maker thereof **h** graven it;	NIH
Zep	1: 7 for the Lord **h** prepared a sacrifice,	NIH
	1: 7 prepared a sacrifice, he **h** bid his guests.	NIH
	3:15 The Lord **h** taken away thy judgments,	NIH
	3:15 thy judgments, he **h** cast out thine enemy:	NIH
Hag	2:19 and the olive tree, **h** not brought forth:	NIH
Zec	1: 2 The Lord **h** been sore displeased with	NIH
	1: 6 to our doings, so **h** he dealt with us.	NIH
	1:10 These *are they* whom the Lord **h** sent to	NIH
	2: 8 After the glory **h** he sent me unto	NIH
	2: 9 ye shall know that the Lord of hosts **h**	NIH
	2:11 thou shalt know that the Lord of hosts **h**	NIH
	3: 2 even the Lord that **h** chosen Jerusalem	NIH
	4: 9 thou shalt know that the Lord of hosts **h**	NIH
	4:10 who **h** despised the day of small *things?*	NIH
	6:15 ye shall know that the Lord of hosts **h**	NIH
	7: 7 the words which the Lord **h** cried by the former prophets,	NIH
	7:12 the words which the Lord of hosts **h** sent	NIH
	10: 3 for the Lord of hosts **h** visited his flock	NIH
	10: 3 **h** made them as his goodly horse in	NIH
	13: 4 one of his vision, when he **h** prophesied;	NIH
Mal	1: 4 The people *against* whom the Lord **h**	NIH
	1: 9 this **h** been by your means: will he regard	NIH
	1:14 which **h** in his flock a male, and voweth, 3426	
	2:10 **h** not one God created us? why do we	NIH
	2:11 Judah **h** dealt treacherously,	NIH
	2:11 for Judah **h** profaned the holiness of	NIH
	2:11 **h** married the daughter of a strange god.	NIH
	2:14 Because the Lord **h** been witness	NIH
Mt	3: 7 who **h** warned you to flee from the wrath	NIG
	5:23 rememberest that thy brother **h** ought	2192
	5:28 **h** committed adultery with her already in	NIG
	5:31 It **h** been said, Whosoever shall put away	2192
	5:33 ye have heard that it **h** been said by them	NIG
	5:38 Ye have heard that it **h** been said, An eye	NIG
	5:43 Ye have heard that it **h** been said,	NIG
	8:20 Son of man **h** not where to lay *his* head.	2192
	9: 6 that ye may know that the Son of man **h**	2192
	9:22 comfort; thy faith **h** made thee whole.	NIG
	11:11 **h** not risen a greater than John the Baptist:	NIG
	11:15 He that **h** ears to hear, let him hear.	2192
	11:18 nor drinking, and they say, He **h** a devil.	2192
	13: 9 Who **h** ears to hear, let him hear.	2192
	13:12 For whosoever **h**, to him shall be given,	2192
	13:12 but whosoever **h** not, from him shall be	2192
	13:12 him shall be taken away even that he **h**.	2192
	13:21 Yet **h** he not root in himself, but dureth	2192
	13:27 in thy field? from whence then **h** it tares?	2192
	13:28 said unto them, An enemy **h** done this.	NIG
	13:43 Who **h** ears to hear, let him hear.	2192
	13:44 which when a man **h** found, he hideth,	2192
	13:44 thereof goeth and selleth all that **h** h,	2192
	13:54 Whence **h** this *man* this wisdom,	NIG
	13:56 Whence then **h** this *man* all these *things?*	NIG
	15:13 which my heavenly Father **h** not planted,	NIG
	16:17 and blood **h** not revealed *it* unto thee,	NIG
	19: 6 What therefore God **h** joined together,	NIG
	19:29 And every one that **h** forsaken houses,	NIG

Mt
20: 7 unto him, Because no *man* h hired us. NIG
21: 3 ye shall say, The Lord h need of them; 2192
24:45 whom his lord h made ruler over his NIG
25:28 give *it* unto him which h ten talents. 2192
25:29 For unto every one that h shall be given, 2192
25:29 from him that h not shall be taken away 2192
25:29 be taken away even *that* which he h. 2192
26:10 for she h wrought a good work upon me. NIG
26:12 For in that she h poured this ointment on NIG
26:13 *there* shall also *this*, that this *woman* h NIG
26:65 clothes, saying, He h spoken blasphemy; NIG
27:23 governor said, Why, what evil he h done? NIG

Mk
2:10 that ye may know that the Son of man h 2192
3:22 He h Beelzebub, and by the prince of 2192
3:26 divided, he cannot stand, but h an end. 2192
3:29 against the Holy Ghost h never 2192
3:30 Because they said, He h an unclean spirit. 2192
4: 9 He that h ears to hear, let him hear. 2192
4:25 For he that h, to him shall be given: 2192
4:25 he that h not, from him shall be taken 2192
4:25 him shall be taken even *that* which he h. 2192
5:19 them how great things the Lord h done NIG
5:19 for thee, and h had compassion on thee. NIG
5:34 Daughter, thy faith h made thee whole; NIG
6: 2 From whence h this *man* these *things?* NIG
7: 6 h Esaias prophesied of you hypocrites, NIG
7:37 saying, He h done all *things* well; NIG
9:17 unto thee my son, which h a dumb spirit: 2192
9:22 And oft h it cast him into the fire, NIG
10: 9 What therefore God h joined together, NIG
10:29 There is no *man* that h left house, NIG
10:52 Go thy way; thy faith h made thee whole. NIG
11: 3 say ye that the Lord h need of him; 2192
12:43 That this poor widow h cast more in, NIG
13:20 for the elect's sake, whom he h chosen, NIG
13:20 he hath chosen, he h shortened the days. NIG
14: 6 she h wrought a good work on me. NIG
14: 8 She h done what she could: she is come 2192
14: 9 *this* also that she h done shall be spoken NIG
15:14 unto them, Why, what evil h he done? NIG

Lk
1:25 Thus h the Lord dealt with me in the days NIG
1:36 she h also conceived a son in her old age: NIG
1:47 And my spirit h rejoiced in God my NIG
1:48 For he h regarded the low estate of his NIG
1:49 For he *that* is mighty h done to me great NIG
1:51 He h shewed strength with his arm; NIG
1:51 he h scattered the proud in the NIG
1:52 He h put down the mighty from *their* NIG
1:53 He h filled the hungry with good *things;* NIG
1:53 and the rich he h sent empty away. NIG
1:54 He h holpen his servant Israel, NIG
1:68 for he h visited and redeemed his people, NIG
1:69 And h raised up a horn of salvation for us NIG
1:78 whereby the dayspring from on high h NIG
2:15 which the Lord h made known unto us. NIG
3: 7 who h warned you to flee from the wrath NIG
3:11 and saith unto them, He that h two coats, 2192
3:11 let him impart to him that h none; 2192
3:11 and he that h meat, let him do likewise. 2192
4:18 he h anointed me to preach the gospel to NIG
4:18 he h sent me to heal the broken-hearted, NIG
5:24 that ye may know that the Son of man h 2192
7: 5 our nation, and h built us a synagogue. NIG
7:16 and, That God h visited his people. NIG
7:20 John Baptist h sent us unto thee, saying, NIG
7:33 drinking wine; and ye say, He h a devil. 2192
7:44 but she h washed my feet with tears, NIG
7:45 *woman* since the time I came in h not NIG
7:46 this *woman* h anointed my feet with NIG
7:50 to the woman, Thy faith h saved thee; NIG
8: 8 He that h ears to hear, let him hear. 2192
8:16 No *man*, when he h lighted a candle, NIG
8:18 for whosoever h, to him shall be given; 2192
8:18 and whosoever h not, from him shall be 2192
8:39 shew how great *things* God h done unto NIG
8:46 And Jesus said, Somebody h touched me: NIG
8:48 thy faith h made thee whole; go in peace.) NIG
9:58 Son of man h not where to lay *his* head. 2192
10:40 thou not care that my sister h left me to NIG
10:42 and Mary h chosen *that* good part, NIG
11:33 No *man*, when he h lighted a candle, NIG
12: 5 which after *he* h killed hath power to cast NIG
12: 5 which after *he* hath killed h power to cast 2192
12:44 he will make him ruler over all that he h. 5225
13:16 whom Satan h bound, lo *these* eighteen NIG
13:25 h shut to the door, and ye begin to stand NIG
14:29 after he h laid the foundation, and is not 5225
14:33 *be* of you that forsaketh not all that he h, 5225
14:35 He that h ears to hear, let him hear. 2192
15: 5 when he h found *it*, he layeth *it* on his NIG
15: 9 And when she h found *it*, she calleth *her* NIG
15:27 and thy father h killed the fatted calf, NIG
15:27 he h received him *safe* and sound. NIG
15:30 which h devoured thy living with harlots, NIG
17:19 go *thy way:* thy faith h made thee whole. NIG
18:29 There is no *man* that h left house, NIG
18:42 Receive thy sight: thy faith h saved thee. NIG
19:16 Lord, thy pound h gained ten pounds. NIG
19:18 Lord, thy pound h gained five pounds. NIG
19:24 and give *it* to him that h ten pounds. 2192
19:25 said unto him, Lord, he h ten pounds.) 2192
19:26 That unto every one which h shall be 2192
19:26 from him that h not, even that he hath 2192
19:26 even that he h shall be taken away from 2192
19:31 him, Because the Lord h need of him. NIG

Lk
19:34 And they said, The Lord h need of him. 2192
20:24 Whose image and superscription h it? 2192
21: 3 that this poor widow h cast in more than NIG
21: 4 she of her penury h cast in all the living NIG
22:29 as my Father h appointed unto me; NIG
22:31 behold, Satan h desired *to have* you, 2192
22:36 now, he that h a purse, let him take *it*, 2192
22:36 and he that h no sword, let him sell his 2192
23:22 the third time, Why, what evil h he done? NIG
23:41 but this *man* h done nothing amiss. NIG
24:34 is risen indeed, and h appeared to Simon. NIG
24:39 for a spirit h not flesh and bones, as ye 2192

Jn
1:18 No *man* h seen God at any time; the only NIG
1:18 bosom of the Father, he h declared *him.* NIG
2:17 The zeal of thine house h eaten me up. NIG
3:13 And no *man* h ascended up to heaven, NIG
3:18 he h not believed in the name of the only NIG
3:29 He that h the bride is the bridegroom: 2192
3:32 And what he h seen and heard, that he NIG
3:33 He that h received his testimony hath set NIG
3:33 He that hath received his testimony h set NIG
3:34 For he whom God h sent speaketh NIG
3:35 and h given all *things* into his hand. NIG
3:36 He that believeth on the Son h everlasting 2192
4:33 H any *man* brought him *ought* to eat? NIG
4:44 that a prophet h no honour in his own 2192
5:22 h committed all judgment unto the Son: NIG
5:23 not the Father which h sent him. NIG
5:24 everlasting life, and shall not come into 2192
5:26 For as the Father h life in himself; 2192
5:26 he h given to the Son to have life in NIG
5:27 And h given him authority to execute NIG
5:30 the will of the Father which h sent me. NIG
5:36 the works which the Father h given me NIG
5:36 witness of me, that the Father h sent me. NIG
5:37 And the Father himself, which h sent me, NIG
5:37 hath sent me, h borne witness of me. NIG
5:38 for whom he h sent, him ye believe not. NIG
6: 9 which h five barley loaves, and two small 2192
6:27 you: for him h God the Father sealed. NIG
6:29 that ye believe on *him* whom h h sent. NIG
6:39 And this is the Father's will which h sent NIG
6:39 that of all which he h given me I should NIG
6:44 except the Father which h sent me draw NIG
6:45 Every *man* therefore that h heard, NIG
6:45 hath heard, and h learned of the Father, NIG
6:46 Not that any *man* h seen the Father, save NIG
6:46 he which is of God, he h seen the Father. NIG
6:47 He that believeth on me h everlasting life. 2192
6:54 and drinketh my blood, h eternal life; 2192
6:57 As the living Father h sent me, and I live NIG
7:29 for I am from him, and he h sent me. NIG
7:31 than these which this *man* h done? NIG
7:38 believeth on me, as the scripture h said, NIG
7:42 H not the scripture said, That Christ NIG
8:10 accusers? h no *man* condemned thee? NIG
8:28 as my Father h taught me, I speak these NIG
8:29 the Father h not left me alone; for I do NIG
8:37 because my word h no *place* in you. 5562
8:40 a man that h told you the truth, which I NIG
9: 3 h this *man* sinned, nor his parents: NIG
9:17 thou of him, that he h opened thine eyes? NIG
9:21 or who h opened his eyes, we know not: NIG
9:30 he is, and *yet* he h opened mine eyes. NIG
10:20 of them said, He h a devil, and is mad; 2192
10:21 are not the words of him that h a devil. 1139
10:36 Say ye *of him,* whom the Father h NIG
11:39 he stinketh: for he h been *dead* four days. NIG
12: 7 against the day of my burying h she kept NIG
12:38 spake, Lord, who h believed our report? NIG
12:38 to whom h the arm of the Lord been NIG
12:40 He h blinded their eyes, and hardened NIG
12:48 not my words, h *one* that judgeth him: 2192
13:18 He that eateth bread with me h lift up his NIG
14: 9 he that h seen me hath seen the Father; NIG
14: 9 he that hath seen h seen the Father; NIG
14:21 He that h my commandments, 2192
14:30 this world cometh, and h nothing in me. 2192
15: 9 As the Father h loved me, so have I loved 2192
15:13 Greater love h no *man* than this, that a 2192
16: 6 unto you, sorrow h filled your heart. NIG
16:15 All *things* that the Father h are mine: 2192
16:21 woman when she is in travail h sorrow, 2192
17:14 and the world h hated them, because NIG
17:25 the world h not known thee: NIG
18:11 the cup which my Father h given me, NIG
19:11 that delivered me unto thee h the greater 2192
21: 7 my Father h sent me, even *so* send I you. NIG

Ac
1: 1 which the Father h put in his own power. NIG
2:24 Whom God h raised up, having loosed NIG
2:32 This Jesus h God raised up, whereof we all NIG
2:33 he h shed forth this, which ye now see NIG
2:36 that God h made that same Jesus, whom NIG
3:13 of our fathers, h glorified his Son Jesus; NIG
3:15 of life, whom God h raised from the dead; NIG
3:16 And his name through faith in his name h NIG
3:16 the faith which is by him h given him this NIG
3:18 that Christ should suffer, he h so fulfilled. NIG
3:21 h spoken by the mouth of all his holy NIG
4:16 for that indeed a notable miracle h been NIG
5: 3 why h Satan filled thine heart to lie to NIG
5:31 Him h God exalted with his right hand *to* NIG
5:32 God h given to them that obey him. NIG
7:50 H not my hand made all these *things?* NIG
9:12 And h seen in a vision a man named NIG

Ac
9:13 how much evil he h done to thy saints at NIG
9:14 And here he h authority from the chief 2192
9:17 h sent me, that thou mightest receive thy NIG
10:15 What God h cleansed, *that* call not thou NIG
10:28 God h shewed me that *I* should not call NIG
11: 8 unclean h at any time entered into my NIG
11: 9 What God h cleansed, *that* call not thou NIG
11:18 Then h God also to the Gentiles granted NIG
12:11 that the Lord h sent his angel, NIG
12:11 h delivered me out of the hand of Herod, NIG
13:23 Of this *man's* seed h God according to *his* NIG
13:33 God h fulfilled the same unto us their NIG
13:33 in that he h raised up Jesus again; NIG
13:47 For so h the Lord commanded us, *saying,* NIG
15:14 Simeon h declared how God at the first NIG
15:21 Moses of old time h in every city them 2192
17: 7 Whom Jason h received: and these all do NIG
17:26 h made of one blood all nations of men NIG
17:26 h determined the times before appointed, NIG
17:31 he h appointed a day, in the which NIG
17:31 by *that* man whom he h ordained; NIG
17:31 he h given assurance unto all *men,* NIG
17:31 in that he h raised him from the dead. NIG
19:26 this Paul h persuaded and turned away NIG
20:28 the which the Holy Ghost h made you NIG
20:28 he h purchased with his own blood. NIG
21:28 temple, and h polluted this holy place. NIG
22:14 The God of our fathers h chosen thee, NIG
23: 9 if a spirit or an angel h spoken to him, NIG
23:17 for he h a certain *thing* to tell him. 2192
23:18 who h something to say unto thee. 2192
24: 6 Who also h gone about to profane NIG
25:25 that he himself h appealed to Augustus, NIG
27:24 God h given thee all them that sail with NIG
28: 4 whom, though he h escaped the sea, NIG

Ro
1:19 in them; for God h shewed *it* unto them. NIG
3: 1 What advantage then h the Jew? NIG
3: 7 For if the truth of God h *more* abounded NIG
3:25 Whom God h set forth *to be* a propitiation NIG
4: 1 as pertaining to the flesh, h found? NIG
4: 2 justified by works, he h whereof to glory; 2192
5:15 Jesus Christ, h abounded unto many. NIG
5:21 That as sin h reigned unto death, even so NIG
6: 9 death h no more dominion over him. NIG
7: 1 that the law h *dominion over* a man, 2961
7: 2 the woman which h a husband is bound NIG
8: 2 Jesus h made me free from the law of sin NIG
8:20 reason of him who h subjected *the same,* NIG
9: 6 Not as though the word of God h taken NIG
9:18 Therefore h he *mercy* on whom he will 1653
9:19 yet find fault? For who h resisted his will? NIG
9:21 H not the potter power over the clay, 2192
9:24 us, whom he h called, not of the Jews NIG
9:31 h not attained to the law of righteousness. NIG
10: 9 believe in thine heart that God h raised NIG
10:16 Lord, who h believed our report? NIG
11: 1 I say then, H God cast away his people? NIG
11: 2 God h not cast away his people which he NIG
11: 7 Israel h not obtained that which he NIG
11: 7 but the election h obtained *it*, and the rest NIG
11: 8 God h given them the spirit of slumber, NIG
11:32 For God h concluded *them* all in unbelief, NIG
11:34 For who h known the mind of the Lord? NIG
11:34 the Lord? or who h been his counseller? NIG
11:35 who h first given to him, and it shall be NIG
12: 3 according as God h dealt to every man NIG
13: 8 he that loveth another h fulfilled the law. NIG
14: 3 him that eateth: for God h received him. NIG
15:18 which Christ h not wrought by me, NIG
15:26 For it h pleased *them of* Macedonia and NIG
15:27 It h pleased them verily; and their debtors NIG
16: 2 in whatsoever business she h need of you: NIG
16: 2 for she h been a succourer of many, NIG

1Co
1:11 For it h been declared unto me of you, NIG
1:20 h not God made foolish the wisdom of this NIG
1:27 But God h chosen the foolish *things of* NIG
1:27 God h chosen the weak *things* of the world NIG
1:28 h God chosen, *yea, and* things which are NIG
2: 9 it is written, Eye h not seen, nor ear heard, NIG
2: 9 *the things* which God h prepared for them NIG
2:10 But God h revealed *them* unto us by his NIG
2:16 For who h known the mind of the Lord, NIG
3:14 If any *man's* work abide which he h built NIG
4: 9 For I think that God h set forth us NIG
5: 2 he that h done this deed might be taken NIG
5: 3 *concerning* him that h so done this *deed,* NIG
6:14 And God h both raised up the Lord, NIG
7: 4 The wife h *power* of her own body, 1850
7: 4 likewise also the husband h not *power* of 1850
7: 7 But every man h his proper gift of God, 2192
7:12 If any brother h a wife that believeth not, 2192
7:13 And the woman which h a husband that 2192
7:15 such *cases:* but God h called us to peace. NIG
7:17 But as God h distributed to every man, NIG
7:17 as the Lord h called every one, so let him NIG
7:25 as one that h obtained mercy of the Lord NIG
7:28 and if a virgin marry, she h not sinned. NIG
7:37 but h power over his own will, and hath 2192
7:37 and so decreed in his heart that *he* will NIG
9:14 h the Lord ordained that they which NIG
10:13 There h no temptation taken you but NIG
12:12 h many members, and all the members 2192
12:18 now h God set the members every one NIG
12:18 of them in the body, as it h pleased him. 2309
12:24 but God h tempered the body together, NIG

H

H

1Co 12:28 And God **h** set some in the church, NIG
14:26 one of you **h** a psalm, hath a doctrine, 2192
14:26 **h** a doctrine, hath a tongue, hath a 2192
14:26 hath a doctrine, **h** a tongue, hath a 2192
14:26 a doctrine, hath a tongue, **h** a revelation, 2192
14:26 hath a revelation, **h** an interpretation. 2192
15:25 till he **h** put all enemies under his feet. NIG
15:27 For he **h** put all *things* under his feet. NIG
15:38 But God giveth it a body as it **h** pleased NIG
16: 2 as *God* **h** prospered him, that there be no NIG
2Co 1:21 you in Christ, and **h** anointed us, *is* God; NIG
1:22 Who **h** also sealed us, and given the NIG
2: 5 he **h** not grieved me, but in part; NIG
3: 6 Who also **h** made us able ministers of NIG
4: 4 In whom the god of this world **h** blinded NIG
4: 6 out of darkness, **h** shined in our hearts, NIG
5: 5 he that **h** wrought us for the selfsame NIG
5: 5 who also **h** given unto us the earnest of NIG
5:10 according to that he **h** done, whether *it be* NIG
5:18 who **h** reconciled us to himself by Jesus NIG
5:18 **h** given to us the ministry of reconciliation NIG
5:19 committed unto us the word of NIG
5:21 For he **h** made him *to be* sin for us, NIG
6:14 for what fellowship **h** righteousness with NIG
6:14 what communion **h** light with darkness? NIG
6:15 And what concord **h** Christ with Belial? NIG
6:15 what part **h** he that believeth with an NIG
6:16 And what agreement **h** the temple of God NIG
6:16 as God **h** said, I will dwell in them, NIG
7: 8 for I perceive that the same epistle **h** made NIG
8:12 *it is* accepted according to that a man **h**, 2192
8:12 and not according to that he **h** not. 2192
9: 2 and your zeal **h** provoked very many. NIG
9: 9 (As it is written, He **h** dispersed abroad; NIG
9: 9 dispersed abroad; he **h** given to the poor: NIG
10: 8 which the Lord **h** given us for edification, NIG
10:13 of the rule which God **h** distributed to us, NIG
13:10 according to the power which the Lord **h** NIG
Gal 3: 1 O foolish Galatians, who **h** bewitched you, NIG
3: 1 before whose eyes Jesus Christ **h** been NIG
3:13 Christ **h** redeemed us from the curse of NIG
3:22 the scripture **h** concluded all under sin, NIG
4: 6 God **h** sent forth the Spirit of his Son into NIG
4:27 the desolate **h** many moe children than NIG
4:27 children than she which **h** a husband. 2192
5: 1 in the liberty wherewith Christ **h** made us NIG
Eph 1: 3 **h** blessed us with all spiritual blessings NIG
1: 4 According as he **h** chosen us in him before NIG
1: 6 wherein he **h** made us accepted in the NIG
1: 8 Wherein he **h** abounded toward us in all NIG
1:22 And **h** put all *things* under his feet, NIG
2: 1 you **h** he quickened, who were dead in NIG
2: 5 **h** quickened *us* together with Christ, NIG
2: 6 **h** raised *us* up together, and made *us* sit NIG
2:10 which God **h** before ordained that we NIG
2:14 who **h** made both one, and hath broken NIG
2:14 **h** broken down the middle wall of NIG
3: 9 which from the beginning of the world **h** NIG
4:32 even as God for Christ's sake **h** forgiven NIG
5: 2 as Christ also **h** loved us, and hath given NIG
5: 2 and **h** given himself for us an offering and NIG
5: 5 **h** *any* inheritance in the kingdom of 2192
Php 1: 6 **h** begun a good work in you will perform NIG
2: 9 Wherefore God also **h** highly exalted him, NIG
2:22 he **h** served with me in the gospel. NIG
3: 4 If any other *man* thinketh that he **h** NIG
4:10 that now at the last your care of me **h** NIG
Col 1:12 which **h** made us meet to be partakers of NIG
1:13 Who **h** delivered us from the power of NIG
1:13 **h** translated *us* into the kingdom of his NIG
1:21 wicked works, yet now **h** he reconciled NIG
1:26 *Even* the mystery which **h** been hid from NIG
2:12 of God, who **h** raised him from the dead. NIG
2:13 he **h** quickened together with him, NIG
2:18 into *those* things which he **h** not NIG
3:25 receive *for* the wrong which he **h** done: NIG
4:13 he **h** a great zeal for you, and them that 2192
1Th 2:12 who **h** called you unto his kingdom and NIG
4: 7 For God **h** not called us unto uncleanness, NIG
4: 8 who **h** also given unto us his holy Spirit. NIG
5: 9 For God **h** not appointed us to wrath, NIG
2Th 2:13 God **h** from the beginning chosen you to NIG
2:16 which **h** loved us, and hath given *us* NIG
2:16 and **h** given *us* everlasting consolation and NIG
1Ti 1:12 who **h** enabled me, for that he counted NIG
4: 3 which God **h** created to be received with NIG
5: 8 he **h** denied the faith, and is worse than NIG
6:16 Who only **h** immortality, dwelling in 2192
6:16 whom no man **h** seen, nor can see: NIG
2Ti 1: 7 For God **h** not given us the spirit of fear; NIG
1: 9 Who **h** saved us, and called *us* with a holy NIG
1:10 who **h** abolished death, and hath brought NIG
1:10 and **h** brought life and immortality to light NIG
2: 4 he may please him who **h** chosen *him* NIG
4:10 Demas **h** forsaken me, having loved *this* NIG
4:15 for he **h** greatly withstood our words. NIG
Tit 1: 3 But **h** in due times manifested his word NIG
1: 9 fast the faithful word as **he h** been NIG
2:11 bringeth salvation **h** appeared to all men, NIG
Phm 1:18 he **h** wronged thee, or oweth *thee* ought, NIG
Heb 1: 2 **H** in these last days spoken unto us by *his* NIG
1: 2 whom he **h** appointed heir of all *things,* NIG
1: 4 as he **h** by inheritance obtained a more NIG
1: 9 **h** anointed thee *with* the oil of gladness NIG
2: 5 For unto *the* angels **h** he not put in NIG

Heb 2:13 and the children which God **h** given me. NIG
2:18 For in that he himself **h** suffered being NIG
3: 3 inasmuch as he who **h** builded the house NIG
3: 3 the house **h** more honour than the house. 2192
4:10 he also **h** ceased from his own works, NIG
7:24 **h** an unchangeable priesthood. 2192
8: 6 But now he **h** obtained a more excellent NIG
8:13 A new *covenant,* he **h** made the first old. NIG
9:20 which God **h** enjoined unto you. NIG
9:26 now once in the end of the world **h** he NIG
10:14 For by one offering he **h** perfected for ever NIG
10:20 living way, which he **h** consecrated for us, NIG
10:29 who **h** trodden under foot the Son of God, NIG
10:29 and **h** counted the blood of the covenant, NIG
10:29 **h** done despite unto the Spirit of grace? NIG
10:30 For we know him that **h** said, NIG
10:35 which **h** great recompence of reward. 2192
11:10 For he looked for a city which **h** 2192
11:16 God: for he **h** prepared for them a city. NIG
12:26 but now he **h** promised, saying, Yet once NIG
13: 5 for he **h** said, I will never leave thee, NIG
Jas 1:12 which the Lord **h** promised to them that NIG
1:15 Then when lust **h** conceived, it bringeth NIG
2: 5 **h** not God chosen the poor of this world NIG
2: 5 of the kingdom which he **h** promised NIG
2:13 without mercy, that **h** shewed no mercy; NIG
2:14 though a man say *he* **h** faith, and have 2192
2:17 Even so faith, if it **h** not works, is dead, 2192
3: 7 is tamed, and **h** been tamed of mankind: NIG
5: 7 **h long patience** for it, until he receive 3114
1Pe 1: 3 which according to his abundant mercy **h** NIG
1:15 But as he which **h** called you is holy, NIG
2: 9 **h** called you out of darkness into his NIG
3:18 For Christ also **h** once suffered for sins, NIG
4: 1 as Christ **h** suffered for us in the flesh, NIG
4: 1 for he that **h** suffered in the flesh hath NIG
4: 1 for he that hath suffered in the flesh **h** NIG
4:10 As every man **h** received *the* gift, *even so* NIG
5:10 who **h** called us into his eternal glory by NIG
2Pe 1: 3 According as his divine power **h** given NIG
1: 3 the knowledge of him that **h** called NIG
1: 9 **h** forgotten that *he* was purged from his NIG
1:14 as our Lord Jesus Christ **h** shewed me. NIG
3:15 given unto him **h** written unto you; NIG
1Jn 2:11 because that darkness **h** blinded his eyes. 2192
2:23 the Son, the same **h** not the Father: NIG
2:23 that acknowledgeth the Son **h** the Father 2192
2:25 this is the promise that he **h** promised NIG
2:27 and is no lie, and even as it **h** taught you, NIG
3: 1 manner of love the Father **h** bestowed NIG
3: 3 And every *man* that **h** this hope in him 2192
3: 6 whosoever sinneth **h** not seen him, NIG
3:15 ye know that no murderer **h** eternal life 2192
3:17 But whoso **h** this world's good, 2192
3:17 and seeth his brother **h** need, 2192
3:24 in us, by the Spirit which he **h** given us. NIG
4:12 No man **h** seen God at any time. If we NIG
4:13 in us, because he **h** given us of his Spirit. NIG
4:16 and believed the love that God **h** to us. 2192
4:18 because fear **h** torment. He that feareth is 2192
4:20 he that loveth not his brother whom he **h** NIG
4:20 can he love God whom he **h** not seen? NIG
5: 9 for this is the witness of God which he **h** NIG
5:10 He that believeth on the Son of God **h** 2192
5:10 that believeth not God **h** made him a liar; NIG
5:11 that God **h** given to us eternal life, 2192
5:12 He that **h** the Son hath life; *and* he that 2192
5:12 He that hath the Son **h** life; *and* he that 2192
5:12 he that **h** not the Son of God hath not life. 2192
5:12 he that hath not the Son of God **h** not life. 2192
5:20 and **h** given us an understanding, that we 2192
2Jn 1: 9 not in the doctrine of Christ, **h** not God. 2192
1: 9 Christ, he **h** both the Father and the Son. 2192
3Jn 1:11 but he that doeth evil **h** not seen God. NIG
1:12 Demetrius **h good report** of all *men,* and 3140
Jude 1: 6 he **h** reserved in everlasting chains under NIG
Rev 1: 6 **h** made us kings and priests unto God NIG
2: 7 He that **h** an ear, let him hear what 2192
2:11 He that **h** an ear, let him hear what NIG
2:12 These *things* saith he which **h** the sharp 2192
2:17 He that **h** an ear, let him hear what NIG
2:18 who **h** his eyes like unto a flame of fire, NIG
2:29 He that **h** an ear, let him hear what NIG
3: 1 These *things* saith he that **h** the seven 2192
3: 6 He that **h** an ear, let him hear what NIG
3: 7 *that is* true, he that **h** the key of David, 2192
3:13 He that **h** an ear, let him hear what NIG
3:22 He that **h** an ear, let him hear what NIG
5: 5 **h** prevailed to open the book, and to loose NIG
9:11 the Greek *tongue* **h** *his* name Apollyon. 2192
10: 7 as he **h** declared to his servants NIG
12: 6 where she **h** a place prepared of God, 2192
12:12 because he knoweth that he **h** *but* a short 2192
13:18 Let him that **h** understanding count NIG
16: 9 God, which **h** power over these plagues: 2192
17: 7 which **h** the seven heads and ten horns. NIG
17: 9 *And* here *is* the mind which **h** wisdom. 2192
17:17 For God **h** put in their hearts to fulfil his NIG
18: 5 and God **h** remembered her iniquities. NIG
18: 6 in the cup which she **h** filled fill to her NIG
18: 7 How much she **h** glorified herself, NIG
18:20 for God **h** avenged you on her. NIG
19: 2 he **h** judged the great whore, which did NIG
19: 2 **h** avenged the blood of his servants at her NIG
19: 7 come, and his wife **h** made herself ready. NIG

Rev 19:16 he **h** on *his* vesture and on his thigh a 2192
20: 6 holy *is* he that **h** part in the first 2192
20: 6 on such the second death **h** no power, 2192

HATHACH See HATACH

HATHATH (1)
1Ch 4:13 and Seraiah: and the sons of Othniel; **H**. 2867

HATING (3) [HATE]
Ex 18:21 fear God, men of truth, **h** covetousness; 8130
Tit 3: 3 and envy, hateful, *and* **h** one another. 3404
Jude 1:23 **h** even the garment spotted by the flesh. 3404

HATIPHA (2)
Ezr 2:54 The children of Neziah, the children of **H**. 2412
Ne 7:56 The children of Neziah, the children of **H**. 2412

HATITA (2)
Ezr 2:42 the children of Akkub, the children of **H**, 2410
Ne 7:45 the children of Akkub, the children of **H**, 2410

HATRED (18) [HATE]
Nu 35:20 if he thrust him of **h**, or hurl at him by 8135
2Sa 13:15 that the **h** wherewith he hated her *was* 8135
Ps 25:19 and they hate me *with* **cruel h.** 2555+8135
109: 3 me about also *with* words of **h**; 8135
109: 5 me evil for good, and **h** for my love. 8135
139:22 I hate them *with* perfect **h**: I count them 8135
Pr 10:12 **H** stirreth up strifes: but love covereth all 8135
10:18 He that hideth **h** *with* lying lips, and he 8135
15:17 love is, than a stalled ox and **h** therewith. 8135
26:26 *Whose* **h** is covered by deceit, 8135
Ecc 9: 1 either love or **h** *by* all *that is* before them. 8135
9: 6 their love, and their **h**, and their envy, 8135
Eze 25:15 despiteful heart, to destroy *it for* the old **h**; 342
35: 5 Because thou hast had a perpetual **h**, 342
35:11 thou hast used out of thy **h** against them; 8135
Hos 9: 7 of thine iniquity, and the great **h**. 4895
9: 8 his ways, *and* **h** in the house of his God. 4895
Gal 5:20 Idolatry, witchcraft, **h**, variance, 2189

HATS (1)
Da 3:21 their **h**, and their *other* garments, 3737

HATTIL (2)
Ezr 2:57 children of Shephatiah, the children of **H**, 2411
Ne 7:59 children of Shephatiah, the children of **H**, 2411

HATTUSH (5)
1Ch 3:22 H, and Igeal, and Bariah, and Neariah, 2407
Ezr 8: 2 Ithamar; Daniel: of the sons of David; **H**. 2407
Ne 3:10 next unto him repaired **H** the son of 2407
10: 4 **H**, Shebaniah, Malluch, 2407
12: 2 Amariah, Malluch, **H**, 2407

HAUGHTILY (1) [HAUGHTY]
Mic 2: 3 remove your necks; neither shall ye go **h**: 7317

HAUGHTINESS (5) [HAUGHTY]
Isa 2:11 the **h** of men shall be bowed down, 7312
2:17 and the **h** of men shall be made low: 7312
13:11 and will lay low the **h** of the terrible. 1346
16: 6 of his **h**, and his pride, and his wrath: 1346
Jer 48:29 and his pride, and the **h** of his heart. 7312

HAUGHTY (10) [HAUGHTINESS]
2Sa 22:28 eyes *are* upon the **h**, *that* thou mayest 7311
Ps 131: 1 LORD, my heart is not **h**, nor mine eyes 1361
Pr 16:18 and a **h** spirit before a fall. 1363
18:12 Before destruction the heart of man is **h**, 1361
21:24 Proud *and* **h** scorner *is* his name, 3093
Isa 3:16 Because the daughters of Zion are **h**, 1361
10:33 hewn down, and the **h** shall be humbled. 1364
24: 4 the **h** people of the earth do languish. 4791
Eze 16:50 they were **h**, and committed abomination 1361
Zep 3:11 thou shalt no more be **h** because of my 1361

HAUNT (3)
1Sa 23:22 know and see his place where his **h** is, 7272
30:31 himself and his men were **wont to h**. 1980
Eze 26:17 cause their terror *to be* on all that **h** 3427

HAURAN (2)
Eze 47:16 which *is* by the coast of **H**. 2362
47:18 the east side ye shall measure from **H**, 2362

HAVE (3902) [HAD, HADST, HAST, HATH, HAVING]
Ge 1:26 let them **h dominion** over the fish of 7287
1:28 **h dominion** over the fish of the sea, 7287
1:29 I **h** given you every herb bearing seed, NIH
1:30 life, *I* **h** *given* every green herb for meat: NIH
4: 1 and said, I **h** gotten a man from the LORD. NIH
4:20 as dwell in tents, and *of such as* **h** cattle. NIH
4:23 for I **h** slain a man to my wounding, NIH
6: 7 I will destroy man whom I **h** created from NIH
6: 7 for it repenteth me that I **h** made them. NIH
7: 1 for thee **h** I seen righteous before me in NIH
7: 4 every living substance that I **h** made will I NIH
8:21 any more every *thing* living, as I **h** done. NIH
9: 3 *even* as the green herb **h** I given you all NIH
9:17 which I **h** established between me and all NIH
11: 6 is one, and they **h** all one language; 3807.1
11: 6 from them, which they **h** imagined to do. NIH
12:19 so I might **h** taken her to me to wife: NIH

Ge	14:22	I **h** lift up mine hand unto the LORD,	NIH
	14:23	thou shouldest say, I **h** made Abram rich:	NIH
	14:24	Save only that which the young men **h**	NIH
	15:18	saying, Unto thy seed **h** I given this land,	NIH
	16: 5	I **h** given my maid into my bosom;	NIH
	16:13	**H** I also here looked after him that seeth	NIH
	17: 5	for a father of many nations **h** I made thee.	NIH
	17:20	as for Ishmael, I **h** heard thee: Behold,	NIH
	17:20	I **h** blessed him, and will make him fruitful	NIH
	18: 3	if now I **h** found favour in thy sight,	NIH
	18:10	and lo, Sarah thy wife shall **h** a son.	3807.1
	18:12	am waxed old shall I **h** pleasure,	1961+3807.1
	18:14	time of life, and Sarah shall **h** a son.	3807.1
	18:21	see whether they **h** done altogether	NIH
	18:27	I **h** taken upon me to speak unto the Lord,	NIH
	18:31	I **h** taken upon me to speak unto the Lord:	NIH
	19: 8	I **h** two daughters which have not	3807.1
	19: 8	I have two daughters which **h** not known	NIH
	19:21	I **h** accepted thee concerning this thing,	NIH
	20: 5	and innocency of my hands **h** I done this.	NIH
	20: 9	what **h** I offended thee, that thou hast	NIH
	20:16	I **h** given thy brother a thousand *pieces* of	NIH
	21: 7	said, Who would **h** said unto Abraham,	NIH
	21: 7	that Sarah should **h** given children suck?	NIH
	21: 7	for I **h** born *him* a son in his old age.	NIH
	21:23	to the kindness that I **h** done unto	NIH
	21:30	witness unto me, that I **h** digged this well.	NIH
	22:16	said, By myself **h** I sworn, saith	NIH
	24:19	camels also, until they **h** done drinking.	NIH
	24:25	We **h** both straw and provender enough,	5973
	24:31	for I **h** prepared the house, and room for	NIH
	24:33	I will not eat, until I **h** told mine errand.	NIH
	26:10	one of the people might lightly **h** lien with	NIH
	26:10	shouldest **h** brought guiltiness upon us.	NIH
	26:27	hate me, and **h** sent me away from you?	NIH
	26:29	as we **h** not touched thee, and as we have	NIH
	26:29	as we **h** done unto thee nothing but good,	NIH
	26:29	but good, and **h** sent thee away in peace:	NIH
	26:32	and said unto him, We **h** found water.	NIH
	27:19	I **h** done according as thou badest me:	NIH
	27:33	I **h** eaten of all before thou camest,	NIH
	27:33	all before thou camest, and **h** blessed him?	NIH
	27:37	I **h** made him thy lord, and all his brethren	NIH
	27:37	all his brethren **h** I given to him for	NIH
	27:37	and with corn and wine **h** I sustained him:	NIH
	27:40	it shall come to pass when thou shalt **h**	NIH
	28:15	until I **h** done *that* which I have spoken to	NIH
	28:15	until I have done *that* which I **h** spoken to	NIH
	28:22	this stone, which I **h** set *for* a pillar, shall	NIH
	29:34	me, because I **h** born him three sons:	NIH
	30: 3	that I may also **h** children by her.	1129
	30: 8	With great wrestlings I **h** wrestled with	NIH
	30: 8	wrestled with my sister, and I **h** prevailed:	NIH
	30:16	for surely I **h** hired thee with my son's	NIH
	30:18	I **h** given my maiden to my husband:	NIH
	30:20	with me, because I **h** born him six sons:	NIH
	30:26	for whom I **h** served thee, and let me go:	NIH
	30:26	thou knowest my service which I **h** done	NIH
	30:27	thee, if I **h** found favour in thine eyes,	NIH
	30:27	*tarry: for* I **h** learned by experience that	NIH
	30:29	Thou knowest how I **h** served thee,	NIH
	31: 6	know that with all my power I **h** served	NIH
	31:12	I **h** seen all that Laban doeth unto thee.	NIH
	31:27	that I might **h** sent thee away with mirth,	NIH
	31:38	This twenty years *h* I *been* with thee;	3807.1
	31:38	and thy she goats **h** not cast their young,	NIH
	31:38	and the rams of thy flock I **h** not eaten.	NIH
	31:41	**h** I been twenty years in thy house;	3807.1
	31:43	or unto their children which they **h** born?	NIH
	31:51	which I **h** cast betwixt me and thee;	NIH
	32: 4	I **h** sojourned with Laban, and stayed	NIH
	32: 5	I **h** oxen, and asses, flocks,	1961+3807.1
	32: 5	I **h** sent to tell my lord, that I may find	NIH
	32:30	for I **h** seen God face to face, and my life	NIH
	33: 9	said, I **h** enough, my brother;	3426+3807.1
	33:10	if now I **h** found grace in thy sight, then	NIH
	33:10	for therefore I **h** seen thy face, as though	3426+3807.1
	33:11	and because I **h** enough.	3426+3807.1
	34:30	Ye **h** troubled me to make me to stink	NIH
	35:17	Fear not; thou shalt **h** this son also.	3807.1
	37: 6	pray you, this dream which I **h** dreamed:	NIH
	37: 8	or shalt thou **indeed h** dominion	4910+4910
	37: 9	said, Behold, I **h** dreamed a dream more;	NIH
	37:32	to their father; and said, This **h** we found:	NIH
	40: 8	We **h** dreamed a dream, and *there is* no	NIH
	40:15	also **h** I done nothing that they should	NIH
	41:15	I **h** dreamed a dream, and *there is* none	NIH
	41:15	I **h** heard say of thee, *that* thou canst	NIH
	41:28	This *is* the thing, which I **h** spoken unto	NIH
	41:41	See, I **h** set thee over all the land of Egypt.	NIH
	42: 2	I **h** heard that there is corn in Egypt:	NIH
	42:36	Me **h** ye bereaved of my children:	NIH
	43: 7	**h** ye *another* brother? and we told	3426+3807.1
	43:21	we **h** brought it again in our hand.	NIH
	43:22	other money **h** we brought down in our	NIH
	44: 4	Wherefore **h** ye rewarded evil for good?	NIH
	44: 5	he divineth? ye **h** done evil in *so* doing.	NIH
	44:15	What deed *is* this that ye **h** done?	NIH
	44:19	**H** ye a father, or a brother?	3426+3807.1
	44:20	We **h** a father, an old man,	3426+3807.1
	45:13	glory in Egypt, and of all that you **h** seen;	NIH
	46:30	I **h** seen thy face, because thou *art* yet	NIH
	46:32	**h** brought their flocks, and their herds,	NIH
	46:32	and their herds, and all that they **h**.	3807.1
	47: 1	and their herds, and all that they **h**,	3807.1

Ge	47: 4	for thy servants **h** no pasture for their	3807.1
	47: 9	evil **h** the days of the years of my life	1961
	47: 9	**h** not attained unto the days of the years	NIH
	47:23	I **h** bought you *this* day and your land for	NIH
	47:26	*that* Pharaoh should **h** the fifth *part;*	3807.1
	47:29	If now I **h** found grace in thy sight, put,	NIH
	48:22	Moreover I **h** given to thee one portion	NIH
	49:18	I **h** waited for thy salvation, O LORD.	NIH
	49:23	The archers **h** sorely grieved him,	NIH
	49:26	The blessings of thy father **h** prevailed	NIH
	50: 4	now I **h** found grace in your eyes, speak,	NIH
	50: 5	in my grave which I **h** digged for me in	NIH
Ex	1:18	Why **h** ye done this thing, and have saved	NIH
	1:18	and **h** saved the men children alive?	NIH
	2:20	why *is it that* ye **h** left the man? call him,	NIH
	2:22	I **h** been a stranger in a strange land.	NIH
	3: 7	I **h** surely seen the affliction of my people	NIH
	3: 7	**h** heard their cry by reason of their	NIH
	3: 9	I **h** also seen the oppression wherewith	NIH
	3:12	*be* a token unto thee, that I **h** sent thee:	NIH
	3:16	I **h** surely visited you, and *seen* that which	NIH
	3:17	I **h** said, I will bring you up out of	NIH
	4:11	or the blind? **h** not I the LORD?	NIH
	4:21	Pharaoh, which I **h** put in thine hand:	NIH
	5:14	Wherefore **h** ye not fulfilled your task in	NIH
	5:21	you **h** made our savour to be abhorred in	NIH
	6: 4	I **h** also established my covenant with	NIH
	6: 5	I **h** also heard the groaning of the children	NIH
	6: 5	and I **h** remembered my covenant.	NIH
	6:12	children of Israel **h** not hearkened unto	NIH
	7: 1	See, I **h** made thee a god to Pharaoh:	NIH
	9:16	in very deed for this cause **h** I raised thee	NIH
	9:27	and said unto them, I **h** sinned *this* time:	NIH
	10: 1	for I **h** hardened his heart, and the heart	NIH
	10: 2	what things I **h** wrought in Egypt, and my	NIH
	10: 2	my signs which I **h** done amongst them;	NIH
	10: 6	thy fathers, nor thy fathers' fathers **h** seen,	NIH
	10:16	I **h** sinned against the LORD your God,	NIH
	12:17	for in this selfsame day **h** I brought your	NIH
	12:31	and go, serve the LORD, as ye **h** said.	NIH
	12:32	and your herds, as ye **h** said, and be gone;	NIH
	14: 5	said, Why **h** we done this, that we have	NIH
	14: 5	that we **h** let Israel go from serving us?	NIH
	14:13	for the Egyptians whom ye **h** seen to day,	NIH
	14:18	I **h** gotten me honour upon Pharaoh,	NIH
	15: 5	The depths **h** covered them: they sank	NIH
	15:17	O Lord, *which* thy hands **h** established.	NIH
	15:26	which I **h** brought upon the Egyptians:	NIH
	16: 3	for ye **h** brought us forth into this	NIH
	16:12	I **h** heard the murmurings of the children	NIH
	16:32	they may see the bread wherewith I **h**	NIH
	17:16	*h* war with Amalek from generation to	NIH
	18: 3	he said, I **h** been an alien in a strange land:	NIH
	18:16	When they **h** a matter, they come	1961+3807.1
	19: 4	Ye **h** seen what I did unto the Egyptians,	NIH
	20: 2	which **h** brought thee out of the land of	NIH
	20: 3	Thou shalt **h** no other gods before	1961+3807.1
	20:22	Ye **h** seen that I have talked with you from	NIH
	20:22	Ye have seen that I **h** talked with you from	NIH
	21: 4	If his master **h** given him a wife,	NIH
	21: 4	and she **h** born him sons or daughters;	NIH
	21: 8	a strange nation he shall **h** no **power**,	4910
	21: 9	if he **h** betrothed her unto his son, he shall	NIH
	21:31	Whether he **h** gored a son, or have	NIH
	21:31	have gored a son, or **h** gored a daughter,	NIH
	22: 3	if he **h** nothing, then he shall be sold for	3807.1
	22: 8	*to see* whether he **h** put his hand unto his	NIH
	23:13	in all *things* that I **h** said unto you be	NIH
	23:20	to bring thee into the place which I **h**	NIH
	24:12	and commandments which I **h** written;	NIH
	24:14	if any man **h** any matters to do, let him	NIH
	26: 2	every one of the curtains shall **h** one	NIH
	28: 3	whom I **h** filled with the spirit of wisdom,	NIH
	28: 7	It shall **h** the two shoulderpieces	1961+3807.1
	28:32	it shall **h** a binding of woven	1961+3807.1
	29:35	according to all *things* which I **h**	NIH
	31: 2	I **h** called by name Bezaleel the son of Uri,	NIH
	31: 3	I **h** filled him *with* the spirit of God,	NIH
	31: 6	I, behold, I **h** given with him Aholiab,	NIH
	31: 6	the hearts of all that are wise hearted I **h**	NIH
	31: 6	they may make all that I **h** commanded	NIH
	31:11	that I **h** commanded thee shall they do.	NIH
	32: 7	land of Egypt, **h** corrupted *themselves:*	NIH
	32: 8	They **h** turned aside quickly out of the	NIH
	32: 8	they **h** made them a molten calf,	NIH
	32: 8	worshipped it, and have sacrificed	NIH
	32: 8	**h** sacrificed thereunto, and said, These *be*	NIH
	32: 8	which **h** brought thee up out of the land	NIH
	32: 9	I **h** seen this people, and, behold, it *is* a	NIH
	32:13	all this land that I **h** spoken of will I give	NIH
	32:30	unto the people, Ye **h** sinned a great sin:	NIH
	32:31	this people **h** sinned a great sin,	NIH
	32:31	a great sin, and **h** made them gods of gold.	NIH
	32:34	the people unto the *place* of which I **h**	NIH
	33:13	I pray thee, if I **h** found grace in thy sight,	NIH
	33:16	and thy people **h** found grace in thy sight?	NIH
	34: 9	If now I **h** found grace in thy sight,	NIH
	34:10	such as **h** not been done in all the earth,	NIH
	34:27	after the tenor of these words I **h** made a	NIH
Lev	4:13	done somewhat against any of	NIH
	4:14	which they **h** sinned against it, is known,	NIH
	6: 3	Or **h** found that which was lost,	NIH
	6:17	**h** given it *unto them for* their portion of	NIH
	7: 7	atonement therewith shall **h** *it.*	1961+3807.1
	7: 8	the priest shall **h** to himself the skin of	1961

Lev	7:10	dry, shall all the sons of Aaron **h**,	1961+3807.1
	7:33	**h** the right shoulder for *his* part.	1961+3807.1
	7:34	heave shoulder **h** I taken of the children	NIH
	7:34	**h** given them unto Aaron the priest and	NIH
	10:17	Wherefore **h** ye not eaten the sin offering	NIH
	10:18	**h** eaten it in the holy *place*, as I	NIH
	10:19	*this* day **h** they offered their sin offering	NIH
	10:19	the LORD; and such things **h** befallen me:	NIH
	10:19	should it **h** been accepted in the sight of	NIH
	11:10	all that **h** not fins nor scales in the seas,	3807.1
	11:11	you shall **h** their carcases in abomination.	NIH
	11:13	these *are they* which **h** in	NIH
	11:21	which **h** legs above their feet, to leap	3807.1
	11:23	which **h** four feet, *shall be* an	3807.1
	12: 2	If a woman **h** conceived seed, and born a	NIH
	13: 2	When a man shall **h** in the skin of his flesh	1961
	13:13	it **h** turned the hair white, and *there be*	NIH
	13:13	*if* the leprosy **h** covered all his flesh,	NIH
	13:24	quick *flesh* that burneth **h** a white bright	1961
	13:38	a woman **h** in the skin of their flesh bright	NIH
	13:55	if the plague **h** not changed his colour,	1961
	15:19	if a woman **h** an issue, *and* her issue in	1961
	15:25	if a woman **h** **an issue** of her blood	2100+2101
	16: 4	shall **h** the linen breeches upon his flesh,	1961
	16:17	**h** made an atonement for himself,	NIH
	17: 7	after whom they **h** gone a whoring.	NIH
	17:11	I **h** given it to you upon the altar to make	NIH
	18:27	(For all these abominations **h** the men of	NIH
	19:23	**h** planted all *manner of* trees for food,	NIH
	19:31	Regard not them that **h** familiar spirits,	NIH
	19:36	and a just hin, shall ye **h**:	1961+3807.1
	20: 6	soul that turneth after such as **h** familiar	NIH
	20:12	they **h** wrought confusion; their blood	NIH
	20:13	of them **h** committed an abomination:	NIH
	20:24	I **h** said unto you, Ye shall inherit their	NIH
	20:24	which **h** separated you from *other* people.	NIH
	20:25	which I **h** separated from you as unclean.	NIH
	20:26	**h** severed you from *other* people, that ye	NIH
	22:13	**h** no child, and is returned unto her	NIH
	23: 7	In the first day ye shall **h** a holy	1961+3807.1
	23:14	the selfsame day that ye **h** brought an	NIH
	23:24	the month, shall ye **h** a sabbath,	1961+3807.1
	23:39	ye **h** gathered in the fruit of the land,	NIH
	24:22	Ye shall **h** one manner of law,	1961+3807.1
	25:26	if the man **h** none to redeem *it*,	1961+3807.1
	25:31	the houses of the villages which **h** no wall	NIH
	25:44	bondmaids, which thou shalt **h**,	1961+3807.1
	26: 9	I will **h** respect unto you, and make you	NIH
	26:13	I **h** broken the bands of your yoke,	NIH
	26:26	*And when* I **h** broken the staff of your	NIH
	26:37	shall **h** no power to stand before	1961+3807.1
	26:40	that also they **h** walked contrary unto me;	NIH
	26:41	*And that* I also **h** walked contrary unto	NIH
	26:41	**h** brought them into the land of their	NIH
	27:20	or if he **h** sold the field to another man,	NIH
Nu	3:12	I **h** taken the Levites from among	NIH
	3:32	*h* the oversight of them that keep the	NIH
	4:15	his sons **h** made an end of covering	NIH
	5: 7	they shall confess their sin which they **h**	NIH
	5: 8	if the man **h** no kinsman to recompense	3807.1
	5:18	priest shall **h** in his hand the bitter water	1961
	5:19	If no man **h** lain with thee, and if thou	NIH
	5:27	and **h** done trespass against her husband,	NIH
	8:16	children of Israel, **h** I taken them unto me.	NIH
	8:18	I **h** taken the Levites for all the firstborn of	NIH
	8:19	I **h** given the Levites *as* a gift to Aaron and	NIH
	9:14	ye shall **h** one ordinance, both for	1961+3807.1
	11:11	**h** I not found favour in thy sight,	NIH
	11:12	**H** I conceived all this people? have I	NIH
	11:12	**h** I begotten them, that thou shouldest say	NIH
	11:13	Whence should I **h** flesh to give unto all	3807.1
	11:15	of hand, if I **h** found favour in thy sight;	NIH
	11:18	for ye **h** wept in the ears of the LORD,	NIH
	11:20	that ye **h** despised the LORD which *is*	NIH
	11:20	**h** wept before him, saying, Why came we	NIH
	12:11	wherein we **h** done foolishly,	NIH
	12:11	done foolishly, and wherein we **h** sinned.	NIH
	13:32	through which we **h** gone to search it,	NIH
	14:11	for all the signs which I **h** shewed among	NIH
	14:14	*for* they **h** heard that thou LORD *art*	NIH
	14:15	nations which **h** heard the fame of thee	NIH
	14:20	I **h** pardoned according to thy word:	NIH
	14:22	Because all *those* men which **h** seen my	NIH
	14:22	**h** tempted me *now* these ten times,	NIH
	14:22	times, and **h** not hearkened to my voice;	NIH
	14:27	I **h** heard the murmurings of the children	NIH
	14:28	as ye **h** spoken in mine ears, so will I do to	NIH
	14:29	upward, which **h** murmured against me,	NIH
	14:31	they shall know the land which ye **h**	NIH
	14:35	I the LORD said, I will surely do it unto	NIH
	14:40	the LORD hath promised: for we **h** sinned.	NIH
	15:22	if ye **h** erred, and not observed all these	NIH
	15:29	You shall **h** one law for him that	1961+3807.1
	16:15	I **h** not taken one ass from them,	NIH
	16:15	from them, neither **h** I hurt one of them.	NIH
	16:28	for *I* **h** not done *them* of mine own mind.	NIH
	16:30	ye shall understand that these men **h**	NIH
	16:41	Ye **h** killed the people of the LORD.	NIH
	18: 6	I **h** taken your brethren the Levites from	NIH
	18: 7	I **h** given your priest's office *unto you as* a	NIH
	18: 8	also **h** given thee the charge of mine heave	NIH
	18: 8	unto thee **h** I given them by reason of	NIH
	18:11	I **h** given them unto thee, and to thy sons	NIH
	18:12	offer unto the LORD, them **h** I given thee.	NIH
	18:19	**h** I given thee, and thy sons and thy	NIH

H

H

Nu 18:20 shalt **h** no **inheritance** in their land, 5157
18:20 thou **h** any part among them: 1961+3807.1
18:21 **h** given the children of Levi all the tenth NIH
18:23 of Israel they **h** no **inheritance**. 5157+5159
18:24 **h** given to the Levites to inherit: NIH
18:24 therefore I **h** said unto them, Among NIH
18:24 Israel they shall **h** no **inheritance**. 5157+5159
18:26 **h** given from them for your NIH
18:30 When ye **h** heaved the best thereof from NIH
18:32 when ye **h** heaved from it the best of it: NIH
20: 4 why **h** ye brought up the congregation of NIH
20: 5 wherefore **h** ye made us to come up out NIH
20:12 into the land which I **h** given them. NIH
20:15 and we **h** dwelt in Egypt a long time; NIH
20:17 to the left, until we **h** passed thy borders. NIH
20:24 he shall not enter into the land which I **h** NIH
21: 5 Wherefore **h** ye brought us up out of NIH
21: 7 came to Moses, and said, We **h** sinned NIH
21: 7 for we **h** spoken against the Lord, NIH
21:30 We **h** shot at them; Heshbon is perished NIH
21:30 we **h** laid *them* waste even unto Nophah, NIH
21:34 I **h** delivered him into thy hand, and all NIH
22:28 unto Balaam, What **h** I done unto thee, NIH
22:34 unto the angel of the Lord, I **h** sinned; NIH
22:38 **h** I now any power at all to say any thing? NIH
23: 4 I **h** prepared seven altars, and I **h** NIH
23: 4 I **h** offered upon *every* altar a bullock and NIH
23:20 I **h** received **commandment** to bless: NIH
24:19 Out of Jacob shall come *he* that shall **h** NIH
25:13 **h** it, and his seed after him, 1961+3807.1
25:18 they **h** beguiled you in the matter NIH
27: 8 no son, then ye shall cause his 3807.1
27: 9 if he **h** no daughter, then ye shall give 3807.1
27:10 if he **h** no brethren, then ye shall give 3807.1
27:11 if his father **h** no brethren, then ye shall 3807.1
27:12 see the land which I **h** given unto NIH
27:17 be not as sheep which **h** no shepherd. 3807.1
28:25 on the seventh day ye shall **h** a 1961+3807.1
28:26 your weeks *be out*, ye shall **h** 1961+3807.1
29: 1 ye shall **h** a holy convocation; 1961+3807.1
29: 7 ye shall **h** on the tenth *day* of 1961+3807.1
29:12 ye shall **h** a holy convocation; 1961+3807.1
29:35 On the eighth day ye shall **h** a 1961+3807.1
30: 9 wherewith they **h** bound their souls, NIH
31:15 them, **H** ye saved all the women alive? NIH
31:18 that **h** not known a man by lying with NIH
31:49 Thy servants **h** taken the sum of the men NIH
31:50 We **h** therefore brought an oblation for NIH
32: 4 land for cattle, and thy servants **h** cattle: 3807.1
32: 5 said they, if we **h** found grace in thy sight, NIH
32:11 because they **h** not wholly followed me: NIH
32:12 for they **h** wholly followed the Lord. NIH
32:17 until we **h** brought them unto their place: NIH
32:18 until the children of Israel **h** inherited NIH
32:23 behold, ye **h** sinned against the Lord: NIH
32:30 they shall **h** **possessions** among you in 270
33:53 for I **h** given you the land to possess it. 1961
34: 6 shall even **h** the great sea for a border; 1961
34:14 **h** received *their inheritance*, and half NIH
34:14 half the tribe of Manasseh **h** received their NIH
34:15 the half tribe **h** received their inheritance NIH
35: 3 the cities shall they **h** to dwell in; 1961+3807.1
35: 8 *them that* **h** many ye shall give many; NIH
35: 8 from *them that* **h** few ye shall give few: NIH
35:13 shall give six cities shall ye **h** for refuge. 1961
35:22 **h** cast upon him any thing without laying NIH
35:28 Because he should **h** remained in the city NIH

Dt 1: 6 Ye **h** dwelt long enough in this mount: NIH
1: 8 Behold, I **h** set the land before you: go in NIH
1:28 our brethren **h** discouraged our heart, NIH
1:28 moreover we **h** seen the sons of NIH
1:41 unto me, We **h** sinned against the Lord, NIH
2: 3 Ye **h** compassed this mountain long 3807.1
2: 5 I **h** given mount Seir unto Esau for a NIH
2: 9 I **h** given Ar unto the children of Lot *for* a NIH
2:19 I **h** given it unto the children of Lot *for* a NIH
2:24 I **h** given into thy hand Sihon the Amorite, NIH
2:31 I **h** begun to give Sihon and his land before NIH
3:19 (*for* I know *that* ye **h** much cattle,) 3807.1
3:19 shall abide in your cities which I **h** given NIH
3:20 Until the Lord **h** given rest unto your 3807.1
3:20 unto his possession, which I **h** given you. NIH
3:21 Thine eyes **h** seen all that the Lord your NIH
4: 3 Your eyes **h** seen what the Lord did NIH
4: 5 I **h** taught you statutes and judgments, NIH
4: 9 forget the things which thine eyes **h** seen, NIH
4:25 ye shall **h** remained long in the land, NIH
5: 7 Thou shalt **h** none other gods 1961+3807.1
5:24 we **h** heard his voice out of the midst of NIH
5:24 we **h** seen this day that God doth talk NIH
5:26 of the midst of the fire, as we **h**, and lived? NIH
5:28 I **h** heard the voice of the words of this NIH
5:28 people, which they **h** spoken unto thee: NIH
5:28 they **h** well *said* all that they **h** spoken. NIH
5:28 they have well *said* all that they **h** spoken. NIH
6:10 when the Lord thy God shall **h** brought NIH
6:11 when thou shalt **h** eaten and be full; NIH
7:16 thine eye shall **h** no pity upon them: NIH
7:16 before thee, until thou **h** destroyed them. NIH
9: 7 ye **h** been rebellious against the Lord. NIH
9: 8 that the Lord was angry with you to **h** NIH
9:12 **h** corrupted *themselves;* they are quickly NIH
9:12 they **h** made them a molten image. NIH
9:13 I **h** seen this people, and, behold, it *is* NIH
9:20 the Lord was very angry with Aaron to **h** NIH

Dt 9:23 and possess the land which I **h** given you; NIH
9:24 You **h** been rebellious against the Lord NIH
10:21 terrible *things*, which thine eyes **h** seen. NIH
11: 2 *I speak* not with your children which **h** NIH
11: 2 which **h** not seen the chastisement of NIH
11: 7 your eyes **h** seen all the great acts of NIH
11:28 after other gods, which ye **h** not known. NIH
12:21 as I **h** commanded thee, and thou shalt NIH
12:31 he hateth, **h** they done unto their gods; NIH
12:31 their daughters they **h** burnt in the fire to NIH
13:13 **h** withdrawn the inhabitants of their city, NIH
13:13 serve other gods, which ye **h** not known; NIH
13:17 **h** **compassion** upon thee, 7355
14: 9 all that **h** fins and scales shall ye eat: 3807.1
15:21 *if it be* lame, or blind, *or* **h** any ill blemish, NIH
17: 3 of heaven, which I **h** not commanded; NIH
17: 5 which **h** committed that wicked thing, NIH
18: 1 **h** no part nor inheritance with 1961+3807.1
18: 2 Therefore shall they **h** no 1961+3807.1
18: 8 They shall **h** like portions to eat, beside NIH
18:17 They **h** well *spoken that* which they have NIH
18:17 They have well *spoken that* which they **h** NIH
18:20 which I **h** not commanded him to speak, NIH
19:14 which they of old time **h** set in thine NIH
19:19 as he had thought to **h** done unto his NIH
20: 9 when the officers **h** made an end of NIH
20:18 which they **h** done unto their gods; NIH
21: 7 and say, Our hands **h** not shed this blood, NIH
21: 7 shed this blood, neither **h** our eyes seen NIH
21:11 that thou wouldest **h** *her* to thy wife; 3947
21:14 if thou **h** no delight in her, then thou shalt NIH
21:15 a man **h** two wives, one beloved, 1961+3807.1
21:15 hated, and they **h** born him children, NIH
21:18 If a man **h** a stubborn and 1961+3807.1
21:18 and *that*, when they **h** chastened him, NIH
21:22 a man **h** committed a sin worthy of death, NIH
23:12 Thou shalt **h** a place also without 1961+3807.1
23:13 thou shalt **h** a paddle upon thy 1961+3807.1
25: 5 and one of them die, and **h** no child, 3807.1
25:13 Thou shalt not **h** in thy bag divers 1961+3807.1
25:14 Thou shalt not **h** in thine house 1961+3807.1
25:15 *But* thou shalt **h** a perfect and 1961+3807.1
25:15 and just measure shalt thou **h**: 1961+3807.1
26:10 I **h** brought the firstfruits of the land, NIH
26:13 I **h** brought away the hallowed *things* out NIH
26:13 also **h** given them unto the Levite, NIH
26:13 I **h** not transgressed thy commandments, NIH
26:13 neither **h** I forgotten *them*: NIH
26:14 I **h** not eaten thereof in my mourning, NIH
26:14 neither **h** I taken away *ought* thereof for NIH
26:14 I **h** hearkened to the voice of the Lord NIH
26:14 **h** done according to all that thou hast NIH
28:21 he **h** consumed thee from off the land, NIH
28:31 and thou shalt **h** none to rescue *them*. 3807.1
28:36 neither thou nor thy fathers **h** known; NIH
28:40 Thou shalt **h** olive trees 1961+3807.1
28:48 upon thy neck, until he **h** destroyed thee. NIH
28:51 of thy sheep, until he **h** destroyed thee. NIH
28:64 neither thou nor thy fathers **h** known, NIH
28:65 shall the sole of thy foot **h** rest: 1961+3807.1
28:66 and shalt **h** none assurance of thy life: NIH
29: 2 Ye **h** seen all that the Lord did before NIH
29: 3 The great temptations which thine eyes **h** NIH
29: 5 I **h** led you forty years in the wilderness: NIH
29: 6 Ye **h** not eaten bread, neither have you NIH
29: 6 neither **h** you drunk wine or strong drink: NIH
29:16 ye know how we **h** dwelt in the land of NIH
29:17 ye **h** seen their abominations, and their NIH
29:19 his heart, saying, I shall **h** peace, 1961+3807.1
29:25 Because they **h** forsaken the covenant of NIH
30: 1 I **h** set before thee, and thou shalt call NIH
30: 3 **h** **compassion** upon thee, and will turn 7355
30:15 I **h** set before thee *this* day life and good, NIH
30:19 that I **h** set before you life and death, NIH
31: 5 commandments which I **h** commanded NIH
31:13 which **h** not known *any thing*, may hear, NIH
31:16 break my covenant which I **h** made with NIH
31:18 all the evils which they shall **h** wrought, NIH
31:20 For when I shall **h** brought them into NIH
31:20 they shall **h** eaten and filled *themselves*, NIH
31:21 I **h** brought them into the land which NIH
31:27 ye **h** been rebellious against the Lord; NIH
31:29 turn aside from the way which I **h** NIH
32: 5 They **h** corrupted themselves, their spot *is* NIH
32:21 They **h** moved me to jealousy with *that* NIH
32:21 they **h** provoked me to anger with their NIH
33: 9 and to his mother, I **h** not seen him; NIH
33: 9 for they **h** observed thy word, and kept NIH
34: 4 I **h** caused thee to see *it* with thine eyes, NIH

Jos 1: 3 I **h** given unto you, as I said unto NIH
1: 8 and then thou shalt **h good success**. 7919
1: 9 **H** not I commanded thee? Be strong and NIH
1:15 Until the Lord **h** given your brethren NIH
1:15 they also **h** possessed the land which NIH
2:10 For we **h** heard how the Lord dried up NIH
2:12 the Lord, since I **h** shewed you kindness, NIH
2:13 all that they **h**, and deliver our lives 3807.1
3: 4 for ye **h** not passed *this* way heretofore. NIH
5: 9 *This* day I **h** rolled away the reproach of NIH
6: 2 I **h** given into thine hand Jericho, NIH
7:11 they **h** also transgressed my covenant NIH
7:11 they **h** even taken of the accursed thing, NIH
7:11 **h** also stolen, and dissembled also, NIH
7:11 **h** put *it* even amongst their own stuff. NIH
7:20 Indeed I **h** sinned against the Lord God NIH

Jos 7:20 God of Israel, and thus and thus **h** I done: NIH
8: 1 I **h** given into thy hand the king of Ai, NIH
8: 6 till we **h** drawn them from the city; for NIH
8: 8 shall be, when ye **h** taken the city, *that* ye NIH
8: 8 shall ye do. See, I **h** commanded you. NIH
9: 9 we **h** heard the fame of him, and all that NIH
9:19 We **h** sworn unto them by the Lord God NIH
9:22 Wherefore **h** ye beguiled us, saying, NIH
9:24 because of you, and **h** done this thing. NIH
10: 8 for I **h** delivered them into thine hand; NIH
11:20 that they might **h** no favour, but that *he* 1961
13: 6 an inheritance, as I **h** commanded thee. NIH
13: 8 the Gadites **h** received their inheritance, NIH
14: 9 the land whereon thy feet **h** trodden NIH
17:16 in the valley **h** chariots of iron, NIH
17:17 thou shalt not **h** one lot *only*: 1961+3807.1
17:18 though they **h** iron chariots, *and* though NIH
18: 7 the Levites **h** no part among you; 3807.1
18: 7 received their inheritance beyond Jordan NIH
22: 2 Ye **h** kept all that Moses the servant of NIH
22: 2 **h** obeyed my voice in all that I NIH
22: 3 Ye **h** not left your brethren these many NIH
22: 3 **h** kept the charge of the commandment of NIH
22:11 the half tribe of Manasseh **h** built an altar NIH
22:16 What trespass *is* this that ye **h** committed NIH
22:16 in that ye **h** builded you an altar, that ye NIH
22:23 That we **h** built us an altar to turn from NIH
22:24 if we **h** *rather* done it for fear of *this* NIH
22:24 What **h** you *to do with* the Lord God 3807.1
22:25 of Gad; ye **h** no part in the Lord: 3807.1
22:27 to come, Ye **h** no part in the Lord. 3807.1
22:31 ye **h** not committed this trespass against NIH
22:31 ye **h** delivered the children of Israel out NIH
23: 3 ye **h** seen all that the Lord your God hath NIH
23: 4 I **h** divided unto you *by lot* these nations NIH
23: 4 with all the nations that I **h** cut off, NIH
23: 8 your God, as ye **h** done unto this day. NIH
23:15 he **h** destroyed you from off this good NIH
23:16 When ye **h** transgressed the covenant of NIH
23:16 **h** gone and served other gods, NIH
24: 7 eyes **h** seen what I have done in Egypt, NIH
24: 7 eyes have seen what I **h** done in Egypt: NIH
24:13 I **h** given you a land for which ye did not NIH
24:22 witnesses against yourselves that ye **h** NIH

Jdg 1: 2 **h** delivered the land into his hand. NIH
1: 7 as I **h** done, so God hath requited me. NIH
2: 1 **h** brought you unto the land which I NIH
2: 2 ye **h** not obeyed my voice: why have ye NIH
2: 2 not obeyed my voice: why **h** ye done this? NIH
2:20 and **h** not hearkened unto my voice; NIH
3:19 I **h** a secret errand unto thee, O king: 3807.1
3:20 I **h** a message from God unto thee. 3807.1
5:13 made him that remaineth
 h dominion over 7287
5:13 the Lord **made** me **h dominion over** 7287
5:30 **H** they not sped? have they *not* divided NIH
5:30 they *not* divided the prey; to every man NIH
6:10 ye dwell: but ye **h** not obeyed my voice. NIH
6:14 hand of the Midianites: **h** not I sent thee? NIH
6:17 If now I **h** found grace in thy sight, then NIH
6:22 I **h** seen an angel of the Lord face to NIH
7: 9 host; for I **h** delivered it into thine hand. NIH
8: 2 What **h** I done now in comparison of you? NIH
9:16 if ye **h** done truly and sincerely, NIH
9:16 in that ye **h** made Abimelech king, and if NIH
9:16 if ye **h** dealt well with Jerubbaal and his NIH
9:16 **h** done unto him according to the NIH
9:18 **h** slain his sons, threescore and ten NIH
9:18 upon one stone, and **h** made Abimelech, NIH
9:19 If ye then **h** dealt truly and sincerely with NIH
9:48 What ye **h** seen me do, make haste, NIH
9:48 me do, make haste, *and* do as I **h** done. NIH
10:10 We **h** sinned against thee, both because NIH
10:10 both because we **h** forsaken our God, NIH
10:13 Yet ye **h** forsaken me, and served other NIH
10:14 and cry unto the gods which ye **h** chosen; NIH
10:15 Israel said unto the Lord, We **h** sinned: NIH
11:27 Wherefore I **h** not sinned against thee, NIH
11:35 for I **h** opened my mouth unto the Lord, NIH
13:15 we shall **h** made ready a kid for thee. NIH
13:22 shall surely die, because we **h** seen God. NIH
13:23 he would not **h** received a burnt offering NIH
13:23 neither would he **h** shewed us all these NIH
13:23 *at this* time **h** told us *such things* as these. NIH
14: 2 I **h** seen a woman in Timnath of NIH
14: 6 he rent him as *he* would **h** rent a kid, NIH
14:15 **h** ye called us to take that we have? *is it* NIH
14:15 have ye called us to **take that** we **h**? *is it* 3423
14:16 I **h** not told *it* my father nor my mother, NIH
15: 7 Though ye **h** done this, yet will I be NIH
15:11 they did unto me, so **h** I done unto them. NIH
15:16 with the jaw of an ass **h** I slain a thousand NIH
16:17 for I **h** *been* a Nazarite unto God from my NIH
17:13 me good, seeing I **h** a Levite to *my* priest. 1961
18: 9 for we **h** seen the land, and behold, it *is* NIH
18:14 now therefore consider what ye **h** to do. NIH
18:24 Ye **h** taken away my gods which I made, NIH
18:24 what **h** I more? and what *is* that *ye* 3807.1
20: 5 me by night, *and* thought to **h** slain me: NIH
20: 5 my concubine **h** they forced, that she is NIH
20: 6 for they **h** committed lewdness and folly NIH
20:10 according to all the folly that they **h** NIH
21: 7 seeing we **h** sworn by the Lord that *we* NIH
21:18 for the children of Israel **h** sworn, saying, NIH

Ru 1: 8 as ye **h** dealt with the dead, and with me. NIH

Ru	1:12 go *your way;* for I am too old to **h**	1961+3807.1
	1:12 If I should say, I **h** hope, *if* I should have	3426
	1:12 *if* I should **h** a husband also to	1961+3807.1
	2: 9 **h** I not charged the young men that *they*	NIH
	2: 9 of *that* which the young men **h** drawn.	NIH
	2:10 Why **h** I found grace in thine eyes,	NIH
	2:21 until they **h** ended all my harvest.	NIH
	3: 3 until he shall **h** done eating and drinking.	NIH
	3:18 rest, until he **h** finished the thing *this* day.	NIH
	4: 9 that I **h** bought all that *was* Elimelech's,	NIH
	4:10 of Mahlon, **h** I purchased to be my wife,	NIH
1Sa	1:15 I **h** drunk neither wine nor strong drink,	NIH
	1:15 **h** poured out my soul before the Lord.	NIH
	1:16 complaint and grief **h** I spoken hitherto.	NIH
	1:20 *saying,* Because I **h** asked him of	NIH
	1:23 thee good; tarry until thou **h** weaned him;	NIH
	1:28 Therefore also I **h** lent him to the Lord;	NIH
	2: 5 *They that were* full **h** hired out themselves	NIH
	2:15 for he will not **h** sodden flesh of thee,	3947
	2:29 which I **h** commanded *in my* habitation;	NIH
	3:12 which I **h** spoken concerning his house:	NIH
	3:13 For I **h** told him that I will judge his house	NIH
	3:14 I **h** sworn unto the house of Eli,	NIH
	4: 9 unto the Hebrews, as they **h** been to you:	NIH
	5:10 They **h** brought about the ark of the God	NIH
	6:21 The Philistines **h** brought again the ark of	NIH
	7: 6 said there, We **h** sinned against the Lord.	NIH
	8: 7 for they **h** not rejected thee, but they have	NIH
	8: 7 not rejected thee, but they **h** rejected me,	NIH
	8: 8 According to all the works which they **h**	NIH
	8: 8 wherewith they **h** forsaken me,	NIH
	8:18 of your king which ye shall **h** chosen you;	NIH
	8:19 Nay, but we will **h** a king over us;	1961
	9: 7 to bring to the man of God: what **h** we?	854
	9: 8 I **h** here at hand the fourth part of a shekel	NIH
	9:16 for I **h** looked upon my people, because	NIH
	9:24 for thee since *I* said, I **h** invited the people.	NIH
	10:19 ye **h** *this* day rejected your God,	NIH
	10:19 We **h** said unto him, Nay, but set a king	NIH
	11: 9 the sun be hot, ye shall **h** help.	1961+3807.1
	12: 1 I **h** hearkened unto your voice in all that	NIH
	12: 1 unto me, and **h** made a king over you.	NIH
	12: 2 I **h** walked before you from my childhood	NIH
	12: 3 whose ox **h** I taken? or whose ass have I	NIH
	12: 3 or whose ass **h** I taken? or whom have I	NIH
	12: 3 or whom **h** I defrauded? whom have I	NIH
	12: 3 whom **h** I oppressed? or of whose hand	NIH
	12: 3 of whose hand **h** I received *any* bribe to	NIH
	12: 5 that ye **h** not found ought in my hand.	NIH
	12:10 said, We **h** sinned, because we have	NIH
	12:10 because we **h** forsaken the Lord,	NIH
	12:10 and **h** served Baalim and Ashtaroth:	NIH
	12:13 behold the king whom ye **h** chosen,	NIH
	12:13 ye have chosen, *and* whom ye **h** desired:	NIH
	12:17 which ye **h** done in the sight of the Lord,	NIH
	12:19 for we **h** added unto all our sins *this* evil,	NIH
	12:20 ye **h** done all this wickedness: yet turn not	NIH
	13:12 I **h** not made supplication unto the Lord:	NIH
	13:13 for now would the Lord **h** established	NIH
	14:29 how mine eyes **h** been enlightened,	NIH
	14:33 said, Ye **h** transgressed: roll a great stone	NIH
	15: 3 utterly destroy all that they **h**,	3807.1
	15:11 It repenteth me that I **h** set up Saul to be	NIH
	15:13 I **h** performed the commandment of the	NIH
	15:15 **h** brought them from the Amalekites:	NIH
	15:15 and the rest we **h** utterly destroyed.	NIH
	15:20 I **h** obeyed the voice of the Lord,	NIH
	15:20 **h** gone the way which the Lord sent me,	NIH
	15:20 **h** brought Agag the king of Amalek,	NIH
	15:20 and **h** utterly destroyed the Amalekites.	NIH
	15:21 chief of the things which should **h** been	NIH
	15:24 Saul said unto Samuel, I **h** sinned: for I	NIH
	15:24 for I **h** transgressed the commandment of	NIH
	15:30 he said, I **h** sinned: *yet* honour me now,	NIH
	16: 1 seeing I **h** rejected him from reigning over	NIH
	16: 1 for I **h** provided me a king among his sons.	NIH
	16: 7 of his stature; because I **h** refused him:	NIH
	16:18 I **h** seen a son of Jesse the Beth-lehemite,	NIH
	17:25 **H** ye seen this man that is come up?	NIH
	17:29 David said, What **h** I now done? *Is there*	NIH
	17:39 for I **h** not proved *them.* And David put	NIH
	18: 8 **h** ascribed unto David ten thousands,	NIH
	18: 8 and to me they **h** ascribed *but* thousands:	NIH
	18: 8 *what* can he **h** more but the kingdom?	3807.1
	18:19 daughter should **h** been given to David,	NIH
	19: 4 his works **h** *been* to thee-ward very good:	NIH
	20: 1 and said before Jonathan, What **h** I done?	NIH
	20: 3 father certainly knoweth that I **h** found	NIH
	20: 7 *It is* well; thy servant shall **h** peace:	NIH
	20:12 when I **h** sounded my father about to	NIH
	20:23 the matter which thou and I **h** spoken of,	NIH
	20:29 now, if I **h** found favour in thine eyes,	NIH
	20:42 forasmuch as we **h** sworn both of us in	NIH
	21: 2 send thee, and what I **h** commanded thee:	NIH
	21: 2 I **h** appointed *my* servants to such and	NIH
	21: 4 the young men **h** kept themselves at least	NIH
	21: 5 a truth women **h** *been* kept from us about	NIH
	21: 8 for I **h** neither brought my sword nor my	NIH
	21:14 *then* **h** ye brought him to me?	NIH
	21:15 **H** I need of mad men, that ye have	NIH
	21:15 ye **h** brought this *fellow* to play the mad	NIH
	22: 8 That all of you **h** conspired against me,	NIH
	22:13 Why **h** ye conspired against me, thou and	NIH
	22:22 I **h** occasioned *the death* of all the persons	NIH
	23:21 the Lord; for ye **h** compassion on me.	2550

1Sa	23:27 for the Philistines **h** invaded the land.	NIH
	24:10 this day thine eyes **h** seen how that	NIH
	24:11 hand, and I **h** not sinned against thee;	NIH
	24:17 me good, whereas I **h** rewarded thee evil.	NIH
	25: 7 now I **h** heard that thou hast shearers:	NIH
	25:11 my flesh that I **h** killed for my shearers,	NIH
	25:21 Surely in vain I kept all that this *fellow*	NIH
	25:30 when the Lord shall **h** done to my lord	NIH
	25:30 shall **h** appointed thee ruler over Israel;	NIH
	25:31 when the Lord shall **h** dealt well with my	NIH
	25:35 I **h** hearkened to thy voice,	NIH
	25:35 to thy voice, and **h** accepted thy person.	NIH
	26:16 to die, because ye **h** not kept your master,	NIH
	26:18 for what **h** I done? or what evil *is* in mine	NIH
	26:19 If the Lord **h** stirred thee up against me,	NIH
	26:19 for they **h** driven me out *this* day from	NIH
	26:21 Saul, I **h** sinned: return, my son David:	NIH
	26:21 I **h** played the fool, and have erred	NIH
	26:21 played the fool, and **h** erred exceedingly.	NIH
	27: 5 If I **h** now found grace in thine eyes,	NIH
	27:10 Whither **h** ye made a road to day?	NIH
	28: 9 how he hath cut off those that **h** familiar	NIH
	28:15 therefore I **h** called thee, that *thou* mayest	NIH
	28:21 I **h** put my life in my hand,	NIH
	28:21 **h** hearkened unto thy words which thou	NIH
	28:22 eat, that thou mayest **h** strength,	1961+871.1
	29: 3 I **h** found no *fault* in him since he fell *unto*	NIH
	29: 6 for I **h** not found evil in thee since the day	NIH
	29: 8 said unto Achish, But what **h** I done?	NIH
	29: 8 long as I **h** been with thee unto this day,	NIH
	29: 9 the princes of the Philistines **h** said,	NIH
	29:10 early in the morning, and **h** **light**, depart.	215
	30:22 *ought* of the spoil that we **h** recovered,	NIH
2Sa	1:10 and **h** brought them hither unto my lord.	NIH
	1:16 **h** slain the Lord's anointed.	NIH
	2: 5 that ye **h** shewed this kindness unto your	NIH
	2: 5 Lord, *even* unto Saul, and **h** buried him.	NIH
	2: 6 kindness, because ye **h** done this thing.	NIH
	2: 7 the house of Judah **h** anointed me king	NIH
	3: 8 **h** not delivered thee into the hand of	NIH
	4: 6 *as though* they would **h** fetched wheat;	NIH
	4:10 dead, thinking to **h** brought good tidings,	NIH
	4:10 who *thought* that I would **h** given him a	NIH
	4:11 wicked men **h** slain a righteous person	NIH
	7: 6 Whereas I **h** not dwelt in *any* house since	NIH
	7: 6 but **h** walked in a tent and in a tabernacle.	NIH
	7: 7 In all *the places* wherein I **h** walked with	NIH
	7: 9 **h** cut off all thine enemies out of thy sight,	NIH
	7: 9 thy sight, and **h** made thee a great name,	NIH
	7:11 **h** caused thee to rest from all thine	NIH
	7:22 according to all that we **h** heard with our	NIH
	9: 1 **h** given unto thy master's son all that	NIH
	9:10 master's son may **h** food to eat:	1961+3807.1
	12: 8 I would moreover **h** given unto thee such	NIH
	12:13 unto Nathan, I **h** sinned against the Lord.	NIH
	12:27 I **h** fought against Rabbah, and have taken	NIH
	12:27 and **h** taken the city of waters.	NIH
	13: 9 Amnon said, **H** out all men from me.	3318
	13:28 he not I commanded you? be courageous,	NIH
	13:32 Let not my lord suppose *that* they **h** slain	NIH
	14:15 *it is* because the people **h** made me afraid:	NIH
	14:21 Joab, Behold now, I **h** done this thing:	NIH
	14:22 To day thy servant knoweth that I **h** found	NIH
	14:29 sent for Joab, to **h** sent him to the king;	NIH
	14:31 Wherefore **h** thy servants set my field on	NIH
	14:32 *been* good for me to **h** been there still:	NIH
	15: 7 which I **h** vowed unto the Lord,	NIH
	15:26 if he thus say, I **h** no delight in thee;	NIH
	15:34 as I **h** *been* thy father's servant hitherto,	NIH
	15:36 they **h** there with them their two sons,	NIH
	16:10 the king said, What **h** I to do with you,	3807.1
	16:19 as I **h** served in thy father's presence,	NIH
	17:15 of Israel; and thus and thus **h** I counselled.	NIH
	18:11 I would **h** given thee ten *shekels* of silver,	NIH
	18:13 Otherwise I should **h** wrought falsehood	NIH
	18:13 thou thyself wouldest **h** set thyself against	NIH
	18:18 I **h** no son to keep my name in	3807.1
	19: 5 which *this* day **h** saved thy life,	NIH
	19:20 thy servant doth know that I **h** sinned:	NIH
	19:22 David said, What **h** I to do with you,	3807.1
	19:28 **h** I yet to cry any more unto the king?	3426
	19:29 I **h** said, Thou and Ziba divide the land.	NIH
	19:34 said unto the king, How long **h** I to live,	NIH
	19:41 Why **h** our brethren the men of Judah	NIH
	19:41 **h** brought the king, and his household,	NIH
	19:42 **h** we eaten at all of the king's *cost?* or	NIH
	19:43 We **h** ten parts in the king, and we have	3807.1
	19:43 we **h** also more *right* in David than ye:	NIH
	20: 1 and said, We **h** no part in David,	3807.1
	20: 1 neither **h** we inheritance in the son of	NIH
	21: 4 We will **h** no silver nor gold of Saul,	3807.1
	21:16 a new *sword,* thought to **h** slain David.	NIH
	22:22 For I **h** kept the ways of the Lord,	NIH
	22:22 **h** not wickedly departed from my God.	NIH
	22:24 and **h** kept myself from mine iniquity.	NIH
	22:30 For by thee I **h** run *through* a troop: by	NIH
	22:30 a troop: by my God I **h** leaped over a wall.	NIH
	22:38 I **h** pursued mine enemies,	NIH
	22:39 I **h** consumed them, and wounded them,	NIH
	24:10 I **h** sinned greatly in *that* I have done:	NIH
	24:10 I have sinned greatly in *that* I **h** done:	NIH
	24:10 of thy servant; for I **h** done very foolishly.	NIH
	24:17 Lo, I **h** sinned, and I **h** done wickedly:	NIH
	24:17 Lo, I have sinned, and I **h** done wickedly:	NIH
	24:17 these sheep, what **h** they done? let thine	NIH

1Ki	1:35 I **h** appointed him to be ruler over Israel	NIH
	1:44 they **h** caused him to ride upon the king's	NIH
	1:45 Nathan the prophet **h** anointed him king	NIH
	1:45 This *is* the noise that ye **h** heard.	NIH
	2:14 I **h** somewhat to say unto thee.	3807.1
	2:23 if Adonijah **h** not spoken this word against	NIH
	2:42 unto me, The word *that* I **h** heard *is* good.	NIH
	2:43 the commandment that I **h** charged thee	NIH
	3:12 Behold, I **h** done according to thy word:	NIH
	3:12 **h** given thee a wise and an understanding	NIH
	3:13 I **h** also given thee *that* which thou hast	NIH
	5: 8 I **h** considered *the things* which thou	NIH
	8:13 I **h** surely built thee a house to dwell in,	NIH
	8:20 **h** built a house for the name of the Lord	NIH
	8:21 I **h** set there a place for the ark, wherein *is*	NIH
	8:27 much less this house that I **h** builded?	NIH
	8:28 Yet **h** thou **respect** unto the prayer of thy	6437
	8:33 because they **h** sinned against thee,	NIH
	8:35 rain, because they **h** sinned against thee;	NIH
	8:43 which I **h** builded, is called by thy name.	NIH
	8:44 the house that I **h** built for thy name:	NIH
	8:47 We **h** sinned, and have done perversely,	NIH
	8:47 We have sinned, and **h** done perversely,	NIH
	8:47 we **h** committed wickedness;	NIH
	8:48 the house which I **h** built for thy name:	NIH
	8:50 forgive thy people that **h** sinned against	NIH
	8:50 all their transgressions wherein they **h**	NIH
	8:50 that they may **h** compassion on them:	7355
	8:59 wherewith I **h** made supplication before	NIH
	9: 3 I **h** heard thy prayer and thy supplication,	NIH
	9: 3 I **h** hallowed this house, which thou hast	NIH
	9: 4 to do according to all that I **h** commanded	NIH
	9: 6 *and* my statutes which I **h** set before you,	NIH
	9: 7 I cut off Israel out of the land which I **h**	NIH
	9: 7 which I **h** hallowed for my name,	NIH
	9: 9 **h** taken hold upon other gods,	NIH
	9: 9 and **h** worshipped them, and served them:	NIH
	11:11 my statutes, which I **h** commanded thee,	NIH
	11:13 for Jerusalem's sake, which I **h** chosen.	NIH
	11:32 (But he shall **h** one tribe for my	1961+3807.1
	11:32 the city which I **h** chosen out of all	NIH
	11:33 Because that they **h** forsaken me,	NIH
	11:33 **h** worshipped Ashtoreth the goddess of	NIH
	11:33 **h** not walked in my ways, to do *that*	NIH
	11:36 that David my servant may **h** a	1961+3807.1
	11:36 the city which I **h** chosen me to put my	NIH
	12: 9 this people, who **h** spoken to me, saying,	NIH
	12:16 What portion **h** we in David?	3807.1
	12:16 *h* we inheritance in the son of Jesse:	NIH
	14:15 because they **h** made their groves,	NIH
	15:19 I **h** sent unto thee a present of silver and	NIH
	17: 4 I **h** commanded the ravens to feed thee	NIH
	17: 9 I **h** commanded a widow woman there to	NIH
	17:12 I **h** not a cake, but a handful of	3426+3807.1
	17:18 What **h** I to do with thee, O thou man	3807.1
	18: 9 he said, What **h** I sinned, that thou	NIH
	18:18 he answered, I **h** not troubled Israel;	NIH
	18:18 in that ye **h** forsaken the commandments	NIH
	18:36 *that* I **h** done all these things at thy word.	NIH
	19:10 I **h** been very jealous for the Lord God of	NIH
	19:10 for the children of Israel **h** forsaken thy	NIH
	19:14 I **h** been very jealous for the Lord God of	NIH
	19:14 the children of Israel **h** forsaken thy	NIH
	19:18 Yet **h** I left *me* seven thousand in Israel,	NIH
	19:18 the knees which **h** not bowed unto Baal,	NIH
	19:20 Go back again: for what **h** I done to thee?	NIH
	20: 4 thy saying, I *am* thine, and all that I **h**.	3807.1
	20: 5 Although I **h** sent unto thee, saying,	NIH
	20:28 the Lord, Because the Syrians **h** said,	NIH
	20:31 we **h** heard that the kings of the house of	NIH
	21: 2 that I may **h** it for a garden of	1961+3807.1
	21:20 I **h** found *thee:* because thou hast sold	NIH
	22:11 the Syrians, until *thou* **h** consumed them.	NIH
	22:17 hills, as sheep that **h** not a shepherd:	3807.1
	22:17 the Lord said, These **h** no master:	3807.1
2Ki	2:21 saith the Lord, I **h** healed these waters;	NIH
	3:13 king of Israel, What **h** I to do with thee?	3807.1
	3:23 slain, and they **h** smitten one another:	NIH
	3:27 took his eldest son that should **h** reigned	NIH
	5: 6 I **h** *therewith* sent Naaman my servant to	NIH
	5:13 wouldest thou not **h** done *it?* how much	NIH
	7:12 I will now shew you what the Syrians **h**	NIH
	7:17 he leaned to **h** **the charge of** the gate:	5921
	9: 3 I **h** anointed thee king over Israel.	NIH
	9: 5 said, I **h** an errand to thee, O captain.	3807.1
	9: 6 I **h** anointed thee king over the people of	NIH
	9: 6 I **h** anointed thee king over Israel.	NIH
	9:26 Surely I **h** seen yesterday the blood of	NIH
	10: 8 **h** brought the heads of the king's sons.	NIH
	10:19 for I **h** a great sacrifice *to do* to Baal;	3807.1
	10:24 *If* any of the men whom I *h* brought into	3318
	11:15 them, **H** her **forth** without the ranges:	3318
	13:17 in Aphek, till *thou* **h** consumed *them.*	NIH
	13:19 *Thou* shouldest **h** smitten five or six times;	NIH
	17:38 the covenant that I **h** made with you ye	NIH
	18:14 of Assyria to Lachish, saying, I **h** offended;	NIH
	18:20 *I* **h** counsel and strength for the war.	NIH
	18:34 they delivered Samaria out of mine	NIH
	18:35 that **h** delivered their country out of mine	NIH
	19: 6 of the king of Assyria **h** blasphemed me.	NIH
	19:11 hast heard what the kings of Assyria **h**	NIH
	19:12 **H** the gods of the nations delivered them	NIH
	19:12 them which my fathers **h** destroyed;	NIH
	19:17 kings of Assyria **h** destroyed the nations	NIH
	19:18 **h** cast their gods into the fire: for they	NIH

2Ki 19:18 stone: therefore they **h** destroyed them.	NIH
19:20 Sennacherib king of Assyria I **h** heard.	NIH
19:24 I **h** digged and drunk strange waters,	NIH
19:24 with the sole of my feet **h** I dried up all	NIH
19:25 thou hast not heard long ago *how* I **h** done	NIH
19:25 *and* of ancient times that I **h** formed it?	NIH
19:25 now **h** I brought it to pass, that thou	NIH
20: 3 now how I **h** walked before thee	NIH
20: 3 **h** done *that* which *is* good in thy sight.	NIH
20: 5 I **h** heard thy prayer, I have seen thy tears:	NIH
20: 5 I have heard thy prayer, I **h** seen thy tears:	NIH
20: 9 This sign shalt thou **h** of the LORD,	3807.1
20:15 he said, What **h** they seen in thine house?	NIH
20:15 *the things* that *are* in mine house **h** they	NIH
20:15 is nothing among my treasures that I **h**	NIH
20:17 *that* which thy fathers **h** laid up in store	NIH
21: 7 which I **h** chosen out of all tribes of Israel,	NIH
21: 8 according to all that I **h** commanded them,	NIH
21:15 Because they **h** done *that* which *was* evil	NIH
21:15 **h** provoked me to anger, since the day	1961
22: 4 the keepers of the door **h** gathered of	NIH
22: 5 that **h** the oversight of the house of	NIH
22: 8 **h** found the book of the law in the house	NIH
22: 9 servants **h** gathered the money that was	NIH
22: 9 delivered it into the hand of them that	NIH
22: 9 that **h** the **oversight** *of* the house of	6485
22:13 fathers **h** not hearkened unto the words	NIH
22:17 they **h** forsaken me, and have burnt	NIH
22:17 and **h** burnt incense unto other gods,	NIH
22:19 I also **h** heard *thee,* saith the LORD.	NIH
23:27 I **h** removed Israel, and will cast off this	NIH
23:27 will cast off this city Jerusalem which I **h**	NIH
1Ch 11:19 men that **h** put their lives **in jeopardy**?	871.1
15:12 Israel unto *the place that* I **h** prepared for	NIH
17: 5 For I **h** not dwelt in a house since the day	NIH
17: 5 **h** gone from tent to tent, and from *one*	NIH
17: 6 Wheresoever I **h** walked with all Israel,	NIH
17: 6 Why **h** ye not built me a house of cedars?	NIH
17: 8 I **h** been with thee whithersoever thou	NIH
17: 8 **h** cut off all thine enemies from before	NIH
17: 8 **h** made thee a name like the name of	NIH
17:20 according to all that we **h** heard with our	NIH
21: 8 I **h** sinned greatly, because I have done	NIH
21: 8 sinned greatly, because I **h** done this thing:	NIH
21: 8 of thy servant; for I **h** done very foolishly.	NIH
21:17 even I *it is* that **h** sinned and done evil	NIH
21:17 *as for* these sheep, what **h** they done?	NIH
22:14 in my trouble I **h** prepared for the house	NIH
22:14 timber also and stone **h** I prepared;	NIH
28: 6 for I **h** chosen him to be my son, and I will	NIH
29: 2 Now I **h** prepared with all my might for	NIH
29: 3 I **h** set my affection to the house of my	NIH
29: 3 I **h** of mine own proper good, *of* gold and	3426
29: 3 *which* I **h** given to the house of my God,	NIH
29: 3 above all *that* I **h** prepared for the holy	NIH
29:14 and of thine own **h** we given thee.	NIH
29:16 all this store that we **h** prepared to build	NIH
29:17 in the uprightness of mine heart I **h**	NIH
29:17 and now **h** I seen with joy thy people,	NIH
29:19 *for* the which I **h** made provision.	NIH
2Ch 1:11 people, over whom I **h** made thee king:	NIH
1:12 such as none of the kings **h** had that *have*	NIH
1:12 such as none of the kings have had that **h**	NIH
1:12 shall there any after thee **h** the like.	1961
2:13 now I **h** sent a cunning man, endued with	NIH
6: 2 I **h** built a house of habitation for thee,	NIH
6: 6 I **h** chosen Jerusalem, that my name might	NIH
6: 6 **h** chosen David to be over my people	NIH
6:10 **h** built the house for the name of	NIH
6:11 **h** I put the ark, wherein *is* the covenant	NIH
6:18 much less this house which I **h** built?	NIH
6:19 **H** respect therefore to the prayer of thy	6437
6:24 because they **h** sinned against thee;	NIH
6:26 rain, because they **h** sinned against thee;	NIH
6:33 may know that this house which I **h** built	NIH
6:34 the house which I **h** built for thy name;	NIH
6:37 We **h** sinned, we have done amiss,	NIH
6:37 we **h** done amiss, and have dealt wickedly	NIH
6:37 we have done amiss, and **h** dealt wickedly	NIH
6:38 whither they **h** carried them captives,	NIH
6:38 toward the house which I **h** built for thy	NIH
6:39 forgive thy people which **h** sinned against	NIH
7:12 I **h** heard thy prayer, and have chosen this	NIH
7:12 **h** chosen this place to myself for a house	NIH
7:16 For now **h** I chosen and sanctified this	NIH
7:17 do according to all that I **h** commanded	NIH
7:18 according as I **h** covenanted with David	NIH
7:19 which I **h** set before you, and shall go and	NIH
7:20 out of my land which I **h** given them;	NIH
7:20 which I **h** sanctified for my name,	NIH
10: 9 which **h** spoken to me, saying,	NIH
10:16 What portion **h** we in David?	3807.1
10:16 *we* **h** none inheritance in the son of Jesse:	NIH
12: 5 Ye **h** forsaken me, and *therefore* have I	NIH
12: 5 **h** I also left you in the hand of Shishak.	NIH
12: 7 They **h** humbled themselves,	NIH
12: 7 **h** strengthened themselves against	NIH
13: 9 **H** ye not cast out the priests of the LORD,	NIH
13: 9 **h** made you priests after the manner of	NIH
13:10 *is* our God, and we **h** not forsaken him.	NIH
13:11 the LORD our God; but ye **h** forsaken him.	NIH
14: 7 because we **h** sought the LORD our God,	NIH
14: 7 we **h** sought *him,* and he hath given us	NIH
14:11 many, *or* with *them* that **h** no power:	NIH
16: 3 behold, I **h** sent thee silver and gold;	NIH

2Ch 16: 9 from henceforth thou shalt **h** wars.	3426+5973
18:16 as sheep that **h** no shepherd:	3807.1
18:16 the LORD said, These **h** no master;	3807.1
20: 8 **h** built thee a sanctuary therein for thy	NIH
20:12 for we **h** no might against this great	871.1
21:15 thou *shalt* **h** great sickness by disease of	NIH
23:14 unto them, **H** her **forth** of the ranges:	3318
24:20 because ye **h** forsaken the LORD, he hath	NIH
25: 9 which I **h** given to the army of Israel?	NIH
28: 9 ye **h** slain them in a rage *that* reacheth up	NIH
28:11 ye **h** taken captive of your brethren:	NIH
28:13 for whereas we **h** offended against	NIH
29: 6 our fathers **h** trespassed, and done *that*	NIH
29: 6 **h** forsaken him, and have turned away	NIH
29: 6 turned away their faces from	NIH
29: 7 they **h** shut up the doors of the porch,	NIH
29: 7 **h** not burnt incense nor offered burnt	NIH
29: 9 our fathers **h** fallen by the sword,	NIH
29:18 We **h** cleansed all the house of the LORD,	NIH
29:19 we prepared and sanctified, and behold,	NIH
29:31 Now ye **h** consecrated yourselves unto	NIH
31:10 *we* **h** had enough to eat, and have left	NIH
31:10 have had enough to eat, and **h** left plenty:	NIH
32:13 my fathers **h** done unto all the people of	NIH
32:17 the gods of the nations of *other* lands **h**	NIH
33: 7 which I **h** chosen before all the tribes of	NIH
33: 8 land which I **h** appointed for your fathers;	NIH
33: 8 that they will take heed to do all that I **h**	NIH
34:15 I **h** found the book of the law in the house	NIH
34:17 they **h** gathered together the money that	NIH
34:17 **h** delivered it into the hand of the	NIH
34:21 our fathers **h** not kept the word of	NIH
34:24 they **h** read before the king of Judah:	NIH
34:25 Because they **h** forsaken me,	NIH
34:25 and **h** burned incense unto other gods,	NIH
34:27 I **h** even heard *thee* also, saith the LORD.	NIH
35:21 saying, What **h** I to do with thee,	3807.1
35:21 but against the house wherewith I **h** war:	NIH
35:23 the king said to his servants, **H** me **away**;	5674
Ezr 4: 3 You **h** nothing to do with us to build a	3807.1
4:12 **h** set up the walls *thereof,* and joined	NIH
4:14 **h** maintenance from *the king's*	4415+4416
4:14 therefore **h** we sent and certified the king;	NIH
4:15 they **h** moved sedition within the same	NIH
4:16 by this means thou shalt **h** no	383+3807.2
4:19 and sedition **h** been made therein.	NIH
4:20 There **h** been mighty kings also over	NIH
4:20 which **h** ruled over all *countries* beyond	NIH
6: 9 that which *they* **h** need of, both young	2818
6:11 Also I **h** made a decree, that whosoever	NIH
6:12 I Darius **h** made a decree; let it be done	NIH
7:15 his counsellers **h** freely offered unto	NIH
7:20 which thou shalt **h** occasion to bestow,	5308
9: 1 **h** not separated themselves from the	NIH
9: 2 For they **h** taken of their daughters for	NIH
9: 2 that the holy seed **h** mingled themselves	NIH
9: 7 Since the days of our fathers **h** we been in	NIH
9: 7 for our iniquities **h** we, our kings,	NIH
9:10 for we **h** forsaken thy commandments,	NIH
9:11 which **h** filled it from one end to another	NIH
10: 2 We **h** trespassed against our God,	NIH
10: 2 **h** taken strange wives of the people of	NIH
10:10 Ye **h** transgressed, and have taken strange	NIH
10:10 and **h** taken strange wives,	NIH
10:13 for we are many that **h** transgressed in	3807.1
10:14 let all *them* which **h** taken strange wives	NIH
Ne 1: 6 of Israel, which we **h** sinned against thee:	NIH
1: 6 both I and my father's house **h** sinned.	NIH
1: 7 We **h** dealt very corruptly against thee,	NIH
1: 7 **h** not kept the commandments,	NIH
1: 9 will bring them unto the place that I **h**	NIH
2: 5 if thy servant **h** found favour in thy sight,	NIH
2:20 you **h** no portion, nor right, nor memorial,	NIH
4: 5 for they **h** provoked *thee* to anger before	NIH
5: 3 We **h** mortgaged our lands, vineyards,	NIH
5: 4 We **h** borrowed money for the king's	NIH
5: 5 *redeem them;* for other men **h** our lands	NIH
5: 8 We after our ability **h** redeemed our	NIH
5:14 my brethren **h** not eaten the bread of	NIH
5:19 *according to* all that I **h** done for this	NIH
6:13 might **h** *matter* for an evil report,	1961+3807.1
6:14 the prophets, that would **h** put me in fear.	1961
9:33 hast done right, but we **h** done wickedly:	NIH
9:34 Neither **h** our kings, our princes,	NIH
9:35 they **h** not served thee in their kingdom,	NIH
9:37 also they **h** dominion over our bodies,	4910
10:37 that the same Levites *might* **h** the tithes in	NIH
13:14 wipe not out my good deeds that I **h** done	NIH
13:29 because they **h** defiled the priesthood,	NIH
Est 1:18 which **h** heard of the deed of the queen.	NIH
3: 9 of those that **h** the charge of the business,	NIH
4:11 I **h** not been called to come in unto the	NIH
5: 4 unto the banquet that I **h** prepared for him.	NIH
5: 8 If I **h** found favour in the sight of the king,	NIH
7: 3 and said, If I **h** found favour in thy sight,	NIH
8: 5 if I **h** found favour in his sight, and the	NIH
8: 7 I **h** given Esther the house of Haman,	NIH
8: 7 him they **h** hanged upon the gallows,	NIH
9: 1 of the Jews hoped to **h** power over them,	7980
9:12 The Jews **h** slain and destroyed five	NIH
9:12 what **h** they done in the rest of the king's	NIH
Job 1: 5 It may be that my sons **h** sinned,	NIH
1:15 they **h** slain the servants with the edge of	NIH
1:17 carried them away, yea, and slain	NIH
3: 9 let it look for light, but *h* none; neither let	NIH

Job 3:13 now should I **h** lien *still* and been quiet,	NIH
3:13 lien *still* and been quiet, I should **h** slept:	NIH
4: 4 words **h** upholden him that was falling,	NIH
4: 8 Even as I **h** seen, they that plow iniquity,	NIH
5: 3 I **h** seen the foolish taking root:	NIH
5:27 we **h** searched it, so it *is;* hear it,	NIH
6: 8 that I might **h** my request; and *that* God	935
6:10 should I yet **h** comfort; yea, I would	1961
6:10 for I **h** not concealed the words of the	NIH
6:15 My brethren **h** dealt deceitfully as a brook,	NIH
6:24 cause me to understand wherein I **h** erred.	NIH
7:20 I **h** sinned; what shall I do unto thee,	NIH
8: 4 If thy children **h** sinned against him,	NIH
8: 4 **h** cast them away for their transgression;	NIH
8:18 shall deny him, *saying,* I **h** not seen thee.	NIH
10: 8 Thine hands **h** made me and fashioned me	NIH
10:19 I should **h** been as though I had not been;	NIH
10:19 I should **h** been carried from the womb to	NIH
12: 3 I **h** understanding as well as you; I *am*	3807.1
13:18 Behold now, I **h** ordered *my* cause; I know	NIH
14:15 thou wilt **h** a *desire* to the work of thine	3700
14:22 his flesh upon him shall **h** **pain**,	3510
15:17 and that which I **h** seen I will declare;	NIH
15:18 Which wise *men* **h** told from their fathers,	NIH
15:18 told from their fathers, and **h** not hid *it;*	NIH
16: 2 I **h** heard many such *things:* miserable	NIH
16: 3 Shall vain words **h** an end?	7093
16:10 They **h** gaped upon me with their mouth;	NIH
16:10 they **h** smitten me upon the cheek	NIH
16:10 they **h** gathered themselves together	NIH
16:15 I **h** sewed sackcloth upon my skin,	NIH
16:18 and let my cry **h** no place.	1961+3807.1
17:13 I **h** made my bed in the darkness.	NIH
17:14 I **h** said to corruption, Thou *art* my father:	NIH
18:17 and he shall **h** no name in the street.	3807.1
18:19 He shall neither **h** son nor nephew	3807.1
19: 3 These ten times **h** ye reproached me:	NIH
19: 4 be it indeed *that* I **h** erred, mine error	NIH
19:14 My kinsfolk **h** failed, and my familiar	NIH
19:14 and my familiar friends **h** forgotten me.	NIH
19:21 **H** pity upon me, have pity upon me,	2603
19:21 **h** pity upon me, O my friends;	2603
20: 3 I **h** heard the check of my reproach,	NIH
20: 7 they which **h** seen him shall say, Where *is*	NIH
21: 3 and after that I **h** spoken, mock on.	NIH
21:15 what profit should we **h**, if we pray unto	NIH
21:29 **H** ye not asked them that go by the way?	NIH
22: 9 the arms of the fatherless **h** been broken.	NIH
22:15 old way which wicked men **h** trodden?	NIH
22:25 and thou shalt **h** plenty of silver.	3807.1
22:26 shalt thou **h** thy *delight* in the Almighty,	6026
23:11 steps, his way I **h** kept, and not declined.	NIH
23:12 Neither **h** I gone back from	NIH
23:12 I **h** esteemed the words of his mouth	NIH
24: 7 that *they* **h** no covering in the cold.	NIH
24:19 *so doth* the grave *those which* **h** sinned.	NIH
27:12 all ye yourselves **h** seen *it;* why then are	NIH
28: 8 The lion's whelps **h** not trodden it,	NIH
28:22 **h** heard the fame thereof with our ears.	NIH
30: 1 *they* that *are* younger than I **h** me in	3807.1
30: 1 whose fathers I would **h** disdained to have	NIH
30: 1 to **h** set with the dogs of my flock.	3807.1
30:11 they **h** also let loose the bridle before me.	NIH
30:13 forward my calamity, they **h** no helper.	3807.1
30:16 days of affliction **h** taken hold upon me.	NIH
31: 5 If I **h** walked with vanity, or *if* my foot	NIH
31: 9 mine heart **h** been deceived by a woman,	NIH
31: 9 or *if* I **h** laid wait at my neighbour's door;	NIH
31:16 If I **h** withheld the poor from *their* desire,	NIH
31:16 or **h** caused the eyes of the widow to fail;	NIH
31:17 Or **h** eaten my morsel myself alone,	NIH
31:18 I **h** guided her from my mother's womb;)	NIH
31:19 If I **h** seen *any* perish for want of clothing,	NIH
31:20 If his loins **h** not blessed me, and *if* he	NIH
31:21 If I **h** lift up my hand against the fatherless,	NIH
31:24 If I **h** made gold my hope, or have said to	NIH
31:24 or **h** said to the fine gold, Thou *art* my	NIH
31:28 I should **h** denied the God *that is* above.	NIH
31:30 (Neither **h** I suffered my mouth to sin by	NIH
31:39 If I **h** eaten the fruits thereof without	NIH
31:39 **h** caused the owners thereof to lose their	NIH
32:13 ye should say, We **h** found out wisdom:	NIH
33: 2 Behold now I **h** opened my mouth,	NIH
33: 8 I **h** heard the voice of *thy* words,	NIH
33:24 down *to* the pit: I **h** found a ransom.	NIH
33:27 I **h** sinned, and perverted *that* which *was*	NIH
34: 2 give ear unto me, ye that **h** knowledge.	3045
34:31 I **h** borne *chastisement,* I will not offend	NIH
34:32 if I **h** done iniquity, I will do no more.	NIH
35: 3 What profit shall I **h**, *if* I *be cleansed*	NIH
36: 2 I will shew thee that *I* **h** yet to speak on	NIH
36: 9 their transgressions that they **h** exceeded.	NIH
36:16 would he **h** removed thee out of the strait	NIH
38:17 **H** the gates of death been opened unto	NIH
38:23 Which I **h** reserved against the time of	NIH
39: 6 Whose house I **h** made the wilderness,	NIH
40: 5 Once **h** I spoken; but I will not answer:	NIH
42: 3 therefore **h** I uttered that I understood not;	NIH
42: 5 I **h** heard of thee by the hearing of the ear:	NIH
42: 7 for ye **h** not spoken of me *the thing that is*	NIH
42: 8 in that ye **h** not spoken of me *the thing*	NIH
Ps 2: 4 the LORD shall **h** them in derision.	3807.1
2: 6 Yet **h** I set my king upon my holy hill of	NIH
2: 7 *art* my Son; *this* day **h** I begotten thee.	NIH
3: 6 that **h** set *themselves* against me round	NIH

Ps
- 4: 1 **h mercy** upon me, and hear my prayer. 2603
- 5:10 for they **h** rebelled against thee. NIH
- 6: 2 **H mercy** upon me, O Lord; for I *am* 2603
- 7: 3 O Lord my God, if I **h** done this; if there NIH
- 7: 4 If I **h** rewarded evil *unto* him that was at NIH
- 7: 4 I **h** delivered him that without cause is NIH
- 8: 6 Thou **madest** him **to h dominion** over 4910
- 9:13 **H mercy** upon me, O Lord; consider my 2603
- 10: 2 them be taken in the devices that they **h** NIH
- 12: 4 Who **h** said, With our tongue will we NIH
- 13: 4 enemy say, I **h** prevailed against him; NIH
- 13: 5 I **h** trusted in thy mercy; my heart shall NIH
- 14: 1 corrupt, they **h** done abominable works, NIH
- 14: 1 **H** all the workers of iniquity no NIH
- 14: 6 You **h** shamed the counsel of the poor, NIH
- 16: 6 pleasant *places; yea,* I **h** a goodly heritage. 5921
- 16: 8 I **h** set the Lord always before me: NIH
- 17: 4 by the word of thy lips I **h** kept *me from* NIH
- 17: 6 I **h** called upon thee, for thou wilt hear NIH
- 17:11 They **h** now compassed us *in* our steps: NIH
- 17:11 they **h** set their eyes bowing down to NIH
- 17:14 *which* **h** their portion in *this* life, NIH
- 18:21 For I **h** kept the ways of the Lord, NIH
- 18:21 **h** not wickedly departed from my God. NIH
- 18:29 For by thee I **h** run *through* a troop; NIH
- 18:29 and by my God I **h** leaped over a wall. NIH
- 18:37 I **h** pursued mine enemies, NIH
- 18:38 I **h** wounded them that they were not able NIH
- 18:43 a people *whom* I **h** not known shall serve NIH
- 19:13 *sins;* let them not **h dominion** over me. 4910
- 22:12 Many bulls **h** compassed me: strong *bulls* NIH
- 22:12 strong *bulls* of Bashan **h** beset me round. NIH
- 22:16 dogs **h** compassed me: the assembly of NIH
- 22:16 the assembly of the wicked **h** inclosed me: NIH
- 25: 6 for they **h** *been* ever of old. NIH
- 25:16 thee unto me, and **h mercy** upon me; 2603
- 26: 1 O Lord; for I **h** walked in mine integrity: NIH
- 26: 1 I **h** trusted also in the Lord; *therefore* NIH
- 26: 3 mine eyes: and I **h** walked in thy truth. NIH
- 26: 4 I **h** not sat with vain persons, neither will NIH
- 26: 5 I **h** hated the congregation of evildoers; NIH
- 26: 8 I **h** loved the habitation of thy house, NIH
- 27: 4 One *thing* I desired of the Lord, that NIH
- 27: 7 **h mercy** also upon me, and answer me. 2603
- 30:10 Hear, O Lord, and **h mercy** upon me: 2603
- 31: 4 Pull me out of the net that they **h** laid NIH
- 31: 6 I **h** hated them that regard lying vanities: NIH
- 31: 9 **H mercy** upon me, O Lord, for I am in 2603
- 31:13 I **h** heard the slander of many: fear *was* NIH
- 31:17 O Lord; for I **h** called upon thee: NIH
- 32: 5 unto thee, and mine iniquity **h** I not hid. NIH
- 32: 9 as the mule, *which* **h** no understanding: NIH
- 33:21 because we **h** trusted in his holy name. NIH
- 35: 7 For without cause **h** they hid for me their NIH
- 35: 7 *which* without cause they **h** digged for my NIH
- 35:25 say in their hearts, Ah, so would we **h** it: NIH
- 35:25 them not say, We **h** swallowed him up. NIH
- 37:14 The wicked **h** drawn out the sword, NIH
- 37:14 bent their bow, to cast down the poor NIH
- 37:25 I **h** been young, and *now* am old; yet have NIH
- 37:25 yet I **h** not seen the righteous forsaken, NIH
- 37:35 I **h** seen the wicked in great power, NIH
- 38: 8 I **h** roared by reason of the disquietness of NIH
- 40: 9 I **h** preached righteousness in the great NIH
- 40: 9 lo, I **h** not refrained my lips, O Lord, NIH
- 40:10 I **h** not hid thy righteousness within my NIH
- 40:10 I **h** declared thy faithfulness and NIH
- 40:10 I **h** not concealed thy lovingkindness and NIH
- 40:12 For innumerable evils **h** compassed me NIH
- 40:12 mine iniquities **h** taken hold upon me, NIH
- 41: 4 heal my soul; for I **h** sinned against thee. NIH
- 42: 3 My tears **h** been my meat day and night, NIH
- 44: 1 We **h** heard with our ears, O God, NIH
- 44: 1 our ears, O God, our fathers **h** told us, NIH
- 44:17 we **h** not forgotten thee, neither have we NIH
- 44:17 neither **h** we dealt falsely in thy covenant. NIH
- 44:18 neither **h** our steps declined from thy way; NIH
- 44:20 If we **h** forgotten the name of our God, NIH
- 45: 1 I speak of the things which I **h** made NIH
- 45: 8 *whereby* they **h** made thee glad. NIH
- 48: 8 we **h** heard, so have we seen in the city NIH
- 48: 8 **h** we seen in the city of the Lord of NIH
- 48: 9 We **h** thought of thy lovingkindness, NIH
- 49:14 upright shall **h dominion** over them in NIH
- 50: 5 that **h** made a covenant with me, by NIH
- 50: 8 *to* **h** *been* continually before me. NIH
- 51: 1 **H mercy** upon me, O God, according to 2603
- 51: 4 I sinned, and done *this* evil in thy sight: NIH
- 53: 1 are they, and **h** done abominable iniquity: NIH
- 53: 4 **H** the workers of iniquity no knowledge? NIH
- 53: 4 eat bread: they **h** not called upon God. NIH
- 54: 3 they **h** not set God before them. Selah. NIH
- 55: 9 for I **h** seen violence and strife in the city. NIH
- 55:12 I could **h** borne *it:* neither *was it* he that NIH
- 55:12 then I would **h** hid myself from him: NIH
- 55:19 Because they **h** no changes, therefore 3807.1
- 56: 4 praise his word, in God I **h** put my trust; NIH
- 56:11 In God I **h** put my trust: I will not be NIH
- 57: 6 They **h** prepared a net for my steps; my NIH
- 57: 6 they **h** digged a pit before me, into the NIH
- 59: 8 thou shalt **h** all the heathen **in derision**. 3932
- 62:11 hath spoken once; twice **h** I heard this; NIH
- 63: 2 so *as* I **h** seen thee in the sanctuary. NIH
- 66:14 Which my lips **h** uttered, and my mouth NIH
- 68:13 Though ye **h** lien among the pots, *yet shall* NIH

Ps
- 68:24 They **h** seen thy goings, O God; *even* NIH
- 69: 7 Because for thy sake I **h** borne reproach; NIH
- 69:22 *which should* **h** been for *their* welfare, NIH
- 69:35 may dwell there, and **h** it **in possession**. 3423
- 71: 6 thee I **h** been holden up from the womb: NIH
- 71:17 hitherto **h** I declared thy wondrous works. NIH
- 71:18 until I **h** shewed thy strength unto *this* NIH
- 72: 8 He shall **h** dominion also from sea to sea, NIH
- 73: 7 **h more than** heart could wish. 5674
- 73:13 Verily I **h** cleansed my heart *in* vain, NIH
- 73:14 For all the day long **h** I been plagued, NIH
- 73:25 Whom **h** I in heaven *but thee?* and 3807.1
- 73:28 I **h** put my trust in the Lord God, that *I* NIH
- 74: 7 They **h** cast fire into thy sanctuary, NIH
- 74: 7 they **h** defiled *by casting down* the NIH
- 74: 8 they **h** burnt up all the synagogues of God NIH
- 74:18 *that* the foolish people **h** blasphemed thy NIH
- 74:20 **H respect** unto the covenant: for the 5027
- 76: 5 are spoiled, they **h** slept their sleep: NIH
- 76: 5 none of the men of might **h** found their NIH
- 77: 5 I **h** considered the days of old, the years of NIH
- 78: 3 Which we **h** heard and known, NIH
- 78: 3 and known, and our fathers **h** told us. NIH
- 79: 1 thy holy temple **h** they defiled; they have NIH
- 79: 1 they **h** laid Jerusalem on heaps. NIH
- 79: 2 The dead bodies of thy servants **h** they NIH
- 79: 3 Their blood **h** they shed like water round NIH
- 79: 6 out thy wrath upon the heathen that **h** NIH
- 79: 6 upon the kingdoms that **h** not called upon NIH
- 79: 7 For they **h** devoured Jacob, and laid waste NIH
- 79:12 wherewith they **h** reproached thee, NIH
- 81:14 I should soon **h** subdued their enemies, NIH
- 81:15 The haters of the Lord should **h** NIH
- 81:15 but their time should **h** endured for ever. NIH
- 81:16 He should **h** fed them also with the finest NIH
- 81:16 *with* honey out of the rock should I **h** NIH
- 82: 6 I **h** said, Ye *are* gods; and all of you are NIH
- 83: 2 and they that hate thee **h** lift up the head. NIH
- 83: 3 They **h** taken crafty counsel against thy NIH
- 83: 4 They **h** said, Come, and let us cut them off NIH
- 83: 5 For they **h** consulted together *with* one NIH
- 83: 8 they **h** holpen the children of Lot. Selah. 1961
- 85:10 and peace **h** kissed *each other.* NIH
- 86:14 the assemblies of violent *men* **h** sought NIH
- 86:14 my soul; and **h** not set thee before them. NIH
- 86:16 O turn unto me, and **h mercy** upon me; 2603
- 88: 1 I **h** cried day *and* night before thee: NIH
- 88: 9 Lord, I **h** called daily upon thee, I have NIH
- 88: 9 I **h** stretched out my hands unto thee. NIH
- 88:13 unto thee I **h** cried, O Lord; and in NIH
- 88:16 goeth over me; thy terrors **h** cut me off. NIH
- 89: 2 For I **h** said, Mercy shall be built up for NIH
- 89: 3 I **h** made a covenant with my chosen, NIH
- 89: 3 I **h** sworn unto David my servant, NIH
- 89:19 I **h** laid help upon *one that is* mighty; NIH
- 89:19 I **h** exalted *one* chosen out of the people. NIH
- 89:20 I **h** found David my servant; with my holy NIH
- 89:20 with my holy oil **h** I anointed him: NIH
- 89:35 Once **h** I sworn by my holiness that I will NIH
- 89:51 Wherewith thine enemies **h** reproached, NIH
- 89:51 they **h** reproached the footsteps NIH
- 90:15 *and* the years *wherein* we **h** seen evil. NIH
- 93: 3 The floods **h** lifted up, O Lord, NIH
- 93: 3 the floods **h** lifted their voice; NIH
- 94:20 Shall the throne of iniquity **h** fellowship NIH
- 95:10 heart, and they **h** not known my ways: NIH
- 98: 3 the ends of the earth **h** seen the salvation NIH
- 102: 9 For I **h** eaten ashes like bread, NIH
- 102:13 shalt arise, *and* **h mercy** upon Zion: 7355
- 102:27 the same, and thy years shall **h** no end. NIH
- 104:12 By them shall the fowls of the heaven **h** NIH
- 104:33 to my God **while** I **h** my being. 5750+871.1
- 106: 6 We **h** sinned with our fathers, we have NIH
- 106: 6 we **h** committed iniquity, we have done NIH
- 106: 6 committed iniquity, we **h** done wickedly. NIH
- 109: 2 they **h** spoken against me *with* a lying NIH
- 109: 5 they **h** rewarded me evil for good, NIH
- 111: 2 sought out of all them that **h** pleasure NIH
- 111:10 a good understanding **h** all they that do 3807.1
- 115: 5 They **h** mouths, but they speak not: NIH
- 115: 5 speak not: eyes **h** they, but they see not: 3807.1
- 115: 6 They **h** ears, but they hear not: 3807.1
- 115: 6 not: noses **h** they, but they smell not: 3807.1
- 115: 7 They **h** hands, but they handle not: feet NIH
- 115: 7 feet **h** they, but they walk not: neither NIH
- 116:10 I believed, therefore **h** I spoken: I was NIH
- 118:26 we **h** blessed you out of the house of NIH
- 119: 6 when I **h** respect unto all thy NIH
- 119: 7 when I shall **h** learned thy righteous NIH
- 119:10 With my whole heart **h** I sought thee: NIH
- 119:11 Thy word **h** I hid in mine heart, that I NIH
- 119:13 my lips **h** I declared all the judgments NIH
- 119:14 I **h** rejoiced in the way of thy testimonies, NIH
- 119:15 precepts, and **h** respect unto thy ways. 5027
- 119:22 contempt; for I **h** kept thy testimonies. NIH
- 119:26 I **h** declared my ways, and thou heardest NIH
- 119:30 I **h** chosen the way of truth: NIH
- 119:30 truth: thy judgments **h** I laid *before me.* NIH
- 119:31 I **h** stuck unto thy testimonies: O Lord, NIH
- 119:40 Behold, I **h** longed after thy precepts: NIH
- 119:42 shall I **h** wherewith to answer him that NIH
- 119:43 mouth; for I **h** hoped in thy judgments. NIH
- 119:47 in thy commandments, which I **h** loved. NIH
- 119:48 thy commandments, which I **h** loved; NIH
- 119:51 The proud **h** had me greatly in derision: NIH

Ps
- 119:51 *yet* **h** I not declined from thy law. NIH
- 119:52 of old, O Lord; and **h** comforted myself. NIH
- 119:54 Thy statutes **h** been my songs in the house NIH
- 119:55 I **h** remembered thy name, O Lord, NIH
- 119:55 O Lord, in the night, and **h** kept thy law. NIH
- 119:57 I **h** said that *I would* keep thy words. NIH
- 119:61 The bands of the wicked **h** robbed me: NIH
- 119:61 robbed me: *but* I **h** not forgotten thy law. NIH
- 119:66 for I **h** believed thy commandments. NIH
- 119:67 I went astray: but now **h** I kept thy word. NIH
- 119:69 The proud **h** forged a lie against me: NIH
- 119:71 *It is* good for me that I **h** been afflicted; NIH
- 119:73 Thy hands **h** made me and fashioned me: NIH
- 119:74 see me; because I **h** hoped in thy word. NIH
- 119:79 and those that **h** known thy testimonies. NIH
- 119:85 The proud **h** digged pits for me, which NIH
- 119:92 should then **h** perished in mine affliction. NIH
- 119:94 save me; for I **h** sought thy precepts. NIH
- 119:95 The wicked **h** waited for me to destroy NIH
- 119:96 I **h** seen an end of all perfection: NIH
- 119:99 I **h** more **understanding** than all my 7919
- 119:101 I **h** refrained my feet from every evil way, NIH
- 119:102 I **h** not departed from thy judgments: NIH
- 119:106 I **h** sworn, and I will perform *it,* that *I* will NIH
- 119:110 The wicked **h** laid a snare for me: yet I NIH
- 119:111 Thy testimonies **h** I taken as an heritage NIH
- 119:112 I **h** inclined mine heart to perform thy NIH
- 119:117 I will **h** respect unto thy statutes 8159
- 119:121 I **h** done judgment and justice: leave me NIH
- 119:126 to work: *for* they **h** made void thy law. NIH
- 119:133 let not any iniquity **h dominion** over me. 7980
- 119:139 mine enemies **h** forgotten thy words. NIH
- 119:143 Trouble and anguish **h** taken hold on me: NIH
- 119:152 I **h** known of old that thou hast founded NIH
- 119:161 Princes **h** persecuted me without a cause: NIH
- 119:165 Great peace **h** they which love thy law: 3807.1
- 119:166 I **h** hoped for thy salvation, and done thy NIH
- 119:168 I **h** kept thy precepts and thy testimonies: NIH
- 119:173 hand help me; for I **h** chosen thy precepts. NIH
- 119:174 I **h** longed for thy salvation, O Lord; NIH
- 119:176 I **h** gone astray like a lost sheep; seek thy NIH
- 123: 2 our God, until that **h** **h mercy** upon us. 2603
- 123: 3 **H mercy** upon us, O Lord, have mercy 2603
- 123: 3 upon us, O Lord, **h mercy** upon us: 2603
- 129: 1 Many a time **h** they afflicted me from my NIH
- 129: 2 Many a time **h** they afflicted me from my NIH
- 129: 2 yet they **h** not prevailed against me. NIH
- 130: 1 Out of the depths **h** I cried unto thee, NIH
- 131: 2 Surely I **h** behaved and quieted myself, NIH
- 132:14 here will I dwell; for I **h** desired it. NIH
- 132:17 I **h** ordained a lamp for mine anointed. NIH
- 135:16 They **h** mouths, but they speak not; 3807.1
- 135:16 not; eyes **h** they, but they see not: 3807.1
- 135:17 They **h** ears, but they hear not; neither 3807.1
- 140: 3 They **h** sharpened their tongues like a NIH
- 140: 4 who **h** purposed to overthrow my goings. NIH
- 140: 5 The proud **h** hid a snare for me, NIH
- 140: 5 they **h** spread a net by the way side; NIH
- 140: 5 by the way side; they **h** set grins for me. NIH
- 141: 9 me from the snare *which* they **h** laid NIH
- 142: 3 the way wherein I walked **h** they privily NIH
- 143: 3 darkness, as those that **h** been long dead. NIH
- 146: 2 my God *while* I **h** *any* being. 5750+871.1
- 147:20 *his* judgments, they **h** not known them. NIH
- 149: 9 this honour **h** all his saints. Praise ye 3807.1

Pr
- 1:14 among us; let us all **h** one purse: 1961+3807.1
- 1:24 Because I **h** called, and ye refused; I have NIH
- 1:24 I **h** stretched out my hand, and no man NIH
- 1:25 ye **h** set at nought all my counsel, NIH
- 3:30 without cause, if he **h** done thee no harm. NIH
- 4:11 I **h** taught thee in the way of wisdom; NIH
- 4:11 way of wisdom; I **h** led thee in right paths. NIH
- 4:16 sleep not, except they **h** done mischief; NIH
- 5:12 How **h** I hated instruction, and my heart NIH
- 5:13 **h** not obeyed the voice of my teachers, NIH
- 7:14 *I* **h** peace offerings with me; *this* day have NIH
- 7:14 with me; *this* day **h** I payed my vows. NIH
- 7:15 to seek thy face, and **h** I found thee. NIH
- 7:16 I **h** deckt my bed with coverings of NIH
- 7:17 I **h** perfumed my bed *with* myrrh, aloes, NIH
- 7:26 many strong *men* **h** been slain by her. NIH
- 8:14 I *am* understanding; I **h** strength. 3807.1
- 9: 5 and drink of the wine *which* I **h** mingled. NIH
- 13: 3 he that openeth wide his lips shall **h** NIH
- 14:26 and his children shall **h** a place of refuge. 1961
- 17: 2 A wise servant shall **h rule** over a son 4910
- 17: 2 shall **h part** of the inheritance among 2505
- 19:10 much less for a servant to **h rule** over 4910
- 20: 4 shall he beg in harvest, and *h* nothing. NIH
- 20: 9 Who can say, I **h** made my heart clean, NIH
- 22:19 I **h** made known to thee *this* day, even *to* NIH
- 22:20 **H** not I written to thee excellent things in NIH
- 22:28 ancient landmark, which thy fathers **h** set. NIH
- 23:24 that begetteth a wise *child* shall **h joy** of 8055
- 23:35 They **h** stricken me, *shalt thou say,* and NIH
- 23:35 they **h** beaten me, *and* I felt *it* not: NIH
- 24:23 *It is* not good to **h** respect of persons in NIH
- 25: 7 of the prince whom thine eyes **h** seen. NIH
- 27:27 *thou shalt* **h** goats' milk enough for thy NIH
- 28:10 the upright shall **h** good *things* in NIH
- 28:13 and forsaketh *them* shall **h mercy**. 7355
- 28:19 He that tilleth his land shall **h plenty** of 7646
- 28:19 vain *persons* shall **h** poverty **enough**. 7646
- 28:21 To **h** respect of persons *is* not good: for NIH
- 28:27 that hideth his eyes shall **h** many a curse. NIH

H

Pr 29:21 shall **h** him become *his* son at the length. NIH
30: 2 and **h** not the understanding of a man. 3807.1
30: 3 nor **h** the **knowledge** of the holy. 1847+3045
30: 7 Two *things* I required of thee; deny me NIH
30:20 and saith, I **h** done no wickedness.
30:27 The locusts **h** no king, yet go they forth 3807.1
31:11 so that he shall **h** no **need** of spoil. 2637
31:29 Many daughters **h** done virtuously,

Ecc 1:14 I **h** seen all the works that are done under NIH
1:16 **h** gotten more wisdom than all *they* that NIH
1:16 *they* that **h** been before me in Jerusalem: NIH
2:19 yet shall he **h** **rule** over all my labour 7980
2:19 over all my labour where*in* I **h** laboured, NIH
2:19 where*in* I **h** shewed myself wise under NIH
3:10 I **h** seen the travail, which God hath given NIH
3:19 they **h** all one breath; so that a man NIH
4: 9 **h** a good reward for their labour. 3426+3807.1
4:11 if two lie together, then they **h heat**: 2552
4:16 *even* of all that **h** been before them: NIH
5:13 There is a sore evil *which* I **h** seen under NIH
5:18 Behold *that* which I **h** seen: *it is* good and NIH
6: 1 There is an evil which I **h** seen under NIH
6: 3 and also *that* he **h** no burial; 1961+3807.1
7:12 *that* wisdom giveth life to **them that h** it. 1167
7:15 *things* **h** I seen in the days of my vanity: NIH
7:23 All this **h** I proved by wisdom: I said, NIH
7:27 Behold, this **h** I found, saith the Preacher, NIH
7:28 one man among a thousand **h** I found; NIH
7:28 a woman among all those **h** I not found. NIH
7:29 this only **h** I found, that God hath made NIH
7:29 but they **h** sought out many inventions. NIH
8: 4 All this **h** I seen, and applied my heart NIH
9: 5 neither **h** they any more a reward; 3807.1
9: 6 neither **h** they any more a portion for 3807.1
9:13 This wisdom **h** I seen also under the sun, NIH
10: 5 There is an evil *which* I **h** seen under NIH
10: 7 I **h** seen servants upon horses, NIH
12: 1 thou shalt say, I **h** no pleasure in them; 3807.1

SS 1: 6 *but* mine own vineyard **h** I not kept. 3807.1
1: 9 I **h** compared thee, O my love, to a NIH
2:15 the vines: for our vines *h* tender grapes. NIH
5: 1 I **h** gathered my myrrh with my spice; NIH
5: 1 I **h** eaten my honeycomb with my honey; NIH
5: 1 I **h** drunk my wine with my milk: NIH
5: 3 I **h** put off my coat; how shall I put it on? NIH
5: 3 I **h** washed my feet; how shall I defile NIH
6: 5 eyes from me, for they **h** overcome me: NIH
7:13 and old, *which* I **h** laid up for thee, NIH
8: 8 We **h** a little sister, and she hath no 3807.1
8:12 *must* **h** a thousand, and those that keep NIH

Isa 1: 2 I **h** nourished and brought up children, NIH
1: 2 children, and they **h** rebelled against me. NIH
1: 4 they **h** forsaken the Lᴏʀᴅ, they have NIH
1: 4 they **h** provoked the Holy One of Israel NIH
1: 6 they **h** not been closed, neither bound up, NIH
1: 9 we should **h** been as Sodom, *and* we NIH
1: 9 we should **h** been like unto Gomorrah. NIH
1:29 ashamed of the oaks which ye **h** desired, NIH
1:29 for the gardens that ye **h** chosen. NIH
2: 8 *that* which their own fingers **h** made: NIH
3: 9 for they **h** rewarded evil unto themselves. NIH
3:14 for ye **h** eaten up the vineyard; the spoil of NIH
4: 4 When the Lord shall **h** washed away NIH
4: 4 shall **h** purged the blood of Jerusalem from NIH
5: 4 What could **h** been done more to my NIH
5: 4 to my vineyard, that I **h** not done in it? NIH
5:13 because *they* **h** no knowledge: NIH
5:24 they **h** cast away the law of the Lᴏʀᴅ of NIH
6: 5 for mine eyes **h** seen the King, the Lᴏʀᴅ NIH
6:12 the Lᴏʀᴅ **h** removed men far away, NIH
7: 5 **h** taken evil counsel against thee, saying, NIH
7:17 thy father's house, days that **h** not come, NIH
8: 4 For before the child shall **h** knowledge to NIH
8:19 Seek unto them that **h** familiar spirits, NIH
9: 2 The people that walked in darkness **h** seen NIH
9:17 Therefore the Lord shall **h** no joy in their NIH
9:17 neither shall **h mercy** on their fatherless 7355
9:17 that write grievousness *which* they **h** NIH
10:11 as I **h** done unto Samaria and her idols, NIH
10:13 By the strength of my hand I **h** done *it,* NIH
10:13 I **h** removed the bounds of the people, NIH
10:13 **h** robbed their treasures, and I have put NIH
10:13 I **h** put down the inhabitants like a valiant NIH
10:14 *that are* left, **h** I gathered all the earth; NIH
10:29 they **h** taken up their lodging at Geba; NIH
13: 3 I **h** commanded my sanctified ones, I have NIH
13: 3 I **h** also called my mighty ones for mine NIH
13:18 they shall **h** no **pity** on the fruit of 7355
14: 1 For the Lᴏʀᴅ will **h mercy** on Jacob, 7355
14:24 Surely as I **h** thought, so shall it come to NIH
14:24 and as I **h** purposed, *so* shall it stand: NIH
15: 7 Therefore the abundance they **h** gotten, NIH
15: 7 gotten, and that which they **h** laid up, NIH
16: 6 We **h** heard of the pride of Moab; *he is* NIH
16: 8 the lords of the heathen **h** broken down NIH
16:10 I **h** made *their* vintage shouting to cease. NIH
17: 7 his eyes shall **h** respect to the Holy One of NIH
17: 8 shall respect *that* which his fingers **h** NIH
18: 2 whose land the rivers **h** spoiled. NIH
18: 2 foot, whose land the rivers **h** spoiled, NIH
19: 3 to them that **h** familiar spirits, and to NIH
19:13 they **h** also seduced Egypt, *even they that* NIH
19:14 they **h** caused Egypt to err in every work NIH
21: 2 all the sighing thereof **h** I made to cease. NIH
21: 3 pangs **h** taken hold upon me, as the pangs NIH

Isa 21:10 that which I **h** heard of the Lᴏʀᴅ of hosts, NIH
21:10 the God of Israel, I declared unto you. NIH
22: 3 are bound together, *which* **h** fled from far. NIH
22: 9 Ye **h** seen also the breaches of the city of NIH
22:10 ye **h** numbered the houses of Jerusalem, NIH
22:10 the houses **h** ye broken down to fortify NIH
22:11 ye **h** not looked unto the Maker thereof, NIH
23: 2 that pass over the sea, *they* replenished. NIH
23:12 Chittim; there also shalt thou **h** no rest. 3807.1
24: 5 because they **h** transgressed the laws, NIH
24:16 From the uttermost part of the earth **h** we NIH
24:16 the treacherous dealers **h** dealt NIH
24:16 the treacherous dealers **h** dealt very NIH
25: 9 we **h** waited for him, and he will save us: NIH
25: 9 we **h** waited for him, we will be glad and NIH
26: 1 We **h** a strong city; salvation will God 3807.1
26: 8 O Lᴏʀᴅ, **h** we waited for thee; NIH
26: 9 *With* my soul **h** I desired thee in the night; NIH
26:13 *other* lords besides thee **h** had dominion NIH
26:16 Lᴏʀᴅ, in trouble **h** they visited thee, NIH
26:17 so **h** we been in thy sight, O Lᴏʀᴅ. NIH
26:18 We **h** been with child, we have been in NIH
26:18 have been with child, we **h** been in pain, NIH
26:18 pain, we **h** as it were brought forth wind; NIH
26:18 we **h** not wrought any deliverance *in* NIH
26:18 **h** the inhabitants of the world fallen. NIH
27:11 he that made them will not **h mercy** on 7355
28: 7 they also **h** erred through wine, NIH
28: 7 the prophet **h** erred through strong drink, NIH
28:15 Because ye **h** said, We have made a NIH
28:15 We **h** made a covenant with death, NIH
28:15 for we **h** made lies our refuge, NIH
28:15 and under falsehood **h** we hid ourselves: NIH
28:22 for I **h** heard from the Lord Gᴏᴅ of hosts NIH
29:13 **h** removed their heart far from me, NIH
30: 2 *into* Egypt, and **h** not asked *at* my mouth; NIH
30: 7 therefore **h** I cried concerning this, NIH
30:18 exalted, that *he* may **h mercy** upon you: 7355
30:29 Ye shall **h** a song, as *in* the night 1961+3807.1
31: 6 the children of Israel **h** deeply revolted. NIH
31: 7 which your own hands **h** made unto you NIH
33: 2 be gracious unto us; we **h** waited for thee: NIH
33:13 Hear, ye *that are* far off, what I **h** done; NIH
36: 5 *I* **h** counsel and strength for war. NIH
36:19 **h** they delivered Samaria out of my hand? NIH
36:20 that **h** delivered their land out of my hand, NIH
37: 6 of the king of Assyria **h** blasphemed me. NIH
37:11 hast heard what the kings of Assyria **h** NIH
37:12 **H** the gods of the nations delivered them NIH
37:12 them which my fathers **h** destroyed, NIH
37:18 the kings of Assyria **h** laid waste all NIH
37:19 **h** cast their gods into the fire: for they NIH
37:19 stone: therefore they **h** destroyed them. NIH
37:25 I **h** digged, and drunk water; and with NIH
37:25 with the sole of my feet **h** I dried up all NIH
37:26 thou not heard long ago, *how* I **h** done it; NIH
37:26 *and* of ancient times, that I **h** formed it? NIH
37:26 now **h** I brought it to pass, that thou NIH
38: 3 how I **h** walked before thee in truth and NIH
38: 3 **h** done *that* which *is* good in thy sight. NIH
38: 5 **h** heard thy prayer, I have seen thy tears: NIH
38: 5 have heard thy prayer, I **h** seen thy tears: NIH
38:12 I **h** cut off like a weaver my life: he will NIH
39: 4 said he, What **h** they seen in thine house? NIH
39: 4 All that *is* in mine house **h** they seen: NIH
39: 6 is nothing among my treasures that I **h** NIH
39: 6 *that* which thy fathers **h** laid up in store NIH
40:21 **H** ye not known? have ye not heard? NIH
40:21 **h** ye not heard? hath it not been told you NIH
40:21 **h** ye not understood *from* the foundations NIH
40:29 to *them* that **h** no might he increaseth NIH
41: 8 *art* my servant, Jacob whom I **h** chosen, NIH
41: 9 *Thou* whom I **h** taken from the ends of NIH
41: 9 I **h** chosen thee, and not cast thee away. NIH
41:25 I **h** raised up *one* from the north, NIH
42: 1 delighteth; I **h** put my spirit upon him: NIH
42: 4 till he **h** set judgment in the earth: NIH
42: 6 I the Lᴏʀᴅ **h** called thee in righteousness, NIH
42:14 I long time holden my peace; I have NIH
42:14 I **h** been still, *and* refrained myself: NIH
42:16 I will lead them in paths *that* they **h** not NIH
42:24 the Lᴏʀᴅ, he against whom we **h** sinned? NIH
43: 1 I **h** redeemed thee, I have called *thee* by NIH
43: 1 thee, I **h** called *thee* by thy name; NIH
43: 4 hast been honourable, and I **h** loved thee: NIH
43: 7 for I **h** created him for my glory, I have NIH
43: 7 created him for my glory, I **h** formed him; NIH
43: 7 I have formed him; yea, I **h** made him. NIH
43: 8 Bring forth the blind people that **h** eyes, 3426
43: 8 that have eyes, and the deaf that **h** ears. 3807.1
43:10 and my servant whom I **h** chosen: NIH
43:12 I **h** declared, and have saved, and I have NIH
43:12 I **h** declared, and have saved, and I have NIH
43:12 and saved, and I have shewed, NIH
43:14 For your sake I **h** sent to Babylon, NIH
43:14 **h** brought down all their nobles, NIH
43:21 This people I **h** formed for myself; NIH
43:23 I **h** not caused thee to serve with an NIH
43:27 thy teachers **h** transgressed against me. NIH
43:28 Therefore I **h** profaned the princes of NIH
43:28 **h** given Jacob to the curse, and Israel to NIH
44: 1 my servant; and Israel, whom I **h** chosen: NIH
44: 2 and *thou,* Jeshurun, whom I **h** chosen. NIH
44: 8 **h** not I told thee from that time, NIH
44: 8 **h** declared *it?* ye *are* even my witnesses. NIH

Isa 44:16 saith, Aha, I am warm, I **h** seen the fire: NIH
44:18 They **h** not known nor understood: for he NIH
44:19 to say, I **h** burnt part of it in the fire; NIH
44:19 I **h** baked bread upon the coals thereof; NIH
44:19 I **h** roasted flesh, and eaten *it:* and shall I NIH
44:21 I **h** formed thee; thou *art* my servant, NIH
44:22 I **h** blotted out, as a thick cloud, NIH
44:22 return unto me; for I **h** redeemed thee. NIH
45: 1 to Cyrus, whose right hand I **h** holden, NIH
45: 4 I **h** even called thee by thy name: NIH
45: 4 I **h** surnamed thee, though thou hast not NIH
45: 8 up together; I the Lᴏʀᴅ **h** created it. NIH
45:12 I **h** made the earth, and created man upon NIH
45:12 **h** stretched out the heavens, and all their NIH
45:12 and all their host **h** I commanded. NIH
45:13 I **h** raised him up in righteousness, NIH
45:19 I **h** not spoken in secret, in a dark place of NIH
45:20 they **h** no knowledge that set up the wood NIH
45:21 *h* not I the Lᴏʀᴅ? and *there is* no God NIH
45:23 I **h** sworn by myself, the word is gone out NIH
45:24 in the Lᴏʀᴅ **h** I righteousness, and 3807.1
46: 4 *even* to hoar hairs will I carry *you:* I **h** NIH
46:11 I **h** spoken *it,* I will also bring it to pass; NIH
46:11 it to pass; I **h** purposed *it,* I will also do it. NIH
47: 6 I **h** polluted mine inheritance, NIH
48: 3 I **h** declared the former *things* from NIH
48: 5 I **h** even from the beginning declared *it* to NIH
48: 6 not ye declare *it?* I **h** shewed thee new NIH
48:10 I **h** refined thee, but not with silver: NIH
48:10 I **h** chosen thee in the furnace of affliction. NIH
48:15 I, *even* I, **h** spoken; yea, I have called him: NIH
48:15 I, *even* I, have spoken; yea, I **h** called him: NIH
48:15 I **h** brought him, and he shall make his NIH
48:16 I **h** not spoken in secret from the NIH
48:19 his name should not **h** been cut off nor NIH
49: 4 I said, I **h** laboured in vain, I have spent NIH
49: 4 I **h** spent my strength for nought, NIH
49: 8 In an acceptable time **h** I heard thee, NIH
49: 8 and in a day of salvation **h** I helped thee: NIH
49:13 and will **h mercy** upon his afflicted. 7355
49:15 that *she* should not **h compassion** on 7355
49:16 I **h** graven thee upon the palms of *my* NIH
49:20 The children which thou shalt **h,** NIH
49:21 seeing I **h** lost my children, NIH
50: 1 divorcement, whom I **h** put away? NIH
50: 1 of my creditors *is it* to whom I **h** sold NIH
50: 1 for your iniquities **h** you sold yourselves, NIH
50: 2 **h** I no power to deliver? behold, at my 871.1
50: 7 therefore **h** I set my face like a flint, NIH
50:11 and in the sparks *that* ye **h** kindled. NIH
50:11 This shall ye **h** of mine hand; 1961+3807.1
51:16 I **h** put my words in thy mouth, NIH
51:16 **h** covered thee in the shadow of mine NIH
51:20 Thy sons **h** fainted, they lie at the head of NIH
51:22 I **h** taken out of thine hand the cup of NIH
51:23 which **h** said to thy soul, Bow down, NIH
52: 3 Ye **h** sold yourselves for nought; NIH
52: 5 Now therefore, what **h** I here, saith 3807.1
53: 6 All we like sheep **h** gone astray; we have NIH
53: 6 we **h** turned every one to his own way; NIH
54: 7 For a small moment **h** I forsaken thee; NIH
54: 8 everlasting kindness will I **h mercy** on 7355
54: 9 for *as* I **h** sworn that the waters of Noah NIH
54: 9 **h** I sworn that *I* would not be wroth with NIH
54:16 I **h** created the smith that bloweth the NIH
54:16 and I **h** created the waster to destroy. NIH
55: 4 I **h** given him *for* a witness to the people, NIH
55: 7 and he will **h mercy** upon him; 7355
56:11 *they are* greedy dogs *which* can never **h** 3045
57:11 **h** not I held my peace even of old, NIH
57:16 before me, and the souls *which* I **h** made. NIH
57:18 I **h** seen his ways, and will heal him: I will NIH
58: 3 Wherefore **h** we fasted, *say they,* and NIH
58: 3 *wherefore* **h** we afflicted our soul, NIH
58: 5 Is it such a fast that I **h** chosen? a day for NIH
58: 6 *Is* not this the fast that I **h** chosen? NIH
59: 2 your iniquities **h** separated between you 1961
59: 2 and your sins **h** hid *his* face from you, NIH
59: 3 your lips **h** spoken lies, your tongue hath NIH
59: 8 they **h** made them crooked paths: NIH
59:21 my words which I **h** put in thy mouth, NIH
60:10 but in my favour **h** I had mercy on thee. NIH
61: 7 For your shame *you shall* **h** double; NIH
62: 6 I **h** set watchmen upon thy walls, NIH
62: 9 they that **h** gathered it shall eat it, NIH
62: 9 they that **h** brought it together shall drink NIH
63: 3 I **h** trodden the winepress alone; and of NIH
63:18 The people of thy holiness **h** possessed *it* NIH
63:18 our adversaries **h** trodden down thy NIH
64: 4 since the beginning of the world *men* **h** NIH
64: 5 behold, thou art wroth; for we **h** sinned: NIH
64: 6 like the wind, **h** taken us away. NIH
65: 2 I **h** spread out mine hands all the day unto NIH
65: 7 **h** burnt incense upon the mountains, NIH
65:10 down in, for my people that **h** sought me. NIH
66: 2 all those *things* **h** been, saith the Lᴏʀᴅ: NIH
66: 3 they **h** chosen their own ways, NIH
66:19 isles afar off, that **h** not heard my fame, NIH
66:19 heard my fame, neither **h** seen my glory; NIH
66:24 look upon the carcases of the men that **h** NIH

Jer 1: 9 Behold, I **h** put my words in thy mouth. NIH
1:10 I **h** this day set thee over the nations and NIH
1:16 **h** forsaken me, and have burnt incense NIH
1:16 **h** burnt incense unto other gods, NIH
1:18 I **h** made thee this day a defenced city, NIH

Jer 2: 5 What iniquity **h** your fathers found in me, NIH
2: 5 **h** walked after vanity, and are become NIH
2:11 my people **h** changed their glory for *that* NIH
2:13 For of my people **h** committed two evils; NIH
2:13 they **h** forsaken me the fountain of living NIH
2:16 Tahapanes **h** broken the crown of thy NIH
2:20 For of old time I **h** broken thy yoke, NIH
2:23 not polluted, I **h** not gone after Baalim? NIH
2:25 for I **h** loved strangers, and after them will NIH
2:27 for they **h** turned *their* back unto me, NIH
2:29 ye all **h** transgressed against me, saith NIH
2:30 In vain **h** I smitten your children; NIH
2:31 **H** I been a wilderness unto Israel? a land NIH
2:32 my people **h** forgotten me days without NIH
2:34 I **h** not found it by secret search, NIH
2:35 because thou sayest, I **h** not sinned. NIH
3: 3 Therefore the showers **h** been withholden, NIH
3:13 ye **h** not obeyed my voice, saith NIH
3:18 **h** given for an inheritance unto your NIH
3:20 so **h** you dealt treacherously with me, NIH
3:21 for they **h** perverted their way, NIH
3:21 *and* they **h** forgotten the Lord their God. NIH
3:25 for we **h** sinned against the Lord our NIH
3:25 **h** not obeyed the voice of the Lord our NIH
4:10 Jerusalem, saying, Ye shall **h** peace; 1961
4:18 thy doings **h** procured these *things* unto NIH
4:22 people *is* foolish, they **h** not known me; NIH
4:22 and they **h** none **understanding**: 995
4:22 but to do good they **h** no knowledge. NIH
4:28 **H** I spoken *it*, I have purposed *it*, and NIH
4:28 I have spoken *it*, I **h** purposed *it*, and NIH
4:31 For I **h** heard a voice as of a woman in NIH
5: 3 stricken them, but they **h** not grieved; NIH
5: 3 *but* they **h** refused to receive correction: NIH
5: 3 **h** made their faces harder than a rock; NIH
5: 3 than a rock; they **h** refused to return. NIH
5: 5 for they **h** known the way of the Lord, NIH
5: 5 these **h** altogether broken the yoke, NIH
5: 7 thy children **h** forsaken me, and sworn by NIH
5:11 the house of Judah **h** dealt very NIH
5:12 They **h** belied the Lord, and said, *It is* NIH
5:19 Like as ye **h** forsaken me, NIH
5:21 which **h** eyes, and see not; which **h** 3807.1
5:21 see not; which **h** ears, and hear not: 3807.1
5:22 which **h** placed the sand *for* the bound of NIH
5:25 Your iniquities **h** turned away these NIH
5:25 your sins **h** withholden good *things* from NIH
5:31 means; and my people love *to h it* so: NIH
6: 2 I **h** likened the daughter of Zion *to* a NIH
6:10 them a reproach; they **h** no delight in it. NIH
6:14 They **h** healed also the hurt of *the* NIH
6:19 they **h** not hearkened unto my words, NIH
6:23 spear; they *are* cruel, and **h** no **mercy**; 7355
6:24 We **h** heard the fame thereof: our hands NIH
6:27 I **h** set thee *for* a tower *and* a fortress NIH
7:11 Behold, even I **h** seen *it*, saith the Lord. NIH
7:13 because ye **h** done all these works, NIH
7:14 and to your fathers, as I **h** done to Shiloh. NIH
7:15 as I **h** cast out all your brethren, *even* NIH
7:23 ye in all the ways that I **h** commanded NIH
7:25 I **h** even sent unto you all my servants NIH
7:30 the children of Judah **h** done evil in my NIH
7:30 they **h** set their abominations in the house NIH
7:31 they **h** built the high places of Tophet, NIH
8: 2 whom they **h** loved, and whom they have NIH
8: 2 they **h** served, and after whom they NIH
8: 2 after whom they **h** walked, and whom NIH
8: 2 whom they **h** sought, and whom they NIH
8: 2 sought, and whom they **h** worshipped: NIH
8: 3 which remain in all the places whither I **h** NIH
8: 6 of his wickedness, saying, What **h** I done? NIH
8: 9 lo, they **h** rejected the word of the Lord; NIH
8:11 they **h** healed the hurt of the daughter of NIH
8:13 *the things that* I **h** given them shall pass NIH
8:14 because we **h** sinned against the Lord. NIH
8:16 He devoured the land, and all that is in it; NIH
8:19 Why **h** they provoked me to anger with NIH
9: 5 They **h** taught their tongue to speak lies, NIH
9:13 they **h** forsaken my law which I set NIH
9:13 not obeyed my voice, neither walked NIH
9:14 **h** walked after the imagination of their NIH
9:16 whom neither they nor their fathers **h** NIH
9:16 sword after them, till I **h** consumed them. NIH
9:19 because we **h** forsaken the land, because NIH
9:19 because our dwellings **h** cast *us* out. NIH
10:11 The gods that **h** not made the heavens NIH
10:21 and **h** not sought the Lord: NIH
10:25 for they **h** eaten up Jacob, NIH
10:25 and **h** made his habitation desolate. NIH
11: 5 That *I* may perform the oath which I **h** NIH
11:10 the house of Judah **h** broken my covenant NIH
11:13 ye **h** set up altars to *that* shameful thing, NIH
11:17 which they **h** done against themselves to NIH
11:20 for unto thee **h** I revealed my cause. NIH
12: 2 planted them, yea, they **h** taken root: NIH
12: 5 thou **h** wearied thee, then how canst thou NIH
12: 6 even they **h** dealt treacherously with thee; NIH
12: 6 yea, they **h** called a multitude after thee NIH
12: 7 I **h** forsaken mine house, I have left mine NIH
12: 7 mine house, I **h** left mine heritage; NIH
12: 7 I **h** given the dearly beloved of my soul NIH
12: 8 out against me: therefore I **h** hated it. NIH
12:10 Many pastors **h** destroyed my vineyard, NIH
12:10 they **h** trodden my portion under foot, NIH
12:10 they **h** made my pleasant portion a NIH

Jer 12:11 They **h** made it desolate, *and being* NIH
12:12 end of the land: no flesh *shall* **h** peace. NIH
12:13 They **h** sown wheat, but shall reap thorns: NIH
12:13 they **h** put themselves to pain, *but shall* NIH
12:14 touch the inheritance which I **h** caused NIH
12:15 that I **h** plucked them out, I will return, NIH
12:15 **h compassion** on them, and will bring 7355
13:11 I caused to cleave unto me the whole NIH
13:14 spare, nor **h mercy**, but destroy them. 7355
13:27 I **h** seen thine adulteries, and thy NIH
14: 3 their nobles **h** sent their little ones to NIH
14: 7 are many; we **h** sinned against thee. NIH
14:10 Thus **h** they loved to wander, they have NIH
14:10 they **h** not refrained their feet, therefore NIH
14:13 neither shall ye **h** famine; 1961+3807.1
14:14 them not, neither **h** I commanded them, NIH
14:16 they *shall* **h** none to bury them, them, 3807.1
14:20 our fathers: for we **h** sinned against thee. NIH
15: 5 For who shall **h** pity upon thee, 2550
15: 8 I **h** brought upon them against the mother NIH
15: 8 I **h** caused *him* to fall upon it suddenly, NIH
15:10 I **h** neither lent on usury, nor *men* have NIH
15:10 on usury, nor *men* **h** lent to me on usury; NIH
15:15 know that for thy sake I **h** suffered rebuke. NIH
16: 2 neither shalt thou **h** sons nor 1961+3807.1
16: 5 for I **h** taken away my peace from this NIH
16:10 what *is* our sin that we **h** committed NIH
16:11 Because your fathers **h** forsaken me, NIH
16:11 walked after other gods, and have NIH
16:11 served them, and have worshipped NIH
16:11 **h** worshipped them, and have forsaken NIH
16:11 **h** forsaken me, and have not kept my law; NIH
16:11 have forsaken me, and **h** not kept my law; NIH
16:12 ye **h** done worse than your fathers; NIH
16:18 because they **h** defiled my land, they have NIH
16:18 they **h** filled mine inheritance with NIH
16:19 Surely our fathers **h** inherited lies, vanity, NIH
17: 4 for ye **h** kindled a fire in mine anger, NIH
17:13 because they **h** forsaken the Lord, NIH
17:16 I **h** not hastened from *being* a pastor to NIH
17:16 neither **h** I desired the woeful day; NIH
18: 8 nation, against whom I **h** pronounced, NIH
18:15 they **h** burnt incense to vanity, NIH
18:15 they **h** caused them to stumble in their NIH
18:20 for they **h** digged a pit for my soul. NIH
18:22 for they **h** digged a pit to take me, NIH
19: 4 Because they **h** forsaken me, NIH
19: 4 **h** estranged this place, and have burnt NIH
19: 4 and **h** burnt incense in it unto other gods, NIH
19: 4 whom neither they nor their fathers **h** NIH
19: 4 **h** filled this place *with* the blood of NIH
19: 5 They **h** built also the high places of Baal, NIH
19:13 of all the houses upon whose roofs they **h** NIH
19:13 **h** poured out drink offerings unto other NIH
19:15 upon all her towns all the evil that I **h** NIH
19:15 because they **h** hardened their necks, NIH
20:12 for unto thee **h** I opened my cause. NIH
20:17 that my mother might **h** been my grave, NIH
21: 7 them, neither **h** pity, nor have mercy. 2550
21: 7 them, neither have pity, nor **h mercy**. 7355
21:10 I **h** set my face against this city for evil, NIH
22: 9 Because they **h** forsaken the covenant of NIH
22:12 shall die in the place whither they **h** led NIH
23: 2 Ye **h** scattered my flock, and driven them NIH
23: 2 them away, and **h** not visited them: NIH
23: 3 of all countries whither I **h** driven them, NIH
23:11 in my house **h** I found their wickedness, NIH
23:13 I **h** seen folly in the prophets of Samaria; NIH
23:14 I **h** seen also in the prophets of Jerusalem NIH
23:17 hath said, Ye shall **h** peace; 1961+3807.1
23:20 until he **h** executed, and till he have NIH
23:20 he **h** performed the thoughts of his heart: NIH
23:21 I **h** not sent *these* prophets, yet they ran: NIH
23:21 **h** not spoken to them, yet they prophesied. NIH
23:22 they should **h** turned them from their evil NIH
23:25 I **h** heard what the prophets said, NIH
23:25 saying, I **h** dreamed, I have dreamed. NIH
23:25 saying, I have dreamed, I **h** dreamed. NIH
23:27 as their fathers **h** forgotten my name for NIH
23:36 for ye **h** perverted the words of the living NIH
23:38 I **h** sent unto you, saying, Ye shall not say, NIH
24: 5 I sent out of this place *into* the land NIH
25: 3 I **h** spoken unto you, rising early and NIH
25: 3 and speaking; but ye **h** not hearkened. NIH
25: 4 sending *them;* but ye **h** not hearkened, NIH
25: 7 Yet ye **h** not hearkened unto me, saith NIH
25: 8 hosts; Because ye **h** not heard my words, NIH
25:13 words which I **h** pronounced against it, NIH
25:35 the shepherds **h** no way to flee, 6+4480
26: 4 walk in my law, which I **h** set before you, NIH
26: 5 sending my servants, but ye **h** not hearkened; NIH
26:11 this city, as ye **h** heard with your ears. NIH
26:12 against this city all the words that ye **h** NIH
27: 5 I **h** made the earth, the man and the beast NIH
27: 5 **h** given it unto whom it seemed meet NIH
27: 6 I **h** given all these lands into the hand NIH
27: 6 the beasts of the field **h** I given him also to NIH
27: 8 until I **h** consumed them by his hand. NIH
27:15 For I **h** not sent them, saith the Lord, NIH
28: 2 I **h** broken the yoke of the king of Babylon. NIH
28: 8 The prophets that **h** been before me and NIH
28:14 I **h** put a yoke of iron upon the neck of all NIH
28:14 I **h** given him the beasts of the field also. NIH
29: 4 whom I **h** caused to be carried away from NIH
29: 7 the peace of the city whither I **h** caused NIH

Jer 29: 7 the peace thereof shall ye **h** peace. 1961+3807.1
29: 9 I **h** not sent them, saith the Lord. NIH
29:14 from all the places whither I **h** driven you, NIH
29:15 Because ye **h** said, The Lord hath raised NIH
29:18 among all the nations whither I **h** driven NIH
29:19 they **h** not hearkened to my words, NIH
29:20 whom I **h** sent from Jerusalem to Babylon: NIH
29:23 they **h** committed villany in Israel, NIH
29:23 **h** committed adultery with their NIH
29:23 **h** spoken lying words in my name, which NIH
29:23 name, which I **h** not commanded them; NIH
29:32 he shall not **h** a man to dwell 1961+3807.1
30: 2 Write thee all the words that I **h** spoken NIH
30: 5 We **h** heard a voice of trembling, of fear, NIH
30:11 of all nations whither I **h** scattered thee, NIH
30:14 All thy lovers **h** forgotten thee; they seek NIH
30:14 I **h** wounded thee with the wound of an NIH
30:15 I **h** done these things unto thee. NIH
30:18 and **h mercy** on his dwelling places; 7355
30:24 until he **h** done *it*, and until he have NIH
30:24 he **h** performed the intents of his heart: NIH
31: 3 I **h** loved thee *with* an everlasting love; NIH
31: 3 *with* lovingkindness **h** I drawn thee. NIH
31:18 I **h** surely heard Ephraim bemoaning NIH
31:20 I will **surely h mercy** upon him, 7355+7355
31:25 For I **h** satiated the weary soul, and I have NIH
31:25 and I **h** replenished every sorrowful soul. NIH
31:28 like as I **h** watched over them, to pluck NIH
31:29 The fathers **h** eaten a sour grape, NIH
31:37 the seed of Israel for all that they **h** done, NIH
32:23 they **h** done nothing of all that thou NIH
32:29 upon whose roofs they **h** offered incense NIH
32:30 the children of Judah **h** only done evil 1961
32:30 for the children of Israel **h** only provoked NIH
32:32 they **h** done to provoke me to anger, NIH
32:33 they **h** turned unto me the back, and not NIH
32:33 teaching *them,* yet they **h** not hearkened NIH
32:37 whither I **h** driven them in mine anger, NIH
32:42 Like as I **h** brought all this great evil upon NIH
32:42 I bring upon them all the good that I **h** NIH
33: 5 whom I **h** slain in mine anger and in my NIH
33: 5 for all whose wickedness I **h** hid my face NIH
33: 8 whereby they **h** sinned against me, NIH
33: 8 whereby they **h** sinned, and whereby they NIH
33: 8 whereby they **h** transgressed against me. NIH
33:14 I will perform *that* good thing which I **h** NIH
33:21 he should not **h** a son to reign 1961+3807.1
33:24 Considerest thou not what this people **h** NIH
33:24 thus they **h** despised my people, that *they* NIH
33:25 *if* I **h** not appointed the ordinances of NIH
33:26 to return, and **h mercy** on them. 7355
34: 5 For I **h** pronounced the word, saith NIH
34:17 Ye **h** not hearkened unto me, NIH
34:18 I will give the men that **h** transgressed my NIH
34:18 which **h** not performed the words of NIH
35: 7 nor **h** *any:* but all your days ye 1961+3807.1
35: 8 Thus **h** we obeyed the voice of Jonadab NIH
35: 9 we **h** vineyard, nor field, 1961+3807.1
35:10 we **h** dwelt in tents, and have obeyed, NIH
35:10 **h** obeyed, and done according to all that NIH
35:14 notwithstanding I **h** spoken unto you, NIH
35:15 I **h** sent also unto you all my servants NIH
35:15 ye shall dwell in the land which I **h** given NIH
35:15 ye **h** not inclined your ear, nor hearkened NIH
35:16 **h** performed the commandment of their NIH
35:17 the evil that I **h** pronounced against them: NIH
35:17 because I **h** spoken unto them, but they NIH
35:17 spoken unto them, but they **h** not heard; NIH
35:17 I **h** called unto them, but they have not NIH
35:17 unto them, but they **h** not answered. NIH
35:18 ye **h** obeyed the commandment of NIH
36: 2 therein all the words that I **h** spoken NIH
36:30 He shall **h** none to sit upon 1961+3807.1
36:31 all the evil that I **h** pronounced against NIH
37:18 What **h** I offended against thee, NIH
37:18 this people, that ye **h** put me in prison? NIH
38: 2 for he shall **h** his life for a prey, 1961
38: 9 men **h** done evil in all that they have NIH
38: 9 men have done evil in all that they **h** NIH
38: 9 whom they **h** cast into the dungeon; NIH
38:22 Thy friends **h** set thee on, NIH
38:22 set thee on, and **h** prevailed against thee: NIH
38:25 the princes hear that I **h** talked with thee, NIH
40: 3 because ye **h** sinned against the Lord, NIH
40: 3 **h** not obeyed his voice, therefore this NIH
40:10 and dwell in your cities that ye **h** taken. NIH
41: 8 for we **h** treasures in the field, 3426+3807.1
42: 4 said unto them, I **h** heard *you;* behold, NIH
42:10 I repent me of the evil that I **h** done unto NIH
42:12 that he may **h mercy** upon you, 7355
42:14 of the trumpet, nor **h** hunger of bread; NIH
42:19 know certainly that I **h** admonished you NIH
42:21 And now I **h** this day declared *it* to you; NIH
42:21 ye **h** not obeyed the voice of the Lord NIH
43:10 set his throne upon these stones that I **h** NIH
44: 2 Ye **h** seen all the evil that I have brought NIH
44: 2 Ye have seen all the evil that I **h** brought NIH
44: 3 Because of their wickedness which they **h** NIH
44: 9 **H** ye forgotten the wickedness of your NIH
44: 9 which they **h** committed in the land of NIH
44:10 they **h** feared, nor walked in my law, NIH
44:12 that **h** set their faces to go *into* the land of NIH
44:13 as I **h** punished Jerusalem, by the sword, NIH
44:14 which they **h a desire** to return 5315+5375
44:17 as we **h** done, we, and our fathers, NIH

H

H

Jer	44:18	we **h** wanted all *things,* and have been	NIH

Jer 44:18 we **h** wanted all *things,* and have been NIH
44:18 **h** been consumed by the sword and by NIH
44:22 the abominations which ye **h** committed; NIH
44:23 Because you **h** burnt incense, and because NIH
44:23 because ye **h** sinned against the LORD, NIH
44:23 **h** not obeyed the voice of the LORD, NIH
44:25 your wives **h** both spoken with your NIH
44:25 will surely perform our vows that we **h** NIH
44:26 Behold, I **h** sworn by my great name, NIH
45: 4 *that* which I **h** built *will* I break down, NIH
45: 4 *that* which I **h** planted I *will* pluck up, NIH
46: 5 Wherefore **h** I seen them dismayed *and* NIH
46:12 The nations **h** heard *of* thy shame, NIH
46:28 of all the nations whither I **h** driven thee: NIH
48: 2 in Heshbon they **h** devised evil against it; NIH
48: 4 her little ones **h** caused a cry to be heard. NIH
48: 5 the enemies **h** heard a cry of destruction. NIH
48:29 We **h** heard the pride of Moab; *he is* NIH
48:33 I **h** caused wine to fail from the wine NIH
48:34 unto Jahaz, **h** they uttered their voice, NIH
48:38 I **h** broken Moab like a vessel wherein *is* NIH
49: 9 they will destroy till they **h** enough. NIH
49:10 I **h** made Esau bare, I have uncovered his NIH
49:10 I **h** uncovered his secret places, and he NIH
49:12 to drink of the cup **h** assuredly drunken; NIH
49:13 For I **h** sworn by myself, saith the LORD, NIH
49:14 I **h** heard a rumour from the LORD, NIH
49:23 for they **h** heard evil tidings: they are NIH
49:24 sorrows **h** taken her as a woman in travail. NIH
49:31 which **h** neither gates nor bars, 3807.1
49:37 sword after them, till I **h** consumed them: NIH
50: 6 shepherds **h** caused them to go astray, NIH
50: 6 they **h** turned them away *on* the mountains: NIH
50: 6 they **h** gone from mountain to hill, NIH
50: 6 hill, they **h** forgotten their resting place. NIH
50: 7 All that found them **h** devoured them: NIH
50: 7 because they **h** sinned against the LORD, NIH
50:17 the lions **h** driven *him* away: NIH
50:18 as I **h** punished the king of Assyria. NIH
50:21 do according to all that I **h** commanded NIH
50:24 I **h** laid a snare for thee, and thou art also NIH
51: 7 the nations **h** drunken of her wine; NIH
51: 9 We would **h** healed Babylon, but she is NIH
51:24 evil that they **h** done in Zion in your sight, NIH
51:30 The mighty *men* of Babylon **h** forborn to NIH
51:30 to fight, they **h** remained in *their* holds: NIH
51:30 they **h** burnt her dwelling places; her bars NIH
51:32 the reeds they **h** burnt with fire, and the NIH
51:50 Ye that **h** escaped the sword, go *away,* NIH
51:51 because we **h** heard reproach: NIH
La 1: 2 her friends **h** dealt treacherously with her, NIH
1: 8 because they **h** seen her nakedness: NIH
1:11 they **h** given their pleasant things for meat NIH
1:18 for I **h** rebelled against his commandment: NIH
1:20 within me; for I **h** grievously rebelled: NIH
1:21 They **h** heard that I sigh; *there is* none to NIH
1:21 all mine enemies **h** heard of my trouble; NIH
2: 7 they **h** made a noise in the house of NIH
2:10 they **h** cast up dust upon their heads; NIH
2:10 they **h** girded themselves with sackcloth: NIH
2:14 Thy prophets **h** seen vain and foolish NIH
2:14 they **h** not discovered thine iniquity, NIH
2:14 **h** seen for thee false burdens and causes NIH
2:16 All thine enemies **h** opened their mouth NIH
2:16 they say, We **h** swallowed *her* up: NIH
2:16 looked for; we **h** found, we **h** seen it. NIH
2:16 looked for; we have found, we **h** seen it. NIH
2:22 that I **h** swaddled and brought up hath NIH
3:21 I recall to my mind, therefore **h** I hope. NIH
3:32 yet will he **h** compassion according to 7355
3:42 We **h** transgressed and have rebelled: NIH
3:42 We have transgressed and **h** rebelled: NIH
3:46 All our enemies **h** opened their mouths NIH
3:53 They **h** cut off my life in the dungeon, NIH
4:10 The hands of the pitiful women **h** sodden NIH
4:12 would not **h** believed that the adversary NIH
4:12 the enemy should **h** entered into the gates NIH
4:13 *h* shed the blood of the just in the midst NIH
4:14 They **h** wandered *as* blind *men* in NIH
4:14 they **h** polluted themselves with blood, NIH
4:17 our watching we **h** watched for a nation NIH
5: 4 We **h** drunken our water for money; NIH
5: 5 we labour, *and* **h** no rest. 3807.1
5: 6 We **h** given the hand *to* the Egyptians, NIH
5: 7 Our fathers **h** sinned, *and are* not; NIH
5: 7 *are* not; *and* we **h** borne their iniquities. NIH
5: 8 Servants **h** ruled over us: *there is* none NIH
5:14 The elders **h** ceased from the gate, NIH
5:16 our head: woe unto us, that we **h** sinned! NIH
Eze 2: 3 their fathers **h** transgressed against me, NIH
3: 6 them, they would **h** hearkened unto thee. NIH
3: 8 **h** made thy face strong against their faces, NIH
3: 9 As an adamant harder than flint **h** I made NIH
3:17 I **h** made thee a watchman unto the house NIH
4: 5 For I **h** laid upon thee the years of their NIH
4: 6 I **h** appointed thee each day for a year. NIH
4:14 from my youth up even till now **h** I not NIH
4:15 **h** given thee cow's dung for man's dung, NIH
5: 5 I **h** set it in the midst of the nations and NIH
5: 6 for they **h** refused my judgments, NIH
5: 6 my statutes, they **h** not walked in them. NIH
5: 7 *and* **h** not walked in my statutes, NIH
5: 7 my statutes, neither **h** I kept my judgments, NIH
5: 7 **h** done according to the judgments NIH
5: 9 I will do in thee that which I **h** not done, NIH

Eze 5:11 mine eye spare, neither will I **h** any **pity**. 2550
5:13 they shall know that I the LORD **h** spoken NIH
5:13 when I **h** accomplished my fury in them. NIH
5:15 furious rebukes. I the LORD **h** spoken *it.* NIH
5:17 sword upon thee. I the LORD **h** spoken *it.* NIH
6: 8 that ye may **h** *some* that shall 1961+3807.1
6:10 Therefore **h** I spoken *it:* it shall come to NIH
6:10 I **h** not said in vain that *I* would do this NIH
7: 4 shall not spare thee, neither will I **h** **pity**: 2550
7: 9 eye shall not spare, neither will I **h** **pity**: 2550
7:14 They **h** blown the trumpet, even to make NIH
7:20 therefore **h** I set it far from them. NIH
8:17 for they **h** filled the land *with* violence, NIH
8:17 and **h** returned to provoke me to anger: NIH
8:18 eye shall not spare, neither will I **h** **pity**: 2550
9: 1 Cause them **that h charge over** the city 6486
9: 5 let not your eye spare, neither **h** ye **pity**: 2550
9:10 will I **h** **pity**, *but* I will recompense 2550
9:11 I **h** done as thou hast commanded me. NIH
11: 5 Thus **h** ye said, O house of Israel: NIH
11: 6 Ye **h** multiplied your slain in this city, NIH
11: 6 **h** filled the streets thereof *with* the slain. NIH
11: 7 slain whom ye **h** laid in the midst of it, NIH
11: 8 Ye **h** feared the sword; and I will bring a NIH
11:12 for ye **h** not walked in my statutes, NIH
11:12 **h** done after the manners of the heathen NIH
11:15 whom the inhabitants of Jerusalem **h** said, NIH
11:16 Although I **h** cast them far off among NIH
11:16 although I **h** scattered them among NIH
11:17 the countries where ye **h** been scattered, NIH
12: 2 which **h** eyes to see, and see not; 3807.1
12: 2 not; they **h** ears to hear, and hear not: 3807.1
12: 6 for I **h** set thee *for* a sign unto the house NIH
12:11 like as I **h** done, so shall it be done unto NIH
12:22 *is* that proverb *that* ye **h** in the land 3807.1
12:28 the word which I **h** spoken shall be done, NIH
13: 3 their own spirit, and **h** seen nothing! 3807.1
13: 5 Ye **h** not gone up into the gaps, NIH
13: 6 They **h** seen vanity and lying divination, NIH
13: 6 they **h** made *others* to hope that *they* NIH
13: 7 **H** ye not seen a vain vision, and have ye NIH
13: 7 **h** ye not spoken a lying divination, NIH
13: 7 The LORD saith *it;* albeit I **h** not spoken? NIH
13: 8 Because ye **h** spoken vanity, and seen lies, NIH
13:10 even because they **h** seduced my people, NIH
13:12 Where *is* the daubing where*with* ye **h** NIH
13:14 So will I break down the wall that ye **h** NIH
13:15 them that **h** daubed it *with* untempered NIH
13:22 Because *with* lies ye **h** made the heart of NIH
13:22 righteous sad, whom I **h** not made sad; NIH
14: 3 men **h** set up their idols in their heart, NIH
14: 9 I the LORD **h** deceived that prophet, NIH
14:22 the evil that I **h** brought upon Jerusalem, NIH
14:22 concerning all that I **h** brought upon it. NIH
14:23 ye shall know that I **h** not done without NIH
14:23 done without cause all that I **h** done in it, NIH
15: 6 which I **h** given to the fire for fuel, so will NIH
15: 8 because they **h** committed a trespass, saith NIH
16: 5 unto thee, to **h** **compassion** upon thee; 2550
16: 7 I **h** caused thee to multiply as the bud of NIH
16:27 I stretched out my hand over thee, NIH
16:27 **h** diminished thine ordinary *food,* and NIH
17:21 ye shall know that I the LORD **h** spoken NIH
17:24 the LORD **h** brought down the high tree, NIH
17:24 **h** exalted the low tree, have dried up NIH
17:24 **h** dried up the green tree, and have made NIH
17:24 and **h** made the dry tree to flourish: NIH
17:24 I the LORD **h** spoken and have done *it.* NIH
17:24 I the LORD **h** have spoken and **h** done *it.* NIH
18: 2 The fathers **h** eaten sour grapes, NIH
18: 3 ye shall not **h** *occasion* any more 1961+3807.1
18:23 **H** I any pleasure at all that the wicked NIH
18:31 whereby ye **h** transgressed; NIH
18:32 I **h** no pleasure in the death of him that NIH
20:27 Yet *in* this your fathers **h** blasphemed me, NIH
20:27 that they **h** committed a trespass against NIH
20:41 you out of the countries wherein ye **h** NIH
20:43 your doings, wherein ye **h** been defiled; NIH
20:43 for all your evils that ye **h** committed. NIH
20:44 I **h** wrought with you for my name's NIH
20:48 all flesh shall see that I the LORD **h** NIH
21: 5 That all flesh may know that I the LORD **h** NIH
21:15 I **h** set the point of the sword against all NIH
21:17 my fury to rest: I the LORD **h** said *it.* NIH
21:23 in their sight, to them that **h** sworn oaths: NIH
21:24 Because ye **h** made your iniquity to be NIH
21:25 day is come, when iniquity *shall h* an end, NIH
21:29 come, when *their* iniquity *shall h* an end. NIH
21:32 for I the LORD **h** spoken *it.* NIH
22: 4 I **h** made thee a reproach unto the NIH
22: 7 In thee **h** they set light by father and NIH
22: 7 in the midst of thee **h** they dealt by NIH
22: 7 in thee **h** they vexed the fatherless and NIH
22:10 In thee **h** they discovered their father's NIH
22:10 In thee **h** they humbled her that was set NIH
22:12 In thee **h** they taken gifts to shed blood; NIH
22:13 I **h** smitten mine hand at thy dishonest NIH
22:14 I the LORD **h** spoken *it,* and will do *it.* NIH
22:22 ye shall know that I the LORD **h** poured NIH
22:25 they **h** devoured souls; they have taken NIH
22:25 they **h** taken the treasure and NIH
22:25 they **h** made her many widows in the NIH
22:26 Her priests **h** violated my law, NIH
22:26 **h** profaned mine holy *things:* they have NIH
22:26 profaned mine holy *things:* they **h** put NIH

Eze 22:26 neither **h** they shewed *difference* between NIH
22:26 **h** hid their eyes from my sabbaths, and I NIH
22:28 her prophets **h** daubed them *with* NIH
22:29 The people of the land **h** used oppression, NIH
22:29 and **h** vexed the poor and needy: NIH
22:29 they **h** oppressed the stranger wrongfully. NIH
22:31 Therefore **h** I poured out mine indignation NIH
22:31 I **h** consumed them with the fire of my NIH
22:31 their own way **h** I recompensed upon their NIH
23: 9 Wherefore I **h** delivered her into the hand NIH
23:34 for I **h** spoken *it,* saith the Lord GOD. NIH
23:37 That they **h** committed adultery, NIH
23:37 their idols **h** they committed adultery, NIH
23:37 **h** also caused their sons, whom they bare NIH
23:38 Moreover this they **h** done unto me: NIH
23:38 they **h** defiled my sanctuary in the same NIH
23:38 same day, and **h** profaned my sabbaths, NIH
23:39 **h** they done in the midst of mine house. NIH
23:40 that ye **h** sent for men to come from far, NIH
24: 8 I **h** set her blood upon the top of a rock, NIH
24:13 I **h** purged thee, and thou wast not NIH
24:13 till I **h** caused my fury to rest upon thee. NIH
24:14 The LORD **h** spoken *it:* it shall come to NIH
24:21 daughters whom ye **h** left shall fall by NIH
24:22 shall do as I **h** done: ye shall not cover NIH
25:15 the Philistines **h** dealt by revenge, NIH
25:15 **h** taken vengeance with a despiteful heart, NIH
26: 5 for I **h** spoken *it,* saith the Lord GOD: NIH
26:14 for I the LORD **h** spoken *it,* saith the Lord NIH
27: 4 thy builders **h** perfected thy beauty. NIH
27: 5 They **h** made all thy *ship* boards of fir NIH
27: 5 they **h** taken cedars from Lebanon to NIH
27: 6 *Of* the oaks of Bashan **h** they made thine NIH
27: 6 the company of the Ashurites **h** made thy NIH
27:11 they **h** made thy beauty perfect. NIH
27:26 Thy rowers **h** brought thee into great NIH
28:10 for I **h** spoken *it,* saith the Lord GOD. NIH
28:14 I **h** set thee *so:* thou wast upon the holy NIH
28:16 the multitude of thy merchandise they **h** NIH
28:22 when I shall **h** executed judgments in her, NIH
28:25 When I shall **h** gathered the house of NIH
28:25 shall they dwell in their land that I **h** given NIH
28:26 I **h** executed judgments upon all those NIH
29: 3 *is* mine own, and I **h** made *it* for myself. NIH
29: 5 I **h** given thee for meat to the beasts of NIH
29: 6 they **h** been a staff of reed to the house of NIH
29: 9 The river *is* mine, and I **h** made *it.* NIH
29:20 I **h** given him the land of Egypt *for* his NIH
30: 8 when I **h** set a fire in Egypt, and *when* all NIH
30:12 of strangers: I the LORD **h** spoken *it.* NIH
30:16 Sin shall **h** great pain, and No 2342+2342
30:16 and Noph *shall h* distresses daily. NIH
30:21 I **h** broken the arm of Pharaoh king of NIH
31: 9 I **h** made him fair by the multitude of his NIH
31:11 I **h** therefore delivered him into the hand NIH
31:11 I **h** driven him out for his wickedness. NIH
31:12 **h** cut him off, and have left him: NIH
31:12 have cut him off, and **h** left him: NIH
31:12 down from his shadow, and **h** left him. NIH
32:24 h they borne their shame with them that NIH
32:25 **h** set her a bed in the midst of the slain NIH
32:25 **h** they borne their shame with them that NIH
32:27 they **h** laid their swords under their heads, NIH
32:32 For I **h** caused my terror in the land of NIH
33: 7 I **h** set thee a watchman unto the house NIH
33:11 I **h** no pleasure in the death of the wicked; NIH
33:29 when I **h** laid the land most desolate NIH
33:29 of all their abominations which they **h** NIH
34: 4 The diseased **h** ye not strengthened, NIH
34: 4 neither **h** ye healed that which was sick, NIH
34: 4 neither **h** ye bound up that which was NIH
34: 4 neither **h** ye brought again that which was NIH
34: 4 neither **h** ye sought that which was lost; NIH
34: 4 force and with cruelty **h** ye ruled them. NIH
34:12 where they **h** been scattered in the cloudy NIH
34:18 a small thing unto you to **h** eaten NIH
34:18 to **h** drunk of the deep waters, but ye must NIH
34:19 eat that which ye **h** trodden with your NIH
34:19 drink that which ye **h** fouled with your NIH
34:21 Because ye **h** thrust with side and NIH
34:21 horns, till ye **h** scattered them abroad; NIH
34:24 among them; I the LORD **h** spoken *it.* NIH
34:27 when I **h** broken the bands of their yoke, NIH
35:11 amongst them, when I **h** judged thee. NIH
35:12 *that* I **h** heard all thy blasphemies which NIH
35:13 with your mouth ye **h** boasted against NIH
35:13 and **h** multiplied your words against me: NIH
35:13 your words against me: I **h** heard *them.* NIH
36: 3 Because *they* **h** made *you* desolate, NIH
36: 5 in the fire of my jealousy **h** I spoken NIH
36: 5 which **h** appointed my land into their NIH
36: 6 I **h** spoken in my jealousy and in my fury, NIH
36: 6 ye **h** borne the shame of the heathen: NIH
36: 7 **h** lifted up mine hand, Surely the heathen NIH
36:22 which ye **h** profaned among the heathen, NIH
36:23 ye **h** profaned in the midst of them; NIH
36:33 In the day that I **h** cleansed you from NIH
36:36 I the LORD **h** spoken *it,* and I will do *it.* NIH
37:13 I **h** opened your graves, O my people, NIH
37:14 shall know that I the LORD **h** spoken *it,* NIH
37:23 wherein they **h** sinned, and will cleanse NIH
37:24 they shall all **h** one shepherd: 1961+3807.1
37:25 they shall dwell in the land that I **h** given NIH
37:25 servant, wherein your fathers **h** dwelt; NIH
38: 8 of Israel, which **h** been always waste: NIH

Eze
38:12 **h** gotten cattle and goods, that dwell NIH
38:17 thou he of whom I **h** spoken in old time NIH
38:19 *and* in the fire of my wrath I **h** spoken, NIH
39: 5 for I **h** spoken *it,* saith the Lord God. NIH
39: 8 this *is* the day whereof I **h** spoken. NIH
39:15 till the buriers **h** buried it in the valley of NIH
39:19 my sacrifice which I **h** sacrificed for you. NIH
39:21 shall see my judgment that I **h** executed, NIH
39:21 and my hand that I **h** laid upon them, NIH
39:24 according to their transgressions **h** I done NIH
39:25 **h** mercy upon the whole house of Israel, 7355
39:26 After that they **h** borne their shame, NIH
39:26 all their trespasses whereby they **h** NIH
39:27 When I **h** brought them again from NIH
39:28 I **h** gathered them unto their own land, NIH
39:28 and **h** left none of them any more there. NIH
39:29 I **h** poured out my spirit upon the house NIH
41: 6 that *they* might **h** hold, but they had not 1961
43: 8 they **h** even defiled my holy name by their NIH
43: 8 their abominations that they **h** committed: NIH
43: 8 wherefore I **h** consumed them in mine NIH
43:11 if they be ashamed of all that they **h** done, NIH
44: 7 In that ye **h** brought *into my sanctuary* NIH
44: 7 they **h** broken my covenant because of all NIH
44: 8 ye **h** not kept the charge of mine holy NIH
44: 8 ye **h** set keepers of my charge in my NIH
44:12 **h** I lift up mine hand against them, NIH
44:13 abominations which they **h** committed. NIH
44:18 They shall **h** linen bonnets upon their 1961
44:18 shall **h** linen breeches upon their loins; 1961
45: 5 of the house, **h**, for themselves, 1961+3807.1
45:10 shall **h** just balances, and a just 1961+3807.1
45:21 ye shall **h** the passover, a feast of 1961+3807.1
47:13 of Israel: Joseph *shall* **h** two portions. NIH
47:22 they shall **h inheritance** with you 5159+5307
48:11 which **h** kept my charge, which went not NIH
48:13 Levites *shall* **h** five and twenty thousand NIH
48:23 the west side, Benjamin *shall* **h** a *portion.* NIH
48:24 the west side, Simeon *shall* **h** a *portion.* NIH

Da
2: 3 I **h** dreamed a dream, and my spirit was NIH
2: 9 ye **h** prepared lying and corrupt words to NIH
2:25 I **h** found a man of the captives of Judah, NIH
2:26 unto me the dream which I **h** seen, NIH
2:30 wisdom that I **h** more than any living, 383
3:12 these men, O king, **h** not regarded thee: NIH
3:14 worship the golden image which I **h** set NIH
3:15 and worship the image which I **h** made; NIH
3:25 the midst of the fire, and they **h** no hurt; 383
3:28 changed the king's word, NIH
4: 9 tell *me* the visions of my dream that I **h** NIH
4:18 dream I king Nebuchadnezzar **h** seen. NIH
4:26 after that thou shalt **h** known that NIH
4:30 that I **h** built for the house of the kingdom NIH
5: 7 **h** a chain of gold about his neck, NIH
5:14 I **h** even heard of thee, that the spirit of NIH
5:15 **h** been brought in before me, that they NIH
5:16 I **h** heard of thee, that thou canst make NIH
5:16 **h** a chain of gold about thy neck, NIH
5:23 they **h** brought the vessels of his house NIH
5:23 thy concubines, **h** drunk wine in them; NIH
6: 2 and the king should **h** no damage. 1934
6: 4 **h** consulted together to establish a royal NIH
6:22 lions' mouths, that they **h** not hurt me: NIH
6:22 also before thee, O king, **h** I done no hurt. NIH
9: 5 **h** sinned, and have committed iniquity, NIH
9: 5 **h** committed iniquity, and have done NIH
9: 5 and **h** done wickedly, and have rebelled, NIH
9: 5 have done wickedly, and **h** rebelled, NIH
9: 6 Neither **h** we hearkened unto thy servants NIH
9: 7 of their trespass that they **h** trespassed NIH
9: 8 because we **h** sinned against thee. NIH
9: 9 though we **h** rebelled against him; NIH
9:10 Neither **h** we obeyed the voice of NIH
9:11 Yea, all Israel **h** transgressed thy law, NIH
9:11 of God, because we **h** sinned against him. NIH
9:15 we **h** sinned, we have done wickedly. NIH
9:15 we have sinned, we **h** done wickedly. NIH
10:16 upon me, and I **h** retained no strength. NIH
11: 5 be strong above him, and **h dominion;** 4910
11:24 he shall do *that* which his fathers **h** not NIH
11:30 indignation against the holy covenant: NIH
11:30 intelligence with them that forsake NIH
11:43 shall **h power** over the treasures of gold 4910
12: 7 when *he* shall **h** accomplished to scatter NIH

Hos
1: 6 I will no more **h mercy** upon the house NIH
1: 6 I will **h mercy** upon the house of Judah, 7355
2: 4 I will not **h mercy** upon her children; 7355
2:12 These *are* my rewards that my lovers **h** NIH
2:23 I will **h mercy** upon her that had not 7355
4:10 For they shall eat, and not **h enough.** 7646
4:10 they **h** left off to take heed to the Lord. NIH
4:12 they **h** gone a whoring from under their NIH
4:18 they **h** committed whoredom continually: NIH
5: 1 because ye **h** been a snare on Mizpah, NIH
5: 2 though I **h** *been* a rebuker of them all. NIH
5: 4 of them, and they **h** not known the Lord. NIH
5: 7 They **h** dealt treacherously against NIH
5: 7 for they **h** begotten strange children: NIH
5: 9 the tribes of Israel **h** I made known NIH
6: 5 **h** I hewed *them* by the prophets; NIH
6: 5 **h** slain them by the words of my mouth: NIH
6: 7 like men **h** transgressed the covenant: NIH
6: 7 **h** they dealt treacherously against me. NIH
6:10 I **h** seen a horrible thing in the house of NIH
7: 1 When I *would* **h** healed Israel, then NIH

Hos
7: 2 now their own doings **h** beset them about; NIH
7: 5 *In* the day of our king the princes **h** made NIH
7: 6 For they **h** made ready their heart like an NIH
7: 7 as an oven, and **h** devoured their judges; NIH
7: 9 Strangers **h** devoured his strength, NIH
7:13 for they **h** fled from me: destruction unto NIH
7:13 because they **h** transgressed against me: NIH
7:13 though I **h** redeemed them, yet they have NIH
7:15 yet they **h** spoken lies against me. NIH
7:14 they **h** not cried unto me with their heart, NIH
8: 1 because they **h** transgressed my covenant, NIH
8: 4 They **h** set up kings, but not by me: NIH
8: 4 they **h** made princes, and I knew *it* not: NIH
8: 4 and their gold **h** they made them idols, NIH
8: 7 For they **h** sown the wind, and they shall NIH
8:10 though they **h** hired among the nations, NIH
8:12 I **h** written to him the great things of my NIH
9: 9 They **h** deeply corrupted *themselves,* as NIH
10: 1 to the goodness of his land they **h** NIH
10: 3 We **h** no king, because we feared not 3807.1
10: 4 They **h** spoken words, swearing falsely in NIH
10:13 Ye **h** plowed wickedness, ye have reaped NIH
10:13 plowed wickedness, ye **h** reaped iniquity; NIH
10:13 reaped iniquity; ye **h** eaten the fruit of lies: NIH
12: 2 become rich, I **h** found me out substance: NIH
12:10 I **h** also spoken by the prophets, and I NIH
12:10 I **h** multiplied visions, and used NIH
13: 2 **h** made them molten images of their silver NIH
13: 6 exalted; therefore **h** they forgotten me. NIH
14: 8 What **h** I **to do** any more **with** idols? 3807.1
14: 8 I **h** heard *him,* and observed him: I *am* NIH

Joel
1:18 perplexed, because they **h** no pasture; 3807.1
3: 2 they **h** scattered among the nations, NIH
3: 3 they **h** cast lots for my people; NIH
3: 3 **h** given a boy for a harlot, and sold a girl NIH
3: 4 and what **h** ye to do with me, O Tyre, NIH
3: 5 ye **h** taken my silver and my gold, NIH
3: 5 **h** carried into your temples my goodly NIH
3: 6 the children of Jerusalem **h** ye sold unto NIH
3: 7 out of the place whither ye **h** sold them, NIH
3:19 they **h** shed innocent blood in their land. NIH
3:21 For I will cleanse their blood *that* I **h** not NIH

Am
1: 3 they **h** threshed Gilead with threshing NIH
1:13 they **h** ript up the women with child at NIH
2: 4 they **h** despised the law of the Lord, NIH
2: 4 not kept his commandments, and their NIH
2: 4 You only **h** I known of all the families of NIH
3: 4 cry out of his den, if he **h** taken nothing? NIH
3: 5 from the earth, and **h** taken nothing at all? NIH
3:15 the great houses shall **h an end,** saith 5486
4: 6 I also **h** given you cleanness of teeth in all NIH
4: 6 yet **h** ye not returned unto me, saith NIH
4: 7 also I **h** withholden the rain from you, NIH
4: 8 yet **h** ye not returned unto me, saith NIH
4: 9 I **h** smitten you with blasting and mildew: NIH
4: 9 the palmerworm devoured *them:* yet **h** ye NIH
4:10 I **h** sent among you the pestilence after NIH
4:10 your young men **h** I slain with the sword, NIH
4:10 the sword, and **h** taken away your horses; NIH
4:10 I **h** made the stink of your camps to come NIH
4:10 yet **h** ye not returned unto me, saith NIH
4:11 I **h** overthrown *some* of you, as God NIH
4:11 yet **h** ye not returned unto me, saith NIH
5:11 ye **h** built houses of hewn stone, but ye NIH
5:11 ye **h** planted pleasant vineyards, but ye NIH
5:14 hosts, shall be with you, as ye **h** spoken. NIH
5:25 **H** ye offered unto me sacrifices and NIH
5:26 ye **h** borne the tabernacle of your Moloch NIH
6:12 for ye **h** turned judgment into gall, NIH
6:13 **H** we not taken to us horns by our own NIH
9: 7 **H** not I brought up Israel out of the land NIH
9:15 up out of their land which I **h** given them, NIH

Ob
1: 1 We **h** heard a rumour from the Lord, NIH
1: 2 I **h** made thee small among the heathen: NIH
1: 5 would they not **h** stolen till they had NIH
1: 7 All the men of thy confederacy **h** brought NIH
1: 7 the men that were at peace with thee **h** NIH
1: 7 *that eat* thy bread **h** laid a wound under NIH
1:12 thou shouldest not **h** looked on the day of NIH
1:12 neither shouldest thou **h** rejoiced over NIH
1:12 neither shouldest thou **h** spoken proudly NIH
1:13 shouldest not **h** entered into the gate NIH
1:13 thou shouldest not **h** looked on their NIH
1:13 nor **h** laid *hands* on their substance in NIH
1:14 Neither shouldest thou **h** stood in NIH
1:14 neither shouldest thou **h** delivered up NIH
1:16 as ye **h** drunk upon my holy mountain, NIH

Jnh
2: 9 I will pay *that* I **h** vowed. NIH

Mic
2: 5 Therefore thou shalt **h** none that 1961+3807.1
2: 9 The women of my people **h** ye cast out NIH
2: 9 from their children **h** ye taken *away* my NIH
2:13 they **h** broken up, and have passed NIH
2:13 **h** passed through the gate, and are gone NIH
3: 4 as they **h** behaved themselves ill in their NIH
3: 6 be unto you, that ye shall not **h** a vision; NIH
4: 6 is driven out, and *her* that I **h** afflicted; NIH
4: 9 for pangs **h** taken thee as a woman in NIH
5: 2 whose goings forth **h** *been* from of old, NIH
5:12 thou shalt **h** no more soothsayers: 1961+3807.1
5:15 the heathen, such as they **h** not heard. NIH
6: 3 O my people, what **h** I done unto thee? NIH
6: 3 wherein **h** I wearied thee? testify against NIH
6:12 the inhabitants thereof **h** spoken lies, NIH

Mic
7: 1 for I am as when they **h** gathered NIH
7: 9 because I **h** sinned against him, until he NIH
7:19 again, he will **h compassion** upon us; 7355

Na
1:12 Though I **h** afflicted thee, I will afflict thee NIH
2: 2 for the emptiers **h** emptied them out, NIH

Hab
1:14 things, that **h** no ruler over them? NIH
3: 2 I **h** heard thy speech, *and* was afraid: NIH

Zep
1: 6 *those* that **h** not sought the Lord, NIH
1:17 because they **h** sinned against the Lord: NIH
2: 3 the earth, which **h** wrought his judgment; NIH
2: 8 I **h** heard the reproach of Moab, NIH
2: 8 whereby they **h** reproached my people, NIH
2:10 This shall they **h** for their pride, because 3807.1
2:10 because they **h** reproached and NIH
3: 4 her priests **h** polluted the sanctuary, NIH
3: 4 they **h** done violence to the law. NIH
3: 6 I **h** cut off *the* nations: their towers are NIH
3:19 fame in every land where they **h** been put NIH

Hag
1: 6 Ye **h** sown much, and bring in little; NIH
1: 6 ye eat, but ye **h** not enough; *ye* drink, 3807.1
2:23 for I **h** chosen thee, saith the Lord of NIH

Zec
1: 4 unto whom the former prophets **h** cried, NIH
1:11 **h** walked to and fro through the earth, NIH
1:12 how long wilt thou not **h mercy** on 7355
1:19 These *are* the horns which **h** scattered NIH
1:21 These *are* the horns which **h** scattered NIH
2: 6 I **h** spread you abroad as the four winds NIH
3: 4 I **h** caused thine iniquity to pass from thee, NIH
3: 9 For behold the stone that I **h** laid before NIH
4: 2 said, I **h** looked, and, behold, a candlestick NIH
4: 9 The hands of Zerubbabel **h** laid NIH
6: 8 these that go toward the north country **h** NIH
7: 3 as I **h** done these so many years? NIH
8:15 So again **h** I thought in these days to do NIH
8:23 for we **h** heard *that* God *is* with you. NIH
9: 8 more: for now **h** I seen with mine eyes. NIH
9:11 the blood of thy covenant I **h** sent forth NIH
9:13 I **h** bent Judah for me, filled the bow NIH
10: 2 For the idols **h** spoken vanity, NIH
10: 2 diviners **h** seen a lie, and have told false NIH
10: 2 have seen a lie, and **h** told false dreams; NIH
10: 6 to place them; for I **h mercy** upon them: 7355
10: 8 and gather them; for I **h** redeemed them: NIH
10: 8 they shall increase as they **h** increased. NIH
12:10 they shall look upon me whom they **h** NIH
14:12 people that **h** fought against Jerusalem; NIH
14:18 that **h** no *rain;* there shall be the plague, NIH

Mal
1: 2 I **h** loved you, saith the Lord. Yet ye say, NIH
1: 6 say, Wherein **h** we despised thy name? NIH
1: 7 and ye say, Wherein **h** we polluted thee? NIH
1:10 I **h** no pleasure in you, saith the Lord 3807.1
1:12 ye **h** profaned it, in that ye say, The table NIH
1:13 a weariness *is it!* and ye **h** snuffed at it, NIH
2: 2 I **h** cursed them already, because ye do NIH
2: 4 ye shall know that I **h** sent this NIH
2: 8 ye **h** caused many to stumble at the law; NIH
2: 8 ye **h** corrupted the covenant of Levi, NIH
2: 9 Therefore **h** I also made you contemptible NIH
2: 9 according as ye **h** not kept my ways, NIH
2: 9 my ways, but **h** been partial in the law. NIH
2:10 **H** we not all one father? hath not one 3807.1
2:13 this **h** ye done again, covering the altar of NIH
2:17 Ye **h** wearied the Lord with your words. NIH
2:17 Wherein **h** we wearied *him?* When ye say, NIH
3: 7 **h** not kept *them.* Return unto me, NIH
3: 8 Yet ye **h** robbed me. But ye say, Wherein NIH
3: 8 say, Wherein **h** we robbed thee? In tithes NIH
3: 9 ye **h** robbed me, *even* this whole nation. NIH
3:13 Your words **h** been stout against me, NIH
3:13 What **h** we spoken so much against thee? NIH
3:14 Ye **h** said, It *is* vain to serve God: NIH
3:14 what profit *is it* that we **h** kept his NIH
3:14 that we **h** walked mournfully before NIH

Mt
2: 2 for we **h** seen his star in the east, NIG
2: 8 ye **h** found *him,* bring me word again, NIG
2:15 saying, Out of Egypt **h** I called my son. NIG
3: 9 We **h** Abraham to *our* father: 2192
3:14 I **h** need to be baptized of thee, 2192
5:13 but if the salt **h** lost his savour, NIG
5:21 Ye **h** heard that it was said by them of old NIG
5:27 Ye **h** heard that it was said by them of old NIG
5:33 Ye **h** heard that it hath been said by them NIG
5:38 Ye **h** heard that it hath been said, An eye NIG
5:40 *away* thy coat, **let** him **h** *thy* cloke also. 863
5:43 Ye **h** heard that it hath been said, Thou NIG
5:46 them which love you, what reward **h** ye? 2192
6: 1 otherwise ye **h** no reward of your Father 2192
6: 2 the streets, that they may **h glory** of men. 1392
6: 2 Verily I say unto you, They **h** their reward. 568
6: 5 Verily I say unto you, They **h** their reward. 568
6: 8 for your Father knoweth what *things* ye **h** 2192
6:16 Verily I say unto you, They **h** their reward. 568
6:32 that ye **h need** of all these *things.* 5535
7:22 Lord, **h** we not prophesied in thy name? NIG
7:22 and in thy name **h** cast out devils? NIG
8:10 not found so great faith, no not in Israel. NIG
8:20 The foxes **h** holes, and the birds of the air 2192
8:20 holes, and the birds of the air **h** nests; NIG
8:29 saying, What **h** we to do with thee, Jesus, NIG
9:13 I will **h** mercy, and not sacrifice: 2309
9:27 Son of David, **h** mercy on us. 1653
10: 8 devils: freely ye **h** received, freely give. NIG
10:23 not gone over the cities of Israel, NIG
10:25 If they **h** called the master of the house NIG
11: 5 the poor **h** the gospel preached to them. NIG

H

H

Ref	Text	Strong's
Mt 11:17	We **h** piped unto you, and ye have not	NIG
11:17	piped unto you, and ye **h** not danced;	NIG
11:17	we **h** mourned unto you, and ye have not	NIG
11:17	unto you, and ye **h** not lamented.	NIG
11:21	Sidon they **would h** repented long ago in	302
11:23	mighty works, which **h** been done in thee,	NIG
11:23	it **would h** remained until this day.	302
12: 3	them, **H** ye not read what David did,	NIG
12: 5	Or **h** ye not read in the law, how that on	NIG
12: 7	I will **h** mercy, and not sacrifice,	2309
12: 7	ye **would** not **h** condemned the guiltless.	302
12:11	that shall **h** one sheep, and if it fall into a	2192
12:18	Behold my servant, whom I **h** chosen;	NIG
13:12	given, and he shall **h** *more* **abundance**:	4052
13:15	of hearing, and their eyes they **h** closed;	NIG
13:17	righteous *men* **h** desired to see *those*	NIG
13:17	and **h** not seen *them;* and to hear *those*	NIG
13:17	which ye hear, and **h** not heard *them.*	NIG
13:35	will utter *things which **h** been* kept secret	NIG
13:51	Ye understood all these *things?*	NIG
14: 4	him, It is not lawful for thee to **h** her.	2192
14: 5	And when he would **h** put him to death,	NIG
14:17	We **h** here but five loaves, and two fishes.	2192
15: 6	*he shall be free.* Thus **h** ye made	NIG
15:22	him, saying, **H mercy** on me, O Lord,	1653
15:32	said, I **h compassion** on the multitude,	4697
15:32	now three days, and **h** nothing to eat:	2192
15:33	Whence should we **h** so much bread in	NIG
15:34	saith unto them, How many loaves **h** ye?	2192
16: 7	saying, *It is* because we **h** taken no bread.	NIG
16: 8	because ye **h** brought no bread?	NIG
17:12	**h** done unto him whatsoever they listed.	NIG
17:15	Lord, **h mercy** on my son: for he is	1653
17:20	If ye **h** faith as a grain of mustard seed,	2192
18:12	if a man **h** an hundred sheep, and one of	1096
18:26	**h patience** with me, and I will pay thee	3114
18:29	**H patience** with me, and I will pay thee	3114
18:33	**Shouldest** not thou also **h** had compassion	1163
19: 4	and said unto them, **H** ye not read,	NIG
19:12	which **h** made themselves eunuchs for	NIG
19:16	*thing* shall I do, that I may **h** eternal life?	2192
19:20	these *things* I **h** kept from my youth up:	NIG
19:21	and thou shalt **h** treasure in heaven.	2192
19:27	we **h** forsaken all, and followed thee;	NIG
19:27	followed thee; what shall we **h** therefore?	1510
19:28	That ye which **h** followed me,	NIG
20:10	they supposed that they should **h** received	NIG
20:12	These last **h** wrought *but* one hour,	NIG
20:12	which **h** borne the burden and heat of	NIG
20:30	cried out, saying, **H mercy** on us, O Lord,	1653
20:31	saying, **H mercy** on us, O Lord, *thou* Son	1653
21:13	prayer; but ye **h** made it a den of thieves.	NIG
21:16	**h** ye never read, Out of the mouth of	NIG
21:21	say unto you, If ye **h** faith, and doubt not,	2192
22: 4	bidden, Behold, I **h** prepared my dinner:	NIG
22:31	**h** ye not read that which was spoken unto	NIG
23:23	**h** omitted the weightier *matters* of the law	NIG
23:23	these **ought** *ye* to **h** done, and not to	1163
23:30	we **would** not **h** been partakers with them	302
23:37	how often would I **h** gathered thy children	NIG
24:25	Behold, I **h** told you before.	NIG
24:43	he **would h** watched, and would not have	302
24:43	**would** not **h** suffered his house to be	302
25:20	I **h** gained besides them five talents moe.	NIG
25:22	I **h** gained two other talents besides them.	NIG
25:26	and gather where I **h** not strawed:	NIG
25:27	Thou **oughtest** therefore to **h** put my	1163
25:27	at my coming I **should h** received mine	302
25:29	be given, and he shall **h abundance**:	4052
25:40	Inasmuch as ye **h** done *it* unto one of	NIG
25:40	these my brethren, ye **h** done *it* unto me.	NIG
26: 9	For this ointment **might h** been sold for	1410
26:11	For ye **h** the poor always with you;	2192
26:11	always with you; but me ye **h** not always.	2192
26:65	what further need **h** we of witnesses?	2192
26:65	behold, now ye **h** heard his blasphemy.	NIG
27: 4	I sinned in that I **h** betrayed	NIG
27: 4	I have sinned in that I **h** betrayed	NIG
27:19	**H** thou nothing to do with that just *man:*	NIG
27:19	I **h** suffered many *things* this day in a	NIG
27:43	let him deliver him now, if he will **h** him:	NIG
27:65	Pilate said unto them, Ye **h** a watch:	2192
28: 7	there shall ye see him: lo, I **h** told you.	NIG
28:20	*things* whatsoever I **h** commanded you:	NIG
Mk 1: 8	I indeed **h** baptized you with water:	NIG
1:24	what **h** we to do with thee, *thou* Jesus of	NIG
2:17	They that are whole **h** no need of	2192
2:19	as long as they **h** the bridegroom with	NIG
2:25	**H** ye never read what David did, when he	NIG
3:15	And to **h** power to heal sicknesses, and to	2192
4:15	but when they **h** heard, Satan cometh	NIG
4:16	who, when they **h** heard the word,	NIG
4:17	**h** no root in themselves, and so endure	2192
4:23	If any *man* **h** ears to hear, let him hear.	2192
4:40	so fearful? how *is it that* you **h** no faith?	2192
5: 7	and said, What **h** I to do with thee, Jesus,	NIG
6:18	It is not lawful for thee to **h** thy brother's	NIG
6:19	against him, and would **h** killed him;	NIG
6:36	bread: for they **h** nothing to eat.	2192
6:38	saith unto them, How many loaves **h** ye?	2192
6:48	the sea, and would **h** passed by them.	NIG
7: 4	which they **h** received to hold,	NIG
7:13	your tradition, which ye **h** delivered:	NIG
7:16	If any *man* **h** ears to hear, let him hear.	2192
7:24	**would h** no *man* know *it:* but he could	2309
Mk 8: 2	I **h compassion** on the multitude,	4697
8: 2	they **h** now been with me three days,	NIG
8: 2	with me three days, and **h** nothing to eat:	2192
8: 5	He asked them, How many loaves **h** ye?	2192
8:16	saying, *It is* because we **h** no bread.	2192
8:17	Why reason ye, because ye **h** no bread?	2192
8:17	**h** ye your heart yet hardened?	2192
9: 1	till they **h** seen the kingdom of God come	NIG
9:13	they **h** done unto him whatsoever they	NIG
9:17	Master, I **h** brought unto thee my son,	NIG
9:22	if thou canst do any *thing,* **h compassion**	4697
9:50	but if the salt **h** lost his saltness,	1096
9:50	**H** salt in yourselves, and have peace one	2192
9:50	and **h peace** one with another.	1514
10:20	all these **h** I observed from my youth.	NIG
10:21	and thou shalt **h** treasure in heaven:	2192
10:23	How hardly shall they that **h** riches enter	2192
10:28	Lo, we **h** left all, and have followed thee.	2192
10:28	Lo, we have left all, and **h** followed thee.	NIG
10:47	Jesus, *thou* Son of David, **h mercy** on me.	1653
10:48	*Thou* Son of David, **h mercy** on me.	1653
11:17	prayer? but ye **h** made it a den of thieves.	NIG
11:22	saith unto them, **H** faith in God.	2192
11:23	to pass; he shall **h** whatsoever he saith.	1510
11:24	ye receive *them,* and ye shall **h** them.	1510
11:25	forgive, if ye **h** ought against any:	2192
12:10	**h** ye not read this scripture; The stone	NIG
12:26	**h** ye not read in the book of Moses, how	NIG
12:43	all they which **h** cast into the treasury:	NIG
13:23	heed: behold, I **h** foretold you all *things.*	NIG
14: 5	it might **h** been sold for more than three	NIG
14: 5	and **h** been given to the poor.	NIG
14: 7	For ye **h** the poor with you always,	2192
14: 7	do them good: but me ye **h** not always.	2192
14:64	Ye **h** heard the blasphemy: what think ye?	NIG
Lk 1: 1	Forasmuch as many **h** taken in hand to set	NIG
1:14	And thou shalt **h** joy and gladness;	1510
1:62	to his father, how he would **h** him called.	2309
1:70	which **h** been since the world began:)	NIG
2:30	For mine eyes **h** seen thy salvation,	NIG
2:44	supposing him to **h** been in the company,	NIG
2:48	thy father and I **h** sought thee sorrowing.	NIG
3: 8	We **h** Abraham to *our* father:	2192
4:23	we **h** heard done in Capernaum,	NIG
4:34	what **h** we to do with thee, *thou* Jesus of	NIG
5: 5	we **h** toiled all the night, and have taken	NIG
5: 5	toiled all the night, and **h** taken nothing:	NIG
5:26	saying, We **h** seen strange *things* to day.	NIG
6: 3	**H** ye not read so much as this, what David	NIG
6:24	rich: for ye **h** received your consolation.	NIG
6:32	them which love you, what thank **h** ye?	1510
6:33	which do good to you, what thank **h** ye?	1510
6:34	ye hope to receive, what thank **h** ye?	1510
7: 9	I **h** not found so great faith, no, not in	NIG
7:22	and tell John what *things* ye **h** seen and	NIG
7:32	We **h** piped unto you, and ye have not	NIG
7:32	piped unto you, and ye **h** not danced;	NIG
7:32	we **h** mourned to you, and ye have not	NIG
7:32	have mourned to you, and ye **h** not wept.	NIG
7:39	**would h** known who and what manner of	302
7:40	Simon, I **h** somewhat to say unto thee.	2192
8:13	and these **h** no root, which for a while	2192
8:14	which, when they **h** heard, go *forth,* and	2192
8:18	taken even *that* which he seemeth to **h**.	2192
8:28	said, What **h** I to do with thee, Jesus,	2192
9: 3	money; neither **h** two coats apiece.	2192
9: 9	And Herod said, John **h** I beheaded:	NIG
9:13	We **h** no more but five loaves and	1510
9:58	Foxes **h** holes, and birds of the air *have*	2192
9:58	have holes, and birds of the air **h** nests;	NIG
10:13	and Sidon, which **h** been done in you,	NIG
10:24	kings **h** desired to see *those things* which	NIG
10:24	and **h** not seen *them;* and to hear *those*	NIG
10:24	which ye hear, and **h** not heard *them.*	NIG
11: 5	Which of you shall **h** a friend, and shall	2192
11: 6	to me, and I **h** nothing to set before him:	2192
11:41	rather give alms *of* such *things* as you **h**;	1751
11:42	ought *ye* to **h** done, and not to leave	NIG
11:52	ye **h** taken away the key of knowledge:	NIG
12: 3	Therefore whatsoever ye **h** spoken in	NIG
12: 3	which ye **h** spoken in the ear in closets	NIG
12: 4	and after that **h** no more that *they* can do.	2192
12:17	I **h** no room where to bestow my fruits?	2192
12:24	which neither **h** storehouse nor barn;	1510
12:30	your Father knoweth that ye **h need** of	5535
12:33	Sell that ye **h**, and give alms;	5225
12:39	he **would h** watched, and not have	302
12:39	not **h** suffered his house to be broken	NIG
12:48	and to whom *men* **h** committed much,	NIG
12:50	But I **h** a baptism to be baptized *with;* and	2192
13:26	We **h** eaten and drunk in thy presence,	NIG
13:34	often would I **h** gathered thy children	NIG
14: 5	of you shall **h** an ass or an ox fallen	NIG
14:10	shalt thou **h** worship in the presence of	1510
14:18	I **h** bought a piece of ground, and I must	NIG
14:18	and see it: I pray thee **h** me excused.	2192
14:19	I **h** bought five yoke of oxen, and I go to	NIG
14:19	to prove them: I pray thee **h** me excused.	2192
14:20	I **h** married a wife, and therefore I cannot	NIG
14:28	whether he **h** sufficient to finish it?	2192
14:34	but if the salt **h** lost his savour,	NIG
15: 6	for I **h** found my sheep which was lost.	NIG
15: 9	for I **h** found the piece which I had lost.	NIG
15:16	And he would fain **h** filled his belly with	NIG
15:17	father's **h** bread **enough and to spare**,	4052
Lk 15:18	I **h** sinned against heaven, and before thee,	NIG
15:21	I **h** sinned against heaven, and in thy sight,	NIG
15:31	art ever with me, and all that I **h** is thine.	1699
16:11	ye **h** not been faithful in the unrighteous	NIG
16:12	And if ye **h** not been faithful in that which	NIG
16:24	**h mercy** on me, and send Lazarus,	1653
16:28	For I **h** five brethren; that he may testify	2192
16:29	him, They **h** Moses and the prophets;	2192
17: 8	and serve me, till I **h** eaten and drunken;	NIG
17:10	when ye shall **h** done all those *things*	NIG
17:10	done *that* which was our duty to do.	NIG
17:13	and said, Jesus, Master, **h mercy** on us.	1653
18:21	All these **h** I kept from my youth up.	NIG
18:22	and thou shalt **h** treasure in heaven:	2192
18:24	How hardly shall they that **h** riches enter	2192
18:28	Then Peter said, Lo, we **h** left all,	NIG
18:38	*thou* Son of David, **h mercy** on me.	1653
18:39	*Thou* Son of David, **h mercy** on me.	1653
19: 8	if I **h** taken any *thing* from any *man* by	NIG
19:14	We will not **h** this *man* to reign over us.	NIG
19:17	little, **h** thou authority over ten cities.	2192
19:20	which I **h** kept laid up in a napkin:	NIG
19:23	that at my coming I **might h** required	302
19:46	prayer: but ye **h** made it a den of thieves.	NIG
21: 4	For all these **h** of their abundance cast in	NIG
22:15	With desire I **h** desired to eat this passover	NIG
22:28	Ye are they which **h** continued with me in	NIG
22:31	behold, Satan hath desired *to h* you,	NIG
22:32	But I **h** prayed for thee, that thy faith fail	NIG
22:37	for the *things* concerning me **h** an end.	2192
22:71	we ourselves **h** heard of his own mouth.	NIG
23: 8	he hoped to **h** seen some miracle done by	NIG
23:14	them, Ye **h** brought this man unto me,	NIG
23:14	**h** found no fault in this man *touching*	NIG
23:22	I **h** found no cause of death in him: I will	NIG
24:17	*are* these that ye **h** one to another,	474
24:20	condemned to death, and crucified him.	NIG
24:21	been he which should **h** redeemed Israel:	NIG
24:25	to believe all that the prophets **h** spoken:	NIG
24:26	Ought not Christ to **h** suffered these	NIG
24:28	made as though *he* would **h** gone further.	NIG
24:39	hath not flesh and bones, as ye see me **h**.	2192
24:41	he said unto them, **H** ye here any meat?	2192
Jn 1:16	And of his fulness **h** all we received,	NIG
1:41	We **h** found the Messias, which is,	NIG
1:45	and saith unto him, We **h** found him,	NIG
2: 3	of Jesus saith unto him, They **h** no wine.	2192
2: 4	her, Woman, what **h** I to do with thee?	NIG
2:10	and when *men* **h** well drunk, then	NIG
3:11	we do know, and testify that we **h** seen;	NIG
3:12	If I **h** told you earthly *things,* and ye	NIG
3:15	him should not perish, but **h** eternal life.	2192
3:16	should not perish, but **h** everlasting life.	2192
4: 9	For the Jews **h** no **dealings with**	4798
4:10	thou **wouldest h** asked of him, and he	302
4:10	and he **would h** given thee living water.	302
4:17	answered and said, I **h** no husband.	2192
4:17	Thou hast well said, I **h** no husband:	2192
4:32	I **h** meat to eat that ye know not of.	2192
4:42	for we **h** heard *him* ourselves,	NIG
5: 7	I **h** no man, when the water is troubled,	NIG
5:26	hath he given to the Son to **h** life in	2192
5:29	that **h** done good, unto the resurrection	NIG
5:29	and they that **h** done evil, unto	NIG
5:36	But I **h** greater witness than *that of* John:	2192
5:37	Ye **h** neither heard his voice at any time,	NIG
5:38	And ye **h** not his word abiding in you:	2192
5:39	for in them ye think ye **h** eternal life:	2192
5:40	will not come to me, that ye might **h** life.	2192
5:42	that ye **h** not the love of God in you.	2192
5:46	believed Moses, ye **would h** believed me:	302
6:36	That ye also **h** seen me, and believe not.	NIG
6:40	believeth on him, may **h** everlasting life:	2192
6:53	and drink his blood, ye **h** no life in you.	2192
6:70	**H** not I chosen you twelve, and one of you	NIG
7:21	I **h** done one work, and ye all marvel.	NIG
7:23	I **h** made a man every whit whole on	NIG
7:44	And some of them would **h** taken him;	NIG
7:45	unto them, Why **h** ye not brought him?	NIG
7:48	**H** any of the rulers or of the Pharisees	NIG
8: 6	that they might **h** to accuse him.	NIG
8:12	in darkness, but shall **h** the light of life.	2192
8:19	ye should **h** known my Father also.	NIG
8:26	**h** many *things* to say and to judge of you:	2192
8:26	speak to the world those *things* which I **h**	NIG
8:28	When ye **h** lift up the Son of man, then	NIG
8:38	speak *that* which I **h** seen with my Father:	NIG
8:38	do *that* which ye **h** seen with your father.	NIG
8:40	you the truth, which I **h** heard of God:	2192
8:41	fornication; we **h** one Father, *even* God.	2192
8:49	Jesus answered, I **h** not a devil;	2192
8:55	Yet ye **h** not known him; but I know him:	NIG
9:27	I **h** told you already, and ye did not hear:	NIG
9:41	If ye were blind, ye should **h** no sin:	2192
10:10	I am come that they might **h** life,	2192
10:10	and that they might **h** *it more* abundantly.	2192
10:16	And other sheep I **h**, which are not of this	2192
10:18	**h** power to lay it down, and I have power	2192
10:18	it down, and I **h** power to take it again.	2192
10:18	This commandment **h** I received of my	NIG
10:32	Many good works **h** I shewed you from	NIG
11:34	And said, Where **h** ye laid him? They say	NIG
11:37	**h** caused that even this *man* should not	NIG
11:37	caused that even this *man* should not **h**	NIG
12: 8	For the poor always ye **h** with you;	2192

Jn		
12: 8	have with you; but me ye **h** not always.	2192
12:28	*saying*, I **h** both glorified *it*, and will glorify	NIG
12:34	We **h** heard out of the law that Christ	NIG
12:35	Walk while ye **h** the light, lest darkness	2192
12:36	While ye **h** light, believe in the light,	2192
12:48	the word that I **h** spoken, the same shall	NIG
12:49	I **h** not spoken of myself; but the Father	NIG
13:12	them, Know ye what I **h** done to you?	NIG
13:14	Lord and Master, **h** washed your feet;	NIG
13:15	For I **h** given you an example, that ye	NIG
13:15	that ye should do as I **h** done to you.	NIG
13:18	I know whom I **h** chosen: but that	NIG
13:26	when I **h** dipped *it*. And when he had	NIG
13:29	Buy *those things* that we **h** need of	2192
13:34	as I **h** loved you, that ye also love one	NIG
13:35	my disciples, if ye **h** love one to another.	2192
14: 2	if *it were* not so, I **would h** told you.	302
14: 7	ye **should h** known my Father also:	302
14: 7	henceforth ye know him, and **h** seen him.	NIG
14: 9	**H** I been so long time with you, and	NIG
14:25	These *things* **h** I spoken unto you, being	NIG
14:26	whatso*ever* I **h** said unto you.	NIG
14:28	ye have how I said unto you, I go away	NIG
14:29	And now I **h** told you before it come to	NIG
15: 3	the word which I **h** spoken unto you.	NIG
15: 9	Father hath loved me, so **h** I loved you:	NIG
15:10	even as I **h** kept my Father's	NIG
15:11	These *things* **h** I spoken unto you, that my	NIG
15:12	That ye love one another, as I **h** loved you.	NIG
15:15	I **h** called you friends; for all *things* that	NIG
15:15	for all *things* that I **h** heard of my Father I	NIG
15:15	of my Father I **h** made known unto you.	NIG
15:16	**h** not chosen me, but I have chosen you,	NIG
15:16	but I **h** chosen you, and ordained you,	NIG
15:19	but I **h** chosen you out of the world,	NIG
15:20	If they **h** persecuted me, they will also	NIG
15:20	if they **h** kept my saying, they will keep	NIG
15:22	but now they **h** no cloke for their sin.	2192
15:24	now **h** they both seen and hated both me	NIG
15:27	ye **h** been with me from the beginning.	NIG
16: 1	These *things* **h** I spoken unto you, that ye	NIG
16: 3	because they **h** not known the Father,	NIG
16: 4	But these *things* **h** I told you, that when	NIG
16: 6	because I **h** said these *things* unto you,	NIG
16:12	I **h** yet many *things* to say unto you,	2192
16:22	ye now therefore **h** sorrow: but I will	2192
16:24	Hitherto **h** ye asked nothing in my name:	NIG
16:25	These *things* **h** I spoken unto you in	NIG
16:27	because ye **h** loved me, and have believed	NIG
16:27	and **h** believed that I came out from God.	NIG
16:33	These *things* I **h** spoken unto you, that in	NIG
16:33	unto you, that in me ye might **h** peace.	2192
16:33	In the world ye shall **h** tribulation: but be	2192
16:33	of good cheer; I **h** overcome the world.	NIG
17: 4	I **h** glorified thee on the earth: I have	NIG
17: 4	I **h** finished the work which thou gavest	NIG
17: 6	I **h** manifested thy name unto the men.	NIG
17: 6	them me; and they **h** kept thy word.	NIG
17: 7	Now they **h** known that all *things*	NIG
17: 8	For I **h** given unto them the words which	NIG
17: 8	they **h** received *them*, and have known	NIG
17: 8	known surely that I came out from thee,	NIG
17: 8	they **h** believed that thou didst send me.	NIG
17:12	*those* that thou gavest me I **h** kept,	NIG
17:13	that they might **h** my joy fulfilled in	2192
17:14	I **h** given them thy word; and the world	NIG
17:18	even *so* **h** I also sent them into the world.	NIG
17:22	And the glory which thou gavest me I **h**	NIG
17:25	I **h** known thee, and these have known	NIG
17:25	these **h** known that thou hast sent me.	NIG
17:26	And I **h** declared unto them thy name,	NIG
18: 8	I **h** told you that I am *he:* if therefore	NIG
18: 9	Of them which thou gavest me **h** I lost	NIG
18:20	resort; and in secret **h** I said nothing.	NIG
18:21	ask them which heard me, what I **h** said	NIG
18:23	Jesus answered him, If I **h** spoken evil,	NIG
18:30	**would** not **h** delivered him up unto thee.	302
18:35	the chief priests **h** delivered thee unto me:	NIG
18:39	But ye **h** a custom, that I should release	1510
19: 7	**h** a law, and by our law he ought to die,	2192
19:10	thou not that I **h** power to crucify	2192
19:10	crucify thee, and **h** power to release thee?	2192
19:11	Thou couldest **h** no power *at all* against	2192
19:15	answered, We **h** no king but Cesar.	2192
19:22	What I **h** written I have written.	NIG
19:22	What I have written I **h** written.	NIG
20: 2	They **h** taken away the Lord out of	NIG
20: 2	and we know not where they **h** laid him.	NIG
20:13	Because they **h** taken away my Lord,	NIG
20:13	and I know not where they **h** laid him.	NIG
20:15	if thou **h** borne him *hence,* tell me where	NIG
20:25	said unto him, We **h** seen the Lord.	NIG
20:29	blessed *are* they that **h** not seen,	NIG
20:29	that have not seen, and *yet* **h** believed.	NIG
20:31	that believing ye might **h** life through his	2192
21: 5	unto him, Children, **h** ye any meat?	2192
21:10	Bring of the fish which ye **h** now caught.	NIG

Ac		
1: 1	former treatise **h** I made, O Theophilus,	NIG
1: 4	which, *saith he,* ye **h** heard of me.	NIG
1:11	come *in* like manner as ye **h** seen him go	NIG
1:16	this scripture must needs **h** been fulfilled,	NIG
1:21	of these men which **h** companied	NIG
2:23	ye **h** taken, and by wicked hands have	NIG
2:23	by wicked hands **h** crucified and slain:	NIG
2:36	ye **h** crucified, both Lord and Christ.	NIG

Ac		
3: 6	Then Peter said, Silver and gold **h** I none;	5225
3: 6	I have none; but such as I **h** give I thee:	2192
3:24	that follow after, as many as **h** spoken,	NIG
3:24	h likewise foretold of these days.	NIG
4: 7	or by what name, **h** ye done this?	NIG
4:20	but speak *the things* which we **h** seen and	NIG
5: 9	How *is it* that ye **h** agreed together to	NIG
5: 9	feet of them which **h** buried thy husband	NIG
5:21	and sent to the prison to **h** them brought.	NIG
5:26	people, lest they should **h** been stoned.	NIG
5:28	ye **h** filled Jerusalem with your doctrine,	NIG
6:11	We **h** heard him speak blasphemous	NIG
6:14	For we **h** heard him say, that this Jesus of	NIG
7:25	For he supposed his brethren would **h**	NIG
7:26	would **h** set them at one *again*, saying,	NIG
7:34	I **h** seen, I have seen the affliction of my	NIG
7:34	I **h** seen the affliction of my people which	NIG
7:34	I **h** heard their groaning, and am come	NIG
7:42	**h** ye offered to me slain beasts and	NIG
7:52	Which of the prophets **h** not your fathers	NIG
7:52	they **h** slain them which shewed before of	NIG
7:52	of whom ye **h** been now the betrayers and	NIG
7:53	Who **h** received the law by the disposition	NIG
7:53	the disposition of angels, and **h** not kept *it.*	NIG
8:24	none of *these things* which ye **h** spoken	NIG
9: 6	Lord, what wilt thou **h** me to do?	2309
9:13	Lord, I **h** heard by many of this man,	NIG
10:10	became very hungry, and would **h** eaten:	NIG
10:14	I **h** never eaten any *thing that is* common	NIG
10:20	doubting nothing: for I **h** sent them.	NIG
10:29	therefore for what intent ye **h** sent for me?	NIG
10:47	which **h** received the Holy Ghost as well	NIG
12: 6	And when Herod **h** brought him	NIG
13: 2	Saul for the work whereunto I **h** called	NIG
13:15	if ye **h** *any* word of exhortation for	1510
13:22	and said, I **h** found David the *son* of Jesse,	NIG
13:27	they **h** fulfilled *them* in condemning *him.*	NIG
13:33	art my Son, this day **h** I begotten thee.	NIG
13:46	of God should first **h** been spoken to you:	NIG
13:47	*saying,* I **h** set thee to be a light of	NIG
14:13	would **h** done sacrifice with the people.	NIG
15:24	Forasmuch as we **h** heard, that certain	NIG
15:24	that certain which went out from us **h**	NIG
15:26	that **h** hazarded their lives for the name	NIG
15:27	We **h** sent therefore Judas and Silas,	NIG
15:36	our brethren in every city where we **h**	NIG
16: 3	Him would Paul **h** to go forth with him;	NIG
16:15	ye **h** judged me to be faithful to the Lord,	NIG
16:27	his sword, and **would h** killed himself,	3195
16:36	The magistrates **h** sent to let you go:	NIG
16:37	They **h** beaten us openly uncondemned,	NIG
16:37	being Romans, and **h** cast *us* into prison;	NIG
17: 3	that Christ must needs **h** suffered,	NIG
17: 6	that **h** turned the world upside down	NIG
17:28	him we live, and move, and **h** our *being;*	1510
17:28	as certain also of your own poets **h** said,	NIG
18:10	hurt thee: for I **h** much people in this city.	1510
19: 2	**H** ye received the Holy Ghost since ye	NIG
19: 2	We **h** not so much as heard whether there	NIG
19:21	to Jerusalem, saying, After I **h** been there,	NIG
19:25	know that by this craft we **h** our wealth.	1510
19:30	And when Paul would **h** entered in unto	NIG
19:33	**h** made *his* defence unto the people.	NIG
19:37	For ye **h** brought *hither* these men,	NIG
19:38	**h** a matter against any *man,* the law is	2192
20:18	after what manner I **h** been with you at	NIG
20:20	profitable *unto you,* but **h** shewed you,	NIG
20:20	**h** taught you publickly, and from house	NIG
20:24	which I **h** received of the Lord Jesus,	NIG
20:25	among whom I **h** gone preaching	NIG
20:27	For I **h** not shunned to declare unto you	NIG
20:33	I **h** coveted no *man's* silver, or gold,	NIG
20:34	that these hands **h** ministered unto my	NIG
20:35	I **h** shewed you all *things,* how that so	NIG
21:23	four men which have a vow on them;	1510
21:23	have four men which **h** a vow on them;	2192
21:25	we **h** written and concluded that they	NIG
22:29	from him which should **h** examined him:	NIG
22:30	would **h** known the certainty wherefore	NIG
23: 1	I lived in all good conscience before God	NIG
23:10	fearing lest Paul should **h** been pulled in	NIG
23:14	bound ourselves under a great curse,	NIG
23:14	that *we* will eat nothing until we **h** slain	NIG
23:20	The Jews **h** agreed to desire thee that thou	NIG
23:21	which **h** bound themselves with an oath,	NIG
23:21	*they* will neither eat nor drink till they **h**	NIG
23:27	Jews, and should **h** been killed of them:	NIG
23:28	And when I would **h** known the cause	NIG
23:29	to nothing laid to his charge worthy of	2192
24: 5	we **h** found this man a pestilent *fellow,*	NIG
24: 6	would **h** judged according to our law.	NIG
24:15	And **h** hope towards God, which they	2192
24:16	to **h** always a conscience void of offence	2192
24:19	Who ought to **h** been here before thee,	NIG
24:20	if they **h** found any evil doing in me,	NIG
24:23	to let *him* **h** liberty, and that *he* should	2192
24:25	when I **h** a convenient season, I will call	3335
24:26	He hoped also that money should **h** been	NIG
25: 8	against Cesar, **h** I offended any *thing at all.*	NIG
25:10	to the Jews **h** I done no wrong, as thou	NIG
25:11	**h** committed any *thing* worthy of death,	NIG
25:11	*me,* desiring to **h** judgment against him.	NIG
25:16	before that he which is accused **h**	2192
25:16	**h** licence to answer for himself concerning	2983
25:24	the multitude of the Jews **h** dealt with me,	NIG

Ac		
25:25	to Augustus, I **h** determined to send him.	NIG
25:26	whom I **h** no certain *thing* to write unto	2192
25:26	Wherefore I **h** brought him forth before	NIG
25:26	I might **h** somewhat to write.	2192
26:16	I **h** appeared unto thee for this *purpose,*	NIG
26:32	This man **might h** been set at liberty,	1410
27:21	ye **should h** hearkened unto me,	1163
27:21	and not **h** loosed from Crete, and to have	NIG
27:21	and to **h** gained this harm and loss.	NIG
27:29	Then fearing lest we should **h** fallen upon	NIG
27:30	colour as though they **would h** cast	3195
27:33	This day is the fourteenth day that ye **h**	NIG
28: 6	Howbeit they looked when he should **h**	NIG
28:17	though I committed nothing against	NIG
28:18	**would h** let me go, because there was no	1014
28:20	For this cause therefore **h** I called for you,	NIG
28:27	of hearing, and their eyes **h** they closed;	NIG

Ro		
1: 5	By whom we **h** received grace and	NIG
1:10	**h** a prosperous journey by the will of	2137
1:13	I would not **h** you ignorant, brethren,	NIG
1:13	that I might **h** some fruit among you also,	2192
1:32	but **h** pleasure in them that do *them.*	NIG
2:12	For as many as **h** sinned without law shall	NIG
2:12	as many as **h** sinned in the law shall be	NIG
2:14	when *the* Gentiles, which **h** not the law,	2192
3: 9	for we **h** before proved both Jews and	NIG
3:13	with their tongues they **h** used deceit;	NIG
3:17	And the way of peace **h** they not known:	NIG
3:23	For all **h** sinned, and come short of	NIG
4:17	I **h** made thee a father of many nations,)	NIG
5: 1	we **h** peace with God through our Lord	2192
5: 2	By whom also we **h** access by faith into	2192
5:11	whom we **h** now received the atonement.	NIG
5:12	passed upon all men, for that all **h** sinned:	NIG
6: 5	For if we **h** been planted together in	NIG
6:14	For sin shall not **h** dominion over you:	NIG
6:17	ye **h** obeyed from the heart *that* form of	NIG
6:19	for as ye **h** yielded your members servants	NIG
6:22	ye **h** your fruit unto holiness, and the end	2192
8: 9	Now if any *man* **h** not the Spirit of Christ,	2192
8:15	ye **h** not received the spirit of bondage	NIG
8:15	but ye **h** received the Spirit of adoption,	NIG
8:23	which **h** the firstfruits of the Spirit,	2192
9: 2	That I **h** great heaviness and	1510
9: 9	time will I come, and Sara shall **h** a son.	1510
9:13	As it is written, Jacob **h** I loved,	NIG
9:13	Jacob have I loved, but Esau **h** I hated.	NIG
9:15	will **h mercy**, on whom I will have mercy,	1653
9:15	will have mercy on whom I will **h** mercy,	1653
9:15	will **h compassion** on whom I will have	3627
9:15	on whom I will **h compassion**.	3627
9:17	for this same *purpose* I raised thee	NIG
9:18	hath he mercy on whom he will **h**	NIG
9:30	**h** attained to righteousness,	NIG
10: 2	I bear them record that they **h** a zeal of	2192
10: 3	**h** not submitted themselves unto	NIG
10:14	they call on *him* in whom they **h** not	NIG
10:14	believe *in* him of whom they **h** not heard?	NIG
10:16	But they **h** not all obeyed the gospel.	NIG
10:18	But I say, **H** they not heard? Yes verily,	NIG
10:21	All day long **h** I stretched forth my hands	NIG
11: 3	they **h** killed thy prophets, and digged	NIG
11: 4	I **h** reserved to myself seven thousand	NIG
11: 4	**h** not bowed the knee to *the image of*	NIG
11:11	**H** they stumbled that they should fall?	NIG
11:30	as ye in times past **h** not believed God,	NIG
11:30	yet **h** now obtained mercy through their	NIG
11:31	*Even* so **h** these also now not believed,	NIG
11:32	unbelief, that he might **h mercy** upon all.	1653
12: 4	For as we **h** many members in one body,	2192
12: 4	and all members **h** not the same office:	2192
13: 3	and thou shalt **h** praise of the same:	2192
14:22	**h** *it* to thyself before God. Happy *is he*	2192
15: 4	comfort of the scriptures might **h** hope.	2192
15:15	I **h** written the more boldly unto you in	NIG
15:17	I **h** therefore whereof *I* may glory through	2192
15:19	I **h** fully preached the gospel of Christ.	NIG
15:20	Yea, so **h** I strived to preach the gospel,	NIG
15:21	they that **h** not heard shall understand.	NIG
15:22	For which cause also I **h** been much	NIG
15:27	For if the Gentiles **h** been made partakers	NIG
15:28	When therefore I **h** performed this,	NIG
15:28	and **h** sealed to them this fruit,	NIG
15:31	that my service which I **h** for Jerusalem	NIG
16: 4	Who **h** for my life laid down their own	NIG
16:17	contrary to the doctrine which ye **h**	NIG
16:19	I would **h** you wise unto *that which is*	1510

1Co		
2: 8	for had they known *it,* they **would** not **h**	302
2: 9	neither **h** entered into the heart of man,	NIG
2:12	Now we **h** received, not the spirit of	NIG
2:16	But we **h** the mind of Christ.	2192
3: 2	I **h** fed you with milk, and not with meat:	NIG
3: 6	I **h** planted, Apollos watered; but God	NIG
3:10	I **h** laid the foundation, and another	NIG
4: 5	and then shall every man **h** praise of God.	1096
4: 6	I **h** in a figure transferred to myself and	NIG
4: 8	are rich, ye **h** reigned as kings without us:	NIG
4:11	and **h** no certain dwelling place;	790
4:15	though you **h** ten thousand instructors	2192
4:15	in Christ, yet **h** ye not many fathers:	NIG
4:15	in Christ Jesus I **h** begotten you through	NIG
4:17	this cause **h** I sent unto you Timotheus,	NIG
5: 1	that one should **h** *his* father's wife.	2192
5: 2	are puffed up, and **h** not rather mourned,	NIG
5: 3	but present in spirit, **h** judged already,	NIG

H

H

1Co
5:11 But now I **h** written unto you not to keep NIG
5:12 For **what h I to do** to judge them 1473+5101
6: 4 ye judgments *of things* pertaining to 2192
6:19 which ye **h** of God, and ye are not your 2192
7: 2 let every man **h** his own wife, and let 2192
7: 2 let every woman **h** her own husband. 2192
7:25 Now concerning virgins I **h** no 2192
7:28 Nevertheless such shall **h** trouble in 2192
7:29 that both they that **h** wives be as though 2192
7:32 But I would **h** you without carefulness. 1510
7:40 and I think also that *I* **h** the Spirit of God. 2192
8: 1 we know that we all **h** knowledge. 2192
9: 1 **h** I not seen Jesus Christ our Lord? NIG
9: 4 **H** we not power to eat and to drink? 2192
9: 5 **H** we not power to lead about a sister, 2192
9: 6 h not we power to forbear working? 2192
9:11 If we **h** sown unto you spiritual *things,* NIG
9:12 Nevertheless we **h** not used this power; NIG
9:15 But I **h** used none of these *things:* neither NIG
9:15 **h** I written these *things,* that it should be NIG
9:16 I preach the gospel, I **h** nothing to glory 1510
9:17 if I do this *thing* willingly, I **h** a reward: 2192
9:19 For though I be free from all *men,* yet **h** I NIG
9:27 any means, when I **h** preached to others, NIG
10:20 I would not that ye should **h** fellowship 1096
11: 3 I would **h** you know, that the head of NIG
11:10 this cause ought the woman to **h** power 2192
11:14 that, if a man **h long hair,** it is a shame 2863
11:15 if a woman **h long hair,** it is a glory to 2863
11:16 **h** no such custom, neither the churches NIG
11:22 **h** ye not houses to eat and to drink *in?* or 2192
11:22 of God, and shame them that **h** not? 2192
11:23 I **h** received of the Lord *that* which also NIG
12: 1 brethren, I would not **h** you ignorant, NIG
12:13 **h** been all made to drink into one Spirit. NIG
12:21 say unto the hand, I **h** no need of thee: 2192
12:21 the head to the feet, I **h** no need of you. 2192
12:23 our uncomely *parts* **h** more abundant 2192
12:24 For our comely *parts* **h** no need: 2192
12:25 the members should **h** the same **care** 3300
12:30 **H** all the gifts of healing? do all speak with 2192
13: 1 of men and of angels, and **h** not charity, 2192
13: 2 And though I **h** *the gift of* prophecy, 2192
13: 2 and though I **h** all faith, so that *I* could 2192
13: 2 and **h** no charity, I am nothing. 2192
13: 3 and **h** not charity, it profiteth me nothing. 2192
15: 1 which also you **h** received, and wherein NIG
15: 2 unto you, unless ye **h** believed in vain. NIG
15:15 we **h** testified of God that he raised up NIG
15:19 If in this life only we **h** hope in Christ, 1510
15:24 when he shall **h** delivered up the kingdom NIG
15:24 when he shall **h** put down all rule and NIG
15:31 I protest by your rejoicing which I **h** in 2192
15:32 If after the manner of men I **h** fought with NIG
15:34 for some **h** not the knowledge of God: 2192
15:49 as we **h** borne the image of the earthy, NIG
15:54 So when this corruptible shall **h** put on NIG
15:54 this mortal shall **h** put on immortality, NIG
16: 1 as I **h** given order to the churches of NIG
16:12 come when he shall **h convenient time.** 2119
16:15 *that* they **h** addicted themselves to NIG
16:17 was lacking on your part they **h** supplied. NIG
16:18 For they **h** refreshed my spirit and yours: NIG

2Co
1: 8 **h** you **ignorant** of our trouble which came 50
1:12 we **h** had our conversation in the world, NIG
1:14 As also you **h** acknowledged us in part, NIG
1:15 that you might **h** a second benefit; 2192
1:24 Not for that we **h dominion over** your 2961
2: 3 I should **h** sorrow from *them of* whom I 2192
2: 4 ye might know the love which I **h** more 2192
2: 5 But if any **h** caused grief, he hath not NIG
3: 4 And such trust **h** we through Christ to 2192
3:12 Seeing then that we **h** such hope, we use 2192
4: 1 Therefore seeing we **h** this ministry, 2192
4: 1 as we **h** received mercy, we faint not; NIG
4: 2 But **h** renounced the hidden *things of* NIG
4: 7 But we **h** this treasure in earthen vessels, 2192
4:13 I believed, *and* therefore **h** I spoken; NIG
5: 1 we **h** a building of God, a house not made 2192
5:12 that you may **h** *somewhat* to **answer** 2192
5:16 though we **h** known Christ after the flesh, NIG
6: 2 I **h** heard thee in a time accepted, and in NIG
6: 2 in the day of salvation **h** I succoured thee: NIG
7: 2 **h** wronged no *man,* we **h** corrupted NIG
7: 2 **h** wronged no *man,* we **h** corrupted NIG
7: 2 no *man,* we **h** defrauded no *man.* NIG
7: 3 speak not *this* to condemn *you:* for I **h** said NIG
7:11 In all *things* ye **h** approved yourselves to NIG
7:14 For if I **h** boasted any *thing* to him of you, NIG
7:16 that I **h confidence** in you in all *things.* 2292
8:10 who **h** begun before, not only to do, NIG
8:11 performance also out of that which *you* **h.** 2192
8:18 And we **h** sent with him the brother, NIG
8:22 And we **h** sent with them our brother, NIG
8:22 whom we **h** oftentimes proved diligent in NIG
8:22 the great confidence which *I* **h** in you. NIG
9: 3 Yet **h** I sent the brethren, lest our boasting NIG
11: 2 I **h** espoused you to one husband, that *I*
11: 4 whom we **h** not preached, or *if* ye receive NIG
11: 4 ye **h** not received, or another gospel, NIG
11: 4 another gospel, which ye **h** not accepted, NIG
11: 6 **h** been throughly made manifest among NIG
11: 7 **H** I committed an offence in abasing NIG
11: 7 I **h** preached to you the gospel of God NIG
11: 9 in all *things* I **h** kept myself from being NIG

2Co
11:25 a night and a day I **h** been in the deep; NIG
12:11 a fool in glorying; ye **h** compelled me: NIG
12:11 for I ought to **h** been commended of you: NIG
12:21 *that* I shall bewail many which **h** sinned NIG
12:21 **h** not repented of the uncleanness and NIG
12:21 lasciviousness which they **h** committed. NIG
13: 2 write to them which heretofore **h** sinned, NIG

Gal
1: 8 than *that* which we **h** preached unto you, NIG
1: 9 gospel unto you than ye **h** received, NIG
1:13 For ye **h** heard of my conversation in time NIG
2: 4 our liberty which we **h** in Christ Jesus, 2192
2:16 even we **h** believed in Jesus Christ, NIG
3: 4 **H** ye suffered so many *things* in vain? if *it* NIG
3:21 been a law given which could **h** given life, NIG
3:21 verily righteousness **should h** been by 302
3:27 For as many of you as **h** been baptized into NIG
3:27 been baptized into Christ **h** put on Christ. NIG
4: 9 after that ye **h** known God, or rather are NIG
4:11 lest I **h** bestowed upon you labour in vain. NIG
4:12 be as I *am;* for I *am* as ye *are:* ye **h** not NIG
4:15 ye would **h** plucked out your own eyes, NIG
4:15 your own eyes, and given *them* to me. NIG
5:10 I **h** confidence in you through the Lord, NIG
5:13 brethren, ye **h** been called unto liberty; NIG
5:21 before, as I **h** also told *you* in time past, NIG
5:24 And they that are Christ's **h** crucified NIG
6: 4 then shall he **h** rejoicing in himself alone, 2192
6:10 As we **h** therefore opportunity, let us do 2192
6:11 Ye see how large a letter I **h** written unto NIG
6:13 but desire to **h** you circumcised, that they NIG

Eph
1: 7 In whom we **h** redemption through his 2192
1:11 whom also we **h** obtained an inheritance, NIG
2:18 For through him we both **h** access by one 2192
3: 2 If ye **h** heard of the dispensation of NIG
3:12 In whom we **h** boldness and access with 2192
4:19 Who being past feeling **h** given themselves NIG
4:20 But ye **h** not so learned Christ; NIG
4:21 If so be that ye **h** heard him, and have NIG
4:21 **h** been taught by him, as the truth is in NIG
4:28 that he may **h** to give to him that needeth. 2192
5:11 And **h** no **fellowship with** the unfruitful 4790
6:22 Whom I **h** sent unto you for the same NIG

Php
1: 7 of you all, because I **h** you in *my* heart; 2192
1:12 the *things* which *happened* unto me **h** NIG
2:12 my beloved, as ye **h** always obeyed, NIG
2:16 that I **h** not run in vain, neither laboured NIG
2:20 For I **h** no *man* likeminded, who will 2192
2:27 lest I should **h** sorrow upon sorrow. 2192
3: 3 and **h** no **confidence** in the flesh. 3982
3: 4 Though I *might* also **h** confidence in 2192
3: 8 whom I **h** suffered the loss of all *things,* NIG
3:13 I count not myself to **h** apprehended: NIG
3:16 whereto we **h** *already* attained, NIG
3:17 which walk so as ye **h** us for an ensample. 2192
3:18 of whom I **h** told you often, and now tell NIG
4: 9 Those *things,* which ye **h** both learned, NIG
4:11 for I **h** learned, in whatsoever *state* I am, NIG
4:14 Notwithstanding ye **h** well done, that ye NIG
4:18 But I **h** all, and abound: I am full, 568

Col
1: 4 of the love which *ye* **h** to all the saints, 2192
1:14 In whom we **h** redemption through his NIG
1:18 that in all *things* he might **h** 1096
1:23 ye heard, *and* which was preached NIG
2: 1 ye knew what great conflict I **h** for you, 2192
2: 1 *for* as many as **h** not seen my face in NIG
2: 6 As ye **h** therefore received Christ Jesus NIG
2: 7 stablished in the faith, as ye **h** been taught, NIG
2:23 Which *things* **h** indeed a shew of wisdom 2192
3: 9 seeing that ye **h** put off the old man with NIG
3:10 And **h** put on the new *man,* which is NIG
3:13 if any *man* **h** a quarrel against any: 2192
4: 1 that ye also **h** a Master in heaven. 2192
4: 8 Whom I **h** sent unto you for the same NIG
4:11 of God, which **h** been a comfort unto me. NIG

1Th
2: 6 when we might **h** been burdensome, NIG
2: 8 we were willing to **h** imparted unto you, NIG
2:14 for ye also **h** suffered like *things* of your NIG
2:14 even as they *h* of the Jews: NIG
2:15 their own prophets, and **h** persecuted us; NIG
2:18 Wherefore we would **h** come unto you, NIG
3: 5 by some means the tempter **h** tempted NIG
3: 6 that ye **h** good remembrance of us always, 2192
4: 1 as ye **h** received of us how ye ought to NIG
4: 6 as we also **h** forewarned you and testified. NIG
4:12 and *that* ye may **h** lack of nothing. 2192
4:13 But I would not **h** you to be ignorant, 2309
4:13 even as others which **h** no hope. 2192
5: 1 ye **h** no need that *I* write unto you. 2192

2Th
2:15 the traditions which ye **h** been taught, NIG
3: 1 the word of the Lord may **h** *free* course, NIG
3: 2 and wicked men: for all *men* **h** not faith. NIG
3: 4 we **h** confidence in the Lord touching NIG
3: 9 Not because we **h** not power, but to make 2192
3:14 that *man,* and **h** no **company with** him, 4874

1Ti
1: 6 which some having swerved **h** turned NIG
1:19 concerning faith **h** made shipwreck: NIG
1:20 whom I **h** delivered unto Satan, that they NIG
2: 4 Who **will h** all men to be saved, 2309
3: 7 Moreover he must **h** a good report of 2192
3:13 they that **h** used the office of a deacon NIG
5: 4 But if any widow **h** children or nephews, 2192
5:10 If she **h** brought up children, if she have NIG
5:10 up children, if she **h** lodged strangers, NIG
5:10 if she **h** washed the saints' feet, NIG
5:10 saints' feet, if she **h** relieved the afflicted, NIG

1Ti
5:10 if she **h** diligently followed every good NIG
5:11 for when they **h begun to** wax wanton NIG
5:12 because they **h** cast off *their* first faith. 2192
5:16 or woman that believeth **h** widows, 2192
6: 2 they that **h** believing masters, let them 2192
6:10 they **h** erred from the faith, NIG
6:21 Which some professing **h** erred NIG

2Ti
1: 3 that without ceasing I **h** remembrance of 2192
1:12 for I know whom I **h** believed, and I am NIG
1:12 I **h** committed unto *him* against that day. NIG
2:18 Who concerning the truth **h** erred, NIG
4: 7 I **h** fought a good fight, I have finished *my* NIG
4: 7 **h** finished *my* course, I have kept the faith: NIG
4: 7 have finished *my* course, I **h** kept the faith: NIG
4:12 And Tychicus **h** I sent to Ephesus. NIG
4:20 but Trophimus **h** I left at Miletum sick. NIG

Tit
3: 5 by works of righteousness which we **h** NIG
3: 8 they which **h** believed in God might be NIG
3:12 for I **h** determined there to winter. NIG

Phm
1: 7 For we **h** great joy and consolation in thy 2192
1:10 whom I **h** begotten in my bonds: NIG
1:12 Whom I **h** sent again: thou therefore NIG
1:13 Whom I would **h** retained with me, that NIG
1:13 in thy stead he might **h** ministered unto NIG
1:19 I Paul **h** written *it* with mine own hand, NIG
1:20 brother, let me **h** joy of thee in the Lord: NIG

Heb
1: 5 art my Son, this day **h** I begotten thee? NIG
2: 1 heed to the *things* which we **h** heard, NIG
3:10 heart; and they **h** not known my ways. NIG
4: 3 we which **h** believed do enter into rest, NIG
4: 3 *he* said, As I **h** sworn in my wrath, if they NIG
4: 8 he **h** not afterward spoken of another NIG
4:13 the eyes of him with whom we **h to do.** 3056
4:14 Seeing then that we **h** a great high priest, 2192
4:15 we **h** not a high priest which cannot be 2192
5: 2 Who can **h compassion** on the ignorant, 3356
5: 5 art my Son, to day **h** I begotten thee. NIG
5:11 Of whom we **h** many things to say, NIG
5:12 ye **h** need that *one* teach you again which 2192
5:12 and are become such as **h** need of milk, 2192
5:14 *even* those who by reason of use **h** their NIG
6: 4 and **h** tasted of the heavenly gift, NIG
6: 5 And **h** tasted the good word of God, NIG
6:10 which ye **h** shewed toward his name, NIG
6:10 in that ye **h** ministered to the saints, NIG
6:18 to lie, we might **h** a strong consolation, 2192
6:18 who **h** fled for refuge to lay hold upon NIG
6:19 hope we **h** as an anchor of the soul, 2192
7: 5 **h** a commandment to take tithes of 2192
7:28 men high priests which **h** infirmity; 2192
8: 1 of the *things* which we **h** spoken *this is* 2192
8: 1 We **h** such a high priest, who is set on 2192
8: 3 *it is* of necessity that this *man* **h** 2192
8: 7 **should** no place **h** been sought for 302
9:26 must he often **h** suffered since NIG
10: 2 **would** they not **h** ceased to be offered? 302
10: 2 the worshippers once purged should **h** NIG
10:26 For if we sin wilfully after that *we* **h** NIG
10:34 knowing in yourselves that *ye* **h** in heaven 2192
10:36 For ye **h** need of patience, that, after ye 2192
10:36 that, after ye **h** done the will of God, NIG
10:38 my soul shall **h** no **pleasure** in him. 2106
11:15 they might **h** had opportunity to have NIG
11:15 they might have had opportunity to **h** NIG
12: 4 Ye **h** not yet resisted unto blood, NIG
12: 5 And ye **h** forgotten the exhortation which NIG
12: 9 Furthermore we **h** had fathers of our flesh NIG
12:17 when he would **h** inherited the blessing, NIG
12:28 us **h** grace, whereby we may serve God 2192
13: 2 for thereby some **h** entertained angels NIG
13: 5 *and be* content with such *things* as ye **h:** 3918
13: 7 Remember them which **h the rule over** 2233
13: 7 who **h** spoken unto you the word of God: NIG
13: 9 which **h** not profited them that have been NIG
13: 9 which have not profited them that **h** been NIG
13:10 We **h** an altar, whereof they have no right 2192
13:10 they **h** no right to eat which serve 2192
13:14 For here **h** we no continuing city, 2192
13:17 Obey them that **h the rule over** you, 2233
13:18 we trust we **h** a good conscience, in all 2192
13:22 for I **h** written a letter unto you in few NIG
13:24 Salute all them that **h the rule over** you, 2233

Jas
1: 4 let patience **h** *her* perfect work, that ye 2192
2: 1 **h** not the faith of our Lord Jesus Christ, 2192
2: 3 And ye **h** respect to him that weareth NIG
2: 6 ye **h** despised the poor. Do not rich *men* NIG
2: 9 if ye **h respect to persons,** ye commit 4380
2:13 For he shall **h** judgment without mercy, NIG
2:14 man say *he* hath faith, and **h** not works? 2192
2:18 may say, Thou hast faith, and I **h** works: 2192
3:14 if ye **h** bitter envying and strife in your 2192
4: 2 Ye lust, and **h** not: ye kill, and desire **to** 2192
4: 2 ye kill, and desire *to* **h,** and cannot obtain: NIG
4: 2 ye fight and war, yet ye **h** not, because ye 2192
5: 3 ye **h** heaped treasure together for the last NIG
5: 4 the hire of the labourers which **h** reaped NIG
5: 4 cries of them which **h** reaped are entered NIG
5: 5 Ye **h** lived in pleasure on the earth, NIG
5: 5 ye **h** nourished your hearts, as in a day of NIG
5: 6 Ye **h** condemned *and* killed the just; NIG
5:10 who **h** spoken in the name of the Lord, NIG
5:11 Ye **h** heard of the patience of Job, NIG
5:11 of Job, and **h** seen the end of the Lord; NIG
5:15 and if he **h** committed sins, they shall be 1510

1Pe
1:10 which salvation the prophets **h** inquired NIG

1Pe	1:12 **h** preached the gospel unto you with	NIG
	1:22 Seeing ye **h** purified your souls in obeying	NIG
	2: 3 so be ye **h** tasted that the Lord *is* gracious.	NIG
	2:10 mercy, but now **h** obtained mercy.	NIG
	4: 3 us to **h** wrought the will of the Gentiles,	NIG
	4: 8 And above all *things* **h** fervent charity	2192
	5:10 after that ye **h** suffered a while, make you	NIG
	5:12 I **h** written briefly, exhorting,	NIG
2Pe	1: 1 to them that **h** obtained like precious faith	NIG
	1:15 to **h** these *things* always in remembrance.	2192
	1:16 For we **h** not followed cunningly devised	NIG
	1:19 We **h** also a more sure word of prophecy;	2192
	2:14 a heart they **h** exercised with covetous	2192
	2:15 Which **h** forsaken the right way,	NIG
	2:20 For if after they **h** escaped the pollutions of	NIG
	2:21 For it had been better for them not to **h**	NIG
	2:21 after they **h** known *it*, to turn from the	NIG
1Jn	1: 1 which we **h** heard, which we have seen	NIG
	1: 1 heard, which we **h** seen with our eyes,	NIG
	1: 1 which we **h** looked upon, and our hands	NIG
	1: 1 and our hands **h** handled, of the Word of	NIG
	1: 2 and we **h** seen *it*, and bear witness,	NIG
	1: 3 *That* which we **h** seen and heard declare	NIG
	1: 3 that ye also may **h** fellowship with us:	2192
	1: 5 is the message which we **h** heard of him,	NIG
	1: 6 If we say that we **h** fellowship with him,	2192
	1: 7 we **h** fellowship one with another,	2192
	1: 8 If we say that we **h** no sin, we deceive	2192
	1:10 If we say that we **h** not sinned, we make	NIG
	2: 1 sin, we **h** an advocate with the Father,	2192
	2: 7 which ye **h** heard from the beginning.	NIG
	2:13 known him that is from the beginning.	NIG
	2:13 because you **h** overcome the wicked one.	NIG
	2:13 because ye **h** known the Father.	NIG
	2:14 I **h** written unto you, fathers, because	NIG
	2:14 known him that is from the beginning.	NIG
	2:14 I **h** written unto you, young men, because	NIG
	2:14 and ye **h** overcome the wicked one.	NIG
	2:18 as ye **h** heard that antichrist shall come,	NIG
	2:19 they **would** *no doubt* **h** continued with us:	302
	2:20 But ye **h** an unction from the Holy One,	2192
	2:21 I **h** not written unto you because ye know	NIG
	2:24 which ye **h** heard from the beginning.	NIG
	2:24 *that* which ye **h** heard from the beginning	NIG
	2:26 These *things* **h** I written unto you	NIG
	2:27 But the anointing which ye **h** received of	NIG
	2:28 may **h** confidence, and be not ashamed	2192
	3:14 We know that we **h** passed from death	NIG
	3:21 *then* **h** we confidence towards God.	2192
	4: 3 whereof you **h** heard that it should come;	NIG
	4: 4 little children, and **h** overcome them:	NIG
	4:14 we **h** seen and do testify that the Father	NIG
	4:16 we **h** known and believed the love that	NIG
	4:17 that we may **h** boldness in the day of	2192
	4:21 And this commandment **h** we from him,	2192
	5:13 These *things* **h** I written unto you	NIG
	5:13 that ye may know that ye **h** eternal life,	2192
	5:14 this is the confidence that we **h** in him,	2192
	5:15 we know that we **h** the petitions that we	2192
2Jn	1: 1 but also all they that **h** known the truth;	NIG
	1: 4 as we **h** received a commandment from	NIG
	1: 6 That, as ye **h** heard from the beginning,	NIG
	1: 8 that we lose not *those things* which we **h**	NIG
3Jn	1: 4 I **h** no greater joy than to hear that my	2192
	1: 6 Which **h** borne witness of thy charity	NIG
	1: 6 **loveth to h** the **preeminence among**	5383
Jude	1:11 for they **h** gone in the way of Cain,	NIG
	1:15 deeds which they **h** ungodly committed,	NIG
	1:15 ungodly sinners **h** spoken against him.	NIG
	1:22 And of some **h** compassion, making a	1653
Rev	1:18 and **h** the keys of hell and of death.	2192
	2: 4 Nevertheless I **h** *somewhat* against thee,	2192
	2:10 tried; and ye shall **h** tribulation ten days:	NIG
	2:14 But I **h** a few *things* against thee, because	2192
	2:20 Notwithstanding I **h** a few *things* against	2192
	2:24 as many as **h** not this doctrine,	2192
	2:24 which **h** not known the depths of Satan,	NIG
	2:25 But *that* which ye **h** *already* hold fast till I	2192
	3: 2 for I **h** not found thy works perfect before	NIG
	3: 4 which **h** not defiled their garments;	NIG
	3: 8 I **h** set before thee an open door, and no	NIG
	3: 9 thy feet, and to know that I **h** loved thee.	NIG
	3:17 with goods, and **h** need of nothing;	2192
	7: 3 till we **h** sealed the servants of our God in	NIG
	7:14 and **h** washed their robes, and made them	2192
	9: 3 as the scorpions of the earth **h** power.	2192
	9: 4 *those* men which **h** not the seal of God	2192
	11: 6 These **h** power to shut heaven, that it	2192
	11: 6 power over waters to turn them to	2192
	11: 7 And when they shall **h** finished their	NIG
	12:17 and **h** the testimony of Jesus Christ.	2192
	13: 9 If any *man* **h** an ear, let him hear.	2192
	14:11 and they **h** no rest day nor night,	2192
	16: 6 For they **h** shed the blood of saints and	NIG
	17: 2 With whom the kings of the earth **h**	NIG
	17: 2 the inhabiters of the earth **h** been made	NIG
	17:12 which **h** received no kingdom as yet;	NIG
	17:13 These **h** one mind, and shall give their	2192
	18: 3 For all nations **h** drunk of the wine of	NIG
	18: 3 the kings of the earth **h** committed	NIG
	18: 5 For her sins **h** reached unto heaven,	NIG
	18: 9 who **h** committed fornication and	NIG
	19:10 of thy brethren that **h** the testimony of	2192
	21: 8 **h** their part in the lake which burneth	NIG
	22:14 that they may **h** right to the tree of life,	1510

Rev	22:16 I Jesus **h** sent mine angel to testify unto	NIG

HAVEN (5) [HAVENS]

Ge	49:13 Zebulun shall dwell at the **h** of the sea;	2348
	49:13 he *shall be* for a **h** of ships; and his border	2348
Ps	107:30 so he bringeth them unto their desired **h**.	4231
Ac	27:12 the **h** was not commodious to winter in,	3040
	27:12 which is a **h** of Crete, and lieth toward	3040

HAVENS (1) [HAVEN]

Ac	27: 8 unto a place *which is* called The **fair h**;	2568

HAVILAH (7)

Ge	2:11 *it* which compasseth the whole land of **H**,	2341
	10: 7 **H**, and Sabtah, and Raamah, and	2341
	10:29 Ophir, and **H**, and Jobab: all these *were*	2341
	25:18 they dwelt from **H** unto Shur, that *is*	2341
1Sa	15: 7 Saul smote the Amalekites from **H** *until*	2341
1Ch	1: 9 **H**, and Sabta, and Raamah, and Sabtecha.	2341
	1:23 Ophir, and **H**, and Jobab. All these *were*	2341

HAVING (193) [HAVE]

Ge	12: 8 **h** Beth-el on the west, and Hai on the east:	NIH
Lev	7:20 the LORD, **h** his uncleanness upon him,	NIH
	20:18 shall lie with a woman **h** her **sickness**,	1739
	22: 3 **h** his uncleanness upon him, that soul	NIH
	22:22 or **h** a wen, or scurvy, or scabbed,	2990
Nu	24: 4 falling *into a trance*, but **h** his eyes open:	NIH
	24:16 falling *into a trance*, but **h** his eyes open:	NIH
Dt	10: 3 mount, **h** the two tables in mine hand.	NIH
Jdg	1: 7 **h** their thumbs and their great toes cut	1961
	19: 3 his servant with him, and a couple of	NIH
Ru	1:13 would ye stay for them from **h**	1961+3807.1
1Sa	22: 6 his spear in his hand, and all his	NIH
	26: 2 **h** three thousand chosen men of Israel	2050.1
1Ki	22:10 each on his throne, **h** put on *their* robes,	NIH
1Ch	4:42 **h** for their captains Pelatiah, and Neariah,	NIH
	21:16 **h** a drawn sword in his hand stretched out	NIH
	26:12 chief men, **h** wards one against another,	NIH
2Ch	5:12 **h** cymbals and psalteries and harps,	871.1
	11:12 **h** Judah and Benjamin on his side.	1961
	23:10 every man **h** his weapon in his hand,	NIH
Ezr	9: 5 **h** rent my garment and my mantle, I fell	NIH
Ne	10:28 every one **h** **knowledge**,	3045
	10:28 having knowledge, *and* **h** **understanding**;	995
	13: 4 **h** the **oversight** of the chamber of	5414+871.1
Est	6:12 house mourning, and **h** his head covered.	NIH
Ps	13: 2 in my soul, **h** sorrow in my heart daily?	NIH
Pr	6: 7 Which **h** no guide, overseer, or ruler,	3807.1
	18: 1 separated himself, seeketh *and*	NIH
Isa	6: 6 unto me, **h** a live coal in his hand,	NIH
	41:15 a new sharp threshing instrument **h** teeth:	1167
Jer	41: 5 **h** their beards shaven, and their clothes	NIH
	41: 5 **h** cut themselves, with offerings and	NIH
Eze	38:11 and **h** neither bars nor gates,	3807.1
	40:44 one at the side of the east gate **h**	NIH
	44:11 **h** charge at the gates of the house,	NIH
Da	8:20 The ram which thou sawest **h** two horns	1167
Mic	1:11 inhabitant of Saphir, **h** *thy* shame naked:	NIH
Zec	9: 9 he *is* just, and **h** **salvation**; lowly,	3467
Mt	7:29 For he taught them as *one* **h** authority,	2192
	8: 9 under authority, **h** soldiers under me:	2192
	9:36 scattered abroad, as sheep **h** no shepherd.	2192
	15:30 **h** with them *those that were* lame, blind,	2192
	18: 8 rather than **h** two hands or two feet to be	2192
	18: 9 rather than **h** two eyes to be cast into hell	2192
	22:12 camest thou in hither not **h** a wedding	2192
	22:24 Moses said, If a man die, **h** no children,	2192
	22:25 and, **h** no issue, left his wife unto his	2192
	26: 7 There came unto him a woman **h** an	2192
Mk	6:34 they were as sheep not **h** a shepherd:	2192
	8: 1 and **h** nothing to eat, Jesus called his	2192
	8:18 **h** eyes, see ye not? and having ears,	2192
	8:18 and **h** ears, hear ye not? and do ye not	2192
	9:43 than **h** two hands to go into hell, into	2192
	9:45 life, than **h** two feet to be cast into hell,	2192
	9:47 than **h** two eyes to be cast into hell fire:	2192
	11:13 And seeing a fig tree afar off **h** leaves,	2192
	12: 6 **H** yet therefore one son, his wellbeloved,	2192
	12:28 and **h** heard them reasoning together,	NIG
	14: 3 there came a woman **h** an alabaster box	2192
	14:51 **h** a linen cloth cast about *his* naked *body*;	NIG
Lk	1: 3 **h** had perfect understanding of all *things*	NIG
	5:39 No *man* also **h** drunk old *wine*	NIG
	7: 8 **h** under me soldiers, and I say unto one,	2192
	8:15 **h** heard the word, keep *it*, and bring forth	1510
	8:43 And a woman **h** an issue of blood twelve	NIG
	9:62 No *man* **h** put his hand to the plough,	NIG
	11:36 therefore **h** no part dark,	2192
	15: 4 What man of you, **h** an hundred sheep,	2192
	15: 8 Either what woman **h** ten pieces of silver,	2192
	17: 7 a servant plowing or feeding cattle,	2192
	19:15 **h** received the kingdom, then	NIG
	20:28 **h** a wife, and **h** die without children,	2192
	23:14 and behold, I, **h** examined *him* before you,	NIG
	23:46 and **h** said thus, he gave up the ghost.	NIG
Jn	4:45 **h** seen all *the things* that he did at	NIG
	5: 2 Hebrew tongue Bethesda, **h** five porches.	2192
	7:15 this *man* letters, **h** never learned?	NIG
	13: 1 loved his own which were in the world,	NIG
	13: 2 devil **h** now put into the heart of Judas	NIG
	13:30 received the sop went immediately out:	NIG
	18: 3 **h** received a band *of men*, and officers	NIG
	18:10 Then Simon Peter **h** a sword drew it,	2192
Ac	2:24 raised up, **h** loosed the pains of death:	NIG

Ac	2:33 **h** received of the Father the promise of	NIG
	2:47 and **h** favour with all the people.	2192
	3:26 you first God, **h** raised up his Son Jesus,	NIG
	4:37 **H** land, sold *it*, and brought the money,	NIG
	12:20 made Blastus the king's chamberlain	NIG
	14:19 **h** stoned Paul, drew *him* out of the city,	NIG
	16:24 **h** received such a charge, thrust them	NIG
	18:18 **h** shorn *his* head in Cenchrea: for he had	NIG
	19: 1 Paul **h** passed through the upper coasts	NIG
	19:29 **h** caught Gaius and Aristarchus, men of	NIG
	22:12 **h** a **good report** of all the Jews which	3140
	23:27 **h** understood that he was a Roman,	NIG
	24:22 when Felix heard these *things*, **h** more	NIG
	26:10 **h** received authority from the chief priests;	NIG
	26:22 **H** therefore obtained help of God,	NIG
	27:33 and continued fasting, **h** taken nothing.	NIG
Ro	2:14 these, **h** not the law, are a law unto	2192
	9:11 yet born, neither **h** done any good or evil,	NIG
	12: 6 **h** then gifts differing according to	2192
	15:23 But now **h** no more place in these parts,	2192
	15:23 **h** a great desire these many years to come	2192
1Co	6: 1 any of you, **h** a matter against another,	2192
	7:37 **h** no necessity, but hath power over his	2192
	11: 4 or prophesying, **h** *his* head covered,	2192
	12:24 given more abundant honour to that	NIG
2Co	2: 3 **h** confidence in you all, that my joy is	NIG
	4:13 We **h** the same spirit of faith, according as	2192
	6:10 nothing, and *yet* possessing all *things*.	2192
	7: 1 **H** therefore these promises, dearly	2192
	9: 8 always **h** all sufficiency in all *things*, may	2192
	10: 6 And **h** in a readiness to revenge all	2192
	10:15 but **h** hope, when your faith is increased,	2192
Gal	3: 3 **h** begun in the Spirit, are ye now made	NIG
Eph	1: 5 **H** predestinated us unto the adoption of	NIG
	1: 9 **H** made known unto us the mystery of his	NIG
	2:12 **h** no hope, and without God in the world:	2192
	2:15 **H** abolished in his flesh the enmity,	NIG
	2:16 by the cross, **h** slain the enmity thereby:	NIG
	4:18 **H** the understanding darkened,	NIG
	5:27 not **h** spot, or wrinkle, or any such *thing*;	2192
	6:13 in the evil day, and **h** done all, to stand.	NIG
	6:14 your loins girt about with truth,	NIG
	6:14 and **h** on the breastplate of righteousness;	1746
Php	1:23 **h** a desire to depart, and to be with Christ;	2192
	1:25 **h** this **confidence**, I know that I shall	3982
	1:30 **H** the same conflict which ye saw in me,	2192
	2: 2 **h** the same love, *being* of one accord,	2192
	3: 9 not **h** mine own righteousness, which is	2192
	4:18 received of Epaphroditus the *things*	NIG
Col	1:20 **h** made peace through the blood of his	NIG
	2:13 with him, **h** forgiven you all trespasses;	NIG
	2:15 *And* **h** spoiled principalities and powers,	NIG
	2:19 and bands **h** nourishment ministered,	NIG
1Th	1: 6 received the word in much affliction,	NIG
1Ti	1: 5 From which some **h** swerved have turned	NIG
	1:19 which some **h** put away, concerning faith	NIG
	3: 4 **h** *his* children in subjection with all	2192
	4: 2 their conscience seared with a hot iron;	NIG
	4: 8 godliness is profitable unto all *things*, **h**	2192
	5: 9 years old, **h** been the wife of one man,	NIG
	5:12 **h** damnation, because they have cast off	2192
	6: 8 **h** food and raiment let us be therewith	2192
2Ti	2:19 **h** this seal, The Lord knoweth them that	2192
	3: 5 **H** a form of godliness, but denying	2192
	4: 3 to themselves teachers, **h** itching ears;	NIG
	4:10 loved *this* present world, and is	2192
Tit	1: 6 **h** faithful children not accused of riot or	2192
	2: 8 be ashamed, **h** no evil *thing* to say of you.	2192
Phm	1:21 **H** **confidence** in thy obedience I wrote	3982
Heb	9:12 **h** obtained eternal redemption *for us*.	NIG
	10: 1 For the law **h** a shadow of good *things* to	2192
	10:19 **h** therefore, brethren, boldness to enter	2192
	10:21 **h** a high priest over the house of God;	NIG
	10:22 **h** our hearts sprinkled from an evil	NIG
	11:13 not **h** received the promises,	NIG
	11:13 but **h** seen them afar off,	NIG
	11:39 **h** obtained a good report through faith,	NIG
	11:40 God **h** provided some better *thing* for us,	NIG
1Pe	2:12 Your conversation honest among	2192
	3: 8 **h** compassion one of another, love as	NIG
	3:16 **H** a good conscience; that, whereas they	2192
2Pe	1: 4 **h** escaped the corruption that is in the	NIG
	2:14 **H** eyes full of adultery and that cannot	2192
2Jn	1:12 **H** many *things* to write unto you, I would	2192
Jude	1: 5 **h** saved the people out of the land of	NIG
	1:16 **h** men's persons in **admiration**	2296+4383
	1:19 sensual, **h** not the Spirit.	NIG
Rev	5: 6 been slain, **h** seven horns and seven eyes,	2192
	5: 8 **h** every one *of them* harps, and golden	2192
	7: 2 the east, **h** the seal of the living God:	2192
	8: 3 and stood at the altar, **h** a golden censer;	2192
	9:17 breastplates of fire, and of jacinth,	2192
	12: 3 **h** seven heads and ten horns,	2192
	12:12 **h** great wrath, because he knoweth that	2192
	13: 1 **h** seven heads and ten horns, and upon	2192
	14: 1 his Father's name written in their	2192
	14: 6 the everlasting gospel to preach unto	2192
	14:14 **h** on his head a golden crown, and in his	2192
	14:17 is in heaven, he also **h** a sharp sickle.	2192
	15: 1 seven angels **h** the seven last plagues;	2192
	15: 6 on the sea of glass, **h** the harps of God.	2192
	15: 6 the seven plagues, clothed in pure and	2192
	15: 6 **h** their breasts girded with golden girdles.	NIG

H

Rev 17: 3 blasphemy, **h** seven heads and ten horns.	2192
17: 4 **h** a golden cup in her hand full of	2192
18: 1 come down from heaven, **h** great power;	2192
20: 1 **h** the key of the bottomless *pit* and a great	2192
21:11 **H** the glory of God: and her light *was* like	2192

HAVOCK (1)

Ac 8: 3 As for Saul, he **made h** of the church,	3075

HAVOTH-JAIR (2) [BASHAN-HAVOTH-JAIR]

Nu 32:41 small towns thereof, and called them **H**.	2334
Jdg 10: 4 which are called **H** unto this day,	2334

HAVVOTH JAIR See BASHAN-HAVOTH-JAIR;
HAVOTH-JAIR

HAWK (5)

Lev 11:16 the **night h**, and the cuckow, and the	8464
11:16 and the cuckow, and the **h** after his kind,	5322
Dt 14:15 the **night h**, and the cuckow, and the	8464
14:15 and the cuckow, and the **h** after his kind,	5322
Job 39:26 Doth the **h** fly by thy wisdom,	5322

HAY (3)

Pr 27:25 The **h** appeareth, and the tender grass	2682
Isa 15: 6 the **h** is withered away, the grass faileth,	2682
1Co 3:12 silver, precious stones, wood, **h**, stubble;	5528

HAZAEL (23)

1Ki 19:15 anoint **H** to be king over Syria:	2371
19:17 him that escapeth the sword of **H** shall	2371
2Ki 8: 8 the king said unto **H**, Take a present in	2371
8: 9 **H** went to meet him, and took a present	2371
8:12 **H** said, Why weepeth my lord? And he	2371
8:13 But, what, *is* thy servant a dog,	2371
8:15 that he died: and **H** reigned in his stead.	2371
8:28 against **H** king of Syria in Ramoth-gilead;	2371
8:29 when he fought against **H** king of Syria;	2371
9:14 and all Israel, because of **H** king of Syria.	2371
9:15 when he fought with **H** king of Syria.)	2371
10:32 **H** smote them in all the coasts of Israel;	2371
12:17 **H** king of Syria went up, and fought	2371
12:17 and **H** set his face to go up to Jerusalem.	2371
12:18 house, and sent *it* to **H** king of Syria:	2371
13: 3 delivered them into the hand of **H**,	2371
13: 3 into the hand of Ben-hadad the son of **H**,	2371
13:22 **H** king of Syria oppressed Israel all	2371
13:24 **H** king of Syria died; and Ben-hadad his	2371
13:25 hand of Ben-hadad the son of **H** the cities,	2371
2Ch 22: 5 against **H** king of Syria at Ramoth-gilead:	2371
22: 6 when he fought with **H** king of Syria.	2371
Am 1: 4 I will send a fire into the house of **H**,	2371

HAZAIAH (1)

Ne 11: 5 the son of **H**, the son of Adaiah, the son	2382

HAZAR-ADDAR (1) [ADDAR]

Nu 34: 4 shall go on *to* **H**, and pass on to Azmon:	2692

HAZARDED (1)

Ac 15:26 Men that have **h** their lives for the name	3860

HAZAR-ENAN (3) [ENAN]

Nu 34: 9 and the goings out of it shall be at **H**:	2704
34:10 shall point out your east border from **H**	2704
Eze 47:17 the border from the sea shall be **H**,	2703
48: 1 as *one* goeth to Hamath, **H**, the border of	2704

HAZAR-GADDAH (1)

Jos 15:27 And **H**, and Heshmon, and Beth-palet,	2693

HAZAR-HATTICON (1)

Eze 47:16 **H**, which *is* by the coast of Hauran.	2691

HAZARMAVETH (2)

Ge 10:26 and Sheleph, and **H**, and Jerah,	2700
1Ch 1:20 and Sheleph, and **H**, and Jerah,	2700

HAZAR-SHUAL (4) [SHUAL]

Jos 15:28 And **H**, and Beer-sheba, and Bizjothjah,	2705
19: 3 And **H**, and Balah, and Azem,	2705
1Ch 4:28 at Beer-sheba, and Moladah, and **H**,	2705
Ne 11:27 at **H**, and at Beer-sheba, and *in* the villages	2705

HAZAR-SUSAH (1) [HAZAR-SUSIM]

Jos 19: 5 And Ziklag, and Beth-marcaboth, and **H**,	2701

HAZAR-SUSIM (1) [HAZAR-SUSAH]

1Ch 4:31 **H**, and at Beth-birei, and at Shaaraim.	2702

HAZAZON-TAMAR (1) [HAZEZON-TAMAR,
TAMAR]

2Ch 20: 2 behold, they *be* in **H**, which *is* En-gedi.	2688

HAZEL (1)

Ge 30:37 poplar, and of the **h** and chesnut tree;	3869

HAZELELPONI (1)

1Ch 4: 3 and the name of their sister *was* **H**:	6753

HAZER HATTICON See HAZAR-HATTICON

HAZERIM (1)

Dt 2:23 the Avims which dwelt in **H**, *even* unto	2699

HAZEROTH (6)

Nu 11:35 journeyed from Kibroth-hattaavah *unto* **H**;	2698

Nu 11:35 *unto* Hazeroth; and abode at **H**.	2698
12:16 afterward the people removed from **H**,	2698
33:17 and encamped at **H**.	2698
33:18 they departed from **H**, and pitched in	2698
Dt 1: 1 and Laban, and **H**, and Dizahab.	2698

HAZEZON-TAMAR (1) [HAZAZON-TAMAR,
TAMAR]

Ge 14: 7 and also the Amorites, that dwelt in **H**.	2688

HAZIEL (1)

1Ch 23: 9 Shelomith, and **H**, and Haran, three.	2381

HAZO (1)

Ge 22:22 **H**, and Pildash, and Jidlaph, and Bethuel.	2375

HAZOR (18) [BAAL-HAZOR, HAZOR HADATTAH]

Jos 11: 1 when Jabin king of **H** had heard *those*	2674
11:10 took **H**, and smote the king thereof with fire.	2674
11:10 **H** beforetime *was* the head of all those	2674
11:11 left to breathe: and he burnt **H** with fire.	2674
11:13 Israel burned none of them, save **H** only;	2674
12:19 king of Madon, one; the king of **H**, one;	2674
15:23 And Kedesh, and **H**, and Ithnan,	2674
15:25 And Kerioth, *and* Hezron, which *is* **H**,	2674
19:36 And Adamah, and Ramah, and **H**,	2674
Jdg 4: 2 Jabin king of Canaan, that reigned in **H**;	2674
4:17 *was* peace between Jabin the king of **H**	2674
1Sa 12: 9 captain of the host of **H**, and into the	2674
1Ki 9:15 and **H**, and Megiddo, and Gezer.	2674
2Ki 15:29 and **H**, and Gilead, and Galilee,	2674
Ne 11:33 **H**, Ramah, Gittaim,	2674
Jer 49:28 and concerning the kingdoms of **H**,	2674
49:30 far off, dwell deep, O ye inhabitants of **H**,	2674
49:33 **H** shall be a dwelling for dragons,	2674

HAZOR HADATTAH (1) [HAZOR]

Jos 15:25 **H**, and Kerioth, *and* Hezron,	2675

HAZZELELPONI See HAZELELPONI

HAZZOBEBAH See ZOBEBAH

HE (10430) [HIM, HIMSELF, HIS] See Index of
Articles, Etc.

HEAD (364) [FOREHEAD, FOREHEADS,
GRAYHEADED, HEADBANDS, HEADLONG,
HEADS, HEADSTONE, HEADY]

Ge 3:15 it shall bruise thy **h**, and thou shalt bruise	7218
24:26 the man **bowed down** his **h**,	6915
24:48 I **bowed down** my **h**, and worshipped	6915
40:13 three days shall Pharaoh lift up thine **h**,	7218
40:16 *I had* three white baskets on my **h**:	7218
40:17 eat them out of the basket upon my **h**.	7218
40:19 shall Pharaoh lift up thy **h** from off thee,	7218
40:20 he lifted up the **h** of the chief butler and	7218
47:31 Israel bowed himself upon the bed's **h**.	7218
48:14 laid *it* upon Ephraim's **h**, who *was*	7218
48:14 and his left hand upon Manasseh's **h**,	7218
48:17 laid his right hand upon the **h** of Ephraim,	7218
48:17 to remove it from Ephraim's **h** unto	7218
48:17 from Ephraim's head unto Manasseh's **h**.	7218
48:18 firstborn; put thy right hand upon his **h**.	7218
49:26 they shall be on the **h** of Joseph, and on	7218
49:26 on the **crown of the h** of him *that was*	6936
Ex 12: 9 **h** with his legs, and with the purtenance	7218
12:27 the people **bowed the h** and worshipped.	6915
26:24 shall be coupled together above the **h**	7218
29: 6 thou shalt put the mitre upon his **h**,	7218
29: 7 and pour *it* upon his **h**, and anoint him.	7218
29:10 sons shall put their hands upon the **h** of	7218
29:15 sons shall put their hands upon the **h** of	7218
29:17 put *them* unto his pieces, and unto his **h**.	7218
29:19 sons shall put their hands upon the **h** of	7218
34: 8 **bowed** his **h** toward the earth,	6915
36:29 coupled together at the **h** thereof, to one	7218
Lev 1: 4 shall put his hand upon the **h** of	7218
1: 8 shall lay the parts, the **h**, and the fat,	7218
1:12 into his pieces, with his **h** and his fat:	7218
1:15 wring off his **h**, and burn *it* on the altar;	7218
3: 2 he shall lay his hand upon the **h** of his	7218
3: 8 he shall lay his hand upon the **h** of his	7218
3:13 he shall lay his hand upon the **h** of it,	7218
4: 4 shall lay his hand upon the bullock's **h**,	7218
4:11 with his **h**, and with his legs,	7218
4:15 the **h** of the bullock before the LORD:	7218
4:24 shall lay his hand upon the **h** of the goat,	7218
4:29 shall lay his hand upon the **h** of the sin	7218
4:33 shall lay his hand upon the **h** of the sin	7218
5: 8 wring off his **h** from his neck, but shall	7218
8: 9 he put the mitre upon his **h**; also upon	7218
8:12 of the anointing oil upon Aaron's **h**,	7218
8:14 his sons laid their hands upon the **h** of	7218
8:18 his sons laid their hands upon the **h** of	7218
8:20 Moses burnt the **h**, and the pieces,	7218
8:22 his sons laid their hands upon the **h** of	7218
9:13 with the pieces thereof, and the **h**:	7218
13:12 the plague from his **h** even to his foot,	7218
13:29 or woman hath a plague upon the **h** or	7218
13:30 *even* a leprosy upon the **h** or beard.	7218
13:40 the man whose hair is fallen off his **h**,	7218
13:41 off from the part of *his* **h** *toward* his face,	NIH
13:42 if there be in the **bald h**, or bald forehead,	7146
13:42 it *is* a leprosy sprung up in his **bald h**,	7146
13:43 of the sore *be* white reddish in the **bald h**,	7146

Lev 13:44 him utterly unclean, his plague *is* in his **h**.	7218
13:45 his **h** bare, and he shall put a covering	7218
14: 9 he shall shave all his hair off his **h** and	7218
14:18 upon the **h** of him that is to be cleansed:	7218
14:29 upon the **h** of him that is to be cleansed,	7218
16:21 Aaron shall lay both his hands upon the **h**	7218
16:21 putting them upon the **h** of the goat,	7218
19:32 Thou shalt rise up before the **hoary h**,	7872
21: 5 shall not make baldness upon their **h**,	7218
21:10 whose **h** the anointing oil was poured,	7218
21:10 shall not uncover his **h**, nor rend his	7218
24:14 heard *him* lay their hands upon his **h**,	7218
Nu 1: 4 every one **h** of the house of his fathers.	7218
5:18 uncover the woman's **h**, and put	7218
6: 5 there shall no rasor come upon his **h**:	7218
6: 5 let the locks of the hair of his **h** grow.	7218
6: 7 the consecration of his God *is* upon his **h**.	7218
6: 9 he hath defiled the **h** of his consecration;	7218
6: 9 he shall shave his **h** in the day of his	7218
6:11 and shall hallow his **h** that *same* day.	7218
6:18 the Nazarite shall shave the **h** of his	7218
6:18 take the hair of the **h** of his separation,	7218
17: 3 for one rod *shall be* for the **h** of the house	7218
22:31 he **bowed down** his **h**, and fell flat on	6915
25:15 he *was* **h** over a people, *and* of a chief	7218
Dt 19: 5 the **h** slippeth from the helve,	1270
21:12 she shall shave her **h**, and pare her nails;	7218
28:13 the LORD shall make thee the **h**,	7218
28:23 heaven that *is* over thy **h** shall be brass,	7218
28:35 the sole of thy foot unto the **top of** thy **h**.	6936
28:44 shall be the **h**, and thou shalt be the tail.	7218
33:16 *the blessing* come upon the **h** of Joseph,	7218
33:16 upon the **top of the h** of him *that was*	6936
33:20 teareth the arm with the **crown of the h**.	6936
Jos 2:19 his blood *shall be* upon his **h**, and we	7218
2:19 his blood *shall be* on our **h**, if *any* hand	7218
11:10 Hazor beforetime *was* the **h** of all those	7218
22:14 each one *was* a **h** of the house of their	7218
Jdg 5:26 smote off his **h**, when she had pierced	7218
9:53 piece of a millstone upon Abimelech's **h**,	7218
10:18 he shall be **h** over all the inhabitants of	7218
11: 8 our **h** over all the inhabitants of Gilead.	7218
11: 9 deliver them before me, shall I be your **h**?	7218
11:11 the people made him **h** and captain over	7218
13: 5 a son; and no rasor shall come on his **h**:	7218
16:13 If thou weavest the seven locks of my **h**	7218
16:17 hath not come a rasor upon mine **h**;	7218
16:19 *him* to shave off the seven locks of his **h**;	7218
16:22 Howbeit the hair of his **h** began to grow	7218
1Sa 1:11 and there shall no rasor come upon his **h**.	7218
4:12 clothes rent, and *with* earth upon his **h**.	7218
5: 4 the **h** of Dagon and both the palms of his	7218
10: 1 poured *it* upon his **h**, and kissed him,	7218
14:45 there shall not one hair of his **h** fall to	7218
15:17 wast thou not **made** the **h** of the tribes of	7218
17: 5 *he had* a helmet of brass upon his **h**,	7218
17: 7 spear's **h** *weighed* six hundred shekels	3852
17:38 and he put a helmet of brass upon his **h**;	7218
17:46 smite thee, and take thine **h** from thee;	7218
17:51 slew him, and cut off his **h** therewith.	7218
17:54 David took the **h** of the Philistine,	7218
17:57 brought him before Saul with the **h** of	7218
25:39 the wickedness of Nabal upon his own **h**.	7218
28: 2 I make thee keeper of mine **h** for ever.	7218
31: 9 they cut off his **h**, and stripped off his	7218
2Sa 1: 2 his clothes rent, and earth upon his **h**:	7218
1:10 I took the crown that *was* upon his **h**,	7218
1:16 said unto him, Thy blood *be* upon thy **h**;	7218
2:16 caught every one his fellow by the **h**,	7218
3: 8 of Ish-bosheth, and said, *Am* I a dog's **h**,	7218
3:29 Let it rest on the **h** of Joab, and on all his	7218
4: 7 took his **h**, and gat them away through	7218
4: 8 they brought the **h** of Ish-bosheth unto	7218
4: 8 the **h** of Ish-bosheth the son of Saul	7218
4:12 they took the **h** of Ish-bosheth, and buried	7218
12:30 he took their king's crown from off his **h**,	7218
12:30 it was *set* on David's **h**. And he brought	7218
13:19 Tamar put ashes on her **h**, and rent her	7218
13:19 laid her hand on her **h**, and went on	7218
14:25 **crown of** his **h** there was no blemish in	6936
14:26 when he polled his **h**, (for it was at every	7218
14:26 weighed the hair of his **h** *at* two hundred	7218
15:30 had his **h** covered, and he went barefoot:	7218
15:30 *was* with him covered every man his **h**,	7218
15:32 with his coat rent, and earth upon his **h**:	7218
16: 9 go over, I pray thee, and take off his **h**.	7218
18: 9 his **h** caught hold of the oak, and he was	7218
20:21 **h** *shall be* thrown to thee over the wall.	7218
20:22 they cut off the **h** of Sheba the son of	7218
22:44 thou hast kept me to be **h** of the heathen:	7218
1Ki 2: 6 let not his **hoar h** go down *to* the grave	7872
2: 9 his **hoar h** bring thou down *to* the grave	7872
2:32 shall return his blood upon his own **h**,	7218
2:33 therefore return upon the **h** of Joab,	7218
2:33 Joab, and upon the **h** of his seed for ever:	7218
2:37 thy blood shall be upon thine own **h**.	7218
2:44 return thy wickedness upon thine own **h**;	7218
8:32 the wicked, to bring his way upon his **h**;	7218
19: 6 the coals, and a cruse of water *at* his **h**.	4763
2Ki 2: 3 take away thy master from thy **h** to day?	7218
2: 5 take away thy master from thy **h** to day?	7218
2:23 and said unto him, Go up, thou **bald h**;	7142
2:23 thou bald head; go up, thou **bald h**.	7142
4:19 he said unto his father, My **h**, my head.	7218
4:19 he said unto his father, My head, my **h**.	7218

H

2Ki	6: 5 a beam, the **axe** h fell into the water:	1270
	6:25 until an ass's h was *sold* for fourscore	7218
	6:31 if the h of Elisha the son of Shaphat shall	7218
	6:32 murderer hath sent to take away mine h?	7218
	9: 3 pour *it* on his h, and say, Thus saith	7218
	9: 6 he poured the oil on his h, and said unto	7218
	9:30 tired her h, and looked out at a window.	7218
	19:21 of Jerusalem hath shaken her h at thee.	7218
	25:27 lift up the h of Jehoiachin king of Judah	7218
1Ch	10: 9 they took his h, and his armour,	7218
	10:10 fastened this h *in* the temple of Dagon.	1538
	20: 2 the crown of their king from off his h,	7218
	20: 2 in it; and it was *set* upon David's h:	7218
	29:11 and *thou* art exalted as h above all.	7218
2Ch	6:23 recompensing his way upon his own h:	7218
	20:18 Jehoshaphat **bowed** his h *with his* face to	6915
Ezr	9: 3 pluckt off the hair of my h and of my	7218
	9: 6 our iniquities are increased over our h,	7218
Ne	4: 4 turn their reproach upon their own h,	7218
Est	2:17 that he set the royal crown upon her h,	7218
	6: 8 the crown royal which is set upon his h:	7218
	6:12 mourning, and having his h covered.	7218
	9:25 should return upon his own h, and that	7218
Job	1:20 shaved his h, and fell down upon	7218
	10:15 I be righteous, *yet* will I not lift up my h.	7218
	16: 4 against you, and shake mine h at you.	7218
	19: 9 glory, and taken the crown *from* my h.	7218
	20: 6 and his h reach unto the clouds;	7218
	29: 3 When his candle shined upon my h,	7218
	41: 7 barbed irons? or his h with fish spears?	7218
Ps	3: 3 my glory, and the lifter up of mine h.	7218
	7:16 His mischief shall return upon his own h,	7218
	18:43 thou hast made me the h of the heathen:	7218
	21: 3 settest a crown of pure gold on his h.	7218
	22: 7 out the lip, they shake the h, *saying,*	7218
	23: 5 thou anointest my h with oil; my cup	7218
	27: 6 now shall mine h be lifted up above mine	7218
	38: 4 For mine iniquities are gone *over* mine h:	7218
	40:12 they are moe than the hairs of mine h:	7218
	44:14 a shaking of the h among the people.	7218
	60: 7 Ephraim also *is* the strength of mine h;	7218
	68:21 God shall wound the h of his enemies,	7218
	69: 4 a cause are moe than the hairs of mine h:	7218
	83: 2 and they that hate thee have lift up the h.	7218
	108: 8 Ephraim also *is* the strength of mine h;	7218
	110: 7 the way: therefore shall he lift up the h.	7218
	118:22 is become the h *stone* of the corner.	7218
	133: 2 *is* like the precious ointment upon the h,	7218
	140: 7 hast covered my h in the day of battle.	7218
	140: 9 *As for* the h of those that compass me	7218
	141: 5 oil, *which* shall not break my h:	7218
Pr	1: 9 *shall* be an ornament of grace unto thy h,	7218
	4: 9 She shall give to thine h an ornament of	7218
	10: 6 Blessings *are* upon the h of the just:	7218
	11:26 blessing *shall* be upon the h of him that	7218
	16:31 the **hoary** h *is* a crown of glory, *if* it be	7872
	20:29 and the beauty of old men *is* the **gray** h.	7872
	25:22 thou shalt heap coals of fire upon his h,	7218
Ecc	2:14 The wise *man's* eyes *are* in his h;	7218
	9: 8 and let thy h lack no ointment.	7218
SS	2: 6 His left hand *is* under my h, and his right	7218
	5: 2 for my h is filled with dew, *and* my locks	7218
	5:11 His h *is as* the most fine gold, his locks	7218
	7: 5 Thine h upon thee *is* like Carmel,	7218
	7: 5 and the hair of thine h like purple;	7218
	8: 3 His left hand *should* be under my h,	7218
Isa	1: 5 the whole h is sick, and the whole heart	7218
	1: 6 From the sole of the foot even unto the h	7218
	3:17 **crown of the** h of the daughters of Zion,	6936
	7: 8 For the h of Syria *is* Damascus,	7218
	7: 8 and the h of Damascus *is* Rezin;	7218
	7: 9 the h of Ephraim *is* Samaria, and the head	7218
	7: 9 the h of Samaria *is* Remaliah's son.	7218
	7:20 of Assyria, the h, and the hair of the feet:	7218
	9:14 the LORD will cut off from Israel h	7218
	9:15 The ancient and honourable, he *is* the h;	7218
	19:15 the h or tail, branch or rush, may do.	7218
	28: 1 which *are* on the h of the fat valleys of	7218
	28: 4 which *is* on the h of the fat valley, shall	7218
	37:22 of Jerusalem hath shaken her h at thee.	7218
	51:11 and everlasting joy *shall* be upon their h:	7218
	51:20 they lie at the h of all the streets, as a	7218
	58: 5 *is it* to bow down his h as a bulrush,	7218
	59:17 and a helmet of salvation upon his h;	7218
Jer	2:16 have broken the **crown** of thy h.	6936
	2:37 from him, and thine hands upon thine h:	7218
	9: 1 that my h were waters, and mine eyes a	7218
	18:16 shall be astonished, and wag his h.	7218
	22: 6 Gilead unto me, *and* the h of Lebanon:	7218
	23:19 it shall fall grievously upon the h of	7218
	30:23 it shall fall with pain upon the h of	7218
	48:37 For every h *shall* be bald, and every beard	7218
	48:45 the **crown of the** h of the tumultuous	6936
	52:31 lifted up the h of Jehoiachin king of Judah,	7218
La	2:15 wag their h at the daughter of Jerusalem;	7218
	3:54 Waters flowed over mine h; *then* I said,	7218
	5:16 The crown is fallen *from* our h: woe unto	7218
Eze	1:22 *cause it* to pass upon thine h and upon	7218
	8: 3 a hand, and took me by a lock of mine h;	7218
	9:10 I will recompense their way upon their h.	7218
	10: 1 in the firmament that *was* above the h of	7218
	10:11 *to* the place whither the h looked they	7218
	13:18 kerchiefs upon the h of every stature	7218
	16:12 and a beautiful crown upon thine h.	7218
	16:25 Thou hast built thy high place at every h	7218

Eze	16:31 thine eminent place in the h of every way,	7218
	16:43 will recompense thy way upon *thine* h,	7218
	17:19 even it will I recompense upon his own h.	7218
	21:19 choose *it, at* the h of the way to the city.	7218
	21:21 the h of the two ways, to use divination:	7218
	24:17 bind the **tire** of thine h upon thee,	6287
	29:18 every h *was* made bald, and every	7218
	33: 4 his blood shall be upon his own h.	7218
	42:12 the south *was* a door in the h of the way,	7218
Da	1:10 shall ye make *me* endanger my h to	7218
	2:28 visions of thy h upon thy bed, *are* these;	7217
	2:32 This image's h *was* of fine gold, his breast	7217
	2:38 over them all. Thou *art* this h of gold.	7217
	3:27 nor was a hair of their h singed,	7217
	4: 5 and the visions of my h troubled me.	7217
	4:10 *were* the visions of mine h in my bed;	7217
	4:13 saw in the visions of my h upon my bed,	7217
	7: 1 dream and visions of his h upon his bed:	7217
	7: 9 and the hair of his h like the pure wool:	7217
	7:15 and the visions of my h troubled me.	7217
	7:20 of the ten horns that *were* in his h,	7217
Hos	1:11 appoint themselves one h, and they shall	7218
Joel	3: 4 your recompence upon your own h;	7218
	3: 7 your recompence upon your own h:	7218
Am	2: 7 the dust of the earth on the h of the poor,	7218
	8:10 all loins, and baldness upon every h;	7218
	9: 1 cut them in the h, all of them; and I will	7218
Ob	1:15 reward shall return upon thine own h.	7218
Jnh	2: 5 the weeds *were* wrapt about my h.	7218
	4: 6 that *it* might be a shadow over his h,	7218
	4: 8 the sun beat upon the h of Jonah, that he	7218
Mic	2:13 and the LORD on the h of them.	7218
Hab	3:13 thou woundedst the h out of the house of	7218
	3:14 with his staves the h of his villages:	7218
Zec	1:21 so that no man did lift up his h:	7218
	3: 5 said, Let them set a fair mitre upon his h.	7218
	3: 5 So they set a fair mitre upon his h,	7218
	6:11 set *them* upon the h of Joshua the son of	7218
Mt	5:36 Neither shalt thou swear by thy h,	2776
	6:17 anoint thine h, and wash thy face;	2776
	8:20 Son of man hath not where to lay *his* h.	2776
	10:30 But the very hairs of your h are all	2776
	14: 8 me here John Baptist's h in a charger.	2776
	14:11 h was brought in a charger,	2776
	21:42 the same is become the h of the corner:	2776
	26: 7 and poured *it* on his h, as he sat at meat.	2776
	27:29 they put *it* upon his h, and a reed in his	2776
	27:30 took the reed, and smote him on the h.	2776
	27:37 and set up over his h his accusation	2776
Mk	6:24 And she said, The h of John the Baptist.	2776
	6:25 by in a charger the h of John the Baptist.	2776
	6:27 and commanded his h to be brought:	2776
	6:28 brought his h in a charger, and gave it	2776
	12: 4 wounded *him* in the h, and sent *him*	2775
	12:10 rejected is become the h of the corner:	2776
	14: 3 she brake the box, and poured *it* on his h.	2776
	15:17 a crown of thorns, and put *it* about his h,	NIG
	15:19 And they smote him on the h with a reed,	2776
Lk	7:38 did wipe *them* with the hairs of her h,	2776
	7:44 and wiped *them* with the hairs of her h.	2776
	7:46 Mine h with oil thou didst not anoint:	2776
	9:58 Son of man hath not where to lay *his* h.	2776
	12: 7 But even the *very* hairs of your h are all	2776
	20:17 the same is become the h of the corner?	2776
	21:18 But there shall not a hair of your h perish.	2776
Jn	13: 9 feet only, but also *my* hands and *my* h.	2776
	19: 2 put *it* on his h, and they put on him a	2776
	19:30 he bowed *his* h, and gave up the ghost.	2776
	20: 7 And the napkin, that was about his h,	2776
	20:12 the one at the h, and the other at the feet,	2776
Ac	4:11 which is become the h of the corner.	2776
	18:18 having shorn *his* h in Cenchrea: for he	2776
	27:34 for there shall not a hair fall from the h of	2776
Ro	12:20 thou shalt heap coals of fire on his h.	2776
1Co	11: 3 that the h of every man is Christ;	2776
	11: 3 and the h of the woman *is* the man;	2776
	11: 3 *is* the man; and the h of Christ *is* God.	2776
	11: 4 or prophesying, having *his* h covered,	2776
	11: 4 *his* head covered, dishonoureth his h.	2776
	11: 5 prophesieth with *her* h uncovered	2776
	11: 5 *her* head uncovered dishonoureth her h:	2776
	11: 7 a man indeed ought not to cover *his* h,	2776
	11:10 the woman to have power on her h	2776
	12:21 again the h to the feet, I have no need	2776
Eph	1:22 gave him *to be* the h over all *things* to	2776
	4:15 *up* into him in all *things,* which is the h,	2776
	5:23 For the husband is the h of the wife,	2776
	5:23 even as Christ *is* the h of the church:	2776
Col	1:18 And he is the h of the body, the church:	2776
	2:10 is the h of all principality and power:	2776
	2:19 And not holding the h, from which all	2776
1Pe	2: 7 the same is made the h of the corner,	2776
Rev	1:14 His h and *his* hairs *were* white like wool,	2776
	10: 1 a rainbow *was* upon his h, and his face	2776
	12: 1 and upon her h a crown of twelve stars:	2776
	14:14 having on his h a golden crown, and in	2776
	19:12 of fire, and on his h *were* many crowns;	2776

HEADBANDS (1) [BAND, HEAD]

Isa	3:20 the h, and the tablets, and the earrings,	7196

HEADDRESSES See BONNETS

HEADLONG (3) [HEAD]

Job	5:13 the counsel of the froward is **carried** h.	4116

Lk	4:29 built, that *they* might **cast** him **down** h.	2630
Ac	1:18 and **falling** h, he burst asunder in	1096+4248

HEADS (110) [HEAD]

Ge	2:10 it was parted, and became into four h.	7218
	43:28 they **bowed down** their h,	6915
Ex	4:31 they **bowed** their h and worshipped.	6915
	6:14 These *are* the h of their fathers' houses:	7218
	6:25 *are* the h of the fathers of the Levites	7218
	18:25 made them h over the people, rulers of	7218
Lev	10: 6 Ithamar his sons, Uncover not your h,	7218
	19:27 Ye shall not round the corners of your h,	7218
Nu	1:16 of their fathers, h of thousands in Israel.	7218
	7: 2 of Israel, h of the house of their fathers,	7218
	8:12 Levites shall lay their hands upon the h	7218
	10: 4 *which are* h of the thousands of Israel,	7218
	13: 3 all those men *which are* h of the children of	7218
	25: 4 Take all the h of the people, and hang	7218
	30: 1 Moses spake unto the h of the tribes	7218
Dt	1:15 and known, and made them h over you,	7218
	5:23 *even* all the h of your tribes,	7218
	33: 5 when the h of the people *and* the tribes	7218
	33:21 he came *with* the h of the people,	7218
Jos	7: 6 of Israel, and put dust upon their h.	7218
	14: 1 the h of the fathers of the tribes of	7218
	19:51 the h of the fathers of the tribes of	7218
	21: 1 came near the h of the fathers of	7218
	21: 1 unto the h of the fathers of the tribes of	7218
	22:21 said unto the h of the thousands of Israel,	7218
	22:30 h of the thousands of Israel which *were*	7218
	23: 2 for their h, and for their judges,	7218
	24: 1 for their h, and for their judges,	7218
Jdg	7:25 brought the h of Oreb and Zeeb to Gideon	7218
	8:28 so that they lifted up their h no more.	7218
	9:57 of Shechem did God render upon their h:	7218
1Sa	29: 4 should it not be with the h of these men?	7218
1Ki	8: 1 elders of Israel, and all the h of the tribes,	7218
	20:31 ropes upon our h, and go out to the king	7218
	20:32 ropes on their h, and came to the king	7218
2Ki	10: 6 take ye the h of the men your master's	7218
	10: 7 put their h in baskets, and sent him *them*	7218
	10: 8 have brought the h of the king's sons.	7218
1Ch	5:24 these *were* the h of the house of their	7218
	5:24 *and* h of the house of their fathers.	7218
	7: 2 and Shemuel, h of their fathers' house,	7218
	7: 7 h of the house of *their* fathers, mighty	7218
	7: 9 h of the house of their fathers, mighty	7218
	7:11 by the h of *their* fathers, mighty *men* of	7218
	7:40 h of *their* fathers' house, choice and	7218
	8: 6 these *are* the h of the fathers of	7218
	8:10 These *were* his sons, h of the fathers.	7218
	8:13 *were* h of the fathers of the inhabitants	7218
	8:28 These *were* h of the fathers, by their	7218
	9:13 h of the house of their fathers, a thousand	7218
	12:19 his master Saul on the jeopardy of our h.	7218
	12:32 the h of them *were* two hundred;	7218
	29:20 **bowed down** their h, and worshipped	6915
2Ch	3:16 and put *them* on the h of the pillars;	7218
	5: 2 elders of Israel, and all the h of the tribes,	7218
	28:12 of the h of the children of Ephraim,	7218
	29:30 and they **bowed** their h, and worshipped.	6915
Ne	8: 6 they **bowed** their h, and worshipped	6915
Job	2:12 dust upon their h toward heaven.	7218
Ps	24: 7 Lift up your h, O ye gates; and be ye lift	7218
	24: 9 Lift up your h, O ye gates; even lift *them*	7218
	66:12 Thou hast caused men to ride over our h;	7218
	74:13 thou brakest the h of the dragons in	7218
	74:14 Thou brakest the h of leviathan in pieces,	7218
	109:25 they looked upon me they shaked their h.	7218
	110: 6 shall wound the h over many countries.	7218
Isa	15: 2 on all their h *shall be* baldness,	7218
	35:10 songs and everlasting joy upon their h:	7218
Jer	14: 3 and confounded, and covered their h.	7218
	14: 4 were ashamed, they covered their h.	7218
La	2:10 they have cast up dust upon their h;	7218
	2:10 virgins of Jerusalem hang down their h	7218
Eze	1:22 the likeness of the firmament upon the h	7218
	1:22 stretched forth over their h above.	7218
	1:25 from the firmament that *was* over their h,	7218
	1:26 the firmament that *was* over their h	7218
	7:18 all faces, and baldness upon all their h.	7218
	11:21 recompense their way upon their own h,	7218
	22:31 way have I recompensed upon their h,	7218
	23:15 exceeding in dyed attire upon their h,	7218
	23:42 and beautiful crowns upon their h.	7218
	24:23 your tires *shall* be upon your h,	7218
	27:30 and shall cast up dust upon their h,	7218
	32:27 they have laid their swords under their h,	7218
	44:18 shall have linen bonnets upon their h,	7218
	44:20 Neither shall they shave their h, nor	7218
	44:20 to grow long; they shall only poll their h.	7218
Da	7: 6 the beast had also four h;	7217
Mic	3: 1 O h of Jacob, and ye princes of the house	7218
	3: 9 ye h of the house of Jacob, and princes of	7218
	3:11 The h thereof judge for reward,	7218
Mt	27:39 passed by, reviled him, wagging their h,	2776
Mk	15:29 wagging their h, and saying, Ah, *thou* that	2776
Lk	21:28 to pass, *then* look up, and lift up your h;	2776
Ac	18: 6 Your blood *be* upon your own h;	2776
	21:24 with them, that they may shave *their* h:	2776
Rev	4: 4 and they had on their h crowns of gold.	2776
	9: 7 their h *were as it were* crowns like gold,	2776
	9:17 the h of the horses *were* as the heads of	2776
	9:17 the heads of the horses *were* as the h of	2776
	9:19 and had h, and with them they do hurt.	2776

Rev 12: 3 having seven **h** and ten horns, *2776*
 12: 3 ten horns, and seven crowns upon his **h**. *2776*
 13: 1 having seven **h** and ten horns, and upon *2776*
 13: 1 upon his **h** the name of blasphemy. *2776*
 13: 3 I saw one of his **h** as *it were* wounded *2776*
 17: 3 having seven **h** and ten horns. *2776*
 17: 7 which hath the seven **h** and ten horns. *2776*
 17: 9 The seven **h** are seven mountains, on *2776*
 18:19 And they cast dust on their **h**, and cried, *2776*

HEADSTONE (1) [HEAD, STONE]
Zec 4: 7 he shall bring forth the **h** *thereof with* *68+7222*

HEADY (1) [HEAD]
2Ti 3: 4 **h**, highminded, lovers of pleasures *4312*

HEAL (40) [HEALED, HEALER, HEALETH, HEALING, HEALINGS, HEALTH]
Nu 12:13 **H** her now, O God, I beseech thee. *7495*
Dt 32:39 I kill, and I make alive; I wound, and I **h**: *7495*
2Ki 20: 5 I will **h** thee: on the third day thou *7495*
 20: 8 *shall be* the sign that the Lord will **h** me, *7495*
2Ch 7:14 forgive their sin, and will **h** their land. *7495*
Ps 6: 2 O Lord, **h** me; for my bones are vexed. *7495*
 41: 4 **h** my soul; for I have sinned against thee. *7495*
 60: 2 **h** the breaches thereof; for it shaketh. *7495*
Ecc 3: 3 A time to kill, and a time to **h**; a time to *7495*
Isa 19:22 shall smite and **h** *it*: and they shall return *7495*
 19:22 be intreated of them, and shall **h** them. *7495*
 57:18 I have seen his ways, and will **h** him: *7495*
 57:19 *is* near, saith the Lord; and I will **h** him. *7495*
Jer 3:22 *and* I will **h** your backslidings. *7495*
 17:14 **H** me, O Lord, and I shall be healed; *7495*
 30:17 I will **h** thee of thy wounds, saith *7495*
La 2:13 *is* great like the sea: who can **h** thee? *7495*
Hos 5:13 yet could he not **h** you nor cure you of *7495*
 6: 1 for he hath torn, and he will **h** us; he hath *7495*
 14: 4 I will **h** their backsliding, I will love them *7495*
Zec 11:16 nor **h** that that is broken, nor feed that *7495*
Mt 8: 7 saith unto him, I will come and **h** him. *2323*
 10: 1 and to **h** all *manner of* sickness and *2323*
 10: 8 **H** the sick, cleanse the lepers, raise *2323*
 12:10 Is it lawful to **h** on the sabbath days? *2323*
 13:15 be converted, and I should **h** them. *2390*
Mk 3: 2 whether he would **h** him on the sabbath *2323*
 3:15 And to have power to **h** sicknesses, and to *2323*
Lk 4:18 he hath sent me to **h** the broken-hearted, *2390*
 4:23 me this proverb, Physician, **h** thyself: *2323*
 5:17 the power of the Lord was *present* to **h** *2390*
 6: 7 whether he would **h** on the sabbath day; *2323*
 7: 3 that he would come and **h** his servant. *1295*
 9: 2 the kingdom of God, and to **h** the sick. *2390*
 10: 9 And **h** the sick that are therein, *2323*
 14: 3 Is it lawful to **h** on the sabbath day? *2323*
Jn 4:47 that he would come down, and **h** his son: *2390*
 12:40 and be converted, and I should **h** them. *2390*
Ac 4:30 By stretching forth thine hand to **h**; *2392*
 28:27 be converted, and I should **h** them. *2390*

HEALED (79) [HEAL]
Ge 20:17 God **h** Abimelech, and his wife, *7495*
Ex 21:19 cause *him* to be thoroughly **h**. *7495+7495*
Lev 13:18 in the skin thereof, was a boil, and is **h**, *7495*
 13:37 the itch; the scall is **h**, he *is* clean: *7495*
 14: 3 *if* the plague of leprosy be **h** in the leper; *7495*
 14:48 the house clean, because the plague is **h**, *7495*
Dt 28:27 the itch, whereof thou canst not be **h**. *7495*
 28:35 legs, with a sore botch that cannot be **h**, *7495*
1Sa 6: 3 ye shall be **h**, and it shall be known to you *7495*
2Ki 2:21 saith the Lord, I have **h** these waters; *7495*
 2:22 So the waters were **h** unto this day, *7495*
 8:29 king Joram went back to be **h** in Jezreel *7495*
 9:15 Joram was returned to be **h** in Jezreel *7495*
2Ch 22: 6 he returned to be **h** in Jezreel because of *7495*
 30:20 hearkened to Hezekiah, and **h** the people. *7495*
Ps 30: 2 I cried unto thee, and thou hast **h** me. *7495*
 107:20 **h** them, and delivered *them* from their *7495*
Isa 6:10 *with* their heart, and convert, and be **h**. *7495*
 53: 5 upon him; and with his stripes we are **h**. *7495*
Jer 6:14 have **h** also the hurt of *the daughter of* *7495*
 8:11 they have **h** the hurt of the daughter of *7495*
 15:18 wound incurable, *which* refuseth to be **h**? *7495*
 17:14 Heal me, O Lord, and I shall be **h**; *7495*
 51: 8 balm for her pain, if so be she may be **h**. *7495*
 51: 9 We would have **h** Babylon, but she is not *7495*
 51: 9 have healed Babylon, but she is not **h**: *7495*
Eze 30:21 it shall not be bound up to be **h**, to put a *7499*
 34: 4 neither have ye **h** that which was sick, *7495*
 47: 8 forth into the sea, the waters shall be **h**. *7495*
 47: 9 for they shall be **h**; and every *thing* shall *7495*
 47:11 the marishes thereof shall not be **h**; *7495*
Hos 7: 1 When I *would have* **h** Israel, then *7495*
 11: 3 arms; but they knew not that I **h** them. *7495*
Mt 4:24 those that had the palsy; and he **h** them. *2323*
 8: 8 the word only, and my servant shall be **h**. *2390*
 8:13 his servant was **h** in the selfsame hour. *2390*
 8:16 with *his* word, and **h** all that were sick: *2323*
 12:15 followed him, and he **h** them all, *2323*
 12:22 he **h** him, insomuch that the blind and *2323*
 14:14 toward them, and he **h** their sick. *2323*
 15:30 them *down* at Jesus' feet; and he **h** them: *2323*
 19: 2 followed him; and he **h** them there. *2323*
 21:14 to him in the temple; and he **h** them. *2323*
Mk 1:34 And he **h** many *that were* sick of divers *2323*
 3:10 For he had **h** many; insomuch that *they* *2323*

Mk 5:23 lay *thy* hands on her, that she may be **h**; *4982*
 5:29 she felt in *her* body that she was **h** of *that* *2390*
 6: 5 hands upon a few sick *folk*, and **h** *them*. *2323*
 6:13 with oil many *that were* sick, and **h** *them*. *2323*
Lk 4:40 hands on every one of them, and **h** them. *2323*
 5:15 and to be **h** by him of their infirmities. *2323*
 6:17 to hear him, and to be **h** of their diseases; *2390*
 6:18 with unclean spirits: and they were **h**. *2323*
 6:19 went virtue out of him, and **h** them all. *2390*
 7: 7 say in a word, and my servant shall be **h**. *2390*
 8: 2 which had been **h** of evil spirits and *2323*
 8:36 he that was possessed of the devils was **h**. *4982*
 8:43 physicians, neither could be **h** of any, *2323*
 8:47 and how she was **h** immediately. *2390*
 9:11 and **h** them that had need of healing. *2390*
 9:42 and he **h** the child, and delivered him again *2390*
 13:14 that Jesus had **h** on the sabbath day, *2323*
 13:14 in them therefore came and be **h**, *2323*
 14: 4 And he took *him*, and **h** him, and let *him* *2390*
 17:15 when he saw that he was **h**, turned back, *2390*
 22:51 And he touched his ear, and **h** him. *2390*
Jn 5:13 And he that was **h** wist not who it was: *2390*
Ac 3:11 As the lame *man* which was **h** held *2390*
 4:14 And beholding the man which was **h** *2323*
 5:16 spirits: and they were **h** every one. *2323*
 8: 7 with palsies, and *that were* lame, were **h**. *2323*
 14: 9 of perceiving that he had faith to be **h**, *4982*
 28: 8 and laid *his* hands on him, and **h** him. *2390*
 28: 9 diseases in the island, came, and were **h**: *2323*
Heb 12:13 out of the way; but let it rather be **h**. *2390*
Jas 5:16 pray one for another, that ye may be **h**. *2390*
1Pe 2:24 by whose stripes ye were **h**. *2390*
Rev 13: 3 to death; and his deadly wound was **h**: *2323*
 13:12 first beast, whose deadly wound was **h**. *2323*

HEALER (1) [HEAL]
Isa 3: 7 shall he swear, saying, I will not be a **h**; *2280*

HEALETH (4) [HEAL]
Ex 15:26 for I *am* the Lord that **h** thee. *7495*
Ps 103: 3 all thine iniquities; who **h** all thy diseases; *7495*
 147: 3 He **h** the broken in heart, and bindeth up *7495*
Isa 30:26 people, and **h** the stroke of their wound. *7495*

HEALING (14) [HEAL]
Jer 14:19 thou smitten us, and *there is* no **h** for us? *4832*
 14:19 for the time of **h**, and behold trouble. *4832*
 30:13 be bound up: thou hast no **h** medicines. *8585*
Na 3:19 *There is* no **h** of thy bruise; thy wound *is* *3545*
Mal 4: 2 of righteousness arise with **h** in his wings; *4832*
Mt 4:23 and **h** all *manner of* sickness and every disease *2323*
 9:35 and **h** every sickness and every disease *2323*
Lk 9: 6 preaching the gospel, and **h** every where. *2323*
 9:11 God, and healed them that had need of **h**. *2322*
Ac 4:22 on whom this miracle of **h** was shewed. *2392*
 10:38 and **h** all that were oppressed of the devil; *2390*
1Co 12: 9 another the gifts of **h** by the same Spirit; *2386*
 12:30 Have all the gifts of **h**? do all speak with *2386*
Rev 22: 2 the leaves of the tree *were* for the **h** of *2322*

HEALINGS (1) [HEAL]
1Co 12:28 then gifts of **h**, helps, governments, *2386*

HEALTH (17) [HEAL]
Ge 43:28 Thy servant our father *is* **in good h**, he *is* *7965*
2Sa 20: 9 said to Amasa, *Art* thou in **h**, my brother? *7965*
Ps 42:11 *who is* the **h** of my countenance, *3444*
 43: 5 *who is* the **h** of my countenance, *3444*
 67: 2 earth, thy **saving h** among all nations. *3444*
Pr 3: 8 It shall be **h** to thy navel, and marrow to *7500*
 4:22 that find them, and **h** to all their flesh. *4832*
 12:18 a sword: but the tongue of the wise *is* **h**. *4832*
 13:17 but a faithful ambassador *is* **h**. *4832*
 16:24 sweet to the soul, and **h** to the bones. *4832*
Isa 58: 8 and thine **h** shall spring forth speedily: *724*
Jer 8:15 no good came; *and* for a time of **h**, *4832*
 8:22 is not the **h** of the daughter of my people *724*
 30:17 I will restore **h** unto thee, and I will heal *724*
 33: 6 I *will* bring it **h** and cure, and I will cure *724*
Ac 27:34 for this is for your **h**: for there shall not a *4991*
3Jn 1: 2 that thou mayest prosper and be in **h**, *5198*

HEAP (38) [HEAPED, HEAPETH, HEAPS]
Ge 31:46 and they took stones, and made a **h**: *1530*
 31:46 heap: and they did eat there upon the **h**. *1530*
 31:48 This **h** *is* a witness between me and thee *1530*
 31:51 Behold this **h**, and behold *this* pillar, *1530*
 31:52 This **h** *be* witness, and *this* pillar *be* *1530*
 31:52 that I will not pass over this **h** to thee, *1530*
 31:52 that thou shalt not pass over this **h** and *1530*
Ex 15: 8 the floods stood upright as a **h**, *5067*
Dt 13:16 shall be a **h** for ever; it shall not be built *8510*
 32:23 I will **h** mischiefs upon them; I will spend *5595*
Jos 3:13 above; and they shall stand upon a **h**. *5067*
 3:16 stood *and* rose up upon a **h** very far, *5067*
 7:26 they raised over him a great **h** of stones *1530*
 8:28 Joshua burnt Ai, and made it a **h** for ever, *8510*
 8:29 raise thereon a great **h** of stones, *1530*
Ru 3: 7 went to lie down at the end of the **h** *of* *6194*
2Sa 18:17 laid a very great **h** of stones upon him: *1530*
Job 8:17 His roots are wrapped about the **h**, *1530*
 16: 4 I could **h** up words against you, *2266*
 27:16 Though he **h** up silver as the dust, *6651*
 36:13 the hypocrites in heart **h** up wrath: *7760*
Ps 33: 7 the waters of the sea together as a **h**: *5067*

Ps 78:13 and he made the waters to stand as a **h**. *5067*
Pr 25:22 thou shalt **h** coals of fire upon his head, *2846*
Ecc 2:26 he giveth travail, to gather and to **h up**, *3664*
SS 7: 2 like a **h** of wheat set about with *6194*
Isa 17: 1 *being* a city, and it shall be a ruinous **h**. *4596*
 17:11 the harvest *shall be* a **h** in the day of grief *5067*
 25: 2 For thou hast made of a city a **h**; *of* a *1530*
Jer 30:18 the city shall be builded upon her own **h**, *8510*
 49: 2 it shall be a desolate **h**, and her daughters *8510*
Eze 24:10 **H** on wood, kindle the fire, consume *7235*
Mic 1: 6 Therefore I will make Samaria as a **h** of *5856*
Hab 1:10 for they shall **h** dust, and take it. *6651*
 3:15 horses, *through* the **h** of great waters. *2563*
Hag 2:16 *one* came to a **h** of twenty *measures*, *6194*
Ro 12:20 thou shalt **h** coals of fire on his head. *4987*
2Ti 4: 3 after their own lusts shall they **h** to *2002*

HEAPED (2) [HEAP]
Zec 9: 3 **h up** silver as the dust, and fine gold as *6651*
Jas 5: 3 ye have **h treasure together** for the last *2343*

HEAPETH (2) [HEAP]
Ps 39: 6 he **h up** *riches*, and knoweth not who *6651*
Hab 2: 5 all nations, and **h** unto him all people: *6908*

HEAPS (20) [HEAP]
Ex 8:14 gathered them together **upon h**: *2563+2563*
Jdg 15:16 With the jawbone of an ass, **h** upon heaps, *2565*
 15:16 With the jawbone of an ass, heaps upon **h**, *2565*
2Ki 10: 8 Lay ye them in two **h** at the entering in *6652*
 19:25 to lay waste fenced cities *into* ruinous **h**. *1530*
2Ch 31: 6 their God, and laid *them* **by h**. *6194+6194*
 31: 7 they began to lay the foundation of the **h**, *6194*
 31: 8 and the princes came and saw the **h**, *6194*
 31: 9 and the Levites concerning the **h**. *6194*
Ne 4: 2 will they revive the stones out of the **h** of *6194*
Job 15:28 which are ready to become **h**. *1530*
Ps 79: 1 defiled; they have laid Jerusalem on **h**. *5856*
Isa 37:26 lay waste defenced cities *into* ruinous **h**. *1530*
Jer 9:11 I will make Jerusalem, *and* a den of *1530*
 26:18 Jerusalem shall become **h**, *5856*
 31:21 Set thee up waymarks, make thee **high h**: *8564*
 50:26 cast her up as **h**, and destroy her utterly: *6194*
 51:37 Babylon shall become **h**, a dwelling place *1530*
Hos 12:11 their altars *are* as **h** in the furrows of *1530*
Mic 3:12 Jerusalem shall become **h**, *5856*

HEAR (550) [HEARD, HEARDEST, HEARER, HEARERS, HEAREST, HEARETH, HEARING]
Ge 4:23 his wives, Adah and Zillah, **H** my voice; *8085*
 21: 6 *so that* all that **h** will laugh with me. *8085*
 23: 6 **H** us, my lord: thou *art* a mighty prince *8085*
 23: 8 **h** me, and intreat for me to Ephron the *8085*
 23:11 Nay, my lord, **h** me: the field give I thee, *8085*
 23:13 But if thou *wilt give it*, I pray thee, **h** me: *8085*
 37: 6 he said unto them, **H**, I pray you, this *8085*
 42:11 he besought us, and we would not **h**; *8085*
 42:22 against the child; and ye would not **h**? *8085*
 49: 2 and **h**, ye sons of Jacob; *8085*
Ex 6:12 then shall Pharaoh **h** me, who *am* of *8085*
 7:16 and behold, hitherto thou wouldest not **h**. *8085*
 15:14 The people shall **h**, *and* be afraid: *8085*
 19: 9 that the people may **h** when I speak with *8085*
 20:19 Speak thou with us, and we will **h**: *8085*
 22:23 unto me, I will **surely h** their cry; *8085+8085*
 22:27 when he crieth unto me, that I will **h**; *8085*
 32:18 *but* the noise of *them that* sing do I **h**. *8085*
Lev 5: 1 **h** the voice of swearing, and *is* a witness, *8085*
Nu 9: 8 I will **h** what the Lord will command *8085*
 12: 6 he said, **H** now my words: If there be a *8085*
 14:13 the Egyptians shall **h** *it*, (for thou *8085*
 16: 8 Korah, **H**, I pray you, ye sons of Levi: *8085*
 20:10 and he said unto them, **H** now, ye rebels; *8085*
 23:18 parable, and said, Rise up, Balak, and **h**; *8085*
 30: 4 her father **h** her vow, and her bond *8085*
Dt 1:16 **H** *the causes* between your brethren, *8085*
 1:17 you shall **h** the small as well as the great; *8085*
 1:17 for you, bring *it* unto me, and I will **h** it. *8085*
 1:43 you would not **h**, but rebelled against *8085*
 2:25 who shall **h** report of thee, *8085*
 3:26 me for your sakes, and would not **h** me: *8085*
 4: 6 which shall **h** all these statutes, and say, *8085*
 4:10 and I will **make** them **h** my words, *8085*
 4:28 neither see, nor **h**, nor eat, nor smell. *8085*
 4:33 Did *ever* people **h** the voice of God *8085*
 4:36 of heaven he **made** thee to **h** his voice, *8085*
 5: 1 **H**, O Israel, the statutes and judgments *8085*
 5:25 if we **h** the voice of the Lord our God *8085*
 5:27 **h** all that the Lord our God shall say: *8085*
 5:27 unto thee; and we will **h** *it*, and do *it*. *8085*
 6: 3 **H** therefore, O Israel, and observe to do *8085*
 6: 4 **H**, O Israel: The Lord our God *is* one *8085*
 9: 1 **H**, O Israel: Thou art to pass over Jordan *8085*
 12:28 **h** all these words which I command thee, *8085*
 13:11 all Israel shall **h**, and fear, and shall do no *8085*
 13:12 If thou shalt **h** *say* in one of thy cities, *8085*
 17:13 all the people shall **h**, and fear, and do no *8085*
 18:16 Let me not **h** again the voice of the Lord *8085*
 19:20 those which remain shall **h**, and fear, *8085*
 20: 3 shall say unto them, **H**, O Israel, *8085*
 21:21 you; and all Israel shall **h**, and fear. *8085*
 29: 4 eyes to see, and ears to **h**, unto this day. *8085*
 30:12 it unto us, that we may **h** it, and do it? *8085*
 30:13 it unto us, that we may **h** it, and do it? *8085*
 30:17 that thou wilt not **h**, but shalt be drawn *8085*

Dt 31:12 that they may **h**, and that they may learn,	8085
31:13 which have not known *any thing*, may **h**,	8085
32: 1 and **h**, O earth, the words of my mouth.	8085
33: 7 and he said, **H**, Lord, the voice of Judah,	8085
Jos 3: 9 and **h** the words of the Lord your God.	8085
6: 5 *and* when ye **h** the sound of the trumpet,	8085
7: 9 all the inhabitants of the land shall **h** *of it,*	8085
Jdg 5: 3 **H**, O ye kings; give ear, O ye princes;	8085
5:16 to **h** the bleatings of the flocks?	8085
7:11 thou shalt **h** what they say;	8085
14:13 Put forth thy riddle, that we may **h** it.	8085
1Sa 2:23 for I **h** of your evil dealings by all this	8085
2:24 my sons; for *it is* no good report that I **h**:	8085
8:18 and the Lord will not **h** you in that day.	6030
13: 3 all the land, saying, Let the Hebrews **h**.	8085
15:14 and the lowing of the oxen which I **h**?	8085
16: 2 if Saul **h** *it,* he will kill me.	8085
22: 7 stood about him, **H** now, ye Benjamites;	8085
22:12 Saul said, **H** now, thou son of Ahitub.	8085
25:24 and **h** the words of thine handmaid.	8085
26:19 let my lord the king **h** the words of his	8085
2Sa 14:16 the king will **h**, to deliver his handmaid	8085
15: 3 *there is* no man *deputed* of the king to **h**	8085
15:10 soon as ye **h** the sound of the trumpet,	8085
15:35 what thing soever thou shalt **h** out of	8085
15:36 send unto me every thing that ye can **h**.	8085
16:21 all Israel shall **h** that thou art abhorred of	8085
17: 5 and let us **h** likewise what he saith.	8085
19:35 can I **h** any more the voice of singing	8085
20:16 a wise woman out of the city, **H**, hear;	8085
20:16 a wise woman out of the city, Hear, **h**;	8085
20:17 him, The words of thine handmaid.	8085
20:17 handmaid. And he answered, I do **h**.	8085
22: 7 he did **h** my voice out of his temple,	8085
22:45 as soon as they **h**, they shall be	241+8085
1Ki 4:34 came of all people to **h** the wisdom of	8085
8:30 thou in heaven thy dwelling place;	8085
8:32 **h** thou *in* heaven, and do, and judge thy	8085
8:34 **h** thou *in* heaven, and forgive the sin of	8085
8:36 **h** thou *in* heaven, and forgive the sin of	8085
8:39 **h** thou *in* heaven thy dwelling place,	8085
8:42 (For they shall **h** of thy great name, and of	8085
8:43 **H** thou *in* heaven thy dwelling place,	8085
8:45 **h** thou *in* heaven their prayer and their	8085
8:49 **h** thou their prayer and their supplication	8085
10: 8 before thee, *and* that **h** thy wisdom.	8085
10:24 to **h** his wisdom, which God had put in	8085
18:26 even until noon, saying, O Baal, **h** us.	6030
18:37 **H** me, O Lord, hear me, that this people	6030
18:37 Hear me, O Lord, **h** me, that this people	6030
22:19 **H** thou therefore the word of the Lord:	8085
2Ki 7: 1 Elisha said, **H** ye the word of the Lord.	8085
7: 6 **made** the host of the Syrians **to h** a noise	8085
14:11 Amaziah would not **h**. Therefore Jehoash	8085
17:14 Notwithstanding they would not **h**,	8085
18:12 and would not **h** *them*, nor do *them*.	8085
18:28 saying, **H** the word of the great king,	8085
19: 4 It may be the Lord thy God will **h** all	8085
19: 7 he shall **h** a rumour, and shall return to	8085
19:16 Lord, bow down thine ear, and **h**: open,	8085
19:16 **h** the words of Sennacherib, which hath	8085
20:16 unto Hezekiah, **H** the word of the Lord.	8085
1Ch 14:15 when thou shalt **h** a sound of going in	8085
28: 2 said, **H** me, my brethren, and my people:	8085
2Ch 6:21 **h** thou from thy dwelling place, *even*	8085
6:23 **h** thou from heaven, and do, and judge	8085
6:25 **h** thou from the heavens, and forgive	8085
6:27 **h** thou *from* heaven, and forgive the sin	8085
6:30 **h** thou from heaven thy dwelling place,	8085
6:33 **h** thou from the heavens, *even* from thy	8085
6:35 **h** thou from the heavens their prayer and	8085
6:39 **h** thou from the heavens, *even* from thy	8085
7:14 I **h** from heaven, and will forgive their	8085
9: 7 before thee, and **h** thy wisdom.	8085
9:23 to **h** his wisdom, that God had put in his	8085
13: 4 said, **H** me, *thou* Jeroboam, and all Israel;	8085
15: 2 **H** ye me, Asa, and all Judah and	8085
18:18 Therefore **h** the word of the Lord;	8085
20: 9 our affliction, then thou wilt **h** and help.	8085
20:20 Jehoshaphat stood and said, **H** me,	8085
25:20 Amaziah would not **h**; for it *came* of God,	8085
28:11 Now **h** me therefore, and deliver	8085
29: 5 said unto them, **H** me, ye Levites,	8085
Ne 1: 6 that *thou* mayest **h** the prayer of thy	8085
4: 4 **H**, O our God; for we are despised:	8085
4:20 *therefore* ye **h** the sound of the trumpet,	8085
8: 2 and all that could **h** with understanding,	8085
9:29 hardened their neck, and would not **h**.	8085
Job 3:18 they **h** not the voice of the oppressor.	8085
5:27 it *is;* **h** it, and know thou *it* for thy good.	8085
13: 6 **H** now my reasoning, and hearken to	8085
13:17 **H** diligently my speech,	8085+8085
15:17 I will shew thee, **h** me; and that which I	8085
21: 2 **H** diligently my speech, and let this	8085+8085
22:27 thou shalt **h** thee, and thou shalt pay thy	8085
27: 9 Will God **h** his cry when trouble cometh	8085
30:20 I cry unto thee, and thou dost not **h** me:	6030
31:35 that one would **h** me! behold, my desire	8085
33: 1 **h** my speeches, and hearken to all my	8085
34: 2 **H** my words, O ye wise *men;* and give ear	8085
34:16 If now *thou hast* understanding, **h** this:	8085
35:13 Surely God will not **h** vanity, neither will	8085
37: 2 **H** attentively the noise of his	8085+8085
42: 4 **H**, I beseech thee, and I will speak: I will	8085
Ps 4: 1 **H** me when I call, O God of my	6030

Ps 4: 1 have mercy upon me, and **h** my prayer.	8085
4: 3 the Lord will **h** when I call unto him.	8085
5: 3 My voice shalt thou **h** in the morning,	8085
10:17 heart, thou wilt **cause** thine ear **to h**:	7181
13: 3 Consider *and* **h** me, O Lord my God:	6030
17: 1 **H** the right, O Lord, attend unto my cry,	8085
17: 6 upon thee, for thou wilt **h** me, O God:	6030
17: 6 thine ear unto me, *and* **h** my speech.	8085
18:44 As soon as they **h** *of me,* they shall obey	8088
20: 1 The Lord **h** thee in the day of trouble;	6030
20: 6 he will **h** him from his holy heaven with	6030
20: 9 Lord: let the king **h** us when we call.	6030
27: 7 **H**, O Lord, *when I cry* with my voice:	8085
28: 2 **H** the voice of my supplications, when I	8085
30:10 **H**, O Lord, and have mercy upon me:	8085
34: 2 the humble shall **h** *thereof,* and be glad.	8085
38:15 do I hope: thou wilt **h**, O Lord my God.	6030
38:16 *H me,* lest *otherwise* they should rejoice	NIH
39:12 **H** my prayer, O Lord, and give ear unto	8085
49: 1 **H** this, all ye people; give ear, all ye	8085
50: 7 **H**, O my people, and I will speak;	8085
51: 8 **Make me to h** joy and gladness; *that*	8085
54: 2 **H** my prayer, O God; give ear to the	8085
55: 2 Attend unto me, and **h** me: I mourn in	6030
55:17 and cry aloud: and he shall **h** my voice.	8085
55:19 God shall **h**, and afflict them, even he	8085
59: 7 in their lips: for who, *say they,* doth **h**?	8085
60: 5 save *with* thy right hand, and **h** me.	6030
61: 1 **H** my cry, O God; attend unto my prayer.	8085
64: 1 **H** my voice, O God, in my prayer:	8085
66:16 Come *and* **h**, all ye that fear God, and I	8085
66:18 in my heart, the Lord will not **h** *me:*	8085
69:13 God, in the multitude of thy mercy **h** me,	6030
69:16 **H** me, O Lord; for thy lovingkindness *is*	6030
69:17 for I am in trouble: **h** me speedily.	6030
81: 8 **H**, O my people, and I will testify unto	8085
84: 8 O Lord God *of* hosts, **h** my prayer:	8085
85: 8 I will **h** what God the Lord will speak:	8085
86: 1 Bow down thine ear, O Lord, **h** me: for I	6030
92:11 mine ears shall **h** *my desire* of the wicked	8085
94: 9 He that planted the ear, shall he not **h**?	8085
95: 7 of his hand. To day if ye will **h** his voice,	8085
102: 1 **H** my prayer, O Lord, and let my cry	8085
102:20 **h** the groaning of the prisoner; to loose	8085
115: 6 have ears, but they **h** not: noses have	8085
119:145 with *my* whole heart; **h** me, O Lord:	6030
119:149 **H** my voice according unto thy	8085
130: 2 **h** my voice: let thine ears be attentive	8085
135:17 They have ears, but they **h**; not; neither is	238
138: 4 when they **h** the words of thy mouth.	8085
140: 6 **h** the voice of my supplications, O Lord.	238
141: 6 in stony places, they shall **h** my words;	8085
143: 1 **H** my prayer, O Lord, give ear to my	8085
143: 7 **H** me speedily, O Lord: my spirit	6030
143: 8 **Cause** me **to h** thy lovingkindness in	8085
145:19 also will **h** their cry, and will save them.	8085
Pr 1: 5 A wise *man* will **h**, and will increase	8085
1: 8 **h** the instruction of thy father,	8085
4: 1 **H**, ye children, the instruction of a father,	8085
4:10 **H**, O my son, and receive my sayings;	8085
5: 7 **H** me now therefore, O ye children,	8085
8: 6 **H**, for I will speak of excellent things;	8085
8:33 **H** instruction, and be wise, and refuse *it*	8085
19:20 **H** counsel, and receive instruction,	8085
19:27 the instruction *that causeth* to err from	8085
22:17 **h** the words of the wise, and apply thine	8085
23:19 **H** thou, my son, and be wise,	8085
Ecc 5: 1 *be* more ready to **h**, than to give	8085
7: 5 *It is* better to **h** the rebuke of the wise,	8085
7: 5 than for a man to **h** the song of fools.	8085
7:21 lest thou **h** thy servant curse thee:	8085
12:13 Let us **h** the conclusion of the whole	8085
SS 2:14 see thy countenance, let me **h** thy voice;	8085
8:13 hearken to thy voice: **cause** me **to h** *it.*	8085
Isa 1: 2 **H**, O heavens, and give ear, O earth:	8085
1:10 **H** the word of the Lord, ye rulers of	8085
1:15 when ye make many prayers, I will not **h**:	8085
6: 9 **H** ye **indeed**, but understand not;	8085+8085
6:10 with their ears, and understand *with*	8085
7:13 he said, **H** ye now, O house of David;	8085
18: 3 and when *he* bloweth a trumpet, **h** ye.	8085
28:12 *is* the refreshing: yet they would not **h**.	8085
28:14 Wherefore **h** the word of the Lord,	8085
28:23 Give ye ear, and **h** my voice; hearken;	8085
28:23 my voice; hearken, and **h** my speech.	8085
29:18 in that day shall the deaf **h** the words of	8085
30: 9 children *that* will not **h** the law of	8085
30:19 when *he* shall **h** it, he will answer thee.	8085
30:21 thine ears shall **h** a word behind thee,	8085
32: 3 the ears of them that **h** shall hearken.	8085
32: 9 ye women that are at ease, **h** my voice;	8085
33:13 **H**, ye *that are* far off, what I have done;	8085
34: 1 near, ye nations, to **h**; and hearken,	8085
34: 1 let the earth **h**, and all that is therein;	8085
36:13 said, **H** ye the words of the great king,	8085
37: 4 It may be the Lord thy God will **H**	8085
37: 7 he shall **h** a rumour, and return to his	8085
37:17 Incline thine ear, O Lord, and **h**;	8085
37:17 **h** all the words of Sennacherib, which	8085
39: 5 **H** the word of the Lord of hosts:	8085
41:17 faileth for thirst, I the Lord will **h** them,	6030
42:18 **H**, ye deaf; and look, ye blind, that *ye*	8085
42:23 will hearken and **h** for the time to come?	8085
43: 9 or let them **h**, and say, *It is* truth.	8085
44: 1 now **h**, O Jacob my servant; and Israel,	8085

Isa 47: 8 Therefore **h** now this, *thou that art* given	8085
48: 1 **H** ye this, O house of Jacob, which are	8085
48:14 All ye, assemble yourselves, and **h**;	8085
48:16 Come ye near unto me, **h** ye this; I have	8085
50: 4 wakeneth mine ear to **h** as the learned.	8085
51:21 Therefore **h** now this, thou afflicted,	8085
55: 3 **h**, and your soul shall live; and I will	8085
59: 1 neither his ear heavy, that *it* cannot **h**:	8085
59: 2 hid *his* face from you, that *he* will not **h**.	8085
65:12 when I spake, ye did not **h**; but did evil	8085
65:24 and whiles they are yet speaking, I will **h**.	8085
66: 4 did answer; when I spake, they did not **h**:	8085
66: 5 **H** the word of the Lord, ye that tremble	8085
Jer 2: 4 **h** ye the word of the Lord, O house of	8085
4:21 *and* **h** the sound of the trumpet?	8085
5:21 **H** now this, O foolish people,	8085
5:21 and see not; which have ears, and **h** not:	8085
6:10 speak, and give warning, that they may **h**?	8085
6:18 Therefore **h**, ye nations, and know,	8085
6:19 O earth: behold, I will bring evil upon	8085
7: 2 say, **H** the word of the Lord, all *ye of*	8085
7:16 intercession to me: for I *will* not **h** thee.	8085
9:10 neither can *men* **h** the voice of the cattle;	8085
9:20 Yet **h** the word of the Lord, O ye	8085
10: 1 **H** ye the word which the Lord speaketh	8085
11: 2 **H** ye the words of this covenant,	8085
11: 6 **H** ye the words of this covenant,	8085
11:10 which refused to **h** my words;	8085
11:14 for I will not **h** *them* in the time that they	8085
13:10 evil people, which refuse to **h** my words,	8085
13:11 and for a glory: but they would not **h**.	8085
13:15 **H** ye, and give ear; be not proud:	8085
13:17 if ye will not **h** it, my soul shall weep in	8085
14:12 When they fast, I will not **h** their cry;	8085
17:20 **H** ye the word of the Lord, ye kings of	8085
17:23 their neck stiff, that *they* might not **h**,	8085
18: 2 there I will **cause** thee **to h** my words.	8085
19: 3 say, **H** ye the word of the Lord, O kings	8085
19:15 that *they* might not **h** my words.	8085
20:16 let him **h** the cry in the morning,	8085
21:11 *say,* **H** ye the word of the Lord.	8085
22: 2 say, **H** the word of the Lord, O king of	8085
22: 5 if ye will not **h** these words, I swear by	8085
22:21 prosperity; *but* thou saidst, I will not **h**.	8085
22:29 earth, earth, **h** the word of the Lord.	8085
23:22 had **caused** my people to **h** my words,	8085
25: 4 not hearkened, nor inclined your ear to **h**.	8085
28: 7 Nevertheless **h** thou now this word that I	8085
28:15 Hananiah the prophet, **H** now, Hananiah;	8085
29:19 and sending *them;* but ye would not **h**,	8085
29:20 **H** ye therefore the word of the Lord,	8085
31:10 **H** the word of the Lord, O ye nations,	8085
33: 9 which shall **h** all the good that I do unto	8085
34: 4 Yet **h** the word of the Lord, O Zedekiah	8085
36: 3 may be that the house of Judah will **h** all	8085
36:25 burn the roll: but he would not **h** them.	8085
37:20 Therefore **h** now, I pray thee, O my lord	8085
38:25 if the princes **h** that I have talked with	8085
42:14 nor **h** the sound of the trumpet, nor have	8085
42:15 therefore **h** the word of the Lord,	8085
44:24 all the women, **H** the word of the Lord,	8085
44:26 Therefore **h** ye the word of the Lord,	8085
49:20 Therefore **h** the counsel of the Lord,	8085
50:45 Therefore **h** ye the counsel of the Lord,	8085
La 1:18 **h**, I pray you, all people, and behold my	8085
Eze 2: 5 whether they will **h**, or whether they will	8085
2: 7 whether they will **h**, or whether they will	8085
2: 8 son of man, **h** what I say unto thee;	8085
3:10 in thine heart, and **h** with thine ears.	8085
3:11 whether they will **h**, or whether they will	8085
3:17 therefore **h** the word at my mouth,	8085
3:27 He that heareth, let him **h**; and he that	8085
6: 3 of Israel, **h** the word of the Lord God;	8085
8:18 *with* a loud voice, *yet* will I not **h** them.	8085
12: 2 see not; they have ears to **h**, and hear not:	8085
12: 2 see not; they have ears to hear, and **h** not:	8085
13: 2 own hearts, **H** ye the word of the Lord;	8085
13:19 your lying to my people that **h** *your* lies?	8085
16:35 O harlot, **h** the word of the Lord:	8085
18:25 **H** now, O house of Israel; Is not my way	8085
20:47 of the south, **H** the word of the Lord;	8085
24:26 to **cause** *thee* **to h** *it* with *thine ears?*	2045
25: 3 **H** the word of the Lord God;	8085
33: 7 thou shalt **h** the word at my mouth,	8085
33:30 **h** what *is* the word that cometh forth	8085
33:31 they **h** thy words, but they will not do	8085
33:32 they **h** thy words, but they do them not.	8085
34: 7 ye shepherds, **h** the word of the Lord;	8085
34: 9 O ye shepherds, **h** the word of the Lord;	8085
36: 1 of Israel, **h** the word of the Lord:	8085
36: 4 of Israel, **h** the word of the Lord God;	8085
36:15 Neither will I **cause** *men* **to h** in thee	8085
37: 4 O ye dry bones, **h** the word of the Lord.	8085
40: 4 **h** with thine ears, and set thine heart	8085
44: 5 **h** with thine ears all that I say unto thee	8085
Da 3: 5 *That* at what time ye **h** the sound of	8086
3:10 that every man *that shall* **h** the sound of	8086
3:15 Now if ye be ready that at what time ye **h**	8086
5:23 stone, which see not, nor **h**, nor know:	8086
9:17 the prayer of thy servant,	8085
9:18 O my God, incline thine ear, and **h**;	8085
9:19 O Lord, **h**; O Lord, forgive; O Lord,	6030
Hos 2:21 I will **h**, saith the Lord, I will hear	6030
2:21 I will **h** the heavens, and they shall hear	6030
2:21 the heavens, and they shall **h** the earth;	6030

H

Hos	2:22	the earth shall **h** the corn, and the wine,	6030

Hos 2:22 the earth shall **h** the corn, and the wine, — 6030
2:22 and the oil; and they shall **h** Jezreel. — 6030
4: 1 **H** the word of the LORD, ye children of — 8085
4: 1 ye this, O priests; and hearken, — 8085
Joel 1: 2 **H** this, ye old men, and give ear, all ye — 8085
Am 3: 1 **H** this word that the LORD hath spoken — 8085
3:13 **H** ye, and testify in the house of Jacob, — 8085
4: 1 **H** this word, ye kine of Bashan, that *are* — 8085
5: 1 **H** ye this word which I take up against — 8085
5:23 for I will not **h** the melody of thy viols. — 8085
7:16 therefore **h** thou the word of the LORD: — 8085
8: 4 **H** this, O ye that swallow up the needy, — 8085
Mic 1: 2 **H**, all ye people; hearken, O earth, — 8085
3: 1 I said, **H**, I pray you, O heads of Jacob, — 8085
3: 4 unto the LORD, but he will not **h** them: — 6030
3: 9 **H** this, I pray you, ye heads of the house — 8085
6: 1 ye now what the LORD saith; Arise, — 8085
6: 1 mountains, and let the hills **h** thy voice. — 8085
6: 2 **H** ye, O mountains, the LORD's — 8085
6: 9 **h** ye the rod, and who hath appointed it. — 8085
7: 7 God of my salvation: my God will **h** me. — 8085
Na 3:19 all that **h** the bruit of thee shall clap — 8085
Hab 1: 2 how long shall I cry, and thou wilt not **h**? — 8085
Zec 1: 4 they did not **h**, nor hearken unto me, — 8085
3: 8 **H** now, O Joshua the high priest, thou, — 8085
7: 7 *Should ye not* **h** the words which — NIH
7:11 stopped their ears, that *they* should not **h**. — 8085
7:12 lest *they* should the law, and the words — 8085
7:13 *that* as he cried, and they would not **h**; — 8085
7:13 so they cried, and I would not **h**, saith — 8085
9: 6 ye that **h** in these days these words by — 8085
10: 6 *am* the LORD their God, and will **h** them. — 6030
13: 9 shall call on my name, and I will **h** them: — 6030
Mal 2: 2 If ye will not **h**, and if ye will not lay *it* to — 8085

Mt 10:14 nor **h** your words, when ye depart out of — 191
10:27 what ye **h** in the ear, *that* preach ye upon — 191
11: 4 John again *those things* which ye do **h**, — 191
11: 5 and the deaf **h**, the dead are raised up, — 191
11:15 He that hath ears to **h**, let him hear. — 191
11:15 He that hath ears to hear, let him **h**. — 191
12:19 neither shall any *man* **h** his voice in — 191
12:42 of the earth to **h** the wisdom of Solomon; — 191
13: 9 Who hath ears to **h**, let him hear. — 191
13: 9 Who hath ears to hear, let him **h**. — 191
13:13 and hearing they **h** not, neither do they — 191
13:14 By hearing ye shall **h**, and shall not — 191
13:15 see with *their* eyes, and **h** with *their* ears, — 191
13:16 for they see: and your ears, for they **h**. — 191
13:17 and to **h** *those things* which ye hear, — 191
13:17 and to hear *those things* which ye **h**, — 191
13:18 **H** ye therefore the parable of the sower. — 191
13:43 Who hath ears to **h**, let him hear. — 191
13:43 Who hath ears to hear, let him **h**. — 191
15:10 and said unto them, **H**, and understand: — 191
17: 5 in whom I am well pleased; **h** ye him. — 191
18:15 if he shall **h** thee, thou hast gained thy — 191
18:16 if he will not **h** *thee*, *then* take with thee — 191
18:17 And if he shall **neglect to h** them, tell *it* — 3878
18:17 if he **neglect to h** the church, let him be — 3878
21:33 **H** another parable: There was a certain — 191
24: 6 ye shall **h** of wars and rumours of wars: — 191
Mk 4: 9 He that hath ears to **h**, let him hear. — 191
4: 9 He that hath ears to hear, let him **h**. — 191
4:12 hearing they may **h**, and not understand; — 191
4:18 sown among thorns; such as **h** the word, — 191
4:20 such as **h** the word, and receive *it*, and — 191
4:23 If any *man* have ears to **h**, let him hear. — 191
4:23 If any *man* have ears to hear, let him **h**. — 191
4:24 he said unto them, Take heed what you **h**: — 191
4:24 and unto you that **h** shall more be given. — 191
4:33 word unto them, as they were able to **h** *it*. — 191
6:11 nor **h** you, when ye depart thence, — 191
7:16 If any *man* have ears to **h**, let him hear. — 191
7:16 If any *man* have ears to hear, let him **h**. — 191
7:37 maketh both the deaf to **h**, and the dumb — 191
8:18 and having ears, **h** ye not? and do ye not — 191
9: 7 saying, This is my beloved Son: **h** him. — 191
12:29 The first of all the commandments *is*, **H**, — 191
13: 7 when ye shall **h** of wars and rumours of — 191
Lk 5: 1 as the people pressed upon him to **h** — 191
5:15 and great multitudes came together to **h**, — 191
6:17 which came to **h** him, and to be healed of — 191
6:27 But I say unto you which **h**, Love your — 191
7:22 cleansed, the deaf **h**, the dead are raised, — 191
8: 8 cried, He that hath ears to **h**, let him hear. — 191
8: 8 cried, He that hath ears to hear, let him **h**. — 191
8:12 Those by the way side are they that **h**; then — 191
8:13 when they **h**, receive the word with joy; — 191
8:18 Take heed therefore how ye **h**: — 191
8:21 my brethren are these which **h** the word of — 191
9: 9 of whom I **h** such *things?* And he desired — 191
9:35 saying, This is my beloved Son: **h** him. — 191
10:24 and to **h** *those things* which ye hear, — 191
10:24 and to hear *those things* which ye **h**, — 191
11:28 blessed *are* they that **h** the word of God, — 191
11:31 of the earth to **h** the wisdom of Solomon; — 191
14:35 it out. He that hath ears to **h**, let him hear. — 191
14:35 it out. He that hath ears to hear, let him **h**. — 191
15: 1 all the publicans and sinners for to **h** him. — 191
16: 2 unto him, How *is it that* I **h** this of thee? — 191
16:29 and the prophets; let them **h** them. — 191
16:31 **h** not Moses and the prophets, — 191
18: 6 Lord said, **H** what the unjust judge saith. — 191
19:48 for all the people were very attentive to **h** — 191
21: 9 But when ye shall **h** of wars and — 191

Lk 21:38 to him in the temple, for to **h** him. — 191
Jn 5:25 when the dead shall **h** the voice of the Son — 191
5:25 the Son of God: and they that **h** shall live. — 191
5:28 the which all that are in the graves shall **h** — 191
5:30 as I **h**, I judge: and my judgment is just; — 191
6:60 This is a hard saying; who can **h** it? — 191
7:51 before it **h** him, and know what he doeth? — 191
8:43 *even* because ye cannot **h** my word. — 191
8:47 therefore **h** *them* not, because ye are not — 191
9:27 I have told you already, and ye did not **h**: — 191
9:27 wherefore would you **h** *it* again? will ye — 191
10: 3 porter openeth; and the sheep **h** his voice: — 191
10: 8 and robbers: but the sheep did not **h** them. — 191
10:16 I must bring, and they shall **h** my voice; — 191
10:20 He hath a devil, and is mad; why **h** ye him? — 191
10:27 My sheep **h** my voice, and I know them, — 191
12:47 And if any *man* **h** my words, — 191
14:24 and the word which you **h** is not mine, — 191
16:13 but whatsoever he shall **h**, *that* shall he — 191
Ac 2: 8 And how **h** we every man in our own — 191
2:11 we do **h** them speak in our tongues — 191
2:22 Ye men of Israel, **h** these words; Jesus of — 191
2:33 shed forth this, which ye now see and **h**. — 191
3:22 him shall ye **h** in all *things* whatsoever he — 191
3:23 every soul, which will not **h** that prophet, — 191
7:37 brethren, like unto me; him shall ye **h**. — 191
10:22 into his house, and to **h** words of thee. — 191
10:33 to **h** all *things* that are commanded thee of — 191
13: 7 Saul, and desired to **h** the word of God. — 191
13:44 whole city together to **h** the word of God. — 191
15: 7 that the Gentiles by my mouth should **h** — 191
17:21 but *either* to tell, or to **h** some new *thing*.) — 191
17:32 We will **h** thee again of this *matter*. — 191
19:26 Moreover ye see and **h**, that not alone at — 191
21:22 for they will **h** that thou art come. — 191
22: 1 **h** ye my defence which *I make* now unto — 191
22:14 and shouldest **h** the voice of his mouth. — 191
23:35 I will **h** thee, said he, when thine accusers — 1251
24: 4 I pray *thee* that thou wouldest **h** us of thy — 191
25:22 Festus, I would also **h** the man myself. — 191
25:22 To morrow, said he, thou shalt **h**. — 191
26: 3 I beseech thee to **h** me patiently. — 191
26:29 but also all that **h** me this day, were both — 191
28:22 But we desire to **h** of thee what thou — 191
28:26 Hearing ye shall **h**, and shall not — 191
28:27 and **h** with *their* ears, and understand with — 191
28:28 unto the Gentiles, and *that* they will **h** it. — 191
Ro 10:14 and how shall they **h** without a preacher? — 191
11: 8 not see, and ears that *they* should **h**;) — 191
1Co 11:18 I **h** that there be divisions among you; — 191
14:21 and yet for all that will they not **h** me, — 1522
Gal 4:21 to be under the law, do ye not **h** the law? — 191
Php 1:27 or *else* be absent, I may **h** of your affairs, — 191
1:30 ye saw in me, and now **h** *to be* in me. — 191
2Th 3:11 For we **h** that *there are* some which walk — 191
1Ti 4:16 both save thyself, and them that **h** thee. — 191
2Ti 4:17 and *that* all the Gentiles might **h**: — 191
Heb 3: 7 Ghost saith, To day if ye will **h** his voice, — 191
3:15 it is said, To day if ye will **h** his voice, — 191
4: 7 as it is said, To day if ye will **h** his voice, — 191
Jas 1:19 let every man be swift to **h**, slow to speak, — 191
1Jn 5:15 if we know that he **h** us, whatsoever we — 191
3Jn 1: 4 I have no greater joy than to **h** that my — 191
Rev 1: 3 they that **h** the words of *this* prophecy, — 191
2: 7 let him **h** what the Spirit saith unto — 191
2:11 let him **h** what the Spirit saith unto — 191
2:17 let him **h** what the Spirit saith unto — 191
2:29 let him **h** what the Spirit saith unto — 191
3: 6 let him **h** what the Spirit saith unto — 191
3:13 let him **h** what the Spirit saith unto — 191
3:20 if any *man* **h** my voice, and open the door, — 191
3:22 let him **h** what the Spirit saith unto — 191
9:20 which neither can see, nor **h**, nor walk: — 191
13: 9 If any *man* have an ear, let him **h**. — 191

HEARD (641) [HEAR]

Ge 3: 8 they **h** the voice of the LORD God — 8085
3:10 I **h** thy voice in the garden, and I was — 8085
14:14 Abram **h** that his brother was taken — 8085
16:11 because the LORD hath **h** thy affliction. — 8085
17:20 as for Ishmael, I have **h** thee: Behold, — 8085
18:10 Sarah **h** *it in* the tent door, which *was* — 8085
21:17 God **h** the voice of the lad; and the angel — 8085
21:17 for God hath **h** the voice of the lad where — 8085
21:26 tell me, neither yet **h** I *of it*, but to day. — 8085
24:30 he **h** the words of Rebekah his sister, — 8085
24:52 when Abraham's servant **h** their words, — 8085
27: 5 Rebekah **h** when Isaac spake to Esau his — 8085
27: 6 **h** thy father speak unto Esau thy brother, — 8085
27:34 when Esau **h** the words of his father, — 8085
29:13 when Laban **h** the tidings of Jacob his — 8085
29:33 Because the LORD hath **h** that I *was* — 8085
30: 6 also **h** my voice, and hath given me a — 8085
31: 1 he **h** the words of Laban's sons, saying, — 8085
34: 5 Jacob **h** that he had defiled Dinah his — 8085
34: 7 came out of the field when they **h** *it:* — 8085
35:22 Israel **h** *it*. Now the sons of Jacob were — 8085
37:17 for I **h** *them* say, Let us go to Dothan. — 8085
37:21 Reuben **h** *it*, and he delivered him out of — 8085
39:15 when he **h** that I lifted up my voice and — 8085
39:19 when his master **h** the words of his wife, — 8085
41:15 I have **h** say of thee, *that* thou canst — 8085
42: 2 I have **h** that there is corn in Egypt: — 8085
43:25 they **h** that they should eat bread there. — 8085
45: 2 Egyptians and the house of Pharaoh **h**. — 8085

Ge 45:16 fame *thereof* was **h** *in* Pharaoh's house, — 8085
Ex 2:15 when Pharaoh **h** this thing, he sought — 8085
2:24 God **h** their groaning, and God — 8085
3: 7 have **h** their cry by reason of their — 8085
4:31 when they **h** that the LORD had visited — 8085
6: 5 I have also **h** the groaning of the children — 8085
16: 9 for he hath **h** your murmurings. — 8085
16:12 I have **h** the murmurings of the children — 8085
18: 1 **h** of all that God had done for Moses, — 8085
23:13 neither let it be **h** out of thy mouth. — 8085
28:35 his sound shall be **h** when he goeth in — 8085
32:17 when Joshua **h** the noise of the people as — 8085
33: 4 when the people **h** these evil tidings, they — 8085
Lev 10:20 And when Moses **h** *that*, he was content. — 8085
24:14 let all that **h** *him* lay their hands upon his — 8085
Nu 7:89 he **h** the voice of one speaking unto him — 8085
11: 1 the LORD **h** *it;* and his anger was kindled; — 8085
11:10 Moses **h** the people weep throughout — 8085
12: 2 spoken also by us? And the LORD **h** *it*. — 8085
14:14 *for* they have **h** that thou LORD *art* — 8085
14:15 nations which have **h** the fame of thee — 8085
14:27 I have **h** the murmurings of the children — 8085
16: 4 when Moses **h** *it*, he fell upon his face: — 8085
20:16 he **h** our voice, and sent an angel, — 8085
21: 1 **h** *tell* that Israel came *by* the way of — 8085
22:36 when Balak **h** that Balaam was come, — 8085
24: 4 He hath said, which **h** the words of God, — 8085
24:16 which **h** the words of God, and knew — 8085
30: 7 husband **h** *it*, and held his peace at her — 8085
30: 7 his peace at her in the day that he **h** *it:* — 8085
30: 8 disallow her on the day that he **h** *it;* — 8085
30:11 husband **h** *it*, and held his peace at her, — 8085
30:12 made them void on the day he **h** *them;* — 8085
30:14 held his peace at her in the day that he **h** — 8085
30:15 them void after *that* he hath **h** *them;* — 8085
33:40 of the coming of the children of Israel. — 8085
Dt 1:34 the LORD **h** the voice of your words, — 8085
4:12 ye **h** the voice of the words, but saw no — 8085
4:12 but saw no similitude; only *ye* **h** a voice. — NIH
4:32 this great thing *is*, or hath been **h** like it? — 8085
4:33 midst of the fire, as thou hast **h**, and live? — 8085
5:23 when ye **h** the voice out of the midst of — 8085
5:24 we have **h** his voice out of the midst of — 8085
5:26 that hath **h** the voice of the living God — 8085
5:28 the LORD **h** the voice of your words, — 8085
5:28 I have **h** the voice of the words of this — 8085
9: 2 *of whom* thou hast **h** *say*, Who can stand — 8085
17: 4 thou hast **h** *of it*, and inquired diligently, — 8085
26: 7 the LORD **h** our voice, and looked on our — 8085
Jos 2:10 For we have **h** how the LORD dried up — 8085
2:11 soon as we had **h** *these things*, our hearts — 8085
5: 1 **h** that the LORD had dried up the waters — 8085
6:20 when the people **h** the sound of — 8085
9: 1 the Hivite, and the Jebusite, **h** *thereof;* — 8085
9: 3 when the inhabitants of Gibeon **h** what — 8085
9: 9 we have **h** the fame of him, and all that — 8085
9:16 they **h** that they *were* their neighbours, — 8085
10: 1 Adoni-zedek king of Jerusalem had **h** — 8085
11: 1 when Jabin king of Hazor had **h** *those* — 8085
22:11 the children of Israel **h** say, Behold, — 8085
22:12 when the children of Israel **h** *of it*, — 8085
22:30 **h** the words that the children of Reuben — 8085
24:27 for it hath **h** all the words of the LORD — 8085
Jdg 7:15 when Gideon **h** the telling of the dream, — 8085
9:30 when Zebul the ruler of the city **h** — 8085
9:46 **h** *that*, they entered into a hold of the — 8085
18:25 Let not thy voice be **h** among us, lest — 8085
20: 3 (Now the children of Benjamin **h** that — 8085
Ru 1: 6 she had **h** in the country of Moab how — 8085
1Sa 1:13 her lips moved, but her voice was not **h**: — 8085
2:22 and **h** all that his sons did unto all Israel; — 8085
4: 6 when the Philistines **h** the noise of — 8085
4:14 Eli **h** the noise of the crying, he said, — 8085
4:19 she **h** the tidings that the ark of God — 8085
7: 7 the Philistines **h** that the children of — 8085
7: 7 the children of Israel **h** *it*, they were — 8085
7: 9 LORD for Israel; and the LORD **h** him. — 6030
8:21 Samuel **h** all the words of the people, — 8085
11: 6 spirit of God came upon Saul when he **h** — 8085
13: 3 the Philistines **h** of it. And Saul blew — 8085
13: 4 all Israel **h** say *that* Saul had smitten a — 8085
14:22 *when* they **h** that the Philistines fled, — 8085
14:27 Jonathan **h** not when his father charged — 8085
17:11 all Israel **h** those words of the Philistine, — 8085
17:23 to the same words: and David **h** *them*. — 8085
17:28 Eliab his eldest brother **h** when he spake — 8085
17:31 the words were **h** which David spake, — 8085
22: 1 his father's house **h** *it*, they went down — 8085
22: 6 When Saul **h** that David was discovered, — 8085
23:10 servant hath **certainly h** that Saul — 8085+8085
23:11 Saul come down, as thy servant hath **h**? — 8085
23:25 when Saul **h** *that*, he pursued after David — 8085
25: 4 David **h** in the wilderness that Nabal did — 8085
25: 7 now I have **h** that thou hast shearers: — 8085
25:39 when David **h** that Nabal was dead, — 8085
31:11 when the inhabitants of Jabesh-gilead **h** — 8085
2Sa 3:28 afterward when David **h** *it*, he said, I and — 8085
4: 1 Saul's son **h** that Abner was dead in — 8085
5:17 when the Philistines **h** that they had — 8085
5:17 David **h** *of it*, and went down to the hold. — 8085
7:22 according to all that we have **h** with our — 8085
8: 9 Toi king of Hamath **h** that David had — 8085
10: 7 when David **h** *of it*, he sent Joab, and all — 8085
11:26 when the wife of Uriah **h** that Uriah her — 8085
13:21 when king David **h** of all these things, — 8085

2Sa	18: 5 all the people **h** when the king gave all	8085
	19: 2 the people **h** say that day *how* the king	8085
1Ki	1:11 Hast thou not **h** that Adonijah the son of	8085
	1:41 all the guests that *were* with him **h** *it* as	8085
	1:41 when Joab **h** the sound of the trumpet,	8085
	1:45 This *is* the noise that ye have **h**	8085
	2:42 unto me, The word *that* I have **h** *is* good.	8085
	3:28 Israel **h** of the judgment which the king	8085
	4:34 of the earth, which had **h** of his wisdom.	8085
	5: 1 for he had **h** that they had anointed him	8085
	5: 7 when Hiram **h** the words of Solomon,	8085
	6: 7 axe *nor* any tool of iron **h** in the house,	8085
	9: 3 I have **h** thy prayer and thy supplication,	8085
	10: 1 the queen of Sheba **h** of the fame of	8085
	10: 6 It was a true report that I **h** in mine own	8085
	10: 7 prosperity exceedeth the fame which I **h**.	8085
	11:21 when Hadad **h** in Egypt that David slept	8085
	12: 2 of *it*, (for he was fled from the	8085
	12:20 all Israel **h** that Jeroboam was come	8085
	13: 4 when king Jeroboam **h** the saying of the	8085
	13:26 back from the way **h** *thereof*, he said,	8085
	14: 6 *so*, when Ahijah **h** the sound of her feet,	8085
	15:21 when Baasha **h** *thereof*, that he left off	8085
	16:16 the people that *were* encamped **h** say,	8085
	17:22 the LORD **h** the voice of Elijah;	8085
	19:13 when Elijah **h** *it*, that he wrapped his face	8085
	20:12 when *Ben-hadad* **h** this message, as he	8085
	20:31 we have **h** that the kings of the house of	8085
	21:15 when Jezebel **h** that Naboth was stoned,	8085
	21:16 when Ahab **h** that Naboth was dead,	8085
	21:27 came to pass, when Ahab **h** those words,	8085
2Ki	3:21 when all the Moabites **h** that the kings	8085
	5: 8 when Elisha the man of God had **h** that	8085
	6:30 the king **h** the words of the woman,	8085
	9:30 Jezebel **h** *of it*; and she painted her face,	8085
	11:13 when Athaliah **h** the noise of the guard	8085
	19: 1 king Hezekiah **h** *it*, that he rent his	8085
	19: 4 words which the LORD thy God hath **h**:	8085
	19: 6 afraid of the words which thou hast **h**,	8085
	19: 8 for he had **h** that he was departed from	8085
	19: 9 when he **h** say of Tirhakah king of	8085
	19:11 thou hast **h** what the kings of Assyria	8085
	19:20 Sennacherib king of Assyria I have **h**.	8085
	19:25 thou not **h** long ago *how* I have done	8085
	20: 5 I have **h** thy prayer, I have seen thy tears:	8085
	20:12 for he had **h** that Hezekiah had been sick.	8085
	22:11 the king had **h** the words of the book	8085
	22:18 *touching* the words which thou hast **h**;	8085
	22:19 I also have **h** *thee*, saith the LORD.	8085
	25:23 that the king of Babylon had made	8085
1Ch	10:11 when all Jabesh-gilead **h** all that	8085
	14: 8 when the Philistines **h** that David was	8085
	14: 8 David **h** *of it*, and went out against them.	8085
	17:20 according to all that we have **h** with our	8085
	18: 9 Now when Tou king of Hamath **h** how	8085
	19: 8 when David **h** *of it*, he sent Joab, and all	8085
2Ch	5:13 to **make** one sound to be **h** in praising	8085
	7:12 I have **h** thy prayer, and have chosen this	8085
	9: 1 when the queen of Sheba **h** of the fame of	8085
	9: 5 *was* a true report which I **h** in mine own	8085
	9: 6 *for* thou exceedest the fame that I **h**.	8085
	10: 2 **h** *it*, that Jeroboam returned out of Egypt.	8085
	15: 8 Asa **h** these words, and the prophecy	8085
	16: 5 Baasha **h** *it*, that he left off building	8085
	20:29 when they had **h** that the LORD fought	8085
	23:12 Now when Athaliah **h** the noise of	8085
	30:27 their voice was **h**, and their prayer came	8085
	33:13 his supplication, and brought him again	8085
	34:16 the king had **h** the words of the law,	8085
	34:26 *concerning* the words which thou hast **h**;	8085
	34:27 I have even **h** *thee* also, saith the LORD.	8085
Ezr	3:13 loud shout, and the noise was **h** afar off.	8085
	4: 1 Benjamin **h** that the children of	8085
	9: 3 when I **h** this thing, I rent my garment	8085
Ne	4: 1 when Sanballat **h** these words, *that* I sat down	8085
	2:10 **h** *of it*, it grieved them exceedingly that	8085
	2:19 **h** *it*, they laughed us to scorn,	8085
	4: 1 when Sanballat **h** that we builded	8085
	4: 7 that the walls of Jerusalem were made	8085
	4:15 when our enemies **h** that it was known	8085
	5: 6 I was very angry when I **h** their cry and	8085
	6: 1 **h** that I had builded the wall, and *that*	8085
	6:16 that when all our enemies **h** *thereof*, and	8085
	8: 9 when they **h** the words of the law.	8085
	12:43 that the joy of Jerusalem was **h** even afar	8085
	13: 3 it came to pass, when they had **h** the law,	8085
Est	1:18 which have **h** of the deed of the queen.	8085
	2: 8 commandment and his decree was **h**,	8085
Job	2:11 Now when Job's three friends **h** of all this	8085
	4:16 *there was* silence, and I **h** a voice, *saying*,	8085
	13: 1 eye hath seen all *this*, mine ear hath **h**	8085
	15: 8 Hast thou **h** the secret of God?	8085
	16: 2 I have **h** many such *things*: miserable	8085
	19: 7 I cry *out* of wrong, but I am not **h**:	6030
	20: 3 I have **h** the check of my reproach,	8085
	26:14 how little a portion is **h** of him?	8085
	28:22 have **h** the fame thereof with our ears.	8085
	29:11 When the ear **h** *me*, then it blessed me;	8085
	33: 8 I have **h** the voice of thy words,	8085
	37: 4 he will not stay them when his voice is **h**.	8085
	42: 5 I have **h** of thee by the hearing of the ear:	8085
Ps	3: 4 voice, and he **h** me out of his holy hill.	6030
	6: 8 for the LORD hath **h** the voice of my	8085
	6: 9 The LORD hath **h** my supplication;	8085
	10:17 thou hast **h** the desire of the humble:	8085

Ps	18: 6 he **h** my voice out of his temple,	8085
	19: 3 nor language, *where* their voice is not **h**.	8085
	22:21 for thou hast **h** me from the horns of	6030
	22:24 but when he cried unto him, he **h**.	8085
	28: 6 he hath **h** the voice of my supplications.	8085
	31:13 For I have **h** the slander of many: fear	8085
	34: 4 he **h** me, and delivered me from all my	6030
	34: 6 the LORD **h** *him*, and saved him out of all	8085
	38:13 I, as a deaf *man*, **h** not; and *I was* as a	8085
	40: 1 and he inclined unto me, and **h** my cry.	8085
	44: 1 We have **h** with our ears, O God,	8085
	48: 8 As we have **h**, so have we seen in the city	8085
	61: 5 thou, O God, hast **h** my vows: thou hast	8085
	62:11 hath spoken once; twice have I **h** this;	8085
	66: 8 and **make** the voice of his praise to be **h**:	8085
	66:19 verily God hath **h** *me*; he hath attended	8085
	76: 8 Thou didst **cause** judgment **to be h** from	8085
	78: 3 Which we have **h** and known,	8085
	78:21 Therefore the LORD **h** *this*, and	8085
	78:59 When God **h** *this*, he was wroth,	8085
	81: 5 I **h** a language *that* I understood not.	8085
	97: 8 Zion **h**, and was glad, and the daughters	8085
	106:44 their affliction, when he **h** their cry:	8085
	116: 1 because he hath **h** my voice *and*	8085
	118:21 for thou hast **h** me, and art become my	6030
	120: 1 I cried unto the LORD, and he **h** me.	8085
	132: 6 Lo, we **h** *of it* at Ephratah: we found it in	8085
Pr	21:13 also shall cry himself, but shall not be **h**.	6030
Ecc	9:16 *is* despised, and his words *are* not **h**.	8085
	9:17 The words of wise *men are* **h** in quiet,	8085
SS	2:12 the voice of the turtle is **h** in our land;	8085
Isa	6: 8 Also I **h** the voice of the Lord, saying,	8085
	10:30 **cause** *it* **to be h** unto Laish, O poor	7181
	15: 4 their voice shall be **h** *even* unto Jahaz:	8085
	16: 6 We have **h** of the pride of Moab; *he is*	8085
	21:10 that which I have **h** of the LORD of hosts,	8085
	24:16 part of the earth have we **h** songs,	8085
	28:22 for I have **h** from the Lord GOD of hosts a	8085
	30:30 shall **cause** his glorious voice **to be h**,	8085
	37: 1 when king Hezekiah **h** *it*, that he rent his	8085
	37: 4 words which the LORD thy God hath **h**:	8085
	37: 6 not afraid of the words that thou hast **h**,	8085
	37: 8 for he had **h** that he was departed from	8085
	37: 9 he **h** say concerning Tirhakah king of	8085
	37: 9 when he **h** *it*, he sent messengers to	8085
	37:11 hast **h** what the kings of Assyria have	8085
	37:26 thou not **h** long ago, *how* I have done	8085
	38: 5 I have **h** thy prayer, I have seen thy tears:	8085
	39: 1 for he had **h** that he had been sick,	8085
	40:21 have ye not? hath it not been told you	8085
	40:28 hast thou not **h**, *that* the everlasting God,	8085
	42: 2 nor **cause** his voice **to be h** in the street.	8085
	48: 6 Thou hast **h**, see all this; and will not ye	8085
	49: 8 In an acceptable time have I **h** thee,	6030
	52:15 *that* which they had not **h** shall they	8085
	58: 4 to **make** your voice **to be h** on high.	8085
	60:18 Violence shall no more be **h** in thy land,	8085
	64: 4 beginning of the world *men* have not **h**,	8085
	65:19 voice of weeping shall be no more **h** in	8085
	66: 8 Who hath **h** such *a thing?* who hath seen	8085
	66:19 isles afar off, that have not **h** my fame,	8085
Jer	3:21 A voice was **h** upon the high places,	8085
	4:19 peace, because thou hast **h**, O my soul,	8085
	4:31 For I have **h** a voice as of a woman in	8085
	6: 7 violence and spoil is **h** in her; before me	8085
	6:24 We have **h** the fame thereof: our hands	8085
	7:13 up early and speaking, but ye **h** not;	8085
	8: 6 I hearkened and **h**, *but* they spake not	8085
	8:16 snorting of his horses was **h** from Dan:	8085
	9:19 For a voice of wailing is **h** out of Zion,	8085
	18:13 hath **h** such things: the virgin of Israel	8085
	18:22 Let a cry be **h** from their houses, when	8085
	20: 1 **h** *that* Jeremiah prophesied these things.	8085
	20:10 For I **h** the defaming of many, fear on	8085
	23:18 and hath perceived and **h** his word?	8085
	23:25 who hath marked his word, and **h** *it?*	8085
	23:25 I have **h** what the prophets said,	8085
	25: 8 hosts; Because ye have not **h** my words,	8085
	25:36 shall be **h**: for the LORD *hath* spoiled their	NIH
	26: 7 all the people **h** Jeremiah speaking these	8085
	26:10 When the princes of Judah **h** these things,	8085
	26:11 this city, as ye have **h** with your ears.	8085
	26:12 this city all the words that ye have **h**.	8085
	26:21 and all the princes, **h** his words,	8085
	26:21 when Urijah **h** *it*, he was afraid, and fled,	8085
	30: 5 We have **h** a voice of trembling, of fear,	8085
	31:15 A voice was **h** in Ramah, lamentation,	8085
	31:18 have **surely h** Ephraim bemoaning	8085+8085
	33:10 there shall be **h** in this place, which	8085
	34:10 **h** that every one should let his	8085
	35:17 spoken unto them, but they have not **h**;	8085
	36:11 had **h** out of the book all the words of	8085
	36:13 unto them all the words that he had **h**,	8085
	36:16 Now it came to pass when they had **h** all	8085
	36:24 nor any of his servants that **h** all these	8085
	37: 5 besieged Jerusalem **h** tidings of them,	8085
	38: 1 the words that Jeremiah had spoken	8085
	38: 7 that they had put Jeremiah in	8085
	40: 7 that the king of Babylon had made	8085
	40:11 that the king of Babylon had left a	8085
	41:11 of all the evil that Ishmael the son of	8085
	42: 4 said unto them, I have **h** *you;* behold,	8085
	46:12 The nations have **h** of thy shame,	8085
	48: 4 little ones have **caused** a cry **to be h**.	8085
	48: 5 the enemies have **h** a cry of destruction.	8085

Jer	48:29 We have **h** the pride of Moab; *he is*	8085
	49: 2 I will **cause** an alarm of war **to be h** in	8085
	49:14 I have **h** a rumour from the LORD,	8085
	49:21 the noise thereof was **h** in the Red sea.	8085
	49:23 for they have **h** evil tidings: they are	8085
	50:43 The king of Babylon hath **h** the report of	8085
	50:46 and the cry is **h** among the nations.	8085
	51:46 ye fear for the rumour that shall be **h** in	8085
	51:51 because we have **h** reproach:	8085
La	1:21 They have **h** that I sigh; *there is* none to	8085
	1:21 all mine enemies have **h** of my trouble;	8085
	3:56 Thou hast **h** my voice: hide not thine ear	8085
	3:61 Thou hast **h** their reproach, O LORD,	8085
Eze	1:24 they went, I **h** the noise of their wings,	8085
	1:28 face, and I **h** a voice of one that spake.	8085
	2: 2 my feet, that I **h** him that spake unto me.	8085
	3:12 I **h** behind me a voice of a great rushing,	8085
	3:13 *I h* also the noise of the wings of the	NIH
	10: 5 the sound of the cherubims' wings was **h**	8085
	19: 4 The nations also **h** of him; he was taken	8085
	19: 9 that his voice should no more be **h** upon	8085
	26:13 sound of thy harps shall be no more **h**.	8085
	27:30 **cause** their voice **to be h** against thee,	8085
	35: 5 He **h** the sound of the trumpet, and took	8085
	35:12 *that* I have **h** all thy blasphemies which	8085
	35:13 your words against me: I have **h** *them*.	8085
	43: 6 **h** *him* speaking unto me out of the house;	8085
Da	3: 7 when all the people **h** the sound of	8086
	5:14 I have even **h** of thee, that the spirit of	8086
	5:16 I have **h** of thee, that thou canst make	8086
	6:14 king, when he **h** *these* words, was sore	8086
	8:13 I **h** one saint speaking, and another saint	8085
	8:16 I **h** a man's voice between *the banks of*	8085
	10: 9 Yet I **h** the voice of his words: and when	8085
	10: 9 when I **h** the voice of his words, then was	8085
	10:12 thy words were **h**, and I am come for thy	8085
	12: 7 I **h** the man clothed in linen, which *was*	8085
	12: 8 I **h**, but I understood not: then said I,	8085
Hos	7:12 them, as their congregation hath **h**.	8088
	14: 8 I have **h** *him*, and observed him: I *am* like	6030
Ob	1: 1 We have **h** a rumour from the LORD,	8085
Jnh	2: 2 affliction unto the LORD, and he **h** me;	6030
Mic	5:15 the heathen, such as they have not **h**.	8085
Na	2:13 of thy messengers shall no more be **h**.	8085
Hab	3: 2 I have **h** thy speech, *and* was afraid:	8085
	3:16 When I **h**, my belly trembled; my lips	8085
Zep	2: 8 I have **h** the reproach of Moab,	8085
Zec	8:23 for we have **h** *that* God *is* with you.	8085
Mal	3:16 **h** *it*, and a book of remembrance was	8085
Mt	2: 3 When Herod the king had **h** *these things,*	191
	2: 9 When they had **h** the king, they departed;	191
	2:18 In Rama was there a voice **h**, lamentation,	191
	2:22 But when he **h** that Archelaus did reign in	191
	4:12 Now when Jesus had **h** that John was cast	191
	5:21 Ye have **h** that it was said by them of old	191
	5:27 Ye have **h** that it was said by them of old	191
	5:33 ye have **h** that it hath been said by them of	191
	5:38 Ye have **h** that it hath been said, An eye	191
	5:43 Ye have **h** that it hath been said, Thou	191
	6: 7 they shall be **h** for their much speaking.	1522
	8:10 When Jesus **h** *it*, he marvelled, and said to	191
	9:12 But when Jesus **h** *that*, he said unto them,	191
	11: 2 Now when John had **h** in the prison	191
	12:24 But when the Pharisees **h** *it*, they said,	191
	13:17 which ye hear, and have not **h** *them*.	191
	14: 1 that time Herod the tetrarch **h** of the fame	191
	14:13 When Jesus **h** *of it*, he departed thence by	191
	14:13 when the people had **h** *thereof*, they	191
	15:12 were offended, after they **h** *this* saying?	191
	17: 6 And when the disciples **h** *it*, they fell on	191
	19:22 But when the young man **h** *that* saying,	191
	19:25 When his disciples **h** *it*, they were	191
	20:24 And when the ten **h** *it*, they were moved	191
	20:30 they **h** that Jesus passed by, cried out,	191
	21:45 and Pharisees had **h** his parables,	191
	22: 7 when the king **h** *thereof*, he was wroth:	191
	22:22 When they had **h** *these words,* they	191
	22:33 And when the multitude **h** *this*, they were	191
	22:34 when the Pharisees had **h** that he had put	191
	26:65 behold, now ye have **h** his blasphemy;	191
	27:47 they **h** *that*, said, This *man* calleth for	191
Mk	2:17 When Jesus **h** *it*, he saith unto them,	191
	3: 8 when they had **h** what great *things* he did,	191
	3:21 when his friends **h** *of it*, they went out	191
	4:15 but when they have **h**, Satan cometh	191
	4:16 who, when they have **h** the word,	191
	5:27 she had **h** of Jesus, came in the press	191
	5:36 As soon as Jesus **h** the word that was	191
	6:14 king Herod **h** *of him;* (for his name was	191
	6:16 But when Herod **h** *thereof*, he said, It is	191
	6:20 and when he **h** him, he did many *things,*	191
	6:20 he did many *things,* and **h** him gladly.	191
	6:29 And when his disciples **h** *of it*, they came	191
	6:55 those that were sick, where they **h** he was.	191
	7:25 daughter had an unclean spirit, **h** of him,	191
	10:41 And when the ten **h** *it*, they began to be	191
	10:47 when he **h** that it was Jesus of Nazareth,	191
	11:14 And his disciples **h** *it*.	191
	11:18 And the scribes and chief priests **h** *it*, and	191
	12:28 and having **h** them reasoning together,	191
	12:37 And the common people **h** him gladly.	191
	14:11 And when they **h** *it*, they were glad,	191
	14:58 We **h** him say, I will destroy this temple	191
	14:64 Ye have **h** the blasphemy: what think ye?	191
	15:35 when they **h** *it*, said, Behold, he calleth	191

H

Mk 16:11 when they had **h** that he was alive, *191*
Lk 1:13 for thy prayer is **h**; and thy wife Elisabeth **h** *1522*
 1:41 it came to pass *that*, when Elisabeth **h** *191*
 1:58 her cousins **h** how the Lord had shewed *191*
 1:66 And all they that **h** *them* laid *them* up in *191*
 2:18 And all they that **h** *it* wondered at those *191*
 2:20 God for all *the things* that they had **h** *191*
 2:47 And all that **h** him were astonished at his *191*
 4:23 whatsoever we have **h** done in Capernaum *191*
 4:28 And when he **h** these *things*, were filled with *191*
 3:32 And what he hath seen and **h**, that he *191*
 7: 9 When Jesus **h** these *things*, he marvelled at *191*
 7:22 tell John what *things* ye have seen and **h**; *191*
 7:29 And all the people that **h** *him*, and *191*
 8:14 which, when they have **h**, go *forth*, and *191*
 8:15 having **h** the word, keep *it*, and bring forth *191*
 8:50 But when Jesus **h** *it*, he answered him, *191*
 9: 7 Now Herod the tetrarch **h** of all that was *191*
 10:24 which ye hear, and have not **h** *them*. *191*
 10:39 also sat at Jesus' feet, and **h** his word. *191*
 12: 3 spoken in darkness shall be **h** in the light; *191*
 14:15 with *him* **h** these *things*, he said unto him, *191*
 15:25 to the house, he **h** musick and dancing. *191*
 16:14 all these *things*: and they derided him. *191*
 18:22 when Jesus **h** these *things*, he said unto *191*
 18:23 when he **h** this, he was very sorrowful: *191*
 18:26 And they that **h** *it* said, Who then can be *191*
 19:11 And as they **h** these *things*, he added and *191*
 20:16 And when they **h** *it*, they said, God forbid. *191*
 22:71 for we ourselves have **h** of his own mouth. *191*
 23: 6 When Pilate **h** of Galilee, he asked whether *191*
 23: 8 because he had **h** many *things* of him; *191*
Jn 1:37 And the two disciples **h** him speak, *191*
 1:40 One of the two which **h** John speak, *191*
 3:32 And what he hath seen and **h**, that he *191*
 4: 1 the Lord knew how the Pharisees had **h** *191*
 4:42 for we have **h** *him* ourselves, and know *191*
 4:47 he **h** that Jesus was come out of Judea *191*
 5:37 Ye have neither **h** his voice at any time, *191*
 6:45 Every *man* therefore that hath **h**, *191*
 6:60 his disciples, when they had **h** *this*, said, *191*
 7:32 The Pharisees that the people murmured *191*
 7:40 when they **h** *this* saying, said, Of a truth *191*
 8: 6 on the ground, *as though he* **h** *them* not. NIG
 8: 9 And they which **h** *it*, being convicted by *191*
 8:26 world those *things* which I have **h** of him. *191*
 8:40 told you the truth, which I have **h** of God: *191*
 9:32 Since the world began was it not **h** that *191*
 9:35 Jesus **h** that they had cast him out; *191*
 9:40 which were with him **h** these *words*, *191*
 11: 4 When Jesus **h** *that*, he said, This sickness is *191*
 11: 6 When he had **h** therefore that he was sick, *191*
 11:20 as soon as she **h** that Jesus was coming, *191*
 11:29 As soon as she **h** *that*, she arose quickly, *191*
 11:41 Father, I thank thee that thou hast **h** me. *191*
 12:12 when they **h** that Jesus was coming to *191*
 12:18 that they **h** that he had done this miracle. *191*
 12:29 stood *by*, and **h** *it*, said that it thundered: *191*
 12:34 have **h** out of the law that Christ abideth *191*
 14:28 Ye have **h** how I said unto you, I go away, *191*
 15:15 for all *things* that I have **h** of my Father I *191*
 18:21 ask them which **h** *me*, what I have said *191*
 19: 8 When Pilate therefore **h** that saying, he *191*
 19:13 When Pilate therefore **h** that saying, *191*
 21: 7 Now when Simon Peter **h** that it was *191*
Ac 1: 4 Father, which, *saith he*, ye have **h** of me. *191*
 2: 6 that every man **h** them speak in his own *191*
 2:37 when they **h** *this*, they were pricked in *191*
 4: 4 Howbeit many of them which **h** the word *191*
 4:20 *the things* which we have seen and **h**. *191*
 4:24 when they **h** *that*, they lift up their voice *191*
 5: 5 great fear came on all them that **h** these *191*
 5:11 and upon as many as **h** these *things*. *191*
 5:21 And when they **h** *that*, they entered into *191*
 5:24 and the chief priests **h** these *things*, *191*
 5:33 they **h** *that*, they were cut *to the heart*, *191*
 6:11 We have **h** him speak blasphemous words *191*
 6:14 For we have **h** him say, that this Jesus of *191*
 7:12 But when Jacob **h** that there was corn in *191*
 7:34 and I have **h** their groaning, and am come *191*
 7:54 When they **h** these *things*, they were cut to *191*
 8:14 **h** that Samaria had received the word of *191*
 8:30 to *him*, and **h** him read the prophet Esaias, *191*
 9: 4 and **h** a voice saying unto him, Saul, Saul, *191*
 9:13 Lord, I have **h** by many of this man, *191*
 9:21 But all that **h** *him* were amazed, and said; *191*
 9:38 the disciples had **h** that Peter was there, *191*
 10:31 thy prayer is **h**, and thine alms are had in *1522*
 10:44 the Holy Ghost fell on all them which **h** *191*
 10:46 For they **h** them speak with tongues, *191*
 11: 1 brethren that were in Judea **h** that *191*
 11: 7 I **h** a voice saying unto me, Arise, Peter; *191*
 11:18 When they **h** these *things*, they held their *191*
 13:48 And when the Gentiles **h** *this*, they were *191*
 14: 9 The same Paul speak: who stedfastly *191*
 14:14 **h** *of*, they rent their clothes, and ran in *191*
 15:24 Forasmuch as we have **h**, that certain *191*
 16:14 **h** *us*: whose heart the Lord opened, *1874*
 16:25 unto God: and the prisoners **h** them. *191*
 16:38 when they **h** that they were Romans, *191*
 17: 8 of the city, when they **h** these *things*. *191*
 17:32 And when they **h** of the resurrection of *191*
 18:26 whom when Aquila and Priscilla had **h**, *191*
 19: 2 as **h** whether there be *any* Holy Ghost. *191*
 19: 5 When they **h** this, they were baptized in *191*

Ac 19:10 all they which dwelt in Asia **h** the word *191*
 19:28 when they **h** *these sayings*, they were *191*
 21:12 And when we **h** these *things*, both we, *191*
 21:20 when they **h** *it*, they glorified the Lord, *191*
 22: 2 (And when they **h** that he spake in *191*
 22: 7 and **h** a voice saying unto me, Saul, Saul, *191*
 22: 9 but **h** not the voice of him that spake to me. *191*
 22:15 unto all men of what thou hast seen and **h**. *191*
 22:26 When the centurion **h** *that*, he went and *191*
 23:16 when Paul's sister's son **h** of *their* lying *191*
 24:22 when Felix **h** these *things*, having more *191*
 24:24 and **h** him concerning the faith in Christ. *191*
 26:14 I **h** a voice speaking unto me, and saying *191*
 28:15 from thence, when the brethren **h** of us, *191*
Ro 10:14 believe *in him* of whom they have not **h**? *191*
 10:18 But I say, Have they not **h**? Yes verily, *191*
 15:21 and they that have not **h** shall understand. *191*
1Co 2: 9 it is written, Eye hath not seen, nor ear **h**, *191*
2Co 6: 2 I have **h** thee in a time accepted, and in *1873*
 12: 4 and **h** unspeakable words, which *it is* not *191*
Gal 1:13 For ye have **h** of my conversation in time *191*
 1:23 But they had **h** only, That he which *191*
Eph 1:13 In whom ye also *trusted*, after that ye **h** *191*
 1:15 after I **h** of your faith in the Lord Jesus, *191*
 3: 2 ye have **h** of the dispensation of the grace *191*
 4:21 If so be that ye have **h** him, and have been *191*
Php 2:26 that ye had **h** that he had been sick. *191*
Col 1: 4 Since ye **h** of your faith in Christ Jesus, *191*
 1: 5 whereof ye **h** before in the word of *4257*
 1: 6 the day ye **h** of *it*, and knew the grace *191*
 1: 9 since the day we **h** *it*, do not cease to pray *191*
 1:23 ye have **h**, *and* which was preached to *191*
1Th 2:13 received the word of God which *ye* **h** of us, *189*
2Ti 1:13 which thou hast **h** of me, in faith and *191*
 2: 2 *the things* that thou hast **h** of me among *191*
Heb 2: 1 heed to the *things* which we have **h**, *191*
 2: 3 confirmed unto us by them that **h** *him*; *191*
 3:16 For some, when they had **h**, did provoke: *191*
 4: 2 being mixed with faith in them that **h** *it*. *191*
 5: 7 from death, and was **h** in that *he* feared; *1522*
 12:19 which *voice* they that **h** intreated that *191*
Jas 5:11 Ye have **h** of the patience of Job, *191*
2Pe 1:18 this voice which came from heaven we **h**, *191*
1Jn 1: 1 we have **h**, which we have seen with *191*
 1: 3 we have seen and **h** declare we unto you, *191*
 1: 5 is the message which we have **h** of him, *191*
 2: 7 word which ye have **h** from the beginning. *191*
 2:18 and as ye have **h** that antichrist shall come, *191*
 2:24 which ye have **h** from the beginning. *191*
 2:24 If *that* which ye have **h** from the beginning *191*
 3:11 For this is the message that ye **h** from *191*
 3: 4 whereof you have **h** that it should come; *191*
2Jn 1: 6 That, as ye have **h** from the beginning, *191*
Rev 1:10 and **h** behind me a great voice, as of a *191*
 3: 3 therefore how thou hast received and **h**, *191*
 4: 1 the first voice which I **h** *was* as *it were* of a *191*
 5:11 I **h** the voice of many angels round about *191*
 5:13 **h** I saying, Blessing, and honour, and glory, *191*
 6: 1 and I **h**, as *it were* the noise of thunder, *191*
 6: 3 I **h** the second beast say, Come and see. *191*
 6: 5 I **h** the third beast say, Come and see. *191*
 6: 6 And I **h** a voice in the midst of the four *191*
 6: 7 I **h** the voice of the fourth beast say, Come *191*
 7: 4 and I **h** the number of them which were *191*
 8:13 **h** an angel flying through the midst of *191*
 9:13 I **h** a voice from the four horns of the *191*
 9:16 and I **h** the number of them. *191*
 10: 4 I **h** a voice from heaven saying unto me, *191*
 10: 8 the voice which I **h** from heaven spake *191*
 11:12 they **h** a great voice from heaven saying *191*
 12:10 And I **h** a loud voice saying in heaven, *191*
 14: 2 I **h** a voice from heaven, as the voice of *191*
 14: 2 I **h** the voice of harpers harping with their *191*
 14:13 And I **h** a voice from heaven saying unto *191*
 16: 1 And I **h** a great voice out of the temple *191*
 16: 5 I **h** the angel of the waters say, Thou art *191*
 16: 7 I **h** another out of the altar say, Even so, *191*
 18: 4 I **h** another voice from heaven, saying, *191*
 18:22 shall be **h** no more at all in thee; *191*
 18:22 sound of a millstone shall be **h** no more *191*
 18:23 the bride shall be **h** no more at all in thee: *191*
 19: 1 And after these *things* I **h** a great voice of *191*
 19: 6 And I **h** as *it were* the voice of a great *191*
 21: 3 And I **h** a great voice out of heaven saying, *191*
 22: 8 **h** *them*. And when I had heard and seen, *191*
 22: 8 heard *them*. And when I had and seen, *191*

HEARDEST (12) [HEAR]

Dt 4:36 thou **h** his words out of the midst of 8085
Jos 14:12 for thou **h** in that day how the Anakims 8085
2Ki 22:19 when thou **h** what I spake against this 8085
2Ch 34:27 when thou **h** his words against this place, 8085
Ne 9: 9 in Egypt, thou **h** their cry by the Red sea; 8085
 9:27 unto thee, thou **h** *them* from heaven; 8085
 9:28 unto thee, thou **h** *them* from heaven; 8085
Ps 31:22 nevertheless thou **h** the voice of my 8085
 119:26 I have declared my ways, and thou **h** me: 6030
Isa 48: 7 before the day when thou **h** them not; 8085
 48: 8 Yea, thou **h** not; yea, thou knewest not; 8085
Jnh 2: 2 belly of hell cried I, *and* thou **h** my voice. 8085

HEARER (2) [HEAR]

Jas 1:23 if any be a **h** of the word, and not a doer, *202*
 1:25 *therein*, he being not a forgetful **h**, *202*

HEARERS (4) [HEAR]

Ro 2:13 not the **h** of the law *are* just before God, *202*
Eph 4:29 that it may minister grace unto the **h**. *191*
2Ti 2:14 no profit, *but* to the subverting of the **h**. *191*
Jas 1:22 not **h** only, deceiving your own selves. *202*

HEAREST (11) [HEAR]

Ru 2: 8 unto Ruth, **H** thou not, my daughter? 8085
1Sa 24: 9 Wherefore **h** thou men's words, saying, 8085
2Sa 5:24 when thou **h** the sound of a going in 8085
1Ki 8:30 place: and when thou **h**, forgive. 8085
2Ch 6:21 from heaven; and when thou **h**, forgive. 8085
Ps 22: 2 I cry in the daytime, but thou **h** not; 6030
 65: 2 O thou that **h** prayer, unto thee shall all 8085
Mt 21:16 said unto him, **H** thou what these say? *191*
 27:13 **H** thou not how many *things* they witness *191*
Jn 3: 8 thou **h** the sound thereof, but canst not *191*
 11:42 And I knew that thou **h** me always: *191*

HEARETH (52) [HEAR]

Ex 16: 7 for that he **h** your murmurings against 8085
 16: 8 for that the LORD **h** your murmurings 8085
Nu 30: 5 father disallow her in the day that he **h**; 8085
Dt 29:19 pass, when he **h** the words of this curse, 8085
1Sa 3: 9 shalt say, Speak, LORD; for thy servant **h**. 8085
 3:10 answered, Speak; for thy servant **h**. 8085
 3:11 which both the ears of every one that **h** it 8085
2Sa 17: 9 first, that whosoever **h** *it* will say, 8085+8085
2Ki 21:12 and Judah, that whosoever **h** of it, 8085
Job 34:28 him, and he **h** the cry of the afflicted. 8085
Ps 34:17 the LORD **h**, and delivereth them out of 8085
 38:14 Thus I was as a man that **h** not, 8085
 69:33 For the LORD **h** the poor, and despiseth 8085
Pr 8:34 Blessed *is* the man that **h** me, watching 8085
 13: 1 A wise son **h** *his* father's instruction: NIH
 13: 1 but a scorner **h** not rebuke. 8085
 13: 8 *are* his riches: but the poor **h** not rebuke. 8085
 15:29 but he **h** the prayer of the righteous. 8085
 15:31 The ear that **h** the reproof of life abideth 8085
 15:32 he that **h** reproof getteth understanding. 8085
 18:13 He that answereth a matter before he **h** *it*, 8085
 21:28 but the man that **h**, speaketh constantly. 8085
 25:10 Lest he that **h** *it* put thee to shame, 8085
 29:24 he **h** cursing, and bewrayeth *it* not. 8085
Isa 41:26 yea, *there is* none that **h** your words. 8085
 42:20 opening the ears, but he **h** not. 8085
Jer 19: 3 the which whosoever **h**, his ears shall 8085
Eze 3:27 He that **h**, let him hear; and he that 8085
 33: 4 whosoever **h** the sound of 8085+8085
Mt 7:24 Therefore whosoever **h** these sayings of *191*
 7:26 every one that **h** these sayings of mine, *191*
 13:19 When any one **h** the word of the kingdom, *191*
 13:20 *places*, the same is he that **h** the word, *191*
 13:22 among the thorns is he that **h** the word; *191*
 13:23 the good ground is he that **h** the word, *191*
Lk 6:47 and **h** my sayings, and doeth them, *191*
 6:49 he that **h**, and doeth not, is like a man *191*
 10:16 He that **h** you heareth me; and he that *191*
 10:16 that heareth you **h** me; and he that *191*
Jn 3:29 standeth and **h** him, rejoiceth greatly *191*
 5:24 He that **h** my word, and believeth on him *191*
 8:47 He that is of God **h** God's words: *191*
 9:31 Now we know that God **h** not sinners: *191*
 9:31 of God, and doeth his will, him he **h**. *191*
 18:37 Every one that is of the truth **h** my voice. *191*
2Co 12: 6 he seeth me *to be*, or that he **h** of me. *191*
1Jn 4: 5 they of the world, and the world **h** them. *191*
 4: 6 he that knoweth God **h** us; *he* that is not *191*
 4: 6 heareth us; *he* that is not of God **h** not us. *191*
 5:14 ask *any thing* according to his will, he **h** us: *191*
Rev 22:17 And let him that **h** say, Come. And let him *191*
 22:18 I testify unto every *man* that **h** the words *191*

HEARING (39) [HEAR]

Dt 31:11 read this law before all Israel in their **h**. 241
2Sa 18:12 for in our **h** the king charged thee and 241
2Ki 4:31 but *there was* neither voice, nor **h**. 7182
Job 33: 8 Surely thou hast spoken in mine **h**, 241
 42: 5 I have heard of thee by the **h** of the ear: 8088
Pr 20:12 The **h** ear, and the seeing eye, the LORD 8085
 28: 9 He that turneth away his ear from **h** 8085
Ecc 1: 8 with seeing, nor the ear filled with **h**. 8085
Isa 11: 3 neither reprove after the **h** of his ears: 4926
 21: 3 I was bowed down at the **h** *of it*; I was 8085
 33:15 that stoppeth his ears from **h** of blood, 8085
Eze 9: 5 the others he said in mine **h**, Go ye after 241
 10:13 it was cried unto them in my **h**, O wheel. 241
Am 8:11 but of **h** the words of the LORD: 8085
Mt 13:13 and **h** they hear not, neither do they *191*
 13:14 **h** ye shall hear, and shall not understand; *180*
 13:15 and *their* ears are dull of **h**, and their eyes *191*
Mk 4:12 and **h** they may hear, and not understand; *191*
 6: 2 and many **h** *him* were astonished, saying, *191*
Lk 2:46 both **h** them, and asking them *questions*. *191*
 8:10 not see, and **h** they might not understand. *191*
 18:36 the multitude pass by, he asked what *191*
Ac 5: 5 And Ananias **h** these words fell down, *191*
 8: 6 **h** and seeing the miracles which he did. *191*
 9: 7 **h** a voice, but seeing no *man*. *191*
 18: 8 and many of the Corinthians **h** believed, *191*
 25:21 to be reserved unto the **h** of Augustus, 1233
 25:23 and were entered into the *place* of **h**, 201
 28:26 Ye shall hear, and shall not understand; 189
 28:27 and *their* ears are dull of **h**, and their eyes *191*
Ro 10:17 So then faith *cometh* by **h**, 189

Ro 10:17 by hearing, and **h** by the word of God. 189
1Co 12:17 body *were* an eye, where *were* the **h**? 189
 12:17 If the whole *were* **h**, where *were* 189
Gal 3: 2 the works of the law, or by the **h** of faith? 189
 3: 5 the works of the law, or by the **h** of faith? 189
Phm 1: 5 **H** of thy love and faith, which thou hast 191
Heb 5:11 hard to be uttered, seeing ye are dull of **h**. 189
2Pe 2: 8 dwelling among them, in seeing and **h**, 189

HEARKEN (153) [HEARKENED, HEARKENEDST, HEARKENETH, HEARKENING]

Ge 4:23 ye wives of Lamech, **h** unto my speech: 238
 21:12 hath said unto thee, **h** unto her voice; 8085
 23:15 lord, **h** unto me: the land *is worth* four 8085
 34:17 ye will not **h** unto us, to be circumcised; 8085
 49: 2 of Jacob; and **h** unto Israel your father. 8085
Ex 3:18 they shall **h** to thy voice: and thou shalt 8085
 4: 1 will not believe me, nor **h** unto my voice: 8085
 4: 8 neither **h** to the voice of the first sign, 8085
 4: 9 these two signs, neither **h** unto thy voice, 8085
 6:30 and how shall Pharaoh **h** unto me? 8085
 7: 4 Pharaoh shall not **h** unto you, that I may 8085
 7:22 hardened, neither did he **h** unto them; 8085
 11: 9 Moses, Pharaoh shall not **h** unto you; 8085
 15:26 thou wilt **diligently h** to the voice 8085+8085
 18:19 **H** now unto my voice, I will give thee 8085
Lev 26:14 if ye will not **h** unto me, and will not do 8085
 26:18 if ye will not yet for *all* this **h** unto me, 8085
 26:21 unto me, and will not **h** unto me; 8085
 26:27 And if ye will not for *all* this **h** unto me, 8085
Nu 23:18 and hear; **h** unto me, thou son of Zippor: 238
Dt 1:45 the Lord would not **h** to your voice, 8085
 4: 1 therefore **h**, O Israel, unto the statutes 8085
 7:12 if ye **h** to these judgments, and keep, 8085
 11:13 if you shall **diligently** unto my 8085+8085
 13: 3 Thou shalt not **h** unto the words of that 8085
 13: 8 not consent unto him, nor **h** unto him; 8085
 13:18 When thou shalt **h** to the voice of 8085
 15: 5 Only if thou **carefully h** unto 8085+8085
 17:12 will not **h** unto the priest that standeth to 8085
 18:15 like unto me; unto him ye shall **h**; 8085
 18:19 *that* whosoever will not **h** unto my words 8085
 21:18 chastened him, will not **h** unto them: 8085
 23: 5 Lord thy God would not **h** unto Balaam: 8085
 26:17 his judgments, and to **h** unto his voice: 8085
 27: 9 saying, Take heed, and **h**, O Israel; 8085
 28: 1 if thou shalt **h diligently** unto 8085+8085
 28: 2 if thou shalt **h** unto the voice of the Lord 8085
 28:13 if that thou **h** unto the commandments of 8085
 28:15 if thou wilt not **h** unto the voice of 8085
 30:10 If thou shalt **h** unto the voice of the Lord 8085
Jos 1:17 in all *things*, so will we **h** unto thee: 8085
 1:18 will not **h** unto thy words in all that thou 8085
 24:10 I would not **h** unto Balaam: therefore 8085
Jdg 2:17 yet they would not **h** unto their judges, 8085
 3: 4 to know whether they would **h unto** 8085
 9: 7 cried, and said unto them, **H** unto me, 8085
 9: 7 of Shechem, that God may **h** unto you. 8085
 11:17 the king of Edom would not **h** *thereto.* 8085
 19:25 the men would not **h** to him: so the man 8085
 20:13 the children of Benjamin would not **h** to 8085
1Sa 8: 7 **H** unto the voice of the people in all that 8085
 8: 9 Now therefore **h** unto their voice: 8085
 8:22 **h** unto their voice, and make them a 8085
 15: 1 **h** thou unto the voice of the words of 8085
 15:22 sacrifice, *and* to **h** than the fat of rams. 7181
 28:22 **h** thou also unto the voice of thine 8085
 30:24 For who will **h** unto you in this matter? 8085
2Sa 12:18 and he would not **h** unto our voice: 8085
 13:14 Howbeit he would not **h** unto her voice: 8085
 13:16 unto me. But he would not **h** unto her. 8085
1Ki 8:28 to **h** unto the cry and to the prayer, 8085
 8:29 that *thou* mayest **h** unto the prayer which 8085
 8:30 **h** thou to the supplication of thy servant, 8085
 8:52 to **h** unto them in all that they call for 8085
 11:38 if thou wilt **h** unto all that I command 8085
 20: 8 unto him, **H** not *unto him*, nor consent. 8085
 22:28 he said, **H**, O people, every one of you. 8085
2Ki 10: 6 *be* mine, and *if* ye will **h** unto my voice, 8085
 17:40 they did not **h**, but they did after 8085
 18:31 **H** not to Hezekiah: for thus saith the king 8085
 18:32 **h** not unto Hezekiah, when he 8085
2Ch 6:19 **h** unto the cry and the prayer which 8085
 6:20 to **h** unto the prayer which thy servant 8085
 6:21 **H** therefore unto the supplications of thy 8085
 10:16 that the king would not **h** unto them, 8085
 18:27 by me. And he said, **H**, all ye people. 8085
 20:15 **H** ye, all Judah, and ye inhabitants of 7181
 33:10 to his people: but they would not **h**. 7181
Ne 13:27 then **h** unto you to do all this great evil, 8085
Job 13: 6 and **h** to the pleadings of my lips. 8085
 32:10 I said, **H** to me; I also will shew 8085
 33: 1 hear my speeches, and **h** to all my words. 238
 33:31 Mark well, O Job, **h** unto me: hold thy 8085
 33:33 If not, **h** unto me: hold thy peace, 8085
 34:10 Therefore **h** unto me, ye men of 8085
 34:16 hear this: **h** to the voice of my words. 238
 34:34 tell me, and let a wise man **h** unto me. 8085
 37:14 **H** unto this, O Job: stand still, 238
Ps 5: 2 **H** unto the voice of my cry, my King, 7181
 34:11 ye children, **h** unto me: I will teach 8085
 45:10 **H**, O daughter, and consider, 8085
 58: 5 will not **h** to the voice of charmers, 8085
 81: 8 thee: O Israel, if thou wilt **h** unto me; 8085
 81:11 my people would not **h** to my voice; 8085

Pr 7:24 **H** unto me now therefore, O ye children, 8085
 8:32 Now therefore **h** unto me, O ye children: 8085
 23:22 **H** unto thy father that begat thee, 8085
 29:12 If a ruler **h** to lies, all his servants *are* 7181
SS 8:13 gardens, the companions **h** to thy voice: 7181
Isa 28:23 hear my voice, **h**, and hear my speech. 7181
 32: 3 and the ears of them that hear shall **h**. 7181
 34: 1 ye nations, to hear; and **h**, ye people: 7181
 36:16 **H** not to Hezekiah: for thus saith the king 8085
 42:23 will **h** and hear for the time to come? 7181
 46: 3 **H** unto me, O house of Jacob, and all 8085
 46:12 **H** unto me, ye stouthearted, that *are* far 8085
 48:12 **H** unto me, O Jacob, and Israel my called; 8085
 49: 1 unto me; and **h**, ye people, from afar; 7181
 51: 1 **H** to me, ye that follow after 8085
 51: 4 **H** unto me, my people; and give ear unto 7181
 51: 7 **H** unto me, ye that know righteousness, 8085
 55: 2 **h diligently** unto me, and eat ye 8085+8085
Jer 6:10 ear *is* uncircumcised, and they cannot **h**: 7181
 6:17 *saying,* **H** to the sound of the trumpet. 7181
 6:17 trumpet. But they said, We will not **h**. 7181
 6:27 unto them; but they will not **h** to thee: 8085
 11:11 shall cry unto me, I will not **h** unto them. 8085
 16:12 evil heart, that *they* may not **h** unto me: 8085
 17:24 if ye **diligently h** unto me, saith 8085+8085
 17:27 if you will not **h** unto me to hallow 8085
 18:19 to the voice of them that contend with 8085
 23:16 **H** not unto the words of the prophets 8085
 26: 3 If so be they will **h**, and turn every man 8085
 26: 4 If ye will not **h** to me, to walk in my law, 8085
 26: 5 To **h** to the words of my servants 8085
 27: 9 Therefore **h** not ye to your prophets, nor 8085
 27:14 Therefore **h** not unto the words of 8085
 27:16 **h** not to the words of your prophets that 8085
 27:17 **H** not unto them; serve the king of 8085
 28: 7 neither **h** to your dreams which ye cause 8085
 29:12 and pray unto me, and I will **h** unto you. 8085
 35:13 Will ye not receive instruction to **h** to my 8085
 37: 2 did **h** unto the words of the Lord, 8085
 38:15 thee counsel, wilt thou not **h** unto me? 8085
 44:16 of the Lord, we will not **h** unto thee. 8085
Eze 3: 7 the house of Israel will not **h** unto thee: 8085
 3: 7 unto thee; for they will not **h** unto me: 8085
 20: 8 against me, and would not **h** unto me: 8085
 20:39 hereafter *also*, if ye will not **h** unto me: 8085
Da 9:19 hear; O Lord, forgive; O Lord, **h** and do; 7181
Hos 5: 1 **h**, ye house of Israel; and give ye ear, 7181
 9:17 because they did not **h** unto him: 8085
Mic 1: 2 people; **h**, O earth, and all that therein is: 7181
Zec 1: 4 they did not hear, nor **h** unto me, saith 7181
 7:11 they refused to **h**, and pulled away 7181
Mk 4: 3 **H**; Behold, there went out a sower to sow: 191
 7:14 **H** unto me every one of you, 191
Ac 2:14 this known unto you, and **h** to my words: 1801
 4:19 it be right in the sight of God to **h** 191
 7: 2 he said, Men, brethren, and fathers, **h**; 191
 12:13 a damsel came to **h**, named Rhoda. 5219
 15:13 saying, Men *and* brethren, **h** unto me: 191
Jas 2: 5 **H**, my beloved brethren, Hath not God 191

HEARKENED (81) [HEARKEN]

Ge 3:17 Because thou hast **h** unto the voice of 8085
 16: 2 And Abram **h** to the voice of Sarai. 8085
 23:16 Abraham **h** unto Ephron; 8085
 30:17 God **h** unto Leah, and she conceived, 8085
 30:22 God **h** to her, and opened her womb. 8085
 34:24 Shechem his son **h** all that went out of 8085
 39:10 that he **h** not unto her, to lie by her, 8085
Ex 6: 9 **h** not unto Moses for anguish of spirit, 8085
 6:12 the children of Israel have not **h** unto me; 8085
 7:13 Pharaoh's heart, that he **h** not unto them; 8085
 8:15 hardened his heart, and **h** not unto them; 8085
 8:19 was hardened, and he **h** not unto them; 8085
 9:12 of Pharaoh, and he **h** not unto them; 8085
 16:20 Notwithstanding they **h** not unto Moses; 8085
 18:24 So Moses **h** to the voice of his father in 8085
Nu 14:22 ten times, and have not **h** to my voice; 8085
 21: 3 the Lord **h** to the voice of Israel, 8085
Dt 9:19 But the Lord **h** unto me at that time also. 8085
 9:23 ye believed him not, nor **h** to his voice. 8085
 10:10 and the Lord **h** unto me at that time also, 8085
 18:14 **h** unto observers of times, 8085
 26:14 I have **h** to the voice of the Lord my 8085
 34: 9 the children of Israel **h** unto him, and did 8085
Jos 1:17 According as we **h** unto Moses in all 8085
 10:14 that the Lord **h** unto the voice of a man: 8085
Jdg 2:20 fathers, and have not **h** unto my voice; 8085
 11:28 **h** not unto the words of Jephthah which 8085
 13: 9 God **h** to the voice of Manoah; 8085
1Sa 2:25 Notwithstanding they **h** not unto the 8085
 12: 1 I have **h** unto your voice in all that ye 8085
 19: 6 Saul **h** unto the voice of Jonathan: 8085
 25:35 I have **h** to thy voice, and have accepted 8085
 28:21 have **h** unto thy words which thou 8085
 28:23 him; and he **h** unto their voice. 8085
1Ki 12:15 the king **h** not unto the people; 8085
 12:16 when all Israel saw that the king **h** not 8085
 12:24 They **h** therefore to the word of 8085
 15:20 So Ben-hadad **h** unto king Asa, and sent 8085
 20:25 And he **h** unto their voice, and did so. 8085
2Ki 13: 4 the Lord, and the Lord **h** unto him: 8085
 16: 9 king of Assyria **h** unto him: for the king 8085
 20:13 Hezekiah **h** unto them, and shewed them 8085
 21: 9 they **h** not: and Manasseh seduced them 8085
 22:13 our fathers have not **h** unto the words of 8085

2Ch 10:15 So the king **h** not unto the people: 8085
 16: 4 Ben-hadad **h** unto king Asa, and sent 8085
 24:17 to the king. Then the king **h** unto them. 8085
 25:16 this, and hast not **h** unto my counsel. 8085
 30:20 the Lord **h** to Hezekiah, and healed 8085
 35:22 **h** not unto the words of Necho from 8085
Ne 9:16 and **h** not to thy commandments, 8085
 9:29 **h** not unto thy commandments, 8085
 9:34 nor **h** unto thy commandments and thy 7181
Est 3: 4 **h** not unto them, that they told Haman, 8085
Job 9:16 would I not believe that he had **h** unto 238
Ps 81:13 O that my people had **h** unto me, 8085
 106:25 *and* **h** not unto the voice of the Lord. 8085
Isa 21: 7 he **h diligently** *with* much heed: 7181+7182
 48:18 that thou hadst **h** to my commandments! 7181
Jer 6:19 because they have not **h** unto my words, 7181
 7:24 they **h** not, nor inclined their ear, 8085
 7:26 Yet they **h** not unto me, nor inclined their 8085
 8: 6 I **h** and heard, *but* they spake not aright: 7181
 25: 3 and speaking; but ye have not **h**. 8085
 25: 4 and sending *them*; but ye have not **h**, 8085
 25: 7 Yet ye have not **h** unto me, saith 8085
 26: 5 and sending *them*, but ye have not **h**; 8085
 29:19 Because they have not **h** to my words, 8085
 32:33 teaching *them*, yet they have not **h** to 8085
 34:14 fathers **h** not unto me, neither inclined 8085
 34:17 Ye have not **h** unto me, in proclaiming 8085
 35:14 and speaking; but ye **h** not unto me. 8085
 35:15 not inclined your ear, nor **h** unto me. 8085
 35:16 but this people hath not **h** unto me: 8085
 36:31 pronounced against them; but they **h** not. 8085
 37:14 he **h** not to him: so Irijah took Jeremiah, 8085
 44: 5 they **h** not, nor inclined their ear to turn 8085
Eze 3: 6 to them, they would have **h** unto thee. 8085
Da 9: 6 Neither have we **h** unto thy servants 8085
Mal 3:16 the Lord **h**, and heard *it*, and a book of 7181
Ac 27:21 ye should have **h** unto me, and not have 3980

HEARKENEDST (1) [HEARKEN]

Dt 28:45 unto the voice of the Lord thy 8085

HEARKENETH (2) [HEARKEN]

Pr 1:33 whoso **h** unto me shall dwell safely, 8085
 12:15 but he that **h** unto counsel *is* wise. 8085

HEARKENING (1) [HEARKEN]

Ps 103:20 **h** unto the voice of his word. 8085

HEART (830) [BROKEN-HEARTED, FAINTHEARTED, HARDHEARTED, HEART'S, HEARTED, HEARTS, MERRYHEARTED, STOUTHEARTED, TENDERHEARTED]

Ge 6: 5 thoughts of his **h** *was* only evil 3820
 6: 6 on the earth, and it grieved him at his **h**. 3820
 8:21 the Lord said in his **h**, I will not again 3820
 8:21 the imagination of man's **h** *is* evil from 3820
 17:17 his face, and laughed, and said in his **h**, 3820
 20: 5 in the integrity of my **h** and innocency of 3824
 20: 6 thou didst this in the integrity of thy **h**; 3824
 24:45 before I had done speaking in mine **h**, 3820
 27:41 Esau said in his **h**, The days of mourning 3820
 42:28 their **h** failed *them*, and they were afraid, 3820
 45:26 **h** fainted, for he believed them not. 3820
Ex 4:14 he seeth thee, he will be glad in his **h**. 3820
 4:21 I will harden his **h**, that he shall not let 3820
 7: 3 I will harden Pharaoh's **h**, and multiply 3820
 7:13 hardened Pharaoh's **h**, that he hearkened 3820
 7:14 Pharaoh's **h** *is* hardened, he refuseth to 3820
 7:22 Pharaoh's **h** was hardened, neither did 3820
 7:23 neither did he set his **h** to this also. 3820
 8:15 he hardened his **h**, and hearkened not 3820
 8:19 Pharaoh's **h** was hardened, 3820
 8:32 Pharaoh hardened his **h** at this time also, 3820
 9: 7 the **h** of Pharaoh was hardened, and he 3820
 9:12 the Lord hardened the **h** of Pharaoh, 3820
 9:14 time send all my plagues upon thine **h**, 3820
 9:34 and hardened his **h**, he and his servants. 3820
 9:35 the **h** of Pharaoh was hardened, 3820
 10: 1 for I have hardened his **h**, and the heart 3820
 10: 1 his heart, and the **h** of his servants, 3820
 10:20 the Lord hardened Pharaoh's **h**, 3820
 10:27 the Lord hardened Pharaoh's **h**, 3820
 11:10 the Lord hardened Pharaoh's **h**, 3820
 14: 4 I will harden Pharaoh's **h**, that he shall 3820
 14: 5 the **h** of Pharaoh and of his servants was 3824
 14: 8 the Lord hardened the **h** of Pharaoh king 3820
 15: 8 the depths were congealed in the **h** of 3820
 23: 9 for ye know the **h** of a stranger, seeing ye 5315
 25: 2 with his **h** ye shall take my offering. 3820
 28:29 the breastplate of judgment upon his **h**, 3820
 28:30 they shall be upon Aaron's **h**, when he 3820
 28:30 upon his **h** before the Lord continually. 3820
 35: 5 whosoever *is* of a willing **h**, let him bring 3820
 35:21 every one whose **h** stirred him up, 3820
 35:26 all the women whose **h** stirred them up 3820
 35:29 whose **h** made them willing to bring for 3820
 35:34 he hath put in his **h** that *he* may teach, 3820
 35:35 Them hath he filled *with* wisdom of **h**, 3820
 36: 2 every one whose **h** the Lord had put wisdom, 3820
 36: 2 *even* every one whose **h** stirred him up to 3820
Lev 19:17 shalt not hate thy brother in thine **h**: 3824
 26:16 consume the eyes, and cause sorrow of **h**: 5315
Nu 15:39 that ye seek not after your own **h** and 3824
 32: 7 wherefore discourage ye the **h** of 3820
 32: 9 they discouraged the **h** of the children of 3820

H

H

Dt
1:28 our brethren have discouraged our **h,** 3824
2:30 made his **h** obstinate, that he might 3824
4: 9 lest they depart from thy **h** all the days of 3824
4:29 find *him,* if thou seek him with all thy **h** 3824
4:39 *this* day, and consider *it* in thine **h.** 3824
5:29 O that there were such a **h** in them, 3824
6: 5 love the LORD thy God with all thine **h,** 3824
6: 6 thee *this* day, shall be in thine **h:** 3824
7:17 If thou shalt say in thine **h,** These nations 3824
8: 2 prove thee, to know what *was* in thine **h,** 3824
8: 5 Thou shalt also consider in thine **h,** that, 3824
8:14 thine **h** be lifted up, and thou forget 3824
8:17 thou say in thine **h,** My power and 3824
9: 4 Speak not thou in thine **h,** after that 3824
9: 5 or for the uprightness of thine **h,** 3824
10:12 to serve the LORD thy God with all thy **h** 3824
10:16 therefore the foreskin of your **h,** 3824
11:13 to serve him with all your **h** and with all 3824
11:16 that your **h** be not deceived, and ye turn 3824
11:18 shall ye lay up these my words in your **h** 3824
13: 3 love the LORD your God with all your **h** 3824
15: 7 shalt not harden thy **h,** nor shut thine 3824
15: 9 there be not a thought in thy wicked **h,** 3824
15:10 thine **h** shall not be grieved when thou 3824
17:17 to himself, that his **h** turn not away: 3824
17:20 That his **h** be not lifted up above his 3824
18:21 thou say in thine **h,** How shall we know 3824
19: 6 while his **h** is hot, and overtake him, 3824
20: 8 lest his brethren's **h** faint as well as his 3824
20: 8 his brethren's heart faint as well as his **h.** 3824
24:15 for he *is* poor, and setteth his **h** upon it: 5315
26:16 keep and do them with all thine **h,** 3824
28:28 and blindness, and astonishment of **h:** 3824
28:47 with gladness of **h,** for the abundance of 3824
28:65 LORD shall give thee there a trembling **h,** 3824
28:67 the fear of thine **h** where*with* thou shalt 3824
29: 4 Yet the LORD hath not given you a **h** to 3820
29:18 whose **h** turneth away *this* day from 3824
29:19 he bless himself in his **h,** saying, I shall 3824
29:19 I walk in the imagination of mine **h,** 3824
30: 2 with all thine **h,** and with all thy soul; 3824
30: 6 LORD thy God will circumcise thine **h,** 3824
30: 6 the **h** of thy seed, to love the LORD thy 3824
30: 6 love the LORD thy God with all thine **h,** 3824
30:10 unto the LORD thy God with all thine **h,** 3824
30:14 mouth, and in thy **h,** that *thou* mayest 3824
30:17 if thine **h** turn away, so that thou wilt not 3824

Jos
5: 1 we were passed over, that their **h** melted, 3824
14: 7 him word again as *it was* in mine **h.** 3824
14: 8 with me made the **h** of the people melt: 3820
22: 5 to serve him with all your **h** and with all 3824
24:23 incline your **h** unto the LORD God of 3824

Jdg
5: 9 My **h** *is* toward the governors of Israel, 3820
5:15 of Reuben *there were* great thoughts of **h.** 3820
5:16 Reuben *there were* great searchings of **h.** 3820
16:15 I love thee, when thine **h** is not with me? 3820
16:17 he told her all his **h,** and said unto her, 3820
16:18 Delilah saw that he had told her all his **h,** 3820
16:18 once, for he hath shewed me all his **h.** 3820
18:20 the priest's **h** was glad, and he took 3820
19: 5 Comfort thine **h** *with* a morsel of bread, 3820
19: 6 tarry all night, and let thine **h** be merry. 3820
19: 8 father said, Comfort thine **h,** I pray thee. 3824
19: 9 lodge here, that thine **h** may be merry: 3824

Ru
3: 7 eaten and drunk, and his **h** was merry, 3820

1Sa
1: 8 why is thy **h** grieved? *am* not I better to 3824
1:13 Hannah, she spake in her **h;** only her 3820
2: 1 and said, My **h** rejoiceth in the LORD, 3820
2:33 thine eyes, and to grieve thine **h:** 5315
2:35 do according to *that* which *is* in my **h** 3824
4:13 for his **h** trembled for the ark of God. 3820
9:19 and will tell thee all that *is* in thine **h.** 3824
10: 9 from Samuel, God gave him another **h:** 3820
12:20 but serve the LORD with all your **h;** 3824
12:24 and serve him in truth with all your **h:** 3824
13:14 hath sought him a man after his own **h,** 3824
14: 7 said unto him, Do all that *is* in thine **h:** 3824
14: 7 I *am* with thee according to thy **h.** 3824
16: 7 but the LORD looketh on the **h.** 3824
17:28 pride, and the naughtiness of thine **h;** 3824
17:32 Saul, Let no man's **h** fail because of him; 3820
21:12 David laid up these words in his **h,** 3824
24: 5 David's **h** smote him, because he had 3820
25:31 unto thee, nor offence of **h** unto my lord, 3820
25:36 Nabal's **h** *was* merry within him, for he 3820
25:37 that his **h** died within him, and he 3820
27: 1 David said in his **h,** I shall now perish 3820
28: 5 he was afraid, and his **h** greatly trembled. 3820

2Sa
3:21 thou mayest reign over all that thine **h** 5315
6:16 the LORD; and she despised him in her **h.** 3820
7: 3 to the king, Go, do all that *is* in thine **h;** 3824
7:21 sake, and according to thine own **h,** 3820
7:27 hath thy servant found in his **h** to pray 3820
13:28 Mark ye now when Amnon's **h** is merry 3820
13:33 my lord the king take the thing to his **h,** 3820
14: 1 that the king's **h** *was* toward Absalom. 3820
17:10 whose **h** *is* as the heart of a lion, 3820
17:10 whose heart *is* as the **h** of a lion, 3820
18:14 thrust them through the **h** of Absalom, 3820
19:14 he bowed the **h** of all the men of Judah, 3824
19:14 men of Judah, *even* as the **h** of one man; NIH
19:19 that the king should take *it* to his **h.** 3820
24:10 David's **h** smote him after that he had 3820

1Ki
2: 4 walk before me in truth with all their **h** 3824
2:44 the wickedness which thine **h** is privy to, 3824

1Ki
3: 6 and in uprightness of **h** with thee; 3824
3: 9 servant an understanding **h** to judge thy 3820
3:12 thee a wise and an understanding **h;** 3820
4:29 exceeding much, and largeness of **h,** 3820
8:17 it was in the **h** of David my father to build 3824
8:18 Whereas it was in thine **h** to build a house 3824
8:18 thou didst well that it was in thine **h.** 3824
8:23 that walk before thee with all their **h:** 3820
8:38 know every man the plague of his own **h,** 3824
8:39 to his ways, whose **h** thou knowest; 3824
8:48 And so return unto thee with all their **h,** 3824
8:61 Let your **h** therefore be perfect with 3824
8:66 glad of **h** for all the goodness that 3820
9: 3 and mine **h** shall be there perpetually. 3820
9: 4 in integrity of **h,** and in uprightness, 3824
10: 2 with him of all that was in her **h.** 3824
10:24 his wisdom, which God had put in his **h.** 3820
11: 2 *for* surely they will turn away your **h** after 3824
11: 3 and his wives turned away his **h.** 3820
11: 4 his wives turned away his **h** after other 3824
11: 4 his **h** was not perfect with the LORD his 3824
11: 4 his God, as *was* the **h** of David his father. 3824
11: 9 his **h** was turned from the LORD God of 3824
12:26 Jeroboam said in his **h,** Now shall 3820
12:27 shall the **h** of this people turn again unto 3820
12:33 which he had devised of his own **h;** 3820
14: 8 and who followed me with all his **h,** 3824
15: 3 his **h** was not perfect with the LORD his 3824
15: 3 his God, as the **h** of David his father. 3824
15:14 nevertheless Asa's **h** was perfect with 3824
18:37 that *thou* hast turned their **h** back again. 3820
21: 7 *and* eat bread, and let thine **h** be merry: 3820

2Ki
5:26 Went not mine **h** *with thee,* when the 3820
6:11 Therefore the **h** of the king of Syria was 3820
9:24 the arrow went out at his **h,** and he sunk 3820
10:15 and said to him, Is thine **h** right, 3824
10:15 heart right, as my **h** *is* with thy heart? 3824
10:15 heart right, as my heart *is* with thy **h?** 3824
10:30 Ahab according to all that *was* in mine **h,** 3824
10:31 of the LORD God of Israel with all his **h:** 3824
12: 4 the money that cometh into any man's **h** 3820
14:10 and thine **h** hath lifted thee up: 3820
20: 3 before thee in truth and with a perfect **h,** 3824
22:19 Because thine **h** was tender, and thou 3824
23: 3 his statutes with all *their* **h** and all *their* 3820
23:25 that turned to the LORD with all his **h,** 3824

1Ch
12:17 to help me, mine **h** shall be knit unto you: 3824
12:33 *were* not of **double h.** 3820+3820+2050.1
12:38 came with a perfect **h** to Hebron, 3824
12:38 all the rest also of Israel *were of* one **h** to 3824
15:29 playing: and she despised him in her **h.** 3820
16:10 let the **h** of them rejoice that seek 3820
17: 2 said unto David, Do all that *is* in thine **h;** 3824
17:19 and according to thine own **h,** 3820
17:25 thy servant hath found in his **h** to pray NIH
22:19 Now set your **h** and your soul to seek 3824
28: 2 *for* me, I *had* in mine **h** to build a house 3824
28: 9 serve him with a perfect **h** and with a 3824
29: 9 with perfect **h** they offered willingly to 3824
29:17 that thou triest the **h,** and hast pleasure 3824
29:17 in the uprightness of mine **h** I have 3824
29:18 of the thoughts of the **h** of thy people, 3824
29:18 thy people, and prepare their **h** unto thee: 3824
29:19 give unto Solomon my son a perfect **h,** 3824

2Ch
1:11 Because this was in thine **h,** and thou 3824
6: 7 Now it was in the **h** of David my father 3824
6: 8 Forasmuch as it was in thine **h** to build a 3824
6: 8 thou didst well *in* that it was in thine **h.** 3824
6:30 unto all his ways, whose **h** thou knowest; 3824
6:38 If they return to thee with all their **h** and 3824
7:10 merry in **h** for the goodness that 3820
7:11 all that came into Solomon's **h** to make in 3820
7:16 and mine **h** shall be there perpetually. 3820
9: 1 with him of all that was in her **h.** 3824
9:23 his wisdom, that God had put in his **h.** 3824
12:14 he prepared not his **h** to seek the LORD. 3820
15:12 LORD God of their fathers with all their **h** 3824
15:15 for they had sworn with all their **h,** 3824
15:17 nevertheless the **h** of Asa was perfect all 3824
16: 9 of *them* whose **h** *is* perfect towards him. 3824
17: 6 his **h** was lift up in the ways of the LORD: 3820
19: 3 and hast prepared thine **h** to seek God. 3824
19: 9 faithfully, and with a perfect **h.** 3824
22: 9 who sought the LORD with all his **h.** 3824
25: 2 of the LORD, but not with a perfect **h.** 3824
25:19 and thine **h** lifteth thee up to boast: 3820
26:16 his **h** was lifted up to *his* destruction: 3820
29:10 Now *it is* in mine **h** to make a covenant 3824
29:31 many as were of a free **h** burnt offerings. 3820
29:34 for the Levites *were* more upright in **h** to 3824
30:12 **h** to do the commandment of the king 3820
30:19 *That* prepareth his **h** to seek God, 3820
31:21 he did *it* with all his **h,** and prospered. 3824
32:25 done unto him; for his **h** was lifted up: 3820
32:26 humbled himself for the pride of his **h,** 3820
32:31 that he might know all *that was* in his **h.** 3824
34:27 Because thine **h** was tender, and thou 3824
34:31 with all his **h,** and with all his soul, 3820
36:13 hardened his **h** from turning unto 3820

Ezr
6:22 turned the **h** of the king of Assyria unto 3820
7:10 Ezra had prepared his **h** to seek the law 3824
7:27 put *such* a thing as this in the king's **h,** 3820

Ne
2: 2 this *nothing* else but sorrow of **h.** 3820
2:12 God had put in my **h** to do at Jerusalem: 3820
6: 8 thou feignest them out of thine own **h.** 3820

Ne
7: 5 God put into mine **h** to gather together 3820
9: 8 And foundest his **h** faithful before thee, 3824

Est
1:10 when the **h** of the king was merry with 3820
5: 9 forth that day joyful and with a glad **h:** 3820
6: 6 Now Haman thought in his **h,** To whom 3820
7: 5 that durst presume in his **h** to do so? 3820

Job
7:17 thou shouldest set thine **h** upon him? 3820
8:10 tell thee, and utter words out of their **h?** 3820
9: 4 *He is* wise in **h,** and mighty in strength: 3824
10:13 these *things* hast thou hid in thine **h:** 3824
11:13 If thou prepare thine **h,** and stretch out 3820
12:24 He taketh away the **h** of the chief of 3820
15:12 Why doth thine **h** carry thee away? 3820
17: 4 For thou hast hid their **h** from 3820
17:11 broken off, *even* the thoughts of my **h.** 3824
22:22 mouth, and lay up his words in thine **h.** 3820
23:16 For God maketh my **h** soft, 3820
27: 6 my **h** shall not reproach *me* so long as I 3824
29:13 I caused the widow's **h** to sing for joy. 3820
31: 7 mine **h** walked after mine eyes, and *if* 3820
31: 9 mine **h** have been deceived by a woman, 3820
31:27 my **h** hath been secretly enticed, 3820
33: 3 *shall be of* the uprightness of my **h:** 3820
34:14 If he set his **h** upon *man, if* he gather 3820
36:13 the hypocrites in **h** heap up wrath: 3820
37: 1 At this also my **h** trembleth, and is moved 3820
37:24 he respecteth not any *that are* wise of **h?** 3820
38:36 who hath given understanding to the **h?** 7907
41:24 His **h** is as firm as a stone; yea, as hard as 3820

Ps
4: 4 commune with your own **h** upon your 3824
4: 7 Thou hast put gladness in my **h,** more 3820
7:10 *is* of God, which saveth the upright in **h.** 3820
9: 1 praise *thee,* O LORD, with my whole **h;** 3820
10: 6 hath said in his **h,** I shall not be moved: 3820
10:11 hath said in his **h,** God hath forgotten: 3820
10:13 hath said in his **h,** Thou wilt not require 3820
10:17 thou wilt prepare their **h,** thou wilt cause 3820
11: 2 *they* may privily shoot at the upright in **h.** 3820
12: 2 a **double h** do they speak. 3820+3820+2050.1
13: 2 in my soul, *having* sorrow in my **h** daily? 3824
13: 5 my **h** shall rejoice in thy salvation. 3820
14: 1 The fool hath said in his **h,** *There is no* 3820
14: 1 and speaketh the truth in his **h.** 3824
16: 9 Therefore my **h** is glad, and my glory 3820
17: 3 hast proved mine **h;** thou hast visited 3820
19: 8 of the LORD *are* right, rejoicing the **h:** 3820
19:14 the meditation of my **h,** be acceptable in 3820
20: 4 Grant thee according to thine own **h,** 3824
22:14 my **h** is like wax; it is melted in the midst 3820
22:26 that seek him: your **h** shall live for ever. 3824
24: 4 He that hath clean hands, and a pure **h;** 3824
25:17 The troubles of my **h** are enlarged: 3824
26: 2 and prove me; try my reins and my **h.** 3820
27: 3 encamp against me, my **h** shall not fear: 3820
27: 8 my **h** said unto thee, Thy face, LORD, 3820
27:14 and he shall strengthen thine **h:** 3820
28: 7 my **h** trusted in him, and I am helped: 3820
28: 7 therefore my **h** greatly rejoiceth; 3820
31:24 and he shall strengthen your **h,** 3824
32:11 shout for joy, all *ye that are* upright in **h.** 3820
33:11 the thoughts of his **h** to all generations. 3820
33:21 For our **h** shall rejoice in him, because 3820
34:18 *is* nigh unto them that are of a broken **h;** 3820
36: 1 of the wicked saith within my **h,** 3820
36:10 and thy righteousness to the upright in **h.** 3820
37: 4 he shall give thee the desires of thine **h.** 3820
37:15 Their sword shall enter into their own **h,** 3820
37:31 The law of his God *is* in his **h;** none of his 3820
38: 8 by reason of the disquietness of my **h.** 3820
38:10 My **h** panteth, my strength faileth me: 3820
39: 3 My **h** was hot within me, while I was 3820
40: 8 O my God: yea, thy law *is* within my **h.** 4578
40:10 not hid thy righteousness within my **h;** 3820
40:12 of mine head: therefore my **h** faileth me. 3820
41: 6 his **h** gathereth iniquity to itself; *when* he 3820
44:18 Our **h** is not turned back, neither have 3820
44:21 for he knoweth the secrets of the **h.** 3820
45: 1 My **h** is inditing a good matter: I speak of 3820
45: 5 Thine arrows *are* sharp in the **h** of 3820
49: 3 the meditation of my **h** *shall be of* 3820
51:10 Create in me a clean **h,** O God; 3820
51:17 a broken and a contrite **h,** O God, thou 3820
53: 1 The fool hath said in his **h,** *There is no* 3820
55: 4 My **h** is sore pained within me: 3820
55:21 than butter, but war *was* in his **h:** 3820
57: 7 My **h** is fixed, O God, my heart is fixed: 3820
57: 7 My heart is fixed, O God, my **h** is fixed: 3820
58: 2 in **h** you work wickedness; you weigh 3820
61: 2 unto thee, when my **h** is overwhelmed: 3820
62: 8 ye people, pour out your **h** before him: 3824
62:10 riches increase, set not *your* **h** *upon them.* 3820
64: 6 *thought* of every one *of them,* and the **h,** 3820
64:10 him; and all the upright in **h** shall glory. 3820
66:18 If I regard iniquity in my **h,** the Lord will 3820
69:20 Reproach hath broken my **h;** and I am full 3820
69:32 and your **h** shall live that seek God. 3824
73: 1 to Israel, *even* to such as are of a clean **h.** 3824
73: 7 they have more than **h** could wish. 3824
73:13 Verily I have cleansed my **h** in vain, 3824
73:21 Thus my **h** was grieved, and I was pricked 3824
73:26 My flesh and my **h** faileth: *but* God *is* 3824
73:26 *but* God *is* the strength of my **h,** 3824
77: 6 I commune with mine own **h:** and my 3824
78: 8 a generation *that* set not their **h** aright, 3824
78:18 tempted God in their **h** by asking meat 3824

H

Ps 78:37 For their **h** was not right with him, 3820
78:72 them according to the integrity of his **h**; 3824
84: 2 **h** and my flesh crieth out for the living 3824
84: 5 thee; in whose **h** *are* the ways of them, 3824
86:11 in thy truth: unite my **h** to fear thy name. 3824
86:12 O Lord my God, with all my **h**: 3824
94:15 and all the upright in **h** shall follow it. 3820
95: 8 Harden not your **h**, as *in* the provocation, 3824
95:10 It *is* a people that do err in *their* **h**, 3824
97:11 and gladness for the upright in **h**. 3820
101: 2 walk within my house with a perfect **h**. 3824
101: 4 A froward **h** shall depart from me: I will 3824
101: 5 high look and a proud **h** will not I suffer. 3824
102: 4 My **h** is smitten, and withered like grass; 3820
104:15 wine *that* maketh glad the **h** of man, 3824
104:15 and bread *which* strengtheneth man's **h**. 3824
105: 3 let the **h** of them rejoice that seek 3820
105:25 He turned their **h** to hate his people, 3820
107:12 Therefore he brought down their **h** with 3820
108: 1 O God, my **h** is fixed; I will sing and 3820
109:16 that *he* might even slay the broken in **h**. 3824
109:22 needy, and my **h** is wounded within me. 3820
111: 1 I will praise the Lord with *my* whole **h**, 3824
112: 7 his **h** is fixed, trusting in the Lord. 3820
112: 8 His **h** *is* established, he shall not be afraid, 3820
119: 2 *and that* seek him with the whole **h**. 3820
119: 7 I will praise thee with uprightness of **h**, 3824
119:10 With my whole **h** have I sought thee: 3820
119:11 Thy word have I hid in mine **h**, that I 3820
119:32 when thou shalt enlarge my **h**. 3820
119:34 yea, I shall observe it with *my* whole **h**. 3820
119:36 Incline my **h** unto thy testimonies, 3820
119:58 I intreated thy favour with *my* whole **h**: 3820
119:69 will keep thy precepts with *my* whole **h**. 3820
119:70 Their **h** is as fat as grease; *but* I delight *in* 3820
119:80 Let my **h** be sound in thy statutes; that I 3820
119:111 ever: for they *are* the rejoicing of my **h**. 3820
119:112 I have inclined mine **h** to perform thy 3820
119:145 I cried with *my* whole **h**; hear me, 3820
119:161 but my **h** standeth in awe of thy word. 3820
131: 1 Lord, my **h** is not haughty, nor mine 3820
138: 1 I will praise thee with my whole **h**: 3820
139:23 Search me, O God, and know my **h**: 3824
140: 2 Which imagine mischiefs in *their* **h**; 3820
141: 4 Incline not my **h** to *any* evil thing, 3820
143: 4 within me; my **h** within me is desolate. 3820
147: 3 He healeth the broken in **h**, and bindeth 3820

Pr 2: 2 *and* apply thine **h** to understanding, 3820
2:10 When wisdom entereth into thine **h**, 3820
3: 1 but let thine **h** keep my commandments; 3820
3: 3 write them upon the table of thine **h**: 3820
3: 5 Trust in the Lord with all thine **h**; 3820
4: 4 unto me, Let thine **h** retain my words: 3820
4:21 keep them in the midst of thine **h**. 3824
4:23 Keep thy **h** with all diligence; for out of it 3820
5:12 and my **h** despised reproof; 3820
6:14 Frowardness *is* in his **h**, he deviseth 3820
6:18 A **h** that deviseth wicked imaginations, 3820
6:21 Bind them continually upon thine **h**, 3820
6:25 Lust not after her beauty in thine **h**; 3824
7: 3 write them upon the table of thine **h**. 3820
7:10 *with* the attire of a harlot, and subtil of **h**. 3820
7:25 Let not thine **h** decline to her ways, go 3820
8: 5 ye fools, be ye of an understanding **h**. 3820
10: 8 wise in **h** will receive commandments: 3820
10:20 the **h** of the wicked *is* little worth. 3820
11:20 *They that are* of a froward **h** are 3820
11:29 the fool *shall be* servant to the wise of **h**. 3820
12: 8 that is of a perverse **h** shall be despised. 3820
12:20 Deceit *is* in the **h** of them that imagine 3820
12:23 but the **h** of fools proclaimeth foolishness. 3820
12:25 Heaviness in the **h** of man maketh it 3820
13:12 Hope deferred maketh the **h** sick: 3820
14:10 The **h** knoweth his own bitterness; 3820
14:13 Even in laughter the **h** is sorrowful; 3820
14:14 The backslider in **h** shall be filled with his 3820
14:30 A sound **h** *is* the life of the flesh: 3820
14:33 Wisdom resteth in the **h** of him that hath 3820
15: 7 but the **h** of the foolish *doeth* not so. 3820
15:13 merry **h** maketh a cheerful countenance: 3820
15:13 by sorrow of the **h** the spirit *is* broken. 3820
15:14 of him that hath understanding 3820
15:15 *he that is* of a merry **h** *hath* a continual 3820
15:28 The **h** of the righteous studieth to answer: 3820
15:30 The light of the eyes rejoiceth the **h**: 3820
16: 1 The preparations of the **h** in man, 3820
16: 5 Every one *that* is proud in **h** *is* an 3820
16: 9 A man's **h** deviseth his way: 3820
16:21 The wise in **h** shall be called prudent: 3820
16:23 The **h** of the wise teacheth his mouth, 3820
17:16 to get wisdom, seeing *he hath* no **h** *to it?* 3820
17:20 He that hath a froward **h** findeth no good: 3820
17:22 A merry **h** doeth good *like* a medicine: 3820
18: 2 but that his **h** may discover itself. 3820
18:12 destruction the **h** of man is haughty, 3820
18:15 The **h** of the prudent getteth knowledge; 3820
19: 3 and his **h** fretteth against the Lord. 3820
19:21 *There are* many devices in a man's **h**; 3820
20: 5 Counsel in the **h** of man *is like* deep 3820
20: 9 Who can say, I have made my **h** clean, 3820
21: 1 The king's **h** *is* in the hand of the Lord, 3820
21: 4 proud **h**, *and* the plowing of the wicked, 3820
22:11 He that loveth pureness of **h**, *for* the grace 3820
22:15 Foolishness *is* bound in the **h** of a child; 3820
22:17 and apply thine **h** unto my knowledge. 3820

Pr 23: 7 For as he thinketh in his **h**, so *is* he: 5315
23: 7 he to thee; but his **h** *is* not with thee. 3820
23:12 Apply thine **h** unto instruction, 3820
23:15 My son, if thine **h** be wise, my heart shall 3820
23:15 be wise, my **h** shall rejoice, even mine. 3820
23:17 Let not thine **h** envy sinners: but *be* thou 3820
23:19 be wise, and guide thine **h** in the way. 3820
23:26 give me thine **h**, and let thine eyes 3820
23:33 and thine **h** shall utter perverse things. 3820
24: 2 For their **h** studieth destruction, 3820
24:12 not he that pondereth the **h** consider 3826
24:17 not thine **h** be glad when he stumbleth: 3820
25: 3 and the **h** of kings *is* unsearchable. 3820
25:20 so *is* he that singeth songs to a heavy **h**. 3820
26:23 a wicked **h** *are like* a potsherd covered 3820
26:25 *there are* seven abominations in his **h**. 3820
27: 9 Ointment and perfume rejoice the **h**: 3820
27:11 My son, be wise, and make my **h** glad, 3820
27:19 to face, so the **h** of man to man. 3820
28:14 he that hardeneth his **h** shall fall into 3820
28:25 He that is of a proud **h** stirreth up strife: 5315
28:26 He that trusteth in his own **h** is a fool: 3820
31:11 The **h** of her husband doth *safely* trust in 3820

Ecc 1:13 I gave my **h** to seek and search out by 3820
1:16 I communed with mine own **h**, saying, 3820
1:16 my **h** had great experience of wisdom and 3820
1:17 gave my **h** to know wisdom, and to know 3820
2: 1 I said in mine **h**, Go to now, I will prove 3820
2: 3 I sought in mine **h** to give myself unto 3820
2: 3 (yet acquainting mine **h** with wisdom) 3820
2:10 withheld not my **h** from any joy; 3820
2:10 joy; for my **h** rejoiced in all my labour: 3820
2:15 I in my **h**, As it happeneth to the fool, 3820
2:15 I said in my **h**, that this also *is* vanity. 3820
2:20 Therefore I went about to cause my **h** to 3820
2:22 his labour, and of the vexation of his **h**, 3820
2:23 yea, his **h** taketh not rest in the night. 3820
3:11 he hath set the world in their **h**, so that 3820
3:17 I said in mine **h**, God shall judge 3820
3:18 I said in my **h** concerning the estate of 3820
5: 2 let not thine **h** be hasty to utter *any* thing 3820
5:20 God answereth *him* in the joy of his **h**. 3820
7: 2 all men; and the living will lay *it* to his **h**. 3820
7: 3 by the sadness of the countenance the **h** 3820
7: 4 The **h** of the wise *is* in the house of 3820
7: 4 but the **h** of fools *is* in the house of mirth. 3820
7: 7 *man* mad; and a gift destroyeth the **h**. 3820
7:22 For oftentimes also thine own **h** knoweth 3820
7:25 I applied mine **h** to know, and to search, 3820
7:26 whose **h** *is* snares and nets, *and* her 3820
8: 5 a wise *man's* **h** discerneth *both* time and 3820
8: 9 applied my **h** unto every work that is 3820
8:11 the **h** of the sons of men is fully set in 3820
8:16 When I applied mine **h** to know wisdom, 3820
9: 1 For all this I considered in my **h** even to 3820
9: 3 the **h** of the sons of men is full *of* evil, 3820
9: 3 madness *is* in their **h** while they live, 3824
9: 7 and drink thy wine with a merry **h**; 3820
10: 2 A wise *man's* **h** *is* at his right hand; 3820
10: 2 at his right hand; but a fool's **h** at his left. 3820
11: 9 let thy **h** cheer thee in the days of thy 3820
11: 9 walk in the ways of thine **h**, and in the 3820
11:10 Therefore remove sorrow from thy **h**, 3820

SS 3:11 and in the day of the gladness of his **h**. 3820
4: 9 Thou hast **ravished** my **h**, my sister, 3823
4: 9 thou hast **ravished** my **h** with one of 3823
5: 2 I sleep, but my **h** waketh: *it is* the voice 3820
6: 8 Set me as a seal upon thine **h**, as a seal 3820

Isa 1: 5 whole head *is* sick, and the whole **h** faint. 3824
6:10 Make the **h** of this people fat, 3820
6:10 understand *with* their **h**, and convert, 3824
7: 2 his **h** was moved, and the heart of his 3824
7: 2 heart was moved, and the **h** of his people, 3824
9: 9 that say in the pride and stoutness of **h**, 3824
10: 7 not so, neither doth his **h** think so; 3824
10: 7 *it is* in his **h** to destroy and cut off nations 3824
10:12 I will punish the fruit of the stout **h** of 3824
13: 7 be faint, and every man's **h** shall melt: 3824
14:13 thou hast said in thine **h**, I will ascend 3820
15: 5 My **h** shall cry out for Moab; his fugitives 3820
19: 1 the **h** of Egypt shall melt in the midst of it. 3824
21: 4 My **h** panted, fearfulness affrighted me: 3824
29:13 have removed their **h** far from me, 3820
30:29 gladness of **h**, as when one goeth with a 3824
32: 4 The **h** also of the rash shall understand 3824
32: 6 his **h** will work iniquity, to practise 3820
33:18 Thine **h** shall meditate terror. Where *is* 3820
35: 4 Say to them that are of a fearful **h**, 3820
38: 3 before thee in truth and with a perfect **h**, 3820
42:25 and it burned him, yet he laid *it* not to **h**. 3820
44:19 none considereth in his **h**, neither *is there* 3820
44:20 a deceived **h** hath turned him aside, 3820
47: 7 thou didst not lay these *things* to thy **h**, 3820
47: 8 that sayest in thine **h**, I *am*, and none 3820
47:10 thou hast said in thine **h**, I *am*, and 3820
49:21 shalt thou say in thine **h**, Who hath 3820
51: 7 the people in whose **h** *is* my law; 3820
57: 1 and no man layeth *it* to **h**: 3820
57:11 not remembered me, nor laid *it* to thy **h**? 3820
57:15 and to revive the **h** of the contrite ones. 3820
57:17 went on frowardly in the way of his **h**. 3820
59:13 uttering from the **h** words of falsehood. 3820
60: 5 flow *together*, and thine **h** shall fear, 3824
63: 4 For the day of vengeance *is* in mine **h**, 3820
63:17 *and* hardened our **h** from thy fear? 3820

Isa 65:14 my servants shall sing for joy of **h**, 3820
65:14 shall cry for sorrow of **h**, and shall howl 3820
66:14 when ye see *this*, your **h** shall rejoice, 3820

Jer 3:10 not turned unto me with her whole **h**, 3820
3:15 will give you pastors according to mine **h**, 3820
3:17 more after the imagination of their evil **h**. 3824
4: 4 take away the foreskins of your **h**, ye men 3824
4: 9 *that* the **h** of the king shall perish, 3820
4: 9 king shall perish, and the **h** of the princes; 3820
4:14 wash thine **h** from wickedness, 3820
4:18 bitter, because it reacheth unto thine **h**. 3820
4:19 I am pained *at* my **very h**; my heart 3820+7023
4:19 my **h** maketh a noise in me; I cannot hold 3820
5:23 people hath a revolting and a rebellious **h**; 3820
5:24 say they in their **h**, Let us now fear 3824
7:24 *and* in the imagination of their evil **h**, 3820
7:31 them not, neither came it into my **h**. 3820
8:18 against sorrow, my **h** is faint in me. 3820
9: 8 his mouth, but in **h** he layeth his wait. 7130
9:14 after the imagination of their own **h**, 3820
9:26 of Israel *are* uncircumcised in the **h**. 3820
11: 8 one in the imagination of their evil **h**: 3820
11:20 that triest the reins, and the **h**, 3820
12: 3 seen me, and tried mine **h** towards thee: 3820
12:11 because no man layeth *it* to **h**. 3820
13:10 which walk in the imagination of their **h**, 3820
13:22 if thou say in thine **h**, Wherefore come 3824
14:14 thing of nought, and the deceit of their **h**. 3820
15:16 unto me the joy and rejoicing of mine **h**: 3824
16:12 one after the imagination of his evil **h**, 3820
17: 1 *it is* graven upon the table of their **h**, 3820
17: 5 and whose **h** departeth from the Lord. 3820
17: 9 The **h** *is* deceitful above all *things*, and 3820
17:10 I the Lord search the **h**, *I* try the reins, 3820
18:12 every one do the imagination of his evil **h**. 3820
20: 9 *his word* was in mine **h** as a burning fire 3820
20:12 righteous, *and* seest the reins and the **h**, 3820
22:17 thine eyes and thine **h** *are* not but for thy 3820
23: 9 Mine **h** within me is broken because of 3820
23:16 they speak a vision of their own **h**, 3820
23:17 after the imagination of his own **h**, 3820
23:20 he have performed the thoughts of his **h**: 3820
23:26 How long shall *this* be in the **h** of 3820
23:26 *are* prophets of the deceit of their own **h**; 3820
24: 7 I will give them a **h** to know me, that I 3820
24: 7 shall return unto me with their whole **h**. 3820
29:13 ye shall search for me with all your **h**. 3824
30:21 for who *is* this that engaged his **h** to 3820
30:24 he have performed the intents of his **h**: 3820
31:21 set thine **h** toward the highway, *even* 3820
32:39 I will give them one **h**, and one way, 3820
32:41 in this land assuredly with my whole **h**. 3820
48:29 his pride, and the haughtiness of his **h**. 3820
48:31 mine **h** shall mourn for the men of NIH
48:36 Therefore mine **h** shall sound for Moab 3820
48:36 mine **h** shall sound like pipes for the men 3820
48:41 shall be as the **h** of a woman in her pangs. 3820
49:16 deceived thee, *and* the pride of thine **h**, 3820
49:22 at that day shall the **h** of the mighty *men* 3820
49:22 Edom be as the **h** of a woman in her 3820
51:46 lest your **h** faint, and ye fear for the 3824

La 1:20 are troubled; mine **h** is turned within me; 3820
1:22 for my sighs *are* many, and my **h** is faint. 3820
2:18 Their **h** cried unto the Lord, O wall of 3820
2:19 pour out thine **h** like water before the face 3820
3:41 Let us lift up our **h** with *our* hands unto 3824
3:51 Mine eye affecteth mine **h** because of all 5315
3:65 Give them sorrow of **h**, thy curse unto 3820
5:15 The joy of our **h** is ceased; our dance is 3820
5:17 For this our **h** is faint; for these *things* our 3820

Eze 3:10 I shall speak unto thee receive in thine **h**, 3824
6: 9 because I am broken with their whorish **h**, 3820
11:19 I will give them one **h**, and I will put a 3820
11:19 I will take the stony **h** out of their flesh, 3820
11:19 flesh, and will give them a **h** of flesh: 3820
11:21 *for them* whose **h** walketh after the heart 3820
11:21 *for them* whose heart walketh after the **h** 3820
13:17 which prophesy out of their own **h**; 3820
13:22 Because *with* lies *ye* have made the **h** of 3820
14: 3 men have set up their idols in his **h**, 3820
14: 4 of Israel that setteth up his idols in his **h**, 3820
14: 5 take the house of Israel in their own **h**, 3820
14: 7 setteth up his idols in his **h**, and putteth 3820
16:30 How weak is thine **h**, saith the Lord God, 3826
18:31 and make you a new **h** and a new spirit: 3820
20:16 for their **h** went after their idols. 3820
21: 7 every **h** shall melt, and all hands shall be 3820
21:15 that *their* **h** may faint, and *their* ruins be 3820
22:14 Can thine **h** endure, or can thine hands 3820
25: 6 rejoiced in **h** with all thy despite against 5315
25:15 have taken vengeance with a despiteful **h**, 5315
27:31 shall weep for thee with bitterness of **h**. 5315
28: 2 Because thine **h** *is* lifted up, and thou hast 3820
28: 2 thou set thine **h** as the heart of God: 3820
28: 2 thou set thine heart as the **h** of God: 3820
28: 5 thine **h** is lifted up because of thy riches: 3820
28: 6 thou hast set thine **h** as the heart of 3824
28: 6 thou hast set thine heart as the **h** of 3820
28:17 Thine **h** was lifted up because of thy 3820
31:10 and his **h** is lifted up in his height; 3820
33:31 *but* their **h** goeth after their covetousness. 3820
36: 5 their possession with the joy of all *their* **h**, 3824
36:26 A new **h** also will I give you, and a new 3820
36:26 I will take away the stony **h** out of your 3820
36:26 your flesh, and I will give you a **h** of flesh. 3820

H

Eze	40: 4 set thine **h** upon all that I shall shew thee;	3820
	44: 7 uncircumcised in **h**, and uncircumcised in	3820
	44: 9 No stranger, uncircumcised in **h**,	3820
Da	1: 8 Daniel purposed in his **h** that he would	3820
	2:30 mightest know the thoughts of thy **h**.	3825
	4:16 Let his **h** be changed from man's, and let	3825
	4:16 let a beast's **h** be given unto him;	3825
	5:20 when his **h** was lifted up, and his mind	3825
	5:21 his **h** was made like the beasts,	3825
	5:22 O Belshazzar, hast not humbled thine **h**,	3825
	6:14 and set *his* **h** on Daniel to deliver him:	1079
	7: 4 as a man, and a man's **h** was given to it.	3825
	7:28 in me: but I kept the matter in my **h**.	3821
	8:25 he shall magnify *himself* in his **h**,	3824
	10:12 that thou didst set thine **h** to understand,	3820
	11:12 the multitude, his **h** shall be lifted up;	3824
	11:28 his **h** *shall be* against the holy covenant;	3824
Hos	4: 8 and they set their **h** on their iniquity.	5315
	4:11 and wine and new wine take *away* the **h**.	3820
	7: 6 For they have made ready their **h** like an	3820
	7:11 also is like a silly dove, without **h**:	3820
	7:14 they have not cried unto me with their **h**,	3820
	10: 2 Their **h** is divided; now shall they be	3820
	11: 8 **h** is turned within me, my repentings	3820
	13: 6 they were filled, and their **h** was exalted;	3820
	13: 8 will rent the caul of their **h**, and there will	3820
Joel	2:12 turn *even* to me with all your **h**,	3824
	2:13 rent your **h**, and not your garments,	3824
Ob	1: 3 The pride of thine **h** hath deceived thee,	3820
	1: 3 that saith in his **h**, Who shall bring me	3820
Na	2:10 the **h** melteth, and the knees smite	3820
Zep	1:12 that say in their **h**, The LORD will not do	3824
	2:15 that said in her **h**, I *am*, and *there is* none	3824
	3:14 be glad and rejoice with all the **h**,	3820
Zec	7:10 imagine evil against his brother in your **h**.	3824
	10: 7 and their **h** shall rejoice as *through* wine:	3820
	10: 7 be glad; their **h** shall rejoice in the LORD.	3820
	12: 5 governors of Judah shall say in their **h**,	3820
Mal	2: 2 will not hear, and if ye will not lay *it* to **h**,	3820
	2: 2 already, because ye do not lay *it* to **h**.	3820
	4: 6 he shall turn the **h** of the fathers to	3820
	4: 6 the **h** of the children to their fathers, lest	3820
Mt	5: 8 Blessed *are* the pure in **h**: for they shall	2588
	5:28 adultery with her already in his **h**.	2588
	6:21 your treasure is, there will your **h** be also.	2588
	11:29 of me; for I am meek and lowly in **h**:	2588
	12:34 abundance of the **h** the mouth speaketh.	2588
	12:35 treasure of the **h** bringeth forth good	2588
	12:40 and three nights in the **h** of the earth.	2588
	13:15 For this people's **h** is waxed gross,	2588
	13:15 and should understand with *their* **h**,	2588
	13:19 away that which was sown in his **h**.	2588
	15: 8 with *their* lips; but their **h** is far from me.	2588
	15:18 out of the mouth come forth from the **h**;	2588
	15:19 For out of the **h** proceed evil thoughts,	2588
	22:37 love the Lord thy God with all thy **h**,	2588
	24:48 *and* if that evil servant shall say in his **h**,	2588
Mk	6:52 of loaves: for their **h** was hardened.	2588
	7: 6 with *their* lips, but their **h** is far from me.	2588
	7:19 Because it entereth not into his **h**,	2588
	7:21 For from within, out of the **h** of men,	2588
	8:17 have ye your **h** yet hardened?	2588
	10: 5 the **hardness** of your **h** he wrote you	4641
	11:23 and shall not doubt in his **h**,	2588
	12:30 love the Lord thy God with all thy **h**,	2588
	12:33 to love him with all the **h**, and with all	2588
	16:14 with their unbelief and **hardness of** **h**,	4641
Lk	2:19 these things, and pondered *them* in her **h**.	2588
	2:51 his mother kept all these sayings in her **h**.	2588
	6:45 of his **h** bringeth forth that which is good;	2588
	6:45 evil man out of the evil treasure of his **h**	2588
	6:45 for of the abundance of the **h** his mouth	2588
	8:15 which in an honest and good **h**,	2588
	9:47 perceiving the thought of their **h**,	2588
	10:27 love the Lord thy God with all thy **h**,	2588
	12:34 your treasure is, there will your **h** be also.	2588
	12:45 and if that servant say in his **h**, My lord	2588
	24:25 slow of **h** to believe all that the prophets	2588
	24:32 to another, Did not our **h** burn within us,	2588
Jn	12:40 blinded their eyes, and hardened their **h**;	2588
	12:40 nor understand with their **h**,	2588
	13: 2 devil having now put into the **h** of Judas	2588
	14: 1 Let not your **h** be troubled: ye believe in	2588
	14:27 Let not your **h** be troubled, neither let it	2588
	16: 6 unto you, sorrow hath filled your **h**.	2588
	16:22 and your **h** shall rejoice, and your joy no	2588
Ac	2:26 Therefore did my **h** rejoice, and my	2588
	2:37 heard *this*, they were pricked in *their* **h**,	2588
	2:46 meat with gladness and singleness of **h**,	2588
	4:32 of them that believed were of one **h**	2588
	5: 3 why hath Satan filled thine **h** to lie to	2588
	5: 4 hast thou conceived this thing in thine **h**?	2588
	5:33 they heard *that*, they were cut *to the* **h**,	NIG
	7:23 it came into his **h** to visit his brethren	2588
	7:51 and uncircumcised in **h** and ears,	2588
	7:54 these *things*, they were cut to the **h**,	2588
	8:21 for thy **h** is not right in the sight of God.	2588
	8:22 if perhaps the thought of thine **h** may be	2588
	8:37 If thou believest with all *thine* **h**,	2588
	11:23 that with purpose of **h** *they* would cleave	2588
	13:22 man after mine own **h**, which shall fulfil	2588
	16:14 heard *us*: whose **h** the Lord opened,	2588
	21:13 mean ye to weep and to break mine **h**?	2588
	28:27 For the **h** of this people is waxed gross,	2588
	28:27 understand with *their* **h**, and should be	2588

Ro	1:21 and their foolish **h** was darkened.	2588
	2: 5 impenitent **h** treasurest up unto thyself	2588
	2:29 and circumcision *is that* of the **h**,	2588
	6:17 ye have obeyed from the **h** *that* form of	2588
	9: 2 and continual sorrow in my **h**.	2588
	10: 6 Say not in thine **h**, Who shall ascend into	2588
	10: 8 thee, *even* in thy mouth, and in thy **h**:	2588
	10: 9 believe in thine **h** that God hath raised	2588
	10:10 For with the **h** *man* believeth unto	2588
1Co	2: 9 neither have entered into the **h** of man,	2588
	7:37 he that standeth stedfast in his **h**,	2588
	7:37 in his **h** that *he* will keep his virgin,	2588
	7:37 And thus are the secrets of his **h** made	2588
2Co	2: 4 anguish of **h** I wrote unto you with many	2588
	3: 3 of stone, but in fleshy tables of the **h**.	2588
	3:15 Moses is read, the vail is upon their **h**.	2588
	5:12 which glory in appearance, and not in **h**.	2588
	6:11 is open unto you, our **h** is enlarged.	2588
	8:16 put the same earnest care into the **h**	2588
	9: 7 man according as he purposeth in *his* **h**,	2588
Eph	4:18 them, because of the blindness of their **h**:	2588
	5:19 and making melody in your **h** to the Lord;	2588
	6: 5 and trembling, in singleness of your **h**,	2588
	6: 6 Christ, doing the will of God from the **h**;	5590
Php	1: 7 of you all, because I have you in my **h**;	2588
Col	3:22 but in singleness of **h**, fearing God:	2588
1Th	2:17 you for a short time in presence, not in **h**,	2588
1Ti	1: 5 commandment is charity out of a pure **h**,	2588
2Ti	2:22 them that call on the Lord out of a pure **h**.	2588
Heb	3:10 and said, They do alway err in *their* **h**;	2588
	3:12 lest there be in any of you an evil **h** of	2588
	4:12 of the thoughts and intents of the **h**.	2588
	10:22 Let us draw near with a true **h** in full	2588
	13: 9 For it is a good *thing* that the **h** be	2588
Jas	1:26 not his tongue, but deceiveth his own **h**,	2588
1Pe	1:22 *that* ye love one another with a pure **h**	2588
	3: 4 But *let it be* the hidden man of the **h**,	2588
2Pe	2:14 they have exercised with covetous	2588
1Jn	3:20 For if *our* **h** condemn us, God is greater	2588
	3:20 God is greater than our **h**, and knoweth	2588
	3:21 if our **h** condemn us not, *then* have we	2588
Rev	18: 7 for she saith in her **h**, I sit a queen,	2588

HEART'S (4) [HEART]

Ps	10: 3 For the wicked boasteth of his **h** desire,	5315
	21: 2 Thou hast given him his **h** desire,	3820
	81:12 So I gave them up unto their own **h** lust:	3820
Ro	10: 1 my **h** desire and prayer to God for Israel	2588

HEARTED (10) [HEART]

Ex	28: 3 thou shalt speak unto all *that are* wise **h**,	3820
	31: 6 in the hearts of all that are wise **h** I have	3820
	35:10 every wise **h** among you shall come,	3820
	35:22 as many as were willing **h**,	3820
	35:25 all the women that were wise **h** did spin	3820
	36: 1 and Aholiab, and every wise **h** man,	3820
	36: 2 and Aholiab, and every wise **h** man,	3820
	36: 8 every wise **h** *man* among them that	3820
2Ch	13: 7 Rehoboam was young and tender **h**,	3824
Eze	2: 4 *they* are impudent children and stiff **h**.	3820

HEARTH (7)

Ge	18: 6 knead *it*, and make cakes upon the **h**.	NIH
Ps	102: 3 smoke, and my bones are burnt as a **h**.	4168
Isa	30:14 of it a sheard to take fire from the **h**,	3344
Jer	36:22 *was a fire* on the **h** burning before him.	254
	36:23 cast *it* into the fire that *was* on the **h**,	254
	36:23 consumed in the fire that *was* on the **h**.	254
Zec	12: 6 of Judah like a **h** of fire among the wood,	3595

HEARTILY (1) [HEARTY]

Col	3:23 **h**, as to the Lord, and not unto men	*1537+5590*

HEARTS (112) [HEART]

Ge	18: 5 a morsel of bread, and comfort ye your **h**;	3820
Ex	14:17 I will harden the **h** of the Egyptians,	3820
	31: 6 in the **h** of all that are wise hearted I have	3820
Lev	26:36 into their **h** in the lands of their enemies;	3824
	26:41 if then their uncircumcised **h** be humbled,	3824
Dt	20: 3 let not your **h** faint, fear not, and do not	3824
	32:46 Set your **h** unto all the words which I	3824
Jos	2:11 soon as we had heard *these things*, our **h**	3824
	7: 5 wherefore the **h** of the people melted,	3824
	11:20 For it was of the LORD to harden their **h**,	3820
	23:14 know in all your **h** and in all your souls,	3824
Jdg	3: 1 their **h** inclined to follow Abimelech;	3820
	16:25 when their **h** were merry, that they said,	3820
	19:22 Now as they were making their **h** merry,	3820
1Sa	6: 6 Wherefore then do ye harden your **h**,	3824
	6: 6 and Pharaoh hardened their **h**?	3820
	7: 3 do return unto the LORD with all your **h**,	3824
	7: 3 prepare your **h** unto the LORD,	3824
	10:26 band of men, whose **h** God had touched.	3820
2Sa	15: 6 Absalom stole the **h** of the men of Israel.	3820
	15:13 The **h** of the men of Israel are after	3820
1Ki	8:39 knowest the **h** of all the children of men;)	3824
	8:58 That *he* may incline our **h** unto him,	3824
1Ch	28: 9 for the LORD searcheth all **h**,	3824
2Ch	6:14 that walk before thee with all their **h**:	3820
	6:30 thou only knowest the **h** of the children	3824
	11:16 to seek the LORD God of Israel came *to*	3824
	20:33 their **h** unto the God of their fathers.	3824
Job	1: 5 have sinned, and cursed God in their **h**.	3824
Ps	7: 9 the righteous God trieth the **h** and reins.	3826
	28: 3 neighbours, but mischief *is* in their **h**.	3824

Ps	33:15 fashioneth their **h** alike; he considereth	3820
	35:25 Let them not say in their **h**,	3820
	74: 8 They said in their **h**, Let us destroy them	3820
	90:12 that we may apply *our* **h** *unto* wisdom.	3824
	125: 4 and to *them that are* upright in their **h**.	3826
Pr	15:11 then the **h** of the children of men?	3826
	3: for gold: but the LORD trieth the **h**.	3826
	21: 2 own eyes: but the LORD pondereth the **h**.	3826
	31: 6 and wine unto those that be of heavy **h**.	5315
Isa	44:18 *and* their **h**, that *they* cannot understand.	3826
Jer	31:33 their inward parts, and write it in their **h**;	3820
	32:40 I will put my fear in their **h**, that they	3824
	42:20 ye dissembled in your **h**, when ye sent	5315
	48:41 the mighty *men's* **h** in Moab at that day	3820
Eze	13: 2 them that prophesy out of their own **h**,	3820
	13: 2 will also vex the **h** of many people,	3820
Da	11:27 these kings' **h** *shall be* to do mischief,	3824
Hos	7: 2 consider not in their **h** that I remember	3824
Zec	7:12 they made their **h** *as* an adamant stone,	3820
	7:12 lest they should hear the law, and the	3824
Mt	9: 4 Wherefore think ye evil in your **h**?	2588
	18:35 if ye from your **h** forgive not every one his	2588
	19: 8 of the **hardness** of your **h** suffered you to	4641
Mk	2: 6 sitting there, and reasoning in their **h**,	2588
	2: 8 Why reason ye these *things* in your **h**?	2588
	3: 5 being grieved for the hardness of their **h**,	2588
	4:15 away the word that was sown in their **h**.	2588
Lk	1:17 to turn the **h** of the fathers to the children,	2588
	1:51 the proud in the imagination of their **h**.	2588
	1:66 that heard *them* laid *them* up in their **h**,	2588
	2:35 that the thoughts of many **h** may be	2588
	3:15 and all *men* mused in their **h** of John,	2588
	5:22 unto them, What reason ye in your **h**?	2588
	8:12 and taketh away the word out of their **h**,	2588
	16:15 before men; but God knoweth your **h**:	2588
	21:14 Settle *it* therefore in your **h**, not to	2588
	21:26 Men's **h** failing them for fear,	674
	21:34 lest at any time your **h** be overcharged	2588
	24:38 and why do thoughts arise in your **h**?	2588
Ac	1:24 which **knowest** the **h** of all *men*, shew	2589
	7:39 in their **h** turned *back again* into Egypt,	2588
	14:17 filling our **h** with food and gladness.	2588
	15: 8 God, which **knoweth** the **h**, bare them	2589
	15: 9 and them, purifying their **h** by faith.	2588
Ro	1:24 through the lusts of their own **h**,	2588
	2:15 the work of the law written in their **h**,	2588
	5: 5 the love of God is shed abroad in our **h**	2588
	8:27 he that searcheth the **h** knoweth what	2588
	16:18 fair speeches deceive the **h** of the simple.	2588
1Co	4: 5 will make manifest the counsels of the **h**:	2588
2Co	1:22 given the earnest of the Spirit in our **h**.	2588
	3: 2 Ye are our epistle written in our **h**,	2588
	4: 6 out of darkness, hath shined in our **h**,	2588
	7: 3 that you are in our **h** to die and live with	2588
Gal	4: 6 forth the Spirit of his Son into your **h**,	2588
Eph	3:17 That Christ may dwell in your **h** by faith;	2588
	6:22 and *that* he might comfort your **h**.	2588
Php	4: 7 keep your **h** and minds through Christ	2588
Col	2: 2 That their **h** might be comforted, being	2588
	3:15 And let the peace of God rule in your **h**,	2588
	3:16 singing with grace in your **h** to the Lord.	2588
	4: 8 know your estate, and comfort your **h**;	2588
1Th	2: 4 men, but God, which trieth our **h**.	2588
	3:13 To the end *he may* stablish your **h**	2588
2Th	2:17 Comfort your **h**, and stablish you in every	2588
	3: 5 the Lord direct your **h** into the love of	2588
Heb	3: 8 Harden not your **h**, as in the provocation,	2588
	3:15 harden not your **h**, as in the provocation.	2588
	4: 7 ye will hear his voice, harden not your **h**.	2588
	8:10 their mind, and write them in their **h**:	2588
	10:16 I will put my laws into their **h**, and in	2588
	10:22 having *our* **h** sprinkled from an evil	2588
Jas	3:14 have bitter envying and strife in your **h**,	2588
	4: 8 and purify your **h**, *ye* double minded.	2588
	5: 5 ye have nourished your **h**, as in a day of	2588
	5: 8 Be ye also patient; stablish your **h**:	2588
1Pe	3:15 But sanctify the Lord God in your **h**:	2588
2Pe	1:19 dawn, and the day star arise in your **h**:	2588
1Jn	3:19 truth, and shall assure our **h** before him.	2588
Rev	2:23 I am he which searcheth the reins and **h**:	2588
	17:17 God hath put in their **h** to fulfil his will,	2588

HEARTY (1) [HEARTILY]

Pr	27: 9 *doth* the sweetness of a man's friend by **h**	5315

HEAT (33) [HEATED]

Ge	8:22 cold and **h**, and summer and winter,	2527
	18: 1 sat *in* the tent door in the **h** of the day;	2527
Dt	29:24 what *meaneth* the **h** of this great anger?	2750
	32:24 devoured with **burning** **h**, and with bitter	7565
1Sa	11:11 the Ammonites until the **h** of the day:	2527
2Sa	4: 5 came about the **h** of the day to the house	2527
1Ki	1: 1 him with clothes, and he **gat** no **h**.	3179
	1: 2 that my lord the king may get **h**.	2552
Job	24:19 Drought and **h** consume the snow waters:	2527
	30:30 upon me, and my bones are burnt with **h**.	2721
Ps	19: 6 there is nothing hid from the **h** thereof.	2535
Ecc	4:11 if two lie together, then they **have h**:	2552
Isa	4: 6 for a shadow in the daytime from the **h**,	2721
	18: 4 dwelling place like a clear **h** upon herbs,	2527
	18: 4 like a cloud of dew in the **h** of harvest.	2721
	25: 4 from the storm, a shadow from the **h**,	2721
	25: 5 noise of strangers, as the **h** in a dry place;	2721
	25: 5 *even* the **h** with the shadow of a cloud:	2721
	49:10 neither shall the **h** nor sun smite them:	8273

Jer 17: 8 not see when **h** cometh, but her leaf 2527
36:30 body shall be cast out in the day to the **h,** 2721
51:39 In their **h** I will make their feasts, and I 2527
Eze 3:14 I went in bitterness, in the **h** of my spirit; 2534
Da 3:19 that *they* should be **h** 228
3:19 *times* more than *it was* wont to be **h.** 228
Mt 20:12 have borne the burden and **h** of the day. 2742
Lk 12:55 south wind blow, ye say, There will be **h;** 2742
Ac 28: 3 there came a viper out of the **h,** 2329
Jas 1:11 sun is no sooner risen with a **burning h,** 2742
2Pe 3:10 the elements shall melt with **fervent h,** 2741
3:12 the elements shall melt with **fervent h?** 2741
Rev 7:16 shall the sun light on them, nor any **h.** 2738
16: 9 And men were scorched *with* great **h,** 2738

HEATED (1) [HEAT]

Hos 7: 4 all adulterers, as an oven by the baker, 1197

HEATH (2)

Jer 17: 6 For he shall be like the **h** in the desert, 6199
48: 6 and be like the **h** in the wilderness. 6176

HEATHEN (150)

Lev 25:44 *be* of the **h** that *are* round about you; 1471
26:33 I will scatter you among the **h,** 1471
26:38 ye shall perish among the **h,** and the land 1471
26:45 of the land of Egypt in the sight of the **h:** 1471
Dt 4:27 shall be left few in number among the **h,** 1471
2Sa 22:44 thou hast kept me to be head of the **h:** 1471
22:50 among the **h,** and I will sing praises unto 1471
2Ki 16: 3 according to the abominations of the **h,** 1471
17: 8 walked in the statutes of the **h,** whom 1471
17:11 as *did* the **h** whom the LORD carried 1471
17:15 *went* after the **h** that *were* round about 1471
21: 2 after the abominations of the **h,** whom 1471
1Ch 16:24 Declare his glory among the **h;** 1471
16:35 us together, and deliver us from the **h,** 1471
2Ch 20: 6 *not* thou over all the kingdoms of the **h?** 1471
28: 3 **h** whom the LORD had cast out before 1471
33: 2 like unto the abominations of the **h,** 1471
33: 9 to err, *and* to do worse than the **h,** 1471
36:14 much after all the abominations of the **h;** 1471
Ezr 6:21 from the filthiness of the **h** of the land, 1471
Ne 5: 8 the Jews, which were sold unto the **h;** 1471
5: 9 of the reproach of the **h** our enemies? 1471
5:17 us from among the **h** that *are* about us. 1471
6: 6 *It is* reported among the **h,** 1471
6:16 all the **h** were about us saw *these* 1471
Ps 2: 1 Why do the **h** rage, and the people 1471
2: 8 shall give *thee* the **h** *for* thine inheritance, 1471
9: 5 Thou hast rebuked the **h,** thou hast 1471
9:15 The **h** are sunk down in the pit *that* they 1471
9:19 let the **h** be judged in thy sight. 1471
10:16 ever: the **h** are perished out of his land. 1471
18:43 thou hast made me the head of the **h:** 1471
18:49 among the **h,** and sing *praises* unto thy 1471
33:10 The LORD bringeth the counsel of the **h** 1471
44: 2 *How* thou didst drive out the **h** *with* thy 1471
44:11 and hast scattered us among the **h.** 1471
44:14 Thou makest us a byword among the **h,** 1471
46: 6 The **h** raged, the kingdoms were moved: 1471
46:10 I will be exalted among the **h,** I will be 1471
47: 8 God reigneth over the **h:** God sitteth upon 1471
59: 5 the God of Israel, awake to visit all the **h:** 1471
59: 8 thou shalt have all the **h** in derision. 1471
78:55 He cast out the **h** also before them, 1471
79: 1 the **h** are come into thine inheritance; 1471
79: 6 Pour out thy wrath upon the **h** that have 1471
79:10 Wherefore should the **h** say, Where *is* 1471
79:10 let him be known among the **h** in our 1471
80: 8 thou hast cast out the **h,** and planted it. 1471
94:10 He that chastiseth the **h,** shall not he 1471
96: 3 Declare his glory among the **h,** 1471
96:10 Say among the **h** *that* the LORD reigneth: 1471
98: 2 he openly shewed in the sight of the **h.** 1471
102:15 So the **h** shall fear the name of the LORD, 1471
105:44 gave them the lands of the **h:** 1471
106:35 were mingled among the **h,** 1471
106:41 he gave them into the hand of the **h;** 1471
106:47 God, and gather us from among the **h,** 1471
110: 6 He shall judge among the **h,** he shall fill 1471
111: 6 *he* may give them the heritage of the **h.** 1471
115: 2 Wherefore should the **h** say, Where *is* 1471
126: 2 said they among the **h,** The LORD hath 1471
135:15 The idols of the **h** *are* silver and gold, 1471
149: 7 To execute vengeance upon the **h,** 1471
Isa 16: 8 the lords of the **h** have broken down 1471
Jer 9:16 I will scatter them also among the **h,** 1471
10: 2 Learn not the way of the **h,** and be not 1471
10: 2 of heaven; for the **h** are dismayed at them. 1471
10:25 Pour out thy fury upon the **h** that know 1471
18:13 Ask ye now among the **h,** who hath heard 1471
49:14 an ambassador *is* sent unto the **h,** 1471
49:15 I will make thee small among the **h,** 1471
La 1: 3 she dwelleth among the **h,** she findeth no 1471
1:10 she hath seen *that* the **h** entered into her 1471
4:15 they said among the **h,** They shall no 1471
4:20 his shadow we shall live among the **h.** 1471
Eze 7:24 Wherefore I will bring the worst of the **h,** 1471
11:12 have done after the manners of the **h** that 1471
11:16 I have cast them far off among the **h,** 1471
12:16 among the **h** whither they come; 1471
16:14 thy renown went forth among the **h** for 1471
20: 9 that *it* should not be polluted before the **h,** 1471
20:14 that *it* should not be polluted before the **h,** 1471

Eze 20:22 not be polluted in the sight of the **h,** 1471
20:23 that *I* would scatter them among the **h,** 1471
20:32 that ye say, We will be as the **h,** 1471
20:41 I will be sanctified in you before the **h.** 1471
22: 4 have I made thee a reproach unto the **h,** 1471
22:15 I will scatter thee among the **h,** 1471
22:16 inheritance in thyself in the sight of the **h,** 1471
23:30 thou hast gone a whoring after the **h,** 1471
25: 7 and will deliver thee for a spoil to the **h;** 1471
25: 8 the house of Judah *is* like unto all the **h;** 1471
28:25 sanctified in them in the sight of the **h,** 1471
30: 3 a cloudy day; it shall be the time of the **h.** 1471
31:11 into the hand of the mighty one of the **h;** 1471
31:17 under his shadow in the midst of the **h.** 1471
34:28 they shall no more be a prey to the **h,** 1471
34:29 neither bear the shame of the **h** any more. 1471
36: 3 be a possession unto the residue of the **h,** 1471
36: 4 derision to the residue of the **h** that *are* 1471
36: 5 have I spoken against the residue of the **h,** 1471
36: 6 because ye have borne the shame of the **h:** 1471
36: 7 hand, Surely the **h** that *are* about you, 1471
36:15 hear in thee the shame of the **h** any more, 1471
36:19 I scattered them among the **h,** 1471
36:20 when they entered unto the **h,** whither 1471
36:21 house of Israel had profaned among the **h,** 1471
36:22 which ye have profaned among the **h,** 1471
36:23 which was profaned among the **h,** 1471
36:23 the **h** shall know that I *am* the LORD, 1471
36:24 For I will take you from among the **h,** 1471
36:30 no more reproach of famine among the **h.** 1471
36:36 the **h** that are left round about you shall 1471
37:21 the children of Israel from among the **h,** 1471
37:28 the **h** shall know that I the LORD do 1471
38:16 my land, that the **h** may know me, 1471
39: 7 the **h** shall know that I *am* the LORD, 1471
39:21 I will set my glory among the **h,** and all 1471
39:21 all the **h** shall see my judgment that I 1471
39:23 the **h** shall know that the house of Israel 1471
39:28 to be led into captivity among the **h:** 1471
Joel 2:17 that the **h** should rule over them: 1471
2:19 more make you a reproach among the **h:** 1471
3:11 all ye **h,** and gather yourselves together 1471
3:12 Let the **h** be wakened, and come up to 1471
3:12 for there will I sit to judge all the **h** round 1471
Am 9:12 of all the **h,** which are called by my name, 1471
Ob 1: 1 an ambassador is sent among the **h,** 1471
1: 2 I have made thee small among the **h:** 1471
1:15 day of the LORD *is* near upon all the **h:** 1471
1:16 *so* shall all the **h** drink continually, yea, 1471
Mic 5:15 vengeance in anger and fury upon the **h,** 1471
Hab 1: 5 Behold ye among the **h,** and regard, 1471
3:12 thou didst thresh the **h** in anger. 1471
Zep 2:11 from his place, *even* all the isles of the **h.** 1471
Hag 2:22 the strength of the kingdoms of the **h;** 1471
Zec 1:15 I am very sore displeased with the **h** that 1471
8:13 *that* as ye were a curse among the **h:** 1471
9:10 he shall speak peace unto the **h:** 1471
14:14 the wealth of all the **h** round about shall 1471
14:18 where*with* the LORD will smite the **h** that 1471
Mal 1:11 for my name *shall be* great among the **h,** 1471
1:14 and my name *is* dreadful among the **h.** 1471
Mt 6: 7 as the **h** *do:* for they think that they shall 1482
18:17 let him be unto thee as a **h** *man* and 1482
Ac 4:25 Why did the **h** rage, and the people 1484
2Co 11:26 *in* perils by the **h,** *in* perils in the city, 1484
Gal 1:16 that I might preach him among the **h,** 1484
2: 9 that we *should go* unto the **h,** and they 1484
3: 8 foreseeing that God would justify the **h** 1484

HEAVE (29) [HEAVED]

Ex 29:27 the shoulder of the **h offering,** which is 8641
29:28 it *is* a **h offering:** and it shall be a heave 8641
29:28 it shall be a **h offering** from the children 8641
29:24 *even* their **h offering** unto the LORD. 8641
Lev 7:14 oblation *for* a **h offering** unto the LORD, 8641
7:32 **h offering** of the sacrifices of your peace 8641
7:34 the **h** shoulder have I taken of the 8641
10:14 shoulder shall ye eat in a clean place; 8641
10:15 The **h** shoulder and the wave breast shall 8641
Nu 6:20 with the wave breast and **h** shoulder: 8641
15:19 ye shall offer up a **h offering** unto 8641
15:20 the first of your dough *for* a **h offering:** 8641
15:20 as *ye do* the **h offering** of 8641
15:20 of the threshingfloor, so shall ye it. 7311
15:21 LORD a **h offering** in your generations. 8641
18: 8 **h offerings** of all the hallowed *things* of 8641
18:11 the **h offering** of their gift, with all 8641
18:19 All the **h offerings** of the holy *things,* 8641
18:24 which they offer *as* a **h offering** unto 8641
18:26 ye shall offer up a **h offering** of it for 8641
18:27 your **h offering** shall be reckoned unto 8641
18:28 you also shall offer a **h offering** unto 8641
18:28 LORD's **h offering** to Aaron the priest. 8641
18:29 shall offer every **h offering** of the LORD, 8641
31:29 the priest, *for* a **h offering** of the LORD. 8641
31:41 *which was* the LORD's **h offering,** 8641
Dt 12: 6 **h offerings** of your hand, and your vows, 8641
12:11 the **h offering** of your hand, and all your 8641
12:17 or **h offering** of thine hand: 8641

HEAVED (3) [HEAVE]

Ex 29:27 which is waved, and which is **h up,** 7311
Nu 18:30 When ye have **h** the best thereof from it, 7311
18:32 when ye have **h** from it the best of it: 7311

HEAVEN (582) [HEAVEN'S, HEAVENLY, HEAVENS]

Ge 1: 1 In the beginning God created the **h** and 8064
1: 8 God called the firmament **H.** 8064
1: 9 Let the waters under the **h** be gathered 8064
1:14 there be lights in the firmament of the **h** to 8064
1:15 of the **h** to give light upon the earth: 8064
1:17 God set them in the firmament of the **h** to 8064
1:20 the earth in the open firmament of **h.** 8064
6:17 *is* the breath of life, from under **h;** 8064
7:11 and the windows of **h** were opened. 8064
7:19 *were* under the whole **h,** were covered. 8064
7:23 creeping things, and the fowl of the **h;** 8064
8: 2 and the windows of **h** were stopped, 8064
8: 2 and the rain from **h** was restrained; 8064
11: 4 a tower, whose top *may reach* unto **h;** 8064
14:19 most high God, possessor of **h** and earth: 8064
14:22 high God, the possessor of **h** and earth, 8064
15: 5 Look now towards **h,** and tell the stars, 8064
19:24 and fire from the LORD out of **h;** 8064
21:17 the angel of God called to Hagar out of **h,** 8064
22:11 of the LORD called unto him out of **h,** 8064
22:15 unto Abraham out of **h** the second time, 8064
22:17 multiply thy seed as the stars of the **h,** 8064
24: 3 the God of **h,** and the God of the earth, 8064
24: 7 The LORD God of **h,** which took me from 8064
26: 4 thy seed to multiply as the stars of **h,** 8064
27:28 Therefore God give thee of the dew of **h,** 8064
27:39 earth, and of the dew of **h** from above; 8064
28:12 the earth, and the top of it reached to **h:** 8064
28:17 house of God, and this *is* the gate of **h.** 8064
49:25 who shall bless thee *with* blessings of **h** 8064
Ex 9: 8 let Moses sprinkle it towards the **h** in 8064
9:10 Moses sprinkled it *up* toward **h;** 8064
9:22 Stretch forth thine hand toward **h,** 8064
9:23 Moses stretched forth his rod toward **h:** 8064
10:21 Stretch out thine hand toward **h,** 8064
10:22 Moses stretched forth his hand toward **h;** 8064
16: 4 Behold, I will rain bread from **h** for you; 8064
17:14 remembrance of Amalek from under **h.** 8064
20: 4 likeness *of any thing* that *is* in **h** above, 8064
20:11 For *in* six days the LORD made **h** and 8064
20:22 seen that I have talked with you from **h.** 8064
24:10 as it were the body of **h** in *his* clearness. 8064
31:17 for *in* six days the LORD made **h** and 8064
32:13 I will multiply your seed as the stars of **h,** 8064
Lev 26:19 I will make your **h** as iron, and your earth 8064
Dt 1:10 you *are this* day as the stars of **h** for 8064
1:28 the cities *are* great and walled up to **h;** 8064
2:25 the nations *that are* under the whole **h,** 8064
3:24 for what God *is there* in **h** or in earth, 8064
4:11 burnt with fire unto the midst of **h,** 8064
4:19 lest thou lift up thine eyes unto **h,** 8064
4:19 and the stars, *even* all the host of **h,** 8064
4:19 unto all nations under the whole **h.** 8064
4:26 I call **h** and earth to witness against you 8064
4:32 *ask* from the one side of **h** unto the other, 8064
4:36 Out of **h** he made thee to hear his voice, 8064
4:39 that the LORD he *is* God in **h** above, 8064
5: 8 likeness *of any thing* that *is* in **h** above, 8064
7:24 shalt destroy their name from under **h:** 8064
9: 1 I thyself, cities great and fenced up to **h,** 8064
9:14 and blot out their name from under **h:** 8064
10:14 the **h** and the heaven of heavens *is* 8064
10:14 the **h** of heavens *is* the LORD's thy God, 8064
10:22 made thee as the stars of **h** for multitude. 8064
11:11 *and* drinketh water of the rain of **h:** 8064
11:17 he shut up the **h,** that there be no rain, 8064
11:21 them, as the days of **h** upon the earth. 8064
17: 3 the sun, or moon, or any of the host of **h,** 8064
25:19 remembrance of Amalek from under **h;** 8064
26:15 from **h,** and bless thy people Israel, 8064
28:12 the **h** to give the rain unto thy land in his 8064
28:23 thy **h** that *is* over thy head shall be brass, 8064
28:24 from **h** shall it come down upon thee, 8064
28:62 whereas ye were as the stars of **h** for 8064
29:20 shall blot out his name from under **h.** 8064
30: 4 driven out unto the outmost parts of **h,** 8064
30:12 It *is* not in **h,** that *thou* shouldest say, 8064
30:12 Who shall go up for us to **h,** and bring it 8064
30:19 call **h** and earth to record *this* day against 8064
31:28 call **h** and earth to record against them. 8064
32:40 For I lift up my hand to **h,** and say, I live 8064
33:13 for the precious things of **h,** for the dew, 8064
33:26 *who* rideth *upon* the **h** in thy help, 8064
Jos 2:11 *is* God in **h** above, and in earth beneath. 8064
8:20 the smoke of the city ascended up to **h,** 8064
10:11 stones from **h** upon them unto Azekah, 8064
10:13 So the sun stood still in the midst of **h,** 8064
Jdg 5:20 They fought from **h;** the stars in their 8064
13:20 the flame went up toward **h** from off 8064
20:40 the flame of the city ascended up to **h.** 8064
1Sa 2:10 out of **h** shall he thunder upon them: 8064
5:12 and the cry of the city went up *to* **h.** 8064
2Sa 18: 9 he was taken up between the **h** and 8064
21:10 until water dropped upon them out of **h,** 8064
22: 8 the foundations of **h** moved and shook, 8064
22:14 The LORD thundered from **h,** 8064
1Ki 8:22 and spread forth his hands *toward* **h:** 8064
8:23 in **h** above, or on earth beneath, 8064
8:27 **h** and heaven of heavens cannot contain 8064
8:27 and **h** of heavens cannot contain thee; 8064
8:30 hear thou in **h** thy dwelling place: 8064
8:32 hear thou in **h,** and do, and judge thy 8064
8:34 hear thou in **h,** and forgive the sin of thy 8064

H

1Ki	8:35	When **h** is shut up, and there is no rain,	8064
	8:36	hear thou *in* **h**, and forgive the sin of thy	8064
	8:39	hear thou *in* **h** thy dwelling place,	8064
	8:43	Hear thou *in* **h** thy dwelling place,	8064
	8:45	hear thou *in* **h** their prayer and their	8064
	8:49	their supplication *in* **h** thy dwelling place,	8064
	8:54	his knees with his hands spread *up to* **h**.	8064
	18:45	the **h** was black *with* clouds and wind,	8064
	22:19	all the host of **h** standing by him on his	8064
2Ki	1:10	let fire come down from **h**,	8064
	1:10	there came down fire from **h**,	8064
	1:12	let fire come down from **h**,	8064
	1:12	the fire of God came down from **h**,	8064
	1:14	came fire down from **h**, and burnt up	8064
	2:1	take up Elijah *into* **h** by a whirlwind,	8064
	2:11	Elijah went up by a whirlwind *into* **h**.	8064
	7:2	*if* the LORD would make windows in **h**,	8064
	7:19	*if* the LORD should make windows in **h**,	8064
	14:27	blot out the name of Israel from under **h**:	8064
	17:16	worshipped all the host of **h**,	8064
	19:15	of the earth; thou hast made **h** and earth.	8064
	21:3	worshipped all the host of **h**,	8064
	21:5	he built altars for all the host of **h** in	8064
	23:4	for the grove, and for all the host of **h**.	8064
	23:5	to the planets, and to all the host of **h**.	8064
1Ch	21:16	LORD stand between the earth and the **h**,	8064
	21:26	he answered him from **h** by fire upon	8064
	29:11	for all *that is* in the **h** and in the earth *is*	8064
2Ch	2:6	seeing the **h** and heaven of heavens	8064
	2:6	and **h** of heavens cannot contain him?	8064
	2:12	God of Israel, that made **h** and earth,	8064
	6:13	and spread forth his hands towards **h**,	8064
	6:14	*there is* no God like thee in the **h**, nor in	8064
	6:18	**h** and the heaven of heavens cannot	8064
	6:18	the **h** of heavens cannot contain thee;	8064
	6:21	from thy dwelling place, *even* from **h**;	8064
	6:23	hear thou from **h**, and do, and judge thy	8064
	6:26	the **h** is shut up, and there is no rain,	8064
	6:27	hear thou *from* **h**, and forgive the sin of	8064
	6:30	hear thou from **h** thy dwelling place,	8064
	7:1	the fire came down from **h**,	8064
	7:13	If I shut up **h** that there be no rain, or if I	8064
	7:14	will I hear from **h**, and will forgive their	8064
	18:18	the host of **h** standing on his right hand	8064
	20:6	of our fathers, *art* not thou God in **h**?	8064
	28:9	them in a rage *that* reacheth up unto **h**.	8064
	30:27	to his holy dwelling place, *even* unto **h**.	8064
	32:20	the son of Amoz, prayed and cried *to* **h**.	8064
	33:3	worshipped all the host of **h**,	8064
	33:5	he built altars for all the host of **h** in	8064
	36:23	earth hath the LORD God of **h** given me;	8064
Ezr	1:2	The LORD God of **h** hath given me all	8064
	5:11	We are the servants of the God of **h** and	8064
	5:12	had provoked the God of **h** unto wrath,	8065
	6:9	for the burnt offerings of the God of **h**,	8065
	6:10	of sweet savours unto the God of **h**,	8065
	7:12	a scribe of the law of the God of **h**,	8065
	7:21	the scribe of the law of the God of **h**,	8065
	7:23	is commanded by the God of **h**,	8065
	7:23	done for the house of the God of **h**:	8065
Ne	1:4	fasted, and prayed before the God of **h**,	8064
	1:5	O LORD God of **h**, the great and terrible	8064
	1:9	cast out unto the uttermost part of the **h**,	8064
	2:4	request? So I prayed to the God of **h**.	8064
	2:20	said unto them, The God of **h**, he will	8064
	9:6	hast made **h**, the heaven of heavens,	8064
	9:6	the **h** of heavens, with all their host,	8064
	9:6	and the host of **h** worshippeth thee.	8064
	9:13	spakest with them from **h**, and gavest	8064
	9:15	them bread from **h** for their hunger,	8064
	9:23	also multipliedst thou as the stars of **h**,	8064
	9:27	unto thee, thou heardest *them* from **h**;	8064
	9:28	unto thee, thou heardest *them* from **h**;	8064
Job	1:16	The fire of God is fallen from **h**,	8064
	2:12	dust upon their heads toward **h**.	8064
	11:8	*It is* as high as **h**; what canst thou do?	8064
	16:19	my witness *is* in **h**, and my record *is*	8064
	20:27	The **h** shall reveal his iniquity;	8064
	22:12	*Is* not God in the height of **h**?	8064
	22:14	and he walketh *in* the circuit of **h**.	8064
	26:11	pillars of **h** tremble and are astonished	8064
	28:24	the earth, *and* seeth under the whole **h**;	8064
	35:11	maketh us wiser than the fowls of **h**?	8064
	37:3	He directeth it under the whole **h**,	8064
	38:29	hoary frost of **h**, who hath gendered it?	8064
	38:33	Knowest thou the ordinances of **h**? canst	8064
	38:37	or who can stay the bottles of **h**,	8064
	41:11	*whatsoever is* under the whole **h** *is* mine.	8064
Ps	11:4	holy temple, the LORD'S throne *is* in **h**:	8064
	14:2	The LORD looked down from **h** upon	8064
	19:6	His going forth *is* from the end of the **h**,	8064
	20:6	he will hear him from his holy **h** with	8064
	33:13	The LORD looketh from **h**; he beholdeth	8064
	53:2	God looked down from **h** upon the	8064
	57:3	He shall send from **h**, and save me *from*	8064
	69:34	Let the **h** and earth praise him, the seas,	8064
	73:25	Whom have I in **h** *but thee*? and *there is*	8064
	76:8	didst cause judgment to be heard from **h**;	8064
	77:18	The voice of thy thunder *was* in the **h**:	1534
	78:23	from above, and opened the doors of **h**,	8064
	78:24	and had given them *of* the corn of **h**.	8064
	78:26	He caused an east wind to blow in the **h**:	8064
	79:2	*given to be* meat unto the fowls of the **h**,	8064
	80:14	look down from **h**, and behold,	8064
	85:11	righteousness shall look down from **h**.	8064

Ps	89:6	For who in the **h** can be compared unto	7834
	89:29	for ever, and his throne as the days of **h**.	8064
	89:37	the moon, and *as* a faithful witness in **h**.	7834
	102:19	from **h** did the LORD behold the earth;	8064
	103:11	For as the **h** is high above the earth,	8064
	104:12	By them shall the fowls of the **h** have	8064
	105:40	and satisfied them *with* the bread of **h**.	8064
	107:26	They mount up to the **h**, they go down	8064
	113:6	to behold the *things that are* in **h**,	8064
	115:15	*are* blessed of the LORD which made **h**	8064
	115:16	The **h**, *even* the heavens, *are* the LORD'S:	8064
	119:89	O LORD, thy word *is* settled in **h**.	8064
	121:2	from the LORD, which made **h** and earth.	8064
	124:8	of the LORD, who made **h** and earth.	8064
	134:3	The LORD that made **h** and earth bless	8064
	135:6	*that* did he in **h**, and in earth, in the seas,	8064
	136:26	O give thanks unto the God of **h**: for his	8064
	139:8	If I ascend up *into* **h**, thou *art* there: if I	8064
	146:6	Which made **h**, and earth, the sea, and all	8064
	147:8	Who covereth the **h** with clouds,	8064
	148:13	his glory *is* above the earth and **h**.	8064
Pr	23:5	they fly away as an eagle *toward* **h**.	8064
	25:3	The **h** for height, and the earth for depth,	8064
	30:4	Who hath ascended up *into* **h**,	8064
Ecc	1:13	all *things* that are done under **h**:	8064
	2:3	which they should do under the **h** all	8064
	3:1	and a time to every purpose under the **h**:	8064
	5:2	for God *is* in **h**, and thou upon earth:	8064
Isa	13:5	from the end of **h**, *even* the LORD,	8064
	13:10	For the stars of the **h** and the constellations	8064
	14:12	How art thou fallen from **h**, O Lucifer,	8064
	14:13	said in thine heart, I will ascend *into* **h**,	8064
	34:4	And all the host of **h** shall be dissolved,	8064
	34:5	For my sword shall be bathed in **h**:	8064
	37:16	of the earth: thou hast made **h** and earth.	8064
	40:12	meted out **h** with the span,	8064
	55:10	snow from **h**, and returneth not thither,	8064
	63:15	Look down from **h**, and behold from	8064
	66:1	The **h** *is* my throne, and the earth *is* my	8064
Jer	7:18	to make cakes to the queen of the **h**,	8064
	7:33	shall be meat for the fowls of the **h**,	8064
	8:2	the moon, and all the host of **h**, whom	8064
	8:7	the stork in the **h** knoweth her appointed	8064
	10:2	and be not dismayed at the signs of **h**;	8064
	15:3	the fowls of the **h**, and the beasts of	8064
	16:4	carcases shall be meat for the fowls of **h**,	8064
	19:7	I give to be meat for the fowls of the **h**,	8064
	19:13	have burnt incense unto all the host of **h**,	8064
	23:24	Do not I fill **h** and earth? saith the LORD.	8064
	31:37	If **h** above can be measured,	8064
	32:17	thou hast made the **h** and the earth by	8064
	33:22	As the host of **h** cannot be numbered,	8064
	33:25	I have not appointed the ordinances of **h**	8064
	34:20	shall be for meat unto the fowls of the **h**,	8064
	44:17	to burn incense unto the queen of **h**,	8064
	44:18	left off to burn incense to the queen of **h**,	8064
	44:19	we burnt incense to the queen of **h**,	8064
	44:25	to burn incense to the queen of **h**,	8064
	49:36	four winds from the four quarters of **h**,	8064
	51:9	for her judgment reacheth unto **h**,	8064
	51:15	hath stretched out the **h** by his	8064
	51:48	**h** and the earth, and all that *is* therein,	8064
	51:53	Though Babylon should mount up *to* **h**,	8064
La	2:1	down from **h** *unto* the earth the beauty	8064
	3:50	The LORD look down, and behold from **h**.	8064
	4:19	are swifter than the eagles of the **h**:	8064
Eze	8:3	lift me up between the earth and the **h**,	8064
	29:5	of the field and to the fowls of the **h**.	8064
	31:6	All the fowls of **h** made their nests in his	8064
	31:13	Upon his ruin shall all the fowls of the **h**	8064
	32:4	will cause all the fowls of the **h** to remain	8064
	32:7	I will cover the **h**, and make the stars	8064
	32:8	All the bright lights of **h** will I make dark	8064
	38:20	the fowls of the **h**, and the beasts of	8064
Da	2:18	of the God of **h** concerning this secret;	8065
	2:19	Then Daniel blessed the God of **h**.	8065
	2:28	there is a God in **h** that revealeth secrets,	8065
	2:37	for the God of **h** hath given thee a	8065
	2:38	the fowls of the **h** hath he given into	8065
	2:44	the days of these kings shall the God of **h**	8065
	4:11	The height thereof reached unto **h**,	8065
	4:12	the fowls of the **h** dwelt in the boughs	8065
	4:13	and a holy one came down from **h**;	8065
	4:15	let it be wet with the dew of **h**, and *let*	8065
	4:20	whose height reached unto the **h**,	8065
	4:21	upon whose branches the fowls of the **h**	8065
	4:22	reacheth unto **h**, and thy dominion to	8065
	4:23	and a holy one coming down from **h**,	8065
	4:23	let it be wet with the dew of **h**, and *let*	8065
	4:25	they *shall* wet thee with the dew of **h**,	8065
	4:31	there fell a voice from **h**, *saying*, O king	8065
	4:33	and his body was wet with the dew of **h**,	8065
	4:34	Nebuchadnezzar lift up mine eyes unto **h**,	8065
	4:35	according to his will in the army of **h**,	8065
	4:37	and extol and honour the King of **h**,	8065
	5:21	and his body was wet with the dew of **h**;	8065
	5:23	hast lifted up thyself against the Lord of **h**;	8065
	6:27	and wonders in **h** and in earth,	8065
	7:2	the four winds of the **h** strove upon	8065
	7:13	Son of man came with the clouds of **h**,	8065
	7:27	of the kingdom under the whole **h**,	8065
	8:8	notable ones toward the four winds of **h**.	8064
	8:10	it waxed great, *even* to the host of **h**;	8064
	9:12	under the whole **h** hath not been done as	8064
	11:4	be divided toward the four winds of **h**;	8064

Da	12:7	his right hand and his left hand unto **h**,	8064
Hos	2:18	with the fowls of **h**, and *with* the creeping	8064
	4:3	of the field, and with the fowls of **h**;	8064
	7:12	bring them down as the fowls of the **h**;	8064
Am	9:2	though they climb up *to* **h**, thence will I	8064
	9:6	*It is* he that buildeth his stories in the **h**,	8064
Jnh	1:9	I fear the LORD, the God of **h**, which hath	8064
Na	3:16	thy merchants above the stars of **h**:	8064
Zep	1:3	I will consume the fowls of the **h**,	8064
	1:5	them that worship the host of **h** upon	8064
Hag	1:10	Therefore the **h** over you is stayed from	8064
Zec	2:6	you abroad as the four winds of the **h**,	8064
	5:9	the ephah between the earth and the **h**.	8064
Mal	3:10	if I will not open you the windows of **h**,	8064
Mt	3:2	ye: for the kingdom of **h** is at hand.	3772
	3:17	lo a voice from **h**, saying, This is my	3772
	4:17	Repent: for the kingdom of **h** is at hand.	3772
	5:3	in spirit: for theirs is the kingdom of **h**.	3772
	5:10	for theirs is the kingdom of **h**.	3772
	5:12	for great *is* your reward in **h**: for so	3772
	5:16	and glorify your Father which is in **h**.	3772
	5:18	Till **h** and earth pass, one jot or one tittle	3772
	5:19	be called the least in the kingdom of **h**:	3772
	5:19	shall be called great in the kingdom of **h**.	3772
	5:20	in no case enter into the kingdom of **h**.	3772
	5:34	unto you, Swear not at all; neither by **h**;	3772
	5:45	the children of your Father which is in **h**:	3772
	5:48	as your Father which is in **h** is perfect.	3772
	6:1	no reward of your Father which is in **h**.	3772
	6:9	Our Father which art in **h**, Hallowed be	3772
	6:10	Thy will be done in earth, as *it is* in **h**.	3772
	6:20	But lay up for yourselves treasures in **h**,	3772
	7:11	**h** give good *things* to them that ask him?	3772
	7:21	Lord, shall enter into the kingdom of **h**;	3772
	7:21	doeth the will of my Father which is in **h**.	3772
	8:11	Isaac, and Jacob, in the kingdom of **h**.	3772
	10:7	saying, The kingdom of **h** is at hand.	3772
	10:32	also before my Father which is in **h**.	3772
	10:33	also deny before my Father which is in **h**.	3772
	11:11	least in the kingdom of **h** is greater than	3772
	11:12	now the kingdom of **h** suffereth violence,	3772
	11:23	Capernaum, which art exalted unto **h**,	3772
	11:25	Lord of **h** and earth, because thou hast	3772
	12:50	do the will of my Father which is in **h**,	3772
	13:11	know the mysteries of the kingdom of **h**,	3772
	13:24	The kingdom of **h** is likened unto a man	3772
	13:31	The kingdom of **h** is like unto a grain of	3772
	13:33	The kingdom of **h** is like unto leaven,	3772
	13:44	the kingdom of **h** is like unto treasure hid	3772
	13:45	the kingdom of **h** is like unto a merchant	3772
	13:47	Again, the kingdom of **h** is like unto a net,	3772
	13:52	**h** is like unto a man *that is* a householder,	3772
	14:19	looking up to **h**, he blessed, and brake,	3772
	16:1	that he would shew them a sign from **h**.	3772
	16:17	unto thee, but my Father which is in **h**.	3772
	16:19	unto thee the keys of the kingdom of **h**:	3772
	16:19	shalt bind on earth shall be bound in **h**:	3772
	16:19	shalt loose on earth shall be loosed in **h**.	3772
	18:1	Who is the greatest in the kingdom of **h**?	3772
	18:3	ye shall not enter into the kingdom of **h**.	3772
	18:4	the same is greatest in the kingdom of **h**.	3772
	18:10	That in **h** their angels do always behold	3772
	18:10	the face of my Father which is in **h**.	3772
	18:14	not the will of your Father which is in **h**,	3772
	18:18	shall bind on earth shall be bound in **h**:	3772
	18:18	shall loose on earth shall be loosed in **h**.	3772
	18:19	done for them of my Father which is in **h**.	3772
	18:23	Therefore is the kingdom of **h** likened	3772
	19:14	unto me: for of such is the kingdom of **h**.	3772
	19:21	poor, and thou shalt have treasure in **h**:	3772
	19:23	shall hardly enter into the kingdom of **h**.	3772
	20:1	the kingdom of **h** is like unto a man	3772
	21:25	from **h**, or of men? And they reasoned	3772
	21:25	saying, If we shall say, From **h**;	3772
	22:2	The kingdom of **h** is like unto a certain	3772
	22:30	but are as *the* angels of God in **h**.	3772
	23:9	for one is your Father, which is in **h**.	3772
	23:13	for ye shut up the kingdom of **h** against	3772
	23:22	And he that shall swear by **h**, sweareth by	3772
	24:29	and the stars shall fall from **h**,	3772
	24:30	appear the sign of the Son of man in **h**:	3772
	24:30	coming in the clouds of **h** with power	3772
	24:31	winds, from one end of **h** to the other.	3772
	24:35	**h** and earth shall pass away, but my	3772
	24:36	not the angels of **h**, but my Father only.	3772
	25:1	Then shall the kingdom of **h** be likened	3772
	25:14	the kingdom of **h** is as a man travelling	NIG
	26:64	of power, and coming in the clouds of **h**.	3772
	28:2	the angel of the Lord descended from **h**,	3772
	28:18	All power is given unto me in **h** and	3772
Mk	1:11	And there came a voice from **h**,	3772
	6:41	he looked up to **h**, and blessed,	3772
	7:34	And looking up to **h**, he sighed,	3772
	8:11	seeking of him a sign from **h**,	3772
	10:21	poor, and thou shalt have treasure in **h**:	3772
	11:25	that your Father also which is in **h** may	3772
	11:26	neither will your Father which is in **h**	3772
	11:30	of John, was *it* from **h**, or of men?	3772
	11:31	saying, If we shall say, From **h**;	3772
	12:25	but are as *the* angels which are in **h**.	3772
	13:25	And the stars of **h** shall fall,	3772
	13:25	the powers that are in **h** shall be shaken.	3772
	13:27	of the earth to the uttermost part of **h**.	3772
	13:31	**H** and earth shall pass away: but my	3772
	13:32	not the angels which are in **h**, neither	3772

Mk	14:62 of power, and coming in the clouds of **h**.	3772
	16:19 he was received up into **h**, and sat on	3772
Lk	2:15 angels were gone away from them into **h**,	3772
	3:21 and praying, the **h** was opened,	3772
	3:22 and a voice came from **h**, which said,	3772
	4:25 when the **h** was shut up three years and	3772
	6:23 joy: for behold, your reward *is* great in **h**:	3772
	9:16 and the two fishes, and looking up to **h**,	3772
	9:54 we command fire to come down from **h**,	3772
	10:15 Capernaum, which art exalted to **h**,	3772
	10:18 I beheld Satan as lightning fall from **h**.	3772
	10:20 because your names are written in **h**.	3772
	10:21 thank thee, O Father, Lord of **h** and earth,	3772
	11: 2 ye pray, say, Our Father which art in **h**,	3772
	11: 2 Thy will be done, as in **h**, so in earth.	3772
	11:16 him, sought of him a sign from **h**.	3772
	15: 7 that likewise joy shall be in **h** over one	3772
	15:18 I have sinned against **h**, and before thee,	3772
	15:21 I have sinned against **h**, and in thy sight,	3772
	16:17 And it is easier for **h** and earth to pass,	3772
	17:24 lighteneth out of the one *part* under **h**,	3772
	17:24 shineth unto the other *part* under **h**;	3772
	17:29 it rained fire and brimstone from **h**,	3772
	18:13 not lift up so much as *his* eyes unto **h**,	3772
	18:22 poor, and thou shalt have treasure in **h**:	3772
	19:38 peace in **h**, and glory in the highest.	3772
	20: 4 of John, was it from **h**, or of men?	3772
	20: 5 saying, If we shall say, From **h**;	3772
	21:11 and great signs shall there be from **h**.	3772
	21:26 for the powers of **h** shall be shaken.	3772
	21:33 **H** and earth shall pass away: but my	3772
	22:43 appeared an angel unto him from **h**,	3772
	24:51 parted from them, and carried up into **h**.	3772
Jn	1:32 I saw the Spirit descending from **h** like a	3772
	1:51 Hereafter ye shall see **h** open,	3772
	3:13 no *man* hath ascended up to **h**, but he	3772
	3:13 but he that came down from **h**, *even*	3772
	3:13 even the Son of man which is in **h**.	3772
	3:27 except it be given him from **h**.	3772
	3:31 he that cometh from **h** is above all.	3772
	6:31 He gave them bread from **h** to eat.	3772
	6:32 Moses gave you not *that* bread from **h**;	3772
	6:32 Father giveth you the true bread from **h**.	3772
	6:33 of God is he which cometh down from **h**,	3772
	6:38 For I came down from **h**, not to do mine	3772
	6:41 I am the bread which came down from **h**.	3772
	6:42 then *that* he saith, I came down from **h**?	3772
	6:50 is the bread which cometh down from **h**,	3772
	6:51 living bread which came down from **h**:	3772
	6:58 is *that* bread which came down from **h**:	3772
	12:28 Then came there a voice from **h**, *saying*,	3772
	17: 1 and lift up his eyes to **h**, and said, Father,	3772
Ac	1:10 while they looked stedfastly toward **h**	3772
	1:11 of Galilee, why stand ye gazing up into **h**?	3772
	1:11 which is taken up from you into **h**, shall	3772
	1:11 manner as ye have seen him go into **h**.	3772
	2: 2 And suddenly there came a sound from **h**	3772
	2: 5 devout men, out of every nation under **h**.	3772
	2:19 And I will shew wonders in **h** above,	3772
	3:21 Whom the **h** must receive until the times	3772
	4:12 there is none other name under **h** given	3772
	4:24 hast made **h**, and earth, and the sea,	3772
	7:42 gave them up to worship the host of **h**;	3772
	7:49 **H** is my throne, and earth *is* my footstool:	3772
	7:55 looked up stedfastly into **h**, and saw	3772
	9: 3 shined round about him a light from **h**:	3772
	10:11 And saw **h** opened, and a certain vessel	3772
	10:16 the vessel was received up again into **h**.	3772
	11: 5 let down from **h** by four corners;	3772
	11: 9 But *the* voice answered me again from **h**,	3772
	11:10 and all were drawn up again into **h**.	3772
	14:15 which made **h**, and earth, and the sea,	3772
	14:17 and gave us rain **from h**,	3771
	17:24 seeing that he is Lord of **h** and earth,	3772
	22: 6 suddenly there shone from **h** a great light	3772
	26:13 O king, I saw in the way a light **from h**,	3771
Ro	1:18 For the wrath of God is revealed from **h**	3772
	10: 6 in thine heart, Who shall ascend into **h**?	3772
1Co	8: 5 whether in **h** or in earth, (as there be gods	3772
	15:47 the second man *is* the Lord from **h**.	3772
2Co	5: 2 upon with our house which is from **h**:	3772
	12: 2 such a one caught up to the third **h**.	3772
Gal	1: 8 But though we, or an angel from **h**,	3772
Eph	1:10 both which are in **h**, and which are on	3772
	3:15 Of whom the whole family in **h** and earth	3772
	6: 9 knowing that your Master also is in **h**;	3772
Php	2:10 of *things* in **h**, and *things* in earth,	2032
	3:20 For our conversation is in **h**; from whence	3772
Col	1: 5 For the hope which is laid up for you in **h**,	3772
	1:16 that are in **h**, and that are in earth, visible	3772
	1:20 *they* be *things* in earth, or *things* in **h**.	3772
	1:23 to every creature which is under **h**;	3772
	4: 1 knowing that ye also have a Master in **h**.	3772
1Th	1:10 And to wait for his Son from **h**, whom he	3772
	4:16 For the Lord himself shall descend from **h**	3772
2Th	1: 7 be revealed from **h** with his mighty angels,	3772
Heb	9:24 but into **h** itself, now to appear in	3772
	10:34 knowing in yourselves that *ye* have in **h** a	3772
	12:23 which are written in **h**, and to God	3772
	12:25 turn away from him that *speaketh* from **h**:	3772
	12:26 I shake not the earth only, but also **h**.	3772
Jas	5:12 swear not, neither by **h**, neither by	3772
	5:18 the gave rain, and the earth brought	3772
1Pe	1: 4 fadeth not away, reserved in **h** for you,	3772
	1:12 with the Holy Ghost sent *down* from **h**;	3772

1Pe	3:22 Who is gone into **h**, and is on the right	3772
2Pe	1:18 And this voice which came from **h** we	3772
1Jn	5: 7 For there are three that bear record in **h**,	3772
Rev	cometh down out of **h** from my God:	3772
	4: 1 and behold, a door *was* opened in **h**:	3772
	4: 2 a throne was set in **h**, and one sat on	3772
	5: 3 And no *man* in **h**, nor in earth,	3772
	5:13 And every creature which is in **h**,	3772
	6:13 And the stars of **h** fell unto the earth,	3772
	6:14 And the **h** departed as a scrole when it is	3772
	8: 1 there was silence in **h** about the space of	3772
	8:10 and there fell a great star from **h**,	3772
	8:13 an angel flying through the **midst of h**,	3321
	9: 1 I saw a star fall from **h** unto the earth:	3772
	10: 1 another mighty angel come down from **h**,	3772
	10: 4 I heard a voice from **h** saying unto me,	3772
	10: 5 upon the earth lifted up his hand to **h**,	3772
	10: 6 created it, and the *things* that therein	3772
	10: 8 And the voice which I heard from **h** spake	3772
	11: 6 have power to shut **h**, that it rain not	3772
	11:12 they heard a great voice from **h** saying	3772
	11:12 And they ascended up to **h** in a cloud;	3772
	11:13 and gave glory to the God of **h**.	3772
	11:15 and there were great voices in **h**, saying,	3772
	11:19 And the temple of God was opened in **h**,	3772
	12: 1 And there appeared a great wonder in **h**;	3772
	12: 3 And there appeared another wonder in **h**;	3772
	12: 4 tail drew the third *part* of the stars of **h**,	3772
	12: 7 And there was war in **h**: Michael and	3772
	12: 8 was their place found any more in **h**.	3772
	12:10 And I heard a loud voice saying in **h**,	3772
	13: 6 his tabernacle, and them that dwell in **h**.	3772
	13:13 he maketh fire come down from **h** on	3772
	14: 2 And I heard a voice from **h**, as the voice	3772
	14: 6 I saw another angel fly in the **midst of h**,	3321
	14: 7 and worship him that made **h**, and earth,	3772
	14:13 I heard a voice from **h** saying unto me,	3772
	14:17 came out of the temple which is in **h**,	3772
	15: 1 And I saw another sign in **h**, great and	3772
	15: 5 of the testimony in **h** was opened:	3772
	16:11 And blasphemed the God of **h** because	3772
	16:21 there fell upon men a great hail out of **h**,	3772
	18: 1 I saw another angel come down from **h**,	3772
	18: 4 And I heard another voice from **h**, saying,	3772
	18: 5 her sins have reached unto **h**, and God	3772
	18:20 and ye holy apostles and prophets;	3772
	19: 1 I heard a great voice of much people in **h**,	3772
	19:11 And I saw **h** opened, and behold a white	3772
	19:14 And the armies which were in **h** followed	3772
	19:17 to all the fowls that fly in the **midst of h**,	3321
	20: 1 And I saw an angel come down from **h**,	3772
	20: 9 and fire came down from God out of **h**,	3772
	20:11 face the earth and the **h** fled *away*; and	3772
	21: 1 And I saw a new **h** and a new earth:	3772
	21: 1 for the first **h** and the first earth were	3772
	21: 2 coming down from God out of **h**,	3772
	21: 3 And I heard a great voice out of **h** saying,	3772
	21:10 descending out of **h** from God,	3772

HEAVEN'S (1) [HEAVEN]

Mt	19:12 eunuchs for the kingdom of **h** sake.	3772

HEAVENLY (23) [HEAVEN]

Mt	6:14 your **h** Father will also forgive you:	3770
	6:26 barns; yet your **h** Father feedeth them.	3770
	6:32 for your **h** Father knoweth that ye have	3770
	15:13 which my **h** Father hath not planted,	3770
	18:35 So likewise shall my **h** Father do *also* unto	2032
Lk	2:13 a multitude of the **h** host praising God,	3770
	11:13 much more shall *your* **h** Father	1537+3772
Jn	3:12 shall ye believe, if I tell you of **h** *things*?	2032
Ac	26:19 not disobedient unto the **h** vision:	3770
1Co	15:48 as *is* the **h**, such *are they* also that are	2032
	15:48 heavenly, such *are they* also *that are* **h**.	2032
	15:49 we shall also bear the image of the **h**.	2032
Eph	1: 3 spiritual blessings in **h** *places* in Christ:	2032
	1:20 set *him* at his own right hand in the **h**	2032
	2: 6 made *us* sit together in **h** *places* in Christ	2032
	3:10 powers in **h** *places* might be known by	2032
2Ti	4:18 and will preserve *me* unto his **h** kingdom:	2032
Heb	3: 1 holy brethren, partakers of the **h** calling,	2032
	6: 4 and have tasted of the **h** gift,	2032
	8: 5 shadow of **h** *things*, as Moses was	2032
	9:23 the **h** *things* themselves with better	2032
	11:16 they desire a better *country*, that is, a **h**:	2032
	12:22 the **h** Jerusalem, and to an innumerable	2032

HEAVENS (133) [HEAVEN]

Ge	2: 1 Thus the **h** and the earth were finished,	8064
	2: 4 These *are* the generations of the **h** and	8064
	2: 4 the Lord God made the earth and the **h**,	8064
Dt	10:14 the heaven of **h** *is* the Lord's thy God,	8064
	32: 1 Give ear, O **h**, and I will speak;	8064
	33:28 wine; also his **h** shall drop down dew.	8064
Jdg	5: 4 the earth trembled, and the **h** dropped,	8064
2Sa	22:10 He bowed the **h** also, and came down;	8064
1Ki	8:27 and heaven of **h** cannot contain thee;	8064
1Ch	16:26 *are* idols: but the Lord made the **h**.	8064
	16:31 the **h** be glad, and let the earth rejoice;	8064
	27:23 increase Israel like to the stars of the **h**.	8064
2Ch	2: 6 and heaven of **h** cannot contain him?	8064
	6:18 and the heaven of **h** cannot contain thee;	8064
	6:25 hear thou from the **h**, and forgive the sin	8064
	6:33 hear thou from the **h**, *even* from thy	8064

2Ch	6:35 hear thou from the **h** their prayer and	8064
	6:39 hear thou from the **h**, *even* from thy	8064
Ezr	9: 6 and our trespass is grown up unto the **h**.	8064
Ne	9: 6 the heaven of **h**, with all their host,	8064
Job	9: 8 Which alone spreadeth out the **h**,	8064
	14:12 the **h** *be* no more, they shall not awake,	8064
	15:15 yea, the **h** are not clean in his sight.	8064
	20: 6 his excellency mount up to the **h**,	8064
	26:13 By his spirit he hath garnished the **h**;	8064
	35: 5 Look unto the **h**, and see; and behold	8064
Ps	2: 4 He that sitteth in the **h** shall laugh:	8064
	8: 1 who hast set thy glory above the **h**.	8064
	8: 3 When I consider thy **h**, the work of thy	8064
	18: 9 He bowed the **h** also, and came down:	8064
	18:13 The Lord also thundered in the **h**,	8064
	19: 1 The **h** declare the glory of God;	8064
	33: 6 By the word of the Lord were the **h**	8064
	36: 5 Thy mercy, O Lord, *is* in the **h**;	8064
	50: 4 He shall call to the **h** from above, and to	8064
	50: 6 the **h** shall declare his righteousness:	8064
	57: 5 Be thou exalted, O God, above the **h**;	8064
	57:10 For thy mercy *is* great unto the **h**,	8064
	57:11 Be thou exalted, O God, above the **h**:	8064
	68: 4 extol him that rideth upon the **h** by his	6160
	68: 8 **h** also dropped at the presence of God:	8064
	68:33 him that rideth upon the **h** of heavens,	8064
	68:33 him that rideth upon the heavens of **h**,	8064
	73: 9 They set their mouth against the **h**,	8064
	89: 2 shalt thou establish in the very **h**.	8064
	89: 5 the **h** shall praise thy wonders, O Lord:	8064
	89:11 The **h** *are* thine, the earth also *is* thine:	8064
	96: 5 *are* idols: but the Lord made the **h**.	8064
	96:11 Let the **h** rejoice, and let the earth be glad	8064
	97: 6 The **h** declare his righteousness, and all	8064
	102:25 and the **h** *are* the work of thy hands.	8064
	103:19 Lord hath prepared his throne in the **h**;	8064
	104: 2 who stretchest out the **h** like a curtain:	8064
	108: 4 For thy mercy *is* great above the **h**:	8064
	108: 5 Be thou exalted, O God, above the **h**:	8064
	113: 4 all nations, *and* his glory above the **h**.	8064
	115: 3 our God *is* in the **h**: he hath done	8064
	115:16 The heaven, *even* the **h**, *are* the Lord's:	8064
	123: 1 mine eyes, O thou that dwellest in the **h**.	8064
	136: 5 To him that by wisdom made the **h**:	8064
	144: 5 Bow thy **h**, O Lord, and come down:	8064
	148: 1 Praise ye the Lord from the **h**:	8064
	148: 4 ye **h** of heavens, and ye waters that *be*	8064
	148: 4 ye heavens of **h**, and ye waters that *be*	8064
	148: 4 ye waters that *be* above the **h**.	8064
Pr	3:19 understanding hath he established the **h**.	8064
	8:27 When he prepared the **h**, I *was* there:	8064
Isa	1: 2 Hear, O **h**, and give ear, O earth:	8064
	5:30 and the light is darkened in the **h** thereof.	6183
	13:13 Therefore I will shake the **h**, and the	8064
	34: 4 the **h** shall be rolled together as a scrole:	8064
	40:22 that stretcheth out the **h** as a curtain,	8064
	42: 5 he that created the **h**, and stretched them	8064
	44:23 Sing, O ye **h**; for the Lord hath done *it*:	8064
	44:24 *things*; that stretcheth forth the **h** alone;	8064
	45: 8 Drop down, ye **h**, from above, and let	8064
	45:12 stretched out the **h**, and all their host	8064
	45:18 thus saith the Lord that created the **h**;	8064
	48:13 and my right hand hath spanned the **h**:	8064
	49:13 Sing, O **h**; and be joyful, O earth;	8064
	50: 3 I clothe the **h** with blackness, and I make	8064
	51: 6 Lift up your eyes to the **h**, and look upon	8064
	51: 6 for the **h** shall vanish away like smoke,	8064
	51:13 that hath stretched forth the **h**, and laid	8064
	51:16 that I may plant the **h**, and lay	8064
	55: 9 For *as* the **h** are higher than the earth,	8064
	64: 1 that thou wouldest rend the **h**, that thou	8064
	65:17 behold, I create new **h** and a new earth:	8064
	66:22 For as the new **h** and the new earth,	8064
Jer	2:12 O ye **h**, at this, and be horribly afraid,	8064
	4:23 void; and the **h**, and they *had* no light.	8064
	4:25 man, and all the birds of the **h** were fled.	8064
	4:28 earth mourn, and the **h** above be black:	8064
	9:10 both the fowl of the **h** and the beast are	8064
	10:11 The gods that have not made the **h** and	8065
	10:11 from the earth, and from under these **h**.	8065
	10:12 hath stretched out the **h** by his discretion.	8064
	10:13 *there is* a multitude of waters in the **h**,	8064
	14:22 can the **h** give showers? *art* not thou, he,	8064
	51:16 *there is* a multitude of waters in the **h**,	8064
La	3:41 heart with *our* hands unto God in the **h**.	8064
	3:66 destroy them in anger from under the **h** of	8064
Eze	1: 1 *that* the **h** were opened, and I saw visions	8064
Da	4:26 that thou shalt have known that the **h**	8065
Hos	2:21 I will hear the **h**, and they shall hear	8064
Joel	2:10 quake before them; the **h** shall tremble:	8064
	2:30 I will shew wonders in the **h** and in	8064
	3:16 and the **h** and the earth shall shake:	8064
Hab	3: 3 His glory covered the **h**, and the earth	8064
Hag	2: 6 I *will* shake the **h**, and the earth,	8064
	2:21 I *will* shake the **h** and the earth;	8064
Zec	6: 5 me, These *are* the four spirits of the **h**,	8064
	8:12 increase, and the **h** shall give their dew;	8064
	12: 1 which stretcheth forth the **h**, and layeth	8064
Mt	3:16 and lo, the **h** were opened unto him,	3772
	24:29 the powers of the **h** shall be shaken:	3772
Mk	1:10 he saw the **h** opened, and the Spirit like a	3772
Lk	12:33 a treasure in the **h** that faileth not, where	3772
Ac	2:34 For David is not ascended into the **h**:	3772
	7:56 And said, Behold, I see the **h** opened,	3772
2Co	5: 1 not made with hand, eternal in the **h**.	3772

H

Eph	4:10 also that ascended up far above all **h**,	3772
Heb	1:10 and the **h** are the works of thine hands:	3772
	4:14 that is passed into the **h**, Jesus the Son of	3772
	7:26 from sinners, and made higher than the **h**;	3772
	8: 1 of the throne of the Majesty in the **h**;	3772
	9:23 in the **h** should be purified with these:	3772
2Pe	3: 5 by the word of God the **h** were of old,	3772
	3: 7 But the **h** and the earth, which are now,	3772
	3:10 in the which the **h** shall pass away with	3772
	3:12 wherein the **h** being on fire shall be	3772
	3:13 look for new **h** and a new earth,	3772
Rev	12:12 ye **h**, and ye that dwell in them.	3772

HEAVIER (3) [HEAVY]

Job	6: 3 For now it would be **h** than the sand of	3513
	23: 2 my stroke is **h** than my groaning.	3513
Pr	27: 3 but a fool's wrath is **h** than them both.	3515

HEAVILY (3) [HEAVY]

Ex	14:25 that they drave them **h**:	3517+871.1
Ps	35:14 I bowed down **h**, as one that mourneth	6937
Isa	47: 6 the ancient hast thou very **h** laid thy	3513

HEAVINESS (14) [HEAVY]

Ezr	9: 5 evening sacrifice I arose up from my **h**;	8589
Job	9:27 I will leave off my **h**, and comfort myself:	6440
Ps	69:20 hath broken my heart; and I am **full of h.**	5136
	119:28 My soul melteth for **h**: strengthen thou	8424
Pr	10: 1 but a foolish son **is the h** of his mother.	8424
	12:25 In the heart of man maketh it stoop:	1674
	14:13 sorrowful; and the end of that mirth **is h**.	8424
Isa	29: 2 and there shall be **h** and sorrow:	8386
	61: 3 the garment of praise for the spirit of **h**;	3544
Ro	9: 2 That I have great **h** and continual sorrow	3077
2Co	2: 1 that I would not come again to you in **h**.	3077
Php	2:26 was **full of h**, because that ye had heard	85
Jas	4: 9 turned to mourning, and your joy to **h**.	2726
1Pe	1: 6 ye are in **h** through manifold temptations:	3076

HEAVY (40) [HEAVIER, HEAVILY, HEAVINESS]

Ex	17:12 Moses' hands were **h**; and they took a	3515
	18:18 this thing is too **h** for thee; thou art not	3515
Nu	11:14 people alone, because it is too **h** for me.	3515
1Sa	4:18 for he was an old man, and **h**.	3515
	5: 6 the hand of the LORD was **h** upon them	3513
	5:11 city; the hand of God was very **h** there.	3513
2Sa	14:26 polled it: because the hair was **h** on him,	3513
1Ki	12: 4 his yoke which he put upon us, lighter,	3515
	12:10 Thy father **made** our yoke, but make	3515
	12:11 My father did lade you with a **h** yoke,	3515
	12:14 My father **made** your yoke, and I will	3515
	14: 6 for I am sent to thee with **h** tidings.	7186
	20:43 the king of Israel went to his house **h** and	5620
	21: 4 came into his house **h** and displeased	5620
2Ch	10: 4 his **h** yoke that he put upon us, and we	3515
	10:10 Thy father **made** our yoke, but make	3515
	10:11 For whereas my father put a **h** yoke upon	3515
	10:14 My father **made** your yoke, but I will	3515
Ne	5:18 the bondage was **h** upon this people.	3513
Job	33: 7 neither shall my hand be **h** upon thee.	3513
Ps	32: 4 day and night thy hand was **h** upon me:	3513
	38: 4 as a burden they are too heavy for me.	3513
	38: 4 as a heavy burden they are too **h** for me.	3513
Pr	25:20 so is he that singeth songs to a **h** heart.	7451
	27: 3 A stone is **h**, and the sand weighty;	3514
	31: 6 and wine unto those that be of **h** hearts.	4751
Isa	6:10 **make** their ears **h**, and shut their eyes;	3513
	24:20 transgression thereof shall be **h** upon it;	3513
	30:27 his anger, and the burden thereof is **h**:	3514
	46: 1 your carriages were **h** loaden; they are a	6006
	58: 6 to undo the **h** burdens, and to let	4133
	59: 1 neither his ear **h**, that it cannot hear:	3513
La	3: 7 get out: he hath **made** my chain **h**.	3513
Mt	11:28 all ye that labour and are **h** laden, and I	5412
	23: 4 they bind **h** burdens and grievous to be	926
	26:37 and began to be sorrowful and very **h**.	85
	26:43 them asleep again: for their eyes were **h**.	916
Mk	14:33 to be sore amazed, and to be very **h**;	85
	14:40 them asleep again, (for their eyes were **h**,)	916
Lk	9:32 that were with him were **h** with sleep:	916

HEBER (13) [EBER, HEBER'S, HEBERITES]

Ge	46:17 and the sons of Beriah; **H**, and Malchiel.	2268
Nu	26:45 of **H**, the family of the Heberites:	2268
Jdg	4:11 Now the Kenite, which was of	2268
	4:17 the tent of Jael the wife of **H** the Kenite.	2268
	4:17 of Hazor and the house of **H** the Kenite.	2268
	5:24 shall Jael the wife of **H** the Kenite be,	2268
1Ch	4:18 **H** the father of Socho, and Jekuthiel	2268
	5:13 Jorai, and Jachan, and Zia, and **H**, seven.	5677
	7:31 **H**, and Malchiel, who is the father of	2268
	7:32 **H** begat Japhlet, and Shomer,	2268
	8:17 and Meshullam, and Hezeki, and **H**,	2268
	8:22 And Ishpan, and **H**, and Eliel,	5677
Lk	3:35 was the son of **H**, which was the son	1443

HEBER'S (1) [HEBER]

Jdg	4:21 Jael **H** wife took a nail of the tent,	2268

HEBERITES (1) [HEBER]

Nu	26:45 of Heber, the family of the **H**: of Malchiel,	2277

HEBREW (26) [HEBREWESS, HEBREWS, HEBREWS']

Ge	14:13 that had escaped, and told Abram the **H**;	5680
	39:14 hath brought in a **H** unto us to mock us;	5680
	39:17 saying, The **H** servant, which thou	5680

Ge	41:12 a **H**, servant to the captain of the guard;	5680
Ex	1:15 king of Egypt spake to the **H** midwives,	5680
	1:16 the office of a midwife to the **H women**,	5680
	1:19 Because the **H women** are not as	5680
	2: 7 and call to thee a nurse of the **H women**,	5680
	2:11 he spied an Egyptian smiting a **H**, one of	5680
	21: 2 If thou buy a **H** servant, six years he shall	5680
Dt	15:12 a **H man**, or a Hebrew woman, be sold	5680
	15:12 a Hebrew man, or a **H woman**, and be sold	5680
Jer	34: 9 being a **H** or a Hebrewess, go free;	5680
	34:14 years let ye go every man his brother a **H**,	5680
Jnh	1: 9 he said unto them, I am a **H**; and I fear	5680
Lk	23:38 and Latin, and **H**, THIS IS THE KING OF	1444
Jn	5: 2 is called **in the H tongue** Bethesda,	1447
	19:13 the Pavement, but **in the H**, Gabbatha.	1447
	19:17 skull, which is called **in the H** Golgotha:	1447
	19:20 and it was written **in H**, and Greek,	1447
Ac	21:40 he spake unto them **in the H** tongue,	1446
	22: 2 that he spake to them **in the H** tongue to them,	1446
	26:14 and saying **in the H** tongue, Saul, Saul,	1446
Php	3: 5 the tribe of Benjamin, an **H** of the Hebrews;	1445
Rev	9:11 name **in the H** tongue is Abaddon.	1447
	16:16 called **in the H** tongue Armageddon.	1447

HEBREWESS (1) [HEBREW]

Jer	34: 9 being a Hebrew or a **H**, go free;	5680

HEBREWS (21) [HEBREW]

Ge	40:15 was stolen away out of the land of the **H**:	5680
	43:32 Egyptians might not eat bread with the **H**;	5680
Ex	2:13 two men of the **H** strove together:	5680
	3:18 The LORD God of the **H** hath met with	5680
	5: 3 The God of the **H** hath met with us:	5680
	7:16 The LORD God of the **H** hath sent me	5680
	9: 1 Thus saith the LORD God of the **H**,	5680
	9:13 Thus saith the LORD God of the **H**,	5680
	10: 3 Thus saith the LORD God of the **H**,	5680
1Sa	4: 6 of this great shout in the camp of the **H**?	5680
	4: 9 that ye be not servants unto the **H**,	5680
	13: 3 all the land, saying, Let the **H** hear.	5680
	13: 7 of the **H** went over Jordan to the land	5680
	13:19 Lest the **H** make them swords or spears:	5680
	14:11 the **H** come forth out of the holes where	5680
	14:21 Moreover the **H** that were with	5680
	29: 3 What do these **H** here? And Achish said	5680
Ac	6: 1 murmuring of the Grecians against the **H**,	1445
2Co	11:22 Are they **H**? so am I. Are they Israelites?	1445
Php	3: 5 the tribe of Benjamin, a Hebrew of the **H**;	1445
Heb	13: S Written to the **H** from Italy by Timothy.	1445

HEBREWS' (1) [HEBREW]

Ex	2: 6 and said, This is one of the **H** children.	5680

HEBRON (73) [HEBRONITES]

Ge	13:18 which is in **H**, and built there an altar	2275
	23: 2 the same is **H** in the land of Canaan:	2275
	23:19 the same is **H** in the land of Canaan.	2275
	35:27 which is **H**, where Abraham and	2275
	37:14 So he sent him out of the vale of **H**,	2275
Ex	6:18 Amram, and Izhar, and **H**, and Uzziel:	2275
Nu	3:19 Amram, and Izehar, and Uzziel.	2275
	13:22 by the south, and came unto **H**;	2275
	13:22 (Now **H** was built seven years before	2275
Jos	10: 3 of Jerusalem sent unto Hoham king of **H**,	2275
	10: 5 the king of **H**, the king of Jarmuth,	2275
	10:23 the king of **H**, the king of Jarmuth,	2275
	10:36 and all Israel with him, unto **H**;	2275
	10:39 as he had done to **H**, so he did to Debir,	2275
	11:21 from **H**, from Debir, from Anab,	2275
	12:10 of Jerusalem, one; the king of **H**, one;	2275
	14:13 gave unto Caleb the son of Jephunneh **H**	2275
	14:14 **H** therefore became the inheritance of	2275
	14:15 the name of **H** before was Kirjath-arba;	2275
	15:13 Arba the father of Anak, which city is **H**.	2275
	15:54 and Kirjath-arba, which is **H**, and Zior;	2275
	19:28 **H**, and Rehob, and Hammon, and Kanah,	5683
	20: 7 Kirjath-arba, which is **H**, in the mountain	2275
	21: 11 which city is **H**, in the hill country of	2275
	21:13 of Aaron the priest **H** with her suburbs,	2275
Jdg	1:10 against the Canaanites that dwelt in **H**:	2275
	1:10 (now the name of **H** before was	2275
	1:20 they gave **H** unto Caleb, as Moses said:	2275
	16: 3 up to the top of a hill that is before **H**.	2275
1Sa	30:31 to them which were in **H**, and to all	2275
2Sa	2: 1 shall I go up? And he said, Unto **H**.	2275
	2: 3 and they dwelt in the cities of **H**.	2275
	2:11 the time that David was king in **H** over	2275
	2:32 and they came to **H** at break of day.	2275
	3: 2 unto David were sons born in **H**:	2275
	3: 5 These were born to David in **H**.	2275
	3:19 David in **H** all that seemed good to Israel,	2275
	3:20 So Abner came to David to **H**,	2275
	3:22 Abner was not with David in **H**; for he	2275
	3:27 when Abner was returned to **H**, Joab took	2275
	3:32 they buried Abner in **H**: and the king lift	2275
	4: 1 son heard that Abner was dead in **H**,	2275
	4: 8 the head of Ish-bosheth unto David to **H**,	2275
	4:12 and hanged them up over the pool in **H**.	2275
	4:12 buried it in the sepulchre of Abner in **H**.	2275
	5: 1 all the tribes of Israel to David unto **H**,	2275
	5: 3 the elders of Israel came to the king to **H**;	2275
	5: 3 David made a league with them in **H**	2275
	5: 5 In **H** he reigned over Judah seven years	2275
	5:13 of Jerusalem, after he was come from **H**:	2275
	15: 7 I have vowed unto the LORD, in **H**.	2275

2Sa	15: 9 Go in peace. So he arose, and went to **H**.	2275
	15:10 then ye shall say, Absalom reigneth in **H**.	2275
1Ki	2:11 seven years reigned he in **H**, and thirty	2275
1Ch	2:42 and the sons of Mareshah the father of **H**.	2275
	2:43 the sons of **H**; Korah, and Tappuah,	2275
	3: 1 David, which were born unto him in **H**;	2275
	3: 4 These six were born unto him in **H**,	2275
	6: 2 Amram, Izhar, and **H**, and Uzziel.	2275
	6:18 and Izhar, and **H**, and Uzziel.	2275
	6:55 they gave them **H** in the land of Judah,	2275
	6:57 namely, **H**, the city of refuge, and Libnah	2275
	11: 1 gathered themselves to David unto **H**,	2275
	11: 3 all the elders of Israel to the king to **H**;	2275
	11: 3 David made a covenant with them in **H**	2275
	12:23 and came to David to **H**, to turn	2275
	12:38 rank, came with a perfect heart to **H**,	2275
	15: 9 Of the sons of **H**; Eliel the chief,	2275
	23:12 Amram, Izhar, and **H**, and Uzziel, four.	2275
	23:19 Of the sons of **H**; Jeriah the first,	2275
	24:23 the sons of **H**; Jeriah the first, Amariah	NIH
	29:27 seven years reigned he in **H**, and thirty	2275
2Ch	11:10 Zorah, and Aijalon, and **H**, which are in	2275

HEBRONITES (6) [HEBRON]

Nu	3:27 the family of the **H**, and the family of	2276
	26:58 family of the Libnites, the family of the **H**,	2276
1Ch	26:23 the Izharites, the **H**, and the Uzzielites:	2276
	26:30 of the **H**, Hashabiah and his brethren,	2276
	26:31 Among the **H** was Jerijah the chief,	2276
	26:31 even among the **H**, according to	2276

HEDGE (9) [HEDGED, HEDGES]

Job	1:10 Hast not thou **made** a **h** about him,	7753
Pr	15:19 The way of the slothful man is as a **h** of	4881
Ecc	10: 8 whoso breaketh a **h**, a serpent shall bite	1447
Isa	5: 5 I will take away the **h** thereof, and it shall	4881
Eze	13: 5 **made up the h** for the house	1443+1447
	22:30 that should **make up the h**,	1443+1447
Hos	2: 6 I will **h** up thy way with thorns, and	7753
Mic	7: 4 most upright is sharper than a **thorn h**:	4534
Mk	12: 1 set a **h** about it, and digged a place for	5418

HEDGED (3) [HEDGE]

Job	3:23 way is hid, and whom God hath **h** in?	5526
La	3: 7 hath **h** me about, that I cannot get out:	1443
Mt	21:33 and **h** it round about, and digged a	5418

HEDGES (6) [HEDGE]

1Ch	4:23 those that dwelt amongst plants and **h**:	1448
Ps	80:12 Why hast thou then broken down her **h**,	1447
	89:40 Thou hast broken down all his **h**; thou	1448
Jer	49: 3 lament, and run to and fro by the **h**;	1448
Na	3:17 which camp in the **h** in the cold day,	1448
Lk	14:23 Go out into the highways and **h**,	5418

HEED (80)

Ge	31:24 **Take h** that thou speak not to Jacob	8104
	31:29 **Take** thou **h** that thou speak not to Jacob	8104
Ex	10:28 Get thee from me, **take h** to thyself, see	8104
	19:12 saying, **Take h** to yourselves, that ye go	8104
	34:12 **Take h** to thyself, lest thou make a	8104
Nu	23:12 Must I not **take h** to speak that which	8104
Dt	2: 4 **take** ye good **h** unto yourselves therefore:	8104
	4: 9 Only **take h** to thyself, and keep thy soul	8104
	4:15 **Take** ye therefore good **h** unto	8104
	4:23 **Take h** unto yourselves, lest ye forget	8104
	11:16 **Take h** to yourselves, that your heart be	8104
	12:13 **Take h** to thyself that thou offer not thy	8104
	12:19 **Take h** to thyself that thou forsake not	8104
	12:30 **Take h** to thyself that thou be not snared	8104
	24: 8 **Take h** in the plague of leprosy, that thou	8104
	27: 9 **Take h**, and hearken, O Israel;	5535
Jos	22: 5 take diligent **h** to do the commandment	8104
	23:11 **Take** good **h** therefore unto yourselves,	8104
1Sa	19: 2 **take h** to thyself until the morning,	8104
2Sa	20:10 Amasa **took** no **h** to the sword that was	8104
1Ki	2: 4 If thy children **take h** to their way,	8104
	8:25 so that thy children **take h** to their way,	8104
2Ki	10:31 Jehu **took** no **h** to walk in the law of	8104
1Ch	22:13 if thou **takest h** to fulfil the statutes and	8104
	28:10 **Take h** now; for the LORD hath chosen	7200
2Ch	6:16 that thy children **take h** to their way to	8104
	19: 6 said to the judges, **Take h** what ye do:	7200
	19: 7 **take h** and do it: for there is no iniquity	8104
	33: 8 that they will **take h** to do all that I have	8104
Ezr	4:22 **Take h** now that ye fail not to do this:	2095
Job	36:21 **Take h**, regard not iniquity: for this hast	8104
Ps	39: 1 I said, I will **take h** to my ways, that I sin	8104
	119: 9 taking **h** thereto according to thy word.	8104
Pr	17: 4 A wicked doer **giveth h** to false lips;	7181
Ecc	7:21 Also **take** no **h** unto all words that 3820+5414	
	12: 9 he **gave** good **h**, and sought out, and set	239
Isa	7: 4 say unto him, **Take h**, and be quiet;	8104
	21: 7 and he hearkened diligently with much **h**.	7182
Jer	9: 4 **Take** ye **h** every one of his neighbour,	8104
	17:21 **Take h** to yourselves, and bear no burden	8104
	18:18 and let us not **give h** to any of his words.	7181
	18:19 **Give h** to me, O LORD, and hearken to	7181
Hos	4:10 they have left off to **take h** to the LORD.	8104
Mal	2:15 Therefore **take h** to your spirit,	8104
	2:16 therefore **take h** to your spirit, that ye	8104
Mt	6: 1 **Take h** that ye do not your alms before	4337
	16: 6 **Take h** and beware of the leaven of	3708
	18:10 **Take h** that ye despise not one of these	3708
	24: 4 them, **Take h** that no man deceive you.	991

Mk	4:24 said unto them, **Take h** what you hear:	991
	8:15 And he charged them, saying, **Take h**,	3708
	13: 5 to say, **Take h** lest any *man* deceive you:	991
	13: 9 But **take h** to yourselves: for they shall	991
	13:23 But **take ye h**: behold, I have foretold you	991
	13:33 **Take ye h**, watch and pray: for ye know	991
Lk	8:18 **Take h** therefore how ye hear:	991
	11:35 **Take h** therefore that the light which is	4648
	12:15 **Take h**, and beware of covetousness:	3708
	17: 3 **Take h** to yourselves: If thy brother	4337
	21: 8 he said, **Take h** that ye be not deceived:	991
	21:34 And **take h** to yourselves, lest at any time	4337
Ac	3: 5 And he gave **h** unto them, expecting to	1907
	5:35 **take h** to yourselves what ye intend to do	4337
	8: 6 And the people with one accord **gave h**	4337
	8:10 To whom they all **gave h**, from the least	4337
	20:28 **Take h** therefore unto yourselves,	4337
	22:26 saying, **Take h** what thou doest:	3708
Ro	11:21 *take* **h** lest he also spare not thee.	NIG
1Co	3:10 But let every man **take h** how he buildeth	991
	8: 9 But **take h** lest by any means this liberty	991
	10:12 thinketh he standeth **take h** lest he fall.	991
Gal	5:15 **take h** ye be not consumed one of another.	991
Col	4:17 **Take h** to the ministry which thou hast	991
1Ti	1: 4 Neither **give h** to fables and	4337
	4: 1 **giving h** to seducing spirits,	4337
	4:16 **Take h** unto thyself, and unto the	1907
Tit	1:14 Not **giving h** to Jewish fables,	4337
Heb	2: 1 **give** the more earnest **h** to the *things*	4337
	3:12 **Take h**, brethren, lest there be in any of	991
2Pe	1:19 whereunto ye do well that ye **take h**,	4337

HEEL (6) [HEELS]

Ge	3:15 thy head, and thou shalt bruise his **h**.	6119
	25:26 and his hand took hold on Esau's **h**;	6119
Job	18: 9 The grin shall take *him* by the **h**,	6119
Ps	41: 9 *of* my bread, hath lift up *his* **h** against me.	6119
Hos	12: 3 **took** his brother **by the h** in the womb,	6117
Jn	13:18 with me hath lift up his **h** against me.	4418

HEELS (4) [HEEL]

Ge	49:17 that biteth the horse, so that his rider	6119
Job	13:27 thou settest a print upon the **h** of my feet,	8328
Ps	49: 5 *when* the iniquity of my **h** shall compass	6120
Jer	13:22 skirts discovered, *and* thy **h** made bare.	6119

HEGAI (3) [HEGE]

Est	2: 8 to the custody of **H**, that Esther was	1896
	2: 8 the custody of **H**, keeper of the women,	1896
	2:15 but what **H** the king's chamberlain,	1896

HEGE (1) [HEGAI]

Est	2: 3 unto the custody of **H** the king's	1896

HEIFER (19) [HEIFER'S]

Ge	15: 9 Take me a **h** of three years old, and a she	5697
Nu	19: 2 that they bring thee a red **h** without spot,	6510
	19: 5 *one* shall burn the **h** in his sight; her skin,	6510
	19: 6 it into the midst of the burning of the **h**.	6510
	19: 9 *is* clean shall gather up the ashes of the **h**,	6510
	19:10 he that gathereth the ashes of the **h** shall	6510
	19:17 ashes of the burnt *h* of purification for sin,	NIH
Dt	21: 3 the elders of that city shall take a **h**,	1241+5697
	21: 4 bring down the **h** unto a rough valley,	5697
	21: 6 over the **h** that is beheaded in the valley:	5697
Jdg	14:18 them, If ye had not plowed with my **h**,	5697
1Sa	16: 2 Take a **h** with thee, and say,	1241+5697
Isa	15: 5 *flee* unto Zoar, an **h** of three years old:	5697
Jer	46:20 Egypt *is* like a very fair **h**,	5697
	48:34 unto Horonaim, *as* a **h** of three years old:	5697
	50:11 because ye are grown fat as the **h** at grass,	5697
Hos	4:16 For Israel slideth back as a backsliding **h**:	6510
	10:11 Ephraim *is as* a **h** *that is* taught,	5697
Heb	9:13 the ashes of a **h** sprinkling the unclean,	1151

HEIFER'S (1) [HEIFER]

Dt	21: 4 shall strike off the **h** neck there in	5697

HEIGHT (62) [HIGH]

Ge	6:15 it fifty cubits, and the **h** of it thirty cubits.	6967
Ex	25:10 and a cubit and a half the **h** thereof.	6967
	25:23 and a cubit and a half the **h** thereof.	6967
	27: 1 and the **h** thereof *shall* be three cubits.	6967
	27:18 the **h** five cubits *of* fine twined linen,	6967
	30: 2 two cubits *shall* be the **h** thereof:	6967
	37: 1 of it, and a cubit and a half the **h** of it:	6967
	37:10 and a cubit and a half the **h** thereof.	6967
	37:25 and two cubits *was* the **h** of it;	6967
	38: 1 and three cubits the **h** thereof.	6967
	38:18 and the **h** in the breadth *was* five cubits,	6967
1Sa	16: 7 countenance, or on the **h** of his stature;	1364
	17: 4 Gath, whose **h** *was* six cubits and a span.	1363
1Ki	6: 2 and the **h** thereof thirty cubits.	6967
	6:20 and twenty cubits in the **h** thereof:	6967
	6:26 The **h** of the one cherub *was* ten cubits,	6967
	7: 2 cubits, and the **h** thereof thirty cubits,	6967
	7:16 the **h** of the one chapiter *was* five cubits:	6967
	7:16 **h** of the other chapiter *was* five cubits:	6967
	7:23 round all about, and his **h** *was* five cubits:	6967
	7:27 thereof, and three cubits the **h** of it.	6967
	7:32 the **h** of a wheel *was* a cubit and a half	6967
2Ki	19:23 I am come up *to* the **h** of the mountains,	4791
	25:17 **h** of the one pillar *was* eighteen cubits,	6967
	25:17 the **h** of the chapiter three cubits:	6967
2Ch	3: 4 and the **h** *was* an hundred and twenty:	1363

2Ch	4: 1 and ten cubits the **h** thereof.	6967
	4: 2 in compass, and five cubits the **h** thereof;	6967
	33:14 **raised** it **up** a very great **h**,	1361
Ezr	6: 3 the **h** thereof threescore cubits,	7314
Job	22:12 *Is not* God *in* the **h** of heaven?	1363
Ps	102:19 he hath looked down from the **h** of his	4791
Pr	25: 3 The heaven for **h**, and the earth for depth,	7312
Isa	7:11 it either in the depth, or in the **h** above.	1361
	37:24 am I come up *to* the **h** of the mountains,	4791
	37:24 I will enter *into* the **h** of his border,	4791
Jer	31:12 they shall come and sing in the **h** of Zion,	4791
	49:16 of the rock, that holdest the **h** of the hill:	4791
	51:53 though she should fortify the **h** of her	4791
	52:21 the **h** of one pillar *was* eighteen cubits;	6967
	52:22 the **h** of one chapiter *was* five cubits,	6967
Eze	17:23 In the mountain of the **h** of Israel will I	4791
	19:11 she appeared in her **h** with the multitude	1363
	20:40 in the mountain of the **h** of Israel, saith	4791
	31: 5 Therefore his **h** was exalted above all	6967
	31:10 Because thou hast lifted up thyself in **h**,	6967
	31:10 and his heart is lifted up in his **h**;	1363
	31:14 the waters exalt themselves for their **h**,	6967
	31:14 neither their trees stand up in their **h**,	1363
	32: 5 and fill the valleys *with* thy **h**.	7419
	40: 5 building, one reed; and the **h**, one reed.	6967
	41: 8 I saw also the **h** of the house round about:	1363
Da	3: 1 whose **h** *was* threescore cubits,	7314
	4:10 of the earth, and the **h** thereof *was* great.	7314
	4:11 the **h** thereof reached unto heaven,	7314
	4:20 whose **h** reached unto heaven,	7314
Am	2: 9 whose **h** *was* like the height of the cedars,	1363
	2: 9 whose height *was* like the height of the cedars,	1363
Ro	8:39 Nor **h**, nor depth, nor any other creature,	5313
Eph	3:18 breadth, and length, and depth, and **h**;	5311
Rev	21:16 and the breadth and the **h** of it are equal.	5311

HEIGHTS (2) [HIGH]

Ps	148: 1 from the heavens: praise him in the **h**.	4791
Isa	14:14 I will ascend above the **h** of the clouds;	1116

HEINOUS (1)

Job	31:11 For this *is* a **h** crime; yea, it *is* an iniquity	2154

HEIR (18) [FELLOWHEIRS, HEIRS, JOINT-HEIRS]

Ge	15: 3 and lo, one born in my house is mine **h**.	3423
	15: 4 him, saying, This shall not be thine **h**;	3423
	15: 4 out of thine own bowels shall be thine **h**.	3423
	21:10 bondwoman shall not be **h** with my son,	3423
2Sa	14: 7 he slew; and we will destroy the **h** also:	3423
Pr	30:23 and a handmaid that is **h** to her mistress.	3423
Jer	49: 1 Hath he no **h**? why *then* doth their king	3423
	49: 2 shall Israel be **h** unto them that were his	3423
Mic	1:15 Yet will I bring an **h** unto thee,	3423
Mt	21:38 said among themselves, This is the **h**;	2818
Mk	12: 7 said amongst themselves, This is the **h**;	2818
Lk	20:14 among themselves, saying, This is the **h**:	2818
Ro	4:13 that he should be the **h** of the world,	2818
Gal	4: 1 Now I say, *That* the **h**, as long as he is a	2818
	4: 7 if a son, then an **h** of God through Christ.	2816
	4:30 not be **h** with the son of the freewoman.	2818
Heb	1: 2 whom he hath appointed **h** of all *things*,	2818
	11: 7 became **h** of the righteousness which is	2818

HEIRS (11) [HEIR]

Jer	49: 2 Israel be heir unto them that were his **h**,	3423
Ro	4:14 if they which are of the law be **h**, faith	2818
	8:17 And if children, then **h**; heirs of God,	2818
	8:17 **h** of God, and joint-heirs with Christ; if	2818
Gal	3:29 and according to the promise.	2818
Tit	3: 7 should be made **h** according to the hope	2818
Heb	1:14 for them who shall be **h** of salvation?	2816
	6:17 more abundantly to shew unto the **h**	2818
	11: 9 the **h** *with him* of the same promise:	4789
Jas	2: 5 **h** of the kingdom which he hath promised	2818
1Pe	3: 7 as *being* **h** **together** of the grace of life;	4789

HELAH (2)

1Ch	4: 5 of Tekoa had two wives, **H** and Naarah.	2458
	4: 7 the sons of **H** *were*, Zereth, and Jezoar,	2458

HELAM (2)

2Sa	10:16 they came *to* **H**; and Shobach the captain	2431
	10:17 and passed over Jordan, and came to **H**.	2431

HELBAH (1)

Jdg	1:31 nor of **H**, nor of Aphik, nor of Rehob:	2462

HELBON (1)

Eze	27:18 in the wine of **H**, and white wool.	2463

HELD (52) [HOLD]

Ge	24:21 the man wondering at her **h** his **peace**,	2790
	34: 5 Jacob **h** his **peace** until they were come.	2790
	48:17 he **h up** his father's hand, to remove it	8551
Ex	17:11 came to pass, when Moses **h up** his hand,	7311
	36:12 the loops **h** one *curtain* to another.	6901
Lev	10: 3 will be glorified. And Aaron **h** his **peace**.	1826
Nu	30: 7 **h** his **peace** at her in the day that he	2790
	30:11 husband heard *it*, and **h** his **peace** at her,	2790
	30:14 he **h** his **peace** at her in the day that he	2790
Jdg	7:20 **h** the lamps in their left hands,	2388
	16:26 Samson said unto the lad that **h** him by	2388
Ru	3:15 when she **h** it, he measured six *measures*	2388
1Sa	10:27 But he **h** his **peace**.	1961+2790+3509.1
	25:36 behold, he **h** a feast in his house, like	3807.1

2Sa	18:16 after Israel: for Joab **h** back the people.	2820
1Ki	8:65 at that time Solomon **h** a feast,	6213
2Ki	18:36 people **h** their **peace**, and answered him	2790
2Ch	4: 5 it received and **h** three thousand baths.	3557
Ne	4:16 the *other* half of them **h** both the spears,	2388
	4:17 and with the other *hand* a weapon.	2388
	4:21 half of them **h** the spears from the rising	2388
	5: 8 they their **peace**, and found nothing *to*	2790
Est	5: 2 king **h out** to Esther the golden sceptre	3447
	7: 4 and bondwomen, I had **h** my **tongue**,	2790
	8: 4 the king **h out** the golden sceptre toward	3447
Job	23:11 My foot hath **h** his steps, his way have I	270
	29:10 The nobles **h** their **peace**,	2244+6963
Ps	32: 9 whose mouth must be **h in** with bit and	1102
	39: 2 I **h** my **peace**, *even* from good;	2814
	94:18 thy mercy, O LORD, **h** me up.	5582
SS	3: 4 I **h** him, and would not let him go, until I	270
	7: 5 like purple; the king *is* **h** in the galleries.	631
Isa	36:21 **h** their **peace**, and answered him not	2790
	57:11 have not I **h** my **peace** even of old,	2814
Jer	50:33 all that took them captives **h** them **fast**;	2388
Da	12: 7 when he **h up** his right hand and his left	7311
Mt	12:14 went out, and **h** a council against him,	2983
	26:63 Jesus **h** his **peace**. And the high priest	4623
	28: 9 And they came and **h** him by the feet,	2902
Mk	3: 4 life, or to kill? But they **h** their **peace**.	4623
	9:34 they **h** their **peace**: for by the way they	4623
	14:61 he **h** his **peace**, and answered nothing.	4623
	15: 1 priests **h** a consultation with the elders	4160
Lk	14: 4 they **h** their **peace**. And he took *him*,	2270
	20:26 at his answer, and **h** their **peace**.	4601
	22:63 And the men that **h** Jesus mocked him,	4912
Ac	3:11 as the lame *man* which was healed **h**	2902
	11:18 heard these *things*, they **h** their **peace**,	2270
	14: 4 and part **h** with the Jews, and part with	1510
	15:13 And after they had **h** their **peace**,	4601
Ro	7: 6 that being dead wherein we were **h**;	2722
Rev	6: 9 God, and for the testimony which they **h**:	2192

HELD FAST See CLEAVE; CLEAVED; CLEAVETH

HELDAI (2)

1Ch	27:15 twelfth month *was* **H** the Netophathite,	2469
Zec	6:10 *even* of **H**, of Tobijah, and of Jedaiah,	2469

HELEB (1)

2Sa	23:29 **H** the son of Baanah, a Netophathite,	2460

HELED (1)

1Ch	11:30 **H** the son of Baanah the Netophathite,	2466

HELEK (2) [HELEKITES]

Nu	26:30 of **H**, the family of the Helekites:	2507
Jos	17: 2 the children of **H**, and for the children	2507

HELEKITES (1) [HELEK]

Nu	26:30 of Helek, the family of the **H**:	2516

HELEM (2)

1Ch	7:35 the son of his brother **H**; Zophah,	1987
Zec	6:14 the crowns shall be to **H**, and to Tobijah,	2494

HELEPH (1)

Jos	19:33 their coast was from **H**, from Allon to	2501

HELEZ (5)

2Sa	23:26 **H** the Paltite, Ira the son of Ikkesh	2503
1Ch	2:39 Azariah begat **H**, and Helez begat Eleasah,	2503
	2:39 Azariah begat Helez, and **H** begat Eleasah,	2503
	11:27 Shammoth the Harorite, **H** the Pelonite,	2503
	27:10 the seventh month *was* **H** the Pelonite,	2503

HELI (1)

Lk	3:23 son of Joseph, which was *the* son of **H**,	2242

HELKAI (1)

Ne	12:15 Of Harim, Adna; of Meraioth, **H**;	2517

HELKATH (2) [HELKATH-HAZZURIM]

Jos	19:25 their border was **H**, and Hali, and Beten,	2520
	21:31 **H** with her suburbs, and Rehob with her	2520

HELKATH-HAZZURIM (1) [HELKATH]

2Sa	2:16 wherefore that place was called **H**, which	2521

HELL (54)

Dt	32:22 shall burn unto the lowest **h**,	7585
2Sa	22: 6 The sorrows of **h** compassed me about;	7585
Job	11: 8 deeper than **h**; what canst thou know?	7585
	26: 6 **h** *is* naked before him, and destruction	7585
Ps	9:17 The wicked shall be turned into **h**,	7585
	16:10 For thou wilt not leave my soul in **h**;	7585
	18: 5 The sorrows of **h** compassed me about:	7585
	55:15 *and* let them go down quick *into* **h**:	7585
	86:13 hast delivered my soul from the lowest **h**.	7585
	116: 3 and the pains of **h** gat hold upon me:	7585
	139: 8 If I make my bed in **h**, behold, thou *art*	7585
Pr	5: 5 down *to* death; her steps take hold on **h**.	7585
	7:27 Her house is the way to **h**, going down to	7585
	9:18 *and* that her guests *are* in the depths of **h**.	7585
	15:11 **H** and destruction *are* before the LORD:	7585
	15:24 that *he* may depart from **h** beneath.	7585
	23:14 the rod, and shalt deliver his soul from **h**.	7585
	27:20 **H** and destruction are never full;	7585
Isa	5:14 Therefore **h** hath enlarged herself,	7585
	14: 9 **H** from beneath is moved for thee to meet	7585

H

Isa 14:15 Yet thou shalt be brought down to **h**, 7585
28:15 death, and with **h** are we at agreement; 7585
28:18 your agreement with **h** shall not stand; 7585
57: 9 and didst debase *thyself even* unto **h**. 7585
Eze 31:16 when I cast him down to **h** with them 7585
31:17 They also went down into **h** with him 7585
32:21 the midst of **h** with them that help him: 7585
32:27 which are gone down *to* **h** with their 7585
Am 9: 2 Though they dig into **h**, thence shall 7585
Jnh 2: 2 out of the belly of **h** cried I, 7585
Hab 2: 5 who enlargeth his desire as **h**, and *is* as 7585
Mt 5:22 *Thou fool,* shall be in danger of **h** fire. 1067
5:29 *that* thy whole body should be cast into **h**. 1067
5:30 *that* thy whole body should be cast into **h**. 1067
10:28 is able to destroy both soul and body in **h**. 1067
11:23 unto heaven, shalt be brought down to **h**: 86
16:18 the gates of **h** shall not prevail against it. 86
18: 9 than having two eyes to be cast into **h** 1067
23:15 ye make him twofold more *the* child of **h** 1067
23:33 how can ye escape the damnation of **h**? 1067
Mk 9:43 than having two hands to go into **h**, into 1067
9:45 than having two feet to be cast into **h**, 1067
9:47 having two eyes to be cast into **h** fire: 1067
Lk 10:15 to heaven, shalt be thrust down to **h**. 86
12: 5 *he* hath killed hath power to cast into **h**; 1067
16:23 And in **h** he lift up his eyes, being in 86
Ac 2:27 Because thou wilt not leave my soul in **h**, 86
2:31 of Christ, that his soul was not left in **h**, 86
Jas 3: 6 course of nature; and it is set on fire of **h**. 1067
2Pe 2: 4 but cast *them* down to **h**, 5020
Rev 1:18 Amen; and have the keys of **h** and of death. 86
6: 8 *was* Death, and **H** followed with him. 86
20:13 **h** delivered up the dead which were in 86
20:14 and **h** were cast into the lake of fire. 86

HELM (1)
Jas 3: 4 they turned about with a very small **h**, 4079

HELMET (8) [HELMETS]
1Sa 17: 5 *he had* a **h** of brass upon his head, 3553
17:38 and he put a **h** of brass upon his head; 6959
Isa 59:17 and a **h** of salvation upon his head; 3553
Eze 23:24 buckler and shield and **h** round about: 6959
27:10 they hanged the shield and **h** in thee; 3553
38: 5 with them; all of them *with* shield and **h**: 3553
Eph 6:17 take the **h** of salvation, and the sword 4030
1Th 5: 8 love; and for a **h**, the hope of salvation. 4030

HELMETS (2) [HELMET]
2Ch 26:14 **h**, and habergeons, and bows, and slings 3553
Jer 46: 4 ye horsemen, and stand forth with *your* **h**; 3553

HELON (5)
Nu 1: 9 Of Zebulun; Eliab the son of **H**. 2497
2: 7 Eliab the son of **H** *shall be* captain of 2497
7:24 On the third day Eliab the son of **H**, 2497
7:29 this *was* the offering of Eliab the son of **H**. 2497
10:16 of Zebulun *was* Eliab the son of **H**. 2497

HELP (126) [FELLOWHELPER, FELLOWHELPERS, HELPED, HELPER, HELPERS, HELPETH, HELPING, HELPS, HOLPEN]
Ge 2:18 alone; I will make him a **h** meet for him. 5828
2:20 for Adam there was not found a **h** meet 5828
49:25 the God of thy father, who shall **h** thee; 5826
Ex 18: 4 *was* mine **h**, and delivered me from 5828
23: 5 wouldest forbear to **h** him, thou shalt 5800
23: 5 thou shalt *surely* **h** with him. 5800+5800
Dt 22: 4 thou shalt surely **h** him to lift *them* up 5973
32:38 let them rise up and **h** you, *and* be your 5826
33: 7 and be thou a **h** *to him* from his enemies. 5828
33:26 *who* rideth upon the heaven in thy **h**, 5828
33:29 the shield of thy **h**, and who *is* the sword 5828
Jos 1:14 all the mighty *men* of valour, and **h** them; 5826
10: 4 Come up unto me, and **h** me, that we 5826
10: 6 up to us quickly, and save us, and **h** us: 5826
10:33 Horam king of Gezer came up to **h** 5826
Jdg 5:23 they came not to the **h** of the LORD, 5833
5:23 to the **h** of the LORD against the mighty. 5833
1Sa 11: 9 *that* time the sun be hot, ye shall have **h**. 8668
2Sa 10:11 for me, then thou shalt **h** me: 1961+3444
10:11 for thee, then I will come and **h** thee, 3467
10:19 So the Syrians feared to **h** the children of 3467
14: 4 and did obeisance, and said, **H**, O king. 3467
2Ki 6:26 unto him, saying, **H**, my lord, O king. 3467
6:27 he said, *If* the LORD do not **h** thee, 3467
6:27 do not help thee, whence shall I **h** thee? 3467
1Ch 12:17 If ye be come peaceably unto me to **h** me, 5826
12:22 day by day there came to David to **h** him, 5826
18: 5 when the Syrians of Damascus came to **h** 5826
19:12 for me, then thou shalt **h** me: 1961+8668
19:12 be too strong for thee, then I will **h** thee. 3467
19:19 neither would the Syrians **h** the children 3467
22:17 the princes of Israel to **h** Solomon his son, 5826
2Ch 14:11 said, LORD, *it is* nothing with thee to **h**, 5826
14:11 **h** us, O LORD our God; for we rest on 5826
19: 2 Shouldest thou **h** the ungodly, 5826
20: 4 to ask **h** of the LORD: NIH
20: 9 our affliction, then thou wilt hear and **h**. 3467
25: 8 God hath power to **h**, and to cast down. 5826
26:13 to **h** the king against the enemy. 5826
28:16 send unto the kings of Assyria to **h** him. 5826
28:23 Because the gods of the kings of Syria **h** 5826
28:23 I sacrifice to them, that they may **h** me. 5826
29:34 their brethren the Levites did **h** 2388

2Ch 32: 3 without the city: and they did **h** him. 5826
32: 8 with us *is* the LORD our God to **h** us, 5826
Ezr 1: 4 let the men of his place **h** him with silver, 5375
8:22 horsemen to **h** us against the enemy in 5833
Job 6:13 *Is* not my **h** in me? and is wisdom driven 5833
8:20 will he **h** the evil doers: 2388+3027+871.1
29:12 and *him that had* none to **h** him. 5826
31:21 fatherless, when I saw my **h** in the gate: 5833
Ps 3: 2 of my soul, *There is* no **h** for him in God. 3444
12: 1 **H**, LORD; for the godly *man* ceaseth; 3467
20: 2 Send thee **h** from the sanctuary, 5828
22:11 for trouble *is* near; for *there is* none to **h**. 5826
22:19 O my strength, haste thee to **h** me. 5833
27: 9 thou hast been my **h**; leave me not, 5833
33:20 for the LORD: he *is* our **h** and our shield. 5828
35: 2 and buckler, and stand up for mine **h**. 5833
37:40 the LORD shall **h** them, and deliver them: 5826
38:22 Make haste to **h** me, O LORD my salvation. 5833
40:13 deliver me: O LORD, make haste to **h** me. 5833
40:17 thou *art* my **h** and my deliverer; make no 5833
42: 5 for I shall yet praise him *for* the **h** of his 3444
44:26 Arise for our **h**, and redeem us for thy 5833
46: 1 and strength, a very present **h** in trouble. 5833
46: 5 God shall **h** her, *and that* right early. 5826
59: 4 *my* fault: awake to **h** me, and behold. 7125
60:11 Give us **h** from trouble; for vain *is* the 8668
60:11 from trouble: for vain *is* the **h** of man. 8668
63: 7 Because thou hast been my **h**, therefore 5833
70: 1 deliver me; make haste to **h** me, O LORD. 5833
70: 5 thou *art* my **h** and my deliverer; O LORD, 5828
71:12 O my God, make haste for my **h**. 5833
79: 9 **H** us, O God of our salvation, for the glory 5826
89:19 I have laid **h** upon *one that is* mighty; 5826
94:17 Unless the LORD *had been* my **h**, my soul 5833
107:12 they fell down, and *there was* none to **h**. 5826
108:12 Give us **h** from trouble: for vain *is* the 5833
108:12 from trouble: for vain *is* the **h** of man. 8668
109:26 **H** me, O LORD my God: O save me 5826
115: 9 the LORD: he *is* their **h** and their shield. 5828
115:10 the LORD: he *is* their **h** and their shield. 5828
115:11 the LORD: he *is* their **h** and their shield. 5828
118: 7 taketh my part with them that **h** me: 5826
119:86 they persecute me wrongfully; **h** thou me. 5826
119:173 Let thine hand **h** me; for I have chosen 5826
119:175 praise thee; and let thy judgments **h** me. 5826
121: 1 the hills, from whence cometh my **h**. 5828
121: 2 My **h** *cometh* from the LORD, 5828
124: 8 Our **h** *is* in the name of the LORD, 5828
146: 3 the son of man, in whom *there is* no **h**. 8668
146: 5 *is* he that *hath* the God of Jacob for his **h**, 5828
Ecc 4:10 for *he* hath none to **h** him **up**. 6965
Isa 10: 3 to whom will ye flee for **h**? and where 5833
20: 6 whither we flee for **h** to be delivered from 5833
30: 5 nor be a **h** nor profit, but a shame, 5826
30: 7 The Egyptians shall **h** in vain, and to no 5826
31: 1 Woe to them that go down *to* Egypt for **h**; 5833
31: 2 against the **h** of them that work iniquity. 5833
41:10 yea, I will **h** thee; yea, I will uphold thee 5826
41:13 saying unto thee, Fear not; I will **h** thee. 5826
41:14 I will **h** thee, saith the LORD, 5826
44: 2 thee from the womb, *which* will **h** thee; 5826
50: 7 For the Lord GOD will **h** me; therefore 5826
50: 9 Behold, the Lord GOD will **h** me; who *is* 5826
63: 5 I looked, and *there was* none to **h**; 5826
Jer 37: 7 which is come forth to **h** you, 5826
La 1: 7 hand of the enemy, and none did **h** her: 5826
1:17 us, our eyes as **h** failed for our vain **h**: 5833
Eze 12:14 wind all that *are* about him to **h** him, 5826
32:21 of the midst of hell with them that **h** him: 5826
Da 10:13 one of the chief princes, came to **h** me; 5826
11:34 they shall be holpen *with* a little **h**: 5828
11:45 come to his end, and none shall **h** him. 5828
Hos 13: 9 destroyed thyself; but in me *is* thine **h**. 5828
Mt 15:25 and worshipped him, saying, Lord, **h** me. 997
Mk 9:22 thing, have compassion on us, and **h** us. 997
9:24 Lord, I believe; **h** thou mine unbelief. 997
Lk 5: 7 that *they* should come and **h** them, 4815
10:40 bid her therefore that she **h** me. 4878
Ac 16: 9 Come over into Macedonia, and **h** us. 997
21:28 Crying out, Men of Israel, **h**: This is 997
26:22 Having therefore obtained **h** of God, 1947
Php 4: 3 **h** those *women* which laboured with me 4815
Heb 4:16 and find grace to **h** in time of need. 996

HELPED (24) [HELP]
Ex 2:17 Moses stood up and **h** them, 3467
1Sa 7:12 Hitherto hath the LORD **h** us. 5826
1Ki 1: 7 and they following Adonijah **h** *him*. 5826
20:16 the thirty and two kings that **h** him. 5826
1Ch 5:20 were **h** against them, and the Hagarites 5826
12:19 they **h** them not: for the lords of 5826
12:21 **h** David against the band *of the rovers*: 5826
15:26 God the Levites that bare the ark of 5826
2Ch 18:31 cried out, and the LORD **h** him; 5826
20:23 of Seir, every one to destroy another. 5826
26: 7 God **h** him against the Philistines, 5826
26:15 for he was marvellously **h**, till he was 5826
28:21 the king of Assyria: but he **h** him not. 5833
Ezr 10:15 and Shabbethai the Levite **h** them. 5826
Est 9: 3 and officers of the king, **h** the Jews; 5375
Job 26: 2 How hast thou **h** *him that is* without 5826
Ps 28: 7 my heart trusted in him, and I am **h**: 5826
116: 6 simple: I was brought low, and he **h** me. 3467
118:13 me that *I* might fall: but the LORD **h** me. 5826
Isa 41: 6 They **h** every one his neighbour; 5826

Isa 49: 8 and in a day of salvation have I **h** thee: 5826
49:8 and they **h** forward the affliction. 5826
Ac 18:27 **h** them much which had believed through 4820
Rev 12:16 And the earth **h** the woman, and the earth 997

HELPER (9) [HELP]
2Ki 14:26 shut up, nor any left, nor any **h** for Israel. 5826
Job 30:13 set forward my calamity, they have no **h**. 5826
Ps 10:14 thee; thou art the **h** of the fatherless. 5826
30:10 mercy upon me: LORD, be thou my **h**. 5826
54: 4 Behold, God *is* mine **h**: the Lord *is* with 5826
72:12 the poor also, and *him* that hath no **h**. 5826
Jer 47: 4 and Zidon every **h** that remaineth: 5826
Ro 16: 9 Salute Urban our **h** in Christ, 4904
Heb 13: 6 The Lord *is* my **h**, and I will not fear what 998

HELPERS (7) [HELP]
1Ch 12: 1 they *were* among the mighty *men,* **h** 5826
12:18 *be* unto thee, and peace *be* to thine **h**; 5826
Job 9:13 anger, the proud **h** do stoop under him. 5826
Eze 30: 8 and *when* all her **h** shall be destroyed. 5826
Na 3: 9 *it was* infinite; Put and Lubim were thy **h**. 5833
Ro 16: 3 and Aquila my **h** in Christ Jesus: 4904
2Co 1:24 over your faith, but are **h** of your joy: 4904

HELPETH (4) [HELP]
1Ch 12:18 *be* to thine helpers; for thy God **h** thee. 5826
Isa 31: 3 both he that **h** shall fall, and he that is 5826
Ro 8:26 Likewise the Spirit also **h** our infirmities: 4878
1Co 16:16 and to every one that **h** with *us,* and 4903

HELPING (3) [HELP]
Ezr 5: 2 with them *were* the prophets of God **h** 5583
Ps 22: 1 *why art thou* so far from **h** me, 3444
2Co 1:11 You also **h** together by prayer for us, 4943

HELPING THE POOR See ALMSDEEDS

HELPS (2) [HELP]
Ac 27:17 they used **h**, undergirding the ship; 996
1Co 12:28 then gifts of healings, **h**, governments, 484

HELVE (1)
Dt 19: 5 the head slippeth from the **h**, 6086

HEM (7) [HEMS]
Ex 28:33 *beneath* upon the **h** of it thou shalt make 7757
28:33 and of scarlet, round about the **h** thereof; 7757
28:34 upon the **h** of the robe round about. 7757
39:25 the pomegranates upon the **h** of the robe, 7757
39:26 round about the **h** of the robe to minister 7757
Mt 9:20 and touched the **h** of his garment: 2899
14:36 might only touch the **h** of his garment: 2899

HEMAM (1)
Ge 36:22 the children of Lotan were Hori and **H**; 1967

HEMAN (17)
1Ki 4:31 **H**, and Chalcol, and Darda, the sons of 1968
1Ch 2: 6 and Ethan, and **H**, and Calcol, and Dara: 1968
6:33 **H** a singer, the son of Joel, the son of 1968
15:17 So the Levites appointed **H** the son of Joel; 1968
15:19 So the singers, **H**, Asaph, and Ethan, 1968
16:41 with them **H** and Jeduthun, and the rest 1968
16:42 with them **H** and Jeduthun *with* trumpets 1968
25: 1 of **H**, and of Jeduthun, who should 1968
25: 4 Of **H**: the sons of Heman; Bukkiah, 1968
25: 4 sons of **H**; Bukkiah, Mattaniah, Uzziel, 1968
25: 5 these *were* the sons of **H** the king's seer 1968
25: 5 God gave to **H** fourteen sons and 1968
25: 6 king's order *to* Asaph, Jeduthun, and **H**. 1968
2Ch 5:12 of **H**, of Jeduthun, with their sons and 1968
29:14 of the sons of **H**; Jehiel, and Shimei; 1968
35:15 and **H**, and Jeduthun the king's seer; 1968
Ps 88: T Maschil of **H** the Ezrahite. 1968

HEMATH (3)
1Ch 2:55 These *are* the Kenites that came of **H**, 2575
13: 5 of Egypt even unto the entering of **H**, 2574
Am 6:14 in of **H** unto the river of the wilderness. 2574

HEMDAN (1)
Ge 36:26 **H**, and Eshban, and Ithran, and Cheran. 2533

HEMLOCK (2)
Hos 10: 4 thus judgment springeth up as **h** in 7219
Am 6:12 and the fruit of righteousness into **h**: 3939

HEMS (1) [HEM]
Ex 39:24 they made upon the **h** of the robe 7757

HEN (3)
Zec 6:14 Jedaiah, and to **H** the son of Zephaniah, 2581
Mt 23:37 even as a **h** gathereth her chickens under 3733
Lk 13:34 as a **h** *doth gather* her brood under her 3733

HENA (3)
2Ki 18:34 *are* the gods of Sepharvaim, **H**, and Ivah? 2012
19:13 of the city of Sepharvaim, *of* **H**, and Ivah? 2012
Isa 37:13 of the city of Sepharvaim, **H**, and Ivah? 2012

HENADAD (4)
Ezr 3: 9 the sons of **H**, *with* their sons and 2582
Ne 3:18 their brethren, Bavai the son of **H**, 2582
3:24 After him repaired Binnui the son of **H** 2582
10: 9 Binnui of the sons of **H**, Kadmiel; 2582

HENCE (30) [HENCEFORTH, HENCEFORWARD]

Ge	37:17 the man said, They are departed h;	2088+4480
	42:15 of Pharaoh ye shall not go forth h,	2088+4480
	50:25 and ye shall carry up my bones from h.	2088
Ex	11: 1 afterwards he will let you go h:	2088+4480
	11: 1 surely thrust you out h altogether.	2088+4480
	13:19 ye shall carry up my bones away h with	2088
	33: 1 and go up h, thou and the people which	2088
	33:15 go not with me, carry us not up h.	2088+4480
Dt	9:12 Arise, get thee down quickly from h;	2088
Jos	4: 3 Take you h out of the midst of Jordan,	NIH
Jdg	6:18 Depart not h, I pray thee, until I	2088+4480
Ru	2: 8 neither go from h, but abide here fast by	2088
1Ki	17: 3 Get thee h, and turn thee eastward,	2088+4480
Ps	39:13 before I go h, and be no more.	NIH
Isa	30:22 thou shalt say unto it, Get thee h.	3318
Jer	38:10 Take from h thirty men with thee,	2088
Zec	6: 7 Get ye h, walk to and fro through the	NIH
Mt	4:10 saith Jesus unto him, Get thee h, Satan:	5217
	17:20 this mountain, Remove to yonder place;	1782
Lk	4: 9 Son of God, cast thyself down from h:	1782
	13:31 unto him, Get thee out, and depart h:	1782
	16:26 they which would pass from h to you	1782
Jn	2:16 that sold doves, Take these things h;	1782
	7: 3 unto him, Depart h, and go into Judea,	1782
	14:31 even so I do. Arise, let us go h.	1782
	18:36 but now is my kingdom not from h.	1782
	20:15 if thou have borne him h, tell me where	NIG
Ac	1: 5 the Holy Ghost not many days h.	3326+3778
	22:21 I will send thee far h unto the Gentiles.	3112
Jas	4: 1 come they not h, even of your lusts that	1782

HENCEFORTH (33) [FORTH, HENCE]

Ge	4:12 shall not h yield unto thee her strength;	3254
Nu	18:22 must the children of Israel h come	5750
Dt	19: 7 Ye shall h return no more that way.	3254
	19:20 shall h commit no more any such evil	3254
Jdg	2:21 I also will not h drive out any from before	3254
2Ki	5:17 for thy servant will h offer neither burnt	5750
2Ch	16: 9 therefore from h thou shalt have wars.	6258
Ps	125: 2 about his people from h even for ever.	6258
	131: 3 Let Israel hope in the LORD from h and	6258
Isa	9: 7 and with justice from h even for ever.	3254
	52: 1 for h there shall no more come into thee	3254
	59:21 saith the LORD, from h and for ever.	6258
Eze	36:12 shalt no more h bereave them of men.	3254
Mic	4: 7 reign over them in mount Zion from h,	6258
Mt	23:39 Ye shall not see me h, till ye shall say,	575+737
	26:29 not drink h of this fruit of the vine,	575+737
Lk	1:48 from h all generations shall call me	3568+3588
	5:10 from h thou shalt catch men.	3568+3588
	12:52 from h there shall be five in one	3568+3588
Jn	14: 7 from h ye know him, and have seen him.	737
	15:15 H I call you not servants; for the servant	3371
Ac	4:17 that they speak h to no man in this name.	3371
	18: 6 from h I will go unto the Gentiles.	3568
Ro	6: 6 that h we should not serve sin.	3371
2Co	5:15 they which live should not h live unto	3371
	5:16 Wherefore h know we no	575+3568+3588
	5:16 flesh, yet now h know we him no more.	3568
Gal	6:17 From h let no man trouble me:	3062+3588
Eph	4:14 That we h be no more children, tossed to	NIG
	4:17 that ye h walk not as other Gentiles walk,	3371
2Ti	4: 8 H there is laid up for me a crown of	3062
Heb	10:13 From h expecting till his enemies	3062+3588
Rev	14:13 are the dead which die in the Lord from h:	534

HENCEFORWARD (2) [FORWARD, HENCE]

Nu	15:23 and h among your generations;	1973
Mt	21:19 Let no fruit grow on thee h for ever.	3371

HENNA See CAMPHIRE

HENOCH (2) [ENOCH]

1Ch	1: 3 H, Methuselah, Lamech,	2585
	1:33 Epher, and H, and Abida, and Eldaah.	2585

HEPHER (9) [GATH-HEPHER, HEPHERITES]

Nu	26:32 and of H, the family of the Hepherites.	2660
	26:33 Zelophehad the son of H had no sons,	2660
	27: 1 the son of H, the son of Gilead, the son	2660
Jos	12:17 king of Tappuah; one; the king of H, one;	2660
	17: 2 for the children of H, and for the children	2660
	17: 3 Zelophehad, the son of H, the son of	2660
1Ki	4:10 pertained Sochoh, and all the land of H:	2660
1Ch	4: 6 and H, and Temeni, and Haahashtari.	2660
	11:36 the Mecherathite, Ahijah the Pelonite,	2660

HEPHERITES (1) [HEPHER]

Nu	26:32 and of Hepher, the family of the H.	2662

HEPHZI-BAH (2)

2Ki	21: 1 And his mother's name was H.	2657
Isa	62: 4 shalt be called H, and thy land Beulah:	2657

HER (1993) [SHE] See Index of Articles, Etc.

HERALD (1)

Da	3: 4 a h cried aloud, To you it is commanded,	3744

HERB (19) [HERBS]

Ge	1:11 h yielding seed, and the fruit tree	6212
	1:12 and h yielding seed after his kind,	6212
	1:29 I have given you every h bearing seed,	6212
	1:30 life, I have given every green h for meat:	6212
	2: 5 and every h of the field before it grew:	6212

Ge	3:18 thee; and thou shalt eat the h of the field,	6212
	9: 3 even as the green h have I given you all	6212
Ex	9:22 upon beast, and upon every h of the field,	6212
	9:25 the hail smote every h of the field,	6212
	10:12 eat every h of the land, even all that the	6212
	10:15 they did eat every h of the land, and all	6212
Dt	32: 2 as the small rain upon the tender h,	1877
2Ki	19:26 as the green h, as the grass on	1877
Job	8:12 down, it withereth before any other h.	2682
	38:27 cause the bud of the tender h to spring	1877
Ps	37: 2 like the grass, and wither as the green h.	1877
	104:14 the cattle, and h for the service of man:	6212
Isa	37:27 as the green h, as the grass on	1877
	66:14 and your bones shall flourish like an h:	1877

HERBS (18) [HERB]

Ex	10:15 in the h of the field, through all the land	6212
	12: 8 and with bitter h they shall eat it.	NIH
Nu	9:11 eat it with unleavened bread and bitter h.	NIH
Dt	11:10 it with thy foot, as a garden of h:	3419
1Ki	21: 2 that I may have it for a garden of h,	3419
2Ki	4:39 one went out into the field to gather h,	219
Ps	105:35 did eat up all the h in their land,	6212
Pr	15:17 Better is a dinner of h where love is, than	3419
	27:25 and h of the mountains are gathered.	6212
Isa	18: 4 my dwelling place like a clear heat upon h,	216
	26:19 thy dew is as the dew of h, and the earth	219
	42:15 and hills, and dry up all their h;	6212
Jer	12: 4 mourn, and the h of every field wither,	6212
Mt	13:32 it is the greatest among h, and becometh	3001
Mk	4:32 and becometh greater than all h,	3001
Lk	11:42 ye tithe mint and rue and all manner of h,	3001
Ro	14: 2 things: another, who is weak, eateth h.	3001
Heb	6: 7 bringeth forth h meet for them by whom	1008

HERD (22) [HERDMAN, HERDMEN, HERDS, SHEPHERD, SHEPHERD'S, SHEPHERDS, SHEPHERDS']

Ge	18: 7 Abraham ran unto the h, and fetch a calf	1241
Lev	1: 2 the cattle, even of the h, and of the flock.	1241
	1: 3 If his offering be a burnt sacrifice of the h,	1241
	3: 1 of peace offering, if he offer it of the h;	1241
	27:32 concerning the tithe of the h, or of	1241
Nu	15: 3 unto the LORD, of the h, or of the flock:	1241
Dt	12:21 thou shalt kill of thy h and of thy flock,	1241
	15:19 All the firstling males that come of thy h	1241
	16: 2 the LORD thy God, of the flock and the h,	1241
1Sa	11: 5 Saul came after the h out of the field;	1241
2Sa	12: 4 to take of his own flock and of his own h,	1241
Jer	31:12 for the young of the flock and of the h:	1241
Jnh	3: 7 nor beast, h nor flock, taste any thing:	1241
Hab	3:17 and there shall be no h in the stalls:	1241
Mt	8:30 there was a good way off from them a h	34
	8:31 suffer us to go away into the h of swine.	34
	8:32 come out, they went into the h of swine:	34
	8:32 the whole h of swine ran violently down a	34
Mk	5:11 there was a great h of swine feeding.	34
	5:13 the h ran violently down a steep place into	34
Lk	8:32 And there was a h of many swine	34
	8:33 the h ran violently down a steep place into	34

HERDMAN (1) [HERD, MAN]

Am	7:14 I was a h, and a gatherer of sycomore fruit:	951

HERDMEN (8) [HERD, MAN]

Ge	13: 7 was a strife between the h of Abram's	7462
	13: 7 Abram's cattle and the h of Lot's cattle:	7462
	13: 8 and between my h and thy herdmen;	7462
	13: 8 and between my h and thy h;	7462
	26:20 the h of Gerar did strive with Isaac's	7462
	26:20 of Gerar did strive with Isaac's h,	7462
1Sa	21: 7 chiefest of the h that belonged to Saul.	7462
Am	1: 1 Amos, who was among the h of Tekoa,	5349

HERDS (33) [HERD]

Ge	13: 5 with Abram, had flocks, and h, and tents.	1241
	24:35 h, and silver, and gold, and menservants,	1241
	26:14 of h, and great store of servants:	1241
	32: 7 flocks, and h, and the camels, into two	1241
	33:13 the flocks and h with young are with me:	1241
	45:10 flocks, and thy h, and all that thou hast:	1241
	46:32 and their h, and all that they have.	1241
	47: 1 and their h, and all that they have,	1241
	47:17 for the cattle of the h, and for the asses:	1241
	47:18 is spent; my lord also had our h of cattle;	4735
	50: 8 little ones, and their flocks, and their h,	1241
Ex	10: 9 our flocks and with our h will we go;	1241
	10:24 only let your flocks and your h be stayed:	1241
	12:32 Also take your flocks and your h, as ye	1241
	12:38 and flocks, and h, even very much cattle.	1241
	34: 3 neither let the flocks nor h feed before	1241
Nu	11:22 Shall the flocks and the h be slain for	1241
Dt	8:13 when thy h and thy flocks multiply,	1241
	12: 6 the firstlings of your h and of your flocks:	1241
	12:17 or the firstlings of thy h or of thy flock,	1241
	14:23 the firstlings of thy h and of thy flocks;	1241
1Sa	30:20 David took all the flocks and the h,	1241
2Sa	12: 2 man had exceeding many flocks and h:	1241
1Ch	27:29 over the h that fed in Sharon was Shitrai	1241
	27:29 over the h that were in the valleys was	1241
2Ch	32:29 possessions of flocks and h in abundance:	1241
Ne	10:36 the firstlings of our h and of our flocks,	1241
Pr	27:23 state of thy flocks, and look well to thy h.	5739
Isa	65:10 the valley of Achor a place for the h to lie	1241
Jer	3:24 their flocks and their h, their sons and	1241

Jer	5:17 they shall eat up thy flocks and thine h:	1241
Hos	5: 6 and with their h to seek the LORD;	1241
Joel	1:18 the h of cattle are perplexed, because	5739

HERE (162) [HEREAFTER, HEREBY, HEREIN, HEREOF, HERETOFORE, HEREUNTO, HEREWITH]

Ge	16:13 Have I also h looked after him that seeth	1988
	19:12 said unto Lot, Hast thou h any besides?	6311
	19:15 and thy two daughters, which are h;	4672
	21:23 swear unto me h by God that thou wilt	2008
	22: 1 Abraham: and he said, Behold, h I am.	NIH
	22: 5 his young men, Abide you h with the ass;	6311
	22: 7 he said, H am I, my son. And he said,	2009
	22:11 Abraham, Abraham: and he said, H am I.	2009
	24:13 Behold, I stand h by the well of water;	NIH
	27: 1 and he said unto him, Behold, h am I?	NIH
	27:18 he said, H am I; who art thou, my son?	2009
	31:11 dream, saying, Jacob: And I said, H am I.	2009
	31:37 set it h before my brethren and	3541
	37:13 unto them. And he said to him, H am I.	2009
	40:15 h also have I done nothing that they	6311
	42:33 leave one of your brethren h with me,	NIH
	46: 2 said, Jacob, Jacob. And he said, H am I.	2009
	47:23 lo, h is seed for you, and ye shall sow	NIH
Ex	3: 4 said, Moses, Moses. And he said, H am I.	2009
	24:14 unto the elders, Tarry ye h for us,	2088+871.1
	33:16 For wherein shall it be known h that I and	645
Nu	14:40 we be h, and will go up unto the place	NIH
	22: 8 Lodge h this night, and I will bring you	6311
	22:19 pray you, tarry ye also h this night,	2088+871.1
	23: 1 Build me h seven altars,	2088+871.1
	23: 1 prepare me h seven oxen and	2088+871.1
	23:15 unto Balak, Stand h by thy burnt offering,	3541
	23:29 Build me h seven altars,	2088+871.1
	23:29 prepare me h seven bullocks and	2088+871.1
	32: 6 brethren go to war, and shall ye sit h?	6311
	32:16 We will build sheepfolds h for our cattle,	6311
Dt	5: 3 us, who are all of us h alive this day.	6311
	5:31 stand thou h by me, and I will speak unto	6311
	12: 8 after all the things that we do h this day,	6311
	29:15 with him that standeth h with us this day	6311
	29:15 with him that is not h with us this day:	6311
Jos	18: 6 that I may cast lots for you h before	6311
	18: 8 that I may h cast lots for you before	6311
	21: 9 cities which are h mentioned by name,	NIH
Jdg	4:20 of thee, and say, Is there any man h?	6311
	18: 3 thou in this place? and what hast thou h?	6311
	19: 9 the day groweth to an end, lodge h,	6311
	19:24 h is my daughter a maiden,	NIH
	20: 7 of Israel; give h your advice and counsel.	1988
Ru	2: 8 but abide h fast by my maidens;	3541
	4: 1 Ho, such a one, turn aside, sit down h.	6311
	4: 2 elders of the city, and said, Sit ye down h.	6311
1Sa	1:26 the woman that stood by thee h,	2088+871.1
	3: 4 called Samuel: and he answered, H am I.	2009
	3: 5 he ran unto Eli, and said, H am I; for thou	2009
	3: 6 and went to Eli, and said, H am I;	2009
	3: 8 arose and went to Eli, and said, H am I;	2009
	3:16 my son. And he answered, H am I.	2009
	9: 8 have h at hand the fourth part of a shekel	4672
	9:11 and said unto them, Is the seer h?	2088
	12: 3 Behold, h I am: witness against me	2009
	14:34 sheep, and slay them h, and eat;	2088+871.1
	16:11 said unto Jesse, Are h all thy children?	NIH
	21: 8 is there not h under thine hand spear or	6311
	21: 9 it is h wrapt in a cloth behind the ephod:	NIH
	21: 9 for there is no other save that h.	2088+871.1
	22:12 And he answered, H I am, my lord.	2009
	23: 3 him, Behold, we be afraid h in Judah:	6311
	29: 3 What do these Hebrews h? And Achish	NIH
2Sa	1: 7 called unto me. And I answered, H am I.	2009
	11:12 Tarry h to day also, and to morrow	2088+871.1
	15:26 h am I, let him do to me as seemeth	NIH
	18:30 said unto him, Turn aside, and stand h.	3541
	20: 4 within three days, and be thou h present.	6311
	24:22 h be oxen for burnt sacrifice,	NIH
1Ki	2:30 he said, Nay; but I will die h.	6311
	18: 8 I am: go, tell thy lord, Behold, Elijah is h.	NIH
	18:11 Go, tell thy lord, Behold, Elijah is h.	NIH
	18:14 Behold, Elijah is h: and he shall slay me.	NIH
	19: 9 said unto him, What doest thou h, Elijah?	6311
	19:13 and said, What doest thou h, Elijah?	6311
	20:40 as thy servant was busy h and there,	2008
	22: 7 Is there not h a prophet of the LORD	6311
2Ki	2: 2 said unto Elisha, Tarry h, I pray thee;	6311
	2: 4 said unto him, Elisha, tarry h, I pray thee;	6311
	2: 6 Elijah said unto him, Tarry, I pray thee, h;	6311
	3:11 Is there not h a prophet of the LORD,	6311
	3:11 and said, H is Elisha the son of Shaphat,	6311
	7: 3 to another, Why sit we h until we die?	6311
	7: 4 if we sit still h, we die also.	6311
	10:23 look that there be h with you none of	6311
1Ch	29:17 which are present h, to offer willingly	6311
2Ch	18: 6 Is there not h a prophet of the LORD	6311
Job	38:11 and h shall thy proud waves be stayed?	6311
	38:35 may go, and say unto thee, H we are?	2009
Ps	132:14 will I dwell; for I have desired it.	6311
Isa	6: 8 go for us? Then I said, H am I; send me.	2009
	21: 9 h cometh a chariot of men, with a	2088
	22:16 What hast thou h? and whom hast thou	6311
	22:16 hast thou h, that thou hast hewed	6311
	22:16 thou hast hewed thee out a sepulchre h,	6311
	28:10 line upon line; h a little, and there a little:	8033
	28:13 line upon line; h a little, and there a little;	8033

H

Isa 52: 5 Now therefore, what have I **h**, saith — 6311
 58: 9 I *am*. If thou take away from the midst — 2009
Eze 6: 8 that the house of Israel committeth **h**, — 6311
 8: 9 the wicked abominations that they do **h**, — 6311
 8:17 the abominations which they commit **h**? — 6311
Hos 9: 9 gray hairs are **h** and **there** upon him, — 2236
Mt 12:41 and behold, a greater than Jonas *is* **h**. — 5602
 12:42 and behold, a greater than Solomon *is* **h**. — 5602
 14: 8 Give me **h** John Baptist's head in a — 5602
 14:17 We have **h** but five loaves, and two fishes. — 5602
 16:28 I say unto you, There be some standing **h**, — 5602
 17: 4 unto Jesus, Lord, it is good for us to be **h**: — 5602
 17: 4 wilt, let us make **h** three tabernacles. — 5602
 20: 6 them, Why stand ye **h** all the day idle? — 5602
 24: 2 There shall not be left **h** one stone upon — 5602
 24:23 say unto you, Lo, **h** *is* Christ; or there; — 5602
 26:36 Sit ye **h**, while I go and pray yonder. — 846
 26:38 death: tarry ye **h**, and watch with me. — 5602
 28: 6 He is not **h**: for he is risen, as he said. — 5602
Mk 6: 3 and are not his sisters **h** with us? — 5602
 8: 4 *men* with bread **h** in the wilderness? — 5602
 9: 1 That there be some of them that stand **h**, — 5602
 9: 5 to Jesus, Master, it is good for us to be **h**: — 5602
 13: 1 of stones and what buildings *are* **h**. — NIG
 13:21 any *man* shall say to you, Lo, **h** *is* Christ; — 5602
 14:32 to his disciples, Sit ye **h**, while I shall pray. — 5602
 14:34 unto death: tarry ye **h**, and watch. — 5602
 16: 6 he is risen; he is not **h**: behold the place — 5602
Lk 4:23 in Capernaum, do also **h** in thy country. — 5602
 9:12 get victuals: for we are **h** in a desert place. — NIG
 9:27 you of a truth, there be some standing **h**, — 5602
 9:33 Jesus, Master, it is good for us to be **h**: — 5602
 11:31 and behold, a greater than Solomon *is* **h**. — 5602
 11:32 and behold, a greater than Jonas *is* **h**. — 5602
 17:21 Neither shall they say, Lo **h**! or, lo there! — 5602
 17:23 And they shall say to you, See **h**; — 5602
 19:20 saying, Lord, behold, **h** *is* thy pound, — NIG
 22:38 said, Lord, behold, **h** *are* two swords. — 5602
 24: 6 He is not **h**, but is risen: remember how — 5602
 24:41 he said unto them, Have ye **h** any meat? — 1759
Jn 6: 9 There is a lad **h**, which hath five barley — 5602
 11:21 if thou hadst been **h**, my brother had — 5602
 11:32 unto him, Lord, if thou hadst been **h**, — 5602
Ac 4:10 by him doth this *man* stand **h** before — 1799
 8:36 and the eunuch said, See, **h** *is* water; — NIG
 9:10 And he said, Behold, I *am* **h**, Lord. — 5602
 9:14 And he **h** hath authority from the chief — 5602
 10:33 are we all **h** present before God, — 3918
 16:28 Do thyself no harm: for we are all **h**. — 1759
 24:19 Who ought to have been **h** before thee, — 3918
 24:20 Or else let these same **h** say, if they have — NIG
 25:24 all men which are **h** present **with** us, — 4840
 25:24 both at Jerusalem, and *also* **h**, crying that — 1759
Col 4: 9 unto you all *things* which *are* done **h**. — 5602
Heb 7: 8 And **h** men that die receive tithes; — 5602
 13:14 For **h** have we no continuing city, — 5602
Jas 2: 3 say unto him, Sit thou **h** in a good *place*; — 5602
 2: 3 thou there, or sit **h** under my footstool: — 5602
1Pe 1:17 pass the time of your sojourning *h* in fear: — NIG
Rev 13:10 **h** is the patience and the faith of the — 5602
 13:18 **h** is wisdom. Let him that hath — 5602
 14:12 **h** is the patience of the saints: here *are* — 5602
 14:12 *are* they that keep the commandments — 5602
 17: 9 And **h** *is* the mind which hath wisdom. — 5602

HEREAFTER (14) [AFTER, HERE]

Isa 41:23 Shew the *things* that are to come **h**, — 268
Eze 20:39 **h** *also*, if ye will not hearken unto me: — 310
Da 2:29 bed, what should come to pass **h**: — 311+1836
 2:45 the king what shall come to pass **h**: — 311+1836
Mt 26:64 **H** shall ye see the Son of man sitting — 575+737
Mk 11:14 No *man* eat fruit of thee **h** for ever. — 3371
Lk 22:69 **H** shall the Son of man sit on — 575+3568+3588
Jn 1:51 **H** ye shall see heaven open, — 575+737
 13: 7 not now; but thou shalt know **h**. — 3326+3778
 14:30 **H** I will **not** talk much with you: — 3765
1Ti 1:16 for a pattern to them which should **h** — 3195
Rev 1:19 and the *things* which shall be **h**; — 3326+3778
 4: 1 thee *things* which must be **h**. — 3326+3778
 9:12 there come two woes more **h**. — 3326+3778

HEREBY (13) [BY, HERE]

Ge 42:15 **H** shall ye be proved: By the life — 2063+871.1
 42:33 said unto us, **H** shall I know that — 2088+871.1
Nu 16:28 Moses said, **H** ye shall know that — 2088+871.1
Jos 3:10 **H** ye shall know that the living — 2088+871.1
1Co 4: 4 by myself; yet am I not **h** justified: — 1722+3778
1Jn 2: 3 And **h** we do know that we know — 1722+3778
 2: 5 **h** know we that we are in him. — 1722+3778
 3:16 **H** perceive we the love *of God*, — 1722+3778
 3:19 And **h** we know that we are of the — 1722+3778
 3:24 **h** we know that he abideth in us, — 1722+3778
 4: 2 **h** know ye the Spirit of God: — 1722+3778
 4: 6 **H** know we the spirit of truth, — 1537+3778
 4:13 **H** know we that we dwell in him, — 1722+3778

HEREIN (9) [HERE, IN]

Ge 34:22 **h** will the men consent unto us — 2063+871.1
2Ch 16: 9 **H** thou hast done foolishly: — 2088+5921
Jn 4:37 And **h** is that saying true, — 1722+3778
 9:30 Why **h** is a marvellous *thing*, that — 1722+3778
 15: 8 **H** is my Father glorified, that ye — 1722+3778
Ac 24:16 And **h** do I exercise myself, to have — 1722+3778
2Co 8:10 And **h** I give *my* advice: for this is — 1722+3778
1Jn 4:10 **H** is love, not that we loved God, — 1722+3778

HEREOF (2) [HERE, OF]

Mt 9:26 the fame **h** went abroad into all that — 3778
Heb 5: 3 And **by reason h** he ought, as for — 1223+3778

HERES (1)

Jdg 1:35 the Amorites would dwell in mount **H** in — 2776

HERESH (1)

1Ch 9:15 **H**, and Galal, and Mattaniah the son of — 2792

HERESIES (3) [HERESY]

1Co 11:19 For there must be also **h** among you, — 139
Gal 5:20 emulations, wrath, strife, seditions, **h**, — 139
2Pe 2: 1 who privily shall bring in damnable **h**, — 139

HERESY (2) [HERESIES, HERETICK]

Ac 24:14 that after the way which they call **h**, — 139

HERETICK (1) [HERESY]

Tit 3:10 A man *that is* a **h** after the first and — 141

HERETOFORE (8) [HERE, TO]

Ex 4:10 neither I, — 1571+4480+4480+8032+8543
 5: 7 straw to make brick, as **h**: — 8032+8543
 5: 8 which they did make **h**, you shall — 8032+8543
 5:14 both yesterday and to day, as **h**? — 8032+8543
Jos 3: 4 have not passed *this* way **h**. — 4480+8032+8543
Ru 2:11 people which thou knewest not **h**. — 8032+8543
1Sa 4: 7 there hath not been such *a thing* **h**. — 865+8032
2Co 13: 2 I write to them which have **sinned**, — 4258

HEREUNTO (2) [HERE, UNTO]

Ecc 2:25 or who else can hasten **h**, more than I? — NIH
1Pe 2:21 For *even* **h** were ye called: because — 1519+3778

HEREWITH (2) [HERE, WITH]

Eze 16:29 and yet thou wast not satisfied **h**, — 2063+871.1
Mal 3:10 prove me now **h**, saith the LORD — 2063+871.1

HERITAGE (30) [HERITAGES]

Ex 6: 8 to Jacob; and I will give it you *for* an **h**: — 4181
Job 20:29 and the appointed unto him by God. — 5159
 27:13 the **h** of oppressors, *which* they shall — 5159
Ps 16: 6 in pleasant *places*; yea, I have a goodly **h**. — 5159
 61: 5 hast given *me* the **h** of those that fear — 3425
 94: 5 thy people, O LORD, and afflict thine **h**. — 5159
 111: 6 he may give them the **h** of the heathen. — 5159
 119:111 Thy testimonies have I **taken as an h** for — 5157
 127: 3 Lo, children *are* an **h** of the LORD: — 5159
 135:12 gave their land *for* an **h**, an heritage unto — 5159
 135:12 an heritage, an **h** unto Israel his people. — 5159
 136:21 gave their land for an **h**: for his mercy — 5159
 136:22 *Even* an **h** unto Israel his servant: for his — 5159
Isa 54:17 This *is* the **h** of the servants of the LORD, — 5159
 58:14 feed thee with the **h** of Jacob thy father: — 5159
Jer 2: 7 land, and made mine **h** an abomination. — 5159
 3:19 a goodly **h** of the hosts of nations? — 5159
 12: 7 forsaken mine house, I have left mine **h**; — 5159
 12: 8 Mine **h** is unto me as a lion in the forest; — 5159
 12: 9 Mine **h** *is* unto me *as* a speckled bird, — 5159
 12:15 every man to his **h**, and every man to his — 5159
 17: 4 shalt discontinue from thine **h** that I gave — 5159
 50:11 O ye destroyers of mine **h**, because ye are — 5159
Joel 2:17 and give not thine **h** to reproach, — 5159
Mic 2: 2 and for my people and *for* my **h**, Israel, — 5159
 2: 2 man and his house, even a man and his **h**. — 5159
 7:14 people with thy rod, the flock of thine **h**, — 5159
 7:18 the transgression of the remnant of his **h**? — 5159
Mal 1: 3 his **h** waste for the dragons of — 5159
1Pe 5: 3 Neither as being lords over *God's* **h**, — 2819

HERITAGES (1) [HERITAGE]

Isa 49: 8 earth, to cause to inherit the desolate; — 5159

HERMAS (1)

Ro 16:14 Phlegon, **H**, Patrobas, Hermes, — 2057

HERMES (1)

Ro 16:14 **H**, and the brethren which are with them. — 2060

HERMOGENES (1)

2Ti 1:15 from me; of whom are Phygellus and **H**. — 2061

HERMON (13) [BAAL-HERMON, HERMONITES]

Dt 3: 8 from the river of Arnon unto mount **H**; — 2768
 3: 9 (*Which* **H** the Sidonians call Sirion; — 2768
 4:48 even unto mount Sion, which *is* **H**, — 2768
Jos 11: 3 to the Hivite under **H** in the land of — 2768
 11:17 in the valley of Lebanon under mount **H**: — 2768
 12: 1 from the river Arnon unto mount **H**, — 2768
 12: 5 reigned in mount **H**, and in Salcah, — 2768
 13: 5 from Baal-gad under mount **H** unto — 2768
 13:11 all mount **H**, and all Bashan unto Salcah: — 2768
1Ch 5:23 and Senir, and *unto* mount **H**. — 2768
Ps 89:12 Tabor and **H** shall rejoice in thy name. — 2768
 133: 3 As the dew of **H**, *and as the dew* that — 2768
SS 4: 8 from the top of Shenir and **H**, from — 2768

HERMONITES (1) [HERMON]

Ps 42: 6 and of the **H**, from the hill Mizar. — 2769

HEROD (40) [HEROD'S, HERODIANS]

Mt 2: 1 of Judea in the days of **H** the king, — 2264
 2: 3 When **H** the king had heard *these things*, — 2264

Mt 2: 7 Then **H**, when he had privily called — 2264
 2:12 a dream that *they* should not return to **H**, — 2264
 2:13 for **H** will seek the young child to destroy — 2264
 2:15 And was there until the death of **H**: that it — 2264
 2:16 Then **H**, when he saw that he was mocked — 2264
 2:19 when **H** was dead, behold, an angel of — 2264
 2:22 reign in Judea in the room of his father **H**, — 2264
 14: 1 At that time **H** the tetrarch heard of — 2264
 14: 3 For **H** had laid hold on John, — 2264
 14: 6 danced before them, and pleased **H**. — 2264
Mk 6:14 And king **H** heard *of him*; (for his name — 2264
 6:16 But when **H** heard *thereof*, he said, It is — 2264
 6:17 For **H** himself had sent forth and laid hold — 2264
 6:18 For John had said unto **H**, It is not lawful — 2264
 6:20 **H** feared John, knowing that he *was* a — 2264
 6:21 **H** on his birthday made a supper to his — 2264
 6:22 pleased **H** and them that sat with him, — 2264
 8:15 of the Pharisees, and *of* the leaven of **H**. — 2264
Lk 1: 5 There was in the days of **H**, the king of — 2264
 3: 1 and **H** being tetrarch of Galilee, — 2264
 3:19 **H** the tetrarch, being reproved by him — 2264
 3:19 and for all the evils which **H** had done, — 2264
 9: 7 Now **H** the tetrarch heard of all that was — 2264
 9: 9 And **H** said, John have I beheaded: — 2264
 13:31 and depart hence: for **H** will kill thee. — 2264
 23: 7 sent him to **H**, who himself also was at — 2264
 23: 8 when **H** saw Jesus, he was exceeding — 2264
 23:11 And **H** with his men of war set him at — 2264
 23:12 Pilate and **H** were made friends together: — 2264
 23:15 No, nor yet **H**: for I sent you to him; — 2264
Ac 4:27 both **H**, and Pontius Pilate, with — 2264
 12: 1 about that time **H** the king stretched — 2264
 12: 6 And when **H** would have brought him — 2264
 12:11 hath delivered me out of the hand of **H**, — 2264
 12:19 And when **H** had sought for him, — 2264
 12:20 **H** was highly displeased with them of — 2264
 12:21 And upon a set day **H**, arrayed in royal — 2264
 13: 1 which had been brought up with **H** — 2264

HEROD'S (4) [HEROD]

Mt 14: 6 But when **H** birthday was kept, — 2264
Lk 8: 3 And Joanna the wife of Chuza **H** steward, — 2264
 23: 7 that he belonged unto **H** jurisdiction. — 2264
Ac 23:35 And he commanded him to be kept in **H** — 2264

HERODIANS (3) [HEROD]

Mt 22:16 out unto him their disciples with the **H**, — 2265
Mk 3: 6 straightway took counsel with the **H** — 2265
 12:13 him certain of the Pharisees and of the **H**, — 2265

HERODIAS (4) [HERODIAS']

Mt 14: 6 the daughter of **H** danced before them, — 2266
Mk 6:19 Therefore **H** had a quarrel against him, — 2266
 6:22 when the daughter of the said **H** came — 2266
Lk 3:19 being reproved by him for **H** his brother — 2266

HERODIAS' (2) [HERODIAS]

Mt 14: 3 and put *him* in prison for **H** sake, — 2266
Mk 6:17 and bound him in prison for **H** sake, — 2266

HERODION (1)

Ro 16:11 Salute **H** my kinsman. Greet them that be — 2267

HERON (2)

Lev 11:19 the **h** after her kind, and the lapwing, — 601
Dt 14:18 the **h** after her kind, and the lapwing, — 601

HERS (4) [SHE]

Dt 21:15 *if* the firstborn son be **h** that was hated: — NIH
1Sa 25:42 five damsels of **h** that went after her; — 1886.3
2Ki 8: 6 Restore all that *was* **h**, and all — 1886.3+3807.1
Job 39:16 as though *they were* not **h**: — 1886.3+3807.1

HERSELF (42) [SELF, SHE]

Ge 18:12 Therefore Sarah laughed within **h**, — 1886.3
 20: 5 she, even she **h** said, He *is* my brother: — 1931
 24:65 therefore she took a vail, and covered **h**. — NIH
 38:14 and wrapped **h**, and sat in an open place, — NIH
Ex 2: 5 came down to wash *h* at the river; — NIH
Lev 15:28 she shall number to **h** seven days, — 1886.3
 21: 9 if she profane **h** by playing the whore, — NIH
Nu 22:25 she thrust **h** unto the wall, — NIH
 30: 3 bind *h* by a bond, *being* in her father's — NIH
Jdg 5:29 *her*, yea, she returned answer to **h**, — 1886.3
Ru 2:10 bowed **h** to the ground, and said unto — NIH
1Sa 4:19 were dead, she bowed **h** and travailed: — NIH
 25:23 on her face, and bowed **h** to the ground, — NIH
 25:41 bowed **h** on her face to the earth, and — NIH
2Sa 11: 2 the roof he saw a woman washing **h**; — NIH
1Ki 14: 5 she shall feign **h** to be another *woman*. — NIH
2Ki 4:37 bowed **h** to the ground, and took up her — NIH
Job 39:18 What time she lifteth up **h** on high, — NIH
Ps 84: 3 swallow a nest for **h**, where she may — 1886.3
Pr 31:22 She maketh **h** coverings of tapestry; — 1886.3
Isa 5:14 Therefore hell hath enlarged **h**, — 5315+1886.3
 34:14 rest there, and find for **h** a place of rest. — 1886.3
 61:10 and as a bride adorneth **h** with her jewels. — NIH
Jer 3:11 **h** more than treacherous Judah. — 5315+1886.3
 4:31 bewaileth **h**, that spreadeth her hands, — NIH
 49:24 turneth **h** to flee, and fear hath seized — 1886.3
Eze 22: 3 maketh idols against **h** to defile *herself*. — 1886.3
 22: 3 maketh idols against herself to defile **h**. — NIH
 23: 7 doted: with all their idols she defiled **h**. — NIH
 24:12 She hath wearied **h** with lies, and her — NIH
Hos 2:13 she decked **h** with her earrings and — NIH
Zec 9: 3 Tyrus did build **h** a strong hold, — 1886.3

Mt	9:21	For she said within **h**, If I may but touch	1438
Mk	4:28	For the earth bringeth forth fruit of **h**;	844
Lk	1:24	and hid **h** five months, saying,	1438
	13:11	and could in no wise lift up **h**.	NIG
Jn	20:14	thus said, she turned **h** back,	NIG
	20:16	She turned **h**, and saith unto him,	NIG
Heb	11:11	through faith also Sara **h** received strength	846
Rev	2:20	which calleth **h** a prophetess, to teach	1438
	18: 7	How much she hath glorified **h**,	1438
	19: 7	is come, and his wife hath made **h** ready.	1438

HESED (1)

1Ki	4:10	The son of **H**, in Aruboth; to him	2618

HESHBON (38)

Nu	21:25	in **H**, and in all the villages thereof.	2809
	21:26	For **H** *was* the city of Sihon the king of	2809
	21:27	Come *into* **H**, let the city of Sihon be	2809
	21:28	For there is a fire gone out of **H**, a flame	2809
	21:30	**H** is perished even unto Dibon,	2809
	21:34	king of the Amorites, which dwelt at **H**,	2809
	32: 3	**H**, and Elealeh, and Shebam, and Nebo,	2809
	32:37	the children of Reuben built **H**,	2809
Dt	1: 4	which dwelt in **H**, and Og the king of	2809
	2:24	Sihon the Amorite, king of **H**, and his	2809
	2:26	Sihon king of **H** *with* words of peace,	2809
	2:30	Sihon king of **H** would not let us pass by	2809
	3: 2	king of the Amorites, which dwelt at **H**.	2809
	3: 6	as we did unto Sihon king of **H**,	2809
	4:46	who dwelt at **H**, whom Moses and	2809
	29: 7	Sihon the king of **H**, and Og the king of	2809
Jos	9:10	to Sihon king of **H**, and to Og king of	2809
	12: 2	who dwelt in **H**, *and* ruled from Aroer,	2809
	12: 5	Gilead, the border of Sihon king of **H**,	2809
	13:10	which reigned in **H**, unto the border of	2809
	13:17	**H**, and all her cities that *are* in the plain;	2809
	13:21	the Amorites, which reigned in **H**,	2809
	13:26	**H** unto Ramath-mizpeh, and Betonim;	2809
	13:27	rest of the kingdom of Sihon king of **H**,	2809
	21:39	**H** with her suburbs, Jazer with her	2809
Jdg	11:19	Sihon king of the Amorites, the king of **H**;	2809
	11:26	While Israel dwelt in **H** and her towns,	2809
1Ch	6:81	with her suburbs, and Jazer with her	2809
Ne	9:22	the land of the king of **H**, and the land of	2809
SS	7: 4	thine eyes *like* the fish-pools in **H**,	2809
Isa	15: 4	**H** shall cry, and Elealeh: their voice shall	2809
	16: 8	the fields of **H** languish, *and* the vine of	2809
	16: 9	water thee *with* my tears, O **H**, and	2809
Jer	48: 2	in **H** they have devised evil against it;	2809
	48:34	From the cry of **H** *even* unto Elealeh,	2809
	48:45	that fled stood under the shadow of **H**	2809
	48:45	a fire shall come forth out of **H**,	2809
	49: 3	Howl, O **H**, for Ai is spoiled: cry,	2809

HESHMON (1)

Jos	15:27	Hazar-gaddah, and **H**, and Beth-palet,	2829

HETH (14)

Ge	10:15	Canaan begat Sidon his firstborn, and **H**,	2845
	23: 3	and spake unto the sons of **H**, saying,	2845
	23: 5	The children of **H** answered Abraham,	2845
	23: 7	of the land, *even* to the children of **H**.	2845
	23:10	Ephron dwelt amongst the children of **H**:	2845
	23:10	in the audience of the children of **H**,	2845
	23:16	named in the audience of the sons of **H**,	2845
	23:18	in the presence of the children of **H**,	2845
	23:20	of a buryingplace by the sons of **H**.	2845
	25:10	Abraham purchased of the sons of **H**:	2845
	27:46	of my life because of the daughters of **H**:	2845
	27:46	if Jacob take a wife of the daughters of **H**,	2845
	49:32	*is* therein *was* from the children of **H**.	2845
1Ch	1:13	Canaan begat Zidon his firstborn, and **H**,	2845

HETHLON (2)

Eze	47:15	from the great sea, the way of **H**, as	2855
	48: 1	north end to the coast of the way of **H**,	2855

HEW (12) [HEWED, HEWER, HEWERS, HEWETH, HEWN]

Ex	34: 1	**H** thee two tables of stone like unto	6458
Dt	10: 1	**H** thee two tables of stone like unto	6458
	12: 3	you shall **h** down the graven images of	1438
	19: 5	the wood with his neighbour to **h** wood,	2404
1Ki	5: 6	command thou that they **h** me cedar trees	3772
	5: 6	skill to **h** timber like unto the Sidonians.	3772
	5:18	Hiram's builders did **h** *them*,	6458
1Ch	22: 2	set masons to **h** wrought stones to build	2672
2Ch	2: 2	fourscore thousand to **h** in the mountain,	2672
Jer	6: 6	ye **h** down trees, and cast a mount	3772
Da	4:14	**H** down the tree, and cut off his	1414
	4:23	saying, **H** the tree *down*, and destroy it;	1414

HEWED (13) [HEW]

Ex	34: 4	he **h** two tables of stone like unto the first	6458
Dt	10: 3	two tables of stone like unto the first	6458
1Sa	11: 7	**h** them **in pieces**, and sent *them*	5408
	15:33	Samuel **h** Agag **in pieces** before	8158
1Ki	5:17	great stones, costly stones, *and* **h** stones,	1496
	6:36	inner court *with* three rows of **h** stones,	1496
	7: 9	according to the measures of **h** stones,	1496
	7:11	the measures of **h** stones, and cedars.	1496
	7:12	about *was* with three rows *of* **h** stones,	1496
2Ki	12:12	**h** stone to repair the breaches of the	4274
Isa	22:16	thou hast **h** thee **out** a sepulchre here,	2672
Jer	2:13	**h** them **out** cisterns, broken cisterns,	2672

Hos	6: 5	Therefore have I **h** *them* by the prophets;	2672

HEWER (1) [HEW]

Dt	29:11	from the **h** of thy wood unto the drawer	2404

HEWERS (9) [HEW]

Jos	9:21	them be **h** of wood and drawers of water	2404
	9:23	**h** of wood and drawers of water for	2404
	9:27	Joshua made them that day **h** of wood	2404
1Ki	5:15	fourscore thousand **h** in the mountains;	2672
2Ki	12:12	**h** of stone, and to buy timber and	2672
1Ch	22:15	**h** and workers of stone and timber,	2672
2Ch	2:10	to thy servants, the **h** that cut timber,	2404
	2:18	fourscore thousand *to be* **h** in the	2672
Jer	46:22	against her with axes, as **h** of wood.	2404

HEWETH (3) [HEW]

Isa	10:15	the axe boast itself against him that **h**	2672
	22:16	*as* he that **h** him out a sepulchre on high,	2672
	44:14	*He* **h** him **down** cedars, and taketh	3772

HEWN (17) [HEW]

Ex	20:25	stone, thou shalt not build it *of* **h** stone:	1496
2Ki	22: 6	timber and **h** stone to repair the house.	4274
2Ch	34:11	and builders gave they *it*, to buy **h** stone,	4274
Pr	9: 1	house, she hath **h** out her seven pillars:	2672
Isa	9:10	but we will build **with h** stones:	1496
	10:33	the high ones of stature *shall be* **h down**,	1438
	33: 9	Lebanon is ashamed *and* **h down**: Sharon	7060
	51: 1	look unto the rock *whence* ye are **h**,	2672
La	3: 9	He hath inclosed my ways with **h** stone,	1496
Eze	40:42	four tables *were* of **h** stone for the burnt	1496
Am	5:11	ye have built houses of **h** stone,	1496
Mt	3:10	bringeth not forth good fruit is **h down**,	1581
	7:19	bringeth not forth good fruit is **h down**,	1581
	27:60	tomb, which he had **h** out in the rock:	2998
Mk	15:46	laid him in a sepulchre which was **h** out	2998
Lk	3: 9	bringeth not forth good fruit is **h down**,	1581
	23:53	laid it in a sepulchre *that was* **h in stone**,	2991

HEZEKI (1)

1Ch	8:17	and Meshullam, and **H**, and Heber,	2395

HEZEKIAH (128) [EZEKIAS]

2Ki	16:20	and **H** his son reigned in his stead.	2396
	18: 1	**H** the son of Ahaz king of Judah *began*	2396
	18: 9	came to pass in the fourth year of king **H**,	2396
	18:10	In the sixth year of **H**, that *is* the ninth	2396
	18:13	Now in the fourteenth year of king **H** did	2396
	18:14	king of Judah sent to the king of	2396
	18:14	king of Assyria appointed unto **H** king	2396
	18:14	gave *him* all the silver that was found	2396
	18:16	At that time did **H** cut off *the gold from*	2396
	18:16	the pillars which **H** king of Judah had	2396
	18:17	Rab-shakeh from Lachish to king **H** with	2396
	18:19	Speak ye now to **H**, Thus saith the great	2396
	18:22	and whose altars **H** hath taken away,	2396
	18:29	saith the king, Let not **H** deceive you:	2396
	18:30	Neither let **H** make you trust in	2396
	18:31	Hearken not to **H**: for thus saith the king	2396
	18:32	hearken not unto **H**, when he persuadeth	2396
	18:37	to **H** with *their* clothes rent, and told him	2396
	19: 1	when king **H** heard *it*, that he rent his	2396
	19: 3	said unto him, Thus saith **H**, This day	2396
	19: 5	So the servants of king **H** came to Isaiah.	2396
	19: 9	he sent messengers again unto **H**, saying,	2396
	19:10	Thus shall ye speak to **H** king of Judah,	2396
	19:14	received the letter of the hand of	2396
	19:14	went up *into* the house of the LORD,	2396
	19:15	And **H** prayed before the LORD, and said,	2396
	19:20	Isaiah the son of Amoz sent to **H**, saying,	2396
	20: 1	In those days was **H** sick unto death.	2396
	20: 3	*is* good in thy sight. And **H** wept sore.	2396
	20: 5	and tell **H** the captain of my people,	2396
	20: 8	And said unto Isaiah, What *shall be* the sign	2396
	20:10	**H** answered, It is a light thing for	3169
	20:12	sent letters and a present unto **H**:	2396
	20:12	for he had heard that **H** had been sick.	2396
	20:13	**H** hearkened unto them, and shewed	2396
	20:13	his dominion, that **H** shewed them not.	2396
	20:14	came Isaiah the prophet unto king **H**,	2396
	20:14	**H** said, They are come from a far country,	2396
	20:15	**H** answered, All *the things* that *are* in	2396
	20:16	Isaiah said unto **H**, Hear the word of	2396
	20:19	said **H** unto Isaiah, Good *is* the word of	2396
	20:20	the rest of the acts of **H**, and all his might,	2396
	20:21	**H** slept with his fathers: and Manasseh	2396
	21: 3	places which **H** his father had destroyed;	2396
1Ch	3:13	Ahaz his son, **H** his son, Manasseh his	2396
	3:23	Elioenai, and **H**, and Azrikam, three.	2396
	4:41	came in the days of **H** king of Judah,	3169
2Ch	28:27	and **H** his son reigned in his stead.	3169
	29: 1	**H** *began* to reign *when he was* five and	2396
	29:18	they went in to **H** the king, and said,	2396
	29:20	the king rose early, and gathered	3169
	29:27	**H** commanded to offer the burnt offering	3169
	29:30	Moreover **H** the king and the princes	3169
	29:31	**H** answered and said, Now ye have	3169
	29:36	**H** rejoiced, and all the people, that God	3169
	30: 1	**H** sent to all Israel and Judah,	3169
	30:18	prayed for them, saying, The good	3169
	30:20	the LORD hearkened to **H**, and healed	3169
	30:22	**H** spake comfortably unto all the Levites	3169
	30:24	For **H** king of Judah did give	2396
	31: 2	**H** appointed the courses of the priests	3169

2Ch	31: 8	when **H** and the princes came and saw	3169
	31: 9	**H** questioned with the priests and	3169
	31:11	**H** commanded to prepare chambers in	3169
	31:13	at the commandment of **H** the king,	3169
	31:20	thus did **H** throughout all Judah,	3169
	32: 2	when **H** saw that Sennacherib was come,	3169
	32: 8	upon the words of **H** king of Judah.	3169
	32: 9	unto **H** king of Judah, and unto all Judah	3169
	32:11	Doth not **H** persuade you to give over	3169
	32:12	Hath not the same **H** taken away his high	3169
	32:15	Now therefore let not **H** deceive you,	2396
	32:16	the LORD God, and against his servant **H**.	2396
	32:17	shall not the God of **H** deliver his people	3169
	32:20	for this *cause* **H** the king, and the prophet	3169
	32:22	Thus the LORD saved **H** and	3169
	32:23	presents to **H** king of Judah:	3169
	32:24	In those days **H** was sick to the death,	3169
	32:25	**H** rendered not again according to	3169
	32:26	Notwithstanding **H** humbled himself for	3169
	32:26	came not upon them in the days of **H**.	3169
	32:27	**H** had exceeding much riches and	3169
	32:30	This same **H** also stopped the upper	3169
	32:30	And **H** prospered in all his works.	3169
	32:32	Now the rest of the acts of **H**,	3169
	32:33	**H** slept with his fathers, and they buried	3169
	33: 3	he built again the high places which **H**	3169
Ezr	2:16	children of Ater of **H**, ninety and eight.	3169
Ne	7:21	children of Ater of **H**, ninety and eight.	2396
Pr	25: 1	which the men of **H** king of Judah copied	2396
Isa	1: 1	Jotham, Ahaz, *and* **H**, kings of Judah.	3169
	36: 1	to pass in the fourteenth year of king **H**,	2396
	36: 2	Jerusalem unto king **H** with a great army.	2396
	36: 7	ye now to **H**, Thus saith the great king,	2396
	36: 7	and whose altars **H** hath taken away,	2396
	36:14	saith the king, Let not **H** deceive you:	2396
	36:15	Neither let **H** make you trust in	2396
	36:16	Hearken not to **H**: for thus saith the king	2396
	36:18	*Beware* lest **H** persuade you, saying,	2396
	36:22	to **H** with *their* clothes rent, and told him	2396
	37: 1	when king **H** heard *it*, that he rent his	2396
	37: 3	said unto him, Thus saith **H**, This day	2396
	37: 5	So the servants of king **H** came to Isaiah.	2396
	37: 9	he heard *it*, he sent messengers to **H**,	2396
	37:10	Thus shall ye speak to **H** king of Judah,	2396
	37:14	received the letter from the hand of	2396
	37:14	**H** went up *unto* the house of the LORD,	2396
	37:15	And **H** prayed unto the LORD, saying,	2396
	37:21	Isaiah the son of Amoz sent unto **H**,	2396
	38: 1	In those days was **H** sick unto death.	2396
	38: 2	turned his face toward the wall,	2396
	38: 3	*is* good in thy sight. And **H** wept sore.	2396
	38: 5	Go and say to **H**, Thus saith the LORD,	2396
	38: 9	The writing of **H**, king of Judah, when he	2396
	38:22	**H** also had said, What *is* the sign that I	2396
	39: 1	Babylon, sent letters and a present to **H**:	2396
	39: 2	was glad of them, and shewed them	2396
	39: 2	his dominion, that **H** shewed them not.	2396
	39: 3	came Isaiah the prophet unto king **H**,	2396
	39: 3	said, They are come from a far country	2396
	39: 4	answered, All that *is* in mine house	2396
	39: 5	said Isaiah to **H**, Hear the word of	2396
	39: 8	said **H** to Isaiah, Good *is* the word of	2396
Jer	15: 4	of Manasseh the son of **H** king of Judah,	3169
	26:18	prophesied in the days of **H** king of Judah,	2396
	26:19	fear the LORD **H** king of Judah and all Judah put	2396
Hos	1: 1	Jotham, Ahaz, *and* **H**, kings of Judah;	3169
Mic	1: 1	*and* **H**, kings of Judah, which he saw	3169

HEZION (1)

1Ki	15:18	of Tabrimon, the son of **H**, king of Syria,	2383

HEZIR (2)

1Ch	24:15	The seventeenth to **H**, the eighteenth to	2387
Ne	10:20	Magpiash, Meshullam, **H**,	2387

HEZRAI (1)

2Sa	23:35	**H** the Carmelite, Paarai the Arbite,	2695

HEZRO (1)

1Ch	11:37	**H** the Carmelite, Naarai the son of Ezbai,	2695

HEZRON (17) [ESROM, HEZRON'S, HEZRONITES]

Ge	46: 9	Hanoch, and Phallu, and **H**, and Carmi.	2696
	46:12	the sons of Pharez were **H** and Hamul.	2696
Ex	6:14	Israel; Hanoch, and Pallu, and Carmi:	2696
Nu	26: 6	Of **H**, the family of the Hezronites:	2696
	26:21	of **H**, the family of the Hezronites:	2696
Jos	15: 3	passed along *to* **H**, and went up to Adar,	2696
	15:25	Hazor, Hadattah, and Kerioth, *and* **H**,	2696
Ru	4:18	generations of Pharez: Pharez begat **H**,	2696
	4:19	**H** begat Ram, and Ram begat	2696
1Ch	2: 5	The sons of Pharez; **H**, and Hamul.	2696
	2: 9	The sons also of **H**, that were born unto	2696
	2:18	Caleb the son of **H** begat *children* of	2696
	2:21	afterward **H** went in to the daughter of	2696
	2:24	after that **H** was dead in Caleb-ephratah,	2696
	2:25	the sons of Jerahmeel the firstborn of **H**	2696
	4: 1	and Carmi, and Hur, and Shobal.	2696
	5: 3	*were*, Hanoch, and Pallu, and Carmi.	2696

HEZRON'S (1) [HEZRON]

1Ch	2:24	Abiah **H** wife bare him Ashur the father	2696

HEZRONITES (2) [HEZRON]

Nu	26: 6	Of Hezron, the family of the **H**: of Carmi,	2697

Nu 26:21 of Hezron, the family of the **H**: 2697

HID (130) [HIDE]

Ge 3: 8 his wife **h** themselves from the presence 2244
 3:10 because I *was* naked; and I **h** myself. 2244
 4:14 from thy face shall I be **h**; and I shall be a 5641
 35: 4 Jacob **h** them under the oak which *was* 2934
Ex 2: 2 *a goodly child,* she **h** him three months. 6845
 2:12 slew the Egyptian, and **h** him in the sand. 2934
 3: 6 Moses **h** his face; for he was afraid to look 5641
Lev 4:13 the thing be **h** from the eyes of 5956
 5: 3 be defiled withal, and it be **h** from him; 5956
 5: 4 with an oath, and it be **h** from him; 5956
Nu 5:13 it be **h** from the eyes of her husband, 5956
Dt 33:19 the seas, and *of* treasures **h** in the sand. 2934
Jos 2: 4 **h** them, and said thus, There came men 2244
 2: 6 **h** them with the stalks of flax, which she 2934
 6:17 she **h** the messengers that we sent. 2244
 6:25 because she **h** the messengers, 2244
 7:21 *are* **h** in the earth in the midst of my 2934
 7:22 *was* **h** in his tent, and the silver under it. 2934
 10:16 and **h** themselves in a cave at Makkedah. 2244
 10:17 The five kings are found **h** in a cave at 2244
 10:27 into the cave wherein they had been **h**, 2244
Jdg 9: 5 of Jerubbaal was left; for he **h** himself. 2244
1Sa 3:18 him every whit, and **h** nothing from him. 3582
 10:22 he hath **h** himself among the stuff. 2244
 14:11 of the holes where they had **h** themselves. 2244
 14:22 all the men of Israel which had **h** 2244
 20:24 So David **h** himself in the field: 5641
2Sa 17: 9 he is **h** now in some pit, or in some *other* 2244
 18:13 for there is no matter **h** from the king, 3582
1Ki 10: 3 there was not *any* thing **h** from the king, 5956
 18: 4 **h** them by fifty in a cave, and fed them 2244
 18:13 how I **h** an hundred men of the Lord's 2244
2Ki 4:27 the Lord hath **h** *it* from me, and hath not 5956
 6:29 we may eat him: and she hath **h** her son. 2244
 7: 8 went and **h** *it;* and came again, 2934
 7: 8 carried thence *also,* and went and **h** *it.* 2934
 11: 2 they **h** him, *even* him and his nurse. 5641
 11: 3 he was with her **h** *in* the house of 2244
1Ch 21:20 and his four sons with him **h** themselves. 2244
2Ch 9: 2 there was nothing **h** from Solomon which 5956
 22: 9 caught him, (for he *was* **h** in Samaria,) 2244
 22:11 **h** him from Athaliah, so that she slew 5641
 22:12 was with them **h** in the house of God six 2244
Job 3:10 nor **h** sorrow from mine eyes. 5641
 3:21 and dig for it more than for **h treasures;** 4301
 3:23 *is light given* to a man whose way is **h**, 5641
 5:21 Thou shalt be **h** from the scourge of 2244
 6:16 of the ice, *and* wherein the snow is **h**: 5956
 10:13 these *things* hast thou **h** in thine heart: 6845
 15:18 told from their fathers, and have not **h** *it:* 3582
 17: 4 For thou hast **h** their heart from 6845
 20:26 darkness *shall* be **h** in his secret places: 2934
 28:11 the **thing that is h** bringeth he forth *to* 8587
 28:21 Seeing it is **h** from the eyes of all living, 5956
 29: 8 young men saw me, and **h** themselves: 2244
 38:30 The waters are **h** as *with* a stone, 2244
Ps 9:15 in the net which they **h** is their own foot 2934
 17:14 belly thou fillest with thy **h** *treasure:* 6845
 19: 6 there is nothing **h** from the heat thereof. 5641
 22:24 neither hath he **h** his face from him; 5641
 32: 5 thee, and mine iniquity have I not **h**. 3680
 35: 7 without cause have they **h** for me their 2934
 35: 8 let his net that he hath **h** catch himself: 2934
 38: 9 and my groaning is not **h** from thee. 5641
 40:10 I have not **h** thy righteousness within my 3680
 55:12 then I would have **h** myself from him: 5641
 69: 5 and my sins are not **h** from thee. 3582
 119:11 Thy word have I **h** in mine heart, that I 6845
 139:15 My substance was not **h** from thee, when 3582
 140: 5 The proud have **h** a snare for me, 2934
Pr 2: 4 and searchest for her as *for* **h treasures;** 4301
Isa 28:15 under falsehood have we **h** ourselves: 5641
 29:14 of their prudent *men* shall be **h**. 5641
 40:27 My way is **h** from the Lord, 5641
 42:22 in holes, and they are **h** in prison houses: 2244
 49: 2 in the shadow of his hand hath he **h** me, 2244
 49: 2 polished shaft; in his quiver hath he **h** me; 5641
 50: 6 I **h** not my face from shame and spitting. 5641
 53: 3 we **h** as it were *our* faces from him; 4564
 54: 8 In a little wrath I **h** my face from thee for 5641
 57:17 I **h** me, and was wroth, and he went on 5641
 59: 2 and your sins have **h** *his* face from you, 5641
 64: 7 for thou hast **h** thy face from us, 5641
 65:16 and because they are **h** from mine eyes. 5641
Jer 13: 5 So I went, and **h** it by Euphrates, 2934
 13: 7 girdle from the place where I had **h** it: 2934
 16:17 they are not **h** from my face, neither is 5641
 16:17 neither is their iniquity **h** from mine eyes. 6845
 18:22 a pit to take me, and **h** snares for my feet. 2934
 33: 5 all whose wickedness I have **h** my face 5641
 36:26 the prophet: but the Lord **h** them. 5641
 43:10 throne upon these stones that I have **h**; 2934
Eze 22:26 have **h** their eyes from my sabbaths, 5956
 39:23 therefore **h** I my face from them, 5641
 39:24 unto them, and **h** my face from them. 5641
Hos 5: 3 Ephraim, and Israel is not **h** from me: 3582
 13:12 of Ephraim *is* bound up; his sin is **h**. 6845
 13:14 repentance shall be **h** from mine eyes. 5641
Am 9: 3 though they be **h** from my sight in 5641
Ob 1: 6 *how* are his **h things** sought up! 4710
Na 3:11 thou shalt be **h**, thou also shalt seek 5956
Zep 2: 3 it may be ye shall be **h** in the day of 5641

Mt 5:14 A city that is set on a hill cannot be **h**. 2928
 10:26 revealed; and **h**, that shall not be known. 2927
 11:25 thou hast **h** these *things* from the wise 613
 13:33 and **h** in three measures of meal, 1470
 13:44 of heaven is like unto treasure **h** in a field; 2928
 25:18 in the earth, and **h** his lord's money. 613
 25:25 and went and **h** thy talent in the earth: 2928
Mk 4:22 For there is nothing **h**, which shall not be 2927
 7:24 no *man* know *it:* but he could not be **h**. 2990
Lk 1:24 and **h** herself five months, saying, 4032
 8:17 *any* thing **h**, that shall not be known 614
 8:47 when the woman saw that she was not **h**, 2990
 9:45 it was **h** from them, that they perceived 3871
 10:21 that thou hast **h** these *things* from 613
 12: 2 neither **h**, that shall not be known. 2927
 13:21 and **h** in three measures of meal, 1470
 18:34 and this saying was **h** from them, 2928
 19:42 but now they are **h** from thine eyes. 2928
Jn 8:59 but Jesus **h** himself, and went out of 2928
2Co 4: 3 But if our gospel be **h**, it is hid to them 2572
 4: 3 gospel be hid, it is **h** to them that are lost: 2572
Eph 3: 9 of the world hath been **h** in God, 613
Col 1:26 mystery which hath been **h** from ages 613
 2: 3 In whom are **h** all the treasures of wisdom 614
 3: 3 and your life is **h** with Christ in God. 2928
1Ti 5:25 and they that are otherwise cannot be **h**. 2928
Heb 11:23 was **h** three months of his parents, 2928
Rev 6:15 every free *man,* **h** themselves in the dens 2928

HIDDAI (1)

2Sa 23:30 the Pirathonite, **H** of the brooks of Gaash, 1914

HIDDEKEL (2)

Ge 2:14 the name of the third river *is* **H**: that *is it* 2313
Da 10: 4 by the side of the great river, which *is* **H**; 2313

HIDDEN (16) [HIDE]

Lev 5: 2 creeping things, and *if* it be **h** from him; 5956
Dt 30:11 it *is* not **h** from thee, neither *is* it far off. 6381
Job 3:16 Or as a **h** untimely birth I had not been; 2934
 15:20 the number of years is **h** to the oppressor. 6845
 24: 1 seeing times are not **h** from the Almighty, 6845
Ps 51: 6 the **h** *part* thou shalt make me to know 5640
 83: 3 and consulted against thy **h ones.** 6845
Pr 28:12 but when the wicked rise, a man is **h**. 2664
Isa 45: 3 **h riches** of secret places, that thou 4301
 48: 6 even **h** *things,* and thou didst not know 5341
Ac 26:26 that none of these *things* are **h** from him; 2990
1Co 2: 7 *even* the **h** wisdom, which God ordained 613
 4: 5 who both will bring to light the **h** *things* 2927
2Co 4: 2 have renounced the **h** *things* of 2927
1Pe 3: 4 *let it be* the **h** man of the heart, in *that* 2927
Rev 2:17 will I give to eat of the **h** manna, 2928

HIDE (83) [HID, HIDDEN, HIDEST, HIDETH, HIDING]

Ge 18:17 Shall I **h** from Abraham *that thing* which 3680
 47:18 unto him, We will not **h** *it* from my lord, 3582
Ex 2: 3 she could not longer **h** him, she took 6845
Lev 8:17 and his **h**, his flesh, and his dung, 5785
 9:11 he burnt with fire without the camp. 5785
 20: 4 **any ways h** their eyes from the 5956+5956
Dt 7:20 **h** themselves from thee, be destroyed. 5641
 22: 1 sheep go astray, and **h** thyself from them: 5956
 22: 3 do likewise: thou mayest not **h** thyself. 5956
 22: 4 by the way, and **h** thyself from them: 5956
 31:17 I will **h** my face from them, and they shall 5641
 31:18 I will **surely h** my face in that day 5641+5641
 32:20 he said, I will **h** my face from them, I will 5641
Jos 2:16 **h** yourselves there three days, until 2244
 7:19 what thou hast done; **h** *it* not from me. 3582
Jdg 6:11 winepress, to **h** *it* from the Midianites. 5127
1Sa 3:17 I pray thee **h** *it* not from me: God do so 3582
 3:17 if thou **h** *any* thing from me of all 3582
 13: 6 the people did **h** themselves in caves, 2244
 19: 2 and abide in a secret place, and **h** thyself: 5641
 20: 2 why should my father **h** this thing from 5641
 20: 5 that I may **h** myself in the fields unto 5641
 20:19 come to the place where thou didst **h** 5641
 23:19 Doth not David **h** himself with us in 5641
 26: 1 Doth not David **h** himself in the hill of 5641
2Sa 14:18 the woman, **H** not from me, I pray thee, 3582
1Ki 17: 3 thyself by the brook Cherith, 5641
 22:25 go into an inner chamber to **h** thyself. 2247
2Ki 7:12 are they gone out of the camp to **h** 2247
2Ch 18:24 go into an inner chamber to **h** thyself. 2244
Job 13:20 me: then will I not **h** myself from thee. 5641
 14:13 O that thou wouldest **h** me in the grave, 6845
 20:12 mouth, *though* he **h** it under his tongue; 3582
 24: 4 poor of the earth **h** themselves together. 2244
 33:17 *from his* purpose, and **h** pride from man. 3680
 34:22 where the workers of iniquity may **h** 5641
 40:13 **H** them in the dust together; *and* bind 2934
Ps 13: 1 how long wilt thou **h** thy face from me? 5641
 17: 8 **h** me under the shadow of thy wings, 5641
 27: 5 For in the time of trouble he shall **h** me in 6845
 27: 5 the secret of his tabernacle shall he **h** me; 5641
 27: 9 **H** not thy face *far* from me; put not thy 5641
 30: 7 thou didst **h** thy face, *and* I was troubled. 5641
 31:20 Thou shalt **h** them in the secret of thy 5641
 51: 9 **H** thy face from my sins, and blot out all 5641
 54: 1 Saul, Doth not David **h** himself with us? 5641
 55: 1 and **h** not thyself from my supplication. 5956
 56: 6 they **h** themselves, they mark my steps, 6845
 64: 2 **H** me from the secret counsel of 5641

Ps 69:17 **h** not thy face from thy servant; for I am 5641
 78: 4 We will not **h** *them* from their children, 3582
 89:46 wilt thou **h** thyself, for ever? shall thy 5641
 102: 2 **H** not thy face from me in the day *when* 5641
 119:19 not thy commandments from me. 5641
 143: 7 **h** not thy face from me, lest I be like unto 5641
 143: 9 mine enemies: I **flee** unto thee **to h** me. 3680
Pr 2: 1 and **h** my commandments with thee; 6845
 28:28 the wicked rise, men **h** themselves: 5641
Isa 1:15 hands, I will **h** mine eyes from you; 5956
 2:10 into the rock, and **h** thee in the dust, 2934
 3: 9 declare their sin as Sodom, they **h** *it* not. 3582
 16: 3 the outcasts; bewray not him that 5641
 26:20 **h** thyself as it were for a little moment, 2247
 29:15 Woe unto them that seek deep to **h** *their* 5641
 58: 7 that thou **h** not thyself from thine own 5956
Jer 13: 4 and **h** it there in a hole of the rock. 2934
 13: 6 which I commanded thee to **h** there. 2934
 23:24 Can any **h** himself in secret places that I 5641
 36:19 Go, **h** thee, thou and Jeremiah; 5641
 38:14 I will ask thee a thing; **h** nothing from me. 3582
 38:25 **h** *it* not from us, and we will not put thee 3582
 43: 9 and **h** them in the clay in the brickkiln, 2934
 49:10 and he shall not be able to **h** himself: 2247
La 3:56 **h** not thine ear at my breathing, at my cry. 5956
Eze 28: 3 no secret *that* they can **h** *from* thee: 6004
 31: 8 in the garden of God could not **h** him: 6004
 39:29 Neither will I **h** my face any more from 5641
Da 10: 7 so that they fled to **h** themselves. 2244
Am 9: 3 though they **h** themselves in the top of 5641
Mic 3: 4 will even **h** his face from them at that 5641
Jn 12:36 departed, and did **h** himself from them. 2928
Jas 5:20 death, and shall **h** a multitude of sins. 2572
Rev 6:16 **h** us from the face of him that sitteth on 2928

HIDEST (6) [HIDE]

Job 13:24 Wherefore **h** thou thy face, and holdest 5641
Ps 10: 1 why **h** thou thyself in times of trouble? 5956
 44:24 Wherefore **h** thou thy face, 5641
 88:14 my soul? why **h** thou thy face from me? 5641
 104:29 Thou **h** thy face, they are troubled: 5641
Isa 45:15 Verily thou *art* a God that **h** thyself, 5641

HIDETH (7) [HIDE]

1Sa 23:23 all the lurking places where he **h** himself, 2244
Job 23: 9 I cannot behold *him:* he **h** *himself on* 5848
 34:29 when he **h** *his* face, who then can behold 5641
 42: 3 Who *is* he that **h** counsel without 5956
Ps 10:11 he **h** his face; he will never see *it.* 5641
 139:12 Yea, the darkness **h** not from thee; 2821
Pr 10:18 He that **h** hatred *with* lying lips, and he 3680
 19:24 A slothful *man* **h** his hand in *his* bosom, 2934
 22: 3 *man* foreseeth the evil, and **h** himself: 5641
 26:15 The slothful **h** his hand in *his* bosom; 2934
 27:12 *man* foreseeth the evil, *and* **h** himself; 5641
 27:16 Whosoever **h** her, hideth the wind, 6845
 27:16 the wind, and the ointment of his right 6845
 28:27 that **h** his eyes shall have many a curse. 5956
Isa 8:17 that **h** his face from the house of Jacob, 5641
Mt 13:44 he **h**, and for joy thereof goeth and 2928

HIDING (6) [HIDE]

Job 31:33 Adam, by **h** mine iniquity in my bosom: 2934
Ps 32: 7 Thou *art* my **h place;** thou shalt preserve 5643
 119:114 Thou *art* my **h place** and my shield: 5643
Isa 28:17 the waters shall overflow the **h place**. 5643
 32: 2 man shall be as a **h place** from the wind, 4224
Hab 3: 4 hand: and there *was* the **h** of his power. 2253

HIEL (1)

1Ki 16:34 In his days did **H** the Bethelite build 2419

HIERAPOLIS (1)

Col 4:13 them that are in Laodicea, and them in **H**. 2404

HIGGAION (1)

Ps 9:16 in the work of his own hands. **H**. Selah. 1902

HIGH (416) [HEIGHT, HEIGHTS, HIGHER, HIGHEST, HIGHLY, HIGHMINDED, HIGH-MINDED, HIGHNESS, HIGHWAY, HIGHWAYS]

Ge 7:19 all the hills, that *were* under the whole 1364
 14:18 and he *was* the priest of the **most h** God. 5945
 14:19 Blessed *be* Abram of the **most h** God, 5945
 14:20 blessed *be* the **most h** God, which hath 5945
 14:22 the **most h** God, the possessor of heaven 5945
 29: 7 said, Lo, *it is* yet **h** day, neither *is it* time 1419
Ex 14: 8 the children of Israel went out with a **h** 7311
 25:20 forth *their* wings **on h**, 4605+1886.5+3807.1
 37: 9 out *their* wings **on h**, 4605+1886.5+3807.1
 39:31 **on h** upon the 4480+4605+1886.5+3807.1
Lev 21:10 *he that is* the **h** priest among his brethren, 1419
Nu 22:41 **h** places of Baal, 1116
 26:30 will destroy your **h places**, and cut down NIH
 11:31 as it were two cubits **h** upon the face of NIH
 20:17 will go *by* the king's **h** way, we will not NIH
 20:19 said unto him, We will go by the **h** way: 4546
 21:22 *but* we will go along by the king's **h** way, NIH
 21:28 *and* the **h** places of Arnon. 1116
 22:41 brought him up *into* the **h** places of Baal, 1116
 23: 3 I will tell thee. And he went to a **h** place, 8205
 24:16 and knew the knowledge of the **most H**, 5945
 33: 3 a **h** hand in the sight of all the Egyptians, 7311
 33:52 and quite pluck down all their **h places**. 1116

Nu 35:25 shall abide in it unto the death of the **h** 1419
35:28 his refuge until the death of the **h** priest: 1419
35:28 after the death of the **h** priest the slayer 1419
Dt 2:27 I will go along by the **h** way, I will 1870
3: 5 All these cities *were* fenced *with* **h** walls, 1364
12: 2 the **h** mountains, and upon the hills, 7311
26:19 to make thee **h** above all nations which 5945
28: 1 that the LORD thy God will set thee on **h** 5945
28:43 thee **very h**; 4605+4605+1886.5+1886.5
28:52 until thy **h** and fenced walls come down, 1364
32: 8 When the **most H** divided to the nations 5945
32:13 He made him ride on the **h** places of 1116
32:27 Our hand *is* **h**, and the LORD hath not 7311
33:29 and thou shalt tread upon their **h** places. 1116
Jos 20: 6 until the death of the **h** priest that shall 1419
Jdg 5:18 the death in the **h** places of the field. 4791
1Sa 9:12 of the people to day in the **h** place: 1116
9:13 before he go up to the **h** place to eat: 1116
9:14 against them, for to go up *to* the **h** place, 1116
9:19 go up before me *unto* the **h** place; for ye 1116
9:25 down from the **h** place *into* the city, 1116
10: 5 down from the **h** place with a psaltery, 1116
10:13 of prophesying, he came *to* the **h** place. 1116
13: 6 in rocks, and in **h** places, and in pits. 6877
2Sa 1:19 of Israel *is* slain upon thy **h** places: 1116
1:25 *thou* wast slain in thine **h** places. 1116
22: 3 my **h** tower, and my refuge, my saviour; 4869
22:14 and the **most H** uttered his voice. 5945
22:34 and setteth me upon my **h** places. 1116
22:49 thou also hast **lifted me up on h** above 7311
23: 1 and the man *who* was raised up on **h**, 5920
1Ki 3: 2 Only the people sacrificed in **h** places, 1116
3: 3 sacrificed and burnt incense in **h** places. 1116
3: 4 for that *was* the great **h** place: 1116
6:10 against all the house, five cubits **h**: 6967
6:23 cherubims *of* olive tree, each ten cubits **h**. 6967
7:15 *of* brass, of eighteen cubits **h** apiece: 6967
7:35 *there* a round compass of half a cubit **h**: 6967
9: 8 *at* this house, which is **h**, every one that 5945
11: 7 Solomon build a **place** for Chemosh, 1116
12:31 he made a house of **h** places, 1116
12:32 priests of the **h** places which he had 1116
13: 2 the **h** places that burn incense upon thee, 1116
13:32 all the houses of the **h** places which 1116
13:33 of the people priests of the **h** places. 1116
13:33 *one of* the priests of the **h** places. 1116
14:23 For they also built them **h** places, 1116
14:23 on every **h** hill, and under every green 1364
15:14 the **h** places were not removed: 1116
21: 9 and set Naboth on **h** among the people. 7218
21:12 and set Naboth on **h** among the people. 7218
22:43 the **h** places were not taken away; 1116
22:43 and burnt incense yet in the **h** places. 1116
2Ki 12: 3 the **h** places were not taken away: 1116
12: 3 and burnt incense in the **h** places. 1116
12:10 king's scribe and the **h** priest came up, 1419
14: 4 the **h** places were not taken away: 1116
14: 4 and burnt incense on the **h** places. 1116
15: 4 that the **h** places were not removed: 1116
15: 4 and burnt incense still on the **h** places. 1116
15:35 the **h** places were not removed: 1116
15:35 and burnt incense still in the **h** places. 1116
16: 4 and burnt incense in the **h** places, 1116
17: 9 built them **h** places in all their cities, 1116
17:10 images and groves in every **h** hill, 1364
17:11 they burnt incense in all the **h** places, 1116
17:29 put *them* in the houses of the **h** places 1116
17:32 lowest of them priests of the **h** places, 1116
17:32 for them in the houses of the **h** places 1116
18: 4 He removed the **h** places, and brake 1116
18:22 **h** places and whose altars Hezekiah 1116
19:22 *thy* voice, and lift up thine eyes on **h**? 4791
21: 3 For he built *up* again the **h** places which 1116
22: 4 Go up to Hilkiah the **h** priest, that he 1419
22: 8 Hilkiah the **h** priest said unto Shaphan 1419
23: 4 the king commanded Hilkiah the **h** priest, 1419
23: 5 in the **h** places in the cities of Judah, 1116
23: 8 defiled the **h** places where the priests 1116
23: 8 brake down the **h** places of the gates that 1116
23: 9 Nevertheless the priests of the **h** places 1116
23:13 the **h** places that *were* before Jerusalem, 1116
23:15 the **h** place which Jeroboam the son of 1116
23:15 that altar and the **h** place he brake down, 1116
23:15 burnt the **h** place, *and* stampt it small to 1116
23:19 all the houses also of the **h** places that 1116
23:20 he slew all the priests of the **h** places 1116
1Ch 11:23 five cubits **h**; and in the Egyptian's hand NIH
14: 2 was lift up on **h**, 4605+1886.5+3807.1
16:39 LORD in the **h** place that *was* at Gibeon, 1116
17:17 to the estate of a man of **h degree**, 4609
21:29 *were* at that season in the **h** place at 1116
2Ch 1: 3 went to the **h** place that *was* at Gibeon; 1116
1:13 **place** that *was* at Gibeon *to* Jerusalem, 1116
3:15 two pillars of thirty and five cubits **h**, 753
6:13 three cubits **h**, and had set it in the midst 6967
7:21 this house, which is **h**, shall be an 5945
11:15 he ordained him priests for the **h** places, 1116
14: 3 of the strange *gods*, and the **h** places, 1116
14: 5 out of all the cities of Judah the **h** places 1116
15:17 the **h** places were not taken away out of 1116
17: 6 moreover he took away the **h** places and 1116
20:19 with a loud voice on **h**. 4605+1886.5+3807.1
20:33 the **h** places were not taken away: 1116
21:11 Moreover he made **h** places in 1116
23:20 they came through the **h** gate *into* 5945

2Ch 24:11 and the **h** priest's officer came and 7218
27: 3 He built the **h** gate of the house of 5945
28: 4 and burnt incense in the **h** places, 1116
28:25 **h** places to burn incense unto other gods, 1116
31: 1 threw down the **h** places and the altars 1116
32:12 same Hezekiah taken away his **h** places 1116
33: 3 For he built again the **h** places which 1116
33:17 people did sacrifice still in the **h** places, 1116
33:19 the places wherein he built **h** places, 1116
34: 3 and Jerusalem from the **h** places, 1116
34: 4 images, that *were* on **h** 4605+1886.5+3807.1
34: 9 when they came to Hilkiah the **h** priest, 1419
Ne 1: 1 Eliashib the **h** priest rose up with his 1419
3:20 door of the house of Eliashib the **h** priest. 1419
3:25 tower which lieth out from the king's **h** 5945
13:28 of Joiada, the son of Eliashib the **h** priest, 1419
Est 5:14 Let a gallows be made of fifty cubits **h**, 1364
7: 9 Behold also, the gallows fifty cubits **h**, 1364
Job 5:11 To set up on **h** those that be low; 4791
11: 8 *It is* as **h** as heaven; what canst thou do? 1363
16:19 is in heaven, and my record *is* on **h**. 4791
21:22 seeing he judgeth those that are **h**. 7311
22:12 the height of the stars, how **h** they are. 7311
25: 2 him, he maketh peace in his **h** places. 4791
31: 2 inheritance of the Almighty from on **h**? 4791
38:15 and the **h** arm shall be broken. 7311
39:18 What time she lifteth up herself on **h**, 4791
39:27 thy command, and **make** her nest on **h**? 7311
41:34 He beholdeth all **h** *things*: he *is* a king 1364
Ps 7: 7 for their sakes therefore return thou on **h**. 4791
7:17 *praise* to the name of the LORD **most H**. 5945
9: 2 sing *praise* to thy name, O thou **most H**. 5945
18: 2 horn of my salvation, *and* my **h** tower. 4869
18:27 but wilt bring down **h** looks. 7311
18:33 and setteth me upon my **h** places. 1116
21: 7 through the mercy of the **most H** he shall 5945
46: 4 *place* of the tabernacles of the **most H**. 5945
47: 2 For the LORD **most H** *is* terrible; he *is* a 5945
49: 2 Both low and **h**, rich and poor, 376+1121
50:14 and pay thy vows unto the **most H**: 5945
56: 2 that fight against me, O thou **most H**. 4791
57: 2 I will cry unto God **most H**; unto God 5945
62: 9 and **men of h degree** *are* a lie: 376+1121
68:15 of Bashan; a **h** hill *as* the hill of Bashan. 1386
68:16 Why leap ye, ye **h** hills? *this is* the hill 1386
68:18 Thou hast ascended on **h**, thou hast led 4791
69:29 let thy salvation, O God, **set me up on h**. 7682
71:19 also, O God, *is* **very h**, 4791+5704
73:11 and *is* there knowledge in the **most H**? 5945
75: 5 Lift not up your horn on **h**: speak *not* with 4791
77:10 the years of the right hand of the **most H**. 5945
78:17 provoking the **most H** in the wilderness. 5945
78:35 their rock, and the **h** God their redeemer. 5945
78:56 and provoked the **most H** God, 5945
78:69 him to anger with their **h** places, 1116
78:69 he built his sanctuary like **h** *palaces*, like 7311
82: 6 and all of you *are* children of the **most H**. 5945
83:18 *art* the **most H** over all the earth. 5945
89:13 is thy hand, *and* **h** is thy right hand. 7311
91: 1 **most H** shall abide under the shadow of 5945
91: 9 refuge, *even* the **most H**, thy habitation; 5945
91:14 I will **set him on h**, because he hath 7682
92: 1 to sing *praises* unto thy name, O **most H**: 5945
92: 8 But thou, LORD, *art* **most h** for evermore. 4791
93: 4 The LORD on **h** *is* 4791+871.1+1886.1
97: 9 LORD, *art* **h** above all the earth: 5945
99: 2 in Zion; and he *is* **h** above all the people. 7311
101: 5 him that hath a **h** look and a proud heart 1362
103:11 For as the heaven is **h** above the earth, 1361
104:18 The hills *are* a refuge for the wild goats; 1364
107:11 contemned the counsel of the **most H**: 5945
107:41 Yet **setteth** he the poor on **h** from 7682
113: 4 The LORD *is* **h** above all nations, 7311
113: 5 The LORD our God, who dwelleth on **h**, 1361
131: 1 great *matters*, or in *things* too **h** for me. 6381
138: 6 Though the LORD *be* **h**, yet hath he 7311
139: 6 for me; it is **h**, I cannot attain unto it. 7682
144: 2 my **h** tower, and my deliverer; my shield, 4869
149: 6 the **h** *praises* of God *be* in their mouth, 7319
150: 5 praise him upon the **h** **sounding** cymbals. 8643
Pr 8: 2 She standeth in the top of **h** places by 4791
9:14 on a seat in the **h** places of the city, 4791
18:11 and as a wall in his own conceit. 7682
21: 4 A **h** look, and a proud heart, 7312
24: 7 Wisdom *is too* **h** for a fool: he openeth 7311
Ecc 12: 5 they shall be afraid of *that which is* **h**, 1364
Isa 2:13 that are **h** and lifted up, and upon all 7311
2:14 upon all the mountains, and upon all 7311
2:15 upon every **h** tower, and upon every 7311
6: 1 **h** and lifted up, and his train filled 7311
10:12 of Assyria, and the glory of his **h** looks. 7312
10:33 **h** ones of stature *shall be* hewn down, 7311
13: 2 Lift ye up a banner upon the **h** mountain, 8192
14:14 of the clouds; I will be like the **most H** 5945
15: 2 and *to* Dibon, the **h** places, to weep: 1116
16:12 seen that Moab is weary on the **h** place, 1116
22:16 he that heweth him out a sepulchre on **h**, 4791
24:18 for the windows from on **h** are open, 4791
24:21 the host of the **h** ones *that are* on high, 4791
24:21 the host of the high ones *that are* on **h**, 4791
25:12 the fortress of the **h** *fort* of thy walls shall 4869
26: 5 he bringeth down them that dwell on **h**; 4791
30:13 swelling out in a wall, whose breaking 7682
30:25 there shall be upon every **h** mountain, 1364
30:25 upon every **h** hill, rivers *and* streams of 5375

H

Isa 32:15 the spirit be poured upon us from on **h**, 4791
33: 5 LORD *is* exalted; for he dwelleth on **h**: 4791
33:16 He shall dwell on **h**: his place of defence 4791
36: 7 **h** places and whose altars Hezekiah 1116
37:23 *thy* voice, and lifted up thine eyes on **h**? 4791
40: 9 get thee up into the **h** mountain; 1364
40:26 Lift up your eyes on **h**, and behold who 4791
41:18 I will open rivers in **h** places, 8205
49: 9 and their pastures *shall be* in all **h** places. 8205
52:13 be exalted and extolled, and be **very h**. 1361
57: 7 and **h** mountain hast thou set thy bed: 5375
57:15 For thus saith the **h** and lofty One that 7311
57:15 I dwell in the **h** and holy *place*, with him 4791
58: 4 to make your voice to be heard on **h**. 4791
58:14 will cause thee to ride upon the **h** places 1116
Jer 2:20 when upon every **h** hill and under every 1364
3: 2 Lift up thine eyes unto the **h** places, 8205
3: 6 she is gone up upon every **h** mountain 1364
3:21 A voice was heard upon the **h** places, 8205
4:11 A dry wind of the **h** places in 8205
7:29 and take up a lamentation on **h** places; 8205
7:31 they have built the **h** places of Tophet, 1116
12:12 The spoilers are come upon all **h** places, 8205
14: 6 the wild asses did stand in the **h** places, 8205
17: 2 groves by the green trees upon the **h** 1364
17: 3 thy **h** places for sin, throughout all thy 1116
17:12 A glorious throne from the beginning *is* 4791
19: 5 They have built also the **h** places of Baal, 1116
20: 2 him in the stocks that *were* in the **h** gate 5945
25:30 The LORD shall roar from on **h**, 4791
26:18 mountain of the house as the **h** places 1116
31:21 thee up waymarks, make thee **h** heaps: 8564
32:35 they built the **h** places of Baal, which *are* 1116
48:35 him that offereth in the **h** places, 1116
49:16 though thou shouldest **make** thy nest as **h** 1361
51:58 her **h** gates shall be burnt with fire; 1364
La 3:35 of a man before the face of the **most H**, 5945
3:38 of the mouth of the **most H** proceedeth 5945
Eze 1:18 they were so **h** that they were dreadful; 1363
6: 3 you, and I will destroy your **h** places. 1116
6: 6 and the **h** places shall be desolate; 1116
6:13 upon every **h** hill, in all the tops of 7311
16:16 thy **h** places with divers colours; 1116
16:24 hast made thee a **h** place in every street. 7413
16:25 Thou hast built thy **h** place at every head 7413
16:31 and makest thou **h** place in every street; 7413
16:39 and shall break down thy **h** places: 7413
17:22 take of the highest branch of the **h** cedar, 7311
17:22 will plant *it* upon a **h** mountain and 1364
17:24 I the LORD have brought down the **h** tree, 1364
20:28 they saw every **h** hill, and all the thick 7311
20:29 What *is* the **h** place whereunto ye go? 1116
21:26 *him that is* low, and abase *him that is* **h**. 1364
31: 3 a shadowing shrowd, and of a **h** stature; 1362
31: 4 the deep set him **up on h** with her rivers 7311
34: 6 all the mountains, and upon every **h** hill: 7311
34:14 upon the mountains of Israel shall their 4791
36: 2 even the ancient **h** places are ours in 1116
40: 2 set me upon a very **h** mountain, by which 1364
40:42 a cubit and a half broad, and one cubit **h**: 1363
41:22 The altar *of* wood *was* three cubits **h**, 1364
43: 7 carcases of their kings *in their* **h** places. 1116
Da 3:26 servants of the **most H** God, come forth, 5943
4: 2 wonders that the **h** God hath wrought 5943
4:17 the **most H** ruleth in the kingdom of 5943
4:24 and this *is* the decree of the **most H**, 5943
4:25 till thou know that the **most H** ruleth in 5943
4:32 till thou know that the **most H** ruleth 5943
4:34 I blessed the **most H**, and I praised and 5943
5:18 the **most h** God gave Nebuchadnezzar 5943
5:21 till he knew that the **most h** God ruled in 5943
7:18 the saints of the **most H** shall take 5946
7:22 *was* given to the saints of the **most H**; 5946
7:25 speak *great* words against the **most H**, 5943
7:25 shall wear out the saints of the **most H**, 5946
7:27 to the people of the saints of the **most H**, 5946
8: 3 two horns *were* **h**; but one *was* higher 1364
Hos 7:16 They return, *but* not to the **most H**: 5920
10: 8 The **h** places also of Aven, the sin of 1116
11: 7 though they called them to the **most H**, 5920
Am 4:13 treadeth upon the **h** places of the earth, 1116
7: 9 the **h** places of Isaac shall be desolate, 1116
Ob 1: 3 clefts of the rock, whose habitation *is* **h**; 4791
Mic 1: 3 and tread upon the **h** places of the earth. 1116
1: 5 what *are* the **h** places of Judah? *are* they 1116
3:12 mountain of the house as the **h** places 1116
6: 6 and bow myself before the **h** God? 4791
Hab 2: 9 that *he* may set his nest on **h**, that *he* may 4791
3:10 his voice, *and* lift up his hands on **h**. 7315
3:19 make me to walk upon mine **h** places. 1116
Zep 1:16 fenced cities, and against the **h** towers. 1364
Hag 1: 1 Joshua the son of Josedech the **h** priest, 1419
1:12 Joshua the son of Josedech the **h** priest, 1419
1:14 Joshua the son of Josedech the **h** priest, 1419
2: 2 Joshua the son of Josedech the **h** priest, 1419
2: 4 O Joshua, son of Josedech the **h** priest, 1419
Zec 3: 1 shewed me Joshua the **h** priest standing 1419
3: 8 Joshua the **h** priest, thou, and thy fellows 1419
6:11 of Joshua the son of Josedech the **h** priest; 1419
Mt 4: 8 devil taketh him *up* into an exceeding **h** 5308
17: 1 bringeth them up into a **h** mountain apart, 5308
26: 3 the people, unto the palace of the **h** priest, 749
26:51 and stroke a servant of the **h** priest's, 749
26:57 led *him* away to Caiaphas the **h** priest, 749
26:58 him afar off unto the **h** priest's palace, 749

Mt 26:62 And the **h priest** arose, and said unto him, 749
26:63 And the **h priest** answered and said unto 749
26:65 Then the **h priest** rent his clothes, 749
Mk 2:26 of God in the days of Abiathar the **h priest**, 749
5: 7 Jesus, *thou* Son of the **most h** God? 5310
6:21 **h captains**, and chief *estates* of Galilee; 5506
9: 2 leadeth them up into a **h mountain** apart 5308
14:47 and smote a servant of the **h priest**, 749
14:53 And they led Jesus away to the **h priest**: 749
14:54 off, even into the palace of the **h priest**: 749
14:60 And the **h priest** stood up in the midst, 749
14:61 Again the **h priest** asked him, and said 749
14:63 Then the **h priest** rent his clothes, 749
14:66 cometh one of the maids of the **h priest**: 749
Lk 1:78 whereby the dayspring from on **h** hath 5311
3: 2 Annas and Caiaphas being the **h priests**, 749
4: 5 devil, taking him up into a **h mountain**, 5308
8:28 thee, Jesus, *thou* Son of God **most h**? 5310
22:50 of them smote the servant of the **h priest**, 749
22:54 brought him into the **h priest's** house. 749
24:49 until ye be endued with power from on **h**. 5311
Jn 11:49 And one of them, *named* Caiaphas, being the **h priest** 749
11:51 but being **h priest** that year, he prophesied 749
18:10 smote the **h priest's** servant, and cut off 749
18:13 which was the **h priest** that *same* year. 749
18:15 that disciple was known unto the **h priest**, 749
18:15 with Jesus into the palace of the **h priest**. 749
18:16 which was known unto the **h priest**, 749
18:19 The **h priest** then asked Jesus of his 749
18:22 saying, Answerest thou the **h priest** so? 749
18:24 him bound unto Caiaphas the **h priest**. 749
18:26 One of the servants of the **h priest**, being 749
18:31 (for that sabbath day was a **h** day,) 3173
Ac 4: 6 And Annas the **h priest**, and Caiaphas, 749
4: 6 as were of the kindred of the **h priest**, 748
5:17 Then the **h priest** rose up, and all they 749
5:21 But the **h priest** came, and they that were 749
5:24 Now when the *h* priest and the captain of NIG
5:27 the council: and the **h priest** asked them, 749
7: 1 said the **h priest**, Are these *things* so? 749
7:48 Howbeit the **most H** dwelleth not in 5310
9: 1 of the Lord, went unto the **h priest**, 749
13:17 with a **h** arm brought them out of it. 5308
16:17 These men are the servants of the **most h** 5310
22: 5 As also the **h priest** doth bear me witness, 749
23: 2 the **h priest** Ananias commanded them 749
23: 4 by said, Revilest thou God's **h priest**? 749
23: 5 not, brethren, that he was the **h priest**: 749
24: 1 And after five days Ananias the **h priest** 749
25: 2 the **h priest** and the chief of the Jews 749
Ro 12:16 Mind not **h** *things*, but condescend to 5308
13:11 now *it is* **h time** to awake out of 2235+5610
2Co 10: 5 every **h** thing that exalteth itself against 5313
Eph 4: 8 *he* saith, When he ascended up on **h**, 5311
6:12 against spiritual wickedness in **h** *places*. 2032
Php 3:14 toward the mark for the prize of the **h** 507
Heb 1: 3 on the right hand of the Majesty on **h**; 5308
2:17 **h priest** *in things* pertaining to God, 749
3: 1 the Apostle and **H Priest** of our profession, 749
4:14 Seeing then that we have a great **h priest**, 749
4:15 we have not a **h priest** which cannot be 749
5: 1 every **h priest** taken from among men is 749
5: 5 glorified not himself to be made a **h priest**; 749
5:10 Called of God a **h priest** after the order of 749
6:20 made a **h priest** for ever after the order of 749
7: 1 king of Salem, priest of the **most h** God, 5310
7:26 such a **h priest** became us, *who is* holy, 749
7:27 as *those* **h priests**, to offer up sacrifice, 749
7:28 For the law maketh men **h priests** which 749
8: 1 We have such a **h priest**, who is set on 749
8: 3 For every **h priest** is ordained to offer gifts 749
9: 7 into the second *went* the **h priest** alone 749
9:11 But Christ being come a **h priest** of good 749
9:25 as the **h priest** entereth into the holy 749
10:21 And *having* a **h priest** over the house of 3173
13:11 into the sanctuary by the **h priest** for sin, 749
Rev 21:10 in the spirit to a great and **h** mountain, 5308
21:12 had a wall great and **h**, and had twelve 5308

HIGHER (21) [HIGH]

Nu 24: 7 his king shall be **h** than Agag, 7311
1Sa 9: 2 upward *he was* **h** than any of the people. 1364
10:23 he was **h** than any of the people from his 1361
2Ki 15:35 He built the **h** gate of the house of 5945
Ne 4:13 behind the wall, *and* on the **h** places, 6706
Job 35: 5 behold the clouds *which* are **h** than thou. 1361
Ps 61: 2 lead me to the rock *that is* **h** than I. 7311
89:27 firstborn, **h** than the kings of the earth. 5945
Ecc 5: 8 *he that is* **h** than the highest regardeth; 1364
5: 8 regardeth; and *there be* **h** than they. 1364
Isa 55: 9 For *as* the heavens are **h** than the earth, 1361
55: 9 so are my ways **h** than your ways, 1361
Jer 36:10 in the **h** court *at* the entry of the new gate 5945
Eze 9: 2 six men came from the way of the **h** gate, 5945
42: 5 for the galleries were **h** than these, than 398
43:13 and this shall be the **h** place of the altar. 1354
Da 8: 3 one *was* **h** than the other, and the higher 1364
8: 3 than the other, and the **h** came up last. 1364
Lk 14:10 he may say unto thee, Friend, go up **h**: 511
Ro 13: 1 Let every soul be subject unto the **h** 5242
Heb 7:26 and made **h** than the heavens; 5308

HIGHEST (18) [HIGH]

Ps 18:13 in the heavens, and the **H** gave his voice; 5945
87: 5 and the **H** himself shall establish her. 5945

Pr 8:26 nor the **h part** of the dust of the world. 7218
9: 3 upon the **h places** of the city, 1610+4791
Ecc 5: 8 for *he that is* higher than the **h** regardeth; 1364
Eze 17: 3 and took the **h branch** of the cedar; 6788
17:22 I will also take of the **h branch** of the 6788
41: 7 *from* the lowest *chamber* to the **h**: 5945
Mt 21: 9 the name of the Lord; Hosanna in the **h**. 5310
Mk 11:10 the name of the Lord: Hosanna in the **h**. 5310
Lk 1:32 and shall be called the Son of the **H**: 5310
1:35 power of the **H** shall overshadow thee: 5310
1:76 child, shalt be called the prophet of the **H**: 5310
2:14 Glory to God in the **h**, and on earth peace, 5310
6:35 and ye shall be the children of the **H**: 5310
14: 8 a wedding, sit not down in the **h room**; 4411
19:38 peace in heaven, and glory in the **h**. 5310
20:46 and the **h seats** in the synagogues, 4410

HIGHLY (6) [HIGH]

Lk 1:28 and said, Hail, *thou that art* **h favoured**, 5487
16:15 that which is **h esteemed** amongst men 5308
Ac 12:20 Herod was **h displeased** with them of 2371
Ro 12: 3 not to **think** *of himself* more **h** than he 5252
Php 2: 9 Wherefore God also hath **h exalted** him, 5251
1Th 5:13 And to esteem them very **h** in love 1537+4053

HIGHMINDED, HIGH-MINDED (3) [HIGH, MIND]

Ro 11:20 thou standest by faith. Be not **h**, but fear: 5309
1Ti 6:17 that *they* be not **h**, nor trust in uncertain 5309
2Ti 3: 4 Traitors, heady, **h**, lovers of pleasures 5187

HIGHNESS (2) [HIGH]

Job 31:23 by reason of his **h** I could not endure. 7613
Isa 13:3 anger, *even* them that rejoice in my **h**. 1346

HIGHWAY (16) [HIGH, WAY]

Jdg 21:19 on the east side of the **h** that goeth up 4546
1Sa 6:12 went along the **h**, lowing as they went, 4546
2Sa 20:12 wallowed in blood in the midst of the **h**. 4546
20:12 he removed Amasa out of the **h** *into* 4546
20:13 When he was removed out of the **h**, 4546
2Ki 18:17 which *is* in the **h** of the fuller's field. 4546
Pr 16:17 The **h** of the upright *is* to depart from evil 4546
Isa 7: 3 upper pool in the **h** of the fuller's field; 4546
11:16 there shall be a **h** for the remnant of his 4546
19:23 In that day shall there be a **h** out of Egypt 4546
35: 8 a **h** shall be there, and a way, and it shall 4547
36: 2 upper pool in the **h** of the fuller's field. 4546
40: 3 straight in the desert a **h** for our God. 4546
62:10 cast up the **h**; gather out the stones; 4546
Jer 31:21 set thine heart toward the **h**, *even* 4546
Mk 10:46 of Timeus, sat by the **h**way side begging. 3598

HIGHWAYS (10) [HIGH, WAY]

Jdg 5: 6 the **h** were unoccupied, and the travellers 734
20:31 *and* kill, as at other times, in the **h**, 4546
20:32 and draw them from the city unto the **h**. 4546
20:45 gleaned of them in the **h** five thousand 4546
Isa 33: 8 The **h** lie waste, the wayfaring man 4546
49:11 a way, and my **h** shall be exalted. 4546
Am 5:16 and they shall say in all the **h**, Alas! 2351
Mt 22: 9 Go ye therefore into the **h**, 1327+3588+3598
22:10 So those servants went out into the **h**, 3598
Lk 14:23 Go out into the **h** and hedges, 3598

HILEN (1)

1Ch 6:58 **H** with her suburbs, Debir with her 2432

HILKIAH (33) [HILKIAH'S]

2Ki 18:18 came out to them Eliakim the son of **H**, 2518
18:26 said Eliakim the son of **H**, and Shebna, 2518
18:37 came Eliakim the son of **H**, which *was* 2518
22: 4 Go up to **H** the high priest, that he may 2518
22: 8 **H** the high priest said unto Shaphan 2518
22: 8 **H** gave the book to Shaphan, and he read 2518
22:10 **H** the priest hath delivered me a book. 2518
22:12 the king commanded the priest, 2518
22:14 So **H** the priest, and Ahikam, and Achbor, 2518
23: 4 the king commanded **H** the high priest, 2518
23:24 **H** the priest found *in* the house of 2518
1Ch 6:13 Shallum begat **H**, and Hilkiah begat 2518
6:13 begat Hilkiah, and **H** begat Azariah, 2518
6:45 the son of Amaziah, the son of **H**, 2518
9:11 Azariah the son of **H**, the son of 2518
26:11 **H** the second, Tebaliah the third, 2518
2Ch 34: 9 when they came to **H** the high priest, 2518
34:14 the priest found a book of the law of 2518
34:15 **H** answered and said to Shaphan the 2518
34:15 And **H** delivered the book to Shaphan. 2518
34:18 **H** the priest hath given me a book. 2518
34:20 the king commanded **H**, and Ahikam, 2518
34:22 **H**, and *they* that the king *had appointed*, 2518
35: 8 **H** and Zechariah and Jehiel, rulers of 2518
Ezr 7: 1 the son of Azariah, the son of **H**, 2518
Ne 8: 4 Anaiah, and Urijah, and **H**, and Maaseiah, 2518
11:11 Seraiah the son of **H**, the son of 2518
12: 7 Sallu, Amok, **H**, Jedaiah. These *were* 2518
12:21 Of **H**, Hashabiah; of Jedaiah, Nethaneel. 2518
Isa 22:20 will call my servant Eliakim the son of **H**: 2518
36:22 came Eliakim, the son of **H**, that *was* 2518
Jer 1: 1 The words of Jeremiah the son of **H**, 2518
29: 3 of Shaphan, and Gemariah the son of **H**, 2518

HILKIAH'S (1) [HILKIAH]

Isa 36: 3 **H** son, which *was* over the house, 2518

HILL (75) [AREOPAGUS, DUNGHILL, DUNGHILLS, HILL'S, HILLS, MARS' HILL]

Ex 17: 9 morrow I will stand on the top of the **h** 1389
17:10 and Hur went up *to* the top of the **h**. 1389
24: 4 builded an altar under the **h**, 2022
Nu 14:44 they presumed to go up unto the **h** top: 2022
14:45 the Canaanites which dwelt in that **h**, 2022
Dt 1:41 war, ye were ready to go up into the **h**. 2022
1:43 and went presumptuously up into the **h**. 2022
Jos 5: 3 circumcised the children of Israel at the **h** 1389
13: 6 All the inhabitants of the **h country** from 2022
15: 9 border was drawn from the top of the **h** 2022
17:16 of Joseph said, The **h** is not enough for us: 2022
18:13 near the **h** that *lieth* on the south side of 2022
18:14 from the **h** that *lieth* before Beth-horon 2022
21:11 *city* is Hebron, in the **h** *country* of Judah, 2022
24:30 on the north side of the **h** of Gaash. 2022
24:33 they buried him in a **h** that pertained to 1389
Jdg 2: 9 on the north side of the **h** Gaash. 1389
7: 1 of them, by the **h** of Moreh, in the valley. 1389
16: 3 carried them up to the top of a **h** that *is* 1389
1Sa 7: 1 it into the house of Abinadab in the **h**, 1389
9:11 as they went up the **h** to the city, they 4608
10: 5 that thou shalt come to the **h** of God, 1389
10:10 when they came thither to the **h**, behold, 1389
23:19 the **h** of Hachilah, which *is* on the south 1389
25:20 she came down by the covert of the **h**, 2022
26: 1 Doth not David hide himself in the **h** of 1389
26: 3 Saul pitched in the **h** of Hachilah, which 1389
26:13 and stood on the top of a **h** afar off; 2022
2Sa 2:24 they were come to the **h** of Ammah, 1389
2:25 one troop, and stood on the top of a **h**. 1389
13:34 by the way of the **h** side behind him. 2022
16: 1 was a little past the top *of the h*, behold, NIH
21: 9 they hanged them in the **h** before 2022
1Ki 11: 7 in the **h** that *is* before Jerusalem, 2022
14:23 on every high **h**, and under every green 1389
16:24 he bought the **h** Samaria of Shemer for 2022
16:24 built *on* the **h**, and called the name of 2022
16:24 of Shemer, owner of the **h**, Samaria. 2022
2Ki 1: 9 behold, he sat on the top of a **h**. 2022
4:27 she came to the man of God to the **h**, 2022
17:10 images and groves in every high **h**, 1389
Ps 2: 6 Yet have I set my king upon my holy **h** of 2022
3: 4 and he heard me out of his holy **h**. 2022
15: 1 who shall dwell in thy holy **h**? 2022
24: 3 Who shall ascend into the **h** of 2022
42: 6 and of the Hermonites, from the **h** Mizar. 2022
43: 3 let them bring me unto thy holy **h**, 2022
68:15 The **h** of God *is as* the hill of Bashan; 2022
68:15 The hill of God *is as* the **h** of Bashan. 2022
68:15 of Bashan; a high **h** *as* the hill of Bashan. 2022
68:15 of Bashan; a high hill *as* the **h** of Bashan. 2022
68:16 *this is* the **h** *which* God desireth to dwell 2022
99: 9 our God, and worship at his holy **h**; 2022
SS 4: 6 of myrrh, and to the **h** of frankincense. 1389
Isa 5: 1 hath a vineyard in a very fruitful **h**: 7161
10:32 the daughter of Zion, the **h** of Jerusalem. 1389
30:17 of a mountain, and as an ensign on a **h**. 1389
30:25 upon every high **h**, rivers *and* streams of 1389
31: 4 for mount Zion, and for the **h** thereof. 1389
40: 4 every mountain and **h** shall be made low: 1389
Jer 2:20 when upon every high **h** and under every 1389
16:16 from every **h**, and out of the holes of 1389
31:39 go forth over against it upon the **h** Gareb, 1389
49:16 the rock, that holdest the height of the **h**: 1389
50: 6 they have gone from mountain to **h**, 1389
Eze 6:13 upon every high **h**, in all the tops of 1389
20:28 they saw every high **h**, and all the thick 1389
34: 6 all the mountains, and upon every high **h**: 1389
34:26 the places round about my **h** a blessing; 1389
Mt 5:14 A city that is set on a **h** cannot be hid. 3735
Lk 1:39 and went into the **h country** with haste, 3714
1:65 throughout all the **h country** of Judea. 3714
3: 5 mountain and **h** shall be brought low; 1015
4:29 led him unto the brow of the **h** whereon 3735
9:37 when they were come down from the **h**, 3735

HILL'S (1) [HILL]

2Sa 16:13 Shimei went along on the **h** side over 2022

HILLEL (2)

Jdg 12:13 after him Abdon the son of **H**, 1985
12:15 Abdon the son of **H** the Pirathonite died, 1985

HILLS (65) [HILL]

Ge 7:19 all the high **h**, that *were* under the whole 2022
49:26 the utmost bound of the everlasting **h**: 1389
Nu 23: 9 I see him, and from the **h** I behold him: 1389
Dt 1: 7 in the **h**, and in the vale, and in the south, 2022
8: 7 that spring out of the valleys and **h**; 2022
8: 9 out of whose **h** thou mayest dig brass. 2042
11:11 *is* a land of **h** and valleys, 2022
12: 2 upon the **h**, and under every green tree: 1389
33:15 for the precious things of the lasting **h**, 1389
Jos 9: 1 in the **h**, and in the valleys, and in all 2022
10:40 So Joshua smote all the country of the **h**, 2022
11:16 the **h**, and all the south country, and all 2022
1Ki 20:23 unto him, Their gods *are* gods of the **h**; 2022
20:28 The LORD *is* God of the **h**, but he *is* not 2022
22:17 I saw all Israel scattered upon the **h**, 2022
2Ki 16: 4 and on the **h**, and under every green tree. 1389
2Ch 28: 4 and on the **h**, and under every green tree. 1389
Job 15: 7 or wast thou made before the **h**? 1389
Ps 18: 7 the foundations also of the **h** moved and 2022

Ps	50:10	mine, *and* the cattle upon a thousand **h**.	2042
	65:12	and the **little h** rejoice on every side.	1389
	68:16	Why leap ye, ye high **h**? *this is* the hill	2022
	72: 3	and the **little h**, by righteousness.	1389
	80:10	The **h** were covered *with* the shadow of	2022
	95: 4	the earth: the strength of the **h** *is* his also.	2022
	97: 5	The **h** melted like wax at the presence of	2022
	98: 8	*their* hands: let the **h** be joyful together	2022
	104:10	into the valleys, *which* run among the **h**.	2022
	104:13	He watereth the **h** from his chambers:	2022
	104:18	The high **h** *are* a refuge for the wild goats;	2022
	104:32	He toucheth the **h**, and they smoke.	2022
	114: 4	like rams, *and* the **little h** like lambs.	1389
	114: 6	like rams; *and* ye **little h**, like lambs?	1389
	121: 1	I will lift up mine eyes unto the **h**,	2022
	148: 9	Mountains, and all **h**; fruitful trees,	1389
Pr	8:25	before the **h** was I brought forth:	1389
SS	2: 8	upon the mountains, skipping upon the **h**.	1389
Isa	2: 2	and *shall* be exalted above the **h**;	1389
	2:14	upon all the **h** that are lifted up,	1389
	5:25	the **h** did tremble, and their carcases were	2022
	7:25	*on* all **h** that shall be digged with	2022
	40:12	in scales, and the **h** in a balance?	1389
	41:15	small, and shalt make the **h** as chaff.	1389
	42:15	I will waste mountains and **h**,	1389
	54:10	shall depart, and the **h** be removed;	1389
	55:12	the **h** shall break forth before you *into*	1389
	65: 7	and blasphemed me upon the **h**:	1389
Jer	3:23	in vain *is* salvation hoped for *from* the **h**,	1389
	4:24	trembled, and all the **h** moved lightly.	1389
	13:27	thine abominations on the **h** in the fields.	1389
	17: 2	by the green trees upon the high **h**.	1389
Eze	6: 3	to the **h**, to the rivers, and to the valleys;	1389
	35: 8	mountains *with* his slain *men*: in thy **h**,	1389
	36: 4	to the **h**, to the rivers, and to the valleys,	1389
	36: 6	to the **h**, to the rivers, and to the valleys,	1389
Hos	4:13	burn incense upon the **h**, under oaks and	1389
	10: 8	Cover us; and to the **h**, Fall on us.	1389
Joel	3:18	the **h** shall flow *with* milk, and all the	1389
Am	9:13	drop sweet wine, and all the **h** shall melt.	1389
Mic	4: 1	and *it shall be* exalted above the **h**,	1389
	6: 1	mountains, and let the **h** hear thy voice.	1389
Na	1: 5	The **h** melt, and the earth is burnt at his	1389
Hab	3: 6	were scattered, the perpetual **h** did bow:	1389
Zep	1:10	second, and a great crashing from the **h**.	1389
Lk	23:30	Fall on us; and to the **h**, Cover us.	1015

HIM (6667) [HE] See Index of Articles, Etc.

HIMSELF (528) [HE, SELF]

Ge	14:15	he divided **h** against them, he and	NIH
	18: 2	door, and bowed **h** toward the ground,	NIH
	19: 1	he bowed **h** with his face toward	NIH
	22: 8	God will provide **h** a lamb for a burnt	2050.2
	23: 7	and bowed **h** to the people of the land,	NIH
	23:12	Abraham bowed down **h** before the people	NIH
	24:52	the LORD, *bowing* **h** to the earth.	NIH
	27:42	as touching thee, doth comfort **h**,	NIH
	30:36	set three days' journey betwixt **h** and	2050.2
	32:21	and **h** lodged that night in the company.	1931
	33: 3	and bowed **h** to the ground seven times,	NIH
	41:14	he shaved **h**, and changed his raiment,	NIH
	42: 7	made **h** strange unto them,	NIH
	42:24	he turned **h** about from them, and wept;	NIH
	43:31	went out, and refrained **h**, and said, Set on	NIH
	43:32	they set on for him **by h**,	905+2050.2+3807.1
	45: 1	Joseph could not refrain **h** before all them	NIH
	45: 1	while Joseph made **h** known unto his	NIH
	46:29	to Goshen, and presented **h** unto him;	NIH
	47:31	And Israel bowed **h** upon the bed's head.	NIH
	48: 2	Israel strengthened **h**, and sat upon the	NIH
	48:12	and he bowed **h** with his face to the earth.	NIH
Ex	10: 6	he turned **h**, and went out from Pharaoh.	NIH
	21: 3	If he came in by **h**, he shall go	1610+2050.2
	21: 3	by himself, he shall go out by **h**:	1610+2050.2
	21: 4	and he shall go out by **h**.	1610+2050.2
	21: 8	hath betrothed her to **h**, then shall he	2050.2
Lev	7: 8	the priest shall have to **h** the skin of	2050.2
	9: 8	calf of the sin offering, which *was* for **h**.	2050.2
	14: 8	shave off all his hair, and wash **h** in water,	NIH
	15: 5	bathe **h** in water, and be unclean until	NIH
	15: 6	bathe **h** in water, and be unclean until	NIH
	15: 7	bathe **h** in water, and be unclean until	NIH
	15: 8	bathe **h** in water, and be unclean until	NIH
	15:10	bathe **h** in water, and be unclean until	NIH
	15:11	bathe **h** in water, and be unclean until	NIH
	15:13	he shall number to **h** seven days for his	2050.2
	15:21	bathe **h** in water, and be unclean until	NIH
	15:22	bathe **h** in water, and be unclean until	NIH
	15:27	bathe **h** in water, and be unclean until	2050.2
	16: 6	which *is* for **h**, and make an atonement	2050.2
	16: 6	make an atonement for **h**, and for his	2050.2
	16:11	which *is* for **h**, and shall make an	2050.2
	16:11	shall make an atonement for **h**,	2050.2
	16:11	of the sin offering which *is* for **h**:	2050.2
	16:17	have made an atonement for **h**,	2050.2
	16:24	make an atonement for **h**, and for	2050.2
	17:15	bathe **h** in water, and be unclean until	NIH
	21: 4	He shall not defile **h**, *being* a chief man	2050.2
	21: 4	man among his people, to profane **h**.	2050.2
	21:11	defile **h** for his father, or for his mother;	NIH
	22: 8	he shall not eat to defile **h** therewith:	NIH
	25:26	redeem *it*, and **h** be able to redeem it;	2050.2
	25:47	sell **h** unto the stranger *or* sojourner by	NIH
	25:49	or if he be able, he may redeem **h**.	NIH

Lev	27: 8	he shall present **h** before the priest,	2050.2
Nu	6: 3	He shall separate **h** from wine and	NIH
	6: 5	*in* the which he separateth **h** unto	NIH
	6: 6	All the days that he separateth **h** unto	NIH
	6: 7	He shall not make **h** unclean for his father,	NIH
	16: 9	to bring you near to **h** to do the service	2050.2
	19:12	He shall purify **h** with it on the third day,	NIH
	19:12	if he purify not **h** the third day, then	NIH
	19:13	purifieth not **h**, defileth the tabernacle of	NIH
	19:19	on the seventh day he shall purify **h**,	2050.2
	19:19	bathe **h** in water, and shall be clean at	NIH
	19:20	shall be unclean, and shall not purify **h**,	NIH
	23:24	a great lion, and lift up **h** as a young lion:	NIH
	25: 3	Israel joined **h** unto Baal-peor:	NIH
	31:53	war had taken spoil, every man for **h**.)	2050.2
	35:19	The revenger of blood **h** shall slay	1931
	36: 7	**h** to the inheritance of the tribe of his	NIH
	36: 9	Israel shall keep **h** to his own inheritance.	NIH
Dt	7: 6	thee to be a special people unto **h**,	2050.2
	14: 2	thee to be a peculiar people unto **h**,	2050.2
	17:16	he shall not multiply horses to **h**,	2050.2
	17:17	Neither shall he multiply wives to **h**,	2050.2
	17:17	neither shall he greatly multiply to **h**	2050.2
	23:11	cometh on, he shall wash **h** with water:	NIH
	28: 9	establish thee a holy people unto **h**,	2050.2
	29:13	thee to day for a people unto **h**,	2050.2
	29:19	that he bless **h** in his heart, saying, I shall	NIH
	32:36	his people, and repent **h** for his servants,	NIH
	33:21	he provided the first *part* for **h**, because	2050.2
Jos	22:23	let the LORD **h** require *it*;	1931
Jdg	3:19	he **h** turned again from the quarries that	1931
	3:20	which he had for **h** alone.	2050.2
	4:11	had severed **h** from the Kenites,	NIH
	6:31	let him plead for **h**, because *one* hath	2050.2
	7: 5	lappeth, him shalt thou set **by h**;	905+3807.1
	9: 5	son of Jerubbaal was left; for he hid **h**.	NIH
	16:30	he bowed **h** with *all his* might;	NIH
Ru	3: 8	that the man was afraid, and turned **h**:	2050.2
1Sa	2:14	brought up the priest took for **h**.	2050.2
	3:21	for the LORD revealed **h** to Samuel in	NIH
	8:11	appoint *them* for **h**, for his chariots,	2050.2
	10:19	**h** saved you out of all your adversities	1931
	10:22	Behold, he hath hid **h** among the stuff.	NIH
	14:47	whithersoever he turned **h**, he vexed	NIH
	17:16	and evening, and presented **h** forty days.	NIH
	18: 4	Jonathan stript **h** of the robe that *was*	NIH
	18: 5	Saul sent him, *and* behaved **h** wisely:	1930.2
	18:14	David behaved **h** wisely in all his ways;	NIH
	18:15	Saul saw that he behaved **h** very wisely,	NIH
	18:30	David behaved **h** more wisely than all	NIH
	20:24	So David hid **h** in the field: and when	NIH
	20:41	to the ground, and bowed **h** three times:	NIH
	21:13	feigned **h** mad in their hands,	NIH
	23:19	Doth not David hide **h** with us in strong	NIH
	23:23	all the lurking places where he hideth **h**,	NIH
	24: 8	*with his* face to the earth, and bowed **h**.	NIH
	25:31	or that my lord hath avenged **h**:	2050.2
	26: 1	Doth not David hide **h** in the hill of	NIH
	28: 8	Saul disguised **h**, and put on other	NIH
	28:14	*with his* face to the ground, and bowed **h**.	NIH
	29: 4	for wherewith should he reconcile **h** unto	NIH
	30: 6	David encouraged **h** in the LORD his God.	NIH
	30:31	to all the places where David **h** and his	1931
2Sa	3: 6	that Abner made **h** strong for the house of	NIH
	3:31	And king David **h** followed the bier.	NIH
	6:20	who uncovered **h** to day in the eyes of	NIH
	6:20	vain *fellows* shamelessly uncovereth **h**!	NIH
	7:23	God went to redeem for a people to **h**,	2050.2
	9: 8	he bowed **h**, and said, What *is* thy servant,	NIH
	12:18	how will he then vex **h**, if we tell him *that*	NIH
	12:20	anointed **h**, and changed his apparel,	NIH
	13: 6	So Amnon lay down, and made **h** sick:	NIH
	14:22	and bowed **h**, and thanked the king:	NIH
	14:33	bowed **h** on his face to the ground	2050.2
	15:23	the king also **h** passed over the brook	NIH
	17:23	hanged **h**, and died, and was buried in	NIH
	18:18	had taken and reared up for **h** a pillar,	2050.2
	18:21	And Cushi bowed **h** unto Joab, and ran.	NIH
	24:20	bowed **h** before the king on his face upon	NIH
1Ki	1: 5	Adonijah the son of Haggith exalted **h**,	NIH
	1:23	he bowed **h** before the king with his face	NIH
	1:47	And the king bowed **h** upon the bed.	NIH
	1:52	If he will shew **h** a worthy man,	NIH
	1:53	he came and bowed **h** to king Solomon:	NIH
	2:19	bowed **h** unto her, and sat down on his	NIH
	11:29	he had clad **h** with a new garment;	NIH
	15:15	*the things* which **h** had dedicated, *into*	2050.2
	16: 9	drinking **h** drunk *in* the house of Arza	NIH
	17:21	he stretched **h** upon the child three times,	NIH
	18: 2	Elijah went to shew **h** unto Ahab.	NIH
	18: 6	Ahab went one way **by h**,	905+2050.2+3807.1
	18: 6	went another way **by h**.	905+2050.2+3807.1
	18:42	he cast **h** down upon the earth, and put	NIH
	19: 4	he **h** went a day's journey into	1931
	19: 4	he requested for **h** that he might	5315+2050.2
	20:11	boast **h** as he that putteth *it* off.	NIH
	20:16	Ben-hadad *was* drinking **h** drunk in	NIH
	20:38	and disguised **h** with ashes upon his face.	NIH
	21:25	which did sell **h** to work wickedness in	NIH
	21:29	Seest thou how Ahab humbleth **h** before	NIH
	21:29	he humbleth **h** before me, I will not	NIH
	22:30	the king of Israel disguised **h**, and went	NIH
2Ki	4:34	he stretched **h** upon the child; and the	NIH
	4:35	and went up, and stretched **h** upon him:	NIH
	5:14	and dipped **h** seven times in Jordan,	NIH

2Ki	6:10	and warned him of, and saved **h** there,	NIH
	19: 1	covered **h** with sackcloth, and went *into*	NIH
	23:16	as Josiah turned **h**, he spied the sepulchres	NIH
1Ch	11:19	when he yet kept **h** close because of Saul	NIH
	13:13	David brought not the ark *home* to **h**	2050.2
	21:21	bowed **h** to David *with his* face to	NIH
2Ch	12: 1	had strengthened **h**, he forsook the law	2050.2
	12:12	when he humbled **h**, the wrath of	NIH
	12:13	So king Rehoboam strengthened **h** in	NIH
	13: 9	that whosoever cometh to consecrate **h**	2050.2
	13:12	God **h** is with us for *our* captain,	NIH
	15:18	that he **h** had dedicated, silver, and gold,	NIH
	16: 9	to shew **h** strong in the behalf of *them*	NIH
	16:14	which he had made for **h** in the city of	2050.2
	17: 1	stead, and strengthened **h** against Israel.	NIH
	17:16	who willingly offered **h** unto the LORD;	NIH
	18:29	So the king of Israel disguised **h**,	NIH
	18:34	howbeit the king of Israel stayed **h** up in	NIH
	20: 3	set **h** to seek the LORD,	6440+2050.2
	20:35	Judah join **h** with Ahaziah king of Israel,	NIH
	20:36	joined with him to make ships to go	1930.2
	21: 4	strengthened **h**, and slew all his brethren	NIH
	23: 1	the seventh year Jehoiada strengthened **h**,	NIH
	25:11	Amaziah strengthened **h**, and led forth his	NIH
	25:14	bowed down **h** before them,	NIH
	26: 8	for he strengthened **h** exceedingly.	NIH
	26:20	yea, **h** hasted also to go out, because	2050.2
	32: 1	and thought to win them for **h**.	2050.2
	32: 5	Also he strengthened **h**, and built up all	NIH
	32: 9	(but he **h** laid siege against Lachish,	NIH
	32:26	Notwithstanding Hezekiah humbled **h** for	NIH
	32:27	he made **h** treasuries for silver,	2050.2
	33:12	humbled **h** greatly before the God of his	NIH
	33:23	humbled not **h** before the LORD,	NIH
	33:23	as Manasseh his father had humbled **h**;	NIH
	35:22	disguised **h**, that *he might* fight with him,	NIH
	36:12	humbled not **h** before Jeremiah the	NIH
Ezr	10: 1	casting **h** down before the house of God,	NIH
	10: 8	separated from the congregation of those	1931
Est	5:10	Nevertheless Haman refrained **h**:	NIH
Job	1:12	only upon **h** put not forth thine hand.	2050.2
	2: 1	Satan came also among them to present **h**	NIH
	2: 8	he took him a potsherd to scrape **h** withal;	NIH
	4: 2	but who can withhold **h** from speaking?	NIH
	9: 4	who hath hardened **h** against him,	NIH
	15:25	and strengtheneth **h** against the Almighty.	NIH
	17: 8	the innocent shall stir up **h** against	NIH
	18: 4	He teareth **h** in his anger: shall	5315+2050.2
	22: 2	that is wise may be profitable unto **h**?	4123.1
	23: 9	I cannot behold *him*: he hideth **h** on	NIH
	27:10	Will he delight **h** in the Almighty? will he	NIH
	32: 2	he justified **h** rather than God.	5315+2050.2
	34: 9	that he should delight **h** with God.	2050.2
	34:14	upon *man*, *if* he gather unto **h** his spirit	2050.2
	41:25	he raiseth up **h**, the mighty are afraid:	NIH
Ps	4: 3	hath set apart *him that is* godly for **h**:	2050.2
	10:10	He croucheth, *and* humbleth **h**, that	NIH
	10:14	the poor committeth **h** unto thee; thou art	NIH
	35: 8	and let his net that he hath laid catch **h**:	2050.2
	36: 2	For he flattereth **h** in his own eyes,	2050.2
	36: 4	he setteth **h** in a way *that is* not good;	NIH
	37:35	and spreading **h** like a green bay tree.	NIH
	50: 6	for God *is* judge **h**. Selah.	1931
	52: 7	and strengthened **h** in his wickedness.	NIH
	54: T	To Saul, Doth not David hide **h** with us?	NIH
	55:12	hated me *that* did magnify **h** against me;	NIH
	68:30	*every one* submit **h** with pieces of silver:	NIH
	87: 5	and the Highest **h** shall establish her.	1931
	93: 1	strength, *wherewith* he hath girded **h**:	NIH
	109:18	As he clothed **h** with cursing like as with	NIH
	113: 6	Who humbleth **h** to behold *the things*	NIH
	132:18	but upon **h** shall his crown flourish.	2050.2
	135: 4	the LORD hath chosen Jacob unto **h**,	2050.2
	135:14	he will repent **h** concerning his servants.	NIH
Pr	5:22	own iniquities shall take the wicked **h**,	2050.2
	9: 7	He that reproveth a scorner getteth to **h**	2050.2
	9: 7	that rebuketh a wicked *man* getteth **h** a	2050.2
	11:25	he that watereth shall be watered also **h**.	1931
	12: 9	*is* better than he that honoureth **h**,	NIH
	13: 7	There is that maketh **h** rich, yet *hath*	NIH
	13: 7	*there is* that maketh **h** poor, yet *hath* great	NIH
	14:14	a good man *shall be* satisfied from **h**.	2050.2
	16: 4	LORD hath made all *things* for **h**:	4617+1930.2
	16:26	He that laboureth laboureth for **h**;	2050.2
	18: 1	having separated **h**, seeketh *and*	NIH
	18:24	A man that hath friends must shew **h**	NIH
	21:13	he also shall cry **h**, but shall not be heard.	NIH
	22: 3	*man* foreseeth the evil, and hideth **h**:	NIH
	25: 9	Debate thy cause with thy neighbour **h**;	NIH
	25:14	Whoso boasteth **h** of a false gift *is like*	NIH
	27:12	*man* foreseeth the evil, *and* hideth **h**;	NIH
	28:10	evil way, he shall fall **h** into his own pit:	1931
	29:15	a child left *to* **h** bringeth his mother to	NIH
Ecc	5: 9	*is* for all: the king **h** is served by the field.	NIH
	10:12	but the lips of a fool will swallow up **h**.	5105.2
SS	2: 9	windows, shewing **h** through the lattice.	NIH
	3: 9	King Solomon made **h** a chariot of	2050.2
	5: 6	my beloved had withdrawn **h**,	NIH
Isa	2: 9	and the great man humbleth **h**,	2050.2
	2:20	which they made each one for **h** to	2050.2
	3: 5	the child shall behave **h** proudly against	NIH
	7:14	Therefore the Lord **h** shall give you a sign;	1931
	8:13	Sanctify the LORD of hosts **h**,	2050.2
	19:17	mention thereof shall be afraid in **h**,	2050.2
	22:16	that graveth a habitation for **h** in a rock?	2050.2

H

H

Isa
28:20 than that *a* man can stretch **h** *on it:* NIH
28:20 narrower than that *he* can wrap **h** *in it.* NIH
31: 4 nor abase **h** for the noise of them: NIH
37: 1 covered **h** with sackcloth, and went *into* NIH
38:15 **h** hath done *it:* I shall go softly all my 1931
44: 5 another shall call **h** by the name of Jacob; NIH
44: 5 and surname **h** by the name of Israel. NIH
44:14 which he strengtheneth for **h** among 2050.2
44:15 for he will take thereof, and warm **h;** yea, NIH
44:16 yea, he warmeth **h**, and saith, Aha, I am NIH
44:23 redeemed Jacob, and glorified **h** in Israel. NIH
45:18 God **h** that formed the earth and made it; 1931
56: 3 that hath joined **h** to the LORD, speak, NIH
59:15 *that* departeth from evil maketh **h** a prey: NIH
61:10 a bridegroom decketh **h** with ornaments, NIH
63:12 to make **h** an everlasting name? 2050.2
64: 7 that stirreth up **h** to take hold of thee: NIH
65:16 That he who blesseth **h** in the earth shall NIH
65:16 the earth shall bless **h** in the God of truth; NIH

Jer
10:23 I knew that the way of man *is* not in **h:** 2050.2
16:20 Shall a man make gods unto **h**, 2050.2
23:24 Can any hide **h** in secret places that I shall NIH
29:26 man *that is* mad, and maketh **h** a prophet, NIH
29:27 which maketh **h** a prophet to you? NIH
31:18 I have surely heard Ephraim bemoaning **h** NIH
34: 9 that none should serve **h** of them, *to wit,* NIH
37:12 to separate **h** thence in the midst of NIH
43:12 he shall array **h** with the land of Egypt, NIH
48:26 for he magnified *h* against the LORD: NIH
48:42 he hath magnified *h* against the LORD, NIH
49:10 and he shall not be able to hide **h:** NIH
51: 3 against *him that* lifteth **h** up in his NIH
51:14 LORD of hosts hath sworn by **h**, 5315+2050.2

La
1: 9 for the enemy hath magnified **h.** NIH

Eze
7:13 neither shall any strengthen **h** in the NIH
14: 7 separateth **h** from me, and setteth up NIH
24: 2 the king of Babylon set **h** against Jerusalem NIH
25:12 and revenged **h** upon them; NIH
45:22 that day shall the prince prepare for **h** 2050.2

Da
1: 8 defile **h** with the portion of the king's NIH
1: 8 of the eunuchs that he might not defile **h.** NIH
6:14 was sore displeased with **h**, and set *his* 1958.2
8:11 he magnified **h** even to the prince of NIH
8:25 he shall magnify *h* in his heart, NIH
9:26 shall Messiah be cut off, but not for **h:** 2050.2
11:36 he shall exalt **h**, and magnify himself NIH
11:36 magnify **h** above every god, and shall speak NIH
11:37 any god: for he shall magnify **h** above all. NIH

Hos
5: 6 he hath withdrawn **h** from them. NIH
7: 8 he hath mixed **h** among the people; NIH
8: 9 up *to* Assyria, a wild ass alone by **h:** 2050.2
10: 1 vine, he bringeth forth fruit unto **h.** 2050.2
13: 1 spake trembling, he exalted **h** in Israel; NIH

Am
2:14 neither shall the mighty deliver **h:** 5315+2050.2
2:15 *that is* swift of foot shall not deliver **h:** NIH
2:15 he that rideth the horse deliver **h.** 5315+2050.2
6: 8 The Lord GOD hath sworn by **h**, 5315+2050.2

Jnh
4: 8 and wished in **h** to die, and said, 5315+2050.2

Hab
2: 6 to him that ladeth **h** with thick clay! NIH

Mt
6: 4 thy Father which seeth in secret **h** shall 846
8:17 saying **H** took our infirmities, and bare our 846
12:15 But when Jesus knew *it,* he withdrew **h** NIG
12:26 cast out Satan, he is divided against **h;** 1438
12:45 taketh **h** seven other spirits more 1438
12:45 seven other spirits more wicked than **h**, 1438
13:21 Yet hath he not root in **h**, but dureth for 1438
16:24 let him deny **h**, and take up his cross, 1438
18: 4 shall humble **h** as this little child, 1438
23:12 And whosoever shall exalt **h** shall be 1438
23:12 he that shall humble **h** shall be exalted. 1438
27: 3 repented **h**, and brought again the thirty NIG
27: 5 and departed, and went and hanged **h.** NIG
27:42 He saved others; **h** he cannot save. 1438
27:57 who also **h** was Jesus' disciple: 846

Mk
3: 7 Jesus withdrew **h** with his disciples NIG
3:21 on him: for they said, He is **beside h.** 1839
3:26 And if Satan rise up against **h**, 1438
5: 5 crying, and cutting **h** with stones. 1438
5:30 And Jesus immediately knowing in **h** that 1438
6:17 For Herod **h** had sent forth and laid hold 846
8:34 let him deny **h**, and take up his cross, 846
12:33 strength, and to love *his* neighbour as **h**, 1438
12:36 For David **h** said by the Holy Ghost, 846
12:37 David therefore **h** calleth him Lord; 846
14:54 the servants, and warmed **h** at the fire. NIG
14:67 And when she saw Peter warming **h**, NIG
15:31 He saved others; **h** he cannot save. 1438

Lk
3:23 Jesus **h** began *to be* about thirty years of 846
5:16 And he withdrew **h** into the wilderness, NIG
6: 3 when **h** was a hungred, and they which 846
7:39 had bidden him saw *it,* he spake within **h**, 1438
9:23 let him deny **h**, and take up his cross 1438
9:25 whole world, and lose **h**, or be cast away? 1438
10: 1 and place, whither he **h** would come. 846
10:29 he, willing to justify **h**, said unto Jesus, 1438
11:18 If Satan also be divided against **h**, 1438
11:26 seven other spirits more wicked than **h;** 1438
12:17 And he thought within **h**, saying, 1438
12:21 So *is* he that layeth up treasure for **h**, 1438
12:37 that he shall gird **h**, and make them to sit NIG
14:11 For whosoever exalteth **h** shall be abased; 1438
14:11 and he that humbleth **h** shall be exalted. 1438
15:15 and joined **h** to a citizen of that country; NIG
15:17 And when he came to **h**, he said, 1438

Lk
16: 3 the steward said within **h**, What shall 1438
18: 4 but afterward he said within **h**, Though I 1438
18:11 Pharisee stood and prayed thus with **h**, 1438
18:14 for every one that exalteth **h** shall be 1438
18:14 and he that humbleth **h** shall be exalted. 1438
19:12 a far country to receive for **h** a kingdom, 1438
20:42 And David **h** saith in the book of Psalms, 846
23: 2 to Cesar, saying that **he h** is Christ a King. 1438
23: 7 who **h** also was at Jerusalem at that time. 846
23:35 let him save **h**, if he be Christ, the chosen 1438
23:51 also **h** waited for the kingdom of God. 846
24:12 wondering in **h** at that which was come 1438
24:15 Jesus **h** drew near, and went with them. 846
24:27 all the scriptures the *things* concerning **h.** 846
24:36 Jesus **h** stood in the midst of them, 846

Jn
2:24 But Jesus did not commit **h** unto them, 1438
4: 2 (Though Jesus **h** baptized not, 846
4:12 and drank thereof **h**, and his children, 846
4:44 Jesus **h** testified, that a prophet hath no 846
4:53 and **h** believed, and his whole house. 846
5:13 Jesus had conveyed **h** away, a multitude NIG
5:18 his Father, making **h** equal with God. 846
5:19 The Son can do nothing of **h**, but what he 1438
5:20 and sheweth him all *things* that **h** doeth: 846
5:26 For as the Father hath life in **h;** so hath he 1438
5:26 hath he given to the Son to have life in **h;** 1438
5:37 And the Father **h**, which hath sent me, 846
6: 6 for he **h** knew what he would do. 846
6:15 departed again into a mountain **h** alone. 846
6:61 When Jesus knew in **h** that his disciples 1438
7: 4 and he **h** seeketh to be known openly. 846
7:18 he that speaketh of **h** seeketh his own 1438
8: 7 he lift up *h*, and said unto them, He that is NIG
8:10 Jesus had lift up **h**, and saw none but 1438
8:22 Then said the Jews, Will he kill **h?** 1438
8:59 Jesus hid **h**, and went out of the temple, 846
9:21 he is of age; ask him: he shall speak for **h.** 846
11:38 again groaning in **h** cometh to the grave. 1438
11:51 And this spake he not of **h:** but being high 1438
12:36 and departed, and did hide **h** from them. NIG
13: 4 and took a towel, and girded **h.** 1438
13:32 in him, God shall also glorify him in **h**, 1438
16:13 for he shall not speak of **h;** 1438
16:27 the Father **h** loveth you, because ye have 846
18:18 Peter stood with them, and warmed **h.** NIG
18:25 And Simon Peter stood and warmed **h.** NIG
19: 7 to die, because he made **h** the Son of God. 1438
19:12 whosoever maketh **h** a king speaketh 846
21: 1 After these *things* Jesus shewed **h** again to 1438
21: 1 of Tiberias; and on this wise shewed he *h.* 1438
21: 7 he was naked,) and did cast **h** into the sea. 1438
21:14 time *that* Jesus shewed **h** to his disciples, 1438

Ac
1: 3 To whom also he shewed **h** alive after his 1438
2:34 but he saith **h**, The LORD said unto my 846
5:13 of the rest durst no man join **h** to them: NIG
5:36 up Theudas, boasting **h** to be somebody; 1438
7:26 the next day he shewed **h** unto them as 1438
8: 9 giving out that **h** was some great one: 1438
8:13 Then Simon **h** believed also: and when he 846
8:34 prophet this? of **h**, or of some other *man?* 1438
9:26 he assayed to join **h** to the disciples: NIG
10:17 Now while Peter doubted in **h** what *this* 1438
12:11 And when Peter was come to **h**, he said, 1438
14:17 he left not **h** without witness, 1438
16:27 out his sword, and would have killed **h**, 1438
18:19 but he **h** entered into the synagogue, 846
19:22 but he **h** stayed in Asia for a season. 846
19:31 *him* that he would not adventure **h** 846
20:13 had he appointed, minding **h** to go afoot. 846
21:26 next day purifying **h** with them entered NIG
25: 4 that he **h** would depart shortly *thither.* NIG
25: 8 While he **answered for h**, Neither against 626
25:16 have licence to answer for **h** concerning NIG
25:25 and *that* he **h** hath appealed to Augustus, 846
26: 1 forth the hand, and answered for **h.** NIG
26:24 And as he thus spake for **h**, Festus said NIG
27: 3 liberty to go unto *his* friends to refresh **h.** NIG
28:16 Paul was suffered to dwell by **h** with a 1438

Ro
12: 3 to think *of h* more highly than he ought NIG
14: 7 none of us liveth to **h**, and no man dieth 1438
14: 7 liveth to himself, and no man dieth to **h.** 1438
14:12 every one of us shall give account of **h** to 1438
14:22 Happy *is* he that condemneth not **h** in 1438
15: 3 For even Christ pleased not **h**; but, as it is 1438

1Co
2:15 all *things*, yet **he h** is judged of no man. 846
3:15 but he **h** shall be saved; yet so as by fire. 846
3:18 Let no man deceive **h.** If any man among 1438
7:36 But if any *man* think that *he* behaveth **h** NIG
11:28 let a man examine **h**, and so let him eat 1438
11:29 eateth and drinketh damnation to **h**, 1438
14: 4 in an *unknown* tongue edifieth **h;** 1438
14: 8 who shall prepare **h** to the battle? 1438
14:28 and let him speak to **h**, and to God. 1438
14:37 If any *man* think **h** to be a prophet, NIG
15:28 shall the Son also **h** be subject unto him 846

2Co
5:18 who hath reconciled us to **h** by Jesus 1438
5:19 in Christ reconciling the world unto **h**, 1438
10: 7 If any *man* trust to **h** that *he is* Christ's, 1438
10: 7 let him of **h** think this again, that, as he *is* 1438
10:18 not he that commendeth **h** is approved, 1438
11:14 for Satan **h** is transformed into an angel of 1438
11:20 you, if a man take *of you*, if a man exalt **h**, NIG

Gal
1: 4 Who gave **h** for our sins, that he might 1438
2:12 were come, he withdrew and separated **h**, 1438
2:20 of God, who loved me, and gave **h** for me. 1438

Gal
6: 3 For if a man think **h** to be something, NIG
6: 3 when he is nothing, he deceiveth **h.** 1438
6: 4 and then shall he have rejoicing in **h** alone, 1438

Eph
1: 5 adoption of children by Jesus Christ to **h**, 846
1: 9 pleasure which he had purposed in **h:** 846
2:15 for to make in **h** of twain one new man, 1438
2:20 Jesus Christ **h** being the chief corner *stone;* 846
5: 2 and hath given **h** for us an offering and 1438
5:25 also loved the church, and gave **h** for it; 1438
5:27 That he might present it to **h** a glorious 1438
5:28 He that loveth his wife loveth **h.** 1438
5:33 in particular so love his wife even as **h;** 1438

Php
2: 7 made **h** of no reputation, and took *upon* 1438
2: 8 he humbled **h**, and became obedient unto 1438
3:21 able even to subdue all *things* unto **h.** 1438

Col
1:20 by him to reconcile all *things* unto **h;** 846

1Th
3:11 Now God **h** and our Father, and our Lord 1438
4:16 For the Lord **h** shall descend from heaven 846

2Th
2: 4 and exalteth **h** above all that is called God, NIG
2: 4 temple of God, shewing **h** that he is God. 1438
2:16 Now our Lord Jesus Christ **h**, and God, 846
3:16 Now the Lord of peace **h** give you peace 846

1Ti
2: 6 gave **h** a ransom for all, to be testified 1438

2Ti
2: 4 No *man* that warreth entangleth **h** with NIG
2:13 *yet* he abideth faithful: he cannot deny **h.** 1438
2:21 If a man therefore purge **h** from these, 1438

Tit
2:14 gave **h** for us, that he might redeem us 1438
2:14 and purify unto **h** a peculiar people, 1438
3:11 and sinneth, being **condemned of h.** 843

Heb
1: 3 when he had by **h** purged our sins, 1438
2:14 he also **h** likewise took part of the same; 1438
2:18 in that he **h** hath suffered being tempted, 846
5: 2 for that he **h** also is compassed with 846
5: 3 the people, so also for **h**, to offer for sins. 1438
5: 4 And no *man* taketh *this* honour unto **h**, 1438
5: 5 also Christ glorified not **h** to be made a 1438
6:13 could swear by no greater, he sware by **h**, 1438
7:27 this he did once, when he offered up **h.** 1438
9: 7 which he offered for **h**, and *for* the errors 1438
9:14 who through the eternal Spirit offered **h** 1438
9:25 Nor yet that he should offer **h** often, 1438
9:26 to put away sin by the sacrifice of **h.** 846
12: 3 such contradiction of sinners against **h**, 1438

Jas
1:24 For he beholdeth **h**, and goeth his way, 1438
1:27 *and* to keep **h** unspotted from the world. 1438

1Pe
2:23 committed *h* to him that judgeth NIG

1Jn
2: 6 He that saith *he* abideth in him ought **h** 846
3: 3 that hath this hope in him purifieth **h**, 1438
5:10 on the Son of God hath the witness in **h:** 846
5:18 but he that is begotten of God keepeth **h**, 1438

3Jn
1:10 neither doth **h** receive the brethren, 846

Rev
19:12 name written, that no *man* knew, but he **h.** 846
21: 3 God **h** shall be with them, *and be* their 846

HIN (22)

Ex
29:40 with the fourth part of a **h** of beaten oil; 1969
29:40 the fourth *part* of a **h** of wine for a drink 1969
30:24 of the sanctuary, and of oil olive a **h:** 1969

Lev
19:36 just weights, a just ephah, and a just **h**, 1969
23:13 *shall be of* wine, the fourth *part* of a **h.** 1969

Nu
15: 4 mingled with the fourth *part* of a **h** of oil. 1969
15: 5 for to make in **h** *of* wine for a drink of 1969
15: 6 mingled with the third *part* of a **h** of oil. 1969
15: 7 shalt offer the third *part* of a **h** *of* wine, 1969
15: 9 deals *of* flour mingled with half a **h** of oil. 1969
15:10 shalt bring for a drink offering half a **h** 1969
28: 5 mingled with the fourth *part* of a **h** of 1969
28: 7 be the fourth *part* of a **h** for the one lamb: 1969
28:14 their drink offerings shall be half a **h** of 1969
28:14 the third *part* of a **h** unto a ram, 1969
28:14 ram, and a fourth *part* of a **h** unto a lamb: 1969

Eze
4:11 water by measure, the sixth *part* of a **h:** 1969
45:24 for a ram, and a **h** of oil for an ephah. 1969
46: 5 be able to give, and a **h** of oil to an ephah. 1969
46: 7 attain unto, and a **h** of oil to an ephah. 1969
46:11 is able to give, and a **h** of oil to an ephah. 1969
46:14 an ephah, and the third *part* of a **h** of oil, 1969

HIND (3) [HINDS, HINDS']

Ge
49:21 Naphtali *is* a **h** let loose: he giveth goodly 355

Pr
5:19 *her be as* the loving **h** and pleasant roe; 365

Jer
14: 5 the **h** also calved in the field, and forsook 365

HINDER (16) [HINDERED, HINDERETH, HINDERMOST, HINDMOST]

Ge
24:56 he said unto them, **H** me not, seeing 309

Nu
22: 16 I pray thee, **h** thee from coming unto me: 4513

2Sa
2:23 Abner with the **h** end of the spear 310

1Ki
7:25 and all their **h** parts *were* inward. 268

2Ch
4: 4 and all their **h** parts *were* inward. 268

Ne
4: 8 fight against Jerusalem, and to **h** it. 6213+8442

Job
9:12 Behold, he taketh away, who can **h** him? 7725
11:10 or gather together, then who can **h** him? 7725

Ps
78:66 he smote his enemies in the **h** parts: 268

Joel
2:20 his **h** part towards the utmost sea, 5490

Zec
14: 8 and half of them toward the **h** sea: 314

Mk
4:38 And he was in the **h** part of the **ship**, 4403

Ac
8:36 *is* water; what doth **h** me to be baptized? 2967
27:41 the **h** part was broken with the violence 4403

1Co
9:12 suffer all *things*, lest we should **h** 1325+1464

Gal
5: 7 who did **h** you that *ye* should not obey 348

HINDERED (5) [HINDER]

Ezr
6: 8 given unto these men, that *they* be not **h.** 989

Lk
11:52 and them that were entering in ye **h.** 2967

Ro 15:22 I have been much **h** from coming to you. *1465*
1Th 2:18 I Paul, once and again; but Satan **h** us. *1465*
1Pe 3: 7 grace of life; that your prayers be not **h**. *1581*

HINDERETH (1) [HINDER]
Isa 14: 6 in anger, *is* persecuted, *and* none **h**. *2820*

HINDERMOST (2) [HINDER]
Ge 33: 2 children after, and Rachel and Joseph **h**. *314*
Jer 50:12 the **h** of the nations *shall be* a wilderness, *319*

HINDMOST (3) [HINDER]
Nu 2:31 They shall go **h** with their standards. *314*
Dt 25:18 by the way, and **smote the h** of thee, *2179*
Jos 10:19 your enemies, and **smite the h** of them; *2179*

HINDS (4) [HIND]
Job 39: 1 *or* canst thou mark when the **h** do calve? *355*
Ps 29: 9 The voice of the LORD maketh the **h** to *355*
SS 2: 7 by the roes, and by the **h** of the field, *355*
3: 5 by the roes, and by the **h** of the field, *355*

HINDS' (3) [HIND]
2Sa 22:34 He maketh my feet like **h** *feet:* and *355*
Ps 18:33 He maketh my feet like **h** *feet,* and *355*
Hab 3:19 he will make my feet like **h** *feet,* *355*

HINGES (2)
1Ki 7:50 the **h** of gold, *both* for the doors of *6596*
Pr 26:14 *As* the door turneth upon his **h**, so *doth* *6735*

HINNOM (13)
Jos 15: 8 unto the south side of the Jebusite; *2011*
15: 8 *lieth* before the valley of **H** westward, *2011*
18:16 *lieth* before the valley of the son of **H**, *2011*
18:16 descended *to* the valley of **H**, to the side *2011*
2Ki 23:10 *is* in the valley of the children of **H**, *2011*
2Ch 28: 3 incense in the valley of the son of **H**, *2011*
33: 6 the fire in the valley of the son of **H**: *2011*
Ne 11:30 from Beer-sheba unto the valley of **H**. *2011*
Jer 7:31 which *is* in the valley of the son of **H**, *2011*
7:32 nor the valley of the son of **H**, *2011*
19: 2 go forth unto the valley of the son of **H**, *2011*
19: 6 nor The valley of the son of **H**, but The *2011*
32:35 which *are* in the valley of the son of **H**, *2011*

HIP (1)
Jdg 15: 8 he smote them **h** and thigh *with* a great *7785*

HIRAH (2)
Ge 38: 1 certain Adullamite, whose name *was* **H**. *2437*
38:12 he and his friend **H** the Adullamite. *2437*

HIRAM (22) [HIRAM'S]
2Sa 5:11 **H** king of Tyre sent messengers to David, *2438*
1Ki 5: 1 **H** king of Tyre sent his servants unto *2438*
5: 1 father: for **H** was ever a lover of David. *2438*
5: 2 And Solomon sent to **H**, saying, *2438*
5: 7 when **H** heard the words of Solomon, *2438*
5: 8 sent to Solomon, saying, I have *2438*
5:10 So **H** gave Solomon cedar trees and *2438*
5:11 Solomon gave **H** twenty thousand *2438*
5:11 thus gave Solomon to **H** year by year. *2438*
5:12 was peace between **H** and Solomon; *2438*
7:13 king Solomon sent and fet **H** out of Tyre. *2438*
7:40 the lavers, and the shovels, *2438*
7:40 So **H** made an end of doing all the work *2438*
7:45 which **H** made to king Solomon *for* *2438*
9:11 (*Now* **H** the king of Tyre had furnished *2438*
9:11 king Solomon gave **H** twenty cities in *2438*
9:12 **H** came out from Tyre to see the cities *2438*
9:14 **H** sent to the king sixscore talents of gold. *2438*
9:27 **H** sent in the navy his servants, *2438*
10:11 the navy also of **H**, that brought gold from *2438*
10:22 a navy of Tharshish with the navy of **H**: *2438*
1Ch 14: 1 Now **H** king of Tyre sent messengers to *2438*

HIRAM'S (1) [HIRAM]
1Ki 5:18 **H** builders did hew *them,* and *2438*

HIRE (23) [HIRED, HIRELING, HIRES, HIREST]
Ge 30:18 God hath given *me* my **h**, because I have *7939*
30:32 the goats: and *of such* shall be my **h**. *7939*
30:33 when it shall come for my **h** before thy *7939*
31: 8 said thus, The **h**straked shall be thy **h**; *7939*
Ex 22:15 if it *be* a hired *thing,* it came for his **h**. *7939*
Dt 23:18 Thou shalt not bring the **h** of a whore, *868*
24:15 At his day thou shalt give *him* his **h**, *7939*
1Ki 5: 6 unto thee will I give **h** for thy servants *7939*
1Ch 19: 6 talents of silver to **h** them chariots *7936*
Isa 23:17 she shall turn to her **h**, and shall commit *868*
23:18 and her **h** shall be holiness to the LORD: *868*
46: 6 silver in the balance, and **h** a goldsmith; *7936*
Eze 16:31 been as a harlot, in that *thou* scornest **h**; *868*
16:41 and thou also shalt give no **h** any more. *868*
Mic 1: 7 for she gathered *it* of the **h** of a harlot, *868*
1: 7 and they shall return to the **h** of a harlot. *868*
3:11 the priests thereof teach for **h**, *4242*
Zec 8:10 For before these days there was no **h** for *7939*
8:10 was no hire for man, nor any **h** for beast; *7939*
Mt 20: 1 *which* went out early in the morning to **h** *3409*
20: 7 Call the labourers, and give them *their* **h**, *3408*
Lk 10: 7 for the labourer is worthy of his **h**. Go not *3408*
Jas 5: 4 of the labourers which have reaped *3408*

HIRED (34) [HIRE]
Ge 30:16 for **surely** I have **h** thee with my *7936+7936*
Ex 12:45 and a **h servant** shall not eat thereof. *7916*
22:15 if it *be* a **h** thing, it came for his hire. *7916*
Lev 19:13 rob *him:* the wages of **him that is h** *7916*
22:10 or a **h servant**, shall not eat *of* the holy *7916*
25: 6 for thy **h servant**, and for thy stranger *7916*
25:40 *But* as a **h servant**, *and* as a sojourner, *7916*
25:50 according to the time of a **h servant** shall *7916*
25:53 as a yearly **h servant** shall he be with *7916*
Dt 15:18 he hath been worth a double **h servant** *7916*
23: 4 **h** against thee Balaam the son of Beor *7916*
24:14 Thou shalt not oppress a **h servant** *that* *7916*
Jdg 9: 4 wherewith Abimelech **h** vain and *7936*
18: 4 and hath **h** me, and I am his priest. *7936*
1Sa 2: 5 *that were* full have **h** out themselves *7936*
2Sa 10: 6 and the Syrians of Beth-rehob, *7936*
2Ki 7: 6 the king of Israel hath **h** against us *7936*
1Ch 19: 7 they **h** thirty and two thousand chariots, *7936*
2Ch 24:12 masons and carpenters to repair the *7936*
25: 6 He **h** also an hundred thousand mighty *7936*
Ezr 4: 5 **h** counsellers against them, to frustrate *7936*
Ne 6:12 for Tobiah and Sanballat had **h** him. *7936*
6:13 *was* he **h**, that I should be afraid, *7936*
13: 2 with water, but **h** Balaam against them, *7936*
Isa 7:20 shall the Lord shave with a rasor that is **h**, *7917*
Jer 46:21 her **h** men *are* in the midst of her like *7916*
Hos 8: 9 alone by himself: Ephraim hath **h** lovers. *8566*
8:10 though they have **h** among the nations, *8566*
Mt 20: 7 say unto him, Because no man hath **h** us. *3409*
20: 9 And when they came that were **h** about *NIG*
Mk 1:20 Zebedee in the ship with the **h servants**, *3411*
Lk 15:17 How many **h** *servants* of my father's have *3407*
15:19 son: make me as one of thy **h** *servants.* *3407*
Ac 28:30 two whole years in his own **h house**, *3410*

HIRED HAND; HIRED MAN See HIRELING

HIRELING (9) [HIRE]
Job 7: 1 *are not* his days also like the days of a **h**? *7916*
7: 2 as a **h** looketh for the reward of his work: *7916*
14: 6 till he shall accomplish, as a **h**, his day. *7916*
Isa 16:14 as the years of a **h**, and the glory of Moab *7916*
21:16 according to the years of a **h**, and all *7916*
Mal 3: 5 against those that oppress the **h** in *his* *7916*
Jn 10:12 But he that is an **h**, and not the shepherd, *3411*
10:13 The **h** fleeth, because he is a hireling, *3411*
10:13 because he is a **h**, and careth not for *3411*

HIRES (1) [HIRE]
Mic 1: 7 the **h** thereof shall be burnt with the fire, *868*

HIREST (1) [HIRE]
Eze 16:33 thy gifts to all thy lovers, and **h** them, *7809*

HIS (8478) [HE] See Index of Articles, Etc.

HISS (12) [HISSING]
1Ki 9: 8 by it shall be astonished, and shall **h**; *8319*
Job 27:23 at him, and shall **h** him out of his place. *8319*
Isa 5:26 **h** unto them from the end of the earth: *8319*
7:18 *that* the LORD shall **h** for the fly that *is* in *8319*
Jer 19: 8 and because of all the plagues thereof. *8319*
49:17 and shall **h** at all the plagues thereof. *8319*
50:13 be astonished, and **h** at all her plagues. *8319*
La 2:15 **h** and wag their head at the daughter *8319*
2:16 they **h** and gnash the teeth: they say, *8319*
Eze 27:36 The merchants among the people shall **h** *8319*
Zep 2:15 every one that passeth by her shall **h**, *8319*
Zec 10: 8 I will **h** for them, and gather them; for I *8319*

HISSING (8) [HISS]
2Ch 29: 8 to astonishment, and to **h**, as ye see with *8322*
Jer 18:16 their land desolate, *and* a perpetual **h**; *8292*
19: 8 I will make this city desolate, and a **h**; *8322*
25: 9 and a **h**, and perpetual desolations. *8322*
25:18 an astonishment, a **h**, and a curse; *8322*
29:18 an astonishment, and a **h**, and a reproach, *8322*
51:37 an astonishment, and a **h**, without an *8322*
Mic 6:16 and the inhabitants thereof a **h**: *8322*

HIT (2)
1Sa 31: 3 sore against Saul, and the archers **h** him; *4672*
1Ch 10: 3 the archers **h** him, and he was wounded *4672*

HITHER (67) [HITHERTO]
Ge 15:16 generation they shall come **h** *2008+1886.5*
42:15 except your youngest brother come **h**. *2008*
45: 5 angry with yourselves, that ye sold me **h**: *2008*
45: 8 So now *it was* not you *that* sent me **h**, *2008*
45:13 shall haste and bring down my father in *2008*
Ex 3: 5 said, Draw not nigh **h**: put off thy shoes *1988*
Jos 2: 2 there came men in **h** to night of *2008*
3: 9 Come **h**, and hear the words of the LORD *2008*
18: 6 and bring the *description* **h** to me, *2008*
Jdg 16: 2 the Gazites, saying, Samson is come **h**. *2008*
18: 3 and said unto him, Who brought thee **h**? *1988*
19:12 We will not turn aside **h** into the city of a *NIH*
Ru 2:14 At mealtime come thou **h**, and eat of *1988*
1Sa 9:22 **Bring h** a burnt offering to me, and peace *5066*
14:18 said unto Ahiah, **Bring h** the ark of God. *5066*
14:34 **Bring** me **h** every man his ox, *5066*
14:36 the priest, Let us draw near **h** unto God. *1988*
14:38 Saul said, Draw ye near **h**, all the chief of *1988*
15:32 **Bring** you **h** to me Agag the king of *5066*
16:11 for we will not sit down till he come **h**. *6311*

1Sa 17:28 and he said, Why camest thou down **h**? *2088*
23: 9 to Abiathar the priest, **Bring h** the ephod. *5066*
30: 7 I pray thee, **bring** me **h** the ephod. *5066*
2Sa 1:10 and have brought them **h** unto my lord. *2008*
5: 6 and the lame, thou shalt not come in **h**: *2008*
5: 6 hither: thinking, David cannot come in **h**. *2008*
14:32 Behold, I sent unto thee, saying, Come **h**, *2008*
20:16 pray you, unto Joab, Come near **h**, *2008+5704*
1Ki 22: 9 said, Hasten **h** Micaiah the son of Imlah. *NIH*
2Ki 2: 8 they were divided **h** and thither, *2008*
2:14 the waters, they parted **h** and thither: *2008*
8: 7 The man of God is come **h**. *2008+5704*
1Ch 11: 5 said to David, Thou shalt not come **h**. *2008*
2Ch 28:13 Ye shall not bring in the captives **h**: *2008*
Ezr 4: 2 king of Assur, which brought us up **h**. *6311*
Ps 73:10 Therefore his people return **h**: *1988*
81: 2 Take a psalm, and bring **h** the timbrel, *NIH*
Pr 9: 4 Whoso *is* simple, let him turn in **h**: *as for* *2008*
9:16 Whoso *is* simple, let him turn in **h**: *2008*
25: 7 *it is* that it be said unto thee, Come up **h**; *2008*
Isa 57: 3 draw near **h**, ye sons of the sorceress, *2008*
Eze 40: 4 shew *them* unto thee that I should bring **h**: *2008*
Da 3:26 come **h**. Then Shadrach, Meshach, *NIH*
Mt 8:29 art thou come **h** to torment us before *5602*
14:18 He said, **Bring** them **h** to me. *5602*
17:17 long shall I suffer you? bring him **h** to me. *5602*
22:12 camest thou in **h** not having a wedding *5602*
Mk 11: 3 him; and straightway he will send him **h**. *5602*
Lk 9:41 with you, and suffer you? Bring thy son **h**. *5602*
14:21 and bring in **h** the poor, and the maimed, *5602*
15:23 And **bring h** the fatted calf, and kill *it;* *5342*
19:27 bring **h**, and slay *them* before me. *5602*
19:30 man sat: loose him, and bring *him* **h**. *NIG*
Jn 4:15 that I thirst not, neither come **h** to draw. *1759*
4:16 her, Go, call thy husband, and come **h**. *1759*
6:25 unto him, Rabbi, when camest thou **h**? *5602*
20:27 Reach **h** thy finger, and behold my hands; *5602*
20:27 reach **h** thy hand, and thrust *it into* my *NIH*
Ac 9:21 came **h** for that *intent,* that he might bring *5602*
10:32 Send therefore to Joppa, and **call h** Simon, *3333*
17: 6 the world upside down are come **h** also; *1759*
19:37 For ye have brought **h** these men, *which* *NIG*
25:17 Therefore, when they were come **h**, *1759*
Rev 4: 1 Come up **h**, and I will shew thee *things* *5602*
11:12 heaven saying unto them, Come up **h**. *5602*
17: 1 I talked with me, saying unto me, Come **h**; *1204*
21: 9 talked with me, saying, Come **h**, I will *1204*

HITHERTO (19) [HITHER, TO]
Ex 7:16 behold, **h** thou wouldest not hear. *3541+5704*
Jos 17:14 as the LORD hath blessed me **h**? *3541+5704*
Jdg 16:13 **H** thou hast mocked me, and told *2008+5704*
1Sa 1:16 and grief have I spoken **h**. *2008+5704*
7:12 **H** hath the LORD helped us. *2008+5704*
2Sa 7:18 that thou hast brought me **h**? *1988+5704*
15:34 I *have been* thy father's servant **h**, *227+4480*
1Ch 9:18 **h** waited in the king's *2008+5704+2050.1*
12:29 for **h** the greatest part of them had *2008+5704*
17:16 that thou hast brought me **h**? *1988+5704*
Job 38:11 **H** shalt thou come, but no further: *5704+6311*
Ps 71:17 have I declared thy wondrous *2008+5704*
Isa 18: 2 a people terrible from their beginning **h**; *1973*
18: 7 a people terrible from their beginning **h**; *1973*
Da 7:28 **H** *is* the end of the matter. *As for* *3542+5705*
Jn 5:17 them, My Father worketh **h**, *737+2193*
16:24 **H** have ye asked nothing in my *737+2193*
Ro 1:13 unto you, (but was let **h**,) *891+1204+3588*
1Co 3: 2 for **h** ye were **not** able *to bear it,* neither *3768*

HITTITE (26) [HITTITES]
Ge 23:10 Ephron the **H** answered Abraham in *2850*
25: 9 field of Ephron the son of Zohar the **H**, *2850*
26:34 to wife Judith the daughter of Beeri the **H**, *2850*
26:34 Bashemath the daughter of Elon the **H**: *2850*
36: 2 Adah the daughter of Elon the **H**, *2850*
49:29 cave that *is* in the field of Ephron the **H**, *2850*
49:30 the **H** for a possession of a buryingplace. *2850*
50:13 of a buryingplace of Ephron the **H**, *2850*
Ex 23:28 Canaanite, and the **H**, from before thee. *2850*
33: 2 and the **H**, and the Perizzite, the Hivite, *2850*
34:11 the **H**, and the Perizzite, and the Hivite, *2850*
Jos 9: 1 the **H**, and the Amorite, the Canaanite, *2850*
11: 3 the **H**, and the Perizzite, and the Jebusite *2850*
1Sa 26: 6 and said to Ahimelech the **H**, *2850*
2Sa 11: 3 the wife of Uriah the **H**? *2850*
11: 6 to Joab, *saying,* Send me Uriah the **H**. *2850*
11:17 of David; and Uriah the **H** died also. *2850*
11:21 Thy servant Uriah the **H** is dead also. *2850*
11:24 and thy servant Uriah the **H** is dead also. *2850*
12: 9 thou hast killed Uriah the **H** with *2850*
12:10 hast taken the wife of Uriah the **H** to be *2850*
23:39 Uriah the **H**: thirty and seven *in* all. *2850*
1Ki 15: 5 save only in the matter of Urijah the **H**. *2850*
1Ch 11:41 Uriah the **H**, Zabad the son of Ahlai, *2850*
Eze 16: 3 *was* an Amorite, and thy mother a **H**. *2850*
16:45 your mother *was* a **H**, and your father an *2850*

HITTITES (22) [HITTITE]
Ge 15:20 the **H**, and the Perizzites, *2850*
Ex 3: 8 the **H**, and the Amorites, and the Perizzites, *2850*
3:17 the **H**, and the Amorites, and the Perizzites, *2850*
13: 5 the **H**, and the Amorites, and the Hivites, *2850*
23:23 the **H**, and the Perizzites, *2850*
Nu 13:29 **H**, and the Jebusites, and the Amorites, *2850*
Dt 7: 1 the **H**, and the Girgashites, *2850*

Dt	20:17	*namely,* the **H,** and the Amorites,	2850
Jos	1: 4	the land of the **H,** and unto the great sea	2850
	3:10	the **H,** and the Hivites, and the Perizzites,	2850
	12: 8	in the south *country;* the **H,** the Amorites,	2850
	24:11	the **H,** and the Girgashites, the Hivites,	2850
Jdg	1:26	the man went *into* the land of the **H,**	2850
	3: 5	**H,** and the Amorites, and Perizzites,	2850
1Ki	9:20	**H,** Perizzites, Hivites, and Jebusites,	2850
	10:29	so for all the kings of the **H,** and for	2850
	11: 1	Ammonites, Edomites, Zidonians, *and* **H;**	2850
2Ki	7: 6	hath hired against us the kings of the **H,**	2850
2Ch	1:17	they out *horses* for all the kings of the **H,**	2850
	8: 7	*for* all the people that were left of the **H,**	2850
Ezr	9: 1	the **H,** the Perizzites, the Jebusites,	2850
Ne	9: 8	the **H,** the Amorites, and the Perizzites,	2850

HIVITE (9) [HIVITES]

Ge	10:17	the **H,** and the Arkite, and the Sinite,	2340
	34: 2	when Shechem the son of Hamor the **H,**	2340
	36: 2	of Anah the daughter of Zibeon the **H;**	2340
Ex	23:28	shall drive out the **H,** the Canaanite,	2340
	34:11	the Perizzite, the **H,** and the Jebusite:	2340
Jos	9: 1	the Perizzite, the **H,** and the Jebusite,	2340
	11: 3	*to* the **H** under Hermon in the land of	2340
1Ch	1:15	And the **H,** and the Arkite, and the Sinite,	2340

HIVITES (16) [HIVITE]

Ex	3: 8	Perizzites, and the **H,** and the Jebusites,	2340
	3:17	Perizzites, and the **H,** and the Jebusites,	2340
	13: 5	Amorites, and the **H,** and the Jebusites,	2340
	23:23	the Canaanites, the **H,** and the Jebusites:	2340
Dt	7: 1	Perizzites, the **H,** and the Jebusites,	2340
	20:17	Perizzites, the **H,** and the Jebusites,	2340
Jos	3:10	the **H,** and the Perizzites,	2340
	9: 7	the men of Israel said unto the **H,**	2340
	11:19	save the **H** the inhabitants of Gibeon:	2340
	12: 8	the Perizzites, the **H,** and the Jebusites;	2340
	24:11	the Girgashites, the **H,** and the Jebusites,	2340
Jdg	3: 3	and the **H** that dwelt in mount Lebanon,	2340
	3: 5	and Perizzites, and the **H,** and Jebusites:	2340
2Sa	24: 7	*to* all the cities of the **H,** and of	2340
1Ki	9:20	Hittites, Perizzites, and Jebusites,	2340
2Ch	8: 7	Perizzites, and the **H,** and the Jebusites,	2340

HIZKI See HEZEKI

HIZKIAH (1)

Zep	1: 1	the son of Amariah, the son of **H,**	2396

HIZKIJAH (1)

Ne	10:17	Ater, **H,** Azzur,	2396

HO (4)

Ru	4: 1	**H,** such a one, turn aside, sit down here.	NIH
Isa	55: 1	**H,** every one that thirsteth, come ye to	1945
Zec	2: 6	**H,** ho, *come forth,* and flee from the land	1945
	2: 6	Ho, **h,** *come forth,* and flee from the land	1945

HOAR (4) [HOARFROST, HOARY]

Ex	16:14	*as* small as the **h** frost on the ground.	3713
1Ki	2: 6	let not his **h** head go down *to* the grave	7872
	2: 9	his **h** head bring thou down *to* the grave	7872
Isa	46: 4	*even* to **h** hairs will I carry *you:* I have	7872

HOARFROST (1) [FROST, HOAR]

Ps	147:16	like wool: he scattereth the **h** like ashes.	3713

HOARY (4) [HOAR]

Lev	19:32	Thou shalt rise up before the **h** head,	7872
Job	38:29	the **h** frost of heaven, who hath gendered	3713
	41:32	*one* would think the deep to be **h.**	7872
Pr	16:31	The **h** head *is* a crown of glory, *if* it be	7872

HOBAB (2)

Nu	10:29	Moses said unto **H,** the son of Raguel	2246
Jdg	4:11	which *was* of the children of **H** the father	2246

HOBAH (1)

Ge	14:15	smote them, and pursued them unto **H,**	2327

HOBAIAH See HABAIAH

HOD (1)

1Ch	7:37	**H,** and Shamma, and Shilshah, and Ithran,	1936

HODAIAH (1)

1Ch	3:24	the sons of Elioenai *were,* **H,** and Eliashib,	1939

HODAVIAH (3)

1Ch	5:24	Azriel, and Jeremiah, and **H,** and Jahdiel,	1938
	9: 7	the son of **H,** the son of Hasenuah,	1938
Ezr	2:40	of the children of **H,** seventy and four.	1938

HODESH (1)

1Ch	8: 9	he begat of **H** his wife, Jobab, and Zibia,	2321

HODEVAH (1)

Ne	7:43	the children of **H,** seventy and four.	1937

HODIAH (1)

1Ch	4:19	sons of *his* wife **H** the sister of Naham,	1940

HODIJAH (5)

Ne	8: 7	**H,** Maaseiah, Kelita, Azariah, Jozabad,	1941
	9: 5	Sherebiah, **H,** Shebaniah, *and* Pethahiah,	1941
	10:10	Shebaniah, **H,** Kelita, Pelaiah, Hanan,	1941

Ne	10:13	**H,** Bani, Beninu.	1941
	10:18	**H,** Hashum, Bezai,	1941

HOGLAH (4)

Nu	26:33	and Noah, **H,** Milcah, and Tirzah.	2295
	27: 1	and Noah, and **H,** and Milcah, and Tirzah.	2295
	36:11	Tirzah, and **H,** and Milcah, and Noah,	2295
Jos	17: 3	and Noah, **H,** Milcah, and Tirzah.	2295

HOHAM (1)

Jos	10: 3	of Jerusalem sent unto **H** king of Hebron,	1944

HOISED (1)

Ac	27:40	and **h** up the mainsail to the wind,	*1869*

HOLD (185) [HELD, HOLDEN, HOLDEST, HOLDETH, HOLDING, HOLDS]

Ge	19:16	the men **laid h** upon his hand, and upon	2388
	21:18	lift up the lad, and **h** him in thine hand;	2388
	25:26	and his hand **took h** on Esau's heel;	270
Ex	5: 1	that they may **h** a feast unto me in	2287
	9: 2	to let *them* go, and wilt **h** them still,	2388
	10: 9	for we *must* **h** a feast unto the Lord.	NIH
	14:14	fight for you, and ye shall **h** your **peace.**	2790
	15:14	sorrow shall **take h** on the inhabitants of	270
	15:15	Moab, trembling shall **take h** upon them;	270
	20: 7	for the Lord will not **h** him **guiltless** that	5352
	26: 5	that the loops may **take h** one of another.	6901
Nu	30: 4	and her father shall **h** his **peace** at her:	2790
	30:14	altogether **h** his **peace** at her	2790+2790
Dt	5:11	for the Lord will not **h** him **guiltless** that	5352
	21:19	his father and his mother **lay h** on him,	8610
	22:28	**lay h** on her, and lie with her, and they	8610
	32:41	and mine hand **take h** on judgment;	270
Jdg	9:46	into a **h** of the house of the god Berith.	6877
	9:49	put *them* to the **h,** and set the hold on fire	6877
	9:49	the hold, and set the **h** on fire upon them:	6877
	16:29	Samson **took h** of the two middle pillars	3943
	18:19	said unto him, **H** thy **peace,** lay thine	2790
	19:29	**laid h** on his concubine, and divided her,	2388
Ru	3:15	vail that *thou hast* upon thee, and **h** it.	270
1Sa	15:27	he **laid h** upon the skirt of his mantle,	2388
	22: 4	all the while that David was in the **h.**	4686
	22: 5	Gad said unto David, Abide not in the **h;**	4686
	24:22	and his men gat them up unto the **h.**	4686
2Sa	1:11	David **took h** on his clothes, and rent	2388
	2:21	and **lay** thee **h on** one of the young men,	270
	2:22	**h** up my face to Joab thy brother?	5375
	4:10	I **took h** of him, and slew him in Ziklag,	270
	5: 7	Nevertheless David took the **strong h** of	4686
	5:17	heard *of it,* and went down to the **h.**	4686
	6: 6	*hand* to the ark of God, and **took h** of it;	270
	13:11	he **took h** of her, and said unto her,	2388
	13:20	**h** now thy **peace,** my sister: he *is* thy	2790
	18: 9	his head **caught h** of the oak, and he was	2388
	23:14	David *was* then in a **h,** and the garrison	4686
	24: 7	came *to* the **strong h** of Tyre, and *to* all	4013
1Ki	1:50	and **caught h** on the horns of the altar.	2388
	1:51	hath **caught h** on the horns of the altar,	270
	2: 9	Now therefore **h** him not **guiltless:** for	5352
	2:28	and **caught h** on the horns of the altar.	2388
	9: 9	have **taken h** upon other gods,	2388
	13: 4	from the altar, saying, **Lay h on** him.	8610
2Ki	2: 3	said, Yea, I know *it;* **h** you your **peace.**	2814
	2: 5	Yea, I know *it;* **h** you your **peace.**	2814
	2:12	he **took h** of his own clothes, and rent	2388
	6:32	shut the door, and **h** him fast at the door:	3905
	7: 9	day of good tidings, and we **h** our **peace:**	2814
1Ch	11:16	David *was* then in the **h,**	4686
	12: 8	into the **h** to the wilderness men of might,	4679
	12:16	Benjamin and Judah to the **h** unto David.	4679
	13: 9	Uzza put forth his hand to **h** the ark;	270
2Ch	7:22	**laid h** on other gods, and worshipped	2388
Ne	8:11	**H** your **peace,** for the day *is* holy;	2013
Est	4:11	except such to whom the king shall **h out**	3447
Job	6:24	Teach me, and I will **h** my **tongue:**	2790
	8:15	he shall **h** it **fast,** but it shall not endure.	2388
	9:28	I know that thou wilt not **h** me **innocent.**	5352
	11: 3	Should thy lies **make** men **h** their **peace?**	2790
	13: 5	would **altogether h** your **peace,**	2790+2790
	13:13	**H** your **peace,** let me alone, that I may	2790
	13:19	for now, if I **h** my **tongue,** I shall give up	2790
	17: 9	The righteous also shall **h** on his way,	2388
	21: 6	and trembling **taketh h** on my flesh.	270
	27: 6	My righteousness I **h fast,** and will not let	2388
	27:20	Terrors **take h on** him as waters,	5381
	30:16	days of affliction have **taken h upon** me.	270
	33:31	unto me: **h** thy **peace,** and I will speak.	2790
	33:33	**h** thy **peace,** and I shall teach thee	2790
	36:17	judgment and justice **take h on** *thee.*	8551
	38:13	*it* might **take h** of the ends of the earth,	270
	41:26	sword of him that layeth at him cannot **h:**	6965
Ps	17: 5	**H** up my goings in thy paths, *that* my	8551
	35: 2	**Take h** of shield and buckler, and stand	270
	39:12	unto my cry; **h** not thy **peace** at my tears:	2790
	40:12	mine iniquities have **taken h upon** me,	5381
	48: 6	Fear **took h** upon them there, *and* pain,	270
	69:24	let thy wrathful anger **take h** of them.	5381
	83: 1	**h** not thy **peace,** and be not still, O God.	2790
	109: 1	**H** not thy **peace,** O God of my praise;	2790
	116: 3	and the pains of hell **gat h** upon me:	4672
	119:53	Horror hath **taken h** upon me because	270
	119:117	**H** thou me **up,** and I shall be safe:	5582
	119:143	and anguish have **taken h on** me:	4672
	139:10	lead me, and thy right hand shall **h** me.	270

Pr	2:19	neither **take** they **h** of the paths of life.	5381
	3:18	*is* a tree of life to them that **lay h** upon	2388
	4:13	**Take fast h** of instruction; let *her* not go:	2388
	5: 5	down *to* death; her steps **take h** on hell.	8551
	30:28	The spider **taketh h** with her hands,	8610
	31:19	the spindle, and her hands **h** the distaff.	8551
Ecc	2: 3	to **lay h** on folly, till I might see what *was*	270
	7:18	*is* good that thou shouldest **take h** of this;	270
SS	3: 8	They all **h** swords, *being* expert in war:	270
	7: 8	I will **take h** of the boughs thereof:	270
Isa	3: 6	When a man shall **take h** of his brother	8610
	4: 1	in that day seven women shall **take h** of	2388
	5:29	lay **h** of the prey, and shall carry *it* away	270
	13: 8	sorrows shall **take h** of *them;* they shall	270
	21: 3	pangs have **taken h** upon me, as the	270
	27: 5	Or let him **take h** of my strength, *that* he	2388
	31: 9	he shall pass over *to* his **strong h** for fear,	5553
	41:13	For I the Lord thy God will **h** thy right	2388
	42: 6	will **h** thine hand, and will keep thee,	2388
	56: 2	and the son of man *that* **layeth h** on it;	2388
	56: 4	please me, and **take h** of my **covenant;**	2388
	56: 6	and **taketh h** of my **covenant;**	2388
	62: 1	For Zion's sake will I not **h** my **peace,**	2814
	62: 6	which shall never **h** their **peace** day nor	2814
	64: 7	that stirreth up himself to **take h** of thee:	2388
	64:12	wilt thou **h** thy **peace,** and afflict us very	2814
Jer	2:13	broken cisterns, that can **h** no water.	3557
	4:19	I cannot **h** my **peace,** because thou hast	2790
	6:23	They shall **lay h** on bow and spear; they	2388
	6:24	anguish hath **taken h** of us, *and* pain, as	2388
	8: 5	they **h** fast deceit, they refuse to return.	2388
	8:21	astonishment hath **taken h** on me.	2388
	50:42	They shall **h** the bow and the lance:	2388
	50:43	anguish **took h** of him, *and* pangs as of a	2388
Eze	29: 7	When they **took h** of thee by thy hand,	8610
	30:21	bind it, to make it strong to **h** the sword.	8610
	41: 6	*they* might have **h,** but they had not hold	270
	41: 6	they had not **h** in the wall of the house.	270
Am	6:10	shall he say, **H** thy **tongue:** for *we may*	2013
Mic	4: 8	the **strong h** of the daughter of Zion,	6077
	6:14	thou shalt **take h,** but shalt not deliver;	5253
Na	1: 7	*is* good, a **strong h** in the day of trouble;	4581
Hab	1:10	they shall deride every **strong h;** for they	4013
Zep	1: 7	**H** thy **peace** at the presence of the Lord	2013
Zec	7: 6	did they not **take h** of your fathers?	5381
	8:23	**take h** out of all languages of the nations,	2388
	8:23	even shall **take h** of the skirt of him that	2388
	9: 3	And Tyrus did build herself a **strong h,**	4692
	9:12	Turn ye to the **strong h,** ye prisoners of	1225
	11: 5	slay them, and **h** themselves not **guilty:**	816
	14:13	they shall **lay** every one on the hand of	2388
Mt	6:24	or else he will **h** to the one, and despise	*472*
	2:11	will he not **lay h** on it, and lift *it* out?	*2902*
	14: 3	For Herod had **laid h** on John,	*2902*
	20:31	because they should **h** their **peace:**	*4623*
	21:26	the people; for all **h** John as a prophet.	*2192*
	26:48	I shall kiss, that *same* is he: **h** him **fast.**	*2902*
	26:55	in the temple, and ye **laid** no **h** on me.	*2902*
	26:57	they that had **laid h** on Jesus led *him*	*2902*
Mk	1:25	**H** thy **peace,** and come out of him.	*5392*
	3:21	*of it,* they went out to **lay h** on him:	*2902*
	6:17	had sent forth and **laid h** upon John,	*2902*
	7: 4	which they have received to **h,**	*2902*
	7: 8	ye **h** the tradition of men, *as* the washing	*2902*
	10:48	charged him that he should **h** his **peace:**	*4623*
	12:12	And they sought to **lay h** on him,	*2902*
	14:51	and the young men **laid h** on him:	*2902*
Lk	4:35	**H** thy **peace,** and come out of him.	*5392*
	16:13	or else he will **h** to the one, and despise	*472*
	18:39	rebuked him, that he should **h** his **peace:**	*4623*
	19:40	you that, if these should **h** their **peace,**	*4623*
	20:20	that they might **take h** of his words,	*1949*
	20:26	And they could not **take h** of his words	*1949*
	23:26	they **laid h** upon one Simon, a Cyrenian,	*1949*
Ac	4: 3	and put *them* in **h** unto the next day:	*5084*
	12:17	them with the hand to **h** their **peace,**	*4601*
	18: 9	but speak, and **h** not thy **peace:**	*4623*
Ro	1:18	men, who **h** the truth in unrighteousness;	*2722*
1Co	14:30	that sitteth *by,* let the first **h** his **peace.**	*4601*
Php	2:29	all gladness; and **h** such in reputation:	*2192*
1Th	5:21	all *things;* **h** fast *that which* is good.	*2722*
2Th	2:15	**h** the traditions which ye have been	*2902*
1Ti	6:12	good fight of faith, **lay h on** eternal life,	*1949*
	6:19	come, that they may **lay h on** eternal life.	*1949*
2Ti	1:13	**H** fast the form of sound words,	*2192*
Heb	3: 6	if we **h** fast the confidence and	*2722*
	3:14	if we **h** the beginning of *our* confidence	*2722*
	4:14	Son of God, let us **h** fast *our* profession.	*2902*
	6:18	who have fled for refuge to **lay h** upon	*2902*
	10:23	Let us **h** fast the profession of *our* hope	*2722*
Rev	2:14	thou hast there them that **h** the doctrine	*2902*
	2:15	hast thou also them that **h** the doctrine	*2902*
	2:25	But *that* which ye have *already* **h** fast till	NIG
	3: 3	and heard, and **h** fast, and repent.	*5083*
	3:11	**h** *that* fast which thou hast, that no *man*	*2902*
	18: 2	the **h** of every foul spirit, and a cage of	*5438*
	20: 2	And he **laid h** on the dragon, *that* old	*2902*

HOLD FAST See CLEAVE; CLEAVED; CLEAVETH

HOLD GUILTY See IMPUTE; IMPUTED; IMPUTETH; IMPUTING

HOLDEN (12) [HOLD]

2Ki	23:22	Surely there was not **h** such a passover	6213

2Ki	23:23 *wherein* this passover was **h** to the Lord	6213
Job	36: 8 in fetters, *and* be **h** in cords of affliction;	3920
Ps	18:35 thy right hand hath **h** me **up**,	5582
	71: 6 By thee have I been **h** **up** from the womb:	5564
	73:23 thee: thou hast **h** me by my right hand.	270
Pr	5:22 he shall be **h** with the cords of his sins.	8551
Isa	42:14 I have long time **h** my **peace**, I have been	2814
	45: 1 to Cyrus, whose right hand I have **h**,	2388
Lk	24:16 their eyes were **h** that *they* should not	2902
Ac	2:24 was not possible that he should be **h** of it.	2902
Ro	14: 4 Yea, he shall be **h up**: for God is able to	2476

HOLDEST (6) [HOLD]

Est	4:14 if thou **altogether h** thy **peace** at	2790+2790
Job	13:24 thou thy face, and **h** me for thine enemy?	2803
Ps	77: 4 Thou **h** mine eyes waking: I am *so*	270
Jer	49:16 of the rock, that **h** the height of the hill:	8610
Hab	1:13 **h** thy **tongue** when the wicked devoureth	2790
Rev	2:13 Satan's seat *is*: and thou **h fast** my name,	2902

HOLDETH (9) [HOLD]

Job	2: 3 still he **h fast** his integrity, although thou	2388
	26: 9 He **h back** the face of *his* throne,	270
Ps	66: 9 Which **h** our soul in life, and suffereth not	7760
Pr	11:12 but a man of understanding **h** his **peace**.	2790
	17:28 Even a fool, when he **h** his **peace**,	2790
Da	10:21 *is* none that **h** with me in these *things*,	2388
Am	1: 5 him that **h** the sceptre from the house of	8551
	1: 8 him that **h** the sceptre from Ashkelon,	8551
Rev	2: 1 *things* saith he that **h** the seven stars	2902

HOLDING (9) [HOLD]

Isa	33:15 that shaketh his hands from **h** of bribes,	8551
Jer	6:11 fury of the Lord; I am weary with **h in**:	3557
Mk	7: 3 eat not, **h** the tradition of the elders.	2902
Php	2:16 **H forth** the word of life; that I may rejoice	1907
Col	2:19 And not **h** the head, from which all	2902
1Ti	1:19 **H** faith, and a good conscience;	2192
	3: 9 **H** the mystery of the faith in a pure	2192
Tit	1: 9 **H fast** the faithful word as *he* hath been	472
Rev	7: 1 the four winds of the earth, that the	2902

HOLDS (21) [HOLD]

Nu	13:19 dwell in, whether in tents, or in **strong h**;	4013
Jdg	6: 2 the mountains, and caves, and **strong h**.	4679
1Sa	23:14 abode in the wilderness in **strong h**,	4679
	23:19 himself with us in **strong h** in the wood,	4679
	23:29 and dwelt in **strong h** at En-gedi.	4679
2Ki	8:12 their **strong h** wilt thou set on fire,	4013
2Ch	11:11 fortified the **strong h**, and put captains	4694
Ps	89:40 thou hast brought his **strong h** to ruin.	4013
Isa	23:11 *city*, to destroy the **strong h** thereof.	4581
Jer	48:18 *and* he shall destroy thy **strong h**.	4013
	48:41 the **strong h** are surprised, and the	4679
	51:30 to fight, they have remained in *their* **h**:	4679
La	2: 2 the **strong h** of the daughter of Judah;	4013
	2: 5 he hath destroyed his **strong h**,	4013
Eze	19: 9 they brought him into **h**, that his voice	4685
Da	11:24 forecast his devices against the **strong h**,	4013
	11:39 shall he do in the most strong **h** with a	4013
Mic	5:11 land, and throw down all thy **strong h**:	4013
Na	3:12 All thy **strong h** *shall be like* fig trees	4013
	3:14 waters for the siege, fortify thy **strong h**,	4013
2Co	10: 4 God to the pulling down of **strong h**;)	3794

HOLE (12) [ARMHOLES, HOLE'S, HOLES]

Ex	28:32 there shall be a **h** in the top of it,	6310
	28:32 of woven work round about the **h** of it,	6310
	28:32 as it were the **h** of an habergeon, *that* it	6310
	39:23 *there was* a **h** in the midst of the robe,	6310
	39:23 as the **h** of an habergeon, *with* a band	6310
	39:23 *with* a band round about the **h**, *that* it	6310
2Ki	12: 9 bored a **h** in the lid of it, and set it beside	2356
SS	5: 4 My beloved put in his hand by the **h** *of*	2356
Isa	11: 8 the sucking child shall play on the **h** of	2352
	51: 1 to the **h** of the pit *whence* ye are digged.	4718
Jer	13: 4 and hide it there in a **h** of the rock.	5357
Eze	8: 7 when I looked, behold a **h** in the wall.	2356

HOLE'S (1) [HOLE]

Jer	48:28 her nest in the sides of the **h** mouth.	6354

HOLES (11) [HOLE]

1Sa	14:11 Hebrews come forth out of the **h** where	2356
Isa	2:19 they shall go into the **h** of the rocks,	4631
	7:19 in the **h** of the rocks, and upon all thorns,	5357
	42:22 *they are* all of them snared in **h**,	2352
Jer	16:16 every hill, and out of the **h** of the rocks.	5357
Mic	7:17 they shall move out of their **h** like worms	4526
Na	2:12 filled his **h** *with* prey, and his dens *with*	2356
Hag	1: 6 earneth wages *to put it* into a bag with **h**.	5344
Zec	14:12 their eyes shall consume away in their **h**,	2356
Mt	8:20 The foxes have **h**, and the birds of the air	5454
Lk	9:58 Foxes have **h**, and birds of the air *have*	5454

HOLIER (1) [HOLY]

Isa	65: 5 not near to me; for I am **h** than thou.	6942

HOLIEST (3) [HOLY]

Heb	9: 3 tabernacle which is called the **h** of all;	40+40
	9: 8 the way into the **h** *of all* was not yet made	40
	10:19 boldness to enter into the **h** by the blood of	40

HOLILY (1) [HOLY]

1Th	2:10 and God also, how **h** and justly and	3743

HOLINESS (43) [HOLY]

Ex	15:11 who *is* like thee, glorious in **h**, fearful *in*	6944
	28:36 engravings of a signet, **H** TO THE LORD.	6944
	39:30 engravings of a signet, **H** TO THE LORD.	6944
1Ch	16:29 worship the Lord in the beauty of **h**.	6944
2Ch	20:21 should praise the beauty of **h**, as *they*	6944
	31:18 set office they sanctified themselves *in* **h**:	6944
Ps	29: 2 worship the Lord in the beauty of **h**.	6944
	30: 4 give thanks at the remembrance of his **h**.	6944
	48: 1 city of our God, *in* the mountain of his **h**.	6944
	60: 6 God hath spoken in his **h**; I will rejoice,	6944
	89:35 Once have I sworn by my **h** that I will not	6944
	93: 5 **h** becometh thine house, O Lord,	6944
	96: 9 O worship the Lord in the beauty of **h**:	6944
	97:12 give thanks at the remembrance of his **h**.	6944
	108: 7 God hath spoken in his **h**; I will rejoice,	6944
	110: 3 in the beauties of **h** from the womb of	6944
Isa	23:18 and her hire shall be **h** to the Lord:	6944
	35: 8 way, and it shall be called The way of **h**;	6944
	62: 9 shall drink it in the courts of my **h**.	6944
	63:15 behold from the habitation of thy **h** and	6944
	63:18 The people of thy **h** have possessed *it* but	6944
Jer	2: 3 Israel *was* **h** unto the Lord,	6944
	23: 9 and because of the words of his **h**.	6944
	31:23 habitation of justice, *and* mountain of **h**.	6944
Am	4: 2 The Lord God hath sworn by his **h**,	6944
Ob	1:17 shall be deliverance, and there shall be **h**;	6944
Zec	14:20 bells of the horses, **H** UNTO THE LORD;	6944
	14:21 in Judah shall be **h** unto the Lord of	6944
Mal	2:11 for Judah hath profaned the **h** of	6944
Lk	1:75 In **h** and righteousness before him,	3742
Ac	3:12 or **h** we had made this *man* to walk?	2150
Ro	1: 4 according to the Spirit of **h**,	42
	6:19 members servants to righteousness unto **h**.	38
	6:22 ye have your fruit unto **h**, and the end	38
2Co	7: 1 and spirit, perfecting **h** in the fear of God.	42
Eph	4:24 is created in righteousness and true **h**.	3742
1Th	3:13 your hearts unblameable in **h** before God,	42
	4: 7 called us unto uncleanness, but unto **h**.	38
1Ti	2:15 in faith and charity and **h** with sobriety.	38
Tit	2: 3 *that they be* in behaviour **as becometh h**,	2412
Heb	12:10 profit, that *we* might be partakers of his **h**.	41
	12:14 Follow peace with all *men*, and **h**,	38

HOLLOW (10)

Ge	32:25 him, he touched the **h** of his thigh;	3709
	32:25 the **h** of Jacob's thigh was out of joint,	3709
	32:32 which *is* upon the **h** of the thigh, unto	3709
	32:32 he touched the **h** of Jacob's thigh in	3709
Ex	27: 8 **H** with boards shalt thou make it: as it	5014
	38: 7 withal; he made the *altar* with boards.	5014
Lev	14:37 in the walls of the house with **h** strakes,	8258
Jdg	15:19 God clave a **h** place *that was* in the jaw,	4388
Isa	40:12 the waters in the **h** of his **hand**,	8168
Jer	52:21 thereof *was* four fingers: *it was* **h**.	5014

HOLON (3)

Jos	15:51 Goshen, and **H**, and Giloh; eleven cities	2473
	21:15 **H** with her suburbs, and Debir with her	2473
Jer	48:21 upon **H**, and upon Jahazah,	2473

HOLPEN (5) [HELP]

Ps	83: 8 they have **h** the children of Lot. Selah.	2220
	86:17 Lord, hast **h** me, and comforted me.	5826
Isa	31: 3 he that is **h** shall fall down, and they all	5826
Da	11:34 shall fall, they shall be **h** *with* a little help:	5826
Lk	1:54 hath **h** his servant Israel, in remembrance	482

HOLY (611) [HOLIER, HOLIEST, HOLILY, HOLINESS, HOLYDAY, UNHOLY]

Ex	3: 5 for the place whereon thou standest *is* **h**	6944
	12:16 in the first day *there shall be* a **h**	6944
	12:16 in the seventh day there shall be a **h**	6944
	15:13 in thy strength unto thy **h** habitation.	6944
	16:23 To morrow *is* the rest of the **h** sabbath	6944
	19: 6 me a kingdom of priests, and a nation.	6918
	20: 8 Remember the sabbath day, to **keep** it **h**.	6942
	22:31 ye shall be **h** men unto me: neither shall	6944
	26:33 vail shall divide unto you between the **h**	6944
	26:33 the holy *place* and the **most h**.	6944+6944
	26:34 the Testimony in the **most h** *place*.	6944+6944
	28: 2 thou shalt make **h** garments for Aaron thy	6944
	28: 4 they shall make **h** garments for Aaron they	6944
	28:29 when he goeth in unto the **h** *place*, for a	6944
	28:35 in unto the **h** *place* before the Lord,	6944
	28:38 that Aaron may bear the iniquity of the **h**	6944
	28:38 of Israel shall hallow in all their **h** gifts;	6944
	28:43 in the **h** *place*; that they bear not iniquity,	6944
	29: 6 and put the **h** crown upon the mitre.	6944
	29:29 the **h** garments of Aaron shall be his sons'	6944
	29:30 congregation to minister in the **h** *place*.	6944
	29:31 and seethe his flesh in the **h** place.	6918
	29:33 shall not eat *thereof*, because they *are* **h**.	6944
	29:34 it shall not be eaten, because it *is* **h**.	6944
	29:37 and it shall be an altar **most h**:	6944+6944
	29:37 whatsoever toucheth the altar shall be **h**.	6942
	30:10 it *is* **most h** unto the Lord.	6944+6944
	30:25 thou shalt make it an oil of the **h** ointment,	6944
	30:25 apothecary: it shall be a **h** anointing oil.	6944
	30:29 that they may be **most h**:	6944+6944
	30:29 whatsoever toucheth them shall be **h**.	6942
	30:31 This shall be a **h** anointing oil unto me	6944
	30:32 of it: it *is* **h**, *and* it shall be holy unto you.	6944
	30:32 of it: it *is* holy, *and* it shall be **h** unto you.	6944

Ex	30:35 tempered together, pure *and* **h**:	6944
	30:36 it shall be unto you **most h**.	6944
	30:37 it shall be unto thee **h** for the Lord.	6944
	31:10 the **h** garments for Aaron the priest,	6944
	31:11 sweet incense for the **h** *place*: according	6944
	31:14 the sabbath therefore; for it *is* **h** unto you:	6944
	31:15 *is* the sabbath of rest, **h** to the Lord:	6944
	35: 2 the seventh day there shall be to you a **h**	6944
	35:19 to do service in the **h** *place*, the holy	6944
	35:19 to do service in the holy *place*, the **h**	6944
	35:21 for all his service, and for the **h** garments.	6944
	37:29 he made the **h** anointing oil, and the pure	6944
	38:24 the **h** *place*, even the gold of the offering,	6944
	39: 1 to do service in the **h** *place*, and made	6944
	39: 1 and made the **h** garments for Aaron;	6944
	39:30 made the plate of the **h** crown *of* pure	6944
	39:41 clothes of service to do service in the **h**	6944
	39:41 and the **h** garments for Aaron the priest,	6944
	40: 9 all the vessels thereof; and it shall be **h**.	6944
	40:10 and it shall be an altar **most h**.	6944+6944
	40:13 shalt put upon Aaron the **h** garments,	6944
Lev	2: 3 *it is* a thing **most h** of the offerings	6944+6944
	2:10 *it is* a **thing most h** of the offerings	6944+6944
	5:15 in the **h** *things* of the Lord;	6944
	5:16 harm that he hath done in the **h** *thing*,	6944
	6:16 bread shall it be eaten in the **h** place;	6918
	6:17 it *is* **most h**, as *is* the sin offering;	6944+6944
	6:18 every one that toucheth them shall be **h**.	6942
	6:25 before the Lord: it *is* **most h**.	6944+6944
	6:26 the **h** place shall it be eaten, in the court	6918
	6:27 shall touch the flesh thereof shall be **h**:	6942
	6:27 whereon it was sprinkled in the **h** place.	6918
	6:29 shall eat thereof: it *is* **most h**.	6944+6944
	6:30 *withal* in the **h** *place*, shall be eaten:	6944
	7: 1 the trespass offering: it *is* **most h**.	6944+6944
	7: 6 it shall be eaten in the **h** place: it *is* most	6918
	7: 6 in the **h** place: it *is* **most h**.	6944+6944
	8: 9 did he put the golden plate, the **h** crown;	6944
	10:10 that *ye* may put difference between **h** and	6944
	10:12 beside the altar: for it *is* **most h**:	6944+6944
	10:13 ye shall eat it in the **h** place, because it *is*	6918
	10:17 not eaten the sin offering in the **h** place,	6944
	10:17 seeing it *is* **most h**, and *God* hath	6944+6944
	10:18 *h place*: ye should indeed have eaten it in	6944
	10:18 eaten it in the **h** *place*, as I commanded.	6944
	11:44 sanctify yourselves, and ye shall be **h**;	6918
	11:44 and ye shall be holy; for I am **h**:	6918
	11:45 ye shall therefore be **h**, for I *am* holy.	6918
	11:45 ye shall therefore be holy, for I *am* **h**.	6918
	14:13 and the burnt offering, in the **h** place:	6944
	14:13 *is* the trespass offering: it *is* **most h**:	6944+6944
	16: 2 that he come not at all times into the **h**	6944
	16: 3 Thus shall Aaron come into the **h** *place*:	6944
	16: 4 He shall put on the **h** linen coat,	6944
	16: 4 these *are* **h** garments; therefore shall he	6944
	16:16 shall make an atonement for the **h** *place*,	6944
	16:17 atonement in the **h** *place*, until he come	6944
	16:20 made an end of reconciling the **h** *place*,	6944
	16:23 he put on when he went into the **h** *place*,	6944
	16:24 shall wash his flesh with water in the **h**	6918
	16:27 **h** *place*, shall *one* carry forth without	6944
	16:32 the linen clothes, *even* the **h** garments:	6944
	16:33 he shall make an atonement for the **h**	6944
	19: 2 Israel, and say unto them, Ye shall be **h**:	6918
	19: 2 be holy: for I the Lord your God *am* **h**.	6918
	19:24 shall be **h** to praise the Lord *withal*.	6944
	20: 3 my sanctuary, and to profane my **h** name.	6944
	20: 7 Sanctify yourselves therefore, and be ye **h**:	6918
	20:26 ye shall be **h** unto me: for I the Lord *am*	6918
	20:26 for I the Lord *am* **h**, and have severed	6918
	21: 6 They shall be **h** unto their God,	6944
	21: 6 they do offer: therefore they shall be **h**.	6918
	21: 7 her husband: for he *is* **h** unto his God.	6918
	21: 8 he shall be **h** unto thee: for I the Lord,	6918
	21: 8 for I the Lord, which sanctify you, *am* **h**.	6918
	21:22 of the **most h**, and of the holy.	6944+6944
	21:22 *both* of the most holy, and of the **h**.	6944
	22: 2 that they separate themselves from the **h**	6944
	22: 2 that they profane not my **h** name *in those*	6944
	22: 3 that goeth unto the **h** *things* which	6944
	22: 4 shall not eat of the **h** *things*, until he	6944
	22: 6 not eat of the **h** *things*, unless he wash	6944
	22: 7 shall afterward eat of the **h** *things*;	6944
	22:10 There shall no stranger eat *of* the **h** *thing*:	6944
	22:10 hired servant, shall not eat *of* the **h** thing.	6944
	22:12 she may not eat of an offering of the **h**	6944
	22:14 if a man eat *of* the **h** *thing* unwittingly,	6944
	22:14 shall give *it* unto the priest with the **h**	6944
	22:15 they shall not profane the **h** *things* of	6944
	22:16 when they eat their **h** things: for I	6944
	22:32 Neither shall ye profane my **h** name;	6944
	23: 2 which ye shall proclaim *to be* **h**	6944
	23: 3 *is* the sabbath of rest, a **h** convocation;	6944
	23: 4 feasts of the Lord, *even* **h** convocations,	6944
	23: 7 In the first day ye shall have a **h**	6944
	23: 8 in the seventh day *is* a **h** convocation:	6944
	23:20 they shall be **h** to the Lord for the priest.	6944
	23:21 *that* it may be a **h** convocation unto you:	6944
	23:24 of blowing of trumpets, a **h** convocation.	6944
	23:27 it shall be a **h** convocation unto you;	6944
	23:35 On the first day *shall be* a **h** convocation:	6944
	23:36 the eighth day shall be a **h** convocation	6944
	23:37 which ye shall proclaim *to be* **h**	6944
	24: 9 and they shall eat it in the **h** place:	6918
	24: 9 for it *is* **most h** unto him of	6944+6944

H

Lev 25:12 For it *is* the jubile; it shall be **h** unto you: 6944
27: 9 giveth of such unto the LORD shall be **h**. 6944
27:10 it and the exchange thereof shall be **h**. 6944
27:14 a man shall sanctify his house *to be* **h** 6944
27:21 shall be **h** unto the LORD, as a field 6944
27:23 in that day, *as a* **h** thing unto the LORD. 6944
27:28 every devoted thing *is* most **h** unto 6944+6944
27:30 *is* the LORD's: *it is* **h** unto the LORD. 6944
27:32 the tenth shall be **h** unto the LORD. 6944
27:33 both it and the change thereof shall be **h**; 6944
Nu 4: 4 *about* the **most h** things: 6944+6944
4:15 they shall not touch *any* **h** thing, lest they 6944
4:19 unto the **most h** things: Aaron 6944+6944
4:20 they shall not go in to see when the **h** 6944
5: 9 every offering of all the **h** *things of* 6944
5:17 the priest shall take **h** water in an earthen 6918
6: 5 he shall be **h**, *and* shall let the locks of 6918
6: 8 All the days of his separation he *is* **h** unto 6944
6:20 this *is* **h** for the priest, with the wave 6944
15:40 and be **h** unto your God. 6918
16: 3 seeing all the congregation *are* **h**, every 6918
16: 5 will shew who *are* his, and who *is* **h**; 6918
16: 7 the LORD doth choose, he *shall be* **h**: 6918
18: 9 This shall be thine of the **most h** 6944+6944
18: 9 **most h** for thee and for thy sons. 6944+6944
18:10 the **most h** *place* shalt thou eat it; 6944+6944
18:10 male shall eat it: it shall be **h** unto thee. 6944
18:17 a goat, thou shalt not redeem; they *are* **h**: 6944
18:19 All the heave offerings of the **h** things, 6944
18:32 neither shall ye pollute the **h** things of 6944
28: 7 in the *place* shalt thou cause the strong 6944
28:18 In the first day *shall be* an **h** convocation; 6944
28:25 on the seventh day ye shall have a **h** 6944
28:26 after your weeks *be out*, ye shall have a **h** 6944
29: 1 the month, ye shall have a **h** convocation; 6944
29: 7 of this seventh month a **h** convocation; 6944
29:12 month ye shall have a **h** convocation; 6944
31: 6 with the instruments, and the trumpets 6944
35:25 which was anointed with the **h** oil. 6944
Dt 7: 6 For thou *art* a **h** people unto the LORD 6918
12:26 Only thy **h** things which thou hast, 6944
14: 2 For thou *art* a **h** people unto the LORD 6918
14:21 for thou *art* a **h** people unto the LORD thy 6918
23:14 thee; therefore shall thy camp be **h**: 6918
26:15 Look down from thy **h** habitation, 6944
26:19 that thou mayest be a **h** people unto 6918
28: 9 The LORD shall establish thee a **h** people 6918
33: 8 and thy Urim *be* with thy **h** one, 2623
Jos 5:15 for the place whereon thou standest *is* **h**. 6944
24:19 for he *is* a **h** God; he *is* a jealous God; 6918
1Sa 2: 2 *There* is none **h** as the LORD: for *there is* 6918
6:20 Who is able to stand before this **h** LORD 6918
21: 5 and the vessels of the young men are **h**, 6944
1Ki 6:16 *even* for the **most h** place. 6944+6944
7:50 **most h** place, *and* for the doors 6944+6944
8: 4 the **h** vessels that *were* in the tabernacle, 6944
8: 6 to the **most h** place, even under 6944+6944
8: 8 seen out in the **h** place before the oracle, 6944
8:10 when the priests were come out of the **h** 6944
2Ki 4: 9 I perceive that this *is* a **h** man of God, 6918
19:22 *even* against the **H One** of Israel. 6918
1Ch 6:49 all the work of the *place* **most h**, 6944+6944
16:10 Glory ye in his **h** name: let the heart of 6944
16:35 that we may give thanks to thy **h** name, 6944
22:19 of the LORD, and the **h** vessels of God, 6944
23:13 should sanctify the **most h** things, 6944+6944
23:28 in the purifying of all **h** things, and 6944
23:32 the charge of the **h** place, and the charge 6944
29: 3 above all *that* I have prepared for the **h** 6944
29:16 for to build thee an **h** name *cometh* of thine hand, 6944
2Ch 3: 8 made the **most h** house, the length 6944+6944
3:10 in the **h** house he made two 6944+6944
4:22 doors thereof for the **most h** place, 6944+6944
5: 5 the **h** vessels that *were* in the tabernacle, 6944
5: 7 into the **most h** place, even under 6944+6944
5:11 when the priests were come out of the **h** 6944
8:11 *the* places *are* **h**, whereunto the ark 6944
23: 6 Levites; they shall go in, for they *are* **h**: 6944
29: 5 forth the filthiness out of the **h** place. 6944
29: 7 in the **h** place unto the God of Israel. 6944
30:27 their prayer came *up* to his **h** **dwelling** 6944
31: 6 the tithe of **h** things which were 6944
31:14 the LORD, and the **most h** things. 6944+6944
35: 3 all Israel, which were **h** unto the LORD, 6918
35: 3 Put the **h** ark in the house which Solomon 6944
35: 5 stand in the **h** place according to 6944
35:13 the *other* **h** offerings sod they in pots, 6944
Ezr 2:63 **most h** things till there stood *up* a 6944+6944
8:28 said unto them, Ye *are* **h** unto the LORD; 6944
8:28 the vessels *are* **h** also; and the silver and 6944
9: 2 that the **h** seed have mingled themselves 6944
9: 8 and to give us a nail in his **h** place, 6944
Ne 7:65 **most h** things, till there stood *up* a 6944+6944
8: 9 This day *is* **h** unto the LORD your God; 6918
8:10 for this day *is* **h** unto our Lord: neither be 6918
8:11 Hold your peace, for the day *is* **h**; 6918
9:14 madest known unto them thy **h** sabbath, 6944
10:31 of them on the sabbath, or on the **h** day: 6944
10:33 for the **h** things, and for the sin offerings 6944
11: 1 of ten to dwell in Jerusalem the **h** city, 6944
11:18 All the Levites in the **h** city *were* two 6944
12:47 they sanctified *h* things unto the Levites; NIH
Job 6:10 not concealed the words of the **H One**. 6918
Ps 2: 6 Yet have I set my king upon my **h** hill of 6944
3: 4 voice, and he heard me out of his **h** hill. 6944

Ps 5: 7 in thy fear will I worship toward thy **h** 6944
11: 4 The LORD *is* in his **h** temple, 6944
15: 1 who shall dwell in thy **h** hill? 6944
16:10 neither wilt thou suffer thine **H One** to 2623
20: 6 he will hear him from his **h** heaven with 6944
22: 3 *art* **h**, O thou that inhabitest the praises 6918
24: 3 and who shall stand in his **h** place? 6944
28: 2 when I lift up my hands toward thy **h** 6944
33:21 because we have trusted in his **h** name. 6944
43: 3 let them bring me unto thy **h** hill, and to 6944
46: 4 the **h** place of the tabernacles of the most 6918
51:11 and take not thy **h** Spirit from me. 6944
65: 4 of thy house, *even* of thy **h** temple. 6918
68: 5 of the widows, *is* God in his **h** habitation. 6944
68:17 is among them, *as in* Sinai, in the **h** place. 6944
68:35 God, *thou art* terrible out of thy **h** places: 4720
71:22 with the harp, O thou **H One** of Israel. 6918
78:41 and limited the **H One** of Israel. 6918
79: 1 thy **h** temple have they defiled; they have 6944
86: 2 Preserve my soul; for I *am* **h**: O thou my 2623
87: 1 His foundation *is* in the **h** mountains. 6944
89:18 and the **H One** of Israel *is* our king. 6918
89:19 thou spakest in vision to thy **h** one, 2623
89:20 with my **h** oil have I anointed him: 6944
98: 1 his **h** arm, hath gotten him the victory. 6944
99: 3 thy great and terrible name; *for it is* **h**. 6918
99: 5 and worship at his footstool; *for he is* **h**. 6918
99: 9 LORD our God, and worship at his **h** hill; 6944
99: 9 his holy hill; for the LORD our God *is* **h**. 6918
103: 1 all that is within me, *bless* his **h** name. 6944
105: 3 Glory ye in his **h** name: let the heart of 6944
105:42 For he remembered his **h** promise, 6944
106:47 to give thanks unto thy **h** name, 6944
111: 9 for ever: **h** and reverend *is* his name. 6944
138: 2 I will worship toward thy **h** temple, 6944
145:17 in all his ways, and **h** in all his works. 2623
145:21 let all flesh bless his **h** name for ever and 6944
Pr 9:10 the knowledge of the **h** *is* understanding. 6918
20:25 the man *who* devoureth *that which is* **h**, 6944
30: 3 nor have the knowledge of the **h**. 6918
Ecc 8:10 come and gone from the place of the **h**, 6944
Isa 1: 4 they have provoked the **H One** of Israel 6918
4: 3 remaineth in Jerusalem, shall be called **h**, 6918
5:16 God that is **h** shall be sanctified in 6918
5:19 the counsel of the **H One** of Israel draw 6918
5:24 despised the word of the **H One** of Israel. 6918
6: 3 said, **H**, holy, holy, *is* the LORD of hosts: 6918
6: 3 said, Holy, **h**, holy, *is* the LORD of hosts. 6918
6: 3 said, Holy, holy, **h**, *is* the LORD of hosts. 6918
6:13 *so* the **h** seed *shall be* the substance 6944
10:17 be for a fire, and his **H One** for a flame: 6918
10:20 the LORD, the **H One** of Israel, in truth. 6918
11: 9 shall not hurt nor destroy in all my **h** 6944
12: 6 great *is* the **H One** of Israel in the midst 6918
17: 7 eyes shall have respect to the **H One** of 6918
27:13 shall worship the LORD in the **h** mount at 6944
29:19 men shall rejoice in the **H One** of Israel. 6918
29:23 sanctify the **H One** of Jacob, and shall 6918
30:11 cause the **H One** of Israel to cease from 6918
30:12 Wherefore thus saith the **H One** of Israel, 6918
30:15 saith the LORD GOD, the **H One** of Israel, 6918
30:29 *in* the night when a **h** solemnity is **kept**; 6942
31: 1 they look not unto the **H One** of Israel, 6918
37:23 high? *even* against the **H One** of Israel. 6918
40:25 or shall I be equal? saith the **H One**. 6918
41:14 thy redeemer, the **H One** of Israel. 6918
41:16 *and* shalt glory in the **H One** of Israel. 6918
41:20 and the **H One** of Israel hath created it. 6918
43: 3 God, the **H One** of Israel, thy Saviour: 6918
43:14 your redeemer, the **H One** of Israel; 6918
43:15 I *am* the LORD, your **H One**, the creator 6918
45:11 the **H One** of Israel, and his maker, 6918
47: 4 of hosts *is* his name, the **H One** of Israel. 6918
48: 2 For they call themselves of the **h** city, 6944
48:17 thy redeemer, the **H One** of Israel; 6918
49: 7 and the **H One** of Israel, and he shall 6918
49: 7 the redeemer of Israel, *and* his **H One**, 6918
52: 1 garments, O Jerusalem, the **h** city: 6944
52:10 The LORD hath made bare his **h** arm in 6944
54: 5 and thy redeemer the **H One** of Israel; 6918
55: 5 thy God, and for the **H One** of Israel; 6918
56: 7 them will I bring to my **h** mountain, 6944
57:13 land, and shall inherit my **h** mountain; 6944
57:15 inhabiteth eternity, whose name *is* **H**; 6918
57:15 **h** place, with him also *that is* of a contrite 6918
58:13 *from* doing thy pleasure on my **h** day; 6944
58:13 a delight, the **h** of the LORD, honourable; 6918
60: 9 to the **H One** of Israel, because he hath 6918
60:14 The Zion of the **H One** of Israel. 6918
62:12 they shall call them, The **h** people, 6944
63:10 they rebelled, and vexed his **h** Spirit: 6944
63:11 *is* he that put his **h** Spirit within him? 6944
64:10 Thy **h** cities are a wilderness, Zion is a 6944
64:11 Our **h** and our beautiful house, where our 6944
65:11 that forget my **h** mountain, that prepare a 6944
65:25 They shall not hurt nor destroy in all my **h** 6944
66:20 to my **h** mountain Jerusalem, saith 6944
Jer 11:15 and the **h** flesh is passed from thee? 6944
25:30 and utter his voice from his **h** habitation; 6944
31:40 the east, *shall be* **h** unto the LORD; 6944
50:29 the LORD, against the **H One** of Israel. 6918
51: 5 filled *with* sin against the **H One** of Israel. 6918
Eze 7:24 cease; and their **h** places shall be defiled. 6942
20:39 pollute ye my **h** name no more with your 6944
20:40 in mine **h** mountain, in the mountain of 6944

Eze 20:40 of your oblations, with all your **h** things. 6944
21: 2 drop *thy word* toward the **h** places, 4720
22: 8 Thou hast despised mine **h** *things*, and 6944
22:26 have profaned mine **h** *things*: they have 6944
22:26 have put no difference between the **h** 6944
28:14 thou wast upon the **h** mountain of God; 6944
36:20 they went, they profaned my **h** name, 6944
36:21 I had pity for mine **h** name, which 6944
36:22 of Israel, but for mine **h** name's sake, 6944
36:38 As the **h** flock, as the flock of Jerusalem 6944
39: 7 So will I make my **h** name known in 6944
39: 7 I will not let *them* pollute my **h** name any 6944
39: 7 that I *am* the LORD, the **H One** in Israel. 6918
39:25 and will be jealous for my **h** name; 6944
41: 4 unto me, This *is* the **most h** place. 6944+6944
42:13 the separate place, they *be* **h** chambers, 6944
42:13 **most h** *things*: there shall they lay 6944+6944
42:13 shall they lay the **most h** things, 6944+6944
42:13 the trespass offering; for the place *is* **h**. 6918
42:14 shall they not go out of the **h** place into 6944
42:14 for they *are* **h**; and shall put on other 6944
43: 7 my **h** name, shall the house of Israel no 6944
43: 8 they have even defiled my **h** name by 6944
43:12 round about *shall be* **most h**. 6944+6944
44: 8 ye have not kept the charge of mine **h** 6944
44:13 nor to come near to any of my **h** *things*, 6944
44:13 holy *things*, in the **most h** *place*: 6944+6944
44:19 lay them in the **h** chambers, and they shall 6944
44:23 my people the *difference* between the **h** 6944
45: 1 unto the LORD, a **h** *portion* of the land: 6944
45: 1 This *shall be* **h** in all the borders thereof 6944
45: 3 sanctuary *and* the **most h** *place*. 6944+6944
45: 4 The **h** *portion* of the land shall be for 6944
45: 4 a **h** place for the sanctuary. 4720
45: 6 over against the oblation of the **h** *portion*: 6944
45: 7 on the other side of the oblation of the **h** 6944
45: 7 before the oblation of the **h** *portion*, and 6944
46:19 into the **h** chambers of the priests, 6944
48:10 for the priests, shall be *this* **h** oblation: 6944
48:12 **most h** by the border of the Levites 6944+6944
48:14 of the land: for *it is* **h** unto the LORD. 6944
48:18 **h** *portion* shall be ten thousand eastward, 6944
48:18 shall be over against the oblation of the **h** 6944
48:20 ye shall offer the **h** oblation foursquare, 6944
48:21 side and on the other of the **h** oblation, 6944
48:21 shall be the **h** oblation; and the sanctuary 6944
Da 4: 8 and in whom *is* the spirit of the **h** gods: 6922
4: 9 I know that the spirit of the **h** gods *is* in 6922
4:13 and a **h** one came down from heaven; 6922
4:17 the demand *by* the word of the **h** ones: 6922
4:18 for the spirit of the **h** gods *is* in thee. 6922
4:23 and a **h** one coming down from heaven, 6922
5:11 in whom *is* the spirit of the **h** gods; 6922
8:24 shall destroy the mighty and the **h** people. 6918
9:16 from thy city Jerusalem, thy **h** mountain: 6944
9:20 my God for the **h** mountain of my God; 6944
9:24 upon thy people and upon thy **h** city, 6944
9:24 and to anoint the **most H**. 6944+6944
11:28 his heart *shall be* against the **h** covenant; 6944
11:30 have indignation against the **h** covenant: 6944
11:30 with them that forsake the **h** covenant. 6944
11:45 the seas in the glorious **h** mountain; 6944
12: 7 to scatter the power of the **h** people, 6944
Hos 11: 9 not man; the **H One** in the midst of thee: 6918
Joel 2: 1 and sound an alarm in my **h** mountain: 6944
3:17 God dwelling in Zion, my **h** mountain: 6944
3:17 shall Jerusalem be **h**, and there shall no 6944
Am 2: 7 the *same* maid, to profane my **h** name: 6944
Ob 1:16 as ye have drunk upon my **h** mountain, 6944
Jnh 2: 4 yet I will look again toward thy **h** temple. 6944
2: 7 came in unto thee, into thine **h** temple. 6944
Mic 1: 2 against you, the Lord from his **h** temple. 6944
Hab 1:12 O LORD my God, mine **H One**? 6918
2:20 the LORD *is* in his **h** temple: let all 6944
3: 3 and the **H One** from mount Paran. 6918
Zep 3:11 be haughty because of my **h** mountain. 6944
Hag 2:12 If one bear **h** flesh in the skirt of his 6944
2:12 or wine, or oil, or any meat, shall it be **h**? 6942
Zec 2:12 inherit Judah his portion in the **h** land, 6944
2:13 for he is raised up out of his **h** habitation. 6944
8: 3 the mountain of the LORD of hosts the **h** 6944
Mt 1:18 she was found with child of the **H** Ghost. 40
1:20 that which is conceived in her is of the **H** 40
3:11 he shall baptize you with the **H** Ghost, 40
4: 5 the devil taketh him *up* into the **h** city, 40
7: 6 **Give not that which is h unto the dogs,** 40
12:31 **blasphemy against the *H* Ghost shall not** NIG
12:32 **whosoever speaketh against the H Ghost,** 40
24:15 **stand in the h place, (whoso readeth, let** 40
25:31 **all the h angels with him, then shall he sit** 40
27:53 **went into the h city, and appeared unto** 40
28:19 **and of the Son, and of the H Ghost:** 40
Mk 1: 8 **he shall baptize you with the H Ghost.** 40
1:24 **thee who thou art, the H One of God.** 40
3:29 **But he that shall blaspheme against the H** 40
6:20 **knowing that he was a just man and a h,** 40
8:38 **in the glory of his Father with the h. angels.** 40
12:36 **For David himself said by the H Ghost,** 40
13:11 **for it is not ye that speak, but the H Ghost.** 40
Lk 1:15 **and he shall be filled with the H Ghost,** 40
1:35 **The H Ghost shall come upon thee,** 40
1:35 *that* **h thing which shall be born of thee** 40
1:41 **and Elisabeth was filled with the H Ghost:** 40
1:49 **done to me great things; and h is his name.** 40
1:67 **his father Zacharias was filled with the H** 40

Lk
1:70 he spake by the mouth of his **h** prophets, 40
1:72 fathers, and to remember his **h** covenant; 40
2:23 the womb shall be called **h** to the Lord;) 40
2:25 of Israel: and the **H** Ghost was upon him. 40
2:26 it was revealed unto him by the **H** Ghost, 40
3:16 he shall baptize you with the **H** Ghost and 40
3:22 the **H** Ghost descended in a bodily shape 40
4: 1 Jesus being full of the **H** Ghost returned 40
4:34 who thou art, the **H** One of God. 40
9:26 and in his Father's, and of the **h** angels. 40
11:13 Father give the **H** Spirit to them that ask 40
12:10 unto him that blasphemeth against the **H** 40
12:12 the **H** Ghost shall teach you in the same 40

Jn
1:33 the same is he which baptizeth with the **H** 40
7:39 for the **H** was not yet given; because 40
14:26 But the Comforter, which is the **H** Ghost, 40
17:11 **H** Father, keep through thine own name 40
20:22 saith unto them, Receive ye the **H** Ghost: 40

Ac
1: 2 that he through the **H** Ghost had given 40
1: 5 ye shall be baptized with the **H** Ghost not 40
1: 8 after that the **H** Ghost is come upon you: 40
1:16 which the **H** Ghost by the mouth of David 40
2: 4 And they were all filled with the **H** Ghost, 40
2:27 neither wilt thou suffer thine **H** One to 3741
2:33 of the Father the promise of the **H** Ghost, 40
2:38 and ye shall receive the gift of the **H** Ghost. 40
3:14 But ye denied the **H** One and the Just, 40
3:21 of all his **h** prophets since the world began. 40
4: 8 Peter, filled with the **H** Ghost, said unto 40
4:27 For of a truth against thy **h** child Jesus, 40
4:30 wonders may be done by the name of thy **h** 40
4:31 and they were all filled with the **H** Ghost, 40
5: 3 hath Satan filled thine heart to lie to the **H** 40
5:32 and so is also the **H** Ghost, whom God hath 40
6: 3 full of the **H** Ghost and wisdom, whom we 40
6: 5 a man full of faith and of the **H** Ghost, 40
6:13 blasphemous words against this **h** place, 40
7:33 the place where thou standest is **h** ground. 40
7:51 and ears, ye do always resist the **H** Ghost: 40
7:55 But he, being full of the **H** Ghost, looked up 40
8:15 them, that they might receive the **H** Ghost. 40
8:17 on them, and that they received the **H** Ghost. 40
8:18 the apostles' hands the **H** Ghost was given, 40
8:19 I lay hands, he may receive the **H** Ghost. 40
9:17 thy sight, and be filled with the **H** Ghost. 40
9:31 and in the comfort of the **H** Ghost, 40
10:22 was warned from God by a **h** angel to send 40
10:38 Jesus of Nazareth with the **H** Ghost 40
10:44 the **H** Ghost fell on all them which heard 40
10:45 also was poured out the gift of the **H** Ghost. 40
10:47 which have received the **H** Ghost as well as 40
11:15 I began to speak, the **H** Ghost fell on them, 40
11:16 but ye shall be baptized with the **H** Ghost. 40
11:24 and full of the **H** Ghost and of faith. 40
13: 2 and fasted, the **H** Ghost said, Separate me 40
13: 4 So they, being sent forth by the **H** Ghost, 40
13: 9 filled with the **H** Ghost, set his eyes on 40
13:35 not suffer thine **H** One to see corruption. 3741
13:52 were filled with joy, and with the **H** Ghost, 40
15: 8 them witness, giving them the **H** Ghost, 40
15:28 it seemed good to the **H** Ghost, and to us, 40
16: 6 were forbidden of the **H** Ghost to preach 40
19: 2 Have ye received the **H** Ghost since ye 40
19: 2 as heard whether there be any **H** Ghost. 40
19: 6 upon them, the **H** Ghost came on them; 40
20:23 Save that the **H** Ghost witnesseth in every 40
20:28 over the which the **H** Ghost hath made you 40
21:11 and feet, and said, Thus saith the **H** Ghost, 40
21:28 the temple, and hath polluted this **h** place. 40
28:25 Well spake the **H** Ghost by Esaias the 40

Ro
1: 2 afore by his prophets in the **h** scriptures,) 40
5: 5 by the **H** Ghost which is given unto us. 40
7:12 Wherefore the law is **h**, 40
7:12 the commandment **h**, and just, and good. 40
9: 1 also bearing me witness in the **H** Ghost, 40
11:16 if the firstfruit be **h**, the lump is also holy: 40
11:16 the lump is also **h**: and if the root be holy, NIG
11:16 the lump is also holy: and if the root be **h**, 40
12: 1 **h**, acceptable unto God, which is your 40
14:17 and peace, and joy in the **H** Ghost. 40
15:13 in hope, through the power of the **H** Ghost. 40
15:16 being sanctified by the **H** Ghost. 40
16:16 Salute one another with a **h** kiss. 40

1Co
2:13 but which the **H** Ghost teacheth; 40
3:17 the temple of God is **h**, which temple ye 40
6:19 the temple of the **H** Ghost which is in you, 40
7:14 your children unclean; but now are they **h**. 40
7:34 she may be both in body and in spirit: 40
9:13 **h** things live of the things of the temple? 2413
12: 3 that Jesus is the Lord, but by the **H** Ghost. 40
16:20 Greet one another with a **h** kiss. 40

2Co
6: 6 by kindness, by the **H** Ghost, 40
13:12 Greet one another with a **h** kiss. 40
13:14 the communion of the **H** Ghost, be with 40

Eph
1: 4 that we should be **h** and without blame 40
1:13 ye were sealed with that **h** Spirit of promise, 40
2:21 groweth unto a **h** temple in the Lord: 40
3: 5 as it is now revealed unto his **h** apostles and 40
4:30 And grieve not the **h** Spirit of God, 40
5:27 any such thing; but that it should be **h** and 40

Col
1:22 to present you **h** and unblameable and 40
3:12 And beloved, bowels of mercies, kindness, 40

1Th
1: 5 in the **H** Ghost, and in much assurance; 40
1: 6 in much affliction, with joy of the **H** Ghost: 40
4: 8 who hath also given unto us his **h** Spirit. 40

1Th
5:26 Greet all the brethren with a **h** kiss. 40
5:27 this epistle be read unto all the **h** brethren. 40

1Ti
2: 8 lifting up **h** hands, without wrath and 3741

2Ti
1: 9 saved us, and called us with a **h** calling, 40
1:14 keep by the **H** Ghost which dwelleth in us. 40
3:15 a child thou hast known the **h** scriptures, 2413

Tit
1: 8 of good men, sober, just, **h**, temperate; 3741
3: 5 regeneration, and renewing of the **H** Ghost; 40

Heb
2: 4 divers miracles, and gifts of the **H** Ghost, 40
3: 1 Wherefore, **h** brethren, partakers of 40
3: 7 Wherefore, as the **H** Ghost saith, To day if 40
6: 4 and were made partakers of the **H** Ghost, 40
7:26 who is **h**, harmless, undefiled, 3741
9: 8 The **H** Ghost this signifying, that the way 40
9:12 **h** place, having obtained eternal redemption 40
9:24 For Christ is not entered into the **h** places 40
9:25 as the high priest entereth into the **h** place 40
10:15 Whereof the **H** Ghost also is a witness to us: 40

1Pe
1:12 with the **H** Ghost sent down from heaven; 40
1:15 But as he which hath called you is **h**, so be 40
1:15 so be ye **h** in all manner of conversation; 40
1:16 Because it is written, Be ye **h**; for I am holy. 40
1:16 Because it is written, Be ye holy; for I am **h**. 40
2: 5 are built up a spiritual house, a **h** priesthood, 40
2: 9 a **h** nation, a peculiar people; 40
3: 5 For after this manner in the old time the **h** 40

2Pe
1:18 when we were with him in the **h** mount. 40
1:21 **h** men of God spake as they were moved NIG
1:21 spake as they were moved by the **H** Ghost. 40
2:21 they have known it, to turn from the **h** 40
3: 2 were spoken before by the **h** prophets, 40
3:11 persons ought ye to be in all **h** conversation 40

1Jn
2:20 But ye have an unction from the **H** One, 40
5: 7 the Father, the Word, and the **H** Ghost: 40

Jude
1:20 up yourselves on your **most h** faith, 40
1:20 most holy faith, praying in the **H** Ghost, 40

Rev
3: 7 things saith he that is **h**, he that is true, 40
4: 8 rest not day and night, saying, **H**, holy, holy, 40
4: 8 rest not day and night, saying, Holy, **h**, holy, 40
4: 8 rest not day and night, saying, Holy, holy, **h**, 40
6:10 saying, How long, O Lord, **h** and true, 40
11: 2 the **h** city shall they tread under foot forty 40
14:10 and brimstone in the presence of the **h** angels, 40
15: 4 for thou only art **h**: for all nations shall 3741
18:20 heaven, and ye **h** apostles and prophets; 40
20: 6 **h** is he that hath part in the first 40
21: 2 And I John saw the **h** city, new Jerusalem, 40
21:10 shewed me that great city, the **h** Jerusalem, 40
22: 6 Lord God of the **h** prophets sent his angel 40
22:11 and he that is **h**, let him be holy still. 40
22:11 and he that is holy, let him be **h** still. 37
22:19 and out of the **h** city, and from the things 40

HOLY [SPIRIT] See HOLY [GHOST]

HOLYDAY (2) [DAY, HOLY]
Ps 42: 4 and praise, with a multitude that kept **h**. 2287
Col 2:16 or in respect of a **h**, or of the new moon, 1859

HOMAM (1)
1Ch 1:39 the sons of Lotan; Hori, and **H**: 1950

HOME (51) [HOMEBORN]
Ge 39:16 his garment by her, until his lord came **h**. 1004
43:16 Bring these men **h**, and slay, 1004
43:26 when Joseph came **h**, they brought him 1004
Ex 9:19 not be brought **h**, the hail shall come 1004
Lev 18: 9 she be born at **h**, or born abroad, 1004
Dt 21:12 thou shalt bring her **h** to thine house; 1004
24: 5 but he shall be free at **h** one year, 1004
Jos 2:18 all thy father's household, **h** unto thee. 1004
Jdg 11: 9 If ye bring me **h** again to fight against NIH
19: 9 on your way, that thou mayest go **h**. 168
Ru 1:21 the LORD hath brought me **h** again empty: NIH
1Sa 2:20 And they went unto their own **h**. 4725
6: 7 and bring their calves **h** from them: 1004
6:10 to the cart, and shut up their calves at **h**: 1004
10:26 Saul also went **h** to Gibeah; and there 1004
18: 2 let him go no more **h** to his father's 7725
24:22 Saul went; but David and his men gat 1004
2Sa 5: 7 David sent **h** to Tamar, saying, Go now to 1004
14:13 in that the king doth not fetch **h** again his NIH
17:23 arose, and gat him **h** to his house, to his NIH
1Ki 5:14 were in Lebanon, and two months at **h**: 1004
13: 7 Come **h** with me, and refresh thyself, and 1004
13:15 him, Come **h** with me, and eat bread. 1004
2Ki 14:10 glory of this, and tarry at **h**: for why 1004
1Ch 13:12 How shall I bring the ark of God **h** to me? NIH
13:13 David brought not the ark **h** to himself to NIH
2Ch 25:10 to go **h** again: wherefore their anger was 4725
25:10 and they returned **h** in great anger. 4725
25:19 abide now at **h**; why shouldest thou 1004
Est 5:10 when he came **h**, he sent and called for 1004
Job 39:12 he will bring **h** thy seed, and gather it 7725
Ps 68:12 she that tarried at **h** divided the spoil. 1004
Pr 7:19 For the goodman is not at **h**, he is gone a 1004
7:20 and will come **h** at the day appointed. 1004
Ecc 12: 5 because man goeth to his long **h**, 1004
Jer 39:14 of Shaphan, that he should carry him **h**: 1004
La 1:20 sword bereaveth, at **h** there is as death. 5115
Hab 2: 5 he is a proud man, neither **keepeth at h**, 1004
Hag 1: 9 when ye brought it **h**, I did blow upon it. NIH
Mt 8: 6 my servant lieth at **h** sick of the palsy, 3614
Mk 5:19 Go **h** to thy friends, and tell them how 3624
Lk 9:61 farewell, which are at **h** in my house. NIG

Lk 15: 6 when he cometh **h**, he calleth together 3624
Jn 19:27 that disciple took her unto his own **h**. NIG
20:10 went away again unto their own **h**. 40
Ac 21: 6 and they returned **h** again. 1519+2398+3588
1Co 11:34 And if any man hunger, let him eat at **h**; 3624
14:35 thing, let them ask their husbands at **h**: 3624
2Co 5: 6 whilst we are at **h** in the body, 1736
1Ti 5: 4 let them learn first to shew piety at **h**, 3624
Tit 2: 5 To be discreet, chaste, **keepers at h**, 3626

HOMEBORN (2) [BEAR, HOME]
Ex 12:49 One law shall be to him that is **h**, 249
Jer 2:14 is he a **h** slave? why is he spoiled? 1004+3211

HOMELAND See HABITATION; NATIVITY

HOMER (11) [HOMERS]
Lev 27:16 a **h** of barley seed shall be valued at fifty 2563
Isa 5:10 and the seed of a **h** shall yield an ephah. 2563
Eze 45:11 bath may contain the tenth part of a **h**, 2563
45:11 and the ephah the tenth part of a **h**: 2563
45:11 the measure thereof shall be after the **h**. 2563
45:13 sixth part of an ephah of a **h** of wheat, 2563
45:13 sixth part of an ephah of a **h** of barley: 2563
45:14 out of the cor, which is a **h** of ten baths; 2563
45:14 ten baths; for ten baths are a **h**: 2563
Hos 3: 2 for a **h** of barley, and a half homer of 2563
3: 2 a homer of barley, and a **half h** of barley: 3963

HOMERS (1) [HOMER]
Nu 11:32 he that gathered least gathered ten **h**: 2563

HONEST (7) [HONESTLY, HONESTY]
Lk 8:15 in an **h** and good heart, having heard 2570
Ac 6: 3 out among you seven men of **h** report, 3140
Ro 12:17 Provide things **h** in the sight of all men. 2570
2Co 8:21 Providing for **h** things, not only in the 2570
13: 7 but that ye should do that which is **h**, 2570
Php 4: 8 whatsoever things are **h**, whatsoever 4586
1Pe 2:12 Having your conversation **h** among 2570

HONESTLY (3) [HONEST]
Ro 13:13 Let us walk **h**, as in the day; not in rioting 2156
1Th 4:12 That ye may walk **h** toward them that are 2156
Heb 13:18 in all things willing to live **h**. 2573

HONESTY (1) [HONEST]
1Ti 2: 2 and peaceable life in all godliness and **h**. 4587

HONEY (56) [HONEYCOMB]
Ge 43:11 a little **h**, spices, and myrrh, nuts, 1706
Ex 3: 8 unto a land flowing with milk and **h**. 1706
3:17 unto a land flowing with milk and **h**. 1706
13: 5 thee, a land flowing with milk and **h**, 1706
16:31 taste of it was like wafers made with **h**. 1706
33: 3 Unto a land flowing with milk and **h**: for 1706
Lev 2:11 for ye shall burn no leaven, nor any **h**, 1706
20:24 a land that floweth with milk and **h**: 1706
Nu 13:27 and surely it floweth with milk and **h**; 1706
14: 8 a land which floweth with milk and **h**, 1706
16:13 of a land that floweth with milk and **h**, 1706
16:14 into a land that floweth with milk and **h**, 1706
Dt 6: 3 in the land that floweth with milk and **h**; 1706
8: 8 pomegranates; a land of oil olive, and **h**; 1706
11: 9 a land that floweth with milk and **h**. 1706
26: 9 even a land that floweth with milk and **h**. 1706
26:15 a land that floweth with milk and **h**. 1706
27: 3 a land that floweth with milk and **h**; 1706
31:20 fathers, that floweth with milk and **h**; 1706
32:13 he made him to suck **h** out of the rock, 1706
Jos 5: 6 a land that floweth with milk and **h**. 1706
Jdg 14: 8 of bees and **h** in the carcase of the lion. 1706
14: 9 he told not them that he had taken the **h** 1706
14:18 sun went down, What is sweeter than **h**? 1706
1Sa 14:25 wood; and there was **h** upon the ground. 1706
14:26 into the wood, behold the **h** dropped; 1706
14:29 because I tasted a little of this **h**. 1706
14:43 taste a little **h** with the end of the rod 1706
2Sa 17:29 **h**, and butter, and sheep, and cheese of 1706
1Ki 14: 3 and a cruse of **h**, and go to him: 1706
2Ki 18:32 and vineyards, a land of oil olive and of **h**, 1706
2Ch 31: 5 oil, and **h**, and of all the increase of 1706
Job 20:17 the floods, the brooks of **h** and butter. 1706
Ps 19:10 sweeter also than **h** and the honeycomb. 1706
81:16 with **h** out of the rock should I have 1706
119:103 taste! yea, sweeter than **h** to my mouth! 1706
Pr 24:13 My son, eat thou **h**, because it is good; 1706
25:16 Hast thou found **h**? eat so much as is 1706
25:27 It is not good to eat much **h**: so for men 1706
SS 4:11 **h** and milk are under thy tongue; 1706
5: 1 I have eaten my honeycomb with my **h**; 1706
Isa 7:15 Butter and **h** shall he eat, that he may 1706
7:22 **h** shall every one eat that is left in the 1706
Jer 11: 5 them a land flowing with milk and **h**, 1706
32:22 them, a land flowing with milk and **h**; 1706
41: 8 and of barley, and of oil, and of **h**. 1706
Eze 3: 3 it was in my mouth as **h** for sweetness. 1706
16:13 thou didst eat fine flour, and **h**, and oil: 1706
16:19 fine flour, and oil, and **h**, wherewith I fed 1706
20: 6 with milk and **h**, which is the glory 1706
20:15 had given them, flowing with milk and **h**, 1706
27:17 and Pannag, and **h**, and oil, and balm. 1706
Mt 3: 4 and his meat was locusts and wild **h**. 3192
Mk 1: 6 and he did eat locusts and wild **h**; 3192
Rev 10: 9 but it shall be in thy mouth sweet as **h**: 3192
10:10 it up; and it was in my mouth sweet as **h**: 3192

H

HONEYCOMB (9) [HONEY]

1Sa	14:27 dipt it in a **h**, and put his	1706+3295+1886.1
Ps	19:10 sweeter also than honey and the **h**.	5317+6688
Pr	5: 3 the lips of a strange woman drop *as* a **h**,	5317
	16:24 Pleasant words *are as* a **h**, sweet to	1706+6688
	24:13 and the **h**, which *is* sweet to thy taste:	5317
	27: 7 The full soul loatheth a **h**; but *to* the	5317
SS	4:11 Thy lips, O *my* spouse, drop *as* the **h**:	5317
	5: 1 I have eaten my **h** with my honey; I have	3293
Lk	24:42 him a piece of a broiled fish, and of a **h**.	3193

HONOR See UPPERMOST

HONOUR (146) [HONOURABLE, HONOURED, HONOUREST, HONOURETH, HONOURS]

Ge	49: 6 assembly, mine **h**, be not thou united:	3519
Ex	14:17 I will **get** me **h** upon Pharaoh, and upon	3513
	14:18 when I have **gotten** me **h** upon Pharaoh,	3513
	20:12 **H** thy father and thy mother: that thy days	3513
Lev	19:15 the poor, nor **h** the person of the mighty:	1921
	19:32 the face of the old man, and fear thy	1921
Nu	22:17 **promote** thee **unto** very great **h**,	3513+3513
	22:37 I not able indeed to **promote** thee **to h**?	3513
	24:11 to **promote** thee **unto** great **h**;	3513+3513
	24:11 lo, the LORD hath kept thee back from **h**.	3519
	27:20 thou shalt put *some* of thine **h** upon him,	1935
Dt	5:16 **H** thy father and thy mother, as the LORD	3513
	26:19 made, in praise, and in name, and in **h**;	8597
Jdg	4: 9 that thou takest shall not be for thine **h**;	8597
	9: 9 wherewith by me they **h** God and man,	3513
	13:17 sayings come to pass we may **do** thee **h**?	3513
1Sa	2:30 for them that **h** me I will honour,	3513
	2:30 for them that honour me I will **h**,	3513
	15:30 **h** me now, I pray thee, before the elders	3513
2Sa	6:22 spoken of, of them shall I be **had in h**.	3513
	10: 3 thou that David doth **h** thy father,	3513
1Ki	3:13 thou hast not asked, both riches, and **h**:	3519
1Ch	16:27 Glory and **h** *are* in his presence; strength	1926
	17:18 more to thee for the **h** of thy servant?	3519
	19: 3 thou that David doth **h** thy father,	3513
	29:12 Both riches and **h** *come* of thee,	3519
	29:28 a good old age, full of days, riches, and **h**:	3519
2Ch	1:11 thou hast not asked riches, wealth, or **h**,	3519
	1:12 will give thee riches, and wealth, and **h**,	3519
	17: 5 and he had riches and **h** in abundance.	3519
	18: 1 Jehoshaphat had riches and **h** in	3519
	26:18 neither *shall it be* for thine **h** from	3519
	32:27 had exceeding much riches and **h**:	3519
	32:33 the inhabitants of Jerusalem did him **h** at	3519
Est	1: 4 the **h** of his excellent majesty many days,	3366
	1:20 the wives shall give to their husbands **h**,	3366
	6: 3 What **h** and dignity hath been done to	3366
	6: 6 the man whom the king delighteth to **h**?	3366
	6: 6 To whom would the king delight to do **h**	3366
	6: 7 the man whom the king delighteth to **h**,	3366
	6: 9 *withal* whom the king delighteth to **h**,	3366
	6: 9 the man whom the king delighteth to **h**.	3366
	8:16 had light, and gladness, and joy, and **h**.	3366
Job	14:21 sons **come to h**, and he knoweth *it* not;	3513
Ps	7: 5 the earth, and lay mine **h** in the dust.	3519
	8: 5 and hast crowned him with glory and **h**.	1926
	21: 5 **h** and majesty hast thou laid upon him.	1935
	26: 8 and the place where thine **h** dwelleth.	3519
	49:12 Nevertheless man *being* in **h** abideth not:	3366
	49:20 Man *that* is in **h**, and understandeth not,	3366
	66: 2 Sing forth the **h** of his name: make his	3519
	71: 8 *with* thy praise *and with* thy **h** all the day.	8597
	91:15 in trouble; I will deliver him, and **h** him.	3513
	96: 6 **H** and majesty *are* before him: strength	1935
	104: 1 thou art clothed with **h** and majesty.	1935
	112: 9 for ever; his horn shall be exalted with **h**.	3519
	145: 5 I will speak of the glorious **h** of thy	1926
	149: 9 this **h** have all his saints. Praise ye	1926
Pr	3: 9 **H** the LORD with thy substance,	3513
	3:16 and in her left hand riches and **h**.	3519
	4: 8 she shall **bring** thee **to h**, when thou dost	3513
	5: 9 Lest thou give thine **h** unto others,	1935
	8:18 Riches and **h** *are* with me; *yea*, durable	3519
	11:16 A gracious woman retaineth **h**:	3519
	14:28 In the multitude of people *is* the king's **h**:	1927
	15:33 of wisdom; and before **h** *is* humility.	3519
	18:12 man is haughty, and before **h** *is* humility.	3519
	20: 3 *It is* an **h** for a man to cease from strife:	3519
	21:21 mercy findeth life, righteousness, and **h**.	3519
	22: 4 of the LORD *are* riches, and **h**, and life.	3519
	25: 2 the **h** of kings *is* to search out a matter.	3519
	26: 1 in harvest, so **h** *is* not seemly for a fool.	3519
	26: 8 in a sling, so *is* he that giveth **h** to a fool.	3519
	29:23 but **h** shall uphold the humble in spirit.	3519
	31:25 Strength and **h** *are* her clothing.	1926
Ecc	6: 2 **h**, so that he wanteth nothing for his soul	3519
	10: 1 *that is* in reputation for wisdom *and* **h**.	3519
Isa	29:13 their lips do **h** me, but have removed	3513
	43:20 The beast of the field shall **h** me,	3513
	58:13 shalt **h** him, not doing thine own ways,	3513
Jer	33: 9 an **h** before all the nations of the earth,	8597
Da	2: 6 of me gifts and rewards and great **h**:	3367
	4:30 my power, and for the **h** of my majesty?	3367
	4:36 mine **h** and brightness returned unto me;	1923
	4:37 and extol and **h** the King of heaven,	1922
	5:18 a kingdom, and majesty, and glory, and **h**:	1923
	11:21 to whom they shall not give the **h** of	1935
	11:38 in his estate shall he **h** the God of forces:	3513
	11:38 god whom his fathers knew not shall he **h**	3513

Mal	1: 6 if then I *be* a father, where *is* mine **h**?	3519
Mt	13:57 A prophet is not **without h**, save in his	820
	15: 4 saying, **H** thy father and mother:	5091
	15: 6 **h** not his father or his mother, *he shall*	5091
	19:19 **H** thy father and *thy* mother: and,	5091
Mk	6: 4 A prophet is not **without h**, but in his	820
	7:10 Moses said, **H** thy father and thy mother;	5091
	10:19 Defraud not, **H** thy father and mother.	5091
Lk	18:20 witness, **H** thy father and thy mother.	5092
Jn	4:44 a prophet hath no **h** in his own country.	5092
	5:23 That all *men* should **h** the Son, even as	5091
	5:23 the Son, even as they **h** the Father.	5091
	5:41 I receive not **h** from men.	1391
	5:44 which receive **h** one of another,	1391
	5:44 seek not the **h** that *cometh* from God	1391
	8:49 I **h** my Father, and ye do dishonour me.	5091
	8:54 Jesus answered, If I **h** myself, my honour	1392
	8:54 If I honour myself, my **h** is nothing;	1391
	12:26 any *man* serve me, him will *my* Father **h**.	5091
Ro	2: 7 seek for glory and **h** and immortality,	5092
	2:10 glory, **h**, and peace, to every *man* that	5092
	9:21 same lump to make one vessel unto **h**,	5092
	12:10 love; in **h** preferring one another;	5092
	13: 7 fear to whom fear; **h** to whom honour.	5092
	13: 7 fear to whom fear; honour to whom **h**.	5092
1Co	12:23 upon these we bestow more abundant **h**;	5092
	12:24 having given more abundant **h** to that	5092
2Co	6: 8 By **h** and dishonour, by evil report and	1391
Eph	6: 2 **H** thy father and mother; (which is the	5091
Col	2:23 not in any **h** to the satisfying of the flesh.	5092
1Th	4: 4 possess his vessel in sanctification and **h**;	5092
1Ti	1:17 God, *be* **h** and glory for ever and ever.	5092
	5: 3 **H** widows that are widows indeed.	5091
	5:17 rule well be counted worthy of double **h**,	5092
	6: 1 count their own masters worthy of all **h**,	5092
	6:16 to whom *be* **h** and power everlasting.	5092
2Ti	2:20 and some to **h**, and some to dishonour.	5092
	2:21 he shall be a vessel unto **h**, sanctified,	5092
Heb	2: 7 thou crownedst him with glory and **h**,	5092
	2: 9 of death, crowned with glory and **h**;	5092
	3: 3 the house hath more **h** than the house.	5092
	5: 4 And no *man* taketh *this* **h** unto himself,	5092
1Pe	1: 7 might be found unto praise and **h** and	5092
	2:17 **H** all *men*. Love the brotherhood.	5091
	2:17 the brotherhood. Fear God. **H** the king.	5091
	3: 7 giving **h** unto the wife, as unto the weaker	5092
2Pe	1:17 For he received from God the Father **h**	5092
Rev	4: 9 when *those* beasts give glory and **h** and	5092
	4:11 O Lord, to receive glory and **h** and power:	5092
	5:12 strength, and **h**, and glory, and blessing.	5092
	5:13 Blessing, and **h**, and glory, and power,	5092
	7:12 and **h**, and power, and might,	5092
	19: 1 Alleluia; Salvation, and glory, and **h**,	5092
	19: 7 us be glad and rejoice, and give **h** to him:	1391
	21:24 the earth do bring their glory and **h** into it.	5092
	21:26 bring the glory and **h** of the nations into it.	5092

HONOURABLE (30) [HONOUR]

Ge	34:19 he *was* more **h** than all the house of his	3513
Nu	22:15 princes, more, and more **h** than they.	3513
1Sa	9: 6 city a man of God, and *he is* an **h** man;	3513
	22:14 at thy bidding, and *is* **h** in thine house?	3513
2Sa	23:19 Was he not most **h** of three? therefore	3513
	23:23 He was more **h** than the thirty,	3513
2Ki	5: 1 **h**, because by him the LORD had	5375+6440
1Ch	4: 9 Jabez was more **h** than his brethren:	3513
	11:21 the three, he was more **h** than the two;	3513
	11:25 he was **h** among the thirty, but attained	3513
	11:25 the *man* dwelt in it.	5375+6440
Job	22: 8 earth; and the **h** man dwelt in it.	5375+6440
Ps	45: 9 Kings' daughters *were* among thy **h**	3368
	111: 3 His work *is* **h** and glorious:	1935
Isa	3: 3 the **h** man, and the counseller,	5375+6440
	3: 5 the ancient, and the base against the **h**.	3513
	5:13 their **h** men *are* famished,	3513
	9:15 The ancient and **h**, he *is* the head;	5375+6440
	23: 8 whose traffickers *are* the **h** of the earth?	3513
	23: 9 bring into contempt all the **h** of the earth.	3513
	42:21 he will magnify the law, and make *it* **h**.	142
	43: 4 thou hast been **h**, and I have loved thee:	3513
	58:13 a delight, the holy of the LORD, **h**;	3513
Na	3:10 they cast lots for her **h** men, and all her	3513
Mk	15:43 Joseph of Arimathea, an **h** counseller,	2158
Lk	14: 8 lest **a more h** *man* than thou be bidden	1784
Ac	13:50 Jews stirred up the devout and **h** women,	2158
	17:12 also of **h** women which were Greeks,	2158
1Co	4:10 *are* strong; ye *are* **h**, but we *are* despised.	1741
	12:23 of the body, which we think to be **less h**,	820
Heb	13: 4 Marriage *is* **h** in all, and the bed undefiled:	5093

HONOURED (9) [HONOUR]

Ex	14: 4 I will be **h** upon Pharaoh, and upon all his	3513
Pr	13:18 but he that regardeth reproof shall be **h**.	3513
	27:18 he that waiteth on his master shall be **h**.	3513
Isa	43:23 neither hast thou **h** me *with* thy sacrifices.	3513
La	1: 8 all that **h** her despise her, because they	3513
	5:12 their hand: the faces of elders were not **h**.	1921
Da	4:34 I praised and **h** him that liveth for ever,	1922
Ac	28:10 Who also **h** us with many honours;	5091
1Co	12:26 suffer with *it*; or one member be **h**,	1392

HONOUREST (1) [HONOUR]

1Sa	2:29 **h** thy sons above me, to make yourselves	3513

HONOURETH (9) [HONOUR]

Ps	15: 4 but he **h** them that fear the LORD.	3513

Pr	12: 9 *is* better than he that **h** himself,	3513
	14:31 but he that **h** him hath mercy on the poor.	3513
Mal	1: 6 son *his* father, and a servant his master:	3513
Mt	15: 8 their mouth, and **h** me with *their* lips;	5091
Mk	7: 6 This people **h** me with *their* lips,	5091
Jn	5:23 He that **h** not the Son honoureth not	5091
	5:23 He that honoureth not the Son **h** not	5091
	8:54 it is my Father that **h** me; of whom ye say,	1392

HONOURS (1) [HONOUR]

Ac	28:10 Who also honoured us with many **h**;	5092

HOODS (1)

Isa	3:23 the fine linen, and the **h**, and the vails.	6797

HOOF (12) [HOOFS, HORSEHOOFS]

Ex	10:26 us; there shall not a **h** be left behind;	6541
Lev	11: 3 Whatsoever parteth the **h**,	6541
	11: 4 the cud, or of them that divide the **h**:	6541
	11: 4 cheweth the cud, but divideth not the **h**;	6541
	11: 5 cheweth the cud, but divideth not the **h**;	6541
	11: 6 cheweth the cud, but divideth not the **h**;	6541
	11: 7 though he divide the **h**,	6541
	11:26 of every beast which divideth the **h**,	6541
Dt	14: 6 every beast that parteth the **h**,	6541
	14: 7 cud, or of them that divide the cloven **h**;	6541
	14: 7 they chew the cud, but divide not the **h**,	6541
	14: 8 the swine, because it divideth the **h**,	6541

HOOFS (6) [HOOF]

Ps	69:31 an ox *or* bullock that hath horns *and* **h**.	6536
Isa	5:28 their horses' **h** shall be counted like flint,	6541
Jer	47: 3 At the noise of the stamping of the **h** of	6541
Eze	26:11 With the **h** of his horses shall he tread	6541
	32:13 more, nor the **h** of beasts trouble them.	6541
Mic	4:13 horn iron, and I will make thy **h** brass:	6541

HOOK (5) [FISHHOOKS, FLESHHOOK, FLESHHOOKS, HOOKS, PRUNINGHOOKS]

2Ki	19:28 therefore I will put my **h** in thy nose,	2397
Job	41: 1 Canst thou draw out leviathan with a **h**?	2443
	41: 2 Canst thou put a **h** into his nose? or bore	100
Isa	37:29 therefore will I put my **h** in thy nose,	2397
Mt	17:27 and cast a **h**, and take up the fish that first	44

HOOKS (18) [HOOK]

Ex	26:32 their **h** *shall be* of gold, upon the four	2053
	26:37 with gold, *and* their **h** *shall be* of gold:	2053
	27:10 the **h** of the pillars and their fillets *shall*	2053
	27:11 **h** of the pillars and their fillets *of* silver.	2053
	27:17 **h** *shall be* of silver, and their sockets	2053
	36:36 **h** *were* of gold; and he cast for them	2053
	36:38 the five pillars of it with their **h**:	2053
	38:10 **h** of the pillars and their fillets *were* of	2053
	38:11 **h** of the pillars and their fillets *of* silver.	2053
	38:12 **h** of the pillars and their fillets *of* silver.	2053
	38:17 **h** of the pillars and their fillets *of* silver.	2053
	38:19 their **h** *of* silver, and the overlaying of	2053
	38:28 and five *shekels* he made **h** for the pillars,	2053
Isa	18: 5 both cut off the sprigs with **pruning h**,	4211
Eze	29: 4 I will put **h** in thy jaws, and I will cause	2397
	38: 4 put **h** into thy jaws, and I will bring thee	2397
	40:43 within *were* **h**, a hand broad,	8240
Am	4: 2 he will take you away with **h**,	6793

HOOPOE See LAPWING

HOPE (130) [HOPE'S, HOPED, HOPETH, HOPING]

Ru	1:12 If I should say, I have **h**, *if* I should have	8615
Ezr	10: 2 yet now there is in Israel concerning	4723
Job	4: 6 *Is* not this *thy* fear, thy confidence, thy **h**;	8615
	5:16 So the poor hath **h**, and iniquity stoppeth	8615
	6:11 What *is* my strength, that I should **h**?	3176
	7: 6 weaver's shuttle, and are spent without **h**.	8615
	8:13 and the hypocrite's **h** shall perish:	8615
	8:14 Whose **h** shall be cut off, and whose trust	3689
	11:18 thou shalt be secure, because there is **h**;	8615
	11:20 their **h** *shall be as* the giving up of	8615
	14: 7 For there is **h** of a tree, if it be cut down,	8615
	14:19 earth; and thou destroyest the **h** of man.	8615
	17:15 where *is* now my **h**? as for my hope,	8615
	17:15 my hope? as for my **h**, who shall see it?	8615
	19:10 and mine **h** hath he removed like a tree.	8615
	27: 8 For what *is* the **h** of the hypocrite,	8615
	31:24 If I have made gold my **h**, or have said to	3689
	41: 9 Behold, the **h** of him is in vain: shall *not*	8431
Ps	16: 9 rejoiceth: my flesh also shall rest in **h**.	983
	22: 9 thou didst **make** me **h** *when I was* upon	982
	31:24 your heart, all ye that **h** in the LORD.	3176
	33:18 fear him, upon them that **h** in his mercy;	3176
	33:22 be upon us, according as we **h** in thee.	3176
	38:15 For in thee, O LORD, do I **h**: thou wilt	3176
	39: 7 Lord, what wait I for? my **h** *is* in thee.	8431
	42: 5 **h** thou in God: for I shall yet praise him	3176
	42:11 **h** thou in God: for I shall yet praise him,	3176
	43: 5 **h** in God: for I shall yet praise him, *who*	3176
	71: 5 For thou *art* my **h**, O Lord GOD: thou *art*	8615
	71:14 will **h** continually, and will yet praise thee	3176
	78: 7 That they might set their **h** in God,	3689
	119:49 upon which thou hast **caused** me **to h**.	3176
	119:81 for thy salvation: *but* I **h** in thy word.	3176
	119:114 place and my shield: I **h** in thy word.	7664
	119:116 and let me not be ashamed of my **h**.	7664
	130: 5 soul doth wait, and in his word do I **h**.	3176
	130: 7 Let Israel **h** in the LORD: for with	3176
	131: 3 Let Israel **h** in the LORD from henceforth	3176

Ps 146: 5 his help, whose **h** *is* in the LORD his God: 7664
147:11 fear him, in those that **h** in his mercy. 3176
Pr 10:28 The **h** of the righteous *shall be* gladness: 8431
11: 7 and the **h** of unjust *men* perisheth. 8431
13:12 **H** deferred maketh the heart sick: 8431
14:32 but the righteous hath **h** in his death. 2620
19:18 Chasten thy son while there is **h**, and let 8615
26:12 *there is* more **h** of a fool than of him. 8615
29:20 *there is* more **h** of a fool than of him. 8615
Ecc 9: 4 that is joined to all the living there is **h**: 986
Isa 38: 18 they that go down into the pit cannot **h** 7663
57:10 way; *yet* saidst thou not, There is **no h**: 2976
Jer 2:25 thou saidst, There is **no h**: no; for I have 2976
14: 8 O the **h** of Israel, the saviour thereof in 4723
17: 7 in the LORD, and whose **h** the LORD is. 4009
17:13 LORD, the **h** of Israel, all that forsake 4723
17:17 unto me: thou *art* my **h** in the day of evil. 4268
18:12 said, There is **no h**: but we will walk 2976
31:17 there is **h** in thine end, saith the LORD, 8615
50: 7 even the LORD, the **h** of their fathers. 4723
La 3:18 and my **h** is perished from the LORD: 8431
3:21 I recall to my mind, therefore have I **h**. 3176
3:24 saith my soul; therefore will I **h** in him. 3176
3:26 *It is* good that a man should both **h** and 3175
3:29 in the dust; if so be there may be **h**. 8615
Eze 13: 6 have **made** *others* **to h** that *they* would 3176
19: 5 her **h** was lost, then she took another of 8615
37:11 Our bones are dried, and our **h** is lost: 8615
Hos 2:15 and the valley of Achor for a door of **h**: 8615
Joel 3:16 the LORD *will be* the **h** of his people, 4268
Zec 9:12 ye to the strong hold, ye prisoners of **h**: 8615
Lk 6:34 And if ye lend *to whom* ye **h** to 1679
Ac 2:26 moreover also my flesh shall rest in **h**: 1680
16:19 And when her masters saw that the **h** of 1680
23: 6 of the **h** and resurrection of the dead I am 1680
24:15 And have **h** towards God, which they 1680
26: 6 judged for the **h** of the promise made of 1680
26: 7 serving *God* day and night, **h** to come. 1679
27:20 no small tempest lay on *us*, all **h** that we 1680
28:20 for the **h** of Israel I am bound with this 1680
Ro 4:18 Who against **h** believed in hope, that he 1680
4:18 Who against hope believed in **h**, that he 1680
5: 2 and rejoice in **h** of the glory of God. 1680
5: 4 experience; and experience, **h**: 1680
5: 5 And **h** maketh not ashamed; because 1680
8:20 him who hath subjected *the same*, in **h**, 1680
8:24 we are saved by **h**: but hope that is seen 1680
8:24 but **h** that is seen is not hope: for what a 1680
8:24 but hope that is seen is not **h**: for what a 1680
8:24 what a man seeth, why doth he yet **h for**? 1679
8:25 if we **h for** that we see not, *then* do we 1679
12:12 Rejoicing in **h**; patient in tribulation; 1680
15: 4 comfort of the scriptures might have **h**. 1680
15:13 Now the God of **h** fill you with all joy and 1680
15:13 in believing, that ye may abound in **h**, 1680
1Co 9:10 that he that ploweth should plow in **h**; 1680
9:10 that he that thresheth in **h** should be 1680
9:10 in hope should be partaker of his **h**. 1680
13:13 now abideth faith, **h**, charity, these three; 1680
15:19 If in this life only we have **h** in Christ, 1679
2Co 1: 7 And our **h** of you *is* stedfast, knowing, 1680
3:12 Seeing then that we have such **h**, we use 1680
10:15 having, when your faith is increased, 1680
Gal 5: 5 we through the Spirit wait for the **h** of 1680
Eph 1:18 that ye may know what is the **h** of his 1680
2:12 no **h**, and without God in the world: 1680
4: 4 even as ye are called in one **h** of your 1680
Php 1:20 to my earnest expectation and *my* **h**, 1680
2:23 Him therefore I **h** to send presently, 1679
Col 1: 5 For the **h** which is laid up for you in 1680
1:23 *be* not moved away from the **h** of 1680
1:27 which is Christ in you, the **h** of glory: 1680
1Th 1: 3 patience of **h** in our Lord Jesus Christ, 1680
2:19 For what *is* our **h**, or joy, or crown of 1680
4:13 even as others which have no **h**. 1680
5: 8 love; and for a helmet, the **h** of salvation. 1680
2Th 2:16 and good **h** through grace, 1680
1Ti 1: 1 and Lord Jesus Christ, *which is* our **h**; 1680
Tit 1: 2 In **h** of eternal life, which God, that 1680
2:13 Looking for *that* blessed **h**, and the 1680
3: 7 should be made heirs according to the **h** 1680
Heb 3: 6 the rejoicing of the **h** firm unto the end. 1680
6:11 to the full assurance of the **h** unto the end: 1680
6:18 to lay hold upon the **h** set before us: 1680
6:19 Which *h* we have as an anchor of the soul, NIG
7:19 the bringing in of a better **h** *did*; 1680
10:23 Let us hold fast the profession of *our* **h** 1680
1Pe 1: 3 **h** by the resurrection of Jesus Christ from 1680
1:13 **h** to the end for the grace that is *to be* 1679
1:21 that your faith and **h** might be in God. 1680
3:15 reason of the **h** that is in you with 1680
1Jn 3: 3 And every *man* that hath this **h** in him 1680

HOPE'S (1) [HOPE]
Ac 26: 7 For which **h** sake, king Agrippa, I am 1680

HOPED (11) [HOPE]
Est 9: 1 the day that the enemies of the Jews **h** to 7663
Job 6:20 were confounded because they had **h**; 982
Ps 119:43 my mouth; for I have **h** in thy judgments. 3176
119:74 see me; because I have **h** in thy word. 3176
119:147 the morning, and cried: I **h** in thy word. 3176
119:166 I have **h** for thy salvation, and done thy 7663
Jer 3:23 Truly in vain *is* salvation **h** for from NIH
Lk 23: 8 he **h** to have seen some miracle done by 1679

Ac 24:26 He **h** also that money should have been 1679
2Co 8: 5 And *this* they did, not as we **h**, 1679
Heb 11: 1 faith is the substance of *things* **h** for, 1679

HOPETH (1) [HOPE]
1Co 13: 7 Beareth all *things*, believeth all *things*, **h** 1679

HOPHNI (5)
1Sa 1: 3 the two sons of Eli, **H** and Phinehas, 2652
2:34 upon thy two sons, on **H** and Phinehas; 2652
4: 4 the two sons of Eli, **H** and Phinehas, 2652
4:11 sons of Eli, **H** and Phinehas, were slain. 2652
4:17 **H** and Phinehas, are dead, and the ark of 2652

HOPING (2) [HOPE]
Lk 6:35 do good, and lend, **h for** nothing again; 560
1Ti 3:14 unto thee, **h** to come unto thee shortly: 1679

HOR (12)
Nu 20:22 from Kadesh, and came *unto* mount **H**. 2023
20:23 spake unto Moses and Aaron in mount **H**. 2023
20:25 son, and bring them up *unto* mount **H**: 2023
20:27 they went up into mount **H** in the sight of 2023
21: 4 they journeyed from mount **H** by the way 2023
33:37 pitched in mount **H**, in the edge of the 2023
33:38 Aaron the priest went up into mount **H** at 2023
33:39 three years old when he died in mount **H**. 2023
33:41 they departed from mount **H**, 2023
34: 7 sea you shall point out for you mount **H**: 2023
34: 8 From mount **H** ye shall point out *your* 2023
Dt 32:50 as Aaron thy brother died in mount **H**, 2023

HOR HAGGIDGAD See HOR-HAGIDGAD

HORAM (1)
Jos 10:33 king of Gezer came up to help Lachish; 2036

HOREB (17) [SINAI]
Ex 3: 1 came to the mountain of God, *even* to **H**. 2722
17: 6 before thee there upon the rock in **H**; 2722
33: 6 of their ornaments by the mount **H**. 2722
Dt 1: 2 (*There are* eleven days' *journey* from **H** 2722
1: 6 The LORD our God spake unto us in **H**, 2722
1:19 when we departed from **H**, we went 2722
4:10 stoodest before the LORD thy God in **H**, 2722
4:15 unto you in **H** out of the midst of the fire: 2722
5: 2 our God made a covenant with us in **H**. 2722
9: 8 Also in **H** ye provoked the LORD to 2722
18:16 thy God in **H** in the day of the assembly, 2722
29: 1 which he made with them in **H**. 2722
1Ki 8: 9 of stone, which Moses put there at **H**, 2722
19: 8 forty nights unto **H** the mount of God. 2722
2Ch 5:10 two tables which Moses put *therein* at **H**, 2722
Ps 106:19 They made a calf in **H**, and worshipped 2722
Mal 4: 4 which I commanded unto him in **H** for all 2722

HOREM (1)
Jos 19:38 **H**, and Beth-anath, and Beth-shemesh; 2765

HOR-HAGIDGAD (2)
Nu 33:32 from Bene-jaakan, and encamped at **H**. 2735
33:33 they went from **H**, and pitched in 2735

HORI (4) [HORIMS, HORITE, HORITES]
Ge 36:22 children of Lotan were **H** and Hemam; 2753
36:30 these *are* the dukes *that came* of **H**, 2753
Nu 13: 5 tribe of Simeon, Shaphat the son of **H**. 2753
1Ch 1:39 And the sons of Lotan; **H**, and Homam: 2753

HORIMS (2) [HORI]
Dt 2:12 The **H** also dwelt in Seir beforetime; 2752
2:22 he destroyed the **H** from before them; 2752

HORITE (1) [HORI]
Ge 36:20 These *are* the sons of Seir the **H**, 2752

HORITES (3) [HORI]
Ge 14: 6 the **H** in their mount Seir, unto El-paran, 2752
36:21 these *are* the dukes of the **H**, the children 2752
36:29 These *are* the dukes *that came* of the **H**; 2752

HORMAH (9)
Nu 14:45 them, and discomfited them, *even* unto **H**. 2767
21: 3 and he called the name of the place **H**. 2767
Dt 1:44 and destroyed you in Seir, *even* unto **H**. 2767
Jos 12:14 The king of **H**, one; the king of Arad, one; 2767
15:30 And Eltolad, and Chesil, and **H**, 2767
19: 4 And Eltolad, and Bethul, and **H**, 2767
Jdg 1:17 and the name of the city was called **H**. 2767
1Sa 30:30 to *them* which *were* in **H**, and to *them* 2767
1Ch 4:30 And at Bethuel, and at **H**, and at Ziklag, 2767

HORN (36) [HORNS, INKHORN]
Ex 21:29 if the ox *were* wont to push with his **h** 5056
Jos 6: 5 *they* make a long blast with the ram's **h**, 7161
1Sa 2: 1 mine **h** is exalted in the LORD: 7161
2:10 his king, and exalt the **h** of his anointed. 7161
16: 1 fill thine **h** *with* oil, and go, I will send 7161
16:13 Samuel took the **h** of oil, and anointed 7161
2Sa 22: 3 the **h** of my salvation, my high tower, 7161
1Ki 1:39 Zadok the priest took a **h** of oil out of 7161
1Ch 25: 5 seer in the words of God, to lift up the **h**. 7161
Job 16:15 my skin, and defiled my **h** in the dust. 7161
Ps 18: 2 the **h** of my salvation, *and* my high tower. 7161
75: 4 and to the wicked, Lift not up the **h**: 7161
75: 5 Lift not up your **h** on high: speak *not* with 7161

Ps 89:17 and in thy favour our **h** shall be exalted. 7161
89:24 and in my name shall his **h** be exalted. 7161
92:10 my **h** shalt thou exalt like *the horn* of an 7161
92:10 my horn shalt thou exalt like *the h* of an NIH
112: 9 ever; his **h** shall be exalted with honour. 7161
132:17 There will I make the **h** of David to bud: 7161
148:14 He also exalteth the **h** of his people, 7161
Jer 48:25 The **h** of Moab is cut off, and his arm is 7161
La 2: 3 hath cut off in *his* fierce anger all the **h** 7161
2:17 he hath set up the **h** of thine adversaries. 7161
Eze 29:21 In that day will I cause the **h** of the house 7161
Da 7: 8 came up among them another little **h**, 7162
7: 8 in this **h** *were* eyes like the eyes of man, 7162
7:11 the voice of the great words which the **h** 7162
7:20 even *of* that **h** that had eyes, and a mouth 7162
7:21 the same **h** made war with the saints, 7162
8: 5 goat *had* a notable **h** between his eyes. 7161
8: 8 he was strong, the great **h** was broken; 7161
8: 9 out of one of them came forth a little **h**, 7161
8:21 the great **h** *that is* between his eyes *is* 7161
Mic 4:13 for I will make thine **h** iron, and I will 7161
Zec 1:21 lift up *their* **h** over the land of Judah 7161
Lk 1:69 And hath raised up a **h** of salvation for us 2768

HORNET (2) [HORNETS]
Dt 7:20 thy God will send the **h** among them, 6880
Jos 24:12 sent the **h** before you, which drave them 6880

HORNETS (1) [HORNET]
Ex 23:28 will send **h** before thee, which shall drive 6880

HORNS (67) [HORN]
Ge 22:13 him a ram caught in a thicket by his **h**: 7161
Ex 27: 2 thou shalt make the **h** of it upon the four 7161
27: 2 his **h** shall be of the same: and thou shalt 7161
29:12 put *it* upon the **h** of the altar with thy 7161
30: 2 the **h** thereof *shall be* of the same. 7161
30: 3 thereof round about, and the **h** thereof; 7161
30:10 shall make an atonement upon the **h** 7161
37:25 of it; the **h** thereof were of the same. 7161
37:26 thereof round about, and the **h** of it: 7161
38: 2 made the **h** thereof on the four corners 7161
38: 2 of it; the **h** thereof were of the same: 7161
Lev 4: 7 the altar of sweet incense before 7161
4:18 shall put *some* of the blood upon the **h** 7161
4:25 put *it* upon the **h** of the altar of burnt 7161
4:30 put *it* upon the **h** of the altar of burnt 7161
4:34 put *it* upon the **h** of the altar of burnt 7161
8:15 put *it* upon the **h** of the altar round about 7161
9: 9 put *it* upon the **h** of the altar, and poured 7161
16:18 put *it* upon the **h** of the altar round about. 7161
Dt 33:17 and his **h** *are* like the horns of unicorns: 7161
33:17 and his horns *are* like the **h** of unicorns: 7161
Jos 6: 4 before the ark seven trumpets of **rams' h**: 3104
6: 6 of **rams' h** before the ark of the LORD. 3104
6: 8 of **rams' h** passed on before the LORD, 3104
6:13 **rams' h** before the ark of the LORD went 3104
1Ki 1:50 and caught hold on the **h** of the altar. 7161
1:51 he hath caught hold on the **h** of the altar, 7161
2:28 and caught hold on the **h** of the altar. 7161
22:11 son of Chenaanah made him **h** of iron: 7161
2Ch 18:10 of Chenaanah had made him **h** of iron, 7161
Ps 22:21 for thou hast heard me from the **h** of 7160
69:31 an ox *or* bullock that hath **h** and hoofs. 7161
75:10 All the **h** of the wicked also will I cut off; 7161
75:10 *but* the **h** of the righteous shall be exalted. 7161
118:27 with cords, *even* unto the **h** of the altar. 7161
Jer 17: 1 their heart, and upon the **h** of your altars; 7161
Eze 27:15 they brought thee *for* a present **h** of ivory 7161
34:21 and pusht all the diseased with your **h**, 7161
43:15 from the altar and upward *shall be* four **h**. 7161
43:20 put *it* on the four **h** of it, and on the four 7161
Da 7: 7 that *were* before it; and it had ten **h**. 7162
7: 8 I considered the **h**, and, behold, there 7162
7: 8 whom there were three of the first **h** 7162
7:20 of the ten **h** that *were* in his head, 7162
7:24 ten **h** out of this kingdom *are* ten kings 7162
8: 3 before the river a ram which had **two h**: 7161
8: 3 the **two h** *were* high; but one *was* higher 7161
8: 6 he came to the ram that had **two h**, 7161
8: 7 and smote the ram, and brake his **two h**: 7161
8:20 The ram which thou sawest having **two h** 7161
Am 3:14 the **h** of the altar shall be cut off, and fall 7161
6:13 Have we not taken to us **h** by our own 7161
Hab 3: 4 light; he had **h** *coming* out of his hand: 7161
Zec 1:18 mine eyes, and saw, and behold four **h**. 7161
1:19 These *are* the **h** which have scattered 7161
1:21 These *are* the **h** which have scattered 7161
1:21 them, to cast out the **h** of the Gentiles, 7161
Rev 5: 6 slain, having seven **h** and seven eyes, 2768
9:13 I heard a voice from the four **h** of 2768
12: 3 having seven heads and ten **h**, 2768
13: 1 having seven heads and ten **h**, and upon 2768
13: 1 and upon his **h** ten crowns, and upon his 2768
13:11 he had two **h** like a lamb, and he spake 2768
17: 3 having seven heads and ten **h**. 2768
17: 7 which hath the seven heads and ten **h**. 2768
17:12 And the ten **h** which thou sawest are ten 2768
17:16 And the ten **h** which thou sawest upon 2768

HORONAIM (4)
Isa 15: 5 *in* the way of **H** they shall raise up a cry 2773
Jer 48: 3 voice of crying *shall be* from **H**, spoiling 2773
48: 5 for in the going down of **H** the enemies 2773
48:34 from Zoar *even* unto **H**, *as* a heifer of 2773

HORONITE (3)

Ne	2:10 When Sanballat the **H**, and Tobiah	2772
	2:19 when Sanballat the **H**, and Tobiah	2772
	13:28 *was* son in law to Sanballat the **H**:	2772

HORRIBLE (6) [HORROR]

Ps	11: 6 fire and brimstone, and a **h** tempest:	2152
	40: 2 He brought me up also out of a **h** pit, out	7588
Jer	5:30 and **h** thing is committed in the land;	8186
	18:13 virgin of Israel hath done a very **h** thing.	8186
	23:14 in the prophets of Jerusalem a **h** thing:	8186
Hos	6:10 have seen a **h** thing in the house of Israel:	8186

HORRIBLY (2) [HORROR]

Jer	2:12 O ye heavens, at this, and be **h** afraid,	8175
Eze	32:10 and their kings shall be **h** afraid for thee,	8178

HORROR (4) [HORRIBLE, HORRIBLY]

Ge	15:12 lo, **h** of great darkness fell upon him.	367
Ps	55: 5 upon me, and **h** hath overwhelmed me.	6427
	119:53 **H** hath taken hold upon me because of	2152
Eze	7:18 with sackcloth, and **h** shall cover them;	6427

HORSE (43) [HORSEBACK, HORSEHOOFS, HORSELEACH, HORSEMAN, HORSEMEN, HORSES, HORSES']

Ge	49:17 that biteth the **h** heels, so that his rider	5483
Ex	15: 1 the **h** and his rider hath he thrown into	5483
	15:19 For the **h** of Pharaoh went in with his	5483
	15:21 the **h** and his rider hath he thrown into	5483
1Ki	10:29 of silver, and a **h** for an hundred and fifty:	5483
	20:20 the king of Syria escaped on a **h**	5483
	20:25 **h** for horse, and chariot for chariot;	5483
	20:25 horse for **h**, and chariot for chariot:	5483
2Ch	1:17 of silver, and a **h** for an hundred and fifty:	5483
	23:15 she was come to the entering of the **h**	5483
Ne	3:28 above the **h** gate repaired the priests,	5483
Est	6: 8 the **h** that the king rideth upon,	5483
	6: 9 be delivered to the hand of one of	5483
	6:10 haste, *and* take the apparel and the **h**,	5483
	6:11 took Haman the apparel and the **h**,	5483
Job	39:18 on high, she scorneth the **h** and his rider.	5483
	39:19 Hast thou given the **h** strength? hast thou	5483
Ps	32: 9 Be ye not as the mule, *or* as the mule,	5483
	33:17 A **h** *is* a vain thing for safety: neither shall	5483
	76: 6 chariot and **h** *are* cast into a dead sleep.	5483
	147:10 delighteth not in the strength of the **h**:	5483
Pr	21:31 **h** *is* prepared against the day of battle:	5483
	26: 3 A whip for the **h**, a bridle for the ass,	5483
Isa	43:17 Which bringeth forth the chariot and **h**,	5483
	63:13 as a **h** in the wilderness, *that* they should	5483
Jer	8: 6 course, as the **h** rusheth into the battle.	5483
	31:40 unto the corner of the **h** gate towards	5483
	51:21 with thee will I break in pieces the **h** and	5483
Am	2:15 shall he that rideth the **h** deliver himself.	5483
Zec	1: 8 behold a man riding upon a red **h**,	5483
	9:10 the **h** from Jerusalem, and the battle bow	5483
	10: 3 hath made them as his goodly **h** in	5483
	12: 4 I will smite every **h** with astonishment,	5483
	12: 4 will smite every **h** of the people with	5483
	14:15 shall be the plague of the **h**, of the mule,	5483
Rev	6: 2 And I saw, and behold a white **h**:	2462
	6: 4 there went out another **h** *that was* red:	2462
	6: 5 I beheld, and lo a black **h**; and he that	2462
	6: 8 And I looked, and behold a pale **h**:	2462
	14:20 *even* unto the **h** bridles, by the space of a	2462
	19:11 heaven opened, and behold a white **h**;	2462
	19:19 make war against him that sat on the **h**,	2462
	19:21 the sword of him that sat upon the **h**,	2462

HORSEBACK (5) [BACK, HORSE]

2Ki	9:18 went one on **h** to meet him,	5483+7392
	9:19 he sent *out* a second on **h**, which	5483+7392
Est	6: 9 bring him on **h** through the street of	5483
	6:11 **brought** him on **h** through the street of	7392
	8:10 sent letters by posts on **h**, *and* riders on	5483

HORSEHOOFS (1) [HOOF, HORSE]

Jdg	5:22 were the **h** broken by the means of	5483+6119

HORSELEACH (1) [HORSE]

Pr	30:15 The **h** hath two daughters, *crying*, Give,	5936

HORSEMAN (2) [HORSE, MAN]

2Ki	9:17 Take a **h**, and send to meet them,	7395
Na	3: 3 The **h** lifteth up both the bright sword and	6571

HORSEMEN (59) [HORSE, MAN]

Ge	50: 9 went up with him both chariots and **h**:	6571
Ex	14: 9 of Pharaoh, and his **h**, and his army)	6571
	14:17 host, upon his chariots, and upon his **h**.	6571
	14:18 upon his chariots, and upon his **h**.	6571
	14:23 Pharaoh's horses, his chariots, and his **h**.	6571
	14:26 upon their chariots, and upon their **h**.	6571
	14:28 the **h**, and all the host of Pharaoh that	6571
	15:19 his chariots and with his **h** into the sea,	6571
Jos	24: 6 with chariots and **h** *unto* the Red sea.	6571
1Sa	8:11 himself, for his chariots, and to be his **h**;	6571
	13: 5 six thousand **h**, and people as the sand	6571
2Sa	1:6 and followed hard after him.	1167+6571
	8: 4 thousand *chariots*, and seven hundred **h**,	6571
	10:18 forty thousand **h**, and smote Shobach	6571
1Ki	1: 5 he prepared him chariots and **h**,	6571
	4:26 for his chariots, and twelve thousand **h**.	6571
	9:19 cities for his **h**, and that which Solomon	6571
	9:22 and rulers of his chariots, and his **h**.	6571
	10:26 gathered together chariots and **h**:	6571
	10:26 hundred chariots, and twelve thousand **h**,	6571
	20:20 of Syria escaped on a horse with the **h**.	6571
2Ki	2:12 the chariot of Israel, and the **h** thereof.	6571
	13: 7 *of* the people to Jehoahaz but fifty **h**,	6571
	13:14 the chariot of Israel, and the **h** thereof.	6571
	18:24 thy trust on Egypt for chariots and for **h**?	6571
1Ch	18: 4 seven thousand **h**, and twenty thousand	6571
	19: 6 them chariots and **h** out of Mesopotamia,	6571
2Ch	1:14 Solomon gathered chariots and **h**:	6571
	1:14 hundred chariots, and twelve thousand **h**,	6571
	8: 6 the cities of the **h**, and all that Solomon	6571
	8: 9 and captains of his chariots and **h**.	6571
	9:25 and chariots, and twelve thousand **h**;	6571
	12: 3 and threescore thousand **h**:	6571
	16: 8 host, with very many chariots and **h**?	6571
Ezr	8:22 **h** to help us against the enemy in the	6571
Ne	2: 9 sent captains of the army and **h** with me.	6571
Isa	21: 7 he saw a chariot *with* a couple of **h**,	6571
	21: 9 a chariot of men, *with* a couple of **h**.	6571
	22: 6 the quiver with chariots of men *and* **h**,	6571
	22: 7 the **h** shall set themselves in array at	6571
	28:28 wheel of his cart, nor bruise it *with* his **h**.	6571
	31: 1 in **h**, because they are very strong;	6571
	36: 9 thy trust on Egypt for chariots and for **h**?	6571
Jer	4:29 whole city shall flee for the noise of the **h**	6571
	46: 4 ye **h**, and stand forth with *your* helmets;	6571
Eze	23: 6 young men, **h** riding upon horses.	6571
	23:12 most gorgeously, **h** riding upon horses,	6571
	26: 7 with **h**, and companies, and much people.	6571
	26:10 thy walls shall shake at the noise of the **h**,	6571
	27:14 in thy fairs with horses and **h** and mules.	6571
	38: 4 forth, and all thine army, horses and **h**,	6571
Da	11:40 and with **h**, and with many ships;	6571
Hos	1: 7 nor by battle, by horses, nor by **h**.	6571
Joel	2: 4 of horses; and as **h**, so shall they run.	6571
Hab	1: 8 their **h** shall spread themselves,	6571
	1: 8 and their **h** shall come from far;	6571
Ac	23:23 **h** threescore *and* ten, and spearmen two	2460
	23:32 On the morrow they left the **h** to go with	2460
Rev	9:16 the number of the army of the **h** were	2461

HORSES (109) [HORSE]

Ge	47:17 gave them bread *in exchange* for **h**,	5483
Ex	9: 3 upon the **h**, upon the asses, upon	5483
	14: 9 Egyptians pursued after them [all the **h**	5483
	14:23 *even* all Pharaoh's **h**, his chariots,	5483
Dt	11: 4 Egypt, unto their **h**, and to their chariots;	5483
	17:16 he shall not multiply **h** to himself,	5483
	17:16 to the end that he should multiply **h**:	5483
	20: 1 seest **h**, and chariots, *and* a people more	5483
Jos	11: 4 with **h** and chariots very many.	5483
	11: 6 thou shalt hough their **h**, and burn their	5483
	11: 9 houghed their **h**, and burnt their chariots	5483
2Sa	8: 4 David houghed all the chariot **h**,	NIH
	15: 1 Absalom prepared him chariots and **h**,	5483
1Ki	4:26 Solomon had forty thousand stalls of **h** for	5483
	4:28 Barley also and straw for the **h** and	5483
	10:25 and armour, and spices, **h**, and mules,	5483
	10:28 Solomon had **h** brought out of Egypt,	5483
	18: 5 we may find grass to save the **h**	5483
	20: 1 two kings with him, and **h**, and chariots:	5483
	20:21 smote the **h** and chariots, and slew	5483
	22: 4 people as thy people, my **h** as thy horses.	5483
	22: 4 people as thy people, my horses as thy **h**.	5483
2Ki	2:11 **h** of fire, and parted them both asunder;	5483
	3: 7 as thy people, *and* my **h** as thy horses.	5483
	3: 7 as thy people, and my horses as thy **h**.	5483
	5: 9 So Naaman came with his **h** and with his	5483
	6:14 Therefore sent he thither **h**, and chariots,	5483
	6:15 host compassed the city both with **h** and	5483
	6:17 the mountain was full of **h** and chariots of	5483
	7: 6 noise of **h**, *even* the noise of a great host:	5483
	7: 7 their tents, and their **h**, and their asses,	5483
	7:10 **h** tied, and asses tied, and the tents as	5483
	7:13 I pray thee, five of the **h** that remain,	5483
	7:14 They took therefore two chariot **h**;	5483
	9:33 was sprinkled on the wall, and on the **h**:	5483
	10: 2 *are* with you chariots and **h**, a fenced	5483
	11:16 she went *by* the way by the which the **h**	5483
	14:20 brought him on **h**: and he was buried	5483
	18:23 and I will deliver thee two thousand **h**,	5483
	23:11 took away the **h** that the kings of Judah	5483
1Ch	18: 4 David also houghed all the chariot **h**,	NIH
2Ch	1:16 Solomon had **h** brought out of Egypt,	5483
	1:17 brought they out **h** for all the kings of	NIH
	9:24 harness, and spices, **h**, and mules,	5483
	9:25 Solomon had four thousand stalls for **h**	5483
	9:28 brought unto Solomon **h** out of Egypt,	5483
	25:28 brought him upon **h**, and buried him	5483
Ezr	2:66 **h** *were* seven hundred thirty and six;	5483
Ne	7:68 Their **h**, seven hundred thirty and six:	5483
Ps	20: 7 Some *trust* in chariots, and some in **h**:	5483
Ecc	10: 7 I have seen servants upon **h**,	5483
SS	1: 9 to a **company of h** in Pharaoh's chariots.	5484
Isa	2: 7 their land is also full *of* **h**, neither *is there*	5483
	30:16 ye said, No; for we will flee upon **h**;	5483
	31: 1 stay on **h**, and trust in chariots, because	5483
	31: 3 not God; and their **h** flesh, and not spirit.	5483
	36: 8 and I will give thee two thousand **h**,	5483
	66:20 unto the Lord out of all nations upon **h**,	5483
Jer	4:13 **h** are swifter than eagles. Woe unto us!	5483
	5: 8 They were *as* fed **h** in the morning:	5483
	6:23 they ride upon **h**, set in array as men for	5483
	8:16 snorting of his **h** was heard from Dan:	5483
	12: 5 then how canst thou contend with **h**?	5483
	17:25 riding in chariots and on **h**, they,	5483
	22: 4 riding in chariots and on **h**, he,	5483
	46: 4 Harness the **h**; and get up, ye horsemen,	5483
	46: 9 Come up, ye **h**; and rage, ye chariots;	5483
	47: 3 his strong **h**, at the rushing of his chariots,	NIH
	50:37 A sword *is* upon their **h**, and upon their	5483
	50:42 they shall ride upon **h**, *every one* put in	5483
	51:27 cause the **h** to come up as the rough	5483
Eze	17:15 that *they* might give him **h** and	5483
	23: 6 young men, horsemen riding upon **h**,	5483
	23:12 gorgeously, horsemen riding upon **h**,	5483
	23:20 whose issue *is* like the issue of **h**.	5483
	23:23 renowned, all of them riding upon **h**.	5483
	26: 7 with **h**, and with chariots,	5483
	26:11 With the hoofs of his **h** shall he tread	5483
	27:14 of Togarmah traded in thy fairs with **h**	5483
	38: 4 and all thine army, and horsemen,	5483
	38:15 of them riding upon **h**, a great company,	5483
	39:20 Thus ye shall be filled at my table *with* **h**	5483
Hos	1: 7 nor by sword, nor by battle, by **h**, nor by	5483
	14: 3 will not ride upon **h**: neither will we say	5483
Joel	2: 4 of them *is* as the appearance of **h**;	5483
Am	4:10 the sword, and have taken away your **h**;	5483
	6:12 Shall **h** run upon the rock? will *one* plow	5483
Mic	5:10 that I will cut off thy **h** out of the midst of	5483
Na	3: 2 of the prancing **h**, and of the jumping	5483
Hab	1: 8 Their **h** also are swifter than the leopards,	5483
	3: 8 that thou didst ride upon thine **h** *and*	5483
	3:15 didst walk through the sea *with* thine **h**,	5483
Hag	2:22 the **h** and their riders shall come down,	5483
Zec	1: 8 behind him *were* there red **h**, speckled,	5483
	6: 2 In the first chariot *were* red **h**; and in	5483
	6: 2 and in the second chariot black **h**;	5483
	6: 3 in the third chariot white **h**; and in	5483
	6: 3 in the fourth chariot grisled *and* bay **h**.	5483
	6: 6 The black **h** which *are* therein go forth	5483
	10: 5 and the riders on **h** shall be confounded.	5483
	14:20 day shall there be upon the bells of the **h**,	5483
Rev	9: 7 *were* like unto **h** prepared unto battle;	2462
	9: 9 of chariots of many **h** running to battle.	2462
	9:17 And thus I saw the **h** in the vision,	2462
	9:17 the heads of the **h** *were* as the heads of	2462
	18:13 and **h**, and chariots, and slaves, and souls	2462
	19:14 in heaven followed him upon white **h**,	2462
	19:18 flesh of mighty *men*, and the flesh of **h**,	2462

HORSES' (2) [HORSE]

Isa	5:28 their **h** hoofs shall be counted like flint,	5483
Jas	3: 3 Behold, we put bits in the **h** mouths,	2462

HOSAH (5)

Jos	19:29 the coast turneth to **H**; and the outgoings	2621
1Ch	16:38 the son of Jeduthun and **H** to be porters:	2621
	26:10 **H**, of the children of Merari, had sons;	2621
	26:11 the sons and brethren of **H** *were* thirteen.	2621
	26:16 and **H** *the lot came forth* westward,	2621

HOSANNA (6)

Mt	21: 9 cried, saying, **H** to the Son of David:	5614
	21: 9 in the name of the Lord; **H** in the highest.	5614
	21:15 and saying, **H** to the Son of David;	5614
Mk	11: 9 and they that followed, cried, saying, **H**;	5614
	11:10 in the name of the Lord: **H** in the highest.	5614
Jn	12:13 and went forth to meet him, and cried, **H**:	5614

HOSEA (3) [OSEE]

Hos	1: 1 The word of the Lord that came unto **H**,	1954
	1: 2 beginning of the word of the Lord by **H**.	1954
	1: 2 the Lord said to **H**, Go, take unto thee a	1954

HOSEN (1)

Da	3:21 their **h**, and their hats, and their *other*	6361

HOSHAIAH (2)

Ne	12:32 after them went **H**, and half of the princes	1955
Jer	42: 1 Jezaniah the son of **H**, and all the people	1955
	43: 2 spake Azariah the son of **H**,	1955

HOSHAMA (1)

1Ch	3:18 Shenazar, Jecamiah, **H**, and Nedabiah.	1953

HOSHEA (11) [JOSHUA]

Dt	32:44 of the people, he and **H** the son of Nun.	1954
2Ki	15:30 **H** the son of Elah made a conspiracy	1954
	17: 1 **H** the son of Elah to reign in Samaria over	1954
	17: 3 **H** became his servant, and gave him	1954
	17: 4 the king of Assyria found conspiracy in **H**:	1954
	17: 6 In the ninth year of **H**, the king of Assyria	1954
	18: 1 Now it came to pass in the third year of **H**	1954
	18: 9 which *was* the seventh year of **H** son of	1954
	18:10 that in the ninth year of **H** king of Israel,	1954
1Ch	27:20 of Ephraim, **H** the son of Azaziah:	1954
Ne	10:23 **H**, Hananiah, Hashub,	1954

HOSPITALITY (4)

Ro	12:13 to the necessity of saints; given to **h**.	5381
1Ti	3: 2 good behaviour, **given to h**, apt to teach;	5382
Tit	1: 8 But a **lover of h**, a lover of good *men*,	5382
1Pe	4: 9 Use **h** one to another without grudging.	5382

HOST (192) [HOSTS]

Ge	2: 1 were finished, and all the **h** of them.	6635
	21:22 Phichol the chief captain of his **h** spake	6635

Ge	21:32 Phichol the chief captain of his **h**,	6635
	32: 2 Jacob saw them, he said, This *is* God's **h**:	4264
Ex	14: 4 upon Pharaoh, and upon all his **h**;	2428
	14:17 upon all his **h**, upon his chariots,	2428
	14:24 **h** of the Egyptians through the pillar of	4264
	14:24 and troubled the **h** of the Egyptians,	2428
	14:28 the **h** of Pharaoh that came into the sea	2428
	15: 4 and his **h** hath he cast into the sea:	2428
	16:13 morning the dew lay round about the **h**.	4264
Nu	2: 4 his **h**, and those that were numbered of	6635
	2: 6 his **h**, and those that were numbered	6635
	2: 8 his **h**, and those that were numbered	6635
	2:11 his **h**, and those that were numbered	6635
	2:13 his **h**, and those that were numbered	6635
	2:15 his **h**, and those that were numbered	6635
	2:19 his **h**, and those that were numbered	6635
	2:21 his **h**, and those that were numbered	6635
	2:23 his **h**, and those that were numbered	6635
	2:26 his **h**, and those that were numbered	6635
	2:28 his **h**, and those that were numbered	6635
	2:30 his **h**, and those that were numbered	6635
	4: 3 fifty years old, all that enter into the **h**,	6635
	10:14 over his **h** *was* Nahshon the son of	6635
	10:15 over the **h** of the tribe of the children of	6635
	10:16 over the **h** of the tribe of the children of	6635
	10:18 over his **h** *was* Elizur the son of Shedeur.	6635
	10:19 over the **h** of the tribe of the children of	6635
	10:20 over the **h** of the tribe of the children of	6635
	10:22 over his **h** *was* Elishama the son of	6635
	10:23 over the **h** of the tribe of the children of	6635
	10:24 over the **h** of the tribe of the children of	6635
	10:25 over his **h** *was* Ahiezer the son of	6635
	10:26 over the **h** of the tribe of the children of	6635
	10:27 over the **h** of the tribe of the children of	6635
	31:14 was wroth with the officers of the **h**,	2428
	31:48 which *were* over thousands of the **h**,	6635
Dt	2:14 war were wasted out from among the **h**,	4264
	2:15 to destroy them from among the **h**,	6635
	4:19 and the stars, *even* all the **h** of heaven,	6635
	17: 3 sun, or moon, or any of the **h** of heaven,	6635
	23: 9 When the **h** goeth against thine	4264
Jos	1:11 Pass through the **h**, and command	4264
	3: 2 that the officers went through the **h**;	4264
	5:14 *as* captain of the **h** of the LORD am I now	6635
	5:15 the captain of the LORD's **h** said unto	6635
	8:13 *even* all the **h** that *was* on the north of	4264
	18: 9 came *again* to Joshua to the **h** at Shiloh.	4264
Jdg	4: 2 the captain of whose **h** *was* Sisera, which	6635
	4:15 and all *his* chariots, and all *his* **h**,	4264
	4:16 the **h**, unto Harosheth of the Gentiles:	4264
	4:16 all the **h** of Sisera fell upon the edge of	4264
	7: 1 that the **h** of the Midianites were on	4264
	7: 8 the **h** of Midian was beneath him in	4264
	7: 9 him, Arise, get thee down unto the **h**;	4264
	7:10 with Phurah thy servant down to the **h**:	4264
	7:11 be strengthened to go down unto the **h**.	4264
	7:11 of the armed *men* that *were* in the **h**.	4264
	7:13 a cake of barley bread tumbled into the **h**	4264
	7:14 hath God delivered Midian, and all the **h**.	4264
	7:15 returned into the **h** of Israel, and said,	4264
	7:15 delivered into your hand the **h** of Midian.	4264
	7:21 and all the **h** ran, and cried, and fled.	4264
	7:22 his fellow, *even* throughout all the **h**:	4264
	7:22 the **h** fled to Beth-shittah in Zererath,	4264
	8:11 of Nobah and Jogbehah, and smote the **h**:	4264
	8:11 and smote the host: for the **h** was secure.	4264
	8:12 and Zalmunna, and discomfited all the **h**.	4264
1Sa	11:11 they came into the midst of the **h** in	4264
	12: 9 captain of the **h** of Hazor, and into the	6635
	14:15 there was trembling in the **h**, in the field,	4264
	14:19 that the noise that *was* in the **h** of	4264
	14:48 gathered a **h**, and smote the Amalekites,	2428
	14:50 name of the captain of his **h** *was* Abner,	6635
	17:20 as the **h** was going forth to the fight,	2428
	17:46 I will give the carcases of the **h** of	4264
	17:55 unto Abner, the captain of the **h**, Abner,	6635
	26: 5 Abner the son of Ner, the captain of his **h**:	6635
	28: 5 when Saul saw the **h** of the Philistines,	4264
	28:19 the **h** also shall deliver the **h** of Israel	4264
	29: 6 thy coming in with me in the **h** *is* good in	4264
2Sa	2: 8 Abner the son of Ner, captain of Saul's **h**,	6635
	3:23 all the **h** that *was* with him were come,	4264
	5:24 to smite the **h** of the Philistines.	4264
	8: 9 David had smitten all the **h** of Hadadezer,	2428
	8:16 Joab the son of Zeruiah *was* over the **h**;	6635
	10: 7 Joab, and all the **h** *of* the mighty *men.*	6635
	10:16 Shobach the captain of the **h** of Hadarezer	6635
	10:18 smote Shobach the captain of their **h**,	6635
	17:25 Absalom made Amasa captain of the **h**	6635
	19:13 if thou be not captain of the **h** before me	6635
	20:23 Now Joab *was* over all the **h** of Israel:	6635
	23:16 three mighty *men* brake through the **h**	4264
	24: 2 the king said to Joab the captain of the **h**,	2428
	24: 4 and against the captains of the **h**.	2428
	24: 4 the captains of the **h** went out from	2428
1Ki	1:19 the priest, and Joab the captain of the **h**:	6635
	1:25 the captains of the **h**, and Abiathar	6635
	2:32 captain of the **h** of Israel, and Amasa	6635
	2:32 son of Jether, captain of the **h** of Judah.	6635
	2:35 son of Jehoiada in his room over the **h**:	6635
	4: 4 the son of Jehoiada *was* over the **h**:	6635
	11:15 Joab the captain of the **h** was gone up to	6635
	11:21 that Joab the captain of the **h** was dead,	6635
	16:16 Israel made Omri, the captain of the **h**,	6635
	20: 1 king of Syria gathered all his **h** together:	2428

1Ki	22:19 all the **h** of heaven standing by him on	6635
	22:34 thine hand, and carry me out of the **h**;	4264
	22:36 went a proclamation throughout the **h**	4264
2Ki	3: 9 there was no water for the **h**, and for	6635
	4:13 for to the king, or to the captain of the **h**?	6635
	5: 1 captain of the **h** of the king of Syria,	6635
	6:14 horses, and chariots, and a great **h**:	2428
	6:15 a **h** compassed the city both with horses	2428
	6:24 Ben-hadad king of Syria gathered all his **h**,	4264
	7: 4 and let us fall unto the **h** of the Syrians:	4264
	7: 6 the Lord had made the **h** of the Syrians	4264
	7: 6 of horses, *even* the noise of a great **h**:	2428
	7:14 the king sent after the **h** of the Syrians,	4264
	9: 5 the captains of the **h** *were* sitting;	2428
	11:15 the officers of the **h**, and said unto them,	2428
	17:16 worshipped all the **h** of heaven,	6635
	18:17 with a great *against* Jerusalem.	2426
	21: 3 worshipped all the **h** of heaven.	6635
	21: 5 he built altars for all the **h** of heaven in	6635
	23: 4 for the grove, and for all the **h** of heaven:	6635
	23: 5 to the planets, and to all the **h** of heaven.	6635
	25: 1 he, and all his **h**, against Jerusalem,	2428
	25:19 the city, and the principal scribe of the **h**,	6635
1Ch	9:19 *being* over the **h** of the LORD,	4264
	11:15 the **h** of the Philistines encamped in	4264
	11:18 the three brake through the **h** of	4264
	12:14 of the sons of Gad, captains of the **h**:	6635
	12:21 of valour, and were captains in the **h**.	6635
	12:22 it was a great **h**, like the host of God.	4264
	12:22 it was a great host, like the **h** of God.	4264
	14:15 thee to smite the **h** of the Philistines.	4264
	14:16 they smote the **h** of the Philistines from	4264
	18: 9 all the **h** of Hadarezer king of Zobah;	2428
	18:15 Joab the son of Zeruiah *was* over the **h**;	6635
	19: 8 Joab, and all the **h** *of* the mighty *men.*	6635
	19:16 the captain of the **h** of Hadarezer	6635
	19:18 killed Shophach the captain of the **h**.	6635
	25: 1 the captains of the **h** separated to	6635
	26:26 and hundreds, and the captains of the **h**,	6635
	27: 3 the captains of the **h** for the first month.	6635
	27: 5 The third captain of the **h** for the third	6635
2Ch	14: 9 with a **h** of a thousand thousand,	2428
	14:13 before the LORD, and before his **h**;	4264
	16: 7 is the **h** of the king of Syria escaped out	2428
	16: 8 the Ethiopians and the Lubims a huge **h**,	2428
	18:18 all the **h** of heaven standing on his right	6635
	18:33 that thou mayest carry me out of the **h**.	4264
	23:14 of hundreds that were set over the **h**,	2428
	24:23 *that* the **h** of Syria came up against him:	2428
	24:24 the LORD delivered a very great **h** into	2428
	26:11 Uzziah had a **h** of fighting *men*,	2428
	26:14 for them throughout all the **h** shields,	6635
	28: 9 he went out before the **h** that came to	6635
	33: 3 worshipped all the **h** of heaven,	6635
	33: 5 he built altars for all the **h** of heaven in	6635
	33:11 captains of the **h** of the king of Assyria,	6635
Ne	9: 6 with all their **h**, the earth, and all *things*	6635
	9: 6 and the **h** of heaven worshippeth thee.	6635
Ps	27: 3 Though a **h** should encamp against me,	4264
	33: 6 all the **h** of them by the breath of his	6635
	33:16 is no king saved by the multitude of a **h**:	2428
	136:15 and his **h** in the Red sea:	2428
Isa	13: 4 the LORD of hosts mustereth the **h** of	6635
	24:21 *that* the LORD shall punish the **h** of	6635
	34: 4 all the **h** of heaven shall be dissolved,	6635
	34: 4 their **h** shall fall down, as the leaf falleth	6635
	40:26 that bringeth out their **h** by number:	6635
	45:12 and all their **h** have I commanded.	6635
Jer	8: 2 the moon, and all the **h** of heaven,	6635
	19:13 burnt incense unto all the **h** of heaven,	6635
	33:22 As the **h** of heaven cannot be numbered,	6635
	51: 3 young men; destroy ye utterly all her **h**.	6635
	52:25 principal scribe of the **h**, who mustered	6635
Eze	1:24 the voice of speech, as the noise of a **h**:	4264
Da	8:10 it waxed great, *even* to the **h** of heaven;	6635
	8:10 cast down *some* of the **h** and of the stars	6635
	8:11 *himself even* to the prince of the **h**,	6635
	8:12 a was given *him* against the daily	6635
	8:13 and the **h** to be trodden under foot?	6635
Ob	1:20 the captivity of this **h** of the children of	2426
Zep	1: 5 them that worship the **h** of heaven upon	6635
Lk	2:13 multitude of the heavenly **h** praising God,	4756
	10:35 gave them to the **h**, and said unto him,	3830
Ac	7:42 gave them up to worship the **h** of heaven;	4756
Ro	16:23 Gaius mine **h**, and of the whole church,	3581

HOSTAGES (2)

| 2Ki | 14:14 and **h**, and returned to Samaria. | 1121+8594 |
| 2Ch | 25:24 **h** also, and returned *to* Samaria. | 1121+8594 |

HOSTILE See VEX; VEXATION; VEXED

HOSTS (299) [HOST]

Ex	12:41 *that* all the **h** of the LORD went out from	6635
Nu	1:52 by his own standard, throughout their **h**.	6635
	2:32 their **h** *were* six hundred thousand	6635
	2:32 of all the camps throughout their **h**:	6635
Jos	10: 5 they and all their **h**, and encamped before	4264
	11: 4 they and all their **h** with them,	4264
Jdg	8:10 *were* in Karkor, and their **h** with them,	4264
	8:10 left of all the **h** of the children of the east:	4264
1Sa	1: 3 to sacrifice unto the LORD of **h** in Shiloh.	6635
	1:11 she vowed a vow, and said, O LORD of **h**,	6635
	4: 4 the ark of the covenant of the LORD of **h**,	6635
	15: 2 Thus saith the LORD of **h**, I remember	6635

1Sa	17:45 to thee in the name of the LORD of **h**,	6635
2Sa	5:10 and the LORD God of **h** *was* with him.	6635
	6: 2 **h** that dwelleth *between* the cherubims.	6635
	6:18 the people in the name of the LORD of **h**,	6635
	7: 8 Thus saith the LORD of **h**, I took thee	6635
	7:26 The LORD of **h** *is* the God over Israel:	6635
	7:27 For thou, O LORD of **h**, God of Israel,	6635
1Ki	2: 5 what he did to the two captains of the **h**	6635
	15:20 sent the captains of the **h** which he had	2428
	18:15 Elijah said, *As* the LORD of **h** liveth,	6635
	19:10 been very jealous for the LORD God of **h**:	6635
	19:14 been very jealous for the LORD God of **h**.	6635
2Ki	3:14 And Elisha said, *As* the LORD of **h** liveth,	6635
	19:31 the zeal of the LORD *of* **h** shall do this.	NIH
1Ch	11: 9 greater: for the LORD of **h** *was* with him.	6635
	17: 7 Thus saith the LORD of **h**, I took thee	6635
	17:24 The LORD of **h** *is* the God of Israel,	6635
Ps	24:10 The LORD of **h**, he *is* the King of glory.	6635
	46: 7 The LORD of **h** *is* with us; the God of	6635
	46:11 The LORD of **h** *is* with us; the God of	6635
	48: 8 we seen in the city of the LORD of **h**,	6635
	59: 5 Thou therefore, O LORD God *of* **h**,	6635
	69: 6 O Lord GOD of **h**, be ashamed for my	6635
	80: 4 O LORD God *of* **h**, how long wilt thou be	6635
	80: 7 O God *of* **h**, and cause thy face to shine;	6635
	80:14 Return, we beseech thee, O God *of* **h**:	6635
	80:19 Turn us again, O LORD God *of* **h**,	6635
	84: 1 *are* thy tabernacles, O LORD of **h**!	6635
	84: 3 O LORD of **h**, my King, and my God.	6635
	84: 8 O LORD God *of* **h**, hear my prayer:	6635
	84:12 O LORD of **h**, blessed *is* the man that	6635
	89: 8 O LORD God of **h**, who *is* a strong	6635
	103:21 Bless ye the LORD, all ye his **h**;	6635
	108:11 not thou, O God, go forth with our **h**?	6635
	148: 2 all his angels: praise ye him, all his **h**.	6635
Isa	1: 9 Except the LORD of **h** had left unto us a	6635
	1:24 Therefore saith the Lord, the LORD of **h**,	6635
	2:12 For the day of the LORD of **h** *shall be*	6635
	3: 1 For behold, the Lord, the LORD of **h**,	6635
	3:15 of the poor? saith the Lord GOD of **h**.	6635
	5: 7 For the vineyard of the LORD of **h** *is*	6635
	5: 9 In mine ears *said* the LORD of **h**, Of a	6635
	5:16 the LORD of **h** shall be exalted in	6635
	5:24 have cast away the law of the LORD of **h**,	6635
	6: 3 said, Holy, holy, holy, *is* the LORD of **h**:	6635
	6: 5 eyes have seen the King, the LORD of **h**.	6635
	8:13 Sanctify the LORD of **h** himself;	6635
	8:18 for wonders in Israel from the LORD of **h**,	6635
	9: 7 The zeal of the LORD of **h** will perform	6635
	9:13 neither do they seek the LORD of **h**.	6635
	9:19 Through the wrath of the LORD of **h** is	6635
	10:16 Therefore shall the Lord, the Lord of **h**,	6635
	10:23 For the Lord GOD of **h** shall make a	6635
	10:24 Therefore thus saith the Lord GOD of **h**,	6635
	10:26 the LORD of **h** shall stir up a scourge for	6635
	10:33 Behold, the Lord, the LORD of **h**,	6635
	13: 4 the LORD of **h** mustereth the host of	6635
	13:13 in the wrath of the LORD of **h**, and in	6635
	14:22 saith the LORD of **h**, and cut off from	6635
	14:23 of destruction, saith the LORD of **h**.	6635
	14:24 The LORD of **h** hath sworn, saying,	6635
	14:27 For the LORD of **h** hath purposed,	6635
	17: 3 children of Israel, saith the LORD of **h**.	6635
	18: 7 unto the LORD of **h** *of* a people scattered	6635
	18: 7 the place of the name of the LORD of **h**,	6635
	19: 4 over them, saith the Lord, the LORD of **h**.	6635
	19:12 let them know what the LORD of **h** hath	6635
	19:16 the shaking of the hand of the LORD of **h**,	6635
	19:17 because of the counsel of the LORD of **h**,	6635
	19:18 of Canaan, and swear to the LORD of **h**:	6635
	19:20 for a witness unto the LORD of **h** in	6635
	19:25 Whom the LORD of **h** shall bless, saying,	6635
	21:10 that which I have heard of the LORD of **h**,	6635
	22: 5 of perplexity by the Lord GOD of **h** in	6635
	22:12 in that day did the Lord GOD of **h** call to	6635
	22:14 revealed in mine ears *by* the LORD of **h**,	6635
	22:14 you till ye die, saith the Lord GOD of **h**.	6635
	22:15 Thus saith the Lord GOD of **h**,	6635
	22:25 In that day, saith the LORD of **h**, shall	6635
	23: 9 The LORD of **h** hath purposed it, to stain	6635
	24:23 when the LORD of **h** shall reign in mount	6635
	25: 6 in this mountain shall the LORD of **h**	6635
	28: 5 In that day shall the LORD of **h** be for a	6635
	28:22 for I have heard from the Lord GOD of **h**,	6635
	28:29 also cometh forth from the LORD of **h**,	6635
	29: 6 Thou shalt be visited of the LORD of **h**	6635
	31: 4 shall the LORD of **h** come down to fight	6635
	31: 5 so will the LORD of **h** defend Jerusalem;	6635
	37:16 O LORD of **h**, God of Israel, that dwellest	6635
	37:32 the zeal of the LORD of **h** shall do this.	6635
	39: 5 Hear the word of the LORD of **h**:	6635
	44: 6 and his redeemer the LORD of **h**;	6635
	45:13 for price nor reward, saith the LORD of **h**.	6635
	47: 4 our redeemer, the LORD of **h** *is* his name,	6635
	48: 2 of Israel; The LORD of **h** *is* his name.	6635
	51:15 The LORD of **h** *is* his name.	6635
	54: 5 the LORD of **h** *is* his name;	6635
Jer	2:19 is not in thee, saith the LORD GOD of **h**.	6635
	3:19 a goodly heritage of the **h** of nations?	6635
	5:14 Wherefore thus saith the LORD God of **h**,	6635
	6: 6 For thus hath the LORD of **h** said, Hew ye	6635
	6: 9 Thus saith the LORD of **h**, They shall	6635
	7: 3 Thus saith the LORD of **h**, the God of	6635
	7:21 Thus saith the LORD of **h**, the God of	6635
	8: 3 I have driven them, saith the LORD of **h**.	6635

Jer	9: 7 Therefore thus saith the Lord of **h**,	6635
	9:15 Therefore thus saith the Lord of **h**,	6635
	9:17 Thus saith the Lord of **h**, Consider ye,	6635
	10:16 The Lord of **h** is his name.	6635
	11:17 For the Lord of **h**, that planted thee,	6635
	11:20 But, O Lord of **h**, that judgest	6635
	11:22 Therefore thus saith the Lord of **h**,	6635
	15:16 called by thy name, O Lord God of **h**.	6635
	16: 9 For thus saith the Lord of **h**, the God of	6635
	19: 3 Thus saith the Lord of **h**, the God of	6635
	19:11 say unto them, Thus saith the Lord of **h**;	6635
	19:15 Thus saith the Lord of **h**, the God of	6635
	20:12 But, O Lord of **h**, that triest	6635
	23:15 Therefore thus saith the Lord of **h**,	6635
	23:16 Thus saith the Lord of **h**, Hearken not	6635
	23:36 living God, of the Lord of **h** our God.	6635
	25: 8 Therefore thus saith the Lord of **h**;	6635
	25:27 Thus saith the Lord of **h**, the God of	6635
	25:28 say unto them, Thus saith the Lord of **h**;	6635
	25:29 of the earth, saith the Lord of **h**.	6635
	25:32 Thus saith the Lord of **h**, Behold,	6635
	26:18 saying, Thus saith the Lord of **h**;	6635
	27: 4 Thus saith the Lord of **h**, the God of	6635
	27:18 now make intercession to the Lord of **h**	6635
	27:19 For thus saith the Lord of **h** concerning	6635
	27:21 Yea, thus saith the Lord of **h**, the God of	6635
	28: 2 Thus speaketh the Lord of **h**, the God of	6635
	28:14 For thus saith the Lord of **h**, the God of	6635
	29: 4 Thus saith the Lord of **h**, the God of	6635
	29: 8 For thus saith the Lord of **h**, the God of	6635
	29:17 Thus saith the Lord of **h**; Behold, I will	6635
	29:21 Thus saith the Lord of **h**, the God of	6635
	29:25 Thus speaketh the Lord of **h**, the God of	6635
	30: 8 to pass in that day, saith the Lord of **h**,	6635
	31:23 Thus saith the Lord of **h**, the God of	6635
	31:35 thereof roar; The Lord of **h** is his name:	6635
	32:14 Thus saith the Lord of **h**, the God of	6635
	32:15 For thus saith the Lord of **h**, the God of	6635
	32:18 Mighty God, the Lord of **h**, is his name,	6635
	33:11 them that say, Praise the Lord of **h**:	6635
	33:12 Thus saith the Lord of **h**, Again in this	6635
	35:13 Thus saith the Lord of **h**, the God of	6635
	35:17 Therefore thus saith the Lord God of **h**,	6635
	35:18 Thus saith the Lord of **h**, the God of	6635
	35:19 Therefore thus saith the Lord of **h**,	6635
	38:17 the God of **h**, the God of Israel;	6635
	39:16 saying, Thus saith the Lord of **h**,	6635
	42:15 Thus saith the Lord of **h**, the God of	6635
	42:18 For thus saith the Lord of **h**, the God of	6635
	43:10 Thus saith the Lord of **h**, the God of	6635
	44: 2 Thus saith the Lord of **h**, the God of	6635
	44: 7 the God of **h**, the God of Israel;	6635
	44:11 Therefore thus saith the Lord of **h**,	6635
	44:25 Thus saith the Lord of **h**, the God of	6635
	46:10 For this is the day of the Lord God of **h**,	6635
	46:10 for the Lord God of **h** hath a sacrifice in	6635
	46:18 the King, whose name is the Lord of **h**,	6635
	46:25 The Lord of **h**, the God of Israel, saith;	6635
	48: 1 Against Moab thus saith the Lord of **h**,	6635
	48:15 the King, whose name is the Lord of **h**.	6635
	49: 5 a fear upon thee, saith the Lord God of **h**,	6635
	49: 7 thus saith the Lord of **h**;	6635
	49:26 cut off in that day, saith the Lord of **h**.	6635
	49:35 Thus saith the Lord of **h**; Behold, I will	6635
	50:18 Therefore thus saith the Lord of **h**,	6635
	50:25 for this is the work of the Lord God of **h**	6635
	50:31 most proud, saith the Lord God of **h**:	6635
	50:33 Thus saith the Lord of **h**; The children	6635
	50:34 is strong; the Lord of **h** is his name:	6635
	51: 5 nor Judah of his God, of the Lord of **h**;	6635
	51:14 The Lord of **h** hath sworn by himself,	6635
	51:19 the Lord of **h** is his name.	6635
	51:33 For thus saith the Lord of **h**, the God of	6635
	51:57 the King, whose name is the Lord of **h**.	6635
	51:58 Thus saith the Lord of **h**; The broad	6635
Hos	12: 5 Even the Lord God of **h**; the Lord is	6635
Am	3:13 saith the Lord God, the God of **h**,	6635
	4:13 The Lord, The God of **h**, is his name.	6635
	5:14 so the Lord, the God of **h**, shall be with	6635
	5:15 it may be that the Lord God of **h** will be	6635
	5:16 the God of **h**, the Lord, saith thus;	6635
	5:27 the Lord, whose name is The God of **h**.	6635
	6: 8 saith the Lord God of **h**, I abhor	6635
	6:14 of Israel, saith the Lord God of **h**;	6635
	9: 5 the Lord God of **h** is he that toucheth	6635
Mic	4: 4 for the mouth of the Lord of **h**	6635
Na	2:13 saith the Lord of **h**, and I will burn her	6635
	3: 5 I am against thee, saith the Lord of **h**;	6635
Hab	2:13 is it not of the Lord of **h** that the people	6635
Zep	2: 9 saith the Lord of **h**, the God of Israel,	6635
	2:10 against the people of the Lord of **h**.	6635
Hag	1: 2 Thus speaketh the Lord of **h**, saying,	6635
	1: 5 Now therefore thus saith the Lord of **h**;	6635
	1: 7 Thus saith the Lord of **h**; Consider your	6635
	1: 9 saith the Lord of **h**. Because of mine	6635
	1:14 did work in the house of the Lord of **h**	6635
	2: 4 for I am with you, saith the Lord of **h**:	6635
	2: 6 For thus saith the Lord of **h**; Yet once,	6635
	2: 7 house with glory, saith the Lord of **h**.	6635
	2: 8 and the gold is mine, saith the Lord of **h**.	6635
	2: 9 than of the former, saith the Lord of **h**:	6635
	2: 9 will I give peace, saith the Lord of **h**.	6635
	2:11 Thus saith the Lord of **h**; Ask now	6635
	2:23 In that day, saith the Lord of **h**, will I	6635
	2:23 I have chosen thee, saith the Lord of **h**.	6635

Zec	1: 3 unto them, Thus saith the Lord of **h**;	6635
	1: 3 saith the Lord of **h**, and I will turn unto	6635
	1: 3 I will turn unto you, saith the Lord of **h**.	6635
	1: 4 saying, Thus saith the Lord of **h**,	6635
	1: 6 Like as the Lord of **h** thought to do unto	6635
	1:12 and said, O Lord of **h**,	6635
	1:14 saying, Thus saith the Lord of **h**;	6635
	1:16 saith the Lord of **h**, and a line shall be	6635
	1:17 saying, Thus saith the Lord of **h**;	6635
	2: 8 For thus saith the Lord of **h**; After	6635
	2: 9 ye shall know that the Lord of **h** hath	6635
	2:11 thou shalt know that the Lord of **h** hath	6635
	3: 7 Thus saith the Lord of **h**; If thou wilt	6635
	3: 9 saith the Lord of **h**, and I will remove	6635
	3:10 In that day, saith the Lord of **h**, shall ye	6635
	4: 6 but by my spirit, saith the Lord of **h**.	6635
	4: 9 thou shalt know that the Lord of **h** hath	6635
	5: 4 saith the Lord of **h**, and it shall enter	6635
	6:12 Thus speaketh the Lord of **h**, saying,	6635
	6:15 ye shall know that the Lord of **h** hath	6635
	7: 3 were in the house of the Lord of **h**,	6635
	7: 4 came the word of the Lord of **h** unto me,	6635
	7: 9 Thus speaketh the Lord of **h**, saying,	6635
	7:12 the words which the Lord of **h** hath sent	6635
	7:12 came a great wrath from the Lord of **h**.	6635
	7:13 I would not hear, saith the Lord of **h**:	6635
	8: 1 Again the word of the Lord of **h** came to	6635
	8: 2 Thus saith the Lord of **h**; I was jealous	6635
	8: 3 the mountain of the Lord of **h** the holy	6635
	8: 4 Thus saith the Lord of **h**; There shall yet	6635
	8: 6 Thus saith the Lord of **h**; If it be	6635
	8: 6 in my eyes? saith the Lord of **h**.	6635
	8: 7 Thus saith the Lord of **h**; Behold, I will	6635
	8: 9 Thus saith the Lord of **h**; Let your hands	6635
	8: 9 of the house of the Lord of **h** was laid,	6635
	8:11 in the former days, saith the Lord of **h**.	6635
	8:14 For thus saith the Lord of **h**,	6635
	8:14 saith the Lord of **h**, and I repented not:	6635
	8:18 the word of the Lord of **h** came unto me,	6635
	8:19 Thus saith the Lord of **h**; The fast of	6635
	8:20 Thus saith the Lord of **h**; It shall yet	6635
	8:21 the Lord, and to seek the Lord of **h**:	6635
	8:22 come to seek the Lord of **h** in Jerusalem,	6635
	8:23 Thus saith the Lord of **h**; In those days it	6635
	9:15 The Lord of **h** shall defend them;	6635
	10: 3 for the Lord of **h** hath visited his flock	6635
	12: 5 my strength in the Lord of **h** their God.	6635
	13: 2 to pass in that day, saith the Lord of **h**,	6635
	13: 7 that is my fellow, saith the Lord of **h**:	6635
	14:16 the Lord of **h**, and to keep the feast of	6635
	14:17 the Lord of **h**, even upon them shall be	6635
	14:21 shall be holiness unto the Lord of **h**:	6635
	14:21 Canaanite in the house of the Lord of **h**.	6635
Mal	1: 4 thus saith the Lord of **h**, They shall	6635
	1: 6 saith the Lord of **h** unto you, O priests,	6635
	1: 8 accept thy person? saith the Lord of **h**.	6635
	1: 9 your persons? saith the Lord of **h**.	6635
	1:10 no pleasure in you, saith the Lord of **h**,	6635
	1:11 among the heathen, saith the Lord of **h**.	6635
	1:13 have snuffed at it, saith the Lord of **h**;	6635
	1:14 saith the Lord of **h**, and my name is	6635
	2: 2 glory unto my name, saith the Lord of **h**,	6635
	2: 4 might be with you, saith the Lord of **h**.	6635
	2: 7 for he is the messenger of the Lord of **h**.	6635
	2: 8 covenant of Levi, saith the Lord of **h**.	6635
	2:12 offereth an offering unto the Lord of **h**.	6635
	2:16 with his garment, saith the Lord of **h**:	6635
	3: 1 he shall come, saith the Lord of **h**.	6635
	3: 5 and fear not me, saith the Lord of **h**.	6635
	3: 7 will return unto you, saith the Lord of **h**,	6635
	3:10 me now herewith, saith the Lord of **h**,	6635
	3:11 the time in the field, saith the Lord of **h**.	6635
	3:12 a delightsome land, saith the Lord of **h**?	6635
	3:14 mournfully before the Lord of **h**?	6635
	3:17 they shall be mine, saith the Lord of **h**,	6635
	4: 1 shall burn them up, saith the Lord of **h**,	6635
	4: 3 that I shall do this, saith the Lord of **h**.	6635

HOT (31) [HOTLY, HOTTEST]

Ex	16:21 and when the sun waxed **h**, it melted.	2552
	22:24 my wrath shall wax **h**, and I will kill you	2734
	32:10 that my wrath may wax **h** against them,	2734
	32:11 why doth thy wrath wax **h** against thy	2734
	32:19 Moses' anger waxed **h**, and he cast	2734
	32:22 Let not the anger of my lord wax **h**:	2734
Lev	13:24 in the skin whereof there is a **h** burning,	784
Dt	9:19 afraid of the anger and **h** displeasure,	2534
	19: 6 while his heart is **h**, and overtake him,	3179
Jos	9:12 our bread we took **h** for our provision	2525
Jdg	2:14 the anger of the Lord was **h** against	2734
	2:20 the anger of the Lord was **h** against	2734
	3: 8 Therefore the anger of the Lord was **h**	2734
	6:39 Let not thine anger be **h** against me,	2734
	10: 7 the anger of the Lord was **h** against	2734
1Sa	11: 9 To morrow, by that time the sun be **h**,	2527
	21: 6 to put **h** bread in the day when it was	2527
Ne	7: 3 Jerusalem be opened until the sun be **h**;	2527
Job	6:17 when it is **h**, they are consumed out of	2527
Ps	6: 1 neither chasten me in thy **h** displeasure.	2534
	38: 1 neither chasten me in thy **h** displeasure.	2534
	39: 3 My heart was **h** within me, while I was	2552
	78:48 hail, and their flocks to **h** thunderbolts.	7565
Pr	6:28 Can one go upon **h** coals, and his feet not	1513
Eze	24:11 the brass of it may be **h**, and may burn,	3179
Da	3:22 was urgent, and the furnace exceeding **h**,	228

Hos	7: 7 They are all **h** as an oven,	2552
1Ti	4: 2 their conscience seared with a **h** iron;	2743
Rev	3:15 works, that thou art neither cold nor **h**:	2200
	3:15 nor hot: I would thou wert cold or **h**.	2200
	3:16 art lukewarm, and neither cold nor **h**,	2200

HOTHAM (1)

1Ch	7:32 and Shomer, and **H**, and Shua their sister.	2369

HOTHAN (1)

1Ch	11:44 and Jehiel the sons of **H** the Aroerite,	2369

HOTHIR (2)

1Ch	25: 4 Mallothi, **H**, and Mahazioth:	1956
	25:28 The one and twentieth to **H**, he, his sons,	1956

HOTLY (1) [HOT]

Ge	31:36 that thou hast so **h** pursued after me?	1814

HOTTEST (1) [HOT]

2Sa	11:15 Uriah in the forefront of the **h** battle,	2389

HOUGH (1) [HOUGHED]

Jos	11: 6 thou shalt **h** their horses, and burn their	6131

HOUGHED (3) [HOUGH]

Jos	11: 9 he **h** their horses, and burnt their chariots	6131
2Sa	8: 4 David **h** all the chariot horses, but	6131
1Ch	18: 4 David also **h** all the chariot horses, but	6131

HOUR (94) [HOURS]

Da	3: 6 worshipped shall the same **h** be cast into	8160
	3:15 ye shall be cast the same **h** into the midst	8160
	4:19 was astonied for one **h**, and his thoughts	8160
	4:33 The same **h** was the thing fulfilled upon	8160
	5: 5 the same **h** came forth fingers of a man's	8160
Mt	8:13 his servant was healed in the selfsame **h**.	5610
	9:22 the woman was made whole from that **h**.)	5610
	10:19 for it shall be given you in that same **h**	5610
	15:28 was made whole from that very **h**.	5610
	17:18 and the child was cured from that very **h**.	5610
	20: 3 And he went out about the third **h**,	5610
	20: 5 he went out about the sixth and ninth **h**,	5610
	20: 6 And about the eleventh **h** he went out,	5610
	20: 9 that were hired about the eleventh **h**,	5610
	20:12 These last have wrought but one **h**,	5610
	24:36 But of that day and **h** knoweth no man,	5610
	24:42 for ye know not what **h** your Lord doth	5610
	24:44 in such an **h** as you think not the Son of	5610
	24:50 him, and in an **h** that he is not ware of,	5610
	25:13 for ye know neither the day nor the **h**	5610
	26:40 could ye not watch with me one **h**?	5610
	26:45 the **h** is at hand, and the Son of man is	5610
	26:55 that same **h** said Jesus to the multitudes,	5610
	27:45 Now from the sixth **h** there was darkness	5610
	27:45 over all the land unto the ninth **h**.	5610
	27:46 And about the ninth **h** Jesus cried with a	5610
Mk	13:11 whatsoever shall be given you in that **h**,	5610
	13:32 of that day and that **h** knoweth no man,	5610
	14:35 were possible, the th might pass from him.	5610
	14:37 couldest not thou watch one **h**?	5610
	14:41 it is enough, the **h** is come; behold, the Son	5610
	15:25 And it was the third **h**, and they crucified	5610
	15:33 And when the sixth **h** was come, there	5610
	15:33 over the whole land until the ninth **h**.	5610
	15:34 And at the ninth **h** Jesus cried with a loud	5610
Lk	7:21 In that same **h** he cured many of	5610
	10:21 In that **h** Jesus rejoiced in spirit, and said,	5610
	12:12 you in the same **h** what ye ought to say.	5610
	12:39 had known what **h** the thief would come,	5610
	12:40 the Son of man cometh at an **h** when ye	5610
	12:46 for him, and at an **h** when he is not ware,	5610
	20:19 the scribes the same **h** sought to lay hands	5610
	22:14 And when the **h** was come, he sat down,	5610
	22:53 but this is your **h**, and the power of	5610
	22:59 about the space of one **h** after another	5610
	23:44 it was about the sixth **h**, and there was	5610
	23:44 over all the earth until the ninth **h**.	5610
	24:33 And they rose up the same **h**,	5610
Jn	1:39 him that day: for it was about the tenth **h**.	5610
	2: 4 I to do with thee? mine **h** is not yet come.	5610
	4: 6 on the well: and it was about the sixth **h**.	5610
	4:21 Woman, believe me, the **h** cometh,	5610
	4:23 But the **h** cometh, and now is, when	5610
	4:52 Then inquired he of them the **h** when he	5610
	4:52 Yesterday at the seventh **h** the fever left	5610
	4:53 the father knew that it was at the same **h**,	5610
	5:25 unto you, The **h** is coming, and now is,	5610
	5:28 the **h** is coming, in the which all that are	5610
	7:30 on him, because his **h** was not yet come.	5610
	8:20 on him; for his **h** was not yet come.	5610
	12:23 answered them, saying, The **h** is come,	5610
	12:27 Father, save me from this **h**: but for this	5610
	12:27 but for this cause came I unto this **h**.	5610
	13: 1 when Jesus knew that his **h** was come	5610
	16:21 hath sorrow, because her **h** is come:	5610
	16:32 Behold, the **h** cometh, yea, is now come,	5610
	17: 1 heaven, and said, Father, the **h** is come;	5610
	19:14 of the passover, and about the sixth **h**:	5610
	19:27 from that **h** that disciple took her unto	5610
Ac	2:15 seeing it is but the third **h** of the day.	5610
	3: 1 into the temple at the **h** of prayer,	5610
	3: 1 at the hour of prayer, being the ninth **h**.	NIG
	10: 3 about the ninth **h** of the day,	5610
	10: 9 upon the house to pray about the sixth **h**:	5610
	10:30 Four days ago I was fasting until this **h**;	5610

Ac 10:30 and at the ninth **h** I prayed in my house, *5610*
16:18 out of her. And he came out the same **h**. *5610*
16:33 And he took them the same **h** of the night, *5610*
22:13 And the same **h** I looked up upon him. *5610*
23:23 two hundred, at the third **h** of the night; *5610*
1Co 4:11 Even unto this present **h** we both hunger, *5610*
8: 7 with conscience of the idol unto **this h**, *737*
15:30 And why stand we in jeopardy every **h**? *5610*
Gal 2: 5 gave place by subjection, no, not for an **h**; *5610*
Rev 3: 3 thou shalt not know what **h** I will come *5610*
3:10 I also will keep thee from the **h** of *5610*
8: 1 in heaven about the space of **half an h**. *2256*
9:15 which were prepared for an **h**, and a day, *5610*
11:13 And the same **h** was there a great *5610*
14: 7 to him; for the **h** of his judgment is come: *5610*
17:12 receive power as kings one **h** with *5610*
18:10 for in one **h** is thy judgment come. *5610*
18:17 For in one **h** so great riches is come to *5610*
18:19 For in one **h** is she made desolate. *5610*

HOURS (3) [HOUR]
Jn 11: 9 Are there not twelve **h** in the day? *5610*
Ac 5: 7 And it was about the space of three **h** after, *5610*
19:34 all with one voice about the space of two **h** *5610*

HOUSE (2025) [HOUSE OF APHRAH, HOUSEHOLD, HOUSEHOLDER, HOUSEHOLDS, HOUSES, HOUSETOP, HOUSETOPS, STOREHOUSE, STOREHOUSES, WINTERHOUSE]
Ge 7: 1 Come thou and all thy **h** into the ark; 1004
12: 1 from thy kindred, and from thy father's **h**, 1004
12:15 the woman was taken into Pharaoh's **h**. 1004
12:17 his **h** with great plagues because of Sarai 1004
14:14 his trained *servants*, born in his own **h**, 1004
15: 2 the steward of my **h** *is* this Eliezer of 1004
15: 3 and lo, one born in my **h** is mine heir. 1004
17:12 he that is born in the **h**, or bought with 1004
17:13 He that is born in thy **h**, and he that is 1004
17:23 all that were born in his **h**, and all that 1004
17:23 male among the men of Abraham's **h**; 1004
17:27 all the men of his **h**, born in the house, 1004
17:27 born in the **h**, and bought with money of 1004
19: 2 into your servant's **h**, and tarry all night, 1004
19: 3 in unto him, and entered into his **h**; 1004
19: 4 compassed the **h** round, both old and 1004
19:10 pulled Lot into the **h** to them, and shut to 1004
19:11 *were at* the door of the **h** with blindness, 1004
20:13 caused me to wander from my father's **h**, 1004
20:18 up all the wombs of the **h** of Abimelech, 1004
24: 2 of his **h** that ruled over all that he had, 1004
24: 7 which took me from my father's **h**, 1004
24:23 is there room *in* thy father's **h** for us to 1004
24:27 the Lord led me to the **h** of my master's 1004
24:28 told *them of* her mother's **h** these things. 1004
24:31 for I have prepared the **h**, and room for 1004
24:32 the man came into the **h**: and he ungirded 1004
24:38 thou shalt go unto my father's **h**, and to 1004
24:40 son of my kindred, and of my father's **h**: 1004
27:15 which *were* with her in the **h**, and put 1004
28: 2 to the **h** of Bethuel thy mother's father; 1004
28:17 this *is* none other but the **h** of God, 1004
28:21 So that I come again to my father's **h** in 1004
28:22 I have set *for* a pillar, shall be God's **h**: 1004
29:13 and kissed him, and brought him to his **h**. 1004
30:30 now when shall I provide for mine own **h** 1004
31:14 or inheritance for us in our father's **h**? 1004
31:30 thou sore longedst after thy father's **h**, 1004
31:41 Thus have I been twenty years in thy **h**; 1004
33:17 built him a **h**, and made booths for his 1004
34:19 he *was* more honourable than all the **h** of 1004
34:26 took Dinah out of Shechem's **h**, 1004
34:29 and spoiled even all that *was* in the **h**. 1004
34:30 and I shall be destroyed, I and my **h**. 1004
36: 6 all the persons of his **h**, and his cattle, 1004
38:11 Remain a widow *at* thy father's **h**, 1004
38:11 Tamar went and dwelt *in* her father's **h**. 1004
39: 2 was in the **h** of his master the Egyptian. 1004
39: 4 he made him overseer over his **h**, 1004
39: 5 *that* he had made him overseer in his **h**, 1004
39: 5 that the Lord blessed the Egyptian's **h** 1004
39: 5 Lord was upon all that he had in the **h**, 1004
39: 8 wotteth not what *is* with me in the **h**, 1004
39: 9 *There is* none greater in this **h** than I; 1004
39:11 that *Joseph* went into the **h** to do his 1004
39:11 *there was* none of the men of the **h** there 1004
39:14 That she called unto the men of her **h**, 1004
40: 3 put them in ward *in* the **h** of the captain 1004
40: 7 *were* with him in the ward of his lord's **h**, 1004
40:14 unto Pharaoh, and bring me out of this **h**: 1004
41:10 in ward *in* the captain of the guard's **h**, 1004
41:40 Thou shalt be over my **h**, 1004
41:51 forget all my toil, and all my father's **h**. 1004
42:19 brethren be bound in the **h** of your prison: 1004
43:16 he said to the ruler of his **h**, Bring *these* 1004
43:17 the man brought the men into Joseph's **h**. 1004
43:18 they were brought into Joseph's **h**; 1004
43:19 came near to the steward of Joseph's **h**, 1004
43:19 communed with him *at* the door of the **h**, 1004
43:24 the man brought the men into Joseph's **h**, 1004
43:26 which *was* in their hand into the **h**, 1004
44: 1 he commanded the steward of his **h**, 1004
44: 8 should we steal out of thy lord's **h** silver 1004
44:14 and his brethren came to Joseph's **h**; 1004
45: 2 the Egyptians and the **h** of Pharaoh heard. 1004
45: 8 lord of all his **h**, and a ruler throughout all 1004

Ge 45:16 fame *thereof* was heard *in* Pharaoh's **h**, 1004
46:27 all the souls of the **h** of Jacob, which came 1004
46:31 unto his father's **h**, I will go up, 1004
46:31 him, My brethren, and my father's **h**, 1004
47:14 brought the money into Pharaoh's **h**. 1004
50: 4 Joseph spake unto the **h** of Pharaoh, 1004
50: 7 the elders of his **h**, and all the elders of 1004
50: 8 all the **h** of Joseph, and his brethren, 1004
50: 8 and his brethren, and his father's **h**: 1004
50:22 dwelt in Egypt, he, and his father's **h**: 1004
Ex 2: 1 there went a man of the **h** of Levi, 1004
3:22 of her that sojourneth in her **h**, jewels of 1004
7:23 Pharaoh turned and went into his **h**, 1004
8: 3 which shall go up and come into thine **h**, 1004
8: 3 into the **h** of thy servants, and upon thy 1004
8:24 swarm *of flies* into the **h** of Pharaoh, 1004
12: 3 according to the **h** of *their* fathers, a lamb 1004
12: 3 the house of *their* fathers, a lamb for a **h**: 1004
12: 4 his neighbour next unto his **h** take *it* 1004
12:22 of you shall go out at the door of his **h** 1004
12:30 *there was* not a **h** where *there* was not 1004
12:46 in one **h** shall it be eaten; thou shalt not 1004
12:46 *ought* of the flesh abroad out of the **h**; 1004
13: 3 out from Egypt, out of the **h** of bondage; 1004
13:14 us out from Egypt, from the **h** of bondage: 1004
16:31 the **h** of Israel called the name thereof 1004
19: 3 Thus shalt thou say to the **h** of Jacob, 1004
20: 2 the land of Egypt, out of the **h** of bondage. 1004
20:17 Thou shalt not covet thy neighbour's **h**, 1004
22: 7 keep, and it be stolen out of the man's **h**; 1004
22: 8 the master of the **h** shall be brought unto 1004
23:19 bring *into* the **h** of the Lord thy God. 1004
34:26 bring *unto* the **h** of the Lord thy God. 1004
40:38 by night, in the sight of all the **h** of Israel, 1004
Lev 10: 6 let your brethren, the whole **h** of Israel, 1004
14:34 put the plague of leprosy in a **h** of the land 1004
14:35 he that owneth the **h** shall come and tell 1004
14:35 to me *there is* as it were a plague in the **h**: 1004
14:36 shall command that they empty the **h**, 1004
14:36 all that *is in* the **h** be not *made* unclean: 1004
14:36 the priest shall go in to see the **h**: 1004
14:37 *if* the plague *be* in the walls of the **h** with 1004
14:38 the priest shall go out of the **h** to the door 1004
14:38 go out of the house to the door of the **h**; 1004
14:38 the house, and shut up the **h** seven days: 1004
14:39 the plague be spread in the walls of the **h**; 1004
14:41 he shall cause the **h** to be scraped within 1004
14:42 take other morter, and shall plaister the **h**. 1004
14:43 come again, and break out in the **h**, 1004
14:43 after he hath scraped the **h**, and after it is 1004
14:44 behold, *if* the plague be spread in the **h**: 1004
14:44 the house, it *is* a fretting leprosy in the **h**: 1004
14:45 shall break down the **h**, the stones of it, 1004
14:45 thereof, and all the morter of the **h**; 1004
14:46 Moreover he that goeth into the **h** all 1004
14:47 that lieth in the **h** shall wash his clothes; 1004
14:47 he that eateth in the **h** shall wash his 1004
14:48 the plague hath not spread in the **h**, 1004
14:48 in the house, after the **h** was plaistered: 1004
14:48 the priest shall pronounce the **h** clean, 1004
14:49 he shall take to cleanse the **h** two birds, 1004
14:51 and sprinkle the **h** seven times: 1004
14:52 he shall cleanse the **h** with the blood of 1004
14:53 and make an atonement for the **h**: 1004
14:55 for the leprosy of a garment, and of a **h**, 1004
16: 6 an atonement for himself, and for his **h**. 1004
16:11 for his **h**, and shall kill the bullock of 1004
17: 3 What man soever *there be* of the **h** of 1004
17: 8 man *there be* of the **h** of Israel, 1004
17:10 man *there be* of the **h** of Israel, 1004
22:11 eat of it, and he that is born in his **h**: 1004
22:13 and is returned unto her father's **h**, 1004
22:18 Whatsoever *he be* of the **h** of Israel, 1004
25:29 if a man sell a dwelling **h** in a walled city, 1004
25:30 the **h** that *is* in the walled city shall be 1004
25:33 the **h** that was sold, and the city of his 1004
27:14 when a man shall sanctify his **h** *to be* holy 1004
27:15 if he that sanctified *it* will redeem his **h**, 1004
Nu 1: 2 their families, by the **h** of their fathers, 1004
1: 4 every one head of the **h** of his fathers. 1004
1:18 by the **h** of their fathers, according to 1004
1:20 their families, by the **h** of their fathers, 1004
1:22 their families, by the **h** of their fathers, 1004
1:24 their families, by the **h** of their fathers, 1004
1:26 their families, by the **h** of their fathers, 1004
1:28 their families, by the **h** of their fathers, 1004
1:30 their families, by the **h** of their fathers, 1004
1:32 their families, by the **h** of their fathers, 1004
1:34 their families, by the **h** of their fathers, 1004
1:36 their families, by the **h** of their fathers, 1004
1:38 their families, by the **h** of their fathers, 1004
1:40 their families, by the **h** of their fathers, 1004
1:42 their families, by the **h** of their fathers, 1004
1:44 each one was for the **h** of his fathers. 1004
1:45 by the **h** of their fathers, from twenty 1004
2: 2 with the ensign of their father's **h**: 1004
2:32 children of Israel by the **h** of their fathers: 1004
2:34 according to the **h** of their fathers. 1004
3:15 Number the children of Levi after the **h** of 1004
3:20 Levites according to the **h** of their fathers. 1004
3:24 the chief of the **h** of the father of 1004
3:30 the chief of the **h** of the father of 1004
3:35 the chief of the **h** of the father of 1004
4: 2 their families, by the **h** of their fathers, 1004
4:29 their families, by the **h** of their fathers; 1004

Nu 4:34 and after the **h** of their fathers, 1004
4:38 families, and by the **h** of their fathers, 1004
4:40 the **h** of their fathers, were two thousand 1004
4:42 their families, by the **h** of their fathers, 1004
4:46 and after the **h** of their fathers, 1004
7: 2 of Israel, heads of the **h** of their fathers, 1004
12: 7 *is* not so, who *is* faithful in all mine **h**. 1004
17: 2 a rod according to the **h** of *their* fathers, 1004
17: 2 of all their princes according to the **h** of 1004
17: 3 one rod *shall be* for the head of the **h** of 1004
17: 8 the rod of Aaron for the **h** of Levi was 1004
18: 1 thy father's **h** with thee shall bear 1004
18:11 every one *that is* clean in thy **h** shall eat 1004
18:13 every one *that is* clean in thine **h** shall eat 1004
20:29 Aaron thirty days, *even* all the **h** of Israel. 1004
22:18 If Balak would give me his **h** full *of* silver 1004
24:13 If Balak would give me his **h** full *of* silver 1004
25:14 prince of a chief **h** among the Simeonites. 1004
25:15 over a people, *and of* a chief **h** in Midian. 1004
26: 2 and upward, throughout their father's **h**, 1004
30: 3 bond, *being* in her father's **h** in her youth; 1004
30:10 if she vowed *in* her husband's **h**, 1004
30:16 *being yet* in her youth *in* her father's **h**. 1004
34:14 Reuben according to the **h** of their fathers, 1004
34:14 of Gad according to the **h** of their fathers, 1004
Dt 5: 6 the land of Egypt, from the **h** of bondage. 1004
5:21 shalt thou covet thy neighbour's **h**, 1004
6: 7 talk of them when thou sittest in thine **h**, 1004
6: 9 shalt write them upon the posts of thy **h**, 1004
6:12 the land of Egypt, from the **h** of bondage. 1004
7: 8 redeemed you out of the **h** of bondmen, 1004
7:26 thou bring an abomination into thine **h**, 1004
8:14 the land of Egypt, from the **h** of bondage; 1004
11:19 of them when thou sittest in thine **h**, 1004
11:20 them upon the door posts of thine **h**, 1004
13: 5 redeemed you out of the **h** of bondage, 1004
13:10 the land of Egypt, from the **h** of bondage. 1004
15:16 because he loveth thee and thine **h**, 1004
20: 5 man *is there* that hath built a new **h**, 1004
20: 5 let him go and return to his **h**, lest he die 1004
20: 6 let him *also* go and return unto his **h**, lest 1004
20: 7 let him go and return unto his **h**, lest he 1004
20: 8 let him go and return unto his **h**, lest his 1004
21:12 thou shalt bring her home to thine **h**, 1004
21:13 shall remain in thine **h**, and bewail her 1004
22: 2 thou shalt bring it unto thine own **h**, 1004
22: 8 When thou buildest a new **h**, then 1004
22: 8 that thou bring not blood upon thine **h**, 1004
22:21 the damsel to the door of her father's **h**, 1004
22:21 to play the whore in her father's **h**: 1004
23:18 *into* the **h** of the Lord thy God for any 1004
24: 1 *it* in her hand, and send her out of his **h**. 1004
24: 2 when she is departed out of his **h**, she 1004
24: 3 in her hand, and sendeth her out of his **h**; 1004
24:10 thou shalt not go into his **h** to fetch his 1004
25: 9 man that will not build up his brother's **h**. 1004
25:10 The **h** of him that hath his shoe loosed. 1004
25:14 Thou shalt not have in thine **h** divers 1004
26:11 unto thine **h**, thou, and the Levite, 1004
26:13 away the hallowed *things* out of *mine* **h**, 1004
28:30 thou shalt build a **h**, and thou shalt not 1004
Jos 2: 1 came *into* a harlot's **h**, named Rahab, 1004
2: 3 to thee, which are entered into thine **h**: 1004
2: 6 had brought them up to the **roof** of the **h**, 1406
2:12 also shew kindness unto my father's **h**, 1004
2:15 for her **h** *was* upon the town wall, 1004
2:19 out of the doors of thy **h** into the street, 1004
2:19 whosoever shall be with thee in the **h**, 1004
6:17 she and all that *are* with her in the **h**, 1004
6:22 Go *into* the harlot's **h**, and bring out 1004
6:24 they put *into* the treasury of the **h** of 1004
9:23 drawers of water for the **h** of my God. 1004
17:17 Joshua spake unto the **h** of Joseph, *even* 1004
18: 5 of Joseph shall abide in their coasts 1004
20: 6 win his own city, and unto his own **h**, 1004
21:45 Lord had spoken unto the **h** of Israel; 1004
22:14 of each chief **h** a prince throughout all 1004
22:14 each one *was* a head of the **h** of their 1004
24:15 as for me and my **h**, we will serve 1004
24:17 from the **h** of bondage, and which did 1004
Jdg 1:22 the **h** of Joseph, they also went up *against* 1004
1:23 the **h** of Joseph sent to descry Beth-el. 1004
1:35 yet the hand of the **h** of Joseph prevailed, 1004
4:17 of Hazor and the **h** of Heber the Kenite. 1004
6: 8 brought you forth out of the **h** of bondage; 1004
6:15 and I *am* the least in my father's **h**. 1004
8:27 became a snare unto Gideon, and to his **h**. 1004
8:29 son of Joash went and dwelt in his own **h**. 1004
8:35 Neither shewed they kindness to the **h** of 1004
9: 1 with all the family of the **h** of his mother's 1004
9: 4 ten *pieces* of silver out of the **h** of 1004
9: 5 he went unto his father's **h** at Ophrah, 1004
9: 6 all the **h** of Millo, and went, 1004
9:16 have dealt well with Jerubbaal and his **h**, 1004
9:18 ye are risen up against my father's **h** *this* 1004
9:19 with Jerubbaal and with his **h** this day, 1004
9:20 the men of Shechem, and the **h** of Millo; 1004
9:20 from the **h** of Millo, 1004
9:27 went *into* the **h** of their god, and did eat 1004
9:46 into a hold of the **h** of the god Berith. 1004
10: 9 and against the **h** of Ephraim. 1004
11: 2 Thou shalt not inherit in our father's **h**; 1004
11: 7 and expel me out of my father's **h**? 1004
11:31 forth of the doors of my **h** to meet me, 1004
11:34 Jephthah came *to* Mizpeh unto his **h**, 1004

H

Jdg 12: 1 we will burn thine **h** upon thee with fire. 1004
14:15 we burn thee and thy father's **h** with fire: 1004
14:19 and he went up *to* his father's **h**. 1004
16:21 of brass; and he did grind in the prison **h**. 1004
16:25 called for Samson out of the prison **h**; 1004
16:26 feel the pillars whereupon the **h** standeth, 1004
16:27 Now the **h** was full *of* men and women; 1004
16:29 middle pillars upon which the **h** stood, 1004
16:30 the **h** fell upon the lords, and upon all 1004
16:31 and all the **h** of his father came down, 1004
17: 4 and they were in the **h** of Micah. 1004
17: 5 the man Micah had a **h** of gods, 1004
17: 8 he came *to* mount Ephraim to the **h** of 1004
17:12 his priest, and was in the **h** of Micah. 1004
18: 2 to the **h** of Micah, they lodged there. 1004
18: 3 When they *were* by the **h** of Micah, they 1004
18:13 and came unto the **h** of Micah. 1004
18:15 to the **h** of the young man the Levite, 1004
18:15 *unto* the **h** of Micah, and saluted him. 1004
18:18 these went *into* Micah's **h**, and fetched 1004
18:19 *it* better for thee to be a priest unto the **h** 1004
18:22 were a good way from the **h** of Micah, 1004
18:22 near to Micah's **h** were gathered together, 1004
18:26 he turned and went back unto his **h**. 1004
18:31 the time that the **h** of God was in Shiloh. 1004
19: 2 went away from him unto her father's **h** 1004
19: 3 she brought him *into* her father's **h**: 1004
19:15 man that took them into *his* **h** to lodging. 1004
19:18 I am *now* going *to* the **h** of the LORD; 1004
19:18 there *is* no man that receiveth me to **h**. 1004
19:21 So he brought him into his **h**, 1004
19:22 beset the **h** round about, *and* beat at 1004
19:22 spake to the master of the **h**, the old man, 1004
19:22 forth the man that came into thine **h**, 1004
19:23 man, the master of the **h**, went out unto 1004
19:23 seeing that this man is come into mine **h**, 1004
19:26 down *at* the door of the man's **h** where 1004
19:27 opened the doors of the **h**, and went out 1004
19:27 *was* fallen down *at* the door of the **h**, 1004
19:29 when he was come into his **h**, he took a 1004
20: 5 the **h** round about upon me by night, 1004
20: 8 neither will we any *of us* turn into his **h**. 1004
20:18 went up *to* the **h** of God, and asked 1004
20:26 came *unto* the **h** of God, and wept, 1004
20:31 *of* which one goeth up *to* the **h** of God, 1004
21: 2 the people came *to* the **h** of God, 1004

Ru 1: 8 in law, Go, return each to her mother's **h**: 1004
1: 9 each *of you* in the **h** of her husband. 1004
2: 7 until now, that she tarried a little in the **h**. 1004
4:11 that is come into thine **h** like Rachel 1004
4:11 which two did build the **h** of Israel: 1004
4:12 let thy **h** be like the house of Pharez, 1004
4:12 let thy house be like the **h** of Pharez, 1004

1Sa 1: 7 when she went up to the **h** of the LORD, 1004
1:19 returned, and came to their **h** to Ramah: 1004
1:21 the man Elkanah, and all his **h**, went up to 1004
1:24 brought him *unto* the **h** of the LORD *in* 1004
2:11 Elkanah went to Ramah to his **h**. 1004
2:27 Did I plainly appear unto the **h** of thy 1004
2:27 when they were in Egypt in Pharaoh's **h**? 1004
2:28 did I give unto the **h** of thy father all 1004
2:30 I said indeed *that* thy **h**, and the house of 1004
2:30 *that* thy house, and the **h** of thy father, 1004
2:31 thine arm, and the arm of thy father's **h**, 1004
2:31 there shall not be an old man in thine **h**. 1004
2:32 there shall not be an old man in thine **h** 1004
2:33 all the increase of thine **h** shall die in 1004
2:35 will build him a sure **h**; and he shall walk 1004
2:36 *that* every one that is left in thine **h** shall 1004
3:12 which I have spoken concerning his **h**: 1004
3:13 For I have told him that I will judge his **h** 1004
3:14 I have sworn unto the **h** of Eli, 1004
3:14 that the iniquity of Eli's **h** shall not be 1004
3:15 opened the doors of the **h** of the LORD. 1004
5: 2 they brought it *into* the **h** of Dagon, 1004
5: 5 nor any that come *into* Dagon's **h**, 1004
7: 1 it into the **h** of Abinadab in the hill, 1004
7: 2 all the **h** of Israel lamented after 1004
7: 3 Samuel spake unto all the **h** of Israel, 1004
7:17 for there *was* his **h**; and there he judged 1004
9:18 Tell me, I pray thee, where the seer's **h** *is*. 1004
9:20 *Is it* not on thee, and on all thy father's **h**? 1004
9:25 with Saul from the **top** of the **h**, 1406
9:26 Samuel called Saul to the **top** of the **h**, 1406
10:25 all the people away, every man to his **h**. 1004
15:34 Saul went up to his **h** *to* Gibeah of Saul. 1004
17:25 and make his father's **h** free in Israel. 1004
18: 2 let him go no more home *to* his father's **h**. 1004
18:10 and he prophesied in the midst of the **h**: 1004
19: 9 as he sat in his **h** with his javelin in his 1004
19:11 Saul also sent messengers unto David's **h**, 1004
20:15 cut off thy kindness from my **h** for ever: 1004
20:16 Jonathan made a *covenant* with the **h** of 1004
21:15 shall this *fellow* come into my **h**? 1004
22: 1 all his father's **h** heard *it*, they went down 1004
22:11 the son of Ahitub, and all his father's **h**, 1004
22:14 thy bidding, and *is* honourable in thine **h**? 1004
22:15 his servant, *nor* to all the **h** of my father: 1004
22:16 Ahimelech, thou, and all thy father's **h**. 1004
22:22 *death* of all the persons of thy father's **h**. 1004
23:18 in the wood, and Jonathan went to his **h**. 1004
24:21 not destroy my name out of my father's **h**. 1004
25: 1 and buried him in his **h** at Ramah. 1004
25: 3 doings; and he *was* **of the h of Caleb**. 3614
25: 6 peace *be* to thine **h**, and peace *be unto* all 1004

1Sa 25:28 will certainly make my lord a sure **h**; 1004
25:35 said unto her, Go up in peace to thine **h**; 1004
25:36 behold, he held a feast in his **h**, like 1004
28:24 the woman had a fat calf in the **h**; 1004
31: 9 to publish *it* in the **h** of their idols, 1004
31:10 they put his armour *in the* **h** of Ashtaroth: 1004

2Sa 1:12 of the LORD, and for the **h** of Israel; 1004
2: 4 they anointed David king over the **h** 1004
2: 7 the **h** of Judah have anointed me king 1004
2:10 But the **h** of Judah followed David. 1004
2:11 over the **h** of Judah was seven years 1004
3: 1 Now there was long war between the **h** 1004
3: 1 the house of Saul and the **h** of David: 1004
3: 1 the **h** of Saul waxed weaker and weaker. 1004
3: 6 there was war between the **h** of Saul 1004
3: 6 the house of Saul and the **h** of David, 1004
3: 6 Abner made himself strong for the **h** of 1004
3: 8 *this* day unto the **h** of Saul thy father, 1004
3:10 To translate the kingdom from the **h** of 1004
3:19 that seemed *good* to the whole **h** of 1004
3:29 the head of Joab, and on all his father's **h**; 1004
3:29 let there not fail from the **h** of Joab one 1004
4: 5 came about the heat of the day to the **h** of 1004
4: 6 they came thither into the midst of the **h**, 1004
4: 7 For when they came *into* the **h**, he lay on 1004
4:11 person in his own **h** upon his bed? 1004
5: 8 and the lame shall not come into the **h**. 1004
5:11 masons: and they built David a **h**. 1004
6: 3 brought it out of the **h** of Abinadab that 1004
6: 4 they brought it out of the **h** of Abinadab 1004
6: 5 all the **h** of Israel played before the LORD 1004
6:10 David carried it aside *into* the **h** of 1004
6:11 the ark of the LORD continued *in* the **h** of 1004
6:12 The LORD hath blessed the **h** of 1004
6:12 brought up the ark of God from the **h** of 1004
6:15 all the **h** of Israel brought up the ark of 1004
6:19 all the people departed every one to his **h**. 1004
6:21 me before thy father, and before all his **h**, 1004
7: 1 when the king sat in his **h**, and the LORD 1004
7: 2 I dwell in a **h** of cedar, but the ark of God 1004
7: 5 thou build me a **h** for me to dwell in? 1004
7: 6 Whereas I have not dwelt in *any* **h** since 1004
7: 7 Why build ye not me a **h** of cedar? 1004
7:11 telleth thee that he will make thee a **h**. 1004
7:13 He shall build a **h** for my name, and I will 1004
7:16 **h** and thy kingdom shall be stablished 1004
7:18 what *is* my **h**, that thou hast brought me 1004
7:19 thou hast spoken also of thy servant's **h** 1004
7:25 concerning his **h**, establish *it* for ever, 1004
7:26 let the **h** of thy servant David be 1004
7:27 thy servant, saying, I will build thee a **h**: 1004
7:29 it please thee to bless the **h** of thy servant, 1004
7:29 with thy blessing let the **h** of thy servant 1004
9: 1 Is there yet *any* that is left of the **h** of Saul, 1004
9: 2 there was of the **h** of Saul a servant whose 1004
9: 3 *Is there* not yet any of the **h** of Saul, 1004
9: 4 Behold, he *is* in the **h** of Machir, the son 1004
9: 5 fet him out of the **h** of Machir, the son of 1004
9: 9 all that pertained to Saul and to all his **h**. 1004
9:12 that dwelt in the **h** of Ziba *were* servants 1004
11: 2 walked upon the roof of the king's **h**: 1004
11: 4 and she returned unto her **h**. 1004
11: 8 Go down to thy **h**, and wash thy feet. 1004
11: 8 And Uriah departed out of the king's **h**, 1004
11: 9 Uriah slept *at* the door of the king's **h** 1004
11: 9 of his lord, and went not down to his **h**. 1004
11:10 saying, Uriah went not down unto his **h**, 1004
11:10 didst thou not go down unto thine **h**? 1004
11:11 shall I then go into mine **h**, to eat and 1004
11:13 of his lord, but went not down to his **h**. 1004
11:27 David sent and fet her to his **h**, 1004
12: 8 gave thee thy master's **h**, and thy master's 1004
12: 8 and gave thee the **h** of Israel and of Judah; 1004
12:10 the sword shall never depart from thine **h**; 1004
12:11 up evil against thee out of thine own **h**, 1004
12:15 Nathan departed unto his **h**. 1004
12:17 the elders of his **h** arose, *and went* to him, 1004
12:20 came *into* the **h** of the LORD, 1004
12:20 he came to his own **h**; and when he 1004
13: 7 Go now *to* thy brother Amnon's **h**, 1004
13: 8 So Tamar went *to* her brother Amnon's **h**; 1004
13:20 desolate *in* her brother Absalom's **h**. 1004
14: 8 Go to thine **h**, and I will give charge 1004
14: 9 iniquity *be* on me, and on my father's **h**: 1004
14:24 Let him turn to his own **h**, and let him 1004
14:24 So Absalom returned to his own **h**, 1004
14:31 came to Absalom unto *his* **h**, and said 1004
15:16 *which were* concubines, to keep the **h**. 1004
15:35 soever thou shalt hear out of the king's **h**, 1004
16: 3 To day shall the **h** of Israel restore me 1004
16: 5 out a man of the family of the **h** of Saul, 1004
16: 8 upon thee all the blood of the **h** of Saul, 1004
16:21 which he hath left to keep the **h**; 1004
16:22 Absalom a tent upon the **top** of the **h**; 1406
17:18 came to a man's **h** in Bahurim, which had 1004
17:20 servants came to the woman to the **h**, 1004
17:23 arose, and gat him *home* to his **h**, to his 1004
19: 5 Joab came *into* the **h** to the king, and said, 1004
19:11 ye the last to bring the king back to his **h**? 1004
19:11 Israel is come to the king, *even* to his **h**. 1004
19:17 Ziba the servant of the **h** of Saul, 1004
19:20 I am come the first *this* day of all the **h** of 1004
19:28 all *of* my father's **h** were but dead men 1004
19:30 is come *again* in peace unto his own **h**. 1004
20: 3 David came to his **h** *at* Jerusalem; 1004

2Sa 20: 3 whom he had left to keep the **h**, 1004
21: 1 for his bloody **h**, because he slew 1004
21: 4 no silver nor gold of Saul, nor of his **h**; 1004
23: 5 Although my **h** *be* not so with God; yet 1004
24:17 be against me, and against my father's **h**. 1004

1Ki 1:53 Solomon said unto him, Go to thine **h**. 1004
2:24 who hath made me a **h**, as he promised, 1004
2:27 which he spake concerning the **h** of Eli in 1004
2:31 from me, and from the **h** of my father. 1004
2:33 and upon his **h**, and upon his throne, 1004
2:34 he was buried in his own **h** in 1004
2:36 Build thee a **h** in Jerusalem, 1004
3: 1 had made an end of building his own **h**, 1004
3: 1 the **h** of the LORD, and the wall of 1004
3:17 lord, I and this woman dwell in one **h**; 1004
3:17 was delivered of a child with her in the **h**. 1004
3:18 *there was* no stranger with us in the **h**, 1004
3:18 us in the house, save we two in the **h**. 1004
5: 3 unto the name of the LORD his God for 1004
5: 5 I purpose to build a **h** unto the name of 1004
5: 5 room, he shall build a **h** unto my name. 1004
5:17 to lay the foundation of the **h**. 1004
5:18 prepared timber and stones to build the **h**. 1004
6: 1 that he *began* to build the **h** of the LORD. 1004
6: 2 the **h** which king Solomon built for 1004
6: 3 the porch before the temple of the **h**, 1004
6: 3 according to the breadth of the **h**; 1004
6: 3 *was* the breadth thereof before the **h**. 1004
6: 4 for the **h** he made windows of narrow 1004
6: 5 against the wall of the **h** he built 1004
6: 5 *against* the walls of the **h** round about, 1004
6: 6 for without *in the wall* of the **h** he made 1004
6: 6 not be fastened in the walls of the **h**. 1004
6: 7 the **h**, when it was in building, was built 1004
6: 7 axe *nor* any tool of iron heard in the **h**, 1004
6: 8 chamber *was* in the right side of the **h**: 1004
6: 9 So he built the **h**, and finished it; 1004
6: 9 covered the **h** with beams and boards of 1004
6:10 *then* he built chambers against all the **h**, 1004
6:10 they rested on the **h** with timber of cedar. 1004
6:12 *Concerning* this **h** which thou art in 1004
6:14 So Solomon built the **h**, and finished it. 1004
6:15 he built the walls of the **h** within with 1004
6:15 both the floor of the **h**, and the walls of 1004
6:15 covered the floor of the **h** with planks of 1004
6:16 built twenty cubits on the sides of the **h**, 1004
6:17 the **h**, that *is*, the temple before it, 1004
6:18 the cedar of the **h** within *was* carved with 1004
6:19 the oracle he prepared in the **h** within, 1004
6:21 Solomon overlaid the **h** within with pure 1004
6:22 the whole **h** he overlaid with gold, until 1004
6:22 with gold, until *he* had finished all the **h**: 1004
6:27 he set the cherubims within the inner **h**: 1004
6:27 touched one another in the midst of the **h**. 1004
6:29 he carved all the walls of the **h** round 1004
6:30 the floor of the **h** he overlaid with gold, 1004
6:37 the foundation of the **h** of the LORD laid, 1004
6:38 he finished throughout all the parts 1004
7: 1 Solomon was building his own **h** thirteen 1004
7: 1 thirteen years, and he finished all his **h**. 1004
7: 2 built also the **h** of the forest of Lebanon; 1004
7: 8 his **h** where he dwelt *had* another court 1004
7: 8 Solomon made also a **h** for Pharaoh's 1004
7:12 both for the inner court of the **h** of 1004
7:12 of the LORD, and for the porch of the **h**. 1004
7:39 put five bases on the right side of the **h**, 1004
7:39 house, and five on the left side of the **h**: 1004
7:39 he set the sea on the right side of the **h** 1004
7:40 king Solomon *for* the **h** of the LORD: 1004
7:45 to king Solomon *for* the **h** of the LORD: 1004
7:48 that *pertained unto* the **h** of the LORD: 1004
7:50 *of* gold, *both* for the doors of the inner **h**, 1004
7:50 holy *place, and* for the doors of the **h**, 1004
7:51 Solomon made *for* the **h** of the LORD. 1004
7:51 he put among the treasures of the **h** of 1004
8: 6 into the oracle of the **h**, to the most holy 1004
8:10 that the cloud filled the **h** of the LORD, 1004
8:11 for the glory of the LORD had filled the **h** 1004
8:13 I have surely built thee a **h** to dwell in, 1004
8:16 out of all the tribes of Israel to build a **h**, 1004
8:17 **h** for the name of the LORD God of 1004
8:18 Whereas it was in thine heart to build a **h** 1004
8:19 Nevertheless thou shalt not build the **h**; 1004
8:19 he shall build the **h** unto my name. 1004
8:20 have built a **h** for the name of the LORD 1004
8:27 how much less this **h** that I have builded? 1004
8:29 thine eyes may be open toward this **h** 1004
8:31 the oath come before thine altar in this **h**: 1004
8:33 and make supplication unto thee in this **h**: 1004
8:38 spread forth his hands towards this **h**: 1004
8:42 he shall come and pray towards this **h**; 1004
8:43 that *they* may know that this **h**, which I 1004
8:44 the **h** that I have built for thy name: 1004
8:48 the **h** which I have built for thy name: 1004
8:63 all the children of Israel dedicated the **h** 1004
8:64 court that *was* before the **h** of the LORD: 1004
9: 1 the building of the **h** of the LORD, 1004
9: 1 the king's **h**, and all Solomon's desire 1004
9: 3 I have hallowed this **h**, which thou hast 1004
9: 7 **h**, which I have hallowed for my name, 1004
9: 8 *at* this **h**, *which* is high, every one that 1004
9: 8 done thus unto this land, and to this **h**? 1004
9:10 the **h** of the LORD, and the king's house, 1004
9:10 the house of the LORD, and the king's **h**, 1004

1Ki
9:15 for to build the **h** of the LORD, and his	1004
9:15 his own **h**, and Millo, and the wall of	1004
9:24 her **h** which *Solomon* had built for her:	1004
9:25 before the LORD. So he finished the **h**.	1004
10: 4 and the **h** that he had built,	1004
10: 5 ascent *by* which he went up *unto* the **h**	1004
10:12 almug trees pillars for the **h** of the LORD,	1004
10:12 for the king's **h**, harps also and	1004
10:17 the king put them *in* the **h** of the forest of	1004
10:21 all the vessels of the **h** of the forest of	1004
11:18 which gave him a **h**, and appointed him	1004
11:20 whom Tahpenes weaned in Pharaoh's **h**:	1004
11:28 over all the charge of the **h** of Joseph.	1004
11:38 build thee a sure **h**, as I built for David,	1004
12:16 now see to thine own **h**, David. So Israel	1004
12:19 So Israel rebelled against the **h** of David	1004
12:20 there was none that followed the **h** of	1004
12:21 he assembled all the **h** of Judah, with	1004
12:21 to fight against the **h** of Israel,	1004
12:23 unto all the **h** of Judah and Benjamin,	1004
12:24 return every man to his **h**; for this thing is	1004
12:26 Now shall the kingdom return to the **h** of	1004
12:27 If this people go up to do sacrifice in the **h**	1004
12:31 he made a **h** of high places,	1004
13: 2 a child *shall be* born unto the **h** of David,	1004
13: 8 If thou wilt give me half thine **h**, I will not	1004
13:18 Bring him back with thee into thine **h**,	1004
13:19 did eat bread in his **h**, and drank water.	1004
13:34 this thing became sin unto the **h** of	1004
14: 4 *to* Shiloh, and came *to* the **h** of Ahijah.	1004
14: 8 rent the kingdom away from the **h** of	1004
14:10 I will bring evil upon the **h** of Jeroboam,	1004
14:10 will take away the remnant of the **h** of	1004
14:12 thou therefore, get thee to thine own **h**:	1004
14:13 LORD God of Israel in the **h** of Jeroboam.	1004
14:14 who shall cut off the **h** of Jeroboam that	1004
14:26 he took away the treasures of the **h** of	1004
14:26 and the treasures of the king's **h**;	1004
14:27 which kept the door of the king's **h**.	1004
14:28 when the king went *into* the **h** of	1004
15:15 *into* the **h** of the LORD, silver, and gold,	1004
15:18 left in the treasures of the **h** of the LORD,	1004
15:18 the treasures of the king's **h**,	1004
15:27 the **h** of Issachar, conspired against him;	1004
15:29 *that* he smote all the **h** of Jeroboam;	1004
16: 3 of Baasha, and the posterity of his **h**;	1004
16: 3 make thy **h** like the house of Jeroboam	1004
16: 3 make thy house like the **h** of Jeroboam	1004
16: 7 against his **h**, even for all the evil that he	1004
16: 7 hands, in being like the **h** of Jeroboam;	1004
16: 9 drinking *himself* drunk *in* the **h** of Arza	1004
16: 9 house of Arza steward of *his* **h** in Tirzah.	1004
16:11 throne, *that* he slew all the **h** of Baasha:	1004
16:12 did Zimri destroy all the **h** of Baasha,	1004
16:18 he went into the palace of the king's **h**,	1004
16:18 burnt the king's **h** over him with fire,	1004
16:32 he reared up an altar for Baal *in* the **h** of	1004
17:15 he, and her **h**, did eat *many* days.	1004
17:17 woman, the mistress of the **h**, fell sick;	1004
17:23 him down out of the chamber into the **h**,	1004
18: 3 which *was* the governor of *his* **h**.	1004
18:18 thou, and thy father's **h**, in that ye have	1004
20: 6 they shall search thine **h**, and the houses	1004
20:31 we have heard that the kings of the **h** of	1004
20:43 the king of Israel went to his **h** heavy and	1004
21: 2 of herbs, because it *is* near unto my **h**:	1004
21: 4 Ahab came into his **h** heavy and	1004
21:22 will make thine **h** like the house of	1004
21:22 will make thine house like the **h** of	1004
21:22 like the **h** of Baasha the son of Ahijah,	1004
21:29 son's days will I bring the evil upon his **h**.	1004
22:17 them return every man to his **h** in peace.	1004
22:39 the ivory **h** which he made, and all	1004

2Ki
4: 2 tell me, what hast thou in the **h**? And she	1004
4: 2 handmaid hath not any thing in the **h**,	1004
4:32 when Elisha was come into the **h**, behold,	1004
4:35 returned, and walked in the **h** to and fro;	1004
5: 9 and stood *at* the door of the **h** of Elisha.	1004
5:18 *that* when my master goeth *into* the **h** of	1004
5:18 and I bow myself *in* the **h** of Rimmon:	1004
5:18 when I bow down myself *in* the **h** of	1004
5:24 their hand, and bestowed *them* in the **h**.	1004
6:32 Elisha sat in his **h**, and the elders sat with	1004
7:11 and they told *it to* the king's **h** within.	1004
8: 3 went forth to cry unto the king for her **h**	1004
8: 5 to the king for her **h** and for her land.	1004
8:18 the kings of Israel, as did the **h** of Ahab:	1004
8:27 he walked in the way of the **h** of Ahab,	1004
8:27 sight of the LORD, as *did* the **h** of Ahab:	1004
8:27 he *was* the son in law of the **h** of Ahab.	1004
9: 6 he arose, and went into the **h**;	1004
9: 7 thou shalt smite the **h** of Ahab thy master,	1004
9: 8 For the whole **h** of Ahab shall perish:	1004
9: 9 I will make the **h** of Ahab like the house	1004
9: 9 will make the house of Ahab like the **h** of	1004
9: 9 and like the **h** of Baasha the son of Ahijah:	1004
9:27 *this*, he fled *by* the way of the garden **h**.	1004
10: 3 and fight for your master's **h**.	1004
10: 5 *he that was* over the **h**, and *he* that *was*	1004
10:10 which the LORD spake concerning the **h**	1004
10:11 So Jehu slew all that remained of the **h** of	1004
10:12 as he *was at* the shearing **h** in the way,	1004
10:14 slew them at the pit of the shearing **h**,	1004
10:21 they came *into* the **h** of Baal; and the	1004
10:21 the **h** of Baal was full from one end to	1004

2Ki
10:23 *into* the **h** of Baal, and said unto	1004
10:25 and went to the city of the **h** of Baal.	1004
10:26 brought forth the images out of the **h**	1004
10:27 brake down the **h** of Baal, and made it a	1004
10:27 and made it a **draught h** unto *this* day.	4280
10:30 hast done unto the **h** of Ahab according	1004
11: 3 he was with her hid *in* the **h** of the LORD,	1004
11: 4 brought them to him *into* the **h** of	1004
11: 4 took an oath of them in the **h** of	1004
11: 5 be keepers of the watch of the king's **h**;	1004
11: 6 so shall ye keep the watch of the **h**, that it	1004
11: 7 even they shall keep the watch of the **h** of	1004
11:15 Let her not be slain *in* the **h** of the LORD.	1004
11:16 which the horses came *into* the king's **h**:	1004
11:18 the people of the land went *into* the **h** of	1004
11:18 the priest appointed officers over the **h** of	1004
11:19 they brought down the king from the **h** of	1004
11:19 of the gate of the guard *to* the king's **h**.	1004
11:20 with the sword *beside* the king's **h**.	1004
12: 4 that is brought *into* the **h** of the LORD,	1004
12: 4 heart to bring *into* the **h** of the LORD,	1004
12: 5 let them repair the breaches of the **h**,	1004
12: 6 had not repaired the breaches of the **h**.	1004
12: 7 Why repair ye not the breaches of the **h**?	1004
12: 7 but deliver it for the breaches of the **h**.	1004
12: 8 neither to repair the breaches of the **h**.	1004
12: 9 the right side as one cometh *into* the **h**	1004
12: 9 that was brought *into* the **h** of the LORD.	1004
12:10 told the money that was found *in* the **h** of	1004
12:11 that had the oversight *of* the **h** of the	1004
12:11 that wrought upon the **h** of the LORD,	1004
12:12 stone to repair the breaches of the **h**	1004
12:12 all that was laid out for the **h** to repair	1004
12:13 Howbeit there were not made *for* the **h**.	1004
12:13 the money that was brought *into* the **h** of	1004
12:14 and repaired therewith the **h** of the LORD.	1004
12:16 sin money was not brought *into* the **h** of	1004
12:18 in the treasures of the **h** of the LORD,	1004
12:18 *in* the king's **h**, and sent *it* to Hazael king	1004
12:20 slew Joash *in* the **h** of Millo,	1004
13: 6 not from the sins of the **h** of Jeroboam,	1004
14:14 all the vessels that were found *in* the **h** of	1004
14:14 in the treasures of the king's **h**.	1004
15: 5 day of his death, and dwelt in a several **h**.	1004
15: 5 Jotham the king's son *was* over the **h**,	1004
15:25 in the palace of the king's **h**, with Argob	1004
15:35 He built the higher gate of the **h** of	1004
16: 8 gold that was found *in* the **h** of the LORD,	1004
16: 8 in the treasures of the king's **h**, and sent	1004
16:14 from the forefront of the **h**, from between	1004
16:14 between the altar and the **h** of the LORD,	1004
16:18 the sabbath that they had built in the **h**,	1004
16:18 turned he *from* the **h** of the LORD for	1004
17:21 For he rent Israel from the **h** of David;	1004
18:15 that was found *in* the **h** of the LORD,	1004
18:15 and in the treasures of the king's **h**.	1004
19: 1 and went *into* the **h** of the LORD.	1004
19:14 Hezekiah went up *into* the **h** of the LORD,	1004
19:30 the remnant that is escaped of the **h** of	1004
19:37 as he was worshipping *in* the **h** of Nisroch	1004
20: 1 Thus saith the LORD, Set thine **h** in order;	1004
20: 5 the third day thou shalt go up *unto* the **h**	1004
20: 8 *that* I shall go up *into* the **h** of the LORD	1004
20:13 shewed them all the **h** of his precious	1004
20:13 all the **h** of his armour, and all that was	1004
20:13 there was nothing in his **h**, nor in all his	1004
20:15 he said, What have they seen in thine **h**?	1004
20:15 All *the things* that *are* in mine **h** have	1004
20:17 that all that *is* in thine **h**, and *that* which	1004
21: 4 he built altars in the **h** of the LORD,	1004
21: 5 In the two courts of the **h** of the LORD.	1004
21: 7 of the grove that he had made in the **h**,	1004
21:13 and the plummet of the **h** of Ahab:	1004
21:18 was buried in the garden of his own **h**,	1004
21:23 and slew the king in his own **h**.	1004
22: 3 the scribe, *to* the **h** of the LORD, saying,	1004
22: 4 which is brought *into* the **h** of the LORD,	1004
22: 5 that have the oversight of the **h** of	1004
22: 5 the work which *is* in the **h** of the LORD,	1004
22: 5 the LORD, to repair the breaches of the **h**,	1004
22: 6 timber and hewn stone to repair the **h**.	1004
22: 8 I have found the book of the law in the **h**	1004
22: 9 the money that was found in the **h**,	1004
22: 9 that have the oversight *of* the **h** of	1004
23: 2 the king went up *into* the **h** of the LORD,	1004
23: 2 which was found in the **h** of the LORD,	1004
23: 6 he brought out the grove from the **h** of	1004
23: 7 that *were* by the **h** of the LORD,	1004
23:11 at the entering in of the **h** of the LORD,	1004
23:12 in the two courts of the **h** of the LORD,	1004
23:24 the priest found *in* the **h** of the LORD.	1004
23:27 the **h** of which I said, My name shall be	1004
24:13 all the treasures of the **h** of the LORD,	1004
24:13 the treasures of the king's **h**, and cut in	1004
25: 9 he burnt the **h** of the LORD,	1004
25: 9 the king's **h**, and all the houses of	1004
25: 9 every great *man's* **h** burnt he with fire.	1004
25:13 the pillars of brass that *were* in the **h** of	1004
25:13 the brasen sea that *was* in the **h** of	1004
25:16 had made for the **h** of the LORD;	1004

1Ch
2:54 **h** of Joab, and half of the Manahethites,	1004
2:55 of Hemath, the father of the **h** of Rechab.	1004
4:21 the families of the **h** of them that wrought	1004
4:21 wrought fine linen, of the **h** of Ashbea,	1004

1Ch
4:38 the **h** of their fathers increased greatly.	1004
5:13 brethren of the **h** of their fathers *were*,	1004
5:15 of Guni, chief of the **h** of their fathers.	1004
5:24 these *were* the heads of the **h** of their	1004
5:24 *and* heads of the **h** of their fathers.	1004
6:31 the service of song in the **h** of the LORD,	1004
6:32 until Solomon had built the **h** of	1004
6:48 service of the tabernacle of the **h** of God.	1004
7: 2 and Shemuel, heads of their fathers' **h**,	1004
7: 4 after the **h** of their fathers,	1004
7: 7 heads of the **h** of *their* fathers, mighty	1004
7: 9 heads of their **h** of their fathers, mighty	1004
7:23 because it went evil with his **h**.	1004
7:40 heads of *their* fathers' **h**, choice *and*	1004
9: 9 of the fathers in the **h** of their fathers.	1004
9:11 son of Ahitub, the ruler of the **h** of God;	1004
9:13 heads of their **h** of their fathers, a thousand	1004
9:13 the work of the service of the **h** of God.	1004
9:19 his brethren, of the **h** of his father,	1004
9:23 of the gates of the **h** of the LORD,	1004
9:23 the **h** of the tabernacle, by wards.	1004
9:26 and treasuries of the **h** of God.	1004
9:27 they lodged round about the **h** of God,	1004
10: 6 his three sons, and all his **h** died together.	1004
10:10 they put his armour *in* the **h** of their gods,	1004
12:28 of his father's **h** twenty and two captains.	1004
12:29 them had kept the ward of the **h** of Saul.	1004
12:30 famous throughout the **h** of their fathers.	1004
13: 7 in a new cart out of the **h** of Abinadab:	1004
13:13 carried it aside into the **h** of Obed-edom	1004
13:14 of Obed-edom in his **h** three months.	1004
13:14 LORD blessed the **h** of Obed-edom,	1004
14: 1 and carpenters, to build him a **h**.	1004
15:25 out of the **h** of Obed-edom with joy.	1004
16:43 the people departed every man to his **h**:	1004
16:43 and David returned to bless his **h**.	1004
17: 1 it came to pass, as David sat in his **h**,	1004
17: 1 I dwell in a **h** of cedars, but the ark of	1004
17: 4 Thou shalt not build me a **h** to dwell in:	1004
17: 5 For I have not dwelt in a **h** since the day	1004
17: 6 Why have ye not built me a **h** of cedars?	1004
17:10 thee that the LORD will build thee a **h**.	1004
17:12 He shall build me a **h**, and I will stablish	1004
17:14 I will settle him in mine **h** and in my	1004
17:16 am I, O LORD God, and what *is* mine **h**,	1004
17:17 thou hast *also* spoken of thy servant's **h**	1004
17:23 concerning his **h** be established for ever,	1004
17:24 let the **h** of David thy servant *be*	1004
17:25 thy servant that *thou* wilt build him a **h**:	1004
17:27 let it please thee to bless the **h** of	1004
21:17 my God, be on me, and on my father's **h**;	1004
22: 1 This *is* the **h** of the LORD God, and this *is*	1004
22: 2 wrought stones to build the **h** of God.	1004
22: 5 the **h** that *is* to be builded for the LORD	1004
22: 6 charged him to build a **h** for the LORD	1004
22: 7 it was in my mind to build a **h** unto	1004
22: 8 thou shalt not build a **h** unto my name,	1004
22:10 He shall build a **h** for my name;	1004
22:11 and build the **h** of the LORD thy God,	1004
22:14 my trouble I have prepared for the **h** of	1004
22:19 the **h** that is *to be* built to the name of	1004
23: 4 forward the work of the **h** of the LORD;	1004
23:11 according to their father's **h**.	1004
23:24 *were* the sons of Levi after the **h** of	1004
23:24 did the work for the service of the **h** of	1004
23:28 for the service of the **h** of the LORD,	1004
23:28 the work of the service of the **h** of God;	1004
23:32 in the service of the **h** of the LORD.	1004
24: 4 chief *men* of the **h** of *their* fathers,	1004
24: 4 according to the **h** of their fathers.	1004
24: 5 governors *of the* **h** of God, were of the	NIH
24:19 service to come into the **h** of the LORD,	1004
24:30 of the Levites after the **h** of their fathers.	1004
25: 6 their father for song in the **h** of the LORD,	1004
25: 6 and harps, for the service of the **h** of God,	1004
26: 6 ruled throughout the **h** of their father:	1004
26:12 to minister in the **h** of the LORD,	1004
26:13 according to the **h** of their fathers, for	1004
26:15 to his sons the **h** of Asuppim.	1004
26:20 Ahijah *was* over the treasures of the **h** of	1004
26:22 *which were* over the treasures of the **h** of	1004
26:27 dedicate to maintain the **h** of the LORD.	1004
28: 2 *for me*, I *had* in mine heart to build a **h**	1004
28: 3 Thou shalt not build a **h** for my name,	1004
28: 4 of my father to be king over Israel for	1004
28: 4 of the **h** of Judah, the house of my father;	1004
28: 4 of the house of Judah, the **h** of my father;	1004
28: 6 son, he shall build my **h** and my courts:	1004
28:10 thee to build a **h** for the sanctuary:	1004
28:12 of the courts of the **h** of the LORD,	1004
28:12 of the treasuries of the **h** of God, and of	1004
28:13 for all the work of the service of the **h** of	1004
28:13 for all the vessels of service in the **h** of	1004
28:20 for the service of the **h** of the LORD.	1004
28:21 *thee* for all the service of the **h** of God:	1004
29: 2 of my God the gold for *things to be*	1004
29: 3 have set my affection to the **h** of my God,	1004
29: 3 *which* I have given to the **h** of my God,	1004
29: 3 all *that* I have prepared for the holy **h**,	1004
29: 7 for the service of the **h** of God *of* gold	1004
29: 8 *them* to the treasure of the **h** of the LORD,	1004
29:16 for thine holy name *cometh* of thine	1004

2Ch
2: 1 Solomon determined to build a **h** for	1004
2: 1 of the LORD, and a **h** for his kingdom.	1004
2: 3 didst send me cedars to build him a **h** to	1004

H

2Ch	2: 4 I build a **h** to the name of the Lord my	1004
	2: 5 the **h** which I build *is* great: for great *is*	1004
	2: 6 who is able to build him a **h**, seeing	1004
	2: 6 *am* I then, that I should build him a **h**,	1004
	2: 9 for the **h** which I am about to build shall	1004
	2:12 that might build a **h** for the Lord,	1004
	2:12 for the Lord, and a **h** for his kingdom.	1004
	3: 1 Solomon began to build the **h** of	1004
	3: 3 for the building of the **h** of God.	1004
	3: 4 the porch that *was* in the front *of the h*,	NIH
	3: 4 *it was* according to the breadth of the **h**,	1004
	3: 5 the greater **h** he cieled with fir tree,	1004
	3: 6 he garnished the **h** with precious stones	1004
	3: 7 He overlaid also the **h**, the beams,	1004
	3: 8 he made the most holy **h**, the length	1004
	3: 8 *was* according to the breadth of the **h**,	1004
	3:10 the most holy **h** he made two cherubims	1004
	3:11 five cubits, reaching to the wall of the **h**:	1004
	3:12 five cubits, reaching to the wall of the **h**:	1004
	3:15 Also he made before the **h** two pillars of	1004
	4:11 make for king Solomon for the **h** of God;	1004
	4:16 for the **h** of the Lord *of* bright brass.	1004
	4:19 all the vessels that *were for* the **h** of God,	1004
	4:22 the entry of the **h**, the inner doors thereof	1004
	4:22 and the doors of the **h** of the temple,	1004
	5: 1 made for the **h** of the Lord was finished:	1004
	5: 1 he among the treasures of the **h** of God.	1004
	5: 7 to the oracle of the **h**, into the most holy	1004
	5:13 that *then* the **h** was filled *with* a cloud,	1004
	5:13 *with* a cloud, *even* the **h** of the Lord;	1004
	5:14 for the glory of the Lord had filled the **h**	1004
	6: 2 I have built a **h** of habitation for thee,	1004
	6: 5 build a **h** *in*, that my name might be there	1004
	6: 7 for the name of the Lord God of	1004
	6: 8 in thine heart to build a **h** for my name,	1004
	6: 9 thou shalt not build the **h**;	1004
	6: 9 loins, he shall build the **h** for my name.	1004
	6:10 have built the **h** for the name of the Lord	1004
	6:18 how much less this **h** which I have built?	1004
	6:20 That thine eyes may be open upon this **h**	1004
	6:22 the oath come before thine altar in this **h**;	1004
	6:24 make supplication before thee in this **h**;	1004
	6:29 and shall spread forth his hands in this **h**:	1004
	6:32 out arm; if they come and pray in this **h**;	1004
	6:33 may know that this **h** which I have built	1004
	6:34 the **h** which I have built for thy name;	1004
	6:38 toward the **h** which I have built for thy	1004
	7: 1 and the glory of the Lord filled the **h**.	1004
	7: 2 the priests could not enter into the **h** of	1004
	7: 2 of the Lord had filled the Lord's **h**.	1004
	7: 3 and the glory of the Lord upon the **h**,	1004
	7: 5 all the people dedicated the **h** of God.	1004
	7: 7 court that was before the **h** of the Lord:	1004
	7:11 Thus Solomon finished the **h** of	1004
	7:11 the house of the Lord, and the king's **h**:	1004
	7:11 heart to make in the **h** of the Lord,	1004
	7:11 in his own **h**, he prosperously effected.	1004
	7:12 have chosen this place to myself for a **h** of	1004
	7:16 now have I chosen and sanctified this **h**,	1004
	7:20 this **h**, which I have sanctified for my	1004
	7:21 this **h**, which is high, shall be an	1004
	7:21 done thus unto this land, and unto this **h**?	1004
	8: 1 wherein Solomon had built the **h** of	1004
	8: 1 the house of the Lord, and his own **h**,	1004
	8:11 David unto the **h** that he had built for her	1004
	8:11 My wife shall not dwell in the **h** of David	1004
	8:16 of the foundation of the **h** of the Lord,	1004
	8:16 *So* the **h** of the Lord was perfected.	1004
	9: 3 of Solomon, and the **h** that he had built,	1004
	9: 4 ascent *by* which he went up *into* the **h**	1004
	9:11 algum trees terraces to the **h** of the Lord,	1004
	9:16 the king put them in the **h** of the forest of	1004
	9:20 all the vessels of the **h** of the forest of	1004
	10:16 *and* now, David, see to thine own **h**.	1004
	10:19 Israel rebelled against the **h** of David unto	1004
	11: 1 he gathered *of* the **h** of Judah and	1004
	11: 4 return every man to his **h**, for this thing is	1004
	12: 9 took away the treasures of the **h** of	1004
	12: 9 and the treasures of the king's **h**;	1004
	12:10 that kept the entrance of the king's **h**.	1004
	12:11 when the king entered *into* the **h** of	1004
	15:18 he brought *into* the **h** of God *the things*	1004
	16: 2 gold out of the treasures of the **h** of	1004
	16: 2 house of the Lord and of the king's **h**,	1004
	16:10 with the seer, and put him *in* a prison **h**;	1004
	17:14 them according to the **h** of their fathers:	1004
	18:16 *therefore* every man to his **h** in peace.	1004
	19: 1 returned to his **h** in peace to Jerusalem.	1004
	19:11 the ruler of the **h** of Judah, for all the	1004
	20: 5 and Jerusalem, in the **h** of the Lord,	1004
	20: 9 stand before this **h**, and in thy presence,	1004
	20: 9 thy presence, (for thy name *is* in this **h**,)	1004
	20:28 and trumpets unto the **h** of the Lord.	1004
	21: 6 kings of Israel, like as did the **h** of Ahab:	1004
	21: 7 Lord would not destroy the **h** of David,	1004
	21:13 like to the whoredoms of the **h** of Ahab,	1004
	21:13 hast slain thy brethren of thy father's **h**,	1004
	21:17 substance that was found in the king's **h**,	1004
	22: 3 He also walked in the ways of the **h** of	1004
	22: 4 the sight of the Lord, like the **h** of Ahab:	1004
	22: 7 had anointed to cut off the **h** of Ahab.	1004
	22: 8 executing judgment upon the **h** of Ahab,	1004
	22: 9 the **h** of Ahaziah had no power to keep	1004
	22:10 destroyed all the seed royal of the **h** of	1004
	22:12 he was with them hid in the **h** of God six	1004

2Ch	23: 3 a covenant with the king in the **h** of God.	1004
	23: 5 a third *part shall be* at the king's **h**;	1004
	23: 5 the people *shall be* in the courts of the **h**	1004
	23: 6 let none come *into* the **h** of the Lord,	1004
	23: 7 whosoever *else* cometh into the **h**, he	1004
	23: 9 David's, which *were* in the **h** of God.	1004
	23:12 she came to the people *into* the **h** of	1004
	23:14 Slay her not *in* the **h** of the Lord.	1004
	23:15 entering of the horse gate *by* the king's **h**,	1004
	23:17 all the people went *to* the **h** of Baal,	1004
	23:18 **h** of the Lord by the hand of the priests	1004
	23:18 whom David had distributed in the **h** of	1004
	23:19 he set the porters at the gates of the **h** of	1004
	23:20 brought down the king from the **h** of	1004
	23:20 through the high gate *into* the king's **h**,	1004
	24: 4 *that* Joash was minded to repair the **h** of	1004
	24: 5 of all Israel money to repair the **h** of	1004
	24: 7 had broken up the **h** of God;	1004
	24: 7 also all the dedicate *things* of the **h** of	1004
	24: 8 set it without at the gate of the **h** of	1004
	24:12 work of the service of the **h** of the Lord,	1004
	24:12 carpenters to repair the **h** of the Lord,	1004
	24:12 and brass to mend the **h** of the Lord.	1004
	24:13 they set the **h** of God in his state,	1004
	24:14 whereof were made vessels for the **h** of	1004
	24:14 they offered burnt offerings in the **h** of	1004
	24:16 both towards God, and *towards* his **h**.	1004
	24:18 they left the **h** of the Lord God of their	1004
	24:21 king in the court of the **h** of the Lord.	1004
	24:27 and the repairing of the **h** of God,	1004
	25:24 all the vessels that were found in the **h** of	1004
	25:24 the treasures of the king's **h**, the hostages	1004
	26:19 before the priests in the **h** of the Lord,	1004
	26:21 and dwelt *in* a several **h**, *being* a leper;	1004
	26:21 for he was cut off from the **h** of	1004
	26:21 Jotham his son *was* over the king's **h**,	1004
	27: 3 He built the high gate of the **h** of	1004
	28: 7 Azrikam the governor of the **h**,	1004
	28:21 Ahaz took away a portion *out* of the **h**	1004
	28:21 of the **h** of the king, and of the princes,	1004
	28:24 gathered together the vessels of the **h**	1004
	28:24 cut in pieces the vessels of the **h** of God,	1004
	28:24 shut up the doors of the **h** of the Lord,	1004
	29: 3 opened the doors of the **h** of the Lord,	1004
	29: 5 sanctify the **h** of the Lord God of your	1004
	29:15 to cleanse the **h** of the Lord.	1004
	29:16 priests went into the inner part *of* the **h**	1004
	29:16 into the court of the **h** of the Lord,	1004
	29:17 they sanctified the **h** of the Lord in eight	1004
	29:18 We have cleansed all the **h** of the Lord,	1004
	29:20 and went up *to* the **h** of the Lord.	1004
	29:25 he set the Levites *in* the **h** of the Lord	1004
	29:31 thank offerings into the **h** of the Lord;	1004
	29:35 So the service of the **h** of the Lord was	1004
	30: 1 that *they* should come to the **h** of	1004
	30:15 brought in the burnt offerings *into* the **h**	1004
	31:10 Azariah the chief priest of the **h** of Zadok	1004
	31:10 the offerings *into* the **h** of the Lord,	1004
	31:11 prepare chambers in the **h** of the Lord;	1004
	31:13 and Azariah the ruler of the **h** of God.	1004
	31:16 unto every one that entereth into the **h**	1004
	31:17 of the priests by the **h** of their fathers,	1004
	31:21 he began in the service of the **h** of God,	1004
	32:21 when he was come *into* the **h** of his god,	1004
	33: 4 Also he built altars in the **h** of the Lord,	1004
	33: 5 in the two courts of the **h** of the Lord.	1004
	33: 7 idol which he had made, in the **h** of God,	1004
	33: 7 his son, In this **h**, and in Jerusalem,	1004
	33:15 and the idol out of the **h** of the Lord,	1004
	33:15 built in the mount of the **h** of the Lord,	1004
	33:20 and they buried him *in* his own **h**:	1004
	33:24 against him, and slew him in his own **h**.	1004
	34: 8 when he had purged the land, and the **h**,	1004
	34: 8 to repair the **h** of the Lord his God.	1004
	34: 9 that was brought *into* the **h** of God,	1004
	34:10 had the oversight of the **h** of the Lord,	1004
	34:10 that wrought in the **h** of the Lord,	1004
	34:10 of the Lord, to repair and mend the **h**:	1004
	34:14 that was brought *into* the **h** of the Lord	1004
	34:15 have found the book of the law in the **h** of	1004
	34:17 that was found in the **h** of the Lord,	1004
	34:30 the king went up *into* the **h** of the Lord,	1004
	34:30 that was found *in* the **h** of the Lord.	1004
	35: 2 encouraged them to the service of the **h** of	1004
	35: 3 Put the holy ark in the **h** which Solomon	1004
	35: 8 and Jehiel, rulers of the **h** of God,	1004
	35:21 but against the **h** wherewith I have war:	1004
	36: 7 vessels of the **h** of the Lord to Babylon,	1004
	36:10 with the goodly vessels of the **h** of	1004
	36:14 polluted the **h** of the Lord which he had	1004
	36:17 the sword in the **h** of their sanctuary,	1004
	36:18 all the vessels of the **h** of God, great and	1004
	36:18 the treasures of the **h** of the Lord,	1004
	36:19 they burnt the **h** of God, and brake down	1004
	36:23 he hath charged me to build him a **h** in	1004
Ezr	1: 2 he hath charged me to build him a **h** at	1004
	1: 3 build the **h** of the Lord God of Israel,	1004
	1: 4 besides the freewill offering for the **h** of	1004
	1: 5 to go up to build the **h** of the Lord	1004
	1: 7 forth the vessels of the **h** of the Lord,	1004
	1: 7 and had brought *into* the **h** of his gods;	1004
	2:36 of the **h** of Jeshua, nine hundred seventy	1004
	2:59 they could not shew their fathers' **h**,	1004
	2:68 when they came to the **h** of the Lord	1004
	2:68 offered freely for the **h** of God to set it up	1004

Ezr	3: 8 coming unto the **h** of God at Jerusalem,	1004
	3: 8 to set forward the work of the **h** of	1004
	3: 9 to set forward the workmen in the **h** of	1004
	3:11 the foundation of the **h** of the Lord was	1004
	3:12 ancient men that had seen the first **h**,	1004
	3:12 when the foundation of this **h** was laid	1004
	4: 3 have nothing to do with us to build a **h**	1004
	4:24 ceased the work of the **h** of the God	1005
	5: 2 began to build the **h** of God which *is* at	1005
	5: 3 hath commanded you to build this **h**,	1005
	5: 8 the **h** of the great God, which *is* builded	1005
	5: 9 Who commanded you to build this **h**,	1005
	5:11 build the **h** that was builded these many	1005
	5:12 who destroyed this **h**, and carried	1005
	5:13 made a decree to build this **h** of God.	1005
	5:14 also of gold and silver of the **h** of God,	1005
	5:15 let the **h** of God be builded in his place.	1005
	5:16 laid the foundation of the **h** of God which	1005
	5:17 be search made in the king's treasure **h**,	1005
	5:17 king to build this **h** of God at Jerusalem,	1005
	6: 1 and search was made in the **h** of the rolls,	1005
	6: 3 *concerning* the **h** of God at Jerusalem,	1005
	6: 3 Let the **h** be builded, the place where	1005
	6: 4 the expences be given out of the king's **h**:	1005
	6: 5 and silver vessels of the **h** of God,	1005
	6: 5 his place, and place *them* in the **h** of God.	1005
	6: 7 Let the work of this **h** of God alone;	1005
	6: 7 the elders of the Jews build this **h** of God	1005
	6: 8 Jews for the building of this **h** of God:	1005
	6:11 let timber be pulled down from his **h**,	1005
	6:11 let his **h** be made a dunghill for this.	1005
	6:12 to destroy this **h** of God which *is* at	1005
	6:15 this **h** was finished on the third day of	1005
	6:16 kept the dedication of this **h** of God with	1005
	6:17 offered at the dedication of this **h** of God	1005
	6:22 their hands in the work of the **h** of God,	1004
	7:16 offering willingly for the **h** of their God	1005
	7:17 offer them upon the altar of the **h** of your	1005
	7:19 thee for the service of the **h** of thy God,	1005
	7:20 more *shall be* needful for the **h**	1005
	7:20 bestow *it* out of the king's treasure **h**.	1005
	7:23 it be diligently done for the **h** of the God	1005
	7:24 or ministers of this **h** of God,	1005
	7:27 to beautify the **h** of the Lord which *is* in	1004
	8:17 unto us ministers for the **h** of our God.	1004
	8:25 *even* the offering of the **h** of our God,	1004
	8:29 *in* the chambers of the **h** of the Lord.	1004
	8:30 to bring *them* to Jerusalem unto the **h** of	1004
	8:33 the vessels weighed in the **h** of our God	1004
	8:36 furthered the people, and the **h** of God.	1004
	9: 9 to set up the **h** of our God, and to repair	1004
	10: 1 casting himself down before the **h** of God,	1004
	10: 6 Ezra rose up from before the **h** of God,	1004
	10: 9 all the people sat in the street of the **h** of	1004
	10:16 after the **h** of their fathers, and all of them	1004
Ne	1: 6 both I and my father's **h** have sinned.	1004
	2: 8 of the palace which *appertained* to the **h**,	1004
	2: 8 city, and for the **h** that I shall enter into.	1004
	3:10 of Harumaph, even over against his **h**.	1004
	3:16 was made, and unto the **h** of the mighty.	1004
	3:20 door of the **h** of Eliashib the high priest.	1004
	3:21 from the door of the **h** of Eliashib even to	1004
	3:21 even to the end of the **h** of Eliashib.	1004
	3:23 and Hashub over against their **h**.	1004
	3:23 of Maaseiah the son of Ananiah by his **h**.	1004
	3:24 from the **h** of Azariah unto the turning *of*	1004
	3:25 which lieth out from the king's high **h**,	1004
	3:28 the priests, every one over against his **h**.	1004
	3:29 the son of Immer over against his **h**.	1004
	4:16 the rulers *were* behind all the **h** of Judah.	1004
	5:13 So God shake out every man from his **h**,	1004
	6:10 Afterward I came *unto* the **h** of Shemaiah	1004
	6:10 Let us meet together in the **h** of God,	1004
	7: 3 and every one *to be* over against his **h**.	1004
	7:39 of the **h** of Jeshua, nine hundred seventy	1004
	7:61 they could not shew their fathers' **h**,	1004
	8:16 every one upon the **roof** of his **h**,	1406
	8:16 in the courts of the **h** of God, and in	1004
	10:32 shekel for the service of the **h** of our God;	1004
	10:33 and *for* all the work of the **h** of our God.	1004
	10:34 to bring *it* into the **h** of our God,	1004
	10:35 year by year, unto the **h** of the Lord:	1004
	10:36 of our flocks, to bring to the **h** of our God,	1004
	10:36 unto the priests that minister in the **h** of	1004
	10:37 to the chambers of the **h** of our God;	1004
	10:38 tithe of the tithes unto the **h** of our God,	1004
	10:38 to the chambers, into the treasure **h**.	1004
	10:39 and we will not forsake the **h** of our God.	1004
	11:11 of Ahitub, *was* the ruler of the **h** of God.	1004
	11:12 their brethren that did the work of the **h**	1004
	11:16 of the outward business of the **h** of God,	1004
	11:22 singers *were* over the business of the **h**	1004
	12:29 Also from the **h** of Gilgal, and out of	1004
	12:37 of the wall, above the **h** of David,	1004
	12:40 *of them* that gave thanks in the **h** of God,	1004
	13: 4 of the chamber of the **h** of our God,	1004
	13: 7 a chamber in the courts of the **h** of God.	1004
	13: 9 brought I again the vessels of the **h**	1004
	13:11 and said, Why is the **h** of God forsaken?	1004
	13:14 that I have done for the **h** of my God,	1004
Est	1: 8 had appointed to all the officers of his **h**,	1004
	1: 9 **h** which *belonged* to king Ahasuerus.	1004
	1:22 every man should bear rule in his own **h**,	1004
	2: 3 to the women, unto the custody	1004
	2: 8 Esther was brought *also* unto the king's **h**,	1004

Est	2: 9 meet to be given her, out of the king's **h**:	1004
	2: 9 her maids unto the best *place* of the **h** of	1004
	2:11 day before the court of the women's **h**,	1004
	2:13 **h** of the women unto the king's house.	1004
	2:13 house of the women unto the king's **h**.	1004
	2:14 returned into the second **h** of the women,	1004
	2:16 into his **h** royal in the tenth month,	1004
	4:13 that *thou* shalt escape *in* the king's **h**,	1004
	4:14 and thy father's **h** shall be destroyed:	1004
	5: 1 stood in the inner court of the king's **h**,	1004
	5: 1 king's house, over against the king's **h**:	1004
	5: 1 sat upon his royal throne in the royal **h**,	1004
	5: 1 house, over against the gate of the **h**.	1004
	6: 4 into the outward court of the king's **h**,	1004
	6:12 Haman hasted to his **h** mourning,	1004
	7: 8 force the queen also before me in the **h**?	1004
	7: 9 for the king, standeth in the **h** of Haman.	1004
	8: 1 **h** of Haman the Jews' enemy unto Esther	1004
	8: 2 Esther set Mordecai over the **h** of Haman.	1004
	8: 7 I have given Esther the **h** of Haman,	1004
	9: 4 For Mordecai *was* great in the king's **h**,	1004
Job	1:10 about his **h**, and about all that he hath on	1004
	1:13 drinking wine in their eldest brother's **h**:	1004
	1:18 drinking wine in their eldest brother's **h**:	1004
	1:19 smote the four corners of the **h**, and it fell	1004
	7:10 He shall return no more to his **h**,	1004
	8:15 He shall lean upon his **h**, but it shall not	1004
	17:13 If I wait, the grave *is* mine **h**: I have made	1004
	19:15 They that dwell in mine **h**,	1004
	20:19 he hath violently taken away a **h** which	1004
	20:28 The increase of his **h** shall depart,	1004
	21:21 For what pleasure hath he in his **h** after	1004
	21:28 For ye say, Where *is* the **h** of the prince?	1004
	27:18 He buildeth his **h** as a moth, and as a	1004
	30:23 and *to* the **h** appointed for all living.	1004
	38:20 thou shouldest know the paths to the **h**	1004
	39: 6 Whose **h** I have made the wilderness,	1004
	42:11 and did eat bread with him in his **h**:	1004
Ps	5: 7 I will come *into* thy **h** in the multitude of	1004
	23: 6 I will dwell in the **h** of the LORD for ever.	1004
	26: 8 I have loved the habitation of thy **h**,	1004
	27: 4 that I may dwell in the **h** of the LORD all	1004
	30: T Song *at* the dedication of the **h** of David.	1004
	31: 2 strong rock, for a **h** of defence to save me.	1004
	36: 8 satisfied with the fatness of thy **h**;	1004
	42: 4 I went with them to the **h** of God, with	1004
	45:10 also thine own people, and thy father's **h**;	1004
	49:16 when the glory of his **h** is increased;	1004
	50: 9 I will take no bullock out of thy **h**, *nor* he	1004
	52: T David is come to the **h** of Ahimelech.	1004
	52: 8 like a green olive tree in the **h** of God:	1004
	55:14 walked unto the **h** of God in company.	1004
	55: T sent, and they watcht the **h** to kill him.	1004
	65: 4 be satisfied with the goodness of thy **h**,	1004
	66:13 I will go *into* thy **h** with burnt offerings:	1004
	69: 9 For the zeal of thine **h** hath eaten me up;	1004
	84: 3 the sparrow hath found a **h**,	1004
	84: 4 Blessed *are* they that dwell in thy **h**:	1004
	84:10 I had rather be a doorkeeper in the **h** of	1004
	92:13 Those that be planted in the **h** of	1004
	93: 5 holiness becometh thine **h**, O LORD,	1004
	98: 3 and his truth toward the **h** of Israel:	1004
	101: 2 I will walk within my **h** with a perfect	1004
	101: 7 deceit shall not dwell within my **h**:	1004
	104:17 *as for* the stork, the fir trees *are* her **h**.	1004
	105:21 made him lord of his **h**, and ruler of all	1004
	112: 3 Wealth and riches *shall be* in his **h**:	1004
	113: 9 He maketh the barren *woman* to keep **h**,	1004
	114: 1 the **h** of Jacob from a people of strange	1004
	115:10 O **h** of Aaron, trust in the LORD: he *is*	1004
	115:12 he will bless *us*; he will bless the **h** of	1004
	115:12 of Israel; he will bless the **h** of Aaron.	1004
	116:19 In the courts of the LORD's **h**,	1004
	118: 3 Let the **h** of Aaron now say, that his	1004
	118:26 we have blessed you out of the **h** of	1004
	119:54 Thy statutes have been my songs in the **h**	1004
	122: 1 Let us go *into* the **h** of the LORD.	1004
	122: 5 judgment, the thrones of the **h** of David.	1004
	122: 9 Because of the **h** of the LORD our God I	1004
	127: 1 Except the LORD build the **h**, they labour	1004
	128: 3 as a fruitful vine by the sides of thine **h**:	1004
	132: 3 will not come into the tabernacle of my **h**,	1004
	134: 1 which by night stand in the **h** of	1004
	135: 2 Ye that stand in the **h** of the LORD,	1004
	135: 2 in the courts of the **h** of our God,	1004
	135:19 Bless the LORD, O **h** of Israel: bless	1004
	135:19 of Israel: bless the LORD, O **h** of Aaron.	1004
	135:20 Bless the LORD, O **h** of Levi: ye that fear	1004
Pr	2:18 For her **h** inclineth unto death,	1004
	3:33 The curse of the LORD *is* in the **h** of	1004
	5: 8 and come not nigh the door of her **h**:	1004
	5:10 and thy labours *be* in the **h** of a stranger;	1004
	6:31 he shall give all the substance of his **h**.	1004
	7: 6 For at the window of my **h** I looked	1004
	7: 8 her corner; and he went the way to her **h**,	1004
	7:11 and stubborn; her feet abide not in her **h**:	1004
	7:27 Her **h** *is* the way to hell, going down to	1004
	9: 1 Wisdom hath builded her **h**, she hath	1004
	9:14 For she sitteth at the door of her **h**, on a	1004
	11:29 He that troubleth his own **h** shall inherit	1004
	12: 7 but the **h** of the righteous shall stand.	1004
	14: 1 Every wise woman buildeth her **h**:	1004
	14:11 The **h** of the wicked shall be overthrown:	1004
	15: 6 *In* the **h** of the righteous *is* much treasure:	1004
	15:25 The LORD will destroy the **h** of	1004

Pr	15:27 that is greedy of gain troubleth his own **h**;	1004
	17: 1 than a **h** full *of* sacrifices with strife.	1004
	17:13 for good, evil shall not depart from his **h**.	1004
	19:14 **H** and riches *are* the inheritance of fathers:	1004
	21: 9 than with a brawling woman in a wide **h**.	1004
	21:12 righteous *man* wisely considereth the **h**	1004
	24: 3 Through wisdom is a **h** builded;	1004
	24:27 in the field; and afterwards build thine **h**.	1004
	25:17 thy foot from thy neighbour's **h**;	1004
	25:24 with a brawling woman and in a wide **h**.	1004
	27:10 neither go *into* thy brother's **h** in the day	1004
Ecc	2: 7 maidens, and had servants born in *my* **h**;	1004
	5: 1 Keep thy foot when thou goest to the **h** of	1004
	7: 2 *It is* better to go to the **h** of mourning,	1004
	7: 2 mourning, than to go to the **h** of feasting;	1004
	7: 4 The heart of the wise *is* in the **h** of	1004
	7: 4 but the heart of fools *is* in the **h** of mirth.	1004
	10:18 through idleness of the hands the **h**	1004
	12: 3 In the day when the keepers of the **h** shall	1004
SS	1:17 The beams of our **h** *are* cedar,	1004
	2: 4 He brought me to the banqueting **h**,	1004
	3: 4 I had brought him into my mother's **h**,	1004
	8: 2 *and* bring thee into my mother's **h**,	1004
	8: 7 give all the substance of his **h** for love,	1004
Isa	2: 2 *that* the mountain of the LORD's **h** shall	1004
	2: 3 the LORD, to the **h** of the God of Jacob;	1004
	2: 5 O **h** of Jacob, come ye, and let us walk in	1004
	2: 6 hast forsaken thy people the **h** of Jacob,	1004
	3: 6 hold of his brother *of* the **h** of his father,	1004
	3: 7 for in my **h** *is* neither bread nor clothing:	1004
	5: 7 of the LORD of hosts *is* the **h** of Israel,	1004
	5: 8 Woe unto them that join **h** to house,	1004
	5: 8 Woe unto them that join house to **h**,	1004
	6: 4 cried, and the **h** was filled *with* smoke.	1004
	7: 2 it was told the **h** of David, saying, Syria is	1004
	7:13 he said, Hear ye now, O **h** of David; *Is it*	1004
	7:17 upon thy people, and upon thy father's **h**,	1004
	8:17 that hideth his face from the **h** of Jacob,	1004
	10:20 and such as are escaped of the **h** of Jacob,	1004
	14: 1 and they shall cleave to the **h** of Jacob.	1004
	14: 2 the **h** of Israel shall possess them in	1004
	14:17 *that* opened not the **h** of his prisoners?	1004
	14:18 lie in glory, every one in his own **h**.	1004
	22: 8 day to the armour of the **h** of the forest.	1004
	22:15 Shebna, which *is* over the **h**, *and say*,	1004
	22:18 glory *shall be* the shame of thy lord's **h**.	1004
	22:21 of Jerusalem, and to the **h** of Judah.	1004
	22:22 the key of the **h** of David will I lay upon	1004
	22:23 be for a glorious throne to his father's **h**.	1004
	22:24 upon him all the glory of his father's **h**,	1004
	23: 1 so that *there is* no **h**, no entering in:	1004
	24:10 every **h** is shut up, that no *man may* come	1004
	29:22 concerning the **h** of Jacob,	1004
	31: 2 will arise against the **h** of the evildoers,	1004
	36: 3 which *was* over the **h**, and Shebna	1004
	37: 1 and went *into* the **h** of the LORD.	1004
	37:14 Hezekiah went up *unto* the **h** of	1004
	37:31 the remnant that is escaped of the **h** of	1004
	37:38 he was worshipping *in* the **h** of Nisroch	1004
	38: 1 Thus saith the LORD, Set thine **h** in order:	1004
	38:20 the days of our life in the **h** of the LORD.	1004
	38:22 What *is* the sign that I shall go up *to* the **h**	1004
	39: 2 shewed them the **h** of his precious things,	1004
	39: 2 all the **h** of his armour, and all that was	1004
	39: 2 there was nothing in his **h**, nor in all his	1004
	39: 4 said he, What have they seen in thine **h**?	1004
	39: 4 All that *is* in mine **h** have they seen:	1004
	39: 6 that all that *is* in thine **h**, and *that* which	1004
	42: 7 that sit in darkness out of the prison **h**.	1004
	44:13 of a man; that it may remain *in* the **h**.	1004
	46: 3 O **h** of Jacob, and all the remnant of	1004
	46: 3 and all the remnant of the **h** of Israel,	1004
	48: 1 Hear ye this, O **h** of Jacob, which are	1004
	56: 5 Even unto them will I give in mine **h** and	1004
	56: 7 and make them joyful in my **h** of prayer:	1004
	56: 7 mine **h** shall be called a house of prayer	1004
	56: 7 mine house shall be called a **h** of prayer	1004
	58: 1 and the **h** of Jacob their sins.	1004
	58: 7 bring the poor that are cast out *to* thy **h**?	1004
	60: 7 and I will glorify the **h** of my glory.	1004
	63: 7 the great goodness towards the **h** of Israel,	1004
	64:11 Our holy and our beautiful **h**, where our	1004
	66: 1 where *is* the **h** that ye build unto me?	1004
	66:20 in a clean vessel *into* the **h** of the LORD.	1004
Jer	2: 4 O **h** of Jacob, and all the families of	1004
	2: 4 and all the families of the **h** of Israel:	1004
	2:26 he is found, so is the **h** of Israel ashamed;	1004
	3:18 In those days the **h** of Judah shall walk	1004
	3:18 of Judah shall walk with the **h** of Israel,	1004
	3:20 with me, O **h** of Israel, saith the LORD.	1004
	5:11 For the **h** of Israel and the house of Judah	1004
	5:11 the **h** of Judah have dealt very	1004
	5:15 from far, O **h** of Israel, saith the LORD:	1004
	5:20 Declare this in the **h** of Jacob,	1004
	7: 2 Stand in the gate of the LORD's **h**,	1004
	7:10 come and stand before me in this **h**,	1004
	7:11 Is this **h**, which is called by my name,	1004
	7:14 Therefore will I do unto *this* **h**, which is	1004
	7:30 they have set their abominations in the **h**	1004
	9:26 all the **h** of Israel *are* uncircumcised in	1004
	10: 1 LORD speaketh unto you, O **h** of Israel:	1004
	11:10 the **h** of Israel and the house of Judah	1004
	11:10 of Judah have broken my covenant	1004
	11:15 What hath my beloved to do in mine **h**,	1004
	11:17 for the evil of the **h** of Israel and of	1004

Jer	11:17 the house of Israel and of the **h** of Judah,	1004
	12: 6 even thy brethren, and the **h** of thy father,	1004
	12: 7 have forsaken mine **h**, I have left mine	1004
	12:14 pluck out the **h** of Judah from among	1004
	13:11 to cleave unto me the whole **h** of Israel	1004
	13:11 house of Israel and the whole **h** of Judah,	1004
	16: 5 Enter not *into* the **h** of mourning,	1004
	16: 8 Thou shalt not also go *into* the **h** of	1004
	17:26 *of* praise, *unto* the **h** of the LORD.	1004
	18: 2 go down *to* the potter's **h**, and there I will	1004
	18: 3 went down *to* the potter's **h**, and, behold,	1004
	18: 6 O **h** of Israel, cannot I do with you as this	1004
	18: 6 so are ye in mine hand, O **h** of Israel.	1004
	19:14 he stood in the court of the LORD's **h**;	1004
	20: 1 who *was* also chief governor in the **h** of	1004
	20: 2 which *was* by the **h** of the LORD.	1004
	20: 6 all that dwell in thine **h** shall go into	1004
	21:11 touching the **h** of the king of Judah,	1004
	21:12 O **h** of David, thus saith the LORD;	1004
	22: 1 Go down *to* the **h** of the king of Judah,	1004
	22: 4 shall there enter in by the gates of this **h**	1004
	22: 5 that this **h** shall become a desolation.	1004
	22: 6 For thus saith the LORD unto the king's **h**	1004
	22:13 Woe unto him that buildeth his **h** by	1004
	22:14 I will build me a wide **h** and	1004
	23: 8 led the seed of the **h** of Israel out of	1004
	23:11 in my **h** have I found their wickedness,	1004
	23:34 I will even punish that man and his **h**.	1004
	26: 2 Stand in the court of the LORD's **h**,	1004
	26: 2 which come to worship *in* the LORD's **h**,	1004
	26: 6 will I make this **h** like Shiloh, and will	1004
	26: 7 these words in the **h** of the LORD.	1004
	26: 9 This **h** shall be like Shiloh, and this city	1004
	26: 9 against Jeremiah in the **h** of the LORD.	1004
	26:10 they came up from the king's **h** *unto*	1004
	26:10 the king's house *unto* the **h** of the LORD,	1004
	26:10 entry of the new gate of the LORD's **h**.	NIH
	26:12 LORD sent me to prophesy against this **h**	1004
	26:18 the mountain of the **h** as the high places	1004
	27:16 the vessels of the LORD's **h** *shall* now	1004
	27:18 that the vessels which are left in the **h** of	1004
	27:18 *in* the **h** of the king of Judah,	1004
	27:21 the vessels that remain *in* the **h**	1004
	27:21 *in* the **h** of the king of Judah and	1004
	28: 1 spake unto me in the **h** of the LORD,	1004
	28: 3 this place all the vessels of the LORD's **h**,	1004
	28: 5 people that stood in the **h** of the LORD,	1004
	28: 6 bring again the vessels of the LORD's **h**,	1004
	29:26 that *ye* should be officers in the **h** of	1004
	31:27 I will sow the **h** of Israel and the house	1004
	31:27 the **h** of Judah *with* the seed of man,	1004
	31:31 I will make a new covenant with the **h**	1004
	31:31 house of Israel, and with the **h** of Judah:	1004
	31:33 that I will make with the **h** of Israel;	1004
	32: 2 which *was* in the king of Judah's **h**.	1004
	32:34 they set their abominations in the **h**,	1004
	33:11 sacrifice of praise *into* the **h** of the LORD.	1004
	33:14 I have promised unto the **h** of Israel	1004
	33:14 the house of Israel and to the **h** of Judah.	1004
	33:17 to sit upon the throne of the **h** of Israel;	1004
	34:13 of Egypt, out of the **h** of bondmen, saying,	1004
	34:15 had made a covenant before me in the **h**	1004
	35: 2 Go unto the **h** of the Rechabites,	1004
	35: 2 and bring them *into* the **h** of the LORD,	1004
	35: 3 sons, and the whole **h** of the Rechabites;	1004
	35: 4 I brought them *into* the **h** of the LORD,	1004
	35: 5 I set before the sons of the **h** of	1004
	35: 7 Neither shall ye build **h**, nor sow seed,	1004
	35:18 said unto the **h** of the Rechabites,	1004
	36: 3 It may be that the **h** of Judah will hear all	1004
	36: 5 I cannot go *into* the **h** of the LORD:	1004
	36: 6 *in* the LORD's **h** upon the fasting day:	1004
	36: 8 words of the LORD in the LORD's **h**.	1004
	36:10 words of Jeremiah *in* the **h** of the LORD,	1004
	36:10 entry of the new gate of the LORD's **h**,	1004
	36:12 he went down *into* the king's **h**, into	1004
	37:15 put him *in* prison *in* the **h** of Jonathan	1004
	37:17 and the king asked him secretly in his **h**,	1004
	37:20 thou cause me not to return *to* the **h** of	1004
	38: 7 of the eunuchs which *was* in the king's **h**,	1004
	38: 8 went forth out of the king's **h**,	1004
	38:11 went into the **h** of the king under	1004
	38:14 third entry that *is* in the **h** of the LORD:	1004
	38:17 with fire; and thou shalt live, and thine **h**:	1004
	38:22 **h** *shall be* brought forth to the king of	1004
	38:26 not cause me to return *to* Jonathan's **h**,	1004
	39: 8 the Chaldeans burnt the king's **h**,	1004
	41: 5 to bring *them* to the **h** of the LORD.	1004
	43: 9 which *is* at the entry of Pharaoh's **h** in	1004
	48:13 as the **h** of Israel was ashamed of Beth-el	1004
	51:51 into the sanctuaries of the LORD's **h**.	1004
	52:13 burnt the **h** of the LORD, and the king's	1004
	52:13 the house of the LORD, and the king's **h**;	1004
	52:17 Also the pillars of brass that *were* in the **h**	1004
	52:17 the brasen sea that *was* in the **h** of	1004
	52:20 which king Solomon had made in the **h** of	1004
La	2: 7 they have made a noise in the **h** of	1004
Eze	2: 5 will forbear, (for they *are* a rebellious **h**,)	1004
	2: 6 their looks, though they *be* a rebellious **h**:	1004
	2: 8 not thou rebellious like *that* rebellious **h**:	1004
	3: 1 this roll, and go speak unto the **h** of Israel.	1004
	3: 4 go, get thee unto the **h** of Israel,	1004
	3: 5 of a hard language, *but* to the **h** of Israel;	1004
	3: 7 the **h** of Israel will not hearken unto thee;	1004
	3: 7 for all the **h** of Israel *are* impudent	1004

H

H

Eze	3: 9 their looks, though they *be* a rebellious **h.**	1004
	3:17 I have made thee a watchman unto the **h**	1004
	3:24 unto me, Go, shut thyself within thine **h.**	1004
	3:26 a reprover: for they *are* a rebellious **h.**	1004
	3:27 him forbear: for they *are* a rebellious **h.**	1004
	4: 3 This *shall be* a sign to the **h** of Israel.	1004
	4: 4 lay the iniquity of the **h** of Israel upon it:	1004
	4: 5 shalt thou bear the iniquity of the **h** of	1004
	4: 6 thou shalt bear the iniquity of the **h** of	1004
	5: 4 a fire come forth into all the **h** of Israel.	1004
	6:11 Alas for all the evil abominations of the **h**	1004
	8: 1 as I sat in mine **h,** and the elders of Judah	1004
	8: 6 *even* the great abominations that the **h** of	1004
	8:10 and all the idols of the **h** of Israel,	1004
	8:11 men of the ancients of the **h** of Israel,	1004
	8:12 hast thou seen what the ancients of the **h**	1004
	8:14 Lord's **h** which *was* towards the north;	1004
	8:16 me into the inner court of the Lord's **h,**	1004
	8:17 Is it a light thing to the **h** of Judah that	1004
	9: 3 he was, to the threshold of the **h.**	1004
	9: 6 the ancient men which *were* before the **h.**	1004
	9: 7 Defile the **h,** and fill the courts *with*	1004
	9: 9 The iniquity of the **h** of Israel and Judah *is*	1004
	10: 3 cherubims stood on the right side of the **h,**	1004
	10: 4 *and stood* over the threshold of the **h;**	1004
	10: 4 the **h** was filled with the cloud,	1004
	10:18 departed from off the threshold of the Lord's **h;**	1004
	10:19 the door of the east gate of the Lord's **h,**	1004
	11: 1 me unto the east gate of the Lord's **h,**	1004
	11: 5 Thus have ye said, O **h** of Israel:	1004
	11:15 thy kindred, and all the **h** of Israel wholly,	1004
	12: 2 dwellest in the midst of a rebellious **h,**	1004
	12: 2 and hear not: for they *are* a rebellious **h.**	1004
	12: 3 consider, though they *be* a rebellious **h.**	1004
	12: 6 for I have set thee *for* a sign unto the **h** of	1004
	12: 9 Son of man, hath not the **h** of Israel,	1004
	12: 9 the rebellious **h,** said unto thee, What	1004
	12:10 all the **h** of Israel that *are* among them.	1004
	12:24 flattering divination within the **h** of Israel.	1004
	12:25 for in your days, O rebellious **h,** will I say	1004
	12:27 of man, behold, *they of* the **h** of Israel say,	1004
	13: 5 neither made up the hedge for the **h** of	1004
	13: 9 be written in the writing of the **h** of Israel,	1004
	14: 4 Every man of the **h** of Israel that setteth	1004
	14: 5 *I* may take the **h** of Israel in their own	1004
	14: 6 Therefore say unto the **h** of Israel,	1004
	14: 7 For every one of the **h** of Israel, or of	1004
	14:11 the **h** of Israel may go no more astray	1004
	17: 2 speak a parable unto the **h** of Israel;	1004
	17:12 Say now to the rebellious **h,** Know ye not	1004
	18: 6 up his eyes to the idols of the **h** of Israel,	1004
	18:15 up his eyes to the idols of the **h** of Israel,	1004
	18:25 Hear now, O **h** of Israel; Is not my way	1004
	18:29 Yet saith the **h** of Israel, The way of	1004
	18:29 O **h** of Israel, are not my ways equal?	1004
	18:30 Therefore I will judge you, O **h** of Israel,	1004
	18:31 for why will ye die, O **h** of Israel?	1004
	20: 5 up mine hand unto the seed of the **h**	1004
	20:13 the **h** of Israel rebelled against me in	1004
	20:27 speak unto the **h** of Israel, and say unto	1004
	20:30 Wherefore say unto the **h** of Israel,	1004
	20:31 be inquired of by you, O **h** of Israel?	1004
	20:39 As for you, O **h** of Israel, thus saith	1004
	20:40 Lord God, there shall all the **h** of Israel,	1004
	20:44 O ye **h** of Israel, saith the Lord God.	1004
	22:18 the **h** of Israel is to me become dross:	1004
	23:39 have they done in the midst of mine **h.**	1004
	24: 3 utter a parable unto the rebellious **h,**	1004
	24:21 Speak unto the **h** of Israel, Thus saith	1004
	25: 3 against the **h** of Judah, when they went	1004
	25: 8 the **h** of Judah *is* like unto all the heathen;	1004
	25:12 that Edom hath dealt against the **h**	1004
	27:14 They of the **h** of Togarmah traded in thy	1004
	28:24 more a pricking brier unto the **h** of Israel,	1004
	28:25 When I shall have gathered the **h** of Israel	1004
	29: 6 they have been a staff of reed to the **h** of	1004
	29:16 shall be no more the confidence of the **h**	1004
	29:21 In that day will I cause the horn of the **h**	1004
	33: 7 I have set thee a watchman unto the **h** of	1004
	33:10 son of man, speak unto the **h** of Israel;	1004
	33:11 for why will ye die, O **h** of Israel?	1004
	33:20 ye **h** of Israel, I will judge you every one	1004
	34:30 that they, *even* the **h** of Israel, *are* my	1004
	35:15 at the inheritance of the **h** of Israel,	1004
	36:10 you, all the **h** of Israel, *even* all of it:	1004
	36:17 when the **h** of Israel dwelt in their own	1004
	36:21 which the **h** of Israel had profaned among	1004
	36:22 Therefore say unto the **h** of Israel,	1004
	36:22 O **h** of Israel, but for mine holy name's	1004
	36:32 for your own sakes, O **h** of Israel.	1004
	36:37 I will yet *for* this be inquired of by the **h**	1004
	37:11 these bones *are* the whole **h** of Israel:	1004
	37:16 and *for* all the **h** of Israel his companions:	1004
	38: 6 the **h** of Togarmah *of* the north quarters,	1004
	39:12 seven months shall the **h** of Israel be	1004
	39:22 So the **h** of Israel shall know that I *am*	1004
	39:23 heathen shall know that the **h** of Israel	1004
	39:25 have mercy upon the whole **h** of Israel,	1004
	39:29 I have poured out my spirit upon the **h**	1004
	40: 4 all that thou seest to the **h** of Israel.	1004
	40: 5 a wall on the outside of the **h** round	1004
	40:45 the keepers of the charge of the **h.**	1004
	40:47 and the altar *that was* before the **h.**	1004
	40:48 he brought me to the porch of the **h,**	1004
	41: 5 After he measured the wall of the **h,**	1004

Eze	41: 5 round about the **h** on every side.	1004
	41: 6 for the side chambers round about,	1004
	41: 6 but they had not hold in the wall of the **h.**	1004
	41: 7 for the winding about of the **h** went still	1004
	41: 7 went still upward round about the **h:**	1004
	41: 7 the breadth of the **h** was still upward,	1004
	41: 8 saw also the height of the **h** round about:	1004
	41:10 cubits round about the **h** on every side.	1004
	41:13 So he measured the **h,** an hundred cubits	1004
	41:14 Also the breadth of the face of the **h,**	1004
	41:17 even unto the inner **h,** and without,	1004
	41:19 *was* made through all the **h** round about.	1004
	41:26 *upon* the side chambers of the **h,** and	1004
	42:15 made an end of measuring the inner **h,**	1004
	43: 4 the glory of the Lord came into the **h** by	1004
	43: 5 the glory of the Lord filled the **h.**	1004
	43: 6 heard *him* speaking unto me out of the **h;**	1004
	43: 7 shall the **h** of Israel no more defile,	1004
	43:10 of man, shew the **h** to the house of Israel,	1004
	43:10 of man, shew the house to the **h** of Israel,	1004
	43:11 shew them the form of the **h,**	1004
	43:12 This *is* the law of the **h;** Upon the top of	1004
	43:12 most holy. Behold, this *is* the law of the **h.**	1004
	43:21 burn it in the appointed place of the **h,**	1004
	44: 4 me the way of the north gate before the **h:**	1004
	44: 4 the glory of the Lord filled the **h** of	1004
	44: 5 all the ordinances of the **h** of the Lord,	1004
	44: 5 mark well the entering in of the **h,**	1004
	44: 6 to the **h** of Israel, Thus saith the Lord	1004
	44: 6 O ye **h** of Israel, let it suffice you of all	1004
	44: 7 in my sanctuary, to pollute it, *even* my **h,**	1004
	44:11 *having* charge at the gates of the **h,**	1004
	44:11 of the house, and ministering to the **h:**	1004
	44:12 caused the **h** of Israel to fall into iniquity;	1004
	44:14 make them keepers of the charge of the **h,**	1004
	44:22 shall take maidens of the seed of the **h**	1004
	44:30 may cause the blessing to rest in thine **h.**	1004
	45: 5 ministers of the **h,** have for themselves,	1004
	45: 6 it shall be for the whole **h** of Israel.	1004
	45: 8 *rest of* the land shall they give to the **h**	1004
	45:17 the sabbaths in all solemnities of the **h** of	1004
	45:17 to make reconciliation for the **h** of Israel.	1004
	45:19 put *it* upon the posts of the **h,** and upon	1004
	45:20 *that is* simple: so shall ye reconcile the **h.**	1004
	46:24 where the ministers of the **h** shall boil	1004
	47: 1 brought me again unto the door of the **h;**	1004
	47: 1 under the threshold of the **h** eastward:	1004
	47: 1 for the forefront of the **h** *stood toward*	1004
	47: 1 from under the right side of the **h,**	1004
	48:21 the sanctuary of the **h** *shall be* in the	1004
Da	1: 2 with part of the vessels of the **h** of God:	1004
	1: 2 *into* the land of Shinar *to* the **h** of his god;	1004
	1: 2 he brought the vessels *into* the treasure **h**	1004
	2:17 Daniel went to his **h,** and made the thing	1005
	4: 4 I Nebuchadnezzar was at rest in mine **h,**	1005
	4:30 that I have built for the **h** of the kingdom	1005
	5: 3 of the **h** of God which *was* at Jerusalem;	1005
	5:10 and his lords, came into the banquet **h:**	1005
	5:23 they have brought the vessels of his **h**	1005
	6:10 writing *was* signed, he went into his **h;**	1005
Hos	1: 4 the blood of Jezreel upon the **h** of Jehu,	1004
	1: 4 will cause to cease the kingdom of the **h**	1004
	1: 6 for I will no more have mercy upon the **h**	1004
	1: 7 I will have mercy upon the **h** of Judah,	1004
	5: 1 hearken, ye **h** of Israel; and give ye ear,	1004
	5: 1 of Israel; and give ye ear, O **h** of the king;	1004
	5:12 moth, and to the **h** of Judah as rottenness.	1004
	5:14 and as a young lion to the **h** of Judah:	1004
	6:10 I have seen a horrible thing in the **h** of	1004
	8: 1 *He shall come* as an eagle against the **h** of	1004
	9: 4 shall not come *into* the **h** of the Lord.	1004
	9: 8 his ways, *and* hatred in the **h** of his God.	1004
	9:15 doings I will drive them out of mine **h,**	1004
	11:12 with lies, and the **h** of Israel with deceit:	1004
Joel	1: 9 the drink offering is cut off from the **h**	1004
	1:13 drink offering is withholden from the **h**	1004
	1:14 all the inhabitants of the land *into* the **h**	1004
	1:16 and gladness from the **h** of our God?	1004
	3:18 a fountain shall come forth of the **h** of	1004
Am	1: 4 I will send a fire into the **h** of Hazael,	1004
	1: 5 that holdeth the sceptre from the **h** of	1004
	2: 8 of the condemned *in* the **h** of their god.	1004
	3:13 Hear ye, and testify in the **h** of Jacob,	1004
	3:15 will smite the winter **h** with the summer	1004
	3:15 the winter house with the summer **h;**	1004
	5: 1 *even* a lamentation, O **h** of Israel.	1004
	5: 3 hundred shall leave ten, to the **h** of Israel.	1004
	5: 4 For thus saith the Lord, Seek ye me,	1004
	5: 6 he break out like fire *in* the **h** of Joseph,	1004
	5:19 went *into* the **h,** and leaned his hand on	1004
	5:25 the wilderness forty years, O **h** of Israel?	1004
	6: 1 nations, to whom the **h** of Israel came!	1004
	6: 9 if there remain ten men in one **h,** that	1004
	6:10 to bring out the bones out of the **h,**	1004
	6:10 say unto *him* that *is* by the sides of the **h,**	1004
	6:11 he will smite the great **h** *with* breaches,	1004
	6:11 *with* breaches, and the little **h** with clefts.	1004
	6:14 O **h** of Israel, saith the Lord the God of	1004
	7: 9 I will rise against the **h** of Jeroboam with	1004
	7:10 against thee in the midst of the **h** of Israel;	1004
	7:16 drop not *thy word* against the **h** of Isaac.	1004
	9: 8 saving that I will not utterly destroy the **h**	1004
	9: 9 I will sift the **h** of Israel among all nations,	1004
Ob	1:17 the **h** of Jacob shall possess their	1004
	1:18 the **h** of Jacob shall be a fire, and the	1004

Ob	1:18 the **h** of Joseph a flame, and the house of	1004
	1:18 the **h** of Esau for stubble, and they shall	1004
	1:18 shall not be *any* remaining of the **h** of	1004
Mic	1: 5 all this, and for the sins of the **h** of Israel.	1004
	2: 2 so they oppress a man and his **h,** even a	1004
	2: 7 O *thou that art* named the **h** of Jacob,	1004
	3: 1 of Jacob, and ye princes of the **h** of Israel;	1004
	3: 9 ye heads of the **h** of Jacob, and princes of	1004
	3: 9 princes of the **h** of Israel, that abhor	1004
	3:12 the mountain of the **h** as the high places	1004
	4: 1 *that* the mountain of the **h** of the Lord	1004
	4: 2 and to the **h** of the God of Jacob;	1004
	6: 4 redeemed thee out of the **h** of servants;	1004
	6:10 of wickedness *in* the **h** of the wicked,	1004
	6:16 the works of the **h** of Ahab, and ye walk	1004
	7: 6 man's enemies *are* the men of his own **h.**	1004
Na	1:14 out of the **h** of thy gods will I cut off	1004
Hab	2: 9 coveteth an evil covetousness to his **h,**	1004
	2:10 Thou hast consulted shame to thy **h** by	1004
	3:13 thou woundedst the head out of the **h** of	1004
Zep	2: 7 coast shall be for the remnant of the **h**	1004
Hag	1: 2 the time that the Lord's **h** should be	1004
	1: 4 your cieled houses, and this **h** *lie* waste?	1004
	1: 8 and bring wood, and build the **h;**	1004
	1: 9 Because of mine **h** that *is* waste, and ye	1004
	1: 9 and ye run every man unto his own **h.**	1004
	1:14 did work in the **h** of the Lord of hosts,	1004
	2: 3 Who *is* left among you that saw this **h** in	1004
	2: 7 I will fill this **h** *with* glory, saith	1004
	2: 9 The glory of this latter **h** shall be greater	1004
Zec	1:16 my **h** shall be built in it, saith the Lord	1004
	3: 7 thou shalt also judge my **h,** and shalt also	1004
	4: 9 have laid the foundation of this **h;**	1004
	5: 4 it shall enter into the **h** of the thief,	1004
	5: 4 into the **h** of him that sweareth falsely by	1004
	5: 4 it shall remain in the midst of his **h,**	1004
	5:11 To build it a **h** in the land of Shinar:	1004
	6:10 go *into* the **h** of Josiah the son of	1004
	7: 2 When they had sent *unto* the **h** of God	1004
	7: 3 *were* in the **h** of the Lord of hosts,	1004
	8: 9 of the **h** of the Lord of hosts was laid,	1004
	8:13 O **h** of Judah, and house of Israel;	1004
	8:13 O house of Judah, and **h** of Israel;	1004
	8:15 unto Jerusalem and to the **h** of Judah:	1004
	8:19 be to the **h** of Judah joy and gladness,	1004
	9: 8 I will encamp about mine **h** because of	1004
	10: 3 hosts hath visited his flock the **h** of Judah,	1004
	10: 6 I will strengthen the **h** of Judah, and I will	1004
	10: 6 will save the **h** of Joseph, and I will bring	1004
	11:13 cast them to the potter *in* the **h** of	1004
	12: 4 will open mine eyes upon the **h** of Judah,	1004
	12: 7 that the glory of the **h** of David and	1004
	12: 8 the **h** of David *shall be* as God, as the	1004
	12:10 I will pour upon the **h** of David,	1004
	12:12 the family of the **h** of David apart,	1004
	12:12 the family of the **h** of Nathan apart,	1004
	12:13 The family of the **h** of Levi apart,	1004
	13: 1 be a fountain opened to the **h** of David	1004
	13: 6 *with* which I was wounded *in* the **h**	1004
	14:20 the pots in the Lord's **h** shall be like	1004
	14:21 Canaanite in the **h** of the Lord of hosts.	1004
Mal	3:10 that there may be meat in mine **h,**	1004
Mt	2:11 And when they were come into the **h,**	3614
	5:15 it giveth light unto all that are in the **h.**	3614
	7:24 wise man, which built his **h** upon a rock:	3614
	7:25 the winds blew, and beat upon that **h,**	3614
	7:26 which built his **h** upon the sand:	3614
	7:27 the winds blew, and beat upon that **h;**	3614
	8:14 come into Peter's **h,**	3614
	9: 6 take up thy bed, and go unto thine **h.**	3624
	9: 7 And he arose, and departed to his **h.**	3624
	9:10 as Jesus sat at meat in the **h,** behold,	3614
	9:23 And when Jesus came into the ruler's **h,**	3614
	9:28 And when he was come into the **h,**	3614
	10: 6 But go rather to the lost sheep of the **h** of	3624
	10:12 And when ye come into a **h** salute it.	3614
	10:13 And if the **h** be worthy, let your peace	3614
	10:14 when ye depart out of that **h** or city,	3614
	10:25 If they have called the **master of the h**	3617
	12: 4 How he entered into the **h** of God,	3624
	12:25 or **h** divided against itself shall not stand:	3614
	12:29 how can one enter into a strong **man's h.**	3614
	12:29 strong *man?* and then he will spoil his **h.**	3614
	12:44 will return into my **h** from whence I came	3624
	13: 1 The same day went Jesus out of the **h,**	3614
	13:36 the multitude away, and went into the **h:**	3614
	13:57 in his own country, and in his own **h.**	3614
	15:24 but unto the lost sheep of the **h** of Israel.	3624
	17:25 And when he was come into the **h,**	3614
	20:11 against the **goodman of the h,**	3617
	21:13 My **h** shall be called the house of prayer;	3624
	21:13 My house shall be called the **h** of prayer;	3624
	23:38 Behold, your **h** is left unto you desolate.	3624
	24:17 come down to take any *thing* out of his **h:**	3614
	24:43 if the **goodman of the h** had known	3617
	24:43 not have suffered his **h** to be broken	3614
	26: 6 in Bethany, in the **h** of Simon the leper,	3614
	26:18 I will keep the passover at thy **h** with my	NIG
Mk	1:29 they entered into the **h** of Simon and	3614
	2: 1 it was noised that he was in the **h.**	3624
	2:11 up thy bed, and go thy way into thine **h.**	3624
	2:15 that as *Jesus* sat at meat in his **h,**	3614
	2:26 How he went into the **h** of God in the	3624
	3:19 betrayed him. And they went into a **h.**	3624
	3:25 And if a **h** be divided against itself,	3614

Mk
3:25 divided against itself, that **h** cannot stand. 3614
3:27 No *man* can enter into a strong *man's* **h**, 3614
3:27 strong *man*; and then he will spoil his **h**. 3614
5:35 of the synagogue's **h** certain which said, NIG
5:38 And he cometh to the **h** of the ruler of 3624
6: 4 among his own kin, and in his own **h**. 3614
6:10 In what place soever ye enter into a **h**, 3614
7:17 when he was entered into *the* **h** from 3624
7:24 and entered into a **h**, and would have no 3614
7:30 And when she was come to her **h**, 3624
8:26 And he sent him away to his **h**, saying, 3624
9:28 And when he was come into the **h**, 3624
9:33 and being in the **h** he asked them, 3614
10:10 in the **h** his disciples asked him again 3614
10:29 There is no *man* that hath left **h**, 3614
11:17 My **h** shall be called of all nations 3624
11:17 be called of all nations the **h** of prayer? 3624
13:15 on the housetop not go down into the **h** 3614
13:15 *therein*, to take any *thing* out of his **h**: 3614
13:34 who left his **h**, and gave authority to his 3614
13:35 ye know not when the master of the **h** 3614
14: 3 And being in Bethany in the **h** of Simon 3614
14:14 say ye to the **goodman of the h**, 3617

Lk
1:23 he departed to his own **h**. 3624
1:27 name was Joseph, of the **h** of David; 3624
1:33 And he shall reign over the **h** of Jacob for 3624
1:40 And entered into the **h** of Zacharias, 3624
1:56 months, and returned to her own **h**. 3624
1:69 for us in the **h** of his servant David; 3624
2: 4 (because he was of the **h** and lineage of 3624
4:38 synagogue, and entered into Simon's **h**. 3614
5:24 take up thy couch, and go into thine **h**. 3624
5:25 departed to his own **h**, glorifying God. 3624
5:29 Levi made him a great feast in his own **h**: 3624
6: 4 How he went into the **h** of God, 3624
6:48 He is like a man which built a **h**, 3614
6:48 the stream beat vehemently upon that **h**, 3614
6:49 a foundation built a **h** upon the earth; 3614
6:49 it fell; and the ruin of that **h** was great. 3614
7: 6 And when he was now not far from the **h**, 3614
7:10 they that were sent, returning to the **h**, 3624
7:36 And he went into the Pharisee's **h**, 3624
7:37 that *Jesus* sat at meat in the Pharisee's **h**, 3614
7:44 I entered into thine **h**, thou gavest me no 3614
8:27 neither abode in *any* **h**, but in the tombs. 3614
8:39 Return to thine own **h**, and shew how 3624
8:41 him that *he* would come into his **h**: 3624
8:49 ruler of the synagogue's **h**, saying to him, NIG
8:51 when he came into the **h**, he suffered 3614
9: 4 And whatsoever **h** ye enter into, 3614
9:61 farewell, which are *at home* in my **h**. 3624
10: 5 And into whatsoever **h** ye enter, first say, 3624
10: 5 ye enter, first say, Peace *be* to this **h**. 3624
10: 7 And in the same **h** remain, eating and 3614
10: 7 of his hire. Go not from **h** to house. 3614
10: 7 of his hire. Go not from house to **h**. 3614
10:38 named Martha received him into her **h**. 3624
11:17 and a **h** *divided* against a house falleth. 3624
11:17 and a house *divided* against a **h** falleth. 3624
11:24 will return unto my **h** whence I came out. 3624
12:39 that if the **goodman of the h** had known 3617
12:39 not have suffered his **h** to be broken 3624
12:52 there shall be five in one **h** divided, 3624
13:25 once the **master of the h** is risen up, 3617
13:35 Behold, your **h** is left unto you desolate: 3624
14: 1 as he went into the **h** of one of the chief 3624
14:21 **master of the h** being angry said to his 3617
14:23 *them* to come in, that my **h** may be filled. 3614
15: 8 and sweep the **h**, and seek diligently till 3614
15:25 and as he came and drew nigh to the **h**, 3614
16:27 thou wouldest send him to my father's **h**: 3624
17:31 upon the housetop, and his stuff in the **h**, 3614
18:14 this man went down to his **h** justified 3624
18:29 no *man* that hath left **h**, or parents, 3624
19: 5 for to day I must abide at thy **h**. 3624
19: 9 This day is salvation come to this **h**, 3624
19:46 It is written, My **h** is the house of prayer: 3624
19:46 It is written, My house is the **h** of prayer? 3624
22:10 him into the **h** where he entereth in. 3614
22:11 ye shall say unto the goodman of the **h**, 3614
22:54 and brought him into the high priest's **h**. 3614

Jn
2:16 make not my Father's **h** a house of 3624
2:16 make not my Father's house a **h** of 3624
2:17 The zeal of thine **h** hath eaten me up. 3624
4:53 himself believed, and his whole **h**. 3614
7:53 And every man went unto his own **h**. 3624
8:35 And the servant abideth not in the **h** for 3614
11:20 and met him: but Mary sat *still* in the **h**, 3624
11:31 then which were with her in the **h**, 3614
12: 3 the **h** was filled with the odour of 3614
14: 2 In my Father's **h** are many mansions: if *it* 3614

Ac
2: 2 it filled all the **h** where they were sitting. 3624
2:36 Therefore let all the **h** of Israel know 3624
2:46 breaking bread from **h** to house, 2596+3624
2:46 breaking bread from house to **h**, 2596+3624
5:42 and in every **h**, they ceased not to 2596+3624
7:10 him governor over Egypt and all his **h**. 3624
7:20 up in his father's **h** three months: 3624
7:42 O ye **h** of Israel, have I offered to me 3624
7:47 But Solomon built him a **h**. 3624
7:49 what **h** will ye build me? saith the Lord: 3624
8: 3 the church, entering into every **h**, 2596+3624
9:11 inquire in the **h** of Judas for *one* called 3614
9:17 went his way, and entered into the **h**; 3614
10: 2 and one that feared God with all his **h**, 3624

Ac
10: 6 Simon a tanner, whose **h** is by the sea 3614
10: 9 Peter went up upon the **h** to pray about 1430
10:17 had made inquiry for Simon's **h**, 3614
10:22 a holy angel to send for thee into his **h**, 3624
10:30 and at the ninth hour I prayed in my **h**, 3624
10:32 is lodged in the **h** of *one* Simon a tanner 3614
11:11 already come unto the **h** where I was, 3614
11:12 and we entered into the man's **h**: 3624
11:13 us how he had seen an angel in his **h**, 3624
11:14 whereby thou and all thy **h** shall be saved. 3624
12:12 came to the **h** of Mary the mother of John, 3614
16:15 come into my **h**, and abide *there*. 3624
16:31 and thou shalt be saved, and thy **h**. 3624
16:32 of the Lord, and to all that were in his **h**. 3614
16:34 when he had brought them into his **h**, 3624
16:34 rejoiced, believing in God with **all** his **h**. 3832
16:40 prison, and entered into the **h** of Lydia: NIG
17: 5 assaulted the **h** of Jason, and sought to 3614
18: 7 and entered into a certain man's **h**, 3614
18: 7 whose **h** joined hard to the synagogue. 3614
18: 8 believed on the Lord with all his **h**; 3624
19:16 so that *they* fled out of that **h** naked and 3624
20:20 publicly, and **from h to house**, 2596+3624
20:20 publicly, and **from house to h**, 2596+3624
21: 8 we entered into the **h** of Philip 3624
28:30 two whole years in his own **hired h**. 3410
Ro
16: 5 greet the church that is in their **h**. 3624
1Co
1:11 by them which are of the **h** of Chloe, NIG
16:15 brethren, (ye know the **h** of Stephanas, 3614
16:19 Lord, with the church that is in their **h**. 3624
2Co
5: 1 For we know that if our earthly **h** of *this* 3614
5: 1 a **h** not made with hand, eternal in 3614
5: 2 upon with our **h** which is from heaven: 3613
Col
4:15 and the church which is in his **h**. 3624
1Ti
3: 4 One that ruleth well his own **h**, having 3624
3: 5 if a man know not how to rule his own **h**, 3624
3:15 oughtest to behave thyself in the **h** of God, 3624
5: 8 and specially for those of his own **h**, 3609
5:13 wandering about **from h to house**; 3588+3614
5:13 wandering about **from house to h**; 3588+3614
5:14 marry, bear children, **guide the h**, 3616
2Ti
1:16 The Lord give mercy unto the **h** of 3624
2:20 But in a great **h** there are not only vessels 3614
Phm
1: 2 and to the church in thy **h**: 3624
Heb
3: 2 as also Moses *was faithful* in all his **h**. 3624
3: 3 inasmuch as he who hath builded **the h**[s] 846
3: 3 the house hath more honour than the **h**. 3624
3: 4 For every **h** is builded by some *man*; but 3624
3: 5 And Moses verily *was* faithful in all his **h**, 3624
3: 6 But Christ as a Son over his own **h**; 3624
3: 6 whose **h** are we, if we hold fast 3624
8: 8 make a new covenant with the **h** of Israel 3624
8: 8 the house of Israel and with the **h** of Judah: 3624
8:10 make with the **h** of Israel after those days, 3624
10:21 *having* a high priest over the **h** of God; 3624
11: 7 prepared an ark to the saving of his **h**; 3624
1Pe
2: 5 as lively stones, are built *up* a spiritual **h**, 3624
4:17 that judgment must begin at the **h** of God: 3624
2Jn
1:10 this doctrine, receive him not into your **h**, 3614

HOUSE OF APHRAH (1) [HOUSE]
Mic 1:10 in the **h** roll thyself *in* the dust. 1036

HOUSEHOLD (61) [HOUSE]
Ge 18:19 his children and his **h** after him, 1004
31:37 what hast thou found of all thy **h** stuff? 1004
35: 2 Jacob said unto his **h**, and to all that 1004
45:11 thou, and thy **h**, and all that thou hast, 1004
47:12 and all thy father's **h**, *with* bread, 1004
Ex 1: 1 every man and his **h** came with Jacob. 1004
12: 4 if the **h** be too little for the lamb, let him 1004
Lev 16:17 for his **h**, and for all the congregation of 1004
Dt 6:22 upon Pharaoh, and upon all his **h**, 1004
14:26 and thou shalt rejoice, thou and thine **h**, 1004
15:20 the Lord shall choose, thou and thy **h**. 1004
Jos 2:18 and thy brethren, and all thy father's **h**, 1004
6:25 and her father's **h**, and all that she had; 1004
7:14 the **h** which the Lord shall take shall 1004
7:18 brought his **h** man by man; and Achan, 1004
Jdg 6:27 because he feared his father's **h**, 1004
18:25 thou lose thy life, with the lives of thy **h**. 1004
1Sa 25:17 against our master, and against all his **h**: 1004
27: 3 he and his men, every man with his **h**: 1004
2Sa 2: 3 did David bring up, every man with his **h**: 1004
6:11 Lord blessed Obed-edom, and all his **h**. 1004
6:20 David returned to bless his **h**. And Michal 1004
15:16 king went forth, and all his **h** after him. 1004
16: 2 The asses *be* for the king's **h** to ride on; 1004
17:23 put his **h** in order, and hanged himself, 1004
19:18 a ferry boat to carry over the king's **h**, 1004
19:41 his **h**, and all David's men with him, 1004
1Ki 4: 6 Ahishar *was* over the **h**: and Adoniram 1004
4: 7 provided victuals for the king and his **h**: 1004
5: 9 my desire, in giving food for my **h**. 1004
5:11 measures of wheat *for* food to his **h**, 1004
11:20 Genubath *was* in Pharaoh's **h** among 1004
2Ki 7: 9 that we may go and tell the king's **h**. 1004
8: 1 go thou and thine **h**, 1004
8: 2 she went with her **h**, and sojourned in 1004
18:18 which *was* over the **h**, and Shebna 1004
18:37 which *was* over the **h**, and Shebna 1004
19: 2 which *was* over the **h**, and Shebna 1004
1Ch 24: 6 one principal **h** being taken for Eleazar, 1004
Ne 13: 8 I cast forth all the **h** stuff of Tobiah out of 1004
Job 1: 3 five hundred she asses, and a very great **h**; 5657

Pr
27:27 for the food of thy **h**, and *for* 1004
31:15 giveth meat to her **h**, and a portion to her 1004
31:21 She is not afraid of the snow for her **h**: 1004
31:21 for all her **h** *are* clothed with scarlet. 1004
31:27 She looketh well to the ways of her **h**, 1004
Isa 36:22 *was* over the **h**, and Shebna the scribe, 1004
37: 2 *was* over the **h**, and Shebna the scribe, 1004
Mt 10:25 much more *shall* they call them **of** his **h**? 3615
10:36 a man's foes *shall be* they of his own **h**. 3615
24:45 his lord hath made ruler over his **h**, 2322
Lk 12:42 his lord shall make ruler over his **h**, 2322
Ac 10: 7 he called two of his **h servants**, 3610
16:15 and her **h**, she besought *us*, saying, 3624
Ro 16:10 Salute them which are of Aristobulus' **h**. NIG
16:11 Greet them that be of the **h** of Narcissus, NIG
1Co 1:16 And I baptized also the **h** of Stephanas, 3624
Gal 6:10 unto them who are of the **h** of faith. 3609
Eph 2:19 with the saints, and of the **h** of God; 3609
Php 4:22 chiefly they that are of Cesar's **h**. 3614
2Ti 4:19 and Aquila, and the **h** of Onesiphorus. 3614

HOUSEHOLDER (4) [HOUSE]
Mt 13:27 the servants of the **h** came and said unto 3617
13:52 of heaven is like unto a man *that is* a **h**, 3617
20: 1 of heaven is like unto a man *that is* a **h**, 3617
21:33 was a certain **h**, which planted a 444+3617

HOUSEHOLDS (7) [HOUSE]
Ge 42:33 take *food* for the famine of your **h**, 1004
45:18 take your father and your **h**, and come 1004
47:24 for them of your **h**, and for food for your 1004
Nu 18:31 shall eat it in every place, ye and your **h**: 1004
Dt 11: 6 their **h**, and their tents, and all 1004
12: 7 ye and your **h**, where*in* the Lord thy 1004
Jos 7:14 the Lord shall take shall come by **h**; 1004

HOUSES (136) [HOUSE]
Ge 42:19 go ye, carry corn *for* the famine of your **h**: 1004
Ex 1:21 feared God, that he made them **h**. 1004
6:14 These *be* the heads of their fathers' **h**: 1004
8: 9 to destroy the frogs from thee and thy **h**, 1004
8:11 from thy **h**, and from thy servants, 1004
8:13 the frogs died out of the **h**, out of 1004
8:21 and upon thy people, and into thy **h**: 1004
8:21 the **h** of the Egyptians shall be full of 1004
8:24 his servants' **h**, and into all the land of 1004
9:20 his servants and his cattle flee into the **h**: 1004
10: 6 they shall fill thy **h**, and the houses of all 1004
10: 6 the **h** of all thy servants, and the houses 1004
10: 6 servants, and the **h** of all the Egyptians; 1004
12: 7 and on the upper door post of the **h**, 1004
12:13 for a token upon the **h** where you *are*: 1004
12:15 ye shall put away leaven out of your **h**: 1004
12:19 shall there be no leaven found in your **h**: 1004
12:23 to come in unto your **h** to smite *you*. 1004
12:27 who passed over the **h** of the children of 1004
12:27 smote the Egyptians, and delivered our **h**. 1004
Lev 25:31 the **h** of the villages which have no wall 1004
25:32 *and* the **h** of the cities of their possession, 1004
25:33 for the **h** of the cities of the Levites *are* 1004
Nu 4:22 throughout the **h** of their fathers, by their 1004
16:32 their **h**, and all the men that *appertained* 1004
17: 6 according to their fathers' **h**, *even* twelve 1004
32:18 We will not return unto our **h**, until 1004
Dt 6:11 **h** full *of* all good things, which thou 1004
8:12 hast built goodly **h**, and dwelt *therein*; 1004
19: 1 and dwellest in their cities, and in their **h**; 1004
Jos 9:12 **h** on the day we came forth to go unto 1004
Jdg 18:14 Do ye know that there is in these **h** an 1004
18:22 men that *were* in the **h** near to Micah's 1004
1Ki 9:10 when Solomon had built the two **h**, 1004
13:32 against all the **h** of the high places which 1004
20: 6 thine house, and the **h** of thy servants; 1004
2Ki 17:29 put *them* in the **h** of the high places 1004
17:32 which sacrificed for them in the **h** of 1004
23: 7 he brake down the **h** of the sodomites, 1004
23:19 all the **h** also of the high places that *were* 1004
25: 9 all the **h** of Jerusalem, and every great 1004
1Ch 15: 1 David made him **h** in the city of David, 1004
28:11 of the **h** thereof, and of the treasuries 1004
29: 4 to overlay the walls of the **h** *withal*: 1004
2Ch 25: 5 according to the **h** of *their* fathers, 1004
34:11 to floor the **h** which the kings of Judah 1004
35: 4 *yourselves* by the **h** of your fathers, 1004
Ne 4:14 your daughters, your wives, and your **h**. 1004
5: 3 vineyards, and **h**, that we might buy corn, 1004
5:11 their oliveyards, and their **h**, 1004
7: 4 few therein, and the **h** *were* not builded, 1004
9:25 fat land, and possessed **h** full *of* all goods, 1004
10:34 after the **h** of our fathers, at times 1004
Job 1: 4 his sons went and feasted *in their* **h**, 1004
3:15 had gold, who filled their **h** *with* silver: 1004
4:19 How much less *in* them that dwell in **h** of 1004
15:28 and in **h** which no man inhabiteth, 1004
21: 9 Their **h** *are* safe from fear, neither *is* the 1004
22:18 Yet he filled their **h** with good *things*: but 1004
24:16 In the dark they dig through **h**, which 1004
Ps 49:11 Their inward thought *is, that* their **h** *shall* 1004
83:12 Let us take to ourselves the **h** of God in 4999
Pr 1:13 We shall fill our **h** *with* spoil: 1004
30:26 yet make they their **h** in the rocks; 1004
Ecc 2: 4 I builded me **h**; I planted me vineyards: 1004
Isa 3:14 the spoil of the poor *is* in your **h**. 1004
5: 9 Of a truth many **h** shall be desolate, 1004
6:11 the **h** without man, and the land be 1004

H

H

Isa	8:14 a rock of offence to both the **h** of Israel,	1004
	13:16 their **h** shall be spoiled, and their wives	1004
	13:21 their **h** shall be full of doleful creatures;	1004
	13:22 the islands shall cry in their desolate **h**,	490
	15: 3 on the tops of their **h**, and in their streets,	1406
	22:10 ye have numbered the **h** of Jerusalem,	1004
	22:10 the **h** have ye broken down to fortify	1004
	32:13 upon all the **h** of joy in the joyous city:	1004
	42:22 in holes, and they are hid in prison **h**.	1004
	65:21 they shall build **h**, and inhabit them; and	1004
Jer	5: 7 themselves by troops in the harlots' **h**.	1004
	5:27 is full of birds, so are their **h** full of deceit:	1004
	6:12 their **h** shall be turned unto others,	1004
	17:22 Neither carry forth a burden out of your **h**	1004
	18:22 Let a cry be heard from their **h**, when	1004
	19:13 the **h** of Jerusalem, and the houses	1004
	19:13 and the **h** of the kings of Judah,	1004
	19:13 of all the **h** upon whose roofs they have	1004
	29: 5 Build ye **h**, and dwell in them; and	1004
	29:28 build ye **h**, and dwell in them; and	1004
	32:15 **H** and fields and vineyards shall be	1004
	32:29 fire on this city, and burn it with the **h**,	1004
	33: 4 concerning the **h** of this city,	1004
	33: 4 concerning the **h** of the kings of Judah,	1004
	35: 9 Nor to build **h** for us to dwell in:	1004
	39: 8 the **h** of the people, with fire, and brake	1004
	43:12 I will kindle a fire in the **h** of the gods of	1004
	43:13 the **h** of the gods of the Egyptians shall he	1004
	52:13 all the **h** of Jerusalem, and all the houses	1004
	52:13 all the **h** of the great men, burnt he with	1004
La	5: 2 is turned to strangers, our **h** to aliens.	1004
Eze	7:24 heathen, and they shall possess their **h**:	1004
	11: 3 Which say, It is not near; let us build **h**:	1004
	16:41 they shall burn thine **h** with fire,	1004
	23:47 and burn up their **h** with fire.	1004
	26:12 thy walls, and destroy thy pleasant **h**:	1004
	28:26 shall build **h**, and plant vineyards;	1004
	33:30 by the walls and in the doors of the **h**,	1004
	45: 4 it shall be a place for their **h**, and a holy	1004
Da	2: 5 and your **h** shall be made a dunghill.	1005
	3:29 and their **h** shall be made a dunghill;	1005
Hos	11:11 I will place them in their **h**, saith	1004
Joel	2: 9 the wall, they shall climb up upon the **h**;	1004
Am	3:15 the **h** of ivory shall perish, and the great	1004
	3:15 the great **h** shall have an end, saith	1004
	5:11 ye have built **h** of hewn stone, but ye	1004
Mic	1:14 the **h** of Achzib shall be a lie to the kings	1004
	2: 2 by violence; and **h**, and take them away:	1004
	2: 9 have ye cast out from their pleasant **h**;	1004
Zep	1: 9 which fill their masters' **h** with violence	1004
	1:13 become a booty, and their **h** a desolation:	1004
	1:13 they shall also build **h**, but not inhabit	1004
	2: 7 in the **h** of Ashkelon shall they lie down	1004
Hag	1: 4 to dwell in your cieled **h**, and this house	1004
Zec	14: 2 and the **h** rifled, and the women ravished;	1004
Mt	11: 8 that wear soft clothing are in kings' **h**.	3624
	19:29 And every one that hath forsaken **h**,	3614
	23:14 ye devour widows' **h**, and for a pretence	3614
Mk	8: 3 I send them away fasting to their own **h**,	3624
	10:30 **h**, and brethren, and sisters, and mothers,	3614
	12:40 Which devour widows' **h**, and for a	3614
Lk	16: 4 they may receive me into their **h**.	3624
	20:47 Which devour widows' **h**, and for a shew	3614
Ac	4:34 were possessors of lands or **h** sold them,	3614
1Co	11:22 have ye not **h** to eat and to drink in? or	3614
1Ti	3:12 their children and their own **h** well.	3614
2Ti	3: 6 of this sort are they which creep into **h**,	3614
Tit	1:11 must be stopped, who subvert whole **h**,	3624

HOUSETOP (7) [HOUSE, TOP]

Ps	102: 7 and am as a sparrow alone upon the **h**.	1406
Pr	21: 9 It is better to dwell in a corner of the **h**,	1406
	25:24 It is better to dwell in a corner of the **h**,	1406
Mt	24:17 him which is on the **h** not come down	1430
Mk	13:15 And let him that is on the **h** not go down	1430
Lk	5:19 they went upon the **h**, and let him down	1430
	17:31 which shall be upon the **h**, and his stuff	1430

HOUSETOPS (8) [HOUSE, TOP]

2Ki	19:26 as the grass on the **h**, and as corn blasted	1406
Ps	129: 6 Let them be as the grass upon the **h**?	1406
Isa	22: 1 that thou art wholly gone up to the **h**?	1406
	37:27 as the grass on the **h**, and as corn blasted	1406
Jer	48:38 generally upon all the **h** of Moab,	1406
Zep	1: 5 worship the host of heaven upon the **h**;	1406
Mt	10:27 hear in the ear, that preach ye upon the **h**.	1430
Lk	12: 3 in closets shall be proclaimed upon the **h**.	1430

HOW (543) [HOWBEIT, HOWSOEVER]

Ge	26: 9 **h** saidst thou, She is my sister? And Isaac	349
	27:20 **H** is it that thou hast found it so quickly,	4100
	28:17 and said, **H** dreadful is this place!	4100
	30:29 Thou knowest **h** I have served thee, and	834
	30:29 and how **h** thy cattle was with me.	834
	38:29 she said, **H** hast thou broken forth?	4100
	39: 9 then can I do this great wickedness,	349
	44: 8 **h** then should we steal out of thy lord's	349
	44:16 or **h** shall we clear ourselves? God hath	4100
	44:34 For **h** shall I go up to my father, and the	349
	47: 8 Pharaoh said unto Jacob, **H** old	4100+3509.1
	47:18 from my lord, **h** that our money is spent;	518
Ex	2:18 **H** is it that you are come so soon to day?	4069
	6:12 **h** then shall Pharaoh hear me, who am of	349
	6:30 and **h** shall Pharaoh hearken unto me?	349
	9:29 that thou mayest know **h** that the earth	3588

Ex	10: 2 that ye may know **h** that I am the Lord.	3588
	10: 3 Lord God of the Hebrews, **H** long	4970+5704
	10: 7 servants said unto him, **H** long	4970+5704
	11: 7 that ye may know **h** that the Lord doth	834
	16:28 said unto Moses, **H** long	575+5704+1886.5
	18: 8 the way, and **h** the Lord delivered them.	NIH
	19: 4 **h** I bare you on eagles' wings,	NIH
	36: 1 to know **h** to work all manner	NIH
Nu	10:31 forasmuch as thou knowest **h** we are to	NIH
	14:11 said unto Moses, **H** long	575+5704+1886.5
	14:11 **h** long will it be ere they	575+5704+1886.5
	14:27 **H** long shall I bear with this evil	4970+5704
	20:15 H our fathers went down into Egypt,	2050.1
	23: 8 H shall I curse, whom God hath not	4100
	23: 8 or **h** shall I defy, whom the Lord hath	4100
	24: 5 H goodly are thy tents, O Jacob,	4100
Dt	1:12 **H** can I myself alone bear your cumbrance,	349
	1:31 where thou hast seen **h** that the Lord thy	834
	7:17 are moe than I; **h** can I dispossess them?	349
	9: 7 **h** thou provokedst the Lord thy God to	834
	11: 4 **h** he made the water of the Red sea to	834
	11: 4 **h** the Lord hath destroyed them unto this	NIH
	11: 6 the earth opened her mouth,	834
	12:30 **h** did these nations serve their gods?	349
	18:21 shall we know the word which	349
	25:18 **h** he met thee by the way, and smote	834
	29:16 ye know **h** we have dwelt in the land of	834
	29:16 **h** we came through the nations which ye	834
	31:27 and **h** much more after my death?	637+3588
	32:30 **H** should one chase a thousand, and two	349
Jos	2:10 For we have heard **h** the Lord dried up	834
	9: 7 and **h** shall we make a league with you?	834
	9:24 **h** that the Lord thy God commanded his	834
	10: 1 Jerusalem had heard **h** Joshua had taken	3588
	10: 1 **h** the inhabitants of Gibeon had made	3588
	14:12 thou heardest in that day **h** the Anakims	3588
Jdg	13:12 **H** shall we order the child, and how shall	4100
	13:12 the child, and **h** shall we do unto him?	NIH
	16:15 unto him, **H** canst thou say, I love thee,	349
	18: 7 that were therein, **h** they dwelt careless,	NIH
	20: 3 of Israel, Tell us, **h** was this wickedness?	349
	21: 7 **H** shall we do for wives for them that	4100
	21:16 **H** shall we do for wives for them that	4100
Ru	1: 6 **h** that the Lord had visited his people in	3588
	2:11 **h** thou hast left thy father and thy mother,	834
	3:18 until thou know **h** the matter will fall:	349
1Sa	1:14 said unto her, **H** long wilt thou be	4970+5704
	2:22 **h** they lay with the women that assembled	834
	10:27 of Belial said, **H** shall this man save us?	4100
	12:24 for consider **h** great things he hath done	834
	14:29 **h** mine eyes have been enlightened,	3588
	14:30 **H** much more, if haply the people	637+3588
	15: 2 **h** he laid wait for him in the way, when he	834
	16: 1 Lord said unto Samuel, **H** long	4970+5704
	16: 2 Samuel said, **H** can I go? if Saul hear it, he	349
	17:18 look **h** thy brethren fare, and take their	3807.1
	23: 3 **h** much more then if we come to Keilah	637
	24:10 this day thine eyes have seen **h** that	834
	24:18 thou hast shewed this day **h** that thou	834
	28: 9 thou hast cut off those that have familiar	834
2Sa	1: 4 David said unto him, **H** went the matter?	4100
	1: 5 **H** knowest thou that Saul and Jonathan	349
	1:14 **H** wast thou not afraid to stretch forth	349
	1:19 thy high places: **h** are the mighty fallen!	349
	1:25 **H** are the mighty fallen in the midst of	349
	1:27 **H** are the mighty fallen, and the weapons	349
	2:22 **h** then should I hold up my face to Joab	349
	2:26 bitterness in the latter end? **h** long	4970+5704
	4:11 **H** much more, when wicked men have	637
	6: 9 **H** shall the ark of the Lord come to me?	349
	6:20 **H** glorious was the king of Israel to day,	4100
	11: 7 demanded of him **h** Joab did,	7965+3807.1
	11: 7 the people did, and **h** the war	7965+3807.1
	11: 7 and **h** the war prospered.	7965+3807.1
	12:18 **h** will he then vex himself, if we tell him	349
	16:11 **h** much more now may this	637+3588
	18:19 **h** that the Lord hath avenged him of his	3588
	19: 2 the people heard say that day **h** the king	NIH
	19:34 the king, **H** long	3117+4100+8141+3605.1
	24: 3 **h** many soever they be, an hundredfold,	3509.1
1Ki	3: 7 I know not **h** to go out or come in.	NIH
	3: 3 Thou knowest **h** that David my father	3588
	8:27 **h** much less this house that I have	637+3588
	12: 6 **H** do you advise that I may answer this	349
	14:19 **h** he warred, and how he reigned,	834
	14:19 how he warred, and **h** he reigned,	834
	18:13 **h** I hid an hundred men of the Lord's	2050.1
	18:21 **H** long halt ye between two	4970+5704
	19: 1 withal **h** he had slain all the prophets with	834
	20: 7 and see **h** this man seeketh mischief:	3588
	21:29 Seest thou **h** Ahab humbleth himself	3588
	22:16 said unto him, **H** many	4100+5704+3509.1
	22:45 might that he shewed, and **h** he warred,	834
2Ki	5: 7 see **h** he seeketh a quarrel against me.	3588
	5:13 not have done it? **h** much rather then,	637
	6:15 unto him, Alas, my master, **h** shall we do?	349
	6:32 See ye **h** this son of a murderer hath sent	3588
	8: 5 he was telling the king **h** he had restored	834
	9:25 remember **h** that, when I and thou rode	NIH
	10: 4 not before him: **h** then shall we stand?	349
	14:15 he fought with Amaziah king of Judah,	834
	14:28 he warred, and how he recovered	834
	14:28 he recovered Damascus, and Hamath,	834
	17:28 taught them **h** they should fear the Lord.	349

2Ki	18:24 **H** then wilt thou turn away the face of	349
	19:25 thou not heard long ago **h** I have done	NIH
	20: 3 now **h** I have walked before thee	834
	20:20 **h** he made a pool, and a conduit,	834
1Ch	13:12 **H** shall I bring the ark of God home to	1963
	18: 9 Now when Tou king of Hamath heard **h**	3588
	19: 5 and told David **h** the men were served.	5921
2Ch	6:18 **h** much less this house which I	637+3588
	7: 3 when all the children of Israel saw **h**	871.1
	18:15 king said to him, **H** many	4100+5704+3509.1
	20:11 Behold, I say, **h** they reward us, to come	NIH
	32:15 **h** much less shall your God	637+3588+3808
	33:19 **h** God was intreated of him, and all his sin,	NIH
Ezr	7:22 oil, and salt without prescribing **h** much.	NIH
Ne	2: 6 For **h** long shall thy journey be?	4970+5704
	2:17 Jerusalem lieth waste, and the gates	834
Est	2:11 to know **h** Esther did, and what should	NIH
	5:11 **h** he had advanced him above the princes	834
	8: 6 For **h** can I endure to see the evil that shall	349
	8: 6 **h** can I endure to see the destruction of my	349
Job	4:19 **h** much less in them that dwell in houses	637
	6:25 **H** forcible are right words! but what doth	4100
	7:19 **H** long wilt thou not depart from	575+5704
	8: 2 **H** long wilt thou speak these things?	575+5704
	8: 2 **h** long shall the words of thy mouth be	5704
	9: 2 but **h** should man be just with God?	4100
	9:14 **H** much less shall I answer him,	637+3588
	13:23 **H** many are mine iniquities and	4100+3509.1
	15:16 **H** much more abominable and	637+3588
	18: 2 **H** long will it be ere you	575+5704+1886.5
	19: 2 **H** long will ye vex my soul,	575+5704+1886.5
	21:17 **H** oft is the candle of the wicked	4100+3509.1
	21:17 **h** oft cometh their destruction upon them!	NIH
	21:34 **h** then comfort ye me in vain, seeing in	349
	22:12 the height of the stars, **h** high they are.	3588
	22:13 thou sayest, **H** doth God know? can he	4100
	25: 4 **H** then can man be justified with God?	4100
	25: 4 **h** can he be clean that is born of a	4100
	25: 6 **H** much less man, that is a worm?	637+3588
	26: 2 **H** hast thou helped him that is without	4100
	26: 2 **h** savest thou the arm that hath no	4100
	26: 3 **H** hast thou counselled him that hath no	4100
	26: 3 **h** hast thou plentifully declared the thing	NIH
	26:14 **h** little a portion is heard of him?	NIH
	34:19 **H** much less to him that accepteth not	NIH
	37:17 **H** thy garments are warm, when he	834
Ps	3: 1 **h** are they increased that trouble me!	4100
	4: 2 **h** long will ye turn my glory into	4100+5704
	4: 2 **h** long will ye love vanity, and seek after	NIH
	6: 3 but thou, O Lord, **h** long?	4970+5704
	8: 1 **h** excellent is thy name in all the earth!	4100
	8: 9 **h** excellent is thy name in all the earth!	4100
	11: 1 **h** say ye to my soul, Flee as a bird to your	349
	13: 1 **H** long wilt thou forget me,	575+5704+1886.5
	13: 1 for ever? **h** long wilt thou	575+5704+1886.5
	13: 2 **H** long shall I take counsel	575+5704+1886.5
	13: 2 **h** long shall mine enemy be	575+5704+1886.5
	21: 1 in thy salvation **h** greatly shall he rejoice!	4100
	31:19 **h** great is thy goodness, which thou hast	4100
	35:17 Lord, **h** long wilt thou look on?	4100+3509.1
	36: 7 **H** excellent is thy lovingkindness, O God!	4100
	39: 4 what it is; that I may know **h** frail I am.	4100
	42: 4 **H** thou didst drive out the heathen with	NIH
	44: 2 **h** thou didst afflict the people, and cast	NIH
	62: 3 **H** long will ye imagine	575+5704+1886.5
	66: 3 God, **H** terrible art thou in thy works!	4100
	73:11 they say, **h** doth God know? and is there	349
	73:19 **H** are they brought into desolation, as in a	349
	74: 9 any that knoweth **h** long.	4100+5704
	74:10 **h** long shall the adversary	4970+5704
	74:22 remember **h** the foolish man reproacheth	NIH
	78:40 **H** oft did they provoke him in	4100+3509.1
	78:43 **H** he had wrought his signs in Egypt,	834
	79: 5 **H** long, Lord? wilt thou be angry,	4100+5704
	80: 4 O Lord God of hosts, **h** long wilt	4970+5704
	82: 2 **H** long will ye judge unjustly,	4970+5704
	84: 1 **H** amiable are thy tabernacles, O Lord	4100
	89:46 **H** long, Lord? wilt thou hide	NIH
	89:47 Remember **h** short my time is:	4100
	89:50 **h** I do bear in my bosom the reproach of	NIH
	90:13 Return, O Lord, **h** long? and let it	4970+5704
	92: 5 O Lord, **h** great are thy works! and	4100
	94: 3 Lord, **h** long shall the wicked,	4970+5704
	94: 3 **h** long shall the wicked triumph?	4970+5704
	94: 4 **H** long shall they utter and speak hard	NIH
	104:24 O Lord, **h** manifold are thy works!	4100
	119:84 **H** many are the days of thy	4100+3509.1
	119:97 O **h** love I thy law! it is my meditation all	4100
	119:103 **H** sweet are thy words unto my taste!	4100
	119:159 Consider **h** I love thy precepts: quicken	3588
	132: 2 **H** he sware unto the Lord,	NIH
	133: 1 **H** good and how pleasant it is for brethren	4100
	133: 1 **h** pleasant it is for brethren to dwell	4100
	137: 4 **H** shall we sing the Lord's song in a	349
	139:17 **H** precious also are thy thoughts unto me,	4100
	139:17 O God! **h** great is the sum of them!	4100
Pr	1:22 **H** long, ye simple ones, will ye love	4970+5704
	5:12 **H** have I hated instruction, and my heart	349
	6: 9 **H** long wilt thou sleep, O sluggard?	4970+5704
	15:11 **h** much more then the hearts of	637+3588
	15:23 word spoken in due season, **h** good is it!	4100
	16:16 **H** much better is it to get wisdom than	4100
	19: 7 **h** much more do his friends go far	637+3588
	20:24 **h** can a man then understand his own	4100
	21:27 **h** much more, when he bringeth it	637+3588

Pr	30:13	*is* a generation, O **h** lofty are their eyes!	4100
Ecc	2:16	And **h** dieth the wise *man?* as the fool.	349
	4:11	have heat: but **h** can one be warm *alone?*	349
	10:15	he knoweth not **h** to go to the city.	349
	11: 5	nor **h** the bones *do* grow in the womb	3509.1
SS	4:10	**H** fair is thy love, my sister, *my* spouse!	4100
	4:10	**h much** better is thy love than wine! and	4100
	5: 3	I have put off my coat; **h** shall I put it on?	349
	5: 3	washed my feet; **h** shall I defile them?	349
	7: 1	**H** beautiful are thy feet with shoes,	4100
	7: 6	fair and how pleasant art thou, O love,	4100
	7: 6	How fair and **h** pleasant art thou, O love,	4100
Isa	1:21	**H** is the faithful city become a harlot!	349
	6:11	said I, Lord, **h long?** And he	4970+5704
	14: 4	and say, **H** hath the oppressor ceased!	349
	14:12	**H** art thou fallen from heaven, O Lucifer,	349
	14:12	*h* art thou cut down to the ground,	NIH
	19:11	**h** say unto Pharaoh, I *am* the son of	349
	20: 6	the king of Assyria: and **h** shall we escape?	349
	36: 9	**H** then wilt thou turn away the face of one	349
	37:26	thou not heard long ago, *h* I have done it;	NIH
	38: 3	**h** I have walked before thee in truth and	834
	48:11	will I do *it:* for **h** should *my name* be	349
	50: 4	that *I* should know **h** to speak a word in	349
	52: 7	**H** beautiful upon the mountains are the	4100
Jer	2:21	**h** then art thou turned *into* the degenerate	349
	2:23	**h** canst thou say, I am not polluted, I have	349
	3:19	**h** shall I put thee among the children,	349
	4:14	that thou mayest be saved. **H long**	4970+5704
	4:21	**H long** shall I see the standard,	4970+5704
	5: 7	**H** shall I pardon thee for this? thy children	335
	8: 8	**H** do ye say, We *are* wise, and the law of	349
	9: 7	for **h** shall I do for the daughter of my	349
	9:19	is heard out of Zion, **H** are we spoiled!	349
	12: 4	**H long** shall the land mourn,	4970+5704
	12: 5	then **h** canst thou contend with horses?	349
	12: 5	**h** wilt thou do in the swelling of Jordan?	349
	15: 5	go aside to ask **h** thou **doest?**	7965+3807.1
	22:23	**h** gracious shalt thou be when pangs	4100
	23:26	**H long** shall *this* be in the heart of	4970+5704
	31:22	**H long** wilt thou go about, O thou	4970+5704
	36:17	**h** didst thou write all these words at his	349
	46:13	**h** Nebuchadrezzar king of Babylon should	NIH
	47: 5	the remnant of their valley: **h long**	4970+5704
	47: 6	sword of the Lord, **h long,**	575+5704+1886.5
	47: 7	**H** can it be quiet, seeing the Lord hath	349
	48:14	say ye, We *are* mighty and strong men	349
	48:17	**h** is the strong staff broken,	349
	48:39	shall howl, *saying,* **H** is it broken down!	349
	48:39	**h** hath Moab turned the back with shame!	349
	49:25	**h** is the city of praise not left, the city of	349
	50:23	**H** is the hammer of the whole earth cut	349
	50:23	**h** is Babylon become a desolation among	349
	51:41	**H** is Sheshach taken! and *how* is the praise	349
	51:41	*h* is the praise of the whole earth surprised!	NIH
	51:41	**h** is Babylon become an astonishment	349
La	1: 1	**H** doth the city sit solitary, *that was* full of	349
	1: 1	*h* is she become as a widow! she *that was*	NIH
	1: 1	the provinces, *h* is she become tributary!	349
	2: 1	**H** hath the Lord covered the daughter of	349
	4: 1	**H** is the gold become dim! *how* is the	349
	4: 1	*h* is the most fine gold changed! the stones	NIH
	2: 4	are they esteemed as earthen pitchers,	349
Eze	14:21	**H much more** when I send my four	637+3588
	15: 5	**h much less** that it be meet yet for	637+3588
	16:30	**H** weak is thine heart, saith the Lord	4100
	26:17	to thee, **H** art thou destroyed, *that wast*	349
	33:10	pine away in them, **h** should we then live?	349
Da	4: 3	**H** great *are* his signs! and how	4101+3509.4
	4: 3	mighty *are* his wonders!	4101+3509.4
	8:13	certain *saint* which spake, **H long**	4970+5704
	10:17	For **h** can the servant of this my lord talk	1963
	12: 6	the waters of the river, **H long**	4970+5704
Hos	8: 5	is kindled against them: **h long**	4970+5704
	11: 8	**H** shall I give thee up, Ephraim? *how* shal	349
	11: 8	*h* shall I deliver thee, Israel? how shall I	NIH
	11: 8	**h** shall I make thee as Admah? *how* shal	349
	11: 8	**h** shall I set thee as Zeboim? mine heart is	NIH
Joel	1:18	**h** do the beasts groan! the herds of cattle	4100
Ob	1: 5	if robbers by night, (**h** art thou cut off!)	349
	1: 6	**h** are the *things* of Esau searched out!	349
	1: 6	*h* are his hid things sought up!	NIH
Mic	2: 4	**h** hath he removed *it* from me! turning	349
Hab	1: 2	O Lord, **h long** shall I cry,	575+5704+1886.5
	2: 6	*that which* is not his! **h long?**	4970+5704
Zep	2:15	**h** is she become a desolation, a place for	349
Hag	2: 3	**h** do ye see it now? *is it* not in your eyes	4100
Zec	1:12	O Lord of hosts, **h long** wilt thou	4970+5704
	9:17	**h great** is his goodness, and how great	4100
	9:17	*is* his goodness, and **h great** is his beauty!	4100
Mt	6:23	be darkness, **h great** *is* that darkness?	4214
	6:28	the lilies of the field, **h** they grow;	4459
	7: 4	Or **h** wilt thou say to thy brother, Let me	4459
	7:11	know **h** to give good gifts unto your	1492
	7:11	**h much** more shall your Father which is	4214
	10:19	take no thought **h** or what ye shall speak:	4459
	10:25	**h much** more *shall they call* them of his	4214
	12: 4	he entered into the house of God,	4459
	12: 5	**h that** on the sabbath days the priests in	3754
	12:12	**H much** then is a man better than a	4214
	12:14	against him, **h** they might destroy him.	3704
	12:26	**h** shall then his kingdom stand?	4459
	12:29	else **h** can one enter into a strong *man's*	4459
	12:34	generation of vipers, **h** can ye, being evil,	4459
	15:34	unto them, **H many** loaves have ye?	4214

Mt	16: 9	and **h many** baskets ye took up?	4214
	16:10	and **h many** baskets ye took up?	4214
	16:11	**H** *is it that* ye do not understand that I	4459
	16:12	understood they **h that** he bade *them*	3754
	16:21	**h that** he must go unto Jerusalem,	3754
	17:17	**h long** shall I be with you?	2193+4219
	17:17	**h long** shall I suffer you? bring him	2193+4219
	18:12	**H** think ye? if a man have an hundred	5101
	18:21	**h** oft shall my brother sin against me,	4212
	21:20	**H** soon is the fig tree withered away!	4459
	22:12	**h** camest thou in hither not having a	4459
	22:15	took counsel **h** they might entangle him	3704
	22:43	**H** then doth David in spirit call him Lord,	4459
	22:45	then call him Lord, **h** is he his son?	4459
	23:33	**h** can ye escape the damnation of hell?	4459
	23:37	**h** often would I have gathered thy	4212
	26:54	But **h** then shall the scriptures be fulfilled,	4459
	27:13	Hearest thou not **h** many *things* they	4214
Mk	2:16	**H** *is it* that he eateth and drinketh with	5101
	2:26	**H** he went into the house of God in	4459
	3: 6	against him, **h** they might destroy him.	3704
	3:23	in parables, **H** can Satan cast out Satan?	4459
	4:13	and **h** *then* will ye know all parables?	4459
	4:27	and grow up, **h** he knoweth not **h.**	5613
	4:40	so fearful? **h** *is it that* you have no faith?	4459
	5:16	they that saw *it* told them **h** it befell to	4459
	5:19	them **h great** *things* the Lord hath done	3745
	5:20	began to publish in Decapolis **h great**	3745
	6:38	unto them, **H** many loaves have ye?	4214
	8: 5	he asked them, **H many** loaves have ye?	4214
	8:19	**h many** baskets full of fragments took ye	4214
	8:20	**h many** baskets full of fragments took ye	4214
	8:21	**H** *is it that* ye do not understand?	4459
	9:12	and **h** it is written of the Son of man,	4459
	9:19	**h long** shall I be with you?	2193+4219
	9:19	**h long** shall I suffer you? bring him	2193+4219
	9:21	**H long** is it ago since this came unto him?	4214
	10:23	**H** hardly shall they that have riches enter	4459
	10:24	**h** hard is it for them that trust in riches to	4459
	11:18	and sought **h** they might destroy him:	4459
	12:26	**h** in the bush God spake unto him, saying,	5613
	12:35	**H** say the scribes that Christ is the Son of	4459
	12:41	beheld **h** the people cast money into	4459
	14: 1	the scribes sought **h** they might take him	4459
	14:11	And he sought **h** he might conveniently	4459
	15: 4	**h many** *things* they witness against	4214
Lk	1:34	**H** shall this be, seeing I know not a man?	4459
	1:58	her cousins heard **h** the Lord had shewed	3754
	1:62	to his father, **h** he would have him called.	5101
	2:49	said unto them, **H** *is it* that ye sought me?	5101
	6: 4	**H** he went into the house of God,	5613
	6:42	Either **h** canst thou say to thy brother,	4459
	7:22	**h** that the blind see, the lame walk,	3754
	8:18	Take heed therefore **h** ye hear:	4459
	8:39	shew **h great** *things* God hath done unto	3745
	8:39	throughout the whole city **h great**	3745
	8:47	and **h** she was healed immediately.	5613
	9:41	**h long** shall I be with you,	2193+4219
	10:26	is written in the law? **h** readest thou?	4459
	11:13	know **h** to give good gifts unto your	1492
	11:13	**h much** more shall your heavenly Father	4214
	11:18	himself, **h** shall his kingdom stand?	4459
	12:11	ye no thought **h** or what *thing* ye shall	4459
	12:24	**h much** are ye better than the	4214
	12:27	Consider the lilies **h** they grow: they toil	4459
	12:28	**h much** more *will he clothe* you, O ye of	4214
	12:50	**h** am I straitened till it be accomplished!	4459
	12:56	**h** *is it* that ye do not discern this time?	4459
	13:34	**h** often would I have gathered thy	4212
	14: 7	he marked **h** they chose out the chief	4459
	15:17	**H many** hired *servants* of my father's	4214
	16: 2	unto him, **H** *is it that* I hear this of thee?	5101
	16: 5	first, **H much** owest thou unto my lord?	4214
	16: 7	he to another, And **h much** owest thou?	4214
	18:24	**H** hardly shall they that have riches enter	4459
	19:15	that he might know **h much** every *man*	5101
	20:41	**H** say they that Christ is David's son?	4459
	20:44	calleth him Lord, **h** is he then his son?	4459
	21: 5	**h** it was adorned with goodly stones and	3754
	22: 2	and scribes sought **h** they might kill him;	4459
	22: 4	**h** he might betray him unto them.	4459
	22:61	he had said unto him, Before *the* cock	5613
	23:55	the sepulchre, and **h** his body was laid.	5613
	24: 6	remember **h** he spake unto you when he	5613
	24:20	And **h** the chief priests and our rulers	3704
	24:35	he was known of them in breaking of	5613
Jn	3: 4	**H** can a man be born when he is old?	4459
	3: 9	and said unto him, **H** can these *things* be?	4459
	3:12	and ye believe not, **h** shall ye believe,	4459
	4: 1	the Lord knew **h** the Pharisees had heard	3754
	4: 9	**H** *is it* that thou, being a Jew, askest drink	4459
	5:44	**H** can ye believe, which receive honour	4459
	5:47	his writings, **h** shall ye believe my words?	4459
	6:42	**h** is it then *that* he saith, I came down	4459
	6:52	**H** can this *man* give us *his* flesh to eat?	4459
	7:15	saying, **H** knoweth this *man* letters,	4459
	8:33	never in bondage to any *man:* **h** sayest	4459
	9:10	unto him, **H** were thine eyes opened?	4459
	9:15	again the Pharisees also asked him **h**	4459
	9:16	**H** can a man *that is* a sinner do such	4459
	9:19	was born blind? **h** then doth he now see?	4459
	9:26	did he to thee? **h** opened he thine eyes?	4459
	10:24	**H long** dost thou make us to doubt	2193+4219
	11:36	said the Jews, Behold, **h** he loved him.	5613
	12:19	Perceive ye **h** ye prevail nothing?	3754

Jn	12:34	**h** sayest thou, The Son of man must be	4459
	14: 5	thou goest; and **h** can we know the way?	4459
	14: 9	**h** sayest thou *then,* Shew us the Father?	4459
	14:22	**h** is it that thou wilt manifest thyself unto	5101
	14:28	Ye have heard **h** I said unto you, I go	3754
Ac	2: 8	And **h** hear we every man in our own	4459
	4:21	finding nothing **h** they might punish them,	4459
	5: 9	**H** *is it* that ye have agreed together to	5101
	7:25	would **h** God by his hand would deliver	3754
	8:31	And he said, **H** can I,	302+1063+4459
	9:13	**h** much evil he hath done to thy saints at	3745
	9:16	I will shew him **h great** *things* he must	3745
	9:27	unto them **h** he had seen the Lord	4459
	9:27	he had preached boldly at Damascus in	4459
	10:28	Ye know **h** that it is an unlawful *thing* for	5613
	10:38	**H** God anointed Jesus of Nazareth with	5613
	11:13	And he shewed us **h** he had seen an angel	4459
	11:16	he that he said, **h** John indeed baptized with	5613
	12:14	and told **h** Peter stood before the gate.	518
	12:17	unto them **h** the Lord had brought	4459
	13:32	**h that** the promise which was made unto	3754
	14:27	he had opened **h** the door of faith unto	3754
	15: 7	ye know **h that** a good while ago God	3754
	15:14	Simeon hath declared **h** God at the first	2531
	15:36	the word of the Lord, *and see* **h** they do.	4459
	19:35	what man is there that knoweth not **h** that	NIG
	20:20	And **h** I kept back nothing that was	5613
	20:35	I have shewed you all *things,* **h** that so	3754
	20:35	he said, It is more blessed to give than	3754
	21:20	**h many** thousands of Jews there are	4214
	23:30	And when it was told me **h** that the Jews	NIG
Ro	3: 6	then shall God judge the world?	4459
	4:10	**H** was it then reckoned? when he was in	4459
	6: 2	**h** shall we, that are dead to sin, live any	4459
	7: 1	**h that** the law hath dominion over a man,	3754
	7:18	**h** to perform that which is good I find not.	NIG
	8:32	**h** shall he not with him also freely give us	4459
	10:14	**H** then shall they call on *him* in whom	4459
	10:14	**h** shall they believe *in him* of whom they	4459
	10:14	and **h** shall they hear without a preacher?	4459
	10:15	And **h** shall they preach, except they be	4459
	10:15	**H** beautiful *are* the feet of them that	5613
	11: 2	**h** he maketh intercession to God against	5613
	11:12	the Gentiles; **h much** more their fulness?	4214
	11:24	**h** much more shall these, which be	4214
	11:33	unsearchable *are* his judgments,	5613
1Co	1:26	**h** that not many wise *men* after the flesh,	3754
	3:10	But let every man take heed **h** he buildeth	4459
	6: 3	**h much more** *things* that pertain to *this*	3386
	7:16	or **h** knowest thou, O man, whether thou	5101
	7:32	to the Lord, **h** he may please the Lord:	4459
	7:33	of the world, **h** he may please *his* wife.	4459
	7:34	the world, **h** she may please *her* husband.	4459
	10: 1	**h** that all our fathers were under the	3754
	14: 7	**h** shall it be known what is piped or	4459
	14: 9	**h** shall it be known what is spoken?	4459
	14:16	**h** shall he that occupieth the room of	4459
	14:26	**H** is it then, brethren? when ye come	5101
	15: 3	**h** that Christ died for our sins according	NIG
	15:12	**h** say some among you that there is no	4459
	15:35	*man* will say, **H** are the dead raised up?	4459
2Co	3: 8	**H** shall not the ministration of the spirit	4459
	7:15	with fear and trembling you received	5613
	8: 2	**H that** in a great trial of affliction	3754
	12: 4	**H that** he was caught up into paradise,	3754
	13: 5	**h** that Jesus Christ is in you, except ye be	3754
Gal	1:13	**h that** beyond measure I persecuted	3754
	4: 9	**h** turn ye again to the weak and	4459
	4:13	Ye see **h** through infirmity of the flesh I	3754
	6:11	Ye see **h large** a letter I have written unto	4080
Eph	3: 3	**H that** by revelation he made known unto	3754
	6:21	and **h** I do, Tychicus, a beloved brother	5101
Php	1: 8	**h** *greatly* I long after you all in the bowels	5613
	2:23	as I shall see **h** it will go with me.	3588+4012
	4:12	I know both **h** to be abased, and I know	NIG
	4:12	to be abased, and I know **h** to abound:	NIG
Col	4: 6	that you may know **h** ye ought to answer	4459
1Th	1: 9	ye turned to God from idols to serve	4459
	2:10	and God *also,* **h** holily and justly and	5613
	2:11	As you know **h** we exhorted and	5613
	4: 1	as ye have received of us **h** ye ought to	4459
	4: 4	That every one of you should know **h** to	NIG
2Th	3: 7	For yourselves know **h** *ye* ought to follow	4459
1Ti	3: 5	(For if a man know not **h** to rule his own	4459
	3: 5	shall he take care of the church of God?)	4459
	3:15	that thou mayest know **h** thou oughtest to	4459
2Ti	1: 3	in **h many** *things* he ministered *unto* me	3745
Phm	1:16	to me, but **h** much more unto thee,	4214
	1:19	I will repay *it:* albeit I do not say to thee **h**	3754
Heb	2: 3	**H** shall we escape, if we neglect so	4459
	7: 4	Now consider **h great** this *man was,* unto	4080
	8: 6	by **h** much also he is the mediator of a	3745
	9:14	**H** much more shall the blood of Christ,	4214
	10:29	Of **h** much sorer punishment, suppose ye,	4214
	12:17	For ye know **h** that afterward, when he	3754
Jas	2:22	thou **h** faith wrought with his works,	3754
	2:24	then **h that** by works a man is justified,	3754
	3: 5	**h great** a matter a little fire kindleth.	2245
2Pe	2: 9	The Lord knoweth **h** to deliver the godly	NIG
1Jn	3:17	**h** dwelleth the love of God in him?	4459
	4:20	**h** can he love God whom he hath not	4459
Jude	1: 5	ye once knew this, **h that** the Lord,	3754
	1:18	**H that** they told you there should be	3754
Rev	2: 2	**h** thou canst not bear *them which are* evil	3754
	3: 3	therefore **h** thou hast received and heard,	4459

H

Rev 6:10 saying, **H long**, O Lord, holy and *2193+4219*
 18: 7 **H** much she hath glorified herself, *3745*

HOWBEIT (64) [BE, HOW, IT]

Jdg 4:17 **H** Sisera fled away on his feet to the *2050.1*
 11:28 **H** the king of the children of Ammon *2050.1*
 16:22 **H** the hair of his head began to grow *2050.1*
 18:29 **h** the name of the city *was* Laish at the *199*
 21:18 **H** we may not give them wives of our *2050.1*
Ru 3:12 **h** there is a kinsman nearer than *1571+2050.1*
1Sa 8: 9 **h yet** protest solemnly unto them, *389+3588*
2Sa 2:23 **h** he refused to turn aside: *2050.1*
 12:14 **h**, because by this deed thou hast given *657*
 13:14 **h** he would not hearken unto her *2050.1*
 13:25 **h** he would not go, but blessed him. *2050.1*
 23:19 **h** he attained not unto the *first* three. *2050.1*
1Ki 2:15 **h** the kingdom is turned about, *2050.1*
 10: 7 **H** I believed not the words, until I *2050.1*
 11:13 **H** I will not rend away all the kingdom; *7535*
 11:22 Nothing: **h** let me go in any wise. *3588*
 11:34 **H** I will not take the whole kingdom *2050.1*
2Ki 3:25 **h** the slingers went about *it*, and smote *2050.1*
 8:10 **h** the Lord hath shewed me that he *2050.1*
 10:29 **H** *from* the sins of Jeroboam the son of *7535*
 12:13 **H** there were not made *for* the house of *389*
 14: 4 **H** the high places were not taken away: *7535*
 15:35 **H** the high places were not removed: *7535*
 17:29 **H** every nation made gods of their own, *2050.1*
 17:40 **H** they did not hearken, but they did *2050.1*
 22: 7 **H** there was no reckoning made with *389*
1Ch 11:21 **h** he attained not to the *first* three. *2050.1*
 28: 4 the Lord God of Israel chose me *2050.1*
2Ch 9: 6 **H** I believed not their words, until I *2050.1*
 18:34 the king of Israel stayed *himself* up in *2050.1*
 20:33 the high places were not taken away: *389*
 21: 7 **H** the Lord would not destroy *2050.1*
 21:20 **H** they buried him in the city of David, *2050.1*
 24: 5 the Levites hastened *it* not. *2050.1*
 27: 2 he entered not into the temple of *7535*
 32:31 **H** in *the business of* *3651+2050.1*
Ne 9:33 **H** thou *art* just in all that is brought *2050.1*
 13: 2 **h** our God turned the curse into a *2050.1*
Job 30:24 **H** *he will* not stretch out *his* hand to *389*
Isa 10: 7 **H** he meaneth not so, neither doth his *2050.1*
Jer 4: 1 I sent unto you all my servants *2050.1*
Mt 17:21 H this kind goeth not out but by prayer *1161*
Mk 5:19 **H** Jesus suffered him not, but saith *1161*
 7: 7 H in vain do they worship me, teaching *1161*
Jn 6:23 (**H** there came other boats from Tiberias *235*
 7:13 **H** no *man* spake openly of him for fear of *3305*
 7:27 we know this *man* whence he is: *235*
 11:13 **H** Jesus spake of his death: *1161*
 16:13 H when he, the Spirit of truth, is come, *1161*
Ac 4: 4 **H** many of them which heard the word *1161*
 7:48 the most High dwelleth not in temples *235*
 14:20 **H**, as the disciples stood round about him, *1161*
 17:34 certain men clave unto him, *1161*
 27:26 we must be cast upon a certain island. *1161*
 28: 6 they looked when he should have *1161*
1Co 2: 6 **H** we speak wisdom among *them that are* *1161*
 8: 7 **H** *there is* not in every *man that* *235*
 14: 2 for no *man* understandeth *him*; **h** in *1161*
 14:20 understanding: **h** in malice ye children, *235*
 15:46 **h** that *was* not first *which is* spiritual, *235*
2Co 11:21 **H** whereinsoever any *302+1161+1722+3739*
Gal 4: 8 **H** then, when ye knew not God, *235+3303*
1Ti 1:16 **H** for this cause I obtained mercy, that *235*
Heb 3:16 **h** not all that came out of Egypt by Moses. *235*

HOWL (29) [HOWLED, HOWLING, HOWLINGS]

Isa 13: 6 **H** ye; for the day of the Lord *is* at hand; *3213*
 14:31 **H**, O gate; cry, O city; thou; *3213*
 15: 2 Moab shall **h** over Nebo, and over *3213*
 15: 3 their streets, every one shall **h**, weeping *3213*
 16: 7 Therefore shall Moab **h** for Moab, *3213*
 16: 7 Moab howl for Moab, every one shall **h**: *3213*
 23: 1 **H**, ye ships of Tarshish; for it is laid waste, *3213*
 23: 6 to Tarshish; **h**, ye inhabitants of the isle. *3213*
 23:14 **H**, ye ships of Tarshish: for your strength *3213*
 52: 5 that rule over them **make** *them* to **h**, *3213*
 65:14 of heart, and shall **h** for vexation of spirit. *3213*
Jer 4: 8 gird you with sackcloth, lament and **h**: *3213*
 25:34 **H**, ye shepherds, and cry; *3213*
 47: 2 and all the inhabitants of the land shall **h**. *3213*
 48:20 **h** and cry; tell ye *it* in Arnon, that Moab *3213*
 48:31 will I **h** for Moab, and I will cry *3213*
 48:39 They shall **h**, *saying*, How is it broken *3213*
 49: 3 **H**, O Heshbon, for Ai is spoiled: cry, *3213*
 51: 8 **h** for her; take balm for her pain, if so *3213*
Eze 21:12 Cry and **h**, son of man: for it shall be *3213*
 30: 2 the Lord God; **H** ye, Woe worth the day! *3213*
Joel 1: 5 **h**, all ye drinkers of wine, because of *3213*
 1:11 **h**, O ye vinedressers, for the wheat and *3213*
 1:13 ye ministers of the altar: come, lie all *3213*
Mic 1: 8 Therefore I will wail and **h**, I will go stript *3213*
Zep 1:11 **H**, ye inhabitants of Maktesh, for all *3213*
Zec 11: 2 **h**, fir tree; for the cedar is fallen; because *3213*
 11: 2 **h**, O ye oaks of Bashan; for the forest of *3213*
Jas 5: 1 **h** for your miseries that shall come upon *3649*

HOWLED (1) [HOWL]

Hos 7:14 their heart, when they **h** upon their beds: *3213*

HOWLING (6) [HOWL]

Dt 32:10 land, and in the waste **h** wilderness; *3214*

Isa 15: 8 the **h** thereof unto Eglaim, and the *3215*
 15: 8 the **h** thereof *unto* Beer-elim. *3215*
Jer 25:36 and a **h** of the principal of the flock, *3215*
Zep 2: 1 **h** from the second, and a great crashing *3215*
Zec 11: 3 *There is* a voice of the **h** of the shepherds; *3215*

HOWLINGS (1) [HOWL]

Am 8: 3 the songs of the temple shall be **h** in that *3213*

HOWSOEVER (4) [EVER, HOW, SO]

Jdg 19:20 **h** *let* all thy wants *lie* upon me; *7535*
2Sa 18:22 **h**, let me, I pray thee, also run after *4100*
 18:23 **h**, *said he*, let me run. And he said unto *4100*
Zep 3: 7 not be cut off, **h** I punished them: *834+3605*

HUB See NAVES

HUGE (1)

2Ch 16: 8 and the Lubims a **h** host, *7230+3807.1*

HUGE FISH See WHALE; WHALE'S; WHALES

HUKKOK (1)

Jos 19:34 goeth out from thence to **H**, and reacheth *2712*

HUKOK (1)

1Ch 6:75 **H** with her suburbs, and Rehob with her *2712*

HUL (2)

Ge 10:23 Uz, and, **H**, and Gether, and Mash. *2343*
1Ch 1:17 Uz, and, **H**, and Gether, and Meshech. *2343*

HULDAH (2)

2Ki 22:14 Asahiah, went unto **H** the prophetess, *2468*
2Ch 34:22 that the king *had appointed*, went to **H** *2468*

HUMBLE (25) [HUMBLED, HUMBLEDST, HUMBLENESS, HUMBLETH, HUMBLY]

Ex 10: 3 How long wilt thou refuse to **h** thyself *6031*
Dt 8: 2 to **h** thee, *and* to prove thee, to know *6031*
 8:16 that he might **h** thee, and that he might *6031*
Jdg 19:24 **h** ye them, and do with them what *6031*
2Ch 7:14 **h** themselves, and pray, and seek *3665*
 34:27 and thou didst **h** thyself before God, *3665*
Job 22:29 and he shall save the **h person**. *5869+7807*
Ps 9:12 he forgetteth not the cry of the **h**. *6035*
 10:12 God, lift up thine hand: forget not the **h**. *6035*
 10:17 Lord, thou hast heard the desire of the **h**: *6035*
 34: 2 the **h** shall hear *thereof*, and be glad. *6035*
 69:32 The **h** shall see *this, and* be glad: *6035*
Pr 6: 3 go, **h** thyself, and make sure thy friend. *7511*
 16:19 Better *it is* to be of an **h** spirit with *8217*
 29:23 but honour shall uphold the **h** in spirit. *8217*
Isa 57:15 him also *that is* of a contrite and **h** spirit, *8217*
 57:15 to revive the spirit of the **h**, and to revive *8217*
Jer 13:18 and to the queen, **H** yourselves, sit down: *8213*
Mt 18: 4 shall **h** himself as this little child, *5013*
 23:12 he that shall **h** himself shall be exalted. *5013*
2Co 12:21 my God will **h** *me* among you, and *that* I *5013*
Jas 4: 6 the proud, but giveth grace unto the **h**. *5011*
 4:10 **H** yourselves in the sight of the Lord, *5013*
1Pe 5: 5 the proud, and giveth grace to the **h**. *5011*
 5: 6 **H** yourselves therefore under the mighty *5013*

HUMBLED (28) [HUMBLE]

Lev 26:41 if then their uncircumcised hearts be **h**, *3665*
Dt 8: 3 he **h** thee, and suffered thee to hunger, *6031*
 21:14 of her, because thou hast **h** her. *6031*
 22:24 because he hath **h** his neighbour's wife: *6031*
 22:29 because he hath **h** her, he may not put *6031*
2Ki 22:19 and thou hast **h** thyself before the Lord, *3665*
2Ch 12: 6 of Israel and the king **h** themselves; *3665*
 12: 7 when the Lord saw that they **h** *3665*
 12: 7 saying, They have **h** themselves; *3665*
 12:12 when he **h** himself, the wrath of *3665*
 30:11 Manasseh and of Zebulun **h** themselves, *3665*
 32:26 Notwithstanding Hezekiah **h** himself for *3665*
 33:12 **h** himself greatly before the God of his *3665*
 33:19 and graven images, before he was **h**: *3665*
 33:23 **h** not himself before the Lord, *3665*
 33:23 as Manasseh his father had **h** himself; *3665*
 36:12 **h** not himself before Jeremiah the prophet *3665*
Ps 35:13 I **h** my soul with fasting; and my prayer *6031*
Isa 2:11 The lofty looks of man shall be **h**, *8213*
 5:15 the mighty man shall be **h**, and the eyes *8213*
 5:15 and the eyes of the lofty shall be **h**: *8213*
 10:33 hewn down, and the haughty shall be **h**. *8213*
Jer 44:10 They are not **h** *even* unto this day, *1792*
La 3:20 still in remembrance, and is **h** in me. *7743*
Eze 22:10 in thee have they **h** her that was set apart *6031*
 22:11 another in thee hath **h** his sister, his *6031*
Da 5:22 O Belshazzar, hast not **h** thine heart, *8214*
Php 2: 8 he **h** himself, and became obedient unto *5013*

HUMBLEDST (1) [HUMBLE]

2Ch 34:27 **h** thyself before me, and didst rend thy *3665*

HUMBLENESS (1) [HUMBLE]

Col 3:12 kindness, **h** of mind, meekness, *5012*

HUMBLETH (7) [HUMBLE]

1Ki 21:29 thou how Ahab **h** himself before me? *3665*
 21:29 because he **h** himself before me, I will not *3665*
Ps 10:10 He croucheth, *and* **h** himself, that the *7817*
 113: 6 Who **h** *himself* to behold *the things that* *8213*
Isa 2: 9 down, and the great man **h** himself: *8213*

Lk 14:11 and he that **h** himself shall be exalted. *5013*
 18:14 and he that **h** himself shall be exalted. *5013*

HUMBLY (2) [HUMBLE]

2Sa 6: 4 I **h** beseech thee *that* I may find grace in *7812*
Mic 6: 8 love mercy, and to walk **h** with thy God? *6800*

HUMILIATION (1) [HUMILITY]

Ac 8:33 In his **h** his judgment was taken away: *5014*

HUMILITY (7) [HUMILIATION]

Pr 15:33 of wisdom; and before honour *is* **h**. *6038*
 18:12 man is haughty, and before honour *is* **h**. *6038*
 22: 4 By **h** *and* the fear of the Lord *are* riches, *6038*
Ac 20:19 Serving the Lord with all **h of mind**, *5012*
Col 2:18 you of your reward in a voluntary **h**, *5012*
 2:23 and **h**, and neglecting of the body, not in *5012*
1Pe 5: 5 one to another, and be clothed with **h**: *5012*

HUMTAH (1)

Jos 15:54 **H**, and Kirjath-arba, which *is* Hebron, *2547*

HUNDRED (590) [HUNDREDFOLD, HUNDREDS, HUNDREDTH]

Ge 5: 3 Adam lived an **h** and thirty years, *3967*
 5: 4 he had begotten Seth were eight **h** years: *3967*
 5: 5 all the days that Adam lived were nine **h** *3967*
 5: 6 Seth lived an **h** and five years, *3967*
 5: 7 Seth lived after he begat Enos eight **h** *3967*
 5: 8 all the days of Seth were nine **h** and *3967*
 5:10 Enos lived after he begat Cainan eight **h** *3967*
 5:11 all the days of Enos were nine **h** and *3967*
 5:13 lived after he begat Mahalaleel eight **h** *3967*
 5:14 all the days of Cainan were nine **h** and *3967*
 5:16 lived after he begat Jared eight **h** *3967*
 5:17 all the days of Mahalaleel were eight **h** *3967*
 5:18 Jared lived an **h** sixty and two years, *3967*
 5:19 Jared lived after he begat Enoch eight **h** *3967*
 5:20 all the days of Jared were nine **h** sixty *3967*
 5:22 after he begat Methuselah three **h** years, *3967*
 5:23 all the days of Enoch were three **h** sixty *3967*
 5:25 Methuselah lived an **h** eighty and seven *3967*
 5:26 after he begat Lamech seven **h** eighty *3967*
 5:27 all the days of Methuselah were nine **h** *3967*
 5:28 Lamech lived an **h** eighty and two years, *3967*
 5:30 Lamech lived after he begat Noah five **h** *3967*
 5:31 all the days of Lamech were seven **h** *3967*
 5:32 Noah was five **h** years old: and Noah *3967*
 6: 3 his days shall be an **h** and twenty years. *3967*
 6:15 length of the ark *shall be* three **h** cubits, *3967*
 7: 6 Noah was six **h** years old when the flood *3967*
 7:24 the waters prevailed upon the earth an **h** *3967*
 8: 3 after the end of the **h** and fifty days *3967*
 9:28 Noah lived after the flood three **h** and *3967*
 9:29 all the days of Noah were nine **h** and *3967*
 11:10 Shem *was* an **h** years old, *3967*
 11:11 Shem lived after he begat Arphaxad five **h** *3967*
 11:13 Arphaxad lived after he begat Salah four **h** *3967*
 11:15 Salah lived after he begat Eber four **h** *3967*
 11:17 Eber lived after he begat Peleg four **h** *3967*
 11:19 Peleg lived after he begat Reu two **h** *3967*
 11:21 Reu lived after he begat Serug two **h** *3967*
 11:23 Serug lived after he begat Nahor two **h** *3967*
 11:25 Nahor lived after he begat Terah an **h** *3967*
 11:32 the days of Terah were two **h** and *3967*
 14:14 three **h** and eighteen, and pursued *them* *3967*
 15:13 and they shall afflict them four **h** years; *3967*
 17:17 *a child* born unto him that is an **h** *3967*
 21: 5 Abraham *was* an **h** years old, when his *3967*
 23: 1 Sarah was an **h** and seven and twenty *3967*
 23:15 the land *is worth* four **h** shekels of silver; *3967*
 23:16 four **h** shekels of silver, current *money* *3967*
 25: 7 lived, an **h** threescore and fifteen years. *3967*
 25:17 Ishmael, an **h** and thirty and seven years: *3967*
 32: 6 to meet thee, and four **h** men with him. *3967*
 32:14 **Two h** she goats, and twenty **h** goats, *3967*
 32:14 he goats, **two h** ewes, and twenty rams, *3967*
 33: 1 Esau came, and with him four **h** men. *3967*
 33:19 for an **h** pieces of money. *3967*
 35:28 the days of Isaac were an **h** and *3967*
 45:22 to Benjamin he gave three **h** *pieces* of *3967*
 47: 9 of the years of my pilgrimage *are* an **h** *3967*
 47:28 so the whole age of Jacob was an **h** forty *3967*
 50:22 and Joseph lived an **h** and ten years. *3967*
 50:26 Joseph died, *being* an **h** and ten years old: *3967*
Ex 6:16 years of the life of Levi *were* an **h** thirty *3967*
 6:18 the years of the life of Kohath *were* an **h** *3967*
 6:20 the years of the life of Amram *were* an **h** *3967*
 12:37 six **h** thousand on foot *that were* men, *3967*
 12:40 in Egypt, *was* four **h** and thirty years. *3967*
 12:41 came to pass at the end of the four **h** and *3967*
 14: 7 he took six **h** chosen chariots, and all *3967*
 27: 9 linen of an **h** cubits long for one side: *3967*
 27:11 *shall be* hangings of an **h** *cubits* long, *3967*
 27:18 length of the court *shall be* an **h** cubits, *3967*
 30:23 pure myrrh five **h** *shekels*, and of sweet *3967*
 30:23 **two h** and fifty *shekels*, and of sweet *3967*
 30:23 and of sweet calamus **two h** and *3967*
 30:24 cassia five **h** *shekels*, after the shekel of *3967*
 38: 9 *were of* fine twined linen, an **h** cubits: *3967*
 38:11 the north side *the hangings were* an **h** *3967*
 38:24 talents, and seven **h** and thirty shekels, *3967*
 38:25 of the congregation *was* an **h** talents, *3967*
 38:25 a thousand seven **h** and threescore and *3967*
 38:26 for six **h** thousand and three thousand *3967*

Ex 38:26 three thousand and five **h** and fifty *men*.	3967
38:27 of the **h** talents of silver were cast	3967
38:27 **h** sockets of the hundred talents, a talent	3967
38:27 hundred sockets of the **h** talents, a talent	3967
38:28 thousand and seven **h** seventy and	3967
38:29 and two thousand and four **h** shekels.	3967
Lev 26: 8 five of you shall chase an **h**,	3967
26: 8 **h** of you shall put ten thousand to flight:	3967
Nu 1:21 *were* forty and six thousand and five **h**.	3967
1:23 fifty and nine thousand and three **h**.	3967
1:25 and five thousand six **h** and fifty.	3967
1:27 and fourteen thousand and six **h**.	3967
1:29 *were* fifty and four thousand and four **h**.	3967
1:31 *were* fifty and seven thousand and four **h**.	3967
1:33 Ephraim, *were* forty thousand and five **h**.	3967
1:35 thirty two thousand and **two h**.	3967
1:37 *were* thirty and five thousand and four **h**.	3967
1:39 and two thousand and seven **h**.	3967
1:41 *were* forty and one thousand and five **h**.	3967
1:43 *were* forty and three thousand and four **h**.	3967
1:46 that were numbered were six **h** thousand	3967
1:46 and three thousand and five **h** and fifty.	3967
2: 4 and fourteen thousand and six **h**.	3967
2: 6 *were* four and twenty thousand and four **h**.	3967
2: 8 *were* fifty and seven thousand and four **h**.	3967
2: 9 in the camp of Judah *were* an **h** thousand	3967
2: 9 and six thousand and four **h**,	3967
2:11 *were* forty and six thousand and five **h**.	3967
2:13 *were* fifty and nine thousand and three **h**.	3967
2:15 and five thousand and six **h** and fifty.	3967
2:16 the camp of Reuben *were* an **h** thousand	3967
2:16 and one thousand and four **h** and fifty,	3967
2:19 of them, *were* forty thousand and five **h**.	3967
2:21 *were* thirty and two thousand and **two h**.	3967
2:23 *were* thirty and four thousand and four **h**.	3967
2:24 the camp of Ephraim *were* an **h** thousand	3967
2:24 and eight thousand and an **h**,	3967
2:26 and two thousand and seven **h**.	3967
2:28 *were* forty and one thousand and five **h**.	3967
2:30 *were* fifty and three thousand and four **h**.	3967
2:31 in the camp of Dan *were* an **h** thousand	3967
2:31 and fifty and seven thousand and six **h**.	3967
2:32 their hosts *were* six **h** thousand	3967
2:32 and three thousand and five **h** and fifty.	3967
3:22 of them *were* seven thousand and five **h**.	3967
3:28 upward, *were* eight thousand and six **h**,	3967
3:34 upward, *were* six thousand and **two h**.	3967
3:43 two thousand **two h** and threescore and	3967
3:46 that are *to be* redeemed of the **two h**	3967
3:50 a thousand three **h** and threescore and	3967
4:36 their families were two thousand seven **h**	3967
4:40 were two thousand and six **h** and thirty.	3967
4:44 were three thousand and **two h**.	3967
4:48 eight thousand and five **h** and fourscore.	3967
7:13 the weight thereof *was* an **h** and	3967
7:19 the weight whereof *was* an **h** and	3967
7:25 the weight whereof *was* an **h** and	3967
7:31 one silver charger of the weight of an **h**	3967
7:37 the weight whereof *was* an **h** and	3967
7:43 one silver charger of the weight of an **h**	3967
7:49 the weight whereof *was* an **h** and	3967
7:55 one silver charger of the weight of an **h**	3967
7:61 the weight whereof *was* an **h** and	3967
7:67 the weight whereof *was* an **h** and	3967
7:73 the weight whereof *was* an **h** and	3967
7:79 the weight whereof *was* an **h** and	3967
7:85 Each charger of silver *weighing* an **h** and	3967
7:85 four **h** *shekels*, after the shekel of	3967
7:86 all the gold of the spoons *was* an **h** and	3967
11:21 amongst whom I *am, are* six **h** thousand	3967
16: 2 **two h** and fifty princes of the assembly,	3967
16:17 man his censer, **two h** and fifty censers;	3967
16:35 consumed the **two h** and fifty men that	3967
16:49 were fourteen thousand and seven **h**,	3967
26: 7 three thousand and seven **h** and thirty.	3967
26:10 what time the fire devoured **two h** and	3967
26:14 twenty and two thousand and **two h**.	3967
26:18 of them, forty thousand and five **h**.	3967
26:22 and sixteen thousand and five **h**.	3967
26:25 and four thousand and three **h**.	3967
26:27 of them, threescore thousand and five **h**.	3967
26:34 fifty and two thousand and seven **h**.	3967
26:37 thirty and two thousand and five **h**.	3967
26:41 *were* forty and five thousand and six **h**.	3967
26:43 and four thousand and four **h**.	3967
26:47 *were* fifty and three thousand and four **h**.	3967
26:50 *were* forty and five thousand and four **h**.	3967
26:51 six **h** thousand and a thousand seven	3967
26:51 and a thousand seven **h** and thirty.	3967
31:28 one soul of five **h**, *both* of the persons,	3967
31:32 was six **h** thousand and seventy thousand	3967
31:36 *in* number three **h** thousand and seven	3967
31:36 and thirty thousand and five **h** sheep:	3967
31:37 the LORD'S tribute of the sheep was six **h**	3967
31:39 the asses *were* thirty thousand and five **h**;	3967
31:43 the congregation was three **h** thousand	3967
31:43 *and* seven thousand and five **h** sheep,	3967
31:45 And thirty thousand asses and five **h**,	3967
31:52 was sixteen thousand seven **h** and	3967
33:39 Aaron *was* an **h** and twenty and three	3967
Dt 22:19 they shall amerce him in an **h** *shekels* of	3967
31: 2 I *am* an **h** and twenty years old *this* day;	3967
34: 7 Moses *was* an **h** and twenty years old	3967
Jos 7:21 **two h** shekels *of* silver, and a wedge of	3967
24:29 died, *being* an **h** and ten years old.	3967

Jos 24:32 of Shechem for an **h** pieces of silver:	3967
Jdg 2: 8 died, *being* an **h** and ten years old.	3967
3:31 which slew *of* the Philistines six **h** men	3967
4: 3 for he had nine **h** chariots of iron;	3967
4:13 *even* nine **h** chariots of iron, and all	3967
7: 6 hand to their mouth, were three **h** men:	3967
7: 7 By the three **h** men that lapped will I save	3967
7: 8 his tent, and retained *those* three **h** men:	3967
7:16 he divided the three **h** men into three	3967
7:19 and the **h** men that *were* with him,	3967
7:22 the three **h** blew the trumpets,	3967
8: 4 and the three **h** men that *were* with him,	3967
8:10 there fell an **h** and twenty thousand men	3967
8:26 a thousand and seven **h** *shekels* of gold;	3967
11:26 by the coasts of Arnon, three **h** years?	3967
15: 4 Samson went and caught three **h** foxes,	3967
16: 5 **eleven** *h* *pieces* of silver. 505+3967+2050.1	
17: 2 **eleven** *h shekels* of silver 505+3967+2050.1	
17: 3 **eleven** *shekels* of silver 505+3967+2050.1	
17: 4 his mother took **two h** *shekels* of silver,	3967
18:11 six **h** men appointed *with* weapons of	3967
18:16 six **h** men appointed *with* their weapons	3967
18:17 **h** men that were appointed *with* weapons	3967
20: 2 **h** thousand footmen that drew sword.	3967
20:10 will take ten men of an **h** throughout all	3967
20:10 an **h** of a thousand, and a thousand out of	3967
20:15 were numbered seven **h** chosen men.	3967
20:16 Among all this people *there* were seven **h**	3967
20:17 were numbered four **h** thousand men that	3967
20:35 and five thousand and an **h** men:	3967
20:47 six **h** men turned and fled to the	3967
21:12 of Jabesh-gilead four **h** young virgins,	3967
1Sa 11: 8 the children of Israel were three **h**	3967
13:15 were present with him, about six **h** men.	3967
14: 2 *were* with him *were* about six **h** men;	3967
15: 4 war **h** thousand footmen, and ten	3967
17: 7 his spear's head *weighed* six **h** shekels *of*	3967
18:25 but an **h** foreskins of the Philistines,	3967
18:27 and slew the Philistines **two h** men;	3967
22: 2 there were with him about four **h** men.	3967
23:13 *which were* about six **h**, arose and	3967
25:13 there went up after David about four **h**	3967
25:13 men; and **two h** abode by the stuff.	3967
25:18 **two h** loaves, and two bottles of wine,	3967
25:18 parched *corn*, and an **h** clusters of raisins,	3967
25:18 **two h** cakes *of figs*, and laid *them* on	3967
27: 2 he passed over with the six **h** men that	3967
30: 9 he and the six **h** men that *were* with him,	3967
30:10 David pursued, he and four **h** men:	3967
30:10 for **two h** abode *behind*, which were so	3967
30:17 save four **h** young men, which rode upon	3967
30:21 David came to the **two h** men, which	3967
2Sa 2:31 *so that* three **h** and threescore men died.	3967
3:14 which I espoused to me for an **h** foreskins	3967
8: 4 thousand *chariots*, and seven **h** horsemen,	3967
8: 4 but reserved of them *for* an **h** chariots.	3967
10:18 David slew the men *of* seven **h** chariots	3967
14:26 he weighed the hair of his head *at* **two h**	3967
15:11 with Absalom went **two h** men out of	3967
15:18 six **h** men which came after him from	3967
16: 1 upon them **two h** *loaves of* bread,	3967
16: 1 an **h** bunches of raisins, and an hundred	3967
16: 1 of summer fruits, and a bottle of wine.	3967
21:16 weight of whose spear *weighed* three **h**	3967
23: 8 he lift up his spear *against* eight **h**,	3967
23:18 he lift up his spear against three **h**,	3967
24: 9 were in Israel eight **h** thousand valiant	3967
24: 9 the men of Judah *were* five **h** thousand	3967
1Ki 4:23 an **h** sheep, beside harts, and roebucks,	3967
5:16 three thousand and three **h**, which ruled	3967
6: 1 it came to pass in the four **h** and	3967
7: 2 the length thereof *was* an **h** cubits,	3967
7:20 the pomegranates *were* **two h** *in* rows	3967
7:42 four **h** pomegranates for the two	3967
8:63 and an **h** and twenty thousand sheep.	3967
9:23 five **h** and fifty, which bare rule over	3967
9:28 four **h** and twenty talents, and brought *it*	3967
10:10 gave the king an **h** and twenty talents of	3967
10:14 Solomon in one year was six **h** threescore	3967
10:16 Solomon made **two h** targets *of* beaten	3967
10:16 six **h** *shekels* of gold went to one target.	3967
10:17 he made three **h** shields *of* beaten gold;	3967
10:26 he had a thousand and four **h** chariots,	3967
10:29 went out of Egypt for six **h** *shekels* of	3967
10:29 of silver, and a horse for an **h** and fifty:	3967
11: 3 he had seven **h** wives, princesses,	3967
11: 3 princesses, and three **h** concubines:	3967
12:21 **h** and fourscore thousand chosen *men*,	3967
18: 4 that Obadiah took an **h** prophets,	3967
18:13 how I hid an **h** men of the LORD'S	3967
18:19 the prophets of Baal four **h** and fifty,	3967
18:19 and the prophets of the groves four **h**,	3967
18:22 Baal's prophets *are* four **h** and fifty men.	3967
20:15 and they were **two h** and thirty two:	3967
20:29 Syrians an **h** thousand footmen in one	3967
22: 6 about four **h** men, and said unto them,	3967
2Ki 3: 4 rendered unto the king of Israel an **h**	3967
3: 4 and an **h** thousand rams, *with* the wool.	3967
3:26 he took with him seven **h** men that drew	3967
4:43 What, should I set this before an **h** men?	3967
14:13 unto the corner gate, four **h** cubits.	3967
18:14 king of Judah three **h** talents of silver	3967
19:35 smote in the camp of the Assyrians an **h**	3967
23:33 put the land to a tribute of an **h** talents of	3967
1Ch 4:42 Simeon, five **h** men, went to mount Seir,	3967

1Ch 5:18 four and forty thousand seven **h** and	3967
5:21 *of* sheep **two h** and fifty thousand,	3967
5:21 thousand, and *of* men an **h** thousand.	3967
7: 2 two and twenty thousand and six **h**.	3967
7: 9 valour, *was* twenty thousand and **two h**.	3967
7:11 **two h** *soldiers, fit* to go out *for* war	3967
8:40 many sons, and sons' sons, an **h** and fifty.	3967
9: 6 and their brethren, six **h** and ninety.	3967
9: 9 generations, nine **h** and fifty and six.	3967
9:13 a thousand and seven **h** and threescore;	3967
9:22 to be porters in the gates *were* **two h**	3967
11:11 he lift up his spear against three **h** slain	3967
11:20 for lifting up his spear against three **h**,	3967
12:14 one of the least *was* over an **h**,	3967
12:24 and spear *were* six thousand and eight **h**,	3967
12:25 for the war, seven thousand and one **h**.	3967
12:26 children of Levi four thousand and six **h**.	3967
12:27 him *were* three thousand and seven **h**;	3967
12:30 of Ephraim twenty thousand and eight **h**,	3967
12:32 the heads of them *were* **two h**; and all	3967
12:35 war twenty and eight thousand and six **h**.	3967
12:37 for the battle, an **h** and twenty thousand.	3967
15: 5 chief, and his brethren an **h** and twenty:	3967
15: 6 and his brethren **two h** and twenty:	3967
15: 7 chief, and his brethren an **h** and thirty:	3967
15: 8 the chief, and his brethren **two h**:	3967
15:10 chief, and his brethren an **h** and twelve.	3967
18: 4 but reserved of them an **h** chariots.	3967
21: 3 The LORD make his people an **h** times so	3967
21: 5 and an **h** thousand men that drew sword:	3967
21: 5 Judah *was* four **h** threescore and	3967
21:25 David gave to Ornan for the place six **h**	3967
22:14 the LORD an **h** thousand talents *of* gold,	3967
25: 7 was four **h** fourscore and eight.	3967
26:30 men of valour, a thousand and seven **h**,	3967
26:32 two thousand and seven **h** chief fathers,	3967
29: 7 and **one h** thousand talents *of* iron.	3967
2Ch 1:14 he had a thousand and four **h** chariots,	3967
1:17 Egypt a chariot for six **h** *shekels* of silver,	3967
1:17 of silver, and a horse for an **h** and fifty:	3967
2: 2 three thousand and an **h** to oversee them.	3967
2:17 they were found an **h** and fifty thousand	3967
2:17 thousand and three thousand and six **h**.	3967
2:18 six **h** overseers to set the people a work.	3967
3: 4 and the height *was* an **h** and twenty:	3967
3: 8 with fine gold, *amounting* to six **h** talents.	3967
3:16 made an **h** pomegranates, and put *them*	3967
4: 8 the left. And he made an **h** basons of gold.	3967
4:13 four **h** pomegranates on the two wreaths;	3967
5:12 with them an **h** and twenty priests	3967
7: 5 and an **h** and twenty thousand sheep:	3967
8:10 *even* **two h** and fifty, that bare rule over	3967
8:18 thence four **h** and fifty talents of gold,	3967
9: 9 gave the king an **h** and twenty talents of	3967
9:13 came to Solomon in one year was six **h**	3967
9:15 Solomon made **two h** targets *of* beaten	3967
9:15 six **h** *shekels* of beaten gold went to one	3967
9:16 three **h** shields *made he of* beaten gold:	3967
9:16 three **h** *shekels* of gold went to one shield.	3967
11: 1 the house of Judah and Benjamin an **h**	3967
12: 3 With **twelve h** chariots, 505+3967+2050.1	
13: 3 war, *even* four **h** thousand chosen men,	3967
13: 3 him with eight **h** thousand chosen men,	3967
13:17 there fell down slain of Israel five **h**	3967
14: 8 spears, out of Judah three **h** thousand;	3967
14: 8 bows, **two h** and fourscore thousand:	3967
14: 9 thousand thousand, and three **h** chariots;	3967
15:11 seven **h** oxen and seven thousand sheep.	3967
17:11 seven thousand and seven **h** rams,	3967
17:11 seven thousand and seven **h** he goats.	3967
17:14 with him mighty *men* of valour three **h**	3967
17:15 with him two **h** and fourscore thousand.	3967
17:16 with him **two h** thousand mighty *men* of	3967
17:17 with bow and shield **two h** thousand.	3967
17:18 with him an **h** and fourscore thousand	3967
18: 5 gathered together *of* prophets four **h** men,	3967
24:15 an **h** and thirty years old *was he* when he	3967
25: 5 them three **h** thousand choice *men*,	3967
25: 6 He hired also an **h** thousand mighty *men*	3967
25: 6 out of Israel for an **h** talents of silver.	3967
25: 9 what *shall* we do for the **h** talents which	3967
25:23 Ephraim to the corner gate, four **h** cubits.	3967
26:12 of valour *were* two thousand and six **h**.	3967
26:13 three **h** thousand and seven thousand and	3967
26:13 and seven thousand and five **h**,	3967
27: 5 him the same year an **h** talents of silver,	3967
28: 6 the son of Remaliah slew in Judah an **h**	3967
28: 8 captive of their brethren **two h** thousand,	3967
29:32 an **h** rams, *and* two hundred lambs:	3967
29:32 an hundred rams, *and* **two h** lambs:	3967
29:33 the consecrated *things* were six **h** oxen	3967
35: 8 six **h** *small cattle*, and three hundred	3967
35: 8 hundred *small cattle*, and three **h** oxen.	3967
35: 9 thousand *small cattle*, and five **h** oxen.	3967
36: 3 the land in an **h** talents of silver.	3967
Ezr 1:10 silver basons of a second sort four **h** and	3967
1:11 of silver *were* five thousand and four **h**.	3967
2: 3 two thousand an **h** seventy and two.	3967
2: 4 of Shephatiah, three **h** seventy and two.	3967
2: 5 of Arah, seven **h** seventy and five.	3967
2: 6 Joab, two thousand eight **h** and twelve.	3967
2: 7 of Elam, a thousand **two h** fifty and four.	3967
2: 8 children of Zattu, nine **h** forty and five.	3967
2: 9 of Zaccai, seven **h** and threescore.	3967
2:10 The children of Bani, six **h** forty and two.	3967

Ezr	2:11 children of Bebai, six **h** twenty and three.	3967
	2:12 a thousand **two h** twenty and two.	3967
	2:13 children of Adonikam, six **h** sixty and six.	3967
	2:15 The children of Adin, four **h** fifty and four.	3967
	2:17 of Bezai, three **h** twenty and three.	3967
	2:18 The children of Jorah, an **h** and twelve.	3967
	2:19 of Hashum, **two h** twenty and three.	3967
	2:21 of Beth-lehem, an **h** twenty and three.	3967
	2:23 men of Anathoth, an **h** twenty and eight.	3967
	2:25 and Beeroth, seven **h** and forty and three.	3967
	2:26 Ramah and Gaba, six **h** twenty and one.	3967
	2:27 men of Michmas, an **h** twenty and two.	3967
	2:28 Beth-el and Ai, **two h** twenty and three.	3967
	2:30 children of Magbish, an **h** fifty and six.	3967
	2:31 a thousand **two h** fifty and four.	3967
	2:32 children of Harim, three **h** and twenty.	3967
	2:33 Hadid, and Ono, seven **h** twenty and five.	3967
	2:34 children of Jericho, three **h** forty and five.	3967
	2:35 three thousand and six **h** and thirty.	3967
	2:36 house of Jeshua, nine **h** seventy and three.	3967
	2:38 a thousand **h** forty and seven.	3967
	2:41 of Asaph, an **h** twenty and eight.	3967
	2:42 of Shobai, *in* all an **h** thirty and nine.	3967
	2:58 *were* three **h** ninety and two.	3967
	2:60 children of Nekoda, six **h** fifty and two.	3967
	2:64 *and* two thousand three **h** *and* threescore,	3967
	2:65 whom *there were* seven thousand three **h**	3967
	2:65 among them **two h** singing *men*	3967
	2:66 Their horses *were* seven **h** thirty and six;	3967
	2:66 and six; their mules, **two h** forty and five;	3967
	2:67 Their camels, four **h** thirty and five;	3967
	2:67 six thousand seven **h** and twenty.	3967
	2:69 of silver, and **one h** priests' garments.	3967
	6:17 of this house of God an **h** bullocks,	3969
	6:17 **two h** rams, four hundred lambs;	3969
	6:17 two hundred rams, four **h** lambs;	3969
	7:22 Unto an **h** talents *of* silver, and to an	3969
	7:22 to an **h** measures *of* wheat, and to an	3969
	7:22 to an **h** baths *of* wine, and to an hundred	3969
	7:22 to an **h** baths *of* oil, and salt without	3969
	8: 3 reckoned by genealogy of the males an **h**	3967
	8: 4 of Zerahiah, and with him **two h** males.	3967
	8: 5 of Jahaziel, and with him three **h** males.	3967
	8: 9 and with him **two h** and eighteen males.	3967
	8:10 and with him an **h** and threescore males.	3967
	8:12 and with him an **h** and ten males.	3967
	8:20 the Levites, **two h** and twenty Nethinims:	3967
	8:26 I even weighed unto their hand six **h** and	3967
	8:26 silver vessels an **h** talents, *and of* gold an	3967
	8:26 hundred talents, *and of* gold an **h** talents;	3967
Ne	5:17 Moreover *there were* at my table an **h**	3967
	7: 8 two thousand an **h** seventy and two.	3967
	7: 9 of Shephatiah, three **h** seventy and two.	3967
	7:10 The children of Arah, six **h** fifty and two.	3967
	7:11 two thousand and eight **h** *and* eighteen.	3967
	7:12 of Elam, a thousand **two h** fifty and four.	3967
	7:13 children of Zattu, eight **h** forty and five.	3967
	7:14 of Zaccai, seven **h** and threescore.	3967
	7:15 children of Binnui, six **h** forty and eight.	3967
	7:16 children of Bebai, six **h** twenty and eight.	3967
	7:17 two thousand three **h** twenty and two.	3967
	7:18 of Adonikam, six **h** threescore and seven.	3967
	7:20 The children of Adin, six **h** fifty and five.	3967
	7:22 of Hashum, three **h** twenty and eight.	3967
	7:23 of Bezai, three **h** twenty and four.	3967
	7:24 The children of Hariph, an **h** *and* twelve.	3967
	7:26 of Netophah, an **h** fourscore and eight.	3967
	7:27 men of Anathoth, an **h** twenty and eight.	3967
	7:29 and Beeroth, seven **h** forty and three.	3967
	7:30 Ramah and Geba, six **h** twenty and one.	3967
	7:31 of Michmas, an **h** and twenty and two.	3967
	7:32 of Beth-el and Ai, an **h** twenty and three.	3967
	7:34 a thousand **two h** fifty and four.	3967
	7:35 children of Harim, three **h** and twenty.	3967
	7:36 children of Jericho, three **h** forty and five.	3967
	7:37 Hadid, and Ono, seven **h** twenty and one.	3967
	7:38 Senaah, three thousand nine **h** and thirty.	3967
	7:39 of Jeshua, nine **h** seventy and three.	3967
	7:41 a thousand **two h** forty and seven.	3967
	7:44 children of Asaph, an **h** forty and eight.	3967
	7:45 children of Shobai, an **h** thirty and eight.	3967
	7:60 *were* three **h** ninety and two.	3967
	7:62 children of Nekoda, six **h** forty and two.	3967
	7:66 two thousand three **h** and threescore,	3967
	7:67 *there were* seven thousand three **h**	3967
	7:67 had **two h** forty and five singing *men*	3967
	7:68 Their horses, seven **h** thirty and six:	3967
	7:68 six: their mules, **two h** forty and five:	3967
	7:69 *Their* camels, four **h** thirty and five:	3967
	7:69 six thousand seven **h** and twenty asses.	3967
	7:70 five **h** and thirty priests' garments.	3967
	7:71 two thousand and **two h** pound *of* silver.	3967
	11: 6 dwelt at Jerusalem *were* four **h** threescore	3967
	11: 8 Sallai, nine **h** twenty and eight.	3967
	11:12 work of the house were eight **h** twenty	3967
	11:13 chief of the fathers, **two h** forty and two:	3967
	11:14 *men* of valour, an **h** twenty and eight:	3967
	11:18 the Levites in the holy city *were* **two h**	3967
	11:19 the gates, *were* an **h** seventy and two.	3967
Est	1: 1 an **h** and seven and twenty provinces	3967
	1: 4 many days, *even* an **h** and fourscore days.	3967
	8: 9 an **h** twenty and seven provinces,	3967
	9: 6 the Jews slew and destroyed five **h** men.	3967
	9:12 destroyed five **h** men in Shushan	3967
	9:15 and slew three **h** men at Shushan;	3967

Est	9:30 to the **h** twenty and seven provinces of	3967
Job	1: 3 five yoke of oxen, and five hundred she	3967
	1: 3 five **h** she asses, and a very great	3967
	42:16 After this lived Job an **h** and forty years,	3967
Ecc	6: 3 If a man beget an **h** *children*, and live	3967
	8:12 Though a sinner do evil an **h** *times*, and	3967
SS	8:12 those that keep the fruit thereof **two h**.	3967
Isa	37:36 smote in the camp of the Assyrians an **h**	3967
	65:20 for the child shall die an **h** years old;	3967
	65:20 the sinner *being* an **h** years old shall be	3967
Jer	52:23 the network *were* an **h** round about.	3967
	52:29 captive from Jerusalem eight **h** thirty	3967
	52:30 away captive of the Jews seven **h** forty	3967
	52:30 persons *were* four thousand and six **h**.	3967
Eze	4: 5 of the days, three **h** and ninety days:	3967
	4: 9 three **h** and ninety days shalt thou eat	3967
	40:19 an **h** cubits eastward and northward.	3967
	40:23 measured from gate to gate an **h** cubits.	3967
	40:27 gate to gate toward the south an **h** cubits.	3967
	40:47 an **h** cubits long, and an hundred cubits	3967
	40:47 and an **h** cubits broad, foursquare;	3967
	41:13 he measured the house, an **h** cubits long;	3967
	41:13 with the walls thereof, an **h** cubits long;	3967
	41:14 place toward the east, an **h** cubits.	3967
	41:15 side and on the other side, an **h** cubits,	3967
	42: 2 Before the length of an **h** cubits *was*	3967
	42: 8 lo, before the temple *were* an **h** cubits.	3967
	42:16 five **h** reeds, with the measuring reed	3967
	42:17 He measured the north side, five **h** reeds,	3967
	42:18 five **h** reeds, with the measuring reed.	3967
	42:19 measured five **h** reeds with the measuring	3967
	42:20 five **h** *reeds* long, and five hundred broad,	3967
	42:20 five hundred *reeds* long, and five **h** broad,	3967
	45: 2 **h** in length, with five hundred in breadth,	3967
	45: 2 five **h** in breadth, square round about;	3967
	45:15 one lamb out of the flock, out of **two h**,	3967
	48:16 the north side four thousand and five **h**,	3967
	48:16 the south side four thousand and five **h**,	3967
	48:16 on the east side four thousand and five **h**,	3967
	48:16 the west side four thousand and five **h**.	3967
	48:17 the city shall be toward the north **two h**,	3967
	48:17 toward the south **two h** and fifty,	3967
	48:17 toward the east **two h** and fifty,	3967
	48:17 fifty, and toward the west **two h** and fifty.	3967
	48:30 four thousand and five **h** measures.	3967
	48:32 at the east side four thousand and five **h**:	3967
	48:33 side four thousand and five **h** measures:	3967
	48:34 *At* the west side four thousand and five **h**,	3967
Da	6: 1 Darius to set over the kingdom an **h**	3969
	8:14 Unto two thousand and three **h** days;	3967
	12:11 *there* shall be a thousand **two h** and	3967
	12:12 cometh to the thousand three **h** and five	3967
Am	5: 3 went out *by* a thousand shall leave an **h**,	3967
	5: 3 that which went forth *by* an **h** shall leave	3967
Mt	18:12 if a man have an **h** sheep, and one of	1540
	18:28 which ought him an **h** pence:	1540
Mk	4: 8 thirty, and some sixty, and some an **h**.	1540
	4:20 thirty*fold*, some sixty, and some an **h**.	1540
	6:37 go and buy **two h** pennyworth of bread,	1250
	14: 5 been sold for more than **three h** pence,	5145
Lk	7:41 one ought **five h** pence, and the other	4001
	15: 4 What man of you, having an **h** sheep, if he	1540
	16: 6 And he said, An **h** measures of oil. And he	1540
	16: 7 And he said, An **h** measures of wheat.	1540
Jn	6: 7 **Two h** pennyworth of bread is not	1250
	12: 5 was not this ointment sold for **three h**	5145
	19:39 and aloes, about an **h** pound *weight*.	1540
	21: 8 from land, but as it were **two h** cubits,)	1250
	21:11 of great fishes, an **h** and fifty *and* three:	1250
Ac	1:15 of names together were about an **h**	1540
	5:36 of men, about **four h**, joined themselves:	5071
	7: 6 and entreat *them* evil **four h** years.	5071
	13:20 *them* judges about *the space of* **four h**	5071
	23:23 Make ready **two h** soldiers to go to	1250
	23:23 *and* ten, and spearmen **two h**,	1250
	27:37 And we were in all in the ship **two h**	1250
Ro	4:19 when he was about an **h** year old,	1541
1Co	15: 6 he was seen of above **five h** brethren at	4001
Gal	3:17 which was **four h** and thirty years after,	5071
Rev	7: 4 *there were* sealed an **h** *and* forty *and*	1540
	9:16 were **two h thousand thousand**:	1417+3461
	11: 3 shall prophesy a thousand **two h** *and*	1250
	12: 6 should feed her there a thousand **two h**	1250
	13:18 his number *is* **Six h threescore** *and* **six**.	5516
	14: 1 with him an **h** forty *and* four thousand,	1540
	14: 3 but the **h** *and* forty *and* four thousand,	1540
	14:20 space of a thousand *and* **six h** furlongs.	1812
	21:17 thereof, an **h** *and* forty *and* four cubits,	1540

HUNDREDFOLD (7) [HUNDRED]

Ge	26:12 received in the same year an **h**:	3967+8180
2Sa	24: 3 an **h**, and *that* the eyes of my lord	3967+6471
Mt	13: 8 some an **h**, some sixty*fold*, some	1540
	13:23 some an **h**, some sixty, some thirty.	1540
	19:29 shall receive an **h**, and shall inherit	1542
Mk	10:30 he shall receive an **h** now in this time,	1542
Lk	8: 8 and sprang up, and bare fruit an **h**.	1542

HUNDREDS (28) [HUNDRED]

Ex	18:21 *and* rulers of **h**, rulers of fifties,	3967
	18:25 rulers of **h**, rulers of fifties, and rulers of	3967
Nu	31:14 captains over **h**, which came from	3967
	31:48 and captains of **h**, came near unto Moses:	3967
	31:52 of thousands, and of the captains of **h**,	3967

Nu	31:54 of the captains of thousands and of **h**,	3967
Dt	1:15 captains over **h**, and captains over fifties,	3967
1Sa	22: 7 captains of thousands, and captains of **h**;	3967
	29: 2 the lords of the Philistines passed on by **h**,	3967
2Sa	18: 1 captains of thousands and captains of **h** over them.	3967
	18: 4 all the people came out by **h** and	3967
2Ki	11: 4 Jehoiada sent and fet the rulers over **h**,	3967
	11:10 to the captains over **h** did the priest give	3967
	11:15 priest commanded the captains of the **h**,	3967
	11:19 took the rulers over **h**, and the captains,	3967
1Ch	13: 1 with the captains of thousands and **h**,	3967
	26:26 the captains over thousands and **h**,	3967
	27: 1 and captains over thousands and **h**,	3967
	28: 1 captains over the **h**, and the stewards	3967
	29: 6 and the captains of thousands and of **h**,	3967
2Ch	1: 2 to the captains of thousands and of **h**,	3967
	23: 1 took the captains of **h**, Azariah the son of	3967
	23: 9 delivered to the captains of **h** spears,	3967
	23:14 captains of **h** that were set over the host,	3967
	23:20 he took the captains of **h**, and the nobles,	3967
	25: 5 over thousands, and captains over **h**,	3967
Mk	6:40 sat down in ranks, by **h**, and by fifties.	1540

HUNDREDTH (3) [HUNDRED]

Ge	7:11 In the six **h** year of Noah's life,	3967
	8:13 it came to pass in the six **h** and first year,	3967
Ne	5:11 also the **h** *part* of the money, and *of*	3967

HUNGER (24) [HUNGER-BITTEN, HUNGERED, HUNGRED, HUNGRY]

Ex	16: 3 to kill this whole assembly with **h**.	7458
Dt	8: 3 **suffered** thee to **h**, and fed thee with	7456
	28:48 in **h**, and in thirst, and in nakedness,	7458
	32:24 *They shall be* burnt with **h**,	7458
Ne	9:15 them bread from heaven for their **h**,	7458
Ps	34:10 The young lions do lack, and **suffer h**:	7456
Pr	19:15 sleep; and an idle soul shall **suffer h**.	7456
Isa	49:10 They shall not **h** nor thirst; neither shall	7456
Jer	38: 9 he is like to die for **h** in the place where	7456
	42:14 of the trumpet, nor have **h** of bread;	7456
La	2:19 that faint for **h** in the top of every street.	7458
	4: 9 are better than *they that be* slain with **h**:	7458
Eze	34:29 they shall be no more consumed with **h** in	7458
Mt	5: 6 Blessed *are* they which do **h** and thirst	3983
Lk	6:21 Blessed *are* ye that **h** now: for ye shall be	3983
	6:25 Woe unto you that laugh	3983
	15:17 and to spare, and I perish with **h**?	3042
Jn	6:35 he that cometh to me shall never **h**;	3983
Ro	12:20 Therefore if thine enemy **h**, feed him; if he	3983
1Co	11:34 Even unto this present hour we both **h**,	3983
2Co	11:27 in **h** and thirst, in fastings often, in cold	3042
Rev	6: 8 and with **h**, and with death, and with	3042
	7:16 They shall **h** no more, neither thirst any	3983

HUNGER-BITTEN (1) [BITE, HUNGER]

Job	18:12 His strength shall be **h**,	7457

HUNGERED (2) [HUNGER]

Mt	21:18 as he returned into the city, he **h**.	3983
Lk	4: 2 when they were ended, he afterward **h**.	3983

HUNGRED (9) [HUNGER]

Mt	4: 2 and forty nights, he was afterward a **h**.	3983
	12: 1 and his disciples were a **h**, and began to	3983
	12: 3 when he was a **h**, and they that were	3983
	25:35 I was a **h**, and ye gave me meat: I was	3983
	25:37 when saw we thee a **h**, and fed *thee?* or	3983
	25:42 For I was a **h**, and ye gave me no meat:	3983
	25:44 when saw we thee a **h**, or athirst,	3983
Mk	2:25 and was a **h**, he, and they *that were* with	3983
Lk	6: 3 when himself was a **h**, and they which	3983

HUNGRY (30) [HUNGER]

1Sa	2: 5 for bread; and *they that were* **h** ceased:	7457
2Sa	17:29 The people *is* **h**, and weary, and thirsty,	7457
2Ki	7:12 They know that we *be* **h**; therefore are	7457
Job	5: 5 Whose harvest the **h** eateth up, and taketh	7457
	22: 7 thou hast withholden bread from the **h**,	7457
	24:10 and they take away the sheaf *from* the **h**;	7457
Ps	50:12 If I were **h**, I would not tell thee:	7456
	107: 5 **H** and thirsty, their soul fainted in them.	7457
	107: 9 and filleth the **h** soul *with* goodness.	7457
	107:36 there he maketh the **h** to dwell, that they	7457
	146: 7 which giveth food to the **h**. The LORD	7457
Pr	6:30 if he steal to satisfy his soul when he is **h**;	7456
	25:21 If thine enemy *be* **h**, give him bread to	7457
	27: 7 *to* the **h** soul every bitter *thing* is sweet.	7457
Isa	8:21 pass through it, hardly bestead and **h**:	7457
	8:21 come to pass, that when they shall be **h**,	7457
	9:20 shall snatch on the right hand, and be **h**;	7457
	29: 8 shall even be as when a **h** *man* dreameth,	7457
	32: 6 to make empty the soul of the **h**,	7457
	44:12 yea, he is **h**, and his strength faileth:	7457
	58: 7 *Is it not* to deal thy bread to the **h**,	7457
	58:10 *if* thou draw out thy soul to the **h**,	7456
	65:13 my servants shall eat, but ye shall be **h**;	7456
Eze	18: 7 hath given his bread to the **h**,	7457
	18:16 *but* hath given his bread to the **h**,	7457
Mk	11:12 they were come from Bethany, he was **h**:	3983
Lk	1:53 He hath filled the **h** with good *things*;	3983
Ac	10:10 And he became very **h**, and would have	4361
1Co	11:21 and one is **h**, and another is drunken.	3983
Php	4:12 am instructed both to be full and to be **h**,	3983

HUNT (12) [HUNTED, HUNTER, HUNTERS, HUNTEST, HUNTETH, HUNTING]

Ge	27: 5 Esau went to the field to **h** for venison,	6679
1Sa	26:20 as when *one* doth **h** a partridge in	7291
Job	38:39 Wilt thou **h** the prey for the lion? or fill	6679
Ps	140:11 evil shall **h** the violent man to overthrow	6679
Pr	6:26 the adulteress will **h** *for* the precious life.	6679
Jer	16:16 they shall **h** them from every mountain,	6679
La	4:18 They **h** our steps, that *we* cannot go in	6679
Eze	13:18 upon the head of every stature to **h** souls!	6679
	13:18 Will ye **h** the souls of my people,	6679
	13:20 where*with* ye there **h** the souls to make	6679
	13:20 *even* the souls that ye **h** to make *them* fly.	6679
Mic	7: 2 they **h** every man his brother *with* a net.	6679

HUNTED (1) [HUNT]

Eze	13:21 shall be no more in your hand to be **h**;	4686

HUNTER (4) [HUNT]

Ge	10: 9 He was a mighty **h** before the LORD:	6718
	10: 9 *Even* as Nimrod the mighty **h** before	6718
	25:27 Esau was a cunning **h**, a man of	376+6718
Pr	6: 5 thyself as a roe from the hand of the **h**,	NIH

HUNTERS (1) [HUNT]

Jer	16:16 after will I send for many **h**, and they shall	6719

HUNTEST (2) [HUNT]

1Sa	24:11 against thee; yet thou **h** my soul to take it.	6658
Job	10:16 Thou **h** me as a fierce lion: and again thou	6679

HUNTETH (1) [HUNT]

Lev	17:13 which **h** and catcheth *any* beast or fowl	6679

HUNTING (2) [HUNT]

Ge	27:30 that Esau his brother came in from his **h**.	6718
Pr	12:27 roasteth not that which he **took in h**:	6718

HUPHAM (1) [HUPHAMITES]

Nu	26:39 of **H**, the family of the Huphamites.	2349

HUPHAMITES (1) [HUPHAM]

Nu	26:39 of Hupham, the family of the **H**.	2350

HUPPAH (1)

1Ch	24:13 The thirteenth to **H**, the fourteenth to	2647

HUPPIM (3)

Ge	46:21 Ehi, and Rosh, Muppim, and **H**, and Ard.	2650
1Ch	7:12 Shuppim also, and **H**, the children of Ir,	2650
	7:15 Machir took to wife *the sister* of **H** and	2650

HUR (16)

Ex	17:10 and **H** went up *to* the top of the hill.	2354
	17:12 Aaron and **H** stayed up his hands, the one	2354
	24:14 behold, Aaron and **H** *are* with you: if any	2354
	31: 2 of Uri, the son of **H**, of the tribe of Judah;	2354
	35:30 of Uri, the son of **H**, of the tribe of Judah;	2354
	38:22 of Uri, the son of **H**, of the tribe of Judah,	2354
Nu	31: 8 and Rekem, and Zur, and **H**, and Reba,	2354
Jos	13:21 and Rekem, and Zur, and **H**, and Reba,	2354
1Ki	4: 8 The son of **H**, in mount Ephraim:	2354
1Ch	2:19 unto him Ephrath, which bare him **H**.	2354
	2:20 And **H** begat Uri, and Uri begat Bezaleel.	2354
	2:50 were the sons of Caleb the son of **H**,	2354
	4: 1 Hezron, and Carmi, and **H**, and Shobal.	2354
	4: 4 These *are* the sons of **H**, the firstborn of	2354
2Ch	1: 5 the son of Uri, the son of **H**, had made,	2354
Ne	3: 9 them repaired Rephaiah the son of **H**,	2354

HURAI (1)

1Ch	11:32 **H** of the brooks of Gaash, Abiel	2360

HURAM (12)

1Ch	8: 5 And Gera, and Shephuphan, and **H**.	2361
2Ch	2: 3 Solomon sent to **H** the king of Tyre,	2361
	2:11 the king of Tyre answered in writing,	2361
	2:12 **H** said moreover, Blessed *be* the LORD	2361
	2:13 with understanding, of **H** my father's,	2361
	4:11 **H** made the pots, and the shovels,	2361
	4:11 **H** finished the work that he was to make	2361
	4:16 **H** his father make to king Solomon for	2361
	8: 2 That the cities which **H** had restored to	2361
	8:18 **H** sent him by the hands of his servants	2361
	9:10 the servants also of **H**, and the servants of	2361
	9:21 went *to* Tarshish with the servants of **H**:	2361

HURI (1)

1Ch	5:14 *are* the children of Abihail the son of **H**,	2359

HURL (1) [HURLETH, HURLING]

Nu	35:20 or **h** at him by laying of wait, that he die;	7993

HURLETH (1) [HURL]

Job	27:21 and **as a storm h** him out of his place.	8175

HURLING (1) [HURL]

1Ch	12: 2 the right hand and the left in **h** stones and	NIH

HURRIED See STRAIGHTWAY

HURT (63) [HURTFUL, HURTING]

Ge	4:23 my wounding, and a young man to my **h**.	2250
	26:29 That thou wilt do us no **h**, as we have not	7451
	31: 7 but God suffered him not to **h** me.	7489
	31:29 It is in the power of my hand to do you **h**:	7451
Ex	21:22 **h** a woman with child, so that her fruit	5062
	21:35 if one man's ox **h** another's, that he die;	5062
	22:10 it die, or be **h**, or driven away, no man	7665
	22:14 be **h**, or die, the owner thereof *being* not	7665
Nu	16:15 from them, neither have I **h** one of them.	7489
Jos	24:20 he will turn and **do** you **h**,	7489
1Sa	20:21 for *there* is peace to thee, and no **h**;	1697
	24: 9 Behold, David seeketh thy **h**?	7451
	25: 7 we were not, we **h** them not,	3637
	25:15 we were not **h**, neither missed we any	3637
2Sa	18:32 all that rise against thee to do *thee* **h**,	7451
2Ki	14:10 for why shouldest thou meddle to thy **h**,	7451
2Ch	25:19 why shouldest thou meddle to thine **h**,	7451
Ezr	4:22 why should damage grow to the **h**	5142
Est	9: 2 to lay hand on such as sought their **h**:	7451
Job	35: 8 Thy wickedness *may* **h** a man as thou *art*;	NIH
Ps	15: 4 *He that* sweareth to *his own* **h**,	7489
	35: 4 brought to confusion that devise my **h**.	7451
	35:26 confusion together that rejoice at mine **h**:	7451
	38:12 they that seek my **h** speak mischievous	7451
	41: 7 against me do they devise my **h**.	7451
	70: 2 and put to confusion, that desire my **h**.	7451
	71:13 and dishonour that seek my **h**.	7451
	71:24 are brought unto shame, that seek my **h**.	7451
	105:18 Whose feet they **h** with fetters: he was	6031
Ecc	5:13 kept for the owners thereof to their **h**.	7451
	8: 9 man ruleth over another to his own **h**.	7451
	10: 9 Whoso removeth stones shall be **h**	6087
Isa	11: 9 They shall not **h** nor destroy in all my	7489
	27: 3 lest *any* **h** it, I will keep it night and day.	6485
	65:25 They shall not **h** nor destroy in all my holy	7489
Jer	6:14 have healed also the **h** of *the daughter*	7667
	7: 6 neither walk after other gods to your **h**:	7451
	8:11 they have healed the **h** of the daughter	7667
	8:21 the **h** of the daughter of my people am I	7665
	8:21 hurt of the daughter of my people am I,	7665
	10:19 Woe is me for my **h**! my wound *is*	7667
	24: 9 all the kingdoms of the earth for *their* **h**,	7451
	25: 6 of your hands; and I will do you no **h**.	7489
	25: 7 The works of your hands to your own **h**.	7451
	38: 4 not the welfare of this people, but the **h**.	7451
Da	3:25 the midst of the fire, and they have no **h**;	2257
	6:22 lions' mouths, that they have not **h** me:	2255
	6:22 before thee, O king, have I done no **h**.	2248
	6:23 no manner of **h** was found upon him,	2257
Mk	16:18 they drink any deadly *thing*, it shall not **h**	984
Lk	4:35 he came out of him, and **h** him not.	984
	10:19 and nothing shall by any means **h** you.	91
Ac	18:10 and no *man* shall set on thee to **h** thee:	2559
	27:10 I perceive that *this* voyage will be with **h**	5196
Rev	2:11 He that overcometh shall not be **h** of	91
	6: 6 and *see* thou **h** not the oil and the wine.	91
	7: 2 to whom it was given to **h** the earth and	91
	7: 3 Saying, **H** not the earth, neither the sea,	91
	9: 4 they should not **h** the grass of the earth,	91
	9:10 their power *was* to **h** men five months.	91
	9:19 and had heads, and with them they do **h**.	91
	11: 5 if any *man* will **h** them, fire proceedeth	91
	11: 5 if any *man* will **h** them, he must in this	91

HURTFUL (3) [HURT]

Ezr	4:15 **h** unto kings and provinces, and that they	5142
Ps	144:10 David his servant from the **h** sword.	7451
1Ti	6: 9 a snare, and *into* many foolish and **h** lusts,	983

HURTING (1) [HURT]

1Sa	25:34 which hath kept me back from **h** thee,	7489

HUSBAND (120) [HUSBAND'S, HUSBANDMAN, HUSBANDMEN, HUSBANDRY, HUSBANDS]

Ge	3: 6 did eat, and gave also unto her **h** with her;	376
	3: 6 desire *shall be* to thy **h**, and he shall rule	376
	16: 3 gave her to her **h** Abram to be his wife.	376
	29:32 now therefore my **h** will love me.	376
	29:34 *this* time will my **h** be joined unto me,	376
	30:15 a small matter that thou hast taken my **h**?	376
	30:18 because I have given my maiden to my **h**:	376
	30:20 now will my **h** dwell with me, because	376
Ex	4:25 said, Surely a bloody **h** *art* thou to me.	2860
	4:26 A bloody **h** *thou art*, because of	2860
	21:22 according as the woman's **h** will lay upon	1167
Lev	19:20 betrothed to a **h**, and not at all redeemed,	376
	21: 3 is nigh unto him, which hath had no **h**;	376
	21: 7 they take a woman put away from her **h**:	376
Nu	5:13 be hid from the eyes of her **h**, and be kept	376
	5:19 uncleanness *with another* instead of thy **h**,	376
	5:20 hast gone aside *to another* instead of thy **h**,	376
	5:20 man hath lain with thee beside thine **h**:	376
	5:27 and have done trespass against her **h**,	376
	5:29 goeth aside *to another* instead of her **h**,	376
	30: 6 And if she had a **h**, when she vowed,	376
	30: 7 her **h** heard *it*, and held his peace at her in	376
	30: 8 if her **h** disallow her on the day that he	376
	30:11 her **h** heard *it*, and held his peace at her,	376
	30:12 if her **h** hath utterly made them void on	376
	30:12 her **h** hath made them void; and the LORD	376
	30:13 her **h** may establish it, or her husband may	376
	30:13 may establish it, or her **h** may make it void.	376
	30:14 if her **h** altogether hold his peace at her	376
Dt	21:13 and be her **h**, and she shall be thy wife.	1166
	22:22 found lying with a woman married to a **h**,	1167
	22:23 *that is* a virgin be betrothed unto a **h**,	376
	24: 3 *if* the latter **h** hate her, and write her a bill	376
	24: 3 if the latter **h** die, which took her *to* his	376
	24: 4 Her former **h**, which sent her away,	1167
Dt	25:11 **h** out of the hand of him that smiteth him,	376
	28:56 her eye shall be evil towards the **h** of her	376
Jdg	13: 6 the woman came and told her **h**, saying,	376
	13: 9 but Manoah her **h** *was* not with her.	376
	13:10 ran, and shewed her **h**, and said unto him,	376
	14:15 they said unto Samson's wife, Entice thy **h**,	376
	19: 3 her **h** arose, and went after her, to speak	376
	20: 4 the **h** of the woman that was slain,	376
Ru	1: 3 Elimelech Naomi's **h** died; and she was left,	376
	1: 5 woman was left of her two sons and her **h**.	376
	1: 9 find rest, each of you in the house of her **h**.	376
	1:12 go *your* way; for I am too old to have a **h**.	376
	1:12 *if* I should have a **h** also to night,	376
	2:11 mother in law since the death of thine **h**:	376
1Sa	1: 8 said Elkanah her **h** to her, Hannah,	376
	1:22 she said unto her **h**, I *will not go up* until	376
	1:23 Elkanah her **h** said unto her, Do what	376
	2:19 when she came up with her **h** to offer	376
	4:19 that her father in law and her **h** were dead,	376
	4:21 and because of her father in law and her **h**.	376
	25:19 after you. But she told not her **h** Nabal.	376
2Sa	3:15 Ish-bosheth sent, and took her from *her* **h**,	376
	3:16 her **h** went with her along weeping behind	376
	11:26 of Uriah heard that Uriah her **h** was dead,	376
	11:26 was dead, she mourned for her **h**.	1167
	14: 5 a widow woman, and mine **h** is dead.	376
	14: 7 shall not leave to my **h** *neither* name nor	376
2Ki	4: 1 saying, Thy servant my **h** is dead;	376
	4: 9 said unto her **h**, Behold now, I perceive	376
	4:14 Verily she hath no child, and her **h** is old.	376
	4:22 she called unto her **h**, and said, Send me,	376
	4:26 *is it* well with thy **h**? *is it* well with	376
Pr	12: 4 A virtuous woman *is* a crown to her **h**:	1167
	31:11 The heart of her **h** doth *safely* trust in her,	1167
	31:23 her **h** is known in the gates, when he	1167
	31:28 blessed; her **h** *also*, and he praiseth her.	1167
Isa	54: 5 For thy Maker *is* thine **h**; the LORD is	1166
Jer	3:20 a wife treacherously departeth from her **h**,	7453
	6:11 even the **h** with the wife shall be taken,	376
	31:32 although I was a **h** unto them, saith	1166
Eze	16:32 *which* taketh strangers instead of her **h**.	376
	16:45 that lotheth her **h** and her children;	376
	44:25 brother, or for sister that hath had no **h**,	376
Hos	2: 2 for she *is* not my wife, neither *am* I her **h**:	376
	2: 7 she say, I will go and return to my first **h**;	1167
Joel	1: 8 with sackcloth for the **h** of her youth.	1167
Mt	1:16 And Jacob begat Joseph the **h** of Mary,	435
	1:19 Then Joseph her **h**, being a just *man*, and	435
Mk	10:12 And if a woman shall put away her **h**,	435
Lk	2:36 had lived with an **h** seven years from her	435
	16:18 put away from *her* **h** committeth adultery.	435
Jn	4:16 unto her, Go, call thy **h**, and come hither.	435
	4:17 woman answered and said, I have no **h**.	435
	4:17 Thou hast well said, I have no **h**:	435
	4:18 and he whom thou now hast is not thy **h**:	435
Ac	5: 9 the feet of them which have buried thy **h**	435
	5:10 and, carrying *her* forth, buried *her* by her **h**.	435
Ro	7: 2 the woman which hath a **h** is bound by	5220
	7: 2 a husband is bound by the law to *her* **h**	435
	7: 2 but if the **h** be dead, she is loosed from	435
	7: 3 dead, she is loosed from the law of the **h**.	435
	7: 3 then if, while *her* **h** liveth, she be married	435
	7: 3 but if *her* **h** be dead, she is free from *that*	435
	7: 2 and let every woman have her own **h**.	435
1Co	7: 3 Let the **h** render unto the wife due	435
	7: 3 and likewise also the wife unto the **h**.	435
	7: 4 not power of her own body, but the **h**:	435
	7: 4 likewise also the **h** hath not power of his	435
	7:10 Lord, Let not the wife depart from *her* **h**:	435
	7:11 unmarried, or be reconciled to *her* **h**:	435
	7:11 and let not the **h** put away his wife.	435
	7:13 And the woman which hath a **h** that	435
	7:14 For the unbelieving **h** is sanctified by	435
	7:14 the unbelieving wife is sanctified by the **h**:	435
	7:16 O wife, whether thou shalt save *thy* **h**?	435
	7:34 of the world, how she may please *her* **h**.	435
	7:39 wife is bound by the law as long as her **h**	435
	7:39 but if her **h** be dead, she is at liberty to be	435
2Co	11: 2 I have espoused you to one **h**, that *I* may	435
Gal	4:27 moe children than she which hath a **h**.	435
Eph	5:23 For the **h** is the head of the wife, even as	435
	5:33 and the wife *see* that she reverence *her* **h**.	435
1Ti	3: 2 the **h** of one wife, vigilant, sober, of good	435
Tit	1: 6 If any be blameless, the **h** of one wife,	435
Rev	21: 2 prepared as a bride adorned for her **h**.	435

HUSBAND'S (6) [HUSBAND]

Nu	30:10 if she vowed *in* her **h** house, or bound her	376
Dt	25: 5 her **h** brother shall go in unto her,	2993
	25: 5 **perform the duty of a h brother** unto	2992
	25: 7 My **h** brother refuseth to raise up unto	2993
	25: 7 not **perform the duty of** my **h** brother.	2992
Ru	2: 1 Naomi had a kinsman of her **h**, a mighty	376

HUSBANDMAN (7) [HUSBAND, MAN]

Ge	9:20 Noah began *to be* a **h**,	127+376+1886.1
Jer	51:23 with thee will I break in pieces the **h** and	406
Am	5:16 they shall call the **h** to mourning,	406
Zec	13: 5 I *am* no prophet, I *am* a **h**;	120+376+5647
Jn	15: 1 I am the true vine, and my Father is the **h**.	1092
2Ti	2: 6 The **h** that laboureth must be first partaker	1092
Jas	5: 7 the **h** waiteth for the precious fruit of	1092

HUSBANDMEN (21) [HUSBAND, MAN]

2Ki	25:12 poor of the land to be vinedressers and **h**.	3009

H

2Ch 26:10 *h also*, and vinedressers in the mountains, 406
Jer 31:24 **h**, and they *that* go forth with flocks. 406
 52:16 poor of the land for vinedressers and for **h**. 3009
Joel 1:11 Be ye ashamed, O ye **h**; howl, O ye 406
Mt 21:33 and let it out to **h**, and went into a far 1092
 21:34 he sent his servants to the **h**, that *they* 1092
 21:35 And the **h** took his servants, and beat one, 1092
 21:38 But when the **h** saw the son, they said, 1092
 21:40 what will he do unto those **h**? 1092
 21:41 and will let out *his* vineyard unto other **h**, 1092
Mk 12: 1 and let it out to **h**, and went into a far 1092
 12: 2 at the season he sent to the **h** a servant, 1092
 12: 2 he might receive from the **h** of the fruit 1092
 12: 7 those **h** said amongst themselves, This 1092
 12: 9 he will come and destroy the **h**, 1092
Lk 20: 9 and let it forth to **h**, and went into a far 1092
 20:10 at the season he sent a servant to the **h**, 1092
 20:10 but the **h** beat him, and sent *him* away 1092
 20:14 But when the **h** saw him, they reasoned 1092
 20:16 He shall come and destroy these **h**, 1092

HUSBANDRY (2) [HUSBAND]

2Ch 26:10 and in Carmel: for he loved **h**. 127
1Co 3: 9 ye are God's **h**, *ye are* God's building. 1091

HUSBANDS (19) [HUSBAND]

Ru 1:11 in my womb, that they may be your **h**? 376
 1:13 would ye stay for them from having **h**? 376
Est 1:17 *they* shall despise their **h** in their eyes, 1167
 1:20 all the wives shall give to their **h** honour, 1167
Jer 29: 6 give your daughters to **h**, that they may 376
Eze 16:45 which lothed their **h** and their children: 376
Jn 4:18 thou hast had five **h**; and he whom thou 435
1Co 14:35 any *thing*, let them ask their **h** at home: 435
Eph 5:22 submit yourselves unto your own **h**, 435
 5:24 *let* the wives *be* to their own **h** in every 435
 5:25 love your wives, even as Christ also 435
Col 3:18 submit yourselves unto your own **h**, 435
 3:19 love *your* wives, and be not bitter 435
1Ti 3:12 Let the deacons be the **h** of one wife, 435
Tit 2: 4 **love** their **h**, to love their children, 1510+5362
 2: 5 at home, good, obedient to their own **h**, 435
1Pe 3: 1 ye wives, *be* in subjection to your own **h**; 435
 3: 5 being in subjection unto their own **h**: 435
 3: 7 Likewise, ye **h**, dwell with *them* according 435

HUSHAH (1)

1Ch 4: 4 father of Gedor, and Ezer the father of **H**. 2364

HUSHAI (14)

2Sa 15:32 **H** the Archite *came* to meet him with his 2365
 15:37 So **H** David's friend came *into* the city, 2365
 16:16 when **H** the Archite, David's friend, 2365
 16:16 that **H** said unto Absalom, God save 2365
 16:17 Absalom said to **H**, *Is* this thy kindness to 2365
 16:18 **H** said unto Absalom, Nay; but whom 2365
 17: 5 Call now **H** the Archite also, and let us 2365
 17: 6 when **H** was come to Absalom, 2365
 17: 7 **H** said unto Absalom, The counsel that 2365
 17: 8 For, (said **H**,) thou knowest thy father 2365
 17:14 The counsel of **H** the Archite *is* better 2365
 17:15 said **H** unto Zadok and to Abiathar 2365
1Ki 4:16 Baanah the son of **H** *was* in Asher and 2365
1Ch 27:33 **H** the Archite *was* the king's companion. 2365

HUSHAM (4)

Ge 36:34 **H** of the land of Temani reigned in his 2367
 36:35 **H** died, and Hadad the son of Bedad, 2367
1Ch 1:45 of the land of the Temanites reigned in 2367
 1:46 **H** was dead, Hadad the son of Bedad, 2367

HUSHATHITE (5)

2Sa 21:18 Sibbechai the **H** slew Saph, which *was of* 2843
 23:27 the Anethothite, Mebunnai the **H**, 2843
1Ch 11:29 Sibbecai the **H**, Ilai the Ahohite, 2843
 20: 4 which time Sibbechai the **H** slew Sippai, 2843
 27:11 for the eighth month *was* Sibbecai the **H**, 2843

HUSHIM (4)

Ge 46:23 And the sons of Dan; **H**. 2366
1Ch 7:12 children of Ir, *and* **H**, the sons of Aher. 2366
 8: 8 them away; **H** and Baara *were* his wives. 2366
 8:11 And of **H** he begat Abitub, and Elpaal. 2366

HUSK (2) [HUSKS]

Nu 6: 4 vine tree, from the kernels even to the **h**. 2085
2Ki 4:42 and full ears of corn in the **h** thereof. 6861

HUSKS (1) [HUSK]

Lk 15:16 belly with the **h** that the swine did eat: 2769

HUZ (1)

Ge 22:21 **H** his firstborn, and Buz his brother, 5780

HUZZAB (1)

Na 2: 7 **H** shall be led away captive, she shall be 5324

HYMENEUS (2)

1Ti 1:20 Of whom is **H** and Alexander; whom I 5211
2Ti 2:17 a canker: of whom is **H** and Philetus; 5211

HYMN (2) [HYMNS]

Mt 26:30 when they had **sung a h**, they went out 5214
Mk 14:26 when they had **sung a h**, they went out 5214

HYMNS (2) [HYMN]

Eph 5:19 in psalms and **h** and spiritual songs, 5215
Col 3:16 in psalms and **h** and spiritual songs, 5215

HYPOCRISIES (1) [HYPOCRISY]

1Pe 2: 1 and **h**, and envies, and all evil speakings, 5272

HYPOCRISY (6) [HYPOCRISIES, HYPOCRITE, HYPOCRITE'S, HYPOCRITES, HYPOCRITICAL]

Isa 32: 6 to practise **h**, and to utter error against 2612
Mt 23:28 but within ye are full of **h** and iniquity. 5272
Mk 12:15 But he, knowing their **h**, said unto them, 5272
Lk 12: 1 of the leaven of the Pharisees, which is **h**. 5272
1Ti 4: 2 Speaking lies in **h**, having their conscience 5272
Jas 3:17 without partiality, and **without h**. 505

HYPOCRITE (10) [HYPOCRISY]

Job 13:16 for a **h** shall not come before him. 2611
 17: 8 shall stir up himself against the **h**. 2611
 20: 5 and the joy of the **h** *but* for a moment? 2611
 27: 8 For what *is* the hope of the **h**, though he 2611
 34:30 That the **h** reign not, lest the people 120+2611
Pr 11: 9 A **h** with *his* mouth destroyeth his 2611
Isa 9:17 for every one *is* a **h** and an evildoer, 2611
Mt 7: 5 *Thou* **h**, first cast out the beam out of 5273
Lk 6:42 *Thou* **h**, cast out first the beam out of 5273
 13:15 then answered him, and said, *Thou* **h**, 5273

HYPOCRITE'S (1) [HYPOCRITE]

Job 8:13 forget God; and the **h** hope shall perish. 2611

HYPOCRITES (20) [HYPOCRISY]

Job 15:34 the congregation of **h** *shall be* desolate, 2611
 36:13 the **h** in heart heap up wrath: they cry 2611
Isa 33:14 afraid; fearfulness hath surprised the **h**. 2611
Mt 6: 2 as the **h** do in the synagogues and in 5273
 6: 5 shalt not be as the **h** *are*: for they love 5273
 6:16 be not as the **h**, of a sad countenance: 5273
 15: 7 *Ye* **h**, well did Esaias prophesy of you, 5273
 16: 3 ye **h**, ye can discern the face of the sky; 5273
 22:18 and said, Why tempt ye me, *ye* **h**? 5273
 23:13 woe unto you, scribes and Pharisees, **h**! 5273
 23:14 Woe unto you, scribes and Pharisees, **h**! 5273
 23:15 Woe unto you, scribes and Pharisees, **h**! 5273
 23:23 Woe unto you, scribes and Pharisees, **h**! 5273
 23:25 Woe unto you, scribes and Pharisees, **h**! 5273
 23:27 Woe unto you, scribes and Pharisees, **h**! 5273
 23:29 Woe unto you, scribes and Pharisees, **h**! 5273
 24:51 and appoint *him* his portion with the **h** 5273
Mk 7: 6 Well hath Esaias prophesied of you **h**, as 5273
Lk 11:44 Woe unto you, scribes and Pharisees, **h**! 5273
 12:56 *Ye* **h**, ye can discern the face of the sky 5273

HYPOCRITICAL (2) [HYPOCRISY]

Ps 35:16 With **h** mockers in feasts, *they* gnashed 2611
Isa 10: 6 I will send him against a **h** nation, 2611

HYSSOP (12)

Ex 12:22 ye shall take a bunch of **h**, and dip *it* in 231
Lev 14: 4 clean, and cedar wood, and scarlet, and **h**: 231
 14: 6 **h**, and shall dip them and the living bird 231
 14:49 and cedar wood, and scarlet, and **h**: 231
 14:51 the **h**, and the scarlet, and the living bird, 231
 14:52 and with the **h**, and with the scarlet: 231
Nu 19: 6 and scarlet, and cast *it* into the midst of 231
 19:18 a clean person shall take **h**, and dip *it* in 231
1Ki 4:33 unto the **h** that springeth out of the wall: 231
Ps 51: 7 Purge me with **h**, and I shall be clean: 231
Jn 19:29 put *it* upon **h**, and put *it* to his mouth. 5301
Heb 9:19 and **h**, and sprinkled both the book, 5301

I

I (8851) [ME, MINE, MY, MYSELF] See Index of Articles, Etc.

IBEX See PYGARG

IBHAR (3)

2Sa 5:15 **I** also, and Elishua, and Nepheg, 2984
1Ch 3: 6 **I** also, and Elishama, and Eliphelet, 2984
 14: 5 And **I**, and Elishua, and Elpalet, 2984

IBLEAM (3)

Jos 17:11 **I** and her towns, and the inhabitants of 2991
Jdg 1:27 nor the inhabitants of **I** and her towns, 2991
2Ki 9:27 *so* at the going up to Gur, which *is* by **I**. 2991

IBNEIAH (1)

1Ch 9: 8 **I** the son of Jeroham, and Elah the son of 2997

IBNIJAH (1)

1Ch 9: 8 **I** the son of Reuel, the son of **I**; 2998

IBRI (1)

1Ch 24:27 Beno, and Shoham, and Zaccur, and **I**. 5681

IBSAM See JIBSAM

IBZAN (2)

Jdg 12: 8 after him **I** of Beth-lehem judged Israel. 78
 12:10 Then died **I**, and was buried at Beth-lehem. 78

ICE (3)

Job 6:16 Which are blackish by reason of the **i**, 7140
 38:29 Out of whose womb came the **i**? 7140
Ps 147:17 He casteth forth his **i** like morsels: who 7140

ICHABOD (1) [ICHABOD'S]

1Sa 4:21 she named the child **I**, saying, The glory is 350

ICHABOD'S (1) [ICHABOD]

1Sa 14: 3 Ahiah, the son of Ahitub, **I** brother, the son 350

ICONIUM (6)

Ac 13:51 their feet against them, and came unto **I**. 2430
 14: 1 And it came to pass in **I**, that they went 2430
 14:19 thither *certain* Jews from Antioch and **I**, 2430
 14:21 *again* to Lystra, and to **I**, and Antioch, 2430
 16: 2 by the brethren that were at Lystra and **I**. 2430
2Ti 3:11 came unto me at Antioch, at **I**, at Lystra, 2430

IDALAH (1)

Jos 19:15 and Shimron, and **I**, and Beth-lehem: 3030

IDBASH (1)

1Ch 4: 3 father of Etam; Jezreel, and Ishma, and **I**: 3031

IDDO (14)

1Ki 4:14 Ahinadab the son of **I** *had* Mahanaim. 5714
1Ch 6:21 Joah his son, **I** his son, Zerah his son, 5714
 27:21 in Gilead, **I** the son of Zechariah: 3035
2Ch 9:29 in the visions of **I** the seer against 3260
 12:15 and of **I** the seer concerning genealogies? 5714
 13:22 *are* written in the story of the prophet **I**. 5714
Ezr 5: 1 the prophet, and Zechariah the son of **I**, 5714
 6:14 the prophet and Zechariah the son of **I**. 5714
 8:17 I sent them with commandment unto **I** 112
 8:17 I told them what they should say unto **I** 112
Ne 12: 4 **I**, Ginnetho, Abijah, 5714
 12:16 **I**, Zechariah; of Ginnethon, Meshullam; 5714
Zec 1: 1 the son of **I** the prophet, saying, 5714
 1: 7 the son of **I** the prophet, saying, 5714

IDEA See WIST

IDLE (11) [IDLENESS]

Ex 5: 8 for they *be* **i**; therefore they cry, saying, 7503
 5:17 he said, Ye *are* **i**, ye *are* idle: therefore 7503
 5:17 he said, Ye *are* idle, ye *are* **i**: therefore 7503
Pr 19:15 and an **i** soul shall suffer hunger. 7423
Mt 12:36 That every **i** word that men shall speak, 692
 20: 3 saw others standing **i** in the marketplace, 692
 20: 6 found others standing **i**, and saith unto 692
 20: 6 them, Why stand ye here all the day **i**? 692
Lk 24:11 their words seemed to them as **i tales**, 3026
1Ti 5:13 And withal they learn to be **i**, 692
 5:13 and not only **i**, but tattlers also and 692

IDLENESS (3) [IDLE]

Pr 31:27 household, and eateth not the bread of **i**. 6104
Ecc 10:18 through **i** of the hands the house droppeth 8220
Eze 16:49 abundance of **i** was in her and in her 8252

IDOL (15) [IDOL'S, IDOLATER, IDOLATERS, IDOLATRIES, IDOLATROUS, IDOLATRY, IDOLS]

1Ki 15:13 because she had made an **i** in a grove; 4656
 15:13 Asa destroyed her **i**, and burnt *it* by 4656
2Ch 15:16 because she had made an **i** in a grove: 4656
 15:16 Asa cut down her **i**, and stamped *it*, and 4656
 33: 7 the **i** which he had made, in the house of 5566
 33:15 the **i** out of the house of the LORD, 5566
Isa 48: 5 Mine **i** hath done them, and my graven 6090
 66: 3 that burneth incense, *as if* he blessed an **i**. 205
Jer 22:28 *Is* this man Coniah a despised broken **i**? 6089
Zec 11:17 to the **i** shepherd that leaveth the flock! 457
Ac 7:41 and offered sacrifice unto the **i**, 1497
1Co 8: 4 we know that an **i** *is* nothing in the world, 1497
 8: 7 for some with conscience of the **i** unto this 1497
 8: 7 eat *it* as a **thing offered unto an i**; 1494
 10:19 that the **i** is any *thing*, or that which is 1497

IDOL'S (1) [IDOL]

1Co 8:10 knowledge sit at meat in the **i** temple, 1493

IDOLATER (2) [IDOL]

1Co 5:11 or an **i**, or a railer, or a drunkard, 1496
Eph 5: 5 person, nor covetous man who is an **i**, 1496

IDOLATERS (5) [IDOL]

1Co 5:10 the covetous, or extortioners, or with **i**; 1496
 6: 9 nor **i**, nor adulterers, nor effeminate, 1496
 10: 7 Neither be ye **i**, as *were* some of them; 1496
Rev 21: 8 and whoremongers, and sorcerers, and **i**, 1496
 22:15 and **i**, and whosoever loveth and maketh 1496

IDOLATRIES (1) [IDOL]

1Pe 4: 3 revellings, banquetings, and abominable **i**: 1495

IDOLATROUS (1) [IDOL]

2Ki 23: 5 put down the **i priests**, whom the kings 3649

IDOLATRY (5) [IDOL]

1Sa 15:23 and stubbornness *is as* iniquity and **i**. 8655

Ac 17:16 he saw the city **wholly given to** i. 1510+2712
1Co 10:14 Wherefore, my dearly beloved, flee from i. 1495
Gal 5:20 I, witchcraft, hatred, variance, emulations, 1495
Col 3: 5 and covetousness, which is i: 1495

IDOLS (101) [IDOL]
Lev 19: 4 Turn ye not unto i, nor make to yourselves 457
26: 1 Ye shall make you no i nor graven image, 457
26:30 your carcases upon the carcases of your i, 1544
Dt 29:17 their i, wood and stone, silver and gold, 1544
1Sa 31: 9 to publish *it in* the house of their i, 6091
1Ki 15:12 all the i that his fathers had made. 1544
21:26 he did very abominably in following i, 1544
2Ki 17:12 For they served i, whereof the LORD had 1544
21:11 hath made Judah also to sin with his i: 1544
21:21 and served the i that his father served, 1544
23:24 the i, and all the abominations that were 1544
1Ch 10: 9 to carry tidings unto their i, and to 6091
16:26 For all the gods of the people *are* i: 457
2Ch 15: 8 put away the **abominable** i out of all 8251
24:18 of their fathers, and served groves and i, 6091
34: 7 cut down all the i throughout all the land 2553
Ps 96: 5 For all the gods of the nations *are* i: 457
97: 7 graven images, that boast themselves of i: 457
106:36 they served their i: which were a snare 6091
106:38 they sacrificed unto the i of Canaan: 6091
115: 4 Their i *are* silver and gold, the work of 6091
135:15 The i of the heathen *are* silver and gold, 6091
Isa 2: 8 Their land also is full *of* i; they worship 457
2:18 And the i he shall utterly abolish. 457
2:20 In that day a man shall cast his i of silver, 457
2:20 cast his idols of silver, and his i of gold, 457
10:10 my hand hath found the kingdoms of the i, 457
10:11 as I have done unto Samaria and her i? 457
10:11 her idols, so do to Jerusalem and her i? 6091
19: 1 the i of Egypt shall be moved at his 457
19: 3 shall seek to the i, and to the charmers, 457
31: 7 every man shall cast away his i of silver, 457
31: 7 his i of gold, which your own hands have 457
45:16 confusion together *that are* makers of i. 6736
46: 1 their i were upon the beasts, and upon 6091
57: 5 Inflaming yourselves with i under every 410
Jer 50: 2 her i are confounded, her images are 6091
50:38 and they are mad upon *their* i. 367
Eze 6: 4 cast down your slain *men* before your i. 1544
6: 5 of the children of Israel before their i; 1544
6: 6 your i may be broken and cease, 1544
6: 9 eyes, which go a whoring after their i: 1544
6:13 their slain *men* shall be among their i 1544
6:13 they did offer sweet savour to all their i. 1544
8:10 and all the i of the house of Israel, 1544
14: 3 men have set up their i in their heart, 1544
14: 4 of Israel that setteth up his i in his heart, 1544
14: 4 according to the multitude of his i; 1544
14: 5 are all estranged from me through their i. 1544
14: 6 Repent, and turn *yourselves* from your i; 1544
14: 7 setteth up his i in his heart, and putteth 1544
16:36 with all the i of thy abominations, 1544
18: 6 neither hath lift up his eyes to the i of 1544
18:12 pledge, and hath lift up his eyes to the i, 1544
18:15 neither hath lift up his eyes to the i of 1544
20: 7 defile not yourselves with the i of Egypt: 1544
20: 8 neither did they forsake the i of Egypt: 1544
20:16 for their heart went after their i. 1544
20:18 nor defile yourselves with their i: 1544
20:24 and their eyes were after their fathers' i. 1544
20:31 ye pollute yourselves with all your i, 1544
20:39 serve ye every one his i, and hereafter 1544
20:39 no more with your gifts, and with your i. 1544
22: 3 maketh i against herself to defile *herself.* 1544
22: 4 hast defiled *thyself* in thine i which thou 1544
23: 7 with all their i she defiled herself. 1544
23:30 *and* because thou art polluted with their i. 1544
23:37 with their i have they committed adultery, 1544
23:39 they had slain their children to their i, 1544
23:49 and ye shall bear the sins of your i: 1544
30:13 I will also destroy the i, and I will cause 1544
33:25 lift up your eyes toward your i, 1544
36:18 for their i *wherewith* they had polluted it: 1544
36:25 and from all your i, will I cleanse you. 1544
37:23 defile themselves any more with their i; 1544
44:10 went astray away from me after their i; 1544
44:12 they ministered unto them before their i, 1544
Hos 4:17 Ephraim *is* joined to i: let him alone. 6091
8: 4 and their gold have they made them i, 6091
13: 2 i according to their own understanding, 6091
14: 8 *say,* What have I to do any more with i? 6091
Mic 1: 7 and all the i thereof will I lay desolate: 6091
Hab 2:18 his work trusteth therein, to make dumb i? 457
Zec 10: 2 For the i have spoken vanity, 8655
13: 2 *that* I will cut off the names of the i out of 6091
Ac 15:20 that *they* abstain from pollutions of i, 1497
15:29 That *ye* abstain from **meats offered to** i, 1494
21:25 themselves from **things offered to** i, 1494
Ro 2:22 thou that abhorrest i, dost thou commit 1497
1Co 8: 1 Now as touching **things offered unto** i, 1494
8: 4 **things** that are
 offered in sacrifice unto i, 1494
8:10 eat those **things** which are **offered to** i; 1494
10:19 that which is **offered in sacrifice to** i, 1494
10:28 This is **offered in sacrifice unto** i, 1494
12: 2 carried away unto *these* dumb i, *even* as 1497
2Co 6:16 agreement hath the temple of God with i? 1497
1Th 1: 9 how ye turned to God from i to serve 1497
1Jn 5:21 Little children, keep yourselves from i. 1497

Rev 2:14 to eat **things sacrificed unto** i, 1494
2:20 and to eat **things sacrificed unto** i. 1494
9:20 should not worship devils, and i of gold, 1497

IDUMEA (5)
Isa 34: 5 It shall come down upon I, and upon 123
34: 6 and a great slaughter in the land of I. 123
Eze 35:15 O mount Seir, and all I, *even* all of it: 123
36: 5 residue of the heathen, and against all I, 123
Mk 3: 8 and from I, and *from* beyond Jordan; 2401

IEZER See JEEZER

IEZERITE See JEEZERITES

IF (1595)
Ge 4: 7 i thou doest well, *shalt thou* not be 518
4: 7 i thou doest not well, sin lieth at the door. 518
4:24 Cain shall be avenged sevenfold, 3588
8: 8 to see i the waters were abated from off 1886.2
13: 9 i *thou wilt take* the left hand, then I will go 518
13: 9 or i *thou depart to* the right hand, then I 518
13:16 i a man can number the dust of the earth, 518
15: 5 the stars, i thou be able to number them: 518
18: 3 i now I have found favour in thy sight, 518
18:21 is come unto me; and i not, I will know. 518
18:26 I I find in Sodom fifty righteous within 518
18:28 he said, I I find there forty and five, I will 518
18:30 he said, I will not do *it,* i I find thirty there. 518
20: 7 i thou restore *her* not, know thou that thou 518
23: 8 I it be your mind that I should bury my 518
23:13 saying, But i thou *wilt give it,* I pray thee, 518
24: 8 i the woman will not be willing to follow 518
24:41 i they give not thee *one,* thou shalt be clear 518
24:42 i now thou do prosper my way which I go: 518
24:49 now i ye will deal kindly and truly with my 518
24:49 i not; tell me; that I may turn to the right 518
25:22 she said, I I *it be* **so,** why *am* I thus? 518+3651
27:46 Jacob take a wife of the daughters of Heth, 518
28:20 I God will be with me, and will keep me in 518
30:27 I I have found favour in thine eyes, 518
30:31 i thou wilt do this thing for me, I will again 518
31: 8 i he said thus, The speckled shall be thy 518
31: 8 i he said thus, The ringstraked shall be thy 518
31:50 I thou shalt afflict my daughters, or if thou 518
31:50 i thou shalt take *other* wives beside my 518
32: 8 I Esau come to the one company, 518
33:10 i now I have found grace in thy sight, then 518
33:13 *men* should overdrive them one day, NIH
34:15 I ye will be as we *be,* that every male of 518
34:17 i ye will not hearken unto us, to be 518
34:22 i every male among us be circumcised, 871.1
37:26 What profit *is it* i we slay our brother, 3588
42:19 I ye be true *men,* let one of your brethren 518
42:37 Slay my two sons, i I bring him not to thee: 518
42:38 i mischief befall him by the way in 2050.1
43: 4 I thou wilt send our brother with us, we 518
43: 5 i thou wilt not send *him,* we will not go 518
43: 9 i I bring him not unto thee, and set him 518
43:11 unto them, I *it must* be so now, do this; 518
43:14 I I be bereaved of my children, 834+3509.1
44:22 for i he should leave his father, *his father* NIH
44:26 i our youngest brother be with us, then 518
44:29 **And** i ye take this also from me, 2050.1
44:32 I I bring him not unto thee, then I shall 518
47: 6 i thou knowest *any* man of activity 518
47:16 I will give you for your cattle, i money fail. 518
47:29 I now I have found grace in thy sight, put, 518
50: 4 I now I have found grace in your eyes, 518
Ex 1:16 i it *be* a son, then ye shall kill him: 518
1:16 but i it *be* a daughter, then she shall live. 518
4: 8 come to pass, i they will not believe thee, 518
4: 9 i they will not believe also these two signs, 518
4:23 i *thou* refuse to let him go, behold, I will NIH
8: 2 i thou refuse to let *them* go, behold, I will 518
8:21 Else, i thou wilt not let my people go, 518
9: 2 For i thou refuse to let *them* go, and wilt 518
10: 4 Else, i thou refuse to let my people go, 518
12: 4 i the household be too little for the lamb, 518
13:13 i thou wilt not redeem *it,* then thou shalt 518
15:26 I thou wilt diligently hearken to the voice 518
18:23 I thou shalt do this thing, and God 518
19: 5 i ye will obey my voice indeed, and keep 518
20:25 i thou wilt make me an altar of stone, 518
20:25 for i thou lift up thy tool upon it, thou hast NIH
21: 2 I thou buy a Hebrew servant, six years he 3588
21: 3 I he came in by himself, he shall go out by 518
21: 3 i he *were* married, then his wife shall go 518
21: 4 I his master have given him a wife, 518
21: 5 I the servant shall plainly say, I love my 518
21: 7 i a man sell his daughter to be a 3588
21: 8 I she please not her master, who hath 518
21: 9 I he have betrothed her unto his son, 518
21:10 I he take him another *wife;* her *food,* 518
21:11 I he do not these three unto her, then 518
21:13 i a man lie not in wait, but God deliver NIH
21:14 i a man come presumptuously upon his 3588
21:16 selleth him, *or* i he be found in his hand, NIH
21:18 i men strive together, and one smite 3588
21:19 I he rise again, and walk abroad upon his 518
21:20 i a man smite his servant, or his maid, 3588
21:21 i he continue a day or two, 518
21:22 I men strive, and hurt a woman with 518
21:23 i *any* mischief follow, then thou shalt give 518
21:26 i a man smite the eye of his servant, 3588
21:27 And i he smite out his manservant's tooth, 518

Ex 21:28 I an ox gore a man or a woman, that they 3588
21:29 i the ox *were* wont to push with his horn 518
21:30 I there be laid on him a sum of money, 518
21:32 I the ox shall push a manservant or 518
21:33 i a man shall open a pit, or if a man shall 3588
21:33 or i a man dig a pit, and not cover it, 3588
21:35 i one man's ox hurt another's, that he die; 3588
21:36 Or i it be known that the ox *hath* used to NIH
22: 1 I a man steal an ox, or a sheep, 3588
22: 2 I a thief be found breaking up, 518
22: 3 I the sun be risen upon him, *there shall be* 518
22: 3 i he have nothing, then he shall be sold for 518
22: 4 I the theft be certainly found in his hand 518
22: 5 I a man shall cause a field or vineyard to 3588
22: 6 I fire break out, and catch in thorns, 3588
22: 7 I a man shall deliver unto his neighbour 518
22: 7 i the thief be found, let him pay double. 518
22: 8 I the thief be not found, then the master of 518
22:10 I a man deliver unto his neighbour an ass, 3588
22:12 I it be stolen from him, he shall make 518
22:13 I it be torn in pieces, *then* let him bring it 518
22:14 I a man borrow *ought* of his neighbour, 3588
22:15 *But* i the owner thereof *be* with it, he shall 518
22:15 i it *be* a hired *thing,* it came for his hire. 518
22:16 I a man entice a maid that is not 3588
22:17 I her father utterly refuse to give her unto 518
22:23 I thou afflict them in any wise, and they 518
22:25 I thou lend money to *any of* my people 518
22:26 I thou at all take thy neighbour's raiment 518
23: 4 I thou meet thine enemy's ox or his ass 3588
23: 5 I thou see the ass of him that hateth thee, 518
23:22 i thou shalt indeed obey his voice, and do 518
23:33 for i thou serve their gods, it will surely be NIH
24:14 i any man have any matters to do, let him NIH
29:34 i *ought* of the flesh of the consecrations, 518
32:32 Yet now, i thou wilt forgive their sin; 518
32:32 i not, blot me, I pray thee, out of thy book 518
33:13 pray thee, i I have found grace in thy sight, 518
33:15 I thy presence go not *with me,* carry us not 518
34: 9 I now I have found grace in thy sight, 518
34:20 i thou redeem *him* not, then shalt thou 518
34:37 the cloud were not taken up, then 518
Lev 1: 2 *any* man of you bring an offering unto 3588
1: 3 I his offering *be* a burnt sacrifice of the 518
1:10 i his offering *be* of the flocks, *namely,* of 518
1:14 i the burnt sacrifice for his offering to 518
2: 4 i thou bring an oblation of a meat offering 3588
2: 5 i thy oblation *be* a meat offering *baken* in a 518
2: 7 i thy oblation *be* a meat offering *baken* in 518
2:14 i thou offer a meat offering of *thy* firstfruits 518
3: 1 i his oblation *be* a sacrifice of peace 518
3: 1 of peace offering, i he offer *it* of the herd; 518
3: 6 i his offering for a sacrifice of peace 518
3: 7 I he offer a lamb for his offering, then 518
3:12 i his offering *be* a goat, then he shall offer 518
4: 2 I a soul shall sin through ignorance against 3588
4: 3 I the priest that is anointed do sin 518
4:13 i the whole congregation of Israel sin 176
4:23 Or i his sin, wherein he hath sinned, 176
4:27 i any one of the common people sin 518
4:28 Or i his sin, which he hath sinned, come to 176
4:32 I he bring a lamb for a sin offering, he shall 518
5: 1 i a soul sin, and hear the voice of 3588
5: 1 or known *of it;* i he do not utter *it,* then 518
5: 2 Or i a soul touch any unclean thing, 834
5: 2 and *it* be hidden from him; NIH
5: 3 Or i he touch the uncleanness of man, 518
5: 4 i a soul swear, pronouncing with *his* lips 3588
5: 7 I he be not able to bring a lamb, then he 518
5:11 I he be not able to bring two turtledoves, 518
5:15 I a soul commit a trespass, and sin through 3588
5:17 I a soul sin, and commit any *of these* 518
6: 2 I a soul sin, and commit a trespass against 3588
6:28 i it be sodden in a brasen pot, it shall 518
7:12 I he offer it for a thanksgiving, then he 518
7:16 i the sacrifice of his offering *be* a vow, 518
7:18 i *any* of the flesh of the sacrifice of his 518
10:19 i I had eaten the sin offering to day, should NIH
11:37 i *any part* of their carcase fall upon any 3588
11:38 i *any* water be put upon the seed, 3588
11:39 i any beast, of which ye may eat, die; 3588
12: 2 I a woman have conceived seed, and born 3588
12: 5 i she bear a maid child, then she shall be 518
12: 8 i she be not able to bring a lamb, then 518
13: 4 I the bright spot *be* white in the skin of his 518
13: 5 *i* the plague *be* in his sight be at a stay, NIH
13: 6 *i* the plague *be* somewhat dark, NIH
13: 7 i the scab spread much abroad in the skin, 518
13: 8 i the priest see that behold, the scab NIH
13:10 i the rising *be* white in the skin, and it 518
13:12 i a leprosy break out abroad in the skin, 518
13:13 i the leprosy have covered all his flesh, 518
13:16 Or i the raw flesh turn again, 3588
13:17 behold, *i* the plague be turned into white; NIH
13:20 i, when the priest seeth it, behold, *be in* NIH
13:21 i the priest look on it, and behold, *there* NIH
13:21 *i* it *be* not lower than the skin, but *be* NIH
13:22 i it spread much abroad in the skin, then 518
13:23 i the bright spot stay in his place, 518
13:24 i there be *any* flesh, in the skin whereof 3588
13:25 *i* the hair in the bright spot be turned NIH
13:26 i the priest look on it, and behold, *there* 518
13:27 *and* i it be spread much abroad in the skin, 518
13:28 i the bright spot stay in his place, 518
13:29 I a man or woman hath a plague upon 3588

I

I

Lev	13:30	*i* it *be* in sight deeper than the skin; NIH
	13:31	the priest look on the plague of the scall, NIH
	13:32	*i* the scall spread not, and there be in it no NIH
	13:34	*i* the scall be not spread in the skin, NIH
	13:35	*i* the scall spread much in the skin after his 518
	13:36	behold, *i* the scall be spread in the skin, NIH
	13:37	*i* the scall be in his sight at a stay, 518
	13:38	I a man also or a woman have in the skin 3588
	13:39	*i* the bright spots in the skin of their flesh NIH
	13:42	*i* there be in the bald head, or bald 3588
	13:43	*i* the rising of the sore *be* white reddish in NIH
	13:49	*i* the plague be greenish or reddish in NIH
	13:51	*i* the plague be spread in the garment, 3588
	13:53	*i* the priest shall look, and behold, the 518
	13:55	*i* the plague have not changed his colour, NIH
	13:56	the priest look, and behold, the plague be 518
	13:57	I it appear still in the garment, either in 518
	13:58	*i* the plague be departed from them, then NIH
	14: 3	*i* the plague of leprosy be healed in NIH
	14:21	*i* he *be* poor, and cannot get *so much;* then 518
	14:37	*i* the plague *be* in the walls of the house NIH
	14:39	*i* the plague be spread in the walls of NIH
	14:43	*i* the plague come again, and break out in 518
	14:44	*i* the plague be spread in the house, 518
	14:48	*i* the priest shall come in, and look *upon it,* 518
	15: 8	*i* he that hath the issue spit upon him that 3588
	15:16	*i* any man's seed of copulation go out from 3588
	15:19	*i* a woman have an issue, *and* her issue in 3588
	15:23	*i* it *be* on *her* bed, or on *any* thing 518
	15:24	*i* any man lie with her at all, and her 518
	15:25	*i* a woman have an issue of her blood 3588
	15:25	*i* it run beyond the time of her separation; 3588
	15:28	*i* she be cleansed of her issue, then she 518
	17:16	he wash *them* not, nor bathe his flesh; 518
	18: 5	which *i* a man do, he shall live in them: 2050.1
	19: 5	*i* ye offer a sacrifice of peace offerings unto 3588
	19: 6	*i* ought remain until the third day, it shall NIH
	19: 7	*i* it be eaten at all on the third day, it *is* 518
	19:33	*i* a stranger sojourn with thee in your land, 3588
	20: 4	*i* the people of the land do any ways hide 518
	20:12	**And** *i* a man lie with his daughter in 2050.1
	20:13	A man **also** lie with mankind, as he 2050.1
	20:14	**And** *i* a man take a wife and her 2050.1
	20:15	**And** *i* a man lie with a beast, he shall 2050.1
	20:16	**And** *i* a woman approach unto any 2050.1
	20:17	**And** *i* a man shall take his sister, 2050.1
	20:18	**And** *i* a man shall lie with a woman 2050.1
	20:20	**And** *i* a man shall lie with his uncle's 2050.1
	20:21	**And** *i* a man shall take his brother's 2050.1
	21: 9	*i* she profane herself by playing the whore 3588
	22: 9	for it, and die therefore, *i* they profane it: 3588
	22:11	*i* the priest buy *any* soul with his money, 3588
	22:12	*i* the priest's daughter also be *married* 3588
	22:13	*i* the priest's daughter be a widow, 3588
	22:14	*i* a man eat *of* the holy *thing* unwittingly, 3588
	24:19	*i* a man cause a blemish in his neighbour; 3588
	25:14	*i* thou sell ought unto thy neighbour, 3588
	25:20	*i* ye shall say, What shall we eat 3588
	25:25	I thy brother be waxen poor, and hath 3588
	25:25	*i* any of his kin come to redeem it, then NIH
	25:26	*i* the man have none to redeem *it,* and 3588
	25:28	But *i* he be not able to restore *it* to him, 518
	25:29	*i* a man sell a dwelling house in a walled 3588
	25:30	*i* it be not redeemed within the space of a 518
	25:33	*i* a man purchase of the Levites, then 834
	25:35	*i* thy brother be waxen poor, and fallen in 3588
	25:39	*i* thy brother *that dwelleth* by thee be 3588
	25:47	*i* a sojourner or stranger wax rich by thee, 3588
	25:49	or *i* he be able, he may redeem himself. NIH
	25:51	I *there be* yet many years *behind,* 518
	25:52	*i* there remain but few years unto the year 518
	25:54	*i* he be not redeemed in these *years,* then 518
	26: 3	I ye walk in my statutes, and keep my 518
	26:14	*i* ye will not hearken unto me, and will 518
	26:15	I ye shall despise my statutes, or if your 518
	26:15	or *i* your soul abhor my judgments, 518
	26:18	*i* ye will not yet for *all* this hearken unto 518
	26:21	*i* ye walk contrary unto me, and will not 518
	26:23	*i* ye will not be reformed by me by these 518
	26:27	*i* ye will not for *all* this hearken unto me, 518
	26:40	I they shall confess their iniquity, NIH
	26:41	**i** then their uncircumcised hearts be 176+227
	27: 4	*i* it *be* a female, then thy estimation shall 518
	27: 5	*i* it *be* from five years old even unto twenty 518
	27: 6	*i* it *be* from a month old even unto five 518
	27: 7	*i* it *be* from sixty years old and above; if *it* 518
	27: 7	*i* it *be* a male, then thy estimation shall be 518
	27: 8	*i* he be poorer than thy estimation, then 518
	27: 9	*i* it *be* a beast, whereof *men* bring an 518
	27:10	*i* he shall at all change beast for beast, then 518
	27:11	*i* it *be* any unclean beast, of which they do 518
	27:13	*i* he will at all redeem it, then he shall add 518
	27:15	*i* he that sanctified *it* will redeem his house, 518
	27:16	*i* a man shall sanctify unto the Lord *some* 518
	27:17	*i* he sanctify his field from the year of jubile, 518
	27:18	*i* he sanctify his field after the jubile, then 518
	27:19	*i* he that sanctified the field will in any wise 518
	27:20	*i* he will not redeem the field, or if he have 518
	27:20	or *i* he have sold the field to another man, 518
	27:22	*i* a man sanctify unto the Lord a field 518
	27:27	*i* it *be* of an unclean beast, then he shall 518
	27:27	*i* it be not redeemed, then it shall be sold 518
	27:31	*i* a man will at all redeem *ought* of his 518
	27:33	*i* he change it at all, then both it and 518
Nu	5: 8	*i* the man have no kinsman to recompense 518

Nu	5:12	I any man's wife go aside, and commit a 3588
	5:14	or *i* the spirit of jealousy come upon him, NIH
	5:19	I no man have lain with thee, and if thou 518
	5:19	*i* thou hast not gone aside to uncleanness 518
	5:20	*i* thou hast gone aside *to another* instead 3588
	5:20	*i* thou be defiled, and *some* man hath lain 3588
	5:27	*i* she be defiled, and have done trespass 518
	5:28	*i* the woman be not defiled, but *be* clean; 518
	6: 9	*i* any man die very suddenly by him, 3588
	9:10	I any man of you or of your posterity shall 3588
	9:14	a stranger shall sojourn among you, 3588
	10: 4	*i* they blow *but* with one *trumpet,* then 518
	10: 9	*i* ye go *to* war in your land against 3588
	10:32	shall be, *i* thou go with us, yea, it shall be, 3588
	11:15	*i* thou deal thus with me, kill me, I pray 518
	11:15	of hand, *i* I have found favour in thy sight; 518
	12: 6	I there be a prophet among you, 518
	12:14	her father had but spit in her face, 2050.1
	14: 8	I the Lord delight in us, then he will 518
	14:15	Now *i* thou shalt kill *all* this people as one 518
	15:14	a stranger sojourn with you, 3588
	15:22	*i* ye have erred, and not observed all these 3588
	15:24	*i* ought be committed by ignorance without 518
	15:27	*i* any soul sin through ignorance, then 518
	16:29	I these *men* die the common death of all 518
	16:29	*i* they be visited after the visitation of all NIH
	16:30	*i* the Lord make a new thing, 518
	19:12	but *i* he purify not himself the third day, 518
	20:19	and I I and my cattle drink *of* thy water, 518
	21: 2	I thou wilt indeed deliver this people into 518
	21: 9	to pass, that *i* a serpent had bitten *any* man, 518
	22:18	I Balak would give me his house full of 518
	22:20	I The men come to call thee, rise up, 518
	22:34	now therefore, *i* it displease thee, I will get 518
	24:13	I Balak would give me his house full of 518
	27: 8	I a man die, and have no son, then ye 3588
	27: 9	I he have no daughter, then ye shall give 518
	27:10	I he have no brethren, then ye shall give 518
	27:11	I his father have no brethren, then ye shall 518
	30: 2	I a man vow a vow unto the Lord, 3588
	30: 3	I a woman also vow a vow unto 3588
	30: 5	I her father disallow her in the day that he 518
	30: 6	I she had at all a husband, when she 518
	30: 8	I her husband disallow her on the day that 518
	30:10	And I she vowed *in* her husband's house, 518
	30:12	I her husband hath utterly made them void 518
	30:14	I her husband altogether hold his peace at 518
	30:15	I he shall any ways make them void after 518
	32: 5	they, I we have found grace in thy sight, 518
	32:15	**For** I ye turn away from after him, he will 3588
	32:20	said unto them, I ye will do this thing, 518
	32:20	I ye will go armed before the Lord to war, 518
	32:23	I ye will not do so, behold, ye have sinned 518
	32:29	I The children of Gad and the children of 518
	32:30	I they will not pass over with you armed, 518
	33:55	I ye will not drive out the inhabitants of 518
	35:16	I he smite him with an instrument of iron, 518
	35:17	I he smite him with throwing a stone, 518
	35:18	Or *i* he smite him with a hand weapon of NIH
	35:20	I he thrust him of hatred, or hurl at him by 518
	35:22	I he thrust him suddenly without enmity, 518
	35:26	I the slayer shall at any time come *without* 518
	36: 3	*i* they be married to any of the sons of NIH
Dt	4:29	I from thence thou shalt seek the Lord 3588
	4:29	shalt find *him,* I thou seek him with all 3588
	4:30	I thou turn to the Lord thy God, NIH
	5:25	I we hear the voice of the Lord our God 518
	6:25	I we observe to do all these 3588
	7:12	I ye hearken to these judgments, and 6118
	7:17	I thou shalt say in thine heart, 3588
	8:19	I thou do at all forget the Lord thy God, 518
	11:13	I you shall hearken diligently unto my 518
	11:22	For I ye shall diligently keep all these 518
	11:27	I ye obey the commandments of the Lord 834
	11:28	I ye will not obey the commandments of 518
	12:21	I the place which the Lord thy God hath 3588
	13: 1	I there arise among you a prophet, 3588
	13: 6	I thy brother, the son of thy mother, 3588
	13:12	I thou shalt hear *say* in one of thy cities, 3588
	13:14	behold, *i* it *be* truth, *and* the thing certain, NIH
	14:24	I the way be too long for thee, so that 3588
	14:24	or *i* the place be too far from thee, 3588
	15: 5	I thou carefully hearken unto the voice 518
	15: 7	I there be among you a poor man of one 3588
	15:12	And *i* thy brother, a Hebrew man, 518
	15:16	shall be, *i* he say unto thee, I will not go 518
	15:21	I there be *any* blemish therein, *as if it be* 3588
	15:21	*as i* it *be* lame, or blind, *or have* any ill NIH
	17: 2	I there be found among you, within any 3588
	17: 8	I there arise a matter too hard for thee in 3588
	18: 6	I a Levite come from any of thy gates out 3588
	18:21	thou say in thine heart, How shall we 3588
	18:22	the thing follow not, nor come to pass, 2050.1
	19: 8	And *i* the Lord thy God enlarge thy coast, 518
	19: 9	I thou shalt keep all these commandments 518
	19:11	I any man hate his neighbour, and lie in 3588
	19:16	I a false witness rise up against any man to 3588
	19:18	*i* the witness *be* a false witness, NIH
	20:11	I it make thee answer of peace, 518
	20:12	I it will make no peace with thee, 518
	21: 1	I *one* be found slain in the land which 3588
	21:14	I thou have no delight in her, then thou 518
	21:15	I a man have two wives, one beloved, 3588
	21:15	*i* the firstborn son be hers that was hated: NIH
	21:18	I a man have a stubborn and rebellious 3588

Dt	21:22	*i* a man have committed a sin worthy of 3588
	22: 2	I thy brother *be* not nigh unto thee, or *if* 518
	22: 2	or *i* thou know him not, then thou shalt NIH
	22: 6	I a bird's nest chance to be before thee in 3588
	22: 8	thine house, *i* any man fall from thence. 3588
	22:13	I any man take a wife, and go in unto her, 3588
	22:20	I this thing be true, *and* the tokens of 518
	22:22	I a man be found lying with a woman 3588
	22:23	I a damsel *that is* a virgin be betrothed 3588
	22:25	I a man find a betrothed damsel in the 518
	22:28	I a man find a damsel *that is* a virgin, 3588
	23:10	I there be among you any man, that is not 3588
	23:21	I thou shalt forbear to vow, it shall be no 3588
	24: 3	*i* the latter husband hate her, and write NIH
	24: 3	*i* the latter husband die, which took her 3588
	24: 7	I a man be found stealing any of his 3588
	24:12	I the man *be* poor, thou shalt not sleep 518
	25: 1	I there be a controversy between men, 3588
	25: 2	I the wicked *man* be worthy to be beaten, 518
	25: 3	*i* he should exceed, and beat him above NIH
	25: 5	I brethren dwell together, and one of 3588
	25: 7	*i* the man like not to take his brother's 518
	25: 8	*i* he stand *to it,* and say, I like not to take NIH
	28: 1	I thou shalt hearken diligently unto the 518
	28: 2	*i* thou shalt hearken unto the voice of 3588
	28: 9	I thou shalt keep the commandments of 3588
	28:13	that thou hearken unto the 3588
	28:15	*i* thou wilt not hearken unto the voice of 518
	28:58	I thou wilt not observe to do all the words 518
	30: 4	*any* of thine be driven out unto the 518
	30:10	I thou shalt hearken unto the voice of 3588
	30:10	*i* thou turn unto the Lord thy God with 3588
	30:17	*i* thine heart turn away, so that thou wilt 518
	32:41	I I whet my glittering sword, and mine 518
Jos	2:14	for yours, *i* ye utter not this our business. 518
	2:19	*be* on our head, *i* any hand be upon him. 518
	2:20	*i* thou utter this our business, then we will 518
	8:15	Israel *made as i* they were beaten before NIH
	9: 4	**made as i** they had been **ambassadors,** 6737
	14:12	*i* **so be** the Lord *will be* with me, then 194
	17:15	I thou be a great people, *then* get thee up 518
	17:15	*i* mount Ephraim be too narrow for thee. NIH
	20: 5	I the avenger of blood pursue after him, 3588
	22:19	*i* the land of your possession *be* unclean, 518
	22:22	*i* it *be* in rebellion, or if in transgression 518
	22:22	or *i* in transgression against the Lord, 518
	22:23	or *i* to offer thereon burnt offering or 518
	22:23	or *i* to offer peace offerings thereon, 518
	22:24	*i* we have not *rather* done it for fear of *this* 518
	23:12	Else *i* ye do in any wise go back, 518
	24:15	*i* it seem evil unto you to serve the Lord, 518
	24:20	I ye forsake the Lord, and serve strange 3588
Jdg	4: 8	I thou wilt go with me, then I will go: 518
	4: 8	I thou wilt not go with me, *then* I will not 518
	6:13	the Lord be with us, why then is all 2050.1
	6:17	I now I have found grace in thy sight, then 518
	6:31	I he *be* a god, let him plead for himself, 518
	6:36	I thou wilt save Israel by mine hand, as 518
	6:37	*i* the dew be on the fleece only, and *it be* 518
	7:10	*i* thou fear to go down, go thou with 518
	8:19	I ye had saved them alive, I would not 3863
	9:15	I in truth ye anoint me king over you, *then* 518
	9:15	not, let fire come out of the bramble, 518
	9:16	I ye have done truly and sincerely, 518
	9:16	*i* ye have dealt well with Jerubbaal and his 518
	9:19	I ye then have dealt truly and sincerely 518
	9:20	I not, let fire come out from Abimelech, 518
	9:36	seest the shadow of the mountains as *i* NIH
	11: 9	I ye bring me *home* again to fight against 518
	11:10	I we do not so according to thy words. 518
	11:30	I thou shalt without fail deliver the children 518
	11:36	*i* thou hast opened thy mouth unto NIH
	12: 5	*Art* thou an Ephraimite? I he said, Nay; 2050.1
	13:16	I thou wilt offer a burnt offering, thou 518
	13:23	I the Lord were pleased to kill us, 3863
	14:12	I you can certainly declare *it* me *within* 518
	14:13	I ye cannot declare *it* me, then shall ye give 518
	14:18	I ye had not plowed with my heifer, 3884
	16: 7	I they bind me with seven green withs that 518
	16:11	I they bind me fast with new ropes that 518
	16:13	I thou weavest the seven locks of my head 518
	16:17	*i* I be shaven, then my strength will 518
	21:21	I the daughters of Shiloh come out to 518
Ru	1:12	I I should say, I have hope, *if* I should 3588
	1:12	*i* I should have a husband also to night, NIH
	1:17	*i* ought but death part thee and me. NIH
	3:13	I he will perform unto thee the part of a 518
	3:13	*i* he will not do the part of a kinsman to 518
	4: 4	I thou wilt redeem *it,* redeem *it:* but if thou 518
	4: 4	but *i* thou wilt not redeem *it, then* tell me, 518
1Sa	1:11	*i* thou wilt indeed look on the affliction of 518
	2:16	I *any* man said unto him, Let them not fail 518
	2:16	*it me* now: and *i* not, I will take *it* by force. 518
	2:25	I one man sin against another, the judge 518
	2:25	*i* a man sin against the Lord, who shall 518
	3: 9	shall be, *i* he call thee, that thou shalt say, 518
	3:17	*i* thou hide *any* thing from me of all 518
	6: 3	I ye send away the ark of the God of Israel, 518
	6: 9	*i* it goeth up *by* the way of his own coast to 518
	6: 9	I not, then we shall know that *it is* not his 518
	7: 3	I ye do return unto the Lord with all your 518
	9: 7	behold, *i* we go, what shall we bring NIH
	10:22	*i* the man should yet come thither. 1886.2
	11: 3	then, *i* there *be* no man to save us, we will 518
	12:14	I ye will fear the Lord, and serve him, 518

1Sa
12:15 i ye will not obey the voice of the LORD, 518
12:25 i ye shall still do wickedly, ye shall be 518
14: 9 i they say thus unto us, Tarry until we 518
14:10 i they say thus, Come up unto us; then 518
14:30 i haply the people had eaten freely to day 3863
16: 2 i Saul hear it, he will kill me. NIH
17: 9 i he be able to fight with me, and to kill 518
17: 9 but i I prevail against him, and kill him, 518
19:11 saying, I thou save not thy life to night, 518
20: 6 I thy father at all miss me, then say, 518
20: 7 i he say thus, It is well; thy servant shall 518
20: 7 i he be very wroth, then be sure that evil is 518
20: 8 i there be in me iniquity, slay me thyself, 518
20: 9 for i I knew certainly that evil were 518
20:10 or what i thy father answer thee roughly? NIH
20:12 i there be good toward David, and I then NIH
20:13 but i it please my father to do thee evil, 3588
20:21 I expressly say unto the lad, Behold, 518
20:22 But i I say thus unto the young man, 518
20:29 now, i I have found favour in thine eyes, 518
21: 4 i the young men have kept themselves at 518
21: 9 i thou wilt take that, take it: for there is no 518
23: 3 i we come to Keilah against the armies of 3588
23:23 it shall come to pass, i he be in the land, 518
24:19 i a man find his enemy, will he let him 3588
25:22 I leave of all that pertain to him by 518
26:19 I the LORD have stirred thee up against 518
26:19 i they be the children of men, cursed be 518
27: 5 I have now found grace in thine eyes, 518

2Sa
3:35 more also, i I taste bread, or ought else, 518
7:14 i he commit iniquity, I will chasten him 871.1
10:11 i the Syrians be too strong for me, then 518
10:11 i the children of Ammon be too strong for 518
11:20 i so be that the king's wrath arise, 518
12: 8 i that had been too little, I would moreover 518
12:18 i we tell him that the child is dead? NIH
13:26 said Absalom, I not, I pray thee, let my 2050.1
14:32 i there be any iniquity in me, let him kill 518
15: 8 i the LORD shall bring me again indeed to 518
15:25 i I shall find favour in the eyes of 518
15:26 i he thus say, I have no delight in thee; 518
15:33 i thou passest on with me, then thou shalt 518
15:34 i thou return to the city, and say unto 518
16:23 was as i a man had inquired at 834+3509.1
17: 3 the man whom thou seekest is as i all 3509.1
17: 6 we do after his saying? i not; speak thou. 518
17:13 i he be gotten into a city, then shall all 518
18: 3 for i we flee away, they will not care for us; 518
18: 3 neither i half of us die, will they care for us: 518
18:25 the king said, I he be alone, there is tidings 518
19: 6 that i Absalom had lived, and all we had 3863
19: 7 I swear by the LORD, i thou go not forth, 3588
19:13 i thou be not captain of the host before me 518

1Ki
1:52 i he will shew himself a worthy man, 518
1:52 i wickedness shall be found in him, he 518
2: 4 I thy children take heed to their way, 518
2:23 i Adonijah have not spoken this word 3588
3:14 i thou wilt walk in my ways, to keep my 518
6:12 i thou wilt walk in my statutes, 518
8:31 i any man trespass against his neighbour, 834
8:35 i they pray towards this place, NIH
8:37 i there be in the land famine, if there be 3588
8:37 i there be pestilence, blasting, mildew, 3588
8:37 i mildew, locust, or i there be caterpillar; 3588
8:37 i their enemy besiege them in the land of 3588
8:44 I thy people go out to battle against their 3588
8:46 i they sin against thee, (for there is no 518
8:47 Yet i they shall bethink themselves in 2050.1
9: 4 i thou wilt walk before me, as David thy 518
9: 6 i you shall at all turn from following me, 518
11:38 i thou wilt hearken unto all that I 518
12: 7 I thou wilt be a servant unto this people 518
12:27 I this people go up to do sacrifice in 518
13: 8 I thou wilt give me half thine house, I will 518
16:31 as i it had been a light thing for him to 1886.2
18:21 i the LORD be God, follow him: 518
18:21 i Baal, then follow him. And the people 518
19: 2 I make not thy life as the life of one of 3588
20:10 i the dust of Samaria shall suffice for 518
20:39 i by any means he be missing, then shall 518
21: 2 or, i it seem good to thee, I will give thee 518
21: 6 or else, i it please thee, I will give thee 518
22:28 Micaiah said, I thou return at all in peace, 518

2Ki
1:10 I be a man of God, then let fire come 518
1:12 and said unto them, I I be a man of God, 518
2:10 i thou see me when I am taken 518
2:10 so unto thee; but i not, it shall not be so. 518
4:29 go thy way: i thou meet any man, 3588
4:29 i any salute thee, answer him not again: 3588
5:13 i the prophet had bid thee do some great NIH
6:27 And he said, I the LORD do not help thee, 518
6:31 i the head of Elisha the son of Shaphat 518
7: 2 i the LORD would make windows in NIH
7: 4 I we say, We will enter into the city, then 518
7: 4 i we sit still here, we die also. 518
7: 4 i they save us alive, we shall live; and i 518
7: 4 live; and i they kill us, we shall but die. 518
7: 9 i we tarry till the morning light, 2050.1
7:19 i the LORD should make windows in NIH
9:15 i it be your minds, then let none go forth 518
10: 6 I ye be mine, and if ye will hearken unto 518
10: 6 and i ye will hearken unto my voice, 518
10:15 It be, give me thine hand. And he gave 2050.1
10:24 I any of the men whom I have brought NIH
18:21 even upon Egypt, on which i a man lean, NIH

2Ki
18:22 i ye say unto me, We trust in the LORD 3588
18:23 i thou be able on thy part to set riders upon 518
20:19 Is it not good, i peace and truth be in my 518
21: 8 only i they will observe to do according to 518

1Ch
12:17 i ye be come peaceably unto me to help 518
12:17 i ye be come to betray me to mine enemies, 518
13: 2 I it seem good unto you, and that it be of 518
19:12 I the Syrians be too strong for me, then 518
19:12 i the children of Ammon be too strong for 518
22:13 i thou takest heed to fulfil the statutes and 518
28: 7 i he be constant to do my commandments 518
28: 9 i thou seek him, he will be found of thee; 518
28: 9 i thou forsake him, he will cast thee off for 518

2Ch
6:22 i a man sin against his neighbour, 518
6:24 i thy people Israel be put to the worse 518
6:26 yet i they pray towards this place, NIH
6:28 i there be dearth in the land, if there be 3588
6:28 i there be pestilence, if there be blasting, 3588
6:28 i there be blasting, or mildew, locusts, NIH
6:28 i their enemies besiege them in the cities 3588
6:32 I they come and pray in this house; NIH
6:34 I thy people go out to war against their 3588
6:36 I they sin against thee, (for there is no 3588
6:37 I they bethink themselves in the land 2050.1
6:38 I they return to thee with all their heart NIH
7:13 I shut up heaven that there be no rain, 2005
7:13 i command the locusts to devour the 2005
7:13 or i I send pestilence among my people; 518
7:14 I my people, which are called by my 2050.1
7:17 as for thee, i thou wilt walk before me, 518
7:19 i ye turn away, and forsake my statutes and 518
10: 7 I thou be kind to this people, 518
15: 2 i ye seek him, he will be found of you; 518
15: 2 but i ye forsake him, he will forsake you. 518
18:27 I thou certainly return in peace, then hath 518
20: 9 I, when evil cometh upon us, as the sword, 518
25: 8 i thou wilt go, do it, be strong for the battle 518
30: 9 For i ye turn again unto the LORD, 3588
30: 9 his face from you, i ye return unto him. 518

Ezr
4:13 i this city be builded, and the walls set up 2006
4:16 i this city be builded again, and the walls 2006
5:17 Now therefore, i it seem good to the king, 2006

Ne
1: 8 saying, I ye transgress, I will scatter you NIH
1: 9 i ye turn unto me, and keep my NIH
2: 5 I it please the king, and if thy servant have 518
2: 5 i thy servant have found favour in thy sight, 518
2: 7 I said unto the king, I it please the king, 518
4: 3 Even i that which they build, i a fox go up, 518
9:29 i a man do, he shall live in them;) 2050.1
10:31 i the people of the land bring ware or NIH
13:21 i ye do so again, I will lay hands on you. 518

Est
1:19 I it please the king, let there go a royal 518
3: 9 I it please the king, let it be written that 518
4:14 i thou altogether holdest thy peace at this 518
4:16 to the law: and i I perish, I perish. 834+3509.1
5: 4 I it seem good unto the king, let the king 518
5: 8 I I have found favour in the sight of the 518
5: 8 i it please the king to grant my petition, 518
6:13 I Mordecai be of the seed of the Jews, 518
7: 3 and said, I I have found favour in thy sight, 518
7: 3 thy sight, O king, and i it please the king, 518
7: 4 i we had been sold for bondmen and 432
8: 5 I it please the king, and if I have found 518
8: 5 i I have found favour in his sight, 518
9:13 said Esther, I it please the king, let it be 518

Job
4: 2 I we assay to commune with thee, wilt NIH
5: 1 i there be any that will answer thee; 1886.2
6:28 upon me; for it is evident unto you i I lie. 518
8: 4 I thy children have sinned against him, 518
8: 5 I thou wouldest seek unto God betimes, 518
8: 6 I thou wert pure and upright; surely now 518
8:18 I he destroy him from his place, then it 518
9: 3 I he will contend with him, he cannot 518
9:13 I God will not withdraw his anger, 518
9:16 I I had called, and he had answered me; 518
9:19 I I speak of strength, lo, he is strong: 518
9:19 i of judgment, who shall set me a time to 518
9:20 I I justify myself, mine own mouth shall 518
9:20 i I say, I am perfect, it shall also prove me NIH
9:23 I the scourge slay suddenly, he will laugh 518
9:24 thereof; i not, where, and who is he? 518
9:27 I say, I will forget my complaint, I will 518
9:29 I be wicked, why then labour I in vain? NIH
9:30 I wash myself with snow water, 518
10:14 I I sin, then thou markest me, and thou 518
10:15 I be wicked, woe unto me; and if I be NIH
10:15 i I be righteous, yet will I not lift up my NIH
11:10 I he cut off, and shut up, or gather 518
11:13 I thou prepare thine heart, and stretch out 518
11:14 I iniquity be in thine hand, put it far away, 518
13:10 reprove you, i ye do secretly accept 518
13:19 now, i I hold my tongue, I shall give up NIH
14: 7 I it be cut down, that it will sprout again, 518
14:14 I a man die, shall he live again? 518
16: 4 I also could speak as ye do: i your soul 3863
17:13 I wait, the grave is mine house: I have 518
19: 5 I indeed ye will magnify yourselves against 518
21: 4 i it were so, why should not my spirit be 518
21:15 should we have, i we pray unto him? 3588
22:23 i thou return to the Almighty, thou shalt 518
24:17 i one know them, they are in the terrors 3588
24:25 i it be not so now, who will make me a liar 518
27:14 I his children be multiplied, it is for 518
29:24 I I laughed on them, they believed it not; NIH
31: 5 I I have walked with vanity, or if my foot 518

Job
31: 5 or i my foot hath hasted to deceit; NIH
31: 7 I my step hath turned out of the way, 518
31: 7 and i any blot hath cleaved to my hands; NIH
31: 9 I mine heart have been deceived by a 518
31: 9 i I have laid wait at my neighbour's door; NIH
31:13 I I did despise the cause of my manservant 518
31:16 I I have withheld the poor from their 518
31:19 I I have seen any perish for want of 518
31:20 I his loins have not blessed me, and if he 518
31:20 i he were not warmed with the fleece of NIH
31:21 I I have lift up my hand against 518
31:24 I I have made gold my hope, or have said 518
31:25 I I rejoiced because my wealth was great, 518
31:26 I beheld the sun when it shined, 518
31:29 I I rejoiced at the destruction of him that 518
31:31 I the men of my tabernacle said not, O that 518
31:33 I I covered my transgressions as Adam, 518
31:38 I my land cry against me, or that the 518
31:39 I I have eaten the fruits thereof without 518
33: 5 I thou canst, answer me, set thy words in 518
33:23 I there be a messenger with him, 518
33:27 I any say, I have sinned, and perverted NIH
33:32 I thou hast any thing to say, answer me: 518
33:33 I not, hearken unto me: hold thy peace, 518
34:14 I he set his heart upon man, if he gather 518
34:14 If he set his heart upon man, i he gather NIH
34:16 I now thou hast understanding, hear this: 518
34:32 I I have done iniquity, I will do no more. 518
35: 3 shall I have, i I be cleansed from my sin? NIH
35: 6 I thou sinnest, what doest thou against 518
35: 6 or i thy transgressions be multiplied, 518
35: 7 I thou be righteous, what givest thou him? 518
36: 8 i they be bound in fetters, and be holden in 518
36:11 I they obey and serve him, they shall spend 518
36:12 I they obey not, they shall perish by 518
37:20 i a man speak, surely he shall be 518
38: 4 I declare, i thou hast understanding. 518
38: 5 laid the measures thereof, i thou knowest? 3588
38: 8 as i it had issued out of the womb? 518
38:18 of the earth? declare i thou knowest it all. 518

Ps
7: 3 O LORD my God, i I have done this; 518
7: 3 done this; i there be iniquity in my hands; 518
7: 4 I I have rewarded evil unto him that was at 518
7:12 I he turn not, he will whet his sword; 518
11: 3 I the foundations be destroyed, what can 3588
14: 2 to see i there were any that did 1886.2
28: 1 lest, i thou be silent to me, I become like NIH
40: 5 i I would declare and speak of them, they NIH
41: 6 I he come to see me, he speaketh vanity: 518
44:20 I we have forgotten the name of our God, 518
50:12 I I were hungry, I would not tell thee: 518
53: 2 to see i there were any that did 1886.2
59:15 meat, and grudge i they be not satisfied. 518
62:10 i riches increase, set not your heart upon 3588
66:18 I I regard iniquity in my heart, the Lord 518
73:15 I I say, I will speak thus; behold, I should 518
81: 8 O Israel, i thou wilt hearken unto me; 518
89:30 I his children forsake my law, and walk 518
89:31 I they break my statutes, and keep not my 518
90:10 I by reason of strength they be fourscore 518
95: 7 of his hand. To day i ye will hear his voice, 518
124: 1 I it had not been the LORD who was on 3884
124: 2 I it had not been the LORD who was on 3884
130: 3 I thou, LORD, shouldest mark iniquities, 518
132:12 I thy children will keep my covenant and 518
137: 5 I I forget thee, O Jerusalem, let my right 518
137: 6 I I do not remember thee, let my tongue 518
137: 6 i I prefer not Jerusalem above my chief joy. 518
139: 8 I I ascend up into heaven, thou art there: 518
139: 8 i I make my bed in hell, behold, thou 2050.1
139: 9 I I take the wings of the morning, NIH
139:11 I I say, Surely the darkness shall cover 2050.1
139:18 I I should count them, they are moe in NIH
139:24 see i there be any wicked way in me, 518

Pr
1:10 My son, i sinners entice thee, consent thou 518
1:11 I they say, Come with us, let us lay wait 518
2: 1 i thou wilt receive my words, and hide my 518
2: 3 i thou criest after knowledge, and liftest up 518
2: 4 I thou seekest her as silver, and searchest 518
3:30 i he have done thee no harm. 518
6: 1 My son, i thou be surety for thy friend, 518
6: 1 i thou hast stricken thy hand with a NIH
6:30 i he steal to satisfy his soul when he is 3588
6:31 i he be found, he shall restore sevenfold; NIH
9:12 I thou be wise, thou shalt be wise for 518
9:12 i thou scornest, thou alone shalt bear it. NIH
16:31 i it be found in the way of righteousness. 518
19:19 for i thou deliver him, yet thou must do it 518
22:18 For it is a pleasant thing i thou keep them 3588
22:27 I thou hast nothing to pay, why should he 518
23: 2 throat, i thou be a man given to appetite. 518
23:13 i thou beatest him with the rod, he shall NIH
23:15 son, i thine heart be wise, my heart shall 518
24:10 I thou faint in the day of adversity, 518
24:11 I thou forbear to deliver them that are NIH
24:12 I thou sayest, Behold, we knew it not; 3588
25:21 I thine enemy be hungry, give him bread 518
25:21 i he be thirsty, give him water to drink: 518
29: 9 I a wise man contendeth with a foolish NIH
29:12 I a ruler hearken to lies, all his servants NIH
30: 4 what is his son's name, i thou canst tell? 3588
30:32 I thou hast done foolishly in lifting up 518
30:32 or i thou hast thought evil, lay thine hand 518

Ecc
4:10 i they fall, the one will lift up his fellow: 518
4:11 i two lie together, then they have heat: 518

I

Ref	Text	Strong's
Ecc	4:12 i one prevail against him, two shall	518
	5: 8 I thou seest the oppression of the poor,	518
	6: 3 I a man beget an hundred *children*, and	518
	10: 4 I the spirit of the ruler rise up against thee,	518
	10:10 I the iron be blunt, and he do not whet	518
	11: 3 I the clouds be full *of* rain, they empty	518
	11: 3 i the tree fall toward the south, or toward	518
	11: 8 i a man live many years, *and* rejoice in	518
SS	1: 8 I thou know not, O thou fairest among	518
	5: 8 I ye find my beloved, that ye tell him, that	518
	7:12 let us see i the vine flourish, *whether*	518
	8: 7 i a man would give all the substance of his	518
	8: 9 I she *be* a wall, we will build upon her a	518
	8: 9 i she *be* a door, we will inclose her with	518
Isa	1:19 I ye be willing and obedient, ye shall eat	518
	1:20 i ye refuse and rebel, ye shall be devoured	518
	5:30 i *one* look unto the land, behold darkness	NIH
	7: 9 I ye will not believe, surely ye shall not be	518
	8:20 i they speak not according to this word,	518
	10:15 **as i** the rod should shake *itself against*	3509.1
	10:15 as i the staff should lift up *itself, as if it*	NIH
	10:15 as if the staff should lift up *itself, as i* it	NIH
	21:12 i ye will inquire, inquire ye: return, come.	518
	36: 6 whereon i a man lean, it will go into his	NIH
	36: I thou say to me, We trust in the LORD	3588
	36: 8 I thou be able on thy part to set riders	518
	47:12 i **so be** thou shalt be able to profit, if so	194
	47:12 able to profit, i **so be** thou mayest prevail.	194
	51:13 **as** i he were ready to destroy?	834+3509.1
	58: 9 I am. I thou take away from the midst	518
	58:10 *i* thou draw out thy soul to the hungry,	NIH
	58:13 I thou turn away thy foot from the sabbath,	518
	59:10 blind, and we grope as i *we had* no eyes;	NIH
	66: 3 that killeth an ox *is as* i he slew a man;	NIH
	66: 3 a lamb, *as* i he cut off a dog's neck;	NIH
	66: 3 an oblation, *as* i he offered swine's blood;	NIH
	66: 3 burneth incense, *as* i he blessed an idol.	NIH
Jer	2:10 and see i there be such a *thing*.	2005
	2:28 i they can save thee in the time of thy	518
	3: 1 I a man put away his wife, and she go	2005
	4: 1 I thou wilt return, O Israel, saith	518
	4: 1 i thou wilt put away thine abominations	518
	5: 1 broad places thereof, i ye can find a man,	518
	5: 1 i there be *any* that executeth judgment,	518
	7: 5 For i ye throughly amend your ways and	518
	7: 5 i you throughly execute judgment between	518
	7: 6 I ye oppress not the stranger, the fatherless,	518
	12: 5 I thou hast run with the footmen,	3588
	12: 5 i in the land of peace, *wherein* thou	NIH
	12:16 i they will diligently learn the ways of my	518
	12:17 i they will not obey, I will utterly pluck up	518
	13:17 i ye will not hear it, my soul shall weep in	518
	13:22 i thou say in thine heart, Wherefore come	3588
	14:18 I go forth *into* the field, then behold	518
	14:18 i I enter *into* the city, then behold them	518
	15: 2 it shall come to pass, i they say unto thee,	3588
	15:19 I thou return, then will I bring thee again,	518
	15:19 i thou take forth the precious from the vile,	518
	17:24 i ye diligently hearken unto me, saith	518
	17:27 i you will not hearken unto me to hallow	518
	18: 8 I that nation, against whom I have	518
	18:10 I it do evil in my sight, that *it* obey not my	NIH
	21: 2 i **so be** that the LORD will deal with us	194
	22: 4 I ye do this thing indeed, then shall there	518
	22: 5 i ye will not hear these words, I swear by	518
	23:22 i they had stood in my counsel,	518
	25:28 i they refuse to take the cup at thine hand	3588
	26: 3 I **so be** they will hearken, and turn every	194
	26: 4 i ye will not hearken to me, to walk in my	518
	26:15 ye for certain, that i ye put me to death,	518
	27:18 i they *be* prophets, and if the word of	518
	27:18 and i the word of the LORD be with them,	518
	31:36 I those ordinances depart from before me,	518
	31:37 I heaven above can be measured,	518
	33:20 I you can break my covenant of the day,	518
	33:25 I my covenant *be* not with day and night,	518
	33:25 *i* I have not appointed the ordinances of	NIH
	38:15 unto Zedekiah, I I declare *it* unto thee,	3588
	38:15 I give counsel, wilt thou not	518
	38:17 I thou wilt assuredly go forth unto the king	518
	38:18 i thou wilt not go forth to the king of	518
	38:21 I thou refuse to go forth, this *is* the word	518
	38:25 i the princes hear that I have talked with	3588
	40: 4 I it seem good unto thee to come with me	518
	40: 4 i it seem ill unto thee to come with me	518
	42: 5 i we do not even according to all things	518
	42:10 I ye will still abide in this land, then will I	518
	42:13 i ye say, We will not dwell in this land,	518
	42:15 I ye wholly set your faces to enter *into*	518
	49: 9 I grapegatherers come to thee, would they	518
	49: 9 i thieves by night, they will destroy till they	518
	51: 8 for her pain, i **so be** she may be healed.	194
La	1:12 see i there *be* any sorrow like unto my	518
	2: 6 his tabernacle, as *i it were of* a garden:	NIH
	3:29 in the dust; i **so be** there may be hope.	194
Eze	3:19 i thou warn the wicked, and he turn not	3588
	3:21 Nevertheless i thou warn the righteous	3588
	10:10 as i a wheel had been in the midst of a	NIH
	14: 9 i the prophet be deceived when he hath	3588
	14:15 I I cause noisome beasts to pass through	3863
	14:17 i I bring a sword upon that land, and say,	NIH
	14:19 Or i I send a pestilence into that land,	NIH
	16:47 as *i that were* a very little *thing*, thou wast	NIH
	18: 5 i a man be just, and do that which is	3588
	18:10 I he beget a son *that is* a robber,	2050.1

Ref	Text	Strong's
Eze	18:14 Now lo, *i* he beget a son, that seeth all his	NIH
	18:21 i the wicked will turn from all his sins	3588
	20:11 which *i* a man do, he shall even live in	NIH
	20:13 which *i* a man do, he shall even live in	NIH
	20:21 which *i* a man do, he shall even live in	NIH
	20:39 *also*, i ye will not hearken unto me:	518
	21:13 what *i the sword* contemn even the rod?	518
	33: 2 I the people of the land take a man of their	NIH
	33: 3 I when he seeth the sword come upon	NIH
	33: 4 I the sword come, and take him away,	NIH
	33: 6 I the watchman see the sword come,	3588
	33: 6 I the sword come, and take *any* person	NIH
	33: 8 i thou dost not speak to warn the wicked	NIH
	33: 9 I thou warn the wicked of his way to turn	3588
	33: 9 i he turn not from his way, he shall die	NIH
	33:10 I our transgressions and our sins *be* upon	3588
	33:13 i he trust to his own righteousness,	NIH
	33:14 i he turn from his sin, and do that which	NIH
	33:15 I the wicked restore the pledge, give again	NIH
	33:19 i the wicked turn from his wickedness,	871.1
	43:11 i they be ashamed of all that they have	518
	46:16 I the prince give a gift unto any of his	3588
	46:17 i he give a gift of his inheritance to one of	3588
Da	2: 5 i ye will not make known unto me	2006
	2: 6 i ye shew the dream, and the	2006
	2: 9 i ye will not make known unto me	2006
	3:15 i ye be ready that at what time ye hear	2006
	3:15 *well*: but i ye worship not, ye shall be cast	2006
	3:17 I it be *so*, our God whom we serve *is* able	2006
	3:18 i not, be it known unto thee, O king,	2006
	4:27 i it may be a lengthening of thy	NIH
	5:16 now i thou canst read the writing,	2006
Hos	6: 3 *i* we follow on to know the LORD:	NIH
	8: 7 I **so be** it yield, *the* strangers shall swallow	194
Joel	2:14 Who knoweth *i* he will return and repent,	NIH
	3: 4 i ye recompense me, swiftly *and*	518
Am	3: 4 cry out of his den, i he have taken nothing?	518
	5:19 As i a man did flee from a lion,	834+3509.1
	6: 9 i there remain ten men in one house,	518
Ob	1: 5 I thieves came to thee, if robbers by night,	518
	1: 5 i robbers by night, (how art thou cut off!)	518
	1: 5 i the grape-gatherers came to thee, would	518
Jnh	1: 6 i **so be** that God will think upon us, that	194
	3: 9 Who can tell *i* God will turn and repent,	NIH
Mic	2:11 I a man walking *in* the spirit and	3863
	5: 8 who, i he go through, both treadeth down,	518
Na	3:12 i they be shaken, they shall even fall into	518
Hag	2:12 I one bear holy flesh in the skirt of his	2005
	2:13 I *one that is* unclean *by* a dead body touch	518
Zec	3: 7 I thou wilt walk in my ways, and if thou	518
	3: 7 i thou wilt keep my charge, then thou shalt	518
	6:15 i ye will diligently obey the voice of	518
	8: 6 I it be marvellous in the eyes of	3588
	11:12 I ye think good, give *me* my price;	518
	11:12 give *me* my price; and i not, forbear.	518
	14:18 i the family of Egypt go not up,	518
Mal	1: 6 I then I *be* a father, where *is* mine honour?	NIH
	1: 6 i I *be* a master, where *is* my fear? saith	518
	1: 8 i ye offer the blind for sacrifice, *is it* not	3588
	1: 8 i ye offer the lame and sick, *is it* not evil?	3588
	2: 2 I ye will not hear, and if ye will not lay *it*	518
	2: 2 not hear, and i ye will not lay *it* to heart,	518
	3:10 i I will not open you the windows of	518
Mt	4: 3 to him, he said, I thou be the Son of God,	1487
	4: 6 I thou be the Son of God, cast thyself	1487
	4: 9 i thou wilt fall down and worship me.	1437
	5:13 but i the salt have lost his savour,	1437
	5:23 Therefore i thou bring thy gift to the altar,	1437
	5:29 And i thy right eye offend thee, pluck it	1487
	5:30 And i thy right hand offend thee, cut it off,	1487
	5:40 And i any man will sue thee at the law,	NIG
	5:46 For i ye love them which love you,	1437
	5:47 i ye salute your brethren only, what do	1437
	6:14 For i ye forgive men their trespasses,	1437
	6:15 But i ye forgive not men their trespasses,	1437
	6:22 i therefore thine eye be single, thy whole	1437
	6:23 But i thine eye be evil, thy whole body	1437
	6:23 I therefore the light that is in thee be	1487
	6:30 I God so clothe the grass of the field,	1487
	7: 9 his son ask bread, will he give him	1437
	7:10 Or i he ask a fish, will he give him a	1437
	7:11 I ye then, being evil, know how to give	1487
	8: 2 worshipped him, saying, Lord, i thou wilt,	1437
	8:31 besought him, saying, I thou cast us out,	1487
	9:21 I may but touch his garment, I shall be	1437
	10:13 And i the house be worthy, let your peace	1437
	10:13 i it be **not** worthy, let your peace return	3362
	10:25 I they have called the master of the house	1487
	11:14 And i ye will receive *it*, this is Elias,	1487
	11:21 i the mighty works which were done in	1487
	11:23 for i the mighty works, which have been	1487
	12: 7 But i ye had known what *this* meaneth,	1487
	12:11 and i it fall into a pit on the sabbath day,	1437
	12:26 And i Satan cast out Satan, he is divided	1487
	12:27 And i I by Beelzebub cast out devils,	1487
	12:28 But i I cast out devils by the Spirit of God,	1487
	14:28 answered him and said, Lord, i it be thou,	1487
	15:14 And i the blind lead the blind, both shall	NIG
	16:24 I any man will come after me, let him	1536
	16:26 i he shall gain the whole world, and lose	1437
	17: 4 i thou wilt, let us make here three	1487
	17:20 I ye have faith as a grain of mustard seed,	1437
	18: 8 Wherefore i thy hand or thy foot offend	1487
	18: 9 And i thine eye offend thee, pluck it out,	1487
	18:12 i a man have an hundred sheep, and one	1437

Ref	Text	Strong's
Mt	18:13 i so be that he find it, verily I say unto	1437
	18:15 Moreover i thy brother shall trespass	1437
	18:15 i he shall hear thee, thou hast gained thy	1437
	18:16 i he will not *hear thee, then* take with	1437
	18:17 And i he shall neglect to hear them, tell *it*	1437
	18:17 i he neglect to hear the church, let him	1437
	18:19 That i two of you shall agree on earth as	1437
	18:35 i ye from your hearts forgive not every	1437
	19:10 The case of the man be so with *his* wife,	1487
	19:17 but i thou wilt enter into life, keep	1487
	19:21 I thou wilt be perfect, go *and* sell that	1487
	21: 3 i any *man* say ought unto you, ye shall	1437
	21:21 unto you, I ye have faith, and doubt not,	1437
	21:21 but also i ye shall say unto this mountain,	2579
	21:24 will ask you one thing, which i ye tell me,	1437
	21:25 saying, I we shall say, From heaven;	1437
	21:26 But i we shall say, Of men; we fear	1437
	22:24 Saying, Master, Moses said, I a man die,	1437
	22:45 I David then call him Lord, how is he his	1487
	23:30 I we had been in the days of our fathers,	1487
	24:23 Then i any *man* shall say unto you,	1437
	24:24 insomuch that, i *it were* possible, *they*	1487
	24:26 Wherefore i they shall say unto you,	1437
	24:43 i the goodman of the house had known	1487
	24:48 I that evil servant shall say in his heart,	1437
	26:24 it had been good for that man i he had	1487
	26:39 saying, O my Father, i it be possible,	1487
	26:42 i this cup may not pass away from me,	1487
	27:40 I thou be the Son of God, come down	1487
	27:42 I he be the King of Israel, let him now	1487
	27:43 him deliver him now, i he will have him:	1487
	28:14 And i this come to the governor's ears,	1437
Mk	1:40 to him, and saying unto him, I thou wilt,	1437
	3:24 And i a kingdom be divided against itself,	1437
	3:25 And i a house be divided against itself,	1437
	3:26 And i Satan rise up against himself,	1487
	4:23 I any *man* have ears to hear, let him hear.	1536
	4:26 i a man should cast seed into the ground,	1437
	5:28 she said, I I may touch **but** his clothes,	2579
	6:56 him that they might touch i it were **but**	2579
	7:11 I a man shall say to *his* father or mother,	1437
	7:16 I any *man* have ears to hear, let him hear.	1536
	8: 3 i I send them away fasting to their own	1437
	8:23 upon him, he asked him i he saw ought.	1487
	8:36 i he shall gain the whole world, and lose	1437
	9:22 i thou canst do any *thing*, have	1487
	9:23 Jesus said unto him, I thou canst believe,	1487
	9:35 unto them, I any *man* desire to be first,	1536
	9:43 And i thy hand offend thee, cut it off: it is	1437
	9:45 And i thy foot offend thee, cut it off: it is	1487
	9:47 And i thine eye offend thee, pluck it out:	1437
	9:50 but i the salt have lost his saltness,	1437
	10:12 i a woman shall put away her husband,	1437
	11: 3 And i any *man* say unto you, Why do ye	1437
	11:13 i haply he might find any *thing* thereon:	1487
	11:25 forgive, i ye have ought against any:	1487
	11:26 But i ye do not forgive, neither will your	1487
	11:31 saying, I we shall say, From heaven;	1437
	11:32 But i we shall say, Of men; they feared	1437
	12:19 I a man's brother die, and leave *his* wife	1437
	13:21 And then i any *man* shall say to you,	1437
	13:22 wonders, to seduce, i *it were* possible,	1487
	14:21 good were it for that man i he had never	1487
	14:31 I I should die with thee, I will not deny	1437
	14:35 and prayed that, i it were possible,	1487
	15:44 And Pilate marvelled i he were already	1487
	16:18 and i they drink any deadly *thing*, it shall	2579
Lk	4: 3 said unto him, I thou be the Son of God,	1487
	4: 7 I thou therefore wilt worship me, all shall	1437
	4: 9 said unto him, I thou be the Son of God,	1487
	5:12 besought him, saying, Lord, i thou wilt,	1437
	5:36 i **otherwise**, *then* both the new maketh a	1490
	6:32 For i ye love them which love you,	1487
	6:33 i ye do good to them which do good to	1437
	6:34 i ye lend *to them* of whom ye hope to	1437
	7:39 saying, This *man*, i he were a prophet,	1487
	9:23 I any *man* will come after me, let him	1487
	9:25 i he gain the whole world, and lose	NIG
	10: 6 i the son of peace be there, your peace	1437
	10: 6 upon it: i *not*, it shall turn to you again.	1490
	10:13 for i the mighty works had been done in	1487
	11:11 I a son shall ask bread of any of you that is	NIG
	11:11 i he ask a fish, will he for a fish give him	1487
	11:12 i he shall ask an egg, will he offer him a	1487
	11:13 I ye then, being evil, know how to give	1487
	11:18 I Satan also be divided against himself,	1487
	11:19 And I I by Beelzebub cast out devils,	1487
	11:20 But i I with the finger of God cast out	1487
	11:36 I thy whole body therefore *be* full of light,	1487
	12:26 I ye then be not able *to do that thing*	1487
	12:28 I then God so clothe the grass, which is to	1487
	12:38 And i he shall come in the second watch,	1437
	12:39 i the goodman of the house had known	1437
	12:45 But and i that *servant* say in his heart,	1437
	12:49 and what will I, i it be already kindled?	1487
	13: 9 And i it bear fruit, *well*: and if not, *then*	2579
	13: 9 *well*: **and i not**, *then* after that thou shalt	1490
	14:26 I any *man* come to me, and hate not his	1536
	14:34 but i the salt have lost his savour,	1437
	15: 4 i he lose one of them, doth not leave	2532
	15: 8 i she lose one piece, doth not light a	1437
	16:11 I therefore ye have not been faithful in	1487
	16:12 And i ye have not been faithful in that	1487
	16:30 but i one went unto them from the dead,	1437
	16:31 I they hear not Moses and the prophets,	1487

Lk 17: 3 **I** thy brother trespass against thee,	1437
17: 3 rebuke him; and **i** he repent, forgive him.	1437
17: 4 And **i** he trespass against thee seven times	1437
17: 6 **I** ye had faith as a grain of mustard seed,	1487
19: 8 **i** I have taken any *thing* from any *man* by	1487
19:31 And **i** any *man* ask you, Why do ye loose	1437
19:40 you that, **i** these should hold their peace,	1437
19:42 Saying, **I** thou hadst known, even thou,	1487
20: 5 saying, **I** we shall say, From heaven;	1437
20: 6 But *and* **i** we say, Of men; all the people	1437
20:28 them, **I** any *man's* brother die, having a wife,	1437
22:42 Saying, Father, **i** thou be willing,	1487
22:67 them, **I** I tell you, you will not believe:	1487
22:68 And **i** I also ask *you*, you will not answer	1437
23:31 For **i** they do these *things* in a green tree,	1487
23:35 he be Christ, the chosen of God.	1487
23:37 saying, **I** thou be the King of the Jews,	1487
23:39 saying, **I** thou be Christ, save thyself and	1487
Jn 1:25 **i** thou be not *that* Christ, nor Elias,	1487
3:12 **I** I have told you earthly *things*, and	1487
3:12 believe, **i** I tell you of heavenly *things*?	1437
4:10 **I** thou knewest the gift of God, and who	1487
5:31 **I** bear witness of myself, my witness is	1437
5:43 **i** another shall come in his own name,	1437
5:47 **i** ye believe not his writings, how shall	1487
6:51 **i** any *man* eat of this bread, he shall live	1437
6:62 **i** ye shall see the Son of man ascend up	1437
7: 4 **I** thou do these *things*, shew thyself to	1487
7:17 **I** any *man* will do his will, he shall know	1437
7:23 **I** a man on the sabbath day receive	1487
7:37 and cried, saying, **I** any *man* thirst,	1437
8:16 And yet **i** I judge, my judgment is true: for	1437
8:19 **i** ye had known me, ye should have	1487
8:24 for **i** ye believe not that I am *he*, ye shall	1437
8:31 **I** ye continue in my word, *then* are ye my	1437
8:36 **I** the Son therefore shall make you free,	1487
8:39 them, **I** ye were Abraham's children,	1487
8:42 **I** God were your Father, ye would love	1487
8:46 **i** I say the truth, why do ye not believe	1487
8:51 **I** say unto you, **I** a man keep my saying,	1437
8:52 and thou sayest, **I** a man keep my saying,	1437
8:54 Jesus answered, **I** I honour myself,	1487
8:55 **and i** I should say, I know him not, I shall	2579
9:22 that **i** any *man* did confess that he *was*	1437
9:31 but **i** any *man* be a worshipper of God,	1487
9:33 **I** this *man* were not of God, he could do	1487
9:41 Jesus said unto them, **I** ye were blind,	1487
10: 9 me **i** any *man* enter in, he shall be saved,	1437
10:24 be the Christ, tell us plainly.	1487
10:35 **I** he called them gods, unto whom the	1487
10:37 **I** I do not the works of my Father,	1487
10:38 But **i** I do, though ye believe not me,	1487
11: 9 **I** any *man* walk in the day, he stumbleth	1437
11:10 **i** a man walk in the night, he stumbleth,	1487
11:12 Lord, **i** he sleep, he shall do well.	1487
11:21 Lord, **i** thou hadst been here, my brother	1487
11:32 unto him, Lord, **i** thou hadst been here,	1487
11:40 unto thee, that, **i** thou wouldest believe,	1437
11:48 We let him thus alone, all *men* will	1487
11:57 that, **i** any *man* knew where he were,	1437
12:24 but **i** it die, it bringeth forth much fruit.	1437
12:26 **I** any *man* serve me, let him follow me;	1437
12:26 **i** any *man* serve me, him will *my* Father	1437
12:32 And **I**, **i** I be lifted up from the earth,	1437
12:47 And **i** any *man* hear my words,	1437
13: 8 Jesus answered him, **I** I wash thee not,	1437
13:14 **I** then, *your* Lord and Master,	1487
13:17 **I** ye know these *things*, happy are ye if ye	1487
13:17 If ye know these *things*, happy are ye **i** ye	1487
13:32 **I** God be glorified in him, God shall also	1487
13:35 disciples, **i** ye have love one to another.	1490
14: 2 **i** it *were* not so, I would have told you.	1437
14: 3 And **i** I go and prepare a place for you,	1437
14: 7 **I** ye had known me, ye should have	1487
14:14 **I** ye shall ask any *thing* in my name, I will	1437
14:15 **I** ye love me, keep my commandments.	1437
14:23 and said unto him, **I** a man love me,	1437
14:28 **I** ye loved me, ye would rejoice, because	1487
15: 4 **I** ye abide not in me, he is cast forth	1437
15: 7 **I** ye abide in me, and my words abide in	1437
15:10 **I** ye keep my commandments, ye shall	1437
15:14 **i** ye do whatsoever I command you.	1437
15:18 **I** the world hate you, ye know that it	1487
15:19 **I** ye were of the world, the world would	1487
15:20 They have persecuted me, they will also	1487
15:20 **i** they have kept my saying, they will keep	1487
15:22 **I** I had not come and spoken unto them,	1487
15:24 **I** I had not done among them the works	1437
16: 7 for **i** I go not away, the Comforter will not	1437
16: 7 but **i** I depart, I will send him unto you.	1437
18: 8 **I** have told you that I am *he*: **i** therefore	1487
18:23 Jesus answered him, **I** I have spoken evil,	1487
18:23 the evil: but **i** I well, why smitest thou me?	1487
18:30 said unto him, **I** he were not a malefactor,	1487
18:36 **i** my kingdom were of this world,	1487
19:12 cried out, saying, **I** thou let this *man* go,	1437
20:15 **i** thou have borne him *hence*, tell mee	1487
21:22 **I** I will that he tarry till I come, what *is*	1437
21:23 **I** I will that he tarry till I come, what *is*	1437
21:25 **i** they should be written every one,	1487
Ac 4: 9 **I** we this day be examined of the good	1487
5:38 for **i** this counsel or this work be of men,	1487
5:39 But **i** it be of God, ye cannot overthrow it;	1487
8:22 **i** perhaps the thought of thine heart may	1487
8:37 **I** thou believest with all *thine* heart,	1487

Ac 9: 2 that **i** he found any of *this* way,	1437
13:15 **i** ye have *any* word of exhortation for	1487
15:29 from which **i** ye keep yourselves, ye shall	NIG
16:15 **I** ye have judged me to be faithful to	1487
17:27 **i** haply they might feel after him,	1487
18:14 **I** it were a matter of wrong or	1487
18:15 But **i** it be a question of words and names,	1487
18:21 I will return again unto you, **i** God will.	NIG
19:38 Wherefore **i** Demetrius, and the craftsmen	1487
19:39 **i** ye inquire any *thing* concerning other	1487
20:16 for he hasted, **i** it were possible for him,	1487
23: 9 but **i** a spirit or an angel hath spoken to	1487
24:19 and object, **i** they had **ought** against me.	1536
24:20 **i** they have found **any** evil doing in me,	1536
25: 5 man, **i** there be **any** *wickedness* in him.	1536
25:11 For **i** I be an offender, or have committed	1487
25:11 **i** there be none *of these things* whereof	1487
26: 5 from the beginning, **i** they would testify,	1437
26:32 liberty, **i** he had not appealed unto Cesar.	1513
27:12 **i** **by any means** they might attain to	1513
27:39 **i** it were possible, to thrust in the ship.	1487
Ro 1:10 **i** **by any means** now at length I might	1513
2:25 verily profiteth, **i** thou keep the law:	1437
2:25 but **i** thou be a breaker of the law,	1437
2:26 Therefore **i** the uncircumcision keep	1437
2:27 it fulfil the law, judge thee, who by	NIG
3: 3 what **i** some did not believe? shall their	1487
3: 5 But **i** our unrighteousness commend	1487
3: 7 For **i** the truth of God hath *more*	1487
4: 2 For **i** Abraham were justified by works,	1487
4:14 For **i** they which are of the law *be* heirs,	1487
4:24 **i** we believe on him that raised up Jesus	NIG
5:10 For **i**, when we were enemies, we were	1487
5:15 For **i** through the offence of one man be	1487
5:17 For **i** by one man's offence death reigned	1487
6: 5 For **i** we have been planted together in	1487
6: 8 **i** we be dead with Christ, we believe	1487
7: 2 but **i** the husband be dead, she is loosed	1437
7: 3 So then **i**, while *her* husband liveth, she	1437
7: 3 **i** *her* husband be dead, she is free from	1437
7:16 **I** then I do that which I would not,	1487
7:20 Now **i** I do that I would not, it is no more	1487
8: 9 **i** so be **that** the Spirit of God dwell in you.	1512
8: 9 Now **i** any *man* have not the Spirit of	1536
8:10 And **i** Christ *be* in you, the body *is* dead	1487
8:11 But **i** the Spirit of him that raised up Jesus	1487
8:13 For **i** ye live after the flesh, ye shall die:	1487
8:13 but **i** ye through the Spirit do mortify the	1487
8:17 And **i** children, then heirs; heirs of God,	1487
8:17 **i** so be **that** we suffer with *him*, that we	1512
8:25 But **i** we hope for that we see not, then	1487
8:31 then say to these *things*? **I** God *be* for us,	1487
9:22 **What** *i* God, willing to shew *his* wrath,	1487
10: 9 That **i** thou shalt confess with thy mouth	1437
11: 6 **i** by grace, *then* is *it* no more of works:	1487
11: 6 But **i** *it be* of works, *then* is it no more	1487
11:12 Now **i** the fall of them *be* the riches of	1487
11:14 **I** **by any means** I may provoke to	1513
11:15 For **i** the casting away of them *be*	1487
11:16 For **i** the firstfruit *be* holy, the lump *is* also	1487
11:16 lump *is* also *holy*: and **i** the root *be* holy,	1487
11:17 **i** some of the branches be broken off,	1487
11:18 **i** thou boast, thou bearest not the root,	1487
11:21 **i** God spared not the natural branches,	1487
11:22 **i** thou continue in *his* goodness,	1437
11:23 they also, **i** they bide not still in unbelief,	1437
11:24 For **i** thou wert cut out of the olive tree	1487
12:18 **I** *it be* possible, as much as lieth in you,	1487
12:20 Therefore **i** thine enemy hunger, feed him;	1437
12:20 feed him; **i** he thirst, give him drink:	1437
13: 4 But **i** thou do *that which* is evil, be afraid;	1437
13: 9 and **i** *there be* **any** other commandment,	1536
14:15 But **i** thy brother be grieved with *thy* meat,	1487
14:23 And he that doubteth is damned **i** he eat,	1437
15:24 **i** first I be somewhat filled with your	1437
15:27 For **i** the Gentiles have been made	1487
1Co 3:12 **i any** *man* build upon this foundation	1536
3:14 **I any** *man's* work abide which he hath	1536
3:15 **I any** *man's* work shall be burnt, he shall	1536
3:17 **I any** *man* defile the temple of God,	1536
3:18 **I any** *man* among you seemeth to be wise	1536
4: 7 now **i** thou didst receive *it*, why dost thou	1487
4: 7 glory, as **i** thou hadst not received *it*?	NIG
4:19 shortly, **i** the Lord will, and will know,	1437
5:11 any *man* that is called a brother be a	1437
6: 2 and **i** the world shall be judged by you,	1487
6: 4 **I** then ye have judgments *of things*	1437
7: 8 It is good for them **i** they abide even as I.	1437
7: 9 But **i** they cannot contain, let them marry:	1487
7:11 But and **i** she depart, let her remain	1437
7:12 **I any** brother hath a wife that believeth	1536
7:13 the woman which hath an husband that	NIG
7:15 **i** the unbelieving depart, let him depart.	1487
7:21 but **i** thou mayest be made free, use *it*	1487
7:28 and **i** thou marry, thou hast not sinned;	1437
7:28 and **i** a virgin marry, she hath not sinned.	1437
7:36 But **i** any *man* think that he behaveth	1487
7:36 his virgin, **i** she pass the flower of *her* age,	1437
7:39 **i** her husband be dead, she is at liberty	1437
7:40 But she is happier **i** she so abide, after my	1487
8: 2 And **i** any *man* think that *he* knoweth any	1487
8: 3 any *man* love God, the same is known	1487
8: 8 for neither, **i** we eat, are we the better;	1437
8: 8 neither, **i** we eat not, are we the worse.	1437
8:10 For **i** any *man* see thee which hast	1437

1Co 8:13 **i** meat make my brother to offend,	1487
9: 2 **I** I be not an apostle unto others,	1487
9:11 **I** we have sown unto you spiritual *things*,	1487
9:11 *thing* **i** we shall reap your carnal *things*?	1487
9:12 **I** others be partakers of *this* power over	1487
9:16 woe is unto me, **i** I preach not the gospel!	1437
9:17 For **i** I do this *thing* willingly, I have a	1487
9:17 but **i** against my will, a dispensation *of*	1487
10:27 **I** any of them that believe not bid you *to a*	1487
10:28 any *man* say unto you, This is offered	1487
10:30 For **i** I by grace be a partaker, why am I	1487
11: 5 **even all one as i** she 846+1520+2532+3588	
11: 6 For **i** the woman be not covered, let her	1487
11: 6 *i it* be a shame for a woman to be shorn or	NIG
11:14 that, **i** a man have long hair, it is a shame	1437
11:15 But **i** a woman have long hair, it is a glory	1437
11:16 But **i** any *man* seem to be contentious,	1487
11:31 **i** we would judge ourselves, we should	1487
11:34 **i** any *man* hunger, let him eat at home;	1487
12:15 The foot shall say, Because I am not	1437
12:16 And **i** the ear shall say, Because I am not	1437
12:17 **I** the whole body *were* an eye, where	1487
12:17 **I** the whole *were* hearing, where *were*	1487
12:19 they were all one member,	1487
14: 6 **i** I come unto you speaking with tongues,	1437
14: 8 For **i** the trumpet give an uncertain sound,	1437
14:11 Therefore **i** I know not the meaning of	1437
14:14 For **i** I pray in an *unknown* tongue,	1437
14:23 **i** therefore the whole church be come	1437
14:24 But **i** all prophesy, and there come in one	1437
14:27 **I** any *man* speak in an *unknown* tongue,	1535
14:28 But **i** there be no interpreter, let him keep	1437
14:30 **I** any *thing* be revealed to another that	1437
14:35 And **i** they will learn any *thing*, let them	1487
14:37 **I** any *man* think himself to be a prophet,	1536
14:38 But **i** any *man* be ignorant, let him be	1536
15: 2 ye keep in memory what I preached unto	1487
15:12 **i** Christ be preached that he rose from	1487
15:13 But **i** there be no resurrection of the dead,	1487
15:14 And **i** Christ be not risen, *then is* our	1487
15:15 not up, **i** so be **that** the dead rise not. 686+1512	
15:16 For **i** the dead rise not, then is not Christ	1487
15:17 And **i** Christ be not raised, your faith *is*	1487
15:19 **I** in this life only we have hope in Christ,	1487
15:29 for the dead, **i** the dead rise not at all?	1487
15:32 **I** after the manner of men I have fought	1487
15:32 advantageth it me, **i** the dead rise not?	1487
16: 4 **i** it be meet that I go also, they shall go	1437
16: 7 tarry a while with you, **i** the Lord permit.	1437
16:10 **I** Timotheus come, see that he may be	1437
16:22 **I** any *man* love not the Lord Jesus Christ,	1536
2Co 2: 2 For **i** I make you sorry, who is he then	1487
2: 5 But **i** any have caused grief, he hath not	1487
2:10 for **i** I forgave **any** *thing*, to whom I	1536
3: 7 **i** the ministration of death, written *and*	1487
3: 9 For **i** the ministration of condemnation *be*	1487
3:11 **i** that which is done away *was* glorious,	1487
4: 3 But **i** our gospel be hid, it is hid to them	1437
5: 1 we know that **i** our earthly house of *this*	1437
5: 3 **I** so be that being clothed we shall not be	1489
5:14 that **i** one died for all, then were all dead:	1487
5:17 Therefore **i** any *man* be in Christ, *he is* a	1536
7:14 For **i** I have boasted **any** *thing* to him of	1536
8:12 For **i** there be first a willing mind, *it is*	1487
9: 4 Lest haply **i** they of Macedonia come with	1437
10: 2 think of us as **i** we walked according	NIG
10: 7 **I** any *man* trust to himself that *he* is	1536
10: 9 I may not seem as **i** / would terrify you	302
11: 4 For **i** he that cometh preacheth another	1487
11: 4 **i** ye receive another spirit, which ye have	NIG
11:15 his ministers **also** be transformed as	1499
11:16 **i** **otherwise**, yet as a fool receive me,	1490
11:20 ye suffer, **i** a **man** bring you into bondage,	1536
11:20 **i** a **man** devour *you*, if a man take *of you*,	1536
11:20 if a man devour *you*, **i** a **man** take *of you*,	1536
11:20 a man take *of you*, **i** a **man** exalt himself,	1536
11:20 **i** a **man** smite you on the face.	1536
11:30 **I** I must needs glory, I will glory of	1487
13: 2 foretell *you*, **as i** I were present the second	5613
13: 2 and to all other, that, **i** I come again, I will	1437
Gal 1: 9 **I any** *man* preach any other gospel unto	1536
1:10 for **i** I yet pleased men, I should not be	1487
2:14 Peter before *them* all, **I** thou, being a Jew,	1487
2:17 But **i**, while we seek to be justified by	1487
2:18 For **i** I build again the *things* which I	1487
2:21 for **i** righteousness *come* by the law, then	1487
3: 4 so many *things* in vain? **i** *it be* yet in vain.	1489
3:15 a man's covenant, *yet* **i** *it be* confirmed,	NIG
3:18 For **i** the inheritance *be* of the law, *it is* no	1487
3:21 for **i** there had been a law given which	1487
3:29 And **i** ye *be* Christ's, then are ye	1487
4: 7 **i** a son, then an heir of God through	1487
4:15 you record, that **i** *it had been* possible,	1487
5: 2 say unto you, that **i** ye be circumcised,	1437
5:11 I, brethren, **i** I yet preach circumcision,	1487
5:15 But **i** ye bite and devour one another,	1487
5:18 But **i** ye be led of the Spirit, ye are not	1487
5:25 We live in the Spirit, let us also walk in	1437
6: 1 Brethren, **i** a man be overtaken in a fault,	1437
6: 3 For **i** a man think himself to be something,	1487
6: 9 in due season we shall reap, **i** we faint not.	NIG
Eph 3: 2 ye have heard of the dispensation of	1489
4:21 **I** so be **that** ye have heard him,	1489
Php 1:22 But **i** I / live in the flesh, this *is* the fruit of	1487
2: 1 **I** *there be* therefore **any** consolation in	1536

Php	2: 1 in Christ, **i** any comfort of love,	1536
	2: 1 **i** any fellowship of the Spirit, if any	1536
	2: 1 of the Spirit, **i** any bowels and mercies,	1536
	2:17 **and** if **I** be offered upon the sacrifice and	1499
	3: 4 **I** any other *man* thinketh that *he* hath	1536
	3:11 **I by any means** I might attain unto	1513
	3:12 I follow *after*, **i that** I may apprehend *that*	1499
	3:15 **i** in any *thing* ye be otherwise minded,	1536
	4: 8 **i** there be any virtue, and if *there be* any	1536
	4: 8 be any virtue, and **i** there be any praise,	1536
Col	1:23 **i** ye continue in the faith grounded and	1489
	2:20 Wherefore **i** ye be dead with Christ from	1487
	3: 1 **I** ye then be risen with Christ, seek those	1487
	3:13 **i** any *man* have a quarrel against any:	1437
	4:10 **i** he come unto you, receive him;)	1437
1Th	3: 8 now we live, **i** ye stand fast in the Lord.	1437
	4:14 For **i** we believe that Jesus died and	1487
2Th	3:10 that **i** any would not work, neither should	1536
	3:14 And **i** any *man* obey not our word by this	1487
1Ti	1: 8 the law *is* good, **i** a man use it lawfully;	1437
	1:10 **i** there be any other *thing that* is contrary	1536
	2:15 **i** they continue in faith and charity and	1437
	3: 1 **I** a man desire the office of a bishop,	1536
	3: 5 **i** a man know not how to rule his own	1487
	3:15 But **i** I tarry long, that thou mayest know	1437
	4: 4 **i** it be received with thanksgiving:	NIG
	4: 6 **i** thou put the brethren in remembrance	NIG
	5: 4 **i** any widow have children or nephews,	1487
	5: 8 But **i** any provide not for his own,	1487
	5:10 **i** she have brought up children, if she	1487
	5:10 up children, **i** she have lodged strangers,	1487
	5:10 **i** she have washed the saints' feet,	1487
	5:10 **i** she have relieved the afflicted,	1487
	5:10 **i** she have diligently followed every good	1487
	5:16 **I** any man or woman that believeth have	1536
	6: 3 **I** any man teach otherwise, and consent	1536
2Ti	2: 5 a man also strive for masteries, *yet* is	1437
	2:11 For **i** we be dead with *him*,	1487
	2:12 **I** we suffer, we shall also reign with *him*:	1487
	2:12 we shall also reign with **i** we deny	1487
	2:13 **I** we believe not, *yet* he abideth faithful:	1487
	2:21 **I** a man therefore purge himself from	1437
	2:25 **i** God **peradventure** will give them	3379
Tit	1: 6 **I** any be blameless, the husband of one	1487
Phm	1:17 **I** thou count me therefore a partner,	1487
	1:18 **I** he hath wronged thee, or oweth *thee*	1487
Heb	2: 2 For **i** the word spoken by angels was	NIG
	2: 3 we escape, **i** we neglect so great salvation;	NIG
	3: 6 **i** we hold fast the confidence and	1437+4007
	3: 7 Ghost saith, To day **i** ye will hear his voice,	1437
	3:14 we hold the beginning of our	1437+4007
	3:15 it is said, To day **i** ye will hear his voice,	1437
	4: 3 my wrath, **i** they shall enter into my rest:	1487
	4: 5 *place* again, **I** they shall enter into my rest.	1487
	4: 7 as it is said, To day **i** ye will hear his voice,	1437
	4: 8 For **i** Jesus had given them rest, *then*	1487
	6: 3 And this will we do, **i** God permit.	1437+4007
	6: 6 **i** they shall fall away, to renew *them* again	NIG
	7:11 **I** therefore perfection were by the Levitical	1487
	8: 4 For **i** he were on earth, he should not be a	1487
	8: 7 For **i** that first *covenant* had been faultless,	1487
	9:13 the blood of bulls and of goats,	1487
	10:26 For **i** we sin wilfully after that *we* have	NIG
	10:38 but **i** any *man* draw back, my soul shall	1437
	11:15 **i** they had been mindful of that *country*	1487
	12: 7 **I** ye endure chastening, God dealeth with	1487
	12: 8 But **i** ye be without chastisement,	1487
	12:20 **And i** so much as a beast touch	2579
	12:25 **i** they escaped not who refused him that	1487
	12:25 much more *shall not* we *escape*, **i** we turn	NIG
	13:23 with whom, **i** he come shortly, I will see	1437
Jas	1: 5 **I** any of you lack wisdom, let him ask of	1487
	1:23 **i** any be a hearer of the word, and not a	1536
	1:26 **I** any *man* among you seem to be	1536
	2: 2 **i** there come unto your assembly a man	1437
	2: 8 **I** ye fulfil the royal law according to	1487+3305
	2: 9 **i** ye have respect to persons, ye commit	1487
	2:11 **i** thou commit no adultery, yet *i* thou kill,	1487
	2:11 if thou commit no adultery, yet *i* thou kill,	NIG
	2:15 **I** a brother or sister be naked,	1437
	2:17 Even so faith, **i** it hath not works, is dead,	1437
	3: 2 **I** any *man* offend not in word, the same	1536
	3:14 But **i** ye have bitter envying and strife in	1487
	4:11 **i** thou judge the law, thou art not a doer	1487
	4:15 The Lord will, we shall live, and do this,	1437
	5:15 **and i** he have committed sins, they shall	2579
	5:19 **i** any of you do err from the truth,	1437
1Pe	1: 6 though now for a season, **i** need be,	1487
	1:17 And **i** ye call on the Father, who without	1487
	2: 3 **I so** be ye have tasted that the Lord *is*	1512
	2:19 **i** a man for conscience toward God endure	1487
	2:20 For what glory *is it*, **i**, when ye be buffeted	1487
	2:20 **i**, when ye do well, and suffer *for it*, ye	1487
	3: 1 that, **i** any obey not the word, they also	1487
	3:13 ye be followers of *that which* is good?	1437
	3:14 But and **i** ye suffer for righteousness' sake,	1487
	3:17 For *it is* better, **i** the will of God be so,	1487
	4:11 **I** any *man* speak, *let him speak* as	1536
	4:11 **I** any minister, *let him do it* as of	1536
	4:14 **I** ye be reproached for the name of Christ,	1487
	4:16 Yet **i** any *man suffer* as a Christian, let	1487
	4:17 **i** *it first* *begin* at us, what *shall* the end	1487
	4:18 And **i** the righteous scarcely be saved,	1487
2Pe	1: 8 For **i** these *things* be in you, and abound,	NIG
	1:10 for **i** ye do these *things*, ye shall never fall:	NIG

2Pe	2: 4 **i** God spared not the angels that sinned,	1487
	2:20 **i** after they have escaped the pollutions	1487
1Jn	1: 6 **I** we say that we have fellowship with	1437
	1: 7 But **i** we walk in the light, as he is in	1437
	1: 8 **I** we say that we have no sin, we deceive	1437
	1: 9 **I** we confess our sins, he is faithful and	1437
	1:10 **I** we say that we have not sinned,	1437
	2: 1 And **i** any *man* sin, we have an advocate	1437
	2: 3 know him, **i** we keep his commandments.	1437
	2:15 **I** any man love the world, the love of	1487
	2:19 for **i** they had been of us, they would *no*	1487
	2:24 **I** *that* which ye have heard from	1437
	2:29 **I** ye know that he is righteous, ye know	1437
	3:13 my brethren, **i** the world hate you.	1487
	3:20 For **i** *our* heart condemn us, God is greater	1437
	3:21 **i** our heart condemn us not, *then* have we	1437
	4:11 Beloved, **i** God so loved us, we ought also	1487
	4:12 **I** we love one another, God dwelleth in	1437
	4:20 **I** a man say, I love God, and hateth his	1437
	5: 9 **I** we receive the witness of men,	1487
	5:14 we ask any *thing* according to his will,	1437
	5:15 And **i** we know that he hear us,	1437
	5:16 **I** any *man* see his brother sin a sin *which*	1437
2Jn	1:10 **I** there come any unto you, and bring not	1487
3Jn	1: 6 **i** thou bring forward on their journey	NIG
	1:10 Wherefore, **i** I come, I will remember his	1437
Rev	1:15 fine brass, as **i** they burned in a furnace;	NIG
	3: 3 I therefore thou shalt not watch, I will	1437
	3:20 **i** any *man* hear my voice, and open	1437
	11: 5 And **i** any *man* will hurt them,	1536
	11: 5 any *man* will hurt them, he must in	1536
	13: 9 **I** any *man* have an ear, let him hear.	1536
	14: 9 **I** any *man* worship the beast and his	1536
	22:18 **I** any *man* shall add unto these *things*,	1437
	22:19 And **i** any *man* shall take away from	1437

IGAL (2)

Nu	13: 7 the tribe of Issachar, **I** the son of Joseph.	3008
2Sa	23:36 **I** the son of Nathan of Zobah, Bani	3008

IGDALIAH (1)

Jer	35: 4 sons of Hanan, the son of **I**, a man of God,	3012

IGEAL (1)

1Ch	3:22 **I**, and Bariah, and Neariah, and Shaphat,	3008

IGNOMINY (1)

Pr	18: 3 cometh also contempt, and with **i** reproach.	7036

IGNORANCE (18) [IGNORANT, IGNORANTLY]

Lev	4: 2 If a soul shall sin through **i** against any of	7684
	4:13 congregation of Israel **sin through i**,	7686
	4:22 done somewhat through **i** against any of	7684
	4:27 one of the common people sin through **i**,	7684
	5:15 soul commit a trespass, and sin through **i**,	7684
	5:18 for him concerning his **i** wherein he erred	7684
Nu	15:24 if *ought* be committed by **i** without	7684
	15:25 and it shall be forgiven them; for it *is* **i**:	7684
	15:25 sin offering before the LORD, for their **i**:	7684
	15:26 seeing all the people were in **i**.	7684
	15:27 **I** if any soul sin through **i**, then he shall	7684
	15:28 when he sinneth by **i** before the LORD,	7684
	15:29 that **sinneth through i**,	6213+7684+871.1
Ac	3:17 I wot that through **i** ye did *it, as did* also	52
	17:30 And the times of *this* **i** God winked at;	52
Eph	4:18 life of God through the **i** that is in them,	52
1Pe	1:14 according to the former lusts in your **i**:	52
	2:15 with well doing *ye* may put to silence the **i**	56

IGNORANT (17) [IGNORANCE]

Ps	73:22 So foolish *was* I, and **i**: I was *as* a	3045+3808
Isa	56:10 are all **i**, they *are* all dumb dogs,	3045+3808
	63:16 though Abraham be **i** of us,	3045+3808
Ac	4:13 that they were unlearned and **i** men,	2399
Ro	1:13 Now I would not have you **i**, brethren,	50
	10: 3 For they being **i** of God's righteousness,	50
	11:25 brethren, that ye should be **i** of this mystery,	50
1Co	10: 1 I would not that ye should be **i**,	50
	12: 1 *gifts*, brethren, I would not have you **i**.	50
	14:38 But if any *man* be **i**, let him be ignorant.	50
	14:38 But if any *man* be ignorant, let him be **i**.	50
2Co	1: 8 **have** you **i** of our trouble which came to us	50
	2:11 of us: for we are not **i** of his devices.	50
1Th	4:13 But I would not have you to be **i**, brethren,	50
Heb	5: 2 Who can have compassion on the **i**,	50
2Pe	3: 5 For this they willingly are **i** of, that by	2990
	3: 8 be **i** of this one *thing*, that one day *is*	2990

IGNORANTLY (4) [IGNORANCE]

Nu	15:28 an atonement for the soul that **sinneth i**,	7683
Dt	19: 4 killeth his neighbour **i**,	1097+1847+871.1
Ac	17:23 Whom therefore ye **i** worship, him declare I	50
1Ti	1:13 obtained mercy, because I did *it* **i** in unbelief.	50

IIM (2)

Nu	33:45 they departed from **I**, and pitched in	5864
Jos	15:29 Baalah, and **I**, and Azem,	5864

IJE-ABARIM (2) [ABARIM]

Nu	21:11 journeyed from Oboth, and pitched at **I**,	5863
	33:44 and pitched in **I**, in the border of Moab.	5863

IJON (2)

1Ki	15:20 **I**, and Dan, and Abel-beth-maachah,	5859
2Ki	15:29 took **I**, and Abel-beth-maachah,	5859
2Ch	16: 4 they smote **I**, and Dan, and Abel-maim,	5859

IKKESH (3)

2Sa	23:26 the Paltite, Ira the son of **I** the Tekoite,	6142
1Ch	11:28 Ira the son of **I** the Tekoite, Abi-ezer,	6142
	27: 9 month *was* Ira the son of **I** the Tekoite:	6142

ILAI (1)

1Ch	11:29 Sibbecai the Hushathite, **I** the Ahohite,	5866

ILL (15)

Ge	41: 3 of the river, **i** favoured and leanfleshed;	7451
	41: 4 the **i** favoured and leanfleshed kine did	7451
	41:19 poor and very **i** favoured and leanfleshed,	7451
	41:20 the **i favoured** kine did eat up the first	7451
	41:21 they *were* still **i** favoured, as at	7451
	41:27 **i favoured** kine that came up after them	7451
	43: 6 Wherefore **dealt** ye so **i** with me,	7489
Dt	15:21 *be* lame, or blind, *or have* any **i** blemish,	7451
Job	20:26 it shall **go i** with him that is left in his	3415
Ps	106:32 that it went **i** with Moses for their sakes:	3415
Isa	3:11 it shall be **i** with him: for the reward of	7451
Jer	40: 4 if it seem **i** unto thee to come with me	7489
Joel	2:20 his **i savour** shall come up, because he	6709
Mic	3: 4 as they have **behaved** themselves **i** in	7489
Ro	13:10 Love worketh no **i** to *his* neighbour:	2556

ILLUMINATED (1)

Heb	10:32 which, after ye were **i**, ye endured a great	5461

ILLYRICUM (1)

Ro	15:19 from Jerusalem, and round about unto **I**,	2437

IMAGE (100) [IMAGE'S, IMAGERY, IMAGES]

Ge	1:26 God said, Let us make man in our **i**,	6754
	1:27 So God created man in his own **i**,	6754
	1:27 image, in the **i** of God created he him;	6754
	5: 3 *a son* in his own likeness, after his **i**;	6754
	9: 6 shed: for in the **i** of God made he man.	6754
Ex	20: 4 shalt not make unto thee *any* **graven i**,	6459
Lev	26: 1 Ye shall make you no idols nor **graven i**,	6459
	26: 1 neither rear you up a **standing i**,	4676
	26: 1 neither shall ye set up *any* **i** of stone in	4906
Dt	4:16 and make you a **graven i**,	6459
	4:23 make you a **graven i**, *or* the likeness of	6459
	4:25 corrupt *yourselves*, and make a **graven i**,	6459
	5: 8 Thou shalt not make thee *any* **graven i**,	6459
	9:12 they have made them a **molten i**.	4541
	16:22 Neither shalt thou set thee up *any* **i**;	4676
	27:15 man that maketh *any* graven or **molten i**,	4541
Jdg	17: 3 to make a **graven i** and a molten image:	6459
	17: 3 to make a graven image and a **molten i**:	4541
	17: 4 made thereof a **graven i** and a molten	6459
	17: 4 thereof a graven image and a **molten i**:	4541
	18:14 a **graven i**, and a molten image?	6459
	18:14 and a graven image, and a **molten i**?	4541
	18:17 *and* took the **graven i**, and the ephod,	6459
	18:18 fetched the **carved i**, the ephod,	6459
	18:18 and the teraphim, and the **molten i**.	4541
	18:20 the **graven i**, and went in the midst of	6459
	18:30 the children of Dan set up the **graven i**:	6459
	18:31 then they set up Micah's **graven i**,	6459
1Sa	19:13 Michal took an **i**, and laid *it* in the bed,	8655
	19:16 in, behold *there was* an **i** in the bed,	8655
2Ki	3: 2 put away the **i** of Baal that his father	4676
	10:27 they brake down the **i** of Baal,	4676
	21: 7 he set a **graven i** of the grove that he had	6459
2Ch	3:10 house he made two cherubims of **i** work,	6816
	33: 7 he set a **carved i**, the idol which he had	6459
Job	4:16 an **i** *was* before mine eyes, there was	8544
Ps	73:20 *thou* awakest, thou shalt despise their **i**.	6754
	106:19 in Horeb, and worshipped the **molten i**.	4541
Isa	40:19 The workman melteth a **graven i**,	6459
	40:20 cunning workman to prepare a **graven i**,	6459
	44: 9 They that make a **graven i** *are* all of them	6459
	44:10 molten a **graven i** *that* is profitable for	6459
	44:15 worshippeth *it*; he maketh it a **graven i**,	6459
	44:17 he maketh a god, *even* his **graven i**:	6459
	45:20 that set up the wood of their **graven i**,	6459
	48: 5 my **graven i**, and my molten image,	6459
	48: 5 my graven image, and my **molten i**,	5262
Jer	10:14 founder is confounded by the **graven i**:	6459
	10:14 for his **molten i** *is* falsehood, and *there is*	5262
	51:17 founder is confounded by the **graven i**:	6459
	51:17 for his **molten i** *is* falsehood, and *there is*	5262
Eze	8: 3 where *was* the seat of the **i** of jealousy,	5566
	8: 5 northward at the gate of the altar this **i** of	5566
Da	2:31 O king, sawest, and behold a great **i**.	6755
	2:31 This great **i**, whose brightness *was*	6755
	2:34 smote the **i** upon his feet *that were* of	6755
	2:35 the stone that smote the **i** became a great	6755
	3: 1 Nebuchadnezzar the king made an **i** of	6755
	3: 2 to come to the dedication of the **i** which	6755
	3: 3 that Nebuchadnezzar the king had set	6755
	3: 3 they stood before the **i** that	6755
	3: 5 worship the golden **i** that	6755
	3: 7 worshipped the golden **i** that	6755
	3:10 shall fall down and worship the golden **i**:	6755
	3:12 nor worship the golden **i** which thou hast	6755
	3:14 nor worship the golden **i** which I have set	6755
	3:15 worship the **i** which I have made;	6755
	3:18 nor worship the golden **i** which thou hast	6755
Hos	3: 4 and without an **i**, and without an ephod,	4676
Na	1:14 of thy gods will I cut off the **graven i**	6459
	1:14 off the graven image and the **molten i**:	4541
Hab	2:18 What profiteth the **graven i** that the	6459

I *(margin tab)*

Hab	2:18 the **molten i**, and a teacher of lies, that	4541
Mt	22:20 Whose *is* this **i** and superscription?	1504
Mk	12:16 Whose **i** and superscription?	1504
Lk	20:24 Whose **i** and superscription hath it?	1504
Ac	19:35 and of the **i** which fell down from Jupiter?	NIG
Ro	1:23 God into an **i** made like to corruptible	1504
	8:29 *to be* conformed to the **i** of his Son,	1504
	11: 4 who have not bowed the knee to *the* **i** of	NIG
1Co	11: 7 forasmuch as he is the **i** and glory of God:	1504
	15:49 and as we have borne the **i** of the earthy,	1504
	15:49 we shall also bear the **i** of the heavenly.	1504
2Co	3:18 are changed *into* the same **i** from glory to	1504
	4: 4 who is the **i** of God, should shine unto	1504
Col	1:15 Who is the **i** of the invisible God,	1504
	3:10 after the **i** of him that created him:	1504
Heb	1: 3 and the **express i** of his person,	5481
	10: 1 to come, *and* not the very **i** of the things,	1504
Rev	13:14 that *they* should make an **i** to the beast,	1504
	13:15 he had power to give life unto the **i** of	1504
	13:15 that the **i** of the beast should both speak,	1504
	13:15 worship the **i** of the beast should be killed.	1504
	14: 9 If any *man* worship the beast and his **i**,	1504
	14:11 who worship the beast and his **i**,	1504
	15: 2 beast, and over his **i**, and over his mark,	1504
	16: 2 and *upon* them which worshipped his **i**.	1504
	19:20 the beast, and them that worshipped his **i**.	1504
	20: 4 not worshipped the beast, neither his **i**,	1504

IMAGE'S (1) [IMAGE]

Da	2:32 This head *was* of fine gold, his breast and	6755

IMAGERY (1) [IMAGE]

Eze	8:12 every man in the chambers of his **i**?	4906

IMAGES (71) [IMAGE]

Ge	31:19 Rachel had stolen the **i** that *were* her	8655
	31:34 Rachel had taken the **i**, and put them	8655
	31:35 And he searched, but found not the **i**.	8655
Ex	23:24 and quite break down their **i**.	4676
	34:13 break their **i**, and cut down their groves:	4676
Lev	26:30 cut down your **i**, and cast your carcases	2553
Nu	33:52 destroy all their molten **i**, and quite pluck	6754
Dt	7: 5 break down their **i**, and cut down their	4676
	7: 5 and burn their **graven i** with fire.	6456
	7:25 The **graven i** of their gods shall ye burn	6456
	12: 3 you shall hew down the **graven i** of their	6456
1Sa	6: 5 Wherefore ye shall make **i** of your	6754
	6: 5 and **i** of your mice that mar the land;	6754
	6:11 mice of gold and the **i** of their emerods.	6754
2Sa	5:21 there they left their **i**, and David and	6091
1Ki	14: 9 and made thee other gods, and **molten i**,	4541
	14:23 **i**, and groves, on every high hill,	4676
2Ki	10:26 they brought forth the **i** out of the house	4676
	11:18 and his **i** brake they in pieces throughly,	6754
	17:10 they set them up **i** and groves in every	4676
	17:16 made them **molten i**, *even* two calves,	4541
	17:41 served their **graven i**, both their children,	6456
	18: 4 brake the **i**, and cut down the groves,	4676
	23:14 he brake in pieces the **i**, and cut down	4676
	23:24 the **i**, and the idols, and all	8655
2Ch	14: 3 brake down the **i**, and cut down the	4676
	14: 5 cities of Judah the high places and the **i**:	2553
	23:17 brake his altars and his **i** in pieces,	6754
	28: 2 and made also **molten i** for Baalim.	4541
	31: 1 brake the **i** *in pieces*, and cut down	4676
	33:19 set up groves and **graven i**, before he was	6456
	33:22 for Amon sacrificed unto all the **carved i**	6456
	34: 3 and the **carved i**, and the molten images.	6456
	34: 3 and the carved images, and the **molten i**.	4541
	34: 4 the **i**, that *were* on high above them,	2553
	34: 4 and the **carved i**, and the molten images,	6456
	34: 4 the **molten i**, he brake *in pieces*, and	4541
	34: 7 had beaten the **graven i** into powder,	6456
Ps	78:58 him to jealousy with their **graven i**,	6456
	97: 7 be all they that serve **graven i**,	6459
Isa	10:10 whose **graven i** did excel *them* of	6456
	17: 8 have made, either the groves, or the **i**.	2553
	21: 9 all the **graven i** of her gods hath	6456
	27: 9 the groves and **i** shall not stand up.	2553
	30:22 also the covering of thy **graven i** of silver,	6456
	30:22 and the ornament of thy **molten i** of gold:	4541
	41:29 their **molten i** *are* wind and confusion.	5262
	42: 8 to another, neither my praise to **graven i**.	6456
	42:17 trust in **graven i**, that say to the molten	6459
	42:17 that say to the **molten i**, Ye *are* our gods.	4541
Jer	8:19 provoked me to anger with their **graven i**,	6456
	43:13 He shall break also the **i** of Beth-shemesh,	4676
	50: 2 confounded, her **i** are broken in pieces.	1544
	50:38 for it *is* the land of **graven i**, and they are	6456
	51:47 I will do judgment upon the **graven i**	6456
	51:52 I will do judgment upon her **graven i**:	6456
Eze	6: 4 be desolate, and your **i** shall be broken:	2553
	6: 6 your **i** may be cut down, and your works	2553
	7:20 they made the **i** of their abominations *and*	6754
	16:17 madest to thyself **i** of men,	6754
	21:21 consulted with **i**, he looked in the liver.	8655
	23:14 the **i** of the Chaldeans pourtrayed with	6754
	30:13 I will cause *their* **i** to cease out of Noph;	457
Hos	10: 1 of his land they have made goodly **i**.	4676
	10: 2 down their altars, he shall spoil their **i**.	2553
	11: 2 and burned incense to **graven i**.	6456
	13: 2 have made them **molten i** of their silver,	4541
Am	5:26 of your Moloch and Chiun your **i**,	6754
Mic	1: 7 all the **graven i** thereof shall be beaten to	6456
	5:13 Thy **graven i** also I will cut off,	6456
Mic	5:13 thy **standing i** out of the midst of thee;	4676

IMAGINATION (14) [IMAGINE]

Ge	6: 5 *that* every **i** of the thoughts of his heart	3336
	8:21 for the **i** of man's heart *is* evil from his	3336
Dt	29:19 though I walk in the **i** of mine heart,	8307
	31:21 for I know their **i** which they go about,	3336
1Ch	29:18 keep this for ever in the **i** of the thoughts	3336
Jer	3:17 shall they walk any more after the **i**	8307
	7:24 counsels *and* in the **i** of their evil heart,	8307
	9:14 have walked after the **i** of their own heart,	8307
	11: 8 every one in the **i** of their evil heart:	8307
	13:10 which walk in the **i** of their heart,	8307
	16:12 ye walk every one after the **i** of his evil	8307
	18:12 will every one do the **i** of his evil heart.	8307
	23:17 that walketh after the **i** of his own heart,	8307
Lk	1:51 hath scattered the proud in the **i** of their	1271

IMAGINATIONS (6) [IMAGINE]

1Ch	28: 9 understandeth all the **i** of the thoughts:	3336
Pr	6:18 A heart that deviseth wicked **i**, feet that	4284
La	3:60 their vengeance *and* all their **i** against me.	4284
	3:61 O Lord, *and* all their **i** against me;	4284
Ro	1:21 became vain in their **i**, and their foolish	1261
2Co	10: 5 Casting down **i**, and every high thing that	3053

IMAGINE (12) [IMAGINATION, IMAGINATIONS, IMAGINED, IMAGINETH]

Job	6:26 Do ye **i** to reprove words, and the	2803
	21:27 devices *which* ye **wrongfully i** against	2554
Ps	2: 1 and the people **i** a vain *thing*?	1897
	38:12 and **i** deceits all the day long.	1897
	62: 3 long will ye **i** **mischief** against a man?	2050
	140: 2 Which **i** mischiefs in *their* heart;	2803
Pr	12:20 Deceit *is* in the heart of them that **i** evil:	2790
Hos	7:15 yet do they **i** mischief against me.	2803
Na	1: 9 What do ye **i** against the Lord? he *will*	2803
Zec	7:10 let none of you **i** evil against his brother	2803
	8:17 let none of you **i** evil in your hearts	2803
Ac	4:25 rage, and the people **i** vain *things*?	3191

IMAGINED (3) [IMAGINE]

Ge	11: 6 from them, which they have **i** to do.	2161
Ps	10: 2 be taken in the devices that they have **i**.	2803
	21:11 they **i** a mischievous device, *which* they	2803

IMAGINETH (1) [IMAGINE]

Na	1:11 that **i** evil against the Lord, a wicked	2803

IMLA (2) [IMLAH]

2Ch	18: 7 the same *is* Micaiah the son of **I**.	3229
	18: 8 said, Fetch quickly Micaiah the son of **I**.	3229

IMLAH (2) [IMLA]

1Ki	22: 8 *is* yet one man, Micaiah the son of **I**,	3229
	22: 9 said, Hasten *hither* Micaiah the son of **I**.	3229

IMMANUEL (2) [EMMANUEL]

Isa	7:14 and bear a Son, and shall call his name **I**.	6005
	8: 8 shall fill the breadth of thy land, O **I**.	6005

IMMEDIATELY (55)

Mt	4:22 And they **i** left the ship and their father,	2112
	8: 3 And **i** his leprosy was cleansed.	2112
	14:31 And **i** Jesus stretched forth *his* hand,	2112
	20:34 and **i** their eyes received sight,	2112
	24:29 **i** after the tribulation of those days shall	2112
	26:74 I know not the man. And **i** the cock crew.	2112
Mk	1:12 And **i** the Spirit driveth him into	2112
	1:28 And **i** his fame spread abroad throughout	2112
	1:31 and **i** the fever left her, and she ministered	2112
	1:42 **i** the leprosy departed from him, and he	2112
	2: 8 And **i** when Jesus perceived in his spirit	2112
	2:12 And **i** he arose, took up the bed,	2112
	4: 5 **i** it sprang up, because *it* had no depth	2112
	4:15 Satan cometh **i**, and taketh away the word	2112
	4:16 heard the word, **i** receive it with gladness;	2112
	4:17 for the word's sake, **i** they are offended.	2112
	4:29 **i** he putteth in the sickle, because	2112
	5: 2 **i** there met him out of the tombs a man	2112
	5:30 Jesus **i** knowing in himself that virtue	2112
	6:27 And **i** the king sent an executioner,	2112
	6:50 And **i** he talked with them, and saith unto	2112
	10:52 And **i** he received his sight,	2112
	14:43 And **i**, while he yet spake, cometh Judas,	2112
Lk	1:64 And his mouth was opened **i**,	3916
	4:39 and **i** she arose and ministered unto them.	3916
	5:13 And **i** the leprosy departed from him.	2112
	5:25 **i** he rose up before them, and took up	3916
	6:49 stream did beat vehemently, and **i** it fell;	2112
	8:44 and **i** her issue of blood stanched.	3916
	8:47 touched him, and how she was healed **i**.	3916
	12:36 knocketh, they may open unto him **i**.	2112
	13:13 and **i** she was made straight,	3916
	18:43 And **i** he received his sight,	3916
	19:11 that the kingdom of God should **i** appear.	3916
	19:40 their peace, the stones would **i** cry out.	NIG
	22:60 And **i**, while he yet spake, the cock crew.	3916
Jn	5: 9 And **i** the man was made whole,	2112
	6:21 the ship was at the land whither they	2112
	13:30 then having received the sop went **i** out:	2112
	18:27 then denied again: and **i** the cock crew.	2112
	21: 3 went forth, and entered into a ship **i**;	2112
Ac	3: 7 and **i** his feet and ankle bones received	3916
	9:18 **i** there fell from his eyes as it had been	2112
	9:34 arise, and make thy bed. And he arose **i**.	2112

Ac	10:33 I therefore I sent to thee; and thou hast	1824
	11:11 here were three men **already** come	1824
	12:23 And **i** *the* angel of the Lord smote him,	3916
	13:11 And there fell on him a mist and	3916
	16:10 we endeavoured to go into Macedonia,	2112
	16:26 and **i** all the doors were opened,	3916
	17:10 the brethren **i** sent away Paul and Silas	2112
	17:14 the brethren **i** sent away Paul to go as *it*	2112
	21:32 Who **i** took soldiers and centurions,	1824
Gal	1:16 **i** I conferred not with flesh and blood:	2112
Rev	4: 2 And **i** I was in the spirit: and behold,	2112

IMMER (10)

1Ch	9:12 the son of Meshillemith, the son of **I**;	564
	24:14 The fifteenth to Bilgah, the sixteenth to **I**,	564
Ezr	2:37 The children of **I**, a thousand fifty and two.	564
	2:59 Tel-harsa, Cherub, Addan, *and* **I**:	564
	10:20 And of the sons of **I**; Hanani, and Zebadiah.	564
Ne	3:29 After them repaired Zadok the son of **I** over	564
	7:40 The children of **I**, a thousand fifty and two.	564
	7:61 Tel-haresha, Cherub, Addon, and **I**:	564
	11:13 the son of Meshillemoth, the son of **I**,	564
Jer	20: 1 Now Pashur the son of **I** the priest, who	564

IMMORAL See WHOREMONGER; WHOREMONGERS

IMMORALITY See LASCIVIOUSNESS

IMMORTAL (1) [IMMORTALITY]

1Ti	1:17 **i**, invisible, the only wise God, *be* honour	862

IMMORTALITY (5) [IMMORTAL]

Ro	2: 7 well doing seek for glory and honour and **i**,	861
1Co	15:53 and this mortal *must* put on **i**.	110
	15:54 and this mortal shall have put on **i**, then	110
1Ti	6:16 Who only hath **i**, dwelling in the light	110
2Ti	1:10 life and **i** to light through the gospel:	861

IMMUTABILITY (1) [IMMUTABLE]

Heb	6:17 the heirs of promise the **i** of his counsel,	276

IMMUTABLE (1) [IMMUTABILITY]

Heb	6:18 That by two **i** things, in which *it* was	276

IMNA (1)

1Ch	7:35 Zophah, and **I**, and Shelesh, and Amal.	3234

IMNAH (2)

1Ch	7:30 **I**, and Isuah, and Ishuai, and Beriah,	3232
2Ch	31:14 Kore the son of **I** the Levite, the porter	3232

IMNITE See JIMNITES

IMPART (2) [IMPARTED]

Lk	3:11 two coats, let him **i** to him that hath none;	3330
Ro	1:11 that I may **i** unto you some spiritual gift,	3330

IMPARTED (1) [IMPART]

Job	39:17 neither hath he **i** to her understanding,	2505
1Th	2: 8 we were willing to have **i** unto you,	3330

IMPEDIMENT (1)

Mk	7:32 *that was* deaf, and had an **i** **in** his **speech**;	3424

IMPENITENT (1)

Ro	2: 5 **i** heart treasurest up unto thyself wrath	279

IMPERIOUS (1)

Eze	16:30 *things*, the work of an **i** whorish woman;	7986

IMPERISHABLE See INCORRUPTIBLE; INCORRUPTION

IMPLACABLE (1)

Ro	1:31 without natural affection, **i**, unmerciful:	786

IMPLEAD (1)

Ac	19:38 there are deputies: let them **i** one another.	1458

IMPORTUNITY (1)

Lk	11: 8 because of his **i** he will rise and give him	335

IMPOSE (1) [IMPOSED]

Ezr	7:24 it *shall* not *be* lawful to **i** toll, tribute,	7412

IMPOSED (1) [IMPOSE]

Heb	9:10 *on them* until the time of reformation.	1945

IMPOSING See STOUT

IMPOSSIBLE (5) [UNPOSSIBLE]

Mk	10:27 With men *it is* **i**, but not with God:	102
Lk	17: 1 It is **i** but that offences will come:	418
Heb	6: 4 For *it is* **i** for those who were once	102
	6:18 in which *it was* **i** for God to lie,	102
	11: 6 But without faith *it is* **i** to please *him*: for	102

IMPOTENT (4)

Jn	5: 3 In these lay a great multitude of **i** *folk*, of	770
	5: 7 **i** *man* answered him, Sir, I have no man,	770
Ac	4: 9 of the good deed done to the **i** man,	772
	14: 8 sat a certain man at Lystra, **i** in *his* feet,	102

IMPOVERISH (1) [POVERTY]

Jer	5:17 they shall **i** thy fenced cities, wherein thou	7567

IMPOVERISHED (3) [POVERTY]
Jdg	6: 6 Israel was greatly i because of	1809
Isa	40:20 so i that he hath no oblation chooseth a	5533
Mal	1: 4 We are i, but we will return and build	7567

IMPRISONED (1) [PRISON]
Ac	22:19 they know that I i and beat in every	5439

IMPRISONMENT (2) [PRISON]
Ezr	7:26 or to confiscation of goods, or to i.	613
Heb	11:36 scourgings, yea, moreover of bonds and i:	5438

IMPRISONMENTS (1) [PRISON]
2Co	6: 5 In stripes, in i, in tumults, in labours,	5438

IMPROPERLY See UNCOMELY

IMPUDENT (3)
Pr	7:13 and with an i face said unto him,	5810
Eze	2: 4 For they are i children and	6440+7186
	3: 7 for all the house of Israel are i	2389+4696

IMPUTE (3) [IMPUTED, IMPUTETH, IMPUTING]
1Sa	22:15 not the king i any thing unto his servant,	7760
2Sa	19:19 Let not my lord i iniquity unto me,	2803
Ro	4: 8 the man to whom the Lord will not i sin.	3049

IMPUTED (8) [IMPUTE]
Lev	7:18 shall it be unto him that offereth i:	2803
	17: 4 blood shall be i unto that man; he hath	2803
Ro	4:11 that righteousness might be i unto them	3049
	4:22 therefore it was i to him for righteousness.	3049
	4:23 for his sake alone, that it was i to him;	3049
	4:24 But for us also, to whom it shall be i, if we	3049
	5:13 but sin is not i when there is no law.	1677
Jas	2:23 and it was i unto him for righteousness:	3049

IMPUTETH (2) [IMPUTE]
Ps	32: 2 man unto whom the Lord i not iniquity,	2803
Ro	4: 6 unto whom God i righteousness without	3049

IMPUTING (2) [IMPUTE]
Hab	1:11 and offend, i this his power unto his god.	NIH
2Co	5:19 not i their trespasses unto them;	3049

IMRAH (1)
1Ch	7:36 Harnepher, and Shual, and Beri, and I,	3236

IMRI (2)
1Ch	9: 4 son of Omri, the son of I, the son of Bani,	566
Ne	3: 2 next to them builded Zaccur the son of I.	566

IN (12674) [HEREIN, INASMUCH, INSOMUCH, INTO, THEREIN, WHEREIN, WHEREINSOEVER, WITHIN] See Index of Articles, Etc.

INASMUCH (9) [AS, IN, MUCH]
Dt	9: 6 death, i as he hated him not in time past.	3588
Ru	3:10 i as thou followedst not young men,	3807.1
Mt	25:40 I as ye have done it unto one of	1909+3745
	25:45 I as ye did it not to one of the least	1909+3745
Ro	11:13 i as I am the apostle	1909+3303+3745+3767
Php	1: 7 i as both in my bonds, and in the defence	5037
Heb	3: 3 i as he who hath builded the house	2596+3745
	7:20 i as not without an oath he was	2596+3745
1Pe	4:13 i as ye are partakers of Christ's sufferings;	2526

INCENSE (129) [FRANKINCENSE]
Ex	25: 6 spices for anointing oil, and for sweet i,	7004
	30: 1 thou shalt make an altar to burn i upon:	7004
	30: 7 Aaron shall burn thereon sweet i every	7004
	30: 7 the lamps, he shall burn i upon it.	6999
	30: 8 the lamps at even, he shall burn i upon it,	6999
	30: 8 a perpetual i before the Lord throughout	7004
	30: 9 Ye shall offer no strange i thereon,	7004
	30:27 and his vessels, and the altar of i,	7004
	31: 8 with all his furniture, and the altar of i,	7004
	31:11 sweet i for the holy place: according to all	7004
	35: 8 for anointing oil, and for the sweet i,	7004
	35:15 i altar and his staves, and the anointing	7004
	35:15 sweet i, and the hanging for the door at	7004
	35:28 for the anointing oil, and for the sweet i.	7004
	37:25 he made the i altar of shittim wood:	7004
	37:29 and the pure i of sweet spices,	7004
	39:38 the sweet i, and the hanging for	7004
	40: 5 thou shalt set the altar of gold for the i	7004
	40:27 he burnt sweet i thereon; as the Lord	7004
Lev	4: 7 of the altar of sweet i before the Lord,	7004
	10: 1 put i thereon, and offered strange fire	7004
	16:12 his hands full of sweet i beaten small,	7004
	16:13 he shall put the i upon the fire before	7004
	16:13 the cloud of the i may cover the mercy	7004
Nu	4:16 the sweet i, and the daily meat offering,	7004
	7:14 One spoon of ten shekels of gold, full of i:	7004
	7:20 One spoon of gold of ten shekels, full of i:	7004
	7:26 One golden spoon of ten shekels, full of i:	7004
	7:32 One golden spoon of ten shekels, full of i:	7004
	7:38 One golden spoon of ten shekels, full of i:	7004
	7:44 One golden spoon of ten shekels, full of i:	7004
	7:50 One golden spoon of ten shekels, full of i:	7004
	7:56 One golden spoon of ten shekels, full of i:	7004
	7:62 One golden spoon of ten shekels, full of i:	7004
	7:68 One golden spoon of ten shekels, full of i:	7004
	7:74 One golden spoon of ten shekels, full of i:	7004
	7:80 One golden spoon of ten shekels, full of i:	7004
	7:86 full of i, weighing ten shekels apiece,	7004

Nu	16: 7 put i in them before the Lord to morrow:	7004
	16:17 put i in them, and bring ye before	7004
	16:18 laid i thereon, and stood in the door of	7004
	16:35 two hundred and fifty men that offered i.	7004
	16:40 come near to offer i before the Lord;	7004
	16:46 put on i, and go quickly unto	7004
	16:47 he put on i, and made an atonement for	7004
Dt	33:10 they shall put i before thee,	6988
1Sa	2:28 offer upon mine altar, to burn i, to wear	7004
1Ki	3: 3 he sacrificed and burnt i in high places.	6999
	9:25 he burnt upon the altar that was before	6999
	11: 8 which burnt i and sacrificed unto their	6999
	12:33 he offered upon the altar, and burnt i.	6999
	13: 1 Jeroboam stood by the altar to burn i.	6999
	13: 2 of the high places that burn i upon thee,	6999
	22:43 for the people offered and burnt i	4480
2Ki	12: 3 and burnt i in the high places.	6999
	14: 4 sacrifice and burnt i on the high places.	6999
	15: 4 and burnt i still on the high places.	6999
	15:35 and burnt i still in the high places.	6999
	16: 4 sacrificed and burnt i in the high places,	6999
	17:11 there they burnt i in all the high places,	6999
	18: 4 the children of Israel did burn i to it:	6999
	22:17 and have burnt i unto other gods,	6999
	23: 5 burn i in the high places in the cities of	6999
	23: 5 also that burnt i unto Baal, to the sun,	6999
	23: 8 high places where the priests had burnt i,	6999
1Ch	6:49 on the altar of i, and were appointed for	7004
	23:13 sons for ever, to burn i before the Lord,	6999
	28:18 for the altar of i refined gold by weight;	7004
2Ch	2: 4 and to burn before him sweet i, and for	7004
	13:11 every evening burnt sacrifices and sweet i:	7004
	25:14 before them, and burned i unto them.	6999
	26:16 Lord to burn i upon the altar of incense.	6999
	26:16 Lord to burn incense upon the altar of i.	7004
	26:18 to burn i unto the Lord, but to	6999
	26:18 of Aaron, that are consecrated to burn i:	6999
	26:19 and had a censer in his hand to burn i:	6999
	26:19 of the Lord, from beside the i altar.	7004
	28: 3 Moreover he burnt i in the valley of	6999
	28: 4 and burnt i in the high places,	6999
	28:25 high places to burn i unto other gods,	6999
	29: 7 have not burnt i nor offered burnt	6999+7004
	29:11 should minister unto him, and burn i.	6999
	30:14 all the altars for i took they away,	6999
	32:12 before one altar, and burn i upon it?	6999
	34:25 and have burned i unto other gods,	6999
Ps	66:15 sacrifices of fatlings, with the i of rams;	7004
	141: 2 my prayer be set forth before thee as i;	7004
Isa	1:13 is an abomination unto me; the new	7004
	43:23 with an offering, nor wearied thee with i.	3828
	60: 6 they shall bring gold and i; and they shall	3828
	65: 3 and burneth i upon altars of brick;	6999
	65: 7 which have burnt i upon the mountains,	6999
	66: 3 he that burneth i, as if he blessed an idol.	3828
Jer	1:16 have burnt i unto other gods,	6999
	6:20 To what purpose cometh there to me i	3828
	7: 9 burn i unto Baal, and walk after other	6999
	11:12 cry unto the gods to whom they offer i:	6999
	11:13 even altars to burn i unto Baal.	6999
	11:17 me to anger in offering i unto Baal.	6999
	17:26 and i, and bringing sacrifices of praise,	3828
	18:15 they have burnt i to vanity, and they have	6999
	19: 4 and have burnt i in it unto other gods,	6999
	19:13 have burnt i unto all the host of heaven,	6999
	32:29 upon whose roofs they have offered i	6999
	41: 5 with offerings and i in their hand,	3828
	44: 3 in that they went to burn i, and to serve	6999
	44: 5 to burn no i unto other gods.	6999
	44: 8 burning i unto other gods in the land of	6999
	44:15 their wives had burnt i unto other gods,	6999
	44:17 to burn i unto the queen of heaven,	6999
	44:18 since we left off to burn i to the queen of	6999
	44:19 when we burnt i to the queen of heaven,	6999
	44:21 The i that ye burnt in the cities of Judah,	7002
	44:23 Because you have burnt i, and because	6999
	44:25 to burn i to the queen of heaven,	6999
	48:35 and him that burneth i to his gods.	6999
Eze	8:11 his hand; and a thick cloud of i went up.	7004
	16:18 hast set mine oil and mine i before them.	7004
	23:41 whereupon thou hast set mine i and	7004
Hos	2:13 wherein she burnt i to them,	6999
	4:13 burn i upon the hills, under oaks and	6999
	11: 2 and burned i to graven images.	6999
Mal	1:11 in every place i shall be offered unto my	6999
Lk	1: 9 his lot was to burn i when he went into	2370
	1:10 were praying without at the time of i.	2368
	1:11 standing on the right side of the altar of i.	2368
Rev	8: 3 and there was given unto him much i,	2368
	8: 4 And the smoke of the i, which came with	2368

INCENSED (2)
Isa	41:11 all they that were i against thee shall be	2734
	45:24 that are i against him shall be ashamed.	2734

INCLINE (16) [INCLINED, INCLINETH]
Jos	24:23 i your heart unto the Lord God of Israel.	5186
1Ki	8:58 he may i our hearts unto him, to walk	5186
Ps	17: 6 i thine ear unto me, and hear my speech.	5186
	45:10 O daughter, and consider, and i thine ear;	5186
	49: 4 I will i mine ear to a parable: I will	5186
	71: 2 escape: i thine ear unto me, and save me.	5186
	78: 1 i your ears to the words of my mouth.	5186
	88: 2 before thee: i thine ear unto my cry;	5186

Ps	102: 2 when I am in trouble; i thine ear unto me:	5186
	119:36 I my heart unto thy testimonies, and not	5186
	141: 4 I not my heart to any evil thing, to practise	5186
Pr	2: 2 So that thou i thine ear unto wisdom,	7181
	4:20 to my words; i thine ear unto my sayings.	5186
Isa	37:17 I thine ear, O Lord, and hear; open thine	5186
	55: 3 I your ear, and come unto me: hear,	5186
Da	9:18 my God, i thine ear, and hear; open thine	5186

INCLINED (13) [INCLINE]
Jdg	9: 3 their hearts i to follow Abimelech; for	5186
Ps	40: 1 and he i unto me, and heard my cry.	5186
	116: 2 Because he hath i his ear unto me,	5186
	119:112 I have i mine heart to perform thy statutes	5186
Pr	5:13 nor i mine ear to them that instructed me!	5186
Jer	7:24 nor i their ear, but walked in the counsels	5186
	7:26 nor i their ear, but hardened their neck:	5186
	11: 8 nor i their ear, but walked every one in	5186
	17:23 i their ear, but made their neck stiff,	5186
	25: 4 not hearkened, nor i your ear to hear.	5186
	34:14 hearkened not unto me, neither i their ear.	5186
	35:15 ye have not i your ear, nor hearkened	5186
	44: 5 nor i their ear to turn from their	5186

INCLINETH (1) [INCLINE]
Pr	2:18 For her house i unto death, and her paths	7743

INCLOSE (1) [INCLOSED, INCLOSINGS]
SS	8: 9 a door, we will i her with boards of cedar.	6696

INCLOSED (8) [INCLOSE]
Ex	39: 6 they wrought onyx stones i in ouches of	5437
	39:13 they were i in ouches of gold in their	5437
Jdg	20:43 Thus they i the Benjamites round about,	3803
Ps	17:10 They are i in their own fat: with their	5462
	22:16 the assembly of the wicked have i me:	5362
SS	4:12 A garden i is my sister, my spouse:	5274
La	3: 9 He hath i my ways with hewn stone,	1443
Lk	5: 6 done, they i a great multitude of fishes:	4788

INCLOSINGS (2) [INCLOSE]
Ex	28:20 a jasper: they shall be set in gold in their i.	4396
	39:13 were inclosed in ouches of gold in their i.	4396

INCONTINENCY (1) [INCONTINENT]
1Co	7: 5 that Satan tempt you not for your i.	192

INCONTINENT (1) [INCONTINENCY]
2Ti	3: 3 trucebreakers, false accusers, i, fierce,	193

INCORRUPTIBLE (4) [INCORRUPTION]
1Co	9:25 to obtain a corruptible crown; but we an i.	862
	15:52 and the dead shall be raised i, and we shall	862
1Pe	1: 4 To an inheritance i, and undefiled,	862
	1:23 but of i, by the word of God, which liveth	862

INCORRUPTION (4) [INCORRUPTIBLE]
1Co	15:42 It is sown in corruption; it is raised in i:	861
	15:50 of God; neither doth corruption inherit i.	861
	15:53 For this corruptible must put on i,	861
	15:54 when this corruptible shall have put on i,	861

INCREASE (88) [INCREASED, INCREASEST, INCREASETH, INCREASING]
Ge	47:24 shall come to pass in the i, that you shall	8393
Lev	19:25 That it may yield unto you the i thereof:	8393
	25: 7 in thy land, shall all the i thereof be meat.	8393
	25:12 ye shall eat the i thereof out of the field.	8393
	25:16 of years thou shalt i the price thereof,	7235
	25:20 we shall not sow, nor gather in our i:	8393
	25:36 Take thou no usury of him, or i:	8636
	25:37 usury, nor lend him thy victuals for i.	4768
	26: 4 the land shall yield her i, and the trees of	2981
	26:20 for your land shall not yield her i, neither	2981
Nu	18:30 shall be counted unto the Levites as the i	8393
	18:30 and as the i of the winepress.	8393
	32:14 in your fathers' stead, an i of sinful men,	8635
Dt	6: 3 with thee, and that ye may i mightily,	7235
	7:13 the i of thy kine, and the flocks of thy	7698
	7:22 lest the beasts of the field i upon thee.	7235
	14:22 Thou shalt truly tithe all the i of thy seed,	8393
	14:28 forth all the tithe of thine i the same year,	8393
	16:15 thy God shall bless thee in all thy i,	8393
	26:12 all the tithes of thine i the third year,	8393
	28: 4 the i of thy kine, and the flocks of thy	7698
	28:18 the i of thy kine, and the flocks of thy	7698
	28:51 or the i of thy kine, or flocks of thy sheep,	7698
	32:13 that he might eat the i of the fields;	8570
	32:22 shall consume the earth with her i,	2981
Jdg	6: 4 destroyed the i of the earth, till thou come	2981
	9:29 to Abimelech, I thine army, and come out.	7235
1Sa	2:33 all the i of thine house shall die in	4768
1Ch	27:23 the Lord had said he would i Israel like	7235
	27:27 over the i of the vineyards for the wine	7945
2Ch	31: 5 oil, and honey, and of all the i of the field;	8393
	32:28 Storehouses also for the i of corn,	8393
Ezr	10:10 to i the trespass of Israel.	3254+5921
Ne	9:37 it yieldeth much i unto the kings whom	8393
Job	8: 7 yet thy latter end should greatly i.	7685
	20:28 The i of his house shall depart,	2981
	31:12 and would root out all mine i.	8393
Ps	44:12 and dost not i thy wealth by their price.	7235
	62:10 if riches i, set not your heart upon them.	5107
	67: 6 Then shall the earth yield her i; and God,	2981
	71:21 Thou shalt i my greatness, and comfort	7235
	73:12 who prosper in the world; they i in riches.	7685

Ps 78:46 He gave also their **i** unto the caterpillar, 2981
85:12 *is* good; and our land shall yield her **i**, 2981
107:37 vineyards, which may yield fruits of **i**. 8393
115:14 The LORD shall **i** you **more and more,** 3254
Pr 1: 5 A wise *man* will hear, and will **i** learning; 3254
3: 9 and with the firstfruits of all thine **i**: 8393
9: 9 teach a just *man*, and he will **i** in learning. 3254
13:11 but he that gathereth by labour shall **i**. 7235
14: 4 but much **i** *is* by the strength of the ox. 8393
18:20 *and with* the **i** of his lips shall he be filled. 8393
22:16 that oppresseth the poor to **i** his *riches*, 7235
28:28 but when they perish, the righteous **i**. 7235
Ecc 5:10 nor he that loveth abundance *with* **i**: 8393
5:11 When goods **i**, they are increased that eat 7235
6:11 Seeing there be many things that **i** vanity, 7235
Isa 9: 7 the **i** of *his* government and peace *there* 4766
29:19 The meek also shall **i** *their* joy in 3254
30:23 bread of the **i** of the earth, and it shall be 8393
57: 9 didst **i** thy perfumes, and didst send thy 7235
Jer 2: 3 unto the LORD, *and* the firstfruits of his **i**: 8393
23: 3 their folds; and they shall be fruitful and **i**. 7235
Eze 5:16 I *will* **i** the famine upon you, and will 3254
18: 8 upon usury, neither hath taken any **i**, 8636
18:13 given forth upon usury, and hath taken **i**: 8636
18:17 *that* hath not received usury nor **i**, 8636
22:12 thou hast taken usury and **i**, and thou 8636
34:27 the earth shall yield her **i**, and they shall 2981
36:11 and beast; and they shall **i** and bring fruit: 7235
36:29 and will **i** it, and lay no famine upon you. 7235
36:30 the fruit of the tree, and the **i** of the field, 8570
36:37 I will **i** them *with* men like a flock. 7235
48:18 the **i** thereof shall be for food unto them 8393
Da 11:39 he shall acknowledge *and* **i** with glory: 7235
Hos 4:10 shall commit whoredom, and shall not **i**: 6555
Zec 8:12 ground shall give her **i**, and the heavens 2981
10: 8 and they shall **i** as they have increased. 7235
Lk 17: 5 apostles said unto the LORD, **I** our faith. 4369
Jn 3:30 He must **i**, but I *must* decrease. 837
1Co 3: 6 Apollos watered; but God **gave** the **i**. 837
3: 7 that watereth; but God that **giveth** the **i**. 837
2Co 9:10 and **i** the fruits of your righteousness;) 837
Eph 4:16 maketh **i** of the body unto the edifying of 838
Col 2:19 knit together, increaseth *with* the **i** of God. 838
1Th 3:12 the Lord **make** you to **i** and abound in 4121
4:10 brethren, that ye **i** *more and more;* 4052
2Ti 2:16 for they will **i** unto more ungodliness. 4298

INCREASED (49) [INCREASE]
Ge 7:17 the waters **i**, and bare up the ark, and it 7235
7:18 and were **i** greatly upon the earth; 7235
30:30 I *came*, and it is *now* **i** unto a multitude; 6555
30:43 man **i** exceedingly, and had much cattle, 6555
Ex 1: 7 **i** abundantly, and multiplied, 8317
23:30 until thou be **i**, and inherit the land. 6509
1Sa 14:19 the host of the Philistines went on and **i**: 7227
2Sa 15:12 for the people **i** continually with Absalom. 7227
1Ki 22:35 the battle **i** that day: and the king was 5927
1Ch 4:38 and the house of their fathers **i** greatly. 6555
5:23 they **i** from Bashan unto Baal-hermon and 7235
2Ch 18:34 the battle **i** that day: howbeit the king of 5927
Ezr 9: 6 for our iniquities are **i** over *our* head, 7235
Job 1:10 hands, and his substance is **i** in the land. 6555
Ps 3: 1 LORD, how are they **i** that trouble me! 7231
4: 7 the time *that* their corn and their wine **i**. 7231
49:16 rich, when the glory of his house is **i**; 7235
105:24 he **i** his people greatly; and made them 6509
Pr 9:11 and the years of thy life shall be **i**. 3254
Ecc 2: 9 **i more** than all that were before me in 3254
5:11 goods increase, they are **i** that eat them: 7231
Isa 9: 3 multiplied the nation, *and* not **i** the joy: 1431
26:15 Thou hast **i** the nation, O LORD, thou hast 3254
26:15 O LORD, thou hast **i** the nation: 3254
51: 2 him alone, and blessed him, and **i** him. 7235
Jer 3:16 when ye be multiplied and **i** in the land, 6509
5: 6 are many, *and* their backslidings are **i**. 6105
15: 8 Their widows are **i** to me above the sand 6105
29: 6 ye may be **i** there, and not diminished. 7235
30:14 of thine iniquity; because thy sins were **i**. 6105
30:15 because thy sins were **i**, I have done these 6105
La 2: 5 hath **i** in the daughter of Judah mourning 7235
Eze 16: 7 thou hast **i** and waxen great, and thou art 7235
16:26 hast **i** thy whoredoms, to provoke me to 7235
23:14 *that* she **i** her whoredoms: for when she 3254
28: 5 *and* by thy traffick hast thou **i** thy riches, 7235
41: 7 **i** *from* the lowest *chamber* to the highest 5927
Da 12: 4 run to and fro, and knowledge shall be **i**. 7235
Hos 4: 7 As they were **i**, so they sinned against me: 7230
10: 1 multitude of his fruit he hath **i** the altars; 7235
Am 4: 9 and your fig trees and your olive trees **i**, 7235
Zec 10: 8 and they shall increase as they have **i**. 7235
Mk 4: 8 and did yield fruit that sprang up and **i**; 837
Lk 2:52 And Jesus **i** in wisdom and stature, 4298
Ac 6: 7 And the word of God **i**; and the number of 837
9:22 But Saul **i** the more in **strength,** 1743
16: 5 in the faith, and **i** in number daily. 4052
2Co 10:15 but having hope, when your faith is **i**, 837
Rev 3:17 and **i with goods, and have need of** 4147

INCREASEST (1) [INCREASE]
Job 10:17 and **i** thine indignation upon me; 7235

INCREASETH (15) [INCREASE]
Job 10:16 For it **i**. Thou huntest me as a fierce lion: 1342
12:23 He **i** the nations, and destroyeth them: 7679
Ps 74:23 that rise up against thee **i** continually. 5927

Pr 11:24 There is that scattereth, and yet **i**; 3254
16:21 and the sweetness of the lips **i** learning. 3254
23:28 prey, and **i** the transgressors among men. 3254
24: 5 yea, a man of knowledge **i** strength. 553
28: 8 by usury and unjust gain **i** his substance, 7235
29:16 the wicked are multiplied, transgression **i**: 7235
Ecc 1:18 he that **i** knowledge increaseth sorrow. 3254
1:18 that increaseth knowledge **i** sorrow. 3254
Isa 40:29 to *them that have* no might he **i** strength. 7235
Hos 12: 1 he daily **i** lies and desolation; and they do 7235
Hab 2: 6 Woe to him that **i** *that which* is not his! 7235
Col 2:19 knit together, **i** *with* the increase of God. 837

INCREASING (1) [INCREASE]
Col 1:10 good work, and **i** in the knowledge of God; 837

INCREDIBLE (1)
Ac 26: 8 should it be thought *a thing* **i** with you, 571

INCURABLE (6)
2Ch 21:18 him in his bowels with an **i** disease. 369+4832
Job 34: 6 my wound *is* **i** without transgression. 605
Jer 15:18 is my pain perpetual, and my wound **i**, 605
30:12 Thy bruise is **i**, *and* thy wound is grievous. 605
30:15 thy sorrow is **i** for the multitude of thine 605
Mic 1: 9 her wound is **i**; for it is come unto Judah; 605

INDEBTED (1) [DEBT]
Lk 11: 4 we also forgive every one *that is* **i** to us. 3784

INDECENT See UNSEEMLY

INDECISIVE See TENDERHEARTED

INDEED (70)
Ge 17:19 Sarah thy wife shall bear thee a son **i**; 61
20:12 yet **i** *she is* my sister; she *is* the daughter of 546
37: 8 to him, Shalt thou **i reign** over us? 4427+4427
37: 8 shalt thou **i have dominion** over 4910+4910
37:10 thy brethren **i come** to bow down 935+935
40:15 For I was **i stolen away** out of 1589+1589
43:20 we **came i down** at the first time 3381+3381
44: 5 and whereby **i** he **divineth?** 5172+5172
Ex 15: 5 if ye will **obey** my voice **i**, 8085+8085+871.1
23:22 if thou shalt **i obey** his voice, 8085+8085
Lev 10:18 have **i eaten** it in the holy *place*, as I 398+398
Nu 12: 2 the LORD **i** spoken **only** by Moses? 5414+5414
21: 2 If thou wilt **i deliver** this people 5414+5414
22:37 am I not able **i** to promote thee to honour? 552
Dt 2:15 For **i** the hand of the LORD was against 1571
21:16 son of the hated, *which is* **i** the firstborn: NIH
Jos 7:20 I have sinned against the LORD God of 546
1Sa 1:11 if thou wilt **i look** on the affliction 7200+7200
2:30 I **said** **i** *that* thy house, and the house 559+559
2Sa 5: 1 am **i** a widow woman, and mine husband 61
15: 8 If the LORD shall **bring** me **again i** 7725+7725
1Ki 8:27 will God **i** dwell on the earth? behold, 552
2Ki 4:10 Thou hast **i smitten** Edom, 5221+5221
1Ch 4:10 Oh that thou wouldest **bless** me **i**, 1288+1288
21:17 that have sinned and **done evil i**; 7489+7489
Job 19: 4 if *that* I have erred, mine error remaineth 551
19: 5 If ye will magnify *yourselves* against me, 551
Ps 58: 1 Do ye **i** speak righteousness, 552
Isa 6: 9 **Hear** ye **i**, but understand not; 8085+8085
6: 9 and **see** ye **i**, but perceive not. 7200+7200
Jer 22: 4 For if ye **do** this thing **i**, then 6213+6213
Mt 3:11 I baptize you with water unto repentance: 3303
13:32 Which **i** is the least of all seeds: but when 3303
20:23 shall drink **i** *of* my cup, and be baptized 3303
23:27 which **i** appear beautiful outward, 3303
26:41 spirit **i** *is* willing, but the flesh *is* weak. 3303
Mk 1: 8 I have baptized you with water: 3303
9:13 That Elias is **i** come, and they have done 2532
10:39 Ye shall **i** drink *of* the cup that I drink *of;* 3303
11:32 counted John, that he was a prophet **i**. 3689
14:21 The Son of man **i** goeth, as it is written of 3303
Lk 3:16 unto *them* all, I **i** baptize you with water; 3303
11:48 for they **i** killed them, and ye build their 3303
23:41 And we **i** justly; for we receive the due 3303
24:34 The Lord is risen **i**, and hath appeared to 3689
Jn 1:47 and saith of him, Behold an Israelite **i**, 230
4:42 know that this is **i** the Christ, the Saviour 230
6:55 For my flesh is meat **i**, 230
6:55 is meat indeed, and my blood is drink **i**. 230
7:26 Do the rulers know **i** that this is the very 230
8:31 in my word, *then* are ye my disciples **i**; 230
8:36 shall make you free, ye shall be free **i**. 3689
Ac 4:16 that a notable miracle hath been done 3303
11:16 that he said, John **i** baptized with water; 3303
22: 9 they that were with me saw **i** the light, 3303
Ro 6:11 ye also yourselves to be dead **i** unto sin, 3303
8: 7 to the law of God, neither **i** can be. 1063
14:20 All *things* **i** *are* pure; but *it is* evil for that 3303
1Co 11: 7 For a man ought not to cover *his* head, 3303
2Co 8:17 For he accepted the exhortation; 3303
11: 1 me a little in *my* folly: and **i** bear with me. 2532
Php 1:15 Some **i** preach Christ even of envy and 3303
2:27 For he was sick nigh unto death: 2532
3: 1 to me **i** *is* not grievous, but for you **i** *is* 3303
Col 2:23 Which *things* have **i** a shew of wisdom in 3303
1Th 4:10 And **i** ye do it toward all the brethren 2532
1Ti 5: 3 Honour widows that are widows **i**. 3689
5: 5 Now she that is a widow **i**, and desolate, 3689
5:16 that it may relieve them that are widows **i**. 3689
1Pe 2: 4 disallowed **i** of men, but chosen of God, 3303

INDESCRIBABLE See UNSPEAKABLE

INDIA (2)
Est 1: 1 I even unto Ethiopia, *over* an hundred 1912
8: 9 rulers of the provinces which *are* from **I** 1912

INDIGNATION (41)
Dt 29:28 great **i**, and cast them into another land, 7110
2Ki 3:27 there was great **i** against Israel: 7110
Ne 4: 1 **took** great **i**, and mocked the Jews. 3707
Est 5: 9 for him, he was full of **i** against Mordecai. 2534
Job 10:17 and increasest thine **i** upon me; 3708
Ps 69:24 Pour out thine **i** upon them, and let thy 2195
78:49 wrath, and **i**, and trouble, *by* sending evil 2195
102:10 Because of thine **i** and thy wrath: for thou 2195
Isa 10: 5 and the staff in their hand is mine **i**. 2195
10:25 the **i** shall cease, and mine anger in their 2195
13: 5 *even* the LORD, and the weapons of his **i**, 2195
26:20 a little moment, until the **i** be overpast. 2195
30:27 his lips are full of **i**, and his tongue as a 2195
30:30 with the **i** of *his* anger, and with the flame 2197
34: 2 For the **i** of the LORD *is* upon all nations, 7110
66:14 servants, and *his* **i** towards his enemies. 2194
Jer 10:10 nations shall not be able to abide his **i**. 2195
15:17 of thy hand: for thou hast filled me *with* **i**. 2195
50:25 hath brought forth the weapons of his **i**: 2195
La 2: 6 despised in the **i** of his anger the king 2195
Eze 21:31 I will pour out mine **i** upon thee, I will 2195
22:24 nor rained upon in the day of **i**. 2195
22:31 Therefore have I poured out mine **i** upon 2195
Da 8:19 what shall be in the last end of the **i**: 2195
11:30 and have **i** against the holy covenant: 2194
11:36 shall prosper till the **i** be accomplished: 2195
Mic 7: 9 I will bear the **i** of the LORD, because 2197
Na 1: 6 Who can stand before his **i**? and who can 2195
Hab 3:12 Thou didst march through the land in **i**, 2195
Zep 3: 8 to pour upon them mine **i**, *even* all my 2195
Zec 1:12 *against* which thou hast had **i** these 2194
Mal 1: 4 *against* whom the LORD hath **i** for ever. 2194
Mt 20:24 were **moved with i** against the two 23
26: 8 But when his disciples saw it, they **had i**, 23
Mk 14: 4 And there were some that **had i** within 23
Lk 13:14 ruler of the synagogue answered with **i**, 23
Ac 5:17 of the Sadducees,) and were filled with **i**, 2205
Ro 2: 8 but obey unrighteousness, **i** and wrath, 2372
2Co 7:11 yea, *what* **i**, yea, *what* fear, yea, 24
Heb 10:27 fearful looking for of judgment and fiery **i**, 2205
Rev 14:10 out without mixture into the cup of his **i**; 3709

INDITING (1)
Ps 45: 1 My heart is **i** a good matter: I speak of 7370

INDUSTRIOUS (1)
1Ki 11:28 the young man that he was **i**, 4399+6213

INEXCUSABLE (1)
Ro 2: 1 Therefore thou art **i**, O man, whosoever 379

INEXPRESSIBLE See UNSPEAKABLE

INFALLIBLE (1)
Ac 1: 3 alive after his passion by many **i proofs,** 5039

INFAMOUS (1) [INFAMY]
Eze 22: 5 *art* **i** *and* much vexed. 2931+8034+1886.1

INFAMY (2) [INFAMOUS]
Pr 25:10 thee to shame, and thine **i** turn not away. 1681
Eze 36: 3 lips of talkers, and *are* an **i** of the people: 1681

INFANT (2) [INFANTS]
1Sa 15: 3 **i** and suckling, ox and sheep, camel and 5768
Isa 65:20 shall be no more thence an **i** of days, 5764

INFANTS (3) [INFANT]
Job 3:16 had not been; as **i** *which* never saw light. 5768
Hos 13:16 their **i** shall be dashed in pieces, 5768
Lk 18:15 And they brought unto him also **i**, that he 1025

INFERIOR (4)
Job 12: 3 as well as you; I *am* not **i** to you: 5307
13: 2 *same* do I know also. I *am* not **i** unto you. 5307
Da 2:39 after thee shall arise another kingdom **i** to 772
2Co 12:13 For what is it wherein ye were **i** to other 2274

INFIDEL (2)
2Co 6:15 what part hath he that believeth with an **i**? 571
1Ti 5: 8 denied the faith, and is worse than an **i**. 571

INFINITE (3)
Job 22: 5 and thine iniquities **i**? 369+7093
Ps 147: 5 great power: his understanding *is* **i**. 369+4557
Na 3: 9 *were* her strength, and *it was* **i**; 369+7097

INFIRMITIES (12) [INFIRMITY]
Mt 8:17 saying Himself took our **i**, and bare our 769
Lk 5:15 to hear, and to be healed by him of their **i**. 769
7:21 in that *same* hour he cured many of *their* **i** 3554
8: 2 which had been healed of evil spirits and **i**, 769
Ro 8:26 Likewise the Spirit also helpeth our **i**: 769
15: 1 that are strong ought to bear the **i** of 771
2Co 11:30 glory of the *things* which concern mine **i**. 769
12: 5 yet of myself I will not glory, but in mine **i**. 769
12: 9 therefore will I rather glory in my **i**, 769
12:10 I take pleasure in, in reproaches, 769
1Ti 5:23 for thy stomach's sake and thine often **i**. 769

I

Heb 4:15 be touched with the feeling of our **i**; 769

INFIRMITY (10) [INFIRMITIES]
Lev 12: 2 separation for her **i** shall she be unclean. 1738
Ps 77:10 I said, This **is** my **i**: *but* I will remember 2470
Pr 18:14 The spirit of a man will sustain his **i**; 4245
Lk 13:11 there was a woman which had a spirit of **i** 769
13:12 her, Woman, thou art loosed from thy **i**. 769
Jn 5: 5 which had an **i** thirty *and* eight years. 769
Ro 6:19 men because of the **i** of your flesh: 769
Gal 4:13 Ye know how through **i** of the flesh I 769
Heb 5: 2 that he himself also is compassed with **i**, 769
7:28 law maketh men high priests which have **i**; 769

INFLAME (1) [INFLAMING, INFLAMMATION]
Isa 5:11 that continue until night, *till* wine **i** them! 1814

INFLAMING (1) [INFLAME]
Isa 57: 5 I yourselves with idols under every green 2552

INFLAMMATION (2) [INFLAME]
Lev 13:28 him clean: for it *is* an **i** of the burning. 6867
Dt 28:22 with an **i**, and with an extreme burning, 1816

INFLICTED (1)
2Co 2: 6 *is* this punishment, which *was* **i** of many. NIG

INFLUENCES (1)
Job 38:31 Canst thou bind the **sweet i** of Pleiades, 4575

INFOLDING (1)
Eze 1: 4 fire **i** itself, and a brightness *was* about it, 3947

INFORM (1) [INFORMED]
Dt 17:10 to do according to all that they **i** thee: 3384

INFORMED (6) [INFORM]
Da 9:22 he **i** *me*, and talked with me, and said, 995
Ac 21:21 they are **i** of thee, that thou teachest all 2727
21:24 whereof they were **i** concerning thee, 2727
24: 1 who **i** the governor against Paul. 1718
25: 2 the chief of the Jews **i** him against Paul, 1718
25:15 elders of the Jews **i** *me*, desiring *to* have 1718

INGATHERING (2) [GATHER]
Ex 23:16 feast of **i**, *which is* in the end of the year, 614
34:22 and the feast of **i** *at* the year's end. 614

INHABIT (10) [HABITABLE, HABITATION, HABITATIONS, INHABITANT, INHABITANTS, INHABITED, INHABITERS, INHABITEST, INHABITETH, INHABITING]
Nu 35:34 therefore the land which ye shall **i**, 3427
Pr 10:30 but the wicked shall not **i** the earth. 7931
Isa 42:11 *their voice*, the villages *that* Kedar doth **i**: 3427
65:21 **i** *them;* and they shall plant vineyards, 3427
65:22 They shall not build, and another **i**; 3427
Jer 17: 6 **i** the parched places in the wilderness, 7931
48:18 Thou daughter that dost **i** Dibon, 3427
Eze 33:24 that **i** those wastes of the land of Israel 3427
Am 9:14 **i** *them;* and they shall plant vineyards, 3427
Zep 1:13 not **i** *them;* and they shall plant vineyards, 3427

INHABITANT (33) [INHABIT]
Job 28: 4 The flood breaketh out from the **i**; *even* 1481
Isa 5: 9 be desolate, *even* great and fair, without **i**. 3427
6:11 Until the cities be wasted without **i**, 3427
9: 9 Ephraim and the **i** of Samaria, that say 3427
12: 6 Cry out and shout, thou **i** of Zion: 3427
20: 6 the **i** of this isle shall say in that day, 3427
24:17 the snare, *are* upon thee, O **i** of the earth. 3427
33:24 the **i** shall not say, I am sick: the people 7934
Jer 2:15 land waste: his cities are burnt without **i**. 3427
4: 7 thy cities shall be laid waste, without an **i**. 3427
9:11 the cities of Judah desolate, without an **i**. 3427
10:17 wares out of the land, O **i** of the fortress. 3427
21:13 O **i** of the valley, *and* rock of the plain, 3427
22:23 O **i** of Lebanon, that makest thy nest in 3427
26: 9 this city shall be desolate without an **i**? 3427
33:10 and without **i**, and without beast, 3427
34:22 cities of Judah a desolation without an **i**. 3427
44:22 and a curse, without an **i**, as *at* this day. 3427
46:19 shall be waste and desolate without an **i**. 3427
48:19 O **i** of Aroer, stand by the way and espy; 3427
48:43 upon thee, O **i** of Moab, saith the Lord. 3427
51:29 land of Babylon a desolation without an **i**. 3427
51:35 *be* upon Babylon, shall the **i** of Zion say; 3427
51:37 and a hissing, without an **i**. 3427
Am 1: 5 cut off the **i** from the plain of Aven, 3427
1: 8 I will cut off the **i** from Ashdod, 3427
Mic 1:11 Pass ye away, thou **i** of Saphir, having thy 3427
1:11 the **i** of Zaanan came not forth *in* 3427
1:12 For the **i** of Maroth waited carefully for 3427
1:13 O thou **i** of Lachish, bind the chariot to 3427
1:15 I bring an heir unto thee, O **i** of Mareshah: 3427
Zep 2: 5 even destroy thee, that there shall be no **i**. 3427
3: 6 that there is no man, that there is none **i**. 3427

INHABITANTS (201) [INHABIT]
Ge 19:25 all the **i** of the cities, and that which grew 3427
34:30 make me to stink among the **i** of the land, 3427
50:11 when the **i** of the land, the Canaanites, 3427
Ex 15:14 shall take hold on the **i** of Palestina. 3427
15:15 all the **i** of Canaan shall melt away. 3427
23:31 for I will deliver the **i** of the land into your 3427
34:12 lest thou make a covenant with the **i** 3427

Ex 34:15 Lest thou make a covenant with the **i** of 3427
Lev 18:25 and the land *itself* vomiteth out her **i**. 3427
25:10 *all* the land unto all the **i** thereof: 3427
Nu 13:32 *is* a land that eateth up the **i** thereof; 3427
14:14 will tell *it* to the **i** of this land: *for* they 3427
32:17 fenced cities because of the **i** of the land. 3427
33:52 ye shall drive out all the **i** of the land from 3427
33:53 ye shall dispossess *the* **i** *of* the land, NIH
33:55 if ye will not drive out the **i** of the land 3427
Dt 13:13 have withdrawn the **i** of their city, saying, 3427
13:15 Thou shalt surely smite the **i** of that city 3427
Jos 2: 9 that all the **i** of the land faint because of 3427
2:24 for even all the **i** of the country do faint 3427
7: 9 all the **i** of the land shall hear *of it*, and 3427
8:24 an end of slaying all the **i** of Ai in the field, 3427
8:26 *he* had utterly destroyed all the **i** of Ai. 3427
9: 3 when the **i** of Gibeon heard what Joshua 3427
9:11 and all the **i** of our country spake to us, 3427
9:24 to destroy all the **i** of the land from before 3427
10: 1 how the **i** of Gibeon had made peace with 3427
11:19 of Israel, save the Hivites the **i** of Gibeon: 3427
13: 6 All the **i** of the hill country from Lebanon 3427
15:15 he went up thence to the **i** of Debir: 3427
15:63 As for the Jebusites the **i** of Jerusalem, 3427
17: 7 the right hand unto the **i** of En-tappuah. 3427
17:11 the **i** of Dor and her towns, 3427
17:11 the **i** of Endor and her towns, 3427
17:11 the **i** of Taanach and her towns, 3427
17:11 and the **i** of Megiddo and her towns, 3427
17:12 could not drive out *the* **i** *of* those cities; NIH
Jdg 1:11 thence he went against the **i** of Debir: 3427
1:19 he drave out *the* **i** *of* the mountain; NIH
1:19 could not drive out the **i** of the valley, 3427
1:27 Neither did Manasseh drive out *the* **i** *of* NIH
1:27 towns, nor the **i** of Dor and her towns, 3427
1:27 nor the **i** of Ibleam and her towns, 3427
1:27 nor the **i** of Megiddo and her towns: 3427
1:30 Neither did Zebulun drive out the **i** of 3427
1:30 inhabitants of Kitron, nor the **i** of Nahalol; 3427
1:31 Neither did Asher drive out the **i** of Accho 3427
1:31 nor the **i** of Zidon, nor of Ahlab, nor of 3427
1:32 among the Canaanites, the **i** of the land: 3427
1:33 Neither did Naphtali drive out the **i** of 3427
1:33 of Beth-shemesh, nor the **i** of Beth-anath; 3427
1:33 among the Canaanites, the **i** of the land: 3427
1:33 nevertheless the **i** of Beth-shemesh and 3427
2: 2 ye shall make no league with the **i** of this 3427
5: 7 The **i** of the villages ceased, they ceased in NIH
5:11 the righteous acts *towards* the **i** of his NIH
5:23 the Lord, curse ye bitterly the **i** thereof; 3427
10:18 he said be head over all the **i** of Gilead. 3427
11: 8 and be our head over all the **i** of Gilead. 3427
11:21 of the Amorites, the **i** of that country. 3427
20:15 that drew sword, beside the **i** of Gibeah, 3427
21: 9 *there were* none of the **i** of Jabesh-gilead 3427
21:10 smite the **i** of Jabesh-gilead with the edge 3427
21:12 they found among the **i** of Jabesh-gilead 3427
Ru 4: 4 Buy *it* before the **i**, and before the elders 3427
1Sa 6:21 they sent messengers to the **i** of 3427
6:21 So David saved the **i** of Keilah. 3427
27: 8 for those *nations were* of old the **i** of 3427
31:11 when the **i** of Jabesh-gilead heard of that 3427
2Sa 5: 6 unto the Jebusites, the **i** of the land: 3427
1Ki 17: 1 *was* of the **i** of Gilead, said unto Ahab, 8453
21:11 and the nobles who *were* the **i** in his city, 3427
2Ki 19:26 Therefore their **i** *were* of small power, 3427
22:16 upon this place, and upon the **i** thereof, 3427
22:19 against the **i** thereof, that *they* should 3427
23: 2 and all the **i** of Jerusalem with him, 3427
1Ch 8: 6 *are* the heads of the fathers of the **i** of 3427
8:13 who *were* the heads of the fathers of the **i** 3427
8:13 of Aijalon, who drove away the **i** of Gath: 3427
9: 2 Now the first **i** that *dwelt* in their 3427
11: 4 the Jebusites *were*, the **i** of the land. 3427
11: 5 **i** of Jebus said to David, Thou shalt not 3427
22:18 he hath given the **i** of the land into mine 3427
2Ch 15: 5 great vexations *were* upon all the **i** of 3427
20: 7 didst drive out the **i** of this land before 3427
20:15 ye **i** of Jerusalem, and thou king 3427
20:18 the **i** of Jerusalem fell before the Lord, 3427
20:20 Hear me, O Judah, and ye **i** of Jerusalem; 3427
20:23 Moab stood up against the **i** of mount Seir 3427
20:23 they had made an end of the **i** of Seir, 3427
21:11 caused the **i** of Jerusalem to commit 3427
21:13 and the **i** of Jerusalem to go a whoring, 3427
22: 1 the **i** of Jerusalem made Ahaziah his 3427
32:22 the **i** of Jerusalem from the hand of 3427
32:26 *both* he and the **i** of Jerusalem, so that 3427
32:33 the **i** of Jerusalem did him honour at his 3427
33: 9 made Judah and the **i** of Jerusalem to err, 3427
34:24 upon this place, and upon the **i** thereof, 3427
34:27 the **i** thereof, and humbledst thyself 3427
34:28 this place, and upon the **i** of the same. 3427
34:30 the **i** of Jerusalem, and the priests, 3427
34:32 Benjamin to stand *to it*. And the **i** of 3427
35:18 that were present, and the **i** of Jerusalem. 3427
Ezr 4: 6 *him* an accusation against the **i** of Judah 3427
Ne 3:13 gate repaired Hanun, and the **i** of Zanoah; 3427
7: 3 and appoint watches of the **i** of Jerusalem, 3427
9:24 thou subduedst before them the **i** of 3427
Job 26: 5 from under the waters, and the **i** thereof. 7931
Ps 33: 8 let all the **i** of the world stand in awe of 3427
33:14 he looketh upon all the **i** of the earth. 3427
49: 1 ye people; give ear, all ye **i** of the world: 3427
75: 3 and all the **i** thereof *are* dissolved: 3427

Ps 83: 7 Amalek; the Philistines with the **i** of Tyre; 3427
Isa 5: 3 O **i** of Jerusalem, and men of Judah, judge, 3427
8:14 a gin and for a snare to the **i** of Jerusalem. 3427
10:13 I have put down the **i** like a valiant *man*: 3427
10:31 the **i** of Gebim gather themselves to flee. 3427
18: 3 All ye **i** of the world, and dwellers on 3427
21:14 The **i** of the land of Tema brought water 3427
22:21 he shall be a father to the **i** of Jerusalem, 3427
23: 2 Be still, ye **i** of the isle; thou whom 3427
23: 6 ye over to Tarshish; howl, ye **i** of the isle. 3427
24: 1 and scattereth abroad the **i** thereof. 3427
24: 5 earth also is defiled under the **i** thereof; 3427
24: 6 therefore the **i** of the earth are burned, 3427
26: 9 the **i** of the world will learn righteousness. 3427
26:18 neither have the **i** of the world fallen. 3427
26:21 punish the **i** of the earth for their iniquity: 3427
37:27 Therefore their **i** *were* of small power, 3427
38:11 I shall behold man no more with the **i** of 3427
40:22 and the **i** thereof *are* as grasshoppers; 3427
42:10 that is therein; the isles, and the **i** thereof. 3427
42:11 let the **i** of the rock sing, let them shout 3427
49:19 now be too narrow by reason of the **i**, 3427
Jer 1:14 shall break forth upon all the **i** of the land. 3427
4: 4 ye men of Judah and **i** of Jerusalem: 3427
6:12 I will stretch out my hand upon the **i** of 3427
8: 1 bones of the **i** of Jerusalem, out of their 3427
10:18 will sling out the **i** of the land at this once, 3427
11: 2 men of Judah, and to the **i** of Jerusalem; 3427
11: 9 of Judah, and among the **i** of Jerusalem. 3427
11:12 the cities of Judah and **i** of Jerusalem go, 3427
13:13 Behold, I *will* fill all the **i** of this land, 3427
13:13 the prophets, and all the **i** of Jerusalem, 3427
17:20 and all Judah, and all the **i** of Jerusalem, 3427
17:25 the men of Judah, and the **i** of Jerusalem: 3427
18:11 to the **i** of Jerusalem, saying, Thus saith 3427
19: 3 O kings of Judah, and **i** of Jerusalem; 3427
19:12 to the **i** thereof, and *even* make this city 3427
21: 6 I will smite the **i** of this city, both man 3427
23:14 as Sodom, and the **i** thereof as Gomorrah. 3427
25: 2 and to all the **i** of Jerusalem, saying, 3427
25: 9 against the **i** thereof, and against all these 3427
25:29 for I *will* call for a sword upon all the **i** of 3427
25:30 *the grapes*, against all the **i** of the earth. 3427
26:15 and upon this city, and upon the **i** thereof: 3427
32:32 the men of Judah, and the **i** of Jerusalem, 3427
35:13 the men of Judah and the **i** of Jerusalem, 3427
35:17 upon all the **i** of Jerusalem all the evil that 3427
36:31 upon the **i** of Jerusalem, and upon the men 3427
42:18 my fury hath been poured forth upon the **i** 3427
46: 8 I will destroy the city and the **i** thereof. 3427
47: 2 and all the **i** of the land shall howl. 3427
49: 8 turn back, dwell deep, O **i** of Dedan; 3427
49:20 that he hath purposed against the **i** of 3427
49:30 you far off, dwell deep, O ye **i** of Hazor, 3427
50:21 *even* against it, and against the **i** of Pekod: 3427
50:34 to the land, and disquiet the **i** of Babylon. 3427
50:35 upon the **i** of Babylon, and upon her 3427
51:12 done that which he spake against the **i** of 3427
51:24 to all the **i** of Chaldea all their evil that 3427
51:35 my blood upon the **i** of Chaldea, 3427
La 4:12 of the earth, and all the **i** of the world, 3427
Eze 11:15 they unto whom the **i** of Jerusalem have 3427
12:19 of Jerusalem, *and* of the land of 3427
15: 6 for fuel, so will I give the **i** of Jerusalem. 3427
26:17 wast strong in the sea, she and her **i**, 3427
27: 8 The **i** of Zidon and Arvad were thy 3427
27:35 All the **i** of the isles shall be astonished at 3427
29: 6 all the **i** of Egypt shall know that I *am* 3427
Da 4:35 the earth *are* reputed as nothing: 1753
4:35 of heaven, and *among* the **i** of the earth: 1753
9: 7 to the **i** of Jerusalem, and unto all Israel, 3427
Hos 4: 1 hath a controversy with the **i** of the land, 3427
10: 5 The **i** of Samaria shall fear because of 7934
Joel 1: 2 old men, and give ear, all ye **i** of the land. 3427
1:14 all the **i** of the land *into* the house of 3427
2: 1 let all the **i** of the land tremble: for the day 3427
Mic 6:12 the **i** thereof have spoken lies, 3427
6:16 a desolation, and the **i** thereof a hissing: 3427
Zep 1: 4 and upon all the **i** of Jerusalem; 3427
1:11 Howl, ye **i** of Maktesh, for all the 3427
1:11 Woe unto the **i** of the sea coast, the nation 3427
Zec 8:20 come people, and the **i** of many cities: 3427
8:21 the **i** of one *city* shall go to another, 3427
11: 6 For I will no more pity the **i** of the land, 3427
12: 5 The **i** of Jerusalem *shall be* my strength in 3427
12: 7 the glory of the **i** of Jerusalem do not 3427
12: 8 In that day shall the Lord defend the **i** of 3427
12:10 upon the **i** of Jerusalem, the spirit of grace 3427
13: 1 to the **i** of Jerusalem for sin and 3427

INHABITED (32) [INHABIT]
Ge 36:20 sons of Seir the Horite, who **i** the land; 3427
Ex 16:35 forty years, until they came to a land **i**; 3427
Lev 16:22 him all their iniquities unto a land **not i**: 1509
Jdg 1:17 they slew the Canaanites that **i** Zephath, 3427
1:21 drive out the Jebusites that **i** Jerusalem; 3427
1Ch 5: 9 eastward he **i** unto the entering in of 3427
Isa 13:20 It shall never be **i**, neither shall it be dwelt 3427
44:26 that saith to Jerusalem, Thou shalt be **i**; 3427
45:18 created it not in vain, he formed it to be **i**: 3427
54: 3 and **make** the desolate cities **to be i**. 3427
Jer 6: 8 lest I make thee desolate, a land not **i**. 3427
17: 6 in the wilderness, *in* a salt land and not **i**. 3427
22: 6 a wilderness *and* cities *which* are not **i**. 3427
46:26 afterwards it shall be **i**, as *in* the days of 7931

Jer 50:13 of the wrath of the LORD it shall not be i, 3427
50:39 it shall be no more i for ever; neither shall 3427
Eze 12:20 the cities that are i shall be laid waste, 3427
26:17 *wast* i of seafaring men, the renowned 3427
26:19 desolate city, like the cities that are not i; 3427
26:20 go down to the pit, that thou be not i; 3427
29:11 through it, neither shall it be i forty years. 3427
34:13 and in all the **i places** of the country. 4186
36:10 the cities shall be i, and the wastes shall 3427
36:35 cities *are become* fenced, *and* are i. 3427
38:12 upon the desolate places *that are now* i, 3427
Zec 2: 4 Jerusalem shall be i *as* towns without 3427
7: 7 when Jerusalem was i and in prosperity, 3427
7: 7 *when men* i the south and the plain? 3427
9: 5 from Gaza, and Ashkelon shall not be i. 3427
12: 6 Jerusalem shall be i again in her own 3427
14:10 it shall be lifted up, and i in her place, 3427
14:11 but Jerusalem shall be safely i. 3427

INHABITERS (3) [INHABIT]
Rev 8:13 to the i of the earth by reason of the other 2730
12:12 Woe to the i of the earth and of the sea! 2730
17: 2 the i of the earth have been made drunk 2730

INHABITEST (1) [INHABIT]
Ps 22: 3 art holy, O thou that i the praises of Israel. 3427

INHABITETH (2) [INHABIT]
Job 15:28 *and* in houses which no man i, which are 3427
Isa 57:15 saith the high and lofty One that i eternity, 7931

INHABITING (1) [INHABIT]
Ps 74:14 *be* meat to the people i **the wilderness**. 6728

INHERIT (62) [INHERITANCE, INHERITANCES, INHERITED, INHERITETH, INHERITOR]
Ge 15: 7 the Chaldees, to give thee this land to i it. 3423
15: 8 whereby shall I know that I shall i it? 3423
28: 4 that thou mayest i the land wherein thou 3423
Ex 23:30 until thou be increased, and i the land. 5157
32:13 unto your seed, and they shall i *it* for ever. 5157
Lev 20:24 Ye shall i their land, and I will give it unto 3423
25:46 after you, to i *them for* a possession; 3423
Nu 18:24 I have given to the Levites to i: 5159
26:55 of the tribes of their fathers they shall i. 5157
32:19 we will not i with them on *yonder* side 5157
33:54 to the tribes of your fathers ye shall i. 5157
34:13 This *is* the land which ye shall i by lot, 5157
Dt 1:38 for he shall **cause** Israel **to** i it. 5157
2:31 to possess, that *thou* mayest i his land. 3423
3:28 he shall **cause** him to i the land which 5157
12:10 the LORD your God **giveth** you **to** i, 5157
16:20 i the land which the LORD thy God 3423
19: 3 which the LORD thy God **giveth** thee **to** i, 5157
19:14 which thou shalt i in the land that 5157
21:16 when he **maketh** his sons **to** i *that* which 5157
31: 7 and thou shalt **cause** them **to** i it. 5157
Jos 17: 14 given me *but* one lot and one portion to i, 5159
Jdg 11: 2 Thou shalt not i in our father's house; 5157
1Sa 2: 8 and to **make** them i the throne of glory; 5157
2Ch 20:11 which thou hast **given** us **to** i. 3423
Ps 25:13 at ease; and his seed shall i the earth. 3423
37: 9 upon the LORD, they shall i the earth. 3423
37:11 meek shall i the earth; and shall delight 3423
37:22 For such as be blessed of him shall i 3423
37:29 The righteous shall i the land, 3423
37:34 and he shall exalt thee to i the land: 3423
69:36 The seed also of his servants shall i it: 5157
82: 8 the earth: for thou shalt i all nations. 5157
Pr 3:35 The wise shall i glory: but shame shall be 5157
8:21 That *I* may **cause** those that love me **to** i 5157
11:29 He that troubleth his own house shall i 5157
14:18 The simple i folly: but the prudent are 5157
Isa 49: 8 to **cause to** i the desolate heritages; 5157
54: 3 thy seed shall i the Gentiles, and make 3423
57:13 the land, and shall i my holy mountain; 3423
60:21 they shall i the land for ever, the branch 3423
65: 9 mine elect shall i it, and my servants shall 3423
Jer 8:10 their fields to them that *shall* i them: for 3423
12:14 I have **caused** my people Israel **to** i; 5157
49: 1 why *then* doth their king i Gad, 3423
Eze 47:13 whereby ye shall i the land according to 5157
47:14 ye shall i it, one as well as another: 5157
Zec 2:12 the LORD shall i Judah his portion in 5157
Mt 5: 5 are the meek: for they shall i the earth. 2816
19:29 hundredfold, and shall i everlasting life. 2816
25:34 i the kingdom prepared for you from 2816
Mk 10:17 what shall I do that I may i eternal life? 2816
Lk 10:25 Master, what shall I do to i eternal life? 2816
18:18 shall I do to i eternal life? 2816
1Co 6: 9 ye not that the unrighteous shall not i 2816
6:10 shall i the kingdom of God. 2816
15:50 and blood cannot i the kingdom of God; 2816
15:50 neither doth corruption i incorruption. 2816
Gal 5:21 that they which do such *things* shall not i 2816
Heb 6:12 through faith and patience i the promises. 2816
1Pe 3: 9 called, that ye should i a blessing. 2816
Rev 21: 7 He that overcometh shall i all *things;* and 2816

INHERITANCE (239) [INHERIT]
Ge 31:14 or i for us in our father's house? 5159
48: 6 after the name of their brethren in their i. 5159
Ex 15:17 plant them in the mountain of thine i, 5159
34: 9 and our sin, and **take** us **for** thine i. 5157
Lev 25:46 shall **take** them **as** an i for your children 5157

Nu 16:14 or given us i of fields and vineyards: 5159
18:20 Thou shalt **have** no i in their land, 5157
18:20 and thine i among the children of Israel. 5159
18:21 of Levi all the tenth in Israel for an i, 5159
18:23 children of Israel they **have** no i. 5157+5159
18:24 of Israel they shall **have** no i. 5157+5159
18:26 I have given you from them for your i, 5159
26:53 these the land shall be divided for an i 5159
26:54 To many thou shalt give the more i, 5159
26:54 to few thou shalt give the less i: 5159
26:54 every one shall his i be given according 5159
26:62 there was no i given them among 5159
27: 7 of an i among their father's brethren; 5159
27: 7 shall **cause** the i of their father to pass 5159
27: 8 ye shall **cause** his i to pass unto his 5159
27: 9 then ye shall give his i unto his brethren. 5159
27:10 shall give his i unto his father's brethren. 5159
27:11 ye shall give his i unto his kinsman that is 5159
32:18 of Israel have inherited every man his i. 5159
32:19 our i is fallen to us on *this* side Jordan 5159
32:32 that the possession of our i on *this* side 5159
33:54 **divide** the land by lot for **an** i **among** 5157
33:54 *and* to the moe ye shall give the more i, 5159
33:54 and to the fewer ye shall give the less i: 5159
33:54 many man's *i* shall be in the place where NIH
34: 2 *is* the land that shall fall unto you for an i, 5159
34:14 have received *their* i, and half the tribe of NIH
34:14 tribe of Manasseh have received their i: 5159
34:15 The half tribe have received their i on *this* 5159
34:18 of every tribe, to **divide** the land **by** i. 5157
34:29 **divide** the i **unto** the children of Israel in 5157
35: 2 that they give unto the Levites of the i of 5159
35: 8 according to his i which he inheriteth. 5159
36: 2 land for an i by lot to the children of Israel: 5159
36: 3 their i be taken from the inheritance of 5159
36: 3 their inheritance be taken from the i of 5159
36: 3 shall be put to the i of the tribe whereinto 5159
36: 3 shall it be taken from the lot of our i. 5159
36: 4 shall their i be put unto the inheritance of 5159
36: 4 shall their inheritance be put unto the i of 5159
36: 4 shall their i be taken away from 5159
36: 4 away from the i of the tribe of our fathers. 5159
36: 7 So shall not the i of the children of Israel 5159
36: 7 himself to the i of the tribe of his fathers. 5159
36: 8 that possesseth an i in any tribe of 5159
36: 8 may enjoy every man the i of his fathers. 5159
36: 9 Neither shall the i remove from *one* tribe 5159
36: 9 of Israel shall keep himself to his own i. 5159
36:12 their i remained in the tribe of the family 5159
Dt 4:20 to be unto him a people of i, as *ye are* this 5159
4:21 the LORD thy God **sware** *for* an i: 5159
4:38 to give thee their land *for* an i, as *it is* this 5159
9:26 destroy not thy people and thine i, 5159
9:29 Yet they *are* thy people and thine i, 5159
10: 9 Wherefore Levi hath no part nor i with 5159
10: 9 the LORD is his i, according as 5159
12: 9 not as yet come to the rest and to the i, 5159
12:12 forasmuch as he hath no part nor i with 5159
14:27 for he hath no part nor i with thee. 5159
14:29 (because he hath no part nor i with thee,) 5159
15: 4 thy God giveth thee *for* an i to possess it: 5159
18: 1 Levi, shall have no part nor i with Israel: 5159
18: 1 of the LORD made by fire, and his i. 5159
18: 2 Therefore shall they have no i among their 5159
18: 2 the LORD *is* their i, as he hath said unto 5159
19:10 the LORD thy God giveth thee *for* an i, 5159
19:14 which they of old time have set in thine i, 5159
20:16 the LORD thy God doth give thee *for* an i, 5159
21:23 the LORD thy God giveth thee *for* an i. 5159
24: 4 the LORD thy God giveth thee *for* an i. 5159
25:19 thy God giveth thee *for* an i to possess it, 5159
26: 1 the LORD thy God giveth thee *for* an i. 5159
29: 8 gave it for an i unto the Reubenites, 5159
32: 8 most High **divided** to the nations their i, 5157
32: 9 is his people; Jacob *is* the lot of his i. 5159
33: 4 *even* the i of the congregation of Jacob. 4181
Jos 1: 6 people shalt thou **divide for an** i the land, 5157
11:23 Joshua gave it for an i unto Israel 5159
13: 6 thou it *by lot* unto the Israelites for an i, 5159
13: 7 this land for an i unto the nine tribes, 5159
13: 8 and the Gadites have received their i, 5159
13:14 unto the tribe of Levi he gave none i; 5159
13:14 God of Israel made by fire *are* their i, 5159
13:15 of Reuben i according to their families. NIH
13:23 the border *thereof.* This *was* the i of NIH
13:24 Moses gave i unto the tribe of Gad, NIH
13:28 This *is* the i of the children of Gad after 5159
13:29 Moses gave *i* unto the half tribe of NIH
13:32 did **distribute for** i in the plains of Moab, 5157
13:33 the tribe of Levi Moses gave not *any* i: 5159
13:33 the LORD God of Israel *was* their i, as he 5157
14: 1 of Israel, **distributed for** i to them. 5159
14: 2 By lot was their i, as the LORD 5159
14: 3 Moses had given the i of two tribes and 5159
14: 3 unto the Levites he gave none i among 5159
14: 9 thy feet have trodden shall be thine i, 5159
14:13 the son of Jephunneh Hebron for an i. 5159
14:14 the i of Caleb the son of Jephunneh 5159
15:20 This *is* the i of the tribe of the children of 5159
16: 4 Manasseh and Ephraim, **took** their i. 5159
16: 5 their i on the east side was Ataroth-addar, 5159
16: 8 This *is* the i of the tribe of the children of 5159
16: 9 among the i of the children of Manasseh, 5159
17: 4 Moses to give us an i among our brethren. 5159

Jos 17: 4 an i among the brethren of their father. 5159
17: 6 the daughters of Manasseh had an i 5159
18: 2 which had not *yet* received their i. 5159
18: 4 describe it according to the i of their 5159
18: 7 for the priesthood of the LORD *is* their i: 5159
18: 7 have received their i beyond Jordan on 5159
18:20 *was* the i of the children of Benjamin, 5159
18:28 This *is* the i of the children of Benjamin 5159
19: 1 their i was within the inheritance of 5159
19: 1 their inheritance was within the i of 5159
19: 2 they had in their i Beer-sheba, or Sheba, 5159
19: 8 This *is* the i of the tribe of the children of 5159
19: 9 Judah *was* the i of the children of Simeon: 5159
19: 9 the children of Simeon had their i within 5157
19: 9 their inheritance within the i of them. 5159
19:10 and the border of their i was unto Sarid: 5159
19:16 This *is* the i of the children of Zebulun 5159
19:23 This *is* the i of the tribe of the children of 5159
19:31 This *is* the i of the tribe of the children of 5159
19:39 This *is* the i of the tribe of the children of 5159
19:41 coast of their i was Zorah, and Eshtaol, 5159
19:48 This *is* the i of the tribe of the children of 5159
19:49 of **dividing** the land **for** i by their coasts, 5157
19:49 the children of Israel gave an i to Joshua 5159
19:51 **divided for an** i by lot in Shiloh before 5157
21: 3 Israel gave unto the Levites out of their i, 5159
23: 4 to be an i for your tribes, from Jordan, 5159
24:28 the people depart, every man unto his i. 5159
24:30 they buried him in the border of his i in 5159
24:32 it became the i of the children of Joseph. 5159
Jdg 2: 6 every man unto his i to possess the land. 5159
2: 9 they buried him in the border of his i in 5159
18: 1 to dwell *in;* for unto that day *all* their 5159
18: 1 had not fallen unto them among the 5159
20: 6 sent her throughout all the country of the i 5159
21:17 *must be* an i for them that be escaped 3425
21:23 they went and returned unto their i, 5159
21:24 went out from thence every man to his i. 5159
Ru 4: 5 raise up the name of the dead upon his i. 5159
4: 6 *it* for myself, lest I mar mine own i: 5159
4:10 raise up the name of the dead upon his i, 5159
1Sa 10: 1 anointed thee to be captain over his i? 5159
26:19 day from abiding in the i of the LORD, 5159
2Sa 14:16 and my son together out of the i of God. 5159
20: 1 neither have we i in the son of Jesse: 5159
20:19 why wilt thou swallow up the i of 5159
21: 3 that ye may bless the i of the LORD? 5159
1Ki 8:36 thou hast given to thy people for an i. 5159
8:51 For they *be* thy people, and thine i, 5159
8:53 to be thine i, as thou spakest by the hand 5159
12:16 neither *have* we i in the son of Jesse: 5159
21: 3 that I should give the i of my fathers unto 5159
21: 4 I will not give thee the i of my fathers. 5159
2Ki 21:14 I will forsake the remnant of mine i, 5159
1Ch 16:18 give the land of Canaan, the lot of your i; 5159
28: 8 **leave** *it* for an i for your children after 5157
2Ch 6:27 thou hast given unto thy people for an i. 5159
10:16 we *have* none i in the son of Jesse: 5159
Ezr 9:12 **leave** *it* for an i to your children for ever. 3423
Ne 11:20 all the cities of Judah, every one in his i. 5159
Job 31: 2 and *what* i of the Almighty from on high? 5159
42:15 their father gave them i among their 5159
Ps 2: 8 I shall give *thee* the heathen *for* thine i, 5159
16: 5 The LORD *is* the portion of mine i and 2506
28: 9 Save thy people, and bless thine i: 5159
33:12 *whom* he hath chosen for his own i. 5159
37:18 the upright: and their i shall be for ever. 5159
47: 4 shall choose our i for us, the excellency 5159
68: 9 whereby thou didst confirm thine i, when 5159
74: 2 the rod of thine i, *which* thou hast 5159
78:55 divided them an i by line, and made 5159
78:62 unto the sword; and was wroth with his i. 5159
78:71 to feed Jacob his people, and Israel his i. 5159
79: 1 God, the heathen are come into thine i; 5159
94:14 his people, neither will he forsake his i. 5159
105:11 give the land of Canaan, the lot of your i: 5159
106: 5 thy nation, that *I* may glory with thine i. 5159
106:40 insomuch that he abhorred his own i. 5159
Pr 13:22 A good *man* **leaveth an** i to *his* children's 5157
17: 2 have part of the i among the brethren. 5159
19:14 House and riches *are* the i of fathers: 5159
20:21 i *may be* gotten hastily at the beginning; 5159
Ecc 7:11 Wisdom *is* good with an i: and *by it there* 5159
Isa 19:25 the work of my hands, and Israel mine i. 5159
47: 6 I have polluted mine i, and given them 5159
63:17 for thy servants' sake, the tribes of thine i. 5159
Jer 3:18 I have **given for an** i unto your fathers. 5157
10:16 of all *things;* and Israel *is* the rod of his i: 5159
12:14 that touch the i which I have caused my 5159
16:18 they have filled mine i with the carcases 5159
32: 8 for the right of i *is* thine, 3425
51:19 of all *things;* and *Israel is* the rod of his i: 5159
La 22: 2 Our i is turned to strangers, our houses to 5159
Eze 22:16 shalt **take** thine i in thyself in the sight 2490
33:24 we *are* many; the land is given us for i. 4181
35:15 As thou didst rejoice at the i of the house 5159
36:12 shalt be their i, and thou shalt no more 5159
44:28 it shall be unto them for an i: I *am* their 5159
44:28 I *am* their i: and ye shall give them no 5159
45: 1 when ye shall divide *by lot* the land for i, 5159
46: 16 his sons, the i thereof shall be his sons'; 5159
46:16 his sons'; it *shall be* their possession by i. 5159
46:17 if he give a gift of his i to one of his 5159
46:17 but his i shall be his sons' for them. 5159
46:18 the prince shall not take of the people's i, 5159

Eze	46:18 he shall **give** his sons i out of his own	5157
	47:14 and this land shall fall unto you for i.	5159
	47:22 *that* ye shall divide it *by lot* for an i unto	5159
	47:22 they shall **have** i with you among	5159+5307
	47:23 there shall ye give *him* his i, saith the Lord	5159
	48:29 divide *by lot* unto the tribes of Israel for i,	5159
Mt	21:38 let us kill him, and let us seize on his i.	2817
Mk	12: 7 let us kill him, and i. shall be ours.	2817
Lk	12:13 my brother, that *he* divide the i with me.	2817
	20:14 let us kill him, that the i may be ours.	2817
Ac	7: 5 And he gave him none i in it, no, not so	2817
	20:32 to give you an i among all them which are	2817
	26:18 i among them which are sanctified by faith	2819
Gal	3:18 For if the i *be* of the law, *it is* no more of	2817
Eph	1:11 In whom also we have **obtained an i**,	2820
	1:14 Which is the earnest of our i, until	2817
	1:18 what the riches of the glory of his i	2817
	5: 5 hath *any* i in the kingdom of Christ and	2817
Col	1:12 be partakers of the i of the saints in light:	2819
	3:24 Lord ye shall receive the reward of the i.	2817
Heb	1: 4 as he hath by i **obtained** a more excellent	2816
	9:15 might receive the promise of eternal i,	2817
	11: 8 which he should after receive for an i,	2817
1Pe	1: 4 To an i incorruptible, and undefiled,	2817

INHERITANCES (1) [INHERIT]

Jos	19:51 These *are* the i, which Eleazar the priest,	5159

INHERITED (6) [INHERIT]

Nu	32:18 the children of Israel have i every man	5157
Jos	14: 1 children of Israel i in the land of Canaan,	5157
Ps	105:44 and they i the labour of the people;	3423
Jer	16:19 Surely our fathers have i lies, vanity,	5157
Eze	33:24 Abraham was one, and he i the land:	3423
Heb	12:17 when he would have i the blessing,	2816

INHERITETH (1) [INHERIT]

Nu	35: 8 according to his inheritance which he i.	5157

INHERITOR (1) [INHERIT]

Isa	65: 9 and out of Judah an i of my mountains:	3423

INIQUITIES (56) [INIQUITY]

Lev	16:21 confess over him all the i of the children	5771
	16:22 goat shall bear upon him all their i unto	5771
	26:39 in the i of their fathers shall they pine	5771
Nu	14:34 shall ye bear your i, *even* forty years,	5771
Ezr	9: 6 for our i are increased over *our* head,	5771
	9: 7 for our i have we, our kings,	5771
	9:13 hast punished us less than our i *deserve,*	5771
Ne	9: 2 their sins, and the i of their fathers.	5771
Job	13:23 How many *are* mine i and sins? make me	5771
	13:26 makest me to possess the i of my youth.	5771
	22: 5 thy wickedness great? and thine i infinite?	5771
Ps	38: 4 For mine i are gone *over* mine head: as a	5771
	40:12 mine i have taken hold upon me, so that I	5771
	51: 9 face from my sins, and blot out all mine i.	5771
	64: 6 They search out i; they accomplish a	5766
	65: 3 I prevail against me: *as for our*	1697+5771
	79: 8 O remember not against us former i: let	5771
	90: 8 Thou hast set our i before thee, our secret	5771
	103: 3 Who forgiveth all thine i; who healeth all	5771
	103:10 nor rewarded us according to our i.	5771
	107:17 because of their i, are afflicted.	5771
	130: 3 If thou, Lord, shouldest mark i, O Lord,	5771
	130: 8 And he shall redeem Israel from all his i.	5771
Pr	5:22 His own i shall take the wicked himself,	5771
Isa	43:24 sins, thou hast wearied me with thine i.	5771
	50: 1 for your i have you sold yourselves,	5771
	53: 5 transgressions, *he was* bruised for our i:	5771
	53:11 justify many; for he shall bear their i.	5771
	59: 2 your i have separated between you	5771
	59:12 with us; and *as for* our i, we know them;	5771
	64: 6 our i, like the wind, have taken us away.	5771
	64: 7 and hast consumed us, because of our i.	5771
	65: 7 Your i, and the iniquities of your fathers	5771
	65: 7 and the i of your fathers together,	5771
Jer	5:25 Your i have turned away these *things,*	5771
	11:10 They are turned back to the i of their	5771
	14: 7 O Lord, though our i testify against us,	5771
	33: 8 I will pardon all their i, whereby they	5771
La	4:13 of her prophets, *and* the i of her priests,	5771
	5: 7 *are* not; and we have borne their i.	5771
Eze	24:23 ye shall pine away for your i,	5771
	28:18 sanctuaries by the multitude of thine i,	5771
	32:27 but their i shall be upon their bones,	5771
	36:31 yourselves in your own sight for your i	5771
	36:33 I shall have cleansed you from all your i,	5771
	43:10 that they may be ashamed of their i:	5771
Da	4:27 and thine i by shewing mercy to the poor;	5758
	9:13 that *we* might turn from our i,	5771
	9:16 for the i of our fathers, Jerusalem and	5771
Am	3: 2 I will punish you for all your i.	5771
Mic	7:19 he will subdue our i; and thou wilt cast all	5771
Ac	3:26 turning away every one of you from *his* i.	4189
Ro	4: 7 *Saying,* Blessed *are they* whose i are	458
Heb	8:12 and their i will I remember no more.	458
	10:17 their sins and i will I remember no more.	458
Rev	18: 5 heaven, and God hath remembered her i.	92

INIQUITY (278) [INIQUITIES]

Ge	15:16 for the i of the Amorites *is* not yet full.	5771
	19:15 lest thou be consumed in the i of the city.	5771
	44:16 God hath found out the i of thy servants:	5771
Ex	20: 5 visiting the i of the fathers upon	5771

Ex	28:38 that Aaron may bear the i of the holy	5771
	28:43 in the holy *place;* that they bear not i,	5771
	34: 7 forgiving i and transgression and sin,	5771
	34: 7 the i of the fathers upon the children,	5771
	34: 9 pardon our i and our sin, and take us for	5771
Lev	5: 1 he do not utter *it,* then he shall bear his i.	5771
	5:17 *it* not, yet is he guilty, and shall bear his i.	5771
	7:18 the soul that eateth of it shall bear his i.	5771
	10:17 God hath given it you to bear the i of	5771
	17:16 bathe his flesh; then he shall bear his i.	5771
	18:25 therefore I do visit the i thereof upon it,	5771
	19: 8 *every* one that eateth it shall bear his i,	5771
	20:17 his sister's nakedness; he shall bear his i.	5771
	20:19 his near kin: they shall bear their i.	5771
	22:16 Or suffer them to bear the i of trespass,	5771
	26:39 away in their i in your enemies' lands;	5771
	26:40 they shall confess their i, and the iniquity	5771
	26:40 their iniquity, and the i of their fathers,	5771
	26:41 then accept of the **punishment of** their i:	5771
	26:43 shall accept of the **punishment of** their i:	5771
Nu	5:15 of memorial, bringing i to remembrance.	5771
	5:31 shall the man be guiltless from i, and this	5771
	5:31 and this woman shall bear her i.	5771
	14:18 forgiving i and transgression, and by no	5771
	14:18 i of the fathers upon the children unto	5771
	14:19 the i of this people according unto	5771
	15:31 utterly be cut off; his i *shall be* upon him.	5771
	18: 1 father's house with thee shall bear the i	5771
	18: 1 thy sons with thee shall bear the i of your	5771
	18:23 and they shall bear their i:	5771
	23:21 hath not beheld i in Jacob, neither hath	205
	30:15 hath heard *them;* then he shall bear her i.	5771
Dt	5: 9 visiting the i of the fathers upon	5771
	19:15 shall not rise up against a man for any i,	5771
	32: 4 a God of truth and without i, just and	5766
Jos	22:17 *Is* the i of Peor too little for us, from	5771
	22:20 and that man perished not alone in his i.	5771
1Sa	3:13 for ever for the i which he knoweth;	5771
	3:14 the i of Eli's house shall not be purged	5771
	15:23 and stubbornness *is as* i and idolatry.	205
	20: 1 what *is* mine i? and what *is* my sin before	5771
	20: 8 if there be in me i, slay me thyself;	5771
	25:24 *upon me let this* i *be:* and let thine	5771
2Sa	7:14 If he **commit** i, I will chasten him with	5753
	14: 9 the i *be* on me, and on my father's house:	5771
	14:32 if there be *any* i in me, let him kill me.	5771
	19:19 king, Let not my lord impute i unto me,	5771
	22:24 and have kept myself from mine i.	5771
	24:10 O Lord, take away the i of thy servant;	5771
1Ch	21: 8 beseech thee, do away the i of thy servant;	5771
2Ch	19: 7 do *it:* for *there is* no i with the Lord our	5766
Ne	4: 5 cover not their i, and let not their sin be	5771
Job	4: 8 they that plow i, and sow wickedness,	205
	5:16 hath hope, and i stoppeth her mouth.	5766
	6:29 Return, I pray you, let it not be i; yea,	5766
	6:30 Is there i in my tongue? cannot my taste	5766
	7:21 my transgression, and take away mine i?	5771
	10: 6 That thou inquirest after mine i,	5771
	10:14 and thou wilt not acquit me from mine i.	5771
	11: 6 God exacteth of thee *less* than thine i	5771
	11:14 If i *be* in thine hand, put it far away,	205
	14:17 up in a bag, and thou sewest up mine i.	5771
	15: 5 For thy mouth uttereth thine i,	5771
	15:16 filthy *is* man, which drinketh i like water?	5766
	20:27 The heaven shall reveal his i; and the	5771
	21:19 God layeth up his i for his children:	205
	22:23 shalt be built *up,* thou shalt put away i	5766
	31: 3 a strange punishment to the workers of i?	205
	31:11 it *is* an i *to be punished by* the judges.	5771
	31:28 This also *were* an i *to be punished by*	5771
	31:33 as Adam, by hiding mine i in my bosom:	5771
	33: 9 I *am* innocent; neither *is there* i in me.	5771
	34: 8 goeth in company with the workers of i,	205
	34:10 the Almighty, *that he should commit* i.	5766
	34:22 the workers of i may hide themselves.	205
	34:32 if I have done i, I will do no more.	5766
	36:10 and commandeth that they return from i.	205
	36:21 Take heed, regard not i: for this hast thou	205
	36:23 or who can say, Thou hast wrought i?	5766
Ps	5: 5 in thy sight: thou hatest all workers of i.	205
	6: 8 Depart from me, all ye workers of i;	205
	7: 3 have done this; if there be i in my hands;	5766
	7:14 he travaileth with i, and hath conceived	205
	14: 4 Have all the workers of i no knowledge?	205
	18:23 him, and I kept myself from mine i.	5771
	25:11 thy name's sake, O Lord, pardon mine i;	5771
	28: 3 the wicked, and with the workers of i,	205
	31:10 my strength faileth because of mine i,	5771
	32: 2 unto whom the Lord imputeth not i,	5771
	32: 5 sin unto thee, and mine i have I not hid.	5771
	32: 5 and thou forgavest the i of my sin.	5771
	36: 2 eyes, until his i be found to be hateful.	5771
	36: 3 The words of his mouth *are* i and deceit:	205
	36:12 There are the workers of i fallen: they are	205
	37: 1 be thou envious against the workers of i.	5766
	38:18 For I will declare mine i; I will be sorry for	5771
	39:11 thou with rebukes dost correct man for i,	5771
	41: 6 heart gathereth to itself; *when* he goeth	205
	49: 5 *when* the i of my heels shall compass me	205
	51: 2 Wash me throughly from mine i,	5771
	51: 5 Behold, I was shapen in i; and in sin did	5771
	53: 1 are they, and have done abominable i:	5766
	53: 4 Have the workers of i no knowledge?	205
	55: 3 for they cast i upon me, and in wrath they	205
	56: 7 *Shall* they escape by? in *thine* anger cast	205

Ps	59: 2 Deliver me from the workers of i,	205
	64: 2 from the insurrection of the workers of i.	205
	66:18 If I regard i in my heart, the Lord will not	205
	69:27 Add i unto their iniquity: and let them not	5771
	69:27 Add iniquity unto their i: and let them not	5771
	78:38 forgave *their* i, and destroyed *them* not:	5771
	85: 2 Thou hast forgiven the i of thy people,	5771
	89:32 with the rod, and their i with stripes.	5771
	92: 7 and when all the workers of i do flourish;	205
	92: 9 all the workers of i shall be scattered.	205
	94: 4 *and* all the workers of i boast themselves?	205
	94:16 stand up for me against the workers of i?	205
	94:20 Shall the throne of i have fellowship *with*	1942
	94:23 he shall bring upon them their own i,	205
	106: 6 we have **committed** i, we have done	5753
	106:43 and were brought low for their i.	5771
	107:42 and rejoice: and all i shall stop her mouth.	5766
	109:14 Let the i of his fathers be remembered	5771
	119: 3 They also do no i: they walk in his ways.	5766
	119:133 and let not any i have dominion over me.	205
	125: 3 the righteous put forth their hands unto i.	5766
	125: 5 lead them forth with the workers of i:	205
	141: 4 wicked works with men that work i:	205
	141: 9 for me, and the gins of the workers of i.	205
Pr	10:29 destruction *shall be* to the workers of i.	205
	16: 6 By mercy and truth i is purged: and by	5771
	19:28 and the mouth of the wicked devoureth i.	205
	21:15 destruction *shall be* to the workers of i.	205
	22: 8 He that soweth i shall reap vanity:	5766
Ecc	3:16 place of righteousness, *that i was* there.	7562
Isa	1: 4 Ah sinful nation, a people laden with i,	5771
	1:13 with; *it is* i, even the solemn meeting.	5771
	5:18 Woe unto them that draw i with cords of	5771
	6: 7 thine i is taken away, and thy sin purged.	5771
	13:11 for *their* evil, and the wicked for their i;	5771
	14:21 Prepare slaughter for his children for the i	5771
	22:14 Surely this i shall not be purged from you	5771
	26:21 the inhabitants of the earth for their i:	5771
	27: 9 therefore shall the i of Jacob be purged;	5771
	29:20 and all that watch for i are cut off:	205
	30:13 Therefore this i shall be to you as a breach	5771
	31: 2 and against the help of them that work i.	205
	32: 6 heart will work i, to practise hypocrisy,	205
	33:24 dwell therein *shall be* forgiven *their* i.	5771
	40: 2 is accomplished, that her i is pardoned:	5771
	53: 6 the Lord hath laid on him the i of us all.	5771
	57:17 For the i of his covetousness was I wroth,	5771
	59: 3 with blood, and your fingers with i;	5771
	59: 4 *they* conceive mischief, and bring forth i.	205
	59: 6 their works *are* works of i, and the act of	205
	59: 7 their thoughts *are* thoughts of i; wasting	205
	64: 9 O Lord, neither remember i for ever:	5771
Jer	2: 5 What i have your fathers found in me,	5766
	2:22 yet thine i *is* marked before me,	5771
	3:13 Only acknowledge thine i, that thou hast	5771
	9: 5 and weary themselves to **commit** i.	5753
	13:22 For the greatness of thine i are thy skirts	5771
	14:10 he will now remember their i,	5771
	14:20 our wickedness, *and* the i of our fathers:	5771
	16:10 what *is* our i? or what *is* our sin that we	5771
	16:17 neither is their i hid from mine eyes.	5771
	16:18 first I will recompense their i and their sin	5771
	18:23 against me to slay *me:* forgive not their i,	5771
	25:12 for their i, and the land of the Chaldeans,	5771
	30:14 a cruel one, for the multitude of thine i;	5771
	30:15 *is* incurable for the multitude of thine i:	5771
	31:30 every one shall die for his own i: every	5771
	31:34 for I will forgive their i, and I will	5771
	32:18 recompensest the i of the fathers into	5771
	33: 8 I will cleanse them from all their i,	5771
	36: 3 that I may forgive their i and their sin.	5771
	36:31 and his seed and his servants for their i;	5771
	50:20 the i of Israel shall be sought for,	5771
	51: 6 be not cut off in her i; for this *is* the time	5771
La	2:14 they have not discovered thine i, to turn	5771
	4: 6 the **punishment of** the i of the daughter	5771
	4:22 The **punishment of** thine i is	5771
	4:22 he will visit thine i, O daughter of Edom;	5771
Eze	3:18 the same wicked *man* shall die in his i;	5771
	3:19 from his wicked way, he shall die in his i;	5771
	3:20 commit i, and I lay a stumblingblock	5766
	4: 4 lay the i of the house of Israel upon it:	5771
	4: 4 shalt lie upon it thou shalt bear their i.	5771
	4: 5 I have laid upon thee the years of their i,	5771
	4: 5 shalt thou bear the i of the house of Israel.	5771
	4: 6 thou shalt bear the i of the house of Judah	5771
	4:17 another, and consume away for their i.	5771
	7:13 shall any strengthen himself in the i	5771
	7:16 all of them mourning, every one for his i.	5771
	7:19 because it is the stumblingblock of their i.	5771
	9: 9 The i of the house of Israel and Judah *is*	5771
	14: 3 put the stumblingblock of their i before	5771
	14: 4 putteth the stumblingblock of his i before	5771
	14: 7 putteth the stumblingblock of his i before	5771
	14:10 they shall bear the **punishment of** their i:	5771
	16:49 this was the i of thy sister Sodom, pride,	5771
	18: 8 *that* hath withdrawn his hand from i,	5766
	18:17 he shall not die for the i of his father,	5771
	18:18 his people, lo, even he shall die in his i.	5771
	18:19 doth not the son bear the i of the father?	5771
	18:20 The son shall not bear the i of the father,	5771
	18:20 shall the father bear the i of the son:	5771
	18:24 committeth i, *and* doeth according to all	5766
	18:26 and committeth i, and dieth in them;	5766
	18:26 for his i that he hath done shall he die.	5766

Eze 18:30 so **i** shall not be your ruin. 5771
 21:23 he will call to remembrance the **i**, that 5771
 21:24 Because ye have made your **i** to be 5771
 21:25 day is come, when **i** *shall* have an end, 5771
 21:29 is come, when *their* **i** *shall* have an end. 5771
 28:15 wast created, till **i** was found in thee. 5766
 28:18 of thine iniquities, by the **i** of thy traffick; 5766
 29:16 which bringeth *their* **i** to remembrance, 5771
 33: 6 among them, he is taken *away* in his **i**; 5771
 33: 8 way, that wicked *man* shall die in his **i**; 5771
 33: 9 turn from his way, he shall die in his **i**; 5771
 33:13 to his own righteousness, and commit **i**, 5766
 33:13 for his **i** that he hath committed, he shall 5766
 33:15 the statutes of life, without committing **i**; 5766
 33:18 committeth **i**, he shall even die thereby. 5766
 35: 5 in the time *that their* **i** *had* an end: 5771
 39:23 of Israel went into captivity for their **i**: 5771
 44:10 their idols; they shall even bear their **i**. 5771
 44:12 caused the house of Israel to fall into **i**; 5771
 44:12 the Lord God, and they shall bear their **i**. 5771
Da 9: 5 have **committed** **i**, and have done 5753
 9:24 to make reconciliation for **i**, and to bring 5771
Hos 4: 8 and they set their heart on their **i**. 5771
 5: 5 shall Israel and Ephraim fall in their **i**; 5771
 6: 8 Gilead *is* a city of them that work **i**, 205
 7: 1 the **i** of Ephraim was discovered, 5771
 8:13 now will he remember their **i**, 5771
 9: 7 for the multitude of thine **i**, and the great 5771
 9: 9 *therefore* he will remember their **i**, 5771
 10: 9 battle in Gibeah against the children of **i** 5932
 10:13 plowed wickedness, ye have reaped **i**; 5766
 12: 8 in all my labours they shall find none **i** in 5771
 12:11 there **i** *in* Gilead? surely they are vanity: 205
 13:12 **i** of Ephraim *is* bound up; his sin *is* hid. 5771
 14: 1 thy God; for thou hast fallen by thine **i**. 5771
 14: 2 Take away all **i**, and receive *us* graciously: 5771
Mic 2: 1 Woe to them that devise **i**, and work evil 205
 3:10 up Zion with blood, and Jerusalem with **i**. 5766
 7:18 that pardoneth **i**, and passeth by 5771
Hab 1: 3 Why dost thou shew me **i**, and cause *me* 205
 1:13 to behold evil, and canst not look on **i**: 5999
 2:12 with blood, and stablisheth a city by **i**! 5766
Zep 3: 5 *is* in the midst thereof; he will not do **i**: 5766
 3:13 The remnant of Israel shall not do **i**, 5766
Zec 3: 4 I have caused thine **i** to pass from thee, 5771
 3: 9 I will remove the **i** of that land in one day. 5771
Mal 2: 6 his mouth, and **i** was not found in his lips: 5766
 2: 6 equity, and did turn many away from **i**. 5771
Mt 7:23 knew you: depart from me, ye that work **i**. 458
 13:41 things that offend, and them which do **i**; 458
 23:28 but within ye are full of hypocrisy and **i**. 458
 24:12 And because **i** shall abound, the love of 458
Lk 13:27 depart from me, all *ye* workers of **i**. 93
Ac 1:18 purchased a field with the reward of **i**; 93
 8:23 the gall of bitterness, and *in* the bond of **i**. 93
Ro 6:19 to uncleanness and to **i** unto iniquity; 458
 6:19 to uncleanness and to iniquity unto **i**; 93
1Co 13: 6 Rejoiceth not in **i**, but rejoiceth in the truth; 93
2Th 2: 7 For the mystery of **i** doth already work: 458
2Ti 2:19 nameth the name of Christ depart from **i**. 93
Tit 2:14 that he might redeem us from all **i**, 458
Heb 1: 9 hast loved righteousness, and hated **i**; 458
Jas 3: 6 And the tongue *is* a fire, a world of **i**: so is 93
2Pe 2:16 But was rebuked for his **i**: the dumb ass 3892

INJURED (1) [INJURIOUS]

Gal 4:12 as I *am*; for I *am* as ye *are*: ye have not **i** 91

INJURIOUS (1) [INJURED]

1Ti 1:13 a blasphemer, and a persecutor, and **i**: 5197

INJUSTICE (1)

Job 16:17 Not for *any* **i** in mine hands: also my 2555

INK (4) [INKHORN]

Jer 36:18 and I wrote *them* with **i** in the book. 1773
2Co 3: 3 written not with **i**, but with the Spirit of 3188
2Jn 1:12 I would not *write* with paper and **i**; 3188
3Jn 1:13 but I will not write with **i** and pen write unto 3188

INKHORN (3) [HORN, INK]

Eze 9: 2 *with* linen, with a writer's **i** by his side: 7083
 9: 3 which *had* the writer's **i** by his side; 7083
 9:11 which *had* the **i** by his side, reported 7083

INN (5)

Ge 42:27 his sack to give his ass provender in the **i**, 4411
 43:21 it came to pass, when we came to the **i**, 4411
Ex 4:24 it came to pass by the way in the **i**, that 4411
Lk 2: 7 there was no room for them in the **i**. 2646
 10:34 and brought him to an **i**, and took care of 3829

INNER (37) [INNERMOST]

1Ki 6:27 he set the cherubims within the **i** house: 6442
 6:36 he built the **i** court *with* three rows of 6442
 7:12 both for the **i** court of the house of 6442
 7:50 *of* gold, *both* for the doors of the **i** house, 6442
 20:30 city, into an **i chamber**. 2315+2315+871.1
 22: 25 an **i chamber** to hide 2315+2315+871.1
2Ki 9: 2 carry him *to* an **i chamber**: 2315+2315+871.1
1Ch 28:11 of the **i** parlours thereof, and of the place 6442
2Ch 4:22 **i** doors thereof for the most holy *place*, 6442
 18:24 an **i chamber** to hide 2315+2315+871.1
 29:16 priests went into the **i part** *of* the house 6441
Est 4:11 shall come unto the king into the **i** court, 6442

Est 5: 1 stood in the **i** court of the king's house, 6442
Eze 8: 3 the door of the **i** gate that looketh toward 6442
 8:16 he brought me into the **i** court of 6442
 10: 3 went in; and the cloud filled the **i** court. 6442
 40:15 the porch of the **i** gate *were* fifty cubits. 6442
 40:19 unto the forefront of the **i** court without, 6442
 40:23 the gate of the **i** court *was* over against 6442
 40:27 *there was* a gate in the **i** court toward 6442
 40:28 he brought me to the **i** court by the south 6442
 40:32 he brought me into the **i** court toward 6442
 40:44 without the **i** gate *were* the chambers of 6442
 40:44 the chambers of the singers in the **i** court, 6442
 41:15 with the temple, and the porches of 6442
 41:17 even unto the **i** house, and without, 6442
 42: 3 twenty *cubits* which *were* for the **i** court, 6442
 42:15 made an end of measuring the **i** house, 6442
 43: 5 me up, and brought me into the **i** court; 6442
 44:17 when they enter in at the gates of the **i** 6442
 44:17 whiles they minister in the gates of the **i** 6442
 44:21 wine, when they enter into the **i** court. 6442
 44:27 unto the **i** court, to minister in 6442
 45:19 upon the posts of the gate of the **i** court. 6442
 46: 1 The gate of the **i** court that looketh 6442
Ac 16:24 thrust them into the **i** prison, and made 2082
Eph 3:16 with might by his Spirit in the **i** man; 2080

INNERMOST (2) [INNER]

Pr 18: 8 they go down *into* the **i parts** of the belly. 2315
 26:22 they go down *into* the **i parts** of the belly. 2315

INNOCENCY (5) [INNOCENT, INNOCENTS]

Ge 20: 5 and **i** of my hands have I done this. 5356
Ps 26: 6 I will wash mine hands in **i**: so will I 5356
 73:13 heart *in* vain, and washed my hands in **i**. 5356
Da 6:22 forasmuch as before him **i** was found in 2136
Hos 8: 5 how long *will it be* ere they attain to **i**? 5356

INNOCENT (38) [INNOCENCY]

Ex 23: 7 and the **i** and righteous slay thou not: 5355
Dt 19:10 That **i** blood be not shed in thy land, 5355
 19:13 thou shalt put away the **guilt** *of* **i** blood 5355
 21: 8 lay not **i** blood unto thy people of Israel's 5355
 21: 9 So shalt thou put away the **guilt** *of* **i** blood 5355
 27:25 *be* he that taketh reward to slay an **i** 5355
1Sa 19: 5 then wilt thou sin against **i** blood, 5355
1Ki 2:31 that thou mayest take away the **i** blood, 2600
2Ki 21:16 Moreover Manasseh shed **i** blood very 5355
 24: 4 also *for* the **i** blood that he shed: for he 5355
 24: 4 for he filled Jerusalem *with* **i** blood; 5355
Job 4: 7 I pray thee, who *ever* perished, being **i**? 5355
 9:23 he will laugh at the trial of the **i**. 5355
 9:28 I know that thou wilt not **hold me i**. 5352
 17: 8 the **i** shall stir up himself against 5355
 22:19 are glad: and the **i** laugh them to scorn. 5355
 22:30 He shall deliver the island of the **i**: and it 5355
 27:17 put *it* on, and the **i** shall divide the silver. 5355
 33: 9 I am clean without transgression, **I am i**; 2643
Ps 10: 8 in the secret places doth he murder the **i**: 5355
 15: 5 to usury, nor taketh reward against the **i**. 5355
 19:13 I shall be **i** from *the* great transgression. 5352
 94:21 the righteous, and condemn the **i** blood. 5355
 106:38 shed **i** blood, *even* the blood of their sons 5355
Pr 1:11 let us lurk privily for the **i** without cause: 5355
 6:17 lying tongue, and hands that shed **i** blood, 5355
 6:29 whosoever toucheth her shall not be **i**. 5352
 28:20 maketh haste to be rich shall not be **i**. 5352
Isa 59: 7 and they make haste to shed **i** blood: 5355
Jer 2:35 Yet thou sayest, Because I am **i**, surely his 5352
 7: 6 and shed not **i** blood in this place, 5355
 22: 3 neither shed **i** blood in this place. 5355
 22:17 for to shed **i** blood, and for oppression, 5355
 26:15 ye shall surely bring **i** blood upon 5355
Joel 3:19 they have shed **i** blood in their land. 5355
Jnh 1:14 man's life, and lay not upon us **i** blood: 5355
Mt 27: 4 I have sinned in that I have betrayed the **i** 121
 27:24 I am **i** of the blood of this just *person*: see 121

INNOCENTS (2) [INNOCENCY]

Jer 2:34 found the blood of the souls of the poor **i**: 5355
 19: 4 have filled this place *with* the blood of **i**; 5355

INNUMERABLE (7)

Job 21:33 after him, as *there are* **i** before him. 369+4557
Ps 40:12 For **i** evils have compassed me 369+4557+5704
 104:25 wherein *are* things creeping **i**, 369+4557
Jer 46:23 than the grasshoppers, and *are* **i**. 369+4557
Lk 12: 1 together an **i multitude** of people, 3461
Heb 11:12 as the sand which is by the sea shore **i**. 382
 12:22 and to an **i company** of angels, 3461

INORDINATE (2)

Eze 23:11 she was more corrupt in her **i love** than 5691
Col 3: 5 fornication, uncleanness, **i affection**, 3806

INQUIRE (52) [INQUIRED, INQUIREST, INQUIRY]

Ge 24:57 will call the damsel, and **i** at her mouth. 7592
 25:22 I thus? And she went to **i** of the LORD. 1875
Ex 18:15 Because the people come unto me to **i** of 1875
Dt 12:30 that thou **i** not after their gods, saying, 1875
 13:14 shalt thou **i**, and make search, 1875
 17: 9 judge that shall be in those days, and **i**, 1875
Jdg 4:20 when any man doth come and **i** of thee, 7592
1Sa 9: 9 when a man went to **i** of God, thus he 1875
 17:56 said, **I** thou whose son the stripling *is*. 7592
 22:15 Did I then begin to **i** of God for him? 7592

1Sa 28: 7 that I may go to her, and **i** of her. 1875
1Ki 22: 5 **I**, I pray thee, at the word of the LORD to 1875
 22: 7 LORD besides, that we might **i** of him? 1875
 22: 8 by whom *we* may **i** of the LORD: 1875
2Ki 1: 2 **i** of Baal-zebub the god of Ekron whether 1875
 1: 3 *that* ye go to **i** of Baal-zebub the god of 1875
 1: 6 thou sendest to **i** of Baal-zebub the god 1875
 1:16 to **i** of Baal-zebub the god of Ekron, 1875
 1:16 *there is* no God in Israel to **i** of his word? 1875
 3:11 that we may **i** of the LORD by him? 1875
 8: 8 and **i** of the LORD by him, saying, 1875
 16:15 the brasen altar shall be for me to **i** *by*. 1239
 22:13 of me, and for the people, 1875
 22:18 the king of Judah which sent you to **i** of 1875
1Ch 10:13 of *one that had* a familiar spirit, to **i** *of it*; 1875
 18:10 of his welfare, and to congratulate him, 7592
 21:30 David could not go before it to **i** of God: 1875
2Ch 18: 4 **I**, I pray thee, at the word of the LORD to 1875
 18: 6 LORD besides, that we might **i** of him? 1875
 18: 7 by whom *we* may **i** of the LORD: 1875
 32:31 who sent unto him to **i** of the wonder that 1875
 34:21 of me, and for them that 1875
 34:26 who sent you to **i** of the LORD, 1875
Ezr 7:14 to **i** concerning Judah and Jerusalem, 1240
Job 8: 8 For **i**, I pray thee, of the former age, 7592
Ps 27: 4 of the LORD, and to **i** in his temple. 1239
Ecc 7:10 for thou dost not **i** wisely concerning this. 7592
Isa 21:12 if ye will **i**, inquire ye: return, come. 1158
 21:12 if ye will **inquire**, **i** ye: return, come. 1158
Jer 21: 2 **I**, I pray thee, of the LORD for us; 1875
 37: 7 Judah, that sent you unto me to **i** of me; 1875
Eze 14: 7 cometh to a prophet to **i** of him 1875
 20: 1 elders of Israel came to **i** of the LORD, 1875
 20: 3 the Lord GOD; Are ye come to **i** of me? 1875
Mt 10:11 town ye shall enter, **i** who in it is worthy; 1833
Lk 22:23 And they began to **i** among themselves, 4802
Jn 16:19 Do ye **i** among yourselves of that I said, 2212
Ac 9:11 in the house of Judas for *one* called Saul, 2212
 19:39 But if ye **i** any *thing* concerning other 1934
 23:15 as though ye would **i** something more 1231
 23:20 as though they would **i** somewhat of him 4441
2Co 8:23 Whether *any do* **i** of Titus, *he is* my NIG

INQUIRED (34) [INQUIRE]

Dt 17: 4 thou hast heard *of it*, and **i** diligently, 1875
Jdg 6:29 when they **i** and asked, they said, 1875
 8:14 man of the men of Succoth, and **i** of him: 7592
 20:27 the children of Israel **i** of the LORD, 7592
1Sa 10:22 Therefore they **i** of the LORD further, 7592
 22:10 he **i** of the LORD for him, and gave him 7592
 22:13 him a sword, and hast **i** of God for him, 7592
 23: 2 Therefore David **i** of the LORD, saying, 7592
 23: 4 David **i** of the LORD yet again. 7592
 28: 6 when Saul **i** of the LORD, the LORD 7592
 30: 8 David **i** at the LORD, saying, Shall I 7592
2Sa 2: 1 that David **i** of the LORD, saying, 7592
 5:19 David **i** of the LORD, saying, Shall I go 7592
 5:23 when David **i** of the LORD, he said, 7592
 11: 3 David sent and **i** after the woman. 1875
 16:23 as if a man had **i** at the oracle of God: 7592
 21: 1 and David **i** of the LORD. 1245+6440
1Ch 10:14 **i** not of the LORD: therefore he slew him, 1875
 13: 3 for we **i** not *at* it in the days of Saul. 1875
 14:10 David **i** of God, saying, Shall I go up 7592
 14:14 Therefore David **i** again of God; and God 7592
Ps 78:34 and they returned and **i** early after God. 7836
Eze 14: 3 should I be **i** of at all by them? 1875+1875
 20: 3 the Lord GOD, I will not be **i** of by you. 1875
 20:31 shall I be **i** of by you, O house of Israel? 1875
 20:31 the Lord GOD, I will not be **i** of by you. 1875
 36:37 I will yet *for* this be **i** of by the house of 1875
Da 1:20 understanding, that the king **i** of them, 1245
Zep 1: 6 have not sought the LORD, nor **i** for him. 1875
Mt 2: 7 **i** of them **diligently** what time the star 198
 2:16 which he had **diligently i** of the wise men. 198
Jn 4:52 Then **i** he of them the hour when he 4441
2Co 8:23 brethren *be i of*, they are the messengers NIG
1Pe 1:10 which salvation the prophets have **i** and 1567

INQUIREST (1) [INQUIRE]

Job 10: 6 That thou **i** after mine iniquity, 1245

INQUIRY (2) [INQUIRE]

Pr 20:25 *which is* holy, and after vows to **make i**. 1239
Ac 10:17 Cornelius had **made i** for Simon's house, 1331

INQUISITION (3)

Dt 19:18 the judges shall **make** diligent **i**: 1875
Est 2:23 when **i was made** of the matter, it was 1245
Ps 9:12 When he **maketh i** for blood, 1875

INSATIABLE See UNSATIABLE

INSCRIBED See GRAVED; GRAVEN

INSCRIPTION (1)

Ac 17:23 devotions, I found an altar with this **i**, 1924

INSIDE (1)

1Ki 6:15 he covered *them* on the **i** with wood, 1004

INSOMUCH (20) [IN, MUCH, SO]

Ps 106:40 **i** that he abhorred his own inheritance. 2050.1
Mal 2:13 that *he* regardeth not the offering any 4480
Mt 8:24 **i that** the ship was covered with the 5620
 12:22 **i that** the blind and dumb both spake and 5620

Mt	13:54 **i that** they were astonished, and said,	5620
	15:31 **I that** the multitude wondered, when	5620
	24:24 **i that**, if it were possible, they shall	5620
	27:14 **i that** the governor marvelled greatly.	5620
Mk	1:27 **i that** they questioned among themselves,	5620
	1:45 **i that** Jesus could no more openly enter	5620
	2: 2 **i that** there was no room to receive them,	5620
	2:12 **i that** they were all amazed,	5620
	3:10 **i that** they pressed upon him for to touch	5620
	9:26 as one dead; **i that** many said, He is dead.	5620
Lk	12: 1 **i that** they trode one upon another,	5620
Ac	1:19 **as that** field is called in their proper	5620
	5:15 **I that** they brought forth the sick into	2532
2Co	1: 8 **i that** we despaired even of life:	5620
	8: 6 **I that** we desired Titus, that as he	1519+3588
Gal	2:13 **i that** Barnabas also was carried away	5620

INSPECTION GATE See MIPHKAD

INSPIRATION (2)

Job	32: 8 the **i** of the Almighty giveth them	5397
2Ti	3:16 All scripture is given by **i** of God,	2315

INSTANT (8) [INSTANTLY]

Isa	29: 5 yea, it shall be at an **i** suddenly.	6621
	30:13 whose breaking cometh suddenly at an **i**.	6621
Jer	18: 7 At what **I** shall speak concerning a	7281
	18: 9 at what **I** shall speak concerning a nation	7281
Lk	2:38 And she coming in that **i** gave thanks	5610
	23:23 And they were **i** with loud voices,	1945
Ro	12:12 in tribulation; **continuing i** in prayer;	4342
2Ti	4: 2 be **i** in season, out of season; reprove,	2186

INSTANTLY (2) [INSTANT]

Lk	7: 4 to Jesus, they besought him **i**, saying,	4709
Ac	26: 7 **i** serving God day and night, hope	1616+1722

INSTEAD (39)

Ge	2:21 his ribs, and closed up the flesh **i** thereof;	8478
	4:25 hath appointed me another seed **i** of Abel,	8478
	44:33 let thy servant abide **i** of the lad a	8478
Ex	4:16 even he shall be to thee **i** of a mouth,	3807.1
	4:16 and thou shalt be to him **i** of God,	3807.1
	5:12 of Egypt to gather stubble **i** of straw.	3807.1
Nu	3:12 **i** of all the firstborn that openeth the	8478
	3:41 **i** of all the firstborn among the children	8478
	3:41 cattle of the Levites **i** of all the firstlings	8478
	3:45 Take the Levites **i** of all the firstborn	8478
	3:45 the cattle of the Levites **i** of their cattle;	8478
	5:19 with another **i** of thy husband,	8478
	5:20 if thou hast gone aside to another **i** of thy	8478
	5:29 a wife goeth aside to another **i** of her	8478
	8:16 of such as open every womb, even	8478
	8:16 even **i** of the firstborn of all the children	NIH
	10:31 and they brought forth **i** of eyes.	3807.1
Jdg	15: 2 than she? take her, I pray thee, **i** of her.	8478
2Sa	17:25 made Amasa captain of the host **i** of Joab;	8478
1Ki	3: 7 hast made thy servant king **i** of David	8478
2Ki	14:21 made him king **i** of his father Amaziah.	8478
	17:24 placed them in the cities of Samaria **i** of	8478
1Ch	29:23 of the LORD as king **i** of David his father,	8478
2Ch	12:10 **I** of which king Rehoboam made shields	8478
Est	2: 4 pleaseth the king be queen **i** of Vashti.	8478
	2:17 her head, and made her queen **i** of Vashti.	8478
Job	31:40 Let thistles grow **i** of wheat,	8478
	31:40 instead of wheat, and cockle **i** of barley.	8478
Ps	45:16 **I** of thy fathers shall be thy children,	8478
Isa	3:24 that **i** of sweet smell there shall be stink;	8478
	3:24 **i** of a girdle a rent; and instead of well set	8478
	3:24 **i** of well set hair baldness; and instead of	8478
	3:24 **i** of a stomacher a girding of sackcloth;	8478
	3:24 of sackcloth; and burning **i** of beauty.	8478
	55:13 **I** of the thorn shall come up the fir tree,	8478
	55:13 **i** of the brier shall come up the myrtle	8478
Jer	22:11 which reigned **i** of Josiah his father,	8478
	37: 1 Zedekiah the son of Josiah reigned **i** of	8478
Eze	16:32 which taketh strangers **i** of her husband.	8478

INSTRUCT (9) [INSTRUCTED, INSTRUCTING, INSTRUCTION, INSTRUCTOR, INSTRUCTORS]

Dt	4:36 to hear his voice, that he might **i** thee:	3256
Ne	9:20 Thou gavest also thy good spirit to **i** them,	7919
Job	40: 2 Almighty **i** him? he that reproveth God,	3250
Ps	16: 7 my reins also **i** me in the night seasons.	3256
	32: 8 I will **i** thee and teach thee in the way	7919
SS	8: 2 my mother's house, who would **i** me:	3925
Isa	28:26 For his God doth **i** him to discretion,	3256
Da	11:33 among the people shall **i** many:	995
1Co	2:16 the mind of the Lord, that he may **i** him?	4822

INSTRUCTED (19) [INSTRUCT]

Dt	32:10 he led him about, he **i** him, he kept him as	995
2Ki	12: 2 days where in Jehoiada the priest **i** him.	3384
1Ch	15:22 **i** about the song, because he was skilful.	3256
	25: 7 their brethren that were **i** in the songs	3925
2Ch	3: 3 was **i** for the building of the house of God.	3245
Job	4: 3 thou hast **i** many, and thou hast	3256
Ps	2:10 O ye kings; be ye judges of the earth.	3256
Pr	5:13 nor inclined mine ear to them that **i** me!	3925
	21:11 the wise is **i**, he receiveth knowledge.	7919
Isa	8:11 me that **I** should not walk in the way of	3256
	40:14 who **i** him, and taught him in the path of	995
Jer	6: 8 Be thou **i**, O Jerusalem, lest my soul	3256
	31:19 after that I was **i**, I smote upon my thigh:	3045
Mt	13:52 Therefore every scribe which is **i** unto	3100
	14: 8 she, being **before i** of her mother, said,	4264

Lk	1: 4 of those things, wherein thou hast been **i**.	2727
Ac	18:25 This man was **i** in the way of the Lord;	2727
Ro	2:18 are more excellent, being **i** out of the law;	2727
Php	4:12 and in all things I am **i** both to be full and	3453

INSTRUCTING (1) [INSTRUCT]

2Ti	2:25 In meekness **i** those that oppose	3811

INSTRUCTION (33) [INSTRUCT]

Job	33:16 the ears of men, and sealeth their **i**.	4561
Ps	50:17 Seeing thou hatest **i**, and castest my	4148
Pr	1: 2 To know wisdom and **i**; to perceive	4148
	1: 3 To receive the **i** of wisdom, justice,	4148
	1: 7 but fools despise wisdom and **i**.	4148
	1: 8 hear the **i** of thy father, and forsake not	4148
	4: 1 the **i** of a father, and attend to know	4148
	4:13 Take fast hold of **i**; let her not go: keep	4148
	5:12 How have I hated **i**, and my heart	4148
	5:23 shall die without **i**; and in the greatness	4148
	6:23 and reproofs of **i** are the way of life:	4148
	8:10 Receive my **i**, and not silver;	4148
	8:33 Hear **i**, and be wise, and refuse it not.	4148
	9: 9 Give **i** to a wise man, and he will be yet	NIH
	10:17 He is in the way of life that keepeth **i**:	4148
	12: 1 Whoso loveth **i** loveth knowledge:	4148
	13: 1 A wise son heareth his father's **i**:	4148
	13:18 shame shall be to him that refuseth **i**:	4148
	15: 5 A fool despiseth his father's **i**: but he that	4148
	15:32 He that refuseth **i** despiseth his own soul:	4148
	15:33 The fear of the LORD is the **i** of wisdom;	4148
	16:22 him that hath it: but the **i** of fools is folly.	4148
	19:20 Hear counsel, and receive **i**, that thou	4148
	19:27 to hear the **i** that causeth to err from	4148
	23:12 Apply thine heart unto **i**, and thine ears to	4148
	23:23 also wisdom, and **i**, and understanding.	4148
	24:32 it well: I looked upon it, and received **i**.	4148
Jer	17:23 that they might not hear, nor receive **i**.	4148
	32:33 yet they have not hearkened to receive **i**.	4148
	35:13 Will ye not receive **i** to hearken to my	4148
Eze	5:15 an **i** and an astonishment unto the nations	4148
Zep	3: 7 thou wilt fear me, thou wilt receive **i**;	4148
2Ti	3:16 for correction, for **i** in righteousness:	3809

INSTRUCTOR (2) [INSTRUCT]

Ge	4:22 an **i** of every artificer in brass and iron:	3913
Ro	2:20 An **i** of the foolish, a teacher of babes,	3810

INSTRUCTORS (1) [INSTRUCT]

1Co	4:15 For though you have ten thousand **i** in	3807

INSTRUMENT (8) [INSTRUMENTS]

Nu	35:16 if he smite him with an **i** of iron, so that	3627
Ps	33: 2 with the psaltery and an **i** of ten strings.	6218
	92: 3 Upon an **i** of ten strings,	6218
	144: 9 an **i** of ten strings will I sing praises unto	6218
Isa	28:27 **i**, neither is a cart wheel turned about	NIH
	41:15 I will make thee a new sharp **threshing i**.	4173
	54:16 and that bringeth forth an **i** for his work;	3627
Eze	33:32 pleasant voice, and can **play** well on an **i**:	5059

INSTRUMENTS (51) [INSTRUMENT]

Ge	49: 5 **i** of cruelty are in their habitations.	3627
Ex	25: 9 the pattern of all the **i** thereof, even so	3627
Nu	3: 8 they shall keep all the **i** of the tabernacle	3627
	4:12 they shall take all the **i** of ministry,	3627
	4:26 the **i** of their service, and all that is made	3627
	4:32 with all their **i**, and with all their service:	3627
	4:32 name ye shall reckon the **i** of the charge	3627
	7: 1 sanctified it, and all the **i** thereof, both	3627
	31: 6 with the holy **i**, and the trumpets to blow	3627
1Sa	8:12 to make his **i** of war, and instruments of	3627
	8:12 instruments of war, and **i** his chariots.	3627
	18: 6 with joy, and with **i** of musick.	7991
2Sa	6: 5 on all manner of **i** made of fir wood,	NIH
	24:22 **threshing i** and other instruments of	4173
	24:22 and other **i** of the oxen for wood.	3627
1Ki	19:21 boiled their flesh with the **i** of the oxen,	3627
1Ch	9:29 the **i** of the sanctuary, and the fine flour,	3627
	12:33 expert in war, with all **i** of war,	3627
	12:37 with all manner of **i** of war for the battle,	3627
	15:16 to be the singers with **i** of musick,	3627
	16:42 make a sound, and with musical **i** of God.	3627
	21:23 the **threshing i** for wood, and the wheat	4173
	23: 5 the LORD with the **i** which I made,	3627
	28:14 of gold, for all **i** of all manner of service;	3627
	28:14 silver also for all **i** of silver by weight,	3627
	28:14 weight, for all **i** of every kind of service:	3627
2Ch	4:16 and the fleshhooks, and all their **i**	3627
	5: 1 the silver, and the gold, and all the **i**, put	3627
	5:13 the trumpets and cymbals and **i** of musick,	3627
	7: 6 the Levites also with **i** of musick of	3627
	23:13 also the singers with **i** of musick,	3627
	29:26 the Levites stood with the **i** of David,	3627
	29:27 the **i** ordained by David king of Israel.	3627
	30:21 singing with loud **i** unto the LORD.	3627
	34:12 all that could skill of **i** of musick.	3627
Ne	12:36 with the musical **i** of David the man of	3627
Ps	7:13 He hath also prepared for him the **i** of	3627
	68:25 the **players on i** followed after;	5059
	87: 7 well the singers as the **players on i** shall	2490
	150: 4 praise him with **stringed i** and organs.	4482
Ecc	2: 8 as musical **i**, and that of all sorts.	7705+7705
Isa	32: 7 The **i** also of the churl are evil: he	3627
	38:20 we will **sing** my songs to the **stringed i**	5059
Eze	40:42 whereupon also they laid the **i** wherewith	3627

Da	6:18 neither were **i** of **musick** brought before	1761
Am	1: 3 have threshed Gilead with threshing **i**	NIH
	6: 5 and invent to themselves **i** of musick,	3627
Hab	3:19 To the chief singer on my **stringed i**.	5058
Zec	11:15 Take unto thee yet the **i** of a foolish	3627
Ro	6:13 Neither yield ye your members as **i** of	3696
	6:13 your members as **i** of righteousness unto	3696

INSURRECTION (5)

Ezr	4:19 city of old time hath **made i** against kings,	5376
Ps	64: 2 from the **i** of the workers of iniquity:	7285
Mk	15: 7 with him, who had committed **i**	4955
	15: 7 him, who had committed murder in the **i**.	4714
Ac	18:12 the Jews **made i** with one accord **against**	2721

INTEGRITY (16)

Ge	20: 5 in the **i** of my heart and innocency of my	8537
	20: 6 I know that thou didst this in the **i** of thy	8537
1Ki	9: 4 in **i** of heart, and in uprightness,	8537
Job	2: 3 still he holdeth fast his **i**, although thou	8538
	2: 9 unto him, Dost thou still retain thine **i**?	8538
	27: 5 till I die I will not remove my **i** from me.	8538
	31: 6 even balance, that God may know mine **i**.	8538
Ps	7: 8 according to mine **i** that is in me.	8537
	25:21 Let **i** and uprightness preserve me; for I	8537
	26: 1 O LORD; for I have walked in mine **i**:	8537
	26:11 for me, I will walk in mine **i**: redeem me,	8537
	41:12 upholdest me in mine **i**, and settest me	8537
	78:72 So he fed them according to the **i** of his	8537
Pr	11: 3 The **i** of the upright shall guide them:	8538
	19: 1 Better is the poor that walketh in his **i**,	8537
	20: 7 The just man walketh in his **i**: his	8537

INTELLIGENCE (1)

Da	11:30 have **i** with them that forsake the holy	995

INTEND (4) [INTENDED, INTENDEST, INTENDING, INTENT, INTENTS]

Jos	22:33 did not **i** to go up against them in battle,	559
2Ch	28:13 LORD already, ye **i** to add more to our sins	559
Ac	5:28 and **i** to bring this man's blood upon us.	1014
	5:35 take heed to yourselves what ye **i** to do as	3195

INTENDED (1) [INTEND]

Ps	21:11 they **i** evil against thee: they imagined a	5186

INTENDEST (1) [INTEND]

Ex	2:14 **i** thou to kill me, as thou killedst	559

INTENDING (3) [INTEND]

Lk	14:28 For which of you, **i** to build a tower,	2309
Ac	12: 4 **i** after Easter to bring him forth to	1014
	20:13 sailed unto Assos, there to take in Paul:	3195

INTENT (11) [INTEND]

2Sa	17:14 **to the i** that the LORD might bring evil	3807.1
2Ki	10:19 did it in subtilty, **to the i** that	4616+3807.1
2Ch	16: 1 **to the i** that he might let none go out	3807.1
Eze	40: 4 **to the i** that I might shew them	4616+3807.1
Da	4:17 to the **i** that the living may know that	1701
Jn	11:15 I was not there, **to the i** ye may believe;	2443
	13:28 no man at the table knew for what he	NIG
Ac	9:21 came hither for that **i**, that he might bring	NIG
	10:29 therefore for what **i** ye have sent for me?	3056
1Co	10: 6 **to the i** we should not lust after	1519+3588
Eph	3:10 **To the i** that now unto the principalities	2443

INTENTS (2) [INTEND]

Jer	30:24 until he have performed the **i** of his heart:	4209
Heb	4:12 of the thoughts and **i** of the heart.	1771

INTERCEDE; INTERCEDED See INTREAT; INTREATED; INTREATIES; INTREATY

INTERCESSION (9) [INTERCESSIONS, INTERCESSOR]

Isa	53:12 many, and **made i** for the transgressors.	6293
Jer	7:16 prayer for them, neither **make i** to me:	6293
	27:18 let them now **make i** to the LORD of	6293
	36:25 Gemariah had **made i** to the king that he	6293
Ro	8:26 the Spirit itself **maketh i** for us with	5241
	8:27 he **maketh i** for the saints according to	1793
	8:34 hand of God, who also **maketh i** for us.	1793
	11: 2 how he **maketh i** to God against Israel,	1793
Heb	7:25 seeing he ever liveth to make **i** for them.	1793

INTERCESSIONS (1) [INTERCESSION]

1Ti	2: 1 prayers, **i**, and giving of thanks,	1783

INTERCESSOR (1) [INTERCESSION]

Isa	59:16 and wondered that there was no **i**:	6293

INTERCOURSE See CARNALLY

INTERMARRY See AFFINITY

INTERMEDDLE (1) [INTERMEDDLETH]

Pr	14:10 and a stranger doth not **i** with his joy.	6148

INTERMEDDLETH (1) [INTERMEDDLE]

Pr	18: 1 seeketh and **i** with all wisdom.	1566

INTERMISSION (1)

La	3:49 and ceaseth not, without any **i**,	2014

I

INTERPRET (8) [INTERPRETATION, INTERPRETATIONS, INTERPRETED, INTERPRETER, INTERPRETING]

Ge	41: 8 *there was* none that could **i** them unto	6622
	41:12 man according to his dream he did **i**.	6622
	41:15 a dream, and *there is* none that can **i** it:	6622
	41:15 thou canst understand a dream to **i** it.	6622
1Co	12:30 do all speak with tongues? do all **i**?	1329
	14: 5 except **he i**, that the church may receive	1329
	14:13 in an *unknown* tongue pray that he may **i**.	1329
	14:27 *by* three, and *that* by course; and let one **i**.	1329

INTERPRETATION (46) [INTERPRET]

Ge	40: 5 each man according to the **i** of his dream,	6623
	40:12 Joseph said unto him, This *is* the **i** of it:	6623
	40:16 When the chief baker saw that the **i** was	6622
	40:18 and said, This *is* the **i** thereof:	6623
	41:11 dreamed each man according to the **i** of	6623
Jdg	7:15 the **i** thereof, that he worshipped,	7667
Pr	1: 6 To understand a proverb, and the **i**;	4426
Ecc	8: 1 and who knoweth the **i** of a thing?	6592
Da	2: 4 the dream, and we will shew the **i**.	6591
	2: 5 the **i** thereof, ye shall be cut in pieces,	6591
	2: 6 if ye shew the dream, and the **i** thereof,	6591
	2: 6 shew me the dream, and the **i** thereof.	6591
	2: 7 the dream, and we will shew the **i** of it.	6591
	2: 9 I shall know that ye can shew me the **i**	6591
	2:16 and that *he* would shew the king the **i**.	6591
	2:24 and I will shew unto the king the **i**.	6591
	2:25 will make known unto the king the **i**.	6591
	2:26 which I have seen, and the **i** thereof?	6591
	2:30 *their* sakes that shall make known the **i**	6591
	2:36 we will tell the **i** thereof before the king.	6591
	2:45 dream *is* certain, and the **i** thereof sure.	6591
	4: 6 they might make known unto me the **i**	6591
	4: 7 they *did* not make known unto me the **i**	6591
	4: 9 dream that I have seen, and the **i** thereof.	6591
	4:18 O Belteshazzar, declare the **i** thereof,	6591
	4:18 not able to make known unto me the **i**:	6591
	4:19 the dream, or the **i** thereof, trouble thee.	6591
	4:19 and the **i** thereof to thine enemies.	6591
	4:24 *is* the **i**, O king, and this *is* the decree	6591
	5: 7 shew me the **i** thereof, shall be clothed	6591
	5: 8 make known to the king the **i** thereof.	6591
	5:12 Daniel be called, and he will shew the **i**.	6591
	5:15 make known unto me the **i** thereof:	6591
	5:15 they could not shew the **i** of the thing:	6591
	5:16 make known to me the **i** thereof, thou	6591
	5:17 the king, and make known to him the **i**.	6591
	5:26 This *is* the **i** of the thing: MENE; God	6591
	7:16 and made me know the **i** of the things.	6591
Jn	1:42 be called Cephas, which is **by i**, A stone.	2059
	9: 7 the pool of Siloam, (which is **by i**, Sent.)	2059
Ac	9:36 which is **i** called Dorcas;	1329
	13: 8 the sorcerer (for so is his name **by i**)	3177
1Co	12:10 of tongues; to another the **i** of tongues:	2058
	14:26 a tongue, hath a revelation, hath an **i**.	2058
Heb	7: 2 first being **by i** King of righteousness,	2059
2Pe	1:20 of the scripture is of *any* private **i**.	1955

INTERPRETATIONS (2) [INTERPRET]

Ge	40: 8 said unto them, *Do* not **i** *belong* to God?	6623
Da	5:16 thou canst **make i**, and dissolve	6590+6591

INTERPRETED (11) [INTERPRET]

Ge	40:22 the chief baker: as Joseph had **i** to them.	6622
	41:12 we told him, and he **i** to us our dreams;	6622
	41:13 it came to pass, as he **i** to us, so it was;	6622
Ezr	4: 7 Syrian tongue, and **i** in the Syrian tongue.	8638
Mt	1:23 which being **i** is, God with us.	3177
Mk	5:41 which is, being **i**, Damsel (I say unto thee)	3177
	15:22 which is, being **i**, The place of a skull.	3177
	15:34 which is, being **i**, My God, my God,	3177
Jn	1:38 Rabbi, (which is to say, being **i**, Master,)	2059
	1:41 the Messias, which is, being **i**, the Christ.	3177
Ac	4:36 (which is, being **i**, The son of consolation,)	3177

INTERPRETER (4) [INTERPRET]

Ge	40: 8 dreamed a dream, and *there is* no **i** of it.	6622
	42:23 *them*; for he spake unto them by an **i**.	3887
Job	33:23 with him, an **i**, one among a thousand,	3887
1Co	14:28 But if there be no **i**, let him keep silence	1328

INTERPRETING (1) [INTERPRET]

Da	5:12 **i** of dreams, and shewing of hard	6590

INTO (2015) [IN, TO, THEREINTO, WHEREINTO]

Ge	2: 7 breathed **i** his nostrils the breath of life;	871.1
	2:10 it was parted, and became **i** four heads.	3807.1
	2:15 put him **i** the garden of Eden to dress it	871.1
	6:18 shalt come **i** the ark, thou, and thy sons,	413
	6:19 of every *sort* shalt thou bring **i** the ark,	413
	7: 1 Come thou and all thy house **i** the ark;	413
	7: 7 **i** the ark, because of the waters of the	413
	7: 9 went in two and two unto Noah **i** the ark,	413
	7:13 wives of his sons with them, **i** the ark;	413
	7:15 they went in unto Noah **i** the ark, two	413
	8: 9 she returned unto him **i** the ark,	413
	8: 9 and pulled her **i** unto him **i** the ark.	413
	9: 2 the sea; **i** your hand are they delivered.	871.1
	11:31 Chaldees, to go **i** the land of Canaan;	1886.5
	12: 5 went forth to go **i** the land of Canaan;	1886.5
	12: 5 and **i** the land of Canaan they came.	1886.5
	12:10 went down **i** Egypt to sojourn there;	1886.5
	12:11 he was come near to enter **i** Egypt,	1886.5

Ge	12:14 that, when Abram was come **i** Egypt,	1886.5
	12:15 the woman was taken **i** Pharaoh's house.	NIH
	13: 1 he had, and Lot with him, **i** the south.	1886.5
	14:20 which hath delivered thine enemies **i** thy	871.1
	16: 5 I have given my maid **i** thy bosom;	871.1
	18: 6 Abraham hastened **i** the tent unto Sarah,	1886.5
	19: 2 **i** your servant's house, and tarry all night,	413
	19: 3 in unto him, and entered **i** his house;	413
	19:10 pulled Lot **i** the house to them, and shut	1886.5
	19:23 upon the earth when Lot entered **i** Zoar.	1886.5
	21:32 they returned **i** the land of the Philistines.	413
	22: 2 and get thee **i** the land of Moriah;	413
	24:20 emptied her pitcher **i** the trough,	413
	24:32 the man came **i** the house:	1886.5
	24:67 Isaac brought her **i** his mother Sarah's	1886.5
	26: 2 him, and said, Go not down **i** Egypt;	1886.5
	27:17 prepared, **i** the hand of her son Jacob.	871.1
	28:15 and will bring thee again **i** this land;	413
	29: 1 came **i** the land of the people of the east.	1886.5
	30:35 and gave *them* **i** the hand of his sons.	871.1
	31:33 Laban went **i** Jacob's tent, and into	871.1
	31:33 **i** Leah's tent, and into the two	871.1
	31:33 and **i** the two maidservants' tents;	871.1
	31:33 Leah's tent, and entered **i** Rachel's tent.	871.1
	32: 7 and herds, and the camels, **i** two bands;	3807.1
	32:16 he delivered *them* **i** the hand of his	871.1
	36: 6 went **i** the country from the face of his	413
	37:20 and cast him **i** some pit, and we will say,	871.1
	37:22 cast him **i** this pit that *is* in the wilderness,	413
	37:24 they took him, and cast him **i** a pit:	1886.5
	37:28 and they brought Joseph **i** Egypt.	1886.5
	37:35 For I will go down **i** the grave unto my	1886.5
	37:36 the Medanites sold him **i** Egypt unto	413
	39: 4 and all *that* he had he put **i** his hand.	871.1
	39:11 that *Joseph* went **i** the house to do his	1886.5
	39:20 master took him, and put him **i** the prison,	413
	40: 3 **i** the prison, the place where Joseph *was*	413
	40:11 pressed them **i** Pharaoh's cup, and I gave	413
	40:11 and I gave the cup **i** Pharaoh's hand.	5921
	40:13 shalt deliver Pharaoh's cup **i** his hand,	871.1
	40:15 that they should put me **i** the dungeon.	871.1
	40:21 and he gave the cup **i** Pharaoh's hand:	5921
	41:57 all countries came **i** Egypt to Joseph for	1886.5
	42:17 put them all together **i** ward three days.	413
	42:25 to restore every man's money **i** his sack,	413
	42:37 deliver him **i** my hand, and I will bring	5921
	43:17 man brought the men **i** Joseph's house.	1886.5
	43:18 they were **brought i** Joseph's house;	935
	43:24 the man brought the men **i** Joseph's	1886.5
	43:26 which *was* in their hand **i** the house,	1886.5
	43:30 entered **i** *his* chamber, and wept there.	1886.5
	45: 4 your brother, whom ye sold **i** Egypt.	1886.5
	45:25 came **i** the land of Canaan unto Jacob	NIH
	46: 3 fear not to go down **i** Egypt; for I will	1886.5
	46: 4 I will go down with thee **i** Egypt;	1886.5
	46: 6 came **i** Egypt, Jacob, and all his seed	1886.5
	46: 7 his seed brought he with him **i** Egypt.	1886.5
	46: 8 which came **i** Egypt, Jacob and his sons:	1886.5
	46:26 All the souls that came with Jacob **i**	1886.5
	46:27 came **i** Egypt, *were* threescore and	1886.5
	46:28 and they came **i** the land of Goshen.	1886.5
	47:14 Joseph brought the money **i** Pharaoh's	1886.5
	48: 5 Egypt before I came unto thee **i** Egypt,	1886.5
	48:16 let them grow **i** a multitude in the midst	3807.1
	49: 6 O my soul, come not thou **i** their secret;	871.1
	49:33 he gathered up his feet **i** the bed,	413
	50:13 For his sons carried him **i** the land of	1886.5
	50:14 Joseph returned **i** Egypt, he,	1886.5
Ex	1: 1 children of Israel, which came **i** Egypt;	1886.5
	1:22 Every son that is born ye shall cast **i**	1886.5
	3:18 three days' journey **i** the wilderness,	871.1
	4: 6 him, Put now thine hand **i** thy bosom.	871.1
	4: 6 he put his hand **i** his bosom: and when	871.1
	4: 7 he said, Put thine hand **i** thy bosom again.	413
	4: 7 he put his hand **i** his bosom again;	413
	4:19 unto Moses in Midian, Go, return **i** Egypt:	NIH
	4:21 When thou goest to return **i** Egypt,	1886.5
	4:27 Go **i** the wilderness to meet Moses.	1886.5
	5: 3 three days' journey **i** the desert,	871.1
	7:23 Pharaoh turned and went **i** his house,	413
	8: 3 shall go up and come **i** thine house,	871.1
	8: 3 **i** thy bedchamber, and upon thy bed,	871.1
	8: 3 **i** the house of thy servants, and upon thy	871.1
	8: 3 **i** thine ovens, and into thy	871.1
	8: 3 thine ovens, and into thy kneadingtroughs:	871.1
	8:21 and upon thy people, and **i** thy houses:	871.1
	8:24 there came a grievous swarm *of flies* **i**	1886.5
	8:24 **i** his servants' houses, and into all the	NIH
	8:24 and **i** all the land of Egypt:	871.1
	8:27 We will go three days' journey **i**	871.1
	9:20 servants and his cattle flee **i** the houses:	413
	10: 4 to morrow will I bring the locusts **i** thy	871.1
	10:19 the locusts, and cast them **i** the Red sea;	1886.5
	11: 4 About midnight will I go out **i** the midst	871.1
	13: 5 bring thee **i** the land of the Canaanites,	413
	13:11 bring thee **i** the land of the Canaanites,	413
	14:22 the children of Israel went **i** the midst of	871.1
	14:28 the host of Pharaoh that came **i** the sea	871.1
	15: 1 and his rider hath he thrown **i** the sea.	871.1
	15: 4 and his host hath he cast **i** the sea:	871.1
	15: 5 they sank **i** the bottom as a stone.	871.1
	15:19 with his horsemen **i** the sea,	871.1
	15:21 and his rider hath he thrown **i** the sea.	871.1
	15:22 they went out **i** the wilderness of Shur;	413
	15:25 *which* when he had cast **i** the waters,	413

Ex	16: 3 for ye have brought us forth **i** this	413
	18: 5 and his wife unto Moses **i** the wilderness,	413
	18: 7 *their* welfare; and they came **i** the tent.	1886.5
	18:27 and he went his way **i** his own land.	413
	19: 1 the same day came they **i** the wilderness	NIH
	19:12 *that ye go not* up **i** the mount, or touch	871.1
	21:13 in wait, but God deliver *him* **i** his hand;	3807.1
	23:19 bring **i** the house of the LORD thy God.	NIH
	23:20 to bring thee **i** the place which I have	413
	23:31 the inhabitants of the land **i** your hand;	871.1
	24:12 Come up to me **i** the mount, and be	1886.5
	24:13 and Moses went up **i** the mount of God.	413
	24:15 Moses went up **i** the mount, and a cloud	413
	24:18 Moses went **i** the midst of the cloud,	871.1
	24:18 of the cloud, and gat him up **i** the mount:	413
	25:14 thou shalt put the staves **i** the rings by	871.1
	25:16 thou shalt put **i** the ark the Testimony	413
	26:11 put the taches **i** the loops, and couple	871.1
	27: 7 the staves shall be put **i** the rings,	871.1
	29: 3 thou shalt put them **i** one basket,	5921
	29:30 when he cometh **i** the tabernacle of	413
	30:20 When they go **i** the tabernacle of	413
	32:24 I cast it **i** the fire, and there came out this	871.1
	33: 5 I will come up **i** the midst of thee in a	871.1
	33: 8 until he was gone **i** the tabernacle.	1886.5
	33: 9 pass, as Moses entered **i** the tabernacle,	1886.5
	33:11 turned again **i** the camp: but his servant	413
	37: 5 put the staves **i** the rings by the sides of	871.1
	38: 7 put the staves **i** the rings on the sides of	871.1
	39: 3 And they did beat the gold **i** thin plates,	NIH
	39: 3 cut *it* **i** wires, to work *it* in the blue,	NIH
	40:20 he took and put the Testimony **i** the ark,	413
	40:21 And he brought the ark **i** the tabernacle,	413
	40:32 When they went **i** the tent of	413
	40:35 Moses was not able to enter **i** the tent of	413
Lev	1: 6 burnt offering, and cut it **i** his pieces.	3807.1
	1:12 he shall cut it **i** his pieces, with his head	3807.1
	6:30 whereof *any* of the blood is brought **i**	413
	8:20 cut the ram **i** pieces; and Moses burnt	3807.1
	9:23 Aaron went **i** the tabernacle of	413
	10: 9 when ye go **i** the tabernacle of	413
	11:32 it must be put **i** water, and it shall be	871.1
	12: 4 hallowed *thing*, nor come **i** the sanctuary,	413
	13:17 behold, *if* the plague be turned **i** white;	3807.1
	14: 7 shall let the living bird loose **i** the open	5921
	14: 8 after *that* he shall come **i** the camp,	413
	14:15 pour *it* **i** the palm of his own left hand:	5921
	14:26 priest shall pour of the oil **i** the palm of	5921
	14:34 When ye be come **i** the land of Canaan,	413
	14:36 before the priest go **i** *it* to see the plague,	NIH
	14:40 they shall cast them **i** an unclean place	413
	14:41 off without the city **i** an unclean place:	413
	14:45 shall carry *them* forth out of the city **i** an	413
	14:46 Moreover he that goeth **i** the house all	413
	14:53 shall let go the living bird out of the city **i**	413
	16: 2 he come not at all times **i** the holy *place*	413
	16: 3 Thus shall Aaron come **i** the holy *place:*	413
	16:10 to let him go for a scapegoat **i**	1886.5
	16:21 the hand of a fit man **i** the wilderness:	1886.5
	16:23 Aaron shall come **i** the tabernacle of	413
	16:23 which he put on when he went **i** the holy	413
	16:26 in water, and afterward come **i** the camp.	413
	16:28 and afterward he shall come **i** the camp.	413
	19:23 when ye shall come **i** the land,	413
	23:10 When ye be come **i** the land which I give	413
	25: 2 When ye come **i** the land which I give you,	413
	26:25 ye shall be delivered **i** the hand of	871.1
	26:32 I will **bring** the land **i** desolation:	8074
	26:36 their hearts in the lands of their	871.1
	26:41 have brought them **i** the land of their	871.1
Nu	4: 3 fifty years old, all that enter **i** the host,	3807.1
	4:30 every one that entereth **i** the service,	3807.1
	4:35 every one that entereth **i** the service,	3807.1
	4:39 every one that entereth **i** the service,	3807.1
	4:43 every one that entereth **i** the service,	3807.1
	5:17 priest shall take, and put *it* **i** the water:	413
	5:22 water that causeth the curse shall go **i**	871.1
	5:24 that causeth the curse shall enter **i** her,	871.1
	5:27 that causeth the curse shall enter **i** her,	871.1
	7:89 when Moses was gone **i** the tabernacle of	413
	11:30 Moses gat him **i** the camp, he and the	413
	13:17 *way* southward, and go up **i** the mountain:	NIH
	14: 3 it not better for us to return **i** Egypt?	1886.5
	14: 3 a captain, and let us return **i** Egypt.	1886.5
	14: 8 he will bring us **i** this land, and give it us;	413
	14:16 in the land which he sware unto them,	413
	14:24 him will I bring **i** the land whereinto he	413
	14:25 get you **i** the wilderness *by* the way of	NIH
	14:30 Doubtless ye shall not come **i** the land,	413
	14:40 gat them up **i** the top of the mountain,	413
	15: 2 When ye be come **i** the land of your	413
	15:18 When ye come **i** the land whither I bring	413
	16:14 thou hast not brought us **i** a land	413
	16:30 and they go down quick **i** the pit;	1886.5
	16:33 went down alive **i** the pit, and the earth	1886.5
	16:47 and ran **i** the midst of the congregation;	413
	17: 8 that on the morrow Moses went **i**	413
	19: 6 cast *it* **i** the midst of the burning of	413
	19: 7 and afterward he shall come **i** the camp,	413
	19:14 all that come **i** the tent, and all that *is* in	413
	20: 1 **i** the desert of Zin in the first month:	NIH
	20: 4 of the LORD **i** this wilderness,	413
	20:12 ye shall not bring this congregation **i**	413
	20:15 How our fathers went down **i** Egypt,	1886.5
	20:24 he shall not enter **i** the land which I have	413

I

Nu 20:27 went up i mount Hor in the sight of all 413
21: 2 If thou wilt indeed deliver this people i 871.1
21:22 we will not turn i the fields, or into 871.1
21:22 turn into the fields, or i the vineyards; 871.1
21:23 went out against Israel i the wilderness: 1886.5
21:27 Come i Heshbon, let the city of Sihon be NIH
21:29 daughters i captivity unto Sihon king of 871.1
21:34 I have delivered him i thy hand, and all 871.1
22:13 the princes of Balak, Get you i your land: 413
22:23 out of the way, and went i the field: 871.1
22:23 smote the ass, to turn her i the way. NIH
22:41 brought him up i the high places of Baal, NIH
23:14 he brought him i the field of Zophim, NIH
24: 4 falling i a trance, but having his eyes open: NIH
24:16 falling i a trance, but having his eyes open: NIH
25: 8 he went after the man of Israel i the tent, 413
27:12 Get thee up i this mount Abarim, and see 413
31:24 and afterward ye shall come i the camp. 413
31:27 **divide** the prey i **two parts**; between 2673
31:54 brought it i the tabernacle of 413
32: 7 i the land which the Lord hath given 413
32: 9 that *they* should not go i the land which 413
32:32 before the Lord i the land of Canaan, NIH
33: 8 passed through the midst of the sea i 1886.5
33:38 Aaron the priest went up i mount Hor at 413
33:51 When ye are passed over Jordan i the land 413
34: 2 When ye come i the land of Canaan; 413
35:10 When ye be come over Jordan i the land 1886.5
35:28 shall return i the land of his possession. 413
36:12 *And* they were married i the families of 4480

Dt 1:22 go up, and i what cities we shall come. 871.1
1:24 turned and went up i the mountain, 1886.5
1:27 to deliver us i the hand of the Amorites, 871.1
1:31 that ye went, until ye came i this place. 5704
1:40 take your journey i the wilderness *by* 1886.5
1:41 of war, ye were ready to go up i the hill. 1886.5
1:43 and went presumptuously up i the hill. 1886.5
2: 1 took our journey i the wilderness *by* 1886.5
2:24 have given i thy hand Sihon the Amorite, 871.1
2:29 until I shall pass over Jordan i the land 413
2:30 that he might deliver him i thy hand, 871.1
3: 2 all his people, and his land, i thy hand; 871.1
3: 3 So the Lord our God delivered i our 871.1
3:27 Get thee up i the top of Pisgah, and lift NIH
5: 5 the fire, and went not up i the mount;) 413
5:30 say to them, Get you i your tents again. 3807.1
6:10 i the land which he sware unto thy fathers, 413
7: 1 When the Lord thy God shall bring thee i 413
7:24 he shall deliver their kings i thine hand, 871.1
7:26 Neither shalt thou bring an abomination i 413
8: 7 For the Lord thy God bringeth thee i a 413
9: 9 When I was gone up i the mount to 1886.5
9:21 I cast the dust thereof i the brook that 413
9:28 them i the land which he promised them, 413
10: 1 come up unto me i the mount, 1886.5
10: 3 went up i the mount, having the two 1886.5
10:22 Thy fathers went down i Egypt with 1886.5
11: 5 the wilderness, until ye came i this place; 5704
13:16 shalt gather all the spoil of it i the midst 413
14: 6 cleaveth the cleft i two claws, NIH
14:25 shalt thou turn *it* i money, and bind up 871.1
17: 8 get thee up i the place which the Lord thy 413
18: 9 When thou art come i the land which 413
19: 3 **divide** the coasts . . . , i **three parts**, 8027
19: 5 As when *a man* goeth i the wood with 871.1
19:11 he die, and fleeth i one of these cities: 413
19:12 deliver him i the hand of the avenger of 871.1
20:13 thy God hath delivered it i thine hands, 871.1
21:10 the Lord thy God hath delivered them i 871.1
23: 1 shall not enter i the congregation of 871.1
23: 2 bastard shall not enter i the congregation 871.1
23: 2 not enter i the congregation of the Lord. 871.1
23: 3 shall not enter i the congregation 871.1
23: 8 **enter** i the congregation of the Lord for 935
23: 5 thy God turned the curse i a 3807.1
23: 8 i the congregation of the Lord in their 871.1
23:11 he shall come i the camp again. 413+8432
23:18 i the house of the Lord thy God for any NIH
23:24 When thou comest i thy neighbour's 871.1
23:25 When thou comest i the standing corn of 871.1
24:10 thou shalt not go i his house to fetch his 413
26: 5 he went down i Egypt, 1886.5
26: 9 he hath brought us i this place, 413
28:25 shalt be removed i all the kingdoms of 3807.1
28:38 shalt carry much seed out i the field, NIH
28:41 enjoy them; for they shall go i captivity. 871.1
28:68 the Lord shall bring thee i Egypt again NIH
29:12 That thou shouldest enter i covenant 871.1
29:12 i his oath, which the Lord thy God 871.1
29:28 cast them i another land, as *it is* this day. 413
30: 5 the Lord thy God will bring thee i 413
31:20 *For* when I shall have brought them i 413
31:21 before I have brought them i the land 413
31:23 for thou shalt bring the children of Israel i 413
32:26 I said, I would **scatter** them i **corners**, 6284
32:49 Get thee up i this mountain Abarim, 413

Jos 2: 1 came i a harlot's house, named Rahab, NIH
2: 3 thee, which are entered i thine house: 3807.1
2:18 Behold, *when* we come i the land, 871.1
2:19 of the doors of thy house i the street, 1886.5
2:24 Truly the Lord hath delivered i our 871.1
3:11 earth passeth over before you i Jordan. 413
4: 5 the Lord your God i the midst of Jordan, 413
6: 2 I have given i thine hand Jericho, 871.1
6:11 they came i the camp, and lodged in NIH

Jos 6:14 the city once, and returned i the camp: NIH
6:19 they shall come i the treasury of NIH
6:20 so that the people went up i the city, 1886.5
6:22 Go i the harlot's house, and bring out NIH
6:24 they put i the treasury of the house of NIH
7: 7 to deliver us i the hand of the Amorites, 871.1
8: 1 I have given i thy hand the king of Ai, 871.1
8: 7 for the Lord your God will deliver it i 871.1
8:13 Joshua that night i the midst of 871.1
8:18 toward Ai; for I will give it i thine hand. 871.1
8:19 they entered i the city, and took it, NIH
10: 8 for I have delivered them i thine hand; 871.1
10:19 suffer them not to enter i their cities: 413
10:19 God hath delivered them i your hand. 871.1
10:20 remained of them entered i fenced cities. 413
10:27 cast them i the cave wherein they had 413
10:30 the king thereof, i the hand of Israel; 871.1
10:32 the Lord delivered Lachish i the hand of 871.1
11: 8 the Lord delivered them i the hand of 871.1
13: 5 Hermon unto the entering i Hamath. 871.1
18: 5 they shall divide it i seven parts: 3807.1
18: 6 therefore describe the land i seven parts, NIH
18: 9 described it by cities i seven parts in a 3807.1
20: 4 they shall take him i the city unto them, 1886.5
20: 5 they shall not deliver the slayer up i his 871.1
21:44 the Lord delivered all their enemies i 871.1
22:13 tribe of Manasseh, i the land of Gilead, 413
24: 4 Jacob and his children went down i Egypt. NIH
24: 8 I brought you i the land of the Amorites, 413
24: 8 I gave them i your hand, that ye might 871.1
24:11 and I delivered them i your hand. 871.1

Jdg 1: 2 I have delivered the land i his hand. 871.1
1: 3 his brother, Come up with me i my lot, 871.1
1: 3 and I likewise will go with thee i thy lot. 871.1
1: 4 and the Perizzites i their hand: 871.1
1:16 of Judah i the wilderness of Judah, NIH
1:24 the entrance i the city, and we will shew NIH
1:25 when he shewed them the entrance i NIH
1:26 the man went i the land of the Hittites, NIH
1:34 Amorites forced the children of Dan i 1886.5
2:14 he delivered them i the hands of spoilers 871.1
2:14 sold them i the hands of their enemies 871.1
2:23 neither delivered he them i the hand of 871.1
3: 8 he sold them i the hand of 871.1
3:10 king of Mesopotamia i his hand; 871.1
3:21 his right thigh, and thrust it i his belly: 871.1
3:28 your enemies the Moabites i your hand. 871.1
4: 2 the Lord sold them i the hand of Jabin 871.1
4: 7 and I will deliver him i thine hand. 871.1
4: 9 for the Lord shall sell Sisera i the hand 871.1
4:14 Lord hath delivered Sisera i thine hand: 871.1
4:18 he had turned in unto her i the tent, 1886.5
4:21 the nail i his temples, and fastened *it* 871.1
4:21 his temples, and fastened *it* i the ground: 871.1
4:22 he came i her *tent*, behold, Sisera lay 413
5:15 he was sent on foot i the valley. 871.1
6: 1 the Lord delivered them i the hand of 871.1
6: 5 and they entered i the land to destroy it. 871.1
6:13 us i the hands of the Midianites. 871.1
7: 2 me to give the Midianites i their hands, 871.1
7: 7 and deliver the Midianites i thine hand: 871.1
7: 9 for I have delivered it i thine hand. 871.1
7:13 a cake of barley bread tumbled i the host 871.1
7:14 *for* i his hand hath God delivered Midian, 871.1
7:15 returned i the host of Israel, and said, 413
7:15 for the Lord hath delivered i your hand 871.1
7:16 he divided the three hundred men i three NIH
8: 3 God hath delivered i your hands 871.1
8: 7 and Zalmunna i mine hand, 871.1
9:27 they went out i the fields, and gathered NIH
9:27 went i the house of their god, and did eat NIH
9:42 that the people went out i the field; NIH
9:43 divided them i three companies, 3807.1
9:46 i a hold of the house of the god Berith. 413
10: 7 sold them i the hands of the Philistines, 871.1
10: 7 i the hands of the children of Ammon. 871.1
11:19 pray thee, through thy land i my place. 5704
11:21 and all his people i the hand of Israel, 871.1
11:30 the children of Ammon i mine hands, 871.1
11:32 the Lord delivered them i his hands. 871.1
12: 3 and the Lord delivered them i my hand: 871.1
13: 1 the Lord delivered them i the hand of 871.1
15: 1 I will go in to my wife i the chamber. 413
15: 5 he let *them* go i the standing corn of 871.1
15:12 that we may deliver thee i the hand of 871.1
15:13 thee fast, and deliver thee i their hand: 871.1
15:18 Thou hast given this great deliverance i NIH
15:18 and fall i the hand of the uncircumcised? 871.1
16:23 delivered Samson our enemy i our hand. 871.1
16:24 Our god hath delivered i our hands our 871.1
18:10 God hath given it i your hands; a place 871.1
18:18 these went i Micah's house, and fetched NIH
19: 3 she brought him i her father's house: NIH
19:11 let us turn in i this city of the Jebusites, 413
19:12 We will not turn aside hither i the city of a 413
19:15 *there was* no man that took them i *his* 1886.5
19:21 So he brought him i his house, 3807.1
19:22 forth the man that came i thine house, 413
19:23 seeing that this man is come i mine house, 413
19:29 when he was come i his house, he took a 413
19:29 i twelve pieces, and sent her into all 3807.1
19:29 and sent her i all the coasts of Israel. 871.1
20: 4 I came i Gibeah that *belongeth* to 1886.5
20: 8 will we any *of us* turn i his house. 3807.1
20:28 for to morrow I will deliver them i thine 871.1

Ru 1: 2 they came i the country of Moab, NIH
2:18 she took *it* up, and went i the city: NIH
3:14 Let it not be known that a woman came i NIH
3:15 and laid *it* on her: and he went i the city. NIH
4:11 The Lord make the woman that is come i 413

1Sa 2:14 strooke *it* i the pan, or kettle, or caldron, 871.1
2:36 I pray thee, i one of the priests' offices, 413
4: 3 when the people were come i the camp, 413
4: 5 covenant of the Lord came i the camp, 413
4: 6 the ark of the Lord was come i the camp. 413
4: 7 for they said, God is come i the camp. 413
4:10 and they fled every man i his tent: 3807.1
4:13 the man came i the city, and told *it*, 871.1
5: 2 they brought it i the house of Dagon, NIH
5: 5 nor any that come i Dagon's house, NIH
6:14 the cart came i the field of Joshua, 413
6:19 they had looked i the ark of the Lord, 871.1
7: 1 it i the house of Abinadab in the hill, 413
7:13 they came no more i the coast of Israel: 871.1
9:13 As soon as ye be come i the city, ye shall NIH
9:14 they went up i the city: *and* when they NIH
9:14 when they were come i the city, 8432+871.1
9:22 brought them i the parlour, 1886.5
9:25 down from the high place i the city, NIH
10: 6 and shalt be turned i another man. 3807.1
11:11 they came i the midst of the host in 871.1
12: 8 When Jacob was come i Egypt, NIH
12: 9 he sold them i the hand of Sisera, 871.1
12: 9 i the hand of the Philistines, and into 871.1
12: 9 i the hand of the king of Moab, 871.1
14:10 for the Lord hath delivered them i our 871.1
14:12 for the Lord hath delivered them i the 871.1
14:21 which went up with them i the camp 871.1
14:26 when the people were come i the wood, 413
14:37 thou deliver them i the hand of Israel? 871.1
17:22 ran i the army, and came and saluted his NIH
17:46 This day will the Lord deliver thee i 871.1
17:47 and he will give you i our hands. 871.1
17:49 that the stone sunk i his forehead; 871.1
19:10 and he smote the javelin i the wall: 871.1
20: 8 for thou hast brought thy servant i a 871.1
20:11 Come, and let us go out i the field. NIH
20:11 they went out both of them i the field. NIH
20:35 Jonathan went out i the field at the time NIH
20:42 departed: and Jonathan went i the city. NIH
21:15 shall i this *fellow* come i my house? 413
22: 5 depart, and get thee i the land of Judah. NIH
22: 5 and came i the forest of Hareth. NIH
23: 4 for I will deliver the Philistines i thine 871.1
23: 7 God hath delivered him i mine hand; 871.1
23: 7 by entering i a town that hath gates and 871.1
23:11 the men of Keilah deliver me up i his 871.1
23:12 me and my men i the hand of Saul? 871.1
23:14 but God delivered him not i his hand. 871.1
23:16 went to David i the wood, NIH
23:20 part *shall* be to deliver him i the king's 871.1
23:25 wherefore he came down i a rock, NIH
24: 4 I will deliver thine enemy i thine hand, 871.1
24:10 thee to day i mine hand in the cave: 871.1
24:18 the Lord had delivered me i thine hand, 871.1
26: 3 he saw that Saul came after him i 1886.5
26: 8 God hath delivered thine enemy i thine 871.1
26:10 or he shall descend i battle, and perish. 871.1
26:23 for the Lord delivered thee i *my* hand to 871.1
27: 1 escape i the land of the Philistines; 413
28:19 with thee i the hand of the Philistines: 871.1
28:19 host of Israel i the hand of the Philistines. 871.1
29:11 to return i the land of the Philistines. 413
30:15 nor deliver me i the hands of my master, 871.1
30:23 company that came against us i our hand. 871.1
31: 9 sent i the land of the Philistines round NIH

2Sa 2: 1 Shall I go up i any of the cities of Judah? 871.1
3: 8 have not delivered thee i the hand of 871.1
3:34 not bound, nor thy feet put i fetters: 3807.1
4: 6 came thither i the midst of the house, 5704
4: 7 when they came i the house, he lay on NIH
5: 8 and the lame shall not come i the house. 413
5:19 wilt thou deliver them i mine hand? 871.1
5:19 I will doubtless deliver the Philistines i 871.1
6:10 of the Lord unto him i the city of David: 5921
6:10 David carried it aside i the house of NIH
6:12 i the city of David with gladness. NIH
6:16 as the ark of the Lord came i the city of NIH
10: 2 David's servants came i the land of NIH
10:10 the rest of the people he delivered i 871.1
10:14 before Abishai, and entered i the city. NIH
11:11 shall I then go i mine house, to eat and 413
11:23 came out unto us i the field, and we were NIH
12: 8 thy master's wives i thy bosom, 871.1
12:20 came i the house of the Lord, NIH
13:10 Bring the meat i the chamber, that I may NIH
13:10 brought *them* i the chamber to Amnon 1886.5
15:25 Carry back the ark of God i the city: NIH
15:27 return i the city in peace, and your two NIH
15:31 **turn** the counsel of Ahithophel
 i **foolishness**. 5528
15:37 So Hushai David's friend came i the city, NIH
15:37 the city, and Absalom came i Jerusalem. NIH
16: 8 the Lord hath delivered the kingdom i 871.1
17:13 if he be gotten i a city, then shall all Israel 413
17:13 that city, and we will draw it i the river, 5704
17:17 for they might not be seen to come i 1886.5
18: 6 So the people went out i the field against NIH
18:17 cast him i a great pit in the wood, and laid 413
19: 2 the victory that day was *turned* i 3807.1

2Sa 19: 3 the people gat them by stealth that day *i* NIH
19: 5 Joab came *i* the house to the king, NIH
20:12 he removed Amasa out of the highway *i* NIH
21: 9 he delivered them *i* the hands of 871.1
22: 7 temple, and my cry *did enter i* his ears. 871.1
22:20 He brought me forth also *i* a large place: 3807.1
23:11 Philistines were gathered together *i* a 3807.1
24:14 let us fall now *i* the hand of the LORD; 871.1
24:14 and let me not fall *i* the hand of man. 871.1

1Ki 1:15 Bath-sheba went in unto the king *i* 1886.5
1:28 she came *i* the king's presence, 3807.1
3: 1 and brought her *i* the city of David, 413
6: 8 they went up with winding stairs *i* 5921
6: 8 and out of the middle *i* the third. 413
8: 6 *i* the oracle of the house, to the most holy 413
11:17 father's servants with him, to go *i* Egypt; NIH
11:40 Jeroboam arose, and fled *i* Egypt, NIH
13:18 Bring him back with thee *i* thine house, 413
14:12 *and* when thy feet enter *i* the city, 1886.5
14:28 when the king went *i* the house of NIH
14:28 brought them back *i* the guard chamber. 413
15:15 *i* the house of the LORD, silver, and gold, NIH
15:18 delivered them *i* the hand of his servants; 871.1
16:18 he went *i* the palace of the king's house, 413
16:21 were the people of Israel divided *i* two 3807.1
17:19 carried him up *i* a loft, where he abode, 413
17:21 this child's soul come *i* him again. 5921+7130
17:22 the soul of the child came *i* him 5921+7130
17:23 brought him down out of the chamber *i* 1886.5
18: 5 Go *i* the land, unto all fountains of water, 871.1
18: 9 that thou wouldest deliver thy servant *i* 871.1
19: 4 he himself went a day's journey *i* 871.1
20: 2 to Ahab king *i* the city, 1886.5
20:13 I will deliver it *i* thine hand *this* day; 871.1
20:28 I deliver all this great multitude *i* thine 871.1
20:30 rest fled to Aphek, *i* the city; and *there* a 413
20:30 Ben-hadad fled, and came *i* the city, into 413
20:30 came into the city, *i* an inner chamber. NIH
20:33 he caused him to come up *i* the chariot. 5921
20:39 Thy servant went out *i* the midst of 871.1
21: 4 Ahab came *i* his house heavy and 413
22: 6 for the Lord shall deliver *it i* the hand of 871.1
22:12 for the LORD shall deliver *it i* the king's 871.1
22:15 for the LORD shall deliver *it i* the king's 871.1
22:25 when thou shalt **go** *i* an inner chamber to 935
22:30 disguise myself, and enter *i* the battle; NIH
22:30 disguised himself, and went *i* the battle. 871.1
22:35 blood ran out of the wound *i* the midst of 413

2Ki 2: 1 when the LORD would take up Elijah *i* NIH
2:11 Elijah went up by a whirlwind *i* heaven. NIH
2:16 upon some mountain, or *i* some valley. 871.1
3:10 to deliver them *i* the hand of Moab. 871.1
3:13 to deliver them *i* the hand of Moab. 871.1
3:18 he will deliver the Moabites also *i* your 871.1
4: 4 shalt pour out *i* all those vessels, 5921
4:11 he turned *i* the chamber, and lay there. 413
4:32 when Elisha was come *i* the house, 1886.5
4:39 one went out *i* the field to gather herbs, 413
4:39 came and shred *them i* the pot of pottage: 413
4:41 he cast *it i* the pot; and he said, Pour out 413
5:18 *that* when my master goeth *i* the house of NIH
6: 5 a beam, the axe head fell *i* the water: 413
6:20 they were come *i* Samaria, that Elisha NIH
6:23 So the bands of Syria came no more *i* 871.1
7: 4 We will enter *i* the city, then the famine NIH
7: 8 went *i* one tent, and did eat and drink, 413
7: 8 entered *i* another tent, and carried thence 413
7:12 shall catch them alive, and get *i* the city. 413
8:21 and the people fled *i* their tents. 3807.1
9: 6 he arose, and went *i* the house; 1886.5
9:26 cast him the plat *of ground,* according 871.1
10:15 and he took him up to him *i* the chariot. 413
10:21 they came *i* the house of Baal; NIH
10:23 *i* the house of Baal, and said unto NIH
10:24 *If* any of the men whom I *have* brought *i* 5921
11: 4 brought them to him *i* the house of NIH
11:13 she came to the people *i* the temple of NIH
11:16 which the horses came *i* the king's house: NIH
11:18 all the people of the land went *i* the house NIH
12: 4 that is brought *i* the house of the LORD, NIH
12: 4 the money that cometh *i* any man's heart 5921
12: 4 heart to bring *i* the house of the LORD, NIH
12: 9 the right side as one cometh *i* the house NIH
12: 9 that was brought *i* the house of the LORD. NIH
12:11 *i* the hands of *them* that did the work, 5921
12:13 the money that was brought *i* the house NIH
12:15 *i* whose hand they delivered the money to 5921
12:16 sin money was not brought *i* the house of NIH
13: 3 he delivered them *i* the hand of Hazael 871.1
13: 3 the hand of Ben-hadad the son of 871.1
13:21 cast the man *i* the sepulchre of Elisha: NIH
17: 6 carried Israel away *i* Assyria, 1886.5
17:20 delivered them *i* the hand of spoilers, 871.1
18:21 it will go *i* his hand, and pierce it: 871.1
18:30 city shall not be delivered *i* the hand of 871.1
19: 1 and went *i* the house of the LORD. NIH
19:10 shall not be delivered *i* the hand 871.1
19:14 Hezekiah went up *i* the house of 871.1
19:18 have cast their gods *i* the fire: for they 871.1
19:23 I will enter *i* the lodgings of his borders, NIH
19:23 his borders, *and i* the forest of his Carmel. NIH
19:25 to lay waste fenced cities *i* ruinous heaps. NIH
19:28 and thy tumult is come up *i* mine ears, 871.1
19:32 He shall not come *i* this city, nor shoot an 413
19:33 shall not come *i* this city, saith the LORD. 413

2Ki 19:37 they escaped *i* the land of Armenia. NIH
20: 4 Isaiah was gone out *i* the middle court, NIH
20: 8 *that* I shall go up *i* the house of the LORD 1886.5
20:20 a conduit, and brought water *i* the city, 871.1
21:14 deliver them *i* the hand of their enemies; 871.1
22: 4 which is brought *i* the house of the LORD, NIH
22: 5 let them deliver it *i* the hand of the doers 5921
22: 7 the money that was delivered *i* their hand, 5921
22: 9 delivered it *i* the hand of them that do 5921
22:20 shalt be gathered *i* thy grave in peace; 413
23: 2 the king went up *i* the house of the LORD, NIH
23:12 cast the dust of them *i* the brook Kidron. 413
24:15 carried he *i* captivity from Jerusalem NIH

1Ch 5:20 the Hagarites were delivered *i* their hand, 871.1
6:15 Jehozadak went *i* *captivity,* when NIH
10: 9 sent *i* the land of the Philistines round 871.1
11:15 the rock to David, *i* the cave of Adullam; 413
12: 8 *i* the hold to the wilderness men of 3807.1
13:13 carried it aside *i* the house of Obed-edom 413
14:10 wilt thou deliver them *i* mine hand? 871.1
14:10 for I will deliver them *i* thine hand. 871.1
14:17 the fame of David went out *i* all lands; 871.1
16: 7 to thank the LORD *i* the hand of Asaph 871.1
19: 2 So the servants of David came *i* the land 413
19:15 his brother, and entered *i* the city. 1886.5
21:13 let me fall now *i* the hand of the LORD; 871.1
21:13 but let me not fall *i* the hand of man. 871.1
21:27 he put up his sword again *i* the sheath 413
22:18 the inhabitants of the land *i* mine hand; 871.1
22:19 *i* the house that is *to be* built to the 3807.1
23: 6 David divided *i* courses among NIH
24:19 to come *i* the house of the LORD, 3807.1

2Ch 5: 7 *i* the most holy *place,* even under the 413
6:41 thy resting place, thou, and the ark of 3807.1
7: 2 the priests could not enter *i* the house of 413
7:10 he sent the people away *i* their tents, 3807.1
7:11 all that came *i* Solomon's heart to make in 5921
9: 4 ascent *by* which he went up *i* the house NIH
12:11 when the king entered *i* the house of NIH
12:11 brought them again *i* the guard chamber. 413
13:16 and God delivered them *i* their hand. 871.1
15:12 they entered *i* a covenant to seek 871.1
15:18 he brought *i* the house of God *the things* NIH
16: 8 he delivered them *i* thine hand. 871.1
18: 5 for God will deliver *it i* the king's hand. 871.1
18:11 for the LORD shall deliver *it i* the hand 871.1
18:14 and they shall be delivered *i* your hand. 871.1
18:24 shalt see on that day when thou shalt **go** *i* 935
20:20 went forth *i* the wilderness of Tekoa: 3807.1
21:17 they came up *i* Judah, and brake into it, 871.1
21:17 **brake** *i* it, and carried away all 1234
23: 1 the son of Zichri, *i* covenant with him. 871.1
23: 6 let none come *i* the house of the LORD, NIH
23: 7 whosoever *else* cometh *i* the house, he 413
23:12 she came to the people *i* the house of NIH
23:20 came through the high gate *i* the king's NIH
24:10 and brought in, and cast *i* the chest, 3807.1
24:24 the LORD delivered a very great host *i* 871.1
25:20 that *he* might deliver them *i* the hand *of* 871.1
26:16 went *i* the temple of the LORD to burn 413
27: 2 howbeit he entered not *i* the temple of 413
28: 5 him *i* the hand of the king of Syria; 871.1
28: 5 he was also delivered *i* the hand of 871.1
28: 9 he hath delivered them *i* your hand, 871.1
28:27 they brought him not *i* the sepulchres of 3807.1
29: 4 gathered them together *i* the east street, 3807.1
29:16 the priests went *i* the inner part *of* 3807.1
29:16 *i* the court of the house of the LORD. 3807.1
29:16 Levites took *it,* to carry *it* out abroad *i* 3807.1
29:31 offerings *i* the house of the LORD. 3807.1
30: 8 enter *i* his sanctuary, which he hath 3807.1
30: 9 so that *they* shall come again *i* this land: 3807.1
30:14 and cast *i* the brook Kidron. 3807.1
30:15 brought in the burnt offerings *i* the house NIH
31: 1 man to his possession, *i* their own cities. 3807.1
31:10 the offerings *i* the house of the LORD, NIH
31:16 *even* unto every one that entereth *i* 3807.1
32: 1 entered *i* Judah, and encamped against 871.1
32:21 when he was come *i* the house of his god, NIH
33:13 brought him again *i* Jerusalem *i* his 3807.1
34: 7 had beaten the graven images *i* powder, 3807.1
34: 9 delivered the money that was brought *i* NIH
34:14 that was brought *i* the house of the LORD, NIH
34:17 have delivered it *i* the hand of 5921
34:30 the king went up *i* the house of the LORD, NIH
36:17 for age: he gave *them* all *i* his hand. 871.1

Ezr 5: 8 that we went *i* the province of Judea, 3807.2
5:12 he gave them *i* the hand of 871.2
5:12 carried the people away *i* Babylon. 3807.2
5:14 brought them *i* the temple of Babylon, 3807.2
5:15 them *i* the temple that *is in* Jerusalem, 871.2
9: 7 been delivered *i* the hand of the kings of 871.1
10: 6 went *i* the chamber of Johanan the son of 413

Ne 2: 7 they may convey me over till I come *i.* 413
2: 8 city, and for the house that I shall enter *i.* 413
5: 5 we **bring bondage** our sons and our 3533
6:11 as I *am,* would go *i* the temple to save 413
7: 5 God put *i* mine heart to gather together 413
8: 1 *i* the street that *was* before the water gate; 413
9:11 persecutors thou threwest *i* the deeps, 871.1
9:11 deeps, as a stone *i* the mighty waters. 871.1
9:22 nations, and didst divide them *i* corners: 3807.1
9:23 brought them *i* the land, *concerning* 413
9:24 and gavest them *i* their hands, 871.1
9:27 thou deliveredst them *i* the hand 871.1

Ne 9:30 gavest thou them *i* the hand of the people 871.1
10:29 and entered *i* a curse, and into an oath, 871.1
10:29 and entered into a curse, and *i* an oath, 871.1
10:34 to bring *it i* the house of our God, 3807.1
10:38 to the chambers, *i* the treasure house. 3807.1
12:44 to gather *i* them out of the fields of 871.1
13: 1 The Moabite should not come *i* 871.1
13: 2 howbeit our God turned the curse *i* a 3807.1
13:15 which they brought *i* Jerusalem on NIH

Est 1:22 he sent letters *i* all the king's provinces, 413
1:22 *i* every province according to the writing 413
2:14 on the morrow she returned *i* the second 413
2:16 So Esther was taken unto king Ahasuerus *i* 413
3: 9 to bring *it i* the king's treasuries. 413
3:13 letters were sent by posts *i* all the king's 413
4: 1 went out *i* the midst of the city, 871.1
4: 2 none might enter *i* the king's gate clothed 413
4:11 shall come unto the king *i* the inner court, 413
6: 4 Now Haman was come *i* the outward 3807.1
7: 7 in his wrath *went i* the palace garden: 413
7: 8 king returned out of the palace garden *i* 413
9:22 to joy, and from mourning *i* a good day: 3807.1

Job 3: 6 it not come *i* the number of the months. 871.1
9:24 The earth is given *i* the hand of 871.1
10: 9 clay; and wilt thou bring me *i* dust again? 413
12: 6 *i* whose hand God bringeth *abundantly.* 871.1
14: 3 and bringest me *i* judgment with thee? 871.1
16:11 turned me over *i* the hands of the wicked. 5921
17:12 They change the night *i* day: the light *is* 3807.1
18: 8 For he is cast *i* a net by his own feet, 871.1
18:18 He shall be driven from light *i* darkness, 413
22: 4 will he enter with thee *i* judgment? 871.1
30: 3 flying *i* the wilderness in former time NIH
30:19 He hath cast me *i* the mire, and I am 3807.1
30:31 my organ *i* the voice of them that weep. 3807.1
33:28 He will deliver his soul from going *i* 871.1
34:23 *he* should enter *i* judgment with God. 413
36:16 thee out of the strait *i* a broad place, NIH
37: 8 the beasts go *i* dens, and remain in their 1119
38:16 Hast thou entered *i* the springs of the sea? 5704
38:22 Hast thou entered *i* the treasures of 413
38:38 When the dust groweth *i* hardness, 3807.1
39:12 home thy seed, and gather *it i* thy barn? NIH
40:23 trusteth that he can draw up Jordan *i* his 413
41: 2 Canst thou put a hook *i* his nose? 871.1
41:22 and sorrow is **turned** *i* **joy** before him. 1750
41:28 slingstones are **turned** with him *i* stubble. 2015

Ps 4: 2 how long *will ye turn* my glory *i* shame? 3807.1
5: 7 I will come *i* thy house in the multitude NIH
7:15 and is fallen *i* the ditch *which* he made. 871.1
9:17 The wicked shall be turned *i* hell, 1886.5
10: 9 poor, when he draweth him *i* his net. 871.1
16: 4 offer, nor take up their names, *i* my lips. 5921
18: 6 my cry came before him, *even i* his ears. 871.1
18:19 brought me forth also *i* a large place; 3807.1
22:15 hast brought me *i* the dust of death. 3807.1
24: 3 Who shall ascend *i* the hill of the LORD? 871.1
28: 1 become like them that go down *i* the pit. NIH
30:11 Thou hast turned for me my mourning *i* 3807.1
31: 5 I thine hand I commit my spirit: thou 871.1
31: 8 hast not shut me up *i* the hand of 871.1
32: 4 my moisture is turned *i* the drought of 871.1
35: 8 *i* that *very* destruction let him fall. 871.1
35:13 my prayer returned *i* mine own bosom. 5921
37:15 Their sword shall enter *i* their own heart, 871.1
37:20 *i* smoke shall they consume *away.* 871.1
45: 2 grace is poured *i* thy lips: therefore 871.1
45:15 they shall enter *i* the king's palace. 871.1
46: 2 though the mountains be carried *i* 871.1
55:15 *and* let them go down quick *i* hell: NIH
55:23 shalt bring them down *i* the pit of 3807.1
56: 8 put thou my tears *i* thy bottle: *are they* NIH
57: 6 *i* the midst whereof they are fallen 871.1
60: 9 Who will bring me *i* the strong city? NIH
60: 9 strong city? who will lead me *i* Edom? 5704
63: 9 to destroy *it,* shall go *i* the lower parts of 871.1
66: 6 He turned the sea *i* dry *land:* they went 3807.1
66:11 Thou broughtest us *i* the net; thou laidst 871.1
66:12 broughtest us out *i* a wealthy *place.* 3807.1
66:13 I will go *i* thy house with burnt offerings: NIH
69: 2 am come *i* deep waters, where the floods 871.1
69:27 let them not come *i* thy righteousness. 871.1
73:17 Until I went *i* the sanctuary of God; *then* 413
73:18 thou castedst them down *i* destruction. 3807.1
73:19 How are they *brought i* desolation, as 3807.1
74: 7 They have cast fire *i* thy sanctuary, NIH
76: 6 and horse *are* **cast** *i* **a dead sleep.** 7290
78:44 had turned their rivers *i* blood; 3807.1
78:61 delivered his strength *i* captivity, 3807.1
78:61 and his glory *i* the enemy's hand. 3807.1
79: 1 the heathen are come *i* thine inheritance; 871.1
79:12 render unto our neighbours sevenfold *i* 413
88: 4 I am counted with them that go down *i* NIH
88:18 *and* mine acquaintance *i* darkness. NIH
95:11 wrath that they should not enter *i* my rest. 413
96: 8 bring an offering, and come *i* his courts. 3807.1
100: 4 Enter *i* his gates with thanksgiving, NIH
100: 4 *and i* his courts with praise: NIH
104:10 He sendeth the springs *i* the valleys, 871.1
105:23 Israel also came *i* Egypt; NIH
105:29 He turned their waters *i* blood, 3807.1
106:15 request; but sent leanness *i* their soul. 871.1
106:20 Thus they changed their glory *i* 871.1
106:41 he gave them *i* the hand of the heathen; 871.1
106:42 they were **brought** *i* **subjection** under 3665

I

Ps	107:33 He turneth rivers i a wilderness,	3807.1
	107:33 and the watersprings i dry ground;	3807.1
	107:34 A fruitful land i barrenness,	3807.1
	107:35 He turneth the wilderness i a standing	3807.1
	107:35 and dry ground i watersprings:	3807.1
	108:10 Who will bring me i the strong city?	NIH
	108:10 the strong city? who will lead me i Edom?	5704
	109:18 so let it come i his bowels like water,	871.1
	109:18 like water, and like oil i his bones.	871.1
	114: 8 turned the rock i a standing water,	NIH
	114: 8 the flint i a fountain of waters.	3807.1
	115:17 neither any that go down i silence.	NIH
	118:19 I will go i them, and I will praise	871.1
	118:20 i which the righteous shall enter.	871.1
	122: 1 Let us go i the house of the Lord.	NIH
	132: 3 Surely I will not come i the tabernacle of	871.1
	132: 3 of my house, nor go up i my bed;	5921
	132: 7 We will go i his tabernacles: we will	935
	132: 8 Arise, O Lord, i thy rest; thou,	3807.1
	135: 9 and wonders i the midst of thee,	871.1
	136:13 him which divided the Red sea i parts.	3807.1
	139: 8 If I ascend up i heaven, thou art there:	NIH
	140:10 let them be cast i the fire; into deep pits,	871.1
	140:10 i deep pits, that they rise not up again.	871.1
	141:10 Let the wicked fall i their own nets,	871.1
	143: 2 enter not i judgment with thy servant:	871.1
	143: 7 lest I be like unto them that go down i	NIH
	143:10 good; lead me i the land of uprightness.	871.1
Pr	1:12 whole, as those that go down i the pit:	NIH
	2:10 When wisdom entereth i thine heart,	871.1
	4:14 Enter not i the path of the wicked,	871.1
	6: 3 when thou art come i the hand of thy	871.1
	13:17 A wicked messenger falleth i mischief:	871.1
	16:29 leadeth him i the way that is not good.	871.1
	16:33 The lot is cast i the lap; but the whole	871.1
	17:10 A reproof entereth more i a wise man	871.1
	17:10 wise man than an hundred stripes i a fool.	NIH
	17:20 he that hath a perverse tongue falleth i	871.1
	18: 6 A fool's lips enter i contention,	871.1
	18: 8 they go down i the innermost parts of	NIH
	18:10 the righteous runneth i it, and is safe.	871.1
	19:15 Slothfulness casteth i a deep sleep;	5307
	23:10 enter not i the fields of the fatherless:	871.1
	24:16 but the wicked shall fall i mischief.	871.1
	26: 9 As a thorn goeth up i the hand of a	871.1
	26:22 they go down i the innermost parts of	NIH
	27:10 neither go i thy brother's house in the day	NIH
	28:10 way, he shall fall himself i his own pit:	871.1
	28:14 he that hardeneth his heart shall fall i	871.1
	29: 8 Scornful men bring a city i a snare:	6315
	30: 4 Who hath ascended up i heaven, yea,	NIH
Ecc	1: 7 All the rivers run i the sea; yet the sea is	413
	10: 8 He that diggeth a pit shall fall i it;	871.1
	11: 9 things God will bring thee i judgment.	871.1
	12:14 For God shall bring every work i	871.1
SS	1: 4 the king hath brought me i his chambers:	NIH
	3: 4 I had brought him i my mother's house,	413
	3: 4 i the chamber of her that conceived me.	413
	4:16 Let my beloved come i his garden,	3807.1
	5: 1 I am come i my garden, my sister,	3807.1
	6: 2 My beloved is gone down i his garden,	3807.1
	6:11 I went down i the garden of nuts to see	NIH
	7:11 my beloved, let us go forth i the field;	NIH
	8: 2 and bring thee i my mother's house,	413
Isa	2: 4 shall beat their swords i plowshares,	3807.1
	2: 4 and their spears i pruninghooks:	3807.1
	2:10 Enter i the rock, and hide thee in the	871.1
	2:19 they shall go i the holes of the rocks,	871.1
	2:19 i the caves of the earth, for fear of	871.1
	2:21 To go i the clifts of the rocks, and into	871.1
	2:21 i the tops of the ragged rocks, for fear of	871.1
	3:14 The Lord will enter i judgment with	871.1
	5:13 my people are gone i captivity,	1540
	5:14 and he that rejoiceth, shall descend i it.	NIH
	9: 8 The Lord sent a word i Jacob, and it hath	871.1
	9:10 down, but we will change them i cedars.	NIH
	13: 2 that they may go i the gates of the nobles.	NIH
	13:14 and flee every one i his own land.	413
	14: 7 and is quiet: they break forth i singing.	NIH
	14:13 said in thine heart, I will ascend i heaven,	NIH
	19: 1 a swift cloud, and shall come i Egypt:	NIH
	19: 4 the Egyptians will I give over i the hand	871.1
	19: 8 all they that cast angle i the brooks shall	871.1
	19:23 the Assyrian shall come i Egypt,	871.1
	19:23 the Egyptian i Assyria, and the Egyptians	871.1
	21: 4 night of my pleasure hath he turned i	3807.1
	22:18 and toss thee like a ball i a large country:	413
	22:21 I will commit thy government i his hand:	871.1
	23: 9 to bring i contempt all the honourable	7043
	24:18 the noise of the fear shall fall i the pit;	413
	26:20 enter thou i thy chambers, and shut thy	871.1
	29:17 Lebanon shall be turned i a fruitful field,	3807.1
	30: 2 That walk to go down i Egypt, and have	NIH
	30: 6 i the land of trouble and anguish,	871.1
	30:20 be removed i a corner any more,	3670
	30:29 as when one goeth with a pipe to come i	871.1
	34: 9 streams thereof shall be turned i pitch,	3807.1
	34: 9 the dust thereof i brimstone, and the	3807.1
	36: 6 it will go i his hand, and pierce it:	871.1
	36:15 city shall not be delivered i the hand of	871.1
	37: 1 and went i the house of the Lord.	NIH
	37:10 Jerusalem shall not be given i the hand of	871.1
	37:19 have cast their gods i the fire: for they	NIH
	37:24 I will enter i the height of his border,	NIH
	37:26 lay waste defenced cities i ruinous heaps.	NIH

Isa	37:29 come up i mine ears, therefore will I put	871.1
	37:33 He shall not come i this city, nor shoot an	413
	37:34 shall not come i this city, saith the Lord.	413
	37:38 and they escaped i the land of Armenia.	NIH
	38:18 they that go down i the pit cannot hope	NIH
	40: 9 get thee up i the high mountain;	5921
	44:23 break forth i singing, ye mountains,	NIH
	46: 2 but themselves are gone i captivity.	871.1
	47: 5 Sit thou silent, and get thee i darkness,	871.1
	47: 6 and given them i thine hand:	871.1
	49:13 and break forth i singing, O mountains:	NIH
	51:23 I will put it i the hand of them that afflict	871.1
	52: 1 henceforth there shall no more come i	871.1
	52: 4 My people went down aforetime i Egypt	NIH
	52: 9 Break forth i joy, sing together, ye waste	7442
	54: 1 break forth i singing, and cry aloud,	NIH
	55:12 the hills shall break forth before you i	NIH
	57: 2 He shall enter i peace: they shall rest in	NIH
	59: 5 which is crushed breaketh out i a viper.	NIH
	63:14 As a beast goeth down i the valley,	871.1
	65: 6 even recompense i their bosom,	5921
	65: 7 will I measure their former work i their	413
	65:17 not be remembered, nor come i mind.	5921
	66:20 in a clean vessel i the house of the Lord.	NIH
Jer	2: 7 I brought you i a plentiful country, to eat	413
	2:21 art thou turned i the degenerate plant of a	NIH
	4: 5 and let us go i the defenced cities.	413
	4:29 they shall go i thickets, and climb up	871.1
	6: 9 turn back thine hand as a grapegatherer i	5921
	6:25 Go not forth i the field, nor walk by	NIH
	7:31 them not, neither came it i my heart.	5921
	8: 6 course, as the horse rusheth i the battle.	NIH
	8:14 let us enter i the defenced cities, and let	413
	9:21 For death is come up i our windows,	871.1
	9:21 and is entered i our palaces, to cut off	871.1
	10: 9 Silver spread i plates is brought from	7554
	12: 7 of my soul i the hand of her enemies.	871.1
	13:16 he turn it i the shadow of death,	3807.1
	14:18 If I go forth i the field, then behold the	NIH
	14:18 if I enter i the city, then behold them that	NIH
	14:18 priest go about i a land that they know	413
	15: 4 I will cause them to be removed i all	3807.1
	15:14 enemies i a land which thou knowest	871.1
	16: 5 Enter not i the house of mourning,	NIH
	16: 8 Thou shalt not also go i the house of	NIH
	16:13 Therefore will I cast you out of this land i	5921
	16:15 I will bring them again i their land that I	5921
	17:25 shall there enter i the gates of this city	871.1
	19: 5 nor spake it, neither came it i my mind:	5921
	20: 4 I will give all Judah i the hand of the	871.1
	20: 4 he shall carry them captive i Babylon,	1886.5
	20: 5 will I give i the hand of their enemies,	871.1
	20: 6 all that dwell in thine house shall go i	871.1
	21: 4 will assemble them i the midst of this city.	413
	21: 7 i the hand of Nebuchadrezzar king of	871.1
	21: 7 i the hand of their enemies, and into	871.1
	21: 7 i the hand of those that seek their life:	871.1
	21:10 it shall be given i the hand of the king of	871.1
	21:13 or who shall enter i our habitations?	871.1
	22: 7 choice cedars, and cast them i the fire.	5921
	22:22 and thy lovers shall go i captivity:	871.1
	22:25 I will give thee i the hand of them that	871.1
	22:25 i the hand of them whose face thou	871.1
	22:25 even i the hand of Nebuchadrezzar king	871.1
	22:25 and i the hand of the Chaldeans.	871.1
	22:26 i another country, where ye were not	5921
	22:28 are cast i a land which they know not?	5921
	23:15 is profaneness gone forth i all the land.	3807.1
	24: 5 I have sent out of this place i the land	NIH
	24: 9 I will deliver them to be removed i all	3807.1
	26:21 he was afraid, and fled, and went i Egypt;	NIH
	26:22 Jehoiakim the king sent men i Egypt,	NIH
	26:22 and certain men with him i Egypt.	413
	26:23 cast his dead body i the graves of	413
	26:24 they should not give him i the hand of	NIH
	27: 6 have I given all these lands i the hand	871.1
	28: 3 two full years will I bring again i this	413
	28: 4 that went i Babylon, saith the Lord:	1886.5
	28: 6 away captives, from Babylon i this place.	413
	29:14 I will bring you again i the place whence I	413
	29:16 are not gone forth with you i captivity;	871.1
	29:21 I will deliver them i the hand of	871.1
	30: 6 and all faces are turned i paleness?	3807.1
	30:16 every one of them, shall go i captivity;	871.1
	31:13 for I will turn their mourning i joy,	3807.1
	32: 3 I will give this city i the hand of the king	NIH
	32: 4 shall surely be delivered i the hand of	871.1
	32:18 recompensest the iniquity of the fathers i	413
	32:24 the city is given i the hand of	871.1
	32:25 for the city is given i the hand of	871.1
	32:28 I will give this city i the hand of	871.1
	32:28 i the hand of Nebuchadrezzar king of	871.1
	32:35 them not, neither came it i my mind,	5921
	32:36 shall be delivered i the hand of the king	871.1
	32:43 it is given i the hand of the Chaldeans.	871.1
	33:11 of praise i the house of the Lord.	NIH
	34: 2 I will give this city i the hand of the king	871.1
	34: 3 surely be taken, and delivered i his hand;	871.1
	34:10 which had entered i the covenant,	871.1
	34:11 brought i subjection for servants	3533
	34:16 return, and brought them i subjection,	3533
	34:17 I will make you to be removed i all	3807.1
	34:20 I will even give them i the hand of their	871.1
	34:20 i the hand of them that seek their life:	871.1
	34:21 his princes will I give i the hand of their	871.1

Jer	34:21 i the hand of them that seek their life,	871.1
	34:21 i the hand of the king of Babylon's army,	871.1
	35: 2 and bring them i the house of the Lord,	NIH
	35: 2 i one of the chambers, and give them wine	413
	35: 4 I brought them i the house of the Lord,	NIH
	35: 4 i the chamber of the sons of Hanan, the son	413
	35:11 king of Babylon came up i the land,	413
	36: 5 I cannot go i the house of the Lord:	NIH
	36:12 he went down i the king's house, into	NIH
	36:12 the king's house, i the scribe's chamber:	5921
	36:20 they went in to the king i the court,	1886.5
	36:23 cast it i the fire that was on the hearth,	413
	37: 4 for they had not put him i prison.	NIH
	37: 7 shall return i Egypt i their own land.	3807.1
	37:12 went forth out of Jerusalem to go i	NIH
	37:16 Jeremiah was entered i the dungeon,	413
	37:16 i the cabins, and Jeremiah had remained	413
	37:17 thou shalt be delivered i the hand of	871.1
	37:21 Jeremiah i the court of the prison,	871.1
	38: 3 city shall surely be given i the hand of	871.1
	38: 6 cast him i the dungeon of Malchiah the	413
	38: 6 whom they have cast i the dungeon:	413
	38:11 went i the house of the king under	NIH
	38:11 let them down by cords i the dungeon to	413
	38:14 took Jeremiah the prophet unto him i	413
	38:16 neither will I give thee i the hand of	871.1
	38:18 shall this city be given i the hand of	871.1
	38:19 lest they deliver me i their hand,	871.1
	39: 9 i Babylon the remnant of the people that	NIH
	39:17 thou shalt not be given i the hand of	NIH
	40: 4 it seem good unto thee to come with me i	NIH
	40: 4 if it seem ill unto thee to come with me i	NIH
	41: 7 so, when they came i the midst of the city,	413
	41: 7 and cast them i the midst of the pit, he,	413
	41:17 is by Beth-lehem, to go to enter i Egypt,	NIH
	42:14 we will go i the land of Egypt, where we	NIH
	42:15 If ye wholly set your faces to enter i Egypt,	NIH
	42:17 their faces to go i Egypt to sojourn there;	NIH
	42:18 upon you, when ye shall enter i Egypt:	NIH
	42:19 O ye remnant of Judah; Go ye not i Egypt:	NIH
	43: 2 to say, Go not i Egypt to sojourn there:	NIH
	43: 3 for to deliver us i the hand of	871.1
	43: 3 and carry us away captives i Babylon.	NIH
	43: 7 So they came i the land of Egypt: for they	NIH
	44:12 that have set their faces to go i the land of	NIH
	44:14 which are gone i the land of Egypt to	871.1
	44:14 they should return i the land of Judah,	NIH
	44:21 and came it not i his mind?	5921
	44:28 of the land of Egypt i the land of Judah,	NIH
	44:28 that are gone i the land of Egypt to	3807.1
	44:30 will give Pharaoh-hophra king of Egypt i	NIH
	44:30 and i the hand of them that seek his life;	871.1
	44:30 as I gave Zedekiah king of Judah i	871.1
	46:11 Go up i Gilead, and take balm, O virgin,	NIH
	46:19 in Egypt, furnish thyself to go i captivity:	1473
	46:24 she shall be delivered i the hand of	NIH
	46:26 will deliver them i the hand of those that	871.1
	46:26 i the hand of Nebuchadrezzar king of	871.1
	46:26 Babylon, and i the hand of his servants:	871.1
	47: 6 put up thyself i thy scabbard, rest,	413
	48: 7 Chemosh shall go forth i captivity with	871.1
	48:11 to vessel, neither hath he gone i captivity:	871.1
	48:44 He that fleeth from the fear shall fall i	413
	49: 3 for their king shall go i captivity,	871.1
	49:32 I will scatter i all winds those that are	3807.1
	51: 9 let us go every one i his own country:	3807.1
	51:50 and let Jerusalem come i your mind.	5921
	51:51 for strangers are come i the sanctuaries	5921
	51:59 i Babylon in the fourth year of his reign.	NIH
	51:63 to it, and cast it i the midst of Euphrates:	NIH
	52:12 served the king of Babylon, i Jerusalem,	871.1
La	1: 3 Judah is gone i captivity because	1540
	1: 5 her children are gone i captivity before	NIH
	1: 7 when her people fell i the hand of	871.1
	1:10 she hath seen that the heathen entered i	935
	1:10 they should not enter i thy congregation.	871.1
	1:13 From above hath he sent fire i my bones,	NIH
	1:14 the Lord hath delivered me i their hands,	871.1
	1:18 and my young men are gone i captivity.	871.1
	2: 7 he hath given up i the hand of the enemy	871.1
	2: 9 Her gates are sunk i the ground; he hath	871.1
	2:12 when their soul was poured out i their	413
	3: 2 brought me i darkness, but not into light.	NIH
	3: 2 brought me into darkness, but not i light.	NIH
	3:13 arrows of his quiver to enter i my reins.	871.1
	4:12 enemy should have entered i the gates	871.1
	4:22 no more carry thee away i captivity;	1540
	5:15 ceased; our dance is turned i mourning.	3807.1
Eze	2: 2 the spirit entered i me when he spake	871.1
	3:22 go forth i the plain, and I will there talk	413
	3:23 Then I arose, and went forth i the plain:	413
	3:24 the spirit entered i me, and set me upon	871.1
	4:14 neither came there abominable flesh i my	871.1
	5: 4 cast them i the midst of the fire,	413
	5: 4 for thereof shall a fire come forth i all	413
	5: 6 she hath changed my judgments i	3807.1
	5:10 whole remnant of thee will I scatter i	3807.1
	5:12 I will scatter i third part i all the winds,	3807.1
	7:11 Violence is risen up i a rod of	3807.1
	7:21 I will give it i the hand of the strangers	871.1
	7:22 place: for the robbers shall enter i it,	871.1
	8:16 he brought me i the inner court of	413
	10: 7 put it i the hands of him that was clothed	413
	11: 5 for I know the things that come i your	4609
	11: 9 deliver you i the hands of strangers,	871.1

Eze 11:24 in vision by the Spirit of God **i** Chaldea,	1886.5
12: 4 their sight, as they that go forth **i** captivity.	NIH
12:11 they shall remove *and* go **i** captivity.	871.1
13: 5 Ye have not gone up **i** the gaps,	871.1
13: 9 neither shall they enter **i** the land of Israel;	413
14:19 Or *if* I send a pestilence **i** that land,	413
15: 4 Behold, it is cast **i** the fire for fuel;	3807.1
16: 8 and entered **i** a covenant with thee,	871.1
16:13 and thou didst prosper **i** a kingdom.	3807.1
16:39 I will also give thee **i** their hand,	871.1
17: 4 and carried it **i** a land of traffick;	413
17:15 him in sending his ambassadors **i** Egypt,	NIH
19: 9 they brought him **i** holds, that his voice	871.1
20: 6 to bring them forth of the land of Egypt **i** a	413
20:10 Egypt, and brought them **i** the wilderness.	413
20:15 that *I* would not bring them **i** the land	413
20:28 *For* when I had brought them **i** the land,	413
20:32 which cometh **i** your mind shall not be	5921
20:35 I will bring you **i** the wilderness of	413
20:37 will bring you **i** the bond of the covenant:	871.1
20:38 and they shall not enter **i** the land of Israel:	413
20:42 when I shall bring you **i** the land of Israel,	413
20:42 **i** the country *for* the which I lifted up mine	413
21:11 to give **i** the hand of the slayer.	871.1
21:14 which **entereth i** their **privy chambers**.	2314
21:30 Shall I cause *it* to return **i** his sheath? I will	413
21:31 deliver thee **i** the hand of brutish men,	871.1
22:19 I will gather you **i** the midst of Jerusalem.	413
22:20 lead, and tin, **i** the midst of the furnace,	413
23: 9 I have delivered her **i** the hand	871.1
23: 9 **i** the hand of the Assyrians, upon whom	871.1
23:16 sent messengers unto them **i** Chaldea.	1886.5
23:17 the Babylonians came to her **i** the bed of	3807.1
23:28 I *will* deliver thee **i** the hand of them	871.1
23:28 **i** the hand of *them* from whom thy mind	871.1
23:31 therefore will I give her cup **i** thine hand.	871.1
23:39 they came the same day **i** my sanctuary to	413
24: 3 a pot, set *it* on, and also pour water **i** it:	871.1
24: 4 Gather the pieces thereof **i** it, *even* every	413
25: 3 of Judah, when they went **i** captivity;	871.1
26:10 when he shall enter **i** thy gates,	871.1
26:10 as men **enter i** a city wherein is made a	3996
26:20 down with them that descend **i** the pit,	NIH
27:26 Thy rowers have brought thee **i** great	871.1
27:27 fall **i** the midst of the seas in the day	871.1
28: 4 gotten gold and silver **i** thy treasures:	871.1
28:23 For I will send **i** her pestilence,	871.1
28:23 her pestilence, and blood **i** her streets;	871.1
29: 5 will leave thee *thrown* **i** the wilderness,	1886.5
29:14 will cause them to return *i* the land of	NIH
29:14 of Pathros, **i** the land of their habitation;	5921
30:12 sell the land **i** the hand of the wicked:	871.1
30:17 and these *cities* shall go **i** captivity.	871.1
30:18 and her daughters shall go **i** captivity.	871.1
30:25 when I shall put my sword **i** the hand of	871.1
31:11 delivered him **i** the hand of the mighty	871.1
31:16 to hell with them that descend **i** the pit:	NIH
31:17 They also went down **i** hell with him	1886.5
32: 9 the countries which thou hast not	5921
32:18 earth, with them that go down **i** the pit.	NIH
32:24 which are gone down uncircumcised **i**	413
36:24 and will bring you **i** your own land.	413
37: 5 I *will* cause breath to enter **i** you,	871.1
37:10 the breath came **i** them, and they lived,	871.1
37:12 and bring you **i** the land of Israel.	413
37:17 join them one to another **i** one stick;	3807.1
37:21 side, and bring them **i** their own land:	413
37:22 neither shall they be divided **i** two	3807.1
38: 4 put hooks **i** thy jaws, and I will bring thee	871.1
38: 8 the latter years thou shalt come **i** the land	413
38:10 at the same time shall things come **i** thy	5921
39:23 Israel **went i** captivity for their iniquity:	1540
39:23 gave them **i** the hand of their enemies:	871.1
39:28 which **caused** them **to be led i captivity**	1540
40: 2 In the visions of God brought he me **i**	413
40:17 Then brought he me **i** the outward court,	413
40:32 he brought me **i** the inner court toward	413
41: 6 they entered **i** the wall which *was* of	871.1
42: 1 brought me forth **i** the utter court, the way	413
42: 1 brought me **i** the chamber that *was* over	413
42: 9 one goeth **i** them from the utter court.	3807.1
42:12 toward the east, as *one* **entereth i** them.	935
42:14 shall they not go out of the holy *place* **i**	413
43: 4 the glory of the Lord came **i** the house by	413
43: 5 me up, and brought me **i** the inner court;	413
44: 7 In that ye have brought *i* my sanctuary	NIH
44: 9 in flesh, shall enter **i** my sanctuary,	413
44:12 caused the house of Israel to fall **i** iniquity;	NIH
44:16 They shall enter **i** my sanctuary,	413
44:19 when they go forth **i** the utter court,	413
44:19 *even* **i** the utter court to the people,	413
44:21 wine, when they enter **i** the inner court.	413
44:27 in the day that he goeth **i** the sanctuary,	413
46:19 **i** the holy chambers of the priests,	413
46:20 *they* bear *them* not out **i** the utter court,	413
46:21 he brought me forth **i** the utter court,	413
47: 8 go down **i** the desert, and go into the sea:	5921
47: 8 down into the desert, and go **i** the sea:	1886.5
47: 8 *which* being brought forth **i** the sea,	413
Da 1: 2 the Lord gave Jehoiakim king of Judah **i**	871.1
1: 2 which he carried **i** the land of Shinar *to*	NIH
1: 2 brought the vessels *i* the treasure house	NIH
1: 9 Now God had brought Daniel **i** favour	3807.1
2:29 thoughts came *i* thy *mind* upon thy bed,	NIH

Da 2:38 the fowls of the heaven hath he given **i**	871.2
3: 6 shall the same hour be cast **i**	3807.2
3: 11 *that* he should be cast **i** the midst of a	3807.2
3:15 shall be cast the same hour **i** the midst	3807.2
3:20 to cast *them* **i** the burning fiery furnace.	3807.2
3:21 cast **i** the midst of the burning fiery	3807.2
3:23 fell down bound **i** the midst of	3807.2
3:24 Did not we cast three men bound **i**	3807.2
3:10 his lords, came **i** the banquet house:	3807.2
6: 7 king, he shall be cast **i** the den of lions.	3807.2
6:10 writing *was* signed, he went **i** his house;	3807.2
6:12 king, shall be cast **i** the den of lions?	3807.2
6:16 and cast *him* **i** the den of lions.	3807.2
6:24 they cast *them* **i** the den of lions, them,	3807.2
7:25 shall be given **i** his hand until a time	871.2
10: 8 for my comeliness was turned in me **i**	3807.1
11: 7 shall enter **i** the fortress of the king of	871.1
11: 8 also carry captives *i* Egypt their gods,	NIH
11: 9 So the king of the south shall come **i** *his*	871.1
11: 9 kingdom, and shall return **i** his own land.	413
11:11 the multitude shall be given **i** his hand.	871.1
11:28 shall he return *i* his land with great riches;	NIH
11:40 he shall enter **i** the countries,	871.1
11:41 He shall enter also **i** the glorious land,	871.1
Hos 2:14 bring her **i** the wilderness,	NIH
4: 7 will I change their glory **i** shame.	871.1
9: 4 their bread for their soul shall not come **i**	NIH
11: 5 He shall not return **i** the land of Egypt,	413
11: 9 of thee: and I will not enter **i** the city.	871.1
12: 1 the Assyrians, and oil is carried **i** Egypt.	3807.1
12:12 Jacob fled *i* the country of Syria,	NIH
Joel 1:14 the inhabitants of the land *i* the house of	NIH
2:20 will drive him **i** a land barren and desolate,	413
2:31 The sun shall be turned **i** darkness,	3807.1
2:31 the moon **i** blood, before the great and	3807.1
3: 2 will bring them down **i** the valley of	413
3: 5 have **carried i** your temples my goodly	935
3: 8 your daughters **i** the hand of the children	871.1
3:10 Beat your plowshares **i** swords,	3807.1
3:10 and your pruninghooks **i** spears:	3807.1
Am 1: 4 I will send a fire **i** the house of Hazael,	871.1
1: 5 people of Syria shall **go i captivity** unto	1540
1:15 their king shall go **i** captivity, he and	871.1
2: 1 burnt the bones of the king of Edom **i**	3807.1
4: 3 ye shall cast *them* **i** the palace, saith	1886.5
5: 5 nor enter *i* Gilgal, and pass not *to*	413
5: 5 Gilgal shall **surely go i captivity**,	1540+1540
5: 8 the shadow of death **i** the morning,	3807.1
5:19 went **i** the house, and leaned his hand on	NIH
5:27 will I **cause** you **to go i captivity**	1540
6:12 for ye have turned judgment **i** gall,	3807.1
6:12 and the fruit of righteousness **i** hemlock:	3807.1
7:12 go, flee thee away **i** the land of Judah,	413
7:17 Israel shall **surely go i captivity**	1540+1540
8:10 I will turn your feasts **i** mourning,	3807.1
8:10 and all your songs **i** lamentation;	3807.1
9: 2 Though they dig **i** hell, thence shall mine	871.1
9: 4 though they go **i** captivity before their	871.1
Ob 1:11 foreigners entered *i* his gates, and cast lots	NIH
1:13 shouldest not have entered **i** the gate	871.1
Jnh 1: 3 paid the fare thereof, and went down **i** it,	871.1
1: 4 the Lord sent out a great wind **i** the sea,	413
1: 5 cast forth the wares that *were* in the ship **i**	413
1: 5 was gone down **i** the sides of the ship;	413
1:12 Take me up, and cast me forth **i** the sea;	413
1:15 took up Jonah, and cast him forth **i** the sea:	413
2: 3 For thou hadst cast me **i** the deep,	NIH
2: 7 came in unto thee, **i** thine holy temple.	413
3: 4 Jonah began to enter **i** the city a day's	871.1
Mic 1: 6 I will pour down the stones thereof **i**	3807.1
1:16 for they are **gone i** captivity from thee.	1540
3: 5 he that putteth not **i** their mouths, they	5921
4: 3 shall beat their swords **i** plowshares,	3807.1
4: 3 and their spears **i** pruninghooks:	3807.1
4:12 for he shall gather them as the sheaves **i**	1886.5
5: 5 when the Assyrian shall come **i** our land:	871.1
5: 6 when he cometh **i** our land, and when he	871.1
7:19 thou wilt cast all their sins **i** the depths of	871.1
Na 3:10 she carried away, she went **i** captivity:	871.1
3:12 shall even fall **i** the mouth of the eater.	5921
3:14 go **i** clay, and tread the mortar,	871.1
Hab 3:16 rottenness entered **i** my bones,	871.1
Hag 1: 6 earneth wages *to put it* **i** a bag with holes.	413
Zec 5: 4 and it shall enter **i** the house of the thief,	413
5: 4 **i** the house of him that sweareth falsely by	413
5: 8 he cast it **i** the midst of the ephah;	413
6: 6 black horses which *are* therein go forth **i**	413
6:10 go **i** the house of Josiah the son of	NIH
10:10 I will bring them **i** the land of Gilead and	413
11: 6 I *will* deliver the men every one **i** his	871.1
11: 6 and **i** the hand of his king:	871.1
14: 2 half of the city shall go forth **i** captivity,	871.1
Mal 3:10 Bring ye all the tithes **i** the storehouse, that	413
Mt 1:17 from David until the carrying away **i**	NIG
1:17 from the carrying away **i** Babylon unto	NIG
2:11 And when they were come **i** the house,	1519
2:12 they departed **i** their own country another	1519
2:13 and flee **i** Egypt, and be thou there until I	1519
2:14 his mother by night, and departed **i** Egypt:	1519
2:20 his mother, and go **i** the land of Israel:	1519
2:21 his mother, and came **i** the land of Israel.	1519
2:22 he turned aside **i** the parts of Galilee:	1519
3:10 fruit is hewn down, and cast **i** the fire.	1519
3:12 floor, and gather his wheat **i** the garner;	1519
4: 1 Then was Jesus led up of the Spirit **i**	1519

Mt 4: 5 the devil taketh him *up* **i** the holy city,	*1519*
4: 8 the devil taketh him *up* **i** an exceeding	*1519*
4:12 had heard that John was **cast i prison**,	*3860*
4:12 cast into prison, he departed **i** Galilee;	*1519*
4:18 his brother, casting a net **i** the sea;	*1519*
5: 1 the multitudes, he went up **i** a mountain:	*1519*
5:20 ye shall in no case enter **i** the kingdom of	*1519*
5:25 to the officer, and thou be cast **i** prison.	*1519*
5:29 not *that* thy whole body should be cast **i**	*1519*
5:30 not *that* thy whole body should be cast **i**	*1519*
6: 6 enter **i** thy closet, and when thou hast	*1519*
6:13 lead us not **i** temptation, but deliver us	*1519*
6:26 neither do they reap, nor gather **i** barns;	*1519*
6:30 and to morrow is cast **i** the oven,	*1519*
7:19 fruit is hewn down, and cast **i** the fire.	*1519*
7:21 shall enter **i** the kingdom of heaven,	*1519*
8: 5 when Jesus was entered **i** Capernaum,	*1519*
8:12 shall be cast out **i** outer darkness:	*1519*
8:14 when Jesus was come **i** Peter's house,	*1519*
8:23 And when he was entered **i** a ship,	*1519*
8:28 when he was come to the other side **i**	*1519*
8:31 suffer us to go away **i** the herd of swine.	*1519*
8:32 come out, they went **i** the herd of swine:	*1519*
8:32 ran violently down a steep place **i** the sea,	*1519*
8:33 and went their ways **i** the city,	*1519*
9: 1 And he entered **i** a ship, and passed over,	*1519*
9: 1 and passed over, and came **i** his own city.	*1519*
9:17 do *men* put new wine **i** old bottles:	*1519*
9:17 but they put new wine **i** new bottles,	*1519*
9:23 And when Jesus came **i** the ruler's house,	*1519*
9:26 And the fame hereof went abroad **i** all	*1519*
9:28 And when he was come **i** the house,	*1519*
9:38 that he will send forth labourers **i** his	*1519*
10: 5 Go not **i** the way of the Gentiles,	*1519*
10: 5 *any* city of the Samaritans enter ye not:	*1519*
10:11 And **i** whatsoever city or town ye shall	*1525*
10:12 And when ye **come i** a house salute	*1525*
10:23 you in this city, flee ye **i** another:	*1519*
11: 7 What went ye out **i** the wilderness to see?	*1519*
12: 4 How he entered **i** the house of God,	*1519*
12: 9 thence, he went **i** their synagogue:	*1519*
12:11 and if it fall **i** a pit on the sabbath day,	*1519*
12:29 else how can one enter **i** a strong *man's*	*1519*
12:44 I will return **i** my house from whence I	*1519*
13: 2 him, so that he went **i** a ship, and sat;	*1519*
13: 8 But other fell **i** good ground,	*1909*
13:20 he that received the seed **i** stony *places*,	*1909*
13:23 he that received seed **i** the good ground	*1909*
13:30 them: but gather the wheat **i** my barn.	*1519*
13:36 multitude away, and went **i** the house:	*1519*
13:42 And shall cast them **i** a furnace of fire:	*1519*
13:47 *that was* cast **i** the sea, and gathered of	*1519*
13:48 and gathered the good **i** vessels, but cast	*1519*
13:50 And shall cast them **i** the furnace of fire:	*1519*
13:54 when he was come **i** his own country,	*1519*
14:13 thence by ship **i** a desert place apart:	*1519*
14:15 that they may go **i** the villages,	*1519*
14:22 constrained his disciples to get **i** a ship,	*1519*
14:23 he went up **i** a mountain apart to pray:	*1519*
14:32 And when they were come **i** the ship,	*1519*
14:34 they came **i** the land of Gennesaret.	*1519*
14:35 sent out **i** all that country round about,	*1519*
15:11 Not that which **goeth i** the mouth	*1525*
15:14 lead the blind, both shall fall **i** the ditch.	*1519*
15:17 entereth in at the mouth goeth **i** the belly,	*1519*
15:17 the belly, and is cast out **i** the draught?	*1519*
15:21 departed **i** the coasts of Tyre and Sidon.	*1519*
15:29 and went up **i** a mountain, and sat down	*1519*
15:39 and came **i** the coasts of Magdala.	*1519*
16:13 When Jesus came **i** the coasts of Cesarea	*1519*
17: 1 bringeth them up **i** a high mountain apart,	*1519*
17:15 ofttimes he falleth **i** the fire, and oft into	*1519*
17:15 he falleth into the fire, and oft **i** the water.	*1519*
17:22 The Son of man shall be betrayed **i**	*1519*
17:25 And when he was **come i** the house,	*1525*
18: 3 shall not enter **i** the kingdom of heaven.	*1519*
18: 8 it is better for thee to enter **i** life halt or	*1519*
18: 8 or two feet to be cast **i** everlasting fire.	*1519*
18: 9 it is better for thee to enter **i** life with one	*1519*
18: 9 than having two eyes to be cast **i** hell	*1519*
18:12 goeth **i** the mountains, and seeketh that	*1909*
18:30 but went and cast him **i** prison, till he	*1519*
19: 1 came **i** the coasts of Judea beyond Jordan;	*1519*
19:17 but if thou wilt enter **i** life, keep	*1519*
19:23 That a rich *man* shall hardly enter **i**	*1519*
19:24 for a rich *man* to enter **i** the kingdom	*1519*
20: 1 morning to hire labourers **i** his vineyard.	*1519*
20: 2 penny a day, he sent them **i** his vineyard.	*1519*
20: 4 Go ye also **i** the vineyard.	*1519*
20: 7 unto them, Go ye also **i** the vineyard;	*1519*
21: 2 Go **i** the village over against you,	*1519*
21:10 And when he was **come i** Jerusalem,	*1525*
21:12 And Jesus **went i** the temple of God,	*1525*
21:17 and went out of the city **i** Bethany;	*1519*
21:18 Now in the morning as he returned **i**	*1519*
21:21 thou removed, and be thou cast **i** the sea;	*1519*
21:23 And when he was come **i** the temple,	*1519*
21:31 harlots go **i** the kingdom of God before	*1519*
21:33 husbandmen, and **went i a far country**:	*589*
22: 9 Go ye therefore **i** the highways,	*1909*
22:10 those servants went out **i** the *highways*,	*1519*
22:13 him away, and cast **i** outer darkness;	*1519*
24:16 Then let them which be in Judea flee **i**	*1909*
24:38 until the day that Noe entered **i** the ark,	*1519*
25:14 *is* as a man **travelling i a far country**,	*589*

I

Mt	25:21	*things:* enter thou i the joy of thy lord.	1519
	25:23	*things:* enter thou i the joy of thy lord.	1519
	25:30	cast ye the unprofitable servant i outer	1519
	25:41	from me, ye cursed, i everlasting fire,	1519
	25:46	And these shall go away i everlasting	1519
	25:46	but the righteous i life eternal.	1519
	26:18	Go i the city to such a man, and say unto	1519
	26:30	they went out i the mount of Olives.	1519
	26:32	risen *again,* I will go before you i Galilee.	1519
	26:41	and pray, that ye enter not i temptation:	1519
	26:45	the Son of man is betrayed i the hands of	1519
	26:52	Put up again thy sword i his place:	1519
	26:71	And when he was gone out i the porch,	1519
	27: 6	It is not lawful for to put them i	1519
	27:27	governor took Jesus i the common hall,	1519
	27:53	and **went** i the holy city,	1525
	28: 7	behold, he goeth before you i Galilee;	1519
	28:10	go tell my brethren that they go i Galilee,	1519
	28:11	some of the watch came i the city,	1519
	28:16	Then the eleven disciples went *away* i	1519
	28:16	i a mountain where Jesus had appointed	1519
Mk	1:12	And immediately the Spirit driveth him i	1519
	1:14	was put in prison, Jesus came i Galilee,	1519
	1:16	Andrew his brother casting a net i the sea:	1519
	1:21	And they **went** i Capernaum;	1531
	1:21	on the sabbath day he entered i	1519
	1:29	they entered the house of Simon and	1519
	1:35	and departed i a solitary place,	1519
	1:38	unto them, Let us go i the next towns,	1519
	1:45	could no more openly enter i the city,	1519
	2: 1	And again he entered i Capernaum after	1519
	2:11	up thy bed, and go thy way i thine house.	1519
	2:22	no *man* putteth new wine i old bottles:	1519
	2:22	but new wine must be put i new bottles.	1519
	2:26	How he **went** i the house of God in	1525
	3: 1	And he entered i the synagogue;	1519
	3:13	And he goeth up i a mountain,	1519
	3:19	betrayed him. And they went i a house.	1519
	3:27	No *man* can enter i a strong *man's* house,	1519
	4: 1	so that he entered i a ship, and sat in	1519
	4:26	as if a man should cast seed i the ground,	1909
	4:37	the waves beat the ship, so that it was	1519
	5: 1	of the sea, i the country of the Gadarenes.	1519
	5:12	saying, Send us i the swine, that we may	1519
	5:12	into the swine, that we may enter i them.	1519
	5:13	spirits went out, and entered i the swine:	1519
	5:13	herd ran violently down a steep place i	1519
	5:18	And when he was come i the ship, he that	1519
	6: 1	from thence, and came i his own country;	1519
	6:10	In what place soever ye enter i a house,	1519
	6:31	Come ye yourselves apart i a desert place,	1519
	6:32	And they departed i a desert place by ship	1519
	6:36	they may go i the country round about,	1519
	6:36	and i the villages, and buy themselves	NIG
	6:45	constrained his disciples to get i the ship,	1519
	6:46	he departed i a mountain to pray.	1519
	6:51	And he went up unto them i the ship;	1519
	6:53	they came i the land of Genesaret,	1909
	6:56	he entered, i villages, or cities, or country,	1519
	7:15	a man, that entering i him can defile him:	1519
	7:17	when he was entered i *the* house from	1519
	7:18	*thing* from without entereth i the man,	1519
	7:19	Because it entereth not i his heart,	1519
	7:19	entereth not into his heart, but i the belly,	1519
	7:19	into the belly, and goeth out i the draught,	1519
	7:24	and went i the borders of Tyre and Sidon,	1519
	7:24	and entered i a house, and would have no	1519
	7:33	and put his fingers i his ears, and he spit,	1519
	8:10	And straightway he entered i a ship with	1519
	8:10	and came i the parts of Dalmanutha.	1519
	8:13	entering i the ship again departed to	1519
	8:26	saying, Neither **go** i the town, nor tell *it* to	1525
	8:27	i the towns of Cesarea Philippi:	1519
	9: 2	leadeth them up i a high mountain apart	1519
	9:22	And ofttimes it hath cast him i the fire,	1519
	9:22	the fire, and i the waters, to destroy him:	1519
	9:25	out of him, and enter no more i him.	1519
	9:28	And when he was **come** i *the* house,	1525
	9:31	The Son of man is delivered i the hands	1519
	9:42	about his neck, and he were cast i the sea.	1519
	9:43	it is better for thee to enter i life maimed,	1519
	9:43	than having two hands to go i hell, into	1519
	9:43	i the fire that never shall be quenched:	1519
	9:45	it is better for thee to enter halt i life,	1519
	9:45	than having two feet to be cast i hell,	1519
	9:45	i the fire that never shall be quenched:	1519
	9:47	it is better for thee to enter i the kingdom	1519
	9:47	than having two eyes to be cast i hell fire:	1519
	10: 1	cometh i the coasts of Judea by the farther	1519
	10:17	And when he was gone forth i the way,	1519
	10:23	have riches enter i the kingdom of God!	1519
	10:24	in riches to enter i the kingdom of God!	1519
	10:25	for a rich *man* to enter i the kingdom	1519
	11: 2	Go your way i the village over against you:	1519
	11: 2	and as soon as ye be entered i it, ye shall	1519
	11:11	And Jesus entered i Jerusalem, and into	1519
	11:11	into Jerusalem, and i the temple:	1519
	11:15	Jesus **went** i the temple, and began to	1525
	11:23	thou removed, and be thou cast i the sea;	1519
	12: 1	husbandmen, and **went** i a far country.	589
	12:41	beheld how the people cast money i	1519
	12:43	all they which have cast i the treasury:	1519
	13:15	on the housetop not go down i the house,	1519
	14:13	Go ye i the city, and there shall meet you	1519
	14:16	and came i the city, and found as he had	1519

Mk	14:26	they went out i the mount of Olives.	1519
	14:28	I am risen, I will go before you i Galilee.	1519
	14:38	and pray, lest ye enter i temptation.	1519
	14:41	the Son of man is betrayed i the hands of	1519
	14:54	off, even i the palace of the high priest:	2080
	14:68	he went out i the porch; and *the* cock	1519
	15:16	And the soldiers led him away i the hall,	2080
	16: 5	And entering i the sepulchre, they saw a	1519
	16: 7	Peter that he goeth before you i Galilee:	1519
	16:12	as they walked, and went i the country.	1519
	16:15	Go ye i all the world, and preach the	1519
	16:19	he was received up i heaven, and sat on	1519
Lk	1: 9	he **went** i the temple of the Lord.	1525
	1:39	and went i the hill country with haste,	1519
	1:39	the hill country with haste, i a city of Juda;	1519
	1:40	And entered i the house of Zacharias,	1519
	1:79	to guide our feet i the way of peace.	1519
	2: 3	to be taxed, every one i his own city.	1519
	2: 4	Nazareth, i Judea, unto the city of David,	1519
	2:15	as the angels were gone away from them i	1519
	2:39	they returned i Galilee, to their own city	1519
	3: 3	he came i all the country about Jordan,	1519
	3: 9	fruit is hewn down, and cast i the fire.	1519
	3:17	and will gather the wheat i his garner;	1519
	4: 1	and was led by the Spirit i the wilderness,	1519
	4: 5	devil, taking him up i a high mountain,	1519
	4:14	in the power of the Spirit i Galilee:	1519
	4:16	he **went** i the synagogue on	1525
	4:37	the fame of him went out i every place	1519
	4:38	and entered i Simon's house.	1519
	4:42	he departed and went i a desert place:	1519
	5: 3	And he entered i one of the ships,	1519
	5: 4	Launch out i the deep, and let down your	1519
	5:16	He withdrew himself i the wilderness,	1722
	5:19	with *his* couch i the midst before Jesus.	1519
	5:24	take up thy couch, and go i thine house.	1519
	5:37	no *man* putteth new wine i old bottles;	1519
	5:38	But new wine must be put i new bottles;	1519
	6: 4	How he **went** i the house of God,	1525
	6: 6	he entered i the synagogue and taught:	1519
	6:12	*that* he went out i a mountain to pray,	1519
	6:38	over, shall *men* give i your bosom.	1519
	6:39	shall they not both fall i the ditch?	1519
	7: 1	of the people, he entered i Capernaum.	1519
	7:11	after, *that* he went i a city called Nain;	1519
	7:24	What went ye out i the wilderness for to	1519
	7:36	And he **went** i the Pharisee's house,	1525
	7:44	I entered i thine house, thou gavest me no	1519
	8:22	that he went i a ship with his disciples:	1519
	8:29	was driven of the devil i the wilderness.)	1519
	8:30	because many devils were entered i him.	1519
	8:31	not command them to go out i the deep.	1519
	8:32	that he would suffer them to enter i them.	1519
	8:33	out of the man, and entered i the swine:	1519
	8:33	herd ran violently down a steep place i	1519
	8:37	and he went *up* i the ship,	1519
	8:41	besought him that *he* would **come** i	1525
	8:51	And when he **came** i the house,	1525
	9: 4	And whatsoever house ye enter i,	1519
	9:10	went aside privately i a desert place	1519
	9:12	that they may go i the towns and	1519
	9:28	James, and went up i a mountain to pray.	1519
	9:34	they feared as they entered i the cloud.	1519
	9:44	Let these sayings sink down i your ears:	1519
	9:44	for the Son of man shall be delivered i	1519
	9:52	and entered i a village of the Samaritans,	1519
	10: 1	and two before his face i every city and	1519
	10: 2	that he would send forth labourers i his	1519
	10: 5	And whatsoever house ye enter, first say,	1519
	10: 8	And i whatsoever city ye enter,	1519
	10:10	But i whatsoever city ye enter,	1519
	10:10	go your ways out i the streets of the same,	1519
	10:38	that he entered i a certain village:	1519
	10:38	named Martha received him i her house.	1519
	11: 4	And lead us not i temptation;	1533
	12: 5	*he* hath killed hath power to cast i hell;	1519
	12:28	the field, and to morrow is cast i the oven;	1519
	12:58	and the officer cast thee i prison.	1519
	13:19	which a man took, and cast i his garden;	1519
	14: 1	as he went i the house of one of the chief	1519
	14: 5	shall have an ass or an ox fallen i a pit,	1519
	14:21	Go out quickly i the streets and lanes of	1519
	14:23	Go out i the highways and hedges,	1519
	15:13	and took his journey i a far country,	1519
	15:15	and he sent him i his fields to feed swine.	1519
	16: 4	they may receive me i their houses.	1519
	16: 9	they may receive you i everlasting	1519
	16:16	is preached, and every *man* presseth i it.	1519
	16:22	was carried by the angels i Abraham's	1519
	16:28	lest they also come i this place of torment.	1519
	17: 2	and he cast i the sea, than that he should	1519
	17:12	And as he entered i a certain village,	1519
	17:27	until the day that Noe entered i the ark,	1519
	18:10	Two men went up i the temple to pray;	1519
	18:24	have riches enter i the kingdom of God!	1519
	18:25	than for a rich *man* to enter i the kingdom	1519
	19: 4	climbed up i a sycomore tree to see him:	1909
	19:12	certain nobleman went i a far country to	1519
	19:23	gavest not thou my money i the bank,	1909
	19:30	Go ye i the village over against *you;* in	1519
	19:45	And he **went** i the temple,	1525
	20: 9	and **went** i a far country for a long time.	589
	21: 1	saw the rich *men* casting their gifts i	1519
	21:12	and i prisons, being brought before kings	NIG

Lk	21:24	and shall be led away captive i all nations:	1519
	22: 3	Then entered Satan i Judas surnamed	1519
	22:10	Behold, when ye are entered i the city,	1519
	22:10	follow him i the house where he entereth	1519
	22:33	go with thee, both i prison, and to death.	1519
	22:40	Pray that *ye* enter not i temptation.	1519
	22:46	rise and pray, lest ye enter i temptation.	1519
	22:54	**brought** him i the high priest's	1521
	22:66	and led him i their council, saying,	1519
	23:19	city, and *for* murder, was cast i prison.)	1519
	23:25	for sedition and murder was cast i prison,	1519
	23:42	remember me when thou comest i thy	1722
	23:46	Father, i thy hands I commend my spirit:	1519
	24: 7	The Son of man must be delivered i	1519
	24:26	these *things,* and to enter i his glory?	1519
	24:51	from them, and carried up i heaven.	1519
Jn	1: 9	which lighteth every man *that* cometh i	1519
	1:43	The day following Jesus would go forth i	1519
	3: 4	he enter the second time i his mother's	1519
	3: 5	he cannot enter i the kingdom of God.	1519
	3:17	For God sent not his Son i the world to	1519
	3:19	that light is come i the world, and men	1519
	3:22	and his disciples the land of Judea;	1519
	3:24	For John was not yet cast i prison.	1519
	3:35	and hath given all *things* i his hand.	1722
	4: 3	left Judea, and departed again i Galilee.	1519
	4:14	of water springing up i everlasting life;	1519
	4:28	and went her way i the city, and saith to	1519
	4:38	and ye are entered i their labours.	1519
	4:43	he departed thence, and went i Galilee.	1519
	4:45	Then when he was come i Galilee,	1519
	4:46	So Jesus came again i Cana of Galilee,	1519
	4:47	Jesus was come out of Judea i Galilee,	1519
	4:54	he was come out of Judea i Galilee.	1519
	5: 4	went down at a *certain* season i the pool,	1722
	5: 7	water is troubled, to put me i the pool:	1519
	5:24	and shall not come i condemnation;	1519
	6: 3	And Jesus went up i a mountain,	1519
	6:14	prophet that should come i the world.	1519
	6:15	he departed again i a mountain himself	1519
	6:17	entered i a ship, and went over the sea	1519
	6:21	they willingly received him i the ship:	1519
	6:22	that Jesus went not with his disciples i	1519
	7: 3	unto him, Depart hence, and go i Judea,	1519
	7:14	of the feast Jesus went up i the temple,	1519
	8: 2	early in the morning he came again i	1519
	9:39	For judgment I am come i this world,	1519
	10: 1	He that entereth not by the door i	1519
	10:36	and sent i the world, Thou blasphemest;	1519
	10:40	And went away again beyond Jordan i	1519
	11: 7	to *his* disciples, Let us go i Judea again.	1519
	11:27	of God, which should come i the world.	1519
	11:30	Now Jesus was not yet come i the town,	1519
	11:54	i a city called Ephraim, and there	1519
	12:24	Except a corn of wheat fall i the ground	1519
	12:46	I am come a light i the world,	1519
	13: 2	the devil having now put i the heart of	1519
	13: 3	the Father had given all *things* i his hands,	1519
	13: 5	he poureth water i a bason, and began to	1519
	13:27	And after the sop Satan entered i him.	1519
	15: 6	and cast *them* i the fire, and they are	1519
	16:13	is come, he will guide you i all truth:	1519
	16:20	but your sorrow shall be turned i joy.	1519
	16:21	for joy that a man is born i the world.	1519
	16:28	the Father, and am come i the world:	1519
	17:18	As thou hast sent me i the world, even *so*	1519
	17:18	even *so* have I also sent them i the world.	1519
	18: 1	i the which he entered, and his disciples.	1519
	18:11	unto Peter, Put up thy sword i the sheath:	1519
	18:15	went in with Jesus i the palace of the high	1519
	18:28	they themselves went not i the judgment	1519
	18:33	Then Pilate entered i the judgment hall	1519
	18:37	and for this cause came I i the world,	1519
	19: 9	And **went** again i the judgment hall,	1525
	19:17	And he bearing his cross went forth i a	1519
	20: 6	and **went** i the sepulchre, and seeth	1525
	20:11	down, and looked i the sepulchre,	1519
	20:25	and put my finger i the print of the nails,	1519
	20:25	and thrust my hand i his side, I will not	1519
	20:27	hither thy hand, and thrust *it* i my side:	1519
	21: 3	and entered i a ship immediately;	1519
	21: 7	naked,) and did cast himself i the sea.	1519
Ac	1:11	why stand ye gazing up i heaven?	1519
	1:11	which is taken up from you i heaven,	1519
	1:11	manner as ye have seen him go i heaven.	1519
	1:13	they went up i an upper room, where	1519
	2:20	The sun shall be turned i darkness,	1519
	2:20	the moon i blood, before *that* great and	1519
	2:34	For David is not ascended i the heavens:	1519
	3: 1	John went up together i the temple at	1519
	3: 2	to ask alms of them that entered i	1519
	3: 3	and John about to go i the temple,	1519
	3: 8	and entered with them i the temple,	1519
	5:15	that *they* brought forth the sick i	2596
	5:21	when they heard *that,* they entered i	1519
	7: 3	come i the land which I shall shew thee.	1519
	7: 4	he removed him i this land, wherein ye	1519
	7: 6	that they should **bring** them i **bondage,**	1402
	7: 9	moved with envy, sold Joseph i Egypt:	1519
	7:15	So Jacob went down i Egypt, and died,	1519
	7:16	And were carried over i Sychem,	1519
	7:23	it came i his heart to visit his brethren	1909
	7:34	And now come, I will send thee i Egypt.	1519
	7:39	in their hearts turned *back again* i Egypt,	1519
	7:45	with Jesus i the possession of the Gentiles,	1722

Ac	7:55	looked up stedfastly **i** heaven, and saw	1519
	8: 3	of the church, **entering i** every house,	1531
	8:38	and they went down both **i** the water,	1519
	9: 6	*and go* **i** *the city, and it shall be told*	1525
	9: 8	and **brought** *him* **i** Damascus.	1521
	9:11	*go* **i** *the street which is called Straight,*	1909
	9:17	went his way, and entered **i** the house;	1519
	9:39	they brought him **i** the upper chamber:	1519
	10:10	while they made ready, he fell **i** a trance,	1909
	10:16	the vessel was received up again **i** heaven.	1519
	10:22	a holy angel to send for thee **i** his house,	1519
	10:24	And the morrow *after* they entered **i**	1519
	11: 8	unclean hath at any time entered **i** my	1519
	11:10	and all were drawn up again **i** heaven.	1519
	11:12	and we entered **i** the man's house;	1519
	12:17	he departed, and went **i** another place.	1519
	13:14	**went i** the synagogue on the sabbath	1525
	14: 1	that they went **i** both together **i**	1525
	14:20	he rose up, and **came i** the city:	1525
	14:22	tribulation enter **i** the kingdom of God.	1519
	14:25	word in Perga, they went down **i** Attalia:	1519
	16: 7	to Mysia, they assayed to go **i** Bithynia:	2596
	16: 9	Come over **i** Macedonia, and help us.	1519
	16:10	immediately we endeavoured to go **i**	1519
	16:15	**come i** my house, and abide *there*.	1525
	16:19	drew *them* **i** the market-place unto	1519
	16:23	they cast *them* **i** prison, charging the jailor	1519
	16:24	thrust them **i** the inner prison,	1519
	16:34	when he had brought them **i** his house,	1519
	16:37	being Romans, and have cast *us* **i** prison;	1519
	16:40	and entered **i** *the house of* Lydia:	1519
	17:10	who coming *thither* went **i** the synagogue	1519
	18: 7	and entered **i** a certain *man's* house,	1519
	18:18	and sailed thence **i** Syria, and with him	1519
	18:19	but he himself entered **i** the synagogue,	1519
	18:27	when he was disposed to pass **i**	1519
	19: 8	And he **went i** the synagogue,	1525
	19:22	So he sent **i** Macedonia two of them that	1519
	19:29	they rushed with one accord **i** the theatre.	1519
	19:31	would not adventure himself **i** the theatre.	1519
	20: 1	and departed for to go **i** Macedonia.	1519
	20: 2	much exhortation, he came **i** Greece,	1519
	20: 3	for him, as he was about to sail **i** Syria,	1519
	20: 4	there accompanied him **i** Asia Sopater	891
	20: 9	being **fallen i** a deep sleep:	2702
	20:18	from the first day that I came **i** Asia,	1519
	21: 3	and sailed **i** Syria, and landed at Tyre:	1519
	21: 8	we entered **i** the house of Philip	1519
	21:11	shall deliver *him* **i** the hands of	1519
	21:26	himself with them entered **i** the temple,	1519
	21:28	**brought** Greeks also **i** the temple,	1521
	21:29	that Paul had **brought i** the temple.)	1521
	21:34	he commanded him to be carried **i**	1519
	21:37	And as Paul was to be **led i**	1521
	21:38	leddest out **i** the wilderness four thousand	1519
	22: 4	and delivering **i** prisons both men and	1519
	22:10	said unto me, *Arise, and go* **i** *Damascus;*	1519
	22:11	that were with me, I came **i** Damascus.	1519
	22:23	*off* their clothes, and threw dust **i** the air,	1519
	22:24	him to be brought **i** the castle,	1519
	23:10	them, and to bring *him* **i** the castle.	1519
	23:16	he went and entered **i** the castle,	1519
	23:20	bring down Paul to morrow **i** the council,	1519
	23:28	I brought him forth **i** their council:	1519
	24:27	Porcius Festus **came i** Felix' **room**:	1240+2983
	25: 1	when Festus was **come i** the province,	1910
	25:23	and were entered **i** the place of hearing,	1519
	27: 1	was determined that we should sail **i** Italy,	1519
	27: 2	And **entering i** a ship of Adramyttium,	1910
	27: 6	found a ship of Alexandria sailing **i** Italy;	1519
	27:15	could not **bear up i** the wind, we let *her*	503
	27:17	fearing lest they should fall **i**	1519
	27:30	they had let down the boat **i** the sea,	1519
	27:38	the ship, and cast out the wheat **i** the sea.	1519
	27:39	**i** the which they were minded, if it were	1519
	27:41	And falling **i** a place where two seas met,	1519
	27:43	should cast *themselves* first **i** *the sea,*	NIG
	28: 5	And he shook off the beast **i** the fire,	1519
	28:17	from Jerusalem **i** the hands of the Romans.	1519
	28:23	there came many to him **i** his lodging,	1519
Ro	1:23	**i** an image made like to corruptible man,	1722
	1:25	Who changed the truth of God **i** a lie,	1722
	1:26	natural use **i** that which is against nature:	1519
	5: 2	By whom also we have access by faith **i**	1519
	5:12	as by one man sin entered **i** the world,	1519
	6: 3	of us as were baptized **i** Jesus Christ	1519
	6: 3	Jesus Christ were baptized **i** his death?	1519
	6: 4	are buried with him by baptism **i** death:	1519
	7:23	**bringing** me **i captivity** to the law of sin	163
	8:21	**i** the glorious liberty of the children of	1519
	10: 6	in thine heart, Who shall ascend **i** heaven?	1519
	10: 7	Who shall descend **i** the deep? (that is,	1519
	10:18	their sound went **i** all the earth,	1519
	11:24	wert graffed contrary to nature **i** a good	1519
	11:24	be the natural *branches*, be **graffed i**	1461
	15:24	Whensoever I take my journey **i** Spain,	1519
	15:28	them this fruit, I will come by you **i** Spain.	1519
1Co	2: 9	neither have entered **i** the heart of man,	1909
	4:17	shall **bring** you **i remembrance** of my	363
	9:27	my body, and **bring** *it* **i subjection:**	1396
	11:20	therefore **i one place,**	846+1909+3588
	12:13	For by one Spirit are we all baptized **i** one	1519
	12:13	have been all made to drink **i** one Spirit.	1519
	14: 9	is spoken? for ye shall speak **i** the air.	1519
	14:23	be come together **i one place,**	846+1909+3588

2Co	1:16	And to pass by you **i** Macedonia,	1519
	2:13	them, I went from *thence* **i** Macedonia.	1519
	3:18	changed *i* the same image from glory to	NIG
	7: 5	For, when we were come **i** Macedonia,	1519
	8:16	put the same earnest care **i** the heart	1722
	10: 5	**bringing i captivity** every thought to	163
	11:13	transforming themselves **i** the apostles of	1519
	11:14	for Satan himself is transformed **i** an angel	1519
	11:20	ye suffer, if a man **bring** you **i** bondage,	2615
	12: 4	How that he was caught up **i** paradise,	1519
Gal	1: 6	so soon removed from him that called you **i**	1722
	1:17	but I went **i** Arabia, and returned again	1519
	1:21	Afterwards I came **i** the regions of Syria	1519
	2: 4	that they might **bring** us **i bondage:**	2615
	3:27	as many of you as have been baptized **i**	1519
	4: 6	God hath sent forth the Spirit of his Son **i**	1519
Eph	4: 9	he also descended first **i** the lower parts	1519
	4:15	may grow up **i** him *in all things*, which is	1519
Col	1:13	translated *us* **i** the kingdom of his dear	1519
	2:18	**intruding i** *those things* which he hath	1687
2Th	3: 5	And the Lord direct your hearts **i** the love	1519
	3: 5	God, and **i** the patient waiting for Christ.	1519
1Ti	1: 3	at Ephesus, when I went **i** Macedonia,	1519
	1:12	me faithful, putting me **i** the ministry;	1519
	1:15	that Christ Jesus came **i** the world to save	1519
	3: 6	lest being lifted up with pride he fall **i**	1519
	3: 7	lest he fall **i** reproach and the snare of	1519
	3:16	on in the world, received up **i** glory.	1722
	5: 9	Let not a widow be **taken i** the **number**	2639
	6: 7	For we brought nothing **i** *this* world,	1519
	6: 9	But they that will be rich fall **i** temptation	1519
	6: 9	snare, and *i* many foolish and hurtful lusts,	NIG
2Ti	3: 6	For of this sort are they which creep **i**	1519
Heb	1: 6	when he bringeth in the firstbegotten **i**	1519
	3:11	my wrath, They shall not enter **i** my rest.	1519
	3:18	he that *they* should not enter **i** his rest,	1519
	4: 1	a promise being left *us* of entering **i** his	1519
	4: 3	we which have believed do enter **i** rest,	1519
	4: 3	in my wrath, If they shall enter **i** my rest:	1519
	4: 5	*place* again, If they shall enter **i** my rest.	1519
	4:10	For he that is entered **i** his rest, he also	1519
	4:11	Let us labour therefore to enter **i** that rest,	1519
	4:14	that is **passed i** the heavens, Jesus the	1330
	6:19	and which entereth **i** that within the vail;	1519
	8:10	I will put my laws **i** their mind,	1519
	9: 6	the priests went always **i** the first	1519
	9: 7	But **i** the second *went* the high priest	1519
	9: 8	the way **i** the holiest *of all* was not yet	NIG
	9:12	by his own blood he entered in once **i**	1519
	9:24	For Christ is not entered **i** the holy *places*	1519
	9:24	but **i** heaven itself, now to appear in	1519
	9:25	as the high priest entereth **i** the holy *place*	1519
	10: 5	Wherefore when he **cometh i**	1525
	10:16	I will put my laws **i** their hearts, and in	1909
	10:19	to enter **i** the holiest by the blood	1519
	10:31	*It is* a fearful *thing* to fall **i** the hands of	1519
	11: 8	when he was called to go out **i** a place	1519
	13:11	whose blood is brought **i** the sanctuary by	1519
Jas	1: 2	count *it* all joy when ye **fall i** divers	4045
	1:25	But whoso looketh **i** the perfect law of	1519
	4:13	or to morrow we will go **i** such a city,	1519
	5: 4	entered **i** the ears of the Lord of sabaoth.	1519
	5:12	*your* nay, nay; lest ye fall **i** condemnation.	1519
1Pe	1:12	which *things* the angels desire to look **i**.	1519
	2: 9	you out of darkness **i** his marvellous light:	1519
	3:22	Who is gone **i** heaven, and is on the right	1519
	5:10	who hath called us **i** his eternal glory by	1519
2Pe	1:11	**i** the everlasting kingdom of our Lord	1519
	2: 4	and **delivered** *them* **i** chains of darkness,	3860
	2: 6	**turning** the cities of Sodom and Gomorrha **i** ashes	5077
1Jn	4: 1	many false prophets are gone out **i**	1519
	4: 9	that God sent his only begotten Son **i**	1519
2Jn	1: 7	many deceivers are entered **i** the world,	1519
	1:10	doctrine, receive him not **i** *your* house,	1519
Jude	1: 4	the grace of our God **i** lasciviousness,	1519
Rev	2:10	*the devil shall cast* some *of you* **i** *prison,*	1519
	2:22	*I will* cast her **i** a bed, and them that	1519
	2:22	that commit adultery with her **i** great	1519
	5: 6	spirits of God sent forth **i** all the earth.	1519
	8: 5	fire of the altar, and cast *it* **i** the earth:	1519
	8: 8	burning with fire was cast **i** the sea:	1519
	11:11	a half the spirit of life from God entered **i**	1909
	12: 6	And the woman fled **i** the wilderness,	1519
	12: 9	he was cast *out* **i** the earth, and his angels	1519
	12:14	she might fly **i** the wilderness, into her	1519
	12:14	**i** her place, where she is nourished for a	1519
	13:10	He that leadeth **i** captivity *shall* go into	1519
	13:10	He that leadeth into captivity *shall* go **i**	1519
	14:10	which is poured out without mixture **i**	1722
	14:19	And the angel thrust in his sickle **i**	1519
	14:19	cast *it* **i** the great winepress of the wrath	1519
	15: 8	no *man* was able to enter **i** the temple,	1519
	16:16	And he gathered them together **i** a place	1519
	16:19	the seventh angel poured out his vial **i**	1519
	16:19	the great city was **divided i** three parts,	1519
	17: 3	So he carried me away in the spirit **i**	1519
	17: 8	of the bottomless *pit*, and go **i** perdition:	1519
	17:11	and is of the seven, and goeth **i** perdition.	1519
	18:21	great millstone, and cast *it* **i** the sea,	1519
	19:20	*These* both were cast alive **i** a lake of fire	1519
	20: 3	And cast him **i** the bottomless *pit*, and	1519
	20:10	the devil that deceived them was cast **i**	1519
	20:14	and hell were cast **i** the lake of fire.	1519
	20:15	the book of life was cast **i** the lake of fire.	1519

Rev	21:24	earth do bring their glory and honour **i** it.	1519
	21:26	the glory and honour of the nations **i** it.	1519
	21:27	And there shall in no wise enter **i** it any	1519
	22:14	*may enter in through the gates* **i** *the city.*	1519

INTREAT (15) [ENTREAT, INTREATED, INTREATIES, INTREATY]

Ge	23: 8	and **i** for me to Ephron the son of Zohar,	6293
Ex	8: 8	and Aaron, and said, **i** the LORD,	6279
	8: 9	shall **i** for thee, and for thy servants,	6279
	8:28	you shall not go very far away: **i** for me.	6279
	8:29	I will **i** the LORD that the swarms *of flies*	6279
	9:28	**i** the LORD (for *it is* enough) that there be	6279
	10:17	only *this* once, and **i** the LORD your God,	6279
	10:18	I me not to leave thee, *or* to return from	6293
Ru	1:16	**i** me not to leave thee, *or* to return from	6293
1Sa	2:25	against the LORD, who shall **i** for him?	6419
1Ki	13: 6	now the face of the LORD thy God,	2470
Ps	45:12	the people shall **i** thy **favour.**	2470+6440
Pr	19: 6	Many will **i** the favour of the prince:	2470
1Co	4:13	being defamed, we **i**: we are made as	3870
Php	4: 3	And **i** thee also, true yokefellow,	2065
1Ti	5: 1	Rebuke not an elder, but **i** *him* as a father;	3870

INTREATED (18) [INTREAT]

Ge	25:21	Isaac **i** the LORD for his wife, because	6279
	25:21	the LORD was **i** of him, and Rebekah his	6279
Ex	8:30	went out from Pharaoh, and **i** the LORD.	6279
	10:18	went out from Pharaoh, and **i** the LORD.	6279
Jdg	13: 8	Manoah **i** the LORD, and said, O my	6279
2Sa	21:14	And after that God was **i** for the land.	6279
	24:25	So the LORD was **i** for the land,	6279
1Ch	5:20	God in the battle, and he was **i** of them;	6279
2Ch	33:13	was **i** of him, and heard his supplication,	6279
	33:19	how God was **i** of him, and all his sin,	6279
Ezr	8:23	our God for this: and he was **i** of us.	6279
Job	19:16	*me* no answer; I him with my mouth.	2603
	19:17	though I **i** for the children's *sake* of mine	2589
Ps	119:58	I thy favour with *my* whole heart:	2470
Isa	19:22	he shall be **i** of them, and shall heal them.	6279
Lk	15:28	*therefore came his father out and* **i** *him.*	3870
Heb	12:19	voice they that heard **i** that the word	3868
Jas	3:17	then peaceable, gentle, *and* **easy to be i,**	2138

INTREATIES (1) [INTREAT]

Pr	18:23	The poor **useth i**; but the rich	1696+8469

INTREATY (1) [INTREAT]

2Co	8: 4	Praying us with much **i** that we would	3874

INTRUDING (1)

Col	2:18	**i** into *those things* which he hath not	1687

INVADE (2) [INVADED, INVASION]

2Ch	20:10	whom thou wouldest not let Israel **i**,	935+871.1
Hab	3:16	people, he will **i** them **with** his **troops.**	1464

INVADED (5) [INVADE]

1Sa	23:27	come; for the Philistines have **i** the land.	6584
	27: 8	**i** the Geshurites, and the Gezrites,	6584
	30: 1	that the Amalekites had **i** the south,	6584
2Ki	13:20	bands of the Moabites **i** the land	935+871.1
2Ch	28:18	The Philistines also had **i** the cities of	6584

INVALID See IMPOTENT

INVASION (1) [INVADE]

1Sa	30:14	We **made an i** *upon* the south of	6584

INVENT (1) [INVENTED, INVENTIONS, INVENTORS]

Am	6: 5	**i** to themselves instruments of musick,	2803

INVENTED (1) [INVENT]

2Ch	26:15	**i** by cunning *men*, to be on the towers	4284

INVENTIONS (5) [INVENT]

Ps	99: 8	though thou tookest vengeance of their **i**.	5949
	106:29	they provoked *him* to anger with their **i**:	4611
	106:39	and went a whoring with their own **i**.	4611
Pr	8:12	and find out knowledge of **witty i.**	4209
Ecc	7:29	but they have sought out many **i.**	2810

INVENTORS (1) [INVENT]

Ro	1:30	**i** of evil *things*, disobedient to parents,	2182

INVESTIGATION See INQUISITION

INVISIBLE (5)

Ro	1:20	For the **i** *things* of him from the creation of	517
Col	1:15	Who is the image of the **i** God, the firstborn	517
	1:16	heaven, and that are in earth, visible and **i**,	517
1Ti	1:17	immortal, **i**, the only wise God, *be* honour	517
Heb	11:27	for he endured, as seeing *him who is* **i.**	517

INVITED (3)

1Sa	9:24	for thee since *I* said, I have **i** the people.	7121
2Sa	13:23	and Absalom **i** all the king's sons.	7121
Est	5:12	to morrow *am* I **i** unto her also with	7121

INWARD (25) [INWARDLY, INWARDS]

Ex	28:26	*is* in the side of the ephod **i**.	1004+1886.5
	39:19	*was* on the side of the ephod **i**.	1004+1886.5
Lev	13:55	it *is* fret **i**, *whether* it *be* bare within or	871.1
2Sa	5: 9	round about from Millo and **i**.	1004+1886.5
1Ki	7:25	and all their hinder parts *were* **i**.	1004+1886.5
2Ch	3:13	on their feet, and their faces *were* **i**.	1004
	4: 4	and all their hinder parts *were* **i**.	1004+1886.5

Job	19:19	All my **i** friends abhorred me:	5475
	38:36	Who hath put wisdom in the **i parts**?	2910
Ps	5: 9	their **i part is** very wickedness;	7130
	49:11	Their **i** thought is, that their houses shall	7130
	51: 6	Behold, thou desirest truth in the **i parts**:	2910
	64: 6	both the **i** thought of every one of them,	7130
Pr	20:27	searching all the **i parts** of the belly.	2315
	20:30	so do stripes the **i parts** of the belly.	2315
Isa	16:11	Moab, and mine **i parts** for Kir-haresh.	7130
Jer	31:33	I will put my law in their **i parts**,	7130
Eze	40: 9	the porch of the gate was **i.** 1004+4480+1886.1	
	40:16	windows were round about **i:** 6441+3807.1	
	41: 3	went he **i**, and measured the post 6441+3807.1	
	42: 4	walk of ten cubits breadth **i**, 413+6442+1886.1	
Lk	11:39	but your **i part** is full of ravening and	2081
Ro	7:22	For I delight in the law of God after the **i**	2080
2Co	4:16	yet the **i** man is renewed day by day.	2081
	7:15	And his **i affection** is more abundant	4698

INWARDLY (3) [INWARD]

Ps	62: 4	with their mouth, but they curse **i.** 7130+871.1	
Mt	7:15	but **i** they are ravening wolves.	2081
Ro	2:29	he is a Jew, which is one **i;** 1722+2927+3588	

INWARDS (20) [INWARD]

Ex	29:13	shalt take all the fat that covereth the **i,**	7130
	29:17	wash the **i** of him, and his legs,	7130
	29:22	the fat that covereth the **i**, and the caul	7130
Lev	1: 9	his **i** and his legs shall he wash in water:	7130
	1:13	shall wash the **i** and the legs with water:	7130
	3: 3	the fat that covereth the **i**, and all the fat	7130
	3: 3	and all the fat that is upon the **i,**	7130
	3: 9	the fat that covereth the **i**, and all the fat	7130
	3: 9	and all the fat that is upon the **i,**	7130
	3:14	the fat that covereth the **i**, and all the fat	7130
	3:14	and all the fat that is upon the **i,**	7130
	4: 8	the fat that covereth the **i,**	7130
	4: 8	and all the fat that is upon the **i,**	7130
	4:11	and with his legs, and his **i**, and his dung,	7130
	7: 3	the rump, and the fat that covereth the **i,**	7130
	8:16	took all the fat that was upon the **i,**	7130
	8:21	he washed the **i** and the legs in water;	7130
	8:25	the fat that was upon the **i**, and the caul	7130
	9:14	he did wash the **i** and the legs,	7130
	9:19	which covereth the **i,** and the kidneys,	NIH

IPHDEIAH See IPHEDEIAH

IPHEDEIAH (1)

1Ch	8:25	And **I**, and Penuel, the sons of Shashak;	3301

IPHTAH See JIPHTAH

IPHTAH EL See JIPHTHAH-EL

IR (1)

1Ch	7:12	Huppim, the children of **I**, and Hushim,	5893

IRA (6)

2Sa	20:26	**I** also the Jairite was a chief ruler about	5896
	23:26	Paltite, **I** the son of Ikkesh the Tekoite,	5896
	23:38	**I** an Ithrite, Gareb an Ithrite,	5896
1Ch	11:28	**I** the son of Ikkesh the Tekoite,	5896
	11:40	the Ithrite, Gareb the Ithrite,	5896
	27: 9	sixth captain for the sixth month was **I**	5896

IRAD (2)

Ge	4:18	unto Enoch was born **I**: and Irad begat	5897
	4:18	**I** begat Mehujael: and Mehujael begat	5897

IRAM (2)

Ge	36:43	Duke Magdiel, duke **I**: these be the dukes	5902
1Ch	1:54	Duke Magdiel, duke **I**. These are the	5902

IRI (1)

1Ch	7: 7	and Uzziel, and Jerimoth, and **I**, five;	5901

IRIJAH (2)

Jer	37:13	whose name was **I**, the son of Shelemiah,	3376
	37:14	So **I** took Jeremiah, and brought him to	3376

IRNAHASH (1)

1Ch	4:12	and Paseah, and Tehinnah the father of **I.**	5904

IRON (101) [IRONS]

Ge	4:22	instructor of every artificer in brass and **i:**	1270
Lev	26:19	I will make your heaven as **i**, and your	1270
Nu	31:22	the brass, the **i**, the tin, and the lead,	1270
	35:16	if he smite him with an instrument of **i,**	1270
Dt	3:11	behold, his bedstead was a bedstead of **i**;	1270
	4:20	brought you forth out of the **i** furnace,	1270
	8: 9	a land whose stones are **i**, and out of	1270
	27: 5	shalt not lift up any **i** tool upon them.	1270
	28:23	the earth that is under thee shall be **i.**	1270
	28:48	he shall put a yoke of **i** upon thy neck,	1270
	33:25	Thy shoes shall be **i** and brass; and as thy	1270
Jos	6:19	and gold, and vessels of brass and **i,**	1270
	6:24	gold, and the vessels of brass and of **i,**	1270
	8:31	over which no man hath lift up any **i:**	1270
	17:16	the land of the valley have chariots of **i,**	1270
	17:18	though they have **i** chariots,	1270
	19:38	**I**, and Migdal-el, Horem, and Beth-anath,	3375
	22: 8	and with **i**, and with very much raiment:	1270
Jdg	1:19	the valley because they had chariots of **i.**	1270
	4: 3	for he had nine hundred chariots of **i**;	1270
	4:13	even nine hundred chariots of **i**, and all	1270
1Sa	17: 7	head weighed six hundred shekels of **i:**	1270

2Sa	12:31	under harrows of **i**, and under axes of iron,	1270
	12:31	under axes of **i**, and made them pass	1270
	23: 7	shall touch them must be fenced with **i**	1270
1Ki	6: 7	axe nor any tool of **i** heard in the house,	1270
	8:51	Egypt, from the midst of the furnace of **i:**	1270
2Ki	6: 5	the **i** did swim.	
	6: 6	and cast it in thither; and the **i** did swim.	1270
1Ch	20: 3	and with harrows of **i**, and with axes.	1270
	22: 3	prepared **i** in abundance for the nails	1270
	22:14	of brass and **i** without weight; for it is in	1270
	22:16	gold, the silver, and the brass, and the **i,**	1270
	29: 2	the **i** for things of iron, and wood for	1270
	29: 2	the iron for things of **i**, and wood for	1270
	29: 7	and one hundred thousand talents of **i.**	1270
2Ch	2: 7	in **i**, and in purple, and in crimson, and blue,	1270
	2:14	in brass, in **i**, in stone, and in timber,	1270
	18:10	Chenaanah made him horns of **i,**	1270
	24:12	also such as wrought **i** and brass to mend	1270
Job	19:24	That they were graven with an **i** pen and	1270
	20:24	He shall flee from the **i** weapon,	1270
	28: 2	**I** is taken out of the earth, and brass	1270
	40:18	pieces of brass; his bones are like bars of **i.**	1270
	41:27	esteemeth **i** as straw, and brass as rotten	1270
Ps	2: 9	Thou shalt break them with a rod of **i;**	
	105:18	they hurt with fetters: he was laid in **i;**	1270
	107:10	of death, being bound in affliction and **i;**	1270
	107:16	of brass, and cut the bars of **i** in sunder.	1270
	149: 8	and their nobles with fetters of **i.**	1270
Pr	27:17	**I** sharpeneth iron; so a man sharpeneth	1270
	27:17	Iron sharpeneth **i**; so a man sharpeneth	1270
Ecc	10:10	If the **i** be blunt, and he do not whet	1270
Isa	10:34	cut down the thickets of the forest with **i,**	1270
	45: 2	of brass, and cut in sunder the bars of **i:**	1270
	48: 4	neck is an **i** sinew, and thy brow brass:	1270
	60:17	I will bring silver, and for wood brass,	1270
	60:17	and for wood brass, and for stones **i:**	1270
Jer	1:18	an **i** pillar, and brasen walls against	1270
	6:28	are brass and **i**; they are all corrupters.	1270
	11: 4	from the **i** furnace, saying, Obey my voice,	1270
	15:12	Shall **i** break the northern iron and	1270
	15:12	Shall iron break the northern **i** and	1270
	17: 1	sin of Judah is written with a pen of **i,**	1270
	28:13	but thou shalt make for them yokes of **i.**	1270
	28:14	I have put a yoke of **i** upon the neck of	1270
Eze	4: 3	Moreover take thou unto thee an **i** pan,	1270
	4: 3	set it for a wall of **i** between thee and	1270
	22:18	they are brass, and tin, and **i**, and lead,	1270
	22:20	and brass, and **i**, and lead, and tin,	1270
	27:12	with silver, **i**, tin, and lead, they traded in	1270
	27:19	bright **i**, cassia, and calamus, were in thy	1270
Da	2:33	His legs of **i**, his feet part of iron and	6523
	2:33	of iron, his feet part of **i** and part of clay.	6523
	2:34	the image upon his feet that were of **i**	6523
	2:35	was the **i**, the clay, the brass, the silver,	6523
	2:40	the fourth kingdom shall be strong as **i:**	6523
	2:40	forasmuch as **i** breaketh in pieces and	6523
	2:40	all things: and as **i** that breaketh all these,	6523
	2:41	toes, part of potter's clay, and part of **i,**	6523
	2:41	there shall be in it of the strength of the **i,**	6523
	2:41	forasmuch as thou sawest the **i** mixed	6523
	2:42	as the toes of the feet were part of **i,**	6523
	2:43	thou sawest **i** mixt with miry clay,	6523
	2:43	another, even as **i** is not mixed with clay.	6523
	2:45	that it brake in pieces the **i**, the brass,	6523
	4:15	even with a band of **i** and brass,	6523
	4:23	even with a band of **i** and brass,	6523
	5: 4	of brass, of **i**, of wood, of stone.	6523
	5:23	gold, of brass, **i**, wood, and stone, which	6523
	7: 7	exceedingly; and it had great **i** teeth:	6523
	7:19	whose teeth were of **i**, and his nails of **i:**	6523
Am	1: 3	Gilead with threshing instruments of **i:**	1270
Mic	4:13	I will make thine horn **i**, and I will make	1270
Ac	12:10	they came unto the **i** gate that leadeth	4603
1Ti	4: 2	their conscience **seared with a hot i;**	2743
Rev	2:27	And he shall rule them with a rod of **i;**	4603
	9: 9	as it were breastplates of **i;**	4603
	12: 5	was to rule all nations with a rod of **i:**	4603
	18:12	and of brass, and **i**, and marble,	4604
	19:15	and he shall rule them with a rod of **i:**	4603

IRONS (1) [IRON]

Job	41: 7	Canst thou fill his skin with **barbed i**?	7905

IRPEEL (1)

Jos	18:27	And Rekem, and **I**, and Taralah,	3416

IR-SHEMESH (1)

Jos	19:41	inheritance was Zorah, and Eshtaol, and **I,**	5905

IRU (1)

1Ch	4:15	the son of Jephunneh; **I**, Elah, and Naam:	5900

IS (6993) [BE] See Index of Articles, Etc.

ISAAC (128) [ISAAC'S]

Ge	17:19	son indeed; and thou shalt call his name **I:**	3327
	17:21	my covenant will I establish with **I,**	3327
	21: 3	unto him, whom Sarah bare to him, **I.**	3327
	21: 4	Abraham circumcised his son **I** being	3327
	21: 5	when his son **I** was born unto him.	3327
	21: 8	feast the same day that **I** was weaned.	3327
	21:10	not be heir with my son, even with **I.**	3327
	21:12	her voice; for in **I** shall thy seed be called.	3327
	22: 2	said, Take now thy son, thine only son **I,**	3327
	22: 3	his son, and clave the wood for the	3327
	22: 6	burnt offering, and laid it upon his son;	

Ge	22: 7	**I** spake unto Abraham his father, and said,	3327
	22: 9	bound **I** his son, and laid him on the altar	3327
	24: 4	kindred, and take a wife unto my son **I.**	3327
	24:14	that thou hast appointed for thy servant **I;**	3327
	24:62	I came from the way of the well Lahai-roi;	3327
	24:63	**I** went out to meditate in the field at	3327
	24:64	when she saw **I**, she lighted off the camel.	3327
	24:66	the servant told **I** all things that he had	3327
	24:67	brought her into his mother Sarah's tent,	3327
	24:67	**I** was comforted after his mother's death.	3327
	25: 5	And Abraham gave all that he had unto **I.**	3327
	25: 6	sent them away from **I** his son, while he	3327
	25: 9	his sons **I** and Ishmael buried him in	3327
	25:11	of Abraham, that God blessed his son **I;**	3327
	25:11	and **I** dwelt by the well Lahai-roi.	3327
	25:19	these are the generations of **I,**	3327
	25:19	of **I**, Abraham's son: Abraham begat **I:**	3327
	25:20	**I** was forty years old when he took	3327
	25:21	**I** intreated the LORD for his wife,	3327
	25:26	**I** was threescore years old when she bare	3327
	25:28	loved Esau, because he did eat of his	3327
	26: 1	**I** went unto Abimelech king of	3327
	26: 6	And **I** dwelt in Gerar:	3327
	26: 8	**I** was sporting with Rebekah his wife.	3327
	26: 9	Abimelech called **I**, and said, Behold, of a	3327
	26: 9	**I** said unto him, Because I said, Lest I die	3327
	26:12	**I** sowed in that land, and received in	3327
	26:16	Abimelech said unto **I**, Go from us;	3327
	26:17	**I** departed thence, and pitched his tent in	3327
	26:18	**I** digged again the wells of water,	3327
	26:27	said unto them, Wherefore come ye to	3327
	26:31	**I** sent them away, and they departed from	3327
	26:35	Which were a grief of mind unto **I** and	3327
	27: 1	when **I** was old, and his eyes were dim,	3327
	27: 5	Rebekah heard when **I** spake to Esau his	3327
	27:20	**I** said unto his son, How is it that thou	3327
	27:21	**I** said unto Jacob, Come near, I pray thee,	3327
	27:22	Jacob went near unto **I** his father;	3327
	27:26	father **I** said unto him, Come near now,	3327
	27:30	as soon as **I** had made an end of blessing	3327
	27:30	gone out from the presence of **I** his father,	3327
	27:32	**I** his father said unto him, Who art thou?	3327
	27:33	**I** trembled very exceedingly, and said,	3327
	27:37	**I** answered and said unto Esau, Behold,	3327
	27:39	his father answered and said unto him,	3327
	27:46	Rebekah said to **I**, I am weary of my life	3327
	28: 1	**I** called Jacob, and blessed him,	3327
	28: 5	**I** sent away Jacob: and he went to	3327
	28: 6	When Esau saw that **I** had blessed Jacob,	3327
	28: 8	of Canaan pleased not **I** his father;	3327
	28:13	of Abraham thy father, and the God of **I:**	3327
	31:18	for to go to **I** his father in the land	3327
	31:42	and the fear of **I**, had been with me,	3327
	31:53	Jacob sware by the fear of his father **I.**	3327
	32: 9	father Abraham, and God of my father **I,**	3327
	35:12	the land which **I** gave Abraham and **I,**	3327
	35:27	Jacob came unto **I** his father unto Mamre,	3327
	35:27	where Abraham and **I** sojourned.	3327
	35:28	the days of **I** were an hundred	3327
	35:29	**I** gave up the ghost, and died,	3327
	46: 1	sacrifices unto the God of his father **I.**	3327
	48:15	my fathers Abraham and **I** did walk,	3327
	48:16	the name of my fathers Abraham and **I;**	3327
	49:31	there they buried **I** and Rebekah his wife;	3327
	50:24	he sware to Abraham, to **I**, and to Jacob.	3327
Ex	2:24	with Abraham, with **I**, and with Jacob.	3327
	3: 6	the God of **I**, and the God of Jacob.	3327
	3:15	the God of **I**, and the God of Jacob.	3327
	3:16	of **I**, and of Jacob, appeared unto me,	3327
	4: 5	the God of **I**, and the God of Jacob,	3327
	6: 3	**I**, and unto Jacob, by the name of God	3327
	6: 8	to give it to Abraham, to **I**, and to Jacob;	3327
	32:13	**I**, and Israel, thy servants,	3327
	33: 1	to **I**, and to Jacob, saying, Unto thy seed	3327
Lev	26:42	also my covenant with **I**, and also my	3327
Nu	32:11	unto Abraham, unto **I**, and unto Jacob;	3327
Dt	1: 8	Abraham, **I**, and Jacob, to give unto them	3327
	6:10	to Abraham, to **I**, and to Jacob, to give	3327
	9: 5	unto thy fathers, Abraham, **I**, and Jacob.	3327
	9:27	thy servants, Abraham, **I**, and Jacob;	3327
	29:13	fathers, to Abraham, to **I**, and to Jacob.	3327
	30:20	to Abraham, to **I**, and to Jacob, to give	3327
	34: 4	unto **I**, and unto Jacob, saying, I will give	3327
Jos	24: 3	and multiplied his seed, and gave him **I.**	3327
	24: 4	I gave unto **I** Jacob and Esau: and I gave	3327
1Ki	18:36	LORD God of Abraham, **I**, and of Israel,	3327
2Ki	13:23	**I**, and Jacob, and would not destroy them	3327
1Ch	1:28	The sons of Abraham; **I**, and Ishmael.	3327
	1:34	Abraham begat **I**. The sons of Isaac; Esau	3327
	1:34	begat Isaac. The sons of **I**; Esau and Israel.	3327
	16:16	with Abraham, and of his oath unto **I;**	3327
	29:18	of Abraham, **I**, and of Israel, our fathers,	3327
2Ch	30: 6	**I**, and Israel, and he will return to	3327
Ps	105: 9	made with Abraham, and his oath unto **I;**	3446
Jer	33:26	over the seed of Abraham, **I**, and Jacob:	3446
Am	7: 9	the high places of **I** shall be desolate,	3446
	7:16	drop not thy word against the house of **I.**	3446
Mt	1: 2	Abraham begat **I**; and Isaac begat Jacob;	2464
	1: 2	and Isaac begat Jacob; and Jacob begat Judas	2464
	8:11	**I**, and Jacob, in the kingdom of heaven.	2464
	22:32	and the God of **I**, and the God of Jacob?	2464
Mk	12:26	and the God of **I**, and the God of Jacob?	2464
Lk	3:34	the son of Jacob, which was the son of **I,**	2464
	13:28	and **I**, and Jacob, and all the prophets,	2464
	20:37	and the God of **I**, and the God of Jacob.	2464

I

ISAAC'S (continued)

Ac	3:13 God of Abraham, and of I, and of Jacob,	2464
	7: 8 and so *Abraham* begat I,	2464
	7: 8 and I *begat* Jacob; and Jacob *begat*	2464
	7:32 and the God of I, and the God of Jacob.	2464
Ro	9: 7 but, In I shall thy seed be called.	2464
	9:10 conceived by one, *even* by our father I;	2464
Gal	4:28 Now we, brethren, as I was,	2464
Heb	11: 9 *country,* dwelling in tabernacles with I	2464
	11:17 when he was tried, offered up I:	2464
	11:18 said, That in I shall thy seed be called:	2464
	11:20 By faith I blessed Jacob and Esau	2464
Jas	2:21 when he had offered I his son upon	2464

ISAAC'S (4) [ISAAC]

Ge	26:19 I servants digged in the valley,	3327
	26:20 the herdmen of Gerar did strive with I	3327
	26:25 and there I servants digged a well.	3327
	26:32 that I servants came, and told him	3327

ISACHAR (1) [ISSACHAR]

Rev	7: 7 Of the tribe of I *were* sealed twelve	2466

ISAIAH (31) [ESAI, ESAIAS]

2Ki	19: 5 the servants of king Hezekiah came to I.	3470
	19: 6 I said unto them, Thus shall ye say to	3470
	19:20 I the son of Amoz sent to Hezekiah,	3470
	20: 1 prophet I the son of Amoz came to him,	3470
	20: 4 I was gone out *into* the middle court,	3470
	20: 7 I said, Take a lump of figs. And they took	3470
	20: 8 Hezekiah said unto I, What *shall be*	3470
	20: 9 I said, This sign shalt thou have of	3470
	20:11 the prophet cried unto the LORD:	3470
	20:14 came I the prophet unto king Hezekiah,	3470
	20:16 I said unto Hezekiah, Hear the word of	3470
	20:19 said Hezekiah unto I, Good *is* the word	3470
2Ch	26:22 first and last, did I the prophet, the son of	3470
	32:20 the prophet I the son of Amoz, prayed	3470
	32:32 they *are* written in the vision of I	3470
Isa	1: 1 The vision of I the son of Amoz, which	3470
	2: 1 The word that I the son of Amoz saw	3470
	7: 3 said the LORD unto I, Go forth now to	3470
	13: 1 which I the son of Amoz did see.	3470
	20: 2 At the same time spake the LORD by I	3470
	20: 3 Like as my servant I hath walked naked	3470
	37: 2 unto I the prophet the son of Amoz.	3470
	37: 5 the servants of king Hezekiah came to I.	3470
	37: 6 I said unto them, Thus shall ye say unto	3470
	37:21 I the son of Amoz sent unto Hezekiah,	3470
	38: 1 I the prophet the son of Amoz came unto	3470
	38: 4 came the word of the LORD to I, saying,	3470
	38:21 For I had said, Let them take a lump of	3470
	39: 3 came I the prophet unto king Hezekiah,	3470
	39: 5 said I to Hezekiah, Hear the word of	3470
	39: 8 said Hezekiah to I, Good *is* the word of	3470

ISCAH (1)

Ge	11:29 the father of Milcah, and the father of I.	3252

ISCARIOT (11)

Mt	10: 4 Simon the Canaanite, and Judas I, who	2469
	26:14 Then one of the twelve, called Judas I,	2469
Mk	3:19 And Judas I, which also betrayed him.	2469
	14:10 And Judas I, one of the twelve, went unto	2469
Lk	6:16 and Judas I, which also was the traitor.	2469
	22: 3 entered Satan into Judas surnamed I,	2469
Jn	6:71 He spake of Judas I the *son* of Simon:	2469
	12: 4 Then saith one of his disciples, Judas I,	2469
	13: 2 having now put into the heart of Judas I,	2469
	13:26 he gave *it* to Judas I, *the son* of Simon.	2469
	14:22 Judas saith unto him, not I, Lord, how is	2469

ISHBAH (1)

1Ch	4:17 and I the father of Eshtemoa.	3431

ISHBAK (2)

Ge	25: 2 Medan, and Midian, and I, and Shuah.	3435
1Ch	1:32 Medan, and Midian, and I, and Shuah.	3435

ISHBI-BENOB (1)

2Sa	21:16 I, which *was* of the sons of the giant,	3430

ISH-BOSHETH (12) [ESHBAAL]

2Sa	2: 8 took I the son of Saul, and brought him	378
	2:10 I Saul's son *was* forty years old when he	378
	2:12 Ner, and the servants of I the son of Saul,	378
	2:15 which *pertained* to I the son of Saul,	378
	3: 7 I *said* to Abner, Wherefore hast thou gone	NIH
	3: 8 was Abner very wroth for the words of I,	378
	3:14 David sent messengers to I Saul's son,	378
	3:15 I sent, and took her from *her* husband,	378
	4: 5 about the heat of the day to the house of I,	378
	4: 8 they brought the head of I unto David *to*	378
	4: 8 Behold the head of I the son of Saul thine	378
	4:12 they took the head of I, and buried *it* in	378

ISHHOD See ISHOD

ISHI (6)

1Ch	2:31 sons of Appaim; I. And the sons of Ishi;	3469
	2:31 the sons of I; Sheshan. And the children	3469
	4:20 sons of I *were,* Zoheth, and Ben-zoheth.	3469
	4:42 and Rephaiah, and Uzziel, the sons of I.	3469
	5:24 I, and Eliel, and Azriel, and Jeremiah,	3469
Hos	2:16 saith the LORD, *that* thou shalt call *me* I;	376

ISHIAH (1)

1Ch	7: 3 Michael, and Obadiah, and Joel, I, five:	3449

ISHIJAH (1)

Ezr	10:31 Eliezer, I, Malchiah, Shemaiah, Shimeon,	3449

ISHMA (1)

1Ch	4: 3 father of Etam; Jezreel, and I, and Idbash:	3457

ISHMAEL (47) [ISHMAEL'S, ISHMAELITE, ISHMAELITES, ISHMEELITE, ISHMEELITES]

Ge	16:11 shalt bear a son, and shalt call his name I;	3458
	16:15 his son's name, which Hagar bare, I.	3458
	16:16 years old, when Hagar bare I to Abram.	3458
	17:18 unto God, O that I might live before thee!	3458
	17:20 as for I, I have heard thee: Behold, I have	3458
	17:23 Abraham took I his son, and all that were	3458
	17:25 I his son *was* thirteen years old, when he	3458
	17:26 was Abraham circumcised, and I his son.	3458
	25: 9 I buried him in the cave of Machpelah,	3458
	25:12 Now these *are* the generations of I,	3458
	25:13 these *are* the names of the sons of I,	3458
	25:13 the firstborn of I, Nebajoth; and Kedar,	3458
	25:16 These *are* the sons of I, and these *are*	3458
	25:17 these *are* the years of the life of I,	3458
	28: 9 Esau unto I, and took unto the wives	3458
	28: 9 Mahalath the daughter of I Abraham's	3458
2Ki	25:23 even I the son of Nethaniah,	3458
	25:25 *that* I the son of Nethaniah, the son of	3458
1Ch	1:28 The sons of Abraham; Isaac, and I.	3458
	1:29 The firstborn of I, Nebajoth; then Kedar,	3458
	1:31 and Kedemah. These *are* the sons of I.	3458
	8:38 I, and Sheariah, and Obadiah, and Hanan.	3458
	9:44 I, and Sheariah, and Obadiah, and Hanan.	3458
2Ch	19:11 Zebadiah the son of I, the ruler of the	3458
	23: 1 I the son of Jehohanan, and Azariah the	3458
Ezr	10:22 Elioenai, Maaseiah, I, Nethaneel, Jozabad,	3458
Jer	40: 8 even I the son of Nethaniah, and Johanan	3458
	40:14 sent I the son of Nethaniah to slay thee?	3458
	40:15 I will slay I the son of Nethaniah,	3458
	40:16 this thing: for thou speakest falsely of I.	3458
	41: 1 *that* I the son of Nethaniah the son of	3458
	41: 2 arose I the son of Nethaniah, and the ten	3458
	41: 3 I also slew all the Jews that were with	3458
	41: 6 I the son of Nethaniah went forth from	3458
	41: 7 that I the son of Nethaniah slew them,	3458
	41: 8 were found among them that said unto I,	3458
	41: 9 the pit wherein I had cast all the dead	3458
	41: 9 I the son of Nethaniah filled it *with* them	3458
	41:10 I carried away captive all the residue of	3458
	41:10 I the son of Nethaniah carried them away	3458
	41:11 heard of all the evil that I the son of	3458
	41:12 went to fight with I the son of Nethaniah,	3458
	41:13 when all the people which *were* with I	3458
	41:14 So all the people that I had carried away	3458
	41:15 I the son of Nethaniah escaped from	3458
	41:16 recovered from I the son of Nethaniah,	3458
	41:18 I the son of Nethaniah had slain Gedaliah	3458

ISHMAEL'S (1) [ISHMAEL]

Ge	36: 3 Bashemath I daughter, sister of Nebajoth.	3458

ISHMAELITE (1) [ISHMAEL]

1Ch	27:30 Over the camels also *was* Obil the I:	3459

ISHMAELITES (2) [ISHMAEL]

Jdg	8:24 had golden earrings, because they *were* I.)	3459
Ps	83: 6 The tabernacles of Edom, and the I;	3459

ISHMAIAH (1)

1Ch	27:19 Of Zebulun, I the son of Obadiah:	3460

ISHMEELITE (1) [ISHMAEL]

1Ch	2:17 and the father of Amasa *was* Jether the I.	3459

ISHMEELITES (4) [ISHMAEL]

Ge	37:25 a company of I came from Gilead with	3459
	37:27 let us sell him to the I, and let not our	3459
	37:28 sold Joseph to the I for twenty *pieces* of	3459
	39: 1 bought him of the hand of the I,	3459

ISHMERAI (1)

1Ch	8:18 I also, and Jezliah, and Jobab, the sons of	3461

ISHOD (1)

1Ch	7:18 sister Hammoleketh bare I, and Abiezer,	379

ISHPAH See ISPAH

ISHPAN (1)

1Ch	8:22 And I, and Heber, and Eliel,	3473

ISH-TOB (2)

2Sa	10: 6 and of I twelve thousand men.	382
	10: 8 of Zoba, and of Rehob, and I, and Maacah,	382

ISHUAH (1)

Ge	46:17 I, and Ishui, and Beriah, and Serah their	3438

ISHUAI (1)

1Ch	7:30 I, and Beriah, and Serah their sister.	3438

ISHUI (2) [JESUI]

Ge	46:17 and I, and Beriah, and Serah their sister:	3440
1Sa	14:49 were Jonathan, and I, and Melchishua:	3440

ISHVAH See ISHUAH

ISHVI See ISHUAI; ISHUI; JESUI

ISHVITE See JESUITES

ISLAND (9) [ISLANDS, ISLE, ISLES]

Job	22:30 He shall deliver the island of the innocent:	336
Isa	34:14 also meet with the **wild beasts of the i**,	338
Ac	27:16 And running under a certain i *which is*	3519
	27:26 Howbeit we must be cast upon a certain i.	3520
	28: 1 they knew that the i was called Melita.	3520
	28: 7 were possessions of the chief *man* of the i,	3520
	28: 9 which had diseases in the i, came,	3520
Rev	6:14 and i were moved out of their places.	3520
	16:20 And every i fled *away,* and the mountains	3520

ISLANDER See BARBARIANS

ISLANDERS See BARBAROUS

ISLANDS (7) [ISLAND]

Isa	11:11 from Hamath, and from the i of the sea.	339
	13:22 the **wild beasts of the i** shall cry in their	338
	41: 1 Keep silence before me, O i; and let	339
	42:12 the LORD, and declare his praise in the i.	339
	42:15 I will make the rivers i, and I will dry up	339
	59:18 to the i he will repay recompence.	339
Jer	50:39 the **wild beasts of the i** shall dwell *there,*	338

ISLE (6) [ISLAND]

Isa	20: 6 the inhabitant of this i shall say in that day,	339
	23: 2 Be still, ye inhabitants of the i; thou whom	339
	23: 6 to Tarshish; howl, ye inhabitants of the i.	339
Ac	13: 6 when they had gone through the i unto	3520
	28:11 which had wintered in the i, *whose* sign	3520
Rev	1: 9 was in the i that is called Patmos,	3520

ISLES (27) [ISLAND]

Ge	10: 5 By these were the i of the Gentiles divided	339
Est	10: 1 upon the land, and *upon* the i of the sea.	339
Ps	72:10 Tarshish and *of* the i shall bring presents:	339
	97: 1 let the multitude of i be glad *thereof.*	339
Isa	24:15 the God of Israel in the i of the sea.	339
	40:15 he taketh up the i as a very little thing.	339
	41: 5 The i saw *it,* and feared; the ends of the	339
	42: 4 the earth: and the i shall wait for his law.	339
	42:10 therein; the i, and the inhabitants thereof.	339
	49: 1 Listen, O i, unto me; and hearken,	339
	51: 5 the i shall wait upon me, and on mine arm	339
	60: 9 Surely the i shall wait for me, and the ships	339
	66:19 *to* Tubal, and Javan, *to* the i afar off,	339
Jer	2:10 For pass over the i of Chittim, and see;	339
	25:22 kings of the i which *are* beyond the sea,	339
	31:10 and declare *it* in the i afar off, and say,	339
Eze	26:15 not the i shake at the sound of thy fall;	339
	26:18 shall the i tremble *in* the day of thy fall;	339
	26:18 that *are* in the sea shall be troubled at	339
	27: 3 *art* a merchant of the people for many i,	339
	27: 6 *of* ivory, *brought* out of the i of Chittim.	339
	27: 7 purple from the i of Elishah was that which	339
	27:15 many i *were* the merchandise of thine	339
	27:35 All the inhabitants of the i shall be	339
	39: 6 among them that dwell carelessly in the i:	339
Da	11:18 After this shall he turn his face unto the i,	339
Zep	2:11 his place, *even* all the i of the heathen.	339

ISMACHIAH (1)

2Ch	31:13 Eliel, and I, and Mahath, and Benaiah,	3253

ISMAIAH (1)

1Ch	12: 4 I the Gibeonite, a mighty *man* among	3460

ISMAKIAH See ISMACHIAH

ISPAH (1)

1Ch	8:16 Michael, and I, and Joha, the sons of	3472

ISRAEL (2565) [EL-ELOHE-ISRAEL, ISRAEL'S, ISRAELITE, ISRAELITES, ISRAELITISH, JACOB]

Ge	32:28 shall be called no more Jacob, but I:	3478
	32:32 Therefore the children of I eat not *of*	3478
	34: 7 he had wrought folly in I in lying with	3478
	35:10 any more Jacob, but I shall be thy name:	3478
	35:10 be thy name: and he called his name I.	3478
	35:21 I journeyed, and spread his tent beyond	3478
	35:22 I dwelt in that land, that Reuben went	3478
	35:22 I heard *it.* Now the sons of Jacob were	3478
	36:31 reigned *any* king over the children of I.	3478
	37: 3 Now I loved Joseph more than all his	3478
	37:13 I said unto Joseph, Do not thy brethren	3478
	42: 5 the sons of I came to buy *corn* among	3478
	43: 6 I said, Wherefore dealt ye *so* ill with me,	3478
	43: 8 Judah said unto I his father, Send the lad	3478
	43:11 their father I said unto them, If *it must be*	3478
	45:21 the children of I did so: and Joseph gave	3478
	45:28 I said, *It is* enough; Joseph my son *is* yet	3478
	46: 1 I took his journey with all that he had,	3478
	46: 2 God spake unto I in the visions of	3478
	46: 5 the sons of I carried Jacob their father,	3478
	46: 8 these *are* the names of the children of I,	3478
	46:29 went up to meet I his father, to Goshen,	3478
	46:30 I said unto Joseph, Now let me die, since	3478
	47:27 I dwelt in the land of Egypt, in the	3478
	47:29 And the time drew nigh that I must die:	3478
	47:31 I bowed himself upon the bed's head.	3478
	48: 2 I strengthened himself, and sat upon	3478
	48: 8 I beheld Joseph's sons, and said, Who *are*	3478

Ge 48:10 Now the eyes of I were dim for age, 3478
48:11 I said unto Joseph, I had not thought to 3478
48:14 I stretched out his right hand, and laid *it* 3478
48:20 saying, In thee shall I bless, saying, 3478
48:21 I said unto Joseph, Behold, I die: 3478
49: 2 of Jacob; and hearken unto I your father. 3478
49: 7 them in Jacob, and scatter them in I. 3478
49:16 judge his people, as one of the tribes of I. 3478
49:24 thence *is* the shepherd, the stone of I:) 3478
49:28 All these *are* the twelve tribes of I: 3478
50: 2 father: and the physicians embalmed I. 3478
50:25 Joseph took an oath of the children of I, 3478
Ex 1: 1 these *are* the names of the children of I, 3478
1: 7 the children of I were fruitful, 3478
1: 9 the people of the children of I *are* moe 3478
1:12 were grieved because of the children of I. 3478
1:13 the Egyptians made the children of I to 3478
2:23 the children of I sighed by reason of 3478
2:25 And God looked upon the children of I, 3478
3: 9 the cry of the children of I is come unto 3478
3:10 my people the children of I out of Egypt. 3478
3:11 that I should bring forth the children of I 3478
3:13 *when* I come unto the children of I, 3478
3:14 Thus shalt thou say unto the children of I, 3478
3:15 Thus shalt thou say unto the children of I, 3478
3:16 gather the elders of I together, and say 3478
3:18 thou shalt come, thou and the elders of I, 3478
4:22 the LORD, I *is* my son, *even* my firstborn: 3478
4:29 together all the elders of the children of I: 3478
4:31 the LORD had visited the children of I, 3478
5: 1 Thus saith the LORD God of I, 3478
5: 2 that I should obey his voice to let I go? 3478
5: 2 not the LORD, neither will I let I go. 3478
5:14 the officers of the children of I, 3478
5:15 the officers of the children of I came and 3478
5:19 the officers of the children of I did see 3478
6: 5 heard the groaning of the children of I, 3478
6: 6 Wherefore say unto the children of I, 3478
6: 9 Moses spake so unto the children of I: 3478
6:11 that he let the children of I go out of his 3478
6:12 the children of I have not hearkened unto 3478
6:13 gave them a charge unto the children of I, 3478
6:13 bring the children of I out of the land of 3478
6:14 The sons of Reuben the firstborn of I; 3478
6:26 Bring out the children of I from the land 3478
6:27 to bring out the children of I from Egypt: 3478
7: 2 that he send the children of I out of his 3478
7: 4 *and* my people the children of I, 3478
7: 5 bring out the children of I from among 3478
9: 4 LORD shall sever between the cattle of I 3478
9: 4 die of all *that is* the children's of I. 3478
9: 6 of the cattle of the children of I died not 3478
9:26 where the children of I *were,* was there 3478
9:35 neither would he let the children of I go; 3478
10:20 that he would not let the children of I go. 3478
10:23 all the children of I had light in their 3478
11: 7 against any of the children of I shall not a 3478
11: 7 a difference between the Egyptians and I. 3478
11:10 that he would not let the children of I go 3478
12: 3 Speak ye unto all the congregation of I, 3478
12: 6 whole assembly of the congregation of I 3478
12:15 that soul shall be cut off from I. 3478
12:19 shall be cut off from the congregation of I, 3478
12:21 Moses called for all the elders of I, 3478
12:27 the houses of the children of I in Egypt, 3478
12:28 the children of I went away, and did as 3478
12:31 people, both you and the children of I, 3478
12:35 children of I did according to the word 3478
12:37 the children of I journeyed from Rameses 3478
12:40 Now the sojourning of the children of I, 3478
12:42 all the children of I in their generations. 3478
12:47 All the congregation of I shall keep it. 3478
12:50 Thus did all the children of I: 3478
12:51 *that* the LORD did bring the children of I 3478
13: 2 the womb among the children of I 3478
13:18 the children of I went up harnessed out 3478
13:19 for he had straitly sworn the children of I, 3478
14: 2 Speak unto the children of I, that they 3478
14: 3 For Pharaoh will say of the children of I, 3478
14: 5 that we have let I go from serving us? 3478
14: 8 and he pursued after the children of I: 3478
14: 8 children of I went out with a high hand. 3478
14:10 the children of I lift up their eyes, 3478
14:10 the children of I cried out unto the LORD, 3478
14:15 speak unto the children of I, that they go 3478
14:16 the children of I shall go on dry *ground* 3478
14:19 which went before the camp of I, 3478
14:20 camp of the Egyptians and the camp of I; 3478
14:22 the children of I went into the midst of 3478
14:25 Let us flee from the face of I; 3478
14:29 the children of I walked upon dry *land* in 3478
14:30 Thus the LORD saved I that day out of 3478
14:30 the Egyptians dead upon the sea 3478
14:31 I saw *that* great work which the LORD 3478
15: 1 the children of I this song unto the LORD, 3478
15:19 the children of I went on dry *land* in 3478
15:22 So Moses brought I from the Red sea, 3478
16: 1 all the congregation of the children of I 3478
16: 2 whole congregation of the children of I 3478
16: 3 the children of I said unto them, Would 3478
16: 6 and Aaron said unto all the children of I, 3478
16: 9 all the congregation of the children of I, 3478
16:10 whole congregation of the children of I, 3478
16:12 heard the murmurings of the children of I: 3478
16:15 the children of I saw *it,* they said one 3478

Ex 16:17 the children of I did so, and gathered, 3478
16:31 the house of I called the name thereof 3478
16:35 the children of I did eat manna forty years, 3478
17: 1 all the congregation of the children of I 3478
17: 5 and take with thee of the elders of I; 3478
17: 6 Moses did so in the sight of the elders of I. 3478
17: 7 because of the chiding of the children of I, 3478
17: 8 and fought with I in Rephidim. 3478
17:11 Moses held up his hand, that I prevailed: 3478
18: 1 for I his people, *and* that the LORD had 3478
18: 1 that the LORD had brought I out of 3478
18: 9 goodness which the LORD had done to I, 3478
18:12 Aaron came, and all the elders of I, to eat 3478
18:25 Moses chose able men out of all I, 3478
19: 1 when the children of I were gone forth 3478
19: 2 and there I camped before the mount. 3478
19: 3 house of Jacob, and tell the children of I; 3478
19: 6 thou shalt speak unto the children of I. 3478
20:22 Thus thou shalt say unto the children of I, 3478
24: 1 and Abihu, and seventy of the elders of I; 3478
24: 4 according to the twelve tribes of I. 3478
24: 5 he sent young men of the children of I, 3478
24: 9 and Abihu, and seventy of the elders of I: 3478
24:10 they saw the God of I: and *there was* 3478
24:11 the nobles of the children of I he laid 3478
24:17 the mount in the eyes of the children of I. 3478
25: 2 Speak unto the children of I, that they 3478
25:22 in commandment unto the children of I, 3478
27:20 thou shalt command the children of I, 3478
27:21 on the behalf of the children of I. 3478
28: 1 with him, from among the children of I, 3478
28: 9 on them the names of the children of I: 3478
28:11 stones with the names of the children of I: 3478
28:12 stones of memorial unto the children of I, 3478
28:21 be with the names of the children of I, 3478
28:29 I upon his heart before the LORD 3478
28:30 I upon his heart before the LORD 3478
28:38 of I shall hallow in all their holy gifts; 3478
29:28 a statute for ever from the children of I: 3478
29:28 of I of the sacrifice of their peace offerings, 3478
29:43 there I will meet with the children of I, 3478
29:45 I will dwell amongst the children of I, 3478
30:12 of the children of I *after their number,* 3478
30:16 the atonement money of the children of I, 3478
30:16 unto the children of I before the LORD, 3478
30:31 thou shalt speak unto the children of I, 3478
31:13 Speak thou also unto the children of I, 3478
31:16 Wherefore the children of I shall keep 3478
31:17 between me and the children of I for ever: 3478
32: 4 they said, These *be* thy gods, O I, 3478
32: 8 and said, These *be* thy gods, O I, 3478
32:13 Isaac, and I, thy servants, 3478
32:20 and made the children of I drink *of it.* 3478
32:27 unto them, Thus saith the LORD God of I, 3478
33: 5 Say unto the children of I, Ye *are* a 3478
33: 6 the children of I stript themselves of their 3478
34:23 before the Lord GOD, the God of I. 3478
34:27 made a covenant with thee and with I. 3478
34:30 and all the children of I saw Moses, 3478
34:32 afterward all the children of I came nigh: 3478
34:34 spake unto the children of I *that* which he 3478
34:35 the children of I saw the face of Moses, 3478
35: 1 congregation of the children of I together, 3478
35: 4 all the congregation of the children of I, 3478
35:20 all the congregation of the children of I 3478
35:29 The children of I brought a willing 3478
35:30 Moses said unto the children of I, See, 3478
36: 3 which the children of I had brought for 3478
39: 6 with the names of the children of I. 3478
39: 7 stones for a memorial to the children of I; 3478
39:14 to the names of the children of I, 3478
39:32 the children of I did according to all that 3478
39:42 so the children of I made all the work. 3478
40:36 the children of I went onward in all their 3478
40:38 by night, in the sight of all the house of I, 3478
Lev 1: 2 Speak unto the children of I, and say unto 3478
4: 2 Speak unto the children of I, saying, If a 3478
4:13 if the whole congregation of I sin through 3478
7:23 Speak unto the children of I, saying, 3478
7:29 Speak unto the children of I, saying, 3478
7:34 I from off the sacrifices of their peace 3478
7:34 for ever from among the children of I, 3478
7:36 to be given them of the children of I, 3478
7:38 I to offer their oblations unto the LORD, 3478
9: 1 and his sons, and the elders of I; 3478
9: 3 unto the children of I thou shalt speak, 3478
10: 6 let your brethren, the whole house of I, 3478
10:11 that ye may teach the children of I all 3478
10:14 of peace offerings of the children of I. 3478
11: 2 Speak unto the children of I, saying, 3478
12: 2 Speak unto the children of I, saying, If a 3478
15: 2 Speak unto the children of I, and say unto 3478
15:31 Thus shall ye separate the children of I 3478
16: 5 of two kids of the goats for a sin offering, 3478
16:16 of the uncleanness of the children of I, 3478
16:17 and for all the congregation of I. 3478
16:19 from the uncleanness of the children of I. 3478
16:21 him all the iniquities of the children of I, 3478
16:34 make an atonement for the children of I, 3478
17: 2 unto all the children of I, and say unto 3478
17: 3 man soever *there be* of the house of I, 3478
17: 5 the end that the children of I may bring 3478
17: 8 man *there be* of the house of I, 3478
17:10 man *there be* of the house of I, 3478
17:12 Therefore I said unto the children of I, 3478

Lev 17:13 man *there be* of the children of I, 3478
17:14 therefore I said unto the children of I, 3478
18: 2 Speak unto the children of I, and say unto 3478
19: 2 all the congregation of the children of I, 3478
20: 2 Again, thou shalt say to the children of I, 3478
20: 2 Whosoever *he be* of the children of I, 376+3478
20: 2 or of the strangers that sojourn in I, 3478
21:24 to his sons, and unto all the children of I. 3478
22: 2 from the holy *things* of the children of I, 3478
22: 3 the children of I hallow unto the LORD, 3478
22:15 the holy *things* of the children of I, 3478
22:18 unto all the children of I, and say unto 3478
22:18 Whatsoever *he be* of the house of I, 376+3478
22:18 house of Israel, or of the strangers in I, 3478
22:32 will be hallowed among the children of I: 3478
23: 2 Speak unto the children of I, and say unto 3478
23:10 Speak unto the children of I, and say unto 3478
23:24 Speak unto the children of I, saying, 3478
23:34 Speak unto the children of I, saying, 3478
23:43 made the children of I to dwell in booths, 3478
23:44 Moses declared unto the children of I 3478
24: 2 Command the children of I, that they 3478
24: 8 *being taken* from the children of I *by* an 3478
24:10 went out among the children of I: 3478
24:10 a man of I strove together in the camp; 3481
24:15 thou shalt speak unto the children of I, 3478
24:23 Moses spake to the children of I, that they 3478
24:23 the children of I did as the LORD 3478
25: 2 Speak unto the children of I, and say unto 3478
25:33 their possession among the children of I, 3478
25:46 over your brethren the children of I, 3478
25:55 For unto me the children of I *are* servants; 3478
26:46 the children of I in mount Sinai by the 3478
27: 2 Speak unto the children of I, and say unto 3478
27:34 Moses for the children of I in mount Sinai. 3478
Nu 1: 2 of all the congregation of the children of I, 3478
1: 3 all that *are able* to go forth *to* war in I 3478
1:16 of their fathers, heads of thousands in I. 3478
1:44 and Aaron numbered, and the princes of I, 3478
1:45 that were numbered of the children of I, 3478
1:45 all that *were able to* go forth *to* war in I; 3478
1:49 the sum of them among the children of I: 3478
1:52 the children of I shall pitch their tents, 3478
1:53 the congregation of the children of I: 3478
1:54 the children of I did according to all that 3478
2: 2 Every man of the children of I shall pitch 3478
2:32 children of I by the house of their fathers: 3478
2:33 not numbered among the children of I; 3478
2:34 the children of I did according to all that 3478
3: 8 the charge of the children of I, to do 3478
3: 9 given unto him out of the children of I. 3478
3:12 I instead of all the firstborn that openeth 3478
3:12 the matrix among the children of I 3478
3:13 I hallowed unto me all the firstborn in I, 3478
3:38 for the charge of the children of I; 3478
3:40 males of the children of I from a month 3478
3:41 all the firstborn among the children of I; 3478
3:41 among the cattle of the children of I. 3478
3:42 all the firstborn among the children of I, 3478
3:45 all the firstborn among the children of I, 3478
3:46 of the firstborn of the children of I, 3478
3:50 Of the firstborn of the children of I took 3478
4:46 and Aaron and the chief of I numbered, 3478
5: 2 Command the children of I, that they put 3478
5: 4 the children of I did so, and put them out 3478
5: 4 unto Moses, so did the children of I. 3478
5: 6 Speak unto the children of I, When a man 3478
5: 9 of all the holy *things* of the children of I, 3478
5:12 Speak unto the children of I, and say unto 3478
6: 2 Speak unto the children of I, and say unto 3478
6:23 this wise ye shall bless the children of I, 3478
6:27 shall put my name upon the children of I; 3478
7: 2 That the princes of I, heads of the house 3478
7:84 when it was anointed, by the princes of I: 3478
8: 6 the Levites from among the children of I, 3478
8: 9 assembly of the children of I together: 3478
8:10 the children of I shall put their hands 3478
8:11 LORD *for* an offering of the children of I, 3478
8:14 the Levites from among the children of I, 3478
8:16 unto me from among the children of I; 3478
8:16 *of* the firstborn of all the children of I, 3478
8:17 For all the firstborn of the children of I 3478
8:18 for all the firstborn among the children of I. 3478
8:19 to his sons from among the children of I, 3478
8:19 to do the service of the children of I in 3478
8:19 make an atonement for the children of I: 3478
8:19 be no plague among the children of I, 3478
8:19 when the children of I come nigh unto 3478
8:20 all the congregation of the children of I, 3478
8:20 so did the children of I unto them. 3478
9: 2 the children of I also keep the passover 3478
9: 4 Moses spake unto the children of I, 3478
9: 5 so did the children of I. 3478
9: 7 season among the children of I? 3478
9:10 Speak unto the children of I, saying, If 3478
9:17 then after that the children of I journeyed: 3478
9:17 there the children of I pitched their tents. 3478
9:18 of the LORD the children of I journeyed, 3478
9:19 the children of I kept the charge of 3478
9:22 the children of I abode in their tents, 3478
10: 4 *which are* heads of the thousands of I, 3478
10:12 the children of I took their journeys out 3478
10:28 the children of I according to their armies, 3478
10:29 the LORD hath spoken good concerning I. 3478
10:36 O LORD, *unto* the many thousands of I. 3478

Nu	11: 4 the children of I also wept again, and said,	3478
	11:16 unto me seventy men of the elders of I,	3478
	11:30 him into the camp, he and the elders of I.	3478
	13: 2 which I give unto the children of I:	3478
	13: 3 those men *were* heads of the children of I.	3478
	13:24 the children of I cut down from thence.	3478
	13:26 to all the congregation of the children of I,	3478
	13:32 they had searched unto the children of I,	3478
	14: 2 all the children of I murmured against	3478
	14: 5 of the congregation of the children of I.	3478
	14: 7 unto all the company of the children of I,	3478
	14:10 congregation before all the children of I.	3478
	14:27 heard the murmurings of the children of I,	3478
	14:39 these sayings unto all the children of I:	3478
	15: 2 Speak unto the children of I, and say unto	3478
	15:18 Speak unto the children of I, and say unto	3478
	15:25 all the congregation of the children of I,	3478
	15:26 all the congregation of the children of I,	3478
	15:29 that is born amongst the children of I,	3478
	15:32 while the children of I were in	3478
	15:38 Speak unto the children of I, and bid	3478
	16: 2 with certain of the children of I,	3478
	16: 9 that the God of I hath separated you from	3478
	16: 9 separated you from the congregation of I,	3478
	16:25 Abiram; and the elders of I followed him.	3478
	16:34 all I that *were* round about them fled at	3478
	16:38 they shall be a sign unto the children of I.	3478
	16:40 *To be* a memorial unto the children of I,	3478
	16:41 the children of I murmured against Moses	3478
	17: 2 Speak unto the children of I, and take of	3478
	17: 5 me the murmurings of the children of I,	3478
	17: 6 Moses spake unto the children of I,	3478
	17: 9 the LORD unto all the children of I:	3478
	17:12 the children of I spake unto Moses,	3478
	18: 5 no wrath any more upon the children of I.	3478
	18: 6 the Levites from among the children of I,	3478
	18: 8 the hallowed *things* of the children of I;	3478
	18:11 all the wave offerings of the children of I:	3478
	18:14 Every thing devoted in I shall be thine.	3478
	18:19 the children of I offer unto the LORD,	3478
	18:20 thine inheritance among the children of I.	3478
	18:21 Levi all the tenth in I for an inheritance,	3478
	18:22 Neither must the children of I henceforth	3478
	18:23 that among the children of I they have no	3478
	18:24 the tithes of the children of I, which they	3478
	18:24 Among the children of I they shall have	3478
	18:26 ye take of the children of I the tithes	3478
	18:28 which ye receive of the children of I;	3478
	18:32 the holy *things* of the children of I,	3478
	19: 2 saying, Speak unto the children of I,	3478
	19: 9 the children of I for a water of separation:	3478
	19:10 it shall be unto the children of I,	3478
	19:13 and that soul shall be cut off from I.	3478
	20: 1 came the children of I, *even* the whole	3478
	20:12 me in the eyes of the children of I,	3478
	20:13 the children of I strove with the LORD,	3478
	20:14 Thus saith thy brother I, Thou knowest	3478
	20:19 the children of I said unto him, We will	3478
	20:21 Thus Edom refused to give I passage	3478
	20:21 wherefore I turned away from him.	3478
	20:22 the children of I, *even* the whole	3478
	20:24 which I have given unto the children of I,	3478
	20:29 Aaron thirty days, *even* all the house of I.	3478
	21: 1 heard *tell* that I came *by* the way of	3478
	21: 1 he fought against I, and took *some* of	3478
	21: 2 I vowed a vow unto the LORD, and said,	3478
	21: 3 the LORD hearkened to the voice of I,	3478
	21: 6 bit the people; and much people of I died.	3478
	21:10 the children of I set forward, and pitched	3478
	21:17 I sang this song, Spring up, O well; sing	3478
	21:21 I sent messengers unto Sihon king of	3478
	21:23 Sihon would not suffer I to pass through	3478
	21:23 went out against I into the wilderness:	3478
	21:23 he came *to* Jahaz, and fought against I.	3478
	21:24 I smote him with the edge of the sword,	3478
	21:25 I took all these cities: and Israel dwelt in	3478
	21:25 I dwelt in all the cities of the Amorites.	3478
	21:31 Thus I dwelt in the land of the Amorites.	3478
	22: 1 the children of I set forward, and pitched	3478
	22: 2 Balak the son of Zippor saw all that I had	3478
	22: 3 distressed because of the children of I.	3478
	23: 7 curse me Jacob, and come, defy I.	3478
	23:10 and the number *of* the fourth part of I?	3478
	23:21 neither hath he seen perverseness in I:	3478
	23:23 neither *is there* any divination against I:	3478
	23:23 *this* time it shall be said of Jacob and of I,	3478
	24: 1 saw that it pleased the LORD to bless I,	3478
	24: 2 he saw I abiding *in his tents* according to	3478
	24: 5 tents, O Jacob, *and* thy tabernacles, O I!	3478
	24:17 Sceptre shall rise out of I, and shall smite	3478
	24:18 for his enemies; and I shall do valiantly.	3478
	25: 1 I abode in Shittim, and the people begun	3478
	25: 3 I joined himself unto Baal-peor:	3478
	25: 3 anger of the LORD was kindled against I.	3478
	25: 4 of the LORD may be turned away from I.	3478
	25: 5 Moses said unto the judges of I, Slay ye	3478
	25: 6 one of the children of I came and	3478
	25: 6 all the congregation of the children of I,	3478
	25: 8 he went after the man of I into the tent,	3478
	25: 8 the man of I, and the woman through her	3478
	25: 8 plague was stayed from the children of I.	3478
	25:11 my wrath away from the children of I,	3478
	25:11 I consumed not the children of I in my	3478
	25:13 made an atonement for the children of I.	3478
	26: 2 all the congregation of the children of I,	3478

Nu	26: 2 all that *are able* to go *to* war in I.	3478
	26: 4 commanded Moses and the children of I,	3478
	26: 5 Reuben, the eldest son of I: the children	3478
	26:51 were the numbered of the children of I,	3478
	26:62 not numbered among the children of I,	3478
	26:62 given them among the children of I.	3478
	26:63 who numbered the children of I in	3478
	26:64 when they numbered the children of I in	3478
	27: 8 thou shalt speak unto the children of I,	3478
	27:11 it shall be unto the children of I a statute	3478
	27:12 which I have given unto the children of I.	3478
	27:20 all the congregation of the children of I	3478
	27:21 he, and all the children of I with him,	3478
	28: 2 Command the children of I, and say unto	3478
	29:40 Moses told the children of I according to	3478
	30: 1 of the tribes concerning the children of I,	3478
	31: 2 Avenge the children of I of the Midianites:	3478
	31: 4 throughout all the tribes of I, shall ye send	3478
	31: 5 were delivered out of the thousands of I,	3478
	31: 9 the children of I took *all* the women of	3478
	31:12 unto the congregation of the children of I,	3478
	31:16 Behold, these caused the children of I,	3478
	31:54 *for* a memorial for the children of I before	3478
	32: 4 LORD smote before the congregation of I,	3478
	32: 7 I from going over into the land which	3478
	32: 9 discouraged the heart of the children of I,	3478
	32:13 the LORD'S anger was kindled against I,	3478
	32:14 the fierce anger of the LORD toward I.	3478
	32:17 go ready armed before the children of I,	3478
	32:18 until the children of I have inherited	3478
	32:22 guiltless before the LORD, and before I:	3478
	32:28 fathers of the tribes of the children of I:	3478
	33: 1 These *are* the journeys of the children of I,	3478
	33: 3 I went out with a high hand in the sight	3478
	33: 5 the children of I removed from Rameses,	3478
	33:38 in the fortieth year after the children of I	3478
	33:40 heard of the coming of the children of I.	3478
	33:51 Speak unto the children of I, and say unto	3478
	34: 2 Command the children of I, and say unto	3478
	34:13 Moses commanded the children of I,	3478
	34:29 the children of I in the land of Canaan.	3478
	35: 2 Command the children of I, that they give	3478
	35: 8 *be* of the possession of the children of I:	3478
	35:10 Speak unto the children of I, and say unto	3478
	35:15 *both* for the children of I, and for	3478
	35:34 the LORD dwell among the children of I.	3478
	36: 1 the chief fathers of the children of I:	3478
	36: 2 an inheritance by lot to the children of I:	3478
	36: 3 of the *other* tribes of the children of I,	3478
	36: 4 the jubile of the children of I shall be,	3478
	36: 5 Moses commanded the children of I	3478
	36: 7 children of I remove from tribe to tribe:	3478
	36: 7 every one of the children of I shall keep	3478
	36: 8 in any tribe of the children of I,	3478
	36: 8 the children of I may enjoy every man	3478
	36: 9 every one of the children of I shall keep	3478
	36:13 I in the plains of Moab by Jordan *near*	3478
Dt	1: 1 all I on *this* side Jordan in the wilderness,	3478
	1: 3 *that* Moses spake unto the children of I,	3478
	1:38 for he shall cause I to inherit it.	3478
	2:12 as I did unto the land of his possession,	3478
	3:18 before your brethren the children of I,	3478
	4: 1 Now therefore hearken, O I, unto	3478
	4:44 which Moses set before the children of I:	3478
	4:45 which Moses spake unto the children of I,	3478
	4:46 whom Moses and the children of I smote,	3478
	5: 1 Moses called all I, and said unto them,	3478
	5: 1 Hear, O I, the statutes and judgments	3478
	6: 3 O I, and observe to do *it;* that it may be	3478
	6: 4 Hear, O I: The LORD our God *is* one	3478
	9: 1 Hear, O I: Thou art to pass over Jordan	3478
	10: 6 the children of I took their journey from	3478
	10:12 now, I, what doth the LORD thy God	3478
	11: 6 in their possession, in the midst of all I:	3478
	13:11 all I shall hear, and fear, and shall do no	3478
	17: 4 *that* such abomination is wrought in I:	3478
	17:12 and thou shalt put away the evil from I.	3478
	17:20 he, and his children, in the midst of I.	3478
	18: 1 shall have no part nor inheritance with I:	3478
	18: 6 come from any of thy gates out of all I,	3478
	19:13 away *the guilt of* innocent blood from I,	3478
	20: 3 shall say unto them, Hear, O I,	3478
	21: 8 Be merciful, O LORD, unto thy people I,	3478
	21:21 among you; and all I shall hear, and fear.	3478
	22:19 up an evil name upon a virgin of I:	3478
	22:21 because she hath wrought folly in I,	3478
	22:22 so shalt thou put away evil from I.	3478
	23:17 shall be no whore of the daughters of I,	3478
	23:17 of Israel, nor a sodomite of the sons of I.	3478
	24: 7 any of his brethren of the children of I,	3478
	25: 6 is dead, that his name be not put out of I.	3478
	25: 7 to raise up unto his brother a name in I,	3478
	25:10 his name shall be called in I, The house	3478
	26:15 bless thy people I, and the land which	3478
	27: 1 Moses with the elders of I commanded	3478
	27: 9 the priests the Levites spake unto all I,	3478
	27: 9 saying, Take heed, and hearken, O I;	3478
	27:14 unto all the men of I *with* a loud voice,	3478
	29: 1 with the children of I in the land of Moab,	3478
	29: 2 Moses called unto all I, and said unto	3478
	29:10 and your officers, *with* all the men of I,	3478
	29:21 him unto evil out of all the tribes of I,	3478
	31: 1 and spake these words unto all I.	3478
	31: 7 unto him in the sight of all I, Be strong	3478
	31: 9 of the LORD, and unto all the elders of I.	3478

Dt	31:11 When all I is come to appear before	3478
	31:11 shalt read this law before all I in their	3478
	31:19 for you, and teach it the children of I:	3478
	31:19 a witness for me against the children of I.	3478
	31:22 same day, and taught it the children of I.	3478
	31:23 for thou shalt bring the children of I into	3478
	31:30 congregation of I the words of this song,	3478
	32: 8 to the number of the children of I.	3478
	32:45 an end of speaking all these words to all I:	3478
	32:49 which I give unto the children of I for a	3478
	32:51 of I at the waters of Meribah-Kadesh,	3478
	32:51 me not in the midst of the children of I.	3478
	32:52 the land which I give the children of I.	3478
	33: 1 blessed the children of I before his death.	3478
	33: 5 the tribes of I were gathered together.	3478
	33:10 teach Jacob thy judgments, and I thy law:	3478
	33:21 of the LORD, and his judgments with I.	3478
	33:28 I then shall dwell *in* safety alone:	3478
	33:29 Happy *art* thou, O I: who *is* like unto	3478
	34: 8 the children of I wept for Moses in	3478
	34: 9 the children of I hearkened unto him,	3478
	34:10 there arose not a prophet since in I like	3478
	34:12 which Moses shewed in the sight of all I.	3478
Jos	1: 2 do give to them, *even* to the children of I.	3478
	2: 2 children of I to search out the country.	3478
	3: 1 he and all the children of I,	3478
	3: 7 begin to magnify thee in the sight of all I,	3478
	3: 9 Joshua said unto the children of I,	3478
	3:12 take ye twelve men out of the tribes of I,	3478
	4: 4 he had prepared of the children of I,	3478
	4: 5 number of the tribes of the children of I:	3478
	4: 7 a memorial unto the children of I for ever.	3478
	4: 8 the children of I did so as Joshua	3478
	4: 8 number of the tribes of the children of I,	3478
	4:12 over armed before the children of I,	3478
	4:14 magnified Joshua in the sight of all I;	3478
	4:21 he spake unto the children of I, saying,	3478
	4:22 I came over this Jordan on dry *land.*	3478
	5: 1 of Jordan from before the children of I,	3478
	5: 1 any more, because of the children of I.	3478
	5: 2 circumcise again the children of I	3478
	5: 3 circumcised the children of I at the hill of	3478
	5: 6 For the children of I walked forty years in	3478
	5:10 the children of I encamped in Gilgal,	3478
	5:12 neither had the children of I manna any	3478
	6: 1 shut up because of the children of I:	3478
	6:18 make the camp of I a curse, and trouble	3478
	6:23 and left them without the camp of I.	3478
	6:25 she dwelleth in I *even* unto this day;	3478
	7: 1 the children of I committed a trespass in	3478
	7: 1 was kindled against the children of I.	3478
	7: 6 he and the elders of I, and put dust upon	3478
	7: 8 when I turneth *their* backs before their	3478
	7:11 I hath sinned, and they have also	3478
	7:12 the children of I could not stand	3478
	7:13 for thus saith the LORD God of I,	3478
	7:13 accursed thing in the midst of thee, O I:	3478
	7:15 and because he hath wrought folly in I.	3478
	7:16 morning, and brought I by their tribes;	3478
	7:19 glory to the LORD God of I,	3478
	7:20 I have sinned against the LORD God of I,	3478
	7:23 unto all the children of I, and laid them	3478
	7:24 Joshua, and all I with him, took Achan	3478
	7:25 all I stoned him *with* stones,	3478
	8:10 and went up, he and the elders of I,	3478
	8:14 the men of the city went out against I to	3478
	8:15 all I *made as if they* were beaten before	3478
	8:17 in Ai or Beth-el, that went not out after I:	3478
	8:17 left the city open, and pursued after I.	3478
	8:21 all I saw that the ambush had taken	3478
	8:22 so they were in the midst of I, some on	3478
	8:24 when I had made an end of slaying all	3478
	8:27 the spoil of that city I took for a prey unto	3478
	8:30 unto the LORD God of I in mount Ebal,	3478
	8:31 the LORD commanded the children of I,	3478
	8:32 wrote in the presence of the children of I	3478
	8:33 all I, and their elders, and officers,	3478
	8:33 that they should bless the people of I.	3478
	8:35 read not before all the congregation of I,	3478
	9: 2 to fight with Joshua and with I, *with* one	3478
	9: 6 said unto him, and to the men of I, We	3478
	9: 7 the men of I said unto the Hivites,	3478
	9:17 the children of I journeyed, and came	3478
	9:18 the children of I smote them not, because	3478
	9:18 sworn unto them by the LORD God of I.	3478
	9:19 sworn unto them by the LORD God of I:	3478
	9:26 them out of the hand of the children of I,	3478
	10: 1 of Gibeon had made peace with I,	3478
	10: 4 with Joshua and the children of I.	3478
	10:10 And the LORD discomfited them before I,	3478
	10:11 as they fled from before I, *and* were	3478
	10:11 the children of I slew with the sword.	3478
	10:12 up the Amorites before the children of I,	3478
	10:12 he said in the sight of I, Sun, stand thou	3478
	10:14 of a man: for the LORD fought for I.	3478
	10:15 Joshua returned, and all I with him,	3478
	10:20 the children of I had made an end of	3478
	10:21 his tongue against any of the children of I.	3478
	10:24 that Joshua called for all the men of I,	3478
	10:29 all I with him, *unto* Libnah,	3478
	10:30 the king thereof, into the hand of I;	3478
	10:31 all I with him, unto Lachish,	3478
	10:32 delivered Lachish into the hand of I,	3478
	10:34 passed on to Eglon, and all I with him;	3478
	10:36 and all I with him, unto Hebron;	3478

I

Ref	Text	Strong's
Jos	10:38 and all I with him, to Debir;	3478
	10:40 as the LORD God of I commanded.	3478
	10:42 the LORD God of I fought for Israel.	3478
	10:42 the LORD God of Israel fought for I.	3478
	10:43 Joshua returned, and all I with him,	3478
	11: 5 at the waters of Merom, to fight against I.	3478
	11: 6 will I deliver them up all slain before I:	3478
	11: 8 LORD delivered them into the hand of I,	3478
	11:13 I burned none of them, save Hazor only;	3478
	11:14 the children of I took for a prey unto	3478
	11:16 the mountain of I, and the valley of	3478
	11:19 that made peace with the children of I,	3478
	11:20 that *they* should come against I *in* battle,	3478
	11:21 of Judah, and from all the mountains of I:	3478
	11:22 left in the land of the children of I:	3478
	11:23 Joshua gave it for an inheritance unto I	3478
	12: 1 which the children of I smote,	3478
	12: 6 of the LORD and the children of I smite:	3478
	12: 7 the children of I smote on *this* side Jordan	3478
	12: 7 which Joshua gave unto the tribes of I *for*	3478
	13: 6 I drive out from before the children of I:	3478
	13:13 the children of I expelled not	3478
	13:14 the sacrifices of the LORD God of I made	3478
	13:22 did the children of I slay with the sword	3478
	13:33 the LORD God of I *was* their inheritance,	3478
	14: 1 of I inherited in the land of Canaan,	3478
	14: 1 fathers of the tribes of I,	3478
	14: 5 so the children of I did, and they divided	3478
	14:10 while *the children of* I wandered in	3478
	14:14 he wholly followed the LORD God of I.	3478
	17:13 the children of I were waxen strong,	3478
	18: 1 whole congregation of the children of I	3478
	18: 2 there remained among the children of I	3478
	18: 3 Joshua said unto the children of I,	3478
	18:10 children of I according to their divisions.	3478
	19:49 the children of I gave an inheritance to	3478
	19:51 fathers of the tribes of the children of I,	3478
	20: 2 Speak to the children of I, saying,	3478
	20: 9 cities appointed for all the children of I,	3478
	21: 1 fathers of the tribes of the children of I;	3478
	21: 3 the children of I gave unto the Levites	3478
	21: 8 the children of I gave by lot unto	3478
	21:41 possession of the children of I *were* forty	3478
	21:43 the LORD gave unto I all the land which	3478
	21:45 the LORD had spoken unto the house of I;	3478
	22: 9 departed from the children of I out of	3478
	22:11 the children of I heard say, Behold,	3478
	22:11 at the passage of the children of I.	3478
	22:12 when the children of I heard *of it,*	3478
	22:12 I gathered themselves together *at* Shiloh,	3478
	22:13 the children of I sent unto the children of	3478
	22:14 a prince throughout all the tribes of I;	3478
	22:14 of their fathers among the thousands of I,	3478
	22:16 ye have committed against the God of I,	3478
	22:18 wroth with the whole congregation of I.	3478
	22:20 wrath fell on all the congregation of I?	3478
	22:21 said unto the heads of the thousands of I,	3478
	22:22 of gods, he knoweth, and I he shall know;	3478
	22:24 have you to do with the LORD God of I?	3478
	22:30 heads of the thousands of I which *were*	3478
	22:31 ye have delivered the children of I out	3478
	22:32 to the children of I, and brought them	3478
	22:33 the thing pleased the children of I;	3478
	22:33 the children of I blessed God, and did not	3478
	23: 1 unto I from all their enemies round about,	3478
	23: 2 Joshua called for all I, *and* for their elders,	3478
	24: 1 Joshua gathered all the tribes of I to	3478
	24: 1 called for the elders of I, and for their	3478
	24: 2 Thus saith the LORD God of I,	3478
	24: 9 arose and warred against I, and sent and	3478
	24:23 your heart unto the LORD God of I.	3478
	24:31 I served the LORD all the days of Joshua,	3478
	24:31 of the LORD, that he had done for I.	3478
	24:32 which the children of I brought up out of	3478
Jdg	1: 1 that the children of I asked the LORD,	3478
	1:28 it came to pass, when I was strong,	3478
	2: 4 these words unto all the children of I,	3478
	2: 6 the children of I went every man unto his	3478
	2: 7 works of the LORD, that he did for I.	3478
	2:10 yet the works which he had done for I.	3478
	2:11 the children of I did evil in the sight of	3478
	2:14 the anger of the LORD was hot against I,	3478
	2:20 the anger of the LORD was hot against I;	3478
	2:22 That through them I may prove I,	3478
	3: 1 which the LORD left, to prove I by them,	3478
	3: 1 *even* as many of *I* as had not known all	NIH
	3: 2 of the children of I might know,	3478
	3: 4 they were to prove I by them, to know	3478
	3: 5 the children of I dwelt among	3478
	3: 7 the children of I did evil in the sight of	3478
	3: 8 the anger of the LORD was hot against I,	3478
	3: 8 the children of I served	3478
	3: 9 when the children of I cried unto	3478
	3: 9 raised up a deliverer to the children of I,	3478
	3:10 and he judged I, and went out to war:	3478
	3:12 the children of I did evil again in the sight	3478
	3:12 Eglon the king of Moab against I,	3478
	3:13 and smote I, and possessed the city of	3478
	3:14 So the children of I served Eglon the king	3478
	3:15 when the children of I cried unto	3478
	3:15 by him the children of I sent a present	3478
	3:27 the children of I went down with him	3478
	3:30 was subdued that day under the hand of I.	3478
	3:31 with an ox goad: and he also delivered I.	3478
	4: 1 the children of I again did evil in the sight	3478

Ref	Text	Strong's
Jdg	4: 3 the children of I cried unto the LORD:	3478
	4: 3 he mightily oppressed the children of I.	3478
	4: 4 of Lapidoth, she judged I at that time.	3478
	4: 5 the children of I came up to her for	3478
	4: 6 hath not the LORD God of I commanded,	3478
	4:23 king of Canaan before the children of I.	3478
	4:24 the hand of the children of I prospered,	3478
	5: 2 Praise ye the LORD for the avenging of I,	3478
	5: 3 I will sing *praise* to the LORD God of I.	3478
	5: 5 Sinai from before the LORD God of I.	3478
	5: 7 ceased in I, until that I Deborah arose,	3478
	5: 7 Deborah arose, that I arose a mother in I.	3478
	5: 8 or spear seen among forty thousand in I?	3478
	5: 9 My heart *is* toward the governors of I,	3478
	5:11 *the* inhabitants of his villages in I:	3478
	6: 1 the children of I did evil in the sight of	3478
	6: 2 the hand of Midian prevailed against I:	3478
	6: 2 of the Midianites the children of I made	3478
	6: 3 *so* it was, when I had sown, that	3478
	6: 4 left no sustenance for I, neither sheep,	3478
	6: 6 I was greatly impoverished because of	3478
	6: 6 the children of I cried unto the LORD.	3478
	6: 7 when the children of I cried unto	3478
	6: 8 sent a prophet unto the children of I,	3478
	6: 8 unto them, Thus saith the LORD God of I,	3478
	6:14 thou shalt save I from the hand of	3478
	6:15 O my Lord, wherewith shall I save I?	3478
	6:36 If thou wilt save I by mine hand, as thou	3478
	6:37 shall I know that thou wilt save I by mine	3478
	7: 2 lest I vaunt themselves against me, saying,	3478
	7: 8 he sent all *the rest of* I every man unto	3478
	7:14 of Gideon the son of Joash, a man of I:	3478
	7:15 returned into the host of I, and said, Arise,	3478
	7:23 the men of I gathered themselves together	3478
	8:22 the men of I said unto Gideon, Rule thou	3478
	8:27 all I went thither a whoring after it:	3478
	8:28 Midian subdued before the children of I,	3478
	8:33 that the children of I turned again,	3478
	8:34 the children of I remembered not	3478
	8:35 goodness which he had shewed unto I.	3478
	9:22 Abimelech had reigned three years over I,	3478
	9:55 when the men of I saw that Abimelech	3478
	10: 1 after Abimelech there arose to defend I	3478
	10: 2 he judged I twenty and three years.	3478
	10: 3 and judged I twenty and two years.	3478
	10: 6 the children of I did evil again in the sight	3478
	10: 7 the anger of the LORD was hot against I,	3478
	10: 8 vexed and oppressed the children of I:	3478
	10: 8 all the children of I that *were* on the	3478
	10: 9 of Ephraim; so that I was sore distressed.	3478
	10:10 the children of I cried unto the LORD,	3478
	10:11 And the LORD said unto the children of I,	3478
	10:15 And the children of I said unto the LORD,	3478
	10:16 his soul was grieved for the misery of I.	3478
	10:17 the children of I assembled themselves	3478
	11: 4 children of Ammon made war against I.	3478
	11: 5 children of Ammon made war against I,	3478
	11:13 Because I took away my land, when they	3478
	11:15 I took not away the land of Moab,	3478
	11:16 when I came up from Egypt,	3478
	11:17 I sent messengers unto the king of Edom,	3478
	11:17 not consent: and I abode in Kadesh.	3478
	11:19 I sent messengers unto Sihon king of	3478
	11:19 I said unto him, Let us pass, we pray thee,	3478
	11:20 Sihon trusted not I to pass through his	3478
	11:20 pitched in Jahaz, and fought against I.	3478
	11:21 the LORD God of I delivered Sihon and	3478
	11:21 and all his people into the hand of I,	3478
	11:21 I possessed all the land of the Amorites,	3478
	11:23 So now the LORD God of I hath	3478
	11:23 the Amorites from before his people I,	3478
	11:25 did he ever strive against I, or did he ever	3478
	11:26 While I dwelt in Heshbon and her towns,	3478
	11:27 judge *this* day between the children of I	3478
	11:33 were subdued before the children of I.	3478
	11:39 knew no man. And it was a custom in I,	3478
	11:40 *That* the daughters of I went yearly to	3478
	12: 7 Jephthah judged I six years. Then died	3478
	12: 9 for his sons. And he judged I seven years.	3478
	12:11 after him Elon, a Zebulonite, judged I;	3478
	12:11 judged Israel; and he judged I ten years.	3478
	12:13 the son of Hillel, a Pirathonite, judged I.	3478
	12:14 ten ass colts: and he judged I eight years.	3478
	13: 1 the children of I did evil again in the sight	3478
	13: 5 he shall begin to deliver I out of the hand	3478
	14: 4 time the Philistines had dominion over I.	3478
	15:20 he judged I in the days of the Philistines	3478
	16:31 his father. And he judged I twenty years.	3478
	17: 6 In those days *there was* no king in I,	3478
	18: 1 In those days *there was* no king in I:	3478
	18: 1 fallen unto them among the tribes of I.	3478
	18:19 be a priest unto a tribe and a family in I?	3478
	18:29 of Dan their father, who was born unto I:	3478
	19: 1 those days, when *there was* no king in I,	3478
	19:12 a stranger, that *is* not of the children of I;	3478
	19:29 and sent her into all the coasts of I.	3478
	19:30 I came up out of the land of Egypt unto	3478
	20: 1 all the children of I went out,	3478
	20: 2 of all the people, *even* of all the tribes of I,	3478
	20: 3 children of I were gone up *to* Mizpeh.)	3478
	20: 3 said the children of I, Tell *us,* how was	3478
	20: 6 all the country of the inheritance of I.	3478
	20: 6 have committed lewdness and folly in I.	3478
	20: 7 Behold, ye *are* all children of I; give here	3478

Ref	Text	Strong's
Jdg	20:10 an hundred throughout all the tribes of I,	3478
	20:10 all the folly that they have wrought in I.	3478
	20:11 So all the men of I were gathered against	3478
	20:12 tribes of I sent men through all the tribe	3478
	20:13 them to death, and put away evil from I.	3478
	20:13 voice of their brethren the children of I.	3478
	20:14 go out to battle against the children of I.	3478
	20:17 the men of I, beside Benjamin,	3478
	20:18 the children of I arose, and went up *to*	3478
	20:19 the children of I rose up in the morning,	3478
	20:20 the men of I went out to battle against	3478
	20:20 the men of I put *themselves* in array to	3478
	20:22 the people the men of I encouraged	3478
	20:23 (And the children of I went up and	3478
	20:24 the children of I came near against	3478
	20:25 children of I again eighteen thousand	3478
	20:26 all the children of I, and all the people,	3478
	20:27 the children of I inquired of the LORD,	3478
	20:29 I set liers in wait round about Gibeah.	3478
	20:30 the children of I went up against	3478
	20:31 Gibeah in the field, about thirty men of I.	3478
	20:32 the children of I said, Let us flee,	3478
	20:33 all the men of I rose up out of their place,	3478
	20:33 the liers in wait of I came forth out of	3478
	20:34 ten thousand chosen men out of all I,	3478
	20:35 the LORD smote Benjamin before I:	3478
	20:35 the children of I destroyed of	3478
	20:36 for the men of I gave place to	3478
	20:38 an appointed sign between the men of I	3478
	20:39 when the men of I retired in the battle,	3478
	20:39 kill of the men of I about thirty persons:	3478
	20:41 when the men of I turned *again,* the men	3478
	20:42 men of I unto the way of the wilderness;	3478
	20:48 the men of I turned again upon the	3478
	21: 1 Now the men of I had sworn in Mizpeh,	3478
	21: 3 said, O LORD God of I, why is this come	3478
	21: 3 of Israel, why is this come to pass in I,	3478
	21: 3 should be to day one tribe lacking in I?	3478
	21: 5 The children of I said, Who *is there* among	3478
	21: 5 Who *is there* among all the tribes of I that	3478
	21: 6 the children of I repented them for	3478
	21: 6 There is one tribe cut off from I *this* day.	3478
	21: 8 What one *is there* of the tribes of I that	3478
	21:15 had made a breach in the tribes of I.	3478
	21:17 that a tribe be not destroyed out of I.	3478
	21:18 for the children of I have sworn, saying,	3478
	21:24 the children of I departed thence at that	3478
	21:25 In those days *there was* no king in I:	3478
Ru	2:12 be given thee of the LORD God of I,	3478
	4: 7 in former time in I concerning redeeming	3478
	4: 7 and this *was* a testimony in I.	3478
	4:11 which two did build the house of I.	3478
	4:14 that his name may be famous in I.	3478
1Sa	1:17 the God of I grant *thee* thy petition that	3478
	2:22 and heard all that his sons did unto all I;	3478
	2:28 I choose him out of all the tribes of I to	3478
	2:28 offerings made by fire of the children of I?	3478
	2:29 chiefest of all the offerings of I my people?	3478
	2:30 Wherefore the LORD God of I saith,	3478
	2:32 in all *the wealth* which *God* shall give I:	3478
	3:11 to Samuel, Behold, I will do a thing in I,	3478
	3:20 all I from Dan even to Beer-sheba knew	3478
	4: 1 the word of Samuel came to all I.	3478
	4: 1 Now I went out against the Philistines to	3478
	4: 2 put themselves in array against I:	3478
	4: 2 I was smitten before the Philistines:	3478
	4: 3 come into the camp, the elders of I said,	3478
	4: 5 all I shouted *with* a great shout, so that	3478
	4:10 I was smitten, and they fled every man	3478
	4:10 there fell of I thirty thousand footmen.	3478
	4:17 I is fled before the Philistines,	3478
	4:18 heavy. And he had judged I forty years.	3478
	4:21 The glory is departed from I:	3478
	4:22 she said, The glory is departed from I:	3478
	5: 7 The ark of the God of I shall not abide	3478
	5: 8 shall we do with the ark of the God of I?	3478
	5: 8 Let the ark of the God of I be carried	3478
	5: 8 they carried the ark of the God of I about	3478
	5:10 brought about the ark of the God of I to	3478
	5:11 Send away the ark of the God of I,	3478
	6: 3 If ye send away the ark of the God of I,	3478
	6: 5 and ye shall give glory unto the God of I:	3478
	7: 2 all the house of I lamented after	3478
	7: 3 Samuel spake unto all the house of I,	3478
	7: 4 the children of I did put away Baalim and	3478
	7: 5 Gather all I to Mizpeh, and I will pray for	3478
	7: 6 Samuel judged the children of I in	3478
	7: 7 of I were gathered together to Mizpeh,	3478
	7: 7 lords of the Philistines went up against I.	3478
	7: 7 the children of I heard *it,* they were	3478
	7: 8 children of I said to Samuel, Cease not	3478
	7: 9 Samuel cried unto the LORD for I;	3478
	7:10 Philistines drew near to battle against I:	3478
	7:10 and they were smitten before I.	3478
	7:11 the men of I went out of Mizpeh,	3478
	7:13 they came no more into the coast of I:	3478
	7:14 had taken from I were restored to Israel,	3478
	7:14 had taken from Israel were restored to I,	3478
	7:14 the coasts thereof did I deliver out of	3478
	7:14 there was peace between I and	3478
	7:15 Samuel judged I all the days of his life.	3478
	7:16 and judged I in all those places.	3478
	7:17 he judged I; and there he built an altar	3478
	8: 1 that he made his sons judges over I.	3478
	8: 4 all the elders of I gathered themselves	3478

1Sa 8:22 Samuel said unto the men of I, Go ye	3478	
9: 2 *there was* not among the children of I a	3478	
9: 9 (Beforetime in I, when a man went to	3478	
9:16 anoint him to be captain over my people I,	3478	
9:20 on whom *is* all the desire of I? *Is it* not on	3478	
9:21 of the smallest of the tribes of I?	3478	
10:18 said unto the children of I, Thus saith	3478	
10:18 Thus saith the Lord God of I, I brought	3478	
10:18 I brought up I out of Egypt,	3478	
10:20 Samuel had caused all the tribes of I	3478	
11: 2 and lay it *for* a reproach upon all I.	3478	
11: 3 send messengers unto all the coasts of I:	3478	
11: 7 sent *them* throughout all the coasts of I	3478	
11: 8 the children of I were three hundred	3478	
11:13 the Lord hath wrought salvation in I.	3478	
11:15 and all the men of I rejoiced greatly.	3478	
12: 1 Samuel said unto all I, Behold, I have	3478	
13: 1 when he had reigned two years over I,	3478	
13: 2 Saul chose him three thousand *men* of I;	3478	
13: 4 all I heard say *that* Saul had smitten a	3478	
13: 4 *that* I also was had in abomination with	3478	
13: 5 themselves together to fight with I,	3478	
13: 6 When the men of I saw that they were in	3478	
13:13 established thy kingdom upon I for ever.	3478	
13:19 smith found throughout all the land of I:	3478	
14:12 hath delivered them into the hand of I.	3478	
14:18 was at that time with the children of I.	3478	
14:22 Likewise all the men of I which had hid	3478	
14:23 So the Lord saved I that day:	3478	
14:24 the men of I were distressed that day:	3478	
14:37 wilt thou deliver them into the hand of I?	3478	
14:39 For, *as* the Lord liveth, which saveth I,	3478	
14:40 said he unto all I, Be ye on one side,	3478	
14:41 Saul said unto the Lord God of I,	3478	
14:45 hath wrought this great salvation in I?	3478	
14:47 So Saul took the kingdom over I,	3478	
14:48 delivered I out of the hands of them that	3478	
15: 1 thee to be king over his people, over I:	3478	
15: 2 I remember *that* which Amalek did to I,	3478	
15: 6 shewed kindness to all the children of I,	3478	
15:17 thou not *made* the head of the tribes of I,	3478	
15:17 and the Lord anointed thee king over I?	3478	
15:26 hath rejected thee from being king over I.	3478	
15:28 The Lord hath rent the kingdom of I	3478	
15:29 also the Strength of I will not lie nor	3478	
15:30 and before I, and turn again with me,	3478	
15:35 that he had made Saul king over I.	3478	
16: 1 I have rejected him from reigning over I?	3478	
17: 2 and the men of I were gathered together,	3478	
17: 3 I stood on a mountain on the other side:	3478	
17: 8 he stood and cried unto the armies of I,	3478	
17:10 I defy the armies of I this day;	3478	
17:11 all I heard those words of the Philistine,	3478	
17:19 Now Saul, and they, and all the men of I,	3478	
17:21 I and the Philistines had put *the battle*	3478	
17:24 all the men of I, when they saw the man	3478	
17:25 the men of I said, Have ye seen this man	3478	
17:25 surely to defy I is he come up: and it shall	3478	
17:25 and make his father's house free in I.	3478	
17:26 and taketh away the reproach from I?	3478	
17:45 the God of the armies of I, whom thou	3478	
17:46 earth may know that there is a God in I.	3478	
17:52 the men of I and of Judah arose,	3478	
17:53 the children of I returned from chasing	3478	
18: 6 that the women came out of all cities of I,	3478	
18:16 all I and Judah loved David, because	3478	
18:18 what *is* my life, *or* my father's family in I,	3478	
19: 5 Lord wrought a great salvation for all I:	3478	
20:12 said unto David, O Lord God of I,	3478	
23:10 said unto David, O Lord God of I,	3478	
23:11 O Lord God of I, I beseech thee, tell thy	3478	
23:17 thou shalt be king over I, and I shall be	3478	
24: 2 three thousand chosen men out of all I,	3478	
24:14 After whom is the king of I come out?	3478	
24:20 the kingdom of I shall be established in	3478	
25:30 shall have appointed thee ruler over I;	3478	
25:32 Blessed *be* the Lord God of I,	3478	
25:34 very deed, *as* the Lord God of I liveth,	3478	
26: 2 having three thousand chosen men of I	3478	
26:15 who *is* like to thee in I? wherefore then	3478	
26:20 for the king of I is come out to seek a flea,	3478	
27: 1 to seek me any more in any coast of I.	3478	
27:12 hath made his people I utterly to abhor	3478	
28: 1 together for warfare, to fight with I.	3478	
28: 3 all I had lamented him, and buried him in	3478	
28: 4 Saul gathered all I together,	3478	
28:19 Moreover the Lord will also deliver I	3478	
28:19 the Lord also shall deliver the host of I,	3478	
29: 3 David, the servant of Saul the king of I,	3478	
30:25 and an ordinance for I unto this day.	3478	
31: 1 Now the Philistines fought against I:	3478	
31: 1 the men of I fled from before	3478	
31: 7 when the men of I that were on the	3478	
31: 7 saw that the men of I fled, and that Saul	3478	
2Sa 1: 3 Out of the camp of I am I escaped.	3478	
1:12 of the Lord, and for the house of I,	3478	
1:19 The beauty of I *is* slain upon thy high	3478	
1:24 Ye daughters of I, weep over Saul,	3478	
2: 9 and over Benjamin, and over all I.	3478	
2:10 years old when he *began* to reign over I,	3478	
2:17 Abner was beaten, and the men of I,	3478	
2:28 stood still, and pursued after I no more,	3478	
3:10 to set up the throne of David over I and	3478	
3:12 with thee, to bring about all I unto thee.	3478	
3:17 had communication with the elders of I,	3478	

2Sa 3:18 people I out of the hand of the Philistines,	3478	
3:19 in Hebron all that seemed good to I,	3478	
3:21 will gather all I unto my lord the king,	3478	
3:37 all I understood that day that it was not of	3478	
3:38 and a great *man* fallen this day in I?	3478	
5: 1 came all the tribes of I to David unto	3478	
5: 2 he that leddest out and broughtest in I:	3478	
5: 2 Thou shalt feed my people I, and thou	3478	
5: 2 and thou shalt be a captain over I.	3478	
5: 3 So all the elders of I came to the king to	3478	
5: 3 and they anointed David king over I.	3478	
5: 5 and three years over all I and Judah.	3478	
5:12 Lord had established him king over I,	3478	
5:17 that they had anointed David king over I,	3478	
6: 1 gathered together all the chosen *men* of I,	3478	
6: 5 all the house of I played before the Lord	3478	
6:15 all the house of I brought up the ark of	3478	
6:19 *even* among the whole multitude of I,	3478	
6:20 How glorious was the king of I to day,	3478	
6:21 ruler over the people of the Lord, over I:	3478	
7: 6 brought up the children of I out of Egypt,	3478	
7: 7 I spake I a word with any of the tribes of	3478	
7: 7 spake I a word with any of the tribes of I,	3478	
7: 7 whom I commanded to feed my people I,	3478	
7: 8 to be ruler over my people, over I:	3478	
7:10 I will appoint a place for my people I,	3478	
7:11 judges *to be* over my people I,	3478	
7:23 like I, whom God went to redeem for	3478	
7:24 people I to be a people unto thee for ever;	3478	
7:26 The Lord of hosts *is* the God over I:	3478	
7:27 For thou, O Lord of hosts, God of I,	3478	
8:15 David reigned over all I; and David	3478	
10: 9 he chose of all the choice *men* of I,	3478	
10:15 saw that they were smitten before I,	3478	
10:17 gathered all I together, and passed over	3478	
10:18 the Syrians fled before I; and David slew	3478	
10:19 saw that they were smitten before I,	3478	
10:19 made peace with I, and served them.	3478	
11: 1 and his servants with him, and all I;	3478	
11:11 The ark, and I, and Judah, abide in tents;	3478	
12: 7 Thus saith the Lord God of I, I anointed	3478	
12: 7 anointed thee king over I, and I delivered	3478	
12: 8 gave thee the house of I and of Judah;	3478	
12:12 I will do this thing before all I,	3478	
13:12 for no such thing ought to be done in I:	3478	
13:13 thou shalt be as one of the fools in I.	3478	
14:25 in all I there was none to be so	3478	
15: 2 Thy servant *is* of one of the tribes of I.	3478	
15: 6 on this manner did Absalom to all I that	3478	
15: 6 Absalom stole the hearts of the men of I.	3478	
15:10 sent spies throughout all the tribes of I,	3478	
15:13 The hearts of the men of I are after	3478	
16: 3 To day shall the house of I restore me	3478	
16:15 and all the people the men of I,	3478	
16:18 this people, and all the men of I, choose,	3478	
16:21 all I shall hear that thou art abhorred of	3478	
16:22 his father's concubines in the sight of all I.	3478	
17: 4 Absalom well, and all the elders of I.	3478	
17:10 all I knoweth that thy father *is* a mighty	3478	
17:11 Therefore I counsel *that* all I be generally	3478	
17:13 shall all I bring ropes to that city,	3478	
17:14 Absalom and all the men of I said,	3478	
17:15 counsel Absalom and the elders of I;	3478	
17:24 he and all the men of I with him.	3478	
17:26 So I and Absalom pitched *in* the land of	3478	
18: 6 people went out *into* the field against I:	3478	
18: 7 Where the people of I were slain before	3478	
18:16 the people returned from pursuing after I:	3478	
18:17 and all I fled every one to his tent.	3478	
19: 8 for I had fled every man to his tent.	3478	
19: 9 at strife throughout all the tribes of I,	3478	
19:11 seeing the speech of all I came to	3478	
19:22 any man be put to death *this* day in I?	3478	
19:22 not I know that I *am this* day king over I?	3478	
19:40 the king, and also half the people of I.	3478	
19:41 all the men of I came to the king,	3478	
19:42 the men of Judah answered the men of I,	3478	
19:43 the men of I answered the men of Judah,	3478	
19:43 fiercer than the words of the men of I.	3478	
20: 1 son of Jesse: every man to his tents, O I.	3478	
20: 2 So every man of I went up from after	3478	
20:14 he went through all the tribes of I unto	3478	
20:19 *them that are* peaceable *and* faithful in I:	3478	
20:19 to destroy a city and a mother in I:	3478	
20:23 Now Joab *was* over all the host of I:	3478	
21: 2 Gibeonites *were* not of the children of I,	3478	
21: 2 the children of I had sworn unto them:	3478	
21: 2 slay them in his zeal to the children of I	3478	
21: 4 neither for us *shalt thou* kill any man in I.	3478	
21: 5 from remaining in any of the coasts of I,	3478	
21:15 the Philistines had yet war again with I;	3478	
21:17 battle, that thou quench not the light of I.	3478	
21:21 when he defied I, Jonathan the son of	3478	
23: 1 of Jacob, and the sweet psalmist of I, said,	3478	
23: 3 The God of I said, the Rock of Israel spake	3478	
23: 3 of Israel said, the Rock of I spake to me,	3478	
23: 9 battle, and the men of I were gone away:	3478	
24: 1 anger of the Lord was kindled against I,	3478	
24: 1 them to say, Go, number I and Judah.	3478	
24: 2 Go now through all the tribes of I,	3478	
24: 4 of the king, to number the people *of* I.	3478	
24: 9 there were in I eight hundred thousand	3478	
24:15 So the Lord sent a pestilence upon I	3478	
24:25 land, and the plague was stayed from I.	3478	
1Ki 1: 3 fair damsel throughout all the coasts of I,	3478	

1Ki 1:20 O king, the eyes of all I *are* upon thee,	3478	
1:30 I sware unto thee by the Lord God of I,	3478	
1:34 the prophet anoint him there king over I:	3478	
1:35 I have appointed him to be ruler over I	3478	
1:48 the king, Blessed *be* the Lord God of I,	3478	
2: 4 thee (said he) a man on the throne of I.	3478	
2: 5 did to the two captains of the hosts of I,	3478	
2:11 the days that David reigned over I *were*	3478	
2:15 all I set their faces on me, that *I* should	3478	
2:32 captain of the host of I, and Amasa the	3478	
3:28 all I heard of the judgment which the	3478	
4: 1 So king Solomon was king over all I.	3478	
4: 7 Solomon had twelve officers over all I,	3478	
4:20 Judah and I *were* many, as the sand	3478	
4:25 Judah and I dwelt safely, every man under	3478	
5:13 king Solomon raised a levy out of all I;	3478	
6: 1 eightieth year after the children of I were	3478	
6: 1 the fourth year of Solomon's reign over I,	3478	
6:13 I will dwell among the children of I,	3478	
6:13 of Israel, and will not forsake my people I.	3478	
8: 1 Solomon assembled the elders of I,	3478	
8: 1 the chief of the fathers of the children of I,	3478	
8: 2 all the men of I assembled themselves	3478	
8: 3 all the elders of I came, and the priests	3478	
8: 5 and all the congregation of I,	3478	
8: 9 made *a covenant* with the children of I,	3478	
8:14 and blessed all the congregation of I:	3478	
8:14 (and all the congregation of I stood;)	3478	
8:15 he said, Blessed *be* the Lord God of I,	3478	
8:16 I brought forth my people I out of Egypt,	3478	
8:16 I chose no city out of all the tribes of I to	3478	
8:16 but I chose David to be over my people I.	3478	
8:17 for the name of the Lord God of I.	3478	
8:20 sit on the throne of I, as the Lord	3478	
8:20 for the name of the Lord God of I.	3478	
8:22 the presence of all the congregation of I,	3478	
8:23 he said, Lord God of I, *there is* no God	3478	
8:25 Therefore now, Lord God of I,	3478	
8:25 man in my sight to sit on the throne of I;	3478	
8:26 O God of I, let thy word, I pray thee,	3478	
8:30 of thy people I, when they shall pray	3478	
8:33 When thy people I be smitten down	3478	
8:34 forgive the sin of thy people I,	3478	
8:36 the sin of thy servants, and of thy people I,	3478	
8:38 *made* by any man, *or* by all thy people I,	3478	
8:41 that *is* not of thy people I, but cometh out	3478	
8:43 thy name, to fear thee, as *do* thy people I;	3478	
8:52 unto the supplication of thy people I,	3478	
8:55 blessed all the congregation of I *with* a	3478	
8:56 that hath given rest unto his people I,	3478	
8:59 the cause of his people I at all times,	3478	
8:62 the king, and all I with him,	3478	
8:63 all the children of I dedicated the house	3478	
8:65 and all I with him, a great congregation,	3478	
8:66 for David his servant, and for I his people.	3478	
9: 5 throne of thy kingdom upon I for ever,	3478	
9: 5 not fail thee a man upon the throne of I.	3478	
9: 7 will I cut off I out of the land which I	3478	
9: 7 I shall be a proverb and a byword among	3478	
9:20 which *were* not of the children of I,	3478	
9:21 whom the children of I also were not able	3478	
9:22 of the children of I did Solomon make no	3478	
10: 9 in thee, to set thee on the throne of I:	3478	
10: 9 because the Lord loved I for ever,	3478	
11: 2 the Lord said unto the children of I,	3478	
11: 9 was turned from the Lord God of I,	3478	
11:16 months did Joab remain there with all I,	3478	
11:25 he was an adversary to I all the days of	3478	
11:25 that Hadad *did:* and he abhorred I,	3478	
11:31 saith the Lord, the God of I, Behold,	3478	
11:32 I have chosen out of all the tribes of I:)	3478	
11:37 soul desireth, and shalt be king over I.	3478	
11:38 built for David, and will give I unto thee.	3478	
11:42 in Jerusalem over all I *was* forty years.	3478	
12: 1 for all I were come *to* Shechem to make	3478	
12: 3 and all the congregation of I came,	3478	
12:16 when all I saw that the king hearkened	3478	
12:16 to your tents, O I: now see to thine own	3478	
12:16 David. So I departed unto their tents.	3478	
12:17 *as for* the children of I which dwelt in	3478	
12:18 all I stoned him with stones, that he died.	3478	
12:19 So I rebelled against the house of David	3478	
12:20 when all I heard that Jeroboam was come	3478	
12:20 and made him king over all I:	3478	
12:21 to fight against the house of I,	3478	
12:24 against your brethren the children of I:	3478	
12:28 behold thy gods, O I, which brought thee	3478	
12:33 ordained a feast unto the children of I:	3478	
14: 7 Thus saith the Lord God of I,	3478	
14: 7 and made thee prince over my people I,	3478	
14:10 *and him that is* shut up and left in I,	3478	
14:13 all I shall mourn for him, and bury him:	3478	
14:13 Lord God of I in the house of Jeroboam.	3478	
14:14 Lord shall raise him up a king over I,	3478	
14:15 For the Lord shall smite I, as a reed is	3478	
14:15 he shall root up I out of this good land,	3478	
14:16 he shall give I up because of the sins of	3478	
14:16 who did sin, and who made I to sin.	3478	
14:18 all I mourned for him, according to	3478	
14:19 book of the chronicles of the kings of I.	3478	
14:21 Lord did choose out of all the tribes of I,	3478	
14:24 Lord cast out before the children of I.	3478	
15: 9 the twentieth year of Jeroboam king of I	3478	
15:16 and Baasha king of I all their days.	3478	
15:17 Baasha king of I went up against Judah,	3478	

I

1Ki 15:19 break thy league with Baasha king of I, 3478
15:20 hosts which he had against the cities of I, 3478
15:25 I in the second year of Asa king of Judah, 3478
15:25 of Judah, and reigned over I two years. 3478
15:26 in his sin wherewith he made I to sin. 3478
15:27 Nadab and all I laid siege to Gibbethon. 3478
15:30 he sinned, and which he made I sin, 3478
15:30 he provoked the Lord God of I to anger. 3478
15:31 book of the chronicles of the kings of I? 3478
15:32 and Baasha king of I all their days. 3478
15:33 son of Ahijah to reign over all I in Tirzah, 3478
15:34 in his sin wherewith he made I to sin. 3478
16: 2 and made thee prince over my people I; 3478
16: 2 hast made my people I to sin, to provoke 3478
16: 5 book of the chronicles of the kings of I? 3478
16: 8 son of Baasha to reign over I in Tirzah, 3478
16:13 and by which they made I to sin, 3478
16:13 in provoking the Lord God of I to anger 3478
16:14 book of the chronicles of the kings of I? 3478
16:16 wherefore all I made Omri, the captain of 3478
16:16 the host, king over I that day in the camp. 3478
16:17 all I with him, and they besieged Tirzah. 3478
16:19 and in his sin which he did, to make I sin. 3478
16:20 book of the chronicles of the kings of I? 3478
16:21 the people of I divided into two parts: 3478
16:23 king of Judah began Omri to reign over I, 3478
16:26 and in his sin wherewith he made I to sin, 3478
16:26 to provoke the Lord God of I to anger 3478
16:27 book of the chronicles of the kings of I? 3478
16:29 Ahab the son of Omri to reign over I: 3478
16:29 Ahab the son of Omri reigned over I in 3478
16:33 I to anger than all the kings of Israel that 3478
16:33 all the kings of I that were before him. 3478
17: 1 unto Ahab, As the Lord God of I liveth, 3478
17:14 For thus saith the Lord God of I, 3478
18:17 unto him, Art thou he that troubleth I? 3478
18:18 he answered, I have not troubled I; 3478
18:19 gather to me all I unto mount Carmel, 3478
18:20 So Ahab sent unto all the children of I, 3478
18:31 Lord came, saying, I shall be thy name: 3478
18:36 Lord God of Abraham, Isaac, and of I, 3478
18:36 be known this day that thou art God in I, 3478
19:10 for the children of I have forsaken thy 3478
19:14 the children of I have forsaken thy 3478
19:16 shalt thou anoint to be king over I: 3478
19:18 Yet I have left me seven thousand in I, 3478
20: 2 he sent messengers to Ahab king of I into 3478
20: 4 the king of I answered and said, My lord, 3478
20: 7 the king of I called all the elders of 3478
20:11 the king of I said, Tell him, 3478
20:13 there came a prophet unto Ahab king of I, 3478
20:15 even all the children of I, being seven 3478
20:20 the Syrians fled; and I pursued them: 3478
20:21 king of I went out, and smote the horses 3478
20:22 the prophet came to the king of I, 3478
20:26 and went up to Aphek, to fight against I. 3478
20:27 the children of I were numbered, 3478
20:27 the children of I pitched before them like 3478
20:28 spake unto the king of I, and said, 3478
20:29 the children of I slew of the Syrians an 3478
20:31 kings of the house of I are merciful kings: 3478
20:31 our heads, and go out to the king of I: 3478
20:32 and came to the king of I, and said, 3478
20:40 the king of I said unto him, So shall thy 3478
20:41 the king of I discerned him that he was of 3478
20:43 the king of I went to his house heavy and 3478
21: 7 Dost thou now govern the kingdom of I? 3478
21:18 Arise, go down to meet Ahab king of I, 3478
21:21 and him that is shut up and left in I, 3478
21:22 provoked me to anger, and made I to sin. 3478
21:26 Lord cast out before the children of I). 3478
22: 1 years without war between Syria and I. 3478
22: 2 king of Judah came down to the king of I. 3478
22: 3 the king of I said unto his servants, Know 3478
22: 4 Jehoshaphat said to the king of I, I am as 3478
22: 5 Jehoshaphat said unto the king of I, 3478
22: 6 the king of I gathered the prophets 3478
22: 8 the king of I said unto Jehoshaphat, 3478
22: 9 the king of I called an officer, and said, 3478
22:10 the king of I and Jehoshaphat the king of 3478
22:17 said, I saw all I scattered upon the hills, 3478
22:18 the king of I said unto Jehoshaphat, Did I 3478
22:26 the king of I said, Take Micaiah, 3478
22:29 So the king of I and Jehoshaphat the king 3478
22:30 the king of I said unto Jehoshaphat, I will 3478
22:30 the king of I disguised himself, 3478
22:31 nor great, save only with the king of I. 3478
22:32 that they said, Surely it is the king of I. 3478
22:33 perceived that it was not the king of I, 3478
22:34 smote the king of I between the joints of 3478
22:39 book of the chronicles of the kings of I? 3478
22:41 Judah in the fourth year of Ahab king of I. 3478
22:44 made peace with the king of I. 3478
22:51 I in Samaria the seventeenth year of 3478
22:51 of Judah, and reigned two years over I. 3478
22:52 the son of Nebat, who made I to sin: 3478
22:53 provoked to anger the Lord God of I, 3478
2Ki 1: 1 Moab rebelled against I after the death of 3478
1: 3 Is it not because there is not a God in I, 3478
1: 6 Is it not because there is not a God in I, 3478
1:16 is no God in I to inquire of his word? 3478
1:18 book of the chronicles of the kings of I? 3478
2:12 chariot of I, and the horsemen thereof. 3478
3: 1 I in Samaria the eighteenth year of 3478
3: 3 the son of Nebat, which made I to sin; 3478

2Ki 3: 4 rendered unto the king of I an hundred 3478
3: 5 of Moab rebelled against the king of I. 3478
3: 6 the same time, and numbered all I. 3478
3: 9 So the king of I went, and the king of 3478
3:10 the king of I said, Alas, that the Lord 3478
3:12 So the king of I and Jehoshaphat and 3478
3:13 Elisha said unto the king of I, What have 3478
3:13 the king of I said unto him, Nay: 3478
3:24 when they came to the camp of I, 3478
3:27 there was great indignation against I: 3478
5: 2 captive out of the land of I a little maid; 3478
5: 4 thus said the maid that is of the land of I. 3478
5: 5 and I will send a letter unto the king of I. 3478
5: 6 he brought the letter to the king of I, 3478
5: 7 when the king of I had read the letter, 3478
5: 8 that the king of I had rent his clothes, 3478
5: 8 he shall know that there is a prophet in I. 3478
5:12 better than all the waters of I? 3478
5:15 there is no God in all the earth, but in I: 3478
6: 8 the king of Syria warred against I, 3478
6: 9 the man of God sent unto the king of I, 3478
6:10 the king of I sent to the place which 3478
6:11 shew me which of us is for the king of I? 3478
6:12 Elisha, the prophet that is in I, telleth 3478
6:12 telleth the king of I the words that thou 3478
6:21 the king of I said unto Elisha, when he 3478
6:23 of Syria came no more into the land of I. 3478
6:26 as the king of I was passing by upon 3478
7: 6 king of I hath hired against us the kings 3478
7:13 they are as all the multitude of I that are 3478
8:12 that thou wilt do unto the children of I: 3478
8:16 year of Joram the son of Ahab king of I, 3478
8:18 he walked in the way of the kings of I, 3478
8:25 I did Ahaziah the son of Jehoram king of 3478
8:26 the daughter of Omri king of I. 3478
9: 3 I have anointed thee king over I. 3478
9: 6 unto him, Thus saith the Lord God of I, 3478
9: 6 over the people of the Lord, even over I. 3478
9: 8 and him that is shut up and left in I: 3478
9:12 I have anointed thee king over I: 3478
9:14 he and all I, because of Hazael king of 3478
9:21 Joram king of I and Ahaziah king of Judah 3478
10:21 Jehu sent through all I: and all 3478
10:28 Thus Jehu destroyed Baal out of I. 3478
10:29 made I to sin, Jehu departed not from 3478
10:30 generation shall sit on the throne of I. 3478
10:31 of the Lord God of I with all his heart: 3478
10:31 sins of Jeroboam, which made I to sin. 3478
10:32 In those days the Lord began to cut I 3478
10:32 Hazael smote them in all the coasts of I; 3478
10:34 book of the chronicles of the kings of I? 3478
10:36 time that Jehu reigned over I in Samaria 3478
13: 1 of Jehu began to reign over I in Samaria, 3478
13: 2 the son of Nebat, which made I to sin; 3478
13: 3 anger of the Lord was kindled against I, 3478
13: 4 for he saw the oppression of I, because 3478
13: 5 (And the Lord gave I a saviour, 3478
13: 5 the children of I dwelt in their tents, 3478
13: 6 who made I sin, but walked therein: 3478
13: 8 book of the chronicles of the kings of I? 3478
13:10 son of Jehoash to reign over I in Samaria, 3478
13:11 the son of Nebat, who made I sin: 3478
13:12 book of the chronicles of the kings of I? 3478
13:13 was buried in Samaria with the kings of I. 3478
13:14 Joash the king of I came down unto him, 3478
13:14 the chariot of I, and the horsemen thereof. 3478
13:16 he said to the king of I, Put thine hand 3478
13:18 took them. And he said unto the king of I, 3478
13:22 Hazael king of Syria oppressed I all 3478
13:25 beat him, and recovered the cities of I. 3478
14: 1 I reigned Amaziah the son of Joash king 3478
14: 8 son of Jehu, king of I, saying, Come, 3478
14: 9 Jehoash the king of I sent to Amaziah 3478
14:11 Therefore Jehoash king of I went up; 3478
14:12 Judah was put to the worse before I, 3478
14:13 Jehoash king of I took Amaziah king of 3478
14:15 book of the chronicles of the kings of I? 3478
14:16 was buried in Samaria with the kings of I; 3478
14:17 son of Jehoahaz king of I fifteen years. 3478
14:23 Joash king of I began to reign in Samaria, 3478
14:24 the son of Nebat, who made I to sin. 3478
14:25 He restored the coast of I from the 3478
14:25 to the word of the Lord God of I, 3478
14:26 For the Lord saw the affliction of I, 3478
14:26 shut up, nor any left, nor any helper for I. 3478
14:27 blot out the name of I from under heaven: 3478
14:28 which belonged to Judah, for I, 3478
14:28 book of the chronicles of the kings of I? 3478
14:29 with his fathers, even with the kings of I; 3478
15: 1 seventh year of Jeroboam king of I began 3478
15: 8 reign over I in Samaria six months. 3478
15: 9 the son of Nebat, who made I to sin. 3478
15:11 book of the chronicles of the kings of I? 3478
15:12 Thy sons shall sit on the throne of I unto 3478
15:15 book of the chronicles of the kings of I? 3478
15:17 Menahem the son of Gadi to reign over I, 3478
15:18 the son of Nebat, who made I to sin. 3478
15:20 Menahem exacted the money of I, even 3478
15:21 book of the chronicles of the kings of I? 3478
15:23 Menahem began to reign over I in 3478
15:24 the son of Nebat, who made I to sin. 3478
15:26 book of the chronicles of the kings of I? 3478
15:27 Remaliah began to reign over I in Samaria, 3478
15:28 the son of Nebat, who made I to sin. 3478
15:29 In the days of Pekah king of I came 3478

2Ki 15:31 book of the chronicles of the kings of I. 3478
15:32 begat Jotham the son of Uzziah king of I. 3478
16: 3 he walked in the way of the kings of I, 3478
16: 3 cast out from before the children of I. 3478
16: 5 Pekah son of Remaliah king of I came up 3478
16: 7 out of the hand of the king of I, which 3478
17: 1 Elah to reign in Samaria over I nine years. 3478
17: 2 not as the kings of I that were before him. 3478
17: 6 carried I away into Assyria, 3478
17: 7 that the children of I had sinned against 3478
17: 8 cast out from before the children of I, 3478
17: 8 of the kings of I, which they had made. 3478
17: 9 the children of I did secretly those things 3478
17:13 Yet the Lord testified against I, 3478
17:18 the Lord was very angry with I, 3478
17:19 walked in the statutes of I which they 3478
17:20 the Lord rejected all the seed of I, 3478
17:21 For he rent I from the house of David; 3478
17:21 Jeroboam drave I from following 3478
17:22 For the children of I walked in all the sins 3478
17:23 Until the Lord removed I out of his 3478
17:23 was I carried away out of their own land 3478
17:24 of Samaria instead of the children of I: 3478
17:34 the children of Jacob, whom he named I; 3478
18: 1 third year of Hoshea son of Elah king of I, 3478
18: 4 for unto those days the children of I did 3478
18: 5 He trusted in the Lord God of I; 3478
18: 9 year of Hoshea son of Elah king of I, 3478
18:10 that in the ninth year of Hoshea king of I, 3478
18:11 the king of Assyria did carry away I unto 3478
19:15 said, O Lord God of I, which dwellest 3478
19:20 Thus saith the Lord God of I, 3478
19:22 on high? even against the Holy One of I. 3478
21: 2 Lord cast out before the children of I. 3478
21: 3 and made a grove, as did Ahab king of I; 3478
21: 7 which I have chosen out of all tribes of I, 3478
21: 8 Neither will I make the feet of I move any 3478
21: 9 Lord destroyed before the children of I. 3478
21:12 Therefore thus saith the Lord God of I, 3478
22:15 unto them, Thus saith the Lord God of I, 3478
22:18 to him, Thus saith the Lord God of I, 3478
23:13 which Solomon the king of I had builded 3478
23:15 who made I to sin, had made, both that 3478
23:19 which the kings of I had made to provoke 3478
23:22 from the days of the judges that judged I, 3478
23:22 nor in all the days of the kings of I, nor of 3478
23:27 as I have removed I, and will cast off this 3478
24:13 of I had made in the temple of the Lord, 3478
1Ch 1:34 begat Isaac. The sons of Isaac; Esau and I. 3478
1:43 any king reigned over the children of I. 3478
2: 1 These are the sons of I; Reuben, Simeon, 3478
2: 7 Achar, the troubler of I, who transgressed 3478
4:10 Jabez called on the God of I, saying, 3478
5: 1 Now the sons of Reuben the firstborn of I, 3478
5: 1 given unto the sons of Joseph the son of I: 3478
5: 3 I say, of Reuben the firstborn of I were, 3478
5:17 and in the days of Jeroboam king of I. 3478
5:26 God of I stirred up the spirit of Pul king 3478
6:38 of Kohath, the son of Levi, the son of I. 3478
6:49 holy, and to make an atonement for I, 3478
6:64 the children of I gave to the Levites these 3478
7:29 dwelt the children of Joseph the son of I. 3478
9: 1 So all I were reckoned by genealogies; 3478
9: 1 were written in the book of the kings of I 3478
10: 1 Now the Philistines fought against I; 3478
10: 1 the men of I fled from before 3478
10: 7 when all the men of I that were in 3478
11: 1 all I gathered themselves to David unto 3478
11: 2 he that leddest out and broughtest in I: 3478
11: 2 Thou shalt feed my people I, and thou 3478
11: 2 and thou shalt be ruler over my people I. 3478
11: 3 Therefore came all the elders of I to 3478
11: 3 they anointed David king over I, 3478
11: 4 David and all I went to Jerusalem, which 3478
11:10 and with all I, to make him king, 3478
11:10 to the word of the Lord concerning I. 3478
12:32 of the times, to know what I ought to do; 3478
12:38 to Hebron, to make David king over all I: 3478
12:38 all the rest also of I were of one heart to 3478
12:40 sheep abundantly: for there was joy in I. 3478
13: 2 David said unto all the congregation of I, 3478
13: 2 that are left in all the land of I, 3478
13: 5 So David gathered all I together, 3478
13: 6 David went up, and all I, to Baalah, 3478
13: 8 I played before God with all their might, 3478
14: 2 the Lord had confirmed him king over I, 3478
14: 2 lift up on high, because of his people I. 3478
14: 8 that David was anointed king over all I, 3478
15: 3 David gathered all I together to Jerusalem, 3478
15:12 unto the place that I have prepared for 3478
15:14 to bring up the ark of the Lord God of I. 3478
15:25 the elders of I, and the captains over 3478
15:28 Thus all I brought up the ark of 3478
16: 3 he dealt to every one of I, both man and 3478
16: 4 to thank and praise the Lord God of I: 3478
16:13 O ye seed of I his servant, ye children of 3478
16:17 law, and to I for an everlasting covenant, 3478
16:36 Blessed be the Lord God of I for ever 3478
16:40 of the Lord, which he commanded I; 3478
17: 5 the day that I brought up I unto this day; 3478
17: 6 Wheresoever I have walked with all I, 3478
17: 6 spake I a word to any of the judges of I, 3478
17: 7 thou shouldest be ruler over my people I: 3478
17: 9 Also I will ordain a place for my people I, 3478
17:10 judges to be over my people I. 3478

1Ch 17:21 nation in the earth *is* like thy people I,	3478	
17:22 thy people I didst thou make thine own	3478	
17:24 The LORD of hosts *is* the God of I,	3478	
17:24 is the God of Israel, and executed	3478	
18:14 So David reigned over all I, and executed	3478	
19:10 he chose out of all the choice of I,	3478	
19:16 that they were put to the worse before I,	3478	
19:17 he gathered all I, and passed over Jordan,	3478	
19:18 the Syrians fled before I; and David slew	3478	
19:19 that they were put to the worse before I,	3478	
20: 7 when he defied I, Jonathan the son of	3478	
21: 1 Satan stood *up* against I,	3478	
21: 1 and provoked David to number I	3478	
21: 2 number I from Beer-sheba even to Dan;	3478	
21: 3 why will he be a cause of trespass to I?	3478	
21: 4 went throughout all I, and came *to*	3478	
21: 5 all *they* of I were a thousand thousand	3478	
21: 7 with this thing; therefore he smote I.	3478	
21:12 destroying throughout all the coasts of I.	3478	
21:14 So the LORD sent pestilence upon I:	3478	
21:14 and there fell of I seventy thousand men.	3478	
21:16 the elders of I, who were clothed in	NIH	
22: 1 this *is* the altar of the burnt offering for I.	3478	
22: 2 the strangers that *were* in the land of I;	3478	
22: 6 to build a house for the LORD God of I.	3478	
22: 9 peace and quietness unto I in his days.	3478	
22:10 the throne of his kingdom over I for ever.	3478	
22:12 and give thee charge concerning I,	3478	
22:13 LORD charged Moses with concerning I:	3478	
22:17 also commanded all the princes of I	3478	
23: 1 he made Solomon his son king over I.	3478	
23: 2 he gathered together all the princes of I,	3478	
23:25 The LORD God of I hath given rest unto	3478	
24:19 as the LORD God of I had commanded	3478	
26:29 were for the outward business over I.	3478	
26:30 officers among them of I on *this* side	3478	
27: 1 Now the children of I after their number,	3478	
27:16 Furthermore over the tribes of I: the ruler	3478	
27:22 These *were* the princes of the tribes of I.	3478	
27:23 the LORD had said *he* would increase I	3478	
27:24 because there fell wrath for it against I;	3478	
28: 1 David assembled all the princes of I,	3478	
28: 4 Howbeit the LORD God of I chose me	3478	
28: 4 of my father to be king over I for ever:	3478	
28: 4 he liked me to make *me* king over all I:	3478	
28: 5 of the kingdom of the LORD over I.	3478	
28: 8 in the sight of all I the congregation of	3478	
29: 6 the fathers and princes of the tribes of I,	3478	
29:10 LORD God of I our father, for ever and	3478	
29:18 of Abraham, Isaac, and of I, our fathers,	3478	
29:21 and sacrifices in abundance for all I:	3478	
29:23 and prospered; and all I obeyed him.	3478	
29:25 Solomon exceedingly in the sight of all I,	3478	
29:25 had not been on any king before him in I.	3478	
29:26 David the son of Jesse reigned over all I.	3478	
29:27 the time that he reigned over I *was* forty	3478	
29:30 over I, and over all the kingdoms of	3478	
2Ch 1: 2 Solomon spake unto all I, to the captains	3478	
1: 2 the judges, and to every governor in all I,	3478	
1:13 of the congregation, and reigned over I.	3478	
2: 4 This *is an ordinance* for ever to I.	3478	
2:12 Blessed *be* the LORD God of I, that made	3478	
2:17 all the strangers that *were* in the land of I,	3478	
5: 2 Solomon assembled the elders of I,	3478	
5: 2 the chief of the fathers of the children of I,	3478	
5: 3 Wherefore all the men of I assembled	3478	
5: 4 all the elders of I came; and the Levites	3478	
5: 6 all the congregation of I that were	3478	
5:10 made *a covenant* with the children of I,	3478	
6: 3 and blessed the whole congregation of I:	3478	
6: 3 and all the congregation of I stood.	3478	
6: 4 he said, Blessed *be* the LORD God of I,	3478	
6: 5 I to build a house *in*, that my name might	3478	
6: 5 I any man to be a ruler over my people I:	3478	
6: 6 chosen David to be over my people I.	3478	
6: 7 for the name of the LORD God of I.	3478	
6:10 am set on the throne of I, as the LORD	3478	
6:10 for the name of the LORD God of I.	3478	
6:11 that he made with the children of I.	3478	
6:12 the presence of all the congregation of I,	3478	
6:13 his knees before all the congregation of I,	3478	
6:14 said, O LORD God of I, *there is* no God	3478	
6:16 Now therefore, O LORD God of I, let my	3478	
6:16 in my sight to sit upon the throne of I;	3478	
6:17 Now then, O LORD God of I, let thy	3478	
6:21 of thy servant, and of thy people I,	3478	
6:24 if thy people I be put to the worse before	3478	
6:25 forgive the sin of thy people I,	3478	
6:27 sin of thy servants, and of thy people I,	3478	
6:29 of all thy people I, when every one shall	3478	
6:32 which *is* not of thy people I, but is come	3478	
6:33 as *doth* thy people I, and may know that	3478	
7: 3 all the children of I saw how the fire	3478	
7: 6 trumpets before them, and all I stood.	3478	
7: 8 all I with him, a very great congregation,	3478	
7:10 and to Solomon, and to I his people.	3478	
7:18 shall not fail thee a man *to be* ruler in I.	3478	
8: 2 caused the children of I to dwell there.	3478	
8: 7 the Jebusites, which *were* not of I,	3478	
8: 8 whom the children of I consumed not,	3478	
8: 9 of the children of I did Solomon make no	3478	
8:11 not dwell in the house of David king of I,	3478	
9: 8 because thy God loved I, to establish	3478	
9:30 Solomon reigned in Jerusalem over all I	3478	
10: 1 for *to* Shechem were all I come to make	3478	

2Ch 10: 3 So Jeroboam and all I came and spake to	3478	
10:16 when all I saw that the king would not	3478	
10:16 every man to your tents, O I: *and* now,	3478	
10:16 own house. So all I went to their tents.	3478	
10:17 *as for* the children of I that dwelt in	3478	
10:18 the children of I stoned him with stones,	3478	
10:19 I rebelled against the house of David unto	3478	
11: 1 to fight against I, that *he* might bring	3478	
11: 3 and to all I in Judah and Benjamin, saying,	3478	
11:13 Levites that *were* in all I resorted to him	3478	
11:16 after them out of all the tribes of I such as	3478	
11:16 the LORD God of I came *to* Jerusalem,	3478	
12: 1 the law of the LORD, and all I with him.	3478	
12: 6 Whereupon the princes of I and the king	3478	
12:13 had chosen out of all the tribes of I,	3478	
13: 4 said, Hear me, *thou* Jeroboam, and all I;	3478	
13: 5 I gave the kingdom over Israel to David	3478	
13: 5 gave the kingdom over I to David for ever,	3478	
13:12 O children of I, fight ye not against	3478	
13:15 and all I before Abijah and Judah.	3478	
13:16 the children of I fled before Judah:	3478	
13:17 there fell down slain of I five hundred	3478	
13:18 Thus the children of I were brought under	3478	
15: 3 for a long season I *hath been* without	3478	
15: 4 trouble did turn unto the LORD God of I,	3478	
15: 9 for they fell to him out of I in abundance,	3478	
15:13 LORD God of I should be put to death,	3478	
15:17 high places were not taken away out of I:	3478	
16: 1 Baasha king of I came up against Judah,	3478	
16: 3 break thy league with Baasha king of I,	3478	
16: 4 of his armies against the cities of I;	3478	
16:11 in the book of the kings of Judah and I.	3478	
17: 1 and strengthened himself against I.	3478	
17: 4 and not after the doings of I.	3478	
18: 3 Ahab king of I said unto Jehoshaphat king	3478	
18: 4 Jehoshaphat said unto the king of I,	3478	
18: 5 Therefore the king of I gathered together	3478	
18: 7 the king of I said unto Jehoshaphat,	3478	
18: 8 the king of I called for one *of his* officers,	3478	
18: 9 king of I and Jehoshaphat king of Judah	3478	
18:16 see all I scattered upon the mountains,	3478	
18:17 the king of I said to Jehoshaphat, Did I	3478	
18:19 Who shall entice Ahab king of I, that he	3478	
18:25 the king of I said, Take ye Micaiah,	3478	
18:28 So the king of I and Jehoshaphat the king	3478	
18:29 the king of I said unto Jehoshaphat, I will	3478	
18:29 So the king of I disguised himself;	3478	
18:30 or great, save only with the king of I.	3478	
18:31 that they said, It *is* the king of I.	3478	
18:32 perceived that it was not the king of I,	3478	
18:33 smote the king of I between the joints of	3478	
18:34 howbeit the king of I stayed *himself* up in	3478	
19: 8 and of the chief of the fathers of I,	3478	
20: 7 of this land before thy people I,	3478	
20:10 whom thou wouldest not let I invade,	3478	
20:19 stood up to praise the LORD God of I	3478	
20:29 LORD fought against the enemies of I.	3478	
20:34 is mentioned in the book of the kings of I.	3478	
20:35 Judah join himself with Ahaziah king of I,	3478	
21: 2 were the sons of Jehoshaphat king of I.	3478	
21: 4 and *divers* also of the princes of I.	3478	
21: 6 he walked in the way of the kings of I,	3478	
21:13 hast walked in the way of the kings of I,	3478	
22: 5 I to war against Hazael king of Syria at	3478	
23: 2 chief of the fathers of I, and they came	3478	
24: 5 gather of all I money to repair the house	3478	
24: 6 the congregation of I, for the tabernacle	3478	
24: 9 of God laid upon I in the wilderness.	3478	
24:16 because he had done good in I,	3478	
25: 6 out of I for an hundred talents of silver.	3478	
25: 7 king, let not the army of I go with thee;	3478	
25: 7 for the LORD *is* not with I, *to wit, with* all	3478	
25: 9 which I have given to the army of I?	3478	
25:17 the son of Jehu, king of I, saying, Come,	3478	
25:18 Joash king of I sent to Amaziah king of	3478	
25:21 So Joash the king of I went up;	3478	
25:22 Judah was put to the worse before I,	3478	
25:23 Joash the king of I took Amaziah king of	3478	
25:25 son of Jehoahaz king of I fifteen years.	3478	
25:26 in the book of the kings of Judah and I?	3478	
27: 7 *are* written in the book of the kings of I.	3478	
28: 2 he walked in the ways of the kings of I,	3478	
28: 3 had cast out before the children of I.	3478	
28: 5 delivered into the hand of the king of I,	3478	
28: 8 the children of I carried away captive of	3478	
28:13 great, and *there is* fierce wrath against I.	3478	
28:19 Judah low because of Ahaz king of I;	3478	
28:23 they were the ruin of him, and of all I.	3478	
28:26 in the book of the kings of Judah and I.	3478	
28:27 not into the sepulchres of the kings of I:	3478	
29: 7 in the holy *place* unto the God of I.	3478	
29:10 a covenant with the LORD God of I,	3478	
29:24 the altar, to make an atonement for all I:	3478	
29:24 the sin offering *should be made* for all I.	3478	
29:27 instruments ordained by David king of I.	3478	
30: 1 Hezekiah sent to all I and Judah,	3478	
30: 1 the passover unto the LORD God of I.	3478	
30: 5 to make proclamation throughout all I,	3478	
30: 5 unto the LORD God of I at Jerusalem:	3478	
30: 6 his princes throughout all I and Judah,	3478	
30: 6 of the king, saying, Ye children of I,	3478	
30: 6 I, and he will return to the remnant of	3478	
30:21 the children of I that were present at	3478	
30:25 all the congregation that came out of I,	3478	
30:25 strangers that came out of the land of I,	3478	

2Ch 30:26 of I *there was* not the like in Jerusalem.	3478		
31: 1 all I that were present went out to the	3478		
31: 1 *all.* Then all the children of I returned,	3478		
31: 5 the children of I brought in abundance	3478		
31: 6 *concerning* the children of I and Judah,	3478		
31: 8 they blessed the LORD, and his people I.	3478		
32:17 also letters to rail on the LORD God of I,	3478		
32:32 in the book of the kings of Judah and I.	3478		
33: 2 had cast out before the children of I.	3478		
33: 7 I have chosen before all the tribes of I,	3478		
33: 8 will I any more remove the foot of I	3478		
33: 9 had destroyed before the children of I.	3478		
33:16 Judah to serve the LORD God of I.	3478		
33:18 to him in the name of the LORD God of I,	3478		
33:18 *are* written in the book of the kings of I.	3478		
34: 7 all the idols throughout all the land of I,	3478		
34: 9 and the remnant of I, and of all Judah and	3478		
34:21 for them that are left in I and in Judah,	3478		
34:23 Thus saith the LORD God of I,	3478		
34:26 Thus saith the LORD God of I *concerning*	3478		
34:33 that *pertained* to the children of I,	3478		
34:33 made all that were present in I to serve,	3478		
35: 3 said unto the Levites that taught all I,	3478		
35: 3 the son of David king of I did build;	3478		
35: 3 the LORD your God, and his people I,	3478		
35: 4 to the writing of David king of I,	3478		
35:17 the children of I that were present kept	3478		
35:18 kept in I from the days of Samuel	3478		
35:18 neither did all the kings of I keep such a	3478		
35:18 all Judah and I that were present,	3478		
35:25 day, and made them an ordinance in I:	3478		
35:27 *are* written in the book of the kings of I	3478		
36:13 from turning unto the LORD God of I.	3478		
Ezr 1: 3 build the house of the LORD God of I:	3478		
2: 2 The number of the men of the people of I:	3478		
2:59 and their seed, whether they *were* of I.	3478		
2:70 in their cities, and all I in their cities.	3478		
3: 1 and the children of I *were* in the cities,	3478		
3: 2 and builded the altar of the God of I,	3478		
3:10 after the ordinance of David king of I.	3478		
3:11 his mercy *endureth* for ever towards I.	3478		
4: 1 the temple unto the LORD God of I;	3478		
4: 3 the rest of the chief of the fathers of I,	3478		
4: 3 will build unto the LORD God of I,	3478		
5: 1 Jerusalem in the name of the God of I	3478		
5:11 a great king of I builded and set up.	3479		
6:14 to the commandment of the God of I,	3479		
6:16 the children of I, the priests,	3479		
6:17 for a sin offering for all I, twelve he goats,	3479		
6:17 according to the number of the tribes of I.	3479		
6:21 the children of I, which were come again	3478		
6:21 to seek the LORD God of I, did eat,	3478		
6:22 work of the house of God, the God of I.	3478		
7: 6 which the LORD God of I had given:	3478		
7: 7 there went up *some* of the children of I,	3478		
7:10 to do *it*, and to teach in I statutes and	3478		
7:11 of the LORD, and of his statutes to I.	3478		
7:13 that all they of the people of I, and *of* his	3479		
7:15 have freely offered unto the God of I,	3478		
7:28 I gathered together out of I chief *men* to	3478		
8:18 of Mahli, the son of Levi,	3478		
8:25 his lords, and all I *there* present,	3478		
8:29 the Levites, and chief of the fathers of I,	3478		
8:35 offered burnt offerings unto the God of I,	3478		
8:35 twelve bullocks for all I, ninety and	3478		
9: 1 The people of I, and the priests,	3478		
9: 4 trembled at the words of the God of I,	3478		
9:15 O LORD God of I, thou *art* righteous:	3478		
10: 1 there assembled unto him out of I a very	3478		
10: 2 yet now there is hope in I concerning this	3478		
10: 5 the chief priests, the Levites, and all I,	3478		
10:10 wives, to increase the trespass of I.	3478		
10:25 Moreover of I: of the sons of Parosh;	3478		
Ne 1: 6 for the children of I thy servants,	3478		
1: 6 confess the sins of the children of I,	3478		
2:10 to seek the welfare of the children of I.	3478		
7: 7 *I say*, of the men of the people of I *was*	3478		
7:61 nor their seed, whether they *were* of I.	3478		
7:73 the people, and the Nethinims, and all I,	3478		
7:73 the children of I *were* in their cities.	3478		
8: 1 which the LORD had commanded to I.	3478		
8:14 the children of I should dwell in booths	3478		
8:17 day had not the children of I done so.	3478		
9: 1 fourth day of this month the children of I	3478		
9: 2 seed of I separated themselves from all	3478		
10:33 sin offerings to make an atonement for I,	3478		
10:39 For the children of I and the children of	3478		
11: 3 *to wit*, I, the priests, and the Levites,	3478		
11:20 the residue of I, of the priests,	3478		
12:47 all I in the days of Zerubbabel, and in	3478		
13: 2 Because they met not the children of I	3478		
13: 3 that they separated from I all the mixed	3478		
13:18 yet ye bring more wrath upon I by	3478		
13:26 Did not Solomon king of I sin by these	3478		
13:26 God, and God made him king over all I:	3478		
Ps 14: 7 that the salvation of I were come out of	3478		
14: 7 Jacob shall rejoice, *and* I shall be glad.	3478		
22: 3 O thou that inhabitest the praises of I.	3478		
22:23 and fear him, all ye the seed of I.	3478		
25:22 Redeem I, O God, out of all his troubles.	3478		
41:13 Blessed *be* the LORD God of I from	3478		
50: 7 O I, and I will testify against thee:	3478		
53: 6 that the salvation of I were come out of	3478		
53: 6 Jacob shall rejoice, *and* I shall be glad.	3478		

I

Ps 59: 5 O LORD God *of* hosts, the God of I, 3478
68: 8 at the presence of God, the God of I. 3478
68:26 *even* the Lord, from the fountain of I. 3478
68:34 his excellency *is* over I, and his strength 3478
68:35 the God of I *is* he that giveth strength and 3478
69: 6 be confounded for my sake, O God of I. 3478
71:22 sing with the harp, O thou Holy One of I. 3478
72:18 Blessed *be* the LORD God, the God of I, 3478
73: 1 God *is* good to I, *even* to such as are 3478
76: 1 *is* God known: his name *is* great in I. 3478
78: 5 appointed a law in I, which he 3478
78:21 and anger also came up against I; 3478
78:31 and smote down the chosen *men* of I. 3478
78:41 and limited the Holy One of I. 3478
78:55 made the tribes of I to dwell in their tents. 3478
78:59 he was wroth, and greatly abhorred I: 3478
78:71 Jacob his people, and I his inheritance. 3478
80: 1 Give ear, O Shepherd of I, thou that 3478
81: 4 For this *was* a statute for I, *and* a law of 3478
81: 8 O I, if thou wilt hearken unto me; 3478
81:11 to my voice; and I would none of me. 3478
81:13 unto me, *and* I had walked in my ways! 3478
83: 4 that the name of I may be no more in 3478
89:18 and the Holy One of I *is* our king. 3478
98: 3 and his truth toward the house of I: 3478
103: 7 Moses, his acts unto the children of I. 3478
105:10 law, *and* to I *for* an everlasting covenant: 3478
105:23 I also came *into* Egypt; 3478
106:48 Blessed *be* the LORD God of I from 3478
114: 1 When I went out of Egypt, the house of 3478
114: 2 was his sanctuary, *and* I his dominion. 3478
115: 9 O I, trust thou in the LORD: he *is* their 3478
115:12 will bless *us;* he will bless the house of I; 3478
118: 2 Let I now say, that his mercy *endureth* 3478
121: 4 he that keepeth I shall neither slumber 3478
122: 4 of the LORD, *unto* the testimony of I, 3478
124: 1 who was on our side, now may I say; 3478
125: 5 of iniquity: *but* peace *shall be* upon I. 3478
128: 6 thy children's children, *and* peace upon I. 3478
129: 1 me from my youth, may I now say: 3478
130: 7 Let I hope in the LORD: for with 3478
130: 8 he shall redeem I from all his iniquities. 3478
131: 3 Let I hope in the LORD from henceforth 3478
135: 4 himself, *and* I for his peculiar treasure. 3478
135:12 an heritage, an heritage unto I his people. 3478
135:19 Bless the LORD, O house of I: bless 3478
136:11 brought out I from among them: for his 3478
136:14 made I to pass through the midst of it: 3478
136:22 *Even* an heritage unto I his servant: for 3478
147: 2 he gathereth together the outcasts of I. 3478
147:19 his statutes and his judgments unto I. 3478
148:14 of the children of I, a people near unto 3478
149: 2 Let I rejoice in him that made him: 3478
Pr 1: 1 of Solomon the son of David, king of I. 3478
Ecc 1:12 the Preacher was king over I in Jerusalem. 3478
SS 3: 7 *men are* about it, of the valiant of I. 3478
Isa 1: 3 *but* I doth not know, my people doth not 3478
1: 4 they have provoked the Holy One of I 3478
1:24 LORD of hosts, the mighty One of I, 3478
4: 2 comely for them that are escaped of I. 3478
5: 7 of the LORD of hosts *is* the house of I, 3478
5:19 let the counsel of the Holy One of I draw 3478
5:24 despised the word of the Holy One of I. 3478
7: 1 and Pekah the son of Remaliah, king of I, 3478
8:14 a rock of offence to both the houses of I, 3478
8:18 for wonders in I from the LORD of hosts, 3478
9: 8 into Jacob, and it hath lighted upon I. 3478
9:12 they shall devour I with open mouth. 3478
9:14 Therefore the LORD will cut off from I 3478
10:17 the light of I shall be for a fire, 3478
10:20 *that* the remnant of I, and such as are 3478
10:20 the LORD, the Holy One of I, in truth. 3478
10:22 For though thy people I be as the sand of 3478
11:12 shall assemble the outcasts of I, 3478
11:16 like as it was to I in the day that he came 3478
12: 6 for great *is* the Holy One of I in the midst 3478
14: 1 yet choose I, and set them in their own 3478
14: 2 the house of I shall possess them in 3478
17: 3 shall be as the glory of the children of I, 3478
17: 6 saith the LORD God of I. 3478
17: 7 shall have respect to the Holy One of I. 3478
17: 9 they left because of the children of I: 3478
19:24 In that day shall I be the third with Egypt 3478
19:25 of my hands, and I mine inheritance. 3478
21:10 the God of I, have I declared unto you. 3478
21:17 for the LORD God of I hath spoken *it.* 3478
24:15 *even* the name of the LORD God of I in 3478
27: 6 I shall blossom and bud, and fill the face 3478
27:12 gathered one by one, O ye children of I. 3478
29:19 men shall rejoice in the Holy One of I. 3478
29:23 One of Jacob, and shall fear the God of I. 3478
30:11 cause the Holy One of I to cease from 3478
30:12 Wherefore thus saith the Holy One of I, 3478
30:15 saith the Lord GOD, the Holy One of I; 3478
30:29 of the LORD, to the mighty One of I. 3478
31: 1 they look not unto the Holy One of I, 3478
31: 6 the children of I have deeply revolted. 3478
37:16 O LORD of hosts, God of I, that dwellest 3478
37:21 Thus saith the LORD God of I, 3478
37:23 on high? *even* against the Holy One of I. 3478
40:27 sayest thou, O Jacob, and speakest, O I, 3478
41: 8 thou, I, *art* my servant, Jacob whom I 3478
41:14 thou worm Jacob, *and* ye men of I; 3478
41:14 thy redeemer, the Holy One of I. 3478
41:16 *and* shalt glory in the Holy One of I. 3478

Isa 41:17 *I* the God of I will not forsake them. 3478
41:20 and the Holy One of I hath created it. 3478
42:24 Jacob for a spoil, and I to the robbers? 3478
43: 1 that formed thee, O I, Fear not: 3478
43: 3 thy God, the Holy One of I, thy Saviour: 3478
43:14 your redeemer, the Holy One of I; 3478
43:15 Holy One, the creator of I, your King. 3478
43:22 but thou hast been weary of me, O I. 3478
43:28 Jacob to the curse, and I to reproaches. 3478
44: 1 my servant; and I, whom I have chosen: 3478
44: 5 and surname *himself* by the name of I. 3478
44: 6 Thus saith the LORD the King of I, 3478
44:21 Remember these, O Jacob and I; for thou 3478
44:21 O I, thou shalt not be forgotten of me. 3478
44:23 redeemed Jacob, and glorified himself in I. 3478
45: 3 call *thee* by thy name, *am* the God of I. 3478
45: 4 Jacob my servant's sake, and I mine elect, 3478
45:11 the Holy One of I, and his maker, 3478
45:15 hidest thyself, O God of I, the saviour. 3478
45:17 *But* I shall be saved in the LORD *with* an 3478
45:25 In the LORD shall all the seed of I be 3478
46: 3 and all the remnant of the house of I, 3478
46:13 I will place salvation in Zion for I my 3478
47: 4 of hosts *is* his name, the Holy One of I. 3478
48: 1 which are called by the name of I, 3478
48: 1 make mention of the God of I, *but* not in 3478
48: 2 and stay themselves upon the God of I; 3478
48:12 unto me, O Jacob, and I my called; 3478
48:17 thy redeemer, the Holy One of I; 3478
49: 3 said unto me, Thou *art* my servant, O I, 3478
49: 5 again to him, Though I be not gathered, 3478
49: 6 of Jacob, and to restore the preserved of I: 3478
49: 7 the redeemer of I, *and* his Holy One, 3478
49: 7 the Holy One of I, and he shall choose 3478
52:12 and the God of I *will be* your rereward. 3478
54: 5 and thy redeemer the Holy One of I; 3478
55: 5 thy God, and for the Holy One of I; 3478
56: 8 which gathereth the outcasts of I saith, 3478
60: 9 to the Holy One of I, because he hath 3478
60:14 the LORD, The Zion of the Holy One of I. 3478
63: 7 great goodness towards the house of I, 3478
63:16 ignorant of us, and I acknowledge us not: 3478
66:20 as the children of I bring an offering in a 3478
Jer 2: 3 I *was* holiness unto the LORD, 3478
2: 4 and all the families of the house of I: 3478
2:14 *Is* I a servant? *is* he a homeborn *slave?* 3478
2:26 he is found, so is the house of I ashamed; 3478
2:31 Have I been a wilderness unto I? a land 3478
3: 6 Hast thou seen *that* which backsliding I 3478
3: 8 I committed adultery I had put her away, 3478
3:11 The backsliding I hath justified herself 3478
3:12 say, Return, thou backsliding I, saith 3478
3:18 of Judah shall walk with the house of I, 3478
3:20 with me, O house of I, saith the LORD. 3478
3:21 and supplications of the children of I: 3478
3:23 in the LORD our God *is* the salvation of I. 3478
4: 1 O I, saith the LORD, return unto me: 3478
5:11 For the house of I and the house of Judah 3478
5:15 from far, O house of I, saith the LORD: 3478
6: 9 shall throughly glean the remnant of I 3478
7: 3 the God of I, Amend your ways and 3478
7:12 to it for the wickedness of my people I. 3478
7:21 saith the LORD of hosts, the God of I; 3478
9:15 saith the LORD of hosts, the God of I; 3478
9:26 all the house of I *are* uncircumcised in 3478
10: 1 LORD speaketh unto you, O house of I: 3478
10:16 and I *is* the rod of his inheritance: 3478
11: 3 unto them, Thus saith the LORD God of I; 3478
11:10 the house of I and the house of Judah 3478
11:17 for the evil of the house of I and of 3478
12:14 I have caused my people I to inherit; 3478
13:11 to cleave unto me the whole house of I 3478
13:12 Thus saith the LORD God of I, 3478
14: 8 the hope of I, the saviour thereof in time 3478
16: 9 saith the LORD of hosts, the God of I; 3478
16:14 that brought up the children of I out of 3478
16:15 that brought up the children of I from 3478
17:13 O LORD, the hope of I, all that forsake 3478
18: 6 house of I, cannot I do with you as this 3478
18: 6 so *are* ye in mine hand, O house of I. 3478
18:13 hath heard such *things:* the virgin of I 3478
19: 3 saith the LORD of hosts, the God of I; 3478
19:15 saith the LORD of hosts, the God of I; 3478
21: 4 Thus saith the LORD God of I; Behold, 3478
23: 2 Therefore thus saith the LORD God of I 3478
23: 6 shall be saved, and I shall dwell safely: 3478
23: 7 which brought up the children of I out of 3478
23: 8 which led the seed of the house of I out 3478
23:13 in Baal, and caused my people I to err. 3478
24: 5 Thus saith the LORD, the God of I; 3478
25:15 For thus saith the LORD God of I unto 3478
25:27 saith the LORD of hosts, the God of I; 3478
27: 4 saith the LORD of hosts, the God of I; 3478
27:21 saith the LORD of hosts, the God of I, 3478
28: 2 the LORD of hosts, the God of I, saying, 3478
28:14 saith the LORD of hosts, the God of I; 3478
29: 4 saith the LORD of hosts, the God of I, 3478
29: 8 saith the LORD of hosts, the God of I; 3478
29:21 the God of I, of Ahab the son of Kolaiah, 3478
29:23 Because they have committed villany in I, 3478
29:25 the LORD of hosts, the God of I, saying, 3478
30: 2 Thus speaketh the LORD God of I, 3478
30: 3 bring again the captivity of my people I 3478
30: 4 words that the LORD spake concerning I 3478
30:10 saith the LORD; neither be dismayed, O I: 3478

Jer 31: 1 will I be the God of all the families of I, 3478
31: 2 *even* I when *I* went to cause him to rest. 3478
31: 4 and thou shalt be built, O virgin of I: 3478
31: 7 save thy people, the remnant of I. 3478
31: 9 for I am a father to I, and Ephraim *is* my 3478
31:10 He that scattered I will gather him, 3478
31:21 turn again, O virgin of I, turn again to 3478
31:23 saith the LORD of hosts, the God of I; 3478
31:27 I will sow the house of I and the house 3478
31:31 a new covenant with the house of I, 3478
31:33 that I will make with the house of I; 3478
31:36 the seed of I also shall cease from being a 3478
31:37 I will also cast off all the seed of I for all 3478
32:14 saith the LORD of hosts, the God of I; 3478
32:15 saith the LORD of hosts, the God of I; 3478
32:20 day, and in I, and amongst *other* men; 3478
32:21 hast brought forth thy people I out of 3478
32:30 For the children of I and the children of 3478
32:30 for the children of I have only provoked 3478
32:32 Because of all the evil of the children of I 3478
32:36 the God of I, concerning this city, 3478
33: 4 For thus saith the LORD, the God of I, 3478
33: 7 of Judah and the captivity of I to return, 3478
33:14 I have promised unto the house of I 3478
33:17 to sit upon the throne of the house of I; 3478
34: 2 Thus saith the LORD, the God of I; 3478
34:13 Thus saith the LORD, the God of I; 3478
35:13 saith the LORD of hosts, the God of I; 3478
35:17 the LORD God of hosts, the God of I; 3478
35:18 saith the LORD of hosts, the God of I; 3478
35:19 saith the LORD of hosts, the God of I; 3478
36: 2 that I have spoken unto thee against I, 3478
37: 7 Thus saith the LORD, the God of I; 3478
38:17 the LORD, the God of hosts, the God of I; 3478
39:16 saith the LORD of hosts, the God of I; 3478
41: 9 king had made for fear of Baasha king of I: 3478
42: 9 Thus saith the LORD, the God of I, 3478
42:15 saith the LORD of hosts, the God of I; 3478
42:18 saith the LORD of hosts, the God of I; 3478
43:10 saith the LORD of hosts, the God of I; 3478
44: 2 saith the LORD of hosts, the God of I; 3478
44: 7 the LORD, the God of hosts, the God of I; 3478
44:11 saith the LORD of hosts, the God of I; 3478
44:25 the LORD of hosts, the God of I, saying; 3478
45: 2 the God of I, unto thee, O Baruch; 3478
46:25 The LORD of hosts, the God of I, saith; 3478
46:27 servant Jacob, and be not dismayed, O I: 3478
48: 1 saith the LORD of hosts, the God of I; 3478
48:13 as the house of I was ashamed of Beth-el 3478
48:27 For was not I a derision unto thee? 3478
49: 1 thus saith the LORD; Hath I no sons? 3478
49: 2 shall I be heir unto them that were his 3478
50: 4 the children of I shall come, they and 3478
50:17 I *is* a scattered sheep; the lions have 3478
50:18 saith the LORD of hosts, the God of I; 3478
50:19 I will bring I again to his habitation, 3478
50:20 the iniquity of I shall be sought for, 3478
50:29 the LORD, against the Holy One of I. 3478
50:33 children of I and the children of Judah 3478
51: 5 For I *hath been* forsaken, nor Judah 3478
51: 5 filled *with* sin against the Holy One of I. 3478
51:19 *things:* and *I is* the rod of his inheritance: NIH
51:33 saith the LORD of hosts, the God of I; 3478
51:49 As Babylon *hath* caused the slain of I to 3478
La 2: 1 heaven *unto* the earth the beauty of I, 3478
2: 3 cut off in *his* fierce anger all the horn of I: 3478
2: 5 hath swallowed up I, he hath swallowed 3478
Eze 2: 3 of man, I send thee to the children of I, 3478
3: 1 roll, and go speak unto the house of I. 3478
3: 4 go, get thee unto the house of I, 3478
3: 5 of a hard language, *but* to the house of I; 3478
3: 7 The house of I will not hearken unto thee; 3478
3: 7 for all the house of I *are* impudent 3478
3:17 thee a watchman unto the house of I: 3478
4: 3 This *shall be* a sign to the house of I. 3478
4: 4 lay the iniquity of the house of I upon it: 3478
4: 5 thou bear the iniquity of the house of I. 3478
4:13 Even thus shall the children of I eat their 3478
5: 4 a fire come forth into all the house of I. 3478
6: 2 set thy face towards the mountains of I, 3478
6: 3 say, Ye mountains of I, hear the word of 3478
6: 5 of the children of I before their idols, 3478
6:11 the evil abominations of the house of I: 3478
7: 2 saith the Lord GOD unto the land of I; 3478
8: 4 the glory of the God of I *was* there, 3478
8: 6 that the house of I committeth here, 3478
8:10 and all the idols of the house of I, 3478
8:11 men of the ancients of the house of I, 3478
8:12 ancients of the house of I do in the dark, 3478
9: 3 the glory of the God of I was gone up 3478
9: 8 thou destroy all the residue of I in thy 3478
9: 9 The iniquity of the house of I and Judah 3478
10:19 The glory of the God of I *was* over them 3478
10:20 under the God of I by the river of Chebar; 3478
11: 5 Thus have ye said, O house of I: 3478
11:10 I will judge you in the border of I; 3478
11:11 *but* I will judge you in the border of I: 3478
11:13 thou make a full end of the remnant of I? 3478
11:15 kindred, and all the house of I wholly, 3478
11:17 and I will give you the land of I. 3478
11:22 the glory of the God of I *was* over them 3478
12: 6 set thee *for* a sign unto the house of I. 3478
12: 9 Son of man, hath not the house of I, 3478
12:10 all the house of I that *are* among them. 3478
12:19 of Jerusalem, *and* of the land of I; 3478

Eze	12:22	that proverb *that* ye have in the land of I,	3478
	12:23	they shall no more use it as a proverb in I;	3478
	12:24	flattering divination within the house of I.	3478
	12:27	of man, behold, *they of* the house of I say,	3478
	13: 2	prophesy against the prophets of I that	3478
	13: 4	O I, thy prophets are like the foxes in	3478
	13: 5	I to stand in the battle in the day of	3478
	13: 9	written in the writing of the house of I,	3478
	13: 9	neither shall they enter into the land of I;	3478
	13:16	*To wit*, the prophets of I which prophesy	3478
	14: 1	came certain of the elders of I unto me,	3478
	14: 4	Every man of the house of I that setteth	3478
	14: 5	That *I* may take the house of I in their	3478
	14: 6	Therefore say unto the house of I,	3478
	14: 7	For every one of the house of I, or of	3478
	14: 7	or of the stranger that sojourneth in I,	3478
	14: 9	him from the midst of my people I	3478
	14:11	the house of I may go no more astray	3478
	17: 2	speak a parable unto the house of I;	3478
	17:23	In the mountain of the height of I will I	3478
	18: 2	use this proverb concerning the land of I,	3478
	18: 3	any more to use this proverb in I.	3478
	18: 6	up his eyes to the idols of the house of I,	3478
	18:15	up his eyes to the idols of the house of I,	3478
	18:25	Hear now, O house of I; Is not my way	3478
	18:29	Yet saith the house of I, The way of	3478
	18:29	O house of I, are not my ways equal?	3478
	18:30	Therefore I will judge you, O house of I,	3478
	18:31	for why will ye die, O house of I?	3478
	19: 1	thou up a lamentation for the princes of I,	3478
	19: 9	more be heard upon the mountains of I.	3478
	20: 1	*that* certain of the elders of I came to	3478
	20: 3	speak unto the elders of I, and say unto	3478
	20: 5	In the day when I chose I, and lifted up	3478
	20:13	the house of I rebelled against me in	3478
	20:27	speak unto the house of I, and say unto	3478
	20:30	Wherefore say unto the house of I,	3478
	20:31	I be inquired of by you, O house of I?	3478
	20:38	they shall not enter into the land of I:	3478
	20:39	As for you, O house of I, thus saith	3478
	20:40	in the mountain of the height of I, saith	3478
	20:40	Lord GOD, there shall all the house of I,	3478
	20:42	when I shall bring you into the land of I,	3478
	20:44	O ye house of I, saith the Lord GOD.	3478
	21: 2	and prophesy against the land of I,	3478
	21: 3	say to the land of I, Thus saith the LORD;	3478
	21:12	*it shall be* upon all the princes of I,	3478
	21:25	thou, profane wicked prince of I,	3478
	22: 6	Behold, the princes of I, every one were	3478
	22:18	the house of I is to me become dross:	3478
	24:21	Speak unto the house of I, Thus saith	3478
	25: 3	the land of I, when it was desolate;	3478
	25: 6	with all thy despite against the land of I;	3478
	25:14	upon Edom by the hand of my people I;	3478
	27:17	Judah, and the land of I, they *were* thy	3478
	28:24	more a pricking brier unto the house of I,	3478
	28:25	When I shall have gathered the house of I	3478
	29: 6	have been a staff of reed to the house of I,	3478
	29:16	no more the confidence of the house of I,	3478
	29:21	the horn of the house of I to bud forth,	3478
	33: 7	set thee a watchman unto the house of I;	3478
	33:10	son of man, speak unto the house of I;	3478
	33:11	for why will ye die, O house of I?	3478
	33:20	ye house of I, I will judge you every one	3478
	33:24	those wastes of the land of I speak,	3478
	33:28	the mountains of I shall be desolate,	3478
	34: 2	prophesy against the shepherds of I,	3478
	34: 2	Woe *be* to the shepherds of I that do feed	3478
	34:13	feed them upon the mountains of I by	3478
	34:14	upon the high mountains of I shall their	3478
	34:14	shall they feed upon the mountains of I.	3478
	34:30	*that* they, *even* the house of I, *are* my	3478
	35: 5	hast shed *the blood* of the children of I by	3478
	35:12	hast spoken against the mountains of I,	3478
	35:15	rejoice at the inheritance of the house of I,	3478
	36: 1	prophesy unto the mountains of I, and say,	3478
	36: 1	say, Ye mountains of I, hear the word of	3478
	36: 6	therefore concerning the land of I,	3478
	36: 8	ye, O mountains of I, ye shall shoot forth	3478
	36: 8	and yield your fruit to my people I:	3478
	36:10	upon you, all the house of I, *even* all of it:	3478
	36:12	men to walk upon you, *even* my people I;	3478
	36:17	when the house of I dwelt in their own	3478
	36:21	which the house of I had profaned among	3478
	36:22	Therefore say unto the house of I,	3478
	36:22	O house of I, but for mine holy name's	3478
	36:32	for your own ways, O house of I.	3478
	36:37	*for* this be inquired of by the house of I,	3478
	37:11	these bones *are* the whole house of I:	3478
	37:12	and bring you into the land of I.	3478
	37:16	and for the children of I his companions:	3478
	37:16	for all the house of I his companions:	3478
	37:19	the tribes of I his fellows, and will put	3478
	37:21	I will take the children of I from among	3478
	37:22	in the land upon the mountains of I;	3478
	37:28	shall know that I the LORD do sanctify I,	3478
	38: 8	against the mountains of I, which have	3478
	38:14	In that day when my people of I dwelleth	3478
	38:16	shalt come up against my people of I,	3478
	38:17	old time by my servants the prophets of I,	3478
	38:18	Gog shall come against the land of I,	3478
	38:19	shall be a great shaking in the land of I;	3478
	39: 2	will bring thee upon the mountains of I:	3478
	39: 4	Thou shalt fall upon the mountains of I,	3478

Eze	39: 7	name known in the midst of my people I;	3478
	39: 7	that I *am* the LORD, the Holy One in I.	3478
	39: 9	they that dwell in the cities of I shall go	3478
	39:11	give unto Gog a place there of graves in I,	3478
	39:12	seven months shall the house of I be	3478
	39:17	a great sacrifice upon the mountains of I,	3478
	39:22	So the house of I shall know that I *am*	3478
	39:23	heathen shall know that the house of I	3478
	39:25	have mercy upon the whole house of I,	3478
	39:29	poured out my spirit upon the house of I,	3478
	40: 2	of God brought he me into the land of I,	3478
	40: 4	all that thou seest to the house of I.	3478
	43: 2	the glory of the God of I came from	3478
	43: 7	in the midst of the children of I for ever,	3478
	43: 7	shall the house of I no more defile,	3478
	43:10	of man, shew the house to the house of I,	3478
	44: 2	because the LORD, the God of I,	3478
	44: 6	to the house of I, Thus saith the Lord	3478
	44: 6	O ye house of I, let it suffice you of all	3478
	44: 9	stranger that *is* among the children of I.	3478
	44:10	away far from me, when I went astray,	3478
	44:12	caused the house of I to fall into iniquity;	3478
	44:15	the children of I went astray from me,	3478
	44:22	maidens of the seed of the house of I,	3478
	44:28	ye shall give them no possession in I: I *am*	3478
	44:29	every dedicate thing in I shall be theirs.	3478
	45: 6	it shall be for the whole house of I.	3478
	45: 8	In the land shall be his possession in I.	3478
	45: 8	to the house of I according to their tribes.	3478
	45: 9	Let it suffice you, O princes of I:	3478
	45:15	two hundred, out of the fat pastures of I;	3478
	45:16	shall give this oblation for the prince in I.	3478
	45:17	in all solemnities of the house of I.	3478
	45:17	to make reconciliation for the house of I.	3478
	47:13	land according to the twelve tribes of I:	3478
	47:18	and from the land of I *by* Jordan,	3478
	47:21	land unto you according to the tribes of I.	3478
	47:22	in the country among the children of I;	3478
	47:22	with you among the tribes of I.	3478
	48:11	astray when the children of I went astray,	3478
	48:19	city shall serve it out of all the tribes of I.	3478
	48:29	*by lot* unto the tribes of I for inheritance,	3478
	48:31	*shall be* after the names of the tribes of I:	3478
Da	1: 3	should bring *certain* of the children of I,	3478
	9: 7	unto all I, *that are* near, and *that are* far	3478
	9:11	Yea, all I have transgressed thy law,	3478
	9:20	my sin and the sin of my people I,	3478
Hos	1: 1	of Jeroboam the son of Joash, king of I.	3478
	1: 4	to cease the kingdom of the house of I.	3478
	1: 5	that I will break the bow of I in the valley	3478
	1: 6	no more have mercy upon the house of I;	3478
	1:10	the number of the children of I shall be	3478
	1:11	the children of I be gathered together,	3478
	3: 1	of the LORD toward the children of I,	3478
	3: 4	the children of I shall abide many days	3478
	3: 5	Afterward shall the children of I return,	3478
	4: 1	the word of the LORD, ye children of I:	3478
	4:15	Though thou, I, play the harlot, *yet* let not	3478
	4:16	For I slideth back as a backsliding heifer:	3478
	5: 1	hearken, ye house of I; and give ye ear,	3478
	5: 3	I know Ephraim, and I is not hid from me:	3478
	5: 3	committest whoredom, *and* I is defiled.	3478
	5: 5	the pride of I doth testify to his face:	3478
	5: 5	therefore shall I and Ephraim fall in their	3478
	5: 9	among the tribes of I have I made known	3478
	6:10	seen a horrible thing in the house of I:	3478
	6:10	*is* the whoredom of Ephraim, I is defiled.	3478
	7: 1	When I *would have* healed I, then	3478
	7:10	the pride of I testifieth to his face:	3478
	8: 2	I shall cry unto me, My God, we know	3478
	8: 3	I hath cast off *the thing that is* good:	3478
	8: 6	For from I *was* it also: the workman made	3478
	8: 8	I is swallowed up: now shall they be	3478
	8:14	For I hath forgotten his Maker,	3478
	9: 1	Rejoice not, O I, for joy, as *other* people:	3478
	9: 7	I shall know *it*: the prophet *is* a fool,	3478
	9:10	I found I like grapes in the wilderness;	3478
	10: 1	I *is* an empty vine, he bringeth forth fruit	3478
	10: 6	I shall be ashamed of his own counsel.	3478
	10: 8	of Aven, the sin of I, shall be destroyed:	3478
	10: 9	O I, thou hast sinned from the days of	3478
	10:15	in a morning shall the king of I utterly be	3478
	11: 1	When I *was* a child, then I loved him,	3478
	11: 8	*how* shall I deliver thee, I? how shall I	3478
	11:12	with lies, and the house of I with deceit:	3478
	12:12	I served for a wife, and for a wife he kept	3478
	12:13	by a prophet the LORD brought I out of	3478
	13: 1	spake trembling, he exalted *himself* in I;	3478
	13: 9	O I, *thou* hast destroyed thyself; but in me	3478
	14: 1	O I, return unto the LORD thy God;	3478
	14: 5	I will be as the dew unto I: he shall grow	3478
Joel	2:27	ye shall know that I *am* in the midst of I,	3478
	3: 2	there for my people and *for* my heritage I,	3478
	3:16	and the strength of the children of I.	3478
Am	1: 1	which he saw concerning I in the days of	3478
	1: 1	of Jeroboam the son of Joash king of I,	3478
	2: 6	For three transgressions of I, and for four,	3478
	2:11	*Is it* not even thus, O ye children of I?	3478
	3: 1	hath spoken against you, O children of I,	3478
	3:12	shall the children of I be taken out that	3478
	3:14	I upon him I will also visit the altars of	3478
	4: 5	for this liketh you, O ye children of I,	3478
	4:12	Therefore thus will I do unto thee, O I:	3478
	4:12	unto thee, prepare to meet thy God, O I.	3478
	5: 1	*even* a lamentation, O house of I.	3478

Am	5: 2	The virgin of I is fallen; she shall no more	3478
	5: 3	hundred shall leave ten, to the house of I.	3478
	5: 4	thus saith the LORD unto the house of I,	3478
	5:25	the wilderness forty years, O house of I?	3478
	6: 1	nations, to whom the house of I came!	3478
	6:14	O house of I, saith the LORD the God of	3478
	7: 8	a plumbline in the midst of my people I:	3478
	7: 9	the sanctuaries of I shall be laid waste;	3478
	7:10	of Beth-el sent to Jeroboam king of I,	3478
	7:10	against thee in the midst of the house of I:	3478
	7:11	I shall surely be led away captive out of	3478
	7:15	unto me, Go, prophesy unto my people I.	3478
	7:16	Prophesy not against I, and drop not *thy*	3478
	7:17	I shall surely go into captivity forth of his	3478
	8: 2	The end is come upon my people *of* I;	3478
	9: 7	the Ethiopians unto me, O children of I?	3478
	9: 7	Have not I brought up I out of the land of	3478
	9: 9	I will sift the house of I among all nations,	3478
	9:14	bring again the captivity of my people of I,	3478
Ob	1:20	captivity of this host of the children of I	3478
Mic	1: 5	all this, and for the sins of the house of I?	3478
	1:13	for the transgressions of I were found in	3478
	1:14	of Achzib *shall be* a lie to the kings of I.	3478
	1:15	he shall come unto Adullam the glory of I.	3478
	2:12	I will surely gather the remnant of I;	3478
	3: 1	of Jacob, and ye princes of the house of I;	3478
	3: 8	Jacob his transgression, and to I his sin.	3478
	3: 9	princes of the house of I, that abhor	3478
	5: 1	they shall smite the judge of I with a rod	3478
	5: 2	come forth unto me *that is* to be ruler in I;	3478
	5: 3	shall return unto the children of I.	3478
	6: 2	with his people, and he will plead with I.	3478
Na	2: 2	excellency of Jacob, as the excellency of I:	3478
Zep	2: 9	saith the LORD of hosts, the God of I,	3478
	3:13	The remnant of I shall not do iniquity,	3478
	3:14	shout, O I; be glad and rejoice with all	3478
	3:15	the king of I, *even* the LORD, *is* in	3478
Zec	1:19	have scattered Judah, I, and Jerusalem.	3478
	8:13	O house of Judah, and house of I;	3478
	9: 1	the eyes of man, as of all the tribes of I,	3478
	11:14	the brotherhood between Judah and I.	3478
	12: 1	burden of the word of the LORD for I,	3478
Mal	1: 1	The burden of the word of the LORD to I	3478
	1: 5	will be magnified from the border of I.	3478
	2:11	an abomination is committed in I and	3478
	2:16	*For* the LORD, the God of I, saith that he	3478
	4: 4	I commanded unto him in Horeb for all I,	3478
Mt	2: 6	a Governor, that shall rule my people I.	2474
	2:20	and his mother, and go into the land of I:	2474
	2:21	his mother, and came into the land of I.	2474
	8:10	have not found so great faith, no not in I.	2474
	9:33	saying, It was never so seen in I.	2474
	10: 6	rather to the lost sheep of the house of I.	2474
	10:23	Ye shall not have gone over the cities of I,	2474
	15:24	but unto the lost sheep of the house of I.	2474
	15:31	to see: and they glorified the God of I.	2474
	19:28	judging the twelve tribes of I.	2474
	27: 9	whom they of the children of I did value;	2474
	27:42	If he be the King of I, let him now come	2474
Mk	12:29	of all the commandments *is*, Hear, O I;	2474
	15:32	Let Christ the King of I descend now from	2474
Lk	1:16	many of the children of I shall he turn	2474
	1:54	He hath holpen his servant I,	2474
	1:68	Blessed *be* the Lord God of I; for he hath	2474
	1:80	deserts till the day of his shewing unto I.	2474
	2:25	devout, waiting for the consolation of I:	2474
	2:32	Gentiles, and the glory of thy people I.	2474
	2:34	for the fall and rising again of many in I;	2474
	4:25	many widows were in I in the days of	2474
	4:27	And many lepers were in I in the time of	2474
	7: 9	have not found so great faith, no, not in I.	2474
	22:30	on thrones judging the twelve tribes of I.	2474
	24:21	been he which should have redeemed I:	2474
Jn	1:31	but that he should be made manifest to I,	2474
	1:49	art the Son of God; thou art the King of I.	2474
	3:10	Art thou a master of I, and knowest not	2474
	12:13	Blessed *is* the King of I that cometh in	2474
Ac	1: 6	this time restore again the kingdom to I?	2474
	2:22	Ye men of I, hear these words; Jesus of	2475
	2:36	Therefore let all the house of I know	2474
	3:12	Ye men of I, why marvel ye at this?	2475
	4: 8	Ye rulers of the people, and elders of I,	2474
	4:10	unto you all, and to all the people of I,	2474
	4:27	with the Gentiles, and the people of I,	2474
	5:21	and all the senate of the children of I,	2474
	5:31	for to give repentance to I,	2474
	5:35	said unto them, Ye men of I, take heed	2475
	7:23	to visit his brethren the children of I,	2474
	7:37	which said unto the children of I,	2474
	7:42	ye house of I, have ye offered to me slain	2474
	9:15	and kings, and the children of I:	2474
	10:36	which *God* sent unto the children of I,	2474
	13:16	Men of I, and *ye* that fear God,	2475
	13:17	The God of this people of I chose our	2474
	13:23	to *his* promise raised unto I a Saviour,	2474
	13:24	of repentance to all the people of I.	2474
	21:28	out, Men of I, help: This is the man,	2475
	28:20	that for the hope of I I am bound with	2474
Ro	9: 6	For they are not all I, which are of Israel:	2474
	9: 6	For they *are* not all Israel, which are of I:	2474
	9:27	Esaias also crieth concerning I, Though	2474
	9:27	Though the number of the children of I	2474
	9:31	But I, which followed *after* the law of	2474
	10: 1	heart's desire and prayer to God for I is,	2474
	10:19	But I say, Did not I know? First Moses	2474

Ro 10:21 But to I he saith, All day long have I 2474
 11: 2 he maketh intercession to God against I, 2474
 11: 7 I hath not obtained that which he seeketh 2474
 11:25 that blindness in part is happened to I, 2474
 11:26 And so all I shall be saved: as it is written, 2474
1Co 10:18 Behold I after the flesh: are not they 2474
2Co 3: 7 that the children of I could not stedfastly 2474
 3:13 that the children of I could not stedfastly 2474
Gal 6:16 and mercy, and upon the I of God. 2474
Eph 2:12 being aliens from the commonwealth of I, 2474
Php 3: 5 of the stock of I, of the tribe of Benjamin, 2474
Heb 8: 8 make a new covenant with the house of I 2474
 8:10 make with the house of I after those days, 2474
 11:22 of the departing of the children of I; 2474
Rev 2:14 a stumblingblock before the children of I, 2474
 7: 4 of all the tribes of the children of I. 2474
 21:12 of the twelve tribes of the children of I: 2474

ISRAEL'S (10) [ISRAEL]

Ge 48:13 Ephraim in his right hand toward I left 3478
 48:13 Manasseh in his left hand towards I right 3478
Ex 18: 8 and to the Egyptians for I sake, 3478
Nu 1:20 I eldest son, by their generations, after 3478
 31:30 the children of I half, thou shalt take one 3478
 31:42 of the children of I half, which Moses 3478
 31:47 Even of the children of I half, Moses took 3478
Dt 21: 8 not innocent blood unto thy people of I 3478
2Sa 5:12 exalted his kingdom for his people I sake. 3478
2Ki 3:11 one of the king of I servants answered and 3478

ISRAELITE (4) [ISRAEL]

Nu 25:14 the name of the I that was slain, 376+3478
2Sa 17:25 a man's son, whose name was Ithra an I, 3481
Jn 1:47 and saith of him, Behold an I indeed, 2475
Ro 11: 1 I also am an I, of the seed of Abraham, 2475

ISRAELITES (18) [ISRAEL]

Ex 9: 7 was not one of the cattle of the I dead. 3478
Lev 23:42 all that are I born shall dwell in booths: 3478
Jos 3:17 all the I passed over on dry ground, until 3478
 8:24 all the I returned unto Ai, and smote it 3478
 13: 6 only divide thou it by lot unto the I for an 3478
 13:13 the Maachathites dwell among the I until 3478
Jdg 20:21 destroyed down to the ground of the I 3478
1Sa 2:14 So they did in Shiloh unto all the I that 3478
 14:21 all the I went down to to the Philistines, 3478
 14:21 even they also turned to be with the I 3478
 25: 1 all the I were gathered together, 3478
 29: 1 the I pitched by a fountain which is in 3478
2Sa 4: 1 were feeble, and all the I were troubled. 3478
2Ki 3:24 the I rose up and smote the Moabites, 3478
 7:13 the multitude of the I that are consumed:) 3478
1Ch 9: 2 possessions in their cities were, the I, 3478
Ro 9: 4 Who are I; to whom pertaineth 2475
2Co 11:22 Are they I? so am I. Are they the seed of 2475

ISRAELITISH (3) [ISRAEL]

Lev 24:10 the son of an I woman, whose father was 3482
 24:10 son of the I woman and a man of Israel 3482
 24:11 the I woman's son blasphemed the name 3482

ISSACHAR (43) [ISACHAR]

Ge 30:18 my husband: and she called his name I. 3485
 35:23 and Levi, and Judah, and I, and Zebulun: 3485
 46:13 the sons of I; Tola, and Phuvah, and Job, 3485
 49:14 I is a strong ass couching down between 3485
Ex 1: 3 I, Zebulun, and Benjamin, 3485
Nu 1: 8 Of I; Nethaneel the son of Zuar. 3485
 1:28 Of the children of I, by their generations, 3485
 1:29 even of the tribe of I, were fifty and 3485
 2: 5 pitch next unto him shall be the tribe of I: 3485
 2: 5 Zuar shall be captain of the children of I. 3485
 7:18 the son of Zuar, prince of I, did offer: 3485
 10:15 of I was Nethaneel the son of Zuar. 3485
 13: 7 Of the tribe of I, Igal the son of Joseph. 3485
 26:23 Of the sons of I after their families: 3485
 26:25 These are the families of I according to 3485
 34:26 the prince of the tribe of the children of I, 3485
Dt 27:12 Judah, and I, and Joseph, and Benjamin, 3485
 33:18 in thy going out; and, I, in thy tents. 3485
Jos 17:10 Asher on the north, and in I on the east. 3485
 17:11 Manasseh had in I and in Asher 3485
 19:17 And the fourth lot came out to I, 3485
 19:17 for the children of I according to their 3485
 19:23 children of I according to their families, 3485
 21: 6 by lot out of the families of the tribe of I, 3485
 21:28 out of the tribe of I, Kishon with her 3485
Jdg 5:15 the princes of I were with Deborah; 3485
 5:15 with Deborah; even I, and also Barak: 3485
 10: 1 son of Puah, the son of Dodo, a man of I 3485
1Ki 4:17 Jehoshaphat the son of Paruah, in I: 3485
 15:27 of the house of I, conspired against him; 3485
1Ch 2: 1 Simeon, Levi, and Judah, I, and Zebulun, 3485
 6:62 their families out of the tribe of I, 3485
 6:72 out of the tribe of I; Kedesh with her 3485
 7: 1 Now the sons of I were, Tola, and Puah, 3485
 7: 5 their brethren among all the families of I 3485
 12:32 of the children of I, which were men that 3485
 12:40 even unto I and Zebulun and Naphtali, 3485
 26: 5 Ammiel the sixth, I the seventh, 3485
 27:18 of David: of I, Omri the son of Michael: 3485
2Ch 30:18 Ephraim, and Manasseh, I, and Zebulun, 3485
Eze 48:25 east side unto the west side, I a portion. 3485
 48:26 by the border of I, from the west side unto 3485
 48:33 one gate of Simeon, one gate of I, one 3485

ISSHIAH (3)

1Ch 24:21 of the sons of Rehabiah, the first was I. 3449
 24:25 The brother of Michah was I: of the sons 3449
 24:25 was Isshiah: of the sons of I; Zechariah. 3449

ISSUE (40) [ISSUED, ISSUES]

Ge 48: 6 thy i, which thou begettest after them, 4138
Lev 12: 7 she shall be cleansed from the i of her 4726
 15: 2 When any man hath a running i out of 2100
 15: 2 of his flesh, because of his i he is unclean. 2101
 15: 3 this shall be his uncleanness in his i: 2101
 15: 3 his flesh run with his i, or his flesh 2101
 15: 3 or his flesh be stopped from his i, it is his 2101
 15: 4 he lieth that hath the i, is unclean: 2100
 15: 6 sat that hath the i shall wash his clothes, 2100
 15: 7 him that hath the i shall wash his clothes, 2100
 15: 8 if he that hath the i spit upon him that is 2100
 15: 9 upon that hath the i shall be unclean. 2100
 15:11 whomsoever he toucheth that hath the i, 2100
 15:12 that he toucheth which hath the i, shall 2100
 15:13 when that hath an i is cleansed of his 2100
 15:13 he that hath an issue is cleansed of his i; 2101
 15:15 for him before the LORD for his i. 2100
 15:19 if a woman have an i, and her issue in 2100
 15:19 an issue, and her i in her flesh be blood, 2100
 15:25 if a woman have an i of her blood 2100+2101
 15:25 all the days of the i of her uncleanness 2101
 15:26 i shall be unto her as the bed of her 2100
 15:28 if she be cleansed of her i, then she shall 2101
 15:30 the LORD for the i of her uncleanness. 2100
 15:32 This is the law of him that hath an i, 2100
 15:33 of him that hath an i, of the man, and of 2101
 22: 4 of Aaron is a leper, or hath a running i; 2100
Nu 5: 2 every one that hath an i, and whosoever 2100
2Sa 3:29 the house of Joab one that hath an i, 2100
2Ki 20:18 of thy sons that shall i from thee, 3318
Isa 22:24 the offspring and the i, all vessels of small 6849
 39: 7 of thy sons that shall i from thee, 3318
Eze 23:20 and whose i is like the issue of horses. 2231
 23:20 and whose issue is like the i of horses. 2231
 47: 8 waters i out toward the east country, 3318
Mt 9:20 which was diseased with an i of blood 131
 22:25 and, having no i, left his wife unto his 4690
Mk 5:25 which had an i of blood twelve years, 4511
Lk 8:43 a woman having an i of blood twelve 4511
 8:44 and immediately her i of blood stanched. 4511

ISSUED (7) [ISSUE]

Jos 8:22 the other i out of the city against them; 3318
Job 38: 8 forth, as if it had i out of the womb? 3318
Eze 47: 1 waters i out from under the threshold of 3318
 47:12 their waters they i out of the sanctuary. 3318
Da 7:10 A fiery stream i and came forth from 5047
Rev 9:17 and out of their mouths i fire and smoke 1607
 9:18 brimstone, which i out of their mouths. 1607

ISSUES (2) [ISSUE]

Ps 68:20 unto GOD the Lord belong the i from 8444
Pr 4:23 all diligence; for out of it are the i of life. 8444

ISUAH (1)

1Ch 7:30 I, and Ishuai, and Beriah, and Serah their 3440

IT (6132) [HOWBEIT, ITSELF] See Index of Articles, Etc.

ITALIAN (1) [ITALY]

Ac 10: 1 a centurion of the band called the I band, 2483

ITALY (5) [ITALY]

Ac 18: 2 born in Pontus, lately come from I, with 2482
 27: 1 was determined that we should sail into I, 2482
 27: 6 found a ship of Alexandria sailing into I; 2482
Heb 13:24 and all the saints. They of I salute you. 2482
 13: S to the Hebrews from I by Timothy. 2482

ITCH (1) [ITCHING]

Dt 28:27 and with the scab, and with the i, 2775

ITCHING (1) [ITCH]

2Ti 4: 3 to themselves teachers, having i ears; 2833

ITHAI (1)

1Ch 11:31 I the son of Ribai of Gibeah, that pertained 863

ITHAMAR (21)

Ex 6:23 him Nadab, and Abihu, Eleazar, and I. 385
 28: 1 Nadab and Abihu, Eleazar and I, 385
 38:21 by the hand of I, son to Aaron the priest. 385
Lev 10: 6 unto Eleazar and unto I his sons, 385
 10:12 and unto I his sons that were left, 385
 10:16 I the sons of Aaron which were left alive, 385
Nu 3: 2 the firstborn, and Abihu, Eleazar, and I. 385
 3: 4 I ministered in the priest's office in the 385
 4:28 their charge shall be under the hand of I 385
 4:33 under the hand of I the son of Aaron 385
 7: 8 under the hand of I the son of Aaron 385
 26:60 born Nadab, and Abihu, Eleazar, and I. 385
1Ch 6: 3 Aaron; Nadab, and Abihu, Eleazar, and I. 385
 24: 1 Aaron; Nadab, and Abihu, Eleazar, and I. 385
 24: 2 Eleazar and I executed the priest's office. 385
 24: 3 of Eleazar, and Ahimelech of the sons of I, 385
 24: 4 of the sons of Eleazar than of the sons of I, 385
 24: 4 eight among the sons of I according to 385
 24: 5 of the sons of Eleazar, and of the sons of 385
 24: 6 taken for Eleazar, and one taken for I. 385

Ezr 8: 2 of the sons of I; Daniel: of the sons of 385

ITHIEL (3)

Ne 11: 7 Maaseiah, the son of I, the son of Jesaiah. 384
Pr 30: 1 man spake unto I, even unto Ithiel and 384
 30: 1 spake unto Ithiel, even unto I and Ucal. 384

ITHLAH See JETHLAH

ITHMAH (1)

1Ch 11:46 the sons of Elnaam, and I the Moabite, 3495

ITHNAN (1)

Jos 15:23 And Kedesh, and Hazor, and I, 3497

ITHRA (1)

2Sa 17:25 man's son, whose name was I an Israelite, 3501

ITHRAN (1)

Ge 36:26 Hemdan, and Eshban, and I, and Cheran. 3506
1Ch 1:41 Amram, and Eshban, and I, and Cheran. 3506
 7:37 Shamma, and Shilshah, and I, and Beera. 3506

ITHREAM (2)

2Sa 3: 5 the sixth, I, by Eglah David's wife. 3507
1Ch 3: 3 of Abital: the sixth, I by Eglah his wife. 3507

ITHRITE (4)

2Sa 23:38 Ira an I, Gareb an Ithrite, 3505
 23:38 Ira an Ithrite, Gareb an I, 3505
1Ch 11:40 Ira the I, Gareb the Ithrite, 3505
 11:40 Ira the Ithrite, Gareb the I, 3505

ITHRITES (1)

1Ch 2:53 I, and the Puhites, and the Shumathites, 3505

ITSELF (50) [IT, SELF]

Ge 1:11 whose seed is in i, upon the earth: 2050.2
 1:12 whose seed was in i, after his kind: 2050.2
Lev 7:24 the fat of the beast that dieth of i, 5038
 17:15 soul that eateth that which died of i, 5038
 18:25 the land i vomiteth out her inhabitants. NIH
 22: 8 That which dieth of i, or is torn with 5038
 25:11 reap that which groweth of i in it, 5599
Dt 14:21 shall not eat of any thing that dieth of i. 5038
1Ki 7:34 the undersetters were of the very base i. NIH
Job 10:22 A land of darkness, as darkness i; and of NIH
Ps 41: 6 his heart gathereth iniquity to i; when 2050.2
 68: 8 even Sinai i was moved at the presence 2088
Pr 18: 2 but that his heart may discover i. NIH
 23:31 colour in the cup, when it moveth i aright. NIH
 27:16 of his right hand, which bewrayeth i. NIH
 27:25 the tender grass sheweth i, and herbs of NIH
Isa 10:15 Shall the axe boast i against him that NIH
 10:15 shall the saw magnify i against him that NIH
 10:15 as if the rod should shake i against them NIH
 10:15 as if the staff should lift up i, as if it were NIH
 37:30 shall eat this year such as groweth of i; 5599
 55: 2 and let your soul delight i in fatness. NIH
 60:20 down; neither shall thy moon withdraw i: NIH
Jer 31:24 them that dwell in Judah i, and in all 1886.3
Eze 1: 4 a fire infolding i, and a brightness was NIH
 4:14 have I not eaten of that which dieth of i, 5038
 17:14 that it might not lift i up, but that by NIH
 29:15 neither shall it exalt i any more above NIH
 44:31 not eat of any thing that is dead of i, 5038
Da 7: 5 it raised up i on one side, and it had three NIH
Mt 6:34 shall take thought for the things of i. 1438
 12:25 Every kingdom divided against i is 1438
 12:25 or house divided against i shall not stand: 1438
Mk 3:24 And if a kingdom be divided against i, 1438
 3:25 And if a house be divided against i, 1438
Lk 11:17 Every kingdom divided against i is 1438
Jn 15: 4 As the branch cannot bear fruit of i, 1438
 20: 7 but wrapped together in a place by i. 5565
 21:25 I suppose that even the world i could not 846
Ro 8:16 The Spirit i beareth witness with our spirit, 846
 8:21 The creature i also shall be delivered 846
 8:26 the Spirit i maketh intercession for us with 846
 14:14 that there is nothing unclean of i: 846
1Co 11:14 Doth not even nature i teach you, that, if 846
 13: 4 charity vaunteth not i, is not puffed up, NIG
 13: 5 Doth not behave i unseemly, seeketh not NIG
2Co 10: 5 every high thing that exalteth i against NIG
Eph 4:16 of the body unto the edifying of i in love. 1438
Heb 9:24 but into heaven i, now to appear in 846
3Jn 1:12 good report of all men, and of the truth i: 846

ITTAH-KAZIN

Jos 19:13 to I, and goeth out to Remmon-methoar 6278

ITTAI (8)

2Sa 15:19 said the king to I the Gittite, Wherefore 863
 15:21 I answered the king, and said, 863
 15:22 David said to I, Go and pass over. And Ittai 863
 15:22 I the Gittite passed over, and all his men, 863
 18: 2 a third part under the hand of I the Gittite. 863
 18: 5 king commanded Joab and Abishai and I, 863
 18:12 the king charged thee and Abishai and I, 863
 23:29 I the son of Ribai out of Gibeah of 863

ITUREA (1)

Lk 3: 1 and his brother Philip tetrarch of I and 2484

IVAH (3)

2Ki 18:34 are the gods of Sepharvaim, Hena, and I? 5755

2Ki 19:13 of the city of Sepharvaim, *of* Hena, and I?	5755
Isa 37:13 of the city of Sepharvaim, Hena, and I?	5755

IVORY (13)

1Ki 10:18 the king made a great throne of **i**,	8127
10:22 and silver, **i**, and apes, and peacocks.	8143
22:39 the **i** house which he made, and all	8127
2Ch 9:17 the king made a great throne of **i**,	8127
9:21 and silver, **i**, and apes, and peacocks.	8143
Ps 45: 8 aloes, *and* cassia, out of the **i** palaces,	8127
SS 5:14 his belly *is as* bright **i** overlaid *with*	8127
7: 4 Thy neck *is as* a tower of **i**; thine eyes *like*	8127
Eze 27: 6 the Ashurites have made thy benches *of* **i**,	8127
27:15 they brought thee *for* a present horns of **i**	8127
Am 3:15 the houses of **i** shall perish, and the great	8127
6: 4 That lie upon beds of **i**,	8127
Rev 18:12 all *manner* vessels of **i**, and all *manner*	1661

IVVAH See IVAH

IYE ABARIM See IJE-ABARIM

IZEHAR (1) [IZEHARITES]

Nu 3:19 Amram, and I, Hebron, and Uzziel.	3324

IZEHARITES (1) [IZEHAR]

Nu 3:27 the family of the I, and the family of	3325

IZHAR (8) [IZHARITES]

Ex 6:18 Amram, and I, and Hebron, and Uzziel:	3324
6:21 the sons of I; Korah, and Nepheg,	3324
Nu 16: 1 Now Korah, the son of I, the son of	3324
1Ch 6: 2 Amram, I, and Hebron, and Uzziel.	3324
6:18 and I, and Hebron, and Uzziel.	3324
6:38 The son of I, the son of Kohath, the son	3324
23:12 Amram, I, Hebron, and Uzziel, four.	3324
23:18 *Of* the sons of I; Shelomith the chief.	3324

IZHARITES (3) [IZHAR]

1Ch 24:22 Of the I; Shelomoth: of the sons of	3325
26:23 *and* the I, the Hebronites,	3325
26:29 Of the I, Chenaniah and his sons *were* for	3325

IZLIAH See JEZLIAH

IZRAHIAH (2)

1Ch 7: 3 the sons of Uzzi; I: and the sons of	3156
7: 3 the sons of I; Michael, and Obadiah,	3156

IZRAHITE (1)

1Ch 27: 8 for the fifth month *was* Shamhuth the I:	3155

IZRI (1)

1Ch 25:11 The fourth to I, *he*, his sons,	3339

IZZIAH See JEZIAH

J

JAAKAN (1) [BENE-JAAKAN]

Dt 10: 6 Beeroth of the children of J *to* Mosera:	3292

JAAKOBAH (1)

1Ch 4:36 J, and Jeshohaiah, and Asaiah, and Adiel,	3291

JAALA (1) [JAALAH]

Ne 7:58 The children of J, the children of Darkon,	3279

JAALAH (1) [JAALA]

Ezr 2:56 The children of J, the children of Darkon,	3279

JAALAM (4)

Ge 36: 5 Aholibamah bare Jeush, and J, and Korah:	3281
36:14 she bare to Esau Jeush, and J, and Korah.	3281
36:18 duke Jeush, duke J, duke Korah:	3281
1Ch 1:35 Reuel, and Jeush, and J, and Korah.	3281

JAANAI (1)

1Ch 5:12 the next, and J, and Shaphat in Bashan.	3285

JAARE-OREGIM (1)

2Sa 21:19 where Elhanan the son of J,	3296

JAARESHIAH See JARESIAH

JAASAU (1)

Ezr 10:37 Mattaniah, Mattenai, and J,	3299

JAASIEL (1)

1Ch 27:21 of Benjamin, J the son of Abner:	3300

JAASU See JAASAU

JAAZANIAH (4)

2Ki 25:23 J the son of a Maachathite, they and	2970
Jer 35: 3 I took J the son of Jeremiah, the son of	2970
Eze 8:11 in the midst of them stood J the son of	2970
11: 1 among whom I saw J the son of Azur,	2970

JAAZER (2)

Nu 21:32 Moses sent to spy out J, and they took	3270
32:35 Atroth, Shophan, and J, and Jogbehah,	3270

JAAZIAH (2)

1Ch 24:26 Mahli and Mushi: the sons of J; Beno.	3269
24:27 The sons of Merari by J; Beno,	3269

JAAZIEL (1)

1Ch 15:18 J, and Shemiramoth, and Jehiel, and Unni,	3268

JABAL (1)

Ge 4:20 Adah bare J: he was the father of such as	2989

JABBOK (7)

Ge 32:22 eleven sons, and passed over the ford J.	2999
Nu 21:24 possessed his land from Arnon unto J,	2999
Dt 2:37 *nor unto* any place of the river J, nor *unto*	2999
3:16 and the border, even unto the river J,	2999
Jos 12: 2 *from* half Gilead, even unto the river J,	2999
Jdg 11:13 from Arnon even unto J, and unto Jordan:	2999
11:22 from Arnon even unto J, and from	2999

JABESH (12) [JABESH-GILEAD]

1Sa 11: 1 all the men of J said unto Nahash, Make a	3003
11: 3 elders of J said unto him, Give us seven	3003
11: 5 they told him the tidings of the men of J.	3003
11: 9 and shewed *it* to the men of J;	3003
11:10 Therefore the men of J said, To morrow	3003
31:12 and came to J, and burnt them there.	3003
31:13 buried *them* under a tree at J,	3003
2Ki 15:10 Shallum the son of J conspired against	3003
15:13 Shallum the son of J *began* to reign in	3003
15:14 smote Shallum the son of J in Samaria,	3003
1Ch 10:12 brought them to J, and buried their bones	3003
10:12 buried their bones under the oak in J,	3003

JABESH-GILEAD (12) [GILEAD, JABESH]

Jdg 21: 8 there came none to the camp from J to	3003
21: 9 *there were* none of the inhabitants of J	3003
21:10 smite the inhabitants of J with the edge of	3003
21:12 they found among the inhabitants of J four	3003
21:14 they had saved alive of the women of J:	3003
1Sa 11: 1 came up, and encamped against J:	3003
11: 9 Thus shall ye say unto the men of J,	3003
31:11 when the inhabitants of J heard of that	3003
2Sa 2: 4 *That* the men of J *were* they that buried	3003
2: 5 David sent messengers unto the men of J	3003
21:12 of Jonathan his son from the men of J,	3003
1Ch 10:11 when all J heard all that the Philistines	3003

JABEZ (4)

1Ch 2:55 families of the scribes which dwelt at J;	3258
4: 9 J was more honourable than his brethren:	3258
4: 9 his mother called his name J, saying,	3258
4:10 J called on the God of Israel, saying,	3258

JABIN (7) [JABIN'S]

Jos 11: 1 when J king of Hazor had heard *those*	2985
Jdg 4: 2 the LORD sold them into the hand of J	2985
4:17 for *there was* peace between J the king of	2985
4:23 So God subdued on that day J the king of	2985
4:24 prevailed against J the king of Canaan,	2985
4:24 until they had destroyed J king of Canaan.	2985
Ps 83: 9 as *to* Sisera, as *to* J, at the brook of Kison:	2985

JABIN'S (1) [JABIN]

Jdg 4: 7 the captain of J army, with his chariots	2985

JABNEEL (2)

Jos 15:11 *to* mount Baalah, and went out *unto* J;	2995
19:33 and Adami, Nekeb, and J, unto Lakum;	2995

JABNEH (1)

2Ch 26: 6 the wall of J, and the wall of Ashdod,	2996

JACAN See JACHAN

JACHAN (1)

1Ch 5:13 Jorai, and J, and Zia, and Heber, seven.	3275

JACHIN (8) [JACHINITES]

Ge 46:10 J, and Zohar, and Shaul the son of a	3199
Ex 6:15 J, and Zohar, and Shaul the son of a	3199
Nu 26:12 of J, the family of the Jachinites:	3199
1Ki 7:21 right pillar, and called the name thereof J:	3199
1Ch 9:10 the priests; Jedaiah, and Jehoiarib, and J,	3199
24:17 The one and twentieth to J, the two and	3199
2Ch 3:17 the name of that on the right hand J,	3199
Ne 11:10 the priests; Jedaiah the son of Joiarib, J,	3199

JACHINITES (1) [JACHIN]

Nu 26:12 Jaminites: of Jachin, the family of the J:	3200

JACINTH (2)

Rev 9:17 of fire, and of **j**, and brimstone:	5191
21:20 eleventh, a **j**; the twelfth, an amethyst.	5192

JACKAL; JACKALS See DRAGON; DRAGONS; FOXES; MONSTERS

JACOB (358) [ISRAEL, JACOB'S]

Ge 25:26 on Esau's heel; and his name was called J:	3290
25:27 and J *was* a plain man, dwelling in tents.	3290
25:28 eat of *his* venison: but Rebekah loved J.	3290
25:29 J sod pottage: and Esau came from	3290
25:30 Esau said to J, Feed me, I pray thee,	3290
25:31 And J said, Sell me *this* day thy birthright.	3290
25:33 J said, Swear to me *this* day; and he sware	3290
25:33 to him: and he sold his birthright unto J.	3290
25:34 J gave Esau bread and pottage of lentiles;	3290
27: 6 Rebekah spake unto J her son, saying,	3290
27:11 J said to Rebekah his mother, Behold,	3290
27:15 and put them upon J her younger son:	3290
27:17 had prepared, into the hand of her son J.	3290
27:19 J said unto his father, I *am* Esau thy	3290
27:21 Isaac said unto J, Come near, I pray thee,	3290
27:22 J went near unto Isaac his father:	3290
27:30 as Isaac had made an end of blessing J,	3290
27:30 J was yet scarce gone out from	3290
27:36 he said, Is not he rightly named J? for he	3290
27:41 Esau hated J because of the blessing	3290
27:41 are at hand; then will I slay my brother J.	3290
27:42 she sent and called J her younger son,	3290
27:46 if I take a wife of the daughters of Heth,	3290
28: 1 Isaac called J, and blessed him,	3290
28: 5 Isaac sent away J: and he went to	3290
28: 6 When Esau saw that Isaac had blessed J,	3290
28: 7 that J obeyed his father and his mother,	3290
28:10 J went out from Beer-sheba,	3290
28:16 J awaked out of his sleep, and he said,	3290
28:18 J rose up early in the morning, and took	3290
28:20 J vowed a vow, saying, If God will be	3290
29: 1 J went on his journey, and came into	3290
29: 4 J said unto them, My brethren, whence	3290
29:10 when J saw Rachel the daughter of Laban	3290
29:10 J went near, and rolled the stone from	3290
29:11 J kissed Rachel, and lifted up his voice,	3290
29:12 J told Rachel that he *was* her father's	3290
29:13 when Laban heard the tidings of J his	3290
29:15 Laban said unto J, Because thou *art* my	3290
29:18 J loved Rachel; and said, I will serve thee	3290
29:20 J served seven years for Rachel;	3290
29:21 J said unto Laban, Give *me* my wife,	3290
29:28 J did so, and fulfilled her week:	3290
30: 1 when Rachel saw that she bare J no	3290
30: 1 J, Give me children, or else I die.	3290
30: 4 to wife: and J went in unto her.	3290
30: 5 And Bilhah conceived, and bare J a son.	3290
30: 7 conceived again, and bare J a second son.	3290
30: 9 Zilpah her maid, and gave her J to wife.	3290
30:10 And Zilpah Leah's maid bare J a son.	3290
30:12 Zilpah Leah's maid bare J a second son.	3290
30:16 came out of the field in the evening,	3290
30:17 she conceived, and bare J the fifth son.	3290
30:19 conceived again, and bare J the sixth son.	3290
30:25 that J said unto Laban, Send me away,	3290
30:31 J said, Thou shalt not give me any thing:	3290
30:36 three days' journey betwixt himself and J:	3290
30:36 and J fed the rest of Laban's flocks.	3290
30:37 J took him rods of green poplar, and of	3290
30:40 J did separate the lambs, and set the faces	3290
30:41 that J laid the rods before the eyes	3290
31: 1 J hath taken away all that *was* our father's	3290
31: 2 J beheld the countenance of Laban,	3290
31: 3 the LORD said unto J, Return unto	3290
31: 4 J sent and called Rachel and Leah to	3290
31:11 God spake unto me in a dream, *saying*, J:	3290
31:17 J rose up, and set his sons and his wives	3290
31:20 J stale away unawares to Laban the Syrian	3290
31:22 it was told Laban on the third day that J	3290
31:24 Take heed that thou speak not to J either	3290
31:25 Laban overtook J. Now Jacob had pitched	3290
31:25 Now J had pitched his tent in the mount:	3290
31:26 Laban said to J, What hast thou done,	3290
31:29 Take thou heed that thou speak not to J	3290
31:31 J answered and said to Laban, Because I	3290
31:32 For J knew not that Rachel had stolen	3290
31:36 J was wroth, and chode with Laban:	3290
31:36 J answered and said to Laban, What *is* my	3290
31:43 Laban answered and said unto J, These	3290
31:45 J took a stone, and set it up *for* a pillar.	3290
31:46 J said unto his brethren, Gather stones;	3290
31:47 it Jegar-sahadutha: but J called it Galeed.	3290
31:51 Laban said to J, Behold this heap,	3290
31:53 And J sware by the fear of his father Isaac.	3290
31:54 J offered sacrifice upon the mount,	3290
32: 1 J went on his way, and the angels of God	3290
32: 2 when J saw them, he said, This *is* God's	3290
32: 3 J sent messengers before him to Esau his	3290
32: 4 Thy servant J saith thus, I have sojourned	3290
32: 6 the messengers returned to J, saying,	3290
32: 7 J was greatly afraid and distressed:	3290
32: 9 J said, O God of my father Abraham,	3290
32:20 Behold, thy servant J *is* behind us.	3290
32:24 J was left alone; and there wrestled a man	3290
32:27 What *is* thy name? And he said, J.	3290
32:28 Thy name shall be called no more J,	3290
32:29 J asked *him*, and said, Tell me, I pray	3290
32:30 J called the name of the place Peniel: for I	3290
33: 1 J lifted up his eyes, and looked,	3290
33:10 J said, Nay, I pray thee, if now I have	3290
33:17 J journeyed to Succoth, and built him a	3290
33:18 J came to Shalem, a city of Shechem,	3290
34: 1 daughter of Leah, which she bare unto J,	3290
34: 3 soul clave unto Dinah the daughter of J,	3290
34: 5 J heard that he had defiled Dinah his	3290
34: 5 and J held his peace until they were come.	3290
34: 6 went out unto J to commune with him.	3290
34: 7 the sons of J came out of the field when	3290
34:13 the sons of J answered Shechem and	3290
34:25 two of the sons of J, Simeon and Levi,	3290

J

J

Ge	34:27 The sons of J came upon the slain,	3290
	34:30 J said to Simeon and Levi, Ye have	3290
	35: 1 God said unto J, Arise, go up to Beth-el,	3290
	35: 2 J said unto his household, and to all that	3290
	35: 4 gave unto J all the strange gods which	3290
	35: 4 J hid them under the oak which *was* by	3290
	35: 5 they did not pursue after the sons of J.	3290
	35: 6 So J came to Luz, which *is* in the land of	3290
	35: 9 God appeared unto J again, when he	3290
	35:10 God said unto him, Thy name *is* J:	3290
	35:10 thy name shall not be called any more J,	3290
	35:14 I set up a pillar in the place where he	3290
	35:15 J called the name of the place where God	3290
	35:20 J set a pillar upon her grave: that *is*	3290
	35:22 Israel heard *it*. Now the sons of J were	3290
	35:26 these *are* the sons of J, which were born	3290
	35:27 J came unto Isaac his father unto Mamre,	3290
	35:29 and his sons Esau and J buried him.	3290
	36: 6 the country from the face of his brother J.	3290
	37: 1 J dwelt in the land wherein his father was	3290
	37: 2 These *are* the generations of J. Joseph,	3290
	37:34 J rent his clothes, and put sackcloth upon	3290
	42: 1 Now when J saw that there was corn in	3290
	42: 1 J said unto his sons, Why do ye look one	3290
	42: 4 J sent not with his brethren;	3290
	42:29 came unto J their father unto the land	3290
	42:36 J their father said unto them, Me have ye	3290
	45:25 came *into* the land of Canaan unto J their	3290
	45:27 the spirit of J their father revived:	3290
	46: 2 the visions of the night, and said, J, Jacob.	3290
	46: 2 the visions of the night, and said, Jacob, J.	3290
	46: 5 J rose up from Beer-sheba: and the sons	3290
	46: 5 the sons of Israel carried J their father,	3290
	46: 6 into Egypt, J, and all his seed with him:	3290
	46: 8 which came into Egypt, J and his sons:	3290
	46:15 which she bare unto J in Padan-aram,	3290
	46:18 these she bare unto J, *even* sixteen souls.	3290
	46:22 the sons of Rachel, which were born to J:	3290
	46:25 his daughter, and she bare these unto J:	3290
	46:26 All the souls that came with J into Egypt,	3290
	46:27 all the souls of the house of J, which came	3290
	47: 7 Joseph brought in J his father, and set him	3290
	47: 7 before Pharaoh: and J blessed Pharaoh.	3290
	47: 8 Pharaoh said unto J, How old *art* thou?	3290
	47: 9 J said unto Pharaoh, The days of the years	3290
	47:10 J blessed Pharaoh, and went out from	3290
	47:28 J lived in the land of Egypt seventeen	3290
	47:28 the whole age of J was an hundred forty	3290
	48: 2 told J, and said, Behold, thy son Joseph	3290
	48: 3 J said unto Joseph, God Almighty	3290
	49: 1 J called unto his sons, and said,	3290
	49: 2 together, and hear, ye sons of J;	3290
	49: 7 will divide them in J, and scatter them in	3290
	49:24 by the hands of the mighty *God* of J;	3290
	49:33 when J had made an end of commanding	3290
	50:24 he sware to Abraham, to Isaac, and to J.	3290
Ex	1: 1 man and his household came with J.	3290
	1: 5 the souls that came *out of* the loins of J	3290
	2:24 with Abraham, with Isaac, and with J.	3290
	3: 6 the God of Isaac, and the God of J.	3290
	3:15 the God of Isaac, and the God of J,	3290
	3:16 of Isaac, and of J, appeared unto me,	3290
	4: 5 the God of Isaac, and the God of J,	3290
	6: 3 Isaac, and unto J, by *the name of* God	3290
	6: 8 to give it to Abraham, to Isaac, and to J;	3290
	19: 3 Thus shalt thou say to the house of J,	3290
	33: 1 to Isaac, and to J, saying, Unto thy seed	3290
Lev	26:42 will I remember my covenant with J,	3290
Nu	23: 7 curse me J, and come, defy Israel.	3290
	23:10 Who can count the dust of J,	3290
	23:21 He hath not beheld iniquity in J,	3290
	23:23 Surely *there is* no enchantment against J,	3290
	23:23 according to *this* time it shall be said of J	3290
	24: 5 O J, *and* thy tabernacles, O Israel!	3290
	24:17 there shall come a Star out of J,	3290
	24:19 Out of J shall come he that shall have	3290
	32:11 unto Abraham, unto Isaac, and unto J;	3290
Dt	1: 8 Abraham, Isaac, and J, to give unto them	3290
	6:10 Abraham, to Isaac, and to J, to give thee	3290
	9: 5 unto thy fathers, Abraham, Isaac, and J.	3290
	9:27 thy servants, Abraham, Isaac, and J;	3290
	29:13 fathers, to Abraham, to Isaac, and to J.	3290
	30:20 to Abraham, to Isaac, and to J, to give	3290
	32: 9 his people; J *is* the lot of his inheritance.	3290
	33: 4 the inheritance of the congregation of J.	3290
	33:10 They shall teach J thy judgments,	3290
	33:28 the fountain of J *shall be* upon a land of	3290
	34: 4 Isaac, and unto J, saying, I will give it	3290
Jos	24: 4 I gave unto Isaac J and Esau: and I gave	3290
	24: 4 J and his children went down *into* Egypt.	3290
	24:32 in a parcel of ground which J bought of	3290
1Sa	12: 8 When J was come *into* Egypt,	3290
2Sa	23: 1 anointed of the God of J, and the sweet	3290
1Ki	18:31 the number of the tribes of the sons of J,	3290
2Ki	13:23 Isaac, and J, and would not destroy them,	3290
	17:34 the LORD commanded the children of J,	3290
1Ch	16:13 ye children of J, his chosen *ones*.	3290
	16:17 hath confirmed the same to J for a law,	3290
Ps	14: 7 J shall rejoice, *and* Israel shall be glad.	3290
	20: 1 the name of the God of J defend thee;	3290
	22:23 all ye the seed of J, glorify him;	3290
	24: 6 that seek him, that seek thy face, O J.	3290
	44: 4 O God: command deliverances for J.	3290
	46: 7 *is* with us; the God of J *is* our refuge.	3290
	46:11 *is* with us; the God of J *is* our refuge.	3290

Ps	47: 4 us, the excellency of J whom he loved.	3290
	53: 6 J shall rejoice, *and* Israel shall be glad.	3290
	59:13 let them know that God ruleth in J unto	3290
	75: 9 ever; I will sing *praises* to the God of J.	3290
	76: 6 thy rebuke, O God of J, both the chariot	3290
	77:15 thy people, the sons of J and Joseph.	3290
	78: 5 For he established a testimony in J,	3290
	78:21 so a fire was kindled against J,	3290
	78:71 he brought him to feed J his people,	3290
	79: 7 For they have devoured J, and laid waste	3290
	81: 1 make a joyful noise unto the God of J.	3290
	81: 4 for Israel, *and* a law of the God of J.	3290
	84: 8 my prayer: give ear, O God of J. Selah.	3290
	85: 1 thou hast brought back the captivity of J.	3290
	87: 2 of Zion more than all the dwellings of J.	3290
	94: 7 neither shall the God of J regard *it*.	3290
	99: 4 judgment and righteousness in J.	3290
	105: 6 his servant, ye children of J, his chosen.	3290
	105:10 confirmed the same unto J for a law,	3290
	105:23 and J sojourned in the land of Ham.	3290
	114: 1 the house of J from a people of strange	3290
	114: 7 the Lord, at the presence of the God of J;	3290
	132: 2 *and* vowed unto the mighty *God* of J.	3290
	132: 5 a habitation for the mighty *God* of J.	3290
	135: 4 For the LORD hath chosen J unto	3290
	146: 5 Happy *is he* that *hath* the God of J for his	3290
	147:19 He sheweth his word unto J, his statutes	3290
Isa	2: 3 the LORD, to the house of the God of J;	3290
	2: 5 O house of J, come ye, and let us walk in	3290
	2: 6 hast forsaken thy people the house of J,	3290
	8:17 that hideth his face from the house of J,	3290
	9: 8 The Lord sent a word into J, and it hath	3290
	10:20 and such as are escaped of the house of J,	3290
	10:21 *even* the remnant of J, unto the mighty	3290
	14: 1 For the LORD will have mercy on J,	3290
	14: 1 and they shall cleave to the house of J.	3290
	17: 4 *that* the glory of J shall be made thin,	3290
	27: 6 He shall cause them *that come of* J to take	3290
	27: 9 shall the iniquity of J be purged;	3290
	29:22 concerning the house of J,	3290
	29:22 of Jacob, J shall not now be ashamed,	3290
	29:23 sanctify the Holy One of J, and shall fear	3290
	40:27 sayest thou, O J, and speakest, O Israel,	3290
	41: 8 *art* my servant, J whom I have chosen,	3290
	41:14 thou worm J, *and* ye men of Israel;	3290
	41:21 your strong *reasons*, saith the King of J.	3290
	42:24 Who gave J for a spoil, and Israel to	3290
	43: 1 O J, and he that formed thee, O Israel,	3290
	43:22 thou hast not called upon me, O J;	3290
	43:28 have given J to the curse, and Israel to	3290
	44: 1 Yet now hear, O J my servant; and Israel,	3290
	44: 2 Fear not, O J, my servant;	3290
	44: 5 shall call *himself* by the name of J;	3290
	44:21 Remember these, O J and Israel; for thou	3290
	44:23 for the LORD hath redeemed J,	3290
	45: 4 For J my servant's sake, and Israel mine	3290
	45:19 I said not unto the seed of J, Seek ye me	3290
	46: 3 O house of J, and all the remnant of	3290
	48: 1 Hear ye this, O house of J, which are	3290
	48:12 unto me, O J, and Israel my called;	3290
	48:20 The LORD hath redeemed his servant J.	3290
	49: 5 to bring J again to him, Though Israel be	3290
	49: 6 be my servant to raise up the tribes of J,	3290
	49:26 and thy redeemer, the mighty One of J.	3290
	58: 1 and the house of J their sins.	3290
	58:14 feed thee with the heritage of J thy father:	3290
	59:20 them that turn from transgression in J,	3290
	60:16 and thy redeemer, the mighty One of J.	3290
	65: 9 I will bring forth a seed out of J, and out	3290
Jer	2: 4 O house of J, and all the families of	3290
	5:20 Declare this in the house of J,	3290
	10:16 The portion of J is not like them: for he *is*	3290
	10:25 for they have eaten up J,	3290
	30:10 thou not, O my servant J, saith the LORD;	3290
	30:10 J shall return, and shall be in rest,	3290
	31: 7 Sing with gladness for J, and shout among	3290
	31:11 For the LORD hath redeemed J,	3290
	33:26 will I cast away the seed of J,	3290
	33:26 over the seed of Abraham, Isaac, and J:	3290
	46:27 O my servant J, and be not dismayed,	3290
	46:27 J shall return, and be in rest and at ease,	3290
	46:28 Fear thou not, O J my servant, saith	3290
	51:19 The portion of J *is* not like them; for he *is*	3290
La	1:17 the LORD hath commanded concerning J,	3290
	2: 2 swallowed up all the habitations of J,	3290
	2: 3 he burned against J like a flaming fire,	3290
Eze	20: 5 hand unto the seed of the house of J,	3290
	28:25 land that I have given to my servant J,	3290
	37:25 land that I have given unto J my servant,	3290
	39:25 Now will I bring again the captivity of J,	3290
Hos	10:11 shall plow, *and* J shall break his clods.	3290
	12: 2 and *will* punish J according to his ways;	3290
	12:12 J fled *into* the country of Syria,	3290
Am	3:13 Hear ye, and testify in the house of J,	3290
	6: 8 I abhor the excellency of J, and hate his	3290
	7: 2 *by* whom shall J arise? for he *is* small.	3290
	7: 5 *by* whom shall J arise? for he *is* small.	3290
	8: 7 LORD hath sworn by the excellency of J,	3290
	9: 8 I will not utterly destroy the house of J,	3290
Ob	1:10 For *thy* violence against thy brother J	3290
	1:17 the house of J shall possess their	3290
	1:18 the house of J shall be a fire, and the	3290
Mic	1: 5 For the transgression of J *is* all this,	3290
	1: 5 What *is* the transgression of J? *is it* not	3290
	2: 7 O thou that *art* named the house of J,	3290

Mic	2:12 I will surely assemble, O J, all of thee;	3290
	3: 1 heads of J, and ye princes of the house of	3290
	3: 8 to declare unto J his transgression,	3290
	3: 9 ye heads of the house of J, and princes of	3290
	4: 2 to the house of the God of J;	3290
	5: 7 the remnant of J shall be in the midst of	3290
	5: 8 the remnant of J shall be among	3290
	7:20 Thou wilt perform the truth to J,	3290
Na	2: 2 hath turned *away* the excellency of J,	3290
Mal	1: 2 saith the LORD: yet I loved J,	3290
	2:12 out of the tabernacles of J, and him that	3290
	3: 6 therefore ye sons of J are not consumed.	3290
Mt	1: 2 and Isaac begat J; and Jacob begat Judas	2384
	1: 2 and J begat Judas and his brethren;	2384
	1:15 begat Matthan; and Matthan begat J;	2384
	1:16 And J begat Joseph the husband of Mary,	2384
	8:11 Isaac, and J, in the kingdom of heaven.	2384
	22:32 and the God of Isaac, and the God of J?	2384
Mk	12:26 and the God of Isaac, and the God of J?	2384
Lk	1:33 And he shall reign over the house of J for	2384
	3:34 was *the son* of J, which was *the son*	2384
	13:28 and Isaac, and J, and all the prophets,	2384
	20:37 and the God of Isaac, and the God of J.	2384
Jn	4: 5 near to the parcel of ground that J gave to	2384
	4:12 Art thou greater than our father J,	2384
Ac	3:13 God of Abraham, and of Isaac, and of J,	2384
	7: 8 and Isaac *begat* J; and Jacob begat	2384
	7: 8 and J *begat* the twelve patriarchs.	2384
	7:12 But when J heard that there was corn in	2384
	7:14 and called his father J to *him*, and all his	2384
	7:15 So J went down into Egypt, and died,	2384
	7:32 and the God of Isaac, and the God of J.	2384
	7:46 to find a tabernacle for the God of J.	2384
Ro	9:13 As it is written, J have I loved,	2384
	11:26 and shall turn away ungodliness from J:	2384
Heb	11: 9 dwelling in tabernacles with Isaac and J,	2384
	11:20 By faith Isaac blessed J and Esau	2384
	11:21 By faith J, when he was a dying,	2384

JACOB'S (19) [JACOB]

Ge	27:22 The voice *is* J voice, but the hands *are*	3290
	28: 5 brother of Rebekah, J and Esau's mother.	3290
	30: 2 J anger was kindled against Rachel:	3290
	30:42 feebler were Laban's, and the stronger J.	3290
	31:33 Laban went into J tent, and into Leah's	3290
	32:18 thou shalt say, *They be* thy servant J; it *is*	3290
	32:25 the hollow of J thigh was out of joint, as	3290
	32:32 he touched the hollow of J thigh in	3290
	34: 7 folly in Israel in lying with J daughter:	3290
	34:19 because he had delight in J daughter:	3290
	35:23 J firstborn, and Simeon, and Levi,	3290
	45:26 J heart fainted, for he believed them not.	NIH
	46: 8 Jacob and his sons: Reuben, J firstborn.	3290
	46:19 The sons of Rachel J wife; Joseph,	3290
	46:26 out of his loins, besides J sons' wives,	3290
Jer	30: 7 *is* even the time of J trouble; but he shall	3290
	30:18 I *will* bring again the captivity of J tents,	3290
Mal	1: 2 *was* not Esau J brother? saith	3290+3807.1
Jn	4: 6 Now J well was there. Jesus therefore,	2384

JADA (2)

1Ch	2:28 the sons of Onam were, Shammai, and J.	3047
	2:32 the sons of J the brother of Shammai;	3047

JADAU (1)

Ezr	10:43 Zabad, Zebina, J, and Joel, Benaiah.	3035

JADDAI See JADAU

JADDUA (3)

Ne	10:21 Meshezabeel, Zadok, J,	3037
	12:11 begat Jonathan, and Jonathan begat J.	3037
	12:22 Joiada, and Johanan, and J, *were* recorded	3037

JADON (1)

Ne	3: 7 J the Meronothite, the men of Gibeon,	3036

JAEL (6)

Jdg	4:17 the tent of J the wife of Heber the Kenite:	3278
	4:18 J went out to meet Sisera, and said unto	3278
	4:21 Then J Heber's wife took a nail of the tent,	3278
	4:22 as J came out to meet him, and said unto	3278
	5: 6 in the days of J, the highways were	3278
	5:24 Blessed above women shall J the wife of	3278

JAGUR (1)

Jos	15:21 southward were Kabzeel, and Eder, and J,	3017

JAH (1) [LORD*]

Ps	68: 4 rideth upon the heavens by his name J,	3050

JAHATH (8)

1Ch	4: 2 Reaiah the son of Shobal begat J;	3189
	4: 2 and J begat Ahumai, and Lahad.	3189
	6:20 Libni his son, J his son, Zimmah his son,	3189
	6:43 The son of J, the son of Gershom, the son	3189
	23:10 the sons of Shimei were, J, Zina,	3189
	23:11 J was the chief, and Zizah the second:	3189
	24:22 Shelomoth: of the sons of Shelomoth; J.	3189
2Ch	34:12 overseers of them *were* J and Obadiah,	3189

JAHAZ (5)

Nu	21:23 he came *to* J, and fought against Israel.	3096
Dt	2:32 he and all his people, to fight at J.	3096
Jdg	11:20 pitched in J, and fought against Israel.	3096
Isa	15: 4 their voice shall be heard *even* unto J:	3096

JAHAZAH (3)
Jos	13:18 And J, and Kedemoth, and Mephaath,	3096
	21:36 with her suburbs, and J with her suburbs,	3096
Jer	48:21 and upon J, and upon Mephaath,	3096

JAHAZIAH (1)
Ezr	10:15 J the son of Tikvah were employed about	3167

JAHAZIEL (6)
1Ch	12: 4 J, and Johanan, and Josabad	3166
	16: 6 J the priests with trumpets continually	3166
	23:19 the third, and Jekameam the fourth.	3166
	24:23 J the third, Jekameam the fourth.	3166
2Ch	20:14 upon J the son of Zechariah, the son of	3166
Ezr	8: 5 the son of J, and with him three hundred	3166

JAHDAI (1)
1Ch	2:47 the sons of J; Regem, and Jotham,	3056

JAHDIEL (1)
1Ch	5:24 and Jeremiah, and Hodaviah, and J,	3164

JAHDO (1)
1Ch	5:14 of Jeshishai, the son of J, the son of Buz;	3163

JAHLEEL (2) [JAHLEELITES]
Ge	46:14 sons of Zebulun; Sered, and Elon, and J.	3177
Nu	26:26 of J, the family of the Jahleelites.	3177

JAHLEELITES (1) [JAHLEEL]
Nu	26:26 the Elonites: of Jahleel, the family of the J.	3178

JAHMAI (1)
1Ch	7: 2 Jeriel, and J, and Jibsam, and Shemuel,	3181

JAHZAH (1)
1Ch	6:78 with her suburbs, and J with her suburbs,	3096

JAHZEEL (2) [JAHZEELITES, JAHZIEL]
Ge	46:24 J, and Guni, and Jezer, and Shillem.	3183
Nu	26:48 of J, the family of the Jahzeelites: of Guni,	3183

JAHZEELITES (1) [JAHZEEL]
Nu	26:48 of Jahzeel, the family of the J: of Guni,	3184

JAHZEIAH See JAHAZIAH

JAHZERAH (1)
1Ch	9:12 the son of J, the son of Meshullam, the	3170

JAHZIEL (1) [JAHZEEL]
1Ch	7:13 J, and Guni, and Jezer, and Shallum.	3185

JAILOR (1)
Ac	16:23 charging the j to keep them safely:	1200

JAIR (10) [BASHAN-HAVOTH-JAIR]
Nu	32:41 J the son of Manasseh went and took	2971
Dt	3:14 J the son of Manasseh took all the country	2971
Jos	13:30 all the towns of J, which are in Bashan,	2971
Jdg	10: 3 after him arose J, a Gileadite,	2971
	10: 5 And J died, and was buried in Camon.	2971
1Ki	4:13 to him pertained the towns of J the son	2971
1Ch	2:22 Segub begat J, who had three and	2971
	2:23 Aram, with the towns of J, from them,	2971
	20: 5 Elhanan the son of J slew Lahmi	3265
Est	2: 5 the son of J, the son of Shimei, the son of	2971

JAIRITE (1)
2Sa	20:26 Ira also the J was a chief ruler about	2972

JAIRUS (2)
Mk	5:22 of the rulers of the synagogue, J by name;	2383
Lk	8:41 there came a man named J, and he was a	2383

JAKAN (1)
1Ch	1:42 sons of Ezer; Bilhan, and Zavan, and J.	3292

JAKEH (1)
Pr	30: 1 The words of Agur the son of J, even	3348

JAKIM (2)
1Ch	8:19 And J, and Zichri, and Zabdi,	3356
	24:12 The eleventh to Eliashib, the twelfth to J,	3356

JAKIN See JACHIN

JAKINITE See JACHINITES

JALAM See JAALAM

JALON (1)
1Ch	4:17 Jether, and Mered, and Epher, and J:	3210

JAMBRES (1)
2Ti	3: 8 Now as Jannes and J withstood Moses,	2387

JAMES (42)
Mt	4:21 J the son of Zebedee, and John his	2385
	10: 2 J, the son of Zebedee, and John his	2385
	10: 3 the son of Alpheus, and Lebbeus,	2385
	13:55 Mary? and his brethren, J, and Joses,	2385
	17: 1 and John his brother, and bringeth	2385
	27:56 and Mary the mother of J and Joses,	2385
Mk	1:19 he saw J the son of Zebedee, and John his	2385
	1:29 of Simon and Andrew, with J and John.	2385

JAMES (continued)
Mk	3:17 And J the son of Zebedee, and John	2385
	3:17 son of Zebedee, and John the brother of J;	2385
	3:18 and J the son of Alpheus, and Thaddeus,	2385
	5:37 and J, and John the brother of James.	2385
	5:37 and James, and John the brother of J.	2385
	6: 3 the brother of J, and Joses, and of Juda,	2385
	9: 2 and J, and John, and leadeth them up into	2385
	10:35 And J and John, the sons of Zebedee,	2385
	10:41 they began to be much displeased with J	2385
	13: 3 Peter and J and John and Andrew asked	2385
	14:33 he taketh with him Peter and J and John,	2385
	15:40 and Mary the mother of J the less and	2385
	16: 1 and Mary the mother of J, and Salome,	2385
Lk	5:10 And so was also J, and John, the sons of	2385
	6:14 J and John, Philip and Bartholomew,	2385
	6:15 The son of Alpheus, and Simon called	2385
	6:16 And Judas the brother of J,	2385
	8:51 and J, and John, and the father and	2385
	9:28 he took Peter and John and J, and went	2385
	9:54 And when his disciples J and John saw	2385
	24:10 Mary the mother of J, and other	2385
Ac	1:13 and J, and John, and Andrew, Philip,	2385
	1:13 J the son of Alpheus, and Simon Zelotes,	2385
	1:13 Simon Zelotes, and Judas the brother of J.	2385
	12: 2 And he killed J the brother of John with	2385
	12:17 Go shew these things unto J, and to	2385
	15:13 J answered, saying, Men and brethren,	2385
	21:18 day following Paul went in with us unto J;	2385
1Co	15: 7 After that, he was seen of J; then of all	2385
Gal	1:19 saw I none, save J the Lord's brother.	2385
	2: 9 And when J, Cephas, and John,	2385
	2:12 For before that certain came from J, he did	2385
Jas	1: 1 J, a servant of God and of the Lord Jesus	2385
Jude	1: 1 servant of Jesus Christ, and brother of J,	2385

JAMIN (6) [JAMINITES]
Ge	46:10 J, and Ohad, and Jachin, and Zohar,	3226
Ex	6:15 J, and Ohad, and Jachin, and Zohar,	3226
Nu	26:12 of J, the family of the Jaminites: of Jachin,	3226
1Ch	2:27 Jerahmeel were, Maaz, and J, and Eker.	3226
	4:24 and J, Jarib, Zerah, and Shaul:	3226
Ne	8: 7 and Sherebiah, J, Akkub, Shabbethai,	3226

JAMINITES (1) [JAMIN]
Nu	26:12 of Jamin, the family of the J: of Jachin,	3228

JAMLECH (1)
1Ch	4:34 and J, and Joshah the son of Amaziah,	3230

JANAI See JAANAI

JANGLING (1)
1Ti	1: 6 swerved have turned aside unto vain j;	3150

JANIM See JANUM

JANNA (1)
Lk	3:24 was the son of J, which was the son	2388

JANNAI See JANNA

JANNES (1)
2Ti	3: 8 Now as J and Jambres withstood Moses,	2389

JANOAH (1)
2Ki	15:29 J, and Kedesh, and Hazor, and Gilead,	3239

JANOHAH (2)
Jos	16: 6 and passed by it on the east to J;	3239
	16: 7 it went down from J to Ataroth,	3239

JANUM (1)
Jos	15:53 And J, and Beth-tappuah, and Aphekah,	3241

JAPHETH (11)
Ge	5:32 and Noah begat Shem, Ham, and J.	3315
	6:10 Noah begat three sons, Shem, Ham, and J.	3315
	7:13 Shem, and Ham, and J, the sons of Noah,	3315
	9:18 of the ark, were Shem, and Ham, and J:	3315
	9:23 Shem and J took a garment, and laid it	3315
	9:27 God shall enlarge J, and he shall dwell in	3315
	10: 1 of the sons of Noah, Shem, Ham, and J:	3315
	10: 2 The sons of J; Gomer, and Magog,	3315
	10:21 the brother of J the elder, even to him	3315
1Ch	1: 4 Noah, Shem, Ham, and J.	3315
	1: 5 The sons of J; Gomer, and Magog,	3315

JAPHIA (4)
Jos	10: 3 unto J king of Lachish, and unto Debir	3309
	19:12 goeth out to Daberath, and goeth up to J,	3309
2Sa	5:15 also, and Elishua, and Nepheg, and J,	3309
1Ch	3: 7 And Nogah, and Nepheg, and J,	3309
	14: 6 And Nogah, and Nepheg, and J,	3309

JAPHLET (3)
1Ch	7:32 Heber begat J, and Shomer, and Hotham,	3310
	7:33 the sons of J; Pasach, and Bimhal,	3310
	7:33 and Ashvath. These are the children of J.	3310

JAPHLETI (1)
Jos	16: 3 goeth down westward to the coast of J,	3311

JAPHLETITES See JAPHLETI

JAPHO (1)
Jos	19:46 and Rakkon, with the border before J.	3305

JAR; JARS See BARREL; BARRELS; CRUSE; WATERPOT; WATERPOTS

JARAH (2)
1Ch	9:42 Ahaz begat J; and Jarah begat Alemeth,	3294
	9:42 J begat Alemeth, and Azmaveth,	3294

JAREB (2)
Hos	5:13 to the Assyrian, and sent to king J:	3377
	10: 6 unto Assyria for a present to king J:	3377

JARED (6)
Ge	5:15 lived sixty and five years, and begat J:	3382
	5:16 Mahalaleel lived after he begat J eight	3382
	5:18 lived an hundred sixty and two years,	3382
	5:19 J lived after he begat Enoch eight hundred	3382
	5:20 all the days of J were nine hundred sixty	3382
Lk	3:37 the son of Enoch, which was the son of J,	2391

JARESIAH (1)
1Ch	8:27 J, and Eliah, and Zichri, the sons of	3298

JARHA (2)
1Ch	2:34 servant, an Egyptian, whose name was J.	3398
	2:35 Sheshan gave his daughter to J his servant	3398

JARIB (3)
1Ch	4:24 and Jamin, J, Zerah, and Shaul:	3402
Ezr	8:16 for J, and for Elnathan, and for Nathan,	3402
	10:18 and Eliezer, and J, and Gedaliah.	3402

JARMUTH (7)
Jos	10: 3 unto Piram king of J, and unto Japhia king	3412
	10: 5 the king of Hebron, the king of J, the king	3412
	10:23 the king of Hebron, the king of J, the king	3412
	12:11 The king of J, one; the king of Lachish,	3412
	15:35 J, and Adullam, Socoh, and Azekah,	3412
	21:29 J with her suburbs, En-gannim with her	3412
Ne	11:29 at En-rimmon, and at Zareah, and at J,	3412

JAROAH (1)
1Ch	5:14 the son of J, the son of Gilead, the son of	3386

JASHAR See JASHER

JASHEN (1)
2Sa	23:32 the Shaalbonite, of the sons of J, Jonathan,	3464

JASHER (2)
Jos	10:13 Is not this written in the book of J?	3477
2Sa	1:18 it is written in the book of J.)	3477

JASHOBEAM (3)
1Ch	11:11 J, a Hachmonite, the chief of the captains:	3434
	12: 6 and Jesiah, and Azareel, and Joezer, and J,	3434
	27: 2 the first month was J the son of Zabdiel:	3434

JASHUB (3) [JASHUBITES]
Nu	26:24 Of J, the family of the Jashubites:	3437
1Ch	7: 1 Tola, and Puah, J, and Shimron, four.	3437
Ezr	10:29 and Adaiah, J, and Sheal, and Ramoth.	3437

JASHUBI-LEHEM (1)
1Ch	4:22 who had the dominion in Moab, and J.	3433

JASHUBITES (1) [JASHUB]
Nu	26:24 Of Jashub, the family of the J: of Shimron,	3432

JASIEL (1)
1Ch	11:47 Eliel, and Obed, and J the Mesobaite.	3300

JASON (5)
Ac	17: 5 assaulted the house of J, and sought to	2394
	17: 6 they drew J and certain brethren unto	2394
	17: 7 Whom J hath received: and these all do	2394
	17: 9 And when they had taken security of J,	2394
Ro	16:21 and Lucius, and J, and Sosipater,	2394

JASPER (7)
Ex	28:20 fourth row a beryl, and an onyx, and a j:	3471
	39:13 the fourth row, a beryl, an onyx, and a j:	3471
Eze	28:13 beryl, the onyx, and the j, the sapphire,	3471
Rev	4: 3 And he that sat was to look upon like a j	2393
	21:11 even like a j stone, clear as crystal;	2393
	21:18 And the building of the wall of it was of j:	2393
	21:19 The first foundation was j; the second,	2393

JATHNIEL (1)
1Ch	26: 2 second, Zebadiah the third, J the fourth,	3496

JATTIR (4)
Jos	15:48 the mountains, Shamir, and J, and Socoh,	3492
	21:14 J with her suburbs, and Eshtemoa with	3492
1Sa	30:27 and to them which were in J,	3492
1Ch	6:57 and J, and Eshtemoa, with their suburbs,	3492

JAVAN (7)
Ge	10: 2 J, and Tubal, and Meshech, and Tiras.	3120
	10: 4 the sons of J; Elishah, and Tarshish,	3120
1Ch	1: 5 J, and Tubal, and Meshech, and Tiras.	3120
	1: 7 the sons of J; Elishah, and Tarshish,	3120
Isa	66:19 Lud, that draw the bow, to Tubal, and J,	3120
Eze	27:13 Tubal, and Meshech, they were thy	3120
	27:19 Dan also and J going to and fro occupied	3120

JAVELIN (7)
Nu	25: 7 the congregation, and took a j in his hand;	7420

J

1Sa	18:10 and *there was* a **j** in Saul's hand.	2595
	18:11 Saul cast the **j**; for he said, I will smite	2595
	19: 9 he sat in his house with **j** in his hand:	2595
	19:10 smite David even to the wall with the **j**;	2595
	19:10 and he smote the **j** into the wall:	2595
	20:33 Saul cast a **j** at him to smite him:	2595

JAVELINS See DARTS

JAW (4) [JAWBONE, JAWS]

Jdg	15:16 the **j** of an ass have I slain a thousand	3895
	15:19 clave a hollow place that *was* in the **j**,	3895
Job	41: 2 or bore his **j** through with a thorn?	3895
Pr	30:14 *are as* swords, and their **j teeth** *as* knives,	4973

JAWBONE (3) [BONE, JAW]

Jdg	15:15 he found a new **j** of an ass, and put forth	3895
	15:16 Samson said, With the **j** of an ass,	3895
	15:17 that he cast away the **j** out of his hand,	3895

JAWS (6) [JAW]

Job	29:17 I brake the **j** of the wicked, and pluckt	4973
Ps	22:15 my tongue cleaveth to my **j**; and thou	4455
Isa	30:28 *shall be* a bridle in the **j** of the people,	3895
Eze	29: 4 I will put hooks in thy **j**, and I will cause	3895
	38: 4 put hooks into thy **j**, and I will bring thee	3895
Hos	11: 4 as they that take off the yoke on their **j**,	3895

JAZER (11)

Nu	32: 1 when they saw the land of **J**, and the land	3270
	32: 3 J, and Nimrah, and Heshbon, and Elealeh	3270
Jos	13:25 their coast was **J**, and all the cities of	3270
	21:39 with her suburbs, **J** with her suburbs;	3270
2Sa	24: 5 midst of the river of Gad, and toward **J**:	3270
1Ch	6:81 with her suburbs, and **J** with her suburbs.	3270
	26:31 them mighty *men* of valour at **J** of Gilead.	3270
Isa	16: 8 are come *even* unto **J**, they wandered	3270
	16: 9 with the weeping of **J** the vine of Sibmah:	3270
Jer	48:32 will weep for thee with the weeping of **J**:	3270
	48:32 the sea, they reach *even* to the sea of **J**:	3270

JAZIZ (1)

1Ch	27:31 over the flocks *was* **J** the Hagerite.	3151

JEALOUS (19) [JEALOUSY]

Ex	20: 5 for I the Lord thy God *am* a **j** God,	7067
	34:14 for the Lord, whose name *is* **J**, *is* a	7067
	34:14 whose name *is* Jealous, *is* a **j** God:	7067
Nu	5:14 he be **j** of his wife, and she be defiled:	7065
	5:14 he be **j** of his wife, and she be not defiled:	7065
	5:30 he be **j** over his wife, and shall set	7065
Dt	4:24 God *is* a consuming fire, *even* a **j** God,	7067
	5: 9 for I the Lord thy God *am* a **j** God,	7067
	6:15 (For the Lord thy God *is* a **j** God among	7067
Jos	24:19 for he *is* a holy God; he *is* a **j** God; he will	7072
1Ki	19:10 I have been **very j** for the Lord	7065+7065
	19:14 I have been **very j** for the Lord	7065+7065
Eze	39:25 of Israel, and will be **j** for my holy name;	7065
Joel	2:18 will the Lord be **j** for his land,	7065
Na	1: 2 God *is* **j**, and the Lord revengeth;	7072
Zec	1:14 I am **j** for Jerusalem and for Zion *with* a	7065
	8: 2 I was **j** for Zion *with* great jealousy,	7065
	8: 2 and I was **j** for her *with* great fury.	7065
2Co	11: 2 For I am **j** over you with godly jealousy:	2206

JEALOUSIES (1) [JEALOUSY]

Nu	5:29 This *is* the law of **j**, when a wife goeth	7068

JEALOUSY (34) [JEALOUS, JEALOUSIES]

Nu	5:14 the spirit of **j** come upon him, and he be	7068
	5:14 or if the spirit of **j** come upon him,	7068
	5:15 for it *is* an offering of **j**, an offering of	7068
	5:18 in her hands, which *is* the **j** offering:	7068
	5:25 the priest shall take the **j** offering out of	7068
	5:30 Or when the spirit of **j** cometh upon him,	7068
	25:11 not the children of Israel in my **j**.	7068
Dt	29:20 and his **j** shall smoke against that man,	7068
	32:16 **provoked** him to **j** with strange *gods*,	7065
	32:21 have **moved** me to **j** with *that which*	7065
	32:21 I will **move** them to **j** with *those which*	7065
1Ki	14:22 they **provoked** him to **j** with their sins	7065
Ps	78:58 **moved** him to **j** with their graven images.	7065
	79: 5 for ever? shall thy **j** burn like fire?	7068
Pr	6:34 For **j** *is* the rage of a man: therefore he	7068
SS	8: 6 *is* cruel as the grave:	7068
Isa	42:13 *man*, he shall stir up **j** like a man of war:	7068
Eze	8: 3 where *was* the seat of the image of **j**,	7068
	8: 3 image of jealousy, which **provoketh** to **j**.	7069
	8: 5 of the altar this image of **j** in the entry.	7068
	16:38 and I will give thee blood in fury and **j**.	7068
	16:42 my **j** shall depart from thee, and I will be	7068
	23:25 I will set my **j** against thee, and they shall	7068
	36: 5 Surely in the fire of my **j** have I spoken	7068
	36: 6 I have spoken in my **j** and in my fury,	7068
	38:19 For in my **j** and in the fire of my wrath	7068
Zep	1:18 land shall be devoured by the fire of his **j**:	7068
	3: 8 shall be devoured with the fire of my **j**.	7068
Zec	1:14 for Jerusalem and for Zion *with* a great **j**.	7068
	8: 2 I was jealous for Zion *with* great **j**,	7068
Ro	10:19 I will **provoke** you to **j** *by them that are*	3863
	11:11 the Gentiles, for to **provoke** them to **j**.	3863
1Co	10:22 Do we **provoke** the Lord to **j**? are we	3863
2Co	11: 2 For I am jealous over you with godly **j**:	2205

JEARIM (1) [KIRJATH-JEARIM]

Jos	15:10 passed along unto the side of mount **J**,	3297

JEATERAI (1)

1Ch	6:21 Iddo his son, Zerah his son, **J** his son.	2979

JEATHERAI See JEATERAI

JEBERECHIAH (1)

Isa	8: 2 the priest, and Zechariah the son of **J**.	3000

JEBEREKIAH See JEBERECHIAH

JEBUS (4) [JEBUSI, JEBUSITE, JEBUSITES, JERUSALEM]

Jdg	19:10 and departed, and came over against **J**,	2982
	19:11 *And* when they *were* by **J**, the day was far	2982
1Ch	11: 4 all Israel went *to* Jerusalem, which *is* **J**;	2982
	11: 5 the inhabitants of **J** said to David,	2982

JEBUSI (2) [JEBUS]

Jos	18:16 to the side of **J** on the south,	2983
	18:28 Zelah, Eleph, and **J**, which *is* Jerusalem,	2983

JEBUSITE (14) [JEBUS]

Ge	10:16 J, and the Amorite, and the Girgashite,	2983
Ex	33: 2 and the Perizzite, the Hivite, and the **J**:	2983
	34:11 the Perizzite, and the Hivite, and the **J**.	2983
Jos	9: 1 the Perizzite, the Hivite, and the **J**,	2983
	11: 3 the **J** in the mountains, and *to* the Hivite	2983
	15: 8 of Hinnom unto the south side of the **J**;	2983
2Sa	24:16 by the threshingplace of Araunah the **J**.	2983
	24:18 in the threshingfloor of Araunah the **J**.	2983
1Ch	1:14 The **J** also, and the Amorite,	2983
	21:15 by the threshingfloor of Ornan the **J**.	2983
	21:18 in the threshingfloor of Ornan the **J**.	2983
	21:28 him in the threshingfloor of Ornan the **J**.	2983
2Ch	3: 1 in the threshingfloor of Ornan the **J**.	2983
Zec	9: 7 as a governor in Judah, and Ekron as a **J**.	2983

JEBUSITES (25) [JEBUS]

Ge	15:21 and the Girgashites, and the **J**.	2983
Ex	3: 8 the Perizzites, and the Hivites, and the **J**.	2983
	3:17 the Perizzites, and the Hivites, and the **J**.	2983
	13: 5 the Amorites, and the Hivites, and the **J**,	2983
	23:23 the Canaanites, the Hivites, and the **J**:	2983
Nu	13:29 the Hittites, and the **J**, and the Amorites,	2983
Dt	7: 1 the Perizzites, and the Hivites, and the **J**,	2983
	20:17 and the Perizzites, the Hivites, and the **J**,	2983
Jos	3:10 and the Amorites, and the **J**.	2983
	12: 8 the Perizzites, the Hivites, and the **J**:	2983
	15:63 As for the **J** the inhabitants of Jerusalem,	2983
	15:63 the **J** dwell with the children of Judah at	2983
	24:11 the Girgashites, the Hivites, and the **J**;	2983
Jdg	1:21 drive out the **J** that inhabited Jerusalem;	2983
	1:21 the **J** dwell with the children of Benjamin	2983
	3: 5 and Perizzites, and Hivites, and **J**:	2983
	19:11 let us turn in into this city of the **J**,	2983
2Sa	5: 6 his men went *to* Jerusalem unto the **J**,	2983
	5: 8 smiteth the **J**, and the lame and the blind,	2983
1Ki	9:20 Hittites, Perizzites, Hivites, and **J**,	2983
1Ch	11: 4 where the **J** *were*, the inhabitants of	2983
	11: 6 Whosoever smiteth the **J** first shall be	2983
2Ch	8: 7 the Perizzites, and the Hivites, and the **J**,	2983
Ezr	9: 1 the Hittites, the Perizzites, the **J**,	2983
Ne	9: 8 and the **J**, and the Girgashites,	2983

JECAMIAH (1)

1Ch	3:18 Pedaiah, and Shenazar, **J**, Hoshama,	3359

JECHOLIAH (1) [JECOLIAH]

2Ki	15: 2 his mother's name *was* **J** of Jerusalem.	3203

JECHONIAS (2) [JECONIAH]

Mt	1:11 And Josias begat **J** and his brethren,	2423
	1:12 brought to Babylon, **J** begat Salathiel;	2423

JECOLIAH (1) [JECHOLIAH]

2Ch	26: 3 His mother's name also *was* **J** of	3203

JECONIAH (7) [JECHONIAS]

1Ch	3:16 of Jehoiakim: **J** his son, Zedekiah his son.	3204
	3:17 And the sons of **J**; Assir, Salathiel his son,	3204
Est	2: 6 been carried away with **J** king of Judah,	3204
Jer	24: 1 the son of Jehoiakim king of Judah,	3204
	27:20 when he carried away captive **J** the son of	3204
	28: 4 I *will* bring again to this place **J** the son of	3204
	29: 2 (After that **J** the king, and the queen,	3204

JEDAIAH (13)

1Ch	4:37 the son of Allon, the son of **J**, the son of	3042
	9:10 of the priests; **J**, and Jehoiarib, and Jachin,	3048
	24: 7 came forth to Jehoiarib, the second to **J**,	3048
Ezr	2:36 the children of **J**, of the house of Jeshua,	3048
Ne	3:10 next unto them repaired **J** the son of	3042
	7:39 the children of **J**, of the house of Jeshua,	3048
	11:10 Of the priests: **J** the son of Joiarib, Jachin,	3048
	12: 6 Shemaiah, and Joiarib, **J**,	3048
	12: 7 Sallu, Amok, Hilkiah, **J**. These *were*	3048
	12:19 And of Joiarib, Mattenai; of **J**, Uzzi;	3048
	12:21 Of Hilkiah, Hashabiah; of **J**, Nethaneel.	3048
Zec	6:10 *even* of Heldai, of Tobijah, and of **J**,	3048
	6:14 to **J**, and to Hen the son of Zephaniah,	3048

JEDIAEL (6)

1Ch	7: 6 Bela, and Becher, and **J**, three.	3043
	7:10 The sons also of **J**; Bilhan: and the sons of	3043
	7:11 All these the sons of **J**, by the heads of	3043
	11:45 **J** the son of Shimri, and Joha his brother,	3043

1Ch	12:20 J, and Michael, and Jozabad, and Elihu,	3043
	26: 2 **J** the second, Zebadiah the third,	3043

JEDIDAH (1)

2Ki	22: 1 his mother's name *was* **J**, the daughter of	3040

JEDIDIAH (1) [SOLOMON]

2Sa	12:25 he called his name **J**, because of	3041

JEDUTHUN (17)

1Ch	9:16 son of **J**, and Berechiah the son of Asa,	3038
	16:38 Obed-edom also the son of **J** and Hosah to	3038
	16:41 with them Heman and **J**, and the rest that	3038
	16:42 with them Heman and **J** with trumpets	3038
	16:42 of God. And the sons of **J** *were* porters.	3038
	25: 1 of Heman, and of **J**, who should prophesy	3038
	25: 3 Of **J**: the sons of Jeduthun; Gedaliah,	3038
	25: 3 the sons of **J**; Gedaliah, and Zeri,	3038
	25: 3 six, under the hands of their father **J**,	3038
	25: 6 the king's order *to* Asaph, **J**, and Heman.	3038
2Ch	5:12 of Heman, of **J**, with their sons and	3038
	29:14 of the sons of **J**; Shemaiah, and Uzziel.	3038
	35:15 Asaph, and Heman, and **J** the king's seer;	3038
Ne	11:17 Shammua, the son of Galal, the son of **J**.	3038
Ps	39: T *even* to **J**, A Psalm of David.	3038
	62: T the chief Musician, to **J**, A Psalm of David.	3038
	77: T the chief Musician, to **J**, A Psalm of Asaph.	3038

JEEZER (1) [JEEZERITES]

Nu	26:30 *of* **J**, the family of the Jeezerites: of Helek,	372

JEEZERITES (1) [JEEZER]

Nu	26:30 *of* Jeezer, the family of the **J**: of Helek,	373

JEGAR-SAHADUTHA (1)

Ge	31:47 Laban called it **J**: but Jacob called it	3026

JEHALELEEL (1)

1Ch	4:16 the sons of **J**; Ziph, and Ziphah, Tiria,	3094

JEHALELEL (1)

2Ch	29:12 the son of Abdi, and Azariah the son of **J**:	3094

JEHALLELEL See JEHALELEEL; JEHALELEL

JEHDEIAH (2)

1Ch	24:20 Shubael: of the sons of Shubael; **J**.	3165
	27:30 and over the asses *was* **J** the Meronothite:	3165

JEHEZEKEL (1)

1Ch	24:16 to Pethahiah, the twentieth to **J**,	3168

JEHEZKEL See JEHEZEKEL

JEHIAH (1)

1Ch	15:24 and **J** *were* doorkeepers for the ark.	3174

JEHIEL (16)

1Ch	9:35 J, whose wife's name *was* Maachah:	3273
	11:44 and **J** the sons of Hothan the Aroerite,	3273
	15:18 J, and Unni, Eliab, and Benaiah,	3171
	15:20 J, and Unni, and Eliab, and Maaseiah,	3171
	16: 5 J, and Mattithiah, and Eliab, and Benaiah,	3171
	23: 8 the chief *was* **J**, and Zetham, and Joel,	3171
	27:32 the son of Hachmoni *was* with the	3171
	29: 8 by the hand of **J** the Gershonite.	3171
2Ch	21: 2 J, and Zechariah, and Azariah,	3171
	29:14 of the sons of Heman; **J**, and Shimei:	3171
	31:13 J, and Azaziah, and Nahath, and Asahel,	3171
	35: 8 Hilkiah and Zechariah and **J**, rulers of	3171
Ezr	8: 9 Obadiah the son of **J**, and with him two	3171
	10: 2 Shechaniah the son of **J**, *one* of the sons	3171
	10:21 Elijah, and Shemaiah, and **J**, and Uzziah.	3171
	10:26 and **J**, and Abdi, and Jeremoth, and Eliah.	3171

JEHIELI (2)

1Ch	26:21 *even* of Laadan the Gershonite, *were* **J**.	3172
	26:22 The sons of **J**; Zetham, and Joel his	3172

JEHIZKIAH (1)

2Ch	28:12 **J** the son of Shallum, and Amasa the son	3169

JEHOADAH (2)

1Ch	8:36 Ahaz begat **J**; and Jehoadah begat Alemeth	3085
	8:36 **J** begat Alemeth, and Azmaveth,	3085

JEHOADDAH See JEHOADAH

JEHOADDAN (2)

2Ki	14: 2 his mother's name *was* **J** of Jerusalem.	3086
2Ch	25: 1 his mother's name *was* **J** of Jerusalem.	3086

JEHOAHAZ (23)

2Ki	10:35 And **J** his son reigned in his stead.	3059
	13: 1 **J** the son of Jehu *began* to reign over	3059
	13: 4 J besought the Lord, and the Lord	3059
	13: 7 Neither did he leave of the people to **J**	3059
	13: 8 the rest of the acts of **J**, and all that he	3059
	13: 9 J slept with his fathers; and they buried	3059
	13:10 son of **J** to reign over Israel in Samaria,	3059
	13:22 Syria oppressed Israel all the days of **J**.	3059
	13:25 Jehoash the son of **J** took again out of	3059
	13:25 he had taken out of the hand of **J** his	3059
	14: 1 In the second year of Joash son of **J** king	3099
	14: 8 the son of **J** son of Jehu, king of Israel,	3059
	14:17 son of **J** king of Israel fifteen years.	3059
	23:30 the people of the land took **J** the son of	3059

JEHOIAKIM (37) [ELIAKIM]

2Ki	23:34 turned his name to J, and took Jehoahaz	3079
	23:35 J gave the silver and the gold to Pharaoh;	3079
	23:36 J was twenty and five year old when he	3079
	24: 1 and J became his servant three years:	3079
	24: 5 the rest of the acts of J, and all that he	3079
	24: 6 So J slept with his fathers:	3079
	24:19 according to all that J had done.	3079
1Ch	3:15 the second J, the third Zedekiah,	3079
	3:16 the sons of J: Jeconiah his son,	3079
2Ch	36: 4 and Jerusalem, and turned his name to J.	3079
	36: 5 J was twenty and five year old when he	3079
	36: 8 Now the rest of the acts of J,	3079
Jer	1: 3 It came also in the days of J the son of	3079
	22:18 J the son of Josiah king of Judah;	3079
	22:24 though Coniah the son of J king of Judah	3079
	24: 1 Jeconiah the son of J king of Judah,	3079
	25: 1 year of J the son of Josiah king of Judah,	3079
	26: 1 In the beginning of the reign of J the son	3079
	26:21 when J the king, with all his mighty men,	3079
	26:22 the king sent men into Egypt, namely,	3079
	26:23 Egypt, and brought him unto J the king;	3079
	27: 1 In the beginning of the reign of J king	3079
	27:20 J king of Judah from Jerusalem to	3079
	28: 4 place Jeconiah the son of J king of Judah,	3079
	35: 1 days of J the son of Josiah king of Judah,	3079
	36: 1 it came to pass in the fourth year of J	3079
	36: 9 came to pass in the fifth year of J the son	3079
	36:28 which J the king of Judah hath burnt.	3079
	36:29 thou shalt say to J king of Judah,	3079
	36:30 Therefore thus saith the LORD of J king	3079
	36:32 J king of Judah had burnt in the fire:	3079
	37: 1 reigned instead of Coniah the son of J,	3079
	45: 1 In the fourth year of J the son of Josiah	3079
	46: 2 year of J the son of Josiah king of Judah.	3079
	52: 2 according to all that J had done.	3079
Da	1: 1 In the third year of the reign of J king of	3079
	1: 2 the Lord gave J king of Judah into his	3079

JEHOIARIB (2)

1Ch	9:10 of the priests; Jedaiah, and J, and Jachin,	3080
	24: 7 Now the first lot came forth to J,	3080

JEHONADAB (3)

2Ki	10:15 he lighted on J the son of Rechab coming	3082
	10:15 J answered, It is. If it be, give me thine	3082
	10:23 Jehu went, and J the son of Rechab,	3082

JEHONATHAN (3)

1Ch	27:25 in the castles, was J the son of Uzziah:	3083
2Ch	17: 8 J, and Adonijah, and Tobijah,	3083
Ne	12:18 Of Bilgah, Shammua; of Shemaiah, J;	3083

JEHORAM (23)

1Ki	22:50 and J his son reigned in his stead.	3088
2Ki	1:17 J reigned in his stead in the second year	3088
	1:17 of J the son of Jehoshaphat king of Judah;	3088
	3: 1 J the son of Ahab began to reign over	3088
	3: 6 king J went out of Samaria the same time,	3088
	8:16 J the son of Jehoshaphat king of Judah	3088
	8:25 the son of J king of Judah begin to reign.	3088
	8:29 Ahaziah the son of J king of Judah went	3088
	9:24 smote J between his arms, and the arrow	3088
	12:18 J, and Ahaziah, his fathers, kings of Judah,	3088
2Ch	17: 8 and with them Elishama and J, priests.	3088
	21: 1 And J his son reigned in his stead.	3088
	21: 3 the kingdom gave he to J; because he was	3088
	21: 4 Now when J was risen up to the kingdom	3088
	21: 5 J was thirty and two years old when he	3088
	21: 9 J went forth with his princes, and all his	3088
	21:16 Moreover the LORD stirred up against J	3088
	22: 1 So Ahaziah the son of J king of Judah	3088
	22: 5 went with J the son of Ahab king of Israel	3088
	22: 6 Azariah the son of J king of Judah went	3088
	22: 6 down to see J the son of Ahab at Jezreel,	3088
	22: 7 he went out with J against Jehu the son	3088
	22:11 So Jehoshabeath, the daughter of king J,	3088

JEHOSHABEATH (2)

2Ch	22:11 J, the daughter of the king, took Joash	3090
	22:11 So J, the daughter of king Jehoram,	3090

JEHOSHAPHAT (85) [JOSAPHAT]

2Sa	8:16 and J the son of Ahilud was recorder;	3092
	20:24 and J the son of Ahilud was recorder:	3092
1Ki	4: 3 scribes; J the son of Ahilud, the recorder.	3092
	4:17 J the son of Paruah, in Issachar:	3092
	15:24 and J his son reigned in his stead.	3092
	22: 2 that J the king of Judah came down to	3092
	22: 4 he said unto J, Wilt thou go with me to	3092
	22: 4 J said to the king of Israel, I am as thou	3092
	22: 5 J said unto the king of Israel, Inquire,	3092
	22: 7 J said, Is there not here a prophet of	3092
	22: 8 the king of Israel said unto J, There is yet	3092
	22: 8 And J said, Let not the king say so.	3092
	22:10 The king of Judah sat each on his throne,	3092
	22:18 the king of Israel said unto J, Did I not tell	3092
	22:29 J the king of Judah went up to	3092
	22:30 the king of Israel said unto J, I will	3092
	22:32 when the captains of the chariots saw J,	3092
	22:32 aside to fight against him: and J cried out.	3092
	22:41 the son of Asa began to reign over Judah	3092
	22:42 J was thirty and five years old when he	3092
	22:44 And J made peace with the king of Israel.	3092
	22:45 the rest of the acts of J, and his might	3092

1Ki	22:48 J made ships of Tharshish to go to Ophir	3092
	22:49 said Ahaziah the son of Ahab unto J,	3092
	22:49 servants in the ships. But J would not.	3092
	22:50 J slept with his fathers, and was buried	3092
	22:51 the seventeenth year of J king of Judah,	3092
2Ki	1:17 of Jehoram the son of J king of Judah;	3092
	3: 1 the eighteenth year of J king of Judah,	3092
	3: 7 he went and sent to J the king of Judah,	3092
	3:11 J said, Is there not here a prophet of	3092
	3:12 J said, The word of the LORD is with	3092
	3:12 So the king of Israel and J and the king of	3092
	3:14 were it not that I regard the presence of J	3092
	8:16 king of Israel, J being then king of Judah,	3092
	8:16 Jehoram the son of J king of Judah began	3092
	9: 2 look out there Jehu the son of J the son of	3092
	9:14 So Jehu the son of J the son of Nimshi	3092
	12:18 Judah took all the hallowed things that J,	3092
1Ch	3:10 Abia his son, Asa his son, J his son,	3092
	15:24 J, and Nethaneel, and Amasai,	3146
	18:15 host; and J the son of Ahilud, recorder.	3092
2Ch	17: 1 J his son reigned in his stead.	3092
	17: 3 the LORD was with J, because he walked	3092
	17: 5 all Judah brought to J presents; and he	3092
	17:10 so that they made no war against J.	3092
	17:11 Also some of the Philistines brought J	3092
	17:12 J waxed great exceedingly; and he built	3092
	18: 1 Now J had riches and honour in	3092
	18: 3 Ahab king of Israel said unto J king of	3092
	18: 4 J said unto the king of Israel, Inquire,	3092
	18: 6 J said, Is there not here a prophet of	3092
	18: 7 the king of Israel said unto J, There is yet	3092
	18: 7 Imla. And J said, Let not the king say so.	3092
	18: 9 J king of Judah sat either of them on his	3092
	18:17 the king of Israel said to J, Did I not tell	3092
	18:28 J the king of Judah went up to	3092
	18:29 the king of Israel said unto J, I will	3092
	18:31 when the captains of the chariots saw J,	3092
	18:31 J cried out, and the LORD helped him:	3092
	19: 1 J the king of Judah returned to his house	3092
	19: 2 said to king J, Shouldest thou help	3092
	19: 4 J dwelt at Jerusalem: and he went out	3092
	19: 8 Moreover in Jerusalem did J set of	3092
	20: 1 the Ammonites, came against J to battle.	3092
	20: 2 there came some that told J, saying,	3092
	20: 3 J feared, and set himself to seek	3092
	20: 5 J stood in the congregation of Judah and	3092
	20:15 inhabitants of Jerusalem, and thou king J,	3092
	20:18 J bowed his head with his face to	3092
	20:20 J stood and said, Hear me, O Judah,	3092
	20:25 when J and his people came to take away	3092
	20:27 Jerusalem, and J in the forefront of them,	3092
	20:30 So the realm of J was quiet: for his God	3092
	20:31 J reigned over Judah: he was thirty and	3092
	20:34 the rest of the acts of J, first and last,	3092
	20:35 after this did J king of Judah join himself	3092
	20:37 of Mareshah prophesied against J,	3092
	21: 1 Now J slept with his fathers,	3092
	21: 2 he had brethren the sons of J, Azariah,	3092
	21: 2 these were the sons of J king of Israel.	3092
	21:12 not walked in the ways of J thy father,	3092
	22: 9 Because, said they, he is the son of J,	3092
Joel	3: 2 will bring them down into the valley of J,	3092
	3:12 and come up to the valley of J:	3092

JEHOSHEBA (1)

2Ki	11: 2 J, the daughter of king Joram, sister of	3089

JEHOSHUA (2) [JOSHUA]

Nu	13:16 Moses called Oshea the son of Nun, J.	3091
1Ch	7:27 Non his son, J his son.	3091

JEHOVAH (4) [GOD*, JEHOVAH-JIREH,
JEHOVAH-NISSI, JEHOVAH-SHALOM, LORD*]

Ex	6: 3 by my name J was I not known to them.	3068
Ps	83:18 know that thou, whose name alone is J,	3068
Isa	12: 2 for the LORD J is my strength and	3068
	26: 4 for in the LORD J is everlasting strength:	3068

JEHOVAH-JIREH (1) [JEHOVAH]

Ge	22:14 Abraham called the name of that place J:	3070

JEHOVAH-NISSI (1) [JEHOVAH]

Ex	17:15 built an altar, and called the name of it J:	3071

JEHOVAH-SHALOM (1) [JEHOVAH]

Jdg	6:24 altar there unto the LORD, and called it J:	3073

JEHOZABAD (4)

2Ki	12:21 the son of Shomer, his servants,	3075
1Ch	26: 4 the second, Joab the third, and Sacar	3075
2Ch	17:18 next him was J, and with him an hundred	3075
	24:26 and J the son of Shimrith a Moabitess.	3075

JEHOZADAK (2)

1Ch	6:14 Azariah begat Seraiah, and Seraiah begat J,	3087
	6:15 J went into captivity, when the LORD	3087

JEHU (59)

1Ki	16: 1 the word of the LORD came to J the son	3058
	16: 7 also by the hand of the prophet J the son	3058
	16:12 which J spake against Baasha by J	3058
	19:16 J the son of Nimshi shalt thou anoint to	3058
	19:17 escapeth the sword of Hazael shall J slay:	3058
	19:17 that escapeth from the sword of J shall	3058
2Ki	9: 2 look out there J the son of Jehoshaphat	3058
	9: 5 J said, Unto which of all us? And he said,	3058

JEHOASH (17)

2Ki	11:21 Seven years old was J when he began to	3060
	12: 1 In the seventh year of Jehu J began to	3060
	12: 2 J did that which was right in the sight of	3060
	12: 4 J said to the priests, All the money of	3060
	12: 6 twentieth year of king J the priests had	3060
	12: 7 king J called for Jehoiada the priest,	3060
	12:18 J king of Judah took all the hallowed	3060
	13:10 J the son of Jehoahaz to reign over Israel	3060
	13:25 the son of Jehoahaz took again out of	3060
	14: 8 Amaziah sent messengers to J, the son of	3060
	14: 9 the king of Israel sent to Amaziah king	3060
	14:11 Therefore J king of Israel went up; and he	3060
	14:13 J king of Israel took Amaziah king of	3060
	14:13 the son of J the son of Ahaziah,	3060
	14:15 the rest of the acts of J which he did,	3060
	14:16 J slept with his fathers, and was buried in	3060
	14:17 J son of Jehoahaz king of Israel fifteen	3060

JEHOHANAN (6)

1Ch	26: 3 Elam the fifth, J the sixth, Elioenai	3076
2Ch	17:15 next to him was J the captain, and with	3076
	23: 1 Ishmael the son of J, and Azariah the son	3076
Ezr	10:28 of Bebai; J, Hananiah, Zabbai, and Athlai.	3076
Ne	12:13 Of Ezra, Meshullam; of Amariah, J,	3076
	12:42 and J, and Malchijah, and Elam, and Ezer.	3076

JEHOIACHIN (10) [CONIAH, JEHOIACHIN'S]

2Ki	24: 6 and J his son reigned in his stead.	3078
	24: 8 J was eighteen years old when he began	3078
	24:12 the king of Judah went out to the king	3078
	24:15 he carried away J to Babylon,	3078
	25:27 thirtieth year of the captivity of J king of	3078
	25:27 did lift up the head of J king of Judah out	3078
2Ch	36: 8 Judah: and J his son reigned in his stead.	3078
	36: 9 J was eight years old when he began to	3078
Jer	52:31 thirtieth year of the captivity of J king of	3078
	52:31 reign lifted up the head of J king of Judah,	3078

JEHOIACHIN'S (1) [JEHOIACHIN]

Eze	1: 2 was the fifth year of king J captivity,	3112

JEHOIADA (52)

2Sa	8:18 Benaiah the son of J was over both	3077
	20:23 Benaiah the son of J was over	3077
	23:20 Benaiah the son of J, the son of a valiant	3077
	23:22 These things did Benaiah the son of J,	3077
1Ki	1: 8 Benaiah the son of J, and Nathan	3077
	1:26 Benaiah the son of J, and thy servant	3077
	1:32 the prophet, and Benaiah the son of J.	3077
	1:36 Benaiah the son of J answered the king,	3077
	1:38 Benaiah the son of J, and the Cherethites,	3077
	1:44 Benaiah the son of J, and the Cherethites,	3077
	2:25 sent by the hand of Benaiah the son of J;	3077
	2:29 Solomon sent Benaiah the son of J, saying,	3077
	2:34 So Benaiah the son of J went up,	3077
	2:35 the king put Benaiah the son of J in his	3077
	2:46 king commanded Benaiah the son of J;	3077
	4: 4 Benaiah the son of J was over the host:	3077
2Ki	11: 4 the seventh year J sent and fet the rulers	3077
	11: 9 to all things that J the priest commanded:	3077
	11: 9 on the sabbath, and came to J the priest.	3077
	11:15 J the priest commanded the captains of	3077
	11:17 J made a covenant between the LORD	3077
	12: 2 days where J the priest instructed him.	3077
	12: 7 king Jehoash called for J the priest,	3077
	12: 9 J the priest took a chest, and bored a hole	3077
1Ch	11:22 Benaiah the son of J, the son of a valiant	3077
	11:24 These things did Benaiah the son of J,	3077
	12:27 J was the leader of the Aaronites,	3077
	18:17 Benaiah the son of J was over	3077
	27: 5 the third month was Benaiah the son of J,	3077
	27:34 after Ahithophel was J the son of Benaiah,	3077
2Ch	22:11 of king Jehoram, the wife of J the priest,	3077
	23: 1 the seventh year J strengthened himself,	3077
	23: 8 all Judah did according to all things that J	3077
	23: 8 for J the priest dismissed not the courses.	3077
	23: 9 Moreover J the priest delivered to	3077
	23:11 J and his sons anointed him, and said,	3077
	23:14 J the priest brought out the captains of	3077
	23:16 J made a covenant between him,	3077
	23:18 J appointed the offices of the house of	3077
	24: 2 of the LORD all the days of J the priest.	3077
	24: 3 J took for him two wives; and he begat	3077
	24: 6 the king called for J the chief,	3077
	24:12 J gave it to such as did the work of	3077
	24:14 rest of the money before the king and J,	3077
	24:14 of the LORD continually all the days of J.	3077
	24:15 J waxed old, and was full of days when he	3077
	24:17 Now after the death of J came the princes	3077
	24:20 upon Zechariah the son of J the priest,	3077
	24:22 which J his father had done to him,	3077
	24:25 for the blood of the sons of J the priest,	3077
Ne	3: 6 Moreover the old gate repaired J the son	3111
Jer	29:26 thee instead of J the priest,	3077

J

2Ki	9:11	J came forth to the servants of his lord:	3058

2Ki 9:11 J came forth to the servants of his lord: 3058
9:13 and blew with trumpets, saying, J is king. 3058
9:14 So J the son of Jehoshaphat the son of 3058
9:15 J said, If it be your minds, *then* let none 3058
9:16 J rode *in a chariot*, and went to Jezreel; 3058
9:17 he spied the company of J as he came, 3058
9:18 J said, What hast thou to do with peace? 3058
9:19 answered, What hast thou to do with 3058
9:20 The driving *is* like the driving of J the son 3058
9:21 they went out against J, and met him in 3058
9:22 Joram saw J, that he said, *Is it* peace, 3058
9:22 saw Jehu, that he said, *Is it* peace, J? 3058
9:24 J drew a bow with his full strength, 3058
9:25 said J to Bidkar his captain, Take up, NIH
9:27 followed after him, and said, Smite him 3058
9:30 J was come to Jezreel, Jezebel heard 3058
9:31 as J entered in at the gate, she said, 3058
10: 1 J wrote letters, and sent *to* Samaria, 3058
10: 5 the bringers up *of the children*, sent to J, 3058
10:11 J slew all that remained of the house of 3058
10:13 J met with the brethren of Ahaziah king 3058
10:18 J gathered all the people together, 3058
10:18 Baal a little; *but* J shall serve him much. 3058
10:19 J did *it* in subtilty, to the intent that *he* 3058
10:20 J said, Proclaim a solemn assembly for 3058
10:21 J sent through all Israel: and all 3058
10:23 went, and Jehonadab the son of Rechab, 3058
10:24 J appointed fourscore men without, 3058
10:25 J said to the guard and to the captains, 3058
10:28 Thus J destroyed Baal out of Israel. 3058
10:29 to sin, J departed not from after them, 3058
10:30 The Lord said unto J, Because thou hast 3058
10:31 J took no heed to walk in the law of 3058
10:34 the rest of the acts of J, and all that he 3058
10:35 J slept with his fathers: and they buried 3058
10:36 the time that J reigned over Israel in 3058
13: 1 In the seventh year of J Jehoash *began* to 3058
13: 1 of J *began* to reign over Israel in Samaria, 3058
14: 8 son of Jehoahaz son of J, king of Israel, 3058
15:12 word of the Lord which he spake unto J, 3058
1Ch 2:38 Obed begat J, and Jehu begat Azariah, 3058
2:38 Obed begat Jehu, and J begat Azariah, 3058
4:35 Joel, and J the son of Josibiah, the son of 3058
12: 3 and Berachah, and J the Antothite, 3058
2Ch 19: 2 J the son of Hanani the seer went out to 3058
20:34 behold they *are* written in the book of J 3058
22: 7 he went out with Jehoram against J the 3058
22: 8 when J was executing judgment upon 3058
22: 9 hid in Samaria,) and brought him to J: 3058
25:17 the son of J, king of Israel, saying, Come, 3058
Hos 1: 4 the blood of Jezreel upon the house of J, 3058

JEHUBBAH (1)
1Ch 7:34 of Shamer; Ahi, and Rohgah, J, and Aram. 3160

JEHUCAL (1)
Jer 37: 3 Zedekiah the king sent J the son of 3081

JEHUD (1)
Jos 19:45 And J, and Bene-berak, and Gath-rimmon, 3055

JEHUDI (4)
Jer 36:14 Therefore all the princes sent J the son of 3065
36:21 So the king sent J to fet the roll: 3065
36:21 J read it in the ears of the king, and in 3065
36:23 *that* when J had read three or four leaves, 3065

JEHUDIJAH (1)
1Ch 4:18 his wife J bare Jered the father of Gedor, 3057

JEHUSH (1)
1Ch 8:39 J the second, and Eliphelet the third. 3266

JEIEL (11)
1Ch 5: 7 *were* the chief, J, and Zechariah, 3273
15:18 and Obed-edom, and J, the porters. 3273
15:21 and Obed-edom, and J, and Azaziah, 3273
16: 5 J, and Shemiramoth, and Jehiel, 3273
16: 5 J with psalteries and with harps; 3273
2Ch 20:14 the son of Benaiah, the son of J, the son 3273
26:11 their account by the hand of J the scribe 3273
29:13 of the sons of Elizaphan; Shimri, and J: 3273
35: 9 and Hashabiah and J and Jozabad, 3273
Ezr 8:13 J, and Shemaiah, and with them 3273
10:43 J, Mattithiah, Zabad, Zebina, Jadau, 3273

JEKABZEEL (1)
Ne 11:25 and at J, and *in* the villages thereof, 3343

JEKAMEAM (2)
1Ch 23:19 Jahaziel the third, and J the fourth. 3360
24:23 second, Jahaziel the third, J the fourth. 3360

JEKAMIAH (2)
1Ch 2:41 Shallum begat J, and Jekamiah begat 3359
2:41 begat Jekamiah, and J begat Elishama. 3359

JEKUTHIEL (1)
1Ch 4:18 of Socho, and J the father of Zanoah. 3354

JEMIMA (1)
Job 42:14 he called the name of the first, J; 3224

JEMUEL (2)
Ge 46:10 J, and Jamin, and Ohad, and Jachin, 3223
Ex 6:15 J, and Jamin, and Ohad, and Jachin, 3223

JEOPARDED (1) [JEOPARDY]
Jdg 5:18 Naphtali *were* a people *that* j their lives 2778

JEOPARDY (6) [JEOPARDED]
2Sa 23:17 of the men that went in *j* of their lives? NIH
1Ch 11:19 these men that **have put** their lives in j? 871.1
11:19 for with the *j* of their lives they brought it. NIH
12:19 will fall to his master Saul to the *j* of our NIH
Lk 8:23 they were filled *with water*, and were in j. 2793
1Co 15:30 And why **stand** we in j every hour? 2793

JEPHTHAE (1) [JEPHTHAH]
Heb 11:32 and *of* Barak, and *of* Samson, and *of* J; 2422

JEPHTHAH (29) [JEPHTHAE]
Jdg 11: 1 Now J the Gileadite was a mighty *man* of 3316
11: 1 the son of a harlot: and Gilead begat J. 3316
11: 2 and they thrust J, and said unto him, 3316
11: 3 J fled from his brethren, and dwelt in 3316
11: 3 there were gathered vain men to J, 3316
11: 5 the elders of Gilead went to fetch J out of 3316
11: 6 said unto J, Come, and be our captain, 3316
11: 7 J said unto the elders of Gilead, Did not 3316
11: 8 the elders of Gilead said unto J, 3316
11: 9 J said unto the elders of Gilead, If ye bring 3316
11:10 the elders of Gilead said unto J, 3316
11:11 J went with the elders of Gilead, 3316
11:11 J uttered all his words before the Lord 3316
11:12 J sent messengers unto the king of 3316
11:13 answered unto the messengers of J, 3316
11:14 J sent messengers again unto the king of 3316
11:15 unto him, Thus saith J, Israel took not 3316
11:28 unto the words of J which he sent him. 3316
11:29 the spirit of the Lord came upon J, 3316
11:30 J vowed a vow unto the Lord, and said, 3316
11:32 So J passed over unto the children of 3316
11:34 J came to Mizpeh unto his house, 3316
11:40 of J the Gileadite four days in a year. 3316
12: 1 and went northward, and said unto J, 3316
12: 2 J said unto them, I and my people were 3316
12: 4 J gathered together all the men of Gilead, 3316
12: 7 J judged Israel six years. Then died 3316
12: 7 J the Gileadite, and was buried in *one* 3316
1Sa 12:11 J, and Samuel, and delivered you out of 3316

JEPHUNNEH (16)
Nu 13: 6 Of the tribe of Judah, Caleb the son of J, 3312
14: 6 the son of Nun, and Caleb the son of J, 3312
14:30 Caleb the son of J, and Joshua the son 3312
14:38 the son of Nun, and Caleb the son of J. 3312
26:65 Caleb the son of J, and Joshua the son of 3312
32:12 Save Caleb the son of the Kenezite, 3312
34:19 Of the tribe of Judah, Caleb the son of J. 3312
Dt 1:36 Save Caleb the son of J, he shall see it, 3312
Jos 14: 6 Caleb the son of J the Kenezite said unto 3312
14:13 gave unto Caleb the son of J Hebron for 3312
14:14 the inheritance of Caleb the son of J 3312
15:13 unto Caleb the son of J he gave a part 3312
21:12 gave they to Caleb the son of J for his 3312
1Ch 4:15 the sons of Caleb the son of J; Iru, Elah, 3312
6:56 they gave to Caleb the son of J. 3312
7:38 the sons of Jether; J, and Pispah, and Ara. 3312

JERAH (2)
Ge 10:26 and Sheleph, and Hazarmaveth, and J, 3392
1Ch 1:20 and Sheleph, and Hazarmaveth, and J, 3392

JERAHMEEL (8) [JERAHMEELITES]
1Ch 2: 9 born unto him; J, and Ram, and Chelubai. 3396
2:25 the sons of J the firstborn of Hezron were, 3396
2:26 J had also another wife, whose name *was* 3396
2:27 the sons of Ram the firstborn of J were, 3396
2:33 and Zaza. These were the sons of J. 3396
2:42 Now the sons of Caleb the brother of J 3396
24:29 Concerning Kish: the son of Kish *was* J. 3396
Jer 36:26 the king commanded J the son of 3396

JERAHMEELITES (2) [JERAHMEEL]
1Sa 27:10 against the south of the J, and against 3397
30:29 to *them* which *were* in the cities of the J, 3397

JERED (2)
1Ch 1: 2 Kenan, Mahalaleel, J, 3382
4:18 his wife Jehudijah bare J the father of 3382

JEREMAI (1)
Ezr 10:33 Zabad, Eliphelet, J, Manasseh, *and* Shimei. 3413

JEREMIAH (146) [JEREMIAH'S, JEREMIAS, JEREMIE]
2Ki 23:31 *was* Hamutal, the daughter of J of Libnah. 3414
24:18 *was* Hamutal, the daughter of J of Libnah. 3414
1Ch 5:24 Azriel, and J, and Hodaviah, and Jahdiel, 3414
12: 4 and Jahaziel, and Johanan, 3414
12:10 Mishmannah the fourth, J the fifth, 3414
12:13 the tenth, Machbanai the eleventh, 3414
2Ch 35:25 J lamented for Josiah: and all the singing 3414
36:12 humbled not himself before J the prophet 3414
36:21 the word of the Lord by the mouth of J, 3414
36:22 by the mouth of J might be accomplished, 3414
Ezr 1: 1 by the mouth of J might be fulfilled, 3414
Ne 10: 2 Seraiah, Azariah, J, 3414
12: 1 of Shealtiel, and Jeshua: Seraiah, J, Ezra, 3414
12:12 of Seraiah, Meraiah; of J, Hananiah; 3414
12:34 and Benjamin, and Shemaiah, and J, 3414
Jer 1: 1 The words of J the son of Hilkiah, 3414

Jer 1:11 came unto me, saying, J, what seest thou? 3414
7: 1 The word that came to J from the Lord, 3414
11: 1 The word that came to J from the Lord, 3414
14: 1 The word of the Lord that came to J 3414
18: 1 The word which came to J from the 3414
18:18 Come, and let us devise devices against J; 3414
19:14 came J from Tophet, whither the Lord 3414
20: 1 heard *that* J prophesied these things. 3414
20: 2 Pashur smote J the prophet, and put him 3414
20: 3 Pashur brought forth J out of 3414
20: 3 said J unto him, The Lord hath not 3414
21: 1 The word which came to J from 3414
21: 3 said J unto them, Thus shall ye say to 3414
24: 3 the Lord unto me, What seest thou, J? 3414
25: 1 The word that came to J concerning all 3414
25: 2 The which J the prophet spake unto all 3414
25:13 which J hath prophesied against all 3414
26: 7 the people heard J speaking these words 3414
26: 8 when J had made an end of speaking all 3414
26: 9 all the people were gathered against J in 3414
26:12 spake J unto all the princes and to all 3414
26:20 this land according to all the words of J: 3414
26:24 of Ahikam the son of Shaphan was with J, 3414
27: 1 came this word unto J from the Lord, 3414
28: 5 the prophet J said unto the prophet 3414
28: 6 Even the prophet J said, Amen: 3414
28:11 And the prophet J went his way. 3414
28:12 the word of the Lord came unto J, 3414
28:12 yoke from off the neck of the prophet J, 3414
28:15 said the prophet J unto Hananiah 3414
29: 1 these *are* the words of the letter that J 3414
29:27 hast thou not reproved J of Anathoth, 3414
29:29 this letter in the ears of J the prophet. 3414
29:30 came the word of the Lord unto J, 3414
30: 1 The word that came to J from the Lord, 3414
32: 1 The word that came to J from the Lord, 3414
32: 2 J the prophet was shut up in the court of 3414
32: 6 J said, The word of the Lord came unto 3414
32:26 came the word of the Lord unto J, 3414
33: 1 the Lord came unto J the second time, 3414
33:19 the word of the Lord came unto J, 3414
33:23 the word of the Lord came to J, 3414
34: 1 The word which came unto J from 3414
34: 6 J the prophet spake all these words unto 3414
34: 8 *This is* the word that came unto J from 3414
34:12 the word came to J from the Lord, 3414
35: 1 The word which came unto J from 3414
35: 3 I took Jaazaniah the son of J, the son 3414
35:12 came the word of the Lord unto J, 3414
35:18 J said unto the house of the Rechabites, 3414
36: 1 *that* this word came unto J from 3414
36: 4 J called Baruch the son of Neriah: 3414
36: 4 Baruch wrote from the mouth of J all 3414
36: 5 J commanded Baruch, saying, I *am* shut 3414
36: 8 to all that J the prophet commanded him, 3414
36:10 read Baruch in the book the words of J *in* 3414
36:19 unto Baruch, Go, hide thee, thou and J; 3414
36:26 take Baruch the scribe and J the prophet: 3414
36:27 the word of the Lord came to J, 3414
36:27 which Baruch wrote at the mouth of J, 3414
36:32 took J another roll, and gave it to Baruch 3414
36:32 who wrote therein from the mouth of J all 3414
37: 2 which he spake by the prophet J. 3414
37: 3 of Maaseiah the priest to the prophet J, 3414
37: 4 Now J came in and went out among 3414
37: 6 the word of the Lord unto the prophet J, 3414
37:12 J went forth out of Jerusalem to go *into* 3414
37:13 he took J the prophet, saying, Thou fallest 3414
37:14 said J, *It is* false; I fall not away to 3414
37:14 so Irijah took J, and brought him to 3414
37:15 Wherefore the princes were wroth with J, 3414
37:16 When J was entered into the dungeon, 3414
37:16 and J had remained there many days; 3414
37:17 J said, There is: for, said he, thou shalt be 3414
37:18 Moreover J said unto king Zedekiah, 3414
37:21 commit J into the court of the prison, 3414
37:21 remained in the court of the prison. 3414
38: 1 heard the words that J had spoken unto 3414
38: 6 they J, and cast him into the dungeon 3414
38: 6 they let down J with cords. And in 3414
38: 6 no water, but mire: so J sunk in the mire. 3414
38: 7 heard that they had put J in the dungeon; 3414
38: 9 all that they have done to J the prophet, 3414
38:10 take up J the prophet out of the dungeon, 3414
38:11 down by cords into the dungeon to J. 3414
38:12 Ebed-melech the Ethiopian said unto J, 3414
38:12 armholes under the cords. And J did so. 3414
38:13 they drew up J with cords, and took him 3414
38:13 and remained in the court of the prison. 3414
38:14 took J the prophet unto him into the third 3414
38:14 king said unto J, I *will* ask thee a thing; 3414
38:15 J said unto Zedekiah, If I declare *it* unto 3414
38:16 Zedekiah the king sware secretly unto J, 3414
38:17 said J unto Zedekiah, Thus saith 3414
38:19 Zedekiah the king said unto J, I am afraid 3414
38:20 J said, They shall not deliver *thee*. Obey, 3414
38:24 said Zedekiah unto J, Let no man know of 3414
38:27 all the princes came to J, and asked him: 3414
38:28 So J abode in the court of the prison until 3414
39:11 J to Nebuzar-adan the captain of the guard 3414
39:14 took J out of the court of the prison, 3414
39:15 Now the word of the Lord came unto J, 3414
40: 1 The word which came to J from 3414
40: 2 the captain of the guard took J, 3414
40: 6 went J unto Gedaliah the son of Ahikam 3414

Jer	42: 2 said unto J the prophet, Let, we beseech	3414
	42: 4 J the prophet said unto them, I have heard	3414
	42: 5 they said to J, The LORD be a true and	3414
	42: 7 that the word of the LORD came unto J.	3414
	43: 1 that when J had made an end of speaking	3414
	43: 2 all the proud men, saying unto J,	3414
	43: 6 J the prophet, and Baruch the son of	3414
	43: 8 came the word of the LORD unto J in	3414
	44: 1 The word that J concerning all	3414
	44:15 of Egypt, in Pathros, answered J, saying,	3414
	44:20 J said unto all the people, to the men,	3414
	44:24 Moreover J said unto all the people,	3414
	45: 1 The word that J the prophet spake unto	3414
	45: 1 these words in a book at the mouth of J,	3414
	46: 1 The word of the LORD which came to J	3414
	46:13 The word that the LORD spake to J	3414
	47: 1 The word of the LORD that came to J	3414
	49:34 The word of the LORD that came to J	3414
	50: 1 against the land of the Chaldeans by J	3414
	51:59 word which J the prophet commanded	3414
	51:60 J wrote in a book all the evil that should	3414
	51:61 J said to Seraiah, When thou comest *to*	3414
	51:64 Thus far *are* the words of J.	3414
	52: 1 *was* Hamutal the daughter of J of Libnah.	3414
Da	9: 2 where*of* the word of the LORD came to J	3414

JEREMIAH'S (1) [JEREMIAH]
Jer 28:10 took the yoke from off the prophet J neck, 3414

JEREMIAS (1) [JEREMIAH]
Mt 16:14 Elias; and others, J, or one of the prophets. 2408

JEREMIE (2) [JEREMIAH]
Mt 2:17 that which was spoken by J the prophet, 2408
 27: 9 that which was spoken by J the prophet, 2408

JEREMOTH (5)
1Ch 8:14 And Ahio, Shashak, and J, 3406
 23:23 of Mushi; Mahli, and Eder, and J, three. 3406
 25:22 The fifteenth to J, *he*, his sons, 3406
Ezr 10:26 and Jehiel, and Abdi, and J, and Eliah. 3406
 10:27 Mattaniah, and J, and Zabad, and Aziza. 3406

JERIAH (2)
1Ch 23:19 J the first, Amariah the second, Jahaziel 3404
 24:23 the sons of *Hebron;* J *the first,* Amariah 3404

JERIBAI (1)
1Ch 11:46 Eliel the Mahavite, and J, and Joshaviah, 3403

JERICHO (64)
Nu	22: 1 plains of Moab on *this* side Jordan *by* J.	3405
	26: 3 in the plains of Moab by Jordan *near* J.	3405
	26:63 in the plains of Moab by Jordan *near* J.	3405
	31:12 of Moab, which *are* by Jordan *near* J.	3405
	33:48 in the plains of Moab by Jordan *near* J.	3405
	33:50 in the plains of Moab by Jordan *near* J.	3405
	34:15 on *this* side Jordan *near* J eastward,	3405
	35: 1 in the plains of Moab by Jordan *near* J.	3405
	36:13 in the plains of Moab by Jordan *near* J.	3405
Dt	32:49 in the land of Moab, that *is* over against J;	3405
	34: 1 *to* the top of Pisgah, that *is* over against J.	3405
	34: 3 the south, and the plain of the valley of J.	3405
Jos	2: 1 saying, Go view the land, even J.	3405
	2: 2 it was told the king of J, saying, Behold,	3405
	2: 3 the king of J sent unto Rahab, saying,	3405
	3:16 and the people passed over right against J.	3405
	4:13 the LORD unto battle, to the plains of J.	3405
	4:19 in Gilgal, in the east border of J.	3405
	5:10 of the month at even in the plains of J.	3405
	5:13 it came to pass, when Joshua was by J,	3405
	6: 1 Now J was straitly shut up because of	3405
	6: 2 I have given into thine hand J, and the	3405
	6:25 which Joshua sent to spy out J.	3405
	6:26 that riseth up and buildeth this city J:	3405
	7: 2 Joshua sent men from J to Ai, which *is*	3405
	8: 2 her king as thou didst unto J and her king:	3405
	9: 3 heard what Joshua had done unto J	3405
	10: 1 as he had done to J and her king, so he	3405
	10:28 of Makkedah as he did unto the king of J.	3405
	10:30 king thereof as he did unto the king of J.	3405
	12: 9 The king of J, one; the king of Ai, which	3405
	13:32 On the *other* side Jordan, *by* J, eastward.	3405
	16: 1 children of Joseph fell from Jordan *by* J,	3405
	16: 1 Jericho, unto the water of J on the east,	3405
	16: 1 *to* the wilderness that goeth up from J	3405
	16: 7 and came to J, and went out at J Jordan.	3405
	18:12 the border went up to the side of J on	3405
	18:21 according to their families were J,	3405
	20: 8 on the *other* side Jordan *by* J eastward,	3405
	24:11 ye went over Jordan, and came unto J:	3405
	24:11 the men of J fought against you,	3405
2Sa	10: 5 Tarry at J until your beards be grown,	3405
1Ki	16:34 In his days did Hiel the Bethelite build J:	3405
2Ki	2: 4 for the LORD hath sent me *to* J.	3405
	2: 4 I will not leave thee. So they came *to* J.	3405
	2: 5 the sons of the prophets that *were* at J	3405
	2:15 prophets which *were* to view at J saw	3405
	2:18 came again to him, (for he tarried at J,)	3405
	25: 5 and overtook him in the plains of J:	3405
1Ch	6:78 on the *other* side Jordan *by* J, on the east	3405
	19: 5 Tarry at J until your beards be grown,	3405
2Ch	28:15 brought them to J, the city of palm trees,	3405
Ezr	2:34 The children of J, three hundred forty and	3405
Ne	3: 2 next unto him builded the men of J.	3405
Ne	7:36 The children of J, three hundred forty and	3405
Jer	39: 5 and overtook Zedekiah in the plains of J:	3405
	52: 8 and overtook Zedekiah in the plains of J;	3405
Mt	20:29 And as they departed from J, a great	2410
Mk	10:46 And they came to J: and as he went out	2410
	10:46 as he went out of J with his disciples and	2410
Lk	10:30 man went down from Jerusalem to J,	2410
	18:35 to pass, *that* as he was come nigh unto J,	2410
	19: 1 And *Jesus* entered and passed through J.	2410
Heb	11:30 By faith the walls of J fell down, after they	2410

JERIEL (1)
1Ch 7: 2 J, and Jahmai, and Jibsam, and Shemuel, 3400

JERIJAH (1)
1Ch 26:31 Among the Hebronites *was* J the chief, 3404

JERIMOTH (8)
1Ch	7: 7 and Uzzi, and Uzziel, and J, and Iri, five;	3406
	7: 8 J, and Abiah, and Anathoth, and Alameth.	3406
	12: 5 J, and Bealiah, and Shemariah,	3406
	24:30 also of Mushi; Mahli, and Eder, and J.	3406
	25: 4 Uzziel, Shebuel, and J, Hananiah, Hanani,	3406
	27:19 of Naphtali, J the son of Azriel:	3406
2Ch	11:18 the daughter of J the son of David *to* wife,	3406
	31:13 and Jozabad, and Eliel, and Ismachiah,	3406

JERIOTH (1)
1Ch 2:18 *children* of Azubah *his* wife, and of J: 3408

JEROBOAM (102) [JEROBOAM'S]
1Ki	11:26 J the son of Nebat, an Ephrathite of	3379
	11:28 the man J *was* a mighty *man* of valour:	3379
	11:29 to pass at that time when J went out	3379
	11:31 he said to J, Take thee ten pieces: for thus	3379
	11:40 Solomon sought therefore to kill J.	3379
	11:40 J arose, and fled *into* Egypt, unto Shishak	3379
	12: 2 it came to pass, when J the son of Nebat,	3379
	12: 2 of king Solomon, and J dwelt in Egypt;)	3379
	12: 3 J and all the congregation of Israel came,	3379
	12:12 So J and all the people came to Rehoboam	3379
	12:15 the Shilonite unto J the son of Nebat.	3379
	12:20 when all Israel heard that J was come	3379
	12:25 J built Shechem in mount Ephraim,	3379
	12:26 J said in his heart, Now shall the kingdom	3379
	12:32 J ordained a feast in the eighth month,	3379
	13: 1 and J stood by the altar to burn incense.	3379
	13: 4 king J heard the saying of the man of	3379
	13:33 this thing J returned not from his evil	3379
	13:34 this thing became sin unto the house of J,	3379
	14: 1 At that time Abijah the son of J fell sick.	3379
	14: 2 J said to his wife, Arise, I pray thee,	3379
	14: 2 thou be not known to be the wife of J;	3379
	14: 5 the wife of J cometh to ask a thing of thee	3379
	14: 6 that he said, Come in, thou wife of J:	3379
	14: 7 Go, tell J, Thus saith the LORD God of	3379
	14:10 I will bring evil upon the house of J,	3379
	14:10 will cut off from J *him* that pisseth against	3379
	14:10 take away the remnant of the house of J,	3379
	14:11 Him that dieth of J in the city shall	3379
	14:13 for he only of J shall come to the grave,	3379
	14:13 the LORD God of Israel in the house of J.	3379
	14:14 who shall cut off the house of J that day:	3379
	14:16 give Israel up because of the sins of J,	3379
	14:19 the rest of the acts of J, how he warred,	3379
	14:20 the days which J reigned *were* two and	3379
	14:30 between Rehoboam and J all *their* days.	3379
	15: 1 Now in the eighteenth year of king J	3379
	15: 6 and J all the days of his life.	3379
	15: 7 there was war between Abijam and J.	3379
	15: 9 in the twentieth year of J king of Israel	3379
	15:25 Nadab the son of J *began* to reign over	3379
	15:29 reigned, *that* he smote all the house of J;	3379
	15:29 he left not to J any that breathed, until he	3379
	15:30 Because of the sins of J which he sinned,	3379
	15:34 walked in the way of J and in his sin	3379
	16: 2 thou hast walked in the way of J,	3379
	16: 3 will make thy house like the house of J	3379
	16: 7 of his hands, in being like the house of J	3379
	16:19 in walking in the way of J, and in his sin	3379
	16:26 he walked in all the way of J the son of	3379
	16:31 to walk in the sins of J the son of Nebat,	3379
	21:22 will make thine house like the house of J	3379
	22:52 in the way of J the son of Nebat, who	3379
2Ki	3: 3 Nevertheless he cleaved unto the sins of J	3379
	9: 9 Ahab like the house of J the son of Nebat.	3379
	10:29 Howbeit *from* the sins of J the son of	3379
	10:31 *for* he departed not from the sins of J,	3379
	13: 2 followed the sins of J the son of Nebat,	3379
	13: 6 not from the sins of the house of J,	3379
	13:11 he departed not from all the sins of J	3379
	13:13 his fathers; and J sat upon his throne:	3379
	14:16 Israel; and J his son reigned in his stead.	3379
	14:23 J the son of Joash king of Israel *began* to	3379
	14:24 he departed not from all the sins of J	3379
	14:27 he saved them by the hand of J the son of	3379
	14:28 the rest of the acts of J, and all that he	3379
	14:29 J slept with his fathers, *even* with the	3379
	15: 1 seventh year of J king of Israel *began*	3379
	15: 8 J reign over Israel in Samaria six months.	3379
	15:18 not from the sins of J the son	3379
	15:18 days from the sins of J the son of Nebat,	3379
	15:24 not from the sins of J the son	3379
	15:28 not from the sins of J the son	3379
	17:21 and they made J the son of Nebat king:	3379
2Ki	17:21 J drave Israel from following the LORD,	3379
	17:22 walked in all the sins of J which he did;	3379
	23:15 the high place which J the son of Nebat,	3379
1Ch	5:17 and in the days of J king of Israel.	3379
2Ch	9:29 in the visions of Iddo the seer against J	3379
	10: 2 when J the son of Nebat, who *was* in	3379
	10: 2 heard *it*, that J returned out of Egypt.	3379
	10: 3 So J and all Israel came and spake to	3379
	10:12 So J and all the people came to Rehoboam	3379
	10:15 Ahijah the Shilonite to J the son of Nebat.	3379
	11: 4 and returned from going against J.	3379
	11:14 for J and his sons had cast them off from	3379
	12:15 between Rehoboam and J continually.	3379
	13: 1 Now in the eighteenth year of king J	3379
	13: 2 And there was war between Abijah and J.	3379
	13: 3 J also set the battle in array against him	3379
	13: 4 and said, Hear me, *thou* J, and all Israel;	3379
	13: 8 Yet J the son of Nebat, the servant of	3379
	13: 8 golden calves, which J made you for gods.	3379
	13:13 J caused an ambushment to come about	3379
	13:15 that God smote J and all Israel before	3379
	13:19 Abijah pursued after J, and took cities	3379
	13:20 Neither did J recover strength again in	3379
Hos	1: 1 in the days of J the son of Joash, king of	3379
Am	1: 1 in the days of J the son of Joash king of	3379
	7: 9 I will rise against the house of J with	3379
	7:10 Amaziah the priest of Beth-el sent to J	3379
	7:11 J shall die by the sword, and Israel shall	3379

JEROBOAM'S (2) [JEROBOAM]
1Ki 14: 4 J wife did so, and arose, and went *to* 3379
 14:17 J wife arose, and departed, and came to 3379

JEROHAM (10)
1Sa	1: 1 the son of J, the son of Elihu, the son of	3395
1Ch	6:27 Eliab his son, J his son, Elkanah his son.	3395
	6:34 the son of J, the son of Eliel, the son of	3395
	8:27 and Eliah, and Zichri, the sons of J.	3395
	9: 8 Ibneiah the son of J, and Elah the son of	3395
	9:12 Adaiah the son of J, the son of Pashur,	3395
	12: 7 and Zebadiah, the sons of J of Gedor.	3395
	27:22 Of Dan, Azareel the son of J. These *were*	3395
2Ch	23: 1 Azariah the son of J, and Ishmael the son	3395
Ne	11:12 Adaiah the son of J, the son of Pelaliah,	3395

JERUBBAAL (14) [GIDEON, JERUBBESHETH]
Jdg	6:32 Therefore on that day he called him J,	3378
	7: 1 J, who *is* Gideon, and all the people that	3378
	8:29 J the son of Joash went and dwelt in his	3378
	8:35 shewed they kindness to the house of J,	3378
	9: 1 Abimelech the son of J went to Shechem	3378
	9: 2 either that all the sons of J, *which are*	3378
	9: 5 slew his brethren the sons of J,	3378
	9: 5 yet Jotham the youngest son of J was left;	3378
	9:16 if ye have dealt well with J and his house,	3378
	9:19 have dealt truly and sincerely with J and	3378
	9:24 and ten sons of J might come,	3378
	9:28 *is not* he the son of J? and Zebul his	3378
	9:57 came the curse of Jotham the son of J.	3378
1Sa	12:11 the LORD sent J, and Bedan,	3378

JERUBBESHETH (1) [JERUBBAAL]
2Sa 11:21 Who smote Abimelech the son of J? 3380

JERUEL (1)
2Ch 20:16 of the brook, before the wilderness of J. 3385

JERUSALEM (811) [JEBUS, JERUSALEM'S, SALEM]
Jos	10: 1 when Adoni-zedec king of J had heard	3389
	10: 3 Wherefore Adoni-zedek king of J sent	3389
	10: 5 the king of J, the king of Hebron, the king	3389
	10:23 the king of J, the king of Hebron, the king	3389
	12:10 The king of J, one; the king of Hebron,	3389
	15: 8 south side of the Jebusite; the same *is* J.	3389
	15:63 As for the Jebusites the inhabitants of J,	3389
	15:63 the children of Judah at J unto this day.	3389
	18:28 Eleph, and Jebusi, which *is* J, Gibeath,	3389
Jdg	1: 7 they brought him *to* J, and there he died.	3389
	1: 8 the children of Judah had fought against J,	3389
	1:21 drive out the Jebusites that inhabited J;	3389
	1:21 children of Benjamin in J unto this day.	3389
	19:10 and came over against Jebus, which *is* J;	3389
1Sa	17:54 head of the Philistine, and brought it *to* J;	3389
2Sa	5: 5 in J he reigned thirty and three years over	3389
	5: 6 and his men went *to* J unto the Jebusites,	3389
	5:13 *him* mo concubines and wives out of J,	3389
	5:14 of those that were born unto him in J;	3389
	8: 7 of Hadadezer, and brought them *to* J.	3389
	9:13 Mephibosheth dwelt in J: for he did eat	3389
	10:14 the children of Ammon, and came *to* J.	3389
	11: 1 But David tarried *still* at J.	3389
	11:12 So Uriah abode in J that day,	3389
	12:31 and all the people returned *unto* J.	3389
	14:23 to Geshur, and brought Absalom *to* J.	3389
	14:28 So Absalom dwelt two full years in J,	3389
	15: 8 LORD shall bring me again indeed *to* J,	3389
	15:11 Absalom went two hundred men out of J,	3389
	15:14 all his servants that *were* with him at J,	3389
	15:29 Abiathar carried the ark of God again *to* J:	3389
	15:37 *into* the city, and Absalom came *into* J.	3389
	16: 3 unto the king, Behold, he abideth at J:	3389
	16:15 came *to* J, and Ahithophel with him.	3389
	17:20 could not find *them*, they returned *to* J.	3389
	19:19 day that my lord the king went out of J,	3389
	19:25 when he was come *to* J to meet the king,	3389

J

2Sa		
19:33 and I will feed thee with me in J.	3389	
19:34 that I should go up with the king *unto* J?	3389	
20: 2 unto their king, from Jordan even to J.	3389	
20: 3 David came to his house at J; and the	3389	
20: 7 the mighty *men*: and they went out of J,	3389	
20:22 And Joab returned to J unto the king.	3389	
24: 8 they came *to* J at the end of nine months	3389	
24:16 stretched out his hand *upon* J to destroy	3389	
1Ki		
2:11 and thirty and three years reigned he in J.	3389	
2:36 Build thee a house in J, and dwell there,	3389	
2:38 And Shimei dwelt in J many days.	3389	
2:41 that Shimei had gone from J *to* Gath,	3389	
3: 1 the Lord, and the wall of J round about.	3389	
3:15 he came *to* J, and stood before the ark of	3389	
8: 1 children of Israel, unto king Solomon *in* J,	3389	
9:15 the wall of J, and Hazor, and Megiddo,	3389	
9:19 that which Solomon desired to build in J,	3389	
10: 2 she came *to* J with a very great train,	3389	
10:26 cities for chariots, and with the king at J.	3389	
10:27 the king made silver *to be* in J as stones,	3389	
11: 7 in the hill that *is* before J, and for Molech.	3389	
11:29 at that time when Jeroboam went out of J,	3389	
11:36 may have a light alway before me in J,	3389	
11:42 time that Solomon reigned in J over all	3389	
12:18 to get *him* up to *his* chariot, to flee *to* J.	3389	
12:21 when Rehoboam was come *to* J,	3389	
12:27 sacrifice in the house of the Lord at J,	3389	
12:28 *It is* too much for you to go up *to* J:	3389	
14:21 and he reigned seventeen years in J,	3389	
14:25 Shishak king of Egypt came up against J:	3389	
15: 2 Three years reigned he in J. And his	3389	
15: 4 the Lord his God give him a lamp in J,	3389	
15: 4 up his son after him, and to establish J:	3389	
15:10 forty and one years reigned he in J.	3389	
22:42 and he reigned twenty and five years in J.	3389	
2Ki		
8:17 to reign; and he reigned eight years in J.	3389	
8:26 to reign; and he reigned one year in J.	3389	
9:28 his servants carried him *in a chariot* to J,	3389	
12: 1 and forty years reigned he in J.	3389	
12:17 and Hazael set his face to go up to J.	3389	
12:18 king of Syria: and he went away from J.	3389	
14: 2 and reigned twenty and nine years in J.	3389	
14: 2 his mother's name *was* Jehoaddan of J.	3389	
14:13 came *to* J, and brake down the wall of	3389	
14:13 brake down the wall of J from the gate of	3389	
14:19 they made a conspiracy against him in J:	3389	
14:20 he was buried at J with his fathers in	3389	
15: 2 and he reigned two and fifty years in J,	3389	
15: 2 And his mother's name *was* Jecholiah of J.	3389	
15:33 to reign, and he reigned sixteen years in J.	3389	
16: 2 reigned sixteen years in J, and did not	3389	
16: 5 king of Israel came up to J to war:	3389	
18: 2 he reigned twenty and nine years in J.	3389	
18:17 king Hezekiah with a great host *against* J.	3389	
18:17 they went up and came *to* J. And when	3389	
18:22 taken away, and hath said to Judah and J,	3389	
18:22 Ye shall worship before this altar in J?	3389	
18:35 that the Lord should deliver J out of	3389	
19:10 J shall not be delivered into the hand of	3389	
19:21 the daughter of J hath shaken her head at	3389	
19:31 For out of J shall go forth a remnant,	3389	
21: 1 and reigned fifty and five years in J.	3389	
21: 4 the Lord said, In J will I put my name.	3389	
21: 7 Solomon his son, In this house, and in J,	3389	
21:12 I *am* bringing *such* evil upon J and Judah,	3389	
21:13 I will stretch over J the line of Samaria,	3389	
21:13 I will wipe J as *a man* wipeth a dish,	3389	
21:16 he had filled J from one end to another;	3389	
21:19 to reign, and he reigned two years in J.	3389	
22: 1 and he reigned thirty and one years in J.	3389	
22:14 (now she dwelt in J in the college;) and	3389	
23: 1 unto him all the elders of Judah and of J.	3389	
23: 2 and all the inhabitants of J with him,	3389	
23: 4 he burnt them without J in the fields of	3389	
23: 5 of Judah, and in the places round about J;	3389	
23: 6 without J, unto the brook Kidron,	3389	
23: 9 came not up to the altar of the Lord in J,	3389	
23:13 the high places that *were* before J,	3389	
23:20 bones upon them, and returned to J.	3389	
23:23 passover was holden to the Lord in J.	3389	
23:24 were spied in the land of Judah and in J,	3389	
23:27 will cast off this city J which I have	3389	
23:30 brought him *to* J, and buried him in his	3389	
23:31 reign; and he reigned three months in J.	3389	
23:33 of Hamath, that *he* might not reign in J;	3389	
23:36 reign; and he reigned eleven years in J.	3389	
24: 4 for he filled J *with* innocent blood;	3389	
24: 8 reign, and he reigned J three months.	3389	
24: 8 the daughter of Elnathan of J.	3389	
24:10 king of Babylon came up *against* J,	3389	
24:14 he carried away all J, and all the princes,	3389	
24:15 *those* carried he *into* captivity from J to	3389	
24:18 to reign, and he reigned eleven years in J.	3389	
24:20 anger of the Lord it came to pass in J	3389	
25: 1 his host, against J, and pitched against it;	3389	
25: 8 a servant of the king of Babylon, *unto* J:	3389	
25: 9 all the houses of J, and every great *man's*	3389	
25:10 brake down the walls of J round about.	3389	
1Ch		
3: 4 and in J he reigned thirty and three years.	3389	
3: 5 these were born unto him in J; Shimea,	3389	
6:10 in the temple that Solomon built in J:)	3389	
6:15 and J by the hand of Nebuchadnezzar.	3389	
6:32 had built the house of the Lord in J.	3389	
8:28 chief *men*. These dwelt in J.	3389	
8:32 these also dwelt with their brethren in J,	3389	

1Ch		
9: 3 in J dwelt of the children of Judah,	3389	
9:34 their generations; these dwelt at J.	3389	
9:38 they also dwelt with their brethren at J,	3389	
11: 4 David and all Israel went to J, which *is*	3389	
14: 3 David took moe wives at J:	3389	
14: 4 names of *his* children which he had in J;	3389	
15: 3 David gathered all Israel together to J,	3389	
18: 7 of Hadarezer, and brought them *to* J.	3389	
19:15 into the city. Then Joab came *to* J.	3389	
20: 1 David tarried at J. And Joab smote Rabbah	3389	
20: 3 David and all the people returned *to* J.	3389	
21: 4 went throughout all Israel, and came *to* J.	3389	
21:15 God sent an angel unto J to destroy it:	3389	
21:16 sword in his hand stretched out over J.	3389	
23:25 that they may dwell in J for ever:	3389	
28: 1 and with all the valiant men, unto J.	3389	
29:27 and thirty and three *years* reigned he in J.	3389	
2Ch		
1: 4 for it: for he had pitched a tent for it at J.	3389	
1:13 to the high place that *was* at Gibeon *to* J,	3389	
1:14 the chariot cities, and with the king at J.	3389	
1:15 and gold at J *as plenteous* as stones,	3389	
2: 7 *men* that *are* with me in Judah and in J,	3389	
2:16 to Joppa; and thou shalt carry it up *to* J.	3389	
3: 1 house of the Lord at J in mount Moriah,	3389	
5: 2 fathers of the children of Israel, unto J,	3389	
6: 6 I have chosen J, that my name might be	3389	
8: 6 all that Solomon desired to build in J,	3389	
9: 1 prove Solomon with hard questions at J,	3389	
9:25 the chariot cities, and with the king at J.	3389	
9:27 the king made silver in J as stones,	3389	
9:30 Solomon reigned in J over all Israel forty	3389	
10:18 to get *him* up to *his* chariot, to flee *to* J.	3389	
11: 1 when Rehoboam was come *to* J,	3389	
11: 5 Rehoboam dwelt in J, and built cities for	3389	
11:14 their possession, and came to Judah and J:	3389	
11:16 seek the Lord God of Israel came to J,	3389	
12: 2 Shishak king of Egypt came up against J,	3389	
12: 4 which *pertained* to Judah, and came to J.	3389	
12: 5 that were gathered together to J because	3389	
12: 7 my wrath shall not be poured out upon J	3389	
12: 9 Shishak king of Egypt came up against J,	3389	
12:13 king Rehoboam strengthened himself in J,	3389	
12:13 and he reigned seventeen years in J.	3389	
13: 2 He reigned three years in J. His mother's	3389	
14:15 camels in abundance, and returned to J.	3389	
15:10 So they gathered themselves together *at* J	3389	
17:13 of war, mighty *men* of valour, *were* in J.	3389	
19: 1 Judah returned to his house in peace to J.	3389	
19: 4 Jehoshaphat dwelt at J: and he went out	3389	
19: 8 Moreover in J did Jehoshaphat set of	3389	
19: 8 controversies, when they returned to J.	3389	
20: 5 stood in the congregation of Judah and J,	3389	
20:15 ye inhabitants of J, and thou king	3389	
20:17 of the Lord with you, O Judah and J:	3389	
20:18 the inhabitants of J fell before the Lord,	3389	
20:20 Hear me, O Judah, and ye inhabitants of J;	3389	
20:27 every man of Judah and J,	3389	
20:27 of them, to go again to J with joy;	3389	
20:28 they came *to* J with psalteries and harps	3389	
20:31 and he reigned twenty and five years in J.	3389	
21: 5 to reign, and he reigned eight years in J.	3389	
21:11 caused the inhabitants of J to commit	3389	
21:13 and the inhabitants of J to go a whoring,	3389	
21:20 he reigned in J eight years,	3389	
22: 1 the inhabitants of J made Ahaziah his	3389	
22: 2 to reign, and he reigned one year in J.	3389	
23: 2 the fathers of Israel, and they came to J.	3389	
24: 1 to reign, and he reigned forty years in J.	3389	
24: 6 in out of Judah and out of J the collection,	3389	
24: 9 made a proclamation through Judah and J,	3389	
24:18 upon Judah and J for this their trespass.	3389	
24:23 they came to Judah and J, and destroyed	3389	
25: 1 he reigned twenty and nine years in J.	3389	
25: 1 his mother's name *was* Jehoaddan of J.	3389	
25:23 him *to* J, and brake down the wall	3389	
25:23 brake down the wall of J from the gate of	3389	
25:27 they made a conspiracy against him in J;	3389	
26: 3 and he reigned fifty and two years in J.	3389	
26: 3 His mother's name also *was* Jecoliah of J.	3389	
26: 9 Moreover Uzziah built towers in J at	3389	
26:15 made in J, engines, invented by cunning	3389	
27: 1 reign, and he reigned sixteen years in J.	3389	
27: 8 to reign, and he reigned sixteen years in J.	3389	
28: 1 reign, and he reigned sixteen years in J:	3389	
28:10 J for bondmen and bondwomen unto you:	3389	
28:24 he made him altars in every corner of J.	3389	
28:27 and they buried him in the city, *even* in J:	3389	
29: 1 and he reigned nine and twenty years in J.	3389	
29: 8 of the Lord was upon Judah and J,	3389	
30: 1 come to the house of the Lord at J,	3389	
30: 2 his princes, and all the congregation in J,	3389	
30: 3 people gathered themselves together to J.	3389	
30: 5 unto the Lord God of Israel at J:	3389	
30:11 humbled themselves, and came to J.	3389	
30:13 there assembled *at* J much people to keep	3389	
30:14 and took away the altars that *were* in J,	3389	
30:21 children of Israel that were present at J	3389	
30:26 So there was great joy in J: for since	3389	
30:26 king of Israel *there* was not the like in J.	3389	
31: 4 dwelt in J to give the portion of the priests	3389	
32: 2 that he was purposed to fight against J,	3389	
32: 9 king of Assyria send his servants to J,	3389	
32: 9 and unto all Judah that *were* at J, saying,	3389	
32:10 do ye trust, that ye abide in the siege in J?	3389	
32:12 and commanded Judah and J, saying,	3389	

2Ch		
32:18 the people of J that *were* on the wall,	3389	
32:19 they spake against the God of J, as against	3389	
32:22 the inhabitants of J from the hand of	3389	
32:23 many brought gifts unto the Lord to J,	3389	
32:25 wrath upon him, and upon Judah and J.	3389	
32:26 *both* he and the inhabitants of J, so that	3389	
32:33 the inhabitants of J did him honour at his	3389	
33: 1 and he reigned fifty and five years in J:	3389	
33: 4 had said, In J shall my name be for ever.	3389	
33: 7 Solomon his son, In this house, and in J,	3389	
33: 9 Judah and the inhabitants of J to err,	3389	
33:13 brought him again *to* J into his kingdom.	3389	
33:15 and in J, and cast *them* out of the city.	3389	
33:21 to reign, and reigned two years in J.	3389	
34: 1 and he reigned in J one and thirty years.	3389	
34: 3 purge Judah and J from the high places,	3389	
34: 5 their altars, and cleansed Judah and J.	3389	
34: 7 all the land of Israel, he returned to J.	3389	
34: 9 and Benjamin; and they returned *to* J.	3389	
34:22 (now she dwelt in J in the college:) and	3389	
34:29 together all the elders of Judah and J.	3389	
34:30 the inhabitants of J, and the priests,	3389	
34:32 he caused all that were present in J and	3389	
34:32 J did according to the covenant of God,	3389	
35: 1 kept a passover unto the Lord in J:	3389	
35:18 were present, and the inhabitants of J.	3389	
35:24 they brought him *to* J, and he died,	3389	
35:24 And all Judah and J mourned for Josiah.	3389	
36: 1 made him king in his father's stead in J.	3389	
36: 2 reign, and he reigned three months in J.	3389	
36: 3 the king of Egypt put him down at J,	3389	
36: 4 his brother king over Judah and J,	3389	
36: 5 to reign, and he reigned eleven years in J:	3389	
36: 9 reigned three months and ten days in J:	3389	
36:10 his brother king over Judah and J.	3389	
36:11 to reign, and reigned eleven years in J.	3389	
36:14 of the Lord which he had hallowed in J.	3389	
36:19 brake down the wall of J, and burnt all	3389	
36:23 charged me to build him a house in J,	3389	
Ezr		
1: 2 charged me to build him a house in J,	3389	
1: 3 let him go up to J, which *is* in Judah,	3389	
1: 3 of Israel, (he *is* the God,) which *is* in J.	3389	
1: 4 offering for the house of God that *is* in J.	3389	
1: 5 the house of the Lord which *is* in J.	3389	
1: 7 had brought forth out of J,	3389	
1:11 were brought up from Babylon unto J.	3389	
2: 1 came again unto J and Judah, every one	3389	
2:68 to the house of the Lord which *is* at J,	3389	
3: 1 themselves together as one man to J.	3389	
3: 8 their coming unto the house of God at J,	3389	
3: 8 were come out of the captivity *unto* J;	3389	
4: 6 against the inhabitants of Judah and J.	3389	
4: 8 the scribe wrote a letter against J	3389	
4:12 came up from thee to us are come unto J,	3390	
4:20 There have been mighty kings also over J,	3390	
4:23 they went up in haste to the Jews,	3390	
4:24 of the house of the God which is at J.	3390	
5: 1 and J in the name of the God of Israel,	3390	
5: 2 to build the house of God which is at J:	3390	
5:14 took out of the temple that *was* in J,	3390	
5:15 go, carry them into the temple that is in J,	3390	
5:16 of the house of God which *is* in J.	3390	
5:17 the king to build this house of God at J,	3390	
6: 3 decree *concerning* the house of God at J,	3390	
6: 5 took forth out of the temple which *is* at J,	3390	
6: 5 *again* unto the temple which *is* at J.	3390	
6: 9 appointment of the priests which *are* at J,	3390	
6:12 destroy this house of God which *is* at J.	3390	
6:18 for the service of God, which *is* at J,	3390	
7: 7 the porters, and the Nethinims, unto J,	3389	
7: 8 he came to J in the fifth month, which	3389	
7: 9 first *day* of the fifth month came he to J,	3389	
7:13 minded of their own freewill to go *up to* J,	3390	
7:14 to inquire concerning Judah and J,	3390	
7:15 the God of Israel, whose habitation *is* in J,	3390	
7:16 for the house of their God which *is* in J:	3390	
7:17 of the house of your God which *is* in J.	3390	
7:19 *those* deliver thou before the God of J.	3390	
7:27 the house of the Lord which *is* in J:	3389	
8:29 and chief of the fathers of Israel, at J,	3389	
8:30 to bring *them* to J unto the house of our	3389	
8:31 *day* of the first month, to go *unto* J:	3389	
8:32 came to J, and abode there three days.	3389	
9: 9 and to give us a wall in Judah and in J.	3389	
10: 7 J unto all the children of the captivity,	3389	
10: 7 should gather themselves together *unto* J;	3389	
10: 9 together *unto* J within three days.	3389	
Ne		
1: 2 left of the captivity, and concerning J.	3389	
1: 3 the wall of J also *is* broken down,	3389	
2:11 So I came to J, and was there three days.	3389	
2:12 my God had put in my heart to do at J:	3389	
2:13 the dung port, and viewed the walls of J,	3389	
2:17 how J *lieth* waste, and the gates thereof	3389	
2:17 come, and let us build *up* the wall of J,	3389	
2:20 no portion, nor right, nor memorial, in J.	3389	
3: 8 and they fortified J unto the broad wall.	3389	
3: 9 son of Hur, the ruler of the half part of J.	3389	
3:12 the ruler of the half part of J, he and	3389	
4: 7 heard that the walls of J were made up,	3389	
4: 8 together to come *and* to fight against J,	3389	
4:22 every one with his servant lodge within J,	3389	
6: 7 appointed prophets to preach of thee at J,	3389	
7: 2 the ruler of the palace, charge over J:	3389	
7: 3 Let not the gates of J be opened until	3389	
7: 3 appoint watches of the inhabitants of J,	3389	

Ne	7: 6 came again to J and to Judah, every one	3389
	8:15 in J, saying, Go forth *unto* the mount,	3389
	11: 1 rulers of the people dwelt at J: the rest	3389
	11: 1 to bring one of ten to dwell in J the holy	3389
	11: 2 willingly offered themselves to dwell at J.	3389
	11: 3 the chief of the province that dwelt in J:	3389
	11: 4 at J dwelt *certain* of the children of Judah,	3389
	11: 6 All the sons of Perez that dwelt at J *were*	3389
	11:22 The overseer also of the Levites at J *was*	3389
	12:27 at the dedication of the wall of J they	3389
	12:27 to bring them to J, to keep the dedication	3389
	12:28 out of the plain country round about J,	3389
	12:29 had builded them villages round about J.	3389
	12:43 that the joy of J was heard even afar off.	3389
	13: 6 all this *time* was not I at J: for in the two	3389
	13: 7 came to J, and understood of the evil that	3389
	13:15 which they brought *into* J on the sabbath	3389
	13:16 unto the children of Judah, and in J.	3389
	13:19 that when the gates of J began to be dark	3389
	13:20 of all *kind* of ware lodged without J	3389
Est	2: 6 Who had been carried away from J with	3389
Ps	51:18 unto Zion: build thou the walls of J.	3389
	68:29 Because of thy temple at J shall kings	3389
	79: 1 they defiled; they have laid J in heaps.	3389
	79: 3 have they shed like water round about J;	3389
	102:21 of the Lord in Zion, and his praise in J;	3389
	116:19 Lord's house, in the midst of thee, O J.	3389
	122: 2 Our feet shall stand within thy gates, O J.	3389
	122: 3 J *is* builded as a city that is compact	3389
	122: 6 Pray for the peace of J: they shall prosper	3389
	125: 2 *As* the mountains *are* round about J,	3389
	128: 5 thou shalt see the good of J all the days of	3389
	135:21 Lord out of Zion, which dwelleth at J.	3389
	137: 5 If I forget thee, O J, let my right hand	3389
	137: 6 if I prefer not J above my chief joy.	3389
	137: 7 the children of Edom *in* the day of J;	3389
	147: 2 The Lord doth build up J: he gathereth	3389
	147:12 Praise the Lord, O J; praise thy God,	3389
Ecc	1: 1 the Preacher, the son of David, king in J.	3389
	1:12 I the Preacher was king over Israel in J.	3389
	1:16 all *they* that have been before me in J:	3389
	2: 7 small cattle above all that were in J before	3389
	2: 9 more than all that were before me in J	3389
SS	1: 5 black, but comely, O ye daughters of J,	3389
	2: 7 O ye daughters of J, by the roes, and by	3389
	3: 5 O ye daughters of J, by the roes, and by	3389
	3:10 paved *with* love, for the daughters of J.	3389
	5: 8 I charge you, O daughters of J, if ye find	3389
	5:16 and this *is* my friend, O daughters of J.	3389
	6: 4 O my love, as Tirzah, comely as J,	3389
	8: 4 I charge you, O daughters of J, that ye stir	3389
Isa	1: 1 and J in the days of Uzziah,	3389
	2: 1 son of Amoz saw concerning Judah and J.	3389
	2: 3 and the word of the Lord from J.	3389
	3: 1 doth take away from J and from Judah	3389
	3: 8 J is ruined, and Judah is fallen: because	3389
	4: 3 that remaineth in J, shall be called holy,	3389
	4: 3 one that is written among the living in J:	3389
	4: 4 shall have purged the blood of J from	3389
	5: 3 O inhabitants of J, and men of Judah,	3389
	7: 1 went up *towards* J to war against it,	3389
	8:14 gin and for a snare to the inhabitants of J.	3389
	10:10 whose graven images did excel *them of* J	3389
	10:11 and her idols, so do to J and her idols?	3389
	10:12 whole work upon mount Zion and on J,	3389
	10:32 of the daughter of Zion, the hill of J.	3389
	22:10 And ye have numbered the houses of J,	3389
	22:21 he shall be a father to the inhabitants of J,	3389
	24:23 in J, and before his ancients gloriously.	3389
	27:13 worship the Lord in the holy mount at J.	3389
	28:14 that rule this people which *is* in J.	3389
	30:19 For the people shall dwell in Zion at J:	3389
	31: 5 so will the Lord of hosts defend J;	3389
	31: 9 whose fire *is* in Zion, and his furnace in J.	3389
	33:20 thine eyes shall see J a quiet habitation,	3389
	36: 2 J unto king Hezekiah with a great army.	3389
	36: 7 said to Judah and to J, Ye shall worship	3389
	36:20 that the Lord should deliver J out of my	3389
	37:10 J shall not be given into the hand of	3389
	37:22 the daughter of J hath shaken her head at	3389
	37:32 For out of J shall go forth a remnant,	3389
	40: 2 Speak ye comfortably to J, and cry unto	3389
	40: 9 O J, that bringest good tidings, lift up thy	3389
	41:27 I will give to J one that bringeth good	3389
	44:26 that saith to J, Thou shalt be inhabited;	3389
	44:28 even saying to J, Thou shalt be built;	3389
	51:17 Awake, awake, stand up, O J, which hast	3389
	52: 1 thy beautiful garments, O J, the holy city:	3389
	52: 2 from the dust; arise, and sit down, O J:	3389
	52: 9 sing together, ye waste places of J:	3389
	52: 9 comforted his people, he hath redeemed J.	3389
	62: 6 I have set watchmen upon thy walls, O J,	3389
	62: 7 and till he make J a praise in the earth.	3389
	64:10 Zion is a wilderness, J a desolation.	3389
	65:18 I create J a rejoicing, and her people a joy.	3389
	65:19 I will rejoice in J, and joy in my people:	3389
	66:10 Rejoice ye with J, and be glad with her,	3389
	66:13 and ye shall be comforted in J.	3389
	66:20 to my holy mountain J, saith the Lord,	3389
Jer	1: 3 unto the carrying away of J captive in	3389
	1:15 his throne *at* the entering of the gates of J,	3389
	2: 2 Go and cry in the ears of J, saying,	3389
	3:17 At that time they shall call J the throne of	3389
	3:17 unto it, to the name of the Lord, to J:	3389
	4: 3 the Lord to the men of Judah and J,	3389

Jer	4: 4 ye men of Judah and inhabitants of J:	3389
	4: 5 Declare ye in Judah, and publish in J;	3389
	4:10 hast greatly deceived this people and J,	3389
	4:11 time shall it be said to this people and to J,	3389
	4:14 O J, wash thine heart from wickedness,	3389
	4:16 behold, publish against J, *that* watchers	3389
	5: 1 Run ye to and fro through the streets of J,	3389
	6: 1 yourselves to flee out of the midst of J,	3389
	6: 6 ye down trees, and cast a mount against J:	3389
	6: 8 Be thou instructed, O J, lest my soul	3389
	7:17 the cities of Judah and in the streets of J?	3389
	7:29 O J, and cast *it* away, and take up a	NIH
	7:34 from the streets of J, the voice of mirth,	3389
	8: 1 the bones of the inhabitants of J, out of	3389
	8: 5 is this people of J slidden back *by* a	3389
	9:11 I will make J heaps, *and* a den of dragons;	3389
	11: 2 men of Judah, and to the inhabitants of J;	3389
	11: 6 in the streets of J, saying, Hear ye	3389
	11: 9 of Judah, and among the inhabitants of J.	3389
	11:12 the cities of Judah and inhabitants of J go,	3389
	11:13 *to* the number of the streets of J	3389
	13: 9 pride of Judah, and the great pride of J.	3389
	13:13 the prophets, and all the inhabitants of J,	3389
	13:27 Woe unto thee, O J! wilt thou not be	3389
	14: 2 the ground; and the cry of J is gone up.	3389
	14:16 shall be cast out in the streets of J	3389
	15: 4 king of Judah, for *that* which he did in J.	3389
	15: 5 For who shall have pity upon thee, O J?	3389
	17:19 they go out, and in all the gates of J;	3389
	17:20 and all Judah, and all the inhabitants of J,	3389
	17:21 nor bring *it* in by the gates of J;	3389
	17:25 men of Judah, and the inhabitants of J:	3389
	17:26 the places about J, and from the land	3389
	17:27 even entering in at the gates of J on	3389
	17:27 it shall devour the palaces of J, and it shall	3389
	18:11 to the inhabitants of J, saying, Thus saith	3389
	19: 3 O kings of Judah, and inhabitants of J;	3389
	19: 7 the counsel of Judah and J in this place;	3389
	19:13 houses of J, and the houses of the kings	3389
	22:19 and cast forth beyond the gates of J.	3389
	23:14 I have seen also in the prophets of J a	3389
	23:15 for from the prophets of J is profaneness	3389
	24: 1 from J, and had brought them to Babylon.	3389
	24: 8 his princes, and the residue of J,	3389
	25: 2 and to all the inhabitants of J, saying,	3389
	25:18 To wit, J, and the cities of Judah,	3389
	26:18 J shall become heaps, and the mountain	3389
	27: 3 come *to* J unto Zedekiah king of Judah;	3389
	27:18 king of Judah, and at J, go not to Babylon.	3389
	27:20 king of Judah from J to Babylon,	3389
	27:20 and all the nobles of Judah and J;	3389
	27:21 *in* the house of the king of Judah and of J;	3389
	29: 1 J unto the residue of the elders which	3389
	29: 1 carried away captive from J to Babylon;	3389
	29: 2 the princes of Judah and J,	3389
	29: 2 and the smiths, were departed from J;)	3389
	29: 4 to be carried away from J unto Babylon;	3389
	29:20 whom I have sent from J to Babylon:	3389
	29:25 thy name unto all the people that *are* at J,	3389
	32: 2 the king of Babylon's army besieged J:	3389
	32:32 men of Judah, and the inhabitants of J,	3389
	32:44 in the places about J, and in the cities of	3389
	33:10 in the streets of J, that are desolate,	3389
	33:13 in the places about J, and in the cities of	3389
	33:16 Judah be saved, and J shall dwell safely:	3389
	34: 1 fought against J, and against all the cities	3389
	34: 6 words unto Zedekiah king of Judah in J,	3389
	34: 7 king of Babylon's army fought against J,	3389
	34: 8 with all the people which *were* at J,	3389
	34:19 the princes of J, the eunuchs,	3389
	35:11 let us go *to* J for fear of the army of	3389
	35:11 the army of the Syrians: so we dwell at J.	3389
	35:13 the men of Judah and the inhabitants of J,	3389
	35:17 upon all the inhabitants of J all the evil	3389
	36: 9 before the Lord *to* all the people in J,	3389
	36: 9 that came from the cities of Judah unto J.	3389
	36:31 the inhabitants of J, and upon the men	3389
	37: 5 when the Chaldeans that besieged J heard	3389
	37: 5 tidings of them, they departed from J.	3389
	37:11 up from J for fear of Pharaoh's army,	3389
	37:12 Jeremiah went forth out of J to go *into*	3389
	38:28 the prison until the day that J was taken:	3389
	38:28 and he was *there* when J was taken.	3389
	39: 1 king of Babylon and all his army against J,	3389
	39: 8 with fire, and brake down the walls of J.	3389
	40: 1 all that were carried away captive of J	3389
	42:18 poured forth upon the inhabitants of J;	3389
	44: 2 all the evil that I have brought upon J,	3389
	44: 6 the cities of Judah and in the streets of J;	3389
	44: 9 the land of Judah, and in the streets of J?	3389
	44:13 as I have punished J, by the sword,	3389
	44:17 the cities of Judah, and in the streets of J:	3389
	44:21 in the streets of J, ye, and your fathers,	3389
	51:35 the inhabitants of Chaldea, shall J say.	3389
	51:50 afar off, and let J come into your mind.	3389
	52: 1 to reign, and he reigned eleven years in J.	3389
	52: 3 anger of the Lord it came to pass in J	3389
	52: 4 against J, and pitched against it,	3389
	52:12 *which* served the king of Babylon, into J,	3389
	52:13 all the houses of J, and all the houses of	3389
	52:14 brake down all the walls of J round about.	3389
	52:29 away captive from J eight hundred thirty	3389
La	1: 1 I remembered in the days of her affliction	3389
	1: 8 J hath grievously sinned; therefore she is	3389
	1:17 J is as a menstruous *woman* among them.	3389

La	2:10 the virgins of J hang down their heads to	3389
	2:13 *thing* shall I liken to thee, O daughter of J?	3389
	2:15 and wag their head at the daughter of J,	3389
	4:12 should have entered into the gates of J.	3389
Eze	4: 1 and pourtray upon it *the* city, *even* J:	3389
	4: 7 shalt set thy face toward the siege of J,	3389
	4:16 behold, I will break the staff of bread in J:	3389
	5: 5 Thus saith the Lord God; This *is* J:	3389
	8: 3 and brought me in the visions of God to J,	3389
	9: 4 midst of the city through the midst of J,	3389
	9: 8 in thy pouring out of thy fury upon J?	3389
	11:15 *are* they unto whom the inhabitants of J	3389
	12:10 This burden *concerneth* the prince in J,	3389
	12:19 of the inhabitants of J, *and* of the land of	3389
	13:16 of Israel which prophesy concerning J,	3389
	14:21 I send my four sore judgments upon J,	3389
	14:22 the evil that I have brought upon J,	3389
	15: 6 for fuel, so will I give the inhabitants of J.	3389
	16: 2 cause J to know her abominations,	3389
	16: 3 And say, Thus saith the Lord God unto J;	3389
	17:12 the king of Babylon is come *to* J,	3389
	21: 2 set thy face toward J, and drop *thy word*	3389
	21:20 and to Judah in J the defenced.	3389
	21:22 At his right hand was the divination for J,	3389
	22:19 I will gather you into the midst of J.	3389
	23: 4 Samaria *is* Aholah, and J Aholibah.	3389
	24: 2 the king of Babylon set himself against J	3389
	26: 2 because that Tyrus hath said against J,	3389
	33:21 *that* one that had escaped out of J came	3389
	36:38 as the flock of J in her solemn feasts;	3389
Da	1: 1 Nebuchadnezzar king of Babylon *unto* J,	3389
	1: 2 taken out of the temple which *was* in J;	3389
	5: 3 of the house of God which *was* at J;	3390
	6:10 being open in his chamber toward J,	3390
	9: 2 seventy years in the desolations of J.	3389
	9: 7 to the inhabitants of J, and unto all Israel,	3389
	9:12 not been done as hath been done upon J.	3389
	9:16 thy fury be turned away from thy city J,	3389
	9:16 J and thy people *are* become a reproach	3389
	9:25 to build J unto the Messiah the Prince	3389
Joel	2:32 mount Zion and in J shall be deliverance,	3389
	3: 1 bring again the captivity of Judah and J,	3389
	3: 6 the children of J have ye sold unto	3389
	3:16 out of Zion, and utter his voice from J;	3389
	3:17 be holy, and there shall no strangers	3389
	3:20 and J from generation to generation.	3389
Am	1: 2 roar from Zion, and utter his voice from J;	3389
	2: 5 and it shall devour the palaces of J.	3389
Ob	1:11 cast lots upon J, even thou wast as one of	3389
	1:20 the captivity of J, which *is* in Sepharad,	3389
Mic	1: 1 which he saw concerning Samaria and J.	3389
	1: 5 the high places of Judah? *are* they not J?	3389
	1: 9 unto the gate of my people, *even* to J.	3389
	1:12 down from the Lord unto the gate of J.	3389
	3:10 up Zion with blood, and J with iniquity.	3389
	3:12 J shall become heaps, and the mountain	3389
	4: 2 and the word of the Lord from J.	3389
	4: 8 kingdom shall come to the daughter of J.	3389
Zep	1: 4 and upon all the inhabitants of J;	3389
	1:12 *that* I will search J with candles,	3389
	3:14 rejoice with all the heart, O daughter of J.	3389
	3:16 In that day it shall be said to J, Fear thou	3389
Zec	1:12 how long wilt thou not have mercy on J	3389
	1:14 I am jealous for J and for Zion *with* a	3389
	1:16 I am returned to J with mercies:	3389
	1:16 and a line shall be stretched forth upon J.	3389
	1:17 yet comfort Zion, and shall yet choose J.	3389
	1:19 which have scattered Judah, Israel, and J.	3389
	2: 2 said unto me, To measure J, to see what	3389
	2: 4 J shall be inhabited *as* towns without	3389
	2:12 in the holy land, and shall choose J again.	3389
	3: 2 even the Lord that hath chosen J rebuke	3389
	7: when J was inhabited and in prosperity,	3389
	8: 3 Zion, and will dwell in the midst of J:	3389
	8: 3 J shall be called a city of truth;	3389
	8: 4 and old women dwell in the streets of J,	3389
	8: 8 and they shall dwell in the midst of J:	3389
	8:15 I thought in these days to do well unto J	3389
	8:22 come to seek the Lord of hosts in J,	3389
	9: 9 daughter of Zion; shout, O daughter of J:	3389
	9:10 the horse from J, and the battle bow shall	3389
	12: 2 I *will* make J a cup of trembling unto all	3389
	12: 2 siege both against Judah *and* against J.	3389
	12: 3 in that day will I make J a burdensome	3389
	12: 5 The inhabitants of J *shall* be my strength	3389
	12: 6 J shall be inhabited again in her own	3389
	12: 6 again in her own place, *even* in J.	3389
	12: 7 the glory of the inhabitants of J do not	3389
	12: 8 the Lord defend the inhabitants of J;	3389
	12: 9 all the nations that come against J.	3389
	12:10 the inhabitants of J, the spirit of grace	3389
	12:11 day shall there be a great mourning in J,	3389
	13: 1 to the inhabitants of J for sin and	3389
	14: 2 For I will gather all nations against J to	3389
	14: 4 which *is* before J on the east,	3389
	14: 8 *that* living waters shall go out from J:	3389
	14:10 a plain from Geba to Rimmon south of J:	3389
	14:11 but J shall be safely inhabited.	3389
	14:12 all the people that have fought against J;	3389
	14:14 Judah also shall fight at J; and the wealth	3389
	14:16 J shall even go up from year to year to	3389
	14:17 of the earth unto J to worship the King,	3389
	14:21 every pot in J and in Judah shall be	3389
Mal	2:11 is committed in Israel and in J;	3389
	3: 4 and J be pleasant unto the Lord,	3389

J

Mt	2: 1 there came wise men from the east to J,	2414
	2: 3 he was troubled, and all J with him.	2414
	3: 5 Then went out to him J, and all Judea,	2414
	4:25 and *from* J, and *from* Judea,	2414
	5:35 neither by J; for it is the city of the great	2414
	15: 1 and Pharisees, which were of J, saying,	2414
	16:21 how that he must go unto J,	2414
	20:17 And Jesus going up to J took the twelve	2414
	20:18 we go up to J; and the Son of man	2414
	21: 1 And when they drew nigh unto J,	2414
	21:10 when he was come into J, all the city	2414
	23:37 O J, Jerusalem, *thou* that killest	2419
	23:37 O Jerusalem, J, *thou* that killest	2419
Mk	1: 5 they of J, and were all baptized of him	2415
	3: 8 And from J, and from Idumea,	2414
	3:22 And the scribes which came down from J	2414
	7: 1 certain of the scribes, which came from J.	2414
	10:32 And they were in the way going up to J;	2414
	10:33 Behold, we go up to J; and the Son	2414
	11: 1 And when they came nigh to J,	2419
	11:11 And Jesus entered into J, and into	2414
	11:15 And they come to J: and Jesus went into	2414
	11:27 And they come again to J: and as he was	2414
	15:41 *women* which came up with him unto J.	2414
Lk	2:22 they brought him to J, to present *him* to	2414
	2:25 And behold, there was a man in J,	2414
	2:38 all them that looked for redemption in J.	2419
	2:41 Now his parents went to J every year at	2419
	2:42 they went up to J after the custom of	2414
	2:43 the child Jesus tarried behind in J;	2419
	2:45 they turned back again to J, seeking him.	2419
	4: 9 And he brought him to J, and set him on	2419
	5:17 of every town of Galilee, and Judea, and J:	2414
	6:17 multitude of people out of all Judea and J,	2419
	9:31 decease which he should accomplish at J.	2419
	9:51 he stedfastly set his face to go to J,	2419
	9:53 his face was *as though he* would go to J.	2419
	10:30 A certain man went down from J to	2419
	13: 4 sinners above all men that dwelt in J?	2419
	13:22 teaching, and journeying towards J.	2419
	13:33 it cannot be that a prophet perish out of J.	2419
	13:34 O J, Jerusalem, which killest the prophets,	2419
	13:34 O Jerusalem, J, which killest the prophets,	2419
	17:11 And it came to pass, as he went to J,	2419
	18:31 we go up to J, and all *things* that are	2414
	19:11 because he was nigh to J, and *because*	2419
	19:28 he went before, ascending up to J.	2414
	21:20 And when ye shall see J compassed with	2419
	21:24 J shall be trodden down of the Gentiles,	2419
	23: 7 who himself also was at J at that time.	2419
	23:28 said, Daughters of J, weep not for me,	2419
	24:13 which was from J *about* threescore	2419
	24:18 Art thou only a stranger in J, and hast not	2419
	24:33 and returned to J, and found the eleven	2419
	24:47 name among all nations, beginning at J.	2414
	24:49 but tarry ye in the city of J, until ye be	2419
	24:52 and returned to J with great joy:	2419
Jn	1:19 sent priests and Levites from J to ask him,	2414
	2:13 was at hand, and Jesus went up to J,	2414
	2:23 Now when he was in J at the passover,	2414
	4:20 that in J is the place where *men* ought to	2414
	4:21 nor yet at J, worship the Father.	2414
	4:45 seen all *the things* that he did at J at	2414
	5: 1 feast of the Jews; and Jesus went up to J.	2414
	5: 2 Now there is at J by the sheep *market* a	2414
	7:25 said some of them of J, Is not this he,	2415
	10:22 it was at J *the feast of* the dedication,	2414
	11:18 Now Bethany was nigh unto J,	2414
	11:55 many went out of the country up to J	2414
	12:12 they heard that Jesus was coming to J,	2414
Ac	1: 4 them that *they* should not depart from J,	2414
	1: 8 ye shall be witnesses unto me both in J,	2419
	1:12 returned they unto J from the mount	2419
	1:12 which is from J a sabbath day's journey.	2419
	1:19 it was known unto all the dwellers at J;	2419
	2: 5 And there were dwelling at J Jews,	2419
	2:14 men of Judea, and all *ye* that dwell at J,	2419
	4: 6 high priest, were gathered together at J.	2419
	4:16 *is* manifest to all them that dwell in J;	2419
	5:16 *out* of the cities round about unto J,	2419
	5:28 ye have filled J with your doctrine,	2419
	6: 7 the number of the disciples multiplied in J	2419
	8: 1 against the church which was at J;	2414
	8:14 Now when the apostles which were at J	2414
	8:25 returned to J, and preached the gospel in	2419
	8:26 way that goeth down from J unto Gaza,	2419
	8:27 and had come to J for to worship,	2419
	9: 2 he might bring *them* bound unto J.	2419
	9:13 much evil he hath done to thy saints at J:	2419
	9:21 them which called on this name in J,	2419
	9:26 And when Saul was come to J, he assayed	2419
	9:28 With them coming in and going out at J.	2419
	10:39 did both in the land of the Jews, and in J;	2419
	11: 2 And when Peter was come up to J,	2414
	11:22 the ears of the church which was in J:	2414
	11:27 And in these days came prophets from J	2414
	12:25 And Barnabas and Saul returned from J,	2419
	13:13 John departing from them returned to J.	2414
	13:27 For they that dwell at J, and their rulers,	2419
	13:31 came up with him from Galilee to J,	2419
	15: 2 should go up to J unto the apostles and	2419
	15: 4 And when they were come to J, they	2414
	16: 4 of the apostles and elders which were at J.	2419
	18:21 all means keep *this* feast that cometh in J:	2414
	19:21 and Achaia, to go to J, saying,	2419

Ac	20:16 for him, to be at J the day of Pentecost.	2414
	20:22 behold, I go bound in the spirit unto J,	2419
	21: 4 the Spirit, that *he* should not go up to J.	2419
	21:11 So shall the Jews at J bind the man that	2419
	21:12 place, besought him not to go up to J.	2419
	21:13 also to die at J for the name of the Lord	2419
	21:15 took up our carriages, and went up to J.	2414
	21:17 when we were come to J, the brethren	2414
	21:31 of the band, that all J was in an uproar.	2419
	22: 5 bound unto J, for to be punished.	2419
	22:17 to pass that, when I was come again to J,	2419
	22:18 Make haste, and get *thee* quickly out of J:	2419
	23:11 for as thou hast testified of me in J,	2419
	24:11 twelve days since I went up to J for to	2414
	25: 1 three days he ascended from Cesarea to J.	2414
	25: 3 that he would send for him to J,	2419
	25: 7 the Jews which came down from J stood	2414
	25: 9 Wilt thou go up to J, and there be judged	2414
	25:15 About whom, when I was at J, the chief	2419
	25:20 I asked *him* whether he would go to J,	2419
	25:24 both at J, and *also* here, crying that he	2414
	26: 4 at the first among mine own nation at J,	2414
	26:10 Which *thing* I also did in J: and many of	2419
	26:20 and at J, and throughout all the coasts of	2414
	28:17 *yet* was I delivered prisoner from J into	2414
Ro	15:19 so that from J, and round about unto	2419
	15:25 But now I go unto J to minister unto	2419
	15:26 for the poor saints which are at J.	2419
	15:31 that my service which I have for J may be	2419
1Co	16: 3 will I send to bring your liberality unto J.	2419
Gal	1:17 Neither went I up to J to them which	2414
	1:18 after three years I went up to J to see	2414
	2: 1 after I went up again to J with Barnabas,	2414
	4:25 answereth to J which now is, and is in	2419
	4:26 But J which is above is free, which is	2419
Heb	12:22 the heavenly J, and to an innumerable	2419
Rev	3:12 of the city of my God, *which is* new J,	2419
	21: 2 And I John saw the holy city, new J,	2419
	21:10 and shewed me *that* great city, the holy J,	2419

JERUSALEM'S (3) [JERUSALEM]

1Ki	11:13 and for J sake, which I have chosen.	3389
	11:32 My servant David's sake, and for J sake,	3389
Isa	62: 1 my peace, and for J sake I will not rest,	3389

JERUSHA (1) [JERUSHAH]

2Ki	15:33 his mother's name *was* J, the daughter of	3388

JERUSHAH (1) [JERUSHA]

2Ch	27: 1 mother's name also *was* J, the daughter	3388

JESAIAH (2)

1Ch	3:21 the sons of Hananiah; Pelatiah, and J:	3470
Ne	11: 7 Maaseiah, the son of Ithiel, the son of J.	3470

JESARELAH See JESHARELAH

JESHAIAH (5)

1Ch	25: 3 Gedaliah, and Zeri, and J, Hashabiah,	3470
	25:15 The eighth to J, *he*, his sons,	3470
	26:25 his son, and Joram his son, and Zichri	3470
Ezr	8: 7 J the son of Athaliah, and with him	3470
	8:19 with him J of the sons of Merari,	3470

JESHANAH (1)

2Ch	13:19 J with the towns thereof, and Ephrain	3466

JESHARELAH (1)

1Ch	25:14 The seventh to J, *he*, his sons,	3480

JESHEBEAB (1)

1Ch	24:13 thirteenth to Huppah, the fourteenth to J,	3428

JESHER (1)

1Ch	2:18 sons *are* these; J, and Shobab, and Ardon.	3475

JESHIMON (6)

Nu	21:20 top of Pisgah, which looketh toward J.	3452
	23:28 the top of Peor, that looketh toward J.	3452
1Sa	23:19 of Hachilah, which *is* on the south of J?	3452
	23:24 of Maon, in the plain on the south of J.	3452
	26: 1 in the hill of Hachilah, which *is* before J?	3452
	26: 3 Hachilah, which *is* before J, by the way.	3452

JESHISHAI (1)

1Ch	5:14 the son of J, the son of Jahdo, the son of	3454

JESHOHAIAH (1)

1Ch	4:36 J, and Asaiah, and Adiel, and Jesimiel,	3439

JESHUA (30) [JOSHUA]

1Ch	24:11 The ninth to J, the tenth to Shecaniah,	3442
2Ch	31:15 And Shemaiah, Amariah, and	3442
Ezr	2: 2 J, Nehemiah, Seraiah, Reelaiah, Mordecai,	3442
	2: 6 the children of J and Joab, two thousand	3442
	2:36 of the house of J, nine hundred seventy	3442
	2:40 the children of J and Kadmiel,	3442
	3: 2 stood up J the son of Jozadak,	3442
	3: 8 J the son of Jozadak, and the remnant of	3442
	3: 9 stood J *with* his sons and his brethren,	3442
	4: 3 J, and the rest of the chief of the fathers	3442
	5: 2 J the son of Jozadak, and began to build	3443
	8:33 with *them* was Jozabad the son of J,	3442
	10:18 of the sons of J the son of Jozadak,	3442
Ne	3:19 next to him repaired Ezer the son of J,	3442
	7: 7 J, Nehemiah, Azariah, Raamiah,	3442

Ne	7:11 the children of J and Joab, two thousand	3442
	7:39 the house of J, nine hundred seventy and	3442
	7:43 the children of J, of Kadmiel, *and of*	3442
	8: 7 Also J, and Bani, and Sherebiah, Jamin,	3442
	8:17 since the day of J the son of Nun unto	3442
	9: 4 J, and Bani, Kadmiel, Shebaniah, Bunni,	3442
	9: 5 J and Kadmiel, Bani, Hashabniah,	3442
	10: 9 both J the son of Azaniah, Binnui of	3442
	11:26 at J, and at Moladah, and at Beth-phelet,	3442
	12: 1 Zerubbabel the son of Shealtiel, and J;	3442
	12: 7 and of their brethren in the days of J.	3442
	12: 8 J, Binnui, Kadmiel, Sherebiah, Judah,	3442
	12:10 J begat Joiakim, Joiakim also begat	3442
	12:24 Sherebiah, and J the son of Kadmiel,	3442
	12:26 *were* in the days of Joiakim the son of J	3442

JESHURUN (4)

Dt	32:15 J waxed fat, and kicked: thou art waxen	3484
	33: 5 he was king in J, when the heads of	3484
	33:26 *There is* none like unto the God of J,	3484
Isa	44: 2 and thou, J, whom I have chosen.	3484

JESIAH (2)

1Ch	12: 6 J, and Azareel, and Joezer, and Jashobeam	3449
	23:20 Michah the first, and J the second.	3449

JESIMIEL (1)

1Ch	4:36 Asaiah, and Adiel, and J, and Benaiah,	3450

JESSE (47)

Ru	4:17 he *is* the father of J, the father of David.	3448
	4:22 And Obed begat J, and Jesse begat David.	3448
	4:22 And Obed begat Jesse, and J begat David.	3448
1Sa	16: 1 I will send thee to J the Beth-lehemite:	3448
	16: 3 call J to the sacrifice, and I will shew thee	3448
	16: 5 he sanctified J and his sons,	3448
	16: 8 J called Abinadab, and made him pass	3448
	16: 9 J made Shammah to pass by. And he said,	3448
	16:10 J made seven of his sons to pass before	3448
	16:10 Samuel said unto J, The LORD hath not	3448
	16:11 Samuel said unto J, Are here all *thy*	3448
	16:11 Samuel said unto J, Send and fetch him:	3448
	16:18 I have seen a son of J the Beth-lehemite,	3448
	16:19 Wherefore Saul sent messengers unto J,	3448
	16:20 J took an ass *laden* with bread, and a	3448
	16:22 Saul sent to J, saying, Let David, I pray	3448
	17:12 of Beth-lehem-judah, whose name *was* J;	3448
	17:13 the three eldest sons of J went *and*	3448
	17:17 J said unto David his son, Take now for	3448
	17:20 and went, as J had commanded him;	3448
	17:58 *I am* the son of thy servant J	3448
	20:27 cometh not the son of J to meat,	3448
	20:30 chosen the son of J to thine own	3448
	20:31 For as long as the son of J liveth upon	3448
	22: 7 will the son of J give every one of you	3448
	22: 8 son hath made a *league* with the son of J,	3448
	22: 9 said, I saw the son of J coming to Nob,	3448
	22:13 thou and the son of J, in that thou hast	3448
	25:10 *is* the son of J? there be many servants	3448
2Sa	20: 1 have we inheritance in the son of J:	3448
	23: 1 David the son of J said, and the man *who*	3448
1Ki	12:16 *have* we inheritance in the son of J?	3448
1Ch	2:12 And Boaz begat Obed, and Obed begat J,	3448
	2:13 J begat his firstborn Eliab,	3448
	10:14 the kingdom unto David the son of J.	3448
	12:18 *we*, David, and on thy side, thou son of J:	3448
	29:26 Thus David the son of J reigned over all	3448
2Ch	10:16 we have no inheritance in the son of J:	3448
	11:18 Abihail the daughter of Eliab the son of J;	3448
Ps	72:20 The prayers of David the son of J are	3448
Isa	11: 1 come forth a rod out of the stem of J,	3448
	11:10 in that day there shall be a root of J,	3448
Mt	1: 5 begat Obed of Ruth; and Obed begat J;	2421
	1: 6 And J begat David the king; and David	2421
Lk	3:32 was *the son of* J, which was *the son*	2421
Ac	13:22 and said, I have found David the *son of* J,	2421
Ro	15:12 There shall be a root of J, and he that	2421

JESTING (1)

Eph	5: 4 filthiness, nor foolish talking, nor j,	2160

JESUI (1) [ISHUI, JESUITES]

Nu	26:44 of J, the family of the Jesuites: of Beriah,	3440

JESUITES (1) [JESUI]

Nu	26:44 of Jesui, the family of the J: of Beriah,	3441

JESUS (973) [JESUS']

Mt	1: 1 The book of the generation of J Christ,	2424
	1:16 of whom was born J, who is called Christ.	2424
	1:18 the birth of J Christ was on this wise:	2424
	1:21 forth a son, and thou shalt call his name J:	2424
	1:25 firstborn son: and *he* called his name J.	2424
	2: 1 Now when J was born in Bethlehem of	2424
	3:13 cometh J from Galilee to Jordan unto	2424
	3:15 And J answering said unto him, Suffer *it*	2424
	3:16 And J, when he was baptized, went up	2424
	4: 1 Then was J led up of the Spirit into	2424
	4: 7 J said unto him, It is written again,	2424
	4:10 Then saith J unto him, Get thee hence,	2424
	4:12 when J had heard that John was cast	2424
	4:17 From that time J began to preach,	2424
	4:18 And J, walking by the sea of Galilee,	2424
	4:23 And J went about all Galilee, teaching in	2424
	7:28 to pass, when J had ended these sayings,	2424
	8: 3 J put forth *his* hand, and touched him;	2424

Mt	8: 4 J saith unto him, See thou tell no *man;*	2424
	8: 5 when J was entered into Capernaum,	2424
	8: 7 And J saith unto him, I will come and	2424
	8:10 When J heard *it,* he marvelled, and said to	2424
	8:13 J said unto the centurion, Go thy way;	2424
	8:14 And when J was come into Peter's house,	2424
	8:18 Now when J saw great multitudes about	2424
	8:20 And J saith unto him, The foxes have	2424
	8:22 But J said unto him, Follow me; and let	2424
	8:29 we to do with thee, J, *thou* Son of God?	2424
	8:34 the whole city came out to meet J:	2424
	9: 2 J seeing their faith said unto the sick of	2424
	9: 4 And J knowing their thoughts said,	2424
	9: 9 And as J passed forth from thence, he saw	2424
	9:10 as J⁵ sat at meat in the house, behold,	846
	9:12 But when J heard *that,* he said unto them,	2424
	9:15 And J said unto them, Can the children of	2424
	9:19 And J arose, and followed him, and *so*	2424
	9:22 But J turned him about, and when he saw	2424
	9:23 And when J came into the ruler's house,	2424
	9:27 And when J departed thence, two blind	2424
	9:28 J saith unto them, Believe ye that I am	2424
	9:30 and J straitly charged them, saying,	2424
	9:35 J went about all the cities and villages,	2424
	10: 5 These twelve J sent forth,	2424
	11: 1 when J had made an end of commanding	2424
	11: 4 J answered and said unto them, Go and	2424
	11: 7 J began to say unto the multitudes	2424
	11:25 At that time J answered and said, I thank	2424
	12: 1 At that time J went on the sabbath day	2424
	12:15 But when J knew *it,* he withdrew himself	2424
	12:25 And J knew their thoughts, and said unto	2424
	13: 1 The same day went J out of the house,	2424
	13:34 All these *things* spake J unto the	2424
	13:36 Then J sent the multitude away,	2424
	13:51 J saith unto them, Have ye understood all	2424
	13:53 *that* when J had finished these parables,	2424
	13:57 But J said unto them, A prophet is not	2424
	14: 1 Herod the tetrarch heard of the fame of J,	2424
	14:12 and buried it, and went and told J.	2424
	14:13 When J heard *of it,* he departed thence by	2424
	14:14 And J went forth, and saw a great	2424
	14:16 J said unto them, They need not depart;	2424
	14:22 straightway J constrained his disciples	2424
	14:25 in the fourth watch of the night J went	2424
	14:27 straightway J spake unto them, saying,	2424
	14:29 ship, he walked on the water, to go to J.	2424
	14:31 And immediately J stretched forth *his*	2424
	15: 1 Then came to J scribes and Pharisees,	2424
	15:16 And J said, Are ye also yet without	2424
	15:21 Then J went thence, and departed into	2424
	15:28 Then J answered and said unto her,	2424
	15:29 J departed from thence, and came nigh	2424
	15:32 Then J called his disciples unto *him,* and	2424
	15:34 And J saith unto them, How many loaves	2424
	16: 6 Then J said unto them, Take heed and	2424
	16: 8 *Which* when J perceived, he said unto	2424
	16:13 When J came into the coasts of Cesarea	2424
	16:17 And J answered and said unto him,	2424
	16:20 tell no *man* that he was J the Christ.	2424
	16:21 From that time forth began J to shew	2424
	16:24 Then said J unto his disciples, If any *man*	2424
	17: 1 And after six days J taketh Peter, James,	2424
	17: 4 answered Peter, and said unto J, Lord,	2424
	17: 7 And J came and touched them, and said,	2424
	17: 8 their eyes, they saw no *man,* save J only.	2424
	17: 9 from the mountain, J charged them,	2424
	17:11 And J answered and said unto them,	2424
	17:17 Then J answered and said, O faithless and	2424
	17:18 And J rebuked the devil; and he departed	2424
	17:19 Then came the disciples to J apart,	2424
	17:20 And J said unto them, Because of your	2424
	17:22 they abode in Galilee, J said unto them,	2424
	17:25 J prevented him, saying, What thinkest	2424
	17:26 J saith unto him, Then are the children	2424
	18: 1 the same time came the disciples unto J,	2424
	18: 2 And J called a little child unto *him,* and	2424
	18:22 J saith unto him, I say not unto thee,	2424
	19: 1 *that* when J had finished these sayings,	2424
	19:14 But J said, Suffer little children,	2424
	19:18 J said, Thou shalt do no murder, Thou	2424
	19:21 J said unto him, If thou wilt be perfect,	2424
	19:23 Then said J unto his disciples, Verily I say	2424
	19:26 But J beheld *them,* and said unto them,	2424
	19:28 And J said unto them, Verily I say unto	2424
	20:17 And J going up to Jerusalem took	2424
	20:22 But J answered and said, Ye know not	2424
	20:25 But J called them unto *him,* and said,	2424
	20:30 they heard that J passed by, cried out,	2424
	20:32 J stood still, and called them, and said,	2424
	20:34 So J had compassion *on them,* and	2424
	21: 1 mount of Olives, then sent J two disciples,	2424
	21: 6 and did as J commanded them,	2424
	21:11 This is J the prophet of Nazareth of	2424
	21:12 And J went into the temple of God,	2424
	21:16 And J saith unto them, Yea; have ye never	2424
	21:21 J answered and said unto them, Verily	2424
	21:24 And J answered and said unto them,	2424
	21:27 they answered J, and said, We cannot	2424
	21:31 J saith unto them, Verily I say unto you,	2424
	21:42 J saith unto them, Did ye never read in	2424
	22: 1 J answered and spake unto them again	2424
	22:18 J perceived their wickedness, and said,	2424
	22:29 J answered and said unto them, Ye do err,	2424
	22:37 J said unto him, Thou shalt love the Lord	2424

Mt	22:41 were gathered together, J asked them,	2424
	23: 1 Then spake J to the multitude, and to his	2424
	24: 1 And J went out, and departed from	2424
	24: 2 And J said unto them, See ye not all these	2424
	26: 1 when J had finished all these sayings,	2424
	26: 4 And consulted that they might take J by	2424
	26: 6 when J was in Bethany, in the house	2424
	26:10 When J understood *it,* he said unto them,	2424
	26:17 unleavened bread the disciples came to J,	2424
	26:19 And the disciples did as J had appointed	2424
	26:26 J took bread, and blessed *it,* and brake *it,*	2424
	26:31 Then saith J unto them, All ye shall be	2424
	26:34 J said unto him, Verily I say unto thee,	2424
	26:36 Then cometh J with them unto a place	2424
	26:49 forthwith he came to J, and said, Hail,	2424
	26:50 J said unto him, Friend, wherefore art	2424
	26:50 and laid hands on J, and took him.	2424
	26:51 one of them which were with J stretched	2424
	26:52 Then said J unto him, Put up again thy	2424
	26:55 that *same* hour said J to the multitudes,	2424
	26:57 And they that had laid hold on J led *him*	2424
	26:59 the council, sought false witness against J,	2424
	26:63 But J held his peace. And the high priest	2424
	26:64 J saith unto him, Thou hast said:	2424
	26:69 saying, Thou also wast with J of Galilee.	2424
	26:71 This *fellow* was also with J of Nazareth.	2424
	26:75 And Peter remembered the word of J,	2424
	27: 1 elders of the people took counsel against J	2424
	27:11 And J stood before the governor:	2424
	27:11 And J said unto him, Thou sayest.	2424
	27:17 Barabbas, or J which is called Christ?	2424
	27:20 they should ask Barabbas, and destroy J.	2424
	27:22 I do then with J, which is called Christ?	2424
	27:26 and when he had scourged J, he delivered	2424
	27:27 Then the soldiers of the governor took J	2424
	27:37 THIS IS J THE KING OF THE JEWS.	2424
	27:46 And about the ninth hour J cried with a	2424
	27:50 J, when he had cried again with a loud	2424
	27:54 watching J, saw the earthquake,	2424
	27:55 which followed J from Galilee,	2424
	27:58 went to Pilate, and begged the body of J.	2424
	28: 5 for I know that ye seek J, which was	2424
	28: 9 behold, J met them, saying, *All* hail.	2424
	28:10 Then said J unto them, Be not afraid:	2424
	28:16 into a mountain where J had appointed	2424
	28:18 And J came and spake unto them, saying,	2424
Mk	1: 1 The beginning of the gospel of J Christ,	2424
	1: 9 *that* J came from Nazareth of Galilee,	2424
	1:14 was put in prison, J came into Galilee,	2424
	1:17 And J said unto them, Come ye after me,	2424
	1:24 we to do with thee, *thou* J of Nazareth?	2424
	1:25 And J rebuked him, saying, Hold thy	2424
	1:41 And J, moved with compassion, put forth	2424
	1:45 that J could no more openly enter	NIG
	2: 5 When J saw their faith, he said unto	2424
	2: 8 when J perceived in his spirit that they so	2424
	2:15 that as J sat at meat in his house,	NIG
	2:15 and sinners sat also together with J and	2424
	2:17 When J heard *it,* he saith unto them,	2424
	2:19 J said unto them, Can the children of	2424
	3: 7 But J withdrew himself with his disciples	2424
	5: 6 But when he saw J afar off, he ran and	2424
	5: 7 and said, What have I to do with thee, J,	2424
	5:13 And forthwith J gave them leave.	2424
	5:15 And they come to J, and see him that was	2424
	5:19 Howbeit J suffered him not, but saith	2424
	5:20 how great *things* J had done for him:	2424
	5:21 when J was passed over again by ship	2424
	5:24 And J went with him; and much people	NIG
	5:27 she had heard of J, came in the press	2424
	5:30 J immediately knowing in himself that	2424
	5:36 As soon as J heard the word *that was*	2424
	6: 4 But J said unto them, A prophet is not	2424
	6:30 gathered themselves together unto J,	2424
	6:34 And J, when he came out, saw much	2424
	7:27 J said unto her, Let the children first be	2424
	8: 1 J called his disciples unto *him,* and	2424
	8:17 And when J knew *it,* he saith unto them,	2424
	8:27 And J went out, and his disciples, into	2424
	9: 2 after six days J taketh with *him* Peter,	2424
	9: 4 with Moses: and they were talking with J.	2424
	9: 5 And Peter answered and said to J, Master,	2424
	9: 8 any more, save J only with themselves.	2424
	9:23 J said unto him, If thou canst believe,	2424
	9:25 J saw that the people came running	2424
	9:27 J took him by the hand, and lifted him	2424
	9:39 But J said, Forbid him not: for there is no	2424
	10: 5 And J answered and said unto them,	2424
	10:14 But when J saw *it,* he was much	2424
	10:18 J said unto him, Why callest thou me	2424
	10:21 Then J beholding him loved him,	2424
	10:23 And J looked round about, and saith unto	2424
	10:24 J answereth again, and saith unto them,	2424
	10:27 And J looking upon them saith, With men	2424
	10:29 And J answered and said, Verily I say unto	2424
	10:32 up to Jerusalem; and J went before them:	2424
	10:38 J said unto them, Ye know not what ye	2424
	10:39 And J said unto them, Ye shall indeed	2424
	10:42 But J called them to *him,* and saith unto	2424
	10:47 And when he heard that it was J of	2424
	10:47 and say, J, *thou* Son of David, have mercy	2424
	10:49 And J stood still, and commanded him to	2424
	10:50 away his garment, rose, and came to J.	2424
	10:51 And J answered and said unto him,	2424

Mk	10:52 J said unto him, Go thy way; thy faith	2424
	10:52 his sight, and followed J in the way.	2424
	11: 6 And they said unto them even as J had	2424
	11: 7 And they brought the colt to J,	2424
	11:11 And J entered into Jerusalem, and into	2424
	11:14 answered and said unto it, No *man*	2424
	11:15 and J went into the temple, and began to	2424
	11:22 And J answering saith unto them,	2424
	11:29 J answered and said unto them, I will	2424
	11:33 And they answered and said unto J,	2424
	11:33 And J answering saith unto them,	2424
	12:17 And J answering said unto them, Render to	2424
	12:24 J answering said unto them, Do ye not	2424
	12:29 And J answered him, The first of all	2424
	12:34 And when J saw that he answered	2424
	12:35 And J answered and said, while he taught	2424
	12:41 And J sat over against the treasury,	2424
	13: 2 J answering said unto him, Seest thou	2424
	13: 5 And J answering began to say,	2424
	14: 6 J said, Let her alone; why trouble you	2424
	14:18 And as they sat and did eat, J said,	2424
	14:22 J took bread, and blessed, and brake *it,*	2424
	14:27 And J saith unto them, All ye shall be	2424
	14:30 And J saith unto him, Verily I say unto	2424
	14:48 And J answered and said unto them,	2424
	14:53 And they led J away to the high priest:	2424
	14:55 the council sought for witness against J	2424
	14:60 and asked J, saying, Answerest thou	2424
	14:62 And J said, I am: and ye shall see the Son	2424
	14:67 *And* thou also wast with J of Nazareth.	2424
	14:72 And Peter called to mind the word that J	2424
	15: 1 and bound J, and carried *him* away,	2424
	15: 5 But J yet answered nothing; so that Pilate	2424
	15:15 Barabbas unto them, and delivered J,	2424
	15:34 And at the ninth hour J cried with a loud	2424
	15:37 J cried with a loud voice, and gave up	2424
	15:43 unto Pilate, and craved the body of J.	2424
	16: 6 Ye seek J of Nazareth, which was	2424
	16: 9 when J was risen early the first *day* of	NIG
Lk	1:31 forth a son, and shalt call his name J.	2424
	2:21 his name was called J, which was *so*	2424
	2:27 when the parents brought in the child J,	2424
	2:43 the child J tarried behind in Jerusalem;	2424
	2:52 And J increased in wisdom and stature,	2424
	3:21 *that* J also being baptized, and praying,	2424
	3:23 And J himself began *to be* about thirty	2424
	4: 1 And J being full of the Holy Ghost	2424
	4: 4 And J answered him, saying, It is written,	2424
	4: 8 And J answered and said unto him,	2424
	4:12 And J answering said unto him, It is said,	2424
	4:14 And J returned in the power of the Spirit	2424
	4:34 we to do with thee, *thou* J of Nazareth?	2424
	4:35 And J rebuked him, saying, Hold thy	2424
	5:10 And J said unto Simon, Fear not;	2424
	5:12 who seeing J fell on *his* face,	2424
	5:19 with *his* couch into the midst before J.	2424
	5:22 But when J perceived their thoughts,	2424
	5:31 And J answering said unto them,	2424
	6: 3 And J answering them said, Have ye not	2424
	6: 9 Then said J unto them, I will ask you one	2424
	6:11 with another what they might do to J.	2424
	7: 3 when he heard of J, he sent unto him	2424
	7: 4 And when they came to J, they besought	2424
	7: 6 J went with them. And when he was	2424
	7: 9 When J heard these *things,* he marvelled	2424
	7:19 *him* two of his disciples sent *them* to J,	2424
	7:22 J answering said unto them, Go your	2424
	7:37 when she knew that J sat at meat in	NIG
	7:40 And J answering said unto him, Simon,	2424
	8:28 When he saw J, he cried out, and fell	2424
	8:28 with thee, J, *thou* Son of God most high?	2424
	8:30 And J asked him, saying, What is thy	2424
	8:35 and came to J, and found the man, out of	2424
	8:35 sitting at the feet of J, clothed, and in his	2424
	8:38 be with him: but J sent him away, saying,	2424
	8:39 how great *things* J had done unto him.	2424
	8:40 it came to pass that, when J was returned,	2424
	8:45 And J said, Who touched me? When all	2424
	8:46 And J said, Somebody hath touched me:	2424
	8:50 But when J heard *it,* he answered him,	2424
	9:33 from him, Peter said unto J, Master,	2424
	9:36 the voice was past, J was found alone.	2424
	9:41 And J answering said, O faithless and	2424
	9:42 And J rebuked the unclean spirit,	2424
	9:43 every one at all *things* which J did,	2424
	9:50 J said unto him, Forbid *him* not: for he	2424
	9:58 And J said unto him, Foxes have holes,	2424
	9:60 J said unto him, Let the dead bury their	2424
	9:62 And J said unto him, No *man* having put	2424
	10:21 In that hour J rejoiced in spirit, and said,	2424
	10:29 willing to justify himself, said unto J,	2424
	10:30 And J answering said, A certain *man* went	2424
	10:37 Then said J unto him, Go, and do thou	2424
	10:41 And J answered and said unto her,	2424
	13: 2 And J answering said unto them,	2424
	13:12 when J saw her, he called *her* to *him,*	2424
	13:14 that J had healed on the sabbath day,	2424
	14: 3 And J answering spake unto the lawyers	2424
	17:13 and said, J, Master, have mercy on us.	2424
	17:17 And J answering said, Were there not ten	2424
	18:16 But J called them unto *him,* and said,	2424
	18:19 And J said unto him, Why callest thou me	2424
	18:22 Now when J heard these *things,* he said	2424
	18:24 And when J saw that he was very	2424

Lk 18:37	told him, that J of Nazareth passeth by. 2424
18:38	he cried, saying, J, *thou* Son of David, 2424
18:40	And J stood, and commanded him to be 2424
18:42	And J said unto him, Receive thy sight: 2424
19: 1	J entered and passed through Jericho. NIG
19: 3	And he sought to see J who he was; 2424
19: 5	And when J came to the place, he looked 2424
19: 9	And J said unto him, This day is salvation 2424
19:35	And they brought him to J: and they cast 2424
19:35	upon the colt, and they set J thereon. 2424
20: 8	J said unto them, Neither tell I you by 2424
20:34	And J answering said unto them, 2424
22:47	and drew near unto J to kiss him. 2424
22:48	But J said unto him, Judas, betrayest thou 2424
22:51	And J answered and said, Suffer ye thus 2424
22:52	Then J said unto the chief priests, 2424
22:63	And the men that held J mocked him, 2424
23: 8	When Herod saw J, he was exceeding 2424
23:20	Pilate therefore, willing to release J, spake 2424
23:25	desired; but he delivered J to their will. 2424
23:26	laid the cross, that he might bear *it* after J. 2424
23:28	J turning unto them, said, Daughters of 2424
23:34	Then said J, Father, forgive them; for they 2424
23:42	And he said unto J, Lord, remember me 2424
23:43	J said unto him, Verily I say unto thee, 2424
23:46	And when J had cried with a loud voice, 2424
23:52	unto Pilate, and begged the body of J. 2424
24: 3	and found not the body of the Lord J. 2424
24:15	J himself drew near, and went with them. 2424
24:19	Concerning J of Nazareth, which was a 2424
24:36	J himself stood in the midst of them, 2424
Jn 1:17	*but* grace and truth came by J Christ. 2424
1:29	The next day John seeth J coming unto 2424
1:36	looking upon J as he walked, he saith, 2424
1:37	heard him speak, and they followed J. 2424
1:38	Then J turned, 2424
1:42	And he brought him to J. And when Jesus 2424
1:42	And when J beheld him, he said, Thou art 2424
1:43	The day following J would go forth into 2424
1:45	the prophets, did write, J of Nazareth, 2424
1:47	J saw Nathanael coming to him, 2424
1:48	J answered and said unto him, Before that 2424
1:50	J answered and said unto him, Because I 2424
2: 1	of Galilee; and the mother of J was there: 2424
2: 2	And both J was called, and his disciples, 2424
2: 3	the mother of J saith unto him, They have 2424
2: 4	J saith unto her, Woman, what have I to 2424
2: 7	J saith unto them, Fill the waterpots with 2424
2:11	This beginning of miracles did J in Cana 2424
2:13	was at hand, and J went up to Jerusalem. 2424
2:19	J answered and said unto them, 2424
2:22	and the word which J had said. 2424
2:24	But J did not commit himself unto them, 2424
3: 2	The same came to J by night, and said 2424
3: 3	J answered and said unto him, Verily, 2424
3: 5	J answered, Verily, verily, I say unto thee, 2424
3:10	J answered and said unto him, Art thou a 2424
3:22	After *these* things came J and his disciples 2424
4: 1	how the Pharisees had heard that J made 2424
4: 2	(Though J himself baptized not, 2424
4: 6	J therefore, being wearied with *his* 2424
4: 7	J saith unto her, Give me to drink. 2424
4:10	J answered and said unto her, If thou 2424
4:13	J answered and said unto her, 2424
4:16	J saith unto her, Go, call thy husband, 2424
4:17	J said unto her, Thou hast well said, 2424
4:21	J saith unto her, Woman, believe me, 2424
4:26	J saith unto her, I that speak unto thee 2424
4:34	J saith unto them, My meat is to do the 2424
4:44	For J himself testified, that a prophet hath 2424
4:46	So J came again into Cana of Galilee, 2424
4:47	When he heard that J was come out of 2424
4:48	Then said J unto him, Except ye see signs 2424
4:50	J saith unto him, Go thy way; thy son 2424
4:50	the man believed the word that J had 2424
4:53	in the which J said unto him, Thy son 2424
4:54	This *is* again the second miracle that J did, 2424
5: 1	of the Jews; and J went up to Jerusalem. 2424
5: 6	When J saw him lie, and knew that he 2424
5: 8	J saith unto him, Rise, take up thy bed, 2424
5:13	for J had conveyed himself away, 2424
5:14	Afterward J findeth him in the temple, 2424
5:15	and told the Jews that it was J, 2424
5:16	And therefore did the Jews persecute J, 2424
5:17	But J answered them, My Father worketh 2424
5:19	Then answered J and said unto them, 2424
6: 1	After these *things* J went over the sea of 2424
6: 3	And J went up into a mountain, 2424
6: 5	When J then lift up *his* eyes, 2424
6:10	And J said, Make the men sit down. 2424
6:11	And J took the loaves; and when he had 2424
6:14	they had seen the miracle that J did, 2424
6:15	When J therefore perceived that they 2424
6:17	now dark, and J was not come to them. 2424
6:19	see J walking on the sea, and drawing 2424
6:22	that J went not with his disciples into 2424
6:24	there saw that J was not there, 2424
6:24	and came to Capernaum, seeking for J. 2424
6:26	J answered them and said, Verily, verily, 2424
6:29	J answered and said unto them, This is 2424
6:32	J said unto them, Verily, verily, I say 2424
6:35	And J said unto them, I am the bread of 2424
6:42	And they said, Is not this J, the son of 2424
6:43	J therefore answered and said unto them, 2424
6:53	Then J said unto them, Verily, verily, I say 2424

Jn 6:61	When J knew in himself that his disciples 2424
6:64	For J knew from the beginning who they 2424
6:67	Then said J unto the twelve, Will ye also 2424
6:70	J answered them, Have not I chosen you 2424
7: 1	After these *things* J walked in Galilee: 2424
7: 6	J said unto them, My time is not yet 2424
7:14	about the midst of the feast J went up 2424
7:16	J answered them, and said, My doctrine is 2424
7:21	J answered and said unto them, 2424
7:28	Then cried J in the temple as he taught, 2424
7:33	Then said J unto them, Yet a little while 2424
7:37	J stood and cried, saying, If any *man* thirst 2424
7:39	because that J was not yet glorified.) 2424
7:50	(he that came to J by night, being one of NIG
8: 1	J went unto the mount of Olives. 2424
8: 6	But J stooped down, and with *his* finger 2424
8: 9	and J was left alone, and the woman 2424
8:10	When J had lift up *himself*, and saw none 2424
8:11	J said unto her, Neither do I condemn 2424
8:12	spake J again unto them, saying, I am 2424
8:14	J answered and said unto them, Though I 2424
8:19	J answered, Ye neither know me, nor my 2424
8:20	These words spake J in the treasury, as he 2424
8:21	Then said J again unto them, I go my way, 2424
8:25	J saith unto them, Even the same that I 2424
8:28	Then said J unto them, When ye have lift 2424
8:31	Then said J to those Jews which believed 2424
8:34	J answered them, Verily, verily, I say unto 2424
8:39	J saith unto them, If ye were Abraham's 2424
8:42	J said unto them, If God were your Father, 2424
8:49	J answered, I have not a devil; but I 2424
8:54	J answered, If I honour myself, my honour 2424
8:58	J said unto them, Verily, verily, I say unto 2424
8:59	but J hid himself, and went out of 2424
9: 1	And as J passed by, he saw a man *which* NIG
9: 3	J answered, Neither hath this *man* sinned, 2424
9:11	A man *that is* called J made clay, 2424
9:14	And it was the sabbath day when J made 2424
9:35	J heard that they had cast him out; 2424
9:37	And J said unto him, Thou hast both seen 2424
9:39	And J said, For judgment I am come into 2424
9:41	J said unto them, If ye were blind, 2424
10: 6	This parable spake J unto them: 2424
10: 7	said J unto them again, Verily, verily, 2424
10:23	And J walked in the temple in Solomon's 2424
10:25	J answered them, I told you, and ye 2424
10:32	J answered them, Many good works have 2424
10:34	J answered them, Is it not written in your 2424
11: 4	When J heard *that*, he said, This sickness 2424
11: 5	Now J loved Martha, and her sister, 2424
11: 9	J answered, Are there not twelve hours in 2424
11:13	Howbeit J spake of his death: 2424
11:14	Then said J unto them plainly, Lazarus is 2424
11:17	Then when J came, he found that he had 2424
11:20	as soon as she heard that J was coming, 2424
11:21	Then said Martha unto J, Lord, if thou 2424
11:23	J saith unto her, Thy brother shall rise 2424
11:25	J said unto her, I am the resurrection, 2424
11:30	Now J was not yet come into the town, 2424
11:32	Then when Mary was come where J was, 2424
11:33	When J therefore saw her weeping, 2424
11:35	J wept. 2424
11:38	J therefore again groaning in himself 2424
11:39	J said, Take ye away the stone. Martha, 2424
11:40	J saith unto her, Said I not unto thee, 2424
11:41	And J lift up *his* eyes, and said, Father, 2424
11:44	J saith unto them, Loose him, and let him 2424
11:45	and had seen the *things* which J did, 2424
11:46	and told them what *things* J had done. 2424
11:51	he prophesied that J should die for *that* 2424
11:54	J therefore walked no more openly among 2424
11:56	Then sought they for J, and spake among 2424
12: 1	Then J six days before the passover came 2424
12: 3	and anointed the feet of J, and wiped his 2424
12: 7	Then said J, Let her alone: against the day 2424
12:11	of the Jews went away, and believed on J. 2424
12:12	when they heard that J was coming to 2424
12:14	And J, when he had found a young ass, 2424
12:16	but when J was glorified, then 2424
12:21	desired him, saying, Sir, we would see J. 2424
12:22	and again Andrew and Philip tell J. 2424
12:23	And J answered them, saying, The hour is 2424
12:30	J answered and said, This voice came not 2424
12:35	J said unto them, Yet a little while is 2424
12:36	These *things* spake J, and departed, 2424
12:44	J cried and said, He that believeth on me, 2424
13: 1	J knew that his hour was come that 2424
13: 3	J knowing that the Father had given all 2424
13: 7	J answered and said unto him, What I do 2424
13: 8	J answered him, If I wash thee not, 2424
13:10	J saith to him, He that is washed needeth 2424
13:21	When J had thus said, he was troubled in 2424
13:23	bosom one of his disciples, whom J loved. 2424
13:26	J answered, He it is, to whom I shall give 2424
13:27	Then said J unto him, That thou doest, 2424
13:29	Judas had the bag, that J had said unto 2424
13:31	Therefore, when he was gone out, J said, 2424
13:36	J answered him, Whither I go, thou canst 2424
13:38	J answered him, Wilt thou lay down thy 2424
14: 6	J saith unto him, I am the way, the truth, 2424
14: 9	J saith unto him, Have I been so long time 2424
14:23	J answered and said unto him, If a man 2424
16:19	J knew that they were desirous to ask 2424
16:31	J answered them, Do ye now believe? 2424
17: 1	These *words* spake J, and lift up his eyes 2424

Jn 17: 3	and J Christ, whom thou hast sent. 2424
18: 1	When J had spoken these *words*, he went 2424
18: 2	for J ofttimes resorted thither with his 2424
18: 4	J therefore, knowing all *things* that should 2424
18: 5	They answered him, J of Nazareth. 2424
18: 5	J saith unto them, I am he. And Judas 2424
18: 7	seek ye? And they said, J of Nazareth. 2424
18: 8	J answered, I have told you that I am he: 2424
18:11	Then said J unto Peter, Put up thy sword 2424
18:12	the captain and officers of the Jews took J, 2424
18:15	And Simon Peter followed J, and so 2424
18:15	went in with J into the palace of the high 2424
18:19	high priest then asked J of his disciples, 2424
18:20	J answered him, I spake openly to 2424
18:22	one of the officers which stood by stroke J 2424
18:23	J answered him, If I have spoken evil, 2424
18:28	Then led they J from Caiaphas unto 2424
18:32	That the saying of J might be fulfilled, 2424
18:33	and called J, and said unto him, Art thou 2424
18:34	J answered him, Sayest thou this *thing* of 2424
18:36	J answered, My kingdom is not of this 2424
18:37	J answered, Thou sayest that I am a king. 2424
19: 1	Then Pilate therefore took J, 2424
19: 5	Then came J forth, wearing the crown of 2424
19: 9	and saith unto J, Whence art thou? 2424
19: 9	art thou? But J gave him no answer. 2424
19:11	J answered, Thou couldest have no power 2424
19:13	he brought J forth, and sat down in 2424
19:16	And they took J, and led *him* away. 2424
19:18	on either side one, and J in the midst. 2424
19:19	J OF NAZARETH THE KING OF THE 2424
19:20	for the place where J was crucified was 2424
19:23	the soldiers, when they had crucified J, 2424
19:25	Now there stood by the cross of J his 2424
19:26	When J therefore saw *his* mother, 2424
19:28	J knowing that all *things* were now 2424
19:30	J therefore had received the vinegar, 2424
19:33	But when they came to J, and saw that he 2424
19:38	being a disciple of J, but secretly for fear 2424
19:38	that he might take away the body of J: 2424
19:38	came therefore, and took the body of J. 2424
19:39	which at the first came to J by night, 2424
19:40	took they the body of J, and wound it 2424
19:42	There laid they J therefore because of 2424
20: 2	whom J loved, and saith unto them, 2424
20:12	at the feet, where the body of J had lain. 2424
20:14	and saw J standing, and knew not that it 2424
20:14	standing, and knew not that it was J. 2424
20:15	J saith unto her, Woman, why weepest 2424
20:16	J saith unto her, Mary. She turned herself, 2424
20:17	J saith unto her, Touch me not; for I am 2424
20:19	came J and stood in the midst, 2424
20:21	Then said J to them again, Peace *be* unto 2424
20:24	was not with them when J came. 2424
20:26	*then* came J, the doors being shut, 2424
20:29	J saith unto him, Thomas, because 2424
20:30	And many other signs truly did J in 2424
20:31	that ye might believe that J is the Christ, 2424
21: 1	After these *things* J shewed himself again 2424
21: 4	was now come, J stood on the shore: 2424
21: 4	but the disciples knew not that it was J. 2424
21: 5	J saith unto them, Children, have ye 2424
21: 7	Therefore that disciple whom J loved saith 2424
21:10	J saith unto them, Bring of the fish which 2424
21:12	J saith unto them, Come *and* dine. 2424
21:13	J then cometh, and taketh bread, 2424
21:14	This *is* now the third time *that* J shewed 2424
21:15	J saith to Simon Peter, Simon, *son of* 2424
21:17	J saith unto him, Feed my sheep. 2424
21:20	the disciple whom J loved following; 2424
21:21	Peter seeing him saith to J, Lord, 2424
21:22	J saith unto him, If I will that he tarry till 2424
21:23	yet J said not unto him, He shall not die; 2424
21:25	are also many other *things* which J did, 2424
Ac 1: 1	of all that J began both to do and teach, 2424
1:11	this *same* J, which is taken up from you 2424
1:14	and Mary the mother of J, and with his 2424
1:16	which was guide to them that took J. 2424
1:21	with us all the time that the Lord J went 2424
2:22	J of Nazareth, a man approved of God 2424
2:32	This J hath God raised up, whereof we all 2424
2:36	that God hath made that same J, whom 2424
2:38	name of J Christ for the remission of sins, 2424
3: 6	In the name of J Christ of Nazareth rise 2424
3:13	of our fathers, hath glorified his Son J; 2424
3:20	And he shall send J Christ, which before 2424
3:26	you first God, having raised up his Son J, 2424
4: 2	preached through J the resurrection from 2424
4:10	that by the name of J Christ of Nazareth, 2424
4:13	of them, that they had been with J. 2424
4:18	to speak at all nor teach in the name of J. 2424
4:27	For of a truth against thy holy child J, 2424
4:30	be done by the name of thy holy child J. 2424
4:33	witness of the resurrection of the Lord J: 2424
5:30	The God of our fathers raised up J, 2424
5:40	*they* should not speak in the name of J, 2424
5:42	ceased not to teach and preach J Christ. 2424
6:14	that this J of Nazareth shall destroy this 2424
7:45	with J into the possession of the Gentiles, 2424
7:55	and J standing on the right hand of God, 2424
7:59	calling upon *God*, and saying, Lord J, 2424
8:12	and the name of J Christ, they were 2424
8:16	were baptized in the name of the Lord J.) 2424
8:35	same scripture, and preached unto him J. 2424
8:37	I believe that J Christ is the Son of God. 2424

J

Ac	9: 5 Lord said, I am J whom thou persecutest:	2424
	9:17 him said, Brother Saul, the Lord, *even* J,	2424
	9:27 boldly at Damascus in the name of J.	2424
	9:29 he spake boldly in the name of the Lord J,	2424
	9:34 Aeneas, J Christ maketh thee whole:	2424
	10:36 of Israel, preaching peace by J Christ:	2424
	10:38 How God anointed J of Nazareth with	2424
	11:17 us, who believed on the Lord J Christ;	2424
	11:20 unto the Grecians, preaching the Lord J.	2424
	13:23 promise raised unto Israel a Saviour, J:	2424
	13:33 in that he hath raised up J again;	2424
	15:11 of the Lord J Christ *we* shall be saved,	2424
	15:26 lives for the name of our Lord J Christ.	2424
	16:18 I command thee in the name of J Christ	2424
	16:31 Believe on the Lord J Christ, and thou	2424
	17: 3 and that this J, whom I preach unto you,	2424
	17: 7 saying that there is another king, *one* J.	2424
	17:18 because he preached unto them J,	2424
	18: 5 and testified to the Jews *that* J was Christ.	2424
	18:28 by the scriptures that J was Christ.	2424
	19: 4 come after him, that is, on Christ J.	2424
	19: 5 were baptized in the name of the Lord J.	2424
	19:10 in Asia heard the word of the Lord J,	2424
	19:13 had evil spirits the name of the Lord J,	2424
	19:13 We adjure you by J whom Paul preacheth.	2424
	19:15 and said, J I know, and Paul I know;	2424
	19:17 the name of the Lord J was magnified.	2424
	20:21 and faith toward our Lord J Christ.	2424
	20:24 which I have received of the Lord J,	2424
	20:35 and to remember the words of the Lord J,	2424
	21:13 at Jerusalem for the name of the Lord J.	2424
	22: 8 And he said unto me, I am J of Nazareth,	2424
	25:19 of one J, *which* was dead, whom Paul	2424
	26: 9 contrary to the name of J of Nazareth.	2424
	26:15 he said, I am J whom thou persecutest.	2424
	28:23 persuading them concerning J, both out	2424
	28:31 *things* which concern the Lord J Christ,	2424
Ro	1: 1 Paul, a servant of J Christ, called *to be* an	2424
	1: 3 Concerning his Son J Christ our Lord,	2424
	1: 6 Among whom are ye also the called of J	2424
	1: 7 God our Father, and the Lord J Christ.	2424
	1: 8 I thank my God through J Christ for you	2424
	2:16 men by J Christ according to my gospel.	2424
	3:22 God *which is* by faith of J Christ unto all	2424
	3:24 through the redemption that is in Christ J:	2424
	3:26 the justifier of him which believeth in J.	2424
	4:24 if we believe on him that raised up J our	2424
	5: 1 peace with God through our Lord J Christ:	2424
	5:11 we also joy in God through our Lord J	2424
	5:15 by grace, which is by one man, J Christ,	2424
	5:17 shall reign in life by one, J Christ.	2424
	5:21 unto eternal life by J Christ our Lord.	2424
	6: 3 many of us as were baptized into J Christ	2424
	6:11 alive unto God through J Christ our Lord.	2424
	6:23 the gift of God *is* eternal life through J	2424
	7:25 I thank God through J Christ our Lord.	2424
	8: 1 in Christ J who walk not after the flesh,	2424
	8: 2 For the law of the Spirit of life in Christ J	2424
	8:11 But if the Spirit of him that raised up J	2424
	8:39 love of God, which is in Christ J our Lord.	2424
	10: 9 shalt confess with thy mouth the Lord J,	2424
	13:14 But put ye on the Lord J Christ,	2424
	14:14 I know, and am persuaded by the Lord J,	2424
	15: 5 towards another according to Christ J:	2424
	15: 6 even the Father of our Lord J Christ.	2424
	15: 8 Now I say that J Christ was a minister of	2424
	15:16 That I should be the minister of J Christ	2424
	15:17 whereof *I* may glory through J Christ *in*	2424
	15:30 for the Lord J Christ's sake, and for	2424
	16: 3 and Aquila my helpers in Christ J:	2424
	16:18 *they that are* such serve not our Lord J	2424
	16:20 The grace of our Lord J Christ *be* with	2424
	16:24 The grace of our Lord J Christ *be* with	2424
	16:25 the preaching of J Christ, according to	2424
	16:27 *be* glory through J Christ for ever.	2424
1Co	1: 1 called *to be* an apostle of J Christ through	2424
	1: 2 to them that are sanctified in Christ J,	2424
	1: 2 call upon the name of J Christ our Lord,	2424
	1: 3 our Father, and *from* the Lord J Christ.	2424
	1: 4 of God which is given you by J Christ;	2424
	1: 7 waiting for the coming of our Lord J	2424
	1: 8 blameless in the day of our Lord J Christ.	2424
	1: 9 fellowship of his Son J Christ our Lord.	2424
	1:10 by the name of our Lord J Christ,	2424
	1:30 But of him are ye in Christ J, who of God	2424
	2: 2 save J Christ, and him crucified.	2424
	3:11 lay than that is laid, which is J Christ.	2424
	4:15 In Christ J I have begotten you through	2424
	5: 4 In the name of our Lord J Christ, when ye	2424
	5: 4 with the power of our Lord J Christ,	2424
	5: 5 may be saved in the day of the Lord J.	2424
	6:11 ye are justified in the name of the Lord J,	2424
	8: 6 and one Lord J Christ, by whom *are* all	2424
	9: 1 have I not seen J Christ our Lord? are not	2424
	11:23 That the Lord J the *same* night in which	2424
	12: 3 by the Spirit of God calleth J accursed:	2424
	12: 3 that no *man* can say that J is the Lord,	2424
	15:31 which I have in Christ J our Lord,	2424
	15:57 us the victory through our Lord J Christ.	2424
	16:22 If any *man* love not the Lord J Christ,	2424
	16:23 The grace of *our* Lord J Christ *be* with	2424
	16:24 My love *be* with you all in Christ J.	2424
2Co	1: 1 an apostle of J Christ by the will of God,	2424
	1: 2 our Father, and *from* the Lord J Christ.	2424
	1: 3 even the Father of our Lord J Christ,	2424

2Co	1:14 ye also *are* ours in the day of the Lord J.	2424
	1:19 For the Son of God, J Christ, who was	2424
	4: 5 not ourselves, but Christ J the Lord;	2424
	4: 6 of the glory of God in the face of J Christ.	2424
	4:10 about in the body the dying of the Lord J,	2424
	4:10 that the life also of J might be made	2424
	4:11 that the life also of J might be made	2424
	4:14 the Lord J shall raise up us also by Jesus,	2424
	4:14 the Lord Jesus shall raise up us also by J,	2424
	5:18 who hath reconciled us to himself by J	2424
	8: 9 ye know the grace of our Lord J Christ,	2424
	11: 4 For if he that cometh preacheth another J,	2424
	11:31 The God and Father of our Lord J Christ,	2424
	13: 5 how that J Christ is in you, except ye be	2424
	13:14 The grace of the Lord J Christ, and the	2424
Gal	1: 1 but by J Christ, and God the Father,	2424
	1: 3 the Father, and *from* our Lord J Christ,	2424
	1:12 taught *it*, but by the revelation of J Christ.	2424
	2: 4 out our liberty which we have in Christ J,	2424
	2:16 but by the faith of J Christ, even we have	2424
	2:16 even we have believed in J Christ,	2424
	3: 1 before whose eyes J Christ hath been	2424
	3:14 come on the Gentiles through J Christ;	2424
	3:22 that the promise by faith of J Christ might	2424
	3:26 all the children of God by faith in Christ J.	2424
	3:28 nor female: for ye are all one in Christ J.	2424
	4:14 me as an angel of God, *even* as Christ J.	2424
	5: 6 For in J Christ neither circumcision	2424
	6:14 save in the cross of our Lord J Christ,	2424
	6:15 For in Christ J neither circumcision	2424
	6:17 I bear in my body the marks of the Lord J.	2424
	6:18 the grace of our Lord J Christ *be* with your	2424
Eph	1: 1 an apostle of J Christ by the will of God,	2424
	1: 1 at Ephesus, and to the faithful in Christ J:	2424
	1: 2 our Father, and *from* the Lord J Christ.	2424
	1: 3 the God and Father of our Lord J Christ,	2424
	1: 5 adoption of children by J Christ to himself	2424
	1:15 after I heard of your faith in the Lord J,	2424
	1:17 That the God of our Lord J Christ,	2424
	2: 6 sit together in heavenly *places* in Christ J:	2424
	2: 7 *his* kindness towards us through Christ J.	2424
	2:10 created in Christ J unto good works,	2424
	2:13 But now in Christ J ye who sometimes	2424
	2:20 Christ himself being the chief corner	2424
	3: 1 the prisoner of J Christ for you Gentiles,	2424
	3: 9 in God, who created all *things* by J Christ:	2424
	3:11 which he purposed in Christ J our Lord:	2424
	3:14 unto the Father of our Lord J Christ,	2424
	3:21 him *be* glory in the church by Christ J	2424
	4:21 been taught by him, as the truth is in J:	2424
	5:20 Father in the name of our Lord J Christ;	2424
	6:23 God the Father and the Lord J Christ.	2424
	6:24 *be* with all them that love our Lord J	2424
Php	1: 1 and Timotheus, the servants of J Christ,	2424
	1: 1 to all the saints in Christ J which are at	2424
	1: 2 our Father, and *from* the Lord J Christ.	2424
	1: 6 will perform *it* until the day of J Christ:	2424
	1: 8 after you all in the bowels of J Christ.	2424
	1:11 which are by J Christ unto the glory and	2424
	1:19 and the supply of the Spirit of J Christ,	2424
	1:26 J Christ for me by my coming to you	2424
	2: 5 be in you, which *was* also in Christ J:	2424
	2:10 That at the name of J every knee should	2424
	2:11 *that* every tongue should confess that J	2424
	2:19 I trust in the Lord J to send Timotheus	2424
	2:21 not the *things which are* J Christ's.	2424
	3: 3 and rejoice in Christ J, and have no	2424
	3: 8 of the knowledge of Christ J my Lord:	2424
	3:12 which also I am apprehended of Christ J.	2424
	3:14 of the high calling of God in Christ J.	2424
	3:20 we look for the Saviour, the Lord J Christ:	2424
	4: 7 your hearts and minds through Christ J.	2424
	4:19 to his riches in glory by Christ J.	2424
	4:21 Salute every saint in Christ J.	2424
	4:23 The grace of our Lord J Christ *be* with	2424
Col	1: 1 an apostle of J Christ by the will of God,	2424
	1: 2 God our Father and the Lord J Christ.	2424
	1: 3 God and the Father of our Lord J Christ,	2424
	1: 4 Since we heard of your faith in Christ J,	2424
	1:28 may present every man perfect in Christ J:	2424
	2: 6 therefore received Christ J the Lord,	2424
	3:17 or deed, *do* all in the name of the Lord J,	2424
	4:11 And J, which is called Justus, who are of	2424
1Th	1: 1 in God the Father and *in* the Lord J Christ:	2424
	1: 1 God our Father, and the Lord J Christ.	2424
	1: 3 and patience of hope in our Lord J Christ,	2424
	1:10 whom he raised from the dead, *even* J,	2424
	2:14 of God which in Judea are in Christ J:	2424
	2:15 Who both killed the Lord J, and their	2424
	2:19 of our Lord J Christ at his coming?	2424
	3:11 and our Father, and our Lord J Christ,	2424
	3:13 at the coming of our Lord J Christ with	2424
	4: 1 brethren, and exhort *you* by the Lord J,	2424
	4: 2 we gave you by the Lord J.	2424
	4:14 if we believe that J died and rose again,	2424
	4:14 them also which sleep in J will God bring	2424
	5: 9 to obtain salvation by our Lord J Christ,	2424
	5:18 for this *is* the will of God in Christ J	2424
	5:23 unto the coming of our Lord J Christ.	2424
	5:28 The grace of our Lord J Christ *be* with	2424
2Th	1: 1 in God our Father and the Lord J Christ:	2424
	1: 2 God our Father and the Lord J Christ.	2424
	1: 7 when the Lord J shall be revealed from	2424
	1: 8 that obey not the gospel of our Lord J	2424
	1:12 That the name of our Lord J Christ may	2424

2Th	1:12 grace of our God and the Lord J Christ.	2424
	2: 1 by the coming of our Lord J Christ,	2424
	2:14 to the obtaining of the glory of our Lord J	2424
	2:16 Now our Lord J Christ himself, and God,	2424
	3: 6 in the name of our Lord J Christ,	2424
	3:12 and exhort by our Lord J Christ,	2424
	3:18 The grace of our Lord J Christ *be* with	2424
1Ti	1: 1 apostle of J Christ by the commandment	2424
	1: 1 and Lord J Christ, *which is* our hope;	2424
	1: 2 God our Father and J Christ our Lord.	2424
	1:12 And I thank Christ J our Lord, who hath	2424
	1:14 with faith and love which is in Christ J.	2424
	1:15 that Christ J came into the world to save	2424
	1:16 that in me first J Christ might shew forth	2424
	2: 5 between God and men, *the* man Christ J;	2424
	3:13 boldness in the faith which is in Christ J.	2424
	4: 6 thou shalt be a good minister of J Christ,	2424
	5:21 the Lord J Christ, and the elect angels,	2424
	6: 3 *even the words* of our Lord J Christ,	2424
	6:13 quickeneth all *things*, and *before* Christ J,	2424
	6:14 until the appearing of our Lord J Christ:	2424
2Ti	1: 1 an apostle of J Christ by the will of God,	2424
	1: 1 to the promise of life which is in Christ J,	2424
	1: 2 God the Father and Christ J our Lord.	2424
	1: 9 which was given us in Christ J before	2424
	1:10 by the appearing of our Saviour J Christ,	2424
	1:13 in faith and love which is in Christ J.	2424
	2: 1 be strong in the grace that is in Christ J.	2424
	2: 3 as a good soldier of J Christ.	2424
	2: 8 Remember that J Christ of the seed of	2424
	2:10 which is in Christ J with eternal glory.	2424
	3:12 all that will live godly in Christ J shall	2424
	3:15 through faith which is in Christ J.	2424
	4: 1 before God, and the Lord J Christ,	2424
	4:22 The Lord J Christ *be* with thy spirit.	2424
Tit	1: 1 servant of God, and an apostle of J Christ,	2424
	1: 4 and the Lord J Christ our Saviour.	2424
	2:13 of the great God and our Saviour J Christ;	2424
	3: 6 he shed on us abundantly through J	2424
Phm	1: 1 a prisoner of J Christ, and Timothy *our*	2424
	1: 3 God our Father and the Lord J Christ.	2424
	1: 5 which thou hast toward the Lord J,	2424
	1: 6 good *thing* which is in you by Christ J.	2424
	1: 9 and now also a prisoner of J Christ.	2424
	1:23 my fellowprisoner in Christ J;	2424
	1:25 The grace of our Lord J Christ *be* with	2424
Heb	2: 9 But we see J, who was made a little lower	2424
	3: 1 and High Priest of our profession, Christ J;	2424
	4: 8 if J had given them rest, *then* would he	2424
	4:14 J the Son of God, let us hold fast *our*	2424
	6:20 the forerunner is for us entered, *even* J,	2424
	7:22 much was J made a surety of a better	2424
	10:10 of the body of J Christ once for all.	2424
	10:19 to enter into the holiest by the blood of J,	2424
	12: 2 Looking unto J the author and finisher of	2424
	12:24 to J the mediator of the new covenant,	2424
	13: 8 J Christ the same yesterday, and to day,	2424
	13:12 Wherefore J also, that he might sanctify	2424
	13:20 brought again from the dead our Lord J,	2424
	13:21 pleasing in his sight, through J Christ;	2424
Jas	1: 1 a servant of God and of the Lord J Christ,	2424
	2: 1 have not the faith of our Lord J Christ,	2424
1Pe	1: 1 Peter, an apostle of J Christ,	2424
	1: 2 and sprinkling of the blood of J Christ:	2424
	1: 3 the God and Father of our Lord J Christ,	2424
	1: 3 the resurrection of J Christ from the dead,	2424
	1: 7 and glory at the appearing of J Christ:	2424
	1:13 unto you at the revelation of J Christ;	2424
	2: 5 acceptable to God by J Christ.	2424
	3:21 by the resurrection of J Christ:	2424
	4:11 *things* may be glorified through J Christ,	2424
	5:10 called us into his eternal glory by Christ J,	2424
	5:14 Peace *be* with you all that are in Christ J.	2424
2Pe	1: 1 a servant and an apostle of J Christ,	2424
	1: 1 of God and our Saviour J Christ:	2424
	1: 2 the knowledge of God, and of J our Lord.	2424
	1: 8 in the knowledge of our Lord J Christ.	2424
	1:11 kingdom of our Lord and Saviour J Christ.	2424
	1:14 as our Lord J Christ hath shewed me.	2424
	1:16 power and coming of our Lord J Christ,	2424
	2:20 of the Lord and Saviour J Christ,	2424
	3:18 of our Lord and Saviour J Christ.	2424
1Jn	1: 3 the Father, and with his Son J Christ.	2424
	1: 7 the blood of J Christ his Son cleanseth us	2424
	2: 1 with the Father, J Christ *the* righteous:	2424
	2:22 but he that denieth that J is the Christ?	2424
	3:23 believe on the name of his Son J Christ,	2424
	4: 2 Every spirit that confesseth that J Christ is	2424
	4: 3 And every spirit that confesseth not that J	2424
	4:15 Whosoever shall confess that J is the Son	2424
	5: 1 Whosoever believeth that J is the Christ is	2424
	5: 5 he that believeth that J is the Son of God?	2424
	5: 6 came by water and blood, *even* J Christ;	2424
	5:20 him *that is* true, *even* in his Son J Christ.	2424
2Jn	1: 3 the Father, and from the Lord J Christ,	2424
	1: 7 who confess not that J Christ is come in	2424
Jude	1: 1 the servant of J Christ, and brother of	2424
	1: 1 and preserved in J Christ, *and* called:	2424
	1: 4 the only Lord God, and our Lord J Christ.	2424
	1:17 before of the apostles of our Lord J Christ;	2424
	1:21 looking for the mercy of our Lord J Christ	2424
Rev	1: 1 The Revelation of J Christ, which God	2424
	1: 2 and of the testimony of J Christ, and of all	2424
	1: 5 And from J Christ, *who is* the faithful	2424
	1: 9 in the kingdom and patience of J Christ,	2424

J

Rev	1: 9 of God, and for the testimony of J Christ.	2424
	12:17 God, and have the testimony of J Christ.	2424
	14:12 commandments of God, and the faith of J.	2424
	17: 6 and with the blood of the martyrs of J:	2424
	19:10 thy brethren that have the witness of J:	2424
	19:10 for the testimony of J is the spirit of	2424
	20: 4 that were beheaded for the witness of J,	2424
	22:16 I J have sent mine angel to testify unto	2424
	22:20 Amen. Even so, come, Lord J.	2424
	22:21 The grace of our Lord J Christ be with	2424

JESUS' (10) [JESUS]
Mt	15:30 others, and cast them down at J feet;	2424
	27:57 who also himself was J disciple.	2424
Lk	5: 8 Simon Peter saw it, he fell down at J	2424
	8:41 and he fell down at J feet,	2424
	10:39 also sat at J feet, and heard his word.	2424
Jn	12: 9 and they came not for J sake only,	2424
	13:23 Now there was leaning on J bosom one of	2424
	13:25 He then lying on J breast saith unto him,	2424
2Co	4: 5 and ourselves your servants for J sake.	2424
	4:11 are alway delivered unto death for J sake,	2424

JETHER (8)
Jdg	8:20 he said unto J his firstborn, Up,	3500
1Ki	2: 5 unto Amasa the son of J, whom he slew,	3500
	2:32 the host of Israel, and Amasa the son of J,	3500
1Ch	2:17 the father of Amasa was J the Ishmeelite.	3500
	2:32 the brother of Shammai; J, and Jonathan.	3500
	2:32 Jonathan: and J died without children.	3500
	4:17 the sons of Ezra were, J, and Mered,	3500
	7:38 the sons of J; Jephunneh, and Pispah,	3500

JETHETH (2)
| Ge | 36:40 duke Timnah, duke Alvah, duke J, | 3509 |
| 1Ch | 1:51 duke Timnah, duke Aliah, duke J, | 3509 |

JETHLAH (1)
| Jos | 19:42 And Shaalabbin, and Aijalon, and J, | 3494 |

JETHRO (10)
Ex	3: 1 Now Moses kept the flock of J his father	3503
	4:18 and returned to J his father in law,	3500
	4:18 And J said to Moses, Go in peace.	3503
	18: 1 the priest of Midian, Moses' father	3503
	18: 2 J, Moses' father in law, took Zipporah,	3503
	18: 5 J, Moses' father in law, came with his	3503
	18: 6 I thy father in law J am come unto thee,	3503
	18: 9 J rejoiced for all the goodness which	3503
	18:10 said, Blessed be the LORD, who hath	3503
	18:12 Moses' father in law, took a burnt	3503

JETUR (3)
Ge	25:15 Hadar, and Tema, J, Naphish,	3195
1Ch	1:31 J, Naphish, and Kedemah. These are	3195
	5:19 with J, and Nephish, and Nodab.	3195

JEUEL (1)
| 1Ch | 9: 6 J, and their brethren, six hundred and | 3262 |

JEUSH (8)
Ge	36: 5 Aholibamah bare J, and Jaalam,	3266
	36:14 bare to Esau J, and Jaalam, and Korah.	3266
	36:18 duke J, duke Jaalam, duke Korah:	3266
1Ch	1:35 Reuel, and J, and Jaalam, and Korah.	3266
	7:10 J, and Benjamin, and Ehud,	3266
	23:10 were, Jahath, Zina, and J, and Beriah.	3266
	23:11 J and Beriah had not many sons; therefore	3266
2Ch	11:19 J, and Shamariah, and Zaham.	3266

JEUZ (1)
| 1Ch | 8:10 J, and Shachia, and Mirma. These were | 3263 |

JEW (32) [JEWESS, JEWISH, JEWRY, JEWS, JEWS']
Est	2: 5 Shushan the palace there was a certain J,	3064
	3: 4 for he had told them that he was a J.	3064
	5:13 long as I see Mordecai the J sitting at	3064
	6:10 said, and do even so to Mordecai the J,	3064
	8: 7 Esther the queen and to Mordecai the J,	3064
	9:29 daughter of Abihail, and Mordecai the J,	3064
	9:31 appointed, according as Mordecai the J	3064
	10: 3 For Mordecai the J was next unto king	3064
Jer	34: 9 himself of them, to wit, of a J his brother.	3064
Zec	8:23 take hold of the skirt of him that is a J,	3064
Jn	4: 9 it that thou, being a J, askest drink of me,	2453
	18:35 Pilate answered, Am I a J? Thine own	2453
Ac	10:28 for a man that is a J to keep company,	2453
	13: 6 a false prophet, a J, whose name was	2453
	18: 2 And found a certain J named Aquila, born	2453
	18:24 And a certain J named Apollos, born at	2453
	19:14 a J, and chief of the priests, which did so.	2453
	19:34 But when they knew that he was a J,	2453
	21:39 I am a man which am a J of Tarsus,	2453
	22: 3 I am verily a man which am a J, born in	2453
Ro	1:16 to the J first, and also to the Greek.	2453
	2: 9 of the J first, and also of the Gentile;	2453
	2:10 to the J first, and also to the Gentile;	2453
	2:17 thou art called a J, and restest in the law,	2453
	2:28 For he is not a J, which is one outwardly;	2453
	2:29 But he is a J, which is one inwardly;	2453
	3: 1 What advantage then hath the J?	2453
	10:12 For there is no difference between the J	2453
1Co	9:20 And unto the Jews I became as a J, that I	2453
Gal	2:14 Peter before them all, If thou, being a J,	2453
	3:28 There is neither J nor Greek, there is	2453
Col	3:11 Where there is neither Greek nor J,	2453

JEWEL (3) [JEWELS]
Pr	11:22 a j of gold in a swine's snout, so is a fair	5141
	20:15 but the lips of knowledge are a precious j.	3627
Eze	16:12 I put a j on thy forehead, and earrings in	5141

JEWELS (25) [JEWEL]
Ge	24:53 the servant brought forth j of silver,	3627
	24:53 j of gold, and raiment, and gave them to	3627
Ex	3:22 j of silver, and jewels of gold, and raiment	3627
	3:22 jewels of silver, and j of gold, and raiment	3627
	11: 2 j of silver, and jewels of gold.	3627
	11: 2 jewels of silver, and j of gold.	3627
	12:35 they borrowed of the Egyptians j of silver,	3627
	12:35 jewels of silver, and j of gold, and raiment	3627
	35:22 and rings, and tablets, all j of gold:	3627
Nu	31:50 of j of gold, chains, and bracelets, rings,	3627
	31:51 took the gold of them, even all wrought j.	3627
1Sa	6: 8 put the j of gold, which ye return him for	3627
	6:15 the j of gold were, and put them on	3627
2Ch	20:25 precious j, which they strip off for	3627
	32:27 shields, and for all manner of pleasant j;	3627
Job	28:17 the exchange of it shall not be for j of fine	3627
SS	1:10 Thy cheeks are comely with rows of j,	NIH
	7: 1 the joints of thy thighs are like j, the work	2481
Isa	3:21 The rings, and nose j,	5141
	61:10 as a bride adorneth herself with her j.	3627
Eze	16:17 Thou hast also taken thy fair j of my gold	3627
	16:39 shall take thy fair j, and leave thee naked	3627
	23:26 of thy clothes, and take away thy fair j.	3627
Hos	2:13 herself with her earrings and her j,	2484
Mal	3:17 hosts, in that day when I make up my j;	5459

JEWESS (2) [JEW]
| Ac | 16: 1 which was a J, and believed; | 2453 |
| | 24:24 which was a J, he sent for Paul, | 2453 |

JEWISH (1) [JEW]
| Tit | 1:14 not giving heed to J fables, | 2451 |

JEWRY (3) [JEW]
Da	5:13 the king my father brought out of J?	3061
Lk	23: 5 up the people, teaching throughout all J,	2449
Jn	7: 1 for he would not walk in J, because	2449

JEWS (243) [JEW]
2Ki	16: 6 Elath to Syria, and drave the J from Elath:	3064
	25:25 the J and the Chaldees that were with him	3064
Ezr	4:12 that the J which came up from thee to us	3062
	4:23 went up in haste to Jerusalem unto the J,	3062
	5: 1 prophesied unto the J that were in Judah	3062
	5: 5 of their God was upon the elders of the J,	3062
	6: 7 let the governor of the J and the elders of	3062
	6: 7 the elders of the J build this house of God	3062
	6: 8 J for the building of this house of God:	3062
	6:14 the elders of the J builded,	3062
Ne	1: 2 I asked them concerning the J that had	3064
	2:16 neither had I as yet told it to the J, nor to	3064
	4: 1 took great indignation, and mocked the J.	3064
	4: 2 and said, What do these feeble J?	3064
	4:12 when the J which dwelt by them came,	3064
	5: 1 of their wives against their brethren the J.	3064
	5: 8 ability have redeemed our brethren the J,	3064
	5:17 an hundred and fifty of the J and rulers,	3064
	6: 6 saith it, that thou and the J think to rebel:	3064
	13:23 In those days also saw I J that had married	3064
Est	3: 6 J that were throughout the whole	3064
	3:13 all J, both young and old, little children	3064
	4: 3 there was great mourning among the J,	3064
	4: 7 to pay to the king's treasuries for the J,	3064
	4:13 in the king's house, more than all the J	3064
	4:14 deliverance arise to the J from another	3064
	4:16 gather together all the J that are present in	3064
	6:13 If Mordecai be of the seed of the J,	3064
	8: 3 device that he had devised against the J.	3064
	8: 5 which he wrote to destroy the J which	3064
	8: 7 because he laid his hand upon the J.	3064
	8: 8 Write ye also for the J, as it liketh you,	3064
	8: 9 all that Mordecai commanded unto the J,	3064
	8: 9 to the J according to their writing,	3064
	8:11 Wherein the king granted the J which	3064
	8:13 the J should be ready against that day	3064
	8:16 The J had light, and gladness, and joy,	3064
	8:17 many of the people of the land became J;	3054
	8:17 for the fear of the J fell upon them.	3064
	9: 1 in the day that the enemies of the J hoped	3064
	9: 1 the J had rule over them that hated them;)	3064
	9: 2 The J gathered themselves together in	3064
	9: 3 and officers of the king, helped the J;	3064
	9: 5 Thus the J smote all their enemies with	3064
	9: 6 in Shushan the palace the J slew and	3064
	9:10 the enemy of the J, slew they;	3064
	9:12 The J have slain and destroyed five	3064
	9:13 let it be granted to the J which are in	3064
	9:15 For the J that were in Shushan gathered	3064
	9:16 the other J that were in the king's	3064
	9:18 the J that were at Shushan assembled	3064
	9:19 Therefore the J of the villages, that dwelt	3064
	9:20 sent letters unto all the J that were in all	3064
	9:22 As the days wherein the J rested from	3064
	9:23 the J undertook to do as they had begun,	3064
	9:24 the Agagite, the enemy of all the J,	3064
	9:24 had devised against the J to destroy them,	3064
	9:25 which he devised against the J,	3064
	9:27 The J ordained, and took upon them,	3064
Est	9:28 Purim should not fail from among the J,	3064
	9:30 he sent the letters unto all the J,	3064
	10: 3 great among the J, and accepted of	3064
Jer	32:12 before all the J that sat in the court of	3064
	38:19 I am afraid of the J that are fallen to	3064
	40:11 when all the J that were in Moab,	3064
	40:12 Even all the J returned out of all places	3064
	40:15 that all the J which are gathered unto	3064
	41: 3 Ishmael also slew all the J that were with	3064
	44: 1 all the J which dwell in the land of Egypt,	3064
	52:28 in the seventh year three thousand J and	3064
	52:30 away captive of the J seven hundred forty	3064
Da	3: 8 Chaldeans came near, and accused the J.	3062
	3:12 There are certain J whom thou hast set	3062
Mt	2: 2 Where is he that is born King of the J?	2453
	27:11 saying, Art thou the King of the J?	2453
	27:29 mocked him, saying, Hail, King of the J!	2453
	27:37 THIS IS JESUS THE KING OF THE J.	2453
	28:15 reported among the J until this day.	2453
Mk	7: 3 For the Pharisees, and all the J, except	2453
	15: 2 asked him, Art thou the King of the J?	2453
	15: 9 that I release unto you the King of the J?	2453
	15:12 unto him whom ye call the King of the J?	2453
	15:18 began to salute him, Hail, King of the J.	2453
	15:26 was written over, THE KING OF THE J.	2453
Lk	7: 3 he sent unto him the elders of the J,	2453
	23: 3 saying, Art thou the King of the J?	2453
	23:37 And saying, If thou be the King of the J,	2453
	23:38 Hebrew, THIS IS THE KING OF THE J.	2453
	23:51 he was of Arimathea, a city of the J,	2453
Jn	1:19 when the J sent priests and Levites from	2453
	2: 6 after the manner of the purifying of the J,	2453
	2:18 Then answered the J and said unto him,	2453
	2:20 Then said the J, Forty and six years was	2453
	3: 1 named Nicodemus, a ruler of the J:	2453
	3:25 John's disciples and the J about purifying.	2453
	4: 9 For the J have no dealings with	2453
	4:22 what we worship: for salvation is of the J.	2453
	5: 1 After this there was a feast of the J;	2453
	5:10 The J therefore said unto him that was	2453
	5:15 and told the J that it was Jesus,	2453
	5:16 And therefore did the J persecute Jesus,	2453
	5:18 The J sought the more to kill him,	2453
	6: 4 the passover, a feast of the J, was nigh.	2453
	6:41 The J then murmured at him, because	2453
	6:52 The J therefore strove amongst	2453
	7: 1 in Jewry, because the J sought to kill him.	2453
	7:11 Then the J sought him at the feast,	2453
	7:13 man spake openly of him for fear of the J.	2453
	7:15 the J marvelled, saying, How knoweth	2453
	7:35 Then said the J among themselves,	2453
	8:22 Then said the J, Will he kill himself?	2453
	8:31 Then said Jesus to those J which believed	2453
	8:48 Then answered the J, and said unto him,	2453
	8:52 Then said the J unto him, Now we know	2453
	8:57 Then said the J unto him, Thou art not	2453
	9:18 But the J did not believe concerning him,	2453
	9:22 his parents, because they feared the J:	2453
	9:22 for the J had agreed already, that if any	2453
	10:19 again among the J for these sayings.	2453
	10:24 Then came the J round about him,	2453
	10:31 Then the J took up stones again to stone	2453
	10:33 The J answered him, saying, For a good	2453
	11: 8 Master, the J of late sought to stone thee;	2453
	11:19 And many of the J came to Martha and	2453
	11:31 The J then which were with her in	2453
	11:33 the J also weeping which came with her,	2453
	11:36 said the J, Behold, how he loved him.	2453
	11:45 Then many of the J which came to Mary,	2453
	11:54 walked no more openly among the J;	2453
	12: 9 Much people of the J therefore knew that	2453
	12:11 reason of him many of the J went away,	2453
	13:33 and as I said unto the J, Whither I go,	2453
	18:12 captain and officers of the J took Jesus,	2453
	18:14 was he, which gave counsel to the J,	2453
	18:20 the temple, whither the J always resort;	2453
	18:31 The J therefore said unto him, It is not	2453
	18:33 said unto him, Art thou the King of the J?	2453
	18:36 that I should not be delivered to the J:	2453
	18:38 went out again unto the J, and saith unto	2453
	18:39 that I release unto you the King of the J?	2453
	19: 3 And said, Hail, King of the J!	2453
	19: 7 The J answered him, We have a law,	2453
	19:12 but the J cried out, saying, If thou let this	2453
	19:14 and he saith unto the J, Behold your King.	2453
	19:19 OF NAZARETH THE KING OF THE J.	2453
	19:20 This title then read many of the J:	2453
	19:21 Then said the chief priests of the J to	2453
	19:21 to Pilate, Write not, The King of the J;	2453
	19:21 but that he said, I am King of the J.	2453
	19:31 The J therefore, because it was	2453
	19:38 of Jesus, but secretly for fear of the J,	2453
	19:40 spices, as the manner of the J is to bury.	2453
	20:19 disciples were assembled for fear of the J,	2453
Ac	2: 5 And there were dwelling at Jerusalem J,	2453
	2:10 and strangers of Rome, J and proselytes,	2453
	9:22 confounded the J which dwelt at	2453
	9:23 the J took counsel to kill him:	2453
	10:22 good report among all the nation of the J,	2453
	10:39 which he did both in the land of the J,	2453
	11:19 the word to none but unto the J only.	2453
	12: 3 And because he saw it pleased the J,	2453
	12:11 the expectation of the people of the J.	2453
	13: 5 word of God in the synagogues of the J:	2453
	13:42 And when the J were gone out of	2453

Ac	13:43 many of the J and religious proselytes	2453
	13:45 But when the J saw the multitudes,	2453
	13:50 But the J stirred up the devout and	2453
	14: 1 *both* together into the synagogue of the J,	2453
	14: 1 that a great multitude both of the J and	2453
	14: 2 But the unbelieving J stirred up	2453
	14: 4 and part held with the J, and part with	2453
	14: 5 and *also* of the J with their rulers, to use	2453
	14:19 And there came thither *certain* J from	2453
	16: 3 of the J which were in those quarters:	2453
	16:20 These men, being J, do exceedingly	2453
	17: 1 where was a synagogue of the J:	2453
	17: 5 But the J which believed not, moved with	2453
	17:10 *thither* went into the synagogue of the J.	2453
	17:13 But when the J of Thessalonica had	2453
	17:17 disputed he in the synagogue with the J,	2453
	18: 2 that Claudius had commanded all J to	2453
	18: 4 and persuaded *the* J and *the* Greeks.	2453
	18: 5 and testified to the J *that* Jesus *was* Christ.	2453
	18:12 the J made insurrection with one accord	2453
	18:14 Gallio said unto the J, If it were a matter	2453
	18:14 of wrong or wicked lewdness, O *ye* J,	2453
	18:19 the synagogue, and reasoned with the J.	2453
	18:28 For he mightily convinced the J,	2453
	19:10 word of the Lord Jesus, both J and Greeks.	2453
	19:13 Then certain of the vagabond J, exorcists,	2453
	19:17 And this was known to all the J and	2453
	19:33 the multitude, the J putting him forward.	2453
	20: 3 and when the J laid wait for him, as he	2453
	20:19 befell me by the lying in wait of the J:	2453
	20:21 Testifying both to the J, and *also* to	2453
	21:11 So shall the J at Jerusalem bind the man	2453
	21:20 how many thousands of J there are which	2453
	21:21 that thou teachest all the J which are	2453
	21:27 the J which were of Asia, when they saw	2453
	22:12 having a good report of all the J which	2453
	22:30 wherefore he was accused of the J,	2453
	23:12 was day, certain of the J banded together,	2453
	23:20 The J have agreed to desire thee that thou	2453
	23:27 This man was taken of the J,	2453
	23:30 And when it was told me how that the J	2453
	24: 5 a mover of sedition among all the J	2453
	24: 9 And the J also assented, saying that these	2453
	24:18 Whereupon certain J from Asia found me	2453
	24:27 Felix, willing to shew the J a pleasure,	2453
	25: 2 the chief of the J informed him against	2453
	25: 7 the J which came down from Jerusalem	2453
	25: 8 Neither against the law of the J,	2453
	25: 9 But Festus, willing to do the J a pleasure,	2453
	25:10 to the J have I done no wrong, as thou	2453
	25:15 the elders of the J informed *me*, desiring	2453
	25:24 the multitude of the J have dealt with me,	2453
	26: 2 *the things* whereof I am accused of the J:	2453
	26: 3 and questions which are among the J:	2453
	26: 4 own nation at Jerusalem, know all the J;	2453
	26: 7 king Agrippa, I am accused of the J.	2453
	26:21 For these causes the J caught me in	2453
	28:17 Paul called the chief of the J together:	2453
	28:19 But when the J spake against *it*, I was	2453
	28:29 And when he had said these *words*, the J	2453
Ro	3: 9 for we have before proved both J and	2453
	3:29 *Is he* the God of the J only? *is he* not also	2453
	3:29 of the J only, but also of the Gentiles?	2453
1Co	1:22 For the J require a sign, and the Greeks	2453
	1:23 unto the J a stumblingblock, and unto	2453
	1:24 both J and Greeks, Christ the power of	2453
	9:20 And unto the J I became as a Jew, that I	2453
	9:20 I became as a Jew, that I might gain *the* J;	2453
	10:32 Give none offence, neither to the J, nor to	2453
	12:13 whether *we be* J or Gentiles, whether	2453
2Co	11:24 Of the J five times received I forty *stripes*	2453
Gal	2:13 And the other J dissembled likewise with	2453
	2:14 manner of Gentiles, and not **as do the** J,	2452
	2:14 thou the Gentiles to **live as do the** J?	2450
	2:15 We *who are* J by nature, and not sinners	2453
1Th	2:14 even as they *have* of the J:	2453
Rev	2: 9 blasphemy of them which say they are J,	2453
	3: 9 which say they are J, and are not,	2453

JEWS' (14) [JEW]

2Ki	18:26 talk not with us **in the J language** in	3066
	18:28 with a loud voice **in the J language**,	3066
2Ch	32:18 **in the J speech** unto the people of	3066
Ne	13:24 could not speak **in the J language**,	3066
Est	3:10 of Hammedatha the Agagite, the J enemy.	3064
	8: 1 Haman the J enemy unto Esther the	3064
Isa	36:11 and speak not to us **in the J language**,	3066
	36:13 with a loud voice **in the J language**,	3066
Jn	2:13 And the J passover was at hand,	2453
	7: 2 the J feast of tabernacles was at hand.	2453
	11:55 And the J passover was nigh at hand:	2453
	19:42 the J preparation *day*; for the sepulchre	2453
Gal	1:13 in time past in the J religion,	2454
	1:14 profited in the J religion above many	2454

JEZANIAH (2)

Jer	40: 8 J the son of a Maachathite, they and	3153
	42: 1 J the son of Hoshaiah, and all the people	3153

JEZEBEL (22) [JEZEBEL'S]

1Ki	16:31 that he took *to* wife J the daughter of	348
	18: 4 when J cut off the prophets of the Lord,	348
	18:13 Was it not told my lord what I did when J	348
	19: 1 Ahab told J all that Elijah had done,	348
	19: 2 Then J sent a messenger unto Elijah,	348

1Ki	21: 5 J his wife came to him, and said unto him,	348
	21: 7 J his wife said unto him, Dost thou now	348
	21:11 did as J had sent unto them, *and as it was*	348
	21:14 they sent to J, saying, Naboth is stoned,	348
	21:15 when J heard that Naboth was stoned,	348
	21:15 and was dead, that J said to Ahab, Arise,	348
	21:23 Of J also spake the Lord, saying,	348
	21:23 The dogs shall eat J by the wall of Jezreel.	348
	21:25 Of the Lord, whom J his wife stirred up.	348
2Ki	9: 7 the servants of the Lord, at the hand of J.	348
	9:10 dogs shall eat J in the portion of Jezreel,	348
	9:22 so long as the whoredoms of thy mother J	348
	9:30 J heard *of it*; and she painted her face,	348
	9:36 of Jezreel shall dogs eat the flesh of J:	348
	9:37 the carcase of J shall be as dung upon	348
	9:37 *so* that they shall not say, This *is* J.	348
Rev	2:20 because thou sufferest *that* woman J,	2403

JEZEBEL'S (1) [JEZEBEL]

1Ki	18:19 groves four hundred, which eat at J table.	348

JEZER (3) [JEZERITES]

Ge	46:24 Jahzeel, and Guni, and J, and Shillem.	3337
Nu	26:49 Of J, the family of the Jezerites:	3337
1Ch	7:13 Jahziel, and Guni, and J, and Shallum,	3337

JEZERITES (1) [JEZER]

Nu	26:49 Of Jezer, the family of the J: of Shillem,	3340

JEZIAH (1)

Ezr	10:25 J, and Malchiah, and Miamin,	3150

JEZIEL (1)

1Ch	12: 3 and J, and Pelet, the sons of Azmaveth;	3149

JEZLIAH (1)

1Ch	8:18 Ishmerai also, and J, and Jobab, the sons	3152

JEZOAR (1)

1Ch	4: 7 of Helah *were*, Zereth, and J, and Ethnan.	3328

JEZRAHIAH (1)

Ne	12:42 singers sang loud, with J *their* overseer.	3156

JEZREEL (36) [JEZREELITE, JEZREELITESS]

Jos	15:56 And J, and Jokdeam, and Zanoah,	3157
	17:16 and *they* who *are* of the valley of J.	3157
	19:18 border was toward J, and Chesulloth,	3157
Jdg	6:33 went over, and pitched in the valley of J.	3157
1Sa	25:43 David also took Ahinoam of J;	3157
	29: 1 pitched by a fountain which *is* in J.	3157
	29:11 And the Philistines went up *to* J.	3157
2Sa	2: 9 over J, and over Ephraim,	3157
	4: 4 came of Saul and Jonathan out of J,	3157
1Ki	4:12 which *is* by Zartanah beneath J,	3157
	18:45 great rain. And Ahab rode, and went to J.	3157
	18:46 and ran before Ahab to the entrance of J.	3157
	21: 1 Jezreelite had a vineyard, which *was* in J,	3157
	21:23 The dogs shall eat Jezebel by the wall of J.	3157
2Ki	8:29 king Joram went back to be healed in J of	3157
	8:29 down to see Joram the son of Ahab in J,	3157
	9:10 dogs shall eat Jezebel in the portion of J,	3157
	9:15 king Joram was returned to be healed in J	3157
	9:15 escape out of the city to go to tell *it* in J.	3157
	9:16 So Jehu rode *in a chariot*, and went to J;	3157
	9:17 there stood a watchman on the tower in J,	3157
	9:30 when Jehu was come to J, Jezebel heard	3157
	9:36 In the portion of J shall dogs eat the flesh	3157
	9:37 the face of the field in the portion of J,	3157
	10: 1 unto the rulers of J, to the elders,	3157
	10: 6 come to me *to* J by to morrow *this* time.	3157
	10: 7 heads in baskets, and sent him *them* to J.	3157
	10:11 that remained of the house of Ahab in J,	3157
1Ch	4: 3 father of Etam; J, and Ishma, and Idbash:	3157
2Ch	22: 6 he returned to be healed in J because of	3157
	22: 6 down to see Jehoram the son of Ahab at J,	3157
Hos	1: 4 the Lord said unto him, Call his name J;	3157
	1: 4 I will avenge the blood of J upon the	3157
	1: 5 break the bow of Israel in the valley of J.	3157
	1:11 of the land: for great *shall be* the day of J.	3157
	2:22 wine, and the oil; and they shall hear J.	3157

JEZREELITE (8) [JEZREEL]

1Ki	21: 1 *that* Naboth the J had a vineyard,	3158
	21: 4 the word which Naboth the J had spoken	3158
	21: 6 Because I spake unto Naboth the J,	3158
	21: 7 give thee the vineyard of Naboth the J.	3158
	21:15 possession of the vineyard of Naboth the J,	3158
	21:16 go down to the vineyard of Naboth the J,	3158
2Ki	9:21 met him in the portion of Naboth the J.	3158
	9:25 in the portion of the field of Naboth the J:	3158

JEZREELITESS (5) [JEZREEL]

1Sa	27: 3 Ahinoam the J, and Abigail	3159
	30: 5 Ahinoam the J, and Abigail the wife of	3159
2Sa	2: 2 Ahinoam the J, and Abigail Nabal's wife	3159
	3: 2 firstborn was Amnon, of Ahinoam the J;	3159
1Ch	3: 1 the firstborn Amnon, of Ahinoam the J;	3159

JIBSAM (1)

1Ch	7: 2 Jeriel, and Jahmai, and J, and Shemuel,	3005

JIDLAPH (1)

Ge	22:22 Hazo, and Pildash, and J, and Bethuel.	3044

JIMNA (1) [JIMNAH, JIMNITES]

Nu	26:44 of J, the family of the Jimnites: of Jesui,	3232

JIMNAH (1) [JIMNA]

Ge	46:17 J, and Ishuah, and Ishui, and Beriah,	3232

JIMNITES (1) [JIMNA]

Nu	26:44 of Jimna, the family of the J: of Jesui,	3232

JIPHTAH (1)

Jos	15:43 And J, and Ashnah, and Nezib,	3316

JIPHTHAH-EL (2)

Jos	19:14 outgoings thereof are *in* the valley of J:	3317
	19:27 to the valley of J toward the north side *of*	3317

JOAB (138) [JOAB'S]

1Sa	26: 6 the son of Zeruiah, brother to J, saying,	3097
2Sa	2:13 J the son of Zeruiah, and the servants of	3097
	2:14 Abner said to J, Let the young men now	3097
	2:14 play before us. And J said, Let them arise.	3097
	2:18 Zeruiah there, J, and Abishai, and Asahel:	3097
	2:22 should I hold up my face to J thy brother?	3097
	2:24 J also and Abishai pursued after Abner:	3097
	2:26 called to J, and said, Shall the sword	3097
	2:27 J said, *As* God liveth, unless thou hadst	3097
	2:28 So J blew a trumpet, and all the people	3097
	2:30 J returned from following Abner:	3097
	2:32 and his men went all night, and they	3097
	3:22 David and J came from *pursuing* a troop,	3097
	3:23 J and all the host that *was* with him	3097
	3:23 they told J, saying, Abner the son of Ner	3097
	3:24 J came to the king, and said, What hast	3097
	3:26 J was come out from David, he sent	3097
	3:27 J took him aside in the gate to speak with	3097
	3:29 Let it rest on the head of J, and on all his	3097
	3:29 let there not fail from the house of J one	3097
	3:30 So J and Abishai his brother slew Abner,	3097
	3:31 David said to J, and to all the people that	3097
	8:16 J the son of Zeruiah *was* over the host;	3097
	10: 7 when David heard *of it*, he sent J, and all	3097
	10: 9 When J saw that the front of the battle	3097
	10:13 drew nigh, and the people that *were*	3097
	10:14 J returned from the children of Ammon,	3097
	11: 1 kings go forth *to* battle, that David sent J,	3097
	11: 6 David sent to J, *saying*, Send me Uriah	3097
	11: 6 the Hittite. And J sent Uriah to David.	3097
	11: 7 J demanded *of him* how J did,	3097
	11:11 my lord, and the servants of my lord,	3097
	11:14 David wrote a letter to J, and sent *it* by	3097
	11:16 it came to pass, when J observed the city,	3097
	11:17 of the city went out, and fought with J:	3097
	11:18 J sent and told David all the things	3097
	11:22 shewed David all that J had sent him for.	3097
	11:25 Thus shalt thou say unto J, Let not this	3097
	12:26 J fought against Rabbah of the children of	3097
	12:27 J sent messengers to David, and said,	3097
	14: 1 Now J the son of Zeruiah perceived that	3097
	14: 2 J sent to Tekoah, and fetcht thence a wise	3097
	14: 3 So J put the words in her mouth.	3097
	14:19 *Is not* the hand of J with thee in all this?	3097
	14:19 for thy servant J, he bade me, and he put	3097
	14:20 speech hath thy servant J done this thing:	3097
	14:21 the king said unto J, Behold now, I have	3097
	14:22 J fell to the ground on his face,	3097
	14:22 J said, To day thy servant knoweth that I	3097
	14:23 So J arose and went to Geshur,	3097
	14:29 Therefore Absalom sent for J, to have sent	3097
	14:31 J arose, and came to Absalom unto *his*	3097
	14:32 Absalom answered, Behold, I sent unto	3097
	14:33 So J came to the king, and told him:	3097
	17:25 Amasa captain of the host instead of J:	3097
	18: 2 part of the people under the hand of J,	3097
	18: 5 the king commanded J and Abishai and	3097
	18:10 a certain man saw *it*, and told J, and said,	3097
	18:11 J said unto the man that told him,	3097
	18:12 the man said unto J, Though I should	3097
	18:14 said J, I may not tarry thus with thee.	3097
	18:16 J blew the trumpet, and the people	3097
	18:16 after Israel: for J held back the people.	3097
	18:20 J said unto him, Thou *shalt* not bear	3097
	18:21 J to Cushi, Go tell the king what thou	3097
	18:21 Cushi bowed himself unto J, and ran.	3097
	18:22 Ahimaaz the son of Zadok yet again to J,	3097
	18:22 J said, Wherefore wilt thou run, my son,	3097
	18:29 When J sent the king's servant, and *me*	3097
	19: 1 it was told J, Behold, the king weepeth	3097
	19: 5 J came *into* the house to the king, and	3097
	19:13 before me continually in the room of J.	3097
	20: 9 J said to Amasa, *Art* thou in health,	3097
	20: 9 J took Amasa by the beard with the right	3097
	20:10 So J and Abishai his brother pursued after	3097
	20:11 He that favoureth J, and he that *is* for	3097
	20:11 he that *is* for David, *let him go* after J.	3097
	20:13 all the people went on after J, to pursue	3097
	20:15 all the people that *were* with J battered	3097
	20:16 say, I pray you, unto J, Come near hither,	3097
	20:17 unto her, the woman said, *Art* thou J?	3097
	20:20 J answered and said, Far be it, far be it	3097
	20:21 the woman said unto J, Behold, his head	3097
	20:22 the son of Bichri, and cast *it* out to J.	3097
	20:22 J returned *to* Jerusalem unto the king.	3097
	20:23 Now J *was* over all the host of Israel:	3097
	23:18 Abishai, the brother of J, the son of	3097
	23:24 Asahel the brother of J *was* one of	3097

2Sa	23:37 armourbearer to J the son of Zeruiah,	3097
	24: 2 For the king said to J the captain of	3097
	24: 3 J said unto the king, Now the LORD thy	3097
	24: 4 the king's word prevailed against J,	3097
	24: 4 and the captains of the host went out	3097
	24: 9 J gave *up* the sum of the number of	3097
1Ki	1: 7 he conferred with J the son of Zeruiah,	3097
	1:19 the priest, and J the captain of the host:	3097
	1:41 when J heard the sound of the trumpet,	3097
	2: 5 Moreover thou knowest also what J the	3097
	2:22 the priest, and for J the son of Zeruiah.	3097
	2:28 tidings came to J: for Joab had turned	3097
	2:28 for J had turned after Adonijah, though he	3097
	2:28 J fled unto the tabernacle of the LORD,	3097
	2:29 it was told king Solomon that J was fled	3097
	2:30 Thus said J, and thus he answered me.	3097
	2:31 J shed, from me, and from the house	3097
	2:33 therefore return upon the head of J,	3097
	11:15 the captain of the host was gone up to	3097
	11:16 six months did J remain there with all	3097
	11:21 that J the captain of the host was dead,	3097
1Ch	2:16 Abishai, and J, and Asahel, three.	3097
	2:54 the house of J, and half of	3097
	4:14 Seraiah begat J, the father of the valley of	3097
	11: 6 So the son of Zeruiah went first up,	3097
	11: 8 and J repaired the rest of the city.	3097
	11:20 Abishai the brother of J, he was chief of	3097
	11:26 the armies *were,* Asahel the brother of J,	3097
	11:39 the armourbearer of J the son of Zeruiah,	3097
	18:15 the son of Zeruiah *was* over the host;	3097
	19: 8 when David heard *of it,* he sent J, and all	3097
	19:10 Now when J saw that the battle was set	3097
	19:14 So J and the people that *were* with him	3097
	19:15 into the city. Then J came to Jerusalem.	3097
	20: 1 the time that kings go out *to battle,* J led	3097
	20: 1 And J smote Rabbah, and destroyed it.	3097
	21: 2 David said to J and to the rulers of	3097
	21: 3 J answered, The LORD make his people	3097
	21: 4 the king's word prevailed against J.	3097
	21: 4 J departed, and went throughout	3097
	21: 5 J gave the sum of the number of the	3097
	21: 6 for the king's word was abominable to J.	3097
	26:28 and J the son of Zeruiah, had dedicated;	3097
	27: 7 fourth month *was* Asahel the brother of J,	3097
	27:24 J the son of Zeruiah began to number,	3097
	27:34 and the general of the king's army *was* J.	3097
Ezr	2: 6 of the children of Jeshua *and* J,	3097
	8: 9 the sons of J; Obadiah the son of Jehiel,	3097
Ne	7:11 of the children of Jeshua and J,	3097
Ps	60: T when J returned, and smote of Edom in	3097

JOAB'S (8) [JOAB]

2Sa	14:30 J field is near mine, and he hath barley	3097
	17:25 of Nahash, sister to Zeruiah J mother.	3097
	18: 2 J brother, and a third part under the hand	3097
	18:15 ten young men that bare J armour	3097
	20: 7 there went out after him J men,	3097
	20: 8 J garment that he had put on *was* girded	3097
	20:10 no heed to the sword that *was* in J hand:	3097
	20:11 one of J men stood by him, and said,	3097

JOAH (11)

2Ki	18:18 and J the son of Asaph the recorder.	3098
	18:26 Shebna, and J, unto Rab-shakeh, Speak,	3098
	18:37 and J the son of Asaph the recorder,	3098
1Ch	6:21 J his son, Iddo his son, Zerah his son,	3098
	26: 4 the third, and Sacar the fourth,	3098
2Ch	29:12 the son of Zimmah, and Eden the son of	3098
	29:12 son of Zimmah, and Eden the son of J:	3098
	34: 8 and the son of Joahaz the recorder.	3098
Isa	36: 3 scribe, and J, Asaph's son, the recorder.	3098
	36:11 and Shebna and J unto Rabshakeh,	3098
	36:22 and J, the son of Asaph, the recorder,	3098

JOAHAZ (1)

2Ch	34: 8 city, and Joah the son of J the recorder,	3099

JOANNA (3)

Lk	3:27 was *the* son of J, which was *the* son	2490
	8: 3 And J the wife of Chuza Herod's steward,	2489
	24:10 and J, and Mary *the* mother of James,	2489

JOASH (49)

Jdg	6:11 that *pertained* unto J the Abi-ezrite,	3101
	6:29 Gideon the son of J hath done this thing.	3101
	6:30 the men of the city said unto J, Bring out	3101
	6:31 J said unto all that stood against him, Will	3101
	7:14 save the sword of Gideon the son of J,	3101
	8:13 Gideon the son of J returned from battle	3101
	8:29 Jerubbaal the son of J went and dwelt in	3101
	8:32 Gideon the son of J died in a good old age	3101
	8:32 was buried in the sepulchre of J his father,	3101
1Ki	22:26 of the city, and to J the king's son;	3101
2Ki	11: 2 took J the son of Ahaziah, and stale him	3101
	12:19 rest of the acts of J, and all that he did,	3101
	12:20 slew J *in* the house of Millo,	3101
	13: 1 twentieth year of J the son of Ahaziah	3101
	13: 9 and J his son reigned in his stead.	3101
	13:10 seventh year of J king of Judah *began*	3101
	13:12 rest of the acts of J, and all that he did,	3101
	13:13 J slept with his fathers; and Jeroboam sat	3101
	13:13 J was buried in Samaria with the kings of	3101
	13:14 the king of Israel came down unto him,	3101
	13:25 Three times did J beat him,	3101
	14: 1 In the second year of J son of Jehoahaz	3101

2Ki	14: 1 Amaziah the son of J king of Judah.	3101
	14:13 did according to all *things* as J his father	3101
	14:17 Amaziah the son of J king of Judah lived	3101
	14:23 J king of Judah Jeroboam the son of Joash	3101
	14:23 J king of Israel *began* to reign in Samaria,	3101
	14:27 by the hand of Jeroboam the son of J.	3101
1Ch	3:11 Joram his son, Ahaziah his son, J his son,	3101
	4:22 the men of Chozeba, and J, and Saraph,	3101
	7: 8 J, and Eliezer, and Elioenai, and Omri,	3135
	12: 3 The chief *was* Ahiezer, then J, the sons of	3101
	27:28 and over the cellars of oil *was* J:	3135
2Ch	18:25 of the city, and to J the king's son;	3101
	22:11 took J the son of Ahaziah, and stole him	3101
	24: 1 J *was* seven years old when he *began* to	3101
	24: 2 J did *that* which *was* right in the sight of	3101
	24: 4 *that* J was minded to repair the house of	3101
	24:22 Thus J the king remembered not	3101
	24:24 So they executed judgment against J.	3101
	25:17 sent to J, the son of Jehoahaz, the son of	3101
	25:18 J king of Israel sent to Amaziah king of	3101
	25:21 So J the king of Israel went up;	3101
	25:23 J the king of Israel took Amaziah king of	3101
	25:23 the son of J, the son of Jehoahaz,	3101
	25:25 Amaziah the son of J king of Judah lived	3101
	25:25 J king of Jehoahaz king of Israel fifteen	3101
Hos	1: 1 in the days of Jeroboam the son of J,	3101
Am	1: 1 in the days of Jeroboam the son of J king	3101

JOATHAM (2)

Mt	1: 9 And Ozias begat J; and Joatham begat	2488
	1: 9 begat Achaz; and Achaz begat	2488

JOB (59) [JOB'S]

Ge	46:13 Tola, and Phuvah, and J, and Shimron.	3102
Job	1: 1 man in the land of Uz, whose name *was* J;	347
	1: 5 J sent and sanctified them, and rose up	347
	1: 5 for J said, It may be that my sons have	347
	1: 5 God in their hearts. Thus did J continually.	347
	1: 8 Hast thou considered my servant J,	347
	1: 9 and said, Doth J fear God for nought?	347
	1:14 there came a messenger unto J, and said,	347
	1:20 J arose, and rent his mantle, and shaved	347
	1:22 In all this J sinned not, nor charged God	347
	2: 3 Hast thou considered my servant J,	347
	2: 7 smote J with sore boils from the sole of his	347
	2:10 In all this did not J sin with his lips.	347
	3: 1 After this opened J his mouth,	347
	3: 2 And J spake, and said,	347
	6: 1 But J answered and said,	347
	9: 1 Then J answered and said,	347
	12: 1 And J answered and said,	347
	16: 1 Then J answered and said,	347
	19: 1 Then J answered and said,	347
	21: 1 But J answered and said,	347
	23: 1 Then J answered and said,	347
	26: 1 But J answered and said,	347
	27: 1 Moreover J continued his parable, and said,	347
	29: 1 Moreover J continued his parable, and said,	347
	31:40 instead of barley. The words of J are ended.	347
	32: 1 So these three men ceased to answer J,	347
	32: 2 against J was his wrath kindled, because	347
	32: 3 no answer, and *yet* had condemned J.	347
	32: 4 Now Elihu had waited till J had spoken,	347
	32:12 *there was* none of you that convinced J,	347
	33: 1 J, I pray thee, hear my speeches,	347
	33:31 Mark well, O J, hearken unto me: hold thy	347
	34: 5 For J hath said, I am righteous:	347
	34: 7 What man *is* like J, *who* drinketh up	347
	34:35 J hath spoken without knowledge,	347
	34:36 My desire *is that* J may be tried unto the	347
	35:16 Therefore doth J open his mouth in vain;	347
	37:14 Hearken unto this, O J: stand still,	347
	38: 1 the LORD answered J out of	347
	40: 1 Moreover the LORD answered J, and said,	347
	40: 3 Then J answered the LORD, and said,	347
	40: 6 answered the LORD unto J out of	347
	42: 1 Then J answered the LORD, and said,	347
	42: 7 the LORD had spoken these words unto J,	347
	42: 7 the thing that *is* right, as my servant J *hath.*	347
	42: 8 go to my servant J, and offer up for	347
	42: 8 and my servant J shall pray for you:	347
	42: 9 the thing which *is* right, like my servant J.	347
	42: 9 the LORD also accepted J.	347
	42:10 the LORD turned the captivity of J,	347
	42:10 also the LORD gave J twice as much as he	347
	42:12 So the LORD blessed the latter end of J	347
	42:15 women found so fair as the daughters of J:	347
	42:16 this lived J an hundred and forty years,	347
	42:17 So J died, *being* old and full of days.	347
Eze	14:14 Noah, Daniel, and J, were in it, they	347
	14:20 Daniel, and J, *were* in it, *as* I live,	347
Jas	5:11 Ye have heard of the patience of J,	2492

JOB'S (1) [JOB]

Job	2:11 Now when J three friends heard of all this	347

JOBAB (9)

Ge	10:29 Ophir, and Havilah, and J: all these *were*	3103
	36:33 the son of Zerah of Bozrah reigned in his	3103
	36:34 died, and Husham of the land of Temani	3103
Jos	11: 1 *things,* that he sent to J king of Madon,	3103
1Ch	1:23 Ophir, and Havilah, and J. All these *were*	3103
	1:44 J the son of Zerah of Bozrah reigned in	3103

1Ch	1:45 when J was dead, Husham of the land of	3103
	8: 9 Zia, and Mesha, and Malcham,	3103
	8:18 Ishmerai also, and Jezliah, and J, the sons	3103

JOCHEBED (2)

Ex	6:20 Amram took him J his father's sister to	3115
Nu	26:59 the name of Amram's wife *was* J,	3115

JOED (1)

Ne	11: 7 the son of J, the son of Pedaiah, the son	3133

JOEL (20)

1Sa	8: 2 Now the name of his firstborn was J;	3100
1Ch	4:35 J, and Jehu the son of Josibiah, the son of	3100
	5: 4 The sons of J; Shemaiah his son, Gog his	3100
	5: 8 the son of Shema, the son of J, who dwelt	3100
	5:12 J the chief, and Shapham the next,	3100
	6:33 Heman a singer, the son of J, the son of	3100
	6:36 the son of J, the son of Azariah,	3100
	7: 3 Michael, and Obadiah, and J, Ishiah, five:	3100
	11:38 J the brother of Nathan, Mibhar the son	3100
	15: 7 J the chief, and his brethren an hundred	3100
	15:11 for Uriel, Asaiah, and J, Shemaiah,	3100
	15:17 the Levites appointed Heman the son of J;	3100
	23: 8 chief *was* Jehiel, and Zetham, and J, three.	3100
	26:22 and J his brother, *which were* over	3100
	27:20 tribe of Manasseh, J the son of Pedaiah:	3100
2Ch	29:12 son of Amasai, and J the son of Azariah,	3100
Ezr	10:43 Zabad, Zebina, Jadau, and J, Benaiah.	3100
Ne	11: 9 the son of Zichri *was* their overseer;	3100
Joel	1: 1 The word of the LORD that came to	3100
Ac	2:16 that which was spoken by the prophet J;	2493

JOELAH (1)

1Ch	12: 7 J, and Zebadiah, the sons of Jeroham of	3132

JOEZER (1)

1Ch	12: 6 and Azareel, and J, and Jashobeam,	3134

JOGBEHAH (2)

Nu	32:35 And Atroth, Shophan, and Jaazer, and J,	3011
Jdg	8:11 dwelt in tents on the east of Nobah and J,	3011

JOGLI (1)

Nu	34:22 of the children of Dan, Bukki the son of J.	3020

JOHA (2)

1Ch	8:16 Michael, and Ispah, and J, the sons of	3109
	11:45 of Shimri, and J his brother, the Tizite,	3109

JOHANAN (27)

2Ki	25:23 J the son of Careah, and Seraiah the son	3110
1Ch	3:15 the sons of Josiah *were,* the firstborn J,	3110
	3:24 and J, and Dalaiah, and Anani, seven.	3110
	6: 9 begat Azariah, and Azariah begat J,	3110
	6:10 J begat Azariah, (he *it is* that executed	3110
	12: 4 and J, and Josabad the Gederathite,	3110
	12:12 the eighth, Elzabad the ninth,	3110
2Ch	28:12 Azariah the son of J, Berechiah the son of	3076
Ezr	8:12 J the son of Hakkatan, and with him an	3110
	10: 6 went into the chamber of J the son of	3076
Ne	6:18 his son J had taken the daughter of	3076
	12:22 Joiada, and J, and Jaddua, *were* recorded	3110
	12:23 until the days of J the son of Eliashib.	3110
Jer	40: 8 and Jonathan the sons of Kareah,	3110
	40:13 Moreover J the son of Kareah, and all	3110
	40:15 J the son of Kareah spake to Gedaliah in	3110
	40:16 Gedaliah the son of Ahikam said unto	3110
	41:11 when J the son of Kareah, and all	3110
	41:13 with Ishmael saw J the son of Kareah,	3110
	41:14 and went unto J the son of Kareah.	3110
	41:15 Nethaniah escaped from J with eight men,	3110
	41:16 took J the son of Kareah, and all	3110
	42: 1 J the son of Kareah, and Jezaniah the son	3110
	42: 8 called he J the son of Kareah, and all	3110
	43: 2 J the son of Kareah, and all the proud	3110
	43: 4 J the son of Kareah, and all the captains	3110
	43: 5 J the son of Kareah, and all the captains	3110

JOHN (131) [JOHN'S]

Mt	3: 1 In those days came J the Baptist,	2491
	3: 4 the same J had his raiment of camel's	2491
	3:13 Jesus from Galilee to Jordan unto J,	2491
	3:14 J forbad him, saying, I have need to be	2491
	4:12 when Jesus had heard that J was cast	2491
	4:21 the *son* of Zebedee, and J his brother,	2491
	9:14 Then came to him the disciples of J,	2491
	10: 2 the *son* of Zebedee, and J his brother;	2491
	11: 2 Now when J had heard in the prison	2491
	11: 4 shew J again *those things* which ye do	2491
	11: 7 to say unto the multitudes concerning J,	2491
	11:11 hath not risen a greater than J the Baptist:	2491
	11:12 from the days of J the Baptist until now	2491
	11:13 prophets and the law prophesied until J.	2491
	11:18 For J came neither eating nor drinking,	2491
	14: 2 unto his servants, This is J the Baptist;	2491
	14: 3 For Herod had laid hold on J,	2491
	14: 4 said unto him, It is not lawful for thee	2491
	14: 8 Give me here J Baptist's head in a charger.	2491
	14:10 he sent, and beheaded J in the prison.	2491
	16:14 Some *say* that thou art J the Baptist:	2491
	17: 1 his brother, and bringeth them up into	2491
	17:13 that he spake unto them of J the Baptist.	2491
	21:25 The baptism of J, whence was it?	2491
	21:26 fear the people; for all hold J as a prophet.	2491
	21:32 For J came unto you in the way of	2491

J

Mk | 1: 4 | J did baptize in the wilderness, | 2491
| 1: 6 | J was clothed with camel's hair, | 2491
| 1: 9 | Galilee, and was baptized of J in Jordan. | 2491
| 1:14 | Now after that J was put in prison, Jesus | 2491
| 1:19 | the *son* of Zebedee, and J his brother, | 2491
| 1:29 | of Simon and Andrew, with James and J. | 2491
| 2:18 | And the disciples of J and of the Pharisees | 2491
| 2:18 | Why do the disciples of J and of | 2491
| 3:17 | of Zebedee, and J the brother of James; | 2491
| 5:37 | and James, and J the brother of James. | 2491
| 6:14 | J the Baptist was risen from the dead, | 2491
| 6:16 | he said, It is J, whom I beheaded: | 2491
| 6:17 | had sent forth and laid hold upon J, | 2491
| 6:18 | For J had said unto Herod, It is not lawful | 2491
| 6:20 | Herod feared J, knowing that he *was* a | 2491
| 6:24 | And she said, The head of J the Baptist. | 2491
| 6:25 | by in a charger the head of J the Baptist. | 2491
| 8:28 | And they answered, J the Baptist: | 2491
| 9: 2 | and J, and leadeth them up into a high | 2491
| 9:38 | And J answered him, saying, Master, | 2491
| 10:35 | And James and J, the sons of Zebedee, | 2491
| 10:41 | to be much displeased with James and J. | 2491
| 11:30 | The baptism of J, was *it* from heaven, | 2491
| 11:32 | all *men* counted J, that he was a prophet. | 2491
| 13: 3 | Peter and James and J and Andrew asked | 2491
| 14:33 | taketh with him Peter and James and J, | 2491
Lk | 1:13 | thee a son, and thou shalt call his name J. | 2491
| 1:60 | and said, Not *so;* but he shall be called J. | 2491
| 1:63 | and wrote, saying, His name is J. | 2491
| 3: 2 | the word of God came unto J the son of | 2491
| 3:15 | and all *men* mused in their hearts of J, | 2491
| 3:16 | J answered, saying unto *them* all, I indeed | 2491
| 3:20 | this above all, that he shut up J in prison. | 2491
| 5:10 | And so *was* also James, and J, *the* sons of | 2491
| 5:33 | Why do the disciples of J fast often, | 2491
| 6:14 | and J, Philip and Bartholomew, | 2491
| 7:18 | And the disciples of J shewed him of all | 2491
| 7:19 | And J calling unto *him* two of his disciples | 2491
| 7:20 | J Baptist hath sent us unto thee, saying, | 2491
| 7:22 | and tell J what *things* ye have seen and | 2491
| 7:24 | And when the messengers of J were | 2491
| 7:24 | to speak unto the people concerning J, | 2491
| 7:28 | is not a greater prophet than J the Baptist: | 2491
| 7:29 | being baptized *with* the baptism of J. | 2491
| 7:33 | J the Baptist came neither eating bread | 2491
| 8:51 | and J, and the father and the mother of | 2491
| 9: 7 | of some, that J was risen from the dead; | 2491
| 9: 9 | And Herod said, J have I beheaded: | 2491
| 9:19 | They answered, J the Baptist; | 2491
| 9:28 | took Peter and J and James, and went up | 2491
| 9:49 | J answered and said, Master, we saw | 2491
| 9:54 | disciples James and J saw *this,* they said, | 2491
| 11: 1 | us to pray, as J also taught his disciples. | 2491
| 16:16 | The law and the prophets *were* until J: | 2491
| 20: 4 | The baptism of J, was it from heaven, | 2491
| 20: 6 | they be persuaded that J was a prophet. | 2491
| 22: 8 | And he sent Peter and J, saying, Go and | 2491
Jn | 1: 6 | a man sent from God, whose name *was* J. | 2491
| 1:15 | J bare witness of him, and cried, saying, | 2491
| 1:19 | And this is the record of J, when the Jews | 2491
| 1:26 | J answered them, saying, I baptize with | 2491
| 1:28 | beyond Jordan, where J was baptizing. | 2491
| 1:29 | The next day J seeth Jesus coming unto | 2491
| 1:32 | And J bare record, saying, I saw the Spirit | 2491
| 1:35 | Again the next day *after* J stood, | 2491
| 1:40 | One of the two which heard J speak, | 2491
| 3:23 | And J also was baptizing in Aenon near to | 2491
| 3:24 | For J was not yet cast into prison. | 2491
| 3:26 | And they came unto J, and said unto him, | 2491
| 3:27 | J answered and said, A man can receive | 2491
| 4: 1 | and baptized moe disciples than J, | 2491
| 5:33 | Ye sent unto J, and he bare witness unto | 2491
| 5:36 | But I have greater witness than *that of* J: | 2491
| 10:40 | into the place where J at first baptized; | 2491
| 10:41 | unto him, and said, J did no miracle: | 2491
| 10:41 | all *things* that J spake of this *man* were | 2491
Ac | 1: 5 | J truly baptized with water; but ye shall | 2491
| 1:13 | and J, and Andrew, Philip, and Thomas, | 2491
| 1:22 | Beginning from the baptism of J, unto | 2491
| 3: 1 | J went up together into the temple at | 2491
| 3: 3 | and J about to go into the temple, | 2491
| 3: 4 | fastening his eyes upon him with J, said, | 2491
| 3:11 | *man* which was healed held Peter and J, | 2491
| 4: 6 | and J, and Alexander, and as many as | 2491
| 4:13 | they saw the boldness of Peter and J, | 2491
| 4:19 | But Peter and J answered and said unto | 2491
| 8:14 | of God, they sent unto them Peter and J: | 2491
| 10:37 | after the baptism which J preached; | 2491
| 11:16 | he said, J indeed baptized with water; | 2491
| 12: 2 | And he killed James the brother of J with | 2491
| 12:12 | to the house of Mary the mother of J, | 2491
| 12:25 | took with *them* J, whose surname was | 2491
| 13: 5 | and they had also J to *their* minister. | 2491
| 13:13 | J departing from them returned to | 2491
| 13:24 | When J had first preached before his | 2491
| 13:25 | And as J fulfilled *his* course, he said, | 2491
| 15:37 | Barnabas determined to take with *them* J, | 2491
| 18:25 | the Lord, knowing only the baptism of J. | 2491
| 19: 4 | J verily baptized *with* the baptism of | 2491
Gal | 2: 9 | And when James, Cephas, and J, | 2491
Rev | 1: 1 | signified *it* by his angel unto J his servant J: | 2491
| 1: 4 | J to the seven churches which are in Asia: | 2491
| 1: 9 | I J, who also am your brother, | 2491
| 21: 2 | And I J saw the holy city, new Jerusalem, | 2491
| 22: 8 | And I J saw these *things,* and heard *them.* | 2491

JOHN'S (2) [JOHN]

Jn | 3:25 | a question between *some* of J disciples | 2491
Ac | 19: 3 | And they said, Unto J baptism. | 2491

JOIADA (4)

Ne | 12:10 | also begat Eliashib, and Eliashib begat J, | 3111
| 12:11 | J begat Jonathan, and Jonathan begat | 3111
| 12:22 | J, and Johanan, and Jaddua, *were* | 3111
| 13:28 | *one* of the sons of J, the son of Eliashib | 3111

JOIAKIM (4)

Ne | 12:10 | Jeshua begat J, Joiakim also begat Eliashib | 3113
| 12:10 | also begat Eliashib, and Eliashib begat | 3113
| 12:12 | in the days of J were priests, the chief of | 3113
| 12:26 | These *were* in the days of J the son of | 3113

JOIARIB (5)

Ezr | 8:16 | chief *men;* also for J, and for Elnathan, | 3114
Ne | 11: 5 | Hazaiah, the son of Adaiah, the son of J, | 3114
| 11:10 | Of the priests: Jedaiah the son of J, Jachin, | 3114
| 12: 6 | Shemaiah, and J, Jedaiah, | 3114
| 12:19 | And of J, Mattenai; of Jedaiah, Uzzi; | 3114

JOIN (14) [JOINED, JOINING, JOININGS, JOINT, JOINT-HEIRS, JOINTS]

Ex | 1:10 | they j also unto our enemies, | 3254
2Ch | 20:35 | after this did Jehoshaphat king of Judah j | 2266
Ezr | 9:14 | j in affinity with the people of these | 2859
Pr | 11:21 | *Though* hand *j* in hand, the wicked shall | NIH
| 16: 5 | *though* hand *j* in hand, he shall not | NIH
Isa | 5: 8 | Woe unto them that j house to house, | 5060
| 9:11 | against him, and j his enemies **together;** | 5526
| 56: 6 | that j themselves to the LORD, to serve | 3867
Jer | 50: 5 | let us j ourselves to the LORD *in* a | 3867
Eze | 37:17 | j them one to another into one stick; | 7126
Da | 11: 6 | of years they shall j themselves **together;** | 2266
Ac | 5:13 | And of the rest durst no *man* j himself to | 2853
| 8:29 | Go near, and j thyself **to** this chariot. | 2853
| 9:26 | he assayed to j himself to the disciples: | 2853

JOINED (43) [JOIN]

Ge | 14: 3 | All these were j **together** in the vale of | 2266
| 14: 8 | they j battle with them in the vale of | 6186
| 29:34 | Now *this* time will my husband be j unto | 3867
Ex | 28: 7 | *thereof* j at the two edges thereof; | 2266
| 28: 7 | thereof; and *so* it shall be j **together.** | 2266
Nu | 18: 2 | that they may be j unto thee, | 3867
| 18: 4 | they shall be j unto thee, and keep | 3867
| 25: 3 | Israel j himself **unto** Baal-peor: | 6775
| 25: 5 | Slay ye every one his men that were j | 6775
1Sa | 4: 2 | when they j battle, Israel was smitten | 5203
1Ki | 7:32 | the axletrees of the wheels *were* j **to** | 871.1
| 20:29 | that in the seventh day the battle was j: | 7126
2Ch | 18: 1 | in abundance, and j **affinity** with Ahab. | 2859
| 20:36 | he j himself with him to make ships to go | 2266
| 20:37 | Because thou hast j thyself with Ahaziah, | 2266
Ezr | 4:12 | the walls *thereof,* and j the foundations. | 2338
Ne | 4: 6 | all the wall was j **together** unto the half | 7194
Est | 9:27 | upon all such as j themselves unto them, | 3867
Job | 3: 6 | let it not be j unto the days of the year, | 2302
| 41:17 | They are j one to another, they stick | 1692
| 41:23 | The flakes of his flesh are j **together:** | 1692
Ps | 83: 8 | Assur also is j with them: they have | 3867
| 106:28 | They j themselves also unto Baal-peor, | 6775
Ecc | 9: 4 | to him that is j to all the living there is | 2266
Isa | 13:15 | every one that is j unto *them* shall fall by | 5595
| 14: 1 | the strangers shall be j with them, | 3867
| 14:20 | Thou shalt not be j **with** them in burial, | 3161
| 56: 3 | that hath j himself to the LORD, speak, | 3867
Eze | 1: 9 | Their wings *were* j one to another; they | 2266
| 1:11 | two *wings* of every one *were* j one to | 2266
| 46:22 | *there* were courts j *of* forty *cubits* long | 7000
Hos | 4:17 | Ephraim *is* j to idols: let him alone. | 2266
Zec | 2:11 | many nations shall be j to the LORD in | 3867
Mt | 19: 6 | What therefore God hath j **together,** let | 4801
Mk | 10: 9 | What therefore God hath j **together,** let | 4801
Lk | 15:15 | and j himself **to** a citizen of that country; | 2853
Ac | 5:36 | of men, about four hundred, j themselves; | 4347
| 18: 7 | whose house is **hard** to the synagogue. | 4927
1Co | 1:10 | ye be **perfectly** j **together** in the same | 2675
| 6:16 | know ye not that he which is j **to** a harlot | 2853
| 6:17 | But he that is j unto the Lord is one spirit. | 2853
Eph | 4:16 | whom the whole body **fitly** j **together** | 4883
| 5:31 | and shall be j unto his wife, and they two | 4347

JOINING (1) [JOIN]

2Ch | 3:12 | the other wing *was* five cubits *also,* j to | 1695

JOININGS (1) [JOIN]

1Ch | 22: 3 | for the doors of the gates, and for the j; | 4226

JOINT (4) [JOIN]

Ge | 32:25 | the hollow of Jacob's thigh was **out of** j, | 3363
Ps | 22:14 | like water, and all my bones are **out of** j: | 6504
Pr | 25:19 | *is like* a broken tooth, and a foot **out of** j. | 4154
Eph | 4:16 | by that which every j supplieth, | 860

JOINT-HEIRS (1) [HEIR, JOIN]

Ro | 8:17 | heirs of God, and j **with** Christ; if so be | 4789

JOINTS (1) [JOIN]

1Ki | 22:34 | smote the king of Israel between the j of | 1694
2Ch | 18:33 | smote the king of Israel between the j of | 1694
SS | 7: 1 | j of thy thighs *are* like jewels, the work | 2542
Da | 5: 6 | so that the j of his loins were loosed, | 7001

Col | 2:19 | from which all the body by j and | 860
Heb | 4:12 | of the j and marrow, and *is* a discerner | 719

JOKDEAM (1)

Jos | 15:56 | And Jezreel, and J, and Zanoah, | 3347

JOKIM (1)

1Ch | 4:22 | J, and the men of Chozeba, and Joash, | 3137

JOKMEAM (1)

1Ch | 6:68 | J with her suburbs, and Beth-horon with | 3361

JOKNEAM (4)

Jos | 12:22 | one; the king of J of Carmel, one; | 3362
| 19:11 | and reached to the river that *is* before J; | 3362
| 21:34 | J with her suburbs, and Kartah with her | 3362
1Ki | 4:12 | *even* unto *the* place *that is* beyond J: | 3361

JOKSHAN (4)

Ge | 25: 2 | J, and Medan, and Midian, and Ishbak, | 3370
| 25: 3 | J begat Sheba, and Dedan. And the sons | 3370
1Ch | 1:32 | J, and Medan, and Midian, and Ishbak, | 3370
| 1:32 | And the sons of J; Sheba, and Dedan. | 3370

JOKTAN (6)

Ge | 10:25 | and his brother's name *was* J. | 3355
| 10:26 | J begat Almodad, and Sheleph, | 3355
| 10:29 | and Jobab: all these *were* the sons of J. | 3355
1Ch | 1:19 | divided: and his brother's name *was* J. | 3355
| 1:20 | J begat Almodad, and Sheleph, | 3355
| 1:23 | and Jobab. All these *were* the sons of J. | 3355

JOKTHEEL (2)

Jos | 15:38 | And Dilean, and Mizpeh, and J, | 3371
2Ki | 14: 7 | and called the name of it J unto this day. | 3371

JONA (1)

Jn | 1:42 | he said, Thou art Simon the son of J: | 2495

JONADAB (12)

2Sa | 13: 3 | Amnon had a friend, whose name *was* J, | 3122
| 13: 3 | and J *was* a very subtil man. | 3122
| 13: 5 | J said unto him, Lay *thee* down on thy | 3082
| 13:32 | J, the son of Shimeah David's brother, | 3122
| 13:35 | J said unto the king, Behold, the king's | 3122
Jer | 35: 6 | J the son of Rechab our father | 3082
| 35: 8 | Thus have we obeyed the voice of J the | 3082
| 35:10 | done according to all that J our father | 3122
| 35:14 | The words of J the son of Rechab, that he | 3082
| 35:16 | Because the sons of J the son of Rechab | 3082
| 35:18 | the commandment of J your father, | 3082
| 35:19 | J the son of Rechab shall not want a man | 3122

JONAH (19) [JONAS]

2Ki | 14:25 | he spake by the hand of his servant J, | 3124
Jnh | 1: 1 | Now the word of the LORD came unto J | 3124
| 1: 3 | J rose up to flee unto Tarshish from | 3124
| 1: 5 | J was gone down into the sides of the | 3124
| 1: 7 | So they cast lots, and the lot fell upon J. | 3124
| 1:15 | So they took up J, and cast him forth into | 3124
| 1:17 | had prepared a great fish to swallow up J. | 3124
| 1:17 | was in the belly of the fish three days | 3124
| 2: 1 | J prayed unto the LORD his God out of | 3124
| 2:10 | and it vomited out J upon the dry *land.* | 3124
| 3: 1 | the word of the LORD came unto J | 3124
| 3: 3 | So J arose, and went unto Nineveh, | 3124
| 3: 4 | J began to enter into the city a day's | 3124
| 4: 1 | it displeased J exceedingly, and he was | 3124
| 4: 5 | So J went out of the city, and sat on | 3124
| 4: 6 | a gourd, and made *it* to come up over J, | 3124
| 4: 6 | So J was exceeding glad of the gourd. | 3124
| 4: 8 | the sun beat upon the head of J, that he | 3124
| 4: 9 | God said to J, Doest thou well to be angry | 3124

JONAM See JONAN

JONAN (1)

Lk | 3:30 | son of Joseph, which was *the* son of J, | 2494

JONAS (2) [JONAH]

Mt | 12:39 | given to it, but the sign of the prophet J: | 2495
| 12:40 | as J was three days and three nights in | 2495
| 12:41 | they repented at the preaching of J; | 2495
| 12:41 | and behold, a greater than J *is* here. | 2495
| 16: 4 | unto it, but the sign of the prophet J. | 2495
Lk | 11:29 | be given it, but the sign of J the prophet. | 2495
| 11:30 | For as J was a sign unto the Ninevites, | 2495
| 11:32 | for they repented at the preaching of J; | 2495
| 11:32 | and behold, a greater than J *is* here. | 2495
Jn | 21:15 | saith to Simon Peter, Simon, *son* of J, | 2495
| 21:16 | Simon, *son* of J, lovest thou me? | 2495
| 21:17 | Simon, *son* of J, lovest thou me? | 2495

JONATHAN (118) [JONATHAN'S]

Jdg | 18:30 | J, the son of Gershom, the son of | 3083
1Sa | 13: 2 | a thousand were with J in Gibeah of | 3129
| 13: 3 | J smote the garrison of the Philistines that | 3129
| 13:16 | his son, and the people that were | 3129
| 13:22 | of the people that *were* with Saul and J: | 3129
| 13:22 | and with J his son was there found. | 3129
| 14: 1 | that J the son of Saul said unto the young | 3129
| 14: 3 | And the people knew not that J was gone. | 3129
| 14: 4 | *by* which J sought to go over unto | 3129
| 14: 6 | J said to the young man that bare his | 3083
| 14: 8 | said J, Behold, we will pass over unto | 3083
| 14:12 | the men of the garrison answered J and | 3129

Ref	Text	Strong's
1Sa	14:12 J said unto his armourbearer, Come up	3129
	14:13 J climbed up upon his hands and upon his	3129
	14:13 they fell before J; and his armourbearer	3129
	14:14 which J and his armourbearer made,	3129
	14:17 behold J and his armourbearer *were* not	3129
	14:21 the Israelites that *were* with Saul and J.	3129
	14:27 heard not when his father charged	3129
	14:29 said J, My father hath troubled the land:	3129
	14:39 though it be in J my son, he shall surely	3129
	14:40 I and J my son will be on the other side.	3129
	14:41 a perfect *lot.* And Saul and J were taken:	3129
	14:42 Cast *lots* between me and J my son.	3129
	14:42 and Jonathan my son. And J was taken.	3129
	14:43 Saul said to J, Tell me what thou hast	3129
	14:43 J told him, and said, I did but taste a little	3129
	14:44 and more also: for thou shalt surely die, J.	3129
	14:45 the people said unto Saul, Shall J die,	3129
	14:45 So the people rescued J, that he died not.	3129
	14:49 Now the sons of Saul were J, and Ishui,	3129
	18: 1 that the soul of J was knit with the soul of	3083
	18: 1 David, and J loved him as his own soul.	3083
	18: 3 J and David made a covenant, because	3083
	18: 4 J stript himself of the robe that *was* upon	3129
	19: 1 Saul spake to J his son, and to all his	3129
	19: 2 J Saul's son delighted much in David:	3083
	19: 2 J told David, saying, Saul my father	3083
	19: 4 spake good of David unto Saul his father,	3083
	19: 6 Saul hearkened unto the voice of J:	3083
	19: 7 J called David, and Jonathan shewed him	3083
	19: 7 and J shewed him all those things.	3083
	19: 7 brought David to Saul, and he was in	3083
	20: 1 said before J, What have I done?	3083
	20: 3 he saith, Let not J know this, lest he be	3083
	20: 4 said J unto David, Whatsoever thy soul	3083
	20: 5 David said unto J, Behold, to morrow *is*	3083
	20: 9 J said, Far be it from thee: for if I knew	3083
	20:10 Then said David to J, Who shall tell me?	3083
	20:11 J said unto David, Come, and let us go	3083
	20:12 J said unto David, O LORD God of Israel,	3083
	20:13 The LORD do so and much more to J:	3083
	20:16 So J made *a covenant* with the house of	3083
	20:17 J caused David to swear again, because	3083
	20:18 J said to *David,* To morrow *is* the new	3129
	20:25 J arose, and Abner sat by Saul's side,	3083
	20:27 Saul said unto J his son, Wherefore	3083
	20:28 J answered Saul, David earnestly asked	3083
	20:30 Saul's anger was kindled against J,	3083
	20:32 J answered Saul his father, and said unto	3083
	20:33 whereby J knew that it was determined	3083
	20:34 So J arose from the table in fierce anger,	3083
	20:35 that J went out *into* the field at the time	3083
	20:37 the place of the arrow which J had shot,	3083
	20:37 J cried after the lad, and said, *Is* not	3083
	20:38 J cried after the lad, Make speed, haste,	3083
	20:39 only J knew the matter.	3083
	20:40 J gave his artillery unto his lad,	3083
	20:42 J said to David, Go in peace, forasmuch	3083
	20:42 and departed: and J went *into* the city.	3083
	23:16 J Saul's son arose, and went to David *into*	3083
	23:18 in the wood, and J went to his house.	3083
	31: 2 the Philistines slew J, and Abinadab,	3083
2Sa	1: 4 and Saul and J his son are dead also.	3083
	1: 5 thou that Saul and J his son be dead?	3083
	1:12 for J his son, and for the people of	3083
	1:17 lamentation over Saul and over J his son:	3083
	1:22 the bow of J turned not back,	3083
	1:23 Saul and J *were* lovely and pleasant in	3083
	1:25 O J, *thou wast* slain in thine high places.	3083
	1:26 I am distressed for thee, my brother J:	3083
	4: 4 J, Saul's son, had a son *that was* lame of	3083
	4: 4 tidings came of Saul and J out of Jezreel,	3083
	9: 3 J hath yet a son, which *is* lame on *his* feet.	3083
	9: 6 the son of J, the son of Saul, was come	3083
	9: 7 for I will surely shew thee kindness for J	3083
	15:27 thy son, and J the son of Abiathar.	3083
	15:36 Zadok's *son,* and Abiathar's *son;* and	3083
	17:17 Now J and Ahimaaz stayed by En-rogel;	3083
	17:20 they said, Where *is* Ahimaaz and J?	3083
	21: 7 the son of J the son of Saul, because of	3083
	21: 7 between David and J the son of Saul.	3083
	21:12 the bones of J his son from the men of	3083
	21:13 bones of Saul and the bones of J his son;	3083
	21:14 J his son buried they in the country of	3083
	21:21 the son of Shimea the brother of David	3083
	23:32 the Shaalbonite, *of* the sons of Jashen, J,	3083
1Ki	1:42 the son of Abiathar the priest came:	3129
	1:43 J answered and said to Adonijah,	3129
1Ch	2:32 the brother of Shammai; Jether, and J:	3129
	2:33 the sons of J; Peleth, and Zaza. These	3129
	8:33 Saul begat J, and Malchishua,	3083
	8:34 the son of J *was* Merib-baal;	3083
	9:39 Saul begat J, and Malchishua,	3083
	9:40 the son of J *was* Merib-baal:	3083
	10: 2 the Philistines slew J, and Abinadab,	3129
	11:34 the son of Shage the Hararite,	3083
	20: 7 J the son of Shimea David's brother slew	3083
	27:32 Also J David's uncle *was* a counseller,	3083
Ezr	8: 6 the son of J, and with him fifty males.	3129
	10:15 Only J the son of Asahel and Jahaziah	3129
Ne	12:11 Joiada begat J, and Jonathan begat Jaddua.	3129
	12:11 Joiada begat Jonathan, and J begat Jaddua.	3129
	12:14 Of Melicu, J; of Shebaniah, Joseph;	3129
	12:35 *namely,* Zechariah the son of J, the son of	3129
Jer	37:15 put him *in* prison *in* the house of J	3083
	37:20 not to return *to* the house of J the scribe,	

Ref	Text	Strong's
Jer	40: 8 Johanan and J the sons of Kareah,	3129

JONATHAN'S (3) [JONATHAN]

Ref	Text	Strong's
1Sa	20:38 J lad gathered up the arrows, and came to	3083
2Sa	9: 1 that I may shew him kindness for J sake?	3083
Jer	38:26 that *he* would not cause me to return *to* J	3083

JONATH-ELEM-RECHOKIM (1)

Ref	Text	Strong's
Ps	56: T To the chief Musician upon J, Michtam of	3128

JOPPA (13)

Ref	Text	Strong's
2Ch	2:16 will bring it to thee *in* flotes by sea *to* J;	3305
Ezr	3: 7 cedar trees from Lebanon to the sea of J,	3305
Jnh	1: 3 of the LORD, and went down *to* J;	3305
Ac	9:36 Now there was at J a certain disciple	2445
	9:38 And forasmuch as Lydda was nigh to J,	2445
	9:42 And it was known throughout all J;	2445
	9:43 that he tarried many days in J with one	2445
	10: 5 And now send men to J, and call for *one*	2445
	10: 8 *things* unto them, he sent them to J.	2445
	10:23 certain brethren from J accompanied him.	2445
	10:32 Send therefore to J, and call hither Simon,	2445
	11: 5 I was in the city of J praying: and in a	2445
	11:13 Send men to J, and call for Simon,	2445

JORAH (1)

Ref	Text	Strong's
Ezr	2:18 The children of J, an hundred and twelve.	3139

JORAI (1)

Ref	Text	Strong's
1Ch	5:13 J, and Jachan, and Zia, and Heber, seven.	3140

JORAM (29)

Ref	Text	Strong's
2Sa	8:10 Toi sent J his son unto king David,	3141
	8:10 J brought with him vessels of silver,	NIH
2Ki	8:16 in the fifth year of J the son of Ahab king	3141
	8:21 J went over to Zair, and all the chariots	3141
	8:23 rest of the acts of J, and all that he did,	3141
	8:24 J slept with his fathers, and was buried	3141
	8:25 In the twelfth year of J the son of Ahab	3141
	8:28 went with J the son of Ahab to the war	3141
	8:28 and the Syrians wounded J.	3141
	8:29 king J went back to be healed in Jezreel	3141
	8:29 down to see J the son of Ahab in Jezreel,	3141
	9:14 the son of Nimshi conspired against J.	3141
	9:14 (Now J had kept Ramoth-gilead, he and	3141
	9:15 J was returned to be healed in Jezreel	3088
	9:16 and went to Jezreel; for J lay there.	3141
	9:16 king of Judah was come down to see J.	3088
	9:17 J said, Take a horseman, and send to	3088
	9:21 J said, Make ready. And his chariot was	3088
	9:21 J king of Israel and Ahaziah king of Judah	3088
	9:22 when J saw Jehu, that he said, *Is it* peace,	3088
	9:23 J turned his hands, and fled, and said to	3088
	9:29 in the eleventh year of J the son of Ahab	3141
	11: 2 Jehosheba, the daughter of king J, sister	3141
1Ch	3:11 J his son, Ahaziah his son, Joash his son,	3141
	26:25 J his son, and Zichri his son,	3141
2Ch	22: 5 Ramoth-gilead: and the Syrians smote J.	3141
	22: 7 of Ahaziah was of God by coming to J:	3141
Mt	1: 8 and Josaphat begat J; and Joram begat	2496
	1: 8 Josaphat begat Joram; and J begat Ozias;	2496

JORDAN (197)

Ref	Text	Strong's
Ge	13:10 up his eyes, and beheld all the plain of J,	3383
	13:11 Lot chose him all the plain of J;	3383
	32:10 for with my staff I passed over this J;	3383
	50:10 is beyond J, and there they mourned	3383
	50:11 called Abel-mizraim, which *is* beyond J.	3383
Nu	13:29 dwell by the sea, and by the coast of J.	3383
	22: 1 in the plains of Moab on *this* side J	3383
	26: 3 in the plains of Moab by J *near* Jericho.	3383
	26:63 in the plains of Moab by J *near* Jericho.	3383
	31:12 of Moab, which *are* by J *near* Jericho.	3383
	32: 5 for a possession, *and* bring us not over J.	3383
	32:19 not inherit with them on *yonder* side J,	3383
	32:19 inheritance is fallen to us on *this* side J	3383
	32:21 will go all of you armed over J before	3383
	32:29 of Reuben will pass with you over J,	3383
	32:32 inheritance on *this* side J *may be* ours.	3383
	33:48 pitched in the plains of Moab by J *near*	3383
	33:49 they pitched by J, from Beth-jesimoth	3383
	33:50 in the plains of Moab by J *near* Jericho.	3383
	33:51 When ye are passed over J into the land	3383
	34:12 the border shall go down to J,	3383
	34:15 on *this* side J *near* Jericho eastward,	3383
	35: 1 in the plains of Moab by J *near* Jericho,	3383
	35:10 When ye be come over J into the land of	3383
	35:14 Ye shall give three cities on *this* side J,	3383
	36:13 in the plains of Moab by J *near* Jericho.	3383
Dt	1: 1 all Israel on *this* side J in the wilderness,	3383
	1: 5 On *this* side J, in the land of Moab,	3383
	2:29 until I shall pass over J into the land	3383
	3: 8 Amorites the land that *was* on *this* side J,	3383
	3:17 J, and the coast *thereof,* from Chinnereth	3383
	3:20 your God hath given them beyond J:	3383
	3:25 and see the good land that *is* beyond J,	3383
	3:27 eyes: for thou shalt not go over this J.	3383
	4:21 sware that I should not go over J, and	3383
	4:22 die in this land, I *must* not go over J:	3383
	4:26 whereunto ye go over J to possess it;	3383
	4:41 Moses severed three cities on *this* side J	3383
	4:46 On *this* side J, in the valley over against	3383
	4:47 which *were* on *this* side J *toward*	3383
	4:49 all the plain on *this* side J eastward, even	3383
	9: 1 Thou art to pass over J this day, to go in	3383

Ref	Text	Strong's
Dt	11:30 they not on the *other* side J, by the way	3383
	11:31 For ye shall pass over J to go in to possess	3383
	12:10 *when* ye go over J and dwell in the land	3383
	27: 2 unto the land which the LORD thy God	3383
	27: 4 it shall be when ye be gone over J,	3383
	27:12 the people, when ye are come over J;	3383
	30:18 thou passest over J to go to possess	3383
	31: 2 unto me, Thou shalt not go over this J.	3383
	31:13 land whither ye go over J to possess it.	3383
	32:47 land, whither ye go over J to possess it.	3383
Jos	1: 2 go over this J, thou, and all this people,	3383
	1:11 within three days ye shall pass over this J,	3383
	1:14 land which Moses gave you on *this* side J;	3383
	1:15 you on *this* side J *toward* the sunrising.	3383
	2: 7 the men pursued after them the way to J	3383
	2:10 *were* on the *other* side J, Sihon and Og,	3383
	3: 1 came to J, he and all the children of Israel,	3383
	3: 8 ye are come to the brink of the water of J,	3383
	3: 8 water of Jordan, ye shall stand still in J.	3383
	3:11 the earth passeth over before you into J.	3383
	3:13 all the earth, shall rest in the waters of J,	3383
	3:13 *that* the waters of J shall be cut off *from*	3383
	3:14 to pass over J, and the priests bearing	3383
	3:15 they that bare the ark were come unto J,	3383
	3:15 J overfloweth all his banks all the time	3383
	3:17 firm on dry *ground* in the midst of J,	3383
	3:17 all the people were passed clean over J.	3383
	4: 1 all the people were clean passed over J,	3383
	4: 3 Take you hence out of the midst of J,	3383
	4: 5 the LORD your God into the midst of J,	3383
	4: 7 That the waters of J were cut off before	3383
	4: 7 it passed over J, the waters of Jordan	3383
	4: 7 over Jordan, the waters of J were cut off:	3383
	4: 8 twelve stones out of the midst of J,	3383
	4: 9 set up twelve stones in the midst of J,	3383
	4:10 bare the ark stood in the midst of J,	3383
	4:16 Testimony, that they come up out of J.	3383
	4:17 the priests, saying, Come ye up out of J.	3383
	4:18 were come up out of the midst of J,	3383
	4:18 the waters of J returned unto their place,	3383
	4:19 the people came up out of J on the tenth	3383
	4:20 twelve stones, which they took out of J,	3383
	4:22 Israel came over this J on dry *land.*	3383
	4:23 dried up the waters of J from before you,	3383
	5: 1 which *were* on the side of J westward,	3383
	5: 1 beyond J for the children of Israel,	3383
	7: 7 hast thou at all brought this people over J,	3383
	7: 7 content, and dwelt on the *other* side J!	3383
	9: 1 all the kings which *were* on *this* side J,	3383
	9:10 that *were* beyond J, to Sihon king of	3383
	12: 1 possessed their land on the *other* side J	3383
	12: 7 the children of Israel smote on *this* side J	3383
	13: 8 Moses gave them, beyond J eastward,	3383
	13:23 border of the children of Reuben was J,	3383
	13:27 Sihon king of Heshbon, J and *his* border,	3383
	13:27 Cinnereth on the *other* side J eastward.	3383
	13:32 on the *other* side J, by Jericho, eastward.	3383
	14: 3 and a half tribe on the *other* side J:	3383
	15: 5 *was* the salt sea, *even* unto the end of J.	3383
	15: 5 bay of the sea at the uttermost part of J:	3383
	16: 1 lot of the children of Joseph fell from J	3383
	16: 7 and came to Jericho, and went out at J.	3383
	17: 5 which *were* on the *other* side J;	3383
	18: 7 have received their inheritance beyond J	3383
	18:12 their border on the north side was from J;	3383
	18:19 bay of the salt sea at the south end of J:	3383
	18:20 J was the border of it on the east side.	3383
	19:22 the outgoings of their border were *at* J:	3383
	19:33 and the outgoings thereof were *at* J:	3383
	19:34 to Judah upon J *toward* the sunrising.	3383
	20: 8 on the *other* side J *by* Jericho eastward,	3383
	22: 4 of the LORD gave you on the *other* side J.	3383
	22: 7 their brethren on *this* side J westward.	3383
	22:10 when they came unto the borders of J,	3383
	22:10 of Manasseh built there an altar by J,	3383
	22:11 in the borders of J, at the passage of	3383
	22:25 For the LORD hath made J a border	3383
	23: 4 be an inheritance for your tribes, from J,	3383
	24: 8 which dwelt on the *other* side J;	3383
	24:11 ye went over J, and came unto Jericho:	3383
Jdg	3:28 took the fords of J toward Moab,	3383
	5:17 Gilead abode beyond J: and why did Dan	3383
	7:24 them the waters unto Beth-barah and J.	3383
	7:24 took the waters unto Beth-barah and J.	3383
	7:25 and Zeeb to Gideon on the *other* side J.	3383
	8: 4 Gideon came to J, *and* passed over,	3383
	10: 8 *other* side J in the land of the Amorites,	3383
	10: 9 passed over J to fight also against Judah,	3383
	11:13 Arnon even unto Jabbok, and unto J:	3383
	11:22 and from the wilderness even unto J.	3383
	12: 5 Gileadites took the passages of J before	3383
	12: 6 and slew him at the passages of J:	3383
1Sa	13: 7 *some* of the Hebrews went over J to	3383
	31: 7 they that *were* on the *other* side J, saw	3383
2Sa	2:29 passed over J, and went *through* all	3383
	10:17 and passed over J, and came to Helam.	3383
	17:22 *were* with him, and they passed over J:	3383
	17:22 not one of them that was not gone over J.	3383
	17:24 Absalom passed over J, he and all the	3383
	19:15 So the king returned, and came to J.	3383
	19:15 meet the king, to conduct the king over J.	3383
	19:17 and they went over J before the king.	3383
	19:18 before the king, as he was come over J;	3383
	19:31 went over J with the king, to conduct	3383
	19:31 with the king, to conduct him over J.	3383

2Sa 19:36	Thy servant will go a little *way* over J	3383
19:39	all the people went over J. And when	3383
19:41	and all David's men with him, over J?	3383
20: 2	unto their king, from J even to Jerusalem.	3383
24: 5	they passed over J, and pitched in Aroer,	3383
1Ki 2: 8	came down to meet me *at* J, and I sware	3383
7:46	In the plain of J did the king cast them,	3383
17: 3	by the brook Cherith, that *is* before J.	3383
17: 5	by the brook Cherith, that *is* before J.	3383
2Ki 2: 6	here; for the LORD hath sent me to J.	3383
2: 7	to view afar off: and they two stood by J.	3383
2:13	went back, and stood by the bank of J;	3383
5:10	Go and wash in J seven times,	3383
5:14	and dipped *himself* seven times in J,	3383
6: 2	J, and take thence every man a beam,	3383
6: 4	they came to J, they cut down wood.	3383
7:15	they went after them unto J: and lo,	3383
10:33	From J eastward, all the land of Gilead,	3383
1Ch 6:78	on the *other* side J *by* Jericho, on the east	3383
6:78	Jordan *by* Jericho, on the east *side* of J,	3383
12:15	These *are* they that went over J in the	3383
12:37	on the *other* side of J, of the Reubenites,	3383
19:17	passed over J, and came upon them,	3383
26:30	J westward in all the business of	3383
2Ch 4:17	In the plain of J did the king cast them,	3383
Job 40:23	he trusteth that he can draw up J into his	3383
Ps 6	will I remember thee from the land of J,	3383
114: 3	sea saw *it*, and fled: J was driven back.	3383
114: 5	thou J, *that* thou wast driven back?	3383
Isa 9: 1	sea, beyond J, in Galilee of the nations.	3383
Jer 12: 5	how wilt thou do in the swelling of J?	3383
49:19	of J against the habitation of the strong:	3383
50:44	of J unto the habitation of the strong:	3383
Eze 47:18	and from the land of Israel by J,	3383
Zec 11: 3	young lions; for the pride of J is spoiled.	3383
Mt 3: 5	Judea, and all the region round about J,	2446
3: 6	And were baptized of him in J,	2446
3:13	Then cometh Jesus from Galilee to J unto	2446
4:15	*by* the way of the sea, beyond J, Galilee of	2446
4:25	and *from* Judea, and *from* beyond J.	2446
19: 1	unto the coasts of Judea beyond J;	2446
Mk 1: 5	were all baptized of him in the river *of* J,	2446
1: 9	of Galilee, and was baptized of John in J.	2446
3: 8	and from Idumea, and *from* beyond J;	2446
10: 1	coasts of Judea by the farther side of J:	2446
Lk 3: 3	And he came into all the country about J,	2446
4: 1	full of the Holy Ghost returned from J,	2446
Jn 1:28	*things* were done in Bethabara beyond J,	2446
3:26	Rabbi, *he* that was with thee beyond J,	2446
10:40	And went away again beyond J into	2446

JORIM (1)

Lk 3:29	son of Eliezer, which was the son of J,	2497

JORKEAM See JORKOAM

JORKOAM (1)

1Ch 2:44	Shema begat Raham, the father of J:	3421

JOSABAD (1)

1Ch 12: 4	and Johanan, and J the Gederathite,	3107

JOSAPHAT (2) [JEHOSHAPHAT]

Mt 1: 8	And Asa begat J; and Josaphat begat	2498
1: 8	J begat Joram; and Joram begat Ozias;	2498

JOSE (1)

Lk 3:29	was the son of J, which was the son	2499

JOSEDECH (6)

Hag 1: 1	to Joshua the son of J the high priest,	3087
1:12	Joshua the son of J the high priest, with	3087
1:14	the spirit of Joshua the son of J the high	3087
2: 2	to Joshua the son of J the high priest and	3087
2: 4	be strong, O Joshua, son of J, the high	3087
Zec 6:11	head of Joshua the son of J the high priest;	3087

JOSEPH (228) [JOSEPH'S, JOSES]

Ge 30:24	she called his name J; and said,	3130
30:25	it came to pass, when Rachel had born J,	3130
33: 2	and Rachel and J hindermost.	3130
33: 7	after came J near and Rachel,	3130
35:24	The sons of Rachel; J, and Benjamin:	3130
37: 2	J, *being* seventeen years old, was feeding	3130
37: 2	brought unto his father their evil report.	3130
37: 3	Now Israel loved J more than all his	3130
37: 5	J dreamed a dream, and he told it his	3130
37:13	Israel said unto J, Do not thy brethren	3130
37:17	J went after his brethren, and found them	3130
37:23	when J was come unto his brethren,	3130
37:23	that they stript J out of his coat,	3130
37:28	they drew and lift up J out of the pit,	3130
37:28	sold J to the Ishmeelites for twenty *pieces*	3130
37:28	of silver: and they brought J into Egypt.	3130
37:29	J *was* not in the pit; and he rent his	3130
37:33	J is without doubt rent in pieces.	3130
39: 1	was brought down to Egypt;	3130
39: 2	the LORD was with J, and he was a	3130
39: 4	J found grace in his sight, and he served	3130
39: 6	J was *a* goodly *person*, and well favoured.	3130
39: 7	his master's wife cast her eyes upon J;	3130
39:10	pass, as she spake to J day by day,	3130
39:11	that J went into the house to do his	NIH
39:21	the LORD was with J, and shewed him	3130
40: 3	the prison, the place where J *was* bound.	3130
40: 4	the captain of the guard charged J with	3130

Ge 40: 6	came in unto them in the morning,	3130
40: 8	J said unto them, *Do* not interpretations	3130
40: 9	the chief butler told his dream to J,	3130
40:12	J said unto him, This *is* the interpretation	3130
40:16	he said unto J, I also *was* in my dream,	3130
40:18	J answered and said, This *is*	3130
40:22	chief baker: as J had interpreted to them.	3130
40:23	Yet did not the chief butler remember J,	3130
41:14	Pharaoh sent and called J, and they	3130
41:15	Pharaoh said unto J, I have dreamed a	3130
41:16	J answered Pharaoh, saying, *It is* not in	3130
41:17	Pharaoh said unto J, In my dream, behold,	3130
41:25	J said unto Pharaoh, The dream of	3130
41:39	Pharaoh said unto J, Forasmuch as God	3130
41:41	Pharaoh said unto J, See, I have set thee	3130
41:44	Pharaoh said unto J, I *am* Pharaoh,	3130
41:45	And J went out over *all* the land of Egypt.	3130
41:46	J *was* thirty years old when he stood	3130
41:46	J went out from the presence of Pharaoh,	3130
41:49	J gathered corn as the sand of the sea,	3130
41:50	unto J were born two sons before the	3130
41:51	J called the name of the firstborn	3130
41:54	began to come, according as J had said:	3130
41:55	said unto the Egyptians, Go unto J;	3130
41:56	J opened all the storehouses, and sold	3130
41:57	all countries came into Egypt to J for to	3130
42: 6	J was the governor over the land, *and* he	3130
42: 7	J saw his brethren, and he knew them,	3130
42: 8	J knew his brethren, but they knew not	3130
42: 9	J remembered the dreams which he	3130
42:14	J said unto them, That *is it* that I spake	3130
42:18	J said unto them the third day, This do,	3130
42:23	they knew not that J understood *them;* for	3130
42:25	J commanded to fill their sacks *with* corn,	3130
42:36	J *is* not, and Simeon *is* not, and ye will	3130
43:15	went down to Egypt, and stood before J.	3130
43:16	J saw Benjamin with them, he said to	3130
43:17	man did as J bade; and the man brought	3130
43:25	made ready the present against J came	3130
43:26	when J came home, they brought him	3130
43:30	J made haste; for his bowels did yern	3130
44: 2	he did according to the word that J had	3130
44: 4	not *yet* far off, J said unto his steward,	3130
44:15	J said unto them, What deed *is* this that	3130
45: 1	J could not refrain himself before all them	3130
45: 1	while J made himself known unto his	3130
45: 3	J said unto his brethren, I *am* J;	3130
45: 3	Joseph said unto his brethren, I *am* J;	3130
45: 4	J said unto his brethren, Come near to	3130
45: 4	said, I *am* J your brother, whom ye sold	3130
45: 9	and say unto him, Thus saith thy son J,	3130
45:17	Pharaoh said unto J, Say unto thy	3130
45:21	J gave them wagons, according to	3130
45:26	J *is* yet alive, and he *is* governor over all	3130
45:27	they told him all the words of J, which	3130
45:27	he saw the wagons which J had sent	3130
45:28	It is enough; J my son *is* yet alive:	3130
46: 4	and J shall put his hand upon thine eyes.	3130
46:19	of Rachel Jacob's wife; J, and Benjamin.	3130
46:20	unto J in the land of Egypt were born	3130
46:27	the sons of J, which were born him in	3130
46:28	he sent Judah before him unto J, to direct	3130
46:29	J made ready his chariot, and went up to	3130
46:30	Israel said unto J, Now let me die, since I	3130
46:31	J said unto his brethren, and unto his	3130
47: 1	J came and told Pharaoh, and said,	3130
47: 5	Pharaoh spake unto J, saying, Thy father	3130
47: 7	J brought in Jacob his father, and set him	3130
47:11	J placed his father and his brethren,	3130
47:12	J nourished his father, and his brethren,	3130
47:14	J gathered up all the money that was	3130
47:14	J brought the money into Pharaoh's	3130
47:15	all the Egyptians came unto J, and said,	3130
47:16	J said, Give your cattle; and I will give	3130
47:17	they brought their cattle unto J:	3130
47:17	J gave them bread *in exchange* for horses,	3130
47:20	J bought all the land of Egypt for Pharaoh;	3130
47:23	J said unto the people, Behold, I have	3130
47:26	J made it a law over the land of Egypt	3130
47:29	he called his son J, and said unto him,	3130
48: 1	that *one* told J, Behold, thy father *is* sick:	3130
48: 2	said, Behold, thy son J cometh unto thee:	3130
48: 3	Jacob said unto J, God Almighty appeared	3130
48: 9	J said unto his father, They *are* my sons,	3130
48:11	Israel said unto J, I had not thought to see	3130
48:12	J brought them out from between his	3130
48:13	J took them both, Ephraim in his right	3130
48:15	he blessed J, and said, God, before whom	3130
48:17	when J saw that his father laid his right	3130
48:18	J said unto his father, Not so, my father:	3130
48:21	Israel said unto J, Behold, I die:	3130
49:22	J *is* a fruitful bough, *even* a fruitful bough	3130
49:26	they shall be on the head of J, and on	3130
50: 1	J fell upon his father's face, and wept	3130
50: 2	J commanded his servants the physicians	3130
50: 4	J spake unto the house of Pharaoh, saying,	3130
50: 7	J went up to bury his father: and with	3130
50: 8	all the house of J, and his brethren,	3130
50:14	J returned into Egypt, he, and his	3130
50:15	J will peradventure hate us,	3130
50:16	they sent a messenger unto J, saying,	3130
50:17	So shall ye say unto J, Forgive, I pray thee	3130
50:17	And J wept when they spake unto him.	3130
50:19	J said unto them, Fear not: for *am* I in	3130
50:22	J dwelt in Egypt, he, and his father's	3130

Ge 50:22	and J lived an hundred and ten years.	3130
50:23	J saw Ephraim's children of the third	3130
50:24	J said unto his brethren, I die: and God	3130
50:25	J took an oath of the children of Israel,	3130
50:26	So J died, *being* an hundred and ten years	3130
Ex 1: 5	seventy souls: for J was in Egypt already.	3130
1: 6	J died, and all his brethren, and all that	3130
1: 8	a new king over Egypt, which knew not J.	3130
13:19	Moses took the bones of J with him: for	3130
Nu 1:10	Of the children of J: of Ephraim;	3130
1:32	Of the children of J, namely, of	3130
13: 7	Of the tribe of Issachar, Igal the son of J.	3130
13:11	Of the tribe of J, namely, of the tribe of	3130
26:28	The sons of J after their families were	3130
26:37	These *are* the sons of J after their families.	3130
27: 1	of the families of Manasseh the son of J:	3130
32:33	half the tribe of Manasseh the son of J,	3130
34:23	The prince of the children of J, for the	3130
36: 1	of the families of the sons of J, came near,	3130
36: 5	The tribe of the sons of J hath said well.	3130
36:12	of the sons of Manasseh the son of J,	3130
Dt 27:12	Judah, and Issachar, and J, and Benjamin:	3130
33:13	of J he said, Blessed of the LORD *be* his	3130
33:16	let *the blessing* come upon the head of J,	3130
Jos 14: 4	For the children of J were two tribes,	3130
16: 1	the lot of the children of J fell from Jordan	3130
16: 4	So the children of J, Manasseh and	3130
17: 1	for he *was* the firstborn of J; *to wit*, for	3130
17: 2	of Manasseh the son of J by their families.	3130
17:14	children of J spake unto Joshua, saying,	3130
17:16	the children of J said, The hill is not	3130
17:17	Joshua spake unto the house of J, *even* to	3130
18: 5	house of J shall abide in their coasts on	3130
18:11	children of Judah and the children of J.	3130
24:32	bones of J, which the children of Israel	3130
24:32	the inheritance of the children of J.	3130
Jdg 1:22	the house of J, they also went up *against*	3130
1:23	the house of J sent to descry Beth-el.	3130
1:35	yet the hand of the house of J prevailed,	3130
2Sa 19:20	of J to go down to meet my lord the king.	3130
1Ki 11:28	ruler over all the charge of the house of J.	3130
1Ch 2: 2	Dan, J, and Benjamin, Naphtali, Gad,	3130
5: 1	his birthright was given unto the sons of J	3130
7:29	In these dwelt the children of J the son of	3130
25: 2	and J, and Nethaniah, and Asarelah,	3130
25: 9	the first lot came forth for Asaph to J:	3130
Ezr 10:42	Shallum, Amariah, *and* J.	3130
Ne 12:14	Of Melicu, Jonathan; of Shebaniah, J;	3130
Ps 77:15	thy people, the sons of Jacob and J.	3130
78:67	Moreover he refused the tabernacle of J,	3130
80: 1	of Israel, thou that leadest J like a flock;	3130
81: 5	This he ordained in J *for* a testimony,	3084
105:17	*even* J, who was sold for a servant:	3130
Eze 37:16	another stick, and write upon it, For J,	3130
37:19	Behold, I *will* take the stick of J, which *is*	3130
47:13	tribes of Israel: J *shall have* two portions.	3130
48:32	one gate of J, one gate of Benjamin,	3130
Am 5: 6	he break out like fire *in* the house of J,	3130
5:15	will be gracious unto the remnant of J.	3130
6: 6	they are not grieved for the affliction of J.	3130
Ob 1:18	the house of J a flame, and the house of	3130
Zec 10: 6	I will save the house of J, and I will bring	3130
Mt 1:16	And Jacob begat J the husband of Mary,	2501
1:18	as his mother Mary was espoused to J,	2501
1:19	Then J her husband, being a just *man*,	2501
1:20	saying, J, thou son of David, fear not to	2501
1:24	Then J being raised from sleep did as	2501
2:13	*the* angel of the Lord appeareth to J in a	2501
2:19	Lord appeareth in a dream to J in Egypt,	2501
27:57	came a rich man of Arimathea, named J,	2501
27:59	And when J had taken the body,	2501
Mk 15:43	J of Arimathea, an honourable counseller,	2501
15:45	*it* of the centurion, he gave the body to J.	2501
Lk 1:27	espoused to a man whose name was J,	2501
2: 4	And J also went up from Galilee, out of	2501
2:16	and J, and the babe lying in a manger.	2501
2:33	And J and his mother marvelled at those	2501
2:43	and J and his mother knew not of it.	2501
3:23	the son of J, which was *the son* of Heli,	2501
3:24	*the son* of Janna, which was *the son* of J,	2501
3:26	which was *the son* of J, which was *the*	2501
3:30	*the son* of Juda, which was *the son* of J,	2501
23:50	And behold, *there was* a man named J,	2501
Jn 1:45	did write, Jesus of Nazareth, the son of J.	2501
4: 5	of ground that Jacob gave to his son J.	2501
6:42	the son of J, whose father and mother we	2501
19:38	And after this J of Arimathea, being a	2501
Ac 1:23	they appointed two, J called Barsabas,	2501
7: 9	moved with envy, sold J into Egypt:	2501
7:13	at the second time J was made known	2501
7:14	Then sent J, and called his father Jacob to	2501
7:18	another king arose, which knew not J.	2501
Heb 11:21	was a dying, blessed both the sons of J;	2501
11:22	By faith J, when he died, made mention	2501
Rev 7: 8	Of the tribe of J *were* sealed twelve	2501

JOSEPH'S (22) [JOSEPH]

Ge 37:31	they took J coat, and killed a kid of	3130
39: 5	blessed the Egyptian's house for J sake;	3130
39: 6	he left all that he had in J hand;	3130
39:20	J master took him, and put him into	3130
39:22	the keeper of the prison committed to J	3130
41:42	put it upon J hand, and arrayed him in	3130
41:45	Pharaoh called J name Zaphnath-paaneah;	3130
42: 3	J ten brethren went down to buy corn in	3130

Ge	42: 4 Benjamin, J brother, Jacob sent not with	3130
	42: 6 J brethren came, and bowed down	3130
	43:17 the man brought the men into J house.	3130
	43:18 because they were brought into J house;	3130
	43:19 they came near to the steward of J house,	3130
	43:24 the man brought the men into J house;	3130
	44:14 and his brethren came to J house;	3130
	45:16 saying, J brethren are come:	3130
	48: 8 Israel beheld J sons, and said, Who *are*	3130
	50:15 when J brethren saw that their father was	3130
	50:23 Manasseh were brought up upon J knees.	3130
1Ch	5: 2 the chief ruler; but the birthright *was* J:)	3130
Lk	4:22 mouth. And they said, Is not this J son?	2501
Ac	7:13 J kindred was made known unto Pharaoh.	2501

JOSES (6) [BARNABAS, JOSEPH]

Mt	13:55 and his brethren, James, and J,	2500
	27:56 and Mary the mother of James and J,	2500
Mk	6: 3 of James, and J, and of Juda, and Simon?	2500
	15:40 the mother of James the less and of J,	2500
	15:47 Mary *the mother* of J beheld where he	2500
Ac	4:36 J, who by the apostles was surnamed	2500

JOSHAH (1)

1Ch	4:34 and Jamlech, and J the son of Amaziah,	3144

JOSHAPHAT (1)

1Ch	11:43 the son of Maachah, and J the Mithnite,	3146

JOSHAVIAH (1)

1Ch	11:46 Eliel the Mahavite, and Jeribai, and J,	3145

JOSHBEKASHAH (2)

1Ch	25: 4 J, Mallothi, Hothir, *and* Mahazioth:	3436
	25:24 The seventeenth to J, *he*, his sons,	3436

JOSHIBIAH See JOSIBIAH

JOSHUA (216) [HOSHEA, JEHOSHUA, JESHUA, OSHEA]

Ex	17: 9 Moses said unto J, Choose us out men,	3091
	17:10 So J did as Moses had said to him,	3091
	17:13 discomfited Amalek and his people with	3091
	17:14 in a book, and rehearse *it* in the ears of J:	3091
	24:13 Moses rose up, and his minister J:	3091
	32:17 when J heard the noise of the people as	3091
	33:11 servant J, the son of Nun, a young man,	3091
Nu	11:28 the son of Nun, the servant of Moses,	3091
	14: 6 J the son of Nun, and Caleb the son of	3091
	14:30 son of Jephunneh, and J the son of Nun.	3091
	14:38 the son of Nun, and Caleb the son of	3091
	26:65 son of Jephunneh, and J the son of Nun.	3091
	27:18 Take thee J the son of Nun, a man in	3091
	27:22 he took J, and set him before Eleazar	3091
	32:12 the Kenezite, and J the son of Nun:	3091
	32:28 the son of Nun, and the chief fathers of	3091
	34:17 Eleazar the priest, and J the son of Nun.	3091
Dt	1:38 *But* J the son of Nun, which standeth	3091
	3:21 I commanded J at that time, saying,	3091
	3:28 charge J, and encourage him,	3091
	31: 3 *and* J, he shall go over before thee,	3091
	31: 7 Moses called unto J, and said unto him in	3091
	31:14 call J, and present yourselves in	3091
	31:14 Moses and J went,	3091
	31:23 And he gave J the son of Nun a charge,	3091
	34: 9 the son of Nun was full *of* the spirit of	3091
Jos	1: 1 that the Lord spake unto J the son of	3091
	1:10 J commanded the officers of the people,	3091
	1:12 the tribe of Manasseh, spake J, saying,	3091
	1:16 they answered J, saying, All that thou	3091
	2: 1 J the son of Nun sent out of Shittim two	3091
	2:23 came to J the son of Nun, and told him	3091
	2:24 they said unto J, Truly the Lord hath	3091
	3: 1 J rose early in the morning;	3091
	3: 5 J said unto the people, Sanctify yourselves	3091
	3: 6 J spake unto the priests, saying, Take up	3091
	3: 7 the Lord said unto J, This day will I	3091
	3: 9 J said unto the children of Israel,	3091
	3:10 J said, Hereby ye shall know that the	3091
	4: 1 that the Lord spake unto J, saying,	3091
	4: 4 J called the twelve men, whom he had	3091
	4: 5 J said unto them, Pass over before the ark	3091
	4: 8 children of Israel did so as J commanded,	3091
	4: 8 of Jordan, as the Lord spake unto J,	3091
	4: 9 J set up twelve stones in the midst of	3091
	4:10 commanded to speak unto the people,	3091
	4:10 according to all that Moses commanded J:	3091
	4:14 On that day the Lord magnified J in	3091
	4:15 And the Lord spake unto J, saying,	3091
	4:17 J therefore commanded the priests,	3091
	4:20 took out of Jordan, did J pitch in Gilgal.	3091
	5: 2 At that time the Lord said unto J,	3091
	5: 3 J made him sharp knives,	3091
	5: 4 this *is* the cause why J did circumcise:	3091
	5: 7 up in their stead, them J circumcised:	3091
	5: 9 the Lord said unto J, This day have I	3091
	5:13 it came to pass, when J was by Jericho,	3091
	5:13 went unto him, and said unto him,	3091
	5:14 J fell on his face to the earth,	3091
	5:15 captain of the Lord's host said unto J,	3091
	5:15 thou standest *is* holy. And J did so.	3091
	6: 2 the Lord said unto J, See, I have given	3091
	6: 6 And J the son of Nun called the priests,	3091
	6: 8 when J had spoken unto the people,	3091
	6:10 J had commanded the people, saying,	3091
	6:12 J rose early in the morning, and the	3091

Jos	6:16 trumpets, J said unto the people, Shout;	3091
	6:22 J said unto the two men that had	3091
	6:25 J saved Rahab the harlot alive, and her	3091
	6:25 which J sent to spy out Jericho.	3091
	6:26 J adjured *them* at that time, saying,	3091
	6:27 So the Lord was with J; and his fame	3091
	7: 2 J sent men from Jericho *to* Ai, which *is*	3091
	7: 3 they returned to J, and said unto him,	3091
	7: 6 J rent his clothes, and fell to the earth	3091
	7: 7 J said, Alas, O Lord God, wherefore hast	3091
	7:10 the Lord said unto J, Get thee up;	3091
	7:16 So J rose up early in the morning,	3091
	7:19 J said unto Achan, My son, give, I pray	3091
	7:20 Achan answered J, and said, Indeed I	3091
	7:22 So J sent messengers, and they ran unto	3091
	7:23 brought them unto J, and unto all	3091
	7:24 J, and all Israel with him, took Achan	3091
	7:25 J said, Why hast thou troubled us?	3091
	8: 1 the Lord said unto J, Fear not,	3091
	8: 3 J arose, and all the people of war, to go	3091
	8: 3 J chose out thirty thousand mighty *men*	3091
	8: 9 J therefore sent them forth: and they	3091
	8: 9 but J lodged that night among the people.	3091
	8:10 J rose up early in the morning,	3091
	8:13 J went that night into the midst of	3091
	8:15 J and all Israel *made as if they* were	3091
	8:16 pursued after J, and were drawn away	3091
	8:18 the Lord said unto J, Stretch out	3091
	8:18 J stretched out the spear that he *had* in	3091
	8:21 when J and all Israel saw that the ambush	3091
	8:23 Ai they took alive, and brought him to J.	3091
	8:26 For J drew not his hand back, wherewith	3091
	8:27 of the Lord which he commanded J.	3091
	8:28 J burnt Ai, and made it a heap for ever,	3091
	8:29 J commanded that they should take his	3091
	8:30 J built an altar unto the Lord God of	3091
	8:35 which J read not before all	3091
	9: 2 to fight with J and with Israel, *with* one	3091
	9: 3 heard what J had done unto Jericho	3091
	9: 6 they went to J unto the camp *at* Gilgal,	3091
	9: 8 they said unto J, We *are* thy servants.	3091
	9: 8 J said unto them, Who *are* ye?	3091
	9:15 J made peace with them, and made a	3091
	9:22 J called for them, and he spake unto	3091
	9:24 they answered J, and said, Because it was	3091
	9:27 J made them that day hewers of wood	3091
	10: 1 Jerusalem had heard how J had taken Ai,	3091
	10: 4 for it hath made peace with J and with	3091
	10: 6 men of Gibeon sent unto J to the camp	3091
	10: 7 So J ascended from Gilgal, he, and all	3091
	10: 8 the Lord said unto J, Fear them not:	3091
	10: 9 J therefore came unto them suddenly,	3091
	10:12 spake J to the Lord in the day when	3091
	10:15 J returned, and all Israel with him, unto	3091
	10:17 it was told J, saying, The five kings are	3091
	10:18 J said, Roll great stones upon the mouth	3091
	10:20 J and the children of Israel had made	3091
	10:21 all the people returned to the camp to J	3091
	10:22 said J, Open the mouth of the cave,	3091
	10:24 they brought out those kings unto J,	3091
	10:24 that J called for all the men of Israel,	3091
	10:25 J said unto them, Fear not, nor be	3091
	10:26 afterward J smote them, and slew them,	3091
	10:27 *that* J commanded, and they took them	3091
	10:28 that day J took Makkedah, and smote it	3091
	10:29 J passed from Makkedah, and all Israel	3091
	10:31 J passed from Libnah, and all Israel with	3091
	10:33 J smote him and his people, until *he* had	3091
	10:34 from Lachish J passed unto Eglon,	3091
	10:36 J went up from Eglon, and all Israel with	3091
	10:38 J returned, and all Israel with him,	3091
	10:40 So J smote all the country of the hills,	3091
	10:41 J smote them from Kadesh-barnea even	3091
	10:42 and their land did J take at one time,	3091
	10:43 J returned, and all Israel with him, unto	3091
	11: 6 the Lord said unto J, Be not afraid	3091
	11: 7 So J came, and all the people of war with	3091
	11: 9 J did unto them as the Lord bade him:	3091
	11:10 J at that time turned back, and took	3091
	11:12 J take, and smote them with the edge of	3091
	11:13 of them, save Hazor only; *that* did J burn.	3091
	11:15 so did Moses command J, and so	3091
	11:15 did Moses command Joshua, and so did J;	3091
	11:16 So J took all that land, the hills, and all	3091
	11:18 J made war a long time with all those	3091
	11:21 at that time came J, and cut off	3091
	11:21 J destroyed them utterly with their cities.	3091
	11:23 So J took the whole land, according to all	3091
	11:23 J gave it for an inheritance unto Israel	3091
	12: 7 these *are* the kings of the country which J	3091
	12: 7 which J gave unto the tribes of Israel *for* a	3091
	13: 1 Now J was old *and* stricken in years;	3091
	14: 1 J the son of Nun, and the heads of	3091
	14: 6 the children of Judah came unto J in	3091
	14:13 J blessed him, and gave unto Caleb the	3091
	17: 4 to the commandment of the Lord to J,	3091
	17:14 children of Joseph spake unto J, saying,	3091
	17:15 J answered them, If thou *be* a great	3091
	17:17 J spake unto the house of Joseph, *even* to	3091
	18: 3 J said unto the children of Israel, How	3091
	18: 8 J charged them that went to describe	3091
	18: 9 and came again to J to the host at Shiloh.	3091
	18:10 J cast lots for them in Shiloh before	3091
	18:10 J divided the land unto the children of	3091

Jos	19:49 to J the son of Nun among them:	3091
	19:51 J the son of Nun, and the heads of	3091
	20: 1 The Lord also spake unto J, saying,	3091
	21: 1 J the son of Nun, and unto the heads	3091
	22: 1 J called the Reubenites, and the Gadites,	3091
	22: 6 So J blessed them, and sent them away:	3091
	22: 7 unto the *other* half thereof gave J among	3091
	22: 7 when J sent them away also unto their	3091
	23: 1 that J waxed old *and* stricken in age.	3091
	23: 2 J called for all Israel, *and* for their elders,	3091
	24: 1 J gathered all the tribes of Israel to	3091
	24: 2 J said unto all the people, Thus saith	3091
	24:19 J said unto the people, Ye cannot serve	3091
	24:21 the people said unto J, Nay; but we will	3091
	24:22 J said unto the people, Ye *are* witnesses	3091
	24:24 the people said unto J, The Lord our	3091
	24:25 J made a covenant with the people that	3091
	24:26 J wrote these words in the book of the	3091
	24:27 J said unto all the people, Behold, this	3091
	24:28 So J let the people depart, every man unto	3091
	24:29 that J the son of Nun, the servant of	3091
	24:31 Israel served the Lord all the days of J,	3091
	24:31 all the days of the elders that overlived J,	3091
Jdg	1: 1 Now after the death of J it came to pass,	3091
	2: 6 when J had let the people go, the children	3091
	2: 7 people served the Lord all the days of J,	3091
	2: 7 all the days of the elders that outlived J,	3091
	2: 8 J the son of Nun, the servant of	3091
	2:21 of the nations which J left when he died:	3091
	2:23 delivered he them into the hand of J.	3091
1Sa	6:14 the cart came into the field of J,	3091
	6:18 *remaineth* unto this day in the field of J,	3091
1Ki	16:34 which he spake by the son of Nun.	3091
2Ki	23: 8 of the gate of J the governor of the city,	3091
Hag	1: 1 to J the son of Josedech the high priest,	3091
	1:12 the son of Josedech the high priest,	3091
	1:14 the spirit of J the son of Josedech the high	3091
	2: 2 J the son of Josedech the high priest and	3091
	2: 4 be strong, O J, son of Josedech, the high	3091
Zec	3: 1 he shewed me J the high priest standing	3091
	3: 3 Now J was clothed with filthy garments,	3091
	3: 6 the angel of the Lord protested unto J,	3091
	3: 8 O J the high priest, thou, and thy fellows	3091
	3: 9 behold the stone that I have laid before J;	3091
	6:11 set *them* upon the head of J the son of	3091

JOSIAH (53) [JOSIAS]

1Ki	13: 2 born unto the house of David, J by name;	2977
2Ki	21:24 people of the land made J his son king	2977
	21:26 Uzza: and J his son reigned in his stead.	2977
	22: 1 J *was* eight years old when he *began* to	2977
	22: 3 to pass in the eighteenth year of king J,	2977
	23:16 J turned himself, he spied the sepulchres	2977
	23:19 J took away, and did to them according to	2977
	23:23 in the eighteenth year of king J,	2977
	23:24 Judah and in Jerusalem, did J put away,	2977
	23:28 the rest of the acts of J, and all that he	2977
	23:29 king J went against him; and he slew him	2977
	23:30 of the land took Jehoahaz the son of J,	2977
	23:34 made Eliakim the son of J	2977
	23:34 of Josiah king in the room of J his father,	2977
1Ch	3:14 Amon his son, J his son.	2977
	3:15 the sons of J *were*, the firstborn Johanan,	2977
2Ch	33:25 people of the land made J his son king	2977
	34: 1 J *was* eight years old when he *began* to	2977
	34:33 J took away all the abominations out of	2977
	35: 1 Moreover J kept a passover unto	2977
	35: 7 J gave to the people, *of* the flock, lambs	2977
	35:16 according to the commandment of king J.	2977
	35:18 of Israel keep such a passover as J kept,	2977
	35:19 In the eighteenth year of the reign of J	2977
	35:20 all this, when J had prepared the temple,	2977
	35:20 by Euphrates: and J went out against him.	2977
	35:22 Nevertheless J would not turn his face	2977
	35:23 archers shot at king J; and the king said	2977
	35:24 all Judah and Jerusalem mourned for J.	2977
	35:25 Jeremiah lamented for J: and all the	2977
	35:25 the singing *women* spake of J in their	2977
	35:26 Now the rest of the acts of J,	2977
	36: 1 of the land took Jehoahaz the son of J,	2977
Jer	1: 2 days of J the son of Amon king of Judah,	2977
	1: 3 of Jehoiakim the son of J king of Judah,	2977
	1: 3 of Zedekiah the son of J king of Judah,	2977
	3: 6 also unto me in the days of J the king,	2977
	22:11 Shallum the son of J king of Judah,	2977
	22:11 which reigned instead of J his father,	2977
	22:18 Jehoiakim the son of J king of Judah;	2977
	25: 1 of Jehoiakim the son of J king of Judah,	2977
	25: 3 From the thirteenth year of J the son of	2977
	26: 1 J king of Judah came this word from	2977
	27: 1 J king of Judah came this word unto	2977
	35: 1 of Jehoiakim the son of J king of Judah,	2977
	36: 1 of Jehoiakim the son of J king of Judah,	2977
	36: 2 from the days of J, even unto this day.	2977
	36: 9 of Jehoiakim the son of J king of Judah,	2977
	37: 1 Zedekiah the son of J reigned instead	2977
	45: 1 the fourth year of Jehoiakim the son of J	2977
	46: 2 of Jehoiakim the son of J king of Judah.	2977
Zep	1: 1 in the days of J the son of Amon, king of	2977
Zec	6:10 go *into* the house of J the son of	2977

JOSIAS (2) [JOSIAH]

Mt	1:10 Manasses begat Amon; and Amon begat J;	2502
	1:11 And J begat Jechonias and his brethren,	2502

JOSIBIAH (1)
1Ch	4:35 Joel, and Jehu the son of J, the son of	3143

JOSIPHIAH (1)
Ezr	8:10 the son of J, and with him an hundred	3131

JOT (1)
Mt	5:18 one j or one tittle shall in no wise pass	2503

JOTBAH (1)
2Ki	21:19 the daughter of Haruz of J.	3192

JOTBATH (1) [JOTBATHAH]
Dt	10: 7 from Gudgodah to J, a land of rivers of	3193

JOTBATHAH (2) [JOTBATH]
Nu	33:33 went from Hor-hagidgad, and pitched in J.	3193
	33:34 they removed from J, and encamped at	3193

JOTHAM (24)
Jdg	9: 5 notwithstanding yet J the youngest son of	3147
	9: 7 when they told it to J, he went and stood	3147
	9:21 ran away, and fled, and went to Beer,	3147
	9:57 upon them came the curse of J the son of	3147
2Ki	15: 5 the king's son was over the house,	3147
	15: 7 David: and J his son reigned in his stead.	3147
	15:30 the twentieth year of J the son of Uzziah.	3147
	15:32 The son of Uzziah king of Judah to reign.	3147
	15:36 the rest of the acts of J, and all that he	3147
	15:38 slept with his fathers, and was buried	3147
	16: 1 the son of J king of Judah began to reign.	3147
1Ch	2:47 J, and Geshan, and Pelet, and Ephah,	3147
	3:12 his son, Azariah his son, J his son,	3147
	5:17 genealogies in the days of J king of Judah,	3147
2Ch	26:21 his son was over the king's house,	3147
	26:23 a leper: and J his son reigned in his stead.	3147
	27: 1 J was twenty and five years old when he	3147
	27: 6 So J became mighty, because he prepared	3147
	27: 7 Now the rest of the acts of J, and all his	3147
	27: 9 J slept with his fathers, and they buried	3147
Isa	1: 1 J, Ahaz, and Hezekiah, kings of Judah.	3147
	7: 1 to pass in the days of Ahaz the son of J,	3147
Hos	1: 1 J, Ahaz, and Hezekiah, kings of Judah.	3147
Mic	1: 1 to Micah the Morasthite in the days of J,	3147

JOURNEY (60) [JOURNEYED, JOURNEYING, JOURNEYINGS, JOURNEYS]
Ge	24:21 to wit whether the LORD had made his j	1870
	29: 1 Jacob went on his j, and came into	5375+7272
	30:36 he set three days' j betwixt himself and	1870
	31:23 and pursued after him seven days' j;	1870
	33:12 Let us take our j, and let us go, and I will	5265
	46: 1 Israel took his j with all that he had,	5265
Ex	3:18 three days' j into the wilderness,	1870
	5: 3 three days' j into the desert,	1870
	8:27 We will go three days' j into	1870
	13:20 they took their j from Succoth,	5265
	16: 1 they took their j from Elim, and all	5265
Nu	9:10 or be in a j afar off, yet he shall keep	1870
	9:13 is not in a j, and forbeareth to keep	1870
	10: 6 lie on the south side shall take their j:	5265
	10:13 they first took their j according to	5265
	10:33 the mount of the LORD three days' j:	1870
	10:33 went before them in the three days' j,	1870
	11:31 as it were a day's j on this side, and as it	1870
	11:31 as it were a day's j on the other side,	1870
	33: 8 went three days' j in the wilderness of	1870
	33:12 they took their j out of the wilderness of	5265
Dt	1: 2 (There are eleven days' j from Horeb by	NIH
	1: 7 take your j, and go to the mount of	1870
	1:40 take your j into the wilderness by the way	5265
	2: 1 took our j into the wilderness by the way	5265
	2:24 take your j, and pass over the river Arnon	5265
	10: 6 the children of Israel took their j from	5265
	10:11 Arise, take thy j before the people,	4550
Jos	9:11 Take victuals with you for the j, and go to	1870
	9:13 become old by reason of the very long j.	1870
Jdg	4: 9 notwithstanding the j that thou takest	1870
1Sa	15:18 the LORD sent thee on a j, and said,	1870
2Sa	11:10 unto Uriah, Camest thou not from thy j?	1870
1Ki	18:27 he is in a j, or peradventure he sleepeth,	1870
	19: 4 he himself went a day's j into	1870
	19: 7 eat; because the j is too great for thee.	1870
2Ki	3: 9 they fetcht a compass of seven days' j:	1870
2Ch	1:13 Solomon came from his j to the high	NIH
Ne	2: 6 (and, For how long shall thy j be?	4109
Pr	7:19 is not at home, he is gone a long j:	1870
Jnh	3: 3 an exceeding great city of three days' j.	4109
	3: 4 began to enter into the city a day's j,	4109
Mt	10:10 Nor scrip for your j, neither two coats,	3598
	25:15 ability; and straightway took his j.	589
Mk	6: 8 that they should take nothing for their j,	3598
	13:34 Son of man is as a man taking a far j,	590
Lk	2:44 been in the company, went a day's j;	3598
	9: 3 Take nothing for your j, neither staves,	3598
	11: 6 a friend of mine in his j is come to me,	3598
	15:13 and took his j into a far country,	3597
Jn	4: 6 Jesus therefore, being wearied with his j,	3597
Ac	1:12 a sabbath day's j.	2192+3598+4521
	10: 9 they went on their j, and drew nigh unto	3596
	22: 6 as I made my j, and was come nigh unto	4198
Ro	1:10 have a prosperous j by the will of God	2137
	15:24 Whensoever I take my j into Spain, I will	4198
	15:24 for I trust to see you in my j, and to be	1279
1Co	16: 6 that ye may bring me on my j	4311

Tit	3:13 Bring Zenas the lawyer and Apollos on their j	4311
3Jn	1: 6 whom if thou bring forward on their j	4311

JOURNEYED (33) [JOURNEY]
Ge	11: 2 it came to pass, as they j from the east,	5265
	12: 9 Abram j, going on still toward the south.	5265
	13:11 him all the plain of Jordan; and Lot j east:	5265
	20: 1 Abraham j from thence toward the south	5265
	33:17 Jacob j to Succoth, and built him a house,	5265
	35: 5 they j: and the terror of God was upon	5265
	35:16 they j from Beth-el; and there was but	5265
	35:21 Israel j, and spread his tent beyond	5265
Ex	12:37 the children of Israel j from Rameses to	5265
	17: 1 of Israel j from the wilderness of Sin,	5265
	40:37 they j not till the day that it was taken up.	5265
Nu	9:17 then after that the children of Israel j:	5265
	9:18 of the LORD the children of Israel j,	5265
	9:19 kept the charge of the LORD, and j not.	5265
	9:20 to the commandment of the LORD they j.	5265
	9:21 was taken up in the morning, then they j:	5265
	9:21 night that the cloud was taken up, they j.	5265
	9:22 of Israel abode in their tents, and j not:	5265
	9:22 but when it was taken up, they j.	5265
	9:23 at the commandment of the LORD they j:	5265
	11:35 And the people j from Kibroth-hattaavah	5265
	12:15 the people j not till Miriam was brought	5265
	20:22 j from Kadesh, and came unto mount	5265
	21: 4 they j from mount Hor by the way of	5265
	21:11 they j from Oboth, and pitched at	5265
	33:22 they j from Rissah, and pitched in	5265
Dt	10: 7 From thence they j unto Gudgodah;	5265
Jos	9:17 the children of Israel j, and came unto	5265
Jdg	17: 8 to the house of Micah, as he j.	1870+6213
Lk	10:33 as he j, came where he was:	3593
Ac	9: 3 he j, he came near Damascus:	4198
	9: 7 And the men which j with him stood	4922
	26:13 about me and them which j with me.	4198

JOURNEYING (3) [JOURNEY]
Nu	10: 2 the assembly, and for the j of the camps.	4550
	10:29 We are j unto the place of which	5265
Lk	13:22 teaching, and j towards Jerusalem.	4160+4197

JOURNEYINGS (2) [JOURNEY]
Nu	10:28 Thus were the j of the children of Israel	4550
2Co	11:26 In j often, in perils of waters, in perils of	3597

JOURNEYS (9) [JOURNEY]
Ge	13: 3 he went on his j from the south even to	4550
Ex	17: 1 after their j, according to	4550
	40:36 of Israel went onward in all their j:	4550
	40:38 the house of Israel, throughout all their j.	4550
Nu	10: 6 they shall blow an alarm for their j.	4550
	10:12 the children of Israel took their j out of	4550
	33: 1 These are the j of the children of Israel,	4550
	33: 2 j by the commandment of the LORD:	4550
	33: 2 these are their j according to their goings	4550

JOY (165) [JOYED, JOYFUL, JOYFULLY, JOYFULNESS, JOYING, JOYOUS]
1Sa	18: 6 with j, and with instruments of musick.	8057
1Ki	1:40 rejoiced with great j, so that the earth	8057
1Ch	12:40 abundantly: for there was j in Israel.	8057
	15:16 sounding, by lifting up the voice with j.	8057
	15:25 out of the house of Obed-edom with j.	8057
	29: 9 David the king also rejoiced with great j.	8057
	29:17 and now have I seen with j thy people,	8057
2Ch	20:27 them, to go again to Jerusalem with j;	8057
	30:26 there was great j in Jerusalem: for since	8057
Ezr	3:12 loud voice; and many shouted aloud for j:	8057
	3:13 j from the noise of the weeping of	8057
	6:16 dedication of this house of God with j,	2305
	6:22 of unleavened bread seven days with j:	8057
Ne	8:10 for the j of the LORD is your strength.	2304
	12:43 God had made them rejoice with great j:	8057
	12:43 the j of Jerusalem was heard even afar	8057
Est	8:16 light, and gladness, and j, and honour.	8342
	8:17 the Jews had j and gladness, a feast and	8057
	9:22 was turned unto them from sorrow to j,	8057
	9:22 should make them days of feasting and j,	8057
Job	8:19 is the j of his way, and out of the earth	4885
	20: 5 the j of the hypocrite but for a moment?	4885
	29:13 I caused the widow's heart to sing for j.	7442
	33:26 he shall see his face with j: for he will	8643
	38: 7 and all the sons of God shouted for j?	7321
	41:22 and sorrow is turned into j before him.	1750
Ps	5:11 let them ever shout for j, because	7442
	16:11 in thy presence is fulness of j; at thy right	8057
	21: 1 The king shall j in thy strength, O LORD;	8055
	27: 6 will I offer in his tabernacle sacrifices of j;	8643
	30: 5 for a night, but j cometh in the morning.	7440
	32:11 shout for j, all ye that are upright in	7442
	35:27 Let them shout for j, and be glad,	7440
	42: 4 with the voice of j and praise, with a	1524
	43: 4 altar of God, unto God my exceeding j:	8057
	48: 2 the j of the whole earth, is mount Zion,	4885
	51: 8 Make me to hear j and gladness; that	8342
	51:12 Restore unto me the j of thy salvation;	8342
	65:13 corn; they shout for j, they also sing.	7321
	67: 4 O let the nations be glad and sing for j:	7442
	105:43 he brought forth his people with j,	8342
	126: 5 They that sow in tears shall reap in j.	7440
	132: 9 and let thy saints shout for j.	7442
	132:16 her saints shall shout aloud for j.	7442+7444

Ps	137: 6 if I prefer not Jerusalem above my chief j.	8057
Pr	12:20 but to the counsellers of peace is j.	8057
	14:10 stranger doth not intermeddle with his j.	8057
	15:21 Folly is j to him that is destitute of	8057
	15:23 man hath j by the answer of his mouth:	8057
	17:21 and the father of a fool hath no j.	8055
	21:15 It is j to the just to do judgment:	8057
	23:24 that begetteth a wise child shall have j	8055
Ecc	2:10 I withheld not my heart from any j;	8057
	2:26 his sight wisdom, and knowledge, and j:	8057
	5:20 God answereth him in the j of his heart.	8057
	9: 7 Go thy way, eat thy bread with j,	8057
Isa	9: 3 the nation, and not increased the j:	8057
	9: 3 they j before thee according to the joy in	8055
	9: 3 they joy before thee according to the j in	8057
	9:17 Therefore the Lord shall have no j in their	8055
	12: 3 Therefore with j shall ye draw water out	8342
	16:10 away, and j out of the plentiful field;	1524
	22:13 behold and gladness, slaying oxen,	8342
	24: 8 rejoice endeth, the j of the harp ceaseth.	4885
	24:11 all j is darkened, the mirth of the land is	8057
	29:19 The meek also shall increase their j in	8057
	32:13 upon all the houses of j in the joyous city;	4885
	32:14 a joy of wild asses, a pasture of flocks;	4885
	35: 2 rejoice even with j and singing:	1525
	35:10 and everlasting j upon their heads:	8057
	35:10 shall obtain j and gladness, and sorrow	8342
	51: 3 j and gladness shall be found therein,	8342
	51:11 and everlasting j shall be upon their head:	8057
	51:11 shall obtain gladness and j; and sorrow	8057
	52: 9 Break forth into j, sing together, ye waste	7442
	55:12 For ye shall go out with j, and be led forth	8057
	60:15 excellency, a j of many generations.	4885
	61: 3 beauty for ashes, the oil of j for mourning,	8342
	61: 7 double: everlasting j shall be unto them.	8057
	65:14 my servants shall sing for j of heart,	2898
	65:18 Jerusalem a rejoicing, and her people a j.	4885
	65:19 rejoice in Jerusalem, and j in my people:	7797
	66: 5 he shall appear to your j, and they shall	8057
	66:10 rejoice for j with her, all ye that mourn for	4885
Jer	15:16 thy word was unto me the j and rejoicing	8342
	31:13 for I will turn their mourning into j,	8342
	33: 9 it shall be to me a name of joy, a praise and	8342
	33:11 The voice of j, and the voice of gladness,	8342
	48:27 spakest of him, thou skippedst for j.	5110
	48:33 and gladness is taken from the plentiful	8057
	49:25 the city of praise not left, the city of my j!	4885
La	2:15 of beauty, The j of the whole earth?	4885
	5:15 The j of our heart is ceased; our dance is	4885
Eze	24:25 j of their glory, the desire of their eyes,	4885
	36: 5 possession with the j of all their heart,	8057
Hos	9: 1 Rejoice not, O Israel, for j, as other people	1524
Joel	1:12 j is withered away from the sons of men.	8342
	1:16 yea, j and gladness from the house of our	8057
Hab	3:18 I will j in the God of my salvation.	1523
Zep	3:17 will save, he will rejoice over thee with j;	8057
	3:17 his love, he will j over thee with singing.	1523
Zec	8:19 shall be to the house of Judah and	8342
Mt	2:10 they rejoiced with exceeding great j.	5479
	13:20 the word, and anon with j receiveth it;	5479
	13:44 and for j thereof goeth and selleth all that	5479
	25:21 things: enter thou into the j of thy lord.	5479
	25:23 things: enter thou into the j of thy lord.	5479
	28: 8 from the sepulchre with fear and great j;	5479
Lk	1:14 And thou shalt have j and gladness;	5479
	1:44 ears, the babe leaped in my womb for j.	20
	2:10 I bring you good tidings of great j,	5479
	6:23 ye in that day, and leap for j: for behold,	NIG
	8:13 when they hear, receive the word with j;	5479
	10:17 And the seventy returned again with j,	5479
	15: 7 that likewise j shall be in heaven over one	5479
	15:10 there is j in the presence of the angels of	5479
	24:41 And while they yet believed not for j,	5479
	24:52 and returned to Jerusalem with great j:	5479
Jn	3:29 this my j therefore is fulfilled.	5479
	15:11 that my j might remain in you,	5479
	15:11 in you, and that your j might be full.	5479
	16:20 but your sorrow shall be turned into j.	5479
	16:21 for j that a man is born into the world.	5479
	16:22 and your j no man taketh from you.	5479
	16:24 ye shall receive, that your j may be full.	5479
	17:13 that they might have my j fulfilled in	5479
Ac	2:28 thou shalt make me full of j with thy	2167
	8: 8 And there was great j in that city.	5479
	13:52 And the disciples were filled with j,	5479
	15: 3 they caused great j unto all the brethren.	5479
	20:24 so that I might finish my course with j,	5479
Ro	5:11 we also j in God through our Lord Jesus	2744
	14:17 and peace, and j in the Holy Ghost.	5479
	15:13 Now the God of hope fill you with all j	5479
	15:32 That I may come unto you with j by	5479
2Co	1:24 over your faith, but are helpers of your j:	5479
	2: 3 in you all, that my j is the joy of you all.	5479
	2: 3 in you all, that my joy is the j of you all.	NIG
	7:13 exceedingly the more joyed we for the j of	5479
	8: 2 trial of affliction the abundance of their j	5479
Gal	5:22 j, peace, longsuffering, gentleness,	5479
Php	1: 4 of mine for you all making request with j,	5479
	1:25 you all for your furtherance and j of faith;	5479
	2: 2 Fulfil ye my j, that ye be likeminded,	5479
	2:17 of your faith, I j, and rejoice with you all.	5463
	2:18 For the same cause also do ye j,	5463
	4: 1 my j and crown, so stand fast in the Lord,	5479
1Th	1: 6 much affliction, with j of the Holy Ghost:	5479
	2:19 is our hope, or j, or crown of rejoicing?	5479

J

1Th 2:20 For ye are our glory and **j**. — 5479
 3: 9 for all the **j** wherewith we joy for your — 5479
 3: 9 for all the joy wherewith we **j** for your — 5463
2Ti 1: 4 of thy tears, that I may be filled with **j**; — 5479
Phm 1: 7 For we have great **j** and consolation in thy — 5479
 1:20 brother, let me have **j** of thee in the Lord: — 3685
Heb 12: 2 who for the **j** that was set before him — 5479
 13:17 that they may do it with **j**, and not with — 5479
Jas 1: 2 count *it* all **j** when ye fall into divers — 5479
 4: 9 to mourning, and *your* **j** to heaviness. — 5479
1Pe 1: 8 ye rejoice with **j** unspeakable and full of — 5479
 4:13 ye may be glad also with **exceeding j**. — 21
1Jn 1: 4 we unto you, that your **j** may be full. — 5479
2Jn 1:12 speak face to face, that our **j** may be full. — 5479
3Jn 1: 4 I have no greater **j** than to hear that my — 5479
Jude 1:24 presence of his glory with **exceeding j**, — 20

JOYED (1) [JOY]
2Co 7:13 exceedingly the more **j** we for the joy of — 5463

JOYFUL (25) [JOY]
1Ki 8:66 went unto their tents **j** and glad of heart — 8056
Ezr 6:22 for the LORD had **made** them **j**, — 8055
Est 5: 9 went Haman forth that day **j** and with a — 8056
Job 3: 7 be solitary, let no **j voice** come therein. — 7445
Ps 5:11 let them also that love thy name be **j** in — 5970
 35: 9 my soul shall be **j** in the LORD: it shall — 1523
 63: 5 my mouth shall praise *thee with* **j** lips: — 7445
 66: 1 **Make a j noise** unto God, all ye lands: — 7321
 81: 1 **make a j noise** unto the God of Jacob. — 7321
 89:15 *is* the people that know the **j sound**: — 8643
 95: 1 let us **make a j noise** to the rock of our — 7321
 95: 2 **make a j noise** unto him with psalms. — 7321
 96:12 Let the field be **j**, and all that *is* therein: — 5937
 98: 4 **Make a j noise** unto the LORD, — 7321
 98: 6 sound of cornet **make a j noise** before — 7321
 98: 8 clap *their* hands: let the hills be **j** together — 7442
 100: 1 **Make a j noise** unto the LORD, all ye — 7321
 113: 9 keep house, *to be* a **j** mother of children. — 8056
 149: 2 let the children of Zion be **j** in their King. — 1523
 149: 5 Let the saints be **j** in glory: let them sing — 5937
Ecc 7:14 In the day of prosperity be **j**, but in the — 2896
Isa 49:13 be **j**, O earth; and break forth *into* singing, — 1523
 56: 7 and **make** them **j** in my house of prayer: — 8055
 61:10 the LORD, my soul shall be **j** in my God; — 1523
2Co 7: 4 I am **exceeding j** in all our tribulation. — 5479

JOYFULLY (3) [JOY]
Ecc 9: 9 Live **j** with the wife whom thou lovest all — 7200
Lk 19: 6 and came down, and received him **j**. — 5463
Heb 10:34 took **j** the spoiling of your goods, — 3326+5479

JOYFULNESS (2) [JOY]
Dt 28:47 servedst not the LORD thy God with **j**, — 8057
Col 1:11 unto all patience and longsuffering with **j**; — 5479

JOYING (1) [JOY]
Col 2: 5 and beholding your order, — 5463

JOYOUS (4) [JOY]
Isa 22: 2 *art* full *of* stirs, a tumultuous city, a **j** city: — 5947
 23: 7 *Is* this your **j** *city*, whose antiquity *is* of — 5947
 32:13 upon all the houses of joy in the **j** city: — 5947
Heb 12:11 chastening for the present seemeth to be **j**, — 5479

JOZABAD (9)
1Ch 12:20 **J**, and Jediael, and Michael, and Jozabad, — 3107
 12:20 Michael, and **J**, and Elihu, and Zilthai, — 3107
2Ch 17: 8 and Eliel, and Ismachiah, and Mahath, — 3107
 35: 9 and Hashabiah and Jeiel and **J**, — 3107
Ezr 8:33 with them *was* **J** the son of Jeshua, — 3107
 10:22 Ishmael, Nethaneel, **J**, and Elasah. — 3107
 10:23 and Shimei, and Kelaiah, (the same *is* — 3107
Ne 8: 7 **J**, Hanan, Pelaiah, and the Levites, — 3107
 11:16 Shabbethai and **J**, of the chief of — 3107

JOZACHAR (1)
2Ki 12:21 For **J** the son of Shimeath, — 3108

JOZADAK (5)
Ezr 3: 2 stood up Jeshua the son of **J**, — 3136
 3: 8 Jeshua the son of **J**, and the remnant of — 3136
 5: 2 Jeshua the son of **J**, and began to build — 3136
 10:18 *namely*, of the sons of Jeshua the son of **J**, — 3136
Ne 12:26 the son of **J**, and in the days of Nehemiah — 3136

JUBAL (1)
Ge 4:21 brother's name *was* **J**: he was the father — 3106

JUBILE (22)
Lev 25: 9 shalt thou cause the trumpet of the **j** to — 8643
 25:10 shall be a **j** unto you; and ye shall return — 3104
 25:11 A **j** shall that fiftieth year be unto you: — 3104
 25:12 For it *is* the **j**; it shall be holy unto you: — 3104
 25:13 In the year of this **j** ye shall return every — 3104
 25:15 to the number of years after the **j** — 3104
 25:28 him that hath bought it until the year of **j**: — 3104
 25:28 in the **j** it shall go out, and he shall return — 3104
 25:30 his generations: it shall not go out in the **j**. — 3104
 25:31 redeemed, and they shall go out in the **j**. — 3104
 25:33 possession, shall go out in the year *of* **j**: — 3104
 25:40 *and* shall serve unto thee unto the year of **j**: — 3104
 25:50 he was sold to him unto the year of **j**: — 3104
 25:52 but few years unto the year of **j**, — 3104
 25:54 then shall he go out in the year of **j**, — 3104
 27:17 If he sanctify his field from the year of **j**, — 3104
 27:18 if he sanctify his field after the **j**, then — 3104
 27:18 *even* unto the year of the **j**, and it shall be — 3104
 27:21 the field, when it goeth out in the **j**, shall — 3104
 27:23 estimation, *even* unto the year of the **j**: — 3104
 27:24 In the year of the **j** the field shall return — 3104
Nu 36: 4 **j** of the children of Israel shall be, — 3104

JUBILEE See JUBILE

JUCAL (1)
Jer 38: 1 **J** the son of Shelemiah, and Pashur the son — 3116

JUDA (11) [JUDAH]
Mt 2: 6 And thou Bethlehem, *in* the land of **J**, — 2448
 2: 6 art not the least among the princes of **J**: — 2448
Mk 6: 3 of James, and Joses, and of **J**, and Simon? — 2455
Lk 1:39 hill country with haste, into a city of **J**; — 2448
 3:26 son of Joseph, which was *the* son of **J**, — 2455
 3:30 which was *the* son of **J**, which was *the* — 2455
 3:33 son of Phares, which was *the* son of **J**, — 2455
Heb 7:14 *it* is evident that our Lord sprang out of **J**; — 2455
 8: 8 house of Israel and with the house of **J**: — 2455
Rev 5: 5 behold, the Lion of the tribe of **J**, the root — 2455
 7: 5 Of the tribe of **J** *were* sealed twelve — 2455

JUDAH (811) [BAALE OF JUDAH, BETH-LEHEM-JUDAH, JUDA, JUDAH'S, JUDAS, JUDEA]
Ge 29:35 therefore she called his name **J**; — 3063
 35:23 Levi, and **J**, and Issachar, and Zebulun: — 3063
 37:26 **J** said unto his brethren, What profit *is it* — 3063
 38: 1 that **J** went down from his brethren, — 3063
 38: 2 saw there a daughter of a certain — 3063
 38: 6 **J** took a wife for Er his firstborn, — 3063
 38: 8 **J** said unto Onan, Go in unto thy — 3063
 38:11 said **J** to Tamar his daughter in law, — 3063
 38:12 **J** was comforted, and went up unto his — 3063
 38:15 When **J** saw her, he thought her to be a — 3063
 38:20 **J** sent the kid by the hand of his friend — 3063
 38:22 returned to **J**, and said, I cannot find her; — 3063
 38:23 **J** said, Let her take *it* to her, lest we be — 3063
 38:24 months after, that it was told **J**, saying, — 3063
 38:24 said, Bring her forth, and let her be — 3063
 38:26 **J** acknowledged *them*, and said, She hath — 3063
 43: 3 spake unto him, saying, The man did — 3063
 43: 8 **J** said unto Israel his father, Send the lad — 3063
 44:14 and his brethren came to Joseph's house — 3063
 44:16 said, What shall we say unto my lord? — 3063
 44:18 came near unto him, and said, O my — 3063
 46:12 the sons of **J**; Er, and Onan, and Shelah, — 3063
 46:28 sent **J** before him unto Joseph, to direct — 3063
 49: 8 **J**, thou *art he* whom thy brethren shall — 3063
 49: 9 **J** *is* a lion's whelp: from the prey, my son, — 3063
 49:10 The sceptre shall not depart from **J**, nor a — 3063
Ex 1: 2 Reuben, Simeon, Levi, and **J**, — 3063
 31: 2 of Uri, the son of Hur, of the tribe of **J**: — 3063
 35:30 of Uri, the son of Hur, of the tribe of **J**: — 3063
 38:22 of Uri, the son of Hur, of the tribe of **J**: — 3063
Nu 1: 7 Of **J**; Nahshon the son of Amminadab. — 3063
 1:26 Of the children of **J**, *by* their generations, — 3063
 1:27 *even* of the tribe of **J**, *were* threescore — 3063
 2: 3 camp of **J** pitch throughout their armies: — 3063
 2: 3 *shall be* captain of the children of **J**. — 3063
 2: 9 All that were numbered in the camp of **J** — 3063
 7:12 the son of Amminadab, of the tribe of **J**: — 3063
 10:14 children of **J** according to their armies: — 3063
 13: 6 Of the tribe of **J**, Caleb the son of — 3063
 26:19 The sons of **J** *were* Er and Onan: and Er — 3063
 26:20 the sons of **J** after their families were, — 3063
 26:22 These *are* the families of **J** according to — 3063
 34:19 Of the tribe of **J**, Caleb the son of — 3063
Dt 27:12 **J**, and Issachar, and Joseph, and Benjamin — 3063
 33: 7 this *is the blessing* of **J**: and he said, Hear, — 3063
 33: 7 the voice of **J**, and bring him unto his — 3063
 34: 2 Manasseh, and all the land of **J**, unto — 3063
Jos 7: 1 Zabdi, the son of Zerah, of the tribe of **J**, — 3063
 7:16 their tribes; and the tribe of **J** was taken: — 3063
 7:17 he brought the family of **J**; and he took — 3063
 7:18 son of Zerah, of the tribe of **J**, was taken. — 3063
 11:21 from all the mountains of **J**, and from all — 3063
 14: 6 the children of **J** came unto Joshua in — 3063
 15: 1 **J** the lot of the tribe of the children of **J** — 3063
 15:12 **J** round about according to their families. — 3063
 15:13 he gave a part among the children of **J**, — 3063
 15:20 children of **J** according to their families. — 3063
 15:21 toward the coast of Edom southward — 3063
 15:63 children of **J** could not drive them out: — 3063
 15:63 the Jebusites dwell with the children of **J** — 3063
 18: 5 **J** shall abide in their coast on the south, — 3063
 18:11 lot came forth between the children of **J** — 3063
 18:14 Kirjath-jearim, a city of the children of **J**: — 3063
 19: 1 the inheritance of the children of **J**. — 3063
 19: 9 Out of the portion of the children of **J** — 3063
 19: 9 for the part of the children of **J** was too — 3063
 19:34 to **J** upon Jordan *toward* the sunrising. — 3063
 20: 7 which *is* Hebron, in the mountain of **J**, — 3063
 21: 4 had by lot out of the tribe of **J**, and out of — 3063
 21: 9 gave out of the tribe of the children of **J**, — 3063
 21:11 *city* is Hebron, in the hill *country* of **J**, — 3063
Jdg 1: 2 And the LORD said, **J** shall go up: behold, — 3063
 1: 3 **J** said unto Simeon his brother, Come up — 3063
 1: 4 **J** went up; and the LORD delivered — 3063
 1: 8 Now the children of **J** had fought against — 3063
Jdg 1: 9 afterward the children of **J** went down to — 3063
 1:10 **J** went against the Canaanites that dwelt — 3063
 1:16 children of **J** *into* the wilderness of Judah, — 3063
 1:16 children of Judah *into* the wilderness of **J**, — 3063
 1:17 **J** went with Simeon his brother, — 3063
 1:18 Also **J** took Gaza with the coast thereof, — 3063
 1:19 the LORD was with **J**; and he drave out — 3063
 10: 9 passed over Jordan to fight also against **J**, — 3063
 15: 9 in **J**, and spread themselves in Lehi. — 3063
 15:10 the men of **J** said, Why are ye come up — 3063
 15:11 three thousand men of **J** went to the top — 3063
 17: 7 out of Beth-lehem-judah of the family of **J**, — 3063
 18:12 and pitched in Kirjath-jearim, in **J**: — 3063
 20:18 And the LORD said, **J** *shall go up* first. — 3063
Ru 1: 7 on the way to return unto the land of **J**. — 3063
 4:12 of Pharez, whom Tamar bare unto **J**, — 3063
1Sa 11: 8 and the men of **J** thirty thousand. — 3063
 15: 4 and ten thousand men of **J**. — 3063
 17: 1 **belongeth** to **J**, and pitched between — 3063
 17:52 the men of Israel and of **J** arose, — 3063
 18:16 all Israel and **J** loved David, because — 3063
 22: 5 depart, and get thee *into* the land of **J**. — 3063
 23: 3 unto him, Behold, we *be* afraid here in **J**: — 3063
 23:23 out throughout all the thousands of **J**. — 3063
 27: 6 unto the kings of **J** unto this day. — 3063
 27:10 Against the south of **J**, and against the — 3063
 30:14 upon *the coast* which *belongeth* to **J**, — 3063
 30:16 of the Philistines, and out of the land of **J**. — 3063
 30:26 he sent the spoil unto the elders of **J**, — 3063
2Sa 1:18 he bade them teach the children of **J** — 3063
 2: 1 Shall I go up into any of the cities of **J**? — 3063
 2: 4 men of **J** came, and there they anointed — 3063
 2: 4 anointed David king over the house of **J**. — 3063
 2: 7 the house of **J** have anointed me king — 3063
 2:10 But the house of **J** followed David. — 3063
 2:11 over the house of **J** was seven years — 3063
 3: 8 against **J** do shew kindness *this* day — 3063
 3:10 throne of David over Israel and over **J**, — 3063
 5: 5 In Hebron he reigned over **J** seven years — 3063
 5: 5 and three years over all Israel and **J**. — 3063
 11:11 The ark, and Israel, and **J**, abide in tents; — 3063
 12: 8 and gave thee the house of Israel and of **J**; — 3063
 19:11 Speak unto the elders of **J**, saying, — 3063
 19:14 he bowed the heart of all the men of **J**, — 3063
 19:15 came to Gilgal, to go to meet the king, — 3063
 19:16 down with the men of **J** to meet king — 3063
 19:40 all the people of **J** conducted the king, — 3063
 19:41 Why have our brethren the men of **J** — 3063
 19:42 the men of **J** answered the men of Israel, — 3063
 19:43 the men of Israel answered the men of **J**, — 3063
 19:43 the words of the men of **J** were fiercer — 3063
 20: 2 the men of **J** clave unto their king, — 3063
 20: 4 Assemble me the men of **J** *within* three — 3063
 20: 5 So Amasa went to assemble *the men of* **J**: — 3063
 21: 2 in his zeal to the children of Israel and **J**.) — 3063
 24: 1 them to say, Go, number Israel and **J**. — 3063
 24: 7 they went out to the south of **J**, *even* to — 3063
 24: 9 the men of **J** *were* five hundred thousand — 3063
1Ki 1: 9 and all the men of **J** the king's servants; — 3063
 1:35 him to be ruler over Israel and over **J**. — 3063
 2:32 the son of Jether, captain of the host of **J**. — 3063
 4:20 **J** and Israel were many, as the sand which — 3063
 4:25 and Israel dwelt safely, every man under — 3063
 12:17 of Israel which dwelt in the cities of **J**, — 3063
 12:20 the house of David, but the tribe of **J** only. — 3063
 12:21 he assembled all the house of **J**, with — 3063
 12:23 king of **J**, and unto all the house of Judah — 3063
 12:23 unto all the house of **J** and Benjamin, — 3063
 12:27 *even* unto Rehoboam king of **J**, — 3063
 12:27 and go again to Rehoboam king of **J**. — 3063
 12:32 like unto the feast that *is* in **J**, — 3063
 13: 1 there came a man of God out of **J** by — 3063
 13:12 man of God went, which came from **J**. — 3063
 13:14 thou the man of God that camest from **J**? — 3063
 13:21 unto the man of God that came from **J**, — 3063
 14:21 the son of Solomon reigned in **J**. — 3063
 14:22 **J** did evil in the sight of the LORD, — 3063
 14:29 book of the chronicles of the kings of **J**? — 3063
 15: 1 the son of Nebat reigned Abijam over **J**. — 3063
 15: 7 book of the chronicles of the kings of **J**? — 3063
 15: 9 king of Israel reigned Asa over **J**. — 3063
 15:17 Baasha king of Israel went up against **J**, — 3063
 15:17 *any* to go out or come in to Asa king of **J**. — 3063
 15:22 made a proclamation throughout all **J**; — 3063
 15:23 book of the chronicles of the kings of **J**? — 3063
 15:25 Israel in the second year of Asa king of **J**, — 3063
 15:28 Even in the third year of Asa king of **J** did — 3063
 15:33 In the third year of Asa king of **J** began — 3063
 16: 8 sixth year of Asa king of **J** began Elah — 3063
 16:10 and seventh year of Asa king of **J**, — 3063
 16:15 seventh year of Asa king of **J** did Zimri — 3063
 16:23 first year of Asa king of **J** began Omri to — 3063
 16:29 eighth year of Asa king of **J** began Ahab — 3063
 19: 3 which *belongeth* to **J**, and left his servant — 3063
 22: 2 Jehoshaphat the king of **J** came down — 3063
 22:10 Jehoshaphat the king of **J** sat each on his — 3063
 22:29 Jehoshaphat the king of **J** went up *to* — 3063
 22:41 **J** in the fourth year of Ahab king of Israel. — 3063
 22:45 book of the chronicles of the kings of **J**? — 3063
 22:51 seventeenth year of Jehoshaphat king of **J**, — 3063
2Ki 1:17 Jehoram the son of Jehoshaphat king of **J**; — 3063
 3: 1 eighteenth year of Jehoshaphat king of **J**, — 3063
 3: 7 and sent to the king of **J**, saying, — 3063
 3: 9 and the king of **J**, and the king of Edom: — 3063
 3:14 the presence of Jehoshaphat the king of **J**, — 3063

J

2Ki

8:16 Israel, Jehoshaphat *being* then king of J, 3063
8:16 the son of Jehoshaphat king of J 3063
8:19 Yet the LORD would not destroy J for 3063
8:20 Edom revolted from under the hand of J 3063
8:22 Edom revolted from under the hand of J 3063
8:23 book of the chronicles of the kings of J? 3063
8:25 son of Jehoram king of J *begin* to reign. 3063
8:29 Ahaziah the son of Jehoram king of J went 3063
9:16 Ahaziah king of J was come down to see 3063
9:21 of Israel and Ahaziah king of J went out, 3063
9:27 when Ahaziah the king of J saw *this*, he 3063
9:29 of Ahab *began* Ahaziah to reign over J. 3063
10:13 with the brethren of Ahaziah king of J, 3063
12:18 Jehoash king of J took all the hallowed 3063
12:18 and Ahaziah, his fathers, kings of J, 3063
12:19 book of the chronicles of the kings of J? 3063
13: 1 Jehoahaz the son of Jehu *began* to reign 3063
13:10 seventh year of Joash king of J *began* 3063
13:12 he fought against Amaziah king of J. 3063
14: 1 Amaziah the son of Joash king of J. 3063
14: 9 king of Israel sent to Amaziah king of J, 3063
14:10 fall, *even* thou, and J with thee? 3063
14:11 Amaziah king of J looked one another *in* 3063
14:11 at Beth-shemesh, which *belongeth* to J. 3063
14:12 J was put to the worse before Israel; 3063
14:13 king of Israel took Amaziah king of J, 3063
14:15 how he fought with Amaziah king of J, 3063
14:17 Amaziah the son of Joash king of J lived 3063
14:18 book of the chronicles of the kings of J? 3063
14:21 all the people of J took Azariah, which 3063
14:22 He built Elath, and restored it to J, 3063
14:23 J Jeroboam the son of Joash king of Israel 3063
14:28 Hamath, *which belonged* to J, for Israel, 3063
15: 1 Azariah son of Amaziah king of J to reign. 3063
15: 6 book of the chronicles of the kings of J? 3063
15: 8 eighth year of Azariah king of J did 3063
15:13 and thirtieth year of Uzziah king of J 3063
15:17 thirtieth year of Azariah king of J *began* 3063
15:23 In the fiftieth year of Azariah king of J 3063
15:27 fiftieth year of Azariah king of J Pekah 3063
15:32 the son of Uzziah king of J to reign. 3063
15:36 book of the chronicles of the kings of J? 3063
15:37 to send against J Rezin the king of Syria, 3063
16: 1 son of Jotham king of J *began* to reign. 3063
16:19 book of the chronicles of the kings of J? 3063
17: 1 In the twelfth year of Ahaz king of J 3063
17:13 against J, by all the prophets, *and by* all 3063
17:18 there was none left but the tribe of J only. 3063
17:19 Also J kept not the commandments of 3063
18: 1 *that* Hezekiah the son of Ahaz king of J 3063
18: 5 none like him among all the kings of J, 3063
18:13 come up against all the fenced cities of J, 3063
18:14 Hezekiah king of J sent to the king of 3063
18:14 king of J three hundred talents of silver 3063
18:16 *from* the pillars which Hezekiah king of J 3063
18:22 and hath said to J and Jerusalem, 3063
19:10 Thus shall ye speak to Hezekiah king of J, 3063
19:30 remnant that is escaped of the house of J 3063
20:20 book of the chronicles of the kings of J? 3063
21:11 Because Manasseh king of J hath done 3063
21:11 and hath made J also to sin with his idols: 3063
21:12 bringing *such* evil upon Jerusalem and J, 3063
21:16 beside his sin where*with* he made J to sin, 3063
21:17 book of the chronicles of the kings of J? 3063
21:25 book of the chronicles of the kings of J? 3063
22:13 for me, and for the people, and for all J, 3063
22:16 of the book which the king of J hath read: 3063
22:18 to the king of J which sent you to inquire 3063
23: 1 they gathered unto him all the elders of J 3063
23: 2 all the men of J and all the inhabitants of 3063
23: 5 the kings of J had ordained to burn 3063
23: 5 in the high places in the cities of J, 3063
23: 8 all the priests out of the cities of J, 3063
23:11 took away the horses that the kings of J 3063
23:12 which the kings of J had made, 3063
23:17 which came from J, and proclaimed these 3063
23:22 the kings of Israel, nor of the kings of J; 3063
23:24 that were spied in the land of J 3063
23:26 his anger was kindled against J, 3063
23:27 I will remove J also out of my sight, 3063
23:28 book of the chronicles of the kings of J? 3063
24: 2 and sent them against J to destroy it, 3063
24: 3 of the LORD came *this* upon J, 3063
24: 5 book of the chronicles of the kings of J? 3063
24:12 Jehoiachin the king of J went out to 3063
24:20 LORD it came to pass in Jerusalem and J, 3063
25:21 So J was carried away out of their land. 3063
25:22 the people that remained in the land of J, 3063
25:27 of the captivity of Jehoiachin king of J, 3063
25:27 lift up the head of Jehoiachin king of J 3063

1Ch

2: 1 Reuben, Simeon, Levi, and J, Issachar, 3063
2: 3 The sons of J; Er, and Onan, and Shelah: 3063
2: 3 Er, the firstborn of J, was evil in the sight 3063
2: 4 and Zerah. All the sons of J *were* five. 3063
2:10 Nahshon, prince of the children of J; 3063
4: 1 sons of J; Pharez, Hezron, and Carmi, 3063
4:21 The sons of Shelah the son of J *were*, Er 3063
4:27 family multiply, like to the children of J. 3063
4:41 came in the days of Hezekiah king of J, 3063
5: 2 For J prevailed above his brethren, and of 3063
5:17 in the days of Jotham king of J, 3063
6:15 *captivity*, when the LORD carried away J 3063
6:55 they gave them Hebron in the land of J, 3063
6:57 the sons of Aaron they gave the cities of J, NIH
6:65 by lot out of the tribe of the children of J, 3063

1Ch

9: 1 in the book of the kings of Israel and J, 3063
9: 3 in Jerusalem dwelt of the children of J, 3063
9: 4 of the children of Pharez the son of J. 3063
12:16 of Benjamin and J to the hold unto David. 3063
12:24 The children of J that bare shield and 3063
13: 6 *is*, to Kirjath-jearim, which *belonged* to J, 3063
21: 5 J *was* four hundred threescore and 3063
27:18 Of J, Elihu, *one* of the brethren of David: 3063
28: 4 for he hath chosen J to be the ruler; 3063
28: 4 of the house of J, the house of my father; 3063

2Ch

2: 7 the cunning *men* that *are* with me in J 3063
9:11 none such seen before in the land of J. 3063
10:17 of Israel that dwelt in the cities of J, 3063
11: 1 he gathered of the house of J and 3063
11: 3 king of J, and to all Israel in Judah and 3063
11: 3 and to all Israel in J and Benjamin, saying, 3063
11: 5 and built cities for defence in J. 3063
11:10 which *are* in J and in Benjamin, 3063
11:12 having J and Benjamin on his side. 3063
11:14 and came to J and Jerusalem: 3063
11:17 So they strengthened the kingdom of J 3063
11:23 children throughout all the countries of J 3063
12: 4 the fenced cities which *pertained* to J, 3063
12: 5 to the princes of J, that were gathered 3063
12:12 and also in J things went well. 3063
13: 1 Jeroboam *began* Abijah to reign over J. 3063
13:13 they were before J, and the ambushment 3063
13:14 when J looked back, behold, the battle 3063
13:15 men of J gave a shout: and as the men 3063
13:15 as the men of J shouted, it came to pass, 3063
13:15 and all Israel before Abijah and J. 3063
13:16 the children of Israel fled before J: 3063
13:18 the children of J prevailed, because 3063
14: 4 commanded J to seek the LORD God of 3063
14: 5 he took away out of all the cities of J 3063
14: 6 he built fenced cities in J: for the land had 3063
14: 7 Therefore he said unto J, Let us build 3063
14: 8 spears, out of J three hundred thousand; 3063
14:12 the Ethiopians before Asa, and before J; 3063
15: 2 Hear ye me, Asa, and all J and Benjamin; 3063
15: 8 abominable idols out of all the land of J 3063
15: 9 he gathered all J and Benjamin, 3063
15:15 all J rejoiced at the oath: for they had 3063
16: 1 Baasha king of Israel came up against J, 3063
16: 1 none go out or come in to Asa king of J. 3063
16: 6 Asa the king took all J; and they carried 3063
16: 7 Hanani the seer came to Asa king of J, 3063
16:11 *are* written in the book of the kings of J, 3063
17: 2 placed forces in all the fenced cities of J, 3063
17: 2 set garrisons in the land of J, and in 3063
17: 5 all J brought to Jehoshaphat presents; 3063
17: 6 away the high places and groves out of J. 3063
17: 7 to Michaiah, to teach in the cities of J. 3063
17: 9 they taught in J, and *had* the book of 3063
17: 9 went about throughout all the cities of J, 3063
17:10 of the lands that *were* round about J, 3063
17:12 he built in J castles, and cities of store. 3063
17:13 he had much business in the cities of J: 3063
17:14 Of J, the captains of thousands; Adnah 3063
17:19 put in the fenced cities throughout all J. 3063
18: 3 of Israel said unto Jehoshaphat king of J, 3063
18: 9 Jehoshaphat king of J sat either of them 3063
18:28 Jehoshaphat the king of J went up to 3063
19: 1 Jehoshaphat the king of J returned to his 3063
19: 5 land throughout all the fenced cities of J, 3063
19:11 ruler of the house of J, for all the king's 3063
20: 3 and proclaimed a fast throughout all J. 3063
20: 4 J gathered themselves together, to ask 3063
20: 4 even out of all the cities of J they came to 3063
20: 5 Jehoshaphat stood in the congregation of J 3063
20:13 all J stood before the LORD, with their 3063
20:15 all J, and ye inhabitants of Jerusalem, 3063
20:17 the LORD with you, O J and Jerusalem: 3063
20:18 all J and the inhabitants of Jerusalem fell 3063
20:20 O J, and ye inhabitants of Jerusalem; 3063
20:22 mount Seir, which were come against J; 3063
20:24 when J came toward the watch tower in 3063
20:27 every man of J and Jerusalem, 3063
20:31 Jehoshaphat reigned over J: *he was* thirty 3063
20:35 after this did Jehoshaphat king of J join 3063
21: 3 of precious things, with fenced cities in J: 3063
21: 8 revolted from under the dominion of J, 3063
21:10 from under the hand of J unto this day. 3063
21:11 made high places in the mountains of J, 3063
21:11 and compelled J *thereto*. 3063
21:12 father, nor in the ways of Asa king of J, 3063
21:13 hast made J and the inhabitants of 3063
21:17 they came up into J, and brake into it, 3063
22: 1 So Ahaziah the son of Jehoram king of J 3063
22: 6 Azariah the son of Jehoram king of J went 3063
22: 8 found the princes of J, and the sons of 3063
22:10 all the seed royal of the house of J. 3063
23: 2 they went about in J, and gathered 3063
23: 2 the Levites out of all the cities of J, 3063
23: 8 all J did according to all *things* that 3063
24: 5 Go out unto the cities of J, and gather of 3063
24: 6 required of the Levites to bring in out of J 3063
24: 9 they made a proclamation through J and 3063
24:17 death of Jehoiada came the princes of J, 3063
24:18 wrath came upon J and Jerusalem for this 3063
24:23 they came to J and Jerusalem, 3063
25: 5 Moreover Amaziah gathered J together, 3063
25: 5 throughout all J and Benjamin: 3063
25:10 their anger was greatly kindled against J, 3063
25:12 did the children of J carry away captive, 3063

2Ch

25:13 fell upon the cities of J, from Samaria 3063
25:17 Amaziah king of J took advice, and sent to 3063
25:18 king of Israel sent to Amaziah king of J, 3063
25:19 shouldest fall, *even* thou, and J with thee? 3063
25:21 *both* he and Amaziah king of J, 3063
25:21 at Beth-shemesh, which *belongeth* to J. 3063
25:22 J was put to the worse before Israel, 3063
25:23 the king of Israel took Amaziah king of J, 3063
25:25 Amaziah the son of Joash king of J lived 3063
25:26 not written in the book of the kings of J. 3063
25:28 buried him with his fathers in the city of J. 3063
26: 1 all the people of J took Uzziah, who *was* 3063
26: 2 He built Eloth, and restored it to J, 3063
27: 4 he built cities in the mountains of J, 3063
27: 7 in the book of the kings of Israel and J. 3063
28: 6 For Pekah the son of Remaliah slew in J 3063
28: 9 God of your fathers was wroth with J, 3063
28:10 purpose to keep under the children of J 3063
28:17 the Edomites had come and smitten J, 3063
28:18 of the south of J, and had taken 3063
28:19 For the LORD brought J low because 3063
28:19 he made J naked, and transgressed sore 3063
28:25 in every several city of J he made high 3063
28:26 *are* written in the book of the kings of J 3063
29: 8 the wrath of the LORD was upon J 3063
29:21 and for the sanctuary, and for J. 3063
30: 1 Hezekiah sent to all Israel and J, 3063
30: 6 his princes throughout all Israel and J, 3063
30:12 in J the hand of God was to give them 3063
30:24 For Hezekiah king of J did give to 3063
30:25 all the congregation of J, with the priests 3063
30:25 of Israel, and that dwelt in J, rejoiced. 3063
31: 1 were present went out to the cities of J, 3063
31: 1 and the altars out of all J and Benjamin, 3063
31: 6 *concerning* the children of Israel and J, 3063
31: 6 and Judah, that dwelt in the cities of J, 3063
31:20 thus did Hezekiah throughout all J, 3063
32: 1 entered into J, and encamped against 3063
32: 8 upon the words of Hezekiah king of J 3063
32: 9 Hezekiah king of J, and unto all Judah 3063
32: 9 unto all J that *were* at Jerusalem, saying, 3063
32:12 and commanded J and Jerusalem, saying, 3063
32:23 and presents to Hezekiah king of J: 3063
32:25 upon him, and upon J and Jerusalem. 3063
32:32 in the book of the kings of J and Israel. 3063
32:33 all J and the inhabitants of Jerusalem did 3063
33: 9 Manasseh made J and the inhabitants of 3063
33:14 captains of war in all the fenced cities of J. 3063
33:16 commanded J to serve the LORD God of 3063
34: 3 the twelfth year he began to purge J and 3063
34: 5 their altars, and cleansed J and Jerusalem. 3063
34: 9 of Israel, and of all J and Benjamin; 3063
34:11 floor the houses which the kings of J had 3063
34:21 and for them that are left in Israel and in J, 3063
34:24 which they have read before the king of J: 3063
34:26 for the king of J, who sent you to inquire 3063
34:29 gathered together all the elders of J and 3063
34:30 all the men of J, and the inhabitants of 3063
35:18 all J and Israel that were present, 3063
35:21 have I to do with thee, thou king of J? 3063
35:24 all J and Jerusalem mourned for Josiah. 3063
35:27 in the book of the kings of Israel and J. 3063
36: 4 made Eliakim his brother king over J 3063
36: 8 in the book of the kings of Israel and J: 3063
36:10 made Zedekiah his brother king over J 3063
36:23 him a house in Jerusalem, which *is* in J. 3063

Ezr

1: 2 him a house at Jerusalem, which *is* in J. 3063
1: 3 which *is* in J, and build the house of 3063
1: 5 rose up the chief of the fathers of J and 3063
1: 8 them unto Sheshbazzar, the prince of J. 3063
2: 1 came again unto Jerusalem and J, 3063
3: 9 Kadmiel and his sons, the sons of J, 3063
4: 1 Now *when* the adversaries of J and 3063
4: 4 weakened the hands of the people of J, 3063
4: 6 an accusation against the inhabitants of J 3063
5: 1 prophesied unto the Jews that *were* in J 3061
7:14 to inquire concerning J and Jerusalem, 3061
9: 9 to give us a wall in J and in Jerusalem. 3063
10: 7 they made proclamation throughout J and 3063
10: 9 all the men of J and Benjamin gathered 3063
10:23 same *is* Kelita,) Pethahiah, J, and Eliezer. 3063

Ne

1: 2 came, me and *certain* men of J; 3063
2: 5 that thou wouldest send me unto J, unto 3063
2: 7 may convey me over till I come into J; 3063
4:10 J said, The strength of the bearers of 3063
4:16 the rulers *were* behind all the house of J. 3063
5:14 to be their governor in the land of J, 3063
6: 7 at Jerusalem, saying, There is a king in J: 3063
6:17 in those days the nobles of J sent 3063
6:18 *there were* many in J sworn unto him, 3063
7: 6 came again to Jerusalem and to J, 3063
11: 3 in the cities of J dwelt every one in his 3063
11: 4 dwelt *certain* of the children of J, 3063
11: 4 Of the children of J; Athaiah the son of 3063
11: 9 J the son of Senuah *was* second over 3063
11:20 *and* the Levites, *were* in all the cities of J, 3063
11:24 of the children of Zerah the son of J, 3063
11:25 *some* of the children of J dwelt at 3063
11:36 of the Levites *were* divisions in J. 3063
12: 8 Kadmiel, Sherebiah, J, *and* Mattaniah, 3063
12:31 brought up the princes of J upon the wall, 3063
12:32 Hoshaiah, and half of the princes of J, 3063
12:34 J, and Benjamin, and Shemaiah, 3063
12:36 Gilalai, Maai, Nethaneel, and J, Hanani, 3063
12:44 for J rejoiced for the priests and for 3063

J

Ne	13:12 brought all **J** the tithe of the corn and	3063
	13:15 those days saw I in **J** *some* treading wine	3063
	13:16 sold on the sabbath unto the children of **J**,	3063
	13:17 I contended with the nobles of **J**,	3063
Est	2: 6 been carried away with Jeconiah king of **J**,	3063
Ps	48:11 let the daughters of **J** be glad, because	3063
	60: 7 strength of mine head; **J** *is* my lawgiver;	3063
	63: 1 when he was in the wilderness of **J**.	3063
	68:27 the princes of **J** *and* their council,	3063
	69:35 save Zion, and will build the cities of **J**:	3063
	76: 1 In **J** *is* God known: his name *is* great in	3063
	78:68 chose the tribe of **J**, the mount Zion	3063
	97: 8 the daughters of **J** rejoiced, because of thy	3063
	108: 8 strength of mine head; **J** *is* my lawgiver;	3063
	114: 2 **J** was his sanctuary, *and* Israel his	3063
Pr	25: 1 which the men of Hezekiah king of **J**	3063
Isa	1: 1 which he saw concerning **J** and	3063
	1: 1 Jotham, Ahaz, *and* Hezekiah, kings of **J**.	3063
	2: 1 Isaiah the son of Amoz saw concerning **J**	3063
	3: 1 and from **J** the stay and the staff,	3063
	3: 8 For Jerusalem is ruined, and **J** is fallen:	3063
	5: 3 men of **J**, judge, I pray you, betwixt me	3063
	5: 7 and the men of **J** his pleasant plant:	3063
	7: 1 the son of Uzziah king of **J**, *that* Rezin	3063
	7: 6 Let us go up against **J**, and vex it, and let	3063
	7:17 the day that Ephraim departed from **J**;	3063
	8: 8 he shall pass through **J**; he shall overflow	3063
	9:21 *and* they together *shall* be against **J**.	3063
	11:12 gather together the dispersed of **J** from	3063
	11:13 and the adversaries of **J** shall be cut off:	3063
	11:13 Ephraim shall not envy **J**, and **J**udah shall	3063
	11:13 envy Judah, and **J** shall not vex Ephraim.	3063
	19:17 the land of **J** shall be a terror unto Egypt,	3063
	22: 8 he discovered the covering of **J**,	3063
	22:21 of Jerusalem, and to the house of **J**.	3063
	26: 1 shall this song be sung in the land of **J**;	3063
	36: 1 up against all the defenced cities of **J**,	3063
	36: 7 said to **J** and to Jerusalem, Ye shall	3063
	37:10 shall ye speak to Hezekiah king of **J**,	3063
	37:31 remnant that is escaped of the house of **J**	3063
	38: 9 king of **J**, when he had been sick,	3063
	40: 9 say unto the cities of **J**, Behold your God.	3063
	44:26 to the cities of **J**, Ye shall be built,	3063
	48: 1 and are come forth out of the waters of **J**,	3063
	65: 9 and out of **J** an inheritor of my mountains:	3063
Jer	1: 2 days of Josiah the son of Amon king of **J**,	3063
	1: 3 of Jehoiakim the son of Josiah king of **J**,	3063
	1: 3 of Zedekiah the son of Josiah king of **J**,	3063
	1:15 round about, and against all the cities of **J**.	3063
	1:18 against the kings of **J**, against the princes	3063
	2:28 the number of thy cities are thy gods, O **J**.	3063
	3: 7 And her treacherous sister **J** saw *it*.	3063
	3: 8 yet her treacherous sister **J** feared not,	3063
	3:10 yet for all this her treacherous sister **J** hath	3063
	3:11 justified herself more than treacherous **J**.	3063
	3:18 In those days the house of **J** shall walk	3063
	4: 3 For thus saith the LORD to the men of **J**	3063
	4: 4 ye men of **J** and inhabitants of Jerusalem:	3063
	4: 5 Declare ye in **J**, and publish in Jerusalem;	3063
	4:16 give out their voice against the cities of **J**.	3063
	5:11 the house of **J** have dealt very	3063
	5:20 house of Jacob, and publish it in **J**, saying,	3063
	7: 2 Hear the word of the LORD, all *ye of* **J**,	3063
	7:17 thou not what they do in the cities of **J**	3063
	7:30 For the children of **J** have done evil in my	3063
	7:34 will I cause to cease from the cities of **J**,	3063
	8: 1 shall bring out the bones of the kings of **J**,	3063
	9:11 I will make the cities of **J** desolate,	3063
	9:26 **J**, and Edom, and the children of Ammon,	3063
	10:22 to make the cities of **J** desolate, *and* a den	3063
	11: 2 speak unto the men of **J**, and to	3063
	11: 6 Proclaim all these words in the cities of **J**,	3063
	11: 9 conspiracy is found among the men of **J**,	3063
	11:10 the house of **J** have broken my covenant	3063
	11:12 shall the cities of **J** and inhabitants of	3063
	11:13 number of thy cities were thy gods, O **J**;	3063
	11:17 the house of Israel and of the house of **J**,	3063
	12:14 pluck out the house of **J** from among	3063
	13: 9 After this manner will I mar the pride of **J**,	3063
	13:11 house of Israel and the whole house of **J**,	3063
	13:19 none shall open *them:* **J** shall be carried	3063
	14: 2 **J** mourneth, and the gates thereof	3063
	14:19 Hast thou utterly rejected **J**? hath thy soul	3063
	15: 4 Manasseh the son of Hezekiah king of **J**,	3063
	17: 1 The sin of **J** *is* written with a pen of iron,	3063
	17:19 whereby the kings of **J** come in, and by	3063
	17:20 ye kings of **J**, and all **J**udah, and all	3063
	17:20 all **J**, and all the inhabitants of Jerusalem,	3063
	17:25 the men of **J**, and the inhabitants of	3063
	17:26 they shall come from the cities of **J**,	3063
	18:11 speak to the men of **J**, and to	3063
	19: 3 kings of **J**, and inhabitants of Jerusalem;	3063
	19: 4 the kings of **J**, and have filled this place	3063
	19: 7 I will make void the counsel of **J** and	3063
	19:13 and the houses of the kings of **J**,	3063
	20: 4 I will give all **J** into the hand of the king	3063
	20: 5 the treasures of the kings of **J** will I give	3063
	21: 7 I will deliver Zedekiah king of **J**, and his	3063
	21:11 touching the house of the king of **J**,	3063
	22: 1 Go down *to* the house of the king of **J**,	3063
	22: 2 Hear the word of the LORD, O king of **J**,	3063
	22: 6 the LORD unto the king's house of **J**;	3063
	22:11 Shallum the son of Josiah king of **J**,	3063
	22:18 Jehoiakim the son of Josiah king of **J**;	3063
	22:24 of **J** were the signet upon my right hand,	3063
Jer	22:30 of David, and ruling any more in **J**.	3063
	23: 6 In his days shall **J** be saved, and Israel	3063
	24: 1 Jeconiah the son of Jehoiakim king of **J**,	3063
	24: 1 the princes of **J**, with the carpenters and	3063
	24: 5 them that are carried away captive of **J**,	3063
	24: 8 So will I give Zedekiah the king of **J**,	3063
	25: 1 in the fourth year of Jehoiakim the son	3063
	25: 1 of Jehoiakim the son of Josiah king of **J**,	3063
	25: 2 the prophet spake unto all the people of **J**,	3063
	25: 3 year of Josiah the son of Amon king of **J**,	3063
	25:18 the cities of **J**, and the kings thereof,	3063
	26: 1 king of **J** came this word from the LORD,	3063
	26: 2 and speak unto all the cities of **J**,	3063
	26:10 When the princes of **J** heard these things,	3063
	26:18 in the days of Hezekiah king of **J**,	3063
	26:18 spake to all the people of **J**, saying,	3063
	26:19 Did Hezekiah king of **J** and all **J**udah put	3063
	26:19 of Judah and all **J** put him at all to death?	3063
	27: 1 **J** came this word unto Jeremiah from	3063
	27: 3 *to* Jerusalem unto Zedekiah king of **J**;	3063
	27:12 I spake also to Zedekiah king of **J**	3063
	27:18 *in* the house of the king of **J**,	3063
	27:20 king of **J** from Jerusalem to Babylon,	3063
	27:20 and all the nobles of **J** and Jerusalem;	3063
	27:21 *in* the house of the king of **J** and	3063
	28: 1 of the reign of Zedekiah king of **J**,	3063
	28: 4 Jeconiah the son of Jehoiakim king of **J**,	3063
	28: 4 with all the captives of **J**, that went into	3063
	29: 2 the princes of **J** and Jerusalem,	3063
	29: 3 whom Zedekiah king of **J** sent unto	3063
	29:22 all the captivity of **J**, which *are* in Babylon,	3063
	30: 3 the captivity of my people Israel and **J**,	3063
	30: 4 spake concerning Israel and concerning **J**.	3063
	31:23 they shall use this speech in the land of **J**	3063
	31:24 there shall dwell in **J** itself, and *in* all	3063
	31:27 and the house of **J** *with* the seed of man,	3063
	31:31 house of Israel, and with the house of **J**:	3063
	32: 1 in the tenth year of Zedekiah king of **J**,	3063
	32: 3 For Zedekiah king of **J** had shut him up,	3063
	32: 4 Zedekiah king of **J** shall not escape out of	3063
	32:30 the children of **J** have only done evil	3063
	32:32 children of Israel and of the children of **J**,	3063
	32:32 the men of **J**, and the inhabitants of	3063
	32:35 do this abomination, to cause **J** to sin.	3063
	32:44 in the cities of **J**, and in the cities of	3063
	33: 4 concerning the houses of the kings of **J**,	3063
	33: 7 I will cause the captivity of **J** and	3063
	33:10 *even* in the cities of **J**, and in the streets	3063
	33:13 about Jerusalem, and in the cities of **J**,	3063
	33:14 the house of Israel and to the house of **J**.	3063
	33:16 In those days shall **J** be saved,	3063
	34: 2 Go and speak to Zedekiah king of **J**,	3063
	34: 4 word of the LORD, O Zedekiah king of **J**;	3063
	34: 6 unto Zedekiah king of **J** in Jerusalem,	3063
	34: 7 against all the cities of **J** that were left,	3063
	34: 7 defenced cities remained of the cities of **J**.	3063
	34:19 The princes of **J**, and the princes of	3063
	34:21 Zedekiah king of **J** and his princes will I	3063
	34:22 will make the cities of **J** a desolation	3063
	35: 1 of Jehoiakim the son of Josiah king of **J**,	3063
	35:13 and tell the men of **J** and the inhabitants	3063
	35:17 I will bring upon **J** and upon all	3063
	36: 1 of Jehoiakim the son of Josiah king of **J**,	3063
	36: 2 against **J**, and against all the nations,	3063
	36: 3 It may be that the house of **J** will hear all	3063
	36: 6 thou shalt read them in the ears of all **J**	3063
	36: 9 of Jehoiakim the son of Josiah king of **J**,	3063
	36: 9 came from the cities of **J** unto Jerusalem.	3063
	36:28 which Jehoiakim the king of **J** hath burnt.	3063
	36:29 thou shalt say to Jehoiakim king of **J**,	3063
	36:30 saith the LORD of Jehoiakim king of **J**;	3063
	36:31 of Jerusalem, and upon the men of **J**,	3063
	36:32 Jehoiakim king of **J** had burnt in the fire:	3063
	37: 1 of Babylon made king in the land of **J**.	3063
	37: 7 Thus shall ye say to the king of **J**, that sent	3063
	39: 1 In the ninth year of Zedekiah king of **J**,	3063
	39: 4 when Zedekiah the king of **J** saw them,	3063
	39: 6 king of Babylon slew all the nobles of **J**.	3063
	39:10 in the land of **J**, and gave them vineyards	3063
	40: 1 carried away captive of Jerusalem and **J**,	3063
	40: 5 hath made governor over the cities of **J**,	3063
	40:11 king of Babylon had left a remnant of **J**,	3063
	40:12 came *to* the land of **J**, to Gedaliah, unto	3063
	40:15 scattered, and the remnant in **J** perish?	3063
	42:15 the word of the LORD, ye remnant of **J**;	3063
	42:19 said concerning you, O ye remnant of **J**;	3063
	43: 4 of the LORD, to dwell in the land of **J**.	3063
	43: 5 of the forces, took all the remnant of **J**,	3063
	43: 5 had been driven, to dwell in the land of **J**:	3063
	43: 9 In Tahpanhes, in the sight of the men of **J**;	3064
	44: 2 and upon all the cities of **J**;	3063
	44: 6 was kindled in the cities of **J** and in	3063
	44: 7 and woman, child and suckling, out of **J**,	3063
	44: 9 the wickedness of the kings of **J**,	3063
	44: 9 they have committed in the land of **J**,	3063
	44:11 against you for evil, and to cut off all **J**.	3063
	44:12 I will take the remnant of **J**, that have set	3063
	44:14 So that none of the remnant of **J**, which	3063
	44:14 that *they* should return *into* the land of **J**,	3063
	44:17 in the cities of **J**, and in the streets of	3063
	44:21 incense that ye burnt in the cities of **J**,	3063
	44:24 all **J** that *are* in the land of Egypt:	3063
	44:26 all **J** that dwell in the land of Egypt;	3063
	44:26 of any man of **J** in all the land of Egypt,	3063
	44:27 all the men of **J** that *are* in the land of	3063
Jer	44:28 out of the land of Egypt *into* the land of **J**,	3063
	44:28 all the remnant of **J**, that are gone into	3063
	44:30 as I gave Zedekiah king of **J** into the hand	3063
	45: 1 of Jehoiakim the son of Josiah king of **J**,	3063
	46: 2 of Jehoiakim the son of Josiah king of **J**.	3063
	49:34 of the reign of Zedekiah king of **J**,	3063
	50: 4 they and the children of **J** together, going	3063
	50:20 the sins of **J**, and they shall not be found:	3063
	50:33 the children of **J** *were* oppressed together:	3063
	51: 5 nor **J** of his God, of the LORD of hosts;	3063
	51:59 he went with Zedekiah the king of **J**	3063
	52: 3 LORD it came to pass in Jerusalem and **J**,	3063
	52:10 he slew also all the princes of **J** in Riblah.	3063
	52:27 Thus was **J** carried away captive out of his	3063
	52:31 of the captivity of Jehoiachin king of **J**,	3063
	52:31 lifted up the head of Jehoiachin king of **J**,	3063
La	1: 3 **J** is gone into captivity because	3063
	1:15 the daughter of **J**, *as in* a winepress.	3063
	2: 2 the strong holds of the daughter of **J**;	3063
	2: 5 hath increased in the daughter of **J**	3063
	5:11 in Zion, *and* the maids in the cities of **J**.	3063
Eze	4: 6 the iniquity of the house of **J** forty days:	3063
	8: 1 and the elders of **J** sat before me,	3063
	8:17 Is it a light thing to the house of **J** that	3063
	9: 9 house of Israel and of **J** *is* exceeding great,	3063
	21:20 to **J** in Jerusalem the defenced.	3063
	25: 3 against the house of **J**, when they went	3063
	25: 8 the house of **J** *is* like unto all the heathen;	3063
	25:12 the house of **J** by taking vengeance,	3063
	27:17 **J**, and the land of Israel, they *were* thy	3063
	37:16 For **J**, and for the children of Israel his	3063
	37:19 *even* with the stick of **J**, and make them	3063
	48: 7 side unto the west side, *a portion for* **J**.	3063
	48: 8 by the border of **J**, from the east side unto	3063
	48:22 between the border of **J** and the border of	3063
	48:31 of Reuben, one gate of **J**, one gate of Levi.	3063
Da	1: 1 **J** came Nebuchadnezzar king of Babylon	3063
	1: 2 the Lord gave Jehoiakim king of **J** into his	3063
	1: 6 among these were of the children of **J**,	3063
	2:25 I have found a man of the captives of **J**,	3061
	5:13 *art* of the children of the captivity of **J**,	3061
	6:13 *is* of the children of the captivity of **J**,	3061
	9: 7 to the men and to the inhabitants of **J**,	3063
Hos	1: 1 kings of **J**, and in the days of Jeroboam	3063
	1: 7 I will have mercy upon the house of **J**,	3063
	1:11 shall the children of **J** and the children of	3063
	4:15 Israel, play the harlot, *yet* let not **J** offend;	3063
	5: 5 their iniquity; **J** also shall fall with them.	3063
	5:10 The princes of **J** were like them that	3063
	5:12 moth, and to the house of **J** as rottenness.	3063
	5:13 **J** saw his wound, then went Ephraim to	3063
	5:14 and as a young lion to the house of **J**:	3063
	6: 4 O **J**, what shall I do unto thee? for your	3063
	6:11 Also, O **J**, he hath set a harvest for thee,	3063
	8:14 and **J** hath multiplied fenced cities:	3063
	10:11 shall plow, *and* Jacob shall break his	3063
	11:12 yet ruleth with God, and is faithful with **J**,	3063
	12: 2 The LORD hath also a controversy with **J**,	3063
Joel	3: 1 when I shall bring again the captivity of **J**	3063
	3: 6 The children also of **J** and the children of	3063
	3: 8 into the hand of the children of **J**,	3063
	3:18 all the rivers of **J** shall flow *with* waters,	3063
	3:19 for the violence against the children of **J**,	3063
	3:20 **J** shall dwell for ever, and Jerusalem from	3063
Am	1: 1 Israel in the days of Uzziah king of **J**,	3063
	2: 4 For three transgressions of **J**, and for four,	3063
	2: 5 will send a fire upon **J**, and it shall devour	3063
	7:12 go, flee thee away into the land of **J**,	3063
Ob	1:12 of **J** in the day of their destruction;	3063
Mic	1: 1 Ahaz, *and* Hezekiah, kings of **J**, which he	3063
	1: 5 what *are* the high places of **J**? *are* they not	3063
	1: 9 wound *is* incurable; for it is come unto **J**;	3063
	5: 2 *thou* be little among the thousands of **J**,	3063
Na	1:15 O **J**, keep thy solemn feasts, perform thy	3063
Zep	1: 1 days of Josiah the son of Amon, king of **J**,	3063
	1: 4 will I also stretch out mine hand upon **J**,	3063
	2: 7 shall be for the remnant of the house of **J**;	3063
Hag	1: 1 governor of **J**, and to Joshua the son of	3063
	1:14 governor of **J**, and the spirit of Joshua	3063
	2: 2 governor of **J**, and to Joshua the son of	3063
	2:21 Speak to Zerubbabel, governor of **J**,	3063
Zec	1:12 mercy on Jerusalem and on the cities of **J**,	3063
	1:19 *are* the horns which have scattered **J**,	3063
	1:21 *are* the horns which have scattered **J**,	3063
	1:21 which lift up *their* horn over the land of **J**	3063
	2:12 the LORD shall inherit **J** his portion in	3063
	8:13 O house of **J**, and house of Israel;	3063
	8:15 well unto Jerusalem and to the house of **J**:	3063
	8:19 shall be to the house of **J** joy and gladness,	3063
	9: 7 he shall be as a governor in **J**, and Ekron	3063
	9:13 When I have bent **J** for me, filled the bow	3063
	10: 3 hosts hath visited his flock the house of **J**,	3063
	10: 6 I will strengthen the house of **J**, and I will	3063
	11:14 I might break the brotherhood between **J**	3063
	12: 2 they shall be in the siege both against **J**	3063
	12: 4 I will open mine eyes upon the house of **J**,	3063
	12: 5 the governors of **J** shall say in their heart,	3063
	12: 6 In that day will I make the governors of **J**	3063
	12: 7 The LORD also shall save the tents of **J**	3063
	14: 5 do not magnify *themselves* against **J**.	3063
	14: 5 earthquake in the days of Uzziah king of **J**:	3063
	14:14 **J** also shall fight at Jerusalem;	3063
	14:21 in **J** shall be holiness unto the LORD of	3063
Mal	2:11 **J** hath dealt treacherously,	3063
	2:11 for **J** hath profaned the holiness of	3063

Mal 3: 4 shall the offering of **J** and Jerusalem be 3063

JUDAH'S (4) [JUDAH]
Ge 38: 7 Er, **J** firstborn, was wicked in the sight of 3063
 38:12 process of time the daughter of Shuah **J** 3063
Jer 32: 2 which *was in* the king of **J** house. 3063
 38:22 the women that are left in the king of **J** 3063

JUDAS (33) [JUDAH]
Mt 1: 2 and Jacob begat **J** and his brethren; 2455
 1: 3 And **J** begat Phares and Zara of Thamar; 2455
 10: 4 Simon the Canaanite, and **J** Iscariot, 2455
 13:55 James, and Joses, and Simon, and **J**? 2455
 26:14 Then one of the twelve, called **J** Iscariot, 2455
 26:25 **J**, which betrayed him, answered and 2455
 26:47 **J**, one of the twelve, came, and with him 2455
 27: 3 **J**, which had betrayed him, when he 2455
Mk 3:19 And **J** Iscariot, which also betrayed him. 2455
 14:10 And **J** Iscariot, one of the twelve, 2455
 14:43 cometh **J**, one of the twelve, and with him 2455
Lk 6:16 *And* the brother of James, 2455
 6:16 and **J** Iscariot, which also was the traitor. 2455
 22: 3 Then entered Satan into **J** surnamed 2455
 22:47 he that was called **J**, one of the twelve, 2455
 22:48 But Jesus said unto him, **J**, betrayest thou 2455
Jn 6:71 He spake of **J** Iscariot *the son* of Simon: 2455
 12: 4 Then saith one of his disciples, **J** Iscariot, 2455
 13: 2 devil having now put into the heart of **J** 2455
 13:26 he gave *it* to **J** Iscariot, *the son* of Simon. 2455
 13:29 *of them* thought, because **J** had the bag, 2455
 14:22 **J** saith unto him, not Iscariot, Lord, how 2455
 18: 2 And **J** also, which betrayed him, knew 2455
 18: 3 **J** then, having received a band *of men*, 2455
 18: 5 And **J** also, which betrayed him, 2455
Ac 1:13 Zelotes, and **J** the brother of James. 2455
 1:16 of David spake before concerning **J**, 2455
 1:25 from which **J** by transgression fell, 2455
 5:37 After this *man* rose up **J** of Galilee in 2455
 9:11 inquire in the house of **J** for *one* called 2455
 15:22 namely, **J** surnamed Barsabas, and Silas, 2455
 15:27 We have sent therefore **J** and Silas, 2455
 15:32 And **J** and Silas, being prophets also 2455

JUDE (1)
Jude 1 **J**, the servant of Jesus Christ, 2455

JUDEA (44) [JUDAH]
Ezr 5: 8 that we went into the province of **J**, 3061
Mt 2: 1 of **J** in the days of Herod the king, 2449
 2: 5 they said unto him, In Bethlehem of **J**: 2449
 2:22 reign in **J** in the room of his father Herod, 2449
 3: 1 preaching in the wilderness of **J**, 2449
 3: 5 and all **J**, and all the region round about 2449
 4:25 and *from* **J**, and *from* beyond Jordan. 2449
 19: 1 came into the coasts of **J** beyond Jordan; 2449
 24:16 Then let them which be in **J** flee into 2449
Mk 1: 5 there went out unto him all the land of **J**, 2449
 3: 7 From Galilee followed him, and from **J**, 2449
 10: 1 cometh into the coasts of **J** by the farther 2449
 13:14 them that be in **J** flee to the mountains: 2449
Lk 1: 5 was in the days of Herod, the king of **J**, 2449
 1:65 throughout all the hill country of **J**. 2449
 2: 4 of Nazareth, into **J**, unto the city of David, 2449
 3: 1 Pontius Pilate being governor of **J**, 2449
 5:17 town of Galilee, and **J**, and Jerusalem: 2449
 6:17 great multitude of people out of all **J** and 2449
 7:17 of him went forth throughout all **J**, 2449
 21:21 Then let them which are in **J** flee to 2449
Jn 3:22 and his disciples into the land of **J**; 2453
 4: 3 He left **J**, and departed again into Galilee. 2449
 4:47 he heard that Jesus was come out of **J** 2449
 4:54 when he was come out of **J** into Galilee. 2449
 7: 3 unto him, Depart hence, and go into **J**, 2449
 11: 7 he to *his* disciples, Let us go into **J** again. 2449
Ac 1: 8 and in all **J**, and in Samaria, and 2449
 2: 9 and in **J**, and Cappadocia, in Pontus, 2449
 2:14 Ye men of **J**, and all *ye* that dwell at 2453
 8: 1 abroad throughout the regions of **J** 2449
 9:31 had the churches rest throughout all **J** 2449
 10:37 which was published throughout all **J**, 2449
 11: 1 brethren that were in **J** heard that 2449
 11:29 relief unto the brethren which dwelt in **J**: 2449
 12:19 And he went down from **J** to Cesarea, 2449
 15: 1 certain *men* which came down from **J** 2449
 21:10 there came down from **J** a certain prophet, 2449
 26:20 throughout all the coasts of **J**, and *then* 2449
 28:21 We neither received letters out of **J** 2449
Ro 15:31 from them that do not believe in **J**; 2449
2Co 1:16 of you to be brought on *my* way toward **J**. 2449
Gal 1:22 the churches of **J** which were in Christ: 2449
1Th 2:14 of God which in **J** are in Christ Jesus: 2449

JUDEAN See JEHUDIJAH; JUDAH

JUDGE (191) [JUDGED, JUDGES, JUDGEST, JUDGETH, JUDGING, JUDGMENT, JUDGMENTS]
Ge 15:14 nation, whom they shall serve, will I **j**: 1777
 16: 5 the LORD **j** between me and thee. 8199
 18:25 Shall not the **J** of all the earth do right? 8199
 19: 9 sojourn, and he will **needs be a j**: 8199+8199
 31:37 that they may **j** betwixt us both. 3198
 31:53 the God of their father, **j** betwixt us. 8199
 49:16 Dan shall **j** his people, as one of the tribes 1777
Ex 2:14 Who made thee a prince and a **j** over us? 8199
 5:21 The LORD look upon you, and **j**; 8199
 18:13 morrow, that Moses sat to **j** the people: 8199

Ex 18:16 I **j** between one and another, and I do 8199
 18:22 let them **j** the people at all seasons: 8199
 18:22 but every small matter they shall **j**: 8199
Lev 19:15 righteousness shalt thou **j** thy neighbour. 8199
Nu 35:24 congregation shall **j** between the slayer 8199
Dt 1:16 **j** righteously between every man and his 8199
 16:18 they shall **j** the people *with* just judgment. 8199
 17: 9 unto the **j** that shall be in those days, 8199
 17:12 or unto the **j**, even that man shall die: 8199
 25: 1 judgment, that *the judges* may **j** them; 8199
 25: 2 that the **j** shall cause him to lie down, 8199
 32:36 For the LORD shall **j** his people, 1777
Jdg 2:18 the LORD was with the **j**, 8199
 2:18 of their enemies all the days of the **j**: 8199
 2:19 when the **j** was dead, *that* they returned, 8199
 11:27 the LORD the **J** be judge *this* day between 8199
 11:27 the LORD the Judge be *this* day between 8199
1Sa 2:10 the LORD shall **j** the ends of the earth; 1777
 2:25 sin against another, the **j** shall judge him: 430
 2:25 sin against another, the judge shall **j** him: 6419
 3:13 For I have told him that I will **j** his house 8199
 8: 5 now make us a king to **j** us like all 8199
 8: 6 when they said, Give us a king to **j** us. 8199
 8:20 that our king may **j** us, and go out before 8199
 24:12 The LORD **j** between me and thee, 8199
 24:15 The LORD therefore be **j**, 1781
 24:15 **j** between me and thee, and see, 8199
2Sa 15: 4 Oh that I were made **j** in the land, 8199
1Ki 3: 9 servant an understanding heart to **j** thy 8199
 3: 9 for who is able to **j** this thy *so* great a 8199
 7: 7 a porch for the throne where he might **j**, 8199
 8:32 do, and **j** thy servants, condemning 8199
1Ch 16:33 because he cometh to **j** the earth. 8199
2Ch 1:10 for who can **j** this thy people, *that is so* 8199
 1:11 for thyself, that thou mayest **j** my people, 8199
 6:23 do, and **j** thy servants, by requiting 8199
 19: 6 for ye **j** not for man, but for the LORD, 8199
 20:12 O our God, wilt thou not **j** them? for we 8199
Ezr 7:25 may **j** all the people that *are* beyond 1778
Job 9:15 *but* I would make supplication to my **j**. 8199
 22:13 can he **j** through the dark *cloud*? 8199
 23: 7 should I be delivered for ever from my **j**. 8199
 31:28 *were* an iniquity *to be punished by* the **j**: 6416
Ps 7: 8 The LORD shall **j** the people: judge me, 1777
 7: 8 **j** me, O LORD, according to my 8199
 9: 8 he shall **j** the world in righteousness, 8199
 10:18 To **j** the fatherless and the oppressed, 8199
 26: 1 **J** me, O LORD; for I have walked in mine 8199
 35:24 **J** me, O LORD my God, according to thy 8199
 43: 1 **J** me, O God, and plead my cause against 8199
 50: 4 to the earth, that *he* may **j** his people. 1777
 50: 6 for God *is* **j** himself. Selah. 8199
 54: 1 by thy name, and **j** me by thy strength. 1777
 58: 1 do ye **j** uprightly, O ye sons of men? 8199
 67: 4 for thou shalt **j** the people righteously, 8199
 68: 5 of the fatherless, and a **j** of the widows, 1781
 72: 2 He shall **j** thy people with righteousness, 1777
 72: 4 He shall **j** the poor of the people, he shall 8199
 75: 2 receive the congregation I will **j** uprightly. 8199
 75: 7 God *is* the **j**: he putteth down one, 8199
 82: 2 How long will ye **j** unjustly, and accept 8199
 82: 8 Arise, O God, **j** the earth: for thou shalt 8199
 94: 2 Lift up thyself, thou **j** of the earth: render 8199
 96:10 moved: he shall **j** the people righteously. 1777
 96:13 he cometh, for he cometh to **j** the earth: 8199
 96:13 he shall **j** the world with righteousness, 8199
 98: 9 the LORD; for he cometh to **j** the earth: 8199
 98: 9 with righteousness shall he **j** the world, 8199
 110: 6 He shall **j** among the heathen, he shall fill 1777
 135:14 For the LORD will **j** his people, 1777
Pr 31: 9 **j** righteously, and plead the cause of 8199
Ecc 3:17 God shall **j** the righteous and the wicked: 8199
Isa 1:17 the fatherless, plead for the widow. 8199
 1:23 they **j** not the fatherless, neither doth 8199
 2: 4 he shall **j** among the nations, 8199
 3: 2 the **j**, and the prophet, and the prudent, 8199
 3:13 *up* to plead, and standeth to **j** the people. 1777
 5: 3 **j**, I pray you, betwixt me and my 8199
 11: 3 he shall not **j** after the sight of his eyes, 8199
 11: 4 with righteousness shall he **j** the poor, 8199
 33:22 For the LORD *is* our **j**, the LORD *is* our 8199
 51: 5 mine arms shall **j** the people; 8199
Jer 5:28 they **j** not the cause, the cause of 1777
 5:28 and the right of the needy do they not **j**. 8199
La 3:59 hast seen my wrong: **j** thou my cause. 8199
Eze 7: 3 will I **j** thee according to thy ways, 8199
 7: 8 I will **j** thee according to thy ways, 8199
 7:27 according to their deserts will I **j** them; 8199
 11:10 I will **j** you in the border of Israel; 8199
 11:11 *but* I will **j** you in the border of Israel: 8199
 16:38 I will **j** thee, as *women* that break 8199
 18:30 Therefore I will **j** you, O house of Israel, 8199
 20: 4 Wilt thou **j** them, son of man, wilt thou 8199
 20: 4 wilt thou **j** *them?* cause them to know 8199
 21:30 I will **j** thee in the place where thou wast 8199
 22: 2 Now, thou son of man, wilt thou **j**, wilt 8199
 22: 2 thou judge, wilt thou **j** the bloody city? 8199
 23:24 they shall **j** thee according to their 8199
 23:36 of man, wilt thou **j** Aholah and Aholibah? 8199
 23:45 they shall **j** them after the manner of 8199
 24:14 shall they **j** thee, saith the Lord GOD. 8199
 33:20 I will **j** you every one after his ways. 8199
 34:17 Behold, I **j** between cattle and cattle, 8199
 34:20 will **j** between the fat cattle and 8199
 34:22 and I will **j** between cattle and cattle. 8199

Eze 44:24 they shall **j** according to my judgments: 8199
Joel 3:12 there will I sit to **j** all the heathen round 8199
Am 2: 3 I will cut off the **j** from the midst thereof, 8199
Ob 1:21 saviours shall come up on mount Zion to **j** 8199
Mic 3:11 The heads thereof **j** for reward, 8199
 4: 3 he shall **j** among many people, 8199
 5: 1 they shall smite the **j** of Israel with a rod 8199
 7: 3 asketh, and the **j** *asketh* for a reward; 8199
Zec 3: 7 thou shalt also **j** my house, and shalt also 1777
Mt 5:25 time the adversary deliver thee to the **j**, 2923
 5:25 and the **j** deliver thee to the officer, 2923
 7: 1 **J** not, that ye be not judged. 2919
 7: 2 For with what judgment ye **j**, ye shall be 2919
Lk 6:37 **J** not, and ye shall not be judged: 2919
 12:14 who made me a **j** or a divider over you? 1348
 12:57 why even of yourselves **j** ye not what *is* 2919
 12:58 lest he hale thee to the **j**, and the judge 2923
 12:58 and the **j** deliver thee to the officer, 2923
 18: 2 Saying, There was in a city a **j**, 2923
 18: 6 Lord said, Hear what the unjust **j** saith. 2923
 19:22 Out of thine own mouth will I **j** thee, 2919
Jn 5:30 as I hear, I **j**: and my judgment is just; 2919
 7:24 **J** not according to the appearance, 2919
 7:24 the appearance, but **j** righteous judgment. 2919
 7:51 Doth our law **j** any man, before it hear 2919
 8:15 Ye **j** after the flesh; I judge no *man*. 2919
 8:15 Ye judge after the flesh; I **j** no *man*. 2919
 8:16 yet if I **j**, my judgment is true: for I am 2919
 8:26 I have many *things* to say and to **j** of you: 2919
 12:47 my words, and believe not, I **j** him not: 2919
 12:47 for I came not to **j** the world, but to save 2919
 12:48 the same shall **j** him in the last day. 2919
 18:31 ye him, and **j** him according to your law. 2919
Ac 4:19 unto you more than unto God, **j** ye. 2919
 7: 7 to whom they shall be in bondage will I **j**, 2919
 7:27 Who made thee a ruler and a **j** over us? 1348
 7:35 saying, Who made thee a ruler and a **j**? 1348
 10:42 was ordained of God *to be* the **J** of quick 2923
 13:46 **j** yourselves unworthy of everlasting life, 2919
 17:31 in the which he will **j** the world in 2919
 18:15 look ye *to it;* for I will be no **j** of such 2923
 23: 3 for sittest thou to **j** me after the law, 2919
 24:10 been of many years a **j** unto this nation, 2923
Ro 2:16 In the day when God shall **j** the secrets of 2919
 2:27 **j** thee, who by the letter and 2919
 3: 6 for then how shall God **j** the world? 2919
 14: 3 let not him which eateth not **j** him that 2919
 14:10 But why dost thou **j** thy brother? or why 2919
 14:13 us not therefore **j** one another any more: 2919
 14:13 but **j** this rather, that no man put a 2919
1Co 2:15 judgment: yea, I **j** not mine own self. 350
 4: 5 Therefore **j** nothing before the time, 2919
 5:12 what have I to do to **j** them also that are 2919
 5:12 do not ye **j** them that are within? 2919
 6: 2 Do ye not know that the saints shall **j** 2919
 6: 2 are ye unworthy to **j** the smallest matters? 2922
 6: 3 Know ye not that we shall **j** angels? 2919
 6: 4 **set** them **to j** who are least esteemed in 2523
 6: 5 not one that shall be able to **j** between his 1252
 10:15 I speak as to wise *men; ye* what I say. 2919
 11:13 **J** in yourselves: is it comely that a woman 2919
 11:31 if we would **j** ourselves, we should not 1252
 14:29 speak two or three, and let the other **j**. 1252
2Co 5:14 because we thus **j**, that if one died for all, 2919
Col 2:16 Let no *man* therefore **j** you in meat, 2919
2Ti 4: 1 who shall **j** the quick and the dead at his 2919
 4: 8 which the Lord, the righteous, shall give 2923
Heb 10:30 And again, The Lord shall **j** his people. 2919
 12:23 to God the **J** of all, and to the spirits of 2923
 13: 4 whoremongers and adulterers God will **j**. 2919
Jas 4:11 if thou **j** the law, thou art not a doer of 2919
 4:11 thou art not a doer of the law, but a **j**. 2923
 5: 9 the **j** standeth before the door. 2923
1Pe 4: 5 account to him that is ready to **j** the quick 2919
Rev 6:10 dost thou not **j** and avenge our blood on 2919
 19:11 and in righteousness he doth **j** and 2919

JUDGED (63) [JUDGE]
Ge 30: 6 God hath **j** me, and hath also heard my 1777
Ex 18:26 they the people at all seasons: the hard 8199
 18:26 but every small matter they **j** themselves. 8199
Jdg 3:10 and he **j** Israel, and went out to war: 8199
 4: 4 wife of Lapidoth, she **j** Israel at that time. 8199
 10: 2 **j** Israel twenty and three years, and died, 8199
 10: 3 and **j** Israel twenty and two years. 8199
 12: 7 Jephthah **j** Israel six years. Then died 8199
 12: 8 after him Ibzan of Beth-lehem **j** Israel. 8199
 12: 9 for his sons. And he **j** Israel seven years. 8199
 12:11 after him Elon, a Zebulonite, **j** Israel; 8199
 12:11 judged Israel; and he **j** Israel ten years. 8199
 12:13 the son of Hillel, a Pirathonite, **j** Israel. 8199
 12:14 ten ass colts: and he **j** Israel eight years. 8199
 15:20 he **j** Israel in the days of the Philistines 8199
 16:31 his father. And he **j** Israel twenty years. 8199
1Sa 4:18 And he had **j** Israel forty years. 8199
 7: 6 Samuel **j** the children of Israel in Mizpeh. 8199
 7:15 Samuel **j** Israel all the days of his life. 8199
 7:16 Mizpeh, and Israel in all those places. 8199
 7:17 he **j** Israel; and there he built an altar 8199
1Ki 3:28 of the judgment which the king had **j**; 8199
2Ki 23:22 from the days of the judges that **j** Israel, 8199
Ps 9:19 let the heathen be **j** in thy sight. 8199
 37:33 his hand, nor condemn him when he is **j**. 8199
 109: 7 he shall be **j**, let him be condemned: 8199
Jer 22:16 He **j** the cause of the poor and needy; 1777

J

Eze	16:38	that break wedlock and shed blood are j;	4941
	16:52	Thou also, which hast j thy sisters,	6419
	28:23	wounded shall be j in the midst of her	5307
	35:11	whom then, when I have j thee.	8199
	36:19	and according to their doings I j them.	8199
Da	9:12	and against our judges that j us,	8199
Mt	7: 1	Judge not, that ye be not j.	2919
	7: 2	what judgment ye judge, ye shall be j:	2919
Lk	6:37	Judge not, and ye shall not be j:	2919
	7:43	he said unto him, Thou hast rightly j.	2919
Jn	16:11	because the prince of this world is j.	2919
Ac	16:15	If ye have j me to be faithful to the Lord,	2919
	24: 6	and would have j according to our law.	2919
	25: 9	and be j of these things before me?	2919
	25:10	judgment seat, where I ought to be j:	2919
	25:20	and there be j of these matters.	2919
	26: 6	am I for the hope of the promise made of	2919
Ro	2:12	many as have sinned in the law shall be j	2919
	3: 4	and mightest overcome when thou art j.	2919
	3: 7	his glory; why yet am I also j as a sinner?	2919
1Co	2:15	all things, yet he himself is j of no man.	350
	4: 3	very small thing that I should be j of you,	350
	5: 3	but present in spirit, have j already,	2919
	6: 2	and if the world shall be j by you, are ye	2919
	10:29	for why is my liberty j of another man's	2919
	11:31	judge ourselves, we should not be j.	2919
	11:32	But when we are j, we are chastened of	2919
	14:24	he is convinced of all, he is j of all:	350
Heb	11:11	she j him faithful who had promised.	2233
Jas	2:12	they that shall be j by the law of liberty.	2919
1Pe	4: 6	that they might be j according to men in	2919
Rev	11:18	that they should be j, and that thou	2919
	16: 5	and shalt be, because thou hast j thus.	2919
	19: 2	for he hath j the great whore, which did	2919
	20:12	the dead were j out of those things which	2919
	20:13	they were j every man according to their	2919

JUDGES (52) [JUDGE]

Ex	21: 6	his master shall bring him unto the j;	430
	21:22	and he shall pay as the j determine.	6414
	22: 8	of the house shall be brought unto the j,	430
	22: 9	of both parties shall come before the j;	430
	22: 9	whom the j shall condemn, he shall pay	430
Nu	25: 5	Moses said unto the j of Israel, Slay ye	8199
Dt	1:16	I charged your j at that time, saying,	8199
	16:18	J and officers shalt thou make thee in all	8199
	19:17	before the priests and the j, which shall	8199
	19:18	the j shall make diligent inquisition:	8199
	21: 2	thy elders and thy j shall come forth,	8199
	25: 1	judgment, that the j may judge them;	NIH
	32:31	even our enemies themselves being j.	6414
Jos	8:33	and their elders, and officers, and their j,	8199
	23: 2	for their j, and for their officers,	8199
	24: 1	and for their j, and for their officers;	8199
Jdg	2:16	Nevertheless the Lord raised up j,	8199
	2:17	yet they would not hearken unto their j,	8199
	2:18	when the Lord raised them up j, then	8199
Ru	1: 1	it came to pass in the days when the j	8199
1Sa	8: 1	old, that he made his sons j over Israel.	8199
	8: 2	Abiah: they were j in Beer-sheba.	8199
2Sa	7:11	since the time that I commanded j to be	8199
2Ki	23:22	from the days of the j that judged Israel,	8199
1Ch	17: 6	spake I a word to any of the j of Israel,	8199
	17:10	since the time that I commanded j to be	8199
	23: 4	and six thousand were officers and j:	8199
	26:29	business over Israel, for officers and j	8199
2Ch	1: 2	the j, and to every governor in all Israel,	8199
	19: 5	he set j in the land throughout all	8199
	19: 6	said to the j, Take heed what ye do: for	8199
Ezr	7:25	is in thine hand, set magistrates and j,	1782
	10:14	the elders of every city, and the j thereof,	8199
Job	9:24	covereth the faces of the j thereof; if not,	8199
	12:17	away spoiled, and maketh the j fools.	8199
	31:11	it is an iniquity to be punished by the j.	6414
Ps	2:10	ye kings: be instructed, ye j of the earth.	8199
	141: 6	When their j are overthrown in stony	8199
	148:11	all people; princes, and all j of the earth:	8199
Pr	8:16	and nobles, even all the j of the earth.	8199
Isa	1:26	I will restore thy j as at the first,	8199
	40:23	he maketh the j of the earth as vanity.	8199
Da	3: 2	and the captains, the j, the treasurers,	148
	3: 3	the governors and captains, the j,	148
	9:12	us, and against our j that judged us,	8199
Hos	7: 7	as an oven, and have devoured their j;	8199
	13:10	of whom thou saidst, Give me a king	8199
Zep	3: 3	roaring lions; her j are evening wolves;	8199
Mt	12:27	them out? therefore they shall be your j.	2923
Lk	11:19	them out? therefore shall they be your j.	2923
Ac	13:20	And after that he gave unto them j about	2923
Jas	2: 4	And are become j of evil thoughts?	2923

JUDGEST (8) [JUDGE]

Ps	51: 4	thou speakest, and be clear when thou j.	8199
Jer	11:20	that j righteously, that triest the reins and	8199
Ro	2: 1	O man, whosoever thou art that j:	2919
	2: 1	for wherein thou j another,	2919
	2: 1	for thou that j doest the same things.	2919
	2: 3	that j them which do such things, and	2919
	14: 4	art thou that j another man's servant?	2919
Jas	4:12	to destroy: who art thou that j another?	2919

JUDGETH (17) [JUDGE]

Job	21:22	seeing he j those that are high.	8199
	36:31	by them j he the people; he giveth meat	1777
Ps	7:11	God j the righteous, and God is angry	8199
	58:11	verily he is a God that j in the earth.	8199
	82: 1	of the mighty; he j among the gods.	8199
Pr	29:14	The king that faithfully j the poor,	8199
Jn	5:22	For the Father j no man, but	2919
	8:50	own glory: there is one that seeketh and j.	2919
		not my words, hath one that j him:	2919
1Co	2:15	But he that is spiritual j all things, yet he	350
	4: 4	justified: but he that j me is the Lord.	350
	5:13	But them that are without God j.	2919
Jas	4:11	and his brother, speaketh evil of the law,	2919
	4:11	speaketh evil of the law, and j the law:	2919
1Pe	1:17	without respect of persons j according	2919
Rev	18: 8	for strong is the Lord God who j her.	2919

JUDGING (6) [JUDGE]

2Ki	15: 5	over the house, j the people of the land.	8199
2Ch	26:21	the king's house, j the people of the land.	8199
Ps	9: 4	cause; thou satest in the throne j right.	8199
Isa	16: 5	j, and seeking judgment,	8199
Mt	19:28	thrones, j the twelve tribes of Israel.	2919
Lk	22:30	sit on thrones j the twelve tribes of Israel.	2919

JUDGMENT (294) [JUDGE]

Ge	18:19	the way of the Lord, to do justice and	4941
Ex	12:12	all the gods of Egypt I will execute j:	8201
	21:31	according to this j shall it be done unto	4941
	23: 2	a cause to decline after many to wrest j:	NIH
	23: 6	Thou shalt not wrest the j of thy poor in	4941
	28:15	thou shalt make the breastplate of j with	4941
	28:29	in the breastplate of j upon his heart,	4941
	28:30	thou shalt put in the breastplate of j	4941
	28:30	Aaron shall bear the j of the children of	4941
Lev	19:15	Ye shall do no unrighteousness in j:	4941
	19:35	Ye shall do no unrighteousness in j,	4941
Nu	27:11	unto the children of Israel a statute of j,	4941
	27:21	who shall ask counsel for him after the j	4941
	35:12	he stand before the congregation in j.	4941
	35:29	So these things shall be for a statute of j	4941
Dt	1:17	Ye shall not respect persons in j;	4941
	1:17	of the face of man; for the j is God's:	4941
	10:18	He doth execute the j of the fatherless	4941
	16:18	and they shall judge the people with just j.	4941
	16:19	Thou shalt not wrest j; thou shalt not	4941
	17: 8	there arise a matter too hard for thee in j,	4941
	17: 9	they shall shew thee the sentence of j:	4941
	17:11	according to the j which they shall tell	4941
	24:17	shalt not pervert the j of the stranger,	4941
	25: 1	come unto j, that the judges may judge	4941
	27:19	Cursed be he that perverteth the j of	4941
	32: 4	for all his ways are j: a God of truth and	4941
	32:41	and mine hand take hold on j;	4941
Jos	20: 6	he stand before the congregation in j.	4941
Jdg	4: 5	the children of Israel came up to her for j.	4941
	5:10	ye that sit in j, and walk by the way.	4055
1Sa	8: 3	lucre, and took bribes, and perverted j.	4941
2Sa	8:15	David executed j and justice unto all his	4941
	15: 2	had a controversy came to the king for j,	4941
	15: 6	to all Israel that came to the king for j:	4941
1Ki	3:11	for thyself understanding to discern j;	4941
	3:28	all Israel heard of the j which the king had	4941
	3:28	the wisdom of God was in him, to do j.	4941
	7: 7	he might judge, even the porch of j:	4941
	10: 9	made he thee king, to do j and justice.	4941
	20:40	So shall thy j be; thyself hast decided it.	4941
2Ki	25: 6	to Riblah; and they gave j upon him.	4941
1Ch	18:14	executed j and justice among all his	4941
2Ch	9: 8	thee king over them, to do j and justice.	4941
	19: 6	the Lord, who is with you in the j.	1697+4941
	19: 8	for the j of the Lord,	4941
	20: 9	as the sword, j, or pestilence, or famine,	8196
	22: 8	that when Jehu was **executing** j upon	8199
	24:24	So they executed j against Joash.	8201
Ezr	7:26	let j be executed speedily upon him,	1780
Est	1:13	manner towards all that knew law and j:	1779
Job	8: 3	Doth God pervert j? or doth the Almighty	4941
	9:19	if of j, who shall set me a time to plead?	4941
	9:32	and we should come together in j.	4941
	14: 3	a one, and bringest me into j with thee?	4941
	19: 7	not heard: I cry aloud, but there is no j.	4941
	19:29	the sword, that ye may know there is a j.	1779
	22: 4	of thee? will he enter with thee into j?	4941
	27: 2	God liveth, who hath taken away my j;	4941
	29:14	my j was as a robe and a diadem.	4941
	32: 9	neither do the aged understand j.	4941
	34: 4	Let us choose to us j: let us know among	4941
	34: 5	and God hath taken away my j.	4941
	34:12	neither will the Almighty pervert j.	4941
	34:23	that he should enter into j with God.	4941
	35:14	thou shalt not see him, yet j is before him;	4941
	36:17	thou hast fulfilled the j of the wicked:	1779
	36:17	wicked: j and justice take hold on thee.	1779
	37:23	power, and in j, and in plenty of justice:	4941
	40: 8	Wilt thou also disannul my j? wilt thou	4941
Ps	1: 5	The ungodly shall not stand in the j,	4941
	7: 6	awake for me to the j that thou hast	4941
	9: 7	he hath prepared his throne for j.	4941
	9: 8	he shall **minister** j to the people in	1777
	9:16	The Lord is known by the j which he	4941
	25: 9	The meek will he guide in j: and the	4941
	33: 5	He loveth righteousness and j: the earth is	4941
	35:23	Stir up thyself, and awake to my j,	4941
	37: 6	as the light, and thy j as the noonday.	4941
	37:28	For the Lord loveth j, and forsaketh not	4941
	37:30	and his tongue talketh of j.	4941
Ps	72: 2	with righteousness, and thy poor with j.	4941
	76: 8	Thou didst cause j to be heard from	1779
	76: 9	When God arose to j, to save all the meek	4941
	89:14	and j are the habitation of thy throne:	4941
	94:15	j shall return unto righteousness: and all	4941
	97: 2	and j are the habitation of his throne.	4941
	99: 4	The king's strength also loveth j; thou	4941
	99: 4	executest j and righteousness in Jacob.	4941
	101: 1	I will sing of mercy and j: unto thee,	4941
	103: 6	and j for all that are oppressed.	4941
	106: 3	Blessed are they that keep j, and he that	4941
	106:30	stood up Phinehas, and **executed**	6419
	111: 7	The works of his hands are verity and j;	4941
	119:66	Teach me good j and knowledge: for I	2940
	119:84	when wilt thou execute j on them that	4941
	119:121	I have done j and justice: leave me not to	4941
	119:149	O Lord, quicken me according to thy j.	4941
	122: 5	there are set thrones of j, the thrones of	4941
	143: 2	enter not into j with thy servant: for in	4941
	146: 7	Which executeth j for the oppressed:	4941
	149: 9	To execute upon them the j written:	4941
Pr	1: 3	of wisdom, justice, and j, and equity;	4941
	2: 8	He keepeth the paths of j,	4941
	2: 9	understand righteousness, and j,	4941
	8:20	in the midst of the paths of j:	4941
	13:23	but there is that is destroyed for want of j.	4941
	16:10	the king: his mouth transgresseth not in j.	4941
	17:23	out of the bosom to pervert the ways of j.	4941
	18: 5	wicked, to overthrow the righteous in j.	4941
	19:28	An ungodly witness scorneth j:	4941
	20: 8	A king that sitteth in the throne of j	1779
	21: 3	j is more acceptable to the Lord than	4941
	21: 7	destroy them; because they refuse to do j.	4941
	21:15	It is joy to the just to do j:	4941
	24:23	is not good to have respect of persons in j.	4941
	28: 5	Evil men understand not j: but they that	4941
	29: 4	The king by j stablisheth the land:	4941
	29:26	every man's j cometh from the Lord.	4941
	31: 5	and pervert the j of any of the afflicted.	1779
Ecc	3:16	I saw under the sun the place of j,	4941
	5: 8	violent perverting of j and justice in a	4941
	8: 5	man's heart discerneth both time and	4941
	8: 6	to every purpose there is time and j,	4941
	11: 9	all these things God will bring thee into j.	4941
	12:14	For God shall bring every work into j,	4941
Isa	1:17	seek j, relieve the oppressed, judge	4941
	1:21	it was full of j; righteousness lodged in it;	4941
	1:27	Zion shall be redeemed with j,	4941
	3:14	The Lord will enter into j with	4941
	4: 4	from the midst thereof by the spirit of j,	4941
	5: 7	he looked for j, but behold oppression;	4941
	5:16	the Lord of hosts shall be exalted in j,	4941
	9: 7	to stablish it with j and with justice from	4941
	10: 2	To turn aside the needy from j, and to	1779
	16: 3	Take counsel, execute j; make thy	6415
	16: 5	and seeking j, and hasting righteousness.	4941
	28: 6	for a spirit of j to him that sitteth in	4941
	28: 6	spirit of judgment to him that sitteth in j.	4941
	28: 7	they err in vision, they stumble in j.	6417
	28:17	j also will I lay to the line,	4941
	30:18	for the Lord is a God of j: blessed are all	4941
	32: 1	righteousness, and princes shall rule in j.	4941
	32:16	j shall dwell in the wilderness,	4941
	33: 5	he hath filled Zion with j and	4941
	34: 5	and upon the people of my curse, to j.	4941
	40:14	taught him in the path of j, and taught	4941
	40:27	and my j is passed over from my God?	4941
	41: 1	speak: let us come near together to j.	4941
	42: 1	he shall bring forth j to the Gentiles.	4941
	42: 3	quench: he shall bring forth j unto truth.	4941
	42: 4	till he have set j in the earth:	4941
	49: 4	yet surely my j is with the Lord,	4941
	51: 4	I will make my j to rest for a light of	4941
	53: 8	He was taken from prison and from j:	4941
	54:17	tongue that shall rise against thee in j	4941
	56: 1	saith the Lord, Keep ye j, and do justice:	4941
	58: 2	not; and there is no j in their goings:	4941
	59: 8	Therefore is j far from us, neither doth	4941
	59: 9	we look for j, but there is none;	4941
	59:11	j is turned away backward,	4941
	59:14	and it displeased him that there was no j.	4941
	59:15	For I the Lord love j, I hate robbery for	4941
	61: 8	in truth, in j, and in righteousness;	4941
Jer	4: 2	a man, if there be any that executeth j,	4941
	5: 1	way of the Lord, nor the j of their God.	4941
	5: 4	way of the Lord, and the j of their God:	4941
	5: 5	if you throughly execute j between a man	4941
	7: 5	my people know not the j of the Lord.	4941
	8: 7	j, and righteousness, in the earth:	4941
	9:24	O Lord, correct me, but with j; not in	4941
	10:24	Execute j in the morning, and deliver him	4941
	21:12	Execute ye j and righteousness,	4941
	22: 3	do j and justice, and then it was well with	4941
	22:15	shall execute j and justice in the earth.	4941
	23: 5	he shall execute j and righteousness in	4941
	33:15	of Hamath, where he gave j upon him.	4941
	39: 5	is come upon the plain country;	4941
	48:21	saith the Lord. Thus far is the j of Moab.	4941
	48:47	they whose j was not to drink of the cup	4941
	49:12	her j reacheth unto heaven, and is lifted	4941
	51: 9	that I will **do** j upon the graven images of	6485
	51:47	that I will **do** j upon her graven images:	6485
	51:52	of Hamath; where he gave j upon him.	4941
	52: 9	executed true j between man and man,	4941
Eze	18: 8	for they had executed j upon her.	8196
	23:10		

Eze 23:24 I will set **j** before them, and they shall 4941
34:16 and the strong; I will feed them with **j**. 4941
39:21 all the heathen shall see my **j** that I have 4941
44:24 in controversy they shall stand in **j**; 4941
45: 9 and spoil, and execute **j** and justice, 4941
Da 4:37 all whose works *are* truth, and his ways **j**: 1780
7:10 the **j** was set, and the books were opened. 1780
7:22 **j** *was* given to the saints of the most High; 1780
7:26 the **j** shall sit, and they shall take away his 1780
Hos 2:19 **j**, and in lovingkindness, and in mercies. 4941
5: 1 for **j** *is* toward you, because ye have been 4941
5:11 Ephraim *is* oppressed *and* broken in **j**, 4941
10: 4 thus **j** springeth up as hemlock in 4941
12: 6 keep mercy and **j**, and wait on thy God 4941
Am 5: 7 *Ye* who turn **j** to wormwood, and leave 4941
5:15 love the good, and establish **j** in the gate: 4941
5:24 let **j** run down as waters, 4941
6:12 ye have turned **j** into gall, and the fruit 4941
Mic 3: 1 Israel; *is it* not for you to know **j**? 4941
3: 8 of **j**, and of might, to declare unto Jacob 4941
3: 9 that abhor **j**, and pervert all equity. 4941
7: 9 he plead my cause, and execute **j** for me: 4941
Hab 1: 4 law is slacked, and **j** doth never go forth: 4941
1: 4 therefore wrong **j** proceedeth. 4941
1: 7 their **j** and their dignity shall proceed of 4941
1:12 O LORD, thou hast ordained them for **j**; 4941
Zep 2: 3 of the earth, which have wrought his **j**; 4941
3: 5 every morning doth he bring his **j** to light, 4941
Zec 7: 9 Execute true **j**, and shew mercy and 4941
8:16 **execute the j** of truth and peace in 4941+8199
Mal 2:17 in them; or, Where *is* the God of **j**? 4941
3: 5 I will come near to you to **j**; and I will be 4941
Mt 5:21 shall kill shall be in danger of the **j**: 2920
5:22 without a cause shall be in danger of the **j**: 2920
7: 2 For with what **j** ye judge, ye shall be 2917
10:15 of Sodom and Gomorrha in the day of **j**, 2920
11:22 tolerable for Tyre and Sidon at the day of **j** 2920
11:24 for the land of Sodom in the day of **j**, 2920
12:18 and he shall shew **j** to the Gentiles. 2920
12:20 quench, till he send forth **j** unto victory. 2920
12:36 shall give account thereof in the day of **j**. 2920
12:41 men of Nineveh shall rise in **j** with this 2920
12:42 queen of the south shall rise up in the **j** 2920
23:23 *matters* of the law, **j**, mercy, and faith: 2920
27:19 When he was set down on the **j seat**, 968
Mk 6:11 for Sodom and Gomorrha in the day of **j**, 2920
Lk 10:14 more tolerable for Tyre and Sidon at the **j**, 2920
11:31 queen of the south shall rise up in the **j** 2920
11:32 *The* men of Nineveh shall rise up in the **j** 2920
11:42 and pass over **j** and the love of God: 2920
Jn 5:22 but hath committed all **j** unto the Son: 2920
5:27 And hath given him authority to execute **j** 2920
5:30 and my **j** is just; because I seek not mine 2920
7:24 to the appearance, but judge righteous **j**. 2920
8:16 yet if I judge, my **j** is true: for I am not 2920
9:39 said, For **j** I am come into this world, 2917
12:31 Now is the **j** of this world: now shall 2920
16: 8 of sin, and of righteousness, and of **j**: 2920
16:11 Of **j**, because the prince of this world is 2920
18:28 Jesus from Caiaphas unto the **hall of j**: 4232
18:28 they themselves went not into the **j hall**, 4232
18:33 Then Pilate entered into the **j hall** again, 4232
19: 9 And went again into the **j hall**, 4232
19:13 sat down in the **j seat** in a place *that is* 968
Ac 8:33 In his humiliation his **j** was taken away: 2920
18:12 Paul, and brought him to the **j seat**, 968
18:16 And he drave them from the **j seat**. 968
18:17 and beat *him* before the **j seat**. 968
23:35 him to be kept in Herod's **j hall**. 4232
24:25 and **j** to come, Felix trembled, 2917
25: 6 and the next day sitting in the **j seat**, 968
25:10 Then said Paul, I stand at Cesar's **j seat**, 968
25:15 *me*, desiring *to have* **j** against him. 1349
25:17 on the morrow I sat on the **j seat**, 968
Ro 1:32 Who knowing the **j** of God, that they 1345
2: 2 But we are sure that the **j** of God is 2917
2: 3 that thou shalt escape the **j** of God? 2917
2: 5 and revelation of the **righteous j** of God; 1341
5:16 for the **j** *was* by one to condemnation, 2917
5:18 Therefore as by the offence of one **j** *came* NIG
14:10 for we shall all stand before the **j seat** of 968
1Co 1:10 in the same mind and in the same **j**. 1106
4: 3 I should be judged of you, or of man's **j**: 2250
7:25 yet I give *my* **j**, as one that hath obtained 1106
7:40 she is happier if she so abide, after my **j**: 1106
2Co 5:10 we must all appear before the **j seat** of 968
Gal 5:10 but he that troubleth you shall bear *his* **j**, 2917
Php 1: 9 more and more in knowledge and *in* all **j**; 144
2Th 1: 5 a manifest token of the righteous **j** 2920
1Ti 5:24 are open beforehand, going before to **j**; 2920
Heb 6: 2 resurrection of the dead, and of eternal **j**. 2917
9:27 unto men once to die, but after this the **j**: 2920
10:27 But a certain fearful looking for of **j** and 2920
Jas 2: 6 and draw you before the **j seats**? 2922
2:13 For he shall have **j** without mercy, that 2920
2:13 no mercy; and mercy rejoiceth against **j**. 2920
1Pe 4:17 The time *is come* that **j** must begin at 2917
2Pe 2: 3 whose **j** now of a long time lingereth not, 2917
2: 4 chains of darkness, *to be* reserved unto **j**; 2920
2: 9 to reserve the unjust unto the day of **j** *to* 2920
3: 7 reserved unto fire against the day of **j** and 2920
1Jn 4:17 that we may have boldness in the day of **j**: 2920
Jude 1: 6 under darkness unto the **j** of the great day. 2920
1:15 To execute **j** upon all, and to convince all 2920
Rev 14: 7 glory to him; for the hour of his **j** is come: 2920

Rev 17: 1 I will shew unto thee the **j** of the great 2917
18:10 mighty city! for in one hour is thy **j** come. 2920
20: 4 upon them, and **j** was given unto them: 2917

JUDGMENTS (127) [JUDGE]

Ex 6: 6 a stretched out arm, and with great **j**: 8201
7: 4 out of the land of Egypt by great **j**. 8201
21: 1 Now these *are* the **j** which thou shalt set 4941
24: 3 all the words of the LORD, and all the **j**: 4941
Lev 18: 4 Ye shall do my **j**, and keep mine 4941
18: 5 therefore keep my statutes, and my **j**: 4941
18:26 therefore keep my statutes and my **j**, 4941
19:37 all my statutes, and all my **j**, and do them: 4941
20:22 all my statutes, and all my **j**, and do them: 4941
25:18 my statutes, and keep my **j**, and do them; 4941
26:15 or if your soul abhor my **j**, so that *ye* will 4941
26:43 even because they despised my **j**, 4941
26:46 These *are* the statutes and **j** and laws, 4941
Nu 33: 4 their gods also the LORD executed **j**. 8201
35:24 the revenger of blood according to these **j**: 4941
36:13 These *are* the commandments and the **j**, 4941
Dt 4: 1 O Israel, unto the statutes and unto the **j**, 4941
4: 5 Behold, I have taught you statutes and **j**, 4941
4: 8 that hath statutes and **j** *so* righteous as all 4941
4:14 at that time to teach you statutes and **j**, 4941
4:45 testimonies, and the statutes, and the **j**, 4941
5: 1 and **j** which I speak in your ears *this* day, 4941
5:31 the statutes, and the **j**, which thou shalt 4941
6: 1 commandments, the statutes, and the **j**, 4941
6:20 testimonies, and the statutes, and the **j**, 4941
7:11 and the statutes, and the **j**, 4941
7:12 if ye hearken to these **j**, and keep, 4941
8:11 his **j**, and his statutes, which I command 4941
11: 1 and his **j**, and his commandments alway. 4941
11:32 and **j** which I set before you *this* day. 4941
12: 1 These *are* the statutes and **j**, which ye 4941
26:16 thee to do these statutes and **j**: 4941
26:17 and his **j**, and to hearken unto his voice: 4941
30:16 and his statutes and his **j**, 4941
33:10 They shall teach Jacob thy **j**, and Israel thy 4941
33:21 justice of the LORD, and his **j** with Israel. 4941
2Sa 22:23 For all his **j** *were* before me: and *as for* his 4941
1Ki 2: 3 and his **j**, and his testimonies, 4941
6:12 execute my **j**, and keep all my 4941
8:58 and his statutes, and his **j**, 4941
9: 4 *and* wilt keep my statutes and my **j**: 4941
11:33 *keep* my statutes and my **j**, as *did* David 4941
1Ch 16:12 his wonders, and the **j** of his mouth; 4941
16:14 LORD our God; his **j** *are* in all the earth. 4941
22:13 which the LORD charged Moses with 4941
28: 7 to do my commandments, and my **j**, 4941
2Ch 7:17 and shalt observe my statutes and my **j**; 4941
19:10 and commandment, statutes and **j**, 4941
Ezr 7:10 do *it*, and to teach in Israel statutes and **j**. 4941
Ne 1: 7 nor the statutes, nor the **j**, 4941
9:13 gavest them right **j**, and true laws, 4941
9:29 sinned against thy **j**, (which if a man do, 4941
10:29 LORD our Lord, and his **j** and his statutes; 4941
Ps 10: 5 thy **j** *are* far above out of his sight: 4941
18:22 For all his **j** *were* before me, and I did not 4941
19: 9 the **j** of the LORD *are* true and 4941
36: 6 great mountains; thy **j** *are* a great deep: 4941
48:11 of Judah be glad, because of thy **j**. 4941
72: 1 Give the king thy **j**, O God, 4941
89:30 forsake my law, and walk not in my **j**; 4941
97: 8 because of thy **j**, O LORD. 4941
105: 5 his wonders, and the **j** of his mouth; 4941
105: 7 LORD our God: his **j** *are* in all the earth. 4941
119: 7 when I shall have learned thy righteous **j**. 4941
119:13 With my lips have I declared all the **j** of 4941
119:20 longing *that it hath* unto thy **j** at all times. 4941
119:30 way of truth: thy **j** have I laid *before* me. 4941
119:39 reproach which I fear: for thy **j** *are* good. 4941
119:43 of my mouth; for I have hoped in thy **j**. 4941
119:52 I remembered thy **j** of old, O LORD; 4941
119:62 unto thee because of thy righteous **j**. 4941
119:75 that thy **j** *are* right, and *that* thou in 4941
119:102 I have not departed from thy **j**: for thou 4941
119:106 perform *it*, that *I* will keep thy righteous **j**. 4941
119:108 my mouth, O LORD, and teach me thy **j**. 4941
119:120 for fear of thee; and I am afraid of thy **j**. 4941
119:137 art thou, O LORD, and upright *are* thy **j**. 4941
119:156 O LORD: quicken me according to thy **j**. 4941
119:160 every one of thy righteous **j** *endureth* for 4941
119:164 I praise thee because of thy righteous **j**. 4941
119:175 it shall praise thee; and let thy **j** help me. 4941
147:19 his statutes and his **j** unto Israel. 4941
147:20 *as for his* **j**, they have not known them. 4941
Pr 19:29 **j** are prepared for scorners, and stripes for 8201
Isa 26: 8 Yea, *in* the way of thy **j**, O LORD, 4941
26: 9 for when thy **j** *are* in the earth, 4941
Jer 1:16 I will utter my **j** against them touching all 4941
12: 1 yet let me talk with thee of *thy* **j**. 4941
Eze 5: 6 she hath changed my **j** into wickedness 4941
5: 6 they have refused my **j**, and my statutes, 4941
5: 7 in my statutes, neither have kept my **j**, 4941
5: 7 neither have done according to the **j** of 4941
5: 8 will execute **j** in the midst of thee in 8201
5:10 I will execute **j** in thee, and the whole 8201
5:15 when I shall execute **j** in thee in anger 8201
11: 9 strangers, and will execute **j** among you. 8201
11:12 neither executed my **j**, but have done 4941
14:21 much more when I send my four sore **j** 8201
16:41 execute **j** upon thee in the sight of many 8201
18: 9 and hath kept my **j**, to deal truly; 4941

Eze 18:17 hath executed my **j**, hath walked in my 4941
20:11 shewed them my **j**, which *if* a man do, 4941
20:13 they despised my **j**, which *if* a man do, 4941
20:16 Because they despised my **j**, and walked 4941
20:18 neither observe their **j**, nor defile 4941
20:19 my statutes, and keep my **j**, and do them; 4941
20:21 neither kept my **j** to do them, which *if* a 4941
20:24 Because they had not executed my **j**, 4941
20:25 and **j** whereby they should not live; 4941
23:24 they shall judge thee according to their **j**. 4941
25:11 will execute **j** upon Moab; and they shall 8201
28:22 when I shall have executed **j** in her, 8201
28:26 when I have executed **j** upon all those 8201
30:14 set fire in Zoan, and will execute **j** in No. 8201
30:19 Thus will I execute **j** in Egypt: 8201
36:27 and ye shall keep my **j**, and do *them*. 4941
37:24 they shall also walk in my **j**, 4941
44:24 *and* they shall judge it according to my **j**: 4941
Da 9: 5 from thy precepts and from thy **j**: 4941
Hos 6: 5 and thy **j** *are* as the light *that* goeth forth. 4941
Zep 3:15 The LORD hath taken away thy **j**, he hath 4941
Mal 4: 4 for all Israel, *with* the statutes and **j**. 4941
Ro 11:33 how unsearchable *are* his **j**, and his ways 2917
1Co 6: 4 ye have **j** *of things* pertaining to *this* life, 2922
Rev 15: 4 before thee; for thy **j** are made manifest. 1345
16: 7 Almighty, true and righteous *are* thy **j**. 2920
19: 2 true and righteous *are* his **j**: for he hath 2920

JUDITH (1)
Ge 26:34 to wife **J** the daughter of Beeri the Hittite, 3067

JUG See CRUSE

JUICE (1)
SS 8: 2 spiced wine, of the **j** of my pomegranate. 6071

JULIA (1)
Ro 16:15 **J**, Nereus, and his sister, and Olympas, 2456

JULIUS (2)
Ac 27: 1 certain other prisoners unto *one* named **J**, 2457
27: 3 And **J** courteously entreated Paul, 2457

JUMPING (1)
Na 3: 2 the pransing horses, and of the **j** chariots, 7540

JUNIA (1)
Ro 16: 7 Salute Andronicus and **J**, my kinsmen, 2458

JUNIAS See JUNIA

JUNIPER (4)
1Ki 19: 4 and came and sat down under a **j** tree, 7574
19: 5 as he lay and slept under a **j** *tree*, 7574
Job 30: 4 by the bushes, and **j** roots *for* their meat. 7574
Ps 120: 4 arrows of the mighty, with coals of **j**. 7574

JUPITER (3)
Ac 14:12 And they called Barnabas, **J**; and Paul, 2203
14:13 Then the priest of **J**, which was before 2203
19:35 of the *image* which **fell down from J**? 1356

JURISDICTION (1)
Lk 23: 7 he knew that he belonged unto Herod's **j**, 1849

JUSHABHESED (1)
1Ch 3:20 and Berechiah, and Hasadiah, **J**, five. 3142

JUST (94) [JUSTICE, JUSTIFICATION, JUSTIFIED, JUSTIFIER, JUSTIFIETH, JUSTIFY, JUSTIFYING, JUSTLY, UNJUST]

Ge 6: 9 Noah was a **j** man *and* perfect in his 6662
Lev 19:36 **J** balances, just weights, a just ephah, 6664
19:36 just weights, a just ephah, and a just hin, 6664
19:36 just weights, a **j** ephah, and a just hin, 6664
19:36 just weights, a just ephah, and a **j** hin, 6664
Dt 16:18 they shall judge the people *with* **j** 6664
16:20 That which is **altogether j** shalt 6664+6664
25:15 thou shalt have a perfect and *j* weight, 6664
25:15 a perfect and **j** measure shalt thou have: 6664
32: 4 and without iniquity, **j** and right *is* he. 6662
2Sa 23: 3 He that ruleth over men *must be* **j**, ruling 6662
Ne 9:33 Howbeit thou *art* **j** in all that is brought 6662
Job 4:17 Shall mortal man be more **j** than God? 6663
9: 2 truth: but how should man be **j** with God? 6663
12: 4 the **j** upright *man* is laughed to scorn. 6662
27:17 He may prepare *it*, but the **j** shall put *it* on, 6662
33:12 in this thou *art* not **j**: I will answer 6663
34:17 wilt thou condemn him that is most **j**? 6662
Ps 7: 9 come to an end; but establish the **j**: 6662
37:12 The wicked plotteth against the **j**, 6662
Pr 3:33 but he blesseth the habitation of the **j**. 6662
4:18 the path of the **j** *is* as the shining light, 6662
9: 9 teach a *man*, and he will increase in 6662
10: 6 Blessings *are* upon the head of the **j**: 6662
10: 7 The memory of the **j** *is* blessed: 6662
10:20 The tongue of the **j** *is* as choice silver: 6662
10:31 mouth of the **j** bringeth forth wisdom: 6662
11: 1 to the LORD: but a **j** weight *is* his delight. 8003
11: 9 knowledge shall the **j** be delivered. 6662
12:13 lips: but the **j** shall come out of trouble. 6662
12:21 There shall no evil happen to the **j**: 6662
13:22 wealth of the sinner *is* laid up for the **j**. 6662
16:11 A **j** weight and balance *are* the LORD's: 4941
17:15 wicked, and he that condemneth the **j**, 6662
17:26 Also to punish the **j** *is* not good, *nor* to 6662

Pr 18:17 that is first in his own cause seemeth j; 6662
20: 7 The j man walketh in his integrity: 6662
21:15 It is joy to the j to do judgment: 6662
24:16 For a j man falleth seven times, and 6662
29:10 hate the upright: but the j seek his soul. 3477
29:27 An unjust man is an abomination to the j: 6662
Ecc 7:15 there is a j man that perisheth in his 6662
7:20 For there is not a j man upon earth, 6662
8:14 that there be j men, unto whom it 6662
Isa 26: 7 The way of the j is uprightness: thou, 6662
26: 7 most upright, dost weigh the path of the j. 6662
29:21 and turn aside the j for a thing of nought. 6662
45:21 j God and a saviour; there is none beside 6662
La 4:13 that have shed the blood of the j in 6662
Eze 18: 5 if a man be j, and do that which is lawful 6662
18: 9 he is j, he shall surely live, saith the Lord 6662
45:10 Ye shall have j balances, and a just ephah, 6664
45:10 balances, and a j ephah, and a just bath. 6664
45:10 balances, and a just ephah, and a j bath. 6664
Hos 14: 9 are right, and the j shall walk in them: 6662
Am 5:12 they afflict the j, they take a bribe, 6662
Hab 2: 4 in him: but the j shall live by his faith. 6662
Zep 3: 5 The j Lord is in the midst thereof; 6662
Zec 9: 9 he is j, and having salvation; lowly, 6662
Mt 1:19 being a j man, and not willing to make her 1342
5:45 sendeth rain on the j and on the unjust. 1342
13:49 and sever the wicked from among the j, 1342
27:19 Have thou nothing to do with that j man: 1342
27:24 am innocent of the blood of this j person: 1342
Mk 6:20 knowing that he was a j man and a holy, 1342
Lk 1:17 the disobedient to the wisdom of the j; 1342
2:25 and the same man was j and devout, 1342
14:14 recompensed at the resurrection of the j. 1342
15: 7 nine j persons which need no repentance. 1342
20:20 which should feign themselves j men, 1342
23:50 and he was a good man, and a j 1342
Jn 5:30 and my judgment is j; because I seek not 1342
Ac 3:14 But ye denied the Holy One and the J, 1342
7:52 shewed before of the coming of the J One; 1342
10:22 a j man, and one that feareth God, 1342
22:14 and see that J One, and shouldest hear 1342
24:15 of the dead, both of the j and unjust. 1342
Ro 1:17 as it is written, The j shall live by faith. 1342
2:13 (For not the hearers of the law are j before 1342
3: 8 good may come? whose damnation is j. 1738
3:26 that he might be j, and the justifier of him 1342
7:12 the commandment holy, and j, and good. 1342
Gal 3:11 it is evident: for, The j shall live by faith. 1342
Php 4: 8 whatsoever things are j, whatsoever 1342
Col 4: 1 give unto your servants that which is j and 1342
Tit 1: 8 of good men, sober, j, holy, temperate; 1342
Heb 2: 2 disobedience received a j recompence of 1738
10:38 the j shall live by faith: but if any man 1342
12:23 and to the spirits of j men made perfect, 1342
Jas 5: 6 Ye have condemned and killed the j; 1342
1Pe 3:18 the j for the unjust, that he might bring us 1342
2Pe 2: 7 And delivered j Lot, vexed with the filthy 1342
1Jn 1: 9 he is faithful and j to forgive us our sins, 1342
Rev 15: 3 j and true are thy ways, thou King of 1342

JUSTICE (28) [JUST]
Ge 18:19 way of the Lord, to do j and judgment; 6666
Dt 33:21 he executed the j of the Lord, 6666
2Sa 8:15 and j unto all his people. 6666
15: 4 come unto me, and I would do him j. 6663
1Ki 10: 9 made he thee king, to do judgment and j. 6666
1Ch 18:14 and j among all his people. 6666
2Ch 9: 8 king over them, to do judgment and j. 6666
Job 8: 3 or doth the Almighty pervert j? 6664
36:17 judgment and j take hold on thee. 4941
37:23 and in judgment, and in plenty of j: 6666
Ps 82: 3 fatherless: do j to the afflicted and needy. 6663
89:14 J and judgment are the habitation of thy 6664
119:121 I have done judgment and j: leave me not 6664
Pr 1: 3 of wisdom, j, and judgment, and equity; 6664
8:15 By me kings reign, and princes decree j. 6664
21: 3 To do j and judgment is more acceptable 6666
Ecc 5: 8 perverting of judgment and j in a province 6664
Isa 9: 7 and with j from henceforth even for ever. 6666
56: 1 the Lord, Keep ye judgment, and do j: 6666
58: 2 they ask of me the ordinances of j; 6664
59: 4 None calleth for j, nor any pleadeth for 6664
59: 9 far from us, neither doth j overtake us: 6666
59:14 away backward, and j standeth afar off: 6666
Jer 22:15 do judgment and j, and then it was well 6666
23: 5 shall execute judgment and j in the earth. 6666
31:23 habitation of j, and mountain of holiness. 6664
50: 7 the habitation of j, even the Lord, 6664
Eze 45: 9 and spoil, and execute judgment and j, 6666

JUSTIFICATION (3) [JUST]
Ro 4:25 and was raised again for our j. 1347
5:16 but the free gift is of many offences unto j. 1345
5:18 free gift came upon all men unto j of life. 1347

JUSTIFIED (43) [JUST]
Job 11: 2 and should a man full of talk be j? 6663
13:18 ordered my cause; I know that I shall be j. 6663
25: 4 How then can man be j with God? 6663
32: 2 because he j himself rather than God. 6663
Ps 51: 4 thou mightest be j when thou speakest, 6663
143: 2 for in thy sight shall no man living be j. 6663
Isa 43: 9 forth their witnesses, that they may be j: 6663
43:26 declare thou, that thou mayest be j. 6663
45:25 the Lord shall all the seed of Israel be j, 6663

Jer 3:11 The backsliding Israel hath j herself more 6663
Eze 16:51 hast j thy sisters in all thine abominations 6663
16:52 thy shame, in that thou hast j thy sisters. 6663
Mt 11:19 sinners. But wisdom is j of her children. 1344
12:37 For by thy words thou shalt be j, and 1344
Lk 7:29 that heard him, and the publicans, j God, 1344
7:35 But wisdom is j of all her children. 1344
18:14 this man went down to his house j rather 1344
Ac 13:39 And by him all that believe are j from all 1344
13:39 ye could not be j by the law of Moses. 1344
Ro 2:13 but the doers of the law shall be j. 1344
3: 4 That thou mightest be j in thy sayings, 1344
3:20 law there shall no flesh be j in his sight: 1344
3:24 Being j freely by his grace through 1344
3:28 Therefore we conclude that a man is j by 1344
4: 2 For if Abraham were j by works, he hath 1344
5: 1 Therefore being j by faith, we have peace 1344
5: 9 more then, being now j by his blood, 1344
8:30 and whom he called, them he also j: 1344
8:30 and whom he j, them he also glorified. 1344
1Co 4: 4 nothing by myself; yet am I not hereby j: 1344
6:11 but ye are j in the name of the Lord Jesus, 1344
Gal 2:16 Knowing that a man is not j by the works 1344
2:16 that we might be j by the faith of Christ, 1344
2:16 by the works of the law shall no flesh be j. 1344
2:17 But if, while we seek to be j by Christ, 1344
3:11 that no man is j by the law in the sight 1344
3:24 unto Christ, that we might be j by faith. 1344
5: 4 whosoever of you are j by the law; 1344
1Ti 3:16 j in the Spirit, seen of angels, 1344
Tit 3: 7 That being j by his grace, we should be 1344
Jas 2:21 Was not Abraham our father j by works, 1344
2:24 Ye see then how that by works a man is j, 1344
2:25 Likewise also was not Rahab the harlot j 1344

JUSTIFIER (1) [JUST]
Ro 3:26 and the j of him which believeth in Jesus. 1344

JUSTIFIETH (4) [JUST]
Pr 17:15 He that j the wicked, and he that 6663
Isa 50: 8 He is near that j me; who will contend 6663
Ro 4: 5 but believeth on him that j the ungodly, 1344
8:33 the charge of God's elect? It is God that j: 1344

JUSTIFY (11) [JUST]
Ex 23: 7 slay thou not: for I will not j the wicked. 6663
Dt 25: 1 they shall j the righteous, and condemn 6663
Job 9:20 If I j myself, mine own mouth shall 6663
27: 5 God forbid that I should j you: till I die I 6663
33:32 answer me: speak, for I desire to j thee. 6663
Isa 5:23 Which j the wicked for reward, 6663
53:11 shall my righteous servant j many; 6663
Lk 10:29 he, willing to j himself, said unto Jesus, 1344
16:15 are they which j yourselves before men; 1344
Ro 3:30 which shall j the circumcision by faith, 1344
Gal 3: 8 foreseeing that God would j the heathen 1344

JUSTIFYING (2) [JUST]
1Ki 8:32 j the righteous, to give him according to 6663
2Ch 6:23 j the righteous, by giving him according 6663

JUSTLE (1)
Na 2: 4 they shall j one against another in 8264

JUSTLY (3)
Mic 6: 8 to do j, and to love mercy, and to walk 4941
Lk 23:41 And we indeed j; for we receive the due 1346
1Th 2:10 and God also, how holily and j and 1346

JUSTUS (3)
Ac 1:23 who was surnamed J, and Matthias. 2459
18: 7 named J, one that worshipped God, 2459
Col 4:11 And Jesus, which is called J, who are of 2459

JUTTAH (2)
Jos 15:55 Maon, Carmel, and Ziph, and J, 3194
21:16 J with her suburbs, and Beth-shemesh 3194

K

KAB (1)
2Ki 6:25 the fourth part of a k of dove's dung for 6894

KABZEEL (3)
Jos 15:21 the coast of Edom southward were K, 6909
2Sa 23:20 the son of a valiant man, of K, who had 6909
1Ch 11:22 the son of a valiant man, of K, who had 6909

KADESH (17) [KADESH-BARNEA, MERIBAH-KADESH]
Ge 14: 7 which is K, and smote all the country of 6946
16:14 behold, it is between K and Bered. 6946
20: 1 dwelled between K and Shur, 6946
Nu 13:26 unto the wilderness of Paran, to K; 6946
20: 1 the people abode in K; and Miriam died 6946
20:14 Moses sent messengers from K unto 6946

Nu 20:16 we are in K, a city in the uttermost 6946
20:22 journeyed from K, and came unto mount 6946
27:14 that is the water of Meribah in K in 6946
33:36 in the wilderness of Zin, which is K. 6946
33:37 they removed from K, and pitched in 6946
Dt 1:46 So ye abode in K many days, 6946
Jdg 11:16 unto the Red sea, and came to K; 6946
11:17 would not consent: and Israel abode in K. 6946
Ps 29: 8 the Lord shaketh the wilderness of K. 6946
Eze 47:19 Tamar even to the waters of strife in K, 6946
48:28 from Tamar unto to the waters of strife in K, 6946

KADESH-BARNEA (10) [KADESH]
Nu 32: 8 when I sent them from K to see the land. 6947
34: 4 forth thereof shall be from the south to K, 6947
Dt 1: 2 Horeb by the way of mount Seir unto K.) 6947
1:19 God commanded us; and we came to K. 6947
2:14 the space in which we came from K, 6947
9:23 when the Lord sent you from K, 6947
Jos 10:41 smote them from K even unto Gaza, 6947
14: 6 man of God concerning me and thee in K. 6947
14: 7 sent me from K to espy out the land; 6947
15: 3 ascended up on the south side unto K, 6947

KADMIEL (8)
Ezr 2:40 the children of Jeshua and K, 6934
3: 9 his sons and his brethren K and his sons, 6934
Ne 7:43 of K, and of the children of Hodevah, 6934
9: 4 Jeshua, and Bani, K, Shebaniah, Bunni, 6934
9: 5 Jeshua and K, Bani, Hashabniah, 6934
10: 9 Binnui of the sons of Henadad, K; 6934
12: 8 Jeshua, Binnui, K, Sherebiah, Judah, 6934
12:24 Sherebiah, and Jeshua the son of K, 6934

KADMONITES (1)
Ge 15:19 Kenites, and the Kenizzites, and the K, 6935

KALLAI (1)
Ne 12:20 Of Sallai, K; of Amok, Eber; 7040

KAMON See CAMON

KANAH (3)
Jos 16: 8 from Tappuah westward unto the river K; 7071
17: 9 the coast descended unto the river K, 7071
19:28 and Rehob, and Hammon, and K, 7071

KAREAH (13)
Jer 40: 8 Johanan and Jonathan the sons of K, 7143
40:13 Moreover Johanan the son of K, and all 7143
40:15 Johanan the son of K spake to Gedaliah in 7143
40:16 Ahikam said unto Johanan the son of K, 7143
41:11 when Johanan the son of K, and all 7143
41:13 with Ishmael saw Johanan the son of K. 7143
41:14 and went unto Johanan the son of K. 7143
41:16 took Johanan the son of K, and all 7143
42: 1 Johanan the son of K, and Jezaniah the 7143
42: 8 called he Johanan the son of K, and all 7143
43: 2 Johanan the son of K, and all the proud 7143
43: 4 So Johanan the son of K, and all 7143
43: 5 Johanan the son of K, and all the captains 7143

KARKA See KARKAA

KARKAA (1)
Jos 15: 3 up to Adar, and fetched a compass to K: 7173

KARKOR (1)
Jdg 8:10 Now Zebah and Zalmunna were in K, 7174

KARNAIM See ASHTEROTH KARNAIM

KARTAH (1)
Jos 21:34 with her suburbs, and K with her suburbs, 7177

KARTAN (1)
Jos 21:32 with her suburbs, and K with her suburbs; 7178

KATTATH (1)
Jos 19:15 K, and Nahallal, and Shimron, and Idalah, 7005

KEBAR See CHEBAR

KEDAR (12)
Ge 25:13 and K, and Adbeel, and Mibsam, 6938
1Ch 1:29 then K, and Adbeel, and Mibsam, 6938
Ps 120: 5 in Mesech, that I dwell in the tents of K! 6938
SS 1: 5 as the tents of K, as the curtains of 6938
Isa 21:16 a hireling, and all the glory of K shall fail: 6938
21:17 the mighty men of the children of K, 6938
42:11 voice, the villages that K doth inhabit: 6938
60: 7 All the flocks of K shall be gathered 6938
Jer 2:10 send unto K, and consider diligently, 6938
49:28 Concerning K, and concerning 6938
49:28 go up to K, and spoil the men of the east. 6938
Eze 27:21 Arabia, and all the princes of K, 6938

KEDEMAH (2)
Ge 25:15 Hadar, and Tema, Jetur, Naphish, and K: 6929
1Ch 1:31 Jetur, Naphish, and K. These are the sons 6929

KEDEMOTH (4)
Dt 2:26 K to Sihon king of Heshbon with words 6932
Jos 13:18 And Jahazah, and K, and Mephaath, 6932
21:37 K with her suburbs, and Mephaath with 6932
1Ch 6:79 K also with her suburbs, and Mephaath 6932

KEDESH (11) [KEDESH-NAPHTALI]

Jos	12:22 The king of **K**, one; the king of Jokneam	6943
	15:23 And **K**, and Hazor, and Ithnan,	6943
	19:37 And **K**, and Edrei, and En-hazor,	6943
	20: 7 they appointed **K** in Galilee in mount	6943
	21:32 Naphtali, **K** in Galilee with her suburbs,	6943
Jdg	4: 9 Deborah arose, and went with Barak to **K**	6943
	4:10 Barak called Zebulun and Naphtali to **K**;	6943
	4:11 unto the plain of Zaanaim, which *is* by **K**.	6943
2Ki	15:29 **K**, and Hazor, and Gilead, and Galilee,	6943
1Ch	6:72 **K** with her suburbs, Daberath with her	6943
	6:76 **K** in Galilee with her suburbs,	6943

KEDESH-NAPHTALI (1) [KEDESH, NAPHTALI]

Jdg	4: 6 Barak the son of Abinoam out of **K**,	5321+6943

KEDORLAOMER See CHEDORLAOMER

KEEP (362) [DOORKEEPER, DOORKEEPERS, KEEPER, KEEPERS, KEEPEST, KEEPETH, KEEPING, KEPT]

Ge	2:15 the garden of Eden to dress it and to **k** it.	8104
	3:24 every way, to **k** the way of the tree of life.	8104
	6:19 into the ark, to **k** *them* alive with thee;	2421
	6:20 shall come unto thee, to **k** *them* alive.	2421
	7: 3 to **k** seed alive upon the face of all	2421
	17: 9 Thou shalt **k** my covenant therefore, thou,	8104
	17:10 which ye shall **k**, between me and you	8104
	18:19 they shall **k** the way of the LORD, to do	8104
	28:15 **k** thee in all *places* whither thou goest,	8104
	28:20 will **k** me in this way that I go,	8104
	30:31 for me, I will again feed *and* **k** thy flock:	8104
	33: 9 my brother; **k** that thou hast unto thyself.	1961
	41:35 and let them **k** food in the cities.	8104
Ex	6: 5 whom the Egyptians **k** in bondage;	5647
	12: 6 ye shall **k** it *up* until the fourteenth	1961+4931
	12:14 you shall **k** it a feast to the LORD	2287
	12:14 you shall **k** it a feast by an ordinance for	2287
	12:25 hath promised, that ye shall **k** this service.	8104
	12:47 All the congregation of Israel shall **k** it.	6213
	12:48 will **k** the passover to the LORD, let all	6213
	12:48 and then let him come near and **k** it;	6213
	13: 5 thou shalt **k** this service in this month.	5647
	13:10 **k** this ordinance in his season from year	8104
	15:26 his commandments, and **k** all his statutes,	8104
	16:28 How long refuse ye to **k** my	8104
	19: 5 **k** my covenant, then ye shall be a peculiar	8104
	20: 6 that love me, and **k** my commandments.	8104
	20: 8 Remember the sabbath day, to **k** it holy.	6942
	22: 7 unto his neighbour money or stuff to **k**,	8104
	22:10 or an ox, a sheep, or any beast, to **k**;	8104
	23: 7 **K** thee far from a false matter;	7368
	23:14 Three times thou shalt **k** a feast unto me	2287
	23:15 shalt **k** the feast of unleavened bread:	8104
	23:20 to **k** thee in the way, and to bring thee	8104
	31:13 Verily my sabbaths ye shall **k**:	8104
	31:14 Ye shall **k** the sabbath therefore; for it *is*	8104
	31:16 Wherefore the children of Israel shall **k**	8104
	34:18 feast of unleavened bread shalt thou **k**.	8104
Lev	6: 2 in that which was delivered him to **k**,	6487
	6: 4 was delivered him to **k**,	854+6485+6487
	8:35 **k** the charge of the LORD, that ye die not:	8104
	18: 4 and **k** mine ordinances, to walk therein:	8104
	18: 5 Ye shall therefore **k** my statutes, and my	8104
	18:26 Ye shall therefore **k** my statutes and my	8104
	18:30 Therefore ye shall **k** mine ordinance,	8104
	19: 3 and his father, and **k** my sabbaths:	8104
	19:19 Ye shall **k** my statutes. Thou shalt not let	8104
	19:30 Ye shall **k** my sabbaths, and reverence my	8104
	20: 8 ye shall **k** my statutes, and do them: I *am*	8104
	20:22 Ye shall therefore **k** all my statutes, and	8104
	22: 9 They shall therefore **k** mine ordinance,	8104
	22:31 Therefore shall ye **k** my commandments,	8104
	23:39 ye shall **k** a feast unto the LORD seven	2287
	23:41 ye shall **k** it a feast unto the LORD	2282+2287
	25: 2 shall the land **k** a sabbath unto	7673+7676
	25:18 and **k** my judgments, and do them;	8104
	26: 2 Ye shall **k** my sabbaths, and reverence my	8104
	26: 3 and **k** my commandments, and do them;	8104
Nu	1:53 the Levites shall **k** the charge of	8104
	3: 7 they shall **k** his charge, and the charge of	8104
	3: 8 they shall **k** all the instruments of	8104
	3:32 *have* the oversight of them that **k**	8104
	6:24 The LORD bless thee, and **k** thee:	8104
	8:26 to **k** the charge, and shall do no service.	8104
	9: 2 Let the children of Israel also **k**	6213
	9: 3 ye shall **k** it in his appointed season:	6213
	9: 3 to all the ceremonies thereof, shall ye **k** it.	6213
	9: 4 of Israel, that they should **k** the passover.	6213
	9: 6 that they could not **k** the passover on that	6213
	9:10 yet he shall **k** the passover unto	6213
	9:11 The second month at even they shall **k** it,	6213
	9:12 ordinances of the passover they shall **k** it.	6213
	9:13 journey, and forbeareth to **k** the passover,	6213
	9:14 and will **k** the passover unto the LORD;	6213
	18: 3 they shall **k** thy charge, and the charge of	8104
	18: 4 **k** the charge of the tabernacle of	8104
	18: 5 ye shall **k** the charge of the sanctuary,	8104
	18: 7 thy sons with thee shall **k** your priest's	8104
	29:12 ye shall **k** a feast unto the LORD	2282+2287
	31:18 by lying with him, **k** alive for yourselves.	2421
	31:30 which **k** the charge of the tabernacle of	8104
	36: 7 himself to the inheritance of the tribe of	1692
	36: 9 himself to his own inheritance.	1692
Dt	4: 2 that *ye* may **k** the commandments of	8104

Dt	4: 6 **K** therefore and do *them;* for this *is* your	8104
	4: 9 heed to thyself, and **k** thy soul diligently,	8104
	4:40 Thou shalt **k** therefore his statutes, and	8104
	5: 1 ye may learn them, and **k**, and do them.	8104
	5:10 that love me and **k** my commandments.	8104
	5:12 **K** the sabbath day to sanctify it,	8104
	5:15 the LORD thy God commanded thee to **k**	6213
	5:29 and **k** all my commandments always,	8104
	6: 2 **k** all his statutes and his commandments,	8104
	6:17 You shall diligently **k**	8104+8104
	7: 8 he would **k** the oath which he had sworn	8104
	7: 9 **k** his commandments to a thousand	8104
	7:11 shalt therefore **k** the commandments,	8104
	7:12 to these judgments, and **k**, and do them,	8104
	7:12 that the LORD thy God shall **k** unto thee	8104
	8: 2 whether thou wouldest **k** his	8104
	8: 6 Therefore thou shalt **k** the commandments	8104
	10:13 To **k** the commandments of the LORD,	8104
	11: 1 his charge, and his statutes,	8104
	11: 8 shall ye **k** all the commandments	8104
	11:22 For if ye shall diligently **k** all these	8104+8104
	13: 4 **k** his commandments, and obey his voice,	8104
	13:18 to **k** all his commandments which I	8104
	16: 1 **k** the passover unto the LORD thy God:	6213
	16:10 thou shalt **k** the feast of weeks unto	6213
	16:15 Seven days shalt thou **k** a solemn feast	2287
	17:19 to **k** all the words of this law and	8104
	19: 9 thou shalt **k** all these commandments	8104
	23: 9 then **k** thee from every wicked thing.	8104
	23:23 which is gone out of thy lips thou shalt **k**	8104
	26:16 thou shalt therefore **k** and do them with	6213
	26:17 to **k** his statutes, and his commandments,	8104
	26:18 that *thou* shouldest **k** all his	8104
	27: 1 **K** all the commandments which I	8104
	28: 9 if thou shalt **k** the commandments of	8104
	28:45 to **k** his commandments and his statutes	8104
	29: 9 **K** therefore the words of this covenant,	8104
	30:10 to **k** his commandments and his statutes	8104
	30:16 to **k** his commandments and his statutes	8104
Jos	6:18 any wise **k** *yourselves* from the accursed	8104
	10:18 the cave, and set men by it to **k** them:	8104
	22: 5 to **k** his commandments, and to cleave	8104
	23: 6 Be ye therefore very courageous to **k** and	8104
Jdg	2:22 whether they will **k** the way of the LORD	8104
	2:22 as their fathers did **k** *it*, or not.	8104
	3:19 who said, **K** silence. And all that stood	2013
Ru	2:21 Thou shalt **k** fast by my young men,	1692
1Sa	2: 9 He will **k** the feet of his saints,	8104
	7: 1 sanctified Eleazar his son to **k** the ark of	8104
2Sa	8: 2 death, and *with* one full line to **k** alive.	2421
	15:16 which were concubines, to **k** the house.	8104
	16:21 which he had left to **k** the house;	8104
	18:18 no son to **k** my name in remembrance:	2142
	20: 3 whom he had left to **k** the house,	8104
1Ki	2: 3 **k** the charge of the LORD thy God,	8104
	2: 3 to **k** his statutes, *and* his commandments,	8104
	3:14 to **k** my statutes and my commandments,	8104
	6:12 **k** all my commandments to walk in them;	8104
	8:25 with thy servant David my father that	8104
	8:58 to **k** his commandments, and his statutes,	8104
	8:61 to **k** his commandments, as at this day.	8104
	9: 4 and **k** my statutes and my judgments:	8104
	9: 6 will not **k** my commandments *and*	8104
	11:33 *to k* my statutes and my judgments, as *did*	NIH
	11:38 to **k** my statutes and that thou **k** my	8104
	20:39 a man unto me, and said, **K** this man:	8104
2Ki	6: 2 so shall ye **k** the watch of the house, that	8104
	11: 7 they shall **k** the watch of the house of	8104
	17:13 ye my commandments *and* my statutes,	8104
	23: 3 **k** his commandments and his testimonies	8104
	23:21 **K** the passover unto the LORD your God.	6213
1Ch	4:10 that thou wouldest **k** *me* from evil, that it	6213
	12:33 war, fifty thousand, which could **k** rank:	5737
	12:38 All these men of war, that could **k** rank,	5737
	22:12 that *thou* mayest **k** the law of the LORD	8104
	23:32 that they should **k** the charge of	8104
	28: 8 and seek for all the commandments of	8104
	29:18 **k** this for ever in the imagination of	8104
	29:19 to **k** thy commandments, thy testimonies,	8104
2Ch	6:16 with thy servant David my father that	8104
	13:11 for we **k** the charge of the LORD our	8104
	22: 9 had no power to **k** still the kingdom.	6113
	23: 6 all the people shall **k** the watch of	8104
	28:10 ye purpose to **k** under the children of	3533
	30: 1 to **k** the passover unto the LORD God of	6213
	30: 2 to **k** the passover in the second month.	6213
	30: 3 For they could not **k** it at that time,	6213
	30: 5 that *they* should come to **k** the passover	6213
	30:13 to **k** the feast of unleavened bread in	6213
	30:23 whole assembly took counsel to **k** other	6213
	34:31 to **k** his commandments,	8104
	35:16 to **k** the passover, and to offer burnt	6213
	35:18 neither did all the kings of Israel **k** such a	6213
Ezr	8:29 **k** *them*, until ye weigh *them* before	8104
Ne	1: 9 and **k** my commandments, and do them;	8104
	12:27 to **k** the dedication with gladness, both	6213
	13:22 *that* they should come and **k** the gates,	8104
Est	3: 8 all people; neither **k** they the king's laws:	6213
	9:21 that they should **k** the fourteenth day of	6213
	9:27 they would **k** these two days according	4513
Job	14:13 that thou wouldest **k** me secret, until thy	5641
	20:13 it not; but **k** it still within his mouth:	4513
Ps	12: 7 Thou shalt **k** them, O LORD, thou shalt	8104
	17: 8 **K** me as the apple of the eye, hide me	8104
	19:13 **K** back thy servant also from	2820

Ps	22:29 and none can **k** alive his own soul.	2421
	25:10 truth unto such as **k** his covenant and	5341
	25:20 **k** my soul, and deliver me: let me not be	8104
	31:20 thou shalt **k** them secretly in a pavilion	6845
	33:19 death, and to **k** them alive in famine.	2421
	34:13 **K** thy tongue from evil, and thy lips from	5341
	35:22 **k** not silence: O Lord, be not far from	2790
	37:34 **k** his way, and he shall exalt thee to	8104
	39: 1 I will **k** my mouth with a bridle, while	8104
	41: 2 LORD will preserve him, and **k** him alive;	2421
	50: 3 God shall come, and shall not **k** silence:	2790
	78: 7 works of God, but **k** his commandments:	5341
	83: 1 **K** not thou silence, O God: hold not thy	1824
	89:28 My mercy will I **k** for him for evermore,	8104
	89:31 statutes, and **k** not my commandments;	8104
	91:11 charge over thee, to **k** thee in all thy ways.	8104
	103: 9 neither will he **k** *his anger* for ever.	5201
	103:18 To such as **k** his covenant, and to those	8104
	105:45 might observe his statutes, and **k** his laws.	5341
	106: 3 Blessed *are* they that **k** judgment,	8104
	113: 9 **maketh** the barren *woman* to **k** house,	3427
	119: 2 Blessed *are* they that **k** his testimonies,	5341
	119: 4 hast commanded *us* to **k** thy precepts	8104
	119: 5 O that my ways were directed to **k** thy	8104
	119: 8 I will **k** thy statutes: O forsake me not	8104
	119:17 servant, *that* I may live, and **k** thy word.	8104
	119:33 thy statutes; and I shall **k** it *unto* the end.	5341
	119:34 me understanding, and I shall **k** thy law;	5341
	119:44 So shall I **k** thy law continually for ever	8104
	119:57 I have said that *I would* **k** thy words.	8104
	119:60 and delayed not to **k** thy commandments.	8104
	119:63 fear thee, and of them that **k** thy precepts.	8104
	119:69 I will **k** thy precepts with *my* whole heart.	5341
	119:88 so shall I **k** the testimony of thy mouth.	8104
	119:100 the ancients, because I **k** thy precepts.	5341
	119:101 every evil way, that I might **k** thy word.	8104
	119:106 will perform *it*, that *I will* **k** thy righteous	8104
	119:115 will I **k** the commandments of my God.	5341
	119:129 therefore doth my soul **k** them.	5341
	119:134 of man: so will I **k** thy precepts.	8104
	119:136 mine eyes, because they **k** not thy law.	8104
	119:145 hear me, O LORD: I will **k** thy statutes.	5341
	119:146 save me, and I shall **k** thy testimonies.	8104
	127: 1 except the LORD **k** the city,	8104
	132:12 If thy children will **k** my covenant and	8104
	140: 4 **K** me, O LORD, from the hands of	8104
	141: 3 before my mouth; **k** the door of my lips.	5341
	141: 9 **K** me from the snare *which* they have laid	8104
Pr	2:11 preserve thee, understanding shall **k** thee:	5341
	2:20 *men*, and the paths of the righteous.	8104
	3: 1 but let thine heart **k** my commandments:	5341
	3:21 eyes: **k** sound wisdom and discretion:	5341
	3:26 and shall **k** thy foot from being taken.	8104
	4: 4 words: **k** my commandments, and live.	8104
	4: 6 love her, and she shall **k** thee.	5341
	4:13 let *her* not go: **k** her; for she *is* thy life.	5341
	4:21 **k** them in the midst of thine heart.	8104
	4:23 **K** thy heart with all diligence; for out of it	5341
	5: 2 and *that* thy lips may **k** knowledge.	5341
	6:20 **k** thy father's commandment,	5341
	6:22 when thou sleepest, it shall **k** thee;	8104
	6:24 To **k** thee from the evil woman, from	8104
	7: 1 **K** my words, and lay up my	8104
	7: 2 **K** my commandments, and live;	8104
	7: 5 That *they* may **k** thee from the strange	8104
	8:32 for blessed *are they* that **k** my ways.	8104
	22: 5 he that doth **k** his soul shall be far from	8104
	22:18 For *it is* a pleasant *thing* if thou **k** them	8104
	22:18 and such as **k** the law content with them,	8104
Ecc	3: 6 a time to **k**, and a time to cast away;	8104
	3: 7 a time to **k** silence, and a time to speak;	2814
	5: 1 **K** thy foot when thou goest to the house	8104
	8: 2 I counsel *thee* to **k** the king's	8104
	12:13 Fear God, and **k** his commandments:	8104
SS	8:12 that **k** the fruit thereof two hundred.	5201
Isa	26: 3 Thou wilt **k** *him* in perfect peace, *whose*	5341
	27: 3 The LORD do **k** it; I will water it every	5341
	27: 3 lest *any* hurt it, I will **k** it night and day.	5341
	41: 1 **K** silence before me, O islands; and let	2790
	42: 6 will **k** thee, and give thee for a covenant	5341
	43: 6 Give *up*; and to the south, **K** not back:	3607
	56: 1 the LORD, **K** ye judgment, and do justice:	8104
	56: 4 unto the eunuchs that **k** my sabbaths,	8104
	62: 6 mention of the LORD, **k** not silence,	3807.1
	65: 1 I will not **k** silence, but will recompense,	NIH
Jer	3: 5 will he **k** *it* to the end? Behold, thou hast	8104
	3:12 the LORD, *and* I will not **k** *anger* for ever.	5201
	31:10 and **k** him as a shepherd *doth* his flock.	8104
	42: 4 unto you; I will **k** nothing back from you.	4513
La	2:10 Zion sit upon the ground, *and* **k** silence:	1826
Eze	11:20 **k** mine ordinances, and do them:	8104
	18:21 **k** all my statutes, and do that which is	8104
	20:19 and **k** my judgments, and do them:	8104
	36:27 ye shall **k** my judgments, and do *them*.	8104
	43:11 that they may **k** the whole form thereof,	8104
	44:16 unto me, and they shall **k** my charge.	8104
	44:24 they shall **k** my laws and my statutes in	8104
Da	9: 4 and to them that **k** his commandments;	8104
Hos	12: 6 **k** mercy and judgment, and wait on thy	8104
Am	5:13 Therefore the prudent shall **k** silence in	1826
Mic	7: 5 **k** the doors of thy mouth from her that	8104
Na	1:15 O Judah, **k** thy solemn feasts, perform thy	2287
	2: 1 the munition, watch the way, make *thy*	5341
Hab	2:20 let all the earth **k** silence before him.	2013
Zec	3: 7 if thou wilt **k** my charge, and then thou shalt	8104

K

Zec 3: 7 also **k** my courts, and I will give thee　8104
13: 5 for man taught me *to* **k** cattle from my　NIH
14:16 of hosts, and to **k** the feast of tabernacles.　2287
14:18 come not up to **k** the feast of tabernacles.　2287
14:19 come not up to **k** the feast of tabernacles.　2287
Mal 2: 7 For the priest's lips should **k** knowledge,　8104
Mt 19:17 wilt enter into life, **k** the commandments.　5083
26:18 I will **k** the passover at thy house with my　4160
Mk 7: 9 of God, that ye may **k** your own tradition.　5083
Lk 4:10 give his angels charge over thee, to **k** thee:　1314
8:15 **k** *it*, and bring forth fruit with patience.　5442
11:28 they that hear the word of God, and **k** it.　5442
19:43 thee round, and **k** thee **in** on every side,　4912
Jn 8:51 I say unto you, If a man **k** my saying,　5083
8:52 and thou sayest, If a man **k** my saying,　5083
8:55 you: but I know him, and **k** his saying.　5083
12:25 that hateth his life in this world shall **k** it　5442
14:15 If ye love me, **k** my commandments.　5083
14:23 If a man love me, he will **k** my words:　5083
15:10 If ye **k** my commandments, ye shall abide　5083
15:20 kept my saying, they will **k** yours also.　5083
17:11 **k** through thine own name those whom　5083
17:15 that thou shouldest **k** them from the evil.　5083
Ac 5: 3 to **k** back *part* of the price of the land?　3557
10:28 for a man *that is* a Jew to **k** company,　2853
12: 4 to four quaternions of soldiers to **k** him;　5442
15: 5 to command *them* to **k** the law of Moses.　5083
15:24 Ye must be circumcised, and **k** the law:　5083
15:29 from which if ye **k** yourselves, ye shall do　1301
16: 4 they delivered them the decrees for to **k**,　5442
16:23 charging the jailor to **k** them safely:　5083
18:21 I must by all means **k** this feast that　4160
21:25 **k** themselves **from** things offered to idols,　5442
24:23 he commanded a centurion to **k** Paul,　5083
Ro 2:25 verily profiteth, if thou **k** the law:　4238
2:26 Therefore if the uncircumcision **k**　5442
1Co 5: 8 Therefore let us **k** the feast, not with old　1858
5:11 have written unto you not to **k** company,　4874
7:37 decreed in his heart that he will **k** his　5083
9:27 But I **k under** my body, and bring *it* into　5299
11: 2 me in all *things*, and **k** the ordinances,　2722
14:28 let him **k silence** in the church;　4601
14:34 your women **k silence** in the churches:　4601
15: 2 if ye **k** in **memory** what I preached unto　2722
2Co 11: 9 to you, and *so* will I **k** *myself.*　5083
Gal 6:13 who are circumcised **k** the law;　5442
Eph 4: 3 Endeavouring to **k** the unity of the Spirit　5083
Php 4: 7 shall **k** your hearts and minds through　5432
2Th 3: 3 shall stablish you, and **k** *you* from evil.　5442
1Ti 5:22 of other *men's* sins: **k** thyself pure.　5083
6:14 That thou **k** *this* commandment without　5083
6:20 **k** that which is committed to *thy* trust,　5442
2Ti 1:12 I am persuaded that he is able to **k** that　5442
1:14 by the Holy Ghost which dwelleth in　5442
Jas 1:27 to **k** himself unspotted from the world.　5083
2:10 For whosoever shall **k** the whole law,　5083
1Jn 2: 3 know him, if we **k** his commandments.　5083
3:22 because we **k** his commandments,　5083
5: 2 we love God, and **k** his commandments.　5083
5: 3 of God, that we **k** his commandments:　5083
5:21 Little children, **k** yourselves from idols.　5442
Jude 1:21 **K** yourselves in the love of God,　5083
1:24 Now unto him that is able to **k** you **from**　5442
Rev 1: 3 **k** those *things* which are written therein:　5083
3:10 I also will **k** thee from the hour of　5083
12:17 which **k** the commandments of God,　5083
14:12 here *are* they that **k** the commandments　5083
22: 9 of them which **k** the sayings of this book:　5083

KEEPER (21) [KEEP]

Ge 4: 2 Abel was a **k** of sheep, but Cain was a　7462
4: 9 said, I know not: Am I my brother's **k**?　8104
39:21 gave him favour in the sight of the **k** of　8269
39:22 the **k** of the prison committed to Joseph's　8269
39:23 The **k** of the prison looked not to any　8269
1Sa 17:20 left the sheep with a **k**, and took,　8104
17:22 left his carriage in the hand of the **k**　8104
28: 2 will I make thee **k** of mine head　8104
2Ki 22:14 the son of Harhas, **k** of the wardrobe,　8104
2Ch 34:22 the son of Hasrah, **k** of the wardrobe;　8104
Ne 2: 8 a letter unto Asaph the **k** of the king's　8104
3:29 son of Shechaniah, the **k** of the east gate.　8104
Est 2: 3 the king's chamberlain, **k** of the women;　8104
2: 8 to the custody of Hegai, **k** of the women.　8104
2:15 the **k** of the women, appointed.　8104
Job 27:18 a moth, and as a booth *that* the **k** maketh.　5341
Ps 121: 5 The LORD *is* thy **k**: the LORD *is* thy　8104
SS 1: 6 they made me the **k** of the vineyards;　5201
Jer 35: 4 the son of Shallum, the **k** of the　8104
Ac 16:27 And the **k of the prison** awaking out of　1200
16:36 And the **k of the prison** told this saying　1200

KEEPERS (21) [KEEP]

2Ki 11: 5 be **k** of the watch of the king's house;　8104
22: 4 which the **k** of the door have gathered of　8104
23: 4 the **k** of the door, to bring forth out of　8104
25:18 second priest, and the three **k** of the door:　8104
1Ch 9:19 service, **k** of the gates of the tabernacle:　8104
9:19 the host of the LORD, *were* **k** of the entry.　8104
Est 6: 2 king's chamberlains, the **k** of the door,　8104
Ecc 12: 3 In the day when the **k** of the house shall　8104
SS 5: 7 the **k** of the walls took away my vail from　8104
8:11 he let out the vineyard unto **k**;　5201
Jer 4:17 As **k** of a field, are they against her round　5341
52:24 second priest, and the three **k** of the　8104

Eze 40:45 priests, the **k** of the charge of the house.　8104
40:46 priests, the **k** of the charge of the altar;　8104
44: 8 have set **k** of my charge in my sanctuary	8104
44:14 will make them **k** of the charge of	8104
Mt 28: 4 And for fear of him the **k** did shake,　5083
Ac 5:23 the **k** standing without before the doors:　5441
12: 6 and *the* **k** before the door kept the prison.　5441
12:19 he examined the **k**, and commanded that　5441
Tit 2: 5 *To be* discreet, chaste, **k at home**, good,　3626

KEEPEST (4) [KEEP]

1Ki 8:23 who **k** covenant and mercy with thy　8104
2Ch 6:14 which **k** covenant, and *shewest* mercy	8104
Ne 9:32 terrible God, who **k** covenant and mercy,　8104
Ac 21:24 also walkest orderly, and **k** the law.　5442

KEEPETH (46) [KEEP]

Ex 21:18 with *his* fist, and he die not, but **k** *his* bed:　5307
Dt 7: 9 which **k** covenant and mercy with them	8104
1Sa 16:11 the youngest, and, behold, he **k** the sheep.　7462
Ne 1: 5 that **k** covenant and mercy for them that	8104
Job 33:18 He **k** back his soul from the pit, and his	2820
Ps 34:20 He **k** all his bones: not one of them is	8104
121: 3 moved: he that **k** thee will not slumber.	8104
121: 4 he that **k** Israel shall neither slumber nor	8104
146: 6 all that therein is: which **k** truth for ever:	8104
Pr 2: 8 He **k** the paths of judgment,	5341
10:17 He *is in* the way of life that **k** instruction:	8104
13: 3 He that **k** his mouth keepeth his life:	5341
13: 3 He that **k** his mouth **k** his life:	8104
13: 6 Righteousness **k** *him that is* upright in	5341
16:17 he that **k** his way preserveth his soul.	5341
19: 8 he that **k** understanding shall find good.	8104
19:16 He that **k** the commandment keepeth his	8104
19:16 He that **k** the commandment **k** his	8104
21:23 Whoso **k** his mouth and his tongue	8104
21:23 and his tongue **k** his soul from troubles.	8104
24:12 heart consider *it?* and he that **k** thy soul,	5341
27:18 Whoso **k** the fig tree shall eat the fruit	5341
28: 7 Whoso **k** the law *is* a wise son: but he	5341
29: 3 that **k company with** harlots spendeth	7462
29:11 but a wise *man* **k** it **in** till afterwards.	7623
29:18 but he that **k** the law, happy *is* he.	8104
Ecc 8: 5 Whoso **k** the commandment shall feel no	8104
Isa 26: 2 the righteous nation which **k** the truth	8104
56: 2 that **k** the sabbath from polluting it,	8104
56: 2 and **k** his hand from doing any evil.	8104
56: 6 one that **k** the sabbath from polluting	8104
Jer 48:10 cursed *be* he that **k** back his sword from	4513
La 3:28 He sitteth alone and **k** silence, because	1826
Hab 2: 5 he *is* a proud man, neither **k at home**,	5115
Lk 11:21 When a strong *man* armed **k** his palace,	5442
Jn 7:19 the law, and *yet* none of you **k** the law?	4160
9:16 of God, because he **k** not the sabbath day.	5083
14:21 and **k** them, he it is that loveth me:	5083
14:24 He that loveth me not **k** not my sayings:	5083
1Jn 2: 4 and **k** not his commandments, is a liar,	5083
2: 5 But whoso **k** his word, in him verily is	5083
3:24 he that **k** his commandments dwelleth	5083
5:18 but he that is begotten of God **k** himself,	5083
Rev 2:26 and **k** my works unto the end,	5083
16:15 and **k** his garments, lest he walk naked,	5083
22: 7 blessed *is* he that **k** the sayings of	5083

KEEPING (12) [KEEP]

Ex 34: 7 **K** mercy for thousands, forgiving iniquity	5341
Nu 3:28 hundred, **k** the charge of the sanctuary.	8104
3:38 **k** the charge of the sanctuary for the	8104
Dt 8:11 in not **k** his commandments,	8104
1Sa 25:16 all the while we were with them **k**	7462
Ne 12:25 porters **k** the ward at the thresholds of	8104
Ps 19:11 and **in k** of them *there is* great reward.	8104
Eze 17:14 that by **k** of his covenant it might stand.	8104
Da 9: 4 **k** the covenant and mercy to them that	8104
Lk 2: 8 **k watch** over their flock by night.	5438+5442
1Co 7:19 but the **k** of the commandments of God.	5084
1Pe 4:19 **commit the k** of their souls *to him* in	3908

KEHELATHAH (2)

Nu 33:22 journeyed from Rissah, and pitched in **K**.	6954
33:23 they went from **K**, and pitched in mount	6954

KEILAH (18)

Jos 15:44 **K**, and Achzib, and Mareshah; nine cities	7084
1Sa 23: 1 Philistines fight against **K**, and they rob	7084
23: 2 Go, and smite the Philistines, and save **K**.	7084
23: 3 if we come to **K** against the armies of	7084
23: 4 and said, Arise, go down to **K**;	7084
23: 5 So David and his men went to **K**,	7084
23: 5 So David saved the inhabitants of **K**.	7084
23: 6 the son of Ahimelech fled to David *to* **K**,	7084
23: 7 was told Saul that David was come to **K**.	7084
23: 8 to go down to **K**, to besiege David and his	7084
23:10 heard that Saul seeketh to come to **K**,	7084
23:11 Will the men of **K** deliver me up into his	7084
23:12 Will the men of **K** deliver me and my men	7084
23:13 arose and departed out of **K**,	7084
23:13 told Saul that David was escaped from **K**;	7084
1Ch 4:19 the father of **K** the Garmite,	7084
Ne 3:17 the ruler of the half part of **K**, in his part.	7084
3:18 Henadad, the ruler of the half part of **K**.	7084

KELAIAH (1)

Ezr 10:23 Jozabad, and Shimei, and **K**, (the same *is*	7041

KELAL See CHELAL

KELITA (3)

Ezr 10:23 and Shimei, and Kelaiah, (the same *is* **K**,)	7042
Ne 8: 7 **K**, Azariah, Jozabad, Hanan, Pelaiah,	7042
10:10 Shebaniah, Hodijah, **K**, Pelaiah, Hanan,	7042

KELUB See CHELUB

KELUHI See CHELLUH

KEMUEL (3)

Ge 22:21 his brother, and **K** the father of Aram,	7055
Nu 34:24 of Ephraim, **K** the son of Shiphtan.	7055
1Ch 27:17 Of the Levites, Hashabiah the son of **K**:	7055

KENAANAH See CHENAANAH

KENAN (1)

1Ch 1: 2 **K**, Mahalaleel, Jered,	7018

KENANI See CHENANI

KENANIAH See CHENANIAH

KENATH (2)

Nu 32:42 Nobah went and took **K**, and the villages	7079
1Ch 2:23 them, with **K**, and the towns thereof,	7079

KENAZ (11)

Ge 36:11 Omar, Zepho, and Gatam, and **K**.	7073
36:15 duke Omar, duke Zepho, duke **K**,	7073
36:42 Duke **K**, duke Teman, duke Mibzar,	7073
Jos 15:17 Othniel the son of **K**, the brother of Caleb	7073
Jdg 1:13 Othniel the son of **K**, Caleb's younger	7073
3: 9 them, *even* Othniel the son of **K**,	7073
3:11 And Othniel the son of **K** died.	7073
1Ch 1:36 and Gatam, **K**, and Timna, and Amalek.	7073
1:53 Duke **K**, duke Teman, duke Mibzar,	7073
4:13 the sons of **K**; Othniel, and Seraiah:	7073
4:15 and Naam: and the sons of Elah, even **K**.	7073

KENEZITE (3)

Nu 32:12 Save Caleb the son of Jephunneh the **K**,	7074
Jos 14: 6 Caleb the son of Jephunneh the **K** said	7074
14:14 the son of Jephunneh the **K** unto this day,	7074

KENITE (6) [KENITES]

Nu 24:22 Nevertheless the **K** shall be wasted,	7014
Jdg 1:16 children of the **K**, Moses' father in law,	7017
4:11 Now Heber the **K**, *which was* of	7017
4:17 the tent of Jael the wife of Heber the **K**:	7017
4:17 of Hazor and the house of Heber the **K**.	7017
5:24 shall Jael the wife of Heber the **K** be,	7017

KENITES (8) [KENITE]

Ge 15:19 The **K**, and the Kenizzites,	7017
Nu 24:21 he looked on the **K**, and took up his	7017
Jdg 4:11 had severed himself from the **K**,	7014
1Sa 15: 6 Saul said unto the **K**, Go, depart, get you	7017
15: 6 So the **K** departed from among	7017
27:10 and against the south of the **K**.	7017
30:29 them which *were* in the cities of the **K**,	7017
1Ch 2:55 These *are* the **K** that came of Hemath,	7017

KENIZZITES (1)

Ge 15:19 and the **K**, and the Kadmonites,	7074

KEPHAR AMMONI See CHEPHAR-HAAMMONAI

KEPHIRAH See CHEPHIRAH

KEPT (175) [KEEP]

Ge 26: 5 my charge, my commandments,	8104
29: 9 with her father's sheep: for she **k** them.	7462
39: 9 neither hath he **k** back any thing from	2820
42:16 your brother, and ye shall be **k in prison**,	631
Ex 3: 1 Moses **k** the flock of Jethro his father	7462
16:23 lay up for you to be **k** until the morning.	4931
16:32 Fill an omer of it to be **k** for your	4931
16:33 the **k**, to be **k** for your generations.	4931
16:34 laid it up before the Testimony, to be **k**.	4931
21:29 hath not **k** him in, but that he hath killed	8104
21:36 past, and his owner hath not **k** him in;	8104
Nu 5:13 be **k close**, and she be defiled, and *there*	5641
9: 5 they **k** the passover on the fourteenth day	6213
9: 7 wherefore are we **k back**, that *we* may	1639
9:19 the children of Israel **k** the charge of	8104
9:23 they **k** the charge of the LORD,	8104
17:10 to be **k** for a token against the rebels;	4931
19: 9 it shall be **k** for the congregation of	4931
24:11 the LORD hath **k** thee **back** from honour.	4513
31:47 which **k** the charge of the tabernacle of	8104
Dt 32:10 he **k** him as the apple of his eye.	5341
33: 9 observed thy word, and **k** thy covenant.	5341
Jos 5:10 **k** the passover on the fourteenth day of	6213
14:10 the LORD hath **k** me **alive**, as he said,	2421
22: 2 Ye have **k** all that Moses the servant of	8104
22: 3 have **k** the charge of the commandment	8104
Ru 2:23 So she **k fast** by the maidens of Boaz to	1692
1Sa 9:24 for unto *this* time hath *it* been **k** for thee	8104
13:13 thou hast not **k** the commandment of	8104
13:14 thou hast not **k** *that* which the LORD	8104
17:34 Thy servant **k** his father's sheep,	7462
21: 4 if the young men have **k** themselves at	8104
21: 5 Of a truth women *have been* **k** from us	6113
25:21 Surely in vain have I **k** all this *fellow*	8104
25:33 which hast **k** me this day from coming to	3607
25:34 hath **k** me **back** from hurting thee,	4513

1Sa	25:39 Nabal, and hath **k** his servant from evil:	2820
	26:15 then hast thou not **k** thy lord the king?	8104
	26:16 die, because ye have not **k** your master,	8104
2Sa	13:34 young man that **k** the **watch** lift up his	6822
	22:22 For I have **k** the ways of the LORD,	8104
	22:24 and have **k** myself from mine iniquity.	8104
	22:44 thou hast **k** me to be head of the heathen:	8104
1Ki	2:43 hast thou not **k** the oath of the LORD,	8104
	3: 6 thou hast **k** for him this great kindness,	8104
	8:24 Who hast **k** with thy servant David my	8104
	11:10 he **k** not *that* which the LORD	8104
	11:11 thou hast not **k** my covenant and	8104
	11:34 because he **k** my commandments and	8104
	13:21 hast not **k** the commandment which	8104
	14: 8 who **k** my commandments,	8104
	14:27 which **k** the door of the king's house.	8104
2Ki	9:14 how Joram had **k** Ramoth-gilead, he and	8104
	12: 9 the priests that **k** the door put therein all	8104
	17:19 Also Judah **k** not the commandments of	8104
	18: 6 following him, but **k** his commandments,	8104
1Ch	10:13 he **k** not, and also for asking *counsel*	8104
	12: 1 while he yet **k** himself **close** because	6113
	12:29 hitherto the greatest part of them had **k**	8104
2Ch	6:15 which hast **k** with thy servant David	8104
	7: 8 at the same time Solomon **k** the feast	6213
	7: 9 they **k** the dedication of the altar seven	6213
	12:10 that **k** the entrance of the king's house.	8104
	30:21 **k** the feast of unleavened bread seven	6213
	30:23 they **k** *other* seven days *with* gladness.	6213
	34: 9 which the Levites that **k** the doors had	8104
	34:21 our fathers have not **k** the word of	8104
	35: 1 Moreover Josiah **k** a passover unto	6213
	35:17 the children of Israel that were present **k**	6213
	35:18 in Israel from the days of Samuel	6213
	35:18 of Israel keep such a passover as Josiah **k**,	6213
	35:19 of the reign of Josiah was this passover **k**	6213
	36:21 as long as *she* lay desolate she **k sabbath**,	7673
Ezr	3: 4 They **k** also the feast of tabernacles, as it	6213
	6:16 the dedication of this house of God	5648
	6:19 children of the captivity **k** the passover	6213
	6:22 **k** the feast of unleavened bread seven	6213
Ne	1: 7 have not **k** the commandments,	8104
	8:18 they **k** the feast seven days; and on	6213
	9:34 our priests, nor our fathers, **k** thy law,	6213
	11:19 and their brethren that **k** the gates,	8104
	12:45 and the porters **k** the ward of their God,	8104
Est	2:14 which **k** the concubines.	8104
	2:21 and Teresh, of those which **k** the door,	8104
	9:28 and **k** throughout every generation,	6213
Job	23:11 his way have I **k**, and not declined.	8104
	28:21 and **k close** from the fowls of the air.	5641
	29:21 and waited, and **k silence** at my counsel.	1826
	31:34 that I **k silence**, *and* went not out of	1826
Ps	17: 4 by the word of thy lips I have **k** *me from*	8104
	18:21 For I have **k** the ways of the LORD,	8104
	18:23 and I **k** myself from mine iniquity.	8104
	30: 3 thou hast **k** me **alive**, that I should not go	2421
	32: 3 When I **k silence**, my bones waxed old	2790
	42: 4 praise, *with* a multitude that **k holyday**.	2287
	50:21 *things* hast thou done, and I **k silence**;	2790
	78:10 They **k** not the covenant of God,	8104
	78:56 most high God, and **k** not his testimonies:	8104
	99: 7 they **k** his testimonies, and the ordinance	8104
	119:22 contempt; for I have **k** thy testimonies.	5341
	119:55 in the night, and have **k** thy law.	8104
	119:56 This I had, because I **k** thy precepts.	5341
	119:67 went astray: but now have I **k** thy word.	8104
	119:158 grieved; because they **k** not thy word.	8104
	119:167 soul hath **k** thy testimonies; and *I* love	8104
	119:168 I have **k** thy precepts and thy testimonies:	8104
Ecc	2:10 whatsoever mine eyes desired I **k** not	680
	5:13 riches **k** for the owners thereof to	8104
SS	1: 6 *but* mine own vineyard have I not **k**.	5201
Isa	30:29 *in* the night when a **holy** solemnity is **k**;	6942
Jer	16:11 forsaken me, and have not **k** my law;	8104
	35:18 **k** all his precepts, and done according	8104
Eze	5: 7 statutes, neither have **k** my judgments,	6213
	18: 9 and hath **k** my judgments, to deal truly;	8104
	18:19 hath **k** all my statutes, and hath done	8104
	20:21 neither **k** my judgments to do them,	8104
	44: 8 ye have not **k** the charge of mine holy	8104
	44:15 that **k** the charge of my sanctuary when	8104
	48:11 which have **k** my charge, which went not	8104
Da	5:19 whom he would he **k alive**; and whom	2418
	7:28 in me: but I **k** the matter in my heart.	5202
Hos	12:12 for a wife, and for a wife he **k** *sheep*.	8104
Am	1:11 and he **k** his wrath for ever:	8104
	2: 4 have not **k** his commandments,	8104
Mic	6:16 For the statutes of Omri are **k**, and all	8104
Mal	2: 9 according as ye have not **k** my ways,	8104
	3: 7 have not **k** *them*. Return unto me, and	8104
	3:14 what profit *is* it that we have **k** his	8104
Mt	8:33 And they that **k** *them* fled, and went their	1006
	13:35 utter things which have been **k secret**	2928
	14: 6 But when Herod's birthday was **k**,	71
	19:20 these *things* have I **k** from my youth up.	5442
Mk	4:22 neither was *any* thing **k secret**, but that it	614
	9:10 And they **k** *that* saying with themselves,	2902
Lk	2:19 But Mary **k** all these things,	4933
	2:51 his mother **k** all these sayings in her heart.	1301
	8:29 he was **k** bound with chains and	5442
	9:36 and **k** *it* **close**, and told no *man* in	4601
	18:21 All these have I **k** from my youth up.	5442
	19:20 which I have **k** laid up in a napkin:	2192
Jn	2:10 *but* thou hast **k** the good wine until now.	5083

Jn	12: 7 against the day of my burying hath she **k**	5083
	15:10 even as I have **k** my Father's	5083
	15:20 if they have **k** my saying, they will keep	5083
	16: 6 them me; and they have **k** thy word.	5083
	17:12 them in the world, I **k** them in thy name:	5083
	17:12 *those* that thou gavest me I have **k**,	5442
	18:16 and spake unto her that **k the door**,	2377
	18:17 saith the damsel that **k the door** unto	2377
Ac	5: 2 And **k back** *part* of the price, his wife also	3557
	7:53 disposition of angels, and have not **k** *it*.	5442
	9:33 which had **k** his bed eight years,	1909+2621
	12: 5 Peter therefore was **k** in prison:	5083
	12: 6 *the* keepers before the door **k** the prison.	5083
	15:12 Then all the multitude **k silence**,	4601
	20:20 *And* how I **k back** nothing that was	5288
	22: 2 tongue to them, they **k** the more silence:	3930
	22:20 and **k** the raiment of them that slew him.	5442
	23:35 he commanded him to be **k** in Herod's	5442
	25: 4 that Paul should be **k** at Cesarea,	5083
	25:21 commanded to be **k** till I might send	5083
	27:43 to save Paul, **k** them *from their* purpose;	2967
	28:16 by himself with a soldier that **k** him.	5442
Ro	16:25 was **k secret** since the world began,	4601
2Co	11: 9 in all things I have **k** myself from being	5083
	11:32 **k** the city of the Damascenes *with a*	5432
Gal	3:23 faith came, we were **k** under the law,	5432
2Ti	4: 7 finished *my* course, I have **k** the faith:	5083
Heb	11:28 Through faith he **k** the passover,	4160
Jas	5: 4 which is of you **k back by fraud**, crieth:	650
1Pe	1: 5 Who are **k** by the power of God through	5432
2Pe	2: 7 now, by the same word are **k in store**,	2343
Jude	1: 6 And the angels which **k** not their first	5083
Rev	3: 8 and hast **k** my word, and hast not denied	5083
	3:10 Because thou hast **k** the word of my	5083

KERAN See CHERAN

KERCHIEFS (2) [HANDKERCHIEFS]

Eze	13:18 make **k** upon the head of every stature to	4555
	13:21 Your **k** also will I tear, and deliver my	4555

KEREN-HAPPUCH (1)

Job	42:14 Kezia; and the name of the third, **K**.	7163

KERETHITES See CHERETHIMS; CHERETHITES

KERIOTH (4)

Jos	15:25 Hazor, Hadattah, and **K**, *and* Hezron,	7152
Jer	48:24 upon **K**, and upon Bozrah, and upon all	7152
	48:41 **K** is taken, and the strong holds are	7152
Am	2: 2 and it shall devour the palaces of **K**:	7152

KERITH See CHERITH

KERNELS (1)

Nu	6: 4 vine tree, from the **k** even to the husk.	2785

KEROS (2)

Ezr	2:44 The children of **K**, the children of Siaha,	7026
Ne	7:47 The children of **K**, the children of Sia,	7026

KESALON See CHESALON

KESED See CHESED

KESIL See CHESIL

KESULLOTH See CHESULLOTH

KETTLE (1)

1Sa	2:14 *it* into the pan, or **k**, or caldron, or pot;	1731

KETURAH (4)

Ge	25: 1 took a wife, and her name *was* **K**.	6989
	25: 4 Eldaah. All these *were* the children of **K**.	6989
1Ch	1:32 the sons of **K**, Abraham's concubine:	6989
	1:33 and Eldaah. All these *are* the sons of **K**.	6989

KEY (6) [KEYS]

Jdg	3:25 they took a **k**, and opened *them*:	4668
Isa	22:22 the **k** of the house of David will I lay	4668
Lk	11:52 ye have taken away the **k** of knowledge:	2807
Rev	3: 7 *that is* true, he that hath the **k** of David,	2807
	9: 1 to him was given the **k** of the bottomless	2807
	20: 1 having the **k** of the bottomless *pit* and	2807

KEYS (2) [KEY]

Mt	16:19 And I will give unto thee the **k** of	2807
Rev	1:18 and have the **k** of hell and of death.	2807

KEZIA (1)

Job	42:14 the name of the second, **K**; and the name	7103

KEZIAH See KEZIA

KEZIB See CHEZIB

KEZIZ (1)

Jos	18:21 and Beth-hoglah, and the valley of **K**,	7104

KIBROTH-HATTAAVAH (5)

Nu	11:34 he called the name of that place **K**:	6914
	11:35 *And* the people journeyed from **K** *unto*	6914
	33:16 from the desert of Sinai, and pitched at **K**.	6914
	33:17 they departed from **K**, and encamped at	6914
Dt	9:22 at Taberah, and at Massah, and at **K**,	6914

KIBZAIM (1)

Jos	21:22 **K** with her suburbs, and Beth-horon with	6911

KICK (2) [KICKED]

1Sa	2:29 Wherefore **k** ye at my sacrifice and at	1163
Ac	9: 5 *it is* hard for thee to **k** against the pricks.	2979
	26:14 *it is* hard for thee to **k** against the pricks.	2979

KICKED (1) [KICK]

Dt	32:15 Jeshurun waxed fat, and **k**: thou art	1163

KID (43) [KIDS]

Ge	37:31 killed a **k** of the goats, and dipped the	8163
	38:17 I will send *thee* a **k** from the flock.	1423+5795
	38:20 Judah sent the **k** by the hand of his	1423+5795
	38:23 I sent this **k**, and thou hast not found her.	1423
Ex	23:19 Thou shalt not seethe a **k** in his mother's	1423
	34:26 Thou shalt not seethe a **k** in his mother's	1423
Lev	4:23 a **k** of the goats, a male without blemish:	8163
	4:28 a **k** of the goats, a female without blemish	8166
	5: 6 a lamb or a **k** of the goats, for a sin	8166
	9: 3 a **k** of the goats for a sin offering;	8163
	23:19 ye shall sacrifice one **k** of the goats for a	8163
Nu	7:16 One **k** of the goats for a sin offering:	8163
	7:22 One **k** of the goats for a sin offering:	8163
	7:28 One **k** of the goats for a sin offering:	8163
	7:34 One **k** of the goats for a sin offering:	8163
	7:40 One **k** of the goats for a sin offering:	8163
	7:46 One **k** of the goats for a sin offering:	8163
	7:52 One **k** of the goats for a sin offering:	8163
	7:58 One **k** of the goats for a sin offering:	8163
	7:64 One **k** of the goats for a sin offering:	8163
	7:70 One **k** of the goats for a sin offering:	8163
	7:76 One **k** of the goats for a sin offering:	8163
	7:82 One **k** of the goats for a sin offering:	8163
	15:11 for one ram, or for a lamb, or a **k**.	5795
	15:24 and one **k** of the goats for a sin offering.	8163
	28:15 one **k** of the goats for a sin offering unto	8163
	28:30 *And* one **k** of the goats, to make an	8163
	29: 5 one **k** of the goats *for a* sin offering:	8163
	29:11 One **k** of the goats *for a* sin offering,	8163
	29:16 one **k** of the goats *for a* sin offering;	8163
	29:19 one **k** of the goats *for a* sin offering;	8163
	29:25 one **k** of the goats *for a* sin offering;	8163
Dt	14:21 Thou shalt not seethe a **k** in his mother's	1423
Jdg	6:19 made ready a **k**,	1423+5795
	13:15 until we shall have made ready a **k**	1423+5795
	13:19 So Manoah took a **k** with a meat	1423+5795
	14: 6 he rent him as *he* would have rent a **k**,	1423
	15: 1 Samson visited his wife with a **k**;	1423+5795
1Sa	16:20 a **k**, and sent *them* by David his son	1423+5795
Isa	11: 6 and the leopard shall lie down with the **k**;	1423
Eze	43:22 on the second day thou shalt offer a **k** of	8163
	45:23 **k** of the goats daily *for a* sin offering.	8163
Lk	15:29 and yet thou never gavest me a **k**, that I	2056

KIDNEYS (18)

Ex	29:13 the two **k**, and the fat that *is* upon them,	3629
	29:22 the two **k**, and the fat that *is* on them,	3629
Lev	3: 4 the two **k**, and the fat that *is* on them,	3629
	3: 4 liver, with the **k**, it shall take away.	3629
	3:10 the two **k**, and the fat that *is* upon them,	3629
	3:10 liver, with the **k**, it shall take away.	3629
	3:15 the two **k**, and the fat that *is* upon them,	3629
	3:15 liver, with the **k**, it shall take away.	3629
	4: 9 the two **k**, and the fat that *is* upon them,	3629
	4: 9 liver, with the **k**, it shall he take away,	3629
	7: 4 the two **k**, and the fat that *is* on them,	3629
	7: 4 liver, with the **k**, it shall he take away:	3629
	8:16 the two **k**, and their fat, and Moses burned	3629
	8:25 the two **k**, and their fat, and the right	3629
	9:10 the **k**, and the caul above the liver of the	3629
	9:19 which covereth the inwards, and the **k**,	3629
Dt	32:14 and goats, with the fat of **k** of wheat;	3629
Isa	34: 6 and goats, with the fat of the **k** of rams:	3629

KIDON See CHIDON

KIDRON (11)

2Sa	15:23 also *himself* passed over the brook **K**,	6939
1Ki	2:37 goest out, and passest over the brook **K**,	6939
	15:13 her idol, and burnt *it* by the brook **K**.	6939
2Ki	23: 4 without Jerusalem in the fields of **K**,	6939
	23: 6 the brook **K**, and burnt it at the brook	6939
	23: 6 burnt it at the brook **K**, and stampt *it*	6939
	23:12 cast the dust of them into the brook **K**.	6939
2Ch	15:16 stamped *it*, and burnt *it* at the brook **K**.	6939
	29:16 *it*, to carry *it* out abroad into the brook **K**.	6939
	30:14 away, and cast *them* into the brook **K**.	6939
Jer	31:40 and all the fields unto the brook **K**,	6939

KIDS (8) [KID]

Ge	27: 9 fetch me from thence two good **k** of	1423
	27:16 she put the skins of the **k** of the goats	1423
Lev	16: 5 Israel two **k** of the goats for a sin offering,	8163
Nu	7:87 the **k** of the goats for sin offering twelve.	8163
1Sa	10: 3 carrying three **k**, and another carrying	1423
1Ki	20:27 before them like two little flocks of **k**;	5795
2Ch	35: 7 people, *of* the flock, lambs and **k**,	1121+5795
SS	1: 8 feed thy **k** beside the shepherds' tents.	1429

KILEAB See CHILEAB

KILION See CHILION

K

KILL (126) [KILLED, KILLEDST, KILLEST, KILLETH, KILLING]

Ge	4:15 lest any finding him should **k** him.	5221
	12:12 they will **k** me, but they will save thee	2026
	26: 7 the men of the place should **k** me	2026
	27:42 comfort himself, *purposing* to **k** thee.	2026
	37:21 their hands; and said, Let us not **k** him.	5221
Ex	1:16 if it *be* a son, then ye shall **k** him:	4191
	2:14 intendest thou to **k** me, as thou killedst	2026
	4:24 the LORD met him, and sought to **k** him.	4191
	12: 6 of Israel shall **k** it in the evening.	7819
	12:21 to your families, and **k** the passover.	7819
	16: 3 to **k** this whole assembly with hunger.	4191
	17: 3 to **k** us and our children and our cattle	4191
	20:13 Thou shalt not **k**.	7523
	22: 1 steal an ox, or a sheep, and **k** it, or sell it;	2873
	22:24 wax hot, and I will **k** you with the sword;	2026
	29:11 thou shalt **k** the bullock before the LORD,	7819
	29:20 thou **k** the ram, and take of his blood,	7819
Lev	1: 5 he shall **k** the bullock before the LORD:	7819
	1:11 he shall **k** it on the side of the altar	7819
	3: 2 **k** it *at* the door of the tabernacle of	7819
	3: 8 **k** it before the tabernacle of	7819
	3:13 **k** it before the tabernacle of	7819
	4: 4 and **k** the bullock before the LORD.	7819
	4:24 **k** it in the place where they kill the burnt	7819
	4:24 kill it in the place where the burnt	7819
	4:33 the place where they **k** the burnt offering.	7819
	7: 2 In the place where they **k** the burnt	7819
	7: 2 offering shall they **k** the trespass offering:	7819
	14:13 place where he shall **k** the sin offering	7819
	14:19 afterward he shall **k** the burnt offering.	7819
	14:25 shall **k** the lamb of the trespass offering,	7819
	14:50 he shall **k** the one of the birds in an earthen	7819
	16:11 shall **k** the bullock of the sin offering,	7819
	16:15 shall he **k** the goat of the sin offering,	7819
	20: 4 of his seed unto Molech, and **k** him not:	4191
	20:16 thou shalt **k** the woman and the beast;	2026
	22:28 ye shall not **k** it and her young both in	7819
Nu	11:15 **k** me, I pray thee, **out of hand**,	2026+2026
	14:15 Now *if* thou shalt **k** *all* this people as one	4191
	16:13 and honey, to **k** us in the wilderness,	4191
	22:29 in mine hand, for now would I **k** thee.	2026
	31:17 **k** every male among the little ones,	2026
	31:17 **k** every woman that hath known man by	2026
	35:27 and the revenger of blood **k** the slayer;	7523
Dt	4:42 which should **k** his neighbour unawares,	7523
	5:17 Thou shalt not **k**.	7523
	12:15 Notwithstanding thou mayest **k** and	2076
	12:21 thou shalt **k** of thy herd and of thy flock,	2076
	13: 9 thou shalt **surely k** him; thine	2026+2026
	32:39 I **k**, and I make alive; I wound, and I heal:	4191
Jdg	13:23 If the LORD were pleased to **k** us,	4191
	15:13 **surely** we will not **k** thee.	4191+4191
	16: 2 when it is day, we shall **k** him.	2026
	20:31 *and* as, at other times, in the highways,	2491
	20:39 **k** of the men of Israel about thirty persons	2491
1Sa	16: 2 if Saul hear *it*, he will **k** me.	2026
	17: 9 *to* **k** me, then will we be your servants:	5221
	17: 9 **k** him, then shall ye be our servants,	5221
	19: 1 all his servants, that they should **k** David.	4191
	19: 2 Saul my father seeketh to **k** thee:	4191
	19:17 me, Let me go; why should I **k** thee?	4191
	24:10 bade *me* **k** thee: but *mine eye* spared	2026
	30:15 me by God, that thou wilt neither **k** me,	4191
2Sa	13:28 Smite Amnon; then **k** him, fear not:	4191
	14: 7 smote his brother, that we may **k** him,	4191
	14:32 there be *any* iniquity in me, let him **k** me.	4191
	21: 4 neither for us *shalt thou* **k** any man in	4191
1Ki	11:40 Solomon sought therefore to **k** Jeroboam.	4191
	12:27 shall **k** me, and go again to Rehoboam	2026
2Ki	5: 7 said, *Am* I God, to **k** and to make alive,	4191
	7: 4 live; and if they **k** us, we shall but die.	4191
	11:15 him that followeth her **k** with the sword.	4191
2Ch	35: 6 So **k** the passover, and sanctify yourselves,	7819
Est	3:13 to **k**, and to cause to perish, all Jews,	2026
Ps	59: 1 and they watcht the house to **k** him.	4191
Ecc	3: 3 A time to **k**, and a time to heal; a time to	2026
Isa	14:30 I will **k** thy root with famine, and he shall	4191
	29: 1 add ye year to year; let them **k** sacrifices.	5362
Eze	34: 3 with the wool, ye **k** them that are fed:	2076
Mt	5:21 by them of old time, Thou shalt not **k**;	5407
	5:21 whosoever shall **k** shall be in danger of	5407
	10:28 And fear not them which **k** the body,	615
	10:28 **kill** the body, but are not able to **k** the soul:	615
	17:23 And they shall **k** him, and the third day he	615
	21:38 let us **k** him, and let us seize on his	615
	23:34 and *some* of them ye shall **k** and crucify;	615
	24: 9 you up to be afflicted, and shall **k** you:	615
	26: 4 might take Jesus by subtilty, and **k** *him*.	615
Mk	3: 4 to save life, or to **k**? But they held their	615
	9:31 the hands of men, and they shall **k** him:	615
	10:19 commit adultery, Do not **k**, Do not steal,	5407
	10:34 and shall spit upon him, and shall **k** him:	615
Lk	12: 7 let us **k** him, and the inheritance shall be	615
	12: 4 Be not afraid of them that **k** the body,	615
	13:31 and depart hence: for Herod will **k** thee.	615
	15:23 and **k** *it*; and let us eat, and be merry:	2380
	18:20 commit adultery, Do not **k**, Do not steal,	5407
	20:14 come, let us **k** him, that the inheritance	615
	22: 2 and scribes sought how they might **k** him;	337
Jn	5:18 Therefore the Jews sought the more to **k**	615
	7: 1 Jewry, because the Jews sought to **k** him.	615
	7:19 the law? Why go ye about to **k** me?	615

Jn	7:20 hast a devil: who goeth about to **k** thee?	615
	7:25 Is not this he, whom they seek to **k**?	615
	8:22 Then said the Jews, Will he **k** himself?	615
	8:37 ye seek to **k** me, because my word hath	615
	8:40 But now ye seek to **k** me, a man that hath	615
	10:10 but for to steal, and to **k**, and to destroy:	2380
Ac	7:28 Wilt thou **k** me, as thou didst the Egyptian	337
	9:23 the Jews took counsel to **k** him:	337
	9:24 watched the gates day and night to **k** him.	337
	10:13 a voice to him, Rise, Peter; **k**, and eat.	2380
	21:31 And as *they* went about to **k** him,	615
	23:15 or ever he come near, are ready to **k** him.	337
	23:15 laying wait in the way to **k** him.	337
	26:21 in the temple, and went about to **k** *me*.	1315
	27:42 and the soldiers' counsel was to **k**	615
Ro	13: 9 Thou shalt not **k**, Thou shalt not steal,	5407
Jas	2:11 not commit adultery, said also, Do not **k**.	5407
	2:11 if thou commit no adultery, yet *if* thou **k**,	5407
	4: 2 ye **k**, and desire to have, and cannot	5407
Rev	2:23 And I will **k** her children with death;	615
	6: 4 and that they should **k** one another:	4969
	6: 8 to **k** with sword, and with hunger,	615
	9: 5 it was given that they should not **k** them,	615
	11: 7 and shall overcome them, and **k** them.	615

KILLED (67) [KILL]

Ge	37:31 a kid of the goats, and dipped the coat	7819
Ex	21:29 but that he hath **k** a man or a woman;	4191
Lev	4:15 the bullock shall be **k** before the LORD.	7819
	6:25 In the place where the burnt offering is **k**	7819
	6:25 the sin offering be **k** before the LORD:	7819
	8:19 he **k** *it;* and Moses sprinkled the blood	7819
	14: 5 in an earthen vessel over running water:	7819
	14: 6 bird *that was* **k** over the running water.	7819
Nu	16:41 Ye have **k** the people of the LORD.	4191
	31:19 whosoever hath **k** *any* person,	2026
1Sa	24:11 **k** thee not, know thou and see that *there*	2026
	25:11 my flesh that I have **k** for my shearers,	2873
	28:24 and **k** it, and took flour, and kneaded *it*,	2076
2Sa	12: 9 thou hast **k** Uriah the Hittite with	5221
	21:17 and smote the Philistine, and **k** him.	4191
1Ki	16: 7 of Jeroboam; and because he **k** him.	5221
	16:10 Zimri went in and smote him, and **k** him,	4191
	21:19 Hast thou **k**, and also taken possession?	7523
2Ki	15:25 he **k** him, and reigned in his room.	4191
1Ch	19:18 **k** Shophach the captain of the host.	4191
2Ch	18: 2 Ahab **k** sheep and oxen for him in	2076
	25: 3 he slew his servants that had the king	5221
	29:22 So they **k** the bullocks, and the priests	7819
	29:22 likewise, when they had **k** the rams, they	7819
	29:22 they **k** also the lambs, and they sprinkled	7819
	29:24 the priests **k** them, and they made	7819
	30:15 they **k** the passover on the fourteenth *day*	7819
	35: 1 they **k** the passover on the fourteenth *day*	7819
	35:11 they **k** the passover, and the priests	7819
Ezr	6:20 the passover for all the children of	7819
Ps	44:22 for thy sake are we **k** all the day long;	2026
Pr	9: 2 She hath **k** her beasts; she hath mingled	2873
La	2:21 thine anger; thou hast **k**, *and* not pitied.	2873
Mt	16:21 be **k**, and be raised *again* the third day.	615
	21:35 one, and **k** another, and stoned another.	615
	22: 4 my oxen and *my* fatlings *are* **k**,	2380
	23:31 that ye are the children of them which **k**	5407
Mk	6:19 against him, and would have **k** him;	615
	8:31 and be **k**, and after three days rise again.	615
	9:31 after that he is **k**, he shall rise the third	615
	12: 5 and him they **k**, and many others;	615
	12: 8 **k** him, and cast *him* out of the vineyard.	615
	14:12 they **k** the passover, his disciples said	2380
Lk	11:47 of the prophets, and your fathers **k** them.	615
	11:48 for they indeed **k** them, and ye build their	615
	12: 5 which after *he* hath **k** hath power to cast	615
	15:27 and thy father hath **k** the fatted calf,	2380
	15:30 thou hast **k** for him the fatted calf.	2380
	20:15 and **k** *him*. What therefore shall the lord	615
	22: 7 when the passover must be **k**.	2380
Ac	3:15 And the Prince of life, whom God hath	615
	12: 2 And he **k** James the brother of John with	337
	16:27 out his sword, and would have **k** himself,	337
	23:12 neither eat nor drink till they had **k** Paul.	615
	23:21 neither eat nor drink till they have **k** him:	337
	23:27 the Jews, and should have been **k** of them:	337
Ro	8:36 For thy sake we are **k** all the day long;	2289
	11: 3 they have **k** thy prophets, and digged	615
2Co	6: 9 behold, we live; as chastened, and not **k**;	2289
1Th	2:15 Who both **k** the Lord Jesus, and their own	615
Jas	5: 6 Ye have condemned *and* **k** the just;	5407
Rev	6:11 that should be **k** as they *were*, should be	615
	9:18 By these three was the third *part* of men **k**,	615
	9:20 the rest of the men which were not **k** by	615
	11: 5 hurt them, he must in this manner be **k**.	615
	13:10 he that killeth with the sword must be **k**.	615
	13:15 worship the image of the beast should be **k**.	615

KILLEDST (2) [KILL]

Ex	2:14 thou to kill me, as thou **k** the Egyptian?	2026
1Sa	24:18 me into thine hand, thou **k** me not.	2026

KILLEST (2) [KILL]

Mt	23:37 *thou* that **k** the prophets, and stonest them	615
Lk	13:34 which **k** the prophets, and stonest them	615

KILLETH (23) [KILL]

Lev	17: 3 **k** an ox, or lamb, or goat, in the camp,	7819
	17: 3 in the camp, or that **k** *it* out of the camp,	7819

Lev	24:17 he that **k** any man shall surely be	5221+5315
	24:18 he that **k** a beast shall make it good	5221+5315
	24:21 he that **k** a beast, he shall restore it:	5221
	24:21 he that **k** a man, he shall be put to death.	5221
Nu	35:11 which **k** *any* person at unawares.	5221
	35:15 every one that **k** *any* person unawares	5221
	35:30 Whoso **k** *any* person, the murderer shall	5221
Dt	19: 4 Whoso **k** his neighbour ignorantly, whom	5221
Jos	20: 3 the slayer that **k** *any* person unawares	5221
	20: 9 whosoever **k** *any* person at unawares	5221
1Sa	2: 6 The LORD **k**, and maketh alive:	4191
	17:25 it shall be, *that* the man who **k** him,	5221
	17:26 What shall be done to the man that **k** this	5221
	17:27 So shall it be done to the man that **k** him.	5221
Job	5: 2 For wrath **k** the foolish man,	2026
	24:14 The murderer rising with the light **k**	6991
Pr	21:25 The desire of the slothful **k** him; for his	4191
Isa	66: 3 He that **k** an ox is *as if* he slew a man;	7819
Jn	16: 2 that whosoever **k** you will think that he	615
2Co	3: 6 for the letter **k**, but the spirit giveth life.	615
Rev	13:10 he that **k** with the sword must be killed	615

KILLING (5) [KILL]

Jdg	9:24 which aided him in the **k** of his brethren.	2026
2Ch	30:17 the Levites had the charge of the **k** of	7821
Isa	22:13 **k** sheep, eating flesh, and drinking wine:	7819
Hos	4: 2 and stealing, and committing adultery,	7523
Mk	12: 5 many others; beating some, and **k** some.	615

KILMAD See CHILMAD

KIMHAM See CHIMHAM

KIN (8) [KINDRED, KINDREDS, KINSFOLK, KINSFOLKS, KINSMAN, KINSMAN'S, KINSMEN, KINSWOMAN, KINSWOMEN]

Lev	18: 6 approach to any that is near of **k** to him,	1320
	20:19 for he uncovereth his **near k**: their	7607
	21: 2 for his **k**, that is near unto him, *that is*, for	7607
	25:25 *if any of* his **k** come to redeem it, then	7138
	25:49 that is nigh of **k** unto him of his family	1320
Ru	2:20 The man *is* **near of k** unto us, one of our	7138
2Sa	19:42 Because the king *is* **near of k** to us:	7138
Mk	6: 4 and among his own **k**, and in his own	4773

KINAH (1)

Jos	15:22 And **K**, and Dimonah, and Adadah,	7016

KIND (45) [KINDLY, KINDNESS, KINDS, LOVINGKINDNESS, LOVINGKINDNESSES]

Ge	1:11 and the fruit tree yielding fruit after his **k**,	4327
	1:12 *and* herb yielding seed after his **k**:	4327
	1:12 whose seed *was* in itself, after his **k**:	4327
	1:21 after their **k**, and every winged fowl after	4327
	1:21 and every winged fowl after his **k**:	4327
	1:24 bring forth the living creature after his **k**,	4327
	1:24 and beast of the earth after his **k**:	4327
	1:25 made the beast of the earth after his **k**,	4327
	1:25 cattle after their **k**, and every thing that	4327
	1:25 that creepeth upon the earth after his **k**:	4327
	6:20 Of fowls after their **k**, and of cattle after	4327
	6:20 after their kind, and of cattle after their **k**,	4327
	6:20 creeping thing of the earth after his **k**,	4327
	7:14 every beast after his **k**, and all the cattle	4327
	7:14 all the cattle after their **k**,	4327
	7:14 that creepeth upon the earth after his **k**,	4327
	7:14 every fowl after his **k**, every bird of every	4327
Lev	11:14 And the vulture, and the kite after his **k**;	4327
	11:15 Every raven after his **k**;	4327
	11:16 the cuckow, and the hawk after his **k**,	4327
	11:19 the heron after her **k**, and the lapwing,	4327
	11:22 the locust after his **k**, and the bald locust	4327
	11:22 the bald locust after his **k**, and the beetle	4327
	11:22 the beetle after his **k**, and the grasshopper	4327
	11:22 his kind, and the grasshopper after his **k**.	4327
	11:29 the mouse, and the tortoise after his **k**,	4327
	19:19 not let thy cattle gender with a **diverse k**:	3610
Dt	14:13 and the kite, and the vulture after his **k**,	4327
	14:14 And every raven after his **k**,	4327
	14:15 the cuckow, and the hawk after his **k**,	4327
	14:18 the heron after her **k**, and the lapwing,	4327
1Ch	28:14 of **every k of service**:	5656+5656+2050.1
2Ch	10: 7 If thou be to this people, and please	2896
Ne	13:20 sellers of all **k** of ware lodged without	NIH
Ecc	2: 5 I planted trees in them of all **k** of fruits:	NIH
Eze	27:12 reason of the multitude of all **k** of riches,	NIH
Mt	13:47 cast into the sea, and gathered of every **k**:	1085
	17:21 this **k** goeth not out but by prayer	1085
Mk	9:29 This **k** can come forth by nothing, but by	1085
Lk	6:35 for he is **k** unto the unthankful and to	5543
1Co	13: 4 Charity suffereth long, *and* is **k**;	5541
	15:39 but *there* is one **k** of flesh of men,	NIG
Eph	4:32 be ye **k** one to another, tenderhearted,	5543
Jas	1:18 that we should be a **k** of firstfruits of his	5100
	3: 7 For every **k** of beasts, and of birds,	5449

KINDLE (19) [KINDLED, KINDLETH]

Ex	35: 3 Ye shall **k** no fire throughout your	1197
Pr	26:21 fire; so *is* a contentious man to **k** strife.	2787
Isa	9:18 shall **k** in the thickets of the forest,	3341
	10:16 under his glory he shall **k** a burning like	3344
	30:33 like a stream of brimstone, doth **k** it.	1197
	43: 2 neither shall the flame **k** upon thee.	1197
	50:11 Behold, all ye that **k** a fire, that compass	6919
Jer	7:18 fathers the fire, and the women knead	1197
	17:27 will I **k** a fire in the gates thereof,	3341

Jer 21:14 I will **k** a fire in the forest thereof, 3341
33:18 to **k** meat offerings, and to do sacrifice 6999
43:12 I will **k** a fire in the houses of the gods of 3341
49:27 I will **k** a fire in the wall of Damascus, 3341
50:32 I will **k** a fire in his cities, and it shall 3341
Eze 20:47 I *will* **k** a fire in thee, and it shall devour 3341
24:10 Heap on wood, **k** the fire, consume 1814
Am 1:14 I will **k** a fire in the wall of Rabbah, 3341
Ob 1:18 they shall **k** in them, and devour them; 1814
Mal 1:10 neither do ye **k** *fire on* mine altar for 215

KINDLED (66) [KINDLE]
Ge 30: 2 Jacob's anger was **k** against Rachel: 2734
39:19 thy servant to me; that his wrath was **k**. 2734
Ex 4:14 the anger of the Lord was **k** against 2734
22: 6 be consumed *therewith;* he that **k** the fire 1197
Lev 10: 6 the burning which the Lord hath **k**. 8313
Nu 11: 1 the Lord heard *it;* and his anger was **k**; 2734
11:10 the anger of the Lord was **k** greatly; 2734
11:33 the wrath of the Lord was **k** against 2734
12: 9 the anger of the Lord was **k** against 2734
22:22 God's anger was **k** because he went: 2734
22:27 Balaam's anger was **k**, and he smote the 2734
24:10 Balak's anger was **k** against Balaam, 2734
25: 3 the anger of the Lord was **k** against 2734
32:10 the Lord's anger was **k** the same time, 2734
32:13 the Lord's anger was **k** against Israel, 2734
Dt 6:15 lest the anger of the Lord thy God be **k** 2734
7: 4 will the anger of the Lord be **k** against 2734
11:17 *then* the Lord's wrath be **k** against you, 2734
29:27 the anger of the Lord was **k** against this 2734
31:17 my anger shall be **k** against them in that 2734
32:22 For a fire is **k** in my anger, and shall burn 6919
Jos 7: 1 the anger of the Lord was **k** against 2734
23:16 shall the anger of the Lord be **k** against 2734
Jdg 9:30 of Gaal the son of Ebed, his anger was **k** 2734
14:19 his anger was **k**, and he went up *to* his 2734
1Sa 11: 6 those tidings, and his anger was **k** greatly. 2734
17:28 Eliab's anger was **k** against David, 2734
20:30 Saul's anger was **k** against Jonathan, 2734
2Sa 6: 7 anger of the Lord was **k** against 2734
12: 5 David's anger was greatly **k** against 2734
22: 9 his mouth devoured: coals were **k** by it. 1197
22:13 brightness before him were coals of fire **k**. 1197
24: 1 again the anger of the Lord was **k** 2734
2Ki 13: 3 the anger of the Lord was **k** against 2734
22:13 wrath of the Lord that is **k** against us, 3341
22:17 my wrath shall be **k** against this place, 3341
23:26 where*with* his anger was **k** against Judah, 2734
1Ch 13:10 the anger of the Lord was **k** against 2734
2Ch 25:10 their anger was greatly **k** against Judah, 2734
25:15 Wherefore the anger of the Lord was **k** 2734
Job 19:11 He hath also **k** his wrath against me, 2734
32: 2 was **k** the wrath of Elihu the son of 2734
32: 2 against Job was his wrath **k**, because 2734
32: 3 against his three friends was his wrath **k**, 2734
32: 5 *these* three men, then his wrath was **k**. 2734
42: 7 My wrath is **k** against thee, and against 2734
Ps 2:12 the way, when his wrath is **k** but a little: 1197
18: 8 his mouth devoured: coals were **k** by it. 1197
78:21 so a fire was **k** against Jacob, 5400
106:18 a fire was **k** in their company; the flame 1197
106:40 was the wrath of the Lord **k** 2734
124: 3 when their wrath was **k** against us: 2734
Isa 5:25 Therefore is the anger of the Lord **k** 2734
50:11 fire, and in the sparks *that* ye have **k**. 1197
Jer 11:16 the noise of a great tumult he hath **k** 3341
15:14 for a fire is **k** in mine anger, *which* shall 6919
17: 4 for ye have **k** a fire in mine anger, 6919
44: 6 was **k** in the cities of Judah and in 1197
La 4:11 **k** a fire in Zion, and it hath devoured 3341
Eze 20:48 all flesh shall see that I the Lord have **k** 1197
Hos 8: 5 *thee* off; mine anger is **k** against them: 2734
11: 8 within me, my repentings are **k** together. 3648
Zec 10: 3 Mine anger was **k** against the shepherds 2734
Lk 12:49 earth; and what will I, if it be already **k**? 381
22:55 when they had **k** a fire in the midst of 681
Ac 28: 2 they **k** a fire, and received us every one, 381

KINDLETH (3) [KINDLE]
Job 41:21 His breath **k** coals, and a flame goeth out 3857
Isa 44:15 yea, he **k** *it*, and baketh bread; yea, 5400
Jas 3: 5 Behold, how great a matter a little fire **k**. 381

KINDLY (10) [KIND]
Ge 24:49 now if ye will deal **k** and truly with my 2617
34: 3 and spake **k** unto the damsel. 3820+5921
47:29 my thigh, and deal **k** and truly with me; 2617
50:21 comforted them, and spake **k** unto them. 3820
Jos 2:14 that we will deal **k** and truly with thee. 2617
Ru 1: 8 the Lord deal **k** with you, as ye have 2617
1Sa 20: 8 Therefore thou shalt deal **k** with thy 2617
2Ki 25:28 he spake **k** to him, and set his throne 2896
Jer 52:32 spake **k** unto him, and set his throne 2896
Ro 12:10 *Be* **k** affectioned one to another with 5387

KINDNESS (48) [KIND]
Ge 20:13 This *is* thy **k** which thou shalt shew unto 2617
21:23 according to the **k** that I have done unto 2617
24:12 and shew **k** unto my master Abraham. 2617
24:14 that thou hast shewed **k** unto my master. 2617
40:14 shew **k**, I pray thee, unto me, 2617
Jos 2:12 by the Lord, since I have shewed you **k**, 2617
2:12 that ye will also shew **k** unto my father's 2617
Jdg 8:35 Neither shewed they **k** to the house of

Ru 2:20 who hath not left off his **k** to the living 2617
3:10 *for* thou hast shewed more **k** in the latter 2617
1Sa 15: 6 ye shewed **k** to all the children of Israel, 2617
20:14 yet I live shew me the **k** of the Lord, 2617
20:15 *also* thou shalt not cut off thy **k** from my 2617
2Sa 2: 5 ye have shewed this **k** unto your lord, 2617
2: 6 now the Lord shew **k** and truth unto 2617
2: 6 I also will requite you this **k**, because 2896
3: 8 which against Judah do shew **k** *this* day 2617
9: 1 I may shew him **k** for Jonathan's sake? 2617
9: 3 that I may shew the **k** of God unto him? 2617
9: 7 for I will surely shew thee **k** for Jonathan 2617
10: 2 I will shew **k** unto Hanun the son of 2617
10: 2 Nahash, as his father shewed unto me. 2617
16:17 said to Hushai, *Is* this thy **k** to thy friend? 2617
1Ki 2: 7 shew **k** unto the sons of Barzillai 2617
3: 6 thou hast kept for him this great **k**, that 2617
1Ch 19: 2 I will shew **k** unto Hanun the son of 2617
19: 2 because his father shewed **k** to me. 2617
2Ch 24:22 Joash the king remembered not the **k** 2617
Ne 9:17 and of great **k**, and forsookest them not. 2617
Est 2: 9 pleased him, and she obtained **k** of him; 2617
Ps 31:21 he hath shewed me his marvellous **k** in 2617
117: 2 For his **merciful k** is great toward us: 2617
119:76 thy **merciful k** be for my comfort, 2617
141: 5 Let the righteous smite me; *it shall be a* **k**: 2617
Pr 19:22 The desire of a man *is his* **k**: and a poor 2617
31:26 and in her tongue *is* the law of **k**. 2617
Isa 54: 8 with everlasting **k** will I have mercy on 2617
54:10 my **k** shall not depart from thee, 2617
Jer 2: 2 I remember thee, the **k** of thy youth, 2617
Joel 2:13 of great **k**, and repenteth him of the evil. 2617
Jnh 4: 2 of great **k**, and repentest thee of the evil. 2617
Ac 28: 2 barbarous people shewed us no little **k**: 5363
2Co 6: 6 by knowledge, by longsuffering, by **k**, 5544
Eph 2: 7 in *his* **k** towards us through Christ Jesus. 5544
Col 3:12 holy and beloved, bowels of mercies, **k**, 5544
Tit 3: 4 But after that the **k** and love of God our 5544
2Pe 1: 7 And to godliness **brotherly k**; 5360
1: 7 and to **brotherly k** charity. 5360

KINDRED (28) [KIN]
Ge 12: 1 from thy **k**, and from thy father's house, 4138
24: 4 my **k**, and take a wife unto my son Isaac. 4138
24: 7 from the land of my **k**, and which spake 4138
24:38 and to my **k**, and take a wife unto my son. 4940
24:40 thou shalt take a wife for my son of my **k**, 4940
24:41 *this* my oath, when thou comest to my **k**; 4940
31: 3 unto the land of thy fathers, and to thy **k**; 4138
31:13 land, and return unto the land of thy **k**. 4138
32: 9 to thy **k**, and I will deal well with thee: 4138
43: 7 of our **k**, saying, *Is* your father yet alive? 4138
Nu 10:30 depart to mine own land, and to my **k**. 4138
Jos 6:23 they brought out all her **k**, and left them 4940
Ru 2: 3 Boaz, who *was* of the **k** of Elimelech. 4940
2: 3 now *is not* Boaz of our **k**, with whose 4130
1Ch 12:29 Benjamin, the **k** of Saul, three thousand: 251
Est 2:10 had not shewed her people nor her **k**: 4138
2:20 Esther had not *yet* shewed her **k** nor her 4138
8: 6 I endure to see the destruction of my **k**? 4138
Job 32: 2 of Barachel the Buzite, of the **k** of Ram: 4940
Eze 11:15 men of thy **k**, and all the house of Israel 1353
Lk 1:61 There is none of thy **k** that is called by 4772
Ac 4: 6 many as were of the **k** of the high priest, 1085
7: 3 and from thy **k**, and come into the land 4772
7:13 Joseph's **k** was made known unto 1085
7:14 his father Jacob to *him*, and all his **k**, 4772
7:19 The same dealt subtilly with our **k**, 1085
Rev 5: 9 us to God by thy blood out of every **k**, 5443
14: 6 and **k**, and tongue, and people, 5443

KINDREDS (8) [KIN]
1Ch 16:28 Give unto the Lord, ye **k** of the people, 4940
Ps 22:27 all the **k** of the nations shall worship 4940
96: 7 unto the Lord, O ye **k** of the people, 4940
Ac 3:25 And in thy seed shall all the **k** of the earth 3965
Rev 1: 7 and all the **k** of the earth shall wail because 5443
7: 9 nations, and **k**, and people, and tongues, 5443
11: 9 *they* of the people and **k** and tongues and 5443
13: 7 and power was given him over all **k**, 5443

KINDS (10) [KIND]
Ge 8:19 after their **k**, went forth out of the ark. 4940
2Ch 16:14 *divers* **k** *of* spices prepared by 2177
Jer 15: 3 I will appoint over them four **k**, saith 4940
Eze 47:10 their fish shall be according to their **k**, 4327
Da 3: 5 psaltery, dulcimer, and all **k** of musick, 2178
3: 7 sackbut, psaltery, and all **k** of musick, 2178
3:10 and dulcimer, and all **k** of musick, 2178
3:15 and dulcimer, and all **k** of musick, 2178
1Co 12:10 of spirits; to another *divers* **k** of tongues; 1085
14:10 so many **k** of voices in the world, 1085

KINE (24)
Ge 32:15 forty **k**, and ten bulls, twenty she asses, 6510
41: 2 up out of the river seven well favoured **k** 6510
41: 3 seven other **k** came up after them out of 6510
41: 3 stood by the *other* **k** upon the brink of 6510
41: 4 leanfleshed **k** did eat up the seven well 6510
41: 4 eat up the seven well favoured and fat **k**. 6510
41:18 there came up out of the river seven **k**, 6510
41:19 seven other **k** came up after them, poor 6510
41:20 ill favoured **k** did eat up the first seven 6510
41:20 kine did eat up the first seven fat **k**: 6510
41:26 The seven good *are* seven years; 6510

Ge 41:27 ill favoured **k** that came up after them *are* 6510
Dt 7:13 the increase of thy **k**, and the flocks of thy 504
28: 4 the increase of thy **k**, and the flocks of thy 504
28:18 the increase of thy **k**, and the flocks of thy 504
28:51 *or* the increase of thy **k**, or flocks of thy 504
32:14 Butter of **k**, and milk of sheep, with fat of 1241
1Sa 6: 7 make a new cart, and take two milch **k**, 6510
6: 7 tie the **k** to the cart, and bring their calves 6510
6:10 two milch **k**, and tied them to the cart, 6510
6:12 he took the straight way to the way of 6510
6:14 offered the **k** a burnt offering unto 6510
2Sa 17:29 butter, and sheep, and cheese of **k**, 1241
Am 4: 1 Hear this word, ye **k** of Bashan, that *are* 6510

KING (2256) [KING'S, KINGDOM, KINGDOMS, KINGLY, KINGS, KINGS']
Ge 14: 1 it came to pass in the days of Amraphel **k** 4428
14: 1 Arioch **k** of Ellasar, Chedorlaomer king of 4428
14: 1 Chedorlaomer **k** of Elam, and Tidal king 4428
14: 1 king of Elam, and Tidal **k** of nations; 4428
14: 2 *That these* made war with Bera **k** of 4428
14: 2 with Birsha **k** of Gomorrah, Shinab king 4428
14: 2 Shinab **k** of Admah, and Shemeber king 4428
14: 2 Shemeber **k** of Zeboiim, and the king of 4428
14: 2 and the **k** of Bela, which *is* Zoar. 4428
14: 8 there went out the **k** of Sodom, 4428
14: 8 **k** of Gomorrah, and the king of Admah, 4428
14: 8 **k** of Admah, and the king of Zeboiim, 4428
14: 8 **k** of Admah, and the king of Zeboiim, 4428
14: 8 and the **k** of Zeboiim, and the king of Bela 4428
14: 8 and the **k** of Bela (the same *is* Zoar); 4428
14: 9 With Chedorlaomer the **k** of Elam, 4428
14: 9 Tidal **k** of nations, and Amraphel king 4428
14: 9 Amraphel **k** of Shinar, and Arioch king of 4428
14: 9 king of Shinar, and Arioch **k** of Ellasar; 4428
14:17 the **k** of Sodom went out to meet him 4428
14:18 Melchizedek **k** of Salem brought forth 4428
14:21 the **k** of Sodom said unto Abram, Give 4428
14:22 Abram said to the **k** of Sodom, I have lift 4428
20: 2 Abimelech **k** of Gerar sent, and took 4428
26: 1 Isaac went unto Abimelech **k** of 4428
26: 8 that Abimelech **k** of the Philistims looked 4428
36:31 before there reigned *any* **k** over the 4428
40: 1 *that* the butler of the **k** of Egypt and *his* 4428
40: 1 *his* baker had offended their lord the **k** of 4428
40: 5 *butler* and the baker of the **k** of Egypt, 4428
41:46 he stood before Pharaoh **k** of Egypt. 4428
Ex 1: 8 Now there arose up a new **k** over Egypt, 4428
1:15 of Egypt spake to the Hebrew 4428
1:17 not as the **k** of Egypt commanded them, 4428
1:18 the **k** of Egypt called for the midwives, 4428
2:23 process of time, that the **k** of Egypt died: 4428
3:18 unto the **k** of Egypt, and you shall say 4428
3:19 I am sure that the **k** of Egypt will not let 4428
5: 4 the **k** of Egypt said unto them, Wherefore 4428
6:11 Go in, speak unto Pharaoh **k** of Egypt, 4428
6:13 of Israel, and unto Pharaoh **k** of Egypt, 4428
6:27 *are* they which spake to Pharaoh **k** of 4428
6:29 speak thou unto Pharaoh **k** of Egypt all 4428
14: 5 it was told the **k** of Egypt that the people 4428
14: 8 hardened the heart of Pharaoh **k** of Egypt, 4428
Nu 20:14 from Kadesh unto the **k** of Edom, 4428
21: 1 *when* Arad the Canaanite, which dwelt 4428
21:21 Israel sent messengers unto Sihon **k** of 4428
21:26 Heshbon *was* the city of Sihon the **k** of 4428
21:26 who had fought against the former **k** of 4428
21:29 daughters into captivity unto Sihon **k** of 4428
21:33 Og the **k** of Bashan went out against 4428
21:34 thou didst unto Sihon **k** of the Amorites, 4428
22: 4 Balak the son of Zippor *was* **k** of 4428
22:10 Balak the son of Zippor, **k** of Moab, 4428
22:10 of Moab, hath sent unto me, *saying,* 4428
23: 7 Balak the **k** of Moab hath brought me 4428
23:21 and the shout of a **k** *is* among them. 4428
24: 7 his **k** shall be higher than Agag, 4428
32:33 the kingdom of Sihon **k** of the Amorites, 4428
32:33 the kingdom of Og **k** of Bashan, the land, 4428
33:40 **k** Arad the Canaanite, which dwelt in 4428
Dt 1: 4 After he had slain Sihon the **k** of 4428
1: 4 in Heshbon, and Og the **k** of Bashan, 4428
2:24 the Amorite, **k** of Heshbon, and his land: 4428
2:26 Sihon **k** of Heshbon *with* words of peace, 4428
2:30 Sihon **k** of Heshbon would not let us pass 4428
3: 1 Og the **k** of Bashan came out against us, 4428
3: 2 thou didst unto Sihon **k** of the Amorites, 4428
3: 3 the **k** of Bashan, and all his people: 4428
3: 6 as we did unto Sihon **k** of Heshbon, 4428
3:11 For only Og **k** of Bashan remained of 4428
4:46 in the land of Sihon **k** of the Amorites, 4428
4:47 the land of Og **k** of Bashan, two kings of 4428
7: 8 from the hand of Pharaoh **k** of Egypt. 4428
11: 3 of Egypt unto Pharaoh the **k** of Egypt, 4428
17:14 shalt say, I will set a **k** over me, 4428
17:15 shalt in any wise set *him* **k** over thee, 4428
17:15 thy brethren shalt thou set **k** over thee: 4428
28:36 and thy **k** which thou shalt set over thee, 4428
29: 7 Sihon the **k** of Heshbon, and Og the king 4428
29: 7 king of Heshbon, and Og the **k** of Bashan, 4428
33: 5 he was **k** in Jeshurun, when the heads of 4428
Jos 2: 2 was told the **k** of Jericho, saying, Behold, 4428
2: 3 the **k** of Jericho sent unto Rahab, saying, 4428
6: 2 the **k** thereof, *and* the mighty *men* of 4428
8: 1 I have given into thy hand the **k** of Ai, 4428
8: 2 her **k** as thou didst unto Jericho 4428
8: 2 king as thou didst unto Jericho and her **k**: 4428
8:14 when the **k** of Ai saw *it*, that they hasted 4428
8:23 the **k** of Ai they took alive, 4428

Jos	8:29 the **k** of Ai he hanged on a tree until	4428
	9:10 to Sihon **k** of Heshbon, and to Og king of	4428
	9:10 Og **k** of Bashan, which was at Ashtaroth.	4428
	10: 1 when Adoni-zedek **k** of Jerusalem had	4428
	10: 1 as he had done to Jericho and her **k**,	4428
	10: 1 her king, so he had done to Ai and her **k**;	4428
	10: 3 Wherefore Adoni-zedek **k** of Jerusalem	4428
	10: 3 Jerusalem sent unto Hoham **k** of Hebron,	4428
	10: 3 unto Piram **k** of Jarmuth, and unto Japhia	4428
	10: 3 unto Japhia **k** of Lachish, and unto Debir	4428
	10: 3 and unto Debir **k** of Eglon, saying,	4428
	10: 5 the **k** of Jerusalem, the king of Hebron,	4428
	10: 5 the **k** of Hebron, the king of Jarmuth,	4428
	10: 5 the king of Hebron, the **k** of Jarmuth,	4428
	10: 5 the **k** of Lachish, the king of Eglon,	4428
	10: 5 the king of Lachish, the **k** of Eglon,	4428
	10:23 the **k** of Jerusalem, the king of Hebron,	4428
	10:23 the **k** of Hebron, the king of Jarmuth,	4428
	10:23 the king of Hebron, the **k** of Jarmuth,	4428
	10:23 the **k** of Lachish, and the king of Eglon.	4428
	10:23 the king of Lachish, and the **k** of Eglon.	4428
	10:28 the thereof he utterly destroyed, them,	4428
	10:28 he did to the **k** of Makkedah as he did	4428
	10:28 Makkedah as he did unto the **k** of Jericho.	4428
	10:30 the thereof, into the hand of Israel;	4428
	10:30 did unto the **k** thereof as he did unto	4428
	10:30 thereof as he did unto the **k** of Jericho.	4428
	10:33 Horam **k** of Gezer came up to help	4428
	10:37 the thereof, and all the cities thereof,	4428
	10:39 the thereof, and all the cities thereof;	4428
	10:39 so he did to Debir, and to the **k** thereof;	4428
	10:39 he had done also to Libnah, and to her **k**.	4428
	11: 1 when Jabin **k** of Hazor had heard those	4428
	11: 1 things, that he sent to Jobab **k** of Madon,	4428
	11: 1 to the **k** of Shimron, and to the king of	4428
	11: 1 of Shimron, and to the **k** of Achshaph,	4428
	11:10 and smote the **k** thereof with the sword:	4428
	12: 2 Sihon **k** of the Amorites, who dwelt in	4428
	12: 4 the coast of Og **k** of Bashan, which was of	4428
	12: 5 the border of Sihon **k** of Heshbon.	4428
	12: 9 The **k** of Jericho, one; the king of Ai,	4428
	12: 9 the **k** of Ai, which is beside Beth-el, one;	4428
	12:10 The **k** of Jerusalem, one; the king of	4428
	12:10 of Jerusalem, one; the **k** of Hebron, one;	4428
	12:11 The **k** of Jarmuth, one; the king of	4428
	12:11 of Jarmuth, one; the **k** of Lachish, one;	4428
	12:12 The **k** of Eglon, one; the king of Gezer,	4428
	12:12 king of Eglon, one; the **k** of Gezer, one;	4428
	12:13 The **k** of Debir, one; the king of Geder,	4428
	12:13 king of Debir, one; the **k** of Geder, one;	4428
	12:14 The **k** of Hormah, one; the king of Arad,	4428
	12:14 king of Hormah, one; the **k** of Arad, one;	4428
	12:15 The **k** of Libnah, one; the king of Adullam,	4428
	12:15 of Libnah, one; the **k** of Adullam, one;	4428
	12:16 The **k** of Makkedah, one; the king of	4428
	12:16 of Makkedah, one; the **k** of Beth-el, one;	4428
	12:17 The **k** of Tappuah, one; the king of	4428
	12:17 of Tappuah, one; the **k** of Hepher, one;	4428
	12:18 The **k** of Aphek, one; the king of	4428
	12:18 of Aphek, one; the **k** of Lasharon, one;	4428
	12:19 The **k** of Madon, one; the king of Hazor,	4428
	12:19 king of Madon, one; the **k** of Hazor, one;	4428
	12:20 The **k** of Shimron-meron, one; the king of	4428
	12:20 one; the **k** of Achshaph, one;	4428
	12:21 The **k** of Taanach, one; the king of	4428
	12:21 of Taanach, one; the **k** of Megiddo, one;	4428
	12:22 The **k** of Kedesh, one; the king of	4428
	12:22 one; the **k** of Jokneam of Carmel, one;	4428
	12:23 The **k** of Dor in the coast of Dor, one;	4428
	12:23 one; the **k** of the nations of Gilgal, one;	4428
	12:24 The **k** of Tirzah, one: all the kings thirty	4428
	13:10 all the cities of Sihon **k** of the Amorites,	4428
	13:21 the kingdom of Sihon **k** of the Amorites,	4428
	13:27 the rest of the kingdom of Sihon **k** of	4428
	13:30 all the kingdom of Og **k** of Bashan,	4428
	24: 9 **k** of Moab, arose and warred against	4428
Jdg	3: 8 of Chushan-rishathaim **k** of Mesopotamia:	4428
	3:10 LORD delivered Chushan-rishathaim **k** of	4428
	3:12 the LORD strengthened Eglon the **k** of	4428
	3:14 the children of Israel served Eglon the **k**	4428
	3:15 sent a present unto Eglon the **k** of Moab.	4428
	3:17 he brought the present unto Eglon **k** of	4428
	3:19 I have a secret errand unto thee, O **k:**	4428
	4: 2 them into the hand of Jabin **k** of Canaan,	4428
	4:17 there was peace between Jabin the **k** of	4428
	4:23 God subdued on that day Jabin the **k** of	4428
	4:24 prevailed against Jabin the **k** of Canaan,	4428
	4:24 they had destroyed Jabin **k** of Canaan.	4428
	8:18 each one resembled the children of a **k**.	4428
	9: 6 Millo, and went, and made Abimelech **k**,	4428
	9: 8 trees went forth on a time to anoint a **k**	4428
	9:15 If in truth ye anoint me **k** over you, then	4428
	9:16 in that ye have **made** Abimelech **k**,	4427
	9:18 **made** Abimelech, the son of his	
	maidservant, **k**	4427
	11:12 Jephthah sent messengers unto the **k** of	4428
	11:13 the **k** of the children of Ammon answered	4428
	11:14 sent messengers again unto the **k**	4428
	11:17 sent messengers unto the **k** of Edom,	4428
	11:17 **k** of Edom would not hearken thereto.	4428
	11:17 manner they sent unto the **k** of Moab:	4428
	11:19 Israel sent messengers unto Sihon **k** of	4428
	11:19 king of the Amorites, the **k** of Heshbon;	4428
	11:25 than Balak the son of Zippor, **k** of Moab?	4428
	11:28 Howbeit the **k** of the children of Ammon	4428

Jdg	17: 6 In those days there was no **k** in Israel,	4428
	18: 1 In those days there was no **k** in Israel:	4428
	19: 1 days, when there was no **k** in Israel,	4428
	21:25 In those days there was no **k** in Israel:	4428
1Sa	2:10 he shall give strength unto his **k**,	4428
	8: 5 now make us a **k** to judge us like all	4428
	8: 6 when they said, Give us a **k** to judge us.	4428
	8: 9 shew them the manner of the **k** that shall	4428
	8:10 unto the people that asked of him a **k**.	4428
	8:11 This will be the manner of the **k** that shall	4428
	8:18 of your **k** which ye shall have chosen you;	4428
	8:19 Nay, but we will have a **k** over us;	4428
	8:20 our **k** may judge us, and go out before	4428
	8:22 their voice, and **make** them a **k**.	4427+4428
	10:19 said unto him, Nay, but set a **k** over us.	4428
	10:24 people shouted, and said, God save the **k**.	4428
	11:15 there they **made** Saul **k** before the LORD	4427
	12: 1 and have **made** a **k** over you.	4427+4428
	12: 2 now behold, the **k** walketh before you:	4428
	12: 9 into the hand of the **k** of Moab,	4428
	12:12 when ye saw that Nahash the **k** of	4428
	12:12 unto me, Nay; but a **k** shall reign over us:	4428
	12:12 when the LORD your God was your **k**.	4428
	12:13 behold the **k** whom ye have chosen,	4428
	12:13 behold, the LORD hath set a **k** over you.	4428
	12:14 also the **k** that reigneth over you continue	4428
	12:17 the sight of the LORD, in asking you a **k**.	4428
	12:19 unto all our sins this evil, to ask us a **k**.	4428
	12:25 shall be consumed, both ye and your **k**.	4428
	15: 1 The LORD sent me to anoint thee to be **k**	4428
	15: 8 took Agag the **k** of the Amalekites alive,	4428
	15:11 that I have **set up** Saul to be **k**:	4427+4428
	15:17 the LORD anointed thee **k** over Israel?	4428
	15:20 have brought Agag the **k** of Amalek,	4428
	15:23 he hath also rejected thee from being **k**.	4428
	15:26 the LORD hath rejected thee from being **k**	4428
	15:32 Bring you hither to me Agag the **k** of	4428
	15:35 that he had **made** Saul **k** over Israel.	4427
	16: 1 I have provided me a **k** among his sons.	4428
	17:25 the **k** will enrich him with great riches,	4428
	17:55 As thy soul liveth, O **k**, I cannot tell.	4428
	17:56 the **k** said, Inquire thou whose son	4428
	18: 6 singing and dancing, to meet **k** Saul,	4428
	18:18 that I should be son in law to the **k?**	4428
	18:22 The **k** hath delight in thee, and all his	4428
	18:25 The **k** desireth not any dowry, but an	4428
	18:27 and they gave them in full tale to the **k**,	4428
	19: 4 Let not the **k** sin against his servant,	4428
	20: 5 I should not fail to sit with the **k** at meat:	4428
	20:24 come, the **k** sat him down to eat meat.	4428
	20:25 the **k** sat upon his seat, as at other times,	4428
	21: 2 The **k** hath commanded me a business,	4428
	21:10 Saul, and went to Achish the **k** of Gath.	4428
	21:11 Is not this David the **k** of the land?	4428
	21:12 was sore afraid of Achish the **k** of Gath.	4428
	22: 3 he said unto the **k** of Moab, Let my father	4428
	22: 4 he brought them before the **k** of Moab:	4428
	22:11 he sent to call Ahimelech the priest,	4428
	22:11 Nob: and they came all of them to the **k**.	4428
	22:14 Ahimelech answered the **k**, and said,	4428
	22:15 let not the **k** impute any thing unto his	4428
	22:16 the **k** said, Thou shalt surely die,	4428
	22:17 the **k** said unto the footmen that stood	4428
	22:17 the servants of the **k** would not put forth	4428
	22:18 the **k** said to Doeg, Turn thou, and fall	4428
	23:17 thou shalt be **k** over Israel, and I shall be	4427
	23:20 therefore, O **k**, come down according	4428
	24: 8 cried after Saul, saying, My lord the **k**.	4428
	24:14 After whom is the **k** of Israel come out?	4428
	24:20 well that thou shalt **surely be k**,	4427+4427
	25:36 a feast in his house, like the feast of a **k**;	4428
	26:14 said, Who art thou that criest to the **k?**	4428
	26:15 then hast thou not kept thy lord the **k?**	4428
	26:15 of the people in to destroy the **k** thy lord.	4428
	26:17 David said, It is my voice, my lord, O **k**.	4428
	26:19 let my lord the **k** hear the words of his	4428
	26:20 for the **k** of Israel is come out to seek a	4428
	27: 2 Achish, the son of Maoch, **k** of Gath.	4428
	28:13 the **k** said unto her, Be not afraid: for	4428
	29: 3 the servant of Saul the **k** of Israel,	4428
	29: 8 against the enemies of my lord the **k?**	4428
2Sa	2: 4 they anointed David **k** over the house	4428
	2: 9 the house of Judah have anointed me **k**.	4428
	2: 9 he **made** him **k** over Gilead, and over	4427
	2:11 the time that David was **k** in Hebron over	4428
	3: 3 the daughter of Talmai **k** of Geshur;	4428
	3:17 Ye sought for David in times past to be **k**	4428
	3:21 will gather all Israel unto my lord the **k**,	4428
	3:23 Abner the son of Ner came to the **k**,	4428
	3:24 Joab came to the **k**, and said, What hast	4428
	3:31 And **k** David himself followed the bier.	4428
	3:32 the **k** lift up his voice, and wept at the	4428
	3:33 the **k** lamented over Abner, and said,	4428
	3:36 as whatsoever the **k** did, pleased all	4428
	3:37 not of the **k** to slay Abner the son of Ner.	4428
	3:38 the **k** said unto his servants, Know ye not	4428
	3:39 I am this day weak, though anointed **k**;	4428
	4: 8 said to the **k**, Behold the head of	4428
	4: 8 the LORD hath avenged my lord the **k**	4428
	5: 2 in time past, when Saul was **k** over us,	4428
	5: 3 So all the elders of Israel came to the **k** to	4428
	5: 3 **k** David made a league with them in	4428
	5: 3 and they anointed David **k** over Israel.	4428
	5: 6 the **k** and his men went to Jerusalem	4428
	5:11 **k** of Tyre sent messengers to David,	4428

2Sa	5:12 LORD had established him **k** over Israel,	4428
	5:17 they had anointed David **k** over Israel,	4428
	6:12 it was told **k** David, saying, The LORD	4428
	6:16 saw **k** David leaping and dancing before	4428
	6:20 How glorious was the **k** of Israel to day,	4428
	7: 1 when the **k** sat in his house,	4428
	7: 2 That the **k** said unto Nathan the prophet,	4428
	7: 3 Nathan said to the **k**, Go, do all that is in	4428
	7:18 went **k** David in, and sat before	4428
	8: 3 the son of Rehob, **k** of Zobah,	4428
	8: 5 came to succour Hadadezer **k** of Zobah,	4428
	8: 8 **k** David took exceeding much brass.	4428
	8: 9 When Toi **k** of Hamath heard that David	4428
	8:10 Toi sent Joram his son unto **k** David,	4428
	8:11 Which also **k** David did dedicate unto	4428
	8:12 of Hadadezer, son of Rehob, **k** of Zobah.	4428
	9: 2 the **k** said unto him, Art thou Ziba?	4428
	9: 3 the **k** said, Is there not yet any of the	4428
	9: 3 Ziba said unto the **k**, Jonathan hath yet a	4428
	9: 4 the **k** said unto him, Where is he?	4428
	9: 4 Ziba said unto the **k**, Behold, he is in	4428
	9: 5 **k** David sent, and fet him out of the	4428
	9: 9 the **k** called to Ziba, Saul's servant,	4428
	9:11 said Ziba unto the **k**, According to all that	4428
	9:11 According to all that my lord the **k** hath	4428
	9:11 said the **k**, he shall eat at my table,	NIH
	10: 1 that the **k** of the children of Ammon died,	4428
	10: 5 the **k** said, Tarry at Jericho until your	4428
	10: 6 of **k** Maacah a thousand men,	4428
	11: 8 followed him a mess of meat from the **k**.	4428
	11:19 telling the matters of the war unto the **k**,	4428
	12: 7 I anointed thee **k** over Israel,	4428
	13: 6 when the **k** was come to see him, Amnon	4428
	13: 6 Amnon said unto the **k**, I pray thee,	4428
	13:13 I pray thee, speak unto the **k**;	4428
	13:21 when **k** David heard of all these things,	4428
	13:24 Absalom came to the **k**, and said,	4428
	13:24 let the **k**, I beseech thee, and his servants	4428
	13:25 the **k** said to Absalom, Nay, my son, let us	4428
	13:26 the **k** said unto him, Why should he go	4428
	13:31 the **k** arose, and tare his garments,	4428
	13:33 let not my lord the **k** take the thing to his	4428
	13:35 Jonadab said unto the **k**, Behold,	4428
	13:36 the **k** also and all his servants wept very	4428
	13:37 the son of Ammihud, **k** of Geshur.	4428
	13:39 the soul of **k** David longed to go forth	4428
	14: 3 come to the **k**, and speak on this manner	4428
	14: 4 the woman of Tekoah spake to the **k**,	4428
	14: 4 and did obeisance, and said, Help, O **k**.	4428
	14: 5 the **k** said unto her, What aileth thee?	4428
	14: 8 the **k** said unto the woman, Go to thine	4428
	14: 9 the woman of Tekoah said unto the **k**,	4428
	14: 9 My lord, O **k**, the iniquity be on me,	4428
	14: 9 and the **k** and his throne be guiltless.	4428
	14:10 he said, Whosoever saith ought unto	4428
	14:11 let the **k** remember the LORD thy God,	4428
	14:12 speak one word unto my lord the **k**.	4428
	14:13 for the **k** doth speak this thing as one	4428
	14:13 in that the **k** doth not fetch home again	4428
	14:15 to speak of this thing unto my lord the **k**,	4428
	14:15 said, I will now speak unto the **k**;	4428
	14:15 it may be that the **k** will perform	4428
	14:16 the **k** will hear, to deliver his handmaid	4428
	14:17 The word of my lord the **k** shall now be	4428
	14:17 is my lord the **k** to discern good and bad:	4428
	14:18 the **k** answered and said unto the woman,	4428
	14:18 said, Let my lord the **k** now speak.	4428
	14:19 the **k** said, Is not the hand of Joab with	4428
	14:19 said, As thy soul liveth, my lord the **k**,	4428
	14:19 to the left from ought that my lord the **k**	4428
	14:21 the **k** said unto Joab, Behold now, I have	4428
	14:22 and bowed himself, and thanked the **k**:	4428
	14:22 lord, O **k**, in that the king hath fulfilled	4428
	14:22 in that the **k** hath fulfilled the request of	4428
	14:24 the **k** said, Let him turn to his own house,	4428
	14:29 sent for Joab, to have sent him to the **k**;	4428
	14:32 that I may send thee to the **k**, to say,	4428
	14:33 So Joab came to the **k**, and told him:	4428
	14:33 he came to the **k**, and bowed himself on	4428
	14:33 on his face to the ground before the **k**:	4428
	14:33 the king: and the **k** kissed Absalom.	4428
	15: 2 controversy came to the **k** for judgment,	4428
	15: 3 there is no man deputed of the **k** to hear	4428
	15: 6 all Israel that came to the **k** for judgment:	4428
	15: 7 that Absalom said unto the **k**, I pray thee,	4428
	15: 9 the **k** said unto him, Go in peace. So he	4428
	15:15 king's servants said unto the **k**, Behold,	4428
	15:15 whatsoever my lord the **k** shall appoint.	4428
	15:16 the **k** went forth, and all his household	4428
	15:16 the **k** left ten women, which were	4428
	15:17 the **k** went forth, and all the people after	4428
	15:18 him from Gath, passed on before the **k**.	4428
	15:19 said the **k** to Ittai the Gittite, Wherefore	4428
	15:19 return to thy place, and abide with the **k**:	4428
	15:21 Ittai answered the **k**, and said,	4428
	15:21 LORD liveth, and as my lord the **k** liveth,	4428
	15:21 in what place my lord the **k** shall be,	4428
	15:23 the **k** also himself passed over the brook	4428
	15:25 the **k** said unto Zadok, Carry back the ark	4428
	15:27 The **k** said also unto Zadok the priest,	4428
	15:34 unto Absalom, I will be thy servant, O **k**;	4428
	16: 2 the **k** said, And where is thy master's son?	4428
	16: 3 Ziba said unto the **k**, Behold, he abideth	4428
	16: 4 said the **k** to Ziba, Behold, thine are all	4428

2Sa 16: 4 may find grace in thy sight, my lord, O **k**.	4428	
16: 5 when **k** David came to Bahurim, behold,	4428	
16: 6 David, and at all the servants of **k** David:	4428	
16: 9 Abishai the son of Zeruiah unto the **k**,	4428	
16: 9 should this dead dog curse my lord the **k**?	4428	
16:10 the **k** said, What have I to do with you,	4428	
16:14 the **k**, and all the people that were with	4428	
16:16 God save the **k**, God save the king.	4428	
16:16 God save the king, God save the **k**.	4428	
17: 2 him shall flee; and I will smite the **k** only:	4428	
17:16 lest the **k** be swallowed up, and all	4428	
17:17 them; and they went and told David.	4428	
17:21 went and told **k** David, and said unto	4428	
18: 2 the **k** said unto the people, I will surely go	4428	
18: 4 the **k** said unto them, What seemeth you	4428	
18: 4 the **k** stood by the gate side, and all	4428	
18: 5 the **k** commanded Joab and Abishai and	4428	
18: 5 all the people heard when the **k** gave all	4428	
18:12 for in our hearing the **k** charged thee and	4428	
18:13 for there is no matter hid from the **k**,	4428	
18:19 Let me now run, and bear the **k** tidings,	4428	
18:21 Cushi, Go tell the **k** what thou hast seen.	4428	
18:25 the watchman cried, and told the **k**.	4428	
18:25 the **k** said, If he be alone, there is tidings	4428	
18:26 And the **k** said, He also bringeth tidings.	4428	
18:27 the **k** said, He is a good man,	4428	
18:28 and said unto the **k**, All is well.	4428	
18:28 to the earth upon his face before the **k**,	4428	
18:28 lift up their hand against my lord the **k**.	4428	
18:29 said, Is the young man Absalom safe?	4428	
18:30 the **k** said unto him, Turn aside,	4428	
18:31 and Cushi said, Tidings, my lord the **k**:	4428	
18:32 the **k** said unto Cushi, Is the young man	4428	
18:32 The enemies of my lord the **k**, and all that	4428	
18:33 the **k** was much moved, and went up to	4428	
19: 1 weepeth and mourneth for Absalom.	4428	
19: 2 the people heard say that day how the **k**	4428	
19: 4 the **k** covered his face, and the king cried	4428	
19: 4 the **k** cried with a loud voice, O my son	4428	
19: 5 Joab came into the house to the **k**,	4428	
19: 8 the **k** rose, and sat in the gate. And they	4428	
19: 8 Behold, the **k** doth sit in the gate.	4428	
19: 9 the people came before the **k**: for Israel	4428	
19: 9 The **k** saved us out of the hand of our	4428	
19:10 speak ye not a word of bringing the **k**	4428	
19:11 **k** David sent to Zadok and to Abiathar	4428	
19:11 Why are ye the last to bring the **k** back to	4428	
19:11 the speech of all Israel is come to the **k**,	4428	
19:12 then are ye the last to bring back the **k**?	4428	
19:14 so that they sent this word unto the **k**,	4428	
19:15 So the **k** returned, and came to Jordan.	4428	
19:15 Judah came to Gilgal, to go to meet the **k**,	4428	
19:15 the king, to conduct the **k** over Jordan.	4428	
19:16 with the men of Judah to meet **k** David.	4428	
19:17 and they went over Jordan before the **k**.	4428	
19:18 the son of Gera fell down before the **k**,	4428	
19:19 said unto the **k**, Let not my lord impute	4428	
19:19 that my lord the **k** went out of Jerusalem,	4428	
19:19 that the **k** should take it to his heart.	4428	
19:20 Joseph to go down to meet my lord the **k**.	4428	
19:22 for do not I know that I am this day **k**	4428	
19:23 Therefore the **k** said unto Shimei,	4428	
19:23 shalt not die. And the **k** sware unto him.	4428	
19:24 the son of Saul came down to meet the **k**,	4428	
19:24 from the day the **k** departed until the day	4428	
19:25 he was come to Jerusalem to meet the **k**,	4428	
19:25 the **k** said unto him, Wherefore wentest	4428	
19:26 he answered, My lord, O **k**, my servant	4428	
19:26 that I may ride thereon, and go to the **k**;	4428	
19:27 slandered thy servant unto my lord the **k**;	4428	
19:27 but my lord the **k** is as an angel of God:	4428	
19:28 but dead men before my lord the **k**:	4428	
19:28 have I yet to cry any more unto the **k**?	4428	
19:29 the **k** said unto him, Why speakest thou	4428	
19:30 Mephibosheth said unto the **k**, Yea, let	4428	
19:30 forasmuch as my lord the **k** is come again	4428	
19:31 went over Jordan with the **k**, to conduct	4428	
19:32 he had provided the **k** of sustenance while	4428	
19:33 the **k** said unto Barzillai, Come thou over	4428	
19:34 Barzillai said unto the **k**, How long have I	4428	
19:34 that I should go up with the **k** unto	4428	
19:35 be yet a burden unto my lord the **k**?	4428	
19:36 go a little way over Jordan with the **k**:	4428	
19:36 why should the **k** recompense it me with	4428	
19:37 let him go over with my lord the **k**;	4428	
19:38 The **k** answered, Chimham shall go over	4428	
19:39 the **k** was come over, the king kissed	4428	
19:39 the **k** kissed Barzillai, and blessed him;	4428	
19:40 the **k** went on to Gilgal, and Chimham	4428	
19:40 all the people of Judah conducted the **k**,	4428	
19:41 all the men of Israel came to the **k**,	4428	
19:41 came to the king, and said unto the **k**,	4428	
19:41 have brought the **k**, and his household,	4428	
19:42 Israel, Because the **k** is near of kin to us:	4428	
19:43 We have ten parts in the **k**, and we have	4428	
19:43 not be first had in bringing back our **k**?	4428	
20: 2 the men of Judah clave unto their **k**,	4428	
20: 3 **k** took the ten women his concubines,	4428	
20: 4 said the **k** to Amasa, Assemble me the	4428	
20:21 hath lift up his hand against the **k**,	4428	
20:22 Joab returned to Jerusalem unto the **k**.	4428	
21: 2 the **k** called the Gibeonites, and said unto	4428	
21: 5 they answered the **k**, The man that	4428	
21: 6 And the **k** said, I will give them.	4428	
21: 7 the **k** spared Mephibosheth, the son of	4428	

2Sa 21: 8 the **k** took the two sons of Rizpah	4428	
21:14 performed all that the **k** commanded.	4428	
22:51 He is the tower of salvation for his **k**:	4428	
24: 2 For the **k** said to Joab the captain of	4428	
24: 3 Joab said unto the **k**, Now the Lord thy	4428	
24: 3 that the eyes of my lord the **k** may see it:	4428	
24: 3 why doth my lord the **k** delight in this	4428	
24: 4 host went out from the presence of the **k**,	4428	
24: 9 of the number of the people unto the **k**:	4428	
24:20 saw the **k** and his servants coming on	4428	
24:20 bowed himself before the **k** on his face	4428	
24:21 Wherefore is my lord the **k** come to his	4428	
24:22 Let my lord the **k** take and offer up what	4428	
24:23 did Araunah, as a **k**, give unto the king.	4428	
24:23 did Araunah, as a king, give unto the **k**.	4428	
24:23 Araunah said unto the **k**, The Lord thy	4428	
24:24 the **k** said unto Araunah, Nay; but I will	4428	
1Ki 1: 1 **k** David was old and stricken in years;	4428	
1: 2 Let there be sought for my lord the **k** a	4428	
1: 2 let her stand before the **k**, and let her	4428	
1: 2 bosom, that my lord the **k** may get heat.	4428	
1: 3 a Shunammite, and brought her to the **k**.	4428	
1: 4 cherished the **k**, and ministered to him:	4428	
1: 4 to him: but the **k** knew her not.	4428	
1: 5 exalted himself, saying, I will be **k**:	4427	
1:13 Go and get thee in unto **k** David,	4428	
1:13 unto him, Didst not thou, my lord O **k**,	4428	
1:14 while thou yet talkest there with the **k**,	4428	
1:15 Bath-sheba went in unto the **k** into	4428	
1:15 the **k** was very old; and Abishag	4428	
1:15 the Shunammite ministered unto the **k**.	4428	
1:16 and did obeisance unto the **k**.	4428	
1:16 And the **k** said, What wouldest thou?	4428	
1:18 now, my lord the **k**, thou knowest it not:	4428	
1:19 hath called all the sons of the **k**,	4428	
1:20 thou, my lord O **k**, the eyes of all Israel	4428	
1:20 on the throne of my lord the **k** after him.	4428	
1:21 when my lord the **k** shall sleep with his	4428	
1:22 lo, while she yet talked with the **k**,	4428	
1:23 they told the **k**, saying, Behold Nathan	4428	
1:23 when he was come in before the **k**,	4428	
1:23 bowed himself before the **k** with his face	4428	
1:24 Nathan said, My lord O **k**, hast thou said,	4428	
1:25 him, and say, God save **k** Adonijah.	4428	
1:27 Is this thing done by my lord the **k**,	4428	
1:27 on the throne of my lord the **k** after him?	4428	
1:28 **k** David answered and said, Call me	4428	
1:28 king's presence, and stood before the **k**.	4428	
1:29 the **k** sware, and said, As the Lord	4428	
1:31 did reverence to the **k**, and said, Let my	4428	
1:31 said, Let my lord **k** David live for ever.	4428	
1:32 **k** David said, Call me Zadok the priest,	4428	
1:32 of Jehoiada. And they came before the **k**.	4428	
1:33 The **k** also said unto them, Take with you	4428	
1:34 Nathan the prophet anoint him there **k**	4428	
1:34 trumpet, and say, God save **k** Solomon.	4428	
1:35 my throne; for he shall be **k** in my stead:	4427	
1:36 the son of Jehoiada answered the **k**,	4428	
1:36 the Lord God of my lord the **k** say so	4428	
1:37 the Lord hath been with my lord the **k**,	4428	
1:37 than the throne of my lord **k** David.	4428	
1:38 caused Solomon to ride upon **k** David's	4428	
1:39 all the people said, God save **k** Solomon.	4428	
1:43 Verily our lord **k** David hath	4428	
1:43 lord king David hath **made** Solomon **k**.	4427	
1:44 the **k** hath sent with him Zadok the priest,	4428	
1:45 Nathan the prophet have anointed him **k**	4428	
1:47 servants came to bless our lord **k** David,	4428	
1:47 And the **k** bowed himself upon the bed.	4428	
1:48 also thus said the **k**, Blessed be the Lord	4428	
1:51 Behold, Adonijah feareth **k** Solomon:	4428	
1:51 Let **k** Solomon swear unto me to day that	4428	
1:53 So **k** Solomon sent, and they brought him	4428	
1:53 came and bowed himself to **k** Solomon:	4428	
2:17 Speak, I pray thee, unto Solomon the **k**,	4428	
2:18 Well; I will speak for thee unto the **k**.	4428	
2:19 therefore went unto **k** Solomon,	4428	
2:19 the **k** rose up to meet her,	4428	
2:20 the **k** said unto her, Ask on, my mother:	4428	
2:22 **k** Solomon answered and said unto his	4428	
2:23 **k** Solomon sware by the Lord, saying,	4428	
2:25 **k** Solomon sent by the hand of Benaiah	4428	
2:26 Abiathar the priest said the **k**, Get thee	4428	
2:29 it was told **k** Solomon that Joab was fled	4428	
2:30 unto him, Thus saith the **k**, Come forth.	4428	
2:30 Benaiah brought the **k** word again, saying,	4428	
2:31 the **k** said unto him, Do as he hath said,	4428	
2:35 the **k** put Benaiah the son of Jehoiada in	4428	
2:35 Zadok the priest did the **k** put in the room	4428	
2:36 the **k** sent and called for Shimei,	4428	
2:38 said unto the **k**, The saying is good:	4428	
2:38 as my lord the **k** hath said, so will thy	4428	
2:39 unto Achish son of Maachah **k** of Gath.	4428	
2:42 the **k** sent and called for Shimei,	4428	
2:44 The **k** said moreover to Shimei,	4428	
2:45 **k** Solomon shall be blessed, and the	4428	
2:46 So the **k** commanded Benaiah the son of	4428	
3: 1 Solomon made affinity with Pharaoh **k** of	4428	
3: 4 the **k** went to Gibeon to sacrifice there;	4428	
3: 7 thou hast **made** thy servant **k** instead of	4427	
3:16 unto the **k**, and stood before him.	4428	
3:22 is my son. Thus they spake before the **k**.	4428	
3:23 said the **k**, The one saith, This is my son	4428	
3:24 the **k** said, Bring me a sword. And they	4428	
3:24 And they brought a sword before the **k**.	4428	

1Ki 3:25 the **k** said, Divide the living child in two,	4428	
3:26 whose the living child was unto the **k**,	4428	
3:27 the **k** answered and said, Give her	4428	
3:28 Israel heard of the judgment which the **k**	4228	
3:28 king had judged; and they feared the **k**:	4228	
4: 1 So **k** Solomon was king over all Israel.	4428	
4: 1 So king Solomon was **k** over all Israel.	4428	
4: 7 which provided victuals for the **k** and his	4428	
4:19 in the country of Sihon **k** of the Amorites,	4428	
4:19 of the Amorites, and of Og **k** of Bashan;	4428	
4:27 those officers provided victual for **k**	4428	
4:27 for all that came unto **k** Solomon's table,	4428	
5: 1 Hiram **k** of Tyre sent his servants unto	4428	
5: 1 anointed him **k** in the room of his father:	4428	
5:13 Solomon raised a levy out of all Israel;	4428	
5:17 the **k** commanded, and they brought great	4428	
6: 2 the house which **k** Solomon built for	4428	
7:13 Solomon sent and fet Hiram out of Tyre.	4428	
7:14 he came to **k** Solomon, and wrought all	4428	
7:40 **k** Solomon for the house of the Lord:	4428	
7:45 which Hiram made to **k** Solomon for	4428	
7:46 In the plain of Jordan did the **k** cast them,	4428	
7:51 was ended all the work that **k** Solomon	4428	
8: 1 of Israel, unto **k** Solomon in Jerusalem,	4428	
8: 2 **k** Solomon at the feast in the month	4428	
8: 5 **k** Solomon, and all the congregation of	4428	
8:14 the **k** turned his face about, and blessed	4428	
8:62 the **k**, and all Israel with him,	4428	
8:63 So the **k** and all the children of Israel	4428	
8:64 The same day did the **k** hallow the middle	4428	
8:66 blessed the **k**, and went unto their tents	4428	
9:11 (Now Hiram **k** of Tyre had furnished	4428	
9:11 **k** Solomon gave Hiram twenty cities in	4428	
9:14 Hiram sent to the **k** sixscore talents of	4428	
9:15 this is the reason of the levy which **k**	4428	
9:16 For Pharaoh **k** of Egypt had gone up,	4428	
9:26 **k** Solomon made a navy of ships in	4428	
9:28 and brought it to **k** Solomon.	4428	
10: 3 there was not any thing hid from the **k**,	4428	
10: 6 she said to the **k**, It was a true report that	4428	
10: 9 therefore made he thee **k**, to do judgment	4428	
10:10 she gave the **k** an hundred and	4428	
10:10 the queen of Sheba gave to **k** Solomon.	4428	
10:12 the **k** made of the almug trees pillars for	4428	
10:13 **k** Solomon gave unto the queen of Sheba	4428	
10:16 **k** Solomon made two hundred targets of	4428	
10:17 the **k** put them in the house of the forest	4428	
10:18 Moreover the **k** made a great throne of	4428	
10:21 all **k** Solomon's drinking vessels were of	4428	
10:22 For the **k** had at sea a navy of Tharshish	4428	
10:23 So **k** Solomon exceeded all the kings of	4428	
10:26 for chariots, and with the **k** at Jerusalem.	4428	
10:27 the **k** made silver to be in Jerusalem as	4428	
11: 1 **k** Solomon loved many strange women,	4428	
11:18 came to Egypt, unto Pharaoh **k** of Egypt;	4428	
11:23 which fled from his lord Hadadezer **k** of	4428	
11:26 even he lift up his hand against the **k**.	4428	
11:27 that he lift up his hand against the **k**:	4428	
11:37 soul desireth, and shalt be **k** over Israel.	4428	
11:40 Shishak **k** of Egypt, and was in Egypt	4428	
12: 1 were come to Shechem to **make** him **k**.	4427	
12: 2 was fled from the presence of **k** Solomon,	4428	
12: 6 Rehoboam consulted with the old men,	4428	
12:12 as the **k** had appointed, saying, Come to	4428	
12:13 the **k** answered the people roughly,	4428	
12:15 Wherefore the **k** hearkened not unto	4428	
12:16 when all Israel saw that the **k** hearkened	4428	
12:16 the people answered the **k**, saying,	4428	
12:18 **k** Rehoboam sent Adoram, who was over	4428	
12:18 Therefore **k** Rehoboam made speed to get	4428	
12:20 and made him **k** over all Israel:	4427	
12:23 **k** of Judah, and unto all the house of	4428	
12:27 even unto Rehoboam **k** of Judah,	4428	
12:27 and go again to Rehoboam **k** of Judah.	4428	
12:28 Whereupon the **k** took counsel,	4428	
13: 4 when **k** Jeroboam heard the saying of	4428	
13: 6 he answered and said unto the man of	4428	
13: 7 the **k** said unto the man of God,	4428	
13: 8 the man of God said unto the **k**, If thou	4428	
13:11 words which he had spoken unto the **k**,	4428	
14: 2 which told me that I should be **k** over	4428	
14:14 Lord shall raise him up a **k** over Israel,	4428	
14:25 it came to pass in the fifth year of **k**	4428	
14:25 that Shishak **k** of Egypt came up against	4428	
14:27 **k** Rehoboam made in their stead brasen	4428	
14:28 when the **k** went into the house of	4428	
15: 1 Now in the eighteenth year of **k** Jeroboam	4428	
15: 9 in the twentieth year of Jeroboam **k** of	4428	
15:16 and Baasha **k** of Israel all their days.	4428	
15:17 Baasha **k** of Israel went up against Judah,	4428	
15:17 to go out or come in to Asa **k** of Judah.	4428	
15:18 Asa sent them to Ben-hadad, the son of	4428	
15:18 Tabrimon, the son of Hezion, **k** of Syria,	4428	
15:19 break thy league with Baasha **k** of Israel,	4428	
15:20 So Ben-hadad hearkened unto **k** Asa,	4428	
15:22 **k** Asa made a proclamation throughout all	4428	
15:22 Asa built with them Geba of Benjamin,	4428	
15:25 in the second year of Asa **k** of Judah,	4428	
15:28 in the third year of Asa **k** of Judah did	4428	
15:32 and Baasha **k** of Israel all their days.	4428	
15:33 In the third year of Asa **k** of Judah began	4428	
16: 8 sixth year of Asa **k** of Judah began Elah	4428	
16:10 and seventh year of Asa **k** of Judah,	4428	
16:15 seventh year of Asa **k** of Judah did Zimri	4428	
16:16 hath conspired, and hath also slain the **k**:	4428	

K

K

1Ki		
16:16	**made** Omri, the captain of the host, **k**	4427
16:21	Tibni the son of Ginath, to **make** him **k**;	4427
16:23	first year of Asa **k** of Judah *began* Omri to	4428
16:29	eighth year of Asa **k** of Judah *began* Ahab	4428
16:31	daughter of Ethbaal **k** of the Zidonians,	4428
19:15	anoint Hazael to be **k** over Syria:	4428
19:16	shalt thou anoint to be **k** over Israel:	4428
20: 1	Ben-hadad the **k** of Syria gathered all his	4428
20: 2	he sent messengers to Ahab **k** of Israel	4428
20: 4	the **k** of Israel answered and said, My lord,	4428
20: 4	of Israel answered and said, My lord, O **k**,	4428
20: 7	the **k** of Israel called all the elders of	4428
20: 9	of Ben-hadad, Tell my lord the **k**,	4428
20:11	the **k** of Israel answered and said, Tell	4428
20:13	came a prophet unto Ahab **k** of Israel,	4428
20:20	Ben-hadad the **k** of Syria escaped on a	4428
20:21	the **k** of Israel went out, and smote	4428
20:22	the prophet came to the **k** of Israel,	4428
20:22	for at the return of the year the **k** of Syria	4428
20:23	servants of the **k** of Syria said unto him,	4428
20:28	spake unto the **k** of Israel, and said,	4428
20:31	our heads, and go out to the **k** of Israel:	4428
20:32	and came to the **k** of Israel, and said,	4428
20:38	waited for the **k** by the way,	4428
20:39	the **k** passed by, he cried unto the king:	4428
20:39	the king passed by, he cried unto the **k**,	4428
20:40	of Israel said unto him, So *shall* thy	4428
20:41	the **k** of Israel discerned him that he *was*	4428
20:43	the **k** of Israel went to his house heavy	4428
21: 1	hard by the palace of Ahab **k** of Samaria.	4428
21:10	Thou didst blaspheme God and the **k**.	4428
21:13	Naboth did blaspheme God and the **k**.	4428
21:18	Arise, go down to meet Ahab **k** of Israel,	4428
22: 2	Jehoshaphat the **k** of Judah came down	4428
22: 2	of Judah came down to the **k** of Israel.	4428
22: 3	the **k** of Israel said unto his servants,	4428
22: 3	it not out of the hand of the **k** of Syria?	4428
22: 4	Jehoshaphat said to the **k** of Israel, I *am*	4428
22: 5	Jehoshaphat said unto the **k** of Israel,	4428
22: 6	the **k** of Israel gathered the prophets	4428
22: 6	shall deliver *it* into the hand of the **k**.	4428
22: 8	the **k** of Israel said unto Jehoshaphat,	4428
22: 8	Jehoshaphat said, Let not the **k** say so.	4428
22: 9	the **k** of Israel called an officer, and said,	4428
22:10	the **k** of Israel and Jehoshaphat the king	4428
22:10	Jehoshaphat the **k** of Judah sat each on	4428
22:13	*declare* good unto the **k** with one mouth:	4428
22:15	he came to the **k**. And the king said unto	4428
22:15	the **k** said unto him, Micaiah, shall we go	4428
22:15	shall deliver *it* into the hand of the **k**.	4428
22:16	the **k** said unto him, How many times	4428
22:18	the **k** of Israel said unto Jehoshaphat, Did	4428
22:26	the **k** of Israel said, Take Micaiah,	4428
22:27	say, Thus saith the **k**, Put this *fellow in*	4428
22:29	the **k** of Israel and Jehoshaphat the king	4428
22:29	Jehoshaphat the **k** of Judah went up *to*	4428
22:30	the **k** of Israel said unto Jehoshaphat,	4428
22:30	the **k** of Israel disguised himself,	4428
22:31	the **k** of Syria commanded his thirty and	4428
22:31	nor great, save only with the **k** of Israel.	4428
22:32	that they said, Surely it *is* the **k** of Israel.	4428
22:33	perceived that it *was* not the **k** of Israel,	4428
22:34	smote the **k** of Israel between the joints	4428
22:35	the **k** was stayed up in *his* chariot against	4428
22:37	the **k** died, and was brought to Samaria;	4428
22:37	and they buried the **k** in Samaria.	4428
22:41	in the fourth year of Ahab **k** of Israel.	4428
22:44	Jehoshaphat made peace with the **k** of	4428
22:47	*There* was then no **k** in Edom: a deputy	4428
22:47	then no king in Edom: a deputy *was* **k**.	4428
22:51	year of Jehoshaphat **k** of Judah,	4428

2Ki		
1: 3	go up to meet the messengers of the **k** of	4428
1: 6	turn again unto the **k** that sent you,	4428
1: 9	he sent unto him a captain of fifty with	NIH
1: 9	man of God, the **k** hath said, Come down.	4428
1:11	O man of God, thus hath the **k** said,	4428
1:15	and went down with him unto the **k**.	4428
1:17	Jehoram the son of Jehoshaphat **k** of	4428
3: 1	year of Jehoshaphat **k** of Judah,	4428
3: 4	Mesha **k** of Moab was a sheepmaster,	4428
3: 4	rendered unto the **k** of Israel an hundred	4428
3: 5	the **k** of Moab rebelled against the king	4428
3: 5	the king of Moab rebelled against the **k**	4428
3: 6	**k** Jehoram went out of Samaria the same	4428
3: 7	and sent to Jehoshaphat the **k** of Judah,	4428
3: 7	The **k** of Moab hath rebelled against me:	4428
3: 9	So the **k** of Israel went, and the king of	4428
3: 9	the **k** of Judah, and the king of Edom:	4428
3: 9	the king of Judah, and the **k** of Edom:	4428
3:10	the **k** of Israel said, Alas, that the LORD	4428
3:11	one of the **k** of Israel's servants answered	4428
3:12	So the **k** of Israel and Jehoshaphat and	4428
3:12	and the **k** of Edom went down to him.	4428
3:13	Elisha said unto the **k** of Israel, What	4428
3:13	the **k** of Israel said unto him, Nay:	4428
3:14	presence of Jehoshaphat the **k** of Judah,	4428
3:26	when the **k** of Moab saw that the battle	4428
3:26	break through *even* unto the **k** of Edom:	4428
4:13	wouldest thou be spoken for to the **k**,	4428
5: 1	captain of the host of the **k** of Syria,	4428
5: 5	the **k** of Syria said, Go to, go, and I will	4428
5: 5	I will send a letter unto the **k** of Israel.	4428
5: 6	he brought the letter to the **k** of Israel,	4428
5: 7	when the **k** of Israel had read the letter,	4428
5: 8	that the **k** of Israel had rent his clothes,	4428

2Ki		
5: 8	that he sent to the **k**, saying, Wherefore	4428
6: 8	the **k** of Syria warred against Israel,	4428
6: 9	the man of God sent unto the **k** of Israel,	4428
6:10	the **k** of Israel sent to the place which	4428
6:11	Therefore the heart of the **k** of Syria was	4428
6:11	shew me which of us *is* for the **k** of Israel?	4428
6:12	of his servants said, None, my lord, O **k**:	4428
6:12	telleth the **k** of Israel the words that thou	4428
6:21	the **k** of Israel said unto Elisha, when he	4428
6:24	that Ben-hadad **k** of Syria gathered all his	4428
6:26	as the **k** of Israel was passing by upon	4428
6:26	unto him, saying, Help, my lord, O **k**.	4428
6:28	the **k** said unto her, What aileth thee?	4428
6:30	the **k** heard the words of the woman,	4428
6:32	and *the* **k** sent a man from before him:	NIH
7: 2	a lord on whose hand the **k** leaned	4428
7: 6	the **k** of Syria hath hired against us	4428
7:12	the **k** arose in the night, and said unto his	4428
7:14	the **k** sent after the host of the Syrians,	4428
7:15	the messengers returned, and told the **k**.	4428
7:17	the **k** appointed the lord on whose hand	4428
7:17	spake when the **k** came down to him.	4428
7:18	as the man of God had spoken to the **k**,	4428
8: 3	she went forth to cry unto the **k** for her	4428
8: 4	the **k** talked with Gehazi the servant of	4428
8: 5	*as* he was telling the **k** how he had	4428
8: 5	cried to the **k** for her house and for her	4428
8: 5	Gehazi said, My lord, O **k**, this *is*	4428
8: 6	the **k** asked the woman, she told him.	4428
8: 6	So the **k** appointed unto her a certain	4428
8: 7	Ben-hadad the **k** of Syria was sick;	4428
8: 8	the **k** said unto Hazael, Take a present in	4428
8: 9	Thy son Ben-hadad **k** of Syria hath sent	4428
8:13	me *that* thou *shalt be* **k** over Syria.	4428
8:16	the fifth year of Joram the son of Ahab **k**	4428
8:16	Jehoshaphat *being* then **k** of Judah,	4428
8:16	Jehoram the son of Jehoshaphat **k** of	4428
8:20	and **made** a **k** over themselves.	4427+4428
8:25	**k** of Israel did Ahaziah the son of Jehoram	4428
8:25	son of Jehoram **k** of Judah *begin* to reign.	4428
8:26	the daughter of Omri **k** of Israel.	4428
8:28	Hazael **k** of Syria in Ramoth-gilead;	4428
8:29	**k** Joram went back to be healed in Jezreel	4428
8:29	when he fought against Hazael **k** of Syria.	4428
8:29	Ahaziah the son of Jehoram **k** of Judah	4428
9: 3	I have anointed thee **k** over Israel.	4428
9: 6	I have anointed thee **k** over the people of	4428
9:12	I have anointed thee **k** over Israel.	4428
9:13	blew with trumpets, saying, Jehu is **k**.	4427
9:14	all Israel, because of Hazael **k** of Syria.	4428
9:15	**k** Joram was returned to be healed in	4428
9:15	when he fought with Hazael **k** of Syria.)	4428
9:16	Ahaziah **k** of Judah was come down to	4428
9:18	and said, Thus saith the **k**, *Is it* peace?	4428
9:19	and said, Thus saith the **k**, *Is it* peace?	4428
9:21	Joram **k** of Israel and Ahaziah king of	4428
9:21	Israel and Ahaziah **k** of Judah went out,	4428
9:27	when Ahaziah the **k** of Judah saw *this*, he	4428
10: 5	shalt bid us; we will not **make** any **k**:	4427
10:13	Jehu met with the brethren of Ahaziah **k**	4428
10:13	go down to salute the children of the **k**	4428
11: 2	Jehosheba, the daughter of **k** Joram,	4428
11: 7	of the house of the LORD about the **k**.	4428
11: 8	ye shall compass the **k** round about,	4428
11: 8	be ye with the **k** as he goeth out and as	4428
11:10	did the priest give **k** David's spears	4428
11:11	weapons in his hand, round about the **k**,	4428
11:12	they **made** him **k**, and anointed him;	4427
11:12	their hands, and said, God save the **k**.	4428
11:14	behold, the **k** stood by a pillar,	4428
11:14	the princes and the trumpeters by the **k**,	4428
11:17	the LORD and the **k** and the people,	4428
11:17	between the **k** also and the people.	4428
11:19	they brought down the **k** from the house	4428
12: 6	twentieth year of **k** Jehoash the priests	4428
12: 7	**k** Jehoash called for Jehoiada the priest,	4428
12:17	Hazael **k** of Syria went up,	4428
12:18	Jehoash **k** of Judah took all the hallowed	4428
12:18	and sent *it* to Hazael **k** of Syria:	4428
13: 1	**k** of Judah Jehoahaz the son of Jehu	4428
13: 3	delivered them into the hand of Hazael **k**	4428
13: 4	because the **k** of Syria oppressed them.	4428
13: 7	for the **k** of Syria had destroyed them,	4428
13:10	seventh year of Joash **k** of Judah *began*	4428
13:12	he fought against Amaziah **k** of Judah,	4428
13:14	Joash the **k** of Israel came down unto	4428
13:16	he said to the **k** of Israel, Put thine hand	4428
13:18	he took *them*. And he said unto the **k** of	4428
13:22	Hazael **k** of Syria oppressed Israel all	4428
13:24	So Hazael **k** of Syria died;	4428
14: 1	**k** of Israel reigned Amaziah the son of	4428
14: 1	Amaziah the son of Joash **k** of Judah.	4428
14: 5	servants which had slain the **k** his father.	4428
14: 8	son of Jehu, **k** of Israel, saying, Come,	4428
14: 9	Jehoash the **k** of Israel sent to Amaziah	4428
14: 9	king of Israel sent to Amaziah **k** of Judah,	4428
14:11	Therefore Jehoash **k** of Israel went up;	4428
14:11	Amaziah **k** of Judah looked one another	4428
14:13	Jehoash **k** of Israel took Amaziah king of	4428
14:13	Jehoash king of Israel took Amaziah **k** of	4428
14:15	how he fought with Amaziah **k** of Judah,	4428
14:17	Amaziah the son of Joash **k** of Judah lived	4428
14:17	son of Jehoahaz **k** of Israel fifteen years.	4428
14:21	**made** him **k** instead of his father	4427
14:22	after that the **k** slept with his fathers.	4428

2Ki		
14:23	**k** of Judah Jeroboam the son of Joash king	4428
14:23	Joash **k** of Israel *began* to reign in Samaria	4428
15: 1	seventh year of Jeroboam **k** of Israel	4428
15: 1	son of Amaziah **k** of Judah to reign.	4428
15: 5	the LORD smote the **k**, so that he was a	4428
15: 8	eighth year of Azariah **k** of Judah did	4428
15:13	thirtieth year of Uzziah **k** of Judah;	4428
15:17	thirtieth year of Azariah **k** of Judah *began*	4428
15:19	*And* Pul the **k** of Assyria came against	4428
15:20	*of* silver, to give to the **k** of Assyria.	4428
15:20	So the **k** of Assyria turned back,	4428
15:23	In the fiftieth year of Azariah **k** of Judah	4428
15:27	fiftieth year of Azariah **k** of Judah Pekah	4428
15:29	In the days of Pekah **k** of Israel came	4428
15:29	of Israel came Tiglath-pileser **k** of Assyria,	4428
15:32	**k** of Israel *began* Jotham the son of	4428
15:32	the son of Uzziah **k** of Judah to reign.	4428
15:37	to send against Judah Rezin the **k** of Syria,	4428
16: 1	son of Jotham **k** of Judah *began* to reign.	4428
16: 5	Rezin **k** of Syria and Pekah son of	4428
16: 5	Pekah son of Remaliah **k** of Israel came	4428
16: 6	At that time Rezin **k** of Syria recovered	4428
16: 7	messengers to Tiglath-pileser **k** of Assyria,	4428
16: 7	save me out of the hand of the **k** of Syria,	4428
16: 7	of the hand of the **k** of Israel, which rise	4428
16: 8	sent *it* for a present to the **k** of Assyria.	4428
16: 9	the **k** of Assyria hearkened unto him:	4428
16: 9	for the **k** of Assyria went up against	4428
16:10	**k** Ahaz went to Damascus to meet	4428
16:10	to meet Tiglath-pileser **k** of Assyria,	4428
16:10	**k** Ahaz sent to Urijah the priest the	4428
16:11	all that **k** Ahaz had sent from Damascus:	4428
16:11	Urijah the priest made *it* against **k** Ahaz	4428
16:12	when the **k** was come from Damascus,	4428
16:12	come from Damascus, the **k** saw the altar:	4428
16:12	the **k** approached to the altar,	4428
16:15	**k** Ahaz commanded Urijah the priest,	4428
16:16	according to all that **k** Ahaz commanded.	4428
16:17	**k** Ahaz cut off the borders of the bases,	4428
16:18	house of the LORD for the **k** of Assyria.	4428
17: 1	In the twelfth year of Ahaz **k** of Judah	4428
17: 3	Against him came up Shalmaneser **k** of	4428
17: 4	the **k** of Assyria found conspiracy in	4428
17: 4	for he had sent messengers to So **k** of	4428
17: 4	brought no present to the **k** of Assyria,	4428
17: 4	therefore the **k** of Assyria shut him up,	4428
17: 5	the **k** of Assyria came up throughout all	4428
17: 6	the **k** of Assyria took Samaria,	4428
17: 7	under the hand of Pharaoh **k** of Egypt,	4428
17:21	they **made** Jeroboam the son of Nebat **k**:	4427
17:24	the **k** of Assyria brought *men* from	4428
17:26	Wherefore they spake to the **k** of Assyria,	4428
17:27	the **k** of Assyria commanded, saying,	4428
18: 1	year of Hoshea son of Elah **k** of Israel,	4428
18: 1	*that* Hezekiah the son of Ahaz **k** of Judah	4428
18: 7	he rebelled against the **k** of Assyria,	4428
18: 9	it came to pass in the fourth year of **k**	4428
18: 9	year of Hoshea son of Elah **k** of Israel,	4428
18:10	*is* the ninth year of Hoshea **k** of Israel,	4428
18:11	the **k** of Assyria did carry away Israel	4428
18:13	in the fourteenth year of **k** Hezekiah	4428
18:13	of Assyria come up against all the	4428
18:14	Hezekiah **k** of Judah sent to the king of	4428
18:14	Hezekiah king of Judah sent to the **k** of	4428
18:14	the **k** of Assyria appointed unto Hezekiah	4428
18:14	of Judah three hundred talents of silver	4428
18:16	the pillars which Hezekiah **k** of Judah	4428
18:16	and gave it to the **k** of Assyria.	4428
18:17	the **k** of Assyria sent Tartan and Rabsaris	4428
18:17	Rab-shakeh from Lachish to **k** Hezekiah	4428
18:18	they had called to the **k**, there came	4428
18:19	Thus saith the great **k**, the king of Assyria,	4428
18:19	Thus saith the great king, the **k** of Assyria,	4428
18:21	*is* Pharaoh **k** of Egypt unto all that trust on	4428
18:23	give pledges to my lord the **k** of Assyria,	4428
18:28	saying, Hear the word of the great **k**,	4428
18:28	word of the great king, the **k** of Assyria:	4428
18:29	saith the **k**, Let not Hezekiah deceive	4428
18:30	into the hand of the **k** of Assyria.	4428
18:31	for thus saith the **k** of Assyria, Make *an*	4428
18:33	land out of the hand of the **k** of Assyria?	4428
19: 1	when **k** Hezekiah heard *it*, that he rent	4428
19: 4	whom the **k** of Assyria his master hath	4428
19: 5	So the servants of **k** Hezekiah came to	4428
19: 6	which the servants of the **k** of Assyria	4428
19: 8	found the **k** of Assyria warring against	4428
19: 9	when he heard say of Tirhakah **k** of	4428
19:10	Thus shall ye speak to Hezekiah **k** of	4428
19:10	into the hand of the **k** of Assyria.	4428
19:13	Where *is* the **k** of Hamath, and the king	4428
19:13	of Arpad, and the king of the city	4428
19:13	the **k** of the city of Sepharvaim, *of* Hena,	4428
19:20	Sennacherib **k** of Assyria I have heard.	4428
19:32	the LORD concerning the **k** of Assyria,	4428
19:36	So Sennacherib **k** of Assyria departed,	4428
20: 6	city out of the hand of the **k** of Assyria;	4428
20:12	**k** of Babylon, sent letters and a present	4428
20:14	came Isaiah the prophet unto **k** Hezekiah,	4428
20:18	shall be eunuchs in the palace of the **k**	4428
21: 3	and made a grove, as did Ahab **k** of Israel;	4428
21:11	Because Manasseh **k** of Judah hath done	4428
21:23	and slew the **k** in his own house.	4428
21:24	them that had conspired against **k** Amon;	4428
21:24	land **made** Josiah his son **k** in his stead.	4427

2Ki 22: 3	it came to pass in the eighteenth year of **k**	4428
22: 3	sent Shaphan the son of Azaliah,	4428
22: 9	Shaphan the scribe came to the **k**,	4428
22: 9	and brought the **k** word again, and said,	4428
22:10	Shaphan the scribe shewed the **k**, saying,	4428
22:10	a book. And Shaphan read it before the **k**.	4428
22:11	the **k** had heard the words of the book	4428
22:12	the **k** commanded Hilkiah the priest,	4428
22:16	all the words of the book which the **k**	4428
22:18	the **k** of Judah which sent you to inquire	4428
22:20	And they brought the **k** word again.	4428
23: 1	the **k** sent, and they gathered unto him	4428
23: 2	he went up *into* the house of	4428
23: 3	the **k** stood by a pillar, and made a	4428
23: 4	the **k** commanded Hilkiah the high priest,	4428
23:12	the **k** beat down, and brake *them* down	4428
23:13	Solomon the **k** of Israel had builded	4428
23:13	the children of Ammon, did the **k** defile.	4428
23:21	the **k** commanded all the people, saying,	4428
23:23	in the eighteenth year of **k** Josiah,	4428
23:25	like unto him was there no **k** before him,	4428
23:29	In his days Pharaoh-nechoh **k** of Egypt	4428
23:29	the **k** of Assyria to the river Euphrates:	4428
23:29	Josiah went against him; and he slew	4428
23:30	and **made** him **k** in his father's stead.	4427
23:34	**made** Eliakim the son of Josiah **k** in	4427
24: 1	In his days Nebuchadnezzar **k** of Babylon	4428
24: 7	the **k** of Egypt came not again any more	4428
24: 7	for the **k** of Babylon had taken from	4428
24: 7	all that pertained to the **k** of Egypt.	4428
24:10	of Babylon came up *against* Jerusalem,	4428
24:11	Nebuchadnezzar **k** of Babylon came	4428
24:12	Jehoiachin the **k** of Judah went out to	4428
24:12	of Judah went out to the **k** of Babylon,	4428
24:12	the **k** of Babylon took him in the eighth	4428
24:13	**k** of Israel had made in the temple of	4428
24:16	even them the **k** of Babylon brought	4428
24:17	the **k** of Babylon made Mattaniah his	4427
24:17	**made** Mattaniah his father's brother **k** in	4428
24:20	that Zedekiah rebelled against the **k** of	4428
25: 1	*that* Nebuchadnezzar **k** of Babylon came,	4428
25: 2	unto the eleventh year of **k** Zedekiah.	4428
25: 4	and *the* **k** went the way toward the plain.	NIH
25: 5	army of the Chaldees pursued after the **k**,	4428
25: 6	So they took the **k**, and brought him up	4428
25: 6	brought him up to the **k** of Babylon to	4428
25: 8	which *is* the nineteenth year of **k**	4428
25: 8	of king Nebuchadnezzar **k** of Babylon,	4428
25: 8	a servant of the **k** of Babylon,	4428
25:11	the fugitives that fell away to the **k** of	4428
25:20	brought them to the **k** of Babylon to	4428
25:21	the **k** of Babylon smote them,	4428
25:22	whom Nebuchadnezzar **k** of Babylon had	4428
25:23	heard that the **k** of Babylon had made	4428
25:24	in the land, and serve the **k** of Babylon;	4428
25:27	of the captivity of Jehoiachin **k** of Judah,	4428
25:27	*that* Evil-merodach **k** of Babylon,	4428
25:27	did lift up the head of Jehoiachin **k** of	4428
25:30	continual allowance given him of the **k**,	4428
1Ch 1:43	any **k** reigned over the children of Israel;	4428
3: 2	the daughter of Talmai **k** of Geshur:	4428
4:23	there they dwelt with the **k** for his work.	4428
4:41	came in the days of Hezekiah **k** of Judah,	4428
5: 6	Tilgath-pilneser **k** of Assyria carried	4428
5:17	in the days of Jotham **k** of Judah,	4428
5:17	and in the days of Jeroboam **k** of Israel.	4428
5:26	stirred up the spirit of Pul **k** of Assyria,	4428
5:26	the spirit of Tilgath-pilneser **k** of Assyria,	4428
11: 2	in time past, even when Saul was **k**,	4428
11: 3	all the elders of Israel to the **k** to Hebron;	4428
11: 3	they anointed David **k** over Israel,	4428
11:10	*and* with all Israel, to **make** him **k**,	4427
12:31	by name, to come and **make** David **k**.	4427
12:38	Hebron, to **make** David **k** over all Israel:	4427
12:38	*were* of one heart to **make** David **k**.	4427
14: 1	Now Hiram **k** of Tyre sent messengers to	4428
14: 2	LORD had confirmed him **k** over Israel,	4428
14: 8	that David was anointed **k** over all Israel,	4428
15:29	out at a window saw **k** David dancing	4428
17:16	David the **k** came and sat before	4428
18: 3	David smote Hadarezer **k** of Zobah unto	4428
18: 5	came to help Hadarezer **k** of Zobah,	4428
18: 9	Now when Tou **k** of Hamath heard how	4428
18: 9	all the host of Hadarezer **k** of Zobah:	4428
18:10	He sent Hadoram his son to **k** David,	4428
18:11	Them also **k** David dedicated unto	4428
18:17	the sons of David *were* chief about the **k**.	4428
19: 1	that Nahash the **k** of the children of	4428
19: 5	he said, Tarry at Jericho until your	4428
19: 7	and the **k** of Maachah and his people;	4428
20: 2	David took the crown of their **k** from off	4428
21: 3	many moe as they *be:* but, my lord the **k**,	4428
21:23	let my lord the **k** do *that which is* good in	4428
21:24	**k** David said to Ornan, Nay; but I will	4428
23: 1	he **made** Solomon his son **k** over Israel.	4427
24: 6	wrote them before the **k**, and the princes,	4428
24:31	of Aaron in the presence of David the **k**,	4428
25: 2	according to the order of the **k**.	4428
26:26	the dedicate *things,* which David the **k**,	4428
26:30	of the LORD, and in the service of the **k**.	4428
26:32	whom **k** David made rulers over	4428
26:32	pertaining to God, and affairs of the **k**.	4428
27: 1	officers that served the **k** in any matter	4428
27:24	the account of the chronicles of **k** David.	4428
27:31	of the substance which *was* David's.	4428

1Ch 28: 1	that ministered to the **k** by course,	4428
28: 1	all the substance and possession of the **k**,	4428
28: 2	David the **k** stood up upon his feet,	4428
28: 4	the **k** over Israel for ever:	4428
28: 4	of my father to be **k** over all Israel:	4427
28: 4	he liked me to **make** *me* **k** over all Israel:	4427
29: 1	Furthermore David the **k** said unto all	4428
29: 9	David the **k** also rejoiced *with* great joy.	4428
29:20	and worshipped the LORD, and the **k**.	4428
29:22	they **made** Solomon the son of David **k**	4427
29:23	LORD as **k** instead of David his father,	4428
29:24	and all the sons likewise of **k** David,	4428
29:24	themselves unto Solomon the **k**.	4428
29:25	not been on any **k** before him in Israel.	4428
29:29	the acts of David the **k**, first and last,	4428
2Ch 1: 9	for thou hast **made** me **k** over a people	4427
1:11	people, over whom I have **made** thee **k**:	4427
1:14	cities, and with the **k** at Jerusalem.	4428
1:15	the **k** made silver and gold at Jerusalem	4428
2: 3	Solomon sent to Huram the **k** of Tyre,	4428
2:11	Huram the **k** of Tyre answered in writing,	4428
2:11	people, he hath made thee **k** over them.	4428
2:12	hath given to David the **k** a wise son,	4428
4:11	made for **k** Solomon for the house of God;	4428
4:16	did Huram his father make to **k** Solomon	4428
4:17	In the plain of Jordan did the **k** cast them,	4428
5: 3	**k** in the feast which *was in* the seventh	4428
6: 3	Also **k** Solomon, and all the congregation	4428
6: 3	the **k** turned his face, and blessed the	4428
7: 4	the **k** and all the people offered sacrifices	4428
7: 5	**k** Solomon offered a sacrifice of twenty	4428
7: 5	so the **k** and all the people dedicated	4428
7: 6	which David the **k** had made to praise	4428
8:10	these *were* the chief of Solomon's	4428
8:11	dwell in the house of David **k** of Israel,	4428
8:15	commandment of the **k** unto the priests	4428
8:18	of gold, and brought *them* to **k** Solomon.	4428
9: 5	she said to the **k**, It *was* a true report	4428
9: 8	his throne, to be **k** for the LORD thy God:	4428
9: 8	therefore made he thee **k** over them, to	4428
9: 9	she gave the **k** an hundred and	4428
9: 9	as the queen of Sheba gave **k** Solomon.	4428
9:11	the **k** made *of* the algum trees terraces to	4428
9:12	Solomon gave to the queen of Sheba all	4428
9:12	*that* which she had brought unto the **k**.	4428
9:15	**k** Solomon made two hundred targets of	4428
9:16	the **k** put them in the house of the forest	4428
9:17	Moreover the **k** made a great throne of	4428
9:20	the drinking vessels of **k** Solomon *were*	4428
9:22	**k** Solomon passed all the kings of	4428
9:25	cities, and with the **k** at Jerusalem.	4428
9:27	the **k** made silver in Jerusalem as stones,	4428
10: 1	were all Israel come to **make** him **k**.	4427
10: 2	fled from the presence of Solomon the **k**,	4428
10: 6	Rehoboam took counsel with the old	4428
10:12	as the **k** bade, saying, Come again to me	4428
10:13	the **k** answered them roughly; and king	4428
10:13	**k** Rehoboam forsook the counsel of the	4428
10:15	So the **k** hearkened not unto the people:	4428
10:16	when all Israel saw that the **k** would not	4428
10:16	the people answered the **k**, saying,	4428
10:18	Rehoboam sent Hadoram that *was* over	4428
10:18	Rehoboam made speed to get *him* up to	4428
11: 3	**k** of Judah, and to all Israel in Judah and	4428
11:22	brethren: for *he thought* to **make** him **k**.	4427
12: 2	*that* in the fifth year of **k** Rehoboam	4428
12: 2	of Egypt came up against Jerusalem,	4428
12: 6	of Israel and the **k** humbled themselves;	4428
12: 9	So Shishak **k** of Egypt came up against	4428
12:10	of which **k** Rehoboam made shields	4428
12:11	when the **k** entered *into* the house of	4428
12:13	So **k** Rehoboam strengthened himself in	4428
13: 1	in the eighteenth year of **k** Jeroboam	4428
15:16	Maachah the mother of Asa the **k**,	4428
16: 1	thirtieth year of the reign of Asa Baasha **k**	4428
16: 1	none go out or come in to Asa **k** of Judah.	4428
16: 2	and sent to Ben-hadad **k** of Syria,	4428
16: 3	break thy league with Baasha **k** of Israel,	4428
16: 4	Ben-hadad hearkened unto **k** Asa,	4428
16: 6	Asa the **k** took all Judah; and they carried	4428
16: 7	that time Hanani the seer came to Asa **k**	4428
16: 7	Because thou hast relied on the **k** of Syria,	4428
16: 7	is the host of the **k** of Syria escaped out of	4428
17:19	waited on the **k**, besides *those* whom	4428
17:19	besides *those* whom the **k** put in the	4428
18: 3	Ahab **k** of Israel said unto Jehoshaphat	4428
18: 3	king of Israel said unto Jehoshaphat	4428
18: 4	Jehoshaphat said unto the **k** of Israel,	4428
18: 5	Therefore the **k** of Israel gathered	4428
18: 7	the **k** of Israel said unto Jehoshaphat,	4428
18: 7	Jehoshaphat said, Let not the **k** say so.	4428
18: 8	the **k** of Israel called for one of *his* officers	4428
18: 9	the **k** of Israel and Jehoshaphat king of	4428
18: 9	of Israel and Judah sat either of them	4428
18:11	shall deliver *it* into the hand of the **k**.	4428
18:12	*declare* good to the **k** with one assent;	4428
18:14	when he was come to the **k**, the king said	4428
18:14	to the king, the **k** said unto him, Micaiah,	4428
18:15	he said to him, How many times shall	4428
18:17	the **k** of Israel said to Jehoshaphat, Did I	4428
18:19	Who shall entice Ahab **k** of Israel, that he	4428
18:25	the **k** of Israel said, Take ye Micaiah,	4428
18:26	say, Thus saith the **k**, Put this *fellow* in	4428
18:28	the **k** of Israel and Jehoshaphat the **k** of	4428
18:28	Jehoshaphat the **k** of Judah went up to	4428
18:29	the **k** of Israel said unto Jehoshaphat,	4428

2Ch 18:29	So the **k** of Israel disguised himself;	4428
18:30	Now the **k** of Syria had commanded	4428
18:30	or great, save only with the **k** of Israel.	4428
18:31	that they said, It *is* the **k** of Israel.	4428
18:32	perceived that it was not the **k** of Israel,	4428
18:33	smote the **k** of Israel between the joints	4428
18:34	howbeit the **k** of Israel stayed *himself* up	4428
19: 1	Jehoshaphat **k** of Judah returned to	4428
19: 2	to Jehoshaphat, Shouldest thou help	4428
20:15	of Jerusalem, and thou **k** Jehoshaphat,	4428
20:35	after this did Jehoshaphat **k** of Judah join	4428
20:35	join himself with Ahaziah **k** of Israel,	4428
21: 2	all these *were* the sons of Jehoshaphat **k**	4428
21: 8	Judah, and **made** themselves a **k**.	4427+4428
21:12	nor in the ways of Asa **k** of Judah,	4428
22: 1	**made** Ahaziah his youngest son **k** in his	4427
22: 1	So Ahaziah the son of Jehoram **k** of Judah	4428
22: 5	went with Jehoram the son of Ahab **k** of	4428
22: 5	Hazael **k** of Syria at Ramoth-gilead:	4428
22: 6	when he fought with Hazael **k** of Syria.	4428
22: 6	Azariah the son of Jehoram **k** of Judah	4428
22:11	Jehoshabeath, the daughter of the **k**,	4428
22:11	the daughter of **k** Jehoram,	4428
23: 3	covenant with the **k** in the house of God.	4428
23: 7	the Levites shall compass the **k** round	4428
23: 7	be you with the **k** when he cometh in,	4428
23: 9	and shields, that *had been* **k** David's,	4428
23:10	and the temple, by the **k** round about.	4428
23:11	*him* the Testimony, and **made** him **k**.	4427
23:11	anointed him, and said, God save the **k**.	4428
23:12	of the people running and praising the **k**,	4428
23:13	the **k** stood at his pillar at the entering in,	4428
23:13	the princes and the trumpets by the **k**:	4428
23:16	all the people, and between the **k**,	4428
23:20	brought down the **k** from the house of	4428
23:20	set the **k** upon the throne of the kingdom.	4428
24: 6	the **k** called for Jehoiada the chief,	4428
24:12	the **k** and Jehoiada gave it to such as did	4428
24:14	the rest of the money before the **k**	4428
24:17	of Judah, and made obeisance to the **k**.	4428
24:17	Then the **k** hearkened unto them.	4428
24:21	**k** in the court of the house of the LORD.	4428
24:22	Thus Joash the **k** remembered not	4428
24:23	sent all the spoil of them unto the **k** of	4428
25: 3	servants that had killed the **k** his father.	4428
25: 7	came a man of God to him, saying, O **k**,	4428
25:16	talked with him, that *the* **k** said unto him,	NIH
25:17	Amaziah **k** of Judah took advice,	4428
25:17	the son of Jehu, **k** of Israel, saying, Come,	4428
25:18	Joash **k** of Israel sent to Amaziah king of	4428
25:18	Joash **k** of Israel sent to Amaziah **k** of	4428
25:21	So Joash the **k** of Israel went up;	4428
25:21	*both* he and Amaziah **k** of Judah,	4428
25:23	Joash the **k** of Israel took Amaziah king of	4428
25:23	Joash the king of Israel took Amaziah **k** of	4428
25:25	Amaziah the son of Joash **k** of Judah lived	4428
25:25	son of Jehoahaz **k** of Israel fifteen years.	4428
26: 1	**made** him **k** in the room of his father	4427
26: 2	after that he slept with his fathers.	4428
26:13	to help the **k** against the enemy.	4428
26:18	they withstood Uzziah the **k**, and said	4428
26:21	Uzziah the **k** was a leper unto the day of	4428
27: 5	He fought also with the **k** of	4428
28: 5	him into the hand of the **k** of Syria;	4428
28: 5	was also delivered into the hand of the **k**	4428
28: 7	and Elkanah *that was* next to the **k**.	4428
28:16	At that time did **k** Ahaz send unto the	4428
28:19	Judah low because of Ahaz **k** of Israel;	4428
28:20	Tilgath-pilneser **k** of Assyria came unto	4428
28:21	*out* of the house of the **k**, and of	4428
28:21	and gave *it* unto the **k** of Assyria:	4428
28:22	against the LORD: this *is that* **k** Ahaz.	4428
29:15	according to the commandment of the **k**,	4428
29:18	they went in to Hezekiah the **k**, and said,	4428
29:19	which **k** Ahaz in his reign did cast away	4428
29:20	Hezekiah the **k** rose early, and gathered	4428
29:23	he goats for the **k** on offering before the **k**	4428
29:24	for the **k** commanded *that* the burnt	4428
29:27	the instruments ordained by David **k**	4428
29:29	the **k** and all that were present with him	4428
29:30	Moreover Hezekiah the **k** and the princes	4428
30: 2	For the **k** had taken counsel,	4428
30: 4	the thing pleased the **k** and all	4428
30: 6	posts went with the letters from the **k**	4428
30: 6	according to the commandment of the **k**,	4428
30:12	heart to do the commandment of the **k**	4428
30:24	For Hezekiah **k** of Judah did give to	4428
30:26	of Israel *there* was not the like in	4428
31:13	at the commandment of Hezekiah the **k**,	4428
32: 1	the establishment *thereof,* Sennacherib **k**	4428
32: 7	be not afraid nor dismayed for the **k** of	4428
32: 8	upon the words of Hezekiah **k** of Judah.	4428
32: 9	After this did Sennacherib **k** of Assyria	4428
32: 9	unto Hezekiah **k** of Judah, and unto all	4428
32:10	Thus saith Sennacherib **k** of Assyria,	4428
32:11	us out of the hand of the **k** of Assyria?	4428
32:20	for this *cause* Hezekiah the **k**,	4428
32:21	captains in the camp of the **k** of Assyria.	4428
32:22	the hand of Sennacherib the **k** of Assyria,	4428
32:23	and presents to Hezekiah **k** of Judah:	4428
33:11	captains of the host of the **k** of Assyria,	4428
33:25	them that had conspired against **k** Amon;	4428
33:25	land **made** Josiah his son **k** in his stead.	4427
34:16	Shaphan carried the book to the **k**,	4428
34:16	brought the **k** word back again, saying,	4428

K

K

2Ch 34:18	Shaphan the scribe told the **k**, saying,	4428
34:18	And Shaphan read it before the **k**.	4428
34:19	the **k** had heard the words of the law,	4428
34:20	the **k** commanded Hilkiah, and Ahikam	4428
34:22	*they* that the **k** *had appointed*, went to	4428
34:24	they have read before the **k** of Judah:	4428
34:26	as for the **k** of Judah, who sent you to	4428
34:28	So they brought the **k** word again.	4428
34:29	the **k** sent and gathered together all	4428
34:30	the **k** went up *into* the house of	4428
34:31	the **k** stood in his place, and made a	4428
35: 3	the son of David **k** of Israel did build;	4428
35: 4	according to the writing of David **k** of	4428
35:16	to the commandment of **k** Josiah.	4428
35:20	Necho **k** of Egypt came up to fight against	4428
35:21	have I to do with thee, thou **k** of Judah?	4428
35:23	the archers shot at **k** Josiah; and the king	4428
35:23	the **k** said to his servants, Have me away;	4428
36: 1	**made** him **k** in his father's stead in	4427
36: 3	the **k** of Egypt put him down at Jerusalem	4428
36: 4	the **k** of Egypt made Eliakim his brother	4428
36: 4	**made** Eliakim his brother **k** over Judah	4427
36: 6	Against him came up Nebuchadnezzar **k**	4428
36:10	**k** Nebuchadnezzar sent, and brought him	4428
36:10	**made** Zedekiah his brother **k** over Judah	4427
36:13	also rebelled against **k** Nebuchadnezzar,	4428
36:17	Therefore he brought upon them the **k** of	4428
36:18	the treasures of the **k**, and of his princes;	4428
36:22	Now in the first year of Cyrus **k** of Persia,	4428
36:22	the LORD stirred up the spirit of Cyrus **k**	4428
36:23	Thus saith **k** of Persia,	4428
Ezr 1: 1	Now in the first year of Cyrus **k** of Persia,	4428
1: 1	the LORD stirred up the spirit of Cyrus **k**	4428
1: 2	Thus saith Cyrus **k** of Persia, The LORD	4428
1: 7	Also Cyrus the **k** brought forth the vessels	4428
1: 8	Even those did Cyrus **k** of Persia bring	4428
2: 1	whom Nebuchadnezzar the **k** of Babylon	4428
3: 7	grant that they had of Cyrus **k** of Persia.	4428
3:10	after the ordinance of David **k** of Israel.	4428
4: 2	since the days of Esar-haddon **k** of Assur,	4428
4: 3	as **k** Cyrus the king of Persia hath	4428
4: 3	as king Cyrus the **k** of Persia hath	4428
4: 5	all the days of Cyrus **k** of Persia,	4428
4: 5	even until the reign of Darius **k** of Persia.	4428
4: 7	unto Artaxerxes **k** of Persia;	4428
4: 8	Jerusalem to Artaxerxes the **k** in this sort:	4430
4:11	unto him, *even* unto Artaxerxes the **k**:	4430
4:12	Be it known unto the **k**, that the Jews	4430
4:13	Be it known now unto the **k**, that, if this	4430
4:14	have we sent and certified the **k**;	4430
4:16	certify the **k** that, if this city be builded	4430
4:17	*Then* sent the **k** an answer unto Rehum	4430
4:23	when the copy of **k** Artaxerxes' letter	4430
4:24	year of the reign of Darius **k** of Persia.	4430
5: 6	side the river, sent unto Darius the **k**:	4430
5: 7	thus: Unto Darius the **k**, all peace.	4430
5: 8	Be it known unto the **k**, that we went	4430
5:11	a great **k** of Israel builded and set up.	4430
5:12	of Nebuchadnezzar the **k** of Babylon,	4430
5:13	in the first year of Cyrus **k** of Babylon	4430
5:13	**k** Cyrus made a decree to build this house	4430
5:14	did Cyrus the **k** take out of the temple	4430
5:17	Now therefore, if *it seem* good to the **k**,	4430
5:17	that a decree *was* made of Cyrus the **k** to	4430
5:17	let the **k** send his pleasure to us	4430
6: 1	Darius the **k** made a decree, and search	4430
6: 3	In the first year of Cyrus the **k** *the same*	4430
6: 3	**k** made a decree *concerning* the house of	4430
6:10	pray for the life of the **k**, and of his sons.	4430
6:13	according to that which Darius the **k** had	4430
6:14	and Darius, and Artaxerxes **k** of Persia.	4430
6:15	sixth year of the reign of Darius the **k**.	4430
6:22	turned the heart of the **k** of Assyria unto	4428
7: 1	in the reign of Artaxerxes **k** of Persia,	4428
7: 6	the **k** granted him all his request,	4428
7: 7	in the seventh year of Artaxerxes the **k**.	4428
7: 8	which *was in* the seventh year of the **k**.	4428
7:11	this *is* the copy of the letter that the **k**	4428
7:12	Artaxerxes, **k** of kings, unto Ezra the	4430
7:14	Forasmuch as *thou art* sent of the **k**,	4430
7:15	which the **k** and his counsellers have	4430
7:21	I, *even* I Artaxerxes the **k**, do make a	4430
7:23	there be wrath against the realm of the **k**	4430
7:26	law of the **k**, let judgment be executed	4430
7:28	extended mercy unto me before the **k**,	4428
8: 1	in the reign of Artaxerxes the **k**.	4428
8:22	For I was ashamed to require of the **k** a	4428
8:22	because we had spoken unto the **k**,	4428
8:25	which the **k**, and his counsellers,	4428
Ne 2: 1	*in* the twentieth year of Artaxerxes the **k**,	4428
2: 1	I took up the wine, and gave *it* unto the **k**.	4428
2: 2	Wherefore the **k** said unto me, Why *is*	4428
2: 3	said unto the **k**, Let the king live for ever:	4428
2: 3	said unto the king, Let the **k** live for ever:	4428
2: 4	the **k** said unto me, For what dost thou	4428
2: 5	I said unto the **k**, If it please the king,	4428
2: 5	If it please the **k**, and if thy servant have	4428
2: 6	the **k** said unto me, (the queen also	4428
2: 6	So it pleased the **k** to send me; and I set	4428
2: 7	Moreover I said unto the **k**, If it please	4428
2: 7	I said unto the king, If it please the **k**,	4428
2: 8	the **k** granted me, according to the good	4428
2: 9	Now the **k** had sent captains of the army	4428
2:19	that ye do? will ye rebel against the **k**?	4428
5:14	and thirtieth year of Artaxerxes the **k**,	4428

Ne 6: 6	that thou mayest be their **k**, according to	4428
6: 7	Jerusalem, saying, *There* is a **k** in Judah:	4428
6: 7	shall it be reported to the **k** according	4428
6:	whom Nebuchadnezzar the **k** of Babylon	4428
9:22	land of the **k** of Heshbon, and the land	4428
9:22	and the land of Og **k** of Bashan.	4428
13: 6	thirtieth year of Artaxerxes **k** of Babylon	4428
13: 6	**k**ing of Babylon came I unto the **k**,	4428
13: 6	certain days obtained I *leave* of the **k**:	4428
13:26	Did not Solomon **k** of Israel sin by these	4428
13:26	many nations was there no **k** like him,	4428
13:26	and God made him **k** over all Israel:	4428
Est 1: 2	when the **k** Ahasuerus sat on the throne	4428
1: 5	the **k** made a feast unto all the people that	4428
1: 7	according to the state of the **k**.	4428
1: 8	the **k** had appointed to all the officers of	4428
1: 9	house which *belonged* to **k** Ahasuerus.	4428
1:10	when the heart of the **k** was merry with	4428
1:10	in the presence of Ahasuerus the **k**,	4428
1:11	To bring Vashti the queen before the **k**	4428
1:12	therefore was the **k** very wroth,	4428
1:13	the **k** said to the wise *men*, which knew	4428
1:15	of the **k** Ahasuerus by the chamberlains?	4428
1:16	Memucan answered before the **k** and	4428
1:16	queen hath not done wrong to the **k** only,	4428
1:16	in all the provinces of the **k** Ahasuerus.	4428
1:17	The **k** Ahasuerus commanded Vashti	4428
1:19	If it please the **k**, let there go a royal	4428
1:19	That Vashti come no *more* before **k**	4428
1:19	let the **k** give her royal estate unto	4428
1:21	the saying pleased the **k** and the princes;	4428
1:21	the **k** did according to the word of	4428
2: 1	when the wrath of **k** Ahasuerus was	4428
2: 2	be fair young virgins sought for the **k**:	4428
2: 3	let the **k** appoint officers in all	4428
2: 4	let the maiden which pleaseth the **k** be	4428
2: 4	the thing pleased the **k**; and he did so.	4428
2: 6	carried away with Jeconiah **k** of Judah,	4428
2: 6	whom Nebuchadnezzar the **k** of Babylon	4428
2:12	turn was come to go in to **k** Ahasuerus,	4428
2:13	thus came *every* maiden unto the **k**;	4428
2:14	she came in unto the **k** no more, except	4428
2:14	except the **k** delighted in her, and *that*	4428
2:15	come to go in unto the **k**, she required	4428
2:16	Esther was taken unto **k** Ahasuerus into	4428
2:17	the **k** loved Esther above all the women,	4428
2:18	**k** made a great feast unto all his princes	4428
2:18	gave gifts, according to the state of the **k**.	4428
2:21	sought to lay hand on the **k** Ahasuerus.	4428
2:22	Esther certified the **k** *thereof* in	4428
2:23	the book of the chronicles before the **k**.	4428
3: 1	After these things did **k** Ahasuerus	4428
3: 2	for he had so commanded concerning	4428
3: 7	in the twelfth year of **k** Ahasuerus,	4428
3: 8	Haman said unto **k** Ahasuerus, There is a	4428
3: 9	If it please the **k**, let it be written that	4428
3:10	the **k** took his ring from his hand,	4428
3:11	the **k** said unto Haman, The silver *is*	4428
3:12	the name of **k** Ahasuerus was it written,	4428
3:15	the **k** and Haman sat down to drink;	4428
4: 8	her that *she* should go in unto the **k**,	4428
4:11	come unto the **k** into the inner court,	4428
4:11	such to whom the **k** shall hold out	4428
4:11	not been called to come in unto the **k**	4428
4:16	so will I go in unto the **k**, which *is* not	4428
5: 1	**k** sat upon his royal throne in the royal	4428
5: 2	the **k** saw Esther the queen standing	4428
5: 2	the **k** held out to Esther the golden	4428
5: 3	said the **k** unto her, What wilt thou,	4428
5: 4	If *it seem* good unto the **k**, let the king	4428
5: 4	let the **k** and Haman come *this* day unto	4428
5: 5	the **k** said, Cause Haman to make haste,	4428
5: 5	So the **k** and Haman came to the banquet	4428
5: 6	the **k** said unto Esther at the banquet of	4428
5: 8	I have found favour in the sight of the **k**,	4428
5: 8	if it please the **k** to grant my petition,	4428
5: 8	the **k** and Haman come to the banquet	4428
5: 8	I will do to morrow as the **k** hath said.	4428
5:11	*the things* where*in* the **k** had promoted	4428
5:11	above the princes and servants of the **k**.	4428
5:12	**k** unto the banquet that she had prepared	4428
5:12	*am* I invited unto her also with the **k**.	4428
5:14	to morrow speak thou unto the **k** that	4428
5:14	go thou in merrily with the **k** unto	4428
6: 1	On that night could not the **k** sleep,	4428
6: 1	and they were read before the **k**.	4428
6: 2	sought to lay hand on the **k** Ahasuerus.	4428
6: 3	the **k** said, What honour and dignity hath	4428
6: 4	the **k** said, Who *is* in the court?	4428
6: 4	to speak unto the **k** to hang Mordecai on	4428
6: 5	And the **k** said, Let him come in.	4428
6: 6	the **k** said unto him, What shall be done	4428
6: 6	man whom the **k** delighteth to honour?	4428
6: 6	whom would the **k** delight to do honour	4428
6: 7	Haman answered the **k**, *For* the man	4428
6: 7	*For* the man whom the **k** delighteth to	4428
6: 8	be brought which the **k** *useth* to wear,	4428
6: 8	the horse that the **k** rideth upon,	4428
6: 9	*withal* whom the **k** delighteth to honour,	4428
6: 9	shall it be done to the man whom the **k**	4428
6:10	the **k** said to Haman, Make haste,	4428
6:11	man whom the **k** delighteth to honour.	4428
7: 1	So the **k** and Haman came to banquet	4428
7: 2	the **k** said again to Esther on the	4428
7: 3	in thy sight, O **k**, and if it please the king,	4428

Est 7: 3	in thy sight, O king, and if it please the **k**,	4428
7: 5	the **k** Ahasuerus answered and said unto	4428
7: 6	Haman was afraid before the **k** and	4428
7: 7	the **k** arising from the banquet of wine in	4428
7: 7	was evil determined against him by the **k**.	4428
7: 8	the **k** returned out of the palace garden	4428
7: 8	whereon Esther *was*. Then said the **k**,	4428
7: 9	said before the **k**, Behold also,	4428
7: 9	who had spoken good for the **k**, standeth	4428
7: 9	Then the **k** said, Hang him thereon.	4428
8: 1	On that day did the **k** Ahasuerus give	4428
8: 1	Mordecai came before the **k**; for Esther	4428
8: 2	the **k** took off his ring, which he had	4428
8: 3	Esther spake yet again before the **k**,	4428
8: 4	the **k** held out the golden sceptre toward	4428
8: 5	If it please the **k**, and if I have found	4428
8: 5	the thing seem right before the **k**, and I	4428
8: 7	the **k** Ahasuerus said unto Esther the	4428
8:10	he wrote in the **k** Ahasuerus' name,	4428
8:11	Where*in* the **k** granted the Jews which	4428
8:12	Upon one day in all the provinces of the **k**	4428
8:15	presence of the **k** in royal apparel *of* blue	4428
9: 2	all the provinces of the **k** Ahasuerus,	4428
9: 3	and the deputies, and officers of the **k**,	4428
9:11	the palace was brought before the **k**.	4428
9:12	the **k** said unto Esther the queen,	4428
9:13	said Esther, If it please the **k**, let it be	4428
9:14	the **k** commanded it so to be done:	4428
9:20	in all the provinces of the **k** Ahasuerus,	4428
9:25	when Esther came before the **k**,	4428
10: 1	the **k** Ahasuerus laid a tribute upon	4428
10: 2	where*unto* the **k** advanced him,	4428
10: 3	For Mordecai the Jew *was* next unto **k**	4428
Job 15:24	against him, as a **k** ready to the battle.	4428
18:14	and it shall bring him to the **k** of terrors.	4428
29:25	sat chief, and dwelt as a **k** in the army,	4428
34:18	*Is it fit* to say to a **k**, Thou *art* wicked?	4428
41:34	beholdeth all high *things*: he *is* a **k** over	4428
Ps 2: 6	Yet have I set my **k** upon my holy hill of	4428
5: 2	the voice of my cry, my **K**, and my God:	4428
10:16	The LORD *is* **K** for ever and ever:	4428
18:50	Great deliverance giveth he to his **k**;	4428
20: 9	LORD: let the **k** hear us when we call.	4428
21: 1	The **k** shall joy in thy strength, O LORD;	4428
21: 7	For the **k** trusteth in the LORD,	4428
24: 7	and the **K** of glory shall come in.	4428
24: 8	Who *is* this **K** of glory? the LORD strong	4428
24: 9	and the **K** of glory shall come in.	4428
24:10	Who is this **K** of glory? The LORD of	4428
24:10	The LORD of hosts, he *is* the **K** of glory.	4428
29:10	yea, the LORD sitteth **K** for ever.	4428
33:16	There is no **k** saved by the multitude of a	4428
44: 4	Thou *art* my **K**, O God:	4428
45: 1	which I have made touching *the* **k**:	4428
45:11	So shall the **k** greatly desire thy beauty:	4428
45:14	shall be brought unto the **k** in raiment	4428
47: 2	terrible; he *is* a great **K** over all the earth.	4428
47: 6	sing *praises*: sing *praises* unto our **K**.	4428
47: 7	For God *is* the **K** of all the earth: sing ye	4428
48: 2	sides of the north, the city of the great **K**.	4428
63:11	the **k** shall rejoice in God; every one that	4428
68:24	of my God, my **K**, in the sanctuary.	4428
72: 1	Give the **k** thy judgments, O God,	4428
74:12	God *is* my **K** of old, working salvation	4428
84: 3	O LORD of hosts, my **K**, and my God.	4428
89:18	and the Holy One of Israel *is* our **k**.	4428
95: 3	a great God, and a great **K** above all gods.	4428
98: 6	a joyful noise before the LORD, the **K**.	4428
105:20	The **k** sent and loosed him; *even* the ruler	4428
135:11	Sihon **k** of the Amorites, and Og king of	4428
135:11	Og **k** of Bashan, and all the kingdoms of	4428
136:19	Sihon **k** of the Amorites: for his mercy	4428
136:20	Og the **k** of Bashan: for his mercy	4428
145: 1	I will extol thee, my God, O **k**; and I will	4428
149: 2	the children of Zion be joyful in their **K**.	4428
Pr 1: 1	of Solomon the son of David, **k** of Israel.	4428
16:10	A divine sentence in the lips of the **k**:	4428
16:14	wrath of a **k** *is as* messengers of death:	4428
20: 2	The fear of a **k** *is* as the roaring of a lion:	4428
20: 8	A **k** that sitteth in the throne of judgment	4428
20:26	A wise **k** scattereth the wicked,	4428
20:28	Mercy and truth preserve the **k**:	4428
22:11	*for* the grace of his lips the **k** *shall be* his	4428
24:21	My son, fear thou the LORD and the **k**:	4428
25: 1	which the men of Hezekiah **k** of Judah	4428
25: 5	Take away the wicked *from* before the **k**,	4428
25: 6	not forth thyself in the presence of the **k**,	4428
29: 4	The **k** by judgment stablisheth the land:	4428
29:14	The **k** that faithfully judgeth the poor,	4428
30:27	The locusts have no **k**, yet go they forth	4428
30:31	a **k**, against whom *there is* no rising up.	4428
31: 1	The words of **k** Lemuel, the prophecy that	4428
Ecc 1: 1	the son of David, **k** in Jerusalem.	4428
1:12	I the Preacher was **k** over Israel in	4428
2:12	*can* the man *do* that cometh after the **k**?	4428
4:13	a wise child than an old and foolish **k**,	4428
5: 9	for all: the **k** *himself* is served by the field.	4428
8: 4	Where the word of a **k** *is, there is* power:	4428
9:14	there came a great **k** against it,	4428
10:16	when thy **k** *is* a child, and thy princes eat	4428
10:17	when thy **k** *is* the son of nobles,	4428
10:20	Curse not the **k**, no not in thy thought;	4428
SS 1: 4	the **k** hath brought me *into* his chambers:	4428
1:12	While the **k** *sitteth* at his table,	4428

SS
3: 9 **K** Solomon made himself a chariot of — 4428
3:11 behold **k** Solomon with the crown — 4428
7: 5 like purple; the **k** is held in the galleries. — 4428
Isa
6: 1 In the year that **k** Uzziah died I saw also — 4428
6: 5 for mine eyes have seen the **K**, the LORD — 4428
7: 1 the son of Uzziah **k** of Judah, that Rezin — 4428
7: 1 Rezin the **k** of Syria, and Pekah the son — 4428
7: 1 Pekah the son of Remaliah, **k** of Israel, — 4428
7: 6 set a **k** in the midst of it, even — 4427+4428
7:17 from Judah; even the **k** of Assyria. — 4428
7:20 by the **k** of Assyria, the head, and the hair — 4428
8: 4 be taken away before the **k** of Assyria. — 4428
8: 7 even of Assyria, and all his glory: — 4428
8:21 curse their **k** and their God, — 4428
10:12 fruit of the stout heart of the **k** of Assyria, — 4428
14: 4 up this proverb against the **k** of Babylon, — 4428
14:28 In the year that **k** Ahaz died was this — 4428
19: 4 a fierce **k** shall rule over them, saith — 4428
20: 1 (when Sargon the **k** of Assyria sent him,) — 4428
20: 4 So shall the **k** of Assyria lead away — 4428
20: 6 to be delivered from the **k** of Assyria: — 4428
23:15 according to the days of one **k**: — 4428
30:33 for the **k** it is prepared; he hath made it — 4428
32: 1 **k** shall reign in righteousness, and princes — 4428
33:17 Thine eyes shall see the **k** in his beauty: — 4428
33:22 is our lawgiver, the LORD is our **k**; — 4428
36: 1 pass in the fourteenth year of **k** Hezekiah, — 4428
36: 1 that Sennacherib **k** of Assyria came up — 4428
36: 2 the **k** of Assyria sent Rabshakeh from — 4428
36: 2 unto **k** Hezekiah with a great army. — 4428
36: 4 Thus saith the great **k**, the king of Assyria, — 4428
36: 4 Thus saith the great king, the **k** of Assyria, — 4428
36: 6 is Pharaoh **k** of Egypt to all that trust in — 4428
36: 8 to my master the **k** of Assyria, and I will — 4428
36:13 said, Hear ye the words of the great **k**, — 4428
36:13 words of the great king, the **k** of Assyria. — 4428
36:14 saith the **k**, Let not Hezekiah deceive — 4428
36:15 into the hand of the **k** of Assyria. — 4428
36:16 for thus saith the **k** of Assyria, Make an — 4428
36:18 land out of the hand of the **k** of Assyria? — 4428
37: 1 when **k** Hezekiah heard it, that he rent — 4428
37: 4 the **k** of Assyria his master hath sent — 4428
37: 5 So the servants of **k** Hezekiah came to — 4428
37: 6 wherewith the servants of the **k** of Assyria — 4428
37: 8 found the **k** of Assyria warring against — 4428
37: 9 he heard say concerning Tirhakah **k** of — 4428
37:10 Thus shall ye speak to Hezekiah **k** of — 4428
37:10 be given into the hand of the **k** of Assyria. — 4428
37:13 Where is the **k** of Hamath, and the king — 4428
37:13 the **k** of Arphad, and the king of the city — 4428
37:13 the **k** of the city of Sepharvaim, Hena, — 4428
37:21 to me against Sennacherib **k** of Assyria: — 4428
37:33 the LORD concerning the **k** of Assyria, — 4428
37:37 So Sennacherib **k** of Assyria departed, — 4428
38: 6 city out of the hand of the **k** of Assyria: — 4428
38: 9 **k** of Judah, when he had been sick, — 4428
39: 1 **k** of Babylon, sent letters and a present to — 4428
39: 3 came Isaiah the prophet unto **k** Hezekiah, — 4428
39: 7 shall be eunuchs in the palace of the **k** — 4428
41:21 forth your strong reasons, saith the **K** — 4428
43:15 Holy One, the creator of Israel, your **K**. — 4428
44: 6 Thus saith the LORD the **k** of Israel, — 4428
57: 9 thou wentest to the **k** with ointment, — 4428
Jer
1: 2 of Josiah the son of Amon **k** of Judah, — 4428
1: 3 of Jehoiakim the son of Josiah **k** of Judah, — 4428
1: 3 of Zedekiah the son of Josiah **k** of Judah, — 4428
3: 6 also unto me in the days of Josiah the **k**, — 4428
4: 9 that the heart of the **k** shall perish, — 4428
8:19 is not her **k** in her? Why have they — 4428
10: 7 Who would not fear thee, O **K** of nations? — 4428
10:10 he is the living God, and an everlasting **k**: — 4428
13:18 Say unto the **k** and to the queen, — 4428
15: 4 of Manasseh the son of Hezekiah **k** of — 4428
20: 4 I will give all Judah into the hand of the **k** — 4428
21: 1 when **k** Zedekiah sent unto him Pashur — 4428
21: 2 for Nebuchadrezzar **k** of Babylon maketh — 4428
21: 4 wherewith ye fight against the **k** of — 4428
21: 7 I will deliver Zedekiah **k** of Judah, and his — 4428
21: 7 into the hand of Nebuchadrezzar **k** of — 4428
21:10 it shall be given into the hand of the **k** of — 4428
21:11 touching the house of the **k** of Judah, — 4428
22: 1 Go down to the house of the **k** of Judah, — 4428
22: 2 the word of the LORD, O **k** of Judah, — 4428
22:11 Shallum the son of Josiah **k** of Judah, — 4428
22:18 Jehoiakim the son of Josiah **k** of Judah; — 4428
22:24 though Coniah the son of Jehoiakim **k** of — 4428
22:25 into the hand of Nebuchadrezzar **k** of — 4428
23: 5 a **K** shall reign and prosper, — 4428
24: 1 after that Nebuchadrezzar **k** of Babylon — 4428
24: 1 Jeconiah the son of Jehoiakim **k** of Judah, — 4428
24: 8 So will I give Zedekiah **k** of Judah, — 4428
25: 1 of Jehoiakim the son of Josiah **k** of Judah, — 4428
25: 1 was the first year of Nebuchadrezzar **k** — 4428
25: 3 year of Josiah the son of Amon **k** of Judah, — 4428
25: 9 Nebuchadrezzar the **k** of Babylon, — 4428
25:11 these nations shall serve the **k** of Babylon — 4428
25:12 that I will punish the **k** of Babylon, and — 4428
25:19 Pharaoh **k** of Egypt, and his servants, — 4428
25:26 the **k** of Sheshach shall drink after them. — 4428
26: 1 **k** of Judah came this word from — 4428
26:18 in the days of Hezekiah **k** of Judah, — 4428
26:19 Did Hezekiah **k** of Judah and all Judah — 4428
26:21 when Jehoiakim the **k**, with all his mighty — 4428
26:21 words, the **k** sought to put him to death: — 4428
26:22 Jehoiakim the **k** sent men into Egypt, — 4428

Jer
26:23 and brought him unto Jehoiakim the **k**; — 4428
27: 1 **k** of Judah came this word unto Jeremiah — 4428
27: 3 send them to the **k** of Edom, and to the — 4428
27: 3 to the **k** of Moab, and to the king of — 4428
27: 3 to the **k** of the Ammonites, and to the — 4428
27: 3 the **k** of Tyrus, and to the king of Zidon, — 4428
27: 3 to Jerusalem unto Zedekiah **k** of Judah; — 4428
27: 6 of Nebuchadnezzar the **k** of Babylon, — 4428
27: 8 same Nebuchadnezzar the **k** of Babylon, — 4428
27: 8 neck under the yoke of the **k** of Babylon, — 4428
27: 9 Ye shall not serve the **k** of Babylon: — 4428
27:11 neck under the yoke of the **k** of Babylon, — 4428
27:12 I spake also to Zedekiah **k** of Judah — 4428
27:12 Bring your necks under the yoke of the **k** — 4428
27:13 that will not serve the **k** of Babylon? — 4428
27:14 Ye shall not serve the **k** of Babylon: — 4428
27:17 serve the **k** of Babylon, and live: — 4428
27:18 in the house of the **k** of Judah, — 4428
27:20 Which Nebuchadnezzar **k** of Babylon — 4428
27:20 **k** of Judah from Jerusalem to Babylon, — 4428
27:21 in the house of the **k** of Judah and — 4428
28: 1 the beginning of the reign of Zedekiah **k** — 4428
28: 2 have broken the yoke of the **k** of Babylon. — 4428
28: 3 that Nebuchadnezzar **k** of Babylon took — 4428
28: 4 Jeconiah the son of Jehoiakim **k** of Judah, — 4428
28: 4 for I will break the yoke of the **k** of — 4428
28:11 I break the yoke of Nebuchadnezzar **k** — 4428
28:14 that they may serve Nebuchadnezzar **k** of — 4428
29: 2 (After that Jeconiah the **k**, and the queen, — 4428
29: 3 whom Zedekiah **k** of Judah sent unto — 4428
29: 3 Babylon to Nebuchadnezzar **k** of Babylon,) — 4428
29:16 Know that thus saith the LORD of the **k** — 4428
29:21 hand of Nebuchadrezzar **k** of Babylon; — 4428
29:22 the **k** of Babylon roasted in the fire; — 4428
30: 9 David their **k**, whom I will raise up unto — 4428
32: 1 in the tenth year of Zedekiah **k** of Judah, — 4428
32: 2 the **k** of Babylon's army besieged — 4428
32: 2 which was in the **k** of Judah's house. — 4428
32: 3 For Zedekiah **k** of Judah had shut him up, — 4428
32: 3 will give this city into the hand of the **k** of — 4428
32: 4 Zedekiah **k** of Judah shall not escape out — 4428
32: 4 into the hand of the **k** of Babylon, — 4428
32:28 into the hand of Nebuchadrezzar **k** of — 4428
32:36 shall be delivered into the hand of the **k** — 4428
34: 1 when Nebuchadnezzar **k** of Babylon, — 4428
34: 2 Go and speak to Zedekiah **k** of Judah, — 4428
34: 2 I will give this city into the hand of the **k** — 4428
34: 3 thine eyes shall behold the eyes of the **k** — 4428
34: 4 of the LORD, O Zedekiah **k** of Judah; — 4428
34: 6 unto Zedekiah **k** of Judah in Jerusalem, — 4428
34: 7 When the **k** of Babylon's army fought — 4428
34: 8 after that the **k** Zedekiah had made a — 4428
34:21 Zedekiah **k** of Judah and his princes will — 4428
34:21 into the hand of the **k** of Babylon's army, — 4428
35: 1 of Jehoiakim the son of Josiah **k** of Judah, — 4428
35:11 when Nebuchadrezzar **k** of Babylon came — 4428
36: 1 of Jehoiakim the son of Josiah **k** of Judah, — 4428
36: 9 of Jehoiakim the son of Josiah **k** of Judah, — 4428
36:16 will surely tell the **k** of all these words. — 4428
36:20 And they went in to the **k** into the court, — 4428
36:20 told all the words in the ears of the **k**. — 4428
36:21 So the **k** sent Jehudi to fet the roll: — 4428
36:21 Jehudi read it in the ears of the **k**, and in — 4428
36:21 all the princes which stood beside the **k**. — 4428
36:22 Now the **k** sat in the winterhouse in — 4428
36:24 nor rent their garments, neither the **k**, — 4428
36:25 Gemariah had made intercession to the **k** — 4428
36:26 the **k** commanded Jerahmeel the son of — 4428
36:27 after that the **k** had burnt the roll, — 4428
36:28 Jehoiakim the **k** of Judah hath burnt. — 4428
36:29 thou shalt say to Jehoiakim the **k** of — 4428
36:29 The **k** of Babylon shall certainly come — 4428
36:30 saith the LORD of Jehoiakim **k** of Judah; — 4428
36:32 Jehoiakim **k** of Judah had burnt in the — 4428
37: 1 **k** Zedekiah the son of Josiah reigned — 4428
37: 1 Nebuchadrezzar **k** of Babylon made — 4428
37: 1 of Babylon made **k** in the land of Judah. — 4427
37: 3 Zedekiah the **k** sent Jehucal the son of — 4428
37: 7 Thus shall ye say to the **k** of Judah, — 4428
37:17 Zedekiah the **k**, and took him out: — 4428
37:17 and the **k** asked him secretly in his house, — 4428
37:17 into the hand of the **k** of Babylon. — 4428
37:18 Moreover Jeremiah said unto **k** Zedekiah, — 4428
37:19 The **k** of Babylon shall not come against — 4428
37:20 hear now, I pray thee, O my lord the **k**: — 4428
37:21 Zedekiah the **k** commanded that they — 4428
38: 3 into the hand of the **k** of Babylon's army, — 4428
38: 4 Therefore the princes said unto the **k**, — 4428
38: 5 Zedekiah the **k** said, Behold, he is in your — 4428
38: 5 for the **k** is not he that can do any thing — 4428
38: 7 the **k** then sitting in the gate of Benjamin; — 4428
38: 8 king's house, and spake to the **k**, saying, — 4428
38: 9 My lord the **k**, these men have done evil — 4428
38:10 the **k** commanded Ebed-melech, — 4428
38:11 went into the house of the **k** under — 4428
38:14 Zedekiah the **k** sent, and took Jeremiah — 4428
38:14 the **k** said unto Jeremiah, I will ask thee — 4428
38:16 So Zedekiah the **k** sware secretly unto — 4428
38:17 If thou wilt assuredly go forth unto the **k** — 4428
38:18 if thou wilt not go forth to the **k** of — 4428
38:19 Zedekiah said unto Jeremiah, I am — 4428
38:22 all the women that are left in the **k** of — 4428
38:22 brought forth to the **k** of Babylon's — 4428
38:23 shalt be taken by the hand of the **k** of — 4428

Jer
38:25 us now what thou hast said unto the **k**, — 4428
38:25 to death; also what the **k** said unto thee: — 4428
38:26 I presented my supplication before the **k**, — 4428
38:27 these words that the **k** had commanded. — 4428
39: 1 In the ninth year of Zedekiah **k** of Judah, — 4428
39: 1 came Nebuchadrezzar **k** of Babylon and — 4428
39: 3 the princes of the **k** of Babylon came in, — 4428
39: 3 all the residue of the princes of the **k** — 4428
39: 4 that when Zedekiah the **k** of Judah saw — 4428
39: 5 brought him up to Nebuchadnezzar **k** — 4428
39: 6 the **k** of Babylon slew the sons of — 4428
39: 6 also the **k** of Babylon slew all the nobles — 4428
39:11 Now Nebuchadrezzar **k** of Babylon gave — 4428
39:13 and all the **k** of Babylon's princes; — 4428
40: 5 whom the **k** of Babylon hath made — 4428
40: 7 heard that the **k** of Babylon had made — 4428
40: 9 in the land and serve the **k** of Babylon, — 4428
40:11 heard that the **k** of Babylon had left a — 4428
40:14 thou certainly know that Baalis the **k** — 4428
41: 1 the seed royal, and the princes of the **k**, — 4428
41: 2 the **k** of Babylon had made governor — 4428
41: 9 it which Asa the **k** had made for fear of — 4428
41: 9 had made for fear of Baasha **k** of Israel: — 4428
41:18 whom the **k** of Babylon made governor in — 4428
42:11 Be not afraid of the **k** of Babylon, — 4428
43:10 take Nebuchadrezzar **k** of Babylon, — 4428
44:30 I will give Pharaoh-hophra **k** of Egypt into — 4428
44:30 I gave Zedekiah **k** of Judah into the hand — 4428
44:30 hand of Nebuchadrezzar **k** of Babylon, — 4428
45: 1 of Jehoiakim the son of Josiah **k** of Judah, — 4428
46: 2 against the army of Pharaoh-necho **k** of — 4428
46: 2 Nebuchadrezzar **k** of Babylon smote — 4428
46: 2 of Jehoiakim the son of Josiah **k** of Judah. — 4428
46:13 Nebuchadrezzar **k** of Babylon should — 4428
46:17 Pharaoh **k** of Egypt is but a noise; — 4428
46:18 As I live, saith the **K**, whose name is — 4428
46:26 into the hand of Nebuchadrezzar **k** of — 4428
48:15 saith the **K**, whose name is the LORD of — 4428
49: 1 why then doth their **k** inherit Gad, — 4428
49: 3 for their **k** shall go into captivity, — 4428
49:28 Nebuchadrezzar **k** of Babylon shall — 4428
49:30 for Nebuchadrezzar **k** of Babylon hath — 4428
49:34 of the reign of Zedekiah **k** of Judah, — 4428
49:38 will destroy from thence the **k** and — 4428
50:17 first the **k** of Assyria hath devoured him; — 4428
50:17 last this Nebuchadrezzar **k** of Babylon — 4428
50:18 will punish the **k** of Babylon and his land, — 4428
50:18 as I have punished the **k** of Assyria. — 4428
50:43 The **k** of Babylon hath heard the report of — 4428
51:31 to shew the **k** of Babylon that his city is — 4428
51:34 Nebuchadrezzar the **k** of Babylon hath — 4428
51:57 sleep, and not wake, saith the **K**, — 4428
51:59 he went with Zedekiah the **k** of Judah — 4428
52: 3 that Zedekiah rebelled against the **k** of — 4428
52: 4 that Nebuchadrezzar **k** of Babylon came, — 4428
52: 5 unto the eleventh year of **k** Zedekiah. — 4428
52: 8 of the Chaldeans pursued after the **k**, — 4428
52: 9 they took the **k**, and carried him up unto — 4428
52: 9 carried him up unto the **k** of Babylon to — 4428
52:10 **k** of Babylon slew the sons of Zedekiah — 4428
52:11 the **k** of Babylon bound him in chains, — 4428
52:12 year of Nebuchadrezzar **k** of Babylon, — 4428
52:12 which served the **k** of Babylon, — 4428
52:15 fell to the **k** of Babylon, and the rest of — 4428
52:20 **k** Solomon had made in the house of — 4428
52:26 them to the **k** of Babylon to Riblah. — 4428
52:27 the **k** of Babylon smote them, and put — 4428
52:31 of the captivity of Jehoiachin **k** of Judah, — 4428
52:31 Evil-merodach **k** of Babylon in the first — 4428
52:31 up the head of Jehoiachin **k** of Judah, — 4428
52:34 diet given him of the **k** of Babylon, — 4428
La
2: 6 in the indignation of his anger the **k** — 4428
2: 9 her **k** and her princes are among — 4428
Eze
1: 2 was the fifth year of **k** Jehoiachin's — 4428
7:27 The **k** shall mourn, and the prince shall — 4428
17:12 the **k** of Babylon is come to Jerusalem, — 4428
17:12 hath taken the **k** thereof, and the princes — 4428
17:16 surely in the place where the **k** dwelleth — 4428
17:16 the king dwelleth that made him **k**, — 4427
19: 9 and brought him to the **k** of Babylon: — 4428
21:19 that the sword of the **k** of Babylon may — 4428
21:21 For the **k** of Babylon stood at the parting — 4428
24: 2 the **k** of Babylon set himself against — 4428
26: 7 will bring upon Tyrus Nebuchadrezzar **k** — 4428
26: 7 a **k** of kings, from the north, with horses, — 4428
28:12 up a lamentation upon the **k** of Tyrus, — 4428
29: 2 set thy face against Pharaoh **k** of Egypt, — 4428
29: 3 I am against thee, Pharaoh **k** of Egypt, — 4428
29:18 Nebuchadrezzar **k** of Babylon caused his — 4428
29:19 Egypt unto Nebuchadrezzar **k** of Babylon; — 4428
30:10 the hand of Nebuchadrezzar **k** of Babylon. — 4428
30:21 I have broken the arm of Pharaoh **k** of — 4428
30:22 I am against Pharaoh **k** of Egypt, — 4428
30:24 I will strengthen the arms of the **k** of — 4428
30:25 I will strengthen the arms of the **k** of — 4428
30:25 sword into the hand of the **k** of Babylon, — 4428
31: 2 speak unto Pharaoh **k** of Egypt, and to his — 4428
32: 2 take up a lamentation for Pharaoh **k** of — 4428
32:11 The sword of the **k** of Babylon shall come — 4428
37:22 and one **k** shall be king to them all: — 4428
37:22 and one king shall be to them all: — 4428
37:24 David my servant shall be **k** over them; — 4428
Da
1: 1 the third year of the reign of Jehoiakim **k** — 4428
1: 1 **k** of Babylon unto Jerusalem, — 4428
1: 2 the Lord gave Jehoiakim **k** of Judah into — 4428

K

Da	1: 3	the **k** spake unto Ashpenaz the master of	4428
	1: 5	the **k** appointed them a daily provision of	4428
	1: 5	thereof they might stand before the **k**.	4428
	1:10	I fear my lord the **k**, who hath appointed	4428
	1:10	we endanger my head to the **k**.	4428
	1:18	Now at the end of the days that the **k** had	4428
	1:19	he communed with them;	4428
	1:19	therefore stood they before the **k**.	4428
	1:20	that the **k** inquired of them,	4428
	1:21	*even* unto the first year of **k** Cyrus.	4428
	2: 2	the **k** commanded to call the magicians,	4428
	2: 2	for to shew the **k** his dreams.	4428
	2: 2	So they came and stood before the **k**.	4428
	2: 3	the **k** said unto them, I have dreamed a	4428
	2: 4	spake the Chaldeans to the **k** in Syriack,	4428
	2: 4	to the king in Syriack, O **k**, live for ever:	4430
	2: 5	**k** answered and said to the Chaldeans,	4430
	2: 7	Let the **k** tell his servants the dream,	4430
	2: 8	The **k** answered and said, I know of	4430
	2:10	The Chaldeans answered before the **k**,	4430
	2:10	therefore *there is* no **k**, lord, nor ruler,	4430
	2:11	*it is* a rare thing that the **k** requireth,	4430
	2:11	none other that can shew it before the **k**,	4430
	2:12	For this cause the **k** was angry and	4430
	2:15	Why *is* the decree *so* hasty from the **k**?	4430
	2:16	desired of the **k** that he would give him	4430
	2:16	he would shew the **k** the interpretation.	4430
	2:24	whom the **k** had ordained to destroy	4430
	2:24	bring me in before the **k**, and I will shew	4430
	2:24	I will shew unto the **k** the interpretation.	4430
	2:25	Arioch brought in Daniel before the **k** in	4430
	2:25	that will make known unto the **k**	4430
	2:26	The **k** answered and said to Daniel,	4430
	2:27	Daniel answered in the presence of the **k**,	4430
	2:27	The secret which the **k** hath demanded	4430
	2:27	the soothsayers, shew unto the **k**;	4430
	2:28	maketh known to the **k** Nebuchadnezzar	4430
	2:29	*As for* thee, O **k**, thy thoughts came *into*	4430
	2:30	make known the interpretation to the **k**,	4430
	2:31	Thou, O **k**, sawest, and behold a great	4430
	2:36	the interpretation thereof before the **k**.	4430
	2:37	O **k**, *art* a king of kings: for the God	4430
	2:37	O king, *art* a **k** of kings: for the God	4430
	2:45	great God hath made known to the **k**	4430
	2:46	the **k** Nebuchadnezzar fell upon his face,	4430
	2:47	The **k** answered unto Daniel, and said,	4430
	2:48	the **k** made Daniel a great man,	4430
	2:49	Daniel requested of the **k**, and he set	4430
	2:49	but Daniel *sat* in the gate of the **k**.	4430
	3: 1	Nebuchadnezzar the **k** made an image of	4430
	3: 2	Nebuchadnezzar the **k** sent to gather	4430
	3: 2	which Nebuchadnezzar the **k** had set up.	4430
	3: 3	that Nebuchadnezzar the **k** had set up;	4430
	3: 5	that Nebuchadnezzar the **k** hath set up:	4430
	3: 7	that Nebuchadnezzar the **k** had set up;	4430
	3: 9	and said to the **k** Nebuchadnezzar,	4430
	3: 9	king Nebuchadnezzar, O **k**, live for ever.	4430
	3:10	Thou, O **k**, hast made a decree, that every	4430
	3:12	these men, O **k**, have not regarded thee:	4430
	3:13	they brought these men before the **k**.	4430
	3:16	Abed-nego, answered and said to the **k**,	4430
	3:17	he will deliver *us* out of thine hand, O **k**.	4430
	3:18	if not, be it known unto thee, O **k**, that	4430
	3:24	Nebuchadnezzar the **k** was astonied,	4430
	3:24	They answered and said unto the **k**, True,	4430
	3:24	and said unto the king, True, O **k**.	4430
	3:30	the **k** promoted Shadrach, Meshach,	4430
	4: 1	Nebuchadnezzar the **k**, unto all people,	4430
	4:18	dream I Nebuchadnezzar have seen.	4430
	4:19	The **k** spake, and said, Belteshazzar, let	4430
	4:22	It *is* thou, O **k**, that art grown and	4430
	4:23	the **k** saw a watcher and a holy one	4430
	4:24	O **k**, and this *is* the decree of the most	4430
	4:24	which is come upon my lord the **k**:	4430
	4:27	Wherefore, O **k**, let my counsel be	4430
	4:28	this came upon the **k** Nebuchadnezzar.	4430
	4:30	The **k** spake, and said, *Is* not this great	4430
	4:31	*saying*, O **k** Nebuchadnezzar, to thee it is	4430
	4:37	and extol and honour the **K** of heaven,	4430
	5: 1	Belshazzar the **k** made a great feast to a	4430
	5: 2	that the **k**, and his princes, his wives,	4430
	5: 3	and his princes, his wives,	4430
	5: 5	the **k** saw the part of the hand that wrote.	4430
	5: 7	The **k** cried aloud to bring in	4430
	5: 7	The **k** spake, and said to the wise *men*	4430
	5: 8	make known to the **k** the interpretation	4430
	5: 9	*was* **k** Belshazzar greatly troubled,	4430
	5:10	by reason of the words of the **k** and	4430
	5:10	the queen spake and said, O **k**, live for	4430
	5:11	whom the **k** Nebuchadnezzar thy father,	4430
	5:11	the, *I say*, thy father, made master of	4430
	5:12	whom the **k** named Belteshazzar:	4430
	5:13	was Daniel brought in before the **k**.	4430
	5:13	*And* the **k** spake and said unto Daniel,	4430
	5:13	whom the **k** my father brought out of	4430
	5:17	Daniel answered and said before the **k**,	4430
	5:17	yet I will read the writing unto the **k**,	4430
	5:18	O thou **k**, the most high God gave	4430
	5:30	In that night *was* Belshazzar the **k** of	4430
	6: 2	and the **k** should have no damage.	4430
	6: 3	he thought to set him over the whole	4430
	6: 6	princes assembled *together* to the **k**,	4430
	6: 6	thus unto him, **K** Darius, live for ever.	4430
	6: 7	or man for thirty days, save of thee, O **k**,	4430
	6: 8	Now, O **k**, establish the decree,	4430

Da	6: 9	Wherefore **k** Darius signed the writing	4430
	6:12	spake before the **k** concerning the king's	4430
	6:12	within thirty days, save of thee, O **k**,	4430
	6:12	**k** answered and said, The thing *is* true,	4430
	6:13	answered they and said before the **k**,	4430
	6:13	regardeth not thee, O **k**, nor the decree	4430
	6:14	**k**, when he heard *these* words, was sore	4430
	6:15	these men assembled unto the **k**,	4430
	6:15	unto the **k**, Know, O king, that the law	4430
	6:15	unto the king, Know, O **k**, that the law	4430
	6:15	which the **k** establisheth may be changed.	4430
	6:16	the **k** commanded, and they brought	4430
	6:16	*Now* the **k** spake and said unto Daniel,	4430
	6:17	the **k** sealed it with his own signet,	4430
	6:18	the **k** went to his palace, and passed	4430
	6:19	the **k** arose very early in the morning,	4430
	6:20	*and* the **k** spake and said to Daniel,	4430
	6:21	said Daniel unto the **k**, O king, live for	4430
	6:21	Daniel unto the king, O **k**, live for ever.	4430
	6:22	before thee, O **k**, have I done no hurt.	4430
	6:23	Then was the **k** exceeding glad for him,	4430
	6:24	the **k** commanded, and they brought	4430
	6:25	**k** Darius wrote unto all people, nations,	4430
	7: 1	In the first year of Belshazzar **k** of Babylon	4430
	8: 1	In the third year of the reign of **k**	4428
	8:21	the rough goat *is* the **k** of Grecia:	4428
	8:21	that *is* between his eyes *is* the first **k**.	4428
	8:23	a **k** of fierce countenance,	4428
	9: 1	which was **made k** over the realm of	4427
	10: 1	In the third year of Cyrus **k** of Persia a	4428
	11: 3	a mighty **k** shall stand up, that shall rule	4428
	11: 5	the **k** of the south shall be strong,	4428
	11: 6	the **k** of the north to make an agreement:	4428
	11: 7	shall enter into the fortress of the **k** of	4428
	11: 8	he shall continue *more* years than the **k** of	4428
	11: 9	So the **k** of the south shall come into *his*	4428
	11:11	the **k** of the south shall be moved with	4428
	11:11	with him, *even* with the **k** of the north:	4428
	11:13	For the **k** of the north shall return,	4428
	11:14	many stand up against the **k** of the south:	4428
	11:15	So the **k** of the north shall come,	4428
	11:25	his courage against the **k** of the south	4428
	11:25	the **k** of the south shall be stirred up to	4428
	11:36	the **k** shall do according to his will;	4428
	11:40	at the time of the end shall the **k** of	4428
	11:40	the **k** of the north shall come against him	4428
Hos	1: 1	of Jeroboam the son of Joash, **k** of Israel.	4428
	3: 4	Israel shall abide many days without a **k**,	4428
	3: 5	the Lord their God, and David their **k**;	4428
	5: 1	Israel; and give ye ear, O house of the **k**;	4428
	5:13	to the Assyrian, and sent to Jareb:	4428
	7: 3	They make the **k** glad with their	4428
	7: 5	*In* the day of our **k** the princes have made	4428
	8:10	a little for the burden of the **k** of princes.	4428
	10: 3	We have no **k**, because we feared not	4428
	10: 3	the Lord; what then should a **k** do to us?	4428
	10: 6	unto Assyria *for* a present to **k** Jareb:	4428
	10: 7	**k** is cut off as the foam upon the water.	4428
	10:15	in a morning shall the **k** of Israel utterly	4428
	11: 5	the Assyrian shall be his **k**, because	4428
	13:10	I will be thy **k**: where *is any other* that	4428
	13:10	thou saidst, Give me a **k** and princes?	4428
	13:11	I gave thee a **k** in mine anger, and took	4428
Am	1: 1	Israel in the days of Uzziah **k** of Judah,	4428
	1: 1	the days of Jeroboam the son of Joash **k**	4428
	1:15	their **k** shall go into captivity, he and	4428
	2: 1	he burnt the bones of the **k** of Edom into	4428
	7:10	of Beth-el sent to Jeroboam **k** of Israel,	4428
Jnh	3: 6	For word came unto the **k** of Nineveh,	4428
	3: 7	through Nineveh by the decree of the **k**	4428
Mic	2:13	their **k** shall pass before them,	4428
	4: 9	*is there* no **k** in thee? is thy counseller	4428
	6: 5	remember now what Balak **k** of Moab	4428
Na	3:18	Thy shepherds slumber, O **k** of Assyria:	4428
Zep	1: 1	of Josiah the son of Amon, **k** of Judah.	4428
	3:15	the **k** of Israel, *even* the Lord, *is* in	4428
Hag	1: 1	In the second year of Darius the **k**,	4428
	1:15	in the second year of Darius the **k**.	4428
Zec	7: 1	it came to pass in the fourth year of **k**	4428
	9: 5	the **k** shall perish from Gaza,	4428
	9: 9	thy **K** cometh unto thee: he *is* just,	4428
	11: 6	and into the hand of his **k**:	4428
	14: 5	in the days of Uzziah **k** of Judah:	4428
	14: 9	the Lord shall be **k** over all the earth:	4428
	14:16	go up from year to year to worship the **K**,	4428
	14:17	earth unto Jerusalem to worship the **K**,	4428
Mal	1:14	Lord a corrupt thing: for I *am* a great **K**,	4428
Mt	1: 6	And Jesse begat David the **k**; and David	935
	1: 6	David the **k** begat Solomon of *her that had*	935
	2: 1	of Judea in the days of Herod the **k**,	935
	2: 2	Where is he that is born **K** of the Jews?	935
	2: 3	When Herod the **k** had heard *these things*,	935
	2: 9	When they had heard the **k**, they departed;	935
	5:35	by Jerusalem; for it is the city of the great **K**.	935
	14: 9	And the **k** was sorry: nevertheless for	935
	18:23	of heaven likened unto a certain **k**,	935
	21: 5	thy **K** cometh unto thee, meek,	935
	22: 2	of heaven is like unto a certain **k**,	935
	22: 7	when the **k** heard *thereof*, he was wroth:	935
	22:11	And when the **k** came in to see the guests,	935
	22:13	Then said the **k** to the servants, Bind him	935
	25:34	shall the **K** say unto them on his right	935
	25:40	the **K** shall answer and say unto them,	935
	27:11	saying, Art thou the **K** of the Jews?	935
	27:29	mocked him, saying, Hail, **K** of the Jews!	935

Mt	27:37	THIS IS JESUS THE **K** OF THE JEWS.	935
	27:42	If he be the **K** of Israel, let him now come	935
Mk	6:14	And **k** Herod heard *of him*; (for his name	935
	6:22	them that sat with *him*, the **k** said unto	935
	6:25	came in straightway with haste unto the **k**,	935
	6:26	And the **k** was exceeding sorry; *yet* for his	935
	6:27	immediately the **k** sent an executioner,	935
	15: 2	asked him, Art thou the **K** of the Jews?	935
	15: 9	Will ye that I release unto you the **K** of	935
	15:12	I shall do *unto* him whom ye call the **K**	935
	15:18	began to salute him, Hail, **K** of the Jews.	935
	15:26	was written over, THE **K** OF THE JEWS.	935
	15:32	Let Christ the **K** of Israel descend now	935
Lk	1: 5	was in the days of Herod, the **k** of Judea,	935
	14:31	Or what **k**, going to make war against	935
	14:31	going to make war against another **k**,	935
	19:38	Blessed *be* the **K** that cometh in the name	935
	23: 2	saying that he himself is Christ a **K**.	935
	23: 3	saying, Art thou the **K** of the Jews?	935
	23:37	And saying, If thou be the **K** of the Jews,	935
	23:38	Hebrew, THIS IS THE **K** OF THE JEWS.	935
Jn	1:49	the Son of God; thou art the **K** of Israel.	935
	6:15	and take him by force, to make him a **k**,	935
	12:13	Blessed *is* the **K** of Israel that cometh in	935
	12:15	behold, thy **K** cometh, sitting on an ass's	935
	18:33	said unto him, Art thou the **K** of the Jews?	935
	18:37	therefore said unto him, Art thou a **k** then?	935
	18:37	Jesus answered, Thou sayest that I am a **k**.	935
	18:39	*that* I release unto you the **K** of the Jews?	935
	19: 3	And said, Hail, **K** of the Jews:	935
	19:12	whosoever maketh himself a **k** speaketh	935
	19:14	he saith unto the Jews, Behold your **K**!	935
	19:15	saith unto them, Shall I crucify your **K**?	935
	19:15	priests answered, We have no **k** but Cesar.	935
	19:19	JESUS OF NAZARETH THE **K** OF THE	935
	19:21	to Pilate, Write not, The **K** of the Jews;	935
	19:21	but that he said, I am **K** of the Jews.	935
Ac	7:10	wisdom in the sight of Pharaoh **k** of Egypt;	935
	7:18	another **k** arose, which knew not Joseph.	935
	12: 1	about that time Herod the **k** stretched	935
	13:21	And afterward they desired a **k**: and God	935
	13:22	raised up unto them David to be their **k**;	935
	17: 7	saying that there is another **k**, *one* Jesus.	935
	25:13	And after certain days **k** Agrippa and	935
	25:14	Festus declared Paul's cause unto the **k**,	935
	25:24	**K** Agrippa, and all men which are here	935
	25:26	specially before thee, O **k** Agrippa, that,	935
	26: 2	**k** Agrippa, because I shall answer for	935
	26: 7	For which hope's sake, **k** Agrippa, I am	935
	26:13	At midday, O **k**, I saw in the way a light	935
	26:19	Whereupon, O **k** Agrippa, I was not	935
	26:26	For the **k** knoweth of these *things*, before	935
	26:27	**K** Agrippa, believest thou the prophets?	935
	26:30	spoken, the **k** rose up, and the governor,	935
2Co	11:32	**k** kept the city of the Damascenes *with a*	935
1Ti	1:17	unto the **K** eternal, immortal, invisible,	935
	6:15	the **K** of kings, and Lord of lords;	935
Heb	7: 1	For this Melchisedec, **k** of Salem, priest of	935
	7: 2	first being by interpretation **K** of	935
	7: 2	and after that also **K** of Salem, which is,	935
	7: 2	also King of Salem, which is, **K** of peace;	935
	11:27	not fearing the wrath of the **k**:	935
1Pe	2:13	whether *it be* to the **k**, as supreme;	935
	2:17	the brotherhood. Fear God. Honour the **k**.	935
Rev	9:11	And they had a **k** over them, *which is*	935
	15: 3	just and true *are* thy ways, thou **K** of saints.	935
	17:14	for he is Lord of lords, and **K** of kings:	935
	19:16	**K** OF KINGS, AND LORD OF LORDS.	935

KING'S (284) [KING]

Ge	14:17	the valley of Shaveh, which *is* the **k** dale.	4428
	39:20	place where the **k** prisoners *were* bound:	4428
Nu	20:17	we will go *by* the **k** high way, we will not	4428
	21:22	*but* we will go along by the **k** high way,	4428
1Sa	18:22	now therefore be the **k** son in law.	4428+871.1
	18:23	a light *thing* to be a **k** son in law,	4428+871.1
	18:25	to be avenged of the **k** enemies.	4428
	18:26	pleased David well to be the **k** son	4428+871.1
	18:27	that he might be the **k** son in law.	4428+871.1
	20:29	he cometh not unto the **k** table.	4428
	21: 8	because the **k** business required haste.	4428
	22:14	*is* the **k** son in law, and goeth at thy	4428
	23:20	our part *shall be* to deliver him into the **k**	4428
	26:16	see where the **k** spear *is*, and the cruse	4428
	26:22	and said, Behold, the **k** spear;	4428
2Sa	9:11	shall eat at my table, as one of the **k** sons.	4428
	9:13	for he did eat continually at the **k** table;	4428
	11: 2	and walked upon the roof of the **k** house:	4428
	11: 8	Uriah departed out of the **k** house,	4428
	11: 9	Uriah slept *at* the door of the **k** house	4428
	11:20	if so be that the **k** wrath arise, and he say	4428
	11:24	*some* of the **k** servants be dead,	4428
	12:30	he took their **k** crown from off his head,	4428
	13: 4	Why *art* thou, *being* the **k** son, lean from	4428
	13:18	for with such robes were the **k** daughters	4428
	13:23	and Absalom invited all the **k** sons.	4428
	13:27	let Amnon and all the **k** sons go with him.	4428
	13:29	all the **k** sons arose, and every man gat	4428
	13:30	Absalom hath slain all the **k** sons,	4428
	13:32	have slain all the young men the **k** sons;	4428
	13:33	to think that all the **k** sons are dead:	4428
	13:35	unto the king, Behold, the **k** sons come:	4428
	13:36	the **k** sons came, and lift up their voice	4428
	14: 1	that the **k** heart *was* toward Absalom.	4428
	14:24	to his own house, and saw not the **k** face.	4428

2Sa
14:26 two hundred shekels after the k weight. 4428
14:28 in Jerusalem, and saw not the k face. 4428
14:32 now therefore let me see the k face; 4428
15:15 the k servants said unto the king, Behold, 4428
15:35 soever thou shalt hear out of the k house, 4428
16: 2 asses be for the k household to ride on; 4428
18:12 put forth mine hand against the k son: 4428
18:18 for himself a pillar, which is in the k dale: 4428
18:20 bear no tidings, because the k son is dead. 4428
18:29 When Joab sent the k servant, and me 4428
19:18 ferry boat to carry over the k household, 4428
19:42 have we eaten at all of the k cost? or 4428
24: 4 Notwithstanding the k word prevailed 4428
1Ki
1: 9 called all his brethren the k sons, and all 4428
1: 9 and all the men of Judah the k servants: 4428
1:25 called all the k sons, and the captains 4428
1:28 she came into the k presence, 4428
1:44 they have caused him to ride upon the k 4428
1:47 moreover the k servants came to bless 4428
2:19 caused a seat to be set for the k mother; 4428
4: 5 was principal officer, and the k friend: 4428
9: 1 the k house, and all Solomon's desire 4428
9:10 the house of the LORD, and the k house, 4428
10:12 for the k house, harps also and 4428
10:28 the k merchants received the linen yarn 4428
11:14 Edomite: he was of the k seed in Edom. 4428
13: 6 the k hand was restored him again, 4428
14:26 and the treasures of the k house; 4428
14:27 which kept the door of the k house. 4428
15:18 the treasures of the k house, 4428
16:18 he went into the palace of the k house, 4428
16:18 burnt the k house over him with fire, 4428
22:12 for the LORD shall deliver it into the k 4428
22:26 of the city, and to Joash the k son; 4428
2Ki
7: 9 that we may go and tell the k household. 4428
7:11 and they told it to the k house within. 4428
9:34 and bury her: for she is a k daughter. 4428
10: 6 Now the k sons, being seventy persons, 4428
10: 7 they took the k sons, and slew seventy 4428
10: 8 have brought the heads of the k sons. 4428
11: 2 stale him from among the k sons which 4428
11: 4 of the LORD, and shewed them the k son. 4428
11: 5 be keepers of the watch of the k house; 4428
11:12 he brought forth the k son, and put 4428
11:16 which the horses came into the k house: 4428
11:19 of the gate of the guard to the k house. 4428
11:20 with the sword beside the k house. 4428
12:10 that the k scribe and the high priest came 4428
12:18 in the k house, and sent it to Hazael king 4428
13:16 Elisha put his hands upon the k hands. 4428
14:14 in the treasures of the k house, 4428
15: 5 Jotham the k son was over the house, 4428
15:25 in the palace of the k house, with Argob 4428
16: 8 in the treasures of the k house, and sent 4428
16:15 the k burnt sacrifice, and his meat 4428
16:18 in the house, and the k entry without, 4428
18:15 and in the treasures of the k house. 4428
18:36 for the k commandment was, saying, 4428
22:12 and Asahiah a servant of the k, saying, 4428
24:13 the treasures of the k house, and cut in 4428
24:15 and the k mother, and the king's wives, 4428
24:15 the k wives, and his officers, 4428
25: 4 two walls, which is by the k garden: 4428
25: 9 the k house, and all the houses of 4428
25:19 five men of them that were in the k 4428
1Ch
9:18 hitherto waited in the k gate eastward: 4428
21: 4 Nevertheless the k word prevailed against 4428
21: 6 for the k word was abominable to Joab. 4428
25: 5 All these were the sons of Heman the k 4428
25: 6 according to the k order to Asaph, 4428
27:25 over the k treasures was Azmaveth the 4428
27:32 the son of Hachmoni was with the k 4428
27:33 Ahithophel was the k counsellor: 4428+3807.1
27:33 Hushai the Archite was the k companion: 4428
27:34 and the general of the k army was Joab. 4428
29: 6 with the rulers over the k work, 4428
2Ch
1:16 the k merchants received the linen yarn 4428
7:11 the house of the LORD, and the k house: 4428
9:11 to the k palace, and harps and psalteries 4428
9:21 For the k ships went to Tarshish with 4428
12: 9 and the treasures of the k house; 4428
12:10 that kept the entrance of the k house. 4428
16: 2 house of the LORD and of the k house, 4428
18: 5 for God will deliver it into the k hand. 4428
18:25 of the city, and to Joash the k son; 4428
19:11 the house of Judah, for all the k matters: 4428
21:17 substance that was found in the k house, 4428
22:11 stole him from among the k sons that 4428
23: 3 unto them, Behold, the k son shall reign, 4428
23: 3 And a third part shall be at the k house; 4428
23:11 they brought out the k son, and put upon 4428
23:15 entering of the horse gate by the k house, 4428
23:20 came through the high gate into the k 4428
24: 8 the k commandment they made a chest, 4428
24:11 the k office by the hand of the Levites, 4428
24:11 the k scribe and the high priest's officer 4428
25:16 him, Art thou made of the k counsel? 4428
25:24 the treasures of the k house, the hostages 4428
26:11 hand of Hananiah, one of the k captains, 4428
26:21 Jotham his son was over the k house, 4428
28: 7 slew Maaseiah the k son, and Azrikam 4428
29:25 Gad the k seer, and Nathan the prophet: 4428
31: 3 He appointed also the k portion of his 4428
34:20 and Asaiah a servant of the k, saying, 4428
35: 7 these were the k substance. 4428

2Ch
35:10 according to the k commandment. 4428
35:15 Heman, and Jeduthun the k seer; 4428
Ezr
4:14 we have maintenance from the k palace, NIH
4:14 it was not meet for us to see the k 4430
5:17 let there be search made in the k treasure 4430
6: 4 let the expences be given out of the k 4430
6: 8 that of the k goods, even of the tribute 4430
7:20 bestow it out of the k treasure house. 4430
7:27 hath put such a thing as this in the k 4428
7:28 and before all the k mighty princes. 4428
8:36 they delivered the k commissions unto 4428
8:36 commissions unto the k lieutenants, 4428
Ne
1:11 of this man. For I was the k cupbearer. 4428
2: 8 Asaph the keeper of the k forest, 4428+3807.1
2: 9 the river, and gave them the k letters. 4428
2:14 the gate of the fountain, and to the k pool: 4428
2:18 as also the k words that he had spoken 4428
3:15 the wall of the pool of Siloah by the k 4428
3:25 the tower which lieth out from the k high 4428
5: 4 have borrowed money for the k tribute, 4428
11:23 it was the k commandment concerning 4428
11:24 at the k hand in all matters concerning 4428
Est
1: 5 in the court of the garden of the k palace; 4428
1:12 queen Vashti refused to come at the k 4428
1:13 was the k manner towards all that knew 4428
1:14 which saw the k face, and which sat 4428
1:18 Media say this day unto all the k princes, 4428
1:20 when the k decree which he shall make 4428
1:22 For he sent letters into all the k provinces, 4428
2: 2 said the k servants that ministered unto 4428
2: 3 unto the custody of Hege the k 4428
2: 8 the k commandment and his decree 4428
2: 8 that Esther was brought also unto the k 4428
2: 9 meet to be given her, out of the k house: 4428
2:13 house of the women unto the k house. 4428
2:14 the k chamberlain, which kept 4428
2:15 but what Hegai the k chamberlain, 4428
2:19 then Mordecai sat in the k gate. 4428
2:21 while Mordecai sat in the k gate, 4428
2:21 two of the k chamberlains, Bigthan and 4428
3: 2 all the k servants, that were in the king's 4428
3: 2 were in the k gate, bowed, 4428
3: 3 the k servants, which were in the king's 4428
3: 3 which were in the k gate, said unto 4428
3: 3 Why transgressest thou the k 4428
3: 8 all people; neither keep they the k laws; 4428
3: 8 it is not for the k profit to suffer them. 4428
3: 9 to bring it into the k treasuries. 4428
3:12 were the k scribes called on the thirteenth 4428
3:12 had commanded unto the k lieutenants, 4428
3:12 was it written, and sealed with the k ring. 4428
3:13 letters were sent by posts into all the k 4428
3:15 being hastened by the k commandment, 4428
4: 2 came even before the k gate: for none 4428
4: 2 none might enter into the k gate clothed 4428
4: 3 whithersoever the k commandment and 4428
4: 5 for Hatach, one of the k chamberlains, 4428
4: 6 of the city, which was before the k gate. 4428
4: 7 to pay to the k treasuries for the Jews, 4428
4:11 All the k servants, and the people of 4428
4:11 the people of the k provinces, do know, 4428
4:13 that thou escape in the k house, 4428
5: 1 stood in the inner court of the k house, 4428
5: 1 king's house, over against the k house: 4428
5: 9 when Haman saw Mordecai in the k gate, 4428
5:13 Mordecai the Jew sitting at the k gate. 4428
6: 2 and Teresh, two of the k chamberlains, 4428
6: 3 said the k servants that ministered unto 4428
6: 4 into the outward court of the k house, 4428
6: 5 the k servants said unto him, Behold, 4428
6: 9 hand of one of the k most noble princes, 4428
6:10 the Jew, that sitteth at the k gate: 4428
6:12 Mordecai came again to the k gate. 4428
6:14 came the k chamberlains, and hasted to 4428
7: 4 could not countervail the k damage. 4428
7: 8 As the word went out of the k mouth, 4428
7:10 Then was the k wrath pacified. 4428
8: 5 the Jews which are in all the k provinces: 4428
8: 8 in the k name, and seal it with the king's 4428
8: 8 king's name, and seal it with the k ring: 4428
8: 8 for the writing which is written in the k 4428
8: 8 with the k ring, may no man reverse. 4428
8: 9 were the k scribes called at that time in 4428
8:10 sealed it with the k ring, and sent letters 4428
8:14 and pressed on by the k commandment, 4428
8:17 whithersoever the k commandment and 4428
9: 1 the k commandment and his decree 4428
9: 4 For Mordecai was great in the k house, 4428
9:12 what have they done in the rest of the k 4428
9:16 other Jews that were in the k provinces 4428
Ps
45: 5 arrows are sharp in the heart of the k 4428
45:13 The k daughter is all glorious within: 4428
45:15 they shall enter into the k palace. 4428
61: 6 Thou wilt prolong the k life: and his years 4428
72: 1 and thy righteousness unto the k son. 4428
99: 4 The k strength also loveth judgment; 4428
Pr
14:28 The multitude of people is the k honour: 4428
14:35 The favour is toward a wise servant: 4428
16:15 In the light of the k countenance is life; 4428
19:12 The k wrath is as the roaring of a lion; 4428
21: 1 The k heart is in the hand of the LORD, 4428
Ecc
8: 2 thee to keep the k commandment, 4428
Isa
36:21 for the k commandment was, saying, 4428
Jer
22: 6 For thus saith the LORD unto the k house 4428
26:10 they came up from the k house unto 4428

Jer
36:12 he went down into the k house, into 4428
38: 7 one of the eunuchs which was in the k 4428
38: 8 went forth out of the k house, 4428
39: 4 by the way of the k garden, by the gate 4428
39: 8 the Chaldeans burnt the k house, 4428
41:10 even the k daughters, and all the people 4428
43: 6 the k daughters, and every person that 4428
52: 7 two walls, which was by the k garden; 4428
52:13 the house of the LORD, and the k house; 4428
52:25 seven men of them that were near the k 4428
Eze
17:13 hath taken of the k seed, and made a 4410
Da
1: 3 and of the k seed, and of the princes; 4410
1: 4 as had ability in them to stand in the k 4428
1: 5 them a daily provision of the k meat, 4428
1: 8 himself with the portion of the k meat, 4428
1:13 that eat of the portion of the k meat: 4428
1:15 which did eat the portion of the k meat. 4428
2:10 the earth that can shew the k matter: 4430
2:14 wisdom to Arioch the captain of the k 4430
2:15 and said to Arioch the k captain, 4430
2:23 now made known unto us the k matter. 4430
3:22 the k commandment was urgent, 4430
3:27 captains, and the k counsellers, 4430
3:28 have changed the k word, and yielded 4430
4:31 While the word was in the k mouth, 4430
5: 5 the plaister of the wall of the k palace: 4430
5: 6 the k countenance was changed, 4430
5: 8 came in all the k wise men: but they 4430
6:12 spake before the king concerning the k 4430
8:27 I rose up, and did the k business; 4428
11: 6 for the k daughter of the south shall come 4428
Am
7: 1 it was the latter growth after the k 4428
7:13 for it is the k chapel, and it is the king's 4428
7:13 is the king's chapel, and it is the k court. 4467
Zep
1: 8 the k children, and all such as are clothed 4428
Zec
14:10 from the tower of Hananeel unto the k 4428
Ac
12:20 having made Blastus the k chamberlain 935
12:20 their country was nourished by the k 937
Heb
11:23 were not afraid of the k commandment. 935

KINGDOM (342) [KING]
Ge
10:10 the beginning of his k was Babel, 4467
20: 9 brought on me and on my k a great sin? 4467
Ex
19: 6 ye shall be unto me a k of priests, 4467
Nu
24: 7 than Agag, and his k shall be exalted. 4438
32:33 the k of Sihon king of the Amorites, 4467
32:33 the k of Og king of Bashan, the land, 4467
Dt
3: 4 region of Argob, the k of Og in Bashan. 4467
3:10 and Edrei, cities of the k of Og in Bashan. 4467
3:13 and all Bashan, being the k of Og, 4467
17:18 when he sitteth upon the throne of his k, 4467
17:20 end that he may prolong his days in his k, 4467
Jos
13:12 All the k of Og king of Bashan, which reigned 4468
13:21 all the k of Sihon king of the Amorites, 4468
13:27 rest of the k of Sihon king of Heshbon, 4468
13:30 all the k of Og king of Bashan, and all 4468
13:31 and Edrei, cities of the k of Og in Bashan, 4468
1Sa
10:16 of the matter of the k, whereof Samuel 4410
10:25 told the people the manner of the k, 4410
11:14 us go to Gilgal, and renew the k there. 4410
13:13 established thy k upon Israel for ever. 4467
13:14 now thy k shall not continue: the LORD 4467
14:47 So Saul took the k over Israel, 4410
15:28 The LORD hath rent the k of Israel from 4468
18: 8 and what can he have more but the k? 4410
20:31 thou shalt not be stablished, nor thy k. 4438
24:20 that the k of Israel shall be established in 4467
28:17 for the LORD hath rent the k out of thine 4467
2Sa
3:10 To translate the k from the house of Saul, 4467
3:28 my k are guiltless before the LORD for 4467
5:12 that he had exalted his k for his people 4467
7:12 of thy bowels, and I will establish his k. 4467
7:13 I will stablish the throne of his k for ever. 4467
7:16 thy k shall be stablished for ever before 4467
16: 3 of Israel restore me the k of my father. 4468
16: 8 the LORD hath delivered thee into 4410
1Ki
1:46 Solomon sitteth on the throne of the k. 4410
2:12 and his k was established greatly. 4438
2:15 Thou knowest that the k was mine, 4410
2:15 howbeit the k is turned about, 4410
2:22 ask for him the k also; for he is mine 4410
2:46 the k was established in the hand of 4467
9: 5 I will establish the throne of thy k upon 4467
10:20 there was not the like made in any k. 4467
11:11 I will surely rend the k from thee, 4467
11:13 Howbeit I will not rend away all the k; 4467
11:31 I will rent the k out of the hand of 4467
11:34 Howbeit I will not take the whole k out 4467
11:35 I will take the k out of his son's hand, 4410
12:21 to bring the k again to Rehoboam the son 4410
12:26 Now shall the k return to the house of 4467
14: 8 rent the k away from the house of David, 4467
18:10 thy God liveth, there is no nation or k, 4467
18:10 He is not there; he took an oath of the k 4467
21: 7 Dost thou now govern the k of Israel? 4410
2Ki
14: 5 soon as the k was confirmed in his hand, 4467
15:19 be with him to confirm the k in his hand. 4467
1Ch
10:14 turned the k unto David the son of Jesse. 4410
11:10 themselves with him in his k, 4438
12:23 to Hebron, to turn the k of Saul to him, 4438
14: 2 for his k was lift up on high, because of 4438
16:20 and from one k to another people; 4467
17:11 be of thy sons; and I will stablish his k. 4438
17:14 him in mine house and in my k for ever: 4438
22:10 I will establish the throne of his k over 4438

K

1Ch 28: 5 throne of the **k** of the Lord over Israel. 4438
28: 7 Moreover I will establish his **k** for ever, 4438
29:11 and in the earth *is thine;* thine *is* the **k,** 4467
2Ch 1: 1 son of David was strengthened in his **k,** 4438
2: 1 name of the Lord, and a house for his **k.** 4438
2:12 for the Lord, and a house for his **k.** 4438
7:18 will I stablish the throne of thy **k,** 4438
9:19 There was not the like made in any **k.** 4467
11: 1 that *he* might bring the **k** again to 4438
11:17 So they strengthened the **k** of Judah, 4438
12: 1 when Rehoboam had established the **k,** 4438
13: 5 gave the **k** over Israel to David for ever, 4467
13: 8 now ye think to withstand the **k** of 4467
14: 5 images: and the **k** was quiet before him. 4467
17: 5 Therefore the Lord stablished the **k** in 4467
21: 3 the **k** gave he to Jehoram; because he 4467
21: 4 when Jehoram was risen up to the **k** 4467
22: 9 Ahaziah had no power to keep still the **k.** 4467
23:20 and set the king upon the throne of the **k.** 4467
25: 3 pass, when the **k** was established to him, 4467
29:21 for a sin offering for the **k,** and for 4467
32:15 **k** was able to deliver his people out of 4467
33:13 brought him again *to* Jerusalem into his **k.** 4438
36:20 his sons until the reign of the **k** of Persia: 4438
36:22 made a proclamation throughout all his **k,** 4438
Ezr 1: 1 made a proclamation throughout all his **k,** 4438
Ne 9:35 For they have not served thee in their **k,** 4438
Est 1: 2 king Ahasuerus sat on the throne of his **k,** 4438
1: 4 he shewed the riches of his glorious **k** 4438
1:14 *and* which sat the first in the **k;**) 4438
2: 3 officers in all the provinces of his **k,** 4438
3: 6 throughout the whole **k** of Ahasuerus, 4438
3: 8 the people in all the provinces of thy **k;** 4438
4:14 art come to the **k** for *such* a time as this? 4438
5: 3 be even given thee to the half of the **k.** 4438
5: 6 even to the half of the **k** it shall be 4438
7: 2 be performed, *even* to the half of the **k.** 4438
9:30 seven provinces of the **k** of Ahasuerus, 4438
Ps 22:28 For the **k** *is* the Lord's: and *he is* 4410
45: 6 the sceptre of thy **k** *is* a right sceptre. 4438
103:19 in the heavens; and his **k** ruleth over all. 4438
105:13 another, from *one* **k** to another people; 4467
145:11 They shall speak of the glory of thy **k,** 4438
145:12 and the glorious majesty of his **k.** 4438
145:13 Thy **k** *is* an everlasting kingdom, 4438
145:13 Thy kingdom *is* an everlasting **k,** 4438
Ecc 4:14 whereas also *he that is* born in his **k** 4438
Isa 9: 7 upon his **k,** to order it, and to stablish it 4467
17: 3 the **k** from Damascus, and the remnant of 4467
19: 2 city against city, *and* **k** against kingdom. 4467
19: 2 city against city, *and* kingdom against **k.** 4467
34:12 They shall call the nobles thereof *to* the **k,** 4410
60:12 and **k** that will not serve thee shall perish; 4467
Jer 18: 7 concerning a nation and concerning a **k,** 4467
18: 9 concerning a nation, *to* build and *to* plant *it;* 4467
27: 8 **k** which will not serve the same 4467
La 2:2 hath polluted the **k** and the princes 4410
Eze 16:13 and thou didst prosper into a **k.** 4410
17:14 That the **k** might be base, that *it* might 4467
29:14 and they shall be there a base **k.** 4467
Da 2:37 the God of heaven hath given thee a **k,** 4437
2:39 after thee shall arise another **k** inferior to 4437
2:39 another third **k** of brass, which shall bear 4437
2:40 the fourth **k** shall be strong as iron: 4437
2:41 and part of iron, the **k** shall be divided; 4437
2:42 *so* the **k** shall be partly strong, 4437
2:44 kings shall the God of heaven set up a **k,** 4437
2:44 the **k** shall not be left to other people, 4437
4: 3 his **k** *is* an everlasting kingdom, 4437
4: 3 his kingdom *is* an everlasting **k,** 4437
4:17 that the most High ruleth in the **k** of men, 4437
4:18 forasmuch as all the wise *men* of my **k** 4437
4:25 that the most High ruleth in the **k** of men, 4437
4:26 thy **k** *shall be* sure unto thee, after that 4437
4:29 walked in the palace of the **k** of Babylon. 4437
4:30 that I have built for the house of the **k** by 4437
4:31 it is spoken; The **k** is departed from thee. 4437
4:32 the most High ruleth in the **k** of men, 4437
4:34 his **k** *is* from generation to generation: 4437
4:36 for the glory of my **k,** mine honour and 4437
4:36 I was established in my **k,** 4437
5: 7 and shall be the third ruler in the **k.** 4437
5:11 There is a man in thy **k,** in whom *is* 4437
5:16 and shalt be the third ruler in the **k.** 4437
5:18 God gave Nebuchadnezzar thy father a **k,** 4437
5:21 the most high God ruled in the **k** of men, 4437
5:26 God hath numbered thy **k,** and finished it. 4437
5:28 Thy **k** is divided, and given to the Medes 4437
5:29 that *he* should be the third ruler in the **k.** 4437
5:31 Darius the Median took the **k,** *being* 4437
6: 1 It pleased Darius to set over the **k** an 4437
6: 1 which should be over the whole **k;** 4437
6: 4 occasion against Daniel concerning the **k;** 4437
6: 7 All the presidents of the **k,** the governors, 4437
6:26 That in every dominion of my **k** *men* 4437
6:26 his **k** *that* which shall not be destroyed, 4437
7:14 glory, and a **k,** that all people, nations, 4437
7:14 his **k** *that* which shall not be destroyed, 4437
7:18 saints of the most High shall take the **k,** 4437
7:18 possess the **k** for ever, even for ever and 4437
7:22 time came that the saints possessed the **k.** 4437
7:23 The fourth beast shall be the fourth **k** 4437
7:24 the ten horns out of this **k** *are* ten kings 4437
7:27 the **k** and dominion, and the greatness of 4437
7:27 the greatness of the **k** under the whole 4437

Da 7:27 whose **k** *is* an everlasting kingdom, 4437
7:27 whose kingdom *is* an everlasting **k,** 4437
8:23 in the latter time of their **k,** when 4438
10:13 the prince of the **k** of Persia withstood me 4438
11: 4 his **k** shall be broken, and shall be divided 4438
11: 4 his **k** shall be pluckt up, even for others 4438
11: 9 king of the south shall come into his **k,** 4438
11:17 to enter with the strength of his whole **k,** 4438
11:20 a raiser of taxes *in* the glory of the **k:** 4438
11:21 they shall not give the honour of the **k:** 4438
11:21 peaceably, and obtain the **k** by flatteries. 4438
Hos 1: 4 will cause to cease the **k** of the house of 4468
Am 9: 8 of the Lord God *are* upon the sinful **k,** 4467
Ob 1:21 of Esau; and the **k** shall be the Lord's. 4410
Mic 4: 8 the **k** shall come to the daughter of 4467
Mt 3: 2 Repent: for the **k** of heaven is at hand. 932
4:17 Repent: for the **k** of heaven is at hand. 932
4:23 and preaching the gospel of the **k,** 932
5: 3 poor in spirit: for theirs is the **k** of heaven. 932
5:10 for theirs is the **k** of heaven. 932
5:19 he shall be called the least in the **k** of 932
5:19 shall be called great in the **k** of heaven. 932
5:20 shall in no case enter into the **k** of heaven. 932
6:10 Thy **k** come. Thy will be done in earth, as 932
6:13 For thine is the **k,** and the power, 932
6:33 But seek ye first the **k** of God, 932
7:21 Lord, shall enter into the **k** of heaven. 932
8:11 and Isaac, and Jacob, in the **k** of heaven. 932
8:12 But the children of the **k** shall be cast out 932
9:35 and preaching the gospel of the **k,** 932
10: 7 preach, saying, The **k** of heaven is at hand. 932
11:11 notwithstanding he that is least in the **k** of 932
11:12 now the **k** of heaven suffereth violence, 932
12:26 against himself; how shall then his **k** stand? 932
12:28 God, then the **k** of God is come unto you. 932
13:11 to know the mysteries of the **k** of heaven, 932
13:19 When any one heareth the word of the **k,** 932
13:24 The **k** of heaven is likened unto a man 932
13:31 The **k** of heaven is like unto a grain of 932
13:33 The **k** of heaven is like unto leaven, which 932
13:38 the good seed are the children of the **k;** 932
13:41 they shall gather out of his **k** all things that 932
13:43 forth as the sun in the **k** of their Father. 932
13:44 the **k** of heaven is like unto treasure hid in 932
13:45 the **k** of heaven is like unto a merchant 932
13:47 Again, the **k** of heaven is like unto a net, 932
13:52 **k** of heaven is like unto a man *that is* a 932
16:19 I will give unto thee the keys of the **k** of 932
16:28 they see the Son of man coming in his **k.** 932
18: 1 Who is the greatest in the **k** of heaven? 932
18: 3 ye shall not enter into the **k** of heaven. 932
18: 4 the same is greatest in the **k** of heaven. 932
18:23 Therefore is the **k** of heaven likened unto 932
19:12 eunuchs for the **k** of heaven's sake. 932
19:14 unto me: for of such is the **k** of heaven. 932
19:23 a rich *man* shall hardly enter into the **k** 932
19:24 than for a rich *man* to enter into the **k** of 932
20: 1 the **k** of heaven is like unto a man *that is* 932
20:21 hand, and the other on the left, in thy **k.** 932
21:31 harlots go into the **k** of God before you. 932
21:43 The **k** of God shall be taken from you, 932
22: 2 The **k** of heaven is like unto a certain king, 932
23:13 ye shut up the **k** of heaven against men: 932
24: 7 rise against nation, and **k** against kingdom: 932
24: 7 rise against nation, and kingdom against **k:** 932
24:14 this gospel of the **k** shall be preached in 932
25: 1 shall the **k** of heaven be likened unto 932
25:14 For *the* **k** *of heaven is* as a man travelling NIG
25:34 inherit the **k** prepared for you from 932
26:29 I drink it new with you in my Father's **k.** 932
Mk 1:14 preaching the gospel of the **k** of God, 932
1:15 is fulfilled, and the **k** of God is at hand: 932
3:24 And if a **k** be divided against itself, 932
3:24 divided against itself, that **k** cannot stand. 932
4:11 to know the mystery of the **k** of God: 932
4:26 he said, So is the **k** of God, as if a man 932
4:30 Whereunto shall we liken the **k** of God? 932
6:23 I will give *it* thee, unto the half of my **k.** 932
9: 1 till they have seen the **k** of God come with 932
9:47 better for thee to enter into the **k** of God 932
10:14 them not: for of such is the **k** of God. 932
10:15 Whosoever shall not receive the **k** of God 932
10:23 that have riches enter into the **k** of God! 932
10:24 trust in riches to enter into the **k** of God! 932
10:25 than for a rich *man* to enter into the **k** of 932
11:10 Blessed *be* the **k** of our father David, 932
12:34 Thou art not far from the **k** of God. 932
13: 8 rise against nation, and **k** against kingdom: 932
13: 8 rise against nation, and kingdom against **k:** 932
14:25 until that day that I drink it new in the **k** of 932
15:43 which also waited for the **k** of God, came, 932
Lk 1:33 for ever; and of his **k** there shall be no end. 932
4:43 I must preach the **k** of God to other cities 932
6:20 *be ye* poor: for yours is the **k** of God. 932
7:28 he that is least in the **k** of God is greater 932
8: 1 shewing the glad tidings of the **k** of God: 932
8:10 to know the mysteries of the **k** of God, 932
9: 2 And he sent them to preach the **k** of God, 932
9:11 and spake unto them of the **k** of God, 932
9:27 taste of death, till they see the **k** of God. 932
9:60 but go thou and preach the **k** of God. 932
9:62 and looking back, is fit for the **k** of God. 932
10: 9 The **k** of God is come nigh unto you. 932
10:11 that the **k** of God is come nigh unto you. 932

Lk 11: 2 Thy **k** come. Thy will be done, as in 932
11:17 Every **k** divided against itself is brought to 932
11:18 against himself, how shall his **k** stand? 932
11:20 no doubt the **k** of God is come upon you. 932
12:31 But rather seek ye the **k** of God; 932
12:32 Father's good pleasure to give you the **k.** 932
13:18 said he, Unto what is the **k** of God like? 932
13:20 Whereunto shall I liken the **k** of God? 932
13:28 in the **k** of God, and you yourselves thrust 932
13:29 south, and shall sit down in the **k** of God. 932
14:15 Blessed *is he* that shall eat bread in the **k** 932
16:16 since that time the **k** of God is preached, 932
17:20 when the **k** of God should come, 932
17:20 The **k** of God cometh not with observation: 932
17:21 for behold, the **k** of God is within you. 932
18:16 forbid them not: for of such is the **k** of God. 932
18:17 Whosoever shall not receive the **k** of God 932
18:24 that have riches enter into the **k** of God! 932
18:25 than for a rich *man* to enter into the **k** of God! 932
18:29 wife, or children, for the **k** of God's sake, 932
19:11 they thought that the **k** of God should 932
19:12 a far country to receive for himself a **k,** 932
19:15 received the **k,** then he commanded 932
21:10 rise against nation, and **k** against kingdom: 932
21:10 rise against nation, and kingdom against **k:** 932
21:31 know ye that the **k** of God is nigh at hand. 932
22:16 until it be fulfilled in the **k** of God. 932
22:18 of the vine, until the **k** of God shall come. 932
22:29 And I appoint unto you a **k,** as my Father 932
22:30 ye may eat and drink at my table in my **k,** 932
23:42 me when thou comest into thy **k.** 932
23:51 who also himself waited for the **k** of God. 932
Jn 3: 3 be born again, he cannot see the **k** of God. 932
3: 5 Spirit, he cannot enter into the **k** of God. 932
18:36 Jesus answered, My **k** is not of this world: 932
18:36 of this world: if my **k** were of this world, 932
18:36 the Jews: but now is my **k** not from hence. 932
Ac 1: 3 speaking of the *things* pertaining to the **k** 932
1: 6 wilt thou at this time restore again the **k** to 932
8:12 the *things* concerning the **k** of God, 932
14:22 much tribulation enter into the **k** of God. 932
19: 8 persuading the *things* concerning the **k** 932
20:25 among whom I have gone preaching the **k** 932
28:23 he expounded and testified the **k** of God, 932
28:31 Preaching the **k** of God, and teaching those 932
Ro 14:17 For the **k** of God is not meat and drink; 932
1Co 4:20 For the **k** of God *is* not in word, 932
6: 9 unrighteous shall not inherit the **k** of God? 932
6:10 nor extortioners, shall inherit the **k** of God. 932
15:24 when he shall have delivered up the **k** to 932
15:50 and blood cannot inherit the **k** of God; 932
Gal 5:21 such *things* shall not inherit the **k** of God. 932
Eph 5: 5 hath *any* inheritance in the **k** of Christ and 932
Col 1:13 translated *us* into the **k** of his dear Son: 932
4:11 only *are my* fellowworkers unto the **k** 932
1Th 2:12 who hath called you unto his **k** and glory. 932
2Th 1: 5 that ye may be counted worthy of the **k** of 932
2Ti 4: 1 and the dead at his appearing and his **k;** 932
4:18 and will preserve *me* unto his heavenly **k:** 932
Heb 1: 8 of righteousness *is* the sceptre of thy **k.** 932
12:28 Wherefore we receiving a **k** which cannot 932
Jas 2: 5 heirs of the **k** which he hath promised to 932
2Pe 1:11 into the everlasting **k** of our Lord 932
Rev 1: 9 and in the **k** and patience of Jesus Christ, 932
12:10 and the **k** of our God, and the power of his 932
16:10 and his **k** was full of darkness; 932
17:12 ten kings, which have received no **k** as yet; 932
17:17 to agree, and give their **k** unto the beast, 932

KINGDOMS (57) [KING]

Dt 3:21 shall the Lord do unto all the **k** whither 4467
28:25 be removed into all the **k** of the earth. 4467
Jos 11:10 beforetime *was* the head of all those **k.** 4467
1Sa 10:18 out of the hand of all **k,** *and* of them that 4467
1Ki 4:21 Solomon reigned over all **k** from the river 4467
2Ki 19:15 *even* thou alone, of all the **k** of the earth; 4467
19:19 that all the **k** of the earth may know that 4467
1Ch 29:30 and over all the **k** of the countries. 4467
2Ch 12: 8 and the service of the **k** of the countries. 4467
17:10 the fear of the Lord fell upon all the **k** of 4467
20: 6 rulest *not* thou over all the **k** of 4467
20:29 fear of God was on all the **k** of *those* 4467
36:23 All the **k** of the earth hath the Lord God 4467
Ezr 1: 2 hath given me all the **k** of the earth; 4467
Ne 9:22 thou gavest them **k** and nations, 4467
Ps 46: 6 The heathen raged, the **k** were moved: 4467
68:32 Sing unto God, ye **k** of the earth; O sing 4467
79: 6 upon the **k** that have not called upon thy 4467
102:22 and the **k,** to serve the Lord. 4467
135:11 king of Bashan, and all the **k** of Canaan: 4467
Isa 10:10 As my hand hath found the **k** of the idols, 4467
13: 4 a tumultuous noise of the **k** of nations 4467
13:19 Babylon, the glory of **k,** the beauty of 4467
14:16 the earth to tremble, that did shake **k;** 4467
23:11 his hand over the sea, he shook the **k:** 4467
23:17 shall commit fornication with all the **k** of 4467
37:16 *even* thou alone, of all the **k** of the earth: 4467
37:20 that all the **k** of the earth may know that 4467
47: 5 shalt no more be called, The lady of **k.** 4467
Jer 1:10 set thee over the nations and over the **k,** 4467
1:15 I will call all the families of the **k** of 4467
10: 7 in all their **k,** *there is* none like unto thee. 4438
15: 4 I will cause them to be removed into all **k** 4467
24: 9 into all the **k** of the earth for *their* hurt, 4467
25:26 with another, and all the **k** of the world, 4467

Jer	28: 8 against great **k**, of war, and of evil,
	29:18 deliver them to be removed to all the **k**
	34: 1 all the **k** of the earth of his dominion,
	34:17 to be removed into all the **k** of the earth.
	49:28 and concerning the **k** of Hazor,
	51:20 nations, and with thee will I destroy **k**:
	51:27 call together against her the **k** of Ararat,
Eze	29:15 It shall be the basest of the **k**; neither
	37:22 neither shall they be divided into two **k**
Da	2:44 break in pieces and consume all these **k**,
	7:23 which shall be diverse from all **k**,
	8:22 four **k** shall stand up out of the nation,
Am	6: 2 *they* better than these **k**? or their border
Na	3: 5 thy nakedness, and the **k** thy shame.
Zep	3: 8 that I may assemble the **k**, to pour upon
Hag	2:22 I will overthrow the throne of **k**, and I
	2:22 I will destroy the strength of the **k** of
Mt	4: 8 and sheweth him all the **k** of the world,
Lk	4: 5 shewed unto him all the **k** of the world in
Heb	11:33 Who through faith subdued **k**,
Rev	11:15 The **k** of *this* world are become
	11:15 *this* world are become *the* **k** of our Lord,

4467, 4467, 4467, 4467, 4467, 4467, 4467, 4467, 4467, 4437, 4437, 4438, 4467, 4467, 4467, 4467, 4467, 932, 932, 932, 932, NIG

KINGLY (1) [KING]

Da 5:20 he was deposed from his **k** throne, 4437

KINGS (329) [KING]

Ge	14: 5 the **k** that *were* with him, and smote
	14: 9 Arioch king of Ellasar; four **k** with five.
	14:10 the **k** of Sodom and Gomorrah fled,
	14:17 of the **k** that *were* with him, at the valley
	17: 6 of thee, and **k** shall come out of thee.
	17:16 of nations; **k** of people shall be of her.
	35:11 of thee, and **k** shall come out of thy loins;
	36:31 these *are* the **k** that reigned in the land
Nu	31: 8 they slew the **k** of Midian, beside *the rest*
	31: 8 and Hur, and Reba, five **k** of Midian:
Dt	3: 8 **k** of the Amorites the land that *was* on
	3:21 your God hath done unto these two **k**:
	4:47 Og king of Bashan, two **k** of the Amorites,
	7:24 he shall deliver their **k** into thine hand,
	31: 4 **k** of the Amorites, and unto the land of
Jos	2:10 what you did unto the two **k** of
	5: 1 to pass, when all the **k** of the Amorites,
	5: 1 all the **k** of the Canaanites, which *were*
	9: 1 when all the **k** which *were* on *this* side
	9:10 that he did to the two **k** of the Amorites,
	10: 5 Therefore the five **k** of the Amorites,
	10: 6 for all the **k** of the Amorites that dwell in
	10:16 these five **k** fled, and hid themselves in a
	10:17 The five **k** are found hid in a cave at
	10:22 bring out those five **k** unto me out of
	10:23 brought forth those five **k** unto him out
	10:24 they brought out those **k** unto Joshua,
	10:24 put your feet upon the necks of these **k**.
	10:40 vale, and of the springs, and all their **k**:
	10:42 all these **k** and their land did Joshua take
	11: 2 to the **k** that *were* on the north of
	11: 5 when all these **k** were met together,
	11:12 all the cities of those **k**, and all the kings
	11:12 all of them, did Joshua take,
	11:17 and all their **k** he took, and smote them,
	11:18 made war a long time with all those **k**.
	12: 1 Now these *are* the **k** of the land, which
	12: 7 *are* the **k** of the country which Joshua
	12:24 of Tirzah, one: all the **k** thirty and one.
	24:12 you, *even* the two **k** of the Amorites.
Jdg	1: 7 Threescore and ten **k**, having their
	5: 3 Hear, O ye **k**; give ear, O ye princes;
	5:19 The **k** came *and* fought, then fought
	5:19 fought the **k** of Canaan in Taanach by
	8: 5 after Zebah and Zalmunna, **k** of Midian.
	8:12 took the two **k** of Midian, Zebah and
	8:26 raiment that *was* on the **k** of Midian.
1Sa	14:47 against the **k** of Zobah, and against
	27: 6 wherefore Ziklag pertaineth unto the **k** of
2Sa	10:19 when all the **k** *that were* servants to
	11: 1 at the time when **k** go forth *to battle*, that
1Ki	3:13 there shall not be any among the **k** like
	4:24 over all the **k** on *this* side the river:
	4:34 from all **k** of the earth, which had heard
	10:15 all the **k** of Arabia, and *of* the governors
	10:23 So king Solomon exceeded all the **k** of
	10:29 so for all the **k** of the Hittites, and for
	10:29 of the Hittites, and for the **k** of Syria,
	14:19 book of the chronicles of the **k** of Israel.
	14:29 book of the chronicles of the **k** of Judah?
	15: 7 book of the chronicles of the **k** of Judah?
	15:23 book of the chronicles of the **k** of Judah?
	15:31 book of the chronicles of the **k** of Israel?
	16: 5 book of the chronicles of the **k** of Israel?
	16:14 book of the chronicles of the **k** of Israel?
	16:20 book of the chronicles of the **k** of Israel?
	16:27 book of the chronicles of the **k** of Israel?
	16:33 all the **k** of Israel that were before him.
	20: 1 *there were* thirty and two **k** with him,
	20:12 drinking, he and the **k** in the pavilions,
	20:16 he and the **k**, the thirty and two kings
	20:16 the thirty and two **k** that helped him.
	20:24 do this thing, Take the **k** away, every
	20:31 we have heard that the **k** of the house of
	20:31 of the house of Israel *are* merciful **k**:
	22:39 book of the chronicles of the **k** of Israel?
	22:45 book of the chronicles of the **k** of Judah?
2Ki	1:18 book of the chronicles of the **k** of Israel?

Number column: all 4428 except Nu 31:8 entries (4428, 4428), etc. — all 4428

2Ki	3:10 that the LORD hath called these three **k**
	3:13 for the LORD hath called these three **k**
	3:21 when all the Moabites heard that the **k**
	3:23 the **k** are surely slain, and they have
	7: 6 king of Israel hath hired against us the **k**
	7: 6 the **k** of the Egyptians, to come upon us.
	8:18 he walked in the way of the **k** of Israel,
	8:23 book of the chronicles of the **k** of Judah?
	10: 4 said, Behold, two **k** stood not before him:
	10:34 book of the chronicles of the **k** of Israel?
	11:19 And he sat on the throne of the **k**.
	12:18 and Ahaziah, his fathers, **k** of Judah,
	12:19 book of the chronicles of the **k** of Judah?
	13: 8 book of the chronicles of the **k** of Israel?
	13:12 book of the chronicles of the **k** of Israel?
	13:13 Joash was buried in Samaria with the **k**
	14:15 book of the chronicles of the **k** of Israel?
	14:16 buried in Samaria with the **k** of Israel;
	14:18 book of the chronicles of the **k** of Judah?
	14:28 book of the chronicles of the **k** of Israel?
	14:29 his fathers, *even* with the **k** of Israel;
	15: 6 book of the chronicles of the **k** of Judah?
	15:11 book of the chronicles of the **k** of Israel.
	15:15 book of the chronicles of the **k** of Israel?
	15:21 book of the chronicles of the **k** of Israel?
	15:26 book of the chronicles of the **k** of Israel.
	15:31 book of the chronicles of the **k** of Israel.
	15:36 book of the chronicles of the **k** of Judah?
	16: 3 he walked in the way of the **k** of Israel,
	16:19 book of the chronicles of the **k** of Judah?
	17: 2 as the **k** of Israel that were before him.
	17: 8 of the **k** of Israel, which they had made.
	18: 5 none like him among all the **k** of Judah,
	19:11 thou hast heard what the **k** of Assyria
	19:17 **k** of Assyria have destroyed the nations
	20:20 book of the chronicles of the **k** of Judah?
	21:17 book of the chronicles of the **k** of Judah?
	21:25 book of the chronicles of the **k** of Judah?
	23: 5 the **k** of Judah had ordained to burn
	23:11 took away the horses that the **k** of Judah
	23:12 which the **k** of Judah had made,
	23:19 the **k** of Israel had made to provoke
	23:22 nor *in* all the days of the **k** of Israel, nor
	23:22 the kings of Israel, nor of the **k** of Judah;
	23:28 book of the chronicles of the **k** of Judah?
	24: 5 book of the chronicles of the **k** of Judah?
	25:28 set his throne above the throne of the **k**
1Ch	1:43 these *are* the **k** that reigned in the land
	9: 1 they *were* written in the book of the **k** of
	16:21 yea, he reproved **k** for their sakes,
	19: 9 the **k** that were come *were* by themselves
	20: 1 at the time that **k** go out *to battle*, Joab
2Ch	1:12 such as none of the **k** have had that *have*
	1:17 brought they out *horses* for all the **k** of
	1:17 and *for* the **k** of Syria, by their means.
	9:14 all the **k** of Arabia and governors of
	9:22 king Solomon passed all the **k** of the earth
	9:23 all the **k** of the earth sought the presence
	9:26 he reigned over all the **k** from the river
	16:11 they *are* written in the book of the **k** of
	20:34 who is mentioned in the book of the **k** of
	21: 6 he walked in the way of the **k** of Israel,
	21:13 hast walked in the way of the **k** of Israel,
	21:20 David, but not in the sepulchres of the **k**.
	24:16 him in the city of David among the **k**,
	24:25 buried him not in the sepulchres of the **k**.
	24:27 written in the story of the book of the **k**.
	25:26 they not written in the book of the **k** of
	26:23 of the burial which *belonged* to the **k**;
	27: 7 lo they *are* written in the book of the **k** of
	28: 2 For he walked in the ways of the **k** of
	28:16 that time did king Ahaz send unto the **k**
	28:23 Because the gods of the **k** of Syria help
	28:26 they *are* written in the book of the **k** of
	28:27 not into the sepulchres of the **k** of Israel:
	30: 6 are escaped out of the hand of the **k** of
	32: 4 Why should the **k** of Assyria come,
	32:32 *and* in the book of the **k** of Judah and
	33:18 they *are written* in the book of the **k** of
	34:11 to floor the houses which the **k** of Judah
	35:18 neither did all the **k** of Israel keep such a
	35:27 they *are* written in the book of the **k** of
	36: 8 they *are* written in the book of the **k** of
Ezr	4:13 shalt endamage the revenue of the **k**.
	4:15 hurtful unto **k** and provinces, and that
	4:19 old time *hath* made insurrection against **k**,
	4:20 There have been mighty **k** also over
	4:22 should damage grow to the hurt of the **k**?
	6:12 his name to dwell there destroy all **k**
	7:12 Artaxerxes, king of **k**, unto Ezra the
	9: 7 iniquities have we, our **k**, *and* our priests,
	9: 7 been delivered into the hand of the **k** of
	9: 7 unto us in the sight of the **k** of Persia,
Ne	9:24 with their **k**, and the people of the land,
	9:32 our **k**, on our princes, and on our priests,
	9:32 since the time of the **k** of Assyria unto
	9:34 Neither have our **k**, our princes,
	9:37 it yieldeth much increase unto the **k**
Est	10: 2 book of the chronicles of the **k** of Media
Job	3:14 With **k** and counsellors of the earth,
	12:18 He looseth the bond of **k**, and girdeth
	36: 7 with **k** *are they* on the throne; yea, he
Ps	2: 2 The **k** of the earth set themselves,
	2:10 Be wise now therefore, O ye **k**:
	48: 4 For lo, the **k** were assembled, they passed

Number column: all 4428 except Ezr entries 4:13–6:12 are 4430, and 7:12 onward 4428

Ps	68:12 **K** of armies did flee apace: and she that
	68:14 When the Almighty scattered **k** in it,
	68:29 Because of thy temple at Jerusalem shall **k**
	72:10 The **k** of Tarshish and *of* the isles shall
	72:10 the **k** of Sheba and Seba shall offer gifts.
	72:11 Yea, all **k** shall fall down before him:
	76:12 *he is* terrible to the **k** of the earth.
	89:27 firstborn, higher than the **k** of the earth.
	102:15 and all the **k** of the earth thy glory.
	105:14 yea, he reproved **k** for their sakes;
	105:30 in abundance, in the chambers of their **k**.
	110: 5 strike through **k** in the day of his wrath.
	119:46 speak of thy testimonies also before **k**,
	135:10 smote great nations, and slew mighty **k**;
	136:17 him which smote great **k**: for his mercy
	136:18 slew famous **k**: for his mercy *endureth*
	138: 4 All the **k** of the earth shall praise thee,
	144:10 *It is he* that giveth salvation unto **k**:
	148:11 of the earth, and all people; princes,
	149: 8 To bind their **k** with chains,
Pr	8:15 By me **k** reign, and princes decree justice.
	16:12 *It is* an abomination to **k** to commit
	16:13 Righteous lips *are* the delight of **k**;
	22:29 he shall stand before **k**; he shall not stand
	25: 2 the honour of **k** *is* to search out a matter.
	25: 3 and the heart of **k** *is* unsearchable.
	31: 3 nor thy ways to *that which* destroyeth **k**.
	31: 4 *is* not for **k**, O Lemuel, *it is* not for kings
	31: 4 O Lemuel, *it is* not for **k** to drink wine;
Ecc	2: 8 the peculiar treasure of **k** and of
Isa	1: 1 Jotham, Ahaz, *and* Hezekiah, **k** of Judah.
	7:16 abhorrest shall be forsaken of both her **k**?
	10: 8 he saith, *Are* not my princes altogether **k**?
	14: 9 hath raised up from their thrones all the **k**
	14:18 All the **k** of the nations, *even* all of them,
	19:11 the son of the wise, the son of ancient **k**?
	24:21 and the **k** of the earth upon the earth.
	37:11 thou hast heard what the **k** of Assyria
	37:18 the **k** of Assyria have laid waste all
	41: 2 before him, and made *him* rule over **k**?
	45: 1 I will loose the loins of **k**, to open before
	49: 7 a servant of rulers, **K** shall see and arise,
	49:23 **k** shall be thy nursing fathers,
	52:15 the **k** shall shut their mouths at him:
	60: 3 and **k** to the brightness of thy rising.
	60:10 and their **k** shall minister unto thee:
	60:11 and *that their* **k** *may be* brought.
	60:16 Gentiles, and shalt suck the breast of **k**:
	62: 2 see thy righteousness, and all **k** thy glory:
Jer	1:18 against the **k** of Judah, against the princes
	2:26 their **k**, their princes, and their priests,
	8: 1 they shall bring out the bones of the **k** of
	13:13 even the **k** that sit upon David's throne,
	17:19 whereby the **k** of Judah come in, and by
	17:20 ye **k** of Judah, and all Judah, and all
	17:25 there enter into the gates of this city **k**
	19: 3 **k** of Judah, and inhabitants of Jerusalem;
	19: 4 nor the **k** of Judah, and have filled this
	19:13 and the houses of the **k** of Judah,
	20: 5 all the treasures of the **k** of Judah will I
	22: 4 house **k** sitting upon the throne of David,
	25:14 great **k** shall serve themselves of them
	25:18 and the **k** thereof, and the princes thereof,
	25:20 all the **k** of the land of Uz, and all the
	25:20 all the **k** of the land of the Philistines,
	25:22 all the **k** of Tyrus, and all the kings of
	25:22 all the **k** of Zidon, and the kings of the
	25:22 the **k** of the isles which *are* beyond the
	25:24 all the **k** of Arabia, and all the kings of
	25:24 all the **k** of the mingled people that dwell
	25:25 all the **k** of Zimri, and all the kings of
	25:25 all the **k** of Elam, and all the kings of
	25:25 kings of Elam, and all the **k** of the Medes,
	25:26 all the **k** of the north, far and near, one
	27: 7 and great **k** shall serve themselves of him.
	32:32 they, their **k**, their princes, their priests,
	33: 4 concerning the houses of the **k** of Judah,
	34: 5 the former **k** which were before thee,
	44: 9 the wickedness of the **k** of Judah,
	44:17 and our fathers, our **k**, and our princes,
	44:21 your **k**, and your princes, and the people
	46:25 and Egypt, with their gods, and their **k**;
	50:41 many **k** shall be raised up from the coasts
	51:11 raised up the spirit of the **k** of the Medes:
	51:28 Prepare against her the nations with the **k**
	52:32 set his throne above the throne of the **k**
La	4:12 The **k** of the earth, and all the inhabitants
Eze	26: 7 a king of **k**, from the north, with horses,
	27:33 thou didst enrich the **k** of the earth with
	27:35 their **k** shall be sore afraid, they shall be
	28:17 I will lay thee before **k**, that *they* may
	32:10 their **k** shall be horribly afraid for thee,
	32:29 There *is* Edom, her **k**, and all her princes,
	43: 7 *neither* they, nor their **k**, by their
	43: 7 nor by the carcases of their **k** in *their high*
	43: 9 the carcases of their **k**, far from me,
Da	2:21 he removeth **k**, and setteth up kings:
	2:21 he removeth kings, and setteth up **k**:
	2:37 Thou, O king, *art* a king of **k**: for the God
	2:44 in the days of these **k** shall the God of
	2:47 a Lord of **k**, and a revealer of secrets,
	7:17 great beasts, which *are* four, *are* four **k**,
	7:24 ten horns out of this kingdom *are* ten **k**
	7:24 the first, and he shall subdue three **k**.
	8:20 having two horns *are* the **k** of Media

Number column (right): 4428 throughout, except Da 2:21 (4430), 2:21 (4430), 2:37 (4430), 2:44 (4430), 2:47 (4430), 7:17 (4430), 7:24 (4430), 7:24 (4430), 8:20 (4428)

K

Da	9: 6 which spake in thy name to our **k**,	4428
	9: 8 our **k**, to our princes, and to our fathers,	4428
	10:13 and I remained there with the **k** of Persia.	4428
	11: 2 there *shall* stand up yet three in Persia;	4428
Hos	1: 1 **k** of Judah, and in the days of Jeroboam	4428
	7: 7 their judges; all their **k** are fallen:	4428
	8: 4 They have **set up k**, but not by me:	4427
Mic	1: 1 Ahaz, *and* Hezekiah, **k** of Judah, which	4428
	1:14 houses of Achzib *shall be* a lie to the **k**	4428
Hab	1:10 they shall scoff at the **k**, and the princes	4428
Mt	10:18 before governors and **k** for my sake,	935
	17:25 whom do the **k** of the earth take custom	935
Mk	13: 9 be brought before rulers and **k** for my sake,	935
Lk	10:24 **k** have desired to see *those things* which	935
	21:12 being brought before **k** and rulers for my	935
	22:25 The **k** of the Gentiles exercise lordship	935
Ac	4:26 The **k** of the earth stood up, and the rulers	935
	9:15 and **k**, and the children of Israel:	935
1Co	4: 8 are rich, ye have **reigned as k** without us:	936
1Ti	2: 2 For **k**, and *for* all that are in authority;	935
	6:15 the King of **k**, and Lord of lords;	936
Heb	7: 1 returning from the slaughter of the **k**,	935
Rev	1: 5 dead, and the prince of the **k** of the earth.	935
	1: 6 And hath made us **k** and priests unto God	935
	5:10 And hast made us unto our God **k** and	935
	6:15 And the **k** of the earth, and the great men,	935
	10:11 and nations, and tongues, and **k**.	935
	16:12 that the way of the **k** of the east might be	935
	16:14 which go forth unto the **k** of the earth and	935
	17: 2 With whom the **k** of the earth have	935
	17:10 And there are seven **k**: five are fallen,	935
	17:12 the ten horns which thou sawest are ten **k**,	935
	17:12 receive power as **k** one hour with the beast.	935
	17:14 for he is Lord of lords, and King of **k**:	935
	17:18 which reigneth over the **k** of the earth.	935
	18: 3 the **k** of the earth have committed	935
	18: 9 the **k** of the earth, who have committed	935
	19:16 KING OF **K**, AND LORD OF LORDS.	935
	19:18 ye may eat the flesh of **k**, and the flesh	935
	19:19 the **k** of the earth, and their armies,	935
	21:24 the **k** of the earth do bring their glory and	935

KINGS' (5) [KING]

Ps	45: 9 daughters *were* among thy honourable	4428
Pr	30:28 hold with her hands, and *is* in **k** palaces.	4428
Da	11: 7 hearts *shall be* to do mischief,	4428
Mt	11: 8 that wear soft *clothing* are in **k** houses.	935
Lk	7:25 and live delicately, are in **k** courts.	933

KINNERETH See CHINNERETH; CINNERETH

KINNEROTH See CINNEROTH

KINSFOLK (2) [FOLK, KIN]

Job	19:14 My **k** have failed, and my familiar friends	7138
Lk	2:44 and they sought him among *their* **k** and	4773

KINSFOLKS (3) [FOLK, KIN]

1Ki	16:11 a wall, neither of his **k**, nor of his friends.	1350
2Ki	10:11 his great *men*, and his **k**, and his priests,	3045
Lk	21:16 and brethren, and **k**, and friends;	4773

KINSMAN (16) [KIN, MAN]

Nu	5: 8 if the man have no **k** to recompense	1350
	27:11 shall give his inheritance unto his **k** that	7607
Ru	2: 1 Naomi had a **k** of her husband's,	4129
	3: 9 thine handmaid; for thou *art* a **near k**.	1350
	3:12 now it is true that I *am* thy **near k**:	1350
	3:12 howbeit there is a **k** nearer than I.	1350
	3:13 will **perform** unto thee the part of a **k**,	1350
	3:13 if he will not **do the part of a k** to thee,	1350
	3:13 will I **do the part of a k** to thee,	1350
	4: 1 the **k** of whom Boaz spake came by;	1350
	4: 3 he said unto the **k**, Naomi, that is come	1350
	4: 6 the **k** said, I cannot redeem *it* for myself,	1350
	4: 8 Therefore the **k** said unto Boaz, Buy *it* for	1350
	4:14 hath not left thee *this* day without a **k**,	1350
Jn	18:26 being *his* **k** whose ear Peter cut off, saith,	4773
Ro	16:11 Salute Herodion my **k**. Greet them that	4773

KINSMAN'S (1) [KIN, MAN]

Ru	3:13 of a kinsman, well; let him **do the k part**.	1350

KINSMEN (7) [KIN, MAN]

Ru	2:20 *is* near of kin unto us, one of our **next k**.	1350
Ps	38:11 from my sore; and my **k** stand afar off.	7138
Lk	14:12 friends, nor thy brethren, neither thy **k**,	4773
Ac	10:24 and had called together his **k** and near	4773
Ro	9: 3 my brethren, my **k** according to the flesh:	4773
	16: 7 and Junia, my **k**, and my fellowprisoners,	4773
	16:21 Lucius, and Jason, and Sosipater, my **k**,	4773

KINSWOMAN (3) [KIN, WOMAN]

Lev	18:12 father's sister: she *is* thy father's **near k**.	7607
	18:13 for she *is* thy mother's **near k**.	7607
Pr	7: 4 my sister; and call understanding thy **k**:	4129

KINSWOMEN (1) [KIN, WOMAN]

Lev	18:17 her nakedness; *for* they *are* her **near k**.	7608

KIOS See CHIOS

KIR (5) [KIR-HARASETH, KIR-HARESETH, KIR-HARESH, KIR-HERES]

2Ki	16: 9 carried *the* people of it captive to **K**,	7024
Isa	15: 1 in the night **K** of Moab is laid waste,	7024

Isa	22: 6 horsemen, and **K** uncovered the shield.	7024
Am	1: 5 of Syria shall go into captivity unto **K**,	7024
	9: 7 from Caphtor, and the Syrians from **K**?	7024

KIR-HARASETH (1) [KIR]

2Ki	3:25 only in **K** left *they* the stones thereof;	7025

KIR-HARESETH (1) [KIR]

Isa	16: 7 for the foundations of **K** shall ye mourn;	7025

KIR-HARESH (1) [KIR]

Isa	16:11 for Moab, and mine inward parts for **K**.	7025

KIR-HERES (2) [KIR]

Jer	48:31 mine *heart* shall mourn for the men of **K**.	7025
	48:36 shall sound like pipes for the men of **K**:	7025

KIRIATH See KIRJATH

KIRIATH ARBA See KIRJATH-ARBA

KIRIATH ARIM See KIRJATH-ARIM

KIRIATH BAAL See KIRJATH-BAAL

KIRIATH HUZOTH See KIRJATH-HUZOTH

KIRIATH JEARIM See KIRJATH-JEARIM

KIRIATH SANNAH See KIRJATH-SANNAH

KIRIATH SEPHER See KIRJATH-SEPHER

KIRIATHAIM (3) [SHAVEH KIRIATHAIM]

Jer	48: 1 **K** is confounded *and* taken: Misgab is	7156
	48:23 upon **K**, and upon Beth-gamul,	7156
Eze	25: 9 Beth-jeshimoth, Baal-meon, and **K**,	7156

KIRJATH (1)

Jos	18:28 which *is* Jerusalem, Gibeath, *and* **K**;	7157

KIRJATHAIM (3)

Nu	32:37 built Heshbon, and Elealeh, and **K**,	7156
	33:19 **K**, and Sibmah, and Zareth-shahar in	7156
1Ch	6:76 her suburbs, and **K** with her suburbs.	7156

KIRJATH-ARBA (6) [ARBA]

Ge	23: 2 Sarah died in **K**; the same *is* Hebron in	7153
Jos	14:15 the name of Hebron before *was* **K**,	7153
	15:54 and **K**, which *is* Hebron, and Zior;	7153
	20: 7 **K**, which *is* Hebron, in the mountain of	7153
Jdg	1:10 (now the name of Hebron before *was* **K**:)	7153
Ne	11:25 *some* of the children of Judah dwelt at **K**,	7153

KIRJATH-ARIM (1) [KIRJATH-JEARIM]

Ezr	2:25 children of **K**, Chephirah, and Beeroth,	7157

KIRJATH-BAAL (2) [BAAL]

Jos	15:60 **K**, which *is* Kirjath-jearim, and Rabbah;	7154
	18:14 the goings out thereof were at **K**, which	7154

KIRJATH-HUZOTH (1)

Nu	22:39 went with Balak, and they came *unto* **K**.	7155

KIRJATH-JEARIM (18) [JEARIM KIRJATH-ARIM]

Jos	9:17 and Chephirah, and Beeroth, and **K**.	7157
	15: 9 border was drawn *to* Baalah, which *is* **K**:	7157
	15:60 Kirjath-baal, which *is* **K**, and Rabbah;	7157
	18:14 *is* **K**, a city of the children of Judah:	7157
	18:15 the south quarter *was* from the end of **K**,	7157
Jdg	18:12 they went up, and pitched in **K**, in Judah:	7157
	18:12 unto this day: behold, *it is* behind **K**.	7157
1Sa	6:21 sent messengers to the inhabitants of **K**,	7157
	7: 1 men of **K** came, and fetched up the ark	7157
	7: 2 it came to pass, while the ark abode in **K**,	7157
1Ch	2:50 of Ephratah; Shobal the father of **K**,	7157
	2:52 Shobal the father of **K** had sons; Haroeh,	7157
	2:53 the families of **K**; the Ithrites,	7157
	13: 5 Hemath, to bring the ark of God from **K**;	7157
	13: 6 and all Israel, to Baalah, *that is,* to **K**,	7157
2Ch	1: 4 **K** to *the place* which David had prepared	7157
Ne	7:29 The men of **K**, Chephirah, and Beeroth,	7157
Jer	26:20 Urijah the son of Shemaiah of **K**,	7157

KIRJATH-SANNAH (1) [DEBIR]

Jos	15:49 And Dannah, and **K**, which *is* Debir,	7158

KIRJATH-SEPHER (4) [DEBIR]

Jos	15:15 and the name of Debir before *was* **K**.	7158
	15:16 said, He that smiteth **K**, and taketh it,	7158
Jdg	1:11 and the name of Debir before *was* **K**:	7158
	1:12 said, He that smiteth **K**, and taketh it,	7158

KISH (21)

1Sa	9: 1 whose name *was* **K**, the son of Abiel,	7027
	9: 3 the asses of **K** Saul's father were lost.	7027
	9: 3 **K** said to Saul his son, Take now one of	7027
	10:11 *is* this *that* is come unto the son of **K**?	7027
	10:21 and Saul the son of **K** was taken:	7027
	14:51 **K** *was* the father of Saul; and Ner the	7027
2Sa	21:14 in Zelah, in the sepulchre of **K** his father:	7027
1Ch	8:30 and Zur, and **K**, and Baal, and Nadab,	7027
	8:33 Ner begat **K**, and **K** begat Saul,	7027
	8:33 **K** begat Saul, and Saul begat Jonathan,	7027
	9:36 and **K**, and Baal, and Ner, and Nadab,	7027
	9:39 Ner begat **K**; and **K** begat Saul;	7027
	9:39 **K** begat Saul, and Saul begat Jonathan,	7027
	12: 1 close because of Saul the son of **K**:	7027

1Ch	23:21 The sons of Mahli; Eleazar, and **K**.	7027
	23:22 their brethren the sons of **K** took them.	7027
	24:29 Concerning **K**: the son of Kish *was*	7027
	24:29 the son of **K** *was* Jerahmeel.	7027
	26:28 Saul the son of **K**, and Abner the son of	7027
2Ch	29:12 **K** the son of Abdi, and Azariah the son of	7027
Est	2: 5 son of Shimei, the son of **K**, a Benjamite;	7027

KISHI (1)

1Ch	6:44 Ethan the son of **K**, the son of Abdi,	7029

KISHION (1)

Jos	19:20 And Rabbith, and **K**, and Abez,	7191

KISHON (6) [KISON]

Jos	21:28 **K** with her suburbs, Dabareh with her	7191
Jdg	4: 7 will draw unto thee to the river **K** Sisera,	7028
	4:13 of the Gentiles unto the river of **K**.	7028
	5:21 The river of **K** swept them away,	7028
	5:21 away, *that* ancient river, the river **K**.	7028
1Ki	18:40 Elijah brought them down to the brook **K**,	7028

KISLEV See CHISLEU

KISLON See CHISLON

KISLOTH TABOR See CHISLOTH-TABOR

KISON (1) [KISHON]

Ps	83: 9 as *to* Sisera, as *to* Jabin, at the brook of **K**:	7028

KISS (20) [KISSED, KISSES]

Ge	27:26 Come near now, and **k** me, my son.	5401
	31:28 hast not suffered me to **k** my sons and	5401
2Sa	20: 9 the beard with the right hand to **k** him.	5401
1Ki	19:20 **k** my father and my mother, and *then* I	5401
Ps	2:12 **K** the Son, lest he be angry, and ye perish	5401
Pr	24:26 *Every man* shall **k** *his* lips that giveth a	5401
SS	1: 2 Let him **k** me with the kisses of his	5401
	8: 1 I should find thee without, I would **k** thee;	5401
Hos	13: 2 Let the men that sacrifice **k** the calves.	5401
Mt	26:48 Whomsoever I shall **k**, that *same* is	5368
Mk	14:44 Whomsoever I shall **k**, that *same* is	5368
Lk	7:45 gavest me no **k**: but this *woman* since	5370
	7:45 I came in hath not ceased to **k** my feet.	2705
	22:47 and drew near unto Jesus to **k** him.	5368
	22:48 betrayest thou the Son of man with a **k**?	5370
Ro	16:16 Salute one another with a holy **k**.	5370
1Co	16:20 Greet ye one another with a holy **k**.	5370
2Co	13:12 Greet one another with a holy **k**.	5370
1Th	5:26 Greet all the brethren with a holy **k**.	5370
1Pe	5:14 Greet ye one another with a **k** of charity.	5370

KISSED (26) [KISS]

Ge	27:27 he came near, and **k**: and he smelled	5401
	29:11 Jacob **k** Rachel, and lifted up his voice,	5401
	29:13 and **k** him, and brought him to his house.	5401
	31:55 **k** his sons and his daughters,	5401
	33: 4 and fell on his neck, and **k** him:	5401
	45:15 Moreover he **k** all his brethren,	5401
	48:10 and he **k** them, and embraced them.	5401
	50: 1 and wept upon him, and **k** him.	5401
Ex	4:27 met him in the mount of God, and **k** him.	5401
	18: 7 in law, and did obeisance, and **k** him;	5401
Ru	1: 9 she **k** them; and they lift up their voice,	5401
	1:14 Orpah **k** her mother in law; but Ruth	5401
1Sa	10: 1 **k** him, and said, *Is it* not because	5401
	20:41 they **k** one another, and wept one with	5401
2Sa	14:33 before the king: and the king **k** Absalom.	5401
	15: 5 forth his hand, and took him, and **k** him.	5401
	19:39 the king **k** Barzillai, and blessed him;	5401
1Ki	19:18 and every mouth which hath not **k** him.	5401
Job	31:27 or my mouth hath **k** my hand:	5401
Ps	85:10 righteousness and peace have **k** *each*	5401
Pr	7:13 him, and with an impudent face said	5401
Mt	26:49 Jesus, and said, Hail, master; and **k** him.	2705
Mk	14:45 and saith, Master, master; and **k** him.	2705
Lk	7:38 and **k** his feet, and anointed *them* with	2705
	15:20 and ran, and fell on his neck, and **k** him.	2705
Ac	20:37 and fell on Paul's neck, and **k** him,	2705

KISSES (2) [KISS]

Pr	27: 6 but the **k** of an enemy *are* deceitful.	5390
SS	1: 2 Let him kiss me with the **k** of his mouth:	5390

KITE (2)

Lev	11:14 And the vulture, and the **k** after his kind;	344
Dt	14:13 and the **k**, and the vulture after his kind,	344

KITHLISH (1)

Jos	15:40 And Cabbon, and Lahmam, and **K**,	3798

KITLISH See KITHLISH

KITRON (1)

Jdg	1:30 Zebulun drive out the inhabitants of **K**,	7003

KITTIM (2)

Ge	10: 4 Elishah, and Tarshish, **K**, and Dodanim.	3794
1Ch	1: 7 Elishah, and Tarshish, **K**, and Dodanim.	3794

KNEAD (2) [KNEADED, KNEADINGTROUGHS]

Ge	18: 6 **k** *it*, and make cakes upon the hearth.	3888
Jer	7:18 the fire, and the women **k** *their* dough,	3888

KNEADED (3) [KNEAD]

1Sa	28:24 **k** *it*, and did bake unleavened bread	3888

2Sa 13: 8 **k** *it,* and made cakes in his sight,　3888
Hos 7: 4 *who* ceaseth from raising after he hath **k**　3888

KNEADINGTROUGHS (2) [KNEAD, TROUGH]
Ex 8: 3 and into thine ovens, and into thy **k:**　4863
　12:34 their **k** being bound up in their clothes　4863

KNEE (6) [KNEES]
Ge 41:43 and they cried before him, **Bow the k:**　86
Isa 45:23 return, That unto me every **k** shall bow,　1290
Mt 27:29 and they **bowed the k** before him,　1120
Ro 11: 4 have not bowed the **k** to *the image of*　1119
　14:11 every **k** shall bow to me, and every tongue　1119
Php 2:10 That at the name of Jesus every **k** should　1119

KNEEL (2) [KNEELED, KNEELING]
Ge 24:11 he **made** *his* camels **to k down** without　1288
Ps 95: 6 let us **k** before the LORD our Maker.　1288

KNEELED (8) [KNEEL]
2Ch 6:13 **k down** upon his knees before all　1288
Da 6:10 he **k** upon his knees three times a day,　1289
Mk 10:17 **k** to him, and asked him, Good Master,　1120
Lk 22:41 a stone's cast, and **k down,**　1119+3588+5087
Ac 7:60 And he **k down,**　1119+3588+5087
　9:40 and **k down,** and prayed;　1119+3588+5087
　20:36 **k down,** and prayed with　1119+3588+5087
　21: 5 **k down** on the shore,　1119+3588+5087

KNEELING (3) [KNEEL]
1Ki 8:54 from **k** on his knees with his hands spread　3766
Mt 17:14 *certain* man, **k down** to him, and saying,　1120
Mk 1:40 and **k down** to him, and saying unto him,　1120

KNEES (30) [KNEE]
Ge 30: 3 she shall bear upon my **k,** that I may also　1290
　48:12 brought them out from between his **k,**　1290
　50:23 were brought up upon Joseph's **k.**　1290
Dt 28:35 The LORD shall smite the in the **k,**　1290
Jdg 7: 5 that boweth down upon his **k** to drink.　1290
　7: 6 bowed down upon their **k** to drink water.　1290
　16:19 she made him sleep upon her **k;**　1290
1Ki 8:54 from kneeling on his **k** with his hands　1290
　18:42 earth, and put his face between his **k,**　1290
　19:18 the **k** which have not bowed unto Baal,　1290
2Ki 1:13 came and fell on his **k** before Elijah,　1290
　4:20 he sat on her **k** till noon, and *then* died.　1290
2Ch 6:13 kneeled *down* upon his **k** before all　1290
Ezr 9: 5 fell upon my **k,** and spread out my hands　1290
Job 3:12 Why did the **k** prevent me? or why　1290
　4: 4 and thou hast strengthened the feeble **k.**　1290
Ps 109:24 My **k** are weak through fasting;　1290
Isa 35: 3 weak hands, and confirm the feeble **k.**　1290
　66:12 her sides, and be dandled upon *her* **k.**　1290
Eze 7:17 feeble, and all **k** shall be weak *as* water.　1290
　21: 7 faint, and all **k** shall be weak *as* water:　1290
　47: 4 the waters; the waters *were* to the **k.**　1290
Da 5: 6 and his **k** smote one against another.　755
　6:10 he kneeled upon his **k** three times a day,　1291
　10:10 which set me upon my **k** and *upon*　1290
Na 2:10 the **k** smite together, and much pain *is* in　1290
Mk 15:19 and bowing *their* **k** worshipped him.　1119
Lk 5: 8 Peter saw *it,* he fell down at Jesus' **k,**　1119
Eph 3:14 For this cause I bow my **k** unto the Father　1119
Heb 12:12 which hang down, and the feeble **k;**　1119

KNEW (169) [KNOW]
Ge 3: 7 and they **k** that they *were* naked;　3045
　4: 1 Adam **k** Eve his wife; and she conceived,　3045
　4:17 Cain **k** his wife; and she conceived,　3045
　4:25 Adam **k** his wife again; and she bare a son　3045
　8:11 Noah **k** that the waters were abated from　3045
　9:24 **k** what his younger son had done unto　3045
　28:16 the LORD is in this place; and I **k** *it* not.　3045
　31:32 For Jacob **k** not that Rachel had stolen　3045
　37:33 he **k** it, and said, *It is* my son's coat;　5234
　38: 9 Onan **k** that the seed should not be his;　3045
　38:16 (for he **k** not that she *was* his daughter in　3045
　38:26 my son. And he **k** her again no more.　3045
　39: 6 he **k** not ought he had, save the bread　3045
　42: 7 he **k** them, but made himself strange unto　5234
　42: 8 Joseph **k** his brethren, but they knew not　5234
　42: 8 knew his brethren, but they **k** not him.　5234
　42:23 they **k** not that Joseph understood *them;*　3045
Ex 1: 8 new king over Egypt, which **k** not Joseph.　3045
Nu 22:34 for I **k** not that thou stoodest in the way　3045
　24:16 and **k** the knowledge of the most High,　3045
Dt 8:16 which thy fathers **k** not, that he might　3045
　9:24 the LORD from the day that I **k** you.　3045
　29:26 whom they **k** not, and *whom* he　3045
　32:17 *to* gods whom they **k** not, *to* new *gods*　3045
　33: 9 his brethren, nor **k** his own children:　3045
　34:10 whom the LORD **k** face to face,　3045
Jdg 2:10 after them, which **k** not the LORD,　3045
　3: 2 at the least such as before **k** nothing　3045
　11:39 she **k** no man. And it was a custom in　3045
　13:16 For Manoah **k** not that he *was* an angel　3045
　13:21 Manoah **k** that he *was* an angel of　3045
　14: 4 his mother **k** not that it *was* of the LORD,　3045
　18: 3 they **k** the voice of the young man　5234
　19:25 they **k** her, and abused her all the night　3045
　20:34 but they **k** not that evil *was* near them.　3045
1Sa 1:19 Elkanah **k** Hannah his wife;　3045
　2:12 *were* sons of Belial; they **k** not the LORD.　3045
　3:20 all Israel from Dan even to Beer-sheba **k**　3045

1Sa 10:11 when all that **k** him beforetime saw that　3045
　14: 3 the people **k** not that Jonathan was gone.　3045
　18:28 and **k** that the LORD *was* with David,　3045
　20: 9 for if I **k** **certainly** that evil were　3045+3045
　20:33 Jonathan **k** that it was determined　3045
　20:39 the lad **k** not any thing: only Jonathan　3045
　20:39 only Jonathan and David **k** the matter.　3045
　22:15 for thy servant **k** nothing of all this, less　3045
　22:17 because they **k** when he fled, and did not　3045
　22:22 David said unto Abiathar, I **k** *it* that day,　3045
　23: 9 David **k** that Saul secretly practised　3045
　26:12 no man saw *it,* nor **k** *it,* neither awaked:　3045
　26:17 Saul **k** David's voice, and said, *Is* this thy　5234
2Sa 3:26 from the well of Sirah: but David **k** *it* not.　3045
　11:16 place where he **k** that valiant men *were.*　3045
　11:20 ye not that they would shoot from　3045
　15:11 their simplicity, and they **k** not any thing.　3045
　18:29 a great tumult, but I **k** not what *it was.*　3045
　22:44 a people *which* I **k** not shall serve me.　3045
1Ki 1: 4 ministered to him: but the king **k** her not.　3045
　18: 7 he **k** him, and fell on his face, and said,　5234
2Ki 4:39 the pot of pottage: for they **k** *them* not.　3045
2Ch 33:13 Manasseh **k** that the LORD he *was* God.　3045
Ne 2:16 the rulers **k** not whither I went, or what　3045
Est 1:13 the king said to the wise *men,* which **k**　3045
　1:13 *was* the king's manner towards all that **k**　3045
Job 2:12 **k** him not, they lifted up their voice,　5234
　23: 3 O that I **k** where I might find him! *that* I　3045
　29:16 the cause *which* I **k** not I searched out.　3045
　42: 3 too wonderful for me, *which* I **k** not.　3045
Ps 35:11 laid to my charge *things* that I **k** not.　3045
　35:15 together against me, and I **k** *it* not;　3045
Pr 24:12 If thou sayest, Behold, we **k** it not; doth　3045
Isa 42:16 will bring the blind by a way *that* they **k**　3045
　42:25 set him on fire round about, yet he **k** not;　3045
　48: 4 Because I **k** that thou *art* obstinate,　1847
　48: 7 lest thou shouldest say, Behold, I **k** them.　3045
　48: 8 for I **k** *that* thou wouldest deal very　3045
　55: 5 nations *that* **k** not thee shall run unto　3045
Jer 1: 5 Before I formed thee in the belly I **k** thee;　3045
　2: 8 they that handle the law **k** me not:　3045
　11:19 I **k** not that they had devised devices　3045
　32: 8 I **k** that this *was* the word of the LORD.　3045
　41: 4 *he* had slain Gedaliah, and no man **k** *it,*　3045
　44: 3 whom they **k** not, *neither* they, you,　3045
　44:15 all the men which **k** that their wives had　3045
Eze 10:20 and I **k** that they *were* the cherubims.　3045
　19: 7 he **k** their desolate palaces, and he laid　3045
Da 5:21 till he **k** that the most high God ruled in　3045
　6:10 Now when Daniel **k** that the writing *was*　3046
　11:38 a god whom his fathers **k** not shall he　3045
Hos 8: 4 they have made princes, and I **k** *it* not:　3045
　11: 3 but they **k** not that I healed them.　3045
Jnh 1:10 For the men **k** that he fled from　3045
　4: 2 for I **k** that thou *art* a gracious God,　3045
Zec 7:14 among all the nations whom they **k** not:　3045
　11:11 poor of the flock that waited upon me **k**　3045
Mt 1:25 **k** her not till she had brought forth her　1097
　7:23 will I profess unto them, I never **k** you:　1097
　12:15 When Jesus **k** *it,* he withdrew himself　1097
　12:25 And Jesus **k** their thoughts, and said unto　1492
　17:12 they **k** him not, but have done unto him　1921
　24:39 And **k** not until the flood came,　1097
　25:24 Lord, I **k** thee that thou art a hard man,　1097
　27:18 For he **k** that for envy they had delivered　1492
Mk 1:34 the devils to speak, because they **k** him.　1492
　6:33 many **k** him, and ran afoot thither out　1921
　6:38 And when they **k,** they say, Five,　1097
　6:54 out of the ship, straightway they **k** him,　1097
　8:17 And when Jesus **k** *it,* he saith unto them,　1097
　12:12 for they **k** that he had spoken the parable　1097
　15:10 he **k** that the chief priests had delivered　1097
　15:45 when he **k** *it* of the centurion, he gave　1097
Lk 2:43 and Joseph and his mother **k** not *of it.*　1097
　4:41 to speak: for they **k** that he was Christ.　1492
　6: 8 he **k** their thoughts, and said to the man　1492
　7:37 when she **k** that *Jesus* sat at meat in　1921
　9:11 the people, when they **k** *it,* followed him:　1097
　12:47 which **k** his lord's will, and prepared not　1097
　12:48 But he that **k** not, and did commit *things*　1097
　18:34 neither **k** they the *things* which were　1921
　23: 7 as soon as he **k** that he belonged unto　1921
　24:31 their eyes were opened, and they **k** him;　1921
Jn 1:10 made by him, and the world **k** him not.　1097
　1:31 And I **k** him not: but that he should be　1492
　1:33 And I **k** him not: but he that sent me to　1492
　2: 9 made wine, and **k** not whence it was:　1492
　2: 9 the servants which drew the water **k;**)　1492
　2:24 himself unto them, because he **k** all *men,*　1097
　2:25 testify of man: for he **k** what was in man.　1097
　4: 1 the Lord how the Pharisees had heard　1097
　4:53 the father **k** that it *was* at the same hour,　1097
　5: 6 **k** that he had been now a long time　1097
　6: 6 for he himself **k** what he would do.　1492
　6:61 When Jesus **k** in himself that his disciples　1492
　6:64 For Jesus **k** from the beginning who they　1492
　11:42 And I **k** that thou hearest me always:　1492
　11:57 that, if any *man* **k** where he were,　1097
　12: 9 of the Jews therefore **k** that he was there:　1097
　13: 1 Jesus **k** that his hour was come that he　1492
　13:11 For he **k** who should betray him;　1097
　13:28 Now no *man* at the table **k** for what　1097
　16:19 Jesus **k** that they were desirous to ask　1097
　18: 2 which betrayed him, **k** the place:　1492
　20: 9 as yet they **k** not the scripture, that he　1492

Jn 20:14 standing, and **k** not that it was Jesus.　1492
　21: 4 but the disciples **k** not that it was Jesus.　1492
Ac 3:10 And they **k** that it was he which sat for　1921
　7:18 another king arose, which **k** not Joseph.　1492
　9:30 Which when the brethren **k,** they brought　1921
　12:14 when she **k** Peter's voice, she opened　1921
　13:27 and their rulers, because they **k** him **not,**　50
　16: 3 for they **k** all that his father was a Greek.　1492
　19:32 the more part **k** not wherefore they were　1492
　19:34 when they **k** that he was a Jew, all with　1921
　22:29 after he **k** that he was a Roman,　1921
　26: 5 Which **k** me from the beginning, if they　4267
　27:39 when it was day, they **k** not the land:　1921
　28: 1 they **k** that the island was called Melita.　1921
Ro 1:21 Because that, when they **k** God,　1097
1Co 1:21 of God the world by wisdom **k** not God,　1097
　2: 8 none of the princes of this world **k:**　1097
2Co 5:21 made him *to be* sin for us, who **k** no sin;　1097
　12: 2 I **k** a man in Christ above fourteen years　1492
　12: 3 I **k** such a man, (whether in the body,　1492
Gal 4: 8 Howbeit then, when ye **k** not God, ye did　1492
Col 1: 6 of *it,* and knew the grace of God in truth:　1921
　1: 6 For I would that ye **k** what great conflict I　1492
1Jn 3: 1 knoweth us not, because it **k** him not.　1097
Jude 1: 5 though ye once **k** this, how that the Lord,　1492
Rev 19:12 that no *man* **k,** but he himself.　1492

KNEWEST (10) [KNOW]
Dt 8: 3 fed thee with manna, which thou **k** not,　3045
Ru 2:11 art come unto a people which thou **k** not　3045
Ne 9:10 for thou **k** that they dealt proudly against　3045
Ps 142: 3 within me, then thou **k** my path.　3045
Isa 48: 8 yea, thou **k** not; yea, from that time *that*　3045
Da 5:22 thine heart, though thou **k** all this;　3046
Mt 25:26 thou **k** that I reap where I sowed not,　1492
Lk 19:22 Thou **k** that I was an austere man, taking　1492
　19:44 thou **k** not the time of thy visitation.　1097
Jn 4:10 If thou **k** the gift of God, and who it is　1492

KNIFE (6) [KNIVES]
Ge 22: 6 he took the fire in his hand, and a **k;**　3979
　22:10 his hand, and took the **k** to slay his son.　3979
Jdg 19:29 took a **k,** and laid hold on his concubine,　3979
Pr 23: 2 put a **k** to thy throat, if thou *be* a man　7915
Eze 5: 1 thou, son of man, take thee a sharp **k,**　2719
　5: 2 a third *part, and* smite about it with a **k:**　2719

KNIT (6)
Jdg 20:11 against the city, **k together** as one man.　2270
1Sa 18: 1 that the soul of Jonathan was **k** with　7194
1Ch 12:17 mine heart shall be **k** unto you:　3162+3807.1
Ac 10:11 as *it had been* a great sheet **k** at the four　1210
Col 2: 2 being **k together** in love, and unto all　4822
　2:19 and **k together,** increaseth *with*　4822

KNITTED See WOOF

KNIVES (5) [KNIFE]
Jos 5: 2 Make thee sharp **k,** and circumcise again　2719
　5: 3 Joshua made him sharp **k,**　2719
1Ki 18:28 cut themselves after their manner with **k**　2719
Ezr 1: 9 chargers of silver, nine and twenty **k,**　4252
Pr 30:14 *are* as swords, and their jaw teeth as **k,**　3979

KNOCK (4) [KNOCKED, KNOCKETH, KNOCKING]
Mt 7: 7 **k,** and it shall be opened unto you:　2925
Lk 11: 9 **k,** and it shall be opened unto you:　2925
　13:25 and to **k** at the door, saying, Lord, Lord,　2925
Rev 3:20 Behold, I stand at the door, and **k:** if any　2925

KNOCKED (1) [KNOCK]
Ac 12:13 And as Peter **k** at the door of the gate,　2925

KNOCKETH (4) [KNOCK]
SS 5: 2 *it is* the voice of my beloved that **k** *saying,*　1849
Mt 7: 8 and to him that **k** it shall be opened.　2925
Lk 11:10 and to him that **k** it shall be opened.　2925
　12:36 when *he* cometh and **k,** they may open　2925

KNOCKING (1) [KNOCK]
Ac 12:16 But Peter continued **k:** and when they　2925

KNOP (10) [KNOP]
Ex 25:33 *with* a **k** and a flower in one branch;　3730
　25:33 the other branch, *with* a **k** and a flower:　3730
　25:35 *there shall be* a **k** under two branches of　3730
　25:35 a **k** under two branches of the same,　3730
　25:35 a **k** under two branches of the same,　3730
　37:19 almonds in one branch, a **k** and a flower;　3730
　37:19 in another branch, a **k** and a flower:　3730
　37:21 a **k** under two branches of the same,　3730
　37:21 a **k** under two branches of the same,　3730
　37:21 and a **k** under two branches of the same,　3730

KNOPS (9) [KNOP]
Ex 25:31 his bowls, his **k,** and his flowers,　3730
　25:34 **k** with their **k** and their flowers.　3730
　25:36 Their **k** and their branches shall be of　3730
　37:17 his bowls, his **k,** and his flowers:　3730
　37:20 made like almonds, his **k,** and his flowers:　3730
　37:22 Their **k** and their branches were of　3730
1Ki 6:18 of the house within *was* carved with **k**　6497
　7:24 the brim of it round about *there were* **k**　6497
　7:24 the **k** *were* cast *in* two rows, when it was　6497

KNOW (763) [FOREKNEW, FOREKNOW, FOREKNOWLEDGE, KNEWEST, KNOWEST, KNOWETH, KNOWING, KNOWLEDGE, KNOWN, UNKNOWN]

Ge 3: 5 For God doth **k** that in the day ye eat 3045
3:22 become as one of us, to **k** good and evil: 3045
4: 9 said, I **k** not: Am I my brother's keeper? 3045
12:11 I **k** that thou art a fair woman to look 3045
15: 8 whereby shall I **k** that I shall inherit it? 3045
15:13 **K** of a surety that thy seed shall be 3045+3045
18:19 For I **k** him, that he will command his 3045
18:21 is come unto me; and if not, I will **k**. 3045
19: 5 them out unto us, that we may **k** them. 3045
20: 6 I **k** that thou didst this in the integrity of 3045
20: 7 **k** thou that thou shalt surely die, thou, 3045
22:12 for now I **k** that thou fearest God, 3045
24:14 thereby shall I **k** that thou hast shewed 3045
27: 2 I am old, I **k** not the day of my death: 3045
29: 5 unto them, **K** ye Laban the son of Nahor? 3045
29: 5 son of Nahor? And they said, We **k** him. 3045
31: 6 ye **k** that with all my power I have served 3045
37:32 **k** now whether it be thy son's coat or no. 5234
42:33 Hereby shall I **k** that ye are true men; 3045
42:34 shall I **k** that ye are no spies, but that ye 3045
43: 7 could we certainly **k** that he 3045+3045
44:27 Ye **k** that my wife bare me two sons: 3045
48:19 father refused, and said, I **k** it, my son, 3045
48:19 I **k** it: he also shall become a people, 3045
Ex 3: 7 of their taskmasters; for I **k** their sorrows; 3045
4:14 I **k** that he can speak well. And also, 3045
5: 2 I **k** not the LORD, neither will I let Israel 3045
6: 7 ye shall **k** that I am the LORD your God, 3045
7: 5 the Egyptians shall **k** that I am the LORD, 3045
7:17 In this thou shalt **k** that I am the LORD: 3045
8:10 that thou mayest **k** that there is none like 3045
8:22 to the end thou mayest **k** that I am 3045
9:14 that thou mayest **k** that there is none like 3045
9:29 that thou mayest **k** how that the earth is 3045
9:30 **k** that ye will not yet fear the LORD 3045
10: 2 that ye may **k** how that I am the LORD. 3045
10:26 we **k** not with what we must serve 3045
11: 7 that ye may **k** how that the LORD doth 3045
14: 4 that the Egyptians may **k** that I am 3045
14:18 the Egyptians shall **k** that I am the LORD, 3045
16: 6 ye shall **k** that the LORD hath brought 3045
16:12 ye shall **k** that I am the LORD your God. 3045
18:11 Now I **k** that the LORD is greater than all 3045
18:16 I do make them **k** the statutes of God, 3045
23: 9 for ye **k** the heart of a stranger, seeing ye 3045
29:46 they shall **k** that I am the LORD their 3045
31:13 that ye may **k** that I am the LORD that 3045
33: 5 that I may **k** what to do unto thee. 3045
33:12 hast not let me **k** whom thou wilt send 3045
33:12 I **k** thee by name, and thou hast also 3045
33:13 shew me now thy way, that I may **k** thee, 3045
33:17 grace in my sight, and I **k** thee by name. 3045
36: 1 understanding to **k** how to work all 3045
Lev 23:43 That your generations may **k** that I made 3045
Nu 14:31 they shall **k** the land which ye have 3045
14:34 and ye shall **k** my breach of promise. 3045
16:28 Hereby ye shall **k** that the LORD hath 3045
22:19 that I may **k** what the LORD will say unto 3045
Dt 3:19 (for I **k** that ye have much cattle,) 3045
4:35 that thou mightest **k** that the LORD he is 3045
4:39 **K** therefore this day, and consider it in 3045
7: 9 **k** therefore that the LORD thy God, he is 3045
8: 2 prove thee, to **k** what was in thine heart, 3045
8: 3 knewest not, neither did thy fathers **k**; 3045
8: 3 he might make thee **k** that man doth 3045
11: 2 **k** you this day: for I speak not with your 3045
13: 3 to **k** whether ye love the LORD your 3045
18:21 How shall we **k** the word which 3045
22: 2 if thou **k** him not, then thou shalt bring it 3045
29: 6 that ye might **k** that I am the LORD your 3045
29:16 (For ye **k** how we have dwelt in the land 3045
31:21 for I **k** their imagination which they go 3045
31:27 For I **k** thy rebellion, and thy stiff neck: 3045
31:29 For I **k** that after my death ye will utterly 3045
Jos 2: 9 I **k** that the LORD hath given you 3045
3: 4 that ye may **k** the way by which ye must 3045
3: 7 they may **k** that, as I was with Moses, 3045
3:10 Hereby ye shall **k** that the living God is 3045
4:22 ye shall let your children **k**, saying, 3045
4:24 That all the people of the earth might **k** 3045
22:22 gods, he knoweth, and Israel he shall **k**; 3045
23:13 **K** for a certainty that the LORD 3045+3045
23:14 **k** in all your hearts and in all your souls, 3045
Jdg 3: 2 of the children of Israel might **k**, 3045
3: 4 to **k** whether they would harken unto 3045
6:37 shall I **k** that thou wilt save Israel by mine 3045
17:13 Now **k** I that the LORD will do me good, 3045
18:14 that we may **k** whether our way which 3045
18:14 Do ye **k** that there is in these houses an 3045
19:22 into thine house, that we may **k** him. 3045
Ru 3:11 for all the city of my people doth **k** that 3045
3:14 she rose up before one could **k** another. 5234
3:18 until thou **k** how the matter will fall: 3045
4: 4 not redeem it, then tell me, that I may **k**: 3045
1Sa 3: 7 Now Samuel did not yet **k** the LORD, 3045
6: 9 shall **k** that it is not his hand that smote 3045
14:38 and see wherein this sin hath been this 3045
17:28 I **k** thy pride, and the naughtiness of 3045
17:46 all the earth may **k** that there is a God 3045
17:47 all this assembly shall **k** that the LORD 3045

1Sa 20: 3 he saith, Let not Jonathan **k** this, lest he 3045
20:30 **k** that thou hast chosen the son of Jesse 3045
21: 2 Let no man **k** any thing of the business 3045
22: 3 you, till I **k** what God will do for me. 3045
23:22 **k** and see his place where his haunt is, 3045
24:11 **k** thou and see that there is neither evil 3045
24:20 I **k** well that thou shalt surely be king, 3045
25:11 men, whom I **k** not whence they be? 3045
25:17 Now therefore **k** and consider what thou 3045
28: 1 said unto David, **K** thou assuredly, 3045+3045
28: 2 thou shalt **k** what thy servant can do. 3045
29: 9 David, I **k** that thou art good in my sight, 3045
2Sa 3:25 to **k** thy going out and thy coming in, 3045
3:25 coming in, and to **k** all that thou doest. 3045
3:38 **K** ye not that there is a prince and a great 3045
7:21 great things, to make thy servant **k** them. 3045
14:20 God, to **k** all things that are in the earth. 3045
19:20 For thy servant doth **k** that I have sinned; 3045
19:22 for do not I **k** that I am this day king over 3045
24: 2 that I may **k** the number of the people. 3045
1Ki 2:37 thou shalt **k** for certain that thou 3045+3045
2:42 unto thee, saying, **K** for a certain, 3045+3045
3: 7 I **k** not how to go out or come in. 3045
8:38 which shall **k** every man the plague of his 3045
8:43 all people of the earth may **k** thy name, 3045
8:43 that they may **k** that this house, which I 3045
8:60 all the people of the earth may **k** that 3045
17:24 by this I **k** that thou art a man of God, 3045
18:12 the LORD shall carry thee whither I **k** not; 3045
18:37 that this people may **k** that thou art 3045
20:13 and thou shalt **k** that I am the LORD. 3045
20:28 and ye shall **k** that I am the LORD. 3045
22: 3 **K** ye that Ramoth in Gilead is ours, 3045
2Ki 2: 3 he said, Yea, I **k** it; hold you your peace. 3045
2: 5 Yea, I **k** it; hold you your peace. 3045
5: 8 he shall **k** that there is a prophet in Israel. 3045
5:15 I **k** that there is no God in all the earth, 3045
7:12 They **k** that we be hungry; therefore 3045
8:12 Because I **k** the evil that thou wilt do unto 3045
9:11 Ye **k** the man, and his communication. 3045
10:10 **K** now that there shall fall unto the earth 3045
17:26 **k** not the manner of the God of the land: 3045
17:26 they **k** not the manner of the God of 3045
19:19 that all the kingdoms of the earth may **k** 3045
19:27 I **k** thy abode, and thy going out, 3045
1Ch 12:32 of the times, to **k** what Israel ought to do; 3045
21: 2 number of them to me, that I may **k** it. 3045
28: 9 **k** thou the God of thy father, and serve 3045
29:17 **k** also, my God, that thou triest the heart, 3045
2Ch 2: 8 for I **k** that thy servants can skill to cut 3045
6:29 when every one shall **k** his own sore and 3045
6:33 all people of the earth may **k** thy name, 3045
6:33 may **k** that this house which I have built 3045
12: 8 they may **k** my service, and the service 3045
13: 5 Ought you not to **k** that the LORD God of 3045
20:12 against us; neither **k** we what to do: 3045
25:16 **k** that God hath determined to destroy 3045
32:13 **K** ye not what I and my fathers have done 3045
32:31 that he might **k** all that was in his heart. 3045
Ezr 4:15 **k** that this city is a rebellious city, 3045
7:25 river, all such as **k** the laws of thy God; 3046
7:25 and teach ye them that **k** them not. 3046
Ne 4:11 They shall not **k**, neither see, 3045
Est 2:11 to **k** how Esther did, and what should 3045
4: 5 to **k** what it was, and why it was. 3045
4:11 do **k**, that whosoever, whether man or 3045
Job 5:24 thou shalt **k** that thy tabernacle shall be 3045
5:25 Thou shalt **k** also that thy seed shall be 3045
5:27 so it is; hear it, and **k** thou it for thy good. 3045
7:10 neither shall his place **k** him any more. 5234
8: 9 nothing, because our days upon earth 3045
9: 2 I **k** it is so of a truth: but how should man 3045
9: 5 removeth the mountains, and they **k** not: 3045
9:21 I were perfect, yet would I not **k** my soul: 3045
9:28 I **k** that thou wilt not hold me innocent. 3045
10:13 in thine heart: I **k** that this is with thee. 3045
11: 6 **K** therefore that God exacteth of thee less 3045
11: 8 deeper than hell; what canst thou **k**? 3045
13: 2 What ye **k**, the same do I know also. 1847
13: 2 What ye know, the same do I **k** also. 3045
13:18 my cause; I **k** that I shall be justified. 3045
13:23 make me to **k** my transgression and 3045
15: 9 What knowest thou, that we **k** not? 3045
19: 6 **K** now that God hath overthrown me, 3045
19:25 For I **k** that my Redeemer liveth, 3045
19:29 that ye may **k** there is a judgment. 3045
21:19 he rewardeth him, and he shall **k** it. 3045
21:27 I **k** your thoughts, and the devices which 3045
21:29 by the way? and do ye not **k** their tokens, 5234
22:13 thou sayest, How doth God **k**? can he 3045
23: 5 I would **k** the words which he would 3045
24: 1 do they that **k** him not see his days? 3045
24:13 they **k** not the ways thereof, nor abide in 5234
24:16 in the daytime: they **k** not the light. 3045
24:17 if one **k** them, they are in the terrors of 5234
30:23 For I **k** that thou wilt bring me to death, 3045
31: 6 that God may know mine integrity. 3045
32:22 For I **k** not to give flattering titles; in so 3045
34: 4 let us **k** among ourselves what is good. 3045
36:26 Behold, God is great, and we **k** him not, 3045
37: 7 every man; that all men may **k** his work. 3045
37:15 Dost thou **k** when God disposed them, 3045
37:16 Dost thou **k** the balancings of the clouds, 3045
38:12 and caused the dayspring to **k** his place; 3045
38:20 thou shouldest **k** the paths to the house 995

Job 42: 2 I **k** that thou canst do every thing, and 3045
Ps 4: 3 **k** that the LORD hath set apart him that is 3045
9:10 they that **k** thy name will put their trust 3045
9:20 that the nations may **k** themselves to be 3045
20: 6 Now **k** I that the LORD saveth his 3045
36:10 lovingkindness unto them that **k** thee; 3045
39: 4 make me to **k** mine end, and the 3045
39: 4 what it is; that I may **k** how frail I am. 3045
41:11 By this I **k** that thou favourest me, 3045
46:10 Be still, and **k** that I am God: I will be 3045
50:11 I **k** all the fowls of the mountains: 3045
51: 6 the hidden part thou shalt make me to **k** 3045
56: 9 turn back: this I **k**; for God is for me. 3045
59:13 let them **k** that God ruleth in Jacob unto 3045
71:15 the day; for I **k** not the numbers thereof. 3045
73:11 they say, How doth God **k**? and is there 3045
73:16 I thought to **k** this, it was too painful 3045
78: 6 the generation to come might **k** them, 3045
82: 5 They **k** not, neither will they understand; 3045
83:18 That men may **k** that thou, whose name 3045
87: 4 of Rahab and Babylon to them that **k** me: 3045
89:15 Blessed is the people that **k** the joyful 3045
94:10 teacheth man knowledge, shall not he **k**? NIH
100: 3 **K** ye that the LORD he is God: it is he 3045
101: 4 from me: I will not **k** a wicked person. 3045
103:16 and the place thereof shall **k** it no more. 5234
109:27 That they may **k** that this is thy hand; 3045
119:75 I **k**, O LORD, that thy judgments are 3045
119:125 that I may **k** thy testimonies. 3045
135: 5 For I **k** that the LORD is great, 3045
139:23 Search me, O God, and **k** my heart: try 3045
139:23 my heart: try me, and **k** my thoughts: 3045
140:12 I **k** that the LORD will maintain the cause 3045
142: 4 but there was no man that would **k** me: 5234
143: 8 **cause** me to **k** the way wherein I should 3045
Pr 1: 2 To **k** wisdom and instruction; to perceive 3045
4: 1 a father, and attend to **k** understanding. 3045
4:19 they **k** not at what they stumble. 3045
5: 6 moveable, that thou canst not **k** them. 3045
10:32 The lips of the righteous **k** what is 3045
22:21 That I might make thee **k** the certainty 3045
24:12 doth not he **k** it? and shall not he render 3045
25: 8 lest thou **k** not what to do in the end NIH
27:23 Be thou **diligent to k** the state of 3045+3045
29: 7 but the wicked regardeth not to **k** it. 1847
30:18 for me, yea, four which I **k** not: 3045
Ecc 1:17 gave my heart to **k** wisdom, and to know 3045
1:17 wisdom, and to **k** madness and folly: 3045
3:12 I **k** that there is no good in them, but for 3045
3:14 I **k** that, whatsoever God doeth, it shall 3045
7:25 I applied mine heart to **k**, and to search, 3045
7:25 things, and to **k** the wickedness of folly, 3045
8:12 yet surely I **k** that it shall be well with 3045
8:16 When I applied mine heart to **k** wisdom, 3045
8:17 though a wise man think to **k** it, yet shall 3045
9: 5 For the living **k** that they shall die: 3045
9: 5 the dead **k** not any thing, neither have 3045
11: 9 **k** thou, that for all these things God will 3045
SS 1: 8 If thou **k** not, O thou fairest among 3045
Isa 1: 3 but Israel doth not **k**, my people doth not 3045
5:19 draw nigh and come, that we may **k** it. 3045
7:15 that he may **k** to refuse the evil, 3045
7:16 For before the child shall **k** to refuse 3045
9: 9 all the people shall **k**, even Ephraim and 3045
19:12 let them **k** what the LORD of hosts hath 3045
19:21 the Egyptians shall **k** the LORD in that 3045
37:20 that all the kingdoms of the earth may **k** 3045
37:28 I **k** thy abode, and thy going out, and thy 3045
41:20 **k**, and consider, and understand together, 3045
41:22 them, and **k** the latter end of them; 3045
41:23 that we may **k** that ye are gods: 3045
41:26 from the beginning, that we may **k**? 3045
43:10 that ye may **k** and believe me, 3045
43:19 now it shall spring forth; shall ye not **k** it? 3045
44: 8 yea, there is no God; I **k** not any. 3045
44: 9 they see not, nor **k**; that they may be 3045
45: 3 that thou mayest **k** that I, the LORD, 3045
45: 6 they may **k** from the rising of the sun, 3045
47: 8 neither shall **k** the loss of children: 3045
47:11 thou shalt not **k** from whence it riseth: 3045
47:11 thee suddenly, which thou shalt not **k**. 3045
48: 6 hidden things, and thou didst not **k** them. 3045
49:23 and thou shalt **k** that I am the LORD: 3045
49:26 all flesh shall **k** that I the LORD am thy 3045
50: 4 that I should **k** how to speak a word in 3045
50: 7 flint, and I **k** that I shall not be ashamed. 3045
51: 7 Hearken unto me, ye that **k** righteousness, 3045
52: 6 Therefore my people shall **k** my name: 3045
52: 6 they shall **k** in that day that I am he that NIH
58: 2 seek me daily, and delight to **k** my ways, 1847
59: 8 The way of peace they **k** not; and there 3045
59: 8 goeth therein shall not **k** peace. 3045
59:12 and as for our iniquities, we **k** them; 3045
60:16 thou shalt **k** that I the LORD am thy 3045
66:18 For I **k** their works and their thoughts: NIH
Jer 2:19 **k** therefore and see that it is an evil thing 3045
2:23 way in the valley, **k** what thou hast done: 3045
5: 1 **k**, and seek in the broad places thereof, 3045
5: 4 for they **k** not the way of the LORD, 3045
6:18 Therefore hear, ye nations, and **k**, 3045
6:27 that thou mayest **k** and try their way. 3045
7: 9 walk after other gods whom ye **k** not; 3045
8: 7 my people **k** not the judgment of 3045
9: 3 and they **k** not me, saith the LORD. 3045
9: 6 through deceit they refuse to **k** me, saith 3045

Jer 10:23 I **k** that the way of man *is* not in himself: 3045
10:25 Pour out thy fury upon the heathen that **k** 3045
11:18 **k** it: then thou shewedst me their doings. 3045
13:12 Do we not **certainly k** that every 3045+3045
14:18 the priest go about into a land that they **k** 3045
15:15 **k** that for thy sake I have suffered rebuke. 3045
16:13 out of this land into a land that ye **k** not, 3045
16:21 I *will* this once **cause** them to **k**, 3045
16:21 I will **cause** them to **k** mine hand and 3045
16:21 they shall **k** that my name *is* The LORD. 3045
17: 9 and desperately wicked: who can **k** it? 3045
22:16 *was* well *with him: was* not this to **k** me? 1847
22:28 and are cast into a land which they **k** not? 3045
24: 7 I will give them a heart to **k** me, that I 3045
26:15 **k** ye **for certain**, that if ye put me 3045+3045
29:11 For I **k** the thoughts that I think towards 3045
29:16 *K* that thus saith the LORD of the king NIH
29:23 even I **k**, and *am* a witness, saith 3045
31:34 man his brother, saying, **K** the LORD: 3045
31:34 for they shall all **k** me, from the least of 3045
36:19 Jeremiah; and let no man **k** where ye *be.* 3045
38:24 Let no man **k** of these words, and thou 3045
40:14 Dost thou **certainly k** that Baalis 3045+3045
40:15 no man shall **k** *it:* wherefore should he 3045
42:19 **k certainly** that I have admonished 3045+3045
42:22 **k certainly** that ye shall die by 3045+3045
44:28 shall **k** whose words shall stand, mine, 3045
44:29 that ye may **k** that my words shall surely 3045
48:17 all ye that **k** his name, say, How is 3045
48:30 I **k** his wrath, saith the LORD; but *it shall* 3045

Eze 2: 5 yet shall **k** that there hath been a prophet 3045
5:13 they shall **k** that I the LORD have spoken 3045
6: 7 and ye shall **k** that I *am* the LORD. 3045
6:10 they shall **k** that I *am* the LORD. 3045
6:13 shall ye **k** that I *am* the LORD, when their 3045
6:14 and they shall **k** that I *am* the LORD. 3045
7: 4 and ye shall **k** that I *am* the LORD. 3045
7: 9 ye shall **k** that I *am* the LORD that 3045
7:27 and they shall **k** that I *am* the LORD. 3045
11: 5 I **k** the things that come into your mind, 3045
11:10 and ye shall **k** that I *am* the LORD. 3045
11:12 ye shall **k** that I *am* the LORD: for ye 3045
12:15 they shall **k** that I *am* the LORD, when I 3045
12:16 and they shall **k** that I *am* the LORD. 3045
12:20 and ye shall **k** that I *am* the LORD. 3045
13: 9 and ye shall **k** that I *am* the Lord GOD. 3045
13:14 and ye shall **k** that I *am* the LORD. 3045
13:21 and ye shall **k** that I *am* the LORD. 3045
13:23 and ye shall **k** that I *am* the LORD. 3045
14: 8 and ye shall **k** that I *am* the LORD. 3045
14:23 ye shall **k** that I have not done without 3045
15: 7 ye shall **k** that I *am* the LORD, when I set 3045
16: 2 **cause** Jerusalem to **k** her abominations, 3045
16:62 and thou shalt **k** that I *am* the LORD: 3045
17:12 **K** ye not what these *things mean?* tell 3045
17:21 ye shall **k** that I the LORD have spoken 3045
17:24 all the trees of the field shall **k** that I 3045
20: 4 wilt thou judge *them?* **cause** them to **k** 3045
20:12 that *they* might **k** that I *am* the LORD that 3045
20:20 that *ye* may **k** that I *am* the LORD your 3045
20:26 to the end that they might **k** that I *am* 3045
20:38 and ye shall **k** that I *am* the LORD. 3045
20:42 ye shall **k** that I *am* the LORD, when I 3045
20:44 ye shall **k** that I *am* the LORD, when I 3045
21: 5 That all flesh may **k** that I the LORD have 3045
22:16 and thou shalt **k** that I *am* the LORD. 3045
22:22 ye shall **k** that I the LORD have poured 3045
23:49 and ye shall **k** that I *am* the Lord GOD. 3045
24:24 ye shall **k** that I *am* the Lord GOD. 3045
24:27 and they shall **k** that I *am* the LORD. 3045
25: 5 and ye shall **k** that I *am* the LORD. 3045
25: 7 and thou shalt **k** that I *am* the LORD. 3045
25:11 and they shall **k** that I *am* the LORD. 3045
25:14 shall **k** my vengeance, saith the Lord 3045
25:17 they shall **k** that I *am* the LORD, when I 3045
26: 6 and they shall **k** that I *am* the LORD. 3045
28:19 All they that **k** thee among the people 3045
28:22 they shall **k** that I *am* the LORD, when I 3045
28:23 and they shall **k** that I *am* the LORD. 3045
28:24 and they shall **k** that I *am* the Lord GOD. 3045
28:26 they shall **k** that I *am* the LORD their 3045
29: 6 all the inhabitants of Egypt shall **k** that I 3045
29: 9 and they shall **k** that I *am* the LORD: 3045
29:16 but they shall **k** that I *am* the Lord GOD. 3045
29:21 and they shall **k** that I *am* the LORD. 3045
30: 8 they shall **k** that I *am* the LORD, when I 3045
30:19 and they shall **k** that I *am* the LORD. 3045
30:25 they shall **k** that I *am* the LORD, when I 3045
30:26 and they shall **k** that I *am* the LORD. 3045
32:15 shall they **k** that I *am* the LORD. 3045
33:29 shall they **k** that I *am* the LORD, when I 3045
33:33 they **k** that a prophet hath been among 3045
34:27 and shall **k** that I *am* the LORD. 3045
34:30 Thus shall they **k** that I the LORD their 3045
35: 4 and thou shalt **k** that I *am* the LORD. 3045
35: 9 ye shall **k** that I *am* the LORD. 3045
35:12 thou shalt **k** that I *am* the LORD, 3045
35:15 of it: and they shall **k** that I *am* the LORD. 3045
36:11 and ye shall **k** that I *am* the LORD. 3045
36:23 the heathen shall **k** that I *am* the LORD, 3045
36:36 **k** that I the LORD build the ruined *places,* 3045
36:38 and they shall **k** that I *am* the LORD. 3045
37: 6 and ye shall **k** that I *am* the LORD, when I 3045
37:13 ye shall **k** that I *am* the LORD, when I 3045
37:14 shall ye **k** that I the LORD have spoken *it,* 3045

Eze 37:28 the heathen shall **k** that I the LORD do 3045
38:14 Israel dwelleth safely, shalt thou not **k** *it?* 3045
38:16 my land, that the heathen may **k** me, 3045
38:23 and they shall **k** that I *am* the LORD. 3045
39: 6 and they shall **k** that I *am* the LORD. 3045
39: 7 the heathen shall **k** that I *am* the LORD. 3045
39:22 So the house of Israel shall **k** that I *am* 3045
39:23 heathen shall **k** that the house of Israel 3045
39:28 shall they **k** that I *am* the LORD their 3045

Da 2: 3 my spirit was troubled to **k** the dream. 3046
2: 8 **k** of certainty that ye would gain the time, 3046
2: 9 I shall **k** that ye can shew me 3046
2:21 knowledge to them that **k** understanding: 3046
2:30 *that* thou mightest **k** the thoughts of thy 3046
4: 9 I **k** that the spirit of the holy gods *is* in 3046
4:17 to the intent that the living may **k** that 3046
4:25 till thou **k** that the most High ruleth in 3046
4:32 until thou **k** that the most High ruleth in 3046
5:23 stone, which see not, nor hear, nor **k:** 3046
6:15 unto the king, **K**, O king, that the law 3046
7:16 **made** me **k** the interpretation of 3046
7:19 I would **k the truth** of the fourth beast, 3321
8:19 I *will* **make** thee **k** what shall be in the 3045
9:25 **K** therefore and understand, *that* from 3045
11:32 the people that do **k** their God shall be 3045

Hos 2: 8 For she did not **k** that I gave her corn, 3045
2:20 and thou shalt **k** the LORD. 3045
5: 3 I **k** Ephraim, and Israel is not hid from 3045
6: 3 shall we **k**, *if* we follow on to know 3045
6: 3 we know, *if* we follow on to **k** the LORD: 3045
8: 2 shall cry unto me, My God, we **k** thee. 3045
9: 7 Israel shall **k** *it:* the prophet *is* a fool, 3045
13: 4 Egypt, and thou shalt **k** no god but me: 3045
13: 5 I did **k** thee in the wilderness, in the land 3045
14: 9 things? prudent, and he shall **k** them? 3045

Joel 2:27 ye shall **k** that I *am* in the midst of Israel, 3045
3:17 So shall ye **k** that I *am* the LORD your 3045

Am 3:10 For they **k** not to do right, saith 3045
5:12 For I **k** your manifold transgressions and 3045

Jnh 1: 7 that we may **k** for whose cause this evil 3045
1:12 for I **k** that for my sake this great tempest 3045

Mic 3: 1 of Israel; *is it* not for you to **k** judgment? 3045
4:12 they **k** not the thoughts of the LORD, 3045
6: 5 that ye may **k** the righteousness of 3045

Zec 2: 9 ye shall **k** that the LORD of hosts hath 3045
2:11 thou shalt **k** that the LORD of hosts hath 3045
4: 9 thou shalt **k** that the LORD of hosts hath 3045
6:15 ye shall **k** that the LORD of hosts hath 3045

Mal 2: 4 ye shall **k** that I have sent this 3045

Mt 6: 3 let not thy left hand **k** what thy right hand 1097
7:11 **k how** to give good gifts unto your 1492
7:16 Ye shall **k** them by their fruits. Do *men* 1921
7:20 Wherefore by their fruits ye shall **k** them. 1921
9: 6 that ye may **k** that the Son of man hath 1492
9:30 them, saying, See *that* no man **k** *it.* 1097
13:11 Because it is given unto you to **k** 1097
10:22 and said, Ye **k** not what ye ask. 1492
20:25 Ye **k** that the princes of the Gentiles 1492
22:16 we **k** that thou art true, and teachest 1492
24:32 forth leaves, ye **k** that summer *is* nigh: 1097
24:33 when ye shall see all these *things,* **k** that 1492
24:42 for ye **k** not what hour your Lord doth 1492
24:43 **k** this, that if the goodman of the house 1492
25:12 said, Verily I say unto you, I **k** you not. 1492
25:13 for ye **k** neither the day nor the hour 1492
26: 2 Ye **k** that after two days is the *feast of* 1492
26:70 *them* all, saying, I **k** not what thou sayest. 1492
26:72 denied with an oath, I do not **k** the man. 1492
26:74 and to swear, *saying,* I **k** not the man. 1492
28: 5 for I **k** that ye seek Jesus, which was 1492

Mk 1:24 I **k** thee who thou art, the Holy One of 1492
2:10 that ye may **k** that the Son of man hath 1492
4:11 Unto you it is given to **k** the mystery of 1097
4:13 he said unto them, **K** ye not this parable? 1492
4:13 and how **then** will ye **k** all parables? 1097
5:43 them straitly that no *man* should **k** it; 1097
7:24 would have no *man* **k** *it:* but he could 1097
9:30 he would not that any *man* should **k** *it.* 1097
10:38 said unto them, Ye **k** not what ye ask: 1492
10:42 they **k** that which are accounted to rule 1492
12:14 we **k** that thou art true, and carest for no 1492
12:24 because ye **k** not the scriptures, 1492
13:28 forth leaves, ye **k** that summer is near: 1097
13:29 pass, **k** that it is nigh, *even* at the doors. 1097
13:33 and pray: for ye **k** not when the time is. 1492
13:35 ye **k** not when the master of the house 1492
14:68 But he denied, saying, I **k** not, neither 1492
14:71 I **k** not this man of whom ye speak. 1492

Lk 1: 4 That thou mightest **k** the certainty of 1921
1:18 unto the angel, Whereby shall I **k** this? 1097
1:34 How shall this be, seeing I **k** not a man? 1097
4:34 I **k** thee who thou art, the Holy One of 1492
5:24 that ye may **k** that the Son of man hath 1492
8:10 Unto you it is given to **k** the mysteries of 1097
9:55 Ye **k** not what manner of spirit ye are of. 1492
11:13 **k how** to give good gifts unto your 1492
12:39 And this **k**, that if the goodman of 1097
13:25 unto you, I **k** you not whence ye are; 1492
13:27 I tell you, I **k** you not whence you are; 1492
19:15 he might **k** how much every *man* had 1097
20:21 we **k** that thou sayest and teachest rightly, 1492
21:20 then **k** that the desolation thereof is nigh. 1097
21:30 **k** of your own selves that summer is now 1097
21:31 ye **k** that the kingdom of God is nigh at 1097
22:57 denied him, saying, Woman, I **k** him not. 1492

Lk 22:60 Peter said, Man, I **k** not what thou sayest. 1492
23:34 forgive them; for they **k** not what they do. 1492
24:16 were holden that *they* should not **k** him. 1921

Jn 1:26 standeth one among you, whom ye **k** not; 1492
3: 2 we **k** that thou art a teacher come from 1492
3:11 We speak that we do **k**, and testify that 1492
4:22 Ye worship ye **k** not what: we know what 1492
4:22 we **k** what we worship: for salvation is of 1492
4:25 I **k** that Messias cometh, which is called 1492
4:32 I have meat to eat that ye **k** not of. 1492
4:42 and **k** that this is indeed the Christ, 1492
5:32 I **k** that the witness which he witnesseth 1492
5:42 But I **k** you, that ye have not the love of 1097
6:42 of Joseph, whose father and mother we **k?** 1492
7:17 he shall **k** of the doctrine, whether it be of 1097
7:26 Do the rulers **k** indeed that this is the very 1097
7:27 Howbeit we **k** this *man* whence he is: 1492
7:28 Ye both **k** me, and ye know whence I am: 1492
7:28 Ye both know me, and ye **k** whence I am: 1492
7:28 he that sent me is true, whom ye **k** not. 1492
7:29 I **k** him: for I am from him, and he hath 1492
7:51 before it hear him, and **k** what he doeth? 1097
8:14 for I **k** whence I came, and whither I go; 1492
8:19 Ye **k** me, nor my Father: 1492
8:28 then shall ye **k** that I am *he,* and *that* I do 1097
8:32 ye shall **k** the truth, and the truth shall 1097
8:37 I **k** that ye are Abraham's seed; but ye 1097
8:52 him, Now we **k** that thou hast a devil. 1097
8:55 Yet ye have not known him; but I **k** him: 1492
8:55 and if I should say, I **k** him not, I shall be 1492
8:55 you: but I **k** him, and keep his saying. 1492
9:12 unto him, Where is he? He said, I **k** not. 1492
9:20 We **k** that this is our son, and that he was 1492
9:21 by what means he now seeth, we **k** not; 1492
9:21 or who hath opened his eyes, we **k** not: 1492
9:24 the praise: we **k** that this man is a sinner. 1492
9:25 Whether he be a sinner *or no,* I **k** not: 1492
9:25 one thing I **k**, that, whereas I was blind, 1492
9:29 We **k** that God spake unto Moses: *as for* 1492
9:29 *as for* this *fellow,* we **k** not from whence 1492
9:30 herein is a marvellous *thing,* that ye **k** 1492
9:31 Now we **k** that God heareth not sinners: 1492
10: 4 the sheep follow him: for they **k** his voice. 1492
10: 5 for they **k** not the voice of strangers. 1492
10:14 and **k** my *sheep,* and am known of mine. 1097
10:15 knoweth me, even so **k** I the Father: 1097
10:27 and I **k** them, and they follow me: 1097
10:38 ye may **k**, and believe, that the Father 1097
11:22 But I **k**, that even now, whatsoever thou 1492
11:24 I **k** that he shall rise again in 1492
11:49 said unto them, Ye **k** nothing at all, 1492
12:50 And I **k** that his commandment is life 1492
13: 7 not now; but thou shalt **k** hereafter. 1097
13:12 them, **K** ye what I have done to you? 1097
13:17 If ye **k** these *things,* happy are ye if ye do 1492
13:18 I **k** whom I have chosen: but that 1492
13:35 By this shall all *men* **k** that ye are my 1097
14: 4 And whither I go ye **k**, and the way ye 1492
14: 4 whither I go ye **k** know, and the way ye **k**. 1492
14: 5 Lord, we **k** not whither thou goest; 1492
14: 5 thou goest; and how can we **k** the way? 1492
14: 7 and from henceforth ye **k** him, 1097
14:17 ye **k** him; for he dwelleth with you, 1097
14:20 At that day ye shall **k** that I *am* in my 1097
14:31 But that the world may **k** that I love 1097
15:18 ye **k** that it hated me before *it hated* you. 1097
15:21 because they **k** not him that sent me. 1492
17: 3 that they might **k** thee the only true God, 1097
17:23 the world may **k** that thou hast sent me, 1097
18:21 unto them: behold, they **k** what I said. 1492
19: 4 that ye may **k** that I find no fault in him. 1097
20: 2 and we **k** not where they have laid him. 1492
20:13 and I **k** not where they have laid him. 1492
21:24 and we **k** that his testimony is true. 1492

Ac 1: 7 It is not for you to **k** the times or 1097
2:22 the midst of you, as ye yourselves also **k:** 1492
2:36 Therefore let all the house of Israel **k** 1097
3:16 this *man* strong, whom ye see and **k:** 1492
10:28 Ye **k** how that it is an unlawful thing for 1987
10:37 *That* word, I *say,* you **k**, which was 1492
12:11 he said, Now I **k** of a surety, that the Lord 1492
15: 7 ye **k** how that a good while ago God made 1987
17:19 saying, May we **k** what this new doctrine, 1097
17:20 we would **k** therefore what these *things* 1097
19:15 and said, Jesus I **k**, and Paul I know; 1097
19:15 and said, Jesus I know, and Paul I **k**; 1987
19:25 ye **k** that by this craft we have our wealth. 1987
20:18 come to him, he said unto them, Ye **k**, 1987
20:25 And now behold, I **k** that ye all, 1492
20:29 For I **k** this, that after my departing shall 1492
20:34 ye yourselves **k**, that these hands have 1097
21:24 all may **k** that *those things,* whereof they 1097
21:34 when he could not **k** the certainty for 1097
22:14 that *thou* shouldest **k** his will, and see 1097
22:19 they **k** that I imprisoned and beat in every 1987
22:24 that he might **k** wherefore they cried so 1921
24:10 Forasmuch as I **k** that thou hast been of 1987
24:22 I will be the **uttermost** of your matter. 1231
26: 3 I **k** thee to be expert in all customs and NIG
26: 4 own nation at Jerusalem, **k** all the Jews; 2467
26:27 thou the prophets? I **k** that thou believest. 1492
28:22 **k** that every where it is spoken 1110+1510

Ro 3:19 we **k** that what *things* soever the law 1492
6: 3 **K** ye **not**, that so many of us as were 50
6:16 **K** ye **not**, that to whom ye yield 1492

Ro 7: 1 **K** ye not, brethren, (for I speak to them 50
7: 1 (for I speak to them that **k** the law,) 1097
7:14 we **k** that the law is spiritual: but I am 1492
7:18 For I **k** that in me (that is, in my flesh,) 1492
8:22 we **k** that the whole creation groaneth 1492
8:26 we **k** not what we should pray for as we 1492
8:28 we **k** that all *things* work together for 1492
10:19 But I say, Did not Israel **k**? First Moses 1097
14:14 I **k**, and am persuaded by the Lord Jesus, 1492

1Co 1:16 I **k** not whether I baptized any other 1492
2: 2 I determined not to **k** any *thing* among 1492
2:12 that we might **k** the *things* that are freely 1492
2:14 neither can he **k** *them*, because they are 1492
3:16 **K** ye not that ye are the temple of God, 1492
4: 4 For I **k** nothing by myself; yet am I not 4894
4:19 to you shortly, if the Lord will, and will **k**, 1492
5: 6 **K** ye not that a little leaven leaveneth 1492
6: 2 Do ye not **k** that the saints shall judge 1492
6: 3 **K** ye not that we shall judge angels? 1492
6: 9 **K** ye not that the unrighteous shall not 1492
6:15 **K** ye not that your bodies are the 1492
6:16 **k** ye not that he which is joined to a 1492
6:19 **k** ye not that your body is the temple of 1492
8: 1 we **k** that we all have knowledge. 1492
8: 2 he knoweth nothing yet as he ought to **k**. 1097
8: 4 we **k** that an idol *is* nothing in the world, 1492
9:13 Do ye not **k** that they which minister 1492
9:24 **K** ye not that they which run in a race 1492
11: 3 But I would have you **k**, that the head of 1492
12: 2 Ye **k** that ye were Gentiles, carried away 1492
13: 9 For we **k** in part, and we prophesy in part. 1492
13:12 now I **k** in part; but then shall I know 1097
13:12 then shall I **k** even as also I am known. 1921
14:11 Therefore if I **k** not the meaning of 1492
15:58 forasmuch as ye **k** that your labour is 1492
16:15 brethren, (ye **k** the house of Stephanas, 1492

2Co 2: 4 ye might **k** the love which I have more 1097
2: 9 I write, that I might **k** the proof of you, 1097
5: 1 For we **k** that if our earthly house of *this* 1492
5:16 Wherefore henceforth **k** we no *man* after 1492
5:16 yet now henceforth **k** we *him* no more. 1097
8: 9 ye **k** the grace of our Lord Jesus Christ, 1097
9: 2 For I **k** the forwardness of your mind, 1492
13: 5 **k** ye not your own selves, how that Jesus 1921
13: 6 But I trust that ye shall **k** that we are not 1097

Gal 3: 7 **K** ye therefore that they which are of 1097
4:13 Ye **k** how through infirmity of the flesh I 1492

Eph 1:18 that ye may **k** what is the hope of his 1492
3:19 to **k** the love of Christ, which passeth 1097
5: 5 For this ye **k**, that no whoremonger, 1492
6:21 But that ye also may **k** my affairs, 1492
6:22 that ye might **k** our affairs, and *that* he 1097

Php 1:19 For I **k** that this shall turn to my salvation 1492
1:25 I **k** that I shall abide and continue with 1492
2:19 be of good comfort, when I **k** your state. 1097
2:22 But ye **k** the proof of him, that, as a son 1097
3:10 That I *may* **k** him, and the power of his 1097
4:12 I **k** both *how* to be abased, and I know 1492
4:12 *how* to be abased, and I **k** *how* to abound: 1492
4:15 Now ye Philippians **k** also, that in 1492

Col 4: 6 that *you* may **k** how ye ought to answer 1492
4: 8 that he might **k** your estate, 1097

1Th 1: 5 as ye **k** what manner of *men* we were 1492
2: 1 brethren, **k** our entrance in unto you, 1492
2: 2 shamefully entreated, as ye **k**, at Philippi, 1492
2: 5 as ye **k**, nor a cloke of covetousness; 1492
2:11 you **k** how we exhorted and comforted 1492
3: 3 for yourselves that we are appointed 1492
3: 4 even as it came to pass, and ye **k**. 1492
3: 5 no longer forbear, I sent to **k** your faith, 1097
4: 2 ye **k** what commandments we gave you 1492
4: 4 That every one of you should **k** how to 1492
4: 5 even as the Gentiles which **k** not God: 1492
5: 2 For yourselves **k** perfectly that the day of 1492
5:12 to **k** them which labour among you, 1492

2Th 1: 8 taking vengeance on them that **k** not God, 1492
2: 6 And now ye **k** what withholdeth that he 1492
3: 7 For yourselves **k** how ye ought to follow 1492

1Ti 1: 8 we **k** that the law *is* good, if a man use 1492
3: 5 (For if a man **k** not how to rule his own 1492
3:15 that thou mayest **k** how *thou* oughtest to 1492
4: 3 of them which believe and **k** the truth. 1921

2Ti 1:12 for I **k** whom I have believed, and I am 1492
3: 1 This **k** also, that in the last days perilous 1097

Tit 1:16 profess that *they* **k** God; but in works 1492

Heb 8:11 every man his brother, saying, The Lord: 1097
8:11 for all shall **k** me, from the least to 1492
10:30 For we **k** him that hath said, 1492
12:17 For ye **k** how that afterward, when he 2467
13:23 **K** ye that *our* brother Timothy is set at 1097

Jas 2:20 But wilt thou **k**, O vain man, that faith 1097
4: 4 ye **k** not that the friendship of the world 1492
4:14 Whereas ye **k** not what *shall be* on 1987
5:20 Let him **k**, that he which converteth 1097

1Pe 1:18 Forasmuch as ye **k** that ye were not 1492

2Pe 1:12 of these *things*, though ye **k** *them*, 1492
3:17 beloved, seeing ye **k** *these things* **before**, 4267

1Jn 2: 3 And hereby we do **k** that we know him, 1097
2: 3 And hereby we do know that we **k** him, 1097
2: 4 I **k** him, and keepeth not his 1097
2: 5 hereby **k** we that we are in him. 1097
2:18 whereby we **k** that it is the last time. 1097
2:20 from the Holy One, and ye **k** all *things*. 1492
2:21 unto you because ye **k** not the truth, 1492
2:21 but because ye **k** it, and that no lie is of 1492

1Jn 2:29 If ye **k** that he is righteous, ye know that 1492
2:29 ye **k** that every one which doeth 1097
3: 2 but we **k** that, when he shall appear, 1492
3: 5 And ye **k** that he was manifested to take 1492
3:14 We **k** that we have passed from death 1492
3:15 ye **k** that no murderer hath eternal life 1492
3:19 And hereby we **k** that we are of the truth, 1097
3:24 And hereby we **k** that he abideth in us, 1097
4: 2 Hereby **k** ye the Spirit of God: Every spirit 1097
4: 6 Hereby **k** we the spirit of truth, 1097
4:13 Hereby **k** we that we dwell in him, 1097
5: 2 By this we **k** that we love the children of 1097
5:13 that ye may **k** that ye have eternal life, 1492
5:15 if we **k** that he hear us, whatsoever we 1492
5:15 we **k** that we have the petitions that we 1492
5:18 We **k** that whosoever is born of God 1492
5:19 *And* we **k** that we are of God, 1492
5:20 And we **k** that the Son of God is come, 1492
5:20 that we may **k** him *that is* true, and we 1097

3Jn 1:12 and ye **k** that our record is true. 1492

Jude 1:10 evil of those *things* which they **k** not: 1492
1:10 but what they **k** naturally, as brute beasts, 1987

Rev 2: 2 I **k** thy works, and thy labour, 1492
2: 9 I **k** thy works, 1492
2: 9 *I* **k** the blasphemy of them which say they NIG
2:13 I **k** thy works, and where thou dwellest, 1492
2:19 I **k** thy works, and charity, and service, 1492
2:23 all the churches shall **k** that I am he 1097
3: 1 I **k** thy works, that thou hast a name that 1492
3: 3 thou shalt not **k** what hour I will come 1492
3: 8 I **k** thy works: behold, I have set before 1492
3: 9 thy feet, and to **k** that I have loved thee. 1097
3:15 I **k** thy works, that thou art neither cold 1492

KNOWEST (89) [KNOW]

Ge 30:26 for thou **k** my service which I have done 3045
30:29 Thou **k** how I have served thee, and how 3045
47: 6 if thou **k** *any* man of activity amongst 3045
Ex 10: 7 **k** thou not yet that Egypt is destroyed? 3045
32:22 thou **k** the people, that they *are* set on 3045
Nu 10:31 as thou **k** how we are to encamp 3045
11:16 thou **k** to be the elders of the people, 3045
20:14 Thou **k** all the travail that hath befallen 3045
Dt 7:15 diseases of Egypt, which thou **k**, upon 3045
9: 2 thou **k**, and *of whom* thou hast heard 3045
20:20 the trees which thou **k** that they *be* not 3045
28:33 shall a nation which thou **k** not eat up; 3045
Jos 14: 6 Thou **k** the thing that the LORD said unto 3045
Jdg 15:11 **k** thou not that the Philistines *are* rulers 3045
1Sa 28: 9 Behold, thou **k** what Saul hath done, 3045
2Sa 1: 5 How **k** thou that Saul and Jonathan his 3045
2:26 **k** thou not that it will be bitterness in 3045
3:25 Thou **k** Abner the son of Ner, that he 3045
7:20 for thou, Lord GOD, **k** thy servant. 3045
17: 8 thou **k** thy father and his men, that they 3045
1Ki 1:18 and now, my lord the king, thou **k** *it* not: 3045
2: 5 Moreover thou **k** also what Joab the son 3045
2: 9 and **k** what thou oughtest to do unto him; 3045
2:15 Thou **k** that the kingdom was mine, 3045
2:44 Thou **k** all the wickedness which thine 3045
5: 3 Thou **k** how that David my father could 3045
5: 6 for thou **k** that *there is* not among us any 3045
8:39 to his ways, whose heart thou **k**; 3045
8:39 the hearts of all the children of men;) 3045
2Ki 2: 3 **K** thou that the LORD will take away thy 3045
2: 5 **K** thou that the LORD will take away thy 3045
4: 1 thou **k** that thy servant did fear the LORD: 3045
1Ch 17:18 of thy servant? for thou **k** thy servant. 3045
2Ch 6:30 unto all his ways, whose heart thou **k**; 3045
6:30 (for thou only **k** the hearts of the children 3045
Job 10: 7 Thou **k** that I am not wicked; 1847+5921
15: 9 What **k** thou, that we know not? 3045
20: 4 **K** thou *not* this of old, since man was 3045
34:33 and not I: therefore speak what thou **k**. 3045
38: 5 hath laid the measures thereof, if thou **k**? 3045
38:18 of the earth? declare if thou **k** it all. 3045
38:21 **K** thou *it*, because thou wast then born? 3045
38:33 **K** thou the ordinances of heaven? canst 3045
39: 1 **K** thou the time when the wild goats of 3045
39: 2 or **k** thou the time when they bring forth? 3045
Ps 40: 9 not refrained my lips, O LORD, thou **k**. 3045
69: 5 O God, thou **k** my foolishness; and my sins 3045
139: 2 Thou **k** my downsitting and mine 3045
139: 4 *but* lo, O LORD, thou **k** it altogether. 3045
Pr 27: 1 thou **k** not what a day may bring forth. 3045
Ecc 11: 2 for thou **k** not what evil shall be upon 3045
11: 5 thou **k** not what *is* the way of the spirit, 3045
11: 5 thou **k** not the works of God who 3045
11: 6 for thou **k** not whether shall prosper, 3045
Isa 55: 5 thou shalt call a nation *that* thou **k** not, 3045
Jer 12: 3 thou, O LORD, **k** me: thou hast seen me, 3045
15:14 enemies into a land *which* thou **k** not: 3045
15:15 O LORD, thou **k**: remember me, 3045
17: 4 enemies in the land *which* thou **k** not: 3045
17:16 have I desired the woeful day; thou **k**: 3045
18:23 thou **k** all their counsel against me to slay 3045
33: 3 and mighty *things*, which thou **k** not. 3045
Eze 37: 3 And I answered, O Lord GOD, thou **k**. 3045
Da 10:20 **K** thou wherefore I come unto thee? 3045
Zec 4: 5 **K** thou not what these *be*? And I said, 3045
4:13 thou **k** not what these *be*? And I said, 3045
Mt 15:12 **K** thou that the Pharisees were offended, 1492
Mk 10:19 Thou **k** the commandments, Do not 1492
Lk 18:20 Thou **k** the commandments, Do not 1492

Lk 22:34 thou shalt thrice deny that *thou* **k** me. 1492
Jn 1:48 saith unto him, Whence **k** thou me? 1492
3:10 master of Israel, and **k** not these *things*? 1097
13: 7 unto him, What I do thou **k** not now; 1492
16:30 Now are we sure that thou **k** all *things*, 1492
19:10 **k** thou not that I have power to crucify 1492
21:15 Yea, Lord; thou **k** that I love thee. 1492
21:16 Yea, Lord; thou **k** that I love thee. 1492
21:17 thou **k** all *things*; thou knowest that I love 1492
21:17 thou knowest all *things*; thou **k** that I love 1097
Ac 1:24 **k** the hearts of all *men*, shew 2589
25:10 I done no wrong, as thou very well **k**. 1921
Ro 2:18 And **k** *his* will, and approvest the *things* 1097
1Co 7:16 what **k** thou, O wife, whether thou shalt 1492
7:16 how **k** thou, O man, whether thou shalt 1492
2Ti 1:15 thou **k**, that all they which are in Asia 1492
1:18 *unto* me at Ephesus, thou **k** very well. 1097
Rev 3:17 and **k** not that *thou* art wretched, 1492
7:14 And I said unto him, Sir, thou **k**. And he 1492

KNOWETH (104) [KNOW]

Ge 33:13 My lord **k** that the children *are* tender, 3045
Lev 5: 3 when he **k** *of it*, then he shall be guilty. 3045
5: 4 when he **k** *of it*, then he shall be guilty in 3045
Dt 2: 7 he **k** thy walking *through* this great 3045
34: 6 no man **k** of his sepulchre unto this day. 3045
Jos 22:22 of gods, he **k**, and Israel he shall know; 3045
1Sa 3:13 for ever for the iniquity which he **k**; 3045
20: 3 Thy father **certainly** **k** that I have 3045+3045
23:17 unto thee; and that also Saul my father **k**. 3045
2Sa 14:22 To day thy servant **k** that I have found 3045
17:10 for all Israel **k** that thy father *is* a mighty 3045
1Ki 1:11 doth reign, and David our lord **k** *it* not? 3045
Est 4:14 who **k** whether thou art come to 3045
Job 11:11 For he **k** vain men: he seeth wickedness 3045
12: 3 you: yea, who **k** not such *things* as these? 854
12: 9 Who **k** not in all these that the hand of 3045
14:21 His sons come to honour, and he **k** *it* not; 3045
15:23 *saying*, Where *is* it? he **k** that the day of 3045
18:21 this *is* the place *of him that* **k** not God. 3045
23:10 he **k** the way that I take: *when* he hath 3045
28: 7 *There is* a path which no fowl **k**, 3045
28:13 Man **k** not the price thereof; neither is it 3045
28:23 way thereof, and he **k** the place thereof. 3045
34:25 Therefore he **k** their works, 5234
35:15 anger; yet he **k** *it* not in great extremity: 3045
Ps 1: 6 For the LORD **k** the way of the righteous: 3045
37:18 The LORD **k** the days of the upright: 3045
39: 6 *riches*, and **k** not who shall gather them. 3045
44:21 this out? for he **k** the secrets of the heart. 3045
74: 9 neither *is there* among us any that **k** how 3045
90:11 Who **k** the power of thine anger? 3045
92: 6 A brutish man **k** not; neither doth a fool 3045
94:11 The LORD **k** the thoughts of man, 3045
103:14 For he **k** our frame; he remembereth that 3045
104:19 for seasons: the sun **k** his going down. 3045
138: 6 for the lowly: but the proud he **k** afar off. 3045
139:14 thy works; and *that* my soul **k** right well. 3045
Pr 7:23 the snare, and **k** not that it *is* for his life. 3045
9:13 clamorous: *she is* simple, and **k** nothing. 3045
9:18 he **k** not that the dead *are* there; 3045
14:10 The heart **k** his own bitterness; 3045
24:22 and who **k** the ruin of them both? 3045
Ecc 2:19 who **k** whether he shall be a wise *man* or 3045
3:21 **k** the spirit of man that goeth upward, 3045
6: 8 the poor, that **k** to walk before the living? 3045
6:12 who **k** what *is* good for man in *this* life, 3045
7:22 oftentimes also thine own heart **k** that 3045
8: 1 and who **k** the interpretation of a thing? 3045
8: 7 For he **k** not that which shall be: for who 3045
9: 1 no man **k** either love or hatred *by* all that 3045
9: 1 For man also **k** not his time: as the fishes 3045
10:15 because he **k** not how to go to the city. 3045
Isa 1: 3 The ox **k** his owner, and the ass his 3045
29:15 they say, Who seeth us? and who **k** us? 3045
Jer 8: 7 the stork in the heaven **k** her appointed 3045
9:24 in this, that he understandeth and **k** me, 3045
Da 2:22 things: he **k** what *is* in the darkness, 3046
Hos 7: 9 devoured his strength, and he **k** *it* not: 3045
7: 9 here and there upon him, yet he **k** not. 3045
Joel 2:14 Who **k** *if* he will return and repent, 3045
Na 1: 7 trouble; and he **k** them that trust in him. 3045
Zep 3: 5 he faileth not; but the unjust **k** no shame. 3045
Mt 6: 8 your Father **k** what *things* ye have need 1492
6:32 for your heavenly Father **k** that ye have 1492
11:27 and no *man* **k** the Son, but the Father; 1921
11:27 **k** any *man* the Father, save the Son, 1921
24:36 But of that day and hour **k** no man, no, 1492
Mk 4:27 spring and grow up, he **k** not how. 1492
13:32 of that day and *that* hour **k** no man, no, 1492
Lk 10:22 and no man **k** who the Son is, 1097
12:30 your Father **k** that ye have need of these 1492
16:15 before men; but God **k** your hearts: 1097
Jn 7:15 saying, How **k** this *man* letters, 1492
7:27 Christ cometh, no *man* **k** whence he is. 1492
7:49 But this people who **k** not the law are 1097
10:15 As the Father **k** me, *even so* know I 1097
12:35 for he that walketh in darkness **k** not 1492
14:17 because it seeth him not, neither **k** him: 1097
15:15 for the servant **k** not what his lord doeth: 1492
19:35 and he **k** that he saith true, that ye might 1492
Ac 15: 8 And God, which **k** the **hearts**, bare them 2589
19:35 what man is there that **k** not how that 1097
26:26 the king **k** of these *things*, before whom 1987
Ro 8:27 he that searcheth the hearts **k** what *is* 1492

1Co 2:11 For what man **k** the *things* of a man, *1492*
 2:11 even so the *things* of God **k** no man, but *1492*
 3:20 The Lord **k** the thoughts of the wise, *1097*
 8: 2 And if any *man* think that he **k** any *thing*, *1492*
 8: 2 he **k** nothing yet as he ought to know. *1097*
2Co 2: 9 because I love you not? God **k**. *1492*
 11:31 is blessed for evermore, **k** that I lie not. *1492*
 12: 2 God **k**;) such a one caught up to the third *1492*
 12: 3 or out of the body, I cannot tell: God **k**;) *1492*
2Ti 2:19 this seal, The Lord **k** them that are his. *1097*
Jas 4:17 Therefore to him that **k** to do good, *1492*
2Pe 2: 9 The Lord **k** *how* to deliver the godly out *1492*
1Jn 2:11 and **k** not whither he goeth, because *1097*
 3: 1 therefore the world **k** us not, because *1097*
 3:20 is greater than our heart, and **k** all *things*. *1097*
 4: 6 he that **k** God heareth us; *he that is not* *1097*
 4: 7 that loveth is born of God, and **k** God. *1097*
 4: 8 He that loveth not, **k** not God; for God is *1097*
Rev 2:17 no man **k** saving he that receiveth *it*. *1097*
 12:12 he **k** that he hath *but* a short time. *1492*

KNOWING (51) [KNOW]

Ge 3: 5 and ye shall be as gods, **k** good and evil. *3045*
1Ki 2:32 my father David not **k** *thereof, to wit,* *3045*
Mt 9: 4 And Jesus **k** their thoughts said, *1492*
 22:29 them, Ye do err, not **k** the scriptures, *1492*
Mk 5:30 And Jesus immediately **k** in himself that *1921*
 5:33 **k** what was done in her, came and *1492*
 6:20 **k** that he *was* a just man and a holy, *1492*
 12:15 But he, **k** their hypocrisy, said unto them, *1492*
Lk 8:53 him to scorn, **k** that she was dead. *1492*
 9:33 and one for Elias: not **k** what he said. *1492*
 11:17 But he, **k** their thoughts, said unto them, *1492*
Jn 13: 3 Jesus **k** that the Father had given all *1492*
 18: 4 **k** all *things* that should come upon him, *1492*
 19:28 Jesus **k** that all *things* were now *1492*
 21:12 Who art thou? **k** that it was the Lord. *1492*
Ac 2:30 **k** that God had sworn with an oath to *1492*
 5: 7 his wife, not **k** what was done, came in. *1492*
 18:25 of the Lord, **k** only the baptism of John. *1987*
 20:22 not **k** the *things* that shall befall me there: *1492*
Ro 1:32 Who **k** the judgment of God, that they *1921*
 2: 4 **not k** that the goodness of God leadeth *50*
 5: 3 **k** that tribulation worketh patience; *1492*
 6: 6 **k** this, that our old man is crucified with *1097*
 6: 9 **k** that Christ being raised from the dead *1492*
 13:11 And that, **k** the time, that now *it is* high *1492*
2Co 1: 7 And our hope of you *is* stedfast, **k** that as *1492*
 4:14 **k** that he which raised up the Lord Jesus *1492*
 5: 6 **k** that, whilst we are at home in the body, *1492*
 5:11 **k** therefore the terror of the Lord, *1492*
Gal 2:16 **k** that a man is not justified by the works *1492*
Eph 6: 8 **k** that whatsoever good *thing* any man *1492*
 6: 9 **k** that your Master also is in heaven; *1492*
Php 1:17 **k** that I am set for the defence of *1492*
Col 3:24 **k** that of the Lord ye shall receive *1492*
 4: 1 **k** that ye also have a Master in heaven. *1492*
1Th 1: 4 **K**, brethren beloved, your election of God. *1492*
1Ti 1: 9 **K** this, that the law is not made for a *1492*
 6: 4 **k** nothing, but doting about questions and *1987*
2Ti 2:23 **k** that they do gender strifes. *1492*
 3:14 **k** of whom thou hast learned *them;* *1492*
Tit 3:11 **K** that *he that is* such is subverted, *1492*
Phm 1:21 **k** that thou wilt also do more than I say. *1492*
Heb 10:34 **k** in yourselves that *ye* have in heaven a *1097*
 11: 8 and he went out, not **k** whither he went. *1987*
Jas 1: 3 **K** this, that the trying of your faith *1097*
 3: 1 that we shall receive the greater *1492*
1Pe 3: 9 **k** that ye are thereunto called, that ye *1492*
 5: 9 **k** that the same afflictions are *1492*
2Pe 1:14 **k** that shortly *I* must put off *this* my *1492*
 1:20 **K** this first, that no prophecy of *1097*
 3: 3 **K** this first, that there shall come in the *1097*

KNOWLEDGE (172) [KNOW]

Ge 2: 9 and the tree of **k** of good and evil. *1847*
 2:17 of the tree of the **k** of good and evil, *1847*
Ex 31: 3 in **k**, and in all *manner* of workmanship, *1847*
 35:31 in **k**, and in all *manner* of workmanship, *1847*
Lev 4:23 wherein he hath sinned, **come to** his **k**, *3045*
 4:28 **come to** his **k**, then he shall bring his *3045*
Nu 15:24 **without** the **k** of the congregation, *4480+5869*
 24:16 of God, and knew the **k** of the most High, *1847*
Dt 1:39 which *in that day* had no **k** between good *3045*
Ru 2:10 that *thou* shouldest **take k** of me, seeing I *5234*
 2:19 blessed be he that did **take k** of thee. *5234*
1Sa 2: 3 for the Lord *is* a God of **k**, and by him *1844*
 23:23 **take k** of all the lurking places where he *3045*
1Ki 9:27 shipmen that had **k** of the sea, with *3045*
2Ch 1:10 Give me now wisdom and **k**, that I may *4093*
 1:11 hast asked wisdom and **k** for thyself, *4093*
 1:12 Wisdom and **k** *is* granted unto thee; *4093*
 8:18 and servants that had **k** of the sea; *3045*
 30:22 **taught** the good **k** of the Lord: *7919+7922*
Ne 10:28 every one having **k**, *3045*
Job 15: 2 Should a wise *man* utter vain **k**, and fill *1847*
 21:14 for we desire not the **k** of thy ways. *1847*
 21:22 Shall *any* teach God **k**? seeing he judgeth *1847*
 33: 3 my heart: and my lips shall utter **k** clearly. *1847*
 34: 2 and give ear unto me, ye that **have k**. *3045*
 34:35 Job hath spoken without **k**, and his words *1847*
 35:16 in vain; he multiplieth words without **k**. *1847*
 36: 3 will fetch my **k** from afar, and will ascribe *1843*
 36: 4 false: *he that is* perfect in **k** *is* with thee. *1844*
 36:12 the sword, and they shall die without **k**. *1847*

Job 37:16 works of *him which is* perfect in **k**? *1843*
 38: 2 darkeneth counsel by words without **k**? *1847*
 42: 3 Who *is* he that hideth counsel without **k**? *1847*
Ps 14: 4 Have all the workers of iniquity no **k**? *3045*
 19: 2 and night unto night sheweth **k**. *1847*
 53: 4 Have the workers of iniquity no **k**? *3045*
 73:11 and is there **k** in the most High? *1844*
 94:10 that teacheth man **k**, *shall not he know?* *1847*
 119:66 Teach me good judgment and **k**: for I *1847*
 139: 6 *Such* **k** *is* too wonderful for me; it is high, *1847*
 144: 3 what *is* man, that thou **takest k** of him? *3045*
Pr 1: 4 to the young man **k** and discretion. *1847*
 1: 7 fear of the Lord *is* the beginning of **k**: *1847*
 1:22 delight in their scorning, and fools hate **k**? *1847*
 1:29 For that they hated **k**, and did not choose *1847*
 2: 3 if thou criest after **k**, *and* liftest up thy *998*
 2: 5 fear of the Lord, and find the **k** of God. *1847*
 2: 6 out of his mouth *cometh* **k** and *1847*
 2:10 heart, and **k** is pleasant unto thy soul; *1847*
 3:20 By his **k** the depths are broken up, *1847*
 5: 2 and that thy lips may keep **k**. *1847*
 8: 9 and right to them that find **k**. *1847*
 8:10 not silver; and **k** rather than choice gold. *1847*
 8:12 and find out **k** of witty inventions. *1847*
 9:10 and the **k** of the holy *is* understanding. *1847*
 10:14 Wise *men* lay up **k**: but the mouth of *1847*
 11: 9 but through **k** shall the just be delivered. *1847*
 12: 1 Whoso loveth instruction loveth **k**: *1847*
 12:23 A prudent *man* concealeth **k**: but the *1847*
 13:16 Every prudent *man* dealeth with **k**: *1847*
 14: 6 **k** *is* easy unto him that understandeth. *1847*
 14: 7 thou perceivest not *in him* the lips of **k**. *1847*
 14:18 but the prudent are crowned *with* **k**. *1847*
 15: 2 The tongue of the wise useth **k** aright: *1847*
 15: 7 The lips of the wise disperse **k**: *1847*
 15:14 him that hath understanding seeketh **k**: *1847*
 17:27 He that **hath k** spareth his words: *1847+3045*
 18:15 The heart of the prudent getteth **k**; *1847*
 18:15 and the ear of the wise seeketh **k**. *1847*
 19: 2 Also, *that* the soul *be* without **k**, *it is* not *1847*
 19:25 and he will understand **k**. *1847*
 19:27 *that causeth* to err from the words of **k**. *1847*
 20:15 but the lips of **k** *are* a precious jewel. *1847*
 21:11 the wise is instructed, he receiveth **k**. *1847*
 22:12 The eyes of the Lord preserve **k**, *1847*
 22:17 wise, and apply thine heart unto my **k**. *1847*
 22:20 thee excellent things in counsels and **k**, *1847*
 23:12 and thine ears to the words of **k**. *1847*
 24: 4 by **k** shall the chambers be filled *with* all *1847*
 24: 5 yea, a man of **k** increaseth strength. *1847*
 24:14 shall the **k** of wisdom be unto thy soul: *3045*
 28: 2 **k** the state *thereof* shall be prolonged. *1847*
 30: 3 nor **have** I the **k** of the holy. *1847+3045*
Ecc 1:16 had great experience of wisdom and **k**. *1847*
 1:18 he that increaseth **k** increaseth sorrow. *1847*
 2:21 *is* in wisdom, and in **k**, and in equity; *1847*
 2:26 good in his sight wisdom, and **k**, and joy: *1847*
 7:12 the excellency of **k** *is, that* wisdom giveth *1847*
 9:10 device, nor **k**, nor wisdom, in the grave, *1847*
 12: 9 was wise, he still taught the people **k**; *1847*
Isa 5:13 into captivity, because *they have* no **k**: *3045*
 8: 4 For before the child shall have **k** to cry, *3045*
 11: 2 the spirit of **k** and of the fear of *1847*
 11: 9 for the earth shall be full of *the* **k** of *1844*
 28: 9 Whom shall he teach **k**? and whom shall *1847*
 32: 4 heart also of the rash shall understand **k**, *1847*
 33: 6 and **k** shall be the stability of thy times, *1847*
 40:14 taught him **k**, and shewed to him the way *1847*
 44:19 *is there* **k** nor understanding to say, *1847*
 44:25 backward, and maketh their **k** foolish; *1847*
 45:20 they have no **k** that set up the wood of *3045*
 47:10 Thy wisdom and thy **k**, it hath perverted *1847*
 53:11 by his **k** shall my righteous servant justify *1847*
 58: 3 afflicted our soul, and thou **takest** no **k**? *3045*
Jer 3:15 which shall feed you with **k** and *1844*
 4:22 to do evil, but to do good they have no **k**. *3045*
 10:14 Every man is brutish in *his* **k**; *1847*
 11:18 the Lord hath **given** me **k** *of it,* and *1847*
 51:17 Every man is brutish by *his* **k**; *1847*
Da 1: 4 cunning in **k**, and understanding science, *1847*
 1:17 God gave them **k** and skill in all learning *4093*
 2:21 to them that know understanding: *4486*
 5:12 **k**, and understanding, interpreting of *4486*
 12: 4 run to and fro, and **k** shall be increased. *1847*
Hos 4: 1 nor mercy, nor **k** of God in the land. *1847*
 4: 6 My people are destroyed for lack of **k**, *1847*
 4: 6 because thou hast rejected **k**, I will also *1847*
 6: 6 the **k** of God more than burnt offerings. *1847*
Hab 2:14 For the earth shall be filled with the **k** of *3045*
Mal 2: 7 For the priest's lips should keep **k**, *1847*
Mt 14:35 And when the men of that place **had k** of *1921*
Lk 1:77 To give **k** of salvation unto his people by *1108*
 11:52 for ye have taken away the key of **k**: *1108*
Ac 4:13 they **took k** of them, that they had been *1921*
 17:13 But when the Jews of Thessalonica had **k** *1097*
 24: 8 **k** of all these *things,* whereof we accuse *1921*
 24:22 *things,* having more perfect **k** of *that* way, *1492*
Ro 1:28 they did not like to retain God in their **k**, *1922*
 2:20 which hast the form of **k** and of the truth *1108*
 3:20 in his sight: for by the law *is* the **k** of sin. *1922*
 10: 2 a zeal of God, but not according to **k**. *1922*
 11:33 riches both of the wisdom and **k** of God! *1108*
 15:14 also are full of goodness, filled with all **k**, *1108*
1Co 1: 5 by him, in all utterance, and in all **k**; *1108*
 8: 1 unto idols, we know that we all have **k**. *1108*

1Co 8: 1 **K** puffeth up, but charity edifieth. *1108*
 8: 7 Howbeit *there is* not in every *man that* **k**: *1108*
 8:10 For if any *man* see thee which hast **k** sit *1108*
 8:11 And through thy **k** shall the weak brother *1108*
 12: 8 another the word of **k** by the same Spirit; *1108*
 13: 2 and understand all mysteries, and all **k**; *1108*
 13: 8 whether *there be* **k**, it shall vanish away. *1108*
 14: 6 or by **k**, or by prophesying, or by doctrine? *1108*
 15:34 for some have **not** the **k** of God: I speak *56*
2Co 2:14 maketh manifest the savour of his **k** by us *1108*
 4: 6 to give the light of the **k** of the glory of *1108*
 6: 6 By pureness, by **k**, by longsuffering, *1108*
 8: 7 **k**, and in all diligence, and *in* your love *1108*
 10: 5 that exalteth itself against the **k** of God, *1108*
 11: 6 though *I be* rude in speech, yet not in **k**; *1108*
Eph 1:17 of wisdom and revelation in the **k** of him: *1922*
 3: 4 ye may understand my **k** in the mystery *4907*
 3:19 know the love of Christ, which passeth **k**; *1108*
 4:13 and of the **k** of the Son of God, unto a *1922*
Php 1: 9 and more in **k** and *in* all judgment; *1922*
 3: 8 loss for the excellency of the **k** of Christ *1922*
Col 1: 9 to desire that ye might be filled *with the* **k** *1922*
 1:10 work, and increasing in the **k** of God; *1922*
 2: 3 are hid all the treasures of wisdom and **k**. *1108*
 3:10 **k** after the image of him that created him: *1922*
1Ti 2: 4 and to come unto the **k** of the truth. *1922*
2Ti 3: 7 never able to come to the **k** of the truth. *1922*
Heb 10:26 that *we* have received the **k** of the truth, *1922*
Jas 3:13 *man* and endued with **k** amongst you? *1990*
1Pe 3: 7 dwell with *them* according to **k**, *1108*
2Pe 1: 2 be multiplied unto you through the **k** *1922*
 1: 3 through the **k** of him that hath called us *1922*
 1: 5 add to your faith virtue; and to virtue **k**; *1108*
 1: 6 And to **k** temperance; and to temperance *1108*
 1: 8 unfruitful in the **k** of our Lord Jesus Christ. *1922*
 2:20 of the world through the **k** of the Lord *1922*
 3:18 and *in* the **k** of our Lord and Saviour Jesus *1108*

KNOWN (222) [KNOW]

Ge 19: 8 I have two daughters which have not **k** *3045*
 24:16 a virgin, neither had any man **k** her: *3045*
 41:21 could not be **k** that they had eaten them; *3045*
 41:31 the plenty shall not be **k** in the land by *3045*
 45: 1 while Joseph **made** himself **k** unto his *3045*
Ex 2:14 and said, Surely this thing is **k**. *3045*
 6: 3 *by* my name JEHOVAH was I not **k** to *3045*
 21:36 *if* it be **k** that the ox *hath* used to push in *3045*
 33:16 For wherein shall it be **k** here that I and *3045*
Lev 4:14 is **k**, then the congregation shall offer a *3045*
 5: 1 or **k** *of it;* if he do not utter *it,* then *3045*
Nu 12: 6 *I* the Lord will **make** myself **k** unto him *3045*
 31:17 kill every woman that hath **k** man by *3045*
 31:18 that have not **k** a man by lying with him, *3045*
 31:35 women that had not **k** man by lying with *3045*
Dt 1:13 **k** among your tribes, and I will make *3045*
 1:15 and **k**, and made them heads over you, *3045*
 11: 2 not with your children which have not **k**. *3045*
 11:28 go after other gods, which ye have not **k**. *3045*
 13: 2 which thou hast not **k**, and let us serve *3045*
 13: 6 thou hast not **k**, thou, nor thy fathers; *3045*
 13:13 serve other gods, which ye have not **k**; *3045*
 21: 1 *and* it be not **k** who hath slain him: *3045*
 28:36 neither thou nor thy fathers have **k**; *3045*
 28:64 neither thou nor thy fathers have **k**, *3045*
 31:13 which have not **k** *any thing,* may hear, *3045*
Jos 24:31 which had **k** all the works of the Lord, *3045*
Jdg 3: 1 *even* as many of Israel as had not **k** all *3045*
 16: 9 the fire. So his strength was not **k**. *3045*
 21:12 had **k** no man by lying with *any* male: *3045*
Ru 3: 3 but **make** not thyself **k** unto the man, *3045*
 3:14 Let it not be **k** that a woman came *into* *3045*
1Sa 2: 6 *it is* **k** by you why his hand is not *3045*
 28:15 that thou mayest **make k** unto me what *3045*
2Sa 17:19 corn thereon; and the thing was not **k**. *3045*
1Ki 14: 2 that thou be not **k** to be the wife of *3045*
 18:36 let it be **k** this day that thou *art* God in *3045*
1Ch 16: 8 **make k** his deeds among the people. *3045*
 17: 19 in **making k** all *these* great things. *3045*
Ezr 4:12 Be it **k** unto the king, that the Jews which *3046*
 4:13 Be it **k** now unto the king, that, if this city *3046*
 5: 8 Be it **k** unto the king, that we went into *3045*
Ne 4:15 our enemies heard that it was **k** unto *3045*
 9:14 **madest k** unto them thy holy sabbath, *3045*
Est 2:22 the thing was **k** to Mordecai, who told *it* *3045*
Ps 9:16 The Lord is **k** *by* the judgment *which* he *3045*
 18:43 people *whom* I have not **k** shall serve me. *3045*
 31: 7 thou hast **k** my soul in adversities; *3045*
 48: 3 God is **k** in her palaces for a refuge. *3045*
 67: 2 That thy way may be **k** upon earth, *3045*
 69:19 Thou hast **k** my reproach, and my shame, *3045*
 76: 1 In Judah *is* God **k**: his name *is* great in *3045*
 77:19 great waters, and thy footsteps are not **k**. *3045*
 78: 3 Which we have heard and **k**, *3045*
 78: 5 that *they* should **make** them **k** to their *3045*
 79: 6 upon the heathen that have not **k** thee, *3045*
 79:10 let him be **k** among the heathen in our *3045*
 88:12 Shall thy wonders be **k** in the dark? *3045*
 89: 1 with my mouth will I **make k** thy *3045*
 91:14 on high, because he hath **k** my name. *3045*
 95:10 heart, and they have not **k** my ways: *3045*
 98: 2 The Lord hath **made k** his salvation: *3045*
 103: 7 He **made k** his ways unto Moses, his *3045*
 105: 1 **make k** his deeds among the people. *3045*
 106: 8 might **make** his mighty power **to be k**. *3045*
 119:79 and those that have **k** thy testimonies. *3045*

K

Ps 119:152 I have **k** of old that thou hast founded 3045
139: 1 thou hast searched me, and **k** me. 3045
145:12 To **make k** to the sons of men his mighty 3045
147:20 *for his* judgments, they have not **k** them. 3045
Pr 1:23 I will **make k** my words unto you. 3045
10: 9 he that perverteth his ways shall be **k**. 3045
12:16 fool's wrath is presently **k**: but a prudent 3045
14:33 which is in the midst of fools is **made k**. 3045
20:11 Even a child is **k** by his doings, whether 5234
22:19 I have **made k** to thee this day, even to 3045
31:23 Her husband is **k** in the gates, when he 3045
Ecc 5: 3 a fool's voice is **k** by multitude of words. NIH
6: 5 nor **k** any thing: this hath more rest than 3045
6:10 named already, and it is **k** that it is man: 3045
Isa 7: 3 excellent things: this is **k** in all the earth. 3045
19:21 the Lord shall be **k** to Egypt, 3045
38:19 father to the children shall **make k** thy 3045
40:21 Have ye not **k**? have ye not heard? hath it 3045
40:28 Hast thou not **k**? hast thou not heard, 3045
42:16 lead them in paths that they have not **k**: 3045
44:18 They have not **k** nor understood: for he 3045
45: 4 thee, though thou hast not **k** me. 3045
45: 5 I girded thee though thou hast not **k** me: 3045
61: 9 their seed shall be **k** among the Gentiles, 3045
64: 2 to **make** thy name **k** to thine adversaries, 3045
66:14 the hand of the Lord shall be **k** towards 3045
Jer 4:22 my people is foolish, they have not **k** me; 3045
5: 5 for they have **k** the way of the Lord, 3045
9:16 neither they nor their fathers have **k**: 3045
19: 4 neither they nor their fathers have **k**, 3045
28: 9 then shall the prophet be **k**, that the Lord 3045
La 4: 8 than a coal; they are not **k** in the streets: 5234
Eze 20: 5 **made** myself **k** unto them in the land of 3045
20: 9 whose sight I **made** myself **k** unto them, 3045
32: 9 into the countries which thou hast not **k**. 3045
35:11 I will **make** myself **k** amongst them, 3045
36:32 this, saith the Lord God, be it **k** unto you: 3045
38:23 I will be **k** in the eyes of many nations, 3045
39: 7 So will I **make** my holy name **k** in 3045
Da 2: 5 if ye will not **make k** unto me the dream, 3046
2: 9 if ye will not **make k** unto me the dream, 3046
2:15 Then Arioch **made** the thing **k** to Daniel. 3046
2:17 **made** the thing **k** to Hananiah, Mishael, 3046
2:23 **made k** unto me now what we desired 3046
2:23 for thou hast now **made k** unto us 3046
2:25 that will **make k** unto the king 3046
2:26 thou able to **make k** unto me the dream 3046
2:28 **maketh k** to the king Nebuchadnezzar 3046
2:29 that revealeth secrets **maketh k** to thee 3046
2:30 for their sakes that **make k** 3046
2:45 the great God hath **made k** to the king 3046
3:18 if not, be it **k** unto thee, O king, that we 3046
4: 6 that they might **make k** unto me 3046
4: 7 they did not **make k** unto me 3046
4:18 to **make k** unto me the interpretation: 3046
4:26 that thou shalt have **k** that the heavens 3046
5: 8 nor **make k** to the king the interpretation 3046
5:15 **make k** unto me the interpretation 3046
5:16 **make k** to me the interpretation thereof, 3046
5:17 and **make k** to him the interpretation. 3046
Hos 5: 4 of them, and they have not **k** the Lord. 3045
5: 9 among the tribes of Israel have I **made k** 3045
Am 3: 2 You only have I **k** of all the families of 3045
Na 3:17 and their place is not **k** where they are. 3045
Hab 3: 2 years, in the midst of the years **make k**; 3045
Zec 14: 7 it shall be one day which shall be **k** to 3045
Mt 10:26 be revealed; and hid, that shall not be **k**. 1097
12: 7 But if ye had **k** what this meaneth, I will 1097
12:16 them that they should not make him **k**: 5318
12:33 fruit corrupt: for the tree is **k** by his fruit. 1097
24:43 that if the goodman of the house had **k** 1492
Mk 3:12 them that they should not make him **k**. 5318
Lk 2:15 which the Lord hath **made k** unto us. 1107
2:17 **made k** abroad the saying which was 1232
6:44 For every tree is **k** by his own fruit. 1097
7:39 would have **k** who and what manner of 1097
8:17 that shall not be **k** and come abroad. 1097
12: 2 revealed; neither hid, that shall not be **k**. 1097
12:39 that if the goodman of the house had **k** 1492
19:42 If thou hadst **k**, even thou, at least 1097
24:18 hast not **k** the things which are come to 1097
24:35 he was **k** of them in breaking of bread. 1097
Jn 7: 4 he himself seeketh to be **k** openly. 1722+3954
8:19 if ye had **k** me, ye should have known my 1492
8:19 ye should have **k** my Father also. 1492
8:55 Yet ye have not **k** him; but I know him: 1097
10:14 and know my sheep, and am **k** of mine. 1097
14: 7 If ye had **k** me, ye should have known my 1097
14: 7 ye should have **k** my Father also: 1097
14: 9 and yet hast thou not **k** me, Philip? 1097
15:15 of my Father I have **made k** unto you. 1107
16: 3 they have not **k** the Father, nor me. 1097
17: 7 they have **k** that all things whatsoever 1097
17: 8 have **k** surely that I came out from thee, 1097
17:25 Father, the world hath not **k** thee: 1097
17:25 but I have **k** thee, and these have known 1097
17:25 and these have **k** that thou hast sent me. 1097
18:15 that disciple was **k** unto the high priest, 1110
18:16 which was **k** unto the high priest, 1110
Ac 1:19 And it was **k** unto all the dwellers at 1110
2:14 be this **k** unto you, and hearken to my 1110
2:28 Thou hast **made k** to me the ways of life; 1107
4:10 Be it **k** unto you all, and to all the people 1110
7:13 at the second time Joseph was **made k** 319
7:13 Joseph's kindred was **made k** unto 5318

Ac 9:24 But their laying await was **k** of Saul. 1097
9:42 And it was **k** throughout all Joppa; 1110
13:38 Be it **k** unto you therefore, men and 1110
15:18 **K** unto God are all his works from 1110
19:17 And this was **k** to all the Jews and 1097
22:30 he would have **k** the certainty wherefore 1097
23:28 And when I would have **k** the cause 1097
28:28 Be it therefore **k** unto you, that 1110
Ro 1:19 Because that which may be **k** of God is 1110
3:17 And the way of peace have they not **k**: 1097
7: 7 Nay, I had not **k** sin, but by the law: for I 1097
7: 7 I had not **k** lust, except the law had said, 1492
9:22 his wrath, and to **make** his power **k**, 1107
9:23 that he might **make k** the riches of his 1107
11:34 For who hath **k** the mind of the Lord? 1097
16:26 **made k** to all nations for the obedience 1107
1Co 2: 8 for had they **k** it, they would not have 1097
2:16 For who hath **k** the mind of the Lord, 1097
8: 3 if any man love God, the same is **k** of him. 1097
13:12 but then shall I **know** even as also I am **k**. 1921
14: 7 how shall it be **k** what is piped or harped? 1097
14: 9 how shall it be **k** what is spoken? 1097
2Co 3: 2 in our hearts, **k** and read of all men: 1097
5:16 though we have **k** Christ after the flesh, 1097
6: 9 As unknown, and yet well **k**; as dying, 1921
Gal 4: 9 after that ye have **k** God, or rather are 1097
4: 9 rather are **k** of God, how turn ye again to 1097
Eph 1: 9 Having **made k** unto us the mystery of his 1107
3: 3 that by revelation he **made k** unto me 1107
3: 5 in other ages was not **made k** unto 1107
3:10 powers in heavenly places might be **k** by 1107
6:19 to **make k** the mystery of the gospel, 1107
6:21 the Lord, shall **make k** to you all things: 1107
Php 4: 5 Let your moderation be **k** unto all men. 1097
4: 6 let your requests be **made k** unto God. 1107
Col 1:27 To whom God would **make k** what is 1107
4: 9 They shall **make k** unto you all things 1107
2Ti 3:10 But thou hast **fully k** my doctrine, 3877
3:15 that from a child thou hast **k** the holy 1492
4:17 by me the preaching might be **fully k**, 4135
Heb 3:10 heart; and they have not **k** my ways. 1097
2Pe 1:16 when we **made k** unto you the power 1107
2:21 it had been better for them not to have **k** 1921
2:21 after they have **k** it, to turn from the holy 1921
1Jn 2:13 ye have **k** him that is from the beginning. 1097
2:13 because ye have **k** the Father. 1097
2:14 ye have **k** him that is from the beginning. 1097
3: 6 sinneth hath not seen him, neither **k** him. 1097
4:16 And we have **k** and believed the love that 1097
2Jn 1: 1 but also all they that have **k** the truth; 1097
Rev 2:24 which have not **k** the depths of Satan, 1097

KOA (1)
Eze 23:23 the Chaldeans, Pekod, and Shoa, and **K**, 6970

KOHATH (32) [KOHATHITES]
Ge 46:11 sons of Levi; Gershon, **K**, and Merari. 6955
Ex 6:16 Gershon, and **K**, and Merari: 6955
6:18 the sons of **K**; Amram, and Izhar, 6955
6:18 years of the life of **K** were an hundred 6955
Nu 3:17 names; Gershon, and **K**, and Merari. 6955
3:19 the sons of **K** by their families; Amram, 6955
3:27 of **K** was the family of the Amramites, 6955
3:29 The families of the sons of **K** shall pitch 6955
4: 2 Take the sum of the sons of **K** from 6955
4: 4 This shall be the service of the sons of **K** 6955
4:15 the sons of **K** shall come to bear it: but 6955
4:15 **K** in the tabernacle of the congregation. 6955
7: 9 unto the sons of **K** he gave none: because 6955
16: 1 the son of **K**, the son of Levi, and Dathan 6955
26:57 of **K**, the family of the Kohathites: 6955
26:58 the Korahites. And **K** begat Amram. 6955
Jos 21: 5 the rest of the children of **K** had by lot 6955
21:20 the families of the children of **K**, 6955
21:20 which remained of the children of **K**, 6955
21:26 of the children of **K** that remained. 6955
1Ch 6: 1 sons of Levi; Gershon, and Merari. 6955
6: 2 sons of **K**; Amram, Izhar, and Hebron, 6955
6:16 sons of Levi; Gershom, **K**, and Merari. 6955
6:18 the sons of **K** were, Amram, and Izhar, 6955
6:22 The sons of **K**; Amminadab his son, 6955
6:38 the son of **K**, the son of Levi, the son of 6955
6:61 unto the sons of **K**, which were left of 6955
6:66 residue of the families of the sons of **K** 6955
6:70 family of the remnant of the sons of **K**. 6955
15: 5 Of the sons of **K**; Uriel the chief, 6955
23: 6 of Levi, namely, Gershon, **K**, and Merari. 6955
23:12 The sons of **K**; Amram, Izhar, Hebron, 6955

KOHATHITES (15) [KOHATH]
Nu 3:27 these are the families of the **K**. 6956
3:30 **K** shall be Elizaphan the son of Uzziel. 6956
4:18 families of the **K** from among the Levites: 6956
4:34 the sons of the **K** after their families, 6956
4:37 were numbered of the families of the **K**, 6956
10:21 the **K** set forward, bearing the sanctuary, 6956
26:57 of Kohath, the family of the **K**: of Merari, 6956
Jos 21: 4 the lot came out for the families of the **K**: 6956
21:10 of Aaron, being of the families of the **K**, 6956
1Ch 6:33 Of the sons of the **K**: Heman a singer, 6956
6:54 sons of Aaron, of the families of the **K**: 6956
9:32 sons of the **K**, were over 6956
2Ch 20:19 the children of the **K**, and of the children 6956
29:12 the son of Azariah, of the sons of the **K**: 6956
34:12 and Meshullam, of the sons of the **K**, 6956

KOLAIAH (2)
Ne 11: 7 of Joed, the son of Pedaiah, the son of **K**, 6964
Jer 29:21 of Ahab the son of **K**, and of Zedekiah, 6964

KORAH (37) [KORAHITE, KORAHITES, KORHITES]
Ge 36: 5 bare Jeush, and Jaalam, and **K**: 7141
36:14 bare to Esau Jeush, and Jaalam, and **K**. 7141
36:16 Duke **K**, duke Gatam, and duke Amalek: 7141
36:18 duke Jeush, duke Jaalam, duke **K**: 7141
Ex 6:21 sons of Izhar; **K**, and Nepheg, and Zichri. 7141
6:24 the sons of **K**; Assir, and Elkanah, 7141
Nu 16: 1 Now **K**, the son of Izhar, the son of 7141
16: 5 spake unto **K** and unto all his company, 7141
16: 6 Take you censers, **K**, and all his company; 7141
16: 8 Moses said unto **K**, Hear, I pray you, 7141
16:16 Moses said unto **K**, Be thou and all thy 7141
16:19 **K** gathered all the congregation against 7141
16:24 you up from about the tabernacle of **K**, 7141
16:27 So they gat up from the tabernacle of **K**, 7141
16:32 all the men that appertained unto **K**, 7141
16:40 that he be not as **K**, and as his company: 7141
16:49 them that died about the matter of **K**. 7141
26: 9 and against Aaron in the company of **K**, 7141
26:10 swallowed them up together with **K**, 7141
26:11 the children of **K** died not. 7141
27: 3 against the Lord in the company of **K**; 7141
1Ch 1:35 Reuel, and Jeush, and Jaalam, and **K**. 7141
2:43 **K**, and Tappuah, and Rekem, and Shema. 7141
6:22 his son, **K** his son, Assir his son, 7141
6:37 Assir, the son of Ebiasaph, the son of **K**, 7141
9:19 Ebiasaph, the son of **K**, and his brethren, 7141
Ps 42: T chief Musician, Maschil, for the sons of **K**. 7141
44: T To the chief Musician for the sons of **K**, 7141
45: T for the sons of **K**, Maschil, A Song of 7141
46: T To the chief Musician for the sons of **K**, 7141
47: T chief Musician, A Psalm for the sons of **K**. 7141
48: T A Song and Psalm for the sons of **K**. 7141
49: T chief Musician, A Psalm for the sons of **K**. 7141
84: T upon Gittith, A Psalm for the sons of **K**. 7141
85: T chief Musician, A Psalm for the sons of **K**. 7141
87: T A Psalm or Song for the sons of **K**. 7141
88: T A Song or Psalm for the sons of **K**. 7141

KORAHITE (1) [KORAH]
1Ch 9:31 who was the firstborn of Shallum the **K**, 7145

KORAHITES (2) [KORAH]
Nu 26:58 of the Mushites, the family of the **K**. 7145
1Ch 9:19 of the house of his father, the **K**, 7145

KORAZIN See CHORAZIN

KORE (4)
1Ch 9:19 Shallum the son of **K**, the son of Ebiasaph, 6981
26: 1 Korhites was Meshelemiah the son of **K**, 6981
26:19 of the porters among the sons of **K**, 7145
2Ch 31:14 **K** the son of Imnah the Levite, the porter 6981

KORHITES (4) [KORAH]
Ex 6:24 Abiasaph: these are the families of the **K**. 7145
1Ch 12: 6 and Joezer, and Jashobeam, the **K**, 7145
26: 1 Of the **K** was Meshelemiah the son of 7145
2Ch 20:19 and of the children of the **K**, 7145

KOUM See CUMI

KOZ (4)
Ezr 2:61 children of Habaiah, the children of **K**, 6976
Ne 3: 4 the son of Urijah, the son of **K**. 6976
3:21 of Urijah the son of **K** another piece, 6976
7:63 children of Habaiah, the children of **K**, 6976

KUSHAIAH (1)
1Ch 15:17 their brethren, Ethan the son of **K**; 6984

L

LAADAH (1)
1Ch 4:21 **L** the father of Mareshah, and the families 3935

LAADAN (7)
1Ch 7:26 **L** his son, Ammihud his son, Elishama his 3936
23: 7 Of the Gershonites were, **L**, and Shimei. 3936
23: 8 the sons of **L**; the chief was Jehiel, 3936
23: 9 These were the chief of the fathers of **L**. 3936
26:21 As concerning the sons of **L**; the sons of 3936
26:21 the sons of the Gershonite **L**, chief fathers, 3936
26:21 even of **L** the Gershonite, were Jehiel. 3936

LABAN (51) [LABAN'S]
Ge 24:29 had a brother, and his name was **L**: 3837
24:29 **L** ran out unto the man, unto the well. 3837
24:50 **L** and Bethuel answered and said, 3837
25:20 of Padan-aram, the sister to **L** the Syrian. 3837
27:43 arise, flee thou to **L** my brother to Haran; 3837
28: 2 the daughters of **L** thy mother's brother. 3837

Ge	28: 5 he went to Padan-aram unto **L**, son of	3837
	29: 5 unto them, Know ye **L** the son of Nahor?	3837
	29:10 when Jacob saw Rachel the daughter of **L**	3837
	29:10 the sheep of **L** his mother's brother,	3837
	29:10 the flock of **L** his mother's brother.	3837
	29:13 when **L** heard the tidings of Jacob his	3837
	29:13 his house. And he told **L** all these things.	3837
	29:14 said to him, Surely thou *art* my bone	3837
	29:15 **L** said unto Jacob, Because thou *art* my	3837
	29:16 **L** had two daughters: the name of the	3837
	29:19 **L** said, *It is* better that I give her to thee,	3837
	29:21 Jacob said unto **L**, Give *me* my wife,	3837
	29:22 **L** gathered together all the men of	3837
	29:24 **L** gave unto his daughter Leah Zilpah his	3837
	29:25 he said to **L**, What *is* this thou hast done	3837
	29:26 **L** said, It must not be so done in our	3837
	29:29 **L** gave to Rachel his daughter Bilhah his	3837
	30:25 that Jacob said unto **L**, Send me away,	3837
	30:27 **L** said unto him, I pray thee, if I have	3837
	30:34 **L** said, Behold, I would it might be	3837
	30:40 and all the brown in the flock of **L**;	3837
	31: 2 Jacob beheld the countenance of **L**,	3837
	31:12 for I have seen all that **L** doeth unto thee.	3837
	31:19 **L** went to shear his sheep: and Rachel had	3837
	31:20 Jacob **stole** away unawares to **L** the Syrian,	3837
	31:22 it was told **L** on the third day that Jacob	3837
	31:24 God came to **L** the Syrian in a dream by	3837
	31:25 **L** overtook Jacob. Now Jacob had pitched	3837
	31:25 **L** with his brethren pitched in the mount	3837
	31:26 **L** said to Jacob, What hast thou done,	3837
	31:31 Jacob answered and said to **L**, Because I	3837
	31:33 **L** went into Jacob's tent, and into Leah's	3837
	31:34 **L** searched the tent, but found *them*	3837
	31:36 Jacob was wroth, and chode with **L**:	3837
	31:36 Jacob answered and said to **L**, What *is* my	3837
	31:43 **L** answered and said unto Jacob, These	3837
	31:47 **L** called it Jegar-sahadutha:	3837
	31:48 **L** said, This heap *is* a witness between me	3837
	31:51 **L** said to Jacob, Behold this heap,	3837
	31:55 early in the morning **L** rose up,	3837
	31:55 **L** departed, and returned unto his place.	3837
	32: 4 I have sojourned with **L**, and stayed *there*	3837
	46:18 whom **L** gave to Leah his daughter,	3837
	46:25 which **L** gave unto Rachel his daughter,	3837
Dt	1: 1 and **L**, and Hazeroth, and Dizahab.	3837

LABAN'S (4) [LABAN]

Ge	30:36 and Jacob fed the rest of **L** flocks.	3837
	30:40 and put them unto **L** cattle.	3837
	30:42 so the feebler were **L**, and the stronger	3837
	31: 1 he heard the words of **L** sons, saying,	3837

LABOR See TRAVAIL; TRAVAILED; TRAVAILEST; TRAVAILETH

LABORERS See HIRELING

LABOUR (89) [FELLOWLABOURER, FELLOWLABOURERS, LABOURED, LABOURER, LABOURERS, LABOURETH, LABOURING, LABOURS]

Ge	31:42 mine affliction and the **l** of my hands,	3018
	35:16 and Rachel travailed, and she had hard **l**.	3205
	35:17 it came to pass, when she was in hard **l**,	3205
Ex	5: 9 upon the men, that they may **l** therein;	6213
	20: 9 Six days shalt thou **l**, and do all thy work;	5647
Dt	5:13 Six days shalt thou **l**, and do all thy work:	5647
	26: 7 and our **l**, and our oppression:	5999
Jos	7: 3 and **make** not all the people to **l** thither;	3021
	24:13 given you a land for which ye did not **l**,	3021
Ne	4:22 may be a guard to us, and **l** on the day.	4399
	5:13 his **l**, that performeth not this promise.	3018
Job	9:29 *If* I be wicked, why then I **l** in vain?	3021
	39:11 *is* great? or wilt thou leave thy **l** to him?	3018
	39:16 not hers: her **l** *is* in vain without fear;	3018
Ps	78:46 the caterpillar, and their **l** unto the locust.	3018
	90:10 yet *is* their strength and sorrow;	5999
	104:23 his work and to his **l** until the evening.	5656
	105:44 and they inherited the **l** of the people;	5999
	107:12 he brought down their heart with **l**;	5999
	109:11 he hath; and let the strangers spoil his **l**.	3018
	127: 1 the house, they **l** in vain that build it:	5998
	128: 2 For thou shalt eat the **l** of thine hands:	3018
	144:14 *That* our oxen may be **strong to l**;	5445
Pr	10:16 The **l** of the righteous *tendeth* to life:	6468
	13:11 but he that gathereth by **l** shall increase.	3027
	14:23 In all **l** there is profit: but the talk of the	6089
	21:25 killeth him; for his hands refuse to **l**.	6213
	23: 4 **L** not to be rich: cease from thine own	3021
Ecc	1: 3 What profit hath a man of all his **l** which	5999
	1: 8 All things *are* **full of l**; man cannot utter	3023
	2:10 any joy; for my heart rejoiced in all my **l**:	5999
	2:10 and this was my portion of all my **l**.	5999
	2:11 and on the **l** that I had laboured to do:	5999
	2:18 I hated all my **l** which I *had* taken under	5999
	2:19 shall he have rule over all my **l** where*in*	5999
	2:20 of all the **l** which I took under the sun.	5999
	2:21 For there is a man whose **l** *is* in wisdom,	5999
	2:22 For what hath man of all his **l**, and of	5999
	2:24 should make his soul enjoy good in his **l**.	5999
	3:13 and drink, and enjoy the good of all his **l**,	5999
	4: 8 yet *is there* no end of all his **l**; neither is	5999
	4: 8 neither *saith he*, For whom do I **l**,	6001
	4: 9 they have a good reward for their **l**.	5999
	5:15 shall take nothing of his **l**, which he may	5999

Ecc	5:18 enjoy the good of all his **l** that he taketh	5999
	5:19 to take his portion, and to rejoice in his **l**;	5999
	6: 7 All the **l** of man *is* for his mouth,	5999
	8:15 for that shall abide with him of his **l**	5999
	8:17 because though a man **l** to seek *it* out,	5998
	9: 9 in thy **l** which thou hast under the sun.	5999
	10:15 The **l** of the foolish wearieth every one of	5999
Isa	22: 4 **l** not to comfort me, because of the	213
	45:14 The **l** of Egypt, and merchandise of	3018
	55: 2 your **l** for *that which* satisfieth not?	3018
	65:23 They shall not **l** in vain, nor bring forth	3021
Jer	3:24 For shame hath devoured the **l** of our	3018
	20:18 came I forth out of the womb to see **l**	5999
	51:58 the people shall **l** in vain, and the folk in	3021
La	5: 5 under persecution: we **l**, *and* have no rest.	3021
Eze	23:29 shall take *away* all thy **l**, and shall leave	3018
	29:20 have given him the land of Egypt *for* his **l**	6468
Mic	4:10 Be in pain, and **l to bring forth**,	1518
Hab	2:13 that the people shall **l** in the very fire,	3021
	3:17 the **l** of the olive shall fail, and the fields	4639
Hag	1:11 cattle, and upon all the **l** of the hands.	3018
Mt	11:28 all ye that **l** and are heavy laden, and I	2872
Jn	4:38 to reap that whereon ye **bestowed** no **l**:	2872
	6:27 **L** not for the meat which perisheth,	2038
Ro	16: 6 Mary, who **bestowed** much **l** on us.	2872
	16:12 and Tryphosa, who **l** in the Lord.	2872
1Co	3: 8 his own reward according to his own **l**.	2873
	4:12 And **l**, working with our own hands:	2872
	15:58 forasmuch as ye know that your **l** is not	2873
2Co	5: 9 Wherefore we **l**, that, whether present or	5389
Gal	4:11 lest I have **bestowed** upon you **l** in vain.	2872
Eph	4:28 rather let him **l**, working with *his* hands	2872
Php	1:22 *I* live in the flesh, this *is* the fruit of my **l**:	2041
	2:25 and **companion** in **l**, and fellowsoldier,	4904
Col	1:29 Whereunto I also **l**, striving according to	2872
1Th	1: 3 and **l** of love, and patience of hope in our	2873
	2: 9 ye remember, brethren, our **l** and travail:	2873
	3: 5 have tempted you, and our **l** be in vain.	2873
	5:12 to know them which **l** among you,	2873
2Th	3: 8 but wrought with **l** and travail night and	2873
1Ti	4:10 For therefore we both **l** and	2872
	5:17 especially they who **l** in the word and	2872
Heb	4:11 Let us **l** therefore to enter into that rest,	4704
	6:10 to forget your work and **l** of love,	2873
Rev	2: 2 thy **l**, and thy patience, and how thou	2873

LABOURED (19) [LABOUR]

Ne	4:21 So we **l** in the work: and half of them	6213
Job	20:20 That which he **l** for shall he restore,	3022
Ecc	2:11 and on the labour that I had **l** to do:	5998
	2:19 rule over all my labour where*in* I have **l**,	5998
	2:21 yet to a man that hath not **l** therein shall	5998
	2:22 heart, wherein he *hath* **l** under the sun?	6001
	5:16 profit hath he that hath **l** for the wind?	5998
Isa	47:12 wherein thou hast **l** from thy youth;	3021
	47:15 they be unto thee *with* whom thou hast **l**,	3021
	49: 4 I said, I have **l** in vain, I have spent my	3021
	62: 8 drink thy wine, for the which thou hast **l**:	3021
Da	6:14 he **l** till the going down of the sun to	7712
Jnh	4:10 for the which thou hast not **l**, neither	5998
Jn	4:38 other men **l**, and ye are entered into their	2872
Ro	16:12 beloved Persis, which **l** much in the Lord.	2872
1Co	15:10 but I **l** more abundantly than they all:	2872
Php	2:16 I have not run in vain, neither **l** in vain.	2872
	4: 3 help those *women* which **l with** me in	4866
Rev	2: 3 for my name's sake hast **l**, and hast not	2872

LABOURER (2) [LABOUR]

Lk	10: 7 for the **l** is worthy of his hire. Go not from	2040
1Ti	5:18 And, The **l** *is* worthy of his reward.	2040

LABOURERS (9) [LABOUR]

Mt	9:37 truly *is* plenteous, but the **l** *are* few;	2040
	9:38 that he will send forth **l** into his harvest.	2040
	20: 1 in the morning to hire **l** into his vineyard.	2040
	20: 2 And when he had agreed with the **l** for a	2040
	20: 8 Call the **l**, and give them *their* hire,	2040
Lk	10: 2 harvest truly *is* great, but the **l** *are* few:	2040
	10: 2 he would send forth **l** into his harvest.	2040
1Co	3: 9 For we are **together** with God: ye are	4904
Jas	5: 4 the hire of the **l** which have reaped *down*	2040

LABOURETH (5) [LABOUR]

Pr	16:26 He that laboureth for himself; for his	6001
	16:26 He that laboureth for himself; for his	5998
Ecc	3: 9 he that worketh in *that* wherein he **l**?	6001
1Co	16:16 to every one that helpeth with *us*, and	2872
2Ti	2: 6 The husbandman that **l** must be first	2872

LABOURING (4) [LABOUR]

Ecc	5:12 The sleep of a **l** *man* is sweet, whether he	5647
Ac	20:35 that so **l** ye ought to support the weak,	2872
Col	4:12 always **l fervently** for you in prayers,	75
1Th	2: 9 night and day, because *we* would not	2038

LABOURS (13) [LABOUR]

Ex	23:16 the feast of harvest, the firstfruits of thy **l**,	4639
	23:16 when thou hast gathered in thy **l** out of	4639
Dt	28:33 The fruit of thy land, and all thy **l**, shall a	3018
Pr	5:10 and thy **l** *be* in the house of a stranger;	6089
Isa	58: 3 *you* find pleasure, and exact all your **l**.	6092
Jer	20: 5 all the **l** thereof, and all the precious	3018
Hos	12: 8 in all my **l** they shall find none iniquity in	3018
Hag	2:17 and with hail *in* all the **l** of your hands;	4639
Jn	4:38 and ye are entered into their **l**.	2873

2Co	6: 5 in tumults, in **l**, in watchings, in fastings;	2873
	10:15 *our* measure, that is, of other men's **l**;	2873
	11:23 in **l** more abundant, in stripes above	2873
Rev	14:13 the Spirit, that they may rest from their **l**;	2873

LACE (4)

Ex	28:28 the rings of the ephod with a **l** of blue,	6616
	28:37 shalt put it on a blue **l**, that it may be	6616
	39:21 the rings of the ephod with a **l** of blue,	6616
	39:31 they tied unto it a **l** of blue, to fasten *it* on	6616

LACHISH (24)

Jos	10: 3 unto Japhia king of **L**, and unto Debir	3923
	10: 5 the king of **L**, the king of Eglon,	3923
	10:23 the king of **L**, *and* the king of Eglon.	3923
	10:31 unto **L**, and encamped against it,	3923
	10:32 the LORD delivered **L** into the hand of	3923
	10:33 Horam king of Gezer came up to help **L**;	3923
	10:34 from **L** Joshua passed unto Eglon,	3923
	10:35 according to all that he had done to **L**.	3923
	12:11 king of Jarmuth, one; the king of **L**, one;	3923
	15:39 **L**, and Bozkath, and Eglon,	3923
2Ki	14:19 he fled to **L**; but they sent after him to	3923
	14:19 they sent after him to **L**, and slew him	3923
	18:14 of Judah sent to the king of Assyria to **L**,	3923
	18:17 Rab-shakeh from **L** to king Hezekiah with	3923
	19: 8 had heard that he was departed from **L**.	3923
2Ch	11: 9 And Adoraim, and **L**, and Azekah,	3923
	25:27 him in Jerusalem; and he fled to **L**:	3923
	25:27 they sent to **L** after him, and slew him	3923
	32: 9 (but he *himself laid* siege against **L**,	3923
Ne	11:30 at **L**, and the fields thereof, *at* Azekah;	3923
Isa	36: 2 king of Assyria sent Rabshakeh from **L**	3923
	37: 8 had heard that he was departed from **L**.	3923
Jer	34: 7 were left, against **L**, and against Azekah:	3923
Mic	1:13 thou inhabitant of **L**, bind the chariot to	3923

LACK (15) [LACKED, LACKEST, LACKETH, LACKING]

Ge	18:28 Peradventure there shall **l** five of the fifty	2637
	18:28 wilt thou destroy all the city for **l** of five?	NIH
Ex	16:18 and he that gathered little had no **l**;	2637
Dt	8: 9 thou shalt not **l** any *thing* in it;	2637
Job	4:11 The old lion perisheth for **l** of prey,	1097
	38:41 cry unto God, they wander for **l** of meat.	1097
Ps	34:10 The young lions do **l**, and suffer hunger:	7326
Pr	28:27 He that giveth unto the poor *shall* not **l**:	4270
Ecc	9: 8 and let thy head **l** no ointment.	2637
Hos	4: 6 My people are destroyed for **l** of	1097
Mt	19:20 I kept from my youth up: what **l** I yet?	5302
2Co	8:15 and he that *had* gathered little had no **l**.	1641
Php	2:30 to supply your **l** of service toward me.	5303
1Th	4:12 and *that* ye may have **l** of no*thing*.	5532
Jas	1: 5 If any of you **l** wisdom, let him ask of God	3007

LACKED (11) [LACK]

Dt	2: 7 *hath been* with thee; thou hast **l** nothing.	2637
2Sa	2:30 there **l** of David's servants nineteen men	6485
	17:22 by the morning light there **l** not one	5737
1Ki	4:27 every man *in* his month: they **l** nothing.	5737
	11:22 what *hast* thou **l** with me, that behold,	2638
Ne	9:21 in the wilderness, *so* that they **l** nothing;	2637
Lk	8: 6 away, because it **l** moisture.	2192+3361
	22:35 and scrip, and shoes, **l** ye any *thing*?	5302
Ac	4:34 Neither was there any among them that **l**:	1729
1Co	12:24 abundant honour to that *part* which **l**:	5302
Php	4:10 were also careful, but ye **l opportunity**.	170

LACKEST (2) [LACK]

Mk	10:21 and said unto him, One *thing* thou **l**:	5302
Lk	18:22 Yet **l** thou one *thing*: sell all that thou	3007

LACKETH (5) [LACK]

Nu	31:49 our charge, and there **l** not one man of us.	6485
2Sa	3:29 that falleth on the sword, or that **l** bread.	2638
Pr	6:32 adultery with a woman **l** understanding:	2638
	12: 9 he that honoureth himself, and **l** bread.	2638
2Pe	1: 9 But he that **l** these *things* is blind,	3361+3918

LACKING (8) [LACK]

Lev	2:13 **suffer** the salt of the covenant of thy God **to be l**	7673
	22:23 any thing superfluous or **l** in his **parts**,	7038
Jdg	21: 3 that there should be to day one tribe **l** in	6485
1Sa	30:19 there was nothing **l** to them, neither small	5737
Jer	23: 4 nor be dismayed, neither shall they be **l**,	6485
1Co	16:17 that which was **l** on your part they have	5303
2Co	11: 9 to me the brethren which came from	5303
1Th	3:10 might perfect that which is **l** in your faith?	5303

LAD (33) [LAD'S, LADS]

Ge	21:12 be grievous in thy sight because of the **l**,	5288
	21:17 God heard the voice of the **l**; and the	5288
	21:17 God hath heard the voice of the **l** where	5288
	21:18 lift up the **l**, and hold him in thine hand;	5288
	21:19 bottle *with* water, and gave the **l** a drink.	5288
	21:20 God was with the **l**; and he grew,	5288
	22: 5 I and the **l** will go yonder and worship,	5288
	22:12 he said, Lay not thine hand upon the **l**,	5288
	37: 2 he *was* with the sons of Bilhah,	5288
	43: 8 Send the **l** with me, and we will arise and	5288
	44:22 my lord, The **l** cannot leave his father:	5288
	44:30 my father, and the **l** *be* not with us;	5288
	44:31 when he seeth that the **l** *is* not *with us*,	5288
	44:32 thy servant became surety for the **l** unto	5288
	44:33 let thy servant abide instead of the **l** a	5288

Ge 44:33 and let the **l** go up with his brethren. | 5288
44:34 to my father, and the **l** *be* not with me? | 5288
Jdg 16:26 Samson said unto the **l** that held him by | 5288
1Sa 20:21 I will send a **l**, *saying*, Go, find out | 5288
20:21 If I expressly say unto the **l**, Behold, | 5288
20:35 with David, and a little **l** with him. | 5288
20:36 he said unto the **l**, Run, find out now | 5288
20:36 as the **l** ran, he shot an arrow beyond | 5288
20:37 when the **l** was come to the place of | 5288
20:37 Jonathan cried after the **l**, and said, *Is* not | 5288
20:38 Jonathan cried after the **l**, Make speed, | 5288
20:38 Jonathan's **l** gathered up the arrows, | 5288
20:39 the **l** knew not any thing: only Jonathan | 5288
20:40 Jonathan gave his artillery unto his **l**, | 5288
20:41 as soon as the **l** was gone, David arose | 5288
2Sa 17:18 Nevertheless a **l** saw them, | 5288
2Ki 4:19 he said to a **l**, Carry him to his mother. | 5288
Jn 6: 9 There is a **l** here, which hath five barley | 3808

LAD'S (1) [LAD]
Ge 44:30 seeing that his life *is* bound up in *the* **l** life; | NIH

LADAN See LAADAN

LADDER (1)
Ge 28:12 a **l** set up on the earth, and the top of | 5551

LADE (3) [LADED, LADEN, LADETH, LADING, UNLADE]
Ge 45:17 **l** your beasts, and go, get you unto the | 2943
1Ki 12:11 now whereas my father did **l** you with a | 6006
Lk 11:46 for ye **l** men *with* burdens grievous to be | 5412

LADED (4) [LADE]
Ge 42:26 they **l** their asses with the corn, | 5375
44:13 every man his ass, and returned to | 6006
Ne 4:17 they that bare burdens, *with* those that **l**, | 6006
Ac 28:10 they **l** *us with* such *things* as were | 2007

LADEN (6) [LADE]
Ge 45:23 ten asses **l** with the good things of Egypt, | 5375
45:23 ten she asses **l** with corn and bread and | 5375
1Sa 16:20 Jesse took an ass **l** with bread, and a bottle | NIH
Isa 1: 4 Ah sinful nation, a people **l** with iniquity, | 3515
Mt 11:28 all ye that labour and are **heavy l**, and **l** | 5412
2Ti 3: 6 and lead captive silly women **l** with sins, | 4987

LADETH (1) [LADE]
Hab 2: 6 and to him that **l** himself **with** thick clay! | 3513

LADIES (2) [LADY]
Jdg 5:29 wise **l** answered *her*, yea, she returned | 8282
Est 1:18 Likewise shall the **l** of Persia and | 8282

LADING (2) [LADE]
Ne 13:15 bringing in sheaves, and **l** asses; | 5921+6006
Ac 27:10 not only of the **l** and ship, but also of our | 5414

LADS (1) [LAD]
Ge 48:16 redeemed me from all evil, bless the **l**; | 5288

LADY (4) [LADIES]
Isa 47: 5 no more be called, The **l** of kingdoms. | 1404
47: 7 thou saidst, I shall be a **l** for ever: | 1404
2Jn 1: 1 elder unto the elect **l** and her children, | 2959
1: 5 now I beseech thee, **l**, not as though I | 2959

LAEL (1)
Nu 3:24 Gershonites *shall be* Eliasaph the son of **L**. | 3815

LAHAD (1)
1Ch 4: 2 and Jahath begat Ahumai, and **L**. | 3855

LAHAI-ROI (2) [BEER-LAHAI-ROI]
Ge 24:62 Isaac came from the way of the **well L**; | 883
25:11 son Isaac; and Isaac dwelt by the **well L**. | 883

LAHMAM (1)
Jos 15:40 And Cabbon, and **L**, and Kithlish, | 3903

LAHMAS See LAHMAM

LAHMI (1)
1Ch 20: 5 Elhanan the son of Jair slew **L** the brother | 3902

LAID (279) [LAY]
Ge 9:23 **l** *it* upon both their shoulders, | 7760
15:10 and **l** each piece one against another: | 5414
19:16 the men **l** hold upon his hand, and upon | 2388
22: 6 burnt offering, and **l** *it* upon Isaac his son; | 7760
22: 9 **l** the wood **in order**, and bound Isaac his | 6186
22: 9 and **l** him on the altar upon the wood. | 7760
30:41 that Jacob **l** the rods before the eyes of | 7760
38:19 **l** by her vail from her, and put on | 5493
39:16 she **l** up his garment by her, until his lord | 3240
41:48 of Egypt, and **l** up the food in the cities: | 5414
41:48 about every city, **l** he up in the same. | 5414
48:14 **l** *it* upon Ephraim's head, who *was* | 7896
48:17 when Joseph saw that his father **l** his right | 7896
Ex 2: 3 she **l** *it* in the flags by the river's brink. | 7760
5: 9 Let there **more** work be **l** upon the men, | 3513
16:24 they **l** *it* **up** till the morning, as Moses | 4340
16:34 so Aaron **l** *it* **up** before the Testimony, | 3240
19: 7 before their faces all these words which | 7760
21:30 If there be **l** on him a sum of money, then | 7896
21:30 of his life whatsoever *is* **l** upon him. | 7896
24:11 of the children of Israel he **l** not his hand: | 7971

Lev 8:14 his sons **l** their hands upon the head of | 5564
8:18 his sons **l** their hands upon the head of | 5564
8:22 his sons **l** their hands upon the head of | 5564
Nu 16:18 **l** incense thereon, and stood *in* the door | 7760
17: 7 Moses **l** **up** the rods before the Lord in | 4340
21:30 have **l** *them* **waste** even unto Nophah, | 8074
27:23 he **l** his hands upon him, and gave him a | 5564
Dt 26: 6 afflicted us, and **l** upon us hard bondage: | 5414
29:22 the sicknesses which the Lord hath **l** | 2470
32:34 *Is* not this **l** **up** in store with me, | 3647
34: 9 for Moses had **l** his hands upon him: | 5564
Jos 2: 6 which she had **l** **in order** upon the roof. | 6186
2: 8 before they were **l** **down**, she came up | 7901
4: 8 they lodged, and **l** them **down** there. | 3240
7:23 and **l** them **out** before the Lord. | 3332
10:27 a great stone in the cave's mouth, | 7760
Jdg 9:24 their blood be **l** upon Abimelech their | 7760
9:34 they **l** **wait** against Shechem *in* four | 693
9:43 **l** **wait** in the field, and looked, and behold, | 693
9:48 **l** *it* on his shoulder, and said unto | 7760
16: 2 **l** **wait** for him all night in the gate of | 693
19:29 **l** **hold** on his concubine, and divided her, | 2388
19: 7 and uncovered his feet, and **l** her **down**. | 7901
Ru 3:15 six *measures* of barley, and **l** *it* on her: | 7896
4:16 **l** *it* in her bosom, and became nurse unto | 7896
1Sa 3: 2 when Eli *was* **l** **down** in his place, | 7901
3: 3 and Samuel was **l** **down** *to sleep*; | 7901
6:11 they **l** the ark of the Lord upon the cart, | 7760
10:25 *it* in a book, and **l** *it* **up** before the Lord. | 3240
15: 2 how he **l** **wait** for him in the way, when | 7760
15: 5 a city of Amalek, and **l** **wait** in the valley. | 7378
15:27 he **l** **hold** upon the skirt of his mantle, | 2388
19:13 **l** *it* in the bed, and put a pillow of goats' | 7760
21:12 David **l** up these words in his heart, | 7760
25:18 cakes *of figs*, and **l** *them* on asses. | 7760
2Sa 13: 8 Amnon's house; and he was **l** **down**. | 7901
13:19 her hand on her head, and went on | 7760
18:17 **l** a very great heap of stones upon him: | 5324
1Ki 3:20 **l** it in her bosom, and laid her dead child | 7901
3:20 and **l** her dead child in my bosom. | 7901
6:37 **foundation** of the house of the Lord **l**, | 3245
8:31 an oath be **l** upon him to cause him to | 5375
13:29 and **l** it upon the ass, and brought it back: | 3240
13:30 he **l** his carcase in his own grave; | 3240
15:27 and all Israel **l** **siege** to Gibbethon. | 6696
16:34 he **l** the **foundation** thereof in Abiram his | 3245
17:19 he abode, and **l** him upon his own bed. | 7901
18:33 pieces, and **l** *him* on the wood, and said, | 7760
19: 6 did eat and drink, and **l** him **down** again. | 7901
21: 4 he **l** him **down** upon his bed, | 7901
2Ki 4:21 **l** him on the bed of the man of God, | 7901
4:31 and **l** the staff upon the face of the child; | 7760
4:32 the child was dead, *and* **l** upon his bed. | 7901
5:23 and **l** *them* upon two of his servants; | 5414
9:25 the Lord **l** this burden upon him; | 5375
11:16 they **l** hands on her; and she went *by* | 7760
12:11 **l** it **out** to the carpenters and builders, | 3318
12:12 all that was **l** **out** for the house to repair | 3318
20: 7 they took and **l** *it* on the boil, | 7760
20:17 *that* which thy fathers have **l** **up** in store | 686
2Ch 6:22 an oath be **l** upon him to make him swear, | 5375
7:22 **l** **hold** on other gods, and worshipped, | 2388
16:14 him in the bed which was filled *with* | 7901
23:15 So they **l** hands on her; and when she was | 7760
24: 9 of God **l** **upon** Israel in the wilderness. | 5921
24:27 the greatness of the burdens *l* upon him, | NIH
29:23 and **l** their hands upon them: | 5564
31: 6 the Lord their God, and **l** *them* by heaps. | 5414
32: 9 (but he *himself* **l** **siege** against Lachish, | NIH
Ezr 3: 6 **foundation** of the temple of the Lord | 3245
was not *yet* **l**. |
3:10 when the builders **l** the **foundation** of | 3245
3:11 **foundation** of the house of the Lord | 3245
was **l**. |
3:12 when the **foundation** of this house was **l** | 3245
5: 8 timber *is* **l** in the walls, and this work | 7761
5:16 **l** the foundation of the house of God | 3052
6: 1 where the treasures were **l** **up** in Babylon. | 5182
6: 3 *let* the foundations thereof *be* **strongly l**; | 5446
Ne 3: 3 who *also* **l** the **beams** thereof, and set up | 7136
3: 6 they **l** the **beams** thereof, and set up | 7136
13: 5 where aforetime they **l** the meat offerings, | 5414
Est 8: 7 because he **l** his hand upon the Jews. | 7971
9:10 but on the spoil **l** they not their hand. | 7971
9:15 but on the prey they **l** not their hand. | 7971
9:16 but they **l** not their hands on the prey, | 7971
10: 1 the king Ahasuerus **l** a tribute upon | 7760
Job 6: 2 my calamity **l** in the balances together! | 5375
18:10 The snare *is* **l** for him in the ground, | 2934
29: 9 and **l** *their* hand upon their mouth. | 7760
31: 9 or *if* I have **l** **wait** at my neighbour's door; | 693
38: 4 wast thou when I **l** the **foundations** | 3245
38: 5 Who hath **l** the measures thereof, if thou | 7760
38: 6 or who **l** the corner stone thereof; | 3384
Ps 3: 5 I me **down** and slept; I awaked; | 7901
21: 5 honour and majesty hast thou **l** upon him. | 7737
31: 4 of the net that they have **l** **privily** for me: | 2934
31:19 which thou hast **l** **up** for them that fear | 6845
35:11 **l** to my **charge** *things* that I knew not. | 7592
49:14 Like sheep they are **l** in the grave; | 8371
62: 9 to be **l** in the balance, they are altogether | 5927
79: 1 they have **l** Jerusalem on heaps. | 7760
79: 7 and **l** **waste** his dwelling place. | 8074
88: 6 Thou hast **l** me in the lowest pit, | 7896
89:19 I have **l** help upon *one that is* mighty; | 7737

Ps 102:25 Of old hast thou **l** the **foundation** of | 3245
104: 5 *Who* **l** the foundations of the earth, *that* it | 3245
105:18 they hurt with fetters: he was **l** *in* iron: | 935
119:30 truth: thy judgments have I **l** before me. | 7737
119:110 The wicked have **l** a snare for me: yet I | 5414
139: 5 and before, and **l** thine hand upon me. | 7896
141: 9 me from the snare *which* they have **l** | 3369
142: 3 walked have they **privily l** a snare for me. | 2934
Pr 13:22 wealth of the sinner *is* **l** **up** for the just. | 6845
SS 7:13 and old, *which* I have **l** **up** for thee, | 6845
Isa 6: 7 he **l** *it* upon my mouth, and said, | 5060
10:28 at Michmash he hath **l** **up** his carriages: | 6485
14: 8 Lebanon, *saying*, Since thou art **l** **down**, | 7901
15: 1 in the night Ar of Moab is **l** **waste**, | 7703
15: 1 in the night Kir of Moab is **l** **waste**, | 7703
15: 7 gotten, and *that* which they have **l** **up**, | 6486
23: 1 for it is **l** **waste**, so that *there is* no house, | 7703
23:14 of Tarshish: for your strength is **l** **waste**. | 7703
23:18 it shall not be treasured nor **l** **up**; for her | 2630
37:18 the kings of Assyria have **l** **waste** all | 2717
39: 6 *that* which thy fathers have **l** **up** in store | 686
42:25 and it burned him, yet he **l** *it* not to heart. | 7760
44:28 *to* the temple, Thy **foundation** shall be **l**. | 3245
47: 6 upon the ancient hast thou very **heavily l** | 3513
48:13 Mine hand also hath **l** the **foundation** of | 3245
51:13 and the **foundations** of the earth; | 3245
51:23 thou hast **l** thy body as the ground, | 7760
53: 6 the Lord hath **l** on him the iniquity of us | 6293
57:11 not remembered me, nor **l** *it* to thy heart? | 7760
64:11 and all our pleasant things are **l** **waste**. | 2723
Jer 4: 7 *and* thy cities shall be **l** **waste**, without an | 5327
27:17 wherefore should this city be **l** **waste**? | 2723
36:20 they **l** **up** the roll in the chamber of | 6485
50:24 I have **l** a **snare** for thee, and thou art | 3369
La 4:19 they **l** **wait** for us in the wilderness. | 693
Eze 4: 5 For I have **l** upon thee the years of their | 5414
6: 6 dwelling places the cities shall be **l** **waste**, | 2717
6: 6 that your altars may be **l** **waste** and | 2717
11: 7 Your slain whom ye have **l** in the midst of | 7760
12:20 cities that are inhabited shall be **l** **waste**, | 2717
19: 7 palaces, and he **l** **waste** their cities; | 2717
26: 2 I shall be replenished, *now* she is **l** **waste**: | 2717
29:12 cities among the cities *that are* **l** **waste** | 2717
32:19 and be thou **l** with the uncircumcised. | 7901
32:27 have **l** their swords under their heads, | 5414
32:29 which with their might are **l** by *them that* | 5414
32:32 he shall be **l** in the midst of | 7901
33:29 when I have **l** the land most desolate | 8074
35:12 They are **l** **desolate**, they are given | 8074
39:21 and my hand that I have **l** upon them. | 7760
40:42 whereupon also they **l** the instruments | 3240
Da 6:17 and **l** upon the mouth of the den; | 7761
Hos 11: 4 on their jaws, and **l** meat unto them. | 5186
Joel 1: 7 He hath **l** my vine waste, and barked my | 7760
1:17 the garners are **l** **desolate**, the barns are | 8074
Am 2: 8 upon clothes **l** **to pledge** by every altar, | 2254
7: 9 the sanctuaries of Israel shall be **l** **waste**; | 2717
Ob 1: 7 *they that eat* thy bread have **l** a wound | 7760
1:13 nor have **l** *hands* on their substance in | 7971
Jnh 3: 6 he **l** his robe from him, and covered *him* | 5674
Mic 5: 1 he hath **l** **siege** against us: they shall smite | 7760
Na 3: 7 from thee, and say, Nineveh is **l** **waste**: | 7703
Hab 2:19 it *is* **l** **over** *with* gold and silver, and *there* | 8610
Hag 2:15 from before a stone was **l** upon a stone in | 7760
2:18 **foundation** of the Lord's temple was **l**, | 3245
Zec 3: 9 For behold the stone that I have **l** before | 5414
4: 9 have **l** the **foundation** of this house; | 3245
7:14 for they **l** the pleasant land desolate. | 7760
8: 9 **foundation** of the house of the Lord | 3245
of hosts was **l**, |
Mal 1: 3 his mountains and his heritage waste for | 7760
Mt 3:10 And now also the axe is **l** unto the root of | 2749
8:14 he saw his wife's mother **l**, and sick of a | 906
14: 3 For Herod had **l** **hold** on John, | 2902
18:28 and he **l** hands on him, and took *him* by | 2902
19:15 And he **l** *his* hands on them, | 2007
26:50 and **l** hands on Jesus, and took him. | 1911
26:55 in the temple, and ye **l** no **hold** on me. | 2902
26:57 And they that had **l** **hold** on Jesus led *him* | 2902
27:60 And **l** it in his own new tomb, which he | 5087
Mk 6: 5 save that he **l** *his* hands **upon** a few sick | 2007
6:17 had sent forth and **l** **hold** **upon** John, | 2902
6:29 and took up his corpse, and **l** it in a tomb. | 5087
6:56 they **l** the sick in the streets, | 5087
7:30 gone out, and *her* daughter **l** upon the bed. | 906
14:46 And they **l** their hands on him, | 1911
14:51 and the young men **l** **hold** **on** him: | 2902
15:46 **l** him in a sepulchre which was hewn out | 2698
15:47 *mother* of Joses beheld where he was **l**. | 5087
16: 6 here: behold the place where they **l** him. | 5087
Lk 1:66 And all they that heard *them* **l** *them* **up** in | 5087
2: 7 swaddling clothes, and **l** him in a manger; | 347
3: 9 And now also the axe is **l** unto the root of | 2749
4:40 and he **l** *his* hands on every one of them, | 2007
6:48 and **l** the foundation on a rock: | 5087
12:19 hast much goods **l** **up** for many years; | 2749
13:13 And he **l** his hands **on** her: | 2007
14:29 after he hath **l** the foundation, and is not | 5087
16:20 which was **l** at his gate, full of sores, | 906
19:20 which I have kept **l** **up** in a napkin: | 606
19:22 taking up that I **l** not **down**, | 5087
23:26 they **l** **hold** **upon** one Simon, a Cyrenian, | 1949
23:26 the country, and **on** him they **l** the cross, | 2007
23:53 it in a sepulchre that was hewn in stone, | 5087
23:53 in stone, wherein never man before was **l**. | 5087

Lk 23:55 the sepulchre, and how his body was l.	5087
24:12 beheld the linen clothes l by themselves,	2749
Jn 7:30 but no *man* l hands on him, because	1911
7:44 taken him; but no *man* l hands on him.	1911
8:20 and no *man* l hands on him; for his hour	4084
11:34 And said, Where have ye l him? They say	5087
11:41 *from the place* where the dead was l.	2749
13: 4 from supper, and l aside *his* garments;	5087
19:41 wherein was never man yet l.	5087
19:42 There l Jesus therefore because of	5087
20: 2 and we know not where they have l him.	5087
20:13 and I know not where they have l him.	5087
20:15 him *hence,* tell me where thou hast l him,	5087
21: 9 coals there, and fish l thereon, and bread.	1945
Ac 3: 2 they l daily at the gate of the temple	5087
4: 3 they l hands on them, and put *them* in	1911
4:35 And l *them* down at the apostles' feet:	5087
4:37 the money, and l *it* at the apostles' feet.	5087
5: 2 a certain part, and l *it* at the apostles' feet.	5087
5:15 streets, and l *them* on beds and couches,	5087
5:18 And l their hands on the apostles,	1911
6: 6 had prayed, they l *their* hands **on** them,	2007
7:16 l in the sepulchre that Abraham bought	5087
7:58 witnesses l **down** their clothes at a young	659
8:17 Then l they *their* hands **on** them,	2007
9:37 they l *her* in an upper chamber,	5087
13: 3 and prayed, and l *their* hands **on** them,	2007
13:29 from the tree, and l *him* in a sepulchre.	5087
13:36 and was l unto his fathers,	4369
16:23 And when they had l many stripes upon	2007
19: 6 when Paul had l *his* hands **upon** them,	2007
20: and when the Jews l **wait for** him,	1096+1917
21:27 up all the people, and l hands on him,	1911
23:29 to have nothing l to his **charge** worthy of	1462
23:30 me how that the Jews l **wait** for the man,	1917
25: 7 many and grievous complaints against	5342
25:16 concerning the **crime** l *against him.*	1462
25:27 not withal to signify the crimes l *against*	NIG
28: 3 and l *them* on the fire, there came a viper	2007
28: 8 and l *his* hands on him, and healed him.	2007
Ro 16: 4 Who have for my life l **down** their own	5294
1Co 3:10 I have l the foundation,	2749
3:11 foundation can no *man* lay than that is l,	2749
9:16 for necessity is l **upon** me; yea, woe is	1945
Col 1: 5 the hope which is l **up** for you in heaven,	606
2Ti 4: 8 Henceforth there is l **up** for me a crown of	606
4:16 *God* that it may not be l to their **charge.**	3049
Heb 1:10 in the beginning hast l **the foundation** of	2311
1Jn 3:16 of *God,* because he l **down** his life for us:	5087
Rev 1:17 And he l his right hand upon me,	2007
20: 2 and he l **hold on** the dragon, *that* old	2902

LAIDST (1) [LAY]

Ps 66:11 the net; thou l affliction upon our loins.	7760

LAIN (3) [LIE]

Nu 5:19 If no man have l with thee, and if thou	7901
5:20 *some* man hath l with thee beside thine	7903
Jn 20:12 at the feet, where the body of Jesus had l.	2749

LAISH (7)

Jdg 18: 7 came to L, and saw the people that *were*	3919
18:14 that went to spy out the country of L,	3919
18:27 priest which he had, and came unto L,	3919
18:29 howbeit the name of the city *was* L at	3919
1Sa 25:44 David's wife, to Phalti the son of L,	3919
2Sa 3:15 *even* from Phaltiel the son of L.	3919
Isa 10:30 cause *it* to be heard unto L, O poor	3919

LAKE (10)

Lk 5: 1 of God, he stood by the l of Gennesaret,	3041
5: 2 And saw two ships standing by the l:	3041
8:22 Let us go over unto the other side of the l.	3041
8:23 came down a storm of wind on the l;	3041
8:33 ran violently down a steep place into the l,	3041
Rev 19:20 *These* both were cast alive into a l of fire	3041
20:10 deceived them was cast into the l of fire	3041
20:14 and hell were cast into the l of fire.	3041
20:15 the book of life was cast into the l of fire.	3041
21: 8 have their part in the l which burneth	3041

LAKKUM See LAKUM

LAKUM (1)

Jos 19:33 and Adami, Nekeb, and Jabneel, unto L;	3946

LAMA (2)

Mt 27:46 saying, ELI, ELI, L SABACHTHANI?	2982
Mk 15:34 saying, ELOI, ELOI, L SABACHTHANI?	2982

LAMB (105) [LAMB'S, LAMBS]

Ge 22: 7 but where *is* the l for a burnt offering?	7716
22: 8 God will provide himself a l for a burnt	7716
Ex 12: 3 they shall take to them every man a l,	7716
12: 3 the house of *their* fathers, a l for a house:	7716
12: 4 if the household be too little for the l,	7716
12: 4 his eating shall make your count for the l.	7716
12: 5 Your l shall be without blemish, a male of	7716
12:21 take you a l according to your families,	6629
13:13 of an ass thou shalt redeem with a l;	7716
29:39 The one l thou shalt offer in the morning;	3532
29:39 and the other l thou shalt offer at even:	3532
29:40 the one l a tenth deal of flour mingled	3532
29:41 the other l thou shalt offer at even,	3532
34:20 of an ass thou shalt redeem with a l:	7716
Lev 3: 7 If he offer a l for his offering, then he shall	3775

Lev 4:32 if he bring a l for a sin offering, he shall	3532
4:35 as the fat of the l is taken away from	3775
5: 6 a l or a kid of the goats, for a sin offering;	3776
5: 7 if he be not able to bring a l, then he shall	7716
9: 3 a calf and a l, both of the first year,	3532
12: 6 she shall bring a l of the first year for a	3532
12: 8 if she be not able to bring a l, then she	7716
14:10 ewe l of the first year without blemish,	3535
14:12 the priest shall take one **he** l, and offer	3532
14:13 he shall slay the l in the place where he	3532
14:21 he shall take one l *for* a trespass offering	3532
14:24 the priest shall take the l of the trespass	3532
14:25 he shall kill the l of the trespass offering	3532
17: 3 or l, or goat, in the camp, or that killeth *it*	3775
22:23 or a l that hath any thing superfluous or	7716
23:12 **he** l without blemish of the first year for a	3532
Nu 6:12 bring a l of the first year for a trespass	3532
6:14 one **he** l of the first year without blemish	3532
6:14 **ewe** l of the first year without blemish	3535
7:15 one ram, one l of the first year,	3532
7:21 one ram, one l of the first year,	3532
7:27 one ram, one l of the first year,	3532
7:33 one ram, one l of the first year,	3532
7:39 one ram, one l of the first year,	3532
7:45 one ram, one l of the first year,	3532
7:51 one ram, one l of the first year,	3532
7:57 one ram, one l of the first year,	3532
7:63 one ram, one l of the first year,	3532
7:69 one ram, one l of the first year,	3532
7:75 one ram, one l of the first year,	3532
7:81 one ram, one l of the first year,	3532
15: 5 the burnt offering or sacrifice, for one l.	3532
15:11 or for one ram, or for a l, or a kid.	3532+7716
28: 4 The one l shalt thou offer in the morning,	3532
28: 4 and the other l shalt thou offer at even;	3532
28: 7 *be* the fourth *part* of a hin for the one l:	3532
28: 8 the other l shalt thou offer at even:	3532
28:13 with oil *for a* meat offering unto one l;	3532
28:14 a ram, and a fourth *part* of a hin unto a l:	3532
28:21 tenth deal shalt thou offer for every l,	3532
28:29 A several tenth deal unto one l,	3532
29: 4 one tenth deal for one l, throughout	3532
29:10 A several tenth deal for one l, throughout	3532
29:15 several tenth deal to each l of the fourteen	3532
1Sa 7: 9 Samuel took a sucking l, and offered it	2924
17:34 and a bear, and took a l out of the flock:	7716
2Sa 12: 3 one little **ewe** l, which he had bought	3535
12: 4 took the poor man's l, and dressed it for	3535
12: 6 he shall restore the l fourfold, because he	3535
Isa 11: 6 The wolf also shall dwell with the l,	3532
16: 1 Send ye l *to* the ruler of the land from	3733
53: 7 he is brought as a l to the slaughter,	7716
65:25 The wolf and the l shall feed together,	2924
66: 3 he that sacrificeth a l, *as if* he cut off a	7716
Jer 11:19 I *was* like a l *or* an ox *that* is brought to	3532
Eze 45:15 l out of the flock, out of two hundred,	7716
46:13 *of* a l of the first year without blemish:	3532
46:15 shall they prepare the l, and the meat	3532
Hos 4:16 now the LORD will feed them as a l in a	3532
Jn 1:29 saith, Behold, the **L** of God, which taketh	286
1:36 he walked, he saith, Behold the **L** of God.	286
Ac 8:32 and like a l dumb before his shearer,	286
1Pe 1:19 as of a l without blemish and without spot:	286
Rev 5: 6 a **L** as *it had been* slain, having seven	721
5: 8 *and* twenty elders fell down before the **L,**	721
5:12 Worthy is the **L** that was slain to receive	721
5:13 throne, and unto the **L** for ever and ever.	721
6: 1 And I saw when the **L** opened one of	721
6:16 the throne, and from the wrath of the **L:**	721
7: 9 stood before the throne, and before the **L,**	721
7:10 sitteth upon the throne, and unto the **L.**	721
7:14 made them white in the blood of the **L.**	721
7:17 the **L** which is in the midst of the throne	721
12:11 they overcame him by the blood of the **L,**	721
13: 8 **L** slain from the foundation of the world.	721
13:11 he had two horns like a l, and he spake	721
14: 1 and lo, a **L** stood on the mount Sion,	721
14: 4 These are they which follow the **L**	721
14: 4 *being* the firstfruits unto God and to the **L**	721
14:10 holy angels, and in the presence of the **L:**	721
15: 3 and the song of the **L,** saying, Great and	721
17:14 These shall make war with the **L,**	721
17:14 the Lamb, and the **L** shall overcome them:	721
19: 7 for the marriage of the **L** is come,	721
19: 9 called unto the marriage supper of the **L.**	721
21:14 the names of the twelve apostles of the **L.**	721
21:22 Almighty and the **L** are the temple of it.	721
21:23 did lighten it, and the **L** *is* the light thereof.	721
22: 1 out of the throne of God and of the **L.**	721
22: 3 throne of God and of the **L** shall be in it;	721

LAMB'S (2) [LAMB]

Rev 21: 9 I will shew thee the bride, the **L** wife.	721
21:27 which are written in the **L** book of life.	721

LAMBS (81) [LAMB]

Ge 21:28 Abraham set seven **ewe** l of the flock by	3535
21:29 What *mean* these seven **ewe** l which	3535
21:30 For *these* seven **ewe** l shalt thou take of	3535
30:40 Jacob did separate the l, and set the faces	3775
Ex 29:38 two l of the first year day by day	3532
Lev 14:10 on the eighth day he shall take two **he** l	3532
23:18 ye shall offer with the bread seven l	3532
23:19 two l of the first year for a sacrifice of	3532
23:20 offering before the LORD, with the two l:	3532

Nu 7:17 five he goats, five l of the first year:	3532
7:23 five he goats, five l of the first year:	3532
7:29 five he goats, five l of the first year:	3532
7:35 five he goats, five l of the first year:	3532
7:41 five he goats, five l of the first year:	3532
7:47 five he goats, five l of the first year:	3532
7:53 five he goats, five l of the first year:	3532
7:59 five he goats, five l of the first year:	3532
7:65 five he goats, five l of the first year:	3532
7:71 five he goats, five l of the first year:	3532
7:77 five he goats, five l of the first year:	3532
7:83 five he goats, five l of the first year:	3532
7:87 rams twelve, the l of the first year twelve,	3532
7:88 he goats sixty, the l of the first year sixty.	3532
28: 3 two l of the first year without spot day by	3532
28: 9 on the sabbath day two l of the first year	3532
28:11 seven l of the first year without spot:	3532
28:19 and one ram, and seven l of the first year:	3532
28:21 for every lamb, throughout the seven l;	3532
28:27 one ram, seven l of the first year;	3532
28:29 unto one lamb, throughout the seven l;	3532
29: 2 seven l of the first year without blemish:	3532
29: 4 for one lamb, throughout the seven l:	3532
29: 8 one ram, *and* seven l of the first year;	3532
29:10 for one lamb, throughout the seven l:	3532
29:13 two rams, *and* fourteen l of the first year;	3532
29:15 tenth deal to each lamb of the fourteen l:	3532
29:17 fourteen l of the first year without spot:	3532
29:18 for the rams, and for the l, *shall be*	3532
29:20 fourteen l of the first year without blemish	3532
29:21 for the rams, and for the l, *shall be*	3532
29:23 fourteen l of the first year without blemish	3532
29:24 for the rams, and for the l, *shall be*	3532
29:26 fourteen l of the first year without spot:	3532
29:27 for the rams, and for the l, *shall be*	3532
29:29 fourteen l of the first year without blemish	3532
29:30 for the rams, and for the l, *shall be*	3532
29:32 fourteen l of the first year without blemish	3532
29:33 for the rams, and for the l, *shall be*	3532
29:36 seven l of the first year without blemish:	3532
29:37 for the ram, and for the l, *shall be*	3532
Dt 32:14 with fat of l, and rams of the breed of	3733
1Sa 15: 9 the l, and all *that was* good, and would	3733
2Ki 3: 4 the king of Israel an hundred thousand l,	3532
1Ch 29:21 a thousand rams, *and* a thousand l,	3532
2Ch 29:21 and seven l, and seven he goats,	3532
29:22 they killed also the l, and they sprinkled	3532
29:32 an hundred rams, *and* two hundred l:	3532
35: 7 gave to the people, *of* the flock, l and kids,	3532
Ezr 6: 9 both young bullocks, and rams, and l,	563
6:17 two hundred rams, four hundred l;	563
7:17 rams, l, with their meat offerings and	563
8:35 ninety and six rams, seventy and seven l,	3532
Ps 37:20 of the LORD *shall be* as the fat of l:	3733
114: 4 like rams, *and the* little hills like l.	1121+6629
114: 6 like rams; *and ye* little hills, like l?	1121+6629
Pr 27:26 The l *are* for thy clothing, and the goats	3532
Isa 1:11 blood of bullocks, or of l, or of he goats.	3532
5:17 Then shall the l feed after their manner,	3532
34: 6 *and* with the blood of l and goats,	3733
40:11 he shall gather the l with his arm,	2922
Jer 51:40 I will bring them down like l to	3733
Eze 27:21 they occupied with thee in l, and rams,	3733
39:18 of rams, of l, and of goats, of bullocks,	3733
46: 4 day *shall be* six l without blemish,	3532
46: 5 the meat offering for the l as he shall be	3532
46: 6 without blemish, and six l, and a ram:	3532
46: 7 for the l according as his hand shall attain	3532
46:11 to the l as he is able to give, and a hin of	3532
Am 6: 4 eat the l out of the flock, and the calves	3733
Lk 10: 3 I send you forth as l among wolves.	704
Jn 21:15 I love thee. He saith unto him, Feed my l.	721

LAME (27)

Lev 21:18 or a l, or he that hath a flat nose,	6455
Dt 15:21 *as if it be* l, or blind, *or have* any ill	6455
2Sa 4: 4 had a son *that was* l of *his* feet,	5223
4: 4 haste to flee, that he fell, and **became** l.	6452
5: 6 thou take away the blind and the l,	6455
5: 8 the Jebusites, and the l and the blind,	6455
5: 8 and the l shall not come into the house.	6455
9: 3 hath yet a son, *which is* l on *his* feet.	5223
9:13 king's table; and *was* l on both his feet.	6455
19:26 go to the king; because thy servant *is* l.	6455
Job 29:15 eyes to the blind, and feet *was* I to the l.	6455
Pr 26: 7 The legs of the l are not equal: so *is a*	6455
Isa 33:23 of a great spoil divided; the l take the prey.	6455
35: 6 shall the l *man* leap as a hart,	6455
Jer 31: 8 *and* with them the blind and the l,	6455
Mal 1: 8 if ye offer the l and sick, *is it* not evil?	6455
1:13 *which was* torn, and the l, and the sick;	6455
Mt 11: 5 and the l walk, the lepers are cleansed,	5560
15:30 having with them *those that were* l, blind,	5560
15:31 the l to walk, and the blind to see:	5560
21:14 and the l came to him in the temple;	5560
Lk 7:22 that the blind see, the l walk, the lepers	5560
14:13 call the poor, the maimed, the l, the blind:	5560
Ac 3: 2 And a certain man l from his mother's	5560
3:11 And as the l *man* which was healed held	5560
8: 7 with palsies, and *that were* l, were healed.	5560
Heb 12:13 *that which is* l be turned out of the way;	5560

LAMECH (12)

Ge 4:18 begat Methusael: and Methusael begat L.	3929
4:19 L took unto him two wives: the name of	3929

Ge	4:23 **L** said unto his wives, Adah and Zillah,	3929
	4:23 ye wives of **L**, hearken unto my speech:	3929
	4:24 truly **L** seventy and sevenfold.	3929
	5:25 and seven years, and begat **L**:	3929
	5:26 Methuselah lived after he begat **L** seven	3929
	5:28 **L** lived an hundred eighty and two years,	3929
	5:30 **L** lived after he begat Noah five hundred	3929
	5:31 all the days of **L** were seven hundred	3929
1Ch	1: 3 Henoch, Methuselah, **L**,	3929
Lk	3:36 the son of Noe, which was the son of **L**,	2984

LAMENT (21) [LAMENTABLE, LAMENTATION, LAMENTATIONS, LAMENTED]

Jdg	11:40 the daughters of Israel went yearly to **l**	8567
Isa	3:26 gates shall **l** and mourn; and she being	578
	19: 8 they that cast angle into the brooks shall **l**,	56
	32:12 They shall **l** for the teats, for the pleasant	5594
Jer	4: 8 this gird you with sackcloth, **l** and howl:	5594
	16: 5 neither go to **l** nor bemoan them:	5594
	16: 6 neither shall men **l** for them, nor cut	5594
	22:18 They shall not **l** for him, saying, Ah my	5594
	22:18 they shall not **l** for him, saying, Ah lord!	5594
	34: 5 and they will **l** thee, saying, Ah lord!	5594
	49: 3 **l**, and run to and fro by the hedges;	5594
La	2: 8 he made the rampart and the wall to **l**;	56
Eze	27:32 **l** over thee, saying, What city is like	6969
	32:16 lamentation wherewith they shall **l** her:	6969
	32:16 the daughters of the nations shall **l** her:	6969
	32:16 they shall **l** for her, even for Egypt,	6969
Joel	1: 8 **L** like a virgin girded with sackcloth for	421
	1:13 Gird yourselves, and **l**, ye priests: howl,	5594
Mic	2: 4 **l** with a doleful lamentation, and say,	5091
Jn	16:20 That ye shall weep and **l**, but the world	2354
Rev	18: 9 with her, shall bewail her, and **l** for her,	2875

LAMENTABLE (1) [LAMENT]

Da	6:20 den, he cried with a **l** voice unto Daniel:	6088

LAMENTATION (25) [LAMENT]

Ge	50:10 mourned with a great and very sore **l**:	4553
2Sa	1:17 David lamented with this **l** over Saul and	7015
Ps	78:64 the sword; and their widows made no **l**.	1058
Jer	6:26 as for an only son, most bitter **l**:	4553
	7:29 it away, and take up a **l** on high places;	7015
	9:10 for the habitations of the wilderness a **l**,	7015
	9:20 and every one her neighbour a **l**.	7015
	31:15 heard in Ramah, **l**, and bitter weeping;	5092
	48:38 There shall be **l** generally upon all	4553
La	2: 5 in the daughter of Judah mourning and **l**.	592
Eze	19: 1 Moreover take thou up a **l** for the princes	7015
	19:14 This is a **l**, and shall be for a lamentation.	7015
	19:14 This is a lamentation, and shall be for a **l**.	7015
	26:17 they shall take up a **l** for thee, and say to	7015
	27: 2 thou son of man, take up a **l** for Tyrus;	7015
	27:32 in their wailing they shall take up a **l** for	7015
	28:12 take up a **l** upon the king of Tyrus,	7015
	32: 2 take up a **l** for Pharaoh king of Egypt,	7015
	32:16 This is the **l** wherewith they shall lament	7015
Am	5: 1 against you, even a **l**, O house of Israel.	7015
	5:16 and such as are skilful of **l** to wailing.	5092
	8:10 into mourning, and all your songs into **l**;	7015
Mic	2: 4 lament with a doleful **l**, and say, We be	5093
Mt	2:18 **l**, and weeping, and great mourning,	2355
Ac	8: 2 to his burial, and made great **l** over him.	2870

LAMENTATIONS (3) [LAMENT]

2Ch	35:25 singing women spake of Josiah in their **l**	7015
	35:25 and behold, they are written in the **l**.	7015
Eze	2:10 was written therein **l**, and mourning,	7015

LAMENTED (11) [LAMENT]

1Sa	6:19 the people **l**, because the LORD had smitten	56
	7: 2 all the house of Israel **l** after the LORD.	5091
	25: 1 **l** him, and buried him in his house at	5594
	28: 3 all Israel had **l** him, and buried him in	5594
2Sa	1:17 David **l** with this lamentation over Saul	6969
	3:33 king **l** over Abner, and said, Died Abner	6969
2Ch	35:25 Jeremiah **l** for Josiah: and all the singing	6969
Jer	16: 4 they shall not be **l**; neither shall they be	5594
	25:33 they shall not be **l**, neither gathered,	5594
Mt	11:17 mourned unto you, and ye have not **l**.	2875
Lk	23:27 women, which also bewailed and **l** him.	2354

LAMENTS See LAMENTATIONS

LAMP (13) [LAMPS]

Ge	15:17 a burning **l** that passed between those	3940
Ex	27:20 the light, to cause the **l** to burn always.	5216
1Sa	3: 3 ere the **l** of God went out in the temple	5216
2Sa	22:29 For thou art my **l**, O LORD:	5216
1Ki	15: 4 LORD his God give him a **l** in Jerusalem,	5216
Job	12: 5 that is ready to slip with his feet is as a **l**.	3940
Ps	119:105 Thy word is a **l** unto my feet, and a light	5216
	132:17 I have ordained a **l** for mine anointed.	5216
Pr	6:23 the commandment is a **l**; and the law is	5216
	13: 9 but the **l** of the wicked shall be put out.	5216
	20:20 his **l** shall be put out in obscure darkness.	5216
Isa	62: 1 the salvation thereof as a **l** that burneth.	3940
Rev	8:10 burning as it were a **l**, and it fell upon	2985

LAMPS (37) [LAMP]

Ex	25:37 thou shalt make the seven **l** thereof:	5216
	25:37 they shall light the **l** thereof, that they	5216
	30: 7 when he dresseth the **l**, he shall burn	5216
	30: 8 when Aaron lighteth the **l** at even, he	5216
	35:14 his furniture, and his **l**, with the oil for	5216

Ex	37:23 he made his seven **l**, and his snuffers,	5216
	39:37 The pure candlestick, with the **l** thereof,	5216
	39:37 even with the **l** to be set in order, and all	5216
	40: 4 in the candlestick, and light the **l** thereof.	5216
	40:25 he lighted the **l** before the LORD.	5216
Lev	24: 2 light, to cause the **l** to burn continually.	5216
	24: 4 He shall order the **l** upon the pure	5216
Nu	4: 9 his **l**, and his tongs, and his snuffdishes,	5216
	8: 2 say unto him, When thou lightest the **l**,	5216
	8: 2 the seven **l** shall give light over against	5216
	8: 3 he lighted the **l** thereof over against	5216
Jdg	7:16 empty pitchers, and **l** within the pitchers.	3940
	7:20 held the **l** in their left hands,	3940
1Ki	7:49 and the **l**, and the tongs of gold,	5216
1Ch	28:15 for their **l** of gold, by weight for every	5216
	28:15 every candlestick, and for the **l** thereof:	5216
	28:15 the candlestick, and also for the **l** thereof,	5216
2Ch	4:20 Moreover the candlesticks with their **l**,	5216
	4:21 the flowers, and the **l**, and the tongs,	5216
	13:11 the candlestick of gold with the **l** thereof,	5216
	29: 7 put out the **l**, and have not burnt incense	5216
Job	41:19 Out of his mouth go burning **l**,	3940
Eze	1:13 coals of fire, and like the appearance of **l**:	3940
Da	10: 6 his eyes as **l** of fire, and his arms and	3940
Zec	4: 2 seven **l** thereon, and seven pipes to	5216
	4: 2 and seven pipes to the seven **l**,	5216
Mt	25: 1 took their **l**, and went forth to meet	2985
	25: 3 They that were foolish took their **l**,	2985
	25: 4 wise took oil in their vessels with their **l**.	2985
	25: 7 those virgins arose, and trimmed their **l**.	2985
	25: 8 Give us of your oil; for our **l** are gone out.	2985
Rev	5: 3 there were seven **l** of fire burning before	2985

LAMPSTAND; LAMPSTANDS See CANDLESTICK; CANDLESTICKS

LANCE (1) [LANCETS]

Jer	50:42 They shall hold the bow and the **l**: they	3591

LANCETS (1) [LANCE]

1Ki	18:28 after their manner with knives and **l**,	7420

LAND (1717) [LANDED, LANDING, LANDMARK, LANDMARKS, LANDS]

Ge	1: 9 unto one place, and let the dry **l** appear:	NIH
	1:10 God called the dry **l** Earth;	NIH
	2:11 that is it which compasseth the whole **l** of	776
	2:12 the gold of that **l** is good: there is bdellium	776
	2:13 the same is it that compasseth the whole **l** of	776
	4:16 dwelt in the **l** of Nod, on the east of Eden.	776
	7:22 of life, of all that was in the dry **l**, died.	NIH
	10:10 and Accad, and Calneh, in the **l** of Shinar.	776
	10:11 Out of that **l** went forth Asshur,	776
	11: 2 that they found a plain in the **l** of Shinar;	776
	11:28 Haran died before his father Terah in the **l**	776
	11:31 of the Chaldees, to go into the **l** of Canaan;	776
	12: 1 house, unto a **l** that I will shew thee:	776
	12: 5 they went forth to go into the **l** of Canaan;	776
	12: 5 and into the **l** of Canaan they came.	776
	12: 6 Abram passed through the **l** unto the place	776
	12: 6 And the Canaanite was then in the **l**.	776
	12: 7 and said, Unto thy seed will I give this **l**:	776
	12:10 was a famine in the **l**: and Abram went	776
	12:10 for the famine was grievous in the **l**.	776
	13: 6 the **l** was not able to bear them, that they	776
	13: 7 and the Perizzite dwelled then in the **l**.	776
	13: 9 Is not the whole **l** before thee?	776
	13:10 the **l** of Egypt, as thou comest unto Zoar.	776
	13:12 Abram dwelled in the **l** of Canaan,	776
	13:15 For all the **l** which thou seest, to thee will	776
	13:17 walk through the **l** in the length of it and	776
	15: 7 Chaldees, to give thee this **l** to inherit it.	776
	15:13 shall be a stranger in a **l** that is not theirs,	776
	15:18 saying, Unto thy seed have I given this **l**,	776
	16: 3 after Abram had dwelt ten years in the **l** of	776
	17: 8 thee, the **l** wherein thou art a stranger,	776
	17: 8 all the **l** of Canaan, for an everlasting	776
	19:28 and toward all the **l** of the plain, and	776
	20:15 Abimelech said, Behold, my **l** is before	776
	21:21 his mother took him a wife out of the **l** of	776
	21:23 and to the **l** wherein thou hast sojourned.	776
	21:32 they returned into the **l** of the Philistines.	776
	21:34 Abraham sojourned in the Philistines' **l**	776
	22: 2 and get thee into the **l** of Moriah;	776
	23: 2 the same is Hebron in the **l** of Canaan:	776
	23: 7 and bowed himself to the people of the **l**,	776
	23:12 down himself before the people of the **l**.	776
	23:13 in the audience of the people of the **l**,	776
	23:15 **l** is worth four hundred shekels of silver;	776
	23:19 the same is Hebron in the **l** of Canaan.	776
	24: 5 will not be willing to follow me unto this **l**:	776
	24: 5 must I needs bring thy son again unto the **l**	776
	24: 7 from the **l** of my kindred, and which spake	776
	24: 7 saying, Unto thy seed will I give this **l**;	776
	24:37 of the Canaanites, in whose **l** I dwell:	776
	26: 1 there was a famine in the **l**, besides the	776
	26: 2 dwell in the **l** which I shall tell thee of:	776
	26: 3 Sojourn in this **l**, and I will be with thee,	776
	26:12 Isaac sowed in that **l**, and received in	776
	26:22 for us, and we shall be fruitful in the **l**.	776
	27:46 these which are of the daughters of the **l**,	776
	28: 4 thou mayest inherit the **l** wherein thou	776
	28:13 the **l** whereon thou liest, to thee will I give	776
	28:15 and will bring thee again into this **l**;	127
	29: 1 came into the **l** of the people of the east.	776

Ge	31: 3 Return unto the **l** of thy fathers, and to thy	776
	31:13 get thee out from this **l**, and return unto	776
	31:13 and return unto the **l** of thy kindred.	776
	31:18 for to go to Isaac his father in the **l** of	776
	32: 3 him to Esau his brother unto the **l** of Seir,	776
	33:18 of Shechem, which is in the **l** of Canaan,	776
	34: 1 went out to see the daughters of the **l**.	776
	34:10 the **l** shall be before you; dwell and trade	776
	34:21 therefore let them dwell in the **l**,	776
	34:21 the **l**, behold, it is large enough for them;	776
	34:30 me to stink among the inhabitants of the **l**,	776
	35: 6 which is in the **l** of Canaan, that is, Beth-el,	776
	35:12 the **l** which I gave Abraham and Isaac,	776
	35:12 and to thy seed after thee will I give the **l**.	776
	35:22 Israel dwelt in that **l**, that Reuben went	776
	36: 5 which were born unto him in the **l** of	776
	36: 6 which he had got in the **l** of Canaan;	776
	36: 7 the **l** wherein they were strangers could	776
	36:16 that came of Eliphaz in the **l** of Edom;	776
	36:17 dukes that came of Reuel in the **l** of Edom;	776
	36:20 of Seir the Horite, who inhabited the **l**;	776
	36:21 the children of Seir in the **l** of Edom.	776
	36:30 of Hori, among their dukes in the **l** of Seir.	776
	36:31 these are the kings that reigned in the **l** of	776
	36:34 Husham of the **l** of Temani reigned in his	776
	36:43 according to their habitations in the **l** of	776
	37: 1 Jacob dwelt in the **l** wherein his father was	776
	37: 1 father was a stranger, in the **l** of Canaan.	776
	40:15 For indeed I was stolen away out of the **l**	776
	41:19 such as I never saw in all the **l** of Egypt for	776
	41:29 great plenty throughout all the **l** of Egypt:	776
	41:30 all the plenty shall be forgotten in the **l** of	776
	41:30 and the famine shall consume the **l**;	776
	41:31 the plenty shall not be known in the **l** by	776
	41:33 and wise, and set him over the **l** of Egypt.	776
	41:34 and let him appoint officers over the **l**,	776
	41:34 take up the fifth part of the **l** of Egypt in	776
	41:36 that food shall be for store to the **l** against	776
	41:36 of famine, which shall be in the **l** of Egypt;	776
	41:36 that the **l** perish not through the famine.	776
	41:41 See, I have set thee over all the **l** of Egypt.	776
	41:43 he made him ruler over all the **l** of Egypt.	776
	41:44 lift up his hand or foot in all the **l** of Egypt.	776
	41:45 Joseph went out over all the **l** of Egypt.	776
	41:46 and went throughout all the **l** of Egypt.	776
	41:48 which were in the **l** of Egypt, and laid up	776
	41:52 me to be fruitful in the **l** of my affliction.	776
	41:53 that was in the **l** of Egypt, were ended.	776
	41:54 but in all the **l** of Egypt there was bread.	776
	41:55 when all the **l** of Egypt was famished,	776
	41:56 the famine waxed sore in the **l** of Egypt.	776
	42: 5 for the famine was in the **l** of Canaan.	776
	42: 6 And Joseph was the governor over the **l**,	776
	42: 6 it was that sold to all the people of the **l**:	776
	42: 7 said, From the **l** of Canaan to buy food.	776
	42: 9 to see the nakedness of the **l** you are come.	776
	42:12 to see the nakedness of the **l** you are come.	776
	42:13 the sons of one man in the **l** of Canaan;	776
	42:29 came unto Jacob their father unto the **l**	776
	42:30 The man, who is the lord of the **l**,	776
	42:32 this day with our father in the **l** of Canaan.	776
	42:34 your brother, and ye shall traffick in the **l**.	776
	43: 1 And the famine was sore in the **l**.	776
	43:11 of the best fruits in the **l** in your vessels,	776
	44: 8 we brought again unto thee out of the **l** of	776
	45: 6 two years hath the famine been in the **l**:	776
	45: 8 and a ruler throughout all the **l** of Egypt.	776
	45:10 And thou shalt dwell in the **l** of Goshen,	776
	45:17 and go, get you unto the **l** of Canaan;	776
	45:18 I will give you the good of the **l** of Egypt,	776
	45:18 of Egypt, and ye shall eat the fat of the **l**.	776
	45:19 take you wagons out of the **l** of Egypt for	776
	45:20 for the good of all the **l** of Egypt is yours.	776
	45:25 came into the **l** of Canaan unto Jacob their	776
	45:26 and he is governor over all the **l** of Egypt.	776
	46: 6 which they had gotten in the **l** of Canaan,	776
	46:12 Er and Onan died in the **l** of Canaan.	776
	46:20 unto Joseph in the **l** of Egypt were born	776
	46:28 and they came into the **l** of Goshen.	776
	46:31 which were in the **l** of Goshen, are come	776
	46:34 that ye may dwell in the **l** of Goshen;	776
	47: 1 I have, are come out of the **l** of Canaan;	776
	47: 1 and behold, they are in the **l** of Goshen.	776
	47: 4 For to sojourn in the **l** are we come;	776
	47: 4 for the famine is sore in the **l** of Canaan:	776
	47: 4 let thy servants dwell in the **l** of Goshen.	776
	47: 6 The **l** of Egypt is before thee; in the best of	776
	47: 6 in the best of the **l** make thy father and	776
	47: 6 to dwell; in the **l** of Goshen let them dwell:	776
	47:11 gave them a possession in the **l** of Egypt,	776
	47:11 in the best of the **l**, in the land of Rameses,	776
	47:11 in the best of the land, in the **l** of Rameses,	776
	47:13 was no bread in all the **l**; for the famine	776
	47:13 so that the **l** of Egypt and all the land of	776
	47:13 of Egypt and all the **l** of Canaan fainted by reason of	776
	47:14 money that was found in the **l** of Egypt,	776
	47:14 in the **l** of Canaan, for the corn which they	776
	47:15 when money failed in the **l** of Egypt,	776
	47:15 in the **l** of Canaan, all the Egyptians came	776
	47:19 die before thine eyes, both we and our **l**?	127
	47:19 buy us and our **l** for bread, and we and	127
	47:19 and our **l** will be servants unto Pharaoh:	127
	47:19 and not die, that the **l** be not desolate.	127
	47:20 bought all the **l** of Egypt for Pharaoh;	127
	47:20 over them: so the **l** became Pharaoh's.	776

Ge	47:22 Only the l of the priests bought he not;	127
	47:23 you *this* day and your l for Pharaoh:	127
	47:23 *here is* seed for you, and ye shall sow the l.	127
	47:26 Joseph made it a law over the l of Egypt	127
	47:26 fifth *part;* except the l of the priests only,	127
	47:27 Israel dwelt in the l of Egypt, in the	776
	47:28 Jacob lived in the l of Egypt seventeen	776
	48: 3 unto me at Luz in the l of Canaan,	776
	48: 4 will give this l to thy seed after thee *for* an	776
	48: 5 were born unto thee in the l of Egypt	776
	48: 7 Rachel died by me in the l of Canaan in	776
	48:21 bring you again unto the l of your fathers.	776
	49:15 *was* good, and the l that *it was* pleasant;	776
	49:30 which *is* before Mamre, in the l of Canaan,	776
	50: 5 I have digged for me in the l of Canaan,	776
	50: 7 and all the elders of the l of Egypt,	776
	50: 8 their herds, they left in the l of Goshen.	776
	50:11 the inhabitants of the l, the Canaanites,	776
	50:13 his sons carried him into the l of Canaan,	776
	50:24 bring you out of this l unto the land which	776
	50:24 bring you out of this land unto the l which	776
Ex	1: 7 and the l was filled with them.	776
	1:10 against us, and *so* get them up out of the l.	776
	2:15 of Pharaoh, and dwelt in the l of Midian:	776
	2:22 said, I have been a stranger in a strange l.	776
	3: 8 to bring them up out of that l unto a good	776
	3: 8 them up out of that land unto a good l	776
	3: 8 unto a l flowing with milk and honey;	776
	3:17 of Egypt unto the l of the Canaanites,	776
	3:17 unto a l flowing with milk and honey.	776
	4: 9 pour *it* upon the dry *l* and the water	NIH
	4: 9 river shall become blood upon the dry *l*	NIH
	4:20 an ass, and he returned to the l of Egypt:	776
	5: 5 the people of the l now *are* many,	776
	5:12 l of Egypt to gather stubble instead of straw.	776
	6: 1 strong hand shall he drive them out of his l.	776
	6: 4 to give them the l of Canaan, the land of	776
	6: 4 the l of their pilgrimage, wherein they	776
	6: 8 I will bring you in unto the l, *concerning*	776
	6:11 he let the children of Israel go out of his l.	776
	6:13 bring the children of Israel out of the l of	776
	6:26 Bring out the children of Israel from the l	776
	6:28 LORD spake unto Moses in the l of Egypt,	776
	7: 2 he send the children of Israel out of his l.	776
	7: 3 my signs and my wonders in the l of Egypt.	776
	7: 4 out of the l of Egypt by great judgments.	776
	7:19 there may be blood throughout all the l of	776
	7:21 there was blood throughout all the l of	776
	8: 5 frogs to come up upon the l of Egypt.	776
	8: 6 frogs came up, and covered the l of Egypt.	776
	8: 7 and brought up frogs upon the l of Egypt.	776
	8:14 them together upon heaps: and the l stank.	776
	8:16 out thy rod, and smite the dust of the l,	776
	8:16 it may become lice throughout all the l	776
	8:17 the dust of the l became lice throughout	776
	8:17 became lice throughout all the l of Egypt.	776
	8:22 I will sever in that day the l of Goshen,	776
	8:24 houses, and into all the l of Egypt:	776
	8:24 I was corrupted by reason of the swarm	776
	8:25 said, Go ye, sacrifice to your God in the l.	776
	9: 5 the LORD shall do this thing in the l.	776
	9: 9 it shall become small dust in all the l of	776
	9: 9 upon beast, throughout all the l of Egypt.	776
	9:22 that there may be hail in all the l of Egypt,	776
	9:22 of the field, throughout the l of Egypt.	776
	9:23 the LORD rained hail upon the l of Egypt.	776
	9:24 such as there was none like it in all the l of	776
	9:25 the hail smote throughout all the l of Egypt	776
	9:26 Only in the l of Goshen, where the children	776
	10:12 Stretch out thine hand over the l of Egypt	776
	10:12 that they may come up upon the l of Egypt,	776
	10:12 every herb of the l, *even* all that the hail	776
	10:13 Moses stretched forth his rod over the l of	776
	10:13 the LORD brought an east wind upon the l	776
	10:14 the locusts went up over all the l of Egypt,	776
	10:15 whole earth, so that the l was darkened;	776
	10:15 they did eat every herb of the l, and all	776
	10:15 of the field, through all the l of Egypt.	776
	10:21 that there may be darkness over the l of	776
	10:22 there was a thick darkness in all the l of	776
	11: 3 Moses *was* very great in the l of Egypt,	776
	11: 5 all the firstborn in the l of Egypt shall die,	776
	11: 6 shall be a great cry throughout all the l	776
	11: 9 my wonders may be multiplied in the l	776
	11:10 let the children of Israel go out of his l.	776
	12: 1 unto Moses and Aaron in the l of Egypt,	776
	12:12 For I will pass through the l of Egypt this	776
	12:12 will smite all the firstborn in the l of Egypt,	776
	12:13 to destroy *you,* when I smite the l of Egypt.	776
	12:17 I brought your armies out of the l of Egypt:	776
	12:19 whether he be a stranger, or born in the l.	776
	12:25 when ye be come to the l which the LORD	776
	12:29 smote all the firstborn in the l of Egypt,	776
	12:33 that they might send them out of the l in	776
	12:41 of the LORD went out from the l of Egypt.	776
	12:42 for bringing them out from the l of Egypt:	776
	12:48 and he shall be as one that is born in the l:	776
	12:51 Israel out of the l of Egypt by their armies.	776
	13: 5 bring thee into the l of the Canaanites,	776
	13: 5 thee, a l flowing with milk and honey,	776
	13:11 bring thee into the l of the Canaanites,	776
	13:15 that the LORD slew all the firstborn in the l	776
	13:17 *through* the way of the l of the Philistines,	776
	13:18 went up harnessed out of the l of Egypt.	776
	14: 3 *are* entangled in the l, the wilderness	776

Ex	14:21 made the sea dry *l,* and the waters were	NIH
	14:29 the children of Israel walked upon dry *l* in	NIH
	15:19 the children of Israel went on dry *l* in	NIH
	16: 1 after their departing out of the l of Egypt.	776
	16: 3 by the hand of the LORD in the l of Egypt,	776
	16: 6 hath brought you out from the l of Egypt:	776
	16:32 when I brought you forth from the l of	776
	16:35 years, until they came to a l inhabited;	776
	16:35 until they came unto the borders of the l	776
	18: 3 he said, I have been an alien in a strange l:	776
	18:27 and he went his way into his own l.	776
	19: 1 Israel were gone forth out of the l of Egypt,	776
	20: 2 which have brought thee out of the l of	776
	20:12 that thy days may be long upon the l which	127
	22:21 for ye were strangers in the l of Egypt.	776
	23: 9 seeing ye were strangers in the l of Egypt.	776
	23:10 six years thou shalt sow thy l,	776
	23:19 The first of the firstfruits of thy l thou shalt	127
	23:26 cast their young, nor be barren, in thy l:	776
	23:29 lest the l become desolate, and the beast	776
	23:30 until thou be increased, and inherit the l.	776
	23:31 I will deliver the inhabitants of the l into	776
	23:33 shall not dwell in thy l, lest they make	776
	29:46 brought them forth out of the l of Egypt,	776
	32: 1 the man that brought us up out of the l of	776
	32: 4 brought thee up out of the l of Egypt,	776
	32: 7 thou broughtest out of the l of Egypt,	776
	32: 8 have brought thee up out of the l of	776
	32:11 thou hast brought forth out of the l of	776
	32:13 all this l that I have spoken of will I give	776
	32:23 the man that brought us up out of the l of	776
	33: 1 thou hast brought up out of the l of Egypt,	776
	33: 1 unto the l which I sware unto Abraham,	776
	33: 3 Unto a l flowing with milk and honey: for	776
	34:12 the inhabitants of the l whither thou goest,	776
	34:15 a covenant with the inhabitants of the l,	776
	34:24 neither shall any man desire thy l, when	776
	34:26 The first of the firstfruits of thy l thou shalt	127
Lev	11:45 that bringeth you up out of the l of Egypt,	776
	14:34 When ye be come into the l of Canaan,	776
	14:34 put the plague of leprosy in a house of the l	776
	16:22 all their iniquities unto a l not inhabited:	776
	18: 3 After the doings of the l of Egypt,	776
	18: 3 After the doings of the l of Canaan, whither	776
	18:25 the l is defiled: therefore I do visit	776
	18:25 the l *itself* vomiteth out her inhabitants.	776
	18:27 abominations have the men of the l done,	776
	18:27 *were* before you, and the l is defiled;)	776
	18:28 That the l spue not you out also, when ye	776
	19: 9 when ye reap the harvest of your l, thou	776
	19:23 when ye shall come into the l, and shall	776
	19:29 lest the l fall to whoredom, and the land	776
	19:29 and the l become full of wickedness.	776
	19:33 if a stranger sojourn with thee in your l,	776
	19:34 for ye were strangers in the l of Egypt:	776
	19:36 which brought you out of the l of Egypt.	776
	20: 2 the people of the l shall stone him with	776
	20: 4 if the people of the l do any ways hide	776
	20:22 that the l, whither I bring you to dwell	776
	20:24 Ye shall inherit their l, and I will give it	127
	20:24 a l that floweth with milk and honey:	776
	22:24 you make *any* offering *thereof* in your l.	776
	22:33 That brought you out of the l of Egypt, to	776
	23:10 When ye be come into the l which I give	776
	23:22 when ye reap the harvest of your l, thou	776
	23:39 when ye have gathered in the fruit of the l,	776
	23:43 when I brought them out of the l of Egypt:	776
	24:16 the stranger, as he **that is born in** the l,	249
	25: 2 When ye come into the l which I give you,	776
	25: 2 shall the l keep a sabbath unto the LORD.	776
	25: 4 year shall be a sabbath of rest unto the l,	776
	25: 5 for it is a year of rest unto the l.	776
	25: 6 the sabbath of the l shall be meat for you;	776
	25: 7 cattle, and for the beast that *are* in thy l,	776
	25: 9 the trumpet sound throughout all your l.	776
	25:10 proclaim liberty throughout *all* the l unto	776
	25:18 them; and ye shall dwell in the l in safety.	776
	25:19 the l shall yield her fruit, and ye shall eat	776
	25:23 The l shall not be sold for ever: for the land	776
	25:23 for the l *is* mine; for ye *were* strangers and	776
	25:24 in all the l of your possession ye shall grant	776
	25:24 ye shall grant a redemption to the l.	776
	25:38 which brought you forth out of the l of	776
	25:38 to give you the l of Canaan, *and* to be your	776
	25:42 which I brought forth out of the l of Egypt:	776
	25:45 *are* with you, which they begat in your l:	776
	25:55 whom I brought forth out of the l of Egypt:	776
	26: 1 shall ye set up *any* image of stone in your l,	776
	26: 4 the l shall yield her increase, and the trees	776
	26: 5 bread to the full, and dwell in your l safely.	776
	26: 6 I will give peace in the l, and ye shall lie	776
	26: 6 I will rid evil beasts out of the l, neither	776
	26: 6 neither shall the sword go through your l.	776
	26:13 which brought you forth out of the l of	776
	26:20 for your l shall not yield her increase,	776
	26:20 neither shall the trees of the l yield their	776
	26:32 I will bring the l into desolation:	776
	26:33 your l shall be desolate, and your cities	776
	26:34 shall the l enjoy her sabbaths, as long as it	776
	26:34 desolate, and ye *be* in your enemies' l;	776
	26:34 *even* then shall the l rest, and enjoy her	776
	26:38 and the l of your enemies shall eat you up.	776
	26:41 have brought them into the l of their	776
	26:42 I remember; and I will remember the l.	776
	26:43 The l also shall be left of them,	776

Lev	26:44 when they be in the l of their enemies,	776
	26:45 whom I brought forth out of the l of Egypt	776
	27:24 to him to whom the possession of the l	776
	27:30 all the tithe of the l, *whether* of the seed of	776
	27:30 *whether* of the seed of the l, *or* of the fruit	776
Nu	1: 1 after they were come out of the l of Egypt,	776
	3:13 l of Egypt I hallowed unto me all	776
	8:17 smote every firstborn in the l of Egypt,	776
	9: 1 after they were come out of the l of Egypt,	776
	9:14 and for him that was born in the l.	776
	10: 9 if ye go *to* war in your l against the enemy	776
	10:30 I will depart to mine own l, and to my	776
	11:12 unto the l which thou swarest unto their	127
	13: 2 that they may search the l of Canaan,	776
	13:16 men which Moses sent to spy out the l.	776
	13:17 sent them to spy out the l of Canaan,	776
	13:18 see the l, what it *is;* and the people	776
	13:19 what the l *is* that they dwell in, whether it	776
	13:20 what the l *is,* whether it *be* fat or lean,	776
	13:20 courage, and bring of the fruit of the l.	776
	13:21 searched the l from the wilderness of Zin	776
	13:25 they returned from searching of the l after	776
	13:26 and shewed them the fruit of the l.	776
	13:27 came unto the l whither thou sentest us,	776
	13:28 the people *be* strong that dwell in the l,	776
	13:29 The Amalekites dwell in the l of the south:	776
	13:32 they brought up an evil report of the l	776
	13:32 The l, through which we have gone	776
	13:32 *is* a l that eateth up the inhabitants thereof;	776
	14: 2 Would God that we had died in the l of	776
	14: 3 *hath* the LORD brought us unto this l,	776
	14: 6 *which were* of them that searched the l,	776
	14: 7 saying, The l, which we passed through to	776
	14: 7 to search it, *is* an exceeding good l.	776
	14: 8 he will bring us into this l, and give it us;	776
	14: 8 a l which floweth with milk and honey.	776
	14: 9 neither fear ye the people of the l;	776
	14:14 they will tell *it* to the inhabitants of this l:	776
	14:16 into the l which he sware unto them,	776
	14:23 they shall not see the l which I sware	776
	14:24 will I bring into the l whereinto he went;	776
	14:30 Doubtless ye shall not come into the l,	776
	14:31 they shall know the l which ye have	776
	14:34 of the days *in* which ye searched the l,	776
	14:36 the men, which Moses sent to search the l,	776
	14:36 by bringing up a slander upon the l,	776
	14:37 that did bring up the evil report upon the l,	776
	14:38 *were* of the men that went to search the l,	776
	15: 2 When ye be come into the l of your	776
	15:18 When ye come into the l whither I bring	776
	15:19 *that* when ye eat of the bread of the l,	776
	15:30 *whether* he be **born in the** l, or a stranger,	249
	15:41 which brought you out of the l of Egypt,	776
	16:13 us up out of a l that floweth with milk	776
	16:14 Moreover thou hast not brought us into a l	776
	18:13 *And* whatsoever is first ripe in the l,	776
	18:20 Thou shalt have no inheritance in their l,	776
	20:12 shall not bring this congregation into the l	776
	20:23 by the coast of the l of Edom, saying,	776
	20:24 for he shall not enter into the l which I	776
	21: 4 of the Red sea, to compass the l of Edom:	776
	21:22 Let me pass through thy l: we will not turn	776
	21:24 possessed his l from Arnon unto Jabbok,	776
	21:26 taken all his l out of his hand, *even* unto	776
	21:31 Thus Israel dwelt in the l of the Amorites.	776
	21:34 into thy hand, and all his people, and his l;	776
	21:35 left him alive: and they possessed his l.	776
	22: 5 which *is* by the river *of* the l of the children	776
	22: 6 and *that* I may drive them out of the l:	776
	22:13 the princes of Balak, Get you into your l:	776
	26: 4 which went forth out of the l of Egypt.	776
	26:19 and Er and Onan died in the l of Canaan.	776
	26:53 Unto these the l shall be divided for an	776
	26:55 the l shall be divided by lot:	776
	27:12 see the l which I have given unto	776
	32: 1 when they saw the l of Jazer, and the land	776
	32: 1 the l of Gilead, that behold, the place *was* a	776
	32: 4 a l for cattle, and thy servants have cattle:	776
	32: 5 let this l be given unto thy servants for a	776
	32: 7 the l which the LORD hath given them?	776
	32: 8 sent them from Kadesh-barnea to see the l.	776
	32: 9 unto the valley of Eshcol, and saw the l,	776
	32: 9 that *they* should not go into the l which	776
	32:11 see the l which I sware unto Abraham,	127
	32:17 because of the inhabitants of the l.	776
	32:22 the l be subdued before the LORD: then	776
	32:22 this l shall be your possession before	776
	32:29 and the l shall be subdued before you;	776
	32:29 ye shall give them the l of Gilead for a	776
	32:30 possessions among you in the l of Canaan.	776
	32:32 before the LORD *into* the l of Canaan,	776
	32:33 the l, with the cities thereof in the coasts,	776
	33: 1 which went forth out of the l of Egypt with	776
	33:37 mount Hor, in the edge of the l of Edom.	776
	33:38 of Israel were come out of the l of Egypt,	776
	33:40 dwelt in the south in the l of Canaan,	776
	33:51 ye are passed over Jordan into the l of	776
	33:52 shall drive out all the inhabitants of the l	776
	33:53 shall dispossess the inhabitants *of* the l,	776
	33:53 for I have given you the l to possess it.	776
	33:54 shall divide the l by lot for an inheritance	776
	33:55 the inhabitants of the l from before you;	776
	33:55 shall vex you in the l wherein ye dwell.	776
	34: 2 When ye come into the l of Canaan;	776
	34: 2 (this *is* the l that shall fall unto you for an	776

L

Nu 34: 2 *even* the l of Canaan with the coasts 776
34:12 this shall be your l with the coasts thereof 776
34:13 This *is* the l which ye shall inherit by lot, 776
34:17 the men which shall divide the l unto you: 776
34:18 every tribe, to divide the l by inheritance. 776
34:29 the children of Israel in the l of Canaan. 776
35:10 When ye be come over Jordan into the l of 776
35:14 three cities shall ye give in the l of Canaan, 776
35:28 shall return into the l of his possession. 776
35:32 he should come again to dwell in the l, 776
35:33 ye shall not pollute the l wherein ye *are:* 776
35:33 wherein ye *are:* for blood it defileth the l: 776
35:33 the l cannot be cleansed of the blood that 776
35:34 therefore the l which ye shall inhabit, 776
36: 2 l for an inheritance by lot to the children 776

Dt 1: 5 On *this* side Jordan, in the l of Moab, 776
1: 7 the l of the Canaanites, and *unto* Lebanon, 776
1: 8 Behold, I have set the l before you: go in 776
1: 8 possess the l which the Lord sware unto 776
1:21 the Lord thy God hath set the l before 776
1:22 they shall search us out the l, and bring us 776
1:25 took of the fruit of the l in their hands, 776
1:25 *It is* a good l which the Lord our God 776
1:27 he hath brought us forth out of the l of 776
1:35 men of this evil generation see that good l, 776
1:36 him will I give the l that he hath trodden 776
2: 5 for I will not give you of their l, no, not so 776
2: 9 for I will not give thee of their l *for* a 776
2:12 as Israel did unto the l of his possession, 776
2:19 for I will not give thee of the l of 776
2:20 (That also was accounted a l of giants: 776
2:24 the Amorite, king of Heshbon, and his l: 776
2:27 Let me pass through thy l: I will go along 776
2:29 until I shall pass over Jordan into the l 776
2:31 begun to give Sihon and his l before thee: 776
2:31 to possess, that *thou* mayest inherit his l. 776
2:37 Only unto the l of the children of Ammon 776
3: 2 and all his people, and his l, into thy hand; 776
3: 8 Amorites the l that *was* on *this* side Jordan, 776
3:12 this l, *which* we possessed at that time, 776
3:13 Bashan, which was called the l of giants. 776
3:18 The Lord your God hath given you this l 776
3:20 *until* they also possess the l which 776
3:25 and see the good l that *is* beyond Jordan, 776
3:28 he shall cause them to inherit the l which 776
4: 1 possess the l which the Lord God of your 776
4: 5 so in the l whither ye go to possess it. 776
4:14 ye might do them in the l whither ye go 776
4:21 that *I* should not go in unto *that* good l, 776
4:22 I *must* die in this l, I *must* not go over 776
4:22 ye *shall* go over, and possess that good l. 776
4:25 and ye shall have remained long in the l, 776
4:26 ye shall soon utterly perish from off the l 776
4:38 to give thee their l *for* an inheritance, as 776
4:46 in the l of Sihon king of the Amorites, 776
4:47 they possessed his l, and the land of Og 776
4:47 the l of Og king of Bashan, two kings of 776
5: 6 which brought thee out of the l of Egypt, 776
5:15 remember that thou wast a servant in the l 776
5:16 in the l which the Lord thy God giveth 127
5:31 they may do *them* in the l which I give 776
5:33 ye may prolong *your* days in the l which 776
6: 1 ye might do *them* in the l whither ye go 776
6: 3 *in* the l that floweth with milk and honey. 776
6:10 into the l which he sware unto thy fathers, 776
6:12 which brought thee forth out of the l of 776
6:18 possess the good l which the Lord sware 776
6:23 to give us the l which he sware unto our 776
7: 1 into the l whither thou goest to possess it, 776
7:13 the fruit of thy l, thy corn, and thy wine, 127
7:13 in the l which he sware unto thy fathers to 776
8: 1 possess the l which the Lord sware unto 776
8: 7 Lord thy God bringeth thee into a good l, 776
8: 7 a l of brooks of water, of fountains and 776
8: 8 A l of wheat, and barley, and vines, 776
8: 8 pomegranates; a l of oil olive, and honey; 776
8: 9 A l wherein thou shalt eat bread without 776
8: 9 l whose stones *are* iron, and out of whose 776
8:10 God for the good l which he hath given 776
8:14 which brought thee forth out of the l of 776
9: 4 Lord hath brought me in to possess this l: 776
9: 5 thine heart, dost thou go to possess their l: 776
9: 6 good l to possess it for thy righteousness; 776
9: 7 that thou didst depart out of the l of Egypt, 776
9:23 and possess the l which I have given you; 776
9:28 Lest the l whence thou broughtest us out 776
9:28 them into the l which he promised them, 776
10: 7 to Jotbath, a l of rivers of waters. 776
10:11 that they may go in and possess the l, 776
10:19 for ye were strangers in the l of Egypt. 776
11: 3 the king of Egypt, and unto all his l; 776
11: 8 may be strong, and go in and possess the l, 776
11: 9 that ye may prolong *your* days in the l, 127
11: 9 a l that floweth with milk and honey. 776
11:10 the l, whither thou goest in to possess it, 776
11:10 *is* not as the l of Egypt, from whence ye 776
11:11 the l, whither ye go to possess it, *is* a land 776
11:11 a l of hills and valleys, *and* drinketh water 776
11:12 A l which the Lord thy God careth for: 776
11:14 That I will give *you* the rain of your l in his 776
11:17 no rain, and *that* the l yield not her fruit; 127
11:17 *lest* ye perish quickly from off the good l 776
11:21 in the l which the Lord sware unto your 127
11:25 the dread of you upon all the l that ye shall 776
11:29 unto the l whither thou goest to possess it, 776

Dt 11:30 sun goeth down, in the l of the Canaanites, 776
11:31 which the Lord your God giveth you, 776
12: 1 which ye shall observe to do in the l, 776
12:10 dwell in the l which the Lord your God 776
12:29 succeedest them, and dwellest in their l; 776
13: 5 which brought you out of the l of Egypt, 776
13:10 which brought thee out of the l of Egypt, 776
15: 4 l which the Lord thy God giveth thee *for* 776
15: 7 thy l which the Lord thy God giveth thee, 776
15:11 For the poor shall never cease out of the l: 776
15:11 to thy poor, and to thy needy, in thy l. 776
15:15 thou wast a bondman in the l of Egypt, 776
16: 3 for thou camest forth out of the l of Egypt 776
16: 3 out of the l of Egypt all the days of thy life. 776
16:20 inherit the l which the Lord thy God 776
17:14 When thou art come unto the l which 776
18: 9 When thou art come into the l which 776
19: 1 whose l the Lord thy God giveth thee, 776
19: 2 three cities for thee in the midst of thy l, 776
19: 3 thee a way, and divide the coasts of thy l, 776
19: 8 give thee all the l which he promised to 776
19:10 That innocent blood be not shed in thy l, 776
19:14 which thou shalt inherit in the l that 776
20: 1 brought thee up out of the l of Egypt. 776
21: 1 If *one* be found slain in the l, which 127
21:23 that thy l be not defiled, which the Lord 127
23: 7 because thou wast a stranger in his l. 776
23:20 in the l whither thou goest to possess it. 776
24: 4 thou shalt not cause the l to sin, which 776
24:14 of thy strangers that *are* in thy l within thy 776
24:22 thou wast a bondman in the l of Egypt: 776
25:15 that thy days may be lengthened in the l 127
25:19 in the l which the Lord thy God giveth 776
26: 1 when thou art come into the l which 776
26: 2 which thou shalt bring of thy l that 776
26: 9 given us this l, *even* a land that floweth 776
26: 9 *even* a l that floweth with milk and honey. 776
26:10 I have brought the firstfruits of the l, 127
26:15 and the l which thou hast given us, 776
26:15 a l that floweth with milk and honey. 776
27: 2 the l which the Lord thy God giveth thee, 776
27: 3 that thou mayest go in unto the l which 776
27: 3 a l that floweth with milk and honey; 776
28: 8 he shall bless thee in the l which the Lord 776
28:11 in the l which the Lord sware unto thy 776
28:12 the heaven to give the rain unto thy l in 776
28:18 the fruit of thy l, the increase of thy kine, 127
28:21 he have consumed thee from off the l, 127
28:24 The Lord shall make the rain of thy l 776
28:33 The fruit of thy l, and all thy labours, shall 127
28:42 and fruit of thy l shall the locust consume. 776
28:51 the fruit of thy l, until thou be destroyed: 127
28:52 thou trustedst, throughout all thy l: 776
28:52 thee in all thy gates throughout all thy l, 776
28:63 ye shall be plucked from off the l whither 127
29: 1 the children of Israel in the l of Moab, 776
29: 2 your eyes in the l of Egypt unto Pharaoh, 776
29: 2 and unto all his servants, and unto all his l; 776
29: 8 took their l, and gave it for an inheritance 776
29:16 ye know how we have dwelt in the l of 776
29:22 the stranger that shall come from a far l, 776
29:22 when they see the plagues of that l, 776
29:23 *And that* the whole l thereof *is* brimstone, 776
29:24 hath the Lord done thus unto this l? 776
29:25 he brought them forth out of the l of Egypt: 776
29:27 of the Lord was kindled against this l, 776
29:28 the Lord rooted them out of their l in 127
29:28 cast them into another l, as *it is* this day. 776
30: 5 the Lord thy God will bring thee into the l 776
30: 9 cattle, and in the fruit of thy l, for good: 776
30:16 the Lord thy God shall bless thee in the l 776
30:18 ye shall not prolong *your* days upon the l, 127
30:20 that thou mayest dwell in the l which 776
31: 4 unto the l of them, whom he destroyed. 776
31: 7 thou must go with this people unto the l 776
31:13 as long as ye live in the l whither ye go 127
31:16 after the gods of the strangers of the l, 776
31:20 when I shall have brought them into the l 127
31:21 I have brought them into the l which I 776
31:23 Israel into the l which I sware unto them: 776
32:10 found him in a desert l, and in the waste 776
32:43 be merciful *unto* his l, *and to* his people. 127
32:47 thing ye shall prolong *your* days in the l, 127
32:49 mount Nebo, which *is* in the l of Moab, 776
32:49 behold the l of Canaan, which I give unto 776
32:52 Yet thou shalt see the l before *thee;* but 776
32:52 thou shalt not go thither unto the l which 776
33:13 he said, Blessed of the Lord *be* his l, 776
33:28 the fountain of Jacob *shall be* upon a l of 776
34: 1 the Lord shewed him all the l of Gilead, 776
34: 2 the l of Ephraim, and Manasseh, and all 776
34: 2 Manasseh, and all the l of Judah, unto 776
34: 4 This *is* the l which I sware unto Abraham, 776
34: 5 of the Lord died there in the l of Moab, 776
34: 6 he buried him in a valley in the l of Moab, 776
34:11 which the Lord sent him to do in the l of 776
34:11 and to all his servants, and to all his l, 776

Jos 1: 2 unto the l which I do give to them, 776
1: 4 all the l of the Hittites, and unto the great 776
1: 6 shalt thou divide for an inheritance the l, 776
1:11 over this Jordan, to go in to possess the l, 776
1:13 given you rest, and hath given you this l. 776
1:14 shall remain in the l which Moses gave you 776
1:15 they also have possessed the l which 776
1:15 shall return unto the l of your possession, 776

Jos 2: 1 saying, Go view the l, even Jericho. 776
2: 9 I know that the Lord hath given you the l, 776
2: 9 all the inhabitants of the l faint because 776
2:14 when the Lord hath given us the l, 776
2:18 *when* we come into the l, thou shalt 776
2:24 hath delivered into our hands all the l; 776
4:18 *l,* that the waters of Jordan returned unto NIH
4:22 Israel came over this Jordan on dry *L.* NIH
5: 6 sware that he would not shew them the l, 776
5: 6 a l that floweth with milk and honey. 776
5:11 they did eat of the old corn of the l on 776
5:12 they had eaten of the old corn of the l; 776
5:12 they did eat of the fruit of the l of Canaan 776
7: 9 all the inhabitants of the l shall hear *of it,* 776
8: 1 Ai, and his people, and his city, and his l: 776
9:24 his servant Moses to give you all the l, 776
9:24 to destroy all the inhabitants of the l from 776
10:42 and their l did Joshua take *at* one time, 776
11: 3 *to* the Hivite under Hermon in the l of 776
11:16 So Joshua took all that l, the hills, and all 776
11:16 the south *country,* and all the l of Goshen, 776
11:22 was none of the Anakims left in the l 776
11:23 Joshua took the whole l, according to all 776
11:23 by their tribes. And the l rested from war. 776
12: 1 Now these *are* the kings of the l, which 776
12: 1 possessed their l on the *other* side Jordan 776
13: 1 there remaineth *yet* very much l to be 776
13: 2 This *is* the l that *yet* remaineth: 776
13: 4 all the l of the Canaanites, and Mearah 776
13: 5 the l of the Giblites, and all Lebanon, 776
13: 7 divide this l for an inheritance unto the 776
13:25 and half the l of the children of Ammon, 776
14: 1 of Israel inherited in the l of Canaan, 776
14: 4 they gave no part unto the Levites in the l, 776
14: 5 of Israel did, and they divided the l. 776
14: 7 me from Kadesh-barnea to espy out the l; 776
14: 9 the l whereon thy feet have trodden 776
14:15 the Anakims. And the l had rest from war. 776
15:19 blessing; for thou hast given me a south l; 776
17: 5 beside the l of Gilead and Bashan, 776
17: 5 the rest of Manasseh's sons had the l of 776
17: 8 *Now* Manasseh had the l of Tappuah: 776
17:12 but the Canaanites would dwell in that l. 776
17:15 cut down for thyself there in the l of 776
17:16 all the Canaanites that dwell in the l of 776
18: 1 And the l was subdued before them. 776
18: 3 long *are* you slack to go to possess the l, 776
18: 4 go through the l, and describe it according 776
18: 6 therefore describe the l *into* seven parts, 776
18: 8 charged them that went to describe the l, 776
18: 8 Go and walk through the l, and describe it, 776
18: 9 the men went and passed through the l, 776
18:10 Joshua divided the l unto the children 776
19:49 they had made an end of dividing the l 776
21: 2 they spake unto them at Shiloh in the l of 776
21:43 the Lord gave unto Israel all the l which 776
22: 4 tents, *and* unto the l of your possession, 776
22: 9 which *is* in the l of Canaan, to go unto 776
22: 9 to the l of their possession, whereof they 776
22:10 that *are* in the l of Canaan, the children of 776
22:11 built an altar over against the l of Canaan, 776
22:13 half tribe of Manasseh, into the l of Gilead, 776
22:15 unto the l of Gilead, and they spake with 776
22:19 if the l of your possession *be* unclean, *then* 776
22:19 pass ye over unto the l of the possession of 776
22:32 out of the l of Gilead, unto the land of 776
22:32 unto the l of Canaan, to the children of 776
22:33 to destroy the l wherein the children of 776
23: 5 ye shall possess their l, as the Lord your 776
23:13 until ye perish from off this good l which 127
23:15 l which the Lord your God hath given 127
23:16 ye shall perish quickly from off the good l 776
24: 3 led him throughout all the l of Canaan, 776
24: 8 I brought you into the l of the Amorites, 776
24: 8 your hand, that ye might possess their l; 776
24:13 I have given you a l for which ye did not 776
24:15 gods of the Amorites, in whose l ye dwell: 776
24:17 us up and our fathers out of the l of Egypt, 776
24:18 even the Amorites which dwelt in the l: 776

Jdg 1: 2 I have delivered the l into his hand. 776
1:15 for thou hast given me a south l; give me 776
1:26 the man went *into* the l of the Hittites, 776
1:27 but the Canaanites would dwell in that l. 776
1:32 the Canaanites, the inhabitants of the l: 776
1:33 the Canaanites, the inhabitants of the l: 776
2: 1 have brought you unto the l which I sware 776
2: 2 no league with the inhabitants of this l; 776
2: 6 man unto his inheritance to possess the l. 776
2:12 which brought them out of the l of Egypt, 776
3:11 the l had rest forty years. And Othniel 776
3:30 Israel. And the l had rest fourscore years. 776
5:31 in his might. And the l had rest forty years. 776
6: 5 and they entered into the l to destroy it. 776
6: 9 out from before you, and gave you their l; 776
6:10 gods of the Amorites, in whose l ye dwell: 776
9:37 come people down by the middle of the l, 776
10: 4 unto this day, which *are* in the l of Gilead. 776
10: 8 *other* side Jordan in the l of the Amorites, 776
11: 3 his brethren, and dwelt in the l of Tob: 776
11: 5 went to fetch Jephthah out of the l of Tob: 776
11:12 thou art come against me to fight in my l? 776
11:13 Because Israel took away my l, when they 776
11:15 Israel took not away the l of Moab, 776
11:15 nor the l of the children of Ammon: 776
11:17 Let me, I pray thee, pass through thy l: 776

Jdg 11:18 compassed the l of Edom, and the land of 776
11:18 of Moab, and came by the east side 776
11:18 came by the east side of the l of Moab, 776
11:19 we pray thee, through thy l into my place. 776
11:21 Israel possessed all the l of the Amorites, 776
12:15 was buried in Pirathon in the l of Ephraim, 776
18: 2 to spy out the l, and to search it; 776
18: 2 and they said unto them, Go, search the l: 776
18: 7 there was no magistrate in the l, that 776
18: 9 for we have seen the l, and behold, it is 776
18: 9 to go, and to enter to possess the l. 776
18:10 unto a people secure, and to a large l: 776
18:17 five men that went to spy out the l went 776
18:30 Dan until the day of the captivity of the l. 776
19:30 came up out of the l of Egypt unto this day: 776
20: 1 with the l of Gilead, unto the LORD in 776
21:12 to Shiloh, which is in the l of Canaan. 776
21:21 of Shiloh, and go in the l of Benjamin. 776
Ru 1: 1 ruled, that there was a famine in the l. 776
1: 7 they went on the way to return unto the l 776
2:11 the l of thy nativity, and art come unto a 776
4: 3 selleth a parcel of l, which was our 7704
1Sa 6: 5 and images of your mice that mar the l; 776
6: 5 from off your gods, and from off your l. 776
9: 4 passed through the l of Shalisha, 776
9: 4 then they passed through the l of Shalim, 776
9: 4 he passed through the l of the Benjamites, 776
9: 5 when they were come to the l of Zuph, 776
9:16 send thee a man out of the l of Benjamin, 776
12: 6 that brought your fathers up out of the l of 776
13: 3 Saul blew the trumpet throughout all the l, 776
13: 7 Hebrews went over Jordan to the l of Gad 776
13:17 leadeth to Ophrah, unto the l of Shual: 776
13:19 smith found throughout all the l of Israel: 776
14:14 within as it were a half acre of l, 7704
14:25 all they of the l came to a wood; 776
14:29 Jonathan, My father hath troubled the l: 776
21:11 him, Is not this David the king of the l? 776
22: 5 depart, and get thee into the l of Judah. 776
23:23 shall come to pass, if he be in the l, that l 776
23:27 for the Philistines have invaded the l. 776
27: 1 speedily escape into the l of the Philistines; 776
27: 8 inhabitants of the l as thou goest to Shur, 776
27: 8 goest to Shur, even unto the l of Egypt. 776
27: 9 David smote the l, and left neither man 776
28: 3 spirits, and the wizards, out of the l. 776
28: 9 spirits, and the wizards, out of the l? 776
29:11 to return into the l of the Philistines. 776
30:16 had taken out of the l of the Philistines, 776
30:16 of the Philistines, and out of the l of Judah. 776
31: 9 into the l of the Philistines round about, 776
2Sa 3:12 David on his behalf, saying, Whose is the l? 776
5: 6 unto the Jebusites, the inhabitants of the l: 776
7:23 for you great things and terrible, for thy l, 776
9: 7 restore thee all the l of Saul thy father; 7704
9:10 shall till the l for him, and thou shalt bring 127
10: 2 David's servants came into the l of 776
15: 4 Oh that I were made judge in the l, 776
17:26 Absalom pitched in the l of Gilead. 776
19: 9 now he is fled out of the l for Absalom. 776
19:29 I have said, Thou and Ziba divide the l. 7704
21:14 And after that God was intreated for the l. 776
24: 6 to Gilead, and to the l of Tahtim-hodshi; 776
24: 8 So when they had gone through all the l, 776
24:13 years of famine come unto thee in thy l? 776
24:13 there be three days' pestilence in thy l? 776
24:25 So the LORD was intreated for the l, 776
1Ki 4:10 pertained Sochoh, and all the l of Hepher: 776
4:19 he was the only officer which was in the l. 776
4:21 from the river unto the l of the Philistines, 776
6: 1 of Israel were come out of the l of Egypt, 776
8: 9 when they came out of the l of Egypt. 776
8:21 he brought them out of the l of Egypt. 776
8:34 bring them again unto the l which thou 127
8:36 give rain upon thy l, which thou hast given 776
8:37 If there be in the l famine, if there be 776
8:37 if their enemy besiege them in the l of their 776
8:40 in the l which thou gavest unto our fathers. 127
8:46 they carry them away captives unto the l 776
8:47 if they shall bethink themselves in the l 776
8:47 supplication unto thee in the l of them 776
8:48 all their soul, in the l of their enemies, 776
8:48 and pray unto thee toward their l, 776
9: 7 will I cut off Israel out of the l which I have 127
9: 8 Why hath the LORD done thus unto this l, 776
9: 9 brought forth their fathers out of the l of 776
9:11 Hiram twenty cities in the l of Galilee. 776
9:13 called them the l of Cabul unto this day. 776
9:18 and Tadmor in the wilderness, in the l, 776
9:19 Lebanon, and in all the l of his dominion. 776
9:21 children that were left after them in the l, 776
9:26 the shore of the Red sea, in the l of Edom. 776
10: 6 that I heard in mine own l of thy acts 127
11:18 appointed him victuals, and gave him l. 776
12:28 brought thee up out of the l of Egypt. 776
14:15 he shall root up Israel out of this good l, 127
14:24 there were also sodomites in the l: 776
15:12 he took away the sodomites out of the l, 776
15:20 all Cinneroth, with all the l of Naphtali. 776
17: 7 because there had been no rain in the l. 776
18: 5 Go into the l, unto all fountains of water, 776
18: 6 they divided the l between them to pass 776
20: 7 king of Israel called all the elders of the l, 776
22:46 days of his father Asa, he took out of the l. 776
2Ki 2:21 from thence any more death or barren l NIH

2Ki 3:19 mar every good piece of l with stones. 2513
3:25 on every good piece of l cast every man 2513
3:27 from him, and returned to their own l. 776
4:38 there was a dearth in the l; and the sons 776
5: 2 had brought away captive out of the l of 776
5: 4 thus said the maid that is of the l of Israel. 776
6:23 of Syria came no more into the l of Israel. 776
8: 1 it shall also come upon the l seven years. 776
8: 2 sojourned in the l of the Philistines seven 776
8: 3 that the woman returned out of the l of 776
8: 3 unto the king for her house and for her l. 7704
8: 5 to the king for her house and for her l. 7704
8: 6 the field since the day that she left the l, 776
10:33 all the l of Gilead, the Gadites, 776
11: 3 And Athaliah did reign over the l. 776
11:14 all the people of the l rejoiced, 776
11:18 all the people of the l went into the house 776
11:19 and the guard, and all the people of the l; 776
11:20 all the people of the l rejoiced, and the city 776
13:20 the bands of the Moabites invaded the l at 776
15: 5 over the house, judging the people of the l. 776
15:19 Pul the king of Assyria came against the l: 776
15:20 turned back, and stayed not there in the l. 776
15:29 all the l of Naphtali, and carried them 776
16:15 the burnt offering of all the people of the l. 776
17: 5 of Assyria came up throughout all the l, 776
17: 7 which had brought them up out of the l of 776
17:23 was Israel carried away out of their own l 127
17:26 know not the manner of the God of the l: 776
17:26 know not the manner of the God of the l. 776
17:27 teach them the manner of the God of the l. 776
17:36 who brought you up out of the l of Egypt 776
18:25 to me, Go up against this l, and destroy it. 776
18:32 take you away to a l like your own land, 776
18:32 take you away to a land like your own l, 776
18:32 a l of corn and wine, a land of bread and 776
18:32 corn and wine, a l of bread and vineyards, 776
18:32 and vineyards, a l of oil olive and of honey, 776
18:33 his l out of the hand of the king of Assyria? 776
19: 7 a rumour, and shall return to his own l; 776
19: 7 him to fall by the sword in his own l. 776
19:37 they escaped into the l of Armenia. 776
21: 8 out of the l which I gave their fathers; 127
21:24 the people of the l slew all them that had 776
21:24 people of the l made Josiah his son king 776
23:24 the abominations that were spied in the l 776
23:30 the people of the l took Jehoahaz the son 776
23:33 him in bands at Riblah in the l of Hamath, 776
23:33 put the l to a tribute of an hundred talents 776
23:35 he taxed the l to give the money according 776
23:35 silver and the gold of the people of the l, 776
24: 7 came not again any more out of his l: 776
24:14 save the poorest sort of the people of the l. 776
24:15 and his officers, and the mighty of the l, 776
25: 3 there was no bread for the people of the l. 776
25:12 left of the poor of the l to be vinedressers 776
25:19 which mustered the people of the l, 776
25:19 threescore men of the people of the l that 776
25:21 slew them at Riblah in the l of Hamath. 776
25:22 So Judah was carried away out of their l. 127
25:22 as for the people that remained in the l of 776
25:24 in the l, and serve the king of Babylon; 776
1Ch 1:43 these are the kings that reigned in the l 776
1:45 Husham of the l of the Temanites reigned 776
2:22 three and twenty cities in the l of Gilead. 776
4:40 the l was wide, and quiet, and peaceable; 776
5: 9 cattle were multiplied in the l of Gilead. 776
5:10 tents throughout all the east l of Gilead. NIH
5:11 in the l of Bashan unto Salchah: 776
5:23 the half tribe of Manasseh dwelt in the l: 776
5:25 after the gods of the people of the l, 776
6:55 they gave them Hebron in the l of Judah, 776
7:21 men of Gath that were born in that l slew, 776
10: 9 into the l of the Philistines round about, 776
11: 4 the Jebusites were, the inhabitants of the l. 776
13: 2 that are left in all the l of Israel, 776
16:18 Unto thee will I give the l of Canaan, 776
19: 2 So the servants of David came into the l of 776
19: 3 and to overthrow, and to spy out the l? 776
21:12 in the l, and the angel of the LORD 776
22: 2 the strangers that were in the l of Israel; 776
22:18 he hath given the inhabitants of the l into 776
22:18 and the l is subdued before the LORD, 776
28: 8 ye may possess this good l, and leave it 776
2Ch 2:17 all the strangers that were in the l of Israel, 776
6: 5 l of Egypt I chose no city among all 776
6:25 bring them again unto the l which thou 127
6:27 send rain upon thy l, which thou hast 776
6:28 If there be dearth in the l, if there be 776
6:28 besiege them in the cities of their l; 776
6:31 long as they live in the l which thou gavest 127
6:36 they carry them away captives unto a l far 776
6:37 Yet if they bethink themselves in the l 776
6:37 pray unto thee in the l of their captivity, 776
6:38 with all their soul in the l of their captivity, 776
6:38 pray toward their l, which thou gavest 776
7:13 if I command the locusts to devour the l, 776
7:14 will forgive their sin, and will heal their l. 776
7:20 I pluck them up by the roots out of my l 127
7:21 Why hath the LORD done thus unto this l, 776
7:22 which brought them forth out of the l of 776
8: 6 and throughout all the l of his dominion. 776
8: 8 who were left after them in the l, 776
8:17 to Eloth, at the sea side in the l of Edom. 776
9: 5 which I heard in mine own l of thine acts, 776

2Ch 9:11 there were none such seen before in the l 776
9:12 went away to her own l, she and 776
9:26 the river even unto the l of the Philistines, 776
14: 1 In his days the l was quiet ten years. 776
14: 6 the l he had rest, and he had no war in those 776
14: 7 gates, and bars, while the l is yet before us; 776
15: 8 away the abominable idols out of all the l 776
17: 2 set garrisons in the l of Judah, and in 776
19: 3 hast taken away the groves out of the l, 776
19: 5 he set judges in the l throughout all 776
20: 7 didst drive out the inhabitants of this l 776
20:10 when they came out of the l of Egypt, 776
22:12 six years: and Athaliah reigned over the l. 776
23:13 all the people of the l rejoiced, 776
23:20 all the people of the l, and brought down 776
23:21 all the people of the l rejoiced: and the city 776
26:21 king's house, judging the people of the l. 776
30: 9 so that they shall come again into this l: 776
30:25 strangers that came out of the l of Israel, 776
32: 4 brook that ran through the midst of the l, 776
32:21 returned with shame of face to his own l. 776
32:31 of the wonder that was done in the l, 776
33: 8 l which I have appointed for your fathers; 127
33:25 the people of the l slew all them that had 776
33:25 people of the l made Josiah his son king 776
34: 7 cut down all the idols throughout all the l 776
34: 8 when he had purged the l, and the house, 776
36: 1 the people of the l took Jehoahaz the son 776
36: 3 condemned the l in an hundred talents of 776
36:21 until the l had enjoyed her sabbaths. 776
Ezr 4: 4 the people of the l weakened the hands of 776
6:21 from the filthiness of the heathen of the l, 776
9:11 The l, unto which ye go to possess it, 776
9:11 is an unclean l with the filthiness of 776
9:12 eat the good of the l, and leave it for an 776
10: 2 taken strange wives of the people of the l: 776
10:11 yourselves from the people of the l, 776
Ne 4: 4 give them for a prey in the l of captivity: 776
5:14 to be their governor in the l of Judah, 7704
5:16 of this wall, neither bought we any l: 7704
9: 8 madest a covenant with him to give the l 776
9:10 his servants, and on all the people of his l: 776
9:11 through the midst of the sea on the dry l, NIH
9:15 the l which thou hadst sworn to give them. 776
9:22 so they possessed the l of Sihon, 776
9:22 the l of the king of Heshbon, and the land 776
9:22 Heshbon, and the l of Og king of Bashan. 776
9:23 broughtest them into the l, concerning 776
9:24 The children went in and possessed the l, 776
9:24 before them the inhabitants of the l, 776
9:24 with their kings, and the people of the l, 776
9:25 a fat l, and possessed houses full of all 127
9:35 and fat l which thou gavest before them, 776
9:36 the l that thou gavest unto our fathers to 776
10:30 our daughters unto the people of the l, 776
10:31 if the people of the l bring ware or 776
Est 8:17 many of the people of the l became Jews; 776
10: 1 king Ahasuerus laid a tribute upon the l, 776
Job 1: 1 There was a man in the l of Uz, whose 776
1:10 and his substance is increased in the l. 776
10:21 even to the l of darkness and the shadow 776
10:22 A l of darkness, as darkness itself; and of 776
28:13 neither is it found in the l of the living. 776
31:38 If my l cry against me, or that the furrows 127
37:13 for correction, or for his l, or for mercy. 776
39: 6 for the barren l his dwellings. NIH
42:15 in all the l were no women found so fair 776
Ps 10:16 ever: the heathen are perished out of his l. 776
27:13 of the LORD in the l of the living. 776
35:20 against them that are quiet in the l. 776
37: 3 so shalt thou dwell in the l, and verily 776
37:29 The righteous shall inherit the l, 776
37:34 and he shall exalt thee to inherit the l: 776
42: 6 will I remember thee from the l of Jordan, 776
44: 3 they got not the l in possession by their 776
52: 5 root thee out of the l of the living. 776
63: 1 in a dry and thirsty l, where no water is; 776
66: 6 He turned the sea into dry l they went 776 NIH
68: 6 but the rebellious dwell in a dry l 776 NIH
74: 8 all the synagogues of God in the l. 776
78:12 in the l of Egypt, in the field of Zoan. 776
80: 9 it to take deep root, and it filled the l. 776
81: 5 when he went out through the l of Egypt: 776
81:10 which brought thee out of the l of Egypt: 776
85: 1 thou hast been favourable unto thy l: 776
85: 9 fear him; that glory may dwell in our l. 776
85:12 is good; and our l shall yield her increase. 776
88:12 thy righteousness in the l of forgetfulness? 776
95: 5 made it: and his hands formed the dry l 776 NIH
101: 6 eyes shall be upon the faithful of the l, 776
101: 8 I will early destroy all the wicked of the l; 776
105:11 Unto thee will I give the l of Canaan, 776
105:16 he called for a famine upon the l: 776
105:23 and Jacob sojourned in the l of Ham. 776
105:27 among them, and wonders in the l of Ham. 776
105:30 Their l brought forth frogs in abundance, 776
105:32 hail for rain, and flaming fire in their l. 776
105:35 did eat up all the herbs in their l, 776
105:36 He smote also all the firstborn in their l, 776
106:22 Wondrous works in the l of Ham, 776
106:24 Yea, they despised the pleasant l, 776
106:38 and the l was polluted with blood. 776
107:34 A fruitful l into barrenness, 776
116: 9 I will walk before the LORD in the l of 776
135:12 gave their l for an heritage, an heritage 776

L

L

Ps 136:21	gave their l for an heritage: for his mercy	776
137: 4	we sing the Lord's song in a strange l?	127
142: 5	and my portion in the l of the living.	776
143: 6	my soul thirsteth after thee, as a thirsty l.	776
143:10	is good; lead me into the l of uprightness.	776
Pr 2:21	For the upright shall dwell in the l,	776
12:11	He that tilleth his l shall be satisfied with	127
28: 2	For the transgression of a l many are	776
28:19	He that tilleth his l shall have plenty of	127
29: 4	The king by judgment stablisheth the l:	776
31:23	when he sitteth among the elders of the l.	776
Ecc 10:16	Woe to thee, O l, when thy king is a child,	776
10:17	Blessed art thou, O l, when thy king is	776
SS 2:12	the voice of the turtle is heard in our l;	776
Isa 1: 7	l, strangers devour it in your presence,	127
1:19	obedient, ye shall eat the good of the l:	776
2: 7	Their l also is full of silver and gold,	776
2: 7	their l is also full of horses, neither is	776
2: 8	Their l also is full of idols; they worship	776
5:30	if one look unto the l, behold darkness	776
6:11	without man, and the l be utterly desolate,	127
6:12	be a great forsaking in the midst of the l.	776
7:16	the l that thou abhorrest shall be forsaken	776
7:18	and for the bee that is in the l of Assyria.	776
7:22	shall every one eat that is left in the l.	776
7:24	all the l shall become briers and thorns.	776
8: 8	of his wings shall fill the breadth of thy l,	776
9: 1	when at the first he lightly afflicted the l of	776
9: 1	the land of Zebulun and the l of Naphtali,	776
9: 2	they that dwell in the l in the shadow of	776
9:19	of the Lord of hosts is the l darkened,	776
10:23	even determined, in the midst of all the l.	NIH
11:16	day that he came up out of the l of Egypt.	776
13: 5	of his indignation, to destroy the whole l.	776
13: 9	and fierce anger, to lay the l desolate:	776
13:14	and flee every one into his own l.	776
14: 1	choose Israel, and set them in their own l:	776
14: 2	house of Israel shall possess them in the l	127
14:20	because thou hast destroyed thy l,	776
14:21	that they do not rise, nor possess the l,	776
14:25	That I will break the Assyrian in my l,	776
15: 9	of Moab, and upon the remnant of the l.	127
16: 1	Send ye the lamb to the ruler of the l from	776
16: 4	the oppressors are consumed out of the l.	776
18: 1	Woe to the l shadowing with wings, which	776
18: 2	whose l the rivers have spoiled.	776
18: 7	under foot, whose l the rivers have spoiled,	776
19:17	the l of Judah shall be a terror unto Egypt,	127
19:18	In that day shall five cities in the l of Egypt	776
19:19	to the Lord in the midst of the l of Egypt,	776
19:20	unto the Lord of hosts in the l of Egypt:	776
19:24	even a blessing in the midst of the l:	776
21: 1	it cometh from the desert, from a terrible l.	776
21:14	The inhabitants of the l of Tema brought	776
23: 1	from the l of Chittim it is revealed to them.	776
23:10	Pass through thy l as a river, O daughter of	776
23:13	Behold the l of the Chaldeans; this people	776
24: 3	The l shall be utterly emptied,	776
24:11	joy is darkened, the mirth of the l is gone.	776
24:13	When thus it shall be in the midst of the l	776
26: 1	In that day shall this song be sung in the l	776
26:10	the l of uprightness will he deal unjustly,	776
27:13	were ready to perish in the l of Assyria,	776
27:13	the outcasts in the l of Egypt,	776
30: 6	into the l of trouble and anguish,	776
32: 2	as the shadow of a great rock in a weary l.	776
32:13	Upon the l of my people shall come up	127
33:17	they shall behold the l that is very far off.	776
34: 6	and a great slaughter in the l of Idumea.	776
34: 7	their l shall be soaked with blood,	776
34: 9	the l thereof shall become burning pitch.	776
35: 7	a pool, and the **thirsty** l springs of water:	6774
36:10	the Lord against this l to destroy it?	776
36:10	me, Go up against this l, and destroy it.	776
36:17	take you away to a like your own land,	776
36:17	take you away to a land like your own l.	776
36:17	a l of corn and wine, a land of bread and	776
36:17	corn and wine, a l of bread and vineyards.	776
36:18	his l out of the hand of the king of Assyria?	776
36:20	that have delivered their l out of my hand,	776
37: 7	hear a rumour, and return to his own l;	776
37: 7	cause him to fall by the sword in his own l.	776
37:38	and they escaped into the l of Armenia.	776
38:11	even the Lord, in the l of the living:	776
41:18	of water, and the dry l springs of water.	776
49:12	the west; and these from the l of Sinim.	776
49:19	places, and the l of thy destruction,	776
53: 8	for he was cut off out of the l of the living:	776
57:13	putteth his trust in me shall possess the l,	776
60:18	Violence shall no more be heard in thy l,	776
60:21	they shall inherit the l for ever, the branch	776
61: 7	in their l they shall possess the double:	776
62: 4	neither shall thy l any more be termed	776
62: 4	be called Hephzi-bah, and thy l Beulah:	776
62: 4	in thee, and thy l shall be married.	776
Jer 1: 1	the priests that were in Anathoth in the l	776
1:14	forth upon all the inhabitants of the l.	776
1:18	and brasen walls against the whole l,	776
1:18	and against the people of the l.	776
2: 2	in the wilderness, in a l that was not sown.	776
2: 6	that brought us up out of the l of Egypt,	776
2: 6	through a l of deserts and of pits, through	776
2: 6	through a l of drought, and of the shadow	776
2: 6	through a l that no man passed through,	776
2: 7	ye defiled my l, and made mine heritage	776

Jer 2:15	and yelled, and they made his l waste:	776
2:31	a l of darkness? wherefore say my people,	776
3: 1	shall not that l be greatly polluted?	776
3: 2	hast polluted the l with thy whoredoms	776
3: 9	that she defiled the l,	776
3:16	ye be multiplied and increased in the l,	776
3:18	they shall come together out of the l of	776
3:18	l that I have given for an inheritance unto	776
3:19	the children, and give thee a pleasant l,	776
4: 5	and say, Blow ye the trumpet in the l:	776
4: 7	is gone forth from his place to make thy l	776
4:20	is cried; for the whole l is spoiled:	776
4:27	Lord said, The whole l shall be desolate;	776
5:19	served strange gods in your l, so shall ye	776
5:19	shall ye serve strangers in a l that is not	776
5:30	and horrible thing is committed in the l;	776
6: 8	lest I make thee desolate, a l not inhabited.	776
6:12	out my hand upon the inhabitants of the l,	776
7: 7	in the l that I gave to your fathers, for ever	776
7:22	that I brought them out of the l of Egypt,	776
7:25	forth out of the l of Egypt unto this day,	776
7:34	of the bride: for the l shall be desolate.	776
8:16	the whole l trembled at the sound of	776
8:16	have devoured the l, and all that is in it;	776
9:12	for what the l perisheth and is burnt up	776
9:19	because we have forsaken the l, because	776
10:17	Gather up thy wares out of the l,	776
10:18	I will sling out the inhabitants of the l at	776
11: 4	brought them forth out of the l of Egypt,	776
11: 5	to give them a l flowing with milk and	776
11: 7	I brought them up out of the l of Egypt,	776
11:19	let us cut him off from the l of the living,	776
12: 4	How long shall the l mourn, and the herbs	776
12: 5	if in the l of peace, wherein thou trustedst,	776
12:11	the whole l is made desolate, because	776
12:12	of the l even to the other end of the land:	776
12:12	of the land even to the other end of the l.	776
12:14	I will pluck them out of their l, and pluck	127
12:15	man to his heritage, and every man to his l.	776
13:13	I will fill all the inhabitants of this l,	776
14: 8	shouldest thou be as a stranger in the l,	776
14:15	Sword and famine shall not be in this l;	776
14:18	the priest go about into a l that they know	776
15: 7	fan them with a fan in the gates of the l;	776
15:14	enemies into a l which thou knowest not:	776
16: 3	their fathers that begat them in this l;	776
16: 6	the great and the small shall die in this l:	776
16:13	Therefore will I cast you out of this l into a	776
16:13	out of this land into a l that ye know not,	776
16:14	the children of Israel out of the l of Egypt;	776
16:15	children of Israel from the l of the north,	776
16:15	bring them again into their l that I gave	127
16:18	because they have defiled my l, they have	776
17: 4	enemies in the l which thou knowest not:	776
17: 6	the wilderness, in a salt l and not inhabited.	776
17:26	from the l of Benjamin, and from the plain,	776
18:16	To make their l desolate, and a perpetual	776
22:12	him captive, and shall see this l no more.	776
22:27	to the l whereunto they desire to return,	776
22:28	and are cast into a l which they know not?	776
23: 7	the children of Israel out of the l of Egypt;	776
23: 8	and they shall dwell in their own l.	127
23:10	For the l is full of adulterers; for because	776
23:10	for because of swearing the l mourneth;	776
23:15	is profaneness gone forth into all the l.	776
24: 5	I have sent out of this place into the l	776
24: 6	and I will bring them again to this l:	776
24: 8	that remain in this l, and them that dwell	776
24: 8	and them that dwell in the l of Egypt:	776
24:10	till they be consumed from off the l that I	127
25: 5	dwell in the l that the Lord hath given	776
25: 9	will bring them against this l, and against	776
25:11	this whole l shall be a desolation,	776
25:12	the l of the Chaldeans, and will make it	776
25:13	I will bring upon that l all my words which	776
25:20	the kings of the l of Uz, and all the kings	776
25:20	all the kings of the l of the Philistines,	776
25:38	for their l is desolate because of	776
26:17	rose up certain of the elders of the l,	776
26:20	against this l according to all the words of	776
27: 7	son, until the very time of his l come:	776
27:10	unto you, to remove you far from your l;	127
27:11	those will I let remain still in their own l,	776
30: 3	cause them to return to the l that I gave	776
30:10	and thy seed from the l of their captivity;	776
31:16	they shall come again into their l	776
31:23	As yet they shall use this speech in the l of	776
31:32	hand, to bring them out of the l of Egypt;	776
32:15	vineyards shall be possessed again in this l.	776
32:20	set signs and wonders in the l of Egypt,	776
32:21	Israel out of the l of Egypt with signs,	776
32:22	hast given them this l, which thou didst	776
32:22	them, a l flowing with milk and honey;	776
32:41	will plant them in this l assuredly with	776
32:43	fields shall be bought in this l, whereof ye	776
32:44	and take witnesses in the l of Benjamin,	776
33:11	return the captivity of the l as at the first,	776
33:13	in the l of Benjamin, and in the places	776
33:15	judgment and righteousness in the l.	776
34:13	I brought them forth out of the l of Egypt,	776
34:19	and the priests, and all the people of the l,	776
35: 7	that ye may live many days in the l where	127
35:11	king of Babylon came up into the l,	776
35:15	ye shall dwell in the l which I have given	127
36:29	shall certainly come and destroy this l,	776

Jer 37: 1	of Babylon made king in the l of Judah.	776
37: 2	nor his servants, nor the people of the l,	776
37: 7	shall return to Egypt into their own l.	776
37:12	of Jerusalem to go into the l of Benjamin,	776
37:19	not come against you, nor against this l?	776
39: 5	of Babylon to Riblah in the l of Hamath,	776
39:10	in the l of Judah, and gave them vineyards	776
40: 4	behold, all the l is before thee: whither it	776
40: 6	among the people that were left in the l.	776
40: 7	the son of Ahikam governor in the l,	776
40: 7	and children, and of the poor of the l,	776
40: 9	in the l and serve the king of Babylon,	776
40:12	came to the l of Judah, to Gedaliah, unto	776
41: 2	of Babylon had made governor over the l.	776
41:18	king of Babylon made governor in the l.	776
42:10	If ye will still abide in this l, then will I	776
42:12	and cause you to return to your own l.	127
42:13	if ye say, We will not dwell in this l,	776
42:14	we will go into the l of Egypt, where we	776
42:16	shall overtake you there in the l of Egypt,	776
43: 4	of the Lord, to dwell in the l of Judah.	776
43: 5	been driven, to dwell in the l of Judah:	776
43:11	he shall smite the l of Egypt,	776
43:12	he shall array himself with the l of Egypt,	776
43:13	of Beth-shemesh, that is in the l of Egypt;	776
44: 1	all the Jews which dwell in the l of Egypt,	776
44: 8	burning incense unto other gods in the l of	776
44: 9	they have committed in the l of Judah,	776
44:12	that have set their faces to go into the l of	776
44:12	all be consumed, and fall in the l of Egypt;	776
44:13	For I will punish them that dwell in the l of	776
44:14	are gone into the l of Egypt to sojourn	776
44:14	that they should return into the l of Judah,	776
44:15	even all the people that dwelt in the l of	776
44:21	and your princes, and the people of the l,	776
44:22	therefore is your l a desolation, and an	776
44:24	all Judah that are in the l of Egypt:	776
44:26	all Judah that dwell in the l of Egypt;	776
44:26	of any man of Judah in all the l of Egypt,	776
44:27	the men of Judah that are in the l of Egypt	776
44:28	out of the l of Egypt into the land of Judah,	776
44:28	out of the land of Egypt into the l of Judah,	776
44:28	that are gone into the l of Egypt to sojourn	776
45: 4	planted I will pluck up, even this whole l.	776
46:12	of thy shame, and thy cry hath filled the l:	776
46:13	should come and smite the l of Egypt.	776
46:16	to the l of our nativity, from the oppressing	776
46:27	and thy seed from the l of their captivity;	776
47: 2	shall overflow the l, and all that is therein;	776
47: 2	and all the inhabitants of the l shall howl.	776
48:24	upon all the cities of the l of Moab, far or	776
48:33	the plentiful field, and from the l of Moab;	776
50: 1	against the l of the Chaldeans by Jeremiah	776
50: 3	which shall make her l desolate,	776
50: 8	go forth out of the l of the Chaldeans,	776
50:12	be a wilderness, a **dry** l, and a desert.	6723
50:16	and they shall flee every one to his own l.	776
50:18	I will punish the king of Babylon and his l,	776
50:21	Go up against the l of Merethaim,	776
50:22	A sound of battle is in the l, and of great	776
50:25	God of hosts in the l of the Chaldeans.	776
50:28	flee and escape out of the l of Babylon,	776
50:34	that he may give rest to the l,	776
50:38	for it is the l of graven images, and they	776
50:45	that he hath purposed against the l of	776
51: 2	that shall fan her, and shall empty her l:	776
51: 4	Thus the slain shall fall in the l of	776
51: 5	though their l was filled with sin against	776
51:27	Set ye up a standard in the l, blow	776
51:28	thereof, and all the l of his dominion.	776
51:29	the l shall tremble and sorrow: for every	776
51:29	to make the l of Babylon a desolation	776
51:43	are a desolation, a dry l, and a wilderness,	776
51:43	wilderness, a l wherein no man dwelleth,	776
51:46	for the rumour that shall be heard in the l;	776
51:46	and violence in the l, ruler against ruler.	776
51:47	her whole l shall be confounded, and all	776
51:52	through all her l the wounded shall groan.	776
51:54	great destruction from the l of	776
52: 6	there was no bread for the people of the l.	776
52: 9	of Babylon to Riblah in the l of Hamath;	776
52:16	of the poor of the l for vinedressers	776
52:25	host, who mustered the people of the l;	776
52:25	threescore men of the people of the l,	776
52:27	put them to death in Riblah in the l of	776
52:27	was carried away captive out of his own l.	127
La 4:21	of Edom, that dwellest in the l of Uz;	776
Eze 1: 3	in the l of the Chaldeans by the river	776
6:14	upon them, and make the l desolate, yea,	776
7: 2	thus saith the Lord God unto the l of	127
7: 2	end is come upon the four corners of the l.	776
7: 7	unto thee, O thou that dwellest in the l:	776
7:23	The l is full of bloody crimes, and the city	776
7:27	the hands of the people of the l shall be	776
8:17	for they have filled the l with violence,	776
9: 9	The l is full of blood, and the city full of	776
11:15	unto us is this l given in possession.	776
11:17	and I will give you the l of Israel.	127
12:13	I will bring him to Babylon to the l of	776
12:19	say unto the people of the l, Thus saith	776
12:19	of Jerusalem, and of the l of Israel;	127
12:19	that her l may be desolate from all that is	776
12:20	be laid waste, and the l shall be desolate;	776
12:22	what is that proverb that ye have in the l	127

Eze	13: 9 neither shall they enter into the l of Israel; 127
14:13 the l sinneth against me by trespassing 776	
14:15 noisome beasts to pass through the l, 776	
14:16 be delivered, but the l shall be desolate. 776	
14:17 Or *if* I bring a sword upon that l, and say, 776	
14:17 land, and say, Sword, go through the l; 776	
14:19 Or *if* I send a pestilence into that l, 776	
15: 8 I will make the l desolate, because they 776	
16: 3 and thy nativity *is* of the l of Canaan; 776	
16:29 fornication in the l of Canaan unto 776	
17: 4 and carried it into a l of traffick; 776	
17: 5 He took also of the seed of the l, 776	
17:13 he hath also taken the mighty of the l. 776	
18: 2 ye use this proverb concerning the l of 127	
19: 4 they brought him with chains unto the l of 776	
19: 7 the l was desolate, and the fulness thereof, 776	
20: 5 made myself known unto them in the l of 776	
20: 6 to bring them forth of the l of Egypt into a 776	
20: 6 of Egypt into a l that I had espied for them, 776	
20: 8 against them in the midst of the l of Egypt. 776	
20: 9 in bringing them forth out of the l of Egypt. 776	
20:10 them to go forth out of the l of Egypt, 776	
20:15 *I* would not bring them into the l which I 776	
20:28 *For* when I had brought them into the l, 776	
20:36 fathers in the wilderness of the l of Egypt, 776	
20:38 and they shall not enter into the l of Israel: 127	
20:40 of Israel, all of them in the l, serve me: 776	
20:42 when I shall bring you into the l of Israel, 127	
21: 2 and prophesy against the l of Israel, 127	
21: 3 say to the l of Israel, Thus saith the LORD, 127	
21:19 both twain shall come forth out of one l: 776	
21:30 thou wast created, in the l of thy nativity. 776	
21:32 thy blood shall be in the midst of the l; 776	
22:24 her, Thou *art* the l that is not cleansed, 776	
22:29 The people of the l have used oppression, 776	
22:30 stand in the gap before me for the l, that *I* 776	
23:15 of Chaldea, the l of their nativity: 776	
23:19 wherein she had played the harlot in the l 776	
23:27 thy whoredom *brought* from the l of Egypt: 776	
23:48 will I cause lewdness to cease out of the l, 776	
25: 3 the l of Israel, when it was desolate; 127	
25: 6 with all thy despite against the l of Israel; 776	
26:20 and I shall set glory in the l of the living; 776	
27:17 Judah, and the l of Israel, they *were* thy 776	
27:29 their ships, they shall stand upon the l; 776	
28:25 shall they dwell in their l that I have given 127	
29: 9 the l of Egypt shall be desolate and waste; 776	
29:10 I will make the l of Egypt utterly waste 776	
29:12 I will make the l of Egypt desolate in 776	
29:14 will cause them to return *into* the l of 776	
29:14 of Pathros, into the l of their habitation; 776	
29:19 I *will* give the l of Egypt unto 776	
29:20 I have given him the l of Egypt *for* his 776	
30: 5 and the men of the l that is in league, 776	
30:11 nations, *shall be* brought to destroy the l: 776	
30:11 against Egypt, and fill the l *with* the slain. 776	
30:12 and sell the l into the hand of the wicked; 776	
30:12 I will make the l waste, and all that is 776	
30:13 there shall be no more a prince of the l of 776	
30:13 and I will put a fear in the l of Egypt. 776	
30:25 he shall stretch it out upon the l of Egypt. 776	
31:12 boughs are broken by all the rivers of the l; 776	
32: 4 I will leave thee upon the l, I will cast thee 776	
32: 6 I will also water with thy blood the l 776	
32: 8 set darkness upon thy l, saith the Lord 776	
32:15 When I shall make the l of Egypt desolate, 776	
32:23 which caused terror in the l of the living. 776	
32:24 which caused their terror in the l of 776	
32:25 though their terror was caused in the l of 776	
32:26 though they caused their terror in the l of 776	
32:27 terror of the mighty in the l of the living. 776	
32:32 For I have caused my terror in the l of 776	
33: 2 them, When I bring the sword upon a l, 776	
33: 2 if the people of the l take a man of their 776	
33: 3 when he seeth the sword come upon the l, 776	
33:24 they that inhabit those wastes of the l of 127	
33:24 Abraham was one, and he inherited the l: 776	
33:24 *are* many; the l is given us for inheritance. 776	
33:25 and shed blood: and shall ye possess the l? 776	
33:26 wife; and shall ye possess the l? 776	
33:28 For I will lay the l most desolate, 776	
33:29 I have laid the l most desolate because 776	
34:13 bring them to their own l, and feed them 127	
34:25 cause the evil beasts to cease out of the l: 776	
34:27 they shall be safe in their l, and shall know 127	
34:28 neither shall the beast of the l devour 776	
34:29 no more consumed with hunger in the l, 776	
36: 5 which have appointed my l into their 776	
36: 6 therefore concerning the l of Israel, 127	
36:13 Thou *l* devourest up men, and hast NIH	
36:17 the house of Israel dwelt in their own l, 127	
36:18 the blood that they had shed upon the l, 776	
36:20 the LORD, and are gone forth out of his l. 776	
36:24 and will bring you into your own l. 127	
36:28 ye shall dwell in the l that I gave to your 127	
36:34 the desolate l shall be tilled, whereas it lay 776	
36:35 This l that was desolate is become like 776	
37:12 and bring you into the l of Israel. 127	
37:14 and I shall place you in your own l: 127	
37:21 side, and bring them into their own l: 127	
37:22 I will make them one nation in the l upon 776	
37:25 they shall dwell in the l that I have given 127	
38: 2 set thy face against Gog, the l of Magog, 776	
38: 8 the latter years thou shalt come into the l 776	
38: 9 thou shalt be like a cloud to cover the l, 776	

Eze	38:11 I will go up to the l of unwalled villages; 776
38:12 and goods, that dwell in the midst of the l. 776	
38:16 people of Israel, as a cloud to cover the l; 776	
38:16 and I will bring thee against my l, 776	
38:18 Gog shall come against the l of Israel, 127	
38:19 shall be a great shaking in the l of Israel; 776	
39:12 of them, that *they* may cleanse the l. 776	
39:13 all the people of the l shall bury *them;* and 776	
39:14 passing through the l to bury with 776	
39:15 the passengers *that* pass through the l, 776	
39:16 *be* Hamonah. Thus shall they cleanse the l. 776	
39:26 when they dwelt safely in their l, 127	
39:28 I have gathered them unto their own l, 127	
40: 2 of God brought he me into the l of Israel, 776	
45: 1 when ye shall divide *by lot* the l for 776	
45: 1 unto the LORD, a holy *portion* of the l: 776	
45: 4 The holy *portion* of the l shall be for 776	
45: 8 In the l shall be his possession in Israel: 776	
45: 8 *rest* of the l shall they give to the house 776	
45:16 the people of the l shall give this oblation 776	
45:22 all the people of the l a bullock *for* a sin 776	
46: 3 Likewise the people of the l shall worship 776	
46: 9 when the people of the l shall come before 776	
47:13 whereby ye shall inherit the l according to 776	
47:14 this l shall fall unto you for inheritance. 776	
47:15 this *shall be* the border of the l toward 776	
47:18 and from the l of Israel *by* Jordan, 776	
47:21 shall ye divide this l unto you according 776	
48:12 oblation of the l that is offered shall be 776	
48:14 nor alienate the firstfruits of the l: 776	
48:29 This *is* the l which ye shall divide *by lot* 776	
Da	1: 2 which he carried *into* the l of Shinar *to* 776
8: 9 the east, and toward the pleasant *l.* NIH	
9: 6 our fathers, and to all the people of the l. 776	
9:15 hast brought thy people forth out of the l 776	
11: 2 kingdom, and shall return into his own l. 127	
11:16 he shall stand in the glorious l, which by 776	
11:19 turn his face towards the fort of his own l: 776	
11:28 shall he return *into* his l with great riches; 776	
11:28 shall do *exploits,* and return to his own l. 776	
11:39 over many, and shall divide the l for gain. 127	
11:41 He shall enter also into the glorious l, 776	
11:42 and the l of Egypt shall not escape. 776	
Hos	1: 2 for the l hath committed great whoredom, 776
1:11 and they shall come up out of the l: 776	
2: 3 set her like a dry l, and slay her with thirst. 776	
2:15 *in* the day when she came up out of the l 776	
4: 1 a controversy with the inhabitants of the l, 776	
4: 1 nor mercy, nor knowledge of God in the l. 776	
4: 3 Therefore shall the l mourn, and every one 776	
7:16 this *shall be* their derision in the l of Egypt. 776	
9: 3 They shall not dwell in the LORD's l; 776	
10: 1 according to the goodness of his l they 776	
11: 5 He shall not return into the l of Egypt, 776	
11:11 and as a dove out of the l of Assyria: 776	
12: 9 I *that am* the LORD thy God from the l of 776	
13: 4 Yet I *am* the LORD thy God from the l of 776	
13: 5 in the wilderness, in the l of great drought. 776	
Joel	1: 2 and give ear, all ye inhabitants of the l. 776
1: 6 For a nation is come up upon my l, strong, 776	
1:10 The field is wasted, the l mourneth; 127	
1:14 all the inhabitants of the l *into* the house of 776	
2: 1 let all the inhabitants of the l tremble: 776	
2: 3 The l *is as* the garden of Eden before them, 776	
2:18 will the LORD be jealous for his l, 776	
2:20 will drive him into a l barren and desolate, 776	
2:21 Fear not, O l; be glad and rejoice: 127	
3: 2 among the nations, and parted my l. 776	
3:19 they have shed innocent blood in their l. 776	
Am	2:10 Also I brought you up from the l of Egypt, 776
2:10 to possess the l of the Amorite. 776	
3: 1 which I brought up from the l of Egypt, 776	
3: 9 in the palaces in the l of Egypt, and say, 776	
3:11 *there shall be* even round about the l; 776	
5: 2 she is forsaken upon her l; *there is* none to 127	
7: 2 made an end of eating the grass of the l, 776	
7:10 the l is not able to bear all his words. 776	
7:11 be led away captive out of their own l. 127	
7:12 go, flee thee away into the l of Judah, 776	
7:17 sword, and thy l shall be divided by line; 127	
7:17 by line; and thou shalt die in a polluted l: 127	
7:17 shall surely go into captivity forth of his l. 127	
8: 4 even to make the poor of the l to fail, 776	
8: 8 Shall not the l tremble for this, 776	
8:11 that I will send a famine in the l, 776	
9: 5 Lord GOD of hosts *is* he that toucheth the l, 776	
9: 7 Have not I brought up Israel out of the l of 776	
9:15 I will plant them upon their l, and they 127	
9:15 shall no more be pulled up out of their l 127	
Jnh	1: 9 which hath made the sea and the dry *l* NIH
1:13 the men rowed hard to bring *it* to the l; 3004	
2:10 and it vomited out Jonah upon the dry *l* NIH	
Mic	5: 5 when the Assyrian shall come into our l: 776
5: 6 they shall waste the l of Assyria with 776	
5: 6 the l of Nimrod in the entrances thereof: 776	
5: 6 when he cometh into our l, and when he 776	
5:11 I will cut off the cities of thy l, 776	
6: 4 For I brought thee up out of the l of Egypt, 776	
7:13 Notwithstanding the l shall be desolate 776	
7:15 of Egypt will I shew unto thee marvellous 776	
Na	3:13 the gates of thy l shall be set wide open 776
Hab	1: 6 *shall* march through the breadth of the l, 776
2: 8 and *for* the violence of the l, *of* the city, 776	
2:17 and *for* the violence of the l, *of* the city, 776	
3: 7 the curtains of the l of Midian did tremble. 776	

Hab	3:12 Thou didst march through the l in 776
Zep	1: 2 utterly consume all *things* from off the l, 127
1: 3 I will cut off man from off the l, saith 127	
1:18 the whole l shall be devoured by the fire 776	
1:18 riddance of all them that dwell in the l. 776	
2: 5 Canaan, the l of the Philistines, I will even 776	
3:19 fame in every l where they have been put 776	
Hag	1:11 I called *for* a drought upon the l, 776
2: 4 be strong, all ye people of the l, saith 776	
2: 6 and the earth, and the sea, and the dry *l*; NIH	
Zec	1:21 lift up *their* horn over the l of Judah to 776
2: 6 *forth,* and flee from the l of the north, 776	
2:12 inherit Judah his portion in the holy l, 127	
3: 9 I will remove the iniquity of that l in one 776	
5:11 To build it a house in the l of Shinar: 776	
7: 5 Speak unto all the people of the l, and to 776	
7:14 thus was I desolate after them, that no 776	
7:14 for they laid the pleasant l desolate. 776	
9: 1 the word of the LORD in the l of Hadrach, 776	
9:16 a crown, lifted up as an ensign upon his l. 127	
10:10 I will bring them again also out of the l of 776	
10:10 I will bring them into the l of Gilead and 776	
11: 6 I will no more pity the inhabitants of the l, 776	
11: 6 they shall smite the l, and out of their hand 776	
11:16 For lo, I *will* raise up a shepherd in the l, 776	
12:12 the l shall mourn, every family apart; 776	
13: 2 cut off the names of the idols out of the l, 776	
13: 2 and the unclean spirit to pass out of the l. 776	
13: 8 to pass, *that* in all the l, saith the LORD, 776	
14:10 All the l shall be turned as a plain from 776	
Mal	3:12 for ye shall be a delightsome l, saith 776
Mt	2: 6 And thou Bethlehem, *in* the l of Juda, 1093
2:20 and his mother, and go into the l of Israel: 1093	
2:21 his mother, and came into the l of Israel. 1093	
4:15 The l of Zabulon, and the land of 1093	
4:15 land of Zabulon, and the l of Nephthalim, 1093	
9:26 fame hereof went abroad into all that l. 1093	
10:15 shall be more tolerable for the l of Sodom 1093	
11:24 that it shall be more tolerable for the l of 1093	
14:34 they came into the l of Gennesaret. 1093	
23:15 compass sea and l to make one proselyte, 3584	
27:45 darkness over all the l unto the ninth 1093	
Mk	1: 5 And there went out unto him all the l of 5561
4: 1 whole multitude was by the sea on the l. 1093	
6:47 midst of the sea, and he alone on the l. 1093	
6:53 they came into the l of Genesaret, 1093	
15:33 there was darkness over the whole l until 1093	
Lk	4:25 great famine was throughout all the l; 1093
5: 3 *he* would thrust out a little from the l, 1093	
5:11 when they had brought *their* ships to l, 1093	
8:27 when he went forth to l, there met him 1093	
14:35 It is neither fit for the l, nor yet for 1093	
15:14 there arose a mighty famine in that l; 5561	
21:23 for there shall be great distress in the l, 1093	
Jn	3:22 and his disciples into the l of Judea; 1093
6:21 immediately the ship was at the l whither 1093	
21: 8 (for they were not far from l, but as it 1093	
21: 9 As soon then as they were come to l, 1093	
21:11 and drew the net to l full of great fishes, 1093	
Ac	4:37 Having l, sold *it,* and brought the money, 68
5: 3 to keep back *part* of the price of the l? 5564	
5: 8 me whether ye sold the l for so much? 5564	
7: 3 come into the l which I shall shew thee. 1093	
7: 4 came he out of the l of the Chaldeans, 1093	
7: 4 he removed him into this l, wherein ye 1093	
7: 6 his seed should sojourn in a strange l; 1093	
7:11 Now there came a dearth over all the l of 1093	
7:29 and was a stranger in the l of Madian, 1093	
7:36 and signs in the l of Egypt, 1093	
7:40 which brought us out of the l of Egypt, 1093	
10:39 which he did both in the l of the Jews, 5561	
13:17 *they* dwelt as strangers in the l of Egypt, 1093	
13:19 seven nations in the l of Canaan, 1093	
13:19 Canaan, he divided their l to them by lot. 1093	
27:39 when it was day, they knew not the l: 1093	
27:43 *themselves* first into the *sea,* and get to l: 1093	
27:44 to pass, that *they* escaped all safe to l. 1093	
Heb	11: 9 hand to lead them out of the l of Egypt; 1093
11: 9 By faith he sojourned in the l of promise, 1093	
11:29 passed through the Red sea as by dry *l*; NIG	
Jude | 1: 5 having saved the people out of the l of 1093

LANDED (2) [LAND]
Ac 18:22 when he had l at Cesarea, and gone up, 2718
 21: 3 and sailed into Syria, and l at Tyre: 2609

LANDING (1) [LAND]
Ac 28:12 And l at Syracuse, we tarried *there* three 2609

LANDMARK (4) [LAND, MARK]
Dt 19:14 Thou shalt not remove thy neighbour's l, 1366
 27:17 *be* he that removeth his neighbour's l. 1366
Pr 22:28 Remove not the ancient l, which thy 1366
 23:10 Remove not the old l; and enter not into 1366

LANDMARKS (1) [LAND, MARK]
Job 24: 2 *Some* remove the l; they violently take 1367

LANDOWNER See GOODMAN

LANDS (46) [LAND]
Ge 10: 5 the isles of the Gentiles divided in their l; 776
 10:31 their tongues, in their l, after their nations. 776
 41:54 the dearth was in all l; but in all the land 776
 41:57 because that the famine was *so* sore in all l. 776
 47:18 sight of my lord, but our bodies, and our l: 127

L

Ge 47:22 gave them: wherefore they sold not their l. 127
Lev 26:36 into their hearts in the l of their enemies; 776
 26:39 away in their iniquity in your enemies' l; 776
Jdg 11:13 therefore restore those l again peaceably. NIH
2Ki 19:11 the kings of Assyria have done to all l, 776
 19:17 have destroyed the nations and their l, 776
1Ch 14:17 the fame of David went out into all l 776
2Ch 9:28 horses out of Egypt, and out of all l. 776
 13: 9 after the manner of the nations of other l 776
 17:10 of the l that were round about Judah, 776
 32:13 have done unto all the people of other l? 776
 32:13 were the gods of the nations of those l any 776
 32:13 able to deliver their l out of mine hand? 776
 32:17 As the gods of the nations of other l have 776
Ezr 9: 1 themselves from the people of the l, 776
 9: 2 themselves with the people of those l: 776
 9: 7 into the hand of the kings of the l, 776
 9:11 with the filthiness of the people of the l, 776
Ne 5: 3 We have mortgaged our l, vineyards. 7704
 5: 4 and that upon our l and vineyards. 7704
 5: 5 redeem them; for other men have our l 7704
 5:11 I pray you, to them, even this day, their l, 7704
 9:30 them into the hand of the people of the l, 776
 10:28 the people of the l unto the law of God, 776
Ps 49:11 they call their l after their own names. 127
 66: 1 Make a joyful noise unto God, all ye l: 776
 100: 1 a joyful noise unto the Lord, all ye l. 776
 105:44 gave them the l of the heathen: 776
 106:27 the nations, and to scatter them in the l. 776
 107: 3 gathered them out of the l, from the east, 776
Isa 36:20 are they amongst all the gods of these l, 776
 37:11 done to all l by destroying them utterly: 776
Jer 16:15 from all the l whither he had driven them: 776
 27: 6 have l given all these l into the hand of 776
Eze 20: 6 and honey, which is the glory of all l: 776
 20:15 and honey, which is the glory of all l; 776
 39:27 gathered them out of their enemies' l, 776
Mt 19:29 father, or mother, or wife, or children, or l, 68
Mk 10:29 father, or mother, or wife, or children, or l, 68
 10:30 sisters, and mothers, and children, and l, 68
Ac 4:34 for as many as were possessors of l or 5564

LANES (1)
Lk 14:21 quickly into the streets and l of the city, 4505

LANGUAGE (27) [LANGUAGES]
Ge 11: 1 the whole earth was of one l, and of one 8193
 11: 6 the people is one, and they have all one l; 8193
 11: 7 us go down, and there confound their l, 8193
 11: 9 the Lord did there confound the l of all 8193
2Ki 18:26 pray thee, to thy servants in the Syrian l; 762
 18:26 talk not with us in the Jews' l in the ears 3066
 18:28 cried with a loud voice in the Jews' l, 3066
Ne 13:24 could not speak in the Jews' l, 3066
 13:24 but according to the l of each people. 3956
Est 1:22 to every people after their l, that every 3956
 1:22 according to the l of every people. 3956
 3:12 and to every people after their l; 3956
 8: 9 unto every people after their l, and to 3956
 8: 9 to their writing, and according to their l. 3956
Ps 19: 3 There is no speech nor l, where their 1697
 81: 5 where I heard a l that I understood not. 8193
 114: 1 house of Jacob from a people of strange l; 3937
Isa 19:18 in the land of Egypt speak the l of Canaan, 8193
 36:11 thee, unto thy servants in the Syrian l; 762
 36:11 and speak not to us in the Jews' l in the 3066
 36:13 cried with a loud voice in the Jews' l, 3066
Jer 5:15 a nation whose l thou knowest not, 3956
Eze 3: 5 people of a strange speech and of a hard l, 3956
 3: 6 people of a strange speech and of a hard l, 3956
Da 3:29 a decree, That every people, nation, and l, 3961
Zep 3: 9 For then will I turn to the people a pure l, 8193
Ac 2: 6 every man heard them speak in his own l. 1258

LANGUAGES (7) [LANGUAGE]
Da 3: 4 is commanded, O people, nations, and l, 3961
 3: 7 the l, fell down and worshipped the 3961
 4: 1 unto all people, nations, and l, that dwell 3961
 5:19 nations, and l, trembled and feared before 3961
 6:25 and l, that dwell in all the earth; 3961
 7:14 a kingdom, that all people, nations, and l, 3961
Zec 8:23 shall take hold out of all l of the nations, 3956

LANGUISH (5) [LANGUISHED, LANGUISHETH, LANGUISHING]
Isa 16: 8 For the fields of Heshbon l, and the vine of 535
 19: 8 that spread nets upon the waters shall l. 535
 24: 4 the haughty people of the earth do l. 535
Jer 14: 2 Judah mourneth, and the gates thereof l; 535
Hos 4: 3 every one that dwelleth therein shall l, 535

LANGUISHED (1) [LANGUISH]
La 2: 8 and the wall to lament; they l together. 535

LANGUISHETH (8) [LANGUISH]
Isa 24: 4 fadeth away, the world l and fadeth away, 535
 24: 7 The new wine mourneth, the vine l, 535
 33: 9 The earth mourneth and l: Lebanon is 535
Jer 15: 9 She that hath borne seven l: she hath given 535
Joel 1:10 wasted, the new wine is dried up, the oil l. 535
 1:12 The vine is dried up, and the fig tree l; 535
Na 1: 4 Bashan l, and Carmel, and the flower of 535
 1: 4 and Carmel, and the flower of Lebanon l. 535

LANGUISHING (1) [LANGUISH]
Ps 41: 3 will strengthen him upon the bed of l: 1741

LANTERNS (1)
Jn 18: 3 cometh thither with l and torches and 5322

LAODICEA (6) [LAODICEANS]
Col 2: 1 for them at L, and for as many as have 2993
 4:13 and them that are in L, and them in 2993
 4:15 Salute the brethren which are in L, 2993
 4:16 that ye likewise read the epistle from L. 2993
1Ti 6: S The first to Timothy was written from L, 2993
Rev 1:11 and unto Philadelphia, and unto L. 2993

LAODICEANS (2) [LAODICEA]
Col 4:16 that it be read also in the church of the L; 2994
Rev 3:14 And unto the angel of the church of the L 2994

LAP (3) [LAPPED, LAPPETH]
2Ki 4:39 gathered thereof wild gourds his l full, 899
Ne 5:13 Also I shook my l, and said, So God shake 2684
Pr 16:33 The lot is cast into the l; but the whole 2436

LAPIDOTH (1)
Jdg 4: 4 Deborah, a prophetess, the wife of L, 3941

LAPPED (2) [LAP]
Jdg 7: 6 the number of them that l, putting their 3952
 7: 7 the three hundred men that l will I save 3952

LAPPETH (2) [LAP]
Jdg 7: 5 Every one that l of the water with his 3952
 7: 5 as a dog l, him shalt thou set by himself; 3952

LAPPIDOTH See LAPIDOTH

LAPWING (2)
Lev 11:19 after her kind, and the l, and the bat. 1744
Dt 14:18 after his kind, and the l, and the bat. 1744

LARGE (21) [LARGENESS]
Ge 34:21 behold, it is l enough for them; 3027+7342
Ex 3: 8 out of that land unto a good land and a l, 7342
Jdg 18:10 a people secure, and to a l land: 3027+7342
2Sa 22:20 He brought me forth also into a l place. 4800
Ne 7: 4 The work is great and l, and we are 7342
 7: 4 Now the city was l and great: 3027+7342
 9:35 in the l and fat land which thou gavest 7342
Ps 18:19 He brought me forth also into a l place; 4800
 31: 8 thou hast set my feet in a l room. 4800
 118: 5 answered me, and set me in a l place. 4800
Isa 22:18 toss thee like a ball into a l country: 3027+7342
 30:23 in that day shall thy cattle feed in l 7337
 30:33 it is prepared; he hath made it deep and l: 7337
Jer 22:14 build me a wide house and l chambers, 7304
Eze 23:32 shalt drink of thy sister's cup deep and l: 7342
Hos 4:16 will feed them as a lamb in a l place. 4800
Mt 28:12 they gave l money unto the soldiers, 2425
Mk 14:15 And he will shew you a l upper room 3173
Lk 22:12 And he shall shew you a l upper room 3173
Gal 6:11 Ye see how l a letter I have written unto 4080
Rev 21:16 and the length is as l as the breadth: 5118

LARGENESS (1) [LARGE]
1Ki 4:29 exceeding much, and l of heart, 7341

LASCIVIOUSNESS (6)
Mk 7:22 deceit, l, an evil eye, blasphemy, pride, 766
2Co 12:21 and l which they have committed. 766
Gal 5:19 Adultery, fornication, uncleanness, l, 766
Eph 4:19 feeling have given themselves over unto l, 766
1Pe 4: 3 we walked in l, lusts, excess of wine, 766
Jude 1: 4 men, turning the grace of our God into l, 766

LASEA (1)
Ac 27: 8 nigh whereunto was the city of L. 2996

LASH; LASHES See SCOURGES; SCOURGETH; SCOURGING; SCOURGINGS; STRIPE; STRIPES

LASHA (1)
Ge 10:19 and Admah, and Zeboim, even unto L. 3962

LASHARON (1)
Jos 12:18 king of Aphek, one; the king of L, one; 8289

LAST (85) [LASTED, LASTING]
Ge 49: 1 that which shall befall you in the l days. 319
 49:19 but he shall overcome at the l. 6119
Nu 23:10 righteous, and let my l end be like his! 319
2Sa 19:11 Why are ye the l to bring the king back 314
 19:12 then are ye the l to bring back the king? 314
 23: 1 Now these be the l words of David. 314
1Ch 23:27 For by the l words of David, the Levites 314
 29:29 acts of David the king, first and l, behold, 314
2Ch 9:29 the rest of the acts of Solomon, first and l, 314
 12:15 Now the acts of Rehoboam, first and l, 314
 16:11 behold, the acts of Asa, first and l, 314
 20:34 rest of the acts of Jehoshaphat, first and l, 314
 25:26 rest of the acts of Amaziah, first and l, behold, 314
 26:22 first and l, did Isaiah the prophet, the son 314
 28:26 and all his ways, first and l, behold, 314
 35:27 deeds, first and l, behold, they are written 314
Ezr 8:13 of the sons of Adonikam, whose names 314
Ne 8:18 by day, from the first day unto the l day, 314
Pr 5:11 thou mourn at the l, when thy flesh and 319

Pr 23:32 At the l it biteth like a serpent, 319
Isa 2: 2 it shall come to pass in the l days, that 319
 41: 4 I the Lord, the first, and with the l; I am 314
 44: 6 I am the first, and I am the l; and besides 314
 48:12 I am he; I am the first, I also am the l. 314
Jer 12: 4 they said, He shall not see our l end. 319
 50:17 this Nebuchadrezzar king of Babylon hath 314
La 1: 9 she remembereth not her l end; therefore 319
Da 4: 8 at the l Daniel came in before me, 314
 8: 3 and the higher came up l. 314+871.1+1886.1
 8:19 shall be in the l end of the indignation: 319
Am 9: 1 I will slay the l of them with the sword: 319
Mic 4: 1 in the l days it shall come to pass, that 319
Mt 12:45 the l state of that man is worse than 2078
 19:30 But many that are first shall be l; 2078
 19:30 first shall be last; and the l shall be first. 2078
 20: 8 beginning from the l unto the first. 2078
 20:12 These l have wrought but one hour, 2078
 20:14 I will give unto this l, even as unto thee. 2078
 20:16 So the l shall be first, and the first last: 2078
 20:16 So the l shall be first, and the first l: 2078
 21:37 But l of all he sent unto them his son, 5306
 22:27 And l of all the woman died also. 5306
 26:60 At the l came two false witnesses, 5306
 27:64 so the l error shall be worse than the first. 2078
Mk 9:35 same shall be l of all, and servant of all. 2078
 10:31 But many that are first shall be l; 2078
 10:31 that are first shall be last; and the l first. 2078
 12: 6 he sent him also l unto them, saying, 2078
 12:22 left no seed: l of all the woman died also. 2078
Lk 11:26 the l state of that man is worse than 2078
 12:59 till thou hast paid the very l mite. 2078
 13:30 are l which shall be first, and there are 2078
 13:30 first, and there are first which shall be l. 2078
 20:32 L of all the woman died also. 5306
Jn 6:39 but should raise it up again at the l day. 2078
 6:40 and I will raise him up at the l day. 2078
 6:44 and I will raise him up at the l day. 2078
 6:54 and I will raise him up at the l day. 2078
 7:37 In the l day, that great day of the feast, 2078
 8: 9 beginning at the eldest, even unto the l: 2078
 11:24 rise again in the resurrection at the l day. 2078
 12:48 the same shall judge him in the l day. 2078
Ac 2:17 And it shall come to pass in the l days, 2078
1Co 4: 9 that God hath set forth us the apostles l, 2078
 15: 8 And l of all he was seen of me also, as of 2078
 15:26 The l enemy that shall be destroyed is 2078
 15:45 the l Adam was made a quickening spirit. 2078
 15:52 in the twinkling of an eye, at the l trump: 2078
Php 4:10 that now at the l your care of me hath 4218
2Ti 3: 1 in the l days perilous times shall come. 2078
Heb 1: 2 Hath in these l days spoken unto us by 2078
Jas 5: 3 have heaped treasure together for the l 2078
1Pe 1: 5 ready to be revealed in the l time. 2078
 1:20 but was manifest in these l times for you, 2078
2Pe 3: 3 there shall come in the l days scoffers, 2078
1Jn 2:18 Little children, it is the l time: and as ye 2078
 2:18 whereby we know that it is the l time. 2078
Jude 1:18 there should be mockers in the l time, 2078
Rev 1:11 I am Alpha and Omega, the first and the l: 2078
 1:17 unto me, Fear not; I am the first and the l: 2078
 2: 8 These things saith the first and the l, 2078
 2:19 and the l to be more than the first. 2078
 15: 1 seven angels having the seven l plagues; 2078
 21: 9 the seven vials full of the seven l plagues, 2078
 22:13 and the end, the first and the l. 2078

LASTED (1) [LAST]
Jdg 14:17 him the seven days, while their feast l: 1961

LASTING (1) [LAST]
Dt 33:15 and for the precious things of the l hills, 5769

LATCHET (4) [SHOELATCHET]
Isa 5:27 nor the l of their shoes be broken: 8288
Mk 1: 7 the l of whose shoes I am not worthy to 2438
Lk 3:16 the l of whose shoes I am not worthy to 2438
Jn 1:27 shoe's l I am not worthy to unloose. 2438

LATE (3) [LATELY, LATTER]
Ps 127: 2 to sit up l, to eat the bread of sorrows: 309
Mic 2: 8 of l my people is risen up as an enemy: 865
Jn 11: 8 the Jews of l sought to stone thee; 3568

LATELY (1) [LATE]
Ac 18: 2 born in Pontus, l come from Italy, with 4373

LATIN (2)
Lk 23:38 and L, and Hebrew, THIS IS THE KING 4513
Jn 19:20 written in Hebrew, and Greek, and L. 4515

LATRINE See DRAUGHT

LATTER (42) [LATE]
Ex 4: 8 they will believe the voice of the l sign. 314
Nu 24:14 people shall do to thy people in the l days. 319
 24:20 his l end shall be that he perish for ever. 319
Dt 4:30 even in the l days, if thou turn to the Lord 319
 8:16 prove thee, to do thee good at thy l end; 319
 11:14 the first rain and the l rain, that thou 4456
 24: 3 if the l husband hate her, and write her a 314
 24: 3 or if the l husband die, which took her to 314
 31:29 evil befall you in the l days; because 319
 32:29 that they would consider their l end! 319
Ru 3:10 in the l end than at the beginning, 314
2Sa 2:26 not that it will be bitterness in the l end? 314

Job 8: 7 yet thy **l** end should greatly increase. 319
19:25 *that* he shall stand *at* the **l** *day* upon 314
29:23 their mouth wide as for the **l rain**. 4456
42:12 So the Lord blessed the **l** end of Job more 319
Pr 16:15 and his favour *is* as a cloud of the **l rain**. 4456
19:20 that thou mayest be wise in thy **l** end. 319
Isa 41:22 them, and know the **l** end of them; 319
47: 7 neither didst remember the **l** end of it. 319
Jer 3: 3 and there hath been no **l rain**; 4456
5:24 both the former and the **l**, in his season: 4456
23:20 in the **l** days ye shall consider it perfectly. 319
30:24 his heart: in the **l** days ye shall consider it. 319
48:47 again the captivity of Moab in the **l** days, 319
49:39 it shall come to pass in the **l** days, *that* I 319
Eze 38: 8 in the **l** years thou shalt come into the land 319
38:16 it shall be in the **l** days, and I will bring 319
Da 2:28 what shall be in the **l** days. 320
8:23 in the **l time** of their kingdom, when 319
10:14 what shall befall thy people in the **l** days: 319
11:29 it shall not be as the former, or as the **l**. 314
Hos 3: 5 the Lord and his goodness in the **l** days. 319
6: 3 as the **l** *and* former rain *unto* the earth. 4456
Joel 2:23 and the **l rain** in the first *month*. 4456
Am 7: 1 of the shooting up of the **l growth**; 3954
7: 1 *it was* the **l growth** after the king's 3954
Hag 2: 9 The glory of this **l** house shall be greater 314
Zec 10: 1 of the Lord rain in the time of the **l rain**; 4456
1Ti 4: 1 that in the **l** times some shall depart from 5306
Jas 5: 7 for it, until he receive the early and **l rain**. 3797
2Pe 2:20 the **l** end is worse with them than 2078

LATTICE (3)
Jdg 5:28 cried through the **l**, Why is his chariot *so* 822
2Ki 1: 2 Ahaziah fell down through a **l** in his upper 7639
SS 2: 9 shewing himself through the **l**. 2762

LAUD (1)
Ro 15:11 all ye Gentiles; and **l** him, all ye people. 1867

LAUGH (18) [LAUGHED, LAUGHETH, LAUGHING, LAUGHTER]
Ge 18:13 Wherefore did Sarah **l**, saying, 6711
18:15 And he said, Nay; but thou didst **l**. 6711
21: 6 God hath made me to **l**, *so that* all that 6712
21: 6 laugh, *so that* all that hear will **l** with me. 6711
Job 5:22 At destruction and famine thou shalt **l**: 7832
9:23 he will **l** at the trial of the innocent. 3932
22:19 glad: and the innocent **l** them to scorn. 3932
Ps 2: 4 He that sitteth in the heavens shall **l**: 7832
22: 7 All they that see me **l** me to scorn: 3932
37:13 The Lord shall **l** at him: for he seeth that 7832
52: 6 also shall see, and fear, and shall **l** at him: 7832
59: 8 thou, O Lord, shalt **l** at them; thou shalt 7832
80: 6 and our enemies **l** among themselves. 3932
Pr 1:26 I also will **l** at your calamity; I will mock 7832
29: 9 whether he rage or **l**, *there is* no rest. 7832
Ecc 3: 4 A time to weep, and a time to **l**; a time to 7832
Lk 6:21 are ye that weep now: for ye shall **l**. 1070
6:25 Woe unto you that **l** now: for ye shall 1070

LAUGHED (13) [LAUGH]
Ge 17:17 upon his face, and **l**, and said in his heart, 6711
18:12 Therefore Sarah **l** within herself, saying, 6711
18:15 Sarah denied, saying, I **l** not; for she was 6711
2Ki 19:21 hath despised thee, *and* **l** thee **to scorn**; 3932
2Ch 30:10 but they **l** them **to scorn**, and mocked 7832
Ne 2:19 heard *it*, they **l** us **to scorn**, 3932
Job 12: 4 the just upright *man is* **l to scorn**. 7814
29:24 *If* I **l** on them, they believed *it* not; 7832
Isa 37:22 hath despised thee, *and* **l** thee **to scorn**; 3932
Eze 23:32 shalt be **l to scorn** and had in derision; 6712
Mt 9:24 but sleepeth. And they **l** him **to scorn**. 2606
Mk 5:40 they **l** him **to scorn**. But when he had 2606
Lk 8:53 they **l** him **to scorn**, knowing that she 2606

LAUGHETH (1) [LAUGH]
Job 41:29 as stubble: he **l** at the shaking of a spear. 7832

LAUGHING (1) [LAUGH]
Job 8:21 Till he fill thy mouth *with* **l**, and thy lips 7814

LAUGHTER (7) [LAUGH]
Ps 126: 2 our mouth filled *with* **l**, and our tongue 7814
Pr 14:13 in the **l** the heart is sorrowful; and the end 7814
Ecc 2: 2 I said of **l**, *It is* mad: and of mirth, 7814
7: 3 Sorrow *is* better than **l**: for by the sadness 7814
7: 6 thorns under a pot, so *is* the **l** of the fool: 7814
10:19 A feast is made for **l**, and wine maketh 7814
Jas 4: 9 let your **l** be turned to mourning, 1071

LAUNCH (1) [LAUNCHED]
Lk 5: 4 **L** out into the deep, and let down your 1877

LAUNCHED (4) [LAUNCH]
Lk 8:22 the other side of the lake. And they **l** forth. 321
Ac 21: 1 after we were gotten from them, and had **l**, 321
27: 2 we **l**, meaning to sail by the coasts of Asia; 321
27: 4 And when we had **l** from thence, we sailed 321

LAUNDERER'S SOAP See SOPE

LAVER (15) [LAVERS]
Ex 30:18 Thou shalt also make a **l** *of* brass, 3595
30:28 with all his vessels, and the **l** and his foot, 3595
31: 9 all his furniture, and the **l** and his foot, 3595
35:16 and all his vessels, the **l** and his foot, 3595

Ex 38: 8 he made the **l** *of* brass, and the foot of it 3595
39:39 and all his vessels, the **l** and his foot, 3595
40: 7 thou shalt set the **l** between the tent of 3595
40:11 And thou shalt anoint the **l** and his foot, 3595
40:30 he set the **l** between the tent of 3595
Lev 8:11 and all his vessels, both the **l** and his foot, 3595
1Ki 7:30 under the **l** *were* undersetters molten, 3595
7:38 one **l** contained forty baths: *and* every 3595
7:38 *and* every **l** was four cubits: *and* every 3595
7:38 upon every one of the ten bases one **l**. 3595
2Ki 16:17 bases, and removed the **l** from off them; 3595

LAVERS (5) [LAVER]
1Ki 7:38 he ten **l** of brass: one laver contained 3595
7:40 And Hiram made the **l**, and the shovels, 3595
7:43 the ten bases, and ten **l** on the bases; 3595
2Ch 4: 6 made also ten **l**, and put five on the right 3595
4:14 also bases and **l** made he upon the bases; 3595

LAVISH (1)
Isa 46: 6 They **l** gold out of the bag, and weigh 2107

LAW (523) [LAWFUL, LAWFULLY, LAWGIVER, LAWLESS, LAWS, LAWYER, LAWYERS, UNLAWFUL]
Ge 11:31 Sarai his **daughter in l**, his son Abram's 3618
19:12 **son in l**, and thy sons, and thy daughters, 2860
19:14 went out, and spake unto his **sons in l**, 2860
19:14 as one that mocked unto his **sons in l**. 2860
38:11 said Judah to Tamar his **daughter in l**, 3618
38:13 thy **father in l** goeth up to Timnath 2524
38:16 not that she *was* his **daughter in l**:) 3618
38:24 Tamar thy **daughter in l** hath played 3618
38:25 she sent to her **father in l**, saying, 2524
47:26 Joseph made it a **l** over the land of Egypt 2706
Ex 3: 1 kept the flock of Jethro his **father in l**, 2859
4:18 and returned to Jethro his **father in l**, 2859
12:49 One **l** shall be to him that is homeborn, 8451
13: 9 that the Lord's **l** may be in thy mouth: 8451
16: 4 whether they will walk in my **l**, or no. 8451
18: 1 the priest of Midian, Moses' **father in l**, 2859
18: 2 Jethro, Moses' **father in l**, took Zipporah, 2859
18: 5 Jethro, Moses' **father in l**, came with his 2859
18: 6 thy **father in l** Jethro am come unto thee, 2859
18: 7 Moses went out to meet his **father in l**, 2859
18: 8 Moses told his **father in l** all that 2859
18:12 Jethro, Moses' **father in l**, took a burnt 2859
18:12 eat bread with Moses' **father in l** before 2859
18:14 Moses' **father in l** saw all that he did 2859
18:15 Moses said unto his **father in l**, 2859
18:17 Moses' **father in l** said unto him, The 2859
18:24 hearkened to the voice of his **father in l**, 2859
18:27 Moses let his **father in l** depart; 2859
24:12 a **l**, and commandments which I have 8451
Lev 6: 9 This *is* the **l** of the burnt offering: 8451
6:14 this *is* the **l** of the meat offering: the sons 8451
6:25 This *is* the **l** of the sin offering: 8451
7: 1 Likewise this *is* the **l** of the trespass 8451
7: 7 *there is* one **l** for them: the priest 8451
7:11 this *is* the **l** of the sacrifice of peace 8451
7:37 This *is* the **l** of the burnt offering, 8451
11:46 This *is* the **l** of the beasts, and of the fowl, 8451
12: 7 This *is* the **l** for her that hath born a male 8451
13:59 This *is* the **l** of the plague of leprosy in a 8451
14: 2 This shall be the **l** of the leper in the day 8451
14:32 This *is* the **l** *of him* in whom *is* the plague 8451
14:54 This *is* the **l** for all *manner of* plague of 8451
14:57 when *it is* clean: this *is* the **l** of leprosy. 8451
15:32 This *is* the **l** of him that hath an issue, 8451
18:15 the nakedness of thy **daughter in l**: 3618
20:12 if a man lie with his **daughter in l**, both 3618
24:22 Ye shall have one manner of **l**, as well for 4941
Nu 5:29 This *is* the **l** of jealousies, when a wife 8451
5:30 The priest shall execute upon her all this **l**. 8451
6:13 This *is* the **l** of the Nazarite, when the days 8451
6:21 This *is* the **l** of the Nazarite who hath 8451
6:21 he must do after the **l** of his separation. 8451
10:29 Raguel the Midianite, Moses' **father in l**, 2859
15:16 One **l** and one manner shall be for you, 8451
15:29 You shall have one **l** for him that sinneth 8451
19: 2 This *is* the ordinance of the **l** which 8451
19:14 This *is* the **l**, when a man dieth in a tent 8451
31:21 This *is* the ordinance of the **l** which 8451
Dt 1: 5 began Moses to declare this **l**, saying, 8451
4: 8 and judgments *so* righteous as all this **l**, 8451
4:44 and this *is* the **l** which Moses set before 8451
17:11 According to the sentence of the **l** which 8451
17:18 that he shall write him a copy of this **l** in 8451
17:19 to keep all the words of this **l** and 8451
27: 3 write upon them all the words of this **l**, 8451
27: 8 stones all the words of this **l** very plainly. 8451
27:23 be he that lieth with his **mother in l**. 2859
27:26 not *all* the words of this **l** to do them. 8451
28:58 of this **l** that are written in this book, 8451
28:61 which *is* not written in the book of this **l**, 8451
29:21 that are written in this book of the **l** 8451
29:29 that *we* may do all the words of this **l**. 8451
30:10 which are written in this book of the **l**, 8451
31: 9 Moses wrote this **l**, and delivered it unto 8451
31:11 thou shalt read this **l** before all Israel in 8451
31:12 and observe to do all the words of this **l**: 8451
31:24 of writing the words of this **l** in a book, 8451
31:26 Take this book of the **l**, and put it in 8451
32:46 to observe to do, all the words of this **l**. 8451
33: 2 his right hand *went* a fiery **l** for them. 1881

Dt 33: 4 Moses commanded us a **l**, *even* 8451
33:10 Jacob thy judgments, and Israel thy **l**: 8451
Jos 1: 7 observe to do according to all the **l**, 8451
1: 8 This book of the **l** shall not depart out of 8451
8:31 as it is written in the book of the **l** of 8451
8:32 upon the stones a copy of the **l** of Moses, 8451
8:34 afterward he read all the words of the **l**, 8451
8:34 to all that is written in the book of the **l**. 8451
22: 5 heed to do the commandment and the **l**, 8451
23: 6 to do all that is written in the book of the **l** 8451
24:26 these words in the book of the **l** of God, 8451
Jdg 1:16 of the Kenite, Moses' **father in l**, 2859
4:11 of Hobab the **father in l** of Moses, 2859
15: 6 the **son in l** of the Timnite, because he 2860
19: 4 his **father in l**, the damsel's father, 2859
19: 5 the damsel's father said unto his **son in l**, 2860
19: 7 up to depart, his **father in l** urged him: 2859
19: 9 and his servant, his **father in l**, 2859
Ru 1: 6 she arose with her **daughters in l**, that 3618
1: 7 and her two **daughters in l** with her; 3618
1: 8 Naomi said unto her two **daughters in l**, 3618
1:14 Orpah kissed her **mother in l**; 2545
1:15 **sister in l** is gone back unto her people, 2994
1:15 gods: return thou after thy **sister in l**. 2994
1:22 Moabitess, her **daughter in l**, with her, 3618
2:11 that thou hast done unto thy **mother in l** 2545
2:18 **mother in l** saw what she had gleaned: 2545
2:19 **mother in l** said unto her, Where hast 2545
2:19 she shewed her **mother in l** with whom 2545
2:20 Naomi said unto her **daughter in l**, 3618
2:22 Naomi said unto Ruth her **daughter in l**, 3618
2:23 and dwelt with her **mother in l**. 2545
3: 1 Naomi her **mother in l** said unto her, 2545
3: 6 did according to all that her **mother in l** 2545
3:16 she came to her **mother in l**, she said, 2545
3:17 me, Go not empty unto thy **mother in l**. 2545
4:15 for thy **daughter in l**, which loveth thee, 3618
1Sa 4:19 his **daughter in l**, Phinehas' wife, was 3618
4:19 that her **father in l** and her husband 2524
4:21 of her **father in l** and her husband. 2524
18:18 that I should be **son in l** to the king? 2860
18:21 Thou shalt *this* day be my **son in l** in 2860
18:22 now therefore be the king's **son in l**. 2860
18:23 you a light *thing* to be a king's **son in l**, 2860
18:26 David well to be the king's **son in l**: 2860
18:27 that he might be the king's **son in l**. 2860
22:14 which *is* the king's **son in l**, and goeth at 2860
1Ki 2: 3 as *it is* written in the **l** of Moses, 8451
2Ki 8:27 for he *was* the **son in l** of the house of 2860
10:31 Jehu took no heed to walk in the **l** of 8451
14: 6 is written in the book of the **l** of Moses, 8451
17:13 according to all the **l** which I commanded 8451
17:34 or after the **l** and commandment which 8451
17:37 and the **l**, and the commandment, 8451
21: 8 to all the **l** that my servant Moses 8451
22: 8 I have found the book of the **l** in the 8451
22:11 had heard the words of the book of the **l**, 8451
23:24 that he might perform the words of the **l** 8451
23:25 his might, according to all the **l** of Moses; 8451
1Ch 2: 4 Tamar his **daughter in l** bare him Pharez 3618
16:17 hath confirmed the same to Jacob for a **l**, 2706
16:40 *do* according to all that is written in the **l** 8451
22:12 that *thou* mayest keep the **l** of the Lord 8451
2Ch 6:16 take heed to their way to walk in my **l**, 8451
12: 1 he forsook the **l** of the Lord, 8451
14: 4 and to do the **l** and the commandment. 8451
15: 3 without a teaching priest, and without **l**. 8451
17: 9 *had* the book of the **l** of the Lord with 8451
19:10 and blood, between **l** and commandment, 8451
23:18 as it is written in the **l** of Moses, 8451
25: 4 *did* as it is written in the **l** in the book of 8451
30:16 according to the **l** of Moses the man of 8451
31: 3 as it is written in the **l** of the Lord. 8451
31: 4 that they might be encouraged in the **l** of 8451
31:21 in the **l**, and in the commandments, to 8451
33: 8 according to the whole **l** and the statutes 8451
34:14 Hilkiah the priest found a book of the **l** 8451
34:15 I have found the book of the **l** in the 8451
34:19 the king had heard the words of the **l**, 8451
35:26 to that which was written in the **l** 8451
Ezr 3: 2 as it is written in the **l** of Moses the man 8451
7: 6 he was a ready scribe in the **l** of Moses, 8451
7:10 his heart to seek the **l** of the Lord, 8451
7:12 a scribe of the **l** of the God of heaven, 1882
7:14 according to the **l** of thy God which *is* in 1882
7:21 the scribe of the **l** of the God of heaven, 1882
7:26 whosoever will not do the **l** of thy God, 1882
7:26 **l** of the king, let judgment be executed 1882
10: 3 and let it be done according to the **l**. 8451
Ne 6:18 he *was* the **son in l** of Shechaniah the 2860
8: 1 scribe to bring the book of the **l** of Moses, 8451
8: 2 Ezra the priest brought the **l** before 8451
8: 3 *were* attentive unto the book of the **l**. 8451
8: 7 caused the people to understand the **l**: 8451
8: 8 So they read in the book in the **l** of God 8451
8: 9 when they heard the words of the **l**. 8451
8:13 even to understand the words of the **l**. 8451
8:14 they found written in the **l** which 8451
8:18 he read in the book of the **l** of God. 8451
9: 3 read in the book of the **l** of the Lord 8451
9:26 cast thy **l** behind their backs, and slew 8451
9:29 mightest bring them again unto thy **l**: 8451
9:34 our priests, nor our fathers, kept thy **l**, 8451
10:28 the people of the lands unto the **l** of God, 8451
10:29 and into an oath, to walk in God's **l**, 8451

L

Ne 10:34 Lord our God, as it is written in the l: 8451
10:36 as it is written in the l, and the firstlings 8451
12:44 cities the portions of the l for the priests 8451
13: 3 came to pass, when they had heard the l, 8451
13:28 was son in l to Sanballat the Horonite: 2860
Est 1: 8 the drinking was according to the l; 1881
1:13 the king's manner towards all that knew l 1881
1:15 do unto the queen Vashti according to l, 1881
4:11 there is one l of his to put him to death, 1881
4:16 the king, which is not according to the l: 1881
Job 22:22 l from his mouth, and lay up his words 8451
Ps 1: 2 his delight is in the l of the Lord; 8451
1: 2 in his l doth he meditate day and night. 8451
19: 7 The l of the Lord is perfect, 8451
37:31 The l of his God is in his heart; none of 8451
40: 8 O my God: yea, thy l is within my heart. 8451
78: 1 Give ear, O my people, to my l: 8451
78: 5 appointed in Israel, which he 8451
78:10 of God, and refused to walk in his l; 8451
81: 4 For Israel, and a l of the God of Jacob. 4941
89:30 If his children forsake my l, and walk not 8451
94:12 O Lord, and teachest him out of thy l; 8451
94:20 which, with thee, frameth mischief by a l? 2706
105:10 confirmed the same unto Jacob for a l, 2706
119: 1 the way, who walk in the l of the Lord. 8451
119:18 may behold wondrous things out of thy l. 8451
119:29 of lying: and grant me thy l graciously. 8451
119:34 me understanding, and I shall keep thy l; 8451
119:44 So shall I keep thy l continually for ever 8451
119:51 yet have I not declined from thy l. 8451
119:53 because of the wicked that forsake thy l. 8451
119:55 in the night, and have kept thy l. 8451
119:61 robbed me: but I have not forgotten thy l. 8451
119:70 is as fat as grease; but I delight in thy l. 8451
119:72 The l of thy mouth is better unto me than 8451
119:77 that I may live: for thy l is my delight. 8451
119:85 pits for me, which are not after thy l. 8451
119:92 Unless thy l had been my delights, I 8451
119:97 how love I thy l! it is my meditation all 8451
119:109 in my hand: yet do I not forget thy l. 8451
119:113 I hate vain thoughts: but thy l do I love. 8451
119:126 to work: for they have made void thy l. 8451
119:136 mine eyes, because they keep not thy l. 8451
119:142 and thy l is the truth. 8451
119:150 after mischief: they are far from thy l. 8451
119:153 and deliver me: for I do not forget thy l. 8451
119:163 I hate and abhor lying: but thy l do I love. 8451
119:165 Great peace have they which love thy l: 8451
119:174 O Lord; and thy l is my delight. 8451
Pr 1: 8 forsake not the l of thy mother: 8451
3: 1 son, forget not my l; but let thine heart 8451
4: 2 you good doctrine, forsake you not my l. 8451
6:20 and forsake not the l of thy mother: 8451
6:23 the l is light; and reproofs of instruction 8451
7: 2 live; and my l as the apple of thine eye. 8451
13:14 The l of the wise is a fountain of life, 8451
28: 4 They that forsake the l praise the wicked: 8451
28: 4 such as keep the l contend with them. 8451
28: 7 Whoso keepeth the l is a wise son: 8451
28: 9 turneth away his ear from hearing the l, 8451
29:18 but he that keepeth the l, happy is he. 8451
31: 5 forget the l, and pervert the judgment of 2710
31:26 and in her tongue is the l of kindness. 8451
Isa 1:10 give ear unto the l of our God, ye people 8451
2: 3 for out of Zion shall go forth the l, 8451
5:24 they have cast away the l of the Lord of 8451
8:16 seal the l among my disciples. 8451
8:20 the l and to the testimony: if they speak 8451
30: 9 children that will not hear the l of 8451
42: 4 earth: and the isles shall wait for his l. 8451
42:21 he will magnify the l, and make it 8451
42:24 neither were they obedient unto his l. 8451
51: 4 for a l shall proceed from me, and I will 8451
51: 7 the people in whose heart is my l; 8451
Jer 2: 8 they that handle the l knew me not: 8451
6:19 my words, nor to my l, but rejected it. 8451
8: 8 and the l of the Lord is with us? 8451
9:13 Because they have forsaken my l which I 8451
16:11 forsaken me, and have not kept my l; 8451
18:18 for the l shall not perish from the priest, 8451
26: 4 to walk in my l, which I have set before 8451
31:33 I will put my l in their inward parts, 8451
32:11 that which was sealed according to the l 4687
32:23 not thy voice, neither walked in thy l; 8451
44:10 nor walked in my l, nor in my statutes, 8451
44:23 nor walked in his l, nor in his statutes, 8451
La 2: 9 the l is no more; her prophets also find 8451
Eze 7:26 the l shall perish from the priest, 8451
22:11 hath lewdly defiled his daughter in l; 3618
22:26 Her priests have violated my l, 8451
43:12 This is the l of the house; Upon the top of 8451
43:12 Behold, this is the l of the house. 8451
Da 6: 5 against him concerning the l of his God. 1882
6: 8 according to the l of the Medes and 1882
6:12 according to the l of the Medes and 1882
6:15 that the l of the Medes and Persians is, 1882
9:11 Yea, all Israel have transgressed thy l, 8451
9:11 the oath that is written in the l of Moses 8451
9:13 As it is written in the l of Moses, all this 8451
Hos 4: 6 thou hast forgotten the l of thy God, 8451
8: 1 covenant, and trespassed against my l. 8451
8:12 written to him the great things of my l, 8451
Am 2: 4 they have despised the l of the Lord, 8451
Mic 4: 2 for the l shall go forth of Zion, 8451
7: 6 the daughter in l against her mother in 3618

Mic 7: 6 daughter in law against her mother in l; 2545
Hab 1: 4 Therefore the l is slacked, 8451
Zep 3: 4 they have done violence to the l. 8451
Hag 2:11 Ask now the priests concerning the l, 8451
Zec 7:12 lest they should hear the l, and the words 8451
Mal 2: 6 The l of truth was in his mouth, 8451
2: 7 and they should seek the l at his mouth: 8451
2: 8 ye have caused many to stumble at the l; 8451
2: 9 my ways, but have been partial in the l. 8451
4: 4 Remember ye the l of Moses my servant, 8451
Mt 5:17 Think not that I am come to destroy the l, 3551
5:18 one tittle shall in no wise pass from the l, 3551
5:40 And if any man will sue thee at the l, 2919
7:12 for this is the l and the prophets. 3551
10:35 the daughter in l against her mother in 3565
10:35 daughter in law against her mother in l. 3994
11:13 and the l prophesied until John. 3551
12: 5 Or have ye not read in the l, how that on 3551
22:36 which is the great commandment in the l? 3551
22:40 these two commandments hang all the l 3551
23:23 omitted the weightier matters of the l, 3551
Lk 2:22 to the l of Moses were accomplished, 3551
2:23 (As it is written in the l of the Lord, Every 3551
2:24 to that which is said in the l of the Lord, 3551
2:27 to do for him after the custom of the l, 3551
2:39 all things according to the l of the Lord, 3551
5:17 doctors of the l sitting by, which were 3547
10:26 said unto him, What is written in the l? 3551
12:53 mother in l against her daughter in law, 3994
12:53 mother in law against her daughter in l, 3565
12:53 the daughter in l against her mother in 3565
12:53 daughter in law against her mother in l. 3994
16:16 The l and the prophets were until John: 3551
16:17 to pass, than one tittle of the l to fail. 3551
24:44 which were written in the l of Moses, 3551
Jn 1:17 For the l was given by Moses, but grace 3551
1:45 of whom Moses in the l, and the prophets, 3551
7:19 not Moses give you the l, and yet none 3551
7:19 law, and yet none of you keepeth the l? 3551
7:23 that the l of Moses should not be broken; 3551
7:49 this people who knoweth not the l are 3551
7:51 Doth our l judge any man, before it hear 3551
8: 5 Now Moses in the l commanded us, 3551
8:17 It is also written in your l, that 3551
10:34 Is it not written in your l, I said, Ye are 3551
12:34 We have heard out of the l that Christ 3551
15:25 be fulfilled that is written in their l, 3551
18:13 for he was father in l to Caiaphas, 3995
18:31 him, and judge him according to your l. 3551
19: 7 We have a l, and by our law he ought to 3551
19: 7 and by our l he ought to die, because 3551
Ac 5:34 Pharisee, named Gamaliel, a doctor of l, 3547
6:13 words against this holy place, and the l: 3551
7:53 have received the l by the disposition 3551
13:15 And after the reading of the l and 3551
13:39 could not be justified by the l of Moses. 3551
15: 5 command them to keep the l of Moses. 3551
15:24 Ye must be circumcised, and keep the l: 3551
18:13 men to worship God contrary to the l. 3551
18:15 of words and names, and of your l, 3551
19:38 a matter against any man, the l is open, 60
21:20 and they are all zealous of the l: 3551
21:24 also walkest orderly, and keepest the l. 3551
21:28 the people, and the l, and this place: 3551
22: 3 the perfect manner of the l of the fathers, 3551
22:12 a devout man according to the l, 3551
23: 3 for sittest thou to judge me after the l, 3551
23: 3 me to be smitten contrary to the l? 3891
23:29 to be accused of questions of their l, 3551
24: 6 would have judged according to our l. 3551
24:14 all things which are written in the l 3551
25: 8 Neither against the l of the Jews, 3551
28:23 both out of the l of Moses, and out of 3551
Ro 2:12 as many as have sinned without l shall 460
2:12 without law shall also perish without l: 460
2:12 as many as have sinned in the l shall be 3551
2:12 sinned in the law shall be judged by the l; 3551
2:13 (For not the hearers of the l are just before 3551
2:13 but the doers of the l shall be justified. 3551
2:14 when the Gentiles, which have not the l, 3551
2:14 do by nature the things contained in the l, 3551
2:14 these, having not the l, are a law unto 3551
2:14 not the law, are a l unto themselves: 3551
2:15 Which shew the work of the l written in 3551
2:17 restest in the l, and makest thy boast of 3551
2:18 being instructed out of the l; 3551
2:20 of knowledge and of the truth in the l. 3551
2:23 Thou that makest thy boast of the l, 3551
2:23 through breaking the l dishonourest thou 3551
2:25 verily profiteth, if thou keep the l: 3551
2:25 but if thou be a breaker of the l, 3551
2:26 keep the righteousness of the l, 3551
2:27 if it fulfil the l, judge thee, who by the 3551
2:27 and circumcision dost transgress the l? 3551
3:19 we know that what things soever the l 3551
3:19 it saith to them who are under the l: 3551
3:20 Therefore by the deeds of the l there shall 3551
3:20 for by the l is the knowledge of sin. 3551
3:21 of God without the l is manifested, 3551
3:21 witnessed by the l and the prophets; 3551
3:27 By what l? of works? Nay: but by the law 3551
3:27 of works? Nay: but by the l of faith. 3551
3:28 by faith without the deeds of the l. 3551
3:31 Do we then make void the l through faith? 3551
3:31 God forbid: yea, we establish the l. 3551

Ro 4:13 the l, but through the righteousness 3551
4:14 if they which are of the l be heirs, faith 3551
4:15 Because the l worketh wrath: for where 3551
4:15 where no l is, there is no transgression. 3551
4:16 to that only which is of the l, but to that 3551
5:13 For until the l sin was in the world: 3551
5:13 but sin is not imputed when there is no l. 3551
5:20 Moreover the l entered, that the offence 3551
6:14 ye are not under the l, but under grace. 3551
6:15 because we are not under the l, 3551
7: 1 (for I speak to them that know the l,) 3551
7: 1 that the l hath dominion over a man, 3551
7: 2 husband is bound by the l to her husband 3551
7: 2 she is loosed from the l of the husband. 3551
7: 3 husband be dead, she is free from that l; 3551
7: 4 ye also are become dead to the l by the 3551
7: 5 the motions of sins, which were by the l, 3551
7: 6 But now we are delivered from the l, 3551
7: 7 Is the l sin? God forbid. Nay, I had not 3551
7: 7 Nay, I had not known sin, but by the l: 3551
7: 7 the l had said, Thou shalt not covet. 3551
7: 8 For without the l sin was dead. 3551
7: 9 For I was alive without the l once: 3551
7:12 Wherefore the l is holy, 3551
7:14 For we know that the l is spiritual: but I 3551
7:16 I consent unto the l that it is good. 3551
7:21 find then a l, that, when I would do good, 3551
7:22 For I delight in the l of God after 3551
7:23 But I see another l in my members, 3551
7:23 warring against the l of my mind, 3551
7:23 bringing me into captivity to the l of sin 3551
7:25 with the mind I myself serve the l of God; 3551
7:25 law of God; but with the flesh the l of sin. 3551
8: 2 For the l of the Spirit of life in Christ Jesus 3551
8: 2 Jesus hath made me free from the l of sin 3551
8: 3 For what the l could not do, in that it was 3551
8: 4 That the righteousness of the l might be 3551
8: 7 for it is not subject to the l of God, 3551
9: 4 the giving of the l, and the service of 3548
9:31 followed after the l of righteousness, 3551
9:31 not attained to the l of righteousness. 3551
9:32 but as it were by the works of the l. 3551
10: 4 For Christ is the end of the l for 3551
10: 5 the righteousness which is of the l, 3551
13: 8 that loveth another hath fulfilled the l. 3551
13:10 therefore love is the fulfilling of the l. 3551
1Co 6: 1 go to l before the unjust, and not before 2919
6: 6 But brother goeth to l with brother, 2919
6: 7 ye go to l one with another. 2192+2917
7:39 The wife is bound by the l as long as her 3551
9: 8 a man? or saith not the l the same also? 3551
9: 9 For it is written in the l of Moses, 3551
9:20 to them that are under the l, as under 3551
9:20 that are under the law, as under the l, 3551
9:20 I might gain them that are under the l; 3551
9:21 them that are without l, as without law, 459
9:21 them that are without law, as without l, 459
9:21 (being not without l to God, but under 459
9:21 law to God, but under the l to Christ,) 1772
9:21 that I might gain them that are without l. 459
14:21 In the l it is written, With men of other 3551
14:34 to be under obedience, as also saith the l. 3551
15:56 is sin; and the strength of sin is the l. 3551
Gal 2:16 man is not justified by the works of the l, 3551
2:16 of Christ, and not by the works of the l: 3551
2:16 for by the works of the l shall no flesh be 3551
2:19 For I through the l am dead to the law, 3551
2:19 For I through the law am dead to the l, 3551
2:21 for if righteousness come by the l, then 3551
3: 2 ye the Spirit by the works of the l, 3551
3: 5 doeth he it by the works of the l, or by 3551
3:10 For as many as are of the works of the l 3551
3:10 written in the book of the l to do them. 3551
3:11 But that no man is justified by the l in 3551
3:12 And the l is not of faith: but, The man 3551
3:13 hath redeemed us from the curse of the l, 3551
3:17 the l, which was four hundred and 3551
3:18 For if the inheritance be of the l, it is no 3551
3:19 Wherefore then serveth the l? It was 3551
3:21 Is the l then against the promises of God? 3551
3:21 if there had been a l given which could 3551
3:21 righteousness should have been by the l. 3551
3:23 faith came, we were kept under the l, 3551
3:24 Wherefore the l was our schoolmaster to 3551
4: 4 made of a woman, made under the l, 3551
4: 5 To redeem them that were under the l, 3551
4:21 Tell me, ye that desire to be under the l, 3551
4:21 to be under the law, do ye not hear the l? 3551
5: 3 that he is a debtor to do the whole l. 3551
5: 4 whosoever of you are justified by the l; 3551
5:14 For all the l is fulfilled in one word, even 3551
5:18 led of the Spirit, ye are not under the l. 3551
5:23 against such there is no l. 3551
6: 2 and so fulfil the l of Christ. 3551
6:13 who are circumcised keep the l; 3551
Eph 2:15 even the l of commandments contained 3551
Php 3: 5 Hebrews; as touching the l, a Pharisee; 3551
3: 6 the righteousness which is in the l, 3551
3: 9 which is of the l, but that which is 3551
1Ti 1: 7 Desiring to be teachers of the l; 3547
1: 8 But we know that the l is good, if a man 3551
1: 9 that the l is not made for a righteous man, 3551
Tit 3: 9 contentions, and strivings about the l; 3544
Heb 7: 5 tithes of the people according to the l, 3551
7:11 (for under it the people received the l,) 3549

Heb	7:12 made of necessity a change also of the l.	3551
	7:16 not after the l of a carnal commandment,	3551
	7:19 For the l made nothing perfect,	3551
	7:28 For the l maketh men high priests which	3551
	7:28 which was since the l, *maketh* the Son,	3551
	8: 4 priests that offer gifts according to the l:	3551
	9:19 to all the people according to the l,	3551
	9:22 And almost all *things* are by the l purged	3551
	10: 1 For the l having a shadow of good *things*	3551
	10: 8 *therein:* which are offered by the l;	3551
	10:28 He that despised Moses' l died without	3551
Jas	1:25 But whoso looketh into the perfect l of	3551
	2: 8 If ye fulfil the royal l according to	3551
	2: 9 are convinced of the l as transgressors.	3551
	2:10 For whosoever shall keep the whole l,	3551
	2:11 thou art become a transgressor of the l.	3551
	2:12 as they that shall be judged by the l of	3551
	4:11 speaketh evil of the l, and judgeth the law:	3551
	4:11 speaketh evil of the law, and judgeth the l:	3551
	4:11 if thou judge the l, thou art not a doer of	3551
	4:11 thou art not a doer of the l, but a judge.	3551
1Jn	3: 4 sin **transgresseth** also the l:	458+4160
	3: 4 law: for sin is the **transgression of** the l.	458

LAWFUL (39) [LAW]

Ezr	7:24 it *shall* not *be* l to impose toll, tribute,	7990
Isa	49:24 the mighty, or the l captive delivered?	6662
Eze	18: 5 be just, and do **that which is** l and right,	4941
	18:19 the son hath done **that which is** l and	4941
	18:21 do **that which is** l and right, he shall	4941
	18:27 doeth **that which is** l and right, he shall	4941
	33:14 his sin, and do **that which is** l and right;	4941
	33:16 he hath done **that which is** l and right;	4941
	33:19 do **that which is** l and right, he shall live	4941
Mt	12: 2 thy disciples do *that* which is not l to do	1832
	12: 4 which was not l for him to eat,	1832
	12:10 saying, Is it l to heal on the sabbath days?	1832
	12:12 Wherefore it is l to do well on the sabbath	1832
	14: 4 unto him, It is not l for thee to have her.	1832
	19: 3 Is it l for a man to put away his wife for	1832
	20:15 Is it not l for me to do what I will with	1832
	22:17 Is it l to give tribute unto Cesar, or not?	1832
	27: 6 is not l for to put them into the treasury,	1832
Mk	2:24 on the sabbath day *that* which is not l?	1832
	2:26 which is not l to eat but for the priests,	1832
	3: 4 Is it l to do good on the sabbath days,	1832
	6:18 It is not l for thee to have thy brother's	1832
	10: 2 Is it l for a man to put away *his* wife?	1832
	12:14 Is it l to give tribute to Cesar, or not?	1832
Lk	6: 2 Why do ye *that* which is not l to do on	1832
	6: 4 which it is not l to eat but **for** the priests	1832
	6: 9 I will ask you one *thing;* Is it l on	1832
	14: 3 saying, Is it l to heal on the sabbath day?	1832
	20:22 Is it l for us to give tribute unto Cesar, or not?	1832
Jn	5:10 it is not l for thee to carry *thy* bed.	1832
	18:31 It is not l for us to put any *man* to death:	1832
Ac	16:21 which are not l for us to receive, neither	1832
	19:39 it shall be determined in a l assembly.	1772
	22:25 l for you to scourge a man *that is* a Roman	1832
1Co	6:12 All *things* are l unto me, but all *things* are	1832
	6:12 all *things* are l for me, but I will not be	1832
	10:23 All *things* are l for me, but all *things* are	1832
	10:23 all *things* are l for me, but all *things* edify	1832
2Co	12: 4 which *it is* not l for a man to utter.	1832

LAWFULLY (2) [LAW]

1Ti	1: 8 that the law *is* good, if a man use it l;	3545
2Ti	2: 5 *yet* is he not crowned, except he strive l.	3545

LAWGIVER (7) [GIVE, LAW]

Ge	49:10 nor a l from between his feet, until Shiloh	2710
Nu	21:18 by the direction of the l, with their staves.	2710
Dt	33:21 because there, *in* a portion of the l, *was*	2710
Ps	60: 7 the strength of mine head; Judah *is* my l;	2710
	108: 8 the strength of mine head; Judah *is* my l;	2710
Isa	33:22 the LORD *is* our l, the LORD *is* our	2710
Jas	4:12 There is one l, who is able to save and	3550

LAWLESS (1) [LAW]

1Ti	1: 9 *man,* but for the l and disobedient,	459

LAWS (20) [LAW]

Ge	26: 5 commandments, my statutes, and my l.	8451
Ex	16:28 ye to keep my commandments and my l?	8451
	18:16 *them* know the statutes of God, and his l.	8451
	18:20 thou shalt teach them ordinances and l,	8451
Lev	26:46 *are* the statutes and judgments and l,	8451
Ezr	7:25 river, all such as know the l of thy God;	1882
Ne	9:13 true l, good statutes and commandments,	8451
	9:14 them precepts, statutes, and l,	8451
Est	1:19 it be written among the l of the Persians	1881
	3: 8 their *are* diverse from all people;	1881
	3: 8 all people; neither keep they the king's l:	1881
Ps	105:45 might observe his statutes, and keep his l.	8451
Isa	24: 5 because they have transgressed the l,	8451
Eze	43:11 all the forms thereof, and all the l thereof:	8451
	44: 5 house of the LORD, and all the l thereof;	8451
	44:24 they shall keep my l and my statutes in all	8451
Da	7:25 High, and think to change times and l:	1882
	9:10 to walk in his l, which he set before us by	8451
Heb	8:10 I will put my l into their mind,	3551
	10:16 I will put my l into their hearts, and in	3551

LAWYER (3) [LAW]

Mt	22:35 Then one of them, *which was* a l,	3544

Lk	10:25 a certain l stood up, and tempted him,	3544
Tit	3:13 Bring Zenas the l and Apollos on their	3544

LAWYERS (5) [LAW]

Lk	7:30 rejected the counsel of God against	3544
	11:45 Then answered one of the l, and said unto	3544
	11:46 And he said, Woe unto you also, *ye* l!	3544
	11:52 Woe unto you, l! for ye have taken away	3544
	14: 3 And Jesus answering spake unto the l and	3544

LAY (241) [LAID, LAIDST, LAYEDST, LAYEST, LAYETH, LAYING, OVERLAY]

Ge	19: 4 before they l **down,** the men of the city,	7901
	19:33 firstborn went in, and l with her father;	7901
	19:33 he perceived not when she l **down,**	7901
	19:34 Behold, I l yesternight with my father:	7901
	19:35 the younger arose, and l with him;	7901
	19:35 he perceived not when she l **down,**	7901
	22:12 he said, L not thine hand upon the lad,	7971
	28:11 and l down in that place **to sleep.**	7901
	30:16 And he l with her that night.	7901
	34: 7 took her, and l with her, and defiled her.	7901
	35:22 and l with Bilhah his father's concubine:	7901
	37:22 l no hand upon him, that he might rid	7971
	41:35 l up corn under the hand of Pharaoh,	6651
Ex	5: 8 make heretofore, ye shall l upon them;	7760
	7: 4 that I may l my hand upon Egypt,	5414
	16:13 in the morning the dew l round about	7902
	16:14 when the dew that l was gone up,	7902
	16:14 upon the face of the wilderness *there* l a	NIH
	16:23 that which remaineth over l up for you	3240
	16:33 l it up before the LORD, to be kept for	3240
	21:22 according as the woman's husband will l	7896
	22:25 neither shalt thou l upon him usury.	7760
Lev	1: 7 And the wood in **order** upon the fire:	6186
	1: 8 l the parts, the head, and the fat, **in order**	6186
	1:12 priest shall l them **in order** on the wood	6186
	2:15 oil upon it, and l frankincense thereon:	7760
	3: 2 he shall l his hand upon the head of his	5564
	3: 8 he shall l his hand upon the head of his	5564
	3:13 he shall l his hand upon the head of it,	5564
	4: 4 shall l his hand upon the bullock's head,	5564
	4:15 the elders of the congregation shall l their	5564
	4:24 he shall l his hand upon the head of	5564
	4:29 shall l his hand upon the head of the sin	5564
	4:33 shall l his hand upon the head of the sin	5564
	6:12 the burnt offering **in order** upon it;	6186
	16:21 Aaron shall l both his hands upon the	5564
	24:14 let all that heard *him* l their hands upon	5564
Nu	8:12 the Levites shall l their hands upon	5564
	12:11 I beseech thee, l not the sin upon us,	7896
	17: 4 whoso shall l them **up** in the tabernacle of	3240
	19: 9 l *them* **up** without the camp in a clean	3240
	24: 9 he l down as a lion, and as a great lion:	7901
	27:18 is the spirit, and l thine hand upon him;	5564
Dt	7:15 will l them upon all them that hate thee.	5414
	11:18 Therefore shall ye l up these my words in	7760
	11:25 *for* the LORD your God shall l the fear of	5414
	14:28 and shalt l *it* **up** within thy gates:	3240
	21: 8 l not innocent blood unto thy people of	5414
	21:19 his father and his mother l **hold** on him,	8610
	22:22 *both* the man that l with the woman,	7901
	22:25 the man only that l with her shall die:	7901
	22:28 l **hold on** her, and lie with her, and they	8610
	22:29 the man that l with her shall give unto	7901
Jos	6:26 he shall l the **foundation** thereof in his	3245
	8: 2 l thee an ambush for the city behind it.	7760
	15:46 all that *l* near Ashdod, with their villages:	NIH
Jdg	4:22 Sisera l dead, and the nail *was* in his	5307
	5:27 At her feet he bowed, he fell, he l **down:**	7901
	6:20 and l *them* upon this rock,	3240
	7:12 all the children of the east l **along** in	5307
	7:13 and overturned it, that the tent l **along.**	5307
	14:17 told her, because she l **sore upon** him:	6693
	16: 3 Samson l till midnight, and arose at	7901
	18:19 l thine hand upon thy mouth, and go	7760
Ru	3: 4 and uncover his feet, and l thee **down;**	7901
	3: 8 and behold, a woman l *at* his feet.	7901
	3:14 she l *at* his feet until the morning:	7901
1Sa	2:22 they l with the women that assembled	7901
	3: 5 down again. And he went and l **down.**	7901
	3: 9 So Samuel went and l **down** in his place.	7901
	3:15 Samuel l until the morning, and opened	7901
	6: 8 ark of the LORD, and l it upon the cart;	5414
	11: 2 and l it *for* a reproach upon all Israel.	7760
	19:24 l **down** naked all that day and all *that*	5307
	26: 5 David beheld the place where Saul l,	7901
	26: 5 Saul l in the trench, and the people	7901
	26: 7 Saul l sleeping within the trench,	7901
	26: 7 Abner and the people l round about him.	7901
2Sa	2:21 l thee **hold** on one of the young men,	270
	4: 5 who l **on a bed** at noon.	4904+7901
	4: 7 he l on his bed in his bedchamber,	7901
	11: 4 she came in unto him, and he l with her;	7901
	12: 3 l in his bosom, and was unto him as a	7901
	12:16 went in, and l all night upon the earth.	7901
	12:24 and went in unto her, and l with her:	7901
	13: 5 L *thee* **down** on thy bed, and make	7901
	13: 6 Amnon l **down,** and made himself sick:	7901
	13:14 than she, forced her, and l with her.	7901
	13:31 and tare his garments, and l on the earth;	7901
	19:32 of sustenance while he l at Mahanaim;	7871
1Ki	5:17 to l the **foundation** of the house.	3245
	7: 3 that *l* on forty five pillars, fifteen *in* a row.	NIH
	13: 4 from the altar, saying, L **hold on** him.	8610

1Ki	13:31 *is* buried; l my bones beside his bones:	3240
	18:23 l *it* on wood, and put no fire *under:* and	7760
	18:23 and l *it* on wood, and put no fire *under:*	5414
	19: 5 as he l and slept under a juniper tree,	7901
	21:27 and l in sackcloth, and went softly.	7901
2Ki	4:11 he turned into the chamber, and l there.	7901
	4:29 and l my staff upon the face of the child.	7760
	4:34 l upon the child, and put his mouth upon	7901
	9:16 and went to Jezreel; for Joram l there.	7901
	10: 8 L ye them in two heaps at the entering in	7760
	19:25 that thou shouldest be to l **waste** fenced	7582
2Ch	31: 7 began to l the **foundation** of the heaps,	3245
	36:21 *for* as long as *she* l **desolate** she kept	8074
Ezr	8:31 and of such as l **in wait** by the way.	693
Ne	13:21 if ye do *so* again, I will l hands on you.	7971
Est	2:21 sought to l hand on the king Ahasuerus.	7971
	3: 6 he thought scorn to l hands on Mordecai	3331
	4: 3 *and* many l in sackcloth and ashes.	3331
	6: 2 who sought to l hand on the king	7971
	9: 2 to l hand on such as sought their hurt:	7971
Job	9:33 *that* might l his hand upon us both.	7896
	17: 3 L **down** now, put me in a surety with	7760
	21: 5 and l *your* hand upon *your* mouth.	7760
	22:22 and l up his words in thine heart.	7760
	22:24 shalt thou l **up** gold as dust, and *the* gold	7896
	29:19 and the dew l **all night** upon my branch.	3885
	34:23 he will not l upon man more *than* right;	7760
	40: 4 l will l my hand upon my mouth.	7760
	41: 8 L thine hand upon him, remember	7760
Ps	4: 8 will both l me **down** in peace, and sleep:	7901
	7: 5 the earth, and l mine honour in the dust.	7931
	38:12 They also that seek after my life l **snares**	5367
	71:10 they that l wait for my soul take counsel	8104
	84: 3 where she may l her young, *even* thine	7896
	104:22 and them **down** in their dens.	7257
Pr	1:11 Come with us, let us l **wait** for blood,	693
	1:18 they l **wait** for their own blood; they lurk	693
	3:18 She *is* a tree of life to them that l **hold**	2388
	7: 1 and l **up** my commandments with thee.	6845
	10:14 Wise men l **up** knowledge: but the mouth	6845
	24:15 L not **wait,** O wicked *man,* against	693
	30:32 evil, l *thine* hand upon thy mouth.	NIH
Ecc	2: 3 l **hold** on folly, till I might see what *was*	270
	7: 2 men; and the living will l *it* to his heart.	5414
Isa	5: 6 I will l it waste: it shall not be pruned,	7896
	5: 8 *that* l field to field, till *there be* no place,	7126
	5:29 l **hold** of the prey, and shall carry *it* away	270
	11:14 they shall l their hand **upon** Edom	4916
	13: 9 and fierce anger, to l the land desolate:	7760
	13:11 will l **low** the haughtiness of the terrible.	8213
	22:22 the key of the house of David will l l upon	5414
	25:12 l **low,** *and* bring to the ground, *even* to	8213
	28:16 I l in Zion **for a foundation** a stone,	3245
	28:17 Judgment also will I l to the line,	7760
	29: 3 will l **siege** against thee *with* a mount,	6696
	30:32 which the LORD shall l upon him, *it* shall	5117
	34:15 l, and hatch, and gather under her	4422
	35: 7 **where** each l, *shall be* grass with reeds	7258
	37:26 thou shouldest be to l **waste** defenced	7582
	38:21 l *it* **for a plaister** upon the boil,	4799
	47: 7 that thou didst not l these *things* to thy	7760
	51:16 l the **foundations** of the earth, and say	3245
	54:11 I will l thy stones with fair colours,	7257
	54:11 and l thy **foundations** with sapphires.	3245
Jer	5:26 are found wicked *men:* they l **wait,**	7789
	6:21 will l stumblingblocks before this people,	5414
	6:23 They shall l **hold on** bow and spear;	2388
Eze	3:20 I l a stumblingblock before him, he shall	5414
	4: 1 l it before thee, and pourtray upon it	5414
	4: 2 l siege against it, and build a fort against	5414
	4: 3 and thou shalt l **siege** against it.	6696
	4: 4 l the iniquity of the house of Israel upon	7760
	4: 8 I will l **bands** upon thee, and thou shalt	5414
	5: 1 will l the dead carcases of the children	5414
	19: 2 she l **down** among lions, she nourished	7257
	23: 8 for in her youth they l with her,	7901
	25:14 I will l my vengeance upon Edom by	5414
	25:17 when I shall l my vengeance upon them.	5414
	26:12 they shall l thy stones and thy timber and	7760
	26:16 l **away** their robes, and put off their	5493
	28:17 I will l thee before kings, that *they* may	5414
	32: 5 I will l thy flesh upon the mountains,	5414
	33:28 For I will l the land most desolate,	5414
	35: 4 I will l thy cities waste, and thou shalt be	7760
	36:29 will increase it, and l no famine upon you.	5414
	36:34 whereas it l desolate in the sight of all	1961
	37: 6 I will l sinews upon you, and will bring	5414
	42:13 there shall they l the most holy *things,*	3240
	42:14 there they shall l their garments wherein	3240
	44:19 l them in the holy chambers, and they	3240
Am	2: 8 they l *themselves* **down** upon clothes	5186
Jnh	1: 5 of the ship; and he l, and was fast asleep.	7901
	1:14 and l not upon us innocent blood:	5414
Mic	1: 7 and all the idols thereof will I l desolate:	7760
	1: 7 she l *their* hand from *their* mouth,	7760
Zec	14:13 they shall l **hold** every one on the hand	2388
Mal	2: 2 not hear, and if ye will not l *it* to heart,	7760
	2: 2 because ye do not l *it* to heart.	7760
Mt	6:19 L not **up** for yourselves treasures upon	2343
	6:20 l **up** for yourselves treasures in heaven,	2343
	8:20 the Son of man hath not where to l *his*	2827
	9:18 but come and l thy hand upon her,	2007
	12:11 will he not l **hold** on it, and lift *it* out?	2902
	21:46 But when they sought to l **hands on** him,	2902

Mt	23: 4 and l them **on** men's shoulders;	2007
	28: 6 Come, see the place where the Lord l.	2749
Mk	1:30 Simon's wife's mother l sick of a fever,	2621
	2: 4 the bed wherein the sick of the palsy l.	2621
	3:21 *of it,* they went out to l **hold** on him:	2902
	5:23 *I pray thee,* come and l *thy* hands **on** her,	2007
	12:12 And they sought to l **hold** on him,	2902
	15: 7 *which* l bound with them that had made	NIG
	16:18 they shall l hands **on** the sick,	2007
Lk	5:18 to bring him in, and to l *him* before him.	5087
	5:25 and took up *that* whereon he l,	2621
	8:42 twelve years of age, and she l a dying.	NIG
	9:58 the Son of man hath not where to l *his*	2827
	19:44 And shall l thee **even with the ground,**	1474
	20:19 same hour sought to l hands **on** him;	1911
	21:12 they shall l their hands **on** you,	1911
Jn	5: 3 In these l a great multitude of impotent	2621
	10:15 and I l **down** my life for the sheep.	5087
	10:17 I l **down** my life, that I might take	5087
	10:18 it from me, but I l it **down** of myself.	5087
	10:18 I have power to l it **down,** and I have	5087
	11:38 It was a cave, and a stone l upon it.	1945
	13:37 I will l **down** my life for thy sake.	5087
	13:38 Wilt thou l **down** thy life for my sake?	5087
	15:13 that a man l **down** his life for his friends.	5087
Ac	7:60 Lord, l not this sin to their **charge.**	2476
	8:19 power, that **on** whomsoever I l hands,	2007
	15:28 to l **upon** you no greater burden than	2007
	27:20 no small tempest l **on** us, all hope that we	1945
	28: 8 that the father of Publius l sick of a fever	2621
Ro	8:33 Who shall l any thing **to the charge** of	1458
	9:33 I l in Sion a stumblingstone and rock of	5087
1Co	3:11 other foundation can no *man* l than that	5087
	16: 2 let every one of you l by him in store,	5087
2Co	12:14 for the children ought not to l **up** for	2343
1Ti	5:22 L hands suddenly **on** no *man,* neither be	2007
	6:12 good fight of faith, l **hold** on eternal life,	1949
	6:19 that they may l **hold** on eternal life.	1949
Heb	6:18 who have fled for refuge to l **hold upon**	2902
	12: 1 let us l **aside** every weight, and the sin	659
Jas	1:21 Wherefore l **apart** all filthiness and	659
1Pe	2: 1 l in Sion a chief corner stone, elect,	5087
1Jn	3:16 we ought to l **down** *our* lives for	5087

LAYEDST (1) [LAY]
Lk	19:21 thou takest up that thou l not **down,**	5087

LAYEST (2) [LAY]
Nu	11:11 that *thou* l the burden of all this people	7760
1Sa	28: 9 wherefore then l thou **a snare** for my life,	5367

LAYETH (18) [LAY]
Job	21:19 God l up his iniquity for his children:	6845
	24:12 crieth out: yet God l not folly *to them.*	7760
	41:26 sword of him that l at him cannot hold:	5381
Ps	33: 7 a heap: he l **up** the depth in storehouses.	5414
	104: 3 Who l the **beams** of his chambers in	7136
Pr	2: 7 He l **up** sound wisdom for the righteous:	6845
	13:16 knowledge: but a fool l **open** *his* folly.	6566
	26:24 with his lips, and l **up** deceit within him;	7896
	31:19 She l her hands to the spindle,	7971
Isa	26: 5 lofty city, he l it **low;** he layeth it **low,**	8213
	26: 5 it **low;** he l it **low,** *even* to the ground;	8213
	56: 2 and the son of man *that* l **hold** on it;	2388
	57: 1 and no man l *it* to heart:	7760
Jer	9: 8 with his mouth, but in heart he l his wait.	7760
	12:11 desolate, because no man l *it* to heart.	7760
Zec	12: 1 l the **foundation** of the earth,	3245
Lk	12:21 So *is* he that l **up treasure** for himself,	2343
	15: 5 And when he hath found *it,* he l *it* on his	2007

LAYING (13) [LAY]
Nu	35:20 or hurl at him by l **of wait,** that he die;	6660
	35:22 upon him any thing without l **of wait,**	6660
Ps	64: 5 commune of l snares **privily;** they say,	2934
Mk	7: 8 For l **aside** the commandment of God,	863
Lk	11:54 L **wait for** him, and seeking to catch	1748
Ac	8:18 when Simon saw that through l **on** of	1936
	9:24 But their l **await** was known of Saul.	1917
	25: 3 l **wait** in the way to kill him.	1747+4160
1Ti	4:14 the l **on** of the hands of the presbytery.	1936
	6:19 L **up in store** for themselves a good	597
Heb	6: 1 not l **again** the foundation of repentance	2598
	6: 2 of l **on** of hands, and of resurrection of	1936
1Pe	2: 1 Wherefore l **aside** all malice, and all guile,	659

LAZARUS (15)
Lk	16:20 And there was a certain beggar named L,	2976
	16:23 Abraham afar off, and L in his bosom.	2976
	16:24 have mercy on me, and send L,	2976
	16:25 and likewise L evil *things:* but now he is	2976
Jn	11: 1 named L, of Bethany, the town of Mary	2976
	11: 2 with her hair, whose brother L was sick.)	2976
	11: 5 Jesus loved Martha, and her sister, and L.	2976
	11:11 saith unto them, Our friend L sleepeth:	2976
	11:14 said Jesus unto them plainly, L is dead.	2976
	11:43 he cried with a loud voice, L, come forth.	2976
	12: 1 where L was which had been dead,	2976
	12: 2 L was one of them that sat at the table	2976
	12: 9 sake only, but that they might see L also,	2976
	12:10 that they might put L also to death;	2976
	12:17 that was with him when he called L out	2976

LAZINESS See SLOTHFUL

LAZY See SLOTHFUL

LEAD (60) [LEADER, LEADERS, LEADEST, LEADETH, LED, LEDDEST, RINGLEADER]
Ge	33:14 I will l **on softly,** according as the cattle	5095
Ex	13:21 in a pillar of a cloud, to l them the way;	5148
	15:10 they sank as l in the mighty waters.	5777
	32:34 l the people unto *the place* of which I	5148
Nu	27:17 which may l them **out,** and which may	3318
	31:22 the brass, the iron, the tin, and the l,	5777
Dt	4:27 whither the LORD shall l you.	5090
	20: 7 captains of the armies to l the people.	7218
	28:37 all nations whither the LORD shall l thee.	5090
	32:12 *So* the LORD alone did l him,	5148
Jdg	5:12 arise, Barak, and l thy captivity **captive,**	7617
1Sa	30:22 that they may l them **away,** and depart.	5090
2Ch	30: 9 before them that l them **captive,**	7617
Ne	9:19 from them by day, to l them in the way;	5148
Job	19:24 an iron pen and l in the rock for ever!	5777
Ps	5: 8 L me, O LORD, in thy righteousness	5148
	25: 5 L me in thy truth, and teach me: for thou	1869
	27:11 l me in a plain path, because of mine	5148
	31: 3 therefore for thy name's sake l me,	5148
	43: 3 let them l me; let them bring me unto thy	5148
	60: 9 the strong city? who will l me into Edom?	5148
	61: 2 l me to the rock *that* is higher than I.	5148
	108:10 the strong city? who will l me into Edom?	5148
	125: 5 the LORD shall l them **forth** with	1980
	139:10 Even there shall thy hand l me,	5148
	139:24 in me, and l me in the way everlasting.	5148
	143:10 *is* good; l me into the land of uprightness.	5148
Pr	6:22 When thou goest, it shall l thee; when	5148
	8:20 I l in the way of righteousness, in the	1980
SS	8: 2 I would l thee, *and* bring thee into my	5090
Isa	3:12 they which l thee cause *thee* to err,	833
	11: 6 and a little child shall l them.	5090
	20: 4 So shall the king of Assyria l **away**	5090
	40:11 shall *gently* l those that are with young.	5095
	42:16 I will l them in paths *that* they have not	1869
	49:10 he that hath mercy on them shall l them,	5148
	57:18 I will l him also, and restore comforts	5148
	63:14 so didst thou l thy people, to make thyself	5090
Jer	6:29 are burnt, the l is consumed of the fire;	5777
	31: 9 and with supplications will I l them:	2986
	32: 5 he shall l Zedekiah *to* Babylon,	1980
Eze	22:18 all they *are* brass, and tin, and iron, and l,	5777
	22:20 and brass, and iron, and l, and tin,	5777
	27:12 with silver, iron, tin, and l, they traded in	5777
Na	2: 7 her maids *shall* l *her* as with the voice of	5090
Zec	5: 7 behold, there *was* lift up a talent of l:	5777
	5: 8 he cast the weight of l upon the mouth	5777
Mt	6:13 And l us not into temptation, but deliver	1533
	15:14 And if the blind l the blind, both shall fall	3594
Mk	13:11 when they shall l *you,* and deliver you up,	71
	14:44 is he; take him, and l *him* **away** safely.	520
Lk	6:39 unto them, Can the blind l the blind?	3594
	11: 4 And l us not **into** temptation;	1533
	11: 4 the stall, and l *him* **away** to watering?	520
Ac	13:11 about seeking *some* to l him **by the hand.**	5497
1Co	9: 5 Have we not power to l **about** a sister,	4013
1Ti	2: 2 that we may l a quiet and peaceable life in	1236
2Ti	3: 6 and l **captive** silly women laden with sins,	162
Heb	8: 9 hand to l them **out** of the land of Egypt;	1806
Rev	7:17 l them unto living fountains of waters:	3594

LEADER (3) [LEAD]
1Ch	12:27 Jehoiada *was* the l of the Aaronites,	5057
	13: 1 and hundreds, *and* with every l.	5057
Isa	55: 4 a l and commander to the people.	5057

LEADERS (3) [LEAD]
2Ch	32:21 the l and captains in the camp of the king	5057
Isa	9:16 For the l of this people cause *them* to err;	833
Mt	15:14 they be blind l of the blind. And if the	3595

LEADERSHIP See BISHOPRICK

LEADEST (1) [LEAD]
Ps	80: 1 of Israel, thou that l Joseph like a flock;	5090

LEADETH (14) [LEAD]
1Sa	13:17 one company turned unto the way that l	NIH
Job	12:17 He l counsellers **away** spoiled,	1980
	12:19 He l princes **away** spoiled,	1980
Ps	23: 2 he l me beside the still waters.	5095
	23: 3 he l me in the paths of righteousness for	5148
Pr	16:29 and l him into the way *that* is not good.	1980
Isa	48:17 which l thee by the way *that* thou	1869
Mt	7:13 that l to destruction, and many there be	520
	7:14 l unto life, and few there be that find	520
Mk	9: 2 l them **up** into a high mountain apart by	399
Jn	10: 3 his own sheep by name, and l them **out.**	1806
Ac	12:10 they came unto the iron gate that l unto	5342
Ro	2: 4 knowing that the goodness of God l thee	71
Rev	13:10 He that l into captivity *shall* go into	4863

LEAF (11) [LEAVES]
Ge	8:11 lo, in her mouth *was* an olive l pluckt off:	5929
Lev	26:36 the sound of a shaken l shall chase them;	5929
Job	13:25 Wilt thou break a l driven to and fro?	5929
Ps	1: 3 his l also shall not wither;	5929
Isa	1:30 For ye shall be as an oak whose l fadeth,	5929
	34: 4 as the l falleth from the vine, and as a	5929
	64: 6 we all do fade as a l; and our iniquities,	5929
Jer	8:13 figs on the fig tree, nor the l shall fade;	5929
	17: 8 heat cometh, but her l shall be green;	5929
Eze	47:12 all trees for meat, whose l shall not fade,	5929

Eze	47:12 for meat, and the l thereof for medicine.	5929

LEAGUE (19)
Jos	9: 6 now therefore make ye a l with us.	1285
	9: 7 and how shall we make a l with you?	1285
	9:11 therefore make ye a l with us.	1285
	9:15 and made a l with them, to let them live:	1285
	9:16 days after they had made a l with them,	1285
Jdg	2: 2 ye shall make no l with the inhabitants of	1285
1Sa	22: 8 son hath made *a* l with the son of Jesse,	NIH
2Sa	3:12 saying also, Make thy l with me,	1285
	3:13 he said, Well; I will make a l with thee:	1285
	3:21 that they may make a l with thee,	1285
	5: 3 king David made a l with them in Hebron	1285
1Ki	5:12 and they two made a l **together.**	1285
	15:19 *There is* a l between me and thee,	1285
	15:19 *and* break thy l with Baasha king of Israel,	1285
2Ch	16: 3 *There is* a l between me and thee, as	1285
	16: 3 go, break thy l with Baasha king of Israel,	1285
Job	5:23 For thou shalt be **in** l with the stones of	1285
Eze	30: 5 Chub, and the men of the land that is in l,	1285
Da	11:23 after the l *made* with him shall he work	2266

LEAH (29) [LEAH'S]
Ge	29:16 name of the elder *was* L, and the name	3812
	29:17 L *was* tender eyed; but Rachel was	3812
	29:23 that he took L his daughter,	3812
	29:24 Laban gave unto his daughter L Zilpah his	3812
	29:25 that in the morning, behold, it *was* L:	3812
	29:30 he loved also Rachel more than Leah,	3812
	29:31 when the LORD saw that L *was* hated,	3812
	29:32 L conceived, and bare a son, and she	3812
	30: 9 When L saw that she had left bearing,	3812
	30:11 L said, A troop cometh: and she called his	3812
	30:13 L said, Happy am I, for the daughters will	3812
	30:14 and brought them unto his mother L.	3812
	30:14 Rachel said to L, Give me, I pray thee,	3812
	30:16 L went out to meet him, and said,	3812
	30:17 hearkened unto L, and she conceived,	3812
	30:18 L said, God hath given *me* my hire,	3812
	30:19 L conceived again, and bare Jacob the	3812
	30:20 L said, God hath endued me with a good	3812
	31: 4 and L to the field unto his flock,	3812
	31:14 and L answered and said unto him,	3812
	33: 1 he divided the children unto L,	3812
	33: 2 L and her children after, and Rachel and	3812
	33: 7 L also with her children came near,	3812
	34: 1 Dinah the daughter of L, which she bare	3812
	35:23 The sons of L; Reuben, Jacob's firstborn,	3812
	46:15 These *be* the sons of L, which she bare	3812
	46:18 whom Laban gave to L his daughter,	3812
	49:31 Rebekah his wife; and there I buried L.	3812
Ru	4:11 into thine house like Rachel and like L,	3812

LEAH'S (5) [LEAH]
Ge	30:10 And Zilpah L maid bare Jacob a son.	3812
	30:12 Zilpah L maid bare Jacob a second son.	3812
	31:33 L tent, and into the two maidservants'	3812
	31:33 went he out of L tent, and entered into	3812
	35:26 the sons of Zilpah, L handmaid; Gad,	3812

LEAN (11) [LEANED, LEANETH, LEANFLESHED, LEANING, LEANNESS]
Ge	41:20 the l and the ill favoured kine did eat up	7534
Nu	13:20 what the land *is,* whether it *be* fat or l,	7330
Jdg	16:26 house standeth, that I may l upon them.	8172
2Sa	13: 4 *being* the king's son, l from day to day?	1800
2Ki	18:21 *even* upon Egypt, on which if a man l,	5564
Job	8:15 He shall l upon his house, but it shall not	8172
Pr	3: 5 and l not unto thine own understanding.	8172
Isa	17: 4 and the fatness of his flesh shall wax l.	7329
	36: 6 if a man l, it will go into his hand,	5564
Eze	34:20 the fat cattle and between the l cattle.	7330
Mic	3:11 yet will they l upon the LORD, and say,	8172

LEANED (6) [LEAN]
2Sa	1: 6 behold, Saul l upon his spear;	8172
2Ki	7: 2 lord on whose hand the king l answered	8172
	7:17 hand he l to have the charge of the gate:	8172
Eze	29: 7 when they l upon thee, thou brakest,	8172
Am	5:19 l his hand on the wall, and a serpent bit	5564
Jn	21:20 also l on his breast at supper, and said,	377

LEANETH (2) [LEAN]
2Sa	3:29 or that l on a staff, or that falleth on	2388
2Ki	5:18 l on my hand, and I bow myself *in*	8172

LEANFLESHED (3) [FLESH, LEAN]
Ge	41: 3 out of the river, ill favoured and l;	1320+1851
	41: 4 l kine did eat up the seven well	1320+1851
	41:19 poor and very ill favoured and l,	1320+7534

LEANING (3) [LEAN]
SS	8: 5 from the wilderness, l upon her beloved?	7514
Jn	13:23 there was l on Jesus' bosom one of his	345
Heb	11:21 worshipped, *l* upon the top of his staff.	NIG

LEANNESS (5) [LEAN]
Job	16: 8 my l rising up in me beareth witness to	3585
Ps	106:15 their request; but sent l into their soul.	7332
Isa	24:16 Lord of hosts, send among his fat ones l;	7332
	24:16 I said, My l, my leanness, woe unto me!	7334
	24:16 I said, My leanness, my l, woe unto me!	7334

LEANNOTH (1)
Ps	88: T To the chief Musician upon Mahalath L,	6031

LEAP (9) [LEAPED, LEAPING, LEAPT]

Ge	31:12 all the rams which l upon the cattle *are*	5927
Lev	11:21 their feet, to l withal upon the earth;	5425
Dt	33:22 *is* a lion's whelp: he shall l from Bashan.	2187
Job	41:19 burning lamps, *and* sparks of fire l **out.**	4422
Ps	68:16 Why l ye, ye high hills? *this is* the hill	7520
Isa	35: 6 shall the lame man l as a hart,	1801
Joel	2: 5 on the tops of mountains shall they l,	7540
Zep	1: 9 I punish all those that l on the threshold,	1801
Lk	6:23 ye in that day, and l *for joy:* for behold,	4640

LEAPED (6) [LEAP]

Ge	31:10 the rams which l upon the cattle *were*	5927
2Sa	22:30 a troop: by my God have I l **over** a wall.	1801
Ps	18:29 and by my God have I l **over** a wall.	1801
Lk	1:41 of Mary, the babe l in her womb;	4640
	1:44 ears, the babe l in my womb for joy.	4640
Ac	14:10 upright on thy feet. And he l and walked.	242

LEAPING (4) [LEAP]

2Sa	6:16 saw King David l and dancing before	6339
SS	2: 8 behold, he cometh l upon the mountains,	1801
Ac	3: 8 And he l **up** stood, and walked,	1814
	3: 8 temple, walking, and l, and praising God.	242

LEAPT (2) [LEAP]

1Ki	18:26 they l upon the altar which was made.	6452
Ac	19:16 whom the evil spirit was l **on** them,	2177

LEARN (32) [LEARNED, LEARNING, UNLEARNED]

Dt	4:10 that they may l to fear me all the days that	3925
	5: 1 ye may l them, and keep, and do them.	3925
	14:23 that thou mayest l to fear the LORD thy	3925
	17:19 that he may l to fear the LORD his God,	3925
	18: 9 shalt not l to do after the abominations	3925
	31:12 that they may l, and fear the LORD your	3925
	31:13 and l to fear the LORD your God,	3925
Ps	119:71 been afflicted; that I might l thy statutes.	3925
	119:73 that I may l thy commandments.	3925
Pr	22:25 Lest thou l his ways, and get a snare to	502
Isa	1:17 **L** to do well; seek judgment, relieve	3925
	2: 4 neither shall they l war any more.	3925
	26: 9 the inhabitants of the world will l	3925
	26:10 wicked, *yet* will he not l righteousness:	3925
	29:24 and they that murmured shall l doctrine.	3925
Jer	10: 2 L not the way of the heathen, and be not	3925
	12:16 if they will **diligently** l the ways of	3925+3925
Mic	4: 3 neither shall they l war any more.	3925
Mt	9:13 But go ye and l what *that* meaneth, I will	3129
	11:29 Take my yoke upon you, and l of me; for	3129
	24:32 Now l a parable of the fig tree; When his	3129
Mk	13:28 Now l a parable of the fig tree; When her	3129
1Co	4: 6 that ye might l in us not to think of *men*	3129
	14:31 that all may l, and all may be comforted.	3129
	14:35 And if they will l any *thing,* let them ask	3129
Gal	3: 2 This only would I l of you, Received ye	3129
1Ti	1:20 that they may l not to blaspheme.	3811
	2:11 Let the woman l in silence with all	3129
	5: 4 let them l first to shew piety at home,	3129
	5:13 And withal they l to be idle,	3129
Tit	3:14 let ours also l to maintain good works	3129
Rev	14: 3 and no *man* could l *that* song but	3129

LEARNED (22) [LEARN]

Ge	30:27 *tarry: for* I have l **by experience** that	5172
Ps	106:35 among the heathen, and l their works.	3925
	119: 7 when I shall have l thy righteous	3925
Pr	30: 3 neither l wisdom, nor have the knowledge	3925
Isa	29:11 which *men* deliver to one that is l,	3045+5612
	29:12 is delivered to *him* that is not l,	3045+5612
	29:12 pray thee: and he saith, I am not l.	3045+5612
	50: 4 GOD hath given me the tongue of the l,	3928
	50: 4 he wakeneth mine ear to hear as the l.	3928
Eze	19: 3 a young lion, and it l to catch the prey;	3925
	19: 6 l to catch the prey, *and* devoured men.	3925
Jn	6:45 that hath heard, and hath l of the Father,	3129
	7:15 knoweth this *man* letters, having never l?	3129
Ac	7:22 And Moses was l in all the wisdom of	3811
Ro	16:17 contrary to the doctrine which ye have l;	3129
Eph	4:20 But ye have not so l Christ;	3129
Php	4: 9 Those *things,* which ye have both l,	3129
	4:11 for I have l, in whatsoever *state* I am,	3129
Col	1: 7 As ye also l of Epaphras our dear	3129
2Ti	3:14 thou in *the things* which thou hast l	3129
	3:14 knowing of whom thou hast l *them;*	3129
Heb	5: 8 yet l he obedience by the things which	3129

LEARNING (9) [LEARN]

Pr	1: 5 A wise *man* will hear, and will increase l;	3948
	9: 9 teach a just *man,* and he will increase in l.	3948
	16:21 and the sweetness of the lips increaseth l.	3948
	16:23 his mouth, and addeth l to his lips.	3948
Da	1: 4 *they* might teach the l and the tongue	5612
	1:17 and skill in all l and wisdom:	5612
Ac	26:24 thyself; much l doth make thee mad.	1121
Ro	15: 4 written aforetime were written for our l,	1319
2Ti	3: 7 Ever l, and never able to come to	3129

LEASING (2)

Ps	4: 2 *long* will ye love vanity, *and* seek after l?	3577
	5: 6 Thou shalt destroy them that speak l:	3577

LEAST (39) [LESS]

Ge	24:55 abide with us *a few* days, **at the** l ten;	176
	32:10 am not worthy **of the** l of all the mercies,	4480

Nu	11:32 he that **gathered** l gathered ten homers:	4591
Jdg	3: 2 **at the** l such as before knew nothing	7535
	6:15 and l *am* the l in my father's house.	6810
1Sa	9:21 my family the l of all the families of	6810
	21: 4 the young men have kept themselves **at** l	389
2Ki	18:24 captain of the l of my master's servants,	6996
1Ch	12:14 one of the l was over an hundred,	6996
Isa	36: 9 captain of the l of my master's servants,	6996
Jer	6:13 For from the l of them even unto	6996
	8:10 l even unto the greatest is given to	6996
	31:34 from the l of them unto the greatest of	6996
	42: 1 all the people from the l even unto	6996
	42: 8 all the people from the l even to	6996
	44:12 from the l even unto the greatest,	6996
	49:20 Surely the l of the flock shall draw them	6810
	50:45 Surely the l of the flock shall draw them	6810
Am	9: 9 shall not the l **grain** fall *upon* the earth.	6872
Jnh	3: 5 from the greatest of them even to the l of	6996
Mt	2: 6 art not the l among the princes of Juda:	1646
	5:19 shall break one of these l commandments,	1646
	5:19 he shall be called the l in the kingdom of	1646
	11:11 he that is l in the kingdom	3398
	13:32 Which indeed is the l of all seeds:	3398
	25:40 *it* unto one of the l of these my brethren,	1646
	25:45 as ye did *it* not to one of the l of	1646
Lk	7:28 that is l in the kingdom of God is greater	3398
	9:48 for he that is l among you all, the same	3398
	12:26 be not able *to do that thing which is* l,	1646
	16:10 He that is faithful in *that which is* l is	1646
	16:10 He that is unjust in the l is unjust also in	1646
	19:42 even thou, **at** l in this thy day,	1065+2532
Ac	5:15 that **at the** l the shadow of Peter passing	2579
	8:10 from the l to the greatest, saying,	3398
1Co	6: 4 set them to judge who are l **esteemed**	1848
	15: 9 For I am the l of the apostles, that am not	1646
Eph	3: 8 who *am* less than the l of all saints,	1647
Heb	8:11 shall know me, from the l to the greatest.	3398

LEATHER (1) [LEATHERN]

2Ki	1: 8 girt *with* a girdle of l about his loins.	5785

LEATHERN (1) [LEATHER]

Mt	3: 4 camel's hair, and a l girdle about his loins;	1193

LEAVE (115) [LEAVED, LEAVETH, LEAVING, LEFT, LEFTEST]

Ge	2:24 Therefore shall a man l his father and his	5800
	28:15 for I will not l thee, until I have done *that*	5800
	33:15 Let me now l with thee *some* of the folk	3322
	42:33 shall I know that ye *are* true men; l	3240
	44:22 unto my lord, The lad cannot l his father:	5800
	44:22 for *if* he should l his father, *his father*	5800
Ex	16:19 Let no man l of it till the morning.	3498
	23:11 they l the beasts of the field shall eat.	3499
Lev	7:15 he shall not l *any* of it until the morning.	3240
	16:23 the holy *place,* and shall l them there:	3240
	19:10 shalt l them for the poor and stranger:	5800
	22:30 ye shall l none of it until the morrow:	3498
	23:22 thou shalt l them unto the poor, and to	5800
Nu	9:12 They shall l none of it unto the morning,	7604
	10:31 he said, **L** us not, I pray thee; forasmuch	5800
	22:13 for the LORD refuseth to **give** me l to go	5414
	32:15 he will yet again l them in the wilderness;	3240
Dt	28:51 which *also* shall not l thee *either* corn,	7604
	28:54 remnant of his children which he shall l:	3498
Jos	4: 3 l them in the lodging place, where you	3240
Jdg	9: 9 tree said unto them, Should I l my fatness,	2308
	9:13 Should I l my wine, which cheereth God	2308
Ru	1:16 Intreat me not to l thee, *or* to return from	5800
	2:16 l *them,* that she may glean *them,* and	2308
1Sa	5: 5 lest my father l *caring* for the asses,	7604
	14:36 and let us not l a man of them.	7604
	20: 6 David earnestly asked *l* of me that *he*	NIH
	20:28 David earnestly asked *l* of me *to go* to	NIH
	25:22 if I l of all that *pertain* to him by	7604
2Sa	14: 7 shall not l to my husband *neither* name	7760
1Ki	8:57 fathers: let him not l us, nor forsake us:	5800
2Ki	2: 2 and *as* thy soul liveth, I will not l thee.	5800
	2: 4 and *as* thy soul liveth, I will not l thee.	5800
	2: 6 and *as* thy soul liveth, I will not l thee.	5800
	4:30 and *as* thy soul liveth, I will not l thee.	5800
	4:43 They shall eat, and shall l *thereof.*	3498
	13: 7 Neither did he l *of* the people to Jehoahaz	7604
1Ch	28: 8 l it **for an inheritance** for your children	5157
Ezr	9: 8 to l us a remnant to escape, and to give us	7604
	9:12 l it *for* an **inheritance** to your children	3423
Ne	5:10 corn: I pray you, let us l **off** this usury.	5800
	6: 3 whilst I l it, and come down to you?	7503
	10:31 *that* we would l the seventh year,	NIH
	13: 6 after certain days obtained I l of the king:	NIH
Job	9:27 I will l **off** my heaviness,	5800
	10: 1 life; I will l my complaint upon myself;	5800
	39:11 *is* great? or wilt thou l thy labour to him?	5800
Ps	16:10 For thou wilt not l my soul in hell;	5800
	17:14 the rest of their *substance* to their babes.	3240
	27: 9 l me not, neither forsake me, O God of	5203
	37:33 The LORD will not l him in his hand,	5800
	49:10 perish, and l their wealth to others.	5800
	119:121 and justice: l me not to mine oppressors.	3240
	141: 8 thee is my trust; l not my soul **destitute.**	6168
Pr	2:13 Who l the paths of uprightness, to walk in	5800
	17:14 therefore l **off** contention, before *it be*	5203
Ecc	2:18 I should l it unto the man that shall be	3240
	2:21 therein leave he l it *for his* portion.	5414
	10: 4 ruler rise up against thee, l not thy place;	3240

Isa	10: 3 for help? and where will ye l your glory?	5800
	65:15 ye shall l your name for a curse unto my	3240
Jer	9: 2 that I might l my people, and go from	5800
	14: 9 and we are called by thy name; l us not.	5800
	17:11 shall l them in the midst of his days,	5800
	18:14 Will *a man* l the snow of Lebanon *which*	5800
	30:11 l thee **altogether unpunished.**	5352+5352
	44: 7 out of Judah, to l you none to remain;	3498
	46:28 l not l thee **wholly unpunished.**	5352+5352
	48:28 l the cities, and dwell in the rock,	5800
	49: 9 would they not l *some* gleaning grapes?	7604
	49:11 **L** thy fatherless children, I will preserve	5800
Eze	6: 8 Yet will I l **a remnant,** that ye may have	3498
	12:16 will I l a few men of them from the sword,	3498
	16:39 thy fair jewels, and l thee naked and bare.	3240
	22:20 and I will l *you* there, and melt you.	3240
	23:29 labour, and shall l thee naked and bare:	5800
	29: 5 I will l thee *thrown* in the wilderness,	5203
	32: 4 will I l thee upon the land, I will cast thee	5203
	39: 2 I will l the **sixth part** of thee, and will	8338
Da	4:15 Nevertheless l the stump of his roots in	7662
	4:23 yet l the stump of the roots thereof in	7662
	4:26 whereas they commanded to l the stump	7662
Hos	12:14 therefore shall he l his blood upon him,	5203
Joel	2:14 and repent, and l a blessing behind him;	7604
Am	5: 3 city that went out *by* a thousand shall l	7604
	5: 3 which went forth *by* an hundred shall l	7604
	5: 7 and l **off** righteousness in the earth,	3240
Ob	1: 5 to thee, would they not l *some* grapes?	7604
Zep	3:12 will also l in the midst of thee an afflicted	7604
Mal	4: 1 it shall l them neither root nor branch.	5800
Mt	5:24 **L** there thy gift before the altar, and go thy	863
	18:12 doth he not l the ninety and nine,	863
	19: 5 For this cause shall a man l father and	2641
	23:23 have done, and not to l the other **undone.**	863
Mk	5:13 And forthwith Jesus **gave** them l.	2010
	10: 7 For this cause shall a man l his father and	2641
	12:19 and l *his* wife *behind him,* and leave no	2641
	12:19 *his* wife *behind him,* and l no children,	863
Lk	11:42 have done, and not to l the other **undone.**	863
	15: 4 doth not l the ninety and nine in	2641
	19:44 they shall not l in thee one stone upon	863
Jn	14:18 I will not l you comfortless: I will come to	863
	14:27 Peace I l with you, my peace I give unto	863
	16:28 again, I l the world, and go to the Father.	863
	16:32 man to his own, and shall l me alone:	863
	19:38 and Pilate **gave** *him* l. He came therefore,	2010
Ac	2:27 Because thou wilt not l my soul in hell,	1459
	6: 2 It is not reason that we should l the word	2641
	18:18 and then **took** his l of the brethren,	657
	21: 6 And when we had **taken** our l one of	782
1Co	7:13 to dwell with her, let her not l him.	863
2Co	2:13 **taking** my l of them, I went from *thence*	657
Eph	5:31 For this cause shall a man l his father and	2641
Heb	13: 5 for he hath said, I will never l thee,	447
Rev	11: 2 the court which is without the temple l	1544

LEAVED (1) [LEAVE]

Isa	45: 1 to open before him the **two l gates;**	1817

LEAVEN (23) [LEAVENED, LEAVENETH, UNLEAVENED]

Ex	12:15 the first day ye shall put away l out of	7603
	12:19 Seven days shall there be no l found in	7603
	13: 7 neither shall there be l seen with thee in	7603
	34:25 not offer the blood of my sacrifice with l;	2557
Lev	2:11 unto the LORD, shall be made *with* l:	2557
	2:11 for ye shall burn no l, nor any honey, in	7603
	6:17 It shall not be baken *with* l. I have given	2557
	10:12 fire, and eat it *without* l beside the altar,	4682
	23:17 *of* fine flour; they shall be baken *with* l;	2557
Am	4: 5 offer a sacrifice of thanksgiving with l,	2557
Mt	13:33 The kingdom of heaven is like unto l,	2219
	16: 6 and beware of the l of the Pharisees and	2219
	16:11 that *ye* should beware of the l of	2219
	16:12 bade *them* not beware of the l of bread,	2219
Mk	8:15 beware of the l of the Pharisees, and *of*	2219
	8:15 of the Pharisees, and *of* the l of Herod.	2219
Lk	12: 1 *of all,* Beware ye of the l of the Pharisees,	2219
	13:21 It is like l, which a woman took and hid	2219
1Co	5: 6 Know ye not that a little l leaveneth	2219
	5: 7 Purge out therefore the old l, that ye may	2219
	5: 8 let us keep the feast, not with old l,	2219
	5: 8 neither with the l of malice and	2219
Gal	5: 9 A little l leaveneth the whole lump.	2219

LEAVENED (14) [LEAVEN]

Ex	12:15 for whosoever eateth l bread from the	2557
	12:19 for whosoever eateth **that which is** l,	2556
	12:20 Ye shall eat nothing l; in all your	2556
	12:34 people took their dough before it was l,	2556
	12:39 forth out of Egypt, for it was not l;	2556
	13: 3 *place:* there shall no l bread be eaten.	2557
	13: 7 there shall no l bread be seen with thee,	2556
	23:18 the blood of my sacrifice with l bread;	2557
Lev	7:13 he shall offer *for* his offering l bread with	2557
Dt	16: 3 Thou shalt eat no l bread with it;	2557
	16: 4 there shall be no l bread seen with thee	7603
Hos	7: 4 he hath kneaded the dough, until it be l.	2556
Mt	13:33 measures of meal, till the whole was l.	2220
Lk	13:21 measures of meal, till the whole was l.	2220

LEAVENETH (2) [LEAVEN]

1Co	5: 6 Know ye not that a little leaven l the	2220
Gal	5: 9 A little leaven l the whole lump.	2220

L

LEAVES (19) [LEAF]

Ge	3: 7 they sewed fig l together,	5929
1Ki	6:34 the two l of the one door *were* folding,	6763
	6:34 the two l of the other door folding.	7050
Isa	6:13 when they cast *their* l so the holy seed	NIH
Jer	36:23 *that* when Jehudi had read three or four l,	1817
Eze	17: 9 it shall wither *in* all the l of her spring,	2964
	41:24 the doors had two l *apiece,* two turning	1817
	41:24 had two leaves *apiece,* two turning l;	1817
	41:24 two *l* for the one door, and two leaves for	NIH
	41:24 one door, and two l for the other *door.*	1817
Da	4:12 The l thereof *were* fair, and the fruit	6074
	4:14 shake off his l, and scatter his fruit:	6074
	4:21 Whose l *were* fair, and the fruit thereof	6074
Mt	21:19 but l only, and said unto it,	5444
	24:32 putteth forth l, ye know that summer *is*	5444
Mk	11:13 And seeing a fig tree afar off having l,	5444
	11:13 he came to it, he found nothing but l;	5444
	13:28 putteth forth l, ye know that summer *is*	5444
Rev	22: 2 the l of the tree *were* for the healing of	5444

LEAVETH (6) [LEAVE]

Job	39:14 Which l her eggs in the earth,	5800
Pr	13:22 A good *man* l an inheritance to *his*	5157
	28: 3 *is* like a sweeping rain which l no food.	NIH
Zec	11:17 Woe to the idol shepherd that l the flock!	5800
Mt	4:11 Then the devil l him, and behold,	863
Jn	10:12 wolf coming, and l the sheep, and fleeth:	863

LEAVING (5) [LEAVE]

Mt	4:13 And l Nazareth, he came and dwelt in	2641
Lk	10:30 *him,* and departed, l *him* half dead.	863
Ro	1:27 the men, l the natural use of the woman,	863
Heb	6: 1 Therefore l the principles of the doctrine	863
1Pe	2:21 Christ also suffered for us, l us an example	5277

LEBANA (1) [LEBANAH]

Ne	7:48 The children of L, the children of Hagaba,	3838

LEBANAH (1) [LEBANA]

Ezr	2:45 The children of L, the children of Hagabah,	3838

LEBANON (71)

Dt	1: 7 *unto* L, unto the great river, the river	3844
	3:25 that goodly mountain, and L.	3844
	11:24 from the wilderness and L, from the river,	3844
Jos	1: 4 and this L even unto the great river,	3844
	9: 1 the coasts of the great sea over against L,	3844
	11:17 unto Baal-gad in the valley of L under	3844
	12: 7 from Baal-gad in the valley of L even unto	3844
	13: 5 and all L, *toward* the sunrising,	3844
	13: 6 country from L unto Misrephoth-maim,	3844
Jdg	3: 3 and the Hivites that dwelt in mount L,	3844
	9:15 the bramble, and devour the cedars of L.	3844
1Ki	4:33 from the cedar tree that *is* in L even unto	3844
	5: 6 that they hew me cedar trees out of L;	3844
	5: 9 servants shall bring *them* down from L	3844
	5:14 he sent them to L, ten thousand a month	3844
	5:14 month they were in L, *and* two months at	3844
	7: 2 He built also the house of the forest of L;	3844
	9:19 in L, and in all the land of his dominion.	3844
	10:17 put them *in* the house of the forest of L.	3844
	10:21 house of the forest of L *were* of pure gold:	3844
2Ki	14: 9 The thistle that *was* in L sent to the cedar	3844
	14: 9 Lebanon sent to the cedar that *was* in L,	3844
	14: 9 there passed by a wild beast that *was* in L,	3844
	19:23 the sides of L, and will cut down the tall	3844
2Ch	2: 8 fir trees, and algum trees, out of L:	3844
	2: 8 thy servants can skill to cut timber in L;	3844
	2:16 we will cut wood out of L, as much as	3844
	8: 6 in L, and throughout all the land of his	3844
	9:16 put them in the house of the forest of L.	3844
	9:20 house of the forest of L *were* of pure gold:	3844
	25:18 The thistle that *was* in L sent to the cedar	3844
	25:18 Lebanon sent to the cedar that *was* in L,	3844
	25:18 there passed by a wild beast that *was* in L,	3844
Ezr	3: 7 to bring cedar trees from L to the sea of	3844
Ps	29: 5 yea, the LORD breaketh the cedars of L.	3844
	29: 6 a calf; L and Sirion like a young unicorn.	3844
	72:16 the fruit thereof shall shake like L:	3844
	92:12 palm tree: he shall grow like a cedar in L.	3844
	104:16 the LORD are full *of sap;* the cedars of L,	3844
SS	3: 9 made himself a chariot of the wood of L.	3844
	4: 8 Come with me from L, *my* spouse, with	3844
	4: 8 Lebanon, *my* spouse, with me from L:	3844
	4:11 of thy garments *is* like the smell of L.	3844
	4:15 well of living waters, and streams from L.	3844
	5:15 his countenance *is* as L, excellent as	3844
	7: 4 thy nose *is* as the tower of L which	3844
Isa	2:13 upon all the cedars of L, that are high and	3844
	10:34 with iron, and L shall fall by a mighty one.	3844
	14: 8 trees rejoice at thee, *and* the cedars of L,	3844
	29:17 L shall be turned into a fruitful field,	3844
	33: 9 L is ashamed *and* hewn down: Sharon is	3844
	35: 2 the glory of L shall be given unto it,	3844
	37:24 height of the mountains, *to* the sides of L;	3844
	40:16 L *is* not sufficient to burn, nor the beasts	3844
	60:13 The glory of L shall come unto thee,	3844
Jer	18:14 Will *a* man leave the snow of L *which*	3844
	22: 6 *art* Gilead unto me, and the head of L:	3844
	22:20 Go up *to* L, and cry; and lift up thy voice	3844
	22:23 O inhabitant of L, that makest thy nest in	3844
Eze	17: 3 came unto L, and took the highest branch	3844
	27: 5 they have taken cedars from L to make	3844
	31: 3 the Assyrian *was* a cedar in L with fair	3844

Eze	31:15 I caused L to mourn for him, and all	3844
	31:16 the choice and best of L, all that drink	3844
Hos	14: 5 as the lily, and cast forth his roots as L.	3844
	14: 6 be as the olive tree, and his smell as L.	3844
	14: 7 the scent thereof *shall be* as the wine of L.	3844
Na	1: 4 Carmel, and the flower of L languisheth.	3844
Hab	2:17 For the violence of L shall cover thee,	3844
Zec	10:10 bring into the land of Gilead and L;	3844
	11: 1 Open thy doors, O L, that the fire may	3844

LEBAOTH (1)

Jos	15:32 L, and Shilhim, and Ain, and Rimmon:	3822

LEBBEUS (1)

Mt	10: 3 James the *son* of Alpheus, and L,	3002

LEBONAH (1)

Jdg	21:19 to Shechem, and on the south of L.	3829

LECAH (1)

1Ch	4:21 the son of Judah *were,* Er the father of L,	3922

LECTURE HALL See SCHOOL

LED (68) [LEAD]

Ge	24:27 the LORD l me to the house of my	5148
	24:48 which had l me in the right way to take	5148
Ex	3: 1 he l the flock to the backside of the desert,	5090
	13:17 that God l them not *through* the way of	5148
	13:18 God l the people about, *through* the way	5437
	15:13 Thou in thy mercy hast l *forth* the people	5148
Dt	8: 2 l thee these forty years in the wilderness,	1980
	8:15 Who l thee *through that* great and terrible	1980
	29: 5 I have l you forty years in the wilderness,	1980
	32:10 he l him *about,* he instructed him, he	5437
Jos	24: 3 l him throughout all the land of Canaan,	1980
1Ki	8:48 which l them *away captive,* and pray	7617
2Ki	6:19 whom ye seek. But he l them to Samaria.	1980
1Ch	20: 1 *battle,* Joab l forth the power of the army,	5090
2Ch	25:11 l forth his people, and went *to* the valley	5090
Ps	68:18 on high, thou hast l captivity *captive:*	7617
	78:14 the daytime also he l them with a cloud,	5148
	78:53 l them *on* safely, so that they feared not:	5148
	106: 9 so he l them through the depths, as	1980
	107: 7 he l them *forth* by the right way, that	1869
	136:16 To him which l his people through	1980
Pr	4:11 of wisdom; I have l thee in right paths.	1869
Isa	9:16 and *they that are* l of them *are* destroyed.	833
	48:21 they thirsted not *when* he l them through	1980
	55:12 out with joy, and be l *forth* with peace:	2986
	63:12 That l *them* by the right hand of Moses	1980
	63:13 That l them through the deep, as a horse	1980
Jer	2: 6 that l us through the wilderness, through	1980
	2:17 thy God, when he l thee by the way?	1980
	22:12 place whither they have l him *captive,*	1540
	31: 2 the seed of the house of Israel out	935
Eze	39:28 *caused* them to be l into captivity	1540
	47: 2 l me *about* the way without unto the	5437
Am	2:10 l you forty years through the wilderness,	1980
	7:11 shall *surely* be l away captive	1540+1540
Na	2: 7 Huzzab shall be l away captive, she shall	1540
Mt	4: 1 Then was Jesus l up of the Spirit into	321
	26:57 they l *him away* to Caiaphas the high	520
	27: 2 they l *him* away, and delivered him to	520
	27:31 on him, and l him *away* to crucify *him.*	520
Mk	8:23 by the hand, and l him *out* of the town;	1806
	14:53 And they l Jesus *away* to the high priest:	520
	15:16 And the soldiers l him *away* into the hall,	520
	15:20 on him, and l him *out* to crucify him.	1806
Lk	4: 1 and was l by the Spirit into the wilderness,	71
	4:29 l him unto the brow of the hill whereon	71
	21:24 shall be l *away captive* into all nations:	163
	22:54 and l *him,* and brought him into the high	71
	22:66 and l him into their council, saying,	321
	23: 1 l *him* arose, and l him unto Pilate.	71
	23:26 as they l *him away,* they laid hold upon	520
	23:32 malefactors, l with him to be put to death.	71
	24:50 And he l them *out* as far as to	1806
Jn	18:13 And l him *away* to Annas first; for he was	520
	18:28 Then l they Jesus from Caiaphas unto the	71
	19:16 And they took Jesus, and l *him* away.	520
Ac	8:32 this, He was l as a sheep to the slaughter;	71
	9: 8 saw no *man:* but they l him *by the hand,*	5496
	21:37 And as Paul was to be l *into*	1521
	22:11 being l *by the hand* of them that were	5496
Ro	8:14 For as many as are l by the Spirit of God,	71
1Co	12: 2 unto *these* dumb idols, *even* as ye were l.	71
Gal	5:18 But if ye be l of the Spirit, ye are not under	71
Eph	4: 8 he l captivity *captive,* and gave gifts unto	162
2Ti	3: 6 laden with sins, l with divers lusts,	71
2Pe	3:17 l *away with* the error of the wicked,	4879

LEDDEST (5) [LEAD]

2Sa	5: 2 thou wast he that l *out* and broughtest in	3318
1Ch	11: 2 thou *wast* he that l *out* and broughtest in	3318
Ne	9:12 Moreover thou l them in the day by a	5148
Ps	77:20 Thou l thy people like a flock by the hand	5148
Ac	21:38 l *out* into the wilderness four thousand	1806

LEDGES (5)

1Ki	7:28 and the borders *were* between the l:	7948
	7:29 the borders that *were* between the l *were*	7948
	7:29 upon the l *there* was a base above:	7948
	7:35 on the top of the base the l thereof and	3027

1Ki	7:36 For on the plates of the l thereof, and on	3027

LEECH See HORSELEACH

LEEKS (1)

Nu	11: 5 and the l, and the onions, and the garlick:	2682

LEES (4)

Isa	25: 6 feast of **wines on the** l, of fat things full	8105
	25: 6 marrow, of **wines on the** l well refined.	8105
Jer	48:11 hath settled on his l, and hath not been	8105
Zep	1:12 punish the men that are settled on their l:	8105

LEESE (1)

1Ki	18: 5 mules alive, that we l not all the beasts.	3772

LEFT (348) [LEAVE, LEFTHANDED]

Ge	11: 8 the earth: and they l off to build the city.	NIH
	13: 9 *if* thou wilt take the **l hand,** then I will go	8040
	13: 9 *to* the right hand, then I will go to the l.	8041
	14:15 which *is* on the **l hand** of Damascus.	8040
	17:22 he l off talking with him, and God went	3615
	18:33 as soon as he had l communing with	3615
	24:27 who hath not l **destitute** my master of his	5800
	24:49 I may turn to the right hand, or to the l.	8040
	29:35 she called his name Judah; and l bearing.	5975
	30: 9 When Leah saw that she had l bearing,	5975
	32: 8 the *other* company which is l shall escape.	7604
	32:24 Jacob was l alone; and there wrestled a	3498
	39: 6 he l all that he had in Joseph's hand,	5800
	39:12 he l his garment in her hand, and fled,	5800
	39:13 when she saw that he had l his garment	5800
	39:15 that he l his garment with me, and fled,	5800
	39:18 that he l his garment with me, and fled,	5800
	41:49 the sea, very much, until he l numbering;	2308
	42:38 for his brother is dead, and he is l alone:	7604
	44:12 began at the eldest, and l at the youngest:	3615
	44:20 he alone is l his mother, and his father	3498
	47:18 is not ought l in the sight of my lord,	7604
	48:13 in his right hand toward Israel's **l hand,**	8040
	48:13 Manasseh in his l hand toward Israel's	8040
	48:14 and his **l hand** upon Manasseh's head,	8040
	50: 8 their herds, they l in the land of Goshen.	5800
Ex	2:20 why is it *that* ye have l the man? call him,	5800
	9:21 not the word of the LORD l his servants	5800
	10:12 of the land, *even* all that the hail hath l.	7604
	10:15 the fruit of the trees which the hail had l:	3498
	10:26 us; there shall not a hoof be l **behind;**	7604
	14:22 them on their right hand, and on their l.	8040
	14:29 them on their right hand, and on their l.	8040
	16:20 some of them l of it until the morning,	3498
	34:25 of the passover be l unto the morning.	3885
Lev	2:10 that which is l of the meat offering *shall*	3498
	10:12 and unto Ithamar his sons that were l,	3498
	10:16 Ithamar the sons of Aaron which were l	3498
	14:15 pour *it* into the palm of his own l hand:	8042
	14:16 right finger in the oil that *is* in his l hand,	8042
	14:26 of the oil into the palm of his own l hand:	8042
	14:27 his l hand seven times before the LORD:	8042
	26:36 them that are l *alive* of you l will send	7604
	26:39 they that are l of you shall pine away in	7604
	26:43 The land also shall be l of them,	5800
Nu	20:17 not turn *to* the right hand nor *to* the l,	8040
	21:35 people, until there was none l him alive:	7604
	22:26 turn *either* to the right hand or *to* the l.	8040
	26:65 there was not l a man of them, save Caleb	3498
Dt	2:27 turn *unto* the right hand nor *to* the l.	8040
	2:34 of every city, we l none to remain:	7604
	3: 3 we smote him until none was l to him	7604
	4:27 ye shall be l few in number among	7604
	5:32 turn aside to the right hand or *to* the l.	8040
	7:20 until they that are l, and hide themselves	7604
	17:11 shew thee, *to* the right hand, nor *to* the l.	8040
	17:20 *to* the right hand, or to the l:	8040
	28:14 *to* the right hand, or *to* the l, to go after	8040
	28:55 he hath nothing l him in the siege,	7604
	28:62 ye shall be l few in number, whereas ye	7604
	32:36 is gone, and *there is* none shut up, or l.	5800
Jos	1: 7 not from it *to* the right hand or *to* the l,	8040
	6:23 and l them without the camp of Israel.	3240
	8:17 there was not a man l in Ai or Beth-el,	7604
	8:17 they l the city open, and pursued after	5800
	10:33 until he l him none remaining:	7604
	10:37 he l none remaining, according to all that	7604
	10:39 that *were* therein; he l none remaining:	7604
	10:40 he l none remaining, but utterly destroyed	7604
	11: 8 until *they* l them none remaining.	7604
	11:11 destroying *them:* there was not any l	3498
	11:14 neither l they any to breathe.	7604
	11:15 he l nothing **undone** of all that the LORD	5493
	11:22 There was none of the Anakims l in	3498
	19:27 and goeth out to Cabul on the **l hand,**	8040
	22: 3 Ye have not l your brethren these many	5800
	23: 6 therefrom *to* the right hand or *to* the l;	8040
Jdg	2:21 the nations which Joshua l when he died:	5800
	2:23 Therefore the LORD l those nations,	3240
	3: 1 these *are* the nations which the LORD l,	3240
	3:21 Ehud put forth his l hand, and took	8040
	4:16 of the sword; *and* there was not a man l.	7604
	6: 4 l no sustenance for Israel, neither sheep,	7604
	7:20 held the lamps in their l hands,	8040
	8:10 fifteen thousand *men,* all that were l	3498
	8:19 the youngest son of Jerubbaal the l:	3498
	16:29 his right hand, and of the other with his l.	8040
Ru	1: 3 and she was l, and her two sons.	7604

Ru 1: 5 the woman was l of her two sons and 7604
1:18 with her, then she l speaking unto her. 2308
2:11 thou hast l thy father and thy mother, 5800
2:14 she did eat, and was sufficed, and l 3498
2:20 hath not l off his kindness to the living 5800
4:14 which hath not l thee *this* day **without** a 7673
1Sa 2:36 every one that is l in thine house shall 3498
5: 4 only *the stump of* Dagon was l to him. 7604
6:12 not aside to the right hand or to the l; 8040
9:24 *Samuel* said, Behold that which is l; set *it* 7604
10: 2 lo, thy father hath l the care of the asses, 5203
11:11 so that two of them were not l together. 7604
17:20 and l the sheep with a keeper, and took, 5203
17:22 David l his carriage in the hand of 5203
17:28 with whom hast thou l those few sheep 5203
25:34 surely there had not been l unto Nabal by 3498
27: 9 l neither man nor woman **alive**, 2421
30: 9 where those that were l **behind** stayed. 3498
30:13 my master l me, because three days agone 5800
2Sa 2:19 hand nor to the l from following Abner. 8040
2:21 thee aside to thy right hand or to thy l, 8040
5:21 there they l their images, and David and 5800
9: 1 Is there yet *any* that is l of the house of 3498
13:30 sons, and there is not one of them l. 3498
14: 7 *so* they shall quench my coal which is l, 7604
14:19 to the l from ought that my lord the king 8041
15:16 the king l ten women, *which were* 5800
16: 6 *men were* on his right hand and on his l. 8040
16:21 which he hath l to keep the house; 3240
17:12 that *are* with him there shall not be l 3498
20: 3 whom he had l to keep the house, 3240
1Ki 7:21 he set up the l pillar, and called the name 8042
7:39 and five on the l side of the house: 8040
7:47 Solomon l all the vessels *unweighed,* 3240
7:49 five on the l, before the oracle, with 8040
9:20 *And* all the people that were l of 8040
9:21 Their children that were l after them in 3498
14:10 *and him that is* shut up and l in Israel, 5800
15:18 the gold that were l in the treasures of 3498
15:21 when Baasha heard *thereof,* that he l off 2308
15:29 he l not to Jeroboam that breathed, 7604
16:11 he l him not *one that* pisseth against a wall, 7604
17:17 so sore, that there was no breath l in him. 3498
19: 3 to Judah, and l his servant there. 3240
19:10 l, *even* l only, am l; and they seek my life, 3498
19:14 l, *even* l only, am l; and they seek my life, 3498
19:18 Yet I have l *me* seven thousand in Israel, 7604
19:20 he l the oxen, and ran after Elijah, and 5800
20:30 seven thousand of the men that were l. 3498
21:21 and *him that is* shut up and l in Israel, 8040
22:19 by him on his right hand and on his l. 8040
2Ki 3:25 only in Kir-haraseth l *they* the stones 7604
4:44 l *thereof,* according to the word of 3498
7: 7 l their tents, and their horses, and their 5800
7:13 that remain, which are l in the city, 7604
7:13 all the multitude of Israel that are l in it: 7604
8: 6 the field since the day that she l the land, 5800
9: 8 *and him that is* shut up and l in Israel: 5800
10:11 his priests, until *he* l him none remaining. 7604
10:14 and forty men; neither l he any of them. 7604
10:21 that there was not a man l that came not. 7604
11:11 the right corner of the temple to the l 8042
14:26 up, nor any l, nor any helper for Israel. 5800
17:16 they l all the commandments of the LORD 5800
17:18 was none l but the tribe of Judah only. 5800
19: 4 up *thy* prayer for the remnant that are l. 4672
20:17 nothing shall be l, saith the LORD. 3498
22: 2 not aside *to* the right hand or to the l. 8040
23: 8 *were* on a man's l **hand** at the gate 8040
25:11 Now the rest of the people that were l in 7604
25:12 the captain of the guard l of the poor of 7604
25:22 Nebuchadnezzar king of Babylon had l, 7604
1Ch 6:44 the sons of Merari *stood* on the l **hand:** 8040
6:61 which were l of the family of *that* tribe, 3498
12: 2 right hand and the l in *hurling* stones and 8041
13: 2 that are l in all the land of Israel, 7604
14:12 when they had l their gods there, David 5800
16:37 he l there before the ark of the covenant 5800
2Ch 3:17 on the right hand, and the other on the l; 8040
3:17 and the name of *that* on the l Boaz. 8042
4: 6 and five on the l, to wash in them: 8040
4: 7 five on the right hand, and five on the l. 8040
4: 8 five on the right side, and five on the l. 8040
8: 7 *As for* all the people that were l of 3498
8: 8 who were l after them in the land, 3498
11:14 For the Levites l their suburbs and 5800
12: 5 have l also l you in the hand of Shishak. 5800
16: 5 Baasha heard *it,* that he l off building 2308
18:18 standing on his right hand and *on* his l. 8040
21:17 so that there was never a son l him, 7604
23:10 from the right side of the temple to the l 8042
24:18 they l the house of the LORD God of their 5800
24:25 him, (for they l him in great diseases,) 5800
25:12 *other* ten thousand *l* alive did the children NIH
28:14 So the armed men l the captives and 5800
31:10 had enough to eat, and have l plenty. 3498
31:10 and that which is l *is* this great store. 3498
32:31 God l him, to try him, that *he* might 5800
34: 2 neither to the right hand, nor *to* the l. 8040
34:21 for them that are l in Israel and in Judah, 7604
Ne 1: 2 which were l of the captivity, 7604
1: 3 The remnant that are l of the captivity 7604
6: 1 and *that* there was no breach l therein; 3498
8: 4 on his l **hand,** Pedaiah, and Mishael, 8040
Job 20:21 *There* shall none of his meat *be* l; 8300

Job 20:26 it shall go ill with him that is l in his 8300
23: 9 *On* the l **hand,** where he doth work, 8040
32:15 no more: they l *off* speaking. 4480+6275
Ps 36: 3 he hath l off to be wise, *and* to do good. 2308
106:11 enemies: there was not one of them l. 3498
Pr 3:16 and in her l **hand** riches and honour. 8040
4:27 Turn not *to* the right hand nor *to* the l: 8040
29:15 a child l *to himself* bringeth his mother to 7971
Ecc 10: 2 his right hand; but a fool's heart at his l. 8040
SS 2: 6 His l **hand** *is* under my head, and his 8040
2: 6 His l **hand** *should be* under my head, 8040
8: 3 His l **hand** *should be* under my head, 8040
Isa 1: 8 the daughter of Zion is l as a cottage in a 3498
1: 9 Except the LORD of hosts had l unto us a 3498
4: 3 *that* he that is l in Zion, and he that 7604
7:22 honey shall every one eat that is l in 3498
9:20 he shall eat on the l **hand,** and they shall 8040
10:14 as *one* gathereth eggs *that are* l, have l 5800
11:11 which shall be l from Assyria, 7604
11:16 his people, which shall be l from Assyria; 7604
17: 6 Yet gleaning grapes shall be l in it, 5800
17: 9 which they l because of the children of 5800
18: 5 They shall be l together unto the fowls of 5800
24: 6 of the earth are burned, and few men l. 7604
24:12 In the city is l desolation, and the gate is 7604
27:10 forsaken, and l like a wilderness: 5800
30:17 till ye be l as a beacon upon the top of a 3498
30:21 right hand, and when ye **turn to** the l. 8041
32:14 multitude of the city shall be l; the forts 5800
37: 4 lift up *thy* prayer for the remnant that are l. 4672
39: 6 nothing shall be l, saith the LORD. 3498
49:21 Behold, I was l alone; these, where *had* 7604
54: 3 forth *on* the right hand and *on* the l; 8040
Jer 12: 7 mine house, I have l mine heritage; 5203
7: 7 as are l in this city from the pestilence, 7604
27:18 that the vessels which are l in the house 3498
31: 2 The people which were l of the sword 8300
34: 7 against all the cities of Judah that were l, 3498
38:22 all the women that are l in the king of 7604
38:27 So they l *off speaking* with him; 2790
39:10 Nebuzar-adan the captain of the guard l 7604
40: 6 among the people that were l in the land. 7604
40:11 heard that the king of Babylon had l a 5414
42: 2 (for we are l *but* a few of many, as thine 7604
43: 6 l with Gedaliah the son of Ahikam the 3240
44:18 we l *off* to burn incense to the queen 2308
49:25 How is the city of praise not l, the city 5800
50:26 destroy her utterly: let nothing of her be l. 7611
52:16 Nebuzar-adan the captain of the guard l 7604
Eze 1:10 four had the face of an ox on the l **side;** 8040
4: 4 lie thou also upon thy l side, and lay 8042
9: 1 I *was* l, they l fell upon my face, and cried, 7604
14:22 therein shall be l a remnant that shall be 3498
16:46 her daughters that dwell at thy l **hand:** 8040
21:16 *either* on the right hand, *or* **on the l.** 8041
23: 8 Neither l she her whoredoms *brought* 5800
24:21 your daughters whom ye have l shall fall 5800
31:12 have cut him off, and have l him: 5203
31:12 down from his shadow, and have l him. 5203
36:36 the heathen that are l round about you 7604
39: 3 I will smite thy bow out of thy l hand, 8040
39:28 and have l none of them any more there. 3498
41: 9 *that* which *was* l *was* the place of the side 3240
41:11 *were* toward the *place* that *was* l, 3240
41:11 breadth of the *place* that was l *was* five 3240
48:15 that are l in the breadth over against 3498
Da 2:44 kingdom shall not be l to other people, 7662
10: 8 I was l alone, and saw this great 7604
10:17 in me, neither is there breath l in me. 7604
12: 7 right hand and his l hand unto heaven, 8040
Hos 4:10 they have l *off* to take heed to the LORD. 5800
9:12 *that there shall* not *be* a man *l* yea, NIH
Joel 1: 4 That which the palmerworm hath l 3499
1: 4 that which the locust hath l 3499
1: 4 that which the cankerworm hath l hath 3499
Jnh 4:11 their right hand and *their* l **hand;** 8040
Hag 2: 3 Who *is* l among you that saw this house 7604
Zec 4: 3 and the other upon the l *side* thereof. 8040
4:11 candlestick and upon the l *side* thereof? 8040
12: 6 about, on the right hand and on the l: 8040
13: 8 *and* die; but the third shall be l therein. 3498
14:16 *that* every one that is l of all the nations 3498
Mt 4:20 And they straightway l *their* nets, 863
4:22 And they immediately l the ship and 863
6: 3 not thy l **hand** know what thy right hand 710
8:15 he touched her hand, and the fever l her: 863
15:37 took up of the broken *meat* that was l 4052
16: 4 And he l them, and departed. 2641
20:21 and the other on the l, in thy kingdom. 2176
20:23 on my l, is not mine to give, but *it shall* 2176
21:17 he l them, and went out of the city into 2641
22:22 and l him, and went their way. 863
22:25 having no issue, l his wife unto his brother: 863
23:38 Behold, your house is l unto you desolate. 863
24: 2 There shall not be l here one stone upon 863
24:40 the one shall be taken, and the other l. 863
24:41 *the one* shall be taken, and the *other* l. 863
25:33 on his right hand, but the goats on the l. 2176
25:41 he say also unto them on the l **hand,** 2176
26:44 And he l them, and went away again, 2176
27:38 on the right hand, and another on the l. 2176
Mk 1:20 they l their father Zebedee in the ship 863
1:31 and immediately the fever l her, 863
8: 8 took up of the broken *meat* that was l 4051
8:13 And he l them, and entering into the ship 863
10:28 Lo, we have l all, and have followed thee. 863

Mk 10:29 There is no *man* that hath l house, 863
10:37 and the other on thy l **hand,** in thy glory. 2176
10:40 and on my l **hand** is not mine to give; 2176
12:12 thy l him, and went their way. 863
12:20 the first took a wife, and dying l no seed. 863
12:21 took her, and died, neither l he *any* seed: 863
12:22 the seven had her, and l no seed: last of 863
13: 2 shall not be l one stone upon another, 863
13:34 who l his house, and gave authority to his 863
14:52 And he l the linen cloth, and fled from 2641
15:27 on *his* right hand, and the other on his l. 2176
Lk 4:39 her, and rebuked the fever; and it l her: 863
5: 4 Now when he had l speaking, he said 3973
5:28 And he l all, rose up, and followed him. 2641
10:40 thou not care that my sister hath l me 2641
13:35 Behold, your house is l unto you desolate: 863
17:34 one shall be taken, and the other shall be l. 863
17:35 the one shall be taken, and the other l. 863
17:36 the one shall be taken, and the other l. 863
18:28 Then Peter said, Lo, we have l all, 863
18:29 is no *man* that hath l house, or parents, 863
20:31 also: and they l no children, and died. 2641
21: 6 in the which there shall not be l one stone 863
23:33 on the right hand, and the other on the l. 710
Jn 4: 3 Judea, and departed again into Galilee. 863
4:28 The woman then l her waterpot, 863
4:52 Yesterday at the seventh hour the fever l 863
8: 9 and Jesus was l alone, and the woman 2641
8:29 the Father hath not l me alone; for I do 863
Ac 2:31 of Christ, that his soul was not l in hell, 2641
14:17 Nevertheless he l not himself without 863
18:19 he came to Ephesus, and l them there: 2641
21: 3 we l it on the left hand, and sailed into 2641
21: 3 we left it on the l **hand,** and sailed into 2176
21:32 and the soldiers, they l beating of Paul. 3973
23:32 On the morrow they l the horsemen to go 1439
24:27 shew the Jews a pleasure, l Paul bound. 2641
25:14 There is a certain man l in bonds by Felix: 2641
Ro 9:29 the Lord of sabaoth had l us a seed, 1459
11: 3 and I am l alone, and they seek my life. 5275
11: 4 I have l to myself seven thousand men, 2641
2Co 6: 7 on the right hand and on the l, 710
1Th 3: 1 thought it good to be l at Athens alone; 2641
2Ti 4:13 The cloke that I l at Troas with Carpus, 620
4:20 but Trophimus have I l at Miletum sick. 620
Tit 1: 5 For this cause l I thee in Crete, that thou 2641
Heb 2: 8 he l nothing *that is* not put under him. 863
4: 1 a promise being l *us* of entering into his 2641
Jude 1: 6 first estate, but l their own habitation, 620
Rev 2: 4 because thou hast l thy first love. 863
10: 2 upon the sea, and *his* l *foot* on the earth, 2176

LEFTEST (1) [LEAVE]
Ne 9:28 l thou them in the hand of their enemies, 5800

LEFTHANDED (2) [HAND, LEFT]
Jdg 3:15 Gera, a Benjamite, a man l: 334+3027+3225
20:16 seven hundred chosen men l; 334+3027+3225

LEG (1) [LEGS]
Isa 47: 2 make bare the l, uncover the thigh, 7640

LEGION (3) [LEGIONS]
Mk 5: 9 And he answered, saying, My name *is* L: 3003
5:15 and had the l, sitting, and clothed, 3003
Lk 8:30 for they said, L: because many devils were 3003

LEGIONS (1) [LEGION]
Mt 26:53 give me more than twelve l of angels? 3003

LEGS (19) [LEG]
Ex 12: 9 head with his l, and with the purtenance 3767
29:17 his l, and put *them* unto his pieces, 3767
Lev 1: 9 and his l shall he wash in water: 3767
1:13 wash the inwards and the l with water: 3767
4:11 with his l, and his inwards, and his dung, 3767
8:21 he washed the inwards and the l in water; 3767
9:14 he did wash the inwards and the l, 3767
11:21 which have l above their feet, to leap 3767
Dt 28:35 in the l, with a sore botch that cannot be 7785
1Sa 17: 6 *he had* greaves of brass upon his l, 7272
Ps 147:10 he taketh not pleasure in the l of a man. 7785
Pr 26: 7 The l of the lame are not equal: so *is* 7785
SS 5:15 His l *are* as pillars of marble, set upon 7785
Isa 3:20 *ornaments of the* l, and the headbands, 6807
Da 2:33 His l of iron, his feet part of iron and 8243
Am 3:12 taketh out of the mouth of the lion two l, 3767
Jn 19:31 Pilate that their l might be broken, 4628
19:32 brake the l of the first, and of the other 4628
19:33 he was dead already, they brake not his l: 4628

LEHABIM (2)
Ge 10:13 and Anamim, and L, and Naphtuhim, 3853
1Ch 1:11 and Anamim, and L, and Naphtuhim, 3853

LEHABITES See LEHABIM

LEHI (3) [RAMATH-LEHI]
Jdg 15: 9 in Judah, and spread themselves in L. 3896
15:14 when he came unto L, the Philistines 3896
15:19 which *is* in L unto this day. 3896

LEISURE (1)
Mk 6:31 and they **had** no l so much as to eat. 2119

LEMUEL (2)
Pr 31: 1 The words of king L, the prophecy that 3927

Pr 31: 4 *It is* not for kings, O **L**, *it is* not for kings 3927

LEND (16) [LENDER, LENDETH, LENT]

Ex 22:25 If thou **l** money to *any* of my people *that* 3867
Lev 25:37 nor **l** him thy victuals for increase. 5414
Dt 15: 6 thou shalt **l** unto many nations, 5670
 15: 8 **surely** I him sufficient for his need, 5670+5670
 23:19 shalt not **l** **upon usury** to thy brother; 5391
 23:20 a stranger thou mayest **l** **upon usury**; 5391
 23:20 thy brother thou shalt not **l** **upon usury**: 5391
 24:10 When thou dost **l** thy brother any 4859+5383
 24:11 the man to whom thou dost **l** shall bring 5383
 28:12 thou shalt **l** unto many nations, 3867
 28:44 He shall **l** to thee, and thou shalt not lend 3867
 28:44 lend to thee, and thou shalt not **l** to him: 3867
Lk 6:34 And if ye **l** *to them* of whom ye hope to 1155
 6:34 for sinners also **l** to sinners, to receive as 1155
 6:35 and do good, and **l**, hoping for nothing 1155
 11: 5 say unto him, Friend, **l** me three loaves; 5531

LENDER (2) [LEND]

Pr 22: 7 and the borrower *is* servant to the **l**. 376+3867
Isa 24: 2 as *with* the **l**, so *with* the borrower; 3867

LENDETH (4) [LEND]

Dt 15: 2 Every creditor that *ought* unto his 5383
Ps 37:26 *He is* ever merciful, and **l**; and his seed *is* 3867
 112: 5 A good man sheweth favour, and **l**: her 3867
Pr 19:17 He that hath pity upon the poor **l** unto 3867

LENGTH (77) [LENGTHEN, LENGTHENED, LENGTHENING, LONG, LONGER, LONGSUFFERING, LONGWINGED]

Ge 6:15 **l** of the ark *shall be* three hundred cubits, 753
 13:17 walk through the land in the **l** of it and in 753
Ex 25:10 two cubits and a half *shall be* the **l** thereof, 753
 25:17 two cubits and a half *shall be* the **l** thereof, 753
 25:23 two cubits *shall be* the **l** thereof, and a 753
 26: 2 The **l** of one curtain *shall be* eight and 753
 26: 8 The **l** of one curtain *shall be* thirty cubits, 753
 26:13 in the **l** of the curtains of the tent, 753
 26:16 Ten cubits *shall be* the **l** of a board, 753
 27:11 for the north side in **l** *there shall be* 753
 27:18 The **l** of the court *shall be* an hundred 753
 28:16 span *shall be* the **l** thereof, and a span *shall* 753
 30: 2 A cubit *shall be* the **l** thereof, and a cubit 753
 36: 9 The **l** of one curtain *was* twenty and 753
 36:15 The **l** of one curtain *was* thirty cubits, 753
 36:21 The **l** of a board *was* ten cubits, 753
 37: 1 two cubits and a half *was* the **l** of it, 753
 37: 6 two cubits and a half *was* the **l** thereof, 753
 37:10 two cubits *was* the **l** thereof, and a cubit 753
 37:25 the **l** of it *was* a cubit, and the breadth of 753
 38: 1 five cubits *was* the **l** thereof, and five 753
 38:18 twenty cubits *was* the **l**, and the height in 753
 39: 9 a span *was* the **l** thereof, and a span 753
Dt 3:11 nine cubits *was* the **l** thereof, and four 753
 30:20 for he *is* thy life, and the **l** of thy days: 753
Jdg 3:16 a dagger which had two edges, of a cubit **l**; 753
1Ki 6: 2 The **l** thereof *was* threescore cubits, 753
 6: 3 twenty cubits *was* the **l** thereof, according 753
 6:20 in the forepart *was* twenty cubits in **l**, 753
 7: 2 The **l** thereof *was* an hundred cubits, 753
 7: 6 the **l** thereof *was* fifty cubits, and the 753
 7:27 four cubits *was* the **l** of one base, 753
2Ch 3: 3 The **l** *by* cubits after the first measure *was* 753
 3: 4 **l** *of it was* according to the breadth of 753
 3: 8 **l** whereof *was* according to the breadth 753
 4: 1 twenty cubits the **l** thereof, and twenty 753
Job 12:12 *is* wisdom; and *in* **l** of days understanding. 753
Ps 21: 4 *it* him, *even* **l** of days for ever and ever. 753
Pr 3: 2 For **l** of days, and long life, and peace, 753
 3:16 **L** of days *is* in her right hand; and in her 753
 29:21 shall have him become *his* son at the **l**. 319
Eze 31: 7 in his greatness, in the **l** of his branches: 753
 40:11 *and* the **l** of the gate, thirteen cubits. 753
 40:18 the **l** of the gates *was* the lower pavement. 753
 40:20 he measured the **l** thereof, and the breadth 753
 40:21 the **l** thereof *was* fifty cubits, and the 753
 40:25 the **l** *was* fifty cubits, and the breadth five 753
 40:36 the **l** *was* fifty cubits, and the breadth five 753
 40:49 The **l** of the porch *was* twenty cubits, 753
 41: 2 he measured the **l** thereof, forty cubits: 753
 41: 4 he measured the **l** thereof, twenty cubits; 753
 41:12 about, and the **l** thereof ninety cubits. 753
 41:15 he measured the **l** of the building over 753
 41:22 cubits high, and the **l** thereof two cubits; 753
 41:22 the **l** thereof, and the walls thereof, *were* 753
 42: 2 Before the **l** of an hundred cubits *was* 753
 42: 7 the chambers, the **l** thereof *was* fifty cubits. 753
 42: 8 For the **l** of the chambers that *were* in 753
 45: 1 the **l** *shall be* the length *of* five and 753
 45: 1 the length *shall be* the **l** *of* five and 753
 45: 2 **l**, with five hundred *in* breadth, square NIH
 45: 3 of this measure shalt thou measure the **l** of 753
 45: 5 five and twenty thousand of **l**, and *the* ten 753
 45: 7 the **l** *shall be* over against one of 753
 48: 8 breadth, and *in* **l** as one of the *other* parts, 753
 48: 9 *shall be of* five and twenty thousand *in* **l**, 753
 48:10 the north five and twenty thousand *in* **l**, NIH
 48:10 the south five and twenty thousand *in* **l**, 753
 48:13 *shall have* five and twenty thousand *in* **l**, 753
 48:13 all the **l** *shall be* five and twenty thousand, 753
 48:18 the residue in **l** over against the oblation of 753
Zec 2: 2 breadth thereof, and what *is* the **l** thereof. 753

Zec 5: 2 the **l** thereof *is* twenty cubits, and the 753
Ro 1:10 if by any means now **at l** I might have a 4218
Eph 3:18 the breadth, and **l**, and depth, and height; 3372
Rev 21:16 the **l** is as large as the breadth. 3372
 21:16 The **l** and the breadth and the height of it 3372

LENGTHEN (2) [LENGTH]

1Ki 3:14 David did walk, then I will **l** thy days. 748
Isa 54: 2 **l** thy cords, and strengthen thy stakes; 748

LENGTHENED (1) [LENGTH]

Dt 25:15 that thy days may be **l** in the land which 748

LENGTHENING (1) [LENGTH]

Da 4:27 the poor; if it may be a **l** of thy tranquillity. 754

LENT (7) [LEND]

Ex 12:36 that they **l** unto them *such* things as they 7592
Dt 23:19 usury of any thing that is **l** **upon usury**: 5391
1Sa 1:28 Therefore also I have **l** him to the LORD; 7592
 1:28 as long as he liveth he *shall be* **l** to 7592
 2:20 for the loan which is **l** to the LORD. 7592
Jer 15:10 I have neither **l** **on usury**, nor *men* have 5383
 15:10 usury, nor *men* have **l** to me **on usury**; 5383

LENTILES (4)

Ge 25:34 Jacob gave Esau bread and pottage of **l**; 5742
2Sa 17:28 and beans, and **l**, and parched *pulse*, 5742
 23:11 where was a piece of ground full of **l**: 5742
Eze 4: 9 **l**, and millet, and fitches, and put them in 5742

LENTILS See LENTILES

LEOPARD (6) [LEOPARDS]

Isa 11: 6 and the **l** shall lie down with the kid; 5246
Jer 5: 6 them, a **l** shall watch over their cities: 5246
 13:23 change his skin, or the **l** his spots? 5246
Da 7: 6 this I beheld, and lo another, like a **l**, 5245
Hos 13: 7 as a **l** by the way will I observe *them*: 5246
Rev 13: 2 the beast which I saw was like unto a **l**, 3917

LEOPARDS (2) [LEOPARD]

SS 4: 8 lions' dens, from the mountains of the **l**. 5246
Hab 1: 8 Their horses also are swifter than the **l**, 5246

LEPER (17) [LEPROSY]

Lev 13:45 the **l** in whom the plague *is*, his clothes 6879
 14: 2 This shall be the law of the **l** in the day of 6879
 14: 3 *if* the plague of leprosy be healed in the **l**; 6879
 22: 4 man soever of the seed of Aaron *is* a **l**, 6879
Nu 5: 2 that they put out of the camp every **l**, 6879
2Sa 3:29 or that **l**, or that leaneth on a staff, 6879
2Ki 5: 1 a mighty *man* in valour, *but he was* a **l**. 6879
 5:11 hand over the place, and recover the **l**. 6879
 5:27 he went out from his presence a **l** *as* 6879
 15: 5 that he was a **l** unto the day of his death, 6879
2Ch 26:21 Uzziah the king was a **l** unto the day of 6879
 26:21 and dwelt *in* a several house, *being* a **l**; 6879
 26:23 to the kings; for they said, He *is* a **l**: 6879
Mt 8: 2 came a **l** and worshipped him, saying, 3015
 26: 6 in Bethany, in the house of Simon the **l**, 3015
Mk 1:40 there came a **l** to him, beseeching him, 3015
 14: 3 in Bethany in the house of Simon the **l**, 3015

LEPERS (7) [LEPROSY]

2Ki 7: 8 when these **l** came to the uttermost part 6879
Mt 10: 8 Heal the sick, cleanse the **l**, raise the dead, 3015
 11: 5 the **l** are cleansed, and the deaf hear, 3015
Lk 4:27 And many **l** were in Israel in the time of 3015
 7:22 walk, the **l** are cleansed, the deaf hear, 3015
 17:12 there met him ten men that were **l**, 3015

LEPROSY (39) [LEPER, LEPERS, LEPROUS]

Lev 13: 2 in the skin of his flesh like the plague of **l**; 6883
 13: 3 the skin of his flesh, it *is* a plague of **l**: 6883
 13: 8 shall pronounce him unclean: it *is* a **l**. 6883
 13: 9 When the plague of **l** is in a man, then 6883
 13:11 It *is* an old **l** in the skin of his flesh, 6883
 13:12 if a **l** break out abroad in the skin, 6883
 13:12 the **l** cover all the skin of *him that hath* 6883
 13:13 behold, *if* the **l** have covered all his flesh, 6883
 13:15 *for* the raw flesh is unclean: it *is* a **l**. 6883
 13:20 it *is* a plague of **l** broken out of the boil. 6883
 13:25 skin; it *is* a **l** broken out of the burning: 6883
 13:25 him unclean: it *is* the plague of **l**. 6883
 13:27 him unclean: it *is* the plague of **l**. 6883
 13:30 scall, *even* a **l** upon the head or beard. 6883
 13:42 it *is* a **l** sprung up in his bald head, or his 6883
 13:43 as the **l** appeareth in the skin of the flesh; 6883
 13:47 The garment also that the plague of **l** is in, 6883
 13:49 it *is* a plague of **l**, and shall be shewed 6883
 13:51 the plague *is* a fretting **l**; it *is* unclean. 6883
 13:52 for it *is* a fretting **l**; it shall be burnt in 6883
 13:59 This *is* the law of the plague of **l** in a 6883
 14: 3 *if* the plague of **l** be healed in the leper; 6883
 14: 7 is to be cleansed from the **l** seven times, 6883
 14:32 law *of* him in whom *is* the plague of **l**, 6883
 14:34 put the plague of **l** in a house of the land 6883
 14:44 the house, it *is* a fretting **l** in the house: 6883
 14:54 *is* the law for all manner *of* plague of **l**, 6883
 14:55 for the **l** of a garment, and of a house, 6883
 14:57 and when it *is* clean: this *is* the law of **l**. 6883
Dt 24: 8 Take heed in the plague of **l**, that *thou* 6883
2Ki 5: 3 for he would recover him of his **l**. 6883
 5: 6 that thou mayest recover him of his **l**. 6883
 5: 7 send unto me to recover a man of his **l**? 6883

2Ki 5:27 The **l** therefore of Naaman shall cleave 6883
2Ch 26:19 the **l** even rose up in his forehead before 6883
Mt 8: 3 And immediately his **l** was cleansed. 3014
Mk 1:42 immediately the **l** departed from him, 3014
Lk 5:12 in a certain city, behold a man full of **l**: 3014
 5:13 immediately the **l** departed from him. 3014

LEPROUS (6) [LEPROSY]

Ex 4: 6 it out, behold, his hand *was* **l** as snow. 6879
Lev 13:44 He *is* a **l** man, he *is* unclean: the priest 6879
Nu 12:10 Miriam *became* **l**, *white* as snow: 6879
 12:10 upon Miriam, and, behold, *she was* **l**. 6879
2Ki 7: 3 there were four **l** men *at* the entering in 6879
2Ch 26:20 he *was* **l** in his forehead, and they thrust 6879

LESHEM (2) [DAN]

Jos 19:47 of Dan went up to fight against **L**, 3959
 19:47 and dwelt therein, and called **L**, Dan, 3959

LESS (27) [LEAST, LESSER]

Ex 16:17 did so, and gathered, some more, some **l**. 4591
 30:15 poor shall not **give** **l** than half a shekel, 4591
Nu 22:18 of the LORD my God, to do **l** or more. 6996
 26:54 to few thou shalt **give** the **l** inheritance: 4591
 33:54 the fewer ye shall **give** the **l** inheritance: 4591
1Sa 22:15 knew nothing of all this, **l** or more. 6996
 25:36 **l** or more, until the morning light. 6996
1Ki 8:27 **how much l** this house that I have 637+3588
2Ch 6:18 **how much l** this house which I 637+3588
 32:15 **how much l** shall your God 637+3588+3808
Ezr 9:13 that thou our God hast punished us **l** 4295
Job 4:19 **How much l** in them that dwell in houses 637
 9:14 **How much l** shall I answer him, 637+3588
 11: 6 that God exacteth of thee **l** than thine NIH
 25: 6 **How much l** man, *that is* a worm? 637+3588
 34:19 *How much l* to him that accepteth not NIH
Pr 7: 4 fool: **much l** do lying lips a prince. 637+3588
 19:10 **much l** for a servant to have rule 637+3588
Isa 40:17 they are counted to him **l** than nothing, 4480
Eze 15: 5 **how much l** shall it be meet yet for 637+3588
Mk 4:31 is **l** than all the seeds that be in the earth: 3398
 15:40 and Mary the mother of James the **l** and 3398
1Co 12:23 which we think to be **l** **honourable**, 820
2Co 12:15 abundantly I love you, the **l** I be loved. 2276
Eph 3: 8 *who am* I than the least of all saints, NIG
Php 2:28 and *that* I may be the **l** **sorrowful**. 253
Heb 7: 7 And without all contradiction the **l** is 1640

LESSER (3) [LESS]

Ge 1:16 the day, and the **l** light to rule the night: 6996
Isa 7:25 of oxen, and for the treading of **l** **cattle**. 7716
Eze 43:14 from the **l** settle *even* to the greater settle 6996

LEST (240)

Ge 3: 3 eat of it, neither shall ye touch it, **l** ye die. 6435
 3:22 he put forth his hand, and take also of 6435
 4:15 **l** any finding him should kill him. 1115+3807.1
 11: 4 **l** we be scattered abroad upon the face of 6435
 14:23 **l** thou shouldest say, I have made 3808+2050.1
 19:15 **l** thou be consumed in the iniquity of 6435
 19:17 to the mountain, **l** thou be consumed. 6435
 19:19 *some* evil take me, and I die: 6435
 26: 7 *said he*, the men of the place should kill 6435
 32: 9 unto him, Because I said, **L** I die for her. 6435
 32:11 he will come and smite me, 6435
 38: 9 **l** *that* he should give seed to his 1115+3807.1
 38:11 for he said, **L** **peradventure** he die also, 6435
 38:23 Let her take *it* to her, **l** we be shamed: 6435
 42: 4 **L** **peradventure** mischief befall him. 6435
 44:34 **l** **peradventure** I see the evil that shall 6435
 45:11 **l** thou, and thy household, and all that 6435
Ex 1:10 **l** they multiply, and it come to pass, that, 6435
 5: 3 **l** he fall upon us with pestilence, or with 6435
 13:17 **L** **peradventure** the people repent when 6435
 19:21 **l** they break through unto the LORD to 6435
 19:22 **l** the LORD break forth upon them. 6435
 19:24 the LORD, **l** he break forth upon them. 6435
 20:19 but let not God speak with us, **l** we die. 6435
 23:29 the land become desolate, and the beast 6435
 23:33 thy land, **l** they make thee sin against me: 6435
 33: 3 I I consume thee in the way. 6435
 34:12 **l** thou make a covenant with the 6435
 34:12 I it be for a snare in the midst of thee: 6435
 34:15 **L** thou make a covenant with 6435
Lev 10: 6 **l** you die, and lest wrath come 3808+2050.1
 10: 6 and I wrath come upon all the people: NIH
 10: 7 tabernacle of the congregation, **l** you die: 6435
 10: 9 of the congregation, **l** ye die: 3808+2050.1
 19:29 **l** the land fall to whoredom, 3808+2050.1
 22: 9 **l** they bear sin for it, 3808+2050.1
Nu 4:15 shall not touch *any* holy *thing*, **l** they 2050.1
 4:20 the holy *things* are covered, **l** they die. 2050.1
 16:26 theirs, **l** ye be consumed in all their sins. 6435
 16:34 they said, **L** the earth swallow us up *also*. 6435
 18:22 the congregation, **l** they bear sin, and die. NIH
 18:32 of the children of Israel, **l** ye die. 3808+2050.1
 20:18 **l** I come out against thee with the sword. 6435
Dt 1:42 **l** ye be smitten before your 3808+2050.1
 4: 9 **l** thou forget the things which thine eyes 6435
 4: 9 **l** they depart from thy heart all the days of 6435
 4:16 **L** ye corrupt *yourselves*, and make you a 6435
 4:19 **l** thou lift up thine eyes unto heaven, 6435
 4:23 **l** ye forget the covenant of the LORD your 6435
 6:12 *Then* beware **l** thou forget the LORD, 6435
 6:15 the anger of the LORD thy God be 6435

Dt	7:22 I the beasts of the field increase upon thee.	6435
	7:25 take *it* unto thee, I thou be snared therein:	6435
	7:26 I thou be a cursed thing like it:	2050.1
	8:12 L *when* thou hast eaten and art full,	6435
	9:28 L the land whence thou broughtest us out	6435
	11:17 I *ye* perish quickly from off the good land	NIH
	19: 6 L the avenger of the blood pursue	6435
	20: 5 I he die in the battle, and another man	6435
	20: 6 I he die in the battle, and another man eat	6435
	20: 7 I he die in the battle, and another man	6435
	20: 8 I his brethren's heart faint as well	3808+2050.1
	22: 9 I the fruit of *thy* seed which thou hast	6435
	24:15 I he cry against thee unto	3808+2050.1
	25: 3 I, *if* he should exceed, and beat him	6435
	29:18 L there should be among you man,	6435
	29:18 I there should be among you a root that	6435
	32:27 I their adversaries should behave	6435
	32:27 *and* I they should say, Our hand is high,	6435
Jos	2:16 to the mountain, I the pursuers meet you;	6435
	6:18 I ye make *yourselves* accursed, when ye	6435
	9:20 I wrath be upon us, because of	3808+2050.1
	24:27 a witness unto you, I ye deny your God.	6435
Jdg	7: 2 I Israel vaunt themselves against me,	6435
	14:15 I we burn thee and thy father's house	6435
	18:25 I angry fellows run upon thee, and thou	6435
Ru	4: 6 for myself, I I mar mine own inheritance:	6435
1Sa	9: 5 I my father leave *caring* for the asses,	6435
	13:19 L the Hebrews make *them* swords or	6435
	15: 6 Amalekites, I I destroy you with them:	6435
	20: 3 not Jonathan know this, I he be grieved:	6435
	27:11 saying, L they should tell on us, saying,	6435
	29: 4 I in the battle he be an adversary	3808+2050.1
	31: 4 I these uncircumcised come and thrust me	6435
2Sa	1:20 I the daughters of the Philistines rejoice,	6435
	1:20 I the daughters of the uncircumcised	6435
	12:28 I I take the city, and it be called after my	6435
	13:25 I we be chargeable unto thee.	3808+2050.1
	14:11 any more, I they destroy my son.	3808+2050.1
	15:14 I he overtake us suddenly, and bring evil	6435
	17:16 I the king be swallowed up, and all	6435
	20: 6 I he get him fenced cities, and escape us.	6435
2Ki	2:16 I **peradventure** the spirit of the Lord	6435
1Ch	10: 4 I these uncircumcised come and abuse	6435
Job	32:13 L ye should say, We have found out	6435
	34:30 reign not, I the people be ensnared.	4480
	36:18 I he take thee away with *his* stroke:	6435
	42: 8 I *I* deal with you *after your* folly,	1115+3807.1
Ps	2:12 I he be angry, and ye perish *from* the way,	6435
	7: 2 L he tear my soul like a lion, rending *it* in	6435
	13: 3 mine eyes, I I sleep the *sleep* of death;	6435
	13: 4 L mine enemy say, I have prevailed	6435
	28: 1 I, *if* thou be silent to me, I become like	6435
	32: 9 and bridle, I *they* come near unto thee.	1077
	38:16 *Hear me,* I otherwise they should rejoice	6435
	50:22 I I tear *you* in pieces, and *there be* none	6435
	59:11 Slay them not, I my people forget;	6435
	91:12 I thou dash thy foot against a stone.	6435
	106:23 his wrath, I *he* should destroy *them.*	4480
	125: 3 the lot of the righteous; I	3808+4616+3807.1
	140: 8 wicked device; *I* they exalt themselves.	NIH
	143: 7 I I be like unto them that go	5973+2050.1
Pr	5: 6 L thou shouldest ponder the path of life,	6435
	5: 9 L thou give thine honour unto others,	6435
	5:10 L strangers be filled *with* thy wealth;	6435
	9: 8 Reprove not a scorner, I he hate thee:	6435
	20:13 Love not sleep, I thou come to poverty;	6435
	22:25 L thou learn his ways, and get a snare to	6435
	24:18 L the Lord see *it,* and it displease him,	6435
	25: 8 I *thou know not* what to do in the end	6435
	25:10 L he that heareth *it* put thee to shame,	6435
	25:16 I thou be filled there*with,* and vomit it.	6435
	25:17 I he be weary of thee, and *so* hate thee.	6435
	26: 4 to his folly, I thou also be like unto him.	6435
	26: 5 his folly, I he be wise in his own conceit.	6435
	30: 6 I he reprove thee, and thou be found a liar	6435
	30: 9 L I be full, and deny *thee,* and say, Who	6435
	30: 9 I I be poor, and steal, and take the name	6435
	30:10 I he curse thee, and thou be found guilty.	6435
	31: 5 L they drink, and forget the law,	6435
Ecc	7:21 I thou hear thy servant curse thee:	834+3808
Isa	6:10 I they see with their eyes, and hear with	6435
	27: 3 I *any* hurt it, I will keep it night and day.	6435
	28:22 mockers, I your bands be made strong:	6435
	36:18 *Beware* I Hezekiah persuade you, saying,	6435
	48: 5 I thou shouldest say, Mine idol hath done	6435
	48: 7 I thou shouldest say, Behold, I knew	6435
Jer	1:17 their faces, I I confound thee before them.	6435
	4: 4 I my fury come forth like fire, and burn	6435
	6: 8 O Jerusalem, I my soul depart from thee;	6435
	6: 8 I I make thee desolate, a land not	6435
	10:24 thine anger, I thou bring me to nothing.	6435
	21:12 I my fury go out like fire, and burn that	6435
	37:20 Jonathan the scribe, I I die there.	3808+2050.1
	38:19 I they deliver me into their hand,	6435
	51:46 I your heart faint, and ye fear for	6435
Hos	2: 3 L I strip her naked, and set her as *in* the	6435
Am	5: 6 I he break out like fire *in* the house of	6435
Zec	7:12 I *they* should hear the law, and the words	4480
Mal	4: 6 I I come and smite the earth *with* a curse.	6435
Mt	4: 6 I **at any time** thou dash thy foot against a	3379
	5:25 I **at any time** the adversary deliver thee to	3379
	7: 6 I they trample them under their feet,	3379
	13:15 I **at any time** they should see with *their*	3379
	13:29 I while ye gather up the tares, I ye root up	3379
	15:32 them away fasting, I they faint in the way.	3379

Mt	17:27 Notwithstanding, I we should offend	3363
	25: 9 *No so;* I there be not enough for us and	3363
	26: 5 Not on the feast *day,* I there be an uproar	3363
	27:64 I his disciples come by night, and steal	3363
Mk	3: 9 the multitude, I they should throng him,	3363
	4:12 I **at any time** they should be converted,	3379
	13: 5 to say, Take heed I any *man* deceive you:	3361
	13:36 L coming suddenly he find you sleeping.	3361
	14: 2 Not on the feast *day,* I there be an uproar	3379
	14:38 and pray, I ye enter into temptation.	3363
Lk	4:11 I **at any time** thou dash thy foot against a	3379
	8:12 I they should believe and be saved.	3363
	12:58 I he hale thee to the judge, and the judge	3379
	14: 8 I a more honourable *man* than thou be	3379
	14:12 I they also bid thee again,	3379
	14:29 L haply, after he hath laid the foundation,	3379
	16:28 I they also come into this place of torment.	3363
	18: 5 I by her continual coming she weary me.	3363
	21:34 I **at any time** your hearts be overcharged	3379
	22:46 rise and pray, I ye enter into temptation.	3363
Jn	3:20 the light, I his deeds should be reproved.	3363
	5:14 no more, I a worse thing come unto thee.	3363
	12:35 have the light, I darkness come upon you:	3363
	12:42 the Pharisees they did not confess *him,* I	3363
	18:28 judgment hall, I they should be defiled;	3363
Ac	5:26 people, I they should have been stoned.	3363
	5:39 I haply ye be found even to fight against	3379
	13:40 Beware therefore, I that come upon you,	3361
	23:10 fearing I Paul should have been pulled in	3361
	27:17 fearing I they should fall into	3361
	27:29 fearing I we should have fallen upon	3381
	27:42 I any *of them* should swim out, and	3361
	28:27 I they should see with *their* eyes,	3379
Ro	11:21 *take heed* I he also spare not thee.	3381
	11:25 I ye should be wise in your own conceits;	3363
	15:20 I I should build upon another *man's*	3363
1Co	1:15 L any should say that I had baptized in	3363
	1:17 the cross of Christ should be made of	3363
	8: 9 take heed I **by any means** this liberty	3381
	8:13 I I make my brother to offend.	3363
	9:12 suffer all *things,* I we should hinder	3363
	9:27 I **that by any means,** when I have	3381
	10:12 thinketh he standeth take heed I he fall.	3361
2Co	2: 3 wrote this same unto you, I, when I came,	3363
	2: 7 comfort *him,* I *perhaps* such a one should	3363
	2:11 L Satan should get an advantage of us:	3363
	4: 4 I the light of the glorious	1519+3361+3588
	9: 3 I our boasting of you should be in vain in	3363
	9: 4 L haply if they of Macedonia come with	3381
	11: 3 I fear, I **by any means,** as the serpent	3381
	12: 6 I any *man* should think of me above *that*	3361
	12: 7 And I I should be exalted above measure	3361
	12: 7 I I should be exalted above measure.	3363
	12:20 For I fear, I, when I come, I shall not find	3381
	12:20 I *there be* debates, envyings, wraths,	3381
	12:21 *And* I, when I come again, my God will	3361
	13:10 I being present I should use sharpness,	3363
Gal	2: 2 I **by any means** I should run, or had run,	3381
	4:11 I I have bestowed upon you labour in	3381
	6: 1 I thyself, I thou also be tempted.	3361
	6:12 only I they should suffer persecution for	3363
Eph	2: 9 Not of works, I any *man* should boast.	3363
Php	2:27 I I should have sorrow upon sorrow.	3363
Col	2: 4 I any *man* should beguile you with	3363
	2: 8 Beware I any *man* spoil you through	3361
	3:21 provoke not your children to anger, I they	3363
1Th	3: 5 I **by some means** the tempter have	3381
1Ti	3: 6 I being lifted up with pride he fall into	3363
	3: 7 I he fall into reproach and the snare of	3363
Heb	2: 1 I **at any time** we should let *them* slip.	3379
	3:12 I there be in any of you an evil heart of	3363
	3:13 I any of you be hardened through	3363
	4: 1 Let us therefore fear, I, a promise being	3379
	4:11 I any *man* fall after the same example of	3363
	11:28 I he that destroyed the firstborn should	3363
	12: 3 I ye be wearied and faint in your minds.	3363
	12:13 I *that which is* lame be turned out of	3363
	12:15 Looking diligently I any *man* fail of	3361
	12:15 I any root of bitterness springing up	3361
	12:16 L there *be* any fornicator,	3361
Jas	5: 9 brethren, I ye be condemned:	3363
	5:12 *your* nay, nay; I ye fall into condemnation.	3363
2Pe	3:17 know *these things* before, beware I ye	3363
Rev	16:15 I he walk naked, and they see his shame.	3363

LET (1511) [LETTEST, LETTETH, LETTING]

Ge	1: 3 God said, L there be light: and there was	NIH
	1: 6 L there be a firmament in the midst of	NIH
	1: 6 I it divide the waters from the waters.	NIH
	1: 9 L the waters under the heaven be gathered	NIH
	1: 9 unto one place, and I the dry *land* appear:	NIH
	1:11 God said, L the earth bring forth grass,	NIH
	1:14 L there be lights in the firmament of	NIH
	1:14 and I them be for signs, and for seasons,	NIH
	1:15 I them be for lights in the firmament of	NIH
	1:20 L the waters bring forth abundantly	NIH
	1:22 the seas, and I fowl multiply in the earth.	NIH
	1:24 L the earth bring forth the living creature	NIH
	1:26 God said, L us make man in our image,	NIH
	1:26 I them have dominion over the fish of	NIH
	11: 3 I us make brick, and burn *them*	NIH
	11: 4 Go to, I us build us a city and a tower,	NIH
	11: 4 I us make us a name, lest we be scattered	NIH
	11: 7 I us go down, and there confound their	NIH
	13: 8 L there be no strife, I pray thee, between	NIH

Ge	14:24 and Mamre; I them take their portion.	NIH
	18: 4 L a little water, I pray you, be fetched,	NIH
	18:30 he said *unto him,* Oh I not the Lord be	NIH
	18:32 I not the Lord be angry, and I will speak	NIH
	19: 8 I me, I pray you, bring them out unto you,	NIH
	19:20 Oh, I me escape thither, (*is* it not a little	NIH
	19:32 I us make our father drink wine, and we	NIH
	19:34 I us make him drink wine this night also;	NIH
	21:12 L it not be grievous in thy sight because	NIH
	21:16 L me not see the death of the child.	NIH
	24:14 I it come to pass, *that* the damsel to whom	NIH
	24:14 **L down** thy pitcher, I pray thee, that I	5186
	24:14 I *the same be* she *that* thou hast appointed	NIH
	24:17 to meet her, and said, L me, I pray thee,	NIH
	24:18 I **down** her pitcher upon her hand,	3381
	24:44 I the same *be* the woman whom the Lord	NIH
	24:45 I said unto her, L me drink, I pray thee.	NIH
	24:46 I **down** her pitcher from her *shoulder,*	3381
	24:51 go, and I her be thy master's son's wife,	NIH
	24:55 L the damsel abide with us *a few* days,	NIH
	24:60 I thy seed possess the gate of those which	NIH
	26:28 said, L there be now an oath betwixt us,	NIH
	26:28 and I us make a covenant with thee;	NIH
	27:29 L people serve thee, and nations bow	NIH
	27:29 I thy mother's sons bow down to thee:	NIH
	27:31 L my father arise, and eat of his son's	NIH
	30:26 whom I have served thee, and I me go:	NIH
	31:32 thou findest thy gods, I him not live:	NIH
	31:35 L it not displease my lord that I cannot rise	NIH
	31:44 I us make a covenant, I and thou;	NIH
	31:44 I it be for a witness between me and thee.	NIH
	32:26 he said, L me go, for the day breaketh.	7971
	32:26 he said, I will not I thee **go,** except thou	7971
	33:12 L us take our journey, and let us go,	NIH
	33:12 and I us go, and I will go before thee.	NIH
	33:14 L my lord, I pray thee, pass over before	NIH
	33:15 L me now leave with thee *some* of the	NIH
	33:15 I me find grace in the sight of my lord.	NIH
	34:11 L me find grace in your eyes, and what ye	NIH
	34:21 therefore I them dwell in the land,	NIH
	34:21 I us take their daughters to us for wives,	NIH
	34:21 wives, and I us give them our daughters.	NIH
	34:23 I us consent unto them, and they will	NIH
	35: 3 I us arise, and go up to Beth-el; and I will	NIH
	37:17 for I heard *them* say, L us go to Dothan.	NIH
	37:20 I us slay him, and cast him into some pit,	NIH
	37:21 of their hands; and said, L us not kill him.	NIH
	37:27 I us sell him to the Ishmeelites, and let not	NIH
	37:27 and I not our hand be upon him;	NIH
	38:16 I pray thee, I me come in unto thee;	NIH
	38:23 Judah said, L her take *it* to her, lest we be	NIH
	38:24 Bring her forth, and I her be burnt.	NIH
	41:33 I Pharaoh look out a man discreet and	NIH
	41:34 L Pharaoh do *this,* and let him appoint	NIH
	41:34 and I him appoint officers over the land,	NIH
	41:35 and I them gather all the food of those good	NIH
	41:35 and I them keep food in the cities.	NIH
	42:16 I him fetch your brother, and ye shall be	NIH
	42:19 If ye *be* true *men,* I one of your brethren	NIH
	43: 9 then I me bear the blame for ever:	NIH
	44: 9 both I him die, and we also will be my	NIH
	44:10 also *I* it according unto your words:	NIH
	44:18 said, O my lord, I thy servant, I pray thee,	NIH
	44:18 I not thine anger burn against thy servant:	NIH
	44:33 I thy servant abide instead of the lad a	NIH
	44:33 and I the lad go up with his brethren.	NIH
	46:30 Now I me die, since I have seen thy face,	NIH
	47: 4 I thy servants dwell in the land of Goshen.	NIH
	47: 6 in the land of Goshen I them dwell:	NIH
	47:25 I us find grace in the sight of my lord,	NIH
	48:16 I my name be named on them, and the	NIH
	48:16 I them grow into a multitude in the midst	NIH
	49:21 Naphtali *is* a hind I **loose:** he giveth	7971
	50: 5 Now therefore I me go up, I pray thee,	NIH
Ex	1:10 Come on, I us deal wisely with them;	NIH
	3:18 now I us go, we beseech thee, three days'	NIH
	3:19 I am sure that the king of Egypt will not I	5414
	3:20 and after that he will I you **go.**	7971
	4:18 L me go, I pray thee, and return unto my	NIH
	4:21 heart, that he shall not I the people **go.**	7971
	4:23 I say unto thee, L my son **go,** that he may	7971
	4:23 *if* thou refuse to I him **go,** behold, I will	7971
	4:26 So he I him **go:** then she said, A bloody	7503
	5: 1 the Lord God of Israel, L my people **go,**	7971
	5: 2 that I should obey his voice to I Israel **go?**	7971
	5: 2 not the Lord, neither will I I Israel **go.**	7971
	5: 3 I us go, we pray thee, three days' journey	NIH
	5: 4 Aaron, I the people from their works?	6544
	5: 7 I them go and gather straw for themselves.	NIH
	5: 8 L us go *and* sacrifice to our God.	NIH
	5: 9 L there more work be laid upon the men,	NIH
	5: 9 and I them not regard vain words.	NIH
	5:17 L us go *and* do sacrifice to the Lord.	NIH
	6: 1 for with a strong hand shall he I them **go,**	7971
	6:11 he I the children of Israel **go** out of his	7971
	7:14 hardened, he refuseth to I the people **go.**	7971
	7:16 saying, L my people **go,** that they may	7971
	8: 1 Thus saith the Lord, L my people **go,**	7971
	8: 2 if thou refuse to I *them* **go,** behold, I will	7971
	8: 8 I will I the people **go,** that they may do	7971
	8:20 Thus saith the Lord, L my people **go,**	7971
	8:21 Else, if thou wilt not I my people **go,**	7971
	8:28 Pharaoh said, I will I you **go,** that ye may	7971
	8:29 I not Pharaoh deal deceitfully any more in	NIH
	8:32 also, neither would he I the people **go.**	7971

L

Ex	9: 1	**L** my people **go**, that they may serve me.	7971
	9: 2	For if thou refuse to **l** *them* **go**, and wilt	7971
	9: 7	and he did not **l** the people **go**.	7971
	9: 8	**l** Moses sprinkle it towards the heaven in	NIH
	9:13	**L** my people **go**, that they may serve me.	7971
	9:17	my people, that *thou* wilt not **l** them **go**?	7971
	9:28	will **l** you **go**, and ye shall stay no longer.	7971
	9:35	would he **l** the children of Israel **go**;	7971
	10: 3	**l** my people **go**, that they may serve me.	7971
	10: 4	Else, if thou refuse to **l** my people **go**,	7971
	10: 7	**l** the men **go**, that they may serve	7971
	10:10	**L** the LORD be so with you, as I will let	NIH
	10:10	as I will **l** you **go**, and your little ones:	7971
	10:20	he would not **l** the children of Israel **go**.	7971
	10:24	**l** your flocks and your herds be stayed:	NIH
	10:24	**l** your little ones also go with you.	7971
	10:27	and he would not **l** them **go**.	7971
	11: 1	afterwards he will **l** you **go** hence:	NIH
	11: 1	when he shall **l** *you* **go**, he shall surely	7971
	11: 2	**l** every man borrow of his neighbour,	NIH
	11:10	he would not **l** the children of Israel **go**	7971
	12: 4	**l** him and his neighbour next unto his	NIH
	12:10	ye shall **l** nothing of it remain until	NIH
	12:48	**l** all his males be circumcised, and then	NIH
	12:48	and then **l** him come near and keep it;	NIH
	13:15	when Pharaoh would hardly **l** us **go**,	7971
	13:17	pass, when Pharaoh had **l** the people **go**,	7971
	14: 5	that we have **l** Israel **go** from serving us?	7971
	14:12	saying, **L** us alone, that we may serve	NIH
	14:25	**L** us flee from the face of Israel;	NIH
	16:19	**L** no man leave of it till the morning.	NIH
	16:29	**l** no man go out of his place on the	NIH
	17:11	when he **l** **down** his hand,	5117
	18:22	**l** them judge the people at all seasons:	NIH
	18:27	Moses **l** his father in law depart;	NIH
	19:10	to morrow, and **l** them wash their clothes,	NIH
	19:22	the priests also, which come near to	NIH
	19:24	**l** not the priests and the people break	NIH
	20:19	but **l** not God speak with us, lest we die.	NIH
	21: 8	himself, then shall he **l** her be redeemed:	NIH
	21:26	he shall **l** him **go** free for his eye's sake.	7971
	21:27	he shall **l** him **go** free for his tooth's sake.	7971
	22: 7	if the thief be found, **l** him pay double.	NIH
	22:13	*then* **l** him bring it *for* witness, *and* he	NIH
	23:11	the seventh *year* thou shalt **l** it rest and	NIH
	23:13	neither **l** it be heard out of thy mouth.	NIH
	24:14	any matters to do, **l** him come unto them.	NIH
	25: 8	**l** them make me a sanctuary; that I may	NIH
	32:10	Now therefore **l** me **alone**, that my wrath	3240
	32:22	**L** not the anger of my lord wax hot:	NIH
	32:24	hath *any* gold, **l** them break *it* off.	NIH
	32:26	*l* him *come* unto me. And all the sons of	NIH
	33:12	thou hast not **l** me know whom thou wilt	NIH
	34: 3	neither **l** any man be seen throughout all	NIH
	34: 3	neither **l** the flocks nor herds feed before	NIH
	34: 9	O Lord, **l** my Lord, I pray thee, go amongst	NIH
	35: 5	**l** him bring it, an offering of the LORD;	NIH
	36: 6	**L** neither man nor woman make any more	NIH
Lev	1: 3	**l** him offer a male without blemish:	NIH
	4: 3	**l** him bring for his sin, which he hath	NIH
	10: 6	**l** your brethren, the whole house of Israel,	NIH
	14: 7	shall **l** the living bird **loose** into the open	7971
	14:53	he shall **l** **go** the living bird out of the city	7971
	16:10	to **l** him **go** for a scapegoat into	7971
	16:22	he shall **l** **go** the goat in the wilderness.	7971
	16:26	he that **l** **go** the goat for the scapegoat	7971
	18:21	thou shalt not **l** *any* of thy seed	5414+3807.1
	19:19	Thou shalt not **l** thy cattle gender with a	NIH
	21:17	**l** him not approach to offer the bread of	NIH
	24:14	**l** all that heard *him* lay their hands upon	NIH
	24:14	and **l** all the congregation stone him.	NIH
	25:27	**l** him count the years of the sale thereof,	NIH
Nu	5: 8	*l* the trespass *be* recompensed unto	NIH
	6: 5	**l** the locks of the hair of his head grow.	NIH
	8: 7	**l** them shave all their flesh, and let them	NIH
	8: 7	**l** them wash their clothes, and *so*	NIH
	8: 8	**l** them take a young bullock with his meat	NIH
	9: 2	**L** the children of Israel also keep	NIH
	10:35	LORD, and **l** thine enemies be scattered;	NIH
	10:35	and **l** them that hate thee flee before thee.	NIH
	11:15	and **l** me not see my wretchedness.	NIH
	11:31	from the sea, and **l** *them* fall by the camp,	NIH
	12:12	**L** her not be as one dead, of whom the	4994
	12:14	**l** her be shut out from the camp seven	NIH
	12:14	and after *that* **l** her be received in *again*.	NIH
	13:30	said, **L** us go up at once, and possess it;	NIH
	14: 4	**L** us make a captain, and let us return into	NIH
	14: 4	a captain, and **l** us return into Egypt.	NIH
	14:17	the power of my Lord be great,	NIH
	16:38	them make broad plates *for* a	NIH
	20:17	**L** us pass, I pray thee, through thy country	NIH
	21:22	**L** me pass through thy land: we will not	NIH
	21:27	the city of Sihon be built and prepared:	NIH
	22:16	**L** nothing, I pray thee, hinder thee from	NIH
	23:10	**L** me die the death of the righteous,	NIH
	23:10	righteous, and *l* my last end be like his!	NIH
	27:16	**L** the LORD, the God of the spirits of all	NIH
	31: 3	**l** them go against the Midianites,	NIH
	32: 5	**l** this land be given unto thy servants for a	NIH
	33:55	*that those* which ye **l** remain of them	NIH
	36: 6	**L** them marry to whom they think best;	NIH
Dt	2:27	**L** me pass through thy land: I will go	NIH
	2:30	king of Heshbon would not **l** us pass	NIH
	3:25	**l** me go over, and see the good land that	NIH
	3:26	the LORD said unto me, **L** it suffice thee;	NIH

Dt	9:14	**L** me **alone**, that I may destroy them,	7503
	13: 2	**L** us go after other gods, which thou	NIH
	13: 2	thou hast not known, and **l** us serve them;	NIH
	13: 6	**L** us go and serve other gods,	NIH
	13:13	saying, **L** us go and serve other gods,	NIH
	15:12	the seventh year thou shalt **l** him **go** free	7971
	15:13	thou shalt not **l** him **go away** empty:	7971
	18:16	**L** me not hear again the voice of	NIH
	18:16	neither **l** me see this great fire any more,	NIH
	20: 3	**l** not your hearts faint, fear not, and do	NIH
	20: 5	**l** him go and return to his house, lest he	NIH
	20: 6	**l** him *also* go and return unto his house,	NIH
	20: 7	**l** him go and return unto his house, lest	NIH
	20: 8	**l** him go and return unto his house, lest	NIH
	21:14	then thou shalt **l** her **go** whither she will;	7971
	22: 7	shalt **in any wise l** the dam **go**,	7971+7971
	24: 1	**l** him write her a bill of divorcement,	NIH
	25: 7	**l** his brother's wife go up to the gate unto	NIH
	32:38	**l** them rise up and help you, *and* be your	NIH
	33: 6	**L** Reuben live, and not die; and let *not* his	NIH
	33: 6	and not die; and **l** *not* his men be few.	NIH
	33: 7	**l** his hands *be* sufficient for him;	NIH
	33: 8	*L* thy Thummim and thy Urim *be* with thy	NIH
	33:16	**l** *the blessing* come upon the head of	NIH
	33:24	he said, *L* Asher *be* blessed with children;	NIH
	33:24	**l** him be acceptable to his brethren,	NIH
	33:24	and **l** him dip his foot in oil.	NIH
Jos	2:15	she **l** them **down** by a cord through	NIH
	2:18	window which thou didst **l** us **down** by:	3381
	4:22	ye shall **l** your children know, saying,	NIH
	6: 6	**l** seven priests bear seven trumpets of	NIH
	6: 7	**l** him that is armed pass on before the ark	NIH
	7: 3	said unto him, **L** not all the people go up;	NIH
	7: 3	**l** about two or three thousand men go up	NIH
	8:22	so that *they* **l** none of them remain or	7604
	9:15	made a league with them, to **l** them live:	NIH
	9:20	we will even **l** them live, lest wrath be	NIH
	9:21	the princes said unto them, **L** them live;	NIH
	9:21	**l** them be hewers of wood and drawers of	NIH
	10:28	souls that *were* therein; he **l** none remain:	7604
	10:30	he **l** none remain in it; but did unto the	7604
	22:23	**l** the LORD himself require *it*;	NIH
	22:26	**L** us now prepare to build us an altar,	NIH
	24:28	So Joshua **l** the people **depart**, every man	7971
Jdg	1:25	but they **l** **go** the man and all his family.	7971
	2: 6	when Joshua had **l** the people **go**,	7971
	5:31	So **l** all thine enemies perish, O LORD:	NIH
	5:31	*l* them that love him *be* as the sun when	NIH
	6:31	**l** him be put to death whilst *it is* yet	NIH
	6:31	**l** him plead for himself, because *one* hath	NIH
	6:32	saying, **L** Baal plead against him, because	NIH
	6:39	**L** not thine anger be hot against me,	NIH
	6:39	**l** me prove, I pray thee, but *this* once with	NIH
	6:39	**l** it now be dry only upon the fleece,	NIH
	6:39	upon all the ground **l** there be dew.	NIH
	7: 3	him return and depart early from mount	NIH
	7: 7	**l** all the *other* people go every man unto	NIH
	9:15	fire come out of the bramble,	NIH
	9:19	Abimelech, and **l** him also rejoice in you:	NIH
	9:20	**l** fire come out from Abimelech,	NIH
	9:20	**l** fire come out from the men of Shechem,	NIH
	10:14	**l** them deliver you in the time of your	NIH
	11:17	**L** me, I pray thee, pass through thy	NIH
	11:19	said unto him, **L** us pass, we pray thee,	NIH
	11:37	her father, **L** this thing be done for me:	NIH
	11:37	**l** me **alone** two months, that I may go up	7503
	12: 5	which were escaped said, **L** me go over;	NIH
	13: 8	the man of God which thou didst send	4994
	13:12	Now **l** thy words come to pass.	NIH
	13:13	Of all that I said unto the woman **l** her	NIH
	13:14	neither **l** her drink wine or strong drink,	NIH
	13:14	all that I commanded her **l** her observe.	NIH
	13:15	I pray thee, **l** us detain thee, until we shall	NIH
	15: 5	he **l** *them* **go** into the standing corn of	7971
	16:30	Samson said, **L** me die with the Philistines.	NIH
	18:25	**L** not thy voice be heard among us,	NIH
	19: 6	tarry all night, and **l** thine heart be merry.	NIH
	19:11	**l** us turn in into this city of the Jebusites,	NIH
	19:13	**l** us draw near to one of *these* places to	NIH
	19:20	howsoever *l* all thy wants *lie* upon me;	NIH
	19:25	the day began to spring, they **l** her **go**.	7971
	19:28	he said unto her, Up, and **l** us be going.	NIH
	20:32	**L** us flee, and draw them from the city	NIH
Ru	2: 2	**L** me now go *to* the field, and glean ears	NIH
	2: 7	**l** me glean and gather after the reapers	NIH
	2: 9	*L* thine eyes *be* on the field that they do	NIH
	2:13	**L** me find favour in thy sight, my lord;	NIH
	2:15	**l** her glean even among the sheaves,	NIH
	2:16	**l** *fall* also *some* of the	NIH
		handfuls **of purpose**	7997+7997
	3:13	well; **l** him do the kinsman's part:	NIH
	3:14	**L** it not be known that a woman came	NIH
	4:12	**l** thy house be like the house of Pharez,	NIH
1Sa	1:18	**L** thine handmaid find grace in thy sight.	NIH
	2: 3	*l* not arrogancy come out of your mouth:	NIH
	2:16	**L** them not fail to burn the fat presently,	NIH
	3:18	**l** him do what seemeth him good.	NIH
	3:19	did **l** none of his words fall to the ground.	NIH
	4: 3	**L** us fetch the ark of the covenant of	NIH
	5: 8	**L** the ark of the God of Israel be carried	NIH
	5:11	**l** it go again to his own place, that it slay	NIH
	6: 6	did they not **l** the people **go**,	7971
	9: 5	that *was* with him, Come, and **l** us return;	NIH
	9: 6	now **l** us go thither; peradventure he can	NIH
	9: 9	he spake, Come, and **l** us go to the seer:	NIH

1Sa	9:10	to his servant, Well said; come, **l** us go.	NIH
	9:19	to morrow I will **l** thee go, and will tell	7971
	10: 7	**l** it be, when these signs are come unto	NIH
	11:14	**l** us go *to* Gilgal, and renew the kingdom	NIH
	13: 3	all the land, saying, **L** the Hebrews hear.	NIH
	14: 1	**l** us go over to the Philistines' garrison,	NIH
	14: 6	**l** us go over unto the garrison of these	NIH
	14:36	**L** us go down after the Philistines by night,	NIH
	14:36	and **l** us not leave a man of them.	NIH
	14:36	priest, **L** us draw near hither unto God.	NIH
	16:16	**L** our lord now command thy servants	NIH
	16:22	saying, **L** David, I pray thee, stand before	NIH
	17: 8	man for you, and **l** him come down to me.	NIH
	17:32	**L** no man's heart fail because of him;	NIH
	18: 2	would **l** him go no more home *to* his	5414
	18:17	**L** not mine hand be upon him, but let	NIH
	18:17	the hand of the Philistines be upon him.	NIH
	19: 4	**L** not the king sin against his servant,	NIH
	19:12	So Michal **l** David **down** through a	3381
	19:17	answered Saul, He said unto me, **L** me **go**;	7971
	20: 3	he saith, **L** not Jonathan know this, lest he	NIH
	20: 5	**l** me **go**, that I may hide myself in the	7971
	20:11	Come, and **l** us go out *into* the field.	NIH
	20:16	saying, **L** the LORD even require *it* at	NIH
	20:29	he said, **L** me **go**, I pray thee; for our	7971
	20:29	**l** me get away, I pray thee, and see my	NIH
	21: 2	**L** no man know any thing of the business	NIH
	21:13	and **l** his spittle **fall down** upon his beard.	3381
	22: 3	**L** my father and my mother, I pray thee,	NIH
	22:15	**l** not the king impute *any* thing unto his	NIH
	24:19	his enemy, will he **l** him **go** well away?	7971
	25: 8	Wherefore **l** the young men find favour in	NIH
	25:24	*upon* me **l** *this* iniquity *be:* and let thine	NIH
	25:24	*let this* iniquity *be:* and **l** thine handmaid,	NIH
	25:25	**L** not my lord, I pray thee, regard this man	NIH
	25:26	**l** thine enemies, and they that seek evil	NIH
	25:27	**l** it even be given unto the young men	NIH
	25:41	*l* thine handmaid *be* a servant to wash	NIH
	26: 8	now therefore **l** me smite him, I pray thee,	NIH
	26:11	and the cruse of water, and **l** us go.	NIH
	26:19	**l** my lord the king hear the words of his	NIH
	26:19	against me, **l** him accept an offering:	NIH
	26:20	**l** not my blood fall to the earth before	NIH
	26:22	one of the young men come over and	NIH
	26:24	**l** my life be much set by in the eyes of	NIH
	26:24	and **l** him deliver me out of all tribulation.	NIH
	27: 5	**l** them give me a place in some town in	NIH
	28:22	**l** me set a morsel of bread before thee;	NIH
	29: 4	**l** him not go down with us to battle,	NIH
2Sa	1:21	mountains of Gilboa, *l* there *be* no dew,	NIH
	1:21	no dew, neither *l* there *be* rain upon you,	NIH
	2: 7	Therefore now **l** your hands be	NIH
	2:14	the young men now arise, and play	NIH
	2:14	before us. And Joab said, **L** them arise.	NIH
	3:29	**L** it rest on the head of Joab, and on all his	NIH
	3:29	**l** there not fail from the house of Joab one	NIH
	5:24	**l** it be, when thou hearest the sound of a	NIH
	7:26	thy name be magnified for ever, saying,	NIH
	7:26	the house of thy servant David be	NIH
	7:29	Therefore now **l** it please thee to bless	NIH
	7:29	thy blessing **l** the house of thy servant	NIH
	10:12	**l** us play the men for our people, and for	NIH
	11:12	and to morrow I will **l** thee depart.	NIH
	11:25	unto Joab, **L** not this thing displease thee,	NIH
	13: 5	**L** my sister Tamar come, and give me meat,	NIH
	13: 6	**l** Tamar my sister come, and make me *a*	NIH
	13:24	the king, I beseech thee, and his servants	NIH
	13:25	Nay, my son, **l** us not all now go,	NIH
	13:26	pray thee, **l** my brother Amnon go with us.	NIH
	13:27	he **l** Amnon and all the king's sons **go**	7971
	13:32	**L** not my lord suppose *that* they have slain	NIH
	13:33	**l** not my lord the king take the thing to his	NIH
	14:11	**l** the king remember the LORD thy God,	NIH
	14:12	said, **L** thine handmaid, I pray thee,	NIH
	14:18	said, **L** my lord the king now speak.	NIH
	14:24	**L** him turn to his own house, and let him	NIH
	14:24	his own house, and **l** him not see my face.	NIH
	14:32	now therefore **l** me see the king's face;	NIH
	14:32	there be *any* iniquity in me, **l** him kill me.	NIH
	15: 7	I pray thee, **l** me go and pay my vow,	NIH
	15:14	with him at Jerusalem, Arise, and **l** us flee;	NIH
	15:26	**l** him do to me as seemeth good unto him.	NIH
	16: 9	**l** me go over, I pray thee, and take off his	NIH
	16:10	so **l** him curse, because the LORD hath	NIH
	16:11	*may this* Benjamite do it? **l** him **alone**,	3240
	16:11	*do it?* let him alone, and **l** him curse;	NIH
	17: 1	**L** me now choose out twelve thousand	NIH
	17: 5	and **l** us hear likewise what he saith.	NIH
	18:19	**L** me now run, and bear the king tidings,	NIH
	18:22	howsoever, **l** me, I pray thee, also run after	NIH
	18:23	howsoever, *said he*, **l** me run. And he said	NIH
	19:19	**L** not my lord impute iniquity unto me,	NIH
	19:30	said unto the king, Yea, **l** him take all,	NIH
	19:37	**L** thy servant, I pray thee, turn back again,	NIH
	19:37	**l** him go over with my lord the king,	NIH
	20:11	he that *is* for David, *l* him **go** after Joab.	NIH
	21: 6	**L** seven men of his sons be delivered unto	NIH
	24:14	**l** us fall now into the hand of the LORD;	NIH
	24:14	and **l** me not fall into the hand of man.	NIH
	24:17	I have sinned, I pray thee, be against me,	NIH
	24:22	**L** my lord the king take and offer up what	NIH
1Ki	1: 2	**L** there be sought for my lord the king a	NIH
	1: 2	**l** her stand before the king, and let her	NIH
	1: 2	**l** her cherish him, and let her lie in thy	NIH
	1: 2	cherish him, and **l** her lie in thy bosom,	NIH

1Ki

1:12 Now therefore come, I me, I pray thee,	NIH
1:31 said, L my lord king David live for ever.	NIH
1:34 I Zadok the priest and Nathan the prophet	NIH
1:51 L king Solomon swear unto me to day	NIH
2: 6 I not his hoar head go down to the grave	NIH
2: 7 I them be of those that eat at thy table:	NIH
2:21 L Abishag the Shunammite be given to	NIH
3:26 L it be neither mine nor thine, but divide	NIH
8:26 Israel, I thy word, I pray thee, be verified,	NIH
8:57 I him not leave us, nor forsake us:	NIH
8:59 I these my words, wherewith I have made	NIH
8:61 L your heart therefore be perfect with	NIH
11:21 Hadad said to Pharaoh, L me depart,	7971
11:22 howbeit I me go in any wise.	7971+7971
17:21 I this child's soul come into him again.	NIH
18:23 L them therefore give us two bullocks;	NIH
18:23 I them choose one bullock for themselves,	NIH
18:24 God that answereth by fire, I him be God.	NIH
18:36 I it be known this day that thou art God in	NIH
18:40 prophets of Baal; I not one of them escape.	NIH
19: 2 So I the gods do to me, and more also,	NIH
19:20 said, L me, I pray thee, kiss my father and	NIH
20:11 Tell him, L not him that girdeth on his	NIH
20:23 I us fight against them in the plain,	NIH
20:31 I us, I pray thee, put sackcloth on our loins,	NIH
20:32 Ben-hadad saith, I pray thee, I me live.	NIH
20:42 Because thou hast I go out of thy hand a	7971
21: 7 and eat bread, and I thine heart be merry:	NIH
22: 8 Jehoshaphat said, L not the king say so.	NIH
22:13 I thy word, I pray thee, be like the word of	NIH
22:17 I them return every man to his house in	NIH
22:49 L my servants go with my servants in	NIH

2Ki

1:10 I fire come down from heaven,	NIH
1:12 I fire come down from heaven,	NIH
1:13 I my life, and the life of these fifty thy	NIH
1:14 I my life now be precious in thy sight.	NIH
2: 9 I a double portion of thy spirit be upon me.	NIH
2:16 I them go, we pray thee, and seek thy	NIH
4:10 L us make a little chamber, I pray thee,	NIH
4:10 I us set for him there a bed, and a table,	NIH
4:27 the man of God said, L her alone; for her	7503
5: 8 I him come now to me, and he shall know	NIH
5:24 and he I the men go, and they departed.	7971
6: 2 L us go, we pray thee, unto Jordan,	NIH
6: 2 I us make us a place there, where we may	NIH
7: 4 and I us fall unto the host of the Syrians;	NIH
7:13 servants answered and said, L some take,	NIH
7:13 that are consumed:) and I us send and see.	NIH
9:15 I none go forth nor escape out of the city	NIH
9:17 to meet them, and I him say, Is it peace?	NIH
10:19 and all his priests; I none be wanting.	NIH
10:25 Go in, and slay them; I none come forth.	NIH
11: 8 cometh within the ranges, I him be slain:	NIH
11:15 L her not be slain in the house of	NIH
12: 5 the priests take it to them, every man of	NIH
12: 5 I them repair the breaches of the house,	NIH
13:21 when the man was I down, and touched	1980
14: 8 Come, I us look one another in the face.	NIH
17:27 I them go and dwell there, and let him	NIH
17:27 I him teach them the manner of the God	NIH
18:29 the king, L not Hezekiah deceive you:	NIH
18:30 Neither I Hezekiah make you trust in	NIH
19:10 L not thy God in whom thou trustest	NIH
20:10 I the shadow return backward ten degrees.	NIH
22: 5 I them deliver it into the hand of the doers	NIH
22: 5 I them give it to the doers of the work	NIH
23:18 he said, L him alone; let no man move	3240
23:18 I him alone; let no man move his bones.	NIH
23:18 they I his bones alone, with the bones of	4422

1Ch

13: 2 I us send abroad unto our brethren every	NIH
13: 3 I us bring again the ark of our God to us:	NIH
16:10 I the heart of them rejoice that seek	NIH
16:31 L the heavens be glad, and let the earth	NIH
16:31 heavens be glad, and I the earth rejoice:	NIH
16:31 men say among the nations, The LORD	NIH
16:32 L the sea roar, and the fulness thereof:	NIH
16:32 the fields rejoice, and all that is therein.	NIH
17:23 the thing that thou hast spoken	NIH
17:24 L it even be established, that thy name	NIH
17:24 I the house of David thy servant be	NIH
17:27 I it please thee to bless the house of thy	NIH
19:13 I us behave ourselves valiantly for our	NIH
19:13 the LORD do that which is good in his	NIH
21:13 I me fall now into the hand of the LORD;	NIH
21:13 but I me not fall into the hand of man.	NIH
21:17 I thine hand, I pray thee, O LORD my	NIH
21:23 I my lord the king do that which is good	NIH

2Ch

1: 9 I thy promise unto David my father be	NIH
2:15 spoken of, I thy send unto his servants:	NIH
6:17 God of Israel, I thy word be verified,	NIH
6:40 my God, I, I beseech thee, thine eyes	NIH
6:40 I thine ears be attent unto the prayer that	NIH
6:41 I thy priests, O LORD God, be clothed	NIH
6:41 I thy saints rejoice in goodness.	NIH
14: 7 L us build these cities, and make about	NIH
14:11 our God; I not man prevail against thee.	NIH
15: 7 I not your hands be weak:	NIH
16: 1 to the intent that he might I none go out	5414
16: 5 building of Ramah, and I his work cease.	NIH
18: 7 Jehoshaphat said, L not the king say so.	NIH
18:12 I thy word therefore, I pray thee, be like	NIH
18:16 I them return therefore every man to his	NIH
19: 7 Wherefore now I the fear of the LORD be	NIH
20:10 whom thou wouldest not I Israel invade,	5414
23: 6 I none come into the house of the LORD,	NIH

23:14 her, I him be slain with the sword.	NIH
25: 7 I not the army of Israel go with thee;	NIH
25:17 Come, I us see one another in the face.	NIH
32:15 therefore I not Hezekiah deceive you,	NIH
36:23 his God be with him, and I him go up.	NIH

Ezr

1: 3 I him go up to Jerusalem, which is in	NIH
1: 4 I the men of his place help him with silver,	NIH
4: 2 and said unto them, L us build with you:	NIH
5:15 I the house of God be builded in his place.	NIH
5:17 I there be search made in the king's	NIH
5:17 I the king send his pleasure to us	NIH
6: 3 L the house be builded, the place where	NIH
6: 3 I the foundations thereof be strongly laid;	NIH
6: 4 I the expences be given out of the king's	NIH
6: 5 also I the golden and silver vessels of	NIH
6: 7 L the work of this house of God alone;	NIH
6: 7 I the governor of the Jews and the elders	NIH
6: 9 I it be given them day by day without fail:	NIH
6:11 I timber be pulled down from his house,	NIH
6:11 and being set up, I him be hanged thereon;	NIH
6:11 I his house be made a dunghill for this.	NIH
6:12 made a decree; I it be done with speed.	NIH
7:23 I it be diligently done for the house of	NIH
7:26 I judgment be executed speedily upon him,	NIH
10: 3 I us make a covenant with our God to put	NIH
10: 3 and I it be done according to the law.	NIH
10:14 L now our rulers of all the congregation	NIH
10:14 I all them which have taken strange wives	NIH

Ne

1: 6 L thine ear now be attentive, and thine	NIH
1:11 I now thine ear be attentive to the prayer	NIH
2: 3 said unto the king, L the king live for ever:	NIH
2: 7 I letters be given me to the governors	NIH
2:17 and I us build up the wall of Jerusalem,	NIH
2:18 they said, L us rise up and build. So they	NIH
4: 5 I not their sin be blotted out from before	NIH
4:22 L every one with his servant lodge within	NIH
5:10 corn: I pray you, I us leave off this usury.	NIH
6: 2 I us meet together in some one of	NIH
6: 7 and I us take counsel together.	NIH
6:10 L us meet together in the house of God,	NIH
6:10 and I us shut the doors of the temple:	NIH
7: 3 L not the gates of Jerusalem be opened	NIH
7: 3 I them shut the gates, and bar them: and	NIH
9:32 I not all the trouble seem little before thee,	NIH

Est

1:19 I there go a royal commandment from him,	NIH
1:19 I it be written among the laws of	NIH
1:19 the king give her royal estate unto	NIH
2: 2 L there be fair young virgins sought for	NIH
2: 3 I the king appoint officers in all	NIH
2: 3 I their things for purification be given	NIH
2: 4 I the maiden which pleaseth the king be	NIH
3: 9 I it be written that they may be destroyed:	NIH
5: 4 I the king and Haman come this day unto	NIH
5: 8 I the king and Haman come to the	NIH
5:12 Esther the queen did I no man come in	NIH
5:14 L a gallows be made of fifty cubits high,	NIH
6: 5 And the king said, L him come in.	NIH
6: 8 L the royal apparel be brought which	NIH
6: 9 I this apparel and horse be delivered to	NIH
6:10 I nothing fail of all that thou hast spoken.	NIH
7: 3 I my life be given me at my petition,	NIH
8: 5 I it be written to reverse the letters devised	NIH
9:13 I it be granted to the Jews which are in	NIH
9:13 Haman's ten sons be hanged upon	NIH

Job

3: 3 L the day perish wherein I was born,	NIH
3: 4 L that day be darkness; let not God regard	NIH
3: 4 I not God regard it from above, neither let	NIH
3: 4 above, neither I the light shine upon it.	NIH
3: 5 L darkness and the shadow of death stain	NIH
3: 5 of death stain; I a cloud dwell upon it;	NIH
3: 5 upon it; I the blackness of the day terrify it.	NIH
3: 6 As for that night, I darkness seize upon it;	NIH
3: 6 I it be not joined unto the days of the year,	NIH
3: 6 I it not come into the number of the	NIH
3: 7 Lo, I that night be solitary, let no joyful	NIH
3: 7 be solitary, I no joyful voice come therein.	NIH
3: 8 L them curse it that curse the day, who	NIH
3: 9 L the stars of the twilight thereof be dark;	NIH
3: 9 I it look for light, but have none; neither	NIH
3: 9 neither I it see the dawning of the day:	NIH
6: 9 he would I loose his hand, and cut me	NIH
6:10 harden myself in sorrow; I him not spare:	NIH
6:29 Return, I pray you, I it not be iniquity; yea,	NIH
7:16 I me alone; for my days are vanity.	NIH
7:19 nor I me alone till I swallow down my	7503
9:34 L him take his rod away from me,	NIH
9:34 from me, and I not his fear terrify me:	NIH
10:20 cease then, and I me alone, that I may	5204.1
11:14 I not wickedness dwell in thy tabernacles.	NIH
13:13 I me alone, that I may speak, and let	4480
13:13 I may speak, and I come on me what will.	NIH
13:21 and I not thy dread make me afraid.	NIH
13:22 or I me speak, and answer thou me.	NIH
15:31 L not him that is deceived trust in vanity:	NIH
16:18 my blood, and I my cry have no place.	NIH
21: 2 speech, and I this be your consolations.	NIH
27: 6 I hold fast, and will not I it go:	7503
27: 7 I mine enemy be as the wicked, and he	NIH
30:11 they have also I loose the bridle before me.	NIH
31: 6 I me be weighed in an even balance,	NIH
31: 8 Then I me sow, and let another eat; yea,	NIH
31: 8 Then let me sow, and I another eat; yea,	NIH
31: 8 yea, I my offspring be rooted out.	NIH
31:10 Then I my wife grind unto another,	NIH
31:10 and I others bow down upon her.	NIH

31:22 Then I mine arm fall from my shoulder	NIH
31:40 L thistles grow instead of wheat,	NIH
32:21 L me not, I pray you, accept any man's	NIH
32:21 I me give flattering titles unto man.	NIH
34: 4 L us choose to us judgment: let us know	NIH
34: 4 I us know among ourselves what is good.	NIH
34:34 L men of understanding tell me, and let a	NIH
34:34 me, and I a wise man hearken unto me.	NIH
40: 2 he that reproveth God, I him answer it.	NIH

Ps

2: 3 L us break their bands asunder,	NIH
5:10 O God; I them fall by their own counsels;	NIH
5:11 I all those that put their trust in thee	NIH
5:11 I them ever shout for joy, because	NIH
5:11 I them also that love thy name be joyful	NIH
6:10 L all mine enemies be ashamed and	NIH
6:10 I them return and be ashamed suddenly.	NIH
7: 5 L the enemy persecute my soul, and take	NIH
7: 5 I him tread down my life upon the earth,	NIH
7: 9 O I the wickedness of the wicked come to	NIH
9:19 Arise, O LORD; I not man prevail:	NIH
9:19 I the heathen be judged in thy sight.	NIH
10: 2 I them be taken in the devices that they	NIH
17: 2 L my sentence come forth from thy	NIH
17: 2 I thine eyes behold the things that are	NIH
18:46 and I the God of my salvation be exalted.	NIH
19:13 sins; I them not have dominion over me:	NIH
19:14 L the words of my mouth,	NIH
20: 9 LORD: I the king hear us when we call.	NIH
22: 8 I him deliver him, seeing he delighted in	NIH
25: 2 I me not be ashamed, let not mine	NIH
25: 2 I not mine enemies triumph over me.	NIH
25: 3 Yea, I none that wait on thee be ashamed:	NIH
25: 3 I them be ashamed which transgress	NIH
25:20 I me not be ashamed; for I put my trust in	NIH
25:21 I integrity and uprightness preserve me;	NIH
31: 1 do I put my trust; I me never be ashamed:	NIH
31:17 L me not be ashamed, O LORD; for I have	NIH
31:17 I the wicked be ashamed, and let them be	NIH
31:17 and I them be silent in the grave.	NIH
31:18 L the lying lips be put to silence;	NIH
33: 8 L all the earth fear the LORD: let all	NIH
33: 8 I all the inhabitants of the world stand in	NIH
33:22 L thy mercy, O LORD, be upon us,	NIH
34: 3 with me, and I us exalt his name together.	NIH
35: 4 L them be confounded and put to shame	NIH
35: 4 I them be turned back and brought to	NIH
35: 5 L them be as chaff before the wind:	NIH
35: 5 and I the angel of the LORD chase them.	NIH
35: 6 I their way be dark and slippery: and let	NIH
35: 6 I the angel of the LORD persecute them.	NIH
35: 8 L destruction come upon him at unawares;	NIH
35: 8 I his net that he hath hid catch himself:	NIH
35: 8 into that very destruction I him fall.	NIH
35:19 L not them that are mine enemies	NIH
35:19 I them wink with the eye that hate	NIH
35:24 and I them not rejoice over me.	NIH
35:25 L them not say in their hearts,	NIH
35:25 I them not say, We have swallowed him	NIH
35:26 L them be ashamed and brought to	NIH
35:26 I them be clothed with shame and	NIH
35:27 L them shout for joy, and be glad,	NIH
35:27 yea, I them say continually, Let the LORD	NIH
35:27 I the LORD be magnified,	NIH
36:11 L not the foot of pride come against me,	NIH
36:11 I not the hand of the wicked remove me.	NIH
40:11 I thy lovingkindness and thy truth	NIH
40:14 L them be ashamed and	NIH
40:14 I them be driven backward and put to	NIH
40:15 L them be desolate for a reward of their	NIH
40:16 L all those that seek thee rejoice and be	NIH
40:16 I such as love thy salvation say continually,	NIH
43: 3 I them lead me; let them bring me unto	NIH
43: 3 I them bring me unto thy holy hill,	NIH
48:11 L mount Zion rejoice, let the daughters of	NIH
48:11 I the daughters of Judah be glad, because	NIH
55:15 L death seize upon them, and let them go	NIH
55:15 and I them go down quick into hell:	NIH
57: 5 I thy glory be above all the earth.	NIH
57:11 I thy glory be above all the earth.	NIH
58: 7 L them melt away as waters which run	NIH
58: 7 his arrows, I them be as cut in pieces.	NIH
58: 8 I every one of them pass away:	NIH
59:10 God shall I me see my desire upon mine	NIH
59:12 words of their lips I them even be taken	NIH
59:13 I them know that God ruleth in Jacob unto	NIH
59:14 at evening I them return; and let them	NIH
59:14 and I them make a noise like a dog,	NIH
59:15 L them wander up and down for meat,	NIH
66: 7 I not the rebellious exalt themselves.	NIH
67: 3 L the people praise thee, O God; let all	NIH
67: 3 O God; I all the people praise thee.	NIH
67: 4 O I the nations be glad and sing for joy:	NIH
67: 5 L the people praise thee, O God; let all	NIH
67: 5 O God; I all the people praise thee.	NIH
68: 1 L God arise, let his enemies be scattered:	NIH
68: 1 Let God arise, I his enemies be scattered:	NIH
68: 1 I them also that hate him flee before him.	NIH
68: 2 I the wicked perish at the presence of God.	NIH
68: 3 I the righteous be glad; let them rejoice	NIH
68: 3 be glad; I them rejoice before God:	NIH
68: 3 God: yea, I them exceedingly rejoice.	NIH
69: 6 L not them that wait on thee, O LORD GOD	NIH
69: 6 I not those that seek thee be confounded	NIH
69:14 me out of the mire, and I me not sink:	NIH
69:14 I me be delivered from them that hate me,	NIH

L

Ps 69:15 L not the waterflood overflow me, NIH
69:15 neither l the deep swallow me up, NIH
69:15 and l not the pit shut her mouth upon me. NIH
69:22 L their table become a snare before them: NIH
69:22 been for their welfare, l it become a trap. NIH
69:23 L their eyes be darkened, that they see NIH
69:24 l thy wrathful anger take hold of them. NIH
69:25 L their habitation be desolate; and let NIH
69:25 desolate; and l none dwell in their tents. NIH
69:27 l them not come into thy righteousness. NIH
69:28 L them be blotted out of the book of NIH
69:29 l thy salvation, O God, set me up on high. NIH
69:34 L the heaven and earth praise him, NIH
70: 2 L them be ashamed and confounded that NIH
70: 2 l them be turned backward, and put to NIH
70: 3 L them be turned back for a reward of NIH
70: 4 L all those that seek thee rejoice and be NIH
70: 4 l such as love thy salvation say continually, NIH
70: 4 say continually, L God be magnified. NIH
71: 1 my trust: l me never be put to confusion. NIH
71: 8 L my mouth be filled with thy praise and NIH
71:13 L them be confounded and consumed that NIH
71:13 them be covered with reproach and NIH
72:19 l the whole earth be filled with his glory; NIH
74: 8 in their hearts, L us destroy them together; NIH
74:21 O l not the oppressed return ashamed: NIH
74:21 the poor and needy praise thy name. NIH
76:11 l all that be round about him bring presents NIH
78:28 he l it fall in the midst of their camp, NIH
79: 8 l thy tender mercies speedily prevent us: NIH
79:10 l him be known among the heathen in our NIH
79:11 L the sighing of the prisoner come before NIH
80:17 L thy hand be upon the man of thy right NIH
83: 4 and l us cut them off from being a nation; NIH
83:12 L us take to ourselves the houses of God NIH
83:17 L them be confounded and troubled for NIH
83:17 yea, l them be put to shame, and perish: NIH
85: 8 saints: but l them not turn again to folly. NIH
88: 2 L my prayer come before thee: incline NIH
90:13 l it repent thee concerning thy servants. NIH
90:16 L thy work appear unto thy servants, NIH
90:17 L the beauty of the Lord our God be upon NIH
95: 1 O come, l us sing unto the Lord: let us NIH
95: 1 l us make a joyful noise to the rock of our NIH
95: 2 L us come before his presence with NIH
95: 6 come, l us worship and bow down: let us NIH
95: 6 l us kneel before the Lord our Maker. NIH
96:11 L the heavens rejoice, and let the earth be NIH
96:11 heavens rejoice, and l the earth be glad; NIH
96:11 l the sea roar, and the fulness thereof. NIH
96:12 L the field be joyful, and all that is therein: NIH
97: 1 The Lord reigneth; l the earth rejoice; NIH
97: 1 l the multitude of isles be glad thereof. NIH
98: 7 L the sea roar, and the fulness thereof; NIH
98: 8 L the floods clap their hands: let the hills NIH
98: 8 their hands: l the hills be joyful together NIH
99: 1 The Lord reigneth; l the people tremble: NIH
99: 1 the cherubims; l the earth be moved. NIH
99: 3 L them praise thy great and terrible name; NIH
102: 1 O Lord, and l my cry come unto thee. NIH
104:35 L the sinners be consumed out of the, NIH
104:35 of the earth, and l the wicked be no more. NIH
105: 3 l the heart of them rejoice that seek NIH
105:20 the ruler of the people, and l him go free. NIH
106:48 l all the people say, Amen. Praise ye NIH
107: 2 L the redeemed of the Lord say so, NIH
107:22 l them sacrifice the sacrifices of NIH
107:32 L them exalt him also in the congregation NIH
109: 6 and l Satan stand at his right hand. NIH
109: 7 he shall be judged, l him be condemned: NIH
109: 7 condemned: and l his prayer become sin. NIH
109: 8 L his days be few; and let another take his NIH
109: 8 days be few; and l another take his office. NIH
109: 9 L his children be fatherless, and his wife a NIH
109:10 L his children be continually vagabonds, NIH
109:10 l them seek their bread also out of their NIH
109:11 L the extortioner catch all that he hath; NIH
109:11 hath; and l the strangers spoil his labour. NIH
109:12 L there be none to extend mercy unto NIH
109:12 neither l there be any to favour his NIH
109:13 L his posterity be cut off; and in NIH
109:13 in the generation following l their name NIH
109:14 L the iniquity of his fathers be NIH
109:14 l not the sin of his mother be blotted out. NIH
109:15 L them be before the Lord continually, NIH
109:17 he loved cursing, so l it come unto him: NIH
109:17 not in blessing, so l it be far from him. NIH
109:18 so l it come into his bowels like water, NIH
109:19 L it be unto him as the garment which NIH
109:20 L this be the reward of mine adversaries NIH
109:28 L them curse, but bless thou: when they NIH
109:28 when they arise, l them be ashamed; NIH
109:28 be ashamed; but l thy servant rejoice. NIH
109:29 L mine adversaries be clothed with NIH
109:29 l them cover themselves with their own NIH
118: 2 L Israel now say, that his mercy endureth NIH
118: 3 L the house of Aaron now say, that his NIH
118: 4 L them now that fear the Lord say, NIH
119:10 O l me not wander from thy NIH
119:41 L thy mercies come also unto me, NIH
119:76 L, I pray thee, thy merciful kindness be NIH
119:77 L thy tender mercies come unto me, that NIH
119:78 L the proud be ashamed; for they dealt NIH
119:79 L those that fear thee turn unto me, NIH
119:80 L my heart be sound in thy statutes; that I NIH

Ps 119:116 and l me not be ashamed of my hope. NIH
119:122 for good: l not the proud oppress me. NIH
119:133 l not any iniquity have dominion over me. NIH
119:169 L my cry come near before thee, O Lord: NIH
119:170 L my supplication come before thee: NIH
119:173 L thine hand help me; for I have chosen NIH
119:175 L my soul live, and it shall praise thee; NIH
119:175 praise thee; and l thy judgments help me. NIH
122: 1 L us go into the house of the Lord. NIH
129: 5 L them all be confounded and turned NIH
129: 6 L them be as the grass upon the NIH
130: 2 l thine ears be attentive to the voice of NIH
130: 7 L Israel hope in the Lord: for with NIH
131: 3 L Israel hope in the Lord from NIH
132: 9 L thy priests be clothed with NIH
132: 9 and l thy saints shout for joy. NIH
137: 5 l my right hand forget her cunning. NIH
137: 6 l my tongue cleave to the roof of my NIH
140: 9 l the mischief of their own lips cover NIH
140:10 L burning coals fall upon them: let them NIH
140:10 l them be cast into the fire; into deep pits, NIH
140:11 L not an evil speaker be established in NIH
141: 2 L my prayer be set forth before thee as NIH
141: 4 and l me not eat of their dainties. NIH
141: 5 L the righteous smite me; it shall be a NIH
141: 5 l him reprove me; it shall be an excellent NIH
141:10 L the wicked fall into their own nets, NIH
145:21 l all flesh bless his holy name for ever and NIH
148: 5 L them praise the name of the Lord: NIH
148:13 L them praise the name of the Lord: NIH
149: 2 L Israel rejoice in him that made him: NIH
149: 2 l the children of Zion be joyful in their NIH
149: 3 L them praise his name in the dance: NIH
149: 3 l them sing praises unto him with NIH
149: 5 L the saints be joyful in glory: let them NIH
149: 5 glory: l them sing aloud upon their beds. NIH
149: 6 L the high praises of God be in their NIH
150: 6 L every thing that hath breath praise NIH
Pr 1:11 Come with us, l us lay wait for blood, NIH
1:11 l us lurk privily for the innocent without NIH
1:12 L us swallow them up alive as the grave; NIH
1:14 thy lot among us; l us all have one purse: NIH
3: 1 l thine heart keep my commandments: NIH
3: 3 L not mercy and truth forsake thee: NIH
3:21 son, l not them depart from thine eyes; NIH
4: 4 unto me, L thine heart retain my words: NIH
4:13 Take fast hold of instruction; l her not go: NIH
4:21 L them not depart from thine eyes; NIH
4:25 L thine eyes look right on, and let thine NIH
4:25 L thine eyelids look straight before thee. NIH
4:26 thy feet, and l all thy ways be established. NIH
5:16 L thy fountains be dispersed abroad, NIH
5:17 L them be only thine own, NIH
5:18 L thy fountain be blessed: and rejoice with NIH
5:19 L her be as the loving hind and pleasant NIH
5:19 l her breasts satisfy thee at all times; NIH
6:25 neither l her take thee with her eyelids. NIH
7:18 l us take our fill of love until the morning: NIH
7:18 l us solace ourselves with loves. NIH
7:25 L not thine heart decline to her ways, go NIH
9: 4 Whoso is simple, l him turn in hither: NIH
9:16 Whoso is simple, l him turn in hither: NIH
17:12 L a bear robbed of her whelps meet a NIH
19:18 and l not thy soul spare for his crying. NIH
23:17 L not thine heart envy sinners: but be NIH
23:26 and l thine eyes observe my ways. NIH
24:17 l not thine heart be glad when he NIH
27: 2 L another man praise thee, and not thine NIH
28:17 shall flee to the pit; l no man stay him. NIH
31: 7 L him drink, and forget his poverty, NIH
31:31 l her own works praise her in the gates. NIH
Ecc 5: 2 l not thine heart be hasty to utter any NIH
5: 2 upon earth: therefore l thy words be few. NIH
9: 8 L thy garments be always white; and let NIH
9: 8 and l thy head lack no ointment. NIH
11: 8 yet l him remember the days of darkness; NIH
11: 9 l thy heart cheer thee in the days of thy NIH
12:13 L us hear the conclusion of the whole NIH
SS 1: 2 L him kiss me with the kisses of his NIH
2:14 l me see thy countenance, let me hear thy NIH
2:14 see thy countenance, l me hear thy voice; NIH
3: 4 l held him, and would not l him go, until 7503
4:16 L my beloved come into his garden, NIH
7:11 my beloved, l us go forth into the field; NIH
7:11 into the field; l us lodge in the villages. NIH
7:12 L us get up early to the vineyards; let us NIH
7:12 l us see if the vine flourish, whether NIH
8:11 he l out the vineyard unto keepers; 5414
Isa 1:18 Come now, and l us reason together, NIH
2: 3 l us go up to the mountain of the Lord, NIH
2: 5 and l us walk in the light of the Lord. NIH
3: 6 ruler, and l this ruin be under thy hand: NIH
4: 1 only l us be called by thy name, to take NIH
5:19 l him make speed, and hasten his work, NIH
5:19 l the counsel of the Holy One of Israel NIH
7: 6 L us go up against Judah, and vex it, NIH
7: 6 l us make a breach therein for us, and set NIH
8:13 l him be your fear, and let him be your NIH
8:13 him be your fear, and l him be your dread. NIH
16: 4 L mine outcasts dwell with thee, Moab; NIH
19:12 thy wise men? and l them tell thee now, NIH
19:12 l them know what the Lord of hosts hath NIH
21: 6 a watchman, l him declare what he seeth. NIH
22:13 l us eat and drink; for to morrow we shall NIH
26:10 L favour be shewed to the wicked, yet will NIH

Isa 27: 5 Or l him take hold of my strength, that he NIH
29: 1 add ye year to year; l them kill sacrifices. NIH
34: 1 l the earth hear, and all that is therein; NIH
36:14 the king, l not Hezekiah deceive you: NIH
36:15 Neither l Hezekiah make you trust in NIH
37:10 saying, L not thy God, in whom thou NIH
38:21 L them take a lump of figs, and lay it for a NIH
41: 1 and l the people renew their strength: NIH
41: 1 l them come near; then let them speak: NIH
41: 1 l them come near; then l them speak: NIH
41: 1 l us come near together to judgment. NIH
41:22 L them bring them forth, and shew us NIH
41:22 l them shew the former things, what they NIH
42:11 L the wilderness and the cities thereof lift NIH
42:11 l the inhabitants of the rock sing, let them NIH
42:11 l them shout from the top of the NIH
42:12 L them give glory unto the Lord, NIH
43: 9 L all the nations be gathered together, NIH
43: 9 and l the people be assembled: NIH
43: 9 shew us former things? l them bring forth NIH
43: 9 or l them hear, and say, It is truth. NIH
43:13 my hand: I will work, and who shall l it? 7725
43:26 l us plead together: declare thou, that NIH
44: 7 and shall come, l them shew unto them. NIH
44:11 l them all be gathered together, let them NIH
44:11 l them stand up; yet they shall fear, NIH
45: 8 and l the skies pour down righteousness: NIH
45: 8 l the earth open, and let them bring forth NIH
45: 8 l them bring forth salvation, NIH
45: 8 l righteousness spring up together; NIH
45: 9 L the potsherd strive with the potsherds NIH
45:13 my city, and he shall l go my captives, 7971
45:21 yea, l them take counsel together: NIH
47:13 L now the astrologers, the stargazers, NIH
50: 8 l us stand together: who is mine adversary? NIH
50: 8 is mine adversary? l him come near to me. NIH
50:10 l him trust in the name of the Lord, NIH
54: 2 l them stretch forth the curtains of thine NIH
55: 2 and l your soul delight itself in fatness. NIH
55: 7 L the wicked forsake his way, NIH
55: 7 l him return unto the Lord, and he will NIH
56: 3 Neither l the son of the stranger, that hath NIH
56: 3 neither l the eunuch say, Behold, I am a NIH
57:13 thou criest, l thy companies deliver thee; NIH
58: 6 l the oppressed go free, and that ye break 7971
66: 5 said, L the Lord be glorified: NIH
Jer 2:28 l them arise, if they can save thee in NIH
4: 5 and l us go into the defenced cities. NIH
5:24 L us now fear the Lord our God, NIH
6: 4 against her; arise, and l us go up at noon. NIH
6: 5 l us go by night, and let us destroy her NIH
6: 5 go by night, and l us destroy her palaces. NIH
8:14 l us enter into the defenced cities, and let NIH
8:14 defenced cities, and l us be silent there: NIH
9:18 l them make haste, and take up a wailing NIH
9:20 l your ear receive the word of his mouth, NIH
9:23 L not the wise man glory in his wisdom, NIH
9:23 l the mighty man glory in his might, NIH
9:23 l not the rich man glory in his riches: NIH
9:24 him that glorieth glory in this, that he NIH
11:19 saying, L us destroy the tree with the fruit NIH
11:19 l us cut him off from the land of the living, NIH
11:20 heart, l me see thy vengeance on them: NIH
12: 1 yet l me talk with thee of thy judgments. NIH
14:17 L mine eyes run down with tears night NIH
14:17 tears night and day, and l them not cease: NIH
15: 1 them out of my sight, and l them go forth. NIH
15:19 l them return unto thee; but return not NIH
17:15 is the word of the Lord? l it come now. NIH
17:18 L them be confounded that persecute me, NIH
17:18 me, but l not me be confounded: NIH
17:18 l them be dismayed, but let not me be NIH
17:18 be dismayed, but l not me be dismayed: NIH
18:18 and l us devise devices against Jeremiah; NIH
18:18 l us smite him with the tongue, and let us NIH
18:18 and l us not give heed to any of his words. NIH
18:21 Their wives be bereaved of their children, NIH
18:21 widows; and l their men be put to death; NIH
18:21 l their young men be slain by the sword in NIH
18:22 L a cry be heard from their houses, NIH
18:23 but l them be overthrown before thee; NIH
20:12 heart, l me see thy vengeance on them: NIH
20:14 l not the day wherein my mother bare me NIH
20:16 l that man be as the cities which the Lord NIH
20:16 l him hear the cry in the morning, NIH
23:28 that hath a dream, l him tell a dream; NIH
23:28 my word, l him speak my word faithfully. NIH
27:11 those will I l remain still in their own land, NIH
27:18 l them now make intercession to NIH
29: 8 l not your prophets and your diviners, NIH
31: 6 l us go up to Zion unto the Lord our NIH
34: 9 That every man should l his manservant, NIH
34:10 heard that every one should l his NIH
34:10 more, then they obeyed, and l them go. 7971
34:11 whom they had l go free, to return, 7971
34:14 At the end of seven years l ye go every 7971
34:14 thou shalt l him go free from thee: 7971
35:11 l us go to Jerusalem for fear of the army of NIH
36:19 and l no man know where ye be. NIH
37:20 l my supplication, I pray thee, be accepted NIH
38: 4 beseech thee, l this man be put to death: NIH
38: 6 they l down Jeremiah with cords. 7971
38:11 l them down by cords into the dungeon 7971
38:24 L no man know of these words, NIH
40: 1 of the guard had l him go from Ramah, 7971

Jer 40: 5 him victuals and a reward, and I him **go.** 7971
40:15 **L** me go, I pray thee, and I will slay NIH
42: 2 Jeremiah the prophet, **L**, we beseech thee, NIH
46: 6 **L** not the swift flee away, nor the mighty NIH
46: 9 and I the mighty **men** come forth; NIH
46:16 I us go again to our own people, and to NIH
48: 2 and I us cut it off from *being* a nation. NIH
49:11 *them* alive; and I thy widows trust in me. NIH
50: 5 I us join ourselves to the LORD *in a* NIH
50:26 destroy her utterly: I nothing of her be left. NIH
50:27 I them all go down to the slaughter: NIH
50:29 it round about; I none thereof escape: 1961
50:33 held them fast; they refused to I them **go.** 7971
51: 3 *him that* bendeth I the archer bend NIH
51: 9 I us go every one into his own country: NIH
51:10 us declare in Zion the work of the LORD NIH
51:50 and I Jerusalem come into your mind. NIH
La 1:22 **L** all their wickedness come before thee; NIH
2:18 I tears run down like a river day and night: NIH
2:18 no rest; I not the apple of thine eye cease. NIH
3:40 **L** us search and try our ways, and turn NIH
3:41 **L** us lift up our heart with *our* hands unto NIH
Eze 1:24 they stood, they I **down** their wings. 7503
1:25 they stood, *and* had I **down** their wings. 7503
3:27 He that heareth, I him hear; and he that NIH
3:27 and he that forbeareth, I him forbear: NIH
7:12 I not the buyer rejoice, nor the seller NIH
9: 5 I not your eye spare, neither have ye pity: NIH
11: 3 say, *It is* not near; I *us* build houses: NIH
13:20 from your arms, and will I the souls go, NIH
21:14 I the sword be doubled the third time, NIH
24: 5 I them seethe the bones of it therein. NIH
24: 6 it out piece by piece; I no lot fall upon it. NIH
24:10 and spice it well, and I the bones be burnt. NIH
39: 7 I will not I *them* pollute my holy name NIH
43: 9 Now I them put away their whoredom, NIH
43:10 and I them measure the pattern. NIH
44: 6 I it suffice you of all your abominations, NIH
45: 9 **L** it suffice you, O princes of Israel: NIH
Da 1:12 I them give us pulse to eat, and water to NIH
1:13 I our countenances be looked upon before NIH
2: 7 **L** the king tell his servants the dream, NIH
4:14 I the beasts get away from under it, NIH
4:15 I it be wet with the dew of heaven, NIH
4:15 I *his* portion *be* with the beasts in the grass NIH
4:16 **L** his heart be changed from man's, NIH
4:16 I a beast's heart be given unto him; NIH
4:16 unto him; and I seven times pass over him. NIH
4:19 I not the dream, or the interpretation NIH
4:23 I it be wet with the dew of heaven, NIH
4:23 I *his* portion *be* with the beasts of the field, NIH
4:27 I my counsel be acceptable unto thee, NIH
5:10 I not thy thoughts trouble thee, nor let thy NIH
5:10 nor I thy countenance be changed. NIH
5:12 now I Daniel be called, and he will shew NIH
5:17 **L** thy gifts be to thyself, and give thy NIH
9:16 I thine anger and thy fury be turned away NIH
10:19 and said, **L** my lord speak; NIH
Hos 2: 2 I her therefore put away her whoredoms NIH
4: 4 Yet I no man strive, nor reprove another: NIH
4:15 play the harlot, *yet* I not Judah offend; NIH
4:17 Ephraim *is* joined to idols: I him **alone.** 3240
6: 1 Come and I us return unto the LORD: NIH
13: 2 **L** the men that sacrifice kiss the calves. NIH
Joel 1: 3 *I* your children *tell* their children, NIH
1:14 I all the inhabitants of the land tremble: NIH
2:16 I the bridegroom go forth of his chamber, NIH
2:17 **L** the priests, the ministers of the LORD, NIH
2:17 the porch and the altar, and I them say, NIH
3: 9 wake up the mighty *men*, I all the men of NIH
3: 9 men of war draw near; I them come up: NIH
3:10 into spears: I the weak say, I *am* strong. NIH
3:12 **L** the heathen be wakened, and come up NIH
Am 4: 1 say to their masters, Bring, and I us drink. NIH
5:24 I judgment run down as waters, NIH
Ob 1: 1 and I us rise up against her in battle. NIH
Jnh 1: 7 to his fellow, Come, and I us cast lots, NIH
1:14 I us not perish for this man's life, NIH
3: 7 nobles, saying, **L** neither man nor beast, NIH
3: 7 thing: I them not feed, nor drink water: NIH
3: 8 I man and beast be covered with sackcloth NIH
3: 8 I them turn every one from his evil way, NIH
Mic 1: 2 I the Lord GOD be witness against you, NIH
4: 2 I us go up to the mountain of the LORD, NIH
4:11 **L** her be defiled, and let our eye look upon NIH
4:11 be defiled, and I our eye look upon Zion. NIH
6: 1 mountains, and I the hills hear thy voice. NIH
7:14 I them feed in Bashan and Gilead, as *in* NIH
Hab 2:16 also, and I thy foreskin be uncovered: NIH
2:20 I all the earth keep silence before him. NIH
Zep 3:16 *and to* Zion, **L** not thine hands be slack. NIH
Zec 3: 5 said, **L** them set a fair mitre upon his head. NIH
7:10 I none of you imagine evil against his NIH
8: 9 **L** your hands be strong, ye that hear in NIH
8:13 fear not, *but* I your hands be strong. NIH
8:17 I none of you imagine evil in your hearts NIH
8:21 **L** us go speedily to pray before the LORD, NIH
11: 9 that that dieth, I it die; and that that is to NIH
11: 9 that that is to be cut off, I it be cut off; NIH
11: 9 the rest eat every one the flesh of another NIH
Mal 2:15 I none deal treacherously against the wife NIH
Mt 5:16 **L** your light so shine before men, that they NIH
5:31 I him give her a writing of divorcement: NIG
5:37 But I your communication be, Yea, yea; NIG
5:40 *away* thy coat, I him **have** *thy* cloke also. 863

Mt 6: 3 I not thy left hand know what thy right NIG
7: 4 **L** me pull out the mote out of thine eye; 863
8:22 Follow me; and I the dead bury their dead. 863
10:13 be worthy, I your peace come upon it: NIG
10:13 be not worthy, I your peace return to you. NIG
11:15 He that hath ears to hear, I him hear. NIG
13: 9 Who hath ears to hear, I him hear. NIG
13:30 **L** both grow together until the harvest: 863
13:43 Who hath ears to hear, I him hear. NIG
15: 4 or mother, I him die the death. NIG
15:14 **L** them **alone:** they be blind leaders of 863
16:24 I him deny himself, and take up his cross, NIG
17: 4 wilt, I us make here three tabernacles; NIG
18:17 I him be unto thee as a heathen *man* and NIG
19: 6 joined together, I not man put asunder. NIG
19:12 that is able to receive *it*, I him receive *it*. NIG
20:26 great among you, I him be your minister; NIG
20:27 chief among you, I him be your servant; NIG
21:19 **L** no fruit grow on thee henceforward for NIG
21:33 I it out to husbandmen, and went into a 1554
21:38 I us kill him, and let us seize on his NIG
21:38 kill him, and I us seize on his inheritance. NIG
21:41 will I **out** *his* vineyard unto other 1554
(whoso readeth, I him understand:) NIG
24:16 Then I them which be in Judea flee into NIG
24:17 **L** him which is on the housetop not come NIG
24:18 Neither I him which is in the field return NIG
26:39 if it be possible, I this cup pass from me: NIG
26:46 Rise, I us be going: behold, he is at hand NIG
27:22 *They* all say unto him, **L** him be crucified. NIG
27:23 out the more, saying, **L** him be crucified. NIG
27:42 I him now come down from the cross, NIG
27:43 I him deliver him now, if he will have him: NIG
27:49 rest said, **L** be, let us see whether Elias 863
27:49 I us see whether Elias will come to save NIG
Mk 1:24 Saying, **L** *us* **alone**; what have we to do 1436
1:38 unto them, **L** us go into the next towns, NIG
2: 4 they I **down** the bed wherein the sick of 5465
4: 9 He that hath ears to hear, I him hear. NIG
4:23 If any *man* have ears to hear, I him hear. NIG
4:35 **L** us pass over unto the other side. NIG
7:10 or mother, I him die the death. NIG
7:16 If any *man* have ears to hear, I him hear. NIG
7:27 said unto her, **L** the children first be filled: 863
8:34 I him deny himself, and take up his cross, NIG
9: 5 and I us make three tabernacles; one for NIG
10: 9 joined together, I not man put asunder. NIG
11: 6 had commanded: and they I them **go.** 863
12: 1 I it **out** to husbandmen, and went into a 1554
12: 7 I us kill him, and the inheritance shall be NIG
12:14 ought not, (I him that readeth understand,) NIG
13:14 I them that be in Judea flee to NIG
13:15 And I him that is on the housetop not go NIG
13:16 I him that is in the field not turn back NIG
14: 6 And Jesus said, **L** her **alone**; why trouble 863
14:42 Rise up, I us go; lo, he that betrayeth me NIG
15:32 **L** Christ the King of Israel descend now NIG
15:36 and gave him to drink, saying, **L** **alone**, 863
15:36 I us see whether Elias will come to take NIG
Lk 2:15 **L** us now go *even* unto Bethlehem, NIG
3:11 I him impart to him that hath none; NIG
3:11 and he that hath meat, I him do likewise. NIG
4:34 Saying, **L** *us* **alone**; what have we to do 1436
5: 4 and I **down** your nets for a draught. 5465
5: 5 nevertheless at thy word I will **down** 5465
5:19 I him **down** through the tiling with *his* 2524
6:42 I me pull out the mote that is in thine eye, 863
8: 8 He that hath ears to hear, I him hear. NIG
8:22 I us go over unto the other side of the NIG
9:23 I him deny himself, and take up his cross NIG
9:33 and I us make three tabernacles; one for NIG
9:44 **L** these sayings sink down into your ears: NIG
9:60 said unto him, **L** the dead bury their dead: 863
9:61 but I me first go bid them farewell, 2010
12:35 **L** your loins be girded about, and *your* NIG
13: 8 I it **alone** this year also, till I shall dig NIG
14: 4 took *him*, and healed him, and I *him* **go**; 630
14:35 He that hath ears to hear, I him hear. NIG
15:23 and kill *it*; and I us eat, and be merry: NIG
16:29 and the prophets; I them hear them. NIG
17:31 I him not come down to take it away: NIG
17:31 the field, I him likewise not return back. NIG
20: 9 I it **forth** to husbandmen, and went into 1554
20:14 I us kill him, that the inheritance may NIG
21:21 Then I them which are in Judea flee to NIG
21:21 I them which are in the midst of it depart NIG
21:21 I not them that are in the countries enter NIG
22:26 among you, I him be as the younger; NIG
22:36 purse, I him take *it*, and likewise *his* scrip: NIG
22:36 I him sell his garment, and buy one. NIG
22:68 *you*, you will not answer me, nor I me **go.** 630
23:22 I will therefore chastise him, and I *him* **go.** 630
23:35 I him save himself, if he be Christ, NIG
Jn 7:37 thirst, I him come unto me, and drink. NIG
8: 7 among you, I him first cast a stone at her. NIG
11: 7 to *his* disciples, **L** us go into Judea again. NIG
11:15 believe; nevertheless I us go unto him. NIG
11:16 unto *his* fellow-disciples, **L** us also go, NIG
11:44 saith unto them, Loose him, and I *him* **go.** 863
11:48 If we I him thus **alone**, all *men* will believe 863
12: 7 said Jesus, **L** her **alone**: against the day NIG
12:26 If any *man* serve me, I him follow me; NIG
14: 1 **L** not your heart be troubled: ye believe in NIG
14:27 **L** not your heart be troubled, neither let it NIG
14:27 heart be troubled, neither I it be afraid. NIG

Jn 14:31 *even* so I do. Arise, I us go hence. NIG
18: 8 therefore ye seek me, I these go their way: 863
19:12 cried out, saying, If thou I this *man* **go**, 630
19:24 **L** us not rent it, but cast lots for it, whose NIG
Ac 1:20 **L** his habitation be desolate, and let no NIG
1:20 be desolate, and I no man dwell therein: 1510
1:20 and his bishoprick I another take. NIG
2:29 I me freely speak unto you of the patriarch 1832
2:36 Therefore I all the house of Israel know NIG
3:13 when he was determined to I *him* **go.** 630
4:17 the people, I us straitly threaten them, NIG
4:21 further threatened *them*, they I them **go**, 630
4:23 And being I **go**, they went to their own 630
5:38 from these men, and I them **alone**: 1439
5:40 speak in the name of Jesus, and I them **go.** 630
9:25 I *him* **down** by the wall in a basket. 2524+5465
10:11 the four corners, and I **down** to the earth: 2524
11: 5 I **down** from heaven by four corners, 2524
15:33 they were I **go** in peace from the brethren 630
15:36 **L** us go again and visit our brethren in NIG
16:35 sent the sergeants, saying, **L** those men **go.** 630
16:36 The magistrates have sent to I you **go**: 630
16:37 but I them come themselves and fetch us NIG
17: 9 of Jason, and *of* the other, they I them **go.** 630
19:38 are deputies: I them implead one another. NIG
23: 9 spoken to him, I us not fight against God. NIG
23:22 chief captain then I the young man **depart**, 630
24:20 Or else I these same *here* say, if they have NIG
24:23 and to I *him* have liberty, and that he NIG
25: 5 **L** them therefore, said he, which among NIG
27:15 up into the wind, we I *her* **drive.** 1929+5342
27:30 they had I **down** the boat into the sea, 5465
27:32 off the ropes of the boat, and I her fall off. 1439
28:18 would have I me **go**, because there was no 630
Ro 1:13 to come unto you, (but was I hitherto,) 2967
3: 4 I God be true, but every man a liar; as it NIG
3: 8 say,) I us do evil, that good may come? NIG
6:12 **L** not sin therefore reign in your mortal NIG
9: 9 **L** their table be made a snare, and a trap, NIG
11:10 **L** their eyes be darkened, that *they* may NIG
12: 6 I us prophesy according to the proportion NIG
12: 7 Or ministry, I us wait on *our* ministering: NIG
12: 8 he that giveth, I him do it with simplicity; NIG
12: 9 **L** love be without dissimulation. NIG
13: 1 **L** every soul be subject unto the higher NIG
13:12 I us therefore cast off the works of NIG
13:12 and I us put on the armour of light. NIG
13:13 **L** us walk honestly, as in the day; not in NIG
14: 3 I not him that eateth despise him that NIG
14: 5 **L** every man be fully persuaded in his NIG
14:13 **L** us not therefore judge one another any NIG
14:16 **L** not then your good be evil spoken of: NIG
14:19 I us therefore follow *after* the things NIG
15: 2 **L** every one of us please *his* neighbour for NIG
1Co 1:31 He that glorieth, I him glory in the Lord. NIG
3:10 I every man take heed how he buildeth NIG
3:18 **L** no man deceive himself. If any *man* NIG
3:18 I him become a fool, that he may be wise. NIG
3:21 Therefore I no *man* glory in men. For all NIG
5: 8 Therefore I us keep the feast, not with old NIG
7: 2 I every man have his own wife, NIG
7: 2 I every woman have her own husband. NIG
7: 3 **L** the husband render unto the wife due NIG
7: 9 But if they cannot contain, I them marry: NIG
7:10 **L** not the wife depart from *her* husband: NIG
7:11 I her remain unmarried, or be reconciled NIG
7:11 and I not the husband put away his wife. NIG
7:12 to dwell with him, I him not put her away. NIG
7:13 to dwell with her, I her not leave him. NIG
7:15 But if the unbelieving depart, I him depart. NIG
7:17 Lord hath called every one, so I him walk. NIG
7:18 I him not become uncircumcised. Is any NIG
7:18 I him not be circumcised. NIG
7:20 **L** every man abide in the same calling NIG
7:24 I every man, wherein he is called, NIG
7:36 need so require, I him do what he will, NIG
7:36 he will, he sinneth not: I them marry. NIG
10: 8 Neither I us commit fornication, as some NIG
10: 9 Neither I us tempt Christ, as some of them NIG
10:12 Wherefore I him that thinketh he standeth NIG
10:24 I no *man* seek his own, but every man NIG
11: 6 be not covered, I her also be shorn: NIG
11: 6 to be shorn or shaven, I her be covered. NIG
11:28 I a man examine himself, and so let him NIG
11:28 so I him eat of *that* bread, and drink of NIG
11:34 if any *man* hunger, I him eat at home; NIG
14:13 Wherefore I him that speaketh in an NIG
14:26 **L** all *things* be done unto edifying. NIG
14:27 I *it* be by two, or at the most *by* three, NIG
14:27 and *that* by course; and I one interpret. NIG
14:28 I him keep silence in the church; NIG
14:28 and I him speak to himself, and to God. NIG
14:29 **L** the prophets speak two or three, NIG
14:30 **L** the first hold his peace. NIG
14:30 that sitteth *by*, I the first hold his peace. NIG
14:34 **L** your women keep silence in the NIG
14:35 if they will learn any *thing*, I them ask NIG
14:37 I him acknowledge that *the things* that I NIG
14:38 if any *man* be ignorant, I him be ignorant. NIG
14:40 **L** all *things* be done decently and in order. NIG
15:32 I us eat and drink; for to morrow we die. NIG
16: 2 Upon the first *day* of the week I every one NIG
16:11 **L** no *man* therefore despise him: NIG

L

1Co 16:14 **L** all your *things* be done with charity. NIG
16:22 I him be anathema, Maran-atha. NIG
2Co 7: 1 **l** us cleanse ourselves from all filthiness of NIG
9: 7 in *his* heart, so **l** *him give;* not grudgingly, NIG
10: 7 **l** him of himself think this again, that, as NIG
10:11 **L** such a one think this, that, such as we NIG
10:17 he that glorieth, **l** him glory in the Lord. NIG
11:16 I say again, **L** no *man* think me a fool; NIG
11:33 in a basket was I **down** by the wall, 5465
Gal 1: 8 preached unto you, **l** him be accursed. NIG
1: 9 that ye have received, **l** him be accursed. NIG
5:25 in the Spirit, **l** us also walk in the Spirit. NIG
5:26 **L** us not be desirous of vain glory, NIG
6: 4 But **l** every man prove his own work, NIG
6: 6 **L** him that is taught in the word NIG
6: 9 And **l** us not be weary in well doing: for NIG
6:10 **l** us do good unto all *men,* especially unto NIG
6:17 From henceforth **l** no *man* trouble me: for NIG
Eph 4:26 **l** not the sun go down upon your wrath: NIG
4:28 **l** him that stole steal no more: but rather NIG
4:28 but rather **l** him labour, working with *his* NIG
4:29 **L** no corrupt communication proceed out NIG
4:31 **L** all bitterness, and wrath, and anger, NIG
5: 3 **l** it not be once named amongst you, NIG
5: 6 **L** no *man* deceive you with vain words: NIG
5:24 *l* the wives *be* to their own husbands in NIG
5:33 Nevertheless **l** every one of you in NIG
Php 1:27 I your conversation be as it becometh NIG
2: 3 **L** nothing *be done* through strife or NIG
2: 3 in lowliness of mind *l* each esteem other NIG
2: 5 **L** this mind be in you, which *was* also in NIG
3:15 **L** us therefore, as many as *be* perfect, NIG
3:16 *l* us walk by the same rule, *let us* mind NIG
3:16 the same rule, *l us* mind the same *thing.* NIG
4: 5 **L** your moderation be known unto all NIG
4: 6 supplication with thanksgiving **l** your NIG
Col 2:16 **L** no *man* therefore judge you in meat, NIG
2:18 **L** no *man* beguile you of your reward in a NIG
3:15 **l** the peace of God rule in your hearts, NIG
3:16 **L** the word of Christ dwell in you richly NIG
4: 6 **L** your speech *be* alway with grace, NIG
1Th 5: 6 Therefore **l** us not sleep, as *do* others; NIG
5: 6 as *do* others; but **l** us watch and be sober. NIG
5: 8 But **l** us, who are of the day, be sober, NIG
2Th 2: 3 **L** no *man* deceive you by any means: NIG
2: 7 only he who now **l** letteth *will* **l,** until he be NIG
1Ti 2:11 **L** the woman learn in silence with all NIG
3:10 And **l** these also first be proved; then NIG
3:10 then **l** them use the office of a deacon, NIG
3:12 **L** the deacons be the husbands of one wife NIG
4:12 **L** no *man* despise thy youth; but be thou NIG
5: 4 **l** them learn first to shew piety at home, NIG
5: 9 **L** not a widow be taken into the number NIG
5:16 **l** them relieve them, and let not the church NIG
5:16 and **l** not the church be charged; NIG
5:17 **L** the elders that rule well be counted NIG
6: 1 **l** as many servants as are under the yoke NIG
6: 2 **l** them not despise *them,* because they are NIG
6: 8 and raiment **l** us be therewith content. NIG
2Ti 2:19 **L** every one that nameth the name of NIG
Tit 2:15 with all authority. **L** no *man* despise thee. NIG
3:14 And **l** ours also learn to maintain good NIG
Phm 1:20 brother, **l** me have joy of thee in the Lord: NIG
Heb 6: 4 And **l** all the angels of God worship him. NIG
2: 1 lest at any time we should **l** *them* slip. NIG
4: 1 **L** us therefore fear, lest, a promise being NIG
4:11 **L** us labour therefore to enter into that rest NIG
4:14 Son of God, **l** us hold fast *our* profession. NIG
4:16 **L** us therefore come boldly unto the NIG
6: 1 of Christ, **l** us go on unto perfection; NIG
10:22 **l** us draw near with a true heart in full NIG
10:23 **L** us hold fast the profession of *our* hope NIG
10:24 And **l** us consider one another to provoke NIG
12: 1 **l** us lay aside every weight, and the sin NIG
12: 1 **l** us run with patience the race that is set NIG
12:13 out of the way; but **l** it rather be healed. NIG
12:28 **l** us have grace, whereby we may serve NIG
13: 1 **L** brotherly love continue. NIG
13: 5 *L* your conversation *be* without NIG
13:13 **L** us go forth therefore unto him without NIG
13:15 **l** us offer the sacrifice of praise to God NIG
Jas 1: 4 But **l** patience have *her* perfect work, that NIG
1: 5 any of you lack wisdom, **l** him ask of God, NIG
1: 6 But **l** him ask in faith, nothing wavering: NIG
1: 7 **l** not that man think that he shall receive NIG
1: 9 **L** the brother of low degree rejoice in that NIG
1:13 **L** no *man* say when he is tempted, I am NIG
1:19 **l** every man be swift to hear, slow to speak NIG
3:13 **l** him shew out of a good conversation his NIG
4: 9 **l** your laughter be turned to mourning, NIG
5:12 but **l** your yea be yea; and *your* nay, nay; NIG
5:13 **l** him pray. Is any merry? **l** him sing NIG
5:13 him pray. Is any merry? **l** him sing psalms. NIG
5:14 **l** him call for the elders of the church; NIG
5:14 and **l** them pray over him, anointing him NIG
5:20 **L** him know, that he which converteth NIG
1Pe 3: 3 Whose adorning **l** it not be that outward NIG
3: 4 But *l* it be the hidden man of the heart, NIG
3:10 **l** him refrain his tongue from evil, NIG
3:11 **L** him eschew evil, and do good; let him NIG
3:11 do good; **l** him seek peace, and ensue it. NIG
4:11 *l* him speak as the oracles of God; NIG
4:11 *l* him do it as of the ability which God NIG
4:15 But **l** none of you suffer as a murderer, NIG
4:16 as a Christian, **l** him not be ashamed; NIG

1Pe 4:16 but **l** him glorify God on this behalf. NIG
4:19 Wherefore **l** them that suffer according to NIG
1Jn 2:24 **L** *that* therefore abide in you, which ye NIG
3: 7 Little children, **l** no *man* deceive you: NIG
3:18 **l** us not love in word, neither in tongue; NIG
4: 7 Beloved, **l** us love one another: for love is NIG
Rev 2: 7 I him hear what the Spirit saith unto NIG
2:11 I him hear what the Spirit saith unto NIG
2:17 I him hear what the Spirit saith unto NIG
2:29 I him hear what the Spirit saith unto NIG
3: 6 I him hear what the Spirit saith unto NIG
3:13 I him hear what the Spirit saith unto NIG
3:22 I him hear what the Spirit saith unto NIG
13: 9 If any *man* have an ear, **l** him hear. NIG
13:18 **l** him that hath understanding count NIG
19: 7 **L** us be glad and rejoice, and give honour NIG
22:11 He that is unjust, **l** him be unjust still: NIG
22:11 and he which is filthy, **l** him be filthy still: NIG
22:11 *that is* righteous, **l** him be righteous still: NIG
22:11 and *he that is* holy, **l** him be holy still. NIG
22:17 And **l** him that heareth say, Come. NIG
22:17 And **l** him that is athirst come. NIG
22:17 **l** him take the water of life freely. NIG

LETTER (37) [LETTERS]

2Sa 11:14 David wrote a **l** to Joab, and sent *it* by 5612
11:15 he wrote in the **l,** saying, Set ye Uriah in 5612
2Ki 5: 5 and I will send a **l** unto the king of Israel. 5612
5: 6 he brought the **l** to the king of Israel, 5612
5: 6 Now when this **l** is come unto thee, 5612
5: 7 when the king of Israel had read the **l,** 5612
10: 2 Now as soon as this **l** cometh to you, 5612
10: 6 he wrote a **l** the second time to them, 5612
10: 7 it came to pass, when the **l** came to them, 5612
19:14 Hezekiah received the **l** of the hand of 5612
Ezr 4: 7 the writing of the **l** was written in 5406
4: 8 Shimshai the scribe wrote a **l** against 104
4:11 This *is* the copy of the **l** that they sent 104
4:18 The **l** which ye sent unto us *hath been* 5407
4:23 Now when the copy of king Artaxerxes' **l** 5407
5: 5 they returned answer by **l** concerning this 5407
5: 6 The copy of the **l** that Tatnai, governor on 104
5: 7 They sent a **l** unto him, wherein *was* 6600
7:11 Now this *is* the copy of the **l** that the king 5406
Ne 2: 8 a **l** unto Asaph the keeper of the king's 107
6: 5 the fifth time with an open **l** in his hand; 107
Est 9:26 Therefore for all the words of this **l,** 107
9:29 to confirm this second **l** of Purim. 107
Isa 37:14 Hezekiah received the **l** from the hand of 5612
Jer 29: 1 Now these *are* the words of the **l** that 5612
29:29 Zephaniah the priest read this **l** in the ears 5612
Ac 23:25 And he wrote a **l** after this manner: 1992
23:34 And when the governor had read the **l,** NIG
Ro 2:27 who by the **l** and circumcision dost 1121
2:29 of the heart, in the spirit, *and* not *in* the **l;** 1121
7: 6 of spirit, and not *in* the oldness of the **l.** 1121
2Co 3: 6 **l** killeth, but the spirit giveth life. 1121
3: 6 for the **l** killeth, but the spirit giveth life. 1121
7: 8 For though I made you sorry with a **l,** I do 1992
Gal 6:11 Ye see how large a **l** I have written unto 1121
2Th 2: 2 spirit, nor by word, nor by **l** as from us, 1992
Heb 13:22 for I have **written a l** unto you in few 1989

LETTERS (34) [LETTER]

1Ki 21: 8 So she wrote **l** in Ahab's name, 5612
21: 8 sent the **l** unto the elders and to the 5612
21: 9 she wrote in the **l,** saying, Proclaim a fast, 5612
21:11 as *it was* written in the **l** which she had 5612
2Ki 10: 1 Jehu wrote **l,** and sent *to* Samaria, unto 5612
20:12 sent **l** and a present unto Hezekiah: 5612
2Ch 30: 1 wrote **l** also to Ephraim and Manasseh, 107
30: 6 the posts went with the **l** from the king 107
32:17 He wrote also **l** to rail on the Lord God 5612
Ne 2: 7 let **l** be given me to the governors beyond 107
2: 9 the river, and gave them the king's **l.** 107
6:17 nobles of Judah sent many **l** unto Tobiah, 107
6:17 and *the* **l** of Tobiah came unto them. NIH
6:19 *And* Tobiah sent **l** to put me in fear. 107
Est 1:22 For he sent **l** into all the king's provinces, 5612
3:13 the **l** were sent by posts into all the king's 5612
8: 5 let it be written to reverse the **l** devised 5612
8:10 sent **l** by posts on horseback, *and* riders 5612
9:20 sent **l** unto all the Jews that *were* in all 5612
9:25 commanded by **l** *that* his wicked device, 5612
9:30 he sent **l** unto all the Jews, 5612
Isa 39: 1 sent **l** and a present to Hezekiah: 5612
Jer 29:25 Because thou hast sent **l** in thy name unto 5612
Lk 23:38 also was written over him in **l** of Greek, 1121
Jn 7:15 saying, How knoweth this *man* **l,** 1121
Ac 9: 2 And desired of him **l** to Damascus to 1992
15:23 they wrote **l** by them after this manner; NIG
22: 5 from whom also I received **l** unto 1992
28:21 We neither received **l** out of Judea 1121
1Co 16: 3 whomsoever you shall approve by *your* **l,** 1992
2Co 3: 1 to you, or **l** of commendation from you? NIG
10: 9 not seem as if **l** would terrify you by **l.** 1992
10:10 For *his,* I say they, *are* weighty and 1992
10:11 such as we are in word by **l** when we are 1992

LETTEST (3) [LET]

Job 15:13 and *such* words go out of thy mouth? NIH
41: 1 tongue with a cord *which* thou **l down?** 8257
Lk 2:29 now **l** thou thy servant depart in peace, NIG

LETTETH (3) [LET]

2Ki 10:24 *that* **l** *him go,* his life *shall* be for the life NIH
Pr 17:14 beginning of strife *is as* when one **l** out 6362
2Th 2: 7 only he who now **l** *will let,* until he be 2722

LETTING (1) [LET]

Ex 8:29 **l** the people **go** to sacrifice to the Lord. 7971

LETUSHIM (1)

Ge 25: 3 were Asshurim, and **L,** and Leummim. 3912

LETUSHITES See LETUSHIM

LEUMMIM (1)

Ge 25: 3 were Asshurim, and Letushim, and **L.** 3817

LEUMMITES See LEUMMIM

LEVI (72) [LEVITE, LEVITES, LEVITICAL]

Ge 29:34 therefore was his name called **L.** 3878
34:25 Simeon and **L,** Dinah's brethren, took 3878
34:30 Jacob said to Simeon and **L,** Ye have 3878
35:23 **L,** and Judah, and Issachar, and Zebulun: 3878
46:11 the sons of **L;** Gershon, Kohath, 3878
49: 5 Simeon and **L** *are* brethren; instruments 3878
Ex 1: 2 Reuben, Simeon, **L,** and Judah, 3878
2: 1 there went a man of the house of **L,** 3878
2: 1 of Levi, and took *to wife* a daughter of **L.** 3878
6:16 these *are* the names of the sons of **L** 3878
6:16 the years of the life of **L** *were* an hundred 3878
6:19 these *are* the families of **L** according to 3878
32:26 all the sons of **L** gathered themselves 3878
32:28 children of **L** did according to the word 3878
Nu 1:49 thou shalt not number the tribe of **L,** 3878
3: 6 Bring the tribe of **L** near, and present 3878
3:15 Number the children of **L** after the house 3878
3:17 these were the sons of **L** by their names; 3878
4: 2 sons of Kohath from among the sons of **L,** 3878
16: 1 the son of **L,** and Dathan and Abiram, 3878
16: 7 *ye take* too much upon you, ye sons of **L.** 3878
16: 8 Korah, Hear, I pray you, ye sons of **L:** 3878
16:10 all thy brethren the sons of **L** with thee: 3878
17: 3 write Aaron's name upon the rod of **L:** 3878
17: 8 the rod of Aaron for the house of **L** was 3878
18: 2 brethren also *of* the tribe of **L,** the tribe 3878
18:21 have given the children of **L** all the tenth 3878
26:59 the daughter of **L,** whom *her mother* bare 3878
26:59 whom *her mother* bare to **L** in Egypt: 3878
Dt 10: 8 time the Lord separated the tribe of **L,** 3878
10: 9 Wherefore **L** hath no part nor inheritance 3878
18: 1 priests the Levites, *and* all the tribe of **L,** 3878
21: 5 the priests the sons of **L** shall come near; 3878
27:12 **L,** and Judah, and Issachar, and Joseph, 3878
31: 9 delivered it unto the priests the sons of **L,** 3878
33: 8 of **L** he said, *Let* thy Thummim and 3878
Jos 13:14 Only unto the tribe of **L** he gave none 3878
13:33 unto the tribe of **L** Moses gave not *any* 3878
21:10 *who were* of the children of **L,** had: 3878
1Ki 12:31 which were not of the sons of **L.** 3878
1Ch 2: 1 Reuben, Simeon, and Judah, Issachar, 3878
6: 1 The sons of **L;** Gershon, Kohath, 3878
6:16 The sons of **L;** Gershom, Kohath, 3878
6:38 of Kohath, the son of **L,** the son of Israel. 3878
6:43 the son of Gershom, the son of **L.** 3878
6:47 the son of Mushi, the son of Merari, the son of **L.** 3878
9:18 in the companies of the children of **L.** 3878
12:26 Of the children of **L** four thousand and 3878
21: 6 **L** and Benjamin counted he not among 3878
23: 6 them *into* courses among the sons of **L,** 3878
23:14 his sons were named of the tribe of **L.** 3878
23:24 These *were* the sons of **L** after the house 3878
24:20 the rest of the sons of **L** *were these:* Of 3878
Ezr 8:15 and found there none of the sons of **L:** 3878
8:18 of Mahli, the son of **L,** the son of Israel; 3878
Ne 10:39 the children of **L** shall bring the offering 3878
12:23 The sons of **L,** the chief of the fathers, 3878
Ps 135:20 Bless the Lord, O house of **L:** ye that 3878
Eze 40:46 the sons of Zadok among the sons of **L,** 3878
48:31 one gate of Judah, one gate of **L.** 3878
Zec 12:13 The family of the house of **L** apart, 3878
Mal 2: 4 that my covenant might be with **L,** saith 3878
2: 8 ye have corrupted the covenant of **L,** 3878
3: 3 he shall purify the sons of **L,** 3878
Mk 2:14 he saw **L** the *son* of Alpheus sitting at 3018
Lk 3:24 which was the *son* of **L,** which was the 3017
3:29 *son* of Matthat, which was the *son* of **L,** 3017
5:27 and saw a publican, named **L,** sitting at 3018
5:29 And **L** made him a great feast in his own 3018
Heb 7: 5 And verily they that are of the sons of **L,** 3017
7: 9 as *I* may say, **L** also, who receiveth 3017
Rev 7: 7 Of the tribe of **L** *were* sealed twelve 3017

LEVIATHAN (5)

Job 41: 1 Canst thou draw out **l** with a hook? 3882
Ps 74:14 Thou brakest the heads of **l** in pieces, 3882
104:26 *there is* that **l,** *whom* thou hast made to 3882
Isa 27: 1 strong sword shall punish **l** the piercing 3882
27: 1 even **l** *that* crooked serpent; 3882

LEVITE (28) [LEVI]

Ex 4:14 he said, Is not Aaron the **L** thy brother? 3881
Dt 12:12 and the **L** that *is* within your gates; 3881
12:18 and the **L** that *is* within thy gates: 3881
12:19 the **L** as long as thou livest upon the earth. 3881
14:27 the **L** that *is* within thy gates; thou shalt 3881
14:29 the **L,** (because he hath no part nor 3881

Dt 16:11 the **L** that *is* within thy gates, 3881
16:14 the **L**, the stranger, and the fatherless, 3881
18: 6 if a **L** come from any of thy gates out of 3881
26:11 the **L**, and the stranger that *is* among you. 3881
26:12 hast given *it* unto the **L**, the stranger, 3881
26:13 also have given them unto the **L**, 3881
Jdg 17: 7 who *was* a **L** of Beth-lehem-judah, and I go to 3881
17: 9 I *am* a **L** of Beth-lehem-judah, and I go to 3881
17:10 and thy victuals. So the **L** went in. 3881
17:11 the **L** was content to dwell with the man; 3881
17:12 Micah consecrated the **L**; and the young 3881
17:13 me good, seeing I have a **L** to *my* priest. 3881
18: 3 knew the voice of the young man the **L**: 3881
18:15 to the house of the young man the **L**, 3881
19: 1 that there was a certain **L** sojourning on 3881
20: 4 the **L**, the husband of the woman that 3881
2Ch 20:14 of Mattaniah, a **L** of the sons of Asaph, 3881
31:12 over which Cononiah the **L** *was* ruler, 3881
31:14 Kore the son of Imnah the **L**, the porter, 3881
Ezr 10:15 and Shabbethai the **L** helped them. 3881
Lk 10:32 And likewise a **L**, when he was at 3019
Ac 4:36 a **L**, *and* of the country of Cyprus, 3019

LEVITES (265) [LEVI]

Ex 6:25 these *are* the heads of the fathers of the **L** 3881
38:21 *for* the service of the **L**, by the hand of 3881
Lev 25:32 Notwithstanding the cities of the **L**, 3881
25:32 may the **L** redeem at any time. 3881
25:33 if a man purchase of the **L**, then the house 3881
25:33 for the houses of the cities of the **L** *are* 3881
Nu 1:47 the **L** after the tribe of their fathers were 3881
1:50 shalt appoint the **L** over the tabernacle 3881
1:51 setteth forward, the **L** shall take it down: 3881
1:51 is to be pitched, the **L** shall set it up: 3881
1:53 the **L** shall pitch round about the 3881
1:53 the **L** shall keep the charge of 3881
2:17 camp of the **L** in the midst of the camp: 3881
2:33 the **L** were not numbered among 3881
3: 9 thou shalt give the **L** unto Aaron and to 3881
3:12 I have taken the **L** from among the 3881
3:12 of Israel: therefore the **L** shall be mine; 3881
3:20 These *are* the families of the **L** according 3881
3:32 *shall be* chief over the chief of the **L**, 3881
3:39 All that were numbered of the **L**, 3881
3:41 thou shalt take the **L** for me (I *am* 3881
3:41 the cattle of the **L** instead of all 3881
3:45 Take the **L** instead of all the firstborn 3881
3:45 the cattle of the **L** instead of their cattle; 3881
3:45 of their cattle; and the **L** shall be mine: 3881
3:46 of Israel, which are more than the **L**: 3881
3:49 above them that were redeemed by the **L**: 3881
4:18 of the Kohathites from among the **L**: 3881
4:46 All those that were numbered of the **L**, 3881
7: 5 thou shalt give them unto the **L**, to every 3881
7: 6 and the oxen, and gave them unto the **L**. 3881
8: 6 Take the **L** from among the children of 3881
8: 9 shalt bring the **L** before the tabernacle 3881
8:10 thou shalt bring the **L** before the LORD: 3881
8:10 of Israel shall put their hands upon the **L**: 3881
8:11 Aaron shall offer the **L** before the LORD 3881
8:12 the **L** shall lay their hands upon the heads 3881
8:12 to make an atonement for the **L**. 3881
8:13 thou shalt set the **L** before Aaron, 3881
8:14 shalt thou separate the **L** from among 3881
8:14 children of Israel: and the **L** shall be mine. 3881
8:15 that shall the **L** go in to do the service 3881
8:18 I have taken the **L** for all the firstborn of 3881
8:19 I have given the **L** *as* a gift to Aaron and 3881
8:20 did to the **L** according unto all that 3881
8:20 commanded Moses concerning the **L**, 3881
8:21 the **L** were purified, and they washed 3881
8:22 after that went the **L** in to do their service 3881
8:22 had commanded Moses concerning the **L**, 3881
8:24 This *is it* that *belongeth* unto the **L**: 3881
8:26 Thus shalt thou do unto the **L** touching 3881
18: 6 I have taken your brethren the **L** from 3881
18:23 the **L** shall do the service of the tabernacle 3881
18:24 I have given to the **L** to inherit: 3881
18:26 Thus speak unto the **L**, and say unto 3881
18:30 it shall be counted unto the **L** as 3881
26:57 *are* they that were numbered of the **L** 3881
26:58 These *are* the families of the **L**: the family 3881
31:30 *of* beasts, and give them unto the **L**, 3881
31:47 and of beast, and gave them unto the **L**, 3881
35: 2 they give unto the **L** of the inheritance 3881
35: 2 ye shall give *also* unto the **L** suburbs for 3881
35: 4 the cities, which ye shall give unto the **L**, 3881
35: 6 the **L** *there shall be* six cities for refuge, 3881
35: 7 all the cities which ye shall give to the **L** 3881
35: 8 one shall give of his cities unto the **L** 3881
Dt 17: 9 thou shalt come unto the priests the **L**: 3881
17:18 of *that which is* before the priests the **L**: 3881
18: 1 The priests the **L**, *and* all the tribe of Levi, 3881
18: 7 as all his brethren the **L** *do*, which stand 3881
24: 8 do according to all that the priests the **L** 3881
27: 9 and the priests the **L** spake unto all Israel, 3881
27:14 the **L** shall speak, and say unto all the 3881
31:25 Moses commanded the **L**, which bare 3881
Jos 3: 3 the priests the **L** bearing it, then ye shall 3881
8:33 and on that side before the priests the **L**, 3881
14: 3 unto the **L** he gave none inheritance 3881
14: 4 they gave no part unto the **L** in the land, 3881

Jos 18: 7 the **L** have no part among you; 3881
21: 1 near the heads of the fathers of the **L** 3881
21: 3 the children of Israel gave unto the **L** out 3881
21: 4 of Aaron the priest, *which were* of the **L**, 3881
21: 8 children of Israel gave by lot unto the **L** 3881
21:20 the **L** which remained of the children of 3881
21:27 of Gershon, of the families of the **L**, 3881
21:34 the rest of the **L**, out of the tribe of 3881
21:40 were remaining of the families of the **L**, 3881
21:41 the cities of the **L** within the possession 3881
1Sa 6:15 the **L** took down the ark of the LORD, 3881
2Sa 15:24 Zadok also, and all the **L** *were* with him, 3881
1Ki 8: 4 those did the priests and the **L** bring up. 3881
1Ch 6:19 these *are* the families of the **L** according 3881
6:48 Their brethren also the **L** *were* appointed 3881
6:64 the children of Israel gave to the **L** these 3881
9: 2 the priests, and the Nethinims. 3881
9:14 of the **L**; Shemaiah the son of Hasshub, 3881
9:26 For these **L**, the four chief porters, *were* in 3881
9:31 Mattithiah, one of the **L**, who was 3881
9:33 the singers, chief of the fathers of the **L**, 3881
9:34 These chief fathers of the **L** *were* chief 3881
13: 2 **L** *which are* in their cities *and* suburbs, 3881
15: 2 ought to carry the ark of God but the **L**: 3881
15: 4 the children of Aaron, and the **L**: 3881
15:11 for the **L**, for Uriel, Asaiah, and Joel, 3881
15:12 Ye *are* the chief of the fathers of the **L**: 3881
15:14 the **L** sanctified themselves to bring up 3881
15:15 the children of the **L** bare the ark of God 3881
15:16 David spake to the chief of the **L** to 3881
15:17 the **L** appointed Heman the son of Joel; 3881
15:22 chief of the **L**, *was* for song: 3881
15:26 when God helped the **L** that bare the ark 3881
15:27 all the **L** that bare the ark, and the singers, 3881
16: 4 he appointed *certain* of the **L** to minister 3881
23: 2 of Israel, with the priests and the **L**. 3881
23: 3 Now the **L** were numbered from the age 3881
23:26 also unto the **L**; *they* shall no *more* carry 3881
23:27 the **L** *were* numbered from twenty 1121+3878
24: 6 one of the **L**, wrote them before the king, 3881
24: 6 chief of the fathers of the priests and **L**: 3881
24:30 These *were* the sons of the **L** after 3881
24:31 chief of the fathers of the priests and **L**, 3881
26:17 Eastward *were* six **L**, northward four a 3881
26:20 *of* the **L**, Ahijah *was* over the treasures of 3881
27:17 Of the **L**, Hashabiah the son of Kemuel: 3881
28:13 for the courses of the priests and the **L**, 3881
28:21 the courses of the priests and the **L**, 3881
2Ch 5: 4 of Israel came; and the **L** took up the ark. 3881
5: 5 these did the priests *and* the **L** bring up. 3881
5:12 Also the **L** *which were* the singers, all of 3881
7: 6 the **L** also with instruments of musick of 3881
8:14 the **L** to their charges, to praise and 3881
8:15 the priests and **L** concerning any matter, 3881
11:13 the **L** that *were* in all Israel resorted to 3881
11:14 For the **L** left their suburbs and 3881
13: 9 the **L**, and have made you priests after 3881
13:10 and the **L** *wait* upon *their* business: 3881
17: 8 with them *he* sent, *even* Shemaiah, 3881
17: 8 and Tobijah, and Tob-adonijah, **L**; 3881
19: 8 in Jerusalem did Jehoshaphat set of the **L**, 3881
19:11 also the **L** *shall be* officers before you. 3881
20:19 the **L**, of the children of the Kohathites, 3881
23: 2 the **L** out of all the cities of Judah, 3881
23: 4 the priests and of the **L**, *shall be* porters 3881
23: 6 priests, and they that minister of the **L**; 3881
23: 7 the **L** shall compass the king round about, 3881
23: 8 the **L** and all Judah did according to all 3881
23:18 LORD by the hand of the priests the **L**, 3881
24: 5 gathered together the priests and the **L**, 3881
24: 5 Howbeit the **L** hastened *it* not. 3881
24: 6 Why hast thou not required of the **L** to 3881
24:11 the king's office by the hand of the **L**, 3881
29: 4 he brought in the priests and the **L**, 3881
29: 5 said unto them, Hear me, ye **L**, 3881
29:12 the **L** arose, Mahath the son of Amasai, 3881
29:16 the **L** took *it*, to carry *it* out abroad into 3881
29:25 he set the **L** *in* the house of the LORD 3881
29:26 the **L** stood with the instruments of David, 3881
29:30 princes commanded the **L** to *sing* praise 3881
29:34 wherefore their brethren the **L** did help 3881
29:34 for the **L** *were* more upright in heart to 3881
30:15 the priests and the **L** were ashamed, 3881
30:16 *they* received of the hand of the **L**. 3881
30:17 the **L** had the charge of the killing of 3881
30:21 the **L** and the priests praised the LORD 3881
30:22 spake comfortably unto all the **L** 3881
30:25 with the priests and the **L**, and all 3881
30:27 the priests the **L** arose and blessed 3881
31: 2 the priests and the **L** after their courses, 3881
31: 2 the priests and **L** for burnt offerings and 3881
31: 4 give the portion of the priests and the **L**, 3881
31: 9 priests and the **L** concerning the heaps. 3881
31:17 from twenty years old and upward, 3881
31:19 reckoned by genealogies among the **L**. 3881
34: 9 which the **L** that kept the doors had 3881
34:12 of them *were* Jahath and Obadiah, the **L**, 3881
34:12 *other of* the **L**, all that could skill of 3881
34:13 of the **L** *there were* scribes, and officers, 3881
34:30 the **L**, and all the people, great and small: 3881
35: 3 said unto the **L** that taught all Israel, 3881
35: 5 *after* the division of the families of the **L**. 3881
35: 8 the people, to the priests, and to the **L** 3881
35: 9 and Jeiel and Jozabad, chief of the **L**, 3881
35: 9 gave unto the **L** for passover *offerings* five 3881

2Ch 35:10 in their place, and the **L** in their courses, 3881
35:11 from their hands, and the **L** flayed *them*. 3881
35:14 therefore the **L** prepared for themselves, 3881
35:15 for their brethren the **L** prepared for them. 3881
35:18 the **L**, and all Judah and Israel that were 3881
Ezr 1: 5 and Benjamin, and the priests, and the **L**, 3881
2:40 **L**: the children of Jeshua and Kadmiel, 3881
2:70 the **L**, and *some* of the people, 3881
3: 8 of their brethren the priests and the **L**, 3881
3: 8 appointed the **L** from twenty years old 3881
3: 9 *with* their sons and their brethren the **L**, 3881
3:10 the **L** the sons of Asaph with cymbals, 3881
3:12 the priests and **L** and chief of the fathers, 3881
6:16 the **L**, and the rest of the children of 3879
6:18 the **L** in their courses, for the service of 3879
6:20 priests and the **L** were purified together, 3881
7: 7 the **L**, and the singers, and the porters, 3881
7:13 and *of* his priests and **L**, in my realm, 3879
7:24 *touching* any of the priests and **L**, 3879
8:20 had appointed for the service of the **L**, 3881
8:29 before the chief of the priests and the **L**, 3881
8:30 and the **L** the weight of the silver, 3881
8:33 and Noadiah the son of Binnui, **L**; 3881
9: 1 of Israel, and the priests, and the **L**, 3881
10: 5 the chief priests, the **L**, and all Israel, 3881
10:23 Also of the **L**; Jozabad, and Shimei, 3881
Ne 3:17 After him repaired the **L**, Rehum the son 3881
7: 1 and the singers, and the **L** were appointed, 3881
7:43 The **L**: the children of Jeshua, of Kadmiel, 3881
7:73 the **L**, and the porters, and the singers, 3881
8: 7 Jozabad, Hanan, Pelaiah, and the **L**, 3881
8: 9 the **L** that taught the people, said unto all 3881
8:11 So the **L** stilled all the people, saying, 3881
8:13 priests, and the **L**, unto Ezra the scribe, 3881
9: 4 stood up upon the stairs of the **L**, Jeshua, 3881
9: 5 the **L**, Jeshua and Kadmiel, Bani, 3881
9:38 write *it*; and our princes, **L**, *and* priests, 3881
10: 9 the **L**: both Jeshua the son of Azaniah, 3881
10:28 the priests, the **L**, the porters, the singers, 3881
10:34 the **L**, and the people, for the wood 3881
10:37 the tithes of our ground unto the **L**, that 3881
10:37 that the same **L** *might* have the tithes in 3881
10:38 the son of Aaron shall be with the **L**, 3881
10:38 with the Levites, when the **L** take tithes: 3881
10:38 the **L** shall bring up the tithe of the tithes 3881
11: 3 **L**, and the Nethinims, and the children 3881
11:15 of the **L**: Shemaiah the son of Hashub, 3881
11:16 and Jozabad, of the chief of the **L**, 3881
11:18 All the **L** in the holy city *were* two 3881
11:20 residue of Israel, of the priests, *and* the **L**, 3881
11:22 The overseer also of the **L** at Jerusalem 3881
11:36 of the **L** *were* divisions *in* Judah, 3881
12: 1 the **L** that went up with Zerubbabel the 3881
12: 8 Moreover the **L**: Jeshua, Binnui, Kadmiel, 3881
12:22 The **L** in the days of Eliashib, Joiada, 3881
12:24 the chief of the **L**: Hashabiah, Sherebiah, 3881
12:27 they sought the **L** out of all their places, 3881
12:30 the priests and the **L** purified themselves, 3881
12:44 portions of the law for the priests and **L**: 3881
12:44 for the priests and for the **L** that waited. 3881
12:47 they sanctified *holy things* unto the **L**; 3881
12:47 the **L** sanctified *them* unto the children of 3881
13: 5 was commanded *to be given* to the **L**, 3881
13:10 I perceived that the portions of the **L** had 3881
13:10 had not been given *them*: for the **L** 3881
13:13 Zadok the scribe, and of the **L**, Pedaiah: 3881
13:22 I commanded the **L** that they should 3881
13:29 covenant of the priesthood, and of the **L**, 3881
13:30 the wards of the priests and the **L**, 3881
Isa 66:21 also take of them for priests *and* for **L**, 3881
Jer 33:18 Neither shall the priests the **L** want a man 3881
33:21 and with the **L** the priests, my ministers. 3881
33:22 and the **L** that minister unto me. 3881
Eze 43:19 thou shalt give to the priests the **L** that *be* 3881
44:10 the **L** that are gone away far from me, 3881
44:15 the priests the **L**, the sons of Zadok, 3881
45: 5 also the **L**, the ministers of the house, 3881
48:11 Israel went astray, as the **L** went astray. 3881
48:12 *a thing* most holy by the border of the **L**. 3881
48:13 the **L** *shall have* five and twenty thousand 3881
48:22 Moreover from the possession of the **L**, 3881
Jn 1:19 and **L** from Jerusalem to ask him, 3019

LEVITICAL (1) [LEVI]

Heb 7:11 perfection were by the **L** priesthood, 3020

LEVY (6)

Nu 31:28 l a tribute unto the LORD of the men of 7311
1Ki 5:13 king Solomon raised a **l** out of all Israel; 4522
5:13 and the **l** was thirty thousand men. 4522
5:14 at home: and Adoniram *was* over the **l**. 4522
9:15 this *is* the reason of the **l** which king 4522
9:21 **upon** those did Solomon **l** a tribute of 5927

LEWD (3) [LEWDLY, LEWDNESS]

Eze 16:27 are ashamed of thy **l** way. 2154
23:44 and unto Aholibah, the **l** women. 2154
Ac 17: 5 took unto *them* certain **l** fellows of 4190

LEWDLY (1) [LEWD]

Eze 22:11 hath **l** defiled his daughter in law; 2154+871.1

LEWDNESS (17) [LEWD]

Jdg 20: 6 for they have committed **l** and folly in 2154
Jer 11:15 *seeing* she hath wrought **l** *with* many, 4209

L

Jer 13:27 the **l** of thy whoredom, 2154
Eze 16:43 thou shalt not commit *this* l above all 2154
16:58 Thou hast borne thy **l** and thine 2154
22: 9 in the midst of thee they commit **l** 2154
23:21 Thus thou callest to remembrance the **l** 2154
23:27 Thus will I make thy **l** to cease from thee, 2154
23:29 both thy **l** and thy whoredoms. 2154
23:35 therefore bear thou also thy **l** and thy 2154
23:48 will I cause **l** to cease out of the land, 2154
23:48 may be taught not to do after your **l**. 2154
23:49 they shall recompense your **l** upon you, 2154
24:13 thy filthiness *is* **l**: because I have purged 2154
Hos 2:10 will I discover her **l** in the sight of her 5040
6: 9 *in* the way by consent: for they commit **l**. 2154
Ac 18:14 If it were a matter of wrong or wicked **l**, 4467

LIAR (13) [LIE]

Job 24:25 who will **make** me a **l**, and make my 3576
Pr 17: 4 *and* a **l** giveth ear to a naughty tongue. 8267
19:22 and a poor man *is* better than a **l**. 376+3577
30: 6 he reprove thee, and thou be **found** a **l**. 3576
Jer 15:18 wilt thou be altogether unto me as a **l**, 391
Jn 8:44 his own: for he is a **l**, and the father of it. 5583
8:55 know him not, I shall be a **l** like unto you: 5583
Ro 3: 4 let God be true, but every man a **l**; as it 5583
1Jn 1:10 make him a **l**, and his word is not in us. 5583
2: 4 is a **l**, and the truth is not in him. 5583
2:22 Who is a **l** but he that denieth that Jesus 5583
4:20 love God, and hateth his brother, he is a **l**: 5583
5:10 that believeth not God hath made him a **l**; 5583

LIARS (8) [LIE]

Dt 33:29 thine enemies shall be **found** **l** unto thee; 3584
Ps 116:11 I said in my haste, All men *are* **l**. 3576
Isa 44:25 That frustrateth the tokens of the **l**, 907
Jer 50:36 A sword *is* upon the **l**; and they shall dote: 907
1Ti 1:10 menstealers, for **l**, for perjured *persons*, 5583
Tit 1:12 said, The Cretians *are* alway **l**, evil beasts, 5583
Rev 2: 2 and are not, and hast found them **l**: 5571
21: 8 and sorcerers, and idolaters, and all **l**, 5571

LIBERAL (6) [LIBERALITY, LIBERALLY, LIBERTINES]

Pr 11:25 The **l** soul shall be made fat: and he that 1293
Isa 32: 5 The vile person shall be no more called **l**, 5081
32: 8 l deviseth liberal *things*; and by liberal 5081
32: 8 liberal deviseth **l** *things*; and by liberal 5082
32: 8 and by **l** *things* shall he stand. 5082
2Co 9:13 and *for your* **l** distribution unto them, 572

LIBERALITY (2) [LIBERAL]

1Co 16: 3 them will I send to bring your **l** unto 5485
2Co 8: 2 poverty abounded unto the riches of their **l**. 572

LIBERALLY (2) [LIBERAL]

Dt 15:14 Thou shalt **furnish** him **l** out of 6059+6059
Jas 1: 5 giveth to all *men* **l**, and upbraideth not; 574

LIBERTINES (1) [LIBERAL]

Ac 6: 9 which is called *the synagogue* of the **L**, 3032

LIBERTY (27)

Lev 25:10 proclaim **l** throughout *all* the land unto all 1865
Ps 119:45 I will walk at **l**: for I seek thy precepts. 7342
Isa 61: 1 to proclaim **l** to the captives, 1865
Jer 34: 8 at Jerusalem, to proclaim **l** unto them; 1865
34:15 in proclaiming **l** every man to his 1865
34:16 whom ye had set at **l** at their pleasure, 2670
34:17 in proclaiming **l**, every one to his brother, 1865
34:17 behold, I proclaim a **l** for you, saith 1865
Eze 46:17 then it shall be his to the year of **l**; 1865
Lk 4:18 the blind, to set at **l** them that are bruised, 859
Ac 24:23 and to let *him* have **l**, and that *he* should 425
26:32 This man might have been **set at l**, 630
27: 3 **gave** *him* **l** to go unto *his* friends to 2010
Ro 8:21 into the glorious **l** of the children of God. 1657
1Co 7:39 she is at **l** to be married to whom she will; 1658
8: 9 But take heed lest by any means this **l** of 1849
10:29 for why is my **l** judged of another *man's* 1657
2Co 3:17 where the Spirit of the Lord *is*, there *is* **l**. 1657
Gal 2: 4 who came in privily to spy out our **l** which 1657
5: 1 wherewith Christ hath made us free, 1657
5:13 For, brethren, ye have been called unto **l**; 1657
5:13 only *use* not **l** for an occasion to the flesh, 1657
Heb 13:23 ye that our brother Timothy is **set at l**; 630
Jas 1:25 whoso looketh into the perfect law of **l**, 1657
2:12 as they that shall be judged by the law of **l**. 1657
1Pe 2:16 not using *your* **l** for a cloke of 1657
2Pe 2:19 While they promise them **l**, they 1657

LIBNAH (18)

Nu 33:20 from Rimmon-parez, and pitched in **L**. 3841
33:21 they removed from **L**, and pitched at 3841
Jos 10:29 unto **L**, and fought against Libnah: 3841
10:29 *unto* Libnah, and fought against **L**: 3841
10:31 Joshua passed from **L**, and all Israel with 3841
10:32 according to all that he had done to **L**. 3841
10:39 as he had done also to **L**, and to her king. 3841
12:15 The king of **L**, one; the king of Adullam 3841
15:42 **L**, and Ether, and Ashan, 3841
21:13 for the priest; and **L** with her suburbs, 3841
2Ki 8:22 Then **L** revolted at the same time. 3841
19: 8 the king of Assyria warring against **L**: 3841
23:31 the daughter of Jeremiah of **L**. 3841
24:18 the daughter of Jeremiah of **L**. 3841
1Ch 6:57 **L** with her suburbs, and Jattir, 3841
2Ch 21:10 The same time also did **L** revolt from 3841

Isa 37: 8 the king of Assyria warring against **L**: 3841
Jer 52: 1 Hamutal the daughter of Jeremiah of **L**. 3841

LIBNI (5) [LIBNITES]

Ex 6:17 **L**, and Shimi, according to their families. 3845
Nu 3:18 Gershon by their families; **L**, and Shimei. 3845
1Ch 6:17 of the sons of Gershom; **L**, and Shimei. 3845
6:20 Mahli, **L** his son, Jahath his son, Zimmah his son, 3845
6:29 Mahli, **L** his son, Shimei his son, Uzza his 3845

LIBNITES (2) [LIBNI]

Nu 3:21 Of Gershon *was* the family of the **L**, 3846
26:58 the family of the **L**, the family of 3846

LIBYA (3) [LIBYANS]

Eze 30: 5 **L**, and Lydia, and all the mingled people, 6316
38: 5 Persia, Ethiopia, and **L** with them; all of 6316
Ac 2:10 and in the parts of **L** about Cyrene, 3033

LIBYANS (2) [LIBYA]

Jer 46: 9 the Ethiopians and the **L**, that handle 6316
Da 11:43 the **L** and the Ethiopians *shall be* at his 3864

LICE (6)

Ex 8:16 it may become **l** throughout all the land 3654
8:17 and it became **l** in man, and in beast; 3654
8:17 the dust of the land became **l** throughout 3654
8:18 with their enchantments to bring forth **l**, 3654
8:18 there were **l** upon man, and upon beast. 3654
Ps 105:31 sorts *of flies, and* **l** in all their coasts. 3654

LICENCE (2)

Ac 21:40 when he had **given** *him* **l**, Paul stood 2010
25:16 have **l** to answer for himself concerning 5117

LICK (5) [LICKED, LICKETH]

Nu 22: 4 Now shall *this* company **l** up all *that are* 3897
1Ki 21:19 blood of Naboth shall dogs **l** thy blood, 3952
Ps 72: 9 him; and his enemies shall **l** the dust. 3897
Isa 49:23 the earth, and **l** up the dust of thy feet; 3897
Mic 7:17 They shall **l** the dust like a serpent, 3897

LICKED (4) [LICK]

1Ki 18:38 and **l** up the water that *was* in the trench. 3897
21:19 In the place where dogs **l** the blood of 3952
22:38 the dogs **l** up his blood; and they washed 3952
Lk 16:21 moreover the dogs came and **l** his sores. 621

LICKETH (1) [LICK]

Nu 22: 4 as the ox **l** up the grass of the field. 3897

LID (1)

2Ki 12: 9 bored a hole in the **l** of it, and set it beside 1817

LIE (155) [LAIN, LIAR, LIARS, LIED, LIEN, LIERS, LIES, LIEST, LIETH, LYING]

Ge 19:32 father drink wine, and we will **l** with him, 7901
19:34 go thou in, *and* **l** with him, that we may 7901
30:15 Therefore he shall **l** with thee to night for 7901
39: 7 upon Joseph; and she said, **L** with me. 7901
39:10 unto her, to **l** by her, *or* to be with her. 7901
39:12 him by his garment, saying, **L** with me: 7901
39:14 he came in unto me to **l** with me, 7901
47:30 I will **l** with my fathers, and thou shalt 7901
Ex 21:13 if a man **l** not in wait, but God deliver 6658
22:16 If a man **l** with her, he shall surely endow her to be 7901
23:11 *year* thou shalt let it rest and **l** still; 5203
Lev 6: 2 **l** unto his neighbour in that which was 3584
15:18 The woman also with whom man shall **l** 7901
15:24 *if* any man **l** with her at all, 854+7901+7901
18:20 **l** carnally with thy 2233+5414+7903+3807.1
18:22 Thou shalt not **l** with mankind, as with 7901
18:23 Neither shalt thou **l** with any beast 5414+7903
18:23 stand before a beast to **l** **down** thereto: 7250
19:11 deal falsely, neither **l** one to another. 8266
20:12 if a man **l** with his daughter in law, both 7901
20:13 if a man also **l** with mankind, as he **l**eth 7901
20:15 if a man **with** a beast, he shall 5414+7903
20:16 **l** down thereto, thou shalt kill the woman 7250
20:18 if a man shall **l** with a woman having her 7901
20:20 if a man shall **l** with his uncle's wife, 7901
26: ye shall **l** **down**, and none shall make *you* 7901
Nu 5:13 a man **l** with her carnally, and it be hid 7901
10: 5 the camps that **l** on the east parts shall go 2583
10: 6 the camps that **l** on the south side shall 2583
23:19 God *is* not a man, that he should **l**; 3576
23:24 shall not **l** **down** until he eat *of* the prey, 7901
Dt 9:11 **l** in wait for him, and rise up against him, 693
22:23 a man find her in the city, and **l** with her; 7901
22:25 and the man force her, and **l** with her: 7901
22:28 on her, and **l** with her, and they be found; 7901
22:25 that the judge shall **cause** him to **l** down, 5307
28:30 a wife, and another man shall **l** with her: 7901
29:20 are written in this book shall **l** upon him, 7257
Jos 8: 4 Behold, ye shall **l** in **wait against** the city, 693
8: 9 they went to **l** in **ambush** 3993
8:12 set them to **l** in **ambush** between Beth-el 693
Jdg 9:32 that *is* with thee, and **l** in **wait** in the: 693
19:20 howsoever *let* all thy wants *l* upon me; NIH
21:20 Go and **l** in **wait** in the vineyards, 693
Ru 3: 4 thou shalt mark the place where he shall **l**, 7901
3: 7 he went to **l** down at the end of the heap 7901
3:13 **Lord** liveth: **l** **down** until the morning. 7901
1Sa 3: 5 he said, I called not; **l** **down** again. 7901
3: 6 I called not, my son; **l** **down** again. 7901
3: 9 Eli said unto Samuel, Go, **l** **down**: 7901

1Sa 15:29 also the Strength of Israel will not **l** nor 8266
22: 8 against me, to **l** in **wait**, as at this day? 693
22:13 against me, to **l** in **wait**, as at this day? 693
2Sa 11:11 eat and to drink, and to **l** with my wife? 7901
11:13 at even he went out to **l** on his bed with 7901
12:11 he shall **l** with thy wives in the sight of 7901
13:11 said unto her, Come **l** with me, my sister. 7901
1Ki 1: 2 cherish him, and let her **l** in thy bosom, 7901
2Ki 4:16 of God, do not **l** unto thine handmaid. 3576
Job 6:28 upon me; for *it is* evident unto you if I **l**. 3576
7: 4 When I **down**, I say, When shall I arise, 7901
11:19 Also thou shalt **l** **down**, and none shall 7257
20:11 which shall **l** **down** with him in the dust. 7901
21:26 They shall **l** **down** alike in the dust, 7901
27:19 The rich *man* shall **l** **down**, but he shall 7901
34: 6 Should I **l** against my right? my wound *is* 3576
38:40 *and* abide in the covert to **l** in **wait**? 695
Ps 23: 2 He **maketh** me to **l** **down** in green 7257
57: 4 I **l** *even among* them that are set on fire, 7901
59: 3 lo, they **l** in **wait** for my soul: the mighty 693
62: 9 vanity, *and* men of high degree *are* a **l**: 3577
88: 5 the dead, like the slain that **l** in the grave, 7901
89:35 my holiness that I will not **l** unto David. 3576
119:69 The proud have forged a **l** against me: 8267
Pr 3:24 thou shalt **l** **down**, and thy sleep shall be 7901
12: 6 The words of the wicked *are* to **l** in **wait** 693
14: 5 A faithful witness will not **l**: but a false 3576
Ecc 4:11 if two **together**, then they have heat: 7901
SS 1:13 he shall **l** **all night** betwixt my breasts. 3885
Isa 11: 6 the leopard shall **l** **down** with the kid; 7257
11: 7 their young ones shall **l** **down** together: 7257
13:21 wild beasts of the desert shall **l** there; 7257
14:18 of the nations, *even* all of them, **l** in glory, 7901
14:30 and the needy shall **l** **down** in safety: 7257
17: 2 which shall **l** **down**, and none shall make 7257
27:10 there shall he **l** **down**, and consume 7257
33: 8 The highways **l** **waste**, the wayfaring 8074
34:10 generation to generation it shall **l** **waste**; 2717
43:17 they shall **l** **down** together, they shall not 7901
44:20 nor say, *Is there* not a **l** in my right hand? 8267
50:11 in mine hand; ye shall **l** **down** in sorrow. 7901
51:20 they **l** at the head of all the streets, as a 7901
63: 8 *are* my people, children *that* will not **l**: 8266
65:10 Achor a **place** for the herds to **l** **down** in, 7258
Jer 3:25 We **l** **down** in our shame, 7901
27:10 they prophesy a **l** unto you, to remove 8267
27:14 Babylon: for they prophesy a **l** unto you. 8267
27:15 yet they prophesy a **l** in my name; 8267
27:16 for they prophesy a **l** unto you. 8267
28:15 thou makest this people to trust in a **l**. 8267
29:21 which prophesy a **l** unto you in my name; 8267
29:31 not, and he caused you to trust in a **l**: 8267
33:12 shepherds **causing** *their* flocks to **l** **down**. 7257
La 2:21 and the old **l** on the ground in the streets: 7901
Eze 4: 4 **L** thou also upon thy left side, and lay 7901
4: 4 upon it thou shalt bear their iniquity. 7901
4: 6 again on thy right side, and thou shalt 7901
4: 9 of the days that thou shalt **l** upon thy side, 7901
21:29 thee, whiles *they* divine a **l** unto thee, 3577
31:18 thou shalt **l** in the midst of 7901
32:21 they **l** uncircumcised, slain by the sword. 7901
32:27 they shall not **l** with the mighty *that are* 7901
32:28 shalt **l** with *them that are* slain with 7901
32:29 they shall **l** with the uncircumcised, 7901
32:30 **l** uncircumcised with *them that be* 7901
34:14 shall they **l** in a good fold, and *in* a fat 7257
34:15 flock, and I will **cause** them to **l** **down**, 7257
Hos 2:18 and will **make** them to **l** **down** safely. 7901
7: 6 heart like an oven, whiles they **l** in **wait**: 693
Joel 1:13 come, **l** **all night** in sackcloth, ye ministers 3885
Am 6: 4 That **l** upon beds of ivory, 6316
Mic 1:14 houses of Achzib *shall be* a **l** to the kings 391
2:11 walking in the spirit and falsehood do **l**, 3576
7: 2 they all **l** in **wait** for blood; they hunt 693
Hab 2: 3 but at the end it shall speak, and not **l**: 3576
Zep 2: 7 Ashkelon shall they **l** **down** in the 7257
2:14 flocks shall **l** **down** in the midst of her, 7257
2:15 a **place** for beasts to **l** **down** in! 4769
Hag 2: 3 cieled houses, and this house *l* waste? NIH
Zec 10: 2 the diviners have seen a **l**, and have told 8267
Jn 5: 6 When Jesus saw him, and knew that he 2621
8:44 When he speaketh a **l**, he speaketh of his 5574
20: 5 sepulchre, and seeth the linen clothes **l**, 2749
Ac 5: 3 why hath Satan filled thine heart to **l** to 5574
23:21 for they **l** in **wait for** him of them moe 1748
Ro 1:25 Who changed the truth of God into a **l**, 5579
3: 7 abounded through my **l** unto his glory; 5582
9: 1 I say the truth in Christ, I **l** not, 5574
2Co 11:31 for evermore, knoweth that I **l** not. 5574
Gal 1:20 unto you, behold, before God, I **l** not. 5574
Eph 4:14 whereby they **l** in **wait** to deceive; 3180
Col 3: 9 **L** not one to another, seeing that ye have 5574
2Th 2:11 that they should believe a **l**: 5579
1Ti 2: 7 (I speak the truth in Christ, *and* **l** not;) 5574
Tit 1: 2 of eternal life, which God, that **cannot** **l**, 893
Heb 6:18 in which *it was* impossible for God to **l**, 5574
Jas 3:14 glory not, and **l** *not* against the truth. 5574
1Jn 1: 6 in darkness, we **l**, and do not the truth: 5574
2:21 ye know it, and that no **l** is of the truth. 5579
2:27 and is no **l**, and even as it hath taught you, 5579
Rev 3: 9 say they are Jews, and are not, but do **l**; 5574
11: 8 And their dead bodies shall **l** in the street 5574
21:27 worketh abomination, or *maketh* a **l**: 5579
22:15 and whosoever loveth and maketh a **l**. 5579

L

LIED (4) [LIE]

1Ki	13:18 and drink water. *But* he l to him.	3584
Ps	78:36 and they l unto him with their tongues.	3576
Isa	57:11 thou hast l, and hast not remembered	3576
Ac	5: 4 thou hast not l unto men, but unto God.	5574

LIEN (6) [LIE]

Ge	26:10 might lightly have l **with** thy wife,	854+7901
Jdg	21:11 and every woman that hath l by man.	4904
Job	3:13 For now should I have l *still* and	7901
Ps	68:13 Though ye have l among the pots, *yet*	7901
Jer	3: 2 and see where thou hast not been l with.	7693
Jn	11:17 found that he had *l* in the grave four days	NIG

LIERS (10) [LIE]

Jos	8:13 and their l **in wait** on the west of the city,	6119
	8:14 he wist not that *there were* l **in ambush**	693
Jdg	9:25 the men of Shechem set l **in wait** for him	693
	16:12 *were* l **in wait** abiding in the chamber.	693
	20:29 Israel set l **in wait** round about Gibeah.	693
	20:33 the l **in wait** of Israel came forth out of	693
	20:36 they trusted unto the l **in wait** which they	693
	20:37 the l **in wait** hasted, and rushed upon	693
	20:37 and the l **in wait** drew *themselves* along,	693
	20:38 the men of Israel and the l **in wait,**	693

LIES (51) [LIE]

Jdg	16:10 thou hast mocked me, and told me l:	3577
	16:13 thou hast mocked me, and told me l:	3577
Job	11: 3 Should thy l make men hold their peace?	907
	13: 4 ye *are* forgers of l, ye *are* all physicians of	8267
Ps	4: 2 not the proud, nor such as turn aside to l.	3577
	58: 3 astray as soon as they be born, speaking l.	3577
	62: 4 they delight in l: they bless with their	3577
	63:11 the mouth of them that speak l shall be	8267
	101: 7 he that telleth l shall not tarry in my sight.	8267
Pr	6:19 A false witness *that* speaketh l, and he	3577
	14: 5 will not lie: but a false witness will utter l.	3577
	14:25 but a deceitful *witness* speaketh l.	3577
	19: 5 and *he that* speaketh l shall not escape.	3577
	19: 9 and *he that* speaketh l shall perish.	3577
	29:12 If a ruler hearken to l, all his	1697+8267
	30: 8 Remove far from me vanity and l:	1697+3577
Isa	9:15 the prophet that teacheth l, he *is* the tail.	8267
	16: 6 and his wrath: *but* his l *shall* not *be* so.	907
	28:15 for we have made l our refuge,	3577
	28:17 the hail shall sweep away the refuge of l,	3577
	59: 3 your lips have spoken l, your tongue hath	8267
	59: 4 *they* trust in vanity, and speak l;	7723
Jer	9: 3 bend their tongues *like* their bow *for* l:	8267
	9: 5 they have taught their tongue to speak l,	8267
	14:14 The prophets prophesy l in my name:	8267
	16:19 our fathers have inherited l, vanity,	8267
	20: 6 to whom thou hast prophesied l.	8267
	23:14 *they* commit adultery, and walk in l:	8267
	23:25 prophesy l in my name, saying, I have	8267
	23:26 the heart of the prophets that prophesy l?	8267
	23:32 cause my people to err by their l,	8267
	48:30 *shall* not *be* so; his l shall not so effect *it.*	907
Eze	13: 8 seen l, therefore behold, I *am* against you,	3577
	13: 9 prophets that see vanity, and that divine l:	3577
	13:19 your lying to my people that hear *your* l?	3577
	13:22 Because *with* l ye have made the heart of	8267
	22:28 divining l unto them, saying, Thus saith	3577
	24:12 She hath wearied *herself* with l,	8383
Da	11:27 and they shall speak l at one table;	3577
Hos	7: 3 and the princes with their l.	3585
	7:13 yet they have spoken l against me.	3577
	10:13 iniquity; ye have eaten the fruit of l,	3585
	11:12 Ephraim compasseth me about with l,	3585
	12: 1 he daily increaseth l and desolation;	3577
Am	2: 4 and their l caused them to err,	3577
Mic	6:12 the inhabitants thereof have spoken l,	8267
Na	3: 1 it *is* all full of l *and* robbery; the prey	3585
Hab	2:18 the molten image, and a teacher of l,	8267
Zep	3:13 of Israel shall not do iniquity, nor speak l;	3577
Zec	13: 3 for thou speakest l in the name of	8267
1Ti	4: 2 **Speaking** l in hypocrisy, having their	5573

LIEST (5) [LIE]

Ge	28:13 the land whereon thou l, to thee will I	7901
Dt	6: 7 thou l **down,** and when thou risest up.	7901
	11:19 thou l **down,** and when thou risest up.	7901
Jos	7:10 wherefore l thou thus upon thy face?	5307
Pr	3:24 thou l **down,** thou shalt not be afraid.	7901

LIETH (59) [LIE]

Ge	4: 7 if thou doest not well, sin l at the door.	7257
	49:25 blessings of the deep that l under;	7257
Ex	22:19 Whosoever l with a beast shall surely be	7901
Lev	6: 3 and l concerning it, and sweareth falsely;	3584
	14:47 that l in the house shall wash his clothes;	7901
	15: 4 he l that hath the issue, is unclean:	7901
	15:20 *thing* that she l upon in her separation	7901
	15:24 all the bed whereon he l shall be unclean.	7901
	15:26 Every bed whereon she l all the days of	7901
	15:33 that l **with** her which is unclean.	5973+7901
	19:20 I **carnally with** a	854+2233+7901+7902
	20:11 the man that l with his father's wife hath	7901
	20:13 lie with mankind, as he l **with** a woman,	4904
	26:34 as long as it l **desolate,** and *ye be* in your	8074
	26:35 As long as it l **desolate** it shall rest;	8074
	26:34 while it l **desolate** without them:	8074
Nu	21:15 of Ar, and l upon the border of Moab.	8172
Dt	27:20 Cursed *be* he that l with his father's wife;	7901

LIEUTENANTS (4)

Ezr	8:36 the king's commissions unto the king's l,	323
Est	3:12 Haman had commanded unto the king's l,	323
	8: 9 to the l, and the deputies and rulers of	323
	9: 3 the l, and the deputies, and officers of	323

LIFE (450) [LIVE]

Ge	1:20 the moving creature that hath l,	2416
	1:30 wherein *there is* l, *I* have given	2416+5315
	2: 7 breathed into his nostrils the breath of l;	2416
	2: 9 tree of l also in the midst of the garden,	2416
	3:14 dust shalt thou eat all the days of thy l;	2416
	3:17 shalt thou eat *of* it all the days of thy l;	2416
	3:22 take also of the tree of l, and eat,	2416
	3:24 way, to keep the way of the tree of l.	2416
	6:17 all flesh, wherein *is* the breath of l,	2416
	7:11 In the six hundredth year of Noah's l,	2416
	7:15 two of all flesh, wherein *is* the breath of l.	2416
	7:22 All in whose nostrils *was* the breath of l,	2416
	9: 4 flesh with the l thereof, *which is* the blood	5315
	9: 5 man's brother will I require the l of man.	5315
	18:10 unto thee according to the time of l;	2416
	18:14 according to the time of l, and Sarah shall	2416
	19:17 abroad, that he said, Escape for thy l;	5315
	19:19 thou hast shewed unto me in saving my l;	5315
	23: 1 *these were* the years of the l of Sarah.	2416
	25: 7 the years of Abraham's l which he lived,	2416
	25:17 these *are* the years of the l of Ishmael,	2416
	27:46 I am weary of my l because of	2416
	27:46 of the land, what good shall my l do me?	2416
	32:30 God face to face, and my l is preserved.	5315
	42:15 By the l of Pharaoh ye shall not go forth	2416
	42:16 by the l of Pharaoh surely ye *are* spies.	2416
	44:30 seeing that his l *is* bound up in *the* lad's	5315
	44:30 that his life *is* bound up in *the* lad's l;	5315
	45: 5 did send me before you to **preserve** l.	4241
	47: 9 evil have the days of the years of my l	2416
	47: 9 l of my fathers in the days of their	2416
	48:15 God which fed me **all my l long**	4480+5750
Ex	4:19 all the men are dead which sought thy l.	5315
	6:16 the years of the l of Levi *were* an hundred	2416
	6:18 the years of the l of Kohath *were* an	2416
	6:20 the years of the l of Amram *were* an	2416
	21:23 then thou shalt give l for life,	5315
	21:23 then thou shalt give life for l,	5315
	21:30 he shall give *for* the ransom of his l	5315
Lev	17:11 For the l of the flesh *is* in the blood:	5315
	17:14 For *it is* the l of all flesh; the blood of it *is*	5315
	17:14 all flesh; the blood of it *is* for the l thereof:	5315
	17:14 for the l of all flesh *is* the blood thereof:	5315
	18:18 besides the other in her l *time.*	2416
Nu	35:31 no satisfaction for the l of a murderer,	5315
Dt	4: 9 depart from thy heart all the days of thy l:	2416
	6: 2 and thy son's son, all the days of thy l;	2416
	12:23 for the blood *is* the l; and thou mayest not	5315
	12:23 thou mayest not eat the l with the flesh.	5315
	16: 3 of the land of Egypt all the days of thy l.	2416
	17:19 he shall read therein all the days of his l:	2416
	19:21 *but* l shall go for life, eye for eye, tooth for	5315
	19:21 *but* life *shall go* for l, eye for eye, tooth for	5315
	20:19 down (for the tree of the field *is* man's *l*	NIH
	24: 6 pledge: for he taketh a *man's* l to pledge.	5315
	28:66 thy l shall hang in doubt before thee;	2416

Dt	27:21 Cursed *be* he that l with any *manner of*	7901
	27:22 Cursed *be* he that l with his sister.	7901
	27:23 *be* he that l with his mother in law.	7901
Jos	15: 8 l before the valley of Hinnom westward,	NIH
	17: 7 to Michmethah, that l before Shechem;	NIH
	18:13 near the hill that l on the south side of	NIH
	18:14 from the hill that l before Beth-horon	NIH
	18:16 l before the valley of the son of Hinnom,	NIH
	1:16 of Judah, which l in the south of Arad;	NIH
Jdg	16: 5 see wherein his great strength *l,* and by	NIH
	16: 6 wherein thy great strength *l,*	NIH
	16:15 not told me wherein thy great strength *l.*	NIH
	18:28 it was in the valley that *l* by Beth-rehob.	NIH
Ru	3: 4 shall be, when he l **down,** that thou shalt	7901
2Sa	2:24 that *l* before Giah *by* the way of	NIH
	24: 5 *on* the right side of the city *that l* in	NIH
Ne	2: 3 *l* waste, and the gates thereof are	NIH
	2:17 how Jerusalem *l* waste, and the gates	NIH
	3:25 the tower which l out from the king's	3318
	3:26 toward the east, and the tower that l **out.**	3318
	3:27 over against the great tower that l **out,**	3318
Job	14:12 So man l **down,** and riseth not: till	7901
	40:21 He l under the shady trees, in the covert	7901
Ps	10: 9 He l in wait secretly as a lion in his den:	693
	10: 9 he l **in wait** to catch the poor: he doth	693
	41: 8 *now* that he l he shall rise up no more.	7901
	88: 7 Thy wrath l **hard** upon me, and thou hast	5564
Pr	7:12 the streets, and l **in wait** at every corner.)	693
	23:28 She also l **in wait** as *for* a prey,	693
	23:34 shalt be as he that l **down** in the midst	7901
	23:34 or as he that l upon the top of a mast.	7901
Eze	9: 2 which l toward the north, and every man	6437
	29: 3 the great dragon that l in the midst of his	7257
Mic	7: 5 the doors of thy mouth from her that l	7901
Mt	8: 6 my servant l at home sick of the palsy,	906
Mk	5:23 daughter l **at the point of death:**	2079+2192
Ac	14: 6 and *unto* the **region that l** round about:	4066
	27:12 toward the south west and north west.	991
Ro	12:18 If *it be* possible, **as much as** l in you,	1537
1Jn	5:19 and the whole world l in wickedness.	2749
Rev	21:16 And the city l foursquare, and the length	2749

Dt	28:66 and shalt have none assurance of thy l:	2416
	30:15 have set before thee *this* day l and good,	2416
	30:19 *that* I have set before you l and death,	2416
	30:19 therefore choose l, that *both* thou and	2416
	30:20 for he *is* thy l, and the length of thy days:	2416
	32:47 a vain thing for you; because it *is* your l:	2416
Jos	1: 5 *to* stand before thee all the days of thy l:	2416
	2:14 men answered her, Our l for yours,	5315
	4:14 as they feared Moses, all the days of his l.	2416
Jdg	5:18 jeoparded their lives unto the death	5315
	12: 3 I put my l in my hands, and passed over	5315
	16:30 moe than *they* which he slew in his l.	5315
	18:25 thou lose thy l, with the lives of thy	5315
Ru	4:15 he shall be unto thee a restorer of *thy* l,	5315
1Sa	1:11 him unto the LORD all the days of his l,	2416
	7:15 Samuel judged Israel all the days of his l.	2416
	18:18 what *is* my l, *or* my father's family in	2416
	19: 5 For he did put his l in his hand,	5315
	19:11 saying, If thou save not thy l to night,	5315
	20: 1 before thy father, that he seeketh my l?	5315
	22:23 for he that seeketh my l seeketh thy life:	5315
	22:23 for he that seeketh my life seeketh thy l:	5315
	23:15 saw that Saul was come out to seek his l:	5315
	25:29 in the bundle of l with the LORD thy God;	2416
	26:24 as thy l was much set by this day in mine	5315
	26:24 let my l be much set by in the eyes of	5315
	28: 9 then layest thou a snare for my l,	5315
	28:21 I have put my l in my hand,	5315
2Sa	1: 9 me, because my l *is yet* whole in me.	5315
	4: 8 of Saul thine enemy, which sought thy l;	5315
	14: 7 for the l of his brother whom he slew;	5315
	15:21 whether in death or l, even there *also* will	2416
	16:11 came forth of my bowels, seeketh my l:	5315
	18:13 wrought falsehood against mine own l:	5315
	19: 5 which this day have saved thy l,	5315
1Ki	1:12 that thou mayest save thine own l,	5315
	1:12 own life, and the l of thy son Solomon.	5315
	2:23 not spoken this word against his own l.	5315
	3:11 and hast not asked for thyself long l;	3117
	3:11 nor hast asked the l of thine enemies;	5315
	4:21 and served Solomon all the days of his l.	2416
	11:34 I will make him prince all the days of his l,	2416
	15: 5 he commanded him all the days of his l,	2416
	15: 6 and Jeroboam all the days of his l.	2416
	19: 2 I make not thy l as the life of one of them	5315
	19: 2 make not my life as the l of one of them	5315
	19: 3 went for his l, and came to Beer-sheba,	5315
	19: 4 now, O LORD, take away my l;	5315
	19:10 left; and they seek my l, to take it away.	5315
	19:14 left; and they seek my l, to take it away.	5315
	20:31 of Israel: peradventure he will save thy l.	5315
	20:39 shall thy l be for his life, or else thou shalt	5315
	20:39 shall thy life be for his l, or else thou shalt	5315
	20:42 therefore thy l shall go for his life,	5315
	20:42 therefore thy life shall go for his l,	5315
2Ki	1:13 let my l, and the l of these fifty thy	5315
	1:13 life, and the l of these fifty thy servants,	5315
	1:14 let my l now be precious in thy sight.	5315
	4:16 this season, according to the time of l,	2416
	4:17 said unto her, according to the time of l.	2416
	7: 7 the camp as it *was,* and fled for their l.	5315
	8: 1 whose son he had **restored to** l,	2421
	8: 5 how he had **restored** a dead *body* to l,	2421
	8: 5 whose son he had **restored to** l,	2421
	8: 5 *is* her son, whom Elisha **restored to** l.	2421
	10:24 he that letteth him go, his l *shall be* for	5315
	10:24 him go, his life *shall be* for the l of him.	5315
	25:29 before him all the days of his l.	2416
	25:30 rate for every day, all the days of his l.	2416
2Ch	1:11 or honour, nor the l of thine enemies,	5315
	1:11 enemies, neither yet hast asked long l;	3117
Ezr	6:10 pray for the l of the king, and of his sons.	2417
Ne	6:11 would go into the temple to **save** his l?	2421
Est	7: 3 let my l be given me at my petition,	5315
	7: 7 Haman stood *up* to make request for his l	5315
	8:11 to stand for their l, to destroy, to slay,	5315
Job	2: 4 all that a man hath will he give for his l.	5315
	2: 6 Behold, he *is* in thine hand; but save his l.	5315
	3:20 is in misery, and *unto* the bitter in soul;	2416
	6:11 *is* mine end, that I should prolong my l?	5315
	7: 7 O remember that my l *is* wind: mine eye	2416
	7:15 *and* death rather than my l.	6106
	9:21 not know my soul: I would despise my l.	2416
	10: 1 My soul is weary of my l; I will leave my	2416
	10:12 Thou hast granted me l and favour,	2416
	13:14 in my teeth, and put my l in mine hand?	5315
	24:22 he riseth up, and no *man* is sure of l.	2416
	31:39 caused the owners thereof to lose their l:	5315
	33: 4 breath of the Almighty hath **given** me l.	2421
	33:18 and his l from perishing by the sword.	2416
	33:20 So that his l abhorreth bread, and his soul	2416
	33:22 the grave, and his l to the destroyers.	2416
	33:28 into the pit, and his l shall see the light.	2416
	36: 6 He **preserveth** not the l of the wicked:	2421
	36:14 youth, and their l *is* among the unclean.	2416
Ps	7: 5 let him tread down my l upon the earth,	2416
	16:11 Thou wilt shew me the path of l: in thy	2416
	17:14 *which have* their portion in *this* l,	2416
	21: 4 asked l of thee, *and* thou gavest *it* him,	2416
	23: 6 mercy shall follow me all the days of my l:	2416
	26: 9 with sinners, nor my l with bloody men:	2416
	27: 1 the LORD *is* the strength of my l;	2416
	27: 4 house of the LORD all the days of my l,	2416
	30: 5 *but* a moment; in his favour *is* l:	2416
	31:10 For my l is spent with grief, and my years	2416

L

Ps	31:13 me, they devised to take away my l.	5315
	34:12 What man *is he that* desireth l,	2416
	36: 9 For with thee *is* the fountain of l: in thy	2416
	38:12 They also that seek after my l lay snares	5315
	42: 8 *and my* prayer unto the God of my l.	2416
	61: 6 wilt **prolong** the king's l: 3117+3117+5921	
	63: 3 thy lovingkindness *is* better than l,	2416
	64: 1 preserve my l from fear of the enemy.	2416
	66: 9 Which holdeth our soul in l,	2416
	78:50 but gave their l over to the pestilence;	2416
	88: 3 and my l draweth nigh unto the grave.	2416
	91:16 *With* long l will I satisfy him,	3117
	103: 4 Who redeemeth thy l from destruction;	2416
	128: 5 good of Jerusalem all the days of thy l.	2416
	133: 3 the blessing, *even* l for evermore.	2416
	143: 3 hath smitten my l down to the ground;	2416
Pr	1:19 *which* taketh away the l of the owners	5315
	2:19 neither take they hold of the paths of l.	2416
	3: 2 For length of days, and long l, and peace,	2416
	3:18 She *is* a tree of l to them that lay hold	2416
	3:22 So shall they be l unto thy soul,	2416
	4:10 and the years of thy l shall be many.	2416
	4:13 let *her* not go: keep her; for she *is* thy l.	2416
	4:22 For they *are* l unto those that find them,	2416
	4:23 diligence; for out of it *are* the issues of l.	2416
	5: 6 Lest thou shouldest ponder the path of l,	2416
	6:23 reproofs of instruction *are* the way of l:	2416
	6:26 the adulteress will hunt for the precious l.	5315
	7:23 and knoweth not that it *is* for his l.	5315
	8:35 For whoso findeth me findeth l,	2416
	9:11 and the years of thy l shall be increased.	2416
	10:11 mouth of a righteous *man is* a well of l:	2416
	10:16 The labour of the righteous *tendeth* to l:	2416
	10:17 He *is* in the way of l that keepeth	2416
	11:19 As righteousness *tendeth* to l: so he that	2416
	11:30 The fruit of the righteous *is* a tree of l;	2416
	12:10 A righteous *man* regardeth the l of his	5315
	12:28 In the way of righteousness *is* l; and *in*	2416
	13: 3 He that keepeth his mouth keepeth his l:	5315
	13: 8 The ransom of a man's l *are* his riches:	5315
	13:12 *when* the desire cometh, *it is* a tree of l.	2416
	13:14 The law of the wise *is* a fountain of l,	2416
	14:27 The fear of the LORD *is* a fountain of l,	2416
	14:30 A sound heart *is* the l of the flesh:	2416
	15: 4 A wholesome tongue *is* a tree of l:	2416
	15:24 The way of l *is* above to the wise, that *he*	2416
	15:31 ear that heareth the reproof of l abideth	2416
	16:15 In the light of the king's countenance *is* l;	2416
	16:22 Understanding *is* a wellspring of l unto	2416
	18:21 and l *are* in the power of the tongue:	2416
	19:23 The fear of the LORD *tendeth* to l:	2416
	21:21 after righteousness and mercy findeth l,	2416
	22: 4 the LORD *are* riches, and honour, and l.	2416
	31:12 good and not evil all the days of her l.	2416
Ecc	2: 3 under the heaven all the days of their l.	2416
	2:17 Therefore I hated l; because the work that	2416
	3:12 *a man* to rejoice, and to do good in his l.	2416
	5:18 taketh under the sun all the days of his l,	2416
	5:20 not much remember the days of his l;	2416
	6:12 knoweth what *is* good for man in *this* l,	2416
	6:12 the days of his vain l which he spendeth	2416
	7:12 *that* wisdom **giveth** l to them that have it.	2421
	7:15 is a wicked *man* that prolongeth *his* l	NIH
	8:15 with him all the labour the days of his l,	2416
	9: 9 lovest all the days of the l of thy vanity,	2416
	9: 9 for that *is* thy portion in *this* l, and in	2416
Isa	15: 4 cry out; his l shall be grievous unto him.	5315
	38:12 I have cut off like a weaver my l: he will	2416
	38:16 and in all these *things* are the l of my spirit:	2416
	38:20 days of our l in the house of the LORD.	2416
	43: 4 I give men for thee, and people for thy l.	5315
	57:10 thou hast found the l of thine hand;	2416
Jer	4:30 will despise thee, they will seek thy l.	5315
	8: 3 death shall be chosen rather than l by all	2416
	11:21 that seek thy l, saying, Prophesy not in	5315
	21: 7 into the hand of those that seek their l:	5315
	21: 8 I set before you the way of l, and the way	2416
	21: 9 and his l shall be unto him for a prey.	5315
	22:25 thee into the hand of them that seek thy l,	5315
	34:20 into the hand of them that seek their l,	5315
	34:21 into the hand of them that seek their l,	5315
	38: 2 for he shall have his l for a prey,	5315
	38:16 the hand of these men that seek thy l.	5315
	39:18 but thy l shall be for a prey unto thee:	5315
	44:30 and into the hand of them that seek his l;	5315
	44:30 his enemy, and that sought his l.	5315
	45: 5 thy l will I give unto thee for a prey in all	5315
	49:37 and before them that seek their l:	5315
	52:33 eat bread before him all the days of his l.	2416
	52:34 the day of his death, all the days of his l.	2416
La	2:19 lift up thy hands toward him for the l of	5315
	3:53 They have cut off my l in the dungeon,	2416
	3:58 of my soul; thou hast redeemed my l.	2416
Eze	3:18 from his wicked way, to **save** his l;	2421
	7:13 strengthen himself in the iniquity of his l.	2416
	13:22 his wicked way, by **promising** him l.	2421
	32:10 every man for his own l, in the day of thy	5315
	33:15 walk in the statutes of l,	2416
Da	12: 2 some to everlasting l, and some to shame	2416
Jnh	1:14 let us not perish for this man's l,	5315
	2: 6 yet hast thou brought up my l from	2416
	4: 3 take, I beseech thee, my l from me;	2416
Mal	2: 5 covenant was with him of l and peace;	2416
Mt	2:20 dead which sought the young child's l.	5590
	6:25 Take no thought for your l, what ye shall	5590

Mt	6:25 shall put on. Is not the l more than meat,	5590
	7:14 which leadeth unto l, and few there be	2222
	10:39 He that findeth his l shall lose it:	5590
	10:39 that loseth his l for my sake shall find it.	5590
	16:25 For whosoever will save his l shall lose it:	5590
	16:25 whosoever will lose his l for my sake shall	5590
	18: 8 it is better for thee to enter into l halt or	2222
	18: 9 it is better for thee to enter into l with one	2222
	19:16 *thing* shall I do, that I may have eternal l?	2222
	19:17 but if thou wilt enter into l, keep	2222
	19:29 and shall inherit everlasting l.	2222
	20:28 and to give his l a ransom for many.	5590
	25:46 but the righteous into l eternal.	2222
Mk	3: 4 to save l, or to kill? But they held their	5590
	8:35 For whosoever will save his l shall lose it;	5590
	8:35 but whosoever will lose his l for my sake	5590
	9:43 it is better for thee to enter into l maimed,	2222
	9:45 it is better for thee to enter halt into l,	2222
	10:17 what shall I do that I may inherit eternal l?	2222
	10:30 and in the world to come eternal l.	2222
	10:45 and to give his l a ransom for many.	5590
Lk	1:75 before him, all the days of our l.	2222
	6: 9 or to do evil? to save l, or to destroy *it?*	2222
	8:14 cares and riches and pleasures of *this* l,	979
	9:24 For whosoever will save his l shall lose it:	5590
	9:24 but whosoever will lose his l for my sake,	5590
	10:25 Master, what shall I do to inherit eternal l?	2222
	12:15 for a man's l consisteth not in	2222
	12:22 Take no thought for your l, what ye shall	5590
	12:23 The l is more than meat, and the body	5590
	14:26 and sisters, yea, and his own l also,	5590
	17:33 Whosoever shall seek to save his l	5590
	17:33 whosoever shall lose *his* l shall preserve it.	NIG
	18:18 what shall I do to inherit eternal l?	2222
	18:30 and in the world to come l everlasting.	2222
	21:34 and cares of *this* l, and *so* that day come	982
Jn	1: 4 In him was l; and the life was the light of	2222
	1: 4 was life; and the l was the light of men.	2222
	3:15 him should not perish, but have eternal l.	2222
	3:16 should not perish, but have everlasting l.	2222
	3:36 believeth on the Son hath everlasting l:	2222
	3:36 that believeth not the Son shall not see l;	2222
	4:14 of water springing up into everlasting l.	2222
	4:36 and gathereth fruit unto l eternal:	2222
	5:24 hath everlasting l, and shall not come into	2222
	5:24 but is passed from death unto l.	2222
	5:26 For as the Father hath l in himself;	2222
	5:26 hath he given to the Son to have l in	2222
	5:29 done good, unto the resurrection of l;	2222
	5:39 for in them ye think ye have eternal l:	2222
	5:40 will not come to me, that ye might have l.	2222
	6:27 meat which endureth unto everlasting l,	2222
	6:33 from heaven, and giveth l unto the world.	2222
	6:35 Jesus said unto them, I am the bread of l:	2222
	6:40 believeth on him, may have everlasting l:	2222
	6:47 that believeth on me hath everlasting l.	2222
	6:48 I am *that* bread of l.	2222
	6:51 which I will give for the l of the world.	2222
	6:53 and drink his blood, ye have no l in you.	2222
	6:54 and drinketh my blood, hath eternal l;	2222
	6:63 unto you, *they* are spirit, and *they* are l.	2222
	6:68 we go? thou hast the words of eternal l.	2222
	8:12 in darkness, but shall have the light of l.	2222
	10:10 I am come that they might have l,	2222
	10:11 the good shepherd giveth his l for	5590
	10:15 and I lay down my l for the sheep.	5590
	10:17 because I lay down my l, that I might take	5590
	10:28 And I give unto them eternal l;	2222
	11:25 unto her, I am the resurrection, and the l:	2222
	12:25 He that loveth his l shall lose it; and he	5590
	12:25 that hateth his l in this world shall keep	5590
	12:25 in this world shall keep it unto l eternal.	2222
	12:50 And I know that his commandment is l	2222
	13:37 I will lay down my l for thy sake.	5590
	13:38 Wilt thou lay down thy l for my sake?	5590
	14: 6 him, I am the way, the truth, and the l:	2222
	15:13 that a man lay down his l for his friends.	5590
	17: 2 that he should give eternal l to as many as	2222
	17: 3 And this is l eternal, that they might know	2222
	20:31 that believing ye might have l through his	2222
Ac	2:28 hast made known to me the ways of l;	2222
	3:15 killed the Prince of l, whom God hath	2222
	5:20 to the people all the words of this l.	2222
	8:33 for his l is taken from the earth.	2222
	11:18 to the Gentiles granted repentance unto l.	2222
	13:46 yourselves unworthy of everlasting l,	2222
	13:48 as many as were ordained to eternal l	2222
	17:25 any *thing,* seeing he giveth to all l,	2222
	20:10 Trouble not yourselves; for his l is in him.	5590
	20:24 neither count I my l dear unto myself,	5590
	26: 4 My **manner** of l from *my* youth, which	981
	27:22 for there shall be no loss of *any man's* l	5590
Ro	2: 7 and honour and immortality, eternal l:	2222
	5:10 we shall be saved by his l.	2222
	5:17 the gift of righteousness shall reign in l	2222
	5:18 *came* upon all men unto justification of l.	2222
	5:21 unto eternal l by Jesus Christ our Lord.	2222
	6: 4 so we also should walk in newness of l.	2222
	6:22 unto holiness, and the end everlasting l.	2222
	6:23 the gift of God *is* eternal l through Jesus	2222
	7:10 which was *ordained* to l,	2222
	8: 2 the law of the Spirit of l in Christ Jesus	2222
	8: 6 to be spiritually minded *is* l and peace.	2222
	8:10 the Spirit *is* l because of righteousness.	2222
	8:38 nor l, nor angels, nor principalities,	2222

Ro	11: 3 and I am left alone, and they seek my l.	5590
	11:15 receiving *of them be,* but l from the dead?	2222
	16: 4 Who have for my l laid down their own	5590
1Co	3:22 or l, or death, or *things* present, or *things*	2222
	6: 3 much more *things* that pertain to this l?	982
	6: 4 judgments *of things* pertaining to this l,	982
	14: 7 *And even things* **without** l giving sound,	895
	15:19 If in this l only we have hope in Christ,	2222
2Co	1: 8 insomuch that we despaired even of l:	2198
	2:16 and to the other the savour of l unto life.	2222
	2:16 and to the other the savour of life unto l.	2222
	3: 6 the letter killeth, but the spirit **giveth** l.	2227
	4:10 that the l also of Jesus might be made	2222
	4:11 that the l also of Jesus might be made	2222
	4:12 So then death worketh in us, but l in you.	2222
	5: 4 that mortality might be swallowed up of l.	2222
Gal	2:20 *the l* which I now live in the flesh I live	NIG
	3:21 a law given which could have **given** l,	2227
	6: 8 Spirit shall of the Spirit reap l everlasting.	2222
Eph	4:18 being alienated from the l of God through	2222
Php	1:20 my body, whether *it be* by l, or by death.	2222
	2:16 Holding forth the word of l; that I may	2222
	2:30 not regarding *his* l, to supply your lack of	5590
	4: 3 whose names *are* in the book of l.	2222
Col	3: 3 and your l is hid with Christ in God.	2222
	3: 4 *who is* our l, shall appear, then shall ye	2222
1Ti	1:16 hereafter believe on him to l everlasting.	2222
	2: 2 peaceable l in all godliness and honesty.	979
	4: 8 having promise of the l that now is,	2222
	6:12 good fight of faith, lay hold on eternal l,	2222
	6:19 that they may lay hold on eternal l.	2222
2Ti	1: 1 according to the promise of l which is in	2222
	1:10 hath brought l and immortality to light	2222
	2: 4 entangleth with the affairs of *this* l;	979
	3:10 **manner of** l, purpose, faith, longsuffering,	72
Tit	1: 2 In hope of eternal l, which God, that	2222
	3: 7 heirs according to the hope of eternal l.	2222
Heb	7: 3 neither beginning of days, nor end of l;	2222
	7:16 but after the power of an endless l.	2222
	11:35 their dead **raised to l again:** 386+1537	
Jas	1:12 is tried, he shall receive the crown of l,	2222
	4:14 for what *is* your l? It is even a vapour,	2222
1Pe	3: 7 as *being* heirs together of the grace of l;	2222
	3:10 For he that will love l, and see good days,	2222
	4: 3 For the time past of *our* l may suffice us to	979
2Pe	1: 3 unto us all *things* that *pertain* unto l	2222
1Jn	1: 1 our hands have handled, of the Word of l;	2222
	1: 2 (For the l was manifested, and we have	2222
	1: 2 and shew unto you *that* eternal l,	2222
	2:16 and the lust of the eyes, and the pride of l,	979
	2:25 that he hath promised us, *even* eternal l.	2222
	3:14 that we have passed from death unto l,	2222
	3:15 ye know that no murderer hath eternal l	2222
	3:16 *of God,* because he laid down his l for us:	5590
	5:11 that God hath given to us eternal l,	2222
	5:11 to us eternal life, and this l is in his Son.	2222
	5:12 He that hath the Son hath l; *and* he that	2222
	5:12 that hath not the Son of God hath not l.	2222
	5:13 that ye may know that ye have eternal l,	2222
	5:16 he shall give him l for them that sin not	2222
	5:20 This is the true God, and eternal l.	2222
Jude	1:21 of our Lord Jesus Christ unto eternal l.	2222
Rev	2: 7 will I give to eat of the tree of l,	2222
	2:10 and I will give thee a crown of l.	2222
	3: 5 not blot out his name out of the book of l,	2222
	8: 9 which were in the sea, and had l, died;	5590
	11:11 a half the spirit of l from God entered into	2222
	13: 8 names are not written in the book of l	2222
	13:15 he had power to give l unto the image	4151
	17: 8 book of l from the foundation of the world,	2222
	20:12 book was opened, which is *the book* of l:	2222
	20:15 the book of l was cast into the lake of fire.	2222
	21: 6 of the fountain of the water of l freely.	2222
	21:27 which are written in the Lamb's book of l.	2222
	22: 1 he shewed me a pure river of water of l,	2222
	22: 2 side of the river, *was there* the tree of l,	2222
	22:14 that they may have right to the tree of l,	2222
	22:17 let him take the water of l freely.	2222
	22:19 take away his part out of the book of l,	2222

LIFELESS See DUMB

LIFETIME (3) [LIVE, TIME]

2Sa	18:18 Now Absalom in his l had taken and	2416
Lk	16:25 remember that thou in thy l receivedst thy	2222
Heb	2:15 death were all their l subject to bondage.	2198

LIFT (193) [LIFTED, LIFTER, LIFTEST, LIFTETH, LIFTING]

Ge	7:17 the ark, and it was l **up** above the earth.	7311
	13:14 **L up** now thine eyes, and look from	5375
	14:22 I have l **up** mine hand unto the LORD,	7311
	18: 2 he l **up** his eyes and looked, and lo,	5375
	21:16 sat over against *him,* and l **up** her voice,	5375
	21:18 l **up** the lad, and hold him in thine hand;	5375
	22: 4 on the third day Abraham l **up** his eyes,	5375
	24:63 he l **up** his eyes, and saw, and behold,	5375
	24:64 Rebekah l **up** her eyes, and when she	5375
	27:38 And Esau l **up** his voice, and wept.	5375
	31:12 he said, **L up** now thine eyes, and see,	5375
	33: 5 he l **up** his eyes, and saw the women and	5375
	37:25 they l **up** their eyes and looked,	5375
	37:28 they drew and l **up** Joseph out of the pit,	5927
	39:18 to pass, as I l **up** my voice and cried,	7311
	40:13 Yet within three days shall Pharaoh l **up**	5375

Ge 40:19	Yet within three days shall Pharaoh l **up**	5375
41:44	without that no man l **up** his hand	7311
43:29	he l **up** his eyes, and saw his brother	5375
Ex 7:20	he l **up** the rod, and smote the waters that	7311
14:10	the children of Israel l **up** their eyes,	5375
14:16	l thou **up** thy rod, and stretch out thine	7311
20:25	for if thou l **up** thy tool upon it, thou hast	5130
Lev 9:22	Aaron l **up** his hand towards the people,	5375
Nu 6:26	The Lord l **up** his countenance upon	5375
16: 3	l you **up** yourselves above the	5375
20:11	Moses l **up** his hand, and with his rod he	7311
23:24	lion, and l **up** himself as a young lion:	5375
24: 2	Balaam l **up** his eyes, and he saw Israel	5375
Dt 3:27	l **up** thine eyes westward, and northward,	5375
4:19	lest thou l **up** thine eyes unto heaven,	5375
22: 4	**surely** help him to	
	l them **up** again.	6965+6965
27: 5	shalt not l **up** any iron *tool* upon them.	5130
32:40	For l l **up** my hand to heaven, and say,	5375
Jos 4:18	the soles of the priests' feet were l **up**	5423
5:13	that he l **up** his eyes and looked,	5375
8:31	over which no *man* hath l **up** any iron:	5130
Jdg 2: 4	the people l **up** their voice, and wept.	5375
9: 7	l **up** his voice, and cried, and said unto	5375
19:17	when he had l **up** his eyes, he saw a	5375
21: 2	and l **up** their voices, and wept sore;	5375
Ru 1: 9	and they l **up** their voice, and wept.	5375
1:14	they l **up** their voice, and wept again:	5375
1Sa 11: 4	all the people l **up** their voices, and wept.	5375
24:16	And Saul l **up** his voice, and wept.	5375
30: 4	the people that *were* with him l **up** their	5375
2Sa 3:32	the king l **up** his voice, and wept at	5375
13:34	young man that kept the watch l **up** his	5375
13:36	sons came, and l **up** their voice and wept:	5375
18:24	l **up** his eyes, and looked, and behold a	5375
18:28	hath delivered up the men that l **up**	5375
20:21	hath l **up** his hand against the king,	5375
23: 8	he l up *his spear* against eight hundred,	NIH
23:18	l **up** his spear against three hundred,	5782
1Ki 11:26	even he l **up** *his* hand against the king.	7311
11:27	this *was* the cause that he l **up** *his* hand	7311
2Ki 9:32	he l **up** his face to the window, and said,	5375
19: 4	wherefore l **up** *thy* prayer for the remnant	5375
19:22	*thy* voice, and l **up** thine eyes on high?	5375
25:27	did l **up** the head of Jehoiachin king of	5375
1Ch 11:11	l **up** his spear against three hundred	5782
14: 2	for his kingdom was l **up** on high,	5375
21:16	David l **up** his eyes, and saw the angel of	5375
25: 5	in the words of God, to l **up** the horn.	7311
2Ch 5:13	when *they* l **up** *their* voice with	7311
17: 6	his heart was l **up** in the ways of	1361
Ezr 9: 6	and blush to l **up** my face to thee,	7311
Job 2:12	when they l **up** their eyes afar off,	5375
10:15	be righteous, *yet* will l not l **up** my head.	5375
11:15	shalt thou l **up** thy face without spot;	5375
22:26	and shalt l **up** thy face unto God.	5375
31:21	If I have l **up** my hand against	5130
31:29	or l **up** myself when evil found him:	5782
38:34	Canst thou l **up** thy voice to the clouds,	7311
Ps 4: 6	l thou the light of thy countenance	5375
7: 6	l **up** thyself because of the rage of mine	5375
10:12	Arise, O Lord; O God, l **up** thine hand:	5375
24: 4	who hath not l **up** his soul unto vanity,	5375
24: 7	**L up** your heads, O ye gates; and be ye lift	5375
24: 7	be ye l **up**, ye everlasting doors;	5375
24: 9	**L up** your heads, O ye gates; even lift	5375
24: 9	even l them **up**, ye everlasting doors;	5375
25: 1	Unto thee, O Lord, do l l **up** my soul.	5375
28: 2	when l l **up** my hands toward thy holy	5375
28: 9	feed them also, and l them **up** for ever.	5375
41: 9	my bread, hath l **up** *his* heel against me.	1431
63: 4	I live: I will l **up** my hands in thy name.	5375
74: 3	**L up** thy feet unto the perpetual	7311
75: 4	and to the wicked, **L** not **up** the horn:	7311
75: 5	**L** not **up** your horn on high: speak not	7311
83: 2	they that hate thee have l **up** the head.	5375
86: 4	for unto thee, O Lord, do l l **up** my soul.	5375
93: 3	their voice; the floods l **up** their waves.	5375
94: 2	**L up** thyself, thou judge of the earth:	5375
110: 7	the way: therefore shall he l **up** the head.	7311
119:48	My hands also will l l **up** unto thy	5375
121: 1	I will l **up** mine eyes unto the hills,	5375
123: 1	Unto thee l **up** mine eyes, O thou that	5375
134: 2	**L up** your hands *in* the sanctuary,	5375
143: 8	should walk; for l l **up** my soul unto thee.	5375
Ecc 4:10	if they fall, the one will l **up** his fellow:	6965
Isa 2: 4	nation shall not l **up** sword against nation,	5375
5:26	he will l **up** an ensign to the nations from	5375
10:15	shake *itself against* them that l it **up**,	7311
10:15	as if the staff should l **up** *itself, as if* it	7311
10:24	shall l **up** his staff against thee, after	5375
10:26	shall he l it **up** after the manner of Egypt.	5375
10:30	**L up** thy voice, O daughter of Gallim:	6670
13: 2	l **up** a banner upon the high mountain	5375
24:14	They shall l **up** their voice, they shall sing,	5375
33:10	will I be exalted; now will I l **up** myself.	5375
37: 4	wherefore l **up** *thy* prayer for the remnant	5375
40: 9	good tidings, l **up** thy voice with strength;	7311
40: 9	l it **up**, be not afraid; say unto the cities of	7311
40:26	**L up** your eyes on high, and behold who	5375
42: 2	He shall not cry, nor l **up**, nor cause his	5375
42:11	the cities thereof l **up** *their* voice,	5375
49:18	**L up** thine eyes round about, and behold:	5375
49:22	I will l **up** mine hand to the Gentiles,	5375
51: 6	**L up** your eyes to the heavens,	5375
Isa 52: 8	Thy watchmen shall l **up** the voice;	5375
58: 1	l **up** thy voice like a trumpet, and shew	7311
59:19	Lord shall l **up a standard** against him.	5127
60: 4	**L up** thine eyes round about, and see:	5375
62:10	the stones; l **up** a standard for the people.	7311
Jer 3: 2	**L up** thine eyes unto the high places,	5375
7:16	neither l **up** cry nor prayer for them:	5375
11:14	neither l **up** a cry or prayer for them:	5375
13:20	**L up** your eyes, and behold them that	5375
22:20	l **up** thy voice in Bashan, and cry from	5414
51:14	and they shall l **up** a shout against thee.	6030
La 2:19	l **up** thy hands toward him for the life of	5375
3:41	Let us l **up** our heart with *our* hands unto	5375
Eze 1:19	when the living creatures were l **up** from	5375
1:19	up from the earth, the wheels were l **up**.	5375
8: 3	the spirit l me **up** between the earth and	5375
8: 5	l **up** thine eyes now the way towards	5375
8: 5	So l l **up** mine eyes the way toward	5375
10:16	when the cherubims l **up** their wings to	5375
10:17	*these* l **up** themselves *also:* for the spirit	7426
10:19	the cherubims l **up** their wings,	5375
11: 1	Moreover the spirit l me **up**,	5375
11:22	did the cherubims l **up** their wings,	5375
17:14	that *it* might not l itself **up**, *but* that by	5375
18: 6	neither hath l **up** his eyes to the idols of	5375
18:12	and hath l **up** his eyes to the idols,	5375
18:15	neither hath l **up** his eyes to the idols of	5375
21:22	to l **up** the voice with shouting,	7311
23:27	that thou shalt not l **up** thine eyes unto	5375
26: 8	and l **up** the buckler against thee.	6965
33:25	l **up** your eyes toward your idols,	5375
44:12	have l l **up** mine hand against them,	5375
Da 4:34	l **up** mine eyes unto heaven,	5191
10: 5	l l **up** mine eyes, and looked, and behold,	5375
Mic 4: 3	shall not l **up** a sword against nation,	5375
5: 9	Thine hand shall be l **up** upon thine	7311
Hab 3:10	his voice, and l **up** his hands on high.	5375
Zec 1:18	l l **up** mine eyes, and saw, and behold	5375
1:21	so that no man did l **up** his head:	5375
1:21	which l **up** *their* horn over the land of	5375
2: 1	l l **up** mine eyes again, and looked,	5375
5: 1	l **up** mine eyes, and looked, and behold,	5375
5: 5	**L up** now thine eyes, and see what *is* this	5375
5: 7	behold, there *was* l **up** a talent of lead:	5375
5: 9	l **up** mine eyes, and looked, and behold,	5375
5: 9	they l **up** the ephah between the earth	5375
6: 1	l **up** mine eyes, and looked, and behold,	5375
Mt 12:11	will he not lay hold on it, and l *it* **out**?	1453
17: 8	And when they had l **up** their eyes,	1869
Mk 1:31	and took her by the hand, and l her **up**;	1453
Lk 11:27	woman of the company l **up** her voice,	1869
13:11	and could in no wise l **up** herself.	352
16:23	And in hell he l **up** his eyes, being in	1869
18:13	would not l **up** so much as *his* eyes unto	1869
21:28	pass, *then* look up, and l **up** your heads;	1869
24:50	and he l **up** his hands, and blessed them.	1869
Jn 4:35	**L up** your eyes, and look on the fields;	1869
6: 5	When Jesus then l **up** *his* eyes,	1869
8: 7	he l **up** himself, and said unto them,	352
8:10	When Jesus had l **up** *himself,* and saw	352
8:28	When ye have l **up** the Son of man, then	5312
11:41	And Jesus l up *his* eyes, and said, Father,	142
12:34	thou, The Son of man must be l **up**?	5312
13:18	that eateth bread with me hath l **up** his	1869
17: 1	and l **up** his eyes to heaven, and said,	1869
Ac 2:14	l **up** his voice, and said unto them, Ye	1869
3: 7	took him by the right hand, and l *him* **up**:	1453
4:24	And when they heard that, they l **up** their	142
9:41	and l her **up**, and when he had called	450
14:11	they l **up** their voices, saying in the speech	1869
22:22	and *then* l **up** their voices, and said,	1869
Heb 12:12	Wherefore l **up** the hands which hang	461
Jas 4:10	sight of the Lord, and he shall l you **up**.	5312

LIFTED (69) [LIFT]

Ge 13:10	Lot l **up** his eyes, and beheld all the plain	5375
22:13	Abraham l **up** his eyes, and looked,	5375
29:11	Rachel, and l **up** his voice, and wept.	5375
31:10	l l **up** mine eyes, and saw in a dream,	5375
33: 1	Jacob l **up** his eyes, and looked,	5375
39:15	when he heard that l l **up** my voice and	7311
40:20	he l **up** the head of the chief butler and	5375
Nu 14: 1	all the congregation l **up** their voice,	5375
Dt 8:14	thine heart be l **up**, and thou forget	7311
17:20	That his heart be not l **up** above his	5375
Jdg 8:28	so that they l **up** their heads no more.	5375
1Sa 6:13	they l **up** their eyes, and saw the ark,	5375
2Sa 22:49	also hast l me **up on high** above them	7311
2Ki 14:10	and thine heart hath l thee **up**:	5375
2Ch 26:16	his heart was l **up** to *his* destruction,	1361
32:25	*done* unto him; for his heart was l **up**:	1361
Job 2:12	him not, they l **up** their voice, and wept;	5375
Ps 27: 6	now shall mine head be l **up** above mine	7311
30: 1	for thou hast l me **up**, and hast not made	1802
74: 5	*man* was famous according as he had l **up**	935
93: 3	The floods have l **up**, O Lord, the floods	5375
93: 3	O Lord, the floods have l **up** their voice;	5375
102:10	for thou hast l me **up**, and cast me down.	5375
106:26	Therefore he l **up** his hand against them,	5375
Pr 30:13	are their eyes! and their eyelids are l **up**.	5375
Isa 2:12	and lofty, and upon every one that is l **up**;	5375
2:13	are high and l **up**, and upon all the oaks	5375
2:14	upon all the hills that are l **up**,	5375
6: 1	high and l **up**, and his train filled	5375
26:11	Lord, *when* thy hand is l **up**, they will	7311
Isa 37:23	*thy* voice, and l **up** thine eyes on high?	5375
Jer 51: 9	unto heaven, and is l **up** *even* to the skies.	5375
52:31	l **up** the head of Jehoiachin king of Judah,	5375
Eze 1:20	the wheels were l **up** over against them:	5375
1:21	when those were l **up** from the earth,	5375
1:21	the wheels were l **up** over against them:	5375
3:14	So the spirit l me **up**, and took me away,	5375
10:15	the cherubims were l **up**. This *is* the	7426
10:17	when they were l **up**, *these* lift up	7311
20: 5	l **up** mine hand unto the seed of the	5375
20: 5	when l l **up** mine hand unto them, saying,	5375
20: 6	In the day *that* l l **up** mine hand unto	5375
20:15	Yet also l l **up** my hand unto them in	5375
20:23	l l **up** mine hand unto them also in	5375
20:28	*for* the which l l **up** mine hand to give it	5375
20:42	into the country *for* the which l l **up** mine	5375
28: 2	Because thine heart *is* l **up**, and thou hast	1361
28: 5	thine heart is l **up** because of thy riches:	1361
28:17	heart was l **up** because of thy beauty,	1361
31:10	Because thou hast l **up** thyself in height,	1361
31:10	and his heart is l **up** in his height;	7311
36: 7	I have l **up** mine hand, Surely the heathen	5375
47:14	*concerning* the which l l **up** mine hand	5375
Da 5:20	when his heart was l **up**, and his mind	7313
5:23	hast l **up** thyself against the Lord of	7313
7: 4	was l **up** from the earth, and made stand	5191
8: 3	l **up** mine eyes, and saw, and behold,	5375
11:12	the multitude, his heart shall be l **up**;	7311
Hab 2: 4	soul *which* is l **up** is not upright in him:	6075
Zec 9:16	crown, l **up as an ensign** upon his land.	5264
14:10	it shall be l **up**, and inhabited in her place,	7213
Mk 9:27	Jesus took him by the hand, and l him **up**;	1453
Lk 6:20	he l **up** his eyes on his disciples,	1869
17:13	And they l **up** *their* voices, and said, Jesus,	142
Jn 3:14	And as Moses l **up** the serpent in	5312
3:14	*even* so must the Son of man be l **up**:	5312
12:32	l, if l be l **up** from the earth, will draw	5312
1Ti 3: 6	lest being l **up with pride** he fall into	5187
Rev 10: 5	upon the earth l **up** his hand to heaven,	142

LIFTER (1) [LIFT]

Ps 3: 3	my glory, and the l **up** of mine head.	7311

LIFTEST (4) [LIFT]

Job 30:22	Thou l me **up** to the wind; thou causest	5375
Ps 9:13	thou that l me **up** from the gates of death:	7311
18:48	thou l me **up** above those that rise up	7311
Pr 2: 3	*and* l **up** thy voice for understanding;	5414

LIFTETH (10) [LIFT]

1Sa 2: 7	maketh rich: he bringeth low, and l **up**.	7311
2: 8	*and* l **up** the beggar from the dunghill,	7311
2Ch 25:19	and thine heart l thee **up** to boast:	5375
Job 39:19	What time she l **up** herself on high,	4754
Ps 107:25	wind, which l **up** the waves thereof.	7311
113: 7	*and* l the needy out of the dunghill:	5749
147: 6	The Lord l **up** the meek: he casteth	5749
Isa 18: 3	l *he* l **up** an ensign on the mountains;	5375
Jer 51: 3	against *him that* l himself **up** in his	5927
Na 3: 3	The horseman l **up** both the bright sword	5927

LIFTING (9) [LIFT]

1Ch 11:20	for l **up** his spear against three hundred,	5782
15:16	sounding, by l **up** the voice with joy.	7311
Ne 8: 6	Amen, Amen, with l **up** their hands:	4607
Job 22:29	then thou shalt say, *There is* l **up**;	1466
Ps 141: 2	the l **up** of my hands *as* the evening	4864
Pr 30:32	If thou hast done foolishly in l **up** thyself,	5375
Isa 9:18	shall mount up *like* the l **up** of smoke.	1348
33: 3	at the l **up** of thyself the nations were	7427
1Ti 2: 8	l **up** holy hands, without wrath and	1869

LIGHT (272) [ENLIGHTEN, ENLIGHTENED, ENLIGHTENING, LIGHTED, LIGHTEN, ENLIGHTEN, LIGHTED, LIGHTENED, LIGHTENED, LIGHTENETH, LIGHTER, LIGHTEST, LIGHTETH, LIGHTING, LIGHTLY, LIGHTNESS, LIGHTS]

Ge 1: 3	said, Let there be l: and there was light.	216
1: 3	Let there be light: and there was l.	216
1: 4	God saw the l, that *it was* good:	216
1: 4	and God divided the l from the darkness.	216
1: 5	God called the l Day, and the darkness he	216
1:15	of the heaven to **give** l upon the earth:	215
1:16	the greater l to rule the day, and the lesser	3974
1:16	the day, and the lesser l to rule the night:	3974
1:17	of the heaven to **give** l upon the earth,	215
1:18	and to divide the l from the darkness:	216
44: 3	As soon as the morning was l, the men	216
Ex 10:23	all the children of Israel had l in their	216
13:21	by night in a pillar of fire, to **give** them l;	215
14:20	to them, but it **gave** l by night *to these*:	215
25: 6	Oil for the l, spices for anointing oil,	3974
25:37	they shall l the lamps thereof, that they	5927
25:37	that they may **give** l over against it.	215
27:20	bring thee pure oil olive beaten for the l,	3974
35: 8	oil for the l, and spices for anointing oil,	3974
35:14	The candlestick also for the l, and his	3974
35:14	and his lamps, with the oil for the l,	3974
35:28	oil for the l, and for the anointing oil,	3974
39:37	all the vessels thereof, and the l lamps thereof.	5927
40: 4	in the candlestick, and l the lamps thereof.	5927
Lev 24: 2	unto thee pure oil olive beaten for the l,	3974
Nu 4: 9	cover the candlestick of the l, and his	3974
4:16	the priest *pertaineth* the oil for the l,	3974
8: 2	the seven lamps shall **give** l over against	215

L

Nu	21: 5 and our soul loatheth *this* l bread.	7052
Dt	27:16 Cursed *be* he that **setteth** l by his father	7034
Jdg	9: 4 Abimelech hired vain and l persons,	6348
	19:26 know where her lord *was*, till it was l.	216
Ru	2: 3 her hap was to l **on** a part of the field	7136
1Sa	14:36 spoil them until the morning l, and let us	216
	18:23 Seemeth it to you a l *thing* to be a king's	7043
	25:22 morning l *any that* pisseth against the wall.	216
	25:34 morning l *any that* pisseth against the wall.	216
	25:36 less or more, until the morning l.	216
	29:10 early in the morning, and **have** l, depart.	215
2Sa	2:18 and Asahel *was as* l of foot as a wild roe.	7031
	17:12 we *will l* upon him as the dew falleth on	NIH
	17:22 by the morning l there lacked not one *of*	216
	21:17 that thou quench not the l of Israel.	5216
	23: 4 *he shall be* as the l of the morning, *when*	216
1Ki	7: 4 and l *was* against light in three ranks.	4237
	7: 4 and light *was* against l in three ranks.	4237
	7: 5 *was* against light *in* three ranks.	4237
	7: 5 and light *was* against l in three ranks.	4237
	11:36 David my servant may have a l alway	5216
	16:31 as if it had been a **l** *thing* for him to walk	7043
2Ki	3:18 *but* a l *thing* in the sight of the LORD:	7043
	7: 9 we tarry till the morning l, *some* mischief	216
	8:19 he promised him to give to him alway a l,	5216
	20:10 It is a l *thing* for the shadow to go down	7043
2Ch	21: 7 as he promised to give a l to him and to	5216
Ne	9:12 to **give** them l in the way wherein they	215
	9:19 to **shew** them l, and the way wherein	215
Est	8:16 The Jews had l, and gladness, and joy,	219
Job	3: 4 from above, neither let the l shine upon it.	5105
	3: 9 let it look for l, but *have* none; neither let	216
	3:16 not been; as infants *which* never saw l.	216
	3:20 is l given to him that is in misery,	216
	3:23 *Why is l given* to a man whose way is hid,	NIH
	10:22 any order, and *where* the l is as darkness.	3313
	12:22 and bringeth out to l the shadow of death.	216
	12:25 They grope *in* the dark without l,	216
	17:12 day: the l *is* short, because of darkness.	216
	18: 5 the l of the wicked shall be put out,	216
	18: 6 The l shall be dark in his tabernacle,	216
	18:18 He shall be driven from l into darkness,	216
	22:28 and the l shall shine upon thy ways.	216
	24:13 They are of those that rebel against the l;	216
	24:14 The murderer rising with the l killeth	216
	24:16 in the daytime: they know not the l.	216
	25: 3 and upon whom doth not his l arise?	216
	28:11 the thing that is hid bringeth he forth to l.	216
	29: 3 *when* by his l I walked *through* darkness;	216
	29:24 the l of my countenance they cast not	216
	30:26 came *unto me:* and when I waited for l,	216
	33:28 into the pit, and his life shall see the l.	216
	33:30 to be enlightened with the l of the living.	216
	36:30 he spreadeth his l upon it, and covereth	216
	36:32 With clouds he covereth the l;	216
	37:15 and caused the l of his cloud to shine?	216
	37:21 now *men* see not the bright l which *is in*	216
	38:15 from the wicked their l is withholden,	216
	38:19 Where *is* the way *where* l dwelleth?	216
	38:24 what way is the l parted, *which* scattereth	216
	41:18 *By* his neesings a l doth shine, and his eyes	216
Ps	4: 6 lift thou up the l of thy countenance upon	216
	18:28 For thou wilt l my candle: the LORD my	215
	27: 1 The LORD *is* my l and my salvation;	216
	36: 9 fountain of life: in thy l shall we see light.	216
	36: 9 fountain of life: in thy light we shall see l.	216
	37: 6 shall bring forth thy righteousness as the l,	216
	38:10 as for the l of mine eyes, it also is gone	216
	43: 3 send out thy l and thy truth: let them lead	216
	44: 3 the l of thy countenance, because thou	216
	49:19 of his fathers; they shall never see l.	216
	56:13 that *I* may walk before God in the l of	216
	74:16 thou hast prepared the l and the sun.	3974
	78:14 a cloud, and all the night with a l of fire.	216
	89:15 O LORD, in the l of thy countenance.	216
	90: 8 secret *sins* in the l of thy countenance.	3974
	97:11 **L** is sown for the righteous, and gladness	216
	104: 2 Who coverest *thyself with* l as *with* a	216
	105:39 a covering; and fire to **give** l in the night.	215
	112: 4 Unto the upright there ariseth l in	216
	118:27 God *is* the LORD, which hath **shewed** us l:	215
	119:105 a lamp unto my feet, and l unto my path.	216
	119:130 The entrance of thy words **giveth** l;	215
	139:11 even the night *shall be* l about me.	216
	139:12 darkness and the l *are* both alike to thee.	219
	148: 3 sun and moon: praise him, all ye stars of l.	216
Pr	4:18 the path of the just *is* as the shining l,	216
	6:23 the law *is* l; and reproofs of instruction *are*	216
	13: 9 The l of the righteous rejoiceth: but the	216
	15:30 The l of the eyes rejoiceth the heart:	3974
	16:15 In the l of the king's countenance *is* life;	216
Ecc	2:13 folly, as far as l excelleth darkness.	216
	11: 7 l *is* sweet, and a pleasant *thing it is*	216
	12: 2 the sun, or the l, or the moon, or the stars,	216
Isa	2: 5 and let us walk in the l of the LORD.	216
	5:20 that put darkness for l, and light for	216
	5:20 put darkness for light, and l for darkness;	216
	5:30 the l is darkened in the heavens thereof.	216
	8:20 *it is* because *there is* no l in them.	7837
	9: 2 walked in darkness have seen a great l:	216
	9: 2 of death, upon them hath the l shined.	216
	10:17 the l of Israel shall be for a fire, and his	216
	13:10 constellations thereof shall not give their l:	216
	13:10 the moon shall not cause her l to shine.	216
	30:26 Moreover the l of the moon shall be as	216

Isa	30:26 of the moon shall be as the l of the sun,	216
	30:26 the l of the sun shall be sevenfold,	216
	30:26 shall be sevenfold, as the l of seven days,	216
	42: 6 of the people, for a l of the Gentiles;	216
	42:16 I will make darkness l before them,	216
	45: 7 I form the l, and create darkness: I make	216
	49: 6 It is a l thing that thou shouldest be my	7043
	49: 6 I will also give thee for a l to the Gentiles,	216
	50:10 that walketh in darkness, and hath no l?	5051
	50:11 walk in the l of your fire, and in the sparks	217
	51: 4 I will make my judgment to rest for a l of	216
	58: 8 shall thy l break forth as the morning,	216
	58:10 thy l rise in obscurity, and thy darkness	216
	59: 9 we wait for l, but behold obscurity;	216
	60: 1 for thy l is come, and the glory of	216
	60: 3 the Gentiles shall come to thy l, and kings	216
	60:19 The sun shall be no more thy l by day;	216
	60:19 for brightness shall the moon **give** l	215
	60:19 LORD shall be unto thee an everlasting l,	216
	60:20 for the LORD shall be thine everlasting l,	216
Jer	4:23 void; and the heavens, and they *had* no l.	216
	13:16 and, while ye look for l, he turn it into	216
	25:10 of the millstones, and the l of the candle.	216
	31:35 which giveth the sun for a l by day,	216
	31:35 the moon and of the stars for a l by night,	216
La	3: 2 brought *me* into darkness, but not *into* l.	216
Eze	8:17 Is it a l *thing* to the house of Judah that	7043
	22: 7 In thee have they **set** l by father and	7043
	32: 7 and the moon shall not **give** her l.	215+216
Da	2:22 darkness, and the l dwelleth with him.	5094
	5:11 in the days of thy father l and	5094
	5:14 that l and understanding and	5094
Hos	6: 5 judgments *are as* the l *that* goeth forth.	216
Am	5:18 the day of the LORD *is* darkness, and not l.	216
	5:20 day of the LORD *be* darkness, and not l?	216
Mic	2: 1 when the morning is l, they practise it,	216
	7: 8 in darkness, the LORD *shall be* a l unto me.	216
	7: 9 he will bring me forth to the l, *and* I shall	216
Hab	3: 4 *his* brightness was as the l; he had horns	216
	3:11 at the l of thine arrows they went, *and* at	216
Zep	3: 4 prophets *are* l *and* treacherous persons:	6348
	3: 5 morning doth he bring his judgment to l,	216
Zec	14: 6 *that* the l shall not be clear, *nor* dark:	216
	14: 7 to pass, *that* at evening time it shall be l.	216
Mt	4:16 people which sat in darkness saw great l;	5457
	4:16 and shadow of death l is sprung up.	5457
	5:14 Ye are the l of the world. A city that is set	5457
	5:15 Neither do men l a candle, and put it	2545
	5:15 it **giveth** l unto all that are in the house.	2989
	5:16 Let your l so shine before men, that they	5457
	6:22 The l of the body is the eye: if therefore	3088
	6:22 single, thy whole body shall be **full of** l.	5460
	6:23 therefore the l that is in thee be darkness,	5457
	10:27 I tell you in darkness, *that* speak ye in l:	5457
	11:30 For my yoke *is* easy, and my burden is l.	1645
	17: 2 sun, and his raiment was white as the l.	5457
	22: 5 they **made** l of *it*, and went their ways,	272
	24:29 and the moon shall not give her l,	5338
Mk	13:24 and the moon shall not give her l,	5338
Lk	1:79 To **give** l to them that sit in darkness and	2014
	2:32 A l to lighten the Gentiles, and the glory	5457
	8:16 that they which enter in may see the l.	5457
	11:33 that they which come in may see the l.	5338
	11:34 The l of the body is the eye:	3088
	11:34 is single, thy whole body also is **full of** l;	5460
	11:35 the l which is in thee be not darkness.	5457
	11:36 If thy whole body therefore *be* **full of** l,	5460
	11:36 no part dark, the whole shall be **full of** l,	5460
	11:36 bright shining of a candle doth **give** thee l.	5461
	12: 3 spoken in darkness shall be heard in the l;	5457
	15: 8 doth not l a candle, and sweep the house,	681
	16: 8 generation wiser than the children of l.	5457
Jn	1: 4 was life; and the life was the l of men.	5457
	1: 5 And the l shineth in darkness;	5457
	1: 7 for a witness, to bear witness of the L,	5457
	1: 8 He was not that **L**, but *was sent* to bear	5457
	1: 8 but *was sent* to bear witness of that **L**.	5457
	1: 9 *That* was the true **L**, which lighteth every	5457
	3:19 that l is come into the world, and men	5457
	3:19 and men loved darkness rather than l,	5457
	3:20 For every one that doeth evil hateth the l,	5457
	3:20 neither cometh to the l, lest his deeds	5457
	3:21 But he that doeth truth cometh to the l,	5457
	5:35 He was a burning and a shining l:	3088
	5:35 willing for a season to rejoice in his l.	5457
	8:12 unto them, saying, I am the l of the world:	5457
	8:12 in darkness, but shall have the l of life.	5457
	9: 5 I am in the world, I am the l of the world.	5457
	11: 9 because he seeth the l of this world.	5457
	11:10 stumbleth, because there is no l in him.	5457
	12:35 Yet a little while is the l with you.	5457
	12:35 Walk while ye have the l, lest darkness	5457
	12:36 While ye have l, believe in the light, that	5457
	12:36 While ye have light, believe in the l, that	5457
	12:36 the light, that ye may be the children of l.	5457
	12:46 I am come a l into the world,	5457
Ac	9: 3 there shined round about him a l	5457
	12: 7 upon *him*, and a l shined in the prison:	5457
	13:47 *saying*, I have set thee to be a l of	5457
	16:29 Then he called for a l, and sprang in,	5457
	22: 6 there shone from heaven a great l	5457
	22: 9 they that were with me saw indeed the l,	5457
	22:11 I could not see for the glory of that l,	5457
	26:13 O king, I saw in the way a l from heaven,	5457
	26:18 *and* to turn *them* from darkness to l,	5457

Ac	26:23 and should shew l unto the people,	5457
Ro	2:19 blind, which are in darkness,	5457
	13:12 and let us put on the armour of l.	5457
1Co	4: 5 who both will **bring to** l the hidden	5461
2Co	4: 4 lest the l of the glorious gospel of Christ,	5462
	4: 6 who commanded the l to shine out of	5457
	4: 6 to give the l of the knowledge of the glory	5462
	4:17 For our l affliction, which is but for a	1645
	6:14 what communion hath l with darkness?	5457
	11:14 himself is transformed into an angel of l.	5457
Eph	5: 8 how were ye l in the Lord:	5457
	5: 8 *ye* light in the Lord: walk as children of l:	5457
	5:13 are reproved are made manifest by the l:	5457
	5:13 for whatsoever doth make manifest is l.	5457
	5:14 the dead, and Christ shall **give** thee l.	2017
Col	1:12 of the inheritance of the saints in l:	5457
1Th	5: 5 are all the children of l, and the children	5457
1Ti	6:16 dwelling in the l which no *man* can	5457
2Ti	1:10 hath **brought** life and immortality **to** l	5461
1Pe	2: 9 you out of darkness into his marvellous l:	5457
2Pe	1:19 as unto a l that shineth in a dark place,	3088
1Jn	1: 5 that God is l, and in him is no darkness at	5457
	1: 7 if we walk in the l, as he is in the light,	5457
	1: 7 if we walk in the light, as he is in the l,	5457
	2: 8 is past, and the true l now shineth.	5457
	2: 9 He that saith *he* is in the l, and hateth his	5457
	2:10 He that loveth his brother abideth in the l,	5457
Rev	7:16 neither shall the sun l on them, nor any	4098
	18:23 the l of a candle shall shine no more at	5457
	21:11 her l was like unto a stone most precious,	5458
	21:23 lighten it, and the Lamb *is* the l thereof.	3088
	21:24 which are saved shall walk in the l of it:	5457
	22: 5 they need no candle, neither l of the sun;	5457
	22: 5 the sun; for the Lord God **giveth** them l:	5461

LIGHTED (13) [LIGHT]

Ge	24:64 when she saw Isaac, she l off the camel.	5307
	28:11 he l upon a *certain* place, and tarried	6293
Ex	40:25 he l the lamps before the LORD;	5927
Nu	8: 3 he l the lamps thereof over against	5927
Jos	15:18 she l **off** *her* ass;	4480+5921+6795
Jdg	1:14 she l from off *her* ass; and Caleb said unto	6795
	4:15 so that Sisera l **down** off *his* chariot,	3381
1Sa	25:23 l off the ass, and fell before David on her	3381
2Ki	5:21 he l **down** from the chariot to meet him,	5307
	10:15 he l **on** Jehonadab the son of Rechab	4672
Isa	9: 8 word into Jacob, and it hath l upon Israel.	5307
Lk	8:16 No *man*, when he hath l a candle, covereth	681
	11:33 No *man*, when he hath l a candle, putteth	681

LIGHTEN (7) [LIGHT]

1Sa	6: 5 peradventure he will l his hand from off	7043
2Sa	22:29 and the LORD will l my darkness.	5050
Ezr	9: 8 that our God may l our eyes, and give us a	215
Ps	13: 3 l mine eyes, lest I sleep the *sleep of* death;	215
Jnh	1: 5 in the ship into the sea, to l *it* of them.	7043
Lk	2:32 A light to l the Gentiles, and the glory of	602
Rev	21:23 for the glory of God did l it, and the Lamb	5461

LIGHTENED (5) [LIGHT]

Ps	34: 5 They looked unto him, and were l:	5102
	77:18 the lightnings l the world: the earth	215
Ac	27:18 the next *day* they l **the ship**;	1546+4160
	27:38 they l the ship, and cast out the wheat	2893
Rev	18: 1 and the earth was l with his glory.	5461

LIGHTENETH (2) [LIGHT]

Pr	29:13 meet together: the LORD l both their eyes.	215
Lk	17:24 that l out of the one *part* under heaven,	797

LIGHTER (5) [LIGHT]

1Ki	12: 4 **make** thou the grievous service . . . l,	7043
	12: 9 **Make** the yoke which thy father did put upon us l?	7043
	12:10 yoke heavy, but **make** thou *it* l unto us;	7043
2Ch	10:10 but **make** thou *it* somewhat l for us;	7043
Ps	62: 9 they *are* altogether l than vanity.	NIH

LIGHTEST (1) [LIGHT]

Nu	8: 2 and say unto him, When thou l the lamps,	5927

LIGHTETH (3) [LIGHT]

Ex	30: 8 when Aaron l the lamps at even, he shall	5927
Dt	19: 5 and l **upon** his neighbour, that he die;	4672
Jn	1: 9 which l every man *that* cometh into	5461

LIGHTING (2) [LIGHT]

Isa	30:30 shall shew the l **down** of his arm, with	5183
Mt	3:16 descending like a dove, and l upon him:	2064

LIGHTLY (7) [LIGHT]

Ge	26:10 of the people might have lien	4592+3509.1
Dt	32:15 and l **esteemed** the Rock of his salvation.	5034
1Sa	2:30 they that despise me shall be l **esteemed**.	7043
	18:23 that I *am* a poor man, and l **esteemed**?	7034
Isa	9: 1 when at the first he l **afflicted** the land of	7043
Jer	4:24 they trembled, and all the hills **moved** l.	7043
Mk	9:39 in my name, that can l speak evil of me.	5036

LIGHTNESS (3) [LIGHT]

Jer	3: 9 it came to pass through the l of her	6963
	23:32 people to err by their lies, and by their l;	6350
2Co	1:17 therefore was thus minded, did I use l?	1644

LIGHTNING (13) [LIGHTNINGS]

2Sa	22:15 scattered them; l, and discomfited them.	1300

Job 28:26 rain, and a way for the l of the thunder: 2385
37: 3 and his l unto the ends of the earth. 216
38:25 of waters, or a way for the l of thunder; 2385
Ps 144: 6 **Cast forth** l, and scatter them: 1299+1300
Eze 1:13 bright, and out of the fire went forth l. 1300
1:14 returned as the appearance of a **flash of** l. 965
Da 10: 6 his face as the appearance of l, and his 1300
Zec 9:14 and his arrow shall go forth as the l: 1300
Mt 24:27 For as the l cometh out of the east, *796*
28: 3 His countenance was like l, and his raiment *796*
Lk 10:18 I beheld Satan as l fall from heaven. *796*
17:24 For as the l, that lighteneth out of the one *796*

LIGHTNINGS (14) [LIGHTNING]
Ex 19:16 there were thunders and l, and a thick 1300
20:18 the l, and the noise of the trumpet, 3940
Job 38:35 Canst thou send l, that they may go, 1300
Ps 18:14 and he shot out l, and discomfited them. 1300
77:18 the l lightened the world: the earth 1300
97: 4 His l enlightened the world: the earth 1300
135: 7 he maketh l for the rain; he bringeth 1300
Jer 10:13 he maketh l with rain, and bringeth forth 1300
51:16 he maketh l with rain, and bringeth forth 1300
Na 2: 4 seem like torches, they shall run like the l. 1300
Rev 4: 5 And out of the throne proceeded l and *796*
8: 5 thunderings, and l, and an earthquake. *796*
11:19 and there were l, and voices, *796*
16:18 and there were voices, and thunders, and l; *796*

LIGHTS (10) [LIGHT]
Ge 1:14 Let there be l in the firmament of the 3974
1:15 let them be for l in the firmament of 3974
1:16 God made two great l; the greater light to 3974
1Ki 6: 4 the house he made windows of narrow l. 8261
Ps 136: 7 To him that made great l: for his mercy 216
Eze 32: 8 All the bright l of heaven will I make dark 216
Lk 12:35 loins be girded about, and your l burning; *3088*
Ac 20: 8 And there were many l in the upper 2985
Php 2:15 among whom ye shine as l in the world; 5458
Jas 1:17 and cometh down from the Father of l, 5457

LIGN (1)
Nu 24: 6 as the **trees of** l aloes *which* the LORD 174

LIGURE (2)
Ex 28:19 third row a l, an agate, and an amethyst. 3958
39:12 third row, a l, an agate, and an amethyst. 3958

LIKE (669) [ALIKE, LIKED, LIKEMINDED, LIKEN,
LIKENED, LIKENESS, LIKETH, LIKEWISE, LIKING]
Ge 13:10 l the land of Egypt, as thou comest unto 3509.1
25:25 came out red, all over l a hairy garment; 3509.1
Ex 7:11 they also did in l manner with their 3651
8:10 there is none l unto the LORD our God. 3509.1
9:14 thou mayest know that there is none l 3644
9:24 such as there was none l it in all the land 3644
11: 6 such as there was none l it, nor shall be 3644
11: 6 none like it, nor shall be l it any more. NIH
15:11 Who is l unto thee, O LORD, among 3644
15:11 who is l thee, glorious in holiness, 3644
16:31 it was l coriander seed, white; 3509.1
16:31 the taste of it was l wafers made with 3509.1
In l manner thou shalt deal with thy 3651
24:17 the sight of the glory of the LORD was l 3509.1
25:33 Three bowls **made** l **unto almonds,** 8246
25:33 three bowls **made** l **almonds** in the other 8246
25:34 be four bowls **made** l **unto almonds,** 8246
28:11 in stone, l the engravings of a signet, NIH
28:21 to their names, l the engravings of a signet, NIH
28:36 grave upon it, l the engravings of a signet, NIH
30:32 neither shall ye make *any other* l it, 3644
30:33 Whosoever compoundeth *any* l it, 3644
30:34 **each** shall there be a l *weight:* 905+905+871.1
30:38 Whosoever shall make l unto that, 3644
34: 1 Hew thee two tables of stone l **unto** 3509.1
34: 4 he hewed two tables of stone l **unto** 3509.1
37:19 three bowls **made** l **almonds** in another 8246
37:20 *were* four bowls **made** l **almonds,** 8246
39: 8 cunning work, l the work of the ephod; 3509.1
39:14 l the engravings of a signet, every one NIH
39:30 it a writing, l to the engravings of a signet, NIH
Lev 13: 2 it be in the skin of his flesh l the plague 3807.1
Nu 23:10 the righteous, and let my last end be l his! 3644
Dt 4:32 this great thing *is,* or hath been heard l it? 3644
7:26 house, lest thou be a cursed thing l it: 3644
10: 1 Hew thee two tables of stone l **unto** 3509.1
10: 3 two tables of stone l **unto** the first, 3509.1
17:14 l as all the nations that *are* about me; 3651
18: 8 They shall have l portions to eat, beside 3509.1
18:15 midst of thee, of thy brethren, l **unto** me; 3644
18:18 l **unto** thee, and will put my words in his 3644
22: 3 **In** l **manner** shalt thou do with his ass; 3651
25: 7 if the man l not to take his brother's wife, 2654
25: 8 stand to *it,* and say, I l not to take her; 2654
29:23 the overthrow of Sodom, 3644
33:17 His glory is l the firstling of his bullock, NIH
33:17 and his horns *are* l the horns of unicorns; NIH
33:26 is none l **unto** the God of Jeshurun, 3509.1
33:29 who is l **unto** thee, O people saved by 3644
34:10 a prophet since in Israel l **unto** Moses, 3509.1
Jos 10:14 there was no day l that before it or 3509.1
Jdg 7:12 the valley l grasshoppers for multitude; 3509.1
11:17 **in** l **manner** they sent unto the king of 1571
13: 6 his countenance *was* l the countenance 3509.1
16:12 he brake them from off his arms l a 3509.1

Jdg 16:17 become weak, and be l any *other* man. 3509.1
Ru 2:13 though I be not l **unto** one of thy 3509.1
4:11 that is come into thine house l Rachel 3509.1
4:11 into thine house like Rachel and l Leah, 3509.1
4:12 let thy house be l the house of Pharez, 3509.1
1Sa 2: 2 neither *is there* any rock l our God. 3509.1
4: 9 Be strong, and quit yourselves l men, 3807.1
4: 9 to you: quit yourselves l men, and fight 3807.1
8: 5 now make us a king to judge us l all 3509.1
8:20 That we also may be l all the nations; 3509.1
10:24 that *there is* none l him among all 3644
17: 7 the staff of his spear *was* l a weaver's 3509.1
19:24 prophesied before Samuel **in** l **manner,** 1571
21: 9 David said, There is none l that; give it 3644
25:36 a feast in his house, l the feast of a king; 3509.1
26:15 who *is* l to thee in Israel? wherefore then 3644
2Sa 7: 9 l **unto** the name of the great *men* that 3509.1
7:22 for *there is* none l thee, neither *is there* 3644
7:23 what one nation in the earth *is* l thy 3509.1
7:23 l Israel, whom God went to redeem 3509.1
18:27 the running of Ahimaaz the son of 3509.1
21:19 staff of whose spear *was* l a weaver's 3509.1
22:34 He maketh my feet l hinds' *feet:* and 3509.1
1Ki 3:12 that there was none l thee before, 3644
3:12 neither after thee shall any arise l **unto** 3644
3:13 among the kings l **unto** thee all thy days. 3644
5: 6 skill to hew timber l **unto** the Sidonians. 3509.1
7: 8 the porch, *which* was of the l work. 3509.1
7: 8 whom he had taken to *wife,* l **unto** this 3509.1
7:26 the brim thereof was wrought l the brim 3509.1
7:33 the work of the wheels was l the work 3509.1
8:23 *there is* no God l thee, in heaven above, 3644
10:20 there was not the l made in any kingdom. 3651
12:32 l **unto** the feast that *is* in Judah, 3509.1
16: 3 will make thy house l the house of 3509.1
16: 7 in being l the house of Jeroboam, 3509.1
18:44 cloud out of the sea, l a man's hand. 3509.1
20:25 l the army that thou hast lost, horse for 3509.1
20:27 before them l two little flocks of kids; 3509.1
21:22 will make thine house l the house of 3509.1
21:22 l the house of Baasha the son of Ahijah, 3509.1
21:25 (But there was none l **unto** Ahab, 3509.1
22:13 be l the word of one of them, 3509.1
2Ki 3: 2 but not l his father, and like his mother: 3509.1
3: 2 but not like his father, and l his mother: 3509.1
5:14 his flesh came again l **unto** the flesh of a 3509.1
9: 9 will make thine house l the house of 3509.1
9: 9 l the house of Baasha the son of Ahijah: 3509.1
9:20 driving is l the driving of Jehu the son 3509.1
13: 7 had made them l the dust by threshing. 3509.1
14: 3 of the LORD, yet not l David his father: 3509.1
16: 2 the LORD his God, l David his father. 3509.1
17:14 necks, l to the neck of their fathers, 3509.1
17:15 that *they* should not do l them. 3509.1
18: 5 that after him was none l him among all 3644
18:32 take you away to a land l your own land, 3509.1
23:25 l **unto** him was there no king before him, 3644
23:25 neither after him arose there any l him. 3644
25:17 l **unto** these had the second pillar with 3509.1
1Ch 4:27 multiply, l to the children of Judah. 5704
11:23 in the Egyptian's hand *was* a spear l a 3509.1
12: 8 whose faces *were* l the faces of lions, NIH
12:22 it was a great host, l the host of God. 3509.1
14:11 hand l the breaking forth of waters: 3509.1
17: 8 have made thee a name l the name of 3509.1
17:20 O LORD, *there is* none l thee, neither *is* 3644
17:21 what one nation in the earth *is* l thy 3509.1
20: 5 spear staff *was* l a weaver's beam. 3509.1
27:23 Israel l to the stars of the heavens. 3509.1
2Ch 1: 9 l the dust of the earth in multitude. 3509.1
1:12 shall there any after thee have the l. 3651
4: 5 the brim of it l the work of the brim of a 3509.1
6:14 *there is* no God l thee in the heaven, 3644
9:19 was not the l made in any kingdom. 3651
18:12 be l one of theirs, and speak thou good. 3509.1
21: 6 Israel, l **as** did the house of Ahab: 834+3509.1
21:13 l to the whoredoms of the house of 3509.1
21:19 for him, l the burning of his fathers. 3509.1
22: 4 sight of the LORD, l the house of Ahab: 3509.1
28: 1 sight of the LORD, l David his father: 3509.1
30: 7 be not ye l your fathers, and like your 3509.1
30: 7 ye like your fathers, and l your brethren, 3509.1
30:26 Israel *there was* not the l in Jerusalem. 3509.1
33: 2 l **unto** the abominations of the heathen, 3509.1
35:18 there was no passover l to that, kept in 3644
Ne 6: 3 sent Sanballat his servant unto me in l 2088
13:26 among these was there no king l him, 3644
Est 2:20 l **as when** she was brought up 834+3509.1
Job 1: 8 that *there is* none l him in the earth, 3644
2: 3 that *there is* none l him in the earth, 3644
3:24 my roarings are poured out l the waters. 3509.1
5:26 l **as** a shock of corn cometh in in his 3509.1
7: 1 *are not* his days also l the days of a 3509.1
8: 2 *long shall* the words of thy mouth be l NIH
10:10 out as milk, and cruddled me l cheese? 3509.1
11:12 though man be born l a wild ass's colt. NIH
12:25 he maketh them to stagger l a drunken 3509.1
13:12 Your remembrances *are* l **unto** ashes, 4912
14: 2 He cometh forth l a flower, and is cut 3509.1
14: 9 will bud, and bring forth boughs l a plant. 3644
15:16 is man, which drinketh iniquity l water? 3509.1
16:14 he runneth upon me l a giant. 3509.1
19:10 and mine hope hath he removed l a tree. 3509.1
20: 7 *Yet* he shall perish for ever l his own 3509.1
21:11 They send forth their little ones l a flock, 3509.1

Job 30:19 and I am **become** l dust and ashes. 4911
32:19 vent; it is ready to burst l new bottles. 3509.1
34: 7 What man *is* l Job, *who* drinketh up 3509.1
34: 7 *who* drinketh up scorning l water? 3644
36:22 by his power: who teacheth l him? 3644
38: 3 Gird up now thy loins l a man; for I will 3509.1
40: 7 Gird up thy loins now l a man: I will 3509.1
40: 9 Hast thou an arm l God? or, canst thou 3509.1
40: 9 canst thou thunder with a voice l him? 3644
40:17 He moveth his tail l a cedar: the sinews 3644
40:18 of brass; his bones *are* l bars of iron. 3509.1
41:18 his eyes *are* l the eyelids of the morning. 3509.1
41:31 He maketh the deep to boil l a pot: 3509.1
41:31 he maketh the sea l a pot of ointment. 3509.1
41:33 Upon earth there is not his l, who is made 4915
42: 8 *thing which is* right, l my servant Job. 3509.1
Ps 1: 3 he shall be l a tree planted by the rivers 3509.1
1: 4 *are* l the chaff which the wind driveth 3509.1
2: 9 shalt dash them in pieces l a potter's 5310
7: 2 Lest he tear my soul l a lion, rending *it* 3509.1
17:12 L as a lion *that* is greedy of his prey, 1825
18:33 He maketh my feet l hinds' *feet,* and 3509.1
22:14 I am poured out l water, and all my 3509.1
22:14 heart is l wax; it is melted in the midst 3509.1
22:15 My strength is dried up l a potsherd; 3509.1
28: 1 I **become** l them that go down into the 4911
29: 6 He maketh them also to skip l a calf; 3644
29: 6 Lebanon and Sirion l a young unicorn. 3644
31:12 man out of mind: I am l a broken vessel. 3509.1
35:10 shall say, LORD, who *is* l **unto** thee, 3644
36: 6 Thy righteousness *is* l the great 3509.1
37: 2 For they shall soon be cut down l 3509.1
37:35 spreading himself l a green bay tree. 3509.1
39:11 his beauty to consume away l a moth: 3509.1
44:11 Thou hast given us l sheep appointed 3509.1
49:12 abideth not: he is l the beasts *that* perish. 4911
49:14 L sheep they are laid in the grave; 3509.1
49:20 is l the beasts *that* perish. 4911
52: 2 l a sharp rasor, working deceitfully. 3509.1
52: 8 I am l a green olive tree in the house of 3509.1
55: 6 O that I had wings l a dove, *for then* 3509.1
58: 4 Their poison *is* l the poison of a 1823+3509.1
58: 4 they are l the deaf adder *that* stoppeth 3644
58: 8 l the untimely birth of a woman, *that* they NIH
59: 6 they make a noise l a dog, and go round 3509.1
59:14 and let them make a noise l a dog, 3509.1
64: 3 Who whet their tongue l a sword, 3509.1
71:19 great *things:* O God, who *is* l **unto** thee! 3644
72: 6 He shall come down l rain upon 3509.1
72:16 the fruit thereof shall shake l Lebanon: 3509.1
72:16 *they* of the city shall flourish l grass of 5973
73: 5 neither are they plagued l *other* men. 5973
77:20 Thou leddest thy people l a flock by 3509.1
78:16 and caused waters to run down l rivers. 3509.1
78:27 feathered fowls l **as** the sand of the sea: 3509.1
78:52 his own people to go forth l sheep, 3509.1
78:52 guided them in the wilderness l a flock. 3509.1
78:57 and dealt unfaithfully l their fathers: 3509.1
78:57 they were turned aside l a deceitful bow. 3509.1
78:65 l a mighty *man* that shouteth by reason 3509.1
78:69 he built his sanctuary l high *palaces,* like 3644
78:69 built his sanctuary like high *palaces,* l 3509.1
79: 3 Their blood have they shed l water 3509.1
79: 5 for ever? shall thy jealousy burn l fire? 3644
80: 1 thou that leadest Joseph l a flock; 3509.1
80:10 boughs thereof *were* l the goodly cedars. NIH
82: 7 ye shall die l men, and fall like one of 3509.1
82: 7 like men, and fall l one of the princes. 3509.1
83:11 Make their nobles l Oreb, and like Zeeb: 3509.1
83:11 Make their nobles like Oreb, and l Zeeb: 3509.1
83:13 O my God, make them l a wheel; 3509.1
86: 8 Among the gods *there is* none l **unto** thee, 3644
86: 8 neither *are there* any *works* l **unto** thy 3509.1
88: 5 the dead, l the slain that lie in the grave; 3644
88:17 came round about me daily l water; 3509.1
89: 8 who *is* a strong LORD l **unto** thee? 3644
89:46 for ever? shall thy wrath burn l fire? 3644
90: 5 in the morning they are l grass which 3509.1
92:10 my horn shalt thou exalt l *the horn of* 3509.1
92:12 The righteous shall flourish l the palm 3509.1
92:12 he shall grow l a cedar in Lebanon. 3509.1
97: 5 The hills melted l wax at the presence 3509.1
102: 3 For my days are consumed l smoke, 871.1
102: 4 heart is smitten, and withered l grass; 3509.1
102: 6 I am l a pelican of the wilderness: I am 1819
102: 6 I am l an owl of the desert. 3509.1
102: 7 For I have eaten ashes l bread, 3509.1
102:11 My days *are* l a shadow that declineth; 3509.1
102:11 declineth; and I am withered l grass. 3509.1
102:26 of them shall wax old l a garment; 3509.1
103: 5 *that* thy youth is renewed l the eagle's. 3509.1
103:13 L as a father pitieth *his* children, 3509.1
104: 2 stretchest out the heavens l a curtain: 3509.1
105:41 they ran in the dry places l a river. NIH
107:27 stagger l a drunken *man,* and are at 3509.1
107:41 and maketh *him* families l a flock. 3509.1
109:18 As he clothed himself with cursing l **as** 3509.1
109:18 so let it come into his bowels l water, 3509.1
109:18 like water, and l oil into his bones. 3509.1
109:23 gone l the shadow when it declineth: 3509.1
113: 5 Who is l **unto** the LORD our God, 3509.1
114: 4 The mountains skipped l rams, 3509.1
114: 4 like rams, *and* the little hills l lambs. 3509.1
114: 6 Ye mountains, *that* ye skipped l rams; 3509.1
114: 6 like rams; *and* ye little hills, l lambs? 3509.1

L

L

Ref	Text	Strong's
Ps 115: 8	They that make them are **l** unto them;	3644
118:12	They compassed me about **l** bees;	3509.1
119:83	I am become **l** a bottle in the smoke;	3509.1
119:119	away all the wicked of the earth **l** dross;	NIH
119:176	I have gone astray **l** a lost sheep; seek	3509.1
126: 1	of Zion, we were **l** them that dream.	3509.1
128: 3	thy children **l** olive plants round about	3509.1
133: 2	*It is* **l** the precious ointment upon	3509.1
135:18	They that make them are **l** unto them:	3644
140: 3	They have sharpened their tongues **l** a	3644
143: 7	lest I be **l** unto them that go down into	4911
144: 4	is **l** to vanity: his days *are* as a shadow	1819
147:16	He giveth snow **l** wool: he scattereth	3509.1
147:16	he scattereth the hoarfrost **l** ashes.	3509.1
147:17	He casteth forth his ice **l** morsels:	3509.1
Pr 12:18	There is that speaketh **l** the piercings of	3509.1
17:22	A merry heart doeth good *l* a medicine:	NIH
18:19	contentions *are* **l** the bars of a castle.	3509.1
20: 5	Counsel in the heart of man *is* **l** deep	3509.1
23:32	At the last it biteth **l** a serpent,	3509.1
23:32	like a serpent, and stingeth **l** an adder.	3509.1
25:11	A word fitly spoken *is* **l** apples of gold in	NIH
25:14	Whoso boasteth himself of a false gift *is* **l**	NIH
25:19	*man* in time of trouble *is* **l** a broken tooth,	NIH
25:28	that *hath* no rule over his own spirit *is* **l** a	NIH
26: 4	to his folly, lest thou also be **l** unto him.	7737
26:17	*is* **l** one that taketh a dog by the ears.	NIH
26:23	a wicked heart *are* **l** a potsherd covered	NIH
28: 3	A poor man that oppresseth the poor *is* **l** a	NIH
31:14	She is **l** the merchant's ships;	3509.1
SS 2: 9	My beloved *is* **l** a roe or a young hart:	1819
2:17	be thou **l** a roe or a young hart upon	1819
3: 6	out of the wilderness **l** pillars of smoke,	3509.1
4: 2	Thy teeth *are* **l** a flock of *sheep that are*	3509.1
4: 3	Thy lips *are* **l** a thread of scarlet,	3509.1
4: 3	thy temples *are* **l** a piece of a	3509.1
4: 4	Thy neck *is* **l** the tower of David builded	3509.1
4: 5	Thy two breasts *are* **l** two young roes	3509.1
4:11	the smell of thy garments *is* **l** the smell	3509.1
5:13	his lips *l* lilies, dropping sweet smelling	NIH
6:12	my soul made me *l* the chariots of	NIH
7: 1	the joints of thy thighs *are* **l** jewels,	3644
7: 2	Thy navel *is* **l** a round goblet,	NIH
7: 2	thy belly *is* **l** a heap of wheat set about	NIH
7: 3	Thy two breasts *are* **l** two young roes	3509.1
7: 4	thine eyes *l* the *fish*pools in Heshbon,	NIH
7: 5	Thine head upon thee *is* **l** Carmel,	3509.1
7: 5	and the hair of thine head **l** purple;	3509.1
7: 7	This thy stature is **l** to a palm tree,	1819
7: 8	and the smell of thy nose **l** apples;	3509.1
7: 9	the roof of thy mouth **l** the best wine,	3509.1
8:10	I am **l** a wall, and my breasts **l** towers:	3509.1
8:14	be thou **l** to a roe or to a young hart upon	1819
Isa 1: 9	we should have been **l** unto Gomorrah.	1819
1:18	though they be red **l** crimson, they shall	3509.1
2: 6	*are* soothsayers **l** the Philistines,	3509.1
3:18	and *their* **round tires l the moon**,	7720
5:28	their horses' hoofs shall be counted **l**	3509.1
5:28	flint, and their wheels **l** a whirlwind:	3509.1
5:29	Their roaring *shall be* **l** a lion, they shall	3509.1
5:29	like a lion, they shall roar **l** young lions:	3509.1
5:30	that day they shall roar against them **l**	3509.1
9:18	they shall mount up **l** the lifting up of	NIH
10: 6	them down **l** the mire of the streets.	3509.1
10:13	I have put down the inhabitants **l** a	3509.1
10:16	his glory he shall kindle a burning **l**	3509.1
11: 7	and the lion shall eat straw **l** the ox.	3509.1
11:16	as it was to Israel in the day that he	3509.1
13: 4	in the mountains, **l as** of a great people;	1823
14:10	weak as? art thou **become l** unto us?	4911
14:14	of the clouds; I will be **l** the most High.	1819
14:19	thou art cast out of thy grave **l** an	3509.1
16:11	Wherefore my bowels shall sound **l** a	3509.1
17:12	make a noise **l** the noise of the seas;	3509.1
17:12	*that* make a rushing **l** the rushing of	3509.1
17:13	The nations shall rush **l** the rushing of	3509.1
17:13	a rolling thing before the whirlwind.	3509.1
18: 4	I will consider in my dwelling place **l** a	3509.1
18: 4	a cloud of dew in the heat of harvest.	3509.1
19:16	that day shall Egypt be **l** unto women:	3509.1
20: 3	**L as** my servant Isaiah hath	834+3509.1
22:18	toss thee **l** a ball into a large country:	3509.1
24:20	The earth shall reel to and fro **l** a	3509.1
24:20	and shall be removed **l** a cottage;	3509.1
26:17	**L as** a woman with child, *that* draweth	3644
27:10	and left **l** a wilderness:	3509.1
29: 5	of thy strangers shall be **l** small dust,	3509.1
30:33	a stream of brimstone, doth kindle it.	3509.1
31: 4	**L as** the lion and the young lion	834+3509.1
33: 4	your spoil shall be gathered **l** the gathering	NIH
33: 9	Sharon is **l** a wilderness; and Bashan	3509.1
36:17	take you away to a land **l** your own land	3509.1
38:12	I have cut off **l** a weaver my life: he will	3509.1
38:14	a crane *or* a swallow, so did I chatter:	3509.1
40:11	He shall feed his flock **l** a shepherd:	3509.1
42:13	he shall stir up jealousy **l** a man of war:	3509.1
42:14	*now* will I cry **l** a travailing woman;	3509.1
46: 5	and compare me, that we may be **l**?	1819
46: 9	*I am* God, and *there is* none **l** me,	3644
48:19	the offspring of thy bowels **l** the gravel	3509.1
49: 2	hath made my mouth **l** a sharp sword;	3509.1
50: 7	therefore have I set my face **l** a flint,	3509.1
51: 3	he will make her wilderness **l** Eden,	3509.1
51: 3	her desert **l** the garden of the Lord;	3509.1
51: 6	for the heavens shall vanish away **l**	3509.1

Ref	Text	Strong's
Isa 51: 6	the earth shall wax old **l** a garment,	3509.1
51: 6	they that dwell therein shall die in **l**	3644
51: 8	For the moth shall eat them up **l** a	3509.1
51: 8	and the worm shall eat them **l** wool:	3509.1
53: 6	All we **l** sheep have gone astray; we	3509.1
57:20	the wicked *are* **l** the troubled sea, when	3509.1
58: 1	lift up thy voice **l** a trumpet, and shew	3509.1
58:11	thou shalt be **l** a watered garden,	3509.1
58:11	**l** a spring of water, whose waters fail	3509.1
59:10	We grope for the wall **l** the blind,	3509.1
59:11	We roar all **l** bears, and mourn sore like	3509.1
59:11	all like bears, and mourn sore **l** doves:	3509.1
59:19	When the enemy shall come in **l** a flood,	3509.1
63: 2	thy garments **l** him that treadeth in	3509.1
64: 6	our iniquities, **l** the wind, have taken us	3509.1
65:25	the lion shall eat straw **l** the bullock:	3509.1
66:12	I will extend peace to her **l** a river,	3509.1
66:12	the glory of the Gentiles **l** a flowing	3509.1
66:14	and your bones shall flourish **l** an herb:	3509.1
66:15	with his chariots **l** a whirlwind,	3509.1
Jer 2:30	your prophets, **l** a destroying lion.	3509.1
4: 4	lest my fury come forth **l** fire,	3509.1
5:19	**L** as ye have forsaken me,	834+3509.1
6:23	their voice roareth **l** the sea; and they	3509.1
9: 3	bend their tongues **l** their bow *for* lies:	NIH
9:12	and is burnt up **l** a wilderness,	3509.1
10: 6	Forasmuch as *there is* none **l** unto thee,	3644
10: 7	kingdoms, *there is* none **l** unto thee.	3644
10:16	The portion of Jacob *is* not **l** them:	3509.1
11:19	I *was* **l** a lamb *or* an ox *that* is brought	3509.1
12: 3	pull them out **l** sheep for the slaughter,	3509.1
14: 6	they snuffed up the wind **l** dragons;	3509.1
17: 6	For he shall be **l** the heath in the desert,	3509.1
21:12	lest my fury go out **l** fire, and burn that	3509.1
23: 9	I am **l** a drunken man, and **l** a man	3509.1
23: 9	a man whom wine hath overcome,	3509.1
23:29	*Is* not my word **l as** a fire? saith	3509.1
23:29	a hammer *that* breaketh the rock in	3509.1
24: 2	*even* **l** the figs *that are* first ripe:	3509.1
24: 5	**L** these good figs, so will I acknowledge	3509.1
25:34	And ye shall fall **l** a pleasant vessel.	3509.1
26: 6	will I make this house **l** Shiloh, and will	3509.1
26: 9	This house shall be **l** Shiloh, and this	3509.1
26:18	Zion shall be plowed **l** a field,	NIH
29:17	and will make them **l** vile figs,	3509.1
29:22	The Lord make thee **l** Zedekiah and	3509.1
29:22	make thee like Zedekiah and **l** Ahab,	3509.1
30: 7	for that day *is* great, so that none *is* **l** it:	3644
31:28	**l as** I have watched over them,	834+3509.1
32:42	**L as** I have brought all this great	834+3509.1
36:32	added besides unto them many **l** words.	3509.1
38: 9	he is **l** to die for hunger in the place where	NIH
46: 8	Egypt riseth up **l** a flood, and *his* waters	3509.1
46: 8	and *his* waters are moved **l** the rivers;	3509.1
46:20	Egypt *is* **l** a very fair heifer,	NIH
46:21	*are* in the midst of her **l** fatted bullocks;	3509.1
46:22	The voice thereof shall go **l** a serpent;	3509.1
48: 6	and be **l** the heath in the wilderness.	3509.1
48:28	be **l** the dove *that* maketh her nest in	3509.1
48:36	mine heart shall sound for Moab **l** pipes,	3509.1
48:36	heart shall sound **l** pipes for the men	3509.1
48:38	for I have broken Moab **l** a vessel	3509.1
49:19	he shall come up **l** a lion from	3509.1
49:19	for who *is* **l** me? and who will appoint	3644
50:42	their voice shall roar **l** the sea,	3509.1
50:42	**l** a man to the battle, against thee,	3509.1
50:44	he shall come up **l** a lion from	3509.1
50:44	for who *is* **l** me? and who will appoint	3644
51:19	The portion of Jacob *is* not **l** them; for he	3509.1
51:33	The daughter of Babylon *is* **l** a	3509.1
51:34	he hath swallowed me up **l** a dragon,	3509.1
51:38	They shall roar together **l** lions: they	3509.1
51:40	I will bring them down **l** lambs to	3509.1
51:40	to the slaughter, **l** rams with he goats.	3509.1
51:55	when her waves do roar **l** great waters,	3509.1
52:22	the pomegranates *were* **l** unto these.	3509.1
La 1: 6	her princes are become **l** harts *that* find	3509.1
1:12	see if there be any sorrow **l** unto my	3509.1
1:21	hast called, and they shall be **l** unto me.	3644
2: 3	he burned against Jacob **l** a flaming fire,	3509.1
2: 4	He hath bent his bow **l** an enemy:	3509.1
2:13	for thy breach *is* great **l** the sea: who	3509.1
2:18	tears run down **l** a river day and night:	3509.1
2:19	pour out thine heart **l** water before	3509.1
3:52	chased me sore, **l** a bird, without cause.	3509.1
4: 3	**l** the ostriches in the wilderness.	3509.1
4: 8	it is withered, it is become **l** a stick.	3509.1
4: 8	Our skin was black **l** an oven because	3509.1
Eze 1: 7	the sole of their feet *was* **l** the sole of a	3509.1
1: 7	they sparkled **l** the colour of burnished	3509.1
1:13	their appearance *was* **l** burning coals of	3509.1
1:13	of fire, *and* **l** the appearance of lamps:	3509.1
1:16	work *was* **l** unto the colour of a beryl:	3509.1
1:24	the noise of great waters, as the voice	3509.1
2: 8	Be not thou rebellious **l** that rebellious	3509.1
5: 9	whereunto I will not do any more the **l**,	3644
7:16	shall be on the mountains **l** doves of	3509.1
12:11	I have done, so shall it be	834+3509.1
13: 4	prophets are **l** the foxes in the deserts.	3509.1
16:16	the **l** things shall come, neither shall	NIH
18:10	*that* doeth the **l** to *any* one of these *things*,	251
18:14	and considereth, and doeth not **such l**,	3509.1
19:10	Thy mother *is* **l** a vine in thy blood,	3509.1
20:36	**L as** I pleaded with your fathers in	834+3509.1

Ref	Text	Strong's
Eze 22:25	**l** a roaring lion ravening the prey;	3509.1
22:27	Her princes in the midst thereof *are* **l**	3509.1
23:18	**l** as my mind was alienated from	834+3509.1
23:20	and whose issue *is* **l** the issue of horses.	NIH
25: 8	house of Judah *is* **l** unto all the heathen;	3509.1
26: 4	and make her **l** the top of a rock.	3807.1
26:14	I will make thee **l** the top of a rock:	3807.1
26:19	the cities that are not inhabited;	3509.1
27:32	over thee, *saying*, What *city is* **l** Tyrus,	3509.1
27:32	the destroyed in the midst of the sea?	3509.1
31: 2	Whom art thou **l** in thy greatness?	1819
31: 8	the fir trees were not **l** his boughs,	1819
31: 8	chesnut trees were not **l** his branches;	3509.1
31: 8	nor any tree in the garden of God was **l**	1819
31:18	To whom art thou thus **l** in glory and	1819
32: 2	Thou art **l** a young lion of the nations,	1819
32:14	their rivers to run **l** oil, saith	3509.1
36:35	This land that was desolate is become **l**	3509.1
36:37	I will increase them *with* men **l** a flock.	3509.1
38: 9	Thou shalt ascend and come **l** a storm,	3509.1
38: 9	thou shalt be **l** a cloud to cover the land,	3509.1
40: 3	whose appearance *was* **l** the appearance	3509.1
40:25	thereof round about, **l** those windows:	3509.1
41:25	**l as** *were* made upon the walls,	834+3509.1
42:11	way before them *was* **l** the appearance	3509.1
43: 2	his voice *was* **l** a noise of many waters:	3509.1
43: 3	the visions *were* **l** the vision that I saw	3509.1
45:25	shall he do the **l** in the feast of the seven	3509.1
Da 1:19	them all was found none **l** Daniel,	3509.1
2:35	became **l** the chaff of the summer	3509.4
3:25	the form of the fourth *is* **l** the Son of God.	1821
4:33	till his hairs were grown **l** eagles'	3509.4
4:33	and his nails **l** birds' *claws*.	3509.4
5:11	and wisdom, **l** the wisdom of the gods,	3509.4
5:21	his heart was made **l** the beasts,	5974
5:21	they fed him with grass **l** oxen,	3509.4
7: 4	The first *was* **l** a lion, and had eagle's	3509.4
7: 5	**l** to a bear, and it raised up itself on one	1821
7: 6	I beheld, and lo another, **l** a leopard,	3509.4
7: 8	this horn *were* eyes **l** the eyes of man,	3509.4
7: 9	the hair of his head **l** the pure wool:	3509.4
7: 9	his throne *was* **l** the fiery flame,	NIH
7:13	*one* **l** the Son of man came with	3509.4
10: 6	His body also *was* **l** the beryl,	3509.1
10: 6	his feet **l** in colour to polished brass,	3509.1
10: 6	the voice of his words **l** the voice of a	3509.1
10:16	*one* **l** the similitude of the sons of men	3509.1
10:18	me *one* **l** the appearance of a man,	3509.1
11:40	shall **come** against him **l** a whirlwind,	8175
Hos 4: 9	there shall be, **l** people, like priest:	3509.1
4: 9	there shall be, like people, **l** priest:	3509.1
5:10	The princes of Judah were **l** them that	3509.1
5:10	I will pour out my wrath upon them **l**	3509.1
6: 7	they **l** men have transgressed	3509.1
7: 6	For they have made ready their heart **l**	3509.1
7:11	Ephraim also is **l** a silly dove,	3509.1
7:16	they are **l** a deceitful bow: their princes	3509.1
9:10	I found Israel **l** grapes in the wilderness;	3509.1
9:11	their glory shall fly away **l** a bird,	3509.1
11:10	he shall roar **l** a lion: when he shall roar,	3509.1
13: 8	and there will **l** devour them **l** a lion:	3509.1
14: 8	I am **l** a green fir tree. From me is thy	3509.1
Joel 1: 8	Lament **l** a virgin girded with sackcloth	3509.1
2: 2	there hath not been ever **the l**, neither	3644
2: 5	**L** the noise of chariots on the tops of	3509.1
2: 5	**l** the noise of a flame of fire that	3509.1
2: 7	They shall run **l** mighty *men;* they shall	3509.1
2: 7	They shall climb the wall **l** men of war;	3509.1
2: 9	shall enter in at the windows **l** a thief.	3509.1
Am 2: 9	whose height *was* **l** the height of	3509.1
5: 6	lest he break out **l** fire *in* the house of	3509.1
6: 5	instruments of musick, **l** David;	3509.1
9: 5	it shall rise up wholly **l** a flood;	3509.1
9: 9	as *corn* is sifted in a sieve, yet shall not	3509.1
Jnh 1: 4	sea, so that the ship was **l** to be broken.	2803
Mic 1: 8	I will make a wailing **l** the dragons,	3509.1
4:10	daughter of Zion, **l** a woman in travail:	3509.1
7:17	They shall lick the dust **l** a serpent,	3509.1
7:17	they shall move out of their holes **l**	3509.1
7:18	Who *is* a God **l** unto thee, that pardoneth	3644
Na 1: 6	his fury is poured out **l** fire, and the	3509.1
2: 4	they shall seem **l** torches, they shall run	3509.1
2: 4	they shall run **l** the lightnings.	3509.1
2: 8	Nineveh *is* of old **l** a pool of water:	3509.1
3:12	All thy strong holds *shall be* **l** fig trees	NIH
3:15	it shall eat thee up **l** the cankerworm:	3509.1
Hab 3:19	he will make my feet **l** hinds' *feet*, and	3509.1
Zep 1:17	that they shall walk **l** blind *men*,	3509.1
2:13	a desolation, *and* dry **l** a wilderness.	3509.1
Zec 1: 6	**L** as the Lord of hosts thought to do	3509.1
5: 9	they had wings **l** the wings of a stork:	3509.1
9:15	they shall be filled **l** bowls, *and* as	3509.1
10: 7	*of* Ephraim shall be **l** a mighty *man*,	3509.1
12: 6	Judah **l** a hearth of fire among the wood,	3509.1
12: 6	the wood, and **l** a torch of fire in a sheaf;	3509.1
14: 5	**l as** ye fled from before	834+3509.1
14:20	the pots in the Lord's house shall be **l**	3509.1
Mal 3: 2	he is **l** a refiner's fire, and like fullers'	3509.1
3: 2	is like a refiner's fire, and **l** fullers' sope:	3509.1
Mt 3:16	he saw the Spirit of God descending **l** a	5616
6: 8	Be not ye therefore **l** unto them: for your	3666
6:29	his glory was not arrayed **l** one of these.	5613
11:16	It is **l** unto children sitting in the markets,	3664
12:13	and it was restored whole, **l** the other.	NIG

Mt	13:31 The kingdom of heaven is l unto a grain	3664
	13:33 The kingdom of heaven is l unto leaven,	3664
	13:44 the kingdom of heaven is l unto treasure	3664
	13:45 kingdom of heaven is l unto a merchant	3664
	13:47 the kingdom of heaven is l unto a net,	3664
	13:52 is l unto a man *that is* a householder,	3664
	20: 1 the kingdom of heaven is l unto a man	3664
	21:24 I in l wise will tell you by what authority	2504
	22: 2 The kingdom of heaven is l unto a certain	3666
	22:39 the second is l unto, Thou shalt love	3664
	23:27 for ye are l unto whited sepulchres,	3945
	28: 3 His countenance was l lightning,	5613
Mk	1:10 the Spirit l a dove descending upon him:	5616
	4:31 *It is* l a grain of mustard seed, which,	5613
	7: 8 cups: and many other such l *things* ye do.	3946
	7:13 and many such l *things* do ye.	3946
	12:31 the second is l, *namely* this, Thou shalt	3664
	13:29 So ye in l manner, when ye shall	2532+3779
Lk	3:22 in a bodily shape l a dove upon him,	5616
	6:23 for in the l manner did their	846+2596+3588
	6:47 I will shew you to whom he is l:	3664
	6:48 He is l a man which built a house,	3664
	6:49 is l a man that without a foundation built	3664
	7:31 of this generation? and to what are they l?	3664
	7:32 They are l unto children sitting in	3664
	12:27 his glory was not arrayed l one of these.	5613
	12:36 ye yourselves l unto men that wait for	3664
	13:18 Unto what is the kingdom of God l?	3664
	13:19 It is l a grain of mustard seed, which a	3664
	13:21 It is l leaven, which a woman took and	3664
	20:31 took her; and in l manner the seven also:	5615
Jn	1:32 I saw the Spirit descending from heaven l	5616
	7:46 Never man spake l this man.	5613
	8:55 know him not, I shall be a liar l unto you:	3664
	9: 9 others *said,* He is l him: but he said, I am	3664
Ac	1:11 come *in* l manner as ye have seen him go	3739
	2: 3 unto them cloven tongues l as of fire,	5616
	3:22 up unto you of your brethren, l unto me;	5613
	7:37 up unto you of your brethren, l unto me;	5613
	8:32 and l a lamb dumb before his shearer,	2470
	11:17 as God gave them the l gift as he did unto	2470
	14:15 We also are men of l passions with you,	3663
	17:29 to think that the Godhead is l unto gold,	3664
	19:25 with the workmen of l occupation,	5108
Ro	1:23 into an image made l to corruptible man,	3667
	1:28 even as they did not l to retain God in	1381
	6: 4 l as Christ was raised up from the dead	5618
	9:29 and been made l unto Gomorrha.	3666
1Co	16:13 fast in the faith, quit you l men, be strong.	407
Gal	5:21 drunkenness, revellings, and such l:	3664
Php	3:21 it may be fashioned l unto his glorious	4832
1Th	2:14 for ye also have suffered l *things* of your	5024
1Ti	2: 9 In l manner also, that women adorn	5615
Heb	2:17 him to be made l unto his brethren,	3666
	4:15 in all *points* tempted l as we are,	2596+3665
	7: 3 of life; but made l unto the Son of God;	871
Jas	1: 6 for he that wavereth is l a wave of the sea	1503
	1:23 he is l unto a man beholding his natural	1503
	5:17 Elias was a man subject to l passions as	3663
1Pe	3:21 The l figure whereunto *even* baptism doth	499
2Pe	1: 1 them that have obtained l precious faith	2472
1Jn	3: 2 when he shall appear, we shall be l him;	3664
Jude	1: 7 in l manner giving themselves over to	3664
Rev	1:13 candlesticks one l unto the Son of man,	NIG
	1:14 His head and *his* hairs *were* white l wool,	5616
	1:15 And his feet l unto fine brass, as if they	3664
	2:18 who hath his eyes l unto a flame of fire,	5613
	2:18 flame of fire, and his feet *are* l fine brass;	3664
	4: 3 he that sat was to look upon l a jasper	3664
	4: 3 the throne, in sight l unto an emerald.	3664
	4: 6 there *was* a sea of glass l unto crystal:	5613
	4: 7 And the first beast *was* l a lion,	3664
	4: 7 The second beast l a calf, and the third	3664
	4: 7 and the fourth beast *was* l a flying eagle.	3664
	9: 7 the shapes of the locusts *were* l unto	3664
	9: 7 on their heads *were* as *it were* crowns l	3664
	9:10 And they had tails l unto scorpions,	3664
	9:19 for their tails *were* l unto serpents,	3664
	11: 1 there was given me a reed l unto a rod:	3664
	13: 2 And the beast which I saw was l unto a	3664
	13: 4 the beast, saying, Who *is* l unto the beast?	3664
	13:11 and he had two horns l a lamb,	3664
	14:14 upon the cloud one sat l unto the Son of	3664
	16:13 And I saw three unclean spirits l frogs	3664
	18:18 saying, What city *is* l unto this great city?	3664
	18:21 And a mighty angel took up a stone l a	5613
	21:11 her light *was* l unto a stone most precious,	3664
	21:11 *even* l a jasper stone, clear as crystal;	5613
	21:18 the city *was* pure gold, l unto clear glass.	3664

LIKED (1) [LIKE]

1Ch	28: 4 among the sons of my father he l me to	7521

LIKEMINDED (3) [LIKE, MIND]

Ro	15: 5 consolation grant you to be l	846+3588+5426
Php	2: 2 Fulfil ye my joy, that ye be l,	846+3588+5426
	2:20 For I have no man l, who will naturally	2473

LIKEN (9) [LIKE]

Isa	40:18 To whom then will ye l God?	1819
	40:25 To whom then will ye l me, or shall I be	1819
	46: 5 whom will ye l me, and make me equal,	1819
La	2:13 what *thing* shall I l to thee, O daughter of	1819
Mt	7:24 doeth them, I will l him unto a wise man,	3666
	11:16 But whereunto shall I l this generation?	3666
Mk	4:30 shall we l the kingdom of God?	3666
Lk	7:31 then shall I l the men of this generation?	3666
	13:20 Whereunto shall I l the kingdom of God?	3666

LIKENED (6) [LIKE]

Ps	89: 6 among the sons of the mighty can be l	1819
Jer	6: 2 I have l the daughter of Zion *to* a comely	1819
Mt	7:26 them not, shall be l unto a foolish man,	3666
	13:24 The kingdom of heaven is l unto a man	3666
	18:23 Therefore is the kingdom of heaven l unto	3666
	25: 1 shall the kingdom of heaven be l unto	3666

LIKENESS (34) [LIKE]

Ge	1:26 us make man in our image, after our l:	1823
	5: 1 man, in the l of God made he him;	1823
	5: 3 thirty years, and begat *a son* in his own l,	1823
Ex	20: 4 any l of any thing that *is* in heaven above,	8544
Dt	4:16 of any figure, the l of male or female,	8403
	4:17 The l of any beast that *is* on the earth,	8403
	4:17 the l of any winged fowl that flieth in	8403
	4:18 The l of any *thing* that creepeth on	8403
	4:18 the l of any fish that *is* in the waters	8403
	4:23 the l of any *thing,* which the LORD thy	8544
	4:25 or the l of any *thing,* and shall do evil in	8544
	5: 8 l of any *thing* that *is* in heaven above,	8544
Ps	17:15 be satisfied, when I awake, with thy l.	8544
Isa	40:18 or what l will ye compare unto him?	1823
Eze	1: 5 Also out of the midst thereof *came* the l	1823
	1: 5 their appearance; they had the l of a man.	1823
	1:10 As for the l of their faces, they four had	1823
	1:13 As for the l of the living creatures,	1823
	1:16 they four had one l: and their appearance	1823
	1:22 the l of the firmament upon the heads of	1823
	1:26 *was* over their heads *was* the l of a throne,	1823
	1:26 upon the l of the throne was the likeness	1823
	1:26 the likeness of the throne *was* the l as	1823
	1:28 This *was* the appearance of the l of	1823
	8: 2 and lo, a l as the appearance of fire:	1823
	10: 1 as the appearance of the l of a throne.	1823
	10:10 *for* their appearances, they four had one l,	1823
	10:21 the l of the hands of a man *was* under	1823
	10:22 the l of their faces was the same faces	1823
Ac	14:11 The gods are come down to us in the l of	3666
Ro	6: 5 if we have been planted together in the l	3667
	6: 5 shall be also in the l of his resurrection:	NIG
	8: 3 God sending his own Son in the l of sinful	3667
Php	2: 7 a servant, and was made in the l of men:	3667

LIKETH (3) [LIKE]

Dt	23:16 where it l him best:	2896+871.1+1886.1
Est	8: 8 it l you, in the king's name,	2896+5869+871.1
Am	4: 5 for this l you, O ye children of Israel,	157

LIKEWISE (107) [LIKE]

Ex	22:30 l shalt thou do with thine oxen,	3651
	26: 4 l shalt thou make in the uttermost edge	3651
	27:11 l for the north side in length *there shall*	3651
	36:11 l he made in the uttermost side of	3651
Lev	7: 1 L this *is* the law of the trespass offering:	2050.1
Dt	9:23 L when the LORD sent you from	2050.1
	12:30 serve their gods? even so will I do l.	1571
	15:17 unto thy maidservant thou shalt do l.	3651
	22: 3 and thou hast found, shalt thou do l:	NIH
Jdg	1: 3 And I l will go with thee into thy lot.	1571
	7: 5 l every one that boweth down upon his	2050.1
	7:17 said unto them, Look on me, and do l:	3651
	8: 8 Penuel, and spake unto them l:	2088+3509.1
	9:49 all the people l cut down every man his	1571
1Sa	14:22 l all the men of Israel which had hid	2050.1
	19:21 other messengers, and they prophesied l.	1571
	31: 5 l upon his sword, and died with	1571+2050.1
2Sa	1:11 l all the men that *were* with him:	1571
	17: 5 also, and let us hear l what he saith.	1571
1Ki	11: 8 l did he for all his strange wives,	3651
1Ch	10: 5 dead, he fell l on the sword, and died.	1571
	18: 8 L from Tibhath, and from Chun, cities	2050.1
	19:15 they l fled before Abishai his	1571+2050.1
	23:30 and praise the LORD, and l at even;	3651
	24:31 These l cast lots over against their	1571
	27: 4 in his course l *were* twenty and	2050.1
	28:16 and l silver for the tables of silver:	NIH
	28:17 l silver by weight for every bason of silver:	NIH
	29:24 and all the sons l of king David,	1571
2Ch	3:11 the other wing *was* l five cubits, reaching	NIH
	29:22 l, when they had killed the rams, they	2050.1
Ne	4:22 L at the same time said l unto the people,	1571
	5:10 I l, *and* my brethren,	1571+2050.1
Est	1:18 L shall the ladies of Persia and Media	2050.1
	4:16 I also and my maidens will fast l; and so	3651
Job	31:38 or that the furrows l thereof complain;	3162
	37: 6 l to the small rain, and to the great rain	2050.1
Ps	49:10 l the fool and the brutish person perish,	3162
	52: 5 God shall l destroy thee for ever, he shall	1571
Ecc	7:22 that thou thyself l hast cursed others.	1571
Isa	30:24 The oxen l and the young asses that ear	2050.1
Jer	40:11 L when all the Jews that *were* in Moab,	1571
Eze	13:17 l thou son of man, set thy face against	2050.1
	40:16 the gate round about, and l to the arches:	3651
	46: 3 L the people of the land shall worship	2050.1
Na	1:12 Though *they be* quiet, and l many, yet	3651
Mt	17:12 L shall also the Son of man suffer of them.	3779
	18:35 So l shall my heavenly Father do *also* unto	3779
	20: 5 about the sixth and ninth hour, and did l.	5615
	20:10 and they l received every man a penny.	2532
	21:30 And he came to the second, and said l.	5615
Mt	21:36 than the first: and they did unto them l.	5615
	22:26 L the second also, and the third,	2532
	24:33 So l ye, when ye shall see all these *things,*	2532
	25:17 And l he that had received two, he also	5615
	26:35 not deny thee. L also said all the disciples.	3668
	27:41 L also the chief priests mocking *him,* with	3668
Mk	4:16 And these are they l which are sown on	5615
	12:21 neither left he *any* seed: and the third l.	5615
	14:31 deny thee in any wise. L also said they all.	5615
	15:31 L also the chief priests mocking said	3668
Lk	2:38 she coming in that instant gave thanks l	NIG
	3:11 and he that hath meat, let him do l.	3668
	3:14 And the soldiers l demanded of him,	2532
	5:33 and the disciples l of the Pharisees;	3668
	6:31 should do to you, do ye also to them l.	3668
	10:32 And l a Levite, when he was at the place,	3668
	10:37 said Jesus unto him, Go, and do thou l.	3668
	13: 3 but, except ye repent, ye shall all l perish.	5615
	13: 5 but except ye repent, ye shall all l perish.	3668
	14:33 l, whosoever he be of you that forsaketh	3779
	15: 7 l joy shall be in heaven over one sinner	3779
	15:10 L, I say unto you, there is joy in	3779
	16:25 and l Lazarus evil *things:* but now he is	3668
	17:10 l ye, when ye shall have done all those	2532
	17:28 L also as it was in the days of Lot; they	3668
	17:31 is in the field, let him l not return back.	3668
	19:19 he said l to him, Be thou also over five	2532
	21:31 l ye, when ye see these *things* come to	2532
	22:20 L also the cup after supper, saying,	5615
	22:36 a purse, let him take *it,* and l his scrip:	3668
Jn	5: 9 he doeth, these also doeth the Son l.	3668
	6:11 and l of the fishes as much as they would.	3668
	21:13 taketh bread, and giveth them, and fish l.	3668
Ac	3:24 have spoken, have l foretold of these days.	2532
Ro	1:27 l also the men, leaving the natural use	3668
	6:11 L reckon ye also yourselves to be dead	3779
	8:26 L the Spirit also helpeth our infirmities:	5615
	16: 5 L greet the church that is in their house.	2532
1Co	7: 3 and l also the wife unto the husband.	3668
	7: 4 l also the husband hath not power of his	3668
	7:22 l also he that is called, *being* free,	3668
	14: 9 So l you, except ye utter by the tongue	2532
Gal	2:13 the other Jews dissembled l with him;	2532
Col	4:16 that ye l read the *epistle* from Laodicea.	2532
1Ti	3: 8 L *must* the deacons be grave,	5615
	5:25 L also the good works of *some* are	5615
Tit	2: 3 The aged women l, *that they be* in	5615
	2: 6 Young men l exhort to be sober minded.	5615
Heb	2:14 he also himself l took part of the same;	3898
Jas	2:25 L also was not Rahab the harlot justified	3668
1Pe	3: 1 L, ye wives, *be* in subjection to your own	3668
	3: 7 L, ye husbands, dwell with *them*	3668
	4: 1 arm yourselves l with the same mind:	2532
	5: 5 L, ye younger, submit yourselves unto	3668
Jude	1: 8 L also these *filthy* dreamers defile	3305+3668
Rev	8:12 not for a third *part* of it, and the night l.	3668

LIKHI (1)

1Ch	7:19 Ahian, and Shechem, and L, and Aniam.	3949

LIKING (2) [LIKE]

Job	39: 4 Their young ones are in good l, they	2492
Da	1:10 for why should he see your faces worse l	2196

LILIES (10) [LILY]

1Ki	7:26 like the brim of a cup, *with* flowers of l:	7799
2Ch	4: 5 of the brim of a cup, *with* flowers of l;	7799
SS	2:16 and I *am* his: he feedeth among the l.	7799
	4: 5 that are twins, which feed among the l.	7799
	5:13 his lips *like* l, dropping sweet smelling	7799
	6: 2 to feed in the gardens, and to gather l.	7799
	6: 3 beloved is mine: he feedeth among the l.	7799
	7: 2 *is like* a heap of wheat set about with l.	7799
Mt	6:28 Consider the l of the field, how they grow	2918
Lk	12:27 Consider the l how they grow: they toil	2918

LILY (5) [LILIES]

1Ki	7:19 of the pillars *were* of l work in the porch,	7799
	7:22 upon the top of the pillars *was* l work:	7799
SS	2: 1 rose of Sharon, *and* the l of the valleys.	7799
	2: 2 As the l among thorns, so *is* my love	7799
Hos	14: 5 he shall grow as the l, and cast forth his	7799

LIME (2)

Isa	33:12 the people shall be *as* the burnings of l:	7875
Am	2: 1 the bones of the king of Edom into l:	7875

LIMIT (1) [LIMITED, LIMITETH]

Eze	43:12 Upon the top of the mountain the whole l	1366

LIMITED (1) [LIMIT]

Ps	78:41 tempted God, and l the Holy One of Israel.	8428

LIMITETH (1) [LIMIT]

Heb	4: 7 Again he l a certain day, saying in David,	3724

LINE (31) [LINEAGE, LINES, PLUMBLINE]

Jos	2:18 thou shalt bind this l of scarlet thread in	8615
	2:21 she bound the scarlet l in the window.	8615
2Sa	8: 2 Moab, and measured them with a l,	2256
	8: 2 death, and *with* one full l to keep alive.	2256
1Ki	7:15 a l of twelve cubits did compass either of	2339
	7:23 a l of thirty cubits did compass it round	6957
2Ki	21:13 I will stretch over Jerusalem the l	6957
2Ch	4: 2 a l of thirty cubits did compass it round	6957
Job	38: 5 or who hath stretched the l upon it?	6957

Ps 19: 4 Their **l** is gone out through all the earth, 6957
78:55 divided them an inheritance by **l**, 2256
Isa 28:10 **l** upon line, line upon line; here a little, 6957
28:10 line upon line, line upon line; here a little, 6957
28:10 line upon line, line upon **l**; here a little, 6957
28:13 **l** upon line, line upon line; here a little, 6957
28:13 line upon line, **l** upon line; here a little, 6957
28:13 line upon line, line upon **l**; here a little, 6957
28:13 line upon line, line upon line; here a little, 6957
28:17 Judgment also will **l** lay to the **l**, 6957
34:11 he shall stretch out upon it the **l** of 6957
34:17 his hand hath divided it unto them by **l**: 6957
44:13 he marketh it out with a **l**; he fitteth it 8279
Jer 31:39 the measuring **l** shall yet go forth over 6957
La 2: 8 he hath stretched out a **l**, he hath not 6957
Eze 40: 3 a **l** of flax in his hand, and a measuring 6616
47: 3 when the man that had the **l** in his hand 6957
Am 7:17 and thy land shall be divided by **l**; 2256
Zec 1:16 **l** shall be stretched forth upon Jerusalem. 6957
2: 1 a man with a measuring **l** in his hand. 2256
2Co 10:16 not to boast in another *man's* **l** *of things* 2583

LINEAGE (1) [LINE]
Lk 2: 4 he was of the house and **l** of David:) 3965

LINEN (104)
Ge 41:42 arrayed him in vestures of **fine l**, and put 8336
Ex 25: 4 and scarlet, and **fine l**, and goats' *hair*, 8336
26: 1 *with* ten curtains of **fine** twined **l**, 8336
26:31 and **fine** twined **l** of cunning work: 8336
26:36 purple, and scarlet, and **fine** twined **l**, 8336
27: 9 **fine** twined **l** of an hundred cubits long 8336
27:16 purple, and scarlet, and **fine** twined **l**, 8336
27:18 the height five cubits of **fine** twined **l**, 8336
28: 5 blue, and purple, and scarlet, and **fine l**. 8336
28: 6 *of* purple, *of* scarlet, and **fine** twined **l**, 8336
28: 8 *of* purple, *of* scarlet, and **fine** twined **l**, 8336
28:15 and *of* scarlet, and *of* **fine** twined **l**, 8336
28:39 thou shalt embroider the coat of **fine l**, 8336
28:39 thou shalt make the mitre *of* **fine l**, 8336
28:42 thou shalt make them **l** breeches to cover 906
35: 6 and scarlet, and **fine l**, and goats' *hair*, 8336
35:23 **fine l**, and goats' *hair*, and red skins of 8336
35:25 of purple, *and* of scarlet, and of **fine l**. 8336
35:35 scarlet, and in **fine l**, and of the weaver, 8336
36: 8 made ten curtains of **fine** twined **l**, 8336
36:35 purple, and scarlet, and **fine** twined **l**: 8336
36:37 purple, and scarlet, and **fine** twined **l**, 8336
38: 9 of the court *were* of **fine** twined **l**, 8336
38:16 court round about *were* of **fine** twined **l**. 8336
38:18 and purple, and scarlet, and **fine** twined **l**: 8336
38:23 and in purple, and in scarlet, and **fine l**. 8336
39: 2 and purple, and scarlet, and **fine l**. 8336
39: 3 and in the scarlet, and in the **fine l**, 8336
39: 5 and purple, and scarlet, and **fine** twined **l**. 8336
39: 8 and purple, and scarlet, and **fine** twined **l**. 8336
39:24 and purple, and scarlet, and *twined* **L** NIH
39:27 they made coats of **fine l** *of* woven work 8336
39:28 a mitre *of* **fine l**, and goodly bonnets *of* 8336
39:28 goodly bonnets *of* **fine l**, and linen 8336
39:28 and **l** breeches *of* **fine** twined linen, 906
39:28 and linen breeches *of* **fine** twined **l**, 8336
39:29 a girdle *of* **fine** twined **l**, and blue, 8336
Lev 6:10 And the priest shall put on his **l** garment, 906
6:10 *his* **l** breeches shall he put upon his flesh, 906
13:47 *it be* a woollen garment, or a **l** garment; 6593
13:48 in the warp, or woof; of **l**, or of woollen; 6593
13:52 in woollen or in **l**, or any thing of skin, 6593
13:59 of leprosy in a garment of woollen or **l**, 6593
16: 4 He shall put on the holy **l** coat, and 906
16: 4 he shall have the **l** breeches upon his flesh, 906
16: 4 shall be girded with a **l** girdle, and with 906
16: 4 and with the **l** mitre shall he be attired: 906
16:23 shall put off the **l** garments, which he put 906
16:32 shall put on the **l** clothes, *even* the holy 906
19:19 **mingled of l** and woollen 3610+8162
Dt 22:11 divers sorts, *as* of woollen and **l** together. 6593
1Sa 2:18 *being* a child, girded *with* a **l** ephod. 906
22:18 and five persons that did wear a **l** ephod. 906
2Sa 6:14 and David *was* girded *with* a **l** ephod. 906
1Ki 10:28 horses brought out of Egypt, and **l yarn**: 4723
10:28 the king's merchants received the **l yarn** 4723
1Ch 4:21 the house of them that wrought **fine l**, 948
15:27 David *was* clothed with a robe of **fine l**, 948
15:27 David also *had* upon him an ephod of **l**. 906
2Ch 1:16 horses brought out of Egypt, and **l yarn**: 4723
1:16 the king's merchants received the **l yarn** 4723
2:14 in blue, and in **fine l**, and in crimson; 948
3:14 **fine l**, and wrought cherubims thereon. 948
5:12 their brethren, *being* arrayed in **white l**, 948
Est 1: 6 *hangings*, fastened with cords of **fine l** 948
8:15 and *with* a garment of **fine l** and purple: 948
Pr 7:16 *with* carved *works, with* **fine l** of Egypt. 330
31:24 She maketh **fine l**, and selleth *it*; and 5466
Isa 3:23 the **fine l**, and the hoods, and the vails, 5466
Jer 13: 1 Go and get thee a **l** girdle, and put it upon 6593
Eze 9: 2 one man among them *was* clothed *with* **l**, 906
9: 3 he called to the man clothed *with* **l**, 906
9:11 behold, the man clothed *with* **l**, which *had* 906
10: 2 he spake unto the man clothed *with* **l**, 906
10: 6 had commanded the man clothed *with* **l**, 906
10: 7 the hands of *him that was* clothed *with* **l**: 906
16:10 and I girded thee about with **fine l**, 8336
16:13 thy raiment *was* of **fine l**, and silk, 8336

Eze 27: 7 **Fine l** with broidered work from Egypt 8336
27:16 and **fine l**, and coral, and agate. 948
44:17 they shall be clothed with **l** garments; 6593
44:18 They shall have **l** bonnets upon their 6593
44:18 shall have **l** breeches upon their loins; 6593
Da 10: 5 and behold, a certain man clothed *in* **l**, 906
12: 6 said to the man clothed in **l**, which *was* 906
12: 7 I heard the man clothed in **l**, which *was* 906
Mt 27:59 body, he wrapped it in a clean **l cloth**, 4616
Mk 14:51 a **l cloth** cast about *his* naked *body*; 4616
14:52 he left the **l cloth**, and fled from them 4616
15:46 he bought **fine l**, and took him down, 4616
15:46 wrapped *him* in the **l**, and laid him in a 4616
Lk 16:19 which was clothed in purple and **fine l**, *1040*
23:53 and wrapped it in **l**, and laid it in a 4616
24:12 beheld the **l clothes** laid by themselves, 3608
Jn 19:40 wound it in **l clothes** with the spices, 3608
20: 5 and looking in, saw the **l clothes** lying; 3608
20: 6 the sepulchre, and seeth the **l clothes** lie, 3608
20: 7 not lying with the **l clothes**, 3608
Rev 15: 6 clothed in pure and white **l**, 3043
18:12 **fine l**, and purple, and silk, and scarlet, *1040*
18:16 that was clothed in **fine l**, and purple, *1039*
19: 8 that she should be arrayed in **fine l**, *1039*
19: 8 the **fine l** is the righteousness of saints. *1039*
19:14 clothed in **fine l**, white and clean. *1039*

LINES (2) [LINE]
2Sa 8: 2 even *with* two **l** measured he to put to 2256
Ps 16: 6 The **l** are fallen unto me in pleasant 2256

LINGERED (2) [LINGERETH]
Ge 19:16 he **l**, the men laid hold upon his hand, 4102
43:10 For except we had **l**, surely now we had 4102

LINGERETH (1) [LINGERED]
2Pe 2: 3 whose judgment now of a long time **l** not, *691*

LINTEL (4) [LINTELS]
Ex 12:22 strike the **l** and the two side posts with 4947
12:23 and when he seeth the blood upon the **l**, 4947
1Ki 6:31 the **l** *and* side posts *were* a fifth *part* of 352
Am 9: 1 he said, Smite the **l of the door**, that 3730

LINTELS (1) [LINTEL]
Zep 2:14 the bittern shall lodge in the **upper l** of it; 3730

LINUS (1)
2Ti 4:21 **L**, and Claudia, and all the brethren. *3044*

LION (98) [LION'S, LIONESS, LIONESSES, LIONLIKE, LIONS, LIONS']
Ge 49: 9 he couched as a **l**, and as an old lion; 738
49: 9 he couched as a lion, and as an **old l**; 3833
Nu 23:24 the people shall rise up as a **great l**, 3833
23:24 great lion, and lift up himself as a **young l**: 738
24: 9 he lay down as a **l**, and as a great lion: 738
24: 9 he lay down as a lion, and as a **great l**: 3833
Dt 33:20 he dwelleth as a **l**, and teareth the arm 3833
Jdg 14: 5 behold, a **young l** roared against him. 738
14: 8 he turned aside to see the carcase of the **l**: 738
14: 8 of bees and honey in the carcase of the **l**. 738
14: 9 taken the honey out of the carcase of the **l**. 738
14:18 what *is* stronger than a **l**? And he said unto 738
1Sa 17:34 there came a **l** and a bear, and took a lamb 738
17:36 Thy servant slew both the **l** and the bear: 738
17:37 that delivered me out of the paw of the **l**, 738
2Sa 17:10 whose heart *is* as the heart of a **l**, shall 738
23:20 slew a **l** in the midst of a pit in time of 738
1Ki 13:24 a **l** met him by the way, and slew him: 738
13:24 stood by it, the **l** also stood by the carcase. 738
13:25 the way, and the **l** standing by the carcase: 738
13:26 the L<small>ORD</small> hath delivered him unto the **l**, 738
13:28 the ass and the **l** standing by the carcase: 738
13:28 the **l** had not eaten the carcase, nor torn 738
20:36 art departed from me, a **l** shall slay thee. 738
20:36 from him, a **l** found him, and slew him. 738
1Ch 11:22 and slew a **l** in a pit in a snowy day. 738
Job 4:10 The roaring of the **l**, and the voice of 738
4:10 the voice of the **fierce l**, and the teeth of 7826
4:11 The **old l** perisheth for lack of prey, 3918
10:16 Thou huntest me as a **fierce l**: 7826
28: 8 trodden it, nor the **fierce l** passed by it. 7826
38:39 Wilt thou hunt the prey for the **l**? or fill 3833
Ps 7: 2 Lest he tear my soul like a **l**, rending *it in* 738
10: 9 He lieth in wait secretly as a **l** in his den: 738
17:12 Like as a **l** *that* is greedy of his prey, 738
17:12 as it were a **young l** lurking in secret 3715
22:13 mouths, *as* a ravening and a roaring **l**. 738
91:13 Thou shalt tread upon the **l** and adder: 7826
91:13 the **young l** and the dragon shalt thou 3715
Pr 19:12 The king's *wrath is* as the roaring of a **l**; 3715
20: 2 The fear of a king *is* as the roaring of a **l**: 3715
22:13 slothful *man* saith, There is a **l** without, 738
26:13 slothful *man* saith, There *is* a **l** in the way; 7826
26:13 *is* a lion in the way; a **l** *is* in the streets. 738
28: 1 but the righteous are bold as a **l**. 3715
28:15 *As* a roaring **l**, and a ranging bear; *so is* a 738
30:30 A **l** *which is* strongest among beasts, 3918
Ecc 9: 4 for a living dog *is* better than a dead **l**. 738
Isa 5:29 Their roaring *shall* be like a **l**, they shall 3833
11: 6 the calf and the **young l** and the fatling 3715
11: 7 and the **l** shall eat straw like the ox. 738
21: 8 he cried, A **l**: My lord, I stand continually 738
30: 6 from whence *come* the young and **old l**, 3918

Isa 31: 4 Like as the **l** and the young lion roaring on 738
31: 4 and the **young l** roaring on his prey, 3715
35: 9 No **l** shall be there, nor *any* ravenous beast 738
38:13 *that*, as a **l**, so will he break all my bones: 738
65:25 and the **l** shall eat straw like the bullock. 738
Jer 2:30 your prophets, like a destroying **l**. 738
4: 7 The **l** is come up from his thicket, 738
5: 6 Wherefore a **l** out of the forest shall slay 738
12: 8 heritage is unto me as a **l** in the forest; 738
25:38 He hath forsaken his covert, as the **l**: 3715
49:19 he shall come up like a **l** from the swelling 738
50:44 he shall come up like a **l** from the swelling 738
La 3:10 lying in wait, *and as* a **l** in secret places. 738
Eze 1:10 man, and the face of a **l**, on the right side: 738
10:14 the third the face of a **l**, and the fourth 738
19: 3 it became a **young l**, and it learned to 3715
19: 5 of her whelps, *and* made him a **young l**. 3715
19: 6 he became a **young l**, and learned to 3715
22:25 like a roaring **l** ravening the prey; 738
32: 2 Thou art like a **young l** of the nations, 3715
41:19 face of a **l** toward the palm tree 3715
Da 7: 4 first *was* like a **l**, and had eagle's wings: 744
Hos 5:14 For I *will be* unto Ephraim as a **l**, and as a 7826
5:14 and as a **young l** to the house of Judah: 3715
11:10 he shall roar like a **l**: when he shall roar, 738
13: 7 Therefore I will be unto them as a **l**: as a 7826
13: 8 and there will I devour them like a **l**: 3833
Joel 1: 6 whose teeth *are* the teeth of a **l**, and he 738
1: 6 and he hath the cheek-teeth of a **great l**. 3833
Am 3: 4 Will a **l** roar in the forest, when he hath 738
3: 4 will a **young l** cry out of his den, if he 3715
3: 8 The **l** hath roared, who will not fear? 738
3:12 taketh out of the mouth of the **l** two legs, 738
5:19 As if a man did flee from a **l**, and a bear 738
Mic 5: 8 people as a **l** among the beasts of the forest, 738
5: 8 as a **young l** among the flocks of sheep: 3715
Na 2:11 where the **l**, *even* the old lion, walked, 738
2:11 *even* the **old l**, walked, *and* the lion's 3833
2:12 The **l** did tear in pieces enough for his 738
2Ti 4:17 I was delivered out of the mouth of the **l**. 3023
1Pe 5: 8 the devil, as a roaring **l**, walketh about, 3023
Rev 4: 7 And the first beast *was* like a **l**, 3023
5: 5 behold, the **L** of the tribe of Juda, the root 3023
10: 3 with a loud voice, as *when* a **l** roareth: 3023
13: 2 a bear, and his mouth as the mouth of a **l**: 3023

LION'S (6) [LION]
Ge 49: 9 Judah *is* a **l** whelp: from the prey, my son, 738
Dt 33:22 of Dan he said, Dan *is* a **l** whelp: he shall 738
Job 4:11 the **stout l** whelps are scattered abroad. 3833
28: 8 The **l** whelps have not trodden it, 7830
Ps 22:21 Save me from the **l** mouth: for thou hast 738
Na 2:11 the **l** whelp, and none made *them* afraid? 738

LIONESS (1) [LION]
Eze 19: 2 A **l**: she lay down among lions, 3833

LIONESSES (1) [LION]
Na 2:12 strangled for his **l**, and filled his holes *with* 3833

LIONLIKE (2) [LION]
2Sa 23:20 many acts; he slew two **l men** of Moab: 739
1Ch 11:22 many acts; he slew two **l men** of Moab: 739

LIONS (43) [LION]
2Sa 1:23 than eagles, they were stronger than **l**. 738
1Ki 7:29 that *were* between the ledges *were* **l**, 738
7:29 beneath the **l** and the oxen *were* certain 738
7:36 he graved cherubims, **l**, and palm trees, 738
10:19 the seat, and two **l** stood beside the stays. 738
10:20 twelve **l** stood there on the one side and 738
2Ki 17:25 therefore the L<small>ORD</small> sent **l** among them, 738
17:26 therefore he hath sent **l** among them, 738
1Ch 12: 8 whose faces *were like* the faces of **l**, 738
2Ch 9:18 place, and two **l** standing by the stays: 738
9:19 twelve **l** stood there on the one side and 738
Job 4:10 and the teeth of the **young l**, are broken. 3715
38:39 Or fill the appetite of the **young l**, 3715
Ps 34:10 The **young l** do lack, and suffer hunger: 3715
35:17 their destructions, my darling from the **l**. 3715
57: 4 My soul *is* among **l**: *and* I lie *even* among 3833
58: 6 break out the great teeth of the **young l**, 3715
104:21 The **young l** roar after *their* prey, and 3715
Isa 5:29 be like a lion, they shall roar like **young l**: 3715
15: 9 **l** upon him that escapeth of Moab. 738
Jer 2:15 The **young l** roared upon him, *and* yelled, 3715
50:17 sheep; the **l** have driven *him* away: 738
51:38 They shall roar together like **l**: they shall 3715
Eze 19: 2 she lay down among **l**, she nourished her 738
19: 2 nourished her whelps among **young l**. 3715
19: 6 he went up and down among the **l**, 738
38:13 with all the **young l** thereof, shall say 3715
Da 6: 7 O king, he shall be cast into the den of **l**. 744
6:12 O king, shall be cast into the den of **l**? 744
6:16 and cast *him* into the den of **l**. 744
6:19 and went in haste unto the den of **l**: 744
6:20 able to deliver thee from the **l**? 744
6:24 they cast *them* into the den of **l**, them, 744
6:24 the **l** had the mastery of them, and brake 744
6:27 delivered Daniel from the power of the **l**. 744
Na 2:11 Where *is* the dwelling of the **l**, 738
2:11 the feeding place of the **young l**, where 3715
2:13 and the sword shall devour thy **young l**: 3715
Zep 3: 3 Her princes within her *are* roaring **l**; 738
Zec 11: 3 a voice of the roaring of **young l**; 3715

Heb	11:33 promises, stopped the mouths of l,	3023
Rev	9: 8 and their teeth were as the teeth of l.	3023
	9:17 heads of the horses were as the heads of l;	3023

LIONS' (3) [LION]

SS	4: 8 top of Shenir and Hermon, from the l dens,	738
Jer	51:38 like lions: they shall yell as l whelps,	738
Da	6:22 hath shut the l mouths, that they have not	744

LIP (3) [LIPS]

Lev	13:45 he shall put a covering upon his upper l,	8222
Ps	22: 7 they shoot out the l, they shake the head,	8193
Pr	12:19 The l of truth shall be established for ever:	8193

LIPS (119) [LIP]

Ex	6:12 hear me, who am of uncircumcised l?	8193
	6:30 I am of uncircumcised l, and how shall	8193
Lev	5: 4 pronouncing with his l to do evil, or to	8193
Nu	30: 6 she vowed, or uttered ought out of her l,	8193
	30: 8 that which she uttered with her l,	8193
	30:12 whatsoever proceeded out of her l	8193
Dt	23:23 That which is gone out of thy l thou shalt	8193
1Sa	1:13 only her l moved, but her voice was not	8193
2Ki	19:28 my bridle in thy l, and I will turn thee	8193
Job	2:10 In all this did not Job sin with his l.	8193
	8:21 with laughing, and thy l with rejoicing.	8193
	11: 5 would speak, and open his l against thee;	8193
	13: 6 and hearken to the pleadings of my l.	8193
	15: 6 not I; yea, thine own l testify against thee.	8193
	16: 5 the moving of my l should asswage your	8193
	23:12 back from the commandment of his l;	8193
	27: 4 My l shall not speak wickedness, nor my	8193
	32:20 refreshed: I will open my l and answer.	8193
	33: 3 and my l shall utter knowledge clearly.	8193
Ps	12: 2 with flattering l and with a double heart	8193
	12: 3 The LORD shall cut off all flattering l,	8193
	12: 4 tongue will we prevail; our l are our own:	8193
	16: 4 offer, nor take up their names into my l.	8193
	17: 1 prayer, that goeth not out of feigned l.	8193
	17: 4 by the word of thy l I have kept me from	8193
	21: 2 hast not withholden the request of his l.	8193
	31:18 Let the lying l be put to silence;	8193
	34:13 from evil, and thy l from speaking guile.	8193
	40: 9 lo, I have not refrained my l, O LORD,	8193
	45: 2 grace is poured into thy l: therefore	8193
	51:15 O Lord, open thou my l; and my mouth	8193
	59: 7 swords are in their l: for who, say they,	8193
	59:12 the words of their l let them even be	8193
	63: 3 is better than life, my l shall praise thee.	8193
	63: 5 my mouth shall praise thee with joyful l:	8193
	66:14 Which my l have uttered, and my mouth	8193
	71:23 My l shall greatly rejoice when I sing unto	8193
	89:34 alter the thing that is gone out of my l.	8193
	106:33 so that he spake unadvisedly with his l.	8193
	119:13 my l have I declared all the judgments	8193
	119:171 My l shall utter praise, when thou hast	8193
	120: 2 from lying l, and from a deceitful tongue.	8193
	140: 3 a serpent; adder's poison is under their l.	8193
	140: 9 let the mischief of their own l cover them.	8193
	141: 3 before my mouth; keep the door of my l.	8193
Pr	4:24 and perverse l put far from thee.	8193
	5: 2 and that thy l may keep knowledge.	8193
	5: 3 For the l of a strange woman drop as a	8193
	7:21 with the flattering of her l she forced him.	8193
	8: 6 the opening of my l shall be right things.	8193
	8: 7 wickedness is an abomination to my l.	8193
	10:13 In the l of him that hath understanding	8193
	10:18 He that hideth hatred with lying l,	8193
	10:19 sin: but he that refraineth his l is wise.	8193
	10:21 The l of the righteous feed many:	8193
	10:32 The l of the righteous know what is	8193
	12:13 is snared by the transgression of his l:	8193
	12:22 Lying l are abomination to the LORD:	8193
	13: 3 he that openeth wide his l shall have	8193
	14: 3 but the l of the wise shall preserve them.	8193
	14: 7 when thou perceivest not in him the l of	8193
	14:23 the talk of the l tendeth only to penury.	8193
	15: 7 The l of the wise disperse knowledge:	8193
	16:10 A divine sentence is in the l of the king:	8193
	16:13 Righteous l are the delight of kings;	8193
	16:21 the sweetness of the l increaseth learning.	8193
	16:23 his mouth, and addeth learning to his l.	8193
	16:27 and in his l there is as a burning fire.	8193
	16:30 moving his l he bringeth evil to pass.	8193
	17: 4 A wicked doer giveth heed to false l;	8193
	17: 7 not a fool: much less do lying l a prince.	8193
	17:28 he that shutteth his l is esteemed a man	8193
	18: 6 A fool's l enter into contention,	8193
	18: 7 and his l are the snare of his soul.	8193
	18:20 with the increase of his l shall he be filled.	8193
	19: 1 than he that is perverse in his l, and is a	8193
	20:15 the l of knowledge are a precious jewel.	8193
	20:19 not with him that flattereth with his l.	8193
	22:11 for the grace of his l the king shall be his	8193
	22:18 they shall withal be fitted in thy l.	8193
	23:16 rejoice, when thy l speak right things.	8193
	24: 2 and their l talk of mischief.	8193
	24:26 Every man shall kiss his l that giveth a	8193
	24:28 without cause; and deceive not with thy l.	8193
	26:23 Burning l and a wicked heart are like a	8193
	26:24 He that hateth dissembleth with his l,	8193
	27: 2 mouth; a stranger, and not thine own l.	8193
Ecc	10:12 the l of a fool will swallow up himself.	8193
SS	4: 3 Thy l are like a thread of scarlet,	8193
	4:11 Thy l, O my spouse, drop as	8193
	5:13 his l like lilies, dropping sweet smelling	8193
	7: 9 causing the l of those that are asleep to	8193
Isa	6: 5 because I am a man of unclean l,	8193
	6: 5 in the midst of a people of unclean l:	8193
	6: 7 and said, Lo, this hath touched thy l;	8193
	11: 4 with the breath of his l shall he slay	8193
	28:11 with stammering l and another tongue	8193
	29:13 with their l do honour me,	8193
	30:27 his l are full of indignation, and his	8193
	37:29 my bridle in thy l, and I will turn thee	8193
	57:19 I create the fruit of the l; Peace, peace to	8193
	59: 3 your l have spoken lies, your tongue hath	8193
Jer	17:16 that which came out of my l was right	8193
La	3:62 The l of those that rose up against me,	8193
Eze	24:17 cover not thy l, and eat not the bread of	8222
	24:22 shall not cover your l, nor eat the bread	8222
	36: 3 ye are taken up in the l of talkers,	8193
Da	10:16 of the sons of men touched my l:	8193
Hos	14: 2 so will we render the calves of our l.	8193
Mic	3: 7 they shall all cover their l; for there is	8222
Hab	3:16 trembled; my l quivered at the voice:	8193
Mal	2: 6 and iniquity was not found in his l:	8193
	2: 7 For the priest's l should keep knowledge,	8193
Mt	15: 8 mouth, and honoureth me with their l;	5491
Mk	7: 6 This people honoureth me with their l;	5491
Ro	3:13 the poison of asps is under their l:	5491
1Co	14:21 and other l will I speak unto this people;	5491
Heb	13:15 fruit of our l giving thanks to his name.	5491
1Pe	3:10 and his l that they speak no guile:	5491

LIQUOR (2) [LIQUORS]

Nu	6: 3 neither shall he drink any l of grapes,	4952
SS	7: 2 like a round goblet, which wanteth not l:	4197

LIQUORS (1) [LIQUOR]

Ex	22:29 the first of thy ripe fruits, and of thy l:	1831

LISTED (2) [LISTETH]

Mt	17:12 have done unto him whatsoever they l.	2309
Mk	9:13 have done unto him whatsoever they l,	2309

LISTEN (1)

Isa	49: 1 L, O isles, unto me; and hearken,	8085

LISTETH (2) [LISTED]

Jn	3: 8 The wind bloweth where it l,	2309
Jas	3: 4 whithersoever the governor l.	1014+2116

LITTERS (1)

Isa	66:20 in l, and upon mules, and upon swift	6632

LITTLE (242)

Ge	18: 4 Let a l water, I pray you, be fetched,	4592
	19:20 city is near to flee unto, and it is a l one:	4705
	19:20 let me escape thither, (is it not a l one?)	4705
	24:17 I pray thee, drink a l water of thy pitcher.	4592
	24:43 thee, a l water of thy pitcher to drink;	4592
	30:30 For it was l which thou hadst before I	4592
	34:29 all their l ones, and their wives took they	2945
	35:16 l way to come to Ephrath:	776+3530+1886.1
	43: 2 come again, buy us a l food.	4592
	43: 8 both we, and thou, and also our l ones.	2945
	43:11 a balm, and a little honey, spices,	4592
	43:11 a honey, spices, and myrrh, nuts,	4592
	44:20 man, and a child of his old age, a l one;	6996
	44:25 father said, Go again, and buy us a l food.	4592
	45:19 out of the land of Egypt for your l ones,	2945
	46: 5 and their l ones, and their wives,	2945
	47:24 and for food for your l ones.	2945
	48: 7 but a l way to come unto Ephrath:	3530
	50: 8 only their l ones, and their flocks,	2945
	50:21 I will nourish you and your l ones.	2945
Ex	10:10 as I will let you go, and your l ones:	2945
	10:24 stayed: let your l ones also go with you.	2945
	12: 4 if the household be too l for the lamb,	4591
	16:18 and he that gathered l had no lack;	4591
	23:30 By l and little I will drive them out from	4592
	23:30 I I will drive them out from before thee,	4592
Lev	11:17 the owl, and the cormorant, and the	3563
Nu	14:31 your l ones, which ye said should be a	2945
	16:27 and their sons, and their l children.	2945
	31: 9 their l ones, and took the spoil of all their	2945
	31:17 kill every male among the l ones,	2945
	32:16 for our cattle, and cities for our l ones:	2945
	32:17 our l ones shall dwell in the fenced cities	2945
	32:24 Build ye cities for your l ones, and folds	2945
	32:26 Our l ones, our wives, our flocks,	2945
Dt	1:39 Moreover your l ones, which ye said	2945
	2:34 the women, and the l ones, of every city,	2945
	3:19 and your l ones, and your cattle,	2945
	7:22 nations before thee by l and little:	4592+4592
	7:22 nations before thee by little and l:	4592+4592
	14:16 l owl, and the great owl, and the swan,	3563
	20:14 the l ones, and the cattle, and all that is	2945
	28:38 into the field, and shalt gather but l in;	4592
	29:11 Your l ones, your wives, and thy stranger	2945
Jos	1:14 Your wives, your l ones, and your cattle,	2945
	8:35 the l ones, and the strangers that were	2945
	19:47 children of Dan went out too l for them:	NIH
	22:17 Is the iniquity of Peor too l for us, from	4592
Jdg	4:19 Give me, I pray thee, a l water to drink;	4592
	18:21 put the l ones and the cattle and	4592
Ru	2: 7 now, that she tarried a l in the house.	4592
1Sa	2:19 Moreover his mother made him a l coat,	6996
	14:29 because I tasted a l of this honey.	4592
	14:43 taste a l honey with the end of the rod	4592
	15:17 When thou wast l in thine own sight,	6996
	20:35 with David, and a l lad with him.	6996
2Sa	12: 3 save one l ewe lamb, which he had	6996
	12: 8 if that had been too l, I would moreover	4592
	15:22 and all the l ones that were with him.	2945
	16: 1 David was a l past the top of the hill,	4592
	19:36 Thy servant will go a l way over Jordan	4592
1Ki	3: 7 I am but a l child: I know not how to go	6996
	8:64 was too l to receive the burnt offerings,	6996
	11:17 go into Egypt; Hadad being yet a l child.	6996
	12:10 My l finger shall be thicker than my	6995
	17:10 Fetch me, I pray thee, a l water in a	4592
	17:12 of meal in a barrel, and a l oil in a cruse:	4592
	17:13 make me thereof a l cake first, and bring	6996
	18:44 there ariseth a l cloud out of the sea,	6996
	20:27 before them like two l flocks of kids;	2835
2Ki	2:23 came forth l children out of the city,	6996
	4:10 Let us make a l chamber, I pray thee,	6996
	5: 2 captive out of the land of Israel a l maid;	6996
	5:14 came again like unto the flesh of a l child,	6996
	5:19 So he departed from him a l way.	3530
	10:18 said unto them, Ahab served Baal a l;	4592
2Ch	10:10 My l finger shall be thicker than my	6995
	20:13 with their l ones, their wives,	2945
	31:18 to the genealogy of all their l ones,	2945
Ezr	8:21 for our l ones, and for all our substance.	2945
	9: 8 now for a l space grace hath been shewed	4592
	9: 8 and give us a l reviving in our bondage.	4592
Ne	9:32 let not all the trouble seem l before thee,	4591
Est	3:13 young and old, l children and women,	2945
	8:11 both l ones and women, and to take	2945
Job	4:12 to me, and mine ear received a l thereof.	8102
	10:20 let me alone, that I may take comfort a l,	4592
	21:11 They send forth their l ones like a flock,	5759
	24:24 are exalted for a while, but are gone	4592
	26:14 how l a portion is heard of him?	8102
	36: 2 Suffer me a l, and I will shew thee that I	2191
Ps	2:12 way, when his wrath is kindled but a l:	4592
	8: 5 For thou hast made him a l lower than	4592
	37:10 yet a while, and the wicked shall not	4592
	37:16 A l that a righteous man hath is better	4592
	65:12 and the l hills rejoice on every side.	1389
	68:27 There is l Benjamin with their ruler,	6810
	72: 3 people, and the l hills, by righteousness.	1389
	114: 4 like rams, and the l hills like lambs.	1389
	114: 6 like rams; and ye l hills, like lambs?	1389
	137: 9 dasheth thy l ones against the stones.	5768
Pr	6:10 Yet a l sleep, a little slumber, a little	4592
	6:10 Yet a little sleep, a l slumber, a little	4592
	6:10 a l folding of the hands to sleep:	4592
	10:20 heart of the wicked is l worth.	4592+3509.1
	15:16 Better is l with the fear of the LORD than	4592
	16: 8 Better is a l with righteousness than great	4592
	24:33 Yet a l sleep, a little slumber, a little	4592
	24:33 Yet a little sleep, a l slumber, a little	4592
	24:33 a l folding of the hands to sleep:	4592
	30:24 There be four things which are l upon	6996
Ecc	5:12 man is sweet, whether he eat l or much:	4592
	9:14 There was a l city, and few men within it;	6996
	10: 1 doth a l folly him that is in reputation for	4592
SS	2:15 Take us the foxes, the l foxes, that spoil	6996
	3: 4 It was but a l that I passed from them,	4592
	8: 8 have a l sister, and she hath no breasts:	6996
Isa	10:25 For yet a very l while,	4213+4592
	11: 6 and a l child shall lead them.	6996
	26:20 hide thyself as it were for a l moment,	4592
	28:10 line upon line; here a l, and there a little:	2191
	28:10 line upon line; here a little, and there a l:	2191
	28:13 line upon line; here a l, and there a little;	2191
	28:13 line upon line; here a little, and there a l;	2191
	29:17 Is it not yet a very l while,	4213+4592
	40:15 he taketh up the isles as a very l thing.	1851
	54: 8 In a l wrath I hid my face from thee for a	8241
	60:22 A l one shall become a thousand,	6996
	63:18 holiness have possessed it but a while:	4705
Jer	14: 3 their nobles have sent their l ones to	6810
	48: 4 her l ones have caused a cry to be heard.	6810
	51:33 yet a while, and the time of her harvest	4592
Eze	9: 6 both maids, and l children, and women:	2945
	11:16 yet will I be to them as a l sanctuary in	4592
	16:47 as if that were a very l thing, thou	4592+6985
	31: 4 sent out her l rivers unto all the trees of	8585
	40: 7 every l chamber was one reed long,	8372
	40: 7 between the l chambers were five cubits	8372
	40:10 l chambers of the gate eastward were	8372
	40:12 The space also before the l chambers	8372
	40:12 The l chambers were six cubits on this	8372
	40:13 the gate from the roof of one l chamber	8372
	40:16 narrow windows to the l chambers,	8372
	40:21 l chambers thereof were three on	8372
	40:29 the l chambers thereof, and the posts	8372
	40:33 the l chambers thereof, and the posts	8372
	40:36 The l chambers thereof, the posts	8372
Da	7: 8 came up among them another l horn,	2192
	8: 9 out of one of them came forth a l horn,	4704
	11:34 fall, they shall be holpen with a l help:	4592
Hos	1: 4 for yet a l while, and I will avenge	4592
	8:10 they shall sorrow a l for the burden of	4592
Am	6:11 breaches, and the l house with clefts.	6996
Mic	5: 2 though thou be l among the thousands of	6810
Hag	1: 6 have sown much, and bring in l; ye eat,	4592
	1: 9 Ye looked for much, and lo, it came to l;	4592
	2: 6 in a while, and I will shake the heavens,	4592
Zec	1:15 I was but a l displeased, and they helped	4592

L

Zec 13: 7 I will turn mine hand upon the **l** ones. 6819
Mt 6:30 much more *clothe* you, O ye **of l faith**? 3640
8:26 Why are ye fearful, O ye **of l faith**? 3640
10:42 **l** ones a cup of cold *water* only in the 3398
14:31 and said unto him, O thou **of l faith**, 3640
15:34 And they said, Seven, and a few **l fishes**. 2485
16: 8 he said unto them, O ye **of l faith**, 3640
18: 2 And Jesus called a **l child** unto *him*, and 3813
18: 3 be converted, and become as **l children**, 3813
18: 4 shall humble himself as this **l child**, 3813
18: 5 whoso shall receive one such **l child** in 3813
18: 6 whoso shall offend one of these **l ones** 3398
18:10 that ye despise not one of these **l ones**; 3398
18:14 that one of these **l ones** should perish. 3398
19:13 were there brought unto him **l children**, 3813
19:14 Suffer **l children**, and forbid them not, 3813
26:39 And he went a **l** further, and fell on his 3398
Mk 1:19 And when he had gone a **l** further thence, 3641
4:36 there were also with him other **l ships**. 4142
5:23 My **l daughter** lieth at the point of death: 2365
9:42 one of *these* **l** ones that believe in me, 3398
10:14 Suffer the **l children** to come unto me, 3813
10:15 receive the kingdom of God as a **l child**, 3813
14:35 And he went forward a **l**, and fell on 3398
14:70 a **l** after, they that stood by said again 3398
Lk 5: 3 prayed him that *he* would thrust out a **l** 3641
7:47 to whom **l** is forgiven, *the same* loveth 3641
7:47 whom little is forgiven, *the same* loveth **l**. 3641
12:28 *more will he clothe* you, O ye **of l faith**? 3640
12:32 Fear not, **l flock**; for it is your Father's 3398
17: 2 that he should offend one of these **l ones**. 3398
18:16 Suffer **l children** to come unto me, 3813
18:17 as a **l child** shall in no wise enter therein. 3813
19: 3 for the press, because he was **l** of stature. 3398
19:17 thou hast been faithful in a **very l**, 1646
22:58 And after a **l while** another saw him, 1024
Jn 6: 7 that every one of them may take a **l**. 1024
7:33 Yet a **l** while am I with you, and *then* I go 3398
12:35 Yet a **l while** is the light with you. 3398
13:33 **L children**, yet a little while I am with 5040
13:33 Little children, yet a **while** I am with 3398
14:19 Yet a **l while**, and the world seeth me no 3398
16:16 A **l while**, and ye shall not see me: 3398
16:16 and again, a **l while**, and ye shall see me, 3398
16:17 A **l while**, and ye shall not see me: 3398
16:17 and again, a **l while**, and ye shall see me: 3398
16:18 What is this that he saith, A **l while**? 3398
16:19 I said, A **l while**, and ye shall not see me 3398
16:19 and again, a **l while**, and ye shall see me? 3398
21: 8 And the other disciples came in a **l ship**; 4142
Ac 5:34 to put the apostles forth a **l space**, 1024
20:12 man alive, and were not a **l** comforted. 3357
27:28 and when they had gone a **l** further, 1024
28: 2 And the barbarous people shewed us no **l** 5177
1Co 5: 6 Know ye not that a **l** leaven leaveneth 3398
2Co 8:15 and he that *had gathered* **l** had no lack. 3641
11: 1 Would *to God* you could bear with me a **l** 3398
11:16 receive me, that I may boast myself a **l**. 3398
Gal 4:19 My **l children**, of whom I travail in birth 5040
5: 9 A **l** leaven leaveneth the whole lump. 3398
1Ti 4: 8 For bodily exercise profiteth **l**: 3641
5:23 but use a **l** wine for thy stomach's sake 3641
Heb 2: 7 madest him a **l** lower than the angels; 1024
2: 9 who was made a **l** lower than the angels, 1024
10:37 For yet a **l while**, 3398+3745+3745
Jas 3: 5 Even so the tongue is a **l** member, 3398
3: 5 how great a matter a **l** fire kindleth. 3641
4:14 that appeareth for a **l** *time*, and then 3641
1Jn 2: 1 My **l children**, these *things* write I unto 5040
2:12 **l children**, because *your* sins are forgiven 5040
2:13 **l children**, because ye have known 3813
2:18 **L children**, it is the last time: and as ye 3813
2:28 And now, **l children**, abide in him; that, 5040
3: 7 **L children**, let no *man* deceive you: he 5040
3:18 My **l children**, let us not love in word, 5040
4: 4 **l children**, and have overcome them: 5040
5:21 **L children**, keep yourselves from idols. 5040
Rev 3: 8 thou hast a **l strength**, and hast kept my 3398
6:11 that they should rest yet for a **l season**, 3398
10: 2 And he had in his hand a **l book** open: 974
10: 8 take the **l book** which is open in the hand 974
10: 9 and said unto him, Give me the **l book**. 974
10:10 And I took the **l book** out of the angel's 974
20: 3 after that he must be loosed a **l** season. 3398

LIVE (247) [ALIVE, LIFE, LIFETIME, LIVED, LIVELY, LIVES, LIVEST, LIVETH, LIVING, OUTLIVED, OVERLIVED]

Ge 3:22 of the tree of life, and eat, and **l** for ever: 2421
12:13 and my soul shall **l** because of thee. 2421
17:18 O that Ishmael might **l** before thee! 2421
19:20 (*is* it not a little one?) and my soul shall **l**. 2421
20: 7 he shall pray for thee, and thou shalt **l**: 2421
27:40 by thy sword shalt thou **l**, and shalt serve 2421
31:32 thou findest thy gods, let him not **l**: 2421
42: 2 from thence; that we may **l**, and not die. 2421
42:18 unto them the third day, This do, and **l**; 2421
43: 8 that we may **l**, and not die, both we, 2421
45: 3 I *am* Joseph; doth my father yet **l**? 2416
47:19 give *us* seed, that we may **l**, and not die, 2421
Ex 1:16 but if it *be* a daughter, then she shall **l**. 2421
19:13 whether *it* be beast or man, it shall not **l**: 2421
21:35 they shall sell the **l** ox, and divide 2416
22:18 Thou shalt not **suffer** a witch **to l**. 2421
33:20 for there shall no man see me, and **l**. 2421

Lev 16:20 and the altar, he shall bring the **l** goat: 2416
16:21 his hands upon the head of the **l** goat, 2416
18: 5 which if a man do, he shall **l** in them: 2421
25:35 or a sojourner; that he may **l** with thee. 2416
25:36 God; that thy brother may **l** with thee. 2416
Nu 4:19 unto them, that they may **l**, and not die, 2421
14:21 as truly *as* **l** I, all the earth shall be filled 2416
14:28 Say unto them, As truly *as* **l** I, saith 2416
21: 8 bitten, when he looketh upon it, shall **l**. 2421
24:23 Alas, who shall **l** when God doeth this! 2421
Dt 4: 1 for to do *them*, that ye may **l**, and go in 2421
4:10 the days that they shall **l** upon the earth, 2416
4:33 of the fire, as thou hast heard, and **l**? 2421
4:42 unto one of these cities he might **l**: 2421
5:33 that ye may **l**, and *that it may be* well 2421
8: 1 that ye may **l**, and multiply, and go in 2421
8: 3 know that man doth not **l** by bread only, 2421
8: 3 out of the mouth of the LORD doth man **l**. 2416
12: 1 all the days that ye **l** upon the earth. 2416
16:20 that thou mayest **l**, and inherit the land 2421
19: 4 which shall flee thither, that he may **l**: 2421
19: 5 shall flee unto one of those cities, and **l**: 2421
30: 6 and with all thy soul, that thou mayest **l**. 2416
30:16 that thou mayest **l** and multiply: 2421
30:19 that *both* thou and thy seed may **l**: 2421
31:13 as long as ye **l** in the land whither ye go 2416
32:40 my hand to heaven, and say, I **l** for ever. 2416
Jos 33: 6 Let Reuben **l**, and not die; and let *not* his 2421
6:17 only Rahab the harlot shall **l**, she and 2421
9:15 made a league with them, to let them **l**: 2421
9:20 we will even let them **l**, lest wrath be 2421
9:21 the princes said unto them, Let them **l**; 2421
1Sa 20:14 thou shalt not only while yet I **l** shew me 2416
2Sa 1:10 I was sure that he could not **l** after *that* he 2421
12:22 be gracious to me, that the child may **l**? 2421
19:34 said unto the king, How long have I **to l**, 2416
1Ki 1:31 said, Let my lord king David **l** for ever. 2421
8:40 **l** in the land which thou gavest unto our 2421
20:32 Ben-hadad saith, I pray thee, let me **l**. 2421
2Ki 4: 7 and **l** thou and thy children of the rest. 2421
7: 4 if they save us alive, we shall **l**; and if 2421
10:19 shall be wanting, he shall not **l**. 2421
18:32 and of honey, that ye may **l**, and not die: 2421
20: 1 in order; for thou shalt die, and not **l**. 2421
2Ch 6:31 long as they **l** in the land which thou 2421
Ne 3: 2 said unto the king, Let the king **l** for ever: 2421
5: 2 up corn *for them*, that we may eat, and **l**. 2421
9:29 (which if a man do, he shall **l** in them;) 2421
Est 4:11 out the golden sceptre, that he may **l**: 2421
Job 7:16 I loathe *it*; I would not always: let me 2421
14:14 shall he **l** *again*? all the days of my 2421
21: 7 Wherefore do the wicked **l**, become old, 2421
27: 6 heart shall not reproach *me* so long as I **l**. 3117
Ps 22:26 that seek him: your heart shall **l** for ever. 2421
49: 9 That he should still **l** for ever, *and* not see 2421
55:23 deceitful men shall not **l out half** their 2673
63: 4 Thus will I bless thee while I **l**: I will lift 2421
69:32 and your heart shall **l** that seek God. 2421
72:15 he shall **l**, and to him shall be given of 2421
104:33 I will sing unto the LORD as long as I **l**: 2416
116: 2 will I call upon *him* as long as I **l**. 3117
118:17 but I, and declare the works of the LORD. 2421
119:17 *that* I may **l**, and keep thy word. 2421
119:77 mercies come *unto* me, that I may **l**: 2421
119:116 according unto thy word, that I may **l**: 2421
119:144 give me understanding, and I shall **l**. 2421
119:175 Let my soul **l**, and it shall praise thee; 2421
146: 2 While I **l** will I praise the LORD: I will 2416
Pr 4: 4 words: keep my commandments, and **l**. 2421
7: 2 Keep my commandments, and **l**; 2421
9: 6 Forsake the foolish, and **l**; and go in 2421
15:27 house; but he that hateth gifts shall **l**. 2421
Ecc 6: 3 an hundred *children*, and *many* years, 2421
6: 6 though he **l** a thousand years twice *told*, 2421
9: 3 madness *is* in their heart while they **l**, 2421
9: 9 **l** joyfully with the wife whom thou lovest 2416
11: 8 if a man **l** many years, *and* rejoice in them 2421
Isa 6: 6 unto me, having a **l coal** in his hand, 7531
26:14 *They are* dead, they shall not **l**; *they are* 2421
26:19 Thy dead *men* shall **l**, *together* with my 2421
38: 1 in order; for thou shalt die, and not **l**. 2421
38:16 by these *things men* **l**, and in all these 2421
38:16 wilt thou recover me, and **make** me **to l**. 2421
49:18 *As* I, saith the LORD, thou shalt surely 2421
55: 3 and your soul shall **l**; and I will make 2421
Jer 21: 9 he shall **l**, and his life shall be unto him 2421
22:24 *As* I, saith the LORD, though Coniah 2416
27:12 and serve him and his people, and **l**. 2421
27:17 serve the king of Babylon, and **l**: 2421
35: 7 that ye may **l** many days in the land 2421
38: 2 that goeth forth to the Chaldeans shall **l**; 2421
38: 2 shall have his life for a prey, and shall **l**. 2421
38:17 thy soul shall **l**, and this city shall not be 2421
38:17 fire; and thou shalt **l**, and thine house: 2421
38:20 be well unto thee, and thy soul shall **l**. 2421
46:18 *As* I, saith the King, whose name *is* 2416
La 4:20 Under his shadow we shall **l** among 2421
Eze 3:21 **surely l**, because he is warned; 2421+2421
5:11 Wherefore, *as* I **l**, saith the Lord GOD, 2416
13:19 to save the souls alive that should not **l**, 2421
14:16 men *were* in it, *as* I **l**, saith the Lord GOD, 2416
14:18 men *were* in it, *as* I **l**, saith the Lord GOD, 2416
14:20 Daniel, and Job, *were* in it, *as* I **l**, 2416
16: 6 thee *when thou wast* in thy blood, **L**; 2421
16: 6 thee *when thou wast* in thy blood, **L**. 2421

Eze 16:48 *As* I **l**, saith the Lord GOD, Sodom thy 2416
17:16 *As* I **l**, saith the Lord GOD, surely in 2416
17:19 *As* I **l**, surely mine oath that he hath 2416
18: 3 *As* I **l**, saith the Lord GOD, ye shall not 2416
18: 9 he *is* just, he shall **surely l**, saith 2421+2421
18:13 shall he then **l**? he shall not live: he hath 2421
18:13 he shall not **l**: he hath done all these 2421
18:17 of his father, he shall **surely l**. 2421+2421
18:19 hath done them, he shall **surely l**, 2421+2421
18:21 lawful and right, he shall **surely l**, 2421+2421
18:22 righteousness that he hath done he shall **l**. 2421
18:23 he should return from his ways, and **l**? 2421
18:24 that the wicked *man* doeth, shall he **l**? 2421
18:28 he shall **surely l**, he shall not die. 2421+2421
18:32 wherefore turn *yourselves*, and **l** ye. 2421
20: 3 *As* I **l**, saith the Lord GOD, I will not be 2416
20:11 *if* a man do, he shall even **l** in them. 2421
20:13 *if* a man do, he shall even **l** in them. 2421
20:21 *if* a man do, he shall even **l** in them; 2421
20:25 judgments whereby they should not **l**; 2421
20:31 *As* I **l**, saith the Lord GOD, I will not be 2416
20:33 *As* I **l**, saith the Lord GOD, surely with a 2416
33:10 away in them, how should we then **l**? 2421
33:11 Say unto them, *As* I **l**, saith the Lord 2416
33:11 that the wicked turn from his way and **l**: 2421
33:12 neither shall the righteous be able to **l** for 2421
33:13 righteous, *that* he shall **surely l**; 2421+2421
33:15 he shall **surely l**, he shall not die. 2421+2421
33:16 lawful and right; he shall **surely l**. 2421+2421
33:19 is lawful and right, he shall **l** thereby. 2421
33:27 *As* I **l**, surely *they* that *are* in the wastes 2416
34: 8 *As* I **l**, saith the Lord GOD, surely because 2416
35: 6 Therefore, *as* I **l**, saith the Lord GOD, 2416
35:11 Therefore, *as* I **l**, saith the Lord GOD, 2416
37: 3 unto me, Son of man, can these bones **l**? 2421
37: 5 breath to enter into you, and ye shall **l**: 2421
37: 6 and put breath in you, and ye shall **l**; 2421
37: 9 breathe upon these slain, that they may **l**. 2421
37:14 ye shall **l**, and I shall place you in your 2421
47: 9 the rivers shall come, shall **l**: 2421
47: 9 *thing* shall **l** whither the river cometh. 2416
Da 2: 4 to the king in Syriack, O king, **l** for ever: 2418
3: 9 king Nebuchadnezzar, O king, **l** for ever. 2418
5:10 queen spake and said, O king, **l** for ever: 2418
6: 6 thus unto him, King Darius, **l** for ever. 2418
6:21 Daniel unto the king, O king, **l** for ever. 2418
Hos 6: 2 raise us up, and we shall **l** in his sight. 2421
Am 5: 4 of Israel, Seek ye me, and ye shall **l**: 2421
5: 6 Seek the LORD, and ye shall **l**; lest he 2421
5:14 Seek good, and not evil, that ye may **l**: 2421
Jnh 4: 3 for *it is* better for me to die than to **l**. 2416
4: 8 said, *It is* better for me to die than to **l**. 2416
Hab 2: 4 in him: but the just shall **l** by his faith. 2421
Zep 2: 9 Therefore *as* I **l**, saith the LORD of hosts, 2416
Zec 1: 5 and the prophets, do they **l** for ever? 2421
10: 9 they shall **l** with their children, 2421
13: 3 him shall say unto him, Thou shalt not **l**; 2421
Mt 4: 4 Man shall not **l** by bread alone, 2198
9:18 lay thy hand upon her, and she shall **l**. 2198
Mk 5:23 that she may be healed; and she shall **l**. 2198
Lk 4: 4 That man shall not **l** by bread alone, 2198
7:25 and **l** delicately, are in kings' courts. 5225
10:28 answered right: this do, and thou shalt **l**. 2198
20:38 but of the living: for all **l** unto him. 2198
Jn 5:25 the Son of God: and they that hear shall **l**. 2198
6:51 *man* eat of this bread, he shall **l** for ever: 2198
6:57 Father hath sent me, and I **l** by the Father: 2198
6:57 he that eateth me, even he shall **l** by me. 2198
6:58 that eateth *of* this bread shall **l** for ever. 2198
11:25 me, though he were dead, *yet* shall he **l**: 2198
14:19 ye see me: because I **l**, ye shall **live** also. 2198
14:19 ye see me: because I live, ye shall **l** also. 2198
Ac 7:19 children, to the end *they* might not **l**. 2225
17:28 For in him we **l**, and move, and have our 2198
22:22 the earth: for it is not fit that he should **l**. 2198
25:24 crying that he ought not to **l** any longer. 2198
28: 4 the sea, yet Vengeance suffereth not to **l**. 2198
Ro 1:17 as it is written, The just shall **l** by faith. 2198
6: 2 that are dead to sin, **l** any longer therein? 2198
6: 8 we believe that we shall also **l with** him: 4800
8:12 not to the flesh, to **l** after the flesh. 2198
8:13 For if ye **l** after the flesh, ye shall die: 2198
8:13 mortify the deeds of the body, ye shall **l**. 2198
10: 5 which doeth those *things* shall **l** by them. 2198
12:18 as lieth in you, **l peaceably** with all men. 1514
14: 8 For whether we **l**, we live unto the Lord; 2198
14: 8 For whether we live, we **l** unto the Lord; 2198
14: 8 whether we **l** therefore, or die, we are 2198
14:11 For it is written, *As* I **l**, saith the Lord, 2198
1Co 9:13 holy *things* **l** of the things of the temple? 2068
9:14 preach the gospel should **l** of the gospel. 2198
2Co 4:11 For we which **l** are alway delivered unto 2198
5:15 they which **l** should not henceforth live 2198
5:15 they which live should not henceforth **l** 2198
6: 9 as dying, and behold, we **l**; as chastened, 2198
7: 3 are in our hearts to die and **l with** *you*. 4800
13: 4 we shall **l** with him by the power of God 2198
13:11 comfort, be of one mind, **l in peace**; 1514
Gal 2:14 thou the Gentiles to **l as do the Jews**? 2450
2:19 dead to the law, that I might **l** unto God. 2198
2:20 nevertheless I **l**; yet not I, but Christ liveth 2198
2:20 *the life* which I now **l** in the flesh I live by 2198
2:20 *the life* which I now live in the flesh I **l** by 2198
3:11 *it is* evident: for, The just shall **l** by faith. 2198
3:12 The man that doeth them shall **l** in them. 2198

Gal 5:25 If we l in the Spirit, let us also walk in — 2198
Eph 6: 3 thou mayest l **long** on the earth. — 1510+3118
Php 1:21 For to me to l *is* Christ, and to die *is* gain. — 2198
 1:22 But if /l in the flesh, this *is* the fruit of my — 2198
1Th 3: 8 For now we l, if ye stand fast in the Lord. — 2198
 5:10 or sleep, we should l together with him. — 2198
2Ti 2:11 dead with *him*, we shall also l with *him*: — 4800
 3:12 all that will l godly in Christ Jesus shall — 2198
Tit 2:12 and worldly lusts we should l soberly, — 2198
Heb 10:38 the just shall l by faith: but if *any man* — 2198
 12: 9 unto the Father of spirits, and l? — 2198
 13:18 in all *things* willing to l honestly. — 390
Jas 4:15 Lord will, we shall l, and do this, or that. — 2198
1Pe 2:24 dead to sins, should l unto righteousness: — 980
 4: 2 That *he* no longer should l the rest of *his* — 2198
 4: 6 but l according to God in the spirit. — 2198
2Pe 2: 6 unto **those that** after should l **ungodly**; — 764
 2:18 clean escaped from them who l in error. — 390
1Jn 2: 6 the world, that we might l through him. — 2198
Rev 13:14 had the wound by a sword, and did l. — 2198

LIVED (58) [LIVE]

Ge 5: 3 Adam l an hundred and thirty years, — 2421
 5: 5 all the days that Adam l were nine — 2421
 5: 6 Seth l an hundred and five years, — 2421
 5: 7 Seth l after he begat Enos eight hundred — 2421
 5: 9 Enos l ninety years, and begat Cainan: — 2421
 5:10 Enos l after he begat Cainan eight — 2421
 5:12 Cainan l seventy years, — 2421
 5:13 Cainan l after he begat Mahalaleel eight — 2421
 5:15 Mahalaleel l sixty and five years, — 2421
 5:16 Mahalaleel l after he begat Jared eight — 2421
 5:18 Jared l an hundred sixty and two years, — 2421
 5:19 Jared l after he begat Enoch eight — 2421
 5:21 Enoch l sixty and five years, — 2421
 5:25 Methuselah l an hundred eighty and — 2421
 5:26 Methuselah l after he begat Lamech seven — 2421
 5:28 Lamech l an hundred eighty and two — 2421
 5:30 Lamech l after he begat Noah five — 2421
 9:28 Noah l after the flood three hundred and — 2421
 11:11 Shem l after he begat Arphaxad five — 2421
 11:12 Arphaxad l five and thirty years, — 2421
 11:13 Arphaxad l after he begat Salah four — 2421
 11:14 And Salah l thirty years, and begat Eber: — 2421
 11:15 Salah l after he begat Eber four hundred — 2421
 11:16 Eber l four and thirty years, — 2421
 11:17 Eber l after he begat Peleg four hundred — 2421
 11:18 And Peleg l thirty years, and begat Reu: — 2421
 11:19 Peleg l after he begat Reu two hundred — 2421
 11:20 Reu l two and thirty years, and begat — 2421
 11:21 Reu l after he begat Serug two hundred — 2421
 11:22 And Serug l thirty years, and begat Nahor: — 2421
 11:23 Serug l after he begat Nahor two hundred — 2421
 11:24 Nahor l nine and twenty years, — 2421
 11:25 Nahor l after he begat Terah an hundred — 2421
 11:26 Terah l seventy years, and begat Abram, — 2421
 25: 6 while he yet l, eastward, unto the east — 2416
 25: 7 of the years of Abraham's life which he l, — 2421
 47:28 Jacob l in the land of Egypt seventeen — 2421
 50:22 and Joseph l an hundred and ten years. — 2421
Nu 14:38 the men that went to search the land, l — 2421
 21: 9 when he beheld the serpent of brass, he l. — 2421
Dt 5:26 of the midst of the fire, as we *have*, and l? — 2421
2Sa 19: 6 that if Absalom had l, and all we had died — 2416
1Ki 12: 6 Solomon his father while he yet l, — 1961+2416
2Ki 14:17 Amaziah the son of Joash king of Judah l — 2421
2Ch 10: 6 before Solomon his father while he yet l, — 2416
 25:25 Amaziah the son of Joash king of Judah l — 2421
Job 42:16 After this l Job an hundred and forty years — 2421
Ps 49:18 Though whiles he l he blessed his soul: — 2416
Eze 37:10 they l, and stood up upon their feet, — 2421
Lk 2:36 had l with a husband seven years from — 2198
Ac 23: 1 I have l in all good conscience before God — 4176
 26: 5 straitest sect of our religion I l a Pharisee. — 2198
Col 3: 7 walked sometime, when ye l in them. — 2198
Jas 5: 5 Ye have l **in pleasure** on the earth, — 5171
Rev 18: 7 and l **deliciously**, so much torment and — 4763
 18: 9 and l **deliciously** with her, — 4763
 20: 4 and they l and reigned with Christ a — 2198
 20: 5 But the rest of the dead l not **again** until — 326

LIVELY (5) [LIVE]

Ex 1:19 for they *are* l, and are delivered ere — 2422
Ps 38:19 mine enemies *are* l, *and* they are strong: — 2416
Ac 7:38 received the l oracles to give unto us: — 2198
1Pe 1: 3 hope by the resurrection of Jesus Christ — 2198
 2: 5 Ye also, as l stones, are built *up* a spiritual — 2198

LIVER (14)

Ex 29:13 the caul *that is* above the l, and the two — 3516
 29:22 caul *above* the l, and the two kidneys, — 3516
Lev 3: 4 the caul above the l, with the kidneys, — 3516
 3:10 the caul above the l, with the kidneys, — 3516
 3:15 the caul above the l, with the kidneys, — 3516
 4: 9 the caul above the l, with the kidneys, — 3516
 7: 4 the caul *that is* above the l, with — 3516
 8:16 caul *above* the l, and the two kidneys, — 3516
 8:25 caul *above* the l, and the two kidneys, — 3516
 9:10 the caul above the l of the sin offering, — 3516
 9:19 the kidneys, and the caul *above* the l: — 3516
Pr 7:23 Till a dart strike through his l; as a bird — 3516
La 2:11 troubled, my l is poured upon the earth, — 3516
Eze 21:21 consulted with images, he looked in the l. — 3516

LIVES (28) [LIVE]

Ge 9: 5 surely your blood of your l will I require; — 5315
 45: 7 and to **save** your l by a great deliverance. — 2421
 47:25 said, Thou hast **saved** our l: let us find — 2421
Ex 1:14 made their l bitter with hard bondage, — 2416
Jos 2:13 they have, and deliver our l from death. — 5315
 9:24 were sore afraid of our l because of you, — 5315
Jdg 5:18 unto the death in the high places of — 5315
 18:25 lose thy life, with the l of thy household. — 5315
2Sa 1:23 were lovely and pleasant in their l, — 2416
 19: 5 the l of thy sons and of thy daughters, — 5315
 19: 5 the l of thy wives, and the lives of thy — 5315
 19: 5 of thy wives, and the lives of thy — 5315
 19: 5 of thy wives, and the l of thy concubines; — 5315
 23:17 the men that went in *jeopardy of* their l? — 5315
1Ch 11:19 men that have put their l in jeopardy? — 5315
 11:19 with *the jeopardy of* their l they brought — 5315
Est 9:16 stood for their l, and had rest from their — 5315
Pr 1:18 blood; they lurk privily for their own l. — 5315
Jer 19: 7 and by the hands of them that seek their l: — 5315
 19: 9 they that seek their l, shall straiten them. — 5315
 46:26 into the hand of those that seek their l, — 5315
 48: 6 save your l, and be like the heath in — 5315
La 5:9 We gat our bread with *the peril of* our l — 5315
Da 7:12 yet their l were prolonged for a season — 2417
Lk 9:56 Son of man is not come to destroy men's l, — 5590
Ac 15:26 that have hazarded their l for the name — 5590
 27:10 of the lading and ship, but also of our l. — 5590
1Jn 3:16 ought to lay down *our* l for the brethren. — 5590
Rev 12:11 and they loved not their l unto the death. — 5590

LIVEST (4) [LIVE]

Dt 12:19 Levite as long as thou lˢ upon the earth. — 3117
2Sa 11:11 *as* thou l, and *as* thy soul liveth, I will not — 2416
Gal 2:14 l after the manner of Gentiles, and not as — 2198
Rev 3: 1 that thou hast a name that thou l, — 2198

LIVETH (96) [LIVE]

Ge 9: 3 Every moving thing that l shall be meat — 2416
Dt 5:24 that God doth talk with man, and he l. — 2421
Jdg 8:19 *as* the Lord l, if ye had saved them alive, — 2416
Ru 3:13 part of a kinsman to thee, *as the* Lord l: — 2416
1Sa 1:26 said, O my lord, *as* thy soul l, my lord, — 2416
 1:28 as long as he l he *shall be* lent to — 1961
 14:39 For, *as the* Lord l, which saveth Israel, — 2416
 14:45 *as the* Lord l, there shall not one hair of — 2416
 17:55 *As* thy soul l, O king, I cannot tell. — 2416
 19: 6 Saul sware, *As the* Lord l, he shall not — 2416
 20: 3 truly *as the* Lord l, and *as* thy soul — 2416
 20: 3 *as* thy soul l, *there is* but a step between — 2416
 20:21 peace to thee, and no hurt; *as the* Lord l. — 2416
 20:31 For as long as the son of Jesse l upon — 2416
 25: 6 shall ye say to him that l *in prosperity*, — 2416
 25:26 *as the* Lord l, and *as* thy soul liveth, — 2416
 25:26 *as the* Lord liveth, and *as* thy soul l, — 2416
 25:34 in very deed, *as the* Lord God of Israel l, — 2416
 26:10 David said furthermore, *As the* Lord l, — 2416
 26:16 *As the* Lord l, ye *are* worthy to die, — 2416
 28:10 by the Lord, saying, *As the* Lord l, — 2416
 29: 6 said unto him, Surely, *as the* Lord l, — 2416
2Sa 2:27 Joab said, *As* God l, unless thou hadst — 2416
 4: 9 and said unto them, *As the* Lord l, I will not — 2416
 11:11 *as* thou livest, and *as* thy soul l, I will not — 2416
 12: 5 he said to Nathan, *As the* Lord l, — 2416
 14:11 he said, *As the* Lord l, there shall not — 2416
 14:19 woman answered and said, *As* thy soul l, — 2416
 15:21 *As the* Lord l, and *as* my lord the king — 2416
 15:21 Lord l, and *as* my lord the king l, — 2416
 22:47 The Lord l; and blessed *be* my rock; — 2416
1Ki 1:29 the king sware, and said, *As the* Lord l, — 2416
 2:24 Now therefore, *as the* Lord l, which hath — 2416
 3:23 This *is* my son that l, and thy son *is* — 2416
 17: 1 unto Ahab, *As the* Lord God of Israel l, — 2416
 17:12 she said, *As the* Lord thy God l, I have — 2416
 17:23 his mother: and Elijah said, See, thy son l. — 2416
 18:10 *As the* Lord thy God l, there is no nation — 2416
 18:15 Elijah said, *As the* Lord of hosts l, — 2416
 22:14 Micaiah said, *As the* Lord l, what — 2416
2Ki 2: 2 And Elisha said *unto him, As the* Lord l, — 2416
 2: 2 and *as* thy soul l, I will not leave thee. — 2416
 2: 4 *As the* Lord l, and *as* thy soul liveth, — 2416
 2: 4 and *as* thy soul l, I will not leave thee. — 2416
 2: 6 *As the* Lord l, and *as* thy soul liveth, — 2416
 2: 6 and *as* thy soul l, I will not leave thee. — 2416
 3:14 Elisha said, *As the* Lord of hosts l, — 2416
 4:30 *As the* Lord l, and *as* thy soul liveth, — 2416
 4:30 and *as* thy soul l, I will not leave thee. — 2416
 5:16 he said, *As the* Lord l, before whom I — 2416
 5:20 but, *as the* Lord l, I will run after him, — 2416
2Ch 18:13 Micaiah said, *As the* Lord l, even what — 2416
Job 19:25 For I know *that* my Redeemer l, and *that* — 2416
 27: 2 *As* God l, *who* hath taken away my judg- — 2416
Ps 18:46 The Lord l; and blessed *be* my rock; — 2416
 89:48 What man *is he that* l, and shall not see — 2421
Jer 4: 2 The Lord l, in truth, in judgment, — 2416
 5: 2 though they say, The Lord l; surely they — 2416
 12:16 to swear by my name, The Lord l; — 2416
 16:14 that it shall no more be said, The Lord l, — 2416
 16:15 But, The Lord l, which brought up — 2416
 23: 7 that they shall no more say, The Lord l, — 2416
 23: 8 But, The Lord l, which brought up and — 2416
 38:16 saying, *As the* Lord l, that made us this — 2416
 44:26 land of Egypt, saying, The Lord God l. — 2416
Eze 47: 9 *that* every thing that l, which moveth, — 2416
Da 4:34 I praised and honoured him that l for ever, — 2417
 12: 7 sware by him that l for ever that *it* shall — 2416

Hos 4:15 up *to* Beth-aven, nor swear, The Lord l. — 2416
Am 8:14 of Samaria, and say, Thy god, O Dan, l; — 2416
 8:14 liveth; and, The manner of Beer-sheba l, — 2416
Jn 4:50 saith unto him, Go thy way; thy son l. — 2198
 4:51 met him, and told *him*, saying, Thy son l. — 2198
 4:53 the which Jesus said unto him, Thy son l: — 2198
 11:26 whosoever l and believeth in me shall — 2198
Ro 6:10 but in that he l, he l unto God. — 2198
 6:10 but in that he l, he l unto God. — 2198
 7: 1 dominion over a man, as long as he l? — 2198
 7: 2 by the law to *her* husband so long as he l; — 2198
 7: 3 So then if, while *her* husband l, she be — 2198
 7: 3 *her* husband l, she be married to another *man* — 2198
1Co 7:39 by the law as long as her husband l; — 2198
2Co 13: 4 yet he l by the power of God. — 2198
Gal 2:20 I live; yet not I, but Christ l in me: — 2198
1Ti 5: 6 she that l **in pleasure** is dead while she — 4684
 5: 6 that liveth in pleasure is dead while she — 2198
Heb 7: 8 them, of whom it is witnessed that he l. — 2198
 7:25 seeing he ever l to make intercession for — 2198
 9:17 of no strength at all whilst the testator l. — 2198
1Pe 1:23 word of God, which l and abideth for ever. — 2198
Rev 1:18 I am he that l, and was dead; and behold, — 2198
 4: 9 sat on the throne, who l for ever and ever, — 2198
 4:10 and worship him that l for ever and ever, — 2198
 5:14 and worshipped him that l for ever and — 2198
 10: 6 sware by him that l for ever and ever, — 2198
 15: 7 wrath of God, who l for ever and ever. — 2198

LIVING (147) [LIVE]

Ge 1:21 and every l creature that moveth, — 2416
 1:24 Let the earth bring forth the l creature — 2416
 1:28 over every l **thing** that moveth upon — 2416
 2: 7 breath of life; and man became a l soul. — 2416
 2:19 whatsoever Adam called every l creature, — 2416
 3:20 because she was the mother of all l. — 2416
 6:19 of every l *thing* of all flesh, two of every — 2416
 7: 4 every l **substance** that I have made will I — 3351
 7:23 every l **substance** was destroyed which — 3351
 8: 1 every l **thing**, and all the cattle that *was* — 2416
 8:17 Bring forth with thee every l **thing** that *is* — 2416
 8:21 will I again smite any more every l *thing*, — 2416
 9:10 with every l creature that *is* with you, — 2416
 9:12 and every l creature that *is* with you, — 2416
 9:15 and you and every l creature of all flesh; — 2416
 9:16 every l creature of all flesh that *is* upon — 2416
Lev 11:10 and of any l thing which *is* in the waters, — 2416
 11:46 of every l creature that moveth in — 2416
 14: 6 As for the l bird, he shall take it, — 2416
 14: 6 the l bird in the blood of the bird *that was* — 2416
 14: 7 let the l bird loose into the open field. — 2416
 14:51 the l bird, and dip them in the blood of — 2416
 14:52 with the l bird, and with the cedar wood, — 2416
 14:53 shall let go the l bird out of the city into — 2416
 20:25 by any *manner of* l *thing* that creepeth *on* — NIH
Nu 16:48 he stood between the dead and the l; — 2416
Dt 5:26 that hath heard the voice of the l God — 2416
Jos 3:10 Hereby ye shall know that the l God *is* — 2416
Ru 2:20 who hath not left off his kindness to the l — 2416
1Sa 17:36 he should defy the armies of the l God? — 2416
 17:36 seeing he hath defied the armies of the l — 2424
2Sa 20: 3 the day of their death, l in widowhood. — 2424
1Ki 3:22 The l *is* my son, and the dead *is* thy son. — 2416
 3:22 the dead *is* thy son, and the l *is* my son. — 2416
 3:23 thy son *is* the dead, and my son *is* the l. — 2416
 3:25 Divide the l child in two, and give half to — 2416
 3:26 spake the woman whose the l child *was* — 2416
 3:26 give her the l child, and in no wise slay it. — 2416
 3:27 Give her the l child, and in no wise slay it: — 2416
2Ki 19: 4 master hath sent to reproach the l God; — 2416
 19:16 hath sent to reproach the l God. — 2416
Job 12:10 In whose hand *is* the soul of every l *thing*, — 2416
 28:13 neither is it found in the land of the l. — 2416
 28:21 Seeing it is hid from the eyes of all l, — 2416
 30:23 and *to* the house appointed for all l. — 2416
 33:30 to be enlightened with the light of the l. — 2416
Ps 27:13 goodness of the Lord in the land of the l. — 2416
 42: 2 My soul thirsteth for God, for the l God: — 2416
 52: 5 and root thee out of the land of the l. — 2416
 56:13 may walk before God in the light of the l? — 2416
 58: 9 a whirlwind, both l, and in *his* wrath. — 2416
 69:28 them be blotted out of the book of the l, — 2416
 84: 2 and my flesh crieth out for the l God. — 2416
 116: 9 walk before the Lord in the land of the l. — 2416
 142: 5 *and* my portion in the land of the l. — 2416
 143: 2 for in thy sight shall no *man* be justified. — 2416
 145:16 and satisfiest the desire of every l **thing.** — 2416
Ecc 4: 2 dead more than the l which are yet alive. — 2416
 4:15 I considered all the l which walk under — 2416
 6: 8 poor, that knoweth to walk before the l? — 2416
 7: 2 all men; and the l will lay *it* to his heart. — 2416
 9: 4 For to him that is joined to all the l there — 2416
 9: 4 for a dog is better than a dead lion. — 2416
 9: 5 For the l know that they shall die: — 2416
SS 4:15 a well of l waters, and streams from — 2416
Isa 4: 3 every one that is written among the l — 2416
 8:19 unto their God? for the l to the dead? — 2416
 37: 4 master hath sent to reproach the l God, — 2416
 37:17 which hath sent to reproach the l God. — 2416
 38:11 even the Lord, in the land of the l: — 2416
 38:19 The l, the living, he shall praise thee, as I — 2416
 38:19 The living, the l, he shall praise thee, as I — 2416
 53: 8 for he was cut off out of the land of the l: — 2416
Jer 2:13 they have forsaken me the fountain of l — 2416
 10:10 he *is* the l God, and an everlasting king: — 2416

L

Jer	11:19	let us cut him off from the land of the l,	2416
	17:13	the Lord, the fountain of l waters.	2416
	23:36	for ye have perverted the words of the l	2416
La	3:39	Wherefore doth a l man complain, a man	2416
Eze	1: 5	came the likeness of four l creatures.	2416
	1:13	As for the likeness of the l creatures,	2416
	1:13	up and down among the l creatures;	2416
	1:14	the l creatures ran and returned as	2416
	1:15	Now as I beheld the l creatures, behold	2416
	1:15	wheel upon the earth by the l creatures,	2416
	1:19	when the l creatures went, the wheels	2416
	1:19	when the l creatures were lift up from	2416
	1:20	for the spirit of the l creature was in	2416
	1:21	for the spirit of the l creature was in	2416
	1:22	l creature was as the colour of the	2416
	3:13	the l creatures that touched one another,	2416
	10:15	is the l creature that I saw by the river	2416
	10:17	the spirit of the l creature was in them.	2416
	10:20	This is the l creature that I saw under	2416
	26:20	and I shall set glory in the land of the l;	2416
	32:23	which caused terror in the land of the l.	2416
	32:24	caused their terror in the land of the l,	2416
	32:25	terror was caused in the land of the l,	2416
	32:26	caused their terror in the land of the l,	2416
	32:27	terror of the mighty in the land of the l.	2416
	32:32	have caused my terror in the land of the l:	2416
Da	2:30	any wisdom that I have more than any l,	2417
	4:17	to the intent that the l may know that	2417
	6:20	O Daniel, servant of the l God, is thy God,	2417
	6:26	for he is the l God, and stedfast for ever,	2417
Hos	1:10	unto them, Ye are the sons of the l God.	2416
Zec	14: 8	that l waters shall go out from Jerusalem:	2416
Mt	16:16	Thou art the Christ, the Son of the l God.	2198
	22:32	is not the God of the dead, but of the l.	2198
	26:63	said unto him, I adjure thee by the l God,	2198
Mk	12:27	God of the dead, but the God of the l:	2198
	12:44	did cast in all that she had, even all her l.	979
Lk	8:43	which had spent all her l upon physicians,	979
	15:12	to me. And he divided unto them his l.	979
	15:13	there wasted his substance with riotous l.	2198
	15:30	which hath devoured thy l with harlots,	979
	20:38	he is not a God of the dead, but of the l:	2198
	21: 4	she of her penury hath cast in all that l	979
	24: 5	Why seek ye the l among the dead?	2198
Jn	4:10	and he would have given thee l water.	2198
	4:11	from whence then hast thou that l water?	2198
	6:51	I am the l bread which came down from	2198
	6:57	As the l Father hath sent me, and I live by	2198
	6:69	thou art that Christ, the Son of the l God.	2198
	7:38	out of his belly shall flow rivers of l water.	2198
Ac	14:15	turn from these vanities unto the l God,	2198
Ro	9:26	they be called the children of the l God.	2198
	12: 1	that ye present your bodies a l sacrifice,	2198
	14: 9	he might be Lord both of the dead and l.	2198
1Co	15:45	The first man Adam was made a l soul;	2198
2Co	3: 3	with ink, but with the Spirit of the l God;	2198
	6:16	for ye are the temple of the l God; as God	2198
Col	2:20	why, as though l in the world, are ye	2198
1Th	1: 9	ye turned to God from idols to serve the l	2198
1Ti	3:15	is the church of the l God, the pillar	2198
	4:10	because we trust in the l God,	2198
	6:17	trust in uncertain riches, but in the l God,	2198
Tit	3: 3	l in malice and envy, hateful,	1236
Heb	3:12	of unbelief, in departing from the l God.	2198
	9:14	from dead works to serve the l God?	2198
	10:20	By a new and l way, which he hath	2198
	10:31	thing to fall into the hands of the l God.	2198
	12:22	unto the city of the l God, the heavenly	2198
1Pe	2: 4	To whom coming, as unto a l stone,	2198
Rev	7: 2	the east, having the seal of the l God:	2198
	7:17	shall lead them unto l fountains of waters:	2198
	16: 3	man: and every l soul died in the sea.	2198

LIZARD (1)

Lev	11:30	and the l, and the snail, and the mole.	3911

LO (159)

Ge	8:11	l, in her mouth was an olive leaf pluckt	2009
	15: 3	and I, one born in my house is mine heir.	2009
	15:12	and, l, a horror of great darkness fell upon	2009
	18: 2	he lift up his eyes and looked, and, l,	2009
	18:10	and l, Sarah thy wife shall have a son.	2009
	19:28	the land of the plain, and beheld, and, l,	2009
	29: 2	and behold a well in the field, and l,	2009
	29: 7	he said, L, it is yet high day, neither is it	2005
	37: 7	l, my sheaf arose, and also stood upright;	2009
	42:28	is restored; and l, it is even in my sack:	2009
	47:23	l, here is seed for you, and ye shall sow	1887
	48:11	and l, God hath shewed me also thy seed.	2009
	50: 5	father made me swear, saying, L, I die:	2009
Ex	7:15	l, he goeth out unto the water;	2009
	8:20	l, he cometh forth to the water;	2009
	8:26	l, shall we sacrifice the abomination of	2005
	19: 9	L, I come unto thee in a thick cloud,	2009
Nu	14:40	saying, L, we be here, and will go up unto	2009
	22:38	said unto Balak, L, I am come unto thee:	2009
	23: 9	he returned unto him, and l, he stood by	2009
	23: 9	l, the people shall dwell alone, and shall	2005
	24:11	l, the Lord hath kept thee back from	2009
Dt	22:17	l, he hath given occasions of speech	2009
Jos	14:10	now l, I am this day fourscore and	2009
Jdg	7:13	said, Behold, I dreamed a dream, and l,	2009
	13: 5	For l, thou shalt conceive, and bear a son;	2009
1Sa	4:13	when he came, l, Eli sat upon a seat by	2009
	10: 2	l, thy father hath left the care of the asses,	2009
1Sa	14:43	that was in mine hand, and l, I must die.	2009
	21:14	his servants, L, ye see the man is mad:	2009
2Sa	1: 6	l, the chariots and horsemen followed	2009
	15:24	l Zadok also, and all the Levites were	2009
	24:17	said, L, I have sinned, and I have done	2009
1Ki	1:22	l, while she yet talked with the king,	2009
	1:51	for l, he hath caught hold on the horns of	2009
	3:12	l, I have given thee a wise and	2009
2Ki	7: 6	they said one to another, L, the king of	2009
	7:15	l, all the way was full of garments and	2009
1Ch	17: 1	L, I dwell in an house of cedars, but the	2009
	21:23	l, I give thee the oxen also for burnt	7200
2Ch	16:11	behold, the acts of Asa, first and last, l,	2009
	25:19	Thou sayest, L, thou hast smitten	2009
	27: 7	l they are written in the book of the kings	2009
	29: 9	l, our fathers have fallen by the sword,	2009
Ne	5: 5	l, we bring into bondage our sons and our	2009
	6:12	l, I perceived that God had not sent him;	2009
Job	3: 7	L, let that night be solitary, let no joyful	2009
	5:27	L this, we have searched it, so it is; hear	2009
	9:11	l, he goeth by me, and I see him not:	2005
	9:19	If l speak of strength, l, he is strong:	2009
	13: 1	L, mine eye hath seen all this, mine ear	2009
	21:16	L, their good is not in their hand:	2005
	26:14	L, these are parts of his ways: but how	2005
	33:29	L, all these things worketh God	2005
	40:16	L now, his strength is in his loins,	2009
Ps	11: 2	For l, the wicked bend their bow,	2009
	37:36	Yet he passed away, and l, he was not:	2009
	40: 7	l, I come: in the volume of the book	2009
	48: 4	For l, the kings were assembled,	2009
	52: 7	L, this is the man that made not God his	2009
	55: 7	L, then would I wander far off,	2009
	59: 3	For l, they lie in wait for my soul:	2005
	68:33	l, he doth send out his voice, and that a	2005
	73:27	For l, they that are far from thee shall	2009
	83: 2	For l, thine enemies make a tumult:	2009
	92: 9	For l, thine enemies, O Lord, for lo,	2009
	92: 9	For lo, thine enemies, O Lord, for l,	2009
	127: 3	l, children are an heritage of the Lord:	2009
	132: 6	L, we heard of it at Ephratah: we found	2009
	139: 4	but l, O Lord, thou knowest it	2005
Pr	24:31	l, it was all grown over with thorns,	2009
Ecc	1:16	saying, L, I am come to great estate,	2009
	7:29	L, this only have I found, that God hath	7200
SS	2:11	For l, the winter is past, the rain is over	2009
Isa	6: 7	and said, L, this hath touched thy lips;	2009
	25: 9	be said in that day, L, this is our God;	2009
	36: 6	L, thou trustest in the staff of this broken	2009
	49:12	l, these from the north and from the west;	2009
	50: 9	l, they all shall wax old as a garment;	2005
Jer	1:15	For l, I will call all the families of	2009
	4:23	I beheld the earth, and l, it was without	2009
	4:24	l, they trembled, and all the hills moved	2009
	4:25	I beheld, and l, there was no man,	2009
	4:26	I beheld, and l, the fruitful place was a	2009
	5:15	L, I will bring a nation upon you from far,	2009
	8: 8	L, certainly in vain made he it; the pen of	2009
	8: 9	l, they have rejected the word of	2009
	25:29	For l, I begin to bring evil on the city	2009
	30: 3	For l, the days come, saith the Lord,	2009
	30:10	for l, I will save thee from afar, and thy	2009
	36:12	l, all the princes sat there, even Elishama	2009
	49:15	For l, I will make thee small among	2009
	50: 9	For l, I will raise and cause to come up	2009
Eze	2: 9	and l, a roll of a book was therein;	2009
	4:15	said unto me, L, I have given thee cow's	7200
	8: 2	and l, a likeness as the appearance	2009
	8:17	and l, they put the branch to their nose.	2009
	13:10	built up a wall, and l, others daubed it	2009
	13:12	L, when the wall is fallen, shall it not be	2009
	17:18	when l, he had given his hand,	2009
	18:14	Now l, if he beget a son, that seeth all his	2009
	18:18	l, even he shall die in his iniquity.	2009
	23:39	l, thus have they done in the midst of	2009
	23:40	a messenger was sent; and l, they came:	2009
	30: 9	as in the day of Egypt: for l, it cometh.	2009
	30:21	l, it shall not be bound up to be healed,	2009
	33:32	l, thou art unto them as a very lovely song	2009
	33:33	when this cometh to pass, (l, it will come)	2009
	37: 2	the open valley; and l, they were very dry.	2009
	37: 8	l, the sinews and the flesh came up upon	2009
	40:17	l, there were chambers, and a pavement	2009
	42: 8	l, before the temple were an hundred	2009
Da	3:25	He answered and said, L, I see four men	1888
	7: 6	this I beheld, and l another, like a leopard,	718
	10:13	l, Michael, one of the chief princes, came	2009
	10:20	when I am gone forth, l, the prince of	2009
Hos	9: 6	l, they are gone because of destruction:	2009
Am	4: 2	that l, the days shall come upon you, that	2009
	4:13	For l, he that formeth the mountains,	2009
	7: 1	l, it was the latter growth after the king's	2009
	7: 7	l, I will command, and I will sift	2009
Hab	1: 6	For l, I raise up the Chaldeans, that bitter	2009
Hag	1: 9	l looked for much, and l, it came to little;	2009
Zec	2:10	For l, I come, and I will dwell in the midst	2009
	11: 6	l, I will deliver the men every one into his	2009
	11:16	For l, I will raise up a shepherd in the land,	2009
Mt	2: 9	l, the star, which they saw in the east,	2400
	3:16	l, the heavens were opened unto him,	2400
	3:17	And l a voice from heaven, saying, This is	2400
	24:23	say unto you, L, here is Christ, or there;	2400
	25:25	the earth: l, there thou hast that is thine.	2396
	26:47	l, Judas, one of the twelve, came,	2400
Mt	28: 7	there shall ye see him: l, I have told you.	2400
	28:20	l, I am with you alway, even unto	2400
Mk	10:28	L, we have left all, and have followed	2400
	13:21	man shall say to you, L, here is Christ;	2400
	13:21	you, Lo, here is Christ; or l, he is there;	2400
	14:42	go; l, he that betrayeth me is at hand.	2400
Lk	1:44	l, as soon as the voice of thy salutation	2400
	2: 9	And l, the angel of the Lord came upon	2400
	9:39	l, a spirit taketh him, and he suddenly	2400
	13:16	Satan hath bound, l these eighteen years,	2400
	15:29	L, these many years do I serve thee,	2400
	17:21	Neither shall they say, L here is: or, lo there:	2400
	17:21	l there: for behold, the kingdom of God	2400
	18:28	Then Peter said, L, we have left all,	2400
	23:15	and l, nothing worthy of death is done	2400
Jn	7:26	But l, he speaketh boldly, and they say	2396
	16:29	L, now speakest thou plainly,	2396
Ac	13:46	everlasting life, we turn to the Gentiles.	2400
	27:24	l, God hath given thee all them that sail	2400
Heb	10: 7	Then said l, L, I come (in the volume of	2400
	10: 9	Then said he, L, I come to do thy will,	2400
Rev	5: 6	And I beheld, and l, in the midst of	2400
	6: 5	And I beheld, and l a black horse;	2400
	6:12	and l, there was a great earthquake;	2400
	7: 9	I beheld, and l, a great multitude,	2400
	14: 1	And I looked, and l, a Lamb stood on	2400

LOAD See LADE; LADED; LADING

LOADEN (1) [LOADETH]

Isa	46: 1	your carriages were heavy l; they are a	6006

LOADETH (1) [LOADEN]

Ps	68:19	daily l us with benefits, even the God	6006

LOAF (3) [LOAVES]

Ex	29:23	l of bread, and one cake of oiled bread,	3603
1Ch	16: 3	every one a l of bread, and a good piece	3603
Mk	8:14	in the ship with them more than one l.	740

LO-AMMI (1) [AMMI]

Hos	1: 9	said God, Call his name L: for ye are not	3818

LOAN (1)

1Sa	2:20	for the l which is lent to the Lord.	7596

LOATHE (1) [LOATHETH, LOATHSOME, LOTHE]

Job	7:16	I l it; I would not live alway: let me alone;	3988

LOATHETH (2) [LOATHE]

Nu	21: 5	any water; and our soul l this light bread.	6973
Pr	27: 7	The full soul l a honeycomb; but to	947

LOATHSOME (4) [LOATHE]

Nu	11:20	out at your nostrils, and it be l unto you:	2214
Job	6: 7	dust; my skin is broken, and become l.	3988
Ps	38: 7	For my loins are filled with a l disease:	7033
Pr	13: 5	a wicked man is l, and cometh to shame.	887

LOAVES (32) [LOAF]

Lev	23:17	habitations two wave l of two tenth deals:	3899
Jdg	8: 5	l of bread unto the people that follow me;	3603
1Sa	10: 3	another carrying three l of bread,	3603
	10: 4	salute thee, and give thee two l of bread;	NIH
	17:17	of this parched corn, and these ten l,	3899
	21: 3	give me five l of bread in mine hand,	NIH
	25:18	took two hundred l, and two bottles of	3899
2Sa	16: 1	upon them two hundred l of bread,	NIH
1Ki	14: 3	And take with thee ten l, and cracknels,	3899
2Ki	4:42	twenty l of barley, and full ears of corn in	3899
Mt	14:17	We have here but five l, and two fishes.	740
	14:19	and took the five l, and the two fishes,	740
	14:19	and gave the l to his disciples,	740
	15:34	saith unto them, How many l have ye?	740
	15:36	And he took the seven l and the fishes,	740
	16: 9	neither remember the five l of the five	740
	16:10	Neither the seven l of the four thousand,	740
Mk	6:38	He saith unto them, How many l have ye?	740
	6:41	And when he had taken the five l	740
	6:41	and brake the l, and gave them to his	740
	6:44	they that did eat of the l were about five	740
	6:52	they considered not the miracle of the l.	740
	8: 5	And he asked them, How many l have ye?	740
	8: 6	and he took the seven l, and gave thanks,	740
	8:19	When I brake the five l among five	740
Lk	9:13	We have no more but five l and two fishes;	740
	9:16	Then he took the five l and the two fishes,	740
	11: 5	and say unto him, Friend, lend me three l;	740
Jn	6: 9	which hath five barley l, and two small	740
	6:11	Jesus took the l; and when he had given	740
	6:13	with the fragments of the five barley l,	740
	6:26	but because ye did eat of the l,	740

LOCK (2) [LOCKED, LOCKS]

SS	5: 5	smelling myrrh, upon the handles of the l.	4514
Eze	8: 3	a hand, and took me by a l of mine head;	6734

LOCKED (2) [LOCK]

Jdg	3:23	doors of the parlour upon him, and l	5274
	3:24	the doors of the parlour were l, they said,	5274

LOCKS (15) [LOCK]

Nu	6: 5	shall let the l of the hair of his head grow.	6545
Jdg	16:13	If thou weavest the seven l of my head	4253
	16:19	she caused him to shave off the seven l of	4253
Ne	3: 3	l thereof, and the bars thereof.	4514

Ne
3: 6 and the l thereof, and the bars thereof. 4514
3:13 the l thereof, and the bars thereof. 4514
3:14 the l thereof, and the bars thereof. 4514
3:15 the l thereof, and the bars thereof. 4514

SS
4: 1 fair; thou *hast* doves' eyes within thy l: 6777
4: 3 a piece of a pomegranate within thy l. 6777
5: 2 *and* my l *with* the drops of the night. 6977
5:11 his l *are* bushy, *and* black as a raven. 6977
6: 7 pomegranate *are* thy temples within thy l. 6777
Isa 47: 2 uncover thy l, make bare the leg, 6777
Eze 44:20 heads, nor suffer *their* l to grow long; 6545

LOCUST (11) [LOCUSTS]
Ex 10:19 there remained not one l in all the coasts of 697
Lev 11:22 the l after his kind, and the bald locust 697
11:22 the **bald** l after his kind, and the beetle 5556
Dt 28:38 *but* little in; for the l shall consume it. 697
28:42 and fruit of thy land shall the l consume. 6767
1Ki 8:37 mildew, l, *or* if there be caterpillar; 697
Ps 78:46 the caterpillar, and their labour unto the l. 697
109:23 I am tossed up and down as the l. 697
Joel 1: 4 the palmerworm hath left hath the l eaten; 697
1: 4 that which the l hath left hath 697
2:25 will restore to you the years that the l hath 697

LOCUSTS (17) [LOCUST]
Ex 10: 4 to morrow will I bring the l into thy coast: 697
10:12 thine hand over the land of Egypt for the l, 697
10:13 was morning, the east wind brought the l. 697
10:14 the l went up over all the land of Egypt, 697
10:14 before them there were no such l as they, 697
10:19 which took away the l, and cast them into 697
2Ch 6:28 be blasting, or mildew, l, or caterpillars; 697
7:13 or if I command the l to devour the land, 2284
Ps 105:34 the l came, and caterpillars, and that 697
Pr 30:27 The have no king, yet go they forth all of 697
Isa 33: 4 and fro of l shall he run upon them. 1357
Na 3:15 cankerworm, make thyself many as the l. 697
3:17 Thy crowned *are* as the l, and thy captains 697
Mt 3: 4 loins; and his meat was l and wild honey. 200
Mk 1: 6 his loins; and he did eat l and wild honey; 200
Rev 9: 3 And there came out of the smoke l upon 200
9: 7 the shapes of the l *were* like unto horses 200

LOD (4)
1Ch 8:12 and Shamed, who built Ono, and **L**, 3850
Ezr 2:33 The children of **L**, Hadid, and Ono, 3850
Ne 7:37 The children of **L**, Hadid, and Ono, 3850
11:35 **L**, and Ono, the valley of craftsmen. 3850

LO-DEBAR (3)
2Sa 9: 4 house of Machir, the son of Ammiel, in **L**. 3810
9: 5 of Machir, the son of Ammiel, from **L**. 3810
17:27 Machir the son of Ammiel, of **L**, 3810

LODGE (27) [LODGED, LODGEST, LODGETH, LODGING, LODGINGS]
Ge 24:23 room *in* thy father's house for us to l in? 3885
24:25 and provender enough, and room to l in. 3885
Nu 22: 8 **L** here *this* night, and I will bring you 3885
Jos 3: 1 lodging place, where you shall l *this* night. 3885
Jdg 19: 9 behold, the day groweth to an end, l here, 3885
19:11 in into this city of the Jebusites, and l in it. 3885
19:13 near to one of *these* places to l **all night**, 3885
19:15 aside thither, to go in *and* to l in Gibeah: 3885
19:20 *lie* upon me; only l not in the street. 3885
20: 4 to Benjamin, I and my concubine, to l. 3885
Ru 1:16 I will go; and where thou lodgest, I will l: 3885
2Sa 17: 8 of war, and will not l with the people. 3885
17:16 l not *this* night in the plains of 3885
Ne 4:22 Let every one with his servant l within 3885
13:21 said unto them, Why I ye about the wall? 3885
Job 24: 7 **cause** the naked to l without clothing, 3885
31:32 The stranger did not l in the street: 3885
SS 7:11 forth *into* the field; let us l in the villages. 3885
Isa 1: 8 as a l in a garden of cucumbers, as a 4412
21:13 In the forest in Arabia shall ye l, O ye 3885
65: 4 l in the monuments, which eat swine's 3885
Jer 4:14 How long shall thy vain thoughts l within 3885
Zep 2:14 the bittern shall l in the upper lintels of it; 3885
Mt 13:32 air come and l in the branches thereof. 2681
Mk 4:32 that the fowls of the air may l under 2681
Lk 9:12 round about, and l, and get victuals: 2647
Ac 21:16 an old disciple, with whom we should l. 3579

LODGED (21) [LODGE]
Ge 32:13 he l there that *same* night; and took of 3885
32:21 and himself l that night in the company. 3885
Jos 2: 1 harlot's house, named Rahab, and l there. 7901
3: 1 and l there before they passed over. 3885
4: 8 with them unto the **place where** they l, 4411
6:11 came *into* the camp, and l in the camp. 3885
8: 9 but Joshua l that night among the people. 3885
Jdg 18: 2 to the house of Micah, they l there. 3885
19: 4 so they did eat and drink, and l there. 3885
19: 7 urged him: therefore he l there again. 3885
1Ki 19: 9 he came thither unto a cave, and l there; 3885
1Ch 9:27 they l round about the house of God, 3885
Ne 13:20 sellers of all *kind* of ware l without 3885
Isa 1:21 righteousness l in it; but now murderers. 3885
Mt 21:17 of the city into Bethany; and he l there. 835
Lk 13:19 the fowls of the air l in the branches of it. 2681
Ac 10:18 which was surnamed Peter, were l there. 3579
10:23 l them. And on the morrow Peter went 3579
10:32 he is l in the house of *one* Simon a tanner 3579

Ac 28: 7 and l *us* three days courteously. 3579
1Ti 5:10 up children, if she have l **strangers**, 3580

LODGEST (1) [LODGE]
Ru 1:16 I will go; and where thou l, I will lodge: 3885

LODGETH (1) [LODGE]
Ac 10: 6 He l with one Simon a tanner, whose 3579

LODGING (6) [LODGE]
Jos 4: 3 leave them in the **l place**, where you shall 4411
Jdg 19:15 no man that took them into *his* house to l. 3885
Isa 10:29 they have **taken up** their l at Geba; 4411
Jer 9: 2 that I had in the wilderness a l **place** of 4411
Ac 28:23 a day, there came many to him into *his* l; 3578
Phm 1:22 But withal prepare me also a l: for I trust 3578

LODGINGS (1) [LODGE]
2Ki 19:23 and I will enter *into* the l of his borders, 4411

LOFT (2)
1Ki 17:19 carried him up into a l, where he abode, 5944
Ac 20: 9 and fell down from the **third l**, 5152

LOFTILY (1) [LOFTY]
Ps 73: 8 oppression: they speak l. 4480+4791

LOFTINESS (2) [LOFTY]
Isa 2:17 of man shall be bowed down, 1365
Jer 48:29 his l, and his arrogancy, and his pride, 1363

LOFTY (8) [LOFTILY, LOFTINESS]
Ps 131: 1 my heart is not haughty, nor mine eyes l: 7311
Pr 30:13 *is* a generation, O how l are their eyes! 7311
Isa 2:11 The l looks of man shall be humbled, 1365
2:12 *be* upon every one *that is* proud and l, 7311
5:15 and the eyes of the l shall be humbled: 1364
26: 5 l city, he layeth it low; he layeth it low, 7682
57: 7 Upon a l and high mountain hast thou set 1364
57:15 high and l One that inhabiteth eternity, 5375

LOG (5)
Lev 14:10 mingled with oil, and one l of oil. 3849
14:12 the l of oil, and wave them *for* a wave 3849
14:15 the priest shall take *some* of the l of oil, 3849
14:21 with oil for a meat offering, and a l of oil; 3849
14:24 of oil, and the priest shall wave them 3849

LOINS (63)
Ge 35:11 of thee, and kings shall come out of thy l; 2504
37:34 put sackcloth upon his l, and mourned for 4975
46:26 which came out of his l, besides Jacob's 3409
Ex 1: 5 the souls that came *out of* the l of Jacob 3409
12:11 your l girded, your shoes on your feet, 4975
28:42 from the l even unto the thighs they shall 4975
Dt 33:11 smite through the l of them that rise 4975
2Sa 20: 8 fastened upon his l in the sheath thereof; 4975
1Ki 2: 5 war upon his girdle that *was* about his l, 4975
8:19 thy son that shall come forth out of thy l, 2504
12:10 *finger* shall be thicker than my father's l. 4975
18:46 he girded up his l, and ran before Ahab to 4975
20:31 put sackcloth on our l, and ropes upon 4975
20:32 So they girded sackcloth on their l, 4975
2Ki 1: 8 girt with a girdle of leather about his l. 4975
4:29 Gird up thy l, and take my staff in thine 4975
9: 1 Gird up thy l, and take this box of oil in 4975
2Ch 6: 9 son which shall come forth out of thy l, 2504
10:10 *finger* shall be thicker than my father's l. 4975
Job 12:18 of kings, and girdeth their l with a girdle. 2504
31:20 If his l have not blessed me, and *if* he 2504
38: 3 Gird up now thy l like a man; for I will 2504
40: 7 Gird up thy l now like a man: I will 2504
40:16 his strength *is* in his l, and his force is in 4975
Ps 38: 7 For my l are filled *with* a loathsome 3689
66:11 the net; thou laidst affliction upon our l. 4975
69:23 and make their l continually to shake. 4975
Pr 31:17 She girdeth her l with strength, 4975
Isa 5:27 shall the girdle of their l be loosed, 4975
11: 5 righteousness shall be the girdle of his l, 4975
20: 2 Go and loose the sackcloth from off thy l, 4975
21: 3 Therefore are my l filled *with* pain: 4975
32:11 ye bare, and gird *sackcloth upon* your l. 2504
45: 1 will loose the l of kings, to open before 4975
Jer 1:17 Thou therefore gird up thy l, and arise, 4975
13: 1 put it upon thy l, and put it not in water. 4975
13: 2 the word of the Lord, and put *it* on my l. 4975
13: 4 which *is* upon thy l, and arise, go to 4975
13:11 as the girdle cleaveth to the l of a man, 4975
30: 6 I see every man with his hands on his l, 2504
48:37 *be* cuttings, and upon the l sackcloth. 4975
Eze 1:27 from the appearance of his l even 4975
1:27 from the appearance of his l even 4975
8: 2 from the appearance of his l even 4975
8: 2 from his l even upward, as the 4975
21: 6 son of man, with the breaking of *thy* l; 4975
23:15 Girded with girdles upon their l, 4975
29: 7 and madest all their l to be at a stand. 4975
44:18 shall have linen breeches upon their l; 4975
47: 4 me through; the waters *were* to the l. 4975
Da 5: 6 so that the joints of his l were loosed, 2783
10: 5 whose l *were* girded with fine gold of 4975
Am 8:10 I will bring up sackcloth upon all l, 4975
Na 2: 1 watch the way, make *thy* l strong, 4975
2:10 much pain *is in* all l, and the faces of 4975
Mt 3: 4 and a leathern girdle about his l; 3751
Mk 1: 6 and with a girdle of a skin about his l; 3751

Lk 12:35 Let your l be girded about, and *your* lights 3751
Ac 2:30 that of the fruit of his l, according to 3751
Eph 6:14 having your l girt about with truth, 3751
Heb 7: 5 they come out of the l of Abraham: 3751
7:10 For he was yet in the l of his father, 3751
1Pe 1:13 Wherefore gird up the l of your mind, 3751

LOIS (1)
2Ti 1: 5 which dwelt first in thy grandmother **L**, 3090

LONG (211) [LENGTH, LONGED, LONGEDST, LONGETH, LONGING]
Ge 26: 8 to pass, when he had been there a l time, 748
48:15 God which fed me **all** my life l 4480+5750
Ex 10: 3 Lord God of the Hebrews, **How** l 4970+5704
10: 7 servants said unto him, **How** l 4970+5704
16:28 said unto Moses, **How** l 575+5704+1886.5
19:13 when the trumpet **soundeth** l, they shall 4900
19:19 when the voice of the trumpet **sounded** l, 1980
20:12 that thy days may be l upon the land which 748
27: 1 five cubits l, and five cubits broad; 753
27: 9 linen of an hundred cubits l for one side: 753
27:11 *shall be* hangings of an hundred *cubits* l, 753
Lev 18:19 as l as she is put apart for her 871.1
26:34 **as l** as it lieth desolate, and ye *be* 3117+3605
26:35 **As l** as it lieth desolate it shall rest; 3117+3605
Nu 9:18 **as l** as the cloud abode upon 3117+3605
9:19 the cloud **tarried** l upon the tabernacle 748
14:11 said unto Moses, **How** l 575+5704+1886.5
14:11 **how** l will it be ere they 575+5704+1886.5
14:27 **How** l *shall I bear* with this evil 4970+5704
20:15 and we have dwelt in Egypt a l time; 7227
Dt 1: 6 Ye have dwelt l **enough** in this mount: 7227
2: 3 have compassed this mountain l **enough**: 7227
4:25 ye shall have **remained** l in the land, 3462
12:19 Levite **as** l as thou livest upon the earth. 3605
14:24 if the way be too l for thee, so that thou 7235
19: 6 because the way is l, and slay him; 7235
20:19 When thou shalt besiege a city a l time, 7227
28:32 fail *with longing* for them all the day l: NIH
28:59 of l **continuance**, and sore sicknesses, 539
28:59 sore sicknesses, and of l **continuance**. 539
31:13 **as l** as ye live in 834+3117+3605+1886.1
33:12 *the Lord* shall cover him all the day l, NIH
Jos 6: 5 that *when they* **make a l blast** with 4900
9:13 old by reason of the very l journey. 7230
11:18 Joshua made war a l time with all those 7227
18: 3 children of Israel, **How** l 575+5704+1886.5
23: 1 it came to pass a l time after that 7227
24: 7 and ye dwelt in the wilderness a l season. 7227
Jdg 5:28 Why is his chariot so l in coming? 954
1Sa 1:14 Eli said unto her, **How** l wilt thou 4970+5704
1:28 **as** l as he liveth he 834+3117+3605+1886.1
7: 2 in Kirjath-jearim, that the time was l: 7235
16: 1 the Lord said unto Samuel, **How** l 4970+5704
20:31 For **as** l as the son of Jesse 3117+3605+1886.1
25:15 **as** l as we were conversant with 3117+3605
29: 8 **so** l as I have been with thee unto 3117+4480
2Sa 2:26 bitterness in the latter end? **how** l 4970+5704
3: 1 Now there was l war between the house 752
14: 2 as a woman *that had* a l time mourned 7227
19:34 the king, **How** l 3117+4100+8141+3509.1
1Ki 3:11 and hast not asked for thyself l life; 7227
6:17 *is*, the temple before it, was forty cubits *l*. NIH
18:21 **How** l halt ye between two 4970+5704
2Ki 9:22 **so** l as the whoredoms of thy mother 5704
9:25 Hast thou not heard l **ago** 4480+7350+3807.1
2Ch 1:11 enemies, neither yet hast asked l life; 7227
3:11 of the cherubims *were* twenty cubits l: 753
6:13 of five cubits l, and five cubits broad, 753
6:31 **so** l as they live in 3117+3605+1886.1
15: 3 for a l season Israel *hath been* without 7227
26: 5 **as** l as he sought the Lord, 3117+871.1
30: 5 they had not done it of a l *time* in such 7230
36:21 for **as** l as *she* lay desolate she kept 3117+3605
Ne 2: 6 **For how** l shall thy journey be? 4970+5704
Est 5:13 **so** l as I see Mordecai the Jew 3605+871.1
Job 3:21 Which l for death, but it *cometh* not; 2442
6: 8 would grant *me* the thing that I l **for!** 8615
7:19 **How** l wilt thou not depart from 4100+3509.1
8: 2 **How** l wilt thou speak these *things*? 5704
8: 2 *how* l shall the words of thy mouth *be* NIH
18: 2 **How** l will it be *ere* you 575+5704+1886.5
19: 2 **How** l will ye vex my soul, 575+5704+1886.5
27: 6 heart shall not reproach *me* so l as I live. 4480
Ps 4: 2 *how* l *will ye* turn my glory into 5704
4: 2 *how* l will ye love vanity, *and* seek after NIH
6: 3 but thou, O Lord, **how** l? 4970+5704
13: 1 **How** l wilt thou forget me, 575+5704+1886.5
13: 1 **how** l wilt thou hide 575+5704+1886.5
13: 2 **How** l shall I take counsel 575+5704+1886.5
13: 2 **how** l shall mine enemy be 575+5704+1886.5
32: 3 old through my roaring all the day l. NIH
35:17 Lord, **how** l wilt thou look on? 4100+3509.1
35:28 *and* of thy praise all the day l. NIH
38: 6 down greatly; I go mourning all the day l. NIH
38:12 and imagine deceits all the day l. NIH
44: 8 In God we boast all the day l, and praise NIH
44:22 Yea, for thy sake are we killed all the day l; NIH
62: 3 **How** l will ye imagine 575+5704+1886.5
71:24 shall talk of thy righteousness all the day l: NIH
72: 5 They shall fear thee **as l as** the sun and 5973
72: 7 peace **so l as** the moon **endureth**. 1097+5704
72:17 name shall be continued **as l as** 6440+3807.1
73:14 For all the day l have I been plagued, NIH

L

Ps
74: 9 among us any that knoweth **how** l. 4100+5704
74:10 O God, **how** l shall the adversary 4970+5704
79: 5 **How** l, Lord? wilt thou be angry, 4100+5704
80: 4 O Lord God of hosts, **how** l wilt 4970+5704
82: 2 **How** l will ye judge unjustly, 4970+5704
89:46 **How** l, Lord? wilt thou hide 4100+5704
90:13 Return, O Lord, **how** l? and let it 4970+5704
91:16 With l life will I satisfy him, and shew him 753
94: 3 Lord, **how** l shall the wicked, 4970+5704
94: 3 **how** l shall the wicked triumph? 4970+5704
94: 4 How l they utter and speak hard NIH
95:10 Forty years l was I grieved with this NIH
104:33 I will sing unto the Lord **as l as** I live: 871.1
116: 2 will I call upon him **as l as** I live. 871.1
120: 6 My soul hath l dwelt with him that hateth 7227
129: 3 upon my back: they **made** l their furrows. 748
143: 3 darkness, as those that have been l dead. 5769

Pr
1:22 How l, ye simple ones, will ye love 4970+5704
3: 2 For length of days, and l life, and peace, 8141
6: 9 **How** l wilt thou sleep, O sluggard? 4970+5704
7:19 not at home, he is gone a l journey: 4480+7350
21:26 He coveteth greedily all the day l: NIH
23:17 thou in the fear of the Lord all the day l. NIH
23:30 They that **tarry** l at the wine; they that go 309
25:15 By l forbearing is a prince persuaded, 753

Ecc
12: 5 because man goeth to his l home, 5769

Isa
6:11 said l, Lord, **how** l? And he 4970+5704
22:11 unto him that fashioned it l ago. 4480+7350
37:26 Hast thou not heard l ago, 4480+7350+3807.1
42:14 I have l time holden my peace; I have 5769
65:22 mine elect shall l enjoy the work of their 1086

Jer
4:14 that thou mayest be saved. How l 4970+5704
4:21 How l shall I see the standard, 4970+5704
12: 4 How l shall the land mourn, 4970+5704
23:26 How l shall this in the heart of the 4970+5704
29:28 us in Babylon, saying, This captivity is l: 752
31:22 How l wilt thou go about, O thou 4970+5704
47: 5 the remnant of their valley: **how** l 4970+5704
47: 6 sword of the Lord, **how** l 575+5704+1886.5

La
2:20 eat their fruit, and children of a **span** l? 2949
5:20 forget us for ever, and forsake us so l time? 753

Eze
31: 5 his branches became l because of 748
40: 5 measuring reed of six cubits l by the cubit NIH
40: 7 And every little chamber was one reed l, 753
40:29 it was fifty cubits l, and five and 753
40:30 round about were five and twenty cubits l, 753
40:33 it was fifty cubits l, and five and 753
40:42 a cubit and a half l, and a cubit and a half 753
40:47 hundred cubits l, and an hundred cubits 753
41:13 measured the house, an hundred cubits l; 753
41:13 with the walls thereof, an hundred cubits l; 753
42:11 north, as l as they, and as broad as they: 753
42:20 five hundred reeds l, and five hundred 753
43:16 the altar shall be twelve cubits l, twelve 753
43:17 the settle shall be fourteen cubits l and 753
44:20 nor **suffer** their locks to grow l; 7971
45: 6 and five and twenty thousand l, 753
46:22 there were courts joined of forty cubits l 753

Da
8:13 certain saint which spake, How l 4970+5704
10: 1 was true, but the time appointed was l: 1419
12: 6 the waters of the river, How l 4970+5704

Hos
5: 8 is kindled against them: how l 4970+5704
13:13 for he should not stay l in the place of 6256

Hab
1: 2 O Lord, how l shall I cry, 575+5704+1886.5
2: 6 that which is not his! how l? 4970+5704

Zec
1:12 O Lord of hosts, how l wilt thou 4970+5704

Mt
9:15 **as l as** the bridegroom is with them? 1909+3745
11:21 Sidon they would have repented l ago in 3819
17:17 **how** l shall I be with you? 2193+4219
17:17 **how** l shall I suffer you? bring him 2193+4219
23:14 and for a pretence make l prayer: 3117
25:19 After a l time the lord of those servants 4183

Mk
2:19 **as l as** they have the bridegroom 3745+5550
9:19 **how** l shall I be with you? 2193+4219
9:19 **how** l shall I suffer you? bring him 2193+4219
9:21 How l is it ago since this came unto him? 5550
12:38 which love to go in l clothing, 4749
12:40 and for a pretence make l prayers: 3117
16: 5 right side, clothed in a l white **garment**; 4749

Lk
1:21 that he **tarried** so l in the temple. 5549
8:27 which had devils l time, and ware no 2425
9:41 **how** l shall I be with you, 2193+4219
18: 7 unto him, though he **bear** l with them? 3114
20: 9 and went into a far country for a l time. 2425
20:46 which desire to walk in l robes, 4749
20:47 and for a shew make l prayers: 3117
23: 8 he was desirous to see him of a l season, 2425

Jn
5: 6 knew that he had been now a l time 4183
9: 5 **As l as** I am in the world, I am the light 3752
10:24 How l dost thou make us to doubt? 2193+4219
14: 9 Have I been so l time with you, 5118

Ac
8:11 that of l time he had bewitched them 2425
14: 3 **L** time therefore abode they speaking 2425
14:28 And there they abode l time with 3641+3756
20: 9 as Paul was l preaching, he sunk 1909+4183
20:11 and eaten, and talked a l while, 1909+2425
27:14 But not l after there arose against it a 4183
27:21 But after l abstinence Paul stood forth in 4183

Ro
1:11 For I l to see you, that I may impart unto 1971
7: 1 a man, **as l as** he liveth? 1909+3745+5550
7: 2 by the law to her husband so l as he liveth; NIG
8:36 For thy sake we are killed all the day l; NIG
10:21 **All** day l have I stretched forth my hands 3650

1Co
7:39 **as l as** her husband liveth; 1909+3745+5550
11:14 if a man **have** l hair, it is a shame unto 2863
11:15 But if a woman **have** l hair, it is a glory 2863
13: 4 **Charity** suffereth l, and is kind; 3114

2Co
9:14 which l **after** you for the exceeding grace 1971

Gal
4: 1 the heir, **as l as** he is a child, 1909+3745+5550

Eph
6: 3 and thou mayest **live** l on the earth. 1510+3118

Php
1: 8 how **greatly** l **after** you all in the bowels 1971

1Ti
3:15 if l **tarry** l, that thou mayest know how 1019

Heb
4: 7 saying in David, To day, after **so** l a time; 5118

Jas
5: 7 hath l **patience** for it, until he receive 3114

1Pe
3: 6 as l as ye do well, and are not afraid **with** NIG

2Pe
1:13 **as l as** I am in this tabernacle, 1909+3745
3: 2 judgment now of a l time lingereth 1597

Rev
6:10 saying, How l, O Lord, holy and 2193+4219

LONGED (8) [LONG]

2Sa
3:39 the soul of king David l to go forth unto 3615
23:15 David l, and said, Oh that one would give 183
1Ch 11:17 David l, and said, Oh that one would give 183
Ps 119:40 Behold, I have l after thy precepts: 8373
119:131 panted: for I l for thy commandments. 2968
119:174 I have l for thy salvation, O Lord; 8373
Php
2:26 For he l **after** you all, and was full of 1971
4: 1 my brethren dearly beloved and l **for**, 1973

LONGEDST (1) [LONG]

Ge 31:30 thou **sore** l after thy father's house, 3700+3700

LONGER (17) [LENGTH]

Ex
2: 3 when she could not hide l him, she took 5750
9:28 I will let you go, and ye shall stay no l. 3254
Jdg 2:14 that they could not **any** l stand before 5750
2Sa 20: 5 he **tarried** l than the set time which he 309
2Ki 6:33 what should I wait for the Lord **any** l? 5750
Job 11: 9 The measure thereof is l than the earth, 752
Jer 44:22 So that the Lord could no l bear, 5750
Lk 16: 2 for thou mayest be no l steward. 2089
Ac 18:20 When they desired him to tarry l 1909+4183
25:24 crying that he ought not to live **any** l. 3371
Ro 6: 2 that are dead to sin, live **any** l therein? 2089
Gal 3:25 come, we are no l under a schoolmaster. 3765
1Th 3: 1 Wherefore when we could no l forbear, 3371
3: 5 For this cause, when I could no l forbear, 3371
1Ti 5:23 Drink no l water, but use a little wine for 3371
1Pe 4: 2 That he no l should live the rest of his 3371
Rev 10: 6 therein, that there should be time no l: 2089

LONGETH (4) [LONG]

Ge 34: 8 The soul of my son Shechem l for your 2836
Dt 12:20 eat flesh, because thy soul l to eat flesh; 183
Ps 63: 1 my flesh l for thee, in a dry and 3642
84: 2 My soul l, yea, even fainteth for the courts 3700

LONGING (3) [LONG]

Dt 28:32 and fail **with** l for them all the day long: NIH
Ps 107: 9 For he satisfieth the l soul, and filleth 8264
119:20 My soul breaketh for the l that it hath 8375

LONGSUFFERING (17) [LENGTH, SUFFER]

Ex 34: 6 l, and abundant in goodness and truth, 639+750
Nu 14:18 The Lord is l, and of great mercy, 639+750
Ps 86:15 l, and plenteous in mercy and truth. 639+750
Jer 15:15 take me not away in thy l: 639+750
Ro 2: 4 of his goodness and forbearance and l; 3115
9:22 endured with much l the vessels of wrath 3115
2Co 6: 6 by knowledge, by l, by kindness, 3115
Gal 5:22 joy, peace, l, gentleness, goodness, faith, 3115
Eph 4: 2 With all lowliness and meekness, with l, 3115
Col 1:11 unto all patience and l with joyfulness; 3115
3:12 humbleness of mind, meekness, l, 3115
1Ti 1:16 first Jesus Christ might shew forth all l, 3115
2Ti 3:10 of life, purpose, faith, l, charity, patience, 3115
4: 2 rebuke, exhort with all l and doctrine. 3115
1Pe 3:20 once the l of God waited in the days 3114
2Pe 3: 9 but is l to us-ward, not willing that any 3114
3:15 And account that the l of our Lord is 3115

LONGWINGED (1) [LENGTH, WING]

Eze 17: 3 l, full of feathers, which had divers 83+750

LOOK (155) [LOOKED, LOOKEST, LOOKETH, LOOKING, LOOKING-GLASSES, LOOKS]

Ge
9:16 I will l upon it, that I may remember 7200
12:11 that thou art a fair woman to l **upon**: 4758
13:14 l from the place where thou art 7200
15: 5 L now towards heaven, and tell the stars, 5027
19:17 l not behind thee, neither stay thou in all 5027
24:16 damsel was very fair to l **upon**, a virgin, 4758
26: 7 because she was fair to l **upon**. 4758
40: 7 Wherefore l ye so sadly to day? 6440
41:33 Pharaoh l **out** a man discreet and wise, 7200
42: 1 his sons, Why do ye l one upon another? 7200

Ex
3: 6 his face; for he was afraid to l upon God. 5027
5:21 The Lord l upon you, and judge; 7200
10:10 little ones: l to it; for evil is before you. 7200
25:20 and their faces shall l one to another; NIH
25:40 l that thou make them after their pattern, 7200
39:43 Moses did l upon all the work, and 7200

Lev
13: 3 the priest shall l on the plague in the skin 7200
13: 3 the priest shall l on him, 7200
13: 5 the priest shall l on him the seventh day: 7200
13: 6 the priest shall l on him again the seventh 7200
13:21 if the priest l on it, and behold, there be 7200
13:25 the priest shall l upon it: and behold, 7200
13:26 if the priest l on it, and behold, there be 7200
13:27 priest shall l upon him the seventh day: 7200
13:31 if the priest l on the plague of the scall, 7200
13:32 in the seventh day the priest shall l on 7200
13:34 in the seventh day the priest shall l on 7200
13:36 the priest shall l on him: and behold, 7200
13:39 the priest shall l: and behold, if the bright 7200
13:43 the priest shall l upon it: and behold, 7200
13:50 the priest shall l upon the plague, 7200
13:51 shall l on the plague on the seventh day: 7200
13:53 if the priest shall l, and behold, the plague 7200
13:55 the priest shall l on the plague, after that 7200
13:56 if the priest l, and behold, the plague be 7200
14: 3 the priest shall l, and behold, if the plague 7200
14:37 he shall l on the plague, and behold, 7200
14:39 come again the seventh day, and shall l: 7200
14:44 the priest shall come and l, and behold, 7200
14:48 shall come in, and l upon it, and behold, 7200
Nu 15:39 that ye may l upon it, and remember all 7200
Dt 9:27 l not unto the stubbornness of this people, 6437
26:15 L down from thy holy habitation, 8259
28:32 thine eyes shall l, and fail with longing for 6437
Jdg 7:17 said unto them, L on me, and do likewise: 7200
1Sa 1:11 thou wilt **indeed** l on the affliction 7200+7200
16: 7 L not on his countenance, or on the 5027
16:12 beautiful countenance, and goodly to l to. 7210
17:18 l how thy brethren fare, and take their 6485
2Sa 9: 8 thou shouldest l upon such a dead dog 6437
11: 2 the woman was very beautiful to l **upon**. 4758
16:12 It may be that the Lord will l on mine 7200
1Ki 18:43 his servant, Go up now, l toward the sea. 5027
2Ki 3:14 I would not l toward thee, nor see thee. 5027
6:32 l, when the messenger cometh, shut 7200
9: 2 l out there Jehu the son of Jehoshaphat 7200
10: 3 L even out the best and meetest of your 7200
10:23 l that there be here with you none of 7200
14: 8 Come, let us l one another in the face. 7200
1Ch 12:17 the God of our fathers l thereon, and 7200
2Ch 24:22 The Lord l upon it, and require it. 7200
Est 1:11 her beauty: for she was fair to l on. 4758
Job 3: 9 let it l for light, but have none; neither 6960
6:28 therefore be content, l upon me; for it 6437
20:21 therefore shall no **man** l for his goods. 2342
35: 5 L unto the heavens, and see; and behold 5027
40:12 L on every one that is proud, and bring 7200
Ps 5: 3 direct my prayer unto thee, and will l **up**. 6822
22:17 all my bones: they l and stare upon me. 7200
25:18 L upon mine affliction and my pain; 7200
35:17 Lord, how long wilt thou l? rescue my 7200
40:12 I am not able to l **up**; they are moe than 7200
80:14 l **down** from heaven, and behold, 5027
84: 9 and l **upon** the face of thine anointed. 5027
85:11 righteousness shall l **down** from heaven. 8259
101: 5 that hath a high l and a proud heart will 5869
119:132 L thou upon me, and be merciful unto 6437
123: 2 as the eyes of servants l unto the hand of NIH
Pr 4:25 Let thine eyes l right on, and let thine 5027
4:25 let thine eyelids l **straight** before thee. 3474
6:17 A proud l, a lying tongue, and hands that 5869
21: 4 A high l, and a proud heart, 5869
23:31 L not thou upon the wine when it is red, 7200
27:23 of thy flocks, and l well to thy herds. 7896
Ecc 12: 3 those that l out of the windows be 7200
SS 1: 6 L not upon me, because I am black, 7200
4: 8 l from the top of Amana, from the top of 7789
6:13 return, return, that we may l upon thee. 2372
Isa 5:30 if one l unto the land, behold darkness 5027
8:17 the house of Jacob, and I will l for him. 6960
8:21 their king and their God, and l upward. 6437
8:22 they shall l unto the earth; 5027
14:16 they that see thee shall **narrowly** l upon 7688
17: 7 At that day shall a man l to his Maker, 8159
17: 8 he shall not l to the altars, the work of his 8159
22: 4 Therefore said I, L **away** from me; I will 8159
22: 8 thou didst l in that day to the armour of 5027
31: 1 they l not unto the Holy One of Israel, 8159
33:20 L upon Zion, the city of our solemnities: 2372
42:18 ye deaf; and l, ye blind, that ye may see. 5027
45:22 L unto me, and be ye saved, all the ends 6437
51: 1 l unto the rock whence ye are hewn, 5027
51: 2 L unto Abraham your father, 5027
51: 6 heavens, and l upon the earth beneath: 5027
56:11 they all l to their own way, every one for 6437
59:11 we l for judgment, but there is none; 6960
63:15 L **down** from heaven, and behold from 5027
66: 2 to this **man** will I l, even to him that is 5027
66:24 upon the carcases of the men that have 7200
Jer 13:16 and, while ye l for light, he turn it into 6960
39:12 l **well** to him, and do him no harm 5869+7760
40: 4 come; and I will l **well** unto thee; 5869+7760
46: 5 and are fled apace, and l not **back**: 6437
47: 3 fathers shall not l **back** to their children 6437
La 3:50 Till the Lord l **down**, and behold from 8259
Eze 23:15 their heads, all of them princes to l **to**, 4758
29:16 when they shall l after them: 6437
43:17 and his stairs shall l **toward** the east. 6437
Da 7:20 whose l was more stout than his fellows. 2376
Hos 3: 1 who l to other gods, and love flagons of 6437
Jnh 2: 4 yet I will l again toward thy holy temple. 6437
Mic 4:11 be defiled, and let our eye l upon Zion. 2372
7: 7 Therefore I will l unto the Lord; I will 6822
Na 2: 8 shall they cry; but none shall l **back**. 6437
3: 7 that all they that l upon thee shall flee 7200
Hab 1:13 to behold evil, and canst not l on iniquity: 5027
2:15 that thou mayest l on their nakedness! 5027
Zec 12:10 they shall l upon me whom they have 5027
Mt 11: 3 that should come, or do we l **for** another? 4328
Mk 8:25 again upon his eyes, and made him l **up**: 308

Lk	7:19 he that should come? or l we **for** another?	4328
	7:20 he that should come? or l we **for** another?	4328
	9:38 I beseech thee, **l upon** my son:	1914
	21:28 to pass, *then* **l up**, and lift up your heads;	352
Jn	4:35 Lift up your eyes, and **l on** the fields;	2300
	7:52 Search, and **l**: for out of Galilee ariseth no	2396
	19:37 They shall **l** on *him* whom they pierced.	3700
Ac	3: 4 his eyes upon him with John, said, **L** on us.	991
	3:12 why l ye *so* **earnestly** on us, as though by	816
	6: 3 l ye **out** among you seven men of honest	1980
	18:15 l ye *to it*; for I will be no judge of such	3700
1Co	16:11 for l l **for** him with the brethren.	1551
2Co	3:13 **stedfastly l** to the end of that which is	816
	4:18 While we l not **at** the *things* which are	4648
	10: 7 Do ye **l on** *things* after the outward	991
Php	2: 4 L not every man on his own *things*, but	4648
	3:20 from whence also we l **for** the Saviour,	553
Heb	9:28 unto them that l **for** him shall he appear	553
1Pe	1:12 which *things the* angels desire to l into.	3879
2Pe	3:13 l **for** new heavens and a new earth,	4328
	3:14 that ye l **for** such *things*, be diligent	4328
2Jn	1: 8 **L** to yourselves, that we lose not *those*	991
Rev	4: 3 And he that sat was to l upon like a jasper	3706
	5: 3 able to open the book, neither to l thereon.	991
	5: 4 and to read the book, neither to l thereon.	991

LOOKED (143) [LOOK]

Ge	6:12 God l upon the earth, and behold, it was	7200
	8:13 l, and behold, the face of the ground was	7200
	16:13 l also here l after him that seeth me?	7200
	18: 2 lift up his eyes and l, and lo, three men	7200
	18:16 from thence, and l toward Sodom.	8259
	19:26 his wife l back from behind him,	5027
	19:28 And he l toward Sodom and Gomorrah,	8259
	22:13 l, and behold behind *him* a ram caught in	7200
	26: 8 Abimelech king of the Philistims l **out**	8259
	29: 2 And he l, and behold a well in the field,	7200
	29:32 Surely the Lord hath l upon my	7200
	33: 1 l, and behold, Esau came, and with him	7200
	37:35 they lift up their eyes and l, and behold,	7200
	39:23 keeper of the prison l not to any thing	7200
	40: 6 l upon them, and behold, they *were* sad.	7200
Ex	2:11 his brethren, and l on their burdens:	7200
	2:12 he l this way and that way, and when he	6437
	2:25 God l **upon** the children of Israel,	7200
	3: 2 he l, and behold, the bush burned with	7200
	4:31 that he had l **upon** their affliction, then	7200
	14:24 that in the morning watch the Lord l	8259
	16:10 that they l toward the wilderness,	6437
	33: 8 man *at* his tent door, and l after Moses,	5027
Nu	12:10 Aaron l upon Miriam, and behold, *she*	6437
	16:42 that they l toward the tabernacle of	6437
	17: 9 and they l, and took every man his rod.	7200
	24:20 when he l on Amalek, he took up his	7200
	24:21 he l on the Kenites, and took up his	7200
Dt	9:16 l l, and behold, ye had sinned against	7200
	26: 7 l on our affliction, and our labour,	7200
Jos	5:13 that he lift up his eyes and l, and behold,	7200
	8:20 when the men of Ai l behind them, they	6437
Jdg	5:28 The mother of Sisera l **out** at a window,	8259
	6:14 the Lord l upon him, and said, Go in this	6437
	9:43 laid wait in the field, and l, and behold,	7200
	13:19 and Manoah and his wife l **on**.	7200
	13:20 Manoah and his wife l on *it*, and fell on	6437
	20:40 Benjamites l behind them, and behold,	6437
1Sa	6:19 they had l into the ark of the Lord,	7200
	9:16 for I have l upon my people, because	7200
	14:16 of Saul in Gibeah of Benjamin l;	7200
	16: 6 were come, that he l on Eliab, and said,	7200
	17:42 the Philistine l **about**, and saw David,	5027
	24: 8 when Saul l behind him, David stooped	5027
2Sa	1: 7 when he l behind him, he saw me,	6437
	2:20 Abner l behind him, and said, *Art* thou	6437
	6:16 Michal Saul's daughter l through a	8259
	13:34 watch lift up his eyes, and l, and behold,	7200
	18:24 and l, and behold a man running alone.	7200
	22:42 They l, *but there was* none to save;	8159
	24:20 Araunah l, and saw the king and his	8259
1Ki	18:43 he went up, and l, and said, *There is*	5027
	19: 6 he l, and behold, *there was* a cake baken	5027
2Ki	2:24 l on them, and cursed them in the name	7200
	6:30 the wall, and the people l, and behold,	7200
	9:30 tired her head, and l **out** at a window.	8259
	9:32 there l **out** to him two *or* three eunuchs.	8259
	11:14 when she l, behold, the king stood by a	7200
	14:11 Amaziah king of Judah l one another *in*	7200
1Ch	21:21 Ornan l and saw David, and went out of	5027
2Ch	13:14 when Judah l **back**, behold, the battle	6437
	20:24 they l unto the multitude, and behold,	6437
	23:13 she l, and behold, the king stood at his	7200
	26:20 all the priests, l upon him, and behold,	7200
Ne	4:14 l l, and rose up, and said unto the nobles,	7200
Est	2:15 in the sight of all them that l upon her.	5027
Job	6:19 The troops of Tema l, the companies of	5027
	30:26 When I l for good, then evil came *unto*	6960
Ps	14: 2 The Lord l down from heaven upon	8259
	34: 5 They l unto him, and were lightened:	5027
	53: 2 God l down from heaven upon the	8259
	69:20 l l *for some* to take pity, but *there was*	6960
	102:19 For he hath l down from the height of	8259
	109:25 *when* they l upon me they shaked their	7200
	142: 4 l l *on my* right hand, and beheld,	5027
Pr	7: 6 at the window of my house l l through	8259
	24:32 l l upon *it, and* received instruction.	7200
Ecc	2:11 l l on all the works that my hands had	6437

SS	1: 6 black, because the sun hath l upon me:	7805
Isa	5: 2 l that *it* should bring forth grapes,	6960
	5: 4 when I l that *it* should bring forth grapes,	6960
	5: 7 he l for judgment, but behold oppression;	6960
	22:11 ye have not l unto the Maker thereof,	5027
	63: 5 l l, and *there was* none to help;	5027
	64: 3 thou didst terrible things *which* we l	6960
Jer	8:15 We l for peace, but no good *came; and for*	6960
	14:19 we l for peace, and *there is* no good;	6960
La	2:16 certainly this *is* the day that we l **for;**	6960
Eze	1: 4 l l, and behold, a whirlwind came out of	7200
	2: 9 when l l, behold, a hand *was* sent unto	7200
	8: 7 and when l l, behold a hole in the wall.	7200
	10: 1 l l, and behold, in the firmament there *was*	7200
	10: 9 when l l, behold the four wheels by	7200
	10:11 *to* the place whither the head l they	6437
	16: 8 l passed by thee, and l upon thee, behold,	7200
	21:21 consulted with images, he l in the liver.	7200
	40:20 gate of the outward court that l toward	6440
	44: 4 l l, and behold, the glory of the Lord	7200
	46:19 of the priests, which l **toward** the north:	6437
Da	1:13 our countenances be l upon before thee,	7200
	10: 5 l lift up mine eyes, and l, and behold,	7200
	12: 5 l Daniel l, and behold, there stood other	7200
Ob	1:12 shouldest not have l on the day of thy	7200
	1:13 shouldest not have l on their affliction	7200
Hag	1: 9 *Ye* l for much, and lo, *it* came to little;	6437
Zec	1: 8 l l upon mine eyes again, and l,	7200
	4: 2 I have l, and behold, a candlestick all	7200
	5: 1 eyes, and l, and behold, a flying roll.	7200
	5: 9 lift l up mine eyes, and l, and behold,	7200
	6: 1 l lift up mine eyes, and l, and behold,	7200
Mk	3: 5 when he had l **round about** on them	4017
	3:34 And he l round about on them which sat	4017
	5:32 And he l **round about** to see her that	4017
	6:41 he l **up** to heaven, and blessed, and brake	308
	8:24 And he l **up**, and said, I see men as trees,	308
	8:33 had turned about and l **on** his disciples,	1492
	9: 8 when they had l **round about**,	4017
	10:23 And Jesus l **round about**, and saith unto	4017
	11:11 he had l **round about** upon all *things*,	4017
	14:67 warming himself, she l **upon** him,	1689
	16: 4 when they l, they saw that the stone was	308
Lk	1:25 l **on** me, to take away my reproach	1896
	2:38 spake of him to all them that l **for**	4327
	10:32 came and l *on him*, and passed by on	1492
	19: 5 he l **up**, and saw him, and said unto him,	308
	21: 1 he l **up**, and saw the rich *men* casting	308
	22:56 and **earnestly** l upon him, and said,	816
	22:61 And the Lord turned, and l **upon** Peter.	1689
Jn	13:22 Then the disciples l one on another,	991
	20:11 she **stooped down, and l** into	3879
Ac	1:10 while they l **stedfastly** toward heaven	816
	7:55 l up **stedfastly** into heaven, and saw	816
	10: 4 And when he l on him, he was afraid,	816
	22:13 And the same hour l l **up** upon him.	308
	28: 6 Howbeit they l when he should have	4328
	28: 6 but after they had l a great while,	4328
Heb	11:10 he l **for** a city which hath foundations,	1551
1Jn	1: 1 we have l **upon**, and our hands have	2300
Rev	4: 1 After this l l, and behold, a door *was*	1492
	6: 8 And l l, and behold a pale horse:	1492
	14: 1 And l l, and lo, a Lamb stood on the	1492
	14:14 And l l, and behold a white cloud,	1492
	15: 5 And after that l l, and behold, the temple	1492

LOOKEST (2) [LOOK]

Job	13:27 and l **narrowly** unto all my paths;	8104
Hab	1:13 wherefore l thou upon them that deal	5027

LOOKETH (33) [LOOK]

Lev	13:12 his foot, wheresoever the priest l;	4758+5869
Nu	21: 8 is bitten, when he l upon it, shall live.	7200
	21:20 top of Pisgah, which l toward Jeshimon.	8259
	23:28 the top of Peor, that l toward Jeshimon.	8259
Jos	15: 2 salt sea, from the bay that l southward:	6437
1Sa	13:18 l to the valley of Zeboim toward	8259
	16: 7 for man l on the outward appearance,	7200
	16: 7 but the Lord l on the heart.	7200
Job	7: 2 as a hireling l for the reward of his work:	6960
	28:24 For he l to the ends of the earth,	5027
	33:27 He l upon men, and *if any* say, I have	7789
Ps	33:13 The Lord l from heaven; he beholdeth	5027
	33:14 From the place of his habitation he l upon	7688
	104:32 He l on the earth, and it trembleth:	5027
Pr	14:15 but the prudent *man* l **well** to his going.	995
	31:27 She l **well** to the ways of her household,	6822
SS	2: 9 our wall, he l forth at the windows,	7688
	6:10 Who *is* she that l **forth** as the morning,	8259
	7: 4 nose *is* as the tower of Lebanon which l	6822
Isa	28: 4 which *when* he l upon it seeth, while	7200
Eze	8: 3 to the door of the inner gate that l toward	6437
	11: 1 of the Lord's house, which l eastward:	6437
	40: 6 came he unto the gate which l toward	6440
	40:22 *were* after the measure of the gate that l	6440
	43: 1 *even* the gate that l toward the east:	6437
	44: 1 sanctuary which l *toward* the east;	6437
	46: 1 The gate of the inner court that l *toward*	6437
	46:12 open him the gate that l *toward* the east,	6437
	47: 2 the utter gate *by* the way that l eastward;	6437
Mt	5:28 whosoever l **on** a woman to lust after	991
	24:50 come in a day when he l not for *him*,	4328
Lk	12:46 will come in a day when he l not **for** *him*,	4328
Jas	1:25 But whoso l into the perfect law of liberty,	3879

LOOKING (30) [LOOK]

Jos	15: 7 northward, l toward Gilgal, that *is* before	6437
1Ki	7:25 three l toward the north, and three	6437
	7:25 three l toward the west, and three	6437
	7:25 three l toward the south, and three	6437
	7:25 the south, and three l toward the east:	6437
1Ch	15:29 that Michal the daughter of Saul l out at a	8259
2Ch	4: 4 three l toward the north, and three	6437
	4: 4 three l toward the west, and three	6437
	4: 4 three l toward the south, and three	6437
	4: 4 the south, and three l toward the east:	6437
Job	37:18 which *is* strong, *and* as a molten **l** glass?	7209
Isa	38:14 mine eyes fail *with* l upward: O Lord,	NIH
Mt	14:19 and l up to heaven, he blessed, and brake,	308
Mk	7:34 And l **up** to heaven, he sighed,	308
	10:27 And Jesus l **upon** them saith, With men *it*	1689
	15:40 There were also women l **on** afar off:	2334
Lk	6:10 And l **round about** upon them all,	4017
	9:16 and the two fishes, and l **up** to heaven,	308
	9:62 and l back, is fit for the kingdom of God.	991
	21:26 *for* l **after** *those things* which are coming	4329
Jn	1:36 And l **upon** Jesus as he walked, he saith,	1689
	20: 5 And he **stooping down**, and l	3879
Ac	6:15 sat in the council, l **stedfastly** on him,	816
	23:21 are they ready, l **for** a promise from thee.	4327
Tit	2:13 **L for** *that* blessed hope, and the glorious	4327
Heb	10:27 But a certain fearful l **for** of judgment and	1561
	12: 2 l unto Jesus the author and finisher of *our*	872
	12:15 **L diligently** lest any *man* fail of the grace	1983
2Pe	3:12 **L for** and hasting *unto* the coming of	4328
Jude	1:21 l **for** the mercy of our Lord Jesus Christ	4327

LOOKING-GLASSES (1) [GLASS, LOOK]

Ex	38: 8 brass, of the l of *the women* assembling,	4759

LOOKS (5) [LOOK]

Ps	18:27 people; but wilt bring down high l.	5869
Isa	2:11 The lofty l of man shall be humbled,	5869
	10:12 king of Assyria, and the glory of his high l.	5869
Eze	2: 6 of their words, nor be dismayed at their l,	6440
	3: 9 them not, neither be dismayed at their l,	6440

LOOPS (13)

Ex	26: 4 thou shalt make l of blue upon the edge	3924
	26: 5 Fifty l shalt thou make in the one curtain,	3924
	26: 5 fifty l shalt thou make in the edge	3924
	26: 5 that the l may take hold one of another.	3924
	26:10 thou shalt make fifty l on the edge of	3924
	26:10 fifty l in the edge of the curtain which	3924
	26:11 put the taches into the l, and couple the	3924
	36:11 he made l of blue on the edge of one	3924
	36:12 Fifty l made he in one curtain,	3924
	36:12 fifty l made he in the edge of the curtain	3924
	36:12 the l held one *curtain* to another.	3924
	36:17 he made fifty l upon the uttermost edge	3924
	36:17 fifty l made he upon the edge of the	3924

LOOSE (29) [LOOSED, LOOSETH, LOOSING, UNLOOSE]

Ge	49:21 Naphtali *is* a hind **let** l: he giveth goodly	7971
Lev	14: 7 the living bird l into the open field.	7971
Dt	25: 9 l his shoe from off his foot, and spit in his	2502
Jos	5:15 unto Joshua, **L** thy shoe from off thy foot;	5394
Job	6: 9 he would let l his hand, and cut me off!	5425
	30:11 they have also let l the bridle before me.	7971
	38:31 of Pleiades, or l the bands of Orion?	6605
Ps	102:20 l those that are appointed to death;	6605
Isa	20: 2 Go and l the sackcloth from off thy loins,	6605
	45: 1 I will l the loins of kings, to open before	6605
	52: 2 l thyself **from** the bands of thy neck,	6605
	58: 6 to l the bands of wickedness, to undo	6605
Jer	40: 4 l l thee *this* day from the chains which	6605
Da	3:25 answered and said, Lo, I see four men l,	8271
Mt	16:19 whatsoever thou shalt l on earth shall be	3089
	18:18 whatsoever ye shall l on earth shall be	3089
	21: 2 her: l *them*, and bring *them* unto me.	3089
Mk	11: 2 never man sat; l him, and bring him.	3089
	11: 4 where two ways met; and they l	3089
Lk	13:15 doth not each one of you on the sabbath l	3089
	19:30 man sat: l him, and bring him hither.	3089
	19:31 Why do ye l *him?* thus shall ye say unto	3089
	19:33 thereof said unto them, Why l ye the colt?	3089
Jn	11:44 saith unto them, **L** him, and let *him* go.	3089
Ac	13:25 shoes of *his* feet I am not worthy to l.	3089
	24:26 given him of Paul, that he might l him:	3089
Rev	5: 2 open the book, and to l the seals thereof?	3089
	5: 5 the book, and to l the seven seals thereof.	3089
	9:14 **L** the four angels which are bound in	3089

LOOSED (32) [LOOSE]

Ex	28:28 the breastplate be not l from the ephod,	2118
	39:21 that the breastplate might not be l from	2118
Dt	25:10 The house of him that hath his shoe l.	2502
Jdg	15:14 and his bands l from off his hands.	4549
Job	30:11 Because he hath l my cord,	6605
	39: 5 or who hath l the bands of the wild ass?	6605
Ps	105:20 The king sent and l him; *even* the ruler of	5425
	116:16 of thy handmaid: thou hast l my bonds.	6605
Ecc	12: 6 Or ever the silver cord be l, or the golden	7576
Isa	5:27 neither shall the girdle of their loins be l,	6605
	33:23 Thy tacklings are l; they could not well	5203
	51:14 captive exile hasteneth that *he* may be l,	6605
Da	5: 6 so that the joints of his loins were l,	8271
Mt	16:19 shalt loose on earth shall be l in heaven.	3089
	18:18 shall loose on earth shall be l in heaven.	3089

L

Ref	Text	Strong's
Mt	18:27 and I him, and forgave him the debt.	630
Mk	7:35 and the string of his tongue was l,	3089
Lk	1:64 and his tongue l, and he spake,	NIG
	13:12 Woman, thou art l from thy infirmity.	630
	13:16 be l from this bond on the sabbath day?	3089
Ac	2:24 hath raised up, having the pains of death:	3089
	13:13 when Paul and his company l from Paphos,	321
	16:26 opened, and every one's bands were l.	447
	22:30 he l from *his* bands,	3089
	27:21 and not have l from Crete, to have	321
	27:40 and l the rudder bands, and hoised up	447
Ro	7: 2 she is l from the law of the husband.	2673
1Co	7:27 seek not to be l. Art thou loosed from a	3080
	7:27 Art thou l from a wife? seek not a wife.	3089
Rev	9:15 And the four angels were l, which were	3089
	20: 3 and after that he must be l a little season.	3089
	20: 7 Satan shall be l out of his prison,	3089

LOOSETH (2) [LOOSE]

Ref	Text	Strong's
Job	12:18 He l the bond of kings, and girdeth their	6605
Ps	146: 7 to the hungry. The Lord l the prisoners:	5425

LOOSING (4) [LOOSE]

Ref	Text	Strong's
Mk	11: 5 said unto them, What do ye, l the colt?	3089
Lk	19:33 And as they were l the colt, the owners	3089
Ac	16:11 Therefore l from Troas, we came with a	321
	27:13 l *thence,* they sailed close by Crete.	142

LOP (1)

Ref	Text	Strong's
Isa	10:33 of hosts, shall l the bough with terror:	5586

LORD (1367) [LORD'S, LORDLY, LORDS, LORDSHIP; see also LORD*]

Ref	Text	Strong's
Ge	15: 2 Abram said, L God, what wilt thou give	136
	15: 8 he said, L God, whereby shall I know that	136
	18: 3 said, My L, if now I have found favour in	136
	18:12 shall I have pleasure, my l being old also?	113
	18:27 I have taken upon me to speak unto the L,	136
	18:30 said *unto him,* Oh let not the L be angry,	136
	18:31 I have taken upon me to speak unto the L:	136
	18:32 Oh let not the L be angry, and I will speak	136
	19:18 And Lot said unto them, Oh, not so, my L:	113
	20: 4 he said, L, wilt thou slay also a righteous	136
	23: 6 Hear us, my l: thou *art* a mighty prince	113
	23:11 Nay, my l, hear me: the field give I thee,	113
	23:15 My l, hearken unto me: the land *is worth*	113
	24:18 she said, Drink, my l: and she hasted,	113
	27:29 be l over thy brethren, and let thy	1376
	27:37 I have made him thy l, and all his brethren	1376
	31:35 Let it not displease my l that I cannot rise	113
	32: 4 saying, Thus shall ye speak unto my l Esau;	113
	32: 5 have sent to tell my l, that I may find grace	113
	32:18 it *is* a present sent unto my l Esau:	113
	33: 8 *These are* to find grace in the sight of my l.	113
	33:13 My l knoweth that the children *are* tender,	113
	33:14 Let my l, I pray thee, pass over before his	113
	33:14 to endure, until I come unto my l unto Seir.	113
	33:15 let me find grace in the sight of my l.	113
	39:16 his garment by her, until his l came home.	113
	40: 1 *his* baker had offended their l the king of	113
	42:10 l, but to buy food are thy servants come.	113
	42:30 The man, *who is* the l of the land,	113
	42:33 the man, the l of the country, said unto us,	113
	44: 5 *Is* not this *it* in which my l drinketh,	113
	44: 7 him, Wherefore saith my l these words?	113
	44:16 Judah said, What shall we say unto my l?	113
	44:18 said, O my l, let thy servant, I pray thee,	113
	44:19 My l asked his servants, saying, Have ye a	113
	44:20 we said unto my l, We have a father, an	113
	44:22 we said unto my l, The lad cannot leave	113
	44:24 my father, we told him the words of my l.	113
	44:33 abide instead of the lad a bondman to my l;	113
	45: 8 l of all his house, and a ruler throughout all	113
	45: 9 God hath made me l of all Egypt:	113
	47:18 unto him, We will not hide *it* from my l,	113
	47:18 is spent; my l also had our herds of cattle;	113
	47:18 there is not ought left in the sight of my l,	113
	47:25 let us find grace in the sight of my l,	113
Ex	4:10 O my L, I *am* not eloquent, neither	136
	4:13 he said, O my L, send, I pray thee,	136
	5:22 L, wherefore hast thou so evil entreated	136
	15:17 the Sanctuary, O L, *which* thy hands have	136
	23:17 thy males shall appear before the L God.	113
	32:22 Let not the anger of my l wax hot:	113
	34: 9 O L, let my Lord, I pray thee, go amongst	136
	34: 9 O Lord, let my L, I pray thee, go amongst	136
	34:23 men children appear before the L God,	113
Nu	11:28 and said, My l Moses, forbid them.	113
	12:11 Alas, my l, I beseech thee, lay not the sin	113
	14:17 thee, let the power of my L be great,	136
	32:25 Thy servants will do as my l commandeth.	113
	32:27 before the Lord to battle, as my l saith.	113
	36: 2 The Lord commanded my l to give	113
	36: 2 my l was commanded by the Lord to give	113
Dt	3:24 O L God, thou hast begun to shew thy	136
	9:26 unto the Lord, and said, O L God,	136
	10:17 L of lords, a great God, a mighty,	113
Jos	3:11 *even* the L of all the earth passeth over	113
	3:13 L of all the earth, shall rest in the waters	113
	5:14 him, What saith my l unto his servant?	113
	7: 7 Joshua said, Alas, O L God,	136
	7: 8 O L, what shall I say, when Israel turneth	136
Jdg	3:25 their l *was* fallen down dead on the earth.	113
	4:18 said unto him, Turn in, my l, turn in to me;	113
	6:13 O my L, if the Lord be with us, why then	113

Ref	Text	Strong's
Jdg	6:15 he said unto him, O my L, wherewith shall	136
	6:22 the Lord, Gideon said, Alas, O L God!	136
	13: 8 intreated the Lord, and said, O my L,	136
	16:28 said, O L God, remember me, I pray thee,	113
	19:26 house where her l *was,* till it was light.	113
	19:27 her l rose up in the morning, and opened	113
Ru	2:13 Let me find favour in thy sight, my l;	113
1Sa	1:15 Hannah answered and said, No, my l, I *am*	113
	1:26 she said, O my l, *as* thy soul liveth, my lord,	113
	1:26 said, O my lord, *as* thy soul liveth, my l,	113
	16: Let our l now command thy servants	113
	22:12 And he answered, Here I *am,* my l.	113
	24: 8 and cried after Saul, saying, My l the king.	113
	24:10 I will not put forth mine hand against my l;	113
	25:24 fell at his feet, and said, Upon me, my l,	113
	25:25 Let not my l, I pray thee, regard this man	113
	25:25 handmaid saw not the young men of my l,	113
	25:26 Now therefore, my l, *as* the Lord liveth,	113
	25:26 they that seek evil to my l, be as Nabal.	113
	25:27 thine handmaid hath brought unto my l,	113
	25:27 given unto the young men that follow my l.	113
	25:28 for the Lord will certainly make my l a	113
	25:28 my l fighteth the battles of the Lord,	113
	25:29 soul of my l shall be bound in the bundle	113
	25:30 when the Lord shall have done to my l	113
	25:31 unto thee, nor offence of heart unto my l,	113
	25:31 or that my l hath avenged himself:	113
	25:31 the Lord shall have dealt well with my l,	113
	25:41 to wash the feet of the servants of my l.	113
	26:15 then hast thou not kept thy l the king?	113
	26:15 of the people in to destroy the king thy l.	113
	26:17 David said, *It is* my voice, my l, O king.	113
	26:18 Wherefore doth my l thus pursue after his	113
	26:19 let my l the king hear the words of his	113
	29: 8 fight against the enemies of my l the king?	113
2Sa	1:10 and have brought them hither unto my l.	113
	2: 5 ye have shewed this kindness unto your l,	113
	3:21 will gather all Israel unto my l the king,	113
	4: 8 the Lord hath avenged my l the king this	113
	7:18 and he said, Who *am* l, O L God?	136
	7:19 yet a small thing in thy sight, O L God;	136
	7:19 And *is* this the manner of man, O L God?	136
	7:20 for thou, O L God, knowest thy servant.	136
	7:28 And now, O L God, thou *art* that God,	136
	7:29 for thou, O L God, hast spoken *it:* and	136
	9:11 According to all that my l the king hath	113
	10: 3 of Ammon said unto Hanun their l,	113
	11: 9 king's house with all the servants of his l,	113
	11:11 my l Joab, and the servants of my lord,	113
	11:11 my lord Joab, and the servants of my l,	113
	11:13 to lie on his bed with the servants of his l,	113
	13:32 Let not my l suppose *that* they have slain	113
	13:33 let not my l the king take the thing to his	113
	14: 9 My l, O king, the iniquity be on me,	113
	14:12 speak *one* word unto my l the king.	113
	14:15 to speak of this thing unto my l the king,	113
	14:17 The word of my l the king shall now be	113
	14:17 so *is* my l the king to discern good and bad:	113
	14:18 woman said, Let my l the king now speak.	113
	14:19 and said, As thy soul liveth, my l the king,	113
	14:19 the left from ought that my l the king hath	113
	14:20 my l, O king, in that the king hath fulfilled	113
	14:22 my l, O king, in that thy servant hath	113
	15:15 servants *are* ready to do whatsoever my l	113
	15:21 Lord liveth, and *as* my l the king liveth,	113
	15:21 surely in what place my l the king shall be,	113
	16: 4 I may find grace in thy sight, my l, O king.	113
	16: 9 Why should this dead dog curse my l	113
	18:28 that lift up their hand against my l the king.	113
	18:31 and Cushi said, Tidings, my l the king:	113
	18:32 The enemies of my l the king, and all that	113
	19:19 let not my l impute iniquity unto me,	113
	19:19 that my l the king went out of Jerusalem,	113
	19:20 Joseph to go down to meet my l the king.	113
	19:26 he answered, My l, O king, my servant	113
	19:27 he hath slandered thy servant unto my l	113
	19:27 but my l the king *is* as an angel of God:	113
	19:28 but dead men before my l the king:	113
	19:30 forasmuch as my l the king is come *again*	113
	19:35 thy servant be yet a burden unto my l	113
	19:37 let him go over with my l the king; and do	113
	24: 3 *that* the eyes of my l the king may see *it:*	113
	24: 3 doth my l the king delight in this thing?	113
	24:21 Wherefore is my l the king come to his	113
	24:22 Let my l the king take and offer up what	113
1Ki	1: 2 Let there be sought for my l the king a	113
	1: 2 bosom, that my l the king may get heat.	113
	1:11 reign, and David our l knoweth *it* not?	113
	1:13 say unto him, Didst not thou, my l O king,	113
	1:17 she said unto him, My l, thou swarest by	113
	1:18 now, my l the king, thou knowest *it* not:	113
	1:20 thou, my l O king, the eyes of all Israel *are*	113
	1:20 sit on the throne of my l the king after him.	113
	1:21 when my l the king shall sleep with his	113
	1:24 Nathan said, My l O king, hast thou said,	113
	1:27 Is this thing done by my l the king,	113
	1:27 should sit on the throne of my l the king	113
	1:31 and said, Let my l king David live for ever.	113
	1:33 Take with you the servants of your l,	113
	1:36 the Lord God of my l the king say so *too.*	113
	1:37 As the Lord hath been with my l the king,	113
	1:37 greater than the throne of my l king David.	113
	1:43 Verily our l king David hath made Solomon	113
	1:47 servants came to bless our l king David,	113
	2:26 thou barest the ark of the L God before	136

Ref	Text	Strong's
1Ki	2:38 as my l the king hath said, so will thy	113
	3:10 the speech pleased the L, that Solomon	136
	3:17 O my l, I and this woman dwell in one	113
	3:26 she said, O my l, give her the living child,	113
	8:53 our fathers out of Egypt, O L God.	136
	11:23 which fled from his l Hadadezer king of	113
	12:27 heart of this people turn again unto their l,	113
	18: 7 his face, and said, *Art* thou that my l Elijah?	113
	18: 8 I *am:* go, tell thy l, Behold, Elijah *is here.*	113
	18:10 whither my l hath not sent to seek thee:	113
	18:11 Go, tell thy l, Behold, Elijah *is here.*	113
	18:13 it not told my l what I did when Jezebel	113
	18:14 Go, tell thy l, Behold, Elijah *is here:* and	113
	20: 4 the king of Israel answered and said, My l,	113
	20: 9 of Ben-hadad, Tell my l the king,	113
	22: 6 for the L shall deliver *it* into the hand of	136
2Ki	2:19 of *this* city *is* pleasant, as my l seeth:	113
	4:16 said, Nay, my l, thou man of God, do not	113
	4:28 said, Did I desire a son of my l? did I not	113
	5: 3 Would God my l *were* with the prophet	113
	5: 4 told his l, saying, Thus and thus said	113
	6:12 of his servants said, None, my l, O king:	113
	6:26 unto him, saying, Help, my l, O king.	113
	7: 2 a l on whose hand the king leaned	7991
	7: 6 For the L had made the host of the Syrians	136
	7:17 the king appointed the l on whose hand	7991
	7:19 *that* l answered the man of God, and said,	7991
	8: 5 Gehazi said, My l, O king, this *is*	113
	8:12 Hazael said, Why weepeth my l? And he	113
	9:11 Jehu came forth to the servants of his l:	113
	18:23 give pledges to my l the king of Assyria,	113
	19:23 messengers thou hast reproached the L,	136
1Ch	21: 3 many moe as they *be: but,* my l the king,	113
	21: 3 doth my l require this *thing?* why will he	113
	21:23 let my l the king do *that* which *is* good in	113
2Ch	2:14 with the cunning *men* of my l David thy	113
	2:15 and the wine, which my l hath spoken of,	113
	13: 6 is risen up, and hath rebelled against his l.	113
Ezr	10: 3 according to the counsel of my l,	113
Ne	1:11 O L, I beseech thee, let now thine ear be	113
	3: 5 put not their necks to the work of their L.	113
	4:14 remember the L, *which* is great and	136
	8:10 for *this* day *is* holy unto our L: neither be	113
	10:29 all the commandments of the Lord our L,	113
Job	28:28 Behold, the fear of the L, that *is* wisdom;	136
Ps	8: 1 O Lord our L, how excellent *is* thy name	113
	8: 9 O Lord our L, how excellent *is* thy name	113
	12: 4 our lips *are* our own: who *is* l over us?	113
	16: 2 hast said unto the Lord, Thou *art* my L:	136
	22:30 it shall be accounted to the L for a	136
	35:17 L, how long wilt thou look on? rescue my	136
	35:22 keep not silence: O L, be not far from me.	136
	35:23 *even* unto my cause, my God and my L.	136
	37:13 The L shall laugh at him: for he seeth that	136
	38: 9 L, all my desire *is* before thee;	136
	38:15 do I hope: thou wilt hear, O L my God.	136
	38:22 Make haste to help me, O L my salvation.	136
	39: 7 L, what wait I for? my hope *is* in thee.	136
	40:17 and needy; *yet* the L thinketh upon me:	136
	44:23 Awake, why sleepest thou, O L? arise,	136
	45:11 for he *is* thy L; and worship thou him.	113
	51:15 L, open thou my lips; and my mouth shall	136
	54: 4 the L *is* with them that uphold my soul.	136
	55: 9 Destroy, O L, *and* divide their tongues:	136
	57: 9 I will praise thee, O L, among the people:	136
	59:11 and bring them down, O L our shield.	136
	62:12 Also unto thee, O L, *belongeth* mercy:	136
	66:18 in my heart, the L will not hear *me:*	136
	68:11 The L gave the word: great *was*	136
	68:17 The L *is* among them, *as in* Sinai, in the	136
	68:19 Blessed *be* the L, *who* daily loadeth us	136
	68:20 unto God the L *belong* the issues from	136
	68:22 The L said, I will bring again from Bashan,	136
	68:26 *even* the L, from the fountain of Israel.	136
	68:32 the earth; O sing *praises unto* the L; Selah.	136
	69: 6 O L God of hosts, be ashamed for my	136
	71: 5 For thou *art* my hope, O L God: *thou art*	136
	71:16 I will go in the strength of the L God:	136
	73:20 *so,* O L, when *thou* awakest, thou shalt	136
	73:28 I have put my trust in the L God, that *I*	136
	77: 2 In the day of my trouble I sought the L:	136
	77: 7 Will the L cast off for ever? and will he be	136
	78:65 the L awaked as one out of sleep, *and* like	136
	79:12 wherewith they have reproached thee, O L.	136
	86: 3 Be merciful unto me, O L: for I cry unto	136
	86: 4 for unto thee, O L, do I lift up my soul.	136
	86: 5 For thou, L, *art* good, and ready to forgive;	136
	86: 8 the gods *there is* none like unto thee, O L;	136
	86: 9 shall come and worship before thee, O L;	136
	86:12 I will praise thee, O L my God, with all	136
	86:15 thou, O L, *art* a God full of compassion,	136
	89:49 L, *where are* thy former lovingkindnesses,	136
	89:50 Remember, L, the reproach of thy servants	136
	90: 1 L, thou hast been our dwelling place in all	136
	97: 5 at the presence of the L of the whole earth.	113
	105:21 He made him l of his house, and ruler of	113
	109:21 do thou for me, O God the L, for thy	136
	110: 1 The Lord said unto my L, Sit thou at my	113
	110: 5 The L at thy right hand shall strike through	136
	114: 7 thou earth, at the presence of the L,	113
	130: 2 L, hear my voice: let thine ears be attentive	136
	130: 3 mark iniquities, O L, who shall stand?	136
	130: 6 My soul *waiteth* for the L more than they	136
	135: 5 *is* great, and *that* our L *is* above all gods.	113
	136: 3 O give thanks to the L of lords: for his	136

L

Ps 140: 7 O God the L, the strength of my salvation, 136
141: 8 But mine eyes *are* unto thee, O God the L: 136
147: 5 Great *is* our L, and of great power: 113
Isa 1:24 Therefore saith the L, the LORD of hosts, 113
3: 1 For behold, the L, the LORD of hosts, 113
3:15 of the poor? saith the L, God of hosts. 113
3:17 Therefore the L will smite with a scab 136
3:18 In that day the L will take away the 136
4: 4 the L shall have washed away the filth 136
6: 1 died I saw also the L sitting upon a throne, 136
6: 8 Also I heard the voice of the L, saying, 136
6:11 said I, L, how long? And he answered, 136
7: 7 Thus saith the L, It shall not stand, 136
7:14 Therefore the L himself shall give you a 136
7:20 In the same day shall the L shave with a 136
8: 7 the L bringeth up upon them the waters of 136
9: 8 The L sent a word into Jacob, and it hath 136
9:17 Therefore the L shall have no joy in their 136
10:12 *that* when the L hath performed his whole 136
10:16 Therefore shall the L, the Lord of hosts, 113
10:16 Therefore shall the Lord, the L of hosts, 113
10:23 For the L God of hosts shall make a 136
10:24 Therefore thus saith the L God of hosts, 136
10:33 Behold, the L, the LORD of hosts, shall lop 113
11:11 the L shall set his hand again the second 113
19: 4 will I give over into the hand of a cruel l; 113
19: 4 over them, saith the L, God of hosts. 113
21: 6 For thus hath the L said unto me, Go, set 136
21: 8 My l, I stand continually upon 136
21:16 For thus hath the L said unto me, Within a 136
22: 5 of perplexity by the L God of hosts in 136
22:12 in that day did the L God of hosts call to 136
22:14 you till ye die, saith the L God of hosts. 136
22:15 Thus saith the L God of hosts, 136
25: 8 the L God will wipe away tears from off 136
28:16 Therefore thus saith the L God, Behold, 136
28:22 for I have heard from the L God of hosts a 136
29:13 Wherefore the L said, Forasmuch as this 136
30:15 For thus saith the L God, the Holy One of 136
30:20 the L give you the bread of adversity, 136
37:24 thy servants hast thou reproached the L, 136
38:16 O L, by these *things* live, and in all 136
40:10 the L God will come with strong *hand,* 136
48:16 now the L God, and his Spirit, hath sent 136
49:14 forsaken me, and my L hath forgotten me. 136
49:22 saith the L God, Behold, I will lift 136
50: 4 The L God hath given me the tongue of 136
50: 5 The L God hath opened mine ear, 136
50: 7 For the L God will help me; therefore 136
50: 9 Behold, the L God will help me; who *is* he 136
51:22 Thus saith thy L the LORD, and thy God 113
52: 4 For thus saith the L God, My people went 136
56: 8 The L God which gathereth the outcasts of 136
61: 1 The Spirit of the L God *is* upon me; 136
61:11 so the L God will cause righteousness and 136
65:13 Therefore thus saith the L God, Behold, 136
65:15 for the L God shall slay thee, and call his 136
Jer 1: 6 said I, Ah, L God, behold, I cannot speak: 136
2:19 *is* not in thee, saith the L God of hosts. 136
2:22 *is* marked before me, saith the L God. 136
4:10 (Then said I, Ah, L God! surely thou hast 136
7:20 Therefore thus saith the L God; Behold, 136
14:13 said I, Ah L God! behold, the prophets say 136
22:18 they shall not lament for him, *saying,* Ah l! 113
32:17 Ah L God! behold, thou hast made 136
32:25 thou hast said unto me, O L God, 113
34: 5 and they will lament thee, *saying,* Ah l! 113
37:20 hear now, I pray thee, O my l the king: 113
38: 9 My l the king, these men have done evil in 113
44:26 land of Egypt, saying, The L God liveth. 136
46:10 For this *is* the day of the L God of hosts, 136
46:10 for the L God of hosts hath a sacrifice in 136
49: 5 a fear upon thee, saith the L God of hosts. 136
50:25 for this *is* the work of the L God of hosts 136
50:31 *thou* most proud, saith the L God of hosts: 136
La 1:14 The L hath delivered me into *their* hands, 136
1:15 The L hath trodden under foot all my 136
1:15 The L hath trodden the virgin, the daughter 136
2: 1 How hath the L covered the daughter of 136
2: 2 The L hath swallowed up all the habitations 136
2: 5 The L was as an enemy: he hath swallowed 136
2: 7 The L hath cast off his altar, he hath 136
2:18 Their heart cried unto the L, O wall of 136
2:19 heart like water before the face of the L: 136
2:20 prophet be slain in the sanctuary of the L? 136
3:31 For the L will not cast off for ever: 136
3:36 a man in his cause, the L approveth not. 136
3:37 to pass, *when* the L commandeth *it* not? 136
3:58 O L, thou hast pleaded the causes of my 136
Eze 2: 4 shalt say unto them, Thus saith the L God. 136
3:11 and tell them, Thus saith the L God; 136
3:27 shalt say unto them, Thus saith the L God; 136
4:14 said I, Ah L God, behold, my soul *hath* 136
5: 5 Thus saith the L God; This *is* Jerusalem: 136
5: 7 Therefore thus saith the L God; 136
5: 8 Therefore thus saith the L God; Behold, 136
5:11 Wherefore, *as* I live, saith the L God; 136
6: 3 of Israel, hear the word of the L God to 136
6: 3 Thus saith the L God to the mountains, 136
6:11 Thus saith the L God; Smite with thine 136
7: 2 thus saith the L God unto the land of 136
7: 5 Thus saith the L God; An evil, an only 136
8: 1 that the hand of the L God fell there upon 136
9: 8 my face, and cried, and said, Ah L God, 136
11: 7 Therefore thus saith the L God; Your slain 136

Eze 11: 8 bring a sword upon you, saith the L God. 136
11:13 *with* a loud voice, and said, Ah L God, 136
11:16 Therefore say, Thus saith the L God; 136
11:17 Therefore say, Thus saith the L God; 136
11:21 upon their own heads, saith the L God. 136
12:10 Say thou unto them, Thus saith the L God; 136
12:19 Thus saith the L God, of the inhabitants of 136
12:23 Tell them therefore, Thus saith the L God, 136
12:25 and will perform it, saith the L God. 136
12:28 say unto them, Thus saith the L God; 136
12:28 spoken shall be done, saith the L God. 136
13: 3 Thus saith the L God; Woe unto 136
13: 8 Therefore thus saith the L God; 136
13: 8 behold, I *am* against you, saith the L God. 136
13: 9 and ye shall know that I *am* the L God. 136
13:13 Therefore thus saith the L God; I will 136
13:16 and *there is* no peace, saith the L God. 136
13:18 say, Thus saith the L God; Woe to 136
13:20 Wherefore thus saith the L God; Behold, 136
14: 4 and say unto them, Thus saith the L God; 136
14: 6 the house of Israel, Thus saith the L God; 136
14:11 and I may be their God, saith the L God. 136
14:14 by their righteousness, saith the L God. 136
14:16 men *were* in it, *as* I live, saith the L God, 136
14:18 men *were* in it, *as* I live, saith the L God, 136
14:20 Job, *were* in it, *as* I live, saith the L God, 136
14:21 For thus saith the L God; How much more 136
14:23 all that I have done in it, saith the L God. 136
15: 6 Therefore thus saith the L God; 136
15: 8 committed a trespass, saith the L God. 136
16: 3 Thus saith the L God unto Jerusalem; 136
16: 8 saith the L God, and thou becamest mine. 136
16:14 I had put upon thee, saith the L God. 136
16:19 and *thus* it was, saith the L God. 136
16:23 (woe, woe unto thee! saith the L God;) 136
16:30 How weak is thine heart, saith the L God, 136
16:36 Thus saith the L God; Because thy 136
16:43 thy way upon *thine* head, saith the L God: 136
16:48 *As* I live, saith the L God, Sodom thy 136
16:59 For thus saith the L God; I will even deal 136
16:63 all that thou hast done, saith the L God. 136
17: 3 say, Thus saith the L God; A great eagle 136
17: 9 Say thou, Thus saith the L God; Shall it 136
17:16 *As* I live, saith the L God, surely in 136
17:19 Therefore thus saith the L God; *As* I live, 136
17:22 Thus saith the L God; I will also take of 136
18: 3 *As* I live, saith the L God, ye shall not 136
18: 9 he shall surely live, saith the L God. 136
18:23 saith the L God: *and* not that he should 136
18:25 Yet ye say, The way of the L is not equal. 136
18:29 of Israel, The way of the L is not equal. 136
18:30 according to his ways, saith the L God. 136
18:32 death of him that dieth, saith the L God: 136
20: 3 and say unto them, Thus saith the L God; 136
20: 3 *As* I live, saith the L God, I will not be 136
20: 5 And say unto them, Thus saith the L God; 136
20:27 and say unto them, Thus saith the L God; 136
20:30 the house of Israel, Thus saith the L God; 136
20:31 *As* I live, saith the L God, I will not be 136
20:33 *As* I live, saith the L God, surely with a 136
20:36 so will I plead with you, saith the L God. 136
20:39 O house of Israel, thus saith the L God; 136
20:40 saith the L God, there shall all the house 136
20:44 O ye house of Israel, saith the L God. 136
20:47 Thus saith the L God; Behold, I *will* 136
20:49 said I, Ah L God, they say of me, Doth he 136
21: 7 shall be brought to pass, saith the L God. 136
21:13 it shall be no *more,* saith the L God. 136
21:24 Therefore thus saith the L God; 136
21:26 Thus saith the L God; Remove 136
21:28 Thus saith the L God concerning 136
22: 3 say thou, Thus saith the L God, The city 136
22:12 and hast forgotten me, saith the L God. 136
22:19 Therefore thus saith the L God; 136
22:28 unto them, saying, Thus saith the L God, 136
22:31 upon their heads, saith the L God. 136
23:22 O Aholibah, thus saith the L God; 136
23:28 For thus saith the L God; Behold, I *will* 136
23:32 Thus saith the L God; Thou shalt drink *of* 136
23:34 for I have spoken *it,* saith the L God. 136
23:35 Therefore thus saith the L God; 136
23:46 For thus saith the L God; *I will* bring up a 136
23:49 and ye shall know that I *am* the L God; 136
24: 3 and say unto them, Thus saith the L God; 136
24: 6 Wherefore thus saith the L God; Woe to 136
24: 9 Therefore thus saith the L God; Woe to 136
24:14 shall they judge thee, saith the L God. 136
24:21 the house of Israel, Thus saith the L God; 136
24:24 ye shall know that I *am* the L God. 136
25: 3 Hear the word of the L God; 136
25: 3 Thus saith the L God; Because thou 136
25: 6 For thus saith the L God; Because thou 136
25: 8 Thus saith the L God; Because that Moab 136
25:12 Thus saith the L God; Because that Edom 136
25:13 Therefore thus saith the L God; I will also 136
25:14 know my vengeance, saith the L God. 136
25:15 Thus saith the L God; Because 136
25:16 Therefore thus saith the L God; Behold, 136
26: 3 Therefore thus saith the L God; Behold, 136
26: 5 for I have spoken *it,* saith the L God: 136
26: 7 For thus saith the L God; Behold, I *will* 136
26:14 for I the LORD have spoken *it,* saith the L God. 136
26:15 Thus saith the L God to Tyrus; Shall not 136
26:19 For thus saith the L God; When I shall 136
26:21 never be found again, saith the L God. 136

Eze 27: 3 for many isles, Thus saith the L God; 136
28: 2 the prince of Tyrus, Thus saith the L God; 136
28: 6 Therefore thus saith the L God; 136
28:10 for I have spoken *it,* saith the L God. 136
28:12 and say unto him, Thus saith the L God; 136
28:22 say, Thus saith the L God; Behold, I *am* 136
28:24 and they shall know that I *am* the L God. 136
28:25 Thus saith the L God; When I shall have 136
29: 3 Speak, and say, Thus saith the L God; 136
29: 8 Therefore thus saith the L God; Behold, 136
29:13 Yet thus saith the L God; At the end of 136
29:16 but they shall know that I *am* the L God. 136
29:19 Therefore thus saith the L God; Behold, 136
29:20 they wrought for me, saith the L God. 136
30: 2 prophesy and say, Thus saith the L God; 136
30: 6 fall in it by the sword, saith the L God. 136
30:10 Thus saith the L God; I will also make 136
30:13 Thus saith the L God; I will also destroy 136
30:22 Therefore thus saith the L God; Behold, 136
31:10 Therefore thus saith the L God; 136
31:15 Thus saith the L God; In the day when he 136
31:18 and all his multitude, saith the L God. 136
32: 3 Thus saith the L God; I will therefore 136
32: 8 darkness upon thy land, saith the L God. 136
32:11 For thus saith the L God; The sword of 136
32:14 their rivers to run like oil, saith the L God. 136
32:16 and for all her multitude, saith the L God. 136
32:31 army slain by the sword, saith the L God. 136
32:32 and all his multitude, saith the L God. 136
33:11 Say unto them, *As* I live, saith the L God, 136
33:17 people say, The way of the L is not equal: 136
33:20 Yet ye say, The way of the L is not equal. 136
33:25 say unto them, Thus saith the L God; 136
33:27 thus unto them, Thus saith the L God; 136
34: 2 Thus saith the L God unto the shepherds; 136
34: 8 saith the L God, surely because my flock 136
34:10 Thus saith the L God; Behold, I *am* 136
34:11 For thus saith the L God; Behold, 136
34:15 cause them to lie down, saith the L God. 136
34:17 *for you,* O my flock, thus saith the L God; 136
34:20 Therefore thus saith the L God unto them; 136
34:30 of Israel, *are* my people, saith the L God. 136
34:31 *and* I am your God, saith the L God. 136
35: 3 say unto it, Thus saith the L God; Behold, 136
35: 6 Therefore, *as* I live, saith the L God, I will 136
35:11 Therefore, *as* I live, saith the L God, I will 136
35:14 Thus saith the L God; When the whole 136
36: 2 Thus saith the L God; Because the enemy 136
36: 3 and say, Thus saith the L God; 136
36: 4 of Israel, hear the word of the L God; 136
36: 4 Thus saith the L God to the mountains, 136
36: 5 Therefore thus saith the L God; Surely in 136
36: 6 and to the valleys, Thus saith the L God; 136
36: 7 Therefore thus saith the L God; I have 136
36:13 Thus saith the L God; Because they say 136
36:14 thy nations any more, saith the L God. 136
36:15 nations to fall any more, saith the L God. 136
36:22 the house of Israel, Thus saith the L God; 136
36:23 that I *am* the LORD, saith the L God, 136
36:32 Not for your sakes do I *this,* saith the L 136
36:33 Thus saith the L God; In the day that I 136
36:37 Thus saith the L God; I will yet *for* this be 136
37: 3 And I answered, O L God, thou knowest. 136
37: 5 Thus saith the L God unto these bones; 136
37: 9 and say to the wind, Thus saith the L God; 136
37:12 and say unto them, Thus saith the L God; 136
37:19 Say unto them, Thus saith the L God; 136
37:21 And say unto them, Thus saith the L God; 136
38: 3 say, Thus saith the L God; Behold, I *am* 136
38:10 Thus saith the L God; It shall also come to 136
38:14 and say unto Gog, Thus saith the L God; 136
38:17 Thus saith the L God; *Art* thou he of 136
38:18 saith the L God, *that* my fury shall come 136
38:21 all my mountains, saith the L God: 136
39: 1 and say, Thus saith the L God; 136
39: 5 for I have spoken *it,* saith the L God. 136
39: 8 it is come, and it is done, saith the L God; 136
39:10 those that robbed them, saith the L God. 136
39:13 that I shall be glorified, saith the L God. 136
39:17 thou son of man, thus saith the L God; 136
39:20 and *with* all men of war, saith the L God. 136
39:25 Therefore thus saith the L God; Now will 136
39:29 upon the house of Israel, saith the L God. 136
43:18 Son of man, thus saith the L God; 136
43:19 to minister unto me, saith the L God. 136
43:27 and I will accept you, saith the L God. 136
44: 6 the house of Israel, Thus saith the L God; 136
44: 9 Thus saith the L God; No stranger, 136
44:12 saith the L God, and they shall bear their 136
44:15 me the fat and the blood, saith the L God: 136
44:27 offer his sin offering, saith the L God. 136
45: 9 Thus saith the L God; Let it suffice you, 136
45: 9 from my people, saith the L God. 136
45:15 reconciliation for them, saith the L God. 136
45:18 Thus saith the L God; In the first *month,* 136
46: 1 Thus saith the L God; The gate of 136
46:16 Thus saith the L God; If the prince give a 136
47:13 This saith the L God; This *shall* be 136
47:23 give *him* his inheritance, saith the L God. 136
48:29 these *are* their portions, saith the L God. 136
Da 1: 2 he gave Jehoiakim king of Judah into his 136
1:10 I fear my l the king, who hath appointed 113
2:10 therefore *there is* no king, l, nor ruler, 7229
2:47 a L of kings, and a revealer of secrets, 4756
4:19 Belteshazzar answered and said, My l, 4756

Da	4:24 which is come upon my **l** the king:	4756
	5:23 hast lifted up thyself against the **L** of	4756
	9: 3 I set my face unto the **L** God, to seek *by*	136
	9: 4 and said, O **L**, the great and dreadful God,	136
	7 O **L**, righteousness *belongeth* unto thee,	136
	9: 8 O **L**, to us *belongeth* confusion of face,	136
	9: 9 To the **L** our God *belong* mercies and	136
	9:15 now, O **L** our God, that hast brought thy	136
	9:16 O **L**, according to all thy righteousness,	136
	9:19 **L**, hear; O Lord, forgive; O Lord, hearken	136
	9:19 Lord, hear; O **L**, forgive; O Lord, hearken	136
	9:19 O Lord, forgive; O **L**, hearken and do;	136
	10:16 unto him that stood before me, O my **l**,	113
	10:17 For how can the servant of this my **l** talk	113
	10:17 servant of this my lord talk with this my **l**?	113
	10:19 was strengthened, and said, Let my **l** speak;	113
	12: 8 O my **l**, what *shall be* the end of these	113
Hos	12:14 his reproach shall his **L** return unto him.	113
Am	1: 8 Philistines shall perish, saith the **L** God.	136
	3: 7 Surely the **L** God will do nothing, but he	136
	3: 8 the **L** God hath spoken, who can but	136
	3:11 Therefore thus saith the **L** God;	136
	3:13 saith the **L** God, the God of hosts,	136
	4: 2 The **L** God hath sworn by his holiness,	136
	4: 5 O ye children of Israel, saith the **L** God.	136
	5: 3 For thus saith the **L** God; The city that	136
	5:16 the God of hosts, the **L**, saith thus;	136
	6: 8 The **L** God hath sworn by himself, saith	136
	7: 1 Thus hath the **L** God shewed unto me;	136
	7: 2 I said, O **L** God, forgive, I beseech thee:	136
	7: 4 Thus hath the **L** God shewed unto me:	136
	7: 4 the **L** God called to contend by fire,	136
	7: 5 said I, O **L** God, cease, I beseech thee:	136
	7: 6 This also shall not be, saith the **L** God.	136
	7: 7 he stood upon a wall made by a	136
	7: 8 said the **L**, Behold, I *will* set a plumbline in	136
	8: 1 Thus hath the **L** God shewed unto me:	136
	8: 3 be howlings in that day, saith the **L** God:	136
	8: 9 come to pass in that day, saith the **L** God,	136
	8:11 Behold, the days come, saith the **L** God,	136
	9: 1 I saw the **L** standing upon the altar:	136
	9: 5 the **L** God of hosts *is* he that toucheth	136
	9: 8 the eyes of the **L** God *are* upon the sinful	136
Ob	1: 1 Thus saith the **L** God concerning Edom;	136
Mic	1: 2 and let the **L** God be witness against you,	136
	1: 2 against you, the **L** from his holy temple.	136
	4:13 their substance unto the **L** of the whole	113
Hab	3:19 The **L** God *is* my strength, and he will	136
Zep	1: 7 Hold thy peace at the presence of the **L**	136
Zec	1: 9 said I, O my **l**, what *are* these? And the	113
	4: 4 with me, saying, What *are* these, my **l**?	113
	4: 5 not what these *be*? And I said, No, my **l**.	113
	4:13 not what these *be*? And I said, No, my **l**.	113
	4:14 that stand by the **L** of the whole earth.	113
	6: 4 that talked with me, What *are* these, my **l**?	113
	6: 5 *which* go forth from standing before the **L**	113
	9: 4 the **L** will cast her out, and he will smite	136
	9:14 and the **L** God shall blow the trumpet,	136
Mal	1:14 sacrificeth unto the **L** a corrupt *thing*: for I	136
Mt	1:20 *the* angel of the **L** appeared unto him in a	2962
	1:22 was spoken of the **L** by the prophet,	2962
	1:24 did as the angel of the **L** had bidden him,	2962
	2:13 *the* angel of the **L** appeareth to Joseph in	2962
	2:15 was spoken of the **L** by the prophet,	2962
	2:19 an angel of the **L** appeareth in a dream to	2962
	3: 3 Prepare ye the way of the **L**, make his	2962
	4: 7 Thou shalt not tempt the **L** thy God.	2962
	4:10 Thou shalt worship the **L** thy God,	2962
	5:33 but shalt perform unto the **L** thine oaths:	2962
	7:21 every one that saith unto me, **L**, Lord,	2962
	7:21 every one that saith unto me, Lord, **L**,	2962
	7:22 Many will say to me in that day, **L**, Lord,	2962
	7:22 Many will say to me in that day, Lord, **L**,	2962
	8: 2 worshipped him, saying, **L**, if thou wilt,	2962
	8: 6 And saying, O **L**, my servant lieth at home	2962
	8: 8 The centurion answered and said, **L**, I am	2962
	8:21 **L**, suffer me first to go and bury my father.	2962
	8:25 *him*, and awoke him, saying, **L**, save us:	2962
	9:28 to do this? They said unto him, Yea, **L**.	2962
	9:38 Pray ye therefore the **L** of the harvest,	2962
	10:24 *his* master, nor the servant above his **l**.	2962
	10:25 be as his master, and the servant as his **l**.	2962
	11:25 **L** of heaven and earth, because thou hast	2962
	12: 8 the Son of man is **L** even of the sabbath	2962
	13:51 these *things*? They say unto him, Yea, **L**.	2962
	14:28 And Peter answered him and said, **L**, if it	2962
	14:30 to sink, he cried, saying, **L**, save me.	2962
	15:22 mercy on me, O **L**, *thou* Son of David;	2962
	15:25 and worshipped him, saying, **L**, help me.	2962
	15:27 And she said, Truth, **L**: yet the dogs eat of	2962
	16:22 rebuke him, saying, Be it far from thee, **L**:	2962
	17: 4 answered Peter, and said unto Jesus, **L**,	2962
	17:15 **L**, have mercy on my son: for he is	2962
	18:21 Then came Peter to him, and said, **L**,	2962
	18:25 his **l** commanded him to be sold,	2962
	18:26 down, and worshipped him, saying, **L**,	2962
	18:27 Then the **l** of that servant was moved	2962
	18:31 and told unto their **l** all that was done.	2962
	18:32 Then his **l**, after that he had called him,	2962
	18:34 And his **l** was wroth, and delivered him to	2962
	20: 8 **l** of the vineyard saith unto his steward,	2962
	20:30 cried out, saying, Have mercy on us, O **L**,	2962
	20:31 saying, Have mercy on us, O **L**, *thou* Son	2962
	20:33 They say unto him, **L**, that our eyes may	2962
	21: 3 ye shall say, The **L** hath need of them;	2962

Mt	21: 9 *is* he that cometh in the name of the **L**;	2962
	21:40 When the **l** therefore of the vineyard	2962
	22:37 Thou shalt love the **L** thy God with all thy	2962
	22:43 How then doth David in spirit call him **L**,	2962
	22:44 The **L** said unto my Lord, Sit thou on my	2962
	22:44 The LORD said unto my **L**, Sit thou on	2962
	22:45 David then call him **L**, how is he his son?	2962
	23:39 *is* he that cometh in the name of the **L**.	2962
	24:42 for ye know not what hour your **L** doth	2962
	24:45 whom his **l** hath made ruler over his	2962
	24:46 whom his **l** when he cometh shall find so	2962
	24:48 say in his heart, My **l** delayeth his coming;	2962
	24:50 The **l** of that servant shall come in a day	2962
	25:11 other virgins, saying, Lord, open to us.	2962
	25:11 other virgins, saying, Lord, **L**, open to us.	2962
	25:19 After a long time the **l** of those servants	2962
	25:20 and brought other five talents, saying, **L**,	2962
	25:21 His **l** said unto him, Well *done, thou* good	2962
	25:21 *things:* enter thou into the joy of thy **l**.	2962
	25:22 received two talents came and said, **L**,	2962
	25:23 His **l** said unto him, Well *done*, good and	2962
	25:23 *things:* enter thou into the joy of thy **l**.	2962
	25:24 received the one talent came and said, **L**,	2962
	25:26 His **l** answered and said unto him,	2962
	25:37 saying, **L**, when saw we thee a hungred,	2962
	25:44 saying, **L**, when saw we thee a hungred,	2962
	26:22 one of them to say unto him, **L**, is it?	2962
	27:10 the potter's field, as the **L** appointed me.	2962
	28: 2 for *the* angel of the **L** descended from	2962
	28: 6 Come, see the place where the **L** lay.	2962
Mk	1: 3 Prepare ye the way of the **L**, make his	2962
	2:28 Therefore the Son of man is **L** also of	2962
	5:19 them how great *things* the **L** hath done	2962
	7:28 she answered and said unto him, Yes, **L**:	2962
	9:24 cried out, and said with tears, **L**, I believe;	2962
	10:51 him, **L**, that I might receive my sight.	4462
	11: 3 say ye that the **L** hath need of him;	2962
	11: 9 *is* he that cometh in the name of the **L**:	2962
	11:10 that cometh in the name of the **L**:	2962
	12: 9 therefore the **l** of the vineyard do?	2962
	12:29 O Israel; The **L** our God is one Lord:	2962
	12:29 O Israel; The Lord our God is one **L**:	2962
	12:30 thou shalt love the **L** thy God with all	2962
	12:36 The **L** said to my Lord, Sit thou on my	2962
	12:36 The LORD said to my **L**, Sit thou on my	2962
	12:37 David therefore himself calleth him **L**;	2962
	13:20 except that the **L** had shortened *those*	2962
	16:19 then after the **L** had spoken unto them,	2962
	16:20 the **L** working with *them*, and	2962
Lk	1: 6 and ordinances of the **L** blameless.	2962
	1: 9 when he went into the temple of the **L**.	2962
	1:11 **L** standing on the right side of the altar of	2962
	1:15 For he shall be great in the sight of the **L**,	2962
	1:16 of Israel shall he turn to the **L** their God.	2962
	1:17 make ready a people prepared for the **L**.	2962
	1:25 Thus hath the **L** dealt with me in the days	2962
	1:28 *art* highly favoured, the **L** is with thee:	2962
	1:32 The **L** God shall give unto him the throne	2962
	1:38 Mary said, Behold the handmaid of the **L**;	2962
	1:43 that the mother of my **L** should come to	2962
	1:45 *things* which were told her from the **L**.	2962
	1:46 Mary said, My soul doth magnify the **L**,	2962
	1:58 her cousins heard how the **L** had shewed	2962
	1:66 And the hand of the **L** was with him.	2962
	1:68 Blessed *be* the **L** God of Israel; for he hath	2962
	1:76 thou shalt go before the face of the **L** to	2962
	2: 9 *the* angel of the **L** came upon them,	2962
	2: 9 glory of the **L** shone round about them:	2962
	2:11 of David a Saviour, which is Christ the **L**.	2962
	2:15 which the **L** hath made known unto us.	2962
	2:22 to Jerusalem, to present *him* to the **L**;	2962
	2:23 (As it is written in the law of the **L**, Every	2962
	2:23 the womb shall be called holy to the **L**;)	2962
	2:24 to that which is said in the law of the **L**,	2962
	2:29 **L**, now lettest thou thy servant depart in	1203
	2:38 instant gave thanks *likewise* unto the **L**,	2962
	2:39 all *things* according to the law of the **L**,	2962
	3: 4 Prepare ye the way of the **L**, make his	2962
	4: 8 Thou shalt worship the **L** thy God,	2962
	4:12 said, Thou shalt not tempt the **L** thy God.	2962
	4:18 The Spirit of the **L** *is* upon me,	2962
	4:19 To preach the acceptable year of the **L**.	2962
	5: 8 from me; for I am a sinful man, O **L**.	2962
	5:12 and besought him, saying, **L**, if thou wilt,	2962
	5:17 the power of the **L** was *present* to heal	2962
	6: 5 That the Son of man is **L** also of	2962
	6:46 **L**, Lord, and do not *the things* which I	2962
	6:46 Lord, **L**, and do not *the things* which I	2962
	7: 6 saying unto him, **L**, trouble not thyself:	2962
	7:13 And when the **L** saw her, he had	2962
	7:31 And the **L** said, Whereunto then shall I	2962
	9:54 And John saw *this*, they said, **L**,	2962
	9:57 a certain *man* said unto him, **L**, I will	2962
	9:59 But he said, **L**, suffer me first to go and	2962
	9:61 another also said, **L**, I will follow thee;	2962
	10: 1 After these *things* the **L** appointed other	2962
	10: 2 pray ye therefore the **L** of the harvest,	2962
	10:17 returned *again* with joy, saying, **L**,	2962
	10:21 O Father, **L** of heaven and earth,	2962
	10:27 Thou shalt love the **L** thy God with all	2962
	10:40 and came to *him*, and said, **L**,	2962
	11: 1 **L**, teach us to pray, as John also taught his	2962
	11:39 And the **L** said unto him, Now do ye	2962
	12:36 like unto men that wait for their **l**,	2962
	12:37 whom the **l** when he cometh shall find	2962

Lk	12:41 Peter said unto him, **L**, speakest thou	2962
	12:42 And the **L** said, Who then is *that* faithful	2962
	12:42 whom *his* **l** shall make ruler over his	2962
	12:43 whom his **l** when he cometh shall find so	2962
	12:45 in his heart, My **l** delayeth his coming;	2962
	12:46 The **l** of that servant will come in a day	2962
	13: 8 **L**, let it alone this year also, till I shall dig	2962
	13:15 The **L** then answered him, and said,	2962
	13:23 Then said one unto him, **L**, are there few	2962
	13:25 the door, saying, **L**, Lord, open unto us;	2962
	13:25 the door, saying, Lord, **L**, open unto us;	2962
	13:35 *is* he that cometh in the name of the **L**.	2962
	14:21 shewed his **l** these *things*. Then the	2962
	14:22 And the servant said, **L**, it is done as thou	2962
	14:23 And the **l** said unto the servant, Go out	2962
	16: 3 for my **l** taketh away from me	2962
	16: 5 first, How much owest thou unto my **l**?	2962
	16: 8 the **l** commended the unjust steward,	2962
	17: 5 And the apostles said unto the **L**,	2962
	17: 6 And the **L** said, If ye had faith as a grain	2962
	17:37 and said unto him, Where, **L**?	2962
	18: 6 the **L** said, Hear what the unjust judge	2962
	18:41 And he said, **L**, that I may receive my	2962
	19: 8 And Zaccheus stood, and said unto the **L**;	2962
	19: 8 Behold, **L**, the half of my goods I give to	2962
	19:16 Then came the first, saying, **L**, thy pound	2962
	19:18 the second came, saying, **L**, thy pound	2962
	19:20 saying, **L**, behold, *here* is thy pound,	2962
	19:25 said unto him, **L**, he hath ten pounds.)	2962
	19:31 him, Because the **L** hath need of him.	2962
	19:34 And they said, The **L** hath need of him.	2962
	19:38 King that cometh in the name of the **L**:	2962
	20:13 said the **l** of the vineyard, What shall	2962
	20:15 shall the **l** of the vineyard do unto them?	2962
	20:37 he calleth the **L** the God of Abraham,	2962
	20:42 The **L** said to my Lord, Sit thou on my	2962
	20:42 The LORD said to my **L**, Sit thou on my	2962
	20:44 David therefore calleth him **L**, how is he	2962
	22:31 And the **L** said, Simon, Simon, behold,	2962
	22:33 he said unto him, **L**, I am ready to go	2962
	22:38 And they said, **L**, behold, here are two	2962
	22:49 said unto him, **L**, shall we smite with	2962
	22:61 the **L** turned, and looked upon Peter.	2962
	22:61 Peter remembered the word of the **L**,	2962
	23:42 And he said unto Jesus, **L**, remember me	2962
	24: 3 and found not the body of the **L** Jesus.	2962
	24:34 **L** is risen indeed, and hath appeared	2962
Jn	1:23 Make straight the way of the **L**, as said	2962
	4: 1 the **L** knew how the Pharisees had heard	2962
	6:23 after that the **L** had given thanks:)	2962
	6:34 said they unto him, **L**, evermore give	2962
	6:68 answered him, **L**, to whom shall we go?	2962
	8:11 She said, No *man*, **L**. And Jesus said unto	2962
	9:36 He answered and said, Who is he, **L**, that	2962
	9:38 And he said, **L**, I believe. And he	2962
	11: 2 (It was *that* Mary which anointed the **L**	2962
	11: 3 saying, **L**, behold, he whom thou lovest is	2962
	11:12 **L**, if he sleep, he shall do well.	2962
	11:21 **L**, if thou hadst been here, my brother	2962
	11:27 She saith unto him, Yea, **L**: I believe that	2962
	11:32 unto him, **L**, if thou hadst been here,	2962
	11:34 They say unto him, **L**, come and see.	2962
	11:39 unto him, **L**, by this time he stinketh:	2962
	12:13 Israel that cometh in the name of the **L**.	2962
	12:38 which he spake, **L**, who hath believed our	2962
	12:38 to whom hath the arm of the **L** been	2962
	13: 6 *Peter* saith unto him, **L**, dost thou wash	2962
	13: 9 not my feet only, but also *my* hands	2962
	13:13 Ye call me Master and **L**: and ye say well;	2962
	13:14 If I then, *your* **L** and Master, have washed	2962
	13:16 The servant is not greater than his **l**;	2962
	13:25 Jesus' breast saith unto him, **L**, who is it?	2962
	13:36 said unto him, **L**, whither goest thou?	2962
	13:37 said unto him, **L**, why cannot I follow	2962
	14: 5 Thomas saith unto him, **L**, we know not	2962
	14: 8 **L**, shew us the Father, and it sufficeth us.	2962
	14:22 Judas saith unto him, not Iscariot, **L**, how	2962
	15:15 for the servant knoweth not what his **l**	2962
	15:20 The servant is not greater than his **l**.	2962
	20: 2 They have taken away the **L** out of	2962
	20:13 Because they have taken away my **L**,	2962
	20:18 told the disciples that she had seen the **L**,	2962
	20:20 the disciples glad, when they saw the **L**.	2962
	20:25 said unto him, We have seen the **L**.	2962
	20:28 and said unto him, My **L** and my God.	2962
	21: 7 Jesus loved saith unto Peter, It is the **L**.	2962
	21: 7 Simon Peter heard that it was the **L**,	2962
	21:12 Who art thou? knowing that it was the **L**.	2962
	21:15 He saith unto him, Yea, **L**; thou knowest	2962
	21:16 He saith unto him, Yea, **L**; thou knowest	2962
	21:17 he said unto him, **L**, thou knowest all	2962
	21:20 and said, **L**, which is he that betrayeth	2962
	21:21 to Jesus, **L**, and what *shall* this *man* do?	2962
Ac	1: 6 they asked of him, saying, **L**,	2962
	1:21 us all the time that the **L** Jesus went in	2962
	1:24 And they prayed, and said, Thou, **L**,	2962
	2:20 *that* great and notable day of the **L** come:	2962
	2:21 call on the name of the **L** shall be saved.	2962
	2:25 I foresaw the **L** always before my face,	2962
	2:34 saith himself, The **L** said unto my Lord,	2962
	2:34 saith himself, The LORD said unto my **L**,	2962
	2:36 ye have crucified, both **L** and Christ.	2962
	2:39 *even* as many as the **L** our God shall call.	2962
	2:47 the **L** added to the church daily such	2962
	3:19 shall come from the presence of the **L**;	2962

L

Ac	3:22	A prophet shall the L your God raise up	2962
	4:24	said, L, thou *art* God, which hast made	1203
	4:26	were gathered together against the L,	2962
	4:29	And now, L, behold their threatenings:	2962
	4:33	witness of the resurrection of the L Jesus:	2962
	5: 9	together to tempt the Spirit of the L?	2962
	5:14	believers were the more added to the L,	2962
	5:19	But *the* angel of the L by night opened	2962
	7:30	angel of the L in a flame of fire in a bush.	2962
	7:31	the voice of the L came unto him,	2962
	7:33	Then said the L to him, Put off *thy* shoes	2962
	7:37	A prophet shall the L your God raise up	2962
	7:49	saith the L: or what *is* the place of my	2962
	7:59	calling upon *God,* and saying, L Jesus,	2962
	7:60	and cried with a loud voice, L,	2962
	8:16	were baptized in the name of the L Jesus.)	2962
	8:24	and said, Pray ye to the L for me,	2962
	8:25	and preached the word of the L,	2962
	8:26	And *the* angel of the L spake unto Philip,	2962
	8:39	the Spirit of the L caught away Philip,	2962
	9: 1	slaughter against the disciples of the L,	2962
	9: 5	And he said, Who art thou, L?	2962
	9: 5	And he said, I am Jesus whom thou	2962
	9: 6	And he trembling and astonished said, L,	2962
	9: 6	he *said* unto him, Arise, and go into	2962
	9:10	and to him said the L in a vision, Ananias.	2962
	9:10	And he said, Behold, I am here, L.	2962
	9:11	the L *said* unto him, Arise, and go into	2962
	9:13	Ananias answered, L, I have heard by	2962
	9:15	L said unto him, Go thy way: for he	2962
	9:17	him said, Brother Saul, the L, *even* Jesus,	2962
	9:27	unto them how he had seen the L	2962
	9:29	And he spake boldly in the name of the L	2962
	9:31	and walking in the fear of the L, and in	2962
	9:35	and Saron saw him, and turned to the L.	2962
	9:42	all Joppa; and many believed in the L.	2962
	10: 4	he was afraid, and said, What is it, L?	2962
	10:14	But Peter said, Not so, L; for I have never	2962
	10:36	peace by Jesus Christ: (he is L of all:)	2962
	10:48	them to be baptized in the name of the L.	2962
	11: 8	But I said, Not so, L: for nothing common	2962
	11:16	Then remembered I the word of the L,	2962
	11:17	who believed on the L Jesus Christ;	2962
	11:20	unto the Grecians, preaching the L Jesus.	2962
	11:21	And the hand of the L was with them:	2962
	11:21	number believed, and turned unto the L.	2962
	11:23	of heart *they* would cleave unto the L.	2962
	11:24	and much people was added unto the L.	2962
	12: 7	*the* angel of the L came upon *him,* and	2962
	12:11	that the L hath sent his angel,	2962
	12:17	unto them how the L had brought	2962
	12:23	And immediately *the* angel of the L smote	2962
	13: 2	As they ministered to the L, and fasted,	2962
	13:10	cease to pervert the right ways of the L?	2962
	13:11	the hand of the L is upon thee,	2962
	13:12	being astonished at the doctrine of the L.	2962
	13:47	For so hath the L commanded us, *saying,*	2962
	13:48	were glad, and glorified the word of the L:	2962
	13:49	And the word of the L was published	2962
	14: 3	abode they speaking boldly in the L,	2962
	14:23	they commended them to the L, on	2962
	15:11	of the L Jesus Christ we shall be saved,	2962
	15:17	the residue of men might seek after the L,	2962
	15:17	saith the L, who doeth all these *things.*	2962
	15:26	lives for the name of our L Jesus Christ.	2962
	15:35	teaching and preaching the word of the L,	2962
	15:36	we have preached the word of the L,	2962
	16:10	assuredly gathering that the L had called	2962
	16:14	heard *us:* whose heart the L opened,	2962
	16:15	ye have judged me to be faithful to the L,	2962
	16:31	Believe on the L Jesus Christ,	2962
	16:32	they spake unto him the word of the L,	2962
	17:24	seeing that he is L of heaven and earth,	2962
	17:27	That *they* should seek the L, if haply they	2962
	18: 8	believed on the L with all his house;	2962
	18: 9	Then spake the L to Paul in the night by	2962
	18:25	*man* was instructed in the way of the L;	2962
	18:25	and taught diligently the *things* of the L.	2962
	19: 5	were baptized in the name of the L Jesus.	2962
	19:10	in Asia heard the word of the L Jesus,	2962
	19:13	had evil spirits the name of the L Jesus,	2962
	19:17	the name of the L Jesus was magnified.	2962
	20:19	Serving the L with all humility of mind,	2962
	20:21	and faith toward our L Jesus Christ.	2962
	20:24	which I have received of the L Jesus,	2962
	20:35	to remember the words of the L Jesus,	2962
	21:13	at Jerusalem for the name of the L Jesus.	2962
	21:14	saying, The will of the L be done.	2962
	21:20	when they heard *it,* they glorified the L,	2962
	22: 8	And I answered, Who art thou, L?	2962
	22:10	And I said, What shall I do, L?	2962
	22:10	the L said unto me, Arise, and go into	2962
	22:16	thy sins, calling on the name of the L.	2962
	22:19	I said, L, they know that I imprisoned	2962
	23:11	And the night following the L stood by	2962
	25:26	have no certain *thing* to write unto *my* l.	2962
	26:15	And I said, Who art thou, L? And he said,	2962
	28:31	those *things* which concern the L.	2962
Ro	1: 3	Concerning his Son Jesus Christ our L,	2962
	1: 7	God our Father, and the L Jesus Christ.	2962
	4: 8	Blessed *is* the man to whom the L will	2962
	4:24	that raised up Jesus our L from the dead;	2962
	5: 1	we have peace with God through our L	2962
	5:11	we also joy in God through our L Jesus	2962
	5:21	unto eternal life by Jesus Christ our L.	2962

	6:11	alive unto God through Jesus Christ our L.	2962
	6:23	*is* eternal life through Jesus Christ our L.	2962
	7:25	I thank God through Jesus Christ our L.	2962
	8:39	of God, which is in Christ Jesus our L.	2962
	9:28	a short work will the L make upon	2962
	9:29	Except the L of sabaoth had left us a seed,	2962
	10: 9	shalt confess with thy mouth the L Jesus,	2962
	10:12	for the same L over all *is* rich unto all	2962
	10:13	upon the name of the L shall be saved.	2962
	10:16	For Esaias saith, L, who hath believed our	2962
	11: 3	L, they have killed thy prophets,	2962
	11:34	For who hath known the mind of the L?	2962
	12:11	business; fervent in spirit; serving the L;	2962
	12:19	*is* mine; I will repay, saith the L.	2962
	13:14	But put ye on the L Jesus Christ,	2962
	14: 6	the day, regardeth *it* unto the L;	2962
	14: 6	to the L he doth not regard *it.* He that	2962
	14: 6	eateth to the L, for he giveth God thanks;	2962
	14: 6	to the L he eateth not, and giveth God	2962
	14: 8	For whether we live, we live unto the L;	2962
	14: 8	and whether we die, we die unto the L:	2962
	14: 9	that he might be L both of the dead and	2961
	14:11	For it is written, As I live, saith the L,	2962
	14:14	I know, and am persuaded by the L Jesus,	2962
	15: 6	even the Father of our L Jesus Christ.	2962
	15:11	And again, Praise the L, all ye Gentiles;	2962
	15:30	for the L Jesus Christ's sake, and by the	2962
	16: 2	That ye receive her in the L, as becometh	2962
	16: 8	Greet Amplias my beloved in the L.	2962
	16:11	of Narcissus, which are in the L.	2962
	16:12	and Tryphosa, who labour in the L.	2962
	16:12	which laboured much in the L.	2962
	16:13	Salute Rufus chosen in the L,	2962
	16:18	*they that are* such serve not our L Jesus	2962
	16:20	The grace of our L Jesus Christ *be* with	2962
	16:22	wrote *this* epistle, salute you in the L.	2962
	16:24	The grace of our L Jesus Christ *be* with	2962
1Co	1: 2	upon the name of Jesus Christ our L,	2962
	1: 3	our Father, and *from* the L Jesus Christ.	2962
	1: 7	waiting for the coming of our L Jesus	2962
	1: 8	blameless in the day of our L Jesus Christ.	2962
	1: 9	fellowship of his Son Jesus Christ our L.	2962
	1:10	by the name of our L Jesus Christ,	2962
	1:31	He that glorieth, let him glory in the L.	2962
	2: 8	would not have crucified the L of glory.	2962
	2:16	For who hath known the mind of the L,	2962
	3: 5	even as the L gave to every man?	2962
	3:20	The L knoweth the thoughts of the wise,	2962
	4: 4	but he that judgeth me is the L.	2962
	4: 5	nothing before the time, until the L come,	2962
	4:17	is my beloved son, and faithful in the L,	2962
	4:19	shortly, if the L will, and will know,	2962
	5: 4	In the name of our L Jesus Christ, when	2962
	5: 4	with the power of our L Jesus Christ,	2962
	5: 5	may be saved in the day of the L Jesus.	2962
	6:11	ye are justified in the name of the L Jesus,	2962
	6:13	body *is* not for fornication, but for the L;	2962
	6:13	but for the Lord; and the L for the body.	2962
	6:14	And God hath both raised up the L,	2962
	6:17	But he that is joined unto the L is one	2962
	7:10	married I command, *yet* not I, but the L,	2962
	7:12	But to the rest speak I, not the L: If any	2962
	7:17	as the L hath called every one, so let him	2962
	7:22	For he that is called in the L, *being* a	2962
	7:25	virgins I have no commandment of the L:	2962
	7:25	as one that hath obtained mercy of the L	2962
	7:32	careth for the *things* that belong to the L:	2962
	7:32	to the Lord, how he may please the L:	2962
	7:34	*woman* careth for the *things* of the L,	2962
	7:35	that you may attend upon the L without	2962
	7:39	married to whom she will; only in the L.	2962
	8: 6	and one L Jesus Christ, by whom *are* all	2962
	9: 1	have I not seen Jesus Christ our L?	2962
	9: 1	our Lord? are not you my work in the L?	2962
	9: 2	seal of mine apostleship are ye in the L.	2962
	9: 5	and *as* the brethren of the L, and Cephas?	2962
	9:14	the L ordained that they which preach	2962
	10:21	Ye cannot drink the cup of the L,	2962
	10:22	Do we provoke the L to jealousy? are we	2962
	11:11	the woman without the man, in the L.	2962
	11:23	For I have received of the L *that* which	2962
	11:23	That the L Jesus the *same* night in which	2962
	11:27	and drink *this* cup of the L unworthily,	2962
	11:27	be guilty of the body and blood of the L.	2962
	11:32	we are judged, we are chastened of the L,	2962
	12: 3	*that no man* can say that Jesus is the L,	2962
	12: 5	of administrations, but the same L.	2962
	14:21	all that will they not hear me, saith the L.	2962
	14:37	you are the commandments of the L.	2962
	15:31	which I have in Christ Jesus our L,	2962
	15:47	the second man *is* the L from heaven.	2962
	15:57	which giveth us the victory through our L	2962
	15:58	always abounding in the work of the L,	2962
	15:58	that your labour is not in vain in the L.	2962
	16: 7	to tarry a while with you, if the L permit.	2962
	16:10	he worketh the work of the L, as I also	2962
	16:19	and Priscilla salute you much in the L,	2962
	16:22	If any *man* love not the L Jesus Christ,	2962
	16:23	The grace of *our* L Jesus Christ *be* with	2962
2Co	1: 2	our Father, and *from* the L Jesus Christ.	2962
	1: 3	even the Father of our L Jesus Christ,	2962
	1:14	as ye also *are* ours in the day of the L.	2962
	2:12	and a door was opened unto me of the L,	2962
	3:16	Nevertheless when *it* shall turn to the L,	2962
	3:17	Now the L is *that* Spirit: and where	2962

	3:17	the Spirit of the L *is,* there *is* liberty.	2962
	3:18	beholding as in a glass the glory of the L,	2962
	3:18	to glory, even as by the Spirit of the L.	2962
	4: 5	not ourselves, but Christ Jesus the L;	2962
	4:10	in the body the dying of the L Jesus,	2962
	4:14	Knowing that he which raised up the L	2962
	5: 6	in the body, we are absent from the L:	2962
	5: 8	the body, and to be present with the L.	2962
	5:11	Knowing therefore the terror of the L,	2962
	6:17	saith the L, and touch not the unclean	2962
	6:18	and daughters, saith the L Almighty.	2962
	8: 5	but first gave their own selves to the L,	2962
	8: 9	For ye know the grace of our L Jesus	2962
	8:19	by us to the glory of the same L,	2962
	8:21	*things,* not only in the sight of the L,	2962
	10: 8	which the L hath given us for edification,	2962
	10:17	he that glorieth, let him glory in the L.	2962
	10:18	approved, but whom the L commendeth.	2962
	11:17	I speak *it* not after the L, but as *it were*	2962
	11:31	The God and Father of our L Jesus Christ,	2962
	12: 1	come to visions and revelations of the L.	2962
	12: 8	For this *thing* I besought the L thrice, that	2962
	13:10	according to the power which the L hath	2962
	13:14	The grace of the L Jesus Christ,	2962
Gal	1: 3	the Father, and *from* our L Jesus Christ,	2962
	4: 1	from a servant, though he be l of all;	2962
	5:10	I have confidence in you through the L,	2962
	6:14	save in the cross of our L Jesus Christ,	2962
	6:17	for I bear in my body the marks of the L	2962
	6:18	the grace of our L Jesus Christ *be* with	2962
Eph	1: 2	our Father, and *from* the L Jesus Christ.	2962
	1: 3	the God and Father of our L Jesus Christ,	2962
	1:15	after I heard of your faith in the L Jesus,	2962
	1:17	That the God of our L Jesus Christ,	2962
	2:21	groweth unto a holy temple in the L:	2962
	3:11	which he purposed in Christ Jesus our L:	2962
	3:14	unto the Father of our L Jesus Christ,	2962
	4: 1	I therefore, the prisoner of the L,	2962
	4: 5	One L, one faith, one baptism,	2962
	4:17	This I say therefore, and testify in the L,	2962
	5: 8	but now *are* ye light in the L:	2962
	5:10	Proving what is acceptable unto the L.	2962
	5:17	understanding what the will of the L *is.*	2962
	5:19	making melody in your heart to the L;	2962
	5:20	the Father in the name of our L Jesus	2962
	5:22	unto your own husbands, as unto the L.	2962
	5:29	cherisheth it, even as the L the church:	2962
	6: 1	Children, obey your parents in the L:	2962
	6: 4	in the nurture and admonition of the L.	2962
	6: 7	doing service, as to the L, and not to men:	2962
	6: 8	the same shall he receive of the L,	2962
	6:10	be strong in the L, and in the power of his	2962
	6:21	and faithful minister in the L,	2962
	6:23	God the Father and the L Jesus Christ.	2962
	6:24	Grace *be* with all them that love our L	2962
Php	1: 2	our Father, and *from* the L Jesus Christ.	2962
	1:14	And many of the brethren in the L,	2962
	2:11	should confess that Jesus Christ *is* L,	2962
	2:19	I trust in the L Jesus to send Timotheus	2962
	2:24	But I trust in the L that I also myself shall	2962
	2:29	therefore in the L with all gladness;	2962
	3: 1	Finally, my brethren, rejoice in the L.	2962
	3: 8	of the knowledge of Christ Jesus my L:	2962
	3:20	look for the Saviour, the L Jesus Christ:	2962
	4: 1	my joy and crown, so stand fast in the L,	2962
	4: 2	that *they* be of the same mind in the L.	2962
	4: 4	Rejoice in the L alway: *and* again I say,	2962
	4: 5	be known unto all men. The L is at hand.	2962
	4:10	I rejoiced in the L greatly, that now at	2962
	4:23	The grace of our L Jesus Christ *be* with	2962
Col	1: 2	God our Father and the L Jesus Christ.	2962
	1: 3	and the Father of our L Jesus Christ,	2962
	1:10	That ye might walk worthy of the L unto	2962
	2: 6	therefore received Christ Jesus the L,	2962
	3:16	singing with grace in your hearts to the L.	2962
	3:17	or deed, *do* all in the name of the L Jesus,	2962
	3:18	your own husbands, as it is fit in the L.	2962
	3:20	for this is well pleasing unto the L.	2962
	3:23	*it* heartily, as to the L, and not unto men;	2962
	3:24	Knowing that of the L ye shall receive	2962
	3:24	the inheritance: for ye serve the L Christ.	2962
	4: 7	minister and fellowservant in the L:	2962
	4:17	which thou hast received in the L,	2962
1Th	1: 1	God the Father and *in* the L Jesus Christ:	2962
	1: 1	God our Father, and the L Jesus Christ.	2962
	1: 3	and patience of hope in our L Jesus Christ,	2962
	1: 6	ye became followers of us, and of the L,	2962
	1: 8	from you sounded out the word of the L,	2962
	2:15	Who both killed the L Jesus, and their	2962
	2:19	*Are* not even ye in the presence of our L	2962
	3: 8	For now we live, if ye stand fast in the L.	2962
	3:11	and our Father, and our L Jesus Christ,	2962
	3:12	And the L make you to increase and	2962
	3:13	at the coming of our L Jesus Christ with	2962
	4: 1	brethren, and exhort *you* by the L Jesus,	2962
	4: 2	we gave you by the L Jesus.	2962
	4: 6	that the L *is* the avenger of all such,	2962
	4:15	we say unto you by the word of the L,	2962
	4:15	remain unto the coming of the L shall not	2962
	4:16	For the L himself shall descend from	2962
	4:17	in the clouds, to meet the L in the air:	2962
	4:17	and so shall we ever be with the L.	2962
	5: 2	know perfectly that the day of the L	2962
	5: 9	to obtain salvation by our L Jesus Christ,	2962
	5:12	and are over you in the L,	2962

L

L

1Th 5:23 unto the coming of our **L** Jesus Christ. *2962*
5:27 I charge you by the **L** that *this* epistle be *2962*
5:28 The grace of our **L** Jesus Christ *be* with *2962*
2Th 1: 1 in God our Father and the **L** Jesus Christ: *2962*
1: 2 God our Father and the **L** Jesus Christ. *2962*
1: 7 when the **L** Jesus shall be revealed from *2962*
1: 8 that obey not the gospel of our **L** Jesus *2962*
1: 9 destruction from the presence of the **L**, *2962*
1:12 That the name of our **L** Jesus Christ may *2962*
1:12 grace of our God and the **L** Jesus Christ. *2962*
2: 1 by the coming of our **L** Jesus Christ, *2962*
2: 8 whom the **L** shall consume with the spirit *2962*
2:13 brethren beloved of the **L**, because God *2962*
2:14 to the obtaining of the glory of our **L** Jesus *2962*
2:16 Now our **L** Jesus Christ himself, and God, *2962*
3: 1 that the word of the **L** may have *free* *2962*
3: 3 But the **L** is faithful, who shall stablish *2962*
3: 4 we have confidence in the **L** touching *2962*
3: 5 And the **L** direct your hearts into the love *2962*
3: 6 in the name of our **L** Jesus Christ, *2962*
3:12 and exhort by our **L** Jesus Christ, *2962*
3:16 the **L** of peace himself give you peace *2962*
3:16 by all means. The **L** *be* with you all. *2962*
3:18 The grace of our **L** Jesus Christ *be* with *2962*
1Ti 1: 1 and **L** Jesus Christ, *which is* our hope; *2962*
1: 2 God our Father and Jesus Christ our **L**. *2962*
1:12 And I thank Christ Jesus our **L**, who hath *2962*
1:14 And the grace of our **L** was exceeding *2962*
5:21 the **L** Jesus Christ, and the elect angels, *2962*
6: 3 *even the words* of our **L** Jesus Christ, *2962*
6:14 until the appearing of our **L** Jesus Christ: *2962*
6:15 the King of kings, and **L** of lords; *2962*
2Ti 1: 2 God the Father and Christ Jesus our **L**. *2962*
1: 8 ashamed of the testimony of our **L**, *2962*
1:16 The **L** give mercy unto the house of *2962*
1:18 The **L** grant unto him that *he* may find *2962*
1:18 *he* may find mercy of the **L** in that day: *2962*
2: 7 The **L** give thee understanding in all *2962*
2:14 *them* before the **L** that *they* strive *2962*
2:19 seal, The **L** knoweth them that are his. *2962*
2:22 with them that call on the **L** out of a pure *2962*
2:24 And the servant of the **L** must not strive; *2962*
3:11 but out of *them* all the **L** delivered me. *2962*
4: 1 before God, and the **L** Jesus Christ, *2962*
4: 8 the **L**, the righteous judge, shall give *2962*
4:14 the **L** reward him according to his works: *2962*
4:17 Notwithstanding the **L** stood with me, *2962*
4:18 And the **L** shall deliver me from every evil *2962*
4:22 The **L** Jesus Christ *be* with thy spirit. *2962*
Tit 1: 4 and the **L** Jesus Christ our Saviour. *2962*
Phm 1: 3 God our Father and the **L** Jesus Christ. *2962*
1: 5 which thou hast toward the **L** Jesus, *2962*
1:16 thee, both in the flesh, and in the **L**? *2962*
1:20 brother, let me have joy of thee in the **L**: *2962*
1:20 in the Lord: refresh my bowels in the **L**. *2962*
1:25 The grace of our **L** Jesus Christ *be* with *2962*
Heb 1:10 And, Thou, **L**, in the beginning hast laid *2962*
2: 3 at the first began to be spoken by the **L**, *2962*
7:14 For *it is* evident that our **L** sprang out of *2962*
7:21 him, The **L** sware and will not repent, *2962*
8: 2 which the **L** pitched, and not man. *2962*
8: 8 Behold, the days come, saith the **L**, *2962*
8: 9 and I regarded them not, saith the **L**. *2962*
8:10 of Israel after those days, saith the **L**; *2962*
8:11 man his brother, saying, Know the **L**: *2962*
10:16 saith the **L**, I will put my laws into their *2962*
10:30 unto me, I will recompense, saith the **L**. *2962*
10:30 And again, The **L** shall judge his people. *2962*
12: 5 despise not thou the chastening of the **L**, *2962*
12: 6 For whom the **L** loveth he chasteneth, *2962*
12:14 without which no *man* shall see the **L**: *2962*
13: 6 The **L** *is* my helper, and I will not fear *2962*
13:20 that brought again from the dead our **L** *2962*
Jas 1: 1 a servant of God and of the **L** Jesus Christ, *2962*
1: 7 that he shall receive any *thing* of the **L**, *2962*
1:12 which the **L** hath promised to them that *2962*
2: 1 have not the faith of our **L** Jesus Christ, *2962*
2: 1 *the **L*** of glory, with respect of persons. *NIG*
4:10 Humble yourselves in the sight of the **L**, *2962*
4:15 If the **L** will, we shall live, and do this, *2962*
5: 4 entered into the ears of the **L** of sabaoth. *2962*
5: 7 brethren, unto the coming of the **L**. *2962*
5: 8 for the coming of the **L** draweth nigh. *2962*
5:10 who have spoken in the name of the **L**, *2962*
5:11 of Job, and have seen the end of the **L**; *2962*
5:11 that the **L** is very pitiful, and of tender *2962*
5:14 him with oil in the name of the **L**: *2962*
5:15 the sick, and the **L** shall raise him up; *2962*
1Pe 1: 3 the God and Father of our **L** Jesus Christ, *2962*
1:25 But the word of the **L** endureth for ever. *2962*
2: 3 so be ye have tasted that the **L** *is* gracious. *2962*
3: 6 as Sara obeyed Abraham, calling him **l**: *2962*
3:12 the eyes of the **L** *are* over the righteous, *2962*
3:12 the face of the **L** *is* against them that do *2962*
3:15 But sanctify the **L** God in your hearts: *2962*
2Pe 1: 2 the knowledge of God, and of Jesus our **L**. *2962*
1: 8 in the knowledge of our **L** Jesus Christ, *2962*
1:11 into the everlasting kingdom of our **L** *2962*
1:14 as our **L** Jesus Christ hath shewed me. *2962*
1:16 and coming of our **L** Jesus Christ, *2962*
2: 1 even denying the **L** that bought them, *1203*
2: 9 The **L** knoweth *how* to deliver the godly *2962*
2:11 accusation against them before the **L**, *2962*
2:20 world through the knowledge of our **L** *2962*
3: 2 commandment of us the apostles of the **L** *2962*

2Pe 3: 8 one day *is* with the **L** as a thousand years, *2962*
3: 9 The **L** is not slack concerning *his* promise, *2962*
3:10 But the day of the **L** will come as a thief in *2962*
3:15 account *that that* the longsuffering of our **L** *2962*
3:18 and *in* the knowledge of our **L** and *2962*
2Jn 1: 3 the Father, and from the **L** Jesus Christ, *2962*
Jude 1: 4 denying the only **L** God, and our Lord *1203*
1: 4 only Lord God, and our **L** Jesus Christ. *2962*
1: 5 ye once knew this, how that the **L**, *2962*
1: 9 but said, The **L** rebuke thee. *2962*
1:14 The **L** cometh with ten thousands of his *2962*
1:17 of the apostles of our **L** Jesus Christ; *2962*
1:21 for the mercy of our **L** Jesus Christ *2962*
Rev 1: 8 saith the **L**, which is, and which was, *2962*
4: 8 saying, Holy, holy, holy, **L** God Almighty, *2962*
4:11 O **L**, to receive glory and honour and *2962*
6:10 saying, How long, O **L**, holy and true, *1203*
11: 8 Egypt, where also our **L** was crucified. *2962*
11:15 world are become *the kingdoms* of our **L**, *2962*
11:17 O **L** God Almighty, which art, and wast, *2962*
14:13 Blessed *are* the dead which die in the **L** *2962*
15: 3 thy works, **L** God Almighty; *2962*
15: 4 not fear thee, O **L**, and glorify thy name? *2962*
16: 5 O **L**, which art, and wast, and shalt be, *2962*
16: 7 **L** God Almighty, true and righteous *are* *2962*
17:14 for he is **L** of lords, and King of kings: *2962*
18: 8 for strong *is* the **L** God who judgeth her. *2962*
19: 1 honour, and power, unto the **L** our God: *2962*
19: 6 for the **L** God Omnipotent reigneth. *2962*
19:16 KING OF KINGS, AND **L** OF LORDS. *2962*
21:22 for the **L** God Almighty and the Lamb are *2962*
22: 5 the sun; for the **L** God giveth them light: *2962*
22: 6 the **L** God of the holy prophets sent his *2962*
22:20 Amen. Even so, come, **L** Jesus. *2962*
22:21 The grace of our **L** Jesus Christ *be* with *2962*

LORD* (6469) [GOD*, JAH, JEHOVAH, LORD'S*;
this is the proper name of God, *Yahweh* or
Jehovah]
Ge 2: 4 in the day that the **L** God made the earth *3068*
2: 5 for the **L** God had not caused it to rain *3068*
2: 7 the **L** God formed man *of* the dust of *3068*
2: 8 the **L** God planted a garden eastward in *3068*
2: 9 of the ground made the **L** God to grow *3068*
2:15 the **L** God took the man, and put him into *3068*
2:16 the **L** God commanded the man, saying, *3068*
2:18 the **L** God said, *It is* not good that the *3068*
2:19 of the ground the **L** God formed every *3068*
2:21 the **L** God caused a deep sleep to fall *3068*
2:22 which the **L** God had taken from man, *3068*
3: 1 of the field which the **L** God had made. *3068*
3: 8 heard the voice of the **L** God walking *3068*
3: 8 the **L** God amongst the trees of the *3068*
3: 9 the **L** God called unto Adam, and said *3068*
3:13 the **L** God said unto the woman, What *is* *3068*
3:14 the **L** God said unto the serpent, *3068*
3:21 to his wife did the **L** God make coats of *3068*
3:22 the **L** God said, Behold, the man is *3068*
3:23 Therefore the **L** God sent him forth from *3068*
4: 1 and said, I have gotten a man from the **L**. *3068*
4: 3 fruit of the ground an offering unto the **L**. *3068*
4: 4 the **L** had respect unto Abel and to his *3068*
4: 6 the **L** said unto Cain, Why art thou *3068*
4: 9 the **L** said unto Cain, Where *is* Abel thy *3068*
4:13 Cain said unto the **L**, My punishment *is* *3068*
4:15 the **L** said unto him, Therefore *3068*
4:15 the **L** set a mark upon Cain, lest any *3068*
4:16 went out from the presence of the **L**, *3068*
4:26 *men* to call upon the name of the **L**. *3068*
5:29 of the ground which the **L** hath cursed. *3068*
6: 3 the **L** said, My spirit shall not always *3068*
6: 6 it repented the **L** that he had made man *3068*
6: 7 the **L** said, I will destroy man whom I *3068*
6: 8 Noah found grace in the eyes of the **L**. *3068*
7: 1 the **L** said unto Noah, Come thou and *3068*
7: 5 Noah did according unto all that the **L** *3068*
7:16 commanded him: and the **L** shut him in. *3068*
8:20 Noah builded an altar unto the **L**; *3068*
8:21 the **L** smelled a sweet savour; *3068*
8:21 the **L** said in his heart, I will not again *3068*
9:26 he said, Blessed *be* the **L** God of Shem; *3068*
10: 9 He was a mighty hunter before the **L**: *3068*
10: 9 Nimrod the mighty hunter before the **L**. *3068*
11: 5 the **L** came down to see the city and *3068*
11: 6 the **L** said, Behold, the people *is* one, *3068*
11: 8 So the **L** scattered them abroad from *3068*
11: 9 the **L** did there confound the language of *3068*
11: 9 thence did the **L** scatter them abroad *3068*
12: 1 Now the **L** had said unto Abram, Get *3068*
12: 4 as the **L** had spoken unto him; *3068*
12: 7 the **L** appeared unto Abram, and said, *3068*
12: 7 there builded he an altar unto the **L**, *3068*
12: 8 there he builded an altar unto the **L**, *3068*
12: 8 and called upon the name of the **L**. *3068*
12:17 the **L** plagued Pharaoh and his house *3068*
13: 4 there Abram called on the name of the **L**. *3068*
13:10 before the **L** destroyed Sodom and *3068*
13:10 Gomorrah, *even* as the garden of the **L**, *3068*
13:13 and sinners before the **L** exceedingly. *3068*
13:14 the **L** said unto Abram, after that Lot was *3068*
13:18 and built there an altar unto the **L**. *3068*
14:22 I have lift up mine hand unto the **L**, *3068*
15: 1 After these things the word of the **L** came *3068*
15: 4 the word of the **L** *came* unto him, saying, *3068*
15: 6 he believed in the **L**; and he counted it to *3068*

Ge 15: 7 I *am* **the L** that brought thee out of Ur of *3068*
15:18 In the same day the **L** made a covenant *3068*
16: 2 **the L** hath restrained me from bearing: *3068*
16: 5 the **L** judge between me and thee. *3068*
16: 7 the angel of **the L** found her by a fountain *3068*
16: 9 the angel of **the L** said unto her, Return *3068*
16:10 the angel of **the L** said unto her, I will *3068*
16:11 the angel of **the L** said unto her, Behold, *3068*
16:11 because the **L** hath heard thy affliction. *3068*
16:13 she called the name of **the L** that spake *3068*
17: 1 the **L** appeared to Abram, and said unto *3068*
18: 1 the **L** appeared unto him in the plains of *3068*
18:13 the **L** said unto Abraham, Wherefore did *3068*
18:14 Is any thing too hard for **the L**? *3068*
18:17 the **L** said, Shall I hide from Abraham *3068*
18:19 they shall keep the way of the **L**, to do *3068*
18:19 that **the L** may bring upon Abraham that *3068*
18:20 the **L** said, Because the cry of Sodom and *3068*
18:22 but Abraham stood yet before the **L**. *3068*
18:26 the **L** said, If I find in Sodom fifty *3068*
18:33 the **L** went his way, as soon as he had *3068*
19:13 is waxen great before the face of the **L**; *3068*
19:13 and the **L** hath sent us to destroy it. *3068*
19:14 this place; for the **L** will destroy this city. *3068*
19:16 he being merciful unto him: *3068*
19:24 the **L** rained upon Sodom and *3068*
19:24 and fire from the **L** out of heaven; *3068*
19:27 to the place where he stood before **the L**: *3068*
20:18 the **L** had fast closed up all the wombs *3068*
21: 1 the **L** visited Sarah as he had said, *3068*
21: 1 the **L** did unto Sarah as he had spoken. *3068*
21:33 called there on the name of **the L**, *3068*
22:11 the angel of **the L** called unto him out of *3068*
22:14 In the mount of **the L** it shall be seen. *3068*
22:15 the angel of **the L** called unto Abraham *3068*
22:16 saith **the L**, for because thou hast done *3068*
24: 1 the **L** had blessed Abraham in all things. *3068*
24: 3 I will make thee swear by the **L**, the God *3068*
24: 7 The **L** God of heaven, which took me *3068*
24:12 O **L** God of my master Abraham, I pray *3068*
24:21 whether the **L** had made his journey *3068*
24:26 down his head, and worshipped the **L**. *3068*
24:27 Blessed *be* the **L** God of my master *3068*
24:27 **the L** led me to the house of my master's *3068*
24:31 he said, Come in, thou blessed of the **L**; *3068*
24:35 the **L** hath blessed my master greatly; *3068*
24:40 unto me, The **L**, before whom I walk, *3068*
24:42 said, O **L** God of my master Abraham, *3068*
24:44 *let* the same *be* the woman whom **the L** *3068*
24:48 worshipped the **L**, and blessed the Lord *3068*
24:48 the **L** God of my master Abraham, *3068*
24:50 said, The thing proceedeth from the **L**: *3068*
24:51 master's son's wife, as the **L** hath spoken. *3068*
24:52 he worshipped the **L**, *bowing himself* to *3068*
24:56 seeing the **L** hath prospered my way; *3068*
25:21 Isaac intreated the **L** for his wife, because *3068*
25:21 the **L** was intreated of him, *3068*
25:22 I thus? and she went to inquire of the **L**. *3068*
25:23 the **L** said unto her, Two nations *are* in *3068*
26: 2 the **L** appeared unto him, and said, Go *3068*
26:12 an hundredfold: and the **L** blessed him. *3068*
26:22 For now the **L** hath made room for us, *3068*
26:24 the **L** appeared unto him the same night, *3068*
26:25 called upon the name of the **L**, *3068*
26:28 saw certainly that the **L** was with thee: *3068*
26:29 peace: thou *art* now the blessed of the **L**. *3068*
27: 7 bless thee before the **L** before my death. *3068*
27:20 Because the **L** thy God brought *it* to me. *3068*
27:27 smell of a field which the **L** hath blessed: *3068*
28:13 the **L** stood above it, and said, I *am* *3068*
28:13 I *am* the **L** God of Abraham thy father, *3068*
28:16 and he said, Surely the **L** is in this place; *3068*
28:21 in peace; then shall **the L** be my God: *3068*
29:31 when the **L** saw that Leah *was* hated, *3068*
29:32 Surely the **L** hath looked upon my *3068*
29:33 the **L** hath heard that I *was* hated, *3068*
29:35 said, Now will I praise the **L**: therefore *3068*
30:24 said, The **L** shall add to me another son. *3068*
30:27 that the **L** hath blessed me for thy sake. *3068*
30:30 the **L** hath blessed thee since my coming: *3068*
31: 3 the **L** said unto Jacob, Return unto the *3068*
31:49 said, The **L** watch between me and thee, *3068*
32: 9 father Isaac, the **L** which saidst unto me, *3068*
38: 7 was wicked in the sight of the **L**; *3068*
38: 7 sight of the Lord; and **the L** slew him. *3068*
38:10 *the thing* which he did displeased the **L**: *3068*
39: 2 the **L** was with Joseph, and he was a *3068*
39: 3 his master saw that the **L** *was* with him, *3068*
39: 3 the **L** made all that he did to prosper in *3068*
39: 5 the **L** blessed the Egyptian's house for *3068*
39: 5 the blessing of the **L** was upon all that he *3068*
39:21 the **L** was with Joseph, and shewed him *3068*
39:23 because the **L** *was* with him, *3068*
39:23 which he did, the **L** made *it* to prosper. *3068*
49:18 I have waited for thy salvation, O **L**. *3068*
Ex 3: 2 the angel of **the L** appeared unto him in *3068*
3: 4 the **L** saw that he turned aside to see, *3068*
3: 7 the **L** said, I have surely seen the affliction *3068*
3:15 The **L** God of your fathers, the God of *3068*
3:16 unto them, The **L** God of your fathers, *3068*
3:18 The **L** God of the Hebrews hath met with *3068*
3:18 that we may sacrifice to **the L** our God. *3068*
4: 1 The **L** hath not appeared unto thee. *3068*
4: 2 the **L** said unto him, What *is* that in thine *3068*
4: 4 the **L** said unto Moses, Put forth thine *3068*

Ex	4: 5 That they may believe that **the L** God of	3068
	4: 6 **the L** said furthermore unto him, Put	3068
	4:10 Moses said unto **the L**, O my Lord, I *am*	3068
	4:11 said unto him, Who hath made	3068
	4:11 the seeing, or the blind? have not I **the L**?	3068
	4:14 the anger of **the L** was kindled against	3068
	4:19 **the L** said unto Moses in Midian,	3068
	4:21 **the L** said unto Moses, When thou goest	3068
	4:22 saith **the L**, Israel *is* my son, *even* my	3068
	4:24 **the L** met him, and sought to kill him.	3068
	4:27 **the L** said to Aaron, Go into the	3068
	4:28 Moses told Aaron all the words of **the L**	3068
	4:30 Aaron spake all the words which **the L**	3068
	4:31 when they heard that **the L** had visited	3068
	5: 1 Thus saith **the L** God of Israel,	3068
	5: 2 Pharaoh said, Who *is* **the L**, that I should	3068
	5: 2 I know not **the L**, neither will I let Israel	3068
	5: 3 and sacrifice unto **the L** our God;	3068
	5:17 ye say, Let us go *and* do sacrifice to **the L**.	3068
	5:21 **The L** look upon you, and judge;	3068
	5:22 Moses returned unto **the L**, and said,	3068
	6: 1 **the L** said unto Moses, Now shalt thou	3068
	6: 2 Moses, and said unto him, I *am* **the L**:	3068
	6: 6 I *am* **the L**, and I will bring you out from	3068
	6: 7 ye shall know that I *am* **the L** your God,	3068
	6: 8 give it you *for* an heritage: I *am* **the L**.	3068
	6:10 And **the L** spake unto Moses, saying,	3068
	6:12 Moses spake before **the L**, saying, Behold,	3068
	6:13 **the L** spake unto Moses and unto Aaron,	3068
	6:26 Aaron and Moses, to whom **the L** said,	3068
	6:28 it came to pass on the day *when* **the L**	3068
	6:29 That **the L** spake unto Moses, saying,	3068
	6:29 spake unto Moses, saying, I *am* **the L**:	3068
	6:30 Moses said before **the L**, Behold, I *am* of	3068
	7: 1 **the L** said unto Moses, See, I have made	3068
	7: 5 The Egyptians shall know that I *am* **the L**,	3068
	7: 6 Aaron did as **the L** commanded them,	3068
	7: 8 **the L** spake unto Moses and unto Aaron,	3068
	7:10 they did so as **the L** had commanded:	3068
	7:13 not unto them; as **the L** had said.	3068
	7:14 **the L** said unto Moses, Pharaoh's heart *is*	3068
	7:16 **The L** God of the Hebrews hath sent me	3068
	7:17 Thus saith **the L**, In this thou shalt know	3068
	7:17 In this thou shalt know that I *am* **the L**:	3068
	7:19 **the L** said unto Moses, Say unto Aaron,	3068
	7:20 and Aaron did so, as **the L** commanded;	3068
	7:22 he hearken unto them; as **the L** had said.	3068
	7:25 after *that* **the L** had smitten the river.	3068
	8: 1 **the L** spake unto Moses, Go unto	3068
	8: 1 and say unto him, Thus saith **the L**,	3068
	8: 5 **the L** spake unto Moses, Say unto Aaron,	3068
	8: 8 and Aaron, and said, Intreat **the L**,	3068
	8: 8 that they may do sacrifice unto **the L**.	3068
	8:10 *there is* none like unto **the L** our God.	3068
	8:12 Moses cried unto **the L** because of	3068
	8:13 **the L** did according to the word of Moses;	3068
	8:15 not unto them; as **the L** had said.	3068
	8:16 **the L** said unto Moses, Say unto Aaron,	3068
	8:19 not unto them; as **the L** had said.	3068
	8:20 **the L** said unto Moses, Rise up early in	3068
	8:20 say unto him, Thus saith **the L**, Let my	3068
	8:22 that I *am* **the L** in the midst of the earth.	3068
	8:24 **the L** did so; and there came a grievous	3068
	8:26 of the Egyptians to **the L** our God:	3068
	8:27 sacrifice to **the L** our God, as he shall	3068
	8:28 ye may sacrifice to **the L** your God in	3068
	8:29 will intreat **the L** that the swarms *of flies*	3068
	8:29 letting the people go to sacrifice to **the L**.	3068
	8:30 out from Pharaoh, and intreated **the L**.	3068
	8:31 **the L** did according to the word of Moses	3068
	9: 1 **the L** said unto Moses, Go in unto	3068
	9: 1 Thus saith **the L** God of the Hebrews,	3068
	9: 3 the hand of **the L** is upon thy cattle	3068
	9: 4 **the L** shall sever between the cattle of	3068
	9: 5 **the L** appointed a set time, saying,	3068
	9: 5 To morrow **the L** shall do this thing in	3068
	9: 6 **the L** did that thing on the morrow,	3068
	9: 8 **the L** said unto Moses and unto Aaron,	3068
	9:12 **the L** hardened the heart of Pharaoh,	3068
	9:12 as **the L** had spoken unto Moses.	3068
	9:13 **the L** said unto Moses, Rise up early in	3068
	9:13 Thus saith **the L** God of the Hebrews,	3068
	9:20 that feared the word of **the L** amongst	3068
	9:21 that regarded not the word of **the L** left	3068
	9:22 **the L** said unto Moses, Stretch forth thine	3068
	9:23 **the L** sent thunder and hail, and the fire	3068
	9:23 **the L** rained hail upon the land of Egypt.	3068
	9:27 **the L** *is* righteous, and I and my people	3068
	9:28 Intreat **the L** (for *it is* enough) that there	3068
	9:29 I will spread abroad my hands unto **the L**;	3068
	9:30 know that ye will not yet fear **the L** God.	3068
	9:33 spread abroad his hands unto **the L**:	3068
	9:35 Israel go; as **the L** had spoken by Moses.	3068
	10: 1 **the L** said unto Moses, Go in unto	3068
	10: 2 that ye may know how that I *am* **the L**.	3068
	10: 3 Thus saith **the L** God of the Hebrews,	3068
	10: 7 that they may serve **the L** their God:	3068
	10: 8 unto them, Go, serve **the L** your God:	3068
	10: 9 go; for we *must* hold a feast unto **the L**.	3068
	10:10 Let **the L** be so with you, as I will let you	3068
	10:11 go now ye *that are* men, and serve **the L**;	3068
	10:12 **the L** said unto Moses, Stretch out thine	3068
	10:13 **the L** brought an east wind upon the land	3068
	10:16 I have sinned against **the L** your God,	3068
	10:17 *this* once, and intreat **the L** your God,	3068

Ex	10:18 out from Pharaoh, and intreated **the L**.	3068
	10:19 **the L** turned a mighty strong west wind,	3068
	10:20 **the L** hardened Pharaoh's heart, so that	3068
	10:21 **the L** said unto Moses, Stretch out thine	3068
	10:24 unto Moses, and said, Go ye, serve **the L**;	3068
	10:25 that we may sacrifice unto **the L** our God.	3068
	10:26 thereof must we take to serve **the L** our	3068
	10:26 not with what we must serve **the L**,	3068
	10:27 **the L** hardened Pharaoh's heart,	3068
	11: 1 (And **the L** said unto Moses, Yet will I	3068
	11: 3 **the L** gave the people favour in the sight	3068
	11: 4 Moses said, Thus saith **the L**,	3068
	11: 7 ye may know how that **the L** doth put	3068
	11: 9 **the L** said unto Moses, Pharaoh shall not	3068
	11:10 **the L** hardened Pharaoh's heart, so that	3068
	12: 1 **the L** spake unto Moses and Aaron in	3068
	12:12 Egypt I will execute judgment: I *am* **the L**.	3068
	12:14 shall keep it a feast to **the L** throughout	3068
	12:23 For **the L** will pass through to smite	3068
	12:23 **the L** will pass over the door, and will	3068
	12:25 ye be come to the land which **the L**	3068
	12:28 did as **the L** had commanded Moses and	3068
	12:29 that at midnight **the L** smote all	3068
	12:31 and go, serve **the L**, as ye have said.	3068
	12:36 **the L** gave the people favour in the sight	3068
	12:41 *that* all the hosts of **the L** went out from	3068
	12:42 **the L** for bringing them out from the land	3068
	12:42 this *is* that night of **the L** to be observed	3068
	12:43 **the L** said unto Moses and Aaron, This *is*	3068
	12:48 will keep the passover to **the L**, let all his	3068
	12:50 as **the L** commanded Moses and Aaron,	3068
	12:51 *that* **the L** did bring the children of Israel	3068
	13: 1 **the L** spake unto Moses, saying,	3068
	13: 3 by strength of hand **the L** brought you	3068
	13: 5 shall be when **the L** shall bring thee into	3068
	13: 6 the seventh day *shall be* a feast to **the L**.	3068
	13: 8 of that *which* **the L** did unto me when I	3068
	13: 9 with a strong hand hath **the L** brought	3068
	13:11 shall be when **the L** shall bring thee into	3068
	13:12 thou shalt set apart unto **the L** all that	3068
	13:14 By strength of hand **the L** brought us out	3068
	13:15 **the L** slew all the firstborn in the land	3068
	13:15 I sacrifice to **the L** all that openeth	3068
	13:16 for by strength of hand **the L** brought us	3068
	13:21 **the L** went before them by day in a pillar	3068
	14: 1 And **the L** spake unto Moses, saying,	3068
	14: 4 the Egyptians may know that I *am* **the L**.	3068
	14: 8 **the L** hardened the heart of Pharaoh king	3068
	14:10 children of Israel cried out unto **the L**.	3068
	14:13 stand still, and see the salvation of **the L**,	3068
	14:14 **The L** shall fight for you, and ye shall	3068
	14:15 **the L** said unto Moses, Wherefore criest	3068
	14:18 the Egyptians shall know that I *am* **the L**,	3068
	14:21 **the L** caused the sea to go *back* by a	3068
	14:24 that in the morning watch **the L** looked	3068
	14:25 for **the L** fighteth for them against	3068
	14:26 **the L** said unto Moses, Stretch out thine	3068
	14:27 **the L** overthrew the Egyptians in the	3068
	14:30 Thus **the L** saved Israel that day out of	3068
	14:31 Israel saw *that* great work which **the L**	3068
	14:31 the people feared **the L**, and believed	3068
	14:31 believed **the L**, and his servant Moses.	3068
	15: 1 the children of Israel this song unto **the L**,	3068
	15: 1 spake, saying, I will sing unto **the L**,	3068
	15: 2 **The L** *is* my strength and song, and he is	3050
	15: 3 **The L** *is* a man of war: the LORD *is* his	3068
	15: 3 LORD *is* a man of war: **the L** *is* his name.	3068
	15: 6 Thy right hand, O **L**, is become glorious	3068
	15: 6 thy right hand, O **L**, hath dashed in pieces	3068
	15:11 is like unto thee, O **L**, among the gods?	3068
	15:16 pass over, O **L**, till the people pass over,	3068
	15:17 the place, O **L**, *which* thou hast made for	3068
	15:18 **The L** shall reign for ever and ever.	3068
	15:19 **the L** brought again the waters of the sea	3068
	15:21 Miriam answered them, Sing ye to **the L**,	3068
	15:25 he cried unto **the L**; and the LORD	3068
	15:25 **the L** shewed him a tree, *which* when he	3068
	15:26 hearken to the voice of **the L** thy God,	3068
	15:26 for I *am* **the L** that healeth thee.	3068
	16: 3 by the hand of **the L** in the land of Egypt,	3068
	16: 4 said **the L** unto Moses, Behold, I will rain	3068
	16: 6 ye shall know that **the L** hath brought	3068
	16: 7 then ye shall see the glory of **the L**;	3068
	16: 7 heareth your murmurings against **the L**:	3068
	16: 8 *This shall be,* when **the L** shall give you	3068
	16: 8 for that **the L** heareth your murmurings	3068
	16: 8 *are* not against us, but against **the L**.	3068
	16: 9 of Israel, Come near before **the L**:	3068
	16:10 the glory of **the L** appeared in the cloud.	3068
	16:11 **the L** spake unto Moses, saying,	3068
	16:12 ye shall know that I *am* **the L** your God.	3068
	16:15 This *is* the bread which **the L** hath given	3068
	16:16 This *is* the thing which **the L** hath	3068
	16:23 This *is that* which **the L** hath said,	3068
	16:23 *is* the rest of the holy sabbath unto **the L**:	3068
	16:25 to day; for to day *is* a sabbath unto **the L**:	3068
	16:28 **the L** said unto Moses, How long refuse	3068
	16:29 for that **the L** hath given you the sabbath,	3068
	16:32 *is* the thing which **the L** commandeth,	3068
	16:33 lay it up before **the L**, to be kept for your	3068
	16:34 **the L** commanded, so Aaron laid	3068
	17: 1 according to the commandment of **the L**,	3068
	17: 2 with me? wherefore do ye tempt **the L**?	3068
	17: 4 Moses cried unto **the L**, saying, What	3068
	17: 5 **the L** said unto Moses, Go on before	3068

Ex	17: 7 because they tempted **the L**, saying,	3068
	17: 7 Is **the L** amongst us, or not?	3068
	17:14 **the L** said unto Moses, Write this *for* a	3068
	17:16 Because **the L** hath sworn *that* the LORD	3050
	17:16 Because the LORD hath sworn *that* **the L**	3068
	18: 1 that **the L** had brought Israel out of Egypt;	3068
	18: 8 Moses told his father in law all that **the L**	3068
	18: 8 the way, and *how* **the L** delivered them.	3068
	18: 9 goodness which **the L** had done to Israel,	3068
	18:10 Jethro said, Blessed *be* **the L**, who hath	3068
	18:11 Now I know that **the L** *is* greater than all	3068
	19: 3 **the L** called him out of the	3068
	19: 7 words which **the L** commanded him.	3068
	19: 8 All that **the L** hath spoken we will do.	3068
	19: 8 the words of the people unto **the L**.	3068
	19: 9 **the L** said unto Moses, Lo, I come unto	3068
	19: 9 told the words of the people unto **the L**.	3068
	19:10 **the L** said unto Moses, Go unto the	3068
	19:11 for the third day **the L** will come down in	3068
	19:18 **the L** descended upon it in fire:	3068
	19:20 **the L** came down upon mount Sinai,	3068
	19:20 **the L** called Moses *up* to the top of	3068
	19:21 **the L** said unto Moses, Go down,	3068
	19:21 they break through unto **the L** to gaze,	3068
	19:22 which come near to **the L**,	3068
	19:22 lest **the L** break forth upon them.	3068
	19:23 Moses said unto **the L**, The people cannot	3068
	19:24 **the L** said unto him, Away, get thee	3068
	19:24 break through to come up unto **the L**,	3068
	20: 2 I *am* **the L** thy God, which have brought	3068
	20: 5 for I **the L** thy God *am* a jealous God,	3068
	20: 7 Thou shalt not take the name of **the L** thy	3068
	20: 7 for **the L** will not hold him guiltless that	3068
	20:10 seventh day *is* the sabbath of **the L** thy	3068
	20:11 For in six days **the L** made heaven and	3068
	20:11 wherefore **the L** blessed the sabbath day,	3068
	20:12 the land which **the L** thy God giveth thee.	3068
	20:22 **the L** said unto Moses, Thus shalt	3068
	22:11 *Then* shall an oath of **the L** be between	3068
	22:20 save unto **the L** only, he shall be utterly	3068
	23:19 bring *into* the house of **the L** thy God.	3068
	23:25 ye shall serve **the L** your God, and he	3068
	24: 1 Come up unto **the L**, thou, and Aaron,	3068
	24: 2 Moses alone shall come near **the L**:	3068
	24: 3 told the people all the words of **the L**,	3068
	24: 3 All the words which **the L** hath said will	3068
	24: 4 Moses wrote all the words of **the L**,	3068
	24: 5 peace offerings *of* oxen unto **the L**.	3068
	24: 7 All that **the L** hath said will we do,	3068
	24: 8 which **the L** hath made with you	3068
	24:12 **the L** said unto Moses, Come up to me	3068
	24:16 glory of **the L** abode upon mount Sinai,	3068
	24:17 the sight of the glory of **the L** *was* like	3068
	25: 1 And **the L** spake unto Moses, saying,	3068
	27:21 it from evening to morning before **the L**:	3068
	28:12 shall bear their names before **the L**	3068
	28:29 for a memorial before **the L** continually.	3068
	28:30 when he goeth in before **the L**:	3068
	28:30 upon his heart before **the L** continually.	3068
	28:35 in unto the holy *place* before **the L**,	3068
	28:36 of a signet, HOLINESS TO **THE L**.	3068
	28:38 that they may be accepted before **the L**.	3068
	29:11 thou shalt kill the bullock before **the L**,	3068
	29:18 it *is* a burnt offering unto **the L**: it *is* a	3068
	29:18 an offering made by fire unto **the L**.	3068
	29:23 unleavened bread that *is* before **the L**:	3068
	29:24 them *for* a wave offering before **the L**.	3068
	29:25 for a sweet savour before **the L**:	3068
	29:25 it *is* an offering made by fire unto **the L**.	3068
	29:26 wave it *for* a wave offering before **the L**:	3068
	29:28 *even* their heave offering unto **the L**.	3068
	29:41 an offering made by fire unto **the L**.	3068
	29:42 of the congregation before **the L**:	3068
	29:46 shall know that I *am* **the L** their God,	3068
	29:46 amongst them: I *am* **the L** their God.	3068
	30: 8 a perpetual incense before **the L**	3068
	30:10 it *is* most holy unto **the L**.	3068
	30:11 And **the L** spake unto Moses, saying,	3068
	30:12 man a ransom for his soul unto **the L**,	3068
	30:13 half shekel *shall be* the offering of **the L**.	3068
	30:14 above, shall give an offering unto **the L**.	3068
	30:15 when *they* give an offering unto **the L**,	3068
	30:16 unto the children of Israel before **the L**,	3068
	30:17 And **the L** spake unto Moses, saying,	3068
	30:20 to burn offering made by fire unto **the L**:	3068
	30:22 Moreover **the L** spake unto Moses,	3068
	30:34 **the L** said unto Moses, Take unto thee	3068
	30:37 it shall be unto thee holy for **the L**.	3068
	31: 1 And **the L** spake unto Moses, saying,	3068
	31:12 And **the L** spake unto Moses, saying,	3068
	31:13 *ye* may know that I *am* **the L** that doth	3068
	31:15 *is* the sabbath of rest, holy to **the L**:	3068
	31:17 for *in* six days **the L** made heaven and	3068
	32: 5 and said, To morrow *is* a feast to **the L**.	3068
	32: 7 **the L** said unto Moses, Go, get thee	3068
	32: 9 **the L** said unto Moses, I have seen this	3068
	32:11 Moses besought **the L** his God, and said,	3068
	32:11 besought the LORD his God, and said, **L**,	3068
	32:14 **the L** repented of the evil which he	3068
	32:27 them, Thus saith **the L** God of Israel,	3068
	32:29 Consecrate yourselves to day to **the L**,	3068
	32:30 now I will go up unto **the L**;	3068
	32:31 Moses returned unto **the L**, and said,	3068
	32:33 **the L** said unto Moses, Whosoever hath	3068
	32:35 **the L** plagued the people, because they	3068

L

Ex	33: 1	**the L** said unto Moses, Depart, *and* go up	3068

Ex
33: 1 **the L** said unto Moses, Depart, *and* go up 3068
33: 5 For **the L** had said unto Moses, Say unto 3068
33: 7 every one which sought **the L** went out 3068
33: 9 tabernacle, and *the L* talked with Moses. NIH
33:11 **the L** spake unto Moses face to face, as a 3068
33:12 Moses said unto **the L**, See, thou sayest 3068
33:17 **the L** said unto Moses, I will do this 3068
33:19 I will proclaim the name of **the L** 3068
33:21 **the L** said, Behold, *there is* a place by me, 3068
34: 1 **the L** said unto Moses, Hew thee two 3068
34: 4 as **the L** had commanded him, and took 3068
34: 5 **the L** descended in the cloud, 3068
34: 5 and proclaimed the name of **the L.** 3068
34: 6 **the L** passed by before him, 3068
34: 6 proclaimed, **The L,** The L**ORD** God, 3068
34: 6 **The L** God, merciful and gracious, 3068
34:10 thou *art* shall see the work of **the L:** 3068
34:14 for **the L,** whose name *is* Jealous, *is* a 3068
34:24 before **the L** thy God thrice in the year. 3068
34:26 bring *unto* the house of **the L** thy God. 3068
34:27 **the L** said unto Moses, Write thou these 3068
34:28 he was there with **the L** forty days and 3068
34:32 **the L** had spoken with him in mount 3068
34:34 Moses went in before **the L** to speak 3068
35: 1 These *are* the words which **the L** hath 3068
35: 2 you a holy *day,* a sabbath of rest to **the L:** 3068
35: 4 *is* the thing which **the L** commanded, 3068
35: 5 amongst you an offering unto **the L:** 3068
35: 5 let him bring it, an offering of **the L,** 3068
35:10 make all that **the L** hath commanded; 3068
35:22 *offered* an offering of gold unto **the L.** 3068
35:29 brought a willing offering unto **the L,** 3068
35:29 which **the L** had commanded to be made 3068
35:30 **the L** hath called by name Bezaleel the 3068
36: 1 in whom **the L** put wisdom and 3068
36: 1 to all that **the L** had commanded. 3068
36: 2 in whose heart **the L** had put wisdom, 3068
36: 5 which **the L** commanded to make. 3068
38:22 made all that **the L** commanded Moses. 3068
39: 1 for Aaron; as **the L** commanded Moses. 3068
39: 5 linen; as **the L** commanded Moses. 3068
39: 7 of Israel; as **the L** commanded Moses. 3068
39:21 the ephod; as **the L** commanded Moses. 3068
39:26 minister *in;* as **the L** commanded Moses. 3068
39:29 as **the L** commanded Moses. 3068
39:30 of a signet, HOLINESS TO **THE L.** 3068
39:31 the mitre; as **the L** commanded Moses. 3068
39:32 to all that **the L** commanded Moses. 3068
39:42 According to all that **the L** commanded 3068
39:43 had done it as **the L** had commanded, 3068
40: 1 And **the L** spake unto Moses, saying, 3068
40:16 according to all that **the L** commanded 3068
40:19 upon it; as **the L** commanded Moses. 3068
40:21 as **the L** commanded Moses. 3068
40:23 the bread in order upon it before **the L;** 3068
40:23 as **the L** had commanded Moses. 3068
40:25 he lighted the lamps before **the L;** 3068
40:25 the L**ORD**; as **the L** commanded Moses. 3068
40:27 as **the L** commanded Moses. 3068
40:29 offering; as **the L** commanded Moses. 3068
40:32 washed; as **the L** commanded Moses. 3068
40:34 the glory of **the L** filled the tabernacle. 3068
40:35 the glory of **the L** filled the tabernacle. 3068
40:38 For the cloud of **the L** *was* upon 3068

Lev
1: 1 **the L** called unto Moses, and spake unto 3068
1: 2 man of you bring an offering unto **the L,** 3068
1: 3 of the congregation before **the L.** 3068
1: 5 he shall kill the bullock before **the L:** 3068
1: 9 by fire, of a sweet savour unto **the L.** 3068
1:11 side of the altar northward before **the L:** 3068
1:13 by fire, of a sweet savour unto **the L.** 3068
1:14 for his offering to **the L** *be* of fowls, 3068
1:17 by fire, of a sweet savour unto **the L.** 3068
2: 1 any will offer a meat offering unto **the L,** 3068
2: 2 by fire, of a sweet savour unto **the L.** 3068
2: 3 of the offerings of **the L** made by fire. 3068
2: 8 that is made of these *things* unto **the L:** 3068
2: 9 by fire, of a sweet savour unto **the L.** 3068
2:10 of the offerings of **the L** made by fire. 3068
2:11 which ye shall bring unto **the L,** 3068
2:11 *in* any offering of **the L** made by fire. 3068
2:12 ye shall offer them unto **the L:** 3068
2:14 meat offering of *thy* firstfruits unto **the L,** 3068
2:16 *it is* an offering made by fire unto **the L.** 3068
3: 1 offer it without blemish before **the L.** 3068
3: 3 an offering made by fire unto **the L;** 3068
3: 5 by fire, of a sweet savour unto **the L:** 3068
3: 6 peace offering unto **the L** *be* of the flock, 3068
3: 7 then shall he offer it before **the L.** 3068
3: 9 an offering made by fire unto **the L;** 3068
3:11 of the offering made by fire unto **the L.** 3068
3:12 a goat, then he shall offer it before **the L.** 3068
3:14 *even* an offering made by fire unto **the L;** 3068
4: 1 And **the L** spake unto Moses, saying, 3068
4: 2 **the L** *(concerning things)* which ought 3068
4: 3 blemish unto **the L** for a sin offering. 3068
4: 4 of the congregation before **the L,** 3068
4: 4 and kill the bullock before **the L.** 3068
4: 6 of the blood seven times before **the L,** 3068
4: 7 the altar of sweet incense before **the L,** 3068
4:13 **the L** *(concerning things)* which should 3068
4:15 the head of the bullock before **the L:** 3068
4:15 the bullock shall be killed before **the L.** 3068
4:17 sprinkle *it* seven times before **the L,** 3068
4:18 horns of the altar which *is* before **the L,** 3068

Lev
4:22 **the L** his God *concerning things* which 3068
4:24 they kill the burnt offering before **the L:** 3068
4:27 **the L** *concerning things* which ought not 3068
4:31 the altar for a sweet savour unto **the L;** 3068
4:35 to the offerings made by fire unto **the L;** 3068
5: 6 he for his sin in which he hath sinned, 3068
5: 7 or two young pigeons, unto **the L;** 3068
5:12 to the offerings made by fire unto **the L:** 3068
5:14 And **the L** spake unto Moses, saying, 3068
5:15 in the holy *things* of **the L;** 3068
5:15 he shall bring for his trespass unto **the L** a 3068
5:17 be done by the commandments of **the L;** 3068
5:19 he hath certainly trespassed against **the L.** 3068
6: 1 And **the L** spake unto Moses, saying, 3068
6: 2 commit a trespass against **the L,** 3068
6: 6 bring his trespass offering unto **the L,** 3068
6: 7 make an atonement for him before **the L:** 3068
6: 8 And **the L** spake unto Moses, saying, 3068
6:14 sons of Aaron shall offer it before **the L,** 3068
6:15 *even* the memorial of it, unto **the L.** 3068
6:18 the offerings of **the L** made by fire: 3068
6:19 And **the L** spake unto Moses, saying, 3068
6:20 which they shall offer unto **the L** in the 3068
6:21 thou offer *for* a sweet savour unto **the L.** 3068
6:22 *it is* a statute for ever unto **the L;** it shall 3068
6:24 And **the L** spake unto Moses, saying, 3068
6:25 the sin offering be killed before **the L:** 3068
7: 5 *for* an offering made by fire unto **the L:** 3068
7:11 which he shall offer unto **the L.** 3068
7:14 oblation *for* a heave offering unto **the L,** 3068
7:20 that *pertain* unto **the L,** having his 3068
7:21 which *pertain* unto **the L,** even that soul 3068
7:22 And **the L** spake unto Moses, saying, 3068
7:25 offer an offering made by fire unto **the L,** 3068
7:28 And **the L** spake unto Moses, saying, 3068
7:29 **the L** shall bring his oblation unto 3068
7:29 **the L** of the sacrifice of his peace 3068
7:30 bring the offerings of **the L** made by fire, 3068
7:30 waved *for* a wave offering before **the L.** 3068
7:35 out of the offerings of **the L** made by fire, 3068
7:35 minister unto **the L** in the priest's office; 3068
7:36 **the L** commanded to be given them 3068
7:38 **the L** commanded Moses in mount 3068
7:38 Israel to offer their oblations unto **the L,** 3068
8: 1 And **the L** spake unto Moses, saying, 3068
8: 4 Moses did as **the L** commanded him; 3068
8: 5 *is* the thing which **the L** commanded 3068
8: 9 holy crown; as **the L** commanded Moses. 3068
8:13 upon them; as **the L** commanded Moses. 3068
8:17 the camp; as **the L** commanded Moses. 3068
8:21 *and* an offering made by fire unto **the L;** 3068
8:21 the L**ORD**; as **the L** commanded Moses. 3068
8:26 that *was* before **the L,** he took one 3068
8:27 them *for* a wave offering before **the L;** 3068
8:28 it *is* an offering made by fire unto **the L,** 3068
8:29 waved it *for* a wave offering before **the L:** 3068
8:29 Moses' part; as **the L** commanded Moses. 3068
8:34 this day, *so* **the L** hath commanded to do, 3068
8:35 keep the charge of **the L,** that ye die not: 3068
8:36 his sons did all things which **the L** 3068
9: 2 and offer *them* before **the L.** 3068
9: 4 peace offerings, to sacrifice before **the L;** 3068
9: 4 for to day **the L** will appear unto you. 3068
9: 5 drew near and stood before **the L.** 3068
9: 6 *is* the thing which **the L** commanded 3068
9: 6 the glory of **the L** shall appear unto you. 3068
9: 7 for them; as **the L** commanded. 3068
9:10 the altar; as **the L** commanded Moses. 3068
9:21 waved *for* a wave offering before **the L;** 3068
9:23 the glory of **the L** appeared unto all 3068
9:24 there came a fire out from before **the L,** 3068
10: 1 offered strange fire before **the L,** 3068
10: 2 there went out fire from **the L,** 3068
10: 2 them, and they died before **the L.** 3068
10: 3 This *is it* that **the L** spake, saying, 3068
10: 6 bewail the burning which **the L** hath 3068
10: 7 for the anointing oil of **the L** *is* upon you. 3068
10: 8 And **the L** spake unto Aaron, saying, 3068
10:11 **the L** hath spoken unto them by the hand 3068
10:12 of the offerings of **the L** made by fire, 3068
10:13 of the sacrifices of **the L** made by fire: 3068
10:15 wave *it for* a wave offering before **the L;** 3068
10:15 for ever; as **the L** hath commanded. 3068
10:17 make atonement for them before **the L?** 3068
10:19 and their burnt offering before **the L;** 3068
10:19 have been accepted in the sight of **the L?** 3068
11: 1 And **the L** spake unto Moses and to Aaron, 3068
11:44 I *am* **the L** your God: ye shall therefore 3068
11:45 I *am* **the L** that bringeth you up out of 3068
12: 1 And **the L** spake unto Moses, saying, 3068
12: 7 Who shall offer it before **the L,** 3068
13: 1 **the L** spake unto Moses and Aaron, 3068
14: 1 And **the L** spake unto Moses, saying, 3068
14:11 those *things,* before **the L,** at the door of 3068
14:12 them *for* a wave offering before **the L,** 3068
14:16 with his finger seven times before **the L:** 3068
14:18 make an atonement for him before **the L.** 3068
14:23 of the congregation, before **the L.** 3068
14:24 them *for* a wave offering before **the L.** 3068
14:27 in his left hand seven times before **the L:** 3068
14:29 make an atonement for him before **the L.** 3068
14:31 him that is to be cleansed before **the L.** 3068
14:33 **the L** spake unto Moses and unto Aaron, 3068
15: 1 And **the L** spake unto Moses and to Aaron, 3068
15:14 come before **the L** unto the door of 3068

Lev
15:15 for him before **the L** for his issue. 3068
15:30 for the issue of her uncleanness. 3068
16: 1 **the L** spake unto Moses after the death 3068
16: 1 when they offered before **the L,** and died; 3068
16: 2 **the L** said unto Moses, Speak unto Aaron 3068
16: 7 present them before **the L** *at* the door of 3068
16: 8 one lot for **the L,** and the other lot for 3068
16:10 shall be presented alive before **the L,** 3068
16:12 of fire from off the altar before **the L,** 3068
16:13 the incense upon the fire before **the L,** 3068
16:18 go out unto the altar that *is* before **the L,** 3068
16:30 be clean from all your sins before **the L.** 3068
16:34 And he did as **the L** commanded Moses. 3068
17: 1 And **the L** spake unto Moses, saying, 3068
17: 2 This *is* the thing which **the L** hath 3068
17: 4 to offer an offering unto **the L** before 3068
17: 4 the L**ORD** before the tabernacle of **the L;** 3068
17: 5 that they may bring them unto **the L,** 3068
17: 5 offer them *for* peace offerings unto **the L.** 3068
17: 6 **the L** at the door of the tabernacle of 3068
17: 6 the fat for a sweet savour unto **the L.** 3068
17: 9 the congregation, to offer it unto **the L;** 3068
18: 1 And **the L** spake unto Moses, saying, 3068
18: 2 and say unto them, I *am* **the L** your God. 3068
18: 4 to walk therein: I *am* **the L** your God. 3068
18: 5 man do, he shall live in them: I *am* **the L.** 3068
18: 6 to uncover *their* nakedness: I *am* **the L.** 3068
18:21 profane the name of thy God: I *am* **the L.** 3068
18:30 yourselves therein: I *am* **the L** your God. 3068
19: 1 And **the L** spake unto Moses, saying, 3068
19: 2 be holy: for I **the L** your God *am* holy. 3068
19: 3 keep my sabbaths: I *am* **the L** your God. 3068
19: 4 molten gods: I *am* **the L** your God. 3068
19: 5 a sacrifice of peace offerings unto **the L,** 3068
19: 8 profaned the hallowed *thing* of **the L;** 3068
19:10 and stranger: I *am* **the L** your God. 3068
19:12 profane the name of thy God: I *am* **the L.** 3068
19:14 but shalt fear thy God: I *am* **the L.** 3068
19:16 the blood of thy neighbour: I *am* **the L.** 3068
19:18 love thy neighbour as thyself: I *am* **the L.** 3068
19:21 bring his trespass offering unto **the L,** 3068
19:22 **the L** for his sin which he hath done: 3068
19:24 shall be holy to praise **the L** *withal.* 3068
19:25 increase thereof: I *am* **the L** your God. 3068
19:28 print any marks upon you: I *am* **the L.** 3068
19:30 and reverence my sanctuary: I *am* **the L.** 3068
19:31 be defiled by them: I *am* **the L** your God. 3068
19:32 old man, and fear thy God: I *am* **the L.** 3068
19:34 in the land of Egypt: I *am* **the L** your God. 3068
19:36 I *am* **the L** your God, which brought you 3068
19:37 my judgments, and do them: I *am* **the L.** 3068
20: 1 And **the L** spake unto Moses, saying, 3068
20: 7 be ye holy: for I *am* **the L** your God. 3068
20: 8 do them: I *am* **the L** which sanctify you. 3068
20:24 I *am* **the L** your God, which have 3068
20:26 I **the L** *am* holy, and have severed you 3068
21: 1 **the L** said unto Moses, Speak unto 3068
21: 6 for the offerings of **the L** made by fire, 3068
21: 8 for I **the L,** which sanctify you, *am* holy. 3068
21:12 oil of his God *is* upon him: I *am* **the L.** 3068
21:15 his people: for I **the L** do sanctify him. 3068
21:16 And **the L** spake unto Moses, saying, 3068
21:21 offer the offerings of **the L** made by fire: 3068
21:23 for I **the L** do sanctify them. 3068
22: 1 And **the L** spake unto Moses, saying, 3068
22: 2 which they hallow unto me: I *am* **the L.** 3068
22: 3 the children of Israel hallow unto **the L,** 3068
22: 3 be cut off from my presence: I *am* **the L.** 3068
22: 8 to defile *himself* therewith: I *am* **the L.** 3068
22: 9 they profane it: I **the L** do sanctify them. 3068
22:15 of Israel, which they offer unto **the L;** 3068
22:16 they eat their holy *things:* for I **the L** 3068
22:17 And **the L** spake unto Moses, saying, 3068
22:18 they will offer unto **the L** for a burnt 3068
22:21 unto **the L** to accomplish *his* vow, 3068
22:22 ye shall not offer these unto **the L,** 3068
22:22 by fire of them upon the altar unto **the L.** 3068
22:24 Ye shall not offer unto **the L** that which is 3068
22:26 And **the L** spake unto Moses, saying, 3068
22:27 for an offering made by fire unto **the L.** 3068
22:29 a sacrifice of thanksgiving unto **the L,** 3068
22:30 none of it until the morrow: I *am* **the L.** 3068
22:31 and do them: I *am* **the L.** 3068
22:32 of Israel: I *am* **the L** which hallow you, 3068
22:33 of Egypt, to be your God: I *am* **the L.** 3068
23: 1 And **the L** spake unto Moses, saying, 3068
23: 2 them, *Concerning* the feasts of **the L,** 3068
23: 3 the sabbath of **the L** in all your dwellings. 3068
23: 4 These *are* the feasts of **the L,** *even* holy 3068
23: 6 the feast of unleavened bread unto **the L:** 3068
23: 8 made by fire unto **the L** seven days: 3068
23: 9 And **the L** spake unto Moses, saying, 3068
23:11 he shall wave the sheaf before **the L,** 3068
23:12 first year for a burnt offering unto **the L.** 3068
23:13 an offering made by fire unto **the L** *for* a 3068
23:16 shall offer a new meat offering unto **the L.** 3068
23:17 *they are* the firstfruits unto **the L.** 3068
23:18 shall be *for* a burnt offering unto **the L,** 3068
23:18 made by fire, of sweet savour unto **the L.** 3068
23:20 firstfruits *for* a wave offering before **the L,** 3068
23:20 they shall be holy to **the L** for the priest. 3068
23:22 and to the stranger: I *am* **the L** your God. 3068
23:23 And **the L** spake unto Moses, saying, 3068
23:25 offer an offering made by fire unto **the L.** 3068
23:26 And **the L** spake unto Moses, saying, 3068

Lev 23:27 offer an offering made by fire unto **the L**. 3068
23:28 make an atonement for you before **the L** 3068
23:33 And **the L** spake unto Moses, saying, 3068
23:34 of tabernacles *for* seven days unto **the L** 3068
23:36 offer an offering made by fire unto **the L**: 3068
23:36 offer an offering made by fire unto **the L**, 3068
23:37 These *are* the feasts of **the L**, which ye 3068
23:37 offer an offering made by fire unto **the L**, 3068
23:38 Beside the sabbaths of **the L**, 3068
23:38 which ye give unto **the L**. 3068
23:39 shall keep a feast unto **the L** seven days: 3068
23:40 ye shall rejoice before **the L** your God 3068
23:41 ye shall keep it a feast unto **the L** seven 3068
23:43 the land of Egypt: I *am* **the L** your God. 3068
23:44 the children of Israel the feasts of **the L**. 3068
24: 1 And **the L** spake unto Moses, saying, 3068
24: 3 the morning before **the L** continually: 3068
24: 4 pure candlestick before **the L** continually. 3068
24: 6 a row, upon the pure table before **the L**. 3068
24: 7 even *for* a offering made by fire unto **the L** 3068
24: 8 set it in order before **the L** continually, 3068
24: 9 him of the offerings of **the L** made by fire, 3068
24:11 son blasphemed the name *of the L*, NIH
24:12 that the mind of **the L** might be shewed 3068
24:13 And **the L** spake unto Moses, saying, 3068
24:16 he that blasphemeth the name of **the L**, 3068
24:16 when he blasphemeth the name *of the L*, NIH
24:22 own country: for I *am* **the L** your God. 3068
24:23 the children of Israel did as **the L** 3068
25: 1 **the L** spake unto Moses in mount Sinai, 3068
25: 2 shall the land keep a sabbath unto **the L** 3068
25: 4 of rest unto the land, a sabbath for **the L**: 3068
25:17 fear thy God: for I *am* **the L** your God. 3068
25:38 I *am* **the L** your God, which brought you 3068
25:55 of the land of Egypt: I *am* **the L** your God. 3068
26: 1 down unto it: for I *am* **the L** your God. 3068
26: 2 and reverence my sanctuary: I *am* **the L**. 3068
26:13 I *am* **the L** your God, which brought you 3068
26:44 with them: for I *am* **the L** their God. 3068
26:45 that *I* might be their God: I *am* **the L**. 3068
26:46 which **the L** made between him and 3068
27: 1 And **the L** spake unto Moses, saying, 3068
27: 2 the persons *shall be* for **the L** by thy 3068
27: 9 *men* bring an offering unto **the L**, 3068
27: 9 that *any man* giveth of such unto **the L** 3068
27:11 they do not offer a sacrifice unto **the L**, 3068
27:14 sanctify his house *to be* holy unto **the L**, 3068
27:16 if a man shall sanctify unto **the L** *some* 3068
27:21 be holy unto **the L**, as a field devoted; 3068
27:22 if *a man* sanctify unto **the L** a field which 3068
27:23 in that day, *as* a holy *thing* unto **the L**. 3068
27:28 that a man shall devote unto **the L** of all 3068
27:28 devoted thing *is* most holy unto **the L**. 3068
27:30 *is* the LORD's: *it is* holy unto **the L**. 3068
27:32 the tenth shall be holy unto **the L**. 3068
27:34 which **the L** commanded Moses for 3068

Nu 1: 1 **the L** spake unto Moses in the wilderness 3068
1:19 As **the L** commanded Moses, 3068
1:48 For **the L** spake unto Moses, saying, 3068
1:54 to all that **the L** commanded Moses, 3068
2: 1 **the L** spake unto Moses and unto Aaron, 3068
2:33 of Israel; as **the L** commanded Moses. 3068
2:34 to all that **the L** commanded Moses: 3068
3: 1 Moses in the day that **the L** spake with 3068
3: 4 Nadab and Abihu died before **the L**, 3068
3: 4 they offered strange fire before **the L**, 3068
3: 5 And **the L** spake unto Moses, saying, 3068
3:11 And **the L** spake unto Moses, saying, 3068
3:13 beast: mine they shall be: I *am* **the L**. 3068
3:14 **the L** spake unto Moses in the wilderness 3068
3:16 them according to the word of **the L**, 3068
3:39 numbered at the commandment of **the L**, 3068
3:40 **the L** said unto Moses, Number all 3068
3:41 shalt take the Levites for me (I *am* **the L**) 3068
3:42 as **the L** commanded him, 3068
3:44 And **the L** spake unto Moses, saying, 3068
3:45 and the Levites shall be mine: I *am* **the L**. 3068
3:51 his sons, according to the word of **the L**, 3068
3:51 the LORD, as **the L** commanded Moses. 3068
4: 1 **the L** spake unto Moses and unto Aaron, 3068
4:17 **the L** spake unto Moses and unto Aaron, 3068
4:21 And **the L** spake unto Moses, saying, 3068
4:37 of **the L** by the hand of Moses. 3068
4:41 according to the commandment of **the L** 3068
4:45 the word of **the L** by the hand of Moses. 3068
4:49 According to the commandment of **the L** 3068
4:49 of him, as **the L** commanded Moses. 3068
5: 1 And **the L** spake unto Moses, saying, 3068
5: 4 as **the L** spake unto Moses, so did 3068
5: 5 And **the L** spake unto Moses, saying, 3068
5: 6 to do a trespass against **the L**, 3068
5: 8 the trespass *be* recompensed unto **the L**, 3068
5:11 And **the L** spake unto Moses, saying, 3068
5:16 bring her near, and set her before **the L**: 3068
5:18 priest shall set the woman before **the L**, 3068
5:21 **The L** make thee a curse and an oath 3068
5:21 when **the L** doth make thy thigh to rot, 3068
5:25 shall wave the offering before **the L**, 3068
5:30 shall set the woman before **the L**, 3068
6: 1 And **the L** spake unto Moses, saying, 3068
6: 2 to separate *themselves* unto **the L**: 3068
6: 5 which he separateth *himself* unto **the L**, 3068
6: 6 **the L** shall come at no dead body. 3068
6: 8 of his separation he *is* holy unto **the L**. 3068
6:12 he shall consecrate unto **the L** the days 3068

Nu 6:14 he shall offer his offering unto **the L**, 3068
6:16 the priest shall bring *them* before **the L**, 3068
6:17 a sacrifice of peace offerings unto **the L**, 3068
6:20 them for a wave offering before **the L**: 3068
6:21 *of* his offering unto **the L** for his 3068
6:22 And **the L** spake unto Moses, saying, 3068
6:24 **The L** bless thee, and keep thee: 3068
6:25 **The L** make his face shine upon thee, 3068
6:26 **The L** lift up his countenance upon thee, 3068
7: 3 they brought their offering before **the L**, 3068
7: 4 And **the L** spake unto Moses, saying, 3068
7:11 **the L** said unto Moses, They shall offer 3068
8: 1 And **the L** spake unto Moses, saying, 3068
8: 3 as **the L** commanded Moses. 3068
8: 4 according unto the pattern which **the L** 3068
8: 5 And **the L** spake unto Moses, saying, 3068
8:10 thou shalt bring the Levites before **the L**: 3068
8:11 Aaron shall offer the Levites before **the L** 3068
8:11 they may execute the service of **the L**. 3068
8:12 the other *for* a burnt offering, unto **the L**, 3068
8:13 and offer them *for* an offering unto **the L**. 3068
8:20 **the L** commanded Moses concerning 3068
8:21 offered them *as* an offering before **the L**; 3068
8:22 as **the L** had commanded Moses 3068
8:23 And **the L** spake unto Moses, saying, 3068
9: 1 **the L** spake unto Moses in the wilderness 3068
9: 5 according to all that **the L** commanded 3068
9: 7 *we* may not offer an offering of **the L** 3068
9: 8 I will hear what **the L** will command 3068
9: 9 And **the L** spake unto Moses, saying, 3068
9:10 he shall keep the passover unto **the L**. 3068
9:13 he brought not the offering of **the L** in his 3068
9:14 and will keep the passover unto **the L**, 3068
9:18 At the commandment of **the L** the 3068
9:18 at the commandment of **the L** they 3068
9:19 children of Israel kept the charge of **the L**, 3068
9:20 according to the commandment of **the L** 3068
9:20 according to the commandment of **the L** 3068
9:23 At the commandment of **the L** they rested 3068
9:23 at the commandment of **the L** they 3068
9:23 they kept the charge of **the L**, 3068
9:23 at the commandment of **the L** by the hand 3068
10: 1 And **the L** spake unto Moses, saying, 3068
10: 9 ye shall be remembered before **the L** your 3068
10:10 before your God: I *am* **the L** your God. 3068
10:13 of **the L** by the hand of Moses. 3068
10:29 unto the place of which **the L** said, 3068
10:29 for **the L** hath spoken good concerning 3068
10:32 what goodness **the L** shall do unto us, 3068
10:33 they departed from the mount of **the L** 3068
10:33 the ark of the covenant of **the L** went 3068
10:34 cloud of **the L** *was* upon them by day, 3068
10:35 L, and let thine enemies be scattered; 3068
10:36 when it rested, he said, Return, O L, 3068
11: 1 people complained, it displeased **the L**: 3068
11: 1 **the L** heard *it*; and his anger was kindled; 3068
11: 1 the fire of **the L** burnt among them, 3068
11: 2 when Moses prayed unto **the L**, the fire 3068
11: 3 the fire of **the L** burnt among them. 3068
11:10 the anger of **the L** was kindled greatly: 3068
11:11 Moses said unto **the L**, Wherefore hast 3068
11:16 **the L** said unto Moses, Gather unto me 3068
11:18 for you have wept in the ears of **the L**, 3068
11:18 therefore **the L** will give you flesh, 3068
11:20 that ye have despised **the L** which *is* 3068
11:23 **the L** said unto Moses, Is the LORD's 3068
11:24 told the people the words of **the L**, 3068
11:25 **the L** came down in a cloud, 3068
11:29 **the L** would put his spirit upon them! 3068
11:31 there went forth a wind from **the L**, 3068
11:33 the wrath of **the L** was kindled against 3068
11:33 **the L** smote the people *with* a very great 3068
12: 2 **the L** indeed spoken only by Moses? 3068
12: 2 spoken also by us? And **the L** heard *it*. 3068
12: 4 **the L** spake suddenly unto Moses, 3068
12: 5 **the L** came down in the pillar of the 3068
12: 6 **the L** will make myself known unto him 3068
12: 8 the similitude of **the L** shall he behold: 3068
12: 9 the anger of **the L** was kindled against 3068
12:13 Moses cried unto **the L**, saying, Heal her 3068
12:14 **the L** said unto Moses, If her father had 3068
13: 1 And **the L** spake unto Moses, saying, 3068
13: 3 Moses by the commandment of **the L** 3068
14: 3 wherefore *hath* **the L** brought us unto 3068
14: 8 If **the L** delight in us, then he will bring 3068
14: 9 Only rebel not ye against **the L**, 3068
14: 9 from them, and **the L** *is* with us: 3068
14:10 the glory of **the L** appeared in 3068
14:11 **the L** said unto Moses, How long will 3068
14:13 Moses said unto **the L**, Then the 3068
14:14 *for* they have heard that thou L *art* among 3068
14:14 that thou L *art* seen face to face, 3068
14:16 Because **the L** was not able to bring this 3068
14:18 **The L** *is* longsuffering, and of great 3068
14:20 **the L** said, I have pardoned according to 3068
14:21 shall be filled *with* the glory of **the L**. 3068
14:26 **the L** spake unto Moses and unto Aaron, 3068
14:28 unto them, *As truly as* I live, saith **the L**, 3068
14:35 I **the L** have said, I will surely do it unto 3068
14:37 the land, died by the plague before **the L**. 3068
14:40 go up unto the place which **the L** hath 3068
14:41 transgress the commandment of **the L**? 3068
14:42 Go not up, for **the L** *is* not among you; 3068
14:43 because ye are turned away from **the L**, 3068
14:43 therefore **the L** will not be with you. 3068

Nu 14:44 the ark of the covenant of **the L**, 3068
15: 1 And **the L** spake unto Moses, saying, 3068
15: 3 will make an offering by fire unto **the L**, 3068
15: 3 to make a sweet savour unto **the L**, 3068
15: 4 **the L** bring a meat offering of a tenth deal 3068
15: 7 *of* wine, *for* a sweet savour unto **the L**. 3068
15: 8 a vow, or peace offerings unto **the L**: 3068
15:10 by fire, of a sweet savour unto **the L**. 3068
15:13 by fire, of a sweet savour unto **the L**. 3068
15:14 by fire, of a sweet savour unto **the L**; 3068
15:15 so shall the stranger be before **the L**. 3068
15:17 And **the L** spake unto Moses, saying, 3068
15:19 offer up a heave offering unto **the L**. 3068
15:21 **the L** a heave offering in your generations. 3068
15:22 which **the L** hath spoken unto Moses, 3068
15:23 *Even* all that **the L** hath commanded you 3068
15:23 from the day that **the L** commanded 3068
15:24 for a sweet savour unto **the L**, with his 3068
15:25 a sacrifice made by fire unto **the L**, 3068
15:25 their sin offering before **the L**, for their 3068
15:28 he sinneth by ignorance before **the L**, 3068
15:30 a stranger, the same reproacheth **the L**; 3068
15:31 he hath despised the word of **the L**, 3068
15:35 **the L** said unto Moses, The man shall be 3068
15:36 he died; as **the L** commanded Moses. 3068
15:37 And **the L** spake unto Moses, saying, 3068
15:39 all the commandments of **the L**, 3068
15:41 I *am* **the L** your God, which brought you 3068
15:41 to be your God: I *am* **the L** your God. 3068
16: 3 one of them, and **the L** *is* among them: 3068
16: 3 above the congregation of **the L**? 3068
16: 5 Even to morrow **the L** will shew who *are* 3068
16: 7 put incense in them before **the L** to 3068
16: 7 it shall be *that* the man whom **the L** doth 3068
16: 9 do the service of the tabernacle of **the L**, 3068
16:11 *are* gathered together against **the L**: 3068
16:15 was very wroth, and said unto **the L**, 3068
16:16 thou and all thy company before **the L**, 3068
16:17 ye before **the L** every man his censer, 3068
16:19 the glory of **the L** appeared unto all 3068
16:20 **the L** spake unto Moses and unto Aaron, 3068
16:23 And **the L** spake unto Moses, saying, 3068
16:28 Hereby ye shall know that **the L** hath sent 3068
16:29 of all men; *then* **the L** hath not sent me. 3068
16:30 If **the L** make a new thing, and the earth 3068
16:30 that these men have provoked **the L**. 3068
16:35 there came out a fire from **the L**, 3068
16:36 And **the L** spake unto Moses, saying, 3068
16:38 for they offered them before **the L**, 3068
16:40 come near to offer incense before **the L**; 3068
16:40 **the L** said to him by the hand of Moses. 3068
16:41 Ye have killed the people of **the L**. 3068
16:42 and the glory of **the L** appeared. 3068
16:44 And **the L** spake unto Moses, saying, 3068
16:46 for there is wrath gone out from **the L**; 3068
17: 1 And **the L** spake unto Moses, saying, 3068
17: 7 Moses laid up the rods before **the L** in 3068
17: 9 **the L** unto all the children of Israel: 3068
17:10 **the L** said unto Moses, Bring Aaron's rod 3068
17:11 Moses did *so*: as **the L** commanded him, 3068
17:13 unto the tabernacle of **the L** shall die: 3068
18: 1 **the L** said unto Aaron, Thou and thy sons 3068
18: 6 to you *they are* given *as* a gift for **the L**, 3068
18: 8 **the L** spake unto Aaron, Behold, I also 3068
18:12 of them which they shall offer unto **the L**, 3068
18:13 which they shall bring unto **the L**, shall 3068
18:15 which they bring unto **the L**, *whether it* 3068
18:17 by fire, for a sweet savour unto **the L**. 3068
18:19 the children of Israel offer unto **the L** 3068
18:19 *is* a covenant of salt for ever before **the L** 3068
18:20 **the L** spake unto Aaron, Thou shalt have 3068
18:24 they offer *as* a heave offering unto **the L**, 3068
18:25 And **the L** spake unto Moses, saying, 3068
18:26 offer up a heave offering of it for **the L**, 3068
18:28 offering unto **the L** of all your tithes, 3068
18:29 shall offer every heave offering of **the L**, 3068
19: 1 **the L** spake unto Moses and unto Aaron, 3068
19: 2 of the law which **the L** hath commanded, 3068
19:13 defileth the tabernacle of **the L**; 3068
19:20 he hath defiled the sanctuary of **the L**: 3068
20: 3 when our brethren died before **the L**! 3068
20: 4 congregation of **the L** into this wilderness, 3068
20: 6 the glory of **the L** appeared unto them. 3068
20: 7 And **the L** spake unto Moses, saying, 3068
20: 9 Moses took the rod from before **the L**, 3068
20:12 **the L** spake unto Moses and Aaron, 3068
20:13 the children of Israel strove with **the L**, 3068
20:16 when we cried unto **the L**, he heard our 3068
20:23 **the L** spake unto Moses and Aaron in 3068
20:27 Moses did as **the L** commanded: 3068
21: 2 Israel vowed a vow unto **the L**, and said, 3068
21: 3 **the L** hearkened to the voice of Israel, 3068
21: 6 **the L** sent fiery serpents among the 3068
21: 7 for we have spoken against **the L**, 3068
21: 7 pray unto **the L**, that he take away 3068
21: 8 **the L** said unto Moses, Make thee a fiery 3068
21:14 it is said in the book of the wars of **the L**, 3068
21:16 that *is* the well whereof **the L** spake unto 3068
21:34 **the L** said unto Moses, Fear him not: for 3068
22: 8 word again, as **the L** shall speak unto me: 3068
22:13 for **the L** refuseth to give me leave to go 3068
22:18 I cannot go beyond the word of **the L** my 3068
22:19 that I may know what **the L** will say unto 3068
22:22 the angel of **the L** stood in the way for an 3068
22:23 the ass saw the angel of **the L** standing in 3068

L

Nu 22:24 the angel of **the L** stood in a path of 3068
22:25 when the ass saw the angel of **the L,** 3068
22:26 the angel of **the L** went further, 3068
22:27 when the ass saw the angel of **the L,** 3068
22:28 **the L** opened the mouth of the ass, 3068
22:31 Then **the L** opened the eyes of Balaam, 3068
22:31 he saw the angel of **the L** standing in 3068
22:32 the angel of **the L** said unto him, 3068
22:34 Balaam said unto the angel of **the L,** 3068
22:35 the angel of **the L** said unto Balaam, 3068
23: 3 peradventure **the L** will come to meet 3068
23: 5 **the L** put a word in Balaam's mouth, 3068
23: 8 shall I defy, *whom* **the L** hath not defied? 3068
23:12 that which **the L** hath put in my mouth? 3068
23:15 burnt offering, while I meet *the L* yonder. NIH
23:16 **the L** met Balaam, and put a word in his 3068
23:17 said unto him, What hath **the L** spoken? 3068
23:21 **the L** his God *is* with him, and the shout 3068
23:26 All that **the L** speaketh, that I must 3068
24: 1 when Balaam saw that it pleased **the L** to 3068
24: 6 as the trees of lign aloes *which* **the L** hath 3068
24:11 **the L** hath kept thee back from honour. 3068
24:13 go beyond the commandment of **the L,** 3068
24:13 *but* what **the L** saith, that will I speak? 3068
25: 3 the anger of **the L** was kindled against 3068
25: 4 **the L** said unto Moses, Take all the heads 3068
25: 4 them up before **the L** against the sun, 3068
25: 4 the fierce anger of **the L** may be turned 3068
25:10 And **the L** spake unto Moses, saying, 3068
25:16 And **the L** spake unto Moses, saying, 3068
26: 1 that **the L** spake unto Moses and 3068
26: 4 as **the L** commanded Moses and 3068
26: 9 of Korah, when they strove against **the L:** 3068
26:52 And **the L** spake unto Moses, saying, 3068
26:61 they offered strange fire before **the L.** 3068
26:65 For **the L** had said of them, They shall 3068
27: 3 against **the L** in the company of Korah; 3068
27: 5 Moses brought their cause before **the L.** 3068
27: 6 And **the L** spake unto Moses, saying, 3068
27:11 judgment, as **the L** commanded Moses. 3068
27:12 **the L** said unto Moses, Get thee up into 3068
27:15 And Moses spake unto **the L,** saying, 3068
27:16 **the L,** the God of the spirits of all flesh, 3068
27:17 that the congregation of **the L** be not as 3068
27:18 **the L** said unto Moses, Take thee Joshua 3068
27:21 after the judgment of Urim before **the L:** 3068
27:22 Moses did as **the L** commanded him: 3068
27:23 **the L** commanded by the hand of Moses. 3068
28: 1 And **the L** spake unto Moses, saying, 3068
28: 3 by fire which ye shall offer unto **the L;** 3068
28: 6 a sacrifice made by fire unto **the L.** 3068
28: 7 be poured unto **the L** *for* a drink offering. 3068
28: 8 by fire, *of* a sweet savour unto **the L.** 3068
28:11 ye shall offer a burnt offering unto **the L;** 3068
28:13 a sacrifice made by fire unto **the L.** 3068
28:15 a sin offering unto **the L** shall be offered, 3068
28:16 of the first month *is* the passover of **the L.** 3068
28:19 by fire *for* a burnt offering unto **the L:** 3068
28:24 by fire, *of* a sweet savour unto **the L:** 3068
28:26 ye bring a new meat offering unto **the L,** 3068
28:27 offering for a sweet savour unto **the L;** 3068
29: 2 offering made by fire unto **the L;** 3068
29: 6 a sacrifice made by fire unto **the L.** 3068
29: 8 ye shall offer a burnt offering unto **the L** 3068
29:12 shall keep a feast unto **the L** seven days: 3068
29:13 by fire, *of* a sweet savour unto **the L;** 3068
29:36 by fire, *of* a sweet savour unto **the L:** 3068
29:39 These *things* ye shall do unto **the L** in 3068
29:40 to all that **the L** commanded Moses. 3068
30: 1 This *is* the thing which **the L** hath 3068
30: 2 If a man vow a vow unto **the L,** 3068
30: 3 If a woman also vow a vow unto **the L,** 3068
30: 5 **the L** shall forgive her, because her father 3068
30: 8 none effect: and **the L** shall forgive her. 3068
30:12 them void; and **the L** shall forgive her. 3068
30:16 which **the L** commanded Moses, between 3068
31: 1 And **the L** spake unto Moses, saying, 3068
31: 3 and avenge **the L** of Midian. 3068
31: 7 as **the L** commanded Moses; 3068
31:16 to commit trespass against **the L** in 3068
31:16 plague among the congregation of **the L.** 3068
31:21 *is* the ordinance of the law which **the L** 3068
31:25 And **the L** spake unto Moses, saying, 3068
31:28 a tribute unto **the L** of the men of war 3068
31:29 the priest, *for* a heave offering of **the L.** 3068
31:30 keep the charge of the tabernacle of **the L.** 3068
31:31 the priest did as **the L** commanded 3068
31:41 the priest, as **the L** commanded Moses. 3068
31:47 the charge of the tabernacle of **the L;** 3068
31:47 the LORD; as **the L** commanded Moses. 3068
31:50 therefore brought an oblation for **the L,** 3068
31:50 an atonement for our souls before **the L.** 3068
31:52 the offering that they offered up to **the L,** 3068
31:54 for the children of Israel before **the L.** 3068
32: 4 the country which **the L** smote before 3068
32: 7 the land which **the L** hath given them? 3068
32: 9 the land which **the L** had given them. 3068
32:12 for they have wholly followed **the L.** 3068
32:13 that had done evil in the sight of **the L,** 3068
32:14 to augment yet the fierce anger of **the L** 3068
32:20 if ye will go armed before **the L** to war, 3068
32:21 all of you armed over Jordan before **the L,** 3068
32:22 And the land be subdued before **the L,** 3068
32:22 guiltless before **the L,** and before Israel; 3068
32:22 shall be your possession before **the L.** 3068

Nu 32:23 behold, ye have sinned against **the L:** 3068
32:27 before **the L** to battle, as my lord saith. 3068
32:29 before **the L,** and the land shall be 3068
32:31 As **the L** hath said unto thy servants, 3068
32:32 We will pass over armed before **the L** 3068
33: 2 journeys by the commandment of **the L:** 3068
33: 4 which **the L** had smitten among them: 3068
33: 4 upon their gods also the **the L** executed 3068
33:38 Hor at the commandment of **the L,** 3068
33:50 **the L** spake unto Moses in the plains of 3068
34: 1 And **the L** spake unto Moses, saying, 3068
34:13 which **the L** commanded to give unto 3068
34:16 And **the L** spake unto Moses, saying, 3068
34:29 These *are* they whom **the L** commanded 3068
35: 1 **the L** spake unto Moses in the plains of 3068
35: 9 And **the L** spake unto Moses, saying, 3068
35:34 for I **the L** dwell among the children of 3068
36: 2 **the L** commanded my lord to give the 3068
36: 2 my lord was commanded by **the L** to give 3068
36: 5 of Israel according to the word of **the L,** 3068
36: 6 This *is* the thing which **the L** doth 3068
36:10 Even as **the L** commanded Moses, 3068
36:13 which **the L** commanded by the hand of 3068
Dt 1: 3 according unto all that **the L** had given 3068
1: 6 **The L** our God spake unto us in Horeb, 3068
1: 8 possess the land which **the L** sware unto 3068
1:10 **The L** your God hath multiplied you, 3068
1:11 (**The L** God of your fathers make you a 3068
1:19 as **the L** our God commanded us; 3068
1:20 which **the L** our God doth give unto us. 3068
1:21 **the L** thy God hath set the land before 3068
1:21 possess *it,* as **the L** God of thy fathers 3068
1:25 *It is* a good land which **the L** our God 3068
1:26 against the commandment of **the L** 3068
1:27 and said, Because **the L** hated us, 3068
1:30 **The L** your God which goeth before you, 3068
1:31 where thou hast seen how that **the L** thy 3068
1:32 Yet in this thing ye did not believe **the L** 3068
1:34 **the L** heard the voice of your words, 3068
1:36 because he hath wholly followed **the L.** 3068
1:37 Also **the L** was angry with me for your 3068
1:41 unto me, We have sinned against **the L,** 3068
1:41 according to all that **the L** our God 3068
1:42 **the L** said unto me, Say unto them, Go 3068
1:43 against the commandment of **the L,** 3068
1:45 And ye returned and wept before **the L;** 3068
1:45 **the L** would not hearken to your voice, 3068
2: 1 of the Red sea, as **the L** spake unto me: 3068
2: 2 And **the L** spake unto me, saying, 3068
2: 7 For **the L** thy God hath blessed thee in all 3068
2: 7 these forty years **the L** thy God *hath been* 3068
2: 9 **the L** said unto me, Distress not 3068
2:12 which **the L** gave unto them.) 3068
2:14 the host, as **the L** sware unto them. 3068
2:15 For indeed the hand of **the L** was against 3068
2:17 That **the L** spake unto me, saying, 3068
2:21 **the L** destroyed them before them; 3068
2:29 the land which **the L** our God giveth us. 3068
2:30 for **the L** thy God hardened his spirit, 3068
2:31 **the L** said unto me, Behold, I have begun 3068
2:33 **the L** our God delivered him before us; 3068
2:36 **the L** our God delivered all unto us: 3068
2:37 *unto* whatsoever **the L** our God forbad 3068
3: 2 **the L** said unto me, Fear him not: for I 3068
3: 3 **the L** our God delivered into our hands 3068
3:18 **The L** your God hath given you this land 3068
3:20 Until **the L** have given rest unto your 3068
3:20 they also possess the land which **the L** 3068
3:21 Thine eyes have seen all that **the L** your 3068
3:21 shall **the L** do unto all the kingdoms 3068
3:22 for **the L** your God he shall fight for you. 3068
3:23 I besought **the L** at that time, saying, 3068
3:26 **the L** was wroth with me for your sakes, 3068
3:26 **the L** said unto me, Let it suffice thee: 3068
4: 1 possess the land which **the L** God of 3068
4: 2 **the L** your God which I command you. 3068
4: 3 Your eyes have seen what **the L** did 3068
4: 3 **the L** thy God hath destroyed them from 3068
4: 4 ye that did cleave unto **the L** your God 3068
4: 5 even as **the L** my God commanded me, 3068
4: 7 as **the L** our God *is* in all *things that* we 3068
4:10 stoodest before **the L** thy God in Horeb, 3068
4:10 when **the L** said unto me, Gather me 3068
4:12 **the L** spake unto you out of the midst of 3068
4:14 **the L** commanded me at that time to 3068
4:15 **the L** spake unto you in Horeb out of 3068
4:19 **the L** thy God hath divided unto all 3068
4:20 **the L** hath taken you, and brought you 3068
4:21 Furthermore **the L** was angry with me 3068
4:21 which **the L** thy God giveth thee *for* an 3068
4:23 lest ye forget the covenant of **the L** your 3068
4:23 likeness of any *thing,* which **the L** thy 3068
4:24 For **the L** thy God *is* a consuming fire, 3068
4:25 do evil in the sight of **the L** thy God, 3068
4:27 **the L** shall scatter you among the nations, 3068
4:27 heathen, whither **the L** shall lead you. 3068
4:29 If from thence thou shalt seek **the L** thy 3068
4:30 if thou turn to **the L** thy God, and shalt 3068
4:31 (For **the L** thy God *is* a merciful God;) 3068
4:34 according to all that **the L** your God did 3068
4:35 that thou mightest know that **the L** he *is* 3068
4:39 that **the L** he *is* God in heaven above, 3068
4:40 **the L** thy God giveth thee, for ever. 3068
5: 2 **The L** our God made a covenant with us 3068
5: 3 **The L** made not this covenant with our 3068

Dt 5: 4 **The L** talked with you face to face in 3068
5: 5 (I stood between **the L** and you at that 3068
5: 5 that time, to shew you the word of **the L:** 3068
5: 6 I *am* **the L** thy God, which brought thee 3068
5: 9 for I **the L** thy God *am* a jealous God, 3068
5:11 shalt not take the name of **the L** thy 3068
5:11 for **the L** will not hold *him* guiltless that 3068
5:12 as **the L** thy God hath commanded thee. 3068
5:14 seventh day *is* the sabbath of **the L** thy 3068
5:15 **the L** thy God brought thee out thence 3068
5:15 **the L** thy God commanded thee to keep 3068
5:16 as **the L** thy God hath commanded thee; 3068
5:16 in the land which **the L** thy God giveth 3068
5:22 These words **the L** spake unto all your 3068
5:24 **the L** our God hath shewed us his glory 3068
5:25 if we hear the voice of **the L** our God any 3068
5:27 and hear all that **the L** our God shall say: 3068
5:27 speak thou unto us all that **the L** our God 3068
5:28 **the L** heard the voice of your words, 3068
5:28 **the L** said unto me, I have heard the 3068
5:32 as **the L** your God hath commanded you: 3068
5:33 shall walk in all the ways which **the L** 3068
6: 1 **the L** your God commanded to teach 3068
6: 2 That thou mightest fear **the L** thy God, 3068
6: 3 as **the L** God of thy fathers hath promised 3068
6: 4 O Israel: **The L** our God *is* one LORD: 3068
6: 4 O Israel: The LORD our God *is* one L: 3068
6: 5 shalt love **the L** thy God with all thine 3068
6:10 when **the L** thy God shall have brought 3068
6:12 *Then* beware lest thou forget **the L,** 3068
6:13 Thou shalt fear **the L** thy God, 3068
6:15 **the L** thy God *is* a jealous God among 3068
6:15 lest the anger of **the L** thy God be kindled 3068
6:16 Ye shall not tempt **the L** your God, as ye 3068
6:17 the commandments of **the L** your God, 3068
6:18 *is* right and good in the sight of **the L:** 3068
6:18 possess the good land which **the L** sware 3068
6:19 from before thee, as **the L** hath spoken. 3068
6:20 which **the L** our God hath commanded 3068
6:21 **the L** brought us out of Egypt with a 3068
6:22 **the L** shewed signs and wonders, great 3068
6:24 **the L** commanded us to do all these 3068
6:24 fear **the L** our God, for our good always, 3068
6:25 commandments before **the L** our God, 3068
7: 1 When **the L** thy God shall bring thee into 3068
7: 2 when **the L** thy God shall deliver them 3068
7: 4 will the anger of **the L** be kindled against 3068
7: 6 For thou *art* a holy people unto **the L** thy 3068
7: 6 **the L** thy God hath chosen thee to be a 3068
7: 7 **The L** did not set his love upon you, 3068
7: 8 because **the L** loved you, and because 3068
7: 8 **the L** brought you out with a mighty 3068
7: 9 Know therefore that **the L** thy God, he *is* 3068
7:12 that **the L** thy God shall keep unto thee 3068
7:15 **the L** will take away from thee all 3068
7:16 which **the L** thy God shall deliver thee; 3068
7:18 shalt well remember what **the L** thy God 3068
7:19 where*by* **the L** thy God brought thee out: 3068
7:19 **the L** thy God do unto all the people 3068
7:20 Moreover **the L** thy God will send 3068
7:21 **the L** thy God *is* among you, a mighty 3068
7:22 **the L** thy God will put out those nations 3068
7:23 **the L** thy God shall deliver them unto 3068
7:25 for it *is* an abomination to **the L** thy God. 3068
8: 1 possess the land which **the L** sware unto 3068
8: 2 **the L** thy God led thee these forty years 3068
8: 3 out of the mouth of **the L** doth man live. 3068
8: 5 son, *so* **the L** thy God chasteneth thee. 3068
8: 6 the commandments of **the L** thy God, 3068
8: 7 For **the L** thy God bringeth thee into a 3068
8:10 shalt bless **the L** thy God for the good 3068
8:11 that thou forget not **the L** thy God, 3068
8:14 lifted up, and thou forget **the L** thy God, 3068
8:18 thou shalt remember **the L** thy God: for 3068
8:19 if thou do at all forget **the L** thy God, 3068
8:20 As the nations which **the L** destroyeth 3068
8:20 unto the voice of **the L** your God. 3068
9: 3 **the L** thy God *is* he which goeth over 3068
9: 3 quickly, as **the L** hath said unto thee. 3068
9: 4 that **the L** thy God hath cast them out 3068
9: 4 For my righteousness **the L** hath brought 3068
9: 4 for the wickedness of these nations **the L** 3068
9: 5 for the wickedness of these nations **the L** 3068
9: 5 he may perform the word which **the L** 3068
9: 6 that **the L** thy God giveth thee not this 3068
9: 7 how thou provokedst **the L** thy God to 3068
9: 7 ye have been rebellious against **the L.** 3068
9: 8 in Horeb ye provoked **the L** to wrath, 3068
9: 8 that **the L** was angry with you to have 3068
9: 9 the tables of the covenant which **the L** 3068
9:10 **the L** delivered unto me two tables of 3068
9:10 **the L** spake with you in the mount 3068
9:11 **the L** gave me the two tables of stone, 3068
9:12 **the L** said unto me, Arise, get thee down 3068
9:13 Furthermore **the L** spake unto me, saying, 3068
9:16 ye had sinned against **the L** your God, 3068
9:16 way which **the L** had commanded you. 3068
9:18 I fell down before **the L,** as at the first, 3068
9:18 in doing wickedly in the sight of **the L,** 3068
9:19 where*with* **the L** was wroth against you 3068
9:19 **the L** hearkened unto me at that time 3068
9:20 **the L** was very angry with Aaron to have 3068
9:22 ye provoked **the L** to wrath. 3068
9:23 Likewise when **the L** sent you from 3068
9:23 the commandment of **the L** your God, 3068

Dt 9:24	You have been rebellious against the L	3068
9:25	Thus I fell down before the L forty days	3068
9:25	the L had said he would destroy you.	3068
9:26	I prayed therefore unto the L, and said,	3068
9:28	Because the L was not able to bring	3068
10: 1	At that time the L said unto me, Hew	3068
10: 4	which the L spake unto you in the mount	3068
10: 4	and the L gave them unto me.	3068
10: 5	there they be, as the L commanded me.	3068
10: 8	At that time the L separated the tribe of	3068
10: 8	to bear the ark of the covenant of the L,	3068
10: 8	stand before the L to minister unto him,	3068
10: 9	the L is his inheritance, according as	3068
10: 9	according as the L thy God promised	3068
10:10	the L hearkened unto me at that time	3068
10:10	and the L would not destroy thee.	3068
10:11	the L said unto me, Arise, take thy	3068
10:12	what doth the L thy God require of thee,	3068
10:12	to fear the L thy God, to walk in all his	3068
10:12	to serve the L thy God with all thy heart	3068
10:13	To keep the commandments of the L,	3068
10:15	Only the L had a delight in thy fathers to	3068
10:17	For the L your God is God of gods,	3068
10:20	Thou shalt fear the L thy God; him shalt	3068
10:22	now the L thy God hath made thee as	3068
11: 1	Therefore thou shalt love the L thy God,	3068
11: 2	seen the chastisement of the L your God,	3068
11: 4	how the L hath destroyed them unto this	3068
11: 7	all the great acts of the L which he did.	3068
11: 9	which the L sware unto your fathers to	3068
11:12	A land which the L thy God careth for:	3068
11:12	eyes of the L thy God are always upon	3068
11:13	to love the L your God, and to serve him	3068
11:17	off the good land which the L giveth you.	3068
11:21	in the land which the L sware unto your	3068
11:22	do them, to love the L your God, to walk	3068
11:23	will the L drive out all these nations from	3068
11:25	the L your God shall lay the fear of you	3068
11:27	if ye obey the commandments of the L	3068
11:28	the commandments of the L your God,	3068
11:29	the L thy God hath brought thee in	3068
11:31	land which the L your God giveth you,	3068
12: 1	which the L God of thy fathers giveth	3068
12: 4	Ye shall not do so unto the L your God.	3068
12: 5	the place which the L your God shall	3068
12: 7	there ye shall eat before the L your God,	3068
12: 7	wherein the L thy God hath blessed thee.	3068
12: 9	which the L your God giveth you.	3068
12:10	dwell in the land which the L your God	3068
12:11	there shall be a place which the L your	3068
12:11	choice vows which ye vow unto the L:	3068
12:12	ye shall rejoice before the L your God,	3068
12:14	in the place which the L shall choose in	3068
12:15	according to the blessing of the L thy God	3068
12:18	must eat them before the L thy God in	3068
12:18	place which the L thy God shall choose,	3068
12:18	thou shalt rejoice before the L thy God in	3068
12:20	When the L thy God shall enlarge thy	3068
12:21	If the place which the L thy God hath	3068
12:21	of thy flock, which the L hath given thee,	3068
12:25	that which is right in the sight of the L.	3068
12:26	unto the place which the L shall choose:	3068
12:27	blood, upon the altar of the L thy God,	3068
12:27	out upon the altar of the L thy God,	3068
12:28	and right in the sight of the L thy God.	3068
12:29	When the L thy God shall cut off	3068
12:31	Thou shalt not do so unto the L thy God:	3068
12:31	for every abomination to the L, which he	3068
13: 3	for the L your God proveth you, to know	3068
13: 3	know whether you love the L your God	3068
13: 4	Ye shall walk after the L your God,	3068
13: 5	to turn you away from the L your God,	3068
13: 5	thrust thee out of the way which the L	3068
13:10	to thrust thee away from the L thy God,	3068
13:12	which the L thy God hath given thee to	3068
13:16	thereof every whit, for the L thy God:	3068
13:17	that the L may turn from the fierceness	3068
13:18	hearken to the voice of the L thy God,	3068
13:18	is right in the eyes of the L thy God.	3068
14: 1	Ye are the children of the L your God:	3068
14: 2	For thou art a holy people unto the L thy	3068
14: 2	the L hath chosen thee to be a peculiar	3068
14:21	for thou art a holy people unto the L thy	3068
14:23	thou shalt eat before the L thy God,	3068
14:23	that thou mayest learn to fear the L thy	3068
14:24	the L thy God shall choose to set his	3068
14:24	when the L thy God hath blessed thee:	3068
14:25	shalt go unto the place which the L thy	3068
14:26	thou shalt eat there before the L thy God,	3068
14:29	that the L thy God may bless thee in all	3068
15: 4	the L shall greatly bless thee in the land	3068
15: 4	the L thy God giveth thee for an	3068
15: 5	hearken unto the voice of the L thy God,	3068
15: 6	For the L thy God blesseth thee, as he	3068
15: 7	land which the L thy God giveth thee,	3068
15: 9	cry unto the L against thee, and it be sin	3068
15:10	for this thing the L thy God shall bless	3068
15:14	of that wherewith the L thy God hath	3068
15:15	and the L thy God redeemed thee:	3068
15:18	the L thy God shall bless thee in all that	3068
15:19	thy flock thou shalt sanctify unto the L	3068
15:20	shalt eat it before the L thy God year	3068
15:20	in the place which the L shall choose,	3068
15:21	thou shalt not sacrifice it unto the L thy	3068
16: 1	keep the passover unto the L thy God:	3068

Dt 16: 1	for in the month of Abib the L thy God	3068
16: 2	sacrifice the passover unto the L thy God,	3068
16: 2	in the place which the L shall choose to	3068
16: 5	gates, which the L thy God giveth thee:	3068
16: 6	at the place which the L thy God shall	3068
16: 7	eat it in the place which the L thy God	3068
16: 8	be a solemn assembly to the L thy God:	3068
16:10	the L thy God with a tribute of a freewill	3068
16:10	which thou shalt give unto the L thy God,	NIH
16:10	as the L thy God hath blessed thee:	3068
16:11	thou shalt rejoice before the L thy God,	3068
16:11	in the place which the L thy God hath	3068
16:15	the L thy God in the place which	3068
16:15	in the place which the L shall choose:	3068
16:15	the L thy God shall bless thee in all thy	3068
16:16	the L thy God in the place which he shall	3068
16:16	they shall not appear before the L empty:	3068
16:17	to the blessing of the L thy God	3068
16:18	which the L thy God giveth thee,	3068
16:20	the land which the L thy God giveth	3068
16:21	trees near unto the altar of the L thy God,	3068
16:22	any image; which the L thy God hateth.	3068
17: 1	shalt not sacrifice unto the L thy God	3068
17: 1	for that is an abomination unto the L thy	3068
17: 2	within any of thy gates which the L thy	3068
17: 2	wickedness in the sight of the L thy God,	3068
17: 8	thee up into the place which the L thy	3068
17:10	they of that place which the L shall	3068
17:12	to minister there before the L thy God,	3068
17:14	land which the L thy God giveth thee,	3068
17:15	whom the L thy God shall choose:	3068
17:16	forasmuch as the L hath said unto you,	3068
17:19	that he may learn to fear the L his God,	3068
18: 1	they shall eat the offerings of the L made	3068
18: 2	the L is their inheritance, as he hath said	3068
18: 5	the L thy God hath chosen him out of	3068
18: 5	stand to minister in the name of the L,	3068
18: 6	unto the place which the L shall choose;	3068
18: 7	he shall minister in the name of the L his	3068
18: 7	which stand there before the L.	3068
18: 9	land which the L thy God giveth thee,	3068
18:12	things are an abomination unto the L:	3068
18:12	of these abominations the L thy God doth	3068
18:13	Thou shalt be perfect with the L thy God.	3068
18:14	the L thy God hath not suffered thee so	3068
18:15	The L thy God will raise up unto thee a	3068
18:16	the L thy God in Horeb in the day of	3068
18:16	Let me not hear again the voice of the L	3068
18:17	the L said unto me, They have well	3068
18:21	shall we know the word which the L	3068
18:22	a prophet speaketh in the name of the L,	3068
18:22	that is the thing which the L hath not	3068
19: 1	When the L thy God hath cut off	3068
19: 1	whose land the L thy God giveth thee,	3068
19: 2	the L thy God giveth thee to possess	3068
19: 3	the L thy God giveth thee to inherit,	3068
19: 8	if the L thy God enlarge thy coast, as he	3068
19: 9	love the L thy God, and to walk ever in	3068
19:10	which the L thy God giveth thee for an	3068
19:14	the L thy God giveth thee to possess it.	3068
19:17	controversy is, shall stand before the L,	3068
20: 1	for the L thy God is with thee,	3068
20: 4	For the L your God is he that goeth with	3068
20:13	the L thy God hath delivered it into	3068
20:14	which the L thy God hath given thee.	3068
20:16	the L thy God doth give thee for an	3068
20:17	as the L thy God hath commanded thee:	3068
20:18	so should ye sin against the L your God.	3068
21: 1	the L thy God giveth thee to possess it,	3068
21: 5	for them the L thy God hath chosen to	3068
21: 5	him, and to bless in the name of the L;	3068
21: 8	Be merciful, O L, unto thy people Israel,	3068
21: 9	that which is right in the sight of the L.	3068
21:10	the L thy God hath delivered them into	3068
21:23	which the L thy God giveth thee for an	3068
22: 5	so are abomination unto the L thy God.	3068
23: 1	not enter into the congregation of the L.	3068
23: 2	not enter into the congregation of the L;	3068
23: 2	not enter into the congregation of the L;	3068
23: 3	not enter into the congregation of the L;	3068
23: 3	into the congregation of the L for ever:	3068
23: 5	Nevertheless the L thy God would not	3068
23: 5	the L thy God turned the curse into a	3068
23: 5	because the L thy God loved thee.	3068
23: 8	of the L in their third generation.	3068
23:14	the L thy God walketh in the midst of	3068
23:18	into the house of the L thy God for any	3068
23:18	are abomination unto the L thy God.	3068
23:20	that the L thy God may bless thee in all	3068
23:21	When thou shalt vow a vow unto the L	3068
23:21	for the L thy God will surely require it of	3068
23:23	according as thou hast vowed unto the L	3068
24: 4	for that is abomination before the L:	3068
24: 4	which the L thy God giveth thee for an	3068
24: 9	Remember what the L thy God did unto	3068
24:13	unto thee before the L thy God.	3068
24:15	lest he cry against thee unto the L, and it	3068
24:18	and the L thy God redeemed thee thence:	3068
24:19	that the L thy God may bless thee in all	3068
25:15	land which the L thy God giveth thee.	3068
25:16	are an abomination unto the L thy God.	3068
25:19	when the L thy God hath given thee rest	3068
25:19	the land which the L thy God giveth thee	3068
26: 1	the L thy God giveth thee for an	3068
26: 2	thou shalt bring of thy land that the L	3068

Dt 26: 2	shalt go unto the place which the L thy	3068
26: 3	I profess this day unto the L thy God,	3068
26: 3	the L sware unto our fathers for to give	3068
26: 4	set it down before the altar of the L thy	3068
26: 5	shalt speak and say before the L thy God,	3068
26: 7	when we cried unto the L God of our	3068
26: 7	the L heard our voice, and looked on our	3068
26: 8	the L brought us forth out of Egypt with	3068
26:10	land, which thou, O L, hast given me.	3068
26:10	thou shalt set it before the L thy God,	3068
26:10	and worship before the L thy God:	3068
26:11	the L thy God hath given unto thee,	3068
26:13	thou shalt say before the L thy God,	3068
26:14	I have hearkened to the voice of the L my	3068
26:16	This day the L thy God hath commanded	3068
26:17	Thou hast avouched the L this day to be	3068
26:18	the L hath avouched thee this day to be	3068
26:19	be a holy people unto the L thy God,	3068
27: 2	land which the L thy God giveth thee,	3068
27: 3	land which the L thy God giveth thee,	3068
27: 3	as the L God of thy fathers hath promised	3068
27: 5	shalt thou build an altar unto the L	3068
27: 6	shalt build the altar of the L thy God	3068
27: 6	offerings thereon unto the L thy God:	3068
27: 7	there, and rejoice before the L thy God.	3068
27: 9	art become the people of the L thy God.	3068
27:10	obey the voice of the L thy God,	3068
27:15	image, an abomination unto the L,	3068
28: 1	unto the voice of the L thy God,	3068
28: 1	that the L thy God will set thee on high	3068
28: 2	hearken unto the voice of the L thy God.	3068
28: 7	The L shall cause thine enemies that rise	3068
28: 8	The L shall command the blessing upon	3068
28: 8	shall bless thee in the land which the L	3068
28: 9	The L shall establish thee a holy people	3068
28: 9	the commandments of the L thy God,	3068
28:10	that thou art called by the name of the L;	3068
28:11	the L shall make thee plenteous in goods,	3068
28:11	in the land which the L sware unto thy	3068
28:12	The L shall open unto thee his good	3068
28:13	the L shall make thee the head, and not	3068
28:13	the commandments of the L thy God,	3068
28:15	hearken unto the voice of the L thy God,	3068
28:20	The L shall send upon thee cursing,	3068
28:21	The L shall make the pestilence cleave	3068
28:22	The L shall smite thee with a	3068
28:24	The L shall make the rain of thy land	3068
28:25	The L shall cause thee to be smitten	3068
28:27	The L will smite thee with the botch of	3068
28:28	The L shall smite thee with madness,	3068
28:35	The L shall smite thee in the knees,	3068
28:36	The L shall bring thee, and thy king	3068
28:37	among all nations whither the L shall lead	3068
28:45	not unto the voice of the L thy God,	3068
28:47	thou servedst not the L thy God	3068
28:48	which the L shall send against thee,	3068
28:49	The L shall bring a nation against thee	3068
28:52	which the L thy God hath given thee.	3068
28:53	which the L thy God hath given thee,	3068
28:58	and fearful name, THE L THY GOD;	3068
28:59	the L will make thy plagues wonderful,	3068
28:61	them will the L bring upon thee, until	3068
28:62	wouldest not obey the voice of the L	3068
28:63	that as the L rejoiced over you to do you	3068
28:63	the L will rejoice over you to destroy you,	3068
28:64	the L shall scatter thee among all people,	3068
28:65	the L shall give thee there a trembling	3068
28:68	the L shall bring thee into Egypt again	3068
29: 1	which the L commanded Moses to make	3068
29: 2	have seen all that the L did before your	3068
29: 4	Yet the L hath not given you a heart to	3068
29: 6	that ye might know that I am the L your	3068
29:10	Ye stand this day all of you before the L	3068
29:12	enter into covenant with the L thy God,	3068
29:12	which the L thy God maketh with thee	3068
29:15	with us this day before the L our God,	3068
29:18	away this day from the L our God,	3068
29:20	The L will not spare him, but then	3068
29:20	then the anger of the L and his jealousy	3068
29:20	the L shall blot out his name from under	3068
29:21	the L shall separate him unto evil out of	3068
29:22	sicknesses which the L hath laid upon	3068
29:23	which the L overthrew in his anger,	3068
29:24	hath the L done thus unto this	3068
29:25	covenant of the L God of their fathers,	3068
29:27	anger of the L was kindled against this	3068
29:28	the L rooted them out of their land in	3068
29:29	The secret things belong unto the L our	3068
30: 1	whither the L thy God hath driven thee,	3068
30: 2	shalt return unto the L thy God,	3068
30: 3	the L thy God will turn thy captivity,	3068
30: 3	the L thy God hath scattered thee.	3068
30: 4	thence will the L thy God gather thee,	3068
30: 5	the L thy God will bring thee into the	3068
30: 6	the L thy God will circumcise thine heart,	3068
30: 6	to love the L thy God with all thine heart,	3068
30: 7	the L thy God will put all these curses	3068
30: 8	shalt return and obey the voice of the L,	3068
30: 9	the L thy God will make thee plenteous	3068
30: 9	for the L will again rejoice over thee for	3068
30:10	hearken to the voice of the L thy God,	3068
30:10	if thou turn unto the L thy God with all	3068
30:16	thee this day to love the L thy God,	3068
30:16	the L thy God shall bless thee in the land	3068
30:20	That thou mayest love the L thy God,	3068

L

Dt	30:20 land which **the L** sware unto thy fathers,	3068
	31: 2 also **the L** hath said unto me, Thou shalt	3068
	31: 3 **the L** thy God, he will go over before	3068
	31: 3 go over before thee, as **the L** hath said.	3068
	31: 4 **the L** shall do unto them as he did to	3068
	31: 5 **the L** shall give them up before your face,	3068
	31: 6 **the L** thy God, he *it is* that doth go with	3068
	31: 7 **the L** hath sworn unto their fathers to	3068
	31: 8 **the L**, he *it is* that doth go before thee;	3068
	31: 9 bare the ark of the covenant of **the L**,	3068
	31:11 **the L** thy God in the place which he shall	3068
	31:12 fear **the L** your God, and observe to do all	3068
	31:13 hear, and learn to fear **the L** your God,	3068
	31:14 **the L** said unto Moses, Behold, thy days	3068
	31:15 **the L** appeared in the tabernacle in a	3068
	31:16 **the L** said unto Moses, Behold, thou shalt	3068
	31:25 bare the ark of the covenant of **the L**,	3068
	31:26 ark of the covenant of **the L** your God,	3068
	31:27 ye have been rebellious against **the L**;	3068
	31:29 ye will do evil in the sight of **the L**,	3068
	32: 3 Because I will publish the name of **the L**:	3068
	32: 6 ye thus requite **the L**, O foolish people	3068
	32:12 So **the L** alone did lead him, and *there*	3068
	32:19 when **the L** saw *it*, he abhorred *them,*	3068
	32:27 is high, and **the L** hath not done all this.	3068
	32:30 sold them, and **the L** had shut them up?	3068
	32:36 For **the L** shall judge his people,	3068
	32:48 **the L** spake unto Moses that selfsame	3068
	33: 2 **The L** came from Sinai, and rose up from	3068
	33: 7 he said, Hear, **L**, the voice of Judah,	3068
	33:11 Bless, **L**, his substance, and accept	3068
	33:12 The beloved of **the L** shall dwell in safety	3068
	33:12 *the L* shall cover him all the day long,	NIH
	33:13 he said, Blessed of **the L** *be* his land,	3068
	33:21 he executed the justice of **the L**,	3068
	33:23 and full *with* the blessing of **the L**:	3068
	33:29 like unto thee, O people saved by **the L**,	3068
	34: 1 **the L** shewed him all the land of Gilead,	3068
	34: 4 **the L** said unto him, This *is* the land	3068
	34: 5 So Moses the servant of **the L** died there	3068
	34: 5 of Moab, according to the word of **the L**.	3068
	34: 9 and did as **the L** commanded Moses.	3068
	34:10 whom **the L** knew face to face,	3068
	34:11 which **the L** sent him to do in the land of	3068
Jos	1: 1 Moses the servant of **the L** it came to	3068
	1: 1 that **the L** spake unto Joshua the son of	3068
	1: 9 for **the L** thy God *is* with thee	3068
	1:11 which **the L** your God giveth you to	3068
	1:13 the servant of **the L** commanded you,	3068
	1:13 **The L** your God hath given you rest,	3068
	1:15 **the L** have given your brethren rest,	3068
	1:15 land which **the L** your God giveth them:	3068
	1:17 only **the L** thy God be with thee, as he	3068
	2: 9 know that **the L** hath given you the land,	3068
	2:10 For we have heard how **the L** dried up	3068
	2:11 for **the L** your God, he *is* God in heaven	3068
	2:12 I pray you, swear unto me by **the L**,	3068
	2:14 be, when **the L** hath given us the land,	3068
	2:24 **the L** hath delivered into our hands	3068
	3: 3 ark of the covenant of **the L** your God,	3068
	3: 5 for to morrow **the L** will do wonders	3068
	3: 7 **the L** said unto Joshua, This day will I	3068
	3: 9 and hear the words of **the L** your God.	3068
	3:13 of the priests that bear the ark of **the L**,	3068
	3:17 **the L** stood firm on dry *ground* in the	3068
	4: 1 that **the L** spake unto Joshua, saying,	3068
	4: 5 over before the ark of **the L** your God	3068
	4: 7 before the ark of the covenant of **the L**;	3068
	4: 8 of Jordan, as **the L** spake unto Joshua,	3068
	4:10 until every thing was finished that **the L**	3068
	4:11 that the ark of **the L** passed over,	3068
	4:13 ward passed over before **the L** unto battle,	3068
	4:14 On that day **the L** magnified Joshua in	3068
	4:15 And **the L** spake unto Joshua, saying,	3068
	4:18 **the L** were come up out of the midst of	3068
	4:23 For **the L** your God dried up the waters	3068
	4:23 as **the L** your God did to the Red sea,	3068
	4:24 the earth might know the hand of **the L**,	3068
	4:24 ye might fear **the L** your God for ever.	3068
	5: 1 heard that **the L** had dried up the waters	3068
	5: 2 At that time **the L** said unto Joshua,	3068
	5: 6 they obeyed not the voice of **the L**:	3068
	5: 6 whom **the L** sware that *he* would not	3068
	5: 6 which **the L** sware unto their fathers that	3068
	5: 9 **the L** said unto Joshua, *This* day have I	3068
	5:14 *as* captain of the host of **the L** am I now	3068
	6: 2 **the L** said unto Joshua, See, I have given	3068
	6: 6 of rams' horns before the ark of **the L**.	3068
	6: 7 is armed pass on before the ark of **the L**.	3068
	6: 8 of rams' horns passed on before **the L**,	3068
	6: 8 the ark of the covenant of **the L** followed	3068
	6:11 So the ark of **the L** compassed the city,	3068
	6:12 and the priests took up the ark of **the L**.	3068
	6:13 the ark of **the L** went on continually,	3068
	6:13 the rereward came after the ark of **the L**,	3068
	6:16 Shout; for **the L** hath given you the city.	3068
	6:17 *even* it, and all that *are* therein, to **the L**:	3068
	6:19 and iron, *are* consecrated unto **the L**:	3068
	6:19 shall come *into* the treasury of **the L**.	3068
	6:24 *into* the treasury of the house of **the L**.	3068
	6:26 saying, Cursed *be* the man before **the L**,	3068
	6:27 So **the L** was with Joshua; and his fame	3068
	7: 1 the anger of **the L** was kindled against	3068
	7: 6 before the ark of **the L** until the eventide,	3068
	7:10 **the L** said unto Joshua, Get thee up;	3068

Jos	7:13 thus saith **the L** God of Israel, *There is*	3068
	7:14 the tribe which **the L** taketh shall come	3068
	7:14 the family which **the L** shall take shall	3068
	7:14 the household which **the L** shall take	3068
	7:15 hath transgressed the covenant of **the L**,	3068
	7:19 glory to **the L** God of Israel,	3068
	7:20 Indeed I have sinned against **the L** God	3068
	7:23 of Israel, and laid them out before **the L**.	3068
	7:25 **the L** shall trouble thee this day. And all	3068
	7:26 So **the L** turned from the fierceness of his	3068
	8: 1 **the L** said unto Joshua, Fear not, neither	3068
	8: 7 **the L** your God will deliver it into your	3068
	8: 8 according to the commandment of **the L**	3068
	8:18 **the L** said unto Joshua, Stretch out	3068
	8:27 according unto the word of **the L** which	3068
	8:30 Joshua built an altar unto **the L** God of	3068
	8:31 Moses the servant of **the L** commanded	3068
	8:31 thereon burnt offerings unto **the L**,	3068
	8:33 bare the ark of the covenant of **the L**,	3068
	8:33 as Moses the servant of **the L** had	3068
	9: 9 because of the name of **the L** thy God:	3068
	9:14 asked not *counsel* at the mouth of **the L**.	3068
	9:18 sworn unto them by **the L** God of Israel.	3068
	9:19 We have sworn unto them by **the L** God	3068
	9:24 how that **the L** thy God commanded his	3068
	9:27 for the altar of **the L**, *even* unto this day,	3068
	10: 8 **the L** said unto Joshua, Fear them not:	3068
	10:10 **the L** discomfited them before Israel,	3068
	10:11 that **the L** cast down great stones from	3068
	10:12 spake Joshua to **the L** in the day when	3068
	10:12 **the L** delivered up the Amorites before	3068
	10:14 that **the L** hearkened unto the voice of a	3068
	10:14 voice of a man: for **the L** fought for Israel.	3068
	10:19 for **the L** your God hath delivered them	3068
	10:25 thus shall **the L** do to all your enemies	3068
	10:30 **the L** delivered it also, and the king	3068
	10:32 **the L** delivered Lachish into the hand of	3068
	10:40 as **the L** God of Israel commanded.	3068
	10:42 **the L** God of Israel fought for Israel.	3068
	11: 6 **the L** said unto Joshua, Be not afraid	3068
	11: 8 **the L** delivered them into the hand of	3068
	11: 9 Joshua did unto them as **the L** bade him:	3068
	11:12 Moses the servant of **the L** commanded.	3068
	11:15 As **the L** commanded Moses his servant,	3068
	11:15 he left nothing undone of all that **the L**	3068
	11:20 For it was of **the L** to harden their hearts,	3068
	11:20 them, as **the L** commanded Moses.	3068
	11:23 to all that **the L** said unto Moses;	3068
	12: 6 Them did Moses the servant of **the L** and	3068
	12: 6 Moses the servant of **the L** gave it *for* a	3068
	13: 1 **the L** said unto him, Thou art old *and*	3068
	13: 8 *even* as Moses the servant of **the L** gave	3068
	13:14 the sacrifices of **the L** God of Israel made	3068
	13:33 **the L** God of Israel *was* their inheritance,	3068
	14: 2 **the L** commanded by the hand of Moses,	3068
	14: 5 As **the L** commanded Moses,	3068
	14: 6 Thou knowest the thing that **the L** said	3068
	14: 7 **the L** sent me from Kadesh-barnea to	3068
	14: 8 but I wholly followed **the L** my God.	3068
	14: 9 hast wholly followed **the L** my God.	3068
	14:10 **the L** hath kept me alive, as he said,	3068
	14:10 *even* since **the L** spake this word unto	3068
	14:12 whereof **the L** spake in that day;	3068
	14:12 if so be **the L** *will be* with me, then I	3068
	14:12 *be able to* drive them out, as **the L** said.	3068
	14:14 that he wholly followed **the L** God of	3068
	15:13 according to the commandment of **the L**	3068
	17: 4 **The L** commanded Moses to give us an	3068
	17: 4 **the L** he gave them an inheritance among	3068
	17:14 forasmuch as **the L** hath blessed me	3068
	18: 3 **the L** God of your fathers hath given	3068
	18: 6 lots for you here before **the L** our God.	3068
	18: 7 for the priesthood of **the L** *is* their	3068
	18: 7 which Moses the servant of **the L** in Shiloh.	3068
	18: 8 cast lots for you before **the L** in Shiloh.	3068
	18:10 cast lots for them in Shiloh before **the L**:	3068
	19:50 According to the word of **the L** they gave	3068
	19:51 inheritance by lot in Shiloh before **the L**,	3068
	20: 1 **The L** also spake unto Joshua, saying,	3068
	21: 2 **The L** commanded by the hand of Moses	3068
	21: 3 the commandment of **the L**, these cities	3068
	21: 8 **the L** commanded by the hand of Moses.	3068
	21:43 **the L** gave unto Israel all the land which	3068
	21:44 **the L** gave them rest round about,	3068
	21:44 **the L** delivered all their enemies into	3068
	21:45 **the L** had spoken unto the house of	3068
	22: 2 The servant of **the L** commanded you,	3068
	22: 3 of the commandment of **the L** your God.	3068
	22: 4 now **the L** your God hath given rest unto	3068
	22: 4 the servant of **the L** gave you	3068
	22: 5 Moses the servant of **the L** charged	3068
	22: 5 love **the L** your God, and to walk in all	3068
	22: 9 according to the word of **the L** by the	3068
	22:16 saith the whole congregation of **the L**,	3068
	22:16 turn away *this* day from following **the L**,	3068
	22:16 that ye might rebel *this* day against **the L**?	3068
	22:17 a plague in the congregation of **the L**,	3068
	22:18 turn away *this* day from following **the L**?	3068
	22:18 *seeing* ye rebel to day against **the L**,	3068
	22:19 unto the land of the possession of **the L**,	3068
	22:19 rebel not against **the L**, nor rebel against	3068
	22:19 an altar beside the altar of **the L** our God.	3068
	22:22 **The L** God of gods, the LORD God of	3068
	22:22 **the L** God of gods, he knoweth,	3068
	22:22 or if in transgression against **the L**,	3068

Jos	22:23 us an altar to turn from following **the L**;	3068
	22:23 let **the L** himself require *it*;	3068
	22:24 What have you to do with **the L** God of	3068
	22:25 For **the L** hath made Jordan a border	3068
	22:25 children of Gad; ye have no part in **the L**.	3068
	22:25 our children cease from fearing **the L**:	3068
	22:27 that *we* might do the service of **the L**,	3068
	22:27 time to come, Ye have no part in **the L**.	3068
	22:28 Behold the pattern of the altar of **the L**,	3068
	22:29 forbid that we should rebel against **the L**,	3068
	22:29 turn *this* day from following **the L**,	3068
	22:29 besides the altar of **the L** our God that *is*	3068
	22:31 *This* day we perceive that **the L** *is*	3068
	22:31 not committed this trespass against **the L**:	3068
	22:31 of Israel out of the hand of **the L**.	3068
	22:34 a witness between us that **the L** *is* God.	3068
	23: 1 came to pass a long time after that **the L**	3068
	23: 3 have seen all that **the L** your God hath	3068
	23: 3 for **the L** your God *is* he that hath fought	3068
	23: 5 **the L** your God, he shall expel them from	3068
	23: 5 **the L** your God hath promised unto you.	3068
	23: 8 cleave unto **the L** your God, as ye have	3068
	23: 9 For **the L** hath driven out from before you	3068
	23:10 **the L** your God, he *it is* that fighteth for	3068
	23:11 that ye love **the L** your God.	3068
	23:13 Know for a certainty that **the L** your God	3068
	23:13 which **the L** your God hath given you.	3068
	23:14 **the L** your God spake concerning you;	3068
	23:15 which **the L** your God promised you;	3068
	23:15 shall **the L** bring upon you all evil things,	3068
	23:15 which **the L** your God hath given you.	3068
	23:16 the covenant of **the L** your God,	3068
	23:16 shall the anger of **the L** be kindled	3068
	24: 2 people, Thus saith **the L** God of Israel,	3068
	24: 7 when they cried unto **the L**, he put	3068
	24:14 therefore fear **the L**, and serve him in	3068
	24:14 flood, and in Egypt; and serve ye **the L**.	3068
	24:15 if it seem evil unto you to serve **the L**,	3068
	24:15 me and my house, we will serve **the L**.	3068
	24:16 God forbid that we should forsake **the L**,	3068
	24:17 For **the L** our God, he *it is* that brought	3068
	24:18 **the L** drave out from before us all	3068
	24:18 *therefore* will we also serve **the L**; for he	3068
	24:19 unto the people, Ye cannot serve **the L**:	3068
	24:20 ye forsake **the L**, and serve strange gods,	3068
	24:21 Joshua, Nay; but we will serve **the L**.	3068
	24:22 yourselves that ye have chosen you **the L**,	3068
	24:23 your heart unto **the L** God of Israel.	3068
	24:24 **The L** our God will we serve, and his	3068
	24:26 oak, that *was* by the sanctuary of **the L**	3068
	24:27 for it hath heard all the words of **the L**	3068
	24:29 the servant of **the L**, died, *being* an	3068
	24:31 Israel served **the L** all the days of Joshua,	3068
	24:31 which had known all the works of **the L**,	3068
Jdg	1: 1 that the children of Israel asked **the L**,	3068
	1: 2 **the L** said, Judah shall go up: behold,	3068
	1: 4 **the L** delivered the Canaanites and	3068
	1:19 **the L** was with Judah; and he drave out	3068
	1:22 Beth-el: and **the L** *was* with them.	3068
	2: 1 an angel of **the L** came up from Gilgal to	3068
	2: 4 the angel of **the L** spake these words	3068
	2: 5 and they sacrificed there unto **the L**.	3068
	2: 7 the people served **the L** all the days of	3068
	2: 7 had seen all the great works of **the L**,	3068
	2: 8 the servant of **the L**, died, *being* an	3068
	2:10 after them, which knew not **the L**,	3068
	2:11 of Israel did evil in the sight of **the L**,	3068
	2:12 they forsook **the L** God of their fathers,	3068
	2:12 unto them, and provoked **the L** to anger.	3068
	2:13 they forsook **the L**, and served Baal and	3068
	2:14 the anger of **the L** was hot against Israel,	3068
	2:15 hand of **the L** was against them for evil,	3068
	2:15 as **the L** had said, and as the LORD had	3068
	2:15 and as **the L** had sworn unto them:	3068
	2:16 Nevertheless **the L** raised up judges,	3068
	2:17 obeying the commandments of **the L**;	3068
	2:18 when **the L** raised them up judges, then	3068
	2:18 **the L** was with the judge,	3068
	2:18 for it repented **the L** because of their	3068
	2:20 the anger of **the L** was hot against Israel;	3068
	2:22 whether they will keep the way of **the L**	3068
	2:23 Therefore **the L** left those nations,	3068
	3: 1 these *are* the nations which **the L** left,	3068
	3: 4 unto the commandments of **the L**,	3068
	3: 7 of Israel did evil in the sight of **the L**,	3068
	3: 7 forgat **the L** their God, and served Baalim	3068
	3: 8 Therefore the anger of **the L** was hot	3068
	3: 9 the children of Israel cried unto **the L**,	3068
	3: 9 **the L** raised up a deliverer to the children	3068
	3:10 the spirit of **the L** came upon him,	3068
	3:10 **the L** delivered Chushan-rishathaim king	3068
	3:12 Israel did evil again in the sight of **the L**:	3068
	3:12 **the L** strengthened Eglon the king of	3068
	3:12 they had done evil in the sight of **the L**.	3068
	3:15 the children of Israel cried unto **the L**,	3068
	3:15 **the L** raised them up a deliverer, Ehud	3068
	3:28 for **the L** hath delivered your enemies	3068
	4: 1 Israel again did evil in the sight of **the L**,	3068
	4: 2 **the L** sold them into the hand of Jabin	3068
	4: 3 the children of Israel cried unto **the L**:	3068
	4: 6 not **the L** God of Israel commanded,	3068
	4: 9 for **the L** shall sell Sisera into the hand of	3068
	4:14 for this *is* the day, in which **the L** hath	3068
	4:14 is not **the L** gone out before thee?	3068
	4:15 **the L** discomfited Sisera, and all *his*	3068

Jdg	5: 2 Praise ye **the L** for the avenging of Israel,	3068
	5: 3 ye princes; I, *even* I, will sing unto **the L;**	3068
	5: 3 I will sing *praise* to **the L** God of Israel.	3068
	5: 4 **L,** when thou wentest out of Seir,	3068
	5: 5 The mountains melted from before **the L,**	3068
	5: 5 *even* that Sinai from before **the L** God of	3068
	5: 9 among the people. Bless ye **the L.**	3068
	5:11 they rehearse the righteous acts of **the L,**	3068
	5:11 shall the people of **the L** go down to	3068
	5:13 **the L** made me have dominion over	3068
	5:23 Curse ye Meroz, said the angel of **the L,**	3068
	5:23 they came not to the help of **the L,**	3068
	5:23 to the help of **the L** against the mighty.	3068
	5:31 So let all thine enemies perish, O **L:**	3068
	6: 1 of Israel did evil in the sight of **the L:**	3068
	6: 1 **the L** delivered them into the hand of	3068
	6: 6 the children of Israel cried unto **the L.**	3068
	6: 7 the children of Israel cried unto **the L,**	3068
	6: 8 **the L** sent a prophet unto the children	3068
	6: 8 them, Thus saith **the L** God of Israel,	3068
	6:10 I said unto you, I *am* **the L** your God;	3068
	6:11 came an angel of **the L,** and sat under	3068
	6:12 the angel of **the L** appeared unto him,	3068
	6:12 said unto him, **The L** *is* with thee,	3068
	6:13 if **the L** be with us, why then is all this	3068
	6:13 Did not **the L** bring us up from Egypt?	3068
	6:13 now **the L** hath forsaken us,	3068
	6:14 **the L** looked upon him, and said, Go in	3068
	6:16 **the L** said unto him, Surely I will be with	3068
	6:21 the angel of **the L** put forth the end of	3068
	6:21 angel of **the L** departed out of his sight.	3068
	6:22 perceived that he *was* an angel of **the L**	3068
	6:22 I have seen an angel of **the L** face to face.	3068
	6:23 **the L** said unto him, Peace *be* unto thee;	3068
	6:24 Gideon built an altar there unto **the L,**	3068
	6:25 **the L** said unto him, Take thy father's	3068
	6:26 build an altar unto **the L** thy God upon	3068
	6:27 and did as **the L** had said unto him:	3068
	6:34 the spirit of **the L** came upon Gideon,	3068
	7: 2 **the L** said unto Gideon, The people that	3068
	7: 4 **the L** said unto Gideon, The people *are*	3068
	7: 5 **the L** said unto Gideon, Every one that	3068
	7: 7 **the L** said unto Gideon, By the three	3068
	7: 9 that **the L** said unto him, Arise, get thee	3068
	7:15 for **the L** hath delivered into your hand	3068
	7:18 say, *The sword* of **the L,** and of Gideon.	3068
	7:20 The sword of **the L,** and of Gideon.	3068
	7:22 **the L** set every man's sword against his	3068
	8: 7 when **the L** hath delivered Zebah	3068
	8:19 **the L** liveth, if ye had saved them alive,	3068
	8:23 rule over you: **the L** shall rule over you.	3068
	8:34 children of Israel remembered not **the L**	3068
	10: 6 Israel did evil again in the sight of **the L,**	3068
	10: 6 and forsook the **L,** and served not him.	3068
	10: 7 the anger of **the L** was hot against Israel,	3068
	10:10 the children of Israel cried unto **the L,**	3068
	10:11 **the L** said unto the children of Israel,	3068
	10:15 the children of Israel said unto **the L,**	3068
	10:16 from among them, and served **the L:**	3068
	11: 9 **the L** deliver them before me, shall I be	3068
	11:10 **The L** be witness between us, if we do	3068
	11:11 uttered all his words before **the L**	3068
	11:21 **the L** God of Israel delivered Sihon and	3068
	11:23 So now **the L** God of Israel hath	3068
	11:24 whomsoever **the L** our God shall drive	3068
	11:27 **the L** the Judge be judge *this* day	3068
	11:29 the spirit of **the L** came upon Jephthah,	3068
	11:30 And Jephthah vowed a vow unto **the L,**	3068
	11:32 and **the L** delivered them into his hands.	3068
	11:35 for I have opened my mouth unto **the L,**	3068
	11:36 thou hast opened thy mouth unto **the L,**	3068
	11:36 forasmuch as **the L** hath taken vengeance	3068
	12: 3 and **the L** delivered them into my hand:	3068
	13: 1 Israel did evil again in the sight of **the L;**	3068
	13: 1 **the L** delivered them into the hand of	3068
	13: 3 the angel of **the L** appeared unto	3068
	13: 8 Manoah intreated **the L,** and said, O my	3068
	13:13 the angel of **the L** said unto Manoah, Of	3068
	13:15 Manoah said unto the angel of **the L,**	3068
	13:16 the angel of **the L** said unto Manoah,	3068
	13:16 thou must offer it unto **the L.**	3068
	13:16 knew not that he *was* an angel of **the L.**	3068
	13:17 Manoah said unto the angel of **the L,**	3068
	13:18 the angel of **the L** said unto him,	3068
	13:19 and offered *it* upon a rock unto **the L:**	3068
	13:20 that the angel of **the L** ascended in	3068
	13:21 the angel of **the L** did no more appear to	3068
	13:21 knew that he *was* an angel of **the L.**	3068
	13:23 him, If **the L** were pleased to kill us,	3068
	13:24 the child grew, and **the L** blessed him.	3068
	13:25 the spirit of **the L** began to move him at	3068
	14: 4 mother knew not that it *was* of **the L,**	3068
	14: 6 the spirit of **the L** came mightily upon	3068
	14:19 the spirit of **the L** came upon him,	3068
	15:14 the spirit of **the L** came mightily upon	3068
	15:18 sore athirst, and called on **the L,** and said,	3068
	16:20 he wist not that **the L** was departed from	3068
	16:28 Samson called unto **the L,** and said,	3068
	17: 2 Blessed *be* thou of **the L,** my son.	3068
	17: 3 unto **the L** from my hand for my son,	3068
	17:13 Now know I that **the L** will do me good,	3068
	18: 6 before **the L** *is* your way wherein ye go.	3068
	19:18 I am *now* going *to* the house of **the L;**	3068
	20: 1 the land of Gilead, unto **the L** *in* Mizpeh.	3068
	20:18 And **the L** said, Judah *shall go up* first.	3068

Jdg	20:23 up and wept before **the L** until even,	3068
	20:23 and asked *counsel* of **the L,** saying,	3068
	20:23 And **the L** said, Go up against him.)	3068
	20:26 there before **the L,** and fasted that day	3068
	20:26 and peace offerings before **the L.**	3068
	20:27 the children of Israel inquired of **the L,**	3068
	20:28 **the L** said, Go up; for to morrow I will	3068
	20:35 **the L** smote Benjamin before Israel:	3068
	21: 3 O **L** God of Israel, why is this come to	3068
	21: 5 not up with the congregation unto **the L?**	3068
	21: 5 that came not up to **the L** *to* Mizpeh,	3068
	21: 7 we have sworn by **the L** that *we* will	3068
	21: 8 that came not up *to* **the L?**	3068
	21:15 **the L** had made a breach in the tribes	3068
	21:19 is a feast of **the L** in Shiloh yearly *in*	3068
Ru	1: 6 **the L** had visited his people in giving	3068
	1: 8 **the L** deal kindly with you, as ye have	3068
	1: 9 **The L** grant you that you may find rest,	3068
	1:13 the hand of **the L** is gone out against me.	3068
	1:17 If **the L** do so to me, and more also, *if*	3068
	1:21 **the L** hath brought me *home* again	3068
	1:21 seeing **the L** hath testified against me,	3068
	2: 4 unto the reapers, **The L** *be* with you.	3068
	2: 4 they answered him, **The L** bless thee.	3068
	2:12 **The L** recompense thy work, and a full	3068
	2:12 a full reward be given thee of **the L** God	3068
	2:20 daughter in law, Blessed *be* he of **the L,**	3068
	3:10 he said, Blessed *be* thou of **the L,**	3068
	3:13 part of a kinsman to thee, *as* **the L** liveth:	3068
	4:11 **The L** make the woman that is come into	3068
	4:12 of the seed which **the L** shall give thee of	3068
	4:13 **the L** gave her conception, and she bare	3068
	4:14 said unto Naomi, Blessed *be* **the L,**	3068
1Sa	1: 3 to sacrifice unto **the L** of hosts in Shiloh.	3068
	1: 3 and Phinehas, the priests of **the L,**	3068
	1: 5 but **the L** had shut up her womb.	3068
	1: 6 because **the L** had shut up her womb.	3068
	1: 7 she went up to the house of **the L,**	3068
	1: 9 a seat by a post of the temple of **the L.**	3068
	1:10 and prayed unto **the L,** and wept sore.	3068
	1:11 she vowed a vow, and said, O **L** of hosts,	3068
	1:11 I will give him unto **the L** all the days of	3068
	1:12 as she continued praying before **the L,**	3068
	1:15 have poured out my soul before **the L.**	3068
	1:19 worshipped before **the L,** and returned,	3068
	1:19 his wife; and **the L** remembered her.	3068
	1:20 Because I have asked him of **the L.**	3068
	1:21 went up to offer unto **the L** the yearly	3068
	1:22 that he may appear before **the L,**	3068
	1:23 him; only **the L** establish his word.	3068
	1:24 brought him *unto* the house of **the L** *in*	3068
	1:26 stood by thee here, praying unto **the L.**	3068
	1:27 **the L** hath given me my petition which I	3068
	1:28 Therefore also I have lent him to **the L;**	3068
	1:28 as he liveth he *shall be* lent to **the L.**	3068
	1:28 And he worshipped **the L** there.	3068
	2: 1 and said, My heart rejoiceth in **the L,**	3068
	2: 1 the **L,** mine horn is exalted in **the L:**	3068
	2: 2 *There is* none holy as **the L:** for *there is*	3068
	2: 3 for **the L** *is* a God of knowledge,	3068
	2: 6 **The L** killeth, and maketh alive:	3068
	2: 7 **The L** maketh poor, and maketh rich:	3068
	2:10 The adversaries of **the L** shall be broken	3068
	2:10 **the L** shall judge the ends of the earth;	3068
	2:11 child did minister unto **the L** before Eli	3068
	2:12 sons of Belial; they knew not **the L.**	3068
	2:17 young men was very great before **the L:**	3068
	2:17 for men abhorred the offering of **the L.**	3068
	2:18 Samuel ministered before **the L,** *being* a	3068
	2:20 **The L** give thee seed of this woman for	3068
	2:20 for the loan which is lent to **the L.**	3068
	2:21 **the L** visited Hannah, so that she	3068
	2:21 And the child Samuel grew before **the L.**	3068
	2:25 a man sin against **the L,** who shall intreat	3068
	2:25 because **the L** would slay them.	3068
	2:26 was in favour both with **the L,**	3068
	2:27 and said unto him, Thus saith **the L,**	3068
	2:30 Wherefore **the L** God of Israel saith, I said	3068
	2:30 now **the L** saith, Be it far from me;	3068
	3: 1 the child Samuel ministered unto **the L**	3068
	3: 1 the word of **the L** was precious in those	3068
	3: 3 of God went out in the temple of **the L,**	3068
	3: 4 That **the L** called Samuel:	3068
	3: 6 **the L** called yet again, Samuel.	3068
	3: 7 Now Samuel did not yet know **the L,**	3068
	3: 7 was the word of **the L** yet revealed	3068
	3: 8 **the L** called Samuel again the third time.	3068
	3: 8 Eli perceived that **the L** had called	3068
	3: 9 he call thee, that thou shalt say, Speak, **L;**	3068
	3:10 **the L** came, and stood, and called as a	3068
	3:11 **the L** said to Samuel, Behold, I will do a	3068
	3:15 opened the doors of the house of **the L.**	3068
	3:17 What *is* the thing that *the L* hath said	NIH
	3:18 he said, It *is* **the L:** let him do what	3068
	3:19 **the L** was with him, and did let none of	3068
	3:20 *was* established to be a prophet of **the L.**	3068
	3:21 **the L** appeared again in Shiloh:	3068
	3:21 for **the L** revealed himself to Samuel in	3068
	3:21 to Samuel in Shiloh by the word of **the L.**	3068
	4: 3 Wherefore hath **the L** smitten us to day	3068
	4: 3 us fetch the ark of the covenant of **the L**	3068
	4: 4 the ark of the covenant of **the L** of hosts,	3068
	4: 5 the ark of the covenant of **the L** came	3068
	4: 6 they understood that the ark of **the L** was	3068
	5: 3 face to the earth before the ark of **the L.**	3068

1Sa	5: 4 face to the ground before the ark of **the L;**	3068
	5: 6 the hand of **the L** was heavy upon them	3068
	5: 9 the hand of **the L** was against the city	3068
	6: 1 the ark of **the L** was in the country of	3068
	6: 2 What shall we do to the ark of **the L?**	3068
	6: 8 take the ark of **the L,** and lay it upon	3068
	6:11 they laid the ark of **the L** upon the cart,	3068
	6:14 the kine a burnt offering unto **the L.**	3068
	6:15 the Levites took down the ark of **the L,**	3068
	6:15 sacrifices the same day unto **the L.**	3068
	6:17 *for* a trespass offering unto **the L;**	3068
	6:18 whereon they set down the ark of **the L:**	3068
	6:19 they had looked into the ark of **the L,**	3068
	6:19 **the L** had smitten *many* of the people	3068
	6:20 Who is able to stand before this holy **L**	3068
	6:21 have brought again the ark of **the L;**	3068
	7: 1 fetched up the ark of **the L,** and brought	3068
	7: 1 Eleazar his son to keep the ark of **the L.**	3068
	7: 2 the house of Israel lamented after **the L.**	3068
	7: 3 If ye do return unto **the L** with all your	3068
	7: 3 prepare your hearts unto **the L,**	3068
	7: 4 and Ashtaroth, and served **the L** only.	3068
	7: 5 and I will pray for you unto **the L.**	3068
	7: 6 poured *it* out before **the L,** and fasted on	3068
	7: 6 said there, We have sinned against **the L.**	3068
	7: 8 Cease not to cry unto **the L** our God for	3068
	7: 9 it *for* a burnt offering wholly unto **the L:**	3068
	7: 9 Samuel cried unto **the L** for Israel;	3068
	7: 9 the **Lord** for Israel; and **the L** heard him.	3068
	7:10 **the L** thundered with a great thunder on	3068
	7:12 Hitherto hath **the L** helped us.	3068
	7:13 the hand of **the L** was against	3068
	7:17 and there he built an altar unto **the L.**	3068
	8: 6 judge us. And Samuel prayed unto **the L.**	3068
	8: 7 **the L** said unto Samuel, Hearken unto	3068
	8:10 Samuel told all the words of **the L**	3068
	8:18 and **the L** will not hear you in that day.	3068
	8:21 he rehearsed them in the ears of **the L.**	3068
	8:22 **the L** said to Samuel, Hearken unto their	3068
	9:15 **the L** had told Samuel in his ear a day	3068
	9:17 Samuel saw Saul, **the L** said unto him,	3068
	10: 1 **the L** hath anointed thee to be captain	3068
	10: 6 the spirit of **the L** will come upon thee,	3068
	10:17 the people together unto **the L** *to* Mizpeh;	3068
	10:18 Thus saith **the L** God of Israel, I brought	3068
	10:19 present yourselves before **the L** by your	3068
	10:22 Therefore they inquired of **the L** further,	3068
	10:22 **the L** answered, Behold, he hath hid	3068
	10:24 See ye him whom **the L** hath chosen,	3068
	10:25 *it* in a book, and laid *it* up before **the L.**	3068
	11: 7 the fear of **the L** fell on the people,	3068
	11:13 for to day **the L** hath wrought salvation	3068
	11:15 there they made Saul king before **the L** in	3068
	11:15 sacrifices *of* peace offerings before **the L;**	3068
	12: 3 I am: witness against me before **the L,**	3068
	12: 5 **The L** *is* witness against you,	3068
	12: 6 *is* **the L** that advanced Moses and Aaron,	3068
	12: 7 I may reason with you before **the L** of	3068
	12: 7 **Lord** of all the righteous acts of **the L,**	3068
	12: 8 your fathers cried unto **the L,** then	3068
	12: 8 then **the L** sent Moses and Aaron,	3068
	12: 9 they forgat **the L** their God, he sold	3068
	12:10 they cried unto **the L,** and said, We have	3068
	12:10 because we have forsaken **the L,**	3068
	12:11 **the L** sent Jerubbaal, and Bedan,	3068
	12:12 when **the L** your God *was* your king.	3068
	12:13 behold, **the L** hath set a king over you.	3068
	12:14 If ye will fear **the L,** and serve him,	3068
	12:14 rebel against the commandment of **the L,**	3068
	12:14 you continue following **the L** your God:	3068
	12:15 if ye will not obey the voice of **the L,**	3068
	12:15 rebel against the commandment of **the L,**	3068
	12:15 shall the hand of **the L** be against you, as	3068
	12:16 which **the L** will do before your eyes.	3068
	12:17 I will call unto **the L,** and he shall send	3068
	12:17 which ye have done in the sight of **the L,**	3068
	12:18 So Samuel called unto **the L;**	3068
	12:18 and **the L** sent thunder and rain that day:	3068
	12:18 all the people greatly feared **the L** and	3068
	12:19 Pray for thy servants unto **the L** thy God,	3068
	12:20 yet turn not aside from following **the L,**	3068
	12:20 but serve **the L** with all your heart;	3068
	12:22 For **the L** will not forsake his people for	3068
	12:22 it hath pleased **the L** to make you his	3068
	12:23 God forbid that I should sin against **the L**	3068
	12:24 Only fear **the L,** and serve him in truth	3068
	13:12 I have not made supplication unto **the L:**	3068
	13:13 kept the commandment of **the L** thy God,	3068
	13:13 now would **the L** have established thy	3068
	13:14 **the L** hath sought him a man after his	3068
	13:14 **the L** hath commanded him to be captain	3068
	13:14 because thou hast not kept *that* which **the L**	3068
	14: 6 it may be that **the L** will work for us:	3068
	14: 6 *there is* no restraint to **the L** to save by	3068
	14:10 for **the L** hath delivered them into our	3068
	14:12 **the L** hath delivered them into the hand	3068
	14:23 So **the L** saved Israel that day:	3068
	14:33 Behold, the people sin against **the L,**	3068
	14:34 sin not against **the L** in eating with	3068
	14:35 Saul built an altar unto **the L:** the same	3068
	14:35 the first altar that he built unto **the L.**	3068
	14:39 For, *as* **the L** liveth, which saveth Israel,	3068
	14:41 Therefore Saul said unto **the L** God of	3068
	14:45 *As* **the L** liveth, there shall not one hair	3068
	15: 1 **The L** sent me to anoint thee to be king	3068

L

1Sa 15: 1 unto the voice of the words of **the L**.	3068
15: 2 Thus saith **the L** of hosts, I remember	3068
15:10 came the word of **the L** unto Samuel,	3068
15:11 and he cried unto **the L** all night.	3068
15:13 said unto him, Blessed *be* thou of **the L**:	3068
15:13 performed the commandment of **the L**.	3068
15:15 oxen, to sacrifice unto **the L** thy God;	3068
15:16 I will tell thee what **the L** hath said to me	3068
15:17 and **the L** anointed thee king over Israel?	3068
15:18 **the L** sent thee on a journey, and said,	3068
15:19 didst thou not obey the voice of **the L**,	3068
15:19 and didst evil in the sight of **the L**?	3068
15:20 I have obeyed the voice of **the L**,	3068
15:20 have gone the way which **the L** sent me,	3068
15:21 to sacrifice unto **the L** thy God in Gilgal.	3068
15:22 Hath **the L** *as great* delight in burnt	3068
15:22 as in obeying the voice of **the L**?	3068
15:23 thou hast rejected the word of **the L**,	3068
15:24 transgressed the commandment of **the L**,	3068
15:25 again with me, that I may worship **the L**.	3068
15:26 for thou hast rejected the word of **the L**,	3068
15:26 **the L** hath rejected thee from being king	3068
15:28 **The L** hath rent the kingdom of Israel	3068
15:30 me, that I may worship **the L** thy God.	3068
15:31 after Saul; and Saul worshipped **the L**.	3068
15:33 hewed Agag in pieces before **the L**	3068
15:35 **the L** repented that he had made Saul	3068
16: 1 **the L** said unto Samuel, How long wilt	3068
16: 2 **the L** said, Take a heifer with thee,	3068
16: 2 say, I am come to sacrifice to **the L**.	3068
16: 4 Samuel did *that* which **the L** spake:	3068
16: 5 I am come to sacrifice unto **the L**:	3068
16: 7 **the L** said unto Samuel, Look not on his	3068
16: 7 for *the L seeth* not as man seeth; for man	NIH
16: 7 but **the L** looketh on the heart.	3068
16: 8 he said, Neither hath **the L** chosen this.	3068
16: 9 he said, Neither hath **the L** chosen this.	3068
16:10 unto Jesse, **The L** hath not chosen these.	3068
16:12 **the L** said, Arise, anoint him: for this *is*	3068
16:13 the spirit of **the L** came upon David from	3068
16:14 the spirit of **the L** departed from Saul,	3068
16:14 an evil spirit from **the L** troubled him.	3068
16:18 a comely person, and **the L** *is* with him.	3068
17:37 **The L** that delivered me out of the paw	3068
17:37 unto David, Go, and **the L** be with thee.	3068
17:45 I come to thee in the name of **the L** of	3068
17:46 This day will **the L** deliver thee into mine	3068
17:47 all this assembly shall know that **the L**	3068
18:12 because **the L** was with him,	3068
18:14 in all his ways; and **the L** *was* with him.	3068
18:28 and knew that **the L** *was* with David,	3068
19: 5 **the L** wrought a great salvation for all	3068
19: 6 Saul sware, *As* **the L** liveth, he shall not	3068
19: 9 the evil spirit from **the L** was upon Saul,	3068
20: 3 *as* **the L** liveth, and *as* thy soul liveth,	3068
20: 8 into a covenant of **the L** with thee:	3068
20:12 said unto David, O **L** God of Israel,	3068
20:13 **The L** do so and much more to Jonathan:	3068
20:13 **the L** be with thee, as he hath been with	3068
20:14 yet I live shew me the kindness of **the L**,	3068
20:15 not when **the L** hath cut off the enemies	3068
20:16 *saying*, Let **the L** even require it at	3068
20:21 to thee, and no hurt; *as* **the L** liveth.	3068
20:22 *thy way*: for **the L** hath sent thee away.	3068
20:23 **the L** *be* between thee and me for ever.	3068
20:42 sworn both of us in the name of **the L**,	3068
20:42 **The L** be between me and thee,	3068
21: 6 that was taken from before **the L**,	3068
21: 7 there that day, detained before **the L**;	3068
22:10 inquired of **the L** for him, and gave him	3068
22:17 Turn, and slay the priests of **the L**;	3068
22:17 hand to fall upon the priests of **the L**.	3068
23: 2 Therefore David inquired of **the L**,	3068
23: 2 **the L** said unto David, Go, and smite	3068
23: 4 David inquired of **the L** yet again.	3068
23: 4 **the L** answered him and said, Arise,	3068
23:10 David, O **L** God of Israel, thy servant	3068
23:11 O **L** God of Israel, I beseech thee, tell thy	3068
23:11 And **the L** said, He will come down.	3068
23:12 **the L** said, They will deliver *thee* up.	3068
23:18 they two made a covenant before **the L**:	3068
23:21 Saul said, Blessed *be* ye of **the L**; for ye	3068
24: 4 Behold the day of which **the L** said unto	3068
24: 6 **The L** forbid that I should do this thing	3068
24: 6 seeing he *is* the anointed of **the L**.	3068
24:10 day thine eyes have seen how that **the L**	3068
24:12 **The L** judge between me and thee,	3068
24:12 and thee, and **the L** avenge me of thee:	3068
24:15 **The L** therefore be judge,	3068
24:18 as when **the L** had delivered me	3068
24:19 **the L** reward thee good for that	3068
24:21 Swear now therefore unto me by **the L**,	3068
25:26 *as* **the L** liveth, and *as* thy soul liveth,	3068
25:26 seeing **the L** hath withholden thee	3068
25:28 for **the L** will certainly make my lord a	3068
25:28 my lord fighteth the battles of **the L**,	3068
25:29 in the bundle of life with **the L** thy God;	3068
25:30 when **the L** shall have done to my lord	3068
25:31 when **the L** shall have dealt well with	3068
25:32 Abigail, Blessed *be* **the L** God of Israel,	3068
25:34 very deed, *as* **the L** God of Israel liveth,	3068
25:38 ten days *after*, that **the L** smote Nabal,	3068
25:39 was dead, he said, Blessed *be* **the L**,	3068
25:39 **the L** hath returned the wickedness of	3068
26:10 David said furthermore, *As* **the L** liveth,	3068

1Sa 26:10 the LORD liveth, **the L** shall smite him;	3068
26:11 **The L** forbid that *I* should stretch forth	3068
26:12 a deep sleep from **the L** was fallen upon	3068
26:16 *As* **the L** liveth, ye *are* worthy to die,	3068
26:19 If **the L** have stirred thee up against me,	3068
26:19 of men, cursed *be* they before **the L**;	3068
26:19 from abiding in the inheritance of **the L**,	3068
26:20 fall to the earth before the face of **the L**:	3068
26:23 **The L** render to every man his	3068
26:23 for **the L** delivered thee into *my* hand to	3068
26:24 life he much set by in the eyes of **the L**,	3068
28: 6 when Saul inquired of **the L**, the LORD	3068
28: 6 **the L** answered him not, neither by	3068
28:10 Saul sware to her by **the L**, saying,	3068
28:10 her by the LORD, saying, *As* **the L** liveth,	3068
28:16 seeing **the L** is departed from thee,	3068
28:17 **the L** hath done to him, as he spake by	3068
28:17 **the L** hath rent the kingdom out of thine	3068
28:18 thou obeyedst not the voice of **the L**,	3068
28:18 hath **the L** done this thing unto thee this	3068
28:19 Moreover **the L** will also deliver Israel	3068
28:19 **the L** also shall deliver the host of Israel	3068
29: 6 said unto him, Surely, *as* **the L** liveth,	3068
30: 6 David encouraged himself in **the L** his	3068
30: 8 David inquired at **the L**, saying, Shall I	3068
30:23 with *that* which **the L** hath given us,	3068
30:26 you of the spoil of the enemies of **the L**;	3068
2Sa 1:12 for the people of **the L**, and for the house	3068
2: 1 that David inquired of **the L**, saying,	3068
2: 1 **the L** said unto him, Go up. And David	3068
2: 5 said unto them, Blessed *be* ye of **the L**,	3068
2: 6 now **the L** shew kindness and truth unto	3068
3: 9 as **the L** hath sworn to David, even so I	3068
3:18 do *it*: for **the L** hath spoken of David,	3068
3:28 my kingdom *are* guiltless before **the L** for	3068
3:39 **the L** shall reward the doer of evil	3068
4: 8 **the L** hath avenged my lord the king this	3068
4: 9 and said unto them, *As* **the L** liveth,	3068
5: 2 **the L** said to thee, Thou shalt feed my	3068
5: 3 league with them in Hebron before **the L**:	3068
5:10 and **the L** God of hosts *was* with him.	3068
5:12 perceived that **the L** had established	3068
5:19 David inquired of **the L**, saying, Shall I go	3068
5:19 **the L** said unto David, Go up: for I will	3068
5:20 **The L** hath broken forth upon mine	3068
5:23 when David inquired of **the L**, he said,	3068
5:24 for then shall **the L** go out before thee,	3068
5:25 did so, as **the L** had commanded him;	3068
6: 2 name is called *by* the name of **the L**	3068
6: 5 all the house of Israel played before **the L**	3068
6: 7 the anger of **the L** was kindled against	3068
6: 8 **the L** had made a breach upon Uzzah:	3068
6: 9 David was afraid of **the L** that day,	3068
6: 9 How shall the ark of **the L** come to me?	3068
6:10 of **the L** unto him into the city of David:	3068
6:11 the ark of **the L** continued *in* the house	3068
6:11 **the L** blessed Obed-edom, and all his	3068
6:12 **The L** hath blessed the house of	3068
6:13 that when they that bare the ark of **the L**	3068
6:14 David danced before **the L** with all *his*	3068
6:15 up the ark of **the L** with shouting,	3068
6:16 as the ark of **the L** came *into* the city	3068
6:16 David leaping and dancing before **the L**;	3068
6:17 they brought in the ark of **the L**, and set	3068
6:17 and peace offerings before **the L**.	3068
6:18 blessed the people in the name of **the L**	3068
6:21 said unto Michal, *It was* before **the L**,	3068
6:21 me ruler over the people of **the L**,	3068
6:21 therefore will I play before **the L**.	3068
7: 1 **the L** had given him rest round about	3068
7: 3 *is* in thine heart; for **the L** *is* with thee.	3068
7: 4 the word of **the L** came unto Nathan,	3068
7: 5 tell my servant David, Thus saith **the L**,	3068
7: 8 Thus saith **the L** of hosts, I took thee	3068
7:11 Also **the L** telleth thee that he will make	3068
7:18 sat before **the L**, and he said, Who *am* I,	3068
7:22 Wherefore thou art great, O **L** God:	3068
7:24 and thou, **L**, art become their God.	3068
7:25 now, O **L** God, the word that thou hast	3068
7:26 **The L** of hosts *is* the God over Israel:	3068
7:27 For thou, O **L** of hosts, God of Israel,	3068
8: 6 **the L** preserved David whithersoever he	3068
8:11 also king David did dedicate unto **the L**,	3068
8:14 **the L** preserved David whithersoever he	3068
10:12 **the L** do that which seemeth him good.	3068
11:27 that David had done displeased **the L**.	3068
12: 1 **the L** sent Nathan unto David.	3068
12: 5 said to Nathan, *As* **the L** liveth, the man	3068
12: 7 Thus saith **the L** God of Israel, I anointed	3068
12: 9 despised the commandment of **the L**,	3068
12:11 Thus saith **the L**, Behold, I will raise up	3068
12:13 Nathan, I have sinned against **the L**.	3068
12:13 **The L** also hath put away thy sin;	3068
12:14 to the enemies of **the L** to blaspheme,	3068
12:15 **the L** strake the child that Uriah's wife	3068
12:20 came *into* the house of **the L**,	3068
12:24 his name Solomon: and **the L** loved him.	3068
12:25 his name Jedidiah, because of **the L**.	3068
14:11 let the king remember **the L** thy God,	3068
14:11 he said, *As* **the L** liveth, there shall not	3068
14:17 **the L** thy God will be with thee.	3068
15: 7 I have vowed unto **the L**, in Hebron.	3068
15: 8 If **the L** shall bring me again indeed *to*	3068
15: 8 to Jerusalem, then I will serve **the L**.	3068
15:21 *As* **the L** liveth, and *as* my lord the king	3068

2Sa 15:25 if I shall find favour in the eyes of **the L**,	3068
15:31 David said, O **L**, I pray thee, turn	3068
16: 8 **The L** hath returned upon thee all the	3068
16: 8 **the L** hath delivered the kingdom into	3068
16:10 because **the L** hath said unto him,	3068
16:11 let him curse; for **the L** hath bidden him.	3068
16:12 It may be that **the L** will look on mine	3068
16:12 that **the L** will requite me good for his	3068
16:18 whom **the L**, and this people, and all	3068
17:14 **the L** had appointed to defeat the good	3068
17:14 to the intent that **the L** might bring evil	3068
18:19 how that **the L** hath avenged him of his	3068
18:28 and said, Blessed *be* **the L** thy God,	3068
18:31 **the L** hath avenged thee *this* day of all	3068
19: 7 for I swear by **the L**, if thou go not forth,	3068
20:19 swallow up the inheritance of **the L**?	3068
21: 1 after year; and David inquired of **the L**.	3068
21: 1 **The L** answered, *It is* for Saul, and for *his*	3068
21: 3 ye may bless the inheritance of **the L**?	3068
21: 6 will hang them up unto **the L** in Gibeah	3068
21: 6 Gibeah of Saul, whom **the L** did choose.	3068
21: 9 they hanged them in the hill before **the L**:	3068
22: 1 David spake unto **the L** the words of this	3068
22: 1 **the L** had delivered him out of the hand	3068
22: 2 **The L** *is* my rock, and my fortress,	3068
22: 4 I will call on **the L**, who *is worthy* to be	3068
22: 7 In my distress I called upon **the L**,	3068
22:14 **The L** thundered from heaven,	3068
22:16 at the rebuking of **the L**, at the blast of	3068
22:19 of my calamity: but **the L** was my stay.	3068
22:21 **The L** rewarded me according to my	3068
22:22 For I have kept the ways of **the L**,	3068
22:25 Therefore **the L** hath recompensed me	3068
22:29 For thou *art* my lamp, O **L**: and the LORD	3068
22:29 and **the L** will lighten my darkness.	3068
22:31 way *is* perfect; the word of **the L** *is* tried:	3068
22:32 For who *is* God, save **the L**? and who *is*	3068
22:42 unto **the L**, but he answered them not.	3068
22:47 **The L** liveth; and blessed *be* my rock;	3068
22:50 O **L**, among the heathen, and I will sing	3068
23: 2 The Spirit of **the L** spake by me,	3068
23:10 **the L** wrought a great victory that day;	3068
23:12 and **the L** wrought a great victory.	3068
23:16 thereof, but poured it out unto **the L**.	3068
23:17 he said, Be it far from me, O **L**, that I	3068
24: 1 again the anger of **the L** was kindled	3068
24: 3 Now **the L** thy God add unto the people,	3068
24:10 David said unto **the L**, I have sinned	3068
24:10 now, I beseech thee, O **L**, take away	3068
24:11 the word of **the L** came unto the prophet	3068
24:12 Go and say unto David, Thus saith **the L**,	3068
24:14 let us fall now into the hand of **the L**;	3068
24:15 **the L** sent a pestilence upon Israel from	3068
24:16 **the L** repented him of the evil, and said	3068
24:16 the angel of **the L** was by	3068
24:17 David spake unto **the L** when he saw	3068
24:18 rear an altar unto **the L** in	3068
24:19 of Gad, went up as **the L** commanded.	3068
24:21 of thee, to build an altar unto **the L**,	3068
24:23 the king, **The L** thy God accept thee.	3068
24:24 **the L** my God of that which doth cost	3068
24:25 David built there an altar unto **the L**,	3068
24:25 So **the L** was intreated for the land,	3068
1Ki 1:17 thou swarest by **the L** thy God unto	3068
1:29 the king sware, and said, *As* **the L** liveth,	3068
1:30 as I sware unto thee by **the L** God of	3068
1:36 **the L** God of my lord the king say so *too*.	3068
1:37 **the L** hath been with my lord the king,	3068
1:48 the king, Blessed *be* **the L** God of Israel,	3068
2: 3 keep the charge of **the L** thy God, to	3068
2: 4 That **the L** may continue his word which	3068
2: 8 and I sware to him by **the L**, saying,	3068
2:15 my brother's: for it was his from **the L**.	3068
2:23 king Solomon sware by **the L**, saying,	3068
2:24 therefore, *as* **the L** liveth, which hath	3068
2:27 Abiathar from being priest unto **the L**;	3068
2:27 that *he* might fulfil the word of **the L**,	3068
2:28 Joab fled unto the tabernacle of **the L**,	3068
2:29 was fled unto the tabernacle of **the L**;	3068
2:30 Benaiah came to the tabernacle of **the L**,	3068
2:32 **the L** shall return his blood upon his	3068
2:33 shall there be peace for ever from **the L**.	3068
2:42 Did I not make thee to swear by **the L**,	3068
2:43 hast thou not kept the oath of **the L**,	3068
2:44 **the L** shall return thy wickedness upon	3068
2:45 shall be established before **the L** for ever.	3068
3: 1 the house of **the L**, and the wall of	3068
3: 2 no house built unto the name of **the L**,	3068
3: 3 Solomon loved **the L**, walking in	3068
3: 5 In Gibeon **the L** appeared to Solomon in	3068
3: 7 now, O **L** my God, thou hast made thy	3068
3:15 before the ark of the covenant of **the L**,	3068
5: 3 **the L** his God for the wars which were	3068
5: 3 until **the L** put them under the soles of	3068
5: 4 now **the L** my God hath given me rest	3068
5: 5 a house unto the name of **the L** my God,	3068
5: 5 as **the L** spake unto David my father,	3068
5: 7 and said, Blessed *be* **the L** *this* day,	3068
5:12 **the L** gave Solomon wisdom, as he	3068
6: 1 he *began* to build the house of **the L**.	3068
6: 2 which king Solomon built for **the L**,	3068
6:11 the word of **the L** came to Solomon,	3068
6:19 there the ark of the covenant of **the L**.	3068
6:37 the foundation of the house of **the L** laid,	3068
7:12 for the inner court of the house of **the L**,	3068

L

1Ki 7:40 king Solomon *for* the house of **the L**:	3068	
7:45 to king Solomon *for* the house of **the L**	3068	
7:48 that *pertained unto* the house of **the L**:	3068	
7:51 Solomon made *for* the house of **the L**.	3068	
7:51 the treasures of the house of **the L**.	3068	
8: 1 covenant of **the L** out of the city of David,	3068	
8: 4 they brought up the ark of **the L**,	3068	
8: 6 of the covenant of **the L** unto his place,	3068	
8: 9 when **the L** made *a covenant* with	3068	
8:10 that the cloud filled the house of **the L**,	3068	
8:11 for the glory of **the L** had filled the house	3068	
8:11 the LORD had filled the house of **the L**.	3068	
8:12 **The L** said that *he* would dwell in the	3068	
8:15 he said, Blessed *be* **the L** God of Israel,	3068	
8:17 house for the name of **the L** God of Israel.	3068	
8:18 **the L** said unto David my father,	3068	
8:20 **the L** hath performed his word that he	3068	
8:20 **the L** promised, and have built a house	3068	
8:20 have built a house for the name of **the L**	3068	
8:21 wherein *is* the covenant of **the L**, which	3068	
8:22 Solomon stood before the altar of **the L** in	3068	
8:23 he said, **L** God of Israel, *there is* no God	3068	
8:25 Therefore now, **L** God of Israel, keep with	3068	
8:28 to his supplication, O **L** my God,	3068	
8:44 shall pray unto **the L** toward the city	3068	
8:54 this prayer and supplication unto **the L**,	3068	
8:54 he arose from before the altar of **the L**,	3068	
8:56 Blessed *be* **the L**, that hath given rest	3068	
8:57 **The L** our God be with us, as he was	3068	
8:59 I have made supplication before **the L**,	3068	
8:59 nigh unto **the L** our God day and night,	3068	
8:60 of the earth may know that **the L** *is* God,	3068	
8:61 therefore be perfect with **the L** our God,	3068	
8:62 with him, offered sacrifice before **the L**.	3068	
8:63 which he offered unto **the L**, two and	3068	
8:63 of Israel dedicated the house of **the L**.	3068	
8:64 court that *was* before the house of **the L**:	3068	
8:64 the brasen altar that *was* before **the L**	3068	
8:65 before **the L** our God, seven days and	3068	
8:66 of heart for all the goodness that **the L**	3068	
9: 1 the building of the house of **the L**,	3068	
9: 2 **the L** appeared to Solomon the second	3068	
9: 3 **the L** said unto him, I have heard thy	3068	
9: 8 Why hath **the L** done thus unto this land,	3068	
9: 9 Because they forsook **the L** their God,	3068	
9: 9 **the L** brought upon them all this evil.	3068	
9:10 the house of **the L**, and the king's house,	3068	
9:15 to build the house of **the L**, and his own	3068	
9:25 upon the altar which he built unto **the L**,	3068	
9:25 upon the altar that *was* before **the L**.	3068	
10: 1 Solomon concerning the name of **the L**,	3068	
10: 5 he went up *unto* the house of **the L**;	3068	
10: 9 Blessed be **the L** thy God, which	3068	
10: 9 because **the L** loved Israel for ever,	3068	
10:12 almug trees pillars for the house of **the L**,	3068	
11: 2 the nations *concerning* which **the L** said	3068	
11: 4 his heart was not perfect with **the L** his	3068	
11: 6 Solomon did evil in the sight of **the L**,	3068	
11: 6 went not fully after **the L**, as *did* David	3068	
11: 9 **the L** was angry with Solomon, because	3068	
11: 9 his heart was turned from **the L** God of	3068	
11:10 kept not *that* which **the L** commanded.	3068	
11:11 Wherefore **the L** said unto Solomon,	3068	
11:14 **the L** stirred up an adversary unto	3068	
11:31 for thus saith **the L**, the God of Israel,	3068	
12:15 the cause was from **the L**, that *he* might	3068	
12:15 which **the L** spake by Ahijah the Shilonite	3068	
12:24 Thus saith **the L**, Ye shall not go up,	3068	
12:24 therefore to the word of **the L**,	3068	
12:24 depart, according to the word of **the L**.	3068	
12:27 in the house of **the L** at Jerusalem,	3068	
13: 1 Judah by the word of **the L** unto Beth-el:	3068	
13: 2 against the altar in the word of **the L**,	3068	
13: 2 and said, O altar, altar, thus saith **the L**;	3068	
13: 3 This *is* the sign which **the L** hath spoken;	3068	
13: 5 of God had given by the word of **the L**.	3068	
13: 6 Intreat now the face of **the L** thy God,	3068	
13: 6 the man of God besought **the L**,	3068	
13: 9 was it charged me by the word of **the L**,	3068	
13:17 it was said to me by the word of **the L**,	3068	
13:18 spake unto me by the word of **the L**,	3068	
13:20 that the word of **the L** came unto	3068	
13:21 from Judah, saying, Thus saith **the L**,	3068	
13:21 thou hast disobeyed the mouth of **the L**,	3068	
13:21 which **the L** thy God commanded thee,	3068	
13:22 of the which *the L* did say to thee, Eat no	NIH	
13:26 was disobedient unto the word of **the L**:	3068	
13:26 **the L** hath delivered him unto the lion,	3068	
13:26 slain him, according to the word of **the L**,	3068	
13:32 word of **the L** against the altar in Beth-el,	3068	
14: 5 **the L** said unto Ahijah, Behold, the wife	3068	
14: 7 Thus saith **the L** God of Israel,	3068	
14:11 of the air eat: for **the L** hath spoken *it*.	3068	
14:13 **the L** God of Israel in the house of	3068	
14:14 Moreover **the L** shall raise him up a king	3068	
14:15 For **the L** shall smite Israel, as a reed in	3068	
14:15 their groves, provoking **the L** to anger.	3068	
14:18 for him, according to the word of **the L**,	3068	
14:21 the city which **the L** did choose out of all	3068	
14:22 Judah did evil in the sight of **the L**,	3068	
14:24 **the L** cast out before the children of Israel	3068	
14:26 away the treasures of the house of **the L**,	3068	
14:28 the king went into the house of **the L**,	3068	
15: 3 his heart was not perfect with **the L** his	3068	
15: 4 Nevertheless for David's sake did **the L**	3068	

1Ki 15: 5 *that* which *was* right in the eyes of **the L**,	3068	
15:11 *that* which *was* right in the eyes of **the L**,	3068	
15:14 heart was perfect with **the L** all his days.	3068	
15:15 *into* the house of **the L**, silver, and gold,	3068	
15:18 left in the treasures of the house of **the L**,	3068	
15:26 he did evil in the sight of **the L**,	3068	
15:29 according to the saying of **the L**,	3068	
15:30 he provoked **the L** God of Israel to anger.	3068	
15:34 he did evil in the sight of **the L**,	3068	
16: 1 word of **the L** came to Jehu the son of	3068	
16: 7 came the word of **the L** against Baasha,	3068	
16: 7 the evil that he did in the sight of **the L**,	3068	
16:12 Baasha, according to the word of **the L**,	3068	
16:13 in provoking **the L** God of Israel to anger	3068	
16:19 sinned in doing evil in the sight of **the L**,	3068	
16:25 Omri wrought evil in the eyes of **the L**,	3068	
16:26 to provoke **the L** God of Israel to anger	3068	
16:30 **the L** above all that *were* before him.	3068	
16:33 Ahab did more to provoke **the L** God of	3068	
16:34 according to the word of **the L**, which he	3068	
17: 1 unto Ahab, *As* **the L** God of Israel liveth,	3068	
17: 2 the word of **the L** came unto him, saying,	3068	
17: 5 did according to the word of **the L**:	3068	
17: 8 the word of **the L** came unto him, saying,	3068	
17:12 she said, *As* **the L** thy God liveth, I have	3068	
17:14 For thus saith **the L** God of Israel,	3068	
17:14 until the day *that* **the L** sendeth rain	3068	
17:16 according to the word of **the L**, which he	3068	
17:20 he cried unto **the L**, and said, O LORD	3068	
17:20 unto the LORD, and said, O **L** my God,	3068	
17:21 cried unto **the L**, and said, O LORD my	3068	
17:21 and said, O **L** my God, I pray thee,	3068	
17:22 **the L** heard the voice of Elijah;	3068	
17:24 the word of **the L** in thy mouth *is* truth.	3068	
18: 1 that the word of **the L** came to Elijah in	3068	
18: 3 (Now Obadiah feared **the L** greatly:	3068	
18: 4 Jezebel cut off the prophets of **the L**,	3068	
18:10 **the L** thy God liveth, there is no nation	3068	
18:12 that the spirit of **the L** shall carry thee	3068	
18:12 *I* thy servant fear **the L** from my youth.	3068	
18:13 when Jezebel slew the prophets of **the L**,	3068	
18:15 Elijah said, *As* **the L** of hosts liveth,	3068	
18:18 forsaken the commandments of **the L**,	3068	
18:21 if **the L** *be* God, follow him: but if Baal,	3068	
18:22 I, *even* I only, remain a prophet of **the L**;	3068	
18:24 and I will call on the name of **the L**:	3068	
18:30 he repaired the altar of **the L** that was	3068	
18:31 unto whom the word of **the L** came,	3068	
18:32 he built an altar in the name of **the L**:	3068	
18:36 said, **L** God of Abraham, Isaac,	3068	
18:37 Hear me, O **L**, hear me, that this people	3068	
18:37 may know that thou *art* **the L** God,	3068	
18:38 the fire of **the L** fell, and consumed	3068	
18:39 they said, **The L**, he *is* the God;	3068	
18:39 he *is* the God; **the L**, he *is* the God.	3068	
18:46 the hand of **the L** was on Elijah;	3068	
19: 4 enough; now, O **L**, take away my life;	3068	
19: 7 the angel of **the L** came again the second	3068	
19: 9 the word of **the L** *came* to him, and he	3068	
19:10 I have been very jealous for **the L** God of	3068	
19:11 and stand upon the mount before **the L**.	3068	
19:11 **the L** passed by, and a great and	3068	
19:11 brake in pieces the rocks before **the L**;	3068	
19:11 the LORD; *but* **the L** *was* not in the wind:	3068	
19:11 *but* **the L** *was* not in the earthquake:	3068	
19:12 a fire; *but* **the L** *was* not in the fire:	3068	
19:14 I have been very jealous for **the L** God of	3068	
19:15 **the L** said unto him, Go, return on thy	3068	
20:13 Thus saith **the L**, Hast thou seen all	3068	
20:13 and thou shalt know that I *am* **the L**.	3068	
20:14 he said, Thus saith **the L**, *Even* by	3068	
20:28 king of Israel, and said, Thus saith **the L**,	3068	
20:28 **The L** *is* God of the hills, but he *is* not	3068	
20:28 and ye shall know that I *am* **the L**.	3068	
20:35 unto his neighbour in the word of **the L**,	3068	
20:36 thou hast not obeyed the voice of **the L**,	3068	
20:42 he said unto him, Thus saith **the L**,	3068	
21: 3 Naboth said to Ahab, **The L** forbid it me,	3068	
21:17 the word of **the L** came to Elijah	3068	
21:19 saying, Thus saith **the L**, Hast thou killed,	3068	
21:19 speak unto him, saying, Thus saith **the L**,	3068	
21:20 thyself to work evil in the sight of **the L**,	3068	
21:23 of Jezebel also spake **the L**, saying,	3068	
21:25 to work wickedness in the sight of **the L**,	3068	
21:26 **the L** cast out before the children of	3068	
21:28 the word of **the L** came to Elijah	3068	
22: 5 I pray thee, at the word of **the L** to day.	3068	
22: 7 *there* not here a prophet of **the L** besides,	3068	
22: 8 by whom *we* may inquire of **the L**:	3068	
22:11 said, Thus saith **the L**, With these shalt	3068	
22:12 for **the L** shall deliver *it* into the king's	3068	
22:14 Micaiah said, *As* **the L** liveth, what	3068	
22:14 **the L** saith unto me, that will I speak.	3068	
22:15 for **the L** shall deliver *it* into the hand of	3068	
22:16 *that* which *is* true in the name of **the L**?	3068	
22:17 **the L** said, These have no master: let	3068	
22:19 Hear thou therefore the word of **the L**:	3068	
22:19 I saw **the L** sitting on his throne, and all	3068	
22:20 **the L** said, Who shall persuade Ahab,	3068	
22:21 stood before **the L**, and said, I will	3068	
22:22 **the L** said unto him, Wherewith? And he	3068	
22:23 **the L** hath put a lying spirit in the mouth	3068	
22:23 **the L** hath spoken evil concerning thee.	3068	
22:24 Which way went the spirit of **the L** from	3068	
22:28 in peace, **the L** hath not spoken by me.	3068	

1Ki 22:38 according unto the word of **the L** which	3068	
22:43 *that* which *was* right in the eyes of **the L**:	3068	
22:52 he did evil in the sight of **the L**,	3068	
22:53 provoked to anger **the L** God of Israel,	3068	
2Ki 1: 3 the angel of **the L** said to Elijah	3068	
1: 4 therefore thus saith **the L**, Thou shalt	3068	
1: 6 Thus saith **the L**, *Is it* not because *there*	3068	
1:15 the angel of **the L** said unto Elijah,	3068	
1:16 he said unto him, Thus saith **the L**,	3068	
1:17 he died according to the word of **the L**	3068	
2: 1 when **the L** would take up Elijah *into*	3068	
2: 2 for **the L** hath sent me to Beth-el.	3068	
2: 2 Elisha said *unto him*, *As* **the L** liveth,	3068	
2: 3 Knowest thou that **the L** will take away	3068	
2: 4 for **the L** hath sent me *to* Jericho.	3068	
2: 4 *As* **the L** liveth, and *as* thy soul liveth,	3068	
2: 5 Knowest thou that **the L** will take away	3068	
2: 6 here; for **the L** hath sent me to Jordan.	3068	
2: 6 *As* **the L** liveth, and *as* thy soul liveth,	3068	
2:14 and said, Where *is* **the L** God of Elijah?	3068	
2:16 lest peradventure the spirit of **the L** hath	3068	
2:21 salt in there, and said, Thus saith **the L**,	3068	
2:24 and cursed them in the name of **the L**;	3068	
3: 2 he wrought evil in the sight of **the L**;	3068	
3:10 that **the L** hath called these three kings	3068	
3:11 *Is there* not here a prophet of **the L**,	3068	
3:11 that we may inquire of **the L** by him?	3068	
3:12 The word of **the L** is with him.	3068	
3:13 for **the L** hath called these three kings	3068	
3:14 Elisha said, *As* **the L** of hosts liveth,	3068	
3:15 that the hand of **the L** came upon him.	3068	
3:16 said, Thus saith **the L**, Make this valley	3068	
3:17 thus saith **the L**, Ye shall not see wind,	3068	
3:18 is *but* a light thing in the sight of **the L**:	3068	
4: 1 knowest that thy servant did fear **the L**:	3068	
4:27 **the L** hath hid *it* from me, and hath not	3068	
4:30 *As* **the L** liveth, and *as* thy soul liveth,	3068	
4:33 upon them twain, and prayed unto **the L**.	3068	
4:43 for thus saith **the L**, They shall eat,	3068	
4:44 *thereof*, according to the word of **the L**.	3068	
5: 1 by him **the L** had given deliverance unto	3068	
5:11 call on the name of **the L** his God,	3068	
5:16 he said, *As* **the L** liveth, before whom I	3068	
5:17 sacrifice unto other gods, but unto **the L**.	3068	
5:18 In this thing **the L** pardon thy servant,	3068	
5:18 **the L** pardon thy servant in this thing.	3068	
5:20 but, *as* **the L** liveth, I will run after him,	3068	
6:17 said, **L**, I pray thee, open his eyes, that he	3068	
6:17 **the L** opened the eyes of the young man;	3068	
6:18 Elisha prayed unto **the L**, and said,	3068	
6:20 come *into* Samaria, that Elisha said, **L**,	3068	
6:20 **the L** opened their eyes, that they saw;	3068	
6:27 he said, *If* **the L** do not help thee, whence	3068	
6:33 he said, Behold, this evil *is* of **the L**;	3068	
6:33 what should I wait for **the L** any longer?	3068	
7: 1 Elisha said, Hear ye the word of **the L**;	3068	
7: 1 Thus saith **the L**, To morrow about *this*	3068	
7: 2 *if* **the L** would make windows in heaven,	3068	
7:16 a shekel, according to the word of **the L**.	3068	
7:19 *if* **the L** should make windows in heaven,	3068	
8: 1 for **the L** hath called for a famine;	3068	
8: 8 and inquire of **the L** by him, saying,	3068	
8:10 howbeit **the L** hath shewed me that he	3068	
8:13 **The L** hath shewed me *that* thou *shalt be*	3068	
8:18 and he did evil in the sight of **the L**.	3068	
8:19 Yet **the L** would not destroy Judah for	3068	
8:27 did evil in the sight of **the L**, as *did*	3068	
9: 3 it on his head, and say, Thus saith **the L**,	3068	
9: 6 to him, Thus saith **the L** God of Israel,	3068	
9: 6 thee king over the people of **the L**,	3068	
9: 7 the blood of all the servants of **the L**,	3068	
9:12 spake he to me, saying, Thus saith **the L**,	3068	
9:25 father, **the L** laid this burden upon him;	3068	
9:26 and the blood of his sons, saith **the L**;	3068	
9:26 I will requite thee in this plat, saith **the L**.	3068	
9:26 *ground*, according to the word of **the L**.	3068	
9:36 he said, This *is* the word of **the L**, which	3068	
10:10 the earth nothing of the word of **the L**,	3068	
10:10 which **the L** spake concerning the house	3068	
10:10 for **the L** hath done *that* which he spake	3068	
10:16 with me, and see my zeal for **the L**.	3068	
10:17 according to the saying of **the L**, which	3068	
10:23 with you none of the servants of **the L**,	3068	
10:30 **the L** said unto Jehu, Because thou hast	3068	
10:31 of **the L** God of Israel with all his heart:	3068	
10:32 In those days **the L** began to cut Israel	3068	
11: 3 was with her hid *in* the house of **the L**	3068	
11: 4 them to him *into* the house of **the L**,	3068	
11: 4 an oath of them in the house of **the L**,	3068	
11: 7 of the house of **the L** about the king.	3068	
11:10 that *were* in the temple of **the L**.	3068	
11:13 to the people *into* the temple of **the L**.	3068	
11:15 Let her not be slain in the house of **the L**.	3068	
11:17 Jehoiada made a covenant between **the L**	3068	
11:18 officers over the house of **the L**.	3068	
11:19 down the king from the house of **the L**,	3068	
12: 2 **the L** all his days where *in* Jehoiada	3068	
12: 4 that is brought *into* the house of **the L**,	3068	
12: 4 heart to bring *into* the house of **the L**,	3068	
12: 9 as one cometh *into* the house of **the L**.	3068	
12: 9 that was brought *into* the house of **the L**.	3068	
12:10 that was found *in* the house of **the L**,	3068	
12:11 had the oversight *of* the house of **the L**:	3068	
12:11 that wrought upon the house of **the L**,	3068	
12:12 repair the breaches of the house of **the L**,	3068	

2Ki 12:13 *for* the house of **the L** bowls of silver,	3068
12:13 was brought *into* the house of **the L**.	3068
12:14 repaired therewith the house of **the L**.	3068
12:16 was not brought *into* the house of **the L**,	3068
12:18 in the treasures of the house of **the L**,	3068
13: 2 *that* which *was* evil in the sight of **the L**,	3068
13: 3 the anger of **the L** was kindled against	3068
13: 4 Jehoahaz besought **the L**, and the Lᴏʀᴅ	3068
13: 4 and **the L** hearkened unto him:	3068
13: 5 (And **the L** gave Israel a saviour,	3068
13:11 *that* which *was* evil in the sight of **the L**;	3068
13:23 **the L** was gracious unto them,	3068
14: 3 which *was* right in the sight of **the L**,	3068
14: 6 where*in* **the L** commanded, saying,	3068
14:14 that were found *in* the house of **the L**,	3068
14:24 *that* which *was* evil in the sight of **the L**:	3068
14:25 according to the word of **the L** God of	3068
14:26 For **the L** saw the affliction of Israel, *that*	3068
14:27 **the L** said not that *he* would blot out	3068
15: 3 which *was* right in the sight of **the L**,	3068
15: 5 **the L** smote the king, so that he was a	3068
15: 9 *that* which *was* evil in the sight of **the L**,	3068
15:12 *was* the word of **the L** which he spake	3068
15:18 *that* which *was* evil in the sight of **the L**,	3068
15:24 *that* which *was* evil in the sight of **the L**,	3068
15:28 *that* which *was* evil in the sight of **the L**:	3068
15:34 *that* which *was* right in the sight of **the L**:	3068
15:35 the higher gate of the house of **the L**.	3068
15:37 In those days **the L** began to send against	3068
16: 2 *was* right in the sight of **the L** his God,	3068
16: 3 whom **the L** cast out from before	3068
16: 8 that was found *in* the house of **the L**,	3068
16:14 *was* before **the L**, from the forefront	3068
16:14 between the altar and the house of **the L**,	3068
16:18 turned he *from* the house of **the L** for	3068
17: 2 *that* which *was* evil in the sight of **the L**,	3068
17: 7 Israel had sinned against **the L** their God,	3068
17: 8 whom **the L** cast out from before	3068
17: 9 *were* not right against **the L** their God,	3068
17:11 as *did* the heathen whom **the L** carried	3068
17:11 wrought wicked things to provoke **the L**	3068
17:12 whereof **the L** had said unto them,	3068
17:13 Yet **the L** testified against Israel,	3068
17:14 that did not believe in **the L** their God.	3068
17:15 whom **the L** had charged them,	3068
17:16 they left all the commandments of **the L**	3068
17:17 to do evil in the sight of **the L**,	3068
17:18 **the L** was very angry with Israel,	3068
17:19 the commandments of **the L** their God,	3068
17:20 **the L** rejected all the seed of Israel,	3068
17:21 drave Israel from following **the L**,	3068
17:23 **the L** removed Israel out of his sight,	3068
17:25 dwelling there, *that* they feared not **the L**:	3068
17:25 therefore **the L** sent lions among them,	3068
17:28 taught them how they should fear **the L**.	3068
17:32 So they feared **the L**, and made unto	3068
17:33 They feared **the L**, and served their own	3068
17:34 they fear not **the L**, neither do they after	3068
17:34 commandment which **the L** commanded	3068
17:35 With whom **the L** had made a covenant,	3068
17:36 the **L**, who brought you up out of the	3068
17:39 **the L** your God ye shall fear; and he shall	3068
17:41 So these nations feared **the L**, and served	3068
18: 3 *that* which *was* right in the sight of **the L**,	3068
18: 5 He trusted in **the L** God of Israel;	3068
18: 6 For he clave to **the L**, *and* departed not	3068
18: 6 which **the L** commanded Moses.	3068
18: 7 **the L** was with him; *and* he prospered	3068
18:12 they obeyed not the voice of **the L**	3068
18:12 all that Moses the servant of **the L**	3068
18:15 that was found *in* the house of **the L**,	3068
18:16 *from* the doors of the temple of **the L**,	3068
18:22 say unto me, We trust in **the L** our God:	3068
18:25 Am I now come up without **the L** against	3068
18:25 **The L** said to me, Go up against this land,	3068
18:30 let Hezekiah make you trust in **the L**,	3068
18:30 **The L** will surely deliver us, and this city	3068
18:32 saying, **The L** will deliver us.	3068
18:35 that **the L** should deliver Jerusalem out of	3068
19: 1 and went *into* the house of **the L**.	3068
19: 4 It may be **the L** thy God will hear all	3068
19: 4 will reprove the words which **the L** thy	3068
19: 6 ye say to your master, Thus saith **the L**,	3068
19:14 went up *into* the house of **the L**,	3068
19:14 of the Lᴏʀᴅ, and spread it before **the L**.	3068
19:15 Hezekiah prayed before **the L**, and said,	3068
19:15 said, O **L** God of Israel, which dwellest	3068
19:16 **L**, bow down thine ear, and hear: open,	3068
19:16 open, **L**, thine eyes, and see: and hear	3068
19:17 Of a truth, **L**, the kings of Assyria have	3068
19:19 O **L** our God, I beseech thee,	3068
19:19 earth may know that thou *art* **the L** God,	3068
19:20 Thus saith **the L** God of Israel,	3068
19:21 This *is* the word that **the L** hath spoken	3068
19:31 the zeal of **the L** *of hosts* shall do this.	3068
19:32 Therefore thus saith **the L** concerning	3068
19:33 shall not come into this city, saith **the L**.	3068
19:35 that the angel of **the L** went out,	3068
20: 1 said unto him, Thus saith **the L**, Set thine	3068
20: 2 the wall, and prayed unto **the L**, saying,	3068
20: 3 I beseech thee, O **L**, remember now how	3068
20: 4 the word of **the L** came to him, saying,	3068
20: 5 Thus saith **the L**, the God of David thy	3068
20: 5 thou shalt go up *unto* the house of **the L**.	3068
20: 8 *shall be* the sign that **the L** will heal	3068

2Ki 20: 8 *that* I shall go up *into* the house of **the L**	3068
20: 9 This sign shalt thou have of **the L**,	3068
20: 9 that **the L** will do the thing that he hath	3068
20:11 Isaiah the prophet cried unto **the L**:	3068
20:16 unto Hezekiah, Hear the word of **the L**.	3068
20:17 nothing shall be left, saith **the L**.	3068
20:19 Good *is* the word of **the L** which thou	3068
21: 2 *that* which *was* evil in the sight of **the L**,	3068
21: 2 whom **the L** cast out before the children	3068
21: 4 he built altars in the house of **the L**,	3068
21: 4 which **the L** said, In Jerusalem will I put	3068
21: 5 in the two courts of the house of **the L**.	3068
21: 6 much wickedness in the sight of **the L**,	3068
21: 7 of which **the L** said to David,	3068
21: 9 **the L** destroyed before the children of	3068
21:10 **the L** spake by his servants the prophets,	3068
21:12 Therefore thus saith **the L** God of Israel,	3068
21:16 *that* which *was* evil in the sight of **the L**.	3068
21:20 *that* which *was* evil in the sight of **the L**,	3068
21:22 he forsook **the L** God of his fathers,	3068
21:22 and walked not in the way of **the L**.	3068
22: 2 *that* which *was* right in the sight of **the L**,	3068
22: 3 the scribe, *to* the house of **the L**, saying,	3068
22: 4 which is brought *into* the house of **the L**,	3068
22: 5 have the oversight of the house of **the L**:	3068
22: 5 the work which *is* in the house of **the L**,	3068
22: 8 the book of the law in the house of **the L**.	3068
22: 9 have the oversight *of* the house of **the L**.	3068
22:13 inquire of **the L** for me, and for the	3068
22:13 for great *is* the wrath of **the L** that is	3068
22:15 them, Thus saith **the L** God of Israel,	3068
22:16 Thus saith **the L**, Behold, I will bring evil	3068
22:18 Judah which sent you to inquire of **the L**,	3068
22:18 say to him, Thus saith **the L** God of Israel,	3068
22:19 thou hast humbled thyself before **the L**,	3068
22:19 I also have heard *thee*, saith **the L**.	3068
23: 2 the king went up *into* the house of **the L**,	3068
23: 2 which was found in the house of **the L**.	3068
23: 3 made a covenant before **the L**, to walk	3068
23: 3 to walk after **the L**, and to keep his	3068
23: 4 bring forth out of the temple of **the L** all	3068
23: 6 out the grove from the house of **the L**,	3068
23: 7 that *were* by the house of **the L**, where	3068
23: 9 not up to the altar of **the L** in Jerusalem,	3068
23:11 at the entering in of the house of **the L**,	3068
23:12 in the two courts of the house of **the L**,	3068
23:16 according to the word of **the L** which	3068
23:19 Israel had made to provoke *the L* to anger,	NIH
23:21 Keep the passover unto **the L** your God,	3068
23:23 this passover was holden to **the L**	3068
23:24 the priest found *in* the house of **the L**.	3068
23:25 that turned to **the L** with all his heart,	3068
23:26 Notwithstanding **the L** turned not from	3068
23:27 **the L** said, I will remove Judah also out	3068
23:32 *that* which *was* evil in the sight of **the L**,	3068
23:37 *that* which *was* evil in the sight of **the L**,	3068
24: 2 **the L** sent against him bands of	3068
24: 2 destroy it, according to the word of **the L**,	3068
24: 3 at the commandment of **the L** came	3068
24: 4 which **the L** would not pardon.	3068
24: 9 *that* which *was* evil in the sight of **the L**,	3068
24:13 all the treasures of the house of **the L**,	3068
24:13 of Israel had made in the temple of **the L**,	3068
24:13 temple of the Lᴏʀᴅ, as **the L** had said.	3068
24:19 *that* which *was* evil in the sight of **the L**,	3068
24:20 For through the anger of **the L** it came to	3068
25: 9 burnt the house of **the L**, and the king's	3068
25:13 of brass that *were in* the house of **the L**,	3068
25:13 brasen sea that *was* in the house of **the L**,	3068
25:16 had made for the house of **the L**;	3068
1Ch 2: 3 of Judah, *was* evil in the sight of **the L**;	3068
6:15 went *into captivity*, when **the L**	3068
6:31 the service of song *in* the house of **the L**	3068
6:32 Solomon had built the house of **the L**	3068
9:19 their fathers, *being* over the host of **the L**,	3068
9:20 in time past, *and* **the L** was with him.	3068
9:23 of the gates of the house of **the L**,	3068
10:13 which he committed against **the L**,	3068
10:13 *even* against the word of **the L**, which he	3068
10:14 inquired not of **the L**: therefore he slew	3068
11: 2 **the L** thy God said unto thee, Thou shalt	3068
11: 3 with them in Hebron before **the L**;	3068
11: 3 to the word of **the L** by Samuel.	3068
11: 9 greater: for **the L** of hosts *was* with him.	3068
11:10 according to the word of **the L**	3068
11:14 **the L** saved *them by* a great deliverance.	3068
11:18 drink *of* it, but poured it out to **the L**,	3068
12:23 to him, according to the word of **the L**.	3068
13: 2 you, and *that it be* of **the L** our God,	3068
13: 6 to bring up thence the ark of God **the L**,	3068
13:10 the anger of **the L** was kindled against	3068
13:11 **the L** had made a breach upon Uzza:	3068
13:14 **the L** blessed the house of Obed-edom,	3068
14: 2 perceived that **the L** had confirmed	3068
14:10 **the L** said unto him, Go up; for I will	3068
14:17 **the L** brought the fear of him upon all	3068
15: 2 them hath **the L** chosen to carry the ark	3068
15: 3 bring up the ark of **the L** unto his place,	3068
15:12 you may bring up the ark of **the L** God	3068
15:13 **the L** our God made a breach upon us,	3068
15:14 to bring up the ark of **the L** God of Israel.	3068
15:15 according to the word of **the L**.	3068
15:25 **the L** out of the house of Obed-edom	3068
15:26 that bare the ark of the covenant of **the L**,	3068
15:28 of the covenant of **the L** with shouting,	3068

1Ch 15:29 the ark of the covenant of **the L** came to	3068
16: 2 blessed the people in the name of **the L**.	3068
16: 4 to minister before the ark of **the L**,	3068
16: 4 to thank and praise **the L** God of Israel:	3068
16: 7 to thank **the L** into the hand of Asaph	3068
16: 8 Give thanks unto **the L**, call upon his	3068
16:10 the heart of them rejoice that seek **the L**.	3068
16:11 Seek **the L** and his strength, seek his face	3068
16:14 He *is* **the L** our God; his judgments *are* in	3068
16:23 Sing unto **the L**, all the earth; shew forth	3068
16:25 For great *is* **the L**, and greatly to be	3068
16:26 *are* idols: but **the L** made the heavens.	3068
16:28 Give unto **the L**, ye kindreds of the	3068
16:28 give unto **the L** glory and strength.	3068
16:29 Give unto **the L** the glory due unto his	3068
16:29 worship **the L** in the beauty of holiness.	3068
16:31 say among the nations, **The L** reigneth.	3068
16:33 wood sing out at the presence of **the L**,	3068
16:34 O give thanks unto **the L**; for *he is* good;	3068
16:36 Blessed *be* **the L** God of Israel for ever	3068
16:36 the people said, Amen, and praised **the L**.	3068
16:37 the ark of the covenant of **the L** Asaph	3068
16:39 before the tabernacle of **the L** in the high	3068
16:40 To offer burnt offerings unto **the L** upon	3068
16:40 to all that is written in the law of **the L**,	3068
16:41 give thanks to **the L**, because his mercy	3068
17: 1 ark of the covenant of **the L** remaineth	3068
17: 4 tell David my servant, Thus saith **the L**,	3068
17: 7 Thus saith **the L** of hosts, I took thee	3068
17:10 I tell thee that **the L** will build	3068
17:16 David the king came and sat before **the L**,	3068
17:16 said, Who *am* I, O **L** God, and what *is* mine house,	3068
17:17 estate of a man of high degree, O **L** God.	3068
17:19 O **L**, for thy servant's sake,	3068
17:20 **L**, *there is* none like thee, neither *is there*	3068
17:22 for ever; and thou, **L**, becamest their God.	3068
17:23 Therefore now, **L**, let the thing that thou	3068
17:24 saying, **The L** of hosts *is* the God of Israel,	3068
17:26 now, **L**, thou *art* God, and hast promised	3068
17:27 **L**, and *it shall be* blessed for ever.	3068
18: 6 **the L** preserved David whithersoever	3068
18:11 also king David dedicated unto **the L**,	3068
18:13 **the L** preserved David whithersoever	3068
19:13 **the L** do *that* which *is* good in his sight.	3068
21: 3 **The L** make his people an hundred times	3068
21: 9 **the L** spake unto Gad, David's seer,	3068
21:10 and tell David, saying, Thus saith **the L**,	3068
21:11 unto him, Thus saith **the L**, Choose thee	3068
21:12 or else three days the sword of **the L**,	3068
21:12 angel of **the L** destroying throughout all	3068
21:13 let me fall now into the hand of **the L**;	3068
21:14 So **the L** sent pestilence upon Israel:	3068
21:15 **the L** beheld, and he repented him of	3068
21:15 the angel of **the L** stood by	3068
21:16 saw the angel of **the L** stand between	3068
21:17 **L** my God, be on me, and on my father's	3068
21:18 angel of **the L** commanded Gad to say	3068
21:18 set up an altar unto **the L** in	3068
21:19 which he spake in the name of **the L**.	3068
21:22 I may build an altar therein unto **the L**:	3068
21:24 will not take *that* which *is* thine for **the L**,	3068
21:26 David built there an altar unto **the L**,	3068
21:26 peace offerings, and called upon **the L**;	3068
21:27 **the L** commanded the angel; and he put	3068
21:28 At that time when David saw that **the L**	3068
21:29 For the tabernacle of **the L**, which Moses	3068
21:30 of the sword of the angel of **the L**.	3068
22: 1 This *is* the house of **the L** God, and this	3068
22: 5 The house *that is* to be builded for **the L**	3068
22: 6 him to build a house for **the L** God	3068
22: 7 a house unto the name of **the L** my God:	3068
22: 8 the word of **the L** came to me, saying,	3068
22:11 Now, my son, **the L** be with thee;	3068
22:11 and build the house of **the L** thy God,	3068
22:12 Only **the L** give thee wisdom and	3068
22:12 *thou* mayest keep the law of **the L** thy	3068
22:13 judgments which **the L** charged Moses	3068
22:14 **the L** an hundred thousand talents *of*	3068
22:16 and be doing, and **the L** be with thee.	3068
22:18 *Is* not **the L** your God with you?	3068
22:18 the land is subdued before **the L**,	3068
22:19 and your soul to seek **the L** your God;	3068
22:19 and build ye the sanctuary of **the L** God,	3068
22:19 to bring the ark of the covenant of **the L**,	3068
22:19 that is *to be* built to the name of **the L**.	3068
23: 4 forward the work of the house of **the L**;	3068
23: 5 four thousand praised **the L** with	3068
23:13 for ever, to burn incense before **the L**,	3068
23:24 for the service of the house of **the L**,	3068
23:25 **The L** God of Israel hath given rest unto	3068
23:28 for the service of the house of **the L**,	3068
23:30 every morning to thank and praise **the L**,	3068
23:31 to offer all burnt sacrifices unto **the L** in	3068
23:31 unto them, continually before **the L**:	3068
23:32 in the service of the house of **the L**.	3068
24:19 service to come into the house of **the L**,	3068
24:19 as **the L** God of Israel had commanded	3068
25: 3 a harp, to give thanks and to praise **the L**.	3068
25: 6 father for song *in* the house of **the L**,	3068
25: 7 *were* instructed in the songs of **the L**,	3068
26:12 to minister in the house of **the L**.	3068
26:22 over the treasures of the house of **the L**.	3068
26:27 dedicate to maintain the house of **the L**.	3068
26:30 westward in all the business of **the L**,	3068
27:23 **the L** had said *he* would increase Israel	3068

L

1Ch 28: 2 rest for the ark of the covenant of **the L**,	3068	
28: 4 Howbeit **the L** God of Israel chose me	3068	
28: 5 (for **the L** hath given me many sons,)	3068	
28: 5 of the kingdom of **the L** over Israel.	3068	
28: 8 of all Israel the congregation of **the L**,	3068	
28: 8 seek for all the commandments of **the L**	3068	
28: 9 for **the L** searcheth all hearts,	3068	
28:10 **the L** hath chosen thee to build a house	3068	
28:12 of the courts of the house of **the L**,	3068	
28:13 work of the service of the house of **the L**,	3068	
28:13 vessels of service in the house of **the L**.	3068	
28:18 covered the ark of the covenant of **the L**.	3068	
28:19 All *this, said David,* **the L** made me	3068	
28:20 **the L** God, *even* my God, *will be* with	3068	
28:20 for the service of the house of **the L**.	3068	
29: 1 palace *is* not for man, but for **the L** God.	3068	
29: 5 his service *this* day unto **the L**?	3068	
29: 8 to the treasure of the house of **the L**,	3068	
29: 9 heart they offered willingly to **the L:**	3068	
29:10 Wherefore David blessed **the L** before all	3068	
29:10 **L** God of Israel our father, for ever and	3068	
29:11 O **L**, *is* the greatness, and the power,	3068	
29:11 **L**, and *thou* art exalted as head above all.	3068	
29:16 O **L** our God, all this store that we have	3068	
29:18 O **L** God of Abraham, Isaac, and of Israel,	3068	
29:20 Now bless **the L** your God.	3068	
29:20 all the congregation blessed **the L** God of	3068	
29:20 and worshipped **the L**, and the king.	3068	
29:21 they sacrificed sacrifices unto **the L**,	3068	
29:21 offered burnt offerings unto **the L**,	3068	
29:22 drink before **the L** on that day with great	3068	
29:22 anointed *him* unto **the L** to be the chief	3068	
29:23 Solomon sat on the throne of **the L** as	3068	
29:25 **the L** magnified Solomon exceedingly in	3068	
2Ch 1: 1 **the L** his God *was* with him,	3068	
1: 3 which Moses the servant of **the L** had	3068	
1: 5 he put before the tabernacle of **the L:**	3068	
1: 6 thither to the brasen altar before **the L**,	3068	
1: 9 O **L** God, let thy promise unto David	3068	
2: 1 to build a house for the name of **the L**,	3068	
2: 4 I build a house to the name of **the L** my	3068	
2: 4 on the solemn feasts of **the L** our God.	3068	
2:11 Because **the L** hath loved his people,	3068	
2:12 Blessed *be* **the L** God of Israel, that made	3068	
2:12 that might build a house for **the L**,	3068	
3: 1 began to build the house of **the L**	3068	
3: 1 *the L* appeared unto David his father,	NIH	
4:16 for the house of **the L** of bright brass.	3068	
5: 1 made for the house of **the L** was finished:	3068	
5: 2 bring up the ark of the covenant of **the L**	3068	
5: 7 of the covenant of **the L** unto his place,	3068	
5:10 when **the L** made *a covenant* with	3068	
5:13 be heard in praising and thanking **the L;**	3068	
5:13 and praised **the L**, *saying,* For *he is* good;	3068	
5:13 *with* a cloud, *even* the house of **the L;**	3068	
5:14 for the glory of **the L** had filled the house	3068	
6: 1 **The L** hath said that *he* would dwell in	3068	
6: 4 he said, Blessed *be* **the L** God of Israel,	3068	
6: 7 house for the name of **the L** God of Israel.	3068	
6: 8 **the L** said to David my father,	3068	
6:10 **The L** therefore hath performed his word	3068	
6:10 **the L** promised, and have built the house	3068	
6:10 built the house for the name of **the L**	3068	
6:11 the ark, wherein *is* the covenant of **the L**,	3068	
6:12 he stood before the altar of **the L** in	3068	
6:14 said, O **L** God of Israel, *there is* no God	3068	
6:16 Now therefore, O **L** God of Israel,	3068	
6:17 then, O **L** God of Israel, let thy word	3068	
6:19 to his supplication, O **L** my God,	3068	
6:41 Now therefore arise, O **L** God, into thy	3068	
6:41 let thy priests, O **L** God, be clothed *with*	3068	
6:42 O **L** God, turn not away the face of thine	3068	
7: 1 and the glory of **the L** filled the house.	3068	
7: 2 could not enter into the house of **the L**,	3068	
7: 2 the glory of **the L** had filled the LORD'S	3068	
7: 3 and the glory of **the L** upon the house,	3068	
7: 3 worshipped, and praised **the L**, *saying,*	3068	
7: 4 the people offered sacrifices before **the L**.	3068	
7: 6 also with instruments of musick of **the L**,	3068	
7: 6 David the king had made to praise **the L**,	3068	
7: 7 court that *was* before the house of **the L:**	3068	
7:10 in heart for the goodness that **the L**	3068	
7:11 Solomon finished the house of **the L**,	3068	
7:11 heart to make in the house of **the L**,	3068	
7:12 **the L** appeared to Solomon by night,	3068	
7:21 Why hath **the L** done thus unto this land,	3068	
7:22 Because they forsook **the L** God of their	3068	
8: 1 Solomon had built the house of **the L**,	3068	
8:11 whereunto the ark of **the L** hath come.	3068	
8:12 offered burnt offerings unto **the L**	3068	
8:12 unto the LORD on the altar of **the L**,	3068	
8:16 of the foundation of the house of **the L**,	3068	
8:16 *So* the house of **the L** was perfected.	3068	
9: 4 he went up *into* the house of **the L;**	3068	
9: 8 Blessed *be* **the L** thy God, which	3068	
9: 8 his throne, to be king for **the L** thy God:	3068	
9:11 trees terraces to the house of **the L**,	3068	
10:15 God, that **the L** might perform his word,	3068	
11: 2 the word of **the L** came to Shemaiah	3068	
11: 4 Thus saith **the L**, Ye shall not go up,	3068	
11: 4 they obeyed the words of **the L**,	3068	
11:14 executing the priest's office unto **the L:**	3068	
11:16 **the L** God of Israel came *to* Jerusalem,	3068	
11:16 sacrifice unto **the L** God of their fathers.	3068	
12: 1 he forsook the law of **the L**, and all Israel	3068	

2Ch 12: 2 they had transgressed against **the L**,	3068	
12: 5 and said unto them, Thus saith **the L**,	3068	
12: 6 and they said, **The L** *is* righteous.	3068	
12: 7 when **the L** saw that they humbled	3068	
12: 7 the word of **the L** came to Shemaiah,	3068	
12: 9 away the treasures of the house of **the L**,	3068	
12:11 the king entered *into* the house of **the L**,	3068	
12:12 the wrath of **the L** turned from him,	3068	
12:13 city which **the L** had chosen out of all	3068	
12:14 he prepared not his heart to seek **the L**.	3068	
13: 5 Ought you not to know that **the L** God	3068	
13: 8 of **the L** in the hand of the sons of David;	3068	
13: 9 Have ye not cast out the priests of **the L**,	3068	
13:10 **the L** *is* our God, and we have not	3068	
13:10 the priests, which minister unto **the L**,	3068	
13:11 they burn unto **the L** every morning	3068	
13:11 for we keep the charge of **the L** our God;	3068	
13:12 fight ye not against **the L** God of your	3068	
13:14 they cried unto **the L**, and the priests	3068	
13:18 relied upon **the L** God of their fathers.	3068	
13:20 and **the L** struck him, and he died.	3068	
14: 2 and right in the eyes of **the L** God of:	3068	
14: 4 commanded Judah to seek **the L** God of	3068	
14: 6 because **the L** had given him rest.	3068	
14: 7 because we have sought **the L** our God,	3068	
14:11 Asa cried unto **the L** his God, and said,	3068	
14:11 said, **L**, *it is* nothing with thee to help,	3068	
14:11 help us, O **L** our God; for we rest on thee,	3068	
14:11 **L**, thou *art* our God; let not man prevail	3068	
14:12 the **L** smote the Ethiopians before Asa,	3068	
14:13 for they were destroyed before **the L**,	3068	
14:14 for the fear of **the L** came upon them:	3068	
15: 2 **The L** *is* with you, while ye be with him;	3068	
15: 4 trouble did turn unto **the L** God of Israel,	3068	
15: 8 renewed the altar of **the L**, that *was*	3068	
15: 8 that *was* before the porch of **the L**.	3068	
15: 9 they saw that **the L** his God *was* with	3068	
15:11 they offered unto **the L** the same time,	3068	
15:12 entered into a covenant to seek **the L**	3068	
15:13 whosoever would not seek **the L** God	3068	
15:14 they sware unto **the L** with a loud voice,	3068	
15:15 and **the L** gave them rest round about.	3068	
16: 2 out of the treasures of the house of **the L**	3068	
16: 7 not relied on **the L** thy God, therefore is	3068	
16: 8 yet, because thou didst rely on **the L**,	3068	
16: 9 For the eyes of **the L** run to and	3068	
16:12 yet in his disease he sought not *to* **the L**,	3068	
17: 3 **the L** was with Jehoshaphat, because	3068	
17: 4 sought to the *L God* of his father,	NIH	
17: 5 Therefore **the L** stablished the kingdom in	3068	
17: 6 his heart was lift up in the ways of **the L**:	3068	
17: 9 the book of the law of **the L** with them,	3068	
17:10 fear of **the L** fell upon all the kingdoms	3068	
17:16 who willingly offered himself unto **the L;**	3068	
18: 4 I pray thee, at the word of **the L** to day.	3068	
18: 6 *there* not here a prophet of **the L** besides,	3068	
18: 7 by whom *we* may inquire of **the L:**	3068	
18:10 said, Thus saith **the L**, With these thou	3068	
18:11 for **the L** shall deliver *it* into the hand of	3068	
18:13 Micaiah said, *As* **the L** liveth, even what	3068	
18:15 but the truth to me in the name of **the L?**	3068	
18:16 **the L** said, These have no master; let	3068	
18:18 said, Therefore hear the word of **the L**,	3068	
18:18 I saw **the L** sitting upon his throne,	3068	
18:19 **the L** said, Who shall entice Ahab king of	3068	
18:20 stood before **the L**, and said, I will entice	3068	
18:20 And **the L** said unto him, Wherewith?	3068	
18:21 *the L* said, Thou shalt entice *him,* and	NIH	
18:22 **the L** hath put a lying spirit in the mouth	3068	
18:22 and **the L** hath spoken evil against thee.	3068	
18:23 Which way went the spirit of **the L** from	3068	
18:27 peace, *then* hath not **the L** spoken by me.	3068	
18:31 cried out, and **the L** helped him;	3068	
19: 2 ungodly, and love them that hate **the L?**	3068	
19: 2 *is* wrath upon thee from before **the L**.	3068	
19: 4 brought them back unto **the L** God of	3068	
19: 6 for ye judge not for man, but for **the L**,	3068	
19: 7 Wherefore now let the fear of **the L** be	3068	
19: 7 for *there is* no iniquity with **the L** our	3068	
19: 8 for the judgment of **the L**,	3068	
19: 9 Thus shall ye do in the fear of **the L**,	3068	
19:10 them that they trespass not against **the L**,	3068	
19:11 priest *is* over you in all matters of **the L;**	3068	
19:11 and **the L** shall be with the good.	3068	
20: 3 set himself to seek **the L**, and proclaimed	3068	
20: 4 themselves together, to ask *help* of **the L:**	3068	
20: 4 cities of Judah they came to seek **the L**.	3068	
20: 5 and Jerusalem, in the house of **the L**,	3068	
20: 6 said, O **L** God of our fathers, *art* not thou	3068	
20:13 all Judah stood before **the L**, with their	3068	
20:14 came the spirit of **the L** in the midst of	3068	
20:15 Thus saith **the L** unto you,	3068	
20:17 and see the salvation of **the L** with you,	3068	
20:17 against them: for **the L** *will be* with you.	3068	
20:18 inhabitants of Jerusalem fell before **the L**,	3068	
20:18 fell before the LORD, worshipping **the L**.	3068	
20:19 stood up to praise **the L** God of Israel	3068	
20:20 Believe in **the L** your God, so shall you	3068	
20:21 he appointed singers unto **the L**,	3068	
20:21 before the army, and to say, Praise **the L;**	3068	
20:22 that **the L** set ambushments against	3068	
20:26 of Berachah; for there they blessed **the L:**	3068	
20:27 for **the L** had made them to rejoice over	3068	
20:28 and trumpets unto the house of **the L**.	3068	
20:29 when they had heard that **the L** fought	3068	

2Ch 20:32 which *was* right in the sight of **the L**.	3068	
20:37 Ahaziah, **the L** hath broken thy works.	3068	
21: 6 *that* which *was* evil in the eyes of **the L**.	3068	
21: 7 the **L** would not destroy the house	3068	
21:10 he had forsaken **the L** God of his fathers.	3068	
21:12 Thus saith **the L** God of David thy father,	3068	
21:14 *with* a great plague will **the L** smite thy	3068	
21:16 the **L** stirred up against Jehoram	3068	
21:18 all this **the L** smote him in his bowels	3068	
22: 4 he did evil in the sight of **the L**,	3068	
22: 7 whom **the L** had anointed to cut off	3068	
22: 9 who sought **the L** with all his heart.	3068	
23: 3 as **the L** hath said of the sons of David.	3068	
23: 5 be in the courts of the house of **the L**.	3068	
23: 6 let none come *into* the house of **the L**,	3068	
23: 6 the people shall keep the watch of **the L**.	3068	
23:12 to the people *into* the house of **the L**:	3068	
23:14 Slay her not *in* the house of **the L**.	3068	
23:18 **the L** by the hand of the priests the	3068	
23:18 had distributed in the house of **the L**,	3068	
23:18 to offer the burnt offerings of **the L**, as it	3068	
23:19 porters at the gates of the house of **the L**,	3068	
23:20 down the king from the house of **the L**:	3068	
24: 2 **the L** all the days of Jehoiada the priest.	3068	
24: 4 was minded to repair the house of **the L**.	3068	
24: 6 of Moses the servant of **the L**,	3068	
24: 7 of **the L** did they bestow upon Baalim.	3068	
24: 8 without at the gate of the house of **the L**,	3068	
24: 9 to bring in to **the L** the collection that	3068	
24:12 work of the service of the house of **the L**,	3068	
24:12 carpenters to repair the house of **the L**,	3068	
24:12 and brass to mend the house of **the L**.	3068	
24:14 were made vessels for the house of **the L**,	3068	
24:14 **the L** continually all the days of Jehoiada.	3068	
24:18 they left the house of **the L** God of their	3068	
24:19 to them, to bring them again unto **the L;**	3068	
24:20 ye the commandments of **the L**,	3068	
24:20 because ye have forsaken **the L**, he hath	3068	
24:21 king in the court of the house of **the L**.	3068	
24:22 said, **The L** look upon *it,* and require *it.*	3068	
24:24 **the L** delivered a very great host into	3068	
24:24 they had forsaken **the L** God of their	3068	
25: 2 which *was* right in the sight of **the L**,	3068	
25: 4 where **the L** commanded, saying,	3068	
25: 7 **the L** *is* not with Israel, *to wit, with* all	3068	
25: 9 **The L** is able to give thee much more	3068	
25:15 Wherefore the anger of **the L** was kindled	3068	
25:27 **the L** they made a conspiracy against him	3068	
26: 4 *that* which *was* right in the sight of **the L**,	3068	
26: 5 long as he sought **the L**, God made him	3068	
26:16 for he transgressed against **the L** his God,	3068	
26:16 went into the temple of **the L** to burn	3068	
26:17 with him fourscore priests of **the L**,	3068	
26:18 to burn incense unto **the L**, but to	3068	
26:18 *it be* for thine honour from **the L** God.	3068	
26:19 before the priests in the house of **the L**,	3068	
26:20 to go out, because **the L** had smitten him.	3068	
26:21 he was cut off from the house of **the L**:	3068	
27: 2 *that* which *was* right in the sight of **the L**,	3068	
27: 2 he entered not into the temple of **the L**.	3068	
27: 3 built the high gate of the house of **the L**,	3068	
27: 6 prepared his ways before **the L** his God.	3068	
28: 1 which *was* right in the sight of **the L**,	3068	
28: 3 **the L** had cast out before the children of	3068	
28: 5 Wherefore **the L** his God delivered him	3068	
28: 6 they had forsaken **the L** God of their	3068	
28: 9 a prophet of **the L** was there, whose name	3068	
28: 9 **the L** God of your fathers was wroth with	3068	
28:10 with you, sins against **the L** your God?	3068	
28:11 for the fierce wrath of **the L** *is* upon you.	3068	
28:13 **the L** already, ye intend to add *more* to	3068	
28:19 For **the L** brought Judah low because	3068	
28:19 and transgressed sore against **the L**.	3068	
28:21 away a portion *out* of the house of **the L**,	3068	
28:22 did he trespass yet more against **the L:**	3068	
28:24 shut up the doors of the house of **the L**,	3068	
28:25 provoked to anger **the L** God of his	3068	
29: 2 which *was* right in the sight of **the L**,	3068	
29: 3 opened the doors of the house of **the L**,	3068	
29: 5 sanctify the house of **the L** God of your	3068	
29: 6 was evil in the eyes of **the L** our God,	3068	
29: 6 their faces from the habitation of **the L**,	3068	
29: 8 Wherefore the wrath of **the L** was upon	3068	
29:10 a covenant with **the L** God of Israel,	3068	
29:11 for **the L** hath chosen you to stand before	3068	
29:15 the words of **the L**, to cleanse the house	3068	
29:15 the LORD, to cleanse the house of **the L**.	3068	
29:16 into the inner part *of* the house of **the L**,	3068	
29:16 **the L** into the court of the house	3068	
29:16 into into the court of the house of **the L**.	3068	
29:17 month came they to the porch of **the L:**	3068	
29:17 they sanctified the house of **the L** in eight	3068	
29:18 We have cleansed all the house of **the L**,	3068	
29:19 behold, they *are* before the altar of **the L**.	3068	
29:20 city, and went up *to* the house of **the L**.	3068	
29:21 Aaron to offer *them* on the altar of **the L**.	3068	
29:25 he set the Levites *in* the house of **the L**,	3068	
29:25 *was* the commandment of **the L** by his	3068	
29:27 the song of **the L** began *also* with	3068	
29:30 unto **the L** with the words of David,	3068	
29:31 have consecrated yourselves unto **the L**,	3068	
29:31 thank offerings into the house of **the L**.	3068	
29:32 these *were* for a burnt offering to **the L**,	3068	
29:35 the service of the house of **the L** was set	3068	
30: 1 *they* should come to the house of **the L**	3068	

2Ch 30: 1 to keep the passover unto **the L** God of 3068
30: 5 unto the **L** God of Israel at Jerusalem: 3068
30: 6 turn again unto the **L** God of Abraham, 3068
30: 7 which trespassed against the **L** God of 3068
30: 8 *but* yield yourselves unto the **L**, 3068
30: 8 serve **the L** your God, that the fierceness 3068
30: 9 For if ye turn again unto the **L** 3068
30: 9 for the **L** your God *is* gracious and 3068
30:12 and of the princes, by the word of the **L** 3068
30:15 burnt offerings *into* the house of the **L**. 3068
30:17 not clean, to sanctify *them* unto the **L**. 3068
30:18 **The** good **L** pardon every one 3068
30:19 to seek God, the **L** God of his fathers, 3068
30:20 the **L** hearkened to Hezekiah, 3068
30:21 and the priests praised **the L** day by day, 3068
30:21 with loud instruments unto the **L**. 3068
30:22 that taught the good knowledge of the **L**: 3068
30:22 making confession to the **L** God of their 3068
31: 2 to praise in the gates of the tents of the **L**. 3068
31: 3 as it is written in the law of the **L**. 3068
31: 4 might be encouraged in the law of the **L**, 3068
31: 6 were consecrated unto the **L** their God, 3068
31: 8 they blessed the **L**, and his people Israel. 3068
31:10 the offerings *into* the house of the **L**, 3068
31:10 for the **L** hath blessed his people; 3068
31:11 prepare chambers in the house of the **L**; 3068
31:14 to distribute the oblations of the **L**, 3068
31:16 one that entereth into the house of the **L**, 3068
31:20 and right and truth before the **L** his God. 3068
32: 8 but with us *is* the **L** our God to help us, 3068
32:11 **The L** our God shall deliver us out of 3068
32:16 his servants spake yet *more* against the **L** 3068
32:17 He wrote also letters to rail on the **L** God 3068
32:21 the **L** sent an angel, which cut off all 3068
32:22 Thus the **L** saved Hezekiah and 3068
32:23 many brought gifts unto the **L** to 3068
32:24 sick to the death, and prayed unto the **L**: 3068
32:26 the wrath of the **L** came not upon them 3068
33: 2 *that* which *was* evil in the sight of the **L**, 3068
33: 2 whom **the L** had cast out before 3068
33: 4 Also he built altars in the house of the **L**, 3068
33: 4 whereof the **L** had said, In Jerusalem shall 3068
33: 5 in the two courts of the house of the **L**, 3068
33: 6 wrought much evil in the sight of the **L**, 3068
33: 9 whom **the L** had destroyed before 3068
33:10 the **L** spake to Manasseh, and to his 3068
33:11 Wherefore the **L** brought upon them 3068
33:12 he besought the **L** his God, 3068
33:13 Manasseh knew that the **L** he *was* God. 3068
33:15 the idol out of the house of the **L**, 3068
33:15 built in the mount of the house of the **L**, 3068
33:16 he repaired the altar of the **L**, 3068
33:16 commanded Judah to serve the **L** God of 3068
33:17 places, *yet* unto the **L** their God only. 3068
33:18 him in the name of the **L** God of Israel, 3068
33:22 *that* which *was* evil in the sight of the **L**, 3068
33:23 humbled not himself before the **L**, 3068
34: 2 *that* which *was* right in the sight of the **L**, 3068
34: 8 to repair the house of the **L** his God. 3068
34:10 had the oversight of the house of the **L**, 3068
34:10 that wrought in the house of the **L**, 3068
34:14 that was brought *into* the house of the **L**, 3068
34:14 book of the law of the **L** *given* by Moses. 3068
34:15 book of the law in the house of the **L**, 3068
34:17 that was found in the house of the **L**, 3068
34:21 inquire of the **L** for me, and for them that 3068
34:21 for great *is* the wrath of the **L** that is 3068
34:21 fathers have not kept the word of the **L**, 3068
34:23 Thus saith **the L** God of Israel, 3068
34:24 Thus saith the **L**, Behold, I will bring evil 3068
34:26 who sent you to inquire of the **L**, 3068
34:26 Thus saith the **L** God of Israel *concerning* 3068
34:27 I have even heard *thee* also, saith the **L**. 3068
34:30 the king went up *into* the house of the **L**, 3068
34:30 that was found in the house of the **L**. 3068
34:31 made a covenant before the **L**, to walk 3068
34:31 to walk after the **L**, and to keep his 3068
34:33 to serve, *even* to serve the **L** their God. 3068
34:33 they departed not from following the **L**, 3068
35: 1 kept a passover unto the **L** in Jerusalem: 3068
35: 2 them to the service of the house of the **L**, 3068
35: 3 all Israel, which were holy unto the **L**, 3068
35: 3 serve now **the L** your God, and his 3068
35: 6 the word of the **L** by the hand of Moses. 3068
35:12 to offer unto the **L**, as it is written in 3068
35:16 So all the service of the **L** was prepared 3068
35:16 burnt offerings upon the altar of the **L**, 3068
35:26 which was written in the law of the **L**, 3068
36: 5 *was* evil in the sight of the **L** his God. 3068
36: 7 vessels of the house of the **L** to Babylon, 3068
36: 9 *that* which *was* evil in the sight of the **L**, 3068
36:10 the goodly vessels of the house of the **L**, 3068
36:12 *was* evil in the sight of the **L** his God, 3068
36:12 *speaking* from the mouth of the **L**. 3068
36:13 his heart from turning unto the **L** 3068
36:14 polluted the house of the **L** which he had 3068
36:15 the **L** God of their fathers sent to them by 3068
36:16 until the wrath of the **L** arose against his 3068
36:18 the treasures of the house of the **L**, 3068
36:21 To fulfil the word of the **L** by the mouth 3068
36:22 the word of the **L** *spoken* by the mouth 3068
36:22 the **L** stirred up the spirit of Cyrus king of 3068
36:23 All the kingdoms of the earth hath **the L** 3068
36:23 **The L** his God *be* with him, and let him 3068
Ezr 1: 1 that the word of the **L** by the mouth of 3068

Ezr 1: 1 **the L** stirred up the spirit of Cyrus king of 3068
1: 2 **The L** God of heaven hath given me all 3068
1: 3 build the house of the **L** God of Israel, 3068
1: 5 go up to build the house of the **L** which 3068
1: 7 forth the vessels of the house of the **L**, 3068
2:68 when they came to the house of the **L** 3068
3: 3 burnt offerings thereon unto the **L**, 3068
3: 5 of all the set feasts of **the L** that were 3068
3: 5 offered a freewill offering unto the **L**. 3068
3: 6 they to offer burnt offerings unto the **L**. 3068
3: 6 foundation of the temple of the **L** was 3068
3: 8 forward the work of the house of the **L**. 3068
3:10 the foundation of the temple of the **L**, 3068
3:10 to praise the **L**, after the ordinance of 3068
3:11 in praising and giving thanks unto the **L**; 3068
3:11 when they praised the **L**, because 3068
3:11 the foundation of the house of the **L** was 3068
4: 1 the temple unto the **L** God of Israel; 3068
4: 3 ourselves together will build unto the **L** 3068
6:21 to seek **the L** God of Israel, did eat, 3068
6:22 for the **L** had made them joyful, 3068
7: 6 which the **L** God of Israel had given: 3068
7: 6 according to the hand of the **L** his God 3068
7:10 his heart to seek the law of the **L**, 3068
7:11 words of the commandments of the **L**, 3068
7:27 Blessed *be* the **L** God of our fathers, 3068
7:27 to beautify the house of the **L** which *is* in 3068
7:28 I was strengthened as the hand of the **L** 3068
8:28 I said unto them, Ye *are* holy unto the **L**; 3068
8:28 gold *are* a freewill offering unto the **L** 3068
8:29 *in* the chambers of the house of the **L**. 3068
8:35 all *this was* a burnt offering unto the **L**. 3068
9: 5 spread out my hands unto **the L** my God, 3068
9: 8 hath been *shewed* from the **L** our God, 3068
9:15 O **L** God of Israel, thou *art* righteous: 3068
10:11 make confession unto the **L** God of your 3068
Ne 1: 5 O **L** God of heaven, the great and terrible 3068
5:13 Amen, and praised the **L**. 3068
8: 1 which the **L** had commanded to Israel. 3068
8: 6 Ezra blessed the **L**, the great God. 3068
8: 6 worshipped the **L** *with their* faces to 3068
8: 9 This day *is* holy unto the **L** your God; 3068
8:10 for the joy of the **L** *is* your strength. 3068
8:14 found written in the law which the **L** 3068
9: 3 read in the book of the law of the **L** their 3068
9: 3 and worshipped the **L** their God. 3068
9: 4 cried with a loud voice unto the **L** their 3068
9: 5 bless the **L** your God for ever and ever: 3068
9: 6 Thou, *even* thou, *art* **L** alone; thou hast 3068
9: 7 *art* the **L** the God, who didst choose 3068
10:29 do all the commandments of the **L** our 3068
10:34 to burn upon the altar of the **L** our God, 3068
10:35 year by year, unto the house of the **L**: 3068
Job 1: 6 came to present themselves before the **L**, 3068
1: 7 the **L** said unto Satan, Whence comest 3068
1: 7 Satan answered the **L**, and said, 3068
1: 8 the **L** said unto Satan, Hast thou 3068
1: 9 Satan answered the **L**, and said, Doth Job 3068
1:12 the **L** said unto Satan, Behold, all that he 3068
1:12 went forth from the presence of the **L**. 3068
1:21 the **L** gave, and the **LORD** hath taken 3068
1:21 the **L** hath taken *away;* blessed be the 3068
1:21 taken *away;* blessed be the name of the **L**. 3068
2: 1 came to present themselves before the **L**, 3068
2: 1 them to present himself before the **L**. 3068
2: 2 the **L** said unto Satan, From whence 3068
2: 2 Satan answered the **L**, and said, 3068
2: 3 the **L** said unto Satan, Hast thou 3068
2: 4 Satan answered the **L**, and said, Skin for 3068
2: 6 the **L** said unto Satan, Behold, he *is* in 3068
2: 7 Satan forth from the presence of the **L**, 3068
12: 9 that the hand of the **L** hath wrought this? 3068
38: 1 the **L** answered Job out of the whirlwind, 3068
40: 1 Moreover the **L** answered Job, and said, 3068
40: 3 Then Job answered the **L**, and said, 3068
40: 6 answered the **L** unto Job out of 3068
42: 1 Then Job answered the **L**, and said, 3068
42: 7 that after the **L** had spoken these words 3068
42: 7 the **L** said to Eliphaz the Temanite, 3068
42: 9 according as the **L** commanded them: 3068
42: 9 them: the **L** also accepted Job. 3068
42:10 the **L** turned the captivity of Job, when 3068
42:10 also the **L** gave Job twice as much as he 3068
42:11 comforted him over all the evil that the **L** 3068
42:12 the **L** blessed the latter end of Job more 3068
Ps 1: 2 his delight *is* in the law of the **L**; and in 3068
1: 6 For the **L** knoweth the way of 3068
2: 2 against the **L**, and against his anointed, 3068
2: 4 the **L** shall have them in derision. 3068
2: 7 the **L** hath said unto me, Thou *art* my 3068
2:11 Serve the **L** with fear, and rejoice with 3068
3: 1 **L**, how are they increased that trouble 3068
3: 3 thou, O **L**, *art* a shield for me; my glory, 3068
3: 4 I cried unto the **L** *with* my voice, 3068
3: 5 slept; I awaked; for the **L** sustained me. 3068
3: 7 Arise, O **L**; save me, O my God: for thou 3068
3: 8 Salvation *belongeth* unto the **L**: 3068
4: 3 know that the **L** hath set apart *him that* 3068
4: 3 the **L** will hear when I call unto him. 3068
4: 5 and put your trust in the **L**. 3068
4: 6 **L**, lift thou up the light of thy 3068
4: 8 thou, **L**, only makest me dwell in safety. 3068
5: 1 Give ear to my words, O **L**, consider my 3068
5: 3 voice shalt thou hear *in* the morning, O **L**; 3068
5: 6 the **L** will abhor the bloody and 3068

Ps 5: 8 Lead me, O **L**, in thy righteousness 3068
5:12 For thou, **L**, wilt bless the righteous; 3068
6: 1 O **L**, rebuke me not in thine anger, 3068
6: 2 Have mercy upon me, O **L**; for I *am* weak: 3068
6: 2 O **L**, heal me; for my bones are vexed. 3068
6: 3 also sore vexed: but thou, O **L**, how long? 3068
6: 4 Return, O **L**, deliver my soul: O save me 3068
6: 8 for the **L** hath heard the voice of my 3068
6: 9 The **L** hath heard my supplication; 3068
6: 9 the **L** will receive my prayer. 3068
7: T of David, which he sang unto the **L**, 3068
7: 1 O **L** my God, in thee do I put my trust: 3068
7: 3 **L** my God, if I have done this; if there be 3068
7: 6 Arise, O **L**, in thine anger, lift up thyself 3068
7: 8 The **L** shall judge the people: judge me, 3068
7: 8 judge me, O **L**, according to my 3068
7:17 I will praise the **L** according to his 3068
7:17 sing praise to the name of the **L** most 3068
8: 1 O **L** our Lord, how excellent *is* thy name 3068
8: 9 O **L** our Lord, how excellent *is* thy name 3068
9: 1 I will praise *thee*, O **L**, with my whole 3068
9: 7 the **L** shall endure for ever: he hath 3068
9: 9 The **L** also will be a refuge for 3068
9:10 for thou, **L**, hast not forsaken them that 3068
9:11 Sing *praises* to the **L**, which dwelleth in 3068
9:13 Have mercy upon me, O **L**; consider my 3068
9:16 The **L** is known *by* the judgment *which* 3068
9:19 Arise, O **L**; let not man prevail: 3068
9:20 Put them in fear, O **L**: *that* the nations 3068
10: 1 Why standest thou afar off, O **L**? 3068
10: 3 the covetous, *whom* the **L** abhorreth. 3068
10:12 Arise, O **L**; O God, lift up thine hand: 3068
10:16 The **L** *is* King for ever and ever: 3068
10:17 **L**, thou hast heard the desire of the 3068
11: 1 In the **L** put I my trust: how say ye to my 3068
11: 4 The **L** *is* in his holy temple, the **LORD**'s 3068
11: 5 The **L** trieth the righteous: but the 3068
11: 7 For the righteous **L** loveth righteousness; 3068
12: 1 Help, **L**; for the godly *man* ceaseth; 3068
12: 3 The **L** shall cut off all flattering lips, 3068
12: 5 of the needy, now will I arise, saith the **L**; 3068
12: 6 The words of **the L** *are* pure words: 3068
12: 7 Thou shalt keep them, O **L**, thou shalt 3068
13: 1 How long wilt thou forget me, O **L**? 3068
13: 3 Consider *and* hear me, O **L** my God: 3068
13: 6 I will sing unto the **L**, because he hath 3068
14: 2 The **L** looked down from heaven upon 3068
14: 4 they eat bread, *and* call not upon the **L**. 3068
14: 6 of the poor, because the **L** *is* his refuge. 3068
14: 7 when the **L** bringeth back the captivity 3068
15: 1 **L**, who shall abide in thy tabernacle? 3068
15: 4 but he honoureth them that fear the **L**. 3068
16: 2 *O my soul*, thou hast said unto the **L**, 3068
16: 5 The **L** *is* the portion of mine inheritance 3068
16: 7 I will bless the **L**, who hath given me 3068
16: 8 I have set the **L** always before me: 3068
17: 1 Hear the right, O **L**, attend unto my cry, 3068
17:13 Arise, O **L**, disappoint him, cast him 3068
17:14 thy hand, O **L**, from men of the world, 3068
18: T *A Psalm* of David, the servant of the **L**, 3068
18: T who spake unto the **L** the words of this 3068
18: T the **L** delivered him from the hand of all 3068
18: 1 I will love thee, O **L**, my strength. 3068
18: 3 I will call upon the **L**, who is *worthy* to 3068
18: 6 In my distress I called upon the **L**, 3068
18:13 The **L** also thundered in the heavens, 3068
18:15 O **L**, at the blast of the breath of thy 3068
18:18 of my calamity: but the **L** was my stay. 3068
18:20 The **L** rewarded me according to my 3068
18:21 For I have kept the ways of the **L**, 3068
18:24 Therefore hath the **L** recompensed me 3068
18:28 the **L** my God will enlighten my darkness. 3068
18:30 the word of the **L** is tried: he *is* a buckler 3068
18:31 For who *is* God save the **L**? or who *is* a 3068
18:41 *was* none to save *them: even* unto the **L**, 3068
18:46 The **L** liveth; and blessed *be* my rock; 3068
18:49 O **L**, among the heathen, and sing *praises* 3068
19: 7 The law of the **L** *is* perfect, converting 3068
19: 7 testimony of the **L** *is* sure, making wise 3068
19: 8 The statutes of the **L** *are* right, rejoicing 3068
19: 8 the commandment of the **L** *is* pure, 3068
19: 9 The fear of the **L** *is* clean, enduring for 3068
19: 9 the judgments of the **L** *are* true *and* 3068
19:14 O **L**, my strength, and my redeemer. 3068
20: 1 The **L** hear thee in the day of trouble; 3068
20: 5 *our* banners: the **L** fulfil all thy petitions. 3068
20: 6 know I that the **L** saveth his anointed; 3068
20: 7 we will remember the name of the **L** our 3068
20: 9 Save, **L**: let the king hear us when we call. 3068
21: 1 The king shall joy in thy strength, O **L**; 3068
21: 7 For the king trusteth in the **L**, 3068
21: 9 the **L** shall swallow them up in his wrath, 3068
21:13 Be thou exalted, **L**, in thine own strength: 3068
22: 8 He trusted on the **L** *that* he would deliver 3068
22:19 be not thou far *from me*, O **L**: O my 3068
22:23 Ye that fear the **L**, praise him; all ye 3068
22:26 they shall praise the **L** that seek him: 3068
22:27 shall remember and turn unto the **L**: 3068
23: 1 The **L** *is* my shepherd; I shall not want. 3068
23: 6 I will dwell in the house of the **L** for ever. 3068
24: 3 Who shall ascend into the hill of the **L**? 3068
24: 5 He shall receive the blessing from the **L**, 3068
24: 8 the **L** strong and mighty, the **LORD** 3068
24: 8 and mighty, the **L** mighty *in* battle. 3068

Ref	Text	Num
Ps 24:10	**The L** of hosts, he *is* the King of glory.	3068
25: 1	Unto thee, O **L,** do I lift up my soul.	3068
25: 4	Shew me thy ways, O **L;** teach me thy	3068
25: 6	Remember, O **L,** thy tender mercies and	3068
25: 7	thou me for thy goodness' sake, O **L.**	3068
25: 8	Good and upright *is* **the L:** therefore	3068
25:10	All the paths of **the L** *are* mercy and	3068
25:11	For thy name's sake, O **L,** pardon mine	3068
25:12	What man *is* he that feareth **the L?**	3068
25:14	The secret of **the L** *is* with them that fear	3068
25:15	Mine eyes *are* ever towards **the L;** for he	3068
26: 1	Judge me, O **L;** for I have walked in mine	3068
26: 1	I have trusted also in **the L;** *therefore*	3068
26: 2	Examine me, O **L,** and prove me; try my	3068
26: 6	so will I compass thine altar, O **L:**	3068
26: 8	**L,** I have loved the habitation of thy	3068
26:12	in the congregations will I bless **the L.**	3068
27: 1	**The L** *is* my light and my salvation;	3068
27: 1	**the L** *is* the strength of my life; of whom	3068
27: 4	One *thing* have I desired of **the L,** that	3068
27: 4	that I may dwell in the house of **the L** all	3068
27: 4	to behold the beauty of **the L,**	3068
27: 6	yea, I will sing *praises* unto **the L.**	3068
27: 7	Hear, O **L,** *when* I cry *with* my voice:	3068
27: 8	said unto thee, Thy face, **L,** will I seek.	3068
27:10	forsake me, then **the L** will take me up.	3068
27:11	O **L,** and lead me in a plain path, because	3068
27:13	of **the L** in the land of the living.	3068
27:14	Wait on **the L:** be of good courage,	3068
27:14	thine heart: wait, I say, on **the L.**	3068
28: 1	Unto thee will I cry, O **L,** my rock; be not	3068
28: 5	they regard not the works of **the L,**	3068
28: 6	Blessed *be* **the L,** because he hath heard	3068
28: 7	**The L** *is* my strength and my shield;	3068
28: 8	**The L** *is* their strength, and he *is* the	3068
29: 1	Give unto **the L,** O ye mighty, give unto	3068
29: 1	give unto **the L** glory and strength.	3068
29: 2	Give unto **the L** the glory due unto his	3068
29: 2	worship **the L** in the beauty of holiness.	3068
29: 3	The voice of **the L** *is* upon the waters:	3068
29: 3	**the L** *is* upon many waters.	3068
29: 4	The voice of **the L** *is* powerful; the voice	3068
29: 4	the voice of **the L** *is* full of majesty.	3068
29: 5	The voice of **the L** breaketh the cedars;	3068
29: 5	**the L** breaketh the cedars of Lebanon.	3068
29: 7	The voice of **the L** divideth the flames of	3068
29: 8	voice of **the L** shaketh the wilderness;	3068
29: 8	**the L** shaketh the wilderness of Kadesh.	3068
29: 9	The voice of **the L** maketh the hinds to	3068
29:10	**The L** sitteth upon the flood; yea,	3068
29:10	the flood; yea, **the L** sitteth King for ever.	3068
29:11	**The L** will give strength unto his people;	3068
29:11	**the L** will bless his people with peace.	3068
30: 1	I will extol thee, O **L;** for thou hast lifted	3068
30: 2	O **L** my God, I cried unto thee,	3068
30: 3	O **L,** thou hast brought up my soul from	3068
30: 4	Sing unto **the L,** O ye saints of his,	3068
30: 7	**L,** by thy favour thou hast made my	3068
30: 8	I cried to thee, O **L;** and unto the Lᴏʀᴅ I	3068
30: 8	and unto **the L** I made supplication.	3068
30:10	Hear, O **L,** and have mercy upon me:	3068
30:10	mercy upon me: **L,** be thou my helper.	3068
30:12	O **L** my God, I will give thanks unto thee	3068
31: 1	In thee, O **L,** do I put my trust; let me	3068
31: 5	hast redeemed me, O **L** God of truth.	3068
31: 6	regard lying vanities: but I trust in **the L.**	3068
31: 9	mercy upon me, O **L,** for I am in trouble:	3068
31:14	I trusted in thee, O **L:** I said, Thou *art* my	3068
31:17	Let me not be ashamed, O **L;** for I have	3068
31:21	Blessed *be* **the L:** for he hath shewed me	3068
31:23	O love **the L,** all ye his saints:	3068
31:23	*for* **the L** preserveth the faithful,	3068
31:24	your heart, all ye that hope in **the L.**	3068
32: 2	Blessed *is* the man unto whom **the L**	3068
32: 5	confess my transgressions unto **the L;**	3068
32:10	he that trusteth in **the L,** mercy shall	3068
32:11	glad in **the L,** and rejoice, ye righteous:	3068
33: 1	Rejoice in **the L,** O ye righteous: *for*	3068
33: 2	Praise **the L** with harp: sing unto him	3068
33: 4	For the word of **the L** *is* right; and all his	3068
33: 5	the earth is full *of* the goodness of **the L.**	3068
33: 6	By the word of **the L** were the heavens	3068
33: 8	Let all the earth fear **the L:** let all	3068
33:10	**The L** bringeth the counsel of the	3068
33:11	The counsel of **the L** standeth for ever,	3068
33:12	Blessed *is* the nation whose God *is* **the L;**	3068
33:13	**The L** looketh from heaven; he beholdeth	3068
33:18	eye of **the L** *is* upon them that fear him,	3068
33:20	Our soul waiteth for **the L:** he *is* our help	3068
33:22	Let thy mercy, O **L,** be upon us,	3068
34: 1	I will bless **the L** at all times: his praise	3068
34: 2	My soul shall make her boast in **the L:**	3068
34: 3	magnify **the L** with me, and let us exalt	3068
34: 4	I sought **the L,** and he heard me,	3068
34: 6	**the L** heard *him,* and saved him out of all	3068
34: 7	The angel of **the L** encampeth round	3068
34: 8	O taste and see that **the L** *is* good:	3068
34: 9	O fear **the L,** ye his saints: for *there is* no	3068
34:10	they that seek **the L** shall not want any	3068
34:11	I will teach you the fear of **the L.**	3068
34:15	The eyes of **the L** *are* upon the righteous,	3068
34:16	The face of **the L** *is* against them that do	3068
34:17	**the L** heareth, and delivereth them out of	3068
34:18	**The L** *is* nigh unto them that are of a	3068
34:19	but **the L** delivereth him out of them all.	3068

Ref	Text	Num
Ps 34:22	**The L** redeemeth the soul of his servants:	3068
35: 1	Plead *my cause,* O **L,** with them that	3068
35: 5	and let the angel of **the L** chase *them.*	3068
35: 6	let the angel of **the L** persecute them.	3068
35: 9	my soul shall be joyful in **the L:** it shall	3068
35:10	bones shall say, **L,** who *is* like unto thee,	3068
35:22	thou hast seen, O **L:** keep not silence:	3068
35:24	Judge me, O **L** my God, according to thy	3068
35:27	say continually, Let **the L** be magnified,	3068
36: T	*A Psalm* of David the servant of **the L.**	3068
36: 5	Thy mercy, O **L,** *is* in the heavens;	3068
36: 6	O **L,** thou preservest man and beast.	3068
37: 3	Trust in **the L,** and do good; *so* shalt	3068
37: 4	Delight thyself also in **the L;** and he shall	3068
37: 5	Commit thy way unto **the L;** trust also in	3068
37: 7	Rest in **the L,** and wait patiently for him:	3068
37: 9	those that wait upon **the L,** they shall	3068
37:17	but **the L** upholdeth the righteous.	3068
37:18	**The L** knoweth the days of the upright:	3068
37:20	the enemies of **the L** *shall be* as the fat	3068
37:23	steps of a *good* man are ordered by **the L:**	3068
37:24	for **the L** upholdeth *him with* his hand.	3068
37:28	For **the L** loveth judgment,	3068
37:33	**The L** will not leave him in his hand,	3068
37:34	Wait on **the L,** and keep his way,	3068
37:39	the salvation of the righteous *is* of **the L:**	3068
37:40	**the L** shall help them, and deliver them:	3068
38: 1	O **L,** rebuke me not in thy wrath:	3068
38:15	in thee, O **L,** do I hope: thou wilt hear,	3068
38:21	Forsake me not, O **L:** O my God, be not	3068
39: 4	**L,** make me to know mine end,	3068
39:12	prayer, O **L,** and give ear unto my cry;	3068
40: 1	patiently for **the L;** and he inclined	3068
40: 3	see *it,* and fear, and shall trust in **the L.**	3068
40: 4	Blessed *is that* man that maketh **the L** his	3068
40: 5	Many, O **L** my God, *are* thy wonderful	3068
40: 9	not refrained my lips, O **L,** thou knowest.	3068
40:11	thou thy tender mercies from me, O **L:**	3068
40:13	Be pleased, O **L,** to deliver me: O Lᴏʀᴅ,	3068
40:13	deliver me: O **L,** make haste to help me.	3068
40:16	say continually, **The L** be magnified.	3068
41: 1	**the L** will deliver him in time of trouble.	3068
41: 2	**The L** will preserve him, and keep him	3068
41: 3	**The L** will strengthen him upon the bed	3068
41: 4	I said, **L,** be merciful unto me: heal my	3068
41:10	thou, O **L,** be merciful unto me,	3068
41:13	Blessed *be* **the L** God of Israel from	3068
42: 8	*Yet* **the L** will command his	3068
46: 7	**The L** of hosts with us; the God of	3068
46: 8	Come, behold the works of **the L,**	3068
46:11	**The L** of hosts with us; the God of	3068
47: 2	For **the L** most High *is* terrible; *he is* a	3068
47: 5	shout, **the L** with the sound of a trumpet.	3068
48: 1	Great *is* **the L,** and greatly to be praised	3068
48: 8	have we seen in the city of **the L** of hosts,	3068
50: 1	*even* **the L,** hath spoken, and called	3068
54: 6	I will praise thy name, O **L;** for *it is* good.	3068
55:16	call upon God; and **the L** shall save me.	3068
55:22	Cast thy burden upon **the L,** and he shall	3068
56:10	*his* word: in **the L** will I praise *his* word.	3068
58: 6	the great teeth of the young lions, O **L.**	3068
59: 3	*for* my transgression, nor *for* my sin, O **L.**	3068
59: 5	therefore, O **L** God *of* hosts, the God	3068
59: 8	O **L,** shalt laugh at them; thou shalt	3068
64:10	The righteous shall be glad in **the L,**	3068
68:16	yea, **the L** will dwell *in it* for ever.	3068
68:18	that **the L** God might dwell *among them.*	3050
69:13	*is* unto thee, O **L,** *in* an acceptable time:	3068
69:16	Hear me, O **L;** for thy lovingkindness *is*	3068
69:31	*This* also shall please **the L** better than an	3068
69:33	For **the L** heareth the poor, and despiseth	3068
70: 1	deliver me; make haste to help me, O **L.**	3068
70: 5	and my deliverer; O **L,** make no tarrying.	3068
71: 1	In thee, O **L,** do I put my trust: let me	3068
72:18	Blessed *be* **the L** God, the God of Israel,	3068
74:18	O **L,** and *that* the foolish people have	3068
75: 8	For in the hand of **the L** *there is* a cup,	3068
76:11	Vow, and pay unto **the L** your God: let all	3068
77:11	I will remember the works of **the L:**	3050
78: 4	generation to come the praises of **the L,**	3068
78:21	**the L** heard *this,* and was wroth:	3068
79: 5	How long, **L?** wilt thou be angry, for ever?	3068
80: 4	O **L** God *of* hosts, how long wilt thou be	3068
80:19	Turn us again, O **L** God *of* hosts, cause	3068
81:10	I *am* **the L** thy God, which brought thee	3068
81:15	haters of **the L** should have submitted	3068
83:16	that they may seek thy name, O **L.**	3068
84: 1	amiable *are* thy tabernacles, O **L** of hosts!	3068
84: 2	yea, even fainteth for the courts of **the L:**	3068
84: 3	O **L** of hosts, my King, and my God.	3068
84: 8	O **L** God of hosts, hear my prayer: give ear,	3068
84:11	For **the L** God *is* a sun and shield:	3068
84:11	**the L** will give grace and glory: no good	3068
84:12	O **L** of hosts, blessed *is* the man that	3068
85: 1	**L,** thou hast been favourable unto thy	3068
85: 7	mercy, O **L,** and grant us thy salvation.	3068
85: 8	I will hear what God **the L** will speak:	3068
85:12	Yea, **the L** shall give *that which is* good;	3068
86: 1	Bow down thine ear, O **L,** hear me: for I	3068
86: 6	Give ear, O **L,** unto my prayer;	3068
86:11	Teach me thy way, O **L;** I will walk in thy	3068
86:17	because thou, **L,** hast holpen me,	3068
87: 2	**The L** loveth the gates of Zion more than	3068
87: 6	**The L** shall count, when he writeth *up*	3068
88: 1	O **L** God of my salvation, I have cried day	3068

Ref	Text	Num
Ps 88: 9	**L,** I have called daily upon thee, I have	3068
88:13	unto thee have I cried, O **L;** and in	3068
88:14	**L,** why castest thou off my soul?	3068
89: 1	I will sing of the mercies of **the L** for ever:	3068
89: 5	heavens shall praise thy wonders, O **L:**	3068
89: 6	the heaven can be compared unto **the L?**	3068
89: 8	O **L** God of hosts, who *is* a strong Lᴏʀᴅ	3068
89: 8	of hosts, who *is* a strong **L** like unto thee?	3050
89:15	they shall walk, O **L,** in the light of thy	3068
89:18	**the L** is our defence; and the Holy One	3068
89:46	How long, **L?** wilt thou hide thyself,	3068
89:51	thine enemies have reproached, O **L;**	3068
89:52	Blessed *be* **the L** for evermore. Amen,	3068
90:13	Return, O **L,** how long? and let it repent	3068
90:17	the beauty of **the L** our God be upon us:	3068
91: 2	I will say of **the L,** *He is* my refuge and	3068
91: 9	Because thou hast made **the L,** *which is*	3068
92: 1	*is* a good *thing* to give thanks unto **the L,**	3068
92: 4	thou, **L,** hast made me glad through thy	3068
92: 5	O **L,** how great are thy works! and	3068
92: 8	But thou, **L,** *art* most high for evermore.	3068
92: 9	For lo, thine enemies, O **L,** for lo,	3068
92:13	that be planted in the house of **the L**	3068
92:15	To shew that **the L** *is* upright: *he is* my	3068
93: 1	**The L** reigneth, he is clothed with	3068
93: 1	**the L** is clothed with strength,	3068
93: 3	The floods have lifted up, O **L,** the floods	3068
93: 4	**The L** on high *is* mightier than the noise	3068
93: 5	becometh thine house, O **L,** for ever.	3068
94: 1	O **L** God, to whom vengeance belongeth;	3068
94: 3	**L,** how long shall the wicked, how long	3068
94: 5	thy people, O **L,** and afflict thine heritage.	3068
94: 7	Yet they say, **The L** shall not see,	3050
94:11	**The L** knoweth the thoughts of man,	3068
94:12	O **L,** and teachest him out of thy law;	3050
94:14	For **the L** will not cast off his people,	3068
94:17	Unless **the L** *had been* my help, my soul	3068
94:18	foot slippeth; thy mercy, O **L,** held me up.	3068
94:22	my defence; and my God *is*	3068
94:23	*yea,* **the L** our God shall cut them off.	3068
95: 1	come, let us sing unto **the L:** let us make	3068
95: 3	For **the L** *is* a great God, and a great King	3068
95: 6	let us kneel before **the L** our Maker.	3068
96: 1	O sing unto **the L** a new song: sing unto	3068
96: 1	a new song: sing unto **the L,** all the earth.	3068
96: 2	Sing unto **the L,** bless his name; shew	3068
96: 4	For **the L** *is* great, and greatly to be	3068
96: 5	*are* idols: but **the L** made the heavens.	3068
96: 7	Give unto **the L,** O ye kindreds of	3068
96: 7	give unto **the L** glory and strength.	3068
96: 8	Give unto **the L** the glory due unto his	3068
96: 9	worship **the L** in the beauty of holiness:	3068
96:10	among the heathen *that* **the L** reigneth:	3068
96:13	Before **the L:** for he cometh, for he	3068
97: 1	**The L** reigneth; let the earth rejoice;	3068
97: 5	melted like wax at the presence of **the L,**	3068
97: 8	because of thy judgments, O **L.**	3068
97: 9	For thou, **L,** *art* High above all the earth:	3068
97:10	that love **the L,** hate evil: he preserveth	3068
97:12	Rejoice in **the L,** ye righteous;	3068
98: 1	sing unto **the L** a new song; for he hath	3068
98: 2	**The L** hath made known his salvation:	3068
98: 4	Make a joyful noise unto **the L,**	3068
98: 5	Sing unto **the L** with the harp; with	3068
98: 6	cornet make a joyful noise before **the L,**	3068
98: 9	Before **the L;** for he cometh to judge	3068
99: 1	**The L** reigneth; let the people tremble:	3068
99: 2	**The L** *is* great in Zion; and he *is* high	3068
99: 5	Exalt ye **the L** our God, and worship at	3068
99: 6	they called upon **the L,** and he answered	3068
99: 8	Thou answeredst them, O **L** our God:	3068
99: 9	Exalt **the L** our God, and worship at his	3068
99: 9	at his holy hill; for **the L** our God *is* holy.	3068
100: 1	Make a joyful noise unto **the L,** all ye	3068
100: 2	Serve **the L** with gladness: come before	3068
100: 3	Know ye that **the L** he *is* God: *it is* he	3068
100: 5	**the L** *is* good; his mercy *is* everlasting;	3068
101: 1	and judgment: unto thee, O **L,** will I sing.	3068
101: 8	off all wicked doers from the city of **the L.**	3068
102: T	poureth out his complaint before **the L.**	3068
102: 1	O **L,** and let my cry come unto thee.	3068
102:12	thou, O **L,** shalt endure for ever;	3068
102:15	the heathen shall fear the name of **the L,**	3068
102:16	When **the L** shall build up Zion, he shall	3068
102:18	which *shall* be created shall praise **the L.**	3050
102:19	from heaven did **the L** behold the earth;	3068
102:21	To declare the name of **the L** in Zion,	3068
102:22	and the kingdoms, to serve **the L.**	3068
103: 1	Bless **the L,** O my soul: and all that is	3068
103: 2	Bless **the L,** O my soul, and forget not all	3068
103: 6	**The L** executeth righteousness and	3068
103: 8	**The L** *is* merciful and gracious, slow to	3068
103:13	so **the L** pitieth them that fear him.	3068
103:17	the mercy of **the L** *is* from everlasting to	3068
103:19	**The L** hath prepared his throne in	3068
103:20	Bless **the L,** ye his angels, that excel in	3068
103:21	Bless ye **the L,** all ye his hosts;	3068
103:22	Bless **the L,** all his works in all places of	3068
103:22	of his dominion: bless **the L,** O my soul.	3068
104: 1	Bless **the L,** O my soul. O Lᴏʀᴅ my	3068
104: 1	O **L** my God, thou art very great; thou art	3068
104:16	The trees of **the L** are full *of sap;*	3068
104:24	O **L,** how manifold are thy works!	3068
104:31	The glory of **the L** shall endure for ever:	3068

L

Ps 104:31 for ever: **the L** shall rejoice in his works.	3068	
104:33 I will sing unto **the L** as long as I live:	3068	
104:34 shall be sweet: I will be glad in **the L**.	3068	
104:35 Bless thou **the L**, O my soul. Praise ye	3068	
104:35 the LORD, O my soul. Praise ye **the L**.	3050	
105: 1 O give thanks unto **the L**; call upon his	3068	
105: 3 the heart of them rejoice that seek **the L**.	3068	
105: 4 Seek **the L**, and his strength: seek his face	3068	
105: 7 He **is the L** our God: his judgments are in	3068	
105:19 word came: the word of **the L** tried him.	3068	
105:45 and keep his laws. Praise ye **the L**.	3050	
106: 1 Praise ye **the L**. O give thanks unto	3050	
106: 1 O give thanks unto **the L**; for he is good:	3068	
106: 2 Who can utter the mighty acts of **the L**?	3068	
106: 4 Remember me, O **L**, with the favour that	3068	
106:16 in the camp, and Aaron the saint of **the L**.	3068	
106:25 hearkened not unto the voice of **the L**.	3068	
106:34 whom **the L** commanded them:	3068	
106:40 Therefore was the wrath of **the L** kindled	3068	
106:47 O **L** our God, and gather us from among	3068	
106:48 Blessed be **the L** God of Israel from	3068	
106:48 all the people say, Amen. Praise ye **the L**.	3050	
107: 1 O give thanks unto **the L**, for he is good:	3068	
107: 2 Let the redeemed of **the L** say so, whom	3068	
107: 6 they cried unto **the L** in their trouble,	3068	
107: 8 Oh that men would praise **the L** for his	3068	
107:13 they cried unto **the L** in their trouble,	3068	
107:15 Oh that men would praise **the L** for his	3068	
107:19 they cry unto **the L** in their trouble,	3068	
107:21 Oh that men would praise **the L** for his	3068	
107:24 These see the works of **the L**,	3068	
107:28 they cry unto **the L** in their trouble,	3068	
107:31 Oh that men would praise **the L** for his	3068	
107:43 understand the lovingkindness of **the L**.	3068	
108: 3 I will praise thee, O **L**, among the people:	3068	
109:14 of his fathers be remembered with **the L**;	3068	
109:15 Let them be before **the L** continually;	3068	
109:20 reward of mine adversaries from **the L**,	3068	
109:26 Help me, O **L** my God: O save me	3068	
109:27 this is thy hand; that thou, **L**, hast done it.	3068	
109:30 I will greatly praise **the L** with my mouth;	3068	
110: 1 **The L** said unto my Lord, Sit thou at my	3068	
110: 2 **The L** shall send the rod of thy strength	3068	
110: 4 **The L** hath sworn, and will not repent,	3068	
111: 1 Praise ye **the L**. I will praise the LORD	3050	
111: 1 I will praise **the L** with my whole heart,	3068	
111: 2 The works of **the L** are great, sought out	3068	
111: 4 **the L** is gracious and full of compassion.	3068	
111:10 The fear of **the L** is the beginning of	3068	
112: 1 Praise ye **the L**. Blessed is the man that	3050	
112: 1 Blessed is the man that feareth **the L**,	3068	
112: 7 his heart is fixed, trusting in **the L**.	3068	
113: 1 Praise ye **the L**. Praise, O ye servants of	3050	
113: 1 Praise, O ye servants of **the L**, praise	3068	
113: 2 Blessed be the name of **the L** from this	3068	
113: 4 **The L** is high above all nations,	3068	
113: 5 Who is like unto **the L** our God,	3068	
113: 9 joyful mother of children. Praise ye **the L**.	3050	
115: 1 O **L**, not unto us, but unto thy name give	3068	
115: 9 Israel, trust thou in **the L**: he is their help	3068	
115:10 house of Aaron, trust in **the L**: he is their	3068	
115:11 Ye that fear **the L**, trust in the LORD:	3068	
115:11 Ye that fear the LORD, trust in **the L**:	3068	
115:12 **The L** hath been mindful of us: he will	3068	
115:13 He will bless them that fear **the L**, both	3068	
115:14 **The L** shall increase you more and more,	3068	
115:15 You are blessed of **the L** which made	3068	
115:17 The dead praise not **the L**, neither any	3050	
115:18 But we will bless **the L** from this time	3068	
115:18 time forth and for evermore. Praise **the L**.	3050	
116: 1 I love **the L**, because he hath heard my	3068	
116: 4 called I upon the name of **the L**;	3068	
116: 4 O **L**, I beseech thee, deliver my soul.	3068	
116: 5 Gracious is **the L**, and righteous; yea,	3068	
116: 6 **The L** preserveth the simple: I was	3068	
116: 7 for **the L** hath dealt bountifully with thee.	3068	
116: 9 I will walk before **the L** in the land of	3068	
116:12 What shall I render unto **the L** for all his	3068	
116:13 and call upon the name of **the L**.	3068	
116:14 I will pay my vows unto **the L** now in	3068	
116:15 Precious in the sight of **the L** is the death	3068	
116:16 Oh **L**, truly I am thy servant; I am thy	3068	
116:17 and will call upon the name of **the L**.	3068	
116:18 I will pay my vows unto **the L** now in	3068	
116:19 of thee, O Jerusalem. Praise ye **the L**.	3050	
117: 1 O praise **the L**, all ye nations: praise him,	3068	
117: 2 the truth of **the L** endureth for ever.	3068	
117: 2 LORD endureth for ever. Praise ye **the L**.	3050	
118: 1 O give thanks unto **the L**; for he is good:	3068	
118: 4 Let them now that fear **the L** say, that his	3068	
118: 5 I called upon **the L** in distress: the LORD	3050	
118: 5 **the L** answered me, and set me in a large	3050	
118: 6 **The L** is on my side; I will not fear:	3068	
118: 7 **The L** taketh my part with them that help	3068	
118: 8 It is better to trust in **the L** than to put	3068	
118: 9 It is better to trust in **the L** than to put	3068	
118:10 in the name of **the L** will I destroy them.	3068	
118:11 in the name of **the L** I will destroy	3068	
118:12 for in the name of **the L** I will destroy	3068	
118:13 me that I might fall: but **the L** helped me.	3068	
118:14 **The L** is my strength and song,	3050	
118:15 the right hand of **the L** doeth valiantly.	3068	
118:16 The right hand of **the L** is exalted:	3068	
118:16 the right hand of **the L** doeth valiantly.	3068	

Ps 118:17 but live, and declare the works of **the L**.	3050	
118:18 **The L** hath chastened me sore: but he	3050	
118:19 will go into them, and I will praise **the L**:	3050	
118:20 gate of **the L**, into which the righteous	3068	
118:24 This is the day which **the L** hath made;	3068	
118:25 Save now, I beseech thee, O **L**: O LORD,	3050	
118:25 O **L**, I beseech thee, send now prosperity.	3068	
118:26 be he that cometh in the name of **the L**:	3068	
118:26 blessed you out of the house of **the L**.	3068	
118:27 God is **the L**, which hath shewed us light	3068	
118:29 O give thanks unto **the L**; for he is good:	3068	
119: 1 the way, who walk in the law of **the L**.	3068	
119:12 Blessed art thou, O **L**: teach me thy	3068	
119:31 testimonies: O **L**, put me not to shame.	3068	
119:33 Teach me, O **L**, the way of thy statutes;	3068	
119:41 O **L**, even thy salvation, according to thy	3068	
119:52 I remembered thy judgments of old, O **L**;	3068	
119:55 O **L**, in the night, and have kept thy law.	3068	
119:57 Thou art my portion, O **L**: I have said that	3068	
119:64 The earth, O **L**, is full of thy mercy:	3068	
119:65 servant, O **L**, according unto thy word.	3068	
119:75 I know, O **L**, that thy judgments are right,	3068	
119:89 For ever, O **L**, thy word is settled in	3068	
119:107 me, O **L**, according to thy word.	3068	
119:108 O **L**, and teach me thy judgments.	3068	
119:126 It is time for thee, **L**, to work: for they	3068	
119:137 O **L**, and upright are thy judgments.	3068	
119:145 cried with my whole heart; hear me, O **L**:	3068	
119:149 O **L**, quicken me according to thy	3068	
119:151 Thou art near, O **L**; and all thy	3068	
119:156 Great are thy tender mercies, O **L**:	3068	
119:159 quicken me, O **L**, according to thy	3068	
119:166 **L**, I have hoped for thy salvation,	3068	
119:169 Let my cry come near before thee, O **L**:	3068	
119:174 I have longed for thy salvation, O **L**;	3068	
120: 1 In my distress I cried unto **the L**,	3068	
120: 2 O **L**, from lying lips, and from a deceitful	3068	
121: 2 My help cometh from **the L**, which made	3068	
121: 5 **The L** is thy keeper: the LORD is thy	3068	
121: 5 the **L** is thy shade upon thy right hand.	3068	
121: 7 **The L** shall preserve thee from all evil:	3068	
121: 8 **The L** shall preserve thy going out and	3068	
122: 1 me, Let us go into the house of **the L**.	3068	
122: 4 the tribes go up, the tribes of **the L**,	3050	
122: 4 to give thanks unto the name of **the L**.	3068	
122: 9 Because of the house of **the L** our God I	3068	
123: 2 so our eyes wait upon **the L** our God,	3068	
123: 3 mercy upon us, O **L**, have mercy upon us:	3068	
124: 1 If it had not been **the L** who was on our	3068	
124: 2 If it had not been **the L** who was on our	3068	
124: 6 Blessed be **the L**, who hath not given us	3068	
124: 8 Our help is in the name of **the L**, who	3068	
125: 1 They that trust in **the L** shall be as mount	3068	
125: 2 **the L** is round about his people from	3068	
125: 4 Do good, O **L**, unto those that be good,	3068	
125: 5 **the L** shall lead them forth with	3068	
126: 1 When **the L** turned again the captivity of	3068	
126: 2 **The L** hath done great things for them.	3068	
126: 3 **The L** hath done great things for us;	3068	
126: 4 Turn again our captivity, O **L**,	3068	
127: 1 Except **the L** build the house, they labour	3068	
127: 1 except **the L** keep the city, the watchman	3068	
127: 3 Lo, children are an heritage of **the L**:	3068	
128: 1 Blessed is every one that feareth **the L**;	3068	
128: 4 the man be blessed that feareth **the L**.	3068	
128: 5 **The L** shall bless thee out of Zion:	3068	
129: 4 **The L** is righteous: he hath cut asunder	3068	
129: 8 say, The blessing of **the L** be upon you:	3068	
129: 8 we bless you in the name of **the L**.	3068	
130: 1 Out of the depths have I cried unto thee, O **L**.	3068	
130: 3 If thou, **L**, shouldest mark iniquities,	3050	
130: 5 I wait for **the L**, my soul doth wait,	3068	
130: 7 Let Israel hope in **the L**: for with	3068	
130: 7 with **the L** there is mercy, and with him	3068	
131: 1 **L**, my heart is not haughty, nor mine eyes	3068	
131: 3 Let Israel hope in **the L** from henceforth	3068	
132: 1 **L**, remember David, and all his afflictions:	3068	
132: 2 How he sware unto **the L**, and vowed	3068	
132: 5 Until I find out a place for **the L**,	3068	
132: 8 Arise, O **L**, into thy rest; thou, and the ark	3068	
132:11 **The L** hath sworn in truth unto David;	3068	
132:13 For **the L** hath chosen Zion; he hath	3068	
133: 3 for there **the L** commanded the blessing,	3068	
134: 1 Behold, bless ye **the L**, all ye servants of	3068	
134: 1 ye the LORD, all ye servants of **the L**,	3068	
134: 1 by night stand in the house of **the L**.	3068	
134: 2 hands in the sanctuary, and bless **the L**.	3068	
134: 3 **The L** that made heaven and earth bless	3068	
135: 1 Praise ye **the L**. Praise ye the name	3050	
135: 1 Praise ye the name of **the L**; praise him,	3068	
135: 1 praise him, O ye servants of **the L**.	3068	
135: 2 Ye that stand in the house of **the L**,	3068	
135: 3 Praise the **L**; for the LORD is good:	3050	
135: 3 Praise the LORD; for **the L** is good:	3068	
135: 4 **the L** hath chosen Jacob unto himself,	3050	
135: 5 I know that **the L** is great, and that our	3068	
135: 6 Whatsoever **the L** pleased, that did he in	3068	
135:13 Thy name, O **L**, endureth for ever;	3068	
135:13 and thy memorial, O **L**, throughout all	3068	
135:14 For **the L** will judge his people, and he	3068	
135:19 Bless **the L**, O house of Israel: bless	3068	
135:19 of Israel: bless **the L**, O house of Aaron:	3068	
135:20 Bless **the L**, O house of Levi: ye that fear	3068	
135:20 ye that fear **the L**, bless the LORD.	3068	
135:20 ye that fear the LORD, bless **the L**.	3068	

Ps 135:21 Blessed be **the L** out of Zion,	3068	
135:21 dwelleth at Jerusalem. Praise ye **the L**.	3050	
136: 1 O give thanks unto **the L**; for he is good:	3068	
137: 7 Remember, O **L**, the children of Edom in	3068	
138: 4 O **L**, when they hear the words of thy	3068	
138: 5 Yea, they shall sing in the ways of **the L**:	3068	
138: 5 the LORD: for great is the glory of **the L**.	3068	
138: 6 Though **the L** be high, yet hath he respect	3068	
138: 8 **The L** will perfect that which concerneth	3068	
138: 8 thy mercy, O **L**, endureth for ever:	3068	
139: 1 O **L**, thou hast searched me,	3068	
139: 4 but lo, O **L**, thou knowest it altogether.	3068	
139:21 Do not I hate them, O **L**, that hate thee?	3068	
140: 1 Deliver me, O **L**, from the evil man:	3068	
140: 4 Keep me, O **L**, from the hands of	3068	
140: 6 I said unto **the L**, Thou art my God:	3068	
140: 6 hear the voice of my supplications, O **L**.	3068	
140: 8 Grant not, O **L**, the desires of the wicked:	3068	
140:12 I know that **the L** will maintain the cause	3068	
141: 1 **L**, I cry unto thee: make haste unto me;	3068	
141: 3 Set a watch, O **L**, before my mouth;	3068	
142: 1 I cried unto **the L** with my voice; with my	3068	
142: 1 with my voice unto **the L** did I make my	3068	
142: 5 cried unto thee, O **L**: I said, Thou art my	3068	
143: 1 Hear my prayer, O **L**, give ear to my	3068	
143: 7 Hear me speedily, O **L**: my spirit faileth:	3068	
143: 9 Deliver me, O **L**, from mine enemies:	3068	
143:11 Quicken me, O **L**, for thy name's sake:	3068	
144: 1 Blessed be **the L** my strength,	3068	
144: 3 **L**, what is man, that thou takest	3068	
144: 5 Bow thy heavens, O **L**, and come down:	3068	
144:15 happy is that people, whose God is **the L**.	3068	
145: 3 Great is **the L**, and greatly to be praised;	3068	
145: 8 **The L** is gracious, and full of compassion;	3068	
145: 9 **The L** is good to all: and his tender	3068	
145:10 All thy works shall praise thee, O **L**;	3068	
145:14 **The L** upholdeth all that fall, and raiseth	3068	
145:17 **The L** is righteous in all his ways,	3068	
145:18 **The L** is nigh unto all them that call upon	3068	
145:20 **The L** preserveth all them that love him:	3068	
145:21 My mouth shall speak the praise of **the L**:	3068	
146: 1 Praise ye **the L**. Praise the LORD, O my	3050	
146: 1 ye the LORD. Praise **the L**, O my soul.	3068	
146: 2 While I live will I praise **the L**: I will sing	3068	
146: 5 his help, whose hope is in **the L** his God:	3068	
146: 7 the hungry. **The L** looseth the prisoners:	3068	
146: 8 **The L** openeth the eyes of the blind:	3068	
146: 8 **the L** raiseth them that are bowed down:	3068	
146: 8 bowed down: **the L** loveth the righteous:	3068	
146: 9 **The L** preserveth the strangers; he	3068	
146:10 **The L** shall reign for ever, even thy God,	3068	
146:10 unto all generations. Praise ye **the L**.	3050	
147: 1 Praise ye **the L**: for it is good to sing	3068	
147: 2 **The L** doth build up Jerusalem:	3068	
147: 6 **The L** lifteth up the meek: he casteth	3068	
147: 7 Sing unto **the L** with thanksgiving;	3068	
147:11 **The L** taketh pleasure in them that fear	3068	
147:12 Praise **the L**, O Jerusalem; praise thy God,	3068	
147:20 have not known them. Praise ye **the L**.	3050	
148: 1 Praise ye **the L**. Praise ye the LORD from	3050	
148: 1 Praise ye **the L** from the heavens:	3068	
148: 5 Let them praise the name of **the L**: for he	3068	
148: 7 Praise **the L** from the earth, ye dragons,	3068	
148:13 Let them praise the name of **the L**: for his	3068	
148:14 a people near unto him. Praise ye **the L**.	3050	
149: 1 Praise ye **the L**. Sing unto the LORD a	3050	
149: 1 Sing unto **the L** a new song, and his	3068	
149: 4 For **the L** taketh pleasure in his people:	3068	
149: 9 have all his saints. Praise ye **the L**.	3050	
150: 1 Praise ye **the L**. Praise God in his	3050	
150: 6 every thing that hath breath praise **the L**.	3050	
150: 6 breath praise the LORD. Praise ye **the L**.	3050	
Pr 1: 7 The fear of **the L** is the beginning of	3068	
1:29 and did not choose the fear of **the L**:	3068	
2: 5 shalt thou understand the fear of **the L**,	3068	
2: 6 **the L** giveth wisdom: out of his mouth	3068	
3: 5 Trust in **the L** with all thine heart;	3068	
3: 7 eyes: fear **the L**, and depart from evil.	3068	
3: 9 Honour **the L** with thy substance,	3068	
3:11 despise not the chastening of **the L**;	3068	
3:12 For whom **the L** loveth he correcteth;	3068	
3:19 **The L** by wisdom hath founded the earth;	3068	
3:26 For **the L** shall be thy confidence,	3068	
3:32 For the froward is abomination to **the L**:	3068	
3:33 The curse of **the L** is in the house of	3068	
5:21 ways of man are before the eyes of **the L**,	3068	
6:16 These six things doth **the L** hate: yea,	3068	
8:13 The fear of **the L** is to hate evil: pride,	3068	
8:22 **The L** possessed me in the beginning of	3068	
8:35 and shall obtain favour of **the L**.	3068	
9:10 The fear of **the L** is the beginning of	3068	
10: 3 **The L** will not suffer the soul of	3068	
10:22 The blessing of **the L**, it maketh rich,	3068	
10:27 The fear of **the L** prolongeth days:	3068	
10:29 way of **the L** is strength to the upright:	3068	
11: 1 A false balance is abomination to **the L**:	3068	
11:20 heart are abomination unto **the L**:	3068	
12: 2 A good man obtaineth favour of **the L**:	3068	
12:22 Lying lips are abomination to **the L**:	3068	
14: 2 walketh in his uprightness feareth **the L**:	3068	
14:26 In the fear of **the L** is strong confidence:	3068	
14:27 The fear of **the L** is a fountain of life,	3068	
15: 3 The eyes of **the L** are in every place,	3068	
15: 8 of the wicked is an abomination to **the L**:	3068	
15: 9 the wicked is an abomination unto **the L**:	3068	

Pr 15:11 Hell and destruction *are* before **the L**:	3068	
15:16 Better *is* little with the fear of **the L** than	3068	
15:25 **The L** will destroy the house of the proud	3068	
15:26 The wicked *are* an abomination to **the L**:	3068	
15:29 **The L** *is* far from the wicked:	3068	
15:33 The fear of **the L** *is* the instruction of	3068	
16: 1 the answer of the tongue, *is* from **the L**.	3068	
16: 2 own eyes; but **the L** weigheth the spirits.	3068	
16: 3 Commit thy works unto **the L**,	3068	
16: 4 **The L** hath made all *things* for himself:	3068	
16: 5 proud in heart *is* an abomination to **the L**:	3068	
16: 6 by the fear of **the L** *men* depart from evil.	3068	
16: 7 When a man's ways please **the L**,	3068	
16: 9 his way: but **the L** directeth his steps.	3068	
16:20 and whoso trusteth in **the L**, happy *is* he.	3068	
16:33 the whole disposing thereof *is* of **the L**.	3068	
17: 3 for gold: but **the L** trieth the hearts.	3068	
17:15 even they both *are* abomination to **the L**.	3068	
18:10 The name of **the L** *is* a strong tower:	3068	
18:22 thing, and obtaineth favour of **the L**.	3068	
19: 3 and his heart fretteth against **the L**.	3068	
19:14 and a prudent wife *is* from **the L**.	3068	
19:17 pity upon the poor lendeth unto **the L**;	3068	
19:21 nevertheless the counsel of **the L**, that	3068	
19:23 The fear of **the L** *tendeth* to life:	3068	
20:10 of them *are* alike abomination to **the L**.	3068	
20:12 **the L** hath made even both of them.	3068	
20:22 *but* wait on **the L**, and he shall save thee.	3068	
20:23 weights *are* an abomination unto **the L**;	3068	
20:24 Man's goings *are* of **the L**; how can a	3068	
20:27 The spirit of man *is* the candle of **the L**,	3068	
21: 1 The king's heart *is* in the hand of **the L**,	3068	
21: 2 eyes: but **the L** pondereth the hearts.	3068	
21: 3 judgment *is* more acceptable to **the L**	3068	
21:30 understanding nor counsel against **the L**.	3068	
21:31 the day of battle: but safety *is* of **the L**.	3068	
22: 2 **the L** *is* the Maker of them all.	3068	
22: 4 *and* the fear of **the L** *are* riches,	3068	
22:12 The eyes of **the L** preserve knowledge,	3068	
22:14 he that is abhorred of **the L** shall fall	3068	
22:19 That thy trust may be in **the L**, I have	3068	
22:23 For **the L** will plead their cause,	3068	
23:17 *thou* in the fear of **the L** all the day long.	3068	
24:18 Lest **the L** see *it*, and it displease him,	3068	
24:21 My son, fear thou **the L** and the king:	3068	
25:22 his head, and **the L** shall reward thee.	3068	
28: 5 that seek **the L** understand all *things*.	3068	
28:25 he that putteth his trust in **the L** shall be	3068	
29:13 **the L** lighteneth both their eyes.	3068	
29:25 whoso putteth his trust in **the L** shall be	3068	
29:26 man's judgment *cometh* from **the L**.	3068	
30: 9 and deny *thee*, and say, Who *is* **the L**?	3068	
31:30 *but* a woman that feareth **the L**, she shall	3068	
Isa 1: 2 **the L** hath spoken, I have nourished	3068	
1: 4 they have forsaken **the L**, they have	3068	
1: 9 Except **the L** of hosts had left unto us a	3068	
1:10 Hear the word of **the L**, ye rulers of	3068	
1:11 saith **the L**: I am full *of* the burnt offerings	3068	
1:18 and let us reason together, saith **the L**:	3068	
1:20 for the mouth of **the L** hath spoken *it*.	3068	
1:24 Therefore saith the Lord, **the L** shall be	3068	
1:28 that forsake **the L** shall be consumed.	3068	
2: 3 let us go up to the mountain of **the L**,	3068	
2: 3 and the word of **the L** from Jerusalem.	3068	
2: 5 and let us walk in the light of **the L**.	3068	
2:10 for fear of **the L**, and for the glory of his	3068	
2:11 **the L** alone shall be exalted in that day.	3068	
2:12 the day of **the L** of hosts *shall be* upon	3068	
2:17 **the L** alone shall be exalted in that day.	3068	
2:19 for fear of **the L**, and for the glory of his	3068	
2:21 for fear of **the L**, and for the glory of his	3068	
3: 1 For behold, the Lord, **the L** of hosts,	3068	
3: 8 and their doings *are* against **the L**,	3068	
3:13 **The L** standeth *up* to plead, and standeth	3068	
3:14 **The L** will enter into judgment with	3068	
3:16 Moreover **the L** saith, Because	3068	
3:17 and **the L** will discover their secret parts.	3068	
4: 2 In that day shall the branch of **the L** be	3068	
4: 5 **The L** will create upon every dwelling	3068	
5: 7 For the vineyard of **the L** of hosts *is*	3068	
5: 9 In mine ears *said* **the L** of hosts, Of a	3068	
5:12 they regard not the work of **the L**,	3068	
5:16 **the L** of hosts shall be exalted in	3068	
5:24 they have cast away the law of **the L** of	3068	
5:25 Therefore is the anger of **the L** kindled	3068	
6: 3 said, Holy, holy, holy, *is* **the L** of hosts:	3068	
6: 5 eyes have seen the King, **the L** of hosts.	3068	
6:12 **the L** have removed men far away,	3068	
7: 3 said **the L** unto Isaiah, Go forth now to	3068	
7:10 Moreover **the L** spake again unto Ahaz,	3068	
7:11 Ask thee a sign of **the L** thy God; ask it	3068	
7:12 I will not ask, neither will I tempt **the L**.	3068	
7:17 **The L** shall bring upon thee, and upon	3068	
7:18 *that* **the L** shall hiss for the fly that *is* in	3068	
8: 1 Moreover **the L** said unto me, Take thee	3068	
8: 3 said **the L** to me, Call his name	3068	
8: 5 **The L** spake also unto me again, saying,	3068	
8:11 For **the L** spake thus to me with a strong	3068	
8:13 Sanctify **the L** of hosts himself; and *let*	3068	
8:17 I will wait upon **the L**, that hideth his face	3068	
8:18 the children whom **the L** hath given me	3068	
8:18 for wonders in Israel from **the L** of hosts,	3068	
9: 7 The zeal of **the L** of hosts will perform	3068	
9:11 **the L** shall set up the adversaries	3068	
9:13 neither do they seek **the L** of hosts.	3068	

Isa 9:14 Therefore **the L** will cut off from Israel	3068	
9:19 Through the wrath of **the L** of hosts is	3068	
10:20 shall stay upon **the L**, the Holy One of	3068	
10:26 **the L** of hosts shall stir up a scourge for	3068	
10:33 the Lord, **the L** of hosts, shall lop	3068	
11: 2 the Spirit of **the L** shall rest upon him,	3068	
11: 2 of knowledge and of the fear of **the L**;	3068	
11: 3 quick understanding in the fear of **the L**:	3068	
11: 9 shall be full *of* the knowledge of **the L**,	3068	
11:15 **the L** shall utterly destroy the tongue of	3068	
12: 1 day thou shalt say, O **L**, I will praise thee:	3068	
12: 2 for **the L** JEHOVAH *is* my strength and	3050	
12: 4 ye say, Praise **the L**, call upon his name,	3068	
12: 5 Sing unto **the L**; for he hath done	3068	
13: 4 **the L** of hosts mustereth the host of	3068	
13: 5 *even* **the L**, and the weapons of his	3068	
13: 6 Howl ye; for the day of **the L** *is* at hand;	3068	
13: 9 Behold, the day of **the L** cometh,	3068	
13:13 in the wrath of **the L** of hosts, and in	3068	
14: 1 For **the L** will have mercy on Jacob,	3068	
14: 2 them in the land of **the L** for servants	3068	
14: 3 shall come to pass in the day that **the L**	3068	
14: 5 **The L** hath broken the staff of the wicked,	3068	
14:22 saith **the L** of hosts, and cut off from	3068	
14:22 and son, and nephew, saith **the L**.	3068	
14:23 besom of destruction, saith **the L** of hosts.	3068	
14:24 **The L** of hosts hath sworn, saying,	3068	
14:27 For **the L** of hosts hath purposed,	3068	
14:32 That **the L** hath founded Zion, and the	3068	
16:13 This *is* the word that **the L** hath spoken	3068	
16:14 now **the L** hath spoken, saying,	3068	
17: 3 the children of Israel, saith **the L** of hosts.	3068	
17: 6 thereof, saith **the L** God of Israel.	3068	
18: 4 For so **the L** said unto me, I will take my	3068	
18: 7 unto **the L** of hosts *of* a people scattered	3068	
18: 7 the place of the name of **the L** of hosts,	3068	
19: 1 **the L** rideth upon a swift cloud,	3068	
19: 4 over them, saith the Lord, **the L** of hosts.	3068	
19:12 let them know what **the L** of hosts hath	3068	
19:14 **The L** hath mingled a perverse spirit in	3068	
19:16 of the shaking of the hand of **the L** of	3068	
19:17 because of the counsel of **the L** of hosts,	3068	
19:18 of Canaan, and swear to **the L** of hosts:	3068	
19:19 In that day shall there be an altar to **the L**	3068	
19:19 and a pillar at the border thereof to **the L**.	3068	
19:20 a witness unto **the L** of hosts in the land	3068	
19:20 for they shall cry unto **the L** because of	3068	
19:21 **the L** shall be known to Egypt,	3068	
19:21 Egyptians shall know **the L** in that day,	3068	
19:21 they shall vow a vow unto **the L**,	3068	
19:22 **the L** shall smite Egypt: *he* shall smite	3068	
19:22 and they shall return *even* to **the L**,	3068	
19:25 Whom **the L** of hosts shall bless, saying,	3068	
20: 2 At the same time spake **the L** by Isaiah	3068	
20: 3 the **L** said, Like as my servant Isaiah hath	3068	
21:10 that which I have heard of **the L** of hosts,	3068	
21:17 for **the L** God of Israel hath spoken *it*.	3068	
22:14 it was revealed in mine ears *by* **the L** of	3068	
22:17 **the L** will carry thee away with a mighty	3068	
22:25 In that day, saith **the L** of hosts, shall	3068	
22:25 it shall be cut off: for **the L** hath spoken	3068	
23: 9 **The L** of hosts hath purposed it, to stain	3068	
23:11 **the L** hath given a commandment against	3068	
23:17 **The L** will visit Tyre, and she shall turn	3068	
23:18 and her hire shall be holiness to **the L**:	3068	
23:18 shall be for them that dwell before **the L**,	3068	
24: 1 **the L** maketh the earth empty,	3068	
24: 3 for **the L** hath spoken this word.	3068	
24:14 they shall sing, for the majesty of **the L**,	3068	
24:15 Wherefore glorify ye **the L** in the fires,	3068	
24:15 *even* the name of **the L** God of Israel in	3068	
24:21 **the L** shall punish the host of the high	3068	
24:23 when **the L** of hosts shall reign in mount	3068	
25: 1 O **L**, thou *art* my God; I will exalt thee,	3068	
25: 6 in this mountain shall **the L** of hosts make	3068	
25: 8 off all the earth: for **the L** hath spoken *it*.	3068	
25: 9 this *is* **the L**; we have waited for him,	3068	
25:10 in this mountain shall the hand of **the L**	3068	
26: 4 Trust ye in **the L** for ever: for in	3068	
26: 4 for in **the L** JEHOVAH *is* everlasting	3050	
26: 8 O **L**, have we waited for thee;	3068	
26:10 and will not behold the majesty of **the L**.	3068	
26:11 **L**, *when* thy hand is lifted up, they will	3068	
26:12 **L**, thou wilt ordain peace for us: for thou	3068	
26:13 **L** our God, *other* lords besides thee have	3068	
26:15 O **L**, thou hast increased the nation:	3068	
26:16 **L**, in trouble have they visited thee,	3068	
26:17 so have we been in thy sight, O **L**.	3068	
26:21 **the L** cometh out of his place to punish	3068	
27: 1 In that day **the L** with his sore and great	3068	
27: 3 I **the L** do keep it; I will water it every	3068	
27:12 **the L** shall beat off from the channel of	3068	
27:13 shall worship **the L** in the holy mount at	3068	
28: 2 **the L** hath a mighty and strong one,	3068	
28: 5 In that day shall **the L** of hosts be for a	3068	
28:13 the word of **the L** was unto them precept	3068	
28:14 Wherefore hear the word of **the L**,	3068	
28:21 For **the L** shall rise up as *in* mount	3068	
28:29 also cometh forth from **the L** of hosts,	3068	
29: 6 Thou shalt be visited of **the L** of hosts	3068	
29:10 For **the L** hath poured out upon you	3068	
29:15 deep to hide *their* counsel from **the L**,	3068	
29:19 also shall increase *their* joy in **the L**,	3068	
29:22 thus saith **the L**, who redeemed	3068	
30: 1 saith **the L**, that take counsel, but not of	3068	

Isa 30: 9 *that* will not hear the law of **the L**:	3068	
30:18 therefore will **the L** wait, that *he* may be	3068	
30:18 for **the L** *is* a God of judgment: blessed	3068	
30:26 the day that **the L** bindeth up the breach	3068	
30:27 the name of **the L** cometh from far,	3068	
30:29 pipe to come into the mountain of **the L**,	3068	
30:30 **the L** shall cause his glorious voice to be	3068	
30:31 For through the voice of **the L** shall	3068	
30:32 which **the L** shall lay upon him, *it* shall	3068	
30:33 the breath of **the L**, like a stream of	3068	
31: 1 Holy One of Israel, neither seek **the L**.	3068	
31: 3 When **the L** shall stretch out his hand,	3068	
31: 4 For thus hath **the L** spoken unto me,	3068	
31: 4 shall **the L** of hosts come down to fight	3068	
31: 5 so will **the L** of hosts defend Jerusalem;	3068	
31: 9 saith **the L**, whose fire *is* in Zion, and his	3068	
32: 6 and to utter error against **the L**,	3068	
33: 2 O **L**, be gracious unto us; we have waited	3068	
33: 5 **The L** *is* exalted; for he dwelleth on high:	3068	
33: 6 the fear of **the L** *is* his treasure.	3068	
33:10 Now will I rise, saith **the L**; now will I be	3068	
33:21 the glorious **L** *will be* unto us a place	3068	
33:22 For **the L** *is* our judge, the LORD *is* our	3068	
33:22 **the L** *is* our lawgiver, the LORD *is* our	3068	
33:22 LORD *is* our lawgiver, **the L** *is* our king;	3068	
34: 2 For the indignation of **the L** *is* upon all	3068	
34: 6 The sword of **the L** is filled *with* blood,	3068	
34: 6 for **the L** hath a sacrifice in Bozrah,	3068	
34:16 Seek ye out of the book of **the L**, and read	3068	
35: 2 they shall see the glory of **the L**,	3068	
35:10 the ransomed of **the L** shall return,	3068	
36: 7 say to me, We trust in **the L** our God:	3068	
36:10 am I now come up without **the L** against	3068	
36:10 **the L** said unto me, Go up against this	3068	
36:15 let Hezekiah make you trust in **the L**,	3068	
36:15 **The L** will surely deliver us:	3068	
36:18 saying, **The L** will deliver us.	3068	
36:20 that **the L** should deliver Jerusalem out	3068	
37: 1 and went *into* the house of **the L**.	3068	
37: 4 It may be **the L** thy God will hear	3068	
37: 4 will reprove the words which **the L** thy	3068	
37: 6 say unto your master, Thus saith **the L**,	3068	
37:14 went up *unto* the house of **the L**,	3068	
37:14 of the LORD, and spread it before **the L**.	3068	
37:15 And Hezekiah prayed unto **the L**, saying,	3068	
37:16 O **L** of hosts, God of Israel, that dwellest	3068	
37:17 Incline thine ear, O **L**, and hear; open	3068	
37:17 and hear; open thine eyes, O **L**, and see:	3068	
37:18 a truth, **L**, the kings of Assyria have laid	3068	
37:20 Now therefore, O **L** our God, save us from	3068	
37:20 the earth may know that thou *art* **the L**,	3068	
37:21 Thus saith **the L** God of Israel,	3068	
37:22 This *is* the word which **the L** hath spoken	3068	
37:32 the zeal of **the L** of hosts shall do this.	3068	
37:33 Therefore thus saith **the L** concerning	3068	
37:34 shall not come into this city, saith **the L**.	3068	
37:36 the angel of **the L** went forth, and smote	3068	
38: 1 said unto him, Thus saith **the L**, Set thine	3068	
38: 2 toward the wall, and prayed unto **the L**,	3068	
38: 3 Remember now, O **L**, I beseech thee,	3068	
38: 4 came the word of **the L** to Isaiah, saying,	3068	
38: 5 and say to Hezekiah, Thus saith **the L**,	3068	
38: 7 this *shall be* a sign unto thee from **the L**,	3068	
38: 7 that **the L** will do this thing that he hath	3068	
38:11 I said, I shall not see **the L**, *even*	3050	
38:11 *even* **the L**, in the land of the living:	3050	
38:14 O **L**, I am oppressed; undertake for me.	3068	
38:20 **The L** *was ready* to save me: therefore	3068	
38:20 the days of our life in the house of **the L**.	3068	
38:22 that I shall go up *to* the house of **the L**?	3068	
39: 5 Hear the word of **the L** of hosts:	3068	
39: 6 nothing shall be left, saith **the L**.	3068	
39: 8 Good *is* the word of **the L** which thou	3068	
40: 3 Prepare ye the way of **the L**,	3068	
40: 5 the glory of **the L** shall be revealed,	3068	
40: 5 for the mouth of **the L** hath spoken *it*.	3068	
40: 7 because the spirit of **the L** bloweth upon	3068	
40:13 Who hath directed the spirit of **the L**,	3068	
40:27 My way is hid from **the L**,	3068	
40:28 heard, *that* the everlasting God, **the L**,	3068	
40:31 they that wait upon **the L** shall renew	3068	
41: 4 I **the L**, the first, and with the last; I *am*	3068	
41:13 For I **the L** thy God will hold thy right	3068	
41:14 help thee, saith **the L**, and thy redeemer,	3068	
41:16 thou shalt rejoice in **the L**, *and* shalt glory	3068	
41:17 faileth for thirst, I **the L** will hear them,	3068	
41:20 that the hand of **the L** hath done this,	3068	
41:21 Produce your cause, saith **the L**; bring	3068	
42: 5 Thus saith God **the L**, he that created	3068	
42: 6 I **the L** have called thee in righteousness,	3068	
42: 8 I *am* **the L**: that *is* my name: and my	3068	
42:10 Sing unto **the L** a new song, *and* his	3068	
42:12 Let them give glory to **the L**,	3068	
42:13 **The L** shall go forth as a mighty *man*, he	3068	
42:21 **The L** is well pleased for his	3068	
42:24 did not **the L**, he against whom we have	3068	
43: 1 now thus saith **the L** that created thee,	3068	
43: 3 For I *am* **the L** thy God, the Holy One of	3068	
43:10 saith **the L**, and my servant whom I have	3068	
43:11 I, *even* I, *am* **the L**; and beside me *there*	3068	
43:12 my witnesses, saith **the L**, that I *am* God.	3068	
43:14 Thus saith **the L**, your redeemer, the Holy	3068	
43:15 I *am* **the L**, your Holy One, the creator of	3068	
43:16 Thus saith **the L**, which maketh a way in	3068	
44: 2 Thus saith **the L** that made thee,	3068	

L

Isa 44: 5 shall subscribe *with* his hand unto **the L,** 3068
44: 6 Thus saith **the L** the King of Israel, 3068
44: 6 of Israel, and his redeemer **the L** of hosts; 3068
44:23 **the L** hath done *it*: shout, ye lower parts 3068
44:23 for **the L** hath redeemed Jacob, 3068
44:24 Thus saith **the L,** thy redeemer, and he 3068
44:24 I *am* **the L** that maketh all *things; that* 3068
45: 1 Thus saith **the L** to his anointed, to Cyrus, 3068
45: 3 **the L,** which call *thee* by thy name, 3068
45: 5 I *am* **the L,** and *there is* none else, *there* 3068
45: 6 I *am* **the L,** and *there is* none else. 3068
45: 7 and create evil: I **the L** do all these *things.* 3068
45: 8 spring up together; I **the L** have created it. 3068
45:11 Thus saith **the L,** the Holy One of Israel, 3068
45:13 for price nor reward, saith **the L** of hosts. 3068
45:14 Thus saith **the L,** The labour of Egypt, 3068
45:17 *But* Israel shall be saved in **the L** *with* an 3068
45:18 For thus saith **the L** that created 3068
45:18 I *am* **the L;** and *there is* none else. 3068
45:19 I **the L** speak righteousness, I declare 3068
45:21 not I **the L?** and *there is* no God else 3068
45:24 in **the L** have I righteousness and 3068
45:25 In **the L** shall all the seed of Israel be 3068
47: 4 our redeemer, **the L** of hosts *is* his name, 3068
48: 1 which swear by the name of **the L,** 3068
48: 2 God of Israel; **The L** of hosts *is* his name. 3068
48:14 these *things;* **The L** hath loved him: 3068
48:17 Thus saith **the L,** thy redeemer, the Holy 3068
48:17 I *am* **the L** thy God which teacheth thee 3068
48:20 **The L** hath redeemed his servant Jacob. 3068
48:22 *is* no peace, saith **the L,** unto the wicked. 3068
49: 1 **The L** hath called me from the womb; 3068
49: 4 *yet* surely my judgment *is* with **the L,** 3068
49: 5 saith **the L** that formed me from the 3068
49: 5 yet shall I be glorious in the eyes of **the L,** 3068
49: 7 Thus saith **the L,** the redeemer of Israel, 3068
49: 7 because of **the L** that *is* faithful, 3068
49: 8 Thus saith **the L,** In an acceptable time 3068
49:13 for **the L** hath comforted his people, 3068
49:14 **The L** hath forsaken me, and my Lord 3068
49:18 *As* I live, saith **the L,** thou shalt surely 3068
49:23 and thou shalt know that I *am* **the L:** 3068
49:25 thus saith **the L,** Even the captives of 3068
49:26 all flesh shall know that I **the L** *am* thy 3068
50: 1 Thus saith **the L,** Where *is* the bill of your 3068
50:10 Who *is* among you that feareth **the L,** 3068
50:10 let him trust in the name of **the L,** 3068
51: 1 after righteousness, ye that seek **the L:** 3068
51: 3 For **the L** shall comfort Zion: he will 3068
51: 3 and her desert like the garden of **the L;** 3068
51: 9 awake, put on strength, O arm of **the L;** 3068
51:11 Therefore the redeemed of **the L** shall 3068
51:13 forgettest **the L** thy Maker, that hath 3068
51:15 I *am* **the L** thy God, that divided the sea, 3068
51:15 waves roared: **The L** of hosts *is* his name. 3068
51:17 which hast drunk at the hand of **the L** 3068
51:20 *are* full *of* the fury of **the L,** the rebuke 3068
51:22 Thus saith thy Lord **the L,** and thy God 3068
52: 3 For thus saith **the L,** Ye have sold 3068
52: 5 what have I here, saith **the L,** 3068
52: 5 them make *them* to howl, saith **the L;** 3068
52: 8 to eye, when **the L** shall bring again Zion. 3068
52: 9 for **the L** hath comforted his people, 3068
52:10 **The L** hath made bare his holy arm in 3068
52:11 ye clean, that bear the vessels of **the L.** 3068
52:12 for **the L** will go before you; and the God 3068
53: 1 to whom is the arm of **the L** revealed? 3068
53: 6 **the L** hath laid on him the iniquity of us 3068
53:10 Yet it pleased **the L** to bruise him; he hath 3068
53:10 the pleasure of **the L** shall prosper in his 3068
54: 1 children of the married wife, saith **the L.** 3068
54: 5 **the L** of hosts *is* his name; 3068
54: 6 For **the L** hath called thee as a woman 3068
54: 8 mercy on thee, saith **the L** thy redeemer. 3068
54:10 saith **the L** that hath mercy on thee. 3068
54:13 all thy children *shall* be taught of **the L;** 3068
54:17 *is* the heritage of the servants of **the L,** 3068
54:17 their righteousness *is* of me, saith **the L.** 3068
55: 5 run unto thee because of **the L** thy God, 3068
55: 6 Seek ye **the L** while he may be found, 3068
55: 7 let him return unto **the L,** and he will 3068
55: 8 *are* your ways my ways, saith **the L.** 3068
55:13 it shall be to **the L** for a name, for an 3068
56: 1 Thus saith **the L,** Keep ye judgment, 3068
56: 3 that hath joined himself to **the L,** speak, 3068
56: 3 **The L** hath utterly separated me from his 3068
56: 4 For thus saith **the L** unto the eunuchs 3068
56: 6 join themselves to **the L,** to serve him, 3068
56: 6 serve him, and to love the name of **the L,** 3068
57:19 off, and to *him that is* near, saith **the L;** 3068
57:19 a fast, and an acceptable day to **the L?** 3068
58: 8 the glory of **the L** shall be thy rereward. 3068
58: 9 shalt thou call, and **the L** shall answer; 3068
58:11 **the L** shall guide thee continually, 3068
58:13 a delight, the holy of **the L,** honourable; 3068
58:14 shalt thou delight thyself in **the L;** 3068
58:14 for the mouth of **the L** hath spoken it. 3068
59: 1 In transgressing and lying against **the L,** 3068
59:15 **the L** saw *it,* and it displeased him that 3068
59:19 So shall they fear the name of **the L** from 3068
59:19 the spirit of **the L** shall lift up a standard 3068
59:20 from transgression in Jacob, saith **the L.** 3068
59:21 *is* my covenant with them, saith **the L;** 3068
59:21 saith **the L,** from henceforth and for ever. 3068
60: 1 and the glory of **the L** is risen upon thee. 3068

Isa 60: 2 **the L** shall arise upon thee, and his glory 3068
60: 6 they shall shew forth the praises of **the L.** 3068
60: 9 unto the name of **the L** thy God, and to 3068
60:14 they shall call thee, The city of **the L,** 3068
60:16 shalt know that I **the L** *am* thy Saviour 3068
60:19 shall be unto thee an everlasting light, 3068
60:20 for **the L** shall be thine everlasting light, 3068
60:22 I **the L** will hasten it in his time. 3068
61: 1 **the L** hath anointed me to preach good 3068
61: 2 To proclaim the acceptable year of **the L,** 3068
61: 3 the planting of **the L,** that *he* might be 3068
61: 6 ye shall be named the Priests of **the L:** 3068
61: 8 For I **the L** love judgment, I hate robbery 3068
61: 9 that they *are* the seed *which* **the L** hath 3068
61:10 I will greatly rejoice in **the L,** my soul 3068
62: 2 which the mouth of **the L** shall name. 3068
62: 3 be a crown of glory in the hand of **the L,** 3068
62: 4 for **the L** delighteth in thee, and thy land 3068
62: 6 ye that make mention of **the L,** keep not 3068
62: 8 **The L** hath sworn by his right hand, 3068
62: 9 gathered it shall eat it, and praise **the L;** 3068
62:11 **the L** hath proclaimed unto the end of 3068
62:12 The holy people, The redeemed of **the L:** 3068
63: 7 mention the lovingkindnesses of **the L,** 3068
63: 7 of the Lᴏʀᴅ, *and* the praises of **the L,** 3068
63: 7 according to all that **the L** hath bestowed 3068
63:14 the Spirit of **the L** caused him to rest: 3068
63:16 thou, O L, *art* our father, our redeemer; 3068
63:17 L, why hast thou made us to err from thy 3068
64: 8 now, O L, thou *art* our father; we *are* 3068
64: 9 Be not wroth very sore, O L, 3068
64:12 thou refrain thyself for these *things,* O L? 3068
65: 7 of your fathers together, saith **the L,** 3068
65: 8 Thus saith **the L,** As the new wine is 3068
65:11 ye *are* they that forsake **the L,** that forget 3068
65:23 they *are* the seed of the blessed of **the L,** 3068
65:25 in all my holy mountain, saith **the L.** 3068
66: 1 Thus saith **the L,** The heaven *is* my 3068
66: 2 all those *things* have been, saith **the L:** 3068
66: 5 Hear the word of **the L,** ye that tremble 3068
66: 5 name's sake, said, Let **the L** be glorified: 3068
66: 6 voice of **the L** that rendereth recompence 3068
66: 9 saith **the L:** shall I cause to bring forth, 3068
66:12 thus saith **the L,** Behold, I will extend 3068
66:14 hand of **the L** shall be known towards 3068
66:15 **the L** will come with fire, and with his 3068
66:16 his sword will **the L** plead with all flesh: 3068
66:16 and the slain of **the L** shall be many. 3068
66:17 shall be consumed together, saith **the L.** 3068
66:20 unto **the L** out of all nations upon horses, 3068
66:20 my holy mountain Jerusalem, saith **the L,** 3068
66:20 in a clean vessel *into* the house of **the L.** 3068
66:21 for priests *and* for Levites, saith **the L.** 3068
66:22 saith **the L,** so shall your seed and 3068
66:23 come to worship before me, saith **the L.** 3068

Jer 1: 2 To whom the word of **the L** came in 3068
1: 4 the word of **the L** came unto me, saying, 3068
1: 7 **the L** said unto me, Say not, I *am* a child: 3068
1: 8 *am* with thee to deliver thee, saith **the L.** 3068
1: 9 **the L** put forth his hand, and touched my 3068
1: 9 **the L** said unto me, Behold, I have put my 3068
1:11 the word of **the L** came unto me, saying, 3068
1:12 said **the L** unto me, Thou hast well seen: 3068
1:13 word of **the L** came unto me the second 3068
1:14 **the L** said unto me, Out of the north an 3068
1:15 of the kingdoms of the north, saith **the L;** 3068
1:19 *am* with thee, saith **the L,** to deliver thee. 3068
2: 1 Moreover the word of **the L** came to me, 3068
2: 2 of Jerusalem, saying, Thus saith **the L;** 3068
2: 3 Israel *was* holiness unto **the L,** 3068
2: 3 evil shall come upon them, saith **the L.** 3068
2: 4 Hear ye the word of **the L,** O house of 3068
2: 5 Thus saith **the L,** What iniquity have your 3068
2: 6 Where *is* **the L** that brought us up out of 3068
2: 8 The priests said not, Where *is* **the L?** 3068
2: 9 saith **the L,** and with your children's 3068
2:12 be ye very desolate, saith **the L.** 3068
2:17 in that thou hast forsaken **the L** thy God, 3068
2:19 that thou hast forsaken **the L** thy God, 3068
2:29 have transgressed against me, saith **the L.** 3068
2:31 O generation, see ye the word of **the L.** 3068
2:37 for **the L** hath rejected thy confidences, 3068
3: 1 yet return again to me, saith **the L.** 3068
3: 6 **The L** said also unto me in the days of 3068
3:10 whole heart, but feignedly, saith **the L.** 3068
3:11 **the L** said unto me, The backsliding 3068
3:12 thou backsliding Israel, saith **the L;** 3068
3:12 saith **the L,** *and* I will not keep *anger* for 3068
3:13 that thou hast transgressed against **the L** 3068
3:13 ye have not obeyed my voice, saith **the L.** 3068
3:14 Turn, O backsliding children, saith **the L;** 3068
3:16 in the land, in those days, saith **the L,** 3068
3:16 more, The ark of the covenant of **the L:** 3068
3:17 shall call Jerusalem the throne of **the L;** 3068
3:17 it, to the name of **the L,** to Jerusalem: 3068
3:20 with me, O house of Israel, saith **the L.** 3068
3:21 *and* they have forgotten **the L** their God. 3068
3:22 unto thee; for thou *art* **the L** our God. 3068
3:23 truly in **the L** our God *is* the salvation of 3068
3:25 for we have sinned against **the L** our God, 3068
3:25 have not obeyed the voice of **the L** our 3068
4: 1 O Israel, saith **the L,** return unto me: 3068
4: 2 **The L** liveth, in truth, in judgment, 3068
4: 3 For thus saith **the L** to the men of Judah 3068
4: 4 Circumcise yourselves to **the L,** 3068

Jer 4: 8 for the fierce anger of **the L** is not turned 3068
4: 9 shall come to pass at that day, saith **the L,** 3068
4:17 been rebellious against me, saith **the L.** 3068
4:26 broken down at the presence of **the L,** 3068
4:27 For thus hath **the L** said, The whole land 3068
5: 2 though they say, **The L** liveth; surely they 3068
5: 3 O L, *are* not thine eyes upon the truth? 3068
5: 4 for they know not the way of **the L,** 3068
5: 5 for they have known the way of **the L,** 3068
5: 9 I not visit for these *things?* saith **the L:** 3068
5:11 treacherously against me, saith **the L.** 3068
5:12 They have belied **the L,** and said, *It is* not 3068
5:14 Wherefore thus saith **the L** God of hosts, 3068
5:15 from far, O house of Israel, saith **the L:** 3068
5:18 Nevertheless in those days, saith **the L,** 3068
5:19 Wherefore doth **the L** our God all these 3068
5:22 saith **the L:** will ye not tremble at my 3068
5:24 Let us now fear **the L** our God, that 3068
5:29 I not visit for these *things?* saith **the L:** 3068
6: 6 For thus hath **the L** of hosts said, Hew ye 3068
6: 9 Thus saith **the L** of hosts, They shall 3068
6:10 word of **the L** is unto them a reproach; 3068
6:11 Therefore I am full *of* the fury of **the L;** 3068
6:12 the inhabitants of the land, saith **the L.** 3068
6:15 them they shall be cast down, saith **the L.** 3068
6:16 Thus saith **the L,** Stand ye in the ways, 3068
6:21 Therefore thus saith **the L,** Behold, I will 3068
6:22 Thus saith **the L,** Behold, a people 3068
6:30 because **the L** hath rejected them. 3068
7: 1 word that came to Jeremiah from **the L,** 3068
7: 2 say, Hear the word of **the L,** all *ye* of 3068
7: 2 enter in at these gates to worship **the L.** 3068
7: 3 saith **the L** of hosts, the God of Israel, 3068
7: 4 saying, The temple of **the L,** The temple 3068
7: 4 The temple of **the L,** The temple of 3068
7: 4 the Lᴏʀᴅ, The temple of **the L,** *are* these. 3068
7:11 Behold, even I have seen *it,* saith **the L.** 3068
7:13 saith **the L,** and I spake unto you, rising 3068
7:19 saith **the L:** *do they* not provoke 3068
7:21 saith **the L** of hosts, the God of Israel; 3068
7:28 obeyeth not the voice of **the L** their God, 3068
7:29 for **the L** hath rejected and forsaken 3068
7:30 have done evil in my sight, saith **the L:** 3068
7:32 the days come, saith **the L,** 3068
8: 1 At that time, saith **the L,** they shall bring 3068
8: 3 I have driven them, saith **the L** of hosts. 3068
8: 4 shalt say unto them, Thus saith **the L;** 3068
8: 7 people know not the judgment of **the L.** 3068
8: 8 *are* wise, and the law of **the L** *is* with us? 3068
8: 9 lo, they have rejected the word of **the L;** 3068
8:12 they shall be cast down, saith **the L.** 3068
8:13 I will surely consume them, saith **the L:** 3068
8:14 for **the L** our God hath put us to silence, 3068
8:14 because we have sinned against **the L,** 3068
8:17 and they shall bite you, saith **the L.** 3068
8:19 not **the L** in Zion? *is* not her king in her? 3068
9: 3 evil, and they know me not, saith **the L.** 3068
9: 6 they refuse to know me, saith **the L.** 3068
9: 7 Therefore thus saith **the L** of hosts, 3068
9: 9 visit them for these *things?* saith **the L:** 3068
9:12 *who is he* to whom the mouth of **the L** 3068
9:13 **the L** saith, Because they have forsaken 3068
9:15 thus saith **the L** of hosts, the God 3068
9:17 Thus saith **the L** of hosts, Consider ye, 3068
9:20 Yet hear the word of **the L,** O ye women, 3068
9:22 Thus saith **the L,** Let not the wise *man* 3068
9:23 Thus saith **the L,** Let not the wise *man* 3068
9:24 that I *am* **the L** which exercise 3068
9:24 for in these *things* I delight, saith **the L.** 3068
9:25 Behold, the days come, saith **the L,** that I 3068
10: 1 Hear ye the word which **the L** speaketh 3068
10: 2 Thus saith **the L,** Learn not the way of 3068
10: 6 as *there is* none like unto thee, O L; 3068
10:10 **the L** *is* the true God, he *is* the living God 3068
10:16 inheritance: **The L** of hosts *is* his name. 3068
10:18 For thus saith **the L,** Behold, I will sling 3068
10:21 brutish, and have not sought **the L:** 3068
10:23 L, I know that the way of man *is* not in 3068
10:24 L, correct me, but with judgment; not in 3068
11: 1 word that came to Jeremiah from **the L,** 3068
11: 3 them, Thus saith **the L** God of Israel; 3068
11: 5 Then answered I, and said, So be it, O L. 3068
11: 6 **the L** said unto me, Proclaim all these 3068
11: 9 **the L** said unto me, A conspiracy is found 3068
11:16 **The L** called thy name, A green olive tree 3068
11:17 For **the L** of hosts, that planted thee, 3068
11:18 **the L** hath given me knowledge *of it,* and 3068
11:20 But, O L of hosts, that judgest righteously, 3068
11:21 Therefore thus saith **the L** of the men of 3068
11:21 Prophesy not in the name of **the L,** 3068
11:22 Therefore thus saith **the L** of hosts, 3068
12: 1 Righteous *art* thou, O L, when I plead 3068
12: 3 O L, knowest me: thou hast seen *me,* 3068
12:12 for the sword of **the L** *shall* devour from 3068
12:13 because of the fierce anger of **the L.** 3068
12:14 Thus saith **the L** against all mine evil 3068
12:16 to swear by my name, **The L** liveth; 3068
12:17 and destroy that nation, saith **the L.** 3068
13: 1 Thus saith **the L** unto me, Go and get 3068
13: 2 according to the word of **the L,** and put 3068
13: 3 word of **the L** came unto me the second 3068
13: 5 by Euphrates, as **the L** commanded me. 3068
13: 6 that **the L** said unto me, Arise, go to 3068
13: 8 the word of **the L** came unto me, saying, 3068

Jer 13: 9 Thus saith **the L**, After this manner will I 3068
13:11 the whole house of Judah, saith **the L**; 3068
13:12 Thus saith **the L** God of Israel, Every 3068
13:13 say unto them, Thus saith **the L**, Behold, 3068
13:14 and the sons together, saith **the L**: 3068
13:15 be not proud: for **the L** hath spoken. 3068
13:16 Give glory to **the L** your God, before he 3068
13:25 of thy measures from me, saith **the L**; 3068
14: 1 The word of **the L** that came to Jeremiah 3068
14: 7 O **L**, though our iniquities testify against 3068
14: 9 yet thou, O **L**, *art* in the midst of us, 3068
14:10 Thus saith **the L** unto this people, Thus 3068
14:10 therefore **he L** doth not accept them; 3068
14:11 said **the L** unto me, Pray not for this 3068
14:14 **the L** said unto me, The prophets 3068
14:15 Therefore thus saith **the L** concerning 3068
14:20 O **L**, our wickedness, *and* the iniquity of 3068
14:22 *art* not thou he, O **L** our God? therefore 3068
15: 1 said **the L** unto me, Though Moses and 3068
15: 2 thou shalt tell them, Thus saith **the L**; 3068
15: 3 over them four kinds, saith **the L**: 3068
15: 6 Thou hast forsaken me, saith **the L**, 3068
15: 9 sword before their enemies, saith **the L**. 3068
15:11 **The L** said, Verily it shall be well with 3068
15:15 O **L**, thou knowest: remember me, 3068
15:16 am called by thy name, O **L** God of hosts. 3068
15:19 Therefore thus saith **the L**, If thou return, 3068
15:20 save thee and to deliver thee, saith **the L**. 3068
16: 1 The word of **the L** came also unto me, 3068
16: 3 For thus saith **the L** concerning the sons 3068
16: 5 For thus saith **the L**, Enter not *into* 3068
16: 5 saith **the L**, *even* lovingkindness and 3068
16: 9 For thus saith **the L** of hosts, the God of 3068
16:10 Wherefore hath **the L** pronounced all this 3068
16:10 have committed against **the L** our God? 3068
16:11 saith **the L**, and have walked after other 3068
16:14 the days come, saith **the L**, 3068
16:14 that it shall no more be said, **The L** liveth, 3068
16:15 But, **The L** liveth, that brought up 3068
16:16 saith **the L**, and they shall fish them; 3068
16:19 O **L**, my strength, and my fortress, 3068
16:21 they shall know that my name *is* **The L**. 3068
17: 5 Thus saith **the L**; Cursed *be* the man that 3068
17: 5 and whose heart departeth from **the L**. 3068
17: 7 Blessed *is* the man, that trusteth in **the L**, 3068
17: 7 in the Lord, and whose hope **the L** is. 3068
17:10 I **the L** search the heart, *I* try the reins, 3068
17:13 **L**, the hope of Israel, all that forsake thee 3068
17:13 because they have forsaken **the L**, 3068
17:14 Heal me, O **L**, and I shall be healed; 3068
17:15 say unto me, Where *is* the word of **the L**? 3068
17:19 Thus said **the L** unto me; Go and stand in 3068
17:20 Hear ye the word of **the L**, ye kings of 3068
17:21 saith **the L**; Take heed to yourselves, 3068
17:24 diligently hearken unto me, saith **the L**, 3068
17:26 *of* praise, *unto* the house of **the L**. 3068
18: 1 which came to Jeremiah from **the L**, 3068
18: 5 the word of **the L** came to me, saying, 3068
18: 6 saith **the L**. Behold, as the clay *is* in 3068
18:11 of Jerusalem, saying, Thus saith **the L**; 3068
18:13 Therefore thus saith **the L**; Ask ye now 3068
18:19 **L**, and hearken to the voice of them that 3068
18:23 Yet, **L**, thou knowest all their counsel 3068
19: 1 Thus saith **the L**, Go and get a potter's 3068
19: 3 say, Hear ye the word of **the L**, O kings of 3068
19: 3 saith **the L** of hosts, the God of Israel; 3068
19: 6 the days come, saith **the L**, 3068
19:11 say unto them, Thus saith **the L** of hosts; 3068
19:12 saith **the L**, and to the inhabitants thereof 3068
19:14 whither **the L** had sent him to prophesy; 3068
19:15 saith **the L** of hosts, the God of Israel; 3068
20: 1 also chief governor in the house of **the L**, 3068
20: 2 which *was* by the house of **the L**. 3068
20: 3 **The L** hath not called thy name Pashur, 3068
20: 4 For thus saith **the L**, Behold, I will make 3068
20: 7 O **L**, thou hast deceived me, and I was 3068
20: 8 the word of **the L** was made a reproach 3068
20:11 **the L** *is* with me as a mighty terrible one: 3068
20:12 O **L** of hosts, that triest the righteous, 3068
20:13 Sing unto **the L**, praise ye the Lord: 3068
20:13 Sing unto the Lord, praise ye **the L**: 3068
20:16 let that man be as the cities which **the L** 3068
21: 1 which came unto Jeremiah from **the L**, 3068
21: 2 Inquire, I pray thee, of **the L** for us; 3068
21: 2 be that **the L** will deal with us according 3068
21: 4 Thus saith **the L** God of Israel; Behold, 3068
21: 7 afterward, saith **the L**, I will deliver 3068
21: 8 people thou shalt say, Thus saith **the L**; 3068
21:10 for evil, and not for good, saith **the L**: 3068
21:11 of Judah, *say*, Hear ye the word of **the L**. 3068
21:12 O house of David, thus saith **the L**; 3068
21:13 *and* rock of the plain, saith **the L**; 3068
21:14 to the fruit of your doings, saith **the L**: 3068
22: 1 Thus saith **the L**; Go down *to* the house 3068
22: 2 say, Hear the word of **the L**, O king of 3068
22: 3 Thus saith **the L**; Execute ye judgment 3068
22: 5 words, I swear by myself, saith **the L**, 3068
22: 6 thus saith **the L** unto the king's house 3068
22: 8 Wherefore hath **the L** done thus unto 3068
22: 9 forsaken the covenant of **the L** their God, 3068
22:11 For thus saith **the L** touching Shallum 3068
22:16 *was* not this to know me? saith **the L**. 3068
22:18 Therefore thus saith **the L** concerning 3068
22:24 *As* I live, saith **the L**, though Coniah 3068
22:29 earth, earth, hear the word of **the L**. 3068

Jer 22:30 Thus saith **the L**, Write ye this man 3068
23: 1 the sheep of my pasture! saith **the L**. 3068
23: 2 Therefore thus saith **the L** God of Israel 3068
23: 2 you the evil of your doings, saith **the L**. 3068
23: 4 neither shall they be lacking, saith **the L**. 3068
23: 5 Behold, the days come, saith **the L**, that I 3068
23: 6 THE **L** OUR RIGHTEOUSNESS. 3068
23: 7 the days come, saith **the L**, 3068
23: 7 that they shall no more say, **The L** liveth, 3068
23: 8 But, **The L** liveth, which brought up and 3068
23: 9 of **the L**, and because of the words 3068
23:11 I found their wickedness, saith **the L**. 3068
23:12 the year of their visitation, saith **the L**. 3068
23:15 Therefore thus saith **the L** of hosts 3068
23:16 Thus saith **the L** of hosts, Hearken not 3068
23:16 *and* not out of the mouth of **the L**. 3068
23:17 **The L** hath said, Ye shall have peace; 3068
23:18 who hath stood in the counsel of **the L**, 3068
23:19 a whirlwind of **the L** is gone forth *in* fury, 3068
23:20 The anger of **the L** shall not return, until 3068
23:23 saith **the L**, and not a God afar off? 3068
23:24 saith **the L**. Do not I fill heaven and earth? 3068
23:24 not I fill heaven and earth? saith **the L**. 3068
23:28 *is* the chaff to the wheat? saith **the L**. 3068
23:29 saith **the L**; and like a hammer *that* 3068
23:30 I *am* against the prophets, saith **the L**, 3068
23:31 saith **the L**, that use their tongues, 3068
23:32 saith **the L**, and do tell them, and cause 3068
23:32 not profit this people at all, saith **the L**. 3068
23:33 saying, What *is* the burden of **the L**? 3068
23:33 I will even forsake you, saith **the L**. 3068
23:34 that shall say, The burden of **the L**, 3068
23:35 his brother, What hath **the L** answered? 3068
23:35 and, What hath **the L** spoken? 3068
23:36 the burden of **the L** shall ye mention no 3068
23:36 the living God, of **the L** of hosts our God. 3068
23:37 What hath **the L** answered thee? 3068
23:37 and, What hath **the L** spoken? 3068
23:38 sith ye say, The burden of **the L**; 3068
23:38 of **the Lord**; therefore thus saith **the L**; 3068
23:38 The burden of **the L**, and I have sent 3068
23:38 Ye shall not say, The burden of **the L**; 3068
24: 1 **The L** shewed me, and behold, two 3068
24: 1 figs *were* set before the temple of **the L**, 3068
24: 3 said **the L** unto me, What seest thou, 3068
24: 4 Again the word of **the L** came unto me, 3068
24: 5 Thus saith **the L**, the God of Israel; 3068
24: 7 a heart to know me, that I *am* **the L**: 3068
24: 8 surely thus saith **the L**, So will I give 3068
25: 3 the word of **the L** hath come unto me, 3068
25: 4 **the L** hath sent unto you all his servants 3068
25: 5 dwell in the land that **the L** hath given 3068
25: 7 have not hearkened unto me, saith **the L**; 3068
25: 8 Therefore thus saith **the L** of hosts; 3068
25: 9 saith **the L**, and Nebuchadrezzar the king 3068
25:12 that nation, saith **the L**, for their iniquity, 3068
25:15 thus saith **the L** God of Israel unto me; 3068
25:17 to drink, unto whom **the L** had sent me: 3068
25:27 saith **the L** of hosts, the God of Israel; 3068
25:28 say unto them, Thus saith **the L** of hosts; 3068
25:29 of the earth, saith **the L** of hosts. 3068
25:30 The **L** shall roar from on high, and utter 3068
25:31 for **the L** hath a controversy with 3068
25:31 *that are* wicked to the sword, saith **the L**. 3068
25:32 Thus saith **the L** of hosts, Behold, evil 3068
25:33 the slain of **the L** be at that day from 3068
25:36 *shall be heard:* for **the L** *hath* spoiled 3068
25:37 because of the fierce anger of **the L**. 3068
26: 1 king of Judah came this word from **the L**, 3068
26: 2 Thus saith **the L**; Stand in the court of 3068
26: 4 shalt say unto them, Thus saith **the L**; 3068
26: 7 these words in the house of **the L**. 3068
26: 8 **the L** had commanded *him* to speak unto 3068
26: 9 thou prophesied in the name of **the L**, 3068
26: 9 against Jeremiah in the house of **the L**. 3068
26:10 the king's house *unto* the house of **the L**, 3068
26:12 **The L** sent me to prophesy against this 3068
26:13 and obey the voice of **the L** your God; 3068
26:13 **the L** will repent him of the evil that he 3068
26:15 for of a truth **the L** hath sent me unto you 3068
26:16 to us in the name of **the L** our God. 3068
26:18 Judah, saying, Thus saith **the L** of hosts; 3068
26:19 did he not fear **the L**, and besought 3068
26:19 besought **the L**, and the Lord repented 3068
26:19 **the L** repented him of the evil which he 3068
26:20 man that prophesied in the name of **the L**, 3068
27: 1 came this word unto Jeremiah from **the L**, 3068
27: 2 Thus saith **the L** to me; Make thee bonds 3068
27: 4 saith **the L** of hosts, the God of Israel; 3068
27: 8 saith **the L**, with the sword, and with 3068
27:11 remain still in their own land, saith **the L**; 3068
27:13 as **the L** hath spoken against the nation 3068
27:15 For I have not sent them, saith **the L**, 3068
27:16 to all this people, saying, Thus saith **the L**; 3068
27:18 and if the word of **the L** be with them, 3068
27:18 let them now make intercession to **the L** 3068
27:18 which are left in the house of **the L**, 3068
27:19 For thus saith **the L** of hosts concerning 3068
27:21 Yea, thus saith **the L** of hosts, the God of 3068
27:21 vessels that remain in the house of **the L**, 3068
27:22 until the day that I visit them, saith **the L**; 3068
28: 1 spake unto me in the house of **the L**, 3068
28: 2 Thus speaketh **the L** of hosts, the God of 3068
28: 4 that went into Babylon, saith **the L**: 3068
28: 5 people that stood in the house of **the L**, 3068

Jer 28: 6 the **L** do so: the Lord perform thy words 3068
28: 6 **the L** perform thy words which thou hast 3068
28: 9 be known, that **the L** hath truly sent him. 3068
28:11 of all the people, saying, Thus saith **the L**; 3068
28:12 the word of **the L** came unto Jeremiah 3068
28:13 tell Hananiah, saying, Thus saith **the L**; 3068
28:14 For thus saith **the L** of hosts, the God of 3068
28:15 **The L** hath not sent thee; but thou 3068
28:16 Therefore thus saith **the L**; Behold, I will 3068
28:16 thou hast taught rebellion against **the L**. 3068
29: 4 saith **the L** of hosts, the God of Israel, 3068
29: 7 away captives, and pray unto **the L** for it: 3068
29: 8 For thus saith **the L** of hosts, the God of 3068
29: 9 name: I have not sent them, saith **the L**. 3068
29:10 For thus saith **the L**, That after seventy 3068
29:11 saith **the L**, thoughts of peace, and not of 3068
29:14 And I will be found of you, saith **the L**: 3068
29:14 whither I have driven you, saith **the L**; 3068
29:15 **The L** hath raised us up prophets in 3068
29:16 *Know* that thus saith **the L** of the king 3068
29:17 Thus saith **the L** of hosts; Behold, I will 3068
29:19 not hearkened to my words, saith **the L**, 3068
29:19 but ye would not hear, saith **the L**. 3068
29:20 Hear ye therefore the word of **the L**, all 3068
29:21 saith **the L** of hosts, the God of Israel, 3068
29:22 make thee like Zedekiah and 3068
29:23 I know, and *am* a witness, saith **the L**. 3068
29:25 Thus speaketh **the L** of hosts, the God of 3068
29:26 should be officers in the house of **the L**, 3068
29:30 came the word of **the L** unto Jeremiah, 3068
29:31 Thus saith **the L** concerning Shemaiah 3068
29:32 Therefore thus saith **the L**; Behold, I will 3068
29:32 that I will do for my people, saith **the L**; 3068
29:32 he hath taught rebellion against **the L**. 3068
30: 1 word that came to Jeremiah from **the L**, 3068
30: 2 Thus speaketh **the L** God of Israel, saying, 3068
30: 3 For lo, the days come, saith **the L**, that I 3068
30: 3 of my people Israel and Judah, saith **the L**: 3068
30: 4 these *are* the words that **the L** spake 3068
30: 5 For thus saith **the L**; We have heard a 3068
30: 8 to pass in that day, saith **the L** of hosts, 3068
30: 9 they shall serve **the L** their God, and 3068
30:10 thou not, O my servant Jacob, saith **the L**, 3068
30:11 I *am* with thee, saith **the L**, to save thee: 3068
30:12 For thus saith **the L**, Thy bruise *is* 3068
30:17 will heal thee of thy wounds, saith **the L**; 3068
30:18 Thus saith **the L**; Behold, I *will* bring 3068
30:21 heart to approach unto me? saith **the L**. 3068
30:23 the whirlwind of **the L** goeth forth *with* 3068
30:24 The fierce anger of **the L** shall not return, 3068
31: 1 At the same time, saith **the L**, will I be 3068
31: 2 Thus saith **the L**, The people which were 3068
31: 3 **The L** hath appeared of old unto me, 3068
31: 6 let us go up *to* Zion unto **the L** our God. 3068
31: 7 Sing with gladness for 3068
31: 7 publish ye, praise ye, and say, O **L**, save 3068
31:10 Hear the word of **the L**, O ye nations, 3068
31:11 For **the L** hath redeemed Jacob, 3068
31:12 flow *together* to the goodness of **the L**, 3068
31:14 satisfied with my goodness, saith **the L**. 3068
31:15 Thus saith **the L**; A voice was heard in 3068
31:16 Thus saith **the L**, Refrain thy voice from 3068
31:16 thy work shall be rewarded, saith **the L**; 3068
31:17 there is hope in thine end, saith **the L**, 3068
31:18 be turned; for thou *art* **the L** my God. 3068
31:20 surely have mercy upon him, saith **the L**. 3068
31:22 for **the L** hath created a new *thing* in 3068
31:23 saith **the L** of hosts, the God of Israel; 3068
31:23 **The L** bless thee, O habitation of justice, 3068
31:27 Behold, the days come, saith **the L**, that I 3068
31:28 to build, and to plant, saith **the L**. 3068
31:31 Behold, the days come, saith **the L**, that I 3068
31:32 I was a husband unto them, saith **the L**: 3068
31:33 After those days, saith **the L**, I will put 3068
31:34 man his brother, saying, Know **the L**: 3068
31:34 unto the greatest of them, saith **the L**: 3068
31:35 Thus saith **the L**, which giveth the sun 3068
31:35 thereof roar; **The L** of hosts *is* his name: 3068
31:36 saith **the L**, *then* the seed of Israel also 3068
31:37 Thus saith **the L**; If heaven above can be 3068
31:37 for all that they have done, saith **the L**. 3068
31:38 Behold, the days come, saith **the L**, that 3068
31:38 that the city shall be built to **the L** from 3068
31:40 the east, *shall be* holy unto **the L**; 3068
32: 1 word that came to Jeremiah from **the L** 3068
32: 3 and say, Thus saith **the L**, Behold, 3068
32: 5 shall he be until I visit him, saith **the L**: 3068
32: 6 The word of **the L** came unto me, saying, 3068
32: 8 prison according to the word of **the L**, 3068
32: 8 I knew that this *was* the word of **the L**. 3068
32:14 saith **the L** of hosts, the God of Israel; 3068
32:15 For thus saith **the L** of hosts, the God of 3068
32:16 of Neriah, I prayed unto **the L**, saying, 3068
32:18 Mighty God, **the L** of hosts, *is* his name, 3068
32:26 came the word of **the L** unto Jeremiah, 3068
32:27 Behold, I *am* **the L**, the God of all flesh: 3068
32:28 Therefore thus saith **the L**; Behold, I *will* 3068
32:30 with the work of their hands, saith **the L**. 3068
32:36 now therefore thus saith **the L**, the God 3068
32:42 For thus saith **the L**; Like as I have 3068
32:44 their captivity to return, saith **the L**. 3068
33: 1 Moreover the word of **the L** came unto 3068
33: 2 Thus saith **the L** the maker thereof, 3068
33: 2 **the L** that formed it, to establish it; 3068

L

Jer 33: 2 to establish it; the L *is* his name; | 3068
33: 4 For thus saith the L, the God of Israel, | 3068
33:10 Thus saith the L; Again there shall be | 3068
33:11 them that shall say, Praise the L of hosts: | 3068
33:11 for the L *is* good; for his mercy *endureth* | 3068
33:11 sacrifice of praise *into* the house of the L. | 3068
33:11 of the land as at the first, saith the L. | 3068
33:12 Thus saith the L of hosts, Again in this | 3068
33:13 of him that telleth *them*, saith the L. | 3068
33:14 Behold, the days come, saith the L, that I | 3068
33:16 shall be called, The L our righteousness. | 3068
33:17 For thus saith the L; David shall never | 3068
33:19 the word of the L came unto Jeremiah, | 3068
33:20 Thus saith the L; If you can break my | 3068
33:23 Moreover the word of the L came to | 3068
33:24 two families which the L hath chosen, | 3068
33:25 Thus saith the L; If my covenant *be* not | 3068
34: 1 which came unto Jeremiah from the L, | 3068
34: 2 Thus saith the L, the God of Israel; Go | 3068
34: 2 of Judah, and tell him, Thus saith the L, | 3068
34: 4 Yet hear the word of the L, O Zedekiah | 3068
34: 4 Thus saith the L of thee, Thou shalt not | 3068
34: 5 I have pronounced the word, saith the L. | 3068
34: 8 that came unto Jeremiah from the L, | 3068
34:12 Therefore the word of the L came to | 3068
34:12 the LORD came to Jeremiah from the L, | 3068
34:13 Thus saith the L, the God of Israel; | 3068
34:17 Therefore thus saith the L; Ye have not | 3068
34:17 saith the L, to the sword, to the | 3068
34:22 saith the L, and cause them to return to | 3068
35: 1 In the days of Jehoiakim the son of | 3068
35: 2 and bring them *into* the house of the L, | 3068
35: 4 I brought them *into* the house of the L, | 3068
35:12 came the word of the L unto Jeremiah, | 3068
35:13 saith the L of hosts, the God of Israel; | 3068
35:13 to hearken to my words? saith the L. | 3068
35:17 Therefore thus saith the L God of hosts, | 3068
35:18 saith the L, the God of Israel; | 3068
35:19 thus saith the L of hosts, the God | 3068
36: 1 word came unto Jeremiah from the L, | 3068
36: 4 mouth of Jeremiah all the words of the L, | 3068
36: 5 I cannot go *into* the house of the L: | 3068
36: 6 the words of the L in the ears of the | 3068
36: 7 present their supplication before the L, | 3068
36: 7 fury that the L hath pronounced against | 3068
36: 8 reading in the book the words of the L in | 3068
36: 9 they proclaimed a fast before the L to | 3068
36:10 words of Jeremiah *in* the house of the L, | 3068
36:11 out of the book all the words of the L, | 3068
36:26 Jeremiah the prophet: but the L hid them. | 3068
36:27 the word of the L came to Jeremiah, | 3068
36:29 Jehoiakim king of Judah, Thus saith the L; | 3068
36:30 Therefore thus saith the L of Jehoiakim | 3068
37: 2 did hearken unto the words of the L, | 3068
37: 3 Pray now unto the L our God for us. | 3068
37: 6 came the word of the L unto the prophet | 3068
37: 7 Thus saith the L, the God of Israel; | 3068
37: 9 Thus saith the L; Deceive not yourselves, | 3068
37:17 and said, Is there *any* word from the L? | 3068
38: 2 Thus saith the L, He that remaineth in | 3068
38: 3 Thus saith the L; This city shall surely be | 3068
38:14 third entry that *is* in the house of the L: | 3068
38:16 saying, *As* the L liveth, that made us this | 3068
38:17 Thus saith the L, the God of hosts, | 3068
38:20 I beseech thee, the voice of the L, which | 3068
38:21 *is* the word that the L hath shewed me: | 3068
39:15 Now the word of the L came unto | 3068
39:16 saying, Thus saith the L of hosts, the God | 3068
39:17 I will deliver thee in that day, saith the L: | 3068
39:18 thou hast put thy trust in me, saith the L. | 3068
40: 1 which came to Jeremiah from the L, | 3068
40: 2 The L thy God hath pronounced this evil | 3068
40: 3 Now the L hath brought *it*, and | 3068
40: 3 because ye have sinned against the L, | 3068
41: 5 to bring *them into* the house of the L. | 3068
42: 2 pray for us unto the L thy God, *even* for | 3068
42: 3 That the L thy God may shew us the way | 3068
42: 4 I *will* pray unto the L your God according | 3068
42: 4 *that* whatsoever thing the L shall answer | 3068
42: 5 The L be a true and faithful witness | 3068
42: 5 the L thy God shall send thee to us. | 3068
42: 6 we will obey the voice of the L our God, | 3068
42: 6 we obey the voice of the L our God. | 3068
42: 7 the word of the L came unto Jeremiah. | 3068
42: 9 Thus saith the L, the God of Israel, | 3068
42:11 afraid; be not afraid of him, saith the L: | 3068
42:13 neither obey the voice of the L your God, | 3068
42:15 now therefore hear the word of the L, | 3068
42:15 saith the L of hosts, the God of Israel; | 3068
42:18 For thus saith the L of hosts, the God | 3068
42:19 The L hath said concerning you, O ye | 3068
42:20 when ye sent me unto the L your God, | 3068
42:20 Pray for us unto the L our God; | 3068
42:20 according unto all that the L our God | 3068
42:21 have not obeyed the voice of the L your | 3068
43: 1 people all the words of the L their God, | 3068
43: 1 *for* which the L their God had sent him | 3068
43: 2 the L our God hath not sent thee to say, | 3068
43: 4 the people, obeyed not the voice of the L, | 3068
43: 7 for they obeyed not the voice of the L: | 3068
43: 8 came the word of the L unto Jeremiah in | 3068
43:10 saith the L of hosts, the God of Israel; | 3068
44: 2 saith the L of hosts, the God of Israel; | 3068
44: 7 Therefore now thus saith the L, the God | 3068
44:11 thus saith the L of hosts, the God | 3068

Jer 44:16 spoken unto us in the name of the L, | 3068
44:21 did not the L remember them, and came | 3068
44:22 that the L could no longer bear, because | 3068
44:23 because ye have sinned against the L, | 3068
44:23 have not obeyed the voice of the L, | 3068
44:24 all the women, Hear the word of the L, | 3068
44:25 saith the L of hosts, the God of Israel, | 3068
44:26 Therefore hear ye the word of the L, | 3068
44:26 sworn by my great name, saith the L, | 3068
44:29 this *shall be* a sign unto you, saith the L, | 3068
44:30 Thus saith the L; Behold, I will give | 3068
45: 2 Thus saith the L, the God of Israel, | 3068
45: 3 for the L hath added grief to my sorrow; | 3068
45: 4 shalt thou say unto him, The L saith thus; | 3068
45: 5 I *will* bring evil upon all flesh, saith the L: | 3068
46: 1 word of the L which came to Jeremiah | 3068
46: 5 *for* fear *was* round about, saith the L. | 3068
46:13 The word that the L spake to Jeremiah | 3068
46:15 stood not, because the L did drive them. | 3068
46:18 the King, whose name *is* the L of hosts, | 3068
46:23 saith the L, though it cannot be searched; | 3068
46:25 The L of hosts, the God of Israel, saith; | 3068
46:26 as *in* the days of old, saith the L. | 3068
46:28 not, O Jacob my servant, saith the L: | 3068
47: 1 The word of the L that came to Jeremiah | 3068
47: 2 Thus saith the L; Behold, waters rise up | 3068
47: 4 for the L will spoil the Philistines, | 3068
47: 6 thou sword of the L, how long *will it be* | 3068
47: 7 seeing the L hath given it a charge against | 3068
48: 1 Against Moab thus saith the L of hosts, | 3068
48: 8 shall be destroyed, as the L hath spoken. | 3068
48:10 *be* he that doeth the work of the L | 3068
48:12 the days come, saith the L, | 3068
48:15 the King, whose name *is* the L of hosts. | 3068
48:25 and his arm is broken, saith the L. | 3068
48:26 for he magnified *himself* against the L: | 3068
48:30 I know his wrath, saith the L; but *it shall* | 3068
48:35 saith the L, him that offereth *in* the high | 3068
48:38 vessel wherein *is* no pleasure, saith the L. | 3068
48:40 For thus saith the L; Behold, he shall fly | 3068
48:42 he hath magnified *himself* against the L. | 3068
48:43 O inhabitant of Moab, saith the L. | 3068
48:44 the year of their visitation, saith the L. | 3068
48:47 of Moab in the latter days, saith the L. | 3068
49: 1 the Ammonites, thus saith the L; | 3068
49: 2 the days come, saith the L, | 3068
49: 2 them that were his heirs, saith the L. | 3068
49: 6 of the children of Ammon, saith the L. | 3068
49: 7 thus saith the L of hosts; | 3068
49:12 For thus saith the L; Behold, they whose | 3068
49:13 For I have sworn by myself, saith the L, | 3068
49:14 I have heard a rumour from the L, | 3068
49:16 bring thee down from thence, saith the L. | 3068
49:18 saith the L, no man shall abide there, | 3068
49:20 Therefore hear the counsel of the L, that | 3068
49:26 cut off in that day, saith the L of hosts. | 3068
49:28 of Babylon shall smite, thus saith the L; | 3068
49:30 O ye inhabitants of Hazor, saith the L; | 3068
49:31 that dwelleth without care, saith the L, | 3068
49:32 from all sides thereof, saith the L. | 3068
49:34 The word of the L that came to Jeremiah | 3068
49:35 Thus saith the L of hosts; Behold, I *will* | 3068
49:37 *even* my fierce anger, saith the L; | 3068
49:38 the king and the princes, saith the L. | 3068
49:39 again the captivity of Elam, saith the L. | 3068
50: 1 word that the L spake against Babylon | 3068
50: 4 those days, and in that time, saith the L, | 3068
50: 4 they shall go, and seek the L their God. | 3068
50: 5 us join ourselves to the L *in* a perpetual | 3068
50: 7 because they have sinned against the L, | 3068
50: 7 the habitation of justice, even the L, | 3068
50:10 spoil her shall be satisfied, saith the L. | 3068
50:13 Because of the wrath of the L it shall not | 3068
50:14 for she hath sinned against the L. | 3068
50:15 for it *is* the vengeance of the L: | 3068
50:18 thus saith the L of hosts, the God | 3068
50:20 those days, and in that time, saith the L, | 3068
50:21 saith the L, and do according to all that I | 3068
50:24 because thou hast striven against the L. | 3068
50:25 The L hath opened his armoury, | 3068
50:28 to declare in Zion the vengeance of the L | 3068
50:29 for she hath been proud against the L, | 3068
50:30 shall be cut off in that day, saith the L. | 3068
50:33 Thus saith the L of hosts; The children of | 3068
50:34 *is* strong; the L of hosts *is* his name: | 3068
50:35 saith the L, and upon the inhabitants of | 3068
50:40 the neighbour *cities* thereof, saith the L, | 3068
50:45 Therefore hear ye the counsel of the L, | 3068
51: 1 Thus saith the L; Behold, I *will* raise up | 3068
51: 5 nor Judah of his God, of the L of hosts; | 3068
51:10 The L hath brought forth our | 3068
51:10 let us declare in Zion the work of the L | 3068
51:11 the L hath raised up the spirit of the kings | 3068
51:11 because it *is* the vengeance of the L, | 3068
51:12 for the L hath both devised and done that | 3068
51:14 The L of hosts hath sworn by himself, | 3068
51:19 inheritance: the L of hosts *is* his name. | 3068
51:24 done in Zion in your sight, saith the L. | 3068
51:25 O destroying mountain, saith the L, | 3068
51:26 shalt be desolate for ever, saith the L. | 3068
51:29 for every purpose of the L shall be | 3068
51:33 For thus saith the L of hosts, the God of | 3068
51:36 Therefore thus saith the L; Behold, I *will* | 3068
51:39 sleep, and not wake, saith the L. | 3068
51:45 his soul from the fierce anger of the L. | 3068

Jer 51:48 unto her from the north, saith the L. | 3068
51:50 remember the L afar off, and let | 3068
51:52 the days come, saith the L, | 3068
51:53 shall spoilers come unto her, saith the L. | 3068
51:55 Because the L hath spoiled Babylon, | 3068
51:56 The L God of recompences shall surely | 3068
51:57 the King, whose name *is* the L of hosts. | 3068
51:58 Thus saith the L of hosts; The broad walls | 3068
51:62 shalt thou say, O L, thou hast spoken | 3068
52: 2 *that* which *was* evil in the eyes of the L, | 3068
52: 3 For through the anger of the L it came to | 3068
52:13 burnt the house of the L, and the king's | 3068
52:17 of brass that *were* in the house of the L, | 3068
52:17 brasen sea that *was* in the house of the L, | 3068
52:20 Solomon had made in the house of the L: | 3068
La 1: 5 for the L hath afflicted her for | 3068
1: 9 O L, behold my affliction: for the enemy | 3068
1:11 see, O L, and consider; for I am become | 3068
1:12 wherewith the L hath afflicted *me* in | 3068
1:17 the L hath commanded concerning Jacob, | 3068
1:18 The L *is* righteous; for I have rebelled | 3068
1:20 Behold, O L; for I *am* in distress: | 3068
2: 6 the L hath caused the solemn feasts and | 3068
2: 7 have made a noise in the house of the L, | 3068
2: 8 The L purposed to destroy the wall | 3068
2: 9 prophets also find no vision from the L. | 3068
2:17 The L hath done *that* which he had | 3068
2:20 L, and consider to whom thou hast done | 3068
3:18 and my hope is perished from the L: | 3068
3:24 The L *is* my portion, saith my soul; | 3068
3:25 The L *is* good unto them that wait for | 3068
3:26 and quietly wait for the salvation of the L. | 3068
3:40 and try our ways, and turn again to the L. | 3068
3:50 Till the L look down, and behold from | 3068
3:55 I called upon thy name, O L, out of the | 3068
3:59 L, thou hast seen my wrong: judge thou | 3068
3:61 L, *and* all their imaginations against me; | 3068
3:64 Render unto them a recompence, O L, | 3068
3:66 anger from under the heavens of the L. | 3068
4:11 The L hath accomplished his fury; he | 3068
4:16 The anger of the L hath divided them; | 3068
4:20 the anointed of the L, was taken in their | 3068
5: 1 Remember, O L, what is come upon us: | 3068
5:19 Thou, O L, remainest for ever; thy throne | 3068
5:21 unto thee, O L, and we shall be turned; | 3068
Eze 1: 3 The word of the L came expressly unto | 3068
1: 3 the hand of the L was there upon him. | 3068
1:28 of the likeness of the glory of the L. | 3068
3:12 saying, Blessed *be* the glory of the L from | 3068
3:14 the hand of the L was strong upon me. | 3068
3:16 that the word of the L came unto me, | 3068
3:22 the hand of the L was there upon me; | 3068
3:23 behold, the glory of the L stood there, | 3068
4:13 the L said, Even thus shall the children | 3068
5:13 they shall know that I the L have spoken | 3068
5:15 in furious rebukes. I the L have spoken *it*. | 3068
5:17 sword upon thee. I the L have spoken *it*. | 3068
6: 1 the word of the L came unto me, saying, | 3068
6: 7 of you, and ye shall know that I *am* the L. | 3068
6:10 they shall know that I *am* the L, *and that* | 3068
6:13 shall ye know that I *am* the L, when their | 3068
6:14 and they shall know that I *am* the L. | 3068
7: 1 the word of the L came unto me, | 3068
7: 4 thee: and ye shall know that I *am* the L. | 3068
7: 9 shall know that I *am* the L that smiteth. | 3068
7:19 them in the day of the wrath of the L: | 3068
7:27 and they shall know that I *am* the L. | 3068
8:12 for they say, The L seeth us not; | 3068
8:12 us not; the L hath forsaken the earth. | 3068
8:16 *at* the door of the temple of the L, | 3068
8:16 their backs toward the temple of the L, | 3068
9: 4 the L said unto him, Go through the | 3068
9: 9 The L hath forsaken the earth, | 3068
9: 9 forsaken the earth, and the L seeth not. | 3068
10: 4 glory of the L went up from the cherub, | 3068
10:18 the glory of the L departed from off | 3068
11: 5 the Spirit of the L fell upon me, | 3068
11: 5 said unto me, Speak; Thus saith the L. | 3068
11:10 and ye shall know that I *am* the L. | 3068
11:12 shall know that I *am* the L: for ye have | 3068
11:14 Again the word of the L came unto me, | 3068
11:15 have said, Get ye far from the L: | 3068
11:23 the glory of the L went up from the midst | 3068
11:25 all the things that the L had shewed me. | 3068
12: 1 The word of the L also came unto me, | 3068
12: 8 in the morning came the word of the L | 3068
12:15 they shall know that I *am* the L, when I | 3068
12:16 and they shall know that I *am* the L. | 3068
12:17 Moreover the word of the L came to me, | 3068
12:20 and ye shall know that I *am* the L. | 3068
12:21 the word of the L came unto me, saying, | 3068
12:25 For I *am* the L: I will speak, and the | 3068
12:26 Again the word of the L came to me, | 3068
13: 1 the word of the L came unto me, saying, | 3068
13: 2 own hearts, Hear ye the word of the L; | 3068
13: 5 to stand in the battle in the day of the L. | 3068
13: 6 and lying divination, saying, The L saith: | 3068
13: 6 the L hath not sent them: and they have | 3068
13: 7 The L saith *it*; albeit I have not spoken? | 3068
13:14 and ye shall know that I *am* the L. | 3068
13:21 and ye shall know that I *am* the L. | 3068
13:23 and ye shall know that I *am* the L. | 3068
14: 2 the word of the L came unto me, saying, | 3068
14: 4 I the L will answer him that cometh | 3068
14: 7 I the L will answer him by myself: | 3068

Eze	14: 8 and ye shall know that I *am* **the L**.	3068
	14: 9 I **the L** have deceived that prophet,	3068
	14:12 The word of **the L** came again to me,	3068
	15: 1 the word of **the L** came unto me, saying,	3068
	15: 7 ye shall know that I *am* **the L**, when I set	3068
	16: 1 Again the word of **the L** came unto me,	3068
	16:35 O harlot, hear the word of **the L**.	3068
	16:58 and thine abominations, saith **the L**.	3068
	16:62 and thou shalt know that I *am* **the L**.	3068
	17: 1 the word of **the L** came unto me, saying,	3068
	17:11 the word of **the L** came unto me, saying,	3068
	17:21 ye shall know that I **the L** have spoken *it*.	3068
	17:24 I have brought down the high tree,	3068
	17:24 I **the L** have spoken and have done *it*.	3068
	18: 1 the word of **the L** came unto me again,	3068
	20: 1 elders of Israel came to inquire of **the L**,	3068
	20: 2 came the word of **the L** unto me, saying,	3068
	20: 5 unto them, saying, I *am* **the L** your God.	3068
	20: 7 the idols of Egypt: I *am* **the L** your God.	3068
	20:12 *they* might know that I *am* **the L** that	3068
	20:19 I *am* **the L** your God; walk in my statutes,	3068
	20:20 that *ye* may know that I *am* **the L** your	3068
	20:26 that they might know that I *am* **the L**.	3068
	20:38 and ye shall know that I *am* **the L**.	3068
	20:42 ye shall know that I *am* **the L**, when I	3068
	20:44 ye shall know that I *am* **the L**, when I	3068
	20:45 the word of **the L** came unto me,	3068
	20:47 of the south, Hear the word of **the L**;	3068
	20:48 flesh shall see that I **the L** have kindled	3068
	21: 1 the word of **the L** came unto me, saying,	3068
	21: 3 say to the land of Israel, Thus saith **the L**;	3068
	21: 5 That all flesh may know that I **the L** have	3068
	21: 8 Again the word of **the L** came unto me,	3068
	21: 9 prophesy, and say, Thus saith **the L**;	3068
	21:17 cause my fury to rest: I **the L** have said *it*.	3068
	21:18 The word of **the L** came unto me again,	3068
	21:32 for I **the L** have spoken *it*.	3068
	22: 1 the word of **the L** came unto me,	3068
	22:14 I **the L** have spoken *it*, and will do *it*.	3068
	22:16 and thou shalt know that I *am* **the L**.	3068
	22:17 the word of **the L** came unto me, saying,	3068
	22:22 shall know that I **the L** have poured out	3068
	22:23 the word of **the L** came unto me, saying,	3068
	22:28 Lord GOD, when **the L** hath not spoken.	3068
	23: 1 The word of **the L** came again unto me,	3068
	23:36 **The L** said moreover unto me; Son of	3068
	24: 1 the word of **the L** came unto me, saying,	3068
	24:14 I **the L** have spoken *it*: it shall come to	3068
	24:15 Also the word of **the L** came unto me,	3068
	24:20 The word of **the L** came unto me, saying,	3068
	24:27 and they shall know that I *am* **the L**.	3068
	25: 1 The word of **the L** came unto me, saying,	3068
	25: 5 and ye shall know that I *am* **the L**.	3068
	25: 7 and thou shalt know that I *am* **the L**.	3068
	25:11 and they shall know that I *am* **the L**.	3068
	25:17 they shall know that I *am* **the L**, when I	3068
	26: 1 *that* the word of **the L** came unto me,	3068
	26: 6 and they shall know that I *am* **the L**.	3068
	26:14 for I **the L** have spoken *it*, saith the Lord	3068
	27: 1 The word of **the L** came again unto me,	3068
	28: 1 The word of **the L** came again unto me,	3068
	28:11 the word of **the L** came unto me,	3068
	28:20 Again the word of **the L** came unto me,	3068
	28:22 they shall know that I *am* **the L**, when I	3068
	28:23 and they shall know that I *am* **the L**.	3068
	28:26 shall know that I *am* **the L** their God.	3068
	29: 1 the word of **the L** came unto me, saying,	3068
	29: 6 of Egypt shall know that I *am* **the L**,	3068
	29: 9 and they shall know that I *am* **the L**:	3068
	29:17 the word of **the L** came unto me, saying,	3068
	29:21 and they shall know that I *am* **the L**.	3068
	30: 1 The word of **the L** came again unto me,	3068
	30: 3 the day of **the L** is near, a cloudy day;	3068
	30: 6 Thus saith **the L**; They also that uphold	3068
	30: 8 they shall know that I *am* **the L**, when I	3068
	30:12 hand of strangers: I **the L** have spoken *it*.	3068
	30:19 and they shall know that I *am* **the L**.	3068
	30:20 *that* the word of **the L** came unto me,	3068
	30:25 they shall know that I *am* **the L**, when I	3068
	30:26 and they shall know that I *am* **the L**.	3068
	31: 1 *that* the word of **the L** came unto me,	3068
	32: 1 *that* the word of **the L** came unto me,	3068
	32:15 shall they know that I *am* **the L**.	3068
	32:17 *that* the word of **the L** came unto me,	3068
	33: 1 Again the word of **the L** came unto me,	3068
	33:22 Now the hand of **the L** was upon me in	3068
	33:23 the word of **the L** came unto me, saying,	3068
	33:29 shall they know that I *am* **the L**, when I	3068
	33:30 *is* the word that cometh forth from **the L**.	3068
	34: 1 the word of **the L** came unto me, saying,	3068
	34: 7 ye shepherds, hear the word of **the L**;	3068
	34: 9 O ye shepherds, hear the word of **the L**;	3068
	34:24 I **the L** will be their God, and my servant	3068
	34:24 among them; I **the L** have spoken *it*.	3068
	34:27 land, and shall know that I *am* **the L**,	3068
	34:30 shall they know that I **the L** their God	3068
	35: 1 the word of **the L** came unto me,	3068
	35: 4 and thou shalt know that I *am* **the L**.	3068
	35: 9 and ye shall know that I *am* **the L**.	3068
	35:10 will possess *it*; whereas **the L** was there:	3068
	35:12 shalt know that I **the L**, *and that* I	3068
	35:15 and they shall know that I *am* **the L**.	3068
	36: 1 of Israel, hear the word of **the L**:	3068
	36:11 and ye shall know that I *am* **the L**:	3068
	36:16 the word of **the L** came unto me,	3068

Eze	36:20 *are* the people of **the L**, and are gone	3068
	36:23 the heathen shall know that I *am* **the L**,	3068
	36:36 know that I **the L** build the ruined *places*,	3068
	36:36 I **the L** have spoken *it*, and I will do *it*.	3068
	36:38 and they shall know that I *am* **the L**.	3068
	37: 1 The hand of **the L** was upon me,	3068
	37: 1 carried me out in the spirit of **the L**,	3068
	37: 4 O ye dry bones, hear the word of **the L**.	3068
	37: 6 and ye shall know that I *am* **the L**.	3068
	37:13 ye shall know that I *am* **the L**, when I	3068
	37:14 shall ye know that I **the L** have spoken *it*,	3068
	37:14 spoken *it*, and performed *it*, saith **the L**.	3068
	37:15 The word of **the L** came again unto me,	3068
	37:28 the heathen shall know that I **the L** do	3068
	38: 1 the word of **the L** came unto me, saying,	3068
	38:23 and they shall know that I *am* **the L**.	3068
	39: 6 and they shall know that I *am* **the L**.	3068
	39: 7 the heathen shall know that I *am* **the L**,	3068
	39:22 that I *am* **the L** their God from that day	3068
	39:28 they know that I *am* **the L** their God,	3068
	40: 1 in the selfsame day the hand of **the L** was	3068
	40:46 come near to the **L** to minister unto	3068
	41:22 This *is* the table that *is* before **the L**.	3068
	42:13 the priests that approach unto **the L**,	3068
	43: 4 the glory of **the L** came into the house	3068
	43: 5 the glory of **the L** filled the house.	3068
	43:24 And thou shalt offer them before **the L**,	3068
	43:24 them up *for* a burnt offering unto **the L**.	3068
	44: 2 **the L** unto me; This gate shall be shut,	3068
	44: 2 because the **L**, the God of Israel,	3068
	44: 3 he shall sit in it to eat bread before the **L**;	3068
	44: 4 the glory of **the L** filled the house of	3068
	44: 4 of the LORD filled the house of **the L**:	3068
	44: 5 **the L** said unto me, Son of man, mark	3068
	44: 5 all the ordinances of the house of **the L**,	3068
	45: 1 shall offer an oblation unto **the L**, a holy	3068
	45: 4 shall come near to minister unto **the L**:	3068
	45:23 he shall prepare a burnt offering to **the L**,	3068
	46: 3 of this gate before **the L** in the sabbaths	3068
	46: 4 **the L** in the sabbath day *shall* be six	3068
	46: 9 come before **the L** in the solemn feasts,	3068
	46:12 or peace offerings voluntarily unto **the L**,	3068
	46:13 **the L** *of* a lamb of the first year without	3068
	46:14 *by* a perpetual ordinance unto **the L**.	3068
	48: 9 oblation that ye shall offer unto **the L**,	3068
	48:10 sanctuary of **the L** shall be in the midst	3068
	48:14 of the land: for *it is* holy unto **the L**.	3068
	48:35 from *that* day *shall be*, **The L** *is* there.	3068
Da	9: 2 where *of* the word of **the L** came to	3068
	9: 4 I prayed unto **the L** my God, and made	3068
	9:10 have we obeyed the voice of **the L**	3068
	9:13 yet made we not our prayer before **the L**	3068
	9:14 Therefore hath **the L** watched upon	3068
	9:14 for **the L** our God *is* righteous in all his	3068
	9:20 presenting my supplication before **the L**	3068
Hos	1: 1 word of **the L** that came unto Hosea,	3068
	1: 2 The beginning of the word of **the L** by	3068
	1: 2 **the L** said to Hosea, Go, take unto thee a	3068
	1: 2 great whoredom, *departing* from **the L**.	3068
	1: 4 **the L** said unto him, Call his name	3068
	1: 7 will save them by **the L** their God,	3068
	2:13 her lovers, and forgat me, saith **the L**.	3068
	2:16 shall be at that day, saith **the L**, *that* thou	3068
	2:20 faithfulness: and thou shalt know **the L**.	3068
	2:21 I will hear, saith **the L**, I will hear	3068
	3: 1 **the L** unto me, Go yet, love a woman	3068
	3: 1 according to the love of **the L** toward	3068
	3: 5 seek **the L** their God, and David their	3068
	3: 5 shall fear **the L** and his goodness in	3068
	4: 1 Hear the word of **the L**, ye children of	3068
	4: 1 for **the L** hath a controversy with	3068
	4:10 they have left off to take heed to **the L**.	3068
	4:15 up *to* Beth-aven, nor swear, **The L** liveth.	3068
	4:16 now **the L** will feed them as a lamb in a	3068
	5: 4 of them, and they have not known **the L**.	3068
	5: 6 and with their herds to seek **the L**;	3068
	5: 7 have dealt treacherously against **the L**:	3068
	6: 1 Come and let us return unto **the L**: for	3068
	6: 3 we know, *if* we follow on to know **the L**:	3068
	7:10 they do not return to **the L** their God,	3068
	8: 1 as an eagle against the house of **the L**,	3068
	8:13 and eat *it; but* **the L** accepteth them not;	3068
	9: 4 shall not offer wine *offerings* to **the L**,	3068
	9: 4 shall not come *into* the house of **the L**.	3068
	9: 5 and in the day of the feast of **the L**?	3068
	9:14 Give them, O **L**: what wilt thou give?	3068
	10: 3 no king, because we feared not **the L**;	3068
	10:12 for *it is* time to seek **the L**, till he come	3068
	11:10 They shall walk after **the L**: he shall roar	3068
	11:11 place them in their houses, saith **the L**.	3068
	12: 2 **The L** hath also a controversy with Judah	3068
	12: 5 Even **the L** God of hosts; the LORD *is* his	3068
	12: 5 God of hosts; **the L** *is* his memorial.	3068
	12: 9 I *that am* **the L** thy God from the land of	3068
	12:13 by a prophet **the L** brought Israel out of	3068
	13: 4 Yet I *am* **the L** thy God from the land of	3068
	13:15 the wind of **the L** *shall* come up from	3068
	14: 1 O Israel, return unto **the L** thy God;	3068
	14: 2 Take with you words, and turn to **the L**:	3068
	14: 9 the ways of **the L** are right, and the just	3068
Joel	1: 1 The word of **the L** that came to Joel the	3068
	1: 9 offering is cut off from the house of **the L**;	3068
	1:14 land *into* the house of **the L** your God,	3068
	1:14 the LORD your God, and cry unto **the L**,	3068
	1:15 for the day of **the L** *is* at hand, and as a	3068

Joel	1:19 O **L**, to thee will I cry: for the fire hath	3068
	2: 1 for the day of **the L** cometh, for *it is* nigh	3068
	2:11 **the L** shall utter his voice before his army:	3068
	2:11 for the day of **the L** *is* great and	3068
	2:12 Therefore also now, saith **the L**, turn ye	3068
	2:13 and turn unto **the L** your God:	3068
	2:14 a drink offering unto **the L** your God?	3068
	2:17 Let the priests, the ministers of **the L**,	3068
	2:17 O **L**, and give not thine heritage to	3068
	2:18 will **the L** be jealous for his land,	3068
	2:19 **the L** will answer and say unto his people	3068
	2:21 and rejoice: for **the L** will do great things.	3068
	2:23 of Zion, and rejoice in **the L** your God:	3068
	2:26 and praise the name of **the L** your God,	3068
	2:27 *that* I *am* **the L** your God, and none else:	3068
	2:31 and the terrible day of **the L** come.	3068
	2:32 on the name of **the L** shall be delivered:	3068
	2:32 as **the L** hath said, and in the remnant	3068
	2:32 in the remnant whom **the L** *shall* call.	3068
	3: 8 a people far off: for **the L** hath spoken *it*.	3068
	3:11 thy mighty ones to come down, O **L**.	3068
	3:14 for the day of **the L** *is* near in the valley	3068
	3:16 **The L** also shall roar out of Zion,	3068
	3:16 **the L** *will be* the hope of his people,	3068
	3:17 shall ye know that I *am* **the L** your God	3068
	3:18 shall come forth of the house of **the L**,	3068
	3:21 not cleansed: for **the L** dwelleth in Zion.	3068
Am	1: 2 **The L** will roar from Zion, and utter his	3068
	1: 3 Thus saith **the L**; For three transgressions	3068
	1: 5 go into captivity unto Kir, saith **the L**.	3068
	1: 6 Thus saith **the L**; For three transgressions	3068
	1: 9 Thus saith **the L**; For three transgressions	3068
	1:11 Thus saith **the L**; For three transgressions	3068
	1:13 Thus saith **the L**; For three transgressions	3068
	1:15 he and his princes together, saith **the L**.	3068
	2: 1 Thus saith **the L**; For three transgressions	3068
	2: 3 the princes thereof with him, saith **the L**.	3068
	2: 4 Thus saith **the L**; For three transgressions	3068
	2: 4 they have despised the law of **the L**,	3068
	2: 6 Thus saith **the L**; For three transgressions	3068
	2:11 O ye children of Israel? saith **the L**.	3068
	2:16 flee away naked in that day, saith **the L**.	3068
	3: 1 Hear this word that **the L** hath spoken	3068
	3: 6 evil in a city, and **the L** hath not done *it*?	3068
	3:10 saith **the L**, who store up violence and	3068
	3:12 Thus saith **the L**; As the shepherd taketh	3068
	3:15 houses shall have an end, saith **the L**.	3068
	4: 3 cast *them* into the palace, saith **the L**.	3068
	4: 6 ye not returned unto me, saith **the L**.	3068
	4: 8 ye not returned unto me, saith **the L**.	3068
	4: 9 ye not returned unto me, saith **the L**.	3068
	4:10 ye not returned unto me, saith **the L**.	3068
	4:11 ye not returned unto me, saith **the L**.	3068
	4:13 **The L**, The God of hosts, *is* his name.	3068
	5: 4 For thus saith **the L** unto the house of	3068
	5: 6 Seek **the L**, and ye shall live; lest he break	3068
	5: 8 the face of the earth: **The L** *is* his name:	3068
	5:14 so **the L**, the God of hosts, shall be with	3068
	5:15 it may be that **the L** God of hosts will be	3068
	5:16 Therefore **the L**, the God of hosts,	3068
	5:17 for I will pass through thee, saith **the L**.	3068
	5:18 unto *you* that desire the day of **the L**!	3068
	5:18 day of **the L** *is* darkness, and not light.	3068
	5:20 *Shall* not the day of **the L** *be* darkness,	3068
	5:27 saith **the L**, whose name *is* The God of	3068
	6: 8 saith **the L** the God of hosts, I abhor	3068
	6:10 not make mention of the name of **the L**.	3068
	6:11 **the L** commandeth, and he will smite	3068
	6:14 of Israel, saith **the L** the God of hosts;	3068
	7: 3 **The L** repented for this: It shall not be,	3068
	7: 3 for this: It shall not be, saith **the L**.	3068
	7: 6 **The L** repented for this: This also shall	3068
	7: 8 **the L** said unto me, Amos, what seest	3068
	7:15 **the L** took me as I followed the flock,	3068
	7:15 **the L** said unto me, Go, prophesy unto	3068
	7:16 therefore hear thou the word of **the L**:	3068
	7:17 Therefore thus saith **the L**; Thy wife shall	3068
	8: 2 said **the L** unto me, The end is come	3068
	8: 7 **The L** hath sworn by the excellency of	3068
	8:11 but of hearing the words of **the L**:	3068
	8:12 run to and fro to seek the word of **the L**,	3068
	9: 6 the face of the earth: **The L** *is* his name.	3068
	9: 7 saith **the L**. Have not I brought up Israel	3068
	9: 8 destroy the house of Jacob, saith **the L**.	3068
	9:12 by my name, saith **the L** that doeth this.	3068
	9:13 Behold, the days come, saith **the L**, that	3068
	9:15 I have given them, saith **the L** thy God.	3068
Ob	1: 1 We have heard a rumour from **the L**,	3068
	1: 4 will I bring thee down, saith **the L**.	3068
	1: 8 Shall I not in that day, saith **the L**,	3068
	1:15 For the day of **the L** *is* near upon all	3068
	1:18 house of Esau; for **the L** hath spoken *it*.	3068
Jnh	1: 1 Now the word of **the L** came unto Jonah	3068
	1: 3 unto Tarshish from the presence of **the L**,	3068
	1: 3 unto Tarshish from the presence of **the L**,	3068
	1: 4 **the L** sent out a great wind into the sea,	3068
	1: 9 I fear **the L**, the God of heaven, which	3068
	1:10 that he fled from the presence of **the L**,	3068
	1:14 they cried unto **the L**, and said,	3068
	1:14 We beseech thee, O **L**, we beseech thee,	3068
	1:14 thou, O **L**, hast done as it pleased thee.	3068
	1:16 the men feared **the L** exceedingly,	3068
	1:16 offered a sacrifice unto **the L**,	3068
	1:17 Now **the L** had prepared a great fish to	3068
	2: 1 Jonah prayed unto **the L** his God out of	3068

L

Jnh	2: 2 by reason of mine affliction unto **the L**,	3068
	2: 6 up my life from corruption, O L my God.	3068
	2: 7 fainted within me I remembered **the L**:	3068
	2: 9 that I have vowed. Salvation *is* of **the L**.	3068
	2:10 the **L** spake unto the fish, and it vomited	3068
	3: 1 the word of **the L** came unto Jonah	3068
	3: 3 according to the word of **the L**.	3068
	4: 2 prayed unto **the L**, and said, I pray thee,	3068
	4: 2 said, I pray thee, O **L**, *was* not this my	3068
	4: 3 Therefore now, O **L**, take, I beseech thee,	3068
	4: 4 said **the L**, Doest thou well to be angry?	3068
	4: 6 the **L** God prepared a gourd, and made	3068
	4:10 said **the L**, Thou hast had pity on	3068
Mic	1: 1 The word of **the L** that came to Micah	3068
	1: 3 **the L** cometh forth out of his place,	3068
	1:12 evil came down from **the L** unto the gate	3068
	2: 3 Therefore thus saith **the L**; Behold,	3068
	2: 5 cord by lot in the congregation of **the L**.	3068
	2: 7 of Jacob, is the spirit of **the L** straitened?	3068
	2:13 and **the L** on the head of them.	3068
	3: 4 shall they cry unto **the L**, but he will not	3068
	3: 5 Thus saith **the L** concerning the prophets	3068
	3: 8 I am full *of* power by the spirit of **the L**,	3068
	3:11 yet will they lean upon **the L**, and say,	3068
	3:11 and say, *Is* not **the L** among us?	3068
	4: 1 *that* the mountain of the house of **the L**	3068
	4: 2 let us go up to the mountain of **the L**,	3068
	4: 2 and the word of **the L** from Jerusalem.	3068
	4: 4 for the mouth of **the L** of hosts hath	3068
	4: 5 will walk in the name of **the L** our God	3068
	4: 6 In that day, saith **the L**, will I assemble	3068
	4: 7 **the L** shall reign over them in mount Zion	3068
	4:10 there **the L** shall redeem thee from	3068
	4:12 they know not the thoughts of **the L**,	3068
	4:13 I will consecrate their gain unto **the L**,	3068
	5: 4 and feed in the strength of **the L**,	3068
	5: 4 in the majesty of the name of **the L** his	3068
	5: 7 of many people as a dew from **the L**,	3068
	5:10 shall come to pass in that day, saith **the L**,	3068
	6: 1 Hear ye now what **the L** saith; Arise,	3068
	6: 2 for **the L** hath a controversy with his	3068
	6: 5 *ye* may know the righteousness of **the L**.	3068
	6: 6 Wherewith shall I come before **the L**,	3068
	6: 7 Will **the L** be pleased with thousands of	3068
	6: 8 what doth **the L** require of thee, but to	3068
	7: 1 I will look unto **the L**; I will wait	3068
	7: 7 darkness, **the L** *shall be* a light unto me.	3068
	7: 9 I will bear the indignation of **the L**,	3068
	7:10 said unto me, Where is **the L** thy God?	3068
	7:17 they shall be afraid of **the L** our God,	3068
Na	1: 2 God *is* jealous, and **the L** revengeth;	3068
	1: 2 **the L** revengeth, and *is* furious;	3068
	1: 2 **the L** will take vengeance on his	3068
	1: 3 **The L** *is* slow to anger, and great in	3068
	1: 3 will not at all acquit *the wicked:* **the L**	3068
	1: 7 **The L** *is* good, a strong hold in the day of	3068
	1: 9 What do ye imagine against **the L**?	3068
	1:11 imagineth evil against **the L**, a wicked	3068
	1:12 Thus saith **the L**; Though *they be* quiet,	3068
	1:14 **the L** hath given a commandment	3068
	2: 2 **the L** hath turned *away* the excellency	3068
	2:13 saith **the L** of hosts, and I will burn her	3068
	3: 5 I *am* against thee, saith **the L** of hosts;	3068
Hab	1: 2 L, how long shall I cry, and thou wilt not	3068
	1:12 O my God, mine Holy One?	3068
	1:12 **L**, thou hast ordained them for judgment;	3068
	2: 2 **the L** answered me, and said, Write	3068
	2:13 *is it* not of **the L** of hosts that the people	3068
	2:14 with the knowledge of the glory of **the L**,	3068
	2:20 **the L** *is* in his holy temple: let all the	3068
	3: 2 O **L**, I have heard thy speech,	3068
	3: 2 O **L**, revive thy work in the midst of	3068
	3: 8 Was **the L** displeased against the rivers?	3068
	3:18 Yet I will rejoice in **the L**, I will joy in	3068
Zep	1: 1 The word of **the L** which came unto	3068
	1: 2 all *things* from off the land, saith **the L**.	3068
	1: 3 cut off man from off the land, saith **the L**.	3068
	1: 5 that worship *and* that swear by **the L**;	3068
	1: 6 them that are turned back from **the L**;	3068
	1: 6 *those* that have not sought **the L**,	3068
	1: 7 for the day of **the L** *is* at hand:	3068
	1: 7 for **the L** hath prepared a sacrifice, he	3068
	1:10 come to pass in that day, saith **the L**,	3068
	1:12 in their heart, **The L** will not do good,	3068
	1:14 The great day of **the L** *is* near, *it is* near,	3068
	1:14 *even* the voice of the day of **the L**:	3068
	1:17 because they have sinned against **the L**:	3068
	2: 2 before the fierce anger of **the L** come	3068
	2: 3 Seek ye **the L**, all ye meek of the earth,	3068
	2: 5 the word of **the L** *is* against you;	3068
	2: 7 for **the L** their God shall visit them,	3068
	2: 9 saith **the L** of hosts, the God of Israel,	3068
	2:10 against the people of **the L** of hosts.	3068
	2:11 **The L** *will be* terrible unto them: for he	3068
	3: 2 not correction; she trusted not in **the L**;	3068
	3: 5 **The** just **L** *is* in the midst thereof; he will	3068
	3: 8 Therefore wait ye upon me, saith **the L**,	3068
	3: 9 they may all call upon the name of **the L**,	3068
	3:12 and they shall trust in the name of **the L**.	3068
	3:15 **The L** hath taken away thy judgments,	3068
	3:15 the king of Israel, *even* **the L**, *is* in	3068
	3:17 **The L** thy God in the midst of thee *is*	3068
	3:20 captivity before your eyes, saith **the L**.	3068
Hag	1: 1 came the word of **the L** by Haggai	3068
	1: 2 Thus speaketh **the L** of hosts, saying,	3068

Hag	1: 3 came the word of **the L** by Haggai	3068
	1: 5 Now therefore thus saith **the L** of hosts;	3068
	1: 7 Thus saith **the L** of hosts; Consider your	3068
	1: 8 in it, and I will be glorified, saith **the L**.	3068
	1: 9 saith **the L** of hosts. Because of mine	3068
	1:12 obeyed the voice of **the L** their God,	3068
	1:12 as **the L** their God had sent him,	3068
	1:12 and the people did fear before **the L**.	3068
	1:13 saying, I *am* with you, saith **the L**.	3068
	1:14 **the L** stirred up the spirit of Zerubbabel	3068
	1:14 did work in the house of **the L** of hosts,	3068
	2: 1 came the word of **the L** by the prophet	3068
	2: 4 now be strong, O Zerubbabel, saith **the L;**	3068
	2: 4 people of the land, saith **the L**, and work:	3068
	2: 4 for I *am* with you, saith **the L** of hosts:	3068
	2: 6 thus saith **the L** of hosts; Yet once, it *is*	3068
	2: 7 this house *with* glory, saith **the L** of hosts.	3068
	2: 8 and the gold *is* mine, saith **the L** of hosts.	3068
	2: 9 than of the former, saith **the L** of hosts:	3068
	2: 9 will I give peace, saith **the L** of hosts.	3068
	2:10 came the word of **the L** by Haggai	3068
	2:11 Thus saith **the L** of hosts; Ask now	3068
	2:14 so *is* this nation before me, saith **the L;**	3068
	2:15 laid upon a stone in the temple of **the L:**	3068
	2:17 yet *ye turned* not to me, saith **the L**.	3068
	2:20 the word of **the L** came unto Haggai	3068
	2:23 In that day, saith **the L** of hosts, will I	3068
	2:23 saith **the L**, and will make thee as a	3068
	2:23 I have chosen thee, saith **the L** of hosts.	3068
Zec	1: 1 came the word of **the L** unto Zechariah,	3068
	1: 2 **The L** hath been sore displeased with	3068
	1: 3 unto them, Thus saith **the L** of hosts;	3068
	1: 3 saith **the L** of hosts, and I will turn unto	3068
	1: 3 I will turn unto you, saith **the L** of hosts.	3068
	1: 4 saying, Thus saith **the L** of hosts;	3068
	1: 4 hear, nor hearken unto me, saith **the L**.	3068
	1: 6 Like as **the L** of hosts thought to do unto	3068
	1: 7 came the word of **the L** unto Zechariah	3068
	1:10 These *are they* whom **the L** hath sent to	3068
	1:11 answered the angel of **the L** that stood	3068
	1:12 the angel of **the L** answered and said,	3068
	1:12 **L**ORD answered and said, O **L** of hosts,	3068
	1:13 **the L** answered the angel that talked	3068
	1:14 thou, saying, Thus saith **the L** of hosts;	3068
	1:16 Therefore thus saith **the L;** I am returned	3068
	1:16 saith **the L** of hosts, and a line shall be	3068
	1:17 Cry yet, saying, Thus saith **the L** of hosts;	3068
	1:17 **the L** shall yet comfort Zion, and shall yet	3068
	1:20 And **the L** shewed me four carpenters.	3068
	2: 5 I, saith **the L**, will be unto her a wall of	3068
	2: 6 from the land of the north, saith **the L:**	3068
	2: 6 four winds of the heaven, saith **the L**.	3068
	2: 8 For thus saith **the L** of hosts; After	3068
	2: 9 shall know that **the L** of hosts hath sent	3068
	2:10 dwell in the midst of thee, saith **the L**.	3068
	2:11 many nations shall be joined to **the L** in	3068
	2:11 thou shalt know that **the L** of hosts hath	3068
	2:12 **the L** shall inherit Judah his portion in	3068
	2:13 Be silent, O all flesh, before **the L:** for he	3068
	3: 1 priest standing before the angel of **the L**,	3068
	3: 2 **the L** said unto Satan, The **L**ORD rebuke	3068
	3: 2 unto Satan, **The L** rebuke thee, O Satan;	3068
	3: 2 even **the L** that hath chosen Jerusalem	3068
	3: 5 And the angel of **the L** stood *by*.	3068
	3: 6 the angel of **the L** protested unto Joshua,	3068
	3: 7 Thus saith **the L** of hosts; If thou wilt	3068
	3: 9 saith **the L** of hosts, and I will remove	3068
	3:10 In that day, saith **the L** of hosts, shall ye	3068
	4: 6 *is* the word of **the L** unto Zerubbabel,	3068
	4: 6 but by my spirit, saith **the L** of hosts.	3068
	4: 8 the word of **the L** came unto me,	3068
	4: 9 thou shalt know that **the L** of hosts hath	3068
	4:10 they *are* the eyes of **the L**, which run to	3068
	5: 4 saith **the L** of hosts, and it shall enter into	3068
	6: 9 the word of **the L** came unto me, saying,	3068
	6:12 Thus speaketh **the L** of hosts, saying,	3068
	6:12 and he shall build the temple of **the L:**	3068
	6:13 Even he shall build the temple of **the L;**	3068
	6:14 for a memorial in the temple of **the L**.	3068
	6:15 and build in the temple of **the L**,	3068
	6:15 shall know that **the L** of hosts hath sent	3068
	6:15 if ye will diligently obey the voice of **the L**	3068
	7: 1 the word of **the L** came unto Zechariah	3068
	7: 2 and their men, to pray before **the L**,	3068
	7: 3 *were* in the house of **the L** of hosts,	3068
	7: 4 came the word of **the L** of hosts unto me,	3068
	7: 7 *ye* not *hear* the words which **the L**	3068
	7: 8 the word of **the L** came unto Zechariah,	3068
	7: 9 Thus speaketh **the L** of hosts, saying,	3068
	7:12 the words which **the L** of hosts hath sent	3068
	7:12 came a great wrath from **the L** of hosts.	3068
	7:13 and I would not hear, saith **the L** of hosts:	3068
	8: 1 Again the word of **the L** of hosts came to	3068
	8: 2 Thus saith **the L** of hosts; I was jealous for	3068
	8: 3 Thus saith **the L;** I am returned unto Zion,	3068
	8: 3 the mountain of **the L** of hosts the holy	3068
	8: 4 Thus saith **the L** of hosts; There shall yet	3068
	8: 6 Thus saith **the L** of hosts; If it be	3068
	8: 6 in my eyes? saith **the L** of hosts.	3068
	8: 7 Thus saith **the L** of hosts; Behold, I *will*	3068
	8: 9 Thus saith **the L** of hosts; Let your hands	3068
	8: 9 of the house of **the L** of hosts was laid,	3068
	8:11 as *in* the former days, saith **the L** of hosts.	3068
	8:14 For thus saith **the L** of hosts; As I thought	3068
	8:14 saith **the L** of hosts, and I repented not:	3068

Zec	8:17 these *are things* that I hate, saith **the L**.	3068
	8:18 the word of **the L** of hosts came unto me,	3068
	8:19 Thus saith **the L** of hosts; The fast of	3068
	8:20 Thus saith **the L** of hosts; *It shall* yet	3068
	8:21 Let us go speedily to pray before **the L**,	3068
	8:21 the **L**ORD, and to seek **the L** of hosts:	3068
	8:22 strong nations shall come to seek **the L**	3068
	8:22 in Jerusalem, and to pray before **the L**.	3068
	8:23 Thus saith **the L** of hosts; In those days *it*	3068
	9: 1 burden of the word of **the L** in the land	3068
	9: 1 the tribes of Israel, *shall be* toward **the L**.	3068
	9:14 **the L** shall be seen over them,	3068
	9:15 **The L** of hosts shall defend them;	3068
	9:16 **the L** their God shall save them in that	3068
	10: 1 Ask ye of **the L** rain in the time of the	3068
	10: 1 *so* **the L** shall make bright clouds,	3068
	10: 3 for **the L** of hosts hath visited his flock	3068
	10: 5 **the L** *is* with them, and the riders	3068
	10: 6 for I *am* **the L** their God, and will hear	3068
	10: 7 be glad; their heart shall rejoice in **the L**,	3068
	10:12 I will strengthen them in **the L;**	3068
	10:12 up and down in his name, saith **the L**.	3068
	11: 4 Thus saith **the L** my God; Feed the flock	3068
	11: 5 they that sell them say, Blessed *be* **the L;**	3068
	11: 6 the inhabitants of the land, saith **the L**.	3068
	11:11 me knew that it *was* the word of **the L**.	3068
	11:13 **the L** said unto me, Cast it unto the	3068
	11:13 them to the potter *in* the house of **the L**.	3068
	11:15 **the L** said unto me, Take unto thee yet	3068
	12: 1 burden of the word of **the L** for Israel,	3068
	12: 1 saith **the L**, which stretcheth forth	3068
	12: 4 In that day, saith **the L**, I will smite every	3068
	12: 5 my strength in **the L** of hosts their God.	3068
	12: 7 **The L** also shall save the tents of Judah	3068
	12: 8 In that day shall **the L** defend	3068
	12: 8 as God, as the angel of **the L** before them.	3068
	13: 2 to pass in that day, saith **the L** of hosts,	3068
	13: 3 thou speakest lies in the name of **the L:**	3068
	13: 7 *that is* my fellow, saith **the L** of hosts:	3068
	13: 8 to pass, *that* in all the land, saith **the L**,	3068
	13: 9 and they shall say, **The L** *is* my God.	3068
	14: 1 the day of **the L** cometh, and thy spoil	3068
	14: 3 shall **the L** go forth, and fight against	3068
	14: 5 **the L** my God shall come, *and* all the	3068
	14: 7 one day which shall be known to **the L**,	3068
	14: 9 **the L** shall be king over all the earth:	3068
	14: 9 in that day shall there be one **L**,	3068
	14:12 this shall be the plague wherewith **the L**	3068
	14:13 *that* a great tumult from **the L** shall be	3068
	14:16 **the L** of hosts, and to keep the feast of	3068
	14:17 **the L** of hosts, even upon them shall be	3068
	14:18 wherewith **the L** will smite the heathen	3068
	14:20 of the horses, HOLINESS UNTO THE **L**;	3068
	14:21 in Judah shall be holiness unto **the L** of	3068
	14:21 Canaanite in the house of **the L** of hosts.	3068
Mal	1: 1 The burden of the word of **the L** to Israel	3068
	1: 2 I have loved you, saith **the L**. Yet ye say,	3068
	1: 2 saith **the L:** yet I loved Jacob,	3068
	1: 4 thus saith **the L** of hosts, They shall build,	3068
	1: 4 The people *against* whom **the L** hath	3068
	1: 5 **The L** will be magnified from the border	3068
	1: 6 saith **the L** of hosts unto you, O priests,	3068
	1: 7 ye say, The table of **the L** *is* contemptible.	3068
	1: 8 or accept any person? saith **the L** of hosts.	3068
	1: 9 regard your persons? saith **the L** of hosts.	3068
	1:10 no pleasure in you, saith **the L** of hosts,	3068
	1:11 among the heathen, saith **the L** of hosts.	3068
	1:12 that ye say, The table of **the L** *is* polluted;	3068
	1:13 ye have snuffed at it, saith **the L** of hosts;	3068
	1:13 I accept this of your hand? saith **the L**.	3068
	1:14 saith **the L** of hosts, and my name *is*	3068
	2: 2 glory unto my name, saith **the L** of hosts,	3068
	2: 4 might be with Levi, saith **the L** of hosts.	3068
	2: 7 for he *is* the messenger of **the L** of hosts.	3068
	2: 8 the covenant of Levi, saith **the L** of hosts.	3068
	2:11 the holiness of **the L** which he loved,	3068
	2:12 **The L** will cut off the man that doth this,	3068
	2:12 that offereth an offering unto **the L** of	3068
	2:13 covering the altar of **the L** *with* tears,	3068
	2:14 Because **the L** hath been witness	3068
	2:16 *For* **the L**, the God of Israel, saith that he	3068
	2:16 with his garment, saith **the L** of hosts:	3068
	2:17 Ye have wearied **the L** with your words.	3068
	2:17 doeth evil *is* good in the sight of **the L**,	3068
	3: 1 **the L**, whom ye seek, shall suddenly	3068
	3: 1 he *shall* come, saith **the L** of hosts.	3068
	3: 3 they may offer unto **the L** an offering	3068
	3: 4 and Jerusalem be pleasant unto **the L**,	3068
	3: 5 and fear not me, saith **the L** of hosts.	3068
	3: 6 For I *am* **the L**, I change not; therefore	3068
	3: 7 will return unto you, saith **the L** of hosts.	3068
	3:10 me now herewith, saith **the L** of hosts,	3068
	3:11 the time in the field, saith **the L** of hosts.	3068
	3:12 a delightsome land, saith **the L** of hosts.	3068
	3:13 have been stout against me, saith **the L**.	3068
	3:14 walked mournfully before **the L** of hosts?	3068
	3:16 they that feared **the L** spake often one to	3068
	3:16 **the L** hearkened, and heard *it*, and a book	3068
	3:16 before him for them that feared **the L**,	3068
	3:17 they shall be mine, saith **the L** of hosts,	3068
	4: 1 shall burn them up, saith **the L** of hosts,	3068
	4: 3 that I *shall* do *this*, saith **the L** of hosts.	3068
	4: 5 of the great and dreadful day of **the L:**	3068

LORD IS MY BANNER See JEHOVAH-NISSI

L

LORD IS PEACE See JEHOVAH-SHALOM

LORD WILL PROVIDE See JEHOVAH-JIREH

LORD'S (26) [LORD]

Ge	40: 7 *were* with him in the ward of his **l** house,	113
	44: 8 should we steal out of my **l** house silver	113
	44: 9 and we also will be my **l** bondmen.	113+3807.1
	44:16 behold, we *are* my **l** servants, both	113+3807.1
	44:18 speak a word in my **l** ears, and let thine	113
2Sa	20: 6 take thou thy **l** servants, and pursue after	113
1Ch	21: 3 *are* they not all my **l** servants?	113+3807.1
Isa	22:18 thy glory *shall be* the shame of thy **l** house.	113
Da	9:17 sanctuary that is desolate, for the **L** sake.	136
Mt	21:42 this is the **L** doing, and it is marvellous in	2962
	25:18 digged in the earth, and hid his **l** money.	
Mk	12:11 This was the **L** doing, and it is marvellous	2962
Lk	2:26 see death, before he had seen the **L** Christ.	2962
	12:47 which knew his **l** will, and prepared not	2962
	16: 5 he called every one of his **l** debtors unto	2962
Ro	14: 8 we live therefore, or die, we are the **L**.	2962
1Co	7:22 Lord, *being* a servant, is the **L** freeman:	2962
	10:21 ye cannot be partakers of the **L** table,	2962
	10:26 For the earth *is* the **L**, and the fulness	2962
	10:28 conscience *sake:* for the earth *is* the **L**,	2962
	11:20 one place, *this* is not to eat the **L** supper.	2960
	11:26 ye do shew the **L** death till he come.	2962
	11:29 to himself, not discerning the **L** body.	2962
Gal	1:19 saw I none, save James the **L** brother.	2962
1Pe	2:13 to every ordinance of man for the **L** sake:	2962
Rev	1:10 I was in the spirit on the **L** day,	2960

LORD'S* (108) [LORD*]

Ex	9:29 how that the earth *is* the **L**.	3068+3807.1
	12:11 it in haste: it *is* the **L** passover.	3068+3807.1
	12:27 *is* the sacrifice of the **L** passover,	3068+3807.1
	13: 9 that the **L** law may be in thy mouth:	3068
	13:12 the males *shall be* the **L**.	3068+3807.1
	32:26 camp, and said, Who *is* on the **L** side?	3068
	35:21 they brought the **L** offering to the work	3068
	35:24 of silver and brass brought the **L** offering:	3068
Lev	3:16 sweet savour: all the fat *is* the **L**.	3068+3807.1
	16: 9 goat upon which the **L** lot fell,	3068+3807.1
	23: 5 month at even *is* the **L** passover.	3068+3807.1
	27:26 which should be the **L** firstling,	3068+3807.1
	27:26 *it be* ox, or sheep: it *is* the **L**.	3068+3807.1
	27:30 of the fruit of the tree, *is* the **L:**	3068+3807.1
Nu	11:23 unto Moses, Is the **L** hand waxed short?	3068
	11:29 would God that all the **L** people were	3068
	18:28 ye shall give thereof the **L** heave offering	3068
	31:37 the **L** tribute of the sheep was six	3068
	31:38 of which the **L** tribute *was* threescore	3068
	31:39 of which the **L** tribute *was*	3068+3807.1
	31:40 of which the **L** tribute *was* thirty	3068+3807.1
	31:41 which *was* the **L** heave offering,	3068
	32:10 the **L** anger was kindled the same time,	3068
	32:13 the **L** anger was kindled against Israel,	3068
Dt	10:14 of heavens *is* the **L** thy God,	3068+3807.1
	11:17 then the **L** wrath be kindled against you,	3068
	15: 2 because it is called the **L** release.	3068+3807.1
	32: 9 For the **L** portion *is* his people; Jacob *is*	3068
Jos	1:15 which Moses the **L** servant gave you on	3068
	5:15 captain of the **L** host said unto Joshua,	3068
	22:19 wherein the **L** tabernacle dwelleth,	3068
Jdg	11:31 shall surely be the **L**, and I will	3068+3807.1
1Sa	2: 8 the pillars of the earth *are* the **L**,	3068+3807.1
	2:24 hear: ye make the **L** people to transgress.	3068
	14: 3 the son of Eli, the **L** priest in Shiloh,	3068
	16: 6 said, Surely the **L** anointed *is* before him.	3068
	17:47 for the battle *is* the **L**, and he will	3068+3807.1
	18:17 valiant for me, and fight the **L** battles.	3068
	22:21 David that Saul had slain the **L** priests.	3068
	24: 6 this thing unto my master, the **L**	3068+3807.1
	24:10 against my lord; for he *is* the **L** anointed.	3068
	26: 9 forth his hand against the **L** anointed,	3068
	26:11 forth mine hand against the **L** anointed:	3068
	26:16 not kept your master, the **L** anointed.	3068
	26:23 forth mine hand against the **L** anointed.	3068
2Sa	1:14 thine hand to destroy the **L** anointed?	3068
	1:16 saying, I have slain the **L** anointed.	3068
	19:21 this, because he cursed the **L** anointed?	3068
	21: 7 of the **L** oath that *was* between them,	3068
1Ki	18:13 how I hid an hundred men of the **L**	3068
2Ki	11:17 that *they* should be the **L** people;	3068+3807.1
	13:17 The arrow of the **L** deliverance,	3068+3807.1
2Ch	7: 2 the glory of the LORD had filled the **L**	3068
	23:16 that *they* should be the **L** people.	3068+3807.1
Ps	11: 4 holy temple, the **L** throne *is* in heaven:	3068
	22:28 For the kingdom *is* the **L:** and he	3068+3807.1
	24: 1 earth *is* the **L**, and the fulness	3068+3807.1
	113: 3 of the same the **L** name *is* to be praised.	3068
	115:16 *even* the heavens, *are* the **L**:	3068+3807.1
	116:19 In the courts of the **L** house, in the midst	3068
	118:23 This is the **L** doing; it is marvellous in our	3068
	137: 4 How shall we sing the **L** song in a strange	3068
Pr	16:11 weight and balance *are* the **L**.	3068+3807.1
Isa	2: 2 *that* the mountain of the **L** house shall be	3068
	34: 8 For *it is* the day of the **L** vengeance,	3068
	40: 2 she hath received of the **L** hand double	3068
	42:19 is perfect, and blind as the **L** servant?	3068
	44: 5 One shall say, I *am* the **L;**	3068+3807.1
	59: 1 the **L** hand is not shortened, that *it*	3068
Jer	5:10 for *they are* not the **L**.	3068+3807.1
	7: 2 Stand in the gate of the **L** house,	3068
	13:17 the **L** flock is carried away captive.	3068

Jer	19:14 he stood in the court of the **L** house;	3068
	25:17 took I the cup at the **L** hand, and made	3068
	26: 2 Stand in the court of the **L** house,	3068
	26: 2 which come to worship in the **L** house,	3068
	26:10 the entry of the new gate of the **L** *house.*	3068
	27:16 the vessels of the **L** house *shall* now	3068
	28: 3 this place all the vessels of the **L** house,	3068
	28: 6 to bring again the vessels of the **L** house,	3068
	36: 6 in the **L** house upon the fasting day:	3068
	36: 8 the words of the LORD in the **L** house.	3068
	36:10 the entry of the new gate of the **L** house,	3068
	51: 6 for this *is* the time of the **L** vengeance,	3068
	51: 7 Babylon *hath been* a golden cup in the **L**	3068
	51:51 come into the sanctuaries of the **L** house.	3068
La	2:22 in the day of the **L** anger none escaped	3068
	3:22 *It is* of the **L** mercies that we are not	3068
Eze	8:14 the **L** house which *was* towards the	3068
	8:16 brought me into the inner court of the **L**	3068
	10: 4 court was full of the brightness of the **L**	3068
	10:19 the door of the east gate of the **L** house;	3068
	11: 1 brought me unto the east gate of the **L**	3068
Hos	9: 3 They shall not dwell in the **L** land;	3068
Joel	1: 9 the priests, the **L** ministers, mourn.	3068
Ob	1:21 and the kingdom shall be the **L**.	3068+3807.1
Mic	6: 2 The **L** controversy, and ye strong	3068
	6: 9 The **L** voice crieth unto the city,	3068
Hab	2:16 cup of the **L** right hand shall be turned	3068
Zep	1: 8 it shall come to pass in the day of the **L**	3068
	1:18 to deliver them in the day of the **L** wrath;	3068
	2: 2 before the day of the **L** anger come upon	3068
	2: 3 may be ye shall be hid in the day of the **L**	3068
Hag	1: 2 the time that the **L** house should be built.	3068
	1:13 spake Haggai the **L** messenger in	3068
	1:13 in the **L** message unto the people,	3068
	2:18 the foundation of the **L** temple was laid,	3068
Zec	14:20 the pots in the **L** house shall be like	3068

LORDLY (1) [LORD]

Jdg	5:25 milk; she brought forth butter in a **l** dish.	117

LORDS (42) [LORD]

Ge	19: 2 Behold now, my **l**, turn in, I pray you,	113
Nu	21:28 *and* the **l** of the high places of Arnon.	1167
Dt	10:17 Lord of **l**, a great God, a mighty,	113
Jos	13: 3 five **l** of the Philistines; the Gazathites,	5633
Jdg	3: 3 Namely, five **l** of the Philistines, and all	5633
	16: 5 the **l** of the Philistines came up unto her,	5633
	16: 8 the **l** of the Philistines brought up to her	5633
	16:18 and called for the **l** of the Philistines,	5633
	16:18 the **l** of the Philistines came up unto her,	5633
	16:23 the **l** of the Philistines gathered them	5633
	16:27 all the **l** of the Philistines *were* there;	5633
	16:30 the house fell upon the **l**, and upon all	5633
1Sa	5: 8 gathered all the **l** of the Philistines unto	5633
	5:11 together all the **l** of the Philistines,	5633
	6: 4 according to the number of the **l** of	5633
	6: 4 one plague *was* on you all, and on your **l**.	5633
	6:12 the **l** of the Philistines went after them	5633
	6:16 when the five **l** of the Philistines had seen	5633
	6:18 of the Philistines *belonging* to the five **l**,	5633
	7: 7 the **l** of the Philistines went up against	5633
	29: 2 the **l** of the Philistines passed on by	5633
	29: 6 day: nevertheless the **l** favour thee not.	5633
	29: 7 that thou displease not the **l** of	5633
1Ch	12:19 the **l** of the Philistines upon advisement	5633
Ezr	8:25 his **l**, and all Israel *there* present,	8269
Ps	136: 3 give thanks to the Lord of **l**: for his mercy	113
Isa	16: 8 the **l** of the heathen have broken down	1167
	26:13 *other* **l** besides thee have had dominion	113
Jer	2:31 wherefore say my people, We are **l**;	7300
Eze	23:23 and rulers, **great** *l* and renowned,	7991
Da	4:36 my counsellers and my **l** sought unto me;	7261
	5: 1 made a great feast to a thousand of his **l**,	7261
	5: 9 changed in him, and his **l** *were* astonied.	7261
	5:10 reason of the words of the king and his **l**,	7261
	5:23 thou, and thy **l**, thy wives,	7261
	6:17 own signet, and with the signet of his **l**,	7261
Mk	6:21 on his birthday made a supper to his **l**,	3175
1Co	8: 5 (as there be gods many, and **l** many,)	2962
1Ti	6:15 the King of kings, and Lord of **l**;	2961
1Pe	5: 3 Neither as being **l** *over* God's heritage,	2634
Rev	17:14 for he is Lord of **l**, and King of kings:	2962
	19:16 KING OF KINGS, AND LORD OF **L**.	2962

LORDSHIP (2) [LORD]

Mk	10:42 over the Gentiles **exercise l** *over* them;	2634
Lk	22:25 The kings of the Gentiles **exercise l** *over*	2961

LO-RUHAMAH (2) [RUHAMAH]

Hos	1: 6 *God* said unto him, Call her name **L:** for I	3819
	1: 8 Now when she had weaned **L**,	3819

LOSE (23) [LOSETH, LOSS, LOST]

Jdg	18:25 thou **l** thy life, with the lives of thy	622
Job	31:39 have **caused** the owners thereof to **l** their	5301
Pr	23: 8 thou vomit up, and **l** thy sweet words.	7843
Ecc	3: 6 time to get, and a time to **l**; a time to keep,	6
Mt	10:39 that findeth his life shall **l** it: and he that	622
	10:42 unto you, he shall in no wise **l** his reward.	622
	16:25 For whosoever will save his life shall **l** it:	622
	16:25 whosoever will **l** his life for my sake shall	622
	16:26 gain the whole world, and **l** his own soul?	2210
Mk	8:35 For whosoever will save his life shall **l** it;	622
	8:35 but whosoever shall **l** his life for my sake	622
	8:36 gain the whole world, and **l** his own soul?	2210

Mk	9:41 I say unto you, he shall not **l** his reward.	622
Lk	9:24 For whosoever will save his life shall **l** it;	622
	9:24 but whosoever will **l** his life for my sake,	622
	9:25 world, and **l** himself, or be cast away?	622
	15: 4 if he **l** one of them, doth not leave the	622
	15: 8 if she **l** one piece, doth not light a candle,	622
	17:33 Whosoever shall seek to save his life shall **l**	622
	17:33 whosoever shall **l** *his life* shall preserve it.	622
Jn	6:39 of all which he hath given me I should **l**	622
	12:25 He that loveth his life shall **l** it; and he that	622
2Jn	1: 8 that we **l** not *those things* which we have	622

LOSETH (1) [LOSE]

Mt	10:39 he that **l** his life for my sake shall find it.	622

LOSS (10) [LOSE]

Ge	31:39 I **bare** the **l** of it; of my hand didst thou	2398
Ex	21:19 only he shall pay *for* the **l** of his time,	7674
Isa	47: 8 neither shall I know the **l** of children:	7908
	47: 9 day, the **l** of children, and widowhood:	7908
Ac	27:21 and to have gained this harm and **l**.	2209
	27:22 for there shall be no **l** of *any man's* life	580
1Co	3:15 work shall be burnt, he shall **suffer l**:	2210
Php	3: 7 gain to me, those I counted **l** for Christ.	2209
	3: 8 I for the excellency of the knowledge of	2209
	3: 8 for whom I have **suffered** the **l** of all	2210

LOST (33) [LOSE]

Ex	22: 9 for any manner of **l** *thing*, which *another*	9
Lev	6: 3 Or have found **that which was l**,	9
	6: 4 him to keep, or the **l** *thing* which he found,	9
Nu	6:12 the days that were before shall be **l**,	5307
Dt	22: 3 with all **l** *thing* of thy brother's, which	9
	22: 3 which he hath **l**, and thou hast found, shalt	6
1Sa	9: 3 the asses of Kish Saul's father were **l**.	6
	9:20 as for thine asses that were **l** three days ago,	6
1Ki	20:25 like the army that thou hast **l**, horse for	5307
Ps	119:176 I have gone astray like a **l** sheep; seek thy	6
Isa	49:20 after thou hast **l** the other, shall say again	7923
	49:21 seeing I have **l** my **children**,	7921
Jer	50: 6 people hath been **l** sheep: their shepherds	6
Eze	19: 5 her hope was **l**, then she took another of	6
	34: 4 neither have ye sought that which was **l**;	6
	34:16 I will seek that which was **l**, and bring again	6
	37:11 Our bones are dried, and our hope is **l**:	6
Mt	5:13 but if the salt have **l** his **savour**,	3471
	10: 6 go rather to the **l** sheep of the house of	622
	15:24 but unto the **l** sheep of the house of Israel.	622
	18:11 of man is come to save that which was **l**.	622
Mk	9:50 but if the salt have **l** his **saltness**,	358
Lk	14:34 but if the salt have **l** his **savour**,	3471
	15: 4 go after that which is **l**, until he find it?	622
	15: 6 for I have found my sheep which was **l**.	622
	15: 9 for I have found the piece which I had **l**.	622
	15:24 and is alive again; he was **l**, and is found.	622
	15:32 and is alive again; and was **l**, and is found.	622
	19:10 to seek and to save that which was **l**.	622
Jn	6:12 fragments that remain, that nothing be **l**.	622
	17:12 and none of them is **l**, but the son of	622
	18: 9 them which thou gavest me have I **l** none.	622
2Co	4: 3 gospel be hid, it is hid to them that are **l**:	622

LOT (111) [LOT'S, LOTS]

Ge	11:27 and Haran; and Haran begat **L**.	3876
	11:31 **L** the son of Haran his son's son, and Sarai	3876
	12: 4 spoken unto him; and **L** went with him:	3876
	12: 5 **L** his brother's son, and all their	3876
	13: 1 he had, and **L** with him, into the south.	3876
	13: 5 **L** also, which went with Abram,	3876
	13: 8 Abram said unto **L**, Let there be no strife,	3876
	13:10 **L** lifted up his eyes, and beheld all the	3876
	13:11 **L** chose him all the plain of Jordan;	3876
	13:11 the plain of Jordan; and **L** journeyed east:	3876
	13:12 **L** dwelled in the cities of the plain,	3876
	13:14 that **L** was separated from him, Lift up	3876
	14:12 they took **L**, Abram's brother's son,	3876
	14:16 also brought again his brother **L**,	3876
	19: 1 at even; and **L** sat in the gate of Sodom:	3876
	19: 1 **L** seeing *them* rose up to meet them;	3876
	19: 5 they called unto **L**, and said unto him,	3876
	19: 6 **L** went out at the door unto them,	3876
	19: 9 *even* **L**, and came near to break the door.	3876
	19:10 pulled **L** into the house to them, and shut	3876
	19:12 the men said unto **L**, Hast thou here any	3876
	19:14 **L** went out, and spake unto his sons in	3876
	19:15 the angels hastened **L**, saying, Arise,	3876
	19:18 **L** said unto them, Oh, not so, my Lord:	3876
	19:23 The sun was risen upon the earth when **L**	3876
	19:29 sent **L** out of the midst of the overthrow,	3876
	19:29 overthrew the cities in the which **L** dwelt.	3876
	19:30 **L** went up out of Zoar, and dwelt in	3876
	19:36 Thus were both the daughters of **L** with	3876
Lev	16: 8 one **l** for the LORD, and the other **l** for	1486
	16: 8 and the other **l** for the scapegoat.	1486
	16: 9 the goat upon which the LORD'S **l** fell,	1486
	16:10 on which the **l** fell to be the scapegoat,	1486
Nu	26:55 the land shall be divided by **l**:	1486
	26:56 According to the **l** shall the possession	1486
	33:54 ye shall divide the land by **l** for an	1486
	33:54 shall be in the place where his **l** falleth;	1486
	34:13 *is* the land which ye shall inherit by **l**,	1486
	36: 2 inheritance by **l** to the children of Israel:	1486
	36: 3 shall it be taken from the **l** of our	1486
Dt	2: 9 have given Ar unto the children of **L** *for a*	3876
	2:19 have given it unto the children of **L** *for a*	3876

Dt	32: 9	people; Jacob *is* the **l** of his inheritance.	2256
Jos	13: 6	only divide thou it *by* **l** unto the Israelites	NIH
	14: 2	By **l** *was* their inheritance, as the LORD	1486
	15: 1	was the **l** of the tribe of the children of	1486
	16: 1	of the children of Joseph fell from	1486
	17: 1	There was also a **l** for the tribe of	1486
	17: 2	There was also a *l* for the rest of	NIH
	17:14	*but* one **l** and one portion to inherit,	1486
	17:17	thou shalt not have one **l** *only*:	1486
	18:11	of the tribe of the children of	1486
	18:11	the coast of their **l** came forth between	1486
	19: 1	the second **l** came forth to Simeon, *even*	1486
	19:10	the third **l** came up for the children of	1486
	19:17	*And* the fourth **l** came out to Issachar,	1486
	19:24	the fifth **l** came out for the tribe of	1486
	19:32	The sixth **l** came out to the children of	1486
	19:40	the seventh **l** came out for the tribe of	1486
	19:51	divided for an inheritance by **l** in Shiloh	1486
	21: 4	the **l** came out for the families of	1486
	21: 4	had by **l** out of the tribe of Judah,	1486
	21: 5	rest of the children of Kohath had by **l**	1486
	21: 6	the children of Gershon *had* by **l** out of	1486
	21: 8	the children of Israel gave by **l** unto	1486
	21:10	of Levi, had: for theirs was the first **l**.	1486
	21:20	even they had the cities of their **l** out of	1486
	21:40	the Levites, were *by* their **l** twelve cities.	1486
	23: 4	I have divided unto you *by* **l** these nations	NIH
Jdg	1: 3	his brother, Come up with me into my **l**,	1486
	1: 3	and I likewise will go with thee into thy **l**.	1486
	20: 9	to Gibeah; *we will go up* by **l** against it;	1486
1Sa	14:41	Give a perfect **l** And Saul and	NIH
1Ch	6:54	of the Kohathites: for theirs was the **l**.	1486
	6:61	half *tribe* of Manasseh, by **l**, ten cities.	1486
	6:63	Unto the sons of Merari *were given* by **l**,	1486
	6:65	they gave by **l** out of the tribe of	1486
	16:18	land of Canaan, the **l** of your inheritance;	2256
	24: 5	Thus were they divided by **l**, one *sort*	1486
	24: 7	Now the first **l** came forth to Jehoiarib,	1486
	25: 9	Now the first **l** came forth for Asaph to	1486
	26:14	the **l** eastward fell to Shelemiah.	1486
	26:14	cast lots; and his **l** came out northward.	1486
	26:16	and Hosah the *l* came forth westward,	NIH
Est	3: 7	they cast Pur, that *is*, the **l**, before Haman	1486
	9:24	had cast Pur, that *is*, the **l**, to consume	1486
Ps	16: 5	and of my cup: thou maintainest my **l**.	1486
	83: 8	they have holpen the children of **L**. Selah.	3876
	105:11	land of Canaan, the **l** of your inheritance:	2256
	125: 3	shall not rest upon the **l** of the righteous;	1486
Pr	1:14	Cast in thy **l** among us; let us all have one	1486
	16:33	The **l** is cast into the lap; but the whole	1486
	18:18	The **l** causeth contentions to cease,	1486
Isa	17:14	spoil us, and the **l** of them that rob us.	1486
	34:17	he hath cast the **l** for them, and his hand	1486
	57: 6	stream *is* thy portion; they, they *are* thy **l**:	1486
Jer	13:25	*is* thy **l**, the portion of thy measures	1486
Eze	24: 6	it out piece by piece; let no **l** fall upon it.	1486
	45: 1	when ye shall divide *by* **l** the land for	NIH
	47:22	ye shall divide it *by* **l** for an inheritance	NIH
	48:29	*is* the land which ye shall divide *by* **l**	NIH
Da	12:13	and stand in thy **l** at the end of the days.	1486
Jnh	1: 7	they cast lots, and the **l** fell upon Jonah.	1486
Mic	2: 5	by **l** in the congregation of the LORD.	1486
Lk	1: 9	his **l** was to burn incense when he went	2975
	17:28	Likewise also as it was in the days of **L**;	3091
	17:29	the *same* day that **L** went out of Sodom	3091
Ac	1:26	and the **l** fell upon Matthias; and he was	2819
	8:21	hast neither part nor **l** in this matter:	2819
	13:19	he **divided** their land to them by **l**.	2624
2Pe	2: 7	delivered just **L**, vexed with the filthy	3091

LOT'S (2) [LOT]

Ge	13: 7	cattle and the herdmen of **L** cattle:	3876
Lk	17:32	Remember **L** wife.	3091

LOTAN (5) [LOTAN'S]

Ge	36:20	**L**, and Shobal, and Zibeon, and Anah,	3877
	36:22	the children of **L** were Hori and Hemam;	3877
	36:29	duke **L**, duke Shobal, duke Zibeon,	3877
1Ch	1:38	**L**, and Shobal, and Zibeon, and Anah,	3877
	1:39	the sons of **L**; Hori, and Homam:	3877

LOTAN'S (2) [LOTAN]

Ge	36:22	and Hemam; and **L** sister *was* Timna.	3877
1Ch	1:39	and Homam: and Timna *was* **L** sister.	3877

LOTHE (4) [LOATHE, LOATHED, LOTHETH, LOTHING]

Ex	7:18	the Egyptians shall **l** to drink of the water	3811
Eze	6: 9	they shall **l** themselves for the evils which	6962
	20:43	ye shall **l** yourselves in your own sight for	6962
	36:31	shall **l** yourselves in your own sight for	6962

LOTHED (3) [LOTHE]

Jer	14:19	thy soul **l** Zion? why hast thou smitten	1602
Eze	16:45	which **l** their husbands and their children:	1602
Zec	11: 8	soul **l** them, and their soul also abhorred	7114

LOTHETH (1) [LOTHE]

Eze	16:45	that **l** her husband and her children;	1602

LOTHING (1) [LOTHE]

Eze	16: 5	to the **l** of thy person, in the day that thou	1604

LOTS (24) [LOT]

Lev	16: 8	Aaron shall cast **l** upon the two goats;	1486
Jos	18: 6	that I may cast **l** for you here before	1486

Jos	18: 8	that I may here cast **l** for you before	1486
	18:10	Joshua cast **l** for them in Shiloh before	1486
1Sa	14:42	Cast **l** between me and Jonathan my son.	NIH
1Ch	24:31	These likewise cast **l** over against their	1486
	25: 8	they cast **l**, ward against *ward*, as well	1486
	26:13	they cast **l**, as well the small as the great,	1486
	26:14	his son, a wise counseller, they cast **l**;	1486
Ne	10:34	cast the **l** *among* the priests, the Levites,	1486
	11: 1	the rest of the people also cast **l**, to bring	1486
Ps	22:18	among them, and cast **l** upon my vesture.	1486
Joel	3: 3	they have cast **l** for my people;	1486
Ob	1:11	cast **l** upon Jerusalem, even thou *wast* as	1486
Jnh	1: 7	to his fellow, Come, and let us cast **l**,	1486
	1: 7	So they cast **l**, and the lot fell upon Jonah.	1486
Na	3:10	they cast **l** for her honourable *men*, and	1486
Mt	27:35	and parted his garments, casting **l**:	2819
	27:35	upon my vesture did they cast **l**.	2819
Mk	15:24	parted his garments, casting **l** upon them,	2819
Lk	23:34	And they parted his raiment, and cast **l**.	2819
Jn	19:24	Let us not rent it, but **cast l** for it, whose	2975
	19:24	and for my vesture they did cast **l**.	2819
Ac	1:26	they gave forth their **l**; and the lot fell	2819

LOUD (61) [ALOUD, LOUDER]

Ge	39:14	to lie with me, and I cried with a **l** voice:	1419
Ex	19:16	and the voice of the trumpet exceeding **l**;	2389
Dt	27:14	unto all the men of Israel *with* a **l** voice,	7311
1Sa	28:12	saw Samuel, she cried with a **l** voice:	1419
2Sa	15:23	And all the country wept *with* a **l** voice,	1419
	19: 4	the king cried *with* a **l** voice, O my son	1419
1Ki	8:55	the congregation of Israel *with* a **l** voice,	1419
	18:28	they cried **l**,	1419+6963+871.1
2Ki	18:28	cried with a **l** voice in the Jews' language,	1419
2Ch	15:14	they sware unto the LORD with a **l** voice,	1419
	20:19	God of Israel with a **l** voice on high.	1419
	30:21	*singing* with **l** instruments unto	5797
	32:18	they cried with a **l** voice in the Jews'	1419
Ezr	3:12	laid before their eyes, wept with a **l** voice;	1419
	3:13	for the people shouted *with* a **l** shout,	1419
	10:12	and said *with* a **l** voice,	1419
Ne	9: 4	cried with a **l** voice unto the LORD their	1419
	12:42	the singers *sang* **l**, with Jezrahiah *their*	8085
Est	4: 1	city, and cried *with* a **l** and a bitter cry;	1419
Ps	33: 3	a new song; play skilfully with a **l** noise.	8643
	98: 4	**make a l** noise, and rejoice,	6476
	150: 5	Praise him upon the **l** cymbals: praise him	8088
Pr	7:11	(She *is* **l** and stubborn; her feet abide not	1993
	27:14	He that blesseth his friend with a **l** voice,	1419
Isa	36:13	cried with a **l** voice in the Jews' language,	1419
Eze	8:18	they cry in mine ears *with* a **l** voice,	1419
	9: 1	He cried also in mine ears *with* a **l** voice,	1419
	11:13	cried *with* a **l** voice, and said, Ah Lord	1419
Mt	27:46	the ninth hour Jesus cried with a **l** voice,	3173
	27:50	when he had cried again with a **l** voice,	3173
Mk	1:26	and cried with a **l** voice, he came out of	3173
	5: 7	And cried with a **l** voice, and said,	3173
	15:34	at the ninth hour Jesus cried with a **l**	3173
	15:37	Jesus cried with a **l** voice, and gave up	3173
Lk	1:42	And she spake out with a **l** voice,	3173
	4:33	devil, and cried out with a **l** voice,	3173
	8:28	down before him, and with a **l** voice said,	3173
	17:15	and with a **l** voice glorified God,	3173
	19:37	praise God with a **l** voice for all the	3173
	23:23	And they were instant with **l** voices,	3173
	23:46	when Jesus had cried with a **l** voice,	3173
Jn	11:43	he cried with a **l** voice, Lazarus,	3173
Ac	7:57	Then they cried out with a **l** voice,	3173
	7:60	and cried with a **l** voice, Lord,	3173
	8: 7	For unclean spirits, crying with **l** voice,	3173
	14:10	Said with a **l** voice, Stand upright on thy	3173
	16:28	But Paul cried with a **l** voice, saying,	3173
	26:24	Festus said with a **l** voice, Paul, thou art	3173
Rev	5: 2	a strong angel proclaiming with a **l** voice,	3173
	5:12	Saying with a **l** voice, Worthy is the Lamb	3173
	6:10	And they cried with a **l** voice, saying,	3173
	7: 2	he cried with a **l** voice to the four angels,	3173
	7:10	And cried with a **l** voice, saying, Salvation	3173
	8:13	saying with a **l** voice, Woe, woe, woe,	3173
	10: 3	And cried with a **l** voice, as *when* a lion	3173
	12:10	And I heard a **l** voice saying in heaven,	3173
	14: 7	Saying with a **l** voice, Fear God,	3173
	14: 9	saying with a **l** voice, If any *man* worship	3173
	14:15	crying with a **l** voice to him that sat on	3173
	14:18	cried with a **l** cry to him that had the	3173
	19:17	and he cried with a **l** voice, saying to all	3173

LOUDER (2) [LOUD]

Ex	19:19	**waxed l and louder**, Moses spake	2390+3966
	19:19	**waxed louder and l**, Moses spake	2390+3966

LOVE (310) [BELOVED, BELOVED'S, LOVE'S, LOVED, LOVEDST, LOVELY, LOVER, LOVERS, LOVES, LOVEST, LOVETH, LOVING, LOVINGKINDNESS, LOVINGKINDNESSES, WELLBELOVED, WELL-BELOVED]

Ge	27: 4	as I **l**, and bring *it* to me, that I may eat;	157
	29:20	*but* a few days, for the **l** he had to her.	160
	29:32	now therefore my husband will **l** me.	157
Ex	20: 6	mercy unto thousands of them that **l**	157
	21: 5	I **l** my master, my wife, and my children;	157
Lev	19:18	but thou shalt **l** thy neighbour as thyself;	157
	19:34	you, and thou shalt **l** him as thyself;	157
Dt	5:10	mercy unto thousands of them that **l**	157
	6: 5	thou shalt **l** the LORD thy God with all	157
	7: 7	The LORD did not **set** his **l** upon you,	2836

Dt	7: 9	and mercy with them that **l** him and	157
	7:13	he will **l** thee, and bless thee,	157
	10:12	to **l** him, and to serve the LORD thy God	157
	10:15	had a delight in thy fathers to **l** them,	157
	10:19	**L** ye therefore the stranger: for ye were	157
	11: 1	Therefore thou shalt **l** the LORD thy God,	157
	11:13	to **l** the LORD your God, and to serve him	157
	11:22	to do them, to **l** the LORD your God,	157
	13: 3	to know whether you **l** the LORD your God	157
	19: 9	to **l** the LORD thy God, and to walk ever in	157
	30: 6	to **l** the LORD thy God with all thine heart,	157
	30:16	In that I command thee *this* day to **l**	157
	30:20	That thou mayest **l** the LORD thy God,	157
Jos	22: 5	to **l** the LORD your God, and to walk in all	157
	23:11	that ye **l** the LORD your God.	157
Jdg	5:31	*let* them that **l** him *be* as the sun when he	157
	16:15	unto him, How canst thou say, I **l** thee,	157
1Sa	18:22	delight in thee, and all his servants **l** thee:	157
2Sa	1:26	thy **l** to me was wonderful, passing the	160
	1:26	was wonderful, passing the **l** of women.	160
	13: 4	Amnon said unto him, I **l** Tamar, my	157
	13:15	than the **l** wherewith he had loved her.	160
1Ki	11: 2	their gods: Solomon clave unto these in **l**.	157
2Ch	19: 2	and them that hate the LORD?	157
Ne	1: 5	and mercy for them that **l** him and	157
Ps	4: 2	how long will ye **l** vanity, *and* seek after	157
	5:11	let them also that **l** thy name be joyful in	157
	18: 1	I will **l** thee, O LORD, my strength.	7355
	31:23	O **l** the LORD, all ye his saints:	157
	40:16	let such as **l** thy salvation say continually,	157
	69:36	they that **l** his name shall dwell therein.	157
	70: 4	let such as **l** thy salvation say continually,	157
	91:14	Because he hath **set** his **l** upon me,	2836
	97:10	Ye that **l** the LORD, hate evil:	157
	109: 4	For my **l** they are my adversaries: but I	160
	109: 5	me evil for good, and hatred for my **l**.	160
	116: 1	I **l** the LORD, because he hath heard my	157
	119:97	O how I **l** thy law! it *is* my meditation all	157
	119:113	I hate *vain* thoughts: but thy law do I **l**.	157
	119:119	*like* dross: therefore I **l** thy testimonies.	157
	119:127	Therefore I **l** thy commandments above	157
	119:132	as thou usest to do unto those that **l** thy	157
	119:159	Consider how I **l** thy precepts: quicken me,	157
	119:163	I hate and abhor lying: *but* thy law do I **l**.	157
	119:165	Great peace have they which **l** thy law:	157
	119:167	thy testimonies; and I **l** them exceedingly.	157
	122: 6	of Jerusalem: they shall prosper that **l** thee.	157
	145:20	The LORD preserveth all them that **l** him:	157
Pr	1:22	ye simple ones, will ye **l** simplicity?	157
	4: 6	her, and she shall keep thee.	157
	5:19	and be thou ravisht always with her **l**.	160
	7:18	let us take our fill of **l** until the morning:	1730
	8:17	I **l** them that love me; and those that seek	157
	8:17	I love them that me; and those that seek	157
	8:21	That *I* may cause those that **l** me to inherit	157
	8:36	his own soul: all they that hate me **l** death.	157
	9: 8	rebuke a wise *man*, and he will **l** thee.	157
	10:12	stirreth up strifes: but **l** coventh all sins.	160
	15:17	Better *is* a dinner of herbs where **l** is, than	160
	16:13	kings; and *they* **l** him that speaketh right.	157
	17: 9	He that coventh a transgression seeketh **l**;	160
	18:21	and they **l** it that shall eat the fruit thereof.	157
	20:13	**L** not sleep, lest thou come to poverty;	157
	27: 5	Open rebuke *is* better than secret **l**.	157
Ecc	3: 8	A time to **l**, and a time to hate; a time of	157
	9: 1	no man knoweth either **l** or hatred *by* all	157
	9: 6	their **l**, and their hatred, and their envy,	160
SS	1: 2	of his mouth: for thy **l** *is* better than wine.	1730
	1: 3	forth, therefore do the virgins **l** thee.	157
	1: 4	we will remember thy **l** more than wine:	1730
	1: 4	love more than wine: the upright **l** thee.	157
	1: 9	I have compared thee, O my **l**, to a	7474
	1:15	Behold, thou *art* fair, my **l**; behold, thou	7474
	2: 2	so *is* my **l** among the daughters.	7474
	2: 4	and his banner over me *was* **l**.	160
	2: 5	comfort me with apples: for I *am* sick of **l**.	160
	2: 7	stir not up, nor awake *my* **l**, till he please.	160
	2:10	Rise up, my **l**, my fair one, and come	7474
	2:13	Arise, my **l**, my fair one, and come away.	7474
	3: 5	stir not up, nor awake *my* **l**, till he please.	160
	3:10	the midst thereof being paved with **l**,	160
	4: 1	Behold, thou *art* fair, my **l**; behold, thou	7474
	4: 7	Thou *art* all fair, my **l**; *there* is no spot in	7474
	4:10	How fair is thy **l**, my sister, *my* spouse!	1730
	4:10	How much better is thy **l** than wine! and	1730
	5: 2	my sister, my **l**, my dove, my undefiled:	7474
	5: 8	that ye tell him, that I *am* sick of **l**.	160
	6: 4	Thou *art* beautiful, O my **l**, as Tirzah,	7474
	7: 6	how pleasant art thou, O **l**, for delights!	160
	8: 4	not up, nor awake *my* **l**, until he please.	160
	8: 6	for **l** is strong as death; jealousy *is* cruel as	160
	8: 7	Many waters cannot quench **l**, neither can	160
	8: 7	give all the substance of his house for **l**,	160
Isa	38:17	thou hast **in l** to my soul *delivered it* from	2836
	56: 6	serve him, and to **l** the name of the LORD,	157
	61: 8	For the LORD I judgment, I hate robbery	157
	63: 9	in his **l** and in his pity he redeemed them;	157
	66:10	and be glad with her, all ye that **l** her:	157
Jer	2: 2	of thy youth, the **l** of thine espousals,	160
	2:33	Why trimmest thou thy way to seek **l**?	157
	5:31	their means; and my people **l** *to have it* so:	157
	31: 3	I have loved thee with an everlasting **l**;	160
Eze	16: 8	behold, thy time *was* the time of **l**;	1730
	23:11	corrupt in her **inordinate l** than she,	5691
	23:17	Babylonians came to her into the bed of **l**,	1730

L

Eze	33:31 for with their mouth they shew **much l**,	5690
Da	1: 9 **tender l** with the prince of the eunuchs,	7356
	9: 4 covenant and mercy to them that l him,	157
Hos	3: 1 Go yet, l a woman beloved of *her friend*,	157
	3: 1 according to the l of the LORD toward	160
	3: 1 look to other gods, and l flagons of wine.	157
	4:18 her rulers *with* shame do l, Give ye	157
	9:15 out of mine house, I will l them no more:	160
	11: 4 them with cords of a man, with bands of l:	157
	14: 4 heal their backsliding, I will l them freely:	157
Am	5:15 l the good, and establish judgment in	157
Mic	3: 2 Who hate the good, and l the evil; who	157
	6: 8 to l mercy, and to walk humbly with thy	160
Zep	3:17 he will rest in his l, he will joy over thee	160
Zec	8:17 against his neighbour; and l no false oath:	157
	8:19 therefore l the truth and peace.	157
Mt	5:43 Thou shalt l thy neighbour, and hate thine	25
	5:44 But I say unto you, L your enemies,	25
	5:46 if ye l them which love you, what reward	25
	5:46 if ye love them which l you, what reward	25
	6: 5 they l to pray standing in the synagogues	5368
	6:24 either he will hate the one, and l the other;	25
	19:19 and, Thou shalt l thy neighbour as thyself.	25
	22:37 Thou shalt l the Lord thy God with all thy	25
	22:39 Thou shalt l thy neighbour as thyself.	25
	23: 6 And l the uppermost rooms at feasts,	5368
	24:12 shall abound, the l of many shall wax cold.	26
Mk	12:30 thou shalt l the Lord thy God with all thy	25
	12:31 Thou shalt l thy neighbour as thyself.	25
	12:33 to l him with all the heart, and with all	25
	12:33 strength, and to l *his* neighbour as himself,	25
	12:38 which l to go in long clothing,	2309
	12:38 and *l* salutations in the marketplaces,	NIG
Lk	6:27 I say unto you which hear, L your enemies,	25
	6:32 if ye l them which love you, what thank	25
	6:32 if ye love them which l you, what thank	25
	6:32 for sinners also l those that love them.	25
	6:32 for sinners also love those that l them.	25
	6:35 l ye your enemies, and do good, and lend,	25
	7:42 therefore, which of them will l him most?	25
	10:27 Thou shalt l the Lord thy God with all thy	25
	11:42 and pass over judgment and the l of God:	26
	11:43 for ye l the uppermost seats in	25
	16:13 either he will hate the one, and l the other;	25
	20:46 and l greetings in the markets,	5368
Jn	5:42 that ye have not the l of God in you.	26
	8:42 If God were your Father, ye would l me:	25
	10:17 doth *my* Father l me, because I lay	25
	13:34 I give unto you, That ye l one another;	25
	13:34 have loved you, that ye also l one another.	26
	13:35 are my disciples, if ye have l one to another.	26
	14:15 If ye l me, keep my commandments.	25
	14:21 and I will l him, and will manifest myself to	25
	14:23 and said unto him, If a man l me,	25
	14:23 my Father will l him, and we will come	25
	14:31 But that the world may know that I l	25
	15: 9 so have I loved you: continue ye in my l.	25
	15:10 my commandments, ye shall abide in my l;	26
	15:10 Father's commandments, and abide in his l.	26
	15:12 That ye l one another, as I have loved you.	25
	15:13 Greater l hath no *man* than this, that a man	26
	15:17 I command you, that ye l one another.	25
	15:19 of the world, the world would l his own:	5368
	17:26 declare *it*: that the l wherewith thou hast	25
	21:15 Yea, Lord; thou knowest that I l thee.	5368
	21:16 Yea, Lord; thou knowest that I l thee.	5368
	21:17 all *things*; thou knowest that I l thee.	5368
Ro	5: 5 the l of God is shed abroad in our hearts	26
	5: 8 God commendeth his l toward us, in that,	26
	8:28 work together for good to them that l God,	25
	8:35 Who shall separate us from the l of Christ?	26
	8:39 be able to separate us from the l of God,	26
	12: 9 *Let* l *be* without dissimulation. Abhor *that*	26
	12:10 one to another with **brotherly l**;	5360
	13: 8 no *man* any *thing*, but to l one another:	25
	13: 9 Thou shalt l thy neighbour as thyself.	25
	13:10 L worketh no ill to *his* neighbour: therefore	26
	13:10 therefore l *is* the fulfilling of the law.	26
	15:30 Christ's sake, and for the l of the Spirit,	26
1Co	2: 9 God hath prepared for them that l him,	25
	4:21 rod, or in l, and *in* the spirit of meekness?	26
	8: 3 if any *man* l God, the same is known of	25
	16:22 If any *man* l not the Lord Jesus Christ,	5368
	16:24 My l *be* with you all in Christ Jesus. Amen.	26
2Co	2: 4 ye might know the l which I have more	26
	2: 8 *you* would confirm *your* l towards him.	26
	5:14 For the l of Christ constraineth us; because	26
	6: 6 by the Holy Ghost, by l unfeigned,	26
	8: 7 and *in* all diligence, and *in* your l to us,	26
	8: 8 others, and to prove the sincerity of your l.	26
	8:24 the proof of your l, and of our boasting on	26
	11:11 because I l you not? God knoweth.	26
	12:15 though the more abundantly I l you, the less	25
	13:11 the God of l and peace shall be with you.	26
	13:14 and the l of God, and the communion of	26
Gal	5: 6 but faith which worketh by l.	26
	5:13 the flesh, but by l serve one another.	26
	5:14 *even in this*; Thou shalt l thy neighbour as	25
	5:22 But the fruit of the Spirit is l, joy, peace,	26
Eph	1: 4 be holy and without blame before him in l:	26
	1:15 in the Lord Jesus, and l unto all the saints,	26
	2: 4 for his great l wherewith he loved us,	26
	3:17 that ye, being rooted and grounded in l,	26
	3:19 And to know the l of Christ, which passeth	26
	4: 2 forbearing one another in l;	26

Eph	4:15 speaking the truth in l, may grow *up* into	26
	4:16 of the body unto the edifying of itself in l.	26
	5: 2 And walk in l, as Christ also hath loved us,	26
	5:25 Husbands, l your wives, even as Christ also	25
	5:28 So ought men to l their wives as their own	25
	5:33 in particular so l his wife even as himself;	25
	6:23 and l with faith, from God the Father and	26
	6:24 Grace *be* with all them that l our Lord Jesus	25
Php	1: 9 that your l may abound yet more and more	26
	1:17 But the other of l, knowing that I am set for	26
	2: 1 consolation in Christ, if any comfort of l,	26
	2: 2 the same l, *being* of one accord, of one	26
Col	1: 4 and of the l which ye have to all the saints,	26
	1: 8 also declared unto us your l in the Spirit.	26
	2: 2 being knit together in l, and unto all riches	26
	3:19 l *your* wives, and be not bitter against them.	26
1Th	1: 3 and labour of l, and patience of hope in our	26
	3:12 and abound in l one towards another,	26
	4: 9 But as touching **brotherly l** ye need not	5360
	4: 9 for ye yourselves are taught of God to l one	25
	5: 8 putting on the breastplate of faith and l;	26
	5:13 to esteem them very highly in l for their	26
2Th	2:10 because they received not the l of the truth,	26
	3: 5 the Lord direct your hearts into the l of	26
1Ti	1:14 with faith and l which is in Christ Jesus.	26
	6:10 For the l *of money* is the root of all evil:	5365
	6:11 godliness, faith, l, patience, meekness.	26
2Ti	1: 7 of power, and of l, and of a sound mind.	26
	1:13 me, in faith and l which is in Christ Jesus.	26
	4: 8 but unto all them also that l his appearing.	25
Tit	2: 4 l their **husbands**, to love their	1510+5362
	2: 4 love their husbands, to l their **children**,	5388
	3: 4 l of God our Saviour **toward man**	5363
	3:15 Greet them that l us in the faith. Grace *be*	5368
Phm	1: 5 Hearing of thy l and faith, which thou hast	26
	1: 7 we have great joy and consolation in thy l,	26
Heb	6:10 to forget your work and labour of l,	26
	10:24 consider one another to provoke unto l	26
	13: 1 Let **brotherly l** continue.	5360
Jas	1:12 the Lord hath promised to them that l	25
	2: 5 he hath promised to them that l him?	25
	2: 8 Thou shalt l thy neighbour as thyself, ye do	25
1Pe	1: 8 Whom having not seen, ye l; in whom,	25
	1:22 Spirit unto unfeigned l of the **brethren**,	5360
	1:22 *see that* ye l one another with a pure heart	25
	2:17 Honour all *men*. L the brotherhood.	25
	3: 8 l **as brethren**, be pitiful, be courteous:	5361
	3:10 For he that will l life, and see good days,	25
1Jn	2: 5 in him verily is the l of God perfected:	26
	2:15 L not the world, neither the *things* that are	25
	2:15 any *man* l the world, the love of the Father	25
	2:15 the world, the l of the Father is not in him.	26
	3: 1 what manner of l the Father hath bestowed	26
	3:11 the beginning, that we should l one another.	25
	3:14 death unto life, because we l the brethren.	25
	3:16 Hereby perceive we the l *of God*, because	26
	3:17 him, how dwelleth the l of God in him?	26
	3:18 let us not l in word, neither in tongue;	25
	3:23 and l one another, as he gave us	25
	4: 7 Beloved, let us l one another: for love is of	25
	4: 7 l is of God; and every one that loveth is	25
	4: 8 loveth not, knoweth not God; for God is l.	25
	4: 9 In this was manifested the l of God towards	26
	4:10 Herein is l, not that we loved God, but that	26
	4:11 so loved us, we ought also to l one another.	25
	4:12 If we l one another, God dwelleth in us,	25
	4:12 dwelleth in us, and his l is perfected in us.	26
	4:16 and believed the l that God hath to us.	26
	4:16 God is l; and he that dwelleth in love	26
	4:16 and he that dwelleth in l dwelleth in God,	26
	4:17 Herein is our l made perfect, that we may	26
	4:18 There is no fear in l; but perfect love casteth	26
	4:18 no fear in love; but perfect l casteth out fear:	26
	4:18 He that feareth is not made perfect in l.	26
	4:19 We l him, because he first loved us.	25
	4:20 I l God, and hateth his brother, he is a liar:	25
	4:20 how can he l God whom he hath not seen?	25
	4:21 That he who loveth God l his brother also.	25
	5: 2 By this we know that we l the children of	25
	5: 2 we l God, and keep his commandments.	25
	5: 3 For this is the l of God, that we keep his	26
2Jn	1: 1 and her children, whom I l in the truth;	25
	1: 3 the Son of the Father, in truth and l.	26
	1: 5 from the beginning, that we l one another.	25
	1: 6 And this is l, that we walk after his	26
3Jn	1: 1 wellbeloved Gaius, whom I l in the truth.	25
Jude	1: 2 unto you, and peace, and l, be multiplied.	25
	1:21 Keep yourselves in the l of God, looking for	26
Rev	2: 4 thee, because thou hast left thy first l.	26
	3:19 As many as I l, I rebuke and chasten:	5368

LOVE'S (1) [LOVE]

Phm	1: 9 *Yet* for l sake I rather beseech *thee*, being	26

LOVED (98) [LOVE]

Ge	24:67 and she became his wife; and he l her:	157
	25:28 Isaac l Esau, because he did eat of *his*	157
	25:28 eat of *his* venison: but Rebekah l Jacob.	157
	27:14 made savoury meat, such as his father l.	157
	29:18 Jacob l Rachel; and said, I will serve thee	157
	29:30 he l also Rachel more than Leah,	157
	34: 3 he l the damsel, and spake kindly unto	157
	37: 3 Now Israel l Joseph more than all his	157
	37: 4 his brethren saw that their father l him	157
Dt	4:37 because he l thy fathers, therefore he chose	157

Dt	7: 8 because the LORD l you, and because	160
	23: 5 because the LORD thy God l thee.	157
	33: 3 he l the people; all his saints *are* in thy	2245
Jdg	16: 4 that he l a woman in the valley of Sorek,	157
1Sa	1: 5 he gave a worthy portion; for l he l Hannah:	157
	16:21 he l him greatly; and he became his	157
	18: 1 and Jonathan l him as his own soul.	157
	18: 3 because he l him as his own soul.	160
	18:16 all Israel and Judah l David, because he	157
	18:20 Michal Saul's daughter l David:	157
	18:28 *that* Michal Saul's daughter l him.	157
	20:17 David to swear again, because he l him:	160
	20:17 for he l him as he loved his own soul.	160
	20:17 he loved him as he l his own soul.	157
2Sa	12:24 his name Solomon: and the LORD l him.	157
	13: 1 and Amnon the son of David l her.	157
	13:15 than the love wherewith he had l her.	157
1Ki	3: 3 Solomon l the LORD, walking in	157
	10: 9 because the LORD l Israel for ever,	160
	11: 1 king Solomon l many strange women,	157
2Ch	2:11 Because the LORD hath l his people,	160
	9: 8 because thy God l Israel, to establish them	160
	11:21 Rehoboam l Maachah the daughter of	157
	26:10 and in Carmel: for he l husbandry.	157
Est	2:17 the king l Esther above all the women,	157
Job	19:19 and they whom I l are turned against me.	157
Ps	26: 8 I have l the habitation of thy house,	157
	47: 4 for us, the excellency of Jacob whom he l.	157
	78:68 tribe of Judah, the mount Zion which he l.	157
	109:17 As he l cursing, so let it come *unto* him:	157
	119:47 in thy commandments, which I have l.	157
	119:48 unto thy commandments, which I have l;	157
Isa	43: 4 hast been honourable, and I have l thee:	157
	48:14 these *things*? The LORD hath l him:	157
Jer	2:25 for I have l strangers, and after them will l	157
	8: 2 whom they have l, and whom they have	157
	14:10 Thus have they l to wander, they have not	157
	31: 3 I have l thee *with* an everlasting love;	157
Eze	16:37 all *them* that thou hast l, with all *them* that	157
Hos	9: 1 thou hast l a reward upon every cornfloor.	157
	9:10 abominations were according as they l.	157
	11: 1 I l him, and called my son out of Egypt.	157
Mal	1: 2 I have l you, saith the LORD. Yet ye say,	157
	1: 2 Yet ye say, Wherein hast thou l us?	157
	1: 2 saith the LORD: yet I l Jacob,	157
	2:11 the holiness of the LORD which he l,	157
Mk	10:21 Then Jesus beholding him l him,	25
Lk	7:47 are many, are forgiven; for she l much:	25
Jn	3:16 God so l the world, that he gave his only	25
	3:19 men l darkness rather than light, because	25
	11: 5 Now Jesus l Martha, and her sister,	25
	11:36 said the Jews, Behold, how he l him.	5368
	12:43 For they l the praise of men more than	25
	13: 1 having l his own which were in the world,	25
	13: 1 were in the world, he l them unto the end.	25
	13:23 bosom one of his disciples, whom Jesus l.	25
	13:34 I have l you, that ye also love one another.	25
	14:21 he that loveth me shall be l of my Father,	25
	14:28 If ye l me, ye would rejoice, because I said,	25
	15: 9 the Father hath l me, so have I loved you:	25
	15: 9 the Father loved me, so have I l you:	25
	15:12 That ye love one another, as I have l you.	25
	16:27 because ye have l me, and have believed	5368
	17:23 and hast l them, as thou hast loved me.	25
	17:23 and hast loved them, as thou hast l me.	25
	17:26 wherewith thou hast l me may be in them,	25
	19:26 and the disciple standing by, whom he l,	25
	20: 2 whom Jesus l, and saith unto them,	5368
	21: 7 Therefore that disciple whom Jesus l saith	25
	21:20 seeth the disciple whom Jesus l following;	25
Ro	8:37 than conquerors through him that l us.	25
	9:13 As it is written, Jacob have I l,	25
2Co	12:15 more abundantly I love you, the less I be l.	25
Gal	2:20 of God, who l me, and gave himself for me.	25
Eph	2: 4 mercy, for his great love wherewith he l us,	25
	2: 5 as Christ also hath l us, and hath given	25
	5:25 even as Christ also l the church,	25
2Th	2:16 hath l us, and hath given *us* everlasting	25
2Ti	4:10 having l this present world, and is departed	25
Heb	1: 9 hast l righteousness, and hated iniquity;	25
2Pe	2:15 Bosor, who l the wages of unrighteousness;	25
1Jn	4:10 not that we l God, but that he loved us,	25
	4:10 but that he l us, and sent his Son to be	25
	4:11 if God so l us, we ought also to love	25
	4:19 We love him, because he first l us.	25
Rev	1: 5 Unto him that l us, and washed us from	25
	3: 9 thy feet, and to know that I have l thee.	25
	12:11 and they l not their lives unto the death.	25

LOVEDST (2) [LOVE]

Isa	57: 8 thou l their bed where thou sawest *it*.	157
Jn	17:24 for thou l me before the foundation of	25

LOVELY (4) [LOVE]

2Sa	1:23 Saul and Jonathan *were* l and pleasant in	157
SS	5:16 he *is* altogether l. This *is* my beloved,	4261
Eze	33:32 thou *art* unto them as a **very l** song *of*	5690
Php	4: 8 *things* are pure, whatsoever *things are* l,	4375

LOVER (4) [LOVE]

1Ki	5: 1 his father: for Hiram was ever a l of David.	157
Ps	88:18 L and friend hast thou put far from me,	157
Tit	1: 8 a l **of hospitality**, a lover of good *men*,	5382
	1: 8 a l **of good** *men*, sober, just, holy,	5358

L

LOVERS (23) [LOVE]
Ps	38:11 My l and my friends stand aloof from my	157
Jer	3: 1 thou hast played the harlot with many l;	7453
	4:30 *thy* l will despise thee, they will seek thy	5689
	22:20 the passages: for all thy l are destroyed.	157
	22:22 pastors, and thy l shall go into captivity:	157
	30:14 All thy l have forgotten thee; they seek	157
La	1: 2 all her l she hath none to comfort *her:*	157
	1:19 I called for my l, *but* they deceived me:	157
Eze	16:33 thou givest thy gifts to all thy l,	157
	16:36 through thy whoredoms with thy l,	157
	16:37 Behold therefore, I will gather all thy l,	157
	23: 5 she doted on her l, on the Assyrians *her*	157
	23: 9 I have delivered her into the hand of her l,	157
	23:22 Behold, I will raise up thy l against thee,	157
Hos	2: 5 she said, I will go after my l, that give *me*	157
	2: 7 she shall follow after her l, but she shall	157
	2:10 discover her lewdness in the sight of her l,	157
	2:12 These *are* my rewards that my l have given	157
	2:13 and she went after her l, and forgat me,	157
	8: 9 ass alone by himself: Ephraim hath hired l.	158
2Ti	3: 2 For men shall be l of their **own selves**,	5367
	3: 4 l **of pleasures** more than lovers of God;	5369
	3: 4 lovers of pleasures more than l **of God**;	5377

LOVES (3) [LOVE]
Ps	45: T the sons of Korah, Maschil, A Song of l.	3039
Pr	7:18 morning: let us solace ourselves with l.	159
SS	7:12 bud forth: there will I give thee my l.	1730

LOVEST (12) [LOVE]
Ge	22: 2 whom thou l, and get thee into the land of	157
Jdg	14:16 said, Thou dost but hate me, and l me not:	157
2Sa	19: 6 In that thou l thine enemies, and hatest	157
Ps	45: 7 l righteousness, and hatest wickedness:	157
	52: 3 Thou l evil more than good; *and* lying	157
	52: 4 Thou l all devouring words, O thou	157
Ecc	9: 9 Live joyfully with the wife whom thou l all	157
Jn	11: 3 Lord, behold, he whom thou l is sick.	5368
	21:15 *son* of Jonas, l thou me more than these?	25
	21:16 Simon, *son* of Jonas, l thou me?	25
	21:17 Simon, *son* of Jonas, l thou me?	5368
	21:17 said unto him the third time, **L** thou me?	5368

LOVETH (65) [LOVE]
Ge	27: 9 savoury meat for thy father, such as he l:	157
	44:20 is left of his mother, and his father l him.	157
Dt	10:18 fatherless and widow, and l the stranger,	157
	15:16 because he l thee and thine house,	157
Ru	4:15 for thy daughter in law, which l thee,	157
Ps	11: 5 and him that l violence his soul hateth.	157
	11: 7 For the righteous LORD l righteousness;	157
	33: 5 He l righteousness and judgment: the earth	157
	34:12 *and* l many days, that *he* may see good?	157
	37:28 For the LORD l judgment,	157
	87: 2 The LORD l the gates of Zion more than all	157
	99: 4 The king's strength also l judgment;	157
	119:140 word *is* very pure: therefore thy servant l it.	157
	146: 8 are bowed down: the LORD l the righteous:	157
Pr	3:12 For whom the LORD l he correcteth;	157
	12: 1 Whoso l instruction loveth knowledge:	157
	12: 1 Whoso l instruction l knowledge:	157
	13:24 but he that l him chasteneth him betimes.	157
	15: 9 he l him that followeth after righteousness.	157
	15:12 A scorner l not one that reproveth him:	157
	17:17 A friend l at all times, and a brother is born	157
	17:19 He l transgression that l strife:	157
	17:19 He l transgression that l strife:	157
	19: 8 He that getteth wisdom l his own soul:	157
	21:17 He that l pleasure *shall be* a poor man:	157
	21:17 he that l wine and oil shall not be rich.	157
	22:11 He that l pureness of heart, *for* the grace of	157
	29: 3 Whoso l wisdom rejoiceth his father:	157
Ecc	5:10 He that l silver shall not be satisfied *with*	157
	5:10 nor he that l abundance *with* increase:	157
SS	1: 7 Tell me, O thou whom my soul l, where	157
	3: 1 on my bed I sought *him* whom my soul l:	157
	3: 2 ways, I will seek *him* whom my soul l?	157
	3: 3 *I said,* Saw ye *him* whom my soul l?	157
	3: 4 them, but I found *him* whom my soul l:	157
Isa	1:23 every one l gifts, and followeth after	157
Hos	10:11 I to tread out *the corn;* but I passed over	157
	12: 7 of deceit are in his hand: he l to oppress.	157
Mt	10:37 He that l father or mother more than me	5368
	10:37 he that l son or daughter more than me	5368
Lk	7: 5 For he l our nation, and he hath built us a	25
	7:47 to whom little is forgiven, *the same* l little.	25
Jn	3:35 Father l the Son, and hath given all *things*	25
	5:20 the Father l the Son, and sheweth him	5368
	12:25 He that l his life shall lose it; and he that	5368
	14:21 and keepeth them, he it is that l me:	25
	14:21 he that l me shall be loved of my Father,	25
	14:24 He that l me not keepeth not my sayings:	25
	16:27 For the Father himself l you, because	5368
Ro	13: 8 for he that l another hath fulfilled the law.	25
2Co	9: 7 or of necessity: for God l a cheerful giver.	25
Eph	5:28 He that l his wife loveth himself.	25
	5:28 that loveth his wife l himself.	25
Heb	12: 6 For whom the Lord l he chasteneth,	25
1Jn	2:10 He that l his brother abideth in the light,	25
	3:10 not of God, neither he that l not his brother.	25
	3:14 He that l not *his* brother abideth in death.	25
	4: 7 and every one that l is born of God,	25
	4: 8 He that l not, knoweth not God; for God is	25
	4:20 for he that l not his brother whom he hath	25

1Jn	4:21 That he who l God love his brother also.	25
	5: 1 every one that l him that begat loveth him	25
	5: 1 every one that loveth him that begat him	25
3Jn	1: 9 who l **to have** the **preeminence among**	5383
Rev	22:15 and whosoever l and maketh a lie.	5368

LOVING (3) [LOVE]
Pr	5:19 *Let her be as* the l hind and pleasant roe;	158
	22: 1 *and* l favour rather than silver and gold.	2896
Isa	56:10 sleeping, lying down, l to slumber.	157

LOVINGKINDNESS (26) [KIND, LOVE]
Ps	17: 7 Shew thy marvellous l, O thou that savest	2617
	26: 3 For thy l *is* before mine eyes: and I have	2617
	36: 7 How excellent *is* thy l, O God! therefore	2617
	36:10 continue thy l unto them that know thee;	2617
	40:10 I have not concealed thy l and thy truth	2617
	40:11 let thy l and thy truth continually preserve	2617
	42: 8 *Yet* the LORD will command his l in	2617
	48: 9 We have thought of thy l, O God,	2617
	51: 1 upon me, O God, according to thy l:	2617
	63: 3 Because thy l *is* better than life, my lips	2617
	69:16 Hear me, O LORD; for thy l *is* good:	2617
	88:11 Shall thy l be declared in the grave?	2617
	89:33 Nevertheless my l will I not utterly take	2617
	92: 2 To shew forth thy l in the morning,	2617
	103: 4 who crowneth thee *with* l and	2617
	107:43 they shall understand the l of the LORD.	2617
	119:88 Quicken me after thy l; so shall I keep	2617
	119:149 Hear my voice according unto thy l:	2617
	119:159 quicken me, O LORD, according to thy l.	2617
	138: 2 praise thy name for thy l and for thy truth:	2617
	143: 8 Cause me to hear thy l in the morning;	2617
Jer	9:24 that I *am* the LORD which exercise l,	2617
	16: 5 saith the LORD, *even* l and mercies.	2617
	31: 3 therefore *with* l have I drawn thee.	2617
	32:18 Thou shewest l unto thousands,	2617
Hos	2:19 in judgment, and in l, and in mercies.	2617

LOVINGKINDNESSES (4) [KIND, LOVE]
Ps	25: 6 O LORD, thy tender mercies and thy l;	2617
	89:49 Lord, where *are* thy former l, *which* thou	2617
Isa	63: 7 I will mention the l of the LORD,	2617
	63: 7 and according to the multitude of his l.	2617

LOW (46) [LOWER, LOWEST, LOWLINESS, LOWLY]
Dt	28:43 thou shalt come down very l.	4295+4295
Jdg	11:35 thou hast **brought** me very l,	3766+3766
1Sa	2: 7 rich: he **bringeth** l, and lifteth up.	8213
1Ch	27:28 sycomore trees that *were* in the l **plains**	8219
2Ch	9:27 that *are* in the l **plains** in abundance.	8219
	26:10 both in the l **country**, and in the plains:	8219
	28:18 had invaded the cities of the l **country**,	8219
	28:19 For the LORD **brought** Judah l because	3665
Job	5:11 To set up on high those that be l;	8217
	14:21 are **brought** l, but he perceiveth *it* not	6819
	24:24 little while, but are gone and **brought** l,	4355
	40:12 every one *that is* proud, *and* **bring** him l;	3665
Ps	49: 2 Both l and high, rich and poor,	120+1121
	62: 9 Surely **men of l degree** *are* vanity,	120+1121
	79: 8 prevent us: for we are **brought** very l.	1809
	106:43 and were **brought** l for their iniquity.	4355
	107:39 and **brought** l through oppression,	7817
	116: 6 I was **brought** l, and he helped me.	1809
	136:23 Who remembered us in our l **estate:**	8216
	142: 6 unto my cry; for I am **brought** very l:	1809
Pr	29:23 A man's pride shall **bring** him l:	8213
Ecc	10: 6 great dignity, and the rich sit in l **place.**	8216
	12: 4 when the sound of the grinding is l,	8217
	12: 4 daughters of musick shall be **brought** l;	7817
Isa	2:12 is lifted up; and he shall be **brought** l:	8213
	2:17 the haughtiness of men shall be **made** l:	8213
	13:11 will **lay** l the haughtiness of the terrible.	8213
	25: 5 of the terrible ones shall be **brought** l.	6030
	25:12 **lay** l, and bring to the ground, *even* to	8213
	26: 5 the lofty city, he **layeth** it l; he layeth it	8213
	26: 5 it low; he **layeth** it l, *even* to the ground;	8213
	29: 4 thy speech shall be l out of the dust,	7817
	32:19 and the city shall be l in a low place.	8213
	32:19 and the city shall be low in a l **place.**	8218
	40: 4 every mountain and hill shall be **made** l:	8213
La	3:55 thy name, O LORD, out of the l dungeon.	8482
Eze	17: 6 and became a spreading vine of l stature,	8217
	17:24 have exalted the l tree, have dried up	8217
	21:26 exalt *him that is* l, and abase *him that is*	8217
	26:20 shall set thee **in** the l **parts** of the earth,	8482
Lk	1:48 For he hath regarded the l **estate** of his	5014
	1:52 *their* seats, and exalted them of l **degree.**	5011
	3: 5 mountain and hill shall be **brought** l;	5013
Ro	12:16 but condescend to **men of l estate.**	5011
Jas	1: 9 Let the brother of l **degree** rejoice in that	5011
	1:10 the rich, in that he is **made** l: because	5014

LOWBORN See DEGREE; DEGREES

LOWER (18) [LOW]
Ge	6:16 *with* l, second, and third *stories* shalt	8482
Lev	13:20 *it be* in sight l than the skin, and the hair	8217
	13:21 *if* it *be* not l than the skin, but *be*	8217
	13:26 *it be* no l than the *other* skin, but *be*	8217
	14:37 which in sight *are* l than the wall;	8217
Ne	4:13 Therefore set I in the l places behind	8482
Ps	8: 5 For thou hast **made** him a little l than	2637
	63: 9 to destroy *it,* shall go into the l **parts**	8482
Pr	25: 7 than that thou shouldest be **put** l in	8213
Isa	22: 9 ye gathered together the waters of the l	8481

Isa	44:23 done *it:* shout, ye l **parts** of the earth:	8482
Eze	40:18 length of the gates *was* the l pavement.	8481
	40:19 l gate unto the forefront of the inner	8481
	42: 5 than the l, and than the middlemost of	8481
	43:14 *even* to the l settle *shall be* two cubits,	8481
Eph	4: 9 he also descended first into the l **parts**	2737
Heb	2: 7 **madest** him a little l than the angels;	1642
	2: 9 who was **made** a little l than the angels,	1642

LOWEST (11) [LOW]
Dt	32:22 shall burn unto the l **hell,**	8482
1Ki	12:31 made priests of the l of the people,	7098
	13:33 made again of the l of the people priests	7098
2Ki	17:32 made unto themselves of the l of them	7098
Ps	86:13 hast delivered my soul from the l **hell.**	8482
	88: 6 hast laid me in the l pit, in darkness,	8482
	139:15 curiously wrought in the l **parts** of	8482
Eze	41: 7 *from* the l *chamber* to the highest	8481
	42: 6 *building* was straitened more than the l	8481
Lk	14: 9 begin with shame to take the l room.	2078
	14:10 bidden, go and sit down in the l room;	2078

LOWETH (1) [LOWING]
Job	6: 5 he hath grass? or l the ox over his fodder?	1600

LOWING (2) [LOWETH]
1Sa	6:12 l as they went, and turned not aside *to*	1600
	15:14 and the l of the oxen which I hear?	6963

LOWLINESS (2) [LOW]
Eph	4: 2 With all l and meekness, with	5012
Php	2: 3 in l **of mind** *let* each esteem other better	5012

LOWLY (6) [LOW]
Ps	138: 6 be high, yet hath he respect unto the l:	8217
Pr	3:34 scorners: but he giveth grace unto the l.	6035
	11: 2 cometh shame: but with the l *is* wisdom.	6800
	16:19 *it is* to be of an humble spirit with the l,	6035
Zec	9: 9 l, and riding upon an ass, and upon a colt	6041
Mt	11:29 learn of me; for I am meek and l in heart:	5011

LOWRING (1)
Mt	16: 3 for the sky is red and l. O *ye* hypocrites,	4768

LUBIM (1) [LUBIMS]
Na	3: 9 *was* infinite; Put and **L** were thy helpers.	3864

LUBIMS (2) [LUBIM]
2Ch	12: 3 the **L,** the Sukkiims, and the Ethiopians,	3864
	16: 8 not the Ethiopians and the **L** a huge host,	3864

LUCAS (2)
2Co	13: S *a city* of Macedonia, by Titus and **L.**	3065
Phm	1:24 Marcus, Aristarchus, Demas, **L,**	3065

LUCIFER (1)
Isa	14:12 from heaven, O **L,** son of the morning!	1966

LUCIUS (2)
Ac	13: 1 and **L** of Cyrene, and Manaen,	3066
Ro	16:21 and **L,** and Jason, and Sosipater,	3066

LUCRE (5) [LUCRE'S]
1Sa	8: 3 turned aside after l, and took bribes,	1215
1Ti	3: 3 wine, no striker, not **greedy of filthy l;**	146
	3: 8 to much wine, not **greedy of filthy l;**	146
Tit	1: 7 to wine, no striker, not **given to filthy l;**	146
1Pe	5: 2 not **for filthy l,** but of a ready mind;	147

LUCRE'S (1) [LUCRE]
Tit	1:11 which *they* ought not, for filthy l sake.	2771

LUD (4)
Ge	10:22 Asshur, and Arphaxad, and **L,** and Aram.	3865
1Ch	1:17 **L,** and Aram, and Uz, and Hul,	3865
Isa	66:19 Tarshish, Pul, and **L,** that draw the bow,	3865
Eze	27:10 They of Persia and of **L** and of Phut were	3865

LUDIM (2)
Ge	10:13 Mizraim begat **L,** and Anamim,	3865
1Ch	1:11 Mizraim begat **L,** and Anamim,	3865

LUDITES See LUDIM

LUHITH (2)
Isa	15: 5 *by* the mounting up of **L** with weeping	3872
Jer	48: 5 *in* the going up of **L** continual weeping	3872

LUKE (2)
Col	4:14 **L,** the beloved physician, and Demas,	3065
2Ti	4:11 Only **L** is with me. Take Mark,	3065

LUKEWARM (1) [WARM]
Rev	3:16 then because thou art l, and neither cold	5513

LUMP (7)
2Ki	20: 7 Isaiah said, Take a l of figs. And they took	1690
Isa	38:21 Let them take a l of figs, and lay *it* for a	1690
Ro	9:21 of the same l to make one vessel unto	5445
	11:16 the l *is* also *holy:* and if the root *be* holy,	5445
1Co	5: 6 that a little leaven leaveneth the whole l?	5445
	5: 7 the old leaven, that ye may be a new l,	5445
Gal	5: 9 A little leaven leaveneth the whole l.	5445

LUNATICK (2)
Mt	4:24 those which were l, and those that had	4583
	17:15 for he is l, and sore vexed: for ofttimes he	4583

LURK (2) [LURKING]
| Pr | 1:11 let us l **privily** for the innocent without | 6845 |
| | 1:18 they l **privily** for their own lives. | 6845 |

LURKING (3) [LURK]
1Sa	23:23 take knowledge of all the l **places** where	4224
Ps	10: 8 He sitteth in the l **places** of the villages:	3993
	17:12 as it were a young lion l in secret places.	3427

LUST (19) [LUSTED, LUSTETH, LUSTING, LUSTS, LUSTY]
Ex	15: 9 spoil; my l shall be satisfied upon them;	5315
Ps	78:18 in their heart by asking meat for their l.	5315
	78:30 They were not estranged from their l.	8378
	81:12 I gave them up unto their own heart's l.	8307
Pr	6:25 L not **after** her beauty in thine heart;	2530
Mt	5:28 I after her hath committed adultery with	1937
Ro	1:27 burned in their l one towards another;	3715
	7: 7 for I had not known l, except the law had	1939
1Co	10: 6 to the intent we should not l **after** evil	1938
Gal	5:16 and ye shall not fulfil the l of the flesh.	1939
1Th	4: 5 Not in the l of concupiscence, even as	3806
Jas	1:14 when he is drawn away of his own l,	1939
	1:15 Then when l hath conceived, it bringeth	1939
	4: 2 Ye l, and have not: ye kill, and desire *to*	1937
2Pe	1: 4 corruption that is in the world through l:	1939
	2:10 after the flesh in the l of uncleanness,	1939
1Jn	2:16 the l of the flesh, and the lust of the eyes,	1939
	2:16 the l of the eyes, and the pride of life,	1939
	2:17 the world passeth away, and the l thereof:	1939

LUSTED (4) [LUST]
Nu	11:34 there they buried the people that l.	183
Ps	106:14 l **exceedingly** in the wilderness,	183+8378
1Co	10: 6 not lust after evil *things,* as they also l.	1937
Rev	18:14 And the fruits that thy soul l **after** are	1939

LUSTETH (6) [LUST]
Dt	12:15 in all thy gates, whatsoever thy soul l **after**,	185
	12:20 eat flesh, whatsoever thy soul l **after**.	185
	12:21 eat in thy gates whatsoever thy soul l **after**,	185
	14:26 *that* money for whatsoever thy soul l **after**,	183
Gal	5:17 For the flesh l against the Spirit,	1937
Jas	4: 5 the spirit that dwelleth in us to envy?	1971

LUSTING (1) [LUST]
| Nu | 11: 4 that *was* among them **fell a** l: | 183+8378 |

LUSTS (24) [LUST]
Mk	4:19 and the l of other *things* entering in,	1939
Jn	8:44 and the l of your father ye will do.	1939
Ro	1:24 through the l of their own hearts,	1939
	6:12 that *ye* should obey it in the l thereof.	1939
	13:14 for the flesh, to *fulfil* the l *thereof.*	1939
Gal	5:24 the flesh with the affections and l.	1939
Eph	2: 3 in times past in the l of our flesh,	1939
	4:22 is corrupt according to the deceitful l;	1939
1Ti	6: 9 snare, and *into* many foolish and hurtful l,	1939
2Ti	2:22 Flee also youthful l:	1939
	3: 6 laden with sins, led away with divers l,	1939
	4: 3 after their own l shall they heap to	1939
Tit	2:12 and worldly l we should live soberly,	1939
	3: 3 deceived, serving divers l and pleasures,	1939
Jas	4: 1 *even* of your l that war in your members?	2237
	4: 3 that ye may consume *it* upon your l.	2237
1Pe	1:14 to the former l in your ignorance:	1939
	2:11 and pilgrims, abstain from fleshly l,	1939
	4: 2 of *his* time in the flesh to the l of men,	1939
	4: 3 l, excess of wine, revellings, banquetings,	1939
2Pe	2:18 they allure through the l of the flesh,	1939
	3: 3 days scoffers, walking after their own l,	1939
Jude	1:16 complainers, walking after their own l;	1939
	1:18 should walk after their own ungodly l.	1939

LUSTY (1) [LUST]
| Jdg | 3:29 men, all l, and all men of valour; | 8082 |

LUXURY See SUMPTUOUSLY

LUZ (8)
Ge	28:19 the name of *that* city *was* called L at	3870
	35: 6 Jacob came to L, which *is* in the land of	3870
	48: 3 God Almighty appeared unto me at L in	3870
Jos	16: 2 goeth out from Beth-el to L,	3870
	18:13 border went over from thence toward L,	3870
	18:13 to the side of L, which *is* Beth-el,	3870
Jdg	1:23 (Now the name of the city before *was* L.)	3870
	1:26 a city, and called the name thereof L:	3870

LYCAONIA (2)
| Ac | 14: 6 cities of L, and *unto* the region that lieth | 3071 |
| | 14:11 their voices, saying **in the speech** of L, | 3072 |

LYCIA (1)
| Ac | 27: 5 Pamphylia, we came to Myra, *a city* of L. | 3073 |

LYDDA (3)
Ac	9:32 down also to the saints which dwelt at L.	3069
	9:35 all that dwelt at L and Saron saw him,	3069
	9:38 And forasmuch as L was nigh to Joppa,	3069

LYDIA (3) [LYDIANS]
Eze	30: 5 L, and all the mingled people, and Chub,	3865
Ac	16:14 a certain woman named L, a seller of	3070
	16:40 prison, and entered into *the house of* L:	3070

LYDIANS (1) [LYDIA]
| Jer | 46: 9 the L, that handle *and* bend the bow. | 3865 |

LYING (57) [LIE]
Ge	29: 2 there *were* three flocks of sheep l by it;	7257
	34: 7 he had wrought folly in Israel in l with	7901
Ex	23: 5 thou see the ass of him that hateth thee l	7257
Nu	31:17 that hath known man by l **with** him.	4904
	31:18 have not known a man by l **with** him,	4904
	31:35 that had not known man by l **with** him.	4904
Dt	21: 1 l in the field, *and* it be not known who	5307
	22:22 If a man be found l with a woman	7901
Jdg	9:35 that *were* with him, from l **in wait**.	3993
	16: 9 *there were* men l **in wait**, abiding with	693
	21:12 had known no man by l **with** *any* male:	4904
1Ki	22:22 I will be a l spirit in the mouth of all his	8267
	22:23 the LORD hath put a l spirit in the mouth	8267
2Ch	18:21 a l spirit in the mouth of all his prophets.	8267
	18:22 the LORD hath put a l spirit in the mouth	8267
Ps	31: 6 I have hated them that regard l vanities:	7723
	31:18 the l lips be put to silence; which speak	8267
	52: 3 *and* l rather than to speak righteousness.	8267
	59:12 and for cursing and l *which* they speak.	3585
	109: 2 they have spoken against me *with* a l	8267
	119:29 Remove from me the way of l:	8267
	119:163 I hate and abhor l: *but* thy law do I love.	8267
	120: 2 from l lips, *and* from a deceitful tongue.	8267
	139: 3 compassest my path and my l **down**,	7252
Pr	6:17 a l tongue, and hands that shed innocent	8267
	10:18 He that hideth hatred *with* l lips, and he	8267
	12:19 but a l tongue *is* but for a moment.	8267
	12:22 L lips *are* abomination to the LORD:	8267
	13: 5 A righteous *man* hateth l:	1697+8267
	17: 7 not a fool: much less do l lips a prince.	8267
	21: 6 The getting of treasures by a l tongue *is* a	8267
	26:28 A l tongue hateth *those that are* afflicted	8267
Isa	30: 9 That this *is* a rebellious people, l children,	3586
	32: 7 devices to destroy the poor with l words,	8267
	56:10 sleeping, l **down**, loving to slumber.	7901
	59:13 In transgressing and l against the LORD,	3584
Jer	7: 4 Trust ye not in l words, saying,	8267
	7: 8 Behold, ye trust in l words, *that* cannot	8267
	29:23 have spoken l words in my name, which	8267
La	3:10 He *was* unto me as *a* bear l **in wait**, *and*	693
Eze	13: 6 They have seen vanity and l divination,	3577
	13: 7 have ye not spoken a l divination,	3577
	13:19 by your l to my people that hear *your* lies?	3576
Da	2: 9 for ye have prepared l and corrupt words	3538
Hos	4: 2 l, and killing, and stealing,	3584
Jnh	2: 8 They that observe l vanities forsake their	7723
Mt	9: 2 to him a man sick of the palsy, l on a bed:	906
Mk	5:40 and entereth in where the damsel was l.	345
Lk	2:12 in swaddling clothes, l in a manger.	2749
	2:16 and Joseph, and the babe l in a manger.	2749
Jn	13:25 He then l on Jesus' breast saith unto him,	1968
	20: 5 And looking in, saw the linen clothes l;	2749
	20: 7 not l with the linen clothes,	2749
Ac	20:19 which befell me by the l **in wait** of	1917
	23:16 Paul's sister's son heard of *their* l **in wait**,	1747
Eph	4:25 Wherefore putting away l, speak every	5579
2Th	2: 9 with all power and signs and l wonders,	5579

LYRE See SACKBUT

LYSANIAS (1)
| Lk | 3: 1 and L the tetrarch of Abilene, | 3078 |

LYSIAS (3)
Ac	23:26 Claudius L unto the most excellent	3079
	24: 7 But the chief captain L came *upon us,*	3079
	24:22 L the chief captain shall come down,	3079

LYSTRA (6)
Ac	14: 6 ware of *it,* and fled unto L and Derbe,	3082
	14: 8 And there sat a certain man at L,	3082
	14:21 they returned *again* to L, and *to* Iconium,	3082
	16: 1 came he to Derbe and L: and behold,	3082
	16: 2 reported of by the brethren that were at L	3082
2Ti	3:11 unto me at Antioch, at Iconium, at L;	3082

M

MAACAH (3) [MAACHAH]
2Sa	3: 3 Absalom the son of M the daughter of	4601
	10: 6 of king M a thousand men, and of Ish-tob	4601
	10: 8 Zoba, and of Rehob, and Ish-tob, and M,	4601

MAACATHITE; MAACATHITES See MAACHATHI; MAACHATHITE; MAACHATHITES

MAACHAH (18) [MAACAH, MAACHATHI, MAACHATHITE, MAACHATHITES]
Ge	22:24 and Gaham, and Thahash, and M.	4601
1Ki	2:39 away unto Achish son of M king of Gath.	4601
	15: 2 his mother's name *was* M, the daughter	4601
	15:10 his mother's name *was* M, the daughter	4601

1Ki	15:13 also M his mother, even her he removed	4601
1Ch	2:48 M, Caleb's concubine, bare Sheber,	4601
	3: 2 Absalom the son of M the daughter of	4601
	7:15 Shuppim, whose sister's name *was* M;)	4601
	7:16 M the wife of Machir bare a son,	4601
	8:29 of Gibeon; whose wife's name *was* M:	4601
	9:35 Jehiel, whose wife's name *was* M:	4601
	11:43 Hanan the son of M, and Joshaphat	4601
	19: 7 and the king of M and his people;	4601
	27:16 the Simeonites, Shephatiah the son of M:	4601
2Ch	11:20 after her he took M the daughter of	4601
	11:21 Rehoboam loved M the daughter of	4601
	11:22 Rehoboam made Abijah the son of M	4601
	15:16 also *concerning* M the mother of Asa	4601

MAACHATHI (1) [MAACHAH]
| Dt | 3:14 Argob unto the coasts of Geshuri and M; | 4602 |

MAACHATHITE (4) [MAACHAH]
2Sa	23:34 the son of Ahasbai, the son of the M,	4602
2Ki	25:23 Jaazaniah the son of a M, they and	4602
1Ch	4:19 Keilah the Garmite, and Eshtemoa the M.	4602
Jer	40: 8 Jezaniah the son of a M, they and	4602

MAACHATHITES (4) [MAACHAH]
Jos	12: 5 the border of the Geshurites and the M,	4602
	13:11 the border of the Geshurites and M,	4602
	13:13 expelled not the Geshurites, nor the M:	4602
	13:13 M dwell among the Israelites until this	4601

MAADAI (1)
| Ezr | 10:34 Of the sons of Bani; M, Amram, and Uel, | 4572 |

MAADIAH (1)
| Ne | 12: 5 Miamin, M, Bilgah, | 4573 |

MAAI (1)
| Ne | 12:36 and Azarael, Milalai, Gilalai, M, | 4597 |

MAALEH-ACRABBIM (1)
| Jos | 15: 3 it went out to the south side to M, | 4610 |

MAARATH (1)
| Jos | 15:59 M, and Beth-anoth, and Eltekon; six cities | 4638 |

MAASEIAH (25)
1Ch	15:18 M, and Mattithiah, and Elipheleh,	4641
	15:20 and Unni, and Eliab, and M, and Benaiah,	4641
2Ch	23: 1 M the son of Adaiah, and Elishaphat	4641
	26:11 hand of Jeiel the scribe and M the ruler,	4641
	28: 7 slew M the king's son, and Azrikam	4641
	34: 8 M the governor of the city, and Joah	4641
Ezr	10:18 M, and Eliezer, and Jarib, and Gedaliah.	4641
	10:21 M, and Elijah, and Shemaiah, and Jehiel,	4641
	10:22 Elioenai, M, Ishmael, Nethaneel, Jozabad,	4641
	10:30 Adna, and Chelal, Benaiah, M, Mattaniah,	4641
Ne	3:23 After him repaired Azariah the son of M	4641
	8: 4 Anaiah, and Urijah, and Hilkiah, and M,	4641
	8: 7 M, Kelita, Azariah, Jozabad, Hanan,	4641
	10:25 Rehum, Hashabnah, M,	4641
	11: 5 M the son of Baruch, the son of	4641
	11: 7 the son of M, the son of Ithiel, the son of	4641
	12:41 Miniamin, Michaiah, Elioenai,	4641
	12:42 And Shemaiah, and Eleazar, and Uzzi,	4641
Jer	21: 1 Zephaniah the son of M the priest, saying,	4641
	29:21 of Kolaiah, and of Zedekiah, the son of M,	4641
	29:25 to Zephaniah the son of M the priest,	4641
	32:12 the son of M, in the sight of Hanameel	4271
	35: 4 *was* above the chamber of M the son	4641
	37: 3 Zephaniah the son of M the priest to	4641
	51:59 Seraiah the son of Neriah, the son of M,	4271

MAASIAI (1)
| 1Ch | 9:12 M the son of Adiel, the son of Jahzerah, | 4640 |

MAATH (1)
| Lk | 3:26 Which was *the son* of M, which was | 3092 |

MAAZ (1)
| 1Ch | 2:27 Jerahmeel were, M, and Jamin, and Eker. | 4619 |

MAAZIAH (2)
| 1Ch | 24:18 to Delaiah, the four and twentieth to M. | 4590 |
| Ne | 10: 8 M, Bilgai, Shemaiah: these *were* | 4590 |

MACBANNAI See MACHBANAI

MACBENAH See MACHBENAH

MACEDONIA (28) [MACEDONIAN]
Ac	16: 9 There stood a man of M, and prayed him,	3110
	16: 9 Come over into M, and help us.	3109
	16:10 we endeavoured to go into M,	3109
	16:12 which is the chief city of *that* part of M,	3109
	18: 5 and Timotheus were come from M,	3109
	19:21 he had passed through M and Achaia,	3109
	19:22 So he sent into M two of them that	3109
	19:29 caught Gaius and Aristarchus, men **of** M,	3110
	20: 1 and departed for to go into M.	3109
	20: 3 he purposed to return through M.	3109
Ro	15:26 For it hath pleased *them of* M and	3109
1Co	16: 5 unto you, when I shall pass through M:	3109
	16: 5 for I do pass through M.	3109
2Co	1:16 And to pass by you into M, and to come	3109
	1:16 and to come again out of M unto you,	3109
	2:13 leave of them, I went into M.	3109
	7: 5 when we were come into M, our flesh	3109

2Co 8: 1 of God bestowed on the churches of **M**; 3109
 9: 2 for which I boast of you to them of **M**, 3110
 9: 4 Lest haply if they of **M** come with me, 3110
 11: 9 brethren which came from **M** supplied: 3109
 13: S *a city of* **M**, by Titus and Lucas. 3109
Php 4:15 of the gospel, when I departed from **M**, 3109
1Th 1: 7 ye were ensamples to all that believe in **M** 3109
 1: 8 out the word of the Lord not only in **M** 3109
 4:10 all the brethren which are in all **M**: 3109
1Ti 1: 3 abide *still* at Ephesus, when I went into **M**, 3109
Tit 3: S of the Cretians, from Nicopolis of **M**. 3109

MACEDONIAN (1) [MACEDONIA]
Ac 27: 2 a **M** of Thessalonica, being with us. 3110

MACHBANAI (1)
1Ch 12:13 Jeremiah the tenth, **M** the eleventh. 4344

MACHBENAH (1)
1Ch 2:49 Sheva the father of **M**, and the father of 4343

MACHI (1)
Nu 13:15 Of the tribe of Gad, Geuel the son of **M**. 4352

MACHIR (22) [MACHIRITES]
Ge 50:23 the son of Manasseh were brought up 4353
Nu 26:29 of **M**, the family of the Machirites: 4353
 26:29 begat Gilead: of Gilead *come* the 4353
 27: 1 Hepher, the son of Gilead, the son of **M**, 4353
 32:39 the children of **M** the son of Manasseh 4353
 32:40 Moses gave Gilead unto **M** the son of 4353
 36: 1 the son of **M**, the son of Manasseh, 4353
Dt 3:15 And I gave Gilead unto **M**. 4353
Jos 13:31 *were pertaining* unto the children of **M** 4353
 13:31 to the one half of the children of **M** by 4353
 17: 1 *to wit,* for **M** the firstborn of Manasseh, 4353
 17: 3 Hepher, the son of Gilead, the son of **M**, 4353
Jdg 5:14 out of **M** came down governors, and out 4353
2Sa 9: 4 Behold, he *is in* the house of **M**, the son 4353
 9: 5 fet him out of the house of **M**, the son of 4353
 17:27 **M** the son of Ammiel of Lo-debar, 4353
1Ch 2:21 to the daughter of **M** the father of Gilead, 4353
 2:23 All these *belonged to* the sons of **M** 4353
 7:14 his concubine the Aramitess bare **M** 4353
 7:15 **M** took to wife *the sister* of Huppim and 4353
 7:16 Maachah the wife of **M** bare a son, 4353
 7:17 the son of **M**, the son of Manasseh. 4353

MACHIRITES (1) [MACHIR]
Nu 26:29 of Machir, the family of the **M**: 4354

MACHNADEBAI (1)
Ezr 10:40 **M**, Shashai, Sharai, 4367

MACHPELAH (6)
Ge 23: 9 That he may give me the cave of **M**, 4375
 23:17 the field of Ephron, which *was in* **M**, 4375
 23:19 the cave of the field of **M** before Mamre: 4375
 25: 9 and Ishmael buried him in the cave of **M**, 4375
 49:30 In the cave that *is* in the field of **M**, 4375
 50:13 buried him in the cave of the field of **M**, 4375

MACNADEBAI See MACHNADEBAI

MAD (22) [MADNESS]
Dt 28:34 So that thou shalt be **m** for the sight of 7696
1Sa 21:13 feigned himself **m** in their hands, 1984
 21:14 his servants, Lo, you see the man *is* **m**: 7696
 21:15 *Have* I need of **m** men, that ye have 7696
 21:15 to **play the m man** in my presence? 7696
2Ki 9:11 wherefore came this **m** *fellow* to thee? 7696
Ps 102: 8 they that are **m** against me are sworn 1984
Pr 26:18 As a **m** man who casteth firebrands, 3856
Ecc 2: 2 I said of laughter, *It is* **m**: and of mirth, 1984
 7: 7 Surely oppression **maketh** a wise *man* **m**; 1984
Isa 44:25 of the liars, and **maketh** diviners **m**; 1984
Jer 25:16 be **m**, because of the sword that I will 1984
 29:26 for every man that is **m**, 7696
 50:38 and they are **m** upon *their* idols. 1984
 51: 7 of her wine; therefore the nations are **m**. 1984
Hos 9: 7 the spiritual man *is* **m**, for the multitude 7696
Jn 10:20 of them said, He hath a devil, and is **m**; 3105
Ac 12:15 And they said unto her, Thou art **m**. 3105
 26:11 and being exceedingly **m** **against** them, 1693
 26:24 learning doth **make** thee **m**. 1519+3130+4062
 26:25 he said, I am not **m**, most noble Festus; 3105
1Co 14:23 will they not say that ye are **m**? 3105

MADAI (2)
Ge 10: 2 **M**, and Javan, and Tubal, and Meshech, 4074
1Ch 1: 5 **M**, and Javan, and Tubal, and Meshech, 4074

MADE (1406) [MAKE]
Ge 1: 7 God **m** the firmament, and divided 6213
 1:16 God **m** two great lights; the greater light 6213
 1:16 light to rule the night: *he* **m** the stars also. NIH
 1:25 God **m** the beast of the earth after his 6213
 1:31 God saw every thing that he had **m**, 6213
 2: 2 God ended his work which he had **m**; 6213
 2: 2 day from all his work which he had **m**, 6213
 2: 3 all his work which God created and **m**. 6213
 2: 4 in the day that the Lord God **m** the earth 6213
 2: 9 **m** the Lord God **to grow** every tree that 6779
 2:22 he **m** a woman, and brought her unto 1129
 3: 1 of the field which the Lord God had **m**. 6213
 3: 7 together, and **m** themselves aprons. 6213

Ge 5: 1 in the likeness of God **m** he him; 6213
 6: 6 it repented the Lord that he had **m** man 6213
 6: 7 for it repenteth me that I have **m** them. 6213
 7: 4 every living substance that I have **m** will I 6213
 8: 1 God **m** a wind **to pass** over the earth, 5674
 8: 6 the window of the ark which he had **m**: 6213
 9: 6 shed: for in the image of God **m** he man. 6213
 13: 4 altar, which he had **m** there at the first: 6213
 14: 2 *these* **m** war with Bera king of Sodom, 6213
 14:23 thou shouldest say, I have **m** Abram **rich**: 6238
 15:18 In the same day the Lord **m** a covenant 3772
 19: 3 a father of many nations have I **m** thee, 5414
 19: 3 **m** them a feast, and did bake unleavened 6213
 19:33 they **m** their father **drink** wine that night: 8248
 19:35 they **m** their father **drink** wine that night 8248
 21: 6 God hath **m** me to laugh, *so that* all that 6213
 21: 8 Abraham **m** a great feast the *same* day 6213
 21:27 and both of them **m** a covenant. 3772
 21:32 Thus they **m** a covenant at Beer-sheba: 3772
 23:17 all the borders round about, were **m** **sure** 6965
 23:20 were **m** **sure** unto Abraham for a 6965
 24:11 he **m** *his* camels **to kneel down** without 1288
 24:21 the Lord had **m** his journey **prosperous** 6743
 24:37 my master **m** me **swear**, saying, Thou 7650
 24:46 she **m** **haste**, and let down her pitcher 4116
 24:46 I drank, and she **m** the camels **drink** also. 8248
 26:22 For now the Lord hath **m** **room** for us, 7337
 26:30 he **m** them a feast, and they did eat and 6213
 27:14 his mother **m** savoury meat, such as his 6213
 27:30 as soon as Isaac had **m an end** of blessing 3615
 27:31 he also had **m** savoury meat, and brought 6213
 27:37 I have **m** him thy lord, and all his brethren 7760
 29:22 all the men of the place, and **m** a feast. 6213
 30:37 **m** the white **appear** which *was* in the 4286
 31:46 and they took stones, and **m** a heap: 6213
 33:17 him a house, and **m** booths for his cattle: 6213
 37: 3 and he **m** him a coat of many colours. 6213
 37: 7 about, and **m** **obeisance** to my sheaf. 7812
 37: 9 and the eleven stars **m** **obeisance** to me. 7812
 39: 3 **m** all that he did **to prosper** in his hand. 6743
 39: 4 he **m** him **overseer** over his house, 6485
 39: 5 *that* he had **m** him **overseer** in his house, 6485
 39:23 which he did, the Lord **m** *it* **to prosper**. 6743
 40:20 that he **m** a feast unto all his servants: 6213
 41:43 he **m** him **to ride** in the second chariot 7392
 41:43 he **m** him **ruler** over all the land of Egypt. 5414
 41:51 *said he,* hath **m** me **forget** all my toil, 5382
 42: 7 **m** himself **strange** unto them, 5234
 43:25 they **m** **ready** the present against Joseph 3559
 43:28 down their heads, and **m** **obeisance**. 7812
 43:30 Joseph **m** **haste**; for his bowels did yern 4116
 45: 1 while Joseph **m** himself **known** unto his 3045
 45: 8 hath **m** me a father to Pharaoh, and lord 7760
 45: 9 God hath **m** me lord of all Egypt: 7760
 46:29 Joseph **m** **ready** his chariot, and went up 631
 47:26 Joseph **m** it a law over the land of Egypt 7760
 49:24 the arms of his hands were **m** **strong** by 6339
 49:33 Jacob had **m an end** of commanding 3615
 50: 5 My father **m** me **swear**, saying, Lo, I die: 7650
 50: 6 father, according as he **m** thee **swear**. 7650
 50:10 **m** a mourning for his father seven days. 6213
Ex 1:13 **m** the children of Israel **to serve** with 5647
 1:14 they **m** their lives **bitter** with hard 4843
 1:14 service, wherein they **m** them **serve**, 5647
 1:21 feared God, that he **m** them houses. 6213
 2:14 Who **m** thee a prince and a judge over us? 7760
 4:11 unto him, Who hath **m** man's mouth? 7760
 5:21 you have **m** our savour **to be abhorred** in 887
 7: 1 See, I have **m** thee a god to Pharaoh: 5414
 9:20 Pharaoh **m** his servants and his cattle **flee** 5127
 14: 6 **m** **ready** his chariot, and took his people 631
 14:21 **m** the sea dry *land,* and the waters were 6213
 15:17 *which* thou hast **m** for thee to dwell in, 6466
 15:25 the waters, the waters were **m** **sweet**: 4985
 15:25 there he **m** for them a statute and 7760
 16:31 taste of it *was* like wafers *m* with honey. NIH
 18:25 them heads over the people, rulers of 5414
 20:11 For *in* six days the Lord **m** heaven and 6213
 24: 8 which the Lord hath **m** with you 3772
 25:31 beaten work shall the candlestick be **m**: 6213
 25:33 Three bowls **m** **like** unto almonds, *with* 8246
 25:33 three bowls **m** **like almonds** in the other 8246
 25:34 *be* four bowls **m** **like** unto almonds, 8246
 25:31 with cherubims shall it be **m**: 6213
 29:18 an **offering m by fire** unto the Lord. 801
 29:25 it *is* an **offering m by fire** unto the Lord. 801
 29:33 *things* wherewith the **atonement** was **m**, 3722
 29:36 when thou shalt **m an atonement** for it, 3722
 29:41 an **offering m by fire**, of a sweet savour 801
 30:20 to burn **offering m by fire** unto the Lord: 801
 31:17 for *in* six days the Lord **m** heaven and 6213
 31:18 when he had **m an end** of communing 3615
 32: 4 after he had **m** it a molten calf: 6213
 32: 5 Aaron **m** **proclamation**, and said, 7121
 32: 8 they have **m** them a molten calf, 6213
 32:20 And he took the calf which they had **m**, 6213
 32:20 and **m** the children of Israel **drink** *of it.* 8248
 32:25 (for Aaron had **m** them **naked** unto *their* 6544
 32:31 great sin, and have **m** them gods of gold. 6213
 32:35 because they **m** the calf, which Aaron 6213
 32:35 they **m** the calf, which Aaron **m**. 6213
 34: 8 Moses **m** **haste**, and bowed his head 4116
 34:27 after the tenor of these words I have **m** 3772
 35:21 every one whom his spirit **m** **willing**, 5068
 35:29 heart **m** them **willing** to bring for all 5068

Ex 35:29 which the Lord had commanded to be **m** 6213
 36: 4 every man from his work which they **m**; 6213
 36: 8 ten curtains *of* fine twined linen, 6213
 36: 8 *with* cherubims *of* cunning work **m** he 6213
 36:11 he **m** loops of blue on the edge of one 6213
 36:11 likewise he **m** in the uttermost side of 6213
 36:12 Fifty loops **m** he in one curtain, 6213
 36:12 fifty loops **m** he in the edge of the curtain 6213
 36:13 he **m** fifty taches of gold, and coupled 6213
 36:14 he **m** curtains *of* goats' *hair* for the tent 6213
 36:14 tabernacle: eleven curtains he **m** them. 6213
 36:17 he **m** fifty loops upon the uttermost edge 6213
 36:17 fifty loops **m** he upon the edge of 6213
 36:18 he **m** fifty taches of brass to couple the 6213
 36:19 he **m** a covering for the tent *of* rams' skins 6213
 36:20 he **m** boards for the tabernacle *of* shittim 6213
 36:23 he **m** boards for the tabernacle: 6213
 36:24 forty sockets of silver he **m** under 6213
 36:25 the north corner, he **m** twenty boards, 6213
 36:27 the tabernacle westward he **m** six boards. 6213
 36:28 two boards **m** he for the corners of 6213
 36:31 he **m** bars of shittim wood; five for 6213
 36:33 he **m** the middle bar to shoot through 6213
 36:34 **m** rings *of* gold *to be* places for 6213
 36:35 he **m** a vail *of* blue, and purple, and scarlet, 6213
 36:35 *with* cherubims **m** he it *of* cunning work. 6213
 36:36 he **m** thereunto four pillars of shittim 6213
 36:37 he **m** a hanging for the tabernacle door *of* 6213
 37: 1 Bezaleel **m** the ark *of* shittim wood: 6213
 37: 2 **m** a crown *of* gold to it round about. 6213
 37: 4 he **m** staves *of* shittim wood, 6213
 37: 6 he **m** the mercy seat *of* pure gold: 6213
 37: 7 he **m** two cherubims *of* gold, beaten out 6213
 37: 7 beaten out of one piece **m** he them, 6213
 37: 8 out of the mercy seat **m** he the cherubims 6213
 37:10 he **m** the table *of* shittim wood: two cubits 6213
 37:11 he **m** thereunto a crown *of* gold round about. 6213
 37:12 Also he **m** thereunto a border of a 6213
 37:12 **m** a crown of gold for the border thereof 6213
 37:15 he **m** the staves *of* shittim wood, 6213
 37:16 he **m** the vessels which *were* upon 6213
 37:17 he **m** the candlestick *of* pure gold: 6213
 37:17 *of* beaten work **m** he the candlestick; 6213
 37:19 **m** after the fashion of almonds** in one 8246
 37:19 three bowls **m** **like almonds** in another 8246
 37:20 *were* four bowls **m** **like almonds**, 8246
 37:23 he **m** his seven lamps, and his snuffers, 6213
 37:24 *Of* a talent *of* pure gold **m** he it, and all 6213
 37:25 he **m** the incense altar *of* shittim wood: 6213
 37:26 also he **m** unto it a crown *of* gold round 6213
 37:27 he **m** two rings of gold for it under 6213
 37:28 he **m** the staves *of* shittim wood, 6213
 37:29 he **m** the holy anointing oil, and the pure 6213
 38: 1 he **m** the altar of burnt offering *of* shittim 6213
 38: 2 he **m** the horns thereof on the four corners 6213
 38: 3 he **m** all the vessels of the altar, the pots, 6213
 38: 3 all the vessels thereof **m** he *of* brass. 6213
 38: 4 **m** for the altar a brasen grate of network 6213
 38: 5 he **m** the staves *of* shittim wood, 6213
 38: 7 he **m** *the altar* hollow with boards. 6213
 38: 8 he **m** the laver *of* brass, and the foot of it 6213
 38: 9 he **m** the court: on the south side 6213
 38:22 **m** all that the Lord commanded Moses. 6213
 38:28 five *shekels* he **m** hooks for the pillars, 6213
 38:30 therewith he **m** the sockets to the door of 6213
 39: 1 and scarlet, they **m** clothes of service, 6213
 39: 1 and the holy garments for Aaron; 6213
 39: 2 he **m** the ephod *of* gold, blue, and purple, 6213
 39: 4 They **m** shoulderpieces for it, to couple *it* 6213
 39: 8 he **m** the breastplate *of* cunning work, 6213
 39: 9 they **m** the breastplate double: 6213
 39:15 they **m** upon the breastplate chains at 6213
 39:16 they **m** two ouches *of* gold, and two gold 6213
 39:19 they **m** two rings of gold, and put *them* 6213
 39:20 they **m** two *other* golden rings, 6213
 39:22 **m** the robe of the ephod *of* woven work, 6213
 39:24 they **m** upon the hems of the robe 6213
 39:25 they **m** bells of pure gold, and put the 6213
 39:27 they **m** coats *of* fine linen *of* woven work 6213
 39:30 they **m** the plate of the holy crown *of* pure 6213
 39:42 so the children of Israel **m** all the work. 6213
Lev 1: 9 *be* a burnt sacrifice, an **offering m by fire**, 801
 1:13 *is* a burnt sacrifice, an **offering m by fire**, 801
 1:17 *is* a burnt sacrifice, an **offering m by fire**, 801
 2: 2 to be an **offering m by fire**, of a sweet 801
 2: 3 of the **offerings of the Lord m by fire**. 801
 2: 7 it shall be **m** *of* fine flour with oil. 6213
 2: 8 shalt bring the meat offering that is **m** 6213
 2: 9 *is* an **offering m by fire**, of a sweet savour 801
 2:10 of the **offerings of the Lord m by fire**. 801
 2:11 unto the Lord, shall be **m** with leaven: 6213
 2:11 *in* any **offering of the Lord m by fire**. 801
 2:16 it *is* an **offering m by fire** unto the Lord. 801
 3: 3 an **offering m by fire** unto the Lord. 801
 3: 5 *is* an **offering m by fire**, of a sweet savour 801
 3: 9 an **offering m by fire** unto the Lord. 801
 3:11 *is* the food of the **offering m by fire** unto 801
 3:14 *even* an **offering m by fire** unto 801
 3:16 *is* the food of the **offering m by fire** for a 801
 4:35 according to the **offerings m by fire** unto 801
 5:12 according to the **offerings m by fire** unto 801
 6:17 their portion of my **offerings m by fire**; 801
 6:18 the **offerings of the Lord m by fire**: 801
 6:21 In a pan it shall be **m** with oil; *and when* 6213
 7: 5 *for* an **offering m by fire** unto the Lord: 801

Lev	7:25 of which *men* offer an **offering m by fire**	801
	7:30 bring the **offerings** of the Lord **m by fire**,	801
	7:35 of the **offerings** of the Lord **m by fire**,	801
	8:21 *and* an **offering m by fire** unto the Lord;	801
	8:28 it *is* an **offering m by fire** unto the Lord.	801
	10:12 of the **offerings** of the Lord **m by fire**,	801
	10:13 of the **sacrifices** of the Lord **m by fire**:	801
	10:15 with the **offerings m by fire** of the fat,	801
	13:48 in a skin, or in any thing **m** of skin;	4399
	13:51 in a skin, *or* in any work that is **m** of skin;	6213
	14:11 present the man that is to be **m clean**,	2891
	14:36 that all that *is* in the house be not **m**	NIH
	16:17 have **m an atonement** for himself,	3722
	16:20 when he hath **m an end** of reconciling	3615
	21: 6 for the **offerings** of the Lord **m by fire**,	801
	21:21 offer the **offerings** of the Lord **m by fire**:	801
	22: 5 whereby he may be **m unclean**, or a man	2930
	22:27 **offering m by fire** unto the Lord.	801+7133
	23: 8 ye shall offer an **offering m by fire** unto	801
	23:13 an **offering m by fire** unto the Lord *for* a	801
	23:18 offerings, *even* an **offering m by fire** unto	801
	23:25 ye shall offer an **offering m by fire** unto	801
	23:27 offer an **offering m by fire** unto	801
	23:36 an **offering m by fire** unto the Lord:	801
	23:36 ye shall offer an **offering m by fire** unto	801
	23:37 to offer an **offering m by fire** unto	801
	23:43 the children of Israel **to dwell** in	3427
	24: 7 *even* an **offering m by fire** unto the Lord.	801
	24: 9 of the **offerings** of the Lord **m by fire**,	801
	26:13 of your yoke, and m you **go** upright.	1980
	26:46 which the Lord **m** between him and	5414
Nu	4:15 his sons have **m an end** of covering	3615
	4:26 of their service, and all that is **m** for them:	6213
	5: 8 an **atonement** shall be **m** for him.	3722
	5:27 when he hath **m** her **to drink** the water,	8248
	6: 4 he eat nothing that is **m** of the vine tree,	6213
	8: 4 shewed Moses, so he **m** the candlestick.	6213
	8:21 Aaron **m an atonement** for them to	3722
	11: 8 and baked *it* in pans, and **m cakes** of it:	6213
	14:36 **m** all the congregation **to murmur**	3885
	15:10 an **offering m by fire**, of a sweet savour	801
	15:13 offer an **offering m by fire**, of a sweet	801
	15:14 offer an **offering m by fire**, of a sweet	801
	15:25 a **sacrifice m by fire** unto the Lord.	801
	16:31 as he had **m an end** of speaking all these	3615
	16:39 they were **m broad** *plates* for a covering	7554
	16:47 an **m an atonement** for the people.	3722
	18:17 burn their fat *for* an **offering m by fire**,	801
	20: 5 wherefore have ye **m** us **to come up** out	5927
	21: 9 Moses a serpent of brass, and put it	6213
	25:13 **m an atonement** for the children of	3722
	28: 2 my bread for my **sacrifices m by fire**,	801
	28: 3 This *is* the **offering m by fire** which ye	801
	28: 6 a **sacrifice m by fire** unto the Lord.	801
	28: 8 thou shalt offer *it*, a **sacrifice m by fire**,	801
	28:13 a **sacrifice m by fire** unto the Lord.	801
	28:19 ye shall offer a **sacrifice m by fire** *for* a	801
	28:24 the meat of the **sacrifice m by fire**,	801
	29: 6 a **sacrifice m by fire** unto the Lord.	801
	29:13 a burnt offering, a **sacrifice m by fire**,	801
	29:36 a burnt offering, a **sacrifice m by fire**,	801
	30:12 utterly **m** them **void** on the day he	6565+6565
	30:12 her husband hath **m** them **void**;	6565
	31:20 all *that* is **m** of skins, and all work of	3627
	31:20 of goats' *hair*, and all **things m** of wood.	3627
	32:13 **m** them **wander** in the wilderness forty	5128
Dt	1:15 and known, and **m** them heads over you,	5414
	2:30 **m** his heart **obstinate**, that he might	553
	4:23 which he **m** with you, and make you a	3772
	4:36 of heaven he **m** thee **to hear** his voice,	8085
	5: 2 The Lord our God **m** a covenant with us	3772
	5: 3 The Lord **m** not this covenant with our	3772
	9: 9 covenant which the Lord **m** with you,	3772
	9:12 they have **m** them a molten image.	6213
	9:16 your God, *and* had **m** you a molten calf:	6213
	9:21 the calf which ye had **m**, and burnt it	6213
	10: 3 I m an ark of shittim wood, and hewed	6213
	10: 5 put the tables in the ark which I had **m**;	6213
	10:22 now the Lord thy God hath **m** thee	7760
	11: 4 **m** the water of the Red sea to **overflow**	6687
	18: 1 eat the **offerings** of the Lord **m by fire**,	801
	20: 9 when the officers have **m an end** of	3615
	26:12 When thou hast **m an end** of tithing all	3615
	26:19 high above all nations which he hath **m**,	6213
	29: 1 the covenant which he **m** with them	3772
	29:25 which he **m** with them when he brought	3772
	31:16 break my covenant which I have **m** with	3772
	31:24 when Moses had **m an end** of writing	3615
	32: 6 hath he *not* **m** thee, and established thee?	6213
	32:13 He **m** him **ride** on the high places of	7392
	32:13 he **m** him **to suck** honey out of the rock,	3243
	32:15 then he forsook God which **m** him,	6213
	32:45 Moses **m an end** of speaking all these	3615
Jos	2:17 thine oath which thou hast **m** us **swear**.	7650
	2:20 oath which thou hast **m** us **to swear**.	7650
	5: 3 Joshua **m** him sharp knives,	
	8:15 all Israel *m as if they* were beaten before	NIH
	8:24 when Israel had **m an end** of slaying all	3615
	8:28 Joshua burnt Ai, and **m** it a heap for ever,	7760
	9: 4 and **m** as if they had been **ambassadors**,	6737
	9:15 Joshua **m peace** with them, and made a	6213
	9:15 a **league** with them, to let them live:	3772
	9:16 days after they had **m** a **league** with them,	3772
	9:27 **m** them that day hewers of wood	5414
	10: 1 the inhabitants of Gibeon had **m peace**	7999

Jos	10: 4 for it hath **m peace** with Joshua and	7999
	10: 5 before Gibeon, and **m war** against it.	3898
	10:20 the children of Israel had **m an end** of	3615
	11:18 Joshua **m** war a long time with all those	6213
	11:19 There was not a city that **m peace** with	7999
	13:14 **sacrifices** of the Lord God of Israel	
	m by fire	801
	14: 8 with me **m** the heart of the people **melt**:	4529
	19:49 When they had **m** an end of dividing	3615
	19:51 So they **m** an end of dividing the country.	3615
	22:25 For the Lord hath **m** Jordan a border	5414
	22:28 which our fathers **m**, not for burnt	6213
	24:25 So Joshua **m** a covenant with the people	3772
Jdg	2: 1 I m you **to go up** out of Egypt,	5927
	3:16 **m** him a dagger which had two edges,	6213
	3:18 he had **m an end** to offer the present,	3615
	5:13 **m** him that remaineth	
	have **dominion over**	7287
	5:13 the Lord **m** me **have dominion over**	7287
	6: 2 of the Midianites the children of Israel **m**	6213
	6:19 **m ready** a kid, and unleavened *cakes of*	6213
	8:27 Gideon **m** an ephod thereof, and put it in	6213
	8:33 after Baalim, and **m** Baal-berith their god.	7760
	9: 6 and went, and **m** Abimelech king,	4427
	9:16 in that ye have **m** Abimelech **king**,	4427
	9:18 Abimelech, the son of his	
	maidservant, **king**	4427
	9:27 trode *the grapes*, and **m** merry,	6213
	11: 4 the children of Ammon **m war** against	3898
	11: 5 that when the children of Ammon **m war**	3898
	11:11 the people **m** him head and captain over	7760
	13:10 the woman **m haste**, and ran,	4116
	13:15 we shall have **m ready** a kid for thee.	6213
	14:10 Samson **m** there a feast; for so used	6213
	15:17 when he had **m an end** of speaking,	3615
	16:19 she **m** him **sleep** upon her knees;	3462
	16:25 the prison house; and he **m** them **sport**:	6711
	16:27 that beheld while Samson **m sport**.	7832
	17: 4 who **m** thereof a graven image and	6213
	18:24 Ye have taken away my gods which I **m**,	6213
	18:27 they took *the things* which Micah had **m**,	6213
	18:31 up Micah's graven image, which he **m**,	6213
	21: 5 *they* had **m** a great oath concerning *him*	1961
	21:15 that the Lord had **m** a breach in	6213
1Sa	2:19 Moreover his mother **m** him a little coat,	6213
	2:28 **offerings m by fire** of the children of	801
	3:13 because his sons **m** themselves **vile**,	7043
	4:18 when he **m mention** of the ark of God,	2142
	8: 1 that he **m** his sons judges over Israel.	7760
	9:22 **m** them **sit** in the chiefest place among	5414
	10:13 when he had **m an end** of prophesying,	3615
	11:15 there they **m** Saul **king** before the Lord	4427
	12: 1 and have **m** a **king** over you.	4427+4428
	12: 8 of Egypt, and **m** them **dwell** in this place.	3427
	13:10 as soon as he had **m an end** of offering	3615
	13:12 I have not **m supplication** unto	2470
	14:14 **slaughter**, which Jonathan and his	
	armourbearer **m**,	4347+5221
	15:17 *wast* thou not **m** the head of the tribes of	NIH
	15:33 As thy sword hath **m** women **childless**,	7921
	15:35 that he had **m** Saul **king** over Israel.	4427
	16: 8 and **m** him **pass** before Samuel.	5674
	16: 9 Jesse **m** Shammah **to pass by**.	5674
	16:10 Jesse **m** seven of his sons **to pass** before	5674
	18: 1 he **m an end** of speaking unto Saul,	3615
	18: 3 Jonathan and David **m** a covenant,	3772
	18:13 and **m** him his captain over a thousand;	7760
	20:16 So Jonathan **m** *a covenant* with the house	3772
	22: 8 son hath **m** *a league* with the son of Jesse,	3772
	23:18 they two **m** a covenant before the Lord:	3772
	23:26 David **m haste** to get away for fear of	2648
	24:16 when David had **m an end** of speaking	3615
	25:18 Abigail **m haste**, and took two hundred	4116
	27:10 Whither have ye **m** a **road** to day?	6584
	27:12 **m** his people Israel **utterly to abhor**	887+887
	30:11 he did eat; and they **m** him **drink** water;	8248
	30:14 We **m** an **invasion** *upon* the south of	6584
	30:21 whom they had **m** also **to abide** at	3427
	30:25 that he **m** it a statute and an ordinance for	7760
2Sa	2: 9 he **m** him **king** over Gilead, and over	4427
	3: 6 Abner **m** himself **strong** for the house	2388
	3:20 David **m** Abner and the men that *were*	6213
	4: 4 as she **m haste** to flee, that he fell,	2648
	5: 3 king David **m** a league with them in	3772
	5: 5 all *manner of instruments* **m** of fir wood,	NIH
	6: 8 had **a breach** upon Uzzah:	6555+6556
	6:18 soon as David had **m an end** of offering	3615
	7: 9 thy sight, and have **m** thee a great name,	6213
	10:19 they **m peace** with Israel, and served	7999
	11:13 drink before him; and he **m** him **drunk**:	7937
	11:19 When thou hast **m an end** of telling	3615
	12:31 and **m** them **pass** through the brickkiln:	5674
	13: 6 So Amnon lay down, and **m** himself **sick**:	2470
	13: 8 kneaded *it*, and **m cakes** in his sight,	3823
	13:10 Tamar took the cakes which she had **m**,	6213
	13:36 as soon as he had **m an end** of speaking,	3615
	14:15 *is* because the people have **m** me **afraid**:	3372
	15: 4 Oh that I were **m** judge in the land,	7760
	17:25 Absalom **m** Amasa captain of the host	7760
	22: 5 the floods of ungodly men **m** me **afraid**;	1204
	22:12 he **m** darkness pavilions round about him,	7896
	22:36 and thy gentleness hath **m** me **great**.	7235
	23: 5 yet he hath **m** with me an everlasting	7760
1Ki	1:41 heard *it* as they had **m an end** of eating.	3615

1Ki	1:43 lord king David hath **m** Solomon **king**.	4427
	2:24 who hath **m** me a house, as he promised,	6213
	3: 1 Solomon **m affinity** with Pharaoh king of	2859
	3: 1 until he had **m an end** of building his	3615
	3: 7 thou hast **m** thy servant **king** instead of	4427
	3:15 and **m** a feast to all his servants.	6213
	4: 7 man *his* month in a year **m provision**.	3557
	5:12 and they two **m** a league *together*.	3772
	6: 4 for the house he **m** windows of narrow	6213
	6: 5 oracle: and he **m** chambers round about:	6213
	6: 6 for without *in the wall* of the house he **m**	6213
	6: 7 was built *of* stone **m ready** *before* it was	8003
	6:21 he **m** a **partition** by the chains of gold	5674
	6:23 within the oracle he **m** two cherubims of	6213
	6:31 for the entering of the oracle he **m** doors	6213
	6:33 So also he **m** for the door of the temple	6213
	7: 6 he **m** a porch of pillars; the length thereof	6213
	7: 7 he **m** a porch for the throne where he	6213
	7: 8 Solomon **m** also a house for Pharaoh's	6213
	7:16 he **m** two chapiters *of* molten brass, to set	6213
	7:18 he **m** the pillars, and two rows round	6213
	7:23 he **m** a molten sea, ten cubits from the	6213
	7:27 he **m** ten bases of brass; four cubits *was*	6213
	7:29 oxen *were* certain additions **m** of thin	4174
	7:37 After this *manner* he **m** the ten bases: all	6213
	7:38 he **m** ten lavers of brass: one laver	6213
	7:40 Hiram **m** the lavers, and the shovels,	6213
	7:40 So Hiram **m an end** of doing all the work	3615
	7:40 **m** king Solomon *for* the house of	6213
	7:45 which Hiram **m** to king Solomon *for*	6213
	7:48 Solomon **m** all the vessels that *pertained*	6213
	7:51 Solomon **m** *for* the house of the Lord.	6213
	8: 9 when the Lord **m** *a covenant* with	3772
	8:21 the Lord, which he **m** with our fathers,	3772
	8:38 and supplication soever be **m** by any man,	NIH
	8:54 *that* when Solomon had **m an end** of	3615
	8:59 wherewith I have **m supplication** before	2603
	9: 3 thy **supplication**, that thou hast **m**	2603+8467
	9:26 king Solomon **m** a navy *of ships* in	6213
	10: 9 therefore **m** he thee king, to do judgment	7760
	10:12 the king **m** *of* the almug trees pillars for	6213
	10:16 king Solomon **m** two hundred targets *of*	6213
	10:17 **m** three hundred shields *of* beaten gold;	NIH
	10:18 Moreover the king **m** a great throne of	6213
	10:20 there was not the like **m** in any kingdom.	6213
	10:27 the king **m** silver *to be* in Jerusalem as	5414
	10:27 cedars **m** he *to be* as the sycomore trees	5414
	11:28 he **m** him **ruler** over all the charge of	6485
	12: 4 Thy father **m** our yoke **grievous**:	7185
	12:10 Thy father **m** our yoke **heavy**,	3513
	12:14 My father **m** your yoke **heavy**, and I will	3513
	12:18 Therefore king Rehoboam **m speed** to get	553
	12:20 and **m** him **king** over all Israel:	4427
	12:28 **m** two calves of gold, and said unto them,	6213
	12:31 he **m** a house of high places,	6213
	12:31 **m** priests of the lowest of the people,	6213
	12:32 sacrificing unto the calves that he had **m**:	6213
	12:32 priests of the high places which he had **m**.	6213
	12:33 offered upon the altar which he had **m**	6213
	13:33 again of the lowest of the people priests	6213
	14: 7 and **m** thee prince over my people Israel,	5414
	14: 9 for thou hast gone and **m** thee other gods,	6213
	14:15 because they have **m** their groves,	6213
	14:16 who did sin, and **m** Israel **to sin**.	2398
	14:26 shields of gold which Solomon had **m**.	6213
	14:27 king Rehoboam **m** in their stead brasen	6213
	15:12 all the idols that his fathers had **m**.	6213
	15:13 because she had **m** an idol in a grove;	6213
	15:22 Asa a **proclamation** throughout all	8085
	15:26 in his sin wherewith he **m** Israel **to sin**.	2398
	15:30 he sinned, and which he **m** Israel **sin**,	2398
	15:34 in his sin wherewith he **m** Israel **to sin**.	2398
	16: 2 and **m** thee prince over my people Israel;	5414
	16: 2 **m** my people Israel **to sin**, to provoke	2398
	16:13 and *by* which they **m** Israel **to sin**,	2398
	16:16 Omri, the captain of the host, **king**	4427
	16:26 in his sin wherewith he **m** Israel **to sin**,	2398
	16:33 Ahab **m** a grove; and Ahab did more to	6213
	18:26 they leapt upon the altar which was **m**.	6213
	18:32 he **m** a trench about the altar, as great as	6213
	20:34 in Damascus, as my father **m** in Samaria.	7760
	20:34 he **m** a covenant with him, and sent him	3772
	21:22 **m** to anger, and **m** Israel to sin.	2398
	22:11 Zedekiah the son of Chenaanah **m** him	6213
	22:39 the ivory house which he **m**, and all	1129
	22:44 Jehoshaphat **m peace** with the king of	7999
	22:48 Jehoshaphat **m** ships of Tharshish to go to	6213
	22:52 the son of Nebat, who **m** Israel to sin:	2398
2Ki	3: 2 the image of Baal that his father had **m**.	6213
	3: 3 the son of Nebat, which **m** Israel to sin:	2398
	7: 6 m the host of the Syrians **to hear** a noise	8085
	8:20 and **m** a **king** over themselves.	4427+4428
	9:21 his chariot was **m ready**. And Joram king	631
	10:16 So they **m** him **ride** in his chariot.	7392
	10:25 as soon as he had **m an end** of offering	3615
	10:27 and **m** it a draught house unto *this* day.	7760
	10:29 who **m** Israel **to sin**, Jehu departed not	2398
	10:31 sins of Jeroboam, which **m** Israel **to sin**.	2398
	11: 4 **m** a covenant with them, and took an	3772
	11:12 they **m** him **king**, and anointed him	4427
	11:17 Jehoiada **m** a covenant between	3772
	12:13 Howbeit there were not **m** for the house	6213
	12:20 **m a conspiracy**, and slew Joash *in*	7194+7195
	13: 2 the son of Nebat, which **m** Israel **to sin**;	2398
	13: 6 who **m** Israel **sin**, *but* walked therein:	2398

2Ki 13: 7 had **m** them like the dust by threshing. 7760
13:11 the son of Nebat, who **m** Israel **sin:** 2398
14:19 Now they **m** a **conspiracy** against 7194+7195
14:21 **m** him **king** instead of his father Amaziah. 4427
14:24 the son of Nebat, who **m** Israel **to sin.** 2398
15: 9 the son of Nebat, who **m** Israel **to sin.** 2398
15:15 his **conspiracy** which he **m,** 7194+7195
15:18 the son of Nebat, who **m** Israel **to sin.** 2398
15:24 the son of Nebat, who **m** Israel **to sin.** 2398
15:28 the son of Nebat, who **m** Israel **to sin.** 2398
15:30 **m** a **conspiracy** against Pekah 7194+7195
16: 3 and **m** his son **to pass** through the fire, 5674
16:11 Urijah the priest **it** against king Ahaz 6213
17: 8 of the kings of Israel, which they had **m.** 6213
17:15 his covenant that he **m** with their fathers, 3772
17:16 **m** them molten images, *even* two calves, 6213
17:16 **m** a grove, and worshipped all the host of 6213
17:19 in the statutes of Israel which they **m.** 6213
17:21 they **m** Jeroboam the son of Nebat **king:** 4427
17:21 the Lord, and **m** them **sin** a great sin. 2398
17:29 every nation **m** gods of their own, 6213
17:29 high places which the Samaritans had **m,** 6213
17:30 the men of Babylon **m** Succoth-benoth, 6213
17:30 the men of Cuth **m** Nergal, and the men 6213
17:30 and the men of Hamath **m** Ashima, 6213
17:31 the Avites **m** Nibhaz and Tartak, 6213
17:32 **m** unto themselves of the lowest of them 6213
17:35 With whom the Lord had **m** a covenant, 3772
17:38 the covenant that I have **m** with you ye 3772
18: 4 the brasen serpent that Moses had **m:** 6213
19:15 the earth; thou hast **m** heaven and earth. 6213
20:20 how he **m** a pool, and a conduit, 6213
21: 3 and **m** a grove, as did Ahab king of Israel; 6213
21: 6 And he **m** his son **pass** through the fire, 5674
21: 7 of the grove that he had **m** in the house, 6213
21:11 hath **m** Judah also to **sin** with his idols: 2398
21:11 his sin where*with* he **m** Judah **to sin,** 2398
21:24 land **m** Josiah his son **king** in his stead. 4427
22: 7 Howbeit there was no **reckoning m** with 2803
23: 3 **m** a covenant before the Lord, to walk 3772
23: 4 all the vessels that were **m** for Baal, 6213
23:12 which the kings of Judah had **m,** 6213
23:12 the altars which Manasseh had **m** in 6213
23:15 who **m** Israel **to sin,** had made, both that 2398
23:15 had **m,** both that altar and the high place 6213
23:19 the kings of Israel had **m** to provoke 6213
23:30 and **m** him **king** in his father's stead. 4427
23:34 **m** Eliakim the son of Josiah **king** 4427
24:13 Israel had **m** in the temple of the Lord, 6213
24:17 **m** Mattaniah his father's brother **king** 4427
25:16 the bases which Solomon had **m** for 6213
25:22 **m** Gedaliah the son of Ahikam, the son
of Shaphan, **ruler.** 6485
25:23 of Babylon had **m** Gedaliah **governor,** 6485
1Ch 5:10 in the days of Saul they **m** war with 6213
5:19 they **m** war with the Hagarites, with Jetur, 6213
9:30 *some* of the sons of the priests **m** 7543
9:31 over the **things that were m** in the pans. 4639
11: 3 David **m** a covenant with them in Hebron 3772
12:18 and **m** them captains of the band. 5414
14:11 God **m** a **breach** upon Uzza: 6555+6556
15: 1 *David* **m** him houses in the city of David, 6213
15:13 the Lord our God **m** a **breach** upon us, 6555
16: 2 when David had **m** an **end** of offering 3615
16: 5 but Asaph **m** a **sound** with cymbals; 8085
16:16 *Even of the covenant* which he **m** with 3772
16:26 *are* idols: but the Lord **m** the heavens. 6213
17: 8 have **m** thee a name like the name of 6213
18: 8 wherewith Solomon **m** the brasen sea, 6213
19: 6 they had **m** themselves **odious** to David, 887
19:19 they **m peace** with David, and became 7999
21:29 which Moses **m** in the wilderness, 6213
22: 8 blood abundantly, and hast **m** great wars: 6213
23: 1 he **m** Solomon his son **king** over Israel. 4427
23: 5 Lord with the instruments which I **m,** 6213
26:10 yet his father **m** him the chief;) 7760
26:32 whom king David **m rulers** over 6485
28: 2 God, and had **m ready** for the building: 3559
28:19 **m** me **understand** in writing by *his* hand 7919
29: 2 God the gold for **things to be m** of gold, NIH
29: 5 all *manner* of work to be **m** by the hands NIH
29:19 *for* the which I have **m provision.** 3559
29:22 they **m** Solomon the son of David **king** 4427

2Ch 1: 3 of the Lord had **m** in the wilderness. 6213
1: 5 the son of Uri, the son of Hur, had **m,** 6213
1: 8 and hast **m** me to **reign** in his stead. 4427
1: 9 for thou hast **m** me **king** over a people 4427
1:11 people, over whom I have **m** thee **king;** 4427
1:15 the king **m** silver and gold at Jerusalem *as* 5414
1:15 cedar trees he **m** as the sycomore trees 5414
2:11 people, he hath **m** thee **king** over them. 5414
2:12 God of Israel, that **m** heaven and earth, 6213
3: 8 he **m** the most holy house, the length 6213
3:10 the most holy house he **m** two cherubims 6213
3:14 he **m** the vail *of* blue, and purple, 6213
3:15 Also he **m** before the house two pillars of 6213
3:16 he **m** chains, *as* in the oracle, and put 6213
3:16 **m** an hundred pomegranates, and put 6213
4: 1 Moreover he **m** an altar of brass, 6213
4: 2 he **m** a molten sea of ten cubits from 6213
4: 6 He **m** also ten lavers, and put five on 6213
4: 7 he **m** ten candlesticks of gold according to 6213
4: 8 He **m** also ten tables, and placed *them* in 6213
4: 8 And he **m** an hundred basons of gold. 6213
4: 9 Furthermore he **m** the court of priests 6213

2Ch 4:11 Huram **m** the pots, and the shovels, 6213
4:14 He **m** also bases and lavers made he upon 6213
4:14 bases and lavers he **m** upon the bases; 6213
4:18 Thus Solomon **m** all these vessels in great 6213
4:19 Solomon **m** all the vessels that *were for* 6213
4:21 *m* he *of* gold, *and* that perfect gold; NIH
5: 1 Thus all the work that Solomon **m** for 6213
5:10 when the Lord **m** a **covenant** with 3772
6:11 that he **m** with the children of Israel. 3772
6:13 For Solomon had **m** a brasen scaffold, 6213
6:29 supplication soever shall be **m** of any NIH
6:40 unto the prayer *that is* **m** in this place. NIH
7: 1 Now when Solomon had **m** an **end** of 3615
7: 6 which David the king had **m** to praise 6213
7: 7 brasen altar which Solomon had **m** was 6213
7: 9 in the eighth day they **m** a solemn 6213
7:15 ears attent unto the prayer *that is* **m** in NIH
9: 8 therefore he **m** thee king over them, 5414
9:11 the king **m** *of* the algum trees terraces to 6213
9:15 king Solomon **m** two hundred targets *of* 6213
9:16 hundred shields **m** he *of* beaten gold; NIH
9:17 Moreover the king **m** a great throne of 6213
9:19 There was not the like **m** in any kingdom. 6213
9:27 the king **m** silver in Jerusalem as stones, 5414
9:27 cedar trees he **m** as the sycomore trees 5414
10: 4 Thy father **m** our yoke **grievous:** 7185
10:10 Thy father **m** our yoke **heavy,** 3513
10:14 My father **m** your yoke **heavy,** but I will 3513
10:18 king Rehoboam **m speed** to get *him* up to 553
11:12 spears, and **m** them exceeding **strong,** 2388
11:15 and for the calves which he had **m.** 6213
11:17 **m** Rehoboam the son of Solomon **strong,** 553
11:22 Rehoboam **m** Abijah the son of Maachah 5975
12: 9 the shields of gold which Solomon had **m.** 6213
12:10 of which king Rehoboam **m** shields 6213
13: 8 which Jeroboam **m** you for gods. 6213
13: 9 have **m** you priests after the manner of 6213
15:16 because she had **m** an idol in a grove: 6213
16:14 which he had **m** for himself in the city of 3738
16:14 **m** a very great **burning** for him. 8313+8316
17:10 that they **m** no **war** against Jehoshaphat. 3898
18:10 Zedekiah the son of Chenaanah had **m** 6213
20:23 they had **m** an **end** of the inhabitants 3615
20:27 for the Lord had **m** them **to rejoice** over 8055
20:36 and they **m** the ships in Ezion-gaber. 6213
21: 7 the covenant that he had **m** with David, 3772
21: 8 Judah, and **m** themselves **a king.** 4427+4428
21:11 Moreover he **m** high places in 6213
21:13 **m** Judah and the inhabitants of Jerusalem
to go a whoring, 2181
21:19 his people **m** no burning for him, like 6213
22: 1 **m** Ahaziah his youngest son **king** in his 4427
23: 3 all the congregation **m** a covenant with 3772
23:11 *him* the Testimony, and **m** him **king.** 4427
23:16 Jehoiada **m** a covenant between him, 3772
24: 8 the king's commandment they **m** a chest, 6213
24: 9 they **m** a proclamation through Judah and 5414
24:10 into the chest, until *they* had **m** an **end.** 3615
24:14 whereof were **m** vessels for the house of 6213
24:17 of Judah, and **m obeisance** to the king. 7812
25: 5 **m** them captains over thousands, 5975
25:16 him, Art thou **m** of the king's counsel? 5414
25:27 **m** a **conspiracy** against him in 7194+7195
26: 1 **m** him **king** in the room of his father 4427
26: 5 the Lord, God **m** him **to prosper.** 6743
26:13 that **m** war with mighty power, 6213
26:15 he **m** in Jerusalem engines, invented by 6213
28: 2 and **m** also molten images for Baalim. 6213
28:19 for he **m** Judah **naked,** 6544
28:24 he **m** him altars in every corner of 6213
28:25 in every several city of Judah he **m** high 6213
29:17 day of the first month they **m** an **end.** 3615
29:24 they **m reconciliation** with their blood 2398
29:24 the sin offering *should* be **m** for all Israel. NIH
29:29 when *they* had **m** an **end** of offering, 3615
32: 5 and **m** darts and shields in abundance. 6213
32:27 he **m** himself treasuries for silver, 6213
33: 3 **m** groves, and worshipped all the host of 6213
33: 7 the idol which he had **m,** in the house of 6213
33: 9 **m** Judah and the inhabitants of Jerusalem
to err, 8582
33:22 images which Manasseh his father had **m,** 6213
33:25 land **m** Josiah his son **king** in his stead. 4427
34: 4 brake *in pieces,* and **m dust** *of* them, 1854
34:31 **m** a covenant before the Lord, to walk 3772
34:33 **m** all that were present in Israel **to serve,** 5975
35:14 afterward they **m ready** for themselves, 3559
35:25 day, and **m** them an ordinance in Israel: 5414
36: 1 **m** Jehoahaz **king** in his father's stead. 4427
36: 4 Eliakim his brother **king** over Judah 4427
36:10 **m** Zedekiah his brother **king** over Judah 4427
36:13 who had **m** him **swear** by God: 7650
36:22 that he **m** a **proclamation** 5674+6963

Ezr 1: 1 that he **m** a **proclamation** 5674+6963
4:15 That **search** may be **m** in the book of 1240
4:19 **search** hath been **m,** and it is found that 1240
4:19 time *hath* **m insurrection** against kings, 5376
4:19 and sedition *have been* **m** therein. 5648
4:23 and **m** them **to cease** by force and power. 989
5:13 **m** a decree to build this house of God. 7761
5:14 whom he had **m** governor; 7761
5:17 there be **search m** in the king's treasure 1240
5:17 that a decree *was* **m** of Cyrus the king to 7761
6: 1 Darius the king **m** a decree, and search 7761
6: 1 **search** was **m** in the house of the rolls, 1240

Ezr 6: 3 **m** a decree *concerning* the house of God 7761
6:11 Also I have **m** a decree, that whosoever 7761
6:11 let his house be **m** a dunghill for this. 5648
6:12 I Darius have **m** a decree; let it be done 7761
6:22 for the Lord had **m** them **joyful,** 8055
10: 5 **m** the chief priests, the Levites, and
all Israel, **to swear** 7650
10: 7 they **m proclamation** throughout 5674+6963
10:17 they **m** an **end** with all the men that had 3615

Ne 3:16 the pool that was **m,** and unto the house 6213
4: 7 the walls of Jerusalem were **m** up, 724+5927
4: 9 Nevertheless we **m** our **prayer** unto our 6419
6: 9 For they all **m** us **afraid,** saying, 3372
8: 4 wood, which they had **m** for the purpose; 6213
8:16 brought *them,* and **m** themselves booths, 6213
8:17 come again out of the captivity **m** booths, 6213
9: 6 hast **m** heaven, the heaven of heavens, 6213
9:18 when they had **m** them a molten calf, 6213
10:32 Also we **m** ordinances for us, to charge 5975
12:43 God had **m** them **rejoice** with great joy: 8055
13:13 I **m treasurers** over the treasuries, 686
13:25 off their hair, and **m** them **swear** by God, 7650
13:26 and God **m** him king over all Israel: 5414

Est 1: 3 he **m** a **feast** unto all his princes and 6213
1: 5 the king **m** a feast unto all the people that 6213
1: 9 Also Vashti the queen **m** a feast for 6213
2:17 and **m** her **queen** instead of Vashti. 4427
2:18 and king **m** a great feast unto all his princes 6213
2:18 he **m** a release to the provinces, 6213
2:23 when **inquisition** was **m** of the matter, 1245
5:14 Let a gallows be **m** of fifty cubits high, 6213
5:14 and he **caused** the gallows to be **m.** 6213
7: 9 which Haman had **m** for Mordecai, 6213
9:17 and **m** it a day of feasting and gladness. 6213
9:18 and **m** it a day of feasting and gladness. 6213
9:19 **m** the fourteenth day of the month Adar 6213

Job 1:10 Hast not thou **m** a **hedge** about him, 7753
1:17 The Chaldeans **m** out three bands, 7760
2:11 they had **m** an **appointment** together to 3259
4:14 which **m** all my bones to **shake.** 6342
7: 3 So am I **m** to **possess** months of vanity, 5157
10: 8 Thine hands have **m** me and fashioned 6087
10: 9 that thou hast **m** me as the clay; 6213
15: 7 or wast thou **m** before the hills? 2342
16: 7 he hath **m** me **weary:** thou hast made 3811
16: 7 thou hast **m desolate** all my company. 8074
17: 6 hath **m** me also a byword of the people; 3322
17:13 I have **m** my bed in the darkness. 7502
28:18 No **mention** shall be **m** of coral, 2142
28:26 he **m** a decree for the rain, and a way 6213
31: 1 I **m** a covenant with mine eyes; why then 3772
31:15 Did not he that **m** me in the womb make 6213
31:24 If I have **m** gold my hope, or have said to 7760
33: 4 The Spirit of God hath **m** me, 6213
38: 9 When I **m** the cloud the garment thereof, 7760
39: 6 Whose house I have **m** the wilderness, 7760
40:15 now behemoth, which I **m** with thee; 6213
40:19 he that **m** him can make his sword to 6213
41:33 is not his like, who is **m** without fear. 6213

Ps 7:12 he hath bent his bow, and **m** it **ready.** 3559
7:15 He **m** a pit, and digged it, and is fallen 3738
7:15 and is fallen into the ditch *which* he **m.** 6466
8: 5 For thou hast **m** him a little **lower** than 2637
9:15 are sunk down in the pit *that* they **m:** 6213
18: 4 the floods of ungodly men **m** me **afraid;** 1204
18:11 He **m** darkness his secret place; 7896
18:35 and thy gentleness hath **m** me **great.** 7235
18:43 thou hast **m** me the head of the heathen: 7760
21: 6 thou hast **m** him most blessed for ever: 7760
21: 6 thou hast **m** him exceeding glad with thy 2302
30: 1 hast not my foes to **rejoice** over me. 8055
30: 7 hast **m** my mountain **to stand** strong: 5975
30: 8 and unto thee, O Lord I **m supplication.** 2603
33: 6 word of the Lord were the heavens **m;** 6213
39: 5 thou hast **m** my days *as* a handbreadth; 5414
45: 1 I speak of the **things** which I have **m** 4639
45: 8 *whereby* they have **m** thee **glad.** 8055
46: 8 what desolations he hath **m** in the earth. 7760
49:16 Be not thou afraid when one is **m** rich, 6238
50: 5 those that have **m** a covenant with me by 3772
52: 7 *is* the man *that* **m** not God his strength; 7760
60: 2 Thou hast **m** the earth to **tremble:** 7493
60: 3 **m** us to **drink** the wine *of* astonishment. 8248
69:11 I **m** sackcloth also my garment; 5414
72:15 **prayer** also shall be **m** for him 6419
74:17 earth: thou hast **m** summer and winter. 3335
77: 6 and my spirit **m diligent search:** 2664
78:13 and he **m** the waters **to stand** as a heap. 5324
78:50 He **m** a way to his anger; he spared not 6424
78:52 his own people **to go forth** like sheep, 5265
78:55 the tribes of Israel **to dwell** in their 7931
78:64 their widows **m** no **lamentation.** 1058
86: 9 All nations whom thou hast **m** shall come 6213
88: 8 hast **m** me an abomination unto them: 7896
89: 3 I have **m** a covenant with my chosen, 3772
89:39 Thou hast **m void** the covenant of thy 5010
89:42 thou hast **m** all his enemies **to rejoice.** 8055
89:43 hast not **m** him **to stand** in the battle. 6965
89:44 Thou hast **m** his glory **to cease,** and cast 7673
89:47 wherefore hast thou **m** all men in vain? 1254
91: 9 Because thou hast **m** the Lord, *which is* 7760
92: 4 Lord, hast **m** me **glad** through thy work: 8055
95: 5 The sea *is,* and he **m** it: and his hands 6213
96: 5 *are* idols: but the Lord **m** the heavens. 6213
98: 2 The Lord hath **m known** his salvation: 3045

Ps	100: 3 *it is* he *that* hath **m** us, and not we	6213	
	103: 7 He **m known** his ways unto Moses, his	3045	
	104:24 in wisdom hast thou **m** them all: the earth	6213	
	104:26 *whom* thou hast **m** to play therein.	3335	
	105: 9 Which *covenant* he **m** with Abraham,	3772	
	105:21 He **m** him lord of his house, and ruler of	7760	
	105:24 **m** them **stronger** than their enemies.	6105	
	105:28 He sent darkness, and **m** it **dark**;	2821	
	106:19 They **m** a calf in Horeb,	6213	
	106:46 He **m** them also to be pitied of all those	5414	
	111: 4 He hath **m** his wonderful works to be	6213	
	115:15 You *are* blessed of the Lord which **m**	6213	
	118:24 This *is* the day *which* the Lord hath **m**;	6213	
	119:60 I **m haste**, and delayed not to keep thy	2363	
	119:73 Thy hands have **m** me and fashioned me:	6213	
	119:98 hast **m** me **wiser** than mine enemies.	2449	
	119:126 to work: *for* they have **m void** thy law.	6565	
	121: 2 the Lord, which **m** heaven and earth.	6213	
	124: 8 of the Lord, who **m** heaven and earth.	6213	
	129: 3 upon my back: they **m** long their furrows.	748	
	134: 3 The Lord that **m** heaven and earth bless	6213	
	136: 5 To him that by wisdom **m** the heavens:	6213	
	136: 7 To him that **m** great lights: for his mercy	6213	
	136:14 **m** Israel **to pass through** the midst of it:	5674	
	139:14 for I am fearfully and **wonderfully m**:	6381	
	139:15 when I was **m** in secret,	6213	
	143: 3 he hath **m** me to **dwell** in darkness, as	3427	
	146: 6 Which **m** heaven, and earth, the sea, and	6213	
	148: 6 he hath **m** a decree which shall not pass.	5414	
	149: 2 Let Israel rejoice in him that **m** him:	6213	
Pr	8:26 While as yet he had not **m** the earth,	6213	
	11:25 The liberal soul shall be **m fat**: and he	1878	
	13: 4 but the soul of the diligent shall be **m fat**.	1878	
	14:33 *is* in the midst of fools is **m known**.	3045	
	15:19 but the way of the righteous *is* **m plain**.	5549	
	16: 4 The Lord hath **m** all *things* for himself:	6466	
	20: 7 Who can say, I have **m** my heart **clean**,	2135	
	20:12 the Lord hath **m** even both of them.	6213	
	21:11 scorner is punished, the simple is **m wise**:	2449	
	22:19 I have **m known** to thee *this* day, even to	3045	
	28:25 his trust in the Lord shall be **m fat**.	1878	
Ecc	1:15 *which* is crooked cannot be **m straight**:	8626	
	2: 4 I **m** me **great** works; I builded me houses;	1431	
	2: 5 I **m** me gardens and orchards, and I	6213	
	2: 6 I **m** me pools of water, to water therewith	6213	
	3:11 He hath **m** every *thing* beautiful in his	6213	
	7: 3 of the countenance the heart is **m better**.	3190	
	7:13 *that* straight, which he hath **m crooked**?	5791	
	7:29 I found, that God hath **m** man upright;	6213	
	10:19 A feast is **m** for laughter, and wine	6213	
SS	1: 6 they **m** me the keeper of the vineyards;	7760	
	3: 9 King Solomon **m** himself a chariot of	6213	
	3:10 He **m** the pillars thereof *of* silver,	6213	
	6:12 my soul **m** me *like* the chariots of	7760	
Isa	2: 8 *that* which their own fingers have **m**:	6213	
	2:17 the haughtiness of men shall be **m low**:	8213	
	2:20 which they **m** *each one* for himself to	6213	
	5: 2 of it, and also **m** a winepress therein:	2672	
	14: 3 bondage wherein thou wast **m to serve**,	5647	
	14:16 the man that **m** the earth to **tremble**,	7264	
	14:17 *That* **m** the world as a wilderness,	7760	
	16:10 I have **m** *their* vintage shouting **to cease**.	7673	
	17: 4 *that* the glory of Jacob shall be **m thin**,	1809	
	17: 8 respect *that* which his fingers have **m**,	6213	
	21: 2 all the sighing thereof have I **m to cease**.	7673	
	22:11 Ye **m** also a ditch between the two walls	6213	
	25: 2 For thou hast **m** of a city a heap; *of* a	7760	
	26:14 and **m** all their memory **to perish**.	6	
	27:11 he that **m** them will not have mercy on	6213	
	28:15 We have **m** a covenant with death,	3772	
	28:15 for we have **m** lies our refuge,	7760	
	28:22 mockers, lest your bands be **m strong**:	2388	
	28:25 When he hath **m plain** the face thereof,	7737	
	29:16 for shall the work say of him that **m** it,	6213	
	29:16 say of him that made it, He **m** me not?	6213	
	30:33 is prepared; he hath **m** *it* **deep** and large:	6009	
	31: 7 which your own hands have **m** unto you	6213	
	34: 6 is **m fat** with fatness, *and* with the blood	1878	
	34: 7 and their dust **m fat** with fatness.	1878	
	37:16 the earth: thou hast **m** heaven and earth.	6213	
	40: 4 every mountain and hill shall be **m low**:	8213	
	40: 4 the crooked shall be **m straight**,	4334	
	41: 2 before him, and **m** *him* **rule over** kings?	7287	
	43: 7 I have formed him; yea, I have **m** him.	6213	
	43:24 thou hast **m** me to **serve** with thy sins,	5647	
	44: 2 Thus saith the Lord that **m** thee,	6213	
	45:12 I have **m** the earth, and created man upon	6213	
	45:18 himself that formed the earth and **m** it;	6213	
	46: 4 to hoar hairs will I carry *you*: I have **m**,	6213	
	49: 1 mother hath he **m mention** of my name.	2142	
	49: 2 he hath **m** my mouth like a sharp sword;	7760	
	49: 2 he hid me, and **m** me a polished shaft;	7760	
	49:17 they that **m** thee **waste** shall go forth of	2717	
	51:10 that hath **m** the depths of the sea a way	7760	
	51:12 the son of man *which* shall be **m** *as*	5414	
	52:10 The Lord hath **m bare** his holy arm in	2834	
	53: 9 he **m** his grave with the wicked,	5414	
	53:12 and **m intercession** for the transgressors.	6293	
	57: 8 bed, and the **m** *a covenant* with them;	3772	
	57:16 before me, and the souls *which* I have **m**.	6213	
	59: 8 they have **m** their **crooked** paths:	6140	
	63:17 why hast thou **m** us to **err** from thy ways,	8582	
	66: 2 For all those *things* hath mine hand **m**,	6213	
	66: 8 the earth be **m to bring forth** in one day?	2342	
Jer	1:18 I have **m** thee *this* day a defenced city,	5414	

Jer	2: 7 and **m** mine heritage an abomination.	7760	
	2:15 *and* yelled, and they **m** his land waste:	7896	
	2:28 where *are* thy gods that thou hast **m** thee?	6213	
	5: 3 have **m** their faces **harder** than a rock;	6213	
	8: 8 certainly in vain he **m** *it*; the pen of	6213	
	10:11 The gods that have not **m** the heavens	5648	
	10:12 He hath **m** the earth by his power, he	6213	
	10:25 and have **m** his habitation **desolate**.	8074	
	11:10 covenant which I **m** with their fathers.	3772	
	12:10 have **m** my pleasant portion a desolate	5414	
	12:11 have **m** it desolate, *and being* desolate	7760	
	12:11 the whole land is **m desolate**, because	8074	
	13:22 skirts discovered, *and* thy heels **m bare**.	2554	
	13:27 wilt thou not be **m clean**? when *shall it*	2891	
	14:22 thee: for thou hast **m** all these *things*.	6213	
	17:23 their neck **stiff**, that *they* might not	7185	
	18: 4 the vessel that he **m** of clay was marred in	6213	
	18: 4 he **m** it again another vessel, as seemed	6213	
	19:11 that cannot be **m whole** again:	7495	
	20: 8 the word of the Lord was **m** a reproach	1961	
	25:17 **m** all the nations **to drink**, unto whom	8248	
	26: 9 Jeremiah had **m an end** of speaking	3615	
	27: 5 I have **m** the earth, the man and the beast	6213	
	29:26 The Lord hath **m** thee priest in the stead	5414	
	31:32 Not according to the covenant that I **m**	3772	
	32:17 hast **m** the heaven and the earth by thy	6213	
	32:20 and hast **m** thee a name, as *at* this day;	6213	
	34: 8 after that the king Zedekiah had **m** a	3772	
	34:13 I **m** a covenant with your fathers in	3772	
	34:15 ye had **m** a covenant before me in	3772	
	34:18 covenant which they **m** before me,	3772	
	36:25 Gemariah had **m intercession** to the	6293	
	37: 1 of Babylon **m** king in the land of Judah.	4427	
	37:15 the scribe: for they had **m** that the prison.	6213	
	38:16 *As* the Lord liveth, that **m** us this soul,	6213	
	40: 5 hath **m governor** over the cities of Judah,	6485	
	40: 7 Gedaliah the son of Ahikam **governor**	6485	
	41: 2 Babylon had **m governor** over the land.	6485	
	41: 9 *was* it which Asa the king had **m** for fear	6213	
	41:18 the king of Babylon **m governor** in	6485	
	43: 1 *that* when Jeremiah had **m an end** of	3615	
	46:10 be satiate and **m drunk** with their blood:	7301	
	46:16 He **m many** to fall, yea, one fell upon	7235	
	49:10 have **m** Esau **bare**, I have uncovered his	2834	
	51: 7 that **m** all the earth **drunken**:	7937	
	51:15 He hath **m** the earth by his power, he	6213	
	51:34 me, he hath **m** me an empty vessel,	3322	
	51:63 when thou hast **m an end** of reading this	3615	
	52:20 which king Solomon had **m** in the house	6213	
La	1:13 hath **m** me desolate *and* faint all the day.	5414	
	1:14 he hath **m** my strength **to fall**, the Lord	3782	
	2: 7 they have **m** a noise in the house of	5414	
	2: 8 he **m** the rampart and the wall to **lament**;	56	
	3: 4 My flesh and my skin hath he **m old**;	1086	
	3: 7 get out: he hath **m** my chain **heavy**.	3513	
	3: 9 stone, he hath **m** my paths **crooked**.	5753	
	3:11 me in pieces: he hath **m** me desolate.	7760	
	3:15 hath **m** me **drunken** with wormwood.	7301	
	3:45 Thou hast **m** us *as* the offscouring and	7760	
Eze	3: 8 have **m** thy face strong against their faces,	5414	
	3: 9 As an adamant harder than flint have I **m**	5414	
	3:17 I have **m** thee a watchman unto the house	5414	
	6: 6 altars may be laid waste and **m desolate**,	816	
	7:20 they **m** the images of their abominations	6213	
	13: 5 neither **m up the hedge** for	1443+1447	
	13: 6 they have **m** *others* to hope that *they*	3176	
	13:22 *ye* have **m** the heart of the righteous **sad**,	3512	
	13:22 righteous sad, whom I have not **m sad**;	3510	
	16:24 hast **m** thee a high place in every street.	6213	
	16:25 hast **m** thy beauty **to be abhorred**,	8581	
	17:13 **m** a covenant with him, and hath taken	3772	
	17:16 the king *dwelleth* that **m** him **king**,	4427	
	17:24 and have **m** the dry tree to **flourish**:	6524	
	19: 5 of her whelps, *and* **m** him a young lion.	7760	
	20: 5 myself **known** unto them in the land	3045	
	20: 9 sight I **m** myself **known** unto them,	3045	
	20:28 there also they **m** their sweet savour,	7760	
	21:15 ah, *it is* **m** bright, *it is* wrapt up for	6213	
	21:21 he **m** his arrows **bright**, he consulted	7043	
	21:24 your iniquity to be **remembered**,	2142	
	22: 4 *thyself* in thine idols which thou hast **m**;	6213	
	22: 4 I **m** thee a reproach unto the heathen,	5414	
	22: 5 at thy dishonest gain which thou hast **m**,	6213	
	22:25 have **m** her **many** widows in the midst	7235	
	26:10 enter into a city wherein is **m** a **breach**.	1234	
	26:15 the **slaughter** is **m** in the midst	2026+2027	
	27: 5 have **m** all thy **ship** boards of fir trees	1129	
	27: 6 *Of* the oaks of Bashan have they **m** thine	6213	
	27: 6 the company of the Ashurites have **m** thy	6213	
	27:11 they have **m** thy beauty **perfect**.	3634	
	27:24 bound with cords, and **m** of **cedar**,	729	
	27:25 **m** very **glorious** in the midst of the seas.	3513	
	29: 3 *is* mine own, and I have **m** *it* for myself.	6213	
	29: 9 The river *is* mine, and I have **m** it.	6213	
	29:18 head *was* **m** bald, and every shoulder	7139	
	31: 4 The waters **m** him **great**, the deep set	1431	
	31: 6 All the fowls of heaven **m** their **nests** in	7077	
	31: 9 I have **m** him fair by the multitude of his	6213	
	31:16 I **m** the nations **to shake** at the sound of	7493	
	36: 3 Because they have **m** you **desolate**,	8074	
	39:26 in their land, and none **m** them **afraid**.	2729	
	40:14 He **m** also posts *of* threescore cubits,	6213	
	40:17 a pavement **m** for the court round about:	6213	
	41:18 *it was* **m** *with* cherubims and palm trees,	6213	
	41:19 *it was* **m** through all the house round	6213	

Eze	41:20 door *were* cherubims and palm trees **m**,	6213	
	41:25 *there were* **m** on them, on the doors of	6213	
	41:25 trees, like as *were* **m** upon the walls;	6213	
	42:15 when he had **m an end** of measuring	3615	
	43:23 When thou hast **m an end** of cleansing *it*,	3615	
	46:23 *was* **m** with boiling places under the rows	6213	
Da	2: 5 and your houses shall be **m** a dunghill.	7761	
	2:15 Arioch the thing **known** to Daniel.	3046	
	2:17 the thing **known** to Hananiah,	3046	
	2:23 hast **m known** unto me now what we	3046	
	2:23 for thou hast *now* **m known** unto us	3046	
	2:38 and hath **m** thee **ruler** over them all.	7981	
	2:45 the great God hath **m known** to the king	3046	
	2:48 the king **m** Daniel a **great** man,	7236	
	2:48 **m** him **ruler** over the whole province of	7981	
	3: 1 Nebuchadnezzar the king **m** an image of	5648	
	3:10 Thou, O king, hast **m** a decree, that every	7761	
	3:15 and worship the image which I have **m**;	5648	
	3:29 and their houses shall be **m** a dunghill:	7739	
	4: 5 I saw a dream which **m** me **afraid**,	1763	
	4: 6 Therefore **m** I a decree to bring in all	7761	
	5: 1 Belshazzar the king **m** a great feast to a	5648	
	5:11 **m** master of the magicians, astrologers,	6966	
	5:21 his heart was **m** like the beasts,	7739	
	5:29 and **m** a **proclamation** concerning him,	3745	
	7: 4 **m stand** upon the feet as a man,	6966	
	7:16 **m** me **know** the interpretation of the	3046	
	7:21 the same horn **m** war with the saints,	5648	
	9: 1 which was **m king** over the realm of	4427	
	9: 4 **m** my **confession**, and said, O Lord,	3034	
	9:13 yet **m** we not our **prayer** before	2470	
	11:23 after the league **m** with him he shall work	NIH	
	12:10 shall be purified, and **m white**, and tried;	3835	
Hos	5: 9 the tribes of Israel have I **m known**	3045	
	7: 5 have **m** him **sick** *with* bottles of wine;	2470	
	7: 6 For they have **m ready** their heart like	7126	
	8: 4 they have **m princes**, and I knew *it* not:	7786	
	8: 4 and their gold have they **m** them idols,	6213	
	8: 6 the workman **m** it; therefore it *is* not God:	6213	
	8:11 Because Ephraim hath **m many** altars to	7235	
	10: 1 of his land they have **m goodly** images.	2895	
	12: 4 he wept, and **m supplication** unto him:	2603	
	13: 2 **m** them molten images of their silver,	6213	
Joel	1: 7 he hath **m** it **clean** bare, and cast *it* away;	2834	
	1: 7 away; the branches thereof are **m white**.	3835	
	1:18 yea, the flocks of sheep are **m desolate**.	816	
Am	4:10 the stink of your camps **to come up**	5927	
	5:26 of your god, which ye **m** to yourselves.	6213	
	7: 2 *that* when they had **m an end** of eating	3615	
	7: 7 the Lord stood upon a wall **m** by a	NIH	
Ob	1: 2 I have **m** thee small among the heathen:	5414	
Jnh	1: 9 which hath **m** the sea and the dry *land*.	6213	
	1:16 a sacrifice unto the Lord, and **m** vows.	5087	
	4: 5 there **m** him a booth, and sat under it in	6213	
	4: 6 a gourd, and **m** *it* **to come up** over Jonah,	5927	
Na	2: 3 The shield of his mighty men is **m red**,	119	
	2:11 lion's whelp, and none **m** them **afraid**?	2729	
Hab	2:17 *which* them **afraid**, because of men's	2865	
	3: 9 Thy bow was **m quite naked**,	5783+6181	
Zep	3: 6 I **m** their streets **waste**, that none passeth	2717	
Zec	7:12 they **m** their hearts as an adamant stone,	7760	
	9:13 and **m** thee as the sword of a mighty *man*.	7760	
	10: 3 hath **m** them as his goodly horse in	7760	
	11:10 which I had **m** with all the people.	3772	
Mal	2: 9 Therefore have I also **m** you contemptible	5414	
Mt	4: 3 command that these stones be **m** bread.	1096	
	9:16 the garment, and the rent is **m** worse.	1096	
	9:22 comfort; thy faith hath **m** thee **whole**.	4982	
	9:22 And the woman was **m whole** from that	4982	
	11: 1 Jesus had **m an end** of commanding	5055	
	14:36 as touched were **m perfectly whole**.	1295	
	15: 6 **m** the commandment of God of none effect	208	
	15:28 And her daughter was **m whole** from that	2390	
	18:25 all that he had, and **payment** to be **m**.	591	
	19: 4 that he which **m** *them* at the beginning	2936	
	19: 4 made *them* at the beginning **m** them male	4160	
	19:12 which were **m eunuchs** of men:	2134	
	19:12 which have **m** themselves **eunuchs** for	2134	
	20:12 and thou hast **m** them equal unto us,	4160	
	21:13 prayer; but ye have **m** it a den of thieves.	4160	
	22: 2 which **m** a marriage for his son,	4160	
	22: 5 they **m light of** *it*, and went their ways,	272	
	23:15 to make one proselyte, and when he is **m**,	4160	
	24:45 whom his lord hath **m ruler** over his	2525	
	25: 6 at midnight there was a cry **m**, Behold,	1096	
	25:16 the same, and **m** *them* other five talents.	4160	
	26:19 and they **m ready** the passover.	2090	
	27:24 but *that* rather a tumult was **m**, he took	1096	
	27:64 the sepulchre be **m sure** until the third	805	
	27:66 So they went, and **m** the sepulchre **sure**,	805	
Mk	2:21 *from* the old, and the rent is **m** worse.	1096	
	2:27 The sabbath was **m** for man, *and* not man	1096	
	5:34 Daughter, thy faith hath **m** thee **whole**;	4982	
	6:21 that Herod on his birthday **m** a supper to	4160	
	6:56 as many as touched him were **m whole**.	4982	
	8:25 again upon his eyes, and **m** him look up:	4160	
	10: 6 of the creation God **m** them male	4160	
	10:52 thy way; thy faith hath **m** thee **whole**.	4982	
	11:17 but ye have **m** it a den of thieves.	4160	
	14: 4 Why was this waste of the ointment **m**?	1096	
	14:16 them: and they **m ready** the passover.	2090	
	14:58 destroy this temple that is **m with hands**,	5499	
	14:58 I will build another **m without hands**.	886	
	15: 7 **m insurrection with** *him*, who had	4955	

M

Lk
1:62 And they m signs to his father, how he 1770
2: 2 this taxing was first m when Cyrenius 1096
2:15 which the Lord hath m known unto us. 1107
2:17 m known abroad the saying which was 1232
3: 5 and the crooked shall be m straight, NIG
3: 5 and the rough ways shall be m smooth; NIG
4: 3 command this stone that it be m bread. 1096
5:29 And Levi m him a great feast in his own 4160
8:17 is secret, that shall not be m manifest; 1096
8:48 faith hath m thee whole; go in peace.) 4982
8:50 believe only, and she shall be m whole. 4982
9:15 they did so, and m them all sit down. 347
11:40 did not he that m that which is without 1096
12:14 who m me a judge or a divider over you? 2525
13:13 and immediately she was m straight, 461
14:12 thee again, and a recompence be m thee. 1096
14:16 A certain man m a great supper, 4160
17:19 go thy way: thy faith hath m thee whole. 4982
19: 6 And he m haste, and came down, 4692
19:46 prayer: but ye have m it a den of thieves. 4692
22:13 them: and they m ready the passover. 2090
23:12 Pilate and Herod were m friends together; 1096
23:19 (Who for a certain sedition m in the city, 1839
24:22 also of our company m us astonished, 1839
24:28 he m as though he would have gone 4364
Jn
1: 3 All things were m by him; and without 1096
1: 3 without him was not any thing m that 1096
1: 3 him was not any thing made that was m. 1096
1:10 the world was m by him, and the world 1096
1:14 And the Word was m flesh, 1096
1:31 that he should be m manifest to Israel, 5319
2: 9 had tasted the water that was m wine, 1096
2:15 And when he had m a scourge of small 4160
3:21 his deeds may be m manifest, that they 5319
4: 1 how the Pharisees had heard that Jesus m 4160
4:46 of Galilee, where he m the water wine. 4160
5: 4 whole of whatsoever disease he had. 1096
5: 6 saith unto him, Wilt thou be m whole? 1096
5: 9 And immediately the man was m whole, 1096
5:11 He answered them, He that m me whole, 4160
5:14 said unto him, Behold, thou art m whole: 1096
5:15 it was Jesus, which had m him whole. 4160
7:23 I have m a man every whit whole on 4160
8:33 how sayest thou, Ye shall be m free? 1096
9: 3 of God should be m manifest in him. 5319
9: 6 and clay of the spittle, and he anointed 4160
9:11 A man that is called Jesus m clay, 4160
9:14 it was the sabbath day when Jesus m 4160
9:39 that they which see might be m blind. 1096
12: 2 There they m him a supper; and Martha 4160
15:15 of my Father I have m known unto you. 1107
17:23 me, that they may be m perfect in one; 5048
18:18 officers stood there, who had m a fire of 4160
19: 7 because he m himself the Son of God. 4160
19:23 took his garments, and m four parts, 4160
Ac
1: 1 The former treatise have I m, 4160
2:28 thou m known to me the ways of life; 1107
2:36 that God hath m that same Jesus, whom 4160
3:12 or holiness we had m this man to walk? 4160
3:16 faith in his name hath m this man strong, 4732
3:25 of the covenant which God m with our 1303
4: 9 by what means he is m whole; 4982
4:24 which hast m heaven, and earth, 4160
4:35 distribution was m unto every man NIG
7:10 and he m him governor over Egypt and 2525
7:13 at the second time Joseph was m known 319
7:13 Joseph's kindred was m known unto 1096
7:27 Who m thee a ruler and a judge over us? 2525
7:35 saying, Who m thee a ruler and a judge? 2525
7:41 And they m a calf in those days, 3447
7:43 figures which ye m to worship them: 4160
7:48 dwelleth not in temples m with hands; 5499
7:50 Hath not my hand m all these things? 4160
8: 2 and m great lamentation over him. 4160
8: 3 As for Saul, he m havock of the church, 3075
9:39 the coats and garments which Dorcas m, 4160
10:10 but while they m ready, he fell into a 3903
10:17 had m inquiry for Simon's house, 1331
12: 5 prayer was m without ceasing of the 1096
12:20 m Blastus the king's chamberlain their friend, 3982
12:21 his throne, and m an oration unto them. 1215
13:32 how that the promise which was m unto 1096
14: 2 m their minds evil affected against 2559
14: 5 And when there was an assault m both of 1096
14:15 which m heaven, and earth, and the sea, 4160
15: 7 good while ago God m choice among us, 1586
16:13 side, where prayer was wont to be m; NIG
16:24 and m their feet fast in the stocks. 805
17:24 God that m the world and all things 4160
17:24 dwelleth not in temples m with hands; 5499
17:26 hath m of one blood all nations of men 4160
18:12 m insurrection with one accord against 2721
19:24 which m silver shrines for Diana, 4160
19:26 they be no gods, which are m with hands; 1096
19:33 have m his defence unto the people. 626
20:28 the which the Holy Ghost hath m you 5087
21:40 And when there was a great silence, 1096
22: 6 as I m my journey, and was come nigh 4198
23:13 they were more than forty which had m 4160
26: 6 judged for the hope of the promise m of 1096
27:40 to the wind, and m toward shore. 2722
Ro
1: 3 which was m of the seed of David, 1096
1:20 understood by the things that are m, 4161
1:23 into an image m like to corruptible man, NIG

Ro
2:25 thy circumcision is m uncircumcision. 1096
4:14 faith is m void, and the promise made of 2758
4:14 and the promise m of none effect: 2673
4:17 I have m thee a father of many nations,) 5087
5:19 disobedience many were m sinners, 2525
5:19 by the obedience of one shall many be m 2525
6:18 Being then m free from sin, ye became 1659
6:22 But now being m free from sin, 1659
7:13 then that which is good m death unto me? 1096
8: 2 Jesus hath m me free from the law of sin 1659
8:20 For the creature was m subject to vanity, 5293
9:20 that formed it, Why hast thou m me thus? 4160
9:29 and been m like unto Gomorrha. 3666
10:10 with the mouth confession is m unto 3670
10:20 I was m manifest unto them that asked 1096
11: 9 Let their table be m a snare, and a 1096+1519
14:21 or is offended, or is m weak. NIG
15: 8 confirm the promises unto the fathers: NIG
15:27 if the Gentiles have been m partakers 2841
16:26 But now is m manifest, and by 5319
16:26 m known to all nations for the obedience 1107
1Co
1:17 of Christ should be m of none effect. 2758
1:20 not God m foolish the wisdom of this 3471
1:30 who of God is m unto us wisdom, 1096
3:13 Every man's work shall be m manifest: 1096
4: 9 for we are m a spectacle unto the world, 1096
4:13 we are m as the filth of the world, 1096
7:21 but if thou mayest be m free, use it rather. 1096
9:19 yet have I m myself servant unto all, 1402
9:22 I am m all things to all men, that I might 1096
11:19 that they which are approved may be m 1096
12:13 have been all m to drink into one Spirit. 4222
14:25 And thus are the secrets of his heart m 1096
15: 2 even so in Christ shall all be m alive. 2227
15:45 first man Adam was m a living soul; 1096+1519
15:45 the last Adam was m a quickening spirit. NIG
2Co
2: 2 but the same which is m sorry by me? 3076
3: 6 Who also hath m us able ministers of 2427
3:10 even that which was m glorious had in 1392
4:10 Jesus might be m manifest in our body. 5319
4:11 might be m manifest in our mortal flesh. 5319
5: 1 a house not m with hand, eternal in 886
5:11 but we are m manifest unto God; 5319
5:11 I trust also are m manifest in your 5319
5:21 For he hath m him to be sin for us, 4160
5:21 that we might be m the righteousness of 1096
7: 8 For though I m you sorry with a letter, 3076
7: 8 that the same epistle hath m you sorry, 3076
7: 9 not that ye were m sorry, but that ye 3076
7: 9 for ye were m sorry after a godly manner, 3076
7:14 so our boasting, which I m before Titus, NIG
10:16 of things m ready to our hand. 1519+2092
11: 6 we have been throughly m manifest 5319
12: 9 for my strength is m perfect in weakness. 5048
Gal
3: 3 are ye now m perfect by the flesh? 2005
3:13 curse of the law, being m a curse for us: 1096
3:16 and his seed were the promises m. 3004
3:19 come to whom the promise was m; 1861
4: 4 m of a woman, made under the law, 1096
4: 4 made of a woman, made under the law, 1096
5: 1 liberty wherewith Christ hath m us free, 1659
Eph
1: 6 wherein he hath m us accepted in 5487
1: 9 Having m known unto us the mystery of 1107
2: 6 m us sit together in heavenly places in 4776
2:11 Circumcision in the flesh m by hands; 5499
2:13 far off are m nigh by the blood of Christ. 1096
2:14 who hath m both one, and hath broken 4160
3: 3 How that by revelation he m known 1107
3: 5 Which in other ages was not m known 1107
3: 7 Whereof I was m a minister, according to 1096
5:13 are reproved are m manifest by the light: 5319
Php
2: 7 But m himself of no reputation, 2758
2: 7 and was m in the likeness of men: 1096
3:10 being m conformable unto his death; 4833
4: 6 let your requests be m known unto God. 1107
Col
1:12 which hath m us meet to be partakers of 2427
1:20 having m peace through the blood of his 1517
1:23 whereof I Paul am m a minister; 1096
1:25 Whereof I am m a minister, according to 1096
1:26 but now is m manifest to his saints: 5319
2:11 with the circumcision m without hands, 886
2:15 powers, he m a shew of them openly, 1165
1Ti
1: 9 that the law is not m for a righteous man, 2749
1:19 concerning faith have m shipwreck: 3489
2: 1 and giving of thanks, be m for all men; 4160
2Ti
1:10 is now m manifest by the appearing of 5319
Tit
3: 7 should be m heirs according to the hope 1096
Heb
1: 2 things, by whom also he m the worlds; 4160
1: 4 Being m so much better than the angels, 1096
2: 9 who was m a little lower than the angels, 1642
2:17 behoved him to be m like unto his 3666
3:14 For we are m partakers of Christ, if we 1096
5: 5 also Christ glorified not himself to be m 1096
5: 9 being m perfect, he became the author 5048
6: 4 and were m partakers of the Holy Ghost, 1096
6:13 For when God m promise to Abraham, 1861
6:20 a high priest for ever after the order of 1096
7: 3 of life; but m like unto the Son of God; 871
7:12 there is m of necessity a change also of 1096
7:16 Who is m, not after the law of a carnal 1096
7:19 For the law m nothing perfect, 5048
7:20 as not without an oath he was m priest: NIG
7:21 (For those priests were m without an oath; 1096
7:22 much was Jesus m a surety of a better 1096
7:26 and m higher than the heavens; 1096

Heb
8: 9 Not according to the covenant that I m 4160
8:13 A new covenant, he hath m the first old. 3822
9: 2 For there was a tabernacle m; the first, 2680
9: 8 the holiest of all was not yet m manifest, 5319
9:11 not m with hands, that is to say, not of 5499
9:24 into the holy places m with hands, 5499
10: 3 remembrance again m of sins every year. NIG
10:13 till his enemies be m his footstool. 5087
10:33 whilst ye were m a gazingstock both by 2301
11: 3 that things which are seen were not m of 1096
11:22 m mention of the departing of the 3421
11:34 out of weakness were m strong, waxed 1743
11:40 they without us should not be m perfect. 5048
12:23 and to the spirits of just men m perfect, 5048
12:27 as of things that are m, that those things 4160
Jas
1:10 But the rich, in that he is m low: because 5014
2:22 and by works was faith m perfect? 5048
3: 3 which are m after the similitude of God. 1096
1Pe
2: 7 same is m the head of the corner, 1096+1519
3:22 and powers being m subject unto him. 5293
2Pe
1:16 when we m known unto you the power 1107
2:12 brute beasts, m to be taken and destroyed, 1080
1Jn
2:19 m manifest that they were not all of us. 5319
4:17 Herein is our love m perfect, that we may 5048
4:18 He that feareth is not m perfect in love. 5048
5:10 that believeth not God hath m him a liar; 4160
Rev
1: 6 And hath m us kings and priests unto God 4160
5:10 And hast m us unto our God kings and 4160
7:14 m them white in the blood of the Lamb. 3021
8:11 the waters, because they were m bitter. 4087
14: 7 worship him that m heaven, and earth, 4160
14: 8 she m all nations drink of the wine of 4222
15: 4 for thy judgments are m manifest. 5319
17: 2 m drunk with the wine of her fornication. 3184
18:15 these things, which were m rich by her, 4147
18:19 wherein were m rich all that had ships in 4147
18:19 for in one hour is she m desolate. 2049
19: 7 come, and his wife hath m herself ready. 2090

MADEST (10) [MAKE]
Ne 9: 8 m a covenant with him to give the land 3772
 9:14 m known unto them thy holy sabbath, 3045
Ps 8: 6 Thou m him to have dominion over 4910
 80:15 the branch that thou m strong for thyself. 553
 80:17 the son of man whom thou m strong, 553
Eze 16:17 m to thyself images of men, 6213
 29: 7 and m all their loins to be at a stand. 5976
Jnh 4:10 hast not laboured, neither m it grow; 1431
Ac 21:38 which before these days m an uproar, 387
Heb 2: 7 him a little lower than the angels; 1642

MADIAN (1) [MIDIAN]
Ac 7:29 and was a stranger in the land of M, 3099

MADMANNAH (2)
Jos 15:31 And Ziklag, and M, and Sansannah, 4089
1Ch 2:49 She bare also Shaaph the father of M, 4089

MADMEN (1)
Jer 48: 2 Also thou shalt be cut down, O M; 4086

MADMENAH (1)
Isa 10:31 M is removed; the inhabitants of Gebim 4088

MADNESS (9) [MAD]
Dt 28:28 The LORD shall smite thee with m, 7697
Ecc 1:17 know wisdom, and to know m and folly: 1947
 2:12 to behold wisdom, and m, and folly: 1947
 7:25 of folly, even of foolishness and m: 1947
 9: 3 is in their heart while they live, 1947
 10:13 and the end of his talk is mischievous m. 1948
Zec 12: 4 with astonishment, and his rider with m; 7697
Lk 6:11 they were filled with m; 454
2Pe 2:16 man's voice forbad the m of the prophet. 3913

MADON (2)
Jos 11: 1 things, that he sent to Jobab king of M, 4068
 12:19 The king of M, one; the king of Hazor, 4068

MAGADAN See MAGDALA

MAGBISH (1)
Ezr 2:30 The children of M, an hundred fifty and 4019

MAGDALA (1) [MAGDALENE]
Mt 15:39 took ship, and came into the coasts of M. 3093

MAGDALENE (12) [MAGDALA]
Mt 27:56 Among which was Mary M, and Mary 3094
 27:61 And there was Mary M, and the other 3094
 28: 1 came Mary M and the other Mary to see 3094
Mk 15:40 among whom was Mary M, and Mary 3094
 15:47 Mary M and Mary the mother of Joses 3094
 16: 1 Mary M, and Mary the mother of James, 3094
 16: 9 he appeared first to Mary M, out of whom 3094
Lk 8: 2 evil spirits and infirmities, Mary called M, 3094
 24:10 It was Mary M, and Joanna, and Mary 3094
Jn 19:25 Mary the wife of Cleophas, and Mary M. 3094
 20: 1 The first day of the week cometh Mary M 3094
 20:18 Mary M came and told the disciples that 3094

MAGDIEL (2)
Ge 36:43 Duke M, duke Iram: these be the dukes 4025
1Ch 1:54 Duke M, duke Iram. These are the dukes 4025

M

MAGICIAN (1) [MAGICIANS]
Da 2:10 *that* asked such things at any **m**, 2749

MAGICIANS (15) [MAGICIAN]
Ge 41: 8 he sent and called for all the **m** of Egypt, 2748
41:24 told *this* unto the **m**; but *there was* none 2748
Ex 7:11 now the **m** of Egypt, they also did in like 2748
7:22 the **m** of Egypt did so with their 2748
8: 7 the **m** did so with their enchantments, 2748
8:18 the **m** did so with their enchantments to 2748
8:19 **m** said unto Pharaoh, This *is* the finger 2748
9:11 the **m** could not stand before Moses 2748
9:11 for the boil was upon the **m**, and upon all 2748
Da 1:20 them ten times better than all the **m** 2748
2: 2 the king commanded to call the **m**, 2748
2:27 **m**, the soothsayers, shew unto the king; 2749
4: 7 came in the **m**, the astrologers, 2749
4: 9 master of the **m**, because I know that 2749
5:11 made master of the **m**, astrologers, 2749

MAGISTRATE (2) [MAGISTRATES]
Jdg 18: 7 *there was* no **m** in the land, 3423+6114
Lk 12:58 thou goest with thine adversary to the **m**, 758

MAGISTRATES (8) [MAGISTRATE]
Ezr 7:25 that *is* in thine hand, set **m** and judges, 8200
Lk 12:11 unto **m**, and powers, take ye no thought 746
Ac 16:20 And brought them to the **m**, saying, 4755
16:22 and the **m** rent off their clothes, 4755
16:35 the **m** sent the sergeants, saying, Let those 4755
16:36 to Paul, The **m** have sent to let you go: 4755
16:38 sergeants told these words unto the **m**: 4755
Tit 3: 1 to principalities and powers, to **obey m**, 3980

MAGNIFICAL (1) [MAGNIFY]
1Ch 22: 5 for the Lord *must be* exceeding **m**, 1431

MAGNIFICENCE (1) [MAGNIFY]
Ac 19:27 and her **m** should be destroyed, whom all 3168

MAGNIFIED (21) [MAGNIFY]
Ge 19:19 in thy sight, and thou hast **m** thy mercy, 1431
Jos 4:14 On that day the Lord **m** Joshua in 1431
2Sa 7:26 let thy name be **m** for ever, saying, 1431
1Ch 17:24 that thy name may be **m** for ever, saying, 1431
29:25 the Lord **m** Solomon exceedingly in 1431
2Ch 1: 1 *was* with him, and **m** him exceedingly, 1431
32:23 that he was **m** in the sight of all nations 5375
Ps 35:27 say continually, Let the Lord be **m**, 1431
40:16 say continually, The Lord be **m**. 1431
70: 4 salvation say continually, Let God be **m**. 1431
138: 2 for thou hast **m** thy word above all thy 1431
Jer 48:26 for he **m** *himself* against the Lord: 1431
48:42 he hath **m** *himself* against the Lord. 1431
La 1: 9 for the enemy hath **m** *himself.* 1431
Da 8:11 *himself even* to the prince of the host, 1431
Zep 2: 8 and **m** *themselves* against their border. 1431
2:10 **m** *themselves* against the people of 1431
Mal 1: 5 The Lord will be **m** from the border of 1431
Ac 5:13 himself to them: but the people **m** them. 3170
19:17 and the name of the Lord Jesus was **m**. 3170
Php 1:20 *so* now also Christ shall be **m** in my body, 3170

MAGNIFY (19) [MAGNIFICAL, MAGNIFICENCE, MAGNIFIED]
Jos 3: 7 This day will I begin to **m** thee in the sight 1431
Job 7:17 What *is* man, that thou shouldest **m** him? 1431
19: 5 If indeed ye will **m** *yourselves* against me, 1431
36:24 Remember that thou **m** his work, 7679
Ps 34: 3 O **m** the Lord with me, and let us exalt 1431
35:26 dishonour that **m** *themselves* against me. 1431
38:16 they **m** *themselves* against me. 1431
55:12 hated me *that* did **m** *himself* against me; 1431
69:30 a song; and will **m** him with thanksgiving. 1431
Isa 10:15 shall the saw **m** itself against him that 1431
42:21 will **m** the law, and make *it* honourable. 1431
Eze 38:23 Thus will I **m** myself, and sanctify myself; 1431
Da 8:25 he shall **m** *himself* in his heart, 1431
11:36 himself above every god, and shall 1431
11:37 any god: for he shall **m** himself above all. 1431
Zec 12: 7 do not **m** *themselves* against Judah. 1431
Lk 1:46 And Mary said, My soul doth **m** the Lord, 3170
Ac 10:46 them speak with tongues, and **m** God. 3170
Ro 11:13 apostle of the Gentiles, I **m** mine office: 1392

MAGOG (5)
Ge 10: 2 M, and Madai, and Javan, and Tubal, 4031
1Ch 1: 5 M, and Madai, and Javan, and Tubal, 4031
Eze 2 set thy face against Gog, the land of M, 4031
39: 6 I will send a fire on M, and among them 4031
Rev 20: 8 Gog and M, to gather them together to 3098

MAGOR-MISSABIB (1)
Jer 20: 3 hath not called thy name Pashur, but M. 4036

MAGPIASH (1)
Ne 10:20 M, Meshullam, Hezir, 4047

MAHALAH (1)
1Ch 7:18 bare Ishod, and Abiezer, and M. 4244

MAHALALEEL (7)
Ge 5:12 Cainan lived seventy years, and begat M: 4111
5:13 Cainan lived after he begat M eight 4111
5:15 M lived sixty and five years, 4111
5:16 M lived after he begat Jared eight hundred 4111
Ge 5:17 the days of M were eight hundred ninety 4111
1Ch 1: 2 Kenan, M, Jered, 4111
Ne 11: 4 the son of Shephatiah, the son of M, 4111

MAHALALEL See MAHALALEEL; MALELEEL

MAHALATH (4)
Ge 28: 9 took unto the wives which he had M 4258
2Ch 11:18 Rehoboam took him M the daughter of 4258
Ps 53: T To the chief Musician upon M, Maschil, 4257
88: T To the chief Musician upon M Leannoth, 4257

MAHALI (1)
Ex 6:19 the sons of Merari; M and Mushi: these 4249

MAHANAIM (13)
Ge 32: 2 and he called the name of that place M. 4266
Jos 13:26 and from M unto the border of Debir; 4266
13:30 their coast was from M, all Bashan, 4266
21:38 for the slayer; and M with her suburbs, 4266
2Sa 2: 8 son of Saul, and brought him over *to* M; 4266
2:12 son of Saul, went out from M to Gibeon. 4266
2:29 *through* all Bithron, and they came to M. 4266
17:24 David came to M. And Absalom passed 4266
17:27 to pass, when David was come to M, 4266
19:32 the king of sustenance while he lay at M; 4266
1Ki 2: 8 curse in the day when I went *to* M: 4266
4:14 Ahinadab the son of Iddo *had* M. 4266
1Ch 6:80 her suburbs, and M with her suburbs, 4266

MAHANEH-DAN (1) [DAN]
Jdg 18:12 wherefore they called that place M unto 4265

MAHARAI (3)
2Sa 23:28 Zalmon the Ahohite, M the Netophathite, 4121
1Ch 11:30 M the Netophathite, Heled the son of 4121
27:13 tenth month *was* M the Netophathite, 4121

MAHATH (3)
1Ch 6:35 the son of M, the son of Amasai, 4287
2Ch 29:12 M the son of Amasai, and Joel the son of 4287
31:13 Eliel, and Ismachiah, and M, and Benaiah, 4287

MAHAVITE (1)
1Ch 11:46 Eliel the M, and Jeribai, and Joshaviah, 4233

MAHAZIOTH (2)
1Ch 25: 4 Joshbekashah, Mallothi, Hothir, *and* M: 4238
25:30 three and twentieth to M, *he*, his sons, 4238

MAHER-SHALAL-HASH-BAZ (2)
Isa 8: 1 in it with a man's pen concerning M. 4122
8: 3 said the Lord to me, Call his name M. 4122

MAHLAH (4)
Nu 26:33 the daughters of Zelophehad *were* M, 4244
27: 1 M, Noah, and Hoglah, and Milcah, 4244
36:11 For M, Tirzah, and Hoglah, and Milcah, 4244
Jos 17: 3 M, and Noah, Hoglah, Milcah, and 4244

MAHLI (11) [MAHLITES]
Nu 3:20 Merari by their families; M, and Mushi. 4249
1Ch 6:19 The sons of Merari; M, and Mushi. 4249
6:29 M, Libni his son, Shimei his son, Uzza his 4249
6:47 The son of M, the son of Mushi, the son 4249
23:21 The sons of Merari; M, and Mushi. 4249
23:21 Mushi. The sons of M; Eleazar, and Kish. 4249
23:23 M, and Eder, and Jeremoth, three. 4249
24:26 The sons of Merari *were* M and Mushi: 4249
24:28 Of M came Eleazar, who had no sons. 4249
24:30 also of Mushi; M, and Eder, and Jerimoth. 4249
Ezr 8:18 of the sons of M, the son of Levi, the son 4249

MAHLITES (2) [MAHLI]
Nu 3:33 Of Merari *was* the family of the M, 4250
26:58 the family of the M, the family of 4250

MAHLON (3) [MAHLON'S]
Ru 1: 2 the name of his two sons M and Chilion, 4248
1: 5 M and Chilion died also both of them; 4248
4:10 Ruth the Moabitess, the wife of M, 4248

MAHLON'S (1) [MAHLON]
Ru 4: 9 all that *was* Chilion's and M, of the hand 4248

MAHOL (1)
1Ki 4:31 and Chalcol, and Darda, the sons of M: 4235

MAID (36) [BONDMAID, BONDMAIDS, HANDMAID, HANDMAIDEN, HANDMAIDENS, HANDMAIDS, MAID'S, MAIDEN, MAIDENS, MAIDS, MAIDSERVANT, MAIDSERVANT'S, MAIDSERVANTS, MAIDSERVANTS']
Ge 16: 2 I pray thee, go in unto my **m**; it may be 8198
16: 3 Sarai Abram's wife took Hagar her **m** 8198
16: 5 I have given my **m** into thy bosom; 8198
16: 6 unto Sarai, Behold, thy **m** *is* in thy hand; 8198
16: 8 he said, Hagar, Sarai's **m**, whence camest 8198
29:24 Leah Zilpah his **m** *for* a handmaid. 8198
29:29 Bilhah his handmaid to be her **m**. 8198
30: 3 she said, Behold my **m** Bilhah, go in unto 519
30: 7 Bilhah Rachel's **m** conceived again, 8198
30: 9 took Zilpah her **m**, and gave her Jacob 8198
30:10 And Zilpah Leah's **m** bare Jacob a son. 8198
30:12 Zilpah Leah's **m** bare Jacob a second son. 8198
Ex 2: 5 the flags, she sent her **m** to fetch it. 519

MAID ... (continued)
Ex 2: 8 the **m** went and called the child's mother. 5959
21:20 or his **m**, with a rod, and he die under his 519
21:26 or the eye of his **m**, that it perish; 519
22:16 if a man entice a **m** that is not betrothed, 1330
Lev 12: 5 if she bear a **m child**, then she shall be 5347
25: 6 and for thy **m**, and for thy hired servant, 519
Dt 22:14 when I came to her, I found her not a **m**: 1331
22:17 saying, I found not thy daughter a **m**; 1331
2Ki 5: 2 captive out of the land of Israel a little **m**; 5291
5: 4 said the **m** that *is* of the land of Israel. 5291
Est 2: 7 and the **m** *was* fair and beautiful; 5291
Job 31: 1 why then should I think upon a **m**? 1330
Pr 30:19 the sea; and the way of a man with a **m**. 5959
Isa 24: 2 as *with* the **m**, so *with* her mistress; 8198
Jer 2:32 Can a **m** forget her ornaments, *or a* bride 1330
51:22 break in pieces the young man and the **m**; 1330
Am 2: 7 and his father will go in unto the *same* **m**, 5291
Mt 9:24 for the **m** is not dead, but sleepeth. 2877
9:25 took her by the hand, and the **m** arose. 2877
26:71 another **m** saw him, and said unto them NIG
Mk 14:69 And a **m** saw him again, and began to say 3814
Lk 8:54 by the hand, and called, saying, M, arise. 3816
22:56 But a certain **m** beheld him as he sat by 3814

MAID'S (1) [MAID]
Est 2:12 when **every m** turn was 5291+5291+2050.1

MAIDEN (8) [MAID]
Ge 30:18 I have given my **m** to my husband: 8198
Jdg 19:24 *here is* my daughter a **m**, 1330
2Ch 36:17 no compassion upon young man or **m**, 1330
Est 2: 4 the **m** which pleaseth the king be queen 5291
2: 9 the **m** pleased him, and she obtained 5291
2:13 thus came *every* **m** unto the king; 5291
Ps 123: 2 as the eyes of a **m** unto the hand of her 8198
Lk 8:51 and the father and the mother of the **m**. 3816

MAIDENS (19) [MAID]
Ex 2: 5 her **m** walked along by the river's side; 5291
Ru 2: 8 from hence, but abide here fast by my **m**: 5291
2:22 daughter, that thou go out with his **m**, 5291
2:23 So she kept fast by the **m** of Boaz to glean 5291
3: 2 of our kindred, with whose **m** thou wast? 5291
1Sa 9:11 they found **young m** going out to draw 5291
Est 2: 8 when many **m** were gathered together 5291
2: 9 seven **m**, *which were* meet to be given 5291
4:16 I also and my **m** will fast likewise; and so 5291
Job 19:15 and my **m**, count me for a stranger: 519
41: 5 a bird? or wilt thou bind him for thy **m**? 5291
Ps 78:63 and their **m** were not given to marriage. 1330
148:12 Both young men, and **m**; old men, 1330
Pr 9: 3 She hath sent forth her **m**: she crieth 5291
27:27 and *for* the maintenance for thy **m**. 5291
31:15 to her household, and a portion to her **m**. 5291
Ecc 2: 7 I got *me* servants and **m**, and had servants 8198
Eze 44:22 they shall take **m** of the seed of the house 1330
Lk 12:45 begin to beat the menservants and **m**, 3814

MAIDS (8) [MAID]
Ezr 2:65 Beside their servants and their **m**, of 519
Est 2: 9 her **m** unto the best *place* of the house of 5291
4: 4 So Esther's **m** and her chamberlains came 5291
La 5:11 in Zion, *and* the **m** in the cities of Judah. 1330
Eze 9: 6 both **m**, and little children, and women: 1330
Na 2: 7 her **m** *shall* lead *her* as with the voice of 519
Zec 9:17 men cheerful, and new wine the **m**. 1330
Mk 14:66 there cometh one of the **m** of the high 3814

MAIDSERVANT (16) [MAID, SERVE]
Ex 11: 5 *even* unto the firstborn of the **m** that *is* 8198
20:10 thy manservant, nor thy **m**, nor thy cattle, 519
20:17 nor his **m**, nor his ox, nor his ass, 519
21: 7 if a man sell his daughter to be a **m**, she 519
21:32 If the ox shall push a manservant or a **m**; 519
Dt 5:14 nor thy **m**, nor thine ox, nor thine ass, 519
5:14 and thy **m** may rest as well as thou. 519
5:21 his **m**, his ox, or his ass, or any *thing* that 519
12:18 thy **m**, and the Levite that *is* within thy 519
15:17 also unto thy **m** thou shalt do likewise. 519
16:11 thy **m**, and the Levite that *is* within thy 519
16:14 thy **m**, and the Levite, the stranger, 519
Jdg 9:18 have made Abimelech, the son of his **m**, 519
Job 31:13 the cause of my manservant or of my **m**, 519
Jer 34: 9 every man his **m**, *being* a Hebrew or 8198
34:10 and every one his **m**, go free, 8198

MAIDSERVANT'S (1) [MAID, SERVE]
Ex 21:27 out his manservant's tooth, or his **m** tooth; 519

MAIDSERVANTS (9) [MAID, SERVE]
Ge 12:16 and **m**, and she asses, and camels. 8198
20:17 Abimelech, and his wife, and his **m**; 519
24:35 menservants, and **m**, and camels, and 8198
30:43 **m**, and menservants, and camels, and 8198
Dt 12:12 your **m**, and the Levite that *is* within your 519
1Sa 8:16 your **m**, and your goodliest young men, 8198
2Sa 6:22 the **m** which thou hast spoken of, of them 519
2Ki 5:26 and oxen, and menservants, and **m**? 8198
Ne 7:67 Beside their menservants and their **m**, 519

MAIDSERVANTS' (1) [MAID, SERVE]
Ge 31:33 into Leah's tent, and into the two **m** tents; 519

MAIL (2)
1Sa 17: 5 and he *was* armed with a coat of **m**; 7193
17:38 also he armed him with a coat *of* **m**. NIH

MAIMED (7)

Lev 22:22 or **m**, or having a wen, or scurvy,	2782
Mt 15:30 **m**, and many others, and cast them *down*	2948
15:31 the **m** *to be* whole, the lame to walk,	2948
18: 8 better for thee to enter into life halt or **m**,	2948
Mk 9:43 it is better for thee to enter into life **m**,	2948
Lk 14:13 call the poor, the **m**, the lame, the blind:	376
14:21 and the **m**, and the halt, and the blind.	376

MAINSAIL (1)

Ac 27:40 and hoised up the **m** to the wind,	736

MAINTAIN (10) [MAINTAINED, MAINTAINEST, MAINTENANCE]

1Ki 8:45 and their supplication, and **m** their cause,	6213
8:49 thy dwelling place, and **m** their cause,	6213
8:59 that he **m** the cause of his servant,	6213
1Ch 26:27 dedicate to **m** the house of the LORD.	2388
2Ch 6:25 their supplication, and **m** their cause.	6213
6:39 **m** their cause, and forgive thy people	6213
Job 13:15 but I will **m** mine own ways before him.	3198
Ps 140:12 I know that the LORD will **m** the cause of	6213
Tit 3: 8 in God might be careful to **m** good works.	4291
3:14 let ours also learn to **m** good works for	4291

MAINTAINED (1) [MAINTAIN]

Ps 9: 4 For thou hast **m** my right and my cause;	6213

MAINTAINEST (1) [MAINTAIN]

Ps 16: 5 and of my cup: thou **m** my lot.	8551

MAINTENANCE (2) [MAINTAIN]

Ezr 4:14 we **have m** from *the king's* palace,	4415+4416
Pr 27:27 and *for* the **m** for thy maidens.	2416

MAJESTY (29)

1Ch 29:11 and the glory, and the victory, and the **m**:	1935
29:25 bestowed upon him *such* royal **m** as had	1935
Est 1: 4 the honour of his excellent **m** many days,	1420
Job 37:22 out of the north: with God *is* terrible **m**.	1935
40:10 Deck thyself now with **m** and excellency;	1347
Ps 21: 5 honour and **m** hast thou laid upon him.	1926
29: 4 the voice of the LORD *is* **full of m**.	1926
45: 3 O *most* mighty, *with* thy glory and thy **m**.	1926
45: 4 thy **m** ride prosperously because of truth	1926
93: 1 The LORD reigneth, he is clothed with **m**;	1348
96: 6 Honour and **m** *are* before him: strength	1926
104: 1 thou art clothed with honour and **m**.	1926
145: 5 speak of the glorious honour of thy **m**,	1935
145:12 and the glorious **m** of his kingdom.	1926
Isa 2:10 of the LORD, and for the glory of his **m**.	1347
2:19 of the LORD, and for the glory of his **m**,	1347
2:21 of the LORD, and for the glory of his **m**,	1347
24:14 they shall sing, for the **m** of the LORD,	1347
26:10 and will not behold the **m** of the LORD.	1348
Eze 7:20 the beauty of his ornament, he set it in **m**:	1347
Da 4:30 my power, and for the honour of my **m**?	1923
4:36 and excellent **m** was added unto me.	7238
5:18 kingdom, and **m**, and glory, and honour:	7238
5:19 for the **m** that he gave him, all people,	7238
Mic 5: 4 in the **m** of the name of the LORD his	1347
Heb 1: 3 sat down on the right hand of the **M** on	3172
8: 1 of the throne of the **M** in the heavens;	3172
2Pe 1:16 but were eyewitnesses of his **m**.	3168
Jude 1:25 *be* glory and **m**, dominion and power,	3172

MAKAZ (1)

1Ki 4: 9 in **M**, and in Shaalbim, and Beth-shemesh,	4739

MAKE (1055) [MADE, MADEST, MAKER, MAKERS, MAKEST, MAKETH, MAKING, TENTMAKERS]

Ge 1:26 God said, Let us **m** man in our image,	6213
2:18 alone; I will **m** him a help meet for him.	6213
3: 6 a tree to be desired to **m** *one* **wise**, she	7919
3:21 to his wife did the LORD God **m** coats of	6213
6:14 **M** thee an ark of gopher wood; rooms	6213
6:14 rooms shalt thou **m** in the ark,	6213
6:15 *is the fashion* which thou shalt **m** it *of*:	6213
6:16 A window shalt thou **m** to the ark, and in	6213
6:16 second, and third *stories* shalt thou **m** it.	6213
9:12 *is* the token of the covenant which I **m**	5414
11: 3 **m brick**, and burn *them*	3835+3843
11: 4 let us **m** us a name, lest we be scattered	6213
12: 2 I will **m** of thee a great nation, and I will	6213
12: 2 I will bless thee, and **m** thy name **great**;	1431
13:16 I will **m** thy seed as the dust of the earth:	7760
17: 2 I will **m** my covenant between me and	5414
17: 6 I will **m** thee exceeding **fruitful**, and I	6509
17: 6 I will **m** nations of thee, and kings shall	5414
17:20 will **m** him **fruitful**, and will multiply him	6509
17:20 he beget, and I will **m** him a great nation.	5414
18: 6 **M ready quickly** three measures of fine	4116
18: 6 knead *it*, and **m** cakes upon the hearth.	6213
19:32 let us **m** our father **drink** wine, and we	8248
19:34 let us **m** him **drink** wine this night also;	8248
21:13 of the son of the bondwoman will I **m**	7760
21:18 hand; for I will **m** him a great nation.	7760
24: 3 I will **m** thee **swear** by the LORD,	7650
26: 4 I will **m** thy seed to **multiply** as the stars	7235
26:28 thee, and let us **m** a covenant with thee;	3772
27: 4 **m** me savoury meat, such as I love,	6213
27: 7 and **m** me savoury meat, that I may eat,	6213
27: 9 I will **m** them savoury meat for thy father,	6213
28: 3 and **m** thee **fruitful**, and multiply thee,	6509
31:44 thou, let us **m** a covenant, I and thou;	3772

Ge 32:12 and **m** thy seed as the sand of the sea,	7760
34: 9 ye **marriages** with us, *and* give your	2859
34:30 Ye have troubled me to **m** me **to stink**	887
35: 1 **m** there an altar unto God, that appeared	6213
35: 3 I will **m** there an altar unto God,	6213
40:14 **m** mention of me unto Pharaoh,	2142
43:16 *these* men home, and slay, and **m ready**;	3559
46: 3 for I will there **m** of thee a great nation.	7760
47: 6 land **m** thy father and brethren to **dwell**;	3427
47: 6 then **m** them rulers over my cattle.	7760
48: 4 I will **m** thee **fruitful**, and multiply thee,	6509
48: 4 and I will **m** of thee a multitude of people;	5414
48:20 God **m** thee as Ephraim and as Manasseh:	7760
Ex 5: 5 and you **m** them **rest** from their burdens.	7673
5: 7 give the people straw to **m brick**,	3835+3843
5: 8 which they did **m** heretofore, you shall lay	6213
5:16 thy servants, and they say to us, **M** brick:	6213
12: 4 eating shall **m** your **count** for the lamb.	3699
18:16 I do **m** *them* **know** the statutes of God,	3045
20: 4 Thou shalt not **m** unto thee *any* graven	6213
20:23 Ye shall not **m** with me gods of silver,	6213
20:23 neither shall ye **m** unto you gods of gold.	6213
20:24 An altar of earth thou shalt **m** unto me,	6213
20:25 if thou wilt **m** me an altar of stone,	6213
21:34 The owner of the pit shall **m** *it* **good**,	6213
22: 3 *for* he should **m full restitution**;	7999+7999
22: 5 his own vineyard, shall he **m restitution**.	7999
22: 6 the fire shall **surely m restitution**.	7999+7999
22:11 *thereof*, and he shall not **m** *it* **good**.	7999
22:12 he shall **m restitution** unto the owner	7999
22:13 he shall not **m good** that which was torn.	7999
22:14 with it, he shall **surely m** *it* **good**.	7999+7999
22:15 thereof *be* with it, he shall not **m** *it* **good**:	7999
23:13 **m** no mention of the name of other gods,	2142
23:27 I will **m** all thine enemies turn their backs	5414
23:32 Thou shalt **m** no covenant with them,	3772
23:33 thy land, lest they **m** thee **sin** against me:	2398
25: 8 let them **m** me a sanctuary; that I may	6213
25: 9 instruments thereof, even so shall ye **m** *it*.	6213
25:10 they shall **m** an ark of shittim wood:	6213
25:11 shalt **m** upon it a crown of gold round	6213
25:13 thou shalt **m** staves of shittim wood,	6213
25:17 thou shalt **m** a mercy seat *of* pure gold:	6213
25:18 thou shalt **m** two cherubims *of* gold,	6213
25:18 *of* beaten work shalt thou **m** them,	6213
25:19 one cherub on the one end, and the	6213
25:19 *even* of the mercy seat shall ye **m**	6213
25:23 Thou shalt also **m** a table *of* shittim wood:	6213
25:24 thereto a crown *of* gold round about.	6213
25:25 thou shalt **m** unto it a border of a	6213
25:25 thou shalt **m** a golden crown to the	6213
25:26 thou shalt **m** for it four rings of gold,	6213
25:28 thou shalt **m** the staves *of* shittim wood,	6213
25:29 thou shalt **m** the dishes thereof,	6213
25:29 *of* pure gold shalt thou **m** them.	6213
25:31 thou shalt **m** a candlestick of pure gold:	6213
25:37 thou shalt **m** the seven lamps thereof:	6213
25:39 *Of* a talent of pure gold shall he **m** it,	6213
25:40 look that thou **m** *them* after their pattern,	6213
26: 1 Moreover thou shalt **m** the tabernacle	6213
26: 1 *of* cunning work shalt thou **m** them.	6213
26: 4 thou shalt **m** loops of blue upon the edge	6213
26: 4 shalt thou **m** in the uttermost edge	6213
26: 5 Fifty loops shalt thou **m** in the one curtain	6213
26: 5 fifty loops shalt thou **m** in the edge of	6213
26: 6 thou shalt **m** fifty taches of gold,	6213
26: 7 thou shalt **m** curtains *of* goats' *hair* to be	6213
26: 7 eleven curtains shalt thou **m**.	6213
26:10 thou shalt **m** fifty loops on the edge of	6213
26:11 thou shalt **m** fifty taches of brass,	6213
26:14 thou shalt **m** a covering for the tent *of*	6213
26:15 thou shalt **m** boards for the tabernacle of	6213
26:17 thus shalt thou **m** for all the boards of	6213
26:18 shalt thou **m** the boards for the tabernacle,	6213
26:19 thou shalt **m** forty sockets of silver under	6213
26:22 westward thou shalt **m** six boards.	6213
26:23 two boards shalt thou **m** for the corners	6213
26:26 thou shalt **m** bars *of* shittim wood; five	6213
26:29 **m** their rings *of* gold *for* places for the	6213
26:31 thou shalt **m** a vail *of* blue, and purple,	6213
26:36 thou shalt **m** a hanging for the door of	6213
26:37 thou shalt **m** for the hanging five pillars	6213
27: 1 thou shalt **m** an altar *of* shittim wood,	6213
27: 2 thou shalt **m** the horns of it upon the four	6213
27: 3 thou shalt **m** his pans to receive his ashes,	6213
27: 3 the vessels thereof thou shalt **m** *of* brass.	6213
27: 4 thou shalt **m** for it a grate of network *of*	6213
27: 4 the net shalt thou **m** four brasen rings	6213
27: 6 thou shalt **m** staves for the altar, staves of	6213
27: 8 Hollow with boards shalt thou **m** it: as it	6213
27: 8 thee in the mount, so shall they **m** *it*.	6213
27: 9 thou shalt **m** the court of the tabernacle:	6213
28: 2 thou shalt **m** holy garments for Aaron thy	6213
28: 3 that they may **m** Aaron's garments to	6213
28: 4 *are* the garments which they shall **m**;	6213
28: 4 they shall **m** holy garments for Aaron thy	6213
28: 6 they shall **m** the ephod *of* gold, *of* blue,	6213
28:11 shalt thou **m** them to be set *in* ouches *of*	6213
28:13 And thou shalt **m** ouches *of* gold;	6213
28:14 *of* wreathen work shalt thou **m** them,	6213
28:15 thou shalt **m** the breastplate of judgment	6213
28:15 the work of the ephod thou shalt **m** it;	6213
28:15 *of* fine twined linen, shalt thou **m** it.	6213
28:22 thou shalt **m** upon the breastplate chains	6213
28:23 shalt **m** upon the breastplate two rings	6213

Ex 28:26 thou shalt **m** two rings of gold,	6213
28:27 two *other* rings of gold thou shalt **m**,	6213
28:31 thou shalt **m** the robe of the ephod all of	6213
28:33 *beneath* upon the hem of it thou shalt **m**	6213
28:36 thou shalt **m** a plate *of* pure gold,	6213
28:39 thou shalt **m** the mitre *of* fine linen,	6213
28:39 thou shalt **m** the girdle *of* needlework.	6213
28:40 for Aaron's sons thou shalt **m** coats,	6213
28:40 thou shalt **m** for them girdles,	6213
28:40 bonnets shalt thou **m** for them, for glory	6213
28:42 shalt **m** them linen breeches to cover	6213
29: 2 *of* wheaten flour shalt thou **m** them.	6213
29:37 Seven days thou shalt **m** an atonement	3722
30: 1 shalt **m** an altar to burn incense upon:	6213
30: 1 *of* shittim wood shalt thou **m** it.	6213
30: 3 thou shalt **m** unto it a crown *of* gold	6213
30: 4 two golden rings shalt thou **m** to it under	6213
30: 4 upon the two sides of it shalt thou **m** *it*;	6213
30: 5 thou shalt **m** the staves of shittim wood,	6213
30:10 Aaron shall **m** an atonement upon	3722
30:10 **m** atonement upon it throughout your	3722
30:15 to **m** an atonement for your souls.	3722
30:16 to **m** an atonement for your souls.	3722
30:18 Thou shalt also **m** a laver *of* brass,	6213
30:25 thou shalt **m** it an oil of holy ointment,	6213
30:32 neither shall ye **m** *any other* like it, after	6213
30:35 shalt **m** it a perfume, a confection *after*	6213
30:37 *as for* the perfume which thou shalt **m**,	6213
30:37 you shall not **m** to yourselves according to	6213
30:38 Whosoever shall **m** like unto that, to	6213
31: 6 they may **m** all that I have commanded	6213
32: 1 said unto him, Up, **m** us gods, which shall	6213
32:10 and I will **m** of thee a great nation.	6213
32:23 For they said unto me, **M** us gods,	6213
32:30 peradventure I shall **m** an atonement for	3722
33:19 I will **m** all my goodness **pass** before thee,	5674
34:10 he said, Behold, I **m** a covenant: before all	3772
34:12 thou **m** a covenant with the inhabitants	3772
34:15 thou **m** a covenant with the inhabitants	3772
34:16 thy sons **go a whoring** after their gods.	2181
34:17 Thou shalt **m** thee no molten gods.	6213
35:10 **m** all that the LORD hath commanded;	6213
35:33 to **m** any *manner of* cunning work.	6213
36: 3 to **m** *it* **withal**. And they brought yet unto	6213
36: 5 which the LORD commanded to **m**.	6213
36: 7 Let neither man nor woman **m** any more	6213
36: 7 was sufficient for all the work to **m** it,	6213
36:22 thus did he **m** for all the boards of	6213
Lev 1: 4 for him to **m** atonement for him.	3722
4:20 priest shall **m** an atonement for them,	3722
4:26 priest shall **m** an atonement for him as	3722
4:31 priest shall **m** an atonement for him,	3722
4:35 priest shall **m** an atonement for his sin	3722
5: 6 the priest shall **m** an atonement for him	3722
5:10 the priest shall **m** an atonement for him	3722
5:13 the priest shall **m** an atonement for him as	3722
5:16 he shall **m amends** for the harm that he	7999
5:16 the priest shall **m** an atonement for him	3722
5:18 the priest shall **m** an atonement for him	3722
6: 7 the priest shall **m** an atonement for him	3722
8:15 sanctified it, to **m reconciliation** upon it.	3722
8:34 to do, to **m** an atonement for you.	3722
9: 7 **m** an atonement for thyself, and for	3722
9: 7 people, and **m** an atonement for them;	3722
10:17 to **m** atonement for them before	3722
11:43 Ye shall not **m** yourselves **abominable**	8262
11:43 neither shall ye **m** yourselves **unclean**	2933
11:47 To **m** a **difference** between the unclean	914
12: 7 the LORD, and **m** an atonement for her;	3722
12: 8 the priest shall **m** an atonement for her,	3722
14:18 the priest shall **m** an atonement for him	3722
14:19 **m** an atonement for him that is to be	3722
14:20 the priest shall **m** an atonement for him,	3722
14:21 to **m** an atonement for him, and one	3722
14:29 to **m** an atonement for him before	3722
14:31 the priest shall **m** an atonement for him	3722
14:53 and **m** an atonement for the house:	3722
15:15 the priest shall **m** an atonement for him	3722
15:30 the priest shall **m** an atonement for her	3722
16: 6 **m** an atonement for himself, and for his	3722
16:10 to **m** an atonement with him, *and* to let	3722
16:11 shall **m** an atonement for himself,	3722
16:16 he shall **m** an atonement for the holy	3722
16:17 **m** an atonement in the holy *place*, until	3722
16:18 the LORD, and **m** an atonement for it;	3722
16:24 **m** an atonement for himself, and for	3722
16:27 blood was brought in to **m** atonement	3722
16:30 shall *the priest* **m** an atonement for you,	3722
16:32 shall **m** the **atonement**, and shall put on	3722
16:33 he shall **m** an atonement for the holy	3722
16:33 shall **m** an atonement for the tabernacle	3722
16:33 he shall **m** an atonement for the priests,	3722
16:34 to **m** an atonement for the children of	3722
17:11 altar to **m** an atonement for your souls:	3722
19: 4 nor **m** to yourselves molten gods:	6213
19:22 the priest shall **m** an atonement for him	3722
19:28 Ye shall not **m** any cuttings in your flesh	5414
20:25 ye shall not **m** your souls **abominable** by	8262
21: 5 They shall not **m baldness** upon	7139+7144
21: 5 nor **m** any **cuttings** in their flesh.	8295+8296
22:22 nor **m** an offering by fire of them upon	5414
22:24 neither shall you **m** *any* offering *thereof*	6213
23:22 thou shalt not **m clean riddance** of	3615
23:28 to **m** an atonement for you before	3722
24:18 he that killeth a beast shall **m** it **good**;	7999

Lev 25: 9 **m** the trumpet **sound** throughout all your	5674
26: 1 Ye shall **m** you no idols nor graven image,	6213
26: 6 lie down, and none shall **m** *you* **afraid:**	2729
26: 9 **m** you **fruitful,** and multiply you,	6509
26:19 I will **m** your heaven as iron, and your	5414
26:22 your cattle, and **m** you **few in number;**	4591
26:31 I will **m** your cities waste, and bring your	5414
27: 2 a man shall **m** a **singular vow,**	5088+6381
Nu 5:21 The Lord **m** thee a curse and an oath	5414
5:21 when the Lord doth **m** thy thigh to rot,	5414
5:22 to **m** *thy* belly to swell, and *thy* thigh to	6638
6: 7 He shall not **m** himself **unclean** for his	2930
6:11 and **m an atonement** for him,	3722
6:25 The Lord **m** his face **shine** upon thee,	215
8: 7 clothes, and *so* **m** themselves **clean.**	2891
8:12 to **m an atonement** for the Levites.	3722
8:19 to **m an atonement** for the children of	3722
10: 2 **M** thee two trumpets of silver; of a whole	6213
10: 2 of a whole piece thou shalt **m** them:	6213
12: 6 *If* the Lord will **m** myself **known** unto	3045
14: 4 Let us **m** a captain, and let us return into	5414
14:12 will **m** of thee a greater nation and	6213
14:30 which I sware to **m** you **dwell**	7931
15: 3 will **m** an offering by fire unto the Lord,	6213
15: 3 to **m** a sweet savour unto the Lord,	6213
15:25 the priest shall **m an atonement** for all	3722
15:28 the priest shall **m an atonement**	3722
15:28 the Lord, to **m an atonement** for him;	3722
15:38 bid them that they **m** them fringes in	6213
16:13 **m** thyself **altogether a prince** over	8323+8323
16:30 if the Lord **m** a new thing, and the earth	1254
16:38 them **m** them broad plates *for* a covering	6213
16:46 and **m an atonement** for them:	3722
17: 5 will **m** to **cease** from me the murmurings	7918
21: 8 **M** thee a fiery **serpent,** and set it upon a	6213
23:19 he spoken, and shall he not **m** it **good?**	6965
28:22 sin offering, to **m an atonement** for you.	3722
28:30 the goats, to **m an atonement** for you.	3722
29: 5 sin offering, to **m an atonement** for you:	3722
30: 8 he shall **m** her vow which she vowed,	NIH
30:13 or her husband may **m** it **void.**	6565
30:15 if he shall **any ways m** them **void**	6565+6565
31:23 ye shall **m** *it* go the fire, and it shall be	5674
31:23 all that abideth not the fire ye shall **m go**	5674
31:50 to **m an atonement** for our souls before	3722
Dt 1:11 m you a thousand times **so many moe**	3254
1:13 and I will **m** them rulers over you.	7760
4:10 and I will **m** them **hear** my words,	8085
4:16 and **m** you a graven image,	6213
4:23 **m** you a graven image, *or* the likeness of	6213
4:25 *yourselves,* and **m** a graven image,	6213
5: 8 Thou shalt not **m** thee *any* graven image,	6213
7: 2 thou shalt **m** no covenant with them,	3772
7: 3 shalt thou **m marriages** with them;	2859
8: 3 he might **m** thee **know** that man doth	3045
9:14 I will **m** of thee a nation mightier and	6213
10: 1 the mount, and **m** thee an ark of wood.	6213
13:14 and **m search,** and ask diligently;	2713
14: 1 nor **m** *any* baldness between your eyes	7760
15: 1 *every* seven years thou shalt **m** a release.	6213
16:18 officers shalt thou **m** thee in all thy gates,	5414
16:21 Lord thy God, which thou shalt **m** thee.	6213
19:18 the judges shall **m** diligent **inquisition:**	1875
20: 9 that they shall **m** captains of the armies to	6485
20:11 if it **m** thee **answer** of peace, and open	6030
20:12 if it will **m** no **peace** with thee,	7999
20:12 will **m** war against thee, then thou shalt	6213
21:14 thou shalt not **m merchandise** of her,	6014
21:16 the son of the beloved **firstborn** before	1069
22: 8 thou shalt **m** a battlement for thy roof,	6213
22:12 Thou shalt **m** the fringes upon the four	6213
26:19 to **m** thee high above all nations which	5414
28:11 the Lord shall **m** thee **plenteous** in	3498
28:13 the Lord shall **m** thee the head,	5414
28:21 The Lord shall **m** the pestilence **cleave**	1692
28:24 The Lord shall **m** the rain of thy land	5414
28:59 the Lord will **m** thy plagues **wonderful,**	6381
29: 1 which the Lord commanded Moses to **m**	3772
29:14 with you only do I **m** this covenant	3772
30: 9 the Lord thy God will **m** thee **plenteous**	3498
32:26 the remembrance of them to **cease**	7673
32:35 that shall come upon them **m haste.**	2363
32:39 I kill, and I **m alive;** I wound, and I heal:	2421
32:42 I will **m** mine arrows **drunk** with blood,	7937
Jos 1: 8 then thou shalt **m** thy way **prosperous,**	6743
5: 2 **M** thee sharp knives, and circumcise	6213
6: 5 *that* when *they* **m** a long blast with	4900
6:10 shout, nor **m** any **noise** with your voice,	8085
6:18 lest ye **m** *yourselves* **accursed,** when ye	2763
6:18 **m** the camp of Israel a curse, and trouble	7760
7: 3 **m** not all the people to **labour** thither;	3021
7:19 God of Israel, and **m** confession unto him;	5414
9: 6 now therefore **m** ye a league with us.	3772
9: 7 and how shall we **m** a league with you?	3772
9:11 therefore now **m** ye a league with us.	3772
22:25 shall your children **m** our children **cease**	7673
23: 7 neither **m mention** of the name of their	2142
23:12 shall **m marriages** with them, and go in	2859
Jdg 2: 2 ye shall **m** no league with the inhabitants	3772
9:48 me do, **m haste,** *and* do as I *have* done.	4116
16:25 Call for Samson, that he may **m** us **sport.**	7832
17: 3 to **m** a graven image and a molten image:	6213
20:38 was a flame with smoke **rise up** out	5927
Ru 3: 3 *but* **m** not thyself **known** unto the man,	3045
4:11 The Lord **m** the woman that is come	5414

1Sa 1: 6 for to **m** her **fret,** because the Lord had	7481
2: 8 to **m** them **inherit** the throne of glory:	5157
2:24 ye **m** the Lord's people **to transgress.**	5674
2:29 to **m** yourselves fat with the chiefest of	1254
3:12 when I begin, I will also **m** an **end.**	3615
6: 5 Wherefore ye shall **m** images of your	6213
6: 7 therefore **m** a new cart, and take two	6213
8: 5 now **m** us a king to judge us like all	7760
8:12 to **m** his instruments of war,	6213
8:22 their voice, and **m** them a **king.**	4427+4428
9:12 **m** haste now, for he came to day to	4116
11: 1 **M** a covenant with us, and we will serve	3772
11: 2 On this *condition* will I **m** *a covenant*	3772
12:22 it hath pleased the Lord to **m** you his	6213
13:19 the Hebrews **m** *them* swords or spears:	6213
17:25 and **m** his father's house free in Israel.	6213
18:25 Saul thought to **m** David **fall** by the hand	5307
20:38 after the lad, **M** speed, haste, stay not.	4120
22: 7 *and* **m** you all captains of thousands,	7760
25:28 for the Lord will **certainly m** my	6213+6213
28: 2 Therefore will I **m** thee keeper of mine	7760
28:15 for the Philistines **m** war against me,	3898
28:15 *thou* mayest **m known** unto me what I	3045
29: 4 **M** this fellow **return,** that he may go	7725
2Sa 3:12 saying *also,* **M** thy league with me,	3772
3:13 said, Well; I will **m** a league with thee:	3772
3:21 that they may **m** a league with thee,	3772
7:11 Also the Lord telleth thee that he will **m**	6213
7:21 things, to **m** thy servant **know** *them.*	3045
7:23 **m** him a name, and to do for you great	7760
11:25 thy battle **more strong** against the city,	2388
13: 5 down on thy bed, and **m** thyself **sick:**	2470
13: 6 **m** a couple of **cakes** in my	3823+3834
15:14 **m speed** to depart, lest he overtake us	4116
15:20 should I *this* day **m** thee go up and	5128
17: 2 weak handed, and will **m** him **afraid:**	2729
21: 3 wherewith shall I **m** the **atonement,**	3722
23: 5 *my* desire, although he **m** *it* not **to grow.**	6779
1Ki 1:37 in his throne **greater** than the throne of	1431
1:47 God **m** the name of Solomon **better** than	3190
1:47 in his throne **greater** than thy throne.	1431
2:42 Did I not **m** thee to **swear** by the Lord,	7650
8:29 **prayer** which thy servant shall **m**	6419+8605
8:33 **m supplication** unto thee in this house:	2603
8:47 **m supplication** unto thee in the land of	2603
9:22 of the children of Israel did Solomon **m** no	5414
11:34 I will **m** him prince all the days of his life	7896
12: 1 were come *to* Shechem to **m** him **king.**	4427
12: 4 thou the grievous service . . . , **lighter,**	7043
12: 9 **M** the yoke which thy father did put upon	7043
us **lighter?**	
12:10 heavy, but **m** thou *it* **lighter** unto us;	7043
16: 3 will **m** thy house like the house of	5414
16:19 in his sin which he did, to **m** Israel **sin.**	2398
16:21 Tibni the son of Ginath, to **m** him **king;**	4427
17:13 me thereof a little cake first, and bring	6213
17:13 and after **m** for thee and for thy son.	6213
19: 2 **m** not my life as the life of one of them	7760
20:34 thou shalt **m** streets for thee in Damascus,	7760
21:22 will **m** thine house like the house of	5414
2Ki 3:16 the Lord, **M** this valley full of ditches.	6213
4:10 Let us **m** a little chamber, I pray thee,	6213
5: 7 said, *Am* I God, to kill and to **m alive,**	2421
6: 2 let us **m** us a place there, where we may	6213
7: 2 *if* the Lord would **m** windows in	6213
7:19 *if* the Lord **m** windows in	6213
9: 2 **m** him **arise up** from among his brethren,	6965
9: 9 I will **m** the house of Ahab like the house	5414
9:21 Joram said, **M ready.** And his chariot was	631
10: 5 shalt bid us; we will not **m** any **king:**	4427
18:30 Neither let Hezekiah **m** you **trust** in	982
18:31 **M** *an agreement* with me *by* a present,	6213
21: 8 Neither will I **m** the feet of Israel **move**	5110
23:10 might **m** his son or his daughter **to pass**	5674
1Ch 6:49 and to **m an atonement** for Israel,	3722
11:10 and with all Israel, to **m** him **king,**	4427
12:31 by name, to come and **m** David **king.**	4427
12:38 Hebron, to **m** David **king** over all Israel:	4427
12:38 Israel *were* of one heart to **m** David **king.**	4427
16: 8 **m known** his deeds among the people.	3045
16:42 cymbals for those that should **m** a **sound,**	8085
17:21 to **m** thee a name of greatness and	7760
17:22 For thy people Israel didst thou **m** thine	5414
21: 3 **m** his people an hundred times	
so many moe	3254
22: 5 will *therefore* now **m preparation** for it.	3559
28: 4 he liked me to **m** *me* **king** over all Israel:	4427
29:12 in thine hand *it is* to **m great,** and to give	1431
2Ch 4:11 finished the work that he was to **m**	6213
4:16 did Huram his father **m** to king Solomon	6213
5:13 to one sound to **be heard** in praising	8085
6:21 which they shall **m** towards this place:	6419
6:22 oath be laid upon him to **m** him **swear,**	422
6:24 **m supplication** before thee in this house;	2603
7:11 all that came into Solomon's heart to **m**	6213
7:20 will **m** it to be a proverb and a byword	5414
8: 8 them did Solomon **m to pay** tribute until	5927
8: 9 of the children of Israel did Solomon **m** no	5414
10: 1 were all Israel come to **m** him **king.**	4427
10:10 but **m** thou *it* **somewhat lighter** for us	7043
11:22 brethren: for *he* thought to **m** him **king.**	4427
14: 7 **m about** *them* walls, and towers, gates,	5437
20:36 joined himself with him to **m** ships to go	6213
25: 8 God shall **m** thee **fall** before the enemy:	3782
29:10 Now *it is* in mine heart to **m** a covenant	3772

2Ch 29:24 altar, to **m an atonement** for all Israel:	3722
30: 5 **m proclamation** throughout all	5674+6963
35:21 for God commanded me to **m haste:**	926
Ezr 5: 3 build this house, and to **m up** this wall?	3635
5: 4 What are the names of the men that **m**	1124
5: 9 this house, and to **m up** these walls?	3635
6: 8 Moreover I **m** a decree what ye shall do	7761
7:13 I **m** a decree, that all they of the people of	7761
7:21 do **m** a decree to all the treasurers which	7761
10: 3 let us **m** a covenant with our God to put	3772
10:11 **m** confession unto the Lord God of your	5414
Ne 2: 4 unto me, For what dost thou **m request?**	1245
2: 8 he may give me timber to **m beams** for	7136
4: 2 will they **m** an end in a day? will they	3615
8:12 to **m** great mirth, because they had	6213
8:15 thick trees, to **m booths,** as it is written.	6213
9:38 because of all this we **m** a sure **covenant,**	3772
10:33 the sin offerings to **m an atonement** for	3722
Est 1:20 when the king's decree which he shall **m**	6213
4: 8 to **m supplication** unto him, and to	2603
4: 8 to **m request** before him for her people.	1245
5: 5 the king said, **Cause** Haman to **m haste,**	4116
6:10 **M haste,** *and* take the apparel and	4116
7: 7 Haman stood *up* to **m request** for his life	1245
9:22 that *they* should **m** them days of feasting	6213
Job 5:18 he woundeth, and his hands **m whole.**	7495
8: 5 and **m** thy **supplication** to the Almighty;	2603
8: 6 in the habitation of thy righteousness	
prosperous.	7999
9:15 *but* I would **m supplication** to my judge.	2603
9:30 **m** my hands	
never so clean;	1253+2141+871.1
11: 3 Should thy lies **m** men **hold** their **peace?**	2790
11: 3 shall no man **m** *thee* **ashamed?**	3637
11:19 lie down, and none shall **m** *thee* **afraid;**	2729
11:19 yea, many shall **m** suit unto thee.	2470
13:11 Shall not his excellency **m** you **afraid?**	1204
13:21 and let not thy dread **m** me **afraid.**	1204
13:23 **m** me **to know** my transgression and	3045
15:24 Trouble and anguish shall **m** him **afraid;**	1204
18: 2 How long *will it be* ere you **m** an end of	7760
18:11 Terrors shall **m** him **afraid** on every side,	1204
19: 3 *that* you **m** yourselves **strange** to me.	1970
20: 2 me to answer, and for *this* I **m haste.**	2363
22:27 Thou shalt **m** thy **prayer** unto him,	6279
24:11 *Which* **m** oil within their walls,	6671
24:25 will **m** me a **liar,** and make my speech	3576
24:25 a liar, and **m** my speech nothing worth?	7760
28:25 To **m** the weight for the winds;	6213
31:15 Did not he that made me in the womb **m**	6213
33: 7 Behold, my terror shall not **m** thee **afraid,**	1204
34:29 quietness, who then can **m trouble?**	7561
35: 9 oppressions they **m** *the oppressed* to **cry:**	2199
39:20 thou **m** him **afraid** as a grasshopper?	7493
39:27 thy command, and **m** her nest on **high?**	7311
40:19 can **m** his sword *to* **approach** *unto him.*	5066
41: 3 Will he **m many** supplications unto thee?	7235
41: 4 Will he **m** a covenant with thee?	3772
41: 6 the companions **m** a **banquet** of him?	3739
41:28 The arrow cannot **m** him **flee:**	1272
Ps 5: 8 **m** thy way **straight** before my face.	3474
6: 6 all the night I **m** my bed to **swim;**	7811
11: 2 **m ready** their arrow upon the string,	3559
21: 9 Thou shalt **m** them as a fiery oven in	7896
21:12 Therefore shalt thou **m** them **turn** their	7896
21:12 thou shalt **m ready** *thine arrows* upon	3559
22: 9 thou didst **m** me **hope** *when I was* upon	982
31:16 **M** thy face to **shine** upon thy servant:	215
34: 2 My soul shall **m** her **boast** in the Lord:	1984
36: 8 shalt **m** them **drink** *of* the river of thy	8248
38:22 **M haste** to help me, O Lord my salvation.	2363
39: 4 **m** me **to know** mine end, and the	3045
39: 8 **m** me not the reproach of the foolish.	7760
40:13 deliver me: O Lord, **m haste** to help me.	2363
40:17 my deliverer; **m** no **tarrying,** O my God.	309
41: 3 thou wilt **m** all his bed in his sickness.	2015
45:16 whom thou mayest **m** princes in all	7896
45:17 I will **m** thy name **to be remembered** in	2142
46: 4 the streams whereof shall **m glad** the city	8055
51: 6 the hidden *part* thou shalt **m** me **to know**	3045
51: 8 **M** me **to hear** joy and gladness; *that*	8085
55: 2 I mourn in my complaint, and **m** a **noise;**	1949
57: 1 shadow of thy wings will I **m** my **refuge,**	2620
59: 6 they **m** a **noise** like a dog, and go round	1993
59:14 *and* let them **m** a **noise** like a dog,	1993
64: 8 So they shall **m** their own tongue to **fall**	3782
66: 1 **M** a **joyful noise** unto God, all ye lands:	7321
66: 2 honour of his name: **m** his praise glorious.	7760
66: 8 **m** the voice *of* his praise **to be heard:**	8085
69:23 and **m** their loins continually **to shake.**	4571
70: 1 **M haste,** O God, to deliver me; make	NIH
70: 1 deliver me; **m haste** to help me, O Lord.	2363
70: 5 **m haste** unto me, O God: thou *art* my	2363
70: 5 my deliverer; O Lord, **m** no **tarrying.**	309
71:12 O my God, **m haste** for my help.	2363
71:16 I will **m mention** of thy righteousness,	2142
78: 5 that *they* should **m** them **known** to their	3045
81: 1 **m** a **joyful noise** unto the God of Jacob.	7321
83: 2 For lo, thine enemies **m** a **tumult:**	1993
83:11 **M** their nobles like Oreb, and like Zeeb:	7896
83:13 O my God, **m** them like a wheel;	7896
83:15 and **m** them **afraid** with thy storm.	926
84: 6 passing through the valley of Baca **m**	7896
87: 4 I will **m mention** of Rahab and Babylon	2142
89: 1 with my mouth will I **m** known thy	3045

M

M

Ps	89:27 I will **m** him *my* firstborn, higher than	5414
	89:29 His seed also will I **m** *to endure* for ever,	7760
	90:15 **M** us **glad** according to the days *wherein*	8055
	95: 1 let us **m a joyful noise** to the rock of our	7321
	95: 2 **m a joyful noise** unto him with psalms.	7321
	98: 4 **M a joyful noise** unto the LORD.	7321
	98: 4 **m a loud noise**, and rejoice,	6476
	98: 6 sound of cornet **m a joyful noise** before	7321
	100: 1 **M a joyful noise** unto the LORD, all ye	7321
	104:15 *and* oil to **m** *his* face **to shine**,	6670
	104:17 Where the birds **m** their **nests**: *as for*	7077
	105: 1 **m known** his deeds among the people.	3045
	106: 8 might **m** his mighty power **to be known**.	3045
	110: 1 until I **m** thine enemies thy footstool.	7896
	115: 8 They that **m** them are like unto them;	6213
	119:27 **M** me to **understand** the way of thy	995
	119:35 **M** me **to go** in the path of thy	1869
	119:135 **M** thy face **to shine** upon thy servant;	215
	132:17 There will I **m** the horn of David **to bud**	6779
	135:18 They that **m** them are like unto them:	6213
	139: 8 if I **m** my **bed** in hell, behold, thou *art*	3331
	141: 1 **m haste** unto me; give ear unto my voice,	2363
	142: 1 unto the LORD did I **m** my **supplication**.	2603
	145:12 **m known** to the sons of men his mighty	3045
Pr	1:16 run to evil, and **m haste** to shed blood.	4116
	1:23 I will **m known** my words unto you.	3045
	6: 3 humble thyself, and **m sure** thy friend.	7292
	14: 9 Fools **m a mock at** sin: but among	3887
	20:18 by counsel: and with good advice **m** war.	6213
	20:25 *is* holy, and after vows to **m inquiry**.	1239
	22:21 That *I* might **m** thee **know** the certainty	3045
	22:24 **M** no **friendship** with an angry man;	7462
	23: 5 for **riches certainly m** themselves	6213+6213
	24: 6 For by wise counsel thou shalt **m** thy war:	6213
	24:27 and **m** it **fit** for thyself in the field;	6257
	27:11 My son, be wise, and **m** my heart **glad**,	8055
	30:26 yet **m** they their houses in the rocks;	7760
Ecc	2:24 he should **m** his soul **enjoy** good in his	7200
	7:13 for who can **m** *that* **straight**, which he	8626
	7:16 over much; neither **m** thyself over **wise**:	2449
SS	1:11 We will **m** thee borders of gold with studs	6213
	8:14 **M haste**, my beloved, and be thou like to	1272
Isa	1:15 yea, when ye **m many** prayers, I will not	7235
	1:16 Wash ye, **m** you **clean**; put away the evil	2135
	3: 7 **m** me not a ruler of the people.	7760
	5:19 Let him **m speed**, *and* hasten his work,	4116
	6:10 **M** the heart of this people **fat**,	8080
	6:10 their ears **heavy**, and shut their eyes;	3513
	7: 6 let us **m a breach** therein for us, and set	1234
	10:23 For the Lord GOD of hosts shall **m** a	6213
	11: 3 shall **m** him of **quick understanding** in	7306
	11:15 and **m** *men* **go over** dryshod.	1869
	12: 4 **m mention** that his name *is* exalted.	2142
	13:12 I will **m** a man more **precious** than fine	3365
	13:20 neither shall the shepherds **m** their **fold**	7257
	14:23 I will also **m** it a possession for the bittern,	7760
	16: 3 **m** thy shadow as the night in the midst of	7896
	17: 2 lie down, and none shall **m** *them* **afraid**.	2729
	17:11 the day shalt thou **m** thy plant **to grow**,	7735
	17:11 shalt thou **m** thy seed **to flourish**:	6524
	17:12 **m a noise** like the noise of the seas;	1993
	17:12 a **rushing** like the rushing of mighty	7582
	19:10 all that **m** sluces *and* ponds for fish.	6213
	23:16 **m sweet** melody, sing many songs, that	3190
	25: 6 unto all people a feast of fat things,	6213
	26:13 by thee only will we **m mention** of thy	2142
	27: 5 **strength**, *that* he may **m** peace with me;	6213
	27: 5 with me; *and* he shall **m** peace with me.	6213
	28: 9 shall he **m** to **understand** doctrine?	995
	28:16 he that believeth shall not **m haste**.	2363
	29:21 That **m** a man an **offender** for a word,	2398
	32: 6 to **m empty** the soul of the hungry,	7324
	32:11 **m** ye **bare**, and gird *sackcloth* upon your	6209
	33: 1 when thou shalt **m an end** to deal	5239
	34:15 There shall the great owl **m** her **nest**,	7077
	36:15 Neither let Hezekiah **m** you **trust** in	982
	36:16 **M** *an agreement* with me *by* a present,	6213
	37: 9 He is come forth to **m** war with thee.	3898
	38:12 day *even* to night wilt thou **m an end**	7999
	38:13 day *even* to night wilt thou **m an end**	7999
	38:16 wilt thou recover me, and **m** me **to live**.	2421
	38:19 the father to the children shall **m known**	3045
	40: 3 **m straight** in the desert a highway for our	3474
	41:15 I will **m** thee a new sharp threshing	7760
	41:15 *them* small, and shalt **m** the hills as chaff.	7760
	41:18 will **m** the wilderness a pool of water,	7760
	42:15 I will **m waste** mountains and hills,	2717
	42:15 will **m** the rivers islands, and I will dry up	7760
	42:16 I will **m** darkness light before them,	7760
	42:21 magnify the law, and **m** it **honourable**.	142
	43:19 I will even **m** a way in the wilderness,	7760
	44: 9 They that **m** a graven image are all of	3335
	44:19 shall I **m** the residue thereof an	6213
	45: 2 and **m** the crooked places **straight**:	3474
	45: 7 I **m** peace, and create evil: I the LORD do	6213
	45:14 they shall **m supplication** unto thee,	6419
	46: 5 **m** *me* **equal**, and compare me, that we	7737
	47: 2 **m bare** the leg, uncover the thigh,	2834
	48: 1 **m mention** of the God of Israel, *but* not	2142
	48:15 and he shall **m** his way **prosperous**.	6743
	49:11 will **m** all my mountains a way,	7760
	49:17 children shall **m haste**; thy destroyers	4116
	50: 2 the sea, I **m** the rivers a wilderness:	7760
	50: 3 and I **m** sackcloth their covering.	7760
	51: 3 and he will **m** her wilderness like Eden,	7760

Isa	51: 4 I will **m** my judgment **to rest** for a light	7280
	52: 5 that rule over them **m** them to howl,	3213
	53:10 thou shalt **m** his soul an offering for	7760
	54: 3 **m** the desolate cities **to be inhabited**.	3427
	54:12 I will **m** thy windows *of* agates,	7760
	55: 3 will **m** an everlasting covenant with you,	3772
	56: 7 **m** them **joyful** in my house of prayer:	8055
	57: 4 against whom **m** ye a **wide** mouth,	7337
	58: 4 to **m** your voice **to be heard** on high.	8085
	58:11 soul in drought, and **m fat** thy bones:	2502
	59: 7 they **m haste** to shed innocent blood:	4116
	60:13 I will **m** the place of thy feet **glorious**.	3513
	60:15 that no man went through *thee*, I will **m**	7760
	60:17 will also **m** thy officers peace,	7760
	61: 8 will **m** an everlasting covenant with them.	3772
	62: 6 ye that **m mention** of the LORD, keep not	2142
	62: 7 till he **m** Jerusalem a praise in the earth.	7760
	63: 6 **m** them **drunk** in my fury, and I will	7937
	63:12 to himself an everlasting name?	6213
	63:14 thy people, to **m** thyself a glorious name.	6213
	64: 2 thy name **known** to thine adversaries,	3045
	66:22 and the new earth, which I *will* **m**,	6213
Jer	4: 7 he is gone forth from his place to **m** thy	7760
	4:16 **M** ye **mention** to the nations; behold,	2142
	4:27 be desolate; yet will I not **m** a full end.	6213
	4:30 in vain shalt thou **m** thyself **fair**;	3302
	5:10 walls, and destroy; but **m** not a full end:	6213
	5:14 I will **m** my words in thy mouth fire,	5414
	5:18 I will not **m** a full end with you.	6213
	6: 8 I **m** thee desolate, a land not inhabited.	7760
	6:26 **m** thee mourning, *as for* an only *son*,	6213
	7:16 for them, neither **m intercession** to me:	6293
	7:18 to **m** cakes to the queen of heaven,	6213
	9:11 I will **m** Jerusalem heaps, *and* a den of	5414
	9:11 will **m** the cities of Judah desolate,	5414
	9:18 let them **m haste**, and take up a wailing	4116
	10:22 the cities of Judah desolate, *and* a den	7760
	13:16 shadow of death, *and* **m** *it* gross darkness.	7896
	15:14 I will **m** *thee* **to pass** with thine enemies	5674
	15:20 I will **m** thee unto this people a fenced	5414
	16: 6 nor **m** themselves **bald** for them:	7139
	16:20 Shall a man **m** gods unto himself,	6213
	18: 4 as seemed good to the potter to **m** *it*.	6213
	18:11 and your ways and your doings **good**.	3190
	18:16 To **m** their land desolate, *and* a perpetual	7760
	19: 7 I will **m void** the counsel of Judah and	1238
	19: 8 I will **m** this city desolate, and a hissing;	7760
	19:12 and *even* **m** this city as Tophet:	7760
	20: 4 I will **m** thee a terror to thyself, and to all	5414
	20: 9 I said, I will not **m mention** of him,	2142
	22: 6 *yet* surely I will **m** thee a **wilderness** *and*	7896
	23:15 and **m** them **drink** the water of gall:	8248
	23:16 they **m** you **vain**: they speak a vision of	1891
	25: 9 **m** them an astonishment, and a hissing,	7760
	25:12 and will **m** it perpetual desolations.	7760
	25:18 to **m** them a desolation, an astonishment,	5414
	26: 6 will I **m** this house like Shiloh, and will	5414
	26: 6 will **m** this city a curse to all the nations	5414
	27: 2 **M** thee bonds and yokes, and put them	6213
	27:18 let them now **m intercession** to the LORD	6293
	28:13 but thou shalt **m** for them yokes of iron.	6213
	29:17 and will **m** them like vile figs,	5414
	29:22 The LORD **m** thee like Zedekiah and	7760
	30:10 be quiet, and none shall **m** *him* **afraid**.	2729
	30:11 though I **m** a full end of all nations	6213
	30:11 yet will I not **m** a full end of thee:	6213
	30:19 and the voice of them that **m merry**.	7832
	31: 4 forth in the dances of them that **m merry**.	7832
	31:13 and **m** them **rejoice** from their sorrow.	8055
	31:21 Set thee up waymarks, **m** thee high heaps:	7760
	31:31 I will **m** a new covenant with the house	3772
	31:33 *shall be* the covenant that I will **m** with	3772
	32:40 I will **m** an everlasting covenant with	3772
	34:17 I will **m** you to be removed into all	5414
	34:22 I will **m** the cities of Judah a desolation	5414
	44:19 did we **m** her cakes to worship her,	6213
	46:27 at ease, and none shall **m** *him* **afraid**.	2729
	46:28 for I will **m** a full end of all the nations	6213
	46:28 I will not **m** a full end of thee,	6213
	48:26 **M** ye him **drunken**: for he magnified	7937
	49:15 I will **m** thee small among the heathen,	5414
	49:16 though thou shouldest **m** thy nest as **high**	1361
	49:19 I will suddenly **m** him run away from her:	7323
	49:20 he shall **m** their habitations **desolate**.	8074
	50: 3 which shall **m** her land desolate,	7896
	50:44 I will **m** them suddenly **run** away from	7323
	50:45 he shall **m** *their* habitation **desolate**.	8074
	51:11 **M bright** the arrows: gather the shields:	1305
	51:12 the watch **strong**, set up the	2388
	51:25 and will **m** thee a burnt mountain.	5414
	51:29 to **m** the land of Babylon a desolation	7760
	51:36 dry up her sea, and **m** her springs **dry**.	3001
	51:39 In their heat I will **m** their feasts, and I	7896
	51:39 I will **m** them **drunken**, that they may	7937
	51:57 I will **m drunk** her princes, and her wise	7937
La	4:21 be drunken, and shalt **m** thyself **naked**.	6168
Eze	3:26 I will **m** thy tongue **cleave** to the roof of	1692
	4: 9 in one vessel, and **m** thee bread thereof,	6213
	5:14 Moreover I will **m** thee waste,	5414
	6:14 upon them, and **m** the land desolate, yea,	5414
	7:14 blown the trumpet, even to **m** all **ready**;	3559
	7:23 **M** a chain: for the land is full *of* bloody	6213
	7:24 also **m** the pomp of the strong **to cease**;	7673
	11:13 *wilt* thou **m** a full end of the remnant of	6213
	12:23 I will **m** this proverb **to cease**,	7673

Eze	13:18 **m** kerchiefs upon the head of every	6213
	13:20 ye there hunt the souls to **m** *them* **fly**,	6524
	13:20 the souls that ye hunt to **m** *them* **fly**.	6524
	14: 8 will **m** him a sign and a proverb, and I	8074
	15: 8 I will **m** the land desolate, because	5414
	16:42 So will I **m** my fury towards thee **to rest**,	5117
	17:17 and great company **m** for him in the war,	6213
	18:31 and **m** you a new heart and a new spirit:	6213
	20:17 neither did I **m** an end of them in	6213
	20:26 that I might **m** them **desolate**, to the end	8074
	20:31 when ye **m** your sons **to pass** through	5674
	21:10 It is sharpened to **m** a sore slaughter; *it is*	1961
	21:10 should we then **m mirth**? it contemneth	7797
	22:30 that *should* **m up the hedge**,	1443+1447
	23:27 Thus will I **m** thy lewdness **to cease** from	7673
	24: 5 *and* **m** it **boil well**, and let them	7570+7571
	24: 9 I will even **m** the pile for fire **great**.	1431
	24:17 to cry, **m** no mourning *for* the dead,	6213
	25: 4 in them, and **m** their dwellings in thee:	5414
	25: 5 I will **m** Rabbah a stable for camels,	5414
	25:13 I will **m** it desolate from Teman;	5414
	26: 4 from her, and **m** her like the top of a rock.	5414
	26: 8 he shall **m** a fort against thee, and cast a	5414
	26:12 they shall **m a spoil** of thy riches,	7997
	26:12 riches, and **m a prey** of thy merchandise:	962
	26:14 I will **m** thee like the top of a rock:	5414
	26:19 When I shall **m** thee a desolate city, like	5414
	26:21 I will **m** a terror, and thou *shalt* be	5414
	27: 5 have taken cedars from Lebanon to **m**	6213
	27:31 shall **m** themselves **utterly bald**	7139+7139
	29:10 I will **m** the land of Egypt utterly waste	5414
	29:12 I will **m** the land of Egypt desolate in	5414
	30: 9 ships to **m** the careless Ethiopians **afraid**,	2729
	30:10 **m** the multitude of Egypt **to cease** by	7673
	30:12 I will **m** the rivers dry, and sell the land	5414
	30:12 I will **m** the land **waste**, and all that is	8074
	30:14 I will **m** Pathros **desolate**, and will set	8074
	30:21 bind it, to **m** it **strong** to hold the sword.	2388
	32: 7 the heaven, and **m** the stars thereof **dark**;	6937
	32: 8 the bright lights of heaven will I **m dark**	6937
	32:10 I will **m** many people **amazed** at thee,	8074
	32:14 will I **m** their waters **deep**, and cause	8257
	32:15 I shall **m** the land of Egypt desolate,	5414
	34:25 I will **m** with them a covenant of peace,	3772
	34:26 I will **m** them and the places round about	5414
	34:28 safely, and none shall **m** *them* **afraid**.	2729
	35: 3 and I will **m** thee most desolate.	5414
	35: 7 Thus will I **m** mount Seir most desolate,	5414
	35: 9 I will **m** thee perpetual desolations,	5414
	35:11 I will **m** myself **known** amongst them,	3045
	35:14 earth rejoiceth, I will **m** thee desolate.	6213
	37:19 **m** them one stick, and they shall be one	6213
	37:22 I will **m** them one nation in the land upon	6213
	37:26 Moreover I will **m** a covenant of peace	3772
	39: 7 So will I **m** my holy name **known** in	3045
	42:20 to **m a separation** between the sanctuary	914
	43:18 the altar in the day when *they* shall **m** it,	6213
	43:27 the priests shall **m** your burnt offerings	6213
	44:14 I will **m** them keepers of the charge of	5414
	45:15 to **m reconciliation** for them,	3722
	45:17 **m reconciliation** for the house of Israel.	3722
Da	1:10 shall ye **m** *me* **endanger** my head to	2325
	2: 5 ye will not **m known** unto me the dream,	3046
	2: 9 ye will not **m known** unto me the dream,	3046
	2:25 that will **m known** unto the king	3046
	2:26 Art thou able to **m known** unto me	3046
	2:30 for *their* sakes that shall **m known**	3046
	3:29 Therefore I **m** a decree, That every people,	7761
	4: 6 that they might **m known** unto me the	3046
	4: 7 they *did* not **m known** unto me	3046
	4:18 to **m known** unto me the interpretation:	3046
	4:25 they shall **m** thee **to eat** grass as oxen,	2939
	4:32 they shall **m** thee **to eat** grass as oxen,	2939
	5: 8 **m known** to the king the interpretation	3046
	5:15 **m known** unto me the interpretation	3046
	5:16 that thou canst **m interpretations**,	6590+6591
	5:16 **m known** to me the interpretation,	3046
	5:17 and **m known** to him the interpretation.	3046
	6: 7 to **m** a **firm** decree, that whosoever shall	8631
	6:26 I **m** a decree, That in every dominion of	7761
	8:16 **m** this *man* to **understand** the vision.	995
	8:19 I *will* **m** thee **know** what shall be in the	3045
	9:24 to **m** an end of sins, and to make	8552
	9:24 to **m reconciliation** for iniquity,	3722
	9:27 of abominations he *shall* **m** it **desolate**,	8074
	10:14 I am come to **m** thee **understand** what	995
	11: 6 the king of the north to **m** an agreement:	6213
	11:35 and to purge, and to **m** them **white**,	3835
	11:44 to destroy, and **utterly** to **m away** many.	2763
Hos	2: 3 **m** her as a wilderness, and set her like a	7760
	2: 6 **m a wall**, that she shall not find her	1443+1447
	2:12 I will **m** a forest, and the beasts of	7760
	2:18 in that day will I **m** a covenant for them	3772
	2:18 and will **m** them **to lie down** safely.	7901
	5: 2 revolters are **profound to m** slaughter,	6009
	7: 3 They **m** the king **glad** with their	8055
	10:11 will **m** Ephraim **to ride**; Judah shall plow,	7392
	11: 8 how shall I **m** thee as Admah? *how* shall I	5414
	12: 1 they do **m** a covenant with the Assyrians,	3772
	12: 9 will yet **m** thee **to dwell** in tabernacles,	3427
Joel	2:19 I will no more **m** you a reproach among	5414
Am	6:10 for *we* may not **m mention** of the name	2142
	8: 4 even to **m** the poor of the land **to fail**,	7673
	8:10 I will **m** it as the mourning of an only *son*,	7760
	9:14 they shall also **m** gardens, and eat the fruit	6213

Mic		
1: 6	Therefore I will **m** Samaria as a heap of	7760
1: 8	I will **m** a wailing like the dragons,	6213
1:16	**M** thee **bald**, and poll thee for thy delicate	7139
2:12	they shall **m great noise** by reason of	1949
3: 5	the prophets that **m** my people **err**,	8582
4: 4	fig tree; and none shall **m** them **afraid**:	2729
4: 7	I will **m** her that halted a remnant,	7760
4:13	I will **m** thine horn iron, and I will make	7760
4:13	horn iron, and I will **m** thy hoofs brass:	7760
6:13	also will I **m** *thee* **sick** in smiting	2470
6:16	that I should **m** thee a desolation,	5414

Na		
1: 8	with an overrunning flood he will **m** an	6213
1: 9	he *will* **m** an utter end: affliction shall not	6213
1:14	I will **m** thy grave; for thou art vile.	7760
2: 1	watch the way, **m** *thy* loins **strong**,	2388
2: 5	they shall **m haste** to the wall thereof,	4116
3: 6	**m** thee **vile**, and will set thee as a	5034
3:14	tread the morter, **m strong** the brickkiln.	2388
3:15	**m** thyself **many** as the cankerworm,	3513
3:15	**m** thyself **many** as the locusts.	3513

Hab		
2: 2	the vision, and **m** it **plain** upon tables,	874
2:18	work trusteth therein, to **m** dumb idols?	6213
3: 2	in the midst of the years **m known**;	3045
3:19	he will **m** my feet like hinds' *feet*, and	7760
3:19	he will **m** me to **walk** upon mine high	1869

Zep		
1:18	he shall **m** even a speedy riddance of all	6213
2:13	will **m** Nineveh a desolation, *and* dry like	7760
3:13	lie down, and none shall **m** *them* **afraid**.	2729
3:20	will **m** you a name and a praise among	5414

Hag		
2:23	the Lord, and will **m** thee as a signet:	7760

Zec		
6:11	**m** crowns, and set *them* upon the head of	6213
9:15	drink, *and* **m** a noise as through wine;	1993
9:17	corn shall **m** the young men **cheerful**,	5107
10: 1	*so* the Lord *shall* **m** bright clouds,	6213
12: 2	I *will* **m** Jerusalem a cup of trembling unto	7760
12: 3	in that day will I **m** Jerusalem a	7760
12: 6	In that day will I **m** the governors of Judah	7760

Mal		
2:15	did not he **m** one? Yet had he the residue	6213
3:17	in that day when I **m** *up my* jewels;	6213

Mt		
1:19	not willing to **m** her a **publick example**,	3856
3: 3	the way of the Lord, **m** his paths straight.	4160
4:19	and I will **m** you fishers of men.	4160
5:36	thou canst not **m** one hair white or black.	4160
8: 2	Lord, if thou wilt, thou canst **m** me **clean**.	2511
12:16	And charged them that they should not **m**	4160
12:33	Either **m** the tree good, and his fruit good;	4160
12:33	or else **m** the tree corrupt, and his fruit	4160
17: 4	thou wilt, let us **m** here three tabernacles:	4160
22:44	till I **m** thine enemies thy footstool?	5087
23: 5	they **m broad** their phylacteries,	4115
23:14	and for a pretence **m** long **prayer**:	4336
23:15	compass sea and land to **m** one proselyte,	4160
23:15	ye **m** him twofold more *the child of* hell	4160
23:25	for ye **m clean** the outside of the cup and	2511
24:47	That he shall **m** him **ruler** over all his	2525
25:21	**m** thee **ruler** over many *things*: enter	2525
25:23	**m** thee **ruler** over many *things*: enter	2525
27:65	go your way, **m** *it* as **sure** as you can.	805

Mk		
1: 3	the way of the Lord, **m** his paths straight.	4160
1:17	I will **m** you to become fishers of men.	4160
1:40	If thou wilt, thou canst **m** me **clean**.	2511
3:12	them that they should not **m** him **known**.	4160
5:39	then, Why **m** ye *this* **ado**, and weep?	2350
6:39	he commanded them to **m** all **sit down**	347
9: 5	let us **m** three tabernacles; one for thee,	4160
12:36	till I **m** thine enemies thy footstool?	5087
12:40	and for a pretence **m** long **prayers**:	4336
12:42	threw in two mites, which **m** a farthing.	1510
14:15	*and* prepared: there **m ready** for us.	2090

Lk		
1:17	**m ready** a people prepared for the Lord.	2090
3: 4	the way of the Lord, **m** his paths straight.	4160
5:12	if thou wilt, thou canst **m** me **clean**.	2511
5:33	**m** prayers, and likewise the *disciples* of	4160
5:34	ye **m** the children of the bridechamber	4160
9:14	**M** them **sit down** by fifties in a company.	2625
9:33	let us **m** three tabernacles; one for thee,	4160
9:52	of the Samaritans, to **m ready** for him.	2090
11:39	Now do ye Pharisees **m clean** the outside	2511
11:40	is without **m** that *which is* within also?	4160
12:37	and **m** them **to sit down to meat**,	347
12:42	whom *his* lord shall **m ruler** over his	2525
12:44	that he will **m** him **ruler** over all that he	2525
14:18	all with one *consent* began to **m excuse**.	3868
14:31	**m war against** another king	1519+4171+4820
15:19	son: **m** me as one of thy hired *servants*.	4160
15:29	that I might **m merry** with my friends:	2165
15:32	It was meet that *we* should **m merry**,	2165
16: 9	**M** to yourselves friends of the mammon	4160
17: 8	**M ready** wherewith I may sup,	2090
19: 5	Zaccheus, **m haste**, and come down;	4692
20:43	Till I **m** thine enemies thy footstool?	5087
20:47	and for a shew **m** long **prayers**:	4336
22:12	upper room furnished: there **m ready**.	2090

Jn		
1:23	**m straight** the way of the Lord, as said	2116
2:16	**m** not my Father's house a house of	4160
6:10	And Jesus said, **M** the men sit down.	4160
6:15	and take him by force, to **m** him a king,	4160
8:32	the truth, and the truth shall **m** you **free**.	1659
8:36	If the Son therefore shall **m** you **free**,	1659
10:24	dost thou **m** us **to doubt?**	142+3588+5590
14:23	unto him, and **m** our abode with him.	4160

Ac		
2:28	thou shalt **m** me **full** of joy with thy	4137
2:35	Until I **m** thy foes thy footstool.	5087
7:40	unto Aaron, **M** us gods to go before us:	4160
7:44	*he* should **m** it according to the fashion	4160
9:34	arise, and **m** thy **bed**. And he arose	4766
22:18	**M haste**, and get *thee* quickly out of	NIG
22:18	**M haste**, and get *thee* quickly out of	4692
23:23	**M ready** two hundred soldiers to go to	2090
26:16	for this *purpose*, to **m** thee a minister	4400
26:24	learning doth **m** thee mad.	1519+3130+4062

Ro		
1: 9	that without ceasing I **m** mention of you,	4160
3: 3	**m** the faith of God **without effect?**	2673
3:31	we then **m void** the law through faith?	2673
9:21	of the same lump to **m** one vessel unto	4160
9:22	*his* wrath, and to **m** his power **known**,	1107
9:23	And that he might **m known** the riches of	1107
9:28	a short work will the Lord **m** upon	4160
13:14	and **m** not provision for the flesh, to *fulfil*	4160
14: 4	for God is able to **m** him **stand**.	2476
14:19	follow *after the things* which **m** for peace,	NIG
15:18	the Gentiles obedient, by word and	1519
15:26	Achaia to **m** a certain contribution for	4160

1Co		
4: 5	**m manifest** the counsels of the hearts:	5319
6:15	and **m** them the members of a harlot?	4160
8:13	if meat **m** my brother **to offend**,	4624
8:13	lest I **m** my brother **to offend**.	4624
9:15	that any *man* should **m** my glorying **void**.	2758
9:18	I may **m** the gospel of Christ without	5087
10:13	with the temptation also **m** a way to	4160

2Co		
2: 2	For if I **m** you **sorry**, who is he then	3076
9: 5	and **m up beforehand** your bounty,	4294
9: 8	And God *is* able to **m** all grace **abound**	4052
10:12	we dare not **m** ourselves **of the number**,	1469
12:17	Did I **m a gain** of you by any of them	4122
12:18	Did Titus **m a gain** of you? walked we	4122

Gal		
2:18	I destroyed, I **m** myself a transgressor.	4921
3:17	*it* should **m** the promise **of none effect**.	2673
6:12	As many as desire to **m a fair shew** in	2146

Eph		
2:15	**m** in himself of twain one new man,	2936
3: 9	And to **m all men see** what *is*	5461
5:13	for whatsoever doth **m manifest** is light.	5319
6:19	to **m known** the mystery of the gospel,	1107
6:21	Lord, shall **m known** to you all *things*:	1107

Col		
1:27	To whom God would **m known** what *is*	1107
4: 4	That I may **m** it **manifest**, as I ought to	5319
4: 9	They shall **m known** unto you all *things*	1107

1Th		
3:12	And the Lord **m** you **to increase** and	4121

2Th		
3: 9	to **m** ourselves an ensample unto you to	1325

2Ti		
3:15	which are able to **m** thee **wise** unto	4679
4: 5	evangelist, **m full proof** of thy ministry.	4135

Heb		
1:13	until I **m** thine enemies thy footstool?	5087
2:10	the captain of their salvation **perfect**	5048
2:17	to **m reconciliation** for the sins of	2433
7:25	seeing he ever liveth to **m intercession**	1793
8: 5	when he was about to **m** the tabernacle:	2005
8: 5	*he, that* thou **m** all *things* according to	4160
8: 8	when I will **m** a new covenant with	4931
8:10	For this *is* the covenant that I will **m** with	1303
9: 9	not **m** him that did the service **perfect**,	5048
10: 1	the comers *thereunto* **perfect**.	5048
10:16	This *is* the covenant that I will **m** with	1303
12:13	**m** straight paths for your feet, lest *that*	4160
13:21	**M** you **perfect** in every good work to do	2675

Jas		
3:18	is sown in peace of them that **m** peace.	4160

1Pe		
5:10	**m** you **perfect**, stablish, strengthen,	2675

2Pe		
1: 8	they **m** *you that ye shall* neither *be* barren	2525
1:10	give diligence to **m** your calling and	4160
2: 3	feigned words **m merchandise** of you:	1710

1Jn		
1:10	**m** him a liar, and his word is not in us.	4160

Rev		
3: 9	I will **m** *them* of the synagogue of Satan,	1325
3: 9	I will **m** them to come and worship	4160
3:12	Him that overcometh will I **m** a pillar in	4160
10: 9	and it shall **m** thy belly **bitter**, but it shall	4087
11: 7	bottomless *pit* shall **m** war against them,	4160
11:10	and **m merry**, and shall send gifts one to	2165
12:17	went to **m** war with the remnant of her	4160
13: 4	beast? who is able to **m war** with him?	4170
13: 7	And it was given unto him to **m** war with	4170
13:14	that *they* should **m** an image to the beast,	4160
17:14	These shall **m war** with the Lamb,	4170
17:16	and shall **m** her desolate and naked,	4160
19:11	righteousness he doth judge and **m war**.	4170
19:19	gathered together to **m** war against him	4160
21: 5	throne said, Behold, I **m** all *things* new.	4160

MAKER (20) [MAKE]

Job		
4:17	shall a man be more pure than his **M**?	6213
32:22	*doing* my **M** would soon take me away.	6213
35:10	none saith, Where *is* God my **M**,	6213
36: 3	and will ascribe righteousness to my **M**.	6466

Ps		
95: 6	let us kneel before the Lord our **M**.	6213

Pr		
14:31	oppresseth the poor reproacheth his **M**:	6213
17: 5	mocketh the poor reproacheth his **M**:	6213
22: 2	the Lord *is* the **M** of them all.	6213

Isa		
1:31	the **m** of it as a spark, and they shall both	6467
17: 7	At that day shall a man look to his **M**,	6213
22:11	ye have not looked unto the **M** thereof,	6213
45: 9	Woe unto him that striveth with his **m**!	3335
45:11	the Holy One of Israel, and his **m**,	3335
51:13	forgettest the Lord thy **M**, that hath	6213
54: 5	For thy **M** *is* thine husband; the Lord of	6213

Jer		
33: 2	Thus saith the Lord the **m** thereof,	6213

Hos		
8:14	For Israel hath forgotten his **M**,	6213

Hab		
2:18	profiteth the graven image that the **m**	3335
2:18	that the **m** of his work trusteth therein,	3335

Heb		
11:10	whose builder and **m** *is* God.	1217

MAKERS (1) [MAKE]

Isa		
45:16	to confusion together *that are* **m** of idols.	2796

MAKEST (26) [MAKE]

Jdg		
18: 3	what **m** thou in this *place?* and what hast	6213

Job		
13:26	**m** me **to possess** the iniquities of my	3423
22: 3	to him, that thou **m** thy ways **perfect?**	8552

Ps		
4: 8	Lord, only **m** me dwell in safety.	3427
39:11	thou **m** his beauty **to consume away** like	4529
44:10	Thou **m** us **to turn** back from the enemy:	7725
44:13	Thou **m** us a reproach to our neighbours,	7760
44:14	Thou **m** us a byword among the heathen,	7760
65: 8	the outgoings of the morning and	
	evening **to rejoice**.	7442
65:10	thou **m** it **soft** with showers: thou blessest	4127
80: 6	Thou **m** us a strife unto our neighbours:	7760
104:20	Thou **m** darkness, and it is night:	7896
144: 3	son of man, that thou **m account** of him?	2803

SS		
1: 7	where thou **m** *thy flock* **to rest** at noon:	7257

Isa		
45: 9	to him that fashioned it, What **m** thou?	6213

Jer		
22:23	of Lebanon, that **m** thy **nest** in the cedars,	7077
28:15	but thou **m** this people **to trust** in a lie.	982

Eze		
16:31	and **m** thine high place in every street;	6213

Hab		
1:14	**m** men as the fishes of the sea,	6213
2:15	bottle to *him,* and **m** him **drunken** also,	7937

Lk		
14:12	When thou **m** a dinner or a supper, call	4160
14:13	But when thou **m** a feast, call the poor,	4160

Jn		
8:53	prophets are dead: whom **m** thou thyself?	4160
10:33	that thou, being a man, **m** thyself God.	4160

Ro		
2:17	in the law, and **m** thy **boast** of God,	2744
2:23	Thou that **m** thy **boast** of the law,	2744

MAKETH (126) [MAKE]

Ex		
4:11	who **m** the dumb, or deaf, or the seeing,	7760

Lev		
7: 7	the priest that **m atonement** therewith	3722
14:11	the priest that **m** him **clean** shall present	2891
17:11	*it is* the blood that **m an atonement** for	3722

Dt		
18:10	that his son or his daughter	
	to pass through the fire,	5674
20:20	against the city that **m** war with thee,	6213
21:16	when he **m** his sons **to inherit** that which	5157
24: 7	**m merchandise** of him, or selleth him;	6014
27:15	Cursed *be* the man that **m** *any* graven or	6213
27:18	Cursed *be* he that **m** the blind **to wander**	7686
29:12	which the Lord thy God **m** with thee	3772

1Sa		
2: 6	The Lord killeth, and **m alive**:	2421
2: 7	The Lord **m poor**, and maketh rich:	3423
2: 7	The Lord maketh poor, and **m rich**:	6238

2Sa		
22:33	*and* power: and he **m** my way perfect.	5425
22:34	He **m** my feet like hinds' *feet:* and	7737

Job		
5:18	For he **m sore**, and bindeth up:	3510
9: 9	Which **m** Arcturus, Orion, and Pleiades,	6213
12:17	away spoiled, and **m** the judges **fools**.	1984
12:25	**m** them **to stagger** like a drunken *man.*	8582
15:27	and collops of fat on *his* flanks.	6213
33:16	God **m** my heart **soft**, and the Almighty	7401
25: 2	with him, he **m** peace in his high places.	6213
27:18	a moth, and as a booth *that* the keeper **m**.	6213
35:11	and **m** us **wiser** than the fowls of heaven?	2449
36:27	For he **m small** the drops of water:	1639
41:31	He **m** the deep **to boil** like a pot: he	7570
41:31	pot: he **m** the sea like a pot of ointment.	7760
41:32	He **m** a path **to shine** after him; *one*	215

Ps		
9:12	When he **m inquisition** for blood,	1875
18:32	me *with* strength, and **m** my way perfect.	5414
18:33	He **m** my feet like hinds' *feet,* and	7737
23: 2	He **m** me **to lie down** in green pastures:	7257
29: 6	He **m** them also **to skip** like a calf;	7540
29: 9	voice of the Lord **m** the hinds **to calve**,	2342
33:10	**m** the devices of the people	
	of none effect.	5106
40: 4	Blessed *is that* man that **m** the Lord his	7760
46: 9	He **m** wars **to cease** unto the end of	7673
104: 3	who **m** the clouds his chariot: who	7760
104: 4	Who **m** his angels spirits; his ministers a	6213
104:15	And wine *that* **m glad** the heart of man,	8055
107:29	He **m** the storm a calm, so that the waves	6965
107:36	there he **m** the hungry **to dwell**, that they	3427
107:41	and **m** *him* families like a flock.	7760
113: 9	He **m** the barren *woman* **to keep** house,	3427
135: 7	he **m lightnings** for the rain; he bringeth	6779
147: 8	**m** grass **to grow** *upon* the mountains.	6779
147:14	He **m** peace in thy borders, *and* filleth	7760

Pr		
10: 1	A wise son **m** a **glad** father: but a foolish	8055
10: 4	but the hand of the diligent **m rich**.	6238
10:22	**m rich**, and he addeth no sorrow with it.	6238
12: 4	she that **m ashamed** *is* as rottenness in	954
12:25	Heaviness in the heart of man **m** it **stoop**:	7812
12:25	it stoop: but a good word **m** it **glad**.	8055
13: 7	There is that **m** himself **rich**, yet *hath*	6238
13: 7	*there is* that **m** himself **poor**, yet *hath*	7326
13:12	Hope deferred **m** the heart **sick**:	2470
15:13	A merry heart **m** a **cheerful** countenance:	3190
15:20	A wise son **m** a **glad** father: but a foolish	8055
15:30	*and* a good report **m** the bones **fat**.	1878
16: 7	he **m** even his enemies **to be at peace**	7999
18:16	A man's gift **m** room for him,	7337
19: 4	Wealth **m** many friends; but the poor is	3254
28:20	he that **m haste** to be rich shall not be	213
31:22	She **m** herself coverings of tapestry;	6213
31:24	She **m** fine linen, and selleth *it;* and	6213

Ecc		
3:11	God **m** from the beginning to the end.	6213
7: 7	Surely oppression **m** a wise *man* **mad**;	1984
7: 7	and a man's wisdom **m** his face **to shine**,	215
10:19	for laughter, and wine **m merry**:	2416+8055
11: 5	knowest not the works of God who **m**	6213

Isa		
19:17	every one that **m mention** thereof shall	2142
24: 1	the Lord **m** the earth **empty**,	1238

M

Isa 24: 1 m it **waste**, and turneth it upside down, 1110
27: 9 when he m all the stones of the altar as 7760
40:23 he m the judges of the earth as vanity. 6213
43:16 which m a way in the sea, and a path in 5414
44:13 m it after the figure of a man, according 6213
44:15 m a god, and worshippeth *it;* he maketh 6466
44:15 worshippeth *it;* he m it a graven image, 6213
44:17 the residue thereof he m a god, *even* his 6213
44:24 I *am* the LORD that m all *things;* that 6213
44:25 tokens of the liars, and m diviners **mad;** 1984
44:25 and m their knowledge **foolish;** 5528
46: 6 *and* hire a goldsmith; and he m it a god: 6213
55:10 the earth, and m it **bring forth** and bud, 3205
59:15 *that* departeth from evil m himself a **prey;** 7997
Jer 4:19 my heart m a **noise** in me; I cannot hold 1993
10:13 he m lightnings with rain, 6213
17: 5 m flesh his arm, and whose heart 7760
21: 2 king of Babylon m **war** against us; 3898
29:26 *that is* mad, and m himself **a prophet,** 5012
29:27 which m himself **a prophet** to you? 5012
48:28 like the dove *that* m her **nest** in the sides 7077
51:16 he m lightnings with rain, 6213
Eze 22: 3 m idols against herself to defile *herself.* 6213
Da 2:28 m **known** to the king Nebuchadnezzar 3046
2:29 that revealeth secrets m **known** to thee 3046
6:13 m his **petition** three times a day. 1156+1159
11:31 place the abomination that m **desolate.** 8074
12:11 the abomination that m **desolate** set up, 8074
Am 4:13 that m the morning darkness, 6213
5: 8 *him* that m the seven stars and Orion, 6213
5: 8 and m the day **dark** *with* night: 2821
Na 1: 4 and m it **dry,** and drieth up all the rivers: 3001
Mt 5:45 for he m his sun to rise on the evil and 393
Mk 7:37 he m both the deaf to hear, and the dumb 4160
Lk 5:36 both the new m a rent, and the piece 4977
Jn 19:12 whosoever m himself a king speaketh 4160
Ac 9:34 Aeneas, Jesus Christ m thee **whole:** 2390
Ro 5: 5 And hope m not **ashamed;** because 2617
8:26 the Spirit itself m **intercession** for us 5241
8:27 m **intercession** for the saints according 1793
8:34 of God, who also m **intercession** for us. 1793
11: 2 how he m **intercession** to God against 1793
1Co 4: 7 For who m thee **to differ** *from another?* 1252
2Co 2: 2 who is he then that m me **glad,** 2165
2:14 m **manifest** the savour of his knowledge 5319
Gal 2: 6 they were, it m no **matter** to me: 1308
Eph 4:16 m increase of the body unto the edifying 4160
Heb 1: 7 m his angels spirits, and his ministers 4160
7:28 the law m men high priests which have 2525
7:28 which was since the law, *m* the Son, NIG
Rev 13:13 that he m fire come down from heaven 4160
21:27 worketh abomination, or *m* a lie: NIG
22:15 and whosoever loveth and m a lie. 4160

MAKHELOTH (2)
Nu 33:25 from Haradah, and pitched in **M.** 4722
33:26 they removed from **M,** and encamped at 4722

MAKI See MACHI

MAKING (30) [MAKE]
Ex 5:14 your task in m **brick** both yesterday 3835
Dt 20:19 long time, in m **war** against it to take it, 3898
Jdg 19:22 *Now* as they were m their hearts **merry,** 3190
1Ki 4:20 eating and drinking, and m **merry.** 8056
1Ch 15:28 m a **noise** with psalteries and harps. 8085
17:19 in m **known** all *these* great things. 3045
2Ch 30:22 m **confession** to the LORD God of their 3034
Ps 19: 7 of the LORD *is* sure, m **wise** the simple. 2449
Ecc 12:12 of m many books *there is* no end; 6213
Isa 3:16 they go, and m a **tinkling** with their feet: 5913
Jer 20:15 born unto thee; m him **very glad.** 8055+8055
Eze 27:16 of the multitude of the **wares** of thy m: 4639
27:18 in the multitude of the **wares** of thy m, 4639
Da 6:11 and m **supplication** before his God. 2604
Hos 10: 4 swearing falsely in m a covenant. 3772
Am 8: 5 m the ephah **small,** and the shekel great, 6994
Mic 6:13 in m *thee* **desolate** because of thy sins. 8074
Mt 9:23 the minstrels and the people m a **noise,** 2350
Mk 7:13 M the word of God of none effect 208
Jn 5:18 his Father, m himself equal with God. 4160
Ro 1:10 M **request,** if by any means now at length 1189
2Co 6:10 as poor, yet m many **rich;** as having 4148
Eph 1:16 for you, m mention of you in my prayers; 4160
2:15 of twain one new man, *so* m **peace;** 4160
5:19 and m **melody** in your heart to the Lord; 5567
Php 1: 4 of mine for you all m request with joy, 4160
1Th 1: 2 you all, m mention of you in our prayers; 4160
Phm 1: 4 m mention of thee always in my prayers, 4160
2Pe 2: 6 m *them* an ensample unto those that after 5087
Jude 1:22 some have compassion, m a **difference:** 1252

MAKIR See MACHIR

MAKIRITE See MACHIRITES

MAKKEDAH (9)
Jos 10:10 and smote them to Azekah, and unto **M.** 4719
10:16 and hid themselves in a cave at **M.** 4719
10:17 five kings are found hid in a cave at **M.** 4719
10:21 to the camp to Joshua *at* **M** in peace: 4719
10:28 that day Joshua took **M,** and smote it 4719
10:28 he did to the king of **M** as he did unto 4719
10:29 Joshua passed from **M,** and all Israel with 4719
12:16 The king of **M,** one; the king of Beth-el; 4719
15:41 Beth-dagon, and Naamah, and **M;** 4719

MAKTESH (1)
Zep 1:11 Howl, ye inhabitants of **M,** for all 4389

MALACHI (1)
Mal 1: 1 of the word of the LORD to Israel by **M.** 4401

MALCAM See MALCHAM

MALCHAM (2) [MOLOCH]
1Ch 8: 9 Jobab, and Zibia, and Mesha, and **M,** 4445
Zep 1: 5 swear by the LORD, and that swear by **M;** 4445

MALCHIAH (9)
1Ch 6:40 the son of Baaseiah, the son of **M,** 4441
Ezr 10:25 **M,** and Miamin, and Eleazar, 4441
10:31 Eliezer, Ishijah, **M,** Shemaiah, Shimeon, 4441
Ne 3:14 the dung gate repaired the son of **M,** 4441
3:31 After him repaired **M** the goldsmith's son 4441
8: 4 and **M,** and Hashum, and Hashbadana, 4441
11:12 the son of Pashur, the son of **M,** 4441
Jer 38: 1 of Shelemiah, and Pashur the son of **M,** 4441
38: 6 cast him into the dungeon of **M** the son 4441

MALCHIEL (3)
Ge 46:17 and the sons of Beriah; Heber, and **M.** 4439
Nu 26:45 of **M,** the family of the Malchielites. 4439
1Ch 7:31 Heber, and **M,** who *is* the father of 4439

MALCHIELITES (1)
Nu 26:45 of Malchiel, the family of the **M.** 4440

MALCHIJAH (6)
1Ch 9:12 son of **M,** and Maasiai the son of Adiel, 4441
24: 9 The fifth to **M,** the sixth to Mijamin, 4441
Ezr 10:25 and Eleazar, and **M,** and Benaiah. 4441
Ne 3:11 **M** the son of Harim, and Hashub the son 4441
10: 3 Pashur, Amariah, **M,** 4441
12:42 Jehohanan, and **M,** and Elam, and Ezer. 4441

MALCHIRAM (1)
1Ch 3:18 **M** also, and Pedaiah, and Shenazar, 4443

MALCHISHUA (4)
1Sa 31: 2 and Abinadab, and **M,** Saul's sons. 4444
1Ch 8:33 and **M,** and Abinadab, and Eshbaal. 4444
9:39 and **M,** and Abinadab, and Eshbaal. 4444
10: 2 and Abinadab, and **M,** the sons of Saul. 4444

MALCHUS (1)
Jn 18:10 his right ear. The servant's name was **M.** 3124

MALE (46) [MALES]
Ge 1:27 he him; and female created he them. 2145
5: 2 M and female created he them; 2145
6:19 with thee; they shall be m and female. 2145
7: 2 to thee by sevens, the m and his female: 376
7: 2 not clean by two, the m and his female. 376
7: 3 the air by sevens, the m and the female; 2145
7: 9 Noah into the ark, the m and the female, 2145
7:16 went in m and female of all flesh, 2145
17:23 every m among the men of Abraham's 2145
34:15 If ye will be as we *be,* that every m of 2145
34:22 if every m among us be circumcised, 2145
34:24 every m was circumcised, all that went 2145
Ex 12: 5 without blemish, a m of the first year: 2145
34:19 thy cattle, *whether* ox or sheep, *that* is m. 2142
Lev 1: 3 herd, let him offer a m without blemish: 2145
1:10 he shall bring it a m without blemish. 2145
3: 1 whether *it be* a m or female, he shall 2145
3: 6 or female, he shall offer it without 2145
4:23 a kid of the goats, a m without blemish; 2145
7: 6 Every m among the priests shall eat 2145
12: 7 This *is* the law for her that hath born a m 2145
22:19 shall offer at your own will a m without 2145
27: 3 of the m from twenty years old even unto 2145
27: 5 thy estimation shall be of the m twenty 2145
27: 6 thy estimation shall be of the m five 2145
27: 7 if *it be* a m, then thy estimation shall be 2145
Nu 1: 2 of *their* names, every m by their polls; 2145
1:20 m from twenty years old and upward, 2145
1:22 m from twenty years old and upward, 2145
3:15 every m from a month old and 2145
5: 3 Both m and female shall ye put out, 2145
18:10 shalt thou eat it; every m shall eat it: 2145
31:17 kill every m among the little ones, 2145
Dt 4:16 of any figure, the likeness of m or female, 2145
7:14 there shall not be a mS or female barren 6135
20:13 thou shalt smite every m thereof with 2138
Jos 17: 2 these *were* the m children of Manasseh 2145
Jdg 21:11 Ye shall utterly destroy every m, 2145
21:12 had known no man by lying with *any* m: 2145
1Ki 11:15 after he had smitten every m in Edom; 2145
11:16 until he had cut off every m in Edom:) 2145
Mal 1:14 which hath in his flock a m, and voweth, 2145
Mt 19: 4 them at the beginning made them m 730
Mk 10: 6 of the creation God made them m 730
Lk 2:23 Every m that openeth the womb shall be 730
Gal 3:28 nor free, there is neither m nor female: 730

MALE PROSTITUTES See EFFEMINATE

MALE SHRINE PROSTITUTES See SODOMITE; SODOMITES

MALEFACTOR (1) [MALEFACTORS]
Jn 18:30 and said unto him, If he were not a m, 2555

MALEFACTORS (3) [MALEFACTOR]
Lk 23:32 there were also two other, m, led with 2557
23:33 and the m, one on the right hand, 2557
23:39 And one of the m which were hanged 2557

MALELEEL (1)
Lk 3:37 *the son* of Jared, which was *the son* of M, 3121

MALES (32) [MALE]
Ge 34:25 upon the city boldly, and slew all the m. 2145
Ex 12:48 let all his m be circumcised, and then 2145
13:12 thou hast; the m *shall be* the LORD's. 2145
13:15 all that openeth the matrix, being m; 2145
23:17 Three times in the year all thy m shall 2138
Lev 6:18 All the m among the children of Aaron 2145
6:29 All the m among the priests shall eat 2145
Nu 3:22 according to the number of all the m, 2145
3:28 In the number of all the m, from a month 2145
3:34 according to the number of all the m, 2145
3:39 all the m from a month old and upward, 2145
3:40 Number all the firstborn of the m of 2145
3:43 the firstborn m by the number of names, 2145
26:62 all m from a month old and upward: 2145
31: 7 and they slew all the m. 2145
Dt 15:19 All the firstling m that come of thy herd 2145
16:16 Three times in a year shall all thy m 2138
Jos 5: 4 *that were* m, *even* all the men of war, 2145
2Ch 31:16 Beside their genealogy of m, from three 2145
31:19 to give portions to all the m among 2145
Ezr 8: 3 by genealogy of the m an hundred 2145
8: 4 of Zerahiah, and with him two hundred m. 2145
8: 5 Jahaziel, and with him three hundred m. 2145
8: 6 the son of Jonathan, and with him fifty m. 2145
8: 7 son of Athaliah, and with him seventy m. 2145
8: 8 of Michael, and with him fourscore m. 2145
8: 9 with him two hundred and eighteen m. 2145
8:10 with him an hundred and threescore m. 2145
8:11 Bebai, and with him twenty and eight m. 2145
8:12 and with him an hundred and ten m. 2145
8:13 Shemaiah, and with them threescore m. 2145
8:14 and Zabbud, and with them seventy m. 2145

MALICE (6) [MALICIOUS, MALICIOUSNESS]
1Co 5: 8 neither with the leaven of m and 2549
14:20 howbeit in m be ye children, 2549
Eph 4:31 be put away from you, with all m: 2549
Col 3: 8 m, blasphemy, filthy communication 2549
Tit 3: 3 living in m and envy, hateful, 2549
1Pe 2: 1 laying aside all m, and all guile, 2549

MALICIOUS (1) [MALICE]
3Jn 1:10 doeth, prating against us with m words: 4190

MALICIOUSNESS (2) [MALICE]
Ro 1:29 fornication, wickedness, covetousness, m; 2549
1Pe 2:16 and not using *your* liberty for a cloke of m, 2549

MALIGNITY (1)
Ro 1:29 full of envy, murder, debate, deceit, m; 2550

MALKI-SHUA See MELCHISHUA

MALKIEL See MALCHIEL

MALKIELITE See MALCHIELITES

MALKIJAH See MALCHIAH; MALCHIJAH; MELCHIAH

MALKIRAM See MALCHIRAM

MALLOTHI (2)
1Ch 25: 4 Joshbekashah, M, Hothir, *and* Mahazioth; 4413
25:26 The nineteenth to M, *he,* his sons, 4413

MALLOWS (1)
Job 30: 4 Who cut up m by the bushes, 4408

MALLUCH (6)
1Ch 6:44 of Kishi, the son of Abdi, the son of M, 4409
Ezr 10:29 M, and Adaiah, Jashub, and Sheal, 4409
10:32 Benjamin, M, *and* Shemariah. 4409
Ne 10: 4 Hattush, Shebaniah, M, 4409
10:27 M, Harim, Baanah. 4409
12: 2 Amariah, M, Hattush, 4409

MALTA See MELITA

MAMMON (4)
Mt 6:24 the other. Ye cannot serve God and m. 3126
Lk 16: 9 Make to yourselves friends of the m of 3126
16:11 not been faithful in the unrighteous m, 3126
16:13 the other. Ye cannot serve God and m. 3126

MAMRE (10)
Ge 13:18 and dwelt in the plain of M, which *is* 4471
14:13 he dwelt in the plain of M the Amorite, 4471
14:24 went with me, Aner, Eshcol, and M; 4471
18: 1 appeared unto him in the plains of M: 4471
23:17 *was* before M, the field, and the cave 4471
23:19 cave of the field of Machpelah, before M: 4471
25: 9 of Zohar the Hittite, which *is* before M; 4471
35:27 Jacob came unto Isaac his father unto M, 4471
49:30 which *is* before M, in the land of Canaan, 4471
50:13 of Ephron the Hittite, before M. 4471

MAN (2616) [BONDMAN, BONDMEN, BOWMEN, CHAPMEN, COUNTRYMEN, CRAFTSMAN, CRAFTSMEN, DAYSMAN, FISHERMEN, FOOTMEN, FREEMAN, GOODMAN, HARVESTMAN, HERDMAN, HERDMEN, HORSEMAN, HORSEMEN, HUSBANDMAN, HUSBANDMEN, KINSMAN, KINSMAN'S, KINSMEN, MAN'S, MANKIND, MANSERVANT, MANSERVANT'S, MANSERVANTS, MANSLAYER, MANSLAYERS, MEN, MEN'S, MENPLEASERS, MENSERVANTS, MENSTEALERS, NOBLEMAN, PLOWMAN, PLOWMEN, SHIPMEN, SPEARMEN, SPOKESMAN, WATCHMAN, WATCHMAN'S, WATCHMEN, WORKFELLOW, WORKMAN, WORKMANSHIP, WORKMEN, WORKMEN'S]

Ge	1:26	God said, Let us make **m** in our image,	120
	1:27	So God created **m** in his own image,	120
	2: 5	and *there was* not a **m** to till the ground.	120
	2: 7	the Lord God formed **m** *of* the dust of	120
	2: 7	breath of life; and **m** became a living soul.	120
	2: 8	there he put the **m** whom he had formed.	120
	2:15	the Lord God took the **m**, and put him	120
	2:16	the Lord God commanded the **m**, saying,	120
	2:18	*It is* not good that the **m** should be alone;	120
	2:22	which the Lord God had taken from **m**,	120
	2:22	he a woman, and brought her unto the **m**.	120
	2:23	because she was taken out of **M.**	376
	2:24	Therefore shall a **m** leave his father and his	120
	2:25	the **m** and his wife, and were not ashamed.	120
	3:12	the **m** said, The woman whom thou gavest	120
	3:22	Behold, the **m** is become as one of us,	120
	3:24	So he drove out the **m**; and he placed at	120
	4: 1	said, I have gotten a **m** from the Lord.	376
	4:23	for I have slain a **m** to my wounding,	376
	4:23	wounding, and a **young m** to my hurt.	3206
	5: 1	In the day that God created **m**,	120
	6: 3	My spirit shall not always strive with **m**,	120
	6: 5	God saw that the wickedness of **m** *was*	120
	6: 6	it repented the Lord that he had made **m**	120
	6: 7	I will destroy **m** whom I have created from	120
	6: 7	both **m**, and beast, and the creeping thing,	120
	6: 9	Noah was a just **m** *and* perfect in his	376
	7:21	that creepeth upon the earth, and every **m:**	120
	7:23	**m**, and cattle, and the creeping things,	120
	9: 5	will I require it, and at the hand of **m**;	120
	9: 5	**m**'s brother will I require the life of **m**.	120
	9: 6	**m**'s blood, by **m** shall his blood be shed:	120
	9: 6	shed: for in the image of God made he **m**.	120
	13:16	if a **m** can number the dust of the earth,	376
	16:12	will be a wild **m**; his hand *will be* against	120
	16:12	his hand *will be* against every **m**,	3605
	17:10	Every **m** *child* among you shall be	2145
	17:12	every **m** *child* in your generations, he that	2145
	17:14	the uncircumcised **m** *child* whose flesh of	2145
	18: 7	and good, and gave *it* unto a **young m**;	5288
	19: 8	two daughters which have not known **m**;	376
	19: 9	they pressed sore upon the **m**, *even* Lot,	376
	19:31	*there is* not a **m** in the earth to come in	376
	20: 3	said to him, Behold, thou *art but* a dead **m**,	NIH
	20: 7	therefore restore the **m** *his* wife; for he	376
	24:16	a virgin, neither had **any m** known her:	376
	24:21	the **m** wondering at her held his peace, to	376
	24:22	that the **m** took a golden earring of half a	376
	24:26	the **m** bowed down his head,	376
	24:29	Laban ran out unto the **m**, unto the well.	376
	24:30	sister, saying, Thus spake the **m** unto me;	376
	24:30	that he came unto the **m**; and behold,	376
	24:32	the **m** came into the house: and he	376
	24:58	said unto her, Wilt thou go with this **m**?	376
	24:61	upon the camels, and followed the **m**:	376
	24:65	What **m** *is* this that walketh in the field to	376
	25: 8	an **old m**, and full *of years;* and	2205
	25:27	was a cunning hunter, a **m** of the field;	376
	25:27	Jacob *was* a plain **m**, dwelling in tents.	376
	26:11	He that toucheth this **m** or his wife shall	376
	26:13	the **m** waxed great, and went forward,	376
	27:11	Esau my brother *is* a hairy **m**, and I *am* a	376
	27:11	*is* a hairy man, and I *am* a smooth **m:**	376
	29:19	than that I should give her to another **m:**	376
	30:43	the **m** increased exceedingly, and had	376
	31:50	beside my daughters, no **m** *is* with us;	376
	32:24	there wrestled a **m** with him until	376
	34:19	the **young m** deferred not to do the thing,	5288
	34:25	took **each m** his sword, and came upon	376
	37:15	*certain* **m** found him, and behold, *he was*	376
	37:15	the **m** asked him, saying, What seekest	376
	37:17	the **m** said, They are departed hence; for I	376
	38:25	sent to her father in law, saying, By the **m**,	376
	39: 2	with Joseph, and he was a prosperous **m;**	376
	40: 5	of them, **each m** his dream in one night,	376
	40: 5	**each m** according to the interpretation of	376
	41:11	we dreamed **each m** according to	376
	41:12	*there was* there with us a **young m**,	5288
	41:12	to **each m** according to his dream he did	376
	41:33	Pharaoh look out a discreet and wise,	376
	41:38	Can we find *such a one* as this *is*, a **m** in	376
	41:44	without thee shall no **m** lift up his hand or	376
	42:13	the sons of one **m** in the land of Canaan;	376
	42:30	The **m**, *who is* the lord of the land,	376
	42:33	the **m**, the lord of the country, said unto	376
	43: 3	The **m** did solemnly protest unto us,	376
	43: 5	for the **m** said unto us, Ye shall not see my	376
	43: 6	to tell the **m** whether ye had yet a brother?	376
	43: 7	The **m** asked us straitly of our state,	376

Ge	43:11	carry down the **m** a present, a little balm,	376
	43:13	brother, and arise, go again unto the **m:**	376
	43:14	Almighty give you mercy before the **m**,	376
	43:17	the **m** did as Joseph bade; and the man	376
	43:17	**m** brought the men into Joseph's house.	376
	43:24	**m** brought the men into Joseph's house,	376
	43:27	father well, the **old m** of whom ye spake?	2205
	44:11	they speedily took down **every m** his sack	376
	44:11	the ground, and opened **every m** his sack.	376
	44:13	laded **every m** his ass, and returned to	376
	44:15	wot ye not that such a **m** as I can certainly	376
	44:17	*but* the **m** in whose hand the cup is found,	376
	44:20	an **old m**, and a child of *his* old age,	2205
	45: 1	he cried, Cause every **m** to go out from me.	376
	45: 1	there stood no **m** with him, while Joseph	376
	45:22	To all of them he gave **each m** changes of	376
	47: 6	if thou knowest *any* **m** of activity amongst	376
	47:20	for the Egyptians sold **every m** his field,	376
	49: 6	in their anger they slew a **m**, and in their	376
Ex	1: 1	**every m** and his household came with	376
	1: 1	there went a **m** of the house of Levi,	376
	2:12	and when he saw that *there was* no **m**,	376
	2:20	why *is it that* ye have left the **m**? call him,	376
	2:21	Moses was content to dwell with the **m:**	376
	7:12	For they cast down **every m** his rod,	376
	8:17	and it became lice in **m**, and in beast;	120
	8:18	there were lice upon **m**, and upon beast.	120
	9: 9	a boil breaking forth *with* blains upon **m**,	120
	9: 9	a boil breaking forth *with* blains upon **m**,	120
	9:19	*for* upon every **m** and beast which shall be	120
	9:22	upon **m**, and upon beast, and upon every	120
	9:25	all that *was* in the field, both **m** and beast;	120
	10: 7	How long shall this **m** be a snare unto us?	NIH
	11: 2	let **every m** borrow of his neighbour,	376
	11: 3	Moreover the **m** Moses *was* very great in	376
	11: 7	a dog move his tongue, against **m** or beast:	376
	12: 3	they shall take to them **every m** a lamb,	376
	12: 4	**every m** according to his eating shall make	376
	12:12	in the land of Egypt, both **m** and beast;	120
	12:16	save *that* which every **m** must eat, that	5315
	13: 2	children of Israel, *both* of **m** and of beast:	120
	13:13	all the firstborn of **m** amongst thy children	376
	13:15	both the firstborn of **m**, and the firstborn of	120
	15: 3	The Lord *is* a **m** of war: the Lord *is*	376
	16:16	Gather of it **every m** according to his	376
	16:16	an omer for **every m**, *according* to	1538
	16:16	take ye **every m** for *them* which *are* in his	376
	16:18	they gathered **every m** according to his	376
	16:19	Let no **m** leave of it till the morning.	376
	16:21	**every m** according to his eating:	376
	16:22	two omers for one **m**: and all the rulers of	NIH
	16:29	abide ye **every m** in his place, let no man	376
	16:29	let no **m** go out of his place on the seventh	376
	19:13	whether *it be* beast or **m**, it shall not live:	376
	21: 7	if a **m** sell his daughter to be a maidservant,	376
	21:12	He that smiteth a **m**, so that he die, shall	376
	21:13	if a **m** lie not in wait, but God deliver *him*	834
	21:14	if a **m** come presumptuously upon his	376
	21:16	And he that stealeth a **m**, and selleth him,	376
	21:20	if a **m** smite his servant, or his maid, with	376
	21:26	if a **m** smite the eye of his servant, or the	376
	21:28	an ox gore a **m** or a woman, that they die:	376
	21:29	but that he hath killed a **m** or a woman;	376
	21:33	if a **m** shall open a pit, or if a man shall dig	376
	21:33	or if a **m** shall dig a pit, and not cover it,	376
	22: 1	If a **m** shall steal an ox, or a sheep,	376
	22: 5	If a **m** shall cause a field or vineyard to be	376
	22: 7	If a **m** shall deliver unto his neighbour	376
	22:10	If a **m** deliver unto his neighbour an ass,	376
	22:10	or be hurt, or driven away, **no m** seeing *it:*	369
	22:14	if a **m** borrow *ought* of his neighbour,	376
	22:16	if a **m** entice a maid that is not betrothed,	376
	23: 3	Neither shalt thou countenance a poor **m**	NIH
	24:14	if any **m** have any matters to do, let him	1167
	25: 2	of every **m** that giveth it willingly with his	376
	30:12	shall they give **every m** a ransom for his	376
	32: 1	the **m** that brought us up out of the land of	376
	32:23	the **m** that brought us up out of the land of	376
	32:27	Put **every m** his sword by his side, *and* go	376
	32:27	slay **every m** his brother, and every man	376
	32:27	**every m** his companion, and every man	376
	32:27	companion, and every **m** his neighbour.	376
	32:29	even **every m** upon his son, and upon his	376
	33: 4	and no **m** did put on him his ornaments.	376
	33: 8	stood **every m** at his tent door,	376
	33:10	and worshipped, **every m** in his tent door.	376
	33:11	to face, as a **m** speaketh unto his friend.	376
	33:11	Joshua, the son of Nun, a **young m**,	5288
	33:20	for there shall no **m** see me, and live.	120
	34: 3	no **m** shall come up with thee, neither let	376
	34: 3	neither let **any m** be seen throughout all	376
	34:24	neither shall any **m** desire thy land,	376
	35:22	every **m** that offered *offered* an offering of	376
	35:23	every **m**, with whom was found blue,	376
	35:24	**every m**, with whom was found shittim	3605
	35:29	every **m** and woman, whose heart made	376
	36: 1	and Aholiab, and every wise hearted **m**,	376
	36: 2	and Aholiab, and every wise hearted **m**,	376
	36: 4	came **every m** from his work which	376+376
	36: 6	Let neither **m** nor woman make any more	NIH
	36: 8	every wise hearted **m** among them that	NIH
	38:26	A bekah for every **m**, *that is*, half a shekel,	1538
Lev	1: 2	If *any* **m** of you bring an offering unto	120
	5: 3	Or if he touch the uncleanness of **m**,	120
	5: 3	whatsoever uncleanness *it be* that a **m**	NIH

Lev	5: 4	whatsoever *it be* that a **m** shall pronounce	120
	6: 3	in any of all *these* that a **m** doeth, sinning	120
	7:21	unclean *thing, as* the uncleanness of a **m**,	120
	12: 2	have conceived seed, and born a **m child:**	2145
	13: 2	When a **m** shall have in the skin of his flesh	120
	13: 9	When the plague of leprosy is in a **m**, then	120
	13:29	If a **m** or woman hath a plague upon	376
	13:38	If a **m** also or a woman have in the skin of	376
	13:40	And the **m** whose hair is fallen off his head,	376
	13:44	He *is* a leprous **m**, he *is* unclean: the priest	376
	14:11	present the **m** that is to be made clean,	376
	15: 2	When any **m** hath a running issue	376+376
	15:18	The woman also with whom shall lie	376
	15:24	if any **m** lie with her at all, and her	376
	15:33	of the **m**, and of the woman, and of him	2145
	16:17	there shall be no **m** in the tabernacle of	120
	16:21	shall send *him* away by the hand of a fit **m**	376
	17: 3	**What m** soever *there be* of the	376+376
	17: 4	blood shall be imputed unto that **m**; he	376
	17: 4	that **m** shall be cut off from among his	376
	17: 8	**Whatsoever m** *there be* of the house	376+376
	17: 9	that **m** shall be cut off from among his	376
	17:10	**whatsoever m** *there be* of the house	376+376
	17:13	**whatsoever m** *there be* of the	376+376
	18: 5	which if a **m** do, he shall live in them:	120
	19: 3	Ye shall fear **every m** his mother,	376
	19:32	honour the face of the **old m**, and fear	2205
	20: 3	I will set my face against that **m**, and will	376
	20: 4	do any ways hide their eyes from the **m**,	376
	20: 5	I will set my face against that **m**,	376
	20:10	the **m** that committeth adultery with	376
	20:11	the **m** that lieth with his father's wife hath	376
	20:12	if a **m** lie with his daughter in law, both of	376
	20:13	If a **m** also lie with mankind, as he lieth	376
	20:14	if a **m** take a wife and her mother, *it is*	376
	20:15	if a **m** lie with a beast, he shall surely be	376
	20:17	if a **m** shall take his sister, his father's	376
	20:18	if a **m** shall lie with a woman having her	376
	20:20	if a **m** shall lie with his uncle's wife, he	376
	20:21	if a **m** shall take his brother's wife, *it is* an	376
	20:27	A **m** also or woman that hath a familiar	376
	21: 4	*being* a **chief m** among his people,	1167
	21:18	whatsoever **m** *he be* that hath a blemish,	376
	21:18	a blind **m**, or a lame, or he that hath a flat	376
	21:19	Or a **m** that is brokenfooted,	376
	21:21	No **m** that hath a blemish, of the seed of	376
	22: 4	**What m** soever of the seed of Aaron	376+376
	22: 4	dead, or a **m** whose seed goeth from him;	376
	22: 5	or a **m** of whom he may take uncleanness,	120
	22:14	if a **m** eat *of* the holy thing unwittingly,	376
	24:10	a **m** of Israel strove together in the camp;	376
	24:17	he that killeth any **m** shall surely be put to	120
	24:19	if a **m** cause a blemish in his neighbour;	376
	24:20	as he hath caused a blemish in a **m**,	120
	24:21	that killeth a **m**, he shall be put to death.	376
	25:10	shall return **every m** unto his possession,	376
	25:10	ye shall return **every m** unto his family.	376
	25:13	shall return **every m** unto his possession.	376
	25:26	if the **m** have none to redeem *it*, and	376
	25:27	restore the overplus unto the **m** to whom	376
	25:29	if a **m** sell a dwelling house in a walled	376
	25:33	if a **m** purchase of the Levites, then	NIH
	27: 2	When a **m** shall make a singular vow,	376
	27: 9	all that *any* **m** giveth of such unto	NIH
	27:14	a **m** shall sanctify his house *to be* holy	376
	27:16	if a **m** shall sanctify unto the Lord *some*	376
	27:20	or if he have sold the field to another **m**,	376
	27:22	if *a* **m** sanctify unto the Lord a field	NIH
	27:26	Lord's firstling, no **m** shall sanctify it;	376
	27:28	that a **m** shall devote unto the Lord of all	376
	27:28	*both* of **m** and beast, and of the field of his	120
	27:31	if a **m** will at all redeem *ought* of his tithes,	376
Nu	1: 4	with you there shall be a **m** of every tribe;	376
	1:52	**every m** by his own camp, and every man	376
	1:52	**every m** by his own standard,	376
	2: 2	**Every m** of the children of Israel shall	376
	2:17	**every m** in his place by their standards.	376
	3:13	all the firstborn in Israel, both **m** and beast:	120
	5: 6	When a **m** or woman shall commit any sin	376
	5: 8	if the **m** have no kinsman to recompense	376
	5:10	whatsoever **any m** giveth the priest, it shall	376
	5:13	a **m** lie with her **carnally**,	376+2233+7902
	5:15	shall the **m** bring his wife unto the priest,	376
	5:19	If no **m** have lain with thee, and if thou	376
	5:20	*some* **m** hath lain with thee beside thine	376
	5:31	shall the **m** be guiltless from iniquity,	376
	6: 2	When either **m** or woman shall separate	376
	6: 9	And if any **m** die very suddenly by him,	NIH
	7: 5	to **every m** according to his service.	376
	8:17	of Israel *are* mine, *both* **m** and beast:	120
	9: 6	were defiled by the dead body of a **m**,	120
	9: 7	We *are* defiled by the dead body of a **m**:	120
	9:10	If any **m** of you or of your posterity shall	376
	9:13	the **m** that *is* clean, and is not in a journey,	376
	9:13	appointed season, that **m** shall bear his sin.	376
	11:10	**every m** in the door of his tent:	376
	11:27	there ran a **young m**, and told Moses,	5288
	12: 3	the **m** Moses *was* very meek, above all	376
	13: 2	tribe of their fathers shall ye send a **m**,	376
	14:15	*if* thou shalt kill *all* this people as one **m**,	376
	15:32	they found a **m** that gathered sticks upon	376
	15:35	The **m** shall be surely put to death:	376
	16: 7	it shall be *that* the **m** whom the Lord doth	376
	16:17	take **every m** his censer, and put incense	376
	16:17	bring ye before the Lord **every m** his	376

M

M

Nu 16:18 they took **every m** his censer, and put fire	376
16:22 shall one **m** sin, and wilt thou be wroth	376
17: 9 they looked, and took **every m** his rod.	376
18:15 nevertheless the firstborn of **m** shalt thou	120
19: 9 a **m** *that is* clean shall gather up the ashes	376
19:11 any **m** shall be unclean seven days.	120+5315
19:13 the dead *body* of *any* **m** that is dead,	120+5315
19:14 This *is* the law, when a **m** dieth in a tent:	120
19:16 a dead *body*, or a bone of a **m**, or a grave,	120
19:20 the **m** that shall be unclean, and shall not	376
21: 9 to pass, that if a serpent had bitten *any* **m**,	376
23:19 God *is* not a **m**, that he should lie; neither	376
23:19 the son of **m**, that he should repent:	120
24: 3 the **m** whose eyes are open hath said:	1397
24:15 the **m** whose eyes are open hath said:	1397
25: 8 he went after the **m** of Israel into the tent,	376
25: 8 the **m** of Israel, and the woman through	376
26:64 among these there was not a **m** of them	376
26:65 there was not left a **m** of them, save Caleb	376
27: 8 If a **m** die, and have no son, then ye shall	376
27:16 of all flesh, set a **m** over the congregation,	376
27:18 a **m** in whom *is* the spirit, and lay thine	376
30: 2 If a **m** vow a vow unto the LORD,	376
30:16 between a **m** and his wife, between	376
31:17 kill every woman that hath known **m** by	376
31:18 have not known a **m** by lying with him,	2145
31:26 *both* of **m** and of beast, thou, and Eleazar	120
31:35 women that had not known **m** by lying	2145
31:47 *both* of **m** and of beast, and gave them	120
31:49 and there lacketh not **one m** of us.	376
31:50 **every m** hath gotten, *of* jewels of gold,	376
31:53 war had taken spoil, **every m** for himself.)	376
32:18 have inherited **every m** his inheritance.	376
32:27 **every m** armed for war, before the LORD	3605
32:29 **every m** armed to battle, before	3605
35:23 wherewith **m** may die, seeing *him* not,	NIH
36: 8 enjoy **every m** the inheritance of his	376
Dt 1:16 judge righteously between every **m** and	376
1:17 you shall not be afraid of the face of **m**;	376
1:31 a **m** doth bear his son, in all the way that	376
1:41 ye had girded on **every m** his weapons	376
3:11 the breadth of it, after the cubit of a **m**.	376
3:20 ye return **every m** unto his possession,	376
4:32 since the day that God created **m** upon	120
5:24 seen this day that God doth talk with **m**,	120
7:24 shall no **m** *be able* to stand before thee,	376
8: 3 that he might make thee know that **m**	120
8: 3 out of the mouth of the LORD doth **m** live.	120
8: 5 as a **m** chasteneth his son, *so* the LORD thy	376
11:25 There shall no **m** *be able* to stand before	376
12: 8 **every m** whatsoever *is* right in his own	376
15: 7 If there be among you a **poor m** of one of	34
15:12 **Hebrew m**, or a Hebrew woman, be sold	5680
16:17 **Every m** *shall give* as he is able, according	376
17: 2 LORD thy God giveth thee, **m** or woman,	376
17: 5 thou bring forth that **m** or that woman,	376
17: 5 *that* **m** or *that* woman, and shalt stone	376
17:12 And the **m** that will do presumptuously,	376
17:12 or unto the judge, even that **m** shall die:	376
19: 5 As when a **m** goeth into the wood with	NIH
19:11 if **any m** hate his neighbour, and lie in wait	376
19:15 One witness shall not rise up against a **m**	376
19:16 If a false witness rise up against **any m** to	376
20: 5 **m** *is there* that hath built a new house,	376
20: 5 die in the battle, and another **m** dedicate it.	376
20: 6 what **m** *is he* that hath planted a vineyard,	376
20: 6 die in the battle, and another **m** eat of it.	376
20: 7 what **m** *is there* that hath betrothed a wife,	376
20: 7 die in the battle, and another **m** take her.	376
20: 8 What **m** *is there that is* fearful and	376
21: 3 the city *which is* next unto the slain **m**,	NIH
21: 6 *that are* next unto the slain **m**, shall wash	NIH
22:15 If a **m** have two wives, one beloved,	376
22:18 If a **m** have a stubborn and rebellious son,	376
21:22 a **m** have committed a sin worthy of death,	376
22: 5 not wear that which pertaineth unto a **m**,	1397
22: 5 neither shall a **m** put on a woman's	1397
22: 8 thine house, if any **m**S fall from thence.	5307
22:13 If **any m** take a wife, and go in unto her,	376
22:16 I gave my daughter unto this **m** to wife,	376
22:18 the elders of that city shall take *that* **m** and	376
22:22 If a **m** be found lying with a woman	376
22:22 *both* the **m** that lay with the woman,	376
22:23 a **m** find her in the city, and lie with her;	376
22:24 the **m**, because he hath humbled his	376
22:25 if a **m** find a betrothed damsel in the field,	376
22:25 and the **m** force her, and lie with her:	376
22:25 then the **m** only that lay with her shall die:	376
22:26 as when a **m** riseth against his neighbour,	376
22:28 If a **m** find a damsel *that is* a virgin, which	376
22:29 the **m** that lay with her shall give unto	376
22:30 A **m** shall not take his father's wife,	376
23:10 If there be among you **any m**, that is not	376
24: 1 When a **m** hath taken a wife,	376
24: 5 When a **m** hath taken a new wife, he shall	376
24: 6 No **m** shall take the nether or the upper	NIH
24: 7 If a **m** be found stealing any of his brethren	376
24:11 the **m** to whom thou dost lend shall bring	376
24:12 if the **m** *be* poor, thou shalt not sleep with	376
24:16 **every m** shall be put to death for his own	376
25: 2 if the wicked *m* *be* worthy to be beaten,	NIH
25: 7 if the **m** like not to take his brother's wife,	376
25: 9 shall it be done unto *that* **m** that will not	376
27:15 Cursed *be* the **m** that maketh *any* graven	376
28:26 the earth, and **no m** shall fray *them* away.	369

Dt 28:29 evermore, and **no m** shall save *thee*.	369
28:30 a wife, and another **m** shall lie with her:	376
28:54 *So that* the **m** *that is* tender among you,	376
28:68 and bondwomen, and **no m** shall buy *you*.	369
29:18 Lest there should be among you **m**,	376
29:20 his jealousy shall smoke against that **m**,	376
32:25 shall destroy both the **young m** and	970
32:25 the suckling *also* with the **m** of gray hairs.	376
33: 1 wherewith Moses the **m** of God blessed	376
34: 6 no **m** knoweth of his sepulchre unto this	376
Jos 1: 5 There shall not **any m** *be able* to stand	376
2:11 there remain any more courage in **any m**,	376
3:12 the tribes of Israel, out of every tribe a **m**,	376
4: 2 out of the people, out of every tribe a **m**,	376
4: 4 children of Israel, out of every tribe a **m**:	376
4: 5 take ye up **every m** of you a stone upon	376
5:13 there stood a **m** over against him with his	376
6: 5 people shall ascend up **every m** straight	376
6:20 **every m** straight before him, and they	376
6:21 and woman, young and old, and ox,	376
6:26 saying, Cursed *be* the **m** before the LORD,	376
7:14 LORD shall take shall come **m** by man.	1397
7:14 LORD shall take shall come man by **m**.	NIH
7:17 he brought the family of the Zarhites **m** by	1397
7:17 the family of the Zarhites man by **m**;	NIH
7:18 he brought his household **m** by man;	1397
7:18 he brought his household man by **m**;	NIH
8:17 there was not a **m** left in Ai or Beth-el,	376
8:31 over which no **m** hath lift up *any* iron:	NIH
10: 8 there shall not a **m** of them stand before	376
10:14 LORD hearkened unto the voice of a **m**:	376
11:14 every **m** they smote with the edge of	120
14: 6 unto Moses the **m** of God concerning me	376
14:15 which *Arba was* a great **m** among	120
17: 1 because he was a **m** of war, therefore he	376
21:44 there stood not a **m** of all their enemies	376
22:20 that **m** perished not alone in his iniquity.	376
23: 9 no **m** hath *been able* to stand before you	376
23:10 One **m** of you shall chase a thousand:	376
24:28 depart, **every m** unto his inheritance.	376
Jdg 1:24 spies saw a **m** come forth out of the city,	376
1:25 but they let go the **m** and all his family.	376
1:26 the **m** went *into* the land of the Hittites,	376
2: 6 the children of Israel went **every m** unto	376
3:15 son of Gera, a Benjamite, a **m** lefthanded:	376
3:17 king of Moab: and Eglon *was* a very fat **m**.	376
3:28 and suffered not a **m** to pass over.	376
3:29 men of valour; and there escaped not a **m**.	376
4:16 of the sword; *and* there was not a **m** left.	259
4:20 any **m** doth come and inquire of thee,	376
4:20 of thee, and say, Is there any **m** here?	376
4:22 I will shew thee the **m** whom thou seekest.	376
5:30 the prey; to every **m** a damsel *or* two;	1397
6:12 *is* with thee, thou mighty **m** of valour.	NIH
6:16 thou shalt smite the Midianites as one **m**.	376
7: 7 let all the *other* people go **every m** unto	376
7: 8 he sent all *the rest of* Israel **every m** unto	376
7:13 there *was* a **m** that told a dream unto his	376
7:14 of Gideon the son of Joash, a **m** of Israel:	376
7:21 stood **every m** in his place round about	376
8:14 caught a **young m** of the men of Succoth,	5288
8:21 for as the **m** *is, so is* his strength.	376
8:24 you would give me **every m** the earrings	376
8:25 cast therein **every m** the earrings of his	376
9: 9 wherewith by me they honour God and **m**,	376
9:13 which cheereth God and **m**, and go to be	376
9:49 all the people likewise cut down **every m**	376
9:54 he called hastily unto the **young m** his	5288
9:54 his **young m** thrust him through,	5288
9:55 they departed **every m** unto his place.	376
10: 1 of Puah, the son of Dodo, a **m** of Issachar;	376
10:18 What **m** *is he* that will begin to fight	376
11: 1 Jephthah the Gileadite was a mighty **m**	NIH
11:39 she knew no **m**. And it was a custom in	376
13: 2 was a certain **m** of Zorah, of the family	376
13: 6 A **m** of God came unto me,	376
13: 8 let the **m** of God which thou didst send	376
13:10 Behold, the **m** hath appeared unto me,	376
13:11 and came to the **m**, and said unto him,	376
13:11 thou the **m** that spakest unto the woman?	376
16: 7 then shall I be weak, and be as another **m**.	120
16:11 shall I be weak, and be as another **m**.	120
16:17 become weak, and be like any *other* **m**.	120
16:19 she called for a **m**, and she caused *him* to	376
17: 1 there was a **m** of mount Ephraim, whose	376
17: 5 the **m** Micah had a house of gods,	376
17: 6 **every m** did *that* which *was* right in his	376
17: 7 there was a **young m** out of	5288
17: 8 the **m** departed out of the city from	376
17:11 Levite was content to dwell with the **m**;	376
17:11 the **young m** was unto him as one of his	5288
17:12 the **young m** became his priest, and was	5288
18: 3 they knew the voice of the **young m**	5288
18: 7 and had no business with *any* **m**.	120
18:15 came to the house of the **young m**	5288
18:19 to be a priest unto the house of one **m**,	376
18:28 and they had no business with *any* **m**;	120
19: 6 the damsel's father had said unto the **m**,	376
19: 7 when the **m** rose up to depart, his father in	376
19: 9 when the **m** rose up to depart, he,	376
19:10 **m** would not tarry *that* night, but he rose	376
19:15 for *there was* no **m** that took them into *his*	376
19:16 there came an old **m** from his work out of	376
19:17 he saw a wayfaring **m** in the street of	376
19:17 and the old **m** said, Whither goest thou?	376

Jdg 19:18 there *is* no **m** that receiveth me to house.	376
19:19 the **young m** *which is* with thy servants:	5288
19:20 the old **m** said, Peace *be* with thee;	376
19:22 master of the house, the **old m**, saying,	2205
19:22 Bring forth the **m** that came into thine	376
19:23 the **m**, the master of the house, went out	376
19:23 seeing that this **m** is come into mine house,	376
19:24 but unto this **m** do not so vile a thing.	376
19:25 so the **m** took his concubine, and brought	376
19:28 the **m** took her *up* upon an ass, and the	NIH
19:28 the **m** rose up, and gat him unto his place.	376
20: 1 was gathered together as one **m**,	376
20: 8 all the people arose as one **m**, saying,	376
20:11 against the city, knit together as one **m**.	376
21:11 and every woman that hath lien by **m**.	2145
21:12 that had known no **m** by lying with *any*	376
21:21 catch you **every m** his wife of the	376
21:22 we reserved not to **each m** his wife in	376
21:24 **every m** to his tribe and to his family,	376
21:24 they went out from thence **every m** to his	376
21:25 **every m** did *that* which *was* right in his	376
Ru 1: 1 a **certain m** of Beth-lehem-judah went to	376
1: 2 the name of the **m** *was* Elimelech,	376
2: 1 a **mighty m** of wealth, of the family of	376
2:20 The **m** *is* near of kin unto us, one of our	376
3: 3 *but* make not thyself known unto the **m**,	376
3: 8 that the **m** was afraid, and turned himself:	376
3:16 she told her all that the **m** had done to her.	376
3:18 for the **m** will not be in rest, until he have	376
4: 7 a **m** plucked off his shoe, and gave *it* to his	376
1Sa 1: 1 Now there was a certain **m** of	376
1: 3 this **m** went up out of his city yearly to	376
1:11 wilt give unto thine handmaid a **m** child,	376
1:21 the Elkanah, and all his house, went up	376
2: 9 for by strength shall no **m** prevail.	376
2:13 *was, that* when any **m** offered sacrifice,	376
2:15 and said to the **m** that sacrificed,	376
2:16 *if any* **m** said unto him, Let them not fail to	376
2:25 If **one m** sin against another, the judge	376
2:25 if a **m** sin against the LORD, who shall	376
2:27 there came a **m** of God unto Eli.	376
2:31 that there shall not be an **old m** in thine	2205
2:32 there shall not be an **old m** in thine house	2205
2:33 the **m** of thine, *whom* I shall not cut off	376
4:10 and they fled **every m** into his tent:	376
4:12 there ran a **m** of Benjamin out of the army,	376
4:13 when the **m** came into the city, and told *it*,	376
4:14 And the **m** came in hastily, and told Eli.	376
4:16 the **m** said unto Eli, I *am* he that came out	376
4:18 for he was an old **m**, and heavy. And he	376
8:22 men of Israel, Go ye **every m** unto his city.	376
9: 1 Now there was a **m** of Benjamin, whose	376
9: 1 a Benjamite, a mighty **m** of power.	376
9: 2 *was* Saul, a choice **young m**, and a goodly:	NIH
9: 6 there is in this city a **m** of God, and *he is*	376
9: 6 a **m** of God, and *he is* an honourable **m**;	376
9: 7 *if* we go, what shall we bring the **m**?	376
9: 7 *there* is not a present to bring to the **m** of	376
9: 8 will I give to the **m** of God, to tell us our	376
9: 9 when a **m** went to inquire of God, thus he	376
9:10 So they went unto the city where the **m** of	376
9:16 send thee a **m** out of the land of Benjamin,	376
9:17 Behold the **m** whom I spake to thee of:	376
10: 6 and shalt be turned into another **m**.	376
10:22 if the **m** should yet come thither.	376
10:25 all the people away, **every m** to his house.	376
10:27 of Belial said, How shall this *m* save us?	NIH
11: 3 then, *if there be* **no m** to save us, we will	369
11:13 shall not a **m** be put to death this day:	376
13: 2 the rest of the people he sent **every m** to	376
13:14 the LORD hath sought him a **m** after his	376
13:20 to sharpen **every m** his share, and his	376
14: 1 unto the **young m** that bare his armour,	5288
14: 6 Jonathan said to the **young m** that bare	5288
14:24 Cursed *be* the **m** that eateth *any* food until	376
14:26 but no **m** put his hand to his mouth:	369
14:28 Cursed *be* the **m** that eateth *any* food this	376
14:34 Bring me hither **every m** his ox,	376
14:34 **every m** his sheep, and slay *them* here,	376
14:34 all the people brought **every m** his ox with	376
14:36 and let us not leave a **m** of them.	376
14:39 there was not a **m** among all the people	NIH
14:52 Saul saw any strong **m**, or any valiant	376
14:52 or any valiant **m**, he took him unto him.	1121
15: 3 slay both **m** and woman, infant and	376
15:29 for he *is* not a **m**, that *he* should repent.	120
16: 7 for the LORD *seeth* not as **m** seeth; for man	120
16: 7 for **m** looketh on the outward appearance,	120
16:16 to seek out a **m**, *who is* a cunning player	376
16:17 Provide me now a **m** that can play well,	376
16:18 a mighty valiant **m**, and a man of war,	NIH
16:18 a mighty valiant **m**, and a **m** of war,	376
17: 8 choose you a **m** for you, and let him come	376
17:10 give me a **m**, that we may fight together.	376
17:12 the **m** went among men *for* an old man in	376
17:12 the man went among men *for* an **old m**	2204
17:24 when they saw the **m**, fled from him,	376
17:25 Have ye seen this **m** that is come up?	376
17:25 it shall be, *that* the **m** who killeth him	376
17:26 What shall be done to the **m** that killeth	376
17:27 So shall it be done to the **m** that killeth	376
17:33 a youth, and he a **m** of war from his youth.	376
17:41 that bare the shield *went* before him.	376
17:58 him, Whose son *art* thou, *thou* **young m**?	5288
18:23 seeing that I *am* a poor **m**,	376

1Sa 20:22 if I say thus unto the **young m**, Behold, 5958
21: 1 Why *art* thou alone, and no **m** with thee? 376
21: 2 Let no **m** know any thing of the business 376
21: 7 a *certain* **m** of the servants of Saul *was* 376
21:14 his servants, Lo, you see the **m** *is* mad: 376
21:15 to **play the mad m** in my presence? 7696
24:19 if a **m** find his enemy, will he let him go 376
25: 2 *was* a **m** in Maon, whose possessions 376
25: 2 the **m** *was* very great, and he had three 376
25: 3 Now the name of the **m** *was* Nabal; 376
25: 3 the **m** *was* churlish and evil *in* his doings; 376
25:10 that break away **every m** from his master. 376
25:13 his men, Gird you on **every m** his sword; 376
25:13 And they girded on **every m** his sword; 376
25:17 of Belial, that a **m** cannot speak to him. NIH
25:25 I pray thee, regard this **m** of Belial, 376
25:29 a **m** is risen to pursue thee, and to seek 120
26:12 **no m** saw *it*, nor knew *it*, neither awaked: 369
26:15 said to Abner, Art not thou a **valiant m**? 376
26:23 The LORD render to **every m** his 376
27: 3 and his men, **every m** with his household, 376
27: 9 left neither **m** nor woman alive, 376
27:11 David saved neither **m** nor woman alive, 376
28:14 she said, An old **m** cometh up; and he *is* 376
30: 6 **every m** for his sons and for his daughters: 376
30:13 he said, I *am* a **young m** of Egypt, 5288
30:17 there escaped not a **m** of them, save four 376
30:22 save *to* **every m** his wife and his children, 376
2Sa 1: 2 a **m** came out of the camp from Saul with 376
1: 5 David said unto the **young m** that told 5288
1: 6 the **young m** that told him said, As I 5288
1:13 David said unto the **young m** that told 5288
2: 3 bring up, **every m** with his household: 376
3:34 as a **m** falleth before wicked men, NIH
3:38 and a great **m** fallen this day in Israel? NIH
7:19 And *is* this the manner of **m**, O Lord GOD? 120
12: 2 The rich **m** had exceeding many flocks NIH
12: 3 poor **m** had nothing, save one little ewe NIH
12: 4 there came a traveller unto the rich **m**, 376
12: 4 to dress for the **wayfaring m** that was 732
12: 4 dressed it for the **m** that was come to him. 376
12: 5 anger was greatly kindled against the **m**; 376
12: 5 the **m** that hath done this *thing* shall surely 376
12: 7 Nathan said to David, Thou *art* the **m**. 376
13: 3 and Jonadab *was* a very subtil **m**. 376
13: 9 And they went out every **m** from him. 376
13:29 and **every m** gat him up upon his mule, 376
13:34 the **young m** that kept the watch lift up 5288
14:16 the hand of the **m** *that would* destroy me 376
14:21 bring the **young m** Absalom again. 5288
15: 2 *that when* any **m** that had a controversy 376
15: 3 *there is* **no m** deputed of the king to hear 369
15: 4 that **every m** which hath *any* suit or 376
15: 5 that when any **m** came nigh *to him* to do 376
15:30 *was* with him covered **every m** his head, 376
16: 5 thence came out a **m** of the family of 376
16: 7 thou bloody **m**, and thou man of Belial: 376
16: 7 thou bloody **m**, and thou **m** of Belial: 376
16: 8 thy mischief, because thou *art* a bloody **m**. 376
16:23 *was* as if a **m** had inquired at the oracle of 376
17: 3 the **m** whom thou seekest *is* as if all 376
17: 8 thy father *is* a **m** of war, and will not lodge 376
17:10 knoweth that thy father *is* a mighty **m**, NIH
18: 5 gently for my sake with the **young m**, 5288
18:10 a *certain* **m** saw *it*, and told Joab, and said, 376
18:11 Joab said unto the **m** that told him, 376
18:12 the **m** said unto Joab, Though I should 376
18:12 Beware *that* none *touch* the **young m** 5288
18:24 and looked, and behold a **m** running alone. 376
18:26 the watchman saw another **m** running: 376
18:26 and said, Behold *another* **m** running alone. 376
18:27 He *is* a good **m**, and cometh with good 376
18:29 king said, *Is* the **young m** Absalom safe? 5288
18:32 Cushi, *Is* the **young m** Absalom safe? 5288
18:32 to do *thee* hurt, be as *that* **young m** *is.* 5288
19: 8 for Israel had fled **every m** to his tent. 376
19:14 men of Judah, *even* as *the heart of* one **m**, 376
19:22 shall there **any m** be put to death *this* day 376
19:32 Now Barzillai *was* a very **aged m**, 2204
19:32 at Mahanaim; for he *was* a very great **m**. 376
20: 1 there happened to be there a **m** of Belial, 376
20: 1 of Jesse: **every m** to his tents, O Israel. 376
20: 2 So **every m** of Israel went up from after 376
20:12 when the **m** saw that all the people stood 376
20:21 a **m** of mount Ephraim, Sheba the son of 376
20:22 retired from the city, **every m** to his tent. 376
21: 4 ye *shalt* thou kill **any m** in Israel. 376
21: 5 The **m** that consumed us, and that devised 376
21:20 where was a **m** of *great* stature, that had 376
22:26 with the upright **m** thou wilt shew thyself 1368
22:49 hast delivered me from the violent **m**. 376
23: 1 and the **m** *who* was raised up on high, 1397
23: 7 the **m** *that* shall touch them must be 376
23:20 the son of a valiant **m**, of Kabzeel, who 376
23:21 he slew an Egyptian, a goodly **m**: 376
24:14 and let me not fall into the hand of **m**. 120
1Ki 1: 6 he also *was* a very goodly **m**; NIH
1:42 for thou *art* a valiant **m**, and bringest good 376
1:49 and rose up, and went **every m** his way. 376
1:52 If he will shew himself a worthy **m**, 1121
2: 2 strong therefore, and shew thyself a **m**; 376
2: 4 thee (said he) a **m** on the throne of Israel. 376
2: 9 for thou *art* a wise **m**, and knowest what 376
4: 7 **each m** *his* month in a year made 259
4:25 **every m** under his vine and under his fig 376

1Ki 4:27 Solomon's table, **every m** *in* his month: 376
4:28 **every m** according to his charge. 376
7:14 his father *was* a **m** of Tyre, a worker in 376
8:25 There shall not fail thee a **m** in my sight to 376
8:31 If **any m** trespass against his neighbour, 120
8:38 supplication soever be *made* by any **m**, 120
8:38 shall know **every m** the plague of his 376
8:39 give to **every m** according to his ways, 376
8:46 (for *there is* **no m** that sinneth not,) 120
9: 5 shall not fail thee a **m** upon the throne 376
10:25 they brought **every m** his present, vessels 376
11:28 the **m** Jeroboam *was* a mighty *man* of 376
11:28 the man Jeroboam *was* a mighty **m** of NIH
11:28 Solomon seeing the **young m** that he was 5288
12:22 word of God came unto Shemaiah the **m** 376
12:24 return **every m** to his house; for this thing 376
13: 1 there came a **m** of God out of Judah by 376
13: 4 heard the saying of the **m** of God, 376
13: 5 according to the sign which the **m** of God 376
13: 6 answered and said unto the **m** of God, 376
13: 6 And the **m** of God besought the LORD, 376
13: 7 the king said unto the **m** of God, 376
13: 8 the **m** of God said unto the king, If thou 376
13:11 told him all the works that the **m** of God 376
13:12 For his sons had seen what way the **m** of 376
13:14 went after the **m** of God, and found him 376
13:14 *Art* thou the **m** of God that camest from 376
13:21 he cried unto the **m** of God that came 376
13:26 It *is* the **m** of God, who was disobedient 376
13:29 the prophet took up the carcase of the **m** of 376
13:31 bury me in the sepulchre wherein the **m** of 376
14:10 as a **m** taketh away dung, till it be all gone. NIH
17:18 have I to do with thee, O thou **m** of God? 376
17:24 Now *by* this I know that thou *art* a **m** of 376
20: 7 and see how this **m** seeketh mischief: NIH
20:20 they slew every one his **m**: and the Syrians 376
20:24 **every m** out of his place, and put captains 376
20:28 there came a **m** of God, and spake unto 376
20:35 a certain **m** of the sons of the prophets said 376
20:35 pray thee. And the **m** refused to smite him. 376
20:37 he found another **m**, and said, Smite me, 376
20:37 the **m** smote him, so that in smiting he 376
20:39 a **m** turned aside, and brought a man unto 376
20:39 brought a **m** unto me, and said, Keep this 376
20:39 a man unto me, and said, Keep this **m**: 376
20:42 thou hast let go out of *thy* hand a **m** 376
22: 8 *There* is yet one **m**, Micaiah the son of 376
22:17 let them return **every m** to his house in 376
22:34 a *certain* **m** drew a bow at a venture, 376
22:36 **Every m** to his city, and every man to his 376
22:36 his city, and **every m** to his own country. 376
2Ki 1: 6 came a **m** up to meet us, and said unto 376
1: 7 What manner of **m** *was he* which came up 376
1: 8 *He was* a hairy **m**, and girt *with* a girdle of 376
1: 9 Thou **m** of God, the king hath said, 376
1:10 If I *be* a **m** of God, then let fire come down 376
1:11 answered and said unto him, O **m** of God, 376
1:12 and said unto them, If I *be* a **m** of God, 376
1:13 O **m** of God, I pray thee, let my life, 376
3:25 every good piece of land cast **every m** his 376
4: 7 that came and told the **m** of God. And he 376
4: 9 I perceive that this *is* a holy **m** of God, 376
4:16 she said, Nay, my lord, thou **m** of God, 376
4:21 and laid him on the bed of the **m** of God, 376
4:22 that I may run to the **m** of God, 376
4:25 came unto the **m** of God to mount Carmel. 376
4:25 pass, when the **m** of God saw her afar off, 376
4:27 when she came to the **m** of God to the hill, 376
4:27 the **m** of God said, Let her alone; for her 376
4:29 go *thy way:* if thou meet **any m**, salute him 376
4:40 they cried out, and said, O thou **m** of God, 376
4:42 And there came a **m** from Baal-shalisha, 376
4:42 the **m** of God bread of the firstfruits, 376
5: 1 was a great **m** with his master, 376
5: 1 he was also a mighty **m** in valour, NIH
5: 7 that this **m** doth send unto me to recover a NIH
5: 7 Send unto me to recover a **m** of his leprosy? 376
5: 8 when Elisha the **m** of God had heard that 376
5:14 according to the saying of the **m** of God: 376
5:15 he returned to the **m** of God, he and all his 376
5:20 the servant of Elisha the **m** of God, said, 376
5:26 not mine heart *with thee*, when the **m** 376
6: 2 take thence **every m** a beam, and let us 376
6: 6 the **m** of God said, Where fell it? And 376
6: 9 the **m** of God sent unto the king of Israel, 376
6:10 to the place which the **m** of God told him 376
6:15 to the servant of the **m** of God was risen 376
6:17 LORD opened the eyes of the **young m**; 5288
6:19 I will bring you to the **m** whom ye seek. 376
6:32 and *the king* sent a **m** from before him: 376
7: 2 the king leaned answered the **m** of God, 376
7: 5 of Syria, behold, *there was* no **m** there. 376
7:10 *there was* no **m** there, neither voice 376
7:10 neither voice of **m**, but horses tied, and 120
7:17 and he died, as the **m** of God had said, 376
7:18 came to pass as the **m** of God had spoken 376
7:19 *that* lord answered the **m** of God, and said, 376
8: 2 did after the saying of the **m** of God: 376
8: 4 with Gehazi the servant of the **m** of God, 376
8: 7 saying, The **m** of God is come hither. 376
8: 8 go, meet the **m** of God, and inquire of 376
8:11 he was ashamed: and the **m** of God wept. 376
9: 4 So the **young m**, *even* the young man 5288
9: 4 man, *even* the **young m** the prophet, 5288
9:11 Ye know the **m**, and his communication. 376

2Ki 9:13 took **every m** his garment, and put *it* under 376
10:21 that there was not a **m** left that came not. 376
11: 8 **every m** with his weapons in his hand: 376
11: 9 they took **every m** his men that were to 376
11:11 **every m** with his weapons in his hand, 376
12: 4 *account,* the money that *every* **m** is set at, 5315
12: 5 *it* to them, **every m** of his acquaintance: 376
13:19 And the **m** of God was wroth with him, 376
13:21 as they were burying a **m**, that behold, 376
13:21 cast the **m** into the sepulchre of Elisha: 376
13:21 when the **m** was let down, and touched 376
14: 6 **every m** shall be put to death for his own 376
14:12 and they fled **every m** to their tents. 376
15:20 of each **m** fifty shekels *of* silver, to give to 376
18:21 *even* upon Egypt, on which if a **m** lean, 376
18:31 and *then* eat ye **every m** of his own vine, 376
21:13 will wipe Jerusalem as *a* **m** wipeth a dish, NIH
22:15 God of Israel, Tell the **m** that sent you to 376
23:10 that no **m** might make his son or his 376
23:16 the LORD which the **m** of God proclaimed, 376
23:17 *It is* the sepulchre of the **m** of God, 376
23:18 Let him alone; let no **m** move his bones. 376
1Ch 11:22 the son of a valiant **m** of Kabzeel, who had 376
11:23 a **m** of *great* stature, five cubits *high;* and 376
12: 4 a mighty **m** among the thirty, and over NIH
12:28 a **young m** mighty of valour, and *of* his 5288
16: 3 both **m** and woman, to every one a loaf of 376
16:21 He suffered no **m** to do them wrong: yea, 376
16:43 the people departed **every m** to his house: 376
17:17 to the estate of a **m** of high degree, 120
20: 6 where was a **m** of *great* stature, whose 376
21:13 but let me not fall into the hand of **m**. 120
22: 9 be born to thee, who shall be a **m** of rest; 376
23: 3 by **man**, was thirty and eight thousand. NIH
23: 3 man by **m**, was thirty and eight thousand. 1397
23:14 Now *concerning* Moses the **m** of God, 376
27:32 *was* a counsellor, a wise **m**, and a scribe: 376
28: 3 because thou *hast been* a **m** of war, 376
28:21 willing skilful **m**, for any *manner of* NIH
29: 1 for the palace *is* not for **m**, but for 120
2Ch 2: 7 therefore a **m** cunning to work in gold, 376
2:13 now I have sent a cunning **m**, endued with 376
2:14 father *was* a **m** of Tyre, skilful to work in 376
6: 5 neither chose I **any m** to be a ruler over 376
6:16 There shall not fail thee a **m** in my sight to 376
6:22 If a **m** sin against his neighbour, and an 376
6:29 soever shall be *made* of any **m**, 120
6:30 render unto **every m** according unto all his 376
6:36 (for *there is* **no m** which sinneth not,) 120
7:18 There shall not fail thee a **m** *to be* ruler in 376
8:14 so had David the **m** of God commanded. 376
9:24 they brought **every m** his present, vessels 376
10:16 **every m** to your tents, O Israel: *and* now, 376
11: 2 LORD came to Shemaiah the **m** of God, 376
11: 4 return **every m** to his house, for this thing 376
14:11 *art* our God; let not **m** prevail against thee. 582
15:13 or great, whether **m** or woman. 376
17:17 Eliada a mighty **m** of valour, and with him NIH
18: 7 *There* is yet one **m**, by whom *we* may 376
18:16 *therefore* **every m** to his house in peace. 376
18:33 a *certain* **m** drew a bow at a venture, 376
18:33 therefore he said to *his* **chariot m**, 7395
19: 6 for ye judge not for **m**, but for the LORD, 120
20:27 **every m** of Judah and Jerusalem, 376
23: 7 **every m** with his weapons in his hand; 376
23: 8 took **every m** his men that were to come 376
23:10 having **every m** having his weapon in his hand, 376
25: 4 but **every m** shall die for his own sin. 376
25: 7 there came a **m** of God to him, saying, 376
25: 7 Amaziah said to the **m** of God, But what 376
25: 9 the **m** of God answered, The LORD is able 376
25:22 and they fled **every m** to his tent. 376
28: 7 Zichri, a mighty **m** of Ephraim, slew NIH
30:16 to the law of Moses the **m** of God: 376
31: 1 **every m** to his possession, into their own 376
31: 2 **every m** according to his service, the 376
32:19 *which were* the work of the hands of **m**. 120
34:23 of Israel, Tell ye the **m** that sent you to me, 376
36:17 had no compassion upon **young m** or 970
36:17 **old m**, or him that stooped for age: 2205
Ezr 3: 1 themselves together as one **m** to Jerusalem. 376
3: 2 as it is written in the law of Moses the **m** of 376
8:18 us they brought us a **m** of understanding, 376
Ne 1:11 and grant him mercy in the sight of this **m**. 376
2:10 **m** to seek the welfare of the children of 376
2:12 neither told I *any* **m** what my God had put 120
5:13 So God shake out every **m** from his house, 376
6:11 I said, Should such a **m** as I flee? and who 376
7: 2 for he *was* a faithful **m**, and feared God 376
8: 1 in *into* the street that *was* before the water 376
9:29 (which if a **m** do, he shall live in them;) 120
12:24 the commandment of David the **m** of God, 376
12:36 the musical instruments of David the **m** 376
Est 1:22 that every **m** should bear rule in his own 376
4:11 that whosoever, *whether* **m** or woman, 376
5:12 Esther the queen did let no **m** come in NIH
6: 6 What shall be done unto the **m** 376
6: 6 *For* the **m** whom the king delighteth to 376
6: 9 that they may array the **m** *withal* whom 376
6: 9 Thus shall it be done to the **m** whom 376
6:11 Thus shall it be done unto the **m** whom 376
6:11 with the king's ring, may no **m** reverse. 369
9: 2 no **m** could withstand them; for the fear of 376
9: 4 for *this* **m** Mordecai waxed greater and 376
Job 1: 1 There was a **m** in the land of Uz, 376

Job

1: 1 that **m** was perfect and upright, and one	376
1: 3 this **m** was the greatest of all the men of	376
1: 8 perfect and an upright **m**, one that feareth	376
2: 3 perfect and an upright **m**, one that feareth	376
2: 4 all that a **m** hath will he give for his life.	376
3: 3 *it was said,* There is a **child** conceived.	1397
3:23 *Why is light given* to a **m** whose way is	1397
4:17 Shall **mortal m** be more just than God?	582
4:17 shall a **m** be more pure than his Maker?	1397
5: 2 For wrath killeth the **foolish m,**	191
5: 7 Yet **m** is born unto trouble, as the sparks	120
5:17 happy *is* the **m** whom God correcteth:	582
7: 1 *Is there* not an appointed time to **m** upon	582
7:17 What *is* **m**, that thou shouldest magnify	582
8:20 God will not cast away a perfect **m**, neither	NIH
9: 2 truth: but how should **m** be just with God?	582
9:32 For *he is* not a **m**, as I *am, that* I should	376
10: 4 eyes of flesh? or seest thou as **m** seeth?	582
10: 5 thy days as the days of **m**? *are* thy years	582
11: 2 and should a **m** full of talk be justified?	376
11: 3 shall **no m** make *thee* ashamed?	369
11:12 For vain **m** would be wise, though man be	376
11:12 though **m** be born *like* a wild ass's colt.	120
12: 4 the just upright **m** *is* laughed to scorn.	NIH
12:14 cannot be built *again:* he shutteth up a **m**,	376
12:25 them to stagger like a drunken **m.**	NIH
13: 9 or as *one* **m** mocketh another, do ye *so*	NIH
14: 1 **M** *that is* born of a woman of few days,	120
14:10 **m** dieth, and wasteth away: yea, man	1397
14:10 **m** giveth up the ghost, and where *is* he?	120
14:12 So **m** lieth down, and riseth not: till	376
14:14 If a **m** die, shall he live *again?* all the days	1397
14:19 earth; and thou destroyest the hope of **m.**	582
15: 2 Should a wise **m** utter vain knowledge,	NIH
15: 7 *Art* thou the first **m** *that* was born?	120
15:14 What *is* **m**, that he should be clean?	582
15:16 much more abominable and filthy *is* **m**,	376
15:20 The wicked **m** travaileth with pain all his	NIH
15:28 *and in* houses which no **m** inhabiteth,	NIH
16:21 O that *one* might plead for a **m** with God,	1397
16:21 as a **m** *pleadeth* for his neighbour.	120+1121
17:10 for I cannot find *one* wise **m** among you.	NIH
20: 4 this of old, since **m** was placed upon earth,	120
20:21 therefore shall no **m** look for his goods.	NIH
20:29 *is* the portion of a wicked **m** from God,	120
21: 4 *As for me, is* my complaint to **m**? and if *it*	120
21:33 every **m** shall draw after him, as *there are*	120
22: 2 Can a **m** be profitable unto God, as he	1397
22: 8 *as for* the mighty **m**, he had the earth;	376
22: 8 earth; and the honourable **m** dwelt in it.	NIH
24:22 he riseth up, and no **m** *is* sure of life.	NIH
25: 4 How then can **m** be justified with God?	582
25: 6 How much less **m**, *that is* a worm?	582
25: 6 and the son of **m**, which *is* a worm?	120
27:13 *is* the portion of a wicked **m** with God,	120
27:19 The rich **m** shall lie down, but he shall not	NIH
28:13 **M** knoweth not the price thereof; neither	582
28:28 **m** he said, Behold, the fear of the Lord,	120
32: 8 *there is* a spirit in **m**: and the inspiration of	582
32:13 wisdom: God thrusteth him down, not **m.**	376
32:21 neither let me give flattering titles unto **m.**	120
33:12 answer thee, that God is greater than **m.**	582
33:14 yea twice, *yet* **m** perceiveth it not.	NIH
33:17 *he* may withdraw **m** *from his* purpose,	120
33:17 *from his* purpose, and hide pride from **m.**	1397
33:23 thousand, to shew unto **m** his uprightness:	120
33:26 he will render unto **m** his righteousness.	582
33:29 *things* worketh God oftentimes with **m**,	1397
34: 7 What **m** *is* like Job, *who* drinketh up	1397
34: 9 It profiteth a **m** nothing that he should	1397
34:11 For the work of a **m** shall he render unto	120
34:11 **every m** to find according to *his* ways.	376
34:14 If he set his heart upon **m**, *if* he gather	NIH
34:15 and **m** shall turn again unto dust.	120
34:21 For his eyes *are* upon the ways of **m**,	376
34:23 he will not lay upon **m** more *than right;*	376
34:29 *done* against a nation, or against a **m** only:	120
34:34 me, and let a wise **m** hearken unto me.	1397
35: 8 Thy wickedness *may hurt* a **m** as thou *art;*	376
35: 8 thy righteousness *may profit* the son of **m.**	120
36:25 Every **m** may see it; man may behold *it* afar	1167
36:25 man may see it; **m** may behold *it* afar off.	582
36:28 do drop *and* distil upon **m** abundantly.	120
37: 7 He sealeth up the hand of every **m**; that all	120
37:20 if a **m** speak, surely he shall be swallowed	376
38: 3 Gird up now thy loins like a **m**; for I will	1397
38:26 *where* no **m** *is;* on the wilderness,	376
38:26 *on the* wilderness, wherein *there is* no **m**;	120
40: 7 Gird up thy loins now like a **m**: I will	1397
42:11 **every m** also gave him a piece of money,	376

Ps

1: 1 Blessed *is* the **m** that walketh not in	376
5: 6 will abhor the bloody and deceitful **m.**	376
8: 4 What *is* **m**, that thou art mindful of him?	582
8: 4 and the son of **m**, that thou visitest him?	120
9:19 Arise, O Lord; let not **m** prevail:	582
10:15 the evil **m**: seek out his wickedness *till*	NIH
10:18 the **m** of the earth may no more oppress.	582
12: 1 Help, Lord; for the godly **m** ceaseth;	NIH
18:25 with an upright **m** thou wilt shew thyself	1399
18:48 hast delivered me from the violent **m.**	376
19: 5 *and* rejoiceth as a strong **m** to run a race.	NIH
22: 6 a worm, and no **m**; a reproach of men,	376
25:12 What **m** *is* he that feareth the Lord?	376
31:12 I am forgotten as a **dead m** out of mind:	4191
31:20 secret of thy presence from the pride of **m**:	376

Ps

32: 2 Blessed *is* the **m** unto whom the Lord	120
33:16 a mighty **m** is not delivered by much	NIH
34: 6 This poor **m** cried, and the Lord heard	NIH
34: 8 blessed *is* the **m** *that* trusteth in him.	1397
34:12 What **m** *is* he that desireth life,	376
36: 6 O Lord, thou preservest **m** and beast.	120
37: 7 of the **m** who bringeth wicked devices to	376
37:16 A little that a righteous **m** hath *is* better	NIH
37:23 The steps of a *good* **m** are ordered by	1397
37:37 Mark the perfect **m**, and behold the	NIH
37:37 the upright: for the end of *that* **m** *is* peace.	NIH
38:13 I, as a deaf **m**, heard not; and *I was* as a	NIH
38:13 *I was* as a dumb **m** *that* openeth not his	NIH
38:14 Thus I was as a **m** that heareth not,	376
39: 5 verily every **m** at his best state *is* altogether	120
39: 6 Surely **every m** walketh in a vain shew:	376
39:11 thou with rebukes dost correct **m** for	376
39:11 like a moth: surely every **m** *is* vanity.	120
40: 3 Blessed *is that* **m** that maketh the Lord	1397
43: 1 me from the deceitful and unjust **m.**	376
49:12 **M** *being* in honour abideth not:	120
49:20 **M** *that is* in honour, and understandeth	120
52: 1 mighty **m**? the goodness of God *endureth*	NIH
52: 7 *this is* the **m** *that* made not God his	1397
55:13 a **m** mine equal, my guide,	582
56: 1 for **m** would swallow me up; he fighting	582
56:11 will not be afraid what **m** can do unto me.	120
58:11 So that a **m** shall say, Verily *there is* a	120
60:11 from trouble: for vain *is* the help of **m.**	376
62: 3 long will ye imagine mischief against a **m**?	376
62:12 for thou renderest to *every* **m** according to	120
65: 4 Blessed *is* the **m** *whom* thou choosest,	NIH
71: 4 the hand of the unrighteous and cruel **m.**	NIH
74: 5 A **m** was famous according as he had lifted	NIH
74:22 remember how the foolish **m** reproacheth	NIH
76:10 Surely the wrath of **m** shall praise thee:	120
78:25 **M** did eat angels' food: he sent them meat	376
78:65 like a mighty **m** that shouteth by reason of	NIH
80:17 Let thy hand be upon the **m** of thy right	376
80:17 the son of **m** *whom* thou madest strong	120
84: 5 Blessed *is* the **m** whose strength *is* in thee;	120
84:12 blessed *is* the **m** that trusteth in thee.	120
87: 4 with Ethiopia; this **m** was born there.	NIH
87: 5 be said, This and that **m** was born in her:	376
87: 6 *up* the people, that this **m** was born there.	NIH
88: 4 the pit: I am as a **m** *that hath* no strength:	1397
89:48 What **m** *is he that* liveth, and shall not	1397
90: T A Prayer of Moses the **m** of God.	376
90: 3 Thou turnest **m** to destruction; and sayest,	582
92: 6 A brutish **m** knoweth not; neither doth a	376
94:10 he that teacheth **m** knowledge, *shall* not	120
94:11 The Lord knoweth the thoughts of **m**,	120
94:12 Blessed *is* the **m** whom thou chastenest,	1397
103:15 *As for* **m**, his days *are* as grass: as a flower	582
104:14 the cattle, and herb for the service of **m**:	120
104:15 wine *that* maketh glad the heart of **m**,	582
104:23 **M** goeth forth unto his work and to his	120
105:14 He suffered no **m** to do them wrong: yea,	120
105:14 He sent a **m** before them, *even* Joseph,	376
107:27 stagger like a drunken **m**, and are at their	NIH
108:12 from trouble: for vain *is* the help of **m.**	120
109: T Set thou a wicked **m** over him: and let	NIH
109:16 persecuted the poor and needy **m**, that *he*	NIH
112: 1 Blessed *is* the **m** *that* feareth the Lord,	376
112: 5 A good **m** sheweth favour, and lendeth:	376
118: 6 I will not fear: what can **m** do unto me?	120
118: 8 in the Lord than to put confidence in **m.**	120
119: 9 Wherewithal shall a **young m** cleanse his	5288
119:134 Deliver me from the oppression of **m**:	120
127: 4 As arrows *are* in the hand of a mighty **m**;	NIH
127: 5 Happy *is* the **m** that hath his quiver full of	1397
128: 4 thus shall the **m** be blessed that feareth	1397
135: 8 the firstborn of Egypt, both of **m** and beast.	120
140: 1 Deliver me, O Lord, from the evil **m**:	120
140: 1 evil man: preserve me from the violent **m**;	376
140: 4 wicked; preserve me from the violent **m**;	376
140:11 evil shall hunt the violent **m** to overthrow	NIH
142: 4 but *there was* no **m** that would know me:	369
142: 4 refuge failed me; no **m** cared for my soul.	369
143: 2 for in thy sight shall no **m** living be	NIH
144: 3 Lord, what *is* **m**, that thou takest	120
144: 3 *or* the son of **m**, that thou makest account	582
144: 4 **M** is like to vanity: his days *are* as a	120
146: 3 *nor* in the son of **m**, in whom *there is* no	120
147:10 he taketh not pleasure in the legs of a **m.**	376

Pr

1: 4 the **young m** knowledge and discretion.	5288
1: 5 A wise **m** will hear, and will increase	NIH
1: 5 **m** of understanding shall attain unto wise	NIH
1:24 out my hand, and no **m** regarded;	NIH
2:12 deliver thee from the way of the evil **m**,	NIH
2:12 from the **m** that speaketh froward things;	376
3: 4 understanding in the sight of God and **m.**	120
3:13 Happy *is* the **m** *that* findeth wisdom,	120
3:13 and the **m** *that* getteth understanding.	120
3:30 Strive not with a **m** without cause, if he	120
5:21 For the ways of **m** *are* before the eyes of	376
6:11 travelleth; and thy want as an armed **m.**	376
6:12 A naughty person, a wicked **m**, walketh	376
6:26 For by means of a whorish woman *a* **m** *is*	NIH
6:27 Can a **m** take fire in his bosom,	376
6:34 For jealousy *is* the rage of a **m**: therefore	1397
7: 7 a **young m** void of understanding,	5288
8: 4 I call; and my voice *is* to the sons of **m.**	120
8:34 Blessed *is* the **m** that heareth me, watching	120
9: 7 that rebuketh a wicked **m** *getteth* himself	NIH

Pr

9: 8 rebuke a wise **m**, and he will love thee.	NIH
9: 9 Give *instruction* to a wise **m**, and he will	NIH
9: 9 teach a just **m**, and he will increase in	NIH
10:11 mouth of a righteous **m** *is* a well of life:	NIH
10:23 but a **m** of understanding hath wisdom.	376
11: 7 When a wicked **m** dieth, *his* expectation	120
11:12 a **m** of understanding holdeth his peace.	376
11:17 merciful **m** doeth good to his own soul:	376
12: 2 A good **m** obtaineth favour of the Lord:	NIH
12: 2 a **m** of wicked devices will he condemn.	376
12: 3 **m** shall not be established by wickedness:	120
12: 8 A **m** shall be commended according to his	376
12:10 A righteous **m** regardeth the life of his	NIH
12:14 A **m** shall be satisfied *with* good by the	376
12:16 but a prudent **m** covereth shame.	NIH
12:23 A prudent **m** concealeth knowledge:	120
12:25 Heaviness in the heart of **m** maketh it	376
12:27 The slothful **m** roasteth not that which he	120
12:27 the substance of a diligent **m** *is* precious.	120
13: 2 **m** shall eat good by the fruit of *his* mouth:	NIH
13: 5 A righteous **m** hateth lying: but a wicked	376
13: 5 a wicked **m** is loathsome, and cometh to	NIH
13:16 Every prudent **m** dealeth with knowledge:	NIH
13:22 A good **m** leaveth an inheritance to *his*	NIH
14: 7 Go from the presence of a foolish **m**,	376
14:12 is a way which seemeth right unto a **m**,	376
14:14 a good **m** *shall be satisfied* from himself.	376
14:15 the prudent **m** looketh well to his going.	NIH
14:16 A wise **m** feareth, and departeth from evil:	376
14:17 and a **m** of wicked devices is hated.	376
15:18 A wrathful **m** stirreth up strife: but he that	376
15:19 The way of the slothful **m** *is* as a hedge of	376
15:20 but a foolish **m** despiseth his mother.	120
15:21 a **m** of understanding walketh uprightly.	376
15:23 A **m** hath joy by the answer of his mouth:	376
16: 1 The preparations of the heart in **m**,	120
16: 2 All the ways of a **m** *are* clean in his own	376
16:14 of death: but a wise **m** will pacify it.	376
16:25 is a way that seemeth right unto a **m**,	376
16:27 An ungodly **m** diggeth up evil: and in his	376
16:28 A froward **m** soweth strife: and a whisperer	376
16:29 A violent **m** enticeth his neighbour,	376
17:10 A reproof entereth more into a wise **m**	NIH
17:11 An evil **m** seeketh only rebellion: therefore	NIH
17:12 *Let* a bear robbed of her whelps meet a **m**,	120
17:18 A **m** void of understanding striketh hands,	120
17:23 A wicked **m** taketh a gift out of the bosom	NIH
17:27 a **m** of understanding is of an excellent	376
17:28 that shutteth his lips *is esteemed a* **m** of	NIH
18: 1 Through desire a **m**, having separated	376
18:12 destruction the heart of **m** is haughty,	376
18:14 The spirit of a **m** will sustain his infirmity;	376
18:24 A **m** that hath friends must shew himself	376
19: 3 The foolishness of **m** perverteth his way:	120
19: 6 every **m** *is* a friend to him that giveth gifts.	376
19:11 The discretion of a **m** deferreth his anger;	120
19:19 **m** of great wrath *shall* suffer punishment:	120
19:22 The desire of a **m** *is* his kindness: and a	120
19:22 and a poor **m** is better than a liar.	376
19:24 A slothful **m** hideth his hand in *his* bosom,	NIH
20: 3 *It is* an honour for a **m** to cease from strife:	376
20: 5 Counsel in the heart of **m** *is like* deep	376
20: 5 but a **m** of understanding will draw it out.	376
20: 6 but a faithful **m** who can find?	376
20: 7 The just **m** walketh in his integrity:	NIH
20:17 Bread of deceit *is* sweet to a **m**;	120
20:24 can a **m** then understand his own way?	120
20:25 *It is* a snare to the **m** *who* devoureth *that*	120
20:27 The spirit of **m** *is* the candle of the Lord,	120
21: 2 Every way of a **m** *is* right in his own eyes:	376
21: 8 The way of **m** *is* froward and strange:	376
21:12 The righteous **m** wisely considereth	376
21:16 The **m** that wandereth out of the way of	120
21:17 He that loveth pleasure *shall be* a poor **m**:	376
21:20 of the wise; but a foolish **m** spendeth it up.	376
21:22 A wise **m** scaleth the city of the mighty,	NIH
21:28 the **m** that heareth, speaketh constantly.	376
21:29 A wicked **m** hardeneth his face: but *as for*	376
22: 3 A prudent **m** foreseeth the evil,	NIH
22:13 The slothful **m** saith, *There is* a lion	NIH
22:24 Make no friendship with an angry **m**;	1167
22:24 and with a furious **m** thou shalt not go:	376
22:29 Seest thou a **m** diligent in his business?	376
23: 2 throat, if thou *be* a **m** given to appetite.	1167
23:21 and drowsiness shall clothe a **m** with rags.	NIH
24: 5 A wise **m** *is* strong; yea, a man of	1397
24: 5 a **m** of knowledge increaseth strength.	376
24:12 shall *not* he render to *every* **m** according to	120
24:15 O wicked **m**, against the dwelling of	NIH
24:16 For a just **m** falleth seven *times,* and	NIH
24:20 For there shall be no reward to the evil **m**;	NIH
24:26 *Every* **m** shall kiss *his* lips that giveth a	NIH
24:29 render to the **m** according to his work.	376
24:30 by the vineyard of the **m** void of	120
24:34 travel; and thy want as an armed **m.**	376
25:18 A **m** that beareth false witness against his	376
25:19 Confidence in an unfaithful **m** in time of	NIH
25:26 A righteous **m** falling down before	120
26:12 Seest thou a **m** wise in his own conceit?	376
26:13 The slothful **m** saith, *There is* a lion in	NIH
26:18 a mad **m** who casteth firebrands, arrows,	NIH
26:19 So is the **m** that deceiveth his neighbour,	376
26:21 fire; so *is* a contentious **m** to kindle strife.	376
27: 2 Let another **m** praise thee, and not thine	NIH
27: 8 so *is* a **m** that wandereth from his place.	376

M

Pr
27:12 A prudent **m** foreseeth the evil, — NIH
27:17 a **m** sharpeneth the countenance of his — 376
27:19 to face, so the heart of **m** to man. — 120
27:19 to face, so the heart of man to **m**. — 120
27:20 so the eyes of **m** are never satisfied. — 120
27:21 The furnace for gold; so *is a* **m** to his praise. — NIH
28: 1 The wicked flee when no **m** pursueth: — 369
28: 2 by a **m** of understanding *and* knowledge — 376
28: 3 A poor **m** that oppresseth the poor *is like* — 1397
28:11 The rich **m** *is* wise in his own conceit; — 376
28:12 but when the wicked rise, a **m** is hidden. — 120
28:14 Happy *is* the **m** that feareth alway: — 120
28:17 A **m** that doeth violence to the blood of — 120
28:17 shall flee to the pit; let no **m** stay him. — NIH
28:20 A faithful **m** shall abound with blessings: — 376
28:21 for for a piece of bread *that* **m** will — 1397
28:23 that rebuketh a **m**, afterwards shall find — 120
29: 5 **m** that flattereth his neighbour spreadeth — 1397
29: 6 In the transgression of an evil **m** *there is a* — 376
29: 9 If a wise man contendeth with a foolish man, — 376
29: 9 If a wise man contendeth with a foolish **m**, — 376
29:11 but a wise **m** keepeth it in *till* afterwards — NIH
29:13 poor and the deceitful **m** meet together: — 376
29:20 Seest thou a **m** that is hasty in his words? — 376
29:22 An angry **m** stirreth up strife, and a furious — 376
29:22 a furious **m** aboundeth in transgression. — 1167
29:25 The fear of **m** bringeth a snare: — 120
29:27 An unjust **m** is an abomination to the just: — 376
30: 1 the **m** spake unto Ithiel, even unto Ithiel — 1397
30: 2 Surely I *am* more brutish than *any* **m**, — 376
30: 2 and have not the understanding of a **m**. — 120
30:19 the sea; and the way of a **m** with a maid. — 1397

Ecc
1: 3 What profit hath a **m** of all his labour — 120
1: 8 **m** cannot utter *it*: the eye is not satisfied — 376
1:13 to the sons of **m** to be exercised therewith. — 120
2:12 for what *can* the **m** *do* that cometh after — 120
2:16 And how dieth the wise **m**? as the fool. — NIH
2:18 I should leave it unto the **m** that shall be — 120
2:19 knoweth whether he shall be a wise **m** — NIH
2:21 there is a **m** whose labour *is* in wisdom, — 120
2:21 yet to a **m** that hath not laboured therein — 120
2:22 For what hath **m** of all his labour, and of — 120
2:24 *There is* nothing better for a **m**, *than* that — 120
2:26 For *God* giveth to a **m** that *is* good in his — 120
3:11 that no **m** can find out the work that God — 120
3:12 *a* **m** to rejoice, and to do good in his life. — NIH
3:13 also that every **m** should eat and drink, — 120
3:19 a **m** hath no preeminence above a beast: — 120
3:21 Who knoweth the spirit of **m** that — 120+1121
3:22 than that a **m** should rejoice in his own — 120
4: 4 that for this a **m** is envied of his neighbour. — 376
5:12 The sleep of a labouring **m** *is* sweet, — NIH
5:19 Every **m** also to whom God hath given — 120
6: 2 A **m** to whom God hath given riches, — 120
6: 3 If a **m** beget an hundred *children*, and — 376
6: 7 All the labour of **m** is for his mouth, — 120
6:10 already, and *it is* known that it *is* **m**: — 120
6:11 that increase vanity, what *is* **m** the better? — 120
6:12 For who knoweth what *is* good for **m** in — 120
6:12 who can tell a **m** what shall be after him — 120
7: 5 than for a **m** to hear the song of fools. — 376
7: 7 Surely oppression maketh a wise **m** mad; — NIH
7:14 the end that **m** should find nothing after — 120
7:15 there is a just **m** that perisheth in his — 120
7:15 is a wicked **m** that prolongeth *his life* — NIH
7:20 For *there is* not a just **m** upon earth, — 120
7:28 one **m** among a thousand have I found; — 120
7:29 I found, that God hath made **m** upright; — 120
8: 1 Who *is* as the wise **m**? and who knoweth — NIH
8: 6 the misery of **m** *is* great upon him. — 120
8: 8 *is* no **m** that hath power over the spirit — 120
8: 9 *there is* a time wherein one **m** ruleth over — 120
8:15 a **m** hath no better *thing* under the sun, — 120
8:17 that a **m** cannot find out the work that is — 120
8:17 because though a **m** labour to seek *it* out, — 120
8:17 though a wise **m** think to know *it*, yet — NIH
9: 1 no **m** knoweth either love or hatred *by* all — 120
9:12 For **m** also knoweth not his time: — 120
9:15 Now there was found in it a poor wise **m**, — 376
9:15 no **m** remembered that *same* poor man. — 120
9:15 no man remembered that *same* poor **m**. — 376
10:14 a **m** cannot tell what shall be; and what — 120
11: 8 if a **m** live many years, *and* rejoice in them — 120
11: 9 Rejoice, O *young* **m**, in thy youth; — 970
12: 5 because **m** goeth to his long home, — 120
12:13 for this *is* the whole *duty* of **m**. — 120

SS
3: 8 every **m** *hath* his sword upon his thigh — 376
8: 7 if a **m** would give all the substance of his — 376

Isa
2: 9 mean **m** boweth down, and the great man — 120
2: 9 and the great **m** humbleth himself; — 376
2:11 The lofty looks of **m** shall be humbled, — 120
2:17 the loftiness of **m** shall be bowed down, — 120
2:20 In that day a **m** shall cast his idols of silver, — 120
2:22 Cease ye from **m**, whose breath *is* in his — 120
3: 2 The mighty **m**, and the man of war, — NIH
3: 2 The mighty *man*, and the man of war, — 376
3: 3 the honourable **m**, and the counsellor, — NIH
3: 6 When a **m** shall take hold of his brother *of* — 376
4: 1 seven women shall take hold of one **m**, — 376
5:15 And the mean **m** shall be brought down, — 120
5:15 the mighty **m** shall be humbled, and the — 376
6: 5 because I *am* a **m** of unclean lips, — 376
6:11 the houses without **m**, and the land be — 120
7:21 *that* a **m** shall nourish a young cow, — 376
9:19 of the fire: no **m** shall spare his brother. — 376

Isa
9:20 they shall eat **every m** the flesh of his own — 376
10:13 put down the inhabitants like a valiant **m**: — NIH
13:12 I will make a **m** more precious than fine — 582
13:12 even a **m** than the golden wedge of Ophir. — 120
13:14 and as a sheep that no **m** taketh up: — NIH
13:14 they shall **every m** turn to his own people, — 376
14:16 *Is* this the **m** that made the earth to — 376
17: 7 At that day shall a **m** look to his Maker, — 120
19:14 as a drunken **m** staggereth in his vomit. — NIH
24:10 house is shut up, that no **m** may come in. — NIH
28:20 For the bed is shorter than that a **m** can — NIH
29: 8 It shall even be as when a hungry **m** — NIH
29: 8 or as when a thirsty **m** dreameth, — NIH
29:21 That make a **m** an offender for a word, — 120
31: 7 For in that day **every m** shall cast away — 376
31: 8 fall with the sword, not of a mighty **m**; — 376
31: 8 the sword, not of a mean **m**, shall devour — 120
32: 2 **m** shall be as a hiding place from the wind, — 376
33: 8 lie waste, the **wayfaring m** ceaseth: — 734+5674
33: 8 despised the cities, he regardeth no **m**. — 582
35: 6 shall the lame **m** leap as a hart, — NIH
36: 6 if a **m** lean, it will go into his hand, — 376
38:11 I shall behold **m** no more with — 376
41: 2 Who raised up the righteous **m** from — 376
41:28 For I beheld, and *there was* no **m**; — 376
42:13 The LORD shall go forth as a mighty **m**, — NIH
42:13 he shall stir up jealousy like a **m** of war: — 376
44:13 maketh it after the figure of a **m**, — 376
44:13 of a man, according to the beauty of a **m**; — 120
44:15 it be for a **m** to burn: for he will take — 120
45:12 made the earth, and created **m** upon it: — 120
46:11 the **m** that executeth my counsel from a — 376
47: 3 and I will not meet *thee* as a **m**. — 120
49: 7 his Holy One, to him whom **m** despiseth, — 5315
50: 2 when I came, *was there* no **m**? — 376
51:12 thou shouldest be afraid of a **m** *that* shall — 582
51:12 of the son of **m** which shall be made *as* — 120
52:14 his visage *was* so marred more than *any* **m**, — 376
53: 3 a **m** of sorrows, and acquainted with grief: — 376
55: 7 way, and the unrighteous **m** his thoughts: — 376
56: 2 Blessed *is* the **m** that doeth this, and the — 582
56: 2 and the son of **m** *that* layeth hold on it; — 120
57: 1 and no **m** layeth *it* to heart: — 376
58: 5 a day for a **m** to afflict his soul? *is it* to bow — 120
59:16 he saw that *there was* no **m**, — 376
60:15 that no **m** went through *thee*, I will make — 369
62: 5 For *as a* **young m** marrieth a virgin, — 970
65:20 nor an **old m** that hath not filled his days: — 2205
66: 2 to this **m** will I look, *even to him that is* — NIH
66: 3 He that killeth an ox *is as if* he slew a **m**; — 376
66: 7 came, she was delivered of a **m child**. — 2145

Jer
2: 6 through a land that no **m** passed through, — 376
2: 6 passed through, and where no **m** dwelt? — 120
3: 1 If a **m** put away his wife, and she go from — 376
4:25 lo, *there was* no **m**, and all the birds of — 120
4:29 be forsaken, and not a **m** dwell therein. — 376
5: 1 broad places thereof, if ye can find a **m**, — 376
5: 1 throughly execute judgment between a **m** — 376
7:20 upon **m**, and upon beast, and upon the — 376
8: 6 no **m** repented him of his wickedness, — 376
9:12 Who *is* the wise **m**, that may understand — 376
9:23 Let not the wise **m** glory in his wisdom, — NIH
9:23 let the mighty **m** glory in his might, — NIH
9:23 let not the rich **m** glory in his riches: — NIH
10:14 Every **m** is brutish in *his* knowledge; — 120
10:23 know that the way of **m** is not in himself: — 376
10:23 not in **m** that walketh to direct his steps. — 376
11: 3 Cursed *be* the **m** that obeyeth not the — 376
12:11 because no **m** layeth *it* to heart. — 120
12:15 **every m** to his heritage, and every man to — 376
12:15 to his heritage, and **every m** to his land. — 376
13:11 as the girdle cleaveth to the loins of a **m**, — 376
14: 8 as a **wayfaring m** *that* turneth aside to — 732
14: 9 Why shouldest thou be as a **m** astonied, — 376
14: 9 as a mighty **m** *that* cannot save? — NIH
15:10 that thou hast borne me a **m** of strife and — 376
15:10 and a **m** of contention to the whole earth! — 376
16:20 Shall a **m** make gods unto himself, — 120
17: 5 Cursed *be* the **m** that trusteth in man, — 1397
17: 5 Cursed *be* the man that trusteth in **m**, — 120
17: 7 Blessed *is* the **m** that trusteth in — 1397
17:10 to give **every m** according to his ways, — 376
18:14 Will a **m** leave the snow of Lebanon — NIH
20:15 Cursed *be* the **m** who brought tidings to — 376
20:15 saying, A **m** child is born unto thee; — 2145
20:16 let that **m** be as the cities which the LORD — 376
21: 6 inhabitants of this city, both **m** and beast: — 120
22: 8 they shall say **every m** to his neighbour, — 376
22:28 *Is* this **m** Coniah a despised broken idol? — 376
22:30 saith the LORD, Write ye this **m** childless, — 376
22:30 a **m** *that* shall not prosper in his days: — 1397
22:30 for no **m** of his seed shall prosper, — 376
23: 9 I am like a drunken **m**, and like a man — 376
23: 9 like a **m** whom wine hath overcome, — 1397
23:27 which they tell **every m** to his neighbour, — 376
23:34 I will even punish that **m** and his house. — 376
26: 3 and turn **every m** from his evil way, — 376
26:11 people, saying, This **m** *is* worthy to die; — 376
26:16 the prophets; This **m** *is* not worthy to die: — 376
26:20 there was also a **m** that prophesied in — 120
27: 5 the **m** and the beast that *are* upon the — 120
29:26 every **m** *that is* mad, and maketh himself — 376
29:32 he shall not have a **m** to dwell among this — 376
30: 6 see whether a **m** doth travail with child? — 2145
30: 6 do I see every **m** *with* his hands — 1397

Jer
30:17 This *is* Zion, whom no **m** seeketh after. — 369
31:22 in the earth, A woman shall compass a **m**. — 1397
31:27 the house of Judah *with* the seed of **m**, — 120
31:30 every **m** that eateth the sour grape, his — 120
31:34 they shall teach no more **every m** his — 376
31:34 **every m** his brother, saying, Know — 376
32:43 ye say, *It is* desolate without **m** or beast; — 120
33:10 which ye say *shall be* desolate without **m** — 120
33:10 without **m**, and without inhabitant, — 120
33:12 *which is* desolate without **m** and — 120
33:17 David shall never want a **m** to sit upon — 376
33:18 shall the priests the Levites want a **m** — 376
34: 9 That **every m** should let his manservant, — 376
34: 9 **every m** his maidservant, *being* a Hebrew — 376
34:14 the end of seven years let ye go **every m** — 376
34:15 in proclaiming liberty **every m** to his — 376
34:16 caused **every m** his servant, and every — 376
34:16 his servant, and **every m** his handmaid, — 376
34:17 brother, and **every m** to his neighbour: — 376
35: 4 of Hanan, the son of Igdaliah, a **m** of God, — 376
35:15 Return ye now **every m** from his evil way, — 376
35:19 not want a **m** to stand before me for ever. — 376
36: 3 that they may return **every m** from his — 376
36:19 Jeremiah, and let no **m** know where ye *be*. — 376
36:29 shall cause to cease from thence **m** and — 120
37:10 should they rise up **every m** in his tent, — 376
38: 4 beseech thee, let this **m** be put to death: — 376
38: 4 for this **m** seeketh not the welfare of this — 376
38:24 Let no **m** know of these words, — 376
40:15 no **m** shall know *it*: wherefore should he — 376
41: 4 *he* had slain Gedaliah, and no **m** knew *it*, — 376
42: 2 a desolation, and no **m** dwelleth therein, — 369
44: 7 to cut off from you **m** and woman, child — 120
44:26 of any **m** of Judah in all the land of Egypt, — 376
46: 6 swift flee away, nor the mighty **m** escape; — NIH
46:12 for the mighty **m** hath stumbled against — NIH
49: 5 ye shall be driven out **every m** right forth; — 376
49:18 saith the LORD, no **m** shall abide there, — 376
49:18 neither shall a son of **m** dwell in it. — 120
49:19 who *is* a chosen **m**, *that* I may appoint — NIH
49:33 there shall no **m** abide there, nor *any* son — 376
49:33 abide there, nor *any* son of **m** dwell in it. — 120
50: 3 they shall depart, both **m** and beast. — 120
50: 9 expert **m**; none shall return in vain. — NIH
50:40 shall no **m** abide there, neither shall any — 376
50:40 neither shall any son of **m** dwell therein. — 376
50:42 array, like a **m** to the battle, against thee, — 376
50:44 who *is* a chosen **m**, *that* I may appoint — 376
51: 6 of Babylon, and deliver **every m** his soul: — 376
51:17 Every **m** is brutish by his knowledge; — 120
51:22 With thee also will I break in pieces **m** and — 376
51:22 thee will I break in pieces the **young m** — 970
51:43 wilderness, a land wherein no **m** dwelleth, — 120
51:43 neither doth *any* son of **m** pass thereby. — 120
51:45 deliver ye **every m** his soul from the fierce — 376
51:62 neither **m** nor beast, but that it shall be — 120

La
1: 1 I *am* the **m** that hath seen affliction by — 1397
3:26 *It is* good that a **m** *should* both hope and — NIH
3:27 *It is* good for a **m** that he bear the yoke in — 1397
3:35 To turn aside the right of a **m** before — 1397
3:36 To subvert a **m** in his cause, the Lord — 120
3:39 Wherefore doth a living **m** complain, — 120
3:39 a **m** for the punishment of his sins? — 1397

Eze
4: 4 bread, *and* no **m** breaketh *it* unto them. — 369
1: 5 they had the likeness of a **m**. — 120
1: 8 *had* the hands of a **m** under their wings — 120
1:10 they four had the face of a **m**, and the face — 120
1:26 as the appearance of a **m** above upon it. — 120
2: 1 Son of **m**, stand upon thy feet, and I will — 120
2: 3 he said unto me, Son of **m**, I send thee to — 120
2: 6 thou, son of **m**, be not afraid of them, — 120
2: 8 thou, son of **m**, hear what I say unto thee; — 120
3: 1 unto me, Son of **m**, eat that thou findest; — 120
3: 3 he said unto me, Son of **m**, cause thy belly — 120
3: 4 he said unto me, Son of **m**, go, get thee — 120
3:10 Moreover he said unto me, Son of **m**, all — 120
3:17 Son of **m**, I have made thee a watchman — 120
3:18 same wicked **m** shall die in his iniquity; — NIH
3:20 When a righteous **m** doth turn from his — NIH
3:21 if thou warn the righteous **m**, — NIH
3:25 thou, O son of **m**, behold, they shall put — 120
4: 1 Thou also, son of **m**, take thee a tile, — 120
4:12 bake it with dung that cometh out of **m**, — 120
4:16 he said unto me, Son of **m**, behold, — 120
5: 1 thou, son of **m**, take thee a sharp knife, — 120
6: 2 Son of **m**, set thy face towards the — 120
7: 2 Also, thou son of **m**, thus saith the Lord — 120
8: 5 he unto me, Son of **m**, lift up thine eyes — 120
8: 6 me, Son of **m**, seest thou what they do? — 120
8: 8 unto me, Son of **m**, dig now in the wall: — 120
8:11 with **every m** his censer in his hand; — 376
8:12 said he unto me, Son of **m**, hast thou seen — 120
8:12 **every m** in the chambers of his imagery? — 376
8:15 unto me, Hast thou seen *this*, O son of **m**? — 120
8:17 unto me, Hast thou seen *this*, O son of **m**? — 120
9: 1 even **every m** *with* his destroying weapon — 376
9: 2 **every m** a slaughter weapon in his hand; — 376
9: 2 one **m** among them *was* clothed *with* linen, — 376
9: 3 he called to the **m** clothed *with* linen, — 376
9: 6 come not near any **m** upon whom *is* — 376
9:11 the **m** clothed with linen, which *had* — 376
10: 2 he spake unto the **m** clothed with linen, — 376
10: 3 side of the house, when the **m** went in; — 376
10: 6 when he had commanded the **m** clothed — 376
10:14 and the second face *was* the face of a **m**, — 120

M

Col 1	Col 2	Col 3

Eze 10:21 the likeness of the hands of a **m** *was* under 120
11: 2 he unto me, Son of **m**, these *are* the men 120
11: 4 against them, prophesy, O son of **m**. 120
11:15 Son of **m**, thy brethren, *even* thy brethren, 120
12: 2 Son of **m**, thou dwellest in the midst of a 120
12: 3 Therefore thou son of **m**, prepare thee stuff 120
12: 9 Son of **m**, hath not the house of Israel, 120
12:18 Son of **m**, eat thy bread with quaking, 120
12:22 Son of **m**, what *is* that proverb *that* ye 120
12:27 Son of **m**, behold, *they of* the house of 120
13: 2 Son of **m**, prophesy against the prophets 120
13:17 Likewise thou son of **m**, set thy face against 120
14: 3 these men have set up their idols 120
14: 4 **Every m** of the house of Israel that 376+376
14: 8 I will set my face against that **m**, 376
14:13 Son of **m**, when the land sinneth against 120
14:13 and will cut off **m** and beast from it: 120
14:15 that **no m** may pass through because of 1097
14:17 so that I cut off **m** and beast from it: 120
14:19 it in blood, to cut off from it **m** and beast: 120
14:21 to cut off from it **m** and beast? 120
15: 2 Son of **m**, What is the vine tree more than 120
16: 2 Son of **m**, cause Jerusalem to know her 120
17: 2 Son of **m**, put forth a riddle, and speak a 120
18: 5 if a **m** be just, and do that which is lawful 376
18: 8 executed true judgment between **m** and 376
18: 8 true judgment between man and **m**, 376
18:24 abominations that the wicked **m** doeth, NIH
18:26 When a righteous **m** turneth away from NIH
18:27 when the wicked **m** turneth away from NIH
20: 3 Son of **m**, speak unto the elders of Israel, 120
20: 4 Wilt thou judge them, son of **m**, wilt thou 120
20: 7 Cast ye away **every m** the abominations 376
20: 8 they did not **every m** cast away 376
20:11 *if* a **m** do, he shall even live in them. 120
20:13 *if* a **m** do, he shall even live in them; 120
20:21 *if* a **m** do, he shall even live in them; 120
20:27 Therefore, son of **m**, speak unto the house 120
20:46 Son of **m**, set thy face toward the south, 120
21: 2 Son of **m**, set thy face toward Jerusalem, 120
21: 6 Sigh therefore, thou son of **m**, with 120
21: 9 Son of **m**, prophesy, and say, Thus saith 120
21:12 and howl, son of **m**: for it shall be upon 120
21:14 son of **m**, prophesy, and smite *thine* hands 120
21:19 thou son of **m**, appoint thee two ways, 120
21:28 son of **m**, prophesy and say, Thus saith 120
22: 2 Now, thou son of **m**, wilt thou judge, wilt 120
22:18 Son of **m**, the house of Israel is to me 120
22:24 Son of **m**, say unto her, Thou *art* the land 120
22:30 I sought for a **m** among them, that *should* 376
23: 2 Son of **m**, there were two women, 120
23:36 Son of **m**, wilt thou judge Aholah and 120
24: 2 Son of **m**, write thee the name of the day, 120
24:16 Son of **m**, behold, I take away from thee 120
24:25 thou son of **m**, *shall it* not *be* in the day 120
25: 2 Son of **m**, set thy face against 120
25:13 and will cut off **m** and beast from it; 120
26: 2 Son of **m**, because that Tyrus hath said 120
27: 2 thou son of **m**, take up a lamentation 120
28: 2 Son of **m**, say unto the prince of Tyrus, 120
28: 2 thou *art* a **m**, and not God, though thou 120
28: 9 thou *shalt be* a **m**, and no God, in the hand 120
28:12 Son of **m**, take up a lamentation upon 120
28:21 Son of **m**, set thy face against Zidon, 120
29: 2 Son of **m**, set thy face against Pharaoh king 120
29: 8 and cut off **m** and beast out of thee. 120
29:11 No foot of **m** shall pass through it, nor foot 120
29:18 Son of **m**, Nebuchadrezzar king of Babylon 120
30: 2 Son of **m**, prophesy and say, Thus saith 120
30:21 Son of **m**, I have broken the arm of 120
30:24 the groanings of a deadly wounded **m**. NIH
31: 2 Son of **m**, speak unto Pharaoh king of 120
32: 2 Son of **m**, take up a lamentation for 120
32:10 **every m** for his own life, in the day of thy 376
32:13 neither shall the foot of **m** trouble them 120
32:18 Son of **m**, wail for the multitude of Egypt, 120
33: 2 Son of **m**, speak to the children of thy 120
33: 2 if the people of the land take a **m** of their 376
33: 7 So thou, O son of **m**, I have set thee a 120
33: 8 O wicked **m**, thou shalt surely die; NIH
33: 8 that wicked **m** shall die in his iniquity; NIH
33:10 Therefore, O thou son of **m**, speak unto 120
33:12 Therefore, thou son of **m**, say unto 120
33:24 Son of **m**, they that inhabit those wastes of 120
33:30 Also, thou son of **m**, the children of thy 120
34: 2 Son of **m**, prophesy against the shepherds 120
35: 2 Son of **m**, set thy face against mount Seir, 120
36: 1 Also, thou son of **m**, prophesy unto 120
36:11 I will multiply upon you **m** and beast; 120
36:17 Son of **m**, when the house of Israel dwelt 120
37: 3 unto me, Son of **m**, can these bones live? 120
37: 9 prophesy, son of **m**, and say to the wind, 120
37:11 said unto me, Son of **m**, these bones *are* 120
37:16 Moreover, thou son of **m**, take thee one 120
38: 2 Son of **m**, set thy face against Gog, the 120
38:14 son of **m**, prophesy and say unto Gog, 120
39: 1 Therefore thou son of **m**, prophesy against 120
39:17 thou son of **m**, thus saith the Lord GOD; 120
40: 3 me thither, and, behold, *there was* a **m**, 376
40: 4 the **m** said unto me, Son of man, behold 376
40: 4 Son of **m**, behold with thine eyes, 120
41:19 that the face of a **m** *was* toward the palm 120
43: 6 out of the house; and *the* **m** stood by me. 376
43: 7 said unto me, Son of **m**, the place of my 120
43:10 son of **m**, shew the house to the house 120

Eze 43:18 he said unto me, Son of **m**, thus saith 120
44: 2 be opened, and no **m** shall enter in by it; 376
44: 5 Son of **m**, mark well, and behold with 120
46:18 that my people be not scattered **every m** 376
47: 3 when the **m** that had the line in his hand 376
47: 6 he said unto me, Son of **m**, hast thou seen 120
47:20 till *a* **m** come over against Hamath. NIH

Da 2:10 There is not a **m** upon the earth that can 606
2:25 I have found a **m** of the captives of Judah, 1400
2:48 the king made Daniel a great **m**, NIH
3:10 that every **m** that shall hear the sound of 606
5:11 There is a **m** in thy kingdom, in whom *is* 1400
6: 7 a petition of any God or **m** for thirty days, 606
6:12 every **m** that shall ask *a petition* of any 606
6:12 of any God or **m** within thirty days, 606
7: 4 made stand upon the feet as a **m**, 606
8: 4 in this horn *were* eyes like the eyes of **m**, 606
7:13 like the Son of **m** came with the clouds 606
8:15 before me as the appearance of a **m**. 1397
8:16 make this **m** to understand the vision. NIH
8:17 said unto me, Understand, O son of **m**: 120
9:21 speaking in prayer, even the **m** Gabriel, 376
10: 5 and behold, a certain **m** clothed *in* linen, 376
10:11 unto me, O Daniel, a **m** greatly beloved, 376
10:18 me *one* like the appearance of a **m**, 120
10:19 said, O **m** greatly beloved, fear not: peace 376
12: 6 *one* said to the **m** clothed in linen, 376
12: 7 I heard the **m** clothed in linen, which *was* 376

Hos 3: 3 and thou shalt not be for *another* **m**: 376
4: 4 Yet let no **m** strive, nor reprove another: 376
6: 9 as troops *of robbers* wait for a **m**, 376
9: 7 the spiritual **m** *is* mad, for the multitude of 376
9:12 *that there shall* not *be* a **m** *left*: yea, 120
11: 4 I drew them with cords of a **m**, with 120
11: 9 for I *am* God, and not **m**; the Holy One in 376

Am 2: 7 a **m** and his father will go in unto the 376
4:13 and declareth unto **m** what *is* his thought, 376
5:19 As if a **m** did flee from a lion, and a bear 376

Jnh 1: 5 cried **every m** unto his god, and cast forth 376
3: 7 his nobles, saying, Let neither **m** nor beast, 120
3: 8 let **m** and beast be covered with sackcloth, 120

Mic 2: 2 so they oppress a **m** and his house, even a 1397
2: 2 and his house, even a **m** and his heritage. 376
2:11 If a **m** walking *in* the spirit and falsehood 376
4: 4 But they shall sit **every m** under his vine 376
5: 5 this **m** shall be *the* peace, when the NIH
5: 7 upon the grass, that tarrieth not for **m**, 376
6: 8 He hath shewed thee, O **m**, what *is* good; 120
6: 9 and *the* **m** *of* wisdom shall see thy name: NIH
7: 2 The good **m** is perished out of the earth: NIH
7: 2 they hunt **every m** his brother with a net. 376
7: 3 the great **m**, he uttereth his mischievous NIH

Na 3:18 the mountains, and no **m** gathereth *them*. NIH

Hab 1:13 the **m** that *is* more righteous than he? NIH
2: 5 *is* a proud **m**, neither keepeth at home, 1397

Zep 1: 3 will consume **m** and beast; I will consume 120
1: 3 I will cut off **m** from off the land, saith 120
1:14 the mighty **m** shall cry there bitterly. NIH
3: 6 cities are destroyed, so that there is no **m**, 376

Hag 1: 9 and ye run **every m** unto his own house. 376

Zec 1: 8 and behold a **m** riding upon a red horse, 376
1:10 the **m** that stood among the myrtle trees 376
1:21 so that no **m** did lift up his head: 376
2: 1 a **m** with a measuring line in his hand. 376
2: 4 Run, speak to this **young m**, saying, 5288
3:10 shall ye call **every m** his neighbour, under 376
4: 1 as a **m** that is wakened out of his sleep, 376
6:12 the **m** whose name *is* The BRANCH; 376
7: 9 and compassions **every m** to his brother: 376
7:14 that no **m** passed through nor returned: NIH
8: 4 **every m** with his staff in his hand for very 376
8:10 before these days there was no hire for **m**, 120
8:16 ye **every m** the truth to his neighbour; 376
9: 1 when the eyes of **m**, as of all the tribes of 120
9:13 made thee as the sword of a mighty **m**. NIH
10: 7 *they of* Ephraim shall be like a mighty **m**, NIH
12: 1 and formeth the spirit of **m** within him. 120
13: 5 for **m** taught me *to keep* cattle from my 120
13: 7 and against the **m** that is my fellow, 1397

Mal 2:10 why do we deal treacherously **every m** 376
2:12 The LORD will cut off the **m** that doth this, 376
3: 8 Will a **m** rob God? Yet ye *have* robbed me. 120
3:17 as a **m** spareth his own son that serveth 376

Mt 1:19 being a just **m**, and not willing to make her NIG
4: 4 And if any **m** will sue thee at the law, NIG
5:40 And if any **m** will sue thee at the law, NIG
6:24 No **m** can serve two masters: for either he NIG
7: 9 what **m** is there of you, whom if his son 444
7:24 them, I will liken him unto a wise **m**, 435
7:26 not, shall be likened unto a foolish **m**, 435
8: 4 See thou tell no **m**; but go thy way, NIG
8: 9 For I am a **m** under authority, 444
8: 9 and I say to this **m**, Go, and he goeth; NIG
8:20 Son of **m** hath not where to lay *his* head. 444
8:27 saying, **What manner of m** is this, 4217
8:28 so that no **m** might pass by that way. NIG
9: 2 brought to him a **m** sick of the palsy, 3885
9: 3 within themselves, This **m** blasphemeth. NIG
9: 6 that ye may know that the Son of **m** hath 444
9: 9 he saw a **m**, named Matthew, sitting at 444
9:16 No **m** putteth a piece of new cloth unto NIG
9:30 saying, See *that* no **m** know *it*. NIG
9:32 brought to him a dumb **m** possessed 444
10:23 cities of Israel, till the Son of **m** be come. 444
10:35 I am come to set a **m** at variance against 444

Mt 10:41 that receiveth a righteous **m** in the name NIG
10:41 shall receive a righteous **man's** reward. NIG
11: 8 A **m** clothed in soft raiment? behold, 444
11:19 The Son of **m** came eating and drinking, 444
11:19 Behold a **m** gluttonous, and a winebibber, 444
11:27 no **m** knoweth the Son, but the Father; NIG
11:27 neither knoweth any **m** the Father, save NIG
12: 8 the Son of **m** is Lord even of the sabbath 444
12:10 was a **m** which had *his* hand withered. 444
12:11 What **m** shall there be among you, 444
12:12 much then is a **m** better than a sheep? 444
12:13 saith he to the **m**, Stretch forth thine 444
12:19 neither shall any **m** hear his voice in NIG
12:29 except he first bind the strong **m**? 444
12:32 speaketh a word against the Son of **m**, 444
12:35 A good **m** out of the good treasure of 444
12:35 an evil **m** out of the evil treasure bringeth 444
12:40 so shall the Son of **m** be three days and 444
12:43 the unclean spirit is gone out of a **m**, 444
12:45 last *state* of that **m** is worse than the first. 444
13:24 kingdom of heaven is likened unto a **m** 444
13:31 which a **m** took, and sowed in his field: 444
13:37 that soweth the good seed is the Son of **m**; 444
13:41 The Son of **m** shall send forth his angels, 444
13:44 which when a **m** hath found, he hideth, 444
13:45 of heaven is like unto a merchant **m**, 444
13:52 is like unto a **m** *that is* a householder, 444
13:54 Whence hath this **m** this wisdom, 444
13:56 Whence then hath this **m** all these *things*? NIG
15:11 which goeth into the mouth defileth a **m**; 444
15:11 out of the mouth, this defileth a **m**. 444
15:18 from the heart; and they defile the **m**. 444
15:20 These are *the things* which defile a **m**: 444
15:20 eat with unwashen hands defileth not a **m**. 444
16:13 Whom do men say that I the Son of **m** am? 444
16:20 tell no **m** that he was Jesus the Christ. NIG
16:24 If any **m** will come after me, let him deny 444
16:26 For what is a **m** profited, if he shall gain 444
16:26 shall a **m** give in exchange for his soul? 444
16:27 For the Son of **m** shall come in the glory 444
16:27 he shall reward **every m** according to his 1538
16:28 till they see the Son of **m** coming in his NIG
17: 8 eyes, they saw no **m**, save Jesus only. NIG
17: 9 the vision to no **m**, until the Son of man NIG
17: 9 the vision to no **man**, until the Son of **m** 444
17:12 Likewise shall also the Son of **m** suffer of 444
17:14 there came to him a *certain* **m**, 444
17:22 The Son of **m** shall be betrayed into 444
18: 7 to that **m** by whom the offence cometh. 444
18:11 the Son of **m** is come to save that which 444
18:12 if a **m** have an hundred sheep, and one of 444
18:17 let him be unto thee as a heathen **m** and NIG
19: 3 Is it lawful for a **m** to put away his wife 444
19: 5 For this cause shall a **m** leave father and 444
19: 6 joined together, let not **m** put asunder. 444
19:10 If the case of the **m** be so with *his* wife, 444
19:20 The **young m** saith unto him, All these 3495
19:22 when the **young m** heard *that* saying, 3495
19:23 That a rich **m** shall hardly enter into NIG
19:24 for a rich **m** to enter into the kingdom NIG
19:28 when the Son of **m** shall sit in the throne 444
20: 1 the kingdom of heaven is like unto a **m** 444
20: 7 unto him, Because no **m** hath hired us. NIG
20: 9 they received **every m** a penny. 303
20:10 they likewise received **every m** a penny. 303
20:18 the Son of **m** shall be betrayed unto the 444
20:28 Even as the Son of **m** came not to be 444
21: 3 if any **m** say ought unto you, ye shall NIG
21:28 A *certain* **m** had two sons; and he came to 444
22:11 he saw there a **m** which had not on a 444
22:16 neither carest thou for any **m**: for thou NIG
22:24 Saying, Master, Moses said, If a **m** die, 5100
22:46 no **m** was able to answer him a word, NIG
22:46 neither durst any **m** from that day forth NIG
23: 9 And call no **m** your father upon the earth: NIG
24: 4 Take heed that no **m** deceive you. NIG
24:23 Then if any **m** shall say unto you, NIG
24:27 shall also the coming of the Son of **m** be. 444
24:30 shall appear the sign of the Son of **m** in 444
24:30 they shall see the Son of **m** coming in 444
24:36 But of that day and hour knoweth no **m**, NIG
24:37 shall also the coming of the Son of **m** be. 444
24:39 shall also the coming of the Son of **m** be. 444
24:44 as ye think not the Son of **m** cometh. 444
25:13 the hour wherein the Son of **m** cometh. 444
25:14 For *the kingdom of heaven is* as a **m** 444
25:15 **every m** according to his several ability; 1538
25:24 Lord, I knew thee that thou art a hard **m**, 444
25:31 the Son of **m** shall come in his glory, 444
26: 2 the Son of **m** is betrayed to be crucified. 444
26:18 Go into the city to **such a m**, and say 1170
26:24 The Son of **m** goeth as it is written of him: 444
26:24 unto that **m** by whom the Son of man is 444
26:24 unto that man by whom the Son of **m** is 444
26:24 it had been good for that **m** if he had not 444
26:45 the Son of **m** is betrayed into the hands of 444
26:64 Hereafter shall ye see the Son of **m** sitting 444
26:72 denied with an oath, I do not know the **m**. NIG
26:74 and to swear, *saying*, I know not the **m**. NIG
27:19 Have thou nothing to do with that just **m**: NIG
27:32 found a **m** of Cyrene, Simon by name: 444
27:47 heard *that*, said, This **m** calleth for Elias. NIG
27:57 there came a rich **m** of Arimathea, 444

Mk 1:23 there was in their synagogue a **m** with 444
1:44 See thou say nothing to any **m**: but go thy NIG

Mk 2: 7 Why doth this *m* thus speak blasphemies? NIG
2:10 that ye may know that the Son of *m* hath 444
2:21 No *m* also seweth a piece of new cloth on NIG
2:22 no *m* putteth new wine into old bottles: NIG
2:27 sabbath was made for *m*, *and* not man 444
2:27 made for man, *and* not *m* for the sabbath: 444
2:28 Therefore the Son of *m* is Lord also of 444
3: 1 there was a *m* there which had a withered 444
3: 3 And he saith unto the *m* which had 444
3: 5 saith unto the *m*, Stretch forth thine hand. 444
3:27 No *m* can enter into a strong *man's* NIG
3:27 except he will first bind the strong *m*; NIG
4:23 If any *m* have ears to hear, let him hear. NIG
4:26 if a *m* should cast seed into the ground, 444
4:41 **What** *manner of* *m* is this, that even 687+5101
5: 2 of the tombs a *m* with an unclean spirit, 444
5: 3 and no *m* could bind him, no, not with NIG
5: 4 in pieces: neither could any *m* tame him. NIG
5: 8 Come out of the *m*, *thou* unclean spirit. 444
5:37 And he suffered no *m* to follow him, NIG
5:43 And he charged them straitly that no *m* NIG
6: 2 From whence hath this *m* these *things*? NIG
6:20 knowing that he *was* a just *m* and a holy, 435
7:11 If a *m* shall say to *his* father or mother, 444
7:15 There is nothing from without a *m*, 444
7:15 of him, those are they that defile the *m*. 444
7:16 If any *m* have ears to hear, let him hear. NIG
7:18 *thing* from without entereth into the *m*, 444
7:20 he said, That which cometh out of the *m*, 444
7:20 out of the man, that defileth the *m*. 444
7:23 come from within, and defile the *m*. 444
7:24 would have no *m* know *it*: but he could NIG
7:36 charged them that they should tell no *m*: NIG
8: 4 From whence can a *m* satisfy these *men* 5100
8:22 and they bring a **blind** *m* unto him, 5185
8:23 And he took the **blind** *m* by the hand, 5185
8:25 he was restored, and saw every *m* clearly. NIG
8:30 them that they should tell no *m* of him. NIG
8:31 the Son of *m* must suffer many *things*, 444
8:36 what shall it profit a *m*, if he shall gain 444
8:37 what shall a *m* give in exchange for his 444
8:38 of him also shall the Son of *m* be ashamed, 444
9: 8 they saw no *m* any more, save Jesus only NIG
9: 9 charged them that they should tell no *m* NIG
9: 9 till the Son of *m* were risen from the dead. 444
9:12 and how it is written of the Son of *m*, 444
9:30 he would not that any *m* should know *it*. NIG
9:31 The Son of *m* is delivered into the hands 444
9:35 unto them, If any *m* desire to be first, NIG
9:39 there is no *m* which shall do a miracle NIG
10: 2 Is it lawful for a *m* to put away *his* wife? 435
10: 7 For this cause shall a *m* leave his father 444
10: 9 joined together, let not *m* put asunder. 444
10:25 for a rich *m* to enter into the kingdom NIG
10:29 There is no *m* that hath left house, 444
10:33 the Son of *m* shall be delivered unto 444
10:45 For even the Son of *m* came not to be 444
10:49 And they call the **blind** *m*, saying unto 5185
10:51 The **blind** *m* said unto him, Lord, that I 5185
11: 2 find a colt tied, whereon never *m* sat; 444
11: 3 if any *m* say unto you, Why do ye this? NIG
11:14 No *m* eat fruit of thee hereafter for ever. NIG
11:16 And would not suffer that any *m* should NIG
12: 1 A *certain m* planted a vineyard, and set a 444
12:14 carest for no *m*: for thou regardest not NIG
12:34 And no *m* after that durst ask him *any* NIG
13: 5 to say, Take heed lest any *m* deceive you: NIG
13:21 then if any *m* shall say to you, Lo, here NIG
13:26 shall they see the Son of *m* coming in 444
13:32 of that day and *that* hour knoweth no *m*, NIG
13:34 *For the Son of man is* as a *man* taking a far NIG
13:34 *For the Son of man is* as a *m* taking a far 444
13:34 and to **every** *m* his work, 1538
14:13 shall meet you a *m* bearing a pitcher of 444
14:21 The Son of *m* indeed goeth, as it is written 444
14:21 woe to that *m* by whom the Son of man is 444
14:21 woe to that man by whom the Son of *m* is 444
14:21 were it for that *m* if he had never been 444
14:41 the Son of *m* is betrayed into the hands of 444
14:51 there followed him a certain **young** *m*, 3495
14:62 shall see the Son of *m* sitting on the right 444
14:71 I know not this *m* of whom ye speak. NIG
15:24 upon them, what every *m* should take. NIG
15:39 said, Truly this *m* was the Son of God. 444
16: 5 they saw a **young** *m* sitting on the right 3495
16: 8 neither said they any *thing* to any *m*; NIG

Lk 1:18 For I am an **old** *m*, and my wife well 4246
1:27 To a virgin espoused to a *m* whose name 435
1:34 How shall this be, seeing I know not a *m*? 435
2:25 And behold, there was a *m* in Jerusalem, 444
2:25 and the same *m was* just and devout, 444
2:52 stature, and in favour with God and *m*. 444
3:14 he said unto them, Do violence to no *m*, 3367
4: 4 That *m* shall not live by bread alone, 444
4:33 And in the synagogue there was a *m*, 444
5: 8 from me; for I am a sinful *m*, O Lord. 435
5:12 a certain city, behold a *m* full of leprosy: 435
5:14 And he charged him to tell no *m*: but go, 444
5:18 brought in a bed a *m* which was taken 444
5:20 he said unto him, M, thy sins are forgiven 444
5:24 that ye may know that the Son of *m* hath 444
5:36 No *m* putteth a piece of a new garment NIG
5:37 no *m* putteth new wine into old bottles; NIG
5:39 No *m* also having drunk old *wine* NIG
6: 5 That the Son of *m* is Lord also of 444

Lk 6: 6 there was a *m* whose right hand was 444
6: 8 to the *m* which had the withered hand, 444
6:10 said unto the *m*, Stretch forth thy hand. 444
6:30 Give to **every** *m* that asketh of thee; 3956
6:45 A good *m* out of the good treasure of his 444
6:45 an evil *m* out of the evil treasure of his 444
6:48 He is like a *m* which built a house, 444
6:49 like a *m* that without a foundation built a 444
7: 8 For I also am a *m* set under authority, 444
7:12 behold, there was a **dead** *m* carried out, 2348
7:14 And he said, **Young** *m*, I say unto thee, 3495
7:25 A *m* clothed in soft raiment? Behold, 444
7:34 The Son of *m* is come eating and drinking; 444
7:34 Behold a gluttonous *m*, and a winebibber, 444
7:39 saying, This *m*, if he were a prophet, NIG
8:16 No *m*, when he hath lighted a candle, NIG
8:25 to another, What *manner of m* is this? NIG
8:27 there met him out of the city a certain *m*, 435
8:29 the unclean spirit to come out of the *m*. 444
8:33 Then went the devils out of the *m*, 444
8:35 came to Jesus, and found the *m*, out of 444
8:38 Now the *m* out of whom the devils were 435
8:41 there came a *m* named Jairus, and he was 435
8:51 he suffered no *m* to go in, save Peter, NIG
8:56 charged them that they should tell no *m* NIG
9:21 commanded *them* to tell no *m* that *thing*; NIG
9:22 The Son of *m* must suffer many *things*, 444
9:23 If any *m* will come after me, let him deny NIG
9:25 For what is a *m* advantaged, if he gain 444
9:26 of him shall the Son of *m* be ashamed, 444
9:36 no *m* in those days any of *those things* NIG
9:38 a *m* of the company cried out, saying, 435
9:44 for the Son of *m* shall be delivered into 444
9:56 For the Son of *m* is not come to destroy 444
9:57 a certain *m* said unto him, Lord, I will NIG
9:58 Son of *m* hath not where to lay *his* head. 444
9:62 No *m* having put his hand to the plough, NIG
10: 4 nor shoes: and salute no *m* by the way. NIG
10:22 and no *m* knoweth who the Son is, NIG
10:30 certain *m* went down from Jerusalem to 444
11:21 a strong *m* armed keepeth his palace, NIG
11:24 the unclean spirit is gone out of a *m*, 444
11:26 last *state* of that *m* is worse than the first. 444
11:30 also the Son of *m* be to this generation. 444
11:33 No *m*, when he hath lighted a candle, NIG
12: 8 him shall the Son of *m* also confess before 444
12:10 shall speak a word against the Son of *m*, 444
12:14 he said unto him, **M**, who made me a 444
12:16 The ground of a certain rich *m* brought 444
12:40 the Son of *m* cometh at an hour when ye 444
13: 6 A certain *m* had a fig tree planted in his NIG
13:19 which a *m* took, and cast into his garden; 444
14: 2 there was a certain *m* before him, NIG
14: 8 When thou art bidden of any *m* to a NIG
14: 8 lest a more honourable *m* than thou be NIG
14: 9 and say to thee, Give this *m* place; NIG
14:16 A certain *m* made a great supper, NIG
14:26 If any *m* come to me, and hate not his NIG
14:30 This *m* began to build, and was not able NIG
15: 4 What *m* of you, having an hundred sheep, NIG
15:11 And he said, A certain *m* had two sons: 444
15:16 swine did eat: and no *m* gave unto him. NIG
16: 1 There was a certain rich *m*, which had a NIG
16:16 is preached, and every *m* presseth into it. NIG
16:19 There was a certain rich *m*, which was NIG
16:22 the rich *m* also died, and was buried: NIG
17:22 to see one of the days of the Son of *m*, 444
17:24 so shall also the Son of *m* be in his day. 444
17:26 shall it be also in the days of the Son of *m*. 444
17:30 in the day when the Son of *m* is revealed. 444
18: 2 which feared not God, neither regarded *m*: 444
18: 4 Though I fear not God, nor regard *m*; 444
18: 8 Nevertheless when the Son of *m* cometh, NIG
18:14 this *m* went down to his house justified NIG
18:25 for a rich *m* to enter into the kingdom NIG
18:29 There is no *m* that hath left house, 444
18:31 the Son of *m* shall be accomplished. 444
18:35 a certain **blind** *m* sat by the way side 5185
19: 2 behold, *there was* a *m* named Zaccheus, 435
19: 7 That he was gone to be guest with a *m* 435
19: 8 if I have taken any *thing* from any *m* by NIG
19:10 the Son of *m* is come to seek and to save 444
19:14 We will not have this *m* to reign over us. NIG
19:15 he might know how much every *m* had NIG
19:21 feared thee, because thou art an austere *m*: 444
19:22 Thou knewest that I was an austere *m*, 444
19:30 find a colt tied, whereon yet never *m* sat: NIG
19:31 And if any *m* ask you, Why do ye loose 444
20: 9 A certain *m* planted a vineyard, and let it 444
21:27 shall they see the Son of *m* coming in a 444
21:36 to pass, and to stand before the Son of *m*. 444
22:10 there shall a *m* meet you, bearing a pitcher 444
22:22 And truly the Son of *m* goeth, as it was 444
22:22 woe unto that *m* by whom he is betrayed. 444
22:48 betrayest thou the Son of *m* with a kiss? 444
22:56 and said, This *m* was also with him. NIG
22:58 also of them. And Peter said, **M**, I am not. 444
22:60 And Peter said, **M**, I know not what thou 444
22:69 Hereafter shall the Son of *m* sit on the right 444
23: 4 and *to* the people, I find no fault in this *m*. 444
23: 6 he asked whether the *m* were a Galilean. 444
23:14 them, Ye have brought this *m* unto me, 444
23:14 have found no fault in this *m* *touching* 444
23:18 Away with this *m*, and release unto us NIG

Lk 23:41 but this *m* hath done nothing amiss. NIG
23:47 saying, Certainly this was a righteous *m*. 444
23:50 behold, *there was* a *m* named Joseph, 435
23:50 *and he was* a good *m*, and a just: 435
23:52 This *m* went unto Pilate, and begged NIG
23:53 stone, wherein never *m* before was laid. 3762
24: 7 The Son of *m* must be delivered into 444

Jn 1: 6 was a *m* sent from God, whose name 444
1: 9 which lighteth every *m* that cometh into 444
1:13 the flesh, nor of the will of *m*, but of God. 435
1:18 No *m* hath seen God at any time; the only 444
1:30 After me cometh a *m* which is preferred 435
1:51 and descending upon the Son of *m*. 444
2:10 Every *m* at the beginning doth set forth 444
2:25 needed not that any should testify of *m*: 444
2:25 of man: for he knew what was in *m*. 444
3: 1 There was a *m* of the Pharisees, 444
3: 2 for no *m* can do these miracles that thou 444
3: 3 say unto thee, Except a *m* be born again, 5100
3: 4 How can a *m* be born when he is old? 444
3: 5 Except a *m* be born of water and *of* 5100
3:13 And no *m* hath ascended up to heaven, NIG
3:13 *even* the Son of *m* which is in heaven. 444
3:14 *even* so must the Son of *m* be lifted up: 444
3:27 and said, A *m* can receive nothing, 444
3:32 and no *m* receiveth his testimony. NIG
4:27 yet no *m* said, What seekest thou? 444
4:29 Come, see a *m*, which told me all *things* 444
4:33 Hath any *m* brought him *ought* to eat? 444
4:50 the *m* believed the word that Jesus had 444
5: 5 And a certain *m* was there, which had an 444
5: 7 The impotent *m* answered him, Sir, 444
5: 7 I have no *m*, when the water is troubled, 444
5: 9 And immediately the *m* was made whole, 444
5:12 What *m* is that which said unto thee, 444
5:15 The *m* departed, and told the Jews that it 444
5:22 For the Father judgeth no *m*, NIG
5:27 judgment also, because he is the Son of *m*. 444
5:34 But I receive not testimony from *m*: 444
6:27 which the Son of *m* shall give unto you: 444
6:44 No *m* can come to me, except the Father NIG
6:45 Every *m* therefore that hath heard, NIG
6:46 Not that any *m* hath seen the Father, NIG
6:50 from heaven, that a *m* may eat thereof, 5100
6:51 if any *m* eat of this bread, he shall live for NIG
6:52 How can this *m* give us *his* flesh to eat? NIG
6:53 Except ye eat the flesh of the Son of *m*, 444
6:62 if ye shall see the Son of *m* ascend up 444
6:65 I unto you, that no *m* can come unto me, NIG
7: 4 For *there is* no *m* that doeth any *thing* in NIG
7:12 He is a good *m*: others said, Nay; NIG
7:13 no *m* spake openly of him for fear NIG
7:15 saying, How knoweth this *m* letters, NIG
7:17 If any *m* will do his will, he shall know of 444
7:22 and ye on the sabbath day circumcise a *m*. 444
7:23 If a *m* on the sabbath day receive 444
7:23 I have made a *m* every whit whole on 444
7:27 Howbeit we know this *m* whence he is: NIG
7:27 Christ cometh, no *m* knoweth whence NIG
7:30 but no *m* laid hands on him, because NIG
7:31 than these which this *m* hath done? NIG
7:37 and cried, saying, If any *m* thirst, NIG
7:44 taken him; but no *m* laid hands on him. NIG
7:46 Never *m* spake like this man. 444
7:46 Never man spake like this *m*. 444
7:51 Doth our law judge any *m*, before it hear 444
7:53 And **every** *m* went unto his own house. 1538
8:10 accusers? hath no *m* condemned thee? NIG
8:11 She said, No *m*, Lord. And Jesus said unto NIG
8:15 Ye judge after the flesh; I judge no *m*. NIG
8:20 and no *m* laid hands on him; for his hour NIG
8:28 When ye have lift up the Son of *m*, then 444
8:33 were never in bondage to any *m*: NIG
8:40 a *m* that hath told you the truth, which I 444
8:51 I say unto you, If a *m* keep my saying, 5100
8:52 and thou sayest, If a *m* keep my saying, 5100
9: 1 saw a *m* which was blind from *his* birth. 444
9: 2 who did sin, this *m*, or his parents, NIG
9: 3 hath this *m* sinned, nor his parents: NIG
9: 4 the night cometh, when no *m* can work. NIG
9: 6 he anointed the eyes of the **blind** *m* with 5185
9:11 A *m that* is called Jesus made clay, 444
9:16 This *m* is not of God, because he keepeth 444
9:16 How can a *m that* is a sinner do such 444
9:17 They say unto the **blind** *m* again, 5185
9:22 if any *m* did confess that he *was* Christ, NIG
9:24 again called they the *m* that was blind, 444
9:24 praise: we know that this *m* is a sinner. 444
9:30 The *m* answered and said unto them, 444
9:31 but if any *m* be a worshipper of God, NIG
9:32 opened the eyes of one that was born NIG
9:33 If this *m* were not of God, he could do NIG
10: 9 by me if any *m* enter in, he shall be saved, NIG
10:18 No *m* taketh it from me, but I lay it down NIG
10:28 neither shall any *m* pluck them out of my NIG
10:29 no *m* is able to pluck *them* out of my NIG
10:33 and because that thou, being a *m*, 444
10:41 all *things* that John spake of this *m* were 444
11: 1 a certain *m* was sick, *named* Lazarus, NIG
11: 9 if any *m* walk in the day, he stumbleth not, NIG
11:10 if a *m* walk in the night, he stumbleth, 5100
11:37 Could not this *m*, which opened the eyes NIG
11:37 have caused that even this *m* should not NIG
11:47 do we? for this *m* doeth many miracles. 444
11:50 that one *m* should die for the people, 444

M

Jn
11:57 that, if any **m** knew where he were, — NIG
12:23 that the Son of **m** should be glorified. — 444
12:26 If any **m** serve me, let him follow me; — NIG
12:26 if any **m** serve me, him will *my* Father — NIG
12:34 thou, The Son of **m** must be lift up? — 444
12:34 must be lift up? who is this Son of **m**? — 444
12:47 And if any **m** hear my words, — NIG
13:28 no **m** at the table knew for what intent — NIG
13:31 Now is the Son of **m** glorified, and God is — 444
14: 6 no **m** cometh unto the Father, but by me. — NIG
14:23 and said unto him, If a **m** love me, — 5100
15: 6 If a **m** abide not in me, he is cast forth as — 5100
15:13 Greater love hath no **m** than this, that a — NIG
15:13 that a **m** lay down his life for his friends. — 5100
15:24 them the works which none other **m** did, — NIG
16:21 for joy that a **m** is born into the world. — 444
16:22 and your joy no **m** taketh from you. — NIG
16:30 needest not that any **m** should ask thee: — NIG
16:32 every **m** to his own, and shall leave me — NIG
18:14 it was expedient that one **m** should die — NIG
18:29 What accusation bring you against this **m**? — 444
18:31 is not lawful for us to put any **m** to death: — NIG
18:40 again, saying, Not this **m**, but Barabbas. — NIG
19: 5 *Pilate* saith unto them, Behold the **m**. — 444
19:12 cried out, saying, If thou let this **m** go, — NIG
19:41 wherein was never **m** yet laid. — 3762
21:21 to Jesus, Lord, and what *shall* this **m** do? — NIG

Ac
1:18 Now this **m** purchased a field with — NIG
1:20 be desolate, and let no **m** dwell therein: — 3588
2: 6 every **m** heard them speak in his own — 1520
2: 8 And how hear we every **m** in our own — 1538
2:22 a **m** approved of God among you by — 435
2:45 parted them to all *men*, as every **m** had — NIG
3: 2 And a certain **m** lame from his mother's — 435
3:11 as the lame **m** which was healed held — NIG
3:12 or holiness we had made this **m** to walk? — NIG
3:16 in his name hath made this **m** strong, — NIG
4: 9 of the good deed done to the impotent **m**, — 444
4:10 by him doth this **m** stand here before — NIG
4:14 And beholding the **m** which was healed — 444
4:17 that *they* speak henceforth to no **m** in this — 444
4:22 For the **m** was above forty years old, — 444
4:35 distribution was made unto every **m** — 1538
5: 1 But a certain **m** named Ananias, — 435
5:13 And of the rest durst no **m** join himself to — NIG
5:23 we had opened, we found no **m** within. — NIG
5:37 After this **m** rose up Judas of Galilee in — NIG
6: 5 a **m** full of faith and of the Holy Ghost, — 435
6:13 This **m** ceaseth not to speak blasphemous — 444
7:56 the Son of **m** standing on the right hand of — 444
8: 9 But there was a certain **m**, called Simon, — 435
8:10 saying, This **m** is the great power of God. — NIG
8:27 and behold, a **m** of Ethiopia, an eunuch of — 435
8:31 can I, except some **m** should guide me? — NIG
8:34 of himself, or of some other **m**? — NIG
9: 7 hearing a voice, but seeing no **m**. — NIG
9: 8 saw no **m**: but they led him by the hand, — NIG
9:12 And hath seen in a vision a **m** named — 435
9:13 Lord, I have heard by many of this **m**, — 435
9:33 And there he found a certain **m** named — 444
10: 1 There was a certain **m** in Cesarea called — 435
10: 2 A devout **m**, and one that feared God with — NIG
10:22 a just **m**, and one that feareth God, — 435
10:26 saying, Stand up; I myself also am a **m**. — 444
10:28 for a **m** *that is* a Jew to keep company, — 435
10:28 me that I should not call any **m** common — 444
10:30 a **m** stood before me in bright clothing, — 435
10:47 Can any **m** forbid water, that these should — NIG
11:24 For he was a good **m**, and full of the Holy — NIG
11:29 every **m** according to his ability, — 1538
12:22 *It is* the voice of a god, and not of a **m**. — 444
13: 7 *the country*, Sergius Paulus, a prudent **m**; — 435
13:21 a **m** of the tribe of Benjamin, *by the space* — 435
13:22 a **m** after mine own heart, which shall — 435
13:38 that through this **m** is preached unto you — NIG
13:41 though a **m** declare it unto you. — 5100
14: 8 And there sat a certain **m** at Lystra, — 435
16: 9 There stood a **m** of Macedonia, — 435
17:31 by that **m** whom he hath ordained; — 435
18:10 and no **m** shall set on thee to hurt thee: — NIG
18:24 eloquent **m**, *and* mighty in the scriptures, — 435
18:25 This **m** was instructed in the way of — NIG
19:16 the **m** in whom the evil spirit was leapt — 444
19:24 For a certain **m** named Demetrius, — NIG
19:35 what **m** is there that knoweth not how — 444
19:38 have a matter against any **m**, the law is — NIG
20: 9 a certain young **m** named Eutychus, — 3494
20:12 And they brought the young **m** alive, — 3816
21: 9 And the same **m** had four daughters, — NIG
21:11 So shall the Jews at Jerusalem bind the **m** — 435
21:28 This is the **m**, that teacheth all *men* every — 444
21:39 I am a **m** *which am* a Jew of Tarsus, — 444
22: 3 I am verily a **m** *which am* a Jew, born in — 444
22:12 a devout **m** according to the law, — 435
22:25 for you to scourge a **m** *that is* a Roman, — 444
22:26 what thou doest: for this **m** is a Roman. — 444
23: 9 strove, saying, We find no evil in this **m**: — 444
23:17 this young **m** unto the chief captain: — 3494
23:18 *me* to bring this young **m** unto thee, — 3494
23:22 captain then let the young **m** depart, — 3494
23:22 him, *See* thou tell no **m** that thou — NIG
23:27 This **m** was taken of the Jews, — 435
23:30 me how that the Jews laid wait for the **m**, — 435
24: 5 we have found this **m** a pestilent *fellow*, — 435
24:12 with any **m**, neither raising up the people, — NIG

Ac
25: 5 go down with *me,* and accuse this **m**, — 435
25:11 no **m** may deliver me unto them. — NIG
25:14 There is a certain **m** left in bonds by Felix: — 435
25:16 of the Romans to deliver any **m** to die, — 444
25:17 commanded the **m** to be brought *forth.* — 435
25:22 Festus, I would also hear the **m** myself. — 444
25:24 ye see this **m**, about whom all the — NIG
26:31 This **m** doeth nothing worthy of death or — 444
26:32 This **m** might have been set at liberty, — 444
28: 4 No doubt this **m** is a murderer, whom, — 444
28: 7 possessions of the chief **m** of the island, — NIG
28:31 with all confidence, no **m** forbidding him. — NIG

Ro
1:23 into an image made like to corruptible **m**, — 444
2: 1 Therefore thou art inexcusable, O **m**, — 444
2: 3 And thinkest thou this, O **m**, that judgest — 444
2: 6 Who will render to every **m** according to — 444
2: 9 upon every soul of **m** that doeth evil, — 444
2:10 and peace, to every **m** that worketh good, — 444
2:21 thou that preachest *a* **m** should not steal, — 444
2:22 thou that sayest a **m** should not commit — 444
3: 4 let God be true, but every **m** a liar; as it — 444
3: 5 who taketh vengeance? (I speak as a **m**) — 444
3:28 Therefore we conclude that a **m** is justified — 444
4: 6 also describeth the blessedness of the **m**, — 444
4: 8 Blessed *is* the **m** to whom the Lord will — 435
5: 7 scarcely for a righteous **m** will one die: — NIG
5: 7 peradventure for a good **m** some would — NIG
5:12 as by one **m** sin entered into the world, — 444
5:15 By grace, which is by one **m**, Jesus Christ, — 444
6: 6 that our old **m** is crucified with *him,* that — 444
7: 1 how that the law hath dominion over a **m**, — 444
7: 3 liveth, she be married to another **m**, — 435
7: 3 though she be married to another **m**. — 435
7:22 in the law of God after the inward **m**: — NIG
7:24 wretched **m** that I am! who shall deliver — 444
8: 9 if any **m** have not the Spirit of Christ, — NIG
8:24 for what a **m** seeth, why doth he yet hope — 5100
9:20 Nay but, O **m**, who art thou that repliest — 444
10: 5 That the **m** which doeth those *things* shall — 444
10:10 For with the heart **m** believeth unto — NIG
12: 3 unto me, to every **m** that is among you, — NIG
12: 3 according as God hath dealt to every **m** — 1538
12:17 Recompense to no **m** evil for evil. — NIG
13: 8 Owe no **m** any *thing,* but to love one — NIG
14: 5 One esteemeth one day above another: — 3739
14: 5 every **m** be fully persuaded in his own — 1538
14: 7 to himself, and no **m** dieth to himself. — NIG
14:13 that no **m** put a stumblingblock or — NIG
14:20 is evil for that **m** who eateth with offence. — 444

1Co
2: 9 neither have entered into the heart of **m**, — 444
2:11 For what **m** knoweth the *things* of a **m**, — 444
2:11 For what man knoweth the *things* of a **m**, — 444
2:11 man, save the spirit of **m** which is in him? — 444
2:11 so the *things* of God knoweth no **m**, — 444
2:14 the natural **m** receiveth not the *things* of — 444
2:15 *things,* yet he himself is judged of no **m**. — NIG
3: 5 even as the Lord gave to every **m**? — 1538
3: 8 every **m** shall receive his own reward — 1538
3:10 let every **m** take heed how he buildeth — 1538
3:11 other foundation can no **m** lay than that — NIG
3:12 Now if any **m** build upon this foundation — NIG
3:17 If any **m** defile the temple of God, him — NIG
3:18 Let no **m** deceive himself. If any *man* — NIG
3:18 If any **m** among you seemeth to be wise — NIG
3:21 Therefore let no **m** glory in men. For all — NIG
4: 1 Let a **m** so account of us, as of the — 444
4: 2 in stewards, that a **m** be found faithful. — 5100
4: 5 then shall every **m** have praise of God. — 1538
5:11 if any *man that is* called a brother be a — NIG
6: 5 that there is not a wise **m** amongst you? — NIG
6:18 sin that a **m** doeth is without the body; — 444
7: 1 *It is* good for a **m** not to touch a woman. — 444
7: 2 let every **m** have his own wife, — 1538
7: 7 But every **m** hath his proper gift of God, — 1538
7:16 how knowest thou, O **m**, whether thou — 435
7:17 But as God hath distributed to every **m**, — 1538
7:18 any **m** called being circumcised? let him — NIG
7:20 Let every **m** abide in the same calling — 1538
7:24 let every **m**, wherein he is called, — 1538
7:26 I *say,* that *it is* good for a **m** so to be. — 444
7:36 if any **m** think that he behaveth himself — NIG
8: 2 And if any **m** think that he knoweth any — NIG
8: 3 But if any **m** love God, the same is known — NIG
8: 7 Howbeit *there is* not in every **m** that — NIG
8:10 if any **m** see thee which hast knowledge — NIG
9: 8 Say I these *things* as a **m**? or saith not — 444
9:15 than that any **m** should make my glorying — NIG
9:25 every **m** that striveth for the mastery is — NIG
10:13 taken you but such as is **common to m**: — 442
10:24 Let no **m** seek his own, but every man — NIG
10:24 his own, but every **m** another's *wealth.* — 1538
10:28 But if any **m** say unto you, This is offered — NIG
11: 3 that the head of every **m** is Christ; — 435
11: 3 and the head of the woman is the **m**; — 435
11: 4 Every **m** praying or prophesying, having — 435
11: 7 a **m** indeed ought not to cover *his* head, — 435
11: 7 God: but the woman is the glory of the **m**. — 435
11: 8 For the **m** is not of the woman; — 435
11: 8 of the woman; but the woman of the **m**. — 435
11: 9 Neither was the **m** created for the woman; — 435
11: 9 for the woman; but the woman for the **m**. — 435
11:11 Nevertheless neither *is* the **m** without — 435
11:11 neither the woman without the **m**, — 435
11:12 For as the woman *is* of the **m**, *even so is* — 435
11:12 *even so is* the **m** also by the woman; — 435

1Co
11:14 if a **m** have long hair, it is a shame unto — 435
11:16 But if any **m** seem to be contentious, — NIG
11:28 let a **m** examine himself, and so let him — 444
11:34 if any **m** hunger, let him eat at home; — NIG
12: 3 that no **m** speaking by the Spirit of God — NIG
12: 3 *that* no **m** can say that Jesus is the Lord, — NIG
12: 7 Spirit is given to every **m** to profit withal. — 1538
12:11 dividing to every **m** severally as he will. — 1538
13:11 when I became a **m**, I put away childish — 435
14: 2 for no **m** understandeth *him;* howbeit in — NIG
14:27 If any **m** speak in an *unknown* tongue, — NIG
14:37 If any **m** think himself to be a prophet, — NIG
14:38 But if any **m** be ignorant, let him be — NIG
15:21 For since by **m** *came* death, by man *came* — 444
15:21 by **m** *came* also the resurrection of the — 444
15:23 But every **m** in his own order: Christ — 1538
15:35 But some **m** will say, How are the dead — NIG
15:45 The first **m** Adam was made a living soul; — 444
15:47 The first **m** *is* of the earth, earthy: — 444
15:47 the second **m** *is* the Lord from heaven. — 444
16:11 Let no **m** therefore despise him: — NIG
16:22 If any **m** love not the Lord Jesus Christ, — NIG

2Co
2: 6 Sufficient to such a **m** *is* this punishment, — NIG
4:16 but though our outward **m** perish, — 444
4:16 yet the inward **m** is renewed day by day. — 444
5:16 henceforth know we no **m** after — NIG
5:17 if any **m** be in Christ, he *is* a new — NIG
7: 2 have wronged no **m**, we have corrupted — NIG
7: 2 no **m**, we have defrauded no **man**. — NIG
7: 2 no **man**, we have defrauded no **m**. — NIG
8:12 *it is* accepted according to that a **m** hath, — 5100
8:20 that no **m** should blame us in this — NIG
9: 7 **Every m** according as he purposeth in *his* — 1538
10: 7 any **m** trust to himself that *he* is Christ's, — NIG
11: 9 I was chargeable to no **m**: for that which — NIG
11:10 no **m** shall stop me of this boasting in — NIG
11:16 I say again, Let no **m** think me a fool; — NIG
11:20 ye suffer, **if a m** bring you into bondage, — 1536
11:20 **if a m** devour *you,* if a man take *of you,* — 1536
11:20 if a man devour *you,* **if a m** take *of you,* — 1536
11:20 if a man take *of you,* **if a m** exalt himself, — 1536
11:20 himself, **if a m** smite you on the face. — 1536
12: 2 I knew a **m** in Christ above fourteen years — 444
12: 3 I knew such a **m**, (whether in the body, — 444
12: 4 which *it is* not lawful for a **m** to utter. — 444
12: 6 lest any **m** should think of me above *that* — NIG

Gal
1: 1 neither by **m**, but by Jesus Christ, — 444
1: 9 If any **m** preach any other gospel unto you — NIG
1:11 which was preached of me is not after **m**. — 444
1:12 For I neither received it of **m**, neither was — 444
2:16 Knowing that a **m** is not justified by — 444
3:11 But that no **m** is justified by the law in — NIG
3:12 The **m** that doeth them shall live in them. — 444
3:15 no **m** disannulleth, or added thereto. — NIG
5: 3 For I testify again to every **m** that is — 444
6: 1 Brethren, if a **m** be overtaken in a fault, — 444
6: 3 For if a **m** think himself to be something, — 5100
6: 4 But let every **m** prove his own work, — 1538
6: 5 For every **m** shall bear his own burden. — 1538
6: 7 whatsoever a **m** soweth, that shall he also — 444
6:17 From henceforth let no **m** trouble me: — NIG

Eph
2: 9 Not of works, lest any **m** should boast. — NIG
2:15 to make in himself of twain one new **m**, — 444
3:16 with might by his Spirit in the inner **m**; — 444
4:13 of the Son of God, unto a perfect **m**, — 435
4:22 the former conversation the old **m**, — 444
4:24 that *ye* put on the new **m**, which after — 444
4:25 speak every **m** truth with his neighbour: — 1538
5: 5 nor unclean *person,* nor **covetous m** who — 4123
5: 6 Let no **m** deceive you with vain words: — NIG
5:29 For no **m** ever yet hated his own flesh; — NIG
5:31 For this cause shall a **m** leave his father — NIG
6: 8 that whatsoever good *thing* **any m** doeth, — 1538

Php
2: 4 Look not every **m** on his own *things,* but — 1538
2: 4 but every **m** also on the *things* of others. — 1538
2: 8 And being found in fashion as a **m**, — 444
2:20 For I have no **m** likeminded, who will — NIG
3: 4 If any other **m** thinketh that *he* hath — NIG

Col
1:28 warning every **m**, and teaching every man — NIG
1:28 and teaching every **m** in all wisdom; — 444
1:28 that we may present every **m** perfect in — 444
2: 4 lest any **m** should beguile you with — NIG
2: 8 Beware lest any **m** spoil you through — NIG
2:16 Let no **m** therefore judge you in meat, — NIG
2:18 Let no **m** beguile you of your reward in a — NIG
3: 9 seeing that ye have put off the old **m** with — 444
3:10 And have put on the new **m**, which is — NIG
3:13 if any **m** have a quarrel against any: — NIG
4: 6 know ye how ye ought to answer every **m**. — 1520

1Th
3: 3 That no **m** should be moved by these — NIG
4: 6 That no **m** go beyond and defraud his — NIG
4: 8 that despiseth, despiseth not **m**, but God, — NIG
5:15 that none render evil for evil unto any **m**; — NIG

2Th
2: 3 Let no **m** deceive you by any means: — NIG
2: 3 and *that* **m** of sin be revealed, the son of — 444
3:14 And if any **m** obey not our word by this — NIG
3:14 note that **m**, and have no company with — 444

1Ti
1: 8 that the law *is* good, if a **m** use it lawfully; — 5100
1: 9 that the law is not made for a righteous **m**, — NIG
2: 5 between God and men, the **m** Christ Jesus; — 444
2:12 nor to usurp authority over the **m**, but to — 435
3: 1 If a **m** desire the office of a bishop, — 1536
3: 5 (For if a **m** know not how to rule his own — 5100
4:12 Let no **m** despise thy youth; but be thou — NIG
5: 9 years old, having been the wife of one **m**, — 435

1Ti	5:16 If any m^s or woman that believeth have	4103
	5:22 Lay hands suddenly on no m, neither be	NIG
6: 3 If any m teach otherwise, and consent not	NIG	
	6:11 But thou, O m of God, flee these things;	444
	6:16 dwelling in the light which no m can	444
	6:16 whom no m hath seen, nor can see:	444
2Ti	2: 4 No m that warreth entangleth himself	NIG
	2: 5 And if a m also strive for masteries, yet is	5100
	2:21 If a m therefore purge himself from these,	5100
	3:17 That the m of God may be perfect,	444
	4:16 At my first answer no m stood with me,	NIG
Tit	2:15 with all authority. Let no m despise thee.	NIG
	3: 2 To speak evil of no m, to be no brawlers,	NIG
	3: 4 love of God our Saviour toward m.	5363
	3:10 A m that is a heretick after the first and	444
Heb	2: 6 What is m, that thou art mindful of	444
	2: 6 or the son of m, that thou visitest him?	444
	2: 9 of God should taste death for every m.	NIG
	3: 3 For this m was counted worthy of more	444
	3: 4 For every house is builded by some m;	NIG
	4:11 lest any m fall after the same example of	NIG
	5: 4 no m taketh this honour unto himself,	NIG
	7: 4 Now consider how great this m was, unto	NIG
	7:13 which he m gave attendance at the altar.	NIG
	7:24 But this m, because he continueth ever,	NIG
	8: 2 which the Lord pitched, and not m.	444
	8: 3 wherefore it is of necessity that this m	NIG
	8:11 And they shall not teach every m his	1538
	8:11 and every m his brother, saying, Know	1538
	10:12 But this m, after he had offered one	NIG
	10:38 if any m draw back, my soul shall have	NIG
	12:14 without which no m shall see the Lord:	NIG
	12:15 Looking diligently lest any m fail of	NIG
	13: 6 I will not fear what m shall do unto me.	444
Jas	1: 7 let not that m think that he shall receive	444
	1: 8 A double minded m is unstable in all his	435
	1:11 shall the rich m fade away in his ways.	NIG
	1:12 Blessed is the m that endureth temptation:	435
	1:13 Let no m say when he is tempted, I am	NIG
	1:13 with evil, neither tempteth he any m:	NIG
	1:14 every m is tempted, when he is drawn	1538
	1:19 let every m be swift to hear, slow to speak,	444
	1:20 For the wrath of m worketh not	435
	1:23 is like unto a m beholding his natural face	435
	1:24 straightway forgetteth what manner of m	NIG
	1:25 this m shall be blessed in his deed.	NIG
	1:26 If any m among you seem to be religious,	NIG
	2: 2 For if there come unto your assembly a m	435
	2: 2 come in also a poor m in vile raiment;	NIG
	2:14 a m say he hath faith, and have not	5100
	2:18 Yea, a m may say, Thou hast faith, and I	5100
	2:20 But wilt thou know, O vain m, that faith	444
	2:24 then how that by works a m is justified,	444
	3: 2 If any m offend not in word, the same is a	NIG
	3: 2 the same is a perfect m, and able also to	435
	3: 8 But the tongue can no m tame; it is an	444
	3:13 Who is a wise m and endued with	NIG
	5:16 prayer of a righteous m availeth much.	NIG
	5:17 Elias was a m subject to like passions as	444
1Pe	1:24 all the glory of m as the flower of grass.	NIG
	2:13 Submit yourselves to every ordinance of m	442
	2:19 if a m for conscience toward God endure	5100
	3: 4 But let it be the hidden m of the heart, in	444
	3:15 m that asketh you a reason of the hope	NIG
	4:10 As every m hath received the gift, even	1538
	4:11 If any m speak, let him speak as the	NIG
	4:11 if any m minister, let him do it as of	NIG
	4:16 Yet if any m suffer as a Christian, let him	NIG
2Pe	1:21 came not in old time by the will of m:	444
	2: 8 that righteous m dwelling among them,	NIG
	2:19 of whom a m is overcome, of the same	5100
1Jn	2: 1 if any m sin, we have an advocate with	NIG
	2:15 If any m love the world, the love of	NIG
	2:27 and ye need not that any m teach you:	NIG
	3: 3 And every m that hath this hope in him	NIG
	3: 7 Little children, let no m deceive you:	NIG
	4:12 No m hath seen God at any time.	NIG
	4:20 If a m say, I love God, and hateth his	5100
	5:16 If any m see his brother sin a sin which is	NIG
Rev	1:13 candlesticks one like unto the Son of m,	444
	2:17 which no m knoweth saving he that	NIG
	3: 7 he that openeth, and no m shutteth;	NIG
	3: 7 and shutteth, and no m openeth;	NIG
	3: 8 thee an open door, and no m can shut it:	NIG
	3:11 thou hast, that no m take thy crown.	NIG
	3:20 any m hear my voice, and open the door,	NIG
	4: 7 and the third beast had a face as a m,	444
	5: 3 And no m in heaven, nor in earth,	NIG
	5: 4 no m was found worthy to open and	NIG
	6:15 every free m, hid themselves in the dens	NIG
	7: 9 which no m could number, of all nations,	444
	9: 5 of a scorpion, when he striketh a m.	NIG
	11: 5 If any m will hurt them, fire proceedeth	NIG
	11: 5 if any m will hurt them, he must in this	NIG
	12: 5 she brought forth a m child, who was to	730
	12:13 woman which brought forth the m child.	730
	13: 9 If any m have an ear, let him hear.	
	13:17 And that no m might buy or sell, save he	NIG
	13:18 it is the number of a m; and his number	444
	14: 3 and no m could learn that song but	NIG
	14: 9 If any m worship the beast and his image,	NIG
	14:14 the cloud one sat like unto the Son of m,	444
	15: 8 no m was able to enter into the temple,	NIG
	16: 3 and it became as the blood of a dead m:	NIG
	18:11 for no m buyeth their merchandise any	NIG

Rev	19:12 that no m knew, but he himself.	NIG
	20:13 they were judged every m according to	1538
	21:17 according to the measure of a m, that is,	444
	22:12 to give every m according as his work	1538
	22:18 For I testify unto every m that heareth	NIG
	22:18 If any m shall add unto these things, God	NIG
	22:19 And if any m shall take away from	NIG

MAN'S (122) [MAN]

Ge	8:21 curse the ground any more for m sake;	120
	8:21 for the imagination of m heart is evil from	120
	9: 5 the hand of every m brother will I require	376
	9: 6 Whoso sheddeth m blood, by man shall	120
	16:12 man, and every m hand against him;	3605
	20: 3 thou hast taken; for she is a m wife.	1167
	42:11 We are all one m sons; we are true men,	376
	42:25 to restore every m money into his sack,	376
	42:35 every m bundle of money was in his sack:	376
	43:21 every m money was in the mouth of his	376
	44: 1 put every m money in his sack's mouth.	376
	44:26 for we may not see the m face, except our	376
Ex	4:11 said unto him, Who hath made m mouth?	120
	21: 7 every m servant that is bought for money,	376
	21:35 if one m ox hurt another's, that he die;	376
	22: 5 beast, and shall feed in another m field;	312
	22: 7 keep, and it be stolen out of the m house;	376
	30:32 Upon m flesh shall it not be poured,	120
Lev	7: 8 priest that offereth any m burnt offering,	376
	15:16 if any m seed of copulation go out from	376
	20:10 committeth adultery with another m wife,	376
Nu	5:10 every m hallowed things shall be his:	376
	5:12 If any m wife go aside, and commit a	376
	17: 2 write thou every m name upon his rod.	376
	17: 5 that the m rod, whom I shall choose, shall	376
	33:54 every m^s inheritance shall be	2050.2+3807.1
Dt	20:19 (for the tree of the field is m life)	120
	24: 2 she may go and be another m wife.	376
	24: 6 to pledge: for he taketh a m life to pledge.	NIH
Jdg	7:16 he put a trumpet in every m^s hand,	3963.1
	7:22 the Lord set every m sword against his	376
	19:26 fell down at the door of the m house	376
Ru	2:19 The m name with whom I wrought to day	376
1Sa	12: 4 hast thou taken ought of any m hand.	376
	14:20 every m sword was against his fellow,	376
	17:32 Saul, Let no m heart fail because of him;	120
2Sa	12: 4 took the poor m lamb, and dressed it for	376
	17:18 came to a m house in Bahurim, which had	376
	17:25 Amasa was a m son, whose name was	376
1Ki	18:44 a little cloud out of the sea, like a m hand.	376
2Ki	12: 4 the money that cometh into any m heart	376
	23: 8 were on a m left hand at the gate of	376
	25: 9 every great m house burnt he with fire.	376
Est	1: 8 to every m pleasure.	376+376+2050.1
Job	10: 5 the days of man? are thy years as m days,	1397
	32:21 me not, I pray you, accept any m person,	376
Ps	104:15 and bread which strengtheneth m heart.	582
Pr	10:15 The rich m wealth is his strong city:	NIH
	12:14 the recompence of a m hands shall be	120
	13: 8 The ransom of a m life are his riches:	376
	16: 7 When a m ways please the Lord,	376
	16: 9 A m heart deviseth his way: but the Lord	120
	18: 4 words of a m mouth are as deep waters,	376
	18:11 The rich m wealth is his strong city,	NIH
	18:16 A m gift maketh room for him,	120
	18:20 A m belly shall be satisfied with the fruit	376
	19:21 There are many devices in a m heart;	376
	20:24 M goings are of the Lord; how can a	1397
	27: 9 doth the sweetness of a m^s friend by	1930.2
	29:23 A m pride shall bring him low:	120
	29:26 every m judgment cometh from the Lord.	376
Ecc	2:14 The wise m eyes are in his head;	NIH
	8: 1 a m wisdom maketh his face to shine,	120
	8: 5 a wise m heart discerneth both time and	NIH
	9:16 nevertheless the poor m wisdom is	NIH
	10: 2 A wise m heart is at his right hand;	NIH
	10:12 words of a wise m mouth are gracious;	NIH
Isa	8: 1 write in it with a m pen concerning	582
	13: 7 be faint, and every m heart shall melt:	582
Jer	3: 1 she go from him, and become another m,	376
	23:36 for every m word shall be his	376+3807.1
Eze	4:15 I have given thee cow's dung for m dung,	120
	10: 8 the form of a m hand under their wings.	120
	38:21 every m sword shall be against his brother	376
	39:15 any seeth a m bone, then shall he set	120
	40: 5 in the m hand a measuring reed of six	376
Da	4:16 Let his heart be changed from m, and let a	606
	5: 5 In the same hour came forth fingers of a m	606
	7: 4 as a man, and a m heart was given to it,	606
	8:16 I heard a m voice between the banks of	120
Am	6:10 a m^s uncle shall take him up, and he	2050.2
Jnh	1:14 let us not perish for this m life, and lay not	376
Mic	7: 6 enemies are the men of his own house.	376
Mt	10:36 And a m foes shall be they of his own	444
	10:41 man shall receive a righteous m reward.	NIG
	12:29 else how can one enter into a strong m	NIG
Mk	3:27 No man can enter into a strong m house,	NIG
	12:19 If a m brother die, and leave his wife	5100
Lk	6:22 your name as evil, for the Son of m sake.	444
	12:15 a m life consisteth not in the abundance	846
	16:12 m, who shall give you that which is your	NIG
	16:21 crumbs which fell from the rich m table:	NIG
	20:28 If any m brother die, having a wife,	NIG
Jn	18:17 Art thou not also one of this m disciples?	444
Ac	5:28 and intend to bring this m blood upon us.	444
	7:58 down their clothes at a young m feet,	3494

Ac	11:12 and we entered into the m house:	435
	13:23 Of this m seed hath God according to his	NIG
	17:29 or stone, graven by art and m device.	444
	18: 7 and entered into a certain m house,	NIG
	20:33 I have coveted no m silver, or gold,	NIG
	27:22 for there shall be no loss of any m life	NIG
Ro	5:17 For if by one m offence death reigned by	NIG
	5:19 For as by one m disobedience many were	444
	14: 4 Who art thou that judgest another m	NIG
	15:20 lest I should build upon another m	NIG
1Co	2: 4 not with enticing words of m wisdom,	442
	2:13 in the words which m wisdom teacheth,	442
	3:13 Every m work shall be made manifest:	1538
	3:13 fire shall try every m work of what sort	1538
	3:14 If any m work abide which he hath built	NIG
	3:15 If any m work shall be burnt, he shall	NIG
	4: 3 be judged of you, or of m judgment:	442
	10:29 why is my liberty judged of another m	NIG
2Co	4: 2 to every m conscience in the sight of God.	444
	10:16 not to boast in another m line of things	NIG
Gal	2: 6 God accepteth no m person:) for they who	444
	3:15 Though it be but a m covenant, yet if it be	444
2Th	3: 8 Neither did we eat any m bread for	NIG
Jas	1:26 his own heart, this m religion is vain.	NIG
1Pe	1:17 judgeth according to every m work,	1538
2Pe	2:16 the dumb ass speaking with m voice	444

MANAEN (1)

| Ac | 13: 1 Niger, and Lucius of Cyrene, and M, | 3127 |

MANAHATH (3) [MANAHETHITES]

Ge	36:23 Alvan, and M, and Ebal, Shepho,	4506
1Ch	1:40 and M, and Ebal, Shephi, and Onam.	4506
	8: 6 of Geba, and they removed them to M:	4506

MANAHETHITES (2) [MANAHATH]

| 1Ch | 2:52 had sons; Haroeh, and half of the M. | 2679 |
| | 2:54 of Joab, and half of the M, the Zorites. | 2680 |

MANASSEH (143) [MANASSEH'S, MANASSES, MANASSITES]

Ge	41:51 called the name of the firstborn M:	4519
	46:20 Joseph in the land of Egypt were born M	4519
	48: 1 with him his two sons, M and Ephraim.	4519
	48: 5 now thy two sons, Ephraim and M,	4519
	48:13 M in his left hand towards Israel's right	4519
	48:14 hands wittingly; for M was the firstborn.	4519
	48:20 God make thee as Ephraim and as M:	4519
	48:20 Manasseh: and he set Ephraim before M.	4519
	50:23 of M were brought up upon Joseph's	4519
Nu	1:10 of M; Gamaliel the son of Pedahzur.	4519
	1:34 the children of M, by their generations,	4519
	1:35 even of the tribe of M, were thirty and	4519
	2:20 by him shall be the tribe of M:	4519
	2:20 the captain of the children of M shall be	4519
	7:54 of Pedahzur, prince of the children of M:	4519
	10:23 M was Gamaliel the son of Pedahzur.	4519
	13:11 of the tribe of M, Gaddi the son of	4519
	26:28 of Joseph after their families were M	4519
	26:29 the sons of M: of Machir, the family of	4519
	26:34 are the families of M, and those that	4519
	27: 1 Gilead, the son of Machir, the son of M,	4519
	27: 1 of the families of M the son of Joseph:	4519
	32:33 unto half the tribe of M the son of Joseph,	4519
	32:39 children of Machir the son of M went to	4519
	32:40 gave Gilead unto Machir the son of M;	4519
	32:41 Jair the son of M went and took the small	4519
	34:14 half the tribe of M have received their	4519
	34:23 for the tribe of the children of M,	4519
	36: 1 the son of Machir, the son of M,	4519
	36:12 of the sons of M the son of Joseph,	4519
Dt	3:13 of Og, gave I unto the half tribe of M;	4519
	3:14 Jair the son of M took all the country of	4519
	29: 8 to the Gadites, and to the half tribe of M.	4520
	33:17 and they are the thousands of M.	4519
	34: 2 M, and all the land of Judah, unto	4519
Jos	1:12 to half the tribe of M, spake Joshua,	4519
	4:12 children of Gad, and half the tribe of M,	4519
	12: 6 and the Gadites, and the half tribe of M,	4519
	13: 7 the nine tribes, and the half tribe of M,	4519
	13:29 inheritance unto the half tribe of M:	4519
	13:29 of the children of M by their families.	4519
	13:31 unto the children of Machir the son of M,	4519
	14: 4 Joseph were two tribes, M and Ephraim:	4519
	16: 4 M and Ephraim, took their inheritance.	4519
	16: 9 the inheritance of the children of M,	4519
	17: 1 There was also a lot for the tribe of M;	4519
	17: 1 to wit, for Machir the firstborn of M,	4519
	17: 2 rest of the children of M by their families;	4519
	17: 2 were the male children of M the son	4519
	17: 3 the son of M, had no sons, but daughters:	4519
	17: 5 fell ten portions to M, beside the land	4519
	17: 6 Because the daughters of M had an	4519
	17: 7 the coast of M was from Asher to	4519
	17: 8 Now M had the land of Tappuah:	4519
	17: 8 Tappuah on the border of M belonged to	4519
	17: 9 of Ephraim are among the cities of M:	4519
	17: 9 coast of M also was on the north side of	4519
	17:11 M had in Issachar and in Asher	4519
	17:12 the children of M could not drive out	4519
	17:17 even to Ephraim and to M, saying, Thou	4519
	18: 7 Gad, and Reuben, and half the tribe of M,	4519
	20: 8 Golan in Bashan out of the tribe of M.	4519
	21: 5 and out of the half tribe of M, ten cities.	4519
	21: 6 out of the half tribe of M in Bashan,	4519

M (thumb index tab, right margin)

Jos 21:25 out of the half tribe of **M**, Tanach with 4519
21:27 out of the half tribe of **M** *they* gave 4519
22: 1 and the Gadites, and the half tribe of **M**, 4519
22: 7 Now to the *one* half of the tribe of **M** 4519
22: 9 of Gad and the half tribe of **M** returned, 4519
22:10 the half tribe of **M** built there an altar by 4519
22:11 the half tribe of **M** have built an altar over 4519
22:13 of Gad, and to the half tribe of **M**, 4519
22:15 of Gad, and to the half tribe of **M**, 4519
22:21 of Gad and the half tribe of **M** answered, 4519
22:30 of Gad and the children of **M** spake, 4519
22:31 of Gad, and the children of **M**, 4519
Jdg 1:27 Neither did **M** drive out *the inhabitants* 4519
6:15 my family *is* poor in **M**, and I *am* the least 4519
6:35 he sent messengers throughout all **M**; 4519
7:23 out of all **M**, and pursued after 4519
11:29 he passed over Gilead and **M**, 4519
18:30 son of **M**, he and his sons were priests 4519
1Ki 4:13 pertained *the towns* of Jair the son of **M**, 4519
2Ki 20:21 and **M** his son reigned in his stead. 4519
21: 1 **M** *was* twelve years old when he *began* 4519
21: 9 **M** seduced them to do more evil than did 4519
21:11 Because **M** king of Judah hath done these 4519
21:16 Moreover **M** shed innocent blood very 4519
21:17 the rest of the acts of **M**, and all that 4519
21:18 **M** slept with his fathers, and was buried 4519
21:20 sight of the LORD, as his father **M** did. 4519
23:12 the altars which **M** had made in the two 4519
23:26 of all the provocations that **M** had 4519
24: 3 for the sins of **M**, according to all that he 4519
1Ch 3:13 his son, Hezekiah his son, **M** his son, 4519
5:18 the Gadites, and half the tribe of **M**, 4519
5:23 children of the half tribe of **M** dwelt in 4519
5:26 the half tribe of **M**, and brought them 4519
6:61 *namely, out of the* half *tribe* of **M**, by lot, 4519
6:62 out of the tribe of **M** in Bashan, 4519
6:70 out of the half tribe of **M**; Aner with her 4519
6:71 out of the family of the half tribe of **M**, 4519
7:14 The sons of **M**; Ashriel, whom she bare: 4519
7:17 Gilead, the son of Machir, the son of **M**. 4519
7:29 by the borders of the children of **M**, 4519
9: 3 and of the children of Ephraim, and **M**, 4519
12:19 there fell *some* of **M** to David, when he 4519
12:20 fell to him of **M**, Adnah, and Jozabad, 4519
12:20 captains of the thousands that *were* of **M**. 4519
12:31 of the half tribe of **M** eighteen thousand, 4519
12:37 the Gadites, and of the half tribe of **M**, 4519
26:32 the Gadites, and the half tribe of **M**, 4520
27:20 of the half tribe of **M**, Joel the son of 4519
27:21 Of the half *tribe* of **M** in Gilead, Iddo 4519
2Ch 15: 9 with them out of Ephraim and **M**, 4519
30: 1 and wrote letters also to Ephraim and **M**, 4519
30:10 of Ephraim and **M** even unto Zebulun: 4519
30:11 Nevertheless divers of Asher and **M** and 4519
30:18 Ephraim, and **M**, Issachar, and Zebulun, 4519
31: 1 and Benjamin, in Ephraim also and **M**, 4519
32:33 And **M** his son reigned in his stead. 4519
33: 1 **M** *was* twelve years old when he *began* 4519
33: 9 So **M** made Judah and the inhabitants of 4519
33:10 the LORD spake to **M**, and to his people: 4519
33:11 which took **M** among the thorns, 4519
33:13 Then knew that the LORD he *was* God. 4519
33:18 Now the rest of the acts of **M**, 4519
33:20 **M** slept with his fathers, and they buried 4519
33:22 sight of the LORD, as did **M** his father: 4519
33:22 images which **M** his father had made, 4519
33:23 as **M** his father had humbled himself; 4519
34: 6 *so did he* in the cities of **M**, and Ephraim, 4519
34: 9 the doors had gathered of the hand of **M** 4519
Ezr 10:30 Mattaniah, Bezaleel, and Binnui, and **M**. 4519
10:33 Zabad, Eliphelet, Jeremai, **M**, *and* Shimei. 4519
Ps 60: 7 Gilead *is* mine, and **M** *is* mine; 4519
80: 2 and Benjamin and **M** stir up thy strength, 4519
108: 8 Gilead *is* mine; **M** *is* mine; Ephraim also 4519
Isa 9:21 **M**, Ephraim; and Ephraim, Manasseh: 4519
9:21 Manasseh, Ephraim; and Ephraim, **M**: 4519
Jer 15: 4 of **M** the son of Hezekiah king of Judah, 4519
Eze 48: 4 side unto the west side, a *portion* for **M**. 4519
48: 5 by the border of **M**, from the east side 4519

MANASSEH'S (4) [MANASSEH]

Ge 48:14 and his left hand upon **M** head, 4519
48:17 remove it from Ephraim's head unto **M** 4519
Jos 17: 5 the rest of **M** sons had the land of Gilead. 4519
17:10 northward it *was* **M**, and the sea 4519+3807.1

MANASSES (3) [MANASSEH]

Mt 1:10 And Ezekias begat **M**; and Manasses begat 3128
1:10 begat Amon; and Amon begat 3128
Rev 7: 6 Of the tribe of **M** *were* sealed twelve 3128

MANASSITES (3) [MANASSEH]

Dt 4:43 and Golan in Bashan, of the **M**. 4520
Jdg 12: 4 the Ephraimites, *and* among the **M**. 4519
2Ki 10:33 the Reubenites, and the **M**, from Aroer, 4520

MANDRAKES (6)

Ge 30:14 found **m** in the field, and brought them 1736
30:14 Give me, I pray thee, of thy son's **m**. 1736
30:15 take away thy son's **m** also? 1736
30:15 lie with thee to night for thy son's **m**. 1736
30:16 surely I have hired thee with my son's **m**. 1736
SS 7:13 The **m** give a smell, and at our gates *are* 1736

MANEH (1)

Eze 45:12 fifteen shekels, shall be your **m**. 4488

MANGER (3)

Lk 2: 7 in swaddling clothes, and laid him in a **m**; 5336
2:12 in swaddling clothes, lying in a **m**. 5336
2:16 and Joseph, and the babe lying in a **m**. 5336

MANIFEST (39) [MANIFESTATION, MANIFESTED, MANIFESTLY]

Ecc 3:18 that God might **m** them, and that *they* 1305
Lk 8:17 is secret, that shall not be made **m**; 5318
Jn 1:31 but that he should be made **m** to Israel, 5319
3:21 that his deeds may be made **m**, that they 5319
9: 3 the works of God should be made **m** in 5319
14:21 I will love him, and will **m** myself to him. 1718
14:22 how is it that thou wilt **m** thyself unto us, 1718
Ac 4:16 *is* **m** to all them that dwell in Jerusalem; 5318
Ro 1:19 may be known of God is **m** in them; 5318
10:20 I was made **m** unto them that asked not 1717
16:26 now is made **m**, and by the scriptures 5319
1Co 3:13 Every man's work shall be made **m**: 5318
4: 5 will make **m** the counsels of the hearts: 5319
11:19 *are* approved may be made **m** among you. 5318
14:25 thus are the secrets of his heart made **m**; 5318
15:27 all *things* are put under *him, it is* **m** that 1212
2Co 2:14 **maketh m** the savour of his knowledge 5319
4:10 the life also of Jesus might be made **m** 5319
4:11 the life also of Jesus might be made **m** 5319
5:11 we are made **m** unto God; and I trust 5319
5:11 I trust also are made **m** in your 5319
11: 6 we have been throughly made **m** among 5319
Gal 5:19 Now the works of the flesh are **m**, 5318
Eph 5:13 all *things* that are reproved are made **m** 5319
5:13 for whatsoever doth make **m** is light. 5319
Php 1:13 So that my bonds in Christ are **m** in all 5318
Col 1:26 but now is made **m** to his saints: 5319
4: 4 I may make it **m**, as I ought to speak. 5319
2Th 1: 5 *Which is* a **m** token of the righteous 1730
1Ti 3:16 God was in the flesh, justified in 5319
5:25 good works of *some* are **m** beforehand; 4271
2Ti 1:10 is now **made m** by the appearing of our 5319
3: 9 for their folly shall be **m** unto all *men*, as 1552
Heb 4:13 is there any creature *that is* not **m** in 852
9: 8 the holiest *of all* was not yet made **m**, 5319
1Pe 1:20 but was **m** in *these* last times for you, 5319
1Jn 2:19 *went out,* that they might be made **m** 5319
3:10 In this the children of God are **m**, 5318
Rev 15: 4 thee; for thy judgments are made **m**. 5319

MANIFESTATION (3) [MANIFEST]

Ro 8:19 waiteth for the **m** of the sons of God. 602
1Co 12: 7 But the **m** of the Spirit is given to every 5321
2Co 4: 2 by **m** of the truth commending ourselves 5321

MANIFESTED (10) [MANIFEST]

Mk 4:22 is nothing hid, which shall not be **m**; 5319
Jn 2:11 in Cana of Galilee, and **m** forth his glory; 5319
17: 6 I have **m** thy name unto the men which 5319
Ro 3:21 of God without the law is **m**, 5319
Tit 1: 3 But hath in due times **m** his word through 5319
1Jn 1: 2 (For the life was **m**, and we have seen *it*, 5319
1: 2 was with the Father, and was **m** unto us;) 5319
3: 5 And ye know that he was **m** to take away 5319
3: 8 For this purpose the Son of God was **m**, 5319
4: 9 In this was the love of God towards us, 5319

MANIFESTLY (1) [MANIFEST]

2Co 3: 3 Forasmuch as ye are **m** declared to be 5319

MANIFOLD (8)

Ne 9:19 Yet thou in thy **m** mercies forsookest 7227
9:27 according to thy **m** mercies thou gavest 7227
Ps 104:24 O LORD, how **m** are thy works! 7231
Am 5:12 For I know your **m** transgressions and 7227
Lk 18:30 Who shall not receive **m** more in this 4179
Eph 3:10 by the church the **m** wisdom of God, 4182
1Pe 1: 6 are in heaviness through **m** temptations: 4164
4:10 as good stewards of the **m** grace of God. 4164

MANKIND (6) [MAN]

Lev 18:22 Thou shalt not lie with **m**, as with 2145
20:13 If a man also lie with **m**, as he lieth with 2145
Job 12:10 living *thing,* and the breath of all **m**. 376+1320
1Co 6: 9 nor abusers of themselves with **m**, 733
1Ti 1:10 for **them that defile** themselves with **m**, 733
Jas 3: 7 sea, is tamed, and hath been tamed of **m**: 442

MANNA (19)

Ex 16:15 saw *it,* they said one to another, It *is* **m**: 4478
16:31 of Israel called the name thereof **M**: 4478
16:33 put an omer full of **m** therein, and lay it 4478
16:35 children of Israel did eat **m** forty years, 4478
16:35 they did eat **m**, until they came unto 4478
Nu 11: 6 at all, beside *this* **m**, *before* our eyes. 4478
11: 7 the **m** *was* as coriander seed, and the 4478
11: 9 the camp in the night, the **m** fell upon it. 4478
Dt 8: 3 thee to hunger, and fed thee with **m**, 4478
8:16 Who fed thee in the wilderness with **m**, 4478
Jos 5:12 the **m** ceased on the morrow after they 4478
5:12 neither had the children of Israel **m** any 4478
Ne 9:20 withheldest not thy **m** from their mouth, 4478
Ps 78:24 had rained down **m** upon them to eat, 4478
Jn 6:31 Our fathers did eat **m** in the desert; as it 3131
6:49 Your fathers did eat **m** in the wilderness, 3131

Jn 6:58 as your fathers did eat **m**, and are dead: 3131
Heb 9: 4 wherein *was* the golden pot that had **m**, 3131
Rev 2:17 will I give to eat of the hidden **m**, 3131

MANNER (196) [MANNERS]

Ge 18:11 it ceased to be with Sarah after the **m** of 734
18:25 That be far from thee to do after this **m**, 1697
19:31 unto us after the **m** of all the earth: 1870
25:23 two **m** of people shall be separated from NIH
32:19 On this **m** shall you speak unto Esau, 1697
39:19 After this **m** did thy servant to me; 1697
40:13 after the former **m** when thou wast his 4941
40:17 the uppermost basket *there was* of all **m** NIH
45:23 his father he sent after this **m**; ten asses NIH
Ex 1:14 brick, and in **all m** of service in the field: 3605
7:11 they also did in **like m** with their 3651
12:16 no **m** *of* work shall be done in them, NIH
21: 9 he shall deal with her after the **m** of 4941
22: 9 all **m** of trespass, *whether it be* for ox, 1697
22: 9 for **any m** of lost *thing,* which *another* 3605
23:11 In **like m** thou shalt deal with thy 3651
31: 3 knowledge, and in all **m** of workmanship, NIH
31: 5 timber, to work in all **m** of workmanship; NIH
35:29 them willing to bring for all **m** of work, NIH
35:31 knowledge, and in all **m** of workmanship; NIH
35:33 wood, to make any **m** of cunning work. NIH
35:35 to work all **m** of work, of the engraver, NIH
36: 1 understanding to know how to work all **m** NIH
Lev 5:10 for a burnt offering, according to the **m**: 4941
7:23 Ye shall eat no **m** fat, of ox, or of sheep, NIH
7:26 Moreover ye shall eat no **m** of blood, NIH
7:27 Whatsoever soul *it be* that eateth any **m** NIH
9:16 and offered it according to the **m**. 4941
11:27 among all **m** of beasts that go on *all* four, NIH
11:44 shall ye defile yourselves with any **m** NIH
14:54 This *is* the law for all **m** of plague of NIH
17:10 among you, that eateth any **m** of blood; NIH
17:14 Ye shall eat the blood of no **m** of flesh; NIH
19:23 shall have planted all **m** of trees for food, NIH
20:25 by any **m** of *living thing* that creepeth *on* NIH
23:31 Ye shall do no **m** of work: *it shall be a* NIH
24:22 Ye shall have **one m** of law, as well for 259
Nu 5:13 neither she be taken *with the* **m**; NIH
9:14 according to the **m** thereof, so shall he do 4941
15:13 shall do these *things* after this **m**, 3602
15:16 One law and one **m** shall be for you, 4941
15:24 according to the **m**, and one kid of 4941
28:18 ye shall do no **m** of servile work *therein:* NIH
28:24 **After** this **m** ye shall offer daily, 3509.1
29: 6 unto their **m**, for a sweet savour, 4941
29:18 according to their number, after the **m**: 4941
29:21 according to their number, after the **m** 4941
29:24 according to their number, after the **m**: 4941
29:27 according to their number, after the **m**: 4941
29:30 according to their number, after the **m**: 4941
29:33 according to their number, after the **m**: 4941
29:37 according to their number, after the **m**: 4941
31:30 of all **m** of beasts, and give them unto NIH
Dt 4:15 for ye saw no **m** of similitude on the day NIH
15: 2 this *is* the **m** of the release: Every creditor 1697
22: 3 In **like m** shalt thou do with his ass; and 3651
27:21 *be* he that lieth with any **m** of beast. NIH
Jos 6:15 compassed the city after the same **m** NIH
Jdg 8:18 **What m** of men *were they* whom ye slew 375
11:17 they sent unto the king of 1571
18: 7 after the **m** of the Zidonians, quiet and 4941
Ru 4: 7 this *was* the **m** in former time in Israel NIH
1Sa 8: 9 shew them the **m** of the king that shall 4941
8:11 This will be the **m** of the king that shall 4941
10:25 Samuel told the people the **m** of 4941
17:27 the people answered him after this **m**, 1697
17:30 and spake after the same **m**: 1697
17:30 answered him again after the former **m**. 1697
18:24 told them, saying, On this **m** spake David. 1697
19:24 prophesied before Samuel in **like m**, 1571
21: 5 and *the bread is in* a **m** common, yea, 1870
27:11 will *he* be **m** all the while he dwelleth in 4941
2Sa 6: 5 on all **m** of *instruments made of* fir wood, NIH
7:19 And *is* this the **m** of man, O Lord GOD? 8452
14: 3 the king, and speak on this **m**. NIH
15: 6 on this **m** did Absalom to all Israel that 1697
17: 6 Ahithophel hath spoken after this **m**. 1697
1Ki 7:28 the work of the bases *was* on this **m**: they NIH
7:37 After this **m** he made the ten bases: all of 4941
18:28 cut themselves after their **m** with knives 4941
22:20 one said on **this m**, and another said on 3541
22:20 this manner, and another said on that **m**. 3541
2Ki 1: 7 What **m** of man *was* he which came up 4941
11:14 as the **m** *was,* and the princes and 4941
17:26 know not the **m** of the God of the land: 4941
17:26 know not the **m** of the God of the land. 4941
17:27 let him teach them the **m** of the God of 4941
17:33 after the **m** of the nations whom they 4941
17:40 but they did after their former **m**. 4941
1Ch 6:48 *of* service of the tabernacle of the house NIH
12:37 with all **m** of instruments of war for NIH
18:10 *with him* all **m** of vessels of gold and silver NIH
22:15 all **m** of cunning *men* for every manner of NIH
22:15 all manner of cunning *men* for every **m** of NIH
23:29 is fried, and for all **m** of measure and size; NIH
24:19 according to their **m**, under Aaron their NIH
28:14 of all **m** of service; 5656+5656+2050.1
28:21 *there shall be* with thee for all **m** of NIH
28:21 willing skilful *man*, for any **m** of service: NIH
29: 2 all **m** of precious stones, and marble NIH

1Ch	29: 5 for all **m** of work *to be made* by the hands	NIH
2Ch	2:14 also to grave any **m** of graving, and to find	NIH
	4:20 that they should burn after the **m** before	4941
	13: 9 have made you priests **after the m of**	3509.1
	18:19 one spake **after this m,**	3602
	18:19 and another saying **after this m.**	3602
	30:16 they stood in their place after their **m,**	4941
	32:15 nor persuade you on this **m,** neither yet	NIH
	32:27 shields, and for all **m** of pleasant jewels;	NIH
	32:28 stalls for all **m** of beasts, and cotes for	NIH
	34:13 work in **any m of service:**	5656+5656+2050.1
Ezr	5: 4 said we unto them **after this m,** What	3660
Ne	6: 4 and I answered them after the same **m.**	1697
	6: 5 Sanballat his servant unto me in like **m**	1697
	8:18 solemn assembly, according to the **m.**	4941
	10:37 fruit of all **m** of wine and of oil,	NIH
	13:15 grapes, and figs, and all **m** of burdens,	NIH
	13:16 all **m** of ware, and sold on the sabbath	NIH
Est	1:13 the king's **m** towards all that knew law	1697
	2:12 according to the **m** of the women, (for so	1881
Ps	107:18 Their soul abhorreth all **m** of meat;	NIH
	144:13 **all m of store:**	413+2177+2177+4480
SS	7:13 at our gates *are* all **m** of pleasant *fruits,*	NIH
Isa	5:17 shall the lambs feed after their **m,**	1699
	10:24 staff against thee, **after the m** of Egypt.	1870
	10:26 so shall he lift it up after the **m** of Egypt.	1870
	51: 6 that dwell therein shall die in **like m:**	3654
Jer	13: 9 **After this m** will I mar the pride of	3602
	22:21 This *hath been* thy **m** from thy youth,	1870
	30:18 palace shall remain after the **m** thereof.	4941
Eze	20:30 ye polluted after the **m** of your fathers?	1870
	23:15 *after* the **m** of the Babylonians of Chaldea,	1823
	23:45 they shall judge them **after the m** of	4941
	23:45 **after the m** of women that shed blood;	4941
Da	6:23 no **m** of hurt was found upon him,	3606
Am	4:10 you the pestilence after the **m** of Egypt:	1870
	8:14 liveth; and, The **m** of Beer-sheba liveth;	1870
Mt	4:23 and healing all **m** of sickness and	NIG
	4:23 and all **m** of disease among the people.	NIG
	5:11 shall say **all m** of evil against you falsely,	3956
	6: 9 **After this m** therefore pray ye: Our	3779
	8:27 saying, **What m of man** is this, that even	4217
	10: 1 to heal all **m** of sickness and all **manner**	NIG
	10: 1 *manner* of sickness and all **m** of disease.	NIG
	12:31 All **m** of sin and blasphemy shall be	NIG
Mk	4:41 What **m** of man is this, that even the wind	4217
	13: 1 see **what m** of stones and what buildings	4217
	13:29 **So ye in like m,** when ye shall see	2532+3779
Lk	1:29 cast in her mind **what m** of salutation this	4217
	1:66 saying, What **m** of child shall this be!	NIG
	6:23 for **in the like m** did their	846+2596+3588
	7:39 **what m** of woman *this is* that toucheth	4217
	8:25 one to another, What **m** of man is this?	NIG
	9:55 Ye know not **what m** of spirit ye are of.	3634
	11:42 ye tithe mint and rue and all **m** of herbs,	NIG
	20:31 took her; and **in like m** the seven also:	5615
	24:17 **What m** of communications *are* these that	NIG
Jn	2: 6 **after the m** of the purifying of the Jews,	2596
	7:36 What **m** of saying is this that he said,	NIG
	19:40 the spices, as the **m** of the Jews is to bury.	1485
Ac	1:11 come **in like m** as ye have seen him go	5158
	10:12 Wherein were all **m** of fourfooted beasts of	NIG
	15: 1 Except ye be circumcised **after the m**	1485
	15:23 they wrote *letters* by them **after this m;**	3592
	17: 2 Paul, as his **m** was, went in unto them,	1486
	20:18 **after what m** I have been with you at all	4459
	22: 3 according to the **perfect m** of the law	195
	23:25 And he wrote a letter **after this m:**	5179
	25:16 It is not the **m** of the Romans to deliver	1485
	25:20 because I doubted of such **m** of questions,	NIG
	26: 4 My **m of life** from *my* youth, which was	981
Ro	6:19 I speak **after the m of men** because of	442
	7: 8 wrought in me all **m** of concupiscence.	NIG
1Co	7: 7 his proper gift of God, one **after this m,**	3779
	11:25 **After the same m** also *he took* the cup,	5615
	15:32 If **after the m** of men I have fought with	2596
2Co	7: 9 ye were made sorry **after a godly m,**	2596
Gal	2:14 livest **after the m of Gentiles,** and not	1483
	3:15 Brethren, I speak **after the m** of men;	2596
1Th	1: 5 know **what m** of *men* we were among	3634
	1: 9 they themselves shew of us **what m of**	3697
1Ti	2: 9 **In like m** also, that women adorn	5615
2Ti	3:10 **m of life,** purpose, faith, longsuffering,	72
Heb	10:25 as the **m** of some *is;* but exhorting *one*	1485
Jas	1:24 straightway forgetteth **what m of** man he	3697
1Pe	1:11 **what m** of time the Spirit of Christ which	4169
	1:15 so be ye holy in all **m** of conversation;	NIG
	3: 5 For **after this m** in the old time the holy	3779
2Pe	3:11 **what m** of *persons* ought ye to be in all	4217
1Jn	3: 1 **what m** of love the Father hath bestowed	4217
Jude	1: 7 in like **m** giving themselves over to	5158
Rev	11: 5 hurt them, he must **in this m** be killed.	3779
	18:12 and all **m** vessels of ivory, and all **manner**	NIG
	18:12 and all **m** vessels of most precious wood,	NIG
	21:19 garnished with all **m** of precious stones.	NIG
	22: 2 which bare twelve **m** of fruits,	NIG

MANNERS (6) [MANNER]

Lev	20:23 ye shall not walk in the **m** of the nation,	2708
2Ki	17:34 Unto this day they do after the former **m:**	4941
Eze	11:12 have done after the **m** of the heathen that	4941
Ac	13:18 **suffered** he their **m** in the wilderness.	5159
1Co	15:33 evil communications corrupt good **m.**	2239
Heb	1: 1 **in divers m** spake in time past	4187

MANOAH (18)

Jdg	13: 2 of the Danites, whose name *was* M;	4495
	13: 8 **M** intreated the LORD, and said, O my	4495
	13: 9 God hearkened to the voice of **M,**	4495
	13: 9 but **M** her husband *was* not with her.	4495
	13:11 **M** arose, and went after his wife,	4495
	13:12 **M** said, Now let thy words come to pass.	4495
	13:13 the angel of the LORD said unto **M,** Of all	4495
	13:15 **M** said unto the angel of the LORD,	4495
	13:16 the angel of the LORD said unto **M,**	4495
	13:16 For **M** knew not that he *was* an angel of	4495
	13:17 **M** said unto the angel of the LORD,	4495
	13:19 So **M** took a kid with a meat offering,	4495
	13:19 and **M** and his wife looked on.	4495
	13:20 **M** and his wife looked on *it,* and fell on	4495
	13:21 of the LORD did no more appear to **M**	4495
	13:21 **M** knew that he *was* an angel of	4495
	13:22 **M** said unto his wife, We shall surely die,	4495
	16:31 in the buryingplace of **M** his father.	4495

MANSERVANT (12) [MAN, SERVE]

Ex	20:10 nor thy son, nor thy daughter, thy **m,**	5650
	20:17 his **m,** nor his maidservant, nor his ox,	5650
	21:32 If the ox shall push a **m** or a maidservant;	5650
Dt	5:14 nor thy son, nor thy daughter, nor thy **m,**	5650
	5:14 thy **m** and thy maidservant may rest as	5650
	5:21 or his **m,** or his maidservant, his ox,	5650
	12:18 **m,** and thy maidservant, and the Levite	5650
	16:11 **m,** and thy maidservant, and the Levite,	5650
	16:14 **m,** and thy maidservant, and the Levite,	5650
Job	31:13 If I did despise the cause of my **m** or of	5650
Jer	34: 9 That every man should let his **m,**	5650
	34:10 heard that every one should let his **m,**	5650

MANSERVANT'S (1) [MAN, SERVE]

Ex	21:27 if he smite out his **m** tooth,	5650

MANSERVANTS (1) [MAN, SERVE]

Ne	7:67 Beside their **m** and their maidservants,	5650

MANSIONS (1)

Jn	14: 2 In my Father's house are many **m:** if *it*	3438

MANSLAYER (2) [MAN, SLAY]

Nu	35: 6 which ye shall appoint for the **m,** that he	7523
	35:12 that he die not, until he stand before	7523

MANSLAYERS (1) [MAN, SLAY]

1Ti	1: 9 of fathers and murderers of mothers, for **m,**	409

MANTLE (13) [MANTLES]

Jdg	4:18 into the tent, she covered him with a **m.**	8063
1Sa	15:27 he laid hold upon the skirt of his **m,**	4598
	28:14 cometh up; and he *is* covered with a **m.**	4598
1Ki	19:13 heard *it,* that he wrapped his face in his **m,**	155
	19:19 passed by him, and cast his **m** upon him.	155
2Ki	2: 8 Elijah took his **m,** and wrapt *it* together,	155
	2:13 He took up also the **m** of Elijah that fell	155
	2:14 he took the **m** of Elijah that fell from him,	155
Ezr	9: 3 I rent my garment and my **m,**	4598
	9: 5 having rent my garment and my **m,** I fell	4598
Job	1:20 rent his **m,** and shaved his head,	4598
	2:12 they rent every one his **m,**	4598
Ps	109:29 *with* their own confusion, as *with* a **m.**	4598

MANTLES (1) [MANTLE]

Isa	3:22 the **m,** and the wimples, and the crisping	4595

MANURE PILE See DUNGHILL

MANY (556)

Ge	17: 4 and thou shalt be a father of **m** nations.	1995
	17: 5 a father of **m** nations have I made thee.	1995
	21:34 sojourned in the Philistines' land **m** days.	7227
	37: 3 and he made him a coat **of m colours.**	6446
	37:23 *his* coat **of m colours** that *was* on him;	6446
	37:32 they sent the coat **of m colours,**	6446
	37:34 loins, and mourned for his son **m** days.	7227
Ex	5: 5 The people of the land now *are* **m,**	7227
	19:21 the LORD to gaze, and **m** of them perish.	7227
	23: 2 to decline after **m** to wrest *judgment;*	7227
	35:22 **as m as** were willing hearted,	3605
Lev	15:25 if a woman have an issue of her blood **m**	7227
	25:51 If *there be* yet **m** years *behind,* according	7227
Nu	9:19 tarried long upon the tabernacle **m** days,	7227
	10:36 O LORD, *unto* the **m** thousands of Israel.	7233
	13:18 they *be* strong or weak, few or **m;**	7227
	22: 3 of the people, because they *were* **m:**	7227
	24: 7 seed *shall be* in **m** waters, and his king	7227
	26:54 thou shalt give the more inheritance	7227
	26:56 possession thereof be divided between **m**	7227
	35: 8 *them that have* **m** ye shall give many;	7227
	35: 8 *them that have* many ye shall **give m;**	7235
Dt	1:11 **make** you a thousand times **so m moe**	3254
	1:46 So ye abode in Kadesh **m** days,	7227
	2: 1 and we compassed mount Seir **m** days.	7227
	2:10 a people great, and **m,** and tall,	7227
	2:21 A people great, and **m,** and tall,	7227
	3: 5 bars; beside unwalled towns a great **m.**	7235
	7: 1 hath cast out **m** nations before thee,	7227
	15: 6 thou shalt lend unto **m** nations,	7227
	15: 6 thou shalt reign over **m** nations,	7227
	25: 3 beat him above these **with m** stripes,	7227
	28:12 thou shalt lend unto **m** nations,	7227
	31:17 **m** evils and troubles shall befall them;	7227
	31:21 when **m** evils and troubles are befallen	7227

Dt	32: 7 years of **m** generations:	1755+1755+2050.1
Jos	11: 4 with horses and chariots very **m.**	7227
	22: 3 have not left your brethren these **m** days	834+3605
Jdg	3: 1 **as m** of Israel **as** had not known	7227
	7: 2 people that *are* with thee are **too m** for	7227
	7: 4 unto Gideon, The people *are* yet **too m;**	7227
	8:30 his body begotten: for he had **m** wives.	7227
	9:40 and were overthrown *and* wounded,	7235
	16:24 of our country, which slew **m** of us.	7227
1Sa	2: 5 she that hath **m** children is waxed feeble.	7227
	6:19 the LORD had smitten **m** of the people	NIH
	14: 6 is no restraint to the LORD to save by **m**	7227
	25:10 be **m** servants now a days that break	7231
2Sa	1: 4 **m** of the people also are fallen and dead;	7235
	2:23 that **as m as** came to the place where	3605
	12: 2 The rich *man* had exceeding **m** flocks	7235
	22:17 he took me; he drew me out of **m** waters;	7227
	23:20 of Kabzeel, who had done **m** acts,	7227
	24: 3 how **m** soever they be, an hundredfold,	1992.1
1Ki	2:38 And Shimei dwelt in Jerusalem **m** days.	7227
	4:20 Judah and Israel *were* **m,** as the sand	7230
	7:47 because they were exceeding **m:**	7227
	11: 1 king Solomon loved **m** strange women,	7227
	17:15 and he, and her house, did eat **m** days.	NIH
	18: 1 came to pass *after* **m** days, that the word	7227
	18:25 ye *are* **m;** and call on the name of your	7227
	22:16 said unto him, **How m**	4100+5704+3509.1
2Ki	9:22 and her witchcrafts *are* so **m?**	7227
1Ch	4:27 his brethren had not **m** children, neither	7227
	5:22 For there fell down **m** slain, because	7227
	7: 4 thousand *men:* for they had **m** wives	7235
	7:22 Ephraim their father mourned **m** days,	7227
	8:40 archers, and **had m** sons, and sons' sons,	7227
	11:22 man of Kabzeel, who had done **m** acts;	7227
	21: 3 **make** his people an hundred times	
	so m moe	3254
	23:11 Jeush and Beriah had not **m** sons;	7235
	23:17 but the sons of Rehabiah were very **m.**	7235
	28: 5 (for the LORD hath given me **m** sons,)	7227
2Ch	11:23 in abundance. And he desired **m** wives.	1995
	14:11 *whether* with **m,** or with *them that have*	7227
	16: 8 with very **m** chariots and horsemen?	7235
	18:15 king said to him, **How m**	4100+5704+3509.1
	26:10 towers in the desert, and digged **m** wells:	7227
	29:31 **as m as** were of a free heart burnt	3605
	30:17 For *there were* **m** in the congregation that	7227
	30:18 *even* **m** of Ephraim, and Manasseh,	7227
	32:23 **m** brought gifts unto the LORD to	7227
Ezr	3:12 **m** of the priests and Levites and chief of	7227
	3:12 loud voice; and **m** shouted aloud for joy:	7227
	5:11 build the house that was builded these **m**	7690
	10:13 people *are* **m,** and *it is* a time of much	7227
	10:13 we are **m** that have transgressed in this	7235
Ne	5: 2 We, our sons, and our daughters, *are* **m:**	7227
	6:17 of Judah sent **m** letters unto Tobiah,	7235
	6:18 there were **m** in Judah sworn unto him.	7227
	7: 2 a faithful man, and feared God above **m.**	7227
	9:28 **m** times didst thou deliver them	7227
	9:30 Yet **m** years didst thou forbear them,	7227
	13:26 nations was there no king like him,	7227
Est	1: 4 honour of his excellent majesty **m** days,	7227
	2: 8 when **m** maidens were gathered together	7227
	4: 3 and **m** lay in sackcloth and ashes.	7227
	8:17 **m** of the people of the land became Jews;	7227
Job	4: 3 thou hast instructed **m,** and thou hast	7227
	11:19 yea, **m** shall make suit unto thee.	7227
	13:23 **How m** *are* mine iniquities and	4100+3509.1
	16: 2 I have heard **m** such *things:* miserable	7227
	23:14 for me: and **m** such *things are* with him.	7227
	41: 3 Will he **make m** supplications unto thee?	7235
Ps	3: 1 **m** *are* they that rise up against me.	7227
	3: 2 **M** *there be* which say of my soul, *There*	7227
	4: 6 *be* **m** that say, Who will shew us *any*	7227
	18:16 took me, he drew me out of **m** waters.	7227
	22:12 **M** bulls have compassed me: strong bulls	7227
	25:19 they are **m;** and they hate me *with* cruel	7231
	29: 3 the LORD *is* upon **m** waters.	7227
	31:13 I have heard the slander of **m:** fear *was*	7227
	32:10 **M** sorrows *shall be* to the wicked:	7227
	34:12 *and* loveth **m** days, that *he* may see good?	NIH
	34:19 **M** *are* the afflictions of the righteous:	7227
	37:16 *is* better than the riches of **m** wicked.	7227
	40: 3 **m** shall see *it,* and fear, and shall trust in	7227
	40: 5 **M,** O LORD my God, *are* thy wonderful	7227
	55:18 against me: for there were **m** with me.	7227
	56: 2 for *they be* **m** that fight against me,	7227
	61: 6 years as **m** generations.	1755+1755+2050.1
	71: 7 I am as a wonder unto **m;** but thou *art*	7227
	78:38 **m** a time turned he his anger away,	7235
	93: 4 *is* mightier than the noise of **m** waters,	7227
	106:43 **M** times did he deliver them;	7227
	110: 6 shall wound the heads over **m** countries.	7227
	119:84 **How m** *are* the days of thy	4100+3509.1
	119:157 **M** *are* my persecutors and mine enemies;	7227
	129: 1 **M a time** have they afflicted me from my	7227
	129: 2 **M a time** have they afflicted me from my	7227
Pr	4:10 and the years of thy life shall be **m.**	7235
	6:35 rest content, though thou **givest m** gifts.	7235
	7:26 For she hath cast down **m** wounded: yea,	7227
	7:26 **m** strong *men have* been slain by her.	3605
	10:21 The lips of the righteous feed **m:**	7227
	14:20 neighbour: but the rich *hath* **m** friends.	7227
	19: 4 Wealth maketh **m** friends; but the poor is	7227
	19: 6 **M** will intreat the favour of the prince:	7227
	19:21 *There are* **m** devices in a man's heart;	7227

M

Pr 28: 2 For the transgression of a land **m** *are* — 7227	
28:27 that hideth his eyes shall have **m** a curse. — 7227	
29:26 **M** seek the ruler's favour; but *every* — 7227	
31:29 **M** daughters have done virtuously, — 7227	
Ecc 5: 7 **m** words *there are* also *divers* vanities: — 7235	
6: 3 an hundred *children*, and live **m** years, — 7227	
6: 3 so that the days of his years be **m**, — 7227	
6:11 Seeing there be **m** things that increase — 7235	
7:29 but they have sought out **m** inventions. — 7227	
11: 1 for thou shalt find it after **m** days. — 7230	
11: 8 if a man live **m** years, *and* rejoice in them — 7235	
11: 8 the days of darkness; for they shall be **m**. — 7235	
12: 9 sought out, *and* set in order **m** proverbs. — 7235	
12:12 of making **m** books *there is* no end; — 7235	
SS 8: 7 **M** waters cannot quench love, neither — 7227	
Isa 1:15 yea, when ye **make m** prayers, I will not — 7235	
2: 3 **m** people shall go and say, Come ye, — 7227	
2: 4 the nations, and shall rebuke **m** people: — 7227	
5: 9 Of a truth **m** houses shall be desolate, — 7227	
8: 7 strong and **m**, *even* the king of Assyria, — 7227	
8:15 **m** among them shall stumble, and fall, — 7227	
17:12 Woe to the multitude of **m** people, — 7227	
17:13 nations shall rush like the rushing of **m** — 7227	
22: 9 of the city of David, that they are **m**: — 7231	
23:16 make sweet melody, sing **m** songs, that — 7235	
24:22 and after **m** days shall they be visited. — 7227	
31: 1 and trust in chariots, because *they are* **m**; — 7227	
32:10 **M** days and years shall ye be troubled, — NIH	
42:20 Seeing **m** *things*, but thou observest not; — 7227	
52:14 As **m** were astonied at thee; his visage — 7227	
52:15 So shall he sprinkle **m** nations; the kings — 7227	
53:11 shall my righteous servant justify **m**; — 7227	
53:12 bare the sin of **m**, and made intercession — 7227	
58:12 of **m generations**; — 1755+1755+2050.1	
60:15 a joy of **m generations**. — 1755+1755+2050.1	
61: 4 of **m generations**. — 1755+1755+2050.1	
66:16 and the slain of the LORD shall be **m**. — 7231	
Jer 3: 1 hast played the harlot with **m** lovers; — 7227	
5: 6 because their transgressions are **m**, — 7231	
11:15 she hath wrought lewdness **with m**, — 7227	
12:10 **M** pastors have destroyed my vineyard, — 7227	
13: 6 it came to pass after **m** days, that — 7227	
14: 7 our backslidings are **m**; we have sinned — 7231	
16:16 Behold, I will send for **m** fishers, saith — 7227	
16:16 after will I send for **m** hunters, — 7227	
20:10 For I heard the defaming of **m**, fear on — 7227	
22: 8 **m** nations shall pass by this city, — 7227	
25:14 For **m** nations and great kings shall serve — 7227	
27: 7 **m** nations and great kings shall serve — 7227	
28: 8 old prophesied both against **m** countries, — 7227	
32:14 that they may continue **m** days. — 7227	
35: 7 ye may live **m** days in the land where — 7227	
36:32 were added besides unto them **m** like — 7227	
37:16 Jeremiah had remained there **m** days; — 7227	
42: 2 (for we are left *but* a few of **m**, as thine — 7235	
46:11 in vain shalt thou **use m** medicines; — 7235	
46:16 He **made m** to fall, yea, one fell upon — 7227	
50:41 **m** kings shall be raised up from the coasts — 7227	
51:13 O thou that dwellest upon **m** waters, — 7227	
La 1:22 for my sighs *are* **m**, and my heart is faint. — 7227	
Eze 3: 6 Not to **m** people of a strange speech and — 7227	
12:27 The vision that he seeth is for **m** days *to* — 7227	
16:41 upon thee in the sight of **m** women: — 7227	
17: 7 eagle with great wings and **m** feathers: — 7227	
17: 9 **m** people to pluck it up by the roots — 7227	
17:17 and building forts, to cut off **m** persons: — 7227	
19:10 full of branches by reason of **m** waters. — 7227	
22:25 have **made** her **m** widows in the midst — 7235	
26: 3 will cause **m** nations to come up against — 7227	
27: 3 *art* a merchant of the people for **m** — 7227	
27:15 **m** isles *were* the merchandise of thine — 7227	
27:33 out of the seas, thou filledst **m** people; — 7227	
32: 3 over thee with a company of **m** people; — 7227	
32: 9 I will also vex the hearts of **m** people, — 7227	
32:10 I will make **m** people amazed at thee, — 7227	
33:24 we *are* **m**; the land is given us for — 7227	
37: 2 *there were* very **m** in the open valley; — 7227	
38: 6 all his bands: *and* **m** people with thee. — 7227	
38: 8 After **m** days thou shalt be visited: — 7227	
38: 8 *and* is gathered out of **m** people, against — 7227	
38: 9 all thy bands, and **m** people with thee. — 7227	
38:15 and **m** people with thee, all of them — 7227	
38:17 which prophesied in those days **m** years, — NIH	
38:22 upon the **m** people that *are* with him, — 7227	
38:23 I will be known in the eyes of **m** nations, — 7227	
39:27 am sanctified in them in the sight of **m** — 7227	
43: 2 his voice *was* like a noise of **m** waters: — 7227	
47: 7 at the bank of the river *were* very **m** trees — 7227	
47:10 as the fish of the great sea, exceeding **m**. — 7227	
Da 2:48 gave him **m** great gifts, and made him — 7690	
8:25 his heart, and by peace shall destroy **m**: — 7227	
8:26 up the vision; for *it shall be* for **m** days. — 7227	
9:27 he shall confirm the covenant with **m** *for* — 7227	
10:14 latter days: for yet the vision *is* for **m** days. — NIH	
11:12 he shall cast down *m* ten thousands: — NIH	
11:14 in those times there shall **m** stand up — 7227	
11:18 his face unto the isles, and shall take **m**: — 7227	
11:26 overflow: and **m** shall fall down slain. — 7227	
11:33 among the people shall instruct **m**: — 7227	
11:33 by captivity, and by spoil, *m* days. — NIH	
11:34 but **m** shall cleave to them with flatteries. — 7227	
11:39 he shall cause **m** to rule over **m**, — 7227	
11:40 and with horsemen, and with **m** ships; — 7227	
11:41 and **m** *countries* shall be overthrown: — 7227	
11:44 to destroy, and utterly to make away **m**. — 7227	
---	---
Da 12: 2 **m** of them that sleep in the dust of the — 7227	
12: 3 they that turn **m** to righteousness as — 7227	
12: 4 **m** shall run to and fro, and knowledge — 7227	
12:10 **M** shall be purified, and made white, — 7227	
Hos 3: 3 her, Thou shalt abide for me **m** days; — 7227	
3: 4 For the children of Israel shall abide **m** — 7227	
8:11 Because Ephraim hath **made m** altars to — 7235	
Joel 2: 2 years of **m generations**. — 1755+1755+2050.1	
Am 3: 9 *shall be* **m** dead bodies in every place; — 7227	
Mic 4: 2 **m** nations shall come, and say, Come, — 7227	
4: 3 he shall judge among **m** people, — 7227	
4:11 Now also **m** nations are gathered against — 7227	
4:13 thou shalt beat in pieces **m** people: — 7227	
5: 7 of **m** people as a dew from the LORD, — 7227	
5: 8 **m** people as a lion among the beasts of — 7227	
Na 1:12 Though *they be* quiet, and likewise **m**, — 7227	
3:15 make thyself **m** as the cankerworm, — 3513	
3:15 make thyself **m** as the locusts. — 3513	
Hab 2: 8 Because thou hast spoiled **m** nations, — 7227	
2:10 to thy house by cutting off **m** people, — 7227	
Zec 2:11 **m** nations shall be joined to the LORD in — 7227	
7: 3 as I have done these **so m** years? — 4100+3509.1	
8:20 and the inhabitants of **m** cities: — 7227	
8:22 people and strong nations shall come — 7227	
Mal 2: 6 and did turn **m** away from iniquity. — 7227	
2: 8 ye have caused **m** to stumble at the law; — 7227	
Mt 3: 7 But when he saw **m** of the Pharisees and — 4183	
7:13 and there be which go in thereat: — 4183	
7:22 **M** will say to me in that day, Lord, Lord, — 4183	
7:22 in thy name done **m** wonderful works? — 4183	
8:11 shall come from the east and west, — 4183	
8:16 they brought unto him **m** *that were* — 4183	
8:30 from them a herd of **m** swine feeding. — 4183	
9:10 publicans and sinners came and sat — 4183	
10:31 ye are of more value than **m** sparrows. — 4183	
13: 3 And he spake **m** *things* unto them in — 4183	
13:17 That **m** prophets and righteous *men* have — 4183	
13:58 And he did not **m** mighty works there, — 4183	
14:36 **as m as** touched were made perfectly — 3745	
15:30 **m** others, and cast *them down* at Jesus' — 4183	
15:34 saith unto them, How **m** loaves have ye? — 4214	
16: 9 and **how m** baskets ye took up? — 4214	
16:10 and **how m** baskets ye took up? — 4214	
16:21 and suffer **m** *things* of the elders and — 4183	
19:30 But **m** *that are* first shall be last; — 4183	
20:16 first last: for **m** be called, but few chosen. — 4183	
20:28 and to give his life a ransom for **m**. — 4183	
22: 9 and **as m as** ye shall find, — 302+3745	
22:10 gathered together all **as m as** they found, — 3745	
22:14 For **m** are called, but few *are* chosen. — 4183	
24: 5 **m** shall come in my name, saying, I am — 4183	
24: 5 saying, I am Christ; and shall deceive **m**. — 4183	
24:10 And then shall **m** be offended, — 4183	
24:11 And **m** false prophets shall rise, — 4183	
24:11 prophets shall rise, and shall deceive **m**. — 4183	
24:12 abound, the love of **m** shall wax cold. — 4183	
25:21 **m** *things*: enter thou into the joy of thy — 4183	
25:23 **m** *things*: enter thou into the joy of thy — 4183	
26:28 which is shed for **m** for the remission of — 4183	
26:60 yea, though **m** false witnesses came, — 4183	
27:13 Hearest thou not **how m** *things* they — 4214	
27:19 suffered **m** *things* this day in a dream — 4183	
27:52 and **m** bodies of saints which slept arose, — 4183	
27:53 into the holy city, and appeared unto **m**. — 4183	
27:55 And **m** women were there beholding afar — 4183	
Mk 1:34 And he healed **m** *that were* sick of divers — 4183	
1:34 of divers diseases, and cast out **m** devils; — 4183	
2: 2 straightway **m** were gathered together, — 4183	
2:15 **m** publicans and sinners sat also together — 4183	
2:15 for there were **m**, and they followed him. — 4183	
3:10 For he had healed **m**; insomuch that *they* — 4183	
3:10 for to touch him, **as m as** had plagues. — 3745	
4: 2 he taught them **m** *things* by parables, — 4183	
4:33 And with **m** such parables spake he — 4183	
5: 9 saying, My name *is* Legion: for we are **m**. — 4183	
5:26 And had suffered **m** *things* of many — 4183	
5:26 And had suffered **many** *things* of **m** — 4183	
6: 2 and **m** hearing *him* were astonished, — 4183	
6:13 And they cast out **m** devils, — 4183	
6:13 and anointed with oil **m** *that were* sick, — 4183	
6:20 he did **m** *things*, and heard him gladly. — 4183	
6:31 for there were **m** coming and going, — 4183	
6:33 **m** knew him, and ran afoot thither out — 4183	
6:34 and he began to teach them **m** *things*. — 4183	
6:38 saith unto them, How **m** loaves have ye? — 4214	
6:56 **as m as** touched were made — 302+3745	
7: 4 And **m** other *things* there be, which they — 4183	
7: 8 cups: and **m** other such like *things* ye do. — 4183	
7:13 and **m** such like *things* do ye. — 4183	
8: 5 he asked them, How **m** loaves have ye? — 4214	
8:19 **how m** baskets full of fragments took ye — 4214	
8:20 **how m** baskets full of fragments took ye — 4214	
8:31 that the Son of man must suffer **m** *things*, — 4183	
9:12 that he must suffer **m** *things*, and be set — 4183	
9:26 insomuch that **m** said, He is dead. — 4183	
10:31 But **m** *that are* first shall be last; — 4183	
10:45 and to give his life a ransom for **m**. — 4183	
10:48 **m** charged him that he should hold his — 4183	
11: 8 And **m** spread their garments in the way: — 4183	
12:41 and **m** *that were* rich cast in much. — 4183	
13: 6 **m** shall come in my name, saying, — 4183	
13: 6 saying, I am *Christ*; and shall deceive **m**. — 4183	
14:24 the new testament, which is shed for **m**. — 4183	
14:56 For **m** bare false witness against him, — 4183	
---	---
Mk 15: 3 And the chief priests accused him of **m** — 4183
15: 4 **how m** *things* they witness against — 4214
15:41 **m** other *women* which came up with — 4183
Lk 1: 1 Forasmuch **as m** have taken in hand to — 4183
1:14 gladness; and **m** shall rejoice at his birth. — 4183
1:16 And **m** of the children of Israel shall he — 4183
2:34 for the fall and rising again of **m** in Israel; — 4183
2:35 that the thoughts of **m** hearts may be — 4183
3:18 And **m** other *things* in his exhortation — 4183
4:25 **m** widows were in Israel in the days of — 4183
4:27 And **m** lepers were in Israel in the time of — 4183
4:41 devils also came out of **m**, crying out, — 4183
7:11 and **m** of his disciples went with him, — 2425
7:21 in that *same* hour he cured **m** of *their* — 4183
7:21 unto **m** *that were* blind he gave sight. — 4183
7:47 Her sins, which are **m**, are forgiven; — 4183
8: 3 and Susanna, and **m** others, — 4183
8:30 because **m** devils were entered into him. — 4183
8:32 And there was there a herd of **m** swine — 2425
9:22 The Son of man must suffer **m** *things*, — 4183
10:24 that **m** prophets and kings have desired — 4183
10:41 art careful and troubled about **m** *things*: — 4183
11: 8 rise and give him **as m as** he needeth. — 3745
11:53 to provoke him to speak of **m** *things*: — 4183
12: 7 ye are of more value than **m** sparrows. — 4183
12:19 hast much goods laid up for **m** years; — 4183
12:47 his will, shall be beaten with **m** *stripes*. — 4183
13:24 **m**, I say unto you, will seek to enter in, — 4183
14:16 man made a great supper, and bade **m**: — 4183
15:13 And not **m** days after the younger son — 4183
15:17 **How m** hired *servants* of my father's — 4214
15:29 Lo, **these m** years do I serve thee, — 5118
17:25 But first must he suffer **m** *things*, and — 4183
21: 8 **m** shall come in my name, saying, I am — 4183
22:65 And **m** other *things* blasphemously spake — 4183
23: 8 because *he* had heard **m** *things* of him — 4183
23: 9 he questioned *with* him in **m** words; — 2425
Jn 1:12 But **as m as** received him, to them gave — 3745
2:12 and they continued there not **m** days. — 4183
2:23 in the feast *day*, **m** believed in his name, — 4183
4:39 And **m** of the Samaritans of that city — 4183
4:41 And **m** moe believed because of his own — 4183
6: 9 but what are they among **so m**? — 5118
6:60 **M** therefore of his disciples, when they — 4183
6:66 From that *time* **m** of his disciples went — 4183
7:31 And **m** of the people believed on him, — 4183
7:40 **M** of the people therefore, when they — 4183
8:26 I have **m** *things* to say and to judge of — 4183
8:30 As he spake these *words*, **m** believed on — 4183
10:20 And **m** of them said, He hath a devil, — 4183
10:32 **M** good works have I shewed you from — 4183
10:41 and **m** resorted unto him, and said, John — 4183
10:42 and **m** believed on him there. — 4183
11:19 And **m** of the Jews came to Martha and — 4183
11:45 Then **m** of the Jews which came to Mary, — 4183
11:47 do we? for this man doeth **m** miracles. — 4183
11:55 **m** went out of the country up to — 4183
12:11 Because that by reason of him **m** of — 4183
12:37 he had done **so m** miracles before them, — 5118
12:42 among the chief rulers also **m** — 4183
14: 2 In my Father's house are **m** mansions: if — 4183
16:12 I have yet **m** *things* to say unto you, — 4183
17: 2 life to **as m as** thou hast given him. — 3739+3956
19:20 This title then read **m** of the Jews: — 4183
20:30 And **m** other signs truly did Jesus in — 4183
21:11 and for **all** there were **so m**, *yet* was not — 5118
21:25 there are also **m** other *things* which — 4183
Ac 1: 3 after his passion by **m** infallible proofs, — 4183
1: 5 with the Holy Ghost not **m** days hence. — 4183
2:40 And with **m** other words did he testify — 4183
2:43 and **m** wonders and signs were done by — 4183
3:24 that follow after, **as m as** have spoken, — 3745
4: 4 **m** of them which heard the word — 4183
4: 6 as **m** as were of the kindred of the high — 3745
4:34 for **as m as** were possessors of lands or — 3745
5:11 and upon **as m as** heard these *things*. — 3956
5:12 by the hands of the apostles were **m** — 4183
5:36 and all, **as m as** obeyed him, — 3745
5:37 and all, *even* **as m as** obeyed him, — 3745
8: 7 came out of **m** that were possessed *with* — 4183
8: 7 *with them*: and **m** taken with palsies, — 4183
8:25 preached the gospel in **m** villages of — 4183
9:13 Lord, I have heard by **m** of this man, — 4183
9:23 And after that **m** days were fulfilled, — 2425
9:42 all Joppa; and **m** believed in the Lord. — 4183
9:43 that he tarried **m** days in Joppa with one — 2425
10:27 and found **m** *that were* come together. — 4183
10:45 **as m as** came with Peter, because that — 3745
12:12 where **m** were gathered together praying. — 2425
13:31 And he was seen **m** days of them which — 4183
13:43 **m** of the Jews and religious proselytes — 4183
13:48 **as m as** were ordained to eternal life — 3745
14:21 and had taught **m**, they returned *again* to — 2425
15:32 exhorted the brethren with **m** words, — 4183
15:35 the word of the Lord, with **m** others also. — 4183
16:18 And this did she **m** days. But Paul, — 4183
16:23 And when they had laid **m** stripes upon — 4183
17:12 Therefore **m** of them believed; also of — 4183
18: 8 **m** of the Corinthians hearing believed, — 4183
19:18 And **m** that believed came, and confessed, — 4183
19:19 **M** also of them which used curious arts — 2425
20: 8 And there were **m** lights in the upper — 2425
20:19 and *with* **m** tears, and temptations, — 4183
21:10 as we tarried *there* **m** days, there came — 4183

Ac	21:20 **how m** thousands of Jews there are	4214
	24:10 been of **m** years a judge unto this nation,	4183
	24:17 Now after **m** years I came to bring alms to	4183
	25: 7 laid and grievous complaints against	4183
	25:14 And when they had been there **m** days,	4183
	26: 9 that *I* ought to do **m** *things* contrary to	4183
	26:10 **m** of the saints did I shut up in prison,	4183
	27: 7 And when we had sailed slowly **m** days,	2425
	27:20 when neither sun nor stars in **m** days	4183
	28:10 Who also honoured us with **m** honours;	4183
	28:23 there came **m** to him into his lodging;	4183
Ro	2:12 For **as m as** have sinned without law	3745
	2:12 **as m as** have sinned in the law shall be	3745
	4:17 I have made thee a father of **m** nations,)	4183
	4:18 that he might become the father of **m**	4183
	5:15 For if through the offence of one **m** be	4183
	5:15 Jesus Christ, hath abounded unto **m.**	4183
	5:16 the free gift *is* of **m** offences unto	4183
	5:19 as by one man's disobedience **m** were	4183
	5:19 by the obedience of one shall **m** be made	4183
	6: 3 so **m** of us as were baptized into Jesus	3745
	8:14 For **as m as** are led by the Spirit of God,	3745
	8:29 that he might be the firstborn amongst **m**	4183
	12: 4 For as we have **m** members in one body,	4183
	12: 5 So we, being **m**, are one body in Christ,	4183
	15:23 a great desire these **m** years to come	4183
	16: 2 for she hath been a succourer of **m**,	4183
1Co	1:26 how that not **m** wise *men* after the flesh,	4183
	1:26 **m** mighty, not many noble, *are* called:	4183
	1:26 many mighty, not **m** noble, *are* called:	4183
	4:15 In Christ, yet *have ye* not **m** fathers:	4183
	8: 5 (as there be gods **m**, and lords many,)	4183
	8: 5 (as there be gods many, and lords **m**,)	4183
	10: 5 But with **m** of them God was not well	4183
	10:17 For we being **m** are one bread,	4183
	10:33 the *profit* of **m**, that they may be saved.	4183
	11:30 For this cause **m** *are* weak and	4183
	11:30 and sickly among you, and **m** sleep.	2425
	12:12 hath **m** members, and all the members	4183
	12:12 of *that* one body, being **m**, are one body:	4183
	12:14 For the body is not one member, but **m**.	4183
	12:20 But now *are they* **m** members, yet *but*	4183
	14:10 **so m** kinds of voices in the world,	5118
	16: 9 unto me, and *there are* **m** adversaries.	4183
2Co	1:11 **m** persons thanks may be given by many	4183
	1:11 thanks may be given by **m** on our behalf.	4183
	2: 4 anguish of heart I wrote unto you with **m**	4183
	2: 6 punishment, which *was inflicted* of **m**.	4183
	2:17 For we are not as **m**, which corrupt	4183
	4:15 of **m** redound to the glory of God.	4183
	6:10 as poor, yet making **m** rich; as having	4183
	8:22 oftentimes proved diligent in **m** *things*,	4183
	9: 2 and your zeal hath provoked **very m**.	4183
	9:12 is abundant also by **m** thanksgivings unto	4183
	11:18 Seeing that **m** glory after the flesh, I will	4183
	12:21 *that* I shall bewail **m** which have sinned	4183
Gal	1:14 profited in the Jews' religion above **m**	4183
	3: 4 Have ye suffered **so m** *things* in vain?	5118
	3:10 For **as m as** are of the works of the law	3745
	3:16 He saith not, And to seeds, as of **m**;	4183
	3:27 **as m** of you **as** have been baptized into	3745
	4:27 for the desolate hath **moe** children	4183
	6:12 **As m as** desire to make a fair shew in	3745
	6:16 And **as m as** walk according to this rule,	3745
Php	1:14 And **m** of the brethren in the Lord,	4183
	3:15 **as m as** *be* perfect, be thus minded:	3745
	3:18 (For **m** walk, of whom I have told you	4183
Col	2: 1 *for* **as m as** have not seen my face in	3745
1Ti	6: 1 Let **as m** servants **as** are under the yoke	3745
	6: 9 and *into* **m** foolish and hurtful lusts,	4183
	6:10 pierced themselves through with **m**	4183
	6:12 professed a good profession before **m**	4183
2Ti	1:18 in **how m** *things* he ministered *unto* me	3745
	2: 2 hast heard of me among **m** witnesses,	4183
Tit	1:10 For there are **m** unruly and vain talkers	4183
Heb	2:10 whom *all things*, in bringing **m** sons	4183
	5:11 Of whom we have **m things** to say,	4183
	7:23 And they truly were **m** priests, because	4183
	9:28 was once offered to bear the sins of **m**;	4183
	11:12 *so* **m** as the stars of the sky in multitude,	NIG
	12:15 trouble *you*, and thereby **m** be defiled;	4183
Jas	3: 1 My brethren, be not **m** masters,	4183
	3: 2 For in **m** *things* we offend all. If any *man*	4183
2Pe	2: 2 And **m** shall follow their pernicious ways;	4183
1Jn	2:18 even now are there **m** antichrists;	4183
	4: 1 **m** false prophets are gone out into	4183
2Jn	1: 7 **m** deceivers are entered into the world,	4183
	1:12 Having **m things** to write unto you, I	4183
3Jn	1:13 I had **m things** to write,	4183
Rev	1:15 and his voice as the sound of **m** waters.	4183
	2:24 **as m as** have not this doctrine,	3745
	3:19 **As m as** I love, I rebuke and	1437+3745
	5:11 I heard the voice of **m** angels round about	4183
	8:11 and **m** men died of the waters, because	4183
	9: 9 of chariots of **m** horses running to battle.	4183
	10:11 Thou must prophesy again before **m**	4183
	13:15 cause that **as m as** would not worship	3745
	14: 2 as the voice of **m** waters, and as the voice	4183
	17: 1 great whore that sitteth upon **m** waters:	4183
	18:17 and sailors, and **as m as** trade by sea,	3745
	19: 6 and as the voice of **m** waters, and as	4183
	19:12 of fire, and on his head *were* **m** crowns;	4183

MAOCH (1)

1Sa	27: 2 unto Achish, the son of **M**, king of Gath.	4582

MAON (7) [MAONITES]

Jos	15:55 **M**, Carmel, and Ziph, and Juttah,	4584
1Sa	23:24 and his men *were* in the wilderness of **M**,	4584
	23:25 a rock, and abode in the wilderness of **M**.	4584
	25: 2 *there was* a man in **M**, whose possessions	4584
1Ch	2:45 the son of Shammai *was* **M**: and Maon	4584
	2:45 And **M** *was* the father of Beth-zur.	4584

MAONITES (1) [MAON]

Jdg	10:12 the Amalekites, and the **M**, did oppress	4584

MAR (6) [MARRED]

Lev	19:27 neither shalt thou **m** the corners of thy	7843
Ru	4: 6 myself, lest I **m** mine own inheritance:	7843
1Sa	6: 5 and images of your mice that **m** the land;	7843
2Ki	3:19 **m** every good piece of land with stones.	3510
Job	30:13 They **m** my path, they set forward my	5420
Jer	13: 9 After this manner will I **m** the pride of	7843

MARA (1)

Ru	1:20 them, Call me not Naomi, call me **M**:	4755

MARAH (5)

Ex	15:23 they came to **M**, they could not drink	4785
	15:23 they could not drink of the waters of **M**,	4785
	15:23 the name of it was called **M**.	4785
Nu	33: 8 wilderness of Etham, and pitched in **M**.	4785
	33: 9 they removed from **M**, and came unto	4785

MARALAH (1)

Jos	19:11 **M**, and reached to Dabbasheth,	4831

MARAN-ATHA (1)

1Co	16:22 Jesus Christ, let him be anathema, **M**.	3134

MARBLE (5)

1Ch	29: 2 and **m** stones in abundance.	7893
Est	1: 6 purple to silver rings and pillars of **m**:	8336
	1: 6 red, and **blue**, and white, and black **m**.	8336
SS	5:15 His legs *are as* pillars of **m**, set upon	8336
Rev	18:12 of brass, and iron, and **m**,	3139

MARCH (5) [MARCHED, MARCHEDST]

Ps	68: 7 thou didst **m** through the wilderness;	6805
Jer	46:22 for they shall **m** with an army,	1980
Joel	2: 7 they shall **m** every one on his ways,	1980
Hab	1: 6 which *shall* **m** through the breadth of	1980
	3:12 Thou didst **m through** the land in	6805

MARCHED (1) [MARCH]

Ex	14:10 and behold, the Egyptians **m** after them;	5265

MARCHEDST (1) [MARCH]

Jdg	5: 4 when thou **m** out of the field of Edom,	6805

MARCUS (3) [MARK]

Col	4:10 and **M**, sister's son to Barnabas,	3138
Phm	1:24 **M**, Aristarchus, Demas, Lucas,	3138
1Pe	5:13 saluteth you; and *so doth* **M** my son.	3138

MARDUK See MERODACH

MARESHAH (8)

Jos	15:44 Keilah, and Achzib, and **M**; nine cities	4762
1Ch	2:42 and the sons of **M** the father of Hebron.	4762
	4:21 Laadah the father of **M**, and the families	4762
2Ch	11: 8 And Gath, and **M**, and Ziph,	4762
	14: 9 hundred chariots; and came unto **M**.	4762
	14:10 in array in the valley of Zephathah at **M**.	4762
	20:37 Eliezer the son of Dodavah of **M**	4762
Mic	1:15 an heir unto thee, O inhabitant of **M**:	4762

MARINERS (5)

Eze	27: 8 of Zidon and Arvad were thy **m**:	7751
	27: 9 all the ships of the sea with their **m** were	4419
	27:27 thy **m**, and thy pilots, thy calkers,	4419
	27:29 oar, the **m**, *and* all the pilots of the sea,	4419
Jnh	1: 5 the **m** were afraid, and cried every man	4419

MARISHES (1)

Eze	47:11 and the **m** thereof shall not be healed;	1360

MARITAL UNFAITHFULNESS See FORNICATION

MARK (37) [LANDMARK, LANDMARKS, MARCUS, MARKED, MARKEST, MARKETH, MARKS, WAYMARKS]

Ge	4:15 the LORD set a **m** upon Cain, lest any	226
Ru	3: 4 thou shalt **m** the place where he shall	3045
1Sa	20:20 the side *thereof*, as *though* I shot at a **m**.	4307
2Sa	13:28 **M** ye now when Amnon's heart is merry	7200
1Ki	20: 7 **M**, I pray you, and see how this *man*	3045
	20:22 and **m**, and see what thou doest:	3045
Job	7:20 why hast thou set me as a **m** against thee,	4645
	16:12 me to pieces, and set me up for his **m**.	4307
	18: 2 words? **m**, and afterwards we will speak.	995
	21: 5 M me, and be astonished,	413+6437
	33:31 **M** well, O Job, hearken unto me: hold	7181
	39: 1 canst thou **m** when the hinds do calve?	8104
Ps	37:37 **M** the perfect *man*, and behold the	8104
	48:13 **M** ye well her bulwarks, consider her	7896
	56: 6 they hide themselves, they **m** my steps,	8104
	130: 3 LORD, shouldest thou **m** iniquities, O Lord,	8104
La	3:12 bow, and set me as a **m** for the arrow.	4307
Eze	9: 4 **set a m** upon the foreheads of	8420+8427

Eze	9: 6 not near any man upon whom *is* the **m**;	8420
	44: 5 **m** well, and behold with thine	3820+7760
	44: 5 **m** well the entering in of the	3820+7760
Ac	12:12 mother of John, whose surname was **M**;	3138
	12:25 with *them* John, whose surname was **M**.	3138
	15:37 with *them* John, whose surname was **M**.	3138
	15:39 and so Barnabas took **M**, and sailed unto	3138
Ro	16:17 **m** them which cause divisions and	4648
Php	3:14 I press toward the **m** for the prize of	4649
	3:17 and them which walk so as ye have us	4648
2Ti	4:11 Take **M**, and bring *him* with thee: for he	3138
Rev	13:16 to receive a **m** in their right hand, or in	5480
	13:17 save he that had the **m**, or the name of	5480
	14: 9 receive *his* **m** in his forehead, or in his	5480
	14:11 whosoever receiveth the **m** of his name.	5480
	15: 2 and over his image, and over his **m**,	5480
	16: 2 the men which had the **m** of the beast,	5480
	19:20 that had received the **m** of the beast,	5480
	20: 4 neither had received *his* **m** upon their	5480

MARKED (6) [MARK]

1Sa	1:12 before the LORD, that Eli **m** her mouth.	8104
Job	22:15 Hast thou **m** the old way which wicked	8104
	24:16 *which* they had **m** for themselves in	2856
Jer	2:22 *yet* thine iniquity *is* **m** before me,	3799
	23:18 who hath **m** his word, and heard *it*?	7181
Lk	14: 7 when he **m** how they chose out the chief	1907

MARKEST (1) [MARK]

Job	10:14 thou **m** me, and thou wilt not acquit me	8104

MARKET (7) [MARKETPLACE, MARKET-PLACE, MARKETPLACES, MARKETS]

Eze	27:13 of men and vessels of brass in thy **m**.	4627
	27:17 they traded in thy **m** wheat of Minnith,	4627
	27:19 cassia, and calamus, were in thy **m**.	4627
	27:25 of Tarshish did sing of thee *in* thy **m**:	4627
Mk	7: 4 when *they come* from the **m**, except they	59
Jn	5: 2 Now there is at Jerusalem by the sheep **m**	NIG
Ac	17:17 in the **m** daily with them that met with	58

MARKETH (3) [MARK]

Job	33:11 my feet in the stocks, he **m** all my paths.	8104
Isa	44:13 he **m** it *out* with a line; he fitteth it with	8388
	44:13 he **m** it *out* with the compass,	8388

MARKETPLACE, MARKET-PLACE (3) [MARKET, PLACE]

Mt	20: 3 and saw others standing idle in the **m**,	58
Lk	7:32 are like unto children sitting in the **m**,	58
Ac	16:19 and drew *them* into the **m** unto the rulers,	58

MARKETPLACES (1) [MARKET, PLACE]

Mk	12:38 long clothing, and *love* salutations in the **m**,	58

MARKETS (4) [MARKET, PLACE]

Mt	11:16 It is like unto children sitting in the **m**,	58
	23: 7 And greetings in the **m**, and to be called of	58
Lk	11:43 in the synagogues, and greetings in the **m**.	58
	20:46 love greetings in the **m**, and the highest	58

MARKS (2) [MARK]

Lev	19:28 for the dead, nor print any **m** upon you:	7085
Gal	6:17 for I bear in my body the **m** of the Lord	4742

MAROTH (1)

Mic	1:12 the inhabitant of **M** waited carefully for	4796

MARRED (5) [MAR]

Isa	52:14 his visage *was* so **m** more than *any* man,	4893
Jer	13: 7 the girdle was **m**, it was profitable	7843
	18: 4 the vessel that he made of clay was **m** in	7843
Na	2: 2 them out, and **m** their vine branches.	7843
Mk	2:22 wine is spilled, and the bottles will be **m**:	622

MARRIAGE (19) [MARRY]

Ex	21:10 raiment, and her **duty of m**, shall he not	5772
Ps	78:63 and their maidens were not **given to m**.	1984
Mt	22: 2 certain king, which made a **m** for his son,	1062
	22: 4 all *things are* ready: come unto the **m**.	1062
	22: 9 as many as ye shall find, bid to the **m**.	1062
	22:30 they neither marry, nor are given in **m**,	1547
	24:38 and drinking, marrying and **giving in m**,	1547
	25:10 *were* ready went in with him to the **m**:	1062
Mk	12:25 they neither marry, nor are **given in m**;	1061
Lk	17:27 married *wives*, they were **given in m**,	1547
	20:34 of this world marry, and are **given in m**:	1548
	20:35 dead, neither marry, nor are **given in m**:	1548
Jn	2: 1 the third day there was a **m** in Cana of	1062
	2: 2 was called, and his disciples, to the **m**.	1062
1Co	7:38 that he that **giveth** *her* in **m** doeth well;	1547
	7:38 he that **giveth** *her* not in **m** doeth better.	1547
Heb	13: 4 **M** is honourable in all, and the bed	1062
Rev	19: 7 the **m** of the Lamb is come, and his wife	1062
	19: 9 are called unto the **m** supper of the Lamb.	1062

MARRIAGES (3) [MARRY]

Ge	34: 9 **make** ye **m** with us, *and* give your	2859
Dt	7: 3 Neither shalt thou **make m** with them;	2859
Jos	23:12 shall **make m** with them, and go in unto	2859

MARRIED (30) [MARRY]

Ge	19:14 which **m** his daughters, and said, Up,	3947
Ex	21: 3 if he were *m*, then his wife shall go	802+1167
Lev	22:12 If the priest's daughter also *be* **m** unto a	NIH
Nu	12: 1 the Ethiopian woman whom he had **m**:	3947

Nu 12: 1 for he had **m** an Ethiopian woman.	3947
36: 3 *if* they be **m** to any of the sons of	802+3807.1
36:11 **m** unto their father's	802+1961+3807.1
36:12 *And* they were **m** into	802+1961+3807.1
Dt 22:22 If a man be found lying with a woman **m**	1166
24: 1 **m** her, and it come to pass that she find	1166
1Ch 3: 2 he **m** when he *was* threescore years	3947
2Ch 13:21 **m** fourteen wives,	5375+3807.1
Ne 13:23 In those days also saw I Jews *that* had **m**	3427
Pr 30:23 For an odious *woman* when she is **m**;	1166
Isa 54: 1 desolate than the children of the **m** wife,	1166
62: 4 in thee, and thy land shall be **m**.	1166
Jer 3:14 saith the LORD; for I am **m** unto you:	1166
Mal 2:11 hath **m** the daughter of a strange god.	1166
Mt 22:25 when he had **m** *a wife*, deceased, and,	1060
Mk 6:17 brother Philip's wife: for he had **m** her.	1060
10:12 and be **m** to another, she committeth	1060
Lk 14:20 I have **m** a wife, and therefore I cannot	1060
17:27 **m** wives, they were given in marriage,	1060
Ro 7: 3 husband liveth, she be **m** to another man,	1096
7: 3 though she be **m** to another man.	1096
7: 4 ye should be **m** to another, *even* to him	1096
1Co 7:10 And unto the **m** I command, yet not I,	1060
7:33 he that is careth for the *things* that	1060
7:34 she that is **m** careth for the *things* of	1060
7:39 is at liberty to **m** to whom she will;	1060

MARRIETH (4) [MARRY]

Isa 62: 5 *as* a young man **m** a virgin, *so* shall thy	1166
Mt 19: 9 whoso **m** her *which is* put away doth	1060
Lk 16:18 and **m** another, committeth adultery	1060
16:18 whosoever **m** her that is put away from	1060

MARROW (5)

Job 21:24 his bones are moistened with **m**.	4221
Ps 63: 5 My soul shall be satisfied as *with* **m** and	2459
Pr 3: 8 health to thy navel, and **m** to thy bones.	8250
Isa 25: 6 wines on the lees, of fat things full of **m**,	4229
Heb 4:12 of the joints and **m**, and *is* a discerner	3452

MARRY (22) [MARRIAGE, MARRIAGES, MARRIED, MARRIETH, MARRYING, UNMARRIED]

Ge 38: 8 **m** her, and raise up seed to thy brother.	2992
Nu 36: 6 **m** to whom they think best;	802+1961+3807.1
36: 6 of their father shall they **m**.	802+1961+3807.1
Dt 25: 5 the wife of the dead shall not **m** without	1961
Isa 62: 5 a virgin, *so* shall thy sons **m** thee:	1166
Mt 5:32 whosoever shall **m** her that is divorced	1060
19: 9 shall **m** another, committeth adultery:	1060
19:10 so with *his* wife, it is not good to **m**.	1060
22:24 his brother shall **m** his wife, and raise up	1918
22:30 For in the resurrection they neither **m**,	1060
Mk 10:11 **m** another, committeth adultery against	1060
12:25 they neither **m**, nor are given in marriage;	1060
Lk 20:34 The children of this world **m**, and are	1060
20:35 neither **m**, nor are given in marriage:	1060
1Co 7: 9 But if they cannot contain, let them **m**:	1060
7: 9 for it is better to **m** than to burn.	1060
7:28 But and if thou **m**, thou hast not sinned;	1060
7:28 and if a virgin **m**, she hath not sinned.	1060
7:36 what he will, he sinneth not: let them **m**.	1060
1Ti 4: 3 Forbidding to **m**, *and commanding* to	1060
5:11 wax wanton against Christ, they will **m**;	1060
5:14 therefore that the younger women **m**,	1060

MARRYING (2) [MARRY]

Ne 13:27 transgress against our God in **m** strange	3427
Mt 24:38 and drinking, and giving in marriage,	1060

MARS' HILL (1) [AREOPAGUS]

Ac 17:22 Then Paul stood in the midst of **M**,	697

MARSENA (1)

Est 1:14 Tarshish, Meres, **M**, *and* Memucan,	4826

MARSHES See MARISHES

MART (1)

Isa 23: 3 her revenue; and she is a **m** of nations.	5505

MARTHA (13)

Lk 10:38 a certain woman named **M** received him	3136
10:40 **M** was cumbered about much serving,	3136
10:41 and said unto her, **M**, Martha,	3136
10:41 and said unto her, Martha, **M**,	3136
Jn 11: 1 the town of Mary and her sister **M**.	3136
11: 5 Now Jesus loved **M**, and her sister,	3136
11:19 And many of the Jews came to **M** and	3136
11:20 Then **M**, as soon as she heard that Jesus	3136
11:21 Then said **M** unto Jesus, Lord, if thou	3136
11:24 Martha saith unto him, I know that he	3136
11:30 but was in *that* place where **M** met him.	3136
11:39 **M**, the sister of him that was dead, saith	3136
12: 2 they made him a supper; and **M** served;	3136

MARTYR (2) [MARTYRS]

Ac 22:20 when the blood of thy **m** Stephen was	3144
Rev 2:13 days wherein Antipas *was* my faithful **m**,	3144

MARTYRS (1) [MARTYR]

Rev 17: 6 and with the blood of the **m** of Jesus:	3144

MARVEL (11) [MARVELLED, MARVELLOUS, MARVELLOUSLY, MARVELS]

Ecc 5: 8 in a province, **m** not at the matter:	8539
Mk 5:20 had done for him; and all *men* did **m**.	2296

Jn 3: 7 **M** not that I said unto thee, Ye must be	2296
5:20 greater works than these, that ye may **m**.	2296
5:28 **M** not at this: for the hour is coming,	2296
7:21 I have done one work, and ye all **m**.	2296
Ac 3:12 Ye men of Israel, why **m** ye at this?	2296
2Co 11:14 no **m**; for Satan himself is transformed	2298
Gal 1: 6 I **m** that you are so soon removed from	2296
1Jn 3:13 **m** not, my brethren, if the world hate	2296
Rev 17: 7 said unto me, Wherefore didst thou **m**?	2296

MARVELLED (23) [MARVEL]

Ge 43:33 youth: and the men **m** one at another.	8539
Ps 48: 5 They saw *it, and* so they **m**; they were	8539
Mt 8:10 When Jesus heard *it*, he **m**, and said to	2296
8:27 But the men, saying, What manner of	2296
9: 8 But when the multitudes saw *it*, they **m**,	2296
9:33 the multitudes, saying, It was never	2296
21:20 And when the disciples saw *it*, they **m**,	2296
22:22 they had heard *these words*, they **m**,	2296
27:14 insomuch that the governor **m** greatly.	2296
Mk 6: 6 he **m** because of their unbelief.	2296
12:17 *things* that are God's. And they **m** at him.	2296
15: 5 yet answered nothing; so that Pilate **m**.	2296
15:44 And Pilate **m** if he were already dead:	2296
Lk 1:21 **m** that he tarried *so* long in the temple.	2296
1:63 saying, His name is John. And they **m** all.	2296
2:33 his mother **m** at those *things* which were	2296
7: 9 When Jesus heard these *things*, he **m** at	2296
11:38 when the Pharisee saw *it*, he **m** that he	2296
20:26 and they **m** at his answer, and held their	2296
Jn 4:27 and **m** that he talked with *the* woman:	2296
7:15 the Jews **m**, saying, How knoweth this	2296
Ac 2: 7 And they were all amazed and **m**,	2296
4:13 unlearned and ignorant men, they **m**;	2296

MARVELLOUS (24) [MARVEL]

1Ch 16:12 Remember his **m** works that he hath	6381
16:24 his **m** works among all nations.	6381
Job 5: 9 unsearchable; **m** *things* without number:	6381
10:16 again thou **shewest** thyself **m** upon me.	6381
Ps 9: 1 I will shew forth all thy **m** works.	6395
17: 7 **Shew** thy lovingkindness, O thou that	6395
31:21 he hath **shewed** me his **m** kindness in a	6381
78:12 **M** things did he in the sight of their	6382
98: 1 he hath done **m** *things:* his right hand,	6381
105: 5 Remember his **m** works that he hath	6381
118:23 is the LORD's doing; it is **m** in our eyes.	6381
139:14 *are* thy works; and *that* my soul	6395
Isa 29:14 I will proceed to do **a m work** amongst	6381
29:14 people, *even* a **m** work and a wonder.	6381
Da 11:36 shall speak **m** things against the God of	6381
Mic 7:15 of Egypt will I shew unto him **m** *things*.	6381
Zec 8: 6 If it be **m** in the eyes of the remnant of	6381
8: 6 days, should it also be **m** in my eyes?	6381
Mt 21:42 the Lord's doing, and it is **m** in our eyes?	2298
Mk 12:11 the Lord's doing, and it is **m** in our eyes?	2298
Jn 9:30 herein is a **m** *thing*, that ye know not	2298
1Pe 2: 9 you out of darkness into his **m** light:	2298
Rev 15: 1 saw another sign in heaven, great and **m**,	2298
15: 3 saying, Great and **m** *are* thy works,	2298

MARVELLOUSLY (3) [MARVEL]

2Ch 26:15 for he was **m** helped, till he was strong.	6381
Job 37: 5 God thundereth **m** with his voice;	6381
Hab 1: 5 the heathen, and regard, and wonder **m**:	8539

MARVELS (1) [MARVEL]

Ex 34:10 before all thy people I will do **m**, such as	6381

MARY (54)

Mt 1:16 Jacob begat Joseph the husband of **M**,	3137
1:18 When as his mother **M** was espoused to	3137
1:20 fear not to take unto thee **M** thy wife:	3137
2:11 they saw the young child with **M** his	3137
13:55 is not his mother called **M**?	3137
27:56 Among which was **M** Magdalene,	3137
27:56 and **M** the mother of James and Joses,	3137
27:61 there was **M** Magdalene, and the other	3137
27:61 was Mary Magdalene, and the other **M**,	3137
28: 1 came **M** Magdalene and the other Mary	3137
28: 1 and the other **M** to see the sepulchre.	3137
Mk 6: 3 the son of **M**, the brother of James,	3137
15:40 among whom was **M** Magdalene,	3137
15:40 and **M** the mother of James the less and	3137
15:47 **M** Magdalene and Mary the *mother* of	3137
15:47 **M** the *mother* of Joses beheld where he	3137
16: 1 **M** Magdalene, and Mary the *mother* of	3137
16: 1 and the *mother* of James, and Salome,	3137
16: 9 he appeared first to **M** Magdalene, out of	3137
Lk 1:27 of David; and the virgin's name was **M**.	3137
1:30 And the angel said unto her, Fear not, **M**:	3137
1:34 Then said **M** unto the angel, How shall	3137
1:38 And **M** said, Behold the handmaid of	3137
1:39 And **M** arose in those days, and went into	3137
1:41 when Elisabeth heard the salutation of **M**,	3137
1:46 And **M** said, My soul doth magnify	3137
1:56 **M** abode with her about three months,	3137
2: 5 To be taxed with **M** his espoused wife,	3137
2:16 and found **M**, and Joseph, and the babe	3137
2:19 But **M** kept all these things,	3137
2:34 and said unto **M** his mother, Behold,	3137
8: 2 and infirmities, **M** called Magdalene,	3137
10:39 And she had a sister called **M**, which also	3137
10:42 and **M** hath chosen *that* good part,	3137
24:10 It was **M** Magdalene, and Joanna,	3137

Lk 24:10 and **M** *the* mother of James, and other	3137
Jn 11: 1 the town of **M** and her sister Martha.	3137
11: 2 (It was *that* **M** which anointed the Lord	3137
11:19 many of the Jews came to Martha and **M**,	3137
11:20 and met him: but **M** sat *still* in the house.	3137
11:28 and called **M** her sister secretly, saying,	3137
11:31 and comforted her, when they saw **M**,	3137
11:32 when **M** was come where Jesus was,	3137
11:45 Then many of the Jews which came to **M**,	3137
12: 3 Then took **M** a pound of ointment of	3137
19:25 the *wife* of Cleophas,	3137
19:25 the *wife* of Cleophas, and **M** Magdalene.	3137
20: 1 The first *day* of the week cometh **M**	3137
20:11 But **M** stood without at the sepulchre	3137
20:16 Jesus saith unto her, **M**. She turned	3137
20:18 **M** Magdalene came and told the disciples	3137
Ac 1:14 **M** the mother of Jesus, and with his	3137
12:12 to the house of **M** the mother of John,	3137
Ro 16: 6 Greet **M**, who bestowed much labour on	3137

MASCHIL (13)

Ps 32: T A Psalm of David, **M**.	4905
42: T chief Musician, **M**, for the sons of Korah.	4905
44: T chief Musician for the sons of Korah, **M**.	4905
45: T for the sons of Korah, **M**, A Song of loves.	4905
52: T the chief Musician, **M**, A Psalm of David,	4905
53: T upon Mahalath, **M**, A Psalm of David.	4905
54: T **M**, A Psalm of David, when the Ziphims	4905
55: T on Neginoth, **M**, A Psalm of David.	4905
74: T **M** of Asaph.	4905
78: T **M** of Asaph.	4905
88: T **M** of Heman the Ezrahite.	4905
89: T **M** of Ethan the Ezrahite.	4905
142: T **M** of David; A Prayer when he was in	4905

MASH (1)

Ge 10:23 Aram; Uz, and Hul, and Gether, and **M**.	4851

MASHAL (1)

1Ch 6:74 **M** with her suburbs, and Abdon with her	4913

MASONS (7)

2Sa 5:11 and carpenters, and **m**:	68+2796+7023
2Ki 12:12 to **m**, and hewers of stone, and to buy	1443
22: 6 **m**, and to buy timber and hewn stone to	1443
1Ch 14: 1 of cedars, with **m** and carpenters,	2796+7023
22: 2 he set **m** to hew wrought stones to build	2672
2Ch 24:12 **m** and carpenters to repair the house	2672
Ezr 3: 7 They gave money also unto the **m**,	2672

MASREKAH (2)

Ge 36:36 and Samlah of **M** reigned in his stead.	4957
1Ch 1:47 Samlah of **M** reigned in his stead.	4957

MASSA (2)

Ge 25:14 And Mishma, and Dumah, and **M**,	4854
1Ch 1:30 and Dumah, **M**, Hadad, and Tema,	4854

MASSAH (4)

Ex 17: 7 he called the name of the place **M**,	4532
Dt 6:16 LORD your God, as ye tempted *him* in **M**.	4532
9:22 and at **M**, and at Kibroth-hattaavah,	4532
33: 8 whom thou didst prove at **M**,	4532

MAST (2) [MASTS]

Pr 23:34 or as he that lieth upon the top of a **m**.	2260
Isa 33:23 they could not well strengthen their **m**,	8650

MASTER (157) [MASTER'S, MASTERBUILDER, MASTERIES, MASTERS, MASTERS', MASTERY, SCHOOLMASTER, SHEEPMASTER, SHIPMASTER, TASKMASTERS]

Ge 24: 9 hand under the thigh of Abraham his **m**,	113
24:10 took ten camels of the camels of his **m**,	113
24:10 for all the goods of his **m** *were* in his hand:	113
24:12 O LORD God of my **m** Abraham, I pray	113
24:12 and shew kindness unto my **m** Abraham.	113
24:14 thou hast shewed kindness unto my **m**.	113
24:27 Blessed *be* the LORD God of my **m**	113
24:27 who hath not left destitute my **m** of his	113
24:35 And the LORD hath blessed my **m** greatly;	113
24:36 Sarah my master's wife bare a son to my **m**	113
24:37 my **m** made me swear, saying, Thou shalt	113
24:39 said unto my **m**, Peradventure the woman	113
24:42 and said, O LORD God of my **m** Abraham,	113
24:48 blessed the LORD God of my **m** Abraham,	113
24:49 if ye will deal kindly and truly with my **m**,	113
24:54 and he said, Send me away unto my **m**.	113
24:56 send me away that I may go to my **m**.	113
24:65 the servant had said, It *is* my **m**: therefore	113
39: 2 he was in the house of his **m** the Egyptian.	113
39: 3 his **m** saw that the LORD *was* with him,	113
39: 8 my **m** wotteth not what *is* with me in	113
39:19 when his **m** heard the words of his wife,	113
39:20 Joseph's **m** took him, and put him into	113
Ex 21: 4 If his **m** have given him a wife, and she	113
21: 5 I love my **m**, my wife, and my children;	113
21: 6 his **m** shall bring him unto the judges;	113
21: 6 **m** shall bore his ear through with an aul;	113
21: 8 she please not her **m**, who hath betrothed	113
21:32 he shall give unto their **m** thirty shekels *of*	113
22: 8 the **m** of the house shall be brought unto	1167
Dt 23:15 shalt not deliver unto his **m** the servant	113
23:15 which is escaped from his **m** unto thee:	113
Jdg 19:11 the servant said unto his **m**, Come, I pray	113
19:12 his **m** said unto him, We will not turn	113

Jdg 19:22 spake to the **m** of the house, the old 376+1167
19:23 man, the **m** of the house, went out unto 1167
1Sa 20:38 up the arrows, and came to his **m**. 113
24: 6 that I should do this thing unto my **m**, 113
25:10 that break away every man from his **m**. 113
25:14 out of the wilderness to salute our **m**; 113
25:17 for evil is determined against our **m**, 113
26:16 to die, because ye have not kept your **m**, 113
29: 4 should he reconcile himself unto his **m**? 113
30:13 my **m** left me, because three days agone I 113
30:15 nor deliver me into the hands of my **m**, 113
2Sa 2: 7 for your **m** Saul is dead, and also the house 113
1Ki 22:17 the Lord said, These have no **m**: let them 113
2Ki 2: 3 take away thy **m** from thy head to day? 113
2: 5 take away thy **m** from thy head to day? 113
2:16 them go, we pray thee, and seek thy **m**: 113
5: 1 a great man with his **m**, and honourable, 113
5:18 that when my **m** goeth into the house of 113
5:20 my **m** hath spared Naaman this Syrian, 113
5:22 My **m** hath sent me, saying, Behold, 113
5:25 he went in, and stood before his **m**. 113
6: 5 he cried, and said, Alas, **m**, for it was 113
6:15 unto him, Alas, my **m**, how shall we do? 113
6:22 they may eat and drink, and go to their **m**. 113
6:23 sent them away, and they went to their **m**. 113
8:14 departed from Elisha, and came to his **m**, 113
9: 7 thou shalt smite the house of Ahab thy **m**, 113
9:31 said, Had Zimri peace, who slew his **m**? 113
10: 9 I conspired against my **m**, and slew him: 113
18:27 Hath my **m** sent me to thy master, 113
18:27 that my master sent me to thy **m**, 113
19: 4 whom the king of Assyria his **m** hath sent 113
19: 6 Thus shall ye say to your **m**, 113
1Ch 12:19 He will fall to his **m** Saul to the jeopardy 113
15:27 Chenaniah the **m** of the song with 8269
2Ch 18:16 the Lord said, These have no **m**; let them 113
Job 3:19 there; and the servant is free from his **m**. 113
Pr 27:18 that waiteth on his **m** shall be honoured. 113
30:10 Accuse not a servant unto his **m**, lest he 113
Isa 24: 2 priest; as with the servant, so with his **m**; 113
36: 8 to my **m** the king of Assyria, and I will give 113
36:12 Hath my **m** sent me to thy master and to 113
36:12 My **m** hath sent me to thy master and to 113
37: 4 whom the king of Assyria his **m** hath sent 113
37: 6 Thus shall ye say unto your **m**, Thus saith 113
Da 1: 3 king spake unto Ashpenaz the **m** of his 7227
4: 9 **m** of the magicians, because I know that 7229
5:11 made **m** of the magicians, astrologers, 7229
Mal 1: 6 honoureth his father, and a servant his **m**: 113
1: 6 if I be a **m**, where is my fear? saith 113
2:12 the **m** and the scholar, out of 5782
Mt 8:19 scribe came, and said unto him, **M**, 1320
9:11 Why eateth your **M** with publicans and 1320
10:24 The disciple is not above his **m**, 1320
10:25 for the disciple that he be as his **m**, 1320
10:25 If they have called the **m of the house** 3617
12:38 and of the Pharisees answered, saying, **M**, 1320
17:24 and said, Doth not your **m** pay tribute? 1320
19:16 one came and said unto him, Good **M**, 1320
22:16 saying, **M**, we know that thou art true, 1320
22:24 Saying, **M**, Moses said, If a man die, 1320
22:36 **M**, which is the great commandment in 1320
23: 8 for one is your **M**, even Christ; 2519
23:10 for one is your **M**, even Christ. 2519
26:18 say unto him, The **M** saith, My time is 1320
26:25 him, answered and said, **M**, is it I? 4461
26:49 he came to Jesus, and said, Hail, **m**? 4461
Mk 4:38 they awake him, and say unto him, **M**, 1320
5:35 why troublest thou the **M** any further? 1320
9: 5 And Peter answered and said to Jesus, **M**, 4461
9:17 of the multitude answered and said, **M**, 1320
9:38 And John answered him, saying, **M**, 1320
10:17 kneeled to him, and asked him, Good **M**, 1320
10:20 And he answered and said unto him, **M**, 1320
10:35 of Zebedee, come unto him, saying, **M**, 1320
11:21 **M**, behold, the fig tree which thou 4461
12:14 they say unto him, we know that thou 1320
12:19 **M**, Moses wrote unto us, If a man's 1320
12:32 him, Well, **M**, thou hast said the truth: 1320
13: 1 **M**, see what manner of stones and 1320
13:35 ye know not when the **m** of the house 2962
14:14 The **M** saith, Where is the guestchamber, 1320
14:45 straightway to him, and saith, **M**, master; 4461
14:45 straightway to him, and saith, Master, **m**; 4461
Lk 3:12 and said unto him, **M**, what shall we do? 1320
5: 5 we have toiled all the night, 1988
6:40 The disciple is not above his **m**: 1320
6:40 every one that is perfect shall be as his **m**. 1320
7:40 to say unto thee. And he saith, **M**, say on. 1320
8:24 awoke him, saying, **M**, master; we perish. 1988
8:24 awoke him, saying, Master, **m**, we perish. 1988
8:45 **M**, the multitude throng thee and 1988
8:49 Thy daughter is dead; trouble not the **M**. 1320
9:33 from him, Peter said unto Jesus, **M**, 1988
9:38 saying, **M**, I beseech thee, look upon my 1988
9:49 And John answered and said, **M**, we saw 1988
10:25 stood up, and tempted him, saying, **M**, 1320
11:45 one of the lawyers, and said unto him, **M**, 1320
12:13 **M**, speak to my brother, that he divide 1320
13:25 When once the **m of the house** is risen 3617
14:21 **m of the house** being angry said to his 3617
17:13 and said, Jesus, **M**, have mercy on us. 1988
18:18 certain ruler asked him, saying, Good **M**, 1320
19:39 said unto him, **M**, rebuke thy disciples. 1320
20:21 And they asked him, saying, **M**, we know 1320

Lk 20:28 Saying, **M**, Moses wrote unto us, If any 1320
20:39 answering said, **M**, thou hast well said. 1320
21: 7 And they asked him, saying, **M**, 1320
22:11 The **M** saith unto thee, Where is 1320
Jn 1:38 (which is to say, being interpreted, **M**,) 1320
3:10 Art thou a **m** of Israel, and knowest not 1320
4:31 his disciples prayed him, saying, **M**, eat. 4461
8: 4 They say unto him, **M**, this woman was 1320
9: 2 saying, **M**, who did sin, this man, or 4461
11: 8 His disciples say unto him, **M**, the Jews of 4461
11:28 The **M** is come, and calleth for thee. 1320
13:13 Ye call me **M** and Lord: and ye say well; 1320
13:14 If I then, your Lord and **M**, have washed 1320
20:16 unto him, Rabboni; which is to say, **M**. 1320
Ac 27:11 Nevertheless the centurion believed the **m** 2942
Ro 6: 9 to his own **m** he standeth or falleth. Yea, 2962
Eph 6: 9 knowing that your **M** also is in heaven; 2962
Col 4: 1 knowing that ye also have a **M** in heaven. 2962

MASTER'S (24) [MASTER]
Ge 24:27 the Lord led me to the house of my **m** 113
24:36 Sarah my **m** wife bare a son to my master 113
24:44 Lord hath appointed out for my **m** son. 113
24:48 take my **m** brother's daughter unto his son. 113
24:51 and go, and let her be thy **m** son's wife, 113
39: 7 that his **m** wife cast her eyes upon Joseph; 113
39: 8 and said unto his **m** wife, Behold, 113
Ex 21: 4 the wife and her children shall be her **m**, 113
1Sa 29:10 thy **m** servants that are come with thee: 113
2Sa 9: 9 I have given unto thy **m** son all that 113
9:10 shalt bring in the fruits, that thy **m** son 113
9:10 Mephibosheth thy **m** son shall eat bread 113
12: 8 I gave thee thy **m** house, and thy master's 113
12: 8 thy **m** wives into thy bosom, and gave 113
16: 3 the king said, And where is thy **m** son? 113
2Ki 6:32 is not the sound of his **m** feet behind him? 113
10: 2 seeing your **m** sons are with you, 113
10: 3 out the best and meetest of your **m** sons, 113
10: 3 throne, and fight for your **m** house. 113
10: 6 take ye the heads of the men your **m** sons, 113
18:24 one captain of the least of my **m** servants, 113
Isa 1: 3 his owner, and the ass his **m** crib: 1167
36: 9 one captain of the least of my **m** servants, 113
2Ti 2:21 meet for the **m** use, and prepared unto 1203

MASTERBUILDER (1) [BUILD, MASTER]
1Co 3:10 as a wise **m**, I have laid the foundation, 753

MASTERIES (1) [MASTER]
2Ti 2: 5 And if a man also **strive for m**, yet is he not 118

MASTERS (20) [MASTER]
Ps 123: 2 of servants look unto the hand of their **m**, 113
Pr 25:13 him: for he refresheth the soul of his **m**. 113
Ecc 12:11 as nails fastened by the **m** of assemblies, 1167
Jer 27: 4 command them to say unto their **m**, 113
27: 4 of Israel; Thus shall ye say unto your **m**; 113
Am 4: 1 say to them, Bring, and let us drink. 113
Mt 6:24 No **man** can serve two **m**: for either he 2962
23:10 Neither be ye called **m**: for one is your 2519
Lk 16:13 No servant can serve two **m**: for either he 2962
Ac 16:16 which brought her **m** much gain by 2962
16:19 when her **m** saw that the hope of their 2962
Eph 6: 5 be obedient to them that are your **m** 2962
6: 9 ye **m**, do the same things unto them, 2962
Col 3:22 obey in all things your **m** according to 2962
4: 1 **M**, give unto your servants that which is 2962
1Ti 6: 1 count their own **m** worthy of all honour, 1203
6: 2 And they that have believing **m**, let them 1203
Tit 2: 9 servants to be obedient unto their own **m**, 1203
Jas 3: 1 My brethren, be not many **m**, knowing 1320
1Pe 2:18 Servants, be subject to your **m** with all 1203

MASTERS' (2) [MASTER]
Zep 1: 9 which fill their **m** houses with violence 113
Mt 15:27 the crumbs which fall from their **m** table. 2962

MASTERY (3) [MASTER]
Ex 32:18 is not the voice of them that shout for **m**, 1369
Da 6:24 the lions had the **m** of them, and brake all 7981
1Co 9:25 And every man that **striveth for the m** is 75

MASTS (1) [MAST]
Eze 27: 5 cedars from Lebanon to make **m** for thee. 8650

MATE (2)
Isa 34:15 also be gathered, every one with her **m**. 7468
34:16 of these shall fail, none shall want her **m**: 7468

MATERIAL See CARNAL

MATHUSALA (1) [METHUSELAH]
Lk 3:37 Which was the son of **M**, which was 3103

MATRED (2)
Ge 36:39 the daughter of **M**, the daughter of 4308
1Ch 1:50 the daughter of **M**, the daughter of 4308

MATRI (1)
1Sa 10:21 the family of **M** was taken, and Saul 4309

MATRIX (5)
Ex 13:12 unto the Lord all that openeth the **m**, 7358
13:15 to the Lord all that openeth the **m**, 7358
34:19 All that openeth the **m** is mine; 7358
Nu 3:12 openeth the **m** among the children of 7358

Nu 18:15 Every thing that openeth the **m** in all 7358

MATTAN (3)
2Ki 11:18 slew **M** the priest of Baal before the altars. 4977
2Ch 23:17 slew **M** the priest of Baal before the altars. 4977
Jer 38: 1 Shephatiah the son of **M**, and Gedaliah 4977

MATTANAH (2)
Nu 21:18 from the wilderness they went to **M**: 4980
21:19 from **M** to Nahaliel: and from Nahaliel to 4980

MATTANIAH (16)
2Ki 24:17 the king of Babylon made **M** his father's 4983
1Ch 9:15 and Galal, and **M** the son of Micah, 4983
25: 4 M, Uzziel, Shebuel, and Jerimoth, 4983
25:16 The ninth to **M**, he, his sons, 4983
2Ch 20:14 of Benaiah, the son of Jeiel, the son of **M**, 4983
29:13 of the sons of Asaph; Zechariah, and **M**: 4983
Ezr 10:26 Zechariah, and Jehiel, and Abdi, 4983
10:27 M, and Jeremoth, and Zabad, and Aziza. 4983
10:30 M, Bezaleel, and Binnui, and Manasseh. 4983
10:37 M, Mattenai, and Jaasau, 4983
Ne 11:17 M the son of Micha, the son of Zabdi, 4983
11:22 the son of **M**, the son of Micha. 4983
12: 8 Kadmiel, Sherebiah, Judah, and **M**, 4983
12:25 M, and Bakbukiah, Obadiah, Meshullam, 4983
12:35 son of **M**, the son of Michaiah, the son 4983
13:13 Hanan the son of Zaccur, the son of **M**: 4983

MATTATHA (1)
Lk 3:31 son of Menan, which was the son of **M**, 3160

MATTATHAH (1)
Ezr 10:33 Mattenai, **M**, Zabad, Eliphelet, Jeremai, 4992

MATTATHIAS (2)
Lk 3:25 Which was the son of **M**, which was 3161
3:26 was the son of **M**, which was the son 3161

MATTATTAH See MATTATHAH

MATTENAI (3)
Ezr 10:33 Mattenai, Mattathah, Zabad, Eliphelet, Jeremai, 4982
10:37 Mattaniah, **M**, and Jaasau, 4982
Ne 12:19 And of Joiarib, **M**; of Jedaiah, Uzzi; 4982

MATTER (80) [MATTERS]
Ge 24: 9 and sware to him concerning that **m**. 1697
30:15 Is it a **small m** that thou hast taken my 4592
Ex 18:16 they have a **m**, they come unto me; 1697
18:22 that every great **m** they shall bring unto 1697
18:22 but every small **m** they shall judge: 1697
18:26 every small **m** they judged themselves. 1697
23: 7 Keep thee far from a false **m**; 1697
Nu 16:49 beside them that died about the **m** of 1697
25:18 they have beguiled you in the **m** 1697
25:18 the **m** of Cozbi, the daughter of a prince 1697
31:16 against the Lord in the **m** of Peor, 1697
Dt 3:26 speak no more unto me of this **m**. 1697
17: 8 If there arise a **m** too hard for thee in 1697
19:15 witnesses, shall the **m** be established. 1697
22:26 and slayeth him, even so is this **m**: 1697
Ru 3:18 until thou know how the **m** will fall: 1697
1Sa 10:16 the **m** of the kingdom, whereof Samuel 1697
20:23 as touching the **m** which thou and I have 1697
20:39 only Jonathan and David knew the **m**. 1697
30:24 who will hearken unto you in this **m**? 1697
2Sa 1: 4 David said unto him, How went the **m**? 1697
18:13 there is no **m** hid from the king, 1697
19:42 wherefore then be ye angry for this **m**? 1697
20:18 counsel at Abel: and so they ended the **m**. NIH
20:21 The **m** is not so: but a man of mount 1697
1Ki 8:59 at all times, as the **m** shall require: 1697
15: 5 save only in the **m** of Urijah the Hittite. 1697
1Ch 26:32 for every **m** pertaining to God, 1697
27: 1 officers that served the king in any **m**, 1697
2Ch 8:15 the priests and Levites concerning any **m**, 1697
24: 5 year to year, and see that ye haste the **m**. 1697
Ezr 5: 5 them to cease, till the **m** came to Darius: 2941
5: 5 answer by letter concerning this **m**. NIH
5:17 his pleasure to us concerning this **m**. NIH
10: 4 Arise; for this **m** belongeth unto thee: 1697
10: 9 trembling because of this **m**, and for 1697
10:14 the fierce wrath of our God for this **m**. 1697
10:15 of Tikvah were employed about this **m**: NIH
10:16 the tenth month to examine the **m**. 1697
Ne 6:13 that they might have **m** for an evil report, NIH
Est 2:23 inquisition was made of the **m**, it was 1697
9:26 which they had seen concerning this **m**, NIH
Job 19:28 seeing the root of the **m** is found in me; 1697
32:18 For I am full of **m**, the spirit within me 4405
Ps 45: 1 My heart is inditing a good **m**: I speak of 1697
64: 5 They encourage themselves in an evil **m**: 1697
Pr 11:13 is of a faithful spirit concealeth the **m**. 1697
16:20 He that handleth a **m** wisely shall find 1697
17: 9 he that repeateth a **m** separateth very 1697
18:13 He that answereth a **m** before he heareth 1697
25: 2 The honour of kings is to search out a **m**. 1697
Ecc 5: 8 justice in a province, marvel not at the **m**: 2656
10:20 that which hath wings shall tell the **m**. 1697
12:13 us hear the conclusion of the whole **m**: 1697
Jer 38:27 with him, for the **m** was not perceived. 1697
Eze 9:11 by his side, reported the **m**, saying, 1697
16:20 Is this of thy whoredoms a **small m**, 4592
Da 1:14 So he consented to them in this **m**, 1697
2:10 the earth that can shew the king's **m**: 4406

M

M

Da	2:23	*now* made known unto us the king's **m.**	4406
	3:16	*are* not careful to answer thee in this **m.**	6600
	4:17	*This is* by the decree of the watchers,	6600
	7:28	Hitherto *is* the end of the **m.** *As for* me	4406
	7:28	in me: but I kept the **m** in my heart.	4406
	9:23	therefore understand the **m.**	1697
Mk	1:45	*it* much, and to blaze abroad the **m,**	3056
	10:10	disciples asked him again of the same **m.**	NIG
Ac	8:21	Thou hast neither part nor lot in this **m:**	3056
	11: 4	But Peter *rehearsed the* **m** from	NIG
	15: 6	came together for to consider of this **m.**	3056
	17:32	We will hear thee again of this **m.**	NIG
	18:14	If it were a **m** of wrong or	5100
	19:38	a **m** against any *man,* the law is open,	3056
	24:22	will know the uttermost of your **m.**	2596+3588
1Co	6: 1	any of you, having a **m** against another,	4229
2Co	7:11	approved yourselves to be clear in *this* **m.**	4229
	9: 5	as a **m** of bounty, and not as of	NIG
Gal	2: 6	they were, it **maketh** no **m** to me:	1308
1Th	4: 6	and defraud his brother in any **m:**	4229
Jas	3: 5	how great a **m** a little fire kindleth.	5208

MATTERS (23) [MATTER]

Ex	24:14	if any man have any **m** to do, let him	1697
Dt	17: 8	*being* of controversy within thy gates:	1697
1Sa	16:18	and prudent in **m,** and a comely person,	1697
2Sa	11:19	of telling the **m** of the war unto the king,	1697
	15: 3	unto him, See, thy **m** *are* good and right;	1697
	19:29	Why speakest thou any more of thy **m?**	1697
2Ch	19:11	priest *is* over you in all **m** of the LORD;	1697
	19:11	of the house of Judah, for all the king's **m:**	1697
Ne	11:24	at the king's hand in all **m** concerning	1697
Est	3: 4	see whether Mordecai's **m** would stand:	1697
	9:31	the **m** of the fastings and their cry.	1697
	9:32	the decree of Esther confirmed these **m** of	1697
Job	33:13	for he giveth not account of any of his **m.**	1697
Ps	35:20	they devise deceitful **m** against *them that*	1697
	131: 1	neither do I exercise myself in great *m,*	NIH
Da	1:20	*in* all **m** of wisdom *and* understanding,	1697
	7: 1	the dream, *and* told the sum of the **m.**	4406
Mt	23:23	have omitted the weightier **m** of the law,	NIG
Ac	18:15	ye to *it;* for I will be no judge of such **m.**	NIG
	19:39	**m,** it shall be determined in a lawful	NIG
	25:20	and there be judged of these **m.**	NIG
1Co	6: 2	ye unworthy to judge the **smallest m?**	1646
1Pe	4:15	or as a **busybody** in other men's **m.**	244

MATTHAN (2)

Mt	1:15	and Eleazar begat **M;** and Matthan begat	3157
	1:15	begat Matthan; and **M** begat Jacob;	3157

MATTHAT (2)

Lk	3:24	Which was *the son of* **M,** which was	3158
	3:29	was *the son of* **M,** which was *the son*	3158

MATTHEW (5)

Mt	9: 9	he saw a man, named **M,** sitting at	3156
	10: 3	Thomas, and **M** the publican;	3156
Mk	3:18	**M,** and Thomas, and James the *son of*	3156
Lk	6:15	**M** and Thomas, James the *son* of Alpheus,	3156
Ac	1:13	Philip, and Thomas, Bartholomew, and **M,**	3156

MATTHIAS (2)

Ac	1:23	who was surnamed Justus, and **M.**	3159
	1:26	and the lot fell upon **M;** and he was	3159

MATTITHIAH (8)

1Ch	9:31	**M,** *one* of the Levites, who *was*	4993
	15:18	and Elipheleh, and Mikneiah,	4993
	15:21	**M,** and Elipheleh, and Mikneiah,	4993
	16: 5	**M,** and Eliab, and Benaiah,	4993
	25: 3	Zeri, and Jeshaiah, Hashabiah, and **M,** six,	4993
	25:21	The fourteenth *to* **M,** *he,* his sons,	4993
Ezr	10:43	Jeiel, **M,** Zabad, Zebina, Jadau, and Joel,	4993
Ne	8: 4	beside him stood **M,** and Shema,	4993

MATTOCK (2) [MATTOCKS]

1Sa	13:20	and his coulter, and his axe, and his **m.**	4281
Isa	7:25	all hills that shall be digged with the **m,**	4576

MATTOCKS (2) [MATTOCK]

1Sa	13:21	Yet they had a file for the **m,** and for	4281
2Ch	34: 6	unto Naphtali, with their **m** round about.	2719

MAUL (1)

Pr	25:18	false witness against his neighbour *is* a **m,**	4650

MAULED See TARE

MAW (1)

Dt	18: 3	and the two cheeks, and the **m.**	6896

MAY (1027) [MAYEST]

Ge	1:20	fowl *that* **m** fly above the earth in the	NIH
	3: 2	We **m** eat of the fruit of the trees of	NIH
	8:17	they **m** breed abundantly in the earth,	NIH
	9:16	I **m** remember the everlasting covenant	NIH
	11: 4	a tower, whose top **m** reach unto heaven;	NIH
	11: 7	that they **m** not understand one another's	NIH
	12:13	that it **m** be well with me for thy sake;	NIH
	16: 2	it **m** be that I may obtain children by her.	194
	16: 2	it may be that I **m** obtain children by her.	NIH
	18:19	that the LORD **m** bring upon Abraham	NIH
	19: 5	them out unto us, that we **m** know them.	NIH
	19:32	that we **m** preserve seed of our father.	NIH
	19:34	that we **m** preserve seed of our father.	NIH

Ge	21:30	that they **m** be a witness unto me, that I	NIH
	23: 4	that I **m** bury my dead out of my sight.	NIH
	23: 9	That he **m** give me the cave of Machpelah,	NIH
	24:14	thy pitcher, I pray thee, that I **m** drink;	NIH
	24:49	I **m** turn to the right hand, or to the left.	NIH
	24:56	send me away that I **m** go to my master.	NIH
	27: 4	as I love, and bring *it* to me, that I **m** eat;	NIH
	27: 4	that my soul **m** bless thee before I die.	NIH
	27: 7	that I **m** eat, and bless thee before	NIH
	27:10	that he **m** eat, and that he may bless thee	NIH
	27:10	that he **m** bless thee before his death.	NIH
	27:19	of my venison, that thy soul **m** bless me.	NIH
	27:21	I pray thee, that I **m** feel thee, my son,	NIH
	27:25	son's venison, that my soul **m** bless thee.	NIH
	27:31	son's venison, that thy soul **m** bless me.	NIH
	29:21	days are fulfilled, that I **m** go in unto her.	NIH
	30: 3	that I **m** also have children by her.	NIH
	30:25	that I **m** go unto mine own place, and to	NIH
	31:37	that they **m** judge betwixt us both.	NIH
	32: 5	my lord, that I **m** find grace in thy sight.	NIH
	42: 2	from thence; that we **m** live, and not die.	NIH
	42:16	in prison, that your words **m** be proved,	NIH
	43: 8	that we **m** live, and not die, both we,	NIH
	43:14	that he **m** send away your other brother,	NIH
	43:18	he **m** seek occasion against us, and fall	NIH
	44:21	me, that I **m** set mine eyes upon him.	NIH
	44:26	we **m** not see the man's face, except our	3201
	46:34	that ye **m** dwell in the land of Goshen;	NIH
	47:19	give *us* seed, that we **m** live, and not die,	NIH
	49: 1	I **m** tell you *that* which shall befall you	NIH
Ex	2: 7	that she **m** nurse the child for thee?	NIH
	2:20	the man? call him, that he **m** eat bread.	NIH
	3:18	that we **m** sacrifice to the LORD our God.	NIH
	4: 5	That they **m** believe that the LORD God of	NIH
	4:23	Let my son go, that he **m** serve me:	NIH
	5: 1	that they **m** hold a feast unto me in	NIH
	5: 9	upon the men, that they **m** labour therein;	NIH
	7: 4	that I **m** lay my hand upon Egypt,	NIH
	7:16	that they **m** serve me in the wilderness.	NIH
	7:19	pools of water, that they **m** become blood;	NIH
	7:19	that there **m** be blood throughout all	NIH
	8: 1	Let my people go, that they **m** serve me.	NIH
	8: 8	that he **m** take away the frogs from me,	NIH
	8: 8	that they **m** do sacrifice unto the LORD.	NIH
	8: 9	*that* they **m** remain in the river only?	NIH
	8:16	it **m** become lice throughout all the land	NIH
	8:20	Let my people go, that they **m** serve me.	NIH
	8:28	that ye **m** sacrifice to the LORD your God	NIH
	8:29	swarms *of flies* **m** depart from Pharaoh,	NIH
	9: 1	Let my people go, that they **m** serve me.	NIH
	9:13	Let my people go, that they **m** serve me.	NIH
	9:15	that I **m** smite thee and thy people with	NIH
	9:16	my name **m** be declared throughout all	NIH
	9:22	there **m** be hail in all the land of Egypt,	NIH
	10: 2	that ye **m** know how that I *am* the LORD.	NIH
	10: 3	let my people go, that they **m** serve me.	NIH
	10: 7	that they **m** serve the LORD their God:	NIH
	10:12	that they **m** come up upon the land of	NIH
	10:17	that he **m** take away from me this death	NIH
	10:21	that there **m** be darkness over the land of	NIH
	10:21	of Egypt, even darkness *which* **m** be felt.	NIH
	10:25	that we **m** sacrifice unto the LORD our	NIH
	11: 7	that ye **m** know how that the LORD doth	NIH
	11: 9	my wonders **m** be multiplied in the land	NIH
	12:16	must eat, that only **m** be done of you.	NIH
	13: 9	that the LORD's law **m** be in thy mouth:	NIH
	14: 4	that the Egyptians **m** know that I *am*	NIH
	14:12	us alone, that we **m** serve the Egyptians?	NIH
	14:26	that the waters **m** come again upon	NIH
	16: 4	rate every day, that I **m** prove them,	NIH
	16:32	they **m** see the bread wherewith I have	NIH
	17: 2	and said, Give us water that we **m** drink.	NIH
	17: 6	water out of it, that the people **m** drink.	NIH
	19: 9	that the people **m** hear when I speak with	NIH
	20:12	thy days **m** be long upon the land which	NIH
	20:20	his fear **m** be before your faces, that ye	NIH
	21:14	take him from mine altar, that he **m** die.	NIH
	23:11	lie still; that the poor of thy people **m** eat:	NIH
	23:12	that thine ox and thine ass **m** rest,	NIH
	23:12	and the stranger, **m** be refreshed.	NIH
	25: 8	a sanctuary; that I **m** dwell amongst them.	NIH
	25:14	ark, that the ark **m** be borne with them.	NIH
	25:28	that the table **m** be borne with them.	NIH
	25:37	that they **m** give light over against it.	NIH
	26: 5	that the loops **m** take hold one of another.	NIH
	26:11	couple the tent together, that it **m** be one.	NIH
	27: 5	that the net **m** be even to the midst of	NIH
	28: 1	that he **m** minister unto me in the priest's	NIH
	28: 3	that they **m** make Aaron's garments to	NIH
	28: 4	that he **m** minister unto me in the priest's	NIH
	28: 4	that he **m** minister unto me in the priest's	NIH
	28:28	that *it* **m** be above the curious girdle of	NIH
	28:37	a blue lace, that it **m** be upon the mitre;	NIH
	28:38	that Aaron **m** bear the iniquity of the holy	NIH
	28:38	that they **m** be accepted before the LORD.	NIH
	28:41	they **m** minister unto me in the priest's	NIH
	29:46	of Egypt, that I **m** dwell amongst them:	NIH
	30:16	that it **m** be a memorial unto the children	NIH
	30:29	sanctify them, that they **m** be most holy:	NIH
	30:30	*they* **m** minister unto me in the priest's	NIH
	31: 6	that they **m** make all that I have	NIH
	31:13	that ye **m** know that I *am* the LORD that	NIH
	31:15	Six days **m** work be done; but in the	NIH
	32:10	that my wrath **m** wax hot against them,	NIH
	32:10	them, and that I **m** consume them:	NIH

Ex	32:29	he **m** bestow upon you a blessing *this*	NIH
	33: 5	that I **m** know what to do unto thee.	NIH
	33:13	me now thy way, that I **m** know thee,	NIH
	33:13	thee, that I **m** find grace in thy sight:	NIH
	35:34	he hath put in his heart that he **m** teach,	NIH
	40:13	that he **m** minister unto me in the priest's	NIH
	40:15	they **m** minister unto me in the priest's	NIH
Lev	7:24	the fat of that which is torn *with beasts,* **m**	NIH
	7:30	that the breast **m** be waved *for* a wave	NIH
	10:10	that ye **m** put difference between holy and	NIH
	10:11	that ye **m** teach the children of Israel all	NIH
	11:21	these **m** ye eat of every flying creeping	NIH
	11:22	*Even* these of them ye **m** eat; the locust	NIH
	11:34	Of all meat which **m** be eaten, *that* on	NIH
	11:34	all drink that **m** be drunk in every *such*	NIH
	11:39	if any beast, of which ye **m** eat, die; he	NIH
	11:47	between the beast that **m** be eaten and	NIH
	11:47	eaten and the beast that **m** not be eaten.	NIH
	14: 8	*himself* in water, that he **m** be clean:	NIH
	16:13	that the cloud of the incense **m** cover	NIH
	16:30	ye **m** be clean from all your sins before	NIH
	17: 5	To the end that the children of Israel **m**	NIH
	17: 5	even that they **m** bring them unto	NIH
	17:13	*any* beast or fowl that **m** be eaten;	NIH
	19:25	it **m** yield unto you the increase thereof:	NIH
	21: 3	had no husband; for her **m** be defiled.	NIH
	22: 5	whereby he **m** be made unclean, or a man	NIH
	22: 5	a man of whom he **m** take uncleanness,	NIH
	22:12	she **m** not eat of an offering of the holy	NIH
	23:21	that it **m** be a holy convocation unto you:	NIH
	23:43	your generations **m** know that I made	NIH
	24: 7	that it **m** be on the bread for a memorial,	NIH
	25:27	that he **m** return unto his possession.	NIH
	25:29	he **m** redeem it within a whole year after	NIH
	25:29	is sold; *within* a full year **m** he redeem it.	NIH
	25:31	they **m** be redeemed, and they shall go	NIH
	25:32	the Levites redeem at any time.	NIH
	25:34	field of the suburbs of their cities **m** not	NIH
	25:35	or a sojourner; that he **m** live with thee.	NIH
	25:36	God; that thy brother **m** live with thee.	NIH
	25:48	After *that* he is sold he **m** be redeemed	NIH
	25:48	one of his brethren **m** redeem him:	NIH
	25:49	**m** redeem him, or *any* that is nigh of kin	NIH
	25:49	unto him of his family **m** redeem him;	NIH
	25:49	or if he be able, he **m** redeem himself.	NIH
Nu	3: 6	the priest, that they **m** minister unto him.	NIH
	4:19	unto them, that they **m** live, and not die,	NIH
	6:20	and after *that* the Nazarite **m** drink wine.	NIH
	7: 5	That they **m** be to do the service of	NIH
	8:11	that they **m** execute the service of	NIH
	9: 7	that *we* **m** not offer an offering of	NIH
	10:10	that they **m** be to you for a memorial,	NIH
	11:13	saying, Give us flesh, that we **m** eat.	NIH
	11:16	that they **m** stand there with thee.	NIH
	11:21	flesh, that they **m** eat a whole month.	NIH
	13: 2	that they **m** search the land of Canaan,	NIH
	15:39	that ye **m** look upon it, and remember all	NIH
	15:40	That ye **m** remember, and do all my	NIH
	16:21	that I **m** consume them in a moment.	NIH
	16:45	that I **m** consume them as in a moment.	NIH
	18: 2	that they **m** be joined unto thee,	NIH
	19: 3	he **m** bring her forth without the camp,	NIH
	22: 6	we **m** smite them, and *that* I may drive	NIH
	22: 6	and *that* I **m** drive them out of the land:	NIH
	22:19	that I **m** know what the LORD will say	NIH
	25: 4	that the fierce anger of the LORD **m** be	NIH
	27:17	Which **m** go out before them,	NIH
	27:17	which **m** go in before them, and which	NIH
	27:17	which **m** lead them out, and which may	NIH
	27:17	them out, and which **m** bring them in;	NIH
	27:20	of the children of Israel **m** be obedient.	NIH
	30:13	her husband **m** establish it, or her husband	NIH
	30:13	or her husband **m** make it void.	NIH
	31:23	Every thing that **m** abide the fire, ye shall	NIH
	32:32	inheritance on *this* side Jordan **m** be ours.	NIH
	35: 6	for the manslayer, that he **m** flee thither:	NIH
	35:11	the slayer **m** flee thither, which killeth	NIH
	35:15	killeth *any* person unawares **m** flee thither.	NIH
	35:17	wherewith he **m** die, and he die, he *is* a	NIH
	35:18	wherewith he **m** die, and he die, he *is* a	NIH
	35:23	wherewith *a man* **m** die, seeing him not,	NIH
	36: 8	that the children of Israel **m** enjoy every	NIH
Dt	2: 6	meat of them for money, that ye **m** eat;	NIH
	2: 6	water of them for money, that ye **m** drink.	NIH
	2:28	sell me meat for money, that I **m** eat;	NIH
	2:28	give me water for money, that I **m** drink:	NIH
	4: 1	for to do *them,* that ye **m** live, and go in	NIH
	4: 2	that ye **m** keep the commandments of	NIH
	4:10	that they **m** learn to fear me all the days	NIH
	4:10	and *that* they **m** teach their children.	NIH
	4:40	that it **m** go well with thee, and with thy	NIH
	5: 1	that ye **m** learn them, and keep, and do	NIH
	5:14	thy maidservant **m** rest as well as thou.	NIH
	5:16	thy days **m** be prolonged, and that it	NIH
	5:16	and that it **m** go well with thee,	NIH
	5:31	that they **m** do *them* in the land which I	NIH
	5:33	that ye **m** live, and that it may be well	NIH
	5:33	*it* **m** be well with you, and *that* ye may	NIH
	5:33	*that* ye **m** prolong *your* days in the land	NIH
	6: 2	thy life; and that thy days **m** be prolonged.	NIH
	6: 3	to do *it;* that it **m** be well with thee,	NIH
	6: 3	thee, and that ye **m** increase mightily,	NIH
	6:18	that it **m** be well with thee, and *that* thou	NIH
	7: 4	me, that they **m** serve other gods:	NIH
	8: 1	that ye **m** live, and multiply, and go in and	NIH

Dt
8:18 that he **m** establish his covenant which he NIH
9: 5 that he **m** perform the word which NIH
9:14 that I **m** destroy them, and blot out their NIH
10:11 that they **m** go in and possess the land, NIH
11: 8 that ye **m** be strong, and go in and NIH
11: 9 that ye **m** prolong your days in the land, NIH
11:18 that they **m** be as frontlets between your NIH
11:21 That your days **m** be multiplied, NIH
12:15 the unclean and the clean **m** eat thereof, NIH
12:25 that it **m** go well with thee, and with thy NIH
12:28 that it **m** go well with thee, and with thy NIH
13:17 that the LORD **m** turn from the fierceness NIH
14:10 hath not fins and scales ye **m** not eat; NIH
14:20 *But* of all clean fowls ye **m** eat. NIH
14:21 that *is* in thy gates, that he **m** eat it; NIH
14:29 that the LORD thy God **m** bless thee in all NIH
17:19 that he **m** learn to fear the LORD his God, NIH
17:20 the end that he **m** prolong *his* days in his NIH
19: 3 parts, that every slayer **m** flee thither. NIH
19: 4 which shall flee thither, that he **m** live: NIH
19:12 of the avenger of blood, that he **m** die. NIH
19:13 from Israel, that *it* **m** go well with thee. NIH
21:16 that he **m** not make the son of the beloved 3201
22: 7 that it **m** be well with thee, and *that* thou NIH
22:19 he **m** not put her away all his days. 3201
22:29 he **m** not put her away all his days. NIH
23:20 that the LORD thy God **m** bless thee in all NIH
24: 2 she **m** go and be another man's *wife*. NIH
24: 4 **m** not take her again to be his wife, 3201
24:13 that he **m** sleep in his own raiment, NIH
24:19 that the LORD thy God **m** bless thee in all NIH
25: 1 that *the judges* **m** judge them; NIH
25: 3 Forty stripes he **m** give him, NIH
25:15 that thy days **m** be lengthened in the land NIH
26:12 that they **m** eat within thy gates, NIH
29: 9 them, that ye **m** prosper *in* all that ye do. NIH
29:13 he **m** establish thee to day for a people NIH
29:13 *that* he **m** be unto thee a God, as he hath NIH
29:29 that *we* **m** do all the words of this law. NIH
30:12 it unto us, that we **m** hear it, and do it? NIH
30:13 it unto us, that we **m** hear it, and do it? NIH
30:19 that *both* thou and thy seed **m** live: NIH
31: 5 that ye **m** do unto them according unto all NIH
31:12 that they **m** hear, and that they may learn, NIH
31:12 that they **m** learn, and fear the LORD your NIH
31:13 which have not known *any thing,* **m** hear, NIH
31:14 that I **m** give him a charge. NIH
31:19 this song **m** be a witness for me against NIH
31:26 it **m** be there for a witness against thee. NIH
31:28 that I **m** speak these words in their ears, NIH

Jos
2:16 and afterward **m** ye go your way. NIH
3: 4 ye **m** know the way by which ye must NIH
3: 7 they **m** know that, as I was with Moses, NIH
4: 6 That this **m** be a sign among you, *that* NIH
9:19 now therefore we **m** not touch them. 3201
10: 4 and help me, that we **m** smite Gibeon: NIH
18: 6 that I **m** cast lots for you here before NIH
18: 8 that I **m** here cast lots for you before NIH
20: 3 *and* unwittingly **m** flee thither: NIH
20: 4 a place, that he **m** dwell among them. NIH
22:27 it **m** *be* a witness between us, and you, NIH
22:27 your children **m** not say to our children NIH
22:28 that we **m** say *again,* Behold the pattern NIH

Jdg
1: 3 that we **m** fight against the Canaanites; NIH
2:22 That through them I **m** prove Israel, NIH
6:30 Joash, Bring out thy son, that he **m** die: NIH
9: 7 Shechem, that God **m** hearken unto you. NIH
11: 6 that we **m** fight with the children of NIH
11:37 that I **m** go up and down upon NIH
13:14 She **m** not eat of any *thing* that cometh NIH
13:17 that when thy sayings come to pass we **m** NIH
14:13 Put forth thy riddle, that we **m** hear it. NIH
14:15 that he **m** declare unto us the riddle, lest NIH
15:12 that we **m** deliver thee into the hand of NIH
16: 5 by what *means* we **m** prevail against him, NIH
16: 5 that we **m** bind him to afflict him: NIH
16:25 Call for Samson, that he **m** make us sport. NIH
16:26 Suffer me that I **m** feel the pillars NIH
16:26 house standeth, that I **m** lean upon them. NIH
16:28 that I **m** be at once avenged of NIH
17: 9 I go to sojourn where I **m** find *a place.* NIH
18: 5 that we **m** know whether our way which NIH
18: 9 Arise, that we **m** go up against them: NIH
19: 9 lodge here, that thine heart **m** be merry; NIH
19:22 into thine house, that we **m** know him. NIH
20:10 victual for the people, that *they* **m** do, NIH
20:13 we **m** put them to death, and put away NIH
21:18 Howbeit we **m** not give them wives of 3201

Ru
1: 9 The LORD grant you that you **m** find rest, NIH
1:11 my womb, that they **m** be your husbands? NIH
2:16 leave *them,* that she **m** glean *them,* and NIH
3: 1 rest for thee, that it **m** be well with thee? NIH
4: 4 redeem *it, then* tell me, that I **m** know: NIH
4:14 that his name **m** be famous in Israel. NIH

1Sa
1:22 that he **m** appear before the LORD, NIH
2:36 that *I* **m** eat a piece of bread. NIH
4: 3 **m** save us out of the hand of our enemies. NIH
6: 8 thereof; and send it away, that it **m** go. NIH
8:20 That we also **m** be like all the nations; NIH
8:20 our king **m** judge us, and go out before NIH
9:16 he **m** save my people out of the hand of NIH
9:26 saying, Up, that I **m** send thee away. NIH
9:27 that I **m** shew thee the word of God. NIH
11: 2 that *I* **m** thrust out all your right eyes, NIH
11: 3 that we **m** send messengers unto all NIH

1Sa
11:12 the men, that we **m** put them to death. NIH
12: 7 that I **m** reason with you before the LORD NIH
12:17 that ye **m** perceive and see that your NIH
14: 6 it **m** be that the LORD will work for us: 194
14:24 that I **m** be avenged on mine enemies. NIH
15:25 with me, that I **m** worship the LORD. NIH
15:30 that I **m** worship the LORD thy God. NIH
17:10 give me a man, that we **m** fight together. NIH
17:46 all the earth **m** know that there is a God NIH
18:21 that she **m** be a snare to him, and that NIH
18:21 the hand of the Philistines **m** be against NIH
19:15 up to me in the bed, that I **m** slay him. NIH
20: 5 that I **m** hide myself in the fields unto NIH
27: 5 town in the country, that I **m** dwell there: NIH
28: 7 that I **m** go to her, and inquire of her. NIH
29: 4 that he **m** go again to his place, NIH
29: 8 that I **m** not go fight against the enemies NIH
30:22 that they **m** lead *them* away, and depart. NIH

2Sa
3:21 that they **m** make a league with thee, NIH
7:10 that they **m** dwell in a place of their own, NIH
7:29 that *it* **m** continue for ever before thee: NIH
9: 1 I **m** shew him kindness for Jonathan's NIH
9: 3 that I **m** shew the kindness of God unto NIH
9:10 that thy master's son **m** have food to eat: NIH
11:15 from him, that he **m** be smitten, and die. NIH
12:22 be gracious to me, that the child **m** live? NIH
13: 5 that I **m** see *it,* and eat at her hand. NIH
13: 6 in my sight, that I **m** eat at her hand. NIH
13:10 the chamber, that I **m** eat of thine hand. NIH
14: 7 smote his brother, that we **m** kill him, NIH
14:15 it **m** be that the king will perform 194
14:32 that I **m** send thee to the king, to say, NIH
15:20 seeing I go whither I **m**, return thou, 1980
16: 2 that such as be faint in the wilderness **m** NIH
16: 4 I humbly beseech thee *that* I **m** find grace NIH
16:11 much more now **m** this Benjamite *do* NIH
16:12 It **m** be that the LORD will look on mine 194
18:14 said Joab, I **m** not tarry thus with thee. NIH
19:26 that I **m** ride thereon, and go to the king; NIH
19:37 I **m** die in mine own city, *and be buried* NIH
20:16 near hither, that I **m** speak with thee. NIH
21: 3 that we **m** bless the inheritance of NIH
24: 2 that I **m** know the number of the people. NIH
24: 3 *that* the eyes of my lord the king **m** see *it:* NIH
24:12 one of them, that I **m** do *it* unto thee. NIH
24:21 the plague **m** be stayed from the people. NIH

1Ki
1: 2 bosom, that my lord the king **m** get heat. NIH
1:35 that he **m** come and sit upon my throne; NIH
2: 4 That the LORD **m** continue his word NIH
3: 9 that *I* **m** discern between good and bad: NIH
8:29 That thine eyes **m** be open toward this NIH
8:40 That they **m** fear thee all the days that NIH
8:43 that all people of the earth **m** know thy NIH
8:43 that *they* **m** know that this house, which NIH
8:50 that they **m** have compassion on them: NIH
8:52 That thine eyes **m** be open unto NIH
8:58 That he **m** incline our hearts unto him, NIH
8:60 That all the people of the earth **m** know NIH
11:21 depart, that I **m** go to mine own country. NIH
11:36 David my servant **m** have a light alway NIH
12: 6 How do you advise that *I* **m** answer this 7725
12: 9 What counsel give ye that we **m** answer 7725
13: 6 that my hand **m** be restored me again. NIH
13:16 said, I **m** not return with thee, nor go in 3201
13:18 that he **m** eat bread and drink water. NIH
15:19 king of Israel, that he **m** depart from me. NIH
17:10 a little water in a vessel, that I **m** drink. NIH
17:12 that I **m** go in and dress it for me and my NIH
17:12 and my son, that we **m** eat it, and die. NIH
18: 5 peradventure we **m** find grass to save NIH
18:37 that this people **m** know that thou *art* NIH
20: 9 this thing I **m** not do. And the messengers 3201
21: 2 that I **m** have it for a garden of herbs, NIH
21:10 him out, and stone him, that he **m** die. NIH
22: 8 by whom we **m** inquire of the LORD: NIH
22:20 that he **m** go up and fall at Ramoth-gilead? NIH

2Ki
3:11 that we **m** inquire of the LORD by him? NIH
3:17 that ye **m** drink, *both* ye, and your cattle, NIH
4:22 that I **m** run to the man of God, NIH
4:41 Pour out for the people, that they **m** eat. NIH
4:42 Give unto the people, that they **m** eat. NIH
4:43 again, Give the people, that they **m** eat: NIH
5:12 be I **m** not wash in them, and be clean? NIH
6: 2 us a place there, where we **m** dwell. NIH
6:13 Go and spy where he *is,* that I **m** send NIH
6:17 I pray thee, open his eyes, that he **m** see. NIH
6:20 the eyes of these *men,* that they **m** see. NIH
6:22 that they **m** eat and drink, and go to their NIH
6:28 we **m** eat him to day, and we will eat NIH
6:29 day, Give thy son, that we **m** eat him: NIH
7: 9 we **m** go and tell the king's household. NIH
9: 7 that I **m** avenge the blood of my servants NIH
18:27 that they **m** eat their own dung, and drink NIH
18:32 and of honey, that ye **m** live, and not die: NIH
19: 4 It **m** be that the LORD thy God will hear all 194
19:19 all the kingdoms of the earth **m** know NIH
22: 4 that he **m** sum the silver which is brought NIH

1Ch
4:10 *me* from evil, that it **m** not grieve me. NIH
13: 2 that they **m** gather themselves unto us: NIH
15:12 that you **m** bring up the ark of the LORD NIH
16:35 that *we* **m** give thanks to thy holy name, NIH
17:24 that thy name **m** be magnified for ever, NIH
17:27 that *it* **m** be before thee for ever: NIH
21: 2 number of them to me, that I **m** know *it.* NIH
21:10 one of them, that I **m** do *it* unto thee. NIH

1Ch
21:22 that I **m** build an altar therein unto NIH
21:22 the plague **m** be stayed from the people. NIH
23:25 that they **m** dwell in Jerusalem for ever: NIH
28: 8 that ye **m** possess *this* good land, NIH

2Ch
1:10 that I **m** go out and come in before this NIH
6:20 That thine eyes **m** be open upon this NIH
6:31 they **m** fear thee, to walk in thy ways, NIH
6:33 that all people of the earth **m** know thy NIH
6:33 **m** know that this house which I have built NIH
7:16 that my name **m** be there for ever: NIH
10: 9 What advice give ye that we **m** return NIH
12: 8 that they **m** know my service, NIH
13: 9 *the same* **m** be a priest of *them that are* NIH
16: 3 king of Israel, that he **m** depart from me. NIH
18: 7 by whom we **m** inquire of the LORD: NIH
18:19 he **m** go up and fall at Ramoth-gilead? NIH
28:23 I sacrifice to them, that they **m** help me. NIH
29:10 his fierce wrath **m** turn away from us. NIH
30: 8 the fierceness of his wrath **m** turn away NIH
35: 6 that *they* **m** do according to the word of NIH

Ezr
4:15 That search **m** be made in the book of NIH
6:10 That they **m** offer sacrifices of sweet NIH
7:25 which **m** judge all the people that *are* NIH
9: 8 that our God **m** lighten our eyes, and give NIH
9:12 that ye **m** be strong, and eat the good of NIH

Ne
2: 5 of my fathers' sepulchres, that I **m** build it. NIH
2: 7 they **m** convey me over till I come into NIH
2: 8 he **m** give me timber to make beams for NIH
4:22 that in the night they **m** be a guard to us, NIH
5: 2 we take up corn *for them,* that we **m** eat, NIH

Est
2: 3 that they **m** gather together all the fair NIH
3: 9 let it be written that they **m** be destroyed: NIH
4:11 out the golden sceptre, that he **m** live: NIH
5: 5 that *he* **m** do as Esther hath said. NIH
5:14 king that Mordecai **m** be hanged thereon: NIH
6: 9 that they **m** array the man *withal* whom NIH
8: 8 with the king's ring, **m** no man reverse. NIH

Job
1: 5 It **m** be that my sons have sinned, 194
5:11 that those which mourn **m** be exalted *to* NIH
10:20 me alone, that I **m** take comfort a little, NIH
13:13 that I **m** speak, and let come on me what NIH
14: 6 Turn from him, that he **m** rest, till he shall NIH
19:29 that ye **m** know *there is* a judgment. NIH
21: 3 Suffer me that I **m** speak; and after that I NIH
22: 2 as he that is wise **m** be profitable unto NIH
27:17 he **m** prepare *it,* but the just shall put *it* NIH
31: 6 that God **m** know mine integrity. NIH
32:20 I will speak, that I **m** be refreshed: I will NIH
33:17 *he* **m** withdraw man *from his* purpose, NIH
34:22 where the workers of iniquity **m** hide NIH
34:36 My desire *is that* Job **m** be tried unto NIH
35: 8 wickedness **m** hurt a man as thou *art;* NIH
35: 8 thy righteousness **m** *profit* the son of man. NIH
36:25 Every man **m** see it; man may behold *it* NIH
36:25 man may see it; man **m** behold *it* afar off. NIH
37: 7 man; that all men **m** know his work. NIH
37:12 they **m** do whatsoever he commandeth NIH
38:34 that abundance of waters **m** cover thee? NIH
38:35 that they **m** go, and say unto thee, Here NIH
39:15 forgetteth that the foot **m** crush them, NIH
39:15 or *that* the wild beast **m** break them. NIH

Ps
9:14 That I **m** shew forth all thy praise in NIH
9:20 the nations **m** know themselves *to be* NIH
10:10 that the poor **m** fall by his strong *ones.* NIH
10:18 that the man of the earth **m** no more NIH
11: 2 that they **m** privily shoot at the upright in NIH
22:17 I **m** tell all my bones: they look *and* NIH
26: 7 That *I* **m** publish with the voice of NIH
27: 4 that I **m** dwell in the house of the LORD NIH
30: 5 weeping **m** endure for a night, NIH
30:12 To the end that *my* glory **m** sing *praise* to NIH
34:12 loveth *many* days, that he **m** see good? NIH
39: 4 what it *is; that* I **m** know how frail I *am.* NIH
39:13 O spare me, that I **m** recover strength, NIH
41:10 and raise me up, that I **m** requite them. NIH
48:13 ye **m** tell *it* to the generation following. NIH
50: 4 to the earth, that he **m** judge his people. NIH
51: 8 *that* the bones *which* thou hast broken **m** NIH
56:13 that *I* **m** walk before God in the light of NIH
58: 8 of a woman, *that* he **m** not see the sun. NIH
59:13 consume *them,* that they **m** not *be:* and NIH
60: 4 that *it* **m** be displayed because of the truth. NIH
60: 5 That thy beloved **m** be delivered; save NIH
61: 7 and truth, *which* **m** preserve him. NIH
61: 8 for ever, that I **m** daily perform my vows. NIH
64: 4 That *they* **m** shoot in secret at the perfect: NIH
65: 4 causest to approach *unto thee, that* he **m** NIH
67: 2 That thy way **m** be known upon earth, NIH
68:23 That thy foot **m** be dipped in the blood of NIH
69:35 that they **m** dwell there, and have it in NIH
71: 3 whereunto *I* **m** continually resort: NIH
73:28 Lord GOD, *that* I **m** declare all thy works. NIH
76: 7 who **m** stand in thy sight when once thou NIH
83: 4 that the name of Israel **m** be no more in NIH
83:16 that they **m** seek thy name, O LORD. NIH
83:18 That *men* **m** know that thou, whose name NIH
84: 3 where she **m** lay her young, *even* thine NIH
85: 6 us again: that thy people **m** rejoice in thee? NIH
85: 9 fear him; that glory **m** dwell in our land. NIH
86:17 that they which hate me **m** see *it,* and NIH
90:12 that we **m** apply *our* hearts *unto* wisdom. NIH
90:14 that we **m** rejoice and be glad all our days. NIH
101: 6 of the land, that *they* **m** dwell with me: NIH
101: 8 that *I* **m** cut off all wicked doers from NIH
104: 9 hast set a bound *that* they **m** not pass NIH

M

Ps
104:14 *he* **m** bring forth food out of the earth; NIH
106: 5 That *I* **m** see the good of thy chosen, that NIH
106: 5 that *I* **m** rejoice in the gladness of thy NIH
106: 5 that *I* **m** glory with thine inheritance. NIH
107:36 that they **m** prepare a city for habitation; NIH
107:37 which **m** yield fruits of increase. NIH
108: 6 That thy beloved **m** be delivered: save NIH
109:15 that he **m** cut off the memory of them NIH
109:27 That they **m** know that this *is* thy hand; NIH
111: 6 that he **m** give them the heritage of NIH
113: 8 That he **m** set *him* with princes, *even* NIH
119:17 *that* I **m** live, and keep thy word. NIH
119:18 that I **m** behold wondrous *things* out of NIH
119:73 that I **m** learn thy commandments. NIH
119:77 mercies come *unto* me, that I **m** live: NIH
119:116 according unto thy word, that I **m** live: NIH
119:125 that I **m** know thy testimonies. NIH
124: 1 who was on our side, now **m** Israel say: NIH
129: 1 me from my youth, **m** Israel now say: NIH
142: 7 out of prison, that I **m** praise thy name: NIH
144:12 That our sons **m** be as plants grown up in NIH
144:12 that our daughters **m** be as corner stones, NIH
144:13 *That* our garners **m** be full, affording all NIH
144:13 that our sheep **m** bring forth thousands NIH
144:14 *That* our oxen **m** be strong to labour; NIH

Pr
5: 2 and *that* thy lips **m** keep knowledge. NIH
7: 5 That *they* **m** keep thee from the strange NIH
8:11 all the things that **m** be desired are not to NIH
8:21 *I* **m** cause those that love me to inherit NIH
15:24 that *he* **m** depart from hell beneath. NIH
18: 2 but that his heart **m** discover itself. NIH
20:21 An inheritance **m** be gotten hastily at NIH
22:19 That thy trust **m** be in the LORD, I have NIH
27: 1 for thou knowest not what a day **m** bring NIH
27:11 that I **m** answer him that reproacheth me. NIH

Ecc
1:10 Is there *any* thing whereof it **m** be said, NIH
2:26 that he **m** give to *him that is* good before NIH
5:15 which he **m** carry away in his hand. NIH
6:10 neither **m** he contend with him that *is* 3201
8: 4 who **m** say unto him, What doest thou? NIH

SS
4:16 *that* the spices thereof **m** flow out. NIH
6: 1 aside? that we **m** seek him with thee. NIH
6:13 return, return, that we **m** look upon thee. NIH

Isa
5: 8 that they **m** be placed alone in the midst NIH
5:11 *that* they **m** follow strong drink; NIH
5:19 that we **m** see it: and let the counsel of NIH
5:19 draw nigh and come, that we **m** know *it.* NIH
7:15 that he **m** know to refuse the evil, NIH
10: 2 that widows **m** be their prey, and *that* NIH
10: 2 and *that* they **m** rob the fatherless. NIH
10:19 shall be few, that a child **m** write them. NIH
13: 2 they **m** go *into* the gates of the nobles. NIH
19:15 the head or tail, branch or rush, **m** do. NIH
24:10 house is shut up, that no man **m** come in. NIH
26: 2 which keepeth the truth **m** enter in. NIH
27: 5 strength, *that* he **m** make peace with me; NIH
28:12 This *is* the rest *wherewith* ye **m** cause NIH
28:21 that he **m** do his work, his strange work; NIH
30: 1 of my Spirit, that *they* **m** add sin to sin: NIH
30: 8 that it **m** be for the time to come for ever NIH
30:18 that he **m** be gracious unto you, NIH
30:18 exalted, that *he* **m** have mercy upon you: NIH
36:12 that they **m** eat their own dung, and drink NIH
37: 4 **It m be** the LORD thy God will hear 194
37:20 that all the kingdoms of the earth **m** know NIH
41:20 That they **m** see, and know, and consider, NIH
41:22 what they *be,* that we **m** consider *them,* NIH
41:23 that we **m** know that ye *are* gods: NIH
41:23 that we **m** be dismayed, and behold *it* NIH
41:26 from the beginning, that we **m** know? NIH
41:26 that we **m** say, *He is* righteous? NIH
42:18 ye deaf; and look, ye blind, that ye **m** see. NIH
43: 9 their witnesses, that they **m** be justified: NIH
43:10 that ye **m** know and believe me, NIH
44: 9 not, nor know; that they **m** be ashamed. NIH
44:13 of a man; that it **m** remain in the house. NIH
45: 6 That they **m** know from the rising of NIH
46: 5 and compare me, that we **m** be like? NIH
49:15 they **m** forget, yet will I not forget thee. NIH
49:20 for me: give place to me that I **m** dwell. NIH
51:14 The captive exile hasteneth that he **m** be NIH
51:16 that I **m** plant the heavens, and lay NIH
51:23 thy soul, Bow down, that we **m** go over: NIH
55: 6 Seek ye the LORD while he **m** be found, NIH
55:10 that it **m** give seed to the sower, NIH
60:11 that men **m** bring unto thee the forces of NIH
60:11 and *that* their kings **m** be brought. NIH
60:21 work of my hands, that I **m** be glorified. NIH
64: 2 the nations **m** tremble at thy presence. NIH
65: 8 that I **m** not destroy them all. NIH
66:11 That ye **m** suck, and be satisfied with NIH
66:11 that ye **m** milk out, and be delighted with NIH

Jer
6:10 speak, and give warning, that they **m** hear? NIH
7:18 that *they* **m** provoke me to anger. NIH
7:23 commanded you, that it **m** be well unto NIH
9:12 *is* the wise man, that **m** understand this? NIH
9:12 that he **m** declare it, for what the land NIH
9:17 call for the mourning *women,* that they **m** NIH
9:17 for cunning *women,* that they **m** come: NIH
9:18 that our eyes **m** run down with tears, NIH
10:18 will distress them, that they **m** find *it so.* NIH
11: 5 That I **m** perform the oath which I have NIH
11:19 that his name **m** be no more remembered. NIH
13:23 then **m** ye also do good, that are 3201
13:26 upon thy face, that thy shame **m** appear. NIH

Jer
16:12 heart, that *they* **m** not hearken unto me: NIH
21: 2 works, that he **m** go up from us. NIH
26: 3 that I **m** repent me of the evil, which I NIH
28:14 that they **m** serve Nebuchadnezzar king NIH
29: 6 that they **m** bear sons and daughters; NIH
29: 6 that ye **m** be increased there, NIH
32:14 that they **m** continue many days. NIH
32:39 one way, that *they* **m** fear me for ever, NIH
33:21 *Then* **m** also my covenant be broken with NIH
35: 7 ye **m** live many days in the land where NIH
36: 3 **It m be** that the house of Judah will hear 194
36: 3 that they **m** return every man from his evil NIH
36: 3 that I **m** forgive their iniquity and their sin. NIH
36: 7 **It m be** they will present their supplication 194
42: 3 That the LORD thy God **m** shew us NIH
42: 3 shew us the way wherein we **m** walk, NIH
42: 3 may walk, and the thing that we **m** do. NIH
42: 6 that it **m** be well with us, when we obey NIH
42:12 that he **m** have mercy upon you, NIH
44:29 that ye **m** know that my words shall surely NIH
46:10 that *he* **m** avenge him of his adversaries: NIH
48: 9 unto Moab, that it **m** flee and get away: NIH
49:19 *is* a chosen *man, that* I **m** appoint over NIH
50:34 that he **m** give rest to the land, NIH
50:44 *is* a chosen *man, that* I **m** appoint over NIH
51: 8 for her pain, if so be she **m** be healed. NIH
51:39 that they **m** rejoice, and sleep a perpetual NIH

La
2:13 I equal to thee, that I **m** comfort thee, NIH
3:29 in the dust; if so be there **m** be hope. NIH

Eze
4:17 That they **m** want bread and water, NIH
6: 6 that your altars **m** be laid waste and NIH
6: 6 your idols **m** be broken and cease, NIH
6: 6 your images **m** be cut down, NIH
6: 6 down, and your works **m** be abolished. NIH
6: 8 that ye **m** have *some* that shall escape NIH
11:20 That they **m** walk in my statutes, and keep NIH
12: 3 it **m** be they will consider, though they 194
12:16 that they **m** declare all their abominations NIH
12:19 that her land **m** be desolate from all that is NIH
14: 5 That *I* **m** take the house of Israel in their NIH
14:11 That the house of Israel **m** go no more NIH
14:11 that they **m** be my people, and I may be NIH
14:11 and I **m** be their God, saith the Lord GOD. NIH
14:15 that no man **m** pass through because of NIH
16:33 that they **m** come unto thee on every side NIH
16:37 that they **m** see all thy nakedness. NIH
20:20 that ye **m** know that I *am* the LORD your NIH
21: 5 That all flesh **m** know that I the LORD NIH
21:10 *it is* furbished that it **m** glitter: NIH
21:11 it to be furbished, that *it* **m** be handled: NIH
21:15 that *their* heart **m** faint, and *their* ruins be NIH
21:19 that the sword of the king of Babylon **m** NIH
21:20 that the sword **m** come to Rabbath of NIH
21:23 the iniquity, that they **m** be taken. NIH
22: 3 that her time **m** come, and maketh idols NIH
23:48 all women **m** be taught not to do after NIH
24:11 the brass of it **m** be hot, and may burn, NIH
24:11 burn, and *that* the filthiness of it may NIH
24:11 *that* the filthiness of it **m** be molten in it, NIH
24:11 in it, *that* the scum of it **m** be consumed. NIH
25:10 the Ammonites **m** not be remembered NIH
28:17 before kings, that *they* **m** behold thee. NIH
34:10 that they **m** not be meat for them. NIH
37: 9 breathe upon these slain, that they **m** live. NIH
38:16 my land, that the heathen **m** know me, NIH
39:12 of them, that *they* **m** cleanse the land. NIH
39:17 that ye **m** eat flesh, and drink blood. NIH
43:10 that they **m** be ashamed of their iniquities: NIH
43:11 that they **m** keep the whole form thereof, NIH
44:25 no husband, they **m** defile themselves. NIH
44:30 he **m** cause the blessing to rest in thine NIH
45:11 the bath **m** contain the tenth part of a 3807.1

Da
4:17 to the intent that the living **m** know that NIH
4:27 if it **m** be a lengthening of thy tranquillity. NIH
6:15 the king establisheth **m** be changed. NIH

Hos
8: 4 made them idols, that they **m** be cut off. NIH
13:10 where *is* any other that **m** save thee in all NIH

Am
5:14 Seek good, and not evil, that ye **m** live: NIH
5:15 **It m be** that the LORD God of hosts will 194
6:10 *we* **m** not make mention of the name of NIH
8: 5 new moon be gone, that we **m** sell corn? NIH
8: 5 the sabbath, that we **m** set forth wheat, NIH
8: 6 That *we* **m** buy the poor for silver, NIH
9: 1 lintel of the door, that the posts **m** shake: NIH
9:12 That they **m** possess the remnant of Edom, NIH

Ob
1: 9 mount of Esau **m** be cut off by slaughter. NIH

Jnh
1: 7 we **m** know for whose cause this evil *is* NIH
1:11 thee, that the sea **m** be calm unto us? NIH

Mic
6: 5 that *ye* **m** know the righteousness of NIH
7: 3 That they **m** do evil with both hands NIH

Hab
2: 2 upon tables, that he **m** run that readeth it. NIH
2: 9 that he **m** set his nest on high, that he NIH
2: 9 that *he* **m** be delivered from the power of NIH

Zep
2: 3 it **m** be ye shall be hid in the day of 194
3: 8 that I **m** assemble the kingdoms, to pour NIH
3: 9 that they **m** all call upon the name of NIH

Zec
11: 1 that the fire **m** devour thy cedars. NIH

Mal
3: 2 who **m** abide the day of his coming? NIH
3: 3 that they **m** offer unto the LORD an NIH
3:10 that there **m** be meat in mine house, NIH

Mt
2: 8 that I **m** come and worship him also. NIH
5:16 that they **m** see your good works, NIG
5:45 That ye **m** be the children of your Father NIG
6: 2 streets, that they **m** have glory of men. NIG
6: 4 That thine alms **m** be in secret: NIG

Mt
6: 5 the streets, that they **m** be seen of men. 302
6:16 that they **m** appear unto men to fast. NIG
9: 6 But that ye **m** know that the Son of man NIG
9:21 If I **m** but touch his garment, I shall be NIG
14:15 that they **m** go into the villages, NIG
18:16 three witnesses every word **m** be NIG
19:16 *thing* shall I do, that I **m** have eternal life? NIG
20:21 Grant that these my two sons **m** sit, NIG
20:33 him, Lord, that our eyes **m** be opened. NIG
23:26 that the outside of them **m** be clean also. NIG
23:35 That upon you **m** come all the righteous NIG
26:42 if this cup **m** not pass away from me, 1410

Mk
1:38 next towns, that I **m** preach there also: NIG
2:10 But that ye **m** know that the Son of man NIG
4:12 That seeing they **m** see, and not perceive; NIG
4:12 and hearing they **m** hear, NIG
4:32 that the fowls of the air **m** lodge under 1410
5:12 the swine, that we **m** enter into them. NIG
5:23 *thy* hands on her, that she **m** be healed; NIG
5:28 For she said, If I **m** touch but his clothes, NIG
6:36 they **m** go into the country round about, NIG
7: 9 God, that ye **m** keep your own tradition. NIG
10:17 shall I do that I **m** inherit eternal life? NIG
10:37 unto thee, Grant unto us that we **m** sit, NIG
11:25 your Father also which is in heaven **m** NIG
12:15 ye me? bring me a penny, that I **m** see *it.* NIG
14: 7 whensoever ye will ye **m** do them good: 1410
15:32 from the cross, that we **m** see and believe. NIG

Lk
2:35 that the thoughts of many hearts **m** be NIG
5:24 But that ye **m** know that the Son of man NIG
8:16 that they which enter in **m** see the light. NIG
9:12 that they **m** go into the towns and NIG
11:33 that they which come in **m** see the light. NIG
11:50 world, **m** be required of this generation; NIG
12:36 they **m** open unto him immediately. NIG
14:10 he **m** say unto thee, Friend, go up higher: NIG
14:23 to come in, that my house **m** be filled. NIG
16: 4 they **m** receive me into their houses. NIG
16: 9 they **m** receive you into everlasting NIG
16:24 he **m** dip the tip of his finger in water, NIG
16:28 that he **m** testify unto them, lest they also NIG
17: 8 Make ready wherewith I **m** sup, NIG
18:41 he said, Lord, that I **m** receive my sight. NIG
20:13 it **m** be they will reverence *him* when 2481
20:14 us kill him, that the inheritance **m** be ours. NIG
21:22 that all *things* which are written **m** be NIG
21:36 ye **m** be accounted worthy to escape all NIG
22: 8 prepare us the passover, that we **m** eat. NIG
22:30 That ye **m** eat and drink at my table in my NIG
22:31 *to have* you, that he **m** sift *you* as wheat: NIG

Jn
1:22 we **m** give an answer to them that sent NIG
3:21 his deeds **m** be made manifest, that they NIG
4:36 and he that reapeth **m** rejoice together. NIG
5:20 works than these, that ye **m** marvel. NIG
6: 5 shall we buy bread, that these **m** eat? NIG
6: 7 that every one of them **m** take a little. NIG
6:30 then, that we **m** see, and believe thee? NIG
6:40 believeth on him, **m** have everlasting life: NIG
6:50 from heaven, that a man **m** eat thereof, NIG
7: 3 that thy disciples also **m** see the works NIG
10:38 ye **m** know, and believe, that the Father NIG
11:11 but I go, that I **m** awake him out of sleep. NIG
11:15 was not there, to the intent ye **m** believe; NIG
11:16 Let us also go, that we **m** die with him. NIG
11:42 they **m** believe that thou hast sent me. NIG
12:36 light, that ye **m** be the children of light. NIG
13:18 that the scripture **m** be fulfilled, He that NIG
13:19 come to pass, ye **m** believe that I am *he.* NIG
14: 3 that where I am, *there* ye **m** be also. NIG
14:13 that the Father **m** be glorified in the Son. NIG
14:16 that he **m** abide with you for ever; NIG
14:31 But that the world **m** know that I love NIG
15: 2 purgeth it, that it **m** bring forth more fruit. NIG
15:16 the Father in my name, he **m** give it you. NIG
16: 4 ye **m** remember that I told you of them. NIG
16:24 ye shall receive, that your joy **m** be full. NIG
17: 1 thy Son, that thy Son also **m** glorify thee; NIG
17:11 given me, that they **m** be one, as we *are.* NIG
17:21 That they **m** be one; as thou, Father, NIG
17:21 I in thee, that they also **m** be one in us: NIG
17:21 that the world **m** believe that thou hast NIG
17:22 that they **m** be one, even as we are one: NIG
17:23 me, that they **m** be made perfect in one; NIG
17:23 the world **m** know that thou hast sent NIG
17:24 that they **m** behold my glory, which thou NIG
17:26 thou hast loved me **m** be in them, NIG
19: 4 ye **m** know that I find no fault in him. NIG

Ac
1:25 That he **m** take part of this ministry and NIG
3:19 that your sins **m** be blotted out, NIG
4:29 that with all boldness *they* **m** speak thy NIG
4:30 wonders **m** be done by the name of thy NIG
6: 3 whom we **m** appoint over this business. NIG
8:19 I lay hands, he **m** receive the Holy Ghost. NIG
8:20 hast thought that the gift of God **m** be NIG
8:22 if perhaps the thought of thine heart **m** be NIG
17:19 **M** we know what this new doctrine, 1410
19:40 being no cause whereby we **m** give an 1410
21:24 with them, that they **m** shave their heads: NIG
21:24 all **m** know that *those things,* whereof NIG
21:37 the chief captain, **M** I speak unto thee? 1832
23:24 they **m** set Paul on, and bring *him* safe NIG
25:11 no man **m** deliver me unto them. 1410
26:18 that they **m** receive forgiveness of sins, NIG

Ro
1:11 I **m** impart unto you some spiritual gift, NIG
1:11 to the end you **m** be established; NIG

Ro	1:12	that *I* **m** be comforted together with you	NIG
	1:19	Because that which **m** be known of God	NIG
	3: 8	say,) Let us do evil, that good **m** come?	NIG
	3:19	that every mouth be stopped, and all	NIG
	3:19	the world **m** become guilty before God.	NIG
	6: 1	we continue in sin, that grace **m** abound?	NIG
	8:17	that we suffer with *him*, that we **m** be	NIG
	11:10	that *they* **m** not see, and bow down their	NIG
	11:14	If by any means I **m** provoke to emulation	NIG
	11:31	through your mercy they also **m** obtain	NIG
	12: 2	that ye **m** prove what *is that* good,	NIG
	14: 2	For one believeth that *he* **m** eat all *things:*	NIG
	14:19	*things* wherewith one **m** edify another.	NIG
	15: 6	That ye **m** with one mind *and* one mouth	NIG
	15:13	in believing, that ye **m** abound in hope,	NIG
	15:17	whereof *I* **m** glory through Jesus Christ *in*	NIG
	15:31	I **m** be delivered from them that do not	NIG
	15:31	for Jerusalem **m** be accepted of the saints;	NIG
	15:32	That I **m** come unto you with joy by the	NIG
	15:32	will of God, and **m** with you be refreshed.	NIG
1Co	1: 8	*that ye* **m** be blameless in the day of our	NIG
	2:16	mind of the Lord, that he **m** instruct him?	NIG
	3:18	let him become a fool, that he **m** be wise.	NIG
	5: 5	that the spirit **m** be saved in the day of	NIG
	5: 7	the old leaven, that ye **m** be a new lump,	NIG
	7: 5	that ye **m** give yourselves to fasting and	NIG
	7:32	to the Lord, how he **m** please the Lord:	NIG
	7:33	of the world, how he **m** please *his* wife.	NIG
	7:34	that she **m** be holy both in body and	NIG
	7:34	world, how she **m** please *her* husband.	NIG
	7:35	not that I **m** cast a snare upon you,	NIG
	7:35	that you **m** attend upon the Lord without	NIG
	9:18	I **m** make the gospel of Christ without	NIG
	9:24	the prize? So run, that ye **m** obtain.	NIG
	10:13	to escape, that ye **m** be able to bear *it.*	NIG
	10:33	the *profit* of many, that they **m** be saved.	NIG
	11:19	that they *which are* approved **m** be made	NIG
	14: 1	but rather that ye **m** prophesy.	NIG
	14: 5	that the church **m** receive edifying.	3588
	14:10	There are, it **m** be,	1487+5177
	14:12	ye **m** excel to the edifying of the church.	NIG
	14:13	*unknown* tongue pray that he **m** interpret.	NIG
	14:31	For ye **m** all prophesy one by one, that all	1410
	14:31	that all **m** learn, and all may be comforted.	NIG
	14:31	that all may learn, and all **m** be comforted.	NIG
	15:28	*things* under him, that God **m** be all in all.	NIG
	15:37	**it m** chance of wheat, or of some	1487+5177
	16: 6	And it **m** be that I will abide, yea,	5177
	16: 6	that ye **m** bring me on my journey	NIG
	16:10	see that he **m** be with you without fear:	NIG
	16:11	forth in peace, that he **m** come unto me:	NIG
2Co	1: 4	that we **m** be able to comfort them which	NIG
	1:11	thanks **m** be given by many on our behalf.	NIG
	2: 5	in part: that I **m** not overcharge you all.	NIG
	4: 7	that the excellency of the power **m** be of	NIG
	5: 9	or absent, we **m** be accepted of him.	NIG
	5:10	that every one **m** receive the *things done*	NIG
	5:12	you **m** have *somewhat* to *answer* them	NIG
	8:11	*there* **m** be a performance also out of that	NIG
	8:14	now at *this* time your abundance **m** *be a*	NIG
	8:14	that their abundance also **m** be *a supply*	NIG
	8:14	for your want: that there **m** be equality:	NIG
	9: 3	this behalf; that, as I said, ye **m** be ready:	NIG
	9: 8	all *things*, **m** abound to every good work:	NIG
	10: 2	But I beseech *you*, that I **m** not be bold	NIG
	10: 9	I **m** not seem as if *I would* terrify you	NIG
	11: 2	that *I* **m** present *you as* a chaste virgin to	NIG
	11:12	I **m** cut off occasion from them which	NIG
	11:12	they glory, they **m** be found even as we.	NIG
	12: 6	receive me, that I **m** boast myself a little.	NIG
	12: 9	that the power of Christ **m** rest upon me.	NIG
Gal	6:13	that they **m** glory in your flesh.	NIG
Eph	1:17	**m** give unto you the spirit of wisdom and	NIG
	1:18	that ye **m** know what is the hope of his	NIG
	3: 4	ye **m** understand my knowledge in	1410
	3:17	Christ **m** dwell in your hearts by faith;	NIG
	3:18	**M** be able to comprehend with all saints	NIG
	4:15	**m** grow *up* into him *in* all *things,* which	NIG
	4:28	he **m** have to give to him that needeth.	NIG
	4:29	that it **m** minister grace unto the hearers.	NIG
	6: 3	That it **m** be well with thee,	NIG
	6:11	ye **m** be able to stand against the wiles	NIG
	6:13	that ye **m** be able to withstand in the evil	NIG
	6:19	me, that utterance **m** be given unto me,	NIG
	6:19	unto me, that *I* **m** open my mouth boldly,	NIG
	6:20	therein I **m** speak boldly, as I ought to	NIG
	6:21	But that ye also **m** know my affairs,	NIG
Php	1: 9	that your love **m** abound yet more and	NIG
	1:10	ye **m** approve *things* that are excellent;	NIG
	1:10	ye **m** be sincere and without offence till	NIG
	1:26	your rejoicing **m** be *more* abundant in	NIG
	1:27	or *else* be absent, I **m** hear of your affairs,	NIG
	2:15	That ye **m** be blameless and harmless,	NIG
	2:16	that I **m** rejoice in the day of Christ, that I	NIG
	2:19	that I also **m** be of good comfort, when I	NIG
	2:28	ye **m** rejoice, and *that* I may be the less	NIG
	2:28	and *that* I **m** be the less sorrowful.	NIG
	3: 8	count *them but* dung, that I **m** win Christ,	NIG
	3:10	That I **m** know him, and the power of his	NIG
	3:12	follow *after*, if that I **m** apprehend *that* for	NIG
	3:21	it **m** be fashioned like unto his glorious	NIG
	4:17	fruit *that* **m** abound to your account.	NIG
Col	1:28	that we **m** present every man perfect in	NIG
	4: 4	That I **m** make it manifest, as I ought to	NIG
	4: 6	that *you* **m** know how ye ought to answer	NIG

Col	4:12	that ye **m** stand perfect and complete in all	NIG
1Th	3:13	To the end *he* **m** stablish your hearts	NIG
	4:12	That ye **m** walk honestly toward them	NIG
	4:12	and *that* ye **m** have lack of *nothing.*	NIG
2Th	1: 5	that ye **m** be counted worthy of	NIG
	1:12	That the name of our Lord Jesus Christ **m**	NIG
	3: 1	that the word of the Lord **m** have *free*	NIG
	3: 2	And that we **m** be delivered from	NIG
	3:14	with him, that he **m** be ashamed.	NIG
1Ti	1:20	that they **m** learn not to blaspheme.	NIG
	2: 2	that we **m** lead a quiet and peaceable life	NIG
	4:15	them; that thy profiting **m** appear to all.	1510
	5: 7	give in charge, that they **m** be blameless.	NIG
	5:16	that it **m** relieve them that are widows	NIG
	5:20	rebuke before all, that others also **m** fear.	NIG
	6:19	come, that they **m** lay hold on eternal life.	NIG
2Ti	1: 4	of thy tears, that I **m** be filled with joy;	NIG
	1:18	The Lord grant unto him that *he* **m** find	NIG
	2: 4	that he **m** please him who hath chosen	NIG
	2:10	they **m** also obtain the salvation which	NIG
	2:26	And *that* they **m** recover themselves out	NIG
	3:17	That the man of God **m** be perfect,	NIG
	4:16	*I* pray God that it **m** not be laid to their	NIG
Tit	1: 9	that he **m** be able by sound doctrine both	NIG
	1:13	that they **m** be sound in the faith;	NIG
	2: 4	That they **m** teach the young *women* to	NIG
	2: 8	that he that is of the contrary *part* **m** be	NIG
	2:10	that they **m** adorn the doctrine of God our	NIG
Phm	1: 6	That the communication of thy faith **m**	NIG
Heb	4:16	that we **m** obtain mercy, and find grace to	NIG
	5: 1	that he **m** offer both gifts and sacrifices for	NIG
	7: 9	as *I* **m** so say, Levi also, who receiveth	NIG
	10: 9	the first, that he **m** establish the second.	NIG
	12:27	those *things* which cannot be shaken **m**	NIG
	12:28	whereby we **m** serve God acceptably with	NIG
	13: 6	So that we **m** boldly say, The Lord *is* my	NIG
	13:17	that they **m** do it with joy, and not with	NIG
	13:19	that I **m** be restored to you the sooner.	NIG
Jas	1: 4	that ye **m** be perfect and entire,	NIG
	2:18	Yea, a man **m** say, Thou hast faith, and I	NIG
	3: 3	the horses' mouths, that they **m** obey us;	NIG
	4: 3	that ye **m** consume *it* upon your lusts.	NIG
	5:16	pray one for another, that ye **m** be healed.	NIG
1Pe	2: 2	milk of the word, that ye **m** grow thereby;	NIG
	2:12	they **m** by *your* good works, *which* they	NIG
	2:15	that with well doing *ye* **m** put to silence	NIG
	3: 1	they also **m** without the word be won by	NIG
	3:16	**m** be ashamed that falsely accuse your	NIG
	4: 3	the time past of *our* life **m** suffice us to	NIG
	4:11	God in all *things* **m** be glorified through	NIG
	4:13	ye **m** be glad also with exceeding joy.	NIG
	5: 6	of God, that he **m** exalt you in due time:	NIG
	5: 8	about, seeking whom he **m** devour:	NIG
2Pe	1:15	Moreover I **m** endeavour that you **m** be	NIG
	3: 2	That *ye* **m** be mindful of the words which	NIG
	3:14	that ye **m** be found of him in peace,	NIG
1Jn	1: 3	that ye also **m** have fellowship with us:	NIG
	1: 4	we unto you, that your joy **m** be full.	NIG
	2:28	we **m** have confidence, and not be ashamed	NIG
	4:17	that we **m** have boldness in the day of	NIG
	5:13	that ye **m** know that ye have eternal life,	NIG
	5:13	ye **m** believe on the name of the Son of	NIG
	5:20	we **m** know him *that is* true, and we are	NIG
2Jn	1:12	speak face to face, that our joy **m** be full.	NIG
Rev		of you into prison, that ye **m** be tried;	NIG
	14:13	that they **m** rest from their labours;	NIG
	19:18	That ye **m** eat the flesh of kings,	NIG
	22:14	that they **m** have right to the tree of life,	NIG
	22:14	**m** enter in through the gates into the city.	NIG

MAYEST (114) [MAY]

Ge	2:16	Of every tree of the garden thou **m** freely	NIH
	23: 6	but that thou **m** bury thy dead.	NIH
	28: 3	that thou **m** be a multitude of people;	NIH
	28: 4	that thou **m** inherit the land wherein thou	NIH
	38:16	give me, that thou **m** come in unto me?	NIH
Ex	3:10	that thou **m** bring forth my people	NIH
	8:10	that thou **m** know that *there is* none like	NIH
	8:22	to the end thou **m** know that I *am*	NIH
	9:14	thou **m** know that *there is* none like me	NIH
	9:29	that thou **m** know how that the earth *is*	NIH
	10: 2	that thou **m** tell in the ears of thy son,	NIH
	18:19	that thou **m** bring the causes unto God:	NIH
	24:12	I have written; that thou **m** teach them.	NIH
	26:33	thou **m** bring in thither within the vail	NIH
Lev	22:23	that **m** thou offer *for a* freewill offering;	NIH
Nu	10: 2	that thou **m** use them for the calling of	NIH
	10:31	and thou **m** be to us instead of eyes.	NIH
	23:13	from whence thou **m** see them:	NIH
	23:27	it will please God that thou **m**	NIH
Dt	2:31	to possess, that *thou* **m** inherit his land.	NIH
	4:40	thou **m** prolong *thy* days upon the earth,	NIH
	6:18	thou **m** go in and possess the good land	NIH
	7:22	thou **m** not consume them at once, lest	3201
	8: 9	out of whose hills thou **m** dig brass.	NIH
	11:14	that thou **m** gather in thy corn,	NIH
	11:15	for the cattle, that thou **m** eat and be full.	NIH
	12:15	Notwithstanding thou **m** kill and eat flesh	NIH
	12:17	Thou **m** not eat within thy gates the tithe	3201
	12:20	thou **m** eat flesh, whatsoever thy soul	NIH
	12:23	and thou **m** not eat the life with the flesh.	NIH
	14:21	may eat it; or thou **m** sell *it* unto an alien:	NIH
	14:23	that thou **m** learn to fear the LORD thy	NIH
	15: 3	Of a foreigner thou **m** exact *it again:* but	NIH
	16: 3	thou **m** remember the day when thou	NIH

Dt	16: 5	Thou **m** not sacrifice the passover within	3201
	16:20	thou **m** live, and inherit the land which	NIH
	17:15	thou **m** not set a stranger over thee,	3201
	20:19	thou **m** eat of them, and thou shalt not	NIH
	22: 3	thou do likewise: thou **m** not hide thyself.	3201
	22: 7	thee, and *that* thou **m** prolong *thy* days.	NIH
	23:20	Unto a stranger thou **m** lend upon usury;	NIH
	23:24	thou **m** eat grapes thy fill at thine own	NIH
	23:25	thou **m** pluck the ears with thine hand;	NIH
	26:19	that thou **m** be a holy people unto	NIH
	27: 3	that thou **m** go in unto the land which	NIH
	28:58	that *thou* **m** fear this glorious and fearful	NIH
	30: 6	and with all thy soul, that thou **m** live.	NIH
	30:14	and in thy heart, that *thou* **m** do it.	NIH
	30:16	that thou **m** live and multiply;	NIH
	30:20	That thou **m** love the LORD thy God,	NIH
	30:20	*and* that thou **m** obey his voice,	NIH
	30:20	voice, and that thou **m** cleave unto him:	NIH
	30:20	thou **m** dwell in the land which	NIH
Jos	1: 7	that *thou* **m** observe to do according to all	NIH
	1: 7	thou **m** prosper whithersoever thou	NIH
	1: 8	that thou **m** observe to do according to all	NIH
Jdg	9:33	**m** thou do to them as thou shalt find	NIH
	11: 8	that thou **m** go with us, and fight against	NIH
	19: 9	early on your way, that thou **m** go home.	NIH
1Sa	20:13	thee away, that thou **m** go in peace:	NIH
	24: 4	thou **m** do to him as it shall seem good	NIH
	28:15	that *thou* **m** make known unto me what I	NIH
	28:22	that thou **m** have strength, when thou	NIH
2Sa	3:21	that thou **m** reign over all that thine heart	NIH
	15:34	thou for me defeat the counsel of	NIH
	22:28	haughty, *that* thou **m** bring *them* down.	NIH
1Ki	1:12	thou **m** save thine own life, and the life	NIH
	2: 3	that thou **m** prosper *in* all that thou doest,	NIH
	2:31	that thou **m** take away the innocent blood,	NIH
	8:29	that *thou* **m** hearken unto the prayer	NIH
2Ki	5: 6	that thou **m** recover him of his leprosy.	NIH
	8:10	say unto him, Thou **m** certainly recover:	NIH
1Ch	22:12	that *thou* **m** keep the law of the LORD thy	NIH
	22:14	have I prepared; and thou **m** add thereto.	NIH
2Ch	1:11	for thyself, that thou **m** judge my people,	NIH
	18:33	that thou **m** carry me out of the host;	NIH
Ezr	7:17	That thou **m** buy speedily with this money	NIH
Ne	1: 6	that *thou* **m** hear the prayer of thy servant,	NIH
	6: 6	that thou **m** be their king, according to	NIH
Job	40: 8	condemn me, that thou **m** be righteous?	NIH
Ps	32: 6	thee in a time when thou **m** be found:	NIH
	45:16	thou **m** make princes in all the earth.	NIH
	94:13	That *thou* **m** give him rest from the days	NIH
	104:27	that *thou* **m** give *them* their meat in due	NIH
	130: 4	with thee, that thou **m** be feared.	NIH
Pr	2:20	thou **m** walk in the way of good *men,*	NIH
	5: 2	*thou* **m** regard discretion, and *that* thy	NIH
	19:20	that thou **m** be wise in thy latter end.	NIH
Isa	23:16	many songs, that thou **m** be remembered.	NIH
	43:26	declare thou, that thou **m** be justified.	NIH
	45: 3	that thou **m** know that I, the LORD,	NIH
	47:12	be able to profit, if so be thou **m** prevail.	NIH
	49: 6	*thou* **m** be my salvation unto the end of	NIH
	49: 9	thou **m** say to the prisoners, Go forth;	NIH
Jer	4:14	from wickedness, that thou **m** be saved.	NIH
	6:27	that thou **m** know and try their way.	NIH
	30:13	plead thy cause, that thou **m** be bound up:	NIH
Eze	16:54	That thou **m** bear thine own shame,	NIH
	16:54	**m** be confounded in all that thou hast	NIH
	16:63	thou **m** remember, and be confounded,	NIH
Hab	2:15	that thou **m** look on their nakedness!	NIH
Mk	14:12	and prepare that thou **m** eat the passover?	NIG
Lk	12:58	give diligence that *thou* **m** be delivered	NIG
	16: 2	for thou **m** be no longer steward.	1410
Ac	8:37	believest with all *thine* heart, thou **m.**	1832
	24: 8	by examining of whom thyself **m** take	1410
	24:11	Because that thou **m** understand, that	1410
1Co	7:21	but if thou **m** be made free, use *it* rather.	1410
Eph	6: 3	thee, and thou **m** live long on the earth.	NIG
1Ti	3:15	that thou **m** know how *thou* oughtest to	NIG
3Jn	1: 2	wish above all *things* that thou **m** prosper	NIG
Rev	3:18	gold tried in the fire, that thou **m** be rich;	NIG
	3:18	thou **m** be clothed, and *that* the shame	NIG
	3:18	thine eyes *with* eyesalve, that thou **m** see.	NIG

MAZZAROTH (1)

Job	38:32	Canst thou bring forth **M** in his season?	4216

ME (4096) [I] See Index of Articles, Etc.

MEADOW (2) [MEADOWS]

Ge	41: 2	and fatfleshed; and they fed in a **m.**	260
	41:18	well favoured; and they fed in a **m:**	260

MEADOWS (1) [MEADOW]

Jdg	20:33	their places, *even* out of the **m** of Gibeah.	4629

MEAH (2)

Ne	3: 1	unto the tower of **M** they sanctified it,	3968
	12:39	tower of Hananeel, and the tower of **M,**	3968

MEAL (12) [MEALTIME]

Ge	18: 6	ready quickly three measures of fine **m,**	7058
Nu	5:15	the tenth *part of* an ephah of barley **m;**	7058
1Ki	4:22	fine flour, and threescore measures of **m,**	7058
	17:12	a handful of **m** in a barrel, and a little oil	7058
	17:14	The barrel of **m** shall not waste,	7058
	17:16	the barrel of **m** wasted not, neither did	7058
2Ki	4:41	he said, Then bring **m.** And he cast *it* into	7058
1Ch	12:40	on mules, and on oxen, *and* meat, **m,**	7058

M

Isa	47: 2 Take the millstones, and grind **m**:	7058
Hos	8: 7 the bud shall yield no **m**: if so be it yield,	7058
Mt	13:33 and hid in three measures of **m**,	224
Lk	13:21 took and hid in three measures of **m**,	224

MEALTIME (1) [MEAL, TIME]

Ru	2:14 At **m** come thou hither,	400+6256+1886.1

MEAN (22) [MEANEST, MEANETH, MEANING, MEANS, MEANT]

Ge	21:29 What **m** these seven ewe lambs which	NIH
Ex	12:26 unto you, What **m** you by this service?	3807.1
Dt	6:20 What **m** the testimonies, and the statutes,	NIH
Jos	4: 6 What **m** you by these stones?	3807.1
	4:21 to come, saying, What **m** these stones?	NIH
1Ki	18:45 in the **m** while,	3541+3541+5704+5704+2050.1
Pr	22:29 he shall not stand before **m** men.	2823
Isa	2: 9 the **m** man boweth down, and the great	NIH
	3:15 What **m** ye *that* ye beat my people to	3807.1
	5:15 the **m** man shall be brought down,	NIH
	31: 8 the sword, not of a **m** man, shall devour	NIH
Eze	17:12 Know ye not what these *things* **m**? tell	NIH
	18: 2 that ye **m**, that ye use this proverb	3807.1
Mk	9:10 what the rising from the dead should **m**.	1510
Lk	12: 1 In the **m** time, when there were	1722+3739
Jn	4:31 In the **m** while *his* disciples prayed him,	3342
Ac	10:17 *this* vision which he had seen should **m**,	1510
	17:20 know therefore what these *things* **m**.	2309
	21:13 What **m** ye to weep and to break mine	5101
	21:39 *a city* in Cilicia, a citizen of no **m** city:	767
Ro	2:15 *their* thoughts the **m** while accusing or	NIG
2Co	8:13 For *I* **m** not that other *men* be eased,	NIG

MEANEST (4) [MEAN]

Ge	33: 8 **m** thou by all this drove which I met?	3807.1
2Sa	16: 2 said unto Ziba, What **m** thou by these?	3807.1
Eze	37:18 Wilt thou not shew us what thou **m** by	3807.1
Jnh	1: 6 unto him, What **m** thou, O sleeper?	3807.1

MEANETH (8) [MEAN]

Dt	29:24 what **m** the heat of this great anger?	NIH
1Sa	4: 6 What **m** the noise of this great shout in	NIH
	4:14 he said, What **m** the noise of this tumult?	NIH
	15:14 What **m** then this bleating of the sheep in	NIH
Isa	10: 7 he **m** not so, neither doth his heart	1819
Mt	9:13 But go ye and learn what *that* **m**, I will	1510
	12: 7 But if ye had known what *this* **m**, I will	1510
Ac	2:12 one to another, What **m** this?	1510+2309

MEANING (3) [MEAN]

Da	8:15 and sought for the **m**, then behold,	998
Ac	27: 2 **m** to sail by the coasts of Asia;	3195
1Co	14:11 if I know not the **m** of the voice,	1411

MEANINGLESS See VANITIES; VANITY

MEANS (35) [MEAN]

Ex	34: 7 will **by no m** clear *the guilty;* visiting	3808
Nu	14:18 **by no m** clearing *the guilty,* visiting	3808
Jdg	5:22 were the horsehoofs broken **by the m** of	4480
	16: 5 by what *m* we may prevail against him,	NIH
2Sa	14:14 doth he devise **m**, that *his* banished be	4284
1Ki	10:29 did they bring *them* out by their **m**.	3027
	20:39 if **by any m** he be **missing**, then	6485+6485
2Ch	1:17 and for the kings of Syria, by their **m**.	3027
Ezr	4:16 by this **m** thou shalt have no portion on	6903
Ps	49: 7 *of* them can **by any m** redeem	6299+6299
Pr	6:26 For **by m** of a whorish woman *a man is*	1157
Jer	5:31 and the priests bear rule by their **m**;	3027
Mal	1: 9 this hath been by your **m**: will he regard	3027
Mt	5:26 Thou shalt **by no m** come out thence,	3364
Lk	5:18 and they sought *m* to bring him in,	NIG
	8:36 **by what m** he that was possessed of	4459
	10:19 and nothing shall **by any m** hurt you.	3364
Jn	9:21 But **by what m** he now seeth, we know	4459
Ac	4: 9 man, **by what m** he is made whole;	NIG
	18:21 I must **by all m** keep *this* feast that	3843
	27:12 if **by any m** they might attain to Phenice,	1513
Ro	1:10 if **by any m** now at length I might have a	1513
	11:14 If **by any m** I may provoke to emulation	1513
1Co	8: 9 take heed **lest by any m** this liberty of	3381
	9:22 all *men*, that I might **by all m** save some.	3843
	9:27 **lest that by any m**, when I have	3381
2Co	1:11 **by the m** of many persons thanks may be	1537
	11: 3 But I fear, **lest by any m**, as the serpent	3381
Gal	2: 2 **lest by any m** I should run, or had run,	3381
Php	3:11 If **by any m** I might attain unto	1513
1Th	3: 5 **lest by some m** the tempter have	3381
2Th	2: 3 Let no *man* deceive you by any **m**: for	5158
	3:16 himself give you peace always by all **m**.	5158
Heb	9:15 of the new testament, that **by m** of death,	NIG
Rev	13:14 **by the m** of *those* miracles which he had	1223

MEANT (3) [MEAN]

Ge	50:20 but God **m** it unto good, to bring to pass,	2803
Lk	15:26 and asked what these *things* **m**.	1510
	18:36 multitude pass by, he asked what it **m**.	1510

MEARAH (1)

Jos	13: 4 **M** that *is* beside the Sidonians, unto	4632

MEASURE (69) [MEASURED, MEASURES, MEASURING]

Ex	26: 2 one of the curtains shall have one **m**.	4060
	26: 8 the eleven curtains *shall be all* of one **m**.	4060

Lev	19:35 in meteyard, in weight, or in **m**.	4884
Nu	35: 5 shall **m** from without the city *on* the east	4058
Dt	21: 2 shall **m** unto the cities which *are* round	4058
	25:15 a perfect and just **m** shalt thou have:	374
Jos	3: 4 and it, about two thousand cubits by **m**:	4060
1Ki	6:25 both the cherubims *were* of one **m** and	4060
	7:37 had one casting, one **m**, and one size.	4060
2Ki	7: 1 To morrow about *this* time *shall* a **m** of	5429
	7:16 So a **m** of fine flour was *sold* for a shekel,	5429
	7:18 shekel, and a **m** of fine flour for a shekel,	5429
1Ch	23:29 is fried, and for all *manner of* **m** and *for*	4884
2Ch	3: 3 The length *by* cubits after the first **m** *was*	4060
Job	11: 9 The **m** thereof *is* longer than the earth,	4055
	28:25 and he weigheth the waters by **m**.	4060
Ps	39: 4 to know mine end, and the **m** of my days,	4060
	80: 5 and givest them tears to drink *in* great **m**.	7991
Isa	5:14 and opened her mouth without **m**:	2706
	27: 8 In **m**, when it shooteth forth, thou wilt	5432
	40:12 the dust of the earth in a **m**,	7991
	65: 7 will I **m** their former work into their	4058
Jer	30:11 I will correct thee in **m**, and will not	4941
	46:28 a full end of thee, but correct thee in **m**;	4941
	51:13 is come, *and* the **m** of thy covetousness.	520
Eze	4:11 Thou shalt drink also water by **m**, the	4884
	4:16 they shall drink water by **m**,	4884
	40:10 on that side; they three *were* of one **m**:	4060
	40:10 the posts had one **m** on this side and on	4060
	40:21 the arches thereof were after the **m** of	4060
	40:22 *were* after the **m** of the gate that looketh	4060
	41:17 round about within and without, *by* **m**.	4060
	43:10 iniquities: and let them **m** the pattern.	4058
	45: 3 of this **m** shalt thou measure the length of	4060
	45: 3 of this measure shalt thou **m** the length of	4058
	45:11 The ephah and the bath shall be of one **m**,	8506
	45:11 the **m** thereof shall be after the homer.	4971
	46:22 these four corners *were* of one **m**.	4060
	47:18 the east side ye shall **m** from Hauran,	4058
Mic	6:10 and the scant **m** *that is* abominable?	374
Zec	2: 2 he said unto me, To **m** Jerusalem, to see	4058
Mt	7: 2 and with what **m** ye mete, it shall be	3358
	23:32 Fill ye up then the **m** of your fathers.	3358
Mk	4:24 what **m** ye mete, it shall be measured	3358
	6:51 sore amazed in themselves beyond **m**,	4053
	7:37 And were **beyond m** astonished, saying,	5249
	10:26 And they were astonished **out of m**,	4057
Lk	6:38 **good m**, pressed down,	3358
	6:38 with the same **m** that ye mete withal it	3358
Jn	3:34 for God giveth not the Spirit by **m** *unto*	3358
Ro	12: 3 hath dealt to every man the **m** of faith.	3358
2Co	1: 8 that we were pressed **out of m**,	2596+5236
	10:13 will not boast of *things* **without** *our* **m**,	280
	10:13 according to the **m** of the rule which God	3358
	10:13 to us, a **m** to reach even unto you.	3358
	10:14 we stretch not ourselves beyond *our* **m**,	NIG
	10:15 Not boasting of *things* **without** *our* **m**,	280
	11:23 in stripes **above m**, in prisons more	5234
	12: 7 And lest I should be **exalted above m**	5229
	12: 7 lest I should be **exalted above m**	5229
Gal	1:13 how that **beyond m** I persecuted	2596+5236
Eph	4: 7 according to the **m** of the gift of Christ.	3358
	4:13 unto the **m** of the stature of the fulness of	3358
	4:16 to the effectual working in the **m**	3358
Rev	6: 6 A **m** of wheat for a penny,	5518
	11: 1 and **m** the temple of God, and the altar,	3354
	11: 2 the temple leave out, and **m** it not;	3354
	21:15 with me had a golden reed to **m** the city,	3354
	21:17 *according* to the **m** of a man, that is,	3358

MEASURED (46) [MEASURE]

Ru	3:15 the **m** six *measures* of barley, and laid *it*	4058
2Sa	8: 2 he smote Moab, and **m** them with a line,	4058
	8: 2 even *with* two lines **m** he to put to death,	4058
Isa	40:12 Who hath **m** the waters in the hollow of	4058
Jer	31:37 If heaven above can be **m**,	4058
	33:22 neither the sand of the sea **m**:	3808+4058
Eze	40: 5 so he **m** the breadth of the building,	4058
	40: 6 and **m** the threshold of the gate,	4058
	40: 8 He **m** also the porch of the gate within,	4058
	40: 9 **m** he the porch of the gate, eight cubits;	4058
	40:11 he **m** the breadth of the entry of the gate,	4058
	40:13 He then **m** the gate from the roof of *one*	4058
	40:19 he **m** the breadth from the forefront of	4058
	40:20 he **m** the length thereof, and the breadth	4058
	40:23 he **m** from gate to gate an hundred cubits.	4058
	40:24 he **m** the posts thereof and the arches	4058
	40:27 he **m** from gate to gate toward the south	4058
	40:28 he **m** the south gate according to these	4058
	40:32 **m** the gate according to these measures.	4058
	40:35 and **m** *it* according to these measures;	4058
	40:47 he **m** the court, an hundred cubits long,	4058
	40:48 **m** *each* post of the porch, five cubits on	4058
	41: 1 the posts, six cubits broad on the one	4058
	41: 2 he **m** the length thereof, forty cubits:	4058
	41: 3 the **m** the post of the door, two cubits;	4058
	41: 4 he **m** the length thereof, twenty cubits,	4058
	41:13 he **m** the wall of the house, six cubits;	4058
	41:13 the house, an hundred cubits long;	4058
	41:15 he **m** the length of the building over	4058
	42:15 *is* toward the east, and **m** it round about.	4058
	42:16 He **m** the east side with the measuring	4058
	42:17 He **m** the north side, five hundred reeds,	4058
	42:18 He **m** the south side, five hundred reeds,	4058
	42:19 **m** five hundred reeds with the measuring	4058
	42:20 He **m** it by the four sides: it had a wall	4058
	47: 3 forth eastward, he **m** a thousand cubits,	4058

Eze	47: 4 Again he **m** a thousand, and brought me	4058
	47: 4 again he **m** a thousand; and brought me	4058
	47: 5 Afterward he **m** a thousand; *and it was* a	4058
Hos	1:10 sea, which cannot be **m** nor numbered;	4058
Hab	3: 6 He stood, and **m** the earth: he beheld,	4128
Mt	7: 2 ye mete, it shall be **m** to you **again**.	488
Mk	4:24 measure ye mete, it shall be **m** to you:	3354
Lk	6:38 ye mete withal it shall be **m** to you **again**.	488
Rev	21:16 and he **m** the city with the reed,	3354
	21:17 he **m** the wall thereof, an hundred *and*	3354

MEASURES (39) [MEASURE]

Ge	18: 6 Make ready quickly three **m** of fine meal,	5429
Dt	25:14 in thine house *divers* **m**,	374+374+2050.1
Ru	3:15 measured six **m** of barley, and laid *it* on	NIH
	3:17 said, These six **m** of barley gave he me;	NIH
1Sa	25:18 five **m** of parched *corn*, and an hundred	5429
1Ki	4:22 for one day was thirty **m** of fine flour,	3734
	4:22 of fine flour, and threescore **m** of meal,	3734
	5:11 Solomon gave Hiram twenty thousand **m**	3734
	5:11 his household, and twenty **m** of pure oil:	3734
	7: 9 according to the **m** of hewed stones,	4060
	7:11 after the **m** of hewed stones, and cedars.	4060
	18:32 as great as would contain **two m** of seed.	5429
2Ki	7: 1 **two m** of barley for a shekel, in the gate	5429
	7:16 **two m** of barley for a shekel, according to	5429
	7:18 **Two m** of barley for a shekel,	5429
2Ch	2:10 twenty thousand **m** of beaten wheat,	3734
	2:10 twenty thousand **m** of barley,	3734
	27: 5 ten thousand **m** of wheat, and ten	3734
Ezr	7:22 to an hundred **m** *of* wheat, and to an	3734
Job	38: 5 Who hath laid the **m** thereof, if thou	4461
Pr	20:10 weights, *and* divers **m**,	374+374+2050.1
Jer	13:25 *is* thy lot, the portion of thy **m** from me,	4055
Eze	40:24 the arches thereof according to these **m**.	4060
	40:28 the south gate according to these **m**;	4060
	40:29 the arches thereof, according to these **m**:	4060
	40:32 measured the gate according to these **m**.	4060
	40:33 thereof, *were* according to these **m**:	4060
	40:35 and measured *it* according to these **m**;	4060
	43:13 *are* the **m** of the altar after the cubits:	4060
	48:16 *shall be* the **m** thereof; the north side	4060
	48:30 four thousand and five hundred **m**.	4060
	48:33 side four thousand and five hundred **m**:	4060
	48:35 *It was* round about eighteen thousand **m**:	NIH
Hag	2:16 when *one* came to a heap of twenty **m**,	NIH
Mt	13:33 woman took, and hid in three **m** of meal,	4568
Lk	13:21 woman took and hid in three **m** of meal,	4568
	16: 6 And he said, An hundred **m** of oil. And he	943
	16: 7 he said, An hundred **m** of wheat.	2884
Rev	6: 6 penny, and three **m** of barley for a penny;	5518

MEASURING (11) [MEASURE]

Jer	31:39 the **m** line shall yet go forth over against	4060
Eze	40: 3 a line of flax in his hand, and a **m** reed;	4060
	40: 5 in the man's hand a **m** reed of six cubits	4060
	42:15 Now when he had made an end of **m**	4060
	42:16 measured the east side with the **m** reed,	4060
	42:16 with the **m** reed round about.	4060
	42:17 with the **m** reed round about.	4060
	42:18 five hundred reeds, with the **m** reed.	4060
	42:19 measured five hundred reeds with the **m**	4060
Zec	2: 1 behold, a man with a **m** line in his hand.	4060
2Co	10:12 but they **m** themselves by themselves,	3354

MEAT (290) [BAKEMEATS, MEATS]

Ge	1:29 tree yielding seed; to you it shall be for **m**.	402
	1:30 *is* life, *I have given* every green herb for **m**:	402
	9: 3 Every moving thing that liveth shall be **m**	402
	24:33 there was set **m** before him to eat:	NIH
	27: 4 make me **savoury m**, such as I love,	4303
	27: 7 make me **savoury m**, that I may eat,	4303
	27: 9 will make them **savoury m** for thy father,	4303
	27:14 mother made **savoury m**, such as his	4303
	27:17 she gave the **savoury m** and the bread,	4303
	27:31 he also had made **savoury m**,	4303
	45:23 bread and **m** for his father by the way.	4202
Ex	29:41 do thereto according to the **m offering**	4503
	30: 9 nor burnt sacrifice, nor **m offering**;	4503
	40:29 it the burnt offering, and the **m offering**,	4503
Lev	2: 1 when any will offer a **m offering** unto	4503
	2: 3 the remnant of the **m offering** *shall be*	4503
	2: 4 if thou bring an oblation of a **m offering**	4503
	2: 5 if thy oblation *be* a **m offering** baken in	4503
	2: 6 and pour oil thereon: it *is* a **m offering**.	4503
	2: 7 if thy oblation *be* a **m offering** baken in	4503
	2: 8 shalt bring the **m offering** that is made	4503
	2: 9 the priest shall take from the **m offering**	4503
	2:10 which is left of the **m offering** *shall be*	4503
	2:11 No **m offering**, which ye shall bring unto	4503
	2:13 oblation of thy **m offering** shalt thou	4503
	2:13 God to be lacking from thy **m offering**	4503
	2:14 if thou offer a **m offering** of *thy* firstfruits	4503
	2:14 thou shalt offer for the **m offering** of thy	4503
	2:15 frankincense thereon: it *is* a **m offering**.	4503
	5:13 shall be the priest's, as a **m offering**.	4503
	6:14 *is* the law of the **m offering**: the sons	4503
	6:15 of the flour of the **m offering**, and of the	4503
	6:15 which *is* upon the **m offering**,	4503
	6:20 of fine flour *for* a **m offering** perpetual,	4503
	6:21 the baken pieces of the **m offering** shalt	4503
	6:23 every **m offering** for the priest shall be	4503
	7: 9 the **m offering** that is baken in the oven,	4503
	7:10 every **m offering**, mingled with oil,	4503
	7:37 of the **m offering**, and of the sin offering,	4503

M

Lev	9: 4	and a **m offering** mingled with oil:	4503
	9:17	he brought the **m offering**, and took a	4503
	10:12	Take the **m offering** that remaineth of	4503
	11:34	Of all which may be eaten, *that* on	400
	14:10	tenth deals of fine flour *for* a **m offering**,	4503
	14:20	and the **m offering** upon the altar:	4503
	14:21	flour mingled with oil for a **m offering**,	4503
	14:31	*for* a burnt offering, with the **m offering**.	4503
	22:11	born in his house: they shall eat of his **m**.	400
	22:13	her youth, she shall eat of her father's **m**:	3899
	23:13	the **m offering** thereof *shall be* two tenth	4503
	23:16	ye shall offer a new **m offering** unto	4503
	23:18	with their **m offering**, and their drink	4503
	23:37	a **m offering**, a sacrifice,	4503
	25: 6	the sabbath of the land shall be **m** for you;	402
	25: 7	land, shall all the increase thereof be **m**.	398
Nu	4:16	daily **m offering**, and the anointing oil,	4503
	6:15	**m offering**, and their drink offerings.	4503
	6:17	the priest shall offer also his **m offering**,	4503
	7:13	flour mingled with oil for a **m offering**:	4503
	7:19	flour mingled with oil for a **m offering**:	4503
	7:25	flour mingled with oil for a **m offering**:	4503
	7:31	flour mingled with oil for a **m offering**:	4503
	7:37	flour mingled with oil for a **m offering**:	4503
	7:43	flour mingled with oil for a **m offering**:	4503
	7:49	flour mingled with oil for a **m offering**:	4503
	7:55	flour mingled with oil for a **m offering**:	4503
	7:61	flour mingled with oil for a **m offering**:	4503
	7:67	flour mingled with oil for a **m offering**:	4503
	7:73	flour mingled with oil for a **m offering**:	4503
	7:79	flour mingled with oil for a **m offering**:	4503
	7:87	first year twelve, with their **m offering**:	4503
	8: 8	a young bullock with his **m offering**,	4503
	15: 4	**m offering** of a tenth deal *of* flour	4503
	15: 6	thou shalt prepare *for* a **m offering** two	4503
	15: 9	he bring with a bullock a **m offering**	4503
	15:24	his **m offering**, and his drink offering,	4503
	18: 9	every **m offering** of theirs, and every sin	4503
	28: 5	of an ephah *of* flour for a **m offering**,	4503
	28: 8	as the **m offering** of the morning,	4503
	28: 9	two tenth deals *of* flour for a **m offering**,	4503
	28:12	their **m offering** *shall be of* flour mingled	4503
	28:12	two tenth deals *of* flour *for* a **m offering**,	4503
	28:13	with oil *for* a **m offering** unto one lamb;	4503
	28:20	their **m offering** *shall be* of flour mingled	4503
	28:24	the **m** of the sacrifice made by fire,	3899
	28:26	when ye bring a new **m offering** unto	4503
	28:28	**m offering** *of* flour mingled with oil,	4503
	28:31	his **m offering**, (they shall be unto you	4503
	29: 3	their **m offering** *shall be of* flour mingled	4503
	29: 6	his **m offering**, and the daily burnt	4503
	29: 6	his **m offering**, and their drink offerings,	4503
	29: 9	their **m offering** *shall be of* flour mingled	4503
	29:11	the **m offering** of it, and their drink	4503
	29:14	their **m offering** *shall be of* flour mingled	4503
	29:16	his **m offering**, and his drink offering.	4503
	29:18	their **m offering** and their drink offerings	4503
	29:19	the **m offering** thereof, and their drink	4503
	29:21	their **m offering** and their drink offerings	4503
	29:22	his **m offering**, and his drink offering.	4503
	29:24	Their **m offering** and their drink offerings	4503
	29:25	his **m offering**, and his drink offering.	4503
	29:27	their **m offering** and their drink offerings	4503
	29:28	his **m offering**, and his drink offering.	4503
	29:30	their **m offering** and their drink offerings	4503
	29:31	his **m offering**, and his drink offering.	4503
	29:33	their **m offering** and their drink offerings	4503
	29:34	his **m offering**, and his drink offering.	4503
	29:37	Their **m offering** and their drink offerings	4503
	29:38	his **m offering**, and his drink offering.	4503
	29:39	for your **m offerings**, and for your drink	4503
Dt	2: 6	Ye shall buy **m** of them for money, that ye	400
	2:28	Thou shalt sell me **m** for money, that I	400
	20:20	knowest that they *be* not trees for **m**,	3978
	28:26	thy carcase shall be **m** unto all fowls of	3978
Jos	22:23	thereon burnt offering or **m offering**,	4503
	22:29	for **m offerings**, or for sacrifices,	4503
Jdg	1: 7	cut off, gathered *their* **m** under my table:	NIH
	13:19	Manoah took a kid with a **m offering**,	4503
	13:23	and a **m offering** at our hands,	4503
	14:14	Out of the eater came forth **m**, and out of	3978
1Sa	20: 5	I should not fail to sit with the king at **m**:	398
	20:24	come, the king sat him down to eat **m**.	3899
	20:27	cometh not the son of Jesse to **m**,	3899
	20:34	eat no **m** the second day of the month:	3899
2Sa	3:35	David to eat **m** while it was yet day,	3899
	11: 8	there followed him a mess of *m* from	NIH
	12: 3	it did eat of his own **m**, and drank of his	6595
	13: 5	me **m**, and dress the meat in my sight,	3899
	13: 5	me meat, and dress the **m** in my sight,	1279
	13: 7	Amnon's house, and dress him **m**.	1279
	13:10	Bring the **m** *into* the chamber, that I may	1279
1Ki	8:64	**m offerings**, and the fat of the peace	4503
	8:64	**m offerings**, and the fat of the peace	4503
	10: 5	the **m** of his table, and the sitting of his	3978
	19: 8	went in the strength of that **m** forty days	396
2Ki	3:20	when the **m offering** was offered,	4503
	16:13	his burnt offering and his **m offering**,	4503
	16:15	the evening **m offering**, and the king's	4503
	16:15	burnt sacrifice, and his **m offering**,	4503
	16:15	**m offering**, and their drink offerings;	4503
1Ch	12:40	and on mules, and on oxen, *and* **m**, meal,	3978
	21:23	wood, and the wheat for the **m offering**:	4503
	23:29	for the fine flour for **m offering**,	4503
2Ch	7: 7	and the **m offerings**, and the fat.	4503

2Ch	9: 4	the **m** of his table, and the sitting of his	3978
Ezr	3: 7	**m**, and drink, and oil, unto them of Zidon	3978
	7:17	with their **m offerings** and their drink	4504
Ne	10:33	*for* the continual **m offering**, and for	4503
	13: 5	aforetime they laid the **m offerings**,	4503
	13: 9	the **m offering** and the frankincense.	4503
Job	6: 7	refused to touch *are* as my sorrowful **m**.	3899
	12:11	try words? and the mouth taste his **m**?	400
	20:14	*Yet* his **m** in his bowels is turned, *it is*	3899
	20:21	*There shall* none of his **m** *be* left;	400
	30: 4	the bushes, and juniper roots *for* their **m**.	3899
	33:20	abhorreth bread, and his soul dainty **m**.	3978
	34: 3	ear trieth words, as the mouth tasteth **m**.	398
	36:31	he the people; he giveth **m** in abundance.	400
	38:41	cry unto God, they wander for lack of **m**.	400
Ps	42: 3	My tears have been my **m** day and night,	3899
	44:11	hast given us like sheep appointed for **m**;	3978
	59:15	Let them wander up and down for **m**,	400
	69:21	They gave me also gall for my **m**;	1267
	74:14	gavest him *to be* **m** to the people	3978
	78:18	tempted God in their heart by asking **m**	400
	78:25	angels' food: he sent them **m** to the full.	6720
	78:30	while their **m** *was* yet in their mouths,	400
	79: 2	*to be* **m** unto the fowls of the heaven,	3978
	104:21	*their* prey, and seek *their* **m** from God.	400
	104:27	that *thou* mayest give *them* their **m** in due	400
	107:18	Their soul abhorreth all *manner of* **m**;	400
	111: 5	hath given **m** unto them that fear him:	2964
	145:15	thou givest them their **m** in due season.	400
Pr	6: 8	Provideth her **m** in the summer,	3899
	23: 3	of his dainties: for they *are* deceitful **m**.	3899
	30:22	and a fool when he is filled *with* **m**;	3899
	30:25	yet they prepare their **m** in the summer;	3899
	31:15	giveth **m** to her household, and a portion	2964
Isa	57: 6	thou hast offered a **m offering**.	4503
	62: 8	I will no more give thy corn *to be* **m**	3978
	65:25	dust *shall be* the serpent's **m**. They shall	3899
Jer	7:33	the carcases of this people shall be **m** for	3978
	16: 4	their carcases shall be **m** for the fowls of	3978
	17:26	**m offerings**, and incense,	4503
	19: 7	their carcases will I give to be **m** for	3978
	33:18	to kindle **m offerings**, and to do sacrifice	4503
	34:20	their dead bodies shall be for **m** unto	3978
La	1:11	they have given their pleasant things for **m**	400
	1:19	while they sought their **m**, to relieve their	400
	4:10	they were their **m** in the destruction of	1262
Eze	4:10	thy **m** which thou shalt eat *shall be* by	3978
	16:19	My **m** also which I gave thee, fine flour,	3899
	29: 5	I have given thee for **m** to the beasts of	402
	34: 5	became **m** to all the beasts of the field,	402
	34: 8	my flock became **m** to every beast of	402
	34:10	that they may not be **m** for them.	402
	42:13	most holy *things*, and the **m offering**,	4503
	44:29	They shall eat the **m offering**, and the	4503
	45:15	for a **m offering**, and for a burnt offering,	4503
	45:17	**m offerings**, and drink offerings,	4503
	45:17	the **m offering**, and the burnt offering,	4503
	45:24	shall prepare a **m offering** *of* an ephah	4503
	45:25	according to the **m offering**,	4503
	46: 5	**m offering** *shall be* an ephah for a ram,	4503
	46: 5	**m offering** for the lambs as he shall be	4503
	46: 7	he shall prepare a **m offering**, an ephah	4503
	46:11	in the solemnities the **m offering** shall be	4503
	46:14	shalt prepare a **m offering** for it every	4503
	46:14	a **m offering** continually *by* a perpetual	4503
	46:15	lamb, and the **m offering**, and the oil,	4503
	46:20	where they shall bake the **m offering**;	4503
	47:12	on that side, shall grow all trees for **m**,	3978
	47:12	fruit thereof shall be for **m**, and the leaf	3978
Da	1: 5	them a daily provision of the king's **m**,	6598
	1: 8	with the **portion of** the king's **m**,	6598
	1:10	hath appointed your **m** and your drink:	3978
	1:13	that eat *of* the **portion of** the king's **m**:	6598
	1:15	did eat the **portion of** the king's **m**.	6598
	1:16	Melzar took away the **portion of** their **m**,	6598
	4:12	thereof much, and in it *was* **m** for all:	4203
	4:21	thereof much, and in it *was* **m** for all;	4203
	11:26	they that feed of the **portion of** his **m**	6598
Hos	11: 4	on their jaws, and I laid **m** unto them.	398
Joel	1: 9	The **m offering** and the drink offering is	4503
	1:13	the **m offering** and the drink offering is	4503
	1:16	Is not the **m** cut off before our eyes, *yea,*	400
	2:14	a **m offering** and a drink offering unto	4503
Am	5:22	burnt offerings and your **m offerings**,	4503
Hab	1:16	portion *is* fat, and their **m** plenteous.	3978
	3:17	shall fail, and the fields shall yield no **m**;	400
Hag	2:12	pottage, or wine, or oil, or any **m**, shall it	3978
Mal	1:12	fruit thereof, *even* his **m**, *is* contemptible.	400
	3:10	that there may be **m** in mine house,	2964
Mt	3: 4	and his **m** was locusts and wild honey.	5160
	6:25	shall put on. Is not the life more than **m**,	5160
	9:10	as Jesus **sat at m** in the house, behold,	345
	10:10	for the workman is worthy of his **m**.	5160
	14: 9	and them which **sat with** him at **m**,	4873
	15:37	took up of the broken **m** that was left	NIG
	24:45	to give them **m** in due season?	5160
	25:35	For I was a hungred, and ye gave me **m**:	5315
	25:42	I was a hungred, and ye gave me no **m**:	5315
	26: 7	poured *it* on his head, as he **sat at m**.	345
Mk	2:15	that as *Jesus* **sat at m** in his house,	2621
	8: 8	they took up of the broken *m* that was	NIG
	14: 3	house of Simon the leper, as he **sat at m**,	2621
	16:14	unto the eleven as they **sat at m**,	345
Lk	3:11	and he that hath **m**, let him do likewise.	1033
	7:36	Pharisee's house, and **sat down to m**.	347

Lk	7:37	when she knew that *Jesus* **sat at m** in	345
	7:49	that **sat at m** with *him* began to	4873
	8:55	and he commanded to give her **m**.	5315
	9:13	should go and buy **m** for all this people.	1033
	11:37	and he went in, and **sat down to m**.	377
	12:23	The life is more than **m**, and the body *is*	5160
	12:37	and **make** them to **sit down to m**,	347
	12:42	to give *them their* **portion of m** in due	4620
	14:10	presence of them that **sit at m with** thee.	4873
	14:15	when one of them that **sat at m with**	4873
	17: 7	from the field, Go and **sit down to m**?	377
	22:27	he that **sitteth at m**, or he that serveth?	345
	22:27	*is* not he that **sitteth at m**? but I am	345
	24:30	as he **sat at m** with them, he took bread,	2625
	24:41	he said unto them, Have ye here any **m**?	1034
Jn	4: 8	were gone away unto the city to buy **m**.)	5160
	4:32	I have **m** to eat that ye know not of.	1035
	4:34	My **m** is to do the will of him that sent	1033
	6:27	Labour not for the **m** which perisheth,	1035
	6:27	*that* **m** which endureth unto everlasting	1035
	6:55	For my flesh is **m** indeed,	1035
	21: 5	unto them, Children, have ye any **m**?	4371
Ac	2:46	did eat *their* **m** with gladness and	5160
	9:19	And when he had received **m**, he was	5160
	16:34	**set m before** them, and rejoiced,	3908+5132
	27:33	Paul besought *them* all to take **m**, saying,	5160
	27:34	Wherefore I pray you to take *some* **m**:	5160
	27:36	good cheer, and they also took *some* **m**.	5160
Ro	14:15	But if thy brother be grieved with *thy* **m**,	1033
	14:15	Destroy not him with thy **m**, for whom	1033
	14:17	the kingdom of God is not **m** and drink;	1035
	14:20	For **m** destroy not the work of God.	1033
1Co	3: 2	have fed you with milk, and not with **m**:	1033
	8: 8	But **m** commendeth us not to God:	1033
	8:10	knowledge **sit at m** in the idol's temple,	2621
	8:13	if **m** make my brother to offend,	1033
	10: 3	And did all eat the same spiritual **m**;	1033
Col	2:16	Let no *man* therefore judge you in **m**,	1035
Heb	5:12	have need of milk, and not of strong **m**.	5160
	5:14	strong **m** belongeth to *them that are* of	5160
	12:16	who for one **morsel of m** sold his	1035

MEAT MARKET See SHAMBLES

MEATS (8) [MEAT]

Pr	23: 6	eye, neither desire thou his **dainty m**:	4303
Mk	7:19	goeth out into the draught, purging all **m**?	1033
Ac	15:29	That *ye* abstain from **m offered to idols**,	1494
1Co	6:13	**M** for the belly, and the belly for meats:	1033
	6:13	Meats for the belly, and the belly for **m**:	1033
1Ti	4: 3	*and commanding* to abstain from **m**,	1033
Heb	9:10	*Which stood* only in **m** and drinks,	1033
	13: 9	not with **m**, which have not profited	1033

MEBUNNAI (1)

2Sa	23:27	the Anethothite, **M** the Hushathite,	4012

MECHERATHITE (1)

1Ch	11:36	Hepher the **M**, Ahijah the Pelonite,	4382

MECONAH See MEKONAH

MEDAD (2)

Nu	11:26	*was* Eldad, and the name of the other **M**:	4312
	11:27	Eldad and **M** do prophesy in the camp.	4312

MEDAN (2) [MEDANITES]

Ge	25: 2	**M**, and Midian, and Ishbak, and Shuah.	4091
1Ch	1:32	**M**, and Midian, and Ishbak, and Shuah.	4091

MEDANITES (1) [MEDAN]

Ge	37:36	the **M** sold him into Egypt unto Potiphar,	4084

MEDDLE (6) [MEDDLED, MEDDLETH, MEDDLING]

Dt	2: 5	**M** not with them; for I will not give you	1624
	2:19	distress them not, nor **m** with them:	1624
2Ki	14:10	why shouldest thou **m** to *thy* hurt,	1624
2Ch	25:19	why shouldest thou **m** to *thine* hurt,	1624
Pr	20:19	**m** not with him that flattereth *with* his	6148
	24:21	**m** not with them that are given to change	6148

MEDDLED (1) [MEDDLE]

Pr	17:14	leave off contention, before *it* be **m with**.	1566

MEDDLER See BUSYBODY

MEDDLETH (1) [MEDDLE]

Pr	26:17	*and* **m** with strife *belonging* not to him,	5674

MEDDLING (2) [MEDDLE]

2Ch	35:21	forbear thee from **m** with God, who *is*	NIH
Pr	20: 3	from strife: but every fool will be **m**.	1566

MEDE (1) [MEDIA]

Da	11: 1	Also I in the first year of Darius the **M**,	4075

MEDEBA (5)

Nu	21:30	unto Nophah, which *reacheth* unto **M**.	4311
Jos	13: 9	and all the plain of **M** unto Dibon;	4311
	13:16	midst of the river, and all the plain by **M**;	4311
1Ch	19: 7	who came and pitched before **M**.	4311
Isa	15: 2	Moab shall howl over Nebo, and over **M**:	4311

MEDES (5) [MEDIA]

2Ki	17: 6	river of Gozan, and in the cities of the **M**.	4074
	18:11	river of Gozan, and in the cities of the **M**:	4074
Ezr	6: 2	palace that *is* in the province of the **M**,	4076

Est	1:19 the laws of the Persians and the **M**,	4074
Isa	13:17 Behold, I will stir up the **M** against them,	4074
Jer	25:25 kings of Elam, and all the kings of the **M**,	4074
	51:11 raised up the spirit of the kings of the **M**:	4074
	51:28 her the nations with the kings of the **M**,	4074
Da	5:28 divided, and given to the **M** and Persians.	4076
	6: 8 to the law of the **M** and Persians,	4076
	6:12 to the law of the **M** and Persians,	4076
	6:15 that the law of the **M** and Persians *is*,	4076
	9: 1 son of Ahasuerus, of the seed of the **M**,	4074
Ac	2: 9 and **M**, and Elamites, and the dwellers in	3370

MEDIA (6) [MEDE, MEDES, MEDIAN]

Est	1: 3 the power of Persia and **M**, the nobles	4074
	1:14 the seven princes of Persia and **M**,	4074
	1:18 **M** say this day unto all the king's princes,	4074
	10: 2 book of the chronicles of the kings of **M**	4074
Isa	21: 2 besiege, O **M**; all the sighing thereof have	4074
Da	8:20 having two horns *are* the kings of **M**	4074

MEDIAN (1) [MEDIA]

Da	5:31 Darius the **M** took the kingdom,	4076

MEDIATOR (7)

Gal	3:19 ordained by angels in the hand of a **m**.	3316
	3:20 a **m** *is not a mediator* of one, but God	3316
	3:20 a mediator is not *a* **m** of one, but God	NIG
1Ti	2: 5 and one **m** between God and men,	3316
Heb	8: 6 by how much also he is the **m** of a better	3316
	9:15 And for this cause he is the **m** of the new	3316
	12:24 And to Jesus the **m** of the new covenant,	3316

MEDICINE (2) [MEDICINES]

Pr	17:22 A merry heart doeth good *like* a **m**:	1456
Eze	47:12 be for meat, and the leaf thereof for **m**.	8644

MEDICINES (2) [MEDICINE]

Jer	30:13 be bound up: thou hast no healing **m**.	7499
	46:11 in vain shalt thou use many **m**; *for* thou	7499

MEDITATE (14) [MEDITATION]

Ge	24:63 Isaac went out to **m** in the field at	7742
Jos	1: 8 thou shalt **m** therein day and night, that	1897
Ps	1: 2 and in his law doth he **m** day and night.	1897
	63: 6 *and* **m** on thee in the *night* watches.	1897
	77:12 I will **m** also of all thy work, and talk of	1897
	119:15 I will **m** in thy precepts, and have respect	7878
	119:23 *but* thy servant did **m** in thy statutes.	7878
	119:48 I have loved; and I will **m** in thy statutes.	7878
	119:78 a cause: *but* I will **m** in thy precepts.	7878
	119:148 watches, that *I* might **m** in thy word.	7878
	143: 5 the days of old; I **m** on all thy works;	1897
Isa	33:18 Thine heart shall **m** terror. Where *is*	1897
Lk	21:14 not to **m** before *what ye* shall answer:	4304
1Ti	4:15 **M** upon these *things*; give thyself wholly	3191

MEDITATION (6) [MEDITATE]

Ps	5: 1 to my words, O LORD, consider my **m**.	1901
	19:14 the **m** of my heart, be acceptable in thy	1902
	49: 3 the **m** of my heart *shall be of*	1900
	104:34 My **m** of him shall be sweet: I will be glad	7879
	119:97 how love I thy law! it *is* my **m** all the day.	7881
	119:99 my teachers: for thy testimonies *are* my **m**.	7881

MEEK (17) [MEEKNESS]

Nu	12: 3 (Now the man Moses *was* very **m**,	6035
Ps	22:26 The **m** shall eat and be satisfied: they	6035
	25: 9 The **m** will he guide in judgment:	6035
	25: 9 and the **m** will he teach his way.	6035
	37:11 the **m** shall inherit the earth;	6035
	76: 9 judgment, to save all the **m** of the earth.	6035
	147: 6 The LORD lifteth up the **m**: he casteth	6035
	149: 4 he will beautify the **m** with salvation.	6035
Isa	11: 4 with equity for the **m** of the earth:	6035
	29:19 The **m** also shall increase *their* joy in	6035
	61: 1 me to preach good tidings unto the **m**;	6035
Am	2: 7 poor, and turn aside the way of the **m**:	6035
Zep	2: 3 Seek ye the LORD, all ye **m** of the earth,	6035
Mt	5: 5 Blessed *are* the **m**: for they shall inherit	4239
	11:29 of me; for I am **m** and lowly in heart:	4235
	21: 5 **m**, and sitting upon an ass, and a colt	4239
1Pe	3: 4 *the ornament* of a **m** and quiet spirit,	4239

MEEKNESS (14) [MEEK]

Ps	45: 4 of truth and **m** *and* righteousness;	6037
Zep	2: 3 judgment; seek righteousness, seek **m**:	6038
1Co	4:21 a rod, or in love, and *in* the spirit of **m**?	4236
2Co	10: 1 I Paul myself beseech you by the **m**	4236
Gal	5:23 **M**, temperance: against such there is no	4236
	6: 1 restore such a one in the spirit of **m**;	4236
Eph	4: 2 With all lowliness and **m**, with	4236
Col	3:12 humbleness of mind, **m**, longsuffering;	4236
1Ti	6:11 godliness, faith, love, patience, **m**.	4236
2Ti	2:25 In **m** instructing those that oppose	4236
Tit	3: 2 *but* gentle, shewing all **m** unto all men.	4236
Jas	1:21 and receive with **m** the engrafted word,	4240
	3:13 his works with **m** of wisdom.	4240
1Pe	3:15 reason of the hope that is in you with **m**	4240

MEET (132) [MEETEST, MEETETH, MEETING, MET]

Ge	2:18 will make him a help **m** *for* him.	5048+3509.1
	2:20 was not found a help **m for** him.	5048+3509.1
	14:17 the king of Sodom went out to **m** him	7125
	18: 2 he saw *them*, he ran to **m** them from	7125
	19: 1 Lot seeing *them* rose up to **m** them;	7125
	24:17 servant ran to **m** her, and said, Let me,	7125

Ge	24:65 *is* this that walketh in the field to **m** us?	7125
	29:13 that he ran to **m** him, and embraced him,	7125
	30:16 Leah went out to **m** him, and said,	7125
	32: 6 he cometh to **m** thee, and four hundred	7125
	33: 4 Esau ran to **m** him, and embraced him,	7125
	46:29 went up to **m** Israel his father, to Goshen,	7125
Ex	4:14 behold, he cometh forth to **m** thee:	7125
	4:27 Go into the wilderness to **m** Moses.	7125
	8:26 Moses said, It is not **m** so to do; for we	3559
	18: 7 Moses went out to **m** his father in law,	7125
	19:17 people out of the camp to **m** with God;	7125
	23: 4 If thou **m** thine enemy's ox or his ass	6293
	25:22 there I will **m** with thee, and I will	3259
	29:42 where I will **m** you, to speak there unto	3259
	29:43 there I will **m** with the children of Israel,	3259
	30: 6 the Testimony, where I will **m** with thee.	3259
	30:36 congregation, where I will **m** with thee:	3259
Nu	17: 4 the Testimony, where I will **m** with you.	3259
	22:36 went out to **m** him unto a city of Moab,	7125
	23: 3 peradventure the LORD will come to **m**	7125
	23:15 while I *the* LORD yonder.	7136
	31:13 went forth to **m** them without the camp.	7125
Dt	3:18 Israel, all *that are* **m** for the war.	1121+2428
Jos	2:16 to the mountain, lest the pursuers **m** you;	6293
	9:11 go to **m** them, and say unto us, We *are*	7125
Jdg	4:18 Jael went out to **m** Sisera, and said unto	7125
	4:22 Jael came out to **m** him, and said unto	7125
	5:30 **m** for the necks of *them that take*	NIH
	6:35 and they came up to **m** them.	7125
	11:31 forth of the doors of my house to **m** me,	7125
	11:34 his daughter came out to **m** him with	7125
	19: 3 damsel saw him, he rejoiced to **m** him.	7125
Ru	2:22 that they **m** thee not in *any* other field.	6293
1Sa	10: 3 there shall **m** thee three men going up to	4672
	10: 5 that thou shalt **m** a company of prophets	6293
	13:10 Saul went out to **m** him, that he might	7125
	15:12 when Samuel rose early to **m** Saul in	7125
	17:48 and drew nigh to **m** David, that David	7125
	17:48 ran *toward* the army to **m** the Philistine.	7125
	18: 6 singing and dancing, to **m** king Saul,	7125
	25:32 Israel, which sent thee this day to **m** me:	7125
	25:34 thou hadst hasted and come to **m** me,	7125
	30:21 they went forth to **m** David, and to meet	7125
	30:21 and to **m** the people that *were* with him:	7125
2Sa	6:20 the daughter of Saul came out to **m**	7125
	15: 5 sent to them, because the men were	7125
	15:32 Hushai the Archite *came* to **m** him with	7125
	19:15 Judah came to Gilgal, to go to **m** the king,	7125
	19:16 came down with the men of Judah to **m**	7125
	19:20 Joseph to go down to **m** my lord the king.	7125
	19:24 the son of Saul came down to **m** the king,	7125
	19:25 when he was come *to* Jerusalem to **m**	7125
1Ki	2: 8 he came down to **m** me *at* Jordan,	7125
	2:19 the king rose up to **m** her,	7125
	18:16 Obadiah went to **m** Ahab, and told him:	7125
	18:16 and told him: and Ahab went to **m** Elijah.	7125
	21:18 Arise, go down to **m** Ahab king of Israel,	7125
2Ki	1: 3 go up to **m** the messengers of the king of	7125
	1: 6 There came a man up to **m** us,	7125
	1: 7 of man *was he* which came up to **m** you,	7125
	2:15 came to **m** him, and bowed themselves	7125
	4:26 I pray thee, to **m** her, and say unto her,	7125
	4:29 *thy way:* if thou **m** any man, salute him	4672
	4:31 Wherefore he went again to **m** him,	7125
	5:21 lighted down from the chariot to **m** him,	7125
	5:26 turned *again* from his chariot to **m** thee?	7125
	8: 8 go, the man of God, and inquire of	7125
	8: 9 So Hazael went to **m** him, and took a	7125
	9:17 send to **m** them, and let him say, *Is it*	7125
	9:18 there went one on horseback to **m** him,	7125
	10:15 the son of Rechab *coming* to **m** him:	7125
	16:10 king Ahaz went *to* Damascus to **m**	7125
1Ch	12:17 David went out to **m** them, and answered	6440
	19: 5 sent to **m** them: for the men were greatly	7125
2Ch	15: 2 he went out to **m** Asa, and said unto him,	6440
	19: 2 of Hanani the seer went out to **m** him,	6440
Ezr	4:14 *it was* not **m** for us to see the king's	749
Ne	6: 2 let us **m** together in *some one of*	3259
	6:10 Let us **m together** in the house of God,	3259
Est	2: 9 *which were* **m** to be given her,	7200
Job	5:14 They **m** with darkness in the daytime,	6298
	34:31 Surely it is **m** *to be* said unto God, I have	NIH
	39:21 He goeth on to **m** the armed men.	7125
Pr	7:15 Therefore came I forth to **m** thee,	7125
	11:24 *there is* that withholdeth more than is **m**,	3476
	17:12 *Let* a bear robbed of her whelps **m** a man,	6298
	22: 2 The rich and poor **m together:** the LORD	6298
	29:13 and the deceitful man **m together:**	6298
Isa	7: 3 Go forth now to **m** Ahaz, thou,	7125
	14: 9 Hell from beneath is moved for thee to **m**	7125
	34:14 The wild beasts of the desert shall also **m**	6298
	47: 3 and I will not **m** *thee* as a man.	6293
Jer	26:14 me as seemeth good and **m** unto you.	3477
	27: 5 given it unto whom it seemed **m** unto	3474
	41: 6 went forth from Mizpah to **m** them,	7125
	51:31 One post shall run to **m** another,	7125
	51:31 and one messenger to **m** another,	7125
Eze	15: 4 *is* burnt. Is it **m** for *any* work?	6743
	15: 5 it was whole, it was **m** for no work:	6213
	15: 5 how much less shall it be **m** yet for *any*	6213
Hos	13: 8 I will **m** them as a bear *that is* bereaved	6298
Am	4:12 thee, prepare to **m** thy God, O Israel.	
Zec	2: 3 And another angel went out to **m** him,	7125
Mt	3: 8 therefore fruits **m for** repentance:	514
	8:34 the whole city came out to **m** Jesus:	4877

Mt	15:26 It is not **m** to take the children's bread,	2570
	25: 1 and went forth to **m** the bridegroom.	529
	25: 6 bridegroom cometh; go ye out to **m** him.	529
Mk	7:27 for it is not **m** to take the children's bread,	2570
	14:13 there shall **m** you a man bearing a pitcher	528
Lk	14:31 him that cometh against him with	528
	15:32 It was **m** that *we* should make merry,	1163
	22:10 shall a man **m** you, bearing a pitcher	4876
Jn	12:13 and went forth to **m** him, and cried,	5222
Ac	26:20 to God, and do works **m for** repentance.	514
	28:15 they came to **m** us as far as Appii forum,	529
Ro	1:27 recompence of their error which was **m**.	1163
1Co	15: 9 that am not **m** to be called an apostle,	2425
	16: 4 And if it be **m** that I go also, they shall go	514
Php	1: 7 Even as it is **m** for me to think this of you	1342
Col	1:12 hath **made** us **m** to be partakers of	2427
1Th	4:17 in the clouds, to **m** the Lord in the air:	529
2Th	1: 3 as it is **m**, because that your faith groweth	514
2Ti	2:21 and **m** for the master's *use*,	2173
Heb	6: 7 bringeth forth herbs **m** for them by whom	2111
2Pe	1:13 Yea, I think it **m**, as long as I am in this	1342

MEETEST (2) [MEET]

2Ki	10: 3 out the best and **m** of your master's sons,	3477
Isa	64: 5 Thou **m** him that rejoiceth and	6293

MEETETH (3) [MEET]

Ge	32:17 When Esau my brother **m** thee,	6298
Nu	35:19 when he **m** him, he shall slay him.	6293
	35:21 shall slay the murderer, when he **m** him.	6293

MEETING (2) [MEET]

1Sa	21: 1 Ahimelech was afraid at the **m** of David,	7125
Isa	1:13 *it is* iniquity, even the **solemn m**.	6116

MEGIDDO (11) [MEGIDDON]

Jos	12:21 king of Taanach, one; the king of **M**, one;	4023
	17:11 and the inhabitants of **M** and her towns,	4023
Jdg	1:27 nor the inhabitants of **M** and her towns:	4023
	5:19 of Canaan in Taanach by the waters of **M**;	4023
1Ki	4:12 to him pertained Taanach and **M**,	4023
	9:15 and Hazor, and **M**, and Gezer.	4023
2Ki	9:27 And he fled *to* **M**, and died there.	4023
	23:29 slew him at **M**, when he had seen him.	4023
	23:30 carried him *in a chariot* dead from **M**,	4023
1Ch	7:29 **M** and her towns, Dor and her towns.	4023
2Ch	35:22 and came to fight in the valley of **M**.	4023

MEGIDDON (1) [MEGIDDO]

Zec	12:11 of Hadadrimmon in the valley of **M**.	4023

MEHETABEEL (1)

Ne	6:10 the son of Delaiah the son of **M**,	4105

MEHETABEL (2)

Ge	36:39 his wife's name *was* **M**, the daughter of	4105
1Ch	1:50 his wife's name *was* **M**, the daughter of	4105

MEHIDA (2)

Ezr	2:52 the children of **M**, the children of Harsha,	4240
Ne	7:54 the children of **M**, the children of Harsha,	4240

MEHIR (1)

1Ch	4:11 Chelub the brother of Shuah begat **M**,	4243

MEHOLATHITE (2)

1Sa	18:19 that she was given unto Adriel the **M** to	4259
2Sa	21: 8 up for Adriel the son of Barzillai the **M**:	4259

MEHUJAEL (2)

Ge	4:18 Irad begat **M**: and Mehujael begat	4232
	4:18 **M** begat Methusael: and Methusael begat	4232

MEHUMAN (1)

Est	1:10 he commanded **M**, Biztha, Harbona,	4104

MEHUNIM (1) [MEHUNIMS, MEUNIM]

Ezr	2:50 The children of Asnah, the children of **M**,	4586

MEHUNIMS (1) [MEHUNIM]

2Ch	26: 7 that dwelt in Gur-baal, and the **M**.	4586

ME-JARKON (1)

Jos	19:46 **M**, and Rakkon, with the border before	4313

MEKERATHITE See MECHERATHITE

MEKONAH (1)

Ne	11:28 and at **M**, and in the villages thereof,	4368

MELATIAH (1)

Ne	3: 7 next unto them repaired **M** the Gibeonite,	4424

MELCHI (2)

Lk	3:24 the *son* of Levi, which was *the son* of **M**,	3197
	3:28 Which was *the son* of **M**, which was	3197

MELCHIAH (1)

Jer	21: 1 sent unto him Pashur the son of **M**,	4441

MELCHISEDEC (9) [MELCHIZEDEK]

Heb	5: 6 *art* a priest for ever after the order of **M**.	3198
	5:10 of God a high priest after the order of **M**.	3198
	6:20 high priest for ever after the order of **M**.	3198
	7: 1 For this **M**, king of Salem, priest of	3198
	7:10 the loins of his father, when **M** met him.	3198
	7:11 priest should rise after the order of **M**,	3198

Heb	7:15 for that after the similitude of **M** there	3198
	7:17 *art* a priest for ever after the order of **M**.	3198
	7:21 *art* a priest for ever after the order of **M**:)	3198

MELCHISHUA (1)
1Sa	14:49 of Saul were Jonathan, and Ishui, and **M**:	4444

MELCHIZEDEK (2) [MELCHISEDEC]
Ge	14:18 **M** king of Salem brought forth bread and	4442
Ps	110: 4 *art* a priest for ever after the order of **M**.	4442

MELEA (1)
Lk	3:31 Which was *the* son of **M**, which was	3190

MELECH (2)
1Ch	8:35 Pithon, and **M**, and Tarea, and Ahaz.	4429
	9:41 and **M**, and Tahrea, *and Ahaz*.	4429

MELICU (1)
Ne	12:14 Of **M**, Jonathan; of Shebaniah, Joseph;	4409

MELITA (1)
Ac	28: 1 they knew that the island was called **M**.	3194

MELKI See MELCHI

MELODY (4)
Isa	23:16 make sweet **m**, sing many songs, that	5059
	51: 3 thanksgiving, and the voice of **m**.	2172
Am	5:23 for I will not hear the **m** of thy viols.	2172
Eph	5:19 and **making m** in your heart to the Lord;	5567

MELONS (1)
Nu	11: 5 and the **m**, and the leeks, and the onions,	20

MELT (17) [MELTED, MELTETH, MELTING, MOLTEN]
Ex	15:15 the inhabitants of Canaan shall **m** away.	4127
Jos	2:11 had heard *these things*, our hearts did **m**,	4549
	14: 8 with me **made** the heart of the people **m**:	4529
2Sa	17:10 the heart of a lion, shall **utterly m**:	4549+4549
Ps	58: 7 Let them **m** away as waters *which* run	3988
	112:10 shall gnash *with* his teeth, and **m away**:	4549
Isa	13: 7 be faint, and every man's heart shall **m**:	4549
	19: 1 heart of Egypt shall **m** in the midst of it.	4549
Jer	9: 7 Behold, I will **m** them, and try them;	6884
Eze	21: 7 every heart shall **m**, and all hands shall **m**	4549
	22:20 to **m** *it*; so will I gather *you* in mine anger	5413
	22:20 and I will leave *you there*, and **m** you.	5413
Am	9: 5 it shall **m**, and all that dwell therein shall	4127
	9:13 drop sweet wine, and all the hills shall **m**.	4127
Na	1: 5 the hills **m**, and the earth is burnt at his	4127
2Pe	3:10 the elements shall **m** with fervent heat,	3089
	3:12 the elements shall **m** with fervent heat?	5080

MELTED (13) [MELT]
Ex	16:21 and when the sun waxed hot, it **m**.	4549
Jos	5: 1 we were passed over, that their heart **m**,	4549
	7: 5 wherefore the hearts of the people **m**,	4549
Jdg	5: 5 The mountains **m** from before the Lord,	5140
1Sa	14:16 the multitude **m away**, and they went on	4127
Ps	22:14 wax; it is **m** in the midst of my bowels.	4549
	46: 6 he uttered his voice, the earth **m**.	4127
	97: 5 The hills **m** like wax at the presence of	4549
	107:26 their soul is **m** because of trouble.	4127
Isa	34: 3 mountains shall be **m** with their blood.	4549
Eze	22:21 and ye shall be **m** in the midst thereof.	5413
	22:22 As silver is **m** in the midst of the furnace,	2046
	22:22 so shall ye be **m** in the midst thereof;	5413

MELTETH (7) [MELT]
Ps	58: 8 As a snail *which* **m**, let *every one* of	8557
	68: 2 wax **m** before the fire, *so* let the wicked	4549
	119:28 My soul **m** for heaviness: strengthen thou	1811
	147:18 He sendeth out his word, and **m** them:	4529
Isa	40:19 The workman **m** a graven image,	5258
Jer	6:29 of the fire; the founder in vain:	6884
Na	2:10 heart **m**, and the knees smite together,	4549

MELTING (1) [MELT]
Isa	64: 2 As *when* the **m** fire burneth, the fire	2003

MELZAR (2)
Da	1:11 said Daniel to **M**, whom the prince of	4453
	1:16 Thus **M** took away the portion of their	4453

MEMBER (6) [MEMBERS]
Dt	23: 1 in the stones, or hath *his* **privy m** cut off,	8212
1Co	12:14 For the body is not one **m**, but many.	3196
	12:19 And if they were all one **m**, where *were*	3196
	12:26 whether one **m** suffer, all the members	3196
	12:26 suffer *with it*; or one **m** be honoured,	3196
Jas	3: 5 Even so the tongue is a little **m**,	3196

MEMBERS (32) [MEMBER]
Job	17: 7 of sorrow, and all my **m** *are* as a shadow.	3338
Ps	139:16 in thy book all *my* **m** were written,	NIH
Mt	5:29 it is profitable for thee that one of thy **m**	3196
	5:30 it is profitable for thee that one of thy **m**	3196
Ro	6:13 Neither yield ye your **m** *as* instruments	3196
	6:13 your **m** *as* instruments of righteousness	3196
	6:19 for as ye have yielded your **m** servants to	3196
	6:19 yield your **m** servants to righteousness	3196
	7: 5 did work in our **m** to bring forth fruit	3196
	7:23 But I see another law in my **m**,	3196
	7:23 to the law of sin which is in my **m**.	3196

Ro	12: 4 For as we have many **m** in one body,	3196
	12: 4 and all **m** have not the same office:	3196
	12: 5 Christ, and every one **m** one of another.	3196
1Co	6:15 Know ye not that your bodies are the **m**	3196
	6:15 shall I then take the **m** of Christ,	3196
	6:15 and make *them* the **m** of a harlot?	3196
	12:12 hath many **m**, and all the members of	3196
	12:12 all the **m** of *that* one body, being many,	3196
	12:18 But now hath God set the **m** every one of	3196
	12:20 But now *are they* many **m**, yet *but*	3196
	12:22 Nay, much more those **m** of the body,	3196
	12:23 those **m** of the body, which we think to	NIG
	12:25 *that* the **m** should have the same care one	3196
	12:26 all the **m** suffer *with it*; or one member be	3196
	12:26 be honoured, all the **m** rejoice with *it*.	3196
	12:27 the body of Christ, and **m** in particular.	3196
Eph	4:25 neighbour: for we are **m** one of another.	3196
	5:30 For we are **m** of his body, of his flesh,	3196
Col	3: 5 your **m** which are upon the earth;	3196
Jas	3: 6 so is the tongue amongst our **m**, that it	3196
	4: 1 *even* of your lusts that war in your **m**?	3196

MEMORIAL (32)
Ex	3:15 and this *is* my **m** unto all generations.	2143
	12:14 this day shall be unto you for a **m**;	2146
	13: 9 for a **m** between thine eyes, that	2146
	17:14 Write this *for* a **m** in a book, and rehearse	2146
	28:12 stones of **m** unto the children of Israel:	2146
	28:12 Lord upon his two shoulders for a **m**.	2146
	28:29 for a **m** before the Lord continually.	2146
	30:16 that it may be a **m** unto the children of	2146
	39: 7 *that they should be* stones for a **m** to	2146
Lev	2: 2 the priest shall burn the **m** of it upon	234
	2: 9 take from the meat offering a **m** thereof,	234
	2:16 the priest shall burn the **m** of it, *part* of	234
	5:12 *even* a **m** thereof, and burn *it* on the altar,	234
	6:15 *even* the **m** of it, unto the Lord.	234
	23:24 *a day* of blowing of trumpets, a holy	2146
	24: 7 that it may be on the bread for a **m**, *even*	234
Nu	5:15 an offering of jealousy, an offering of **m**,	2146
	5:18 and put the offering in her hands,	2146
	5:26 *even* the **m** thereof, and burn *it* upon	234
	10:10 they may be to you for a **m** before your	2146
	16:40 To be a **m** unto the children of Israel,	2146
	31:54 *for* a **m** for the children of Israel before	2146
Jos	4: 7 these stones shall be for a **m** unto	2146
Ne	2:20 portion, nor right, nor **m**, in Jerusalem.	2146
Est	9:28 nor the **m** of them perish from their seed.	2143
Ps	9: 6 their **m** is perished *with* them.	2143
	135:13 *and* thy **m**, O Lord, throughout all	2143
Hos	12: 5 Lord God of hosts; the Lord *is* his **m**.	2143
Zec	6:14 for a **m** in the temple of the Lord.	2146
Mt	26:13 woman hath done, be told for a **m** of her.	3422
Mk	14: 9 done shall be spoken of for a **m** of her.	3422
Ac	10: 4 alms are come up for a **m** before God.	3422

MEMORY (6)
Ps	109:15 that he may cut off the **m** of them from	2143
	145: 7 They shall abundantly utter the **m** of thy	2143
Pr	10: 7 The **m** of the just *is* blessed: but the name	2143
Ecc	9: 5 a reward; for the **m** of them is forgotten.	2143
Isa	26:14 and made all their **m** to perish.	2143
1Co	15: 2 if ye **keep in m** what I preached unto	2722

MEMPHIS (1)
Hos	9: 6 shall gather them up, **M** shall bury them:	4644

MEMUCAN (3)
Est	1:14 Tarshish, Meres, Marsena, *and* **M**,	4462
	1:16 **M** answered before the king and	4462
	1:21 the king did according to the word of **M**:	4462

MEN (1652) [MAN]
Ge	4:26 began **m** to call upon the name of	NIH
	6: 1 when **m** began to multiply on the face of	120
	6: 2 the sons of God saw the daughters of **m**	120
	6: 4 of God came in unto the daughters of **m**,	120
	6: 4 the same *became* mighty **m** which *were*	NIH
	6: 4 **men** which *were* of old, **m** of renown.	376
	11: 5 tower, which the children of **m** builded.	120
	12:20 Pharaoh commanded *his* **m** concerning	376
	13:13 the **m** of Sodom *were* wicked and	376
	14:24 Save only that which the **young m** have	5288
	14:24 the portion of the **m** which went with me,	376
	17:23 every male among the **m** of Abraham's	376
	17:27 all the **m** of his house, born in the house,	376
	18: 2 and looked, and lo, three **m** stood by him:	376
	18:16 the **m** rose up from thence,	376
	18:22 the **m** turned their faces from thence,	376
	19: 4 the **m** of the city, *even* the men of Sodom,	376
	19: 4 the **men** of the city, *even* the **m** of Sodom,	376
	19: 5 Where *are* the **m** which came in to thee	376
	19: 8 unto these **m** do nothing; for therefore	376
	19:10 the **m** put forth their hand, and pulled Lot	376
	19:11 they smote the **m** that *were* at the door of	376
	19:12 the **m** said unto Lot, Hast thou here any	376
	19:16 the **m** laid hold upon his hand, and upon	376
	20: 8 in their ears: and the **m** were sore afraid.	376
	22: 3 took two of his **young m** with him,	5288
	22: 5 Abraham said unto his **young m**,	5288
	22:19 So Abraham returned unto his **young m**,	5288
	24:13 the daughters of the **m** of the city come	376
	24:54 he and the **m** that *were* with him,	376
	24:59 and Abraham's servant, and his **m**.	376
	26: 7 the **m** of the place asked *him* of his wife;	376

Ge	26: 7 the **m** of the place should kill me for	376
	29:22 Laban gathered together all the **m** of	376
	32: 6 meet thee, and four hundred **m** with him.	376
	32:28 hast thou power with God and with **m**,	376
	33: 1 Esau came, and with him four hundred **m**.	376
	33:13 if **m** should overdrive them one day,	NIH
	34: 7 they heard *it*: and the **m** were grieved,	376
	34:20 communed with the **m** of their city, saying,	376
	34:21 These **m** *are* peaceable with us; therefore	376
	34:22 herein will the **m** consent unto us for to	376
	38:21 he asked the **m** of that place, saying,	376
	38:22 the **m** of the place said, *that* there was	376
	39:11 *was* none of the **m** of the house there	376
	39:14 That she called unto the **m** of her house,	376
	41: 8 of Egypt, and all the **wise m** thereof:	2450
	42:11 we *are* true **m**, thy servants are no spies.	NIH
	42:19 If ye *be* true **m**, let one of your brethren	NIH
	42:31 unto him, We *are* true **m**, we are no spies:	NIH
	42:33 Hereby shall I know that ye *are* true **m**;	NIH
	42:34 ye *are* true **m**: *so* will I deliver you your	NIH
	43:15 the **m** took that present, and they took	376
	43:16 Bring *these* **m** home, and slay,	376
	43:16 for *these* **m** shall dine with me at noon.	376
	43:17 man brought the **m** into Joseph's house.	376
	43:18 the **m** were afraid, because they were	376
	43:24 man brought the **m** into Joseph's house,	376
	43:33 and the **m** marvelled one at another.	376
	44: 3 **m** were sent away, they and their asses.	376
	44: 4 unto his steward, Up, follow after the **m**;	376
	46:32 the **m** *are* shepherds, for their trade hath	376
	47: 2 *even* five **m**, and presented them unto	376
Ex	1:17 but saved the **m children** alive.	3206
	1:18 have saved the **m children** alive?	3206
	2:13 two **m** of the Hebrews strove together:	376
	4:19 all the **m** are dead which sought thy life.	376
	5: 9 Let there more work be laid upon the **m**,	376
	7:11 Pharaoh also called the **wise m** and	2450
	10: 7 let the **m** go, that they may serve the Lord	NIH
	10:11 go now ye *that are* **m**, and serve	1397
	12:33 in haste; for they said, We *be* all dead **m**.	NIH
	12:37 hundred thousand on foot *that were* **m**,	1397
	15:15 the **mighty m** of Moab, trembling shall	352
	17: 9 Choose us out **m**, and go out, fight with	376
	18:21 shalt provide out of all the people able **m**,	376
	18:21 such as fear God, **m** of truth,	376
	18:25 Moses chose able **m** out of all Israel,	376
	21:18 if **m** strive together, and one smite another	376
	21:22 If **m** strive, and hurt a woman with child,	376
	22:31 ye shall be holy **m** unto me: neither shall	376
	24: 5 he sent **young m** of the children of Israel,	5288
	32:28 people that day about three thousand **m**.	376
	34:23 in the year shall all your **m children**	2138
	35:22 they came, both **m** and women, as many	376
	36: 4 all the wise **m**, that wrought all the work	NIH
	38:26 and five hundred and fifty **m**.	NIH
Lev	7:25 of which **m** offer an offering made by fire	NIH
	18:27 (For all these abominations have the **m** of	NIH
	27: 9 whereof **m** bring an offering unto	NIH
	27:29 devoted, which shall be devoted of **m**,	120
Nu	1: 5 *are* the names of the **m** that shall stand	376
	1:17 Aaron took these **m** which are expressed	NIH
	1:44 and the princes of Israel, *being* twelve **m**:	NIH
	5: 6 shall commit any sin that **m** commit,	120
	9: 6 there were *certain* **m**, who were defiled	376
	9: 7 those **m** said unto him, We *are* defiled by	376
	11:16 Gather unto me seventy **m** of the elders of	376
	11:24 gathered the seventy **m** of the elders of	376
	11:26 there remained two *of the* **m** in the camp,	376
	11:28 *one* of his **young m**, answered and said,	979
	12: 3 above all the **m** which *were* upon the face	120
	13: 2 Send thou **m**, that they may search the	376
	13: 3 all those **m** *were* heads of the children of	376
	13:16 *are* the names of the **m** which Moses	376
	13:21 Zin unto Rehob, as **m** come to Hamath.	NIH
	13:31 the **m** that went up with him said, We be	376
	13:32 all the people that we saw in it *are* **m** of a	376
	14:22 Because all *those* **m** which have seen my	376
	14:36 **m**, which Moses sent to search the land,	376
	14:37 *Even* those **m** that did bring up the evil	376
	14:38 *which were* of the **m** that went to search	376
	16: 1 the son of Peleth, sons of Reuben, took **m**:	NIH
	16: 2 famous in the congregation, **m** of renown:	376
	16:14 wilt thou put out the eyes of these **m**?	376
	16:26 from the tents of these wicked **m**,	376
	16:29 If these **m** die the common death of all	NIH
	16:29 these **men** die the common death of all **m**,	120
	16:29 they be visited after the visitation of all **m**;	120
	16:30 ye shall understand that these **m** have	376
	16:32 all the **m** that *appertained* unto Korah,	120
	16:35 and fifty **m** that offered incense.	376
	18:15 *whether it be* of **m** or beasts, shall be thine:	120
	22: 9 and said, What **m** *are* these with thee?	376
	22:20 If the **m** come to call thee, rise up,	376
	22:35 Lord said unto Balaam, Go with the **m**:	376
	25: 5 Slay ye every one his **m** that were joined	376
	26:10 the fire devoured two hundred and fifty **m**:	376
	31:11 and all the prey, *both* of **m** and of beasts.	120
	31:21 Eleazar the priest said unto the **m** of war	376
	31:28 levy a tribute unto the Lord of the **m** of	376
	31:32 *being* the rest of the prey which the **m** of	5971
	31:42 which Moses divided from the **m** that	376
	31:49 servants have taken the sum of the **m** of	376
	31:53 (*For* the **m** of war had taken spoil,	376
	32:11 Surely none of the **m** that came up out of	376
	32:14 your *fathers'* stead, an increase of sinful **m**,	376

M

Nu	34:17 These *are* the names of the **m** which shall	376
	34:19 the names of the **m** *are* these: Of the tribe	376
Dt	1:13 Take ye wise **m**, and understanding,	376
	1:15 wise **m**, and known, and made them heads	376
	1:22 We will send us before us, and they shall	376
	1:23 I took twelve **m** of you, one of a tribe:	376
	1:35 there shall not one of these **m** of this	376
	2:14 all the generation of the **m** of war were	376
	2:16 when all the **m** of war were consumed	376
	2:34 utterly destroyed the **m**, and the women,	4962
	3: 6 utterly destroying the **m**, women,	4962
	4: 3 for all the **m** that followed Baal-peor,	376
	13:13 *Certain* **m**, the children of Belial, are gone	376
	19:17 the **m**, between whom the controversy	376
	21:21 all the **m** of his city shall stone him with	376
	22:21 the **m** of her city shall stone her with	376
	25: 1 If there be a controversy between **m**,	376
	25:11 When **m** strive together one with another,	376
	27:14 say unto all the **m** of Israel *with* a loud	376
	29:10 and your officers, *with* all the **m** of Israel,	376
	29:25 **m** shall say, Because they have forsaken	NIH
	31:12 **m**, and women, and children,	376
	32:26 of them to cease from among **m**:	582
	33: 6 and not die; and let *not* his **m** be few.	4962
Jos	1:14 all the mighty **m** of valour, and help them;	NIH
	2: 1 I sent out of Shittim two **m** to spy secretly,	376
	2: 2 there came **m** in hither to night of	376
	2: 3 Bring forth the **m** that are come to thee,	376
	2: 4 the woman took the two **m**, and hid them,	376
	2: 4 There came **m** unto me, but I wist not	376
	2: 5 when it was dark, that the **m** went out:	376
	2: 5 whither the **m** went I wot not: pursue	376
	2: 7 pursued after them the way to Jordan	376
	2: 9 she said unto the **m**, I know that the LORD	376
	2:14 the **m** answered her, Our life for yours,	376
	2:17 the **m** said unto her, We *will be* blameless	376
	2:23 the two **m** returned, and descended from	376
	3:12 take ye twelve **m** out of the tribes of Israel,	376
	4: 2 Take you twelve **m** out of the people, out	376
	4: 4 Joshua called the twelve **m**, whom he had	376
	5: 4 *that were* males, *even* all the **m** of war,	376
	5: 6 till all the people *that were* **m** of war,	376
	6: 2 king thereof, *and* the mighty **m** of valour.	NIH
	6: 3 all *ye* **m** of war, *and* go round about the	376
	6: 9 the armed **m** went before the priests that	NIH
	6:13 the armed **m** went before them;	NIH
	6:22 Joshua had said unto the two **m** that had	376
	6:23 the **young m** that were spies went in,	5288
	7: 2 Joshua sent **m** from Jericho *to* Ai, which *is*	376
	7: 2 And the **m** went up and viewed Ai.	376
	7: 3 or three thousand **m** go up and smite Ai;	376
	7: 4 of the people about three thousand **m**:	376
	7: 4 and they fled before the **m** of Ai.	376
	7: 5 the **m** of Ai smote of them about thirty	376
	7: 5 Ai smote of them about thirty and six **m**:	376
	8: 3 chose out thirty thousand mighty **m**	NIH
	8:12 he took about five thousand **m**, and set	376
	8:14 the **m** of the city went out against Israel to	376
	8:20 the **m** of Ai looked behind them, they	376
	8:21 they turned again, and slew the **m** of Ai.	376
	8:25 both of **m** and women, *were* twelve	376
	8:25 twelve thousand, *even* all the **m** of Ai.	376
	9: 6 said unto him, and to the **m** of Israel, We	376
	9: 7 the **m** of Israel said unto the Hivites,	376
	9:14 the **m** took of their victuals, and asked not	376
	10: 2 Ai, and all the **m** thereof *were* mighty.	376
	10: 6 the **m** of Gibeon sent unto Joshua to	376
	10: 7 with him, and all the mighty **m** of valour.	NIH
	10:18 the cave, and set **m** by it for to keep them:	376
	10:24 that Joshua called for all the **m** of Israel,	376
	10:24 unto the captains of the **m** of war which	376
	18: 4 Give out from among you three **m** for	376
	18: 8 the **m** arose, and went away:	376
	18: 9 the **m** went and passed through the land,	376
	24:11 the **m** of Jericho fought against you,	1167
Jdg	1: 4 slew *of* them in Bezek ten thousand **m**.	376
	3:29 Moab at that time about ten thousand **m**,	376
	3:29 men, all lusty, and all **m** of valour;	376
	3:31 slew of the Philistines six hundred **m**	376
	4: 6 take with thee ten thousand **m** of	376
	4:10 went up with ten thousand **m** at his feet:	376
	4:14 Tabor, and ten thousand **m** after him.	376
	6:27 Then Gideon took ten **m** of his servants,	376
	6:27 the **m** of the city, that *he* could not do *it*	376
	6:28 when the **m** of the city arose early in	376
	6:30 the **m** of the city said unto Joash, Bring out	376
	7: 6 to their mouth, were three hundred **m**:	376
	7: 7 By the three hundred **m** that lapped will I	376
	7: 8 tent, and retained *those* three hundred **m**:	376
	7:11 of the armed **m** that *were* in the host.	NIH
	7:16 he divided the three hundred **m** *into* three	376
	7:19 and the hundred **m** that *were* with him,	376
	7:23 the **m** of Israel gathered themselves	376
	7:24 all the **m** of Ephraim gathered themselves	376
	8: 1 the **m** of Ephraim said unto him, Why hast	376
	8: 4 the three hundred **m** that *were* with him,	376
	8: 5 he said unto the **m** of Succoth, Give, I	376
	8: 8 the **m** of Penuel answered him as the men	376
	8: 8 men of Penuel answered him as the **m** of	376
	8: 9 spake also unto the **m** of Penuel, saying,	376
	8:10 fifteen thousand **m**, all that were left	NIH
	8:10 and twenty thousand **m** that drew sword.	376
	8:14 caught a young man of the **m** of Succoth,	376
	8:14 *even* threescore and seventeen **m**.	376
	8:15 he came unto the **m** of Succoth, and said,	376

Jdg	8:15 that we should give bread unto thy **m** *that*	376
	8:16 with them he taught the **m** of Succoth,	376
	8:17 of Penuel, and slew the **m** of the city.	376
	8:18 What manner of **m** *were they* whom ye	376
	8:22 of Israel said unto Gideon, Rule	376
	9: 2 in the ears of all the **m** of Shechem,	1167
	9: 3 of all the **m** of Shechem all these words:	1167
	9: 6 all the **m** of Shechem gathered together,	1167
	9: 7 Hearken unto me, you **m** of Shechem,	1167
	9:18 king over the **m** of Shechem, because he	1167
	9:20 devour the **m** of Shechem, and the house	1167
	9:20 let fire come out from the **m** of Shechem,	1167
	9:23 Abimelech and the **m** of Shechem;	1167
	9:23 the **m** of Shechem dealt treacherously	1167
	9:24 the **m** of Shechem, which aided him	1167
	9:25 the **m** of Shechem set liers in wait for	1167
	9:26 the **m** of Shechem put their confidence in	1167
	9:28 serve the **m** of Hamor the father of	376
	9:36 of the mountains as *if they were* **m**.	376
	9:39 Gaal went out before the **m** of Shechem,	1167
	9:46 when all the **m** of the tower of Shechem	1167
	9:47 that all the **m** of the tower of Shechem	1167
	9:49 all the **m** of the tower of Shechem died	376
	9:49 also, about a thousand **m** and women.	376
	9:51 thither fled all the **m** and women,	376
	9:54 and slay me, that *m* say not of me,	NIH
	9:55 when the **m** of Israel saw that Abimelech	376
	9:57 all the evil of the **m** of Shechem did God	376
	11: 3 there were gathered vain **m** to Jephthah,	376
	12: 1 the **m** of Ephraim gathered themselves	376
	12: 3 Jephthah gathered together all the **m** of	376
	12: 4 the **m** of Gilead smote Ephraim, because	376
	12: 5 the **m** of Gilead said unto him, *Art* thou	376
	14:10 a feast; for so used the **young m** to do.	970
	14:18 the **m** of the city said unto him on	376
	14:19 slew thirty of them, and took their spoil,	376
	15:10 the **m** of Judah said, Why are ye come up	376
	15:11 three thousand **m** of Judah went to the top	376
	15:15 took it, and slew a thousand **m** therewith.	376
	15:16 the jaw of an ass have I slain a thousand **m**.	376
	16: 9 Now there were **m** lying in wait,	NIH
	16:27 Now the house was full *of* **m** and women;	376
	16:27 upon the roof about three thousand **m**	376
	18: 2 of their family five **m** from their coasts,	376
	18: 2 **m** of valour, from Zorah and	376+1121
	18: 7 the five **m** departed, and came to Laish,	376
	18:11 six hundred **m** appointed *with* weapons of	376
	18:14 answered the five **m** that went to spy out	376
	18:16 the six hundred **m** appointed *with* their	376
	18:17 five **m** that went to spy out the land went	376
	18:17 **m** that were appointed *with* weapons of	376
	18:22 the **m** that *were* in the houses near to	376
	19:16 but the **m** of the place *were* Benjamites.	376
	19:22 behold, the **m** of the city, certain sons of	376
	19:25 the **m** would not hearken to him: so the	376
	20: 5 the **m** of Gibeah rose against me,	1167
	20:10 will take ten **m** of an hundred throughout	376
	20:11 So all the **m** of Israel were gathered against	376
	20:12 the tribes of Israel sent **m** through all	376
	20:13 therefore deliver *us* the **m**, the children	376
	20:15 and six thousand **m** that drew sword,	376
	20:15 were numbered seven hundred chosen **m**	376
	20:16 *were* seven hundred chosen **m** lefthanded;	376
	20:17 the **m** of Israel, beside Benjamin,	376
	20:17 were numbered four hundred thousand **m**	376
	20:17 that drew sword: all these *were* **m** of war.	376
	20:20 the **m** of Israel went out to battle against	376
	20:20 the **m** of Israel put *themselves* in array to	376
	20:21 that day twenty and two thousand **m**.	376
	20:22 the people the **m** of Israel encouraged	376
	20:25 of Israel again eighteen thousand **m**;	376
	20:31 in the field, about thirty **m** of Israel.	376
	20:33 the **m** of Israel rose up out of their place,	376
	20:34 ten thousand chosen **m** out of all Israel,	376
	20:35 and five thousand and an hundred **m**:	376
	20:36 for the **m** of Israel gave place to	376
	20:38 an appointed sign between the **m** of Israel	376
	20:39 when the **m** of Israel retired in the battle,	376
	20:39 kill of the **m** of Israel about thirty persons:	376
	20:41 the **m** of Israel turned *again*, the men	376
	20:41 the men of Israel turned *again*, the **m**	376
	20:42 **m** of Israel unto the way of the wilderness;	376
	20:44 fell of Benjamin eighteen thousand **m**;	376
	20:44 thousand men; all these *were* **m** of valour.	376
	20:45 of them in the highways five thousand **m**;	376
	20:45 and slew two thousand **m** of them.	376
	20:46 and five thousand **m** that drew the sword;	376
	20:46 the sword; all these *were* **m** of valour.	376
	20:47 six hundred **m** turned and fled to	376
	20:48 the **m** of Israel turned again upon	376
	20:48 as well the **m** of *every* city, as the beast,	4974
	21: 1 the **m** of Israel had sworn in Mizpeh,	376
	21:10 twelve thousand **m** of the valiantest,	376
Ru	2: 9 I not charged the **young m** that *they*	5288
	2: 9 drink of *that* which the **young m** have	5288
	2:15 Boaz commanded his **young m**, saying,	5288
	2:21 Thou shalt keep fast by my **young m**,	5288
	3:10 as *thou* followedst not **young m**,	970
	4: 2 he took ten **m** of the elders of the city,	376
1Sa	2: 4 The bows of the mighty *m are* broken,	NIH
	2:17 Wherefore the sin of the **young m** was	5288
	2:17 for **m** abhorred the offering of the LORD.	NIH
	2:26 both with the LORD, and also with **m**.	376
	4: 2 army in the field about four thousand **m**.	376
	4: 9 Be strong, and quit yourselves like **m**, O	376

1Sa	4: 9 to you: quit yourselves like **m**, and fight.	376
	5: 7 when the **m** of Ashdod saw that *it was* so,	376
	5: 9 he smote the **m** of the city, both small and	376
	5:12 the **m** that died not were smitten with	376
	6:10 the **m** did so; and took two milch kine,	376
	6:15 the **m** of Beth-shemesh offered burnt	376
	6:19 he smote the **m** of Beth-shemesh, because	376
	6:19 fifty thousand and threescore and ten **m**:	376
	6:20 the **m** of Beth-shemesh said, Who is able to	376
	7: 1 the **m** of Kirjath-jearim came,	376
	7:11 And the **m** of Israel went out of Mizpeh,	376
	8:16 your goodliest **young m**, and your asses,	970
	8:22 Samuel said unto the **m** of Israel, Go ye	376
	10: 2 shalt find two **m** by Rachel's sepulchre	376
	10: 3 there shall meet thee three **m** going up to	376
	10:26 there went with him a **band of m**,	2428
	11: 1 all the **m** of Jabesh said unto Nahash,	376
	11: 5 told him the tidings of the **m** of Jabesh.	376
	11: 8 and the **m** of Judah thirty thousand.	376
	11: 9 Thus shall ye say unto the **m** of	376
	11: 9 and shewed *it* to the **m** of Jabesh;	376
	11:10 Therefore the **m** of Jabesh said, To morrow	376
	11:12 the **m**, that we may put them to death.	376
	11:15 and all the **m** of Israel rejoiced greatly.	376
	13: 2 chose him three thousand *m* of Israel;	NIH
	13: 6 the **m** of Israel saw that they were in a	376
	13:15 present with him, about six hundred **m**.	376
	14: 2 *were* with him *were* about six hundred **m**;	376
	14:12 the **m** of the garrison answered Jonathan	376
	14:14 armourbearer made, was about twenty **m**,	376
	14:22 Likewise all the **m** of Israel which had hid	376
	14:24 the **m** of Israel were distressed that day:	376
	15: 4 and ten thousand **m** of Judah.	376
	17: 2 of Israel were gathered together,	376
	17:12 the man went among **m** *for* an old man in	376
	17:19 Saul, and they, and all the **m** of Israel,	376
	17:24 the **m** of Israel, when they saw the man,	376
	17:25 the **m** of Israel said, Have ye seen this man	376
	17:26 David spake to the **m** that stood by him,	376
	17:28 brother heard when he spake unto the **m**;	376
	17:52 the **m** of Israel and of Judah arose,	376
	18: 5 Saul set him over the **m** of war, and he	376
	18:27 he and his **m**, and slew of the Philistines	376
	18:27 slew of the Philistines two hundred **m**;	376
	21: 4 if the **young m** have kept themselves at	5288
	21: 5 the vessels of the **young m** are holy,	5288
	21:15 *Have* I need of **mad m**, that ye have	7696
	22: 2 were with him about four hundred **m**.	376
	22: 6 and the **m** that *were* with him,	376
	22:19 **m** and women, children and sucklings,	376
	23: 3 David's **m** said unto him, Behold, we *be*	376
	23: 5 So David and his **m** went *to* Keilah,	376
	23: 8 *to* Keilah, to besiege David and his **m**.	376
	23:11 Will the **m** of Keilah deliver me up into	1167
	23:12 Will the **m** of Keilah deliver me and my	1167
	23:12 me and my **m** into the hand of Saul?	376
	23:13 David and his **m**, which were about six	376
	23:24 and his **m** *were* in the wilderness of Maon,	376
	23:25 his **m** went to seek *him*. And they told	376
	23:26 and his **m** on that side of the mountain:	376
	23:26 Saul and his **m** compassed David and his	376
	23:26 and his **m** round about to take them.	376
	24: 2 Saul took three thousand chosen **m** out of	376
	24: 2 his **m** upon the rocks of the wild goats.	376
	24: 3 his **m** remained in the sides of the cave.	376
	24: 4 the **m** of David said unto him, Behold	376
	24: 6 he said unto his **m**, The LORD forbid that I	376
	24:22 David and his **m** gat them up unto the	376
	25: 5 David sent out ten **young m**, Get you	5288
	25: 5 David said unto the **young m**, Get you	5288
	25: 8 Ask thy **young m**, and they will shew	5288
	25: 8 Wherefore let the **young m** find favour in	5288
	25: 9 when David's **young m** came, they spake	5288
	25:11 give *it* unto **m**, whom I know not whence	376
	25:12 So David's **young m** turned their way,	5288
	25:13 David said unto his **m**, Gird you on every	376
	25:13 up after David about four hundred **m**;	376
	25:14 one of the **young m** told Abigail,	5288
	25:15 the **m** *were* very good unto us, and we	376
	25:20 David and his **m** came down against her;	376
	25:25 I thine handmaid saw not the **young m** of	5288
	25:27 even be given unto the **young m** that	5288
	26: 2 having three thousand chosen **m** of Israel	376
	26:19 if *they be* the children of **m**, cursed *be*	120
	26:22 let one of the **young m** come over and	5288
	27: 2 passed over with the six hundred **m** that	376
	27: 3 and his **m**, every man with his household,	376
	27: 8 David and his **m** went up, and invaded	376
	28: 1 go out with me to battle, thou and thy **m**.	376
	28: 8 two **m** with him, and they came to	376
	29: 2 **m** passed on in the rereward with Achish.	376
	29: 4 *should it* not *be* with the heads of these **m**?	376
	29:11 **m** rose up early to depart in the morning,	376
	30: 1 **m** were come to Ziklag on the third day,	376
	30: 3 So David and his **m** came to the city,	376
	30: 9 the six hundred **m** that *were* with him,	376
	30:10 David pursued, he and four hundred **m**:	376
	30:17 save four hundred **young m**,	376+5288
	30:21 David came to the two hundred **m**,	376
	30:22 answered all the wicked **m** and *men* of	376
	30:22 all the wicked men, and *m* of Belial,	NIH
	30:31 David himself and his **m** were wont to	376
	31: 1 the **m** of Israel fled from before	376
	31: 6 and his armourbearer, and all his **m**,	376

1Sa 31: 7	the **m** of Israel that *were* on the *other*	376
31: 7	saw that the **m** of Israel fled, and that Saul	376
31:12	All the valiant **m** arose, and went all night,	376
2Sa 1:11	and likewise all the **m** that *were* with him:	376
1:15	David called one of the **young m**, and	5288
2: 3	his **m** that *were* with him did David bring	376
2: 4	the **m** of Judah came, and there they	376
2: 4	*That* the **m** of Jabesh-gilead *were* they that	376
2: 5	David sent messengers unto the **m** of	376
2:14	Let the **young m** now arise, and play	5288
2:17	Abner was beaten, and the **m** of Israel,	376
2:21	lay thee hold on one of the **young m**,	5288
2:29	**m** walked all that night through the plain,	376
2:30	lacked of David's servants nineteen **m**	376
2:31	of Abner's, *so that* three hundred and	376
2:31	*that* three hundred and threescore **m** died.	376
2:32	Joab and his **m** went all night, and they	376
3:20	David *to* Hebron, and twenty **m** with him.	376
3:20	and the **m** that *were* with him a feast.	376
3:34	as *a man* falleth before wicked **m**,	1121
3:39	the sons of Zeruiah *be* too hard for	376
4: 2	Saul's son had two **m** that *were* captains	376
4:11	when wicked **m** have slain a righteous	376
4:12	David commanded *his* **young m**,	5288
5: 6	**m** went *to* Jerusalem unto the Jebusites,	376
5:21	and David and his **m** burnt them.	376
6: 1	David gathered together all the chosen **m**	NIH
6:19	as well to the women as **m**, to every one	376
7: 9	like unto the name of the great **m** that *are*	NIH
7:14	I will chasten him with the rod of **m**,	376
7:14	and with the stripes of the children of **m**:	120
8: 5	the Syrians two and twenty thousand **m**.	376
8:13	valley of salt, *being* eighteen thousand **m**.	NIH
10: 5	because the **m** were greatly ashamed:	376
10: 6	king Maacah a thousand **m**, and of Ish-tob	376
10: 6	and of Ish-tob twelve thousand **m**.	376
10: 7	Joab, and all the host *of* the mighty **m**.	NIH
10: 9	he chose of all the choice **m** of Israel,	376
10:12	let us **play the m** for our people,	2388
10:18	David slew the **m** of *seven* hundred	NIH
11:16	place where he knew that valiant **m** *were*.	376
11:17	the **m** of the city went out, and fought	376
11:23	Surely the **m** prevailed against us,	376
12: 1	unto him, There were two **m** in one city;	376
13: 9	Amnon said, Have out all **m** from me.	376
13:32	slain all the **young m** the king's sons;	5288
15: 1	and horses, and fifty **m** to run before him.	376
15: 6	Absalom stole the hearts of the **m** of Israel.	376
15:11	with Absalom went two hundred **m** out of	376
15:13	The hearts of the **m** of Israel are after	376
15:18	six hundred **m** which came after him from	376
15:22	all his **m**, and all the little ones that *were*	376
16: 2	and summer fruit for the **young m** to eat;	5288
16: 6	all the mighty **m** *were* on his right hand	NIH
16:13	David and his **m** went by the way, Shimei	376
16:15	and all the people the **m** of Israel,	376
16:18	people, and all the **m** of Israel, choose,	376
17: 1	me now choose out twelve thousand **m**,	376
17: 8	thou knowest thy father and his **m**, that	376
17: 8	they *be* mighty **m**, and they *be* chafed	NIH
17:10	*they* which *be* with him *are* valiant **m**.	1121
17:12	all the **m** that *are* with him there shall not	376
17:14	Absalom and all the **m** of Israel said,	376
17:24	he and all the **m** of Israel with him.	376
18: 7	slaughter that day *of* twenty thousand **m**.	NIH
18:15	ten **young m** that bare Joab's armour	5288
18:28	which hath delivered up the **m** that lift up	376
19:14	he bowed the heart of all the **m** of Judah,	376
19:16	came down with the **m** of Judah to meet	376
19:17	*there were* a thousand **m** of Benjamin	376
19:28	but dead **m** before my lord the king:	376
19:35	I hear any more the voice of singing **m**	NIH
19:41	all the **m** of Israel came to the king,	376
19:41	Why have our brethren the **m** of Israel	376
19:41	and all David's **m** with him, over Jordan?	376
19:42	all the **m** of Judah answered the men of	376
19:42	all the men of Judah answered the **m** of	376
19:43	the **m** of Israel answered the men of Judah,	376
19:43	the men of Israel answered the **m** of Judah,	376
19:43	the words of the **m** of Judah were fiercer	376
19:43	fiercer than the words of the **m** of Israel.	376
20: 2	the **m** of Judah clave unto their king,	376
20: 4	Assemble me the **m** of Judah *within* three	376
20: 5	Amasa went to assemble the **m** of Judah:	NIH
20: 7	there went out after him Joab's **m**,	376
20: 7	all the mighty **m**: and they went out of	NIH
20:11	one of Joab's **m** stood by him, and said,	5288
21: 6	seven of his sons be delivered unto us,	376
21:12	the bones of Jonathan his son from the **m**	1167
21:17	the **m** of David sware unto him, saying,	376
22: 5	the floods of **ungodly m** made me afraid;	1100
23: 3	He that ruleth over **m** *must be* just, ruling	120
23: 8	*be* the names of the mighty **m** whom	NIH
23: 9	*one* of the three mighty **m** with David,	NIH
23: 9	and the **m** of Israel were gone away:	376
23:16	the three mighty **m** brake through the host	NIH
23:17	*Is not* this the blood of the **m** that went in	376
23:17	These *things* did *these* three mighty **m**.	NIH
23:20	acts, he slew two **lionlike m** of Moab:	739
23:22	had the name among three mighty **m**.	NIH
24: 9	thousand valiant **m** that drew the sword;	376
24: 9	of Judah *were* five hundred thousand **m**.	376
24: 9	of Judah *were* five hundred thousand **m**.	376
24:15	even to Beer-sheba seventy thousand **m**.	376
1Ki 1: 5	horsemen, and fifty **m** to run before him.	376

1Ki 1: 8	the mighty **m** which *belonged* to David,	NIH
1: 9	and all the **m** of Judah the king's servants,	376
1:10	the mighty **m**, and Solomon his brother,	NIH
2:32	who fell upon two **m** more righteous and	376
4:31	For he was wiser than all **m**; than Ethan	120
5:13	and the levy was thirty thousand **m**.	376
8: 2	all the **m** of Israel assembled themselves	376
8:39	the hearts of all the children of **m**;)	120
9:22	they *were* **m** of war, and his servants,	376
10: 8	Happy *are* thy **m**, happy *are* these thy	376
11:18	and they took **m** with them out of Paran,	376
11:24	gathered **m** unto him, and became captain	376
12: 6	Rehoboam consulted with the **old m**,	2205
12: 8	he forsook the counsel of the **old m**,	2205
12: 8	consulted with the **young m** that were	3206
12:10	**young m** that were grown up with him	3206
12:14	to them after the counsel of the **young m**,	3206
12:21	fourscore thousand chosen **m**, which were	NIH
13:25	**m** passed by, and saw the carcase cast in	376
18:13	how I hid an hundred **m** of the LORD's	376
18:22	prophets *are* four hundred and fifty **m**.	376
20:14	*Even* by the **young m** of the princes of	5288
20:15	numbered the **young m** of the princes of	5288
20:17	**young m** of the princes of the provinces	5288
20:17	There are **m** come out of Samaria.	376
20:19	So these **young m** of the princes of	5288
20:30	seven thousand of the **m** that were left.	376
20:33	the **m** did diligently observe whether	376
2Ki 2: 7	fifty **m** of the sons of the prophets went,	376
2:16	there be with thy servants fifty strong **m**;	376
2:17	They sent therefore fifty **m**; and they	376
2:19	the **m** of the city said unto Elisha, Behold,	376
3:26	took with him seven hundred **m** that drew	376
4:22	one of the **young m**, and one of the asses,	5288
4:40	So they poured out for the **m** to eat. And it	376
4:43	should I set this before an hundred **m**?	376
5:22	two **young m** of the sons of the prophets:	5288
5:24	and he let the **m** go, and they departed.	376
6:20	the eyes of these **m**, that they may see.	NIH
7: 3	were four leprous **m** at the entering in	376
8:12	young **m** wilt thou slay with the sword,	NIH
10: 6	take ye the heads of the **m** your master's	NIH
10: 6	*were* with the great **m** of the city,	NIH
10:11	all his great **m**, and his kinsfolks,	376
10:14	the shearing house, *even* two and forty **m**;	376
10:24	Jehu appointed fourscore **m** without,	376
10:24	*If* any of the **m** whom I *have* brought into	376
11: 9	took every man his **m** that were to come	376
12:15	Moreover they reckoned not with the **m**,	376
13:21	they spied a band *of* **m**; and they cast	NIH
15:20	of all the mighty **m** of wealth, of each	376
15:25	and with him fifty **m** of the Gileadites:	376
17:24	the king of Assyria brought **m** from	NIH
17:30	the **m** of Babylon made Succoth-benoth,	376
17:30	the **m** of Cuth made Nergal, and the men	376
17:30	and the **m** of Hamath made Ashima,	376
18:27	he not *sent me* to the **m** which sit on	376
20:14	and said unto him, What said these **m**?	376
23: 2	all the **m** of Judah and all the inhabitants	376
23:14	and filled their places with the bones of **m**.	120
23:17	**m** of the city told him, *It is* the sepulchre	376
24:14	princes, and all the mighty **m** of valour,	NIH
24:16	all the **m** of might, *even* seven thousand,	376
25: 4	all the **m** of war *fled* by night *by* the way	376
25:19	an officer that was set over the **m** of war,	376
25:19	five **m** of them that were in the king's	376
25:19	threescore **m** of the people of the land that	376
25:23	captains of the armies, they and *their* **m**,	376
25:23	son of a Maachathite, they and their **m**.	376
25:24	them, and to their **m**, and said unto them,	376
25:25	and ten **m** with him, and smote Gedaliah,	376
1Ch 4:12	of Irnahash. These *are* the **m** of Rechah.	376
4:22	the **m** of Chozeba, and Joash, and Saraph,	376
4:42	five hundred **m**, went to mount Seir,	376
5:18	valiant **m**, men *able* to bear buckler and	1121
5:18	**m** *able* to bear buckler and sword,	376
5:21	and *of* **m** an hundred thousand.	120+5315
5:24	and Jahdiel, mighty **m** of valour,	376
5:24	famous **m**, *and* heads of the house of their	376
7: 2	*they were* valiant **m** of might in their	NIH
7: 3	and Joel, Ishiah, five: all of them chief **m**.	NIH
7: 4	thousand **m**: for they had many wives	NIH
7: 5	the families of Issachar **m** of might,	1368
7: 7	house of *their* fathers, mighty **m** of valour;	NIH
7: 9	mighty **m** of valour, *was* twenty thousand	NIH
7:11	mighty **m** of valour, *were* seventeen	NIH
7:21	whom the **m** of Gath that were born in	376
7:40	choice *and* mighty **m** of valour, chief of	NIH
7:40	to battle *was* twenty and six thousand **m**	NIH
8:28	chief **m**. These dwelt in Jerusalem.	NIH
8:40	the sons of Ulam were mighty **m** of valour,	376
9: 9	All these **m** *were* chief of the fathers in	376
9:13	very able **m** *for* the work of the service of	1368
10: 1	the **m** of Israel fled from before	376
10: 7	when all the **m** of Israel that *were* in	376
10:12	all the valiant **m**, and took away the body	376
11:10	These also *are* the chief of the mighty **m**	NIH
11:11	this *is* the number of the mighty **m** whom	NIH
11:19	**m** that have put their lives in jeopardy?	376
11:22	acts; he slew two **lionlike m** of Moab:	739

1Ch 11:26	Also the valiant **m** of the armies were,	NIH
12: 1	they *were* among the mighty **m**, helpers	NIH
12: 8	the hold to the wilderness **m** of might,	1368
12: 8	*and* **m** of war *fit* for the battle, that could	NIH
12:21	for they *were* all mighty **m** of valour,	NIH
12:25	mighty **m** of valour for the war,	NIH
12:30	and eight hundred, mighty **m** of valour,	NIH
12:32	which *were* **m** that had understanding of	376
12:38	All these **m** of war, that could keep rank,	376
16:31	let **m** say among the nations, The LORD	NIH
17: 8	name of the great **m** that *are* in the earth.	NIH
18: 5	the Syrians two and twenty thousand **m**.	NIH
19: 5	and told David how the **m** were served.	376
19: 5	for the **m** were greatly ashamed.	376
19: 8	Joab, and all the host *of* the mighty **m**.	NIH
19:18	slew of the Syrians seven thousand **m**	NIH
21: 5	an hundred thousand **m** that drew sword:	376
21: 5	and ten thousand **m** that drew sword.	376
21:14	there fell of Israel seventy thousand **m**.	376
22:15	all *manner of* cunning **m** for every	NIH
24: 4	there were moe chief **m** found of the sons	1397
24: 4	sixteen chief **m** of the house of *their*	NIH
26: 6	for they *were* mighty **m** of valour.	NIH
26: 7	whose brethren *were* strong **m**, Elihu,	1121
26: 8	able **m** for strength for the service,	376
26: 9	had sons and brethren, strong **m**,	1121
26:12	among the chief **m**, *having* wards one	1397
26:30	**m** of valour, a thousand and seven	1121
26:31	were found among them mighty **m** of	NIH
26:32	his brethren, **m** of valour, *were* two	1121
28: 1	the mighty **m**, and with all the valiant	NIH
28: 1	mighty **men**, and with all the valiant **m**,	1368
29:24	the mighty **m**, and all the sons likewise of	NIH
2Ch 2: 2	and ten thousand **m** to bear burdens,	376
2: 7	can skill to grave with the cunning **m**	NIH
2:14	with thy cunning **m**, and with the	NIH
2:14	with the cunning **m** of my lord David thy	NIH
5: 3	Wherefore all the **m** of Israel assembled	376
6:18	will God in very deed dwell with **m** on	120
6:30	knowest the hearts of the children of **m**:)	120
8: 9	they *were* **m** of war, and chief of his	376
9: 7	Happy *are* thy **m**, and happy *are* these thy	376
10: 6	Rehoboam took counsel with the **old m**	2205
10: 8	he forsook the counsel which the **old m**	2205
10: 8	took counsel with the **young m** that	3206
10:10	the **young m** that were brought up with	3206
10:13	forsook the counsel of the **old m**,	2205
10:14	them after the advice of the **young m**,	3206
11: 1	fourscore thousand chosen **m**, which	NIH
13: 3	in array with an army of valiant **m** of war,	NIH
13: 3	*even* four hundred thousand chosen **m**:	376
13: 3	with eight hundred thousand chosen **m**,	376
13: 3	chosen men, *being* mighty **m** of valour.	NIH
13: 7	there are gathered unto him vain **m**,	376
13:15	the **m** of Judah gave a shout: and as the	376
13:15	as the **m** of Judah shouted, it came to pass,	376
13:17	of Israel five hundred thousand chosen **m**.	376
14: 8	Asa had an army of **m** that bare targets	NIH
14: 8	all these *were* mighty **m** of valour.	NIH
17:13	the **m** of war, mighty **men** of valour,	376
17:13	the men of war, mighty **m** of valour,	NIH
17:14	him mighty **m** of valour three hundred	NIH
17:16	him two hundred thousand mighty **m**	NIH
17:17	him armed **m** with bow and shield two	NIH
18: 5	together *of* prophets four hundred **m**,	376
22: 1	for the band *of* **m** that came with	NIH
23: 8	took every man his **m** that were to come	376
24:24	Syrians came with a small *company* of **m**,	376
25: 5	thousand choice **m**, *able* to go forth *to*	NIH
25: 6	of valour out of Israel for an hundred	NIH
26:11	Uzziah had a host of fighting **m**,	NIH
26:12	mighty **m** of valour *were* two thousand	NIH
26:15	invented by cunning **m**, to be on the	NIH
26:17	priests of the LORD, *that were* valiant **m**:	1121
28: 6	in one day, *which were* all valiant **m**;	1121
28:14	So the armed **m** left the captives and	NIH
28:15	the **m** which were expressed by name rose	376
31:19	the **m** that were expressed by name,	NIH
32: 3	his mighty **m** to stop the waters of	NIH
32:21	which cut off all the mighty **m** of valour,	NIH
34:12	the **m** did the work faithfully:	376
34:30	all the **m** of Judah, and the inhabitants of	376
35:25	all the singing **m** and the singing **women**	NIH
36:17	slew their **young m** with the sword in	970
Ezr 1: 4	let the **m** of his place help him with silver,	376
2: 2	number of the **m** of the people of Israel:	376
2:22	The **m** of Netophah, fifty and six.	376
2:23	The **m** of Anathoth, an hundred twenty	376
2:27	The **m** of Michmas, an hundred twenty	376
2:28	The **m** of Beth-el and Ai, two hundred	376
2:65	among them two hundred singing **m**	NIH
3:12	**ancient m** that had seen the first	2205
4:11	Thy servants the **m** *on this* side the river,	606
4:21	commandment to cause these **m** to cease,	1400
5: 4	What are the names of the **m** that make	1400
5:10	we might write the names of the **m** that	1400
6: 8	expences be given unto these **m**,	1400
7:28	I gathered together out of Israel chief **m** to	NIH
8:16	chief **m**; also for Joiarib, and for Elnathan,	NIH
8:16	and for Elnathan, **m** of understanding.	NIH
10: 1	out of Israel a very great congregation *of* **m**	376
10: 9	all the **m** of Judah and Benjamin gathered	376
10:17	they made an end with all the **m** that had	376
Ne 1: 2	came, he and *certain* **m** of Judah;	376
2:12	in the night, I and *some* few **m** with me;	376

M

M

Ne
3: 2 next unto him builded the **m** of Jericho. 376
3: 7 the **m** of Gibeon, and of Mizpah, 376
3:22 repaired the priests, the **m** of the plain. 376
4:23 nor the **m** of the guard which followed me, 376
5: 5 *redeem them;* for **other m** have our lands 312
7: 7 *I say,* of the **m** of the people of Israel *was* 376
7:26 The **m** of Beth-lehem and Netophah, 376
7:27 The **m** of Anathoth, an hundred twenty 376
7:28 The **m** of Beth-azmaveth, forty and two. 376
7:29 The **m** of Kirjath-jearim, Chephirah, 376
7:30 The **m** of Ramah and Geba, six hundred 376
7:31 The **m** of Michmas, an hundred and 376
7:32 The **m** of Beth-el and Ai, an hundred 376
7:33 The **m** of the other Nebo, fifty and two. 376
7:67 and five singing *m* and singing **women.** NIH
8: 2 the law before the congregation both of **m** 376
8: 3 before the **m** and the women, and those 376
11: 2 the people blessed all the **m**, that willingly 376
11: 6 hundred threescore and eight valiant **m.** 376
11:14 mighty *m* of valour, an hundred twenty NIH
11:14 Zabdiel, the son of *one of* the great **m.** 376
13:16 There dwelt **m of Tyre** also therein, 6876

Est
1:13 the king said to the wise **m**, which knew NIH
6:13 said his wise *m* and Zeresh his wife unto NIH
9: 6 Jews slew and destroyed five hundred **m.** 376
9:12 destroyed five hundred **m** in Shushan 376
9:15 and slew three hundred **m** at Shushan; 376

Job
1: 3 this man was the greatest of all the **m** 1121
1:19 it fell upon the **young m**, and they are 5288
4:13 the night, when deep sleep falleth on **m.** 376
7:20 I do unto thee, O thou preserver of **m?** 120
11: 3 Should thy lies make **m** hold their peace? 4962
11:11 For he knoweth vain **m**: he seeth 4962
15:10 both the grayheaded and **very aged m,** 3453
15:18 wise *m* have told from their fathers, NIH
17: 8 Upright *m* shall be astonied at this, 376
22:15 old way which wicked **m** have trodden? 4962
22:29 *m* are cast down, then thou shalt say, NIH
24:12 **M** groan from out of the city, and the soul 4962
27:23 **M** shall clap their hands at him, NIH
28: 4 are dried up, they are gone away from **m.** 582
29: 8 **young m** saw me, and hid themselves: 5288
29:21 Unto me *m* gave ear, and waited, NIH
30: 5 They were driven forth from among **m**, NIH
30: 8 of fools, yea, children of **base m:** 1097+8034
31:31 If the **m** of my tabernacle said not, O that 4962
32: 1 So these three **m** ceased to answer Job, 376
32: 5 no answer in the mouth of *these* three **m**, 376
32: 9 **Great m** are not *always* wise: neither do 7227
33:15 night, when deep sleep falleth upon **m,** 376
33:16 he openeth the ears of **m**, and sealeth their 376
33:27 He looketh upon **m**, and *if any* say, I have 376
34: 2 O ye wise **m**; and give ear unto me, NIH
34: 8 of iniquity, and walketh with wicked **m.** 376
34:10 hearken unto me, ye **m** of understanding: NIH
34:24 He shall break in pieces mighty **m** without NIH
34:26 He striketh them as wicked *m* in the open NIH
34:34 Let **m** of understanding tell me, and let a 376
34:36 because of *his* answers for wicked **m.** 376
35:12 because of the pride of **evil m.** 7451
36:24 thou magnify his work, which **m** behold. 376
37: 7 every man; that all **m** may know his work. 376
37:21 now **m** see not the bright light which *is* in NIH
37:24 **M** do therefore fear him: he respecteth not 376
39:21 He goeth on to meet the **armed m.** 5402

Ps
4: 2 O ye sons of **m**, how long *will ye* turn my 376
9:20 may know themselves *to be but* **m.** 582
11: 4 his eyelids try, the children of **m.** 120
12: 1 faithful fail from among the children of **m.** 120
12: 8 when the vilest **m** are exalted. 120+1121
14: 2 from heaven upon the children of **m**, 120
4: 4 Concerning the works of **m**, by the word 120
17:14 From *which are* thy hand, O LORD, 4962
17:14 thy hand, O LORD, from **m** of the world, 4962
18: 4 the floods of **ungodly m** made me afraid. 1100
21:10 their seed from among the children of **m.** 120
22: 6 reproach of **m**, and despised of the people. 120
26: 9 with sinners, nor my life with bloody **m**: 376
31:19 that trust in thee before the sons of **m!** 120
33:13 heaven; he beholdeth all the sons of **m.** 120
36: 7 the children of **m** put their trust under 120
45: 2 Thou art fairer than the children of **m:** 120
49:10 For he seeth *that* wise **m** die, likewise NIH
49:18 *m* will praise thee, when thou doest well NIH
53: 2 from heaven upon the children of **m**, 120
55:23 deceitful **m** shall not live out half their 376
57: 4 the sons of **m**, whose teeth *are* spears 120
58: 1 do ye judge uprightly, O ye sons of **m?** 376
59: 2 of iniquity, and save me from bloody **m.** 376
62: 9 Surely **m of low degree** *are* vanity, 120+1121
62: 9 and **m of high degree** *are* a lie: 376+1121
64: 9 all **m** shall fear, and shall declare the work 120
66: 5 *in his* doing toward the children of **m.** 120
66:12 hast caused **m** to ride over our heads; 582
68:18 thou hast received gifts for **m;** yea, 120
72:17 **m** shall be blessed in him: all nations shall NIH
73: 5 They are not in trouble *as other* **m;** 582
73: 5 neither are they plagued like *other* **m.** 120
76: 5 none of the **m** of might have found their 376
78:31 and smote down the chosen **m** of Israel. NIH
78:60 the tent *which* he placed among **m;** 120
78:63 The fire consumed their **young m;** 970
82: 7 ye shall die like **m**, and fall like one of 120
83:18 That *m* may know that thou, whose name NIH
86:14 the assemblies of violent **m** have sought NIH

Ps
89:47 hast thou made all **m** in vain? 120+1121
90: 3 and sayest, Return, ye children of **m.** 120
105:12 When they were *but a few* **m** in number; 4962
107: 8 Oh that **m** would praise the LORD *for* his NIH
107: 8 his wonderful works to the children of **m!** NIH
107:15 Oh that **m** would praise the LORD *for* his 120
107:15 his wonderful works to the children of **m!** 120
107:21 Oh that **m** would praise the LORD *for* his 120
107:21 his wonderful works to the children of **m!** 120
107:31 Oh that **m** would praise the LORD *for* his 120
107:31 his wonderful works to the children of **m!** 120
115:16 earth hath he given to the children of **m.** 120
116:11 I said in my haste, All **m** *are* liars. 120
124: 2 on our side, when **m** rose up against us: 120
139:19 depart from me therefore, ye bloody **m**: 376
141: 4 practise wicked works with **m** that work 376
145: 6 **m** shall speak of the might of thy terrible NIH
145:12 make known to the sons of **m** his mighty 120
148:12 Both **young m**, and maidens; old men, 970
148:12 and maidens; **old m**, and children: 2205

Pr
2:20 thou mayest walk in the way of good **m**, NIH
4:14 and go not in the way of evil **m.** NIH
6:30 **M** do not despise a thief, if he steal to NIH
7:26 many strong **m** *have been* slain by her. NIH
8: 4 Unto you, O **m**, I call; and my voice *is* to 376
8:31 and my delights *were* with the sons of **m.** 120
10:14 Wise **m** lay up knowledge: but the mouth NIH
11: 7 and the hope of unjust *m* perisheth. NIH
11:16 honour: and strong **m** retain riches. NIH
12:12 The wicked desireth the net of evil **m:** NIH
13:20 that walketh with wise **m** shall be wise: NIH
15:11 then the hearts of the children of **m?** 120
16: 6 by the fear of the LORD *m* depart from NIH
17: 6 children *are* the crown of **old m;** 2205
18:16 for him, and bringeth him before great **m.** NIH
20: 5 Most **m** will proclaim every one his own 120
20:29 The glory of **young m** *is* their strength: 970
20:29 and the beauty of **old m** *is* the gray head. 2205
22:29 he shall not stand before mean **m.** NIH
23:28 and increaseth the transgressors among **m.** 120
24: 1 Be not thou envious against evil **m**, 376
24: 9 and the scorner *is* an abomination to **m.** 120
24:19 of evil **m**, neither be thou envious at NIH
25: 1 which the **m** of Hezekiah king of Judah 376
25: 6 and stand not in the place of great **m:** NIH
25:27 *m* to search their own glory *is not* glory. NIH
26:16 than seven *m* that can render a reason. NIH
28: 5 Evil **m** understand not judgment: 376
28: 7 that is a companion of riotous **m** shameth NIH
28:12 When righteous *m* do rejoice, *there is* 120
28:28 When the wicked rise, **m** hide themselves: 120
29: 8 Scornful **m** bring a city into a snare: NIH
29: 8 into a snare: but wise *m* turn away wrath. NIH
30:14 the earth, and the needy from *among* **m.** 120

Ecc
2: 3 see what *was* that good for the sons of **m**, NIH
2: 8 I gat me **m** singers and **women** singers, NIH
2: 8 and the delights of the sons of **m**, 120
3:10 God hath given to the sons of **m** to be 120
3:14 doeth *it*, that **m** should fear before him. 120
3:18 concerning the estate of the sons of **m**, 120
3:19 For that which befalleth the sons of **m** 120
6: 1 the sun, and it *is* common among **m:** 120
7: 2 for that *is* the end of all **m**; and the living 120
7:19 than ten mighty *m* which are in the city. 120
8:11 heart of the sons of **m** is fully set in them 120
8:14 that there be just **m**, unto whom it 120
8:14 there be wicked **m**, to whom it happeneth NIH
9: 3 the heart of the sons of **m** is full *of* evil, 120
9:11 nor yet riches to **m**s of understanding, 1886.1
9:11 nor yet favour to **m**s of skill; 1886.1
9:12 *are* the sons of **m** snared in an evil time, 120
9:14 was a little city, and few **m** within it; 376
9:17 The words of wise **m** *are* heard in quiet, 376
12: 3 and the strong **m** shall bow themselves, 376

SS
3: 7 threescore valiant *m* are about it, NIH
4: 4 bucklers, all shields of mighty **m.** NIH

Isa
2:11 haughtiness of **m** shall be bowed down, 376
2:17 the haughtiness of **m** shall be made low: NIH
3:25 Thy **m** shall fall by the sword, 4962
5: 3 **m** of Judah, judge, I pray you, betwixt me 376
5: 7 and the **m** of Judah his pleasant plant: 376
5:13 their honourable **m** *are* famished, 4962
5:22 and **m** of strength to mingle strong drink: 120
6:12 And the LORD have removed **m** far away, 120
7:13 *Is it* a small thing for you to weary **m**, 376
7:24 and with bows shall **m** come thither; 376
9: 3 as **m** rejoice when they divide the spoil. NIH
9:17 Lord shall have no joy in their **young m**, 970
11:15 and make **m** go over dryshod. NIH
13:18 *Their* bows also shall dash the **young m** 5288
19:12 where *are* thy wise **m?** and let them tell NIH
21: 9 behold, here cometh a chariot of **m**, *with* 376
21:17 the mighty **m** of the children of Kedar, NIH
22: 2 thy slain **m** *are* not slain with the sword, 376
22: 6 Elam bare the quiver with chariots of **m** 120
23: 4 neither do I nourish up **young m**, *nor* 970
24: 6 of the earth are burned, and few **m** left. 582
26:19 Thy dead **m** shall live, *together with* my 5288
28:14 hear the word of the LORD, ye scornful **m**, NIH
29:11 which *m* deliver to one that is learned, 376
29:13 towards me is taught *by* the precept of **m**: 376
29:14 the wisdom of their wise **m** shall perish, NIH
29:14 understanding of their prudent **m** shall NIH
29:19 the poor among **m** shall rejoice in the Holy 120
31: 3 Now the Egyptians *are* **m**, and not God; 120

Isa
31: 8 and his **young m** shall be discomfited. 970
35: 8 the **wayfaring m**, though fools, 1870+1980
36:12 *he* not *sent me* to the **m** that sit upon 376
38:16 by these *things* **m** live, and in all these 376
39: 3 and said unto him, What said these **m?** 376
40:30 weary, and the **young m** shall utterly fall: 970
41: 9 and called thee from the **chief m** thereof, 678
41:14 thou worm Jacob, *and* ye **m** of Israel; 4962
43: 4 therefore will I give **m** for thee, 120
44:11 workmen, they *are* of **m**: let them be all 120
44:25 that turneth wise **m** backward, NIH
45:14 Ethiopia and of the Sabeans, **m** of stature, 376
45:24 to him shall *m* come; and all that are NIH
46: 8 Remember this, and **shew yourselves m**: 377
51: 7 fear ye not the reproach of **m**, neither be 582
52:14 and his form more than the sons of **m:** 376
53: 3 He is despised and rejected of **m**; a man of 376
57: 1 merciful **m** *are* taken away, none 376
59:10 *we are* in desolate places as dead **m.** NIH
60:11 that *m* may bring unto thee the forces of NIH
61: 6 **m** shall call you the Ministers of our God: NIH
64: 4 since the beginning of the world **m** have NIH
66:24 look upon the carcases of the **m** that have NIH

Jer
4: 3 For thus saith the LORD to the **m** of Judah 376
4: 4 **m** of Judah and inhabitants of Jerusalem: 376
5: 1 I will get me unto the **great m**, 1419
5:16 an open sepulchre, they *are* all mighty **m.** NIH
5:26 among my people are found wicked **m**: 376
5:26 snares; they set a trap, they catch **m.** 376
6:11 upon the assembly of **young m** together: 970
6:23 set in array as **m** for war against thee, 376
6:30 Reprobate silver shall **m** call them, NIH
8: 9 wise **m** are ashamed, they are dismayed NIH
9: 2 a lodging place of **wayfaring m;** 732
9: 2 an assembly of treacherous **m.** NIH
9:10 neither can **m** hear the voice of the cattle; NIH
9:21 *and* the **young m** from the streets. 970
9:22 Even the carcases of **m** shall fall as dung 120
10: 7 forasmuch as among all the wise **m** of NIH
10: 9 they *are* all the work of cunning **m.** NIH
11: 2 speak unto the **m** of Judah, and to 376
11: 9 A conspiracy is found among the **m** of 376
11:21 Therefore thus saith the LORD of the **m** of 376
11:22 the **young m** shall die by the sword; 970
11:23 I will bring evil upon the **m** of Anathoth, 376
15: 8 of the **young m** a spoiler at noonday: 970
15:10 usury, nor **m** have lent to me on usury; NIH
16: 6 neither shall **m** lament for them, nor cut NIH
16: 7 Neither shall **m** tear *themselves* for them NIH
16: 7 neither shall **m** give them the cup of NIH
17:25 the **m** of Judah, and the inhabitants of 376
18:11 speak to the **m** of Judah, and to 376
18:21 widows; and let their **m** be put to death; 376
18:21 *let* their **young m** *be* slain by the sword in 970
19:10 in the sight of the **m** that go with thee. 376
20:21 with all his mighty **m**, and all the princes, 376
22:22 Jehoiakim the king sent **m** *into* Egypt, 376
22:22 and *certain* **m** with him into Egypt. 376
31:13 dance, both **young m** and old together: 970
32:19 open upon all the ways of the sons of **m:** 120
32:20 day, and in Israel, and amongst *other* **m;** 120
32:32 the **m** of Judah, and the inhabitants of 376
32:44 **M** shall buy fields for money, NIH
33: 5 *is* to fill them with the dead bodies of **m**, 120
34:18 I will give the **m** that have transgressed NIH
35:13 Go and tell the **m** of Judah and 376
36:31 of Jerusalem, and upon the **m** of Judah, 376
37:10 remained *but* wounded **m** among them, 376
38: 4 thus he weakeneth the hands of the **m** of 376
38: 9 these **m** have done evil in all that they 376
38:10 Take from hence thirty **m** with thee, 376
38:11 So Ebed-melech took the **m** with him, 376
38:16 into the hand of these **m** that seek thy life. 376
39: 4 all the **m** of war, then they fled, 376
39:17 shalt not be given into the hand of the **m** 376
40: 7 *were* in the fields, *even* they and their **m**, 376
40: 7 had committed unto him **m**, and women, 376
40: 8 son of a Maachathite, they and their **m.** 376
40: 9 Shaphan sware unto them and to their **m**, 376
41: 1 princes of the king, even ten **m** with him, 376
41: 2 the ten **m** that were with him, 376
41: 3 that were found there, *and* the **m** of war. 376
41: 5 and from Samaria, *even* fourscore **m**, 376
41: 7 the pit, he, and the **m** that *were* with him. 376
41: 8 ten **m** were found among them that said 376
41: 9 had cast all the dead bodies of the **m**, 376
41:12 they took all the **m**, and went to fight with 376
41:15 escaped from Johanan with eight **m**, 376
41:16 even mighty **m** of war, and the women, 376
42:17 So shall it be with all the **m** that set their 376
43: 2 all the proud **m**, saying unto Jeremiah, 376
43: 6 *Even* **m**, and women, and children, 1397
43: 9 Tahpanhes, in the sight of the **m** of Judah; 376
44:15 all the **m** which knew that their wives 376
44:19 drink offerings unto her, without our **m?** 376
44:20 to the **m**, and to the women, and to all 1397
44:27 all the **m** of Judah that *are* in the land of 376
46: 9 and let the mighty **m** come forth; NIH
46:15 Why are thy valiant **m** swept away? NIH
46:21 Also her **hired m** *are* in the midst of her 7916
47: 2 the **m** shall cry, and all the inhabitants of 120
48:14 We *are* mighty and strong **m** for the war? 376
48:15 his chosen **young m** are gone down to 970
48:31 *mine heart* shall mourn for the **m** of 376
48:36 heart shall sound like pipes for the **m** 376

Jer	49:15 the heathen, *and* despised among **m**.	120
	49:22 that day shall the heart of the mighty *m*	NIH
	49:26 Therefore her **young m** shall fall in her	970
	49:26 the **m** of war shall be cut off in that day,	376
	49:28 up to Kedar, and spoil the **m** of the east.	1121
	50:30 Therefore her **young m** shall fall	970
	50:30 all her **m** of war shall be cut off in that day,	376
	50:35 upon her princes, and upon her wise **m**.	NIH
	50:36 a sword *is* upon her mighty *m*;	NIH
	51: 3 spare ye not her **young m**; destroy ye	970
	51:14 Surely I will fill thee **with m**, as *with*	120
	51:30 The mighty **m** of Babylon have forborn to	NIH
	51:32 with fire, and the **m** of war are affrighted.	376
	51:56 Babylon, and her mighty **m** are taken,	NIH
	51:57 her wise **m**, her captains, and her rulers,	NIH
	51:57 her mighty **m**: and they shall sleep a	NIH
	52: 7 all the **m** of war fled, and went forth out	376
	52:13 the houses of the great **m**, burnt he with	NIH
	52:25 which had the charge of the **m** of war;	376
	52:25 seven of them that were near the king's	376
	52:25 threescore **m** of the people of the land,	376
La	1:15 foot all my mighty *m* in the midst of me:	NIH
	1:15 against me to crush my **young m**:	970
	1:18 and my **young m** are gone into captivity.	970
	2:15 saying, *Is* this the city that *m* call The	NIH
	2:21 and my **young m** are fallen by the sword;	970
	3:33 willingly nor grieve the children of **m**.	376
	4:14 They have wandered *as* blind *m* in	NIH
	4:14 so that **m** could not touch their garments.	NIH
	5:13 They took the **young m** to grind,	970
	5:14 the gate, the **young m** from their musick.	970
Eze	6: 4 I will cast down your slain **m** before your	NIH
	6:13 when their slain **m** shall be among their	NIH
	8:11 there stood before them seventy **m** of	376
	8:16 the altar, *were* about five and twenty **m**,	376
	9: 2 six **m** came from the way of the higher	376
	9: 4 a mark upon the foreheads of the **m** that	376
	9: 6 they began at the ancient **m** which *were*	376
	11: 1 at the door of the gate five and twenty **m**;	376
	11: 2 these *are* the **m** that devise mischief,	376
	11:15 the **m** of thy kindred, and all the house of	376
	12:16 will leave a few **m** of them from the sword,	376
	14: 3 **m** have set up their idols in their heart,	376
	14:14 Though these three **m**, Noah, Daniel,	376
	14:16 *Though* these three **m** *were* in it, *as* I live,	376
	14:18 Though these three **m** *were* in it, *as* I live,	376
	15: 3 will **m** take a pin of it to hang any vessel	NIH
	16:17 madest to thyself images of **m**,	2145
	19: 3 learned to catch the prey; it devoured **m**.	120
	19: 6 to catch the prey, *and* devoured **m**.	120
	21:14 *is* the sword of the great **m** *that are* slain,	NIH
	21:31 deliver thee into the hand of brutish **m**,	376
	22: 9 thee are **m** that carry tales to shed blood:	376
	23: 6 rulers, all of them desirable **young m**,	970
	23: 7 *with* all them *that were* the chosen **m** of	1121
	23:12 horses, all of them desirable **young m**,	970
	23:14 for when she saw **m** pourtrayed upon	376
	23:23 all of them desirable **young m**, captains	970
	23:40 that ye have sent for to come from far,	376
	23:42 the **m** of the common sort *were* brought	376
	23:45 righteous **m**, they shall judge them after	376
	24:17 not *thy* lips, and eat not the bread of **m**.	376
	24:22 cover *your* lips, nor eat the bread of **m**.	376
	25: 4 I *will* deliver thee to the **m** of the east for	1121
	25:10 the **m** of the east with the Ammonites,	1121
	26:10 as **m** enter into a city wherein is made a	NIH
	26:17 *that wast* inhabited of seafaring **m**,	NIH
	27: 8 thy wise **m**, O Tyrus, *that* were in thee,	NIH
	27: 9 wise **m** thereof were in thee thy calkers:	NIH
	27:10 of Phut and Lud in thine army, thy **m** of war:	376
	27:11 The **m** of Arvad with thine army *were*	1121
	27:13 they traded the persons of **m** and vessels	120
	27:15 The **m** of Dedan *were* thy merchants;	1121
	27:27 all thy **m** of war, that *are* in thee, and in	376
	30: 5 and the **m** of the land that is in league,	1121
	30:17 The **young m** of Aven and of Phi-beseth	970
	31:14 earth, in the midst of the children of **m**,	120
	34:31 *are* **m**, *and* I *am* your God, saith the Lord	120
	35: 8 I will fill his mountains *with* his slain **m**:	NIH
	36:10 I will multiply **m** upon you, all the house	120
	36:12 Yea, I will cause **m** to walk upon you,	120
	36:12 no more henceforth **bereave** them of **m**.	7921
	36:13 Thou *land* devourest up **m**,	120
	36:14 Therefore thou shalt devour **m** no more,	120
	36:15 Neither will I cause *m* to hear in thee	NIH
	36:37 I will increase them *with* **m** like a flock.	120
	36:38 the waste cities be filled *with* flocks of **m**:	120
	38:20 the **m** that *are* upon the face of the earth,	120
	39:14 they shall sever out **m** of continual	376
	39:20 with mighty **m**, and *with* all men of war,	NIH
	39:20 with mighty **men**, and *with* all **m** of war,	376
	47:15 the way of Hethlon, as **m** go to Zedad;	NIH
Da	2:12 commanded to destroy all the wise **m** of	NIH
	2:13 the decree went forth that the wise **m**	NIH
	2:14 which was gone forth to slay the wise **m**	NIH
	2:18 with the rest of the wise **m** of Babylon.	NIH
	2:24 to destroy the wise **m** of Babylon:	NIH
	2:24 Destroy not the wise **m**, the astrologians;	NIH
	2:27 cannot the wise **m**, the astrologians	NIH
	2:38 wheresoever the children of **m** dwell,	606
	2:43 mingle themselves with the seed of **m**:	606
	2:48 of the governors over all the wise **m** of	NIH
	3:12 these **m**, O king, have not regarded thee:	1400
	3:13 they brought these **m** before the king.	1400
	3:20 **most mighty m** that *were*	1400+1401+2429

Da	3:21 these **m** were bound in their coats,	1400
	3:22 flame of the fire slew those **m** that took	1400
	3:23 these three **m**, Shadrach, Meshach,	1400
	3:24 Did not we cast three **m** bound into	1400
	3:25 and said, Lo, I see four **m** loose,	1400
	3:27 being gathered together, saw these **m**,	1400
	4: 6 in all the wise **m** of Babylon before me,	NIH
	4:17 most High ruleth in the kingdom of **m**,	606
	4:17 and setteth up over it the basest of **m**.	606
	4:18 as all the wise **m** of my kingdom	NIH
	4:25 That they *shall* drive thee from **m**,	606
	4:25 most High ruleth in the kingdom of **m**,	606
	4:32 they *shall* drive thee from **m**,	606
	4:32 most High ruleth in the kingdom of **m**,	606
	4:33 he *was* driven from **m**, and did eat grass	606
	5: 7 and said to the wise **m** of Babylon,	NIH
	5: 8 came in all the king's wise **m**:	NIH
	5:15 the wise **m**, the astrologers, have been	NIH
	5:21 he *was* driven from the sons of **m**;	606
	5:21 most high God ruled in the kingdom of **m**,	606
	6: 5 said these **m**, We shall not find any	1400
	6:11 these **m** assembled, and found Daniel	1400
	6:15 these **m** assembled unto the king,	1400
	6:24 they brought those **m** which had accused	1400
	6:26 in every dominion of my kingdom **m**	NIH
	9: 7 to the **m** of Judah, and to the inhabitants	376
	10: 7 for the **m** that were with me saw not	376
	10:16 *one* like the similitude of the sons of **m**	120
Hos	6: 7 like as have transgressed the covenant:	120
	10:13 way, in the multitude of thy mighty **m**.	NIH
	13: 2 Let the **m** that sacrifice kiss the calves.	120
Joel	1: 2 Hear this, ye **old m**, and give ear, all ye	2205
	1:12 joy is withered away from the sons of **m**.	120
	2: 7 They shall run like mighty **m**; they shall	NIH
	2: 7 they shall climb the wall like **m** of war;	376
	2:28 your **old m** shall dream dreams,	2205
	2:28 your **young m** shall see visions:	970
	3: 9 wake up the mighty **m**, let all the men of	NIH
	3: 9 up the mighty **men**, let all the **m** of war	376
Am	2:11 and of your **young m** for Nazarites.	970
	4:10 **young m** have I slain with the sword,	970
	6: 9 if there remain ten **m** in one house, that	376
	8:13 fair virgins and **young m** faint for thirst.	970
Ob	1: 7 All the **m** of thy confederacy have brought	376
	1: 7 the **m** that were at peace with thee have	376
	1: 8 even destroy the wise **m** out of Edom,	NIH
	1: 9 mighty **m**, O Teman, shall be dismayed,	NIH
Jnh	1:10 were the **m** exceedingly afraid, and said	376
	1:10 For he knew that he fled from	NIH
	1:13 Nevertheless the **m** rowed hard to bring	NIH
	1:16 Then the **m** feared the Lord exceedingly,	376
Mic	2: 8 pass by securely *as* **m** averse from war.	376
	2:12 noise by reason of *the* multitude of **m**.	120
	5: 5 seven shepherds, and eight principal **m**.	120
	5: 5 for man, nor waiteth for the sons of **m**.	120
	6:12 For the rich **m** thereof are full of violence,	NIH
	7: 2 is none upright among **m**: they all lie in	120
	7: 6 enemies *are* the **m** of his own house.	376
Na	2: 3 The shield of his mighty **m** *is* made red,	NIH
	2: 3 is made red, the valiant **m** *are* in scarlet:	376
	3:10 they cast lots for her honourable **m**,	NIH
	3:10 all her great **m** were bound in chains.	NIH
Hab	1:14 makest **m** as the fishes of the sea,	120
Zep	1:12 punish the **m** that are settled on their lees:	376
	1:17 I will bring distress upon **m**, that they shall	NIH
	1:17 that they shall walk like blind **m**, because	NIH
	2:11 **m** shall worship him, every one from his	NIH
Hag	1:11 upon **m**, and upon cattle, and upon all	120
Zec	2: 4 without walls for the multitude of **m**	120
	3: 8 for they *are* **m** wondered at: for behold,	376
	7: 2 and Regem-melech, and their **m**,	376
	7: 7 **m** inhabited the south and the plain?	NIH
	8: 4 shall yet **old m** and old women dwell	2205
	8:10 for I set all **m** every one against his	120
	8:23 shall take hold out of all languages of	376
	9:17 corn shall make the **young m** cheerful,	970
	10: 5 They shall be as mighty **m**, which tread	NIH
	11: 6 I *will* deliver the **m** every one into his	120
	14:11 **m** shall dwell in it, and there shall be no	NIH
Mt	2: 1 there came **wise m** from the east to	3097
	2: 7 when he had privily called the **wise m**,	3097
	2:16 saw that he was mocked of the **wise m**,	3097
	2:16 he had diligently inquired of the **wise m**,	3097
	4:19 and I will make you fishers of **m**.	444
	5:11 **m** shall revile you, and persecute *you*,	NIG
	5:13 out, and to be trodden under foot of **m**.	444
	5:15 Neither do **m** light a candle, and put it	NIG
	5:16 Let your light so shine before **m**, that they	444
	5:19 commandments, and shall teach **m** so,	444
	6: 1 heed that *ye* do not your alms before **m**,	444
	6: 2 the streets, that they may have glory of **m**.	444
	6: 5 of the streets, that they may be seen of **m**.	444
	6:14 For if ye forgive **m** their trespasses,	444
	6:15 But if ye forgive not **m** their trespasses,	444
	6:16 that they may appear unto **m** to fast.	444
	6:18 That thou appear not unto **m** to fast,	444
	7:12 ye would that **m** should do to you,	444
	7:16 Do **m** gather grapes of thorns, or figs of	NIG
	8:27 the **m** marvelled, saying, What manner	444
	9: 8 which had given such power unto **m**.	NIG
	9:17 do **m** put new wine into old bottles:	NIG
	9:27 two **blind m** followed him, crying,	5185
	9:28 into the house, the **blind m** came to him:	5185
	10:17 But beware of **m**: for they will deliver you	444
	10:22 And ye shall be hated of all **m** for my	NIG

Mt	10:32 therefore shall confess me before **m**,	444
	10:33 But whosoever shall deny me before **m**,	444
	12:31 and blasphemy shall be forgiven unto **m**:	444
	12:31 *Holy* Ghost shall not be forgiven unto **m**.	444
	12:36 That every idle word that **m** shall speak,	444
	12:41 The **m** of Nineveh shall rise in judgment	435
	13:17 righteous **m** have desired to see *those*	NIG
	13:25 But while **m** slept, his enemy came and	444
	14:21 had eaten were about five thousand **m**,	435
	14:35 And when the **m** of that place had	435
	15: 9 for doctrines the commandments of **m**.	444
	15:38 they that did eat were four thousand **m**,	435
	16:13 do **m** say that I the Son of man am?	444
	16:23 that be of God, but *those* that be of **m**.	444
	17:22 shall be betrayed into the hands of **m**:	444
	19:11 them, All **m** cannot receive this saying,	NIG
	19:12 which were made eunuchs of **m**:	444
	19:26 unto them, With **m** this is unpossible;	444
	20:30 two **blind m** sitting by the way side,	5185
	21:25 from heaven, or of **m**? And they reasoned	444
	21:26 But if we shall say, Of **m**; we fear	444
	21:41 will miserably destroy those wicked **m**,	NIG
	22:16 for thou regardest not the person of **m**.	444
	23: 5 their works they do for to be seen of **m**:	444
	23: 7 and to be called of **m**, Rabbi, Rabbi.	444
	23:13 shut up the kingdom of heaven against **m**:	444
	23:28 also outwardly appear righteous unto **m**,	444
	23:34 you prophets, and wise **m**, and scribes:	NIG
	26:33 Though all **m** shall be offended because	NIG
	28: 4 keepers did shake, and became as dead **m**.	NIG
Mk	1:17 I will make you to become fishers of **m**.	444
	1:37 they said unto him, All **m** seek for thee.	NIG
	3:28 sins shall be forgiven unto the sons of **m**,	444
	5:20 had done for him: and all **m** did marvel.	NIG
	6:12 and preached that **m** should repent.	NIG
	6:44 the loaves were about five thousand **m**.	435
	7: 7 for doctrines the commandments of **m**.	444
	7: 8 ye hold the tradition of **m**, *as* the washing	444
	7:21 For from within, out of the heart of **m**,	444
	8: 4 From whence can a man satisfy these **m**	NIG
	8:24 and said, I see **m** as trees, walking.	444
	8:27 unto them, Whom do **m** say that I am?	444
	8:33 be of God, but the *things* that be of **m**.	444
	9:31 of man is delivered into the hands of **m**,	444
	10:27 With **m** *it is* impossible, but not with God:	444
	11:30 of John, was *it* from heaven, or of **m**?	444
	11:32 But if we shall say, Of **m**; they feared	444
	11:32 for all **m** counted John, that he was a	NIG
	12:14 for thou regardest not the person of **m**,	444
	13:13 And ye shall be hated of all **m** for my	NIG
	14:51 and the **young m** laid hold on him:	3495
Lk	1:25 me, to take away my reproach among **m**.	444
	2:14 and on earth peace, good will towards **m**.	444
	3:15 and all **m** mused in their hearts of John,	NIG
	5:10 from henceforth thou shalt catch **m**.	444
	5:18 brought in a bed a man which was	435
	6:22 when **m** shall hate you, and when they	444
	6:26 when all **m** shall speak well of you:	444
	6:31 And as ye would that **m** should do to you,	444
	6:38 over, shall **m** give into your bosom.	NIG
	6:44 For of thorns **m** do not gather figs, nor of	NIG
	7:20 the **m** were come unto him, they said,	435
	7:31 then shall I liken the **m** of this generation?	444
	9:14 For they were about five thousand **m**.	435
	9:30 And behold, there talked with him two **m**,	435
	9:32 glory, and the two **m** that stood with him.	435
	9:44 be delivered into the hands of **m**.	444
	11:31 judgment with the **m** of this generation,	435
	11:32 The **m** of Nineveh shall rise up in	435
	11:44 the **m** that walk over *them* are not aware	444
	11:46 for ye lade **m** *with* burdens grievous to be	444
	12: 8 Whosoever shall confess me before **m**,	444
	12: 9 But he that denieth me before **m** shall be	444
	12:36 ye yourselves like unto **m** that wait for	444
	12:48 and to whom **m** have committed much,	NIG
	13: 4 ye that they were sinners above all **m**	444
	13:14 There are six days in which **m** ought to	NIG
	14:24 That none of those **m** which were bidden	435
	14:35 nor yet for the dunghill; *but* **m** cast it out.	NIG
	16:15 are they which justify yourselves before **m**;	444
	16:15 that which is highly esteemed amongst **m**	444
	17:12 there met him ten **m** *that were* lepers,	435
	17:34 in that night there shall be two **m** in one	NIG
	17:36 Two **m** shall be in the field; the one shall	NIG
	18: 1 to this end, that **m** ought always to pray,	NIG
	18:10 Two **m** went up into the temple to pray;	444
	18:11 that I am not as other **m** *are*, extortioners,	444
	18:27 *things which are* unpossible with **m** are	444
	20: 4 of John, was it from heaven, or of **m**?	444
	20: 6 But *and* if we say, Of **m**; all the people	444
	20:20 which *should* feign themselves just **m**,	NIG
	21: 1 saw the rich **m** casting their gifts into	NIG
	21:17 And ye shall be hated of all **m** for my	NIG
	22:63 And the **m** that held Jesus mocked him,	435
	23:11 And Herod with his **m** of war** set him at	4753
	24: 4 two **m** stood by them in shining garments:	435
	24: 7 be delivered into the hands of sinful **m**,	444
Jn	1: 4 was life; and the life was the light of **m**.	444
	1: 7 that all **m** through him might believe.	NIG
	2:10 and when **m** have well drunk, then	NIG
	2:24 unto them, because he knew all **m**,	NIG
	3:19 and **m** loved darkness rather than light,	444
	3:26 same baptizeth, and all **m** come to him.	NIG
	4:20 that in Jerusalem is the place where **m**	NIG
	4:28 her way into the city, and saith to the **m**,	444

M

M

Jn	4:38 other *m* laboured, and ye are entered into	NIG
	5:23 That all *m* should honour the Son, even as	NIG
	5:41 I receive not honour from *m*.	444
	6:10 And Jesus said, Make the *m* sit down,	444
	6:10 So the *m* sat down, *in* number about five	435
	6:14 Then *those m*, when they had seen	444
	8:17 law, that the testimony of two *m* is true.	444
	11:48 him thus alone, all *m* will believe on him:	NIG
	12:32 from the earth, will draw all *m* unto me.	NIG
	12:43 For they loved the praise of *m* more than	444
	13:35 By this shall all *m* know that ye are my	NIG
	15: 6 and *m* gather them, and cast *them* into	444
	17: 6 I have manifested thy name unto the *m*	444
	18: 3 having received a band of *m*,	NIG
Ac	1:10 two *m* stood by them in white apparel;	435
	1:11 also said, Ye *m* of Galilee, why stand	435
	1:16 M *and* brethren, this scripture must needs	435
	1:21 Wherefore of these *m* which have	435
	1:24 which knowest the hearts of all *m*, shew	NIG
	2: 5 devout *m*, out of every nation under	435
	2:13 *These m* are full of new wine.	NIG
	2:14 Ye *m* of Judea, and all *ye* that dwell at	435
	2:17 and your **young** *m* shall see visions,	3495
	2:17 and your **old** *m* shall dream dreams:	4245
	2:22 Ye *m* of Israel, hear these words; Jesus of	435
	2:29 M *and* brethren, let *me* freely speak unto	435
	2:37 M *and* brethren, what shall we do?	435
	2:45 parted them to all *m*, as every *man* had	NIG
	3:12 Ye *m* of Israel, why marvel ye at this?	435
	4: 4 the number of the *m* was about five	435
	4:12 other name under heaven given among *m*,	444
	4:13 that they were unlearned and ignorant *m*,	444
	4:16 Saying, What shall we do to these *m*?	444
	4:21 for all *m* glorified God for that which was	NIG
	5: 4 thou hast not lied unto *m*, but unto God.	444
	5: 6 And the **young** *m* arose, wound him up,	3501
	5:10 and the **young** *m* came in, and found her	3495
	5:14 Lord, multitudes both of *m* and women.)	435
	5:25 the *m* whom ye put in prison are standing	435
	5:29 said, We ought to obey God rather than *m*.	444
	5:35 And said unto them, Ye *m* of Israel,	435
	5:35 what ye intend to do as touching these *m*.	444
	5:36 to whom a number of *m*, about four	444
	5:38 Refrain from these *m*, and let them alone:	444
	5:38 for if this counsel or this work be of *m*,	444
	6: 3 look ye out among you seven *m* of honest	435
	6:11 they suborned *m*, which said, We have	435
	7: 2 he said, M, brethren, and fathers, hearken;	435
	8: 2 devout *m* carried Stephen *to his burial*,	435
	8: 3 and haling *m* and women committed *them*	435
	8:12 they were baptized, both *m* and women.	435
	9: 2 *this* way, whether they were *m* or women,	435
	9: 7 the *m* which journeyed with him stood	435
	9:38 was there, they sent unto him two *m*,	435
	10: 5 now send *m* to Joppa, and call for *one*	435
	10:17 the *m* which were sent from Cornelius had	435
	10:19 said unto him, Behold, three *m* seek thee:	435
	10:21 Peter went down to the *m* which were	435
	11: 3 Thou wentest in to *m* uncircumcised,	435
	11:11 immediately there were three *m* already	435
	11:13 Send *m* to Joppa, and call for Simon,	435
	11:20 And some of them were *m* of Cyprus and	435
	13:15 saying, Ye *m and* brethren, if ye have *any*	435
	13:16 M of Israel, and *ye* that fear God,	435
	13:26 M *and* brethren, children of the stock of	435
	13:38 unto you therefore, *m and* brethren,	435
	13:50 and the chief *m* of the city,	444
	14:11 are come down to us in the likeness of *m*.	444
	14:15 why do ye these *things?* We also are *m* of	444
	15: 1 And certain *m* which came down from	NIG
	15: 7 and said unto them, M *and* brethren,	435
	15:13 James answered, saying, M *and* brethren,	435
	15:17 That the residue of *m* might seek after	444
	15:22 to send chosen *m* of their own company to	444
	15:22 and Silas, chief *m* among the brethren:	NIG
	15:25 to send chosen *m* unto you with our	435
	15:26 M that have hazarded their lives for	444
	16:17 These *m* are the servants of the most high	444
	16:20 These *m*, being Jews, do exceedingly	444
	16:35 sent the sergeants, saying, Let those *m* go.	444
	17:12 which were Greeks, and of *m*, not a few.	435
	17:22 of Mars' hill, and said, Ye *m* of Athens,	435
	17:26 hath made of one blood all nations of *m*	444
	17:30 now commandeth all *m* every where to	444
	17:31 he hath given assurance unto all *m*,	NIG
	17:34 Howbeit certain *m* clave unto him,	435
	18:13 This *fellow* persuadeth *m* to worship God	444
	19: 7 And all the *m* were about twelve.	435
	19:19 and burned *them* before all *m*:	NIG
	19:29 and Aristarchus, *m* of Macedonia,	NIG
	19:35 the people, he said, Ye *m* of Ephesus,	435
	19:37 For ye have brought *hither* these *m*,	444
	20:26 that I *am* pure from the blood of all *m*.	NIG
	20:30 Also of your own selves shall *m* arise,	435
	21:23 have four *m* which have a vow on them;	435
	21:26 Then Paul took the *m*, and the next day	435
	21:28 Crying out, M of Israel, help: This is	435
	21:28 that teacheth all *m* every where against	NIG
	21:38 four thousand *m* that were murderers?	435
	22: 1 M, brethren, and fathers, hear ye my	435
	22: 4 and delivering into prisons both *m* and	435
	22:15 For thou shalt be his witness unto all *m* of	444
	23: 1 the council, said, M *and* brethren,	435
	23: 6 M *and* brethren, I am a Pharisee, the son	435
	23:21 in wait for him of them moe *than* forty *m*,	435

Ac	24:16 of offence toward God, and *toward m*.	444
	25:23 chief captains, and principal *m* of the city,	435
	25:24 and all *m* which are here present with us,	435
	28:17 he said unto them, M *and* brethren,	435
Ro	1:18 all ungodliness and unrighteousness of *m*,	444
	1:27 likewise also the *m*, leaving the natural	730
	1:27 *m* with men working that which is	730
	1:27 men with *m* working that which is	730
	2:16 by Jesus Christ according to my gospel.	444
	2:29 whose praise *is* not of *m*, but of God.	444
	5:12 and so death passed upon all *m*, for that all	444
	5:18 *came* upon all *m* to condemnation;	444
	5:18 *came* upon all *m* unto justification of life.	444
	6:19 I speak **after the manner of** *m* because	442
	11: 4 reserved to myself seven thousand *m*,	435
	12:16 *things*, but condescend to *m* of low estate.	NIG
	12:17 Provide *things* honest in the sight of all *m*.	444
	12:18 as lieth in you, live peaceably with all *m*.	444
	14:18 *is* acceptable to God, and approved of *m*.	444
	16: 9 is come abroad unto all *m*. I am glad	NIG
1Co	1:25 the foolishness of God is wiser than *m*;	444
	1:25 the weakness of God is stronger than *m*.	444
	1:26 how that not many wise *m* after the flesh,	NIG
	2: 5 should not stand in the wisdom of *m*,	444
	3: 3 are ye not carnal, and walk as *m*?	444
	3:21 Therefore let no *man* glory in *m*. For all	NIG
	4: 6 ye might learn in us not to think of *m*	NIG
	4: 9 unto the world, and to angels, and to *m*.	444
	7: 7 I would that all *m* were even as I myself.	444
	7:23 with a price; be not ye the servants of *m*.	444
	9:19 though I be free from all *m*, yet have I	NIG
	9:22 I am made all *things* to all *m*, that I might	NIG
	10:15 I speak as to wise *m*; judge ye what I say.	NIG
	10:33 Even as I please all *m* in all *things*, not	NIG
	13: 1 Though I speak with the tongues of *m* and	444
	14: 2 an *unknown* tongue speaketh not unto *m*,	444
	14: 3 he that prophesieth speaketh unto *m to*	444
	14:20 ye children, but in understanding be *m*.	5046
	14:21 With *m* of other tongues and other lips	NIG
	15:19 in Christ, we are of all *m* most miserable.	444
	15:32 If after the manner of *m* I have fought with	444
	15:39 but *there is* one *kind of* flesh of *m*,	444
	16:13 in the faith, quit you **like** *m*, be strong.	407
2Co	3: 2 in our hearts, known and read of all *m*:	444
	5:11 the terror of the Lord, we persuade *m*;	444
	8:13 For *I mean* not that other *m* be eased,	NIG
	8:21 of the Lord, but also in the sight of *m*.	444
	9:13 distribution unto them, and unto all *m*;	NIG
Gal	1: 1 Paul, an apostle, (not of *m*, neither by man	444
	1:10 For do I now persuade *m*, or God? or do I	444
	1:10 do I seek to please *m*? for if I yet pleased	444
	1:10 for if I yet pleased *m*, I should not be	444
	3:15 Brethren, I speak after the manner of *m*;	444
	6:10 let us do good unto all *m*, especially unto	NIG
Eph	3: 5 was not made known unto the sons of *m*,	444
	3: 9 And to make all *m* see what *is*	NIG
	4: 8 captivity captive, and gave gifts unto *m*.	444
	4:14 wind of doctrine, by the sleight of *m*,	444
	5:28 So ought *m* to love their wives as their	435
	6: 7 service, as to the Lord, and not to *m*:	444
Php	2: 7 and was made in the likeness of *m*:	444
	4: 5 your moderation be known unto all *m*.	444
Col	2: 8 and vain deceit, after the tradition of *m*,	444
	2:22 the commandments and doctrines of *m*?	444
	3:23 heartily, as to the Lord, and not unto *m*;	444
1Th	1: 5 as ye know what manner of *m* we were	NIG
	2: 4 not as pleasing *m*, but God, which trieth	444
	2: 6 Nor of *m* sought we glory, neither of you,	444
	2:13 ye received *it* not as the word of *m*, but as	444
	2:15 please not God, and are contrary to all *m*:	444
	3:12 towards all *m*, even as we *do* towards	NIG
	5:14 the weak, be patient toward all *m*.	NIG
	5:15 both among yourselves, and to all *m*.	NIG
2Th	3: 2 from unreasonable and wicked *m*:	444
	3: 2 and wicked men: for all *m* have not faith.	NIG
1Ti	2: 1 *and* giving of thanks, be made for all *m*;	444
	2: 4 Who will have all *m* to be saved,	444
	2: 5 and one mediator between God and *m*,	444
	2: 8 I will therefore that *m* pray every where,	435
	4:10 living God, who is the Saviour of all *m*,	444
	5: 1 a father; *and* the younger *m* as brethren;	NIG
	5:24 judgment; and some *m* they follow after.	NIG
	6: 5 Perverse disputings of *m* of corrupt minds,	444
	6: 9 drown in destruction and perdition.	444
2Ti	2: 2 the same commit thou to faithful *m*,	444
	2:24 but be gentle unto all *m*, apt to teach,	NIG
	3: 2 For *m* shall be lovers of their own selves,	444
	3: 8 of corrupt minds, reprobate concerning	444
	3: 9 for their folly shall be manifest unto all *m*,	NIG
	3:13 But evil *m* and seducers shall wax worse	444
	4:16 *man* stood with me, but all *m* forsook me:	NIG
Tit	1: 8 a lover of good *m*, sober, just, holy,	NIG
	1:14 and commandments of *m*, that turn from	444
	2: 2 That the **aged** *m* be sober, grave,	4246
	2: 6 Young *m* likewise exhort to be sober	444
	2:11 bringeth salvation hath appeared to all *m*,	444
	3: 2 shewing all meekness unto all *m*.	444
	3: 8 *things* are good and profitable unto *m*.	444
Heb	5: 1 every high priest taken from among *m* is	444
	5: 1 ordained for *m* in *things* pertaining to God,	444
	6:16 For *m* verily swear by the greater:	444
	7: 8 And here *m* that die receive tithes;	444
	7:28 For the law maketh *m* high priests which	444
	9:17 a testament *is* of force after *m* are dead:	NIG
	9:27 And as it is appointed unto *m* once to die,	444

Heb	12:14 Follow peace with all *m*, and holiness,	NIG
	12:23 and to the spirits of just *m* made perfect,	NIG
Jas	1: 5 that giveth to all *m* liberally,	NIG
	2: 6 Do not rich *m* oppress you, and draw you	NIG
	3: 9 therewith curse we *m*, which are made	444
	5: 1 rich *m*, weep and howl for your miseries	NIG
1Pe	2:15 disallowed indeed of *m*, but chosen of God	444
	2:15 put to silence the ignorance of foolish *m*:	444
	2:17 Honour all *m*. Love the brotherhood.	NIG
	4: 2 of *his* time in the flesh to the lusts of *m*,	444
	4: 6 that they might be judged according to *m*	444
2Pe	1:21 holy *m* of God spake *as they were* moved	444
	3: 7 of judgment and perdition of ungodly *m*.	444
	3: 9 *his* promise, as some *m* count slackness;	NIG
1Jn	2:13 **young** *m*, because ye have overcome	3495
	2:14 **young** *m*, because ye are strong,	3495
	5: 9 If we receive the witness of *m*, the witness	444
3Jn	1:12 Demetrius hath good report of all *m*,	NIG
Jude	1: 4 For there are certain *m* crept in unawares,	444
	1: 4 ungodly *m*, turning the grace of our God	NIG
Rev	6:15 and the **great** *m*, and the rich **men**, and	3175
	6:15 and the rich *m*, and the chief captains,	NIG
	6:15 and the mighty *m*, and every bondman,	NIG
	8:11 and many *m* died of the waters, because	444
	9: 4 *those m* which have not the seal of God	444
	9: 6 And in those days shall *m* seek death,	444
	9: 7 and their faces *were* as the faces of *m*.	444
	9:10 their power *was* to hurt *m* five months.	444
	9:15 and a year, for to slay the third *part* of *m*.	444
	9:18 these three was the third *part* of *m* killed,	444
	9:20 the rest of the *m* which were not killed	444
	11:13 in the earthquake were slain of	444+3686
	13:13 from heaven on the earth in the sight of *m*,	444
	14: 4 These were redeemed from among *m*,	444
	16: 2 grievous sore upon the *m* which had	444
	16: 8 was given unto him to scorch *m* with	444
	16: 9 And *m* were scorched *with* great heat,	444
	16:18 as was not since *m* were upon the earth,	444
	16:21 And there fell upon *m* a great hail out of	444
	16:21 and blasphemed God because of	444
	18:13 and chariots, and slaves, and souls of *m*.	444
	18:23 for thy merchants were the **great** *m* of	3175
	19:18 the flesh of mighty *m*, and the flesh of	NIG
	19:18 the flesh of all *m*, both free and bond,	NIG
	21: 3 the tabernacle of God *is* with *m*, and he	444

MEN OF TOB See ISH-TOB

MEN'S (24) [MAN]

Ge	24:32 feet, and the *m* feet that *were* with him.	376
	44: 1 Fill the *m* sacks *with* food, as much	376
Dt	4:28 the work of *m* hands, wood and stone,	120
1Sa	24: 9 Wherefore hearest thou *m* words, saying,	120
1Ki	12:13 forsook the **old** *m* counsel that they gave	2205
	13: 2 and *m* bones shall be burnt upon thee.	120
2Ki	19:18 the work of *m* hands, wood and stone:	120
	23:20 burnt *m* bones upon them, and returned	120
Ps	115: 4 *are* silver and gold, the work of *m* hands.	120
	135:15 *are* silver and gold, the work of *m* hands.	120
Isa	37:19 but the work of *m* hands, wood and stone:	120
Jer	48:41 the mighty *m* hearts in Moab at that day	NIH
Hab	2: 8 because of *m* blood, and *for* the violence	120
	2:17 because of *m* blood, and *for* the violence	120
Mt	23: 4 be borne, and lay *them* on *m* shoulders;	444
	23:27 but are within full of dead *m* bones,	NIG
Lk	9:56 not the Son of man is not come to destroy *m*	444
	21:26 M hearts failing them for fear,	444
Ac	17:25 Neither is worshipped with hands,	444
2Co	10:15 *our* measure, *that is*, of other *m* labours;	NIG
1Ti	5:22 neither be partaker of other *m* sins:	NIG
	5:24 Some *m* sins are open beforehand,	444
1Pe	4:15 or as a **busybody in other m matters.**	244
Jude	1:16 words, having *m* persons in admiration	NIG

MENAHEM (8)

2Ki	15:14 For M the son of Gadi went up from	4505
	15:16 M smote Tiphsah, and all that *were*	4505
	15:17 M the son of Gadi to reign over Israel,	4505
	15:19 M gave Pul a thousand talents of silver,	4505
	15:20 M exacted the money of Israel, *even* of all	4505
	15:21 rest of the acts of M, and all that he did,	4505
	15:22 M slept with his fathers; and Pekahiah	4505
	15:23 of M *began* to reign over Israel in	4505

MENAN (1)

Lk	3:31 *son of* Melea, which was *the son of* M,	3104

MEND (2) [MENDING]

2Ch	24:12 and brass to *m* the house of the Lord.	2388
	34:10 of the Lord, to repair and *m* the house:	2388

MENDING (2) [MEND]

Mt	4:21 with Zebedee their father, *m* their nets;	2675
Mk	1:19 who also *were* in the ship *m their* nets.	2675

MENE (3)

Da	5:25 M, MENE, TEKEL, UPHARSIN.	4484
	5:25 MENE, MENE, TEKEL, UPHARSIN.	4484
	5:26 M; God hath numbered thy kingdom,	4484

MENNA See MENAN

MENPLEASERS (2) [MAN, PLEASE]

Eph	6: 6 Not with eyeservice, as *m*; but as	441
Col	3:22 not with eyeservice, as *m*; but in	441

MENSERVANTS (10) [MAN, SERVE]
Ge	12:16 m, and maidservants, and she asses,	5650
	20:14 m, and womenservants, and gave them	5650
	24:35 m, and maidservants, and camels,	5650
	30:43 and m, and camels, and asses.	5650
	32: 5 asses, flocks, and m, and womenservants:	5650
Ex	21: 7 she shall not go out as the m do.	5650
Dt	12:12 your m, and your maidservants,	5650
1Sa	8:16 he will take your m, and your	5650
2Ki	5:26 and oxen, and m, and maidservants?	5650
Lk	12:45 shall begin to beat the m and maidens,	3816

MENSTEALERS (1) [MAN, STEAL]
1Ti	1:10 for m, for liars, for perjured persons, and	405

MENSTRUOUS (3)
Isa	30:22 thou shalt cast them away as a m cloth;	1739
La	1:17 Jerusalem is as a m woman among them.	5079
Eze	18: 6 neither hath come near to a m woman,	5079

MENTION (23) [MENTIONED]
Ge	40:14 make m of me unto Pharaoh, and bring	2142
Ex	23:13 make no m of the name of other gods,	2142
Jos	23: 7 make m of the name of their gods,	2142
1Sa	4:18 when he made m of the ark of God,	2142
Job	28:18 No m shall be made of coral, or of pearls:	2142
Ps	71:16 I will make m of thy righteousness,	2142
	87: 4 I will make m of Rahab and Babylon to	2142
Isa	12: 4 make m that his name is exalted.	2142
	19:17 one that maketh m thereof shall be	2142
	26:13 thee only will we make m of thy name.	2142
	48: 1 make m of the God of Israel, but not in	2142
	49: 1 mother hath he made m of my name.	2142
	62: 6 ye that make m of the LORD, keep not	2142
	63: 7 I will m the lovingkindnesses of	2142
Jer	4:16 Make ye m to the nations; behold,	2142
	20: 9 will not make m of him, nor speak	2142
	23:36 the burden of the LORD shall ye m no	2142
Am	6:10 for we may not make m of the name of	2142
Ro	1: 9 that without ceasing I make m of you,	3417
Eph	1:16 for you, making m of you in my prayers;	3417
1Th	1: 2 you all, making m of you in our prayers;	3417
Phm	1: 4 making m of thee always in my prayers,	3417
Heb	11:22 made m of the departing of the children	3421

MENTIONED (7) [MENTION]
Jos	21: 9 these cities which are here m by name,	7121
1Ch	4:38 These m by their names were princes in	935
2Ch	20:34 is m in the book of the kings of Israel.	5927
Eze	16:56 For thy sister Sodom was not m by thy	8052
	18:22 they shall not be m unto him:	2142
	18:24 that he hath done shall not be m:	2142
	33:16 he hath committed shall be m unto him:	2142

MEONENIM (1)
Jdg	9:37 company come along by the plain of M.	6049

MEONOTHAI (1)
1Ch	4:14 M begat Ophrah: and Seraiah begat Joab,	4587

MEPHAATH (4)
Jos	13:18 and Jahazah, and Kedemoth, and M,	4158
	21:37 her suburbs, and M with her suburbs;	4158
1Ch	6:79 her suburbs, and M with her suburbs;	4158
Jer	48:21 and upon Jahazah, and upon M,	4158

MEPHIBOSHETH (15) [MERIB-BAAL]
2Sa	4: 4 and became lame. And his name was M.	4648
	9: 6 when M, the son of Jonathan, the son	4648
	9: 6 David said, M. And he answered,	4648
	9:10 My master's son shall eat bread alway	4648
	9:11 As for M, said the king, he shall eat at my	4648
	9:12 M had a young son, whose name was	4648
	9:12 the house of Ziba were servants unto M.	4648
	9:13 So M dwelt in Jerusalem: for he did eat	4648
	16: 1 Ziba the servant of M met him, with a	4648
	16: 4 thine are all that pertained unto M.	4648
	19:24 the son of Saul came down to meet	4648
	19:25 Wherefore wentest not thou with me, M?	4648
	19:30 M said unto the king, Yea, let him take	4648
	21: 7 the king spared M, the son of Jonathan	4648
	21: 8 she bare unto Saul, Armoni and M;	4648

MERAB (3)
1Sa	14:49 were these; the name of the firstborn M,	4764
	18:17 to David, Behold my elder daughter M,	4764
	18:19 came to pass at the time when M Saul's	4764

MERAIAH (1)
Ne	12:12 of Seraiah, M; of Jeremiah, Hananiah;	4811

MERAIOTH (7)
1Ch	6: 6 begat Zerahiah, and Zerahiah begat M,	4812
	6: 7 M begat Amariah, and Amariah begat	4812
	6:52 M his son, Amariah his son, Ahitub his	4812
	9:11 the son of Zadok, the son of M, the son	4812
Ezr	7: 3 the son of Azariah, the son of M,	4812
Ne	11:11 the son of Zadok, the son of M, the son	4812
	12:15 Of Harim, Adna; of M, Helkai;	4812

MERARI (39) [MERARITES]
Ge	46:11 sons of Levi; Gershon, Kohath, and M.	4847
Ex	6:16 Gershon, and Kohath, and M:	4847
	6:19 the sons of M; Mahli and Mushi: these	4847
Nu	3:17 names; Gershon, and Kohath, and M.	4847
	3:20 the sons of M by their families; Mahli,	4847

Nu	3:33 Of M was the family of the Mahlites,	4847
	3:33 Mushites: these are the families of M.	4847
	3:35 of M was Zuriel the son of Abihail:	4847
	3:36 charge of the sons of M shall be the	4847
	4:29 As for the sons of M, thou shalt number	4847
	4:33 service of the families of the sons of M,	4847
	4:42 of the families of the sons of M,	4847
	4:45 of the families of the sons of M,	4847
	7: 8 eight oxen he gave unto the sons of M,	4847
	10:17 Gershon and the sons of M set forward,	4847
	26:57 of M, the family of the Merarites.	4847
Jos	21: 7 The children of M by their families had	4847
	21:34 unto the families of the children of M,	4847
	21:40 So all the cities for the children of M by	4847
1Ch	6: 1 sons of Levi; Gershon, Kohath, and M.	4847
	6:16 sons of Levi; Gershom, Kohath, and M.	4847
	6:19 The sons of M; Mahli, and Mushi.	4847
	6:29 The sons of M; Mahli, Libni his son,	4847
	6:44 their brethren the sons of M stood on	4847
	6:47 of Mushi, the son of M, the son of Levi.	4847
	6:63 Unto the sons of M were given by lot,	4847
	6:77 Unto the rest of the children of M were	4847
	9:14 the son of Hashabiah, of the sons of M;	4847
	15: 6 Of the sons of M; Asaiah the chief,	4847
	15:17 of the sons of M their brethren, Ethan	4847
	23: 6 Levi, namely, Gershon, Kohath, and M.	4847
	23:21 The sons of M; Mahli, and Mushi.	4847
	24:26 The sons of M were Mahli and Mushi:	4847
	24:27 The sons of M by Jaaziah; Beno,	4847
	26:10 Hosah, of the children of M, had sons;	4847
	26:19 the sons of Kore, and among the sons of M.	4847
2Ch	29:12 of the sons of M, Kish the son of Abdi,	4847
	34:12 Obadiah, the Levites, of the sons of M;	4847
Ezr	8:19 with him Jeshaiah of the sons of M,	4847

MERARITES (1) [MERARI]
Nu	26:57 of Merari, the family of the M.	4848

MERCHANDISE (22) [MERCHANT]
Dt	21:14 thou shalt not make m of her, because	6014
	24: 7 and maketh m of him, or selleth him;	6014
Pr	3:14 For the m of it is better than	5504
	3:14 of it is better than the m of silver,	5505
	31:18 She perceiveth that her m is good:	5504
Isa	23:18 her m and her hire shall be holiness to	5504
	23:18 for her m shall be for them that dwell	5504
	45:14 of Ethiopia and of the Sabeans, men of	5505
Eze	26:12 of thy riches, and make a prey of thy m:	7404
	27: 9 mariners were in thee to occupy thy m.	4627
	27:15 many isles were the m of thine hand:	5506
	27:24 and made of cedar, among thy m.	4819
	27:27 Thy riches, and thy fairs, thy m,	4627
	27:27 the occupiers of thy m, and all thy men	4627
	27:33 the multitude of thy riches and of thy m.	4627
	27:34 thy m and all thy company in the midst	4627
	28:16 By the multitude of thy m they have filled	7404
Mt	22: 5 one to his farm, another to his m:	1711
	21:12 make not my Father's house a house of m.	1712
2Pe	2: 3 with feigned words make m of you:	1710
Rev	18:11 for no man buyeth their m any more:	1117
	18:12 The m of gold, and silver,	1117

MERCHANT (12) [MERCHANDISE, MERCHANT'S, MERCHANTMEN, MERCHANTS]
Ge	23:16 of silver, current money with the m.	5503
Pr	31:24 and delivereth girdles unto the m.	3669
SS	3: 6 frankincense, with all powders of the m?	7402
Isa	23:11 m city, to destroy the strong holds thereof	3667
Eze	27: 3 art a m of the people for many isles,	7402
	27:16 Tarshish was thy m by reason of	5503
	27:18 Damascus was thy m in the multitude of	5503
	27:20 Dedan was thy m in precious clothes for	7402
Hos	12: 7 He is a m, the balances of deceit are in	3667
Zep	1:11 for all the m people are cut down;	3667
Mt	13:45 the kingdom of heaven is like unto a m	1713

MERCHANT'S (1) [MERCHANT]
Pr	31:14 She is like the m ships; she bringeth her	5503

MERCHANTMEN (2) [MERCHANT]
Ge	37:28 there passed by Midianites m;	376+5503
1Ki	10:15 Besides that he had of the m,	376+8446

MERCHANTS (28) [MERCHANT]
1Ki	10:15 of the traffick of the spice m, and of all	7402
	10:28 the king's m received the linen yarn at a	5503
2Ch	1:16 the king's m received the linen yarn at a	5503
	9:14 that which chapmen and m brought.	5503
Ne	3:31 of the m, over against the gate Miphkad,	7402
	3:32 gate repaired the goldsmiths and the m.	7402
	13:20 So the m and sellers of all kind of ware	7402
Job	41: 6 him? shall they part him among the m?	3669
Isa	23: 2 thou whom the m of Zidon, that pass over	5503
	23: 8 the crowning city, whose m are princes,	5503
	47:15 laboured, even thy m, from thy youth:	5503
Eze	17: 4 a land of traffick; he set it in a city of m.	7402
	27:13 Tubal, and Meshech, they were thy m:	7402
	27:15 The men of Dedan were thy m; many	7402
	27:17 and the land of Israel, they were thy m:	7402
	27:21 and goats: in these were they thy m.	5503
	27:22 The m of Sheba and Raamah, they were	7402
	27:22 of Sheba and Raamah, they were thy m:	7402
	27:23 Eden, the m of Sheba, Asshur,	7402
	27:23 Asshur, and Chilmad, were thy m.	7402

Eze	27:24 These were thy m in all sorts of things,	7402
	27:36 The m among the people shall hiss at	5503
	38:13 Sheba, and Dedan, and the m of Tarshish,	5503
Na	3:16 hast multiplied thy m above the stars	7402
Rev	18: 3 the m of the earth are waxed rich	1713
	18:11 And the m of the earth shall weep and	1713
	18:15 The m of these things, which were made	1713
	18:23 thy m were the great men of the earth;	1713

MERCIES (40) [MERCY]
Ge	32:10 I am not worthy of the least of all the m,	2617
2Sa	24:14 hand of the LORD; for his m are great:	7356
1Ch	21:13 of the LORD; for very great are his m:	7356
2Ch	6:42 remember the m of David thy servant.	2617
Ne	9:19 Yet thou in thy manifold m forsookest	7356
	9:27 according to thy manifold m thou gavest	7356
	9:28 thou deliver them according to thy m	7356
Ps	25: 6 thy tender m and thy lovingkindnesses;	7356
	40:11 Withhold not thou thy tender m from	7356
	51: 1 thy tender m blot out my transgressions.	7356
	69:16 to the multitude of thy tender m.	7356
	77: 9 hath he in anger shut up his tender m?	7356
	79: 8 let thy tender m speedily prevent us:	7356
	89: 1 I will sing of the m of the LORD for ever:	2617
	103: 4 thee with lovingkindness and tender m;	7356
	106: 7 remembered not the multitude of thy m;	2617
	106:45 according to the multitude of his m.	2617
	119:41 Let thy m come also unto me, O LORD,	2617
	119:77 Let thy tender m come unto me, that I	7356
	119:156 Great are thy tender m, O LORD:	7356
	145: 9 and his tender m are over all his works.	7356
Pr	12:10 the tender m of the wicked are cruel.	7356
Isa	54: 7 but with great m will I gather thee.	7356
	55: 3 with you, even the sure m of David.	2617
	63: 7 bestowed on them according to his m,	7356
	63:15 of thy bowels and of thy m towards me?	7356
Jer	16: 5 the LORD, even my lovingkindness and m.	7356
	42:12 I will shew unto you, that he may have	7356
La	3:22 It is of the LORD'S m that we are not	2617
	3:32 according to the multitude of his m.	7356
Da	2:18 That they would desire m of the God of	7359
	9: 9 To the Lord our God belong m and	7356
	9:18 our righteousnesses, but for thy great m.	7356
Hos	2:19 and in lovingkindness, and in m.	7356
Zec	1:16 I am returned to Jerusalem with m:	7356
Ac	13:34 I will give you the sure m of David.	3741
Ro	12: 1 you therefore, brethren, by the m of God,	3628
2Co	1: 3 the Father of m, and the God of all	3628
Php	2: 1 of the Spirit, if any bowels and m,	3628
Col	3:12 holy and beloved, bowels of m, kindness,	3628

MERCIES' (1) [MERCY]
Ne	9:31 Nevertheless for thy great m sake thou	7356

MERCIFUL (40) [MERCY]
Ge	19:16 the LORD being m unto him:	2551
Ex	34: 6 m and gracious, longsuffering,	7349
Dt	4:31 (For the LORD thy God is a m God;)	7349
	21: 8 Be m, O LORD, unto thy people Israel,	3722
	32:43 be m unto his land, and to his people.	3722
2Sa	22:26 the m thou wilt shew thyself merciful,	2623
	22:26 the merciful thou wilt shew m,	2616
1Ki	20:31 kings of the house of Israel are m kings:	2617
2Ch	30: 9 the LORD your God is gracious and m,	7349
Ne	9:17 gracious and m, slow to anger, and of	7349
	9:31 for thou art a gracious and m God.	7349
Ps	18:25 the m thou wilt shew thyself merciful;	2623
	18:25 the merciful thou wilt shew thyself m;	2616
	26:11 redeem me, and be m unto me.	2603
	37:26 He is ever m, and lendeth; and his seed	2603
	41: 4 I said, LORD, be m unto me: heal my	2603
	41:10 O LORD, be m unto me, and raise me up,	2603
	56: 1 Be m unto me, O God: for man would	2603
	56: 1 Be m unto me, O God, be merciful unto	2603
	57: 1 merciful unto me, O God, be m unto me:	2603
	59: 5 be not m to any wicked transgressors.	2603
	67: 1 God be m unto us, and bless us;	2603
	86: 3 m unto me, O Lord: for I cry unto	2603
	103: 8 The LORD is m and gracious, slow to	7349
	116: 5 and righteous; yea, our God is m.	7355
	117: 2 For his m kindness is great toward us:	2617
	119:58 be m unto me according to thy word.	2603
	119:76 thy m kindness be for my comfort,	2617
	119:132 Look thou upon me, and be m unto me,	2603
Pr	11:17 The m man doeth good to his own soul:	2617
Isa	57: 1 m men are taken away, none considering	2617
Jer	3:12 for I am m, saith the LORD, and I will not	2623
Joel	2:13 for he is gracious and m, slow to anger,	7349
Jnh	4: 2 m, slow to anger, and of great kindness,	7349
Mt	5: 7 Blessed are the m: for they shall obtain	1655
Lk	6:36 Be ye therefore m, as your Father also is	3629
	6:36 merciful, as your Father also is m.	3629
	18:13 breast, saying, God be m to me a sinner.	2433
Heb	2:17 that he might be a m and faithful high	1655
	8:12 For I will be m to their unrighteousness,	2436

MERCURIUS (1)
Ac	14:12 and Paul, M, because he was the chief	2060

MERCY (277) [MERCIES, MERCIES', MERCIFUL, MERCY'S, UNMERCIFUL]
Ge	19:19 thy sight, and thou hast magnified thy m,	2617
	24:27 hath not left destitute my master of his m	2617
	39:21 shewed him m, and gave him favour in	2617
	43:14 God Almighty give you m before the man,	7356

Ex	15:13	Thou in thy **m** hast led forth the people	2617
	20: 6	shewing **m** unto thousands of them that	2617
	25:17	thou shalt make a **m seat** *of* pure gold;	3727
	25:18	them, in the two ends of the **m seat**.	3727
	25:19	*even* of the **m seat** shall ye make	3727
	25:20	covering the **m seat** with their wings,	3727
	25:20	toward the **m seat** shall the faces of	3727
	25:21	thou shalt put the **m seat** above upon	3727
	25:22	with thee from above the **m seat**,	3727
	26:34	thou shalt put the **m seat** upon the ark of	3727
	30: 6	before the **m seat** that *is* over	3727
	31: 7	the **m seat** that *is* thereupon, and all	3727
	33:19	shew **m** on whom I will shew mercy.	7355
	33:19	shew mercy on whom I will **shew m**.	7355
	34: 7	Keeping **m** for thousands,	2617
	35:12	*with* the **m seat**, and the vail of	3727
	37: 6	he made the **m seat** *of* pure gold;	3727
	37: 7	he them, on the two ends of the **m seat**;	3727
	37: 8	of the **m seat** made he the cherubims on	3727
	37: 9	covered with their wings over the **m seat**,	3727
	37: 9	to the **m seatward** were the faces of	3727
	39:35	and the staves thereof, and the **m seat**,	3727
	40:20	and put the **m seat** above upon the ark:	3727
Lev	16: 2	*place* within the vail before the **m seat**,	3727
	16: 2	will appear in the cloud upon the **m seat**.	3727
	16:13	the **m seat** that *is* upon the Testimony,	3727
	16:14	*it* with his finger upon the **m seat**	3727
	16:14	before the **m seat** shall he sprinkle it	3727
	16:15	sprinkle it upon the **m seat**, and before	3727
	16:15	the mercy seat, and before the **m seat**:	3727
Nu	7:89	**m seat** that *was* upon the ark of	3727
	14:18	of great **m**, forgiving iniquity and	2617
	14:19	according to the greatness of thy **m**,	2617
Dt	5:10	shewing **m** unto thousands of them that	2617
	7: 2	with them, nor **shew m** unto them:	2603
	7: 9	and **m** with them that love him and	2617
	7:12	the **m** which he sware unto thy fathers:	2617
	13:17	shew thee **m**, and have compassion upon	7356
Jdg	1:24	into the city, and we will shew thee **m**.	2617
2Sa	7:15	my **m** shall not depart away from him,	2617
	15:20	thy brethren: **m** and truth *be* with thee.	2617
	22:51	sheweth **m** to his anointed, unto David,	2617
1Ki	3: 6	thy servant David my father great **m**,	2617
	8:23	**m** with thy servants that walk before thee	2617
1Ch	16:34	*he is* good; for his **m** *endureth* for ever.	2617
	16:41	because his **m** *endureth* for ever;	2617
	17:13	I will not take my **m** away from him, as I	2617
	28:11	and of the place of the **m seat**,	3727
2Ch	1: 8	Thou hast shewed great **m** unto David	2617
	5:13	*he is* good; for his **m** *endureth* for ever;	2617
	6:14	and *shewest* **m** unto thy servants,	2617
	7: 3	*he is* good; for his **m** *endureth* for ever.	2617
	7: 6	because the LORD; for his **m** *endureth* for ever,	2617
	20:21	the LORD; for his **m** *endureth* for ever.	2617
Ezr	3:11	his **m** *endureth* for ever towards Israel.	2617
	7:28	extended **m** unto me before the king,	2617
	9: 9	hath extended **m** unto us in the sight of	2617
Ne	1: 5	and **m** for them that love him and	2617
	1:11	and grant him **m** in the sight of this man.	7356
	9:32	God, who keepest covenant and **m**,	2617
	13:22	me according to the greatness of thy **m**.	2617
Job	37:13	for correction, or for his land, or for **m**.	2617
Ps	4: 1	**have m** upon me, and hear my prayer.	2603
	5: 7	*into* thy house in the multitude of thy **m**:	2617
	6: 2	**Have m** upon me, O LORD; for I *am*	2603
	9:13	**Have m** upon me, O LORD; consider my	2603
	13: 5	I have trusted in thy **m**; my heart shall	2617
	18:50	sheweth **m** to his anointed, to David,	2617
	21: 7	through the **m** of the most High he shall	2617
	23: 6	**m** shall follow me all the days of my life:	2617
	25: 7	according to thy **m** remember thou me	2617
	25:10	All the paths of the LORD *are* **m** and	2617
	25:16	thee unto me, and **have m** upon me;	2603
	27: 7	**have m** also upon me, and answer me.	2603
	30:10	Hear, O LORD, and **have m** upon me:	2603
	31: 7	I will be glad and rejoice in thy **m**: for	2617
	31: 9	**Have m** upon me, O LORD, for I am in	2603
	32:10	in the LORD, shall compass him about.	2617
	33:18	fear him, upon them that hope in his **m**;	2617
	33:22	Let thy **m**, O LORD, be upon us,	2617
	36: 5	Thy **m**, O LORD, *is* in the heavens;	2617
	37:21	the righteous **sheweth m**, and giveth.	2603
	51: 1	**Have m** upon me, O God, according to	2603
	52: 8	I trust in the **m** of God for ever and ever.	2617
	57: 3	God shall send forth his **m** and his truth.	2617
	57:10	For thy **m** *is* great unto the heavens,	2617
	59:10	The God of my **m** shall prevent me:	2617
	59:16	I will sing aloud of thy **m** in the morning:	2617
	59:17	*is* my defence, *and* the God of my **m**.	2617
	61: 7	prepare **m** and truth, *which* may preserve	2617
	62:12	Also unto thee, O Lord, *belongeth* **m**:	2617
	66:20	away my prayer, nor his **m** from me.	2617
	69:13	God, in the multitude of thy **m** hear me,	2617
	77: 8	Is his **m** clean gone for ever? doth *his*	2617
	85: 7	Shew us thy **m**, O LORD, and grant us thy	2617
	85:10	**M** and truth are met together;	2617
	86: 5	plenteous in **m** unto all them that call	2617
	86:13	For great *is* thy **m** toward me: and thou	2617
	86:15	plenteous in **m** and truth.	2617
	86:16	O turn unto me, and **have m** upon me;	2603
	89: 2	I have said, **M** shall be built up for ever:	2617
	89:14	and truth shall go before thy face.	2617
	89:24	and my **m** *shall be* with him:	2617
	89:28	My **m** will I keep for him for evermore,	2617
	90:14	satisfy us early *with* thy **m**; that we may	2617

Ps	94:18	thy **m**, O LORD, held me up.	2617
	98: 3	He hath remembered his **m** and his truth	2617
	100: 5	*is* everlasting; and his truth *endureth*	2617
	101: 1	I will sing of **m** and judgment: unto thee,	2617
	102:13	Thou shalt arise, and **have m** upon Zion:	7355
	103: 8	slow to anger, and plenteous in **m**.	2617
	103:11	great is his **m** toward them that fear him.	2617
	103:17	the **m** of the LORD *is* from everlasting to	2617
	106: 1	*he is* good: for his **m** *endureth* for ever.	2617
	107: 1	*he is* good: for his **m** *endureth* for ever.	2617
	108: 4	For thy **m** *is* great above the heavens:	2617
	109:12	Let there be none to extend **m** unto him:	2617
	109:16	that he remembered not to shew **m**,	2617
	109:21	because thy **m** *is* good, deliver thou me.	2617
	109:26	my God: O save me according to thy **m**:	2617
	115: 1	for thy **m**, *and* for thy truth's sake.	2617
	118: 1	*is* good: because his **m** *endureth* for ever.	2617
	118: 2	now say, that his **m** *endureth* for ever.	2617
	118: 3	now say, that his **m** *endureth* for ever.	2617
	118: 4	LORD say, that his **m** *endureth* for ever.	2617
	118:29	for his **m** *endureth* for ever.	2617
	119:64	The earth, O LORD, is full of thy **m**:	2617
	119:124	with thy servant according unto thy **m**,	2617
	123: 2	our God, until that he **have m** upon us.	2603
	123: 3	**Have m** upon us, O LORD, have mercy	2603
	123: 3	upon us, O LORD, have **m** upon us:	2603
	130: 7	for with the LORD *there is* **m**,	2617
	136: 1	*he is* good: for his **m** *endureth* for ever.	2617
	136: 2	God of gods: for his **m** *endureth* for ever.	2617
	136: 3	Lord of lords: for his **m** *endureth* for ever.	2617
	136: 4	wonders: for his **m** *endureth* for ever.	2617
	136: 5	the heavens: for his **m** *endureth* for ever.	2617
	136: 6	the waters: for his **m** *endureth* for ever.	2617
	136: 7	great lights: for his **m** *endureth* for ever:	2617
	136: 8	rule by day: for his **m** *endureth* for ever:	2617
	136: 9	rule by night: for his **m** *endureth* for ever.	2617
	136:10	firstborn: for his **m** *endureth* for ever:	2617
	136:11	among them: for his **m** *endureth* for ever:	2617
	136:12	out arm: for his **m** *endureth* for ever.	2617
	136:13	into parts: for his **m** *endureth* for ever:	2617
	136:14	midst of it: for his **m** *endureth* for ever:	2617
	136:15	the Red sea: for his **m** *endureth* for ever:	2617
	136:16	wilderness: for his **m** *endureth* for ever.	2617
	136:17	great kings: for his **m** *endureth* for ever:	2617
	136:18	kings: for his **m** *endureth* for ever:	2617
	136:19	Amorites: for his **m** *endureth* for ever:	2617
	136:20	of Bashan: for his **m** *endureth* for ever:	2617
	136:21	an heritage: for his **m** *endureth* for ever:	2617
	136:22	his servant: for his **m** *endureth* for ever:	2617
	136:23	low estate: for his **m** *endureth* for ever:	2617
	136:24	our enemies: for his **m** *endureth* for ever:	2617
	136:25	to all flesh: for his **m** *endureth* for ever.	2617
	136:26	of heaven: for his **m** *endureth* for ever.	2617
	138: 8	thy **m**, O LORD, *endureth* for ever:	2617
	143:12	of thy **m** cut off mine enemies,	2617
	145: 8	slow to anger, and of great **m**.	2617
	147:11	that fear him, in those that hope in his **m**.	2617
Pr	3: 3	Let not **m** and truth forsake thee: bind	2617
	14:21	he that **hath m** on the poor, happy *is* he.	2603
	14:22	**m** and truth *shall be* to them that devise	2617
	14:31	that honoureth him **hath m** on the poor.	2603
	16: 6	By **m** and truth iniquity is purged:	2617
	20:28	**M** and truth preserve the king:	2617
	20:28	king: and his throne is upholden by **m**.	2617
	21:21	after righteousness and **m** findeth life,	2617
	28:13	and forsaketh *them* shall **have m**.	7355
Isa	9:17	neither shall **have m** on their fatherless	7355
	14: 1	For the LORD will **have m** on Jacob,	7355
	16: 5	in **m** shall the throne be established:	2617
	27:11	he that made them will not **have m** on	7355
	30:18	exalted, that *he* may **have m** upon you:	7355
	47: 6	thou didst shew them no **m**; upon	7356
	49:10	he that **hath m** on them shall lead them,	7355
	49:13	and will **have m** upon his afflicted.	7355
	54: 8	everlasting kindness will I **have m** on	7355
	54:10	saith the LORD that **hath m** on thee.	7355
	55: 7	the LORD, and he will **have m** upon him;	7355
	60:10	but in my favour have I **had m** on thee.	7355
Jer	6:23	and spear; they *are* cruel, and **have no m**;	7355
	13:14	nor spare, nor have **m**, but destroy them.	7355
	21: 7	them, neither have pity, nor **have m**.	7355
	30:18	and **have m** on his dwelling places;	7355
	31:20	I will **surely have m** upon him,	7355+7355
	33:11	*is* good; for his **m** *endureth* for ever:	2617
	33:26	captivity to return, and **have m** on them.	7355
	42:12	that he may **have m** upon you,	7355
	50:42	they *are* cruel, and will not **shew m**:	7355
Eze	39:25	have **m** upon the whole house of Israel,	7355
Da	4:27	iniquities by **shewing m** to the poor;	2604
	9: 4	covenant and **m** to them that love him,	2617
Hos	1: 6	I will no more **have m** upon the house	7355
	1: 7	I will **have m** upon the house of Judah,	7355
	1: 8	I will not **have m** upon her children;	7355
	2:23	I will **have m** upon her that had not	7355
	2:23	upon her that had not **obtained m**;	7355
	4: 1	because *there is* no truth, nor **m**,	2617
	6: 7	For I desired **m**, and not sacrifice;	2617
	10:12	yourselves in righteousness, reap in **m**;	2617
	12: 6	keep **m** and judgment, and wait on thy	2617
	14: 3	for in thee the fatherless **findeth m**.	7355
Jnh	2: 8	lying vanities forsake their own **m**.	2617
Mic	6: 8	to love **m**, and to walk humbly with thy	2617
	7:18	for ever, because he delighteth in **m**.	2617
	7:20	the truth to Jacob, *and* the **m** to Abraham,	2617
Hab	3: 2	make known; in wrath remember **m**.	7355

Zec	1:12	how long wilt thou not **have m** on	7355
	7: 9	shew **m** and compassions every man to	2617
	10: 6	to place them; for I **have m** upon them:	7355
Mt	5: 7	*are* the merciful: for they shall **obtain m**.	1653
	9:13	I will **have m**, and not sacrifice:	1656
	9:27	*Thou* Son of David, **have m** on us.	1653
	12: 7	I will **have m**, and not sacrifice,	1656
	15:22	him, saying, **Have m** on me, O Lord,	1653
	17:15	**have m** on my son: for he is lunatick,	1653
	20:30	cried out, saying, **Have m** on us, O Lord,	1653
	20:31	**Have m** on us, O Lord, *thou* Son of	1653
	23:23	of the law, judgment, **m**, and faith:	1656
Mk	10:47	Jesus, *thou* Son of David, **have m** on me.	1653
	10:48	*Thou* Son of David, **have m** on me.	1653
Lk	1:50	And his **m** *is* on them that fear him from	1656
	1:54	servant Israel, in remembrance of *his* **m**,	1656
	1:58	the Lord had shewed great **m** upon her;	1656
	1:72	To perform the **m** *promised* to our fathers,	1656
	1:78	Through the **tender m** of our God;	1656+4698
	10:37	And he said, He that shewed **m** on	1656
	16:24	have **m** on me, and send Lazarus,	1653
	17:13	and said, Jesus, Master, **have m** on us.	1653
	18:38	Jesus, *thou* Son of David, **have m** on me.	1653
	18:39	*Thou* Son of David, **have m** on me.	1653
Ro	9:15	will **have m** on whom I will have mercy,	1653
	9:15	will have mercy on whom I will **have m**,	1653
	9:16	runneth, but of God that **sheweth m**.	1653
	9:18	Therefore **hath** he **m** on whom he will	1653
	9:18	hath he mercy on whom he will **have m**,	NIG
	9:23	the riches of his glory on the vessels of **m**,	1656
	11:30	yet have now **obtained m** through their	1653
	11:31	that through your **m** they also may obtain	1656
	11:31	your mercy they also may **obtain m**.	1656
	11:32	unbelief, that he might **have m** upon all.	1653
	12: 8	he that **sheweth m**, with cheerfulness.	1653
	15: 9	the Gentiles might glorify God for *his* **m**;	1656
1Co	7:25	as one that hath **obtained m** of the Lord	1653
2Co	4: 1	as we have **received m**, we faint not;	1653
Gal	6:16	to this rule, peace *be* on them, and **m**,	1656
Eph	2: 4	But God, who is rich in **m**, for his great	1656
Php	2:27	but God **had m** on him; and not on him	1653
1Ti	1: 2	Grace, **m**, *and* peace, from God our Father	1656
	1:13	but I **obtained m**, because I did *it*	1653
	1:16	Howbeit for this cause I **obtained m**,	1653
2Ti	1: 2	Grace, **m**, *and* peace, from God the Father	1656
	1:16	The Lord give **m** unto the house of	1656
	1:18	Lord grant unto him that *he* may find **m**	1656
Tit	1: 4	Grace, **m**, *and* peace, from God the Father	1656
	3: 5	but according to his **m** he saved us,	1656
Heb	4:16	that we may obtain **m**, and find grace to	1656
	9: 5	cherubims of glory shadowing the **m seat**;	2435
	10:28	Moses' law died without **m** under two	3628
Jas	2:13	For he shall have judgment **without m**,	448
	2:13	without mercy, that hath shewed no **m**;	1656
	2:13	and **m** rejoiceth against judgment.	1656
	3:17	full of **m** and good fruits, without	1656
	5:11	the Lord is very pitiful, and of **tender m**.	3629
1Pe	1: 3	which according to his abundant **m** hath	1656
	2:10	which had not **obtained m**, but now have	1653
	2:10	mercy, but now have **obtained m**.	1653
2Jn	1: 3	Grace be with you, **m**, *and* peace, from	1656
Jude	1: 2	**M** unto you, and peace, and love,	1656
	1:21	looking for the **m** of our Lord Jesus Christ	1656

MERCY'S (3) [MERCY]

Ps	6: 4	my soul: O save me for thy **m** sake.	2617
	31:16	thy servant: save me for thy **m** sake.	2617
	44:26	our help, and redeem us for thy **m** sake.	2617

MERED (2)

1Ch	4:17	Jether, and **M**, and Epher, and Jalon:	4778
	4:18	the daughter of Pharaoh, which **M** took.	4778

MEREMOTH (6)

Ezr	8:33	the hand of **M** the son of Uriah the priest;	4822
	10:36	Vaniah, **M**, Eliashib,	4822
Ne	3: 4	next unto them repaired **M** the son of	4822
	3:21	After him repaired **M** the son of Urijah	4822
	10: 5	Harim, **M**, Obadiah,	4822
	12: 3	Shechaniah, Rehum, **M**,	4822

MERES (1)

Est	1:14	Tarshish, **M**, Marsena, *and* Memucan,	4825

MERETHAIM (1)

Jer	50:21	Go up against the land of **M**, *even* against	4850

MERIBAH (6) [MERIBAH-KADESH]

Ex	17: 7	**M**, because of the chiding of the children	4809
Nu	20:13	This *is* the water of **M**; because	4809
	20:24	against my word at the water of **M**.	4809
	27:14	that *is* the water of **M** in Kadesh *in*	4809
Dt	33: 8	thou didst strive at the waters of **M**;	4809
Ps	81: 7	I proved thee at the waters of **M**. Selah.	4809

MERIBAH-KADESH (1) [MERIBAH, KADESH]

Dt	32:51	the children of Israel at the waters of **M**,	4809

MERIB-BAAL (4) [MEPHIBOSHETH]

1Ch	8:34	the son of Jonathan *was* **M**;	4807
	8:34	*was* Merib-baal; and **M** begat Micah.	4807
	9:40	the son of Jonathan *was* **M**:	4807
	9:40	*was* Merib-baal: and **M** begat Micah.	4810

MERODACH (1)

Jer	50: 2	Bel is confounded, **M** is broken in pieces;	4781

M

MERODACH-BALADAN (1)
[BERODACH-BALADAN]
Isa 39: 1 At that time **M**, the son of Baladan, king 4757

MEROM (2)
Jos 11: 5 and pitched together at the waters of **M**, 4792
 11: 7 them by the waters of **M** suddenly; 4792

MERONOTHITE (2)
1Ch 27:30 and over the asses *was* Jehdeiah the **M**: 4824
Ne 3: 7 Jadon the **M**, the men of Gibeon, and of 4824

MEROZ (1)
Jdg 5:23 Curse ye **M**, said the angel of the LORD, 4789

MERRILY (1) [MERRY]
Est 5:14 go thou in **m** with the king unto 8056

MERRY (28) [MERRILY, MERRYHEARTED]
Ge 43:34 And they drunk, and were **m** with him. 7937
Jdg 9:27 trode *the grapes*, and made **m**, 1974
 16:25 when their hearts were **m**, that they said, 2896
 19: 6 tarry all night, and let thine heart be **m**. 3190
 19: 9 lodge here, that thine heart may be **m**; 3190
 19:22 as they were **making** their hearts **m**, 3190
Ru 3: 7 eaten and drunk, and his heart was **m**, 3190
1Sa 25:36 Nabal's heart *was* **m** within him, for he 2896
2Sa 13:28 Mark ye now when Amnon's heart is **m** 2896
1Ki 4:20 eating and drinking, and **making m**. 8056
 21: 7 *and* eat bread, and let thine heart be **m**: 3190
2Ch 7:10 **m** in heart for the goodness that 2896
Est 1:10 when the heart of the king was **m** with 2896
Pr 15:13 **m** heart maketh a cheerful countenance; 8056
 15:15 *he that is* of a **m** heart *hath* a continual 2896
 17:22 A **m** heart doeth good *like* a medicine: 8056
Ecc 8:15 than to eat, and to drink, and to be **m**: 8055
 9: 7 and drink thy wine with a **m** heart; 2896
 10:19 for laughter, and wine **maketh m**: 2416+8055
Jer 30:19 and the voice of them that **make m**. 7832
 31: 4 in the dances of them that **make m**. 7832
Lk 12:19 take thine ease, eat, drink, *and* be **m**. 2165
 15:23 and kill *it*; and let us eat, and be **m**: 2165
 15:24 and is found. And they began to be **m**. 2165
 15:29 that I might **make m** with my friends: 2165
 15:32 It was meet that *we* should **make m**, 2165
Jas 5:13 Is any **m**? let him sing psalms. 2114
Rev 11:10 and **make m**, and shall send gifts one to 2165

MERRYHEARTED (1) [HEART, MERRY]
Isa 24: 7 vine languisheth, all the **m** do sigh. 3820+8056

MESECH (1)
Ps 120: 5 Woe is me, that I sojourn in **M**, *that* I 4902

MESHA (4)
Ge 10:30 their dwelling was from **M**, as thou goest 4852
2Ki 3: 4 **M** king of Moab was a sheepmaster, 4338
1Ch 2:42 of Jerahmeel *were*, **M** his firstborn, 4337
 8: 9 and Zibia, and **M**, and Malcham, 4331

MESHACH (15)
Da 1: 7 to Mishael, of **M**; and to Azariah, 4335
 2:49 and he set Shadrach, **M**, and Abed-nego; 4336
 3:12 of Babylon, Shadrach, **M**, and Abed-nego; 4336
 3:13 to bring Shadrach, **M**, and Abed-nego. 4336
 3:14 *Is it* true, O Shadrach, **M**, and Abed-nego, 4336
 3:16 **M**, and Abed-nego, answered and said to 4336
 3:19 against Shadrach, **M**, and Abed-nego: 4336
 3:20 **M**, and Abed-nego, *and* to cast *them* into 4336
 3:22 took up Shadrach, **M**, and Abed-nego, 4336
 3:23 three men, Shadrach, **M**, and Abed-nego, 4336
 3:26 and said, Shadrach, **M**, and Abed-nego, 4336
 3:26 Then Shadrach, **M**, and Abed-nego, 4336
 3:28 **M**, and Abed-nego, who hath sent his 4336
 3:29 **M**, and Abed-nego, shall be cut in pieces, 4336
 3:30 **M**, and Abed-nego, in the province of 4336

MESHECH (8)
Ge 10: 2 and Javan, and Tubal, and **M**, and Tiras. 4902
1Ch 1: 5 and Javan, and Tubal, and **M**, and Tiras. 4902
 1:17 and Uz, and Hul, and Gether, and **M**. 4902
Eze 27:13 Javan, Tubal, and **M**, they *were* thy 4902
 32:26 There *is* **M**, Tubal, and all her multitude: 4902
 38: 2 the chief prince of **M** and Tubal, 4902
 38: 3 O Gog, the chief prince of **M** and Tubal: 4902
 1 O Gog, the chief prince of **M** and Tubal: 4902

MESHELEMIAH (4)
1Ch 9:21 Zechariah the son of **M** *was* porter of 4920
 26: 1 Of the Korhites *was* **M** the son of Kore, 4920
 26: 2 the sons of **M** *were*, Zechariah 4920
 26: 9 **M** had sons and brethren, strong men, 4920

MESHEZABEEL (3)
Ne 3: 4 the son of Berechiah, the son of **M**. 4898
 10:21 **M**, Zadok, Jaddua, 4898
 11:24 Pethahiah the son of **M**, of the children of 4898

MESHEZABEL See MESHEZABEEL

MESHILLEMITH (1) [MESHILLEMOTH]
1Ch 9:12 the son of **M**, the son of Immer; 4921

MESHILLEMOTH (2) [MESHILLEMITH]
2Ch 28:12 Berechiah the son of **M**, and Jehizkiah 4919
Ne 11:13 Ahasai, the son of **M**, the son of Immer, 4919

MESHOBAB (1)
1Ch 4:34 **M**, and Jamlech, and Joshah the son of 4877

MESHULLAM (25)
2Ki 22: 3 the son of **M**, the scribe, *to* the house of 4918
1Ch 3:19 **M**, and Hananiah, and Shelomith their 4918
 5:13 **M**, and Sheba, and Jorai, and Jachan, 4918
 8:17 and **M**, and Hezeki, and Heber, 4918
 9: 7 Sallu the son of **M**, the son of Hodaviah, 4918
 9: 8 **M** the son of Shephathiah, the son of 4918
 9:11 the son of **M**, the son of Zadok, the son 4918
 9:12 the son of Jahzerah, the son of **M**, the son 4918
2Ch 34:12 Zechariah and **M**, of the sons of 4918
Ezr 8:16 for Nathan, and for Zechariah, and for **M**, 4918
 10:15 **M** and Shabbethai the Levite helped 4918
 10:29 **M**, Malluch, and Adaiah, Jashub, 4918
Ne 3: 4 next unto them repaired **M** the son of 4918
 3: 6 of Paseah, and **M** the son of Besodeiah; 4918
 3:30 him repaired **M** the son of Berechiah. 4918
 6:18 the daughter of **M** the son of Berechiah. 4918
 8: 4 and Hashbadana, Zechariah, *and* **M**. 4918
 10: 7 **M**, Abijah, Mijamin, 4918
 10:20 Magpiash, **M**, Hezir, 4918
 11: 7 Sallu the son of **M**, the son of Joed, the 4918
 11:11 the son of **M**, the son of Zadok, the son 4918
 12:13 Of Ezra, **M**; of Amariah, Jehohanan; 4918
 12:16 Of Iddo, Zechariah; of Ginnethon, **M**; 4918
 12:25 Bakbukiah, Obadiah, **M**, Talmon, Akkub, 4918
 12:33 And Azariah, Ezra, and **M**, 4918

MESHULLEMETH (1)
2Ki 21:19 his mother's name *was* **M**, the daughter 4922

MESOBAITE (1)
1Ch 11:47 Eliel, and Obed, and Jasiel the **M**. 4677

MESOPOTAMIA (7)
Ge 24:10 he arose, and went to **M**, unto the city of 763
Dt 23: 4 Balaam the son of Beor of Pethor of **M**, 763
Jdg 3: 8 the hand of Chushan-rishathaim king of **M**: 763
 3:10 Chushan-rishathaim king of **M** into his 758
1Ch 19: 6 them chariots and horsemen out of **M**, 763
Ac 2: 9 and the dwellers in **M**, and in Judea, 3318
 7: 2 when he was in **M**, before he dwelt in 3318

MESS (2) [MESSES]
Ge 43:34 Benjamin's **m** was five times so much as 4864
2Sa 11: 8 there followed him a **m** *of meat* from 4864

MESSAGE (7) [MESSENGER, MESSENGERS]
Jdg 3:20 said, I have a **m** from God unto thee. 1697
1Ki 20:12 when *Ben-hadad* heard this **m**, as he *was* 1697
Pr 26: 6 He that sendeth a **m** by the hand of a fool 1697
Hag 1:13 in the LORD's **m** unto the people, 4400
Lk 19:14 hated him, and sent a **m** after him, saying, 4242
1Jn 1: 5 is the **m** which we have heard of him, 1860
 3:11 For this is the **m** that ye heard from 31

MESSENGER (34) [MESSAGE]
Ge 50:16 they sent a **m** unto Joseph, saying, 6680
1Sa 4:17 the **m** answered and said, Israel is fled 1319
 23:27 there came a **m** unto Saul, saying, 4397
2Sa 11:19 charged the **m**, saying, When thou hast 4397
 11:22 So the **m** went, and came and 4397
 11:23 the **m** said unto David, Surely the men 4397
 11:25 David said unto the **m**, Thus shalt thou 4397
 15:13 there came a **m** to David, saying, 5046
1Ki 19: 2 Jezebel sent a **m** unto Elijah, saying, So let 4397
 22:13 the **m** that was gone to call Micaiah spake 4397
2Ki 5:10 Elisha sent a **m** unto him, saying, Go and 4397
 6:32 ere the **m** came to him, he said to 4397
 6:32 look, when the **m** cometh, shut the door, 4397
 6:33 behold, the **m** came down unto him: 4397
 9:18 The **m** came to them, but he cometh not 4397
 10: 8 there came a **m**, and told him, saying, 4397
2Ch 18:12 the **m** that went to call Micaiah spake to 4397
Job 1:14 there came a **m** unto Job, and said, 4397
 33:23 If there be a **m** with him, an interpreter, 4397
Pr 17:11 A wicked **m** falleth into mischief: 4397
 17:11 a cruel **m** shall be sent against him. 4397
 25:13 *so is* a faithful **m** to them that send him: 6735
Isa 42:19 or deaf, as my **m** *that* I sent? who *is* blind 4397
Jer 51:31 meet another, and one **m** to meet another, 5046
Eze 23:40 come from far, unto whom a **m** *was* sent; 4397
Hag 1:13 spake Haggai the LORD's **m** in 4397
Mal 2: 7 for he *is* the **m** of the LORD of hosts. 4397
 3: 1 I *will* send my **m**, and he shall prepare 4397
 3: 1 even the **m** of the covenant, whom ye 4397
Mt 11:10 Behold, I send my **m** before thy face, 32
Mk 1: 2 Behold, I send my **m** before thy face, 32
Lk 7:27 Behold, I send my **m** before thy face, 32
2Co 12: 7 the **m** of Satan to buffet me, lest I should 32
Php 2:25 but your **m**, and he that ministered to my 652

MESSENGERS (79) [MESSAGE]
Ge 32: 3 Jacob sent **m** before him to Esau his 4397
 32: 6 the **m** returned to Jacob, saying, We came 4397
Nu 20:14 Moses sent **m** from Kadesh unto the king 4397
 21:21 Israel sent **m** unto Sihon king of 4397
 22: 5 He sent **m** therefore unto Balaam the son 4397
 24:12 Spake I not also to thy **m** which thou 4397
Dt 2:26 sent **m** out of the wilderness of Kedemoth 4397
Jos 6:17 because she hid the **m** that we sent. 4397
 6:25 because she hid the **m**, which Joshua sent 4397
 7:22 So Joshua sent **m**, and they ran unto 4397

Jdg 6:35 he sent **m** throughout all Manasseh; 4397
 6:35 he sent **m** unto Asher, and unto Zebulun, 4397
 7:24 Gideon sent **m** throughout all mount 4397
 9:31 he sent **m** unto Abimelech privily, saying, 4397
 11:12 Jephthah sent **m** unto the king of 4397
 11:13 answered unto the **m** of Jephthah, 4397
 11:14 Jephthah sent **m** again unto the king of 4397
 11:17 Israel sent **m** unto the king of Edom, 4397
 11:19 Israel sent **m** unto Sihon king of 4397
1Sa 6:21 they sent **m** to the inhabitants of 4397
 11: 3 that we may send **m** unto all the coasts of 4397
 11: 4 came the **m** *to* Gibeah of Saul, and told 4397
 11: 7 all the coasts of Israel by the hands of **m**, 4397
 11: 9 they said unto the **m** that came, Thus 4397
 11: 9 the **m** came and shewed *it* to the men of 4397
 16:19 Wherefore Saul sent **m** unto Jesse, 4397
 19:11 Saul also sent **m** unto David's house, 4397
 19:14 when Saul sent **m** to take David, she said, 4397
 19:15 Saul sent the **m** *again* to see David, 4397
 19:16 when the **m** were come in, behold *there* 4397
 19:20 Saul sent **m** to take David: and when they 4397
 19:20 the spirit of God was upon the **m** of Saul, 4397
 19:21 he sent other **m**, and they prophesied 4397
 19:21 Saul sent **m** again the third time, 4397
 25:14 sent **m** out of the wilderness to 4397
 25:42 she went after the **m** of David, 4397
2Sa 2: 5 David sent **m** unto the men of 4397
 3:12 Abner sent **m** to David on his behalf, 4397
 3:14 David sent **m** to Ish-bosheth Saul's son, 4397
 3:26 out from David, he sent **m** after Abner, 4397
 5:11 Hiram king of Tyre sent **m** to David, 4397
 11: 4 David sent **m**, and took her; and she 4397
 12:27 Joab sent **m** to David, and said, I have 4397
1Ki 20: 2 he sent **m** to Ahab king of Israel into 4397
 20: 5 the **m** came again, and said, Thus 4397
 20: 9 Wherefore he said unto the **m** of 4397
 20: 9 the **m** departed, and brought him word 4397
2Ki 1: 2 he sent **m**, and said unto them, 4397
 1: 3 up to meet the **m** of the king of Samaria, 4397
 1: 5 the **m** turned back unto him, he said 4397
 1:16 Forasmuch as thou hast sent **m** to inquire 4397
 7:15 And the **m** returned, and told the king. 4397
 14: 8 Amaziah sent **m** to Jehoash, the son of 4397
 16: 7 So Ahaz sent **m** to Tiglath-pileser king of 4397
 17: 4 for he had sent **m** to So king of Egypt, 4397
 19: 9 he sent **m** again unto Hezekiah, saying, 4397
 19:14 received the letter of the hand of the **m**, 4397
 19:23 By thy **m** thou hast reproached the Lord, 4397
1Ch 14: 1 Now Hiram king of Tyre sent **m** to David, 4397
 19: 2 David sent **m** to comfort him concerning 4397
 19:16 they sent **m**, and drew forth the Syrians 4397
2Ch 36:15 of their fathers sent to them by his **m**, 4397
 36:16 they mocked the **m** of God, 4397
Ne 6: 3 I sent **m** unto them, saying, I *am* doing a 4397
Pr 16:14 The wrath of a king *is as* **m** of death: 4397
Isa 14:32 one then answer the **m** of the nation? 4397
 18: 2 saying, Go, ye swift **m**, to a nation 4397
 37: 9 when he heard *it*, he sent **m** to Hezekiah, 4397
 37:14 the letter from the hand of the **m**, 4397
 44:26 and performeth the counsel of his **m**; 4397
 57: 9 didst send thy **m** far off, and didst debase 6735
Jer 27: 3 by the hand of the **m** which come *to* 4397
Eze 23:16 and sent **m** unto them into Chaldea. 4397
 30: 9 In that day shall **m** go forth from me in 4397
Na 2:13 the voice of thy **m** shall no more be heard. 4397
Lk 7:24 And when the **m** of John were departed, 32
 9:52 sent **m** before his face: and they went, 32
2Co 8:23 our brethren *be inquired of*, they *are* the **m** 652
Jas 2:25 when she had received the **m**, and had sent 32

MESSES (1) [MESS]
Ge 43:34 *and sent* **m** unto them from before him: 4864

MESSIAH (2) [MESSIAS]
Da 9:25 to build Jerusalem unto the **M** the Prince 4899
 9:26 and two weeks shall **M** be cut off, 4899

MESSIAS (2) [MESSIAH]
Jn 1:41 him, We have found the **M**, which is, 3323
 4:25 I know that **M** cometh, which is called 3323

MET (45) [MEET]
Ge 32: 1 on his way, and the angels of God **m** him. 6293
 33: 8 meanest thou by all this drove which I **m**? 6298
Ex 3:18 The LORD God of the Hebrews hath **m** 7136
 4:24 that the LORD **m** him, and sought to kill 6298
 4:27 **m** him in the mount of God, 6298
 5: 3 The God of the Hebrews hath **m** with us: 7122
 5:20 they **m** Moses and Aaron, who stood in 6293
Nu 23: 4 God **m** Balaam: and he said unto him, 7136
 23:16 the LORD **m** Balaam, and put a word in 7136
Dt 23: 4 Because they **m** you not with bread and 6923
 25:18 How he **m** thee by the way, and smote 7136
Jos 11: 5 when all these kings were **m together**, 3259
 17:10 they **m together** in Asher on the north, 6293
1Sa 10:10 behold, a company of prophets **m** him; 7125
 25:20 came down against her; and she **m** them. 6298
2Sa 2:13 and **m together** by the pool of Gibeon; 6298
 16: 1 Ziba the servant of Mephibosheth **m** him, 7125
 18: 9 Absalom **m** the servants of David. 7122
1Ki 13:24 a lion **m** him by the way, and slew him: 4672
 18: 7 was in the way, behold Elijah **m** him: 7125
2Ki 9:21 **m** him in the portion of Naboth 4672
 10:13 Jehu **m** with the brethren of Ahaziah king 4672
Ne 13: 2 Because they **m** not the children of Israel 6923

Ps 85:10 Mercy and truth are **m together**; 6298
Pr 7:10 there **m** him a woman *with* the attire of a 7125
Jer 41: 6 came to pass, as he **m** them, he said unto 6298
Am 5:19 did flee from a lion, and a bear **m** him; 6293
Mt 5:19 there him **m** two possessed with devils, 5221
 28: 9 behold, Jesus **m** them, saying, *All hail.* 528
Mk 5: 2 immediately there **m** him out of the tombs 5221
 11: 4 without in a place where two ways **m**; 296
Lk 8:27 there **m** him out of the city a certain man, 5221
 9:37 down from the hill, much people **m** him, 4876
 17:12 there **m** him ten men *that were* lepers, 528
Jn 4:51 his servants **m** him, and told *him*, saying, 528
 11:20 that Jesus was coming, **went and m** him: 5221
 11:30 was in *that* place where Martha **m** him. 5221
 12:18 For this cause the people also **m** him, 5221
Ac 10:25 Cornelius **m** him, and fell down at *his* 4876
 16:16 possessed with a spirit of divination **m** us, 528
 17:17 the market daily with them that **m with** 3909
 20:14 when he **m with** us at Assos, we took 4820
 27:41 falling into a place **where two seas m**, 1337
Heb 7: 1 who **m** Abraham returning from 4876
 7:10 of his father, when Melchisedec **m** him. 4876

METALWORKER See COPPERSMITH

METE (6) [METED]
Ex 16:18 when they did **m** *it* with an omer, he that 4058
Ps 60: 6 and **m out** the valley of Succoth. 4058
 108: 7 and **m out** the valley of Succoth. 4058
Mt 7: 2 and with what measure ye **m**, it shall be 3354
Mk 4:24 with what measure ye **m**, it shall be 3354
Lk 6:38 with the same measure that ye **m** withal 3354

METED (3) [METE]
Isa 18: 2 a nation **m out** and trodden down, 6978+6978
 18: 7 a nation **m out** and trodden under 6978+6978
 40:12 **m out** heaven with the span, 8505

METEYARD (1)
Lev 19:35 in **m**, in weight, or in measure. 4060

METHEG-AMMAH (1) [AMMAH]
2Sa 8: 1 David took **M** out of the hand of 4964

METHUSAEL (2)
Ge 4:18 Mehujael begat **M:** and Methusael begat 4967
 4:18 begat Methusael: and **M** begat Lamech. 4967

METHUSELAH (6) [MATHUSALA]
Ge 5:21 lived sixty and five years, and begat **M:** 4968
 5:22 Enoch walked with God after he begat **M** 4968
 5:25 **M** lived an hundred eighty and seven 4968
 5:26 **M** lived after he begat Lamech seven 4968
 5:27 all the days of **M** were nine hundred sixty 4968
1Ch 1: 3 Henoch, **M**, Lamech, 4968

METHUSHAEL See METHUSAEL

MEUNIM (1) [MEHUNIM]
Ne 7:52 The children of Besai, the children of **M**, 4586

MEUNITES See MEHUNIMS

MEZAHAB (2)
Ge 36:39 daughter of Matred, the daughter of **M**. 4314
1Ch 1:50 daughter of Matred, the daughter of **M**. 4314

MEZOBAITE See MESOBAITE

MIAMIN (2)
Ezr 10:25 **M**, and Eleazar, and Malchijah, 4326
Ne 12: 5 **M**, Maadiah, Bilgah, 4326

MIBHAR (1)
1Ch 11:38 brother of Nathan, **M** the son of Haggeri, 4006

MIBSAM (3)
Ge 25:13 Nebajoth; and Kedar, and Adbeel, and **M**, 4017
1Ch 1:29 Nebajoth; then Kedar, and Adbeel, and **M**, 4017
 4:25 his son, **M** his son, Mishma his son. 4017

MIBZAR (2)
Ge 36:42 Duke Kenaz, Duke Teman, duke **M**, 4014
1Ch 1:53 Duke Kenaz, duke Teman, duke **M**, 4014

MICAH (27) [MICAH'S, MICHA]
Jdg 17: 1 of mount Ephraim, whose name *was* **M**. 4321
 17: 4 and they were in the house of **M**. 4321
 17: 5 the man **M** had a house of gods, 4318
 17: 8 *to* mount Ephraim to the house of **M**, 4318
 17: 9 **M** said unto him, Whence comest thou? 4318
 17:10 **M** said unto him, Dwell with me, 4318
 17:12 **M** consecrated the Levite; and the young 4318
 17:12 his priest, and was in the house of **M**. 4318
 17:13 said **M**, Now know I that the Lord will 4318
 18: 2 to the house of **M**, they lodged there. 4318
 18: 3 When they *were* by the house of **M**, they 4318
 18: 4 Thus and thus dealeth **M** with me, 4318
 18:13 and came unto the house of **M**. 4318
 18:15 *unto* the house of **M**, and saluted him. 4318
 18:22 were a good way from the house of **M**, 4318
 18:23 and said unto **M**, What aileth thee, 4318
 18:26 **M** saw that they *were* too strong for 4318
 18:27 they took *the things* which **M** had made, 4318
1Ch 5: 5 **M** his son, Reaia his son, Baal his son, 4318
 8:34 *was* Merib-baal; and Merib-baal begat **M**. 4318
 8:35 the sons of **M** *were*, Pithon, and Melech, 4318

1Ch 9:15 and Galal, and Mattaniah the son of **M**, 4316
 9:40 *was* Merib-baal: and Merib-baal begat **M**. 4318
 9:41 the sons of **M** *were*, Pithon, and Melech, 4318
2Ch 34:20 Abdon the son of **M**, and Shaphan. 4318
Mic 1: 1 The word of the Lord that came to **M** 4318

MICAH'S (3) [MICAH]
Jdg 18:18 these went *into* **M** house, and fetched 4318
 18:22 men that *were* in the houses near to **M** 4318
 18:31 set them up **M** graven image, which he 4318

MICAIAH (18)
1Ki 22: 8 *is* yet one man, **M** the son of Imlah, 4321
 22: 9 said, Hasten *hither* **M** the son of Imlah. 4321
 22:13 the messenger that was gone to call **M** 4321
 22:14 **M** said, *As* the Lord liveth, what 4321
 22:15 the king said unto him, **M**, shall we go 4321
 22:24 and smote **M** on the cheek, and said, 4321
 22:25 **M** said, Behold, thou shalt see in that day, 4321
 22:26 Take **M**, and carry him back unto Amon 4321
 22:28 **M** said, If thou return at all in peace, 4321
2Ch 18: 7 the same *is* **M** the son of Imla. 4321
 18: 8 and said, Fetch quickly **M** the son of Imla. 4321
 18:12 the messenger that went to call **M** spake 4321
 18:13 **M** said, *As* the Lord liveth, even what 4321
 18:14 to the king, the king said unto him, **M**, 4318
 18:23 and smote **M** upon the cheek, and said, 4321
 18:24 **M** said, Behold, thou shalt see on that day 4321
 18:25 Take ye **M**, and carry him back to Amon 4321
 18:27 **M** said, If thou certainly return in peace, 4321

MICE (4) [MOUSE]
1Sa 6: 4 Five golden emerods, and five golden **m**, 5909
 6: 5 and images of your **m** that mar the land; 5909
 6:11 the coffer with the **m** of gold and 5909
 6:18 the golden **m**, *according to* the number 5909

MICHA (4) [MICAH]
2Sa 9:12 had a young son, whose name *was* **M**. 4316
Ne 10:11 **M**, Rehob, Hashabiah, 4316
 11:17 Mattaniah the son of **M**, the son of Zabdi, 4316
 11:22 the son of Mattaniah, the son of **M**. 4316

MICHAEL (15)
Nu 13:13 the tribe of Asher, Sethur the son of **M**. 4317
1Ch 5:13 of the house of their fathers *were*, **M**, 4317
 5:14 Jaroah, the son of Gilead, the son of **M**, 4317
 6:40 The son of **M**, the son of Baaseiah, the 4317
 7: 3 **M**, and Obadiah, and Joel, Ishiah, five: 4317
 8:16 And Ispah, and Joha, the sons of 4317
 12:20 and Jozabad, and Elihu, and Zilthai, 4317
 27:18 of David: of Issachar, Omri the son of **M**: 4317
2Ch 21: 2 and Azariah, and **M**, and Shephatiah: 4317
Ezr 8: 8 Zebadiah the son of **M**, and with him 4317
Da 10:13 lo, **M**, one of the chief princes, came to 4317
 10:21 in these *things*, but **M** your prince. 4317
 12: 1 at that time shall **M** stand up, the great 4317
Jude 1: 9 Yet **M** the archangel, when contending 3413
Rev 12: 7 **M** and his angels fought against the 3413

MICHAH (4)
1Ch 23:20 **M** the first, and Jesiah the second. 4318
 24:24 *Of* the sons of Uzziel; **M:** of the sons of 4318
 24:24 Michah: of the sons of **M**; Shamir. 4318
 24:25 The brother of **M** *was* Isshiah: of the sons 4318

MICHAIAH (7)
2Ki 22:12 Achbor the son of **M**, and Shaphan. 4320
2Ch 13: 2 His mother's name also *was* **M** 4322
 17: 7 Zechariah, and to Nethaneel, and to **M**, 4322
Ne 12:35 the son of **M**, the son of Zaccur, the son 4320
 12:41 Maaseiah, Miniamin, **M**, Elioenai, 4320
Jer 36:11 When **M** the son of Gemariah, the son of 4321
 36:13 **M** declared unto them all the words that 4321

MICHAL (18)
1Sa 14:49 and the name of the younger **M:** 4324
 18:20 **M** Saul's daughter loved David: 4324
 18:27 Saul gave him **M** his daughter to wife. 4324
 18:28 and *that* **M** Saul's daughter loved him. 4324
 19:11 **M** David's wife told him, saying, If thou 4324
 19:12 So **M** let David down through a window: 4324
 19:13 **M** took an image, and laid *it* in the bed, 4324
 19:17 said unto **M**, Why hast thou deceived 4324
 19:17 answered Saul, He said unto me, Let 4324
 25:44 Saul had given **M** his daughter, 4324
2Sa 3:13 except thou first bring **M** Saul's daughter, 4324
 3:14 Saul's son, saying, Deliver *me* my wife **M**, 4324
 6:16 **M** Saul's daughter looked through a 4324
 6:20 The daughter of Saul came out to meet 4324
 6:21 David said unto **M**, *It was* before 4324
 6:23 Therefore **M** the daughter of Saul had no 4324
 21: 8 the five sons of **M** the daughter of Saul, 4324
1Ch 15:29 the daughter of Saul looking out at a 4324

MICHMAS (2) [MICHMASH]
Ezr 2:27 men of **M**, an hundred twenty and two. 4363
Ne 7:31 men of **M**, an hundred and twenty and 4363

MICHMASH (9) [MICHMAS]
1Sa 13: 2 two thousand were with Saul in **M** 4363
 13: 5 they came up, and pitched in **M**, 4363
 13:11 gathered themselves together *at* **M**; 4363
 13:16 but the Philistines encamped in **M**. 4363
 13:23 Philistines went out to the passage of **M**. 4363

1Sa 14: 5 *was* situate northward over against **M**, 4363
 14:31 smote the Philistines that day from **M** 4363
Ne 11:31 also of Benjamin from Geba *dwelt at* **M**, 4363
Isa 10:28 at **M** he hath laid up his carriages: 4363

MICHMETHAH (2)
Jos 16: 6 border went out toward the sea *to* **M** on 4366
 17: 7 coast of Manasseh was from Asher *to* **M**, 4366

MICHRI (1)
1Ch 9: 8 the son of **M**, and Meshullam the son of 4381

MICHTAM (6)
Ps 16: T **M** of David. 4387
 56: T **M** of David, when the Philistines took 4387
 57: T chief Musician, Al-taschith, **M** of David, 4387
 58: T chief Musician, Al-taschith, **M** of David. 4387
 59: T chief Musician, Al-taschith, **M** of David; 4387
 60: T Shushan-eduth, **M** of David, to teach; 4387

MICMASH See MICHMAS; MICHMASH

MICMETHATH See MICHMETHAH

MICRI See MICHRI

MIDDAY (3) [DAY, MIDDLE]
1Ki 18:29 when **m** was past, and they prophesied 6672
Ne 8: 3 from the morning until **m**, 3117+4276+1886.1
Ac 26:13 At **m**, O king, I saw in the way a 2250+3319

MIDDIN (1)
Jos 15:61 Beth-arabah, **M**, and Secacah, 4081

MIDDLE (18) [MIDDAY, MIDDLEMOST, MIDNIGHT, MIDST]
Ex 26:28 the **m** bar in the midst of the boards shall 8484
 36:33 he made the **m** bar to shoot through 8484
Jos 12: 2 *from* the **m** of the river, and *from* half 8432
Jdg 7:19 camp in the beginning of the **m** watch; 8484
 9:37 See there come people down by the **m** of 2872
 16:29 Samson took hold of the two **m** pillars 8432
1Sa 25:29 shall he sling out *as out of* the **m** of a 3709
2Sa 10: 4 cut off their garments in the **m**, *even* to 2677
1Ki 6: 6 the **m** *was* six cubits broad, and the third 8484
 6: 8 The door for the **m** chamber *was* in 8484
 6: 8 went up with winding stairs into the **m** 8484
 6: 8 and out of the **m** into the third. 8484
 8:64 The same day did the king hallow the **m** 8432
2Ki 20: 4 Isaiah was gone out *into* the **m** court, 8484
2Ch 7: 7 Moreover Solomon hallowed the **m** of 8432
Jer 39: 3 sat in the **m** gate, *even* Nergal-sharezer, 8432
Eze 1:16 work *was* as it were a wheel in the **m** 8432
Eph 2:14 broken down the **m wall** of partition 3320

MIDDLEMOST (2) [MIDDLE]
Eze 42: 5 lower, and than the **m** of the building. 8484
 42: 6 the lowest and the **m** from the ground. 8484

MIDIAN (39) [MADIAN, MIDIANITE, MIDIANITES, MIDIANITISH]
Ge 25: 2 Medan, and **M**, and Ishbak, and Shuah, 4080
 25: 4 the sons of **M**; Ephah, and Epher, 4080
 36:35 who smote **M** in the field of Moab, 4080
Ex 2:15 of Pharaoh, and dwelt in the land of **M:** 4080
 2:16 Now the priest of **M** had seven daughters: 4080
 3: 1 of Jethro his father in law, the priest of **M:** 4080
 4:19 the Lord said unto Moses in **M**, 4080
 18: 1 When Jethro, the priest of **M**, Moses' 4080
Nu 22: 4 Moab said unto the elders of **M**, Now 4080
 22: 7 the elders of **M** departed with the rewards 4080
 25:15 over a people, *and* of a chief house in **M**. 4080
 25:18 the daughter of a prince of **M**, their sister, 4080
 31: 3 and avenge the Lord of **M**. 4080
 31: 8 slew the kings of **M**, beside *the rest of* 4080
 31: 8 and Hur, and Reba, five kings of **M**: 4080
 31: 9 Israel took *all* the women of **M** captives, 4080
Jos 13:21 Moses smote with the princes of **M**, 4080
Jdg 6: 1 them into the hand of **M** seven years. 4080
 6: 2 the hand of **M** prevailed against Israel: 4080
 7: 8 the host of **M** was beneath him in 4080
 7:13 barley bread tumbled into the host of **M**, 4080
 7:14 for into his hand hath God delivered **M**, 4080
 7:15 delivered into your hand the host of **M**. 4080
 7:25 pursued **M**, and brought the heads of 4080
 8: 3 into your hands the princes of **M**, 4080
 8: 5 after Zebah and Zalmunna, kings of **M**. 4080
 8:12 took the two kings of **M**, Zebah and 4080
 8:22 hast delivered us from the hand of **M**. 4080
 8:26 raiment that *was* on the kings of **M**, 4080
 8:28 Thus was **M** subdued before the children 4080
 9:17 and delivered you out of the hand of **M**: 4080
1Ki 11:18 they arose out of **M**, and came *to* Paran: 4080
1Ch 1:32 Medan, and **M**, and Ishbak, and Shuah. 4080
 1:33 the sons of **M**; Ephah, and Epher, 4080
 1:46 which smote **M** in the field of Moab, 4080
Isa 9: 4 rod of his oppressor, as *in* the day of **M**, 4080
 10:26 to the slaughter of **M** at the rock Oreb: 4080
 60: 6 the dromedaries of **M** and Ephah; 4080
Hab 3: 7 the curtains of the land of **M** did tremble. 4080

MIDIANITE (1) [MIDIAN]
Nu 10:29 the son of Raguel the **M**, Moses' father in 4084

MIDIANITES (23) [MIDIAN]
Ge 37:28 there passed by **M** merchantmen; 4084

Nu	25:17 Vex the **M**, and smite them:	4084
	31: 2 Avenge the children of Israel of the **M**:	4084
	31: 3 let them go against the **M**, and avenge	4080
	31: 7 they warred against the **M**, as the Lord	4080
Jdg	6: 2 the **M** the children of Israel made them	4080
	6: 3 that the **M** came up, and the Amalekites,	4080
	6: 6 greatly impoverished because of the **M**;	4080
	6: 7 cried unto the Lord because of the **M**,	4080
	6:11 by the winepress, to hide *it* from the **M**.	4080
	6:13 and delivered us into the hands of the **M**.	4080
	6:14 shalt save Israel from the hand of the **M**:	4080
	6:16 and thou shalt smite the **M** as one man.	4080
	6:33 all the **M** and the Amalekites and	4080
	7: 1 that the host of the **M** were on the north	4080
	7: 2 for me to give the **M** into their hands,	4080
	7: 7 and deliver the **M** into thine hand:	4080
	7:12 the **M** and the Amalekites and all	4080
	7:23 of all Manasseh, and pursued after the **M**.	4080
	7:24 Come down against the **M**, and take	4080
	7:25 they took two princes of the **M**, Oreb and	4080
	8: 1 when thou wentest to fight with the **M**?	4080
Ps	83: 9 Do unto them as *unto* the **M**; as to Sisera,	4080

MIDIANITISH (3) [MIDIAN]

Nu	25: 6 brought unto his brethren a **M** *woman* in	4084
	25:14 *even* that was slain with the **M woman**,	4084
	25:15 the name of the **M** woman that was slain	4084

MIDNIGHT (14) [MIDDLE, NIGHT]

Ex	11: 4 About **m** will I go out into	2676+3915+1886.1
	12:29 that at **m** the Lord smote	2677+3915+1886.1
Jdg	16: 3 Samson lay till **m**,	2677+3915+1886.1
	16: 3 arose at **m**, and took	2677+3915+1886.1
Ru	3: 8 it came to pass at **m**, that	2677+3915+1886.1
1Ki	3:20 she rose at **m**, and took	3915+8432+1886.1
Job	34:20 the people shall be troubled at **m**,	2676+3915
Ps	119:62 **At m** I will rise to give thanks unto	2676+3915
Mt	25: 6 And **at m** there was a cry made,	3319+3571
Mk	13:35 or **at m**, or at the cockcrowing, or in	3317
Lk	11: 5 and shall go unto him **at m**, and say unto	3317
Ac	16:25 And **at m** Paul and Silas prayed,	3317
	20: 7 and continued *his* speech until **m**.	3317
	27:27 about **m** the shipmen	3319+3571+3588

MIDST (364) [MIDDLE]

Ge	1: 6 Let there be a firmament in the **m** of	8432
	2: 9 tree of life also in the **m** of the garden,	8432
	3: 3 the fruit of the tree which *is* in the **m** of	8432
	15:10 divided them in the **m**, and laid each	8432
	19:29 sent Lot out of the **m** of the overthrow,	8432
	48:16 them grow into a multitude in the **m** of	7130
Ex	3: 2 in a flame of fire out of the **m** of a bush:	8432
	3: 4 God called unto him out of the **m** of	8432
	3:20 wonders which I will do in the **m** thereof:	7130
	8:22 that I *am* the Lord in the **m** of the earth.	7130
	11: 4 midnight will I go out into the **m** of	8432
	14:16 on dry *ground* through the **m** of the sea.	8432
	14:22 the children of Israel went into the **m** of	8432
	14:23 went in after them to the **m** of the sea,	8432
	14:27 the Egyptians in the **m** of the sea.	8432
	14:29 on dry *land* in the **m** of the sea;	8432
	15:19 went on dry *land* in the **m** of the sea.	8432
	23:25 I will take sickness away from the **m** of	7130
	24:16 unto Moses out of the **m** of the cloud.	8432
	24:18 Moses went into the **m** of the cloud,	8432
	26:28 middle bar in the **m** of the boards shall	8432
	27: 5 that the net may be even to the **m** of	2677
	28:32 a hole in the top of it, in the **m** thereof:	8432
	33: 3 for I will not go up in the **m** of thee;	7130
	33: 5 I will come up into the **m** of thee in a	7130
	34:12 lest it be for a snare in the **m** of thee:	7130
	38: 4 thereof beneath unto the **m** of it.	2677
	39:23 *there was* a hole in the **m** of the robe,	8432
Lev	16:16 that remaineth among them in the **m** of	8432
Nu	2:17 camp of the Levites in the **m** of the camp:	8432
	5: 3 not their camps, in the **m** whereof I dwell.	8432
	16:47 and ran into the **m** of the congregation;	8432
	19: 6 cast *it* into the **m** of the burning of	8432
	33: 8 passed through the **m** of the sea	8432+871.1
	35: 5 and the city *shall* be in the **m**:	8432
Dt	4:11 mountain burnt with fire unto the **m** of	3820
	4:12 the Lord spake unto you out of the **m** of	8432
	4:15 you in Horeb out of the **m** of the fire:	8432
	4:33 of God speaking out of the **m** of the fire,	8432
	4:34 take him a nation from the **m** of *another*	7130
	4:36 thou heardest his words out of the **m** of	8432
	5: 4 face in the mount out of the **m** of the fire,	8432
	5:22 in the mount out of the **m** of the fire,	8432
	5:23 when ye heard the voice out of the **m** of	8432
	5:24 we have heard his voice out of the **m** of	8432
	5:26 God speaking out of the **m** of the fire,	8432
	9:10 **m** of the fire in the day of the assembly.	8432
	10: 4 **m** of the fire in the day of the assembly.	8432
	11: 3 which he did in the **m** of Egypt unto	8432
	11: 6 in their possession, in the **m** of all Israel:	7130
	13: 5 shalt thou put the evil away from the **m** of	7130
	13:16 spoil of it, into the **m** of the street thereof,	8432
	17:20 he, and his children, in the **m** of Israel.	7130
	18:15 unto thee a Prophet from the **m** of thee,	7130
	19: 2 three cities for thee in the **m** of thy land,	8432
	23:14 For the Lord thy God walketh in the **m**	7130
	32:51 ye sanctified me not in the **m** of	8432
Jos	3:17 firm on dry *ground* in the **m** of Jordan,	8432
	4: 3 Take you hence out of the **m** of Jordan,	8432
	4: 5 the Lord your God into the **m** of Jordan,	8432
Jos	4: 8 took up twelve stones out of the **m** of	8432
	4: 9 Joshua set up twelve stones in the **m** of	8432
	4:10 bare the ark stood in the **m** of Jordan,	8432
	4:18 were come up out of the **m** of Jordan,	8432
	7:13 *is* an accursed thing in the **m** of thee,	7130
	7:21 they *are* hid in the earth in the **m** of my	8432
	7:23 they took them out of the **m** of the tent,	8432
	8:13 Joshua that night into the **m** of	8432
	8:22 so they were in the **m** of Israel, some on	8432
	10:13 So the sun stood still in the **m** of heaven,	2677
	13: 9 and the city that *is* in the **m** of the river,	8432
	13:16 and the city that *is* in the **m** of the river,	8432
Jdg	15: 4 a firebrand in the **m** between two tails.	8432
	18:20 and went in the **m** of the people.	7130
	20:42 cities they destroyed in the **m** of them.	8432
1Sa	11:11 they came into the **m** of the host in	8432
	16:13 anointed him in the **m** of his brethren:	7130
	18:10 and he prophesied in the **m** of the house:	8432
2Sa	1:25 How are the mighty fallen in the **m** of	8432
	4: 6 came thither into the **m** of the house,	8432
	6:17 in the **m** of the tabernacle that David had	8432
	18:14 he was yet alive in the **m** of the oak.	3820
	20:12 Amasa wallowed in blood in the **m** of	8432
	23:12 he stood in the **m** of the ground,	8432
	23:20 slew a lion in the **m** of a pit in time of	8432
	24: 5 that *lieth* in the **m** of the river of Gad,	8432
1Ki	3: 8 servant *is* in the **m** of thy people which	8432
	6:27 wings touched one another in the **m** of	8432
	8:51 Egypt, from the **m** of the furnace of iron:	8432
	20:39 Thy servant went out into the **m** of	7130
	22:35 blood ran out of the wound into the **m**	2436
2Ki	6:20 behold, *they were* in the **m** of Samaria.	8432
1Ch	11:14 set themselves in the **m** of *that* parcel,	8432
	16: 1 set it in the **m** of the tent that David had	8432
	19: 4 cut off their garments in the **m** hard by	2677
2Ch	6:13 and had set it in the **m** of the court:	8432
	20:14 came the spirit of the Lord in the **m** of	8432
	32: 4 the brook that ran through the **m** of	8432
Ne	4:11 till we come **in the m** among them,	413
	9:11 that they went through the **m** of	8432+871.1
Est	4: 1 went out into the **m** of the city,	8432
Job	21:21 of his months is **cut off** in the **m**?	2686
Ps	22:14 it is melted in the **m** of my bowels.	8432
	22:22 in the **m** of the congregation will I praise	8432
	46: 2 the mountains be carried into the **m**	3820
	46: 5 God *is* in the **m** of her; she shall not be	7130
	48: 9 O God, in the **m** of thy temple.	7130
	55:10 also and sorrow *are* in the **m** of it.	8432
	55:11 Wickedness *is* in the **m** thereof: deceit	7130
	57: 6 into the **m** whereof they are fallen	8432
	74: 4 Thine enemies roar in the **m** of thy	7130
	74:12 working salvation in the **m** of the earth.	7130
	78:28 he let *it* fall in the **m** of their camp,	7130
	102:24 take me not away in the **m** of my days:	2677
	110: 2 rule thou in the **m** of thine enemies.	7130
	116:19 in the **m** of thee, O Jerusalem.	8432
	135: 9 tokens and wonders into the **m** of thee,	8432
	136:14 Israel to pass through the **m** of	8432+871.1
	137: 2 harps upon the willows in the **m** thereof.	8432
	138: 7 Though I walk in the **m** of trouble,	7130
Pr	4:21 keep them in the **m** of thine heart.	8432
	5:14 I was almost in all evil in the **m** of	8432
	8:20 in the **m** of the paths of judgment:	8432
	14:33 *that which is* in the **m** of fools is made	7130
	23:34 be as he that lieth down in the **m** of	3820
	30:19 the way of a ship in the **m** of the sea;	3820
SS	3:10 the **m** thereof being paved *with* love,	8432
Isa	4: 4 the **m** thereof by the spirit of judgment,	7130
	5: 2 built a tower in the **m** of it, and also made	8432
	5: 8 that they may be placed alone in the **m** of	7130
	5:25 their carcases were torn in the **m** of	7130
	6: 5 I dwell in the **m** of a people of unclean	8432
	6:12 *there be* a great forsaking in the **m** of	7130
	7: 6 set a king in the **m** of it, *even* the son of	8432
	10:23 even determined, *in the* **m** of all *the land*.	7130
	12: 6 great *is* the Holy One of Israel in the **m**	7130
	16: 3 thy shadow as the night in the **m** of	8432
	19: 1 heart of Egypt shall melt in the **m** of it.	7130
	19: 3 the spirit of Egypt shall fail in the **m**	7130
	19:14 mingled a perverse spirit in the **m** thereof:	7130
	19:19 the Lord in the **m** of the land of Egypt,	8432
	19:24 *even* a blessing in the **m** of the land:	7130
	24:13 When thus it shall be in the **m** of the land	7130
	24:18 he that cometh up out of the **m** of the pit	8432
	25:11 he shall spread forth his hands in the **m** of	7130
	29:23 the work of mine hands, in the **m** of him,	7130
	30:28 shall reach to the **m** of the neck,	2673
	41:18 and fountains in the **m** of the valleys:	8432
	52:11 no unclean *thing;* go ye out of the **m**	8432
	58: 9 I *am*. If thou take away from the **m** of	8432
	66:17 in the gardens behind one *tree* in the **m**,	8432
Jer	6: 1 gather yourselves to flee out of the **m** of	7130
	6: 6 she *is* wholly oppression in the **m** of her.	8432
	9: 6 Thine habitation *is* in the **m** of deceit;	8432
	12:16 shall they be built in the **m** of my people.	8432
	14: 9 in the **m** of us, and we are called by thy	7130
	17:11 shall leave them in the **m** of his days,	2677
	21: 4 will assemble them into the **m** of this city.	8432
	29: 8 that *be* in the **m** of you, deceive you,	7130
	30:21 governor shall proceed from the **m** of	7130
	37:12 to separate himself thence in the **m** of	8432
	41: 7 when they came into the **m** of the city,	8432
	41: 7 *and* cast them into the **m** of the pit, he,	8432
	46:21 her hired men *are* in the **m** of her like	7130
	48:45 a flame from the **m** of Sihon,	996
Jer	50: 8 Remove out of the **m** of Babylon,	8432
	50:37 mingled people that *are* in the **m** of her;	8432
	51: 1 against them that dwell in the **m** of them	3820
	51: 6 Flee out of the **m** of Babylon,	8432
	51:45 go ye out of the **m** of her, and deliver ye	8432
	51:47 and all her slain shall fall in the **m** of her.	8432
	51:63 to it, and cast it into the **m** of Euphrates:	8432
	52:25 that were found in the **m** of the city.	8432
La	1:15 foot all my mighty *men* in the **m** of me:	7130
	3:45 and refuse in the **m** of the people.	7130
	4:13 *have* shed the blood of the just in the **m**	7130
Eze	1: 4 of the **m** thereof as the colour of amber,	8432
	1: 4 colour of amber, out of the **m** of the fire.	8432
	1: 5 out of the **m** thereof *came* the likeness	8432
	5: 2 with fire a third *part* in the **m** of the city,	8432
	5: 4 cast them into the **m** of the fire,	8432
	5: 5 I have set it in the **m** of the nations and	8432
	5: 8 execute judgments in the **m** of thee in	8432
	5:10 fathers shall eat the sons in the **m** of thee,	8432
	5:12 shall they be consumed in the **m** of thee:	8432
	6: 7 the slain shall fall in the **m** of you,	8432
	7: 4 thine abominations shall be in the **m** of	8432
	7: 9 thine abominations *that are* in the **m** of	8432
	8:11 in the **m** of them stood Jaazaniah the son	8432
	9: 4 Go through the **m** of the city 8432+871.1	
	9: 4 of the city through the **m** of Jerusalem,	8432
	9: 4 abominations that be done in the **m** of	8432
	10:10 if a wheel had been in the **m** of a wheel.	8432
	11: 7 Your slain whom ye have laid in the **m**	8432
	11: 7 *I* will bring you forth out of the **m** of it.	8432
	11: 9 I will bring you out of the **m** thereof,	8432
	11:23 the Lord went up from the **m** of the city,	8432
	12: 2 thou dwellest in the **m** of a rebellious	8432
	13:14 ye shall be consumed in the **m** thereof:	8432
	14: 8 will cut him off from the **m** of my people;	8432
	14: 9 will destroy him from the **m** of my people	8432
	15: 4 the ends of it, and the **m** of it is burnt.	8432
	16:53 captivity of thy captives in the **m** of them:	8432
	17:16 with him in the **m** of Babylon he shall	8432
	20: 8 them in the **m** of the land of Egypt.	8432
	21:32 thy blood shall be in the **m** of the land;	8432
	22: 3 The city sheddeth blood in the **m** of it,	8432
	22: 7 in the **m** of thee have they dealt by	8432
	22: 9 in the **m** of thee they commit lewdness.	8432
	22:13 thy blood which hath been in the **m** of	8432
	22:18 iron, and lead, in the **m** of the furnace;	8432
	22:19 I will gather you into the **m** of Jerusalem.	8432
	22:20 lead, and tin, into the **m** of the furnace,	8432
	22:21 and ye shall be melted in the **m** thereof.	8432
	22:22 silver is melted in the **m** of the furnace,	8432
	22:22 so shall ye be melted in the **m** thereof;	8432
	22:25 conspiracy of her prophets in the **m**	8432
	22:25 have made her many widows in the **m**	8432
	22:27 Her princes in the **m** thereof *are* like	7130
	23:39 thus have they done in the **m** of mine	8432
	24: 7 For her blood is in the **m** of her; she set it	8432
	26: 5 the spreading of nets in the **m** of the sea:	8432
	26:12 and thy dust in the **m** of the water.	8432
	26:15 when the slaughter is made in the **m** of	8432
	27: 4 Thy borders *are* in the **m** of the seas,	3820
	27:25 made very glorious in the **m** of the seas.	3820
	27:26 east wind hath broken thee in the **m** of	3820
	27:27 in all thy company which *is* in the **m** of	3820
	27:27 shall fall into the **m** of the seas in the day	3820
	27:32 like the destroyed in the **m** of the sea?	8432
	27:34 all thy company in the **m** of thee shall fall.	8432
	28: 2 sit in the seat of God, in the **m** of the seas;	3820
	28: 8 of *them that are* slain in the **m** of the seas.	3820
	28:14 and down in the **m** of the stones of fire.	8432
	28:16 have filled the **m** of thee *with* violence,	8432
	28:16 from the **m** of the stones of fire.	8432
	28:18 will I bring forth a fire from the **m** of thee,	8432
	28:22 and I will be glorified in the **m** of thee:	8432
	28:23 the wounded shall be judged in the **m** of	8432
	29: 3 the great dragon that lieth in the **m** of his	8432
	29: 4 I will bring thee up out of the **m** of thy	8432
	29:12 the **m** of the countries *that are* desolate,	8432
	29:21 opening of the mouth in the **m** of them;	8432
	30: 7 they shall be desolate in the **m** of	8432
	30: 7 cities shall be in the **m** of the cities that	8432
	31:14 earth, in the **m** of the children of men,	8432
	31:17 *that* dwelt under his shadow in the **m** of	8432
	31:18 shalt lie in the **m** of the uncircumcised	8432
	32:20 They shall fall in the **m** of *them that are*	8432
	32:21 of the **m** of hell with them that help him:	8432
	32:25 They have set her a bed in the **m** of	8432
	32:25 he is put in the **m** of *them that be* slain.	8432
	32:28 thou shalt be broken in the **m** of	8432
	32:32 he shall be laid in the **m** of	8432
	36:23 ye have profaned in the **m** of them;	8432
	37: 1 me down in the **m** of the valley which	8432
	37:26 will set my sanctuary in the **m** of them	8432
	37:28 when my sanctuary shall be in the **m** of	8432
	38:12 goods, that dwell in the **m** of the land.	2872
	39: 7 known in the **m** of my people Israel;	8432
	41: 7 lowest *chamber* to the highest by the **m**.	8484
	43: 7 I will dwell in the **m** of the children	8432
	43: 9 I will dwell in the **m** of them for ever.	8432
	46:10 prince in the **m** of them, when they go	8432
	48: 8 and the sanctuary shall be in the **m** of it.	8432
	48:10 of the Lord shall be in the **m** thereof.	8432
	48:15 and the city shall be in the **m** thereof.	8432
	48:21 sanctuary of the house *shall* be in the **m**	8432
	48:22 in the **m** *of that* which is the prince's,	8432

M

Da
3: 6 cast into the **m** of a burning fiery furnace. 1459
3:11 *that* he should be cast into the **m** of a 1459
3:15 ye shall be cast the same hour into the **m** 1459
3:21 were cast into the **m** of the burning fiery 1459
3:23 down bound into the **m** of the burning 1459
3:24 not we cast three men bound into the **m** 1459
3:25 walking in the **m** of the fire, and they 1459
3:26 came forth of the **m** of the fire. 1459
4:10 tree in the **m** of the earth, and the height 1459
7:15 Daniel was grieved in my spirit in the **m** 1459
9:27 *in* the week he shall cause 2677

Hos
5: 4 for the spirit of whoredoms *is* in the **m** of 7130
11: 9 not man; the Holy One in the **m** of thee: 7130

Joel
2:27 ye shall know that I *am* in the **m** of Israel, 7130

Am
2: 3 will cut off the judge from the **m** thereof, 7130
3: 9 the great tumults in the **m** thereof, 7130
3: 9 and the oppressed in the **m** thereof. 8432
6: 4 and the calves out of the **m** of the stall; 8432
7: 8 I *will* set a plumbline in the **m** of my 7130
7:10 hath conspired against thee in the **m** of 7130

Jnh
2: 3 me *into* the deep, in the **m** of the seas; 3824

Mic
2:12 as the flock in the **m** of their fold: 8432
5: 7 the remnant of Jacob shall be in the **m** of 7130
5: 8 **m** of many people as a lion among 7130
5:10 I will cut off thy horses out of the **m** of 7130
5:13 thy standing images out of the **m** of thee; 7130
5:14 I will pluck up thy groves out of the **m** of thee; 7130
6:14 casting down *shall be* in the **m** of thee; 7130
7:14 *in* the wood, in the **m** of Carmel: 8432

Na
3:13 thy people in the **m** of thee *are* women; 7130

Hab
2:19 *there* is no breath at all in the **m** of it. 7130
3: 2 revive thy work in the **m** of the years, 7130
3: 2 in the **m** of the years make known; 7130

Zep
2:14 flocks shall lie down in the **m** of her, 8432
3: 5 The just Lord *is* in the **m** thereof; he will 7130
3:11 I will take away out of the **m** of thee 7130
3:12 I will also leave in the **m** of thee an 7130
3:15 *even* the Lord, *is* in the **m** of thee: 7130
3:17 The Lord thy God in the **m** of thee *is* 7130

Zec
2: 5 and will be the glory in the **m** of her. 8432
2:10 I come, and I will dwell in the **m** of thee, 8432
2:11 I will dwell in the **m** of thee, and thou 8432
5: 4 it shall remain in the **m** of his house, 8432
5: 7 this *is* a woman that sitteth in the **m** of 8432
5: 8 he cast it into the **m** of the ephah; 8432
8: 3 and will dwell in the **m** of Jerusalem: 8432
8: 8 they shall dwell in the **m** of Jerusalem: 8432
14: 1 spoil shall be divided in the **m** of thee. 7130
14: 4 the mount of Olives shall cleave in the **m** 2677

Mt
10:16 I send you forth as sheep in the **m** of 3319
14:24 But the ship was now in the **m** of the sea, 3319
18: 2 unto *him*, and set him in the **m** of them. 3319
18:20 in my name, there am I in the **m** of them. 3319

Mk
6:47 the ship was in the **m** of the sea, 3319
7:31 through the **m** of the coasts of Decapolis. 3319
9:36 a child, and set him in the **m** of them: 3319
14:60 And the high priest stood up in the **m**, 3319

Lk
2:46 in the **m** of the doctors, both hearing 3319
4:30 he passing through the **m** of them went 3319
4:35 when the devil had thrown him in the **m**, 3319
5:19 with *his* couch into the **m** before Jesus. 3319
6: 8 Rise up, and stand *forth* in the **m**. 3319
17:11 he passed through the **m** of Samaria 3319
21:21 them which are in the **m** of it depart out; 3319
22:55 when they had kindled a fire in the **m** 3319
23:45 the vail of the temple was rent **in the m**. 3319
24:36 Jesus himself stood in the **m** of them, 3319

Jn
7:14 about the **m** of the feast Jesus went up 3322
8: 3 and when they had set her in the **m**, 3319
8: 9 and the woman standing in the **m**. 3319
8:59 going through the **m** of them, and so 3319
19:18 on either side one, and Jesus in the **m**. 3319
20:19 came Jesus and stood in the **m**, 3319
20:26 stood in the **m**, and said, Peace be unto 3319

Ac
1:15 in those days Peter stood up in the **m** 3319
1:18 he burst asunder in the **m**, and all his 3319
2:22 which God did by him in the **m** of you, 3319
4: 7 And when they had set them in the **m**, 3319
17:22 Then Paul stood in the **m** of Mars' hill, 3319
27:21 Paul stood *forth* in the **m** of them, 3319

Php
2:15 the **m** of a crooked and perverse nation, 3319

Heb
2:12 in the **m** of the church will I sing praise 3319

Rev
1:13 in the **m** of the seven candlesticks one 3319
2: 1 walketh in the **m** of the seven golden 3319
2: 7 which is in the **m** of the paradise of God. 3319
4: 6 in the **m** of the throne, and round about 3319
5: 6 in the **m** of the throne and of the four 3319
5: 6 four beasts, and in the **m** of the elders, 3319
6: 6 And I heard a voice in the **m** of the four 3319
7:17 For the Lamb which is in the **m** of 3319
8:13 an angel flying through the **m of heaven**, 3321
14: 6 saw another angel fly in the **m of heaven**, 3321
19:17 all the fowls that fly in the **m of heaven**, 3321
22: 2 In the **m** of the street of it, and of either 3319

MIDWIFE (3) [MIDWIVES]
Ge
35:17 that the **m** said unto her, Fear not; 3205
38:28 the **m** took and bound upon his hand a 3205
Ex
1:16 When ye **do the office of a m** to 3205

MIDWIVES (7) [MIDWIFE]
Ex
1:15 the king of Egypt spake to the Hebrew **m**, 3205
1:17 the **m** feared God, and did not as the king 3205
1:18 And the king of Egypt called for the **m**, 3205
1:19 the **m** said unto Pharaoh, Because 3205

Ex
1:19 delivered ere the **m** come in unto them. 3205
1:20 Therefore God dealt well with the **m**: 3205
1:21 came to pass, because the **m** feared God, 3205

MIGDAL-EL (1)
Jos
19:38 M, Horem, and Beth-anath, 4027

MIGDAL-GAD (1)
Jos
15:37 Zenan, and Hadashah, and M, 4028

MIGDOL (4)
Ex
14: 2 between M and the sea, over against 4024
Nu
33: 7 and they pitched before M. 4024
Jer
44: 1 which dwell at M, and at Tahpanhes, 4024
46:14 publish in M, and publish in Noph and 4024

MIGHT (475) [ALMIGHTY, MIGHTEST, MIGHTIER, MIGHTIES, MIGHTIEST, MIGHTILY, MIGHTY]
Ge
12:19 so I **m** have taken her to me to wife: NIH
13: 6 to bear them, that they **m** dwell together: NIH
17:18 O that Ishmael **m** live before thee! NIH
26:10 one of the people **m** lightly have lien with NIH
30:34 I would it **m** be according to thy word. NIH
30:41 that they **m** conceive among the rods. NIH
31:27 that I **m** have sent thee away with mirth, NIH
36: 7 their riches were more than that they **m** NIH
37:22 that he **m** rid him out of their hands, NIH
43:32 the Egyptians **m** not eat bread with 3201
49: 3 my **m**, and the beginning of my strength, 3581
Ex
10: 1 that I **m** shew these my signs before him: NIH
12:33 that they **m** send them out of the land in NIH
36:18 couple the tent together, that it **m** be one. NIH
39:21 that it **m** be above the curious girdle of NIH
39:21 that the breastplate **m** not be loosed from NIH
Lev
24:12 that the mind of the Lord **m** be shewed NIH
26:45 of the heathen, that I **m** be their God: NIH
Nu
4:37 all that **m** do service in the tabernacle of NIH
4:41 of all that **m** do service in the tabernacle NIH
14:13 this people in thy **m** from among them;) 3581
22:41 that thence he **m** see the utmost part of NIH
Dt
2:30 that he **m** deliver him into thy hand, NIH
3:24 to thy works, and according to thy **m**? 1369
4:14 that ye **m** do them in the land whither ye NIH
4:36 to hear his voice, that he **m** instruct thee: NIH
4:42 That the slayer **m** flee thither, which NIH
4:42 that fleeing unto one of these cities he **m** NIH
5:29 that it **m** be well with them, and with NIH
6: 1 that ye **m** do *them* in the land whither ye NIH
6: 5 and with all thy soul, and with all thy **m**. 3966
6:23 us out from thence, that he **m** bring us in, NIH
6:24 that he **m** preserve us alive, as *it is* at this NIH
8: 3 that he **m** make thee know that man doth NIH
8:16 that he **m** humble thee, and that he **m** NIH
8:16 humble thee, and that he **m** prove thee, NIH
8:17 the **m** of mine hand hath gotten me this 6108
28:32 and *there shall* be no **m** in thine hand. 410
29: 6 that ye **m** know that I *am* the Lord your NIH
32:13 that he **m** eat the increase of the fields; NIH
Jos
4:24 That all the people of the earth **m** know NIH
4:24 that ye **m** fear the Lord your God for NIH
11:20 that he **m** destroy them utterly, *and* that NIH
11:20 that they **m** have no favour, but that he NIH
11:20 no favour, but that he **m** destroy them, NIH
20: 3 *any* person at unawares **m** flee thither, NIH
22:16 that ye **m** rebel *this* day against NIH
22:24 time to come your children **m** speak unto NIH
22:27 that we **m** do the service of the Lord NIH
24: 8 your hand, that ye **m** possess their land; NIH
Jdg
3: 2 of the children of Israel **m** know, NIH
5:31 as the sun when he goeth forth in his **m**. 1369
6:14 in this thy **m**, and thou shalt save Israel 3581
9:24 and ten sons of Jerubbaal **m** come, NIH
16:30 he bowed *himself* with all his **m**; 3581
18: 7 that **m** put *them* to shame in *any* thing; NIH
Ru
1: 6 she **m** return from the country of Moab; NIH
1Sa
4: 4 that they **m** bring from thence the ark of NIH
13:10 out to meet him, that he **m** salute him. NIH
14:14 of land, which a yoke *of oxen* **m** plow. NIH
18:27 king, that he **m** be the king's son in law. NIH
20: 6 earnestly asked *leave* of me that he **m** NIH
2Sa
6:14 danced before the Lord with all *his* **m**; 5797
10:10 that he **m** put *them* in array against NIH
15: 4 hath *any* suit or cause **m** come unto me, NIH
17:14 to the intent that the Lord **m** bring evil NIH
17:17 for they **m** not be seen to come into 3201
24:21 that he **m** destroy them that hate me. NIH
1Ki
2:27 that he **m** fulfil the word of the Lord, NIH
7: 7 made a porch for the throne where he **m** NIH
8: 1 they **m** bring up the ark of the covenant NIH
8:16 build a house, that my name **m** be therein; NIH
12:15 the Lord, that he **m** perform his saying, NIH
15:17 that he **m** not suffer *any* to go out or NIH
15:23 all his **m**, and all that he did, and the 1369
16: 5 of Baasha, and what he did, and his **m**, 1369
16:27 which he did, and his **m** that he shewed, 1369
19: 4 he requested for himself that he **m** die; NIH
22: 7 Lord besides, that we **m** inquire of him? NIH
22:45 that he shewed, and how he warred, 1369
2Ki
7: 2 windows in heaven, **m** this thing be? NIH
7:19 windows in heaven, **m** such a thing be? NIH
10:19 to the intent that he **m** destroy NIH
10:34 of Jehu, and all that he did, and all his **m**, 1369
13: 8 Jehoahaz, and all that he did, and his **m**, 1369
13:12 his **m** where*with* he fought against 1369
14:15 his **m**, and how he fought with Amaziah 1369

2Ki
14:28 all that he did, and his **m**, how he warred, 1369
15:19 that his hand **m** be with him to confirm NIH
20:20 all his **m**, and how he made a pool, and a 1369
22:17 that they **m** provoke me to anger with all NIH
23:24 that he **m** perform the words of the law NIH
23:25 with all his soul, and with all his **m**, 3966
23:33 that *he* **m** not reign in Jerusalem; NIH
24:16 all the men of *m*, *even* seven thousand, 2428
1Ch
4:10 thine hand **m** be with me, and that thou NIH
7: 2 *they were* valiant *men of* **m** in their 2428
7: 5 the families of Issachar *were* men of **m**, 2428
12: 8 into the hold to the wilderness men of **m**, 2428
13: 8 Israel played before God with all *their* **m**, 5797
29: 2 Now I have prepared with all my **m** for 3581
29:12 in thine hand *is* power and **m**; and in 1369
29:30 With all his reign and his **m**, and the 1369
2Ch
2:12 that build a house for the Lord, NIH
6: 5 a house *in*, that my name **m** be there; NIH
6: 6 Jerusalem, that my name **m** be there; NIH
10:15 that the Lord **m** perform his word, NIH
11: 1 that *he* **m** bring the kingdom again to NIH
16: 1 to the intent that he **m** let none go out or NIH
18: 6 Lord besides, that we **m** inquire of? NIH
20: 6 in thine hand *is there not* power and **m**? 1369
20:12 for we have no **m** against this great 3581
25:20 he **m** deliver them into the hand *of their* NIH
31: 4 that they **m** be encouraged in the law of NIH
32:18 to trouble them; that they **m** take the city. NIH
32:31 that he **m** know all *that was* in his heart. NIH
34:25 that *they* **m** provoke me to anger with all NIH
35:12 that they **m** give according to the divisions NIH
35:15 they **m** not depart from their service; NIH
35:22 he **m** fight with him, and hearkened not NIH
36:22 mouth of Jeremiah **m** be accomplished, NIH
Ezr
1: 1 by the mouth of Jeremiah **m** be fulfilled, NIH
5:10 we **m** write the names of the men that NIH
8:21 we **m** afflict ourselves before our God, NIH
Ne
5: 3 houses, that we **m** buy corn, because of NIH
5:10 **m** exact of them money and corn: NIH
6:13 that they **m** have *matter* for an evil report, NIH
6:13 an evil report, that they **m** reproach me. NIH
7: 5 that *they* **m** be reckoned by genealogy. NIH
9:24 that *they* **m** do with them as they would. NIH
10:37 that the same Levites **m** have the tithes in NIH
Est
4: 2 for none **m** enter into the king's gate NIH
10: 2 all the acts of his power and of his **m**, 1369
Job
6: 8 O that I **m** have my request; and *that* God NIH
9:33 that **m** lay his hand upon us both. NIH
16:21 that *one* **m** plead for a man with God, as NIH
23: 3 O that I knew where I **m** find him! *that* I NIH
23: 3 find him! *that* I **m** come *even* to his seat! NIH
23: 7 There the righteous **m** dispute with him; NIH
30: 2 whereto *m* the strength of their hands NIH
38:13 *it* **m** take hold of the ends of the earth, NIH
38:13 that the wicked **m** be shaken out of it? NIH
Ps
18:40 that I **m** destroy them that hate me. NIH
68:18 that the Lord God **m** dwell *among* them. NIH
76: 5 none of the men of **m** have found their 2428
78: 6 the generation to come **m** know *them*, NIH
78: 7 That they **m** set their hope in God, NIH
78: 8 **m** not be as their fathers, a stubborn NIH
105:45 That they **m** observe his statutes, NIH
106: 8 that *he* **m** make his mighty power to be NIH
107: 7 that *they* **m** go to a city of habitation. NIH
109:16 that *he* **m** even slay the broken in heart. NIH
118:13 Thou hast thrust sore at me that I **m** fall: NIH
119:11 mine heart, that I **m** not sin against thee. NIH
119:71 been afflicted; that I **m** learn thy statutes. NIH
119:101 every evil way, that I **m** keep thy word. NIH
119:148 that I **m** meditate in thy word. NIH
145: 6 men shall speak of the **m** of thy terrible 5807
Pr
22:21 That I **m** make thee know the certainty of NIH
Ecc
2: 3 I **m** see what *was* that good for the sons NIH
3:18 that God **m** manifest them, and that *they* NIH
3:18 that *they* **m** see that they themselves are NIH
9:10 thy hand findeth to do, do *it* with thy **m**; 3581
Isa
11: 2 the spirit of counsel and **m**, 1369
28:13 that they **m** go, and fall backward, NIH
33:13 and ye *that are* near, acknowledge my **m**. 1369
40:26 all by names by the greatness of *his* **m**, 202
40:29 to *them* that have no **m** he increaseth 202
61: 3 they **m** be called trees of righteousness, NIH
61: 3 of the Lord, that he **m** be glorified. NIH
64: 1 that the mountains **m** flow down at thy NIH
Jer
9: 1 that I **m** weep day and night for the slain NIH
9: 2 that I **m** leave my people, and go from NIH
9:23 neither let the mighty *man* glory in his **m**, 1369
10: 6 art great, and thy name *is* great in **m**. 1369
13:11 that *they* **m** be unto me for a people, NIH
16:21 them to know mine hand and my **m**; 1369
17:23 made their neck stiff, that *they* **m** not hear, NIH
19:15 necks, that *they* **m** not hear my words. NIH
20:17 or that my mother **m** have been my grave, NIH
25: 7 that ye **m** provoke me to anger with NIH
26:19 Thus *m* we procure great evil against our NIH
27:15 that I **m** drive you out, and that ye **m** NIH
27:15 that ye **m** perish, ye, and the prophets that NIH
43: 3 that *they* **m** put us to death, and carry us NIH
44: 8 that ye **m** cut yourselves off, and that *ye* NIH
44: 8 **m** be a curse and a reproach NIH
49:35 the bow of Elam, the chief of their **m**. 1369
51:30 hath failed; their **m** became as women: 1369
Eze
17: 7 this **m** water it by the furrows of her NIH
17: 8 that *it* **m** bring forth branches, and that *it* NIH

Eze 17: 8	*it* **m** bear fruit, that *it* might be a goodly	NIH
17: 8	bear fruit, that *it* **m** be a goodly vine.	NIH
17:14	That the kingdom **m** be base, that *it* might	NIH
17:14	that *it* **m** not lift itself up, *but* that by	NIH
17:14	that by keeping of his covenant *it* **m** stand.	NIH
17:15	that *they* **m** give him horses and	NIH
20:12	that *they* **m** know that I *am* the LORD that	NIH
20:26	that I **m** make them desolate, to the end	NIH
20:26	to the end that they **m** know that I *am*	NIH
24: 8	That *it* **m** cause fury to come up to take	NIH
32:29	which with their **m** are laid by *them that*	1369
32:30	their terror *they are* ashamed of their **m**;	1369
36: 3	that ye **m** be a possession unto the residue	NIH
40: 4	for to the intent that *I* **m** shew *them* unto	NIH
41: 6	*they* **m** have hold, but they had not hold	NIH
Da 1: 4	whom *they* **m** teach the learning and	NIH
1: 5	at the end thereof they **m** stand before	NIH
1: 8	the eunuchs that he **m** not defile himself.	NIH
2:20	and ever: for wisdom and **m** are his:	1370
2:23	who hast given me wisdom and **m**,	1370
3:28	they **m** not serve nor worship any god,	NIH
4: 6	that they **m** make known unto me	NIH
4:30	of the kingdom by the **m** of my power,	8632
5: 2	and his concubines, **m** drink therein.	NIH
6: 2	the princes **m** give accounts unto them,	1934
6:17	that the purpose **m** not be changed	NIH
8: 4	so that no beasts **m** stand before him,	NIH
9:11	that *they* **m** not obey thy voice;	NIH
9:13	that *we* **m** turn from our iniquities,	NIH
Joel 3: 3	and sold a girl for wine, that *they* **m** drink.	NIH
3: 6	that *ye* **m** remove them far from their	NIH
Am 1:13	Gilead, that *they* **m** enlarge their border:	NIH
Jnh 4: 5	he **m** see what become of the city.	NIH
4: 6	that *it* **m** be a shadow over his head,	NIH
Mic 3: 8	*of* judgment, and *of* **m**, to declare unto	1369
7:16	see and be confounded at all their **m**:	1369
Hab 3:16	myself, that I **m** rest in the day of trouble:	NIH
Zec 4: 6	Not by **m**, nor by power, but by my	2428
6: 7	sought to go that *they* **m** walk to and	NIH
8: 9	hosts was laid, that the temple **m** be built.	NIH
11:10	that *I* **m** break my covenant which I had	NIH
11:14	that *I* **m** break the brotherhood between	NIH
Mal 2: 4	that my covenant **m** be with Levi, saith	NIH
2:15	That he **m** seek a godly seed. Therefore	NIH
Mt 1:22	that it **m** be fulfilled which was spoken of	NIG
2:15	that it **m** be fulfilled which was spoken of	NIG
2:23	that it **m** be fulfilled which was spoken by	NIG
4:14	That it **m** be fulfilled which was spoken	NIG
8:17	That it **m** be fulfilled which was spoken	3704
8:28	so that no *man* **m** pass by that way.	2480
12:10	the sabbath days? that they **m** accuse him.	NIG
12:14	against him, how they **m** destroy him.	NIG
12:17	That it **m** be fulfilled which was spoken by	NIG
13:35	That it **m** be fulfilled which was spoken by	NIG
14:36	And besought him that they **m** only touch	NIG
21: 4	that it **m** be fulfilled which was spoken by	NIG
21:32	not afterward, that ye **m** believe him.	NIG
21:34	that *they* **m** receive the fruits of it.	NIG
22:15	took counsel how they **m** entangle him in	NIG
26: 4	And consulted that they **m** take Jesus by	NIG
26: 9	For this ointment **m** have been sold for	1410
26:56	that the scriptures of the prophets **m** be	NIG
27:35	that it **m** be fulfilled which was spoken by	NIG
Mk 3: 2	the sabbath day; that they **m** accuse him.	NIG
3: 6	against him, how they **m** destroy him.	NIG
3:14	and that he **m** send them forth to preach,	NIG
5:18	devil prayed him that he **m** be with him.	NIG
6:56	besought him that they **m** touch if it were	NIG
10:51	unto him, Lord, that I **m** receive my sight.	NIG
11:13	if haply he **m** find any *thing* thereon:	NIG
11:18	and sought how they **m** destroy him:	NIG
12: 2	that he **m** receive from the husbandmen	NIG
14: 1	scribes sought how they **m** take him by	NIG
14: 5	it **m** have been sold for more than three	NIG
14:11	And he sought how he **m** conveniently	NIG
14:35	were possible, the hour **m** pass from him.	NIG
16: 1	that they **m** come and anoint him.	NIG
Lk 1:74	of our enemies **m** serve him without fear,	NIG
4:29	that *they* **m** cast him down headlong.	NIG
5:19	not find by what *way* they **m** bring him in	NIG
6: 7	they **m** find an accusation against him.	NIG
6:11	one with another what they **m** do	302
8: 9	him, saying, What **m** this parable be?	NIG
8:10	that seeing they **m** not see, and hearing	NIG
8:10	see, and hearing they **m** not understand.	NIG
8:38	besought him that *he* **m** be with him:	NIG
11:54	out of his mouth, that they **m** accuse him.	NIG
15:29	kid, that I **m** make merry with my friends:	NIG
17: 6	ye say unto this sycamine tree, Be thou	302
19:15	he **m** know how much every *man* had	302
19:23	at my coming I **m** have required *mine*	302
19:48	could not find what they **m** do: for all	NIG
20:20	*men*, that they **m** take hold of his words,	NIG
20:20	*so* they **m** deliver him unto the power and	NIG
22: 2	and scribes sought how they **m** kill him;	NIG
22: 4	captains, how he **m** betray him unto them.	NIG
23:23	requiring that he **m** be crucified.	NIG
23:26	laid the cross, that *he* **m** bear *it* after Jesus.	NIG
24:45	that *they* **m** understand the scriptures,	NIG
Jn 1: 7	that all *men* through him **m** believe.	NIG
3:17	that the world through him **m** be saved.	NIG
5:34	but these *things* I say, that ye **m** be saved.	NIG
5:40	will not come to me, that ye **m** have life.	NIG
6:28	we do, that we **m** work the works of God?	NIG
8: 6	that they **m** have to accuse him.	NIG

Jn 9:36	Who is he, Lord, that I **m** believe on him?	NIG
9:39	this world, that they which see not **m** see;	NIG
9:39	and that they which see **m** be made blind.	NIG
10:10	I am come that they **m** have life,	NIG
10:10	and that they **m** have it *more* abundantly.	NIG
10:17	I lay down my life, that I **m** take it again.	NIG
11: 4	the Son of God **m** be glorified thereby.	NIG
11:57	he should shew *it*, that they **m** take him.	NIG
12: 9	only, but that they **m** see Lazarus also,	NIG
12:10	the chief priests consulted that they **m**	NIG
12:38	That the saying of Esaias the prophet **m** be	NIG
14:29	when it is come to pass, ye **m** believe.	NIG
15:11	my joy **m** remain in you, and *that* your	NIG
15:11	remain in you, and *that* your joy **m** be full.	NIG
15:25	this cometh to pass, that the word **m** be	NIG
16:33	unto you, that in me ye **m** have peace.	NIG
17: 3	that they **m** know thee the only true God,	NIG
17:12	that the scripture **m** be fulfilled.	NIG
17:13	that they **m** have my joy fulfilled in	NIG
17:19	that they also **m** be sanctified through	NIG
18: 9	That the saying **m** be fulfilled, which he	NIG
18:28	defiled; but that they **m** eat the passover.	NIG
18:32	That the saying of Jesus **m** be fulfilled,	NIG
19:24	the scripture **m** be fulfilled, which saith,	NIG
19:28	that the scripture **m** be fulfilled, saith,	NIG
19:31	Pilate that their legs **m** be broken,	NIG
19:31	broken, and *that* they **m** be taken away.	NIG
19:35	that he saith true, that ye **m** believe.	NIG
19:38	besought Pilate that he **m** take away	NIG
20:31	that ye **m** believe that Jesus is the Christ,	NIG
20:31	that believing ye **m** have life through his	NIG
Ac 1:25	that he **m** go to his own place.	NIG
4:21	finding nothing how they **m** punish them,	NIG
5:15	passing by **m** overshadow some of them.	NIG
7:19	children, to the end they **m** not live.	NIG
8:15	that they **m** receive the Holy Ghost:	NIG
9: 2	he **m** bring *them* bound unto Jerusalem.	NIG
9:12	hand on him, that he **m** receive his sight.	NIG
9:21	that *intent*, that he **m** bring	NIG
13:42	Gentiles besought that these words **m** be	NIG
15:17	That the residue of men **m** seek after	NIG
17:27	haply they **m** feel after him, and find *him,*	NIG
20:24	so that *I* **m** finish my course with joy,	NIG
22:24	that he **m** know wherefore they cried so	NIG
24:26	given him of Paul, that he **m** loose him:	NIG
25:21	I commanded him to be kept till I **m** send	NIG
25:26	I have somewhat to write.	NIG
26:32	This man **m** have been set at liberty,	1410
27:12	if by any means they **m** attain to Phenice,	1410
Ro 1:10	if by any means now at length I **m** have a	NIG
1:13	that I **m** have some fruit among you also,	NIG
3:26	that he **m** be just, and the justifier of him	NIG
4:11	that he **m** be the father of all them that	NIG
4:11	righteousness **m** be imputed unto them	NIG
4:16	*it is* of faith, that it **m** *be* by grace;	NIG
4:16	to the end the promise **m** be sure to all	NIG
4:18	that he **m** become the father of many	NIG
5:20	law entered, that the offence **m** abound.	NIG
5:21	grace reign through righteousness unto	NIG
6: 6	*him,* that the body of sin **m** be destroyed,	NIG
7:13	sin, that it **m** appear sin, working death	NIG
7:13	that sin by the commandment **m** become	NIG
8: 4	That the righteousness of the law **m** be	NIG
8:29	that he **m** be the firstborn amongst many	NIG
9:11	of God according to election **m** stand,	NIG
9:17	that I **m** shew my power in thee,	NIG
9:17	my name **m** be declared throughout all	NIG
9:23	that he **m** make known the riches of his	NIG
10: 1	to God for Israel is, that *they* **m** be saved.	NIG
11:14	*are* my flesh, and **m** save some of them.	NIG
11:19	were broken off, that I **m** be graffed in.	NIG
11:32	unbelief, that he **m** have mercy upon all.	NIG
14: 9	that he **m** be Lord both of the dead and	NIG
15: 4	comfort of the scriptures **m** have hope.	NIG
15: 9	that the Gentiles **m** glorify God for *his*	NIG
15:16	that the offering up of the Gentiles **m** be	NIG
1Co 2:12	that we **m** know the *things* that are freely	NIG
4: 6	that ye **m** learn in us not to think *of men*	NIG
4: 8	did reign, that we also **m** reign with you.	NIG
5: 5	that the flesh **m** be taken	NIG
9:19	servant unto all, that I **m** gain the more.	NIG
9:20	I became as a Jew, that I **m** gain the Jews;	NIG
9:20	that I **m** gain them that are under the law;	NIG
9:21	that I **m** gain them *that are* without law.	NIG
9:22	became I as weak, that I **m** gain the weak:	NIG
9:22	I am made all *things* to all *men,* that I **m**	NIG
9:23	that I **m** be partaker thereof with *you.*	NIG
14:19	that *by my voice* I **m** teach others also,	NIG
2Co 1:15	that you **m** have a second benefit;	NIG
2: 4	ye **m** know the love which I have more	NIG
2: 9	I write, that I **m** know the proof of you,	NIG
4:10	that the life also of Jesus **m** be made	NIG
4:11	that the life also of Jesus **m** be made	NIG
4:15	that the abundant grace **m** through	NIG
5: 4	that mortality **m** be swallowed up of life.	NIG
5:21	that we **m** be made the righteousness of	NIG
7: 9	ye **m** receive damage by us in nothing.	NIG
7:12	that our care for you in the sight of God **m**	NIG
8: 9	that ye through his poverty **m** be rich.	NIG
9: 5	that the same **m** be ready, as a matter of	NIG
11: 4	not accepted, ye **m** well bear with *him.*	NIG
11: 7	in abasing myself that you **m** be exalted,	NIG
12: 8	the Lord thrice, that it **m** depart from me.	NIG
Gal 1: 4	that he **m** deliver us from *this* present evil	NIG
1:16	that I **m** preach him among the heathen;	NIG

Gal 2: 4	that they **m** bring us into bondage:	NIG
2: 5	the truth of the gospel **m** continue with	NIG
2:16	we **m** be justified by the faith of Christ,	NIG
2:19	dead to the law, that I **m** live unto God.	NIG
3:14	That the blessing of Abraham **m** come on	NIG
3:14	we **m** receive the promise of the Spirit	NIG
3:22	that the promise by faith of Jesus Christ **m**	NIG
3:24	Christ, that we **m** be justified by faith.	NIG
4: 5	that we **m** receive the adoption of sons.	NIG
4:17	exclude you, that you **m** affect them.	NIG
Eph 1:10	gather together in one all *things* in	NIG
1:21	**m**, and dominion, and every name that	1411
2: 7	That in the ages to come he **m** shew	NIG
2:16	And *that* he **m** reconcile both unto God in	NIG
3:10	powers in heavenly *places* **m** by his Spirit in	NIG
3:16	to be strengthened with **m** by his Spirit in	1411
3:19	that ye **m** be filled with all the fulness of	NIG
4:10	all heavens, that he **m** fill all *things.*)	NIG
5:26	That he **m** sanctify and cleanse *it* with	NIG
5:27	That he **m** present it to himself a glorious	NIG
6:10	in the Lord, and in the power of his **m**.	2479
6:22	that ye **m** know our affairs, and *that he*	NIG
6:22	and *that he* **m** comfort your hearts.	NIG
Php 3: 4	Though I **m** also have confidence in	NIG
3: 4	he hath whereof he **m** trust in the flesh,	NIG
3:11	If by any means I **m** attain unto	NIG
Col 1: 9	to desire that ye **m** be filled *with*	NIG
1:10	That ye **m** walk worthy of the Lord unto	NIG
1:11	Strengthened with all **m**, according to his	1411
1:18	that in all *things* he **m** have	NIG
2: 2	That their hearts **m** be comforted, being	NIG
4: 8	that he **m** know your estate,	NIG
1Th 2: 6	when we **m** have been burdensome,	1410
2:16	to the Gentiles that they **m** be saved,	NIG
3:10	praying exceedingly that *we* **m** see your	NIG
3:10	**m** perfect that which is lacking in your	NIG
2Th 2: 6	that he **m** be revealed in his time.	NIG
2:10	love of the truth, that they **m** be saved.	NIG
2:12	That they all **m** be damned who believed	NIG
3: 8	*we* **m** not be chargeable to any of you:	NIG
1Ti 1:16	in me first Jesus Christ **m** shew forth all	NIG
2Ti 4:17	by me the preaching **m** be fully known,	NIG
4:17	and *that* all the Gentiles **m** hear:	NIG
Tit 2:14	he **m** redeem us from all iniquity,	NIG
3: 8	they which have believed in God **m** be	NIG
Phm 1: 8	be much bold in Christ to enjoin	NIG
1:13	in thy stead the **m** have ministered unto	NIG
Heb 2:14	that through death he **m** destroy him that	NIG
2:17	that he **m** be a merciful and faithful high	NIG
6:18	to lie, we **m** have a strong consolation,	NIG
9:15	which are called **m** receive the promise	NIG
10:36	the will of God, ye **m** receive the promise.	NIG
11:15	they **m** have had opportunity to have	302
11:35	that they **m** obtain a better resurrection:	NIG
12:10	that *we* **m** be partakers of his holiness.	NIG
12:18	ye are not come unto the mount that **m**	NIG
13:12	he **m** sanctify the people with his own	NIG
Jas 5:17	and he prayed earnestly that it **m** not rain:	NIG
1Pe 1: 7	be found unto praise and honour and	NIG
1:21	that your faith and hope **m** be in God.	NIG
3:18	for the unjust, that he **m** bring us to God,	NIG
4: 6	that they **m** be judged according to men	NIG
2Pe 1: 4	that by these you **m** be partakers of	NIG
2:11	which are greater in power and **m**,	1411
1Jn 2:19	*went out,* that they **m** be made manifest	NIG
3: 8	that he **m** destroy the works of the devil.	NIG
4: 9	the world, that we **m** live through him.	NIG
3Jn 1: 8	that we **m** be fellowhelpers to the truth.	NIG
Rev 7:12	and honour, and power, and **m**,	2479
12:14	she **m** fly into the wilderness, into her	NIG
12:15	that the **m** cause her to be carried away of	NIG
13:17	that no *man* **m** buy or sell, save that	1410
16:12	that the way of the kings of the east **m** be	NIG

MIGHTEST (19) [MIGHT]

Dt 4:35	that thou **m** know that the LORD he *is*	NIH
6: 2	That thou **m** fear the LORD thy God,	NIH
Jdg 16: 6	thou **m** be bound to afflict thee.	NIH
16:10	I pray thee, wherewith thou **m** be bound.	NIH
16:13	tell me wherewith thou **m** be bound.	NIH
1Sa 17:28	for thou art come down that thou **m** see	NIH
Ne 9:29	*thou* **m** bring them again unto thy law:	NIH
Ps 8: 2	*thou* **m** still the enemy and the avenger.	NIH
51: 4	*thou* **m** be justified when thou speakest,	NIH
Pr 22:21	that *thou* **m** answer the words *of* truth to	NIH
Da 2:30	*thou* **m** know the thoughts of thy heart,	NIH
Mt 15: 5	*by* whatsoever thou **m** be profited by me;	NIG
Mk 7:11	*by* whatsoever thou **m** be profited by me;	NIG
Lk 1: 4	That thou **m** know the certainty of *those*	NIG
Ac 9:17	thou **m** receive thy sight, and be filled	NIG
Ro 3: 4	That thou **m** be justified in thy sayings,	NIG
3: 4	and overcome when thou art judged.	NIG
1Ti 1: 3	that thou **m** charge some that *they* teach	NIG
1:18	that thou by them **m** war a good warfare;	NIG

MIGHTIER (13) [MIGHT]

Ge 26:16	from us; for thou art much **m** than we.	6105
Ex 1: 9	children of Israel *are* moe and **m** than we.	6099
Nu 14:12	of thee a greater nation and **m** than they.	6099
Dt 4:38	and than thou *art,* to bring thee in,	6099
7: 1	seven nations greater and **m** than thou;	6099
9: 1	nations greater and **m** than thyself,	6099
9:14	I will make of thee a nation and **m** and	6099
11:23	greater nations and **m** than yourselves.	6099
Ps 93: 4	The LORD on high *is* **m** than the noise of	117

M

Ecc	6:10 may he contend with him that *is* **m**	8623	
Mt	3:11 but he that cometh after me is **m than** I,	2478	
Mk	1: 7 There cometh one **m than** I after me,	2478	
Lk	3:16 but one **m than** I cometh, the latchet of	2478	

MIGHTIES (2) [MIGHT]

1Ch	11:12 Ahohite, who *was* one of the three **m**.	1368
	11:24 and had the name among the three **m**.	1368

MIGHTIEST (1) [MIGHT]

1Ch	11:19 drink it. These *things* did *these* three **m**.	1368

MIGHTILY (11) [MIGHT]

Dt	6: 3 with thee, and that ye may increase **m**,	3966
Jdg	4: 3 twenty years he **m** oppressed	2393+871.1
	14: 6 the spirit of the Lord **came m** upon him,	6743
	15:14 the spirit of the Lord **came m** upon him,	6743
Jer	25:30 shall **m** roar upon his habitation;	7580+7580
Jnh	3: 8 sackcloth, and cry **m** unto God:	2394+871.1
Na	2: 1 *thy* loins strong, fortify *thy* power **m**.	3966
Ac	18:28 For he **m** convinced the Jews,	2159
	19:20 So **m** grew the word of God and	2596+2904
Col	1:29 to his working, which worketh in me **m**.	1411
Rev	18: 2 he cried **m** with a strong voice, saying,	2479

MIGHTY (284) [MIGHT]

Ge	6: 4 the same *became* **m men** which *were* of	1368
	10: 8 he began to be a **m** one in the earth.	1368
	10: 9 He was a **m** hunter before the Lord:	1368
	10: 9 *Even* as Nimrod the **m** hunter before	1368
	18:18 shall surely become a great and **m** nation,	6099
	23: 6 *art* a **m** prince among us: in the choice	430
	49:24 by the hands of the **m** *God* of Jacob;	46
Ex	1: 7 and multiplied, and **waxed** exceeding **m**;	6105
	1:20 people multiplied, and **waxed** very **m**.	6105
	3:19 will not let you go, no, not by a **m** hand.	2389
	9:28 there be no *more* **m** thunderings and	430
	10:19 the Lord turned a **m** strong west wind,	3966
	15:10 they sank as lead in the **m** waters.	117
	15:15 the **m** men of Moab, trembling shall take	352
	32:11 with great power, and with a **m** hand?	2389
Lev	19:15 poor, nor honour the person of the **m**:	1419
Nu	22: 6 this people; for they *are* too **m** for me:	6099
Dt	3:24 servant thy greatness, and thy **m** hand:	2389
	4:34 by a **m** hand, and by a stretched out arm,	2389
	4:37 brought thee out in his sight with his **m**	1419
	5:15 thee out thence through a **m** hand	2389
	6:21 brought us out of Egypt with a **m** hand:	2389
	7: 8 hath the Lord brought you out with a **m**	2389
	7:19 the **m** hand, and the stretched out arm,	2389
	7:21 God *is* among you, a **m** God and terrible.	1419
	7:23 shall destroy them *with* a **m** destruction,	1419
	9:26 forth out of Egypt with a **m** hand.	2389
	9:29 thou broughtest out by thy **m** power	1419
	10:17 of lords, a great God, a **m**, and a terrible,	1368
	11: 2 his **m** hand, and his stretched out arm,	2389
	26: 5 there a nation, great, **m**, and populous:	6099
	26: 8 us forth out of Egypt with a **m** hand,	2389
	34:12 in all *that* **m** hand, and in all the great	2389
Jos	1:14 all the **men** of valour, and help them;	1368
	4:24 know the hand of the Lord, that it *is* **m**:	2389
	6: 2 king thereof, *and* the **m** men of valour.	1368
	8: 3 Joshua chose out thirty thousand **m** *men*	1368
	10: 2 than Ai, and all the men thereof *were* **m**.	1368
	10: 7 with him, and all the men **of** valour.	1368
Jdg	5:13 made me have dominion over the **m**.	1368
	5:22 pransings, the pransings of their **m** ones.	47
	5:23 to the help of the Lord against the **m**.	1368
	6:12 Lord *is* with thee, thou **m** *man* of valour.	1368
	11: 1 Jephthah the Gileadite was a **m** *man*	1368
Ru	2: 1 a **m** man of wealth, of the family of	1368
1Sa	2: 4 The bows of the **m** *men* are broken,	1368
	4: 8 us out of the hand of these **m** Gods?	117
	9: 1 Aphiah, a Benjamite, a **m** *man* of power.	1368
	16:18 and a **m** valiant *man*, and a man of war,	1368
2Sa	1:19 thy high places: how are the **m** fallen!	1368
	1:21 for there the shield of the **m** is vilely cast	1368
	1:22 blood of the slain, from the fat of the **m**,	1368
	1:25 How are the **m** fallen in the midst of	1368
	1:27 How are the **m** fallen, and the weapons	1368
	10: 7 sent Joab, and all the host *of* the **m** men.	1368
	16: 6 all the **m** *men* were on his right hand and	1368
	17: 8 they *be* **m** men, and they *be* chafed in	1368
	17:10 all Israel knoweth that thy father *is* a **m**	1368
	20: 7 all the **m** men: and they went out of	1368
	23: 8 These *be* the names of the **m** *men* whom	1368
	23: 9 *one* of the three **m** men with David,	1368
	23:16 the three **m** men brake through the host	1368
	23:17 These *things* did *these* three **m** men.	1368
	23:22 and had the name among three **m** *men*.	1368
1Ki	1: 8 and the **m** men which *belonged* to David,	1368
	1:10 and the **m** men, and Solomon his brother,	1368
	11:28 man Jeroboam *was* a **m** man of valour:	1368
2Ki	5: 1 was also a **m** man in valour, *but he was*	1368
	15:20 *even* of all the **m** men of wealth, of each	1368
	24:14 the princes, and all the **m** men of valour,	1368
	24:15 and his officers, and the **m** of the land,	352
1Ch	1:10 he began to be **m** upon the earth.	1368
	5:24 Hodaviah, and Jahdiel, **m** men of valour,	1368
	7: 5 house of *their* fathers, **m** men of valour;	1368
	7: 9 **m** men of valour, *was* twenty thousand	1368
	7:11 **m** men of valour, *were* seventeen	1368
	7:40 choice *and* **m** men of valour, chief of	1368
	8:40 the sons of Ulam were **m** men of valour,	1368
	11:10 These also *are* the chief of the **m** *men*	1368

1Ch	11:11 this *is* the number of the **m** men whom	1368	
	12: 1 they *were* among the **m** men, helpers of	1368	
	12: 4 a **m** *man* among the thirty, and over	1368	
	12:21 rovers: for they were all **m** *men* of valour,	1368	
	12:25 **m** *men* of valour for the war,	1368	
	12:28 a young man **m** of valour, and *of* his	1368	
	12:30 and eight hundred, **m** *men* of valour,	1368	
	19: 8 sent Joab, and all the host *of* the **m** men.	1368	
	26: 6 father: for they *were* **m** men of valour.	1368	
	26:31 there were found among them **m** *men* of	1368	
	27: 6 who *was* **m** among the thirty, and above	1368	
	28: 1 with the **m** men, and with all the valiant	1368	
	29:24 the **m** men, and all the sons likewise of	1368	
2Ch	6:32 thy **m** hand, and thy stretched out arm;	2389	
	13: 3 chosen men, *being* **m** men of valour.	1368	
	13:21 Abijah **waxed m**, and married fourteen	2388	
	14: 8 all these *were* **m** men of valour.	1368	
	17:13 the men of war, **m** *men* of valour, *were* in	1368	
	17:14 with him **m** *men* of valour three hundred	1368	
	17:16 with him two hundred thousand **m** *men*	1368	
	17:17 Eliada a **m** *man* of valour, and with him	1368	
	25: 6 hired also an hundred thousand **m** *men*	1368	
	26:12 the **m** *men* of valour were two thousand	1368	
	26:13 hundred, that made war with **m** power,	2428	
	27: 6 Jotham prepared **m**, because he prepared	2388	
	28: 7 Zichri, a **m** *man* of Ephraim, slew	1368	
	32: 3 his **m** men to stop the waters of	1368	
	32:21 which cut off all the **m** men of valour,	1368	
Ezr	4:20 There have been **m** kings also over	8624	
	7:28 and before all the king's **m** princes.	1368	
Ne	3:16 was made, and unto the house of the **m**.	1368	
	9:11 the deeps, as a stone into the **m** waters.	5794	
	9:32 the great, the **m**, and the terrible God,	1368	
	11:14 *men* of valour, an hundred twenty and	1368	
Job	5:15 their mouth, and from the hand of the **m**.	2389	
	6:23 or, Redeem me from the hand of the **m**?	6184	
	9: 4 *He is* wise in heart, and **m** in strength:	533	
	12: 9 away spoiled, and overthroweth the **m**.	386	
	12:21 and weakeneth the strength of the **m**.	650	
	21: 7 become old, yea, are **m** in power?	1396	
	22: 8 *as for* the **m** man, he had the earth;	2220	
	24:22 He draweth also the **m** with his power:	47	
	34:20 the **m** shall be taken away without hand.	47	
	34:24 He shall break in pieces **m** *men* without	3524	
	35: 9 cry out by reason of the arm of the **m**.	7227	
	36: 5 God *is* **m**, and despiseth not *any: he is*	3524	
	36: 5 despiseth not *any: he is* **m** in strength	3524	
	41:25 When he raiseth up *himself*, the **m** are	352	
Ps	24: 8 the Lord strong and **m**, the Lord	1368	
	24: 8 and **mighty**, the Lord **m** in battle.	1368	
	29: 1 Give unto the Lord, O ye **m**, give	410+1121	
	33:16 **m** *man* is not delivered by much strength.	1368	
	45: 3 O most **m**, with thy glory and thy majesty.	1368	
	50: 1 The **m** God, *even* the Lord, hath spoken,	410	
	52: 1 O **m** *man*? the goodness of God *endureth*	1368	
	59: 3 the **m** are gathered against me; not *for* my	5794	
	68:33 send out his **m** voice, *and that* a **m** voice.	5797	
	69: 4 *being* mine enemies wrongfully, are **m**;	6105	
	74:15 and the flood: thou driedst up **m** rivers.	386	
	78:65 like a **m** *man* that shouteth by reason of	1368	
	82: 1 standeth in the congregation of the **m**;	410	
	89: 6 among the sons of the **m** can be likened	410	
	89:13 Thou hast a **m** arm: strong is thy	1369+5973	
	89:19 I have laid help upon *one that is* **m**;	1368	
	89:50 bosom *the reproach of* all the **m** people;	7227	
	93: 4 yea, than the **m** waves of the sea.	117	
	106: 2 Who can utter the **m** acts of the Lord?	1369	
	106: 8 that he might make his **m power** to be	1369	
	112: 2 His seed shall be **m** upon earth:	1368	
	120: 4 Sharp arrows of the **m**, with coals of	1368	
	127: 4 As arrows *are* in the hand of a **m** *man;* so	1368	
	132: 2 *and* vowed unto the **m** God of Jacob;	46	
	132: 5 a habitation for the **m** God of Jacob.	46	
	135:10 smote great nations, and slew **m** kings;	6099	
	145: 4 to another, and shall declare thy **m acts**	1369	
	145:12 known to the sons of men his **m acts**,	1369	
	150: 1 Praise him for his **m** acts: praise him	1369	
Pr	16:32 that *is* slow to anger *is* better than the **m**;	1368	
	18:18 to cease, and parteth between the **m**.	6099	
	21:22 A wise *man* scaleth the city of the **m**,	1368	
	23:11 For their Redeemer *is* **m**; he shall plead	2389	
Ecc	7:19 than ten **m** *men* which are in the city.	7989	
SS	4: 4 thousand bucklers, all shields of **m** men.	1368	
Isa	1:24 the Lord of hosts, the **m One** of Israel,	46	
	3: 2 The **m** *man*, and the man of war,,	1368	
	3:25 fall by the sword, and thy **m** in the war.	1369	
	5:15 the **m** man shall be humbled, and the eyes	NIH	
	5:22 Woe unto *them that are* **m** to drink wine,	1368	
	9: 6 Counseller, The **m** God, The everlasting	1368	
	10:21 the remnant of Jacob, unto the **m** God.	410	
	10:34 iron, and Lebanon shall fall by a **m** one.	117	
	11:15 with his **m** wind shall he shake his hand	5868	
	13: 3 I have also called my **m** ones for mine	1368	
	17:12 *that* make a rushing like the rushing of **m**	3524	
	21:17 the **m** men of the children of Kedar,	1368	
	22:17 the Lord will carry thee away with a **m**	1397	
	28: 2 the Lord hath a **m** and strong one,	2389	
	28: 2 as a flood of **m** waters overflowing,	3524	
	30:29 of the Lord, to the **m** One of Israel.	6697	
	31: 8 fall with the sword, not of a **m** man;	NIH	
	42:13 The Lord shall go forth as a **m** *man*,	1368	
	43:16 in the sea, and a path in the **m** waters;	5794	
	49:24 Shall the prey be taken from the **m**,	1368	
	49:25 Even the captives of the **m** shall be taken	1368	
	49:26 and thy redeemer, the **m** One of Jacob.	46	

Isa	60:16 and thy redeemer, the **m** One of Jacob.	46	
	63: 1 I that speak in righteousness, **m** to save.	7227	
Jer	5:15 it *is* a **m** nation, it *is* an ancient nation,	386	
	5:16 as an open sepulchre, they *are* all **m**.	1368	
	9:23 neither let the **m** *man* glory in his might,	1368	
	14: 9 astonied, as a **m** *man* that cannot save?	1368	
	20:11 the Lord *is* with me as a **m** terrible one:	1368	
	26:21 with all his **m** men, and all the princes,	1368	
	32:18 the Great, the **M** God, the Lord of hosts,	1368	
	32:19 Great in counsel, and **m** in work: for	7227	
	33: 3 and **m** things, which thou knowest not.	1219	
	41:16 *even* **m** men of war, and the women,	1397	
	46: 5 **m** ones are beaten down, and are fled	1368	
	46: 6 swift flee away, nor the **m** *man* escape;	1368	
	46: 9 chariots; and let the **m** men come forth;	1368	
	46:12 for the **m** man hath stumbled against	1368	
	46:12 mighty *man* hath stumbled against the **m**,	1368	
	48:14 We *are* **m** and strong men for the war?	1368	
	48:41 the **m** men's hearts in Moab at that day	1368	
	49:22 that day shall the heart of the **m** men of	1368	
	50: 9 arrows *shall be* as of a **m** expert *man;*	1368	
	50:36 a sword *is* upon her **m** men; and they	1368	
	51:30 The **m** men of Babylon have forborn to	1368	
	51:56 upon Babylon, and her **m** men are taken,	1368	
	51:57 her **m** men: and they shall sleep a perpetual	1368	
La	1:15 Lord hath trodden under foot all my **m**	47	
Eze	17:13 him: he hath also taken the **m** of the land:	352	
	17:17 Neither shall Pharaoh with *his* **m** army	1419	
	20:33 with a **m** hand, and with a stretched	2389	
	20:34 with a **m** hand, and with a stretched out	2389	
	31:11 delivered him into the hand of the **m** one	410	
	32:12 By the swords of the **m** will I cause thy	1368	
	32:21 The strong among the **m** shall speak to	1368	
	32:27 shall not lie with the **m** that *are* fallen	1368	
	32:27 though *they were* the terror of the **m** in	1368	
	38:15 a great company, and a **m** army:	7227	
	39:18 Ye shall eat the flesh of the **m**,	1368	
	39:20 with **m** men, and *with* all men of war,	1368	
Da	3:20 **most m** men that *were* in	1400+1401+2429	
	4: 3 how **m** *are* his wonders! his kingdom *is*	8624	
	8:24 his power shall be **m**, but not by his own	6105	
	8:24 shall destroy the **m** and the holy people.	6099	
	9:15 out of the land of Egypt with a **m** hand,	2389	
	11: 3 a **m** king shall stand up, that shall rule	1368	
	11:25 to battle with a very great and **m** army;	6099	
Hos	10:13 thy way, in the multitude of thy **m** men.	1368	
Joel	2: 7 shall run like **m** men; they shall climb	1368	
	3: 9 wake up the **m** men, let all the men of	1368	
	3:11 thither cause thy **m** ones to come down,	1368	
Am	2:14 neither shall the **m** deliver himself:	1368	
	2:16 he *that is* courageous among the **m** shall	1368	
	5:12 manifold transgressions and your **m** sins:	6099	
	5:24 waters, and righteousness as a **m** stream.	386	
Ob	1: 9 thy **m** men, O Teman, shall be dismayed,	1368	
Jnh	1: 4 there was a **m** tempest in the sea, so that	1419	
Na	2: 3 The shield of his **m** men is made red,	1368	
Hab	1:12 O **m** God, thou hast established them	6697	
Zep	1:14 the **m** *man* shall cry there bitterly.	1368	
	3:17 Lord thy God in the midst of thee *is* **m**;	1368	
Zec	9:13 and made thee as the sword of a **m** man.	1368	
	10: 5 shall be as **m** men, which tread down	1368	
	10: 7 *they* of Ephraim shall be like a **m** man,	1368	
	11: 2 cedar is fallen; because the **m** are spoiled:	117	
Mt	11:20 wherein most of his **m works** were done,	1411	
	11:21 for if the **m works** which were done in	1411	
	11:23 if the **m works**, which have been done	1411	
	13:54 *man* this wisdom, and *these* **m works**?	1411	
	13:58 And he did not many **m works** there,	1411	
	14: 2 **m works** do shew forth themselves in	1411	
Mk	6: 2 even such **m works** are wrought by his	1411	
	6: 5 And he could there do no **m work**,	1411	
	6:14 **m works** do shew forth themselves in	1411	
Lk	1:49 For he *that is* **m** hath done to me great	1415	
	1:52 He hath put down the **m** from *their* seats,	1413	
	9:43 they were all amazed at the **m power**	3168	
	10:13 for if the **m works** had been done in Tyre	1411	
	15:14 there arose a **m** famine in that land;	2478	
	19:37 for all the **m works** that they had seen;	1411	
	24:19 which was a prophet **m** in deed and	1415	
Ac	2: 2 from heaven as of a rushing **m** wind,	972	
	7:22 and was **m** in words and in deeds.	1415	
	18:24 an eloquent man, *and* **m** in the scriptures,	1415	
Ro	15:19 Through **m** signs and wonders,	1411	
1Co	1:26 not many **m**, not many noble, *are called*:	1415	
	1:27 to confound the *things which are* **m**;	2478	
2Co	4: 4 through God to the pulling down of	1415	
	12:12 in signs, and wonders, and **m deeds**.	1411	
	13: 3 to you-ward is not weak, but is **m** in you.	1414	
Gal	2: 8 *the same* was **m** in me towards	1754	
Eph	1:19 according to the working of his **m** power,	2904	
2Th	1: 7 revealed from heaven with his **m** angels,	1411	
1Pe	5: 6 therefore under the hand of God,	2900	
Rev	6:13 when she is shaken of a **m** wind.	3173	
	6:15 and the **m** men, and every bondman,	1415	
	10: 1 And I saw another **m** angel come down	2478	
	16:18 earth, so **m** an earthquake, *and* so great.	5082	
	18:10 alas, *that* great city Babylon, *that* **m** city!	2478	
	18:21 And a **m** angel took up a stone like a great	2478	
	19: 6 and as the voice of **m** thunderings, saying,	2478	
	19:18 and the flesh of **m** men, and the flesh of	2478	

MIGRON (2)

1Sa	14: 2 under a pomegranate tree which *is* in **M**:	4051
Isa	10:28 He is come to Aiath, he is passed to **M**;	4051

M

MIJAMIN (2)

1Ch 24:	9 The fifth to Malchijah, the sixth to **M**,	4326
Ne 10:	7 Meshullam, Abijah, **M**,	4326

MIKLOTH (4)

1Ch 8:32	**M** begat Shimeah. And these also dwelt	4732
9:37	and Ahio, and Zechariah, and **M**.	4732
9:38	**M** begat Shimeah. And they also dwelt	4732
27: 4	and of his course was **M** also the ruler:	4732

MIKNEIAH (2)

1Ch 15:18	and **M**, and Obed-edom, and Jeiel,	4737
15:21	**M**, and Obed-edom, and Jeiel,	4737

MILALAI (1)

Ne 12:36	Shemaiah, and Azarael, **M**, Gilalai, Maai,	4450

MILCAH (11)

Ge 11:29	**M**, the daughter of Haran, the father of	4435
11:29	the father of **M**, and the father of Iscah.	4435
22:20	it was told Abraham, saying, Behold, **M**,	4435
22:23	these eight **M** did bear to Nahor,	4435
24:15	son of **M**, the wife of Nahor,	4435
24:24	am the daughter of Bethuel the son of **M**,	4435
24:47	Nahor's son, whom **M** bare unto him:	4435
Nu 26:33	and Noah, Hoglah, **M**, and Tirzah.	4435
27: 1	Noah, and Hoglah, and **M**, and Tirzah.	4435
36:11	Tirzah, and Hoglah, and **M**, and Noah,	4435
Jos 17: 3	and Noah, Hoglah, and **M**, and Tirzah.	4435

MILCH (3) [MILK]

Ge 32:15	Thirty **m** camels with their colts, forty	3243
1Sa 6: 7	make a new cart, and take two **m** kine,	5763
6:10	two **m** kine, and tied them to the cart,	5763

MILCOM (3) [MOLOCH]

1Ki 11: 5	**M** the abomination of the Ammonites.	4445
11:33	**M** the god of the children of Ammon,	4445
2Ki 23:13	for **M** the abomination of the children of	4445

MILDEW (5)

Dt 28:22	sword, and with blasting, and with **m**;	3420
1Ki 8:37	**m**, locust, or if there be caterpillar;	3420
2Ch 6:28	be blasting, or **m**, locusts, or caterpillars;	3420
Am 4: 9	I have smitten you with blasting and **m**:	3420
Hag 2:17	I smote you with blasting and with **m** and	3420

MILE (1)

Mt 5:41	whosoever shall compel thee to go a **m**,	3400

MILES See FURLONGS

MILETUM (1) [MILETUS]

2Ti 4:20	but Trophimus have I left at **M** sick.	3399

MILETUS (2) [MILETUM]

Ac 20:15	and the next day we came to **M**.	3399
20:17	And from **M** he sent to Ephesus,	3399

MILK (48) [MILCH]

Ge 18: 8	**m**, and the calf which he had dressed,	2461
49:12	with wine, and his teeth white with **m**.	2461
Ex 3: 8	unto a land flowing with **m** and honey;	2461
3:17	unto a land flowing with **m** and honey,	2461
13: 5	a land flowing with **m** and honey,	2461
23:19	shalt not seethe a kid in his mother's **m**.	2461
33: 3	Unto a land flowing with **m** and honey:	2461
34:26	shalt not seethe a kid in his mother's **m**.	2461
Lev 20:24	a land that floweth with **m** and honey:	2461
Nu 13:27	and surely it floweth with **m** and honey;	2461
14: 8	a land which floweth with **m** and honey.	2461
16:13	us up out of a land that floweth with **m**	2461
16:14	us into a land that floweth with **m**	2461
Dt 6: 3	the land that floweth with **m** and honey.	2461
11: 9	a land that floweth with **m** and honey.	2461
14:21	shalt not seethe a kid in his mother's **m**.	2461
26: 9	a land that floweth with **m** and honey.	2461
26:15	a land that floweth with **m** and honey;	2461
27: 3	a land that floweth with **m** and honey;	2461
31:20	that floweth with **m** and honey;	2461
32:14	Butter of kine, and **m** of sheep, with fat	2461
Jos 5: 6	a land that floweth with **m** and honey.	2461
Jdg 4:19	she opened a bottle of **m**, and gave him	2461
5:25	He asked water, and she gave him **m**;	2461
Job 10:10	Hast thou not poured me out as **m**,	2461
21:24	His breasts are full of **m**, and his bones	2461
Pr 27:27	thou shalt have goats' **m** enough for thy	2461
30:33	Surely the churning of **m** bringeth forth	2461
SS 4:11	honey and **m** are under thy tongue;	2461
5: 1	I have drunk my wine with my **m**:	2461
5:12	of waters, washed with **m**, and fitly set.	2461
Isa 7:22	the abundance of **m** that they shall give	2461
28: 9	them that are weaned from the **m**,	2461
55: 1	buy wine and **m** without money and	2461
60:16	shalt also suck the **m** of the Gentiles,	2461
66:11	that ye may **m** out, and be delighted with	4711
Jer 11: 5	to give them a land flowing with **m** and	2461
32:22	a land flowing with **m** and honey;	2461
La 4: 7	than snow, they were whiter than **m**,	2461
Eze 25: 4	eat thy fruit, and they shall drink thy **m**.	2461
Joel 3:18	the hills shall flow with **m**, and all	2461
1Co 3: 2	I have fed you with **m**, and not with meat:	1051
9: 7	and eateth not of the **m** of the flock?	1051
Heb 5:12	and are become such as have need of **m**,	1051

Heb 5:13	For every one that useth **m** is unskilful in	1051
1Pe 2: 2	desire the sincere **m** of the word,	1051

MILL (2) [MILLS, MILLSTONE, MILLSTONES]

Ex 11: 5	of the maidservant that is behind the **m**;	7347
Mt 24:41	Two women shall be grinding at the **m**;	3459

MILLET (1)

Eze 4: 9	**m**, and fitches, and put them in one	1764

MILLIONS (1)

Ge 24:60	be thou the mother of thousands of **m**,	7233

MILLO (10)

Jdg 9: 6	all the house of **M**, and went,	4407
9:20	men of Shechem, and the house of **M**;	4407
9:20	from the house of **M**,	4407
2Sa 5: 9	David built round about from **M** and	4407
1Ki 9:15	**M**, and the wall of Jerusalem, and Hazor,	4407
9:24	had built for her: then did he build **M**.	4407
11:27	Solomon built **M**, and repaired the	4407
2Ki 12:20	slew Joash in the house of **M**,	4407
1Ch 11: 8	round about, even from **M** round about:	4407
2Ch 32: 5	repaired **M** in the city of David,	4407

MILLS (1) [MILL]

Nu 11: 8	gathered it, and ground it in **m**, or beat it	7347

MILLSTONE (9) [MILL]

Dt 24: 6	the nether or the **upper m** to pledge:	7393
Jdg 9:53	a certain woman cast a piece of a **m** upon	7393
2Sa 11:21	did not a woman cast a piece of a **m** upon	7393
Job 41:24	yea, as hard as a piece of the nether **m**.	NIH
Mt 18: 6	were better for him that a **m** were	3458+3684
Mk 9:42	it is better for him that a **m** were	3037+3457
Lk 17: 2	were better for him that a **m** were	3458+3684
Rev 18:21	angel took up a stone like a great **m**,	3458
18:22	the sound of a **m** shall be heard no more	3458

MILLSTONES (2) [MILL]

Isa 47: 2	Take the **m**, and grind meal: uncover thy	7347
Jer 25:10	the sound of the **m**, and the light of	7347

MINAH See MANEH

MINCING (1)

Isa 3:16	walking and **m** as they go, and making a	2952

MIND (95) [FEEBLEMINDED, HIGHMINDED, HIGH-MINDED, LIKEMINDED, MINDED, MINDFUL, MINDING, MINDS, UNMINDFUL]

Ge 23: 8	If it be your **m** that I should bury my	5315
26:35	Which were a grief of **m** unto Isaac and	7307
Lev 24:12	that the **m** of the Lord might be shewed	6310
Nu 16:28	I have not done them of mine own **m**.	3820
24:13	to do either good or bad of mine own **m**;	3820
Dt 18: 6	come with all the desire of his **m** unto	5315
28:65	and failing of eyes, and sorrow of **m**:	5315
30: 1	thou shalt call them to **m** among all	3824
1Sa 2:35	that which is in my heart and in my **m**:	5315
9:20	three days ago, set not thy **m** on them;	3820
1Ch 22: 7	it was in my **m** to build a house unto	5315
28: 9	a perfect heart and with a willing **m**:	3824
Ne 4: 6	for the people had a **m** to work.	3820
Job 23:13	he is in one **m**, and who can turn him?	NIH
34:33	Should it be according to thy **m**?	4480+5973
Ps 31:12	I am forgotten as a dead man out of **m**:	3820
Pr 21:27	when he bringeth it with a **wicked** **m**?	2154
29:11	A fool uttereth all his **m**: but a wise man	7307
Isa 26: 3	whose **m** is stayed on thee: because	3336
46: 8	bring it again to **m**, O ye transgressors.	3820
65:17	not be remembered, nor come into **m**.	3820
Jer 3:16	neither shall it come to **m**: neither shall	3820
15: 1	my **m** could not be toward this people:	5315
19: 5	nor spake it, neither came it into my **m**:	3820
32:35	them not, neither came it into my **m**,	3820
44:21	and came it not into his **m**?	3820
51:50	and let Jerusalem come into your **m**.	3824
La 3:21	This I recall to my **m**, therefore have I	3820
Eze 11: 5	I know the things that come into your **m**,	7307
20:32	that which cometh into your **m** shall not	7307
23:17	and her **m** was alienated from them.	5315
23:18	my **m** was alienated from her, like as my	5315
23:18	like as my **m** was alienated from her sister.	5315
23:22	from whom thy **m** is alienated, and I will	5315
23:28	into the hand of them from whom thy **m**	5315
38:10	same time shall things come into thy **m**,	3824
Da 2:29	thoughts came into thy **m** upon thy bed,	NIH
5:20	lifted up, and his **m** hardened in pride,	7308
Hab 1:11	his **m** change, and he shall pass over,	7307
Mt 22:37	and with all thy soul, and with all thy **m**.	1271
Mk 5:15	sitting, and clothed, and in his **right m**,	4993
12:30	and with all thy **m**, and with all thy	1271
14:72	Peter **called** to **m** the word that Jesus	363
Lk 1:29	**cast in** her **m** what manner of salutation	1260
8:35	feet of Jesus, clothed, and in his **right m**,	4993
10:27	with all thy strength, and with all thy **m**;	1271
12:29	shall drink, neither be ye of **doubtful m**.	3349
Ac 17:11	the word with all **readiness of m**,	4288
20:19	Serving the Lord with all **humility of m**,	5012
Ro 1:28	God gave them over to a reprobate **m**,	3563
7:23	warring against the law of my **m**,	3563
7:25	with the **m** I myself serve the law of God;	3563
8: 5	For they that are after the flesh do **m**	5426
8: 7	Because the carnal **m** is enmity against	5427
8:27	knoweth what is the **m** of the Spirit,	5427

Ro 11:34	For who hath known the **m** of the Lord?	3563
12: 2	transformed by the renewing of your **m**,	3563
12:16	Be of the same **m** one towards another.	5426
12:16	**M** not high things, but condescend to	5426
14: 5	man be fully persuaded in his own **m**.	3563
15: 6	That ye may with **one m** and one mouth	3661
15:15	as **putting** you **in m**, because of the grace	1878
1Co 1:10	be perfectly joined together in the same **m**	3563
2:16	For who hath known the **m** of the Lord,	3563
2:16	But we have the **m** of Christ.	3563
2Co 7: 7	mourning, your **fervent m** toward me;	2205
8:12	For if there be first a **willing m**, it is	4288
8:19	and declaration of your **ready m**:	4288
9: 2	For I know the **forwardness of** your **m**,	4288
13:11	good comfort, be of one **m**, live in peace;	5426
Eph 2: 3	the desires of the flesh and of the **m**;	1271
4:17	Gentiles walk, in the vanity of their **m**,	3563
4:23	And be renewed in the spirit of your **m**;	3563
Php 1:27	with one **m** striving together for the faith	5590
2: 2	same love, being of one accord, of one **m**.	5426
2: 3	in **lowliness of m** let each esteem other	5012
2: 5	Let this **m** be in you, which was also in	5426
3:16	by the same rule, let us **m** the same thing.	5426
3:19	is in their shame, who **m** earthly things.)	5426
4: 2	that they be of the same **m** in the Lord.	5426
Col 1:21	and enemies in your **m** by wicked works,	1271
2:18	not seen, vainly puft up by his fleshly **m**,	3563
3:12	kindness, **humbleness of m**, meekness,	5012
2Th 2: 2	That ye be not soon shaken in **m**,	3563
2Ti 1: 7	of power, and of love, and of a **sound m**.	4995
Tit 1:15	even their **m** and conscience is defiled.	3563
3: 1	**Put** them **in m** to be subject to	5279
Phm 1:14	But without thy **m** would I do nothing;	1106
Heb 8:10	I will put my laws into their **m**,	1271
1Pe 1:13	Wherefore gird up the loins of your **m**,	1271
3: 8	Finally, be ye all of **one m**,	3675
4: 1	arm yourselves likewise with the same **m**:	1771
5: 2	not for filthy lucre, but **of a ready m**;	4290
Rev 17: 9	And here is the **m** which hath wisdom.	3563
17:13	These have one **m**, and shall give their	1106

MINDED (15) [MIND]

Ru 1:18	she saw that she was **stedfastly m** to	553
2Ch 24: 4	Joash was **m** to repair the house	3820+5973
Ezr 7:13	are **m** of their **own freewill** to go up	5069
Mt 1:19	was **m** to put her away privily.	1014
Ac 27:39	into the which they were **m**, if it were	1011
Ro 8: 6	For to be carnally **m** is death;	5427
8: 6	but to be spiritually **m** is life and peace.	5427
2Co 1:15	And in this confidence I was **m** to come	1014
1:17	When I therefore was thus **m**, did I use	1011
Gal 5:10	that you will be none otherwise **m**:	5426
Php 3:15	as many as be perfect, be thus **m**:	5426
3:15	and if in any thing ye be otherwise **m**,	5426
Tit 2: 6	men likewise exhort to be **sober m**.	4993
Jas 1: 8	A **double m** man is unstable in all his	1374
4: 8	and purify your hearts, ye **double m**.	1374

MINDFUL (10) [MIND]

1Ch 16:15	Be ye always of his covenant; the word	2142
Ne 9:17	neither were ye **m** of thy wonders that thou	2142
Ps 8: 4	What is man, that thou art **m** of him?	2142
111: 5	he: he will ever be **m** of his covenant.	2142
115:12	The Lord hath been **m** of us: he will	2142
Isa 17:10	not been **m** of the rock of thy strength,	2142
2Ti 1: 4	desiring to see thee, being **m** of thy tears,	3415
Heb 2: 6	What is man, that thou art **m** of him?	3403
11:15	if they had been **m** of that country from	3421
2Pe 3: 2	That ye may be **m** of the words which	3415

MINDING (1) [MIND]

Ac 20:13	had he appointed, **m** himself to go afoot.	3195

MINDS (16) [MIND]

Jdg 19:30	of it, take advice, and speak your **m**.	NIH
2Sa 17: 8	men, and they be chafed in their **m**,	5315
2Ki 9:15	If it be your **m**, then let none go forth	5315
Eze 24:25	whereupon they set their **m**, their sons	5315
36: 5	despiteful **m**, to cast it out for a prey.	5590
Ac 14: 2	made their **m** evil affected against	NIG
28: 6	they changed their **m**, and said that he	3540
2Co 3:14	their **m** were blinded: for until this day	3540
4: 4	blinded the **m** of them which believe not,	3540
11: 3	your **m** should be corrupted from	3540
Php 4: 7	your hearts and **m** through Christ Jesus.	3540
1Ti 6: 5	Perverse disputings of men of corrupt **m**,	3563
2Ti 3: 8	men of corrupt **m**, reprobate concerning	3563
Heb 10:16	and in their **m** will I write them;	1271
12: 3	lest ye be wearied and faint in your **m**.	5590
2Pe 3: 1	both which I stir up your pure **m** by way	1271

MINE (647) [I]

Ge 14:22	have lift up **m** hand unto the Lord,	2967.1
15: 3	and lo, one born in my house is **m** heir.	2967.1
24:33	will not eat, until I have told **m** errand.	2967.1
24:45	before I had done speaking in **m** heart,	2967.1
30:25	that I may go unto **m** own place,	2967.1
30:30	now when shall I provide for **m** own	2967.1
31:10	that I lifted up **m** eyes, and saw in a	2967.1
31:40	and my sleep departed from **m** eyes.	2967.1
31:42	God hath seen **m** affliction and the	2967.1
31:43	and all that thou seest is **m**:	2967.1+3807.1
41:13	he restored unto **m** office, and him he	2967.1
44:21	me, that I may set **m** eyes upon him.	2967.1
48: 5	unto thee into Egypt, are **m**;	2967.1+3807.1

MIJAMIN – MINE

M

Ge 48: 5 and Simeon, they shall be **m**. 2967.1+3807.1
49: 6 **m** honour, be not thou united: 2967.1
Ex 7: 4 bring forth **m** armies, *and* my people 2967.1
7: 5 I stretch forth **m** hand upon Egypt, 2967.1
7:17 will smite with the rod that *is* in **m** hand 2967.1
13: 2 of man and of beast: it *is* **m**. 2967.1+3807.1
17: 9 the hill with the rod of God in **m** hand. 2967.1
18: 4 *said* **m**, *was* **m** help, and delivered me 2967.1
19: 5 all people: for all the earth *is* **m**: 2967.1+3807.1
20:26 shalt thou go up by steps unto **m** 2967.1
21:14 thou shalt take him from **m** altar, that 2967.1
23:23 For **m** Angel shall go before thee, 2967.1
32:34 behold, **m** Angel shall go before thee: 2967.1
33:23 I will take away **m** hand, and thou shalt 2967.1
34:19 that openeth the matrix *is* **m**; 2967.1+3807.1
Lev 18: 4 and keep **m** ordinances, to walk therein: 2967.1
18:30 Therefore ye shall keep **m** ordinance, 2967.1
20:26 that *ye* should be **m**. 2967.1+3807.1
22: 9 They shall therefore keep **m** ordinance, 2967.1
25:23 for the land *is* **m**; for ye were 2967.1+3807.1
Nu 3:12 therefore the Levites shall be **m**; 2967.1+3807.1
3:13 Because all the firstborn *are* **m**; 2967.1+3807.1
3:13 and beast: **m** they shall be: 2967.1+3807.1
3:45 and the Levites shall be **m**: 2967.1+3807.1
8:14 and the Levites shall be **m**. 2967.1+3807.1
8:17 of the children of Israel *are* **m**, 2967.1+3807.1
10:30 I will depart to **m** own land, and to my 2967.1
12: 7 *is* not so, who *is* faithful in all **m** house. 2967.1
14:28 as ye have spoken in **m** ears, so will I do 2967.1
16:28 *I have* not *done them of* **m** own mind. 2967.1
18: 8 I also have given thee the charge of **m** 2967.1
22:29 I would there were a sword in **m** hand, 2967.1
23:11 I took thee to curse **m** enemies, 2967.1
24:10 I called thee to curse **m** enemies, 2967.1
24:13 do *either* good or bad of **m** own mind; 2967.1
Dt 8:17 The might of **m** hand hath gotten me 2967.1
10: 3 having the two tables in **m** hand. 2967.1
26:13 the hallowed *things* out of **m** house, NIH
29:19 though I walk in the imagination of **m** 2967.1
32:23 I will spend **m** arrows upon them. 2967.1
32:41 and **m** hand take hold on judgment; 2967.1
32:41 I will render vengeance to **m** enemies, 2967.1
32:42 I will make **m** arrows drunk with blood, 2967.1
Jos 14: 7 brought him word again as *it was* in **m** 2967.1
Jdg 6:36 If thou wilt save Israel by **m** hand, 2967.1
6:37 that thou wilt save Israel by **m** hand, 2967.1
7: 2 saying, **M** own hand hath saved me. 2967.1
8: 7 and Zalmunna into **m** hand, 2967.1
11:30 the children of Ammon into **m** hands, 2967.1
16:17 hath not come a rasor upon **m** head; 2967.1
17: 2 spakest of also in **m** ears, behold, 2967.1
19:23 seeing that this man is come into **m** 2967.1
Ru 4: 6 myself, lest I mar **m** mine inheritance: 2967.1
1Sa 2: 1 **m** horn is exalted in the LORD: 2967.1
2: 1 my mouth is enlarged over **m** enemies; 2967.1
2:28 to offer upon **m** altar, to burn incense, 2967.1
2:29 ye at my sacrifice and at **m** offering, 2967.1
2:33 *whom* I shall not cut off from **m** altar, 2967.1
2:35 shall walk before **m** anointed for ever. 2967.1
12: 3 *any* bribe to blind **m** eyes therewith? 2967.1
14:24 that I may be avenged on **m** enemies, 2967.1
14:29 how **m** eyes have been enlightened, 2967.1
14:43 the end of the rod that *was* in **m** hand, 2967.1
15:14 this bleating of the sheep in **m** ears, 2967.1
17:46 will the LORD deliver thee into **m** hand; 2967.1
18:17 Let not **m** hand be upon him, but let 2967.1
19:17 sent away **m** enemy, that he is escaped? 2967.1
20: 1 what *is* **m** iniquity? and what *is* my sin 2967.1
21: 3 give *me* five *loaves of* bread in **m** hand, 2967.1
21: 4 *is* no common bread under **m** hand, 2967.1
23: 7 God hath delivered him into **m** hand; 2967.1
24: 6 to stretch forth **m** hand against him, 2967.1
24:10 thee to day into **m** hand in the cave: 2967.1
24:10 *m* eye spared thee; and I said, I will not NIH
24:10 not put forth **m** hand against my lord; 2967.1
24:11 evil nor transgression in **m** hand, 2967.1
24:12 but **m** hand shall not be upon thee. 2967.1
24:13 but **m** hand shall not be upon thee. 2967.1
25:33 avenging myself with **m** own hand. 2967.1
26:11 **m** hand against the LORD's anointed; 2967.1
26:18 have I done? or what evil *is* in **m** hand? 2967.1
26:23 would not stretch forth **m** hand against 2967.1
26:24 thy life was much set by this day in **m** 2967.1
28: 2 Therefore will I make thee keeper of **m** 2967.1
2Sa 5:19 wilt thou deliver them into **m** hand? 2967.1
5:20 The LORD hath broken forth upon **m** 2967.1
6:22 and will be base in **m** own sight: 2967.1
11:11 shall I then go into **m** house, to eat and 2967.1
14: 5 widow woman, and **m** husband is dead. 2967.1
14:30 Joab's field is near **m**, and he hath 2967.1
16:12 It may be that the LORD will look on **m** 2967.1
18:12 a thousand *shekels of* silver in **m** hand, 2967.1
18:12 would I not put forth **m** hand against 2967.1
18:13 wrought falsehood against **m** own life: 2967.1
19:37 that I may die in **m** own city, 2967.1
22: 4 so shall I be saved from **m** enemies. 2967.1
22:24 and have kept myself from **m** iniquity. 2967.1
22:35 a bow of steel is broken by **m** arms. 2967.1
22:38 I have pursued **m** enemies, 2967.1
22:41 hast also given me the necks of **m** 2967.1
22:49 that bringeth me forth from **m** enemies: 2967.1
1Ki 1:33 son to ride upon **m** own mule, 2967.1+3807.1
1:48 throne *this* day, **m** eyes even seeing *it.* 2967.1
2:15 that the kingdom was **m**, 2967.1+3807.1
2:22 for he is **m** elder brother; even for him, 2967.1

1Ki 3:26 **m** nor thine, *but* divide *it.* 2967.1+3807.1
9: 3 **m** eyes and mine heart shall be there 2967.1
9: 3 and **m** heart shall be there perpetually. 2967.1
10: 6 a true report that I heard in **m** own 2967.1
10: 7 and **m** eyes had seen *it*: and behold, 2967.1
11:21 that I may go to **m** own country. 2967.1
11:33 to do *that* which *is* right in **m** eyes, 2967.1
14: 8 do *that* only which *was* right in **m** eyes; 2967.1
20: 3 Thy silver and thy gold *is* **m**; 2967.1+3807.1
20: 3 *even* the goodliest, *are* **m**. 2967.1+3807.1
21:20 Hast thou found me, O **m** enemy? 2967.1
2Ki 4:13 I dwell among **m** own people. 2967.1
5:26 Went not **m** heart *with thee,* when 2967.1
6:32 hath sent to take away **m** head? 2967.1
10: 6 If ye be **m**, and if ye will 2967.1+3807.1
10:30 executing *that* which *is* right in **m** eyes, 2967.1
10:30 according to all that *was* in **m** heart, 2967.1
18:34 have they delivered Samaria out of **m** 2967.1
18:35 have delivered their country out of **m** 2967.1
18:35 deliver Jerusalem out of **m** hand? 2967.1
19:28 and thy tumult is come up into **m** ears, 2967.1
19:34 for **m** own sake, and for my servant 2967.1
20: 6 I will defend this city for **m** own sake, 2967.1
20:15 All *the things* that *are* in **m** house have 2967.1
21:14 will forsake the remnant of **m** 2967.1
1Ch 12:17 unto me to help me, **m** 2967.1+3807.1
12:17 ye be come to betray me to **m** enemies, 2967.1
12:17 seeing *there is* no wrong in **m** hands, 2967.1
14:10 wilt thou deliver them into **m** hand? 2967.1
14:11 God hath broken in upon **m** enemies 2967.1
14:11 **m** hand like the breaking forth of 2967.1
16:22 *Saying,* Touch not **m** anointed, 2967.1
17:14 I will settle him in **m** house and in my 2967.1
17:16 O LORD God, and what *is* **m** house, 2967.1
22:18 the inhabitants of the land into **m** hand; 2967.1
28: 2 *As for me,* I *had* in **m** heart to build a 2967.1
29: 3 I have of **m** own proper good, 2967.1+3807.1
29:17 in the uprightness of **m** heart I have 2967.1
2Ch 7:15 **m** eyes shall be open, and mine ears 2967.1
7:15 **m** ears attent unto the prayer *that is* 2967.1
7:16 **m** eyes and mine heart shall be there 2967.1
7:16 and **m** heart shall be there perpetually. 2967.1
9: 5 I heard in **m** own land of thine acts, 2967.1
9: 6 and **m** eyes had seen *it:* and behold, 2967.1
29:10 *it is* in **m** heart to make a covenant 2967.1
32:13 to deliver their lands out of **m** hand? 2967.1
32:14 that could deliver his people out of **m** 2967.1
32:14 be able to deliver you out of **m** hand? 2967.1
32:15 to deliver his people out of **m** hand, 2967.1
32:15 your God deliver you out of **m** hand? 2967.1
32:17 delivered their people out of **m** hand, 2967.1
32:17 deliver his people out of **m** hand. 2967.1
Ne 5: 7 my God put into **m** heart to gather 2967.1
Job 3:10 nor hid sorrow from **m** eyes. 2967.1
4:12 and **m** ear received a little thereof. 2967.1
4:16 an image *was* before **m** eyes, *there was* 2967.1
6:11 what *is* **m** end, that I should prolong 2967.1
7: 7 *is* wind: **m** eye shall no more see good. 2967.1
7:21 and take away **m** iniquity? 2967.1
9:20 **m** own mouth shall condemn me: 2967.1
9:31 and **m** own clothes shall abhor me. 2967.1
10: 6 That thou inquirest after **m** iniquity, 2967.1
10:14 wilt not acquit me from **m** iniquity. 2967.1
10:15 therefore see thou **m** affliction; 2967.1
13: 1 **m** eye hath seen all *this,* mine ear hath 2967.1
13: 1 mine eye hath seen all *this,* **m** ear hath 2967.1
13:14 in my teeth, and put my life in **m** hand? 2967.1
13:15 will maintain **m** own ways before him. 2967.1
13:23 How many *are* **m** iniquities 2967.1+3807.1
14:17 a bag, and thou sewest up **m** iniquity. 2967.1
16: 4 against you, and shake **m** head at you. 2967.1
16: 9 **m** enemy sharpeneth his eyes upon me. 2967.1
16:16 on **m** eyelids *is* the shadow of death; 2967.1
16:17 Not for *any* injustice in **m** hands: also 2967.1
16:20 *but* **m** eye poureth out *tears* unto God. 2967.1
17: 2 *doth* not **m** eye continue in their 2967.1
17: 7 **M** eye also is dim by reason of sorrow, 2967.1
17:13 If I wait, the grave *is* **m** house: I have 2967.1
19: 4 error remaineth with myself. 2967.1
19:10 **m** hope hath he removed like a tree. 2967.1
19:13 **m** acquaintance are verily estranged 2967.1
19:15 They that dwell in **m** house, 2967.1
19:17 for the children's *sake* of **m** own body. 2967.1
19:27 **m** eyes shall behold, and not another; 2967.1
27: 7 Let **m** enemy be as the wicked, 2967.1
31: 1 I made a covenant with **m** eyes; why 2967.1
31: 6 that God may know **m** integrity. 2967.1
31: 7 **m** heart walked after mine eyes, 2967.1
31: 7 mine heart walked after **m** eyes, 2967.1
31: 9 If **m** heart have been deceived by a 2967.1
31:12 and would root out all **m** increase. 2967.1
31:22 *Then* let **m** arm fall from *my* shoulder 2967.1
31:22 and **m** arm be broken from the bone. 2967.1
31:25 and because **m** hand had gotten much; 2967.1
31:33 by hiding **m** iniquity in my bosom: 2967.1
31:35 *that* **m** adversary had written a book. 2967.1
32: 6 and durst not shew you **m** opinion. 2967.1
32:10 to me; I also will shew **m** opinion. 2967.1
32:17 my part, I also will shew **m** opinion. 2967.1
33: 8 Surely thou hast spoken in **m** hearing, 2967.1
41:11 under the whole heaven is **m**. 2967.1+3807.1
42: 5 of the ear: but now **m** eye seeth thee. 2967.1
Ps 3: 3 my glory, and the lifter up of **m** head. 2967.1
3: 7 for thou hast smitten all **m** enemies 2967.1
5: 8 righteousness because of **m** enemies; 2967.1

Ps 6: 7 **M** eye is consumed because of grief; 2967.1
6: 7 it waxeth old because of all **m** enemies. 2967.1
6:10 Let all **m** enemies be ashamed and 2967.1
7: 4 him that without cause is **m** enemy:) 2967.1
7: 5 earth, and lay **m** honour in the dust. 2967.1
7: 6 because of the rage of **m** enemies: 2967.1
7: 8 according to **m** integrity *that is* in me. 2967.1
9: 3 When **m** enemies are turned back, 2967.1
13: 2 how long shall **m** enemy be exalted 2967.1
13: 3 lighten **m** eyes, lest I sleep the *sleep of* 2967.1
13: 4 Lest **m** enemy say, I have prevailed 2967.1
16: 5 The LORD *is* the portion of **m** 2967.1
17: 3 Thou hast proved **m** heart; thou hast 2967.1
18: 3 so shall I be saved from **m** enemies. 2967.1
18:23 and I kept myself from **m** iniquity. 2967.1
18:34 a bow of steel is broken by **m** arms. 2967.1
18:37 I have pursued **m** enemies, 2967.1
18:40 Thou hast also given me the necks of **m** 2967.1
18:48 He delivereth me from **m** enemies: yea, 2967.1
23: 5 me in the presence of **m** enemies: 2967.1
25: 2 let not **m** enemies triumph over me. 2967.1
25:11 O LORD, pardon **m** iniquity; 2967.1+3807.1
25:15 **M** eyes *are* ever towards the LORD: 2967.1
25:18 Look upon **m** affliction and my pain; 2967.1
25:19 Consider **m** enemies; for they are many 2967.1
26: 1 for I have walked in **m** integrity: 2967.1
26: 3 For thy lovingkindness *is* before **m** eyes: 2967.1
26: 6 I will wash **m** hands in innocency: 2967.1
26:11 *as for* me, I will walk in **m** integrity: 2967.1
27: 2 wicked, *even* **m** enemies and my foes, 2967.1
27: 6 shall **m** head be lifted up above mine 2967.1
27: 6 shall mine head be lifted up above **m** 2967.1
27:11 in a plain path, because of **m** enemies. 2967.1
27:12 Deliver me not over unto the will of **m** 2967.1
31: 9 **m** eye is consumed with grief, *yea,* my 2967.1
31:10 strength faileth because of **m** iniquity, 2967.1
31:11 I was a reproach among all **m** enemies, 2967.1
31:11 and a fear to **m** acquaintance: 2967.1
31:15 deliver me from the hand of **m** enemies, 2967.1
32: 5 thee, and **m** iniquity have I not hid. 2967.1
32: 8 shalt go: I will guide thee with **m** eye. 2967.1
35: 2 and buckler, and stand up for **m** help. 2967.1
35:13 prayer returned into **m** own bosom. 2967.1
35:15 in **m** adversity they rejoiced, 2967.1
35:19 Let not them that are **m** enemies 2967.1
35:26 together that rejoice at **m** hurt: 2967.1
38: 4 **m** iniquities are gone *over* mine head: 2967.1
38: 4 mine iniquities are gone *over* **m** head: 2967.1
38:10 as for the light of **m** eyes, it also is gone 2967.1
38:18 For I will declare **m** iniquity; I will be 2967.1
38:19 **m** enemies are lively, and they are 2967.1
38:20 also that render evil for good are **m** 5204.1
39: 4 make me to know **m** end, 2967.1
39: 5 and **m** age *is* as nothing before thee: 2967.1
40: 6 thou didst not desire; **m** 2967.1+3807.1
40:12 **m** iniquities have taken hold upon me, 2967.1
40:12 they are moe than the hairs of **m** head: 2967.1
41: 5 **M** enemies speak evil of me, When shall 2967.1
41: 9 Yea, **m** own familiar friend, in whom I 2967.1
41:11 **m** enemy doth not triumph over me. 2967.1
42:10 in my bones, **m** enemies reproach me; 2967.1
49: 4 I will incline **m** ear to a parable: I will 2967.1
50:10 every beast of the forest *is* **m**, 2967.1+3807.1
50:11 wild beasts of the field *are* **m**. 5978+2967.1
50:12 *is* **m**, and the fulness thereof. 2967.1+3807.1
51: 2 Wash me throughly from **m** iniquity, 2967.1
51: 9 my sins, and blot out all **m** iniquities. 2967.1
54: 4 Behold, God *is* **m** helper: 2967.1+3807.1
54: 5 He shall reward evil unto **m** enemies: 2967.1
54: 7 **m** eye hath seen *his desire* upon mine 2967.1
54: 7 mine eye hath seen *his desire* upon **m** 2967.1
55:13 a man **m** equal, my guide, 2967.1
55:13 my guide, and **m** acquaintance. 2967.1
56: 2 **M** enemies would daily swallow *me* up: 2967.1
56: 9 then shall **m** enemies turn back: 2967.1
59: 1 Deliver me from **m** enemies, O my God: 2967.1
59:10 God shall let me see *my desire* upon **m** 2967.1
60: 7 Gilead *is* **m**, and Manasseh *is* 2967.1+3807.1
60: 7 *is* mine, and Manasseh *is* **m**; 2967.1+3807.1
60: 7 Ephraim also *is* the strength of **m** head; 2967.1
69: 3 **m** eyes fail while I *wait* for my God. 2967.1
69: 4 cause are moe than the hairs of **m** head: 2967.1
69: 4 **m** enemies wrongfully, are mighty; 2967.1
69:18 deliver me because of **m** enemies. 2967.1
69:19 **m** adversaries *are* all before thee. 2967.1
71:10 For **m** enemies speak against me; 2967.1
77: 4 Thou holdest **m** eyes waking: I am *so* 2967.1
77: 6 I commune with **m** own heart: 2967.1
88: 8 Thou hast put away **m** acquaintance far 2967.1
88: 9 **M** eye mourneth by reason of affliction: 2967.1
88:18 *and* **m** acquaintance *into* darkness. 2967.1
89:21 **m** arm also shall strengthen him. 2967.1
92:11 **M** eye also shall see *my desire* on mine 2967.1
92:11 Mine eye also shall see *my desire* on **m** 2967.1
92:11 **m** ears shall hear *my desire* of the 2967.1
101: 3 will set no wicked thing before **m** eyes: 2967.1
101: 6 **M** eyes *shall be* upon the faithful of 2967.1
102: 3 **M** enemies reproach me all the day; 2967.1
105:15 *Saying,* Touch not **m** anointed, and do 2967.1
108: 8 Gilead *is* **m**; Manasseh *is* mine; 2967.1+3807.1
108: 8 Gilead *is* mine; Manasseh *is* **m**; 2967.1+3807.1
108: 8 Ephraim also *is* the strength of **m** head; 2967.1
109:20 *Let* this *be* the reward of **m** adversaries 2967.1
109:29 **m** adversaries be clothed with shame, 2967.1

Ps 116: 8 m eyes from tears, *and* my feet from 2967.1
119:11 Thy word have I hid in m heart, that I 2967.1
119:18 Open thou m eyes, that I may behold 2967.1
119:37 Turn away m eyes from beholding 2967.1
119:82 M eyes fail for thy word, saying, 2967.1
119:92 then have perished in m affliction. 2967.1
119:98 hast made me wiser than m enemies: 2967.1
119:112 I have inclined m heart to perform thy 2967.1
119:121 justice: leave me not to m oppressors. 2967.1
119:123 M eyes fail for thy salvation, and for 2967.1
119:136 Rivers of waters run down m eyes, 2967.1
119:139 m enemies have forgotten thy words. 2967.1
119:148 M eyes prevent the *night* watches, that 2967.1
119:153 Consider m affliction, and deliver me: 2967.1
119:157 *are* my persecutors and m enemies; 2967.1
121: 1 I will lift up m eyes unto the hills, 2967.1
123: 1 Unto thee lift I up m eyes, O thou that 2967.1
131: 1 heart is not haughty, nor m eyes lofty: 2967.1
132: 4 I will not give sleep to m eyes, 2967.1
132: 4 to mine eyes, *or* slumber to m eyelids, 2967.1
132:17 I have ordained a lamp for m anointed. 2967.1
138: 7 hand against the wrath of m enemies, 2967.1
139: 2 my downsitting and m uprising, 2967.1
139:22 hatred: I count them m enemies. 2967.1
141: 8 m eyes *are* unto thee, O GOD the Lord: 2967.1
143: 9 Deliver me, O LORD, from m enemies: 2967.1
143:12 of thy mercy cut off m enemies, 2967.1
Pr 5:13 inclined m ear to them that instructed 2967.1
8:14 Counsel *is* m, 2967.1+3807.1
23:15 be wise, my heart shall rejoice, even m. 589
Ecc 1:16 I communed with m own heart, saying, 2967.1
2: 1 I said in m heart, Go to now, I will 2967.1
2: 3 I sought in m heart to give myself unto 2967.1
2: 3 (yet acquainting m heart with wisdom) 2967.1
2:10 whatsoever m eyes desired I kept not 2967.1
3:17 I said in m heart, God shall judge 2967.1
7:25 applied m heart to know, and to search, 2967.1
8:16 I applied m heart to know wisdom, 2967.1
SS 1: 6 *but* m own vineyard have I not kept. 2967.1
2:16 My beloved *is* m, and I *am* his: 2967.1+3807.1
6: 3 and my beloved *is* m: 2967.1+3807.1
8:12 My vineyard, which *is* m, 2967.1+3807.1
Isa 1:15 hands, I will hide m eyes from you: 2967.1
1:16 evil of your doings from before m eyes; 2967.1
1:24 I will ease me of m adversaries, 2967.1
1:24 and avenge me of m enemies: 2967.1
5: 9 In m ears *said* the LORD of hosts, Of a 2967.1
6: 5 for m eyes have seen the King, 2967.1
10: 5 the rod of m anger, and the staff in their 2967.1
10: 5 the staff in their hand *is* m indignation. 2967.1
10:25 and m anger in their destruction. 2967.1
13: 3 I have also called my mighty ones for m 2967.1
16: 4 Let m outcasts dwell with thee, Moab; 2967.1
16:11 and m inward parts for Kir-haresh. 2967.1
19:25 of my hands, and Israel m inheritance. 2967.1
22:14 it was revealed in m ears *by* the LORD 2967.1
29:23 work of m hands, in the midst of him, 2967.1
37:29 is come up into m ears, therefore will I 2967.1
37:35 this city to save it for m own sake, 2967.1
38:12 M age is departed, and is removed from 2967.1
38:14 m eyes fail *with looking* upward: 2967.1
39: 4 All that *is* in m house have they seen: 2967.1
42: 1 m elect, *in whom* my soul delighteth; 2967.1
43: 1 *thee* by thy name; thou *art* m. 2967.1+3807.1
43:25 out thy transgressions for m own sake, 2967.1
45: 4 my servant's sake, and Israel m elect, 2967.1
47: 6 I have polluted m inheritance, 2967.1
48: 5 M idol hath done them, and my graven 2967.1
48: 9 my name's sake will I defer m anger, 2967.1
48:11 m own sake, *even* for mine own sake, 2967.1
48:11 mine own sake, *even* for m own sake, 2967.1
48:13 M hand also hath laid the foundation of 2967.1
49:22 I will lift up m hand to the Gentiles, 2967.1
50: 4 m ear to hear as the learned. 2967.1+3807.1
50: 5 The Lord GOD hath opened m 2967.1+3807.1
50: 8 who *is* m adversary? let him come near 2967.1
50:11 shall ye have of m hand; ye shall lie 2967.1
51: 5 and m arms shall judge the people; 2967.1
51: 5 and on m arm shall they trust. 2967.1
51:16 have covered thee in the shadow of m 2967.1
56: 5 Even unto them will I give in m house 2967.1
56: 7 sacrifices *shall be* accepted upon m 2967.1
56: 7 for m house shall be called a house of 2967.1
60: 7 shall come up with acceptance on m 2967.1
63: 3 for I will tread them in m anger, 2967.1
63: 4 For the day of vengeance *is* in m heart, 2967.1
63: 5 m own arm brought salvation unto me; 2967.1
63: 6 will tread down the people in m anger, 2967.1
65: 2 I have spread out m hands all the day 2967.1
65: 9 m elect shall inherit it, and my servants 2967.1
65:12 did evil before m eyes, and did choose 2967.1
65:16 and because they are hid from m eyes. 2967.1
65:22 m elect shall long enjoy the work of 2967.1
66: 2 and made m heritage an abomination. 2967.1
66: 4 they did evil before m eyes, 2967.1
Jer 2: 7 and made m heritage an abomination. 2967.1
3:12 I will not cause m anger to fall upon 2967.1
3:15 I will give you pastors according to m 2967.1
7:20 m anger and my fury *shall be* poured 2967.1
9: 1 m eyes a fountain of tears, that I might 2967.1
11:15 hath my beloved to do in m house, 2967.1
12: 3 me, and tried m heart towards thee: 2967.1
12: 7 I have forsaken m house, I have left 2967.1
12: 7 mine house, I have left m heritage; 2967.1
12: 8 M heritage is unto me as a lion in 2967.1

Jer 12: 9 M heritage *is* unto me *as* a speckled 2967.1
12:14 Thus saith the LORD against all m evil 2967.1
13:17 m eye shall weep sore, and run down 2967.1
14:17 Let m eyes run down *with* tears night 2967.1
15:14 for a fire is kindled in m anger, 2967.1
15:16 me the joy and rejoicing of m heart: 2967.1
16:17 For m eyes *are* upon all their ways: 2967.1
16:17 is their iniquity hid from m eyes. 2967.1
16:18 they have filled m inheritance with 2967.1
16:21 I will cause them to know m hand and 2967.1
17: 4 for ye have kindled a fire in m anger, 2967.1
18: 6 so *are* ye in m hand, O house of Israel. 2967.1
20: 9 *word* was in m heart as a burning fire 2967.1
23: 9 m heart within me is broken because 2967.1
24: 6 I will set m eyes upon them for good, 2967.1
25:15 the wine cup of this fury at m hand, 2967.1
32: 8 Hanameel m uncle's son came to me 2967.1
32:12 in the sight of Hanameel m uncle's *son*, 2967.1
32:31 been to me *as* a provocation of m anger 2967.1
32:37 whither I have driven them in m anger, 2967.1
33: 5 whom I have slain in m anger and in 2967.1
42:18 As m anger and my fury hath been 2967.1
44: 6 my fury and m anger was poured forth, 2967.1
44:28 whose words shall stand, m, 4480+5204.1
48:31 m *heart* shall mourn for the men of NIH
48:36 Therefore m heart shall sound for Moab 2967.1
48:36 m heart shall sound like pipes for the 2967.1
50:11 O ye destroyers of m heritage, because 2967.1
51:25 I will stretch out m hand upon thee, 2967.1
La 1:16 m eye, mine eye runneth down *with* 2967.1
1:16 m eye runneth down *with* water, 2967.1
1:19 m elders gave up the ghost in the city, 2967.1
1:20 troubled; m heart is turned within me; 2967.1
1:21 all m enemies have heard of my trouble; 2967.1
2:11 M eyes do fail with tears, my bowels are 2967.1
2:22 brought up hath m enemy consumed. 2967.1
3:19 Remembering m affliction and 2967.1
3:48 M eye runneth down *with* rivers of 2967.1
3:49 M eye trickleth down, and ceaseth not, 2967.1
3:51 M eye affecteth mine heart because of 2967.1
3:51 Mine eye affecteth m heart 2967.1+3807.1
3:52 M enemies chased me sore, like a bird, 2967.1
3:54 Waters flowed over m head; *then* I said, 2967.1
Eze 5:11 I also diminish *thee*; neither shall m 2967.1
5:13 Thus shall m anger be accomplished, 2967.1
6:14 will I stretch out m hand upon them, 2967.1
7: 3 I will send m anger upon thee, 2967.1
7: 4 m eye shall not spare, neither will 2967.1
7: 8 and accomplish m anger upon thee: 2967.1
7: 9 m eye shall not spare, neither will I 2967.1
8: 1 as I sat in m house, and the elders of 2967.1
8: 3 and took me by a lock of m head; 2967.1
8: 5 So I lift up m eyes the way toward 2967.1
8:18 m eye shall not spare, neither will I 2967.1
8:18 though they cry in m ears *with* a loud 2967.1
9: 1 cried also in m ears *with* a loud voice, 2967.1
9: 5 to the others he said in m hearing, Go 2967.1
9:10 *as for* me also, m eye shall not spare, 2967.1
11:20 and keep m ordinances, and do them: 2967.1
12: 7 through the wall with m hand; 2967.1+3807.1
13: 9 m hand shall be upon the prophets that 2967.1
13:13 be an overflowing shower in m anger, 2967.1
14:13 will I stretch out m hand upon it, 2967.1
16: 8 and thou becamest m. 2967.1+3807.1
16:18 thou hast set m oil and mine incense 2967.1
16:18 mine oil and m incense before them. 2967.1
17:19 surely m oath that he hath despised, 2967.1
18: 4 Behold, all souls are m; 2967.1+3807.1
18: 4 so also the soul of the son is m. 2967.1+3807.1
20: 5 lifted up m hand unto the seed of 2967.1
20: 5 when I lifted up m hand unto them, 2967.1
20: 6 In the day *that* I lifted up m hand unto 2967.1
20:17 Nevertheless m eye spared them from 2967.1
20:22 Nevertheless I withdrew m hand, 2967.1
20:23 I lifted up m hand unto them also in 2967.1
20:28 the which I lifted up m hand to give it 2967.1
20:40 in m holy mountain, in the mountain 2967.1
20:42 up m hand to give it to your fathers. 2967.1
21:17 I will also smite m hands together, 2967.1
21:31 will pour out m indignation upon thee, 2967.1
22: 8 Thou hast despised m holy *things*, and 2967.1
22:13 I have smitten m hand at thy dishonest 2967.1
22:20 so will I gather *you* in m anger and 2967.1
22:26 have profaned m holy *things*: they have 2967.1
22:31 Therefore have I poured out m 2967.1+3807.1
23: 4 were m, and they bare sons 2967.1+3807.1
23: 5 the harlot when she was m; 8478+2967.1
23:39 thus have they done in the midst of m 2967.1
23:41 whereupon thou hast set m incense and 2967.1
23:41 thou hast set mine incense and m oil. 2967.1
25: 7 I will stretch out m hand upon thee, 2967.1
25:13 I will also stretch out m hand upon 2967.1
25:14 they shall do in Edom according to m 2967.1
25:16 I *will* stretch out m hand upon 2967.1
29: 3 My river *is* m own, and I have 2967.1+3807.1
29: 3 river *is* m, and I have made *it*. 2967.1+3807.1
35: 3 I will stretch out m hand against thee, 2967.1
35:10 these two countries shall be m, 2967.1+3807.1
36: 7 I have lifted up m hand, Surely 2967.1
36:21 had pity for m holy name, which 2967.1
36:22 of Israel, but for m holy name's sake, 2967.1
37:19 and they shall be one in m hand. 2967.1
43: 8 wherefore I have consumed them in m 2967.1
44: 8 ye have not kept the charge of m holy 2967.1
44:12 have I lift up m hand against them, 2967.1

Eze 44:24 and my statutes in all m assemblies; 2967.1
47:14 the which I lifted up m hand 2967.1
Da 4: 4 Nebuchadnezzar was at rest in m house 2967.2
4:10 Thus *were* the visions of m head in my 2967.2
4:34 lift up m eyes unto heaven, 2967.2
4:34 understanding returned unto me, 2967.2
4:36 honour and brightness returned unto 2967.2
8: 3 I lifted up m eyes, and saw, and behold, 2967.1
10: 5 I lift up m eyes, and looked, and behold, 2967.1
Hos 2: 5 and my flax, m oil and my drink. 2967.1
2:10 none shall deliver her out of m hand, 2967.1
8: 5 off; m anger is kindled against them: 2967.1
8:13 flesh for the sacrifices of m offerings, 2967.1
9:15 I will drive them out of m house, 2967.1
11: 8 m heart is turned within me, 2967.1
11: 9 I will not execute the fierceness of m 2967.1
13:11 I gave thee a king in m anger, 2967.1
13:14 repentance shall be hid from m eyes. 2967.1
14: 4 for m anger is turned away from him. 2967.1
Am 1: 8 and I will turn m hand against Ekron: 2967.1
9: 2 hell, thence shall m hand take them; 2967.1
9: 4 I will set m eyes upon them for evil, 2967.1
Jnh 2: 2 I cried by reason of m affliction 2967.1+3807.1
Mic 7: 8 Rejoice not against me, O m enemy: 2967.1
7:10 she that is m enemy shall see *it*, and 2967.1
7:10 m eyes shall behold her: now shall she 2967.1
Hab 1:12 O LORD my God, m Holy One? 2967.1
3: 16 he will make me to walk upon m high 2967.1
Zep 1: 4 also stretch out m hand upon Judah, 2967.1
3: 8 to pour upon them m indignation, 2967.1
3:10 of my dispersed, shall bring m offering. 2967.1
Hag 1: 9 Because of m house that *is* waste, 2967.1
2: 8 The silver *is* m, and the gold *is* 2967.1+3807.1
2: 8 *is* mine, and the gold *is* m, 2967.1+3807.1
Zec 1:18 lift I up m eyes again, and saw, and behold 2967.1
2: 1 I lift up m eyes again, and looked, 2967.1
2: 9 I *will* shake m hand upon them, 2967.1
5: 1 lift up m eyes, and looked, and behold, 2967.1
5: 9 lift I up m eyes, and looked, and 2967.1
6: 1 lift up m eyes, and looked, and behold, 2967.1
8: 8 I will encamp about m house because 2967.1
9: 8 for now have I seen with m eyes. 2967.1
10: 3 M anger was kindled against 2967.1
11:14 I cut asunder m other staff, *even* Bands, 2967.1
12: 4 I will open m eyes upon the house of 2967.1
13: 7 I will turn m hand upon the little ones. 2967.1
Mal 1: 6 then I *be* a father, where *is* m honour? 2967.1
1: 7 *Ye* offer polluted bread upon m altar; 2967.1
1:10 do ye kindle *fire on* m altar for nought. 2967.1
3: 7 ye are gone away from m ordinances, 2967.1
3:10 that there may be meat in m house, 2967.1
3:17 they shall be m, saith the LORD 2967.1+3807.1
Mt 7:24 whosoever heareth these sayings of m, 1473
7:26 every one that heareth these sayings of m, 1473
20:15 for me to do what I will with m own? 1699
20:23 is not m to give, but *it shall be* given to 1699
25:27 should have received m own with usury. 1699
Mk 9:24 Lord, I believe; help thou m unbelief. 1473
10:40 and on my left hand is not m to give; 1699
Lk 1:44 voice of thy salutation sounded in m ears, 1473
2:30 For m eyes have seen thy salvation, 1473
7:46 M head with oil thou didst not anoint: 1473
9:38 look upon my son: for he is m only child. 1473
11: 6 For a friend of m in *his* journey is come to 1473
18: 3 saying, Avenge me of m adversary. 1473
19:23 at my coming I might have required *m* NIG
19:27 those m enemies, which would not that 1473
Jn 2: 4 to do with thee? m hour is not yet come. 1473
5:30 I can of m own self do nothing: as I hear, 1683
5:30 is just; because I seek not m own will, 1699
6:38 not to do m own will, but the will of him 1699
7:16 My doctrine is not m, but his that sent 1699
8:50 And I seek not m own glory: there is one 1473
9:11 and anointed m eyes, and said unto me, 1473
9:15 He put clay upon m eyes, and I washed, 1473
9:30 he is, and *yet* he hath opened m eyes. 1473
10:14 know my *sheep*, and am known of m. 1699
14:24 and the word which you hear is not m, 1699
16:14 he shall receive of m, and shall shew *it* 1699
16:15 All *things* that the Father hath are m: 1699
16:15 he shall take of m, and shall shew *it* 1699
17:10 And all are thine, and thine are mine; 1699
17:10 And all mine are thine, and thine are m; 1699
Ac 11: 6 Upon the which when I had fastened m NIG
13:22 man after m own heart, which shall fulfil 1473
21:13 mean ye to weep and to break m heart? 1473
26: 4 was at the first among m own nation 1473
Ro 11:13 apostle of the Gentiles, I magnify m office: 1473
12:19 for it is written, Vengeance *is* m; I will 1473
16:13 in the Lord, and his mother and m. 1473
16:23 Gaius m host, and of the whole church, 1473
1Co 1:15 say that I had baptized in m own name. 1699
4: 3 yea, I judge not m own self. 1683
9: 2 for the seal of m apostleship are ye in 1699
9: 3 M answer to them that do examine me is 1699
10:33 in all *things*, not seeking m own profit, 1683
16:21 The salutation of *me* Paul with m own 1699
2Co 11:30 will glory of the *things* which concern m 1473
12: 5 I will not glory, but in m infirmities. 1473
Gal 1:14 above many *my* equals in m own nation, 1473
6:11 have written unto you with m own hand. 1699
Php 1: 4 Always in every prayer of m for you all 1473
3: 9 not having m own righteousness, which 1699
2Th 3:17 The salutation of Paul with m own hand, 1699
Tit 1: 4 *m* own son after the common faith: NIG

M

Phm 1:12 receive him, that is, **m** own bowels: 1699
 1:18 oweth *thee* ought, put that on **m** account; 1473
 1:19 I Paul have written *it* with **m** own hand, 1699
Rev 22:16 I Jesus have sent **m** angel to testify unto 1473

MINGLE (2) [MINGLED]

Isa 5:22 and men of strength to **m** strong drink: 4537
Da 2:43 they shall **m** themselves with the seed of 6151

MINGLED (55) [MINGLE]

Ex 9:24 and fire **m** with the hail, very grievous, 3947
 29:40 with the one lamb a tenth deal of flour **m** 1101
Lev 2: 4 *shall be* unleavened cakes of fine flour **m** 1101
 2: 5 be *of* fine flour unleavened, **m** with oil. 1101
 7:10 every meat offering, **m** with oil, and dry, 1101
 7:12 unleavened cakes **m** with oil, 1101
 7:12 and cakes **m** with oil, of fine flour, fried. 1101
 9: 4 and a meat offering **m** with oil: 1101
 14:10 **m** with oil, and one log of oil. 1101
 14:21 one tenth deal of fine flour **m** with oil for 1101
 19:19 thou shalt not sow thy field with **m** seed: 3610
 19:19 garment **m of linen and woollen** 3610+8162
 23:13 two tenth deals *of* fine flour **m** with oil, 1101
Nu 6:15 cakes *of* fine flour **m** with oil, 1101
 7:13 of them *were* full *of* fine flour **m** with 1101
 7:19 both of them full *of* fine flour **m** with oil 1101
 7:25 both of them full *of* fine flour **m** with oil 1101
 7:31 both of them full *of* fine flour **m** with oil 1101
 7:37 both of them full *of* fine flour **m** with oil 1101
 7:43 both of them full *of* fine flour **m** with oil 1101
 7:49 both of them full *of* fine flour **m** with oil 1101
 7:55 both of them full *of* fine flour **m** with oil 1101
 7:61 both of them full *of* fine flour **m** with oil 1101
 7:67 both of them full *of* fine flour **m** with oil 1101
 7:73 both of them full *of* fine flour **m** with oil 1101
 7:79 both of them full *of* fine flour **m** with oil 1101
 8: 8 *even* fine flour **m** with oil, 1101
 15: 4 flour **m** with the fourth *part* of a hin of 1101
 15: 6 flour **m** with the third *part* of a hin of oil. 1101
 15: 9 deals *of* flour **m** with half a hin of oil. 1101
 28: 5 **m** with the fourth *part* of a hin of beaten 1101
 28: 9 **m** with oil, and the drink offering thereof: 1101
 28:12 meat offering, **m** with oil, for one bullock; 1101
 28:12 a meat offering, **m** with oil, for one ram; 1101
 28:13 a several tenth deal of flour **m** with oil *for* 1101
 28:20 meat offering *shall be of* flour **m** with oil, 1101
 28:28 their meat offering *of* flour **m** with oil, 1101
 29: 3 meat offering *shall be of* flour **m** with 1101
 29: 9 meat offering *shall be of* flour **m** with 1101
 29:14 meat offering *shall be of* flour **m** with oil 1101
Ezr 9: 2 the holy seed have **m** themselves with 6148
Ps 102: 9 bread, and **m** my drink with weeping, 4537
 106:35 were **m** among the heathen, 6148
Pr 9: 2 killed her beasts; she hath **m** her wine; 4537
 9: 5 and drink of the wine *which* I have **m**. 4537
Isa 19:14 The LORD hath **m** a perverse spirit in 4537
Jer 25:20 all the **m people**, and all the kings of 6153
 25:24 all the kings of the **m people** that dwell 6153
 50:37 all the **m** people that *are* in the midst NIH
Eze 30: 5 all the **m people**, and Chub, and the men 6153
Mt 27:34 They gave him vinegar to drink **m** with 3396
Mk 15:23 gave him to drink wine **m with myrrh:** 4669
Lk 13: 1 whose blood Pilate had **m** with their 3396
Rev 8: 7 there followed hail and fire **m** with blood, 3396
 15: 2 And I saw as *it were* a sea of glass **m** with 3396

MINIAMIN (3)

2Ch 31:15 **M**, and Jeshua, and Shemaiah, Amariah, 4509
Ne 12:17 Abijah, Zichri; of **M**, of Moadiah, Piltai; 4509
 12:41 Maaseiah, **M**, Michaiah, Elioenai, 4509

MINISH (1) [MINISHED]

Ex 5:19 Ye shall not **m** *ought* from your bricks of 1639

MINISHED (1) [MINISH]

Ps 107:39 they are **m** and brought low through 4591

MINISTER (100) [MINISTERED, MINISTERETH, MINISTERING, MINISTERS, MINISTRATION, MINISTRY]

Ex 24:13 Moses rose up, and his **m** Joshua: 8334
 28: 1 may **m** unto me **in the priest's office.** 3547
 28: 3 may **m** unto me **in the priest's office.** 3547
 28: 4 may **m** unto me **in the priest's office.** 3547
 28:35 shall be upon Aaron to **m:** and his sound 8334
 28:41 may **m** unto me **in the priest's office.** 3547
 28:43 they come near unto the altar to **m** in 8334
 29: 1 to **m** unto me **in the priest's office:** 3547
 29:30 the congregation to **m** in the holy *place.* 8334
 29:44 sons, to **m** to me **in the priest's office.** 3547
 30:20 or when they come near to the altar to **m,** 8334
 30:30 may **m** unto me **in the priest's office.** 3547
 31:10 of his sons, to **m in the priest's office.** 3547
 35:19 of his sons, to **m in the priest's office.** 3547
 39:26 round about the hem of the robe to **m** *in;* 8334
 39:41 garments, to **m in the priest's office.** 3547
 40:13 he may **m** unto me **in the priest's office:** 3547
 40:15 may **m** unto me **in the priest's office:** 3547
Lev 7:35 **m** unto the LORD **in the priest's office;** 3547
 16:32 **m** **in the priest's office** in his father's 3547
Nu 1:50 they shall **m** unto it, and shall encamp 8334
 3: 3 consecrated to **m in the priest's office.** 3547
 3: 6 Aaron the priest, that they may **m** unto 8334
 3:31 of the sanctuary wherewith they **m,** 8334
 4: 9 thereof, wherewith they **m** unto it: 8334

Nu 4:12 wherewith they **m** in the sanctuary, 8334
 4:14 wherewith they **m** about it, *even* 8334
 8:26 **m** with their brethren in the tabernacle 8334
 16: 9 stand before the congregation to **m** unto 8334
 18: 2 be joined unto thee, and **m** unto thee: 8334
 18: 2 thy sons with thee *shall* **m** before NIH
Dt 10: 8 to stand before the LORD to **m** unto him, 8334
 17:12 to **m** there before the LORD thy God, 8334
 18: 5 to stand to **m** in the name of the LORD, 8334
 18: 7 he shall **m** in the name of the LORD his 8334
 21: 5 thy God hath chosen to **m** unto him, 8334
Jos 1: 1 Joshua the son of Nun, Moses' **m,** saying, 8334
1Sa 2:11 the child did **m** unto the LORD before Eli 8334
1Ki 8:11 So that the priests could not stand to **m** 8334
1Ch 15: 2 ark of God, and to **m** unto him for ever. 8334
 16: 4 he appointed *certain* of the Levites to **m** 8334
 16:37 to **m** before the ark continually, 8334
 23:13 to **m** unto him, and to bless in his name 8334
 26:12 to **m** in the house of the LORD. 8334
2Ch 5:14 that the priests could not stand to **m** by 8334
 8:14 to praise and **m** before the priests, 8334
 13:10 the priests, which **m** unto the LORD, 8334
 23: 6 priests, and they that **m** of the Levites; 8334
 24:14 vessels to **m,** and to offer *withal,* and 8335
 29:11 that *you* should **m** unto him, 8334
 31: 2 to **m,** and to give thanks, and to praise in 8334
Ne 10:36 the priests that **m** in the house of our 8334
 10:39 the priests that **m,** and the porters, 8334
Ps 9: 8 he shall **m judgment** to the people in 1777
Isa 60: 7 the rams of Nebajoth shall **m** unto thee: 8334
 60:10 walls, and their kings shall **m** unto thee: 8334
Jer 33:22 and the Levites that **m** unto me. 8334
Eze 40:46 which come near to the LORD to **m** unto 8334
 42:14 shall lay their garments wherein they **m;** 8334
 43:19 to **m** unto me, saith the Lord GOD, 8334
 44:11 they shall stand before them to **m** unto 8334
 44:15 they shall come near to me to **m** unto me, 8334
 44:16 to **m** unto me, and they shall keep my 8334
 44:17 whiles they **m** in the gates of the inner 8334
 44:27 the inner court, to **m** in the sanctuary, 8334
 45: 4 which shall come near to **m** unto 8334
Mt 20:26 be great among you, let him be your **m;** 1249
 20:28 but to **m,** and to give his life a ransom for 1247
 25:44 or in prison, and did not **m** unto thee? 1247
Mk 10:43 will be great among you, shall be your **m:** 1249
 10:45 but to **m,** and to give his life a ransom for 1247
Lk 4:20 and he gave *it* again to the **m,** 5257
Ac 13: 5 Jews: and they had also John to *their* **m.** 5257
 24:23 forbid none of his acquaintance to **m** 5256
 26:16 thee for this *purpose,* to make thee a **m** 5257
Ro 13: 4 For he is the **m** of God to thee for good. 1249
 13: 4 for he is the **m** of God, a revenger on 1249
 15: 8 Now I say that Jesus Christ was a **m** of 1249
 15:16 That I should be the **m** of Jesus Christ to 3011
 15:25 But now I go unto Jerusalem to **m** unto 1247
 15:27 is also to **m** unto them in carnal *things.* 3008
1Co 9:13 Do ye not know that they which **m** about 2038
2Co 9:10 to the sower both **m** bread for your food, 5524
Gal 2:17 *is* therefore Christ the **m** of sin? 1249
Eph 3: 7 Whereof I was made a **m,** according to 1249
 4:29 that it may **m** grace unto the hearers. 1325
 6:21 brother and faithful **m** in the Lord, 1249
Col 1: 7 who is for you a faithful **m** of Christ; 1249
 1:23 whereof I Paul am made a **m;** 1249
 1:25 Whereof I am made a **m,** according to 1249
 4: 7 and a faithful **m** and fellowservant in 1249
1Th 3: 2 and **m** of God, and our fellowlabourer in 1249
1Ti 1: 4 endless genealogies, which **m** questions, 3930
 4: 6 thou shalt be a good **m** of Jesus Christ, 1249
Heb 1:14 sent forth to **m** for them who shall be 1248
 6:10 have ministered to the saints, and do **m.** 1247
 8: 2 A **m** of the sanctuary, and of the true 3011
1Pe 1:12 but unto us they did **m** the things, 1247
 4:10 gift, *even so* **m** the same one to another, 1247
 4:11 any *man* **m,** *let him do it* as of the ability 1247

MINISTERED (37) [MINISTER]

Nu 3: 4 Ithamar **m in the priest's office** in the 3547
Dt 10: 6 Eleazar his son **m in the priest's office** 3547
1Sa 2:18 Samuel **m** before the LORD, *being* a 8334
 3: 1 the child Samuel **m** unto the LORD before 8334
2Sa 13:17 he called his servant that **m** unto him, 8334
1Ki 1: 4 and cherished the king, and **m** to him: 8334
 1:15 the Shunammite **m** unto the king. 8334
 19:21 and went after Elijah, and **m** unto him. 8334
2Ki 25:14 the vessels of brass wherewith they **m,** 8334
1Ch 6:32 they **m** before the dwelling place of 8334
 28: 1 the captains of the companies that **m** to 8334
2Ch 22: 8 that **m** to Ahaziah, he slew them. 8334
Est 2: 2 said the king's servants that **m** unto him, 8334
 6: 3 said the king's servants that **m** unto him, 8334
Jer 52:18 all the vessels of brass wherewith they **m,** 8334
Eze 44:12 Because they **m** unto them before their 8334
 44:19 put off their garments wherein they **m,** 8334
Da 7:10 thousand thousands **m** unto him, 8120
Mt 4:11 angels came and **m** unto him. 1247
 8:15 left her: and she arose, and **m** unto them. 1247
 20:28 Even as the Son of man came not to be **m** 1247
Mk 1:13 wild beasts; and the angels **m** unto him. 1247
 1:31 the fever left her, and she **m** unto them. 1247
 10:45 even the Son of man came not to be **m** 1247
 15:41 Galilee, followed him, and **m** unto him;) 1247
Lk 4:39 immediately she arose and **m** unto them. 1247
 8: 3 which **m** unto him of their substance. 1247
Ac 13: 2 As they **m** to the Lord, and fasted, the 3008

Ac 19:22 Macedonia two of them that **m** unto him, 1247
 20:34 that these hands have **m** unto my 5256
2Co 3: 3 to be the epistle of Christ **m** by us, 1247
Php 2:25 and he **m** to my wants. 3011
Col 2:19 and bands having **nourishment m,** 2023
2Ti 1:18 in how many *things* he **m** *unto me* at 1247
Phm 1:13 in thy stead he might have **m** unto me 1247
Heb 6:10 in that ye have **m** to the saints, 1247
2Pe 1:11 entrance shall be **m** unto you abundantly 2023

MINISTERETH (2) [MINISTER]

2Co 9:10 Now he that **m** seed to the sower both 2023
Gal 3: 5 He therefore that **m** to you the Spirit, 2023

MINISTERING (9) [MINISTER]

1Ch 9:28 *certain* of them had the charge of the **m** 5656
Eze 44:11 gates of the house, and **m** to the house: 8334
Mt 27:55 followed Jesus from Galilee, **m** unto him; 1247
Ro 12: 7 ministry, *let us wait* on *our* **m:** or he that 1248
 15:16 the gospel of God, that the offering up 2418
2Co 8: 4 *take upon us* the fellowship of the **m** 1248
 9: 1 For as touching the **m** to the saints, it is 1248
Heb 1:14 Are they not all **m** spirits, sent forth to 3010
 10:11 And every priest standeth daily **m** and 3008

MINISTERS (26) [MINISTER]

1Ki 10: 5 attendance of his **m,** and their apparel, 8334
2Ch 9: 4 attendance of his **m,** and their apparel; 8334
Ezr 7:24 or **m** of this house of God, 6399
 8:17 that *they* should bring unto us **m** for 8334
Ps 103:21 hosts; ye **m** of his, that do his pleasure. 8334
 104: 4 his angels spirits; his **m** a flaming fire: 8334
Isa 61: 6 *men* shall call you the **M** of our God: 8334
Jer 33:21 and with the Levites the priests, my **m.** 8334
Eze 44:11 Yet they shall be **m** in my sanctuary, 8334
 45: 4 be for the priests the **m** of the sanctuary, 8334
 45: 5 the **m** of the house, have for themselves, 8334
 46:24 where the **m** of the house shall boil 8334
Joel 1: 9 the priests, the LORD's **m,** mourn. 8334
 1:13 ye **m** of the altar: come, lie all night 8334
 1:13 lie all night in sackcloth, ye **m** of my God; 8334
 2:17 Let the priests, the **m** of the LORD, 8334
Lk 1: 2 were eyewitnesses, and **m** of the word; 5257
Ro 13: 6 for they are God's **m,** 3011
1Co 3: 5 is Apollos, but **m** by whom ye believed, 1249
 4: 1 as of the **m** of Christ, and stewards of 5257
2Co 3: 6 also hath made us able **m** of the new 1249
 6: 4 approving ourselves as the **m** of God; 1249
 11:15 Therefore *it is* no great *thing* if his **m** also 1249
 11:15 be transformed as the **m** of righteousness; 1249
 11:23 Are they not of Christ? (I speak as a fool) 1249
Heb 1: 7 his angels spirits, and his **m** a flame of fire. 3011

MINISTRATION (7) [MINISTER]

Lk 1:23 as the days of his **m** were accomplished, 3009
Ac 6: 1 widows were neglected in the daily **m.** 1248
2Co 3: 7 But if the **m** of death, written *and* 1248
 3: 8 How shall not the **m** of the spirit be rather 1248
 3: 9 For if the **m** of condemnation *be* glory, 1248
 3: 9 much more doth the **m** of righteousness 1248
 9:13 Whiles by the experiment of this **m** they 1248

MINISTRY (22) [MINISTER]

Nu 4:12 they shall take all the instruments of the **m,** 8335
 4:47 one that came to do the service of the **m,** 5656
2Ch 7: 6 for ever, when David praised by their **m;** 3027
Hos 12:10 used similitudes by the **m** of the prophets. 3027
Ac 1:17 with us, and had obtained part of this **m.** 1248
 1:25 That *he* may take part of this **m** and 1248
 6: 4 to prayer, and to the **m** of the word. 1248
 12:25 when they had fulfilled *their* **m,** 1248
 20:24 finish my course with joy, and the **m,** 1248
 21:19 wrought among the Gentiles by his **m.** 1248
Ro 12: 7 Or **m,** *let us wait* on *our* ministering: 1248
1Co 16:15 they have addicted themselves to the **m** 1248
2Co 4: 1 Therefore seeing we have this **m,** as we 1248
 5:18 hath given to us the **m** of reconciliation; 1248
 6: 3 Giving no offence in any *thing,* that the **m** 1248
Eph 4:12 of the saints for the work of the **m,** 1248
Col 4:17 Take heed to the **m** which thou hast 1248
1Ti 1:12 me faithful, putting *me* into the **m;** 1248
2Ti 4: 5 of an evangelist, make full proof of thy **m.** 1248
 4:11 for he is profitable to me for the **m.** 1248
Heb 8: 6 hath obtained a more excellent **m,** 3009
 9:21 tabernacle, and all the vessels of the **m.** 3009

MINNI (1)

Jer 51:27 kingdoms of Ararat, **M,** and Ashchenaz; 4508

MINNITH (2)

Jdg 11:33 even till thou come *to* **M,** *even* twenty 4511
Eze 27:17 they traded in thy market wheat of **M,** 4511

MINSTREL (2) [MINSTRELS]

2Ki 3:15 now bring me a **m.** And it came to pass, 5059
 3:15 it came to pass, when the **m** played, that 5059

MINSTRELS (1) [MINSTREL]

Mt 9:23 and saw the **m** and the people making a 834

MINT (2)

Mt 23:23 for ye pay tithe of **m** and anise and 2238
Lk 11:42 for ye tithe **m** and rue and all *manner of* 2238

MIPHKAD (1)

Ne 3:31 over against the gate **M,** and to the going 4662

M

MIRACLE (10) [MIRACLES]

Ex	7: 9 unto you, saying, Shew a **m** for you:	4159
Mk	6:52 they considered not *the* **m** of the loaves:	NIG
	9:39 for there is no **man** which shall do a **m** in	1411
Lk	23: 8 he hoped to have seen some **m** done by	4592
Jn	4:54 This *is* again the second **m** *that* Jesus did,	4592
	6:14 when they had seen the **m** that Jesus did,	4592
	10:41 unto him, and said, John did no **m**	4592
	12:18 that they heard that he had done this **m**.	4592
Ac	4:16 that indeed a notable **m** hath been done	4592
	4:22 on whom this **m** of healing was shewed.	4592

MIRACLES (27) [MIRACLE]

Nu	14:22 my **m**, which I did in Egypt and in	226
Dt	11: 3 his **m**, and his acts, which he did in the	226
	29: 3 have seen, the signs, and those great **m**:	4159
Jdg	6:13 *be* all his **m** which our fathers told us	6381
Jn	2:11 This beginning of **m** did Jesus in Cana of	4592
	2:23 when they saw the **m** which he did.	4592
	3: 2 no *man* can do these **m** that thou doest,	4592
	6: 2 they saw his **m** which he did on them	4592
	6:26 not because ye saw *the* **m**, but because	4592
	7:31 will he do moe **m** than these which this	4592
	9:16 can a man *that is* a sinner do such **m**?	4592
	11:47 do we? for this man doeth many **m**.	4592
	12:37 he had done so many **m** before them,	4592
Ac	2:22 a man approved of God among you by **m**	1411
	6: 8 great wonders and **m** among the people.	4592
	8: 6 hearing and seeing the **m** which he did.	4592
	8:13 beholding *the* **m** and signs *which* were	1411
	15:12 declaring what **m** and wonders God had	4592
	19:11 And God wrought special **m** by the hands	4592
1Co	12:10 To another the working of **m**; to another	1411
	12:28 after that **m**, then gifts of healings, helps,	1411
	12:29 *are* all teachers? *are* all **workers of m**?	1411
Gal	3: 5 the Spirit, and worketh **m** among you,	1411
Heb	2: 4 and with divers **m**, and gifts of the Holy	1411
Rev	13:14 **m** which he had power to do in the sight	4592
	16:14 they are the spirits of devils, working **m**,	4592
	19:20 him the false prophet that wrought **m**	4592

MIRE (15) [MIRY]

2Sa	22:43 I did stamp them as the **m** of the street,	2916
Job	8:11 Can the rush grow up without **m**?	1207
	30:19 He hath cast me into the **m**, and I am	2563
	41:30 sharp pointed *things* upon the **m**.	2916
Ps	69: 2 I sink in deep **m**, where *there is* no	3121
	69:14 Deliver me out of the **m**, and let me not	2916
Isa	10: 6 to tread them down like the **m** of	2563
	57:20 whose waters cast up **m** and dirt.	7516
Jer	38: 6 the dungeon *there was* no water, but **m**:	2916
	38: 6 but mire: so Jeremiah sunk in the **m**.	2916
	38:22 thy feet are sunk in the **m**, *and* they are	1206
Mic	7:10 shall she be trodden down as the **m** of	2916
Zec	9: 3 and fine gold as the **m** of the streets.	2916
	10: 5 *enemies* in the **m** of the streets in the	2916
2Pe	2:22 was washed to *her* wallowing in the **m**.	1004

MIRIAM (15)

Ex	15:20 **M** the prophetess, the sister of Aaron,	4813
	15:21 **M** answered them, Sing ye to the LORD,	4813
Nu	12: 1 **M** and Aaron spake against Moses	4813
	12: 4 Moses, and unto Aaron, and unto **M**,	4813
	12: 5 the tabernacle, and called Aaron and **M**:	4813
	12:10 **M** *became* leprous, *white* as snow:	4813
	12:10 Aaron looked upon **M**, and behold, *she*	4813
	12:15 **M** was shut out from the camp seven	4813
	12:15 the people journeyed not till **M** was	4813
	20: 1 and **M** died there, and was buried there.	4813
	26:59 and Moses, and **M** their sister.	4813
Dt	24: 9 LORD thy God did unto **M** by the way,	4813
1Ch	4:17 she bare **M**, and Shammai, and Ishbah	4813
	6: 3 of Amram; Aaron, and Moses, and **M**.	4813
Mic	6: 4 I sent before thee Moses, Aaron, and **M**.	4813

MIRMA (1)

1Ch	8:10 Jeuz, and Shachia, and **M**. These *were* his	4821

MIRROR See GLASSES; LOOKINGGLASSES

MIRTH (15)

Ge	31:27 that I might have sent thee away with **m**,	8057
Ne	8:12 to make great **m**, because they had	8057
Ps	137: 3 they that wasted *us required of us* **m**,	8057
Pr	14:13 and the end of that **m** *is* heaviness.	8057
Ecc	2: 1 I will prove thee with **m**, therefore	8057
	2: 2 *It is* mad: and of **m**, What doeth it?	8057
	7: 4 but the heart of fools *is* in the house of **m**.	8057
	8:15 I commended **m**, because a man hath no	8057
Isa	24: 8 of tabrets ceaseth, the noise of **m**	4885
	24:11 is darkened, the **m** of the land is gone.	4885
Jer	7:34 the voice of **m**, and the voice of gladness,	8342
	16: 9 the voice of **m**, and the voice of gladness,	8342
	25:10 I will take from them the voice of **m**,	8342
Eze	21:10 should we then **make m**? it contemneth	7797
Hos	2:11 I will also cause all her **m** to cease,	4885

MIRY (4) [MIRE]

Ps	40: 2 out of the **m** clay, and set my feet upon a	3121
Eze	47:11 the **m** places thereof and the marishes	1207
Da	2:41 thou sawest the iron mixed with **m** clay.	2917
	2:43 thou sawest iron mixt with **m** clay,	2917

MISCARRYING (1)

Hos	9:14 give them a **m** womb and dry breasts.	7921

MISCHIEF (47) [MISCHIEFS, MISCHIEVOUS]

Ge	42: 4 he said, Lest peradventure **m** befall him.	611
	42:38 if **m** befall him by the way in which ye	611
	44:29 take this also from me, and **m** befall him,	611
Ex	21:22 fruit depart *from her*, and yet no **m** follow:	611
	21:23 if *any* **m** follow, then thou shalt give life	611
	32:12 say, For **m** did he bring them out, to slay	7451
	32:22 the people, that they *are* set on **m**.	7451
1Sa	23: 9 David knew that Saul secretly practised **m**	7451
2Sa	16: 8 and, behold, thou *art taken* to thy **m**,	7451
1Ki	11:25 beside the **m** that Hadad *did*: and	7451
	20: 7 you, and see how this *man* seeketh **m**:	7451
2Ki	7: 9 light, *some* will come upon us:	5771
Ne	6: 2 of Ono. But they thought to do me **m**.	7451
Est	8: 3 him with tears to put away the **m**	7451
Job	15:35 They conceive **m**, and bring forth vanity,	5999
Ps	7:14 hath conceived **m**, and brought forth	5999
	7:16 His **m** shall return upon his own head,	5999
	10: 7 fraud: under his tongue *is* **m** and vanity.	5999
	10:14 hast seen *it*; for thou beholdest **m** and	5999
	26:10 In whose hands *is* **m**, and their right hand	2154
	28: 3 their neighbours, but **m** *is* in their hearts.	7451
	36: 4 He deviseth **m** upon his bed; he setteth	205
	52: 1 Why boastest thou thyself in **m**, O mighty	7451
	55:10 **m** also and sorrow *are* in the midst of it.	205
	62: 3 How long will ye imagine **m** against a	2050
	94:20 *with* thee, which frameth **m** by a law?	5999
	119:150 They draw nigh that follow after **m**:	2154
	140: 9 let the **m** of their own lips cover them.	5999
Pr	4:16 they sleep not, except they have **done m**;	7489
	6:14 *is* in his heart, he deviseth **m** continually;	7451
	6:18 feet that be swift in running to **m**,	7451
	10:23 *It is* as sport to a fool to do: but a man	2154
	11:27 that seeketh **m**, it shall come *unto* him.	7451
	12:21 but the wicked shall be filled *with* **m**.	7451
	13:17 A wicked messenger falleth into **m**:	7451
	17:20 hath a perverse tongue falleth into **m**.	7451
	24: 2 and their lips talk of **m**.	5999
	24:16 up *again*: but the wicked shall fall into **m**.	7451
	28:14 that hardeneth his heart shall fall into **m**.	7451
Isa	47:11 **m** shall fall upon thee; thou shalt not be	1943
	59: 4 *they* conceive **m**, and bring forth iniquity.	5999
Eze	7:26 **M** shall come upon mischief,	1943
	7:26 Mischief shall come upon **m**,	1943
	11: 2 these *are* the men that devise **m**, and give	205
Da	11:27 both these kings' hearts *shall be* to do **m**,	4827
Hos	7:15 yet do they imagine **m** against me.	7451
Ac	13:10 And said, O full of all subtilty and all **m**,	4468

MISCHIEFS (3) [MISCHIEF]

Dt	32:23 I will heap **m** upon them; I will spend	7451
Ps	52: 2 Thy tongue deviseth **m**; like a sharp rasor,	1942
	140: 2 Which imagine **m** in *their* heart;	7451

MISCHIEVOUS (5) [MISCHIEF]

Ps	21:11 they imagined a **m device**, *which* they	4209
	38:12 they that seek my hurt speak **m things**,	1942
Pr	24: 8 to do evil shall be called a **m** person.	4209
Ecc	10:13 and the end of his talk *is* **m** madness.	7451
Mic	7: 3 the great *man*, he uttereth his **m** desire:	1942

MISERABLE (3) [MISERY]

Job	16: 2 I have heard many such *things*: **m**	5999
1Co	15:19 hope in Christ, we are of all men **most m**.	1652
Rev	3:17 and **m**, and poor, and blind, and naked:	1652

MISERABLY (1) [MISERY]

Mt	21:41 He will **m** destroy those wicked *men*, and	2560

MISERIES (2) [MISERY]

La	1: 7 of her **m** all her pleasant things that she	4788
Jas	5: 1 howl for your **m** that shall come upon *you*.	5004

MISERY (7) [MISERABLE, MISERABLY, MISERIES]

Jdg	10:16 his soul was grieved for the **m** of Israel.	5999
Job	3:20 is light given to him that is in **m**,	6001
	11:16 Because thou shalt forget *thy* **m**,	5999
Pr	31: 7 poverty, and remember his **m** no more.	5999
Ecc	8: 6 therefore the **m** of man *is* great upon him.	7451
La	3:19 Remembering mine affliction and my **m**,	4788
Ro	3:16 Destruction and **m** *are* in their ways:	5004

MISFORTUNE See TRAVAIL; TRAVAILED; TRAVAILEST; TRAVAILETH

MISGAB (1)

Jer	48: 1 taken: **M** is confounded and dismayed.	4869

MISHAEL (8)

Ex	6:22 of Uzziel; **M**, and Elzaphan, and Zithri.	4332
Lev	10: 4 Moses called **M** and Elzaphan, the sons	4332
Ne	8: 4 **M**, and Malchiah, and Hashum,	4332
Da	1: 6 Daniel, Hananiah, **M**, and Azariah:	4332
	1: 7 to **M**, of Meshach; and to Azariah,	4332
	1:11 over Daniel, Hananiah, **M**, and Azariah,	4332
	1:19 like Daniel, Hananiah, **M**, and Azariah:	4332
	2:17 **M**, and Azariah, his companions:	4333

MISHAL (1)

Jos	21:30 **M** with her suburbs, Abdon with her	4861

MISHAM (1)

1Ch	8:12 and **M**, and Shamed, who built Ono,	4936

MISHEAL (1)

Jos	19:26 Alammelech, and Amad, and **M**;	4861

MISHMA (4)

Ge	25:14 And **M**, and Dumah, and Massa,	4927
1Ch	1:30 **M**, and Dumah, Massa, Hadad, and	4927
	4:25 his son, Mibsam his son, **M** his son.	4927
	4:26 the sons of **M**; Hamuel his son, Zacchur	4927

MISHMANNAH (1)

1Ch	12:10 **M** the fourth, Jeremiah the fifth,	4925

MISHRAITES (1)

1Ch	2:53 and the Shumathites, and the **M**;	4954

MISPAR See MIZPAR

MISPERETH (1)

Ne	7: 7 Bilshan, **M**, Bigvai, Nehum, Baanah.	4559

MISREPHOTH-MAIM (2)

Jos	11: 8 unto **M**, and unto the valley of Mizpeh	4956
	13: 6 of the hill country from Lebanon unto **M**,	4956

MISS (2) [AMISS, MISSED, MISSING]

Jdg	20:16 sling stones at a hair *breadth*, and not **m**.	2398
1Sa	20: 6 If thy father **at all m** me, then say,	6485+6485

MISSED (3) [MISS]

1Sa	20:18 thou shalt be **m**, because thy seat will be	6485
	25:15 were not hurt, neither **m** we any thing,	6485
	25:21 that nothing was **m** of all that *pertained*	6485

MISSING (2) [MISS]

1Sa	25: 7 neither was there ought **m** unto them,	6485
1Ki	20:39 if **by any means** he be **m**, then	6485+6485

MIST (3)

Ge	2: 6 there went up a **m** from the earth,	108
Ac	13:11 immediately there fell on him a **m** and	887
2Pe	2:17 to whom the **m** of darkness is reserved for	2217

MISTREAT; MISTREATED See VEX; VEXATION; VEXED

MISTRESS (9)

Ge	16: 4 her **m** was despised in her eyes.	1404
	16: 8 I flee from the face of my **m** Sarai.	1404
	16: 9 Return to thy **m**, and submit thyself	1404
1Ki	17:17 the woman, the **m** of the house, fell sick;	1172
2Ki	5: 3 she said unto her **m**, Would God my lord	1404
Ps	123: 2 eyes of a maiden unto the hand of her **m**;	1404
Pr	30:23 and a handmaid that is heir to her **m**.	1404
Isa	24: 2 master; as *with* the maid, so *with* her **m**;	1404
Na	3: 4 the **m** of witchcrafts, that selleth nations	1172

MISUSED (1)

2Ch	36:16 despised his words, and **m** his prophets,	8591

MITE (1) [MITES]

Lk	12:59 till thou hast paid the very last **m**.	3016

MITES (2) [MITE]

Mk	12:42 and she threw in two **m**, which make a	3016
Lk	21: 2 poor widow casting in thither two **m**.	3016

MITHCAH (2)

Nu	33:28 removed from Tarah, and pitched in **M**.	4989
	33:29 they went from **M**, and pitched in	4989

MITHNITE (1)

1Ch	11:43 son of Maachah, and Joshaphat the **M**,	4981

MITHREDATH (2)

Ezr	1: 8 forth by the hand of **M** the treasurer,	4990
	4: 7 **M**, Tabeel, and the rest of their	4990

MITRE (13)

Ex	28: 4 and a broidered coat, a **m**, and a girdle:	4701
	28:37 on a blue lace, that it may be upon the **m**;	4701
	28:37 upon the forefront of the **m** it shall be.	4701
	28:39 thou shalt make the **m** *of* fine linen,	4701
	29: 6 thou shalt put the **m** upon his head,	4701
	29: 6 and put the holy crown upon the **m**.	4701
	39:28 a **m** *of* fine linen, and goodly bonnets *of*	4701
	39:31 of blue, to fasten *it* on high upon the **m**;	4701
Lev	8: 9 he put the **m** upon his head; also upon	4701
	8: 9 also upon the **m**, *even* upon his forefront,	4701
	16: 4 and with the linen **m** shall he be attired:	4701
Zec	3: 5 said, Let them set a fair **m** upon his head.	6797
	3: 5 So they set a fair **m** upon his head,	6797

MITYLENE (1)

Ac	20:14 at Assos, we took him in, and came to **M**.	3412

MIXED (6) [MIXTURE]

Ex	12:38 a **m** multitude went up also with them;	6154
Ne	13: 3 separated from Israel all the **m multitude**.	6154
Da	2:41 forasmuch as thou sawest the iron **m** with	6151
	2:43 another, even as iron is not **m** with clay.	6151
Hos	7: 8 he hath **m** himself among the people;	1101
Heb	4: 2 not being **m** with faith in them that heard	4786

MIXT (4) [MIXTURE]

Nu	11: 4 the **m multitude** that *was* among them fell	628
Pr	23:30 at the wine; they that go to seek **m wine**.	4469
Isa	1:22 is become dross, thy wine **m** with water:	4107
Da	2:43 thou sawest iron **m** with miry clay,	6151

MIXTURE (3) [MIXED, MIXT]
Ps 75: 8 it is full of **m**; and he poureth out of 4538
Jn 19:39 and brought a **m** of myrrh and aloes, 3395
Rev 14:10 is poured out **without m** into the cup 194

MIZAR (1)
Ps 42: 6 and of the Hermonites, from the hill **M**. 4706

MIZPAH (23) [MIZPEH]
Ge 31:49 **M**; for he said, The LORD watch between 4709
1Ki 15:22 with them Geba of Benjamin, and **M**. 4709
2Ki 25:23 came to Gedaliah *to* **M**, even Ishmael 4709
 25:25 the Chaldees that were with him at **M**. 4709
2Ch 16: 6 and he built therewith Geba and **M**. 4709
Ne 3: 7 the men of Gibeon, and of **M**, 4709
 3:15 son of Col-hozeh, the ruler of part of **M**; 4709
 3:19 Ezer the son of Jeshua, the ruler of **M**, 4709
Jer 40: 6 unto Gedaliah the son of Ahikam to **M**; 4708
 40: 8 came to Gedaliah to **M**, even Ishmael 4709
 40:10 I *will* dwell at **M** to serve the Chaldeans, 4709
 40:12 unto **M**, and gathered wine and 4708
 40:13 in the fields, came to Gedaliah to **M**, 4708
 40:15 Kareah spake to Gedaliah in **M** secretly, 4709
 41: 1 unto Gedaliah the son of Ahikam to **M**; 4709
 41: 1 there they did eat bread together in **M**. 4708
 41: 3 *even* with Gedaliah at **M**, 4709
 41: 6 went forth from **M** to meet them, 4709
 41:10 the residue of the people that *were* in **M**, 4709
 41:10 and all the people that remained in **M**, 4709
 41:14 carried away captive from **M** cast about 4709
 41:16 from **M**, after *that* he had slain Gedaliah 4709
Hos 5: 1 because ye have been a snare on **M**, 4709

MIZPAR (1)
Ezr 2: 2 Bilshan, **M**, Bigvai, Rehum, Baanah. 4558

MIZPEH (23) [MIZPAH, RAMATH-MIZPEH]
Jos 11: 3 Hivite under Hermon in the land of **M**. 4709
 11: 8 and unto the valley of **M** eastward; 4708
 15:38 And Dilean, and **M**, and Joktheel, 4708
 18:26 And **M**, and Chephirah, and Mozah, 4708
Jdg 10:17 together, and encamped in **M**. 4709
 11:11 all his words before the LORD in **M**. 4709
 11:29 passed over **M** of Gilead, and from 4708
 11:29 from **M** of Gilead he passed over *unto* 4708
 11:34 Jephthah came *to* **M** unto his house, 4709
 20: 1 the land of Gilead, unto the LORD *unto* 4709
 20: 3 the children of Israel were gone up *to* **M**.) 4709
 21: 1 Now the men of Israel had sworn in **M**, 4709
 21: 5 *him* that came not up to the LORD to **M**, 4709
 21: 8 that came not up *to* **M** to the LORD? 4709
1Sa 7: 5 Gather all Israel to **M**, and I will pray for 4708
 7: 6 they gathered together to **M**, 4709
 7: 6 Samuel judged the children of Israel in **M**. 4708
 7: 7 of Israel were gathered together to **M**, 4708
 7:11 the men of Israel went out of **M**, 4709
 7:12 set *it* between **M** and Shen, and called 4709
 7:16 **M**, and judged Israel in all those places. 4709
 10:17 the people together unto the LORD *to* **M**; 4709
 22: 3 David went thence *to* **M** of Moab: 4708

MIZRAIM (4)
Ge 10: 6 Cush, and **M**, and Phut, and Canaan. 4714
 10:13 **M** begat Ludim, and Anamim, 4714
1Ch 1: 8 of Ham; Cush, and **M**, Put, and Canaan. 4714
 1:11 **M** begat Ludim, and Anamim, 4714

MIZZAH (3)
Ge 36:13 Nahath, and Zerah, Shammah, and **M**: 4199
 36:17 duke Zerah, duke Shammah, duke **M**: 4199
1Ch 1:37 Reuel; Nahath, Zerah, Shammah, and **M**. 4199

MNASON (1)
Ac 21:16 and brought *with them* one **M** of Cyprus, *3416*

MO (1) [= MORE]
2Sa 5:13 David took *him* **m** concubines and 5750

MOAB (168) [MOABITE, MOABITES, MOABITESS, MOABITISH]
Ge 19:37 bare a son, and called his name **M**: 4124
 36:35 who smote Midian in the field of **M**, 4124
Ex 15:15 the mighty men of **M**, trembling shall 4124
Nu 21:11 in the wilderness which *is* before **M**, 4124
 21:13 for Arnon *is* the border of **M**, 4124
 21:13 of Moab, between **M** and the Amorites. 4124
 21:15 of Ar, and lieth upon the border of **M**. 4124
 21:20 that *is* in the country of **M**, *to* the top of 4124
 21:26 had fought against the former king of **M**, 4124
 21:28 hath consumed Ar of **M**, *and* the lords of 4124
 21:29 Woe to thee, **M**! thou art undone, 4124
 22: 1 pitched in the plains of **M** on *this* side 4124
 22: 3 **M** was sore afraid of the people, because 4124
 22: 3 **M** was distressed because of the children 4124
 22: 4 **M** said unto the elders of Midian, 4124
 22: 7 the elders of **M** and the elders of Midian 4124
 22: 8 and the princes of **M** abode with Balaam. 4124
 22:10 king of **M**, hath sent unto me, *saying*, 4124
 22:14 the princes of **M** rose up, and they went 4124
 22:21 his ass, and went with the princes of **M**. 4124
 22:36 went out to meet him unto a city of **M**, 4124
 23: 6 sacrifice, he, and all the princes of **M**. 4124
 23: 7 Balak the king of **M** hath brought me 4124
 23:17 and the princes of **M** with him. 4124
 24:17 shall smite the corners of **M**, 4124

Nu 25: 1 whoredom with the daughters of **M**. 4124
 26: 3 in the plains of **M** by Jordan *near* Jericho. 4124
 26:63 in the plains of **M** by Jordan *near* Jericho. 4124
 31:12 unto the camp at the plains of **M**, which 4124
 33:44 pitched in Ije-abarim, in the border of **M**. 4124
 33:48 pitched in the plains of **M** by Jordan *near* 4124
 33:49 *even* unto Abel-shittim in the plains of **M**. 4124
 33:50 in the plains of **M** by Jordan *near* Jericho, 4124
 35: 1 in the plains of **M** by Jordan *near* Jericho, 4124
 36:13 in the plains of **M** by Jordan *near* Jericho. 4124
Dt 1: 5 On *this* side Jordan, in the land of **M**, 4124
 2: 8 passed *by* the way of the wilderness of **M**. 4124
 2:18 over *through* Ar, the coast of **M**, *this* day: 4124
 29: 1 the children of Israel in the land of **M**, 4124
 32:49 mount Nebo, which *is* in the land of **M**, 4124
 34: 1 Moses went up from the plains of **M** unto 4124
 34: 5 the LORD died there in the land of **M**, 4124
 34: 6 buried him in a valley in the land of **M**, 4124
 34: 8 for Moses in the plains of **M** thirty days: 4124
Jos 13:32 for inheritance in the plains of **M**, 4124
 24: 9 arose and warred against Israel, 4124
Jdg 3:12 Eglon the king of **M** against Israel, 4124
 3:14 Eglon the king of **M** eighteen years. 4124
 3:15 sent a present unto Eglon the king of **M**. 4124
 3:17 the present unto Eglon king of **M**: 4124
 3:28 took the fords of Jordan toward **M**, 4124
 3:29 they slew of **M** at that time about ten 4124
 3:30 **M** was subdued that day under the hand 4124
 10: 6 gods of **M**, and the gods of the children 4124
 11:15 Israel took not away the land of **M**, 4124
 11:17 like manner they sent unto the king of **M**: 4124
 11:18 land of **M**, and came by the east side of 4124
 11:18 came by the east side of the land of **M**, 4124
 11:18 but came not within the border of **M**: 4124
 11:18 of Moab: for Arnon *was* the border of **M**. 4124
 11:25 than Balak the son of Zippor, king of **M**? 4124
Ru 1: 1 went to sojourn in the country of **M**, 4124
 1: 2 they came *into* the country of **M**, 4124
 1: 4 took them wives of the **women of M**; 4125
 1: 6 she might return from the country of **M**: 4124
 1: 6 she had heard in the country of **M** how 4124
 1:22 which returned out of the country of **M**: 4124
 2: 6 back with Naomi out of the country of **M**: 4124
 4: 3 is come again out of the country of **M**, 4124
1Sa 12: 9 into the hand of the king of **M**, 4124
 14:47 against **M**, and against the children of 4124
 22: 3 David went thence *to* Mizpeh of **M**: 4124
 22: 3 he said unto the king of **M**, Let my father 4124
 22: 4 he brought them before the king of **M**: 4124
2Sa 8: 2 he smote **M**, and measured them with a 4124
 8:12 of **M**, and of the children of Ammon, 4124
 23:20 acts, he slew two lionlike men of **M**: 4124
1Ki 11: 7 the abomination of **M**, in the hill that *is* 4124
2Ki 1: 1 **M** rebelled against Israel after the death 4124
 3: 4 Mesha king of **M** was a sheepmaster, 4124
 3: 5 the king of **M** rebelled against the king 4124
 3: 7 The king of **M** hath rebelled against me: 4124
 3: 7 wilt thou go with me against **M** to battle? 4124
 3:10 to deliver them into the hand of **M**. 4124
 3:13 to deliver them into the hand of **M**. 4124
 3:23 another: now therefore, **M**, to the spoil. 4124
 3:26 when the king of **M** saw that the battle 4124
1Ch 1:46 which smote Midian in the field of **M**, 4124
 4:22 who had the dominion in **M**, 4124
 8: 8 begat *children* in the country of **M**, 4124
 11:22 acts; he slew two lionlike men of **M**: 4124
 18: 2 he smote **M**; and the Moabites became 4124
 18:11 **M**, and from the children of Ammon, 4124
2Ch 20: 1 The children of **M**, and the children of 4124
 20:10 of Ammon and **M** and mount Seir, 4124
 20:22 **M**, and mount Seir, which were come 4124
 20:23 **M** stood up against the inhabitants of 4124
Ne 13:23 wives of Ashdod, of Ammon, *and* of **M**: 4125
Ps 60: 8 **M** *is* my washpot; over Edom will I cast 4124
 83: 6 the Ishmaelites; of **M**, and the Hagarenes; 4124
 108: 9 **M** *is* my washpot; over Edom will I cast 4124
Isa 11:14 shall lay their hand upon Edom and **M**; 4124
 15: 1 The burden of **M**. Because in the night Ar 4124
 15: 1 Because in the night Ar of **M** is laid waste, 4124
 15: 1 because in the night Kir of **M** is laid waste, 4124
 15: 2 **M** shall howl over Nebo, and over 4124
 15: 4 the armed soldiers of **M** shall cry out; 4124
 15: 5 My heart shall cry out for **M**; his fugitives 4124
 15: 8 cry is gone round about the borders of **M**; 4124
 15: 9 lions upon him that escapeth of **M**, 4124
 16: 2 the daughters of **M** shall be *at* the fords of 4124
 16: 4 Let mine outcasts dwell with thee, **M**; 4124
 16: 6 We have heard of the pride of **M**; *he is* 4124
 16: 7 Therefore shall **M** howl for Moab, 4124
 16: 7 Therefore shall Moab howl for **M**, 4124
 16:11 my bowels shall sound like a harp for **M**, 4124
 16:12 it is seen that **M** is weary on the high 4124
 16:13 spoken concerning **M** since that time. 4124
 16:14 and the glory of **M** shall be contemned, 4124
 25:10 **M** shall be trodden down under him, 4124
Jer 9:26 **M**, and all *that are* in the utmost corners, 4124
 25:21 and **M**, and all the children of Ammon, 4124
 27: 3 to the king of **M**, and to the king of 4124
 40:11 when all the Jews that *were* in **M**, 4124
 48: 1 Against **M** thus saith the LORD of hosts, 4124
 48: 2 *There shall be* no more praise of **M**: 4124
 48: 4 **M** is destroyed; her little ones have 4124
 48: 9 Give wings unto **M**, that it may flee and 4124
 48:11 **M** hath been at ease from his youth, 4124
 48:13 **M** shall be ashamed of Chemosh, 4124

Jer 48:15 **M** is spoiled, and gone up *out of* her 4124
 48:16 The calamity of **M** *is* near to come, 4124
 48:18 for the spoiler of **M** shall come upon thee, 4124
 48:20 **M** is confounded; for it is broken down: 4124
 48:20 cry; tell ye *it* in Arnon, that **M** is spoiled, 4124
 48:24 upon all the cities of the land of **M**, far or 4124
 48:25 The horn of **M** is cut off, and his arm is 4124
 48:26 **M** also shall wallow in his vomit, 4124
 48:28 O ye that dwell in **M**, leave the cities, 4124
 48:29 We have heard the pride of **M**; *he is* 4124
 48:31 Therefore will I howl for **M**, and I will cry 4124
 48:31 for Moab, and I will cry out for all 4124
 48:33 plentiful field, and from the land of **M**; 4124
 48:35 Moreover I will cause to cease in **M**, 4124
 48:36 Therefore mine heart shall sound for **M** 4124
 48:38 generally upon all the housetops of **M**, 4124
 48:38 for I have broken **M** like a vessel wherein 4124
 48:39 how hath **M** turned the back with shame! 4124
 48:39 so shall **M** be a derision and a dismaying 4124
 48:40 and shall spread his wings over **M**. 4124
 48:41 the mighty *men's* hearts in **M** at that day 4124
 48:42 **M** shall be destroyed from *being* a people, 4124
 48:43 O inhabitant of **M**, saith the LORD. 4124
 48:44 for I will bring upon it, *even* upon **M**, 4124
 48:45 shall devour the corner of **M**, 4124
 48:46 Woe be unto thee, O **M**! the people of 4124
 48:47 Yet will I bring again the captivity of **M** in 4124
 48:47 the LORD. Thus far *is* the judgment of **M**. 4124
Eze 25: 8 Because that **M** and Seir do say, Behold, 4124
 25: 9 I *will* open the side of **M** from the cities, 4124
 25:11 I will execute judgments upon **M**; 4124
Da 11:41 **M**, and the chief of the children of 4124
Am 2: 1 three transgressions of **M**, and for four, 4124
 2: 1 I will send a fire upon **M**, and it shall 4124
 2: 2 **M** shall die with tumult, with shouting, 4124
Mic 6: 5 remember now what Balak king of **M** 4124
Zep 2: 8 I have heard the reproach of **M**, 4124
 2: 9 Surely **M** shall be as Sodom, 4124

MOABITE (3) [MOAB]
Dt 23: 3 **M** shall not enter into the congregation of 4125
1Ch 11:46 the sons of Elnaam, and Ithmah the **M**, 4125
Ne 13: 1 the **M** should not come into 4125

MOABITES (19) [MOAB]
Ge 19:37 the same *is* the father of the **M** unto *this* 4124
Nu 22: 4 Balak the son of Zippor *was* king of the **M** 4124
Dt 2: 9 LORD said unto me, Distress not the **M**, 4124
 2:11 the Anakims; but the **M** call them Emims. 4125
 2:29 the **M** which dwell in Ar, did unto me;) 4125
Jdg 3:28 your enemies the **M** into your hand. 4124
2Sa 8: 2 so the **M** became David's servants, 4124
1Ki 11: 1 women of the **M**, Ammonites, Edomites, 4124
 11:33 Chemosh the god of the **M**, and Milcom 4124
2Ki 3:18 he will deliver the **M** also into your hand. 4124
 3:21 when all the **M** heard that the kings were 4124
 3:22 the **M** saw the water on the other side *as* 4124
 3:24 the Israelites rose up and smote the **M**, 4124
 3:24 they went forward smiting the **M**, even in 4124
 13:20 the bands of the **M** invaded the land *at* 4124
 23:13 for Chemosh the abomination of the **M**, 4124
 24: 2 bands of the **M**, and bands of the children 4124
1Ch 18: 2 the **M** became David's servants, 4124
Ezr 9: 1 the **M**, the Egyptians, and the Amorites. 4125

MOABITESS (6) [MOAB]
Ru 1:22 So Naomi returned, and Ruth the **M**, 4125
 2: 2 Ruth the **M** said unto Naomi, Let me 4125
 2:21 Ruth the **M** said, He said unto me also, 4125
 4: 5 thou must buy *it* also of Ruth the **M**, 4125
 4:10 Ruth the **M**, the wife of Mahlon, 4125
2Ch 24:26 and Jehozabad the son of Shimrith a **M**. 4125

MOABITISH (1) [MOAB]
Ru 2: 6 It *is* the **M** damsel that came back with 4125

MOADIAH (1)
Ne 12:17 Zichri; of Miniamin, of **M**, Piltai, 4153

MOCK (12) [MOCKED, MOCKER, MOCKERS, MOCKEST, MOCKETH, MOCKING, MOCKINGS]
Ge 39:14 hath brought in a Hebrew unto us to **m** 6711
 39:17 unto us, came in unto me to **m** me: 6711
Job 13: 9 man mocketh another, do ye *so* **m** him? 2048
 21: 3 and after that I have spoken, **m** on. 3932
Pr 1:26 I will **m** when your fear cometh; 3932
 14: 9 Fools **make a m** at sin: but among 3887
Jer 38:19 me into their hand, and they **m** me. 5953
La 1: 7 saw her, *and* did **m** at her sabbaths. 7832
Eze 22: 5 **m** thee, *which art* infamous *and* 7048
Mt 20:19 shall deliver him to the Gentiles to **m**, *1702*
Mk 10:34 shall **m** him, and shall scourge *1702*
Lk 14:29 finish *it*, all that behold *it* begin to **m** him, *1702*

MOCKED (21) [MOCK]
Ge 19:14 he seemed as one that **m** unto his sons in 6711
Nu 22:29 unto the ass, Because thou hast **m** me: 5953
Jdg 16:10 thou hast **m** me, and told me lies: 2048
 16:13 thou hast **m** me, and told me lies: 2048
 16:15 thou hast **m** me these three times, 2048
1Ki 18:27 Elijah **m** them, and said, Cry aloud: 2048
2Ki 2:23 **m** him, and said unto him, Go up, thou 7046
2Ch 30:10 they laughed them to scorn, and **m** them. 3931
 36:16 they **m** the messengers of God, 3931
Ne 4: 1 took great indignation, and **m** the Jews. 3932

Job 12: 4 I am *as* **one** of his neighbour, 7814
Mt 27: 16 when he saw that he was **m** of the wise 1702
27:29 **m** him, saying, Hail, King of the Jews! 1702
27:31 And after that they had **m** him, they took 1702
Mk 15:20 And when they had **m** him, they took off 1702
Lk 18:32 and shall be **m**, and spitefully entreated, 1702
22:63 And the men that held Jesus **m** him, 1702
23:11 **m** *him*, and arrayed him in a gorgeous 1702
23:36 And the soldiers also **m** him, coming to 1702
Ac 17:32 of the resurrection of the dead, some **m**: 5512
Gal 6: 7 Be not deceived; God is not **m**: 3456

MOCKER (1) [MOCK]
Pr 20: 1 Wine *is* a **m**, strong drink *is* raging: 3887

MOCKERS (5) [MOCK]
Job 17: 2 *Are there* not **m** with me? and *doth not* 2049
Ps 35:16 hypocritical **m** in feasts, *they* gnashed 3934
Isa 28:22 therefore be ye not **m**, lest your bands 3887
Jer 15:17 I sat not in the assembly of the **m**, 7832
Jude 1:18 that they told you there should be **m** 1703

MOCKEST (1) [MOCK]
Job 11: 3 when thou **m**, shall no man make *thee* 3932

MOCKETH (5) [MOCK]
Job 13: 9 or as *one* man **m** another, do ye *so* 2048
39:22 He **m** at fear, and is not affrighted; 7832
Pr 17: 5 **m** the poor reproacheth his Maker: 3932
30:17 The eye *that* **m** at *his* father, 3932
Jer 20: 7 I am in derision daily, every one **m** me. 3932

MOCKING (5) [MOCK]
Ge 21: 9 which she had born unto Abraham, **m**. 6711
Eze 22: 4 the heathen, and a **m** to all countries. 7048
Mt 27:41 Likewise also the chief priests **m** *him*, 1702
Mk 15:31 Likewise also the chief priests **m** said 1702
Ac 2:13 Others **m** said, *These men* are full of new 5512

MOCKINGS (1) [MOCK]
Heb 11:36 And others had trial of *cruel* **m** and 1701

MODEL See ENSAMPLE

MODERATELY (1) [MODERATION]
Joel 2:23 given you the former rain **m**, 6666+3807.1

MODERATION (1) [MODERATELY]
Php 4: 5 Let your **m** be known unto all men. 1933

MODEST (1)
1Ti 2: 9 women adorn themselves in **m** apparel, 2887

MOE (28) [= MORE]
Ex 1: 9 the people of the children of Israel *are* **m** 7227
Lev 26:21 I will bring seven *times* **m** plagues upon NIH
Nu 33:54 the **m** ye shall give the more inheritance, 7227
Dt 1:11 **make** you a thousand times **so many m** 3254
7: 7 ye were **m** in number *than* any people; 4480
7:17 thine heart, These nations *are* **m** than I; 7227
19: 9 shalt thou add three cities **m** for thee, 5750
Jos 10:11 *they were* **m** which died with hailstones 7227
Jdg 16:30 **m** than *they* which he slew in his life. 7227
Ru 1:11 *are there* yet any **m** sons in my womb, NIH
2Ki 6:16 *they* that *be* with us *are* **m** than *they* that 7227
1Ch 14: 3 David took **m** wives at Jerusalem: 5750
14: 3 and David begat **m** sons and daughters. 5750
21: 3 **make** his people an hundred times
 so many m 3254
24: 4 there were **m** chief men found of the sons 7227
2Ch 32: 7 for *there be* **m** with us than with him: 7227
Ps 40: 5 speak *of* them, they are **m** than can be 6105
40:12 that I am not able to look *up*; they are **m** 6105
69: 4 They that hate me without a cause are **m** 7231
139:18 they are **m** in number *than* the sand: 4480
Mt 21:36 he sent other servants **m than** the first: 4183
22:46 that day forth ask him **any m** questions. 3765
25:20 I have gained besides them five talents **m**. 243
Jn 4: 1 and baptized **m** disciples than John, 4183
4:41 And many **m** believed because of his own 4183
7:31 he do **m** miracles than these which this 4183
Ac 23:21 there lie in wait for him of them **m** *than* 4183
Gal 4:27 the desolate hath **many m** children than 4183

MOIST (1) [MOISTENED, MOISTURE]
Nu 6: 3 of grapes, nor eat **m** grapes, or dried. 3892

MOISTENED (1) [MOIST]
Job 21:24 milk, and his bones are **m** with marrow. 8248

MOISTURE (2) [MOIST]
Ps 32: 4 **m** is turned into the drought of summer. 3955
Lk 8: 6 it withered away, because *it* lacked **m**. 2429

MOLADAH (4)
Jos 15:26 Amam, and Shema, and **M**, 4137
19: 2 inheritance Beer-sheba, or Sheba, and **M**, 4137
1Ch 4:28 at Beer-sheba, and **M**, and Hazar-shual, 4137
Ne 11:26 at Jeshua, and at **M**, and at Beth-phelet, 4137

MOLDY See MOULDY

MOLE (1) [MOLES]
Lev 11:30 and the lizard, and the snail, and the **m**. 8580

MOLECH (8)
Lev 18:21 of thy seed pass through *the* fire to **M**, 4432

Lev 20: 2 that giveth *any* of his seed unto **M**; 4432
20: 3 because he hath given of his seed unto **M**, 4432
20: 4 when he giveth of his seed unto **M**, 4432
20: 5 commit whoredom with **M**, from among 4432
1Ki 11: 7 hill that *is* before Jerusalem, and for **M**, 4432
2Ki 23:10 daughter to pass through the fire to **M**. 4432
Jer 32:35 daughters to pass through *the fire* unto **M** 4432

MOLES (1) [MOLE]
Isa 2:20 worship, to the **m** and to the bats; 2661+6512

MOLID (1)
1Ch 2:29 and she bare him Ahban, and **M**. 4140

MOLLIFIED (1)
Isa 1: 6 bound up, neither **m** with ointment. 7401

MOLOCH (2) [MALCHAM, MILCOM]
Am 5:26 ye have borne the tabernacle of your **M** 4429
Ac 7:43 took up the tabernacle of **M**, and the star 3434

MOLTEN (39) [MELT]
Ex 32: 4 tool, after he had made it a **m** calf: 4541
32: 8 they have made them a **m** calf, 4541
34:17 Thou shalt make thee no **m** gods. 4541
Lev 19: 4 idols, nor make to yourselves **m** gods: 4541
Nu 33:52 destroy all their **m** images, and quite 4541
Dt 9:12 they have made them a **m image**. 4541
9:16 your God, *and* had made you a **m** calf: 4541
27:15 that maketh *any* graven or **m image**, 4541
Jdg 17: 3 to make a graven image and a **m image**: 4541
17: 4 thereof a graven image and a **m image**: 4541
18:14 and a graven image, and a **m image**? 4541
18:17 and the teraphim, and the **m image**: 4541
18:18 and the teraphim, and the **m image**: 4541
1Ki 7:16 he made two chapiters *of* **m** brass, to set 3332
7:23 he made a **m** sea, ten cubits from the one 3332
7:30 under the laver *were* undersetters **m**, 3332
7:33 their felloes, and their spokes, *were* all **m**. 3332
14: 9 made thee other gods, and **m images**, 4541
2Ki 17:16 made them **m images**, *even* two calves, 4541
2Ch 4: 2 Also he made a **m** sea of ten cubits from 3332
4: 2 and made also **m images** for Baalim. 4541
34: 3 the carved images, and the **m images**. 4541
34: 4 the **m images**, he brake *in pieces*, and 4541
Ne 9:18 when they had made them a **m** calf, 4541
Job 28: 2 the earth, and brass is **m** *out of* the stone. 6694
37:18 *which* is strong, *and* as a **m** looking glass? 3332
Ps 106:19 in Horeb, and worshipped the **m image**. 4541
Isa 30:22 the ornament of thy **m images** of gold: 4541
41:29 their **m images** *are* wind and confusion. 5262
42:17 say to the **m images**, Ye *are* our gods. 4541
44:10 a graven image *that* is profitable for 5258
48: 5 my graven image, and my **m image**, 5262
Jer 10:14 his **m image** *is* falsehood, and *there is* 5262
51:17 his **m image** *is* falsehood, and *there is* 5262
Eze 24:11 and *that* the filthiness of it may be **m** in it, 5413
Hos 13: 2 have made them **m images** of their silver, 4541
Mic 1: 4 the mountains shall be **m** under him, 4549
Na 1:14 off the graven image and the **m image**: 4541
Hab 2:18 the **m image**, and a teacher of lies, that 4541

MOMENT (22)
Ex 33: 5 come up into the midst of thee in a **m**, 7281
Nu 16:21 I may consume them **in a m**. 7281+3509.1
16:45 that I may consume them **in a m**. 7281
Job 7:18 him every morning, *and* try him every **m**? 7281
20: 5 and the joy of the hypocrite *but* for a **m**? 7281
21:13 wealth, and in a **m** go down *to* the grave. 7281
34:20 *In a* **m** shall they die, and the people shall 7281
Ps 30: 5 For his anger *endureth but* a **m**; in his 7281
73:19 they *brought* into desolation, as *in a* **m**! 7281
Pr 12:19 for ever: but a lying tongue *is* but for a **m**. 7280
Isa 26:20 hide thyself as it were for a little **m**, 7281
27: 3 keep it; I will water it **every m**: 7281+3807.1
47: 9 two *things* shall come to thee in a **m** 7281
54: 7 For a small **m** have I forsaken thee; 7281
54: 8 wrath I hid my face from thee for a **m**; 7281
Jer 4:20 tents spoiled, *and* my curtains **in a m**. 7281
La 4: 6 that was overthrown as **in a m**, 7281
Eze 26:16 tremble at every **m**, and be astonished 7281
32:10 they shall tremble at every **m**, every *man* 7281
Lk 4: 5 the kingdoms of the world in a **m** of time. 4743
1Co 15:52 In a **m**, in the twinkling of an eye, at the 823
2Co 4:17 our light affliction, which is but **for a m**, 3910

MONEY (140) [MONEYCHANGERS, MONEY-CHANGERS]
Ge 17:12 bought with **m** of any stranger, which *is* 3701
17:13 he that is bought with thy **m**, must needs 3701
17:23 and all that were bought with his **m**, 3701
17:27 and bought with **m** of the stranger, 3701
23: 9 for as much **m** as it is worth he shall give 3701
23:13 I will give *thee* **m** for the field; take *it of* 3701
23:16 of silver, current with the merchant. NIH
31:15 and hath quite devoured also our **m**. 3701
33:19 for an hundred **pieces of m**. 7192
42:25 to restore every man's **m** into his sack, 3701
42:27 ass provender in the inn, he espied his **m**; 3701
42:28 said unto his brethren, My **m** is restored; 3701
42:35 every man's bundle of **m** *was* in his sack: 3701
42:35 and their father saw the bundles of **m**, 3701
43:12 double **m** in your hand; and the money 3701
43:12 the **m** that was brought again in the 3701
43:15 they took double **m** in their hand, 3701

Ge 43:18 Because of the **m** that was returned in our 3701
43:21 every man's **m** *was* in the mouth of his 3701
43:21 mouth of his sack, our **m** in full weight: 3701
43:22 other **m** have we brought down in our 3701
43:22 cannot tell who put our **m** in our sacks. 3701
43:23 I had your **m**. And he brought Simeon 3701
44: 1 put every man's **m** in his sack's mouth. 3701
44: 2 mouth of the youngest, and his corn **m**. 3701
44: 8 Behold, the **m**, which we found in our 3701
47:14 Joseph gathered up all the **m** that was 3701
47:14 Joseph brought the **m** into Pharaoh's 3701
47:15 when **m** failed in the land of Egypt, 3701
47:15 we die in thy presence? for the **m** faileth. 3701
47:16 I will give you for your cattle, if **m** fail. 3701
47:18 *it* from my lord, how that our **m** is spent; 3701
Ex 12:44 every man's servant that is bought for **m**, 3701
21:11 then shall she go out free without **m**. 3701
21:21 he shall not be punished: for he *is* his **m**. 3701
21:30 If there be laid on him a **sum of m**, then 3724
21:34 *and* give **m** unto the owner of them; 3701
21:35 sell the live ox, and divide the **m** of it; 3701
22: 7 a man shall deliver unto his neighbour **m** 3701
22:17 he shall pay **m** according to the dowry of 3701
22:25 If thou lend **m** to *any of* my people that 3701
30:16 thou shalt take the atonement **m** of 3701
Lev 22:11 if the priest buy *any* soul with his **m**, 3701
25:37 shalt not give him thy **m** upon usury, 3701
25:51 out of the **m** that he was bought for. 3701
27:15 he shall add the fifth *part* of the **m** of thy 3701
27:18 the priest shall reckon unto him the **m** 3701
27:19 he shall add the fifth *part* of the **m** of thy 3701
Nu 3:48 thou shalt give the **m**, wherewith the odd 3701
3:49 Moses took the redemption **m** of them 3701
3:50 of the children of Israel took he the **m**; 3701
3:51 Moses gave the **m** of them that were 3701
18:16 thine estimation, *for* the **m** of five shekels, 3701
Dt 2: 6 Ye shall buy meat of them for **m**, that ye 3701
2: 6 ye shall also buy water of them for **m**, 3701
2:28 Thou shalt sell me meat for **m**, that I may 3701
2:28 give me water for **m**, that I may drink: 3701
14:25 shalt thou turn *it* into **m**, and bind up 3701
14:25 bind up the **m** in thine hand, and shalt go 3701
14:26 thou shalt bestow *that* **m** for whatsoever 3701
21:14 thou shalt not sell her at all for **m**, 3701
23:19 usury of **m**, usury of victuals, usury of any 3701
Jdg 5:19 of Megiddo; they took no gain of **m**. 3701
16:18 unto her, and brought **m** in their hand. 3701
17: 4 Yet he restored the **m** unto his mother; 3701
1Ki 21: 2 thee, I will give thee the worth of it *in* **m**. 3701
21: 6 unto him, Give me thy vineyard for **m**; 3701
21:15 which he refused to give thee for **m**: 3701
2Ki 5:26 *Is it* a time to receive **m**, and to receive 3701
12: 4 All the **m** of the dedicated *things* that is 3701
12: 4 *even* the **m** of every one that passeth 3701
12: 4 *account*, the **m** that every man is set at, 3701
12: 4 the **m** that cometh into any man's heart 3701
12: 7 receive no **more** *of* your acquaintance, 3701
12: 8 priests consented to receive no **more m** 3701
12: 9 the **m** that was brought **into** the house of 3701
12:10 when they saw that *there was* much **m** in 3701
12:10 told the **m** that was found *in* the house of 3701
12:11 gave the **m**, being told, into the hands 3701
12:13 the **m** that was brought *into* the house of 3701
12:15 whose hand they delivered the **m** to be 3701
12:16 The trespass and sin **money** was not 3701
12:16 sin **m** was not brought *into* the house of 3701
15:20 Menahem exacted the **m** of Israel, *even* 3701
22: 7 the **m** that was delivered into their hand, 3701
22: 9 Thy servants have gathered the **m** that 3701
23:35 he taxed the land to give the **m** according 3701
2Ch 24: 5 gather of all Israel **m** to repair the house 3701
24:11 when they saw that *there was* much **m**, 3701
24:11 by day, and gathered in abundance. 3701
24:14 brought the rest of the **m** before the king 3701
34: 9 they delivered the **m** that was brought 3701
34:14 when they brought out the **m** that was 3701
34:17 they have gathered together the **m** that 3701
Ezr 3: 7 They gave **m** also unto the masons, 3702
7:17 thou mayest buy speedily with this **m** 3701
Ne 5: 4 have borrowed **m** for the king's tribute, 3701
5:10 *might* exact of them **m** and corn: 3701
5:11 also the hundredth *part* of the **m**, and *of* 3701
Est 4: 7 of the sum of the **m** that Haman had 3701
Job 31:39 have eaten the fruits thereof without **m**, 3701
41:11 every man also gave him a **piece of m**, 7192
Ps 15: 5 *He that* putteth not out his **m** to usury, 3701
Pr 7:20 He hath taken a bag of **m** with him, 3701
Ecc 7:12 wisdom *is* a defence, *and* **m** *is* a defence: 3701
10:19 merry: but **m** answereth all *things*. 3701
Isa 43:24 hast bought me no sweet cane with **m**, 3701
52: 3 and ye shall be redeemed without **m**. 3701
55: 1 to the waters, and he that hath no **m**; 3701
55: 1 buy wine and milk without **m** and 3701
55: 2 Wherefore do ye spend **m** for *that which* 3701
Jer 32: 9 in Anathoth, and weighed him the **m**, 3701
32:10 weighed *him* the **m** in the balances. 3701
32:25 Buy thee the field for **m**, 3701
32:44 *Men* shall buy fields with **m**, 3701
La 4: 4 We have drunken our water for **m**; 3701
Mic 3:11 and the prophets thereof divine for **m**: 3701
Mt 17:24 that received **tribute m** came to Peter, 1323
17:27 his mouth, thou shalt find a **piece of m**: 4715
22:19 Shew me the **tribute m**. And they brought 3546
25:18 digged in the earth, and hid his lord's **m**. 694
25:27 to have put my **m** to the exchangers, 694

M

Mt	28:12 they gave large **m** unto the soldiers,	694
	28:15 So they took the **m**, and did as they were	694
Mk	6: 8 no scrip, no bread, no **m** in *their* purse:	5475
	12:41 beheld how the people cast **m** into	5475
	14:11 were glad, and promised to give him **m**.	694
Lk	9: 3 nor scrip, neither bread, neither **m**;	694
	19:15 unto him, to whom he had given the **m**,	694
	19:23 then gavest not thou my **m** into the bank,	694
	22: 5 were glad, and covenanted to give him **m**.	694
Jn	2:14 doves, and the **changers of m** sitting:	2773
	2:15 and poured out the changers' **m**,	2772
Ac	4:37 sold *it*, and brought the **m**, and laid *it* at	5536
	7:16 the sons of Emmor the *father* of	694
	8:18 Holy Ghost was given, he offered them **m**,	5536
	8:20 Thy **m** perish with thee, because thou	694
	8:20 the gift of God may be purchased with **m**.	5536
	24:26 He hoped also that **m** should have been	5536
1Ti	6:10 For the **love of m** is the root of all evil:	5365

MONEYCHANGERS, MONEY-CHANGERS (2)
[MONEY]

Mt	21:12 and overthrew the tables of the **m**,	2855
Mk	11:15 and overthrew the tables of the **m**,	2855

MONEYLENDER See USURER

MONSTER See WHALE; WHALE'S; WHALES

MONSTERS (1)

La	4: 3 Even the **sea m** draw out the breast,	8577

MONTH (250) [MONTHLY, MONTHS]

Ge	7:11 in the second **m**, the seventeenth day of	2320
	7:11 the seventeenth day of the **m**,	2320
	8: 4 the ark rested in the seventh **m**,	2320
	8: 4 on the seventeenth day of the **m**, upon	2320
	8: 5 decreased continually until the tenth **m**:	2320
	8: 5 tenth **m**, on the first *day* of the month,	NIH
	8: 5 tenth *month*, on the first *day* of the **m**,	2320
	8:13 in the first **m**, the first *day* of the month,	NIH
	8:13 in the first *month*, the first *day* of the **m**,	2320
	8:14 in the second **m**, on the seven and	2320
	8:14 on the seven and twentieth day of the **m**,	2320
	29:14 And he abode with him the space of a **m**.	2320
Ex	12: 2 This **m** *shall be* unto you the beginning	2320
	12: 2 it *shall be* the first **m** of the year to you.	2320
	12: 3 In the tenth *day* of this **m** they shall take	2320
	12: 6 until the fourteenth day of the same **m**:	2320
	12:18 In the first **m**, on the fourteenth day	NIH
	12:18 on the fourteenth day of the **m** at even,	2320
	12:18 one and twentieth day of the **m** at even.	2320
	13: 4 *This* day came ye out in the **m** Abib.	2320
	13: 5 thou shalt keep this service in this **m**.	2320
	16: 1 on the fifteenth day of the second **m** after	2320
	19: 1 the third **m**, when the children of Israel	2320
	23:15 in the time appointed of the **m** Abib;	2320
	34:18 in the time of the **m** Abib:	2320
	34:18 for in the **m** Abib thou camest out from	2320
	40: 2 the first day of the first **m** shalt thou set	2320
	40:17 came to pass in the first **m** in the second	2320
	40:17 the first *day* of the **m**, *that* the tabernacle	2320
Lev	16:29 in the seventh **m**, on the tenth *day*	2320
	16:29 on the tenth *day* of the **m**, ye shall afflict	2320
	23: 5 the fourteenth *day* of the first **m** at even	2320
	23: 6 on the fifteenth day of the same **m** *is*	2320
	23:24 In the seventh **m**, in the first *day* of	2320
	23:24 seventh month, in the first *day* of the **m**,	2320
	23:27 Also on the tenth *day* of this seventh **m**	2320
	23:32 the ninth *day* of the **m** at even, from even	2320
	23:34 The fifteenth *day* of this seventh **m** *shall*	2320
	23:39 Also in the fifteenth day of the seventh **m**,	2320
	23:41 ye shall celebrate it in the seventh **m**.	2320
	25: 9 sound on the tenth *day* of the seventh **m**,	2320
	27: 6 if *it be* from a **m** old even unto five years	2320
Nu	1: 1 on the first *day* of the second **m**,	2320
	1:18 together on the first *day* of the second **m**,	2320
	3:15 every male from a **m** old and upward	2320
	3:22 all the males, from a **m** old and upward,	2320
	3:28 from a **m** old and upward, *were* eight	2320
	3:34 from a **m** old and upward, *were* six	2320
	3:39 all the males from a **m** old and upward,	2320
	3:40 of the children of Israel from a **m** old	2320
	3:43 from a **m** old and upward, of those that	2320
	9: 1 in the first **m** of the second year after they	2320
	9: 3 In the fourteenth day of this **m**, at even,	2320
	9: 5 first **m** at even in the wilderness of Sinai:	2320
	9:11 fourteenth day of the second **m** at even	2320
	9:22 *it were* two days, or a **m**, or a year,	2320
	10:11 on the twentieth *day* of the second **m**,	2320
	11:20 *But* even a whole **m**, until it come out at	2320
	11:21 them flesh, that they may eat a whole **m**.	2320
	18:16 that are *to be* redeemed from a **m** old	2320
	20: 1 *into* the desert of Zin in the first **m**:	2320
	26:62 all males from a **m** old and upward:	2320
	28:14 **every m** throughout 2320+2320+871.1	
	28:16 in the fourteenth day of the first **m** *is*	2320
	28:17 in the fifteenth day of this **m** *is* the feast:	2320
	29: 1 in the seventh **m**, on the first *day* of	2320
	29: 1 seventh month, on the first *day* of the **m**,	2320
	29: 6 Beside the burnt offering of the **m**,	2320
	29: 7 of this seventh **m** a holy convocation;	2320
	29:12 on the fifteenth day of the seventh **m** ye	2320
	33: 3 departed from Rameses in the first **m**,	2320
	33: 3 on the morrow after the passover	2320
	33:38 of Egypt, in the first *day* of the fifth **m**.	2320
Dt	1: 3 in the eleventh **m**, on the first *day* of	2320

Dt	1: 3 month, on the first *day* of the **m**,	2320
	16: 1 Observe the **m** of Abib, and keep	2320
	16: 1 for in the **m** of Abib the Lᴏʀᴅ thy God	2320
	21:13 father and her mother a **full m**:	3117+3391
Jos	4:19 of Jordan on the tenth *day* of the first **m**,	2320
	5:10 of the **m** at even in the plains of Jericho.	2320
1Sa	20:27 which *was* the second *day* of the **m**,	2320
	20:34 did eat no meat the second day of the **m**:	2320
1Ki	4: 7 each man *his* **m** in a year made provision.	2320
	4:27 Solomon's table, every man *in* his **m**:	2320
	5:14 to Lebanon, ten thousand a **m** *by* courses:	2320
	5:14 **m** they were in Lebanon, *and* two months	2320
	6: 1 in the **m** Zif, which *is* the second month,	2320
	6: 1 in the month Zif, which *is* the second **m**,	2320
	6:37 the house of the Lᴏʀᴅ laid, in the **m** Zif:	3391
	6:38 in the eleventh year, in the **m** Bul, which	3391
	6:38 in the month Bul, which *is* the eighth **m**,	2320
	8: 2 Solomon at the feast in the **m** Ethanim,	3391
	8: 2 month Ethanim, which *is* the seventh **m**.	2320
	12:32 ordained a feast in the eighth **m**,	2320
	12:32 on the fifteenth day of the **m**, like unto	2320
	12:33 Beth-el the fifteenth day of the eighth **m**,	2320
	12:33 in the **m** which he had devised of his	2320
2Ki	15:13 and he reigned a **full m** in Samaria. 3117+3391	
	25: 1 in the tenth **m**, in the tenth *day* of	2320
	25: 1 tenth month, in the tenth *day* of the **m**,	2320
	25: 3 the ninth *day* of the *fourth* **m** the famine	2320
	25: 8 in the fifth **m**, on the seventh *day*	2320
	25: 8 fifth month, on the seventh *day* of the **m**,	2320
	25:25 it came to pass in the seventh **m**,	2320
	25:27 in the twelfth **m**, on the seven and	2320
	25:27 on the seven and twentieth *day* of the **m**,	2320
1Ch	12:15 they that went over Jordan in the first **m**,	2320
	27: 1 went out **m** by month throughout all	2320
	27: 1 went out month by **m** throughout all	2320
	27: 2 Over the first course for the first **m** *was*	2320
	27: 3 all the captains of the host for the first **m**.	2320
	27: 4 over the course of the second **m** *was*	2320
	27: 5 third captain of the host for the third **m**	2320
	27: 7 The fourth *captain* for the fourth **m** *was*	2320
	27: 8 The fifth *captain* for the fifth **m** *was*	2320
	27: 9 The sixth *captain* for the sixth **m** *was* Ira	2320
	27:10 The seventh *captain* for the seventh **m**	2320
	27:11 The eighth *captain* for the eighth **m** *was*	2320
	27:12 The ninth *captain* for the ninth **m** *was*	2320
	27:13 The tenth *captain* for the tenth **m** *was*	2320
	27:14 The eleventh *captain* for the eleventh **m**	2320
	27:15 The twelfth *captain* for the twelfth **m**	2320
2Ch	3: 2 build in the second *day* of the second **m**,	2320
	5: 3 in the feast which *was in* the seventh **m**.	2320
	7:10 twentieth day of the seventh **m** he sent	2320
	15:10 together *at* Jerusalem in the third **m**,	2320
	29: 3 in the first year of his reign, in the first **m**,	2320
	29:17 on the first *day* of the first **m** to sanctify,	2320
	29:17 on the eighth day of the **m** came they to	2320
	29:17 in the sixteenth day of the first **m** they	2320
	30: 2 to keep the passover in the second **m**.	2320
	30:13 of unleavened bread in the second **m**,	2320
	30:15 on the fourteenth *day* of the second **m**:	2320
	31: 7 In the third **m** they began to lay	2320
	31: 7 and finished *them* in the seventh **m**.	2320
	35: 1 on the fourteenth *day* of the first **m**.	2320
Ezr	3: 1 when the seventh **m** was come,	2320
	3: 6 From the first day of the seventh **m** began	2320
	3: 8 the second **m**, began Zerubbabel the son	2320
	6:15 finished on the third *day* of the **m** Adar,	3393
	6:19 upon the fourteenth *day* of the first **m**.	2320
	7: 8 he came *to* Jerusalem in the fifth **m**,	2320
	7: 9 For upon the first *day* of the first **m** began	2320
	7: 9 on the first *day* of the fifth **m** came he to	2320
	8:31 of Ahava on the twelfth *day* of the first **m**,	2320
	10: 9 It *was* the ninth **m**, on the twentieth *day*	2320
	10: 9 month, on the twentieth *day* of the **m**;	2320
	10:16 sat down in the first day of the tenth **m** to	2320
	10:17 wives by the first day of the first **m**.	2320
Ne	1: 1 it came to pass in the **m** Chisleu,	2320
	2: 1 it came to pass in the **m** Nisan,	2320
	6:15 in the twenty and fifth *day* of *the* **m** Elul,	NIH
	7:73 when the seventh **m** came, the children	2320
	8: 2 upon the first day of the seventh **m**.	2320
	8:14 in booths in the feast of the seventh **m**:	2320
	9: 1 fourth day of this **m** the children of Israel	2320
Est	2:16 into his house royal in the tenth **m**,	2320
	2:16 which *is the* **m** Tebeth, in the seventh	2320
	3: 7 In the first **m**, that *is*, the month Nisan,	2320
	3: 7 In the first month, that *is*, the **m** Nisan,	2320
	3: 7 from day to day, and from month to **m**,	2320
	3: 7 from day to day, and from **m** to month,	2320
	3: 7 *to* the twelfth **m**, that *is*, the month Adar.	NIH
	3: 7 *to* the twelfth *month*, that *is*, the **m** Adar.	2320
	3:12 called on the thirteenth day of the first **m**,	2320
	3:13 upon the thirteenth *day* of the twelfth **m**,	2320
	3:13 *is* the **m** Adar, and *to take* the spoil	2320
	8: 9 scribes called at that time in the third **m**,	2320
	8: 9 that *is*, the Sivan, on the three and	2320
	8:12 upon the thirteenth *day* of the twelfth **m**,	2320
	8:12 the twelfth month, which *is* the **m** Adar.	2320
	9: 1 Now in the twelfth **m**, that *is*, the month	2320
	9: 1 in the twelfth month, that *is*, the **m** Adar,	2320
	9:15 on the fourteenth day also of the **m** Adar	2320
	9:17 On the thirteenth day of the **m** Adar;	2320
	9:19 made the fourteenth day of the **m** Adar *a*	2320
	9:21 keep the fourteenth day of the **m** Adar,	2320
	9:22 the **m** which was turned unto them from	2320
Jer	1: 3 away of Jerusalem captive in the fifth **m**.	2320

Jer	2:24 in her **m** they shall find her.	2320
	28: 1 in the fourth year, *and* in the fifth **m**,	2320
	28:17 died the same year in the seventh **m**.	2320
	36: 9 the ninth **m**, *that* they proclaimed a fast	2320
	36:22 sat *in* the winterhouse in the ninth **m**:	2320
	39: 1 the tenth **m**, came Nebuchadrezzar king	2320
	39: 2 the fourth **m**, the ninth *day* of the month,	2320
	39: 2 the fourth month, the ninth *day* of the **m**,	2320
	41: 1 Now it came to pass in the seventh **m**,	2320
	52: 4 in the tenth **m**, in the tenth *day* of	2320
	52: 4 tenth month, in the tenth *day* of	2320
	52: 6 in the fourth **m**, in the ninth *day* of	2320
	52: 6 fourth month, in the ninth *day* of	2320
	52:12 Now in the fifth **m**, in the tenth *day* of	2320
	52:12 fifth month, in the tenth *day* of the **m**,	2320
	52:31 in the twelfth **m**, in the five and	2320
	52:31 in the five and twentieth *day* of the **m**,	2320
Eze	1: 1 in the fourth **m**, in the fifth *day* of	NIH
	1: 1 fourth *month*, in the fifth *day* of	2320
	1: 2 In the fifth *day* of the **m**, which *was*	2320
	8: 1 the sixth **m**, in the fifth *day* of the month,	NIH
	8: 1 sixth *month*, in the fifth *day* of the **m**,	2320
	20: 1 In the fifth **m**, the tenth *day* of the month,	NIH
	20: 1 In the fifth *month*, the tenth *day* of the **m**,	2320
	24: 1 Again in the ninth year, in the tenth **m**,	2320
	24: 1 tenth month, in the tenth *day* of the **m**,	2320
	26: 1 eleventh year, in the first *day* of the **m**,	2320
	29: 1 In the tenth **m**, in the twelfth *day* of	NIH
	29: 1 tenth *month*, in the twelfth *day* of the **m**,	2320
	30:20 in the first **m**, in the seventh *day* of	NIH
	30:20 first *month*, in the seventh *day* of the month,	NIH
	31: 1 the third **m**, in the first *day* of the month,	NIH
	31: 1 third *month*, in the first *day* of the **m**,	2320
	32: 1 in the twelfth **m**, in the first *day* of	2320
	32: 1 twelfth month, in the first *day* of the **m**,	2320
	32:17 twelfth year, in the fifteenth *day* of the **m**,	2320
	33:21 the tenth **m**, in the fifth *day* of the month,	NIH
	33:21 the tenth *month*, in the fifth *day* of the **m**,	2320
	40: 1 of the year, in the tenth *day* of	2320
	45:18 the first **m**, in the first *day* of the month,	NIH
	45:18 the first *month*, in the first *day* of the **m**,	2320
	45:20 thou shalt do the seventh *day* of the **m** for	2320
	45:21 In the first **m**, in the fourteenth day of	NIH
	45:21 *month*, in the fourteenth day of the **m**,	2320
	45:25 In the seventh **m**, in the fifteenth *day* of	NIH
	45:25 month, in the fifteenth day of the **m**,	2320
Da	10: 4 the four and twentieth day of the first **m**,	2320
Hos	5: 7 now shall a **m** devour them with their	2320
Joel	2:23 and the latter rain in the first **m**.	NIH
Hag	1: 1 the sixth **m**, in the first day of the month,	2320
	1: 1 the sixth month, in the first day of the **m**,	2320
	1:15 the four and twentieth day of the sixth **m**,	2320
	2: 1 In the seventh **m**, in the one and	NIH
	2: 1 In the one and twentieth *day* of the **m**,	2320
	2:10 twentieth *day* of the ninth **m**, in the	NIH
	2:18 twentieth *day* of the ninth **m**, *even* from	2320
	2:20 in the four and twentieth *day* of the **m**,	2320
Zec	1: 1 In the eighth **m**, in the second year of	2320
	1: 7 four and twentieth day of the eleventh **m**,	2320
	1: 7 *is* the **m** Sebat, in the second year of	2320
	7: 1 in the fourth *day* of the ninth **m**,	2320
	7: 3 Should I weep in the fifth **m**,	2320
	7: 5 and seventh **m**, *even* those seventy years,	NIH
	8:19 The fast of the fourth **m**, and the fast of	2320
	11: 8 Three shepherds also I cut off in one **m**;	3391
Lk	1:26 And in the sixth **m** the angel Gabriel was	3376
	1:36 and this is the sixth **m** with her, who was	3376
Rev	9:15 and a day, and a **m**, and a year, for to slay	3376
	22: 2 *of* fruits, *and* yielded her fruit every **m**:	3376

MONTHLY (1) [MONTH]

Isa	47:13 the **m** prognosticators, stand *up*, and	2320

MONTHS (59) [MONTH]

Ge	38:24 came to pass about three **m** after, that it	2320
Ex	2: 2 *was* a goodly *child*, she hid him three **m**.	3391
	12: 2 *shall be* unto you the beginning of **m**:	2320
Nu	10:10 and in the beginnings of your **m**,	2320
	28:11 In the beginnings of your **m** ye shall offer	2320
	28:14 month throughout the **m** of the year.	2320
Jdg	11:37 let me alone two **m**, that I may go up and	2320
	11:38 sent her away *for* two **m**: and she went	2320
	11:39 to pass at the end of two **m**, that she	2320
	19: 2 was there four whole **m**.	2320
	20:47 and abode in the rock Rimmon four **m**.	2320
1Sa	6: 1 in the country of the Philistines seven **m**.	2320
	27: 7 The Philistines was a full year and four **m**.	2320
2Sa	2:11 of Judah was seven years and six **m**.	2320
	5: 5 over Judah seven years and six **m**:	2320
	6:11 house of Obed-edom the Gittite three **m**:	2320
	24: 8 came *to* Jerusalem at the end of nine **m**	2320
	24:13 thou flee three **m** before thine enemies,	2320
1Ki	5:14 were in Lebanon, *and* two **m** at home:	2320
	11:16 (For six **m** did Joab remain there with all	2320
2Ki	15: 8 reign over Israel in Samaria six **m**.	2320
	23:31 and he reigned three **m** in Jerusalem.	2320
	24: 8 and he reigned in Jerusalem three **m**.	2320
1Ch	3: 4 there he reigned seven years and six **m**:	2320
	13:14 of Obed-edom in his house three **m**.	2320
	21:12 three **m** to be destroyed before thy foes,	2320
	27: 1 month throughout all the **m** of the year,	2320
2Ch	36: 2 and he reigned three **m** in Jerusalem.	2320
	36: 9 he reigned three **m** and ten days in	2320

M

Ref	Text	Strong
Est 2:12	after that she had been twelve **m**,	2320
2:12	to wit, six **m** with oil of myrrh,	2320
2:12	six **m** with sweet odours, and with *other*	2320
Job 3: 6	let it not come into the number of the **m**.	3391
7: 3	So am I made to possess **m** of vanity,	3391
14: 5	the number of his **m** *are* with thee,	2320
21:21	when the number of his **m** is cut off in	2320
29: 2	O that I were as in **m** past, as *in* the days	3391
39: 2	Canst thou number the **m** *that* they fulfil?	3391
Eze 39:12	seven **m** shall the house of Israel be	2320
39:14	after the end of seven **m** shall they search.	2320
47:12	bring forth new fruit according to his **m**,	2320
Da 4:29	At the end of twelve **m** he walked in	3393
Am 4: 7	*there were* yet three **m** to the harvest:	2320
Lk 1:24	and hid herself five **m**, saying,	3376
1:56	And Mary abode with her about three **m**,	3376
4:25	was shut up three years and six **m**,	3376
Jn 4:35	There are yet **four m**, and *then* cometh	5072
Ac 7:20	up in his father's house three **m**:	3376
18:11	he continued *there* a year and six **m**,	3376
19: 8	and spake boldly for the space of three **m**,	3376
20: 3	And *there* abode three **m**: and when	3376
28:11	after three **m** we departed in a ship of	3376
Gal 4:10	days, and **m**, and times, and years.	5150
Heb 11:23	was hid **three m** of his parents, because	3376
Jas 5:17	*by the space of* three years and six **m**.	3376
Rev 9: 5	that they should be tormented five **m**:	3376
9:10	and their power *was* to hurt men five **m**.	3376
11: 2	they tread under foot forty and two **m**.	3376
13: 5	unto him to continue forty and two **m**.	3376

MONUMENTS (1)

Ref	Text	Strong
Isa 65: 4	lodge in the **m**, which eat swine's flesh,	5341

MOON (51) [MOONS]

Ref	Text	Strong
Ge 37: 9	the sun and the **m** and the eleven stars	3394
Dt 4:19	seest the sun, and the **m**, and the stars,	3394
17: 3	sun, or **m**, or any of the host of heaven,	3394
33:14	the precious things put forth by the **m**,	3391
Jos 10:12	and thou, **M**, in the valley of Ajalon.	3394
10:13	the sun stood still, and the **m** stayed,	3394
1Sa 20: 5	to morrow *is* the new **m**, and I should	2320
20:18	said to *David*, To morrow *is* the new **m**:	2320
20:24	when the new **m** was come, the king sat	2320
2Ki 4:23	*it is* neither new **m**, nor sabbath.	2320
23: 5	to the **m**, and to the planets, and to all	3394
Job 25: 5	Behold *even* to the **m**, and it shineth not;	3394
31:26	it shined, or the **m** walking *in* brightness;	3394
Ps 8: 3	work of thy fingers, the **m** and the stars,	3394
72: 5	thee as long as the sun and **m** endure,	3394
72: 7	of peace so long as the **m** endureth.	3394
81: 3	Blow up the trumpet in the new **m**,	2320
89:37	It shall be established for ever as the **m**,	3394
104:19	He appointed the **m** for seasons: the sun	3394
121: 6	smite thee by day, nor the **m** by night.	3394
136: 9	The **m** and stars to rule by night: for his	3394
148: 3	Praise ye him, sun and **m**: praise him, all	3394
Ecc 12: 2	sun, or the light, or the **m**, or the stars,	3842
SS 6:10	fair as the **m**, clear as the sun,	3842
Isa 3:18	and *their* **round tires like the m**,	7720
13:10	the **m** shall not cause her light to shine.	3394
24:23	the **m** shall be confounded, and the	3842
30:26	Moreover the light of the **m** shall be as	3842
60:19	for brightness shall the **m** give light	3394
60:20	neither shall thy **m** withdraw itself:	3391
66:23	*that* from one new **m** to another,	2320
Jer 8: 2	the **m**, and all the host of heaven,	3394
31:35	the ordinances of the **m** and of the stars	3394
Eze 32: 7	cloud, and the **m** shall not give her light.	3394
46: 1	the day of the new **m** it shall be opened.	2320
46: 6	the day of the new **m** *it shall be* a young	2320
Joel 2:10	the sun and the **m** shall be dark,	3394
2:31	the **m** into blood, before the great and	3394
3:15	The sun and the **m** shall be darkened,	3394
Am 8: 5	Saying, When will the **new m** be gone,	2320
Hab 3:11	and the **m** stood still in *their* habitation:	3394
Mt 24:29	and the **m** shall not give her light,	4582
Mk 13:24	and the **m** shall not give her light,	4582
Lk 21:25	in the sun, and in the **m**, and in the stars;	4582
Ac 2:20	into blood, before *that* great and	4582
1Co 15:41	and another glory of the **m**,	4582
Col 2:16	or of the **new m**, or of the sabbath days:	3561
Rev 6:12	of hair, and the **m** became as blood;	4582
8:12	and the third *part* of the **m**, and the third	4582
12: 1	and the **m** under her feet, and upon her	4582
21:23	the sun, neither of the **m**, to shine in it:	4582

MOONS (11) [MOON]

Ref	Text	Strong
1Ch 23:31	in the **new m**, and on the set feasts,	2320
2Ch 2: 4	on the **new m**, and on the solemn feasts,	2320
8:13	on the **new m**, and on the solemn feasts,	2320
31: 3	and for the **new m**, and for the set feasts,	2320
Ezr 3: 5	of the **new m**, and of all the set feasts	2320
Ne 10:33	the sabbaths, of the **new m**, for the set	2320
Isa 1:13	the **new m** and sabbaths, the calling of	2320
1:14	Your **new m** and your appointed feasts	2320
Eze 45:17	in the **new m**, and in the sabbaths in all	2320
46: 3	Lord in the sabbaths and in the **new m**,	2320
Hos 2:11	her feast *days*, her **new m**,	2320

MORASTHITE (2) [MORESHETH-GATH]

Ref	Text	Strong
Jer 26:18	Micah the **M** prophesied in the days of	4183
Mic 1: 1	to Micah the **M** in the days of Jotham,	4183

MORDECAI (58) [MORDECAI'S]

Ref	Text	Strong
Ezr 2: 2	**M**, Bilshan, Mizpar, Bigvai, Rehum,	4782
Ne 7: 7	**M**, Bilshan, Mispereth, Bigvai, Nehum,	4782
Est 2: 5	name *was* **M**, the son of Jair, the son	4782
2: 7	whom **M**, when her father and mother	4782
2:10	**M** had charged her that she should not	4782
2:11	**M** walked every day before the court of	4782
2:15	the daughter of Abihail the uncle of **M**,	4782
2:19	time, then **M** sat in the king's gate.	4782
2:20	nor her people; as **M** had charged her:	4782
2:20	for Esther did the commandment of **M**,	4782
2:21	those days, while **M** sat in the king's gate,	4782
2:22	thing was known to **M**, who told *it* unto	4782
3: 2	But **M** bowed not, nor did *him* reverence.	4782
3: 3	*were* in the king's gate, said unto **M**,	4782
3: 5	when Haman saw that **M** bowed not,	4782
3: 6	thought scorn to lay hands on **M** alone;	4782
3: 6	they had shewed him the people of **M**:	4782
3: 6	of Ahasuerus, *even* the people of **M**.	4782
4: 1	When **M** perceived all that was done,	4782
4: 1	**M** rent his clothes, and put on sackcloth	4782
4: 4	she sent raiment to clothe **M**, and to take	4782
4: 5	gave him a commandment to **M**, to know	4782
4: 6	So Hatach went forth to **M** unto the street	4782
4: 7	And told him of all that had happened unto	4782
4: 9	and told Esther the words of **M**.	4782
4:10	and gave him commandment unto **M**:	4782
4:12	And they told to **M** Esther's words.	4782
4:13	**M** commanded to answer Esther, Think	4782
4:15	Esther bade *them* return **M** this answer:	4782
4:17	So **M** went his way, and did according to	4782
5: 9	when Haman saw **M** in the king's gate,	4782
5: 9	he was full of indignation against **M**.	4782
5:13	as I see **M** the Jew sitting at the king's	4782
5:14	speak thou unto the king that **M**	4782
6: 2	that **M** had told of Bigthana and Teresh,	4782
6: 3	and dignity hath been done to **M** for this?	4782
6: 4	to speak unto the king to hang **M** on	4782
6:10	hast said, and do *even* so to **M** the Jew,	4782
6:11	arrayed **M**, and brought him on horseback	4782
6:12	**M** came again to the king's gate.	4782
6:13	unto him, If **M** *be* of the seed of the Jews,	4782
7: 9	high, which Haman had made for **M**,	4782
7:10	the gallows that he had prepared for **M**.	4782
8: 1	**M** came before the king; for Esther had	4782
8: 2	taken from Haman, and gave it unto **M**.	4782
8: 2	Esther set **M** over the house of Haman.	4782
8: 7	unto Esther the queen and to **M** the Jew,	4782
8: 9	it was written according to all that **M**	4782
8:15	**M** went out from the presence of the king	4782
9: 3	because the fear of **M** fell upon them.	4782
9: 4	For **M** *was* great in the king's house,	4782
9: 4	*this* man **M** waxed greater and greater.	4782
9:20	**M** wrote these things, and sent letters	4782
9:23	and as **M** had written unto them;	4782
9:29	the daughter of Abihail, and **M** the Jew,	4782
9:31	times *appointed*, according as **M** the Jew	4782
10: 2	and the declaration of the greatness of **M**,	4782
10: 3	For **M** the Jew *was* next unto king	4782

MORDECAI'S (2) [MORDECAI]

Ref	Text	Strong
Est 2:22	Esther certified the king *thereof* in **M**	4782
3: 4	to see whether **M** matters would stand:	4782

MORE (657) [= MO, = MOE, MOREOVER, MUCH]

Ref	Text	Strong
Ge 3: 1	Now the serpent was **m** subtil **than** any	4480
8:12	returned not again unto him any **m**.	5750
8:21	I will not again curse the ground any **m**	5750
8:21	neither will I again smite any **m** every	5750
9:11	neither shall all flesh be cut off any **m** by	5750
9:11	neither shall there any **m** be a flood to	5750
9:15	the waters shall no **m** become a flood to	5750
17: 5	Neither shall thy name any **m** be called	5750
29:30	he loved also Rachel **m than** Leah,	4480
32:28	Thy name shall be called no **m** Jacob,	5750
34:19	he *was* **m** honourable **than** all the house	4480
35:10	thy name shall not be called any **m** Jacob,	5750
36: 7	For their riches were **m** than that they	7227
37: 3	Now Israel loved Joseph **m than** all his	4480
37: 4	father loved him **m than** all his brethren,	4480
37: 5	and they hated him **yet the m**.	3254+5750
37: 8	they hated him **yet** the **m** for his	3254+5750
37: 9	said, Behold, I have dreamed a dream **m**;	5750
38:26	said, She hath been **m** righteous **than** I;	4480
38:26	my son. And he knew her again no **m**.	5750
44:23	with you, ye shall see my face no **m**.	3254
Ex 1:12	**the m** they afflicted them,	834+3509.1
1:12	**the m** they multiplied and grew.	3651
5: 7	Ye shall no **m** give the people straw to	3254
5: 9	let there **m** work be laid upon the men,	3513
8:29	let not Pharaoh deal deceitfully any **m** in	3254
9:28	that there be no **m** mighty thunderings	NIH
9:29	neither shall there be any **m** hail;	5750
9:34	he sinned yet **m**, and hardened his heart,	3254
10:28	take heed to thyself, see my face no **m**;	5750
10:29	well, I will see thy face again no **m**.	5750
11: 1	Yet will I bring one plague **m** upon	NIH
11: 6	none like it, nor shall be like it any **m**.	3254
14:13	ye shall see them again no **m** for ever.	5750
16:17	did so, and gathered, some **m**, some less.	7235
30:15	The rich shall not give **m**, and the poor	7235
36: 5	The people bring **much m** than enough	7235
36: 6	Let neither man nor woman make any **m**	5750
Lev 6: 5	shall add the fifth *part* **m** thereto,	5921
11:42	hath **m** feet among all creeping	7235
Lev 13: 5	priest shall shut him up seven days **m**:	8145
13:33	up *him that hath* the scall seven days **m**:	8145
13:54	and that shall shut it up seven days **m**:	8145
17: 7	they shall no **m** offer their sacrifices unto	5750
26:18	I will punish you seven *times* **m** for your	3254
27:20	it shall not be redeemed any **m**.	5750
Nu 3:46	of Israel, which are **m** than the Levites;	5736
8:25	the service *thereof*, and shall serve no **m**:	5750
18: 5	that there be no wrath **any m** upon	5750
22:15	**m**, and more honourable than they.	7227
22:15	more, and more honourable than they.	4480
22:18	of the Lord my God, to do less or **m**.	1419
22:19	know what the Lord will say unto me **m**.	3254
26:54	many thou shalt **give** the **m** inheritance,	7235
33:54	the moe ye shall **give** the **m** inheritance.	7235
Dt 3:26	speak no **m** unto me of this matter.	3254+5750
5:22	he **added** no **m**. And he wrote them in	3254+5750
5:25	voice of the Lord our God **any m**,	3254+5750
10:16	of your heart, and be no **m** stiffnecked.	5750
13:11	shall do no **m** any such wickedness as this	3254
17:13	and fear, and do no **m** presumptuously.	5750
17:16	Ye shall henceforth return no **m** that way.	5750
18:16	neither let me see this great fire **any m**,	5750
19:20	shall henceforth commit no **m** any such	5750
20: 1	and chariots, *and* a people **m** than thou,	7227
28:68	unto thee, Thou shalt see it no **m** again:	5750
31: 2	*this* day; I can no **m** go out and come in:	5750
31:27	and **how much m** after my death?	637+3588
Jos 2:11	neither did there remain **any m** courage	5750
5: 1	neither was there spirit in them **any m**,	5750
5:12	had the children of Israel manna **any m**;	5750
7:12	neither will I be with you **any m**, except	3254
23:13	**m** drive out any of these nations from	3254
Jdg 2:19	corrupted *themselves* **m than** their	4480
8:28	so that they lifted up their heads no **m**.	3254
10:13	wherefore I will deliver you no **m**.	3254
13:21	the angel of the Lord did no **m**	3254+5750
15: 3	Now shall I be **m** blameless **than**	4480
18:24	what have I **m**? and what *is* this *that* ye	4480
Ru 1:17	the Lord do so to me, and **m** also,	3254
3:10	*for* thou hast **shewed m** kindness than	3190
1Sa 1:18	and her countenance was no **m** *sad*.	5750
2: 3	Talk no **m** *so* exceeding proudly; let *not*	7235
3:17	God do so to thee, and **m** also, if thou	3254
7:13	came no **m** into the coast of Israel:	3254+5750
14:30	**How much m**, if haply the people	637+3588
14:44	Saul answered, God do so and **m** also:	3254
15:35	Samuel **came** no **m** to see Saul until	3254
18: 2	let him go no **m** home *to* his father's	3808
18: 8	*what* can he have **m** but the kingdom?	3254
18:29	Saul was yet the **m** afraid of David;	4480
18:30	David behaved himself **m** wisely **than**	4480
20:13	Lord do so and much **m** to Jonathan:	3254
22:15	knew nothing of all this, less or **m**.	1419
23: 3	**how much m** then if we come to Keilah	637
24:17	to David, Thou *art* **m** righteous **than** I:	4480
25:22	**m** also do God unto the enemies of David	3254
25:36	less or **m**, until the morning light.	1419
26:21	for I will no **m** do thee harm, because my	5750
27: 1	to seek me **any m** in any coast of Israel:	5750
27: 4	Gath: and he sought no **m** again for him.	5750
28:15	answereth me no **m**, neither by prophets,	5750
30: 4	until they had **no m** power to weep.	369
2Sa 2:28	stood still, and pursued after Israel no **m**,	3254
2:28	no more, neither fought they **any m**.	5750
3: 9	So do God to Abner, and **m** also, except,	3254
3:35	and also, if I taste bread, or ought else,	5750
4:11	**How much m**, when wicked men have	637
6:22	I will yet be **m** vile **than** thus, and will be	4480
7:10	in a place of their own, and move no **m**;	5750
7:10	of wickedness afflict them **any m**,	3254
7:20	what can David say **m** unto thee?	3254+5750
10:19	to help the children of Ammon **any m**.	5750
11:25	make thy battle ***m*** strong against the city,	NIH
14:10	and he shall not touch thee **any m**.	3254+5750
14:11	the revengers of blood to destroy **any m**,	7235
16:11	**how much m** now *may this*	637+3588
18: 8	the wood devoured **m** people that day	7235
19:13	God do so to me, and **m** also, if	3254+3541
19:28	have I yet to cry **any m** unto the king?	5750
19:29	Why speakest thou **any m** of thy matters?	5750
19:35	can I hear **any m** the voice of singing	5750
19:43	we have also **m** *right* in David **than** ye:	4480
20: 6	Bichri do us **m** harm **than** *did* Absalom:	4480
21:17	Thou shalt go no **m** out with us to battle,	5750
23:23	He was **m** honourable **than** the thirty,	4480
1Ki 2:23	God do so to me, and **m** also,	3254
2:32	two men **m** righteous and better **than**	4480
10: 5	of the Lord; there was no **m** spirit in her.	5750
10:10	came no **m** such abundance of spices	5750
16:33	Ahab did **m** to provoke the Lord God of	3254
19: 2	So let the gods do to *me*, and **m** also,	3254
20:10	said, The gods do so unto me, and **m** also,	3254
2Ki 2:12	he saw him no **m**: and he took hold of his	5750
2:21	shall not be from thence **any m** death	5750
4: 6	he said unto her, *There is* not a vessel **m**.	5750
6:23	So the bands of Syria came no **m**	3254+5750
6:31	he said, God do so and **m** also to me,	3254
9:35	they found no **m** of her than the skull,	3808
12: 7	receive no ***m*** money of your acquaintance,	NIH
12: 8	priests consented to receive no ***m*** money	NIH
21: 8	**any m** out of the land which I gave their	3254
21: 9	seduced them to do **m** evil **than**	4480
24: 7	the king of Egypt came not again **any m**	5750
1Ch 4: 9	was **m** honourable **than** his brethren:	4480

1Ch	11:21 he was **m** honourable **than** the two;	871.1
	17: 9 in their place, and shall be moved no **m**;	5750
	17: 9 of wickedness waste them any **m**,	3254
	17:18 What can David *speak* **m** to thee	3254+5750
	19:19 help the children of Ammon any **m**.	5750
	23:26 *they* shall no **m** carry the tabernacle,	NIH
2Ch	1: 4 of the LORD; there was no **m** spirit in her.	5750
	10:11 yoke upon you, I will **put m** to your yoke:	3254
	15:19 there was no **m** war unto the five and	5750
	20:25 **m than** they could carry away:	369+3807.1
	25: 9 The LORD is able to give thee **much m**	7235
	28:13 *already*, ye intend to add **m** to our sins	NIH
	28:22 did he trespass yet **m** against the LORD:	3254
	29:34 **m** upright in heart to sanctify	
	themselves **than**	4480
	32:16 his servants spake yet **m** against the LORD	NIH
	33: 8 Neither will I any **m** remove the foot of	3254
	33:23 but Amon trespassed **m and more**.	7235
	33:23 but Amon trespassed **more and m**.	7235
Ezr	7:20 whatsoever **m** *shall be* needful for	7606
Ne	2:17 of Jerusalem, that we be no **m** a reproach.	5750
	13:18 yet ye **bring m** wrath upon Israel by	3254
	13:21 From that time forth came they no **m** on	NIH
Est	1:19 That Vashti come no **m** before king	NIH
	2:14 she came in unto the king no **m**, except	5750
	2:17 favour in his sight **m than** all the virgins;	4480
	4:13 *in* the king's house, **m than** all the Jews.	4480
	6: 6 delight to do honour **m than** to myself?	3148
Job	3:21 and dig for it **m than** for hid treasures;	4480
	4:17 Shall mortal man be **m** just **than** God?	4480
	4:17 shall a man be **m** pure **than** his Maker?	4480
	7: 7 *is* wind: mine eye shall no **m** see good.	7725
	7: 8 see me no **m**: thine eyes *are* upon me,	NIH
	7: 9 down *to* the grave shall come up no **m**.	NIH
	7:10 He shall return no **m** to his house,	5750
	7:10 neither shall his place know him any **m**.	5750
	14:12 till the heavens *be* no **m**, they shall not	1115
	15:16 **How much m** abominable and	637+3588
	20: 9 also *which* saw him shall *see him* no **m**;	3254
	20: 9 neither shall his place any **m** behold him.	5750
	23:12 of his mouth **m than** my necessary *food*.	4480
	24:20 he shall be no **m** remembered;	5750
	32:15 They were amazed, they answered no **m**:	5750
	32:16 but stood still, *and* answered no **m**:)	5750
	34:19 the rich **m than** the poor?	6440+3807.1
	34:23 he will not lay upon man **m** *than* right;	5750
	34:31 *chastisement*, I will not offend any **m**:	NIH
	34:32 if I have done iniquity, I will **do** no **m**.	3254
	35: 2 My righteousness **m** *than* God's?	4480
	35:11 Who teacheth us **m than** the beasts of	4480
	41: 8 upon him, remember the battle, **do** no **m**.	3254
	42:12 latter end of Job **m than** his beginning.	4480
M Ps	4: 7 **m than** *in* the time *that* their corn and	4480
	10:18 the man of the earth may no **m**	3254+5750
	19:10 **M** to be desired *are they* **than** gold, yea,	4480
	39:13 before I go hence, and be no **m**.	369
	41: 8 *now* that he lieth he shall rise up no **m**.	3254
	52: 3 Thou lovest evil **m than** good;	4480
	71:14 praise thee **m and more**.	3254+3605+5921
	71:14 praise thee **more and m**.	3254+3605+5921
	73: 7 they **have m** than heart could wish.	5674
	74: 9 *there is* no **m** any prophet: neither *is*	5750
	76: 4 Thou *art* **m** glorious *and* excellent **than**	4480
	77: 7 and will he be favourable no **m**?	3254+5750
	78:17 they sinned yet **m** against him by	3254+5750
	83: 4 that the name of Israel may be no **m** in	5750
	87: 2 of Zion **m than** all the dwellings of Jacob.	4480
	88: 5 grave, whom thou rememberest no **m**:	5750
	103:16 and the place thereof shall know it no **m**.	5750
	104:35 of the earth, and let the wicked be no **m**.	5750
	115:14 LORD shall **increase** you **m and more**,	3254
	115:14 LORD shall **increase** you **more and m**,	3254
	119:99 I have **m** understanding **than** all my	4480
	119:100 I understand **m than** the ancients,	4480
	130: 6 My soul *waiteth* for the Lord **m than** they	4480
	130: 6 I say, **m** than they that watch for	NIH
Pr	3:15 She *is* **m** precious **than** rubies: and all	4480
	4:18 that **shineth m and more** unto	215+1980
	4:18 that **shineth more and m** unto	215+1980
	10:25 so *is* the wicked no **m**: but the righteous	NIH
	11:24 *there is* that withholdeth **m than** is meet,	4480
	11:31 **much m** the wicked and the sinner.	637+3588
	12:26 The righteous *is* **m** excellent **than** his	4480
	15:11 **how much m** then the hearts of	637+3588
	17:10 reproof entereth **m** into a wise *man* **than**	4480
	19: 7 **how much m** do his friends go far	637+3588
	21: 3 is acceptable to the LORD **than** sacrifice.	4480
	21:27 **how much m**, *when* he bringeth it	637+3588
	26:12 *there is* **m** hope of a fool **than** of him.	4480
	28:23 afterwards shall find **m** favour **than** he	4480
	29:20 *there is* **m** hope of a fool **than** of him.	4480
	30: 2 Surely I *am* **m** brutish **than** *any* man,	4480
	30:15 and thy merry no **m**.	5750
Ecc	1:16 have **gotten m** wisdom than all *they* that	3254
	2: 9 **increased m** than all that were before me	3254
	2:15 even to me; and why was I then **m** wise?	3148
	2:16 of the wise **m than** of the fool for ever;	5973
	2:25 who else can hasten *hereunto*, **m** than I?	2351
	4: 2 dead **m than** the living which are yet	4480
	4:13 who will no **m** be admonished.	5750
	5: 1 *be* **m** ready to hear, **than** to give	4480
	6: 3 known *any thing*: this hath **m** rest **than**	4480
	6: 8 For what hath the wise **m than** the fool?	3148
	7:19 Wisdom strengtheneth the wise **m than**	4480
	7:26 I find **m** bitter **than** death the woman,	4480

Ecc	9: 5 neither have they **any m** a reward;	5750
	9: 6 neither have they **any m** a portion for	5750
	9:17 **m than** the cry of him that ruleth among	4480
	10:10 edge, then must he **put** to **m** strength:	1396
SS	1: 4 we will remember thy love **m than** wine:	4480
	5: 9 What *is* thy beloved **m than** *another*	4480
	5: 9 What *is* thy beloved **m than** *another*	4480
Isa	1: 5 Why should ye be stricken **any m**? ye will	5750
	1: 5 will revolt **m and more**: the whole head	3254
	1: 5 will revolt **more and m**: the whole head	3254
	1:13 Bring no **m** vain oblations; incense *is* an	3254
	2: 4 neither shall they learn war **any m**.	5750
	5: 4 What could have been done **m** to my	5750
	9: 1 afterward did **m** grievously afflict *her by*	3513
	10:20 no **m** again stay upon him that smote	3254
	13:12 I will make a man **m** precious **than** fine	3254
	15: 9 I will bring **m** upon Dimon, lions upon	3254
	19: 7 wither, be driven away, and *be* no **m**.	NIH
	23:10 of Tarshish: *there is* no **m** strength.	5750
	23:12 he said, Thou shalt no **m** rejoice,	3254+5750
	26:21 her blood, and shall no **m** cover her slain.	3254
	30:19 thou shalt **weep** no **m**: he will be	1058+1058
	30:20 teachers be removed into a corner **any m**,	3254
	32: 5 vile person be no **m** called liberal,	5750
	38:11 I shall behold man no **m** with	5750
	47: 1 for thou shalt no **m** be called tender and	3254
	47: 5 for thou shalt no **m** be called, The lady of	3254
	51:22 of my fury; thou shalt no **m** drink it again:	3254
	52: 1 for henceforth there shall no **m** come into	5750
	52:14 visage *was* so marred **m than** *any* man,	4480
	52:14 and his form **m than** the sons of men:	4480
	54: 1 for **m** *are* the children of the desolate	7227
	54: 4 the reproach of thy widowhood **any m**.	5750
	54:12 of Noah should no **m** go over the earth;	5750
	56:12 be as this day, *and* much **m** abundant.	1419
	60:18 Violence shall no **m** be heard in thy land,	5750
	60:19 The sun shall be no **m** thy light by day;	5750
	60:20 Thy sun shall no **m** go down; neither shall	5750
	62: 4 Thou shalt no **m** be termed Forsaken;	5750
	62: 4 neither shall thy land **any m** be termed	5750
	62: 8 Surely I will no **m** give thy corn *to be*	5750
	65:19 the voice of weeping shall be no **m** heard	5750
	65:20 There shall be no **m** thence an infant of	5750
Jer	2:31 are lords; we will come no **m** unto thee?	5750
	3:11 herself **m than** treacherous Judah.	4480
	3:16 saith the LORD, they shall say no **m**,	5750
	3:16 visit *it*; neither shall *that* be done **any m**.	5750
	3:17 neither shall they walk **any m** after	5750
	7:32 that it shall no **m** be called Tophet,	5750
	10:20 *is* none to stretch forth my tent **any m**,	5750
	11:19 that his name may be no **m** remembered.	5750
	16:14 saith the LORD, that it shall no **m** be said,	5750
	19: 6 this place shall no **m** be called Tophet,	5750
	20: 9 of him, nor speak **any m** in his name.	5750
	22:10 he shall return no **m**, nor see his native	5750
	22:11 He shall not return thither **any m**.	5750
	22:12 him captive, and shall see this land no **m**.	5750
	22:30 of David, and ruling **any m** in Judah.	5750
	23: 4 they shall fear no **m**, nor be dismayed,	5750
	23: 7 saith the LORD, that they shall no **m** say,	5750
	23:36 of the LORD shall ye mention no **m**:	5750
	25:27 spue, and fall, and rise no **m**, because of	5750
	30: 8 strangers shall no **m** serve themselves of	5750
	31:12 they shall not sorrow **any m at all**.	3254+5750
	31:29 In those days they shall say no **m**,	5750
	31:34 they shall teach no **m** every man his	5750
	31:34 and I will remember their sin no **m**.	5750
	31:40 nor thrown down **any m** for ever.	5750
	33:24 that *they* should be no **m** a nation before	5750
	34:10 should serve themselves of them **any m**,	5750
	38: 9 he is: for *there is* no **m** bread in the city.	5750
	42:18 and ye shall see this place no **m**.	5750
	44:26 that my name shall no **m** be named in	5750
	46:23 because they are **m** than the grasshoppers,	7231
	48: 2 There shall be no **m** praise of Moab:	5750
	49: 7 of hosts; *Is* wisdom no **m** in Teman?	5750
	50:39 it shall be no **m** inhabited for ever;	5750
	51:44 not flow *together* any **m** unto him: **yea**,	1571
La	2: 9 the law *is* no **m**; her prophets also find no	NIH
	4: 7 they were **m** ruddy *in* body **than** rubies,	4480
	4:15 They shall no **m** sojourn *there*.	3254
	4:16 divided them; he will no **m** regard them:	3254
	4:22 will no **m** carry thee away into captivity:	3254
Eze	5: 6 into wickedness **m than** the nations,	4480
	5: 6 my statutes **m than** the countries that *are*	4480
	5: 7 Because ye multiplied **m than** the nations	4480
	5: 9 whereunto I will not do **any m** the like,	5750
	6:14 **m** desolate **than** the wilderness toward	5750
	12:23 shall no **m** use it as a proverb in Israel;	5750
	12:24 For there shall be no **m** any vain vision	5750
	12:25 come to pass; it shall be no **m** prolonged:	5750
	12:28 none of my words be prolonged **any m**,	5750
	13:15 wall *is* no **m**, neither they that daubed	NIH
	13:21 they shall be no **m** in your hand to be	5750
	13:23 Therefore ye shall see no **m** vanity,	5750
	14:11 That the house of Israel may go no **m**	5750
	14:11 neither be polluted **any m** with all their	5750
	14:21 **How much m** when I send my four	637+3588
	15: 2 What is the vine tree **m than** any tree,	4480
	16:41 and thou also shalt give no hire **any m**.	5750
	16:42 I will be quiet, and will be no **m** angry.	5750
	16:47 corrupted **m than** they in all thy ways.	4480
	16:51 thine abominations **m than** they,	4480
	16:52 hast committed **m** abominable **than** they:	4480
	16:52 they are **m** righteous **than** thou: yea,	4480

Eze	16:63 never open thy mouth **any m**, because	5750
	18: 3 ye shall not have *occasion* **any m** to use	5750
	19: 9 that his voice should no **m** be heard upon	5750
	20:39 pollute ye my holy name no **m** with your	5750
	21: 5 of his sheath: it shall not return **any m**.	5750
	21:13 it shall be no **m**, saith the Lord GOD.	NIH
	21:27 it shall be no **m**, until he come whose	NIH
	21:32 the land; thou shalt be no **m** remembered:	NIH
	23:11 **m** corrupt in her inordinate love than she,	NIH
	23:11 in her whoredoms **m than** her sister in	4480
	23:27 unto them, nor remember Egypt **any m**.	5750
	24:13 not be purged from thy filthiness **any m**,	5750
	24:27 and thou shalt speak, and be no **m** dumb:	5750
	26:13 sound of thy harps shall be no **m** heard.	5750
	26:14 nets upon; thou shalt be built no **m**:	5750
	26:21 *shalt* be no **m**: though thou be sought	5750
	27:36 a terror, and never *shalt* be **any m**.	5704+5769
	28:19 and never *shalt* thou be **any m**.	5704+5769
	28:24 there shall be no **m** a pricking brier unto	5750
	29:15 neither shall it exalt itself **any m** above	5750
	29:15 **that** *they* shall no **m** rule over	1115+3807.1
	29:16 shall be no **m** the confidence of the house	5750
	30:13 there shall be no **m** a prince of the land of	5750
	32:13 shall the foot of man trouble them **any m**,	5750
	33:22 was opened, and I was no **m** dumb.	5750
	34:10 the shepherds feed themselves **any m**;	5750
	34:22 my flock, and they shall no **m** be a prey;	5750
	34:28 they shall no **m** be a prey to the heathen,	5750
	34:29 they shall be no **m** consumed with hunger	5750
	34:29 bear the shame of the heathen **any m**.	5750
	36:12 thou shalt no **m** henceforth bereave them	5750
	36:14 Therefore thou shalt devour men no **m**,	5750
	36:14 neither bereave thy nations **any m**, saith	5750
	36:15 in thee the shame of the heathen **any m**,	5750
	36:15 bear the reproach of the people **any m**,	5750
	36:30 that ye shall receive no **m** reproach of	5750
	37:22 they shall be no **m** two nations,	5750
	37:22 into two kingdoms **any m at all**:	5750+5750
	37:23 shall they defile themselves **any m**	5750
	39: 7 let *them* pollute my holy name **any m**:	5750
	39:28 and have left none of them **any m** there.	5750
	39:29 Neither will I hide my face **any m** from	5750
	42: 6 *the building* was straitened **m than**	4480
	43: 7 shall the house of Israel no **m** defile,	5750
	45: 8 my princes shall no **m** oppress my people;	5750
Da	2:30 wisdom that I have **m** than any living,	871.2
	3:19 *times* **m** than *it was* wont to be heat.	5922
	7:20 whose look *was* **m** stout **than** his fellows.	4481
	11: 8 he shall continue *m* years than the king of	NIH
Hos	1: 6 for I will no **m** have mercy upon	3254+5750
	2:16 call *me* Ishi; and shalt call me no **m** Baali.	5750
	2:17 they shall no **m** be remembered by their	5750
	6: 6 the knowledge of God **m than** burnt	4480
	9:15 out of mine house, I will love them no **m**:	3254
	13: 2 they sin **m and more**, and have made	3254
	13: 2 they sin **more and m**, and have made	3254
	14: 3 neither will we say **any m** to the work of	5750
	14: 8 shall *say*, What have I to do **any m**	5750
Joel	2: 2 the like, neither shall be any **m** after it,	3254
	2:19 I will no **m** make you a reproach among	5750
	3:17 no strangers pass through her **any m**.	5750
Am	5: 2 of Israel is fallen; she shall no **m** rise:	3254
	7: 8 I will not again pass by them **any m**:	5750
	7:13 prophesy not again **any m** *at* Beth-el: for	5750
	8: 2 I will not again pass by them **any m**:	5750
	9:15 they shall no **m** be pulled up out of their	5750
Jnh	4:11 wherein are **m than** sixscore thousand	7235
Mic	4: 3 neither shall they learn war **any m**.	5750
	5:12 and thou shalt have no **m** soothsayers:	NIH
	5:13 thou shalt no **m** worship the work of	5750
Na	1:12 afflicted thee, I will afflict thee no **m**.	5750
	1:14 *that* no **m** of thy name be sown:	5750
	1:15 for the wicked shall no **m** pass	3254+5750
	2:13 the voice of thy messengers shall no **m** be	5750
Hab	1: 8 are **m** fierce **than** the evening wolves:	4480
	1:13 *the man that is* **m** righteous **than** he?	4480
Zep	3:11 shalt no **m** be haughty	3254+5750+3807.1
	3:15 of thee: thou shalt not see evil **any m**.	5750
Zec	9: 8 oppressor shall pass through them **any m**:	5750
	11: 6 For I will no **m** pity the inhabitants of	5750
	13: 2 that they shall no **m** be remembered:	5750
	14:11 and there shall be no **m** utter destruction;	5750
	14:21 in that day there shall be no **m**	5750
Mal	2:13 that *he* regardeth not the offering **any m**,	5750
Mt	5:37 for whatsoever is **m than** these cometh of	4053
	5:47 what do ye **m** *than others*? do not even	4053
	6:25 shall put on. Is not the life **m than** meat,	4183
	6:30 *shall* he not much **m** *clothe* you, O ye of	3123
	7:11 how much **m** shall your Father which is in	3123
	10:15 be **m tolerable** for the land of Sodom	414
	10:25 how much **m** *shall they call* them of his	3123
	10:31 ye are of **m** value **than** many sparrows.	1308
	10:37 mother **m than** me is not worthy of me:	5228
	10:37 daughter **m than** me is not worthy of me.	5228
	11: 9 I say unto you, and **m than** a prophet.	4053
	11:22 It shall be **m tolerable** for Tyre and Sidon	414
	11:24 that it shall be **m tolerable** for the land of	414
	12:45 other spirits **m wicked than** himself,	4191
	13:12 be given, and he shall have **m** abundance:	NIG
	18:13 he rejoiceth **m** of that *sheep*, than of	3123
	18:16 *thee*, then take with thee one or two **m**,	2089
	19: 6 Wherefore they are no **m** twain,	3765
	20:10 that they should have received **m**;	4183
	20:31 they cried the **m**, saying, Have mercy	3187

Mt
23:15 **twofold m** *the* child of hell **than** 1362
26:53 he shall presently give me **m** than twelve 4183
27:23 But they cried out the **m**, saying, Let him 4057

Mk
1:45 insomuch that *Jesus* could no **m** openly 3371
4:24 and unto you that hear shall **m** be **given**. 4369
6:11 It shall be **m tolerable** for Sodom and 414
7:12 ye suffer him **no m** to do ought for his 3765
7:36 tell no *man:* but the **m** he charged them, 3745
7:36 **much** the **m** a great deal they published 3123
8:14 in the ship with them **m than** one loaf. 1508
9: 8 they saw no *man* **any m**, save Jesus only 3765
9:25 out of him, and enter **no m** into him. 3371
10: 8 then they are **no m** twain, but one flesh. 3765
10:48 but he cried the **m** a great deal, *Thou* Son 3123
12:33 is **m than** all whole burnt offerings and 4183
12:43 this poor widow hath cast **m** in, **than** 4183
14: 5 For it might have been sold for **m than** 1883
14:25 I will drink **no m** of the fruit of the vine, 3765
14:31 he spake the **m** vehemently, If I should 3123
15:14 And they cried out the **m exceedingly**, 4056

Lk
3:13 Exact no **m** than that which is appointed 4183
5:15 *much* the **m** went there a fame abroad of 3123
7:26 unto you, and **much m than** a prophet. 4054
9:13 We have no **m** but five loaves and 4183
10:12 that it shall be **m tolerable** in that day for 414
10:14 But it shall be **m tolerable** for Tyre and 414
10:35 whatsoever thou **spendest m**, when I 4325
11:13 how much **m** shall *your* heavenly Father 3123
11:26 other spirits **m wicked than** himself, 4191
12: 4 that have no **m** that *they* can do. 4055+5100
12: 7 ye are of **m value than** many sparrows. 1308
12:23 The life is **m than** meat, and the body *is* 4183
12:23 meat, and the body *is* **m** than raiment. NIG
12:24 how much **m** are ye better than the fowls? 3123
12:28 how much **m** *will he clothe* you, O ye of 4054
12:48 of him they will ask the **m**. 4054
14: 8 lest a **m honourable** *man* than thou be 1784
15: 7 **m** than over ninety and nine just *persons* NIG
15:19 am **no m** worthy to be called thy son: 3765
15:21 am **no m** worthy to be called thy son. 3765
18:30 Who shall not receive **manifold m** in this 4179
18:39 but he cried **so** much the **m**, *Thou* Son of 3123
20:36 Neither can they die **any m**: for they are 2089
21: 3 that this poor widow hath cast in **m than** 4183
22:16 unto you, I will not **any m** eat thereof, 3765
22:44 in an agony he prayed **m earnestly**: 1617
23: 5 And they were the **m fierce**, saying, 2001

Jn
5:14 sin **no m**, lest a worse *thing* come unto 3371
5:18 Therefore the Jews sought the **m** to kill 3123
6:66 went back, and walked **no m** with him. 3765
8:11 do I condemn thee: go, and sin **no m**. 3371
10:10 that they might have *it* **m** abundantly. NIG
11:54 walked **no m** openly among the Jews; 3765
12:43 For they loved the praise of men **m** than 3123
14:19 while, and the world seeth me **no m**; 3765
15: 2 purgeth it, that it may bring forth **m** fruit. 4183
15: 4 **no m** can ye, except ye abide in me. 3761
16:10 I go to my Father, and ye see me **no m**; 3765
16:21 she remembereth **no m** the anguish, 3765
16:25 when I shall **no m** speak unto you in 3765
17:11 And *now* I am **no m** in the world, 3765
19: 8 heard that saying, he was the **m** afraid; 3123
21:15 of Jonas, lovest thou me **m than** these? 4183

Ac
4:19 to hearken unto you **m** than unto God, 3123
5:14 And believers were the **m** added to 3123
8:39 that the eunuch saw him **no m**: 3765
9:22 But Saul increased the **m** in strength, 3123
13:34 *now* **no m** to return to corruption, he said 3371
17:11 These were **m noble** than those in 2104
18:26 unto him the way of God **m perfectly**. 197
19:32 the **m part** knew not wherefore they 4183
20:25 kingdom of God, shall see my face **no m**. 3765
20:35 It is **m blessed** to give than to receive. 3123
20:38 that they should see his face **no m**. 3765
22: 2 tongue to them, they kept the **m** silence: 3123
23:13 And they were **m** *than* forty which had 4183
23:15 something **m perfectly** concerning him: 197
23:20 inquire somewhat of him **m perfectly**. 197
24:10 I do the **m cheerfully** answer for myself: 2115
24:22 having **m perfect** knowledge of *that* way, 197
25: 6 And when he had tarried among them **m** 4183
27:11 **m** than those *things* which were spoken 3123
27:12 the **m part** advised to depart thence also, 4183

Ro
1:25 served the creature **m than** the Creator, 3844
2:18 the *things* that are **m excellent**, 1308
3: 7 For if the truth of God hath *m* abounded NIG
5: 9 Much **m** then, being now justified by his 3123
5:10 much **m**, being reconciled, we shall be 3123
5:15 much **m** the grace of God, and the gift by 3123
5:17 much **m** they which receive abundance of 3123
5:20 abounded, grace did **much m abound**: 5248
6: 9 being raised from the dead dieth **no m**; 3765
6: 9 death hath **no m** dominion over him. 3765
7:17 then it is **no m** I that do it, but sin that 3765
7:20 is **no m** I that do it, but sin that dwelleth 3765
8:37 **m than conquerors** through him that 5245
11: 6 And if by grace, *then* is it **no m** of works: 3765
11: 6 otherwise grace is **no m** grace. But if *it be* 3765
11: 6 if *it be* of works, *then* is it **no m** grace: 3765
11: 6 grace: otherwise work is **no m** work. 3765
11:12 the Gentiles; how much **m** their fulness? 3123
11:24 how much **m** shall these, which be 3123
12: 3 not to think *of himself* **m** highly **than** he 3844
14:13 **not** therefore judge one another **any m**: 3371
15:15 I have written the **m boldly** unto you in 5112

Ro
15:23 now having **no m** place in these parts, 3371
1Co
6: 3 how much **m things** that pertain to *this* 3386
9:19 servant unto all, that I might gain the **m**. 4183
12:22 Nay, much **m** those members of the body, 3123
12:22 seem to be **m** feeble, are necessary: 772
12:23 upon these we bestow **m abundant** 4055
12:23 our uncomely *parts* have **m abundant** 4055
12:24 having given **m abundant** honour to 4055
14:18 I speak with tongues **m than** you all: 3123
15:10 I laboured **m abundantly than** they all: 4054
2Co
1:12 and **m abundantly** to you-wards. 4056
4: 1 which I have **m abundantly** unto you. 4056
3: 9 which **m** doth the ministration of 3123
3:11 much **m** that which remaineth *is* glorious. 3123
4:17 a **far m exceeding** 1519+2596+5236+5236
5:16 yet now henceforth know we him **no m**. 3765
7: 7 mind toward me; so that I rejoiced the **m**. 3123
7:13 exceedingly the **m** joyed we for the joy of 3123
7:15 And his inward affection is **m abundant** 4056
8:17 being **m** forward, of his own accord he 4707
8:22 in many *things*, but now much **m** diligent, NIG
10: 8 For though I should boast somewhat **m** of 4054
11:23 (I speak as a fool) I *am* **m**; in labours more 5228
11:23 in labours **abundant**, in stripes above 4056
11:23 in prisons **m frequent**, in deaths oft. 4056
12:15 though the **m abundantly** I love you, 4056

Gal
1:14 being **m exceedingly** zealous of 4056
3:18 *be* of the law, *it is* **no m** of promise: 3765
4: 7 Wherefore thou art **no m** a servant, 3765

Eph
2:19 Now therefore ye are **no m** strangers and 3765
4:14 That we *henceforth* be **no m** children, 3371
4:28 Let him that stole steal **no m**: but rather 3371

Php
1: 9 that your love may abound yet **m** and 3123
1: 9 and in knowledge and *in* all judgment; 3123
1:14 are **much m** bold to speak the word 4056
1:24 to abide in the flesh *is* **m** needful for you. 316
1:26 That your rejoicing may be *m* abundant in NIG
2:12 but now much **m** in my absence, 3123
2:28 I sent him therefore the **m carefully**, that, 4708
3: 4 *whereof* he might trust in the flesh, I **m**: 3123

1Th
2:17 endeavoured the **m abundantly** to see 4056
4: 1 *so* ye would abound **m** and **more**. 3123
4: 1 *so* ye would abound more *and* **m**. NIG
4:10 brethren, that *ye* increase **m** *and more*; 3123
4:10 brethren, that *ye* increase more *and* **m**; 3123

2Ti
2:16 for they will increase unto **m** ungodliness. 4183
3: 4 lovers of pleasures **m** than lovers of God; 3123

Phm
1:16 to me, but how much **m** unto thee, 3123
1:21 knowing that thou wilt also do **m than** I 5228

Heb
1: 4 obtained a **m excellent** name than they. 1313
2: 1 we ought to give the **m earnest** 4056
3: 3 For this *man* was counted worthy of **m** 4183
3: 3 the house hath **m** honour than the house. 4183
6:17 willing **m abundantly** to shew unto 4054
7:15 And it is yet **far m** evident: for that after 4054
8: 6 But now hath he obtained a **m excellent** 1313
8:12 their iniquities will I remember **no m**. 2089
9:11 by a greater and **m perfect** tabernacle, 5046
9:14 How much **m** shall the blood of Christ, 3123
10: 2 have had **no m** conscience of sins. 2089+3367
10:17 and iniquities will I remember **no m**. 2089
10:18 of these *is, there is* **no m** offering for sin. 3765
10:25 one another; and so much the **m**, 3123
10:26 there remaineth **no m** sacrifice for sins, 3765
11: 4 God **m excellent** sacrifice than Cain, 4183
11:32 what shall I **m** say? for the time would 2089
12:19 should not be spoken to them **any m**: 4369
12:25 much **m** *shall not* we *escape*, if we turn 3123
12:26 Yet once **m** I shake not the earth only, NIG
12:27 And this *word*, Yet once **m**, signifieth NIG

Jas
4: 6 he giveth **m** grace. Wherefore he *saith*, 3187

1Pe
1: 7 *being* much **m precious** than of gold that 5093

2Pe
1:19 We have also a **m sure** word of prophecy; 949

Rev
2:19 and the last *to be* **m than** the first. 4183
3:12 of my God, and he shall go no **m** out: 2089
7:16 They shall hunger no **m**, neither thirst any 2089
7:16 hunger no more, neither thirst **any m**; 2089
9:12 there come two woes **m** hereafter. 2089
12: 8 neither was their place found **any m** in 2089
18:11 no *man* buyeth their merchandise **any m**: 3765
18:14 shalt find them **no m at all**. 3361+3756+3765
18:21 and shall be found **no m** at all. 2089
18:22 shall be heard **no m** at all in thee; 2089
18:22 craft *he be*, shall be found **any m** in thee; 2089
18:22 shall be heard **no m** at all in thee; 2089
18:23 And the light of a candle shall shine **no m** 2089
18:23 of the bride shall be heard **no m** at all in 2089
20: 3 that he should deceive the nations **no m**, 2089
21: 1 passed away; and there was **no m** sea. 2089
21: 4 and there shall be **no m death**, 2089
21: 4 neither shall there be **any m** pain: 2089
22: 3 And there shall be **no m** curse: 2089

MOREH (3)
Ge 12: 6 the place of Sichem, unto the plain of **M**. 4176
Dt 11:30 against Gilgal, beside the plains of **M**? 4176
Jdg 7: 1 of them, by the hill of **M**, in the valley. 4176

MOREOVER (171) [MORE]
Ge 24:25 She said **m** unto him, We have both 2050.1
32:20 say **ye, M**, Behold, thy servant Jacob *is* 1571
45:15 **M** he kissed all his brethren, 2050.1
47: 4 said **m** unto Pharaoh, For to sojourn 2050.1
48:22 **M** I have given to thee one portion 2050.1

Ex
3: 6 **M** he said, *I am* the God of thy father, 2050.1
3:15 God said **m** unto Moses, Thus shalt thou 5750
11: 3 **M** the man Moses *was* very great in 1571
18:21 **M** thou shalt provide out of all the 2050.1
26: 1 **M** thou shalt make the tabernacle *with* 2050.1
30:22 **M** the LORD spake unto Moses, saying, 2050.1
Lev
7:21 **M** the soul that shall touch any unclean 2050.1
7:26 **M** ye shall eat no *manner of* blood, 2050.1
14:46 **M** he that goeth into the house all 2050.1
18:20 **M** thou shalt not lie carnally with thy 2050.1
25:45 **M** of the children of the strangers 1571+2050.1
Nu
13:28 **M** we saw the children of Anak there. 1571
16:14 **M** thou hast not brought us into a land 637
33:56 **M** it shall come to pass, *that* I shall do 2050.1
35:31 **M** ye shall take no satisfaction for the 2050.1
Dt
1:28 **M** we have seen the sons of the Anakims 1571
1:39 **M** your little ones, which ye said should 2050.1
7:20 **M** the LORD thy God will send 1571+2050.1
28:45 **M** all these curses shall come upon thee 2050.1
28:60 **M** he will bring upon thee all the 2050.1
Jdg 10: 9 **M** the children of Ammon passed over 2050.1
Ru 4:10 **M** Ruth the Moabitess, the wife 1571+2050.1
1Sa
2:19 **M** his mother made him a little coat, 2050.1
12:23 **M as for** me, God forbid that I should sin 1571
14:21 **M** the Hebrews *that* were with 2050.1
17:37 David said **m**, The LORD that delivered 2050.1
20: 3 David sware **m**, and said, Thy father 5750
24:11 **M**, my father, see, yea see the skirt of 2050.1
28:19 **M** the LORD will also deliver Israel 2050.1
2Sa
7:10 **M** I will appoint a place for my people 2050.1
12: 8 I would **m** have **given** unto thee such 3254
15: 4 Absalom said **m**, Oh that I were made 2050.1
17: 1 **M** Ahithophel said unto Absalom, Let 2050.1
17:13 **M**, if he be gotten into a city, then 2050.1
21:15 the Philistines had yet war again with 2050.1
1Ki
1:47 **M** the king's servants came to bless our 1571
2: 5 **M** thou knowest also what Joab the son 2050.1
2:14 He said **m**, I have somewhat to say unto 2050.1
2:44 king said **m** to Shimei, Thou knowest 2050.1
8:41 **M** concerning a stranger, that *is* 1571+2050.1
10:18 **M** the king made a great throne of ivory 2050.1
14:14 **M** the LORD shall raise him up a king 2050.1
2Ki
12:15 **M** they reckoned not with the men, 2050.1
21:16 **M** Manasseh shed innocent blood 1571+2050.1
23:15 **M** the altar *that was* at Beth-el, 1571+2050.1
23:24 **M** the *workers* with familiar 1571+2050.1
1Ch
1: 2 *And* **m** in time past, even when Saul was 1571
12:40 **M** they *that* were nigh them, 1571+2050.1
17:10 **M** I will subdue all thine enemies. 2050.1
18:12 **M** Abishai the son of Zeruiah slew all 2050.1
22:15 **M** *there are* workmen with thee in 2050.1
23: 5 **M** four thousand *were* porters; 2050.1
25: 1 **M** David and the captains of the host 2050.1
26: 4 **M** the sons of Obed-edom *were*, 2050.1
28: 1 **M** I will establish his kingdom for ever, 2050.1
29: 3 **M**, because I have set my affection to 5750
2Ch
1: 5 **M** the brasen altar, that Bezaleel the 2050.1
2:12 Huram said **m**, Blessed *be* the LORD 2050.1
4: 1 **M** he made an altar of brass, 2050.1
4:20 **M** the candlesticks with their lamps, 2050.1
6:32 **M** concerning the stranger, 1571+2050.1
7: 7 **M** Solomon hallowed the middle of 2050.1
9:17 **M** the king made a great throne of ivory 2050.1
17: 6 he took away the high places 5750+2050.1
19: 8 **M** in Jerusalem did Jehoshaphat 1571+2050.1
21:11 **M** he made high places in the mountains 1571
21:16 **M** the LORD stirred up against Jehoram 2050.1
23: 9 **M** Jehoiada the priest delivered to 2050.1
25: 5 **M** Amaziah gathered Judah together, 2050.1
26: 2 **M** Uzziah built towers in Jerusalem at 2050.1
26:11 **M** Uzziah had a host of fighting *men*, 2050.1
27: 4 **M** he built cities in the mountains of 2050.1
28: 3 **M** he burnt incense in the valley of 2050.1
29:19 **M** all the vessels, which king Ahaz in 2050.1
29:30 Hezekiah the king and the princes 2050.1
31: 4 **M** he commanded the people that dwelt 2050.1
32:29 **M** he provided him cities, 2050.1
35: 1 **M** Josiah kept a passover unto 2050.1
36:14 **M** all the chief of the priests, 1571
Ezr
6: 8 **M** I make a decree what ye shall do to 2050.3
10:25 of Israel: of the sons of Parosh; 2050.1
Ne
2: 7 **M** I said unto the king, If it please 2050.1
3: 6 **M** the old gate repaired Jehoiada the 2050.1
3:26 **M** the Nethinims dwelt in Ophel, unto 2050.1
5:14 **M** from the time that I was appointed 1571
5:17 **M** *there were* at my table an hundred 2050.1
6:17 **M** in those days the nobles of Judah sent 2050.1
9:12 **M** thou leddest them in the day by a 2050.1
9:22 **M** thou gavest them kingdoms and 2050.1
11:19 **M** the porters, Akkub, Talmon, 2050.1
12: 8 **M** the Levites: Jeshua, Binnui, Kadmiel, 2050.1
Est 5:12 Haman said **m**, Yea, Esther the queen 2050.1
Job
27: 1 **M** Job continued his parable, and said, 2050.1
29: 1 **M** Job continued his parable, and said, 2050.1
35: 1 Elihu spake **m**, and said, 2050.1
40: 1 the LORD answered Job, and said, 2050.1
Ps
19:11 **M** by them *is* thy servant warned; 1571
78:67 **M** he refused the tabernacle of Joseph, 2050.1
105:16 **M** he called *for* a famine upon the land: 2050.1
Ecc
3:16 **m** I saw under the sun the place of 5750
5: 9 the profit of the earth is for all: 2050.1
6: 5 **M** he hath not seen the sun, nor known 1571
12: 9 **m**, because the Preacher was wise, he still 3148
Isa
7:10 the LORD saith, Because 2050.1
7:10 **M** the LORD spake again unto Ahaz, 2050.1

M

M

Isa	8: 1 **M** the Lord said unto me, Take thee a	2050.1
	19: 9 **M** they that work in fine flax,	2050.1
	29: 5 **M** the multitude of thy strangers shall	2050.1
	30:26 **M** the light of the moon shall be as	2050.1
	39: 8 He said **m**, For there shall be peace and	3588
Jer	1:11 **M**, the word of the Lord came unto	2050.1
	2: 1 **M** the word of the Lord came to me,	2050.1
	8: 4 **M** thou shalt say unto them, Thus saith	2050.1
	20: 5 **M** I will deliver all the strength of this	2050.1
	25:10 **M** I will take from them the voice of	2050.1
	33: 1 **M** the word of the Lord came unto	2050.1
	33:23 **M** the word of the Lord came to	2050.1
	37:18 Jeremiah said unto king Zedekiah,	2050.1
	39: 7 **M** he put out Zedekiah's eyes,	2050.1
	40:13 **M** Johanan the son of Kareah, and all	2050.1
	44:24 **M** Jeremiah said unto all the people,	2050.1
	48:35 **M** I will cause to cease in Moab, saith	2050.1
Eze	3: 1 **M** he said unto me, Son of man, eat that	2050.1
	3:10 **M** he said unto me, Son of man, all my	2050.1
	4: 3 **M** take thou unto thee an iron pan,	2050.1
	4:16 **M** he said unto me, Son of man, behold,	2050.1
	5:14 **M** I will make thee waste, and a	2050.1
	7: 1 **M** the word of the Lord came unto	2050.1
	11: 1 **M** the spirit lift me up, and brought me	2050.1
	12:17 **M** the word of the Lord came to me,	2050.1
	16:20 **M** thou hast taken thy sons and thy	2050.1
	16:29 Thou hast **m** multiplied thy fornication	2050.1
	17:11 **M** the word of the Lord came unto	2050.1
	19: 1 **M** take thou up a lamentation for	2050.1
	20:12 **M** also I gave them my sabbaths, to be	2050.1
	20:45 **M** the word of the Lord came unto	2050.1
	22: 1 **M** the word of the Lord came unto	2050.1
	23:36 The Lord said **m** unto me; Son of	2050.1
	23:38 **M** this they have done unto me: they	5750
	28:11 **M** the word of the Lord came unto	2050.1
	35: 1 **M** the word of the Lord came unto	2050.1
	36:16 **M** the word of the Lord came unto	2050.1
	37:16 **M**, thou son of man, take thee one	2050.1
	37:26 **M** I will make a covenant of peace with	2050.1
	45: 1 **M**, when ye shall divide *by lot* the land	2050.1
	46:18 **M** the prince shall not take of	2050.1
	48:22 **M** from the possession of the Levites,	2050.1
Zec	4: 8 **M** the word of the Lord came unto	2050.1
	5: 6 He said **m**, This *is* their resemblance	2050.1
Mt	6:16 **M** when ye fast, be not as the hypocrites,	1161
	18:15 **M** if thy brother shall trespass against thee	1161
Lk	16:21 **m** the dogs came and licked his	235+2532
Ac	2:26 **m** also my flesh shall rest in hope:	1161+2089
	11:12 **M** these six brethren accompanied me,	2532
	19:26 **M** ye see and hear, that not alone at	2532
Ro	5:20 **M** the law entered, that the offence might	1161
	8:30 **M** whom he did predestinate, them he	1161
1Co	4: 2 **M** it is required in stewards,	1161+3062+3739
	10: 1 **M**, brethren, I would not that ye should	1161
	15: 1 **M**, brethren, I declare unto you the gospel	1161
2Co	1:23 **M** I call God for a record upon my soul,	1161
	8: 1 **M**, brethren, we do you to wit of the	1161
1Ti	3: 7 **M** he must have a good report of them	1161
Heb	9:21 **M** he sprinkled with blood both	3668
	11:36 yea, **m** of bonds and imprisonment:	2089
2Pe	1:15 **M** I will endeavour that you may be able	2532

MORESHETH-GATH (1) [GATH, MORASTHITE]

Mic	1:14 Therefore shalt thou give presents to **M**:	4182

MORIAH (2)

Ge	22: 2 lovest, and get thee into the land of **M**;	4179
2Ch	3: 1 of the Lord at Jerusalem in mount **M**,	4179

MORNING (227)

Ge	1: 5 the evening and the **m** were the first day.	1242
	1: 8 the evening and the **m** were the second	1242
	1:13 the evening and the **m** were the third day.	1242
	1:19 the evening and the **m** were the fourth	1242
	1:23 the evening and the **m** were the fifth day.	1242
	1:31 the evening and the **m** were the sixth day.	1242
	19:15 the **m** arose, then the angels hastened	7837
	19:27 Abraham gat up early in the **m** to the	1242
	20: 8 Therefore Abimelech rose early in the **m**,	1242
	21:14 Abraham rose up early in the **m**,	1242
	22: 3 Abraham rose up early in the **m**,	1242
	24:54 rose up in the **m**, and he said, Send me	1242
	26:31 they rose up betimes in the **m**,	1242
	28:18 Jacob rose up early in the **m**, and took	1242
	29:25 pass, that in the **m**, behold, it *was* Leah:	1242
	31:55 early in the **m** Laban rose up,	1242
	40: 6 Joseph came in unto them in the **m**,	1242
	41: 8 came to pass in the **m** that his spirit was	1242
	44: 3 As soon as the **m** was light, the men	1242
	49:27 in the **m** he shall devour the prey,	1242
Ex	7:15 Get thee unto Pharaoh in the **m**;	1242
	8:20 Rise up early in the **m**, and stand before	1242
	9:13 Rise up early in the **m**, and stand before	1242
	10:13 *and* when it was **m**, the east wind brought	1242
	12:10 shall let nothing of it remain until the **m**;	1242
	12:10 that which remaineth of it until the **m** ye	1242
	12:22 go out at the door of his house until the **m**.	1242
	14:24 that in the **m** watch the Lord looked	1242
	14:27 sea returned to his strength when the **m**	1242
	16: 7 in the **m**, then ye shall see the glory of	1242
	16: 8 to eat, and in the **m** bread to the full;	1242
	16:12 and in the **m** ye shall be filled *with* bread;	1242
	16:13 the **m** the dew lay round about the host.	1242
	16:19 Let no man leave of it till the **m**.	1242
	16:20 some of them left of it until the **m**,	1242

Ex	16:21 they gathered it **every m**,	1242
	16:23 over lay up for you to be kept until the **m**.	1242
	16:24 they laid it up till the **m**, as Moses bade:	1242
	18:13 people stood by Moses from the **m** unto	1242
	18:14 all the people stand by thee from **m** unto	1242
	19:16 it came to pass on the third day in the **m**,	1242
	23:18 the fat of my sacrifice remain until the **m**.	1242
	24: 4 rose up early in the **m**, and builded an altar	1242
	27:21 his sons shall order it from evening to	1242
	29:34 remain unto the **m**, then thou shalt burn	1242
	29:39 The one lamb thou shalt offer in the **m**;	1242
	29:41 according to the meat offering of the **m**,	1242
	30: 7 burn thereon sweet incense **every m**:	1242+1242+871.1+871.1+1886.1+1886.1
	34: 2 be ready in the **m**, and come up in	1242
	34: 2 come up in the **m** unto mount Sinai,	1242
	34: 4 Moses rose up early in the **m**, and went	1242
	34:25 feast of the passover be left unto the **m**.	1242
	36: 3 free offerings **every m**.	1242+1242+871.1+871.1+1886.1+1886.1
Lev	6: 9 upon the altar all night unto the **m**,	1242
	6:12 burn wood on it **every m**,	1242+1242+871.1+871.1+1886.1+1886.1
	6:20 half of it in the **m**, and half thereof at	1242
	7:15 he shall not leave *any* of it until the **m**.	1242
	9:17 beside the burnt sacrifice of the **m**.	1242
	19:13 not abide with thee all night until the **m**.	1242
	24: 3 unto the **m** before the Lord continually:	1242
Nu	9:12 They shall leave none of it unto the **m**,	1242
	9:15 it were the appearance of fire, until the **m**.	1242
	9:21 the cloud abode from even unto the **m**,	1242
	9:21 the cloud was taken up in the **m**, then	1242
	14:40 they rose up early in the **m**, and gat them	1242
	22:13 Balaam rose up in the **m**, and said unto	1242
	22:21 Balaam rose up in the **m**, and saddled his	1242
	28: 4 The one lamb shalt thou offer in the **m**,	1242
	28: 8 as the meat offering of the **m**, and as	1242
	28:23 these beside the burnt offering in the **m**,	1242
Dt	16: 4 day at even, remain all night until the **m**.	1242
	16: 7 thou shalt turn in the **m**, and go unto thy	1242
	28:67 In the **m** thou shalt say, Would God it	1242
	28:67 thou shalt say, Would God it were **m**!	1242
Jos	3: 1 Joshua rose early in the **m**;	1242
	6:12 Joshua rose early in the **m**, and the priests	1242
	7:14 In the **m** therefore ye shall be brought	1242
	7:16 So Joshua rose up early in the **m**,	1242
	8:10 Joshua rose up early in the **m**,	1242
Jdg	6:28 the men of the city arose early in the **m**,	1242
	6:31 let him be put to death while *it is yet* **m**:	1242
	9:33 shall be, *that* in the **m**, as soon as the sun	1242
	16: 2 saying, In the **m**, when it is day, we shall	1242
	19: 5 they arose early in the **m**, that he rose	1242
	19: 8 he arose early in the **m** on the fifth day to	1242
	19:25 and abused her all the night until the **m**:	1242
	19:27 her lord rose up in the **m**, and opened	1242
	20:19 the children of Israel rose up in the **m**,	1242
Ru	2: 7 continued even from the **m** until now,	1242
	3:13 Tarry this night, and it shall be in the **m**,	1242
	3:13 *as* the Lord liveth: lie down until the **m**.	1242
	3:14 lay *at* his feet until the **m**: and she rose	1242
1Sa	1:19 they rose up in the **m** early,	1242
	3:15 Samuel lay until the **m**, and opened	1242
	5: 4 when they arose early on the morrow **m**,	1242
	11:11 into the midst of the host in the **m** watch,	1242
	14:36 spoil them until the **m** light, and let us	1242
	15:12 Samuel rose early to meet Saul in the **m**,	1242
	17:16 the Philistine drew near **m** and evening,	7925
	17:20 David rose up early in the **m**, and left	1242
	19: 2 take heed to thyself until the **m**,	1242
	19:11 to watch him, and to slay him in the **m**:	1242
	20:35 came to pass in the **m**, that Jonathan went	1242
	25:22 I leave of all that *pertain* to him by the **m**	1242
	25:34 **m** light *any* that pisseth against the wall.	1242
	25:36 nothing, less or more, until the **m** light.	1242
	25:37 it came to pass in the **m**, when the wine	1242
	29:10 Wherefore now rise up early in the **m**	1242
	29:10 as soon as ye be up early in the **m**,	1242
	29:11 his men rose up early to depart in the **m**,	1242
2Sa	2:27 in the **m** the people had gone up every	1242
	11:14 to pass in the **m**, that David wrote a	1242
	17:22 by the **m** light there lacked not one *of*	1242
	23: 4 *he shall be* as the light of the **m**, *when*	1242
	23: 4 the sun riseth, *even* a **m** without clouds;	1242
	24:11 when David was up in the **m**, the word	1242
	24:15 from the **m** even to the time appointed:	1242
1Ki	3:21 I rose in the **m** to give my child suck,	1242
	3:21 when I had considered it in the **m**,	1242
	17: 6 brought him bread and flesh in the **m**,	1242
	18:26 called on the name of Baal from **m** even	1242
2Ki	3:20 it came to pass in the **m**, when the meat	1242
	3:22 they rose up early in the **m**, and the sun	1242
	7: 9 if we tarry till the **m** light, *some* mischief	1242
	10: 8 *at* the entering in of the gate until the **m**.	1242
	10: 9 came to pass in the **m**, that he went out,	1242
	16:15 Upon the great altar burn the **m** burnt	1242
	19:35 when they arose early in the **m**, behold,	1242
1Ch	9:27 the opening *thereof* **every m**	1242+1242+1886.1+1886.1+3807.1+3807.1
	16:40 altar of the burnt offering continually **m**	1242
	23:30 **every m** to thank and praise the Lord,	1242+1242+871.1+871.1+1886.1+1886.1
2Ch	2: 4 *for* the burnt offerings **m** and evening,	1242
	13:11 burn unto the Lord **every m**	1242+1242+871.1+871.1+1886.1+1886.1

2Ch	20:20 they rose early in the **m**, and went forth	1242
	31: 3 *to wit*, for the **m** and evening burnt	1242
Ezr	3: 3 *even* burnt offerings **m** and evening,	1242
Ne	4:21 the rising of the **m** till the stars appeared.	7837
	8: 3 the water gate from the **m** until midday,	216
Job	1: 5 rose up early in the **m**, and offered burnt	1242
	4:20 They are destroyed from **m** to evening:	1242
	7:18 *that* thou shouldest visit him every **m**,	1242
	7:21 shalt **seek** me in the **m**, but I *shall* not	7836
	11:17 shalt shine forth, thou shalt be as the **m**.	1242
	24:17 the **m** *is* to them even as the shadow of	1242
	38: 7 When the **m** stars sang together, and all	1242
	38:12 Hast thou commanded the **m** since thy	1242
	41:18 and his eyes *are* like the eyelids of the **m**.	7837
Ps	5: 3 My voice shalt thou hear *in* the **m**,	1242
	5: 3 *in* the **m** will I direct *my prayer* unto thee	1242
	30: 5 for a night, but joy *cometh* in the **m**.	1242
	49:14 shall have dominion over them in the **m**;	1242
	55:17 Evening, and **m**, and at noon, will I pray,	1242
	59:16 I will sing aloud of thy mercy in the **m**:	1242
	65: 8 thou makest the outgoings of the **m** and	1242
	73:14 I been plagued, and chastened every **m**.	1242
	88:13 and in the **m** shall my prayer prevent thee.	1242
	90: 5 in the **m** they are like grass which	1242
	90: 6 In the **m** it flourisheth, and groweth up;	1242
	92: 2 shew forth thy lovingkindness in the **m**,	1242
	110: 3 of holiness from the womb of the **m**:	4891
	119:147 I prevented the **dawning of the m**,	5399
	130: 6 more than they that watch for the **m**:	1242
	130: 6 *more than* they that watch for the **m**.	1242
	139: 9 *If* I take the wings of the **m**, *and* dwell in	7837
	143: 8 me to hear thy lovingkindness in the **m**;	1242
Pr	7:18 let us take our fill of love until the **m**:	1242
	27:14 rising early in the **m**, it shall be counted a	1242
Ecc	10:16 *is* a child, and thy princes eat in the **m**.	1242
	11: 6 In the **m** sow thy seed, and in the	1242
SS	6:10 Who *is* she that looketh forth as the **m**,	7837
Isa	5:11 unto them that rise up early in the **m**,	1242
	14:12 from heaven, O Lucifer, son of the **m**!	7837
	17:11 In the **m** shalt thou make thy seed to	1242
	17:14 *and* before the **m** he *is* not.	1242
	21:12 The **m** cometh, and also the night:	1242
	28:19 for **m** by morning shall it pass over, by	1242
	28:19 for morning by **m** shall it pass over, by	1242
	33: 2 be thou their arm every **m**, our salvation	1242
	37:36 when they arose early in the **m**, behold,	1242
	38:13 I reckoned till **m**, *that*, as a lion, so will	1242
	50: 4 he wakeneth **m** by morning, he wakeneth	1242
	50: 4 he wakeneth morning by **m**, he wakeneth	1242
	58: 8 shall thy light break forth as the **m**,	7837
Jer	5: 8 They were *as* fed horses in the **m**:	7904
	20:16 let him hear the cry in the **m**,	1242
	21:12 Execute judgment in the **m**,	1242
La	3:23 *They are* new every **m**: great *is* thy	1242
Eze	7: 7 The **m** is come unto thee, O thou that	6843
	7:10 the **m** is gone forth; the rod hath	6843
	12: 8 in the **m** came the word of the Lord unto	1242
	24:18 So I spake unto the people in the **m**:	1242
	24:18 and I did in the **m** as I was commanded.	1242
	33:22 my mouth, until *he* came to me in the **m**;	1242
	46:13 thou shalt prepare it **every m**,	1242+1242+871.1+871.1+1886.1+1886.1
	46:14 a meat offering for it **every m**,	1242+1242+871.1+871.1+1886.1+1886.1
	46:15 **every m** *for* a continual burnt offering.	1242+1242+871.1+871.1+1886.1+1886.1
Da	6:19 the king arose very early in the **m**,	5053
	8:26 and the **m** which was told *is* true:	1242
Hos	6: 3 his going forth *is* prepared as the **m**;	7837
	6: 4 for your goodness *is* as a **m** cloud,	1242
	7: 6 in the **m** it burneth as a flaming fire.	1242
	10:15 in a **m** shall the king of Israel utterly be	7837
	13: 3 Therefore they shall be as the **m** cloud,	1242
Joel	2: 2 as the **m** spread upon the mountains:	7837
Am	4: 4 bring your sacrifices *every* **m**,	1242
	4:13 that maketh the **m** darkness,	7837
	5: 8 turneth the shadow of death into the **m**,	1242
Jnh	4: 7 God prepared a worm when the **m** rose	7837
Mic	2: 1 when the **m** is light, they practise it,	1242
Zep	3: 5 **every m** doth he bring his judgment	1242+1242+871.1+871.1+1886.1+1886.1
Mt	16: 3 And in the **m**, *It will be* foul weather to	4404
	20: 1 went out **early in the m** to hire	260+4404
	21:18 in the **m** as he returned into the city,	4405
	27: 1 the **m** was come, all the chief priests	4405
Mk	1:35 And in the **m**, rising up a great while	4404
	11:20 in the **m**, as they passed by, they saw	4404
	13:35 or at the cockcrowing, or in the **m**:	4404
	15: 1 And straightway in the **m** the chief priests	4404
	16: 2 And very **early in the m** the first *day* of	4404
Lk	21:38 all the people **came early in the m** to	3719
	24: 1 **very early in the m** they came	901+3722
Jn	8: 2 **early in the m** he came again into	3722
	21: 4 But when the **m** was now come,	4405
Ac	5:21 the temple **early in the m**,	3588+3722+5259
	28:23 *out of* the prophets, from **m** till evening.	4404
Rev	2:28 **And I will give him the m** star.	4407
	22:16 of David, *and* the bright and **m** star.	3720

MORROW (103)

Ge	19:34 came to pass on the **m**, that the firstborn	4283
Ex	8:10 he said, To **m**. And he said, Be it	4279
	8:23 and thy people: to **m** shall this sign be.	4279
	8:29 his servants, and from his people, to **m**:	4279
	9: 5 To **m** the Lord shall do this thing in	4279

Ex	9: 6 the Lord did that thing on the **m**,	4283
	9:18 to **m** about *this* time I will cause it to rain	4279
	10: 4 to **m** will I bring the locusts into thy coast	4279
	16:23 **To m** *is* the rest of the holy sabbath unto	4279
	17: 9 to **m** I will stand on the top of the hill	4279
	18:13 came to pass on the **m**, that Moses sat to	4283
	19:10 sanctify them to day and to **m**, and let	4279
	32: 5 and said, **To m** *is* a feast to the Lord.	4279
	32: 6 they rose up early on the **m**,	4283
	32:30 it came to pass on the **m**, that Moses said	4283
Lev	7:16 on the **m** also the remainder of it shall be	4283
	19: 6 the *same* day ye offer it, and on the **m**:	4283
	22:30 ye shall leave none of it until the **m**:	1242
	23:11 on the **m** after the sabbath the priest shall	4283
	23:15 ye shall count unto you from the **m** after	4283
	23:16 unto the **m** after the seventh sabbath	4283
Nu	11:18 Sanctify yourselves against to **m**,	4279
	14:25 To **m** turn you, and get you into	4279
	16: 5 Even to **m** the Lord will shew who *are*	1242
	16: 7 incense in them before the Lord to **m**:	4279
	16:16 thou, and they, and Aaron, to **m**:	4279
	16:41 on the **m** all the congregation of	4283
	17: 8 that on the **m** Moses went into	4283
	22:41 it came to pass on the **m**, that Balak took	1242
	33: 3 on the **m** after the passover the children	4283
Jos	3: 5 for to **m** the Lord will do wonders	4279
	5:11 of the land on the **m** after the passover,	4283
	5:12 the manna ceased on the **m** after they	4283
	7:13 and say, Sanctify yourselves against to **m**:	4279
	11: 6 for to **m** about this time will I deliver	4279
	22:18 to **m** he will be wroth with the whole	4279
Jdg	6:38 for he rose up early on the **m**, and thrust	4283
	9:42 it came to pass on the **m**, that the people	4283
	19: 9 to **m** get you early on your way, that thou	4279
	20:28 to **m** I will deliver them into thine hand.	4279
	21: 4 it came to pass on the **m**, that the people	4283
1Sa	5: 3 they of Ashdod arose early on the **m**,	4283
	5: 4 when they arose early on the **m** morning,	4283
	9:16 To **m** about *this* time I will send thee a	4279
	9:19 to **m** I will let thee go, 1242+871.1+1886.1	
	11: 9 To **m**, by *that* time the sun be hot, ye	4279
	11:10 To **m** we will come out unto you,	4279
	11:11 *so* on the **m**, that Saul put the people	4283
	18:10 came to pass on the **m**, that the evil spirit	4283
	19:11 thy life to night, to **m** thou *shalt be* slain.	4279
	20: 5 to **m** is the new moon, and I should not	4279
	20:12 I have sounded my father about to **m**	4279
	20:18 Jonathan said to *David*, To **m** *is* the new	4279
	20:27 it came to pass on the **m**, *which was*	4283
	28:19 to **m** *shalt* thou and thy sons *be* with me:	4279
	31: 8 it came to pass on the **m**, when	4283
2Sa	11:12 also, and to **m** I will let thee depart.	4279
	11:12 abode in Jerusalem that day, and the **m**.	4283
1Ki	19: 2 of one of them *by* to **m** about *this* time.	4279
	20: 6 I will send my servants unto thee to **m**,	4283
2Ki	6:28 him to day, and we will eat my son to **m**.	4279
	7: 1 To **m** about *this* time *shall* a measure of	4279
	7:18 shall be to **m** about *this* time in the gate	4279
	8:15 it came to pass on the **m**, that he took a	4283
	10: 6 come to me to Jezreel by to **m** *this* time.	4279
1Ch	10: 8 it came to pass on the **m**, when	4283
	29:21 on the **m** after that day, *even* a thousand	4283
2Ch	20:16 To **m** go ye down against them: behold,	4279
	20:17 be dismayed; to **m** go out against them:	4279
Est	2:14 on the **m** she returned into the second	1242
	5: 8 and I will do to **m** as the king hath said.	4279
	5:12 to **m** *am* I invited unto her also with	4279
	5:14 to **m** speak thou unto the king that	1242
	9:13 to **m** also according unto *this* day's	4279
Pr	3:28 Go, and come again, and to **m** I will give;	4279
	27: 1 Boast not thyself of to **m**; for thou 3117+4279	
Isa	22:13 us eat and drink; for to **m** we shall die.	4279
	56:12 to **m** shall be as this day, *and* much more	4279
Jer	20: 3 it came to pass on the **m**, that Pashur	4283
Zep	3: 3 they gnaw not the bones till the **m**.	1242
Mt	6:30 to day is, and to **m** is cast into the oven,	*839*
	6:34 Take therefore no thought for the **m**:	*839*
	6:34 for the **m** shall take thought for the *things*	*839*
Mk	11:12 on the **m**, when they were come from	*1887*
Lk	10:35 on the **m** when he departed, he took out	*839*
	12:28 in the field, and to **m** is cast into the oven;	*839*
	13:32 I do cures to day and to **m**, and the third	*839*
	13:33 to day, and to **m**, and the *day* following:	*839*
Ac	4: 5 And it came to pass on the **m**, that their	*1887*
	10: 9 On the **m**, as they went on their journey,	*1887*
	10:23 lodged *them*. And on the **m** Peter went	*1887*
	10:24 the **m** *after* they entered into Cesarea.	*1887*
	20: 7 unto them, ready to depart on the **m**;	*1887*
	22:30 On the **m**, because he would have known	*1887*
	23:15 that he bring him down unto you to **m**,	*839*
	23:20 bring down Paul to **m** into the council,	*839*
	23:32 On the **m** they left the horsemen to go	*1887*
	25:17 on the **m** I sat on the judgment seat,	*1836*
	25:22 To **m**, said he, thou shalt hear him.	*839*
	25:23 And on the **m**, when Agrippa was come,	*1887*
1Co	15:32 let us eat and drink; for to **m** we die.	*839*
Jas	4:13 To day or to **m** we will go into such a city,	*839*
	4:14 ye know not what *shall be* on the **m**:	*839*

MORSEL (10) [MORSELS]

Ge	18: 5 I will fetch a **m** of bread, and comfort ye	6595
Jdg	19: 5 Comfort thine heart *with* a **m** of bread,	6595
Ru	2:14 the bread, and dip thy **m** in the vinegar.	6595
1Sa	2:36 him for a piece of silver and a **m** of bread,	3603
	28:22 and let me set a **m** of bread before thee;	6595

1Ki	17:11 I pray thee, a **m** of bread in thine hand.	6595
Job	31:17 Or have eaten my **m** myself alone,	6595
Pr	17: 1 Better *is* a dry **m**, and quietness	6595
	23: 8 The **m** *which* thou hast eaten shalt thou	6595
Heb	12:16 for one **m** of meat sold his birthright.	*1035*

MORSELS (1) [MORSEL]

Ps	147:17 He casteth forth his ice like **m**: who can	6595

MORTAL (6) [MORTALITY, MORTALLY]

Job	4:17 Shall **m man** be more just than God? shall	582
Ro	6:12 not sin therefore reign in your **m** body,	*2349*
	8:11 **m** bodies by his Spirit that dwelleth in	*2349*
1Co	15:53 and this **m** *must* put on immortality,	*2349*
	15:54 and this **m** shall have put on immortality,	*2349*
2Co	4:11 might be made manifest in our **m** flesh.	*2349*

MORTALITY (1) [MORTAL]

2Co	5: 4 that **m** might be swallowed up of life.	*2349*

MORTALLY (1) [MORTAL]

Dt	19:11 smite him **m** that he die, and fleeth into	5315

MORTAR (2) [MORTER]

Nu	11: 8 or beat *it* in a **m**, and baked *it* in pans,	4085
Pr	27:22 thou shouldest bray a fool in a **m**	4388

MORTER (11) [MORTAR]

Ge	11: 3 brick for stone, and slime had they for **m**.	2563
Ex	1:14 in **m**, and in brick, and in all manner of	2563
Lev	14:42 he shall take other **m**, and shall plaister	6083
	14:45 thereof, and all the **m** of the house;	6083
Isa	41:25 he shall come *upon* princes as *upon* **m**,	2563
Eze	13:10 lo, others daubed it *with* untempered **m**:	NIH
	13:11 daub *it with* untempered **m**, that it shall	NIH
	13:14 that ye have daubed *with* untempered **m**,	NIH
	13:15 that have daubed *with* untempered **m**,	NIH
	22:28 them *with* untempered **m**, seeing vanity,	NIH
Na	3:14 into clay, and tread the **m**, make strong	2563

MORTGAGED (1)

Ne	5: 3 We have **m** our lands, vineyards,	6148

MORTIFY (2)

Ro	8:13 if ye through the Spirit do **m** the deeds of	*2289*
Col	3: 5 **M** therefore your members which are	*3499*

MOSERA (1)

Dt	10: 6 Beeroth of the children of Jaakan *to* **M**:	4149

MOSEROTH (2)

Nu	33:30 from Hashmonah, and encamped at **M**.	4149
	33:31 they departed from **M**, and pitched in	4149

MOSES (829) [MOSES']

Ex	2:10 she called his name **M**: and she said,	4872
	2:11 pass in those days, when **M** was grown,	4872
	2:14 **M** feared, and said, Surely *this* thing is	4872
	2:15 heard this thing, he sought to slay **M**.	4872
	2:15 fled from the face of Pharaoh,	4872
	2:17 **M** stood up and helped them,	4872
	2:21 **M** was content to dwell with the man:	4872
	2:21 and he gave **M** Zipporah his daughter.	4872
	3: 1 Now **M** kept the flock of Jethro his father	4872
	3: 3 And **M** said, I will now turn aside, and see this	4872
	3: 4 midst of the bush, and said, **M**, Moses.	4872
	3: 4 midst of the bush, and said, Moses, **M**.	4872
	3: 6 **M** hid his face; for he was afraid to look	4872
	3:11 **M** said unto God, Who *am* I, that I	4872
	3:13 **M** said unto God, Behold, *when* I come	4872
	3:14 God said unto **M**, I AM THAT I AM:	4872
	3:15 God said moreover unto **M**, Thus shalt	4872
	4: 1 **M** answered and said, But behold, they	4872
	4: 3 a serpent; and **M** fled from before it.	4872
	4: 4 the Lord said unto **M**, Put forth thine	4872
	4:10 **M** said unto the Lord, O my Lord, I *am*	4872
	4:14 of the Lord was kindled against **M**,	4872
	4:18 **M** went and returned to Jethro his father	4872
	4:18 And Jethro said to **M**, Go in peace.	4872
	4:19 the Lord said unto **M** in Midian,	4872
	4:20 **M** took his wife and his sons, and set	4872
	4:20 and **M** took the rod of God in his hand.	4872
	4:21 the Lord said unto **M**, When thou goest	4872
	4:27 Go into the wilderness to meet **M**.	4872
	4:28 **M** told Aaron all the words of the Lord	4872
	4:29 **M** and Aaron went and gathered together	4872
	4:30 which the Lord had spoken unto **M**,	4872
	5: 1 afterward **M** and Aaron went in,	4872
	5: 4 Wherefore do ye, **M** and Aaron,	4872
	5:20 they met **M** and Aaron, who stood in	4872
	5:22 And **M** returned unto the Lord, and said,	4872
	6: 1 the Lord said unto **M**, Now shalt thou	4872
	6: 2 God spake unto **M**, and said unto him,	4872
	6: 9 **M** spake so unto the children of Israel:	4872
	6: 9 they hearkened not unto **M** for anguish	4872
	6:10 And the Lord spake unto **M**, saying,	4872
	6:12 **M** spake before the Lord, saying,	4872
	6:13 the Lord spake unto **M** and unto Aaron,	4872
	6:20 to wife; and she bare him Aaron and **M**:	4872
	6:26 *These are* that Aaron and **M**, to whom	4872
	6:27 from Egypt: *these are* that **M** and Aaron.	4872
	6:28 the Lord spake unto **M** in the land of Egypt,	4872
	6:29 That the Lord spake unto **M**, saying,	4872
	6:30 **M** said before the Lord, Behold, I *am* of	4872
	7: 1 the Lord said unto **M**, See, I have made	4872
	7: 6 **M** and Aaron did as the Lord	4872

Ex	7: 7 **M** *was* fourscore years old,	4872
	7: 8 the Lord spake unto **M** and unto Aaron,	4872
	7:10 **M** and Aaron went in unto Pharaoh,	4872
	7:14 the Lord said unto **M**, Pharaoh's heart *is*	4872
	7:19 the Lord spake unto **M**, Say unto Aaron,	4872
	7:20 **M** and Aaron did so, as the Lord	4872
	8: 1 the Lord spake unto **M**, Go in	4872
	8: 5 the Lord said unto **M**, Say unto Aaron,	4872
	8: 8 Pharaoh called for **M** and Aaron, and said,	4872
	8: 9 **M** said unto Pharaoh, Glory over me:	4872
	8:12 **M** and Aaron went out from Pharaoh:	4872
	8:12 **M** cried unto the Lord because of	4872
	8:13 Lord did according to the word of **M**;	4872
	8:16 the Lord said unto **M**, Say unto Aaron,	4872
	8:20 the Lord said unto **M**, Rise up early in	4872
	8:25 Pharaoh called for **M** and for Aaron,	4872
	8:26 **M** said, It is not meet so to do; for we	4872
	8:29 **M** said, Behold, I go out from thee,	4872
	8:30 **M** went out from Pharaoh, and intreated	4872
	8:31 Lord did according to the word of **M**;	4872
	9: 1 the Lord said unto **M**, Go in unto	4872
	9: 8 the Lord said unto **M** and unto Aaron,	4872
	9: 8 let **M** sprinkle it towards the heaven in	4872
	9:10 **M** sprinkled it *up* toward heaven;	4872
	9:11 the magicians could not stand before **M**	4872
	9:12 as the Lord had spoken unto **M**.	4872
	9:13 the Lord said unto **M**, Rise up early in	4872
	9:22 the Lord said unto **M**, Stretch forth thine	4872
	9:23 **M** stretched forth his rod toward heaven:	4872
	9:27 called for **M** and Aaron, and said unto	4872
	9:29 **M** said unto him, As soon as I am gone	4872
	9:33 **M** went out of the city from Pharaoh,	4872
	9:35 Israel go; as the Lord had spoken by **M**.	4872
	10: 1 the Lord said unto **M**, Go in unto	4872
	10: 3 **M** and Aaron came in unto Pharaoh,	4872
	10: 8 **M** and Aaron were brought again unto	4872
	10: 9 **M** said, We will go with our young and	4872
	10:12 the Lord said unto **M**, Stretch out thine	4872
	10:13 **M** stretched forth his rod over the land of	4872
	10:16 Pharaoh called for **M** and Aaron in haste;	4872
	10:21 the Lord said unto **M**, Stretch out thine	4872
	10:22 **M** stretched forth his hand toward	4872
	10:24 Pharaoh called unto **M**, and said, Go ye,	4872
	10:25 **M** said, Thou must give us also sacrifices	4872
	10:29 **M** said, Thou hast spoken well, I will see	4872
	11: 1 (And the Lord said unto **M**, Yet will I	4872
	11: 3 Moreover the man **M** *was* very great in	4872
	11: 4 **M** said, Thus saith the Lord,	4872
	11: 9 the Lord said unto **M**, Pharaoh shall not	4872
	11:10 **M** and Aaron did all these wonders	4872
	12: 1 the Lord spake unto **M** and Aaron in	4872
	12:21 **M** called for all the elders of Israel,	4872
	12:28 did as the Lord had commanded **M** and	4872
	12:31 he called for **M** and Aaron by night,	4872
	12:35 of Israel did according to the word of **M**;	4872
	12:43 the Lord said unto **M** and Aaron, This *is*	4872
	12:50 as the Lord commanded **M** and Aaron,	4872
	13: 1 And the Lord spake unto **M**, saying,	4872
	13: 3 **M** said unto the people, Remember this	4872
	13:19 **M** took the bones of Joseph with him:	4872
	14: 1 And the Lord spake unto **M**, saying,	4872
	14:11 they said unto **M**, Because *there were* no	4872
	14:13 **M** said unto the people, Fear ye not,	4872
	14:15 the Lord said unto **M**, Wherefore criest	4872
	14:21 **M** stretched out his hand over the sea;	4872
	14:26 the Lord said unto **M**, Stretch out thine	4872
	14:27 **M** stretched forth his hand over the sea,	4872
	14:31 believed the Lord, and his servant **M**.	4872
	15: 1 sang **M** and the children of Israel this	4872
	15:22 So **M** brought Israel from the Red sea,	4872
	15:24 the people murmured against **M**, saying,	4872
	16: 2 children of Israel murmured against **M**	4872
	16: 4 said the Lord unto **M**, Behold, I will	4872
	16: 6 **M** and Aaron said unto all the children	4872
	16: 8 **M** said, This shall be, when the Lord	4872
	16: 9 **M** spake unto Aaron, Say unto all	4872
	16:11 And the Lord spake unto **M**, saying,	4872
	16:15 they wist not what it *was*. And **M** said	4872
	16:19 **M** said, Let no man leave of it till	4872
	16:20 they hearkened not unto **M**;	4872
	16:20 and stank: and **M** was wroth with them.	4872
	16:22 of the congregation came and told **M**.	4872
	16:24 laid it up till the morning, as **M** bade:	4872
	16:25 **M** said, Eat that to day; for to day *is* a	4872
	16:28 the Lord said unto **M**, How long refuse	4872
	16:32 **M** said, This *is* the thing which the Lord	4872
	16:33 **M** said unto Aaron, Take a pot, and put	4872
	16:34 As the Lord commanded **M**,	4872
	17: 2 Wherefore the people did chide with **M**,	4872
	17: 2 **M** said unto them, Why chide you with	4872
	17: 3 people murmured against **M**, and said,	4872
	17: 4 **M** cried unto the Lord, saying,	4872
	17: 5 the Lord said unto **M**, Go on before	4872
	17: 6 **M** did so in the sight of the elders of	4872
	17: 9 **M** said unto Joshua, Choose us out men,	4872
	17:10 So Joshua did as **M** had said to him,	4872
	17:10 **M**, Aaron, and Hur went up *to* the top of	4872
	17:11 came to pass, when **M** held up his hand,	4872
	17:14 the Lord said unto **M**, Write this *for* a	4872
	17:15 **M** built an altar, and called the name of	4872
	18: 1 heard of all that God had done for **M**,	4872
	18: 5 and his wife unto **M** into the wilderness,	4872
	18: 6 he said unto **M**, I thy father in law Jethro	4872
	18: 7 **M** went out to meet his father in law,	4872
	18: 8 **M** told his father in law all that the Lord	4872

M

Ex	18:13 morrow, that **M** sat to judge the people:	4872
	18:13 the people stood by **M** from the morning	4872
	18:15 **M** said unto his father in law, Because	4872
	18:24 So **M** hearkened to the voice of his father	4872
	18:25 **M** chose able men out of all Israel,	4872
	18:26 the hard causes they brought unto **M**,	4872
	18:27 **M** let his father in law depart; and he	4872
	19: 3 **M** went up unto God, and the Lord	4872
	19: 7 **M** came and called for the elders of	4872
	19: 8 **M** returned the words of the people unto	4872
	19: 9 the Lord said unto **M**, Lo, I come unto	4872
	19: 9 **M** told the words of the people unto	4872
	19:10 the Lord said unto **M**, Go unto	4872
	19:14 **M** went down from the mount unto	4872
	19:17 **M** brought forth the people out of the	4872
	19:19 **M** spake, and God answered him by a	4872
	19:20 the Lord called **M** *up* to the top of	4872
	19:20 to the top of the mount; and **M** went up.	4872
	19:21 the Lord said unto **M**, Go down,	4872
	19:23 **M** said unto the Lord, The people	4872
	19:25 So **M** went down unto the people,	4872
	20:19 they said unto **M**, Speak thou with us,	4872
	20:20 **M** said unto the people, Fear not: for God	4872
	20:21 **M** drew near unto the thick darkness	4872
	20:22 the Lord said unto **M**, Thus thou shalt	4872
	24: 1 he said unto **M**, Come up unto the Lord,	4872
	24: 2 **M** alone shall come near the Lord:	4872
	24: 3 **M** came and told the people all the words	4872
	24: 4 **M** wrote all the words of the Lord,	4872
	24: 6 **M** took half of the blood, and put *it* in	4872
	24: 8 **M** took the blood, and sprinkled *it* on	4872
	24: 9 went up **M**, and Aaron, Nadab, and	4872
	24:12 the Lord said unto **M**, Come up to me	4872
	24:13 **M** rose up, and his minister Joshua:	4872
	24:13 and **M** went up into the mount of God.	4872
	24:15 **M** went up into the mount, and a cloud	4872
	24:16 the seventh day he called unto **M** out of	4872
	24:18 **M** went into the midst of the cloud,	4872
	24:18 **M** was in the mount forty days and	4872
	25: 1 And the Lord spake unto **M**, saying,	4872
	30:11 And the Lord spake unto **M**, saying,	4872
	30:17 And the Lord spake unto **M**, saying,	4872
	30:22 Moreover the Lord spake unto **M**,	4872
	30:34 the Lord said unto **M**, Take unto thee	4872
	31: 1 And the Lord spake unto **M**, saying,	4872
	31:12 And the Lord spake unto **M**, saying,	4872
	31:18 gave unto **M**, when he had made an end	4872
	32: 1 when the people saw that **M** delayed to	4872
	32: 1 *as for* this **M**, the man that brought us	4872
	32: 7 the Lord said unto **M**, Go, get thee	4872
	32: 9 the Lord said unto **M**, I have seen this	4872
	32:11 **M** besought the Lord his God, and said,	4872
	32:15 **M** turned, and went down from the	4872
	32:17 he said unto **M**, There *is* a noise of war in	4872
	32:21 **M** said unto Aaron, What did this people	4872
	32:23 for *as for* this **M**, the man that brought us	4872
	32:25 when **M** saw that the people *were* naked;	4872
	32:26 **M** stood in the gate of the camp, and said,	4872
	32:28 of Levi did according to the word of **M**:	4872
	32:29 For **M** had said, Consecrate yourselves to	4872
	32:30 that **M** said unto the people, Ye have	4872
	32:31 And **M** returned unto the Lord, and said,	4872
	32:33 the Lord said unto **M**, Whosoever hath	4872
	33: 1 the Lord said unto **M**, Depart, *and* go up	4872
	33: 5 For the Lord had said unto **M**, Say unto	4872
	33: 7 **M** took the tabernacle, and pitched it	4872
	33: 8 when **M** went out unto the tabernacle,	4872
	33: 8 man *at* his tent door, and looked after **M**,	4872
	33: 9 to pass, as **M** entered into the tabernacle,	4872
	33: 9 and *the Lord* talked with **M**.	4872
	33:11 And the Lord spake unto **M** face to face,	4872
	33:12 **M** said unto the Lord, See, thou sayest	4872
	33:17 the Lord said unto **M**, I will do this	4872
	34: 1 the Lord said unto **M**, Hew thee two	4872
	34: 4 **M** rose up early in the morning,	4872
	34: 8 **M** made haste, and bowed his head	4872
	34:27 the Lord said unto **M**, Write thou these	4872
	34:29 **M** came down from mount Sinai with	4872
	34:29 that **M** wist not that the skin of his face	4872
	34:30 and all the children of Israel saw **M**,	4872
	34:31 **M** called unto them; and Aaron and all	4872
	34:31 unto him: and **M** talked with them.	4872
	34:33 **M** had done speaking with them, he put	4872
	34:34 when **M** went in before the Lord to	4872
	34:35 the children of Israel saw the face of **M**,	4872
	34:35 **M** put the vail upon his face again, until	4872
	35: 1 **M** gathered all the congregation of	4872
	35: 4 **M** spake unto all the congregation of	4872
	35:20 of Israel departed from the presence of **M**.	4872
	35:29 to be made by the hand of **M**.	4872
	35:30 **M** said unto the children of Israel, See,	4872
	36: 2 **M** called Bezaleel and Aholiab, and every	4872
	36: 3 they received of **M** all the offering,	4872
	36: 5 they spake unto **M**, saying, The people	4872
	36: 6 **M** gave commandment, and they caused	4872
	38:21 according to the commandment of **M**,	4872
	38:22 made all that the Lord commanded **M**.	4872
	39: 1 for Aaron; as the Lord commanded **M**.	4872
	39: 5 as the Lord commanded **M**.	4872
	39: 7 of Israel; as the Lord commanded **M**.	4872
	39:21 the ephod; as the Lord commanded **M**.	4872
	39:26 minister *in;* as the Lord commanded **M**.	4872
	39:29 as the Lord commanded **M**.	4872
	39:31 the mitre; as the Lord commanded **M**.	4872
	39:32 to all that the Lord commanded **M**,	4872

Ex	39:33 they brought the tabernacle unto **M**,	4872
	39:42 to all that the Lord commanded **M**,	4872
	39:43 **M** did look upon all the work, and	4872
	39:43 so had they done it: and **M** blessed them.	4872
	40: 1 And the Lord spake unto **M**, saying,	4872
	40:16 Thus did **M**: according to all that	4872
	40:18 **M** reared up the tabernacle,	4872
	40:19 upon it; as the Lord commanded **M**.	4872
	40:21 as the Lord commanded **M**.	4872
	40:23 as the Lord had commanded **M**.	4872
	40:25 the Lord; as the Lord commanded **M**.	4872
	40:27 as the Lord commanded **M**.	4872
	40:29 as the Lord commanded **M**.	4872
	40:31 **M** and Aaron and his sons washed their	4872
	40:32 as the Lord commanded **M**.	4872
	40:33 the court gate. So **M** finished the work.	4872
	40:35 **M** was not able to enter into the tent of	4872
Lev	1: 1 the Lord called unto **M**, and spake unto	4872
	4: 1 And the Lord spake unto **M**, saying,	4872
	5:14 And the Lord spake unto **M**, saying,	4872
	6: 1 And the Lord spake unto **M**, saying,	4872
	6: 8 And the Lord spake unto **M**, saying,	4872
	6:19 And the Lord spake unto **M**, saying,	4872
	6:24 And the Lord spake unto **M**, saying,	4872
	7:22 And the Lord spake unto **M**, saying,	4872
	7:28 And the Lord spake unto **M**, saying,	4872
	7:38 Which the Lord commanded **M** in	4872
	8: 1 And the Lord spake unto **M**, saying,	4872
	8: 4 **M** did as the Lord commanded him;	4872
	8: 5 **M** said unto the congregation, This *is*	4872
	8: 6 **M** brought Aaron and his sons,	4872
	8: 9 holy crown; as the Lord commanded **M**.	4872
	8:10 **M** took the anointing oil, and anointed	4872
	8:13 **M** brought Aaron's sons, and put coats	4872
	8:13 upon them; as the Lord commanded **M**.	4872
	8:15 slew *it;* and **M** took the blood, and put *it*	4872
	8:16 their fat, and **M** burned *it* upon the altar.	4872
	8:17 the camp; as the Lord commanded **M**.	4872
	8:19 **M** sprinkled the blood upon the altar	4872
	8:20 **M** burnt the head, and the pieces,	4872
	8:21 **M** burnt the whole ram upon the altar:	4872
	8:21 the Lord; as the Lord commanded **M**.	4872
	8:23 he slew *it;* and **M** took of the blood of it,	4872
	8:24 **M** put of the blood upon the tip of their	4872
	8:24 **M** sprinkled the blood upon the altar	4872
	8:28 **M** took them from off their hands,	4872
	8:29 **M** took the breast, and waved it *for* a	4872
	8:29 as the Lord commanded **M**.	4872
	8:30 **M** took of the anointing oil, and of	4872
	8:31 **M** said unto Aaron and to his sons, Boil	4872
	8:36 the Lord commanded by the hand of **M**.	4872
	9: 1 *that* **M** called Aaron and his sons,	4872
	9: 5 they brought *that* which **M** commanded	4872
	9: 6 **M** said, This *is* the thing which the Lord	4872
	9: 7 **M** said unto Aaron, Go unto the altar,	4872
	9:10 the altar; as the Lord commanded **M**.	4872
	9:21 before the Lord; as **M** commanded.	4872
	9:23 **M** and Aaron went into the tabernacle of	4872
	10: 3 **M** said unto Aaron, This *is* it that	4872
	10: 4 **M** called Mishael and Elzaphan, the sons	4872
	10: 5 coats out of the camp; as **M** had said.	4872
	10: 6 **M** said unto Aaron, and unto Eleazar and	4872
	10: 7 And they did according to the word of **M**.	4872
	10:11 hath spoken unto them by the hand of **M**.	4872
	10:12 **M** spake unto Aaron, and unto Eleazar	4872
	10:16 **M** diligently sought the goat of the sin	4872
	10:19 Aaron said unto **M**, Behold, *this* day have	4872
	10:20 And when **M** heard *that,* he was content.	4872
	11: 1 the Lord spake unto **M** and to Aaron,	4872
	12: 1 And the Lord spake unto **M**, saying,	4872
	13: 1 the Lord spake unto **M** and Aaron,	4872
	14: 1 And the Lord spake unto **M**, saying,	4872
	14:33 the Lord spake unto **M** and unto Aaron,	4872
	15: 1 the Lord spake unto **M** and to Aaron,	4872
	16: 1 the Lord spake unto **M** after the death of	4872
	16: 2 the Lord said unto **M**, Speak unto Aaron	4872
	16:34 And he did as the Lord commanded **M**.	4872
	17: 1 And the Lord spake unto **M**, saying,	4872
	18: 1 And the Lord spake unto **M**, saying,	4872
	19: 1 And the Lord spake unto **M**, saying,	4872
	20: 1 And the Lord spake unto **M**, saying,	4872
	21: 1 the Lord said unto **M**, Speak unto	4872
	21:16 And the Lord spake unto **M**, saying,	4872
	21:24 **M** told *it* unto Aaron, and to his sons,	4872
	22: 1 And the Lord spake unto **M**, saying,	4872
	22:17 And the Lord spake unto **M**, saying,	4872
	22:26 And the Lord spake unto **M**, saying,	4872
	23: 1 And the Lord spake unto **M**, saying,	4872
	23: 9 And the Lord spake unto **M**, saying,	4872
	23:23 And the Lord spake unto **M**, saying,	4872
	23:26 And the Lord spake unto **M**, saying,	4872
	23:33 And the Lord spake unto **M**, saying,	4872
	23:44 **M** declared unto the children of Israel	4872
	24: 1 And the Lord spake unto **M**, saying,	4872
	24:11 they brought him unto **M**: (and	4872
	24:13 And the Lord spake unto **M**, saying,	4872
	24:23 **M** spake to the children of Israel, that	4872
	24:23 of Israel did as the Lord commanded **M**.	4872
	25: 1 the Lord spake unto **M** in mount Sinai,	4872
	26:46 Israel in mount Sinai by the hand of **M**.	4872
	27: 1 And the Lord spake unto **M**, saying,	4872
	27:34 which the Lord commanded **M** for	4872
Nu	1: 1 the Lord spake unto **M** in the wilderness	4872
	1:17 **M** and Aaron took these men which are	4872
	1:19 As the Lord commanded **M**,	4872

Nu	1:44 which **M** and Aaron numbered,	4872
	1:48 For the Lord had spoken unto **M**,	4872
	1:54 to all that the Lord commanded **M**,	4872
	2: 1 the Lord spake unto **M** and unto Aaron,	4872
	2:33 of Israel; as the Lord commanded **M**.	4872
	2:34 to all that the Lord commanded **M**:	4872
	3: 1 **M** in the day that the Lord spake with	4872
	3: 1 the Lord spake with **M** in mount Sinai.	4872
	3: 5 And the Lord spake unto **M**, saying,	4872
	3:11 And the Lord spake unto **M**, saying,	4872
	3:14 the Lord spake unto **M** in the wilderness	4872
	3:16 **M** numbered them according to the word	4872
	3:38 *shall be* **M**, and Aaron and his sons,	4872
	3:39 which **M** and Aaron numbered at	4872
	3:40 the Lord said unto **M**, Number all	4872
	3:42 **M** numbered, as the Lord commanded	4872
	3:44 And the Lord spake unto **M**, saying,	4872
	3:49 **M** took the redemption money of them	4872
	3:51 **M** gave the money of them that were	4872
	3:51 the Lord, as the Lord commanded **M**.	4872
	4: 1 the Lord spake unto **M** and unto Aaron,	4872
	4:17 the Lord spake unto **M** and unto Aaron,	4872
	4:21 And the Lord spake unto **M**, saying,	4872
	4:34 **M** and Aaron and the chief of	4872
	4:37 **M** and Aaron did number according	4872
	4:37 of the Lord by the hand of **M**.	4872
	4:41 **M** and Aaron did number according	4872
	4:45 **M** and Aaron numbered according	4872
	4:45 the word of the Lord by the hand of **M**.	4872
	4:46 **M** and Aaron and the chief of Israel	4872
	4:49 they were numbered by the hand of **M**,	4872
	4:49 of him, as the Lord commanded **M**.	4872
	5: 1 And the Lord spake unto **M**, saying,	4872
	5: 4 as the Lord spake unto **M**, so did	4872
	5: 5 And the Lord spake unto **M**, saying,	4872
	5:11 And the Lord spake unto **M**, saying,	4872
	6: 1 And the Lord spake unto **M**, saying,	4872
	6:22 And the Lord spake unto **M**, saying,	4872
	7: 1 came to pass on the day that **M** had fully	4872
	7: 4 And the Lord spake unto **M**, saying,	4872
	7: 6 **M** took the wagons and the oxen,	4872
	7:11 the Lord said unto **M**, They shall offer	4872
	7:89 when **M** was gone into the tabernacle of	4872
	8: 1 And the Lord spake unto **M**, saying,	4872
	8: 3 as the Lord commanded **M**.	4872
	8: 4 pattern which the Lord had shewed **M**,	4872
	8: 5 And the Lord spake unto **M**, saying,	4872
	8:20 **M**, and Aaron, and all the congregation of	4872
	8:20 commanded **M** concerning the Levites,	4872
	8:22 as the Lord had commanded **M**	4872
	8:23 And the Lord spake unto **M**, saying,	4872
	9: 1 the Lord spake unto **M** in the wilderness	4872
	9: 4 **M** spake unto the children of Israel,	4872
	9: 5 to all that the Lord commanded **M**,	4872
	9: 6 they came before **M** and before Aaron on	4872
	9: 8 **M** said unto them, Stand still, and I will	4872
	9: 9 And the Lord spake unto **M**, saying,	4872
	9:23 of the Lord by the hand of **M**.	4872
	10: 1 And the Lord spake unto **M**, saying,	4872
	10:13 of the Lord by the hand of **M**.	4872
	10:29 **M** said unto Hobab, the son of Raguel	4872
	10:35 that **M** said, Rise up, Lord, and let thine	4872
	11: 2 people cried unto **M**; and when Moses	4872
	11: 2 when **M** prayed unto the Lord, the fire	4872
	11:10 **M** heard the people weep throughout	4872
	11:10 kindled greatly; **M** also was displeased.	4872
	11:11 **M** said unto the Lord, Wherefore hast	4872
	11:16 the Lord said unto **M**, Gather unto me	4872
	11:21 **M** said, The people, amongst whom I *am,*	4872
	11:23 the Lord said unto **M**, Is the Lord's	4872
	11:24 **M** went out, and told the people the	4872
	11:27 told **M**, and said, Eldad and Medad do	4872
	11:28 the servant of **M**, *one* of his young men,	4872
	11:28 answered and said, My lord **M**,	4872
	11:29 **M** said unto him, Enviest thou for my	4872
	11:30 **M** gat him into the camp, he and the	4872
	12: 1 and Aaron spake against **M** because	4872
	12: 2 the Lord indeed spoken only by **M**?	4872
	12: 3 (Now the man **M** *was* very meek, above	4872
	12: 4 the Lord spake suddenly unto **M**,	4872
	12: 7 My servant **M** *is* not so, who *is* faithful in	4872
	12: 8 not afraid to speak against my servant **M**?	4872
	12:11 Aaron said unto **M**, Alas, my lord,	4872
	12:13 **M** cried unto the Lord, saying, Heal her	4872
	12:14 the Lord said unto **M**, If her father no	4872
	13: 1 And the Lord spake unto **M**, saying,	4872
	13: 3 **M** by the commandment of the Lord	4872
	13:16 These *are* the names of the men which **M**	4872
	13:16 **M** called Oshea the son of Nun, Jehoshua.	4872
	13:17 **M** sent them to spy out the land of	4872
	13:26 they went and came to **M**, and to Aaron,	4872
	13:30 Caleb stilled the people before **M**, and	4872
	14: 2 children of Israel murmured against **M**	4872
	14: 5 **M** and Aaron fell on their faces before all	4872
	14:11 the Lord said unto **M**, How long will	4872
	14:13 **M** said unto the Lord, Then	4872
	14:26 the Lord spake unto **M** and unto Aaron,	4872
	14:36 men, which **M** sent to search the land,	4872
	14:39 **M** told these sayings unto all the children	4872
	14:41 **M** said, Wherefore now do ye transgress	4872
	14:44 and, he departed not out of the camp.	4872
	15: 1 And the Lord spake unto **M**, saying,	4872
	15:17 And the Lord spake unto **M**, saying,	4872
	15:22 which the Lord hath spoken unto **M**,	4872
	15:23 hath commanded you by the hand of **M**,	4872

Nu 15:23 the day that the LORD commanded **M**,	NIH
15:33 him gathering sticks brought him unto **M**	4872
15:35 the LORD said unto **M**, The man shall be	4872
15:36 and he died; as the LORD commanded **M**.	4872
15:37 And the LORD spake unto **M**, saying,	4872
16: 2 they rose up before **M**, with certain of	
16: 3 gathered themselves together against **M**	
16: 4 when **M** heard *it*, he fell upon his face:	
16: 8 **M** said unto Korah, Hear, I pray you,	
16:12 **M** sent to call Dathan and Abiram, the	
16:15 **M** was very wroth, and said unto	
16:16 **M** said unto Korah, Be thou and all thy	
16:18 the tabernacle of the congregation with **M**	4872
16:20 the LORD spake unto **M** and unto Aaron,	4872
16:23 And the LORD spake unto **M**, saying,	4872
16:25 **M** rose up and went unto Dathan and	
16:28 **M** said, Hereby ye shall know that	
16:36 And the LORD spake unto **M**, saying,	4872
16:40 the LORD said to him by the hand of **M**.	4872
16:41 children of Israel murmured against **M**	4872
16:42 the congregation was gathered against **M**	4872
16:43 **M** and Aaron came before the tabernacle	
16:44 And the LORD spake unto **M**, saying,	4872
16:46 **M** said unto Aaron, Take a censer,	
16:47 Aaron took as **M** commanded, and ran	
16:50 Aaron returned unto **M** unto the door of	
17: 1 And the LORD spake unto **M**, saying,	4872
17: 6 **M** spake unto the children of Israel,	
17: 7 **M** laid up the rods before the LORD in	
17: 8 that on the morrow **M** went into	
17: 9 **M** brought out all the rods from before	
17:10 the LORD said unto **M**, Bring Aaron's	4872
17:11 **M** did *so:* as the LORD commanded him,	
17:12 children of Israel spake unto **M**, saying,	4872
18:25 And the LORD spake unto **M**, saying,	4872
19: 1 the LORD spake unto **M** and unto Aaron,	4872
20: 2 gathered themselves together against **M**	
20: 3 the people chode with **M**, and spake,	
20: 6 And **M** and Aaron went from the presence of	
20: 7 And the LORD spake unto **M**, saying,	4872
20: 9 **M** took the rod from before the LORD,	
20:10 and Aaron gathered the congregation	
20:11 **M** lift up his hand, and with his rod he	
20:12 the LORD spake unto **M** and Aaron,	4872
20:14 **M** sent messengers from Kadesh unto	
20:23 the LORD spake unto **M** and Aaron in	4872
20:27 And **M** did as the LORD commanded:	
20:28 And **M** stripped Aaron of his garments,	
20:28 **M** and Eleazar came down from the	
21: 5 people spake against God, and against **M**,	
21: 7 Therefore the people came to **M**, and	
21: 7 from us. And **M** prayed for the people.	
21: 8 the LORD said unto **M**, Make thee a fiery	4872
21: 9 **M** made a serpent of brass, and put it	
21:16 well whereof the LORD spake unto **M**,	4872
21:32 **M** sent to spy out Jaazer, and they took	
21:34 the LORD said unto **M**, Fear him not:	4872
25: 4 the LORD said unto **M**, Take all the heads	4872
25: 5 **M** said unto the judges of Israel, Slay ye	
25: 6 a Midianitish *woman* in the sight of **M**,	
25:10 And the LORD spake unto **M**, saying,	4872
25:16 And the LORD spake unto **M**, saying,	4872
26: 1 that the LORD spake unto **M** and	
26: 3 **M** and Eleazar the priest spake with them	4872
26: 4 as the LORD commanded **M** and	
26: 9 strove against **M** and against Aaron in	
26:52 And the LORD spake unto **M**, saying,	4872
26:59 she bare unto Amram Aaron and **M**,	4872
26:63 These *are* they that were numbered by **M**	4872
26:64 there was not a man of them whom **M**	4872
27: 2 they stood before **M**, and before Eleazar	
27: 5 **M** brought their cause before the LORD.	
27: 6 And the LORD spake unto **M**, saying,	4872
27:11 as the LORD commanded **M**.	4872
27:12 the LORD said unto **M**, Get thee up into	4872
27:15 And **M** spake unto the LORD, saying,	4872
27:18 the LORD said unto **M**, Take thee Joshua	4872
27:22 And **M** did as the LORD commanded him:	
27:23 the LORD commanded by the hand of **M**.	4872
28: 1 And the LORD spake unto **M**, saying,	4872
29:40 **M** told the children of Israel according to	
29:40 to all that the LORD commanded	
30: 1 **M** spake unto the heads of the tribes	
30:16 which the LORD commanded **M**,	4872
31: 1 And the LORD spake unto **M**, saying,	4872
31: 3 **M** spake unto the people, saying,	
31: 6 **M** sent them to the war, a thousand of	
31: 7 as the LORD commanded **M**;	4872
31:12 unto **M**, and Eleazar the priest, and unto	4872
31:13 **M**, and Eleazar the priest, and all	
31:14 **M** was wroth with the officers of the host	
31:15 **M** said unto them, Have ye saved all	
31:21 the law which the LORD commanded **M**;	4872
31:25 And the LORD spake unto **M**, saying,	4872
31:31 And Eleazar the priest did as the LORD	
31:31 priest did as the LORD commanded **M**.	4872
31:41 **M** gave the tribute, *which was*	
31:41 the priest, as the LORD commanded **M**.	4872
31:42 **M** divided from the men that warred,	
31:47 **M** took one portion of fifty, *both* of man	
31:47 the LORD; as the LORD commanded **M**.	4872
31:48 captains of hundreds, came near unto **M**:	4872
31:49 said unto **M**, Thy servants have taken	
31:51 **M** and Eleazar the priest took the gold of	4872
31:54 **M** and Eleazar the priest took the gold of	4872

Nu 32: 2 of Reuben came and spake unto **M**,	4872
32: 6 **M** said unto the children of Gad and to	4872
32:20 **M** said unto them, If ye will do this thing,	4872
32:25 and the children of Reuben spake unto **M**,	4872
32:28 concerning them **M** commanded Eleazar	4872
32:29 **M** said unto them, If the children of Gad	4872
32:33 **M** gave unto them, *even* to the children	4872
32:40 **M** gave Gilead unto Machir the son of	4872
33: 1 with their armies under the hand of **M**	4872
33: 2 **M** wrote their goings out according to	4872
33:50 the LORD spake unto **M** in the plains of	4872
34: 1 And the LORD spake unto **M**, saying,	4872
34:13 **M** commanded the children of Israel,	4872
34:16 And the LORD spake unto **M**, saying,	4872
35: 1 the LORD spake unto **M** in the plains of	4872
35: 9 And the LORD spake unto **M**, saying,	4872
36: 1 spake before **M**, and before the princes,	4872
36: 5 **M** commanded the children of Israel	4872
36:10 Even as the LORD commanded **M**,	4872
36:13 unto the children of Israel in the plains	4872
Dt 1: 1 These *be* the words which **M** spake unto	4872
1: 3 that **M** spake unto the children of Israel,	4872
1: 5 began **M** to declare this law, saying,	4872
4:41 **M** severed three cities on *this* side Jordan	4872
4:44 this *is* the law which **M** set before	4872
4:45 **M** spake unto the children of Israel,	4872
4:46 and the children of Israel smote,	4872
5: 1 **M** called all Israel, and said unto them,	4872
27: 1 **M** with the elders of Israel commanded	4872
27: 9 **M** and the priests the Levites spake unto	4872
27:11 **M** charged the people the same day,	4872
29: 1 which the LORD commanded **M** to make	4872
29: 2 **M** called unto all Israel, and said unto	4872
31: 1 **M** went and spake these words unto all	4872
31: 7 **M** called unto Joshua, and said unto him	4872
31: 9 **M** wrote this law, and delivered it unto	4872
31:10 **M** commanded them, saying, At the end	4872
31:14 the LORD said unto **M**, Behold, thy days	4872
31:14 **M** and Joshua went,	4872
31:16 the LORD said unto **M**, Behold, thou shalt	4872
31:22 **M** therefore wrote this song the same day,	4872
31:24 when **M** had made an end of writing	4872
31:25 That **M** commanded the Levites,	4872
31:30 **M** spake in the ears of all the	4872
32:44 **M** came and spake all the words of this	4872
32:45 **M** made an end of speaking all these	4872
32:48 the LORD spake unto **M** that selfsame	4872
33: 1 wherewith **M** the man of God blessed	4872
33: 4 **M** commanded us a law, *even*	4872
34: 1 **M** went up from the plains of Moab unto	4872
34: 5 So **M** the servant of the LORD died there	4872
34: 7 **M** *was* an hundred and twenty years old	4872
34: 8 the children of Israel wept for **M** in	4872
34: 8 *and* mourning for **M** were ended.	4872
34: 9 for **M** had laid his hands upon him:	4872
34: 9 and did as the LORD commanded **M**.	4872
34:10 not a prophet since in Israel like unto **M**,	4872
34:12 in all the great terror which **M** shewed in	4872
Jos 1: 1 Now after the death of **M** the servant of	4872
1: 2 **M** my servant is dead; now therefore	4872
1: 3 have I given unto you, as I said unto **M**.	4872
1: 5 as I was with **M**, *so* I will be with thee:	4872
1: 7 which **M** my servant commanded thee:	4872
1:13 Remember the word which **M** the	4872
1:14 remain in the land which **M** gave you	4872
1:15 which the LORD'S servant gave you	4872
1:17 According as we hearkened unto **M** in all	4872
1:17 thy God be with thee, as he was with **M**.	4872
3: 7 as I was with **M**, *so* I will be with thee.	4872
4:10 to all that **M** commanded Joshua:	4872
4:12 children of Israel, as **M** spake unto them:	4872
4:14 they feared him, as they feared **M**,	4872
8:31 As **M** the servant of the LORD	4872
8:31 it is written in the book of the law of **M**,	4872
8:32 upon the stones a copy of the law of **M**,	4872
8:33 as **M** the servant of the LORD had	4872
8:35 There was not a word of all that **M**	4872
9:24 his servant **M** to give you all the land,	4872
11:12 as **M** the servant of the LORD	4872
11:15 As the LORD commanded **M** his servant,	4872
11:15 so did **M** command Joshua, and so	4872
11:15 of all that the LORD commanded **M**.	4872
11:20 as the LORD commanded **M**.	4872
11:23 to all that the LORD said unto **M**;	4872
12: 6 Them did **M** the servant of the LORD and	4872
12: 6 **M** the servant of the LORD gave it *for* a	4872
13: 8 which **M** gave them, beyond Jordan	4872
13: 8 *even* as **M** the servant of the LORD gave	4872
13:12 for these did **M** smite, and cast them out.	4872
13:15 **M** gave unto the tribe of the children of	4872
13:21 **M** smote with the princes of Midian,	4872
13:24 **M** gave *inheritance* unto the tribe of Gad,	4872
13:29 **M** gave *inheritance* unto the half tribe of	4872
13:32 These *are* the countries which **M** did	4872
13:33 unto the tribe of Levi **M** gave not *any*	4872
14: 2 the LORD commanded by the hand of **M**,	4872
14: 3 For **M** had given the inheritance of two	4872
14: 5 As the LORD commanded **M**,	4872
14: 6 said unto the man of God concerning	4872
14: 7 Forty years old *was* I when **M** the servant	4872
14: 9 **M** sware on that day, saying, Surely	4872
14:10 since the LORD spake this word unto **M**,	4872
14:11 day as *I was* in the day that **M** sent me:	4872
17: 4 The LORD commanded **M** to give us an	4872
18: 7 which **M** the servant of the LORD gave	4872

Jos 20: 2 I spake unto you by the hand of **M**:	4872
21: 2 The LORD commanded by the hand of **M**.	4872
21: 8 the LORD commanded by the hand of **M**.	4872
22: 2 Ye have kept all that **M** the servant of	4872
22: 4 which **M** the servant of the LORD gave	4872
22: 5 which **M** the servant of the LORD	4872
22: 7 **M** had given *possession* in Bashan:	4872
22: 9 the word of the LORD by the hand of **M**.	4872
23: 6 is written in the book of the law of **M**,	4872
24: 5 I sent **M** also and Aaron, and I plagued	4872
Jdg 1:20 they gave Hebron unto Caleb, as **M** said:	4872
3: 4 their fathers by the hand of **M**.	4872
4:11 children of Hobab the father in law of **M**,	4872
1Sa 12: 6 *It is* the LORD that advanced **M** and	4872
12: 8 then the LORD sent **M** and Aaron,	4872
1Ki 2: 3 as *it is* written in the law of **M**,	4872
8: 9 of stone, which **M** put there at Horeb,	4872
8:53 as thou spakest by the hand of **M** thy	4872
8:56 which he promised by the hand of **M** his	4872
2Ki 14: 6 is written in the book of the law of **M**,	4872
18: 4 brake in pieces the brasen serpent that **M**	4872
18: 6 which the LORD commanded **M**.	4872
18:12 all that **M** the servant of the LORD	4872
21: 8 to all the law that my servant **M**	4872
23:25 his might, according to all the law of **M**;	4872
1Ch 6: 3 of Amram; Aaron, and **M**, and Miriam.	4872
6:49 according to all that **M** the servant of God	4872
15:15 **M** commanded according to the word of	4872
21:29 which **M** made in the wilderness,	4872
22:13 judgments which the LORD charged **M**	4872
23:13 The sons of Amram; Aaron and **M**:	4872
23:14 Now *concerning* **M** the man of God,	4872
23:15 sons of **M** *were*, Gershom, and Eliezer.	4872
26:24 the son of **M**, *was* ruler of the treasures.	4872
2Ch 1: 3 which **M** the servant of the LORD had	4872
5:10 two tables which **M** put *therein* at Horeb,	4872
8:13 according to the commandment of **M**,	4872
23:18 as it is written in the law of **M**,	4872
24: 6 *according to the commandment* of **M**	4872
24: 9 **M** the servant of God laid upon Israel in	4872
25: 4 it is written in the law in the book of **M**,	4872
30:16 to the law of **M** the man of God:	4872
33: 8 and the ordinances by the hand of **M**.	4872
34:14 book of the law of the LORD *given* by **M**.	4872
35: 6 the word of the LORD by the hand of **M**.	4872
35:12 as it is written in the book of **M**.	4872
Ezr 3: 2 as it is written in the law of **M** the man	4872
6:18 as it is written in the book of **M**.	4873
7: 6 he *was* a ready scribe in the law of **M**,	4872
Ne 1: 7 which thou commandedst thy servant **M**.	4872
1: 8 that thou commandedst thy servant **M**,	4872
8: 1 scribe to bring the book of the law of **M**,	4872
8:14 which the LORD had commanded by **M**,	4872
9:14 and laws, by the hand of **M** thy servant:	4872
10:29 was given by **M** the servant of God,	4872
13: 1 On that day they read in the book of **M** in	4872
Ps 77:20 thy people like a flock by the hand of **M**	4872
90: T A Prayer of **M** the man of God.	4872
99: 6 **M** and Aaron among his priests,	4872
103: 7 made known his ways unto **M**, his acts	4872
105:26 He sent **M** his servant; *and* Aaron whom	4872
106:16 They envied **M** also in the camp,	4872
106:23 had not **M** his chosen stood before him in	4872
106:32 so that it went ill with **M** for their sakes:	4872
Isa 63:11 the days of old, **M**, *and* his people,	4872
63:12 That led *them* by the right hand of **M**	4872
Jer 15: 1 Though **M** and Samuel stood before me,	4872
Da 9:11 the oath that *is* written in the law of **M**,	4872
9:13 *it is* written in the law of **M**, all this evil	4872
Mic 6: 4 I sent before thee **M**, Aaron, and Miriam.	4872
Mal 4: 4 Remember ye the law of **M** my servant,	4872
Mt 8: 4 offer the gift that **M** commanded for a	3475
17: 3 there appeared unto them **M** and	3475
17: 4 for thee, and one for **M**, and one for Elias.	3475
19: 7 Why did **M** then command to give a	3475
19: 8 **M** because of the hardness of your hearts	3475
22:24 Saying, Master, **M** said, If a man die,	3475
Mk 1:44 *those things* which **M** commanded,	3475
7:10 For **M** said, Honour thy father and	3475
9: 4 there appeared unto them Elias with **M**:	3475
9: 5 for thee, and one for **M**, and one for Elias.	3475
10: 3 unto them, What did **M** command you?	3475
10: 4 **M** suffered to write a bill of divorcement,	3475
12:19 Master, **M** wrote unto us, If a man's	3475
12:26 have ye not read in the book of **M**, how	3475
Lk 2:22 to the law of **M** were accomplished,	3475
5:14 cleansing, according as **M** commanded,	3475
9:30 him two men, which were **M** and Elias:	3475
9:33 for thee, and one for **M**, and one for Elias:	3475
16:29 him, They have **M** and the prophets;	3475
16:31 If they hear not **M** and the prophets,	3475
20:28 Saying, Master, **M** wrote unto us, If any	3475
20:37 are raised, even **M** shewed at the bush,	3475
24:27 And beginning at **M** and all the prophets,	3475
24:44 which were written in the law of **M**,	3475
Jn 1:17 For the law was given by **M**, *but* grace	3475
1:45 of whom **M** in the law, and the prophets,	3475
3:14 And as **M** lifted up the serpent in	3475
5:45 accuseth you, *even* **M**, in whom ye trust.	3475
5:46 For had ye believed **M**, ye would have	3475
6:32 **M** gave you not *that* bread from heaven;	3475
7:19 not **M** give you the law, and *yet* none	3475
7:22 **M** therefore gave unto you circumcision;	3475
7:22 not because it is of **M**, but of the fathers;	3475
7:23 that the law of **M** should not be broken;	3475

M

Ref	Text	Strong's
Jn	8: 5 Now **M** in the law commanded us,	3475
	9:29 We know that God spake unto **M:** *as for*	3475
Ac	3:22 **M** truly said unto the fathers, A prophet	3475
	6:11 him speak blasphemous words against **M**,	3475
	6:14 shall change the customs which **M**	3475
	7:20 In which time **M** was born,	3475
	7:22 And **M** was learned in all the wisdom of	3475
	7:29 Then fled **M** at this saying, and was a	3475
	7:31 When **M** saw *it*, he wondered at the sight:	3475
	7:32 and the God of Jacob. Then **M** trembled,	3475
	7:35 This **M** whom they refused, saying,	3475
	7:37 is *that* **M**, which said unto the children	3475
	7:40 for *as for* this **M**, which brought us out of	3475
	7:44 as he had appointed, speaking unto **M**,	3475
	13:39 ye could not be justified by the law of **M**.	3475
	15: 1 ye be circumcised after the manner of **M**,	3475
	15: 5 to command *them* to keep the law of **M**.	3475
	15:21 For **M** of old time hath in every city them	3475
	21:21 are among the Gentiles to forsake **M**,	3475
	26:22 the prophets and **M** did say should come:	3475
	28:23 both out of the law of **M**, and *out of*	3475
Ro	5:14 death reigned from Adam to **M**,	3475
	9:15 For he saith to **M**, I will have mercy on	3475
	10: 5 For **M** describeth the righteousness which	3475
	10:19 First **M** saith, I will provoke you to	3475
1Co	9: 9 For it is written in the law of **M**, Thou	3475
	10: 2 were all baptized unto **M** in the cloud	3475
2Co	3: 7 face of **M** for the glory of his countenance;	3475
	3:13 And not as **M**, *which* put a vail over his	3475
	3:15 But *even* unto this day, when **M** is read,	3475
2Ti	3: 8 Now as Jannes and Jambres withstood **M**,	3475
Heb	3: 2 as also **M** *was faithful* in all his house.	3475
	3: 3 counted worthy of more glory than **M**,	3475
	3: 5 And **M** verily *was* faithful in all his house,	3475
	3:16 not all that came out of Egypt by **M**.	3475
	7:14 which tribe **M** spake nothing concerning	3475
	8: 5 shadow of heavenly *things*, as **M** was	3475
	9:19 For when **M** had spoken every precept to	3475
	11:23 By faith **M**, when he was born, was hid	3475
	11:24 By faith **M**, when he was come to years,	3475
	12:21 *that* **M** said, I exceedingly fear and quake;)	3475
Jude	1: 9 devil he disputed about the body of **M**,	3475
Rev	15: 3 they sing the song of **M** the servant of	3475

MOSES' (19) [MOSES]

Ref	Text	Strong's
Ex	17:12 **M** hands *were* heavy; and they took a	4872
	18: 1 the priest of Midian, **M** father in law,	4872
	18: 2 Jethro, **M** father in law, took Zipporah,	4872
	18: 2 father in law, took Zipporah, **M** wife,	4872
	18: 5 Jethro, **M** father in law, came with his	4872
	18:12 Jethro, **M** father in law, took a burnt	4872
	18:12 to eat bread with **M** father in law before	4872
	18:14 when **M** father in law saw all that he did	4872
	18:17 **M** father in law said unto him, The thing	4872
	32:19 **M** anger waxed hot, and he cast the	4872
	34:29 the two tables of Testimony in **M** hand,	4872
	34:35 of Moses, that the skin of **M** face shone:	4872
Lev	8:29 of consecration it was **M** part;	4872+3807.1
Nu	10:29 of Raguel the Midianite, **M** father in law,	4872
Jos	1: 1 Joshua the son of Nun, **M** minister,	4872
Jdg	1:16 children of the Kenite, **M** father in law,	4872
Mt	23: 2 scribes and the Pharisees sit in **M** seat:	3475
Jn	9:28 art his disciple; but we are **M** disciples.	3475
Heb	10:28 that despised **M** law died without mercy	3475

MOST (135) [MUCH]

Ref	Text	Strong's
Ge	14:18 and he was the priest of the **m high** God.	5945
	14:19 Blessed *be* Abram of the **m high** God,	5945
	14:20 blessed be the **m high** God, which hath	5945
	14:22 the **m high** God, the possessor of heaven	5945
Ex	26:33 the holy *place* and the **m holy**.	6944+6944
	26:34 Testimony in the **m holy** *place*.	6944+6944
	29:37 and it shall be an altar **m holy:**	6944+6944
	30:10 it *is* **m holy** unto the LORD.	6944+6944
	30:29 that they may be **m holy**.	6944+6944
	30:36 it shall be unto you **m holy**,	6944+6944
	40:10 and it shall be an altar **m holy**.	6944+6944
Lev	2: 3 *it is a thing* **m holy** of the offerings	6944+6944
	2:10 *is a* **thing m holy** of the offerings	6944+6944
	6:17 it *is* **m holy**, as *is* the sin offering,	6944+6944
	6:25 before the LORD: it *is* **m holy**.	6944+6944
	6:29 shall eat thereof: it *is* **m holy**.	6944+6944
	7: 1 the trespass offering: it *is* **m holy**.	6944+6944
	7: 6 in the holy place: it *is* **m holy**.	6944+6944
	10:12 beside the altar: for it *is* **m holy**:	6944+6944
	10:17 seeing it *is* **m holy**, and *God* hath	6944+6944
	14:13 the trespass offering: it *is* **m holy**:	6944+6944
	21:22 of the **m holy**, and of the holy.	6944+6944
	24: 9 for it *is* **m holy** unto him of	6944+6944
	27:28 devoted thing *is* **m holy** unto	6944+6944
Nu	4: 4 *about* the **m holy** *things*:	6944+6944
	4:19 unto the **m holy** *things:* Aaron	6944+6944
	18: 9 This shall be thine of the **m holy**,	6944+6944
	18: 9 **m holy** for thee and for thy sons.	6944+6944
	18:10 In the **m holy** *place* shalt thou eat	6944+6944
	24:16 and knew the knowledge of the **m High**,	5945
Dt	32: 8 When the **m High** divided to the nations	5945
2Sa	22:14 and the **m High** uttered his voice.	5945
	23:19 Was he not **m** honourable of three?	3588
1Ki	6:16 *even* for the **m holy** place.	6944+6944
	7:50 **m holy** place, and for the doors	6944+6944
	8: 6 to the **m holy** place, even under	6944+6944
1Ch	6:49 all the work of the *place* **m holy**,	6944+6944
	23:13 should sanctify the **m holy** *things*,	6944+6944
2Ch	3: 8 he made the **m holy** house,	6944+6944

Ref	Text	Strong's
2Ch	3:10 in the **m holy** house he made two	6944+6944
	4:22 doors thereof for the **m holy** *place*,	6944+6944
	5: 7 into the **m holy** *place*, even under	6944+6944
	31:14 the LORD, and the **m holy** *things*.	6944+6944
Ezr	2:63 **m holy** *things* till there stood *up* a	6944+6944
Ne	7:65 **m holy** *things*, till there stood *up* a	6944+6944
Est	6: 9 of one of the king's **m noble** princes,	6579
Job	34:17 wilt thou condemn him that is **m** just?	3524
Ps	7:17 *praise* to the name of the LORD **m High**.	5945
	9: 2 sing *praise* to thy name, O thou **m High**.	5945
	21: 6 thou hast made him blessed for ever:	NIH
	21: 7 through the mercy of the **m High** he shall	5945
	45: 3 O **m** mighty, with thy glory and	NIH
	46: 4 place of the tabernacles of the **m High**.	5945
	47: 2 For the LORD **m High** is terrible; *he is* a	5945
	50:14 and pay thy vows unto the **m High**:	5945
	56: 2 that fight against me, O thou **m High**.	NIH
	57: 2 I will cry unto God **m High**; unto God	5945
	73:11 and is there knowledge in the **m High**?	5945
	77:10 the years of the right hand of the **m High**.	5945
	78:17 provoking the **m High** in the wilderness.	5945
	78:56 and provoked the **m high** God,	5945
	82: 6 and all of you *are* children of the **m High**.	5945
	83:18 *art* the **m High** over all the earth.	5945
	91: 1 **m High** shall abide under the shadow of	5945
	91: 9 even the **m High**, thy habitation;	5945
	92: 1 to sing *praises* unto thy name, O **m High**:	5945
	92: 8 But thou, LORD, *art* **m** high for evermore.	NIH
	107:11 contemned the counsel of the **m High**:	5945
Pr	20: 6 **M** men will proclaim every one his own	7230
SS	5:11 His head *is as* the **m** fine gold, his locks	3800
	5:16 His mouth is **m** sweet: yea, he *is*	4477
	8: 6 fire, *which hath* a **m** vehement flame.	7957
Isa	14:14 of the clouds; I will be like the **m High**.	5945
	26: 7 thou, **m upright**, dost weigh the path of	3477
Jer	6:26 *as for an only son*, **m** bitter lamentation:	NIH
	50:31 I *am* against thee, O thou **m** proud,	NIH
	50:32 the **m proud** shall stumble and fall,	2087
La	3:35 of a man before the face of the **m High**,	5945
	3:38 of the mouth of the **m High** proceedeth	5945
	4: 1 is the **m** fine gold changed! the stones	2896
Eze	2: 7 will forbear: for they *are* **m** rebellious.	NIH
	23:12 and rulers clothed **m** gorgeously,	4358
	33:28 lay the land **m desolate**,	4923+8077+2050.1
	33:29 laid the land **m desolate**	4923+8077+2050.1
	35: 3 make thee **m desolate**,	4923+8077+2050.1
	35: 7 mount Seir **m desolate**,	8077+8077+2050.1
	41: 4 unto me, This *is* the **m holy** place.	6944+6944
	42:13 **m holy** *things:* there shall they lay	6944+6944
	42:13 shall they lay the **m holy** *things*,	6944+6944
	43:12 round about *shall* be **m holy**.	6944+6944
	44:13 holy *things*, in the **m holy** *place:*	6944+6944
	45: 3 sanctuary and the **m holy** place.	6944+6944
	48:12 **m holy** by the border of the	6944+6944
Da	3:20 **m mighty men** that *were* in	1400+1401+2429
	3:26 servants of the **m high** God, come forth,	5943
	4:17 the **m High** ruleth in the kingdom of men,	5943
	4:24 and this *is* the decree of the **m High**,	5943
	4:25 till thou know that the **m High** ruleth in	5943
	4:32 thou know that the **m High** ruleth in	5943
	4:34 I blessed the **m High**, and I praised and	5943
	5:18 the **m high** God gave Nebuchadnezzar	5943
	5:21 till he knew that the **m high** God ruled	5943
	7:18 the saints of the **m High** shall take	5946
	7:22 was given to the saints of the **m High**;	5946
	7:25 speak *great* words against the **m High**,	5943
	7:25 shall wear out the saints of the **m High**,	5946
	7:27 to the people of the saints of the **m High**,	5946
	9:24 and to anoint the **m Holy**.	6944+6944
	11:15 a mount, and take the **m fenced** cities	4013
	11:39 Thus shall he do in the **m strong** holds	4581
Hos	7:16 They return, *but* not to the **m High**:	5920
	11: 7 though they called them to the **m High**,	5920
	12:14 provoked *him* to anger **m** bitterly:	8563
Mic	7: 4 the **m** upright *is sharper* than a thorn	NIH
Mt	11:20 **m** of his mighty works were done,	4183
Mk	5: 7 Jesus, *thou* Son of the **m high** God?	4183
Lk	1: 1 which are **m** surely believed among us,	4135
	1: 3 thee in order, **m** excellent Theophilus,	2903
	7:42 which of them will love him **m**?	4183
	7:43 I suppose that *he*, to whom he forgave **m**.	4183
	8:28 thee, Jesus, *thou* Son of God **m** high?	5310
	7:48 Howbeit the **m High** dwelleth not in	5310
Ac	16:17 men are the servants of the **m high**	5310
	20:38 Sorrowing **m** *of all* for the words which	3122
	23:26 Claudius Lysias unto the **m excellent**	2903
	24: 3 always, and in all places, **m noble** Felix,	2903
	26: 5 after the **m straitest** sect of our religion	196
	26:25 he said, I am not mad, **m noble** Festus;	2903
1Co	15:19 In Christ, we are of all men **m** miserable.	1652
2Co	12: 9 **M** gladly therefore will I rather glory in	2236
Heb	7: 1 king of Salem, priest of the **m high** God,	5310
Jude	1:20 up yourselves on your **m holy** faith,	40
Rev	18:12 all *manner* vessels of **m precious** wood,	5093
	21:11 light *was* like unto a stone **m precious**,	5093

MOTE (6)

Ref	Text	Strong's
Mt	7: 3 why beholdest thou the **m** that is in thy	2595
	7: 4 Let me pull out the **m** out of thine eye;	2595
	7: 5 thou see clearly to cast out the **m** out	2595
Lk	6:41 why beholdest thou the **m** that is in thy	2595
	6:42 let me pull out the **m** that is in thine eye,	2595
	6:42 thou see clearly to pull out the **m** that	2595

MOTH (9) [MOTHEATEN, MOTH-EATEN]

Ref	Text	Strong's
Job	4:19 the dust, which are crushed before the **m**?	6211
	27:18 He buildeth his house as a **m**, and as a	6211
Ps	39:11 his beauty to consume away like a **m**:	6211
Isa	50: 9 old as a garment; the **m** shall eat them up.	6211
	51: 8 the **m** shall eat them up like a garment,	6211
Hos	5:12 Therefore *will* I *be* unto Ephraim as a **m**,	6211
Mt	6:19 where **m** and rust doth corrupt,	4597
	6:20 where neither **m** nor rust doth corrupt,	4597
Lk	12:33 thief approacheth, neither **m** corrupteth.	4597

MOTHEATEN, MOTH-EATEN (2) [MOTH]

Ref	Text	Strong's
Job	13:28 consumeth, as a garment that is **m**.	398+6211
Jas	5: 2 are corrupted, and your garments are **m**.	4598

MOTHER (245) [GRANDMOTHER, MOTHER'S, MOTHERS, MOTHERS']

Ref	Text	Strong's
Ge	2:24 shall a man leave his father and his **m**,	517
	3:20 because she was the **m** of all living.	517
	17:16 bless her, and she shall be *a* **m** of nations;	NIH
	20:12 my father, but not the daughter of my **m**;	517
	21:21 his **m** took him a wife out of the land of	517
	24:53 her brother and to her **m** precious things.	517
	24:55 her brother and her **m** said, Let the damsel	517
	24:60 be thou the **m** of thousands of millions,	NIH
	24:67 Isaac brought her into his **m** Sarah's tent,	517
	27:11 Jacob said to Rebekah his **m**, Behold,	517
	27:13 **m** said unto him, Upon me *be* thy curse,	517
	27:14 and fetched, and brought *them* to his **m**:	517
	27:14 **m** made savoury meat, such as his father	517
	28: 5 brother of Rebekah, Jacob's and Esau's **m**.	517
	28: 7 that Jacob obeyed his father and his **m**,	517
	30:14 field, and brought them unto his **m** Leah.	517
	32:11 smite me, *and* the **m** with the children.	517
	37:10 Shall I and thy **m** and thy brethren indeed	517
	44:20 he alone is left of his **m**, and his father	517
Ex	2: 8 the maid went and called the child's **m**.	517
	20:12 Honour thy father and thy **m**: that thy days	517
	21:15 or his **m**, shall be surely put to death.	517
	21:17 or his **m**, shall surely be put to death.	517
Lev	18: 7 or the nakedness of thy **m**, shalt thou not	517
	18: 7 she *is* thy **m**; thou shalt not uncover her	517
	18: 9 of thy father, or daughter of thy **m**,	517
	19: 3 Ye shall fear every man his **m**,	517
	20: 9 or his **m** shall be surely put to death:	517
	20: 9 hath cursed his father or his **m**; his blood	517
	20:14 if a man take a wife and her **m**, it *is*	517
	21: 2 *that is*, for his **m**, and for his father,	517
	21:11 defile himself for his father, or for his **m**;	517
Nu	6: 7 for his **m**, for his brother, or for his sister,	517
	26:59 Levi, whom *her* **m** bare to Levi in Egypt:	NIH
Dt	5:16 Honour thy father and thy **m**, as the LORD	517
	13: 6 son of thy **m**, or thy son, or thy daughter,	517
	21:13 bewail her father and her **m** a full month:	517
	21:18 or the voice of his **m**, and *that*, when they	517
	21:19 shall his father and his **m** lay hold on him,	517
	22:15 her **m**, take and bring forth the *tokens of*	517
	27:16 he that setteth light by his father or his **m**.	517
	27:22 of his father, or the daughter of his **m**,	517
	27:23 Cursed *be* he that lieth with his **m in law**.	2859
	33: 9 Who said unto his father and to his **m**,	517
Jos	2:13 my **m**, and my brethren, and my sisters,	517
	2:18 **m**, and thy brethren, and all thy father's	517
	6:23 **m**, and her brethren, and all that she had;	517
Jdg	5: 7 I Deborah arose, that I arose a **m** in Israel.	517
	5:28 The **m** of Sisera looked out at a window,	517
	8:19 *were* my brethren, *even* the sons of my **m**:	517
	14: 2 and told his father and his **m**, and said,	517
	14: 3 father and his **m** said unto him, *Is there*	517
	14: 4 his **m** knew not that it *was* of the LORD,	517
	14: 5 his father and his **m**, to Timnath,	517
	14: 6 not his father or his **m** what he had done.	517
	14: 9 to his father and **m**, and he gave them,	517
	14:16 I have not told *it* my father nor my **m**,	517
	17: 2 he said unto his **m**, The eleven hundred	517
	17: 2 his **m** said, Blessed *be* thou of the LORD,	517
	17: 3 eleven hundred *shekels* of silver to his **m**,	517
	17: 3 **m** said, I had wholly dedicated the silver	517
	17: 4 Yet he restored the money unto his **m**;	517
	17: 4 his **m** took two hundred *shekels* of silver,	517
Ru	1:14 Orpah kissed her **m in law**; but Ruth	2545
	2:11 all that thou hast done unto thy **m in law**	2545
	2:11 *how* thou hast left thy father and thy **m**,	517
	2:18 her **m in law** saw what she had gleaned:	2545
	2:19 her **m in law** said unto her, Where hast	2545
	2:19 she shewed her **m in law** with whom	2545
	2:23 and dwelt with her **m in law**.	2545
	3: 1 Naomi her **m in law** said unto her,	2545
	3: 6 according to all that her **m in law** bade	2545
	3:16 she came to her **m in law**, she said,	2545
	3:17 to me, Go not empty unto thy **m in law**.	2545
1Sa	2:19 Moreover his **m** made him a little coat,	517
	15:33 so shall thy **m** be childless among women.	517
	22: 3 Let my father and my **m**, I pray thee,	517
2Sa	17:25 of Nahash, sister to Zeruiah Joab's **m**.	517
	19:37 by the grave of my father and of my **m**.	517
	20:19 seekest to destroy a city and a **m** in Israel:	517
1Ki	1: 6 and *his* **m** bare him after Absalom.	NIH
	1:11 spake unto Bath-sheba the **m** of Solomon,	517
	2:13 came to Bath-sheba the **m** of Solomon.	517
	2:19 caused a seat to be set for the king's **m**;	517
	2:20 the king said unto her, Ask on, my **m**: for I	517
	2:22 Solomon answered and said unto his **m**,	517
	3:27 in no wise slay it: she *is* the **m** thereof.	517
	15:13 Maachah his **m**, even her he removed	517

1Ki	17:23 the house, and delivered him unto his **m**:	517
	19:20 kiss my father and my **m**, and *then* I will	517
	22:52 in the way of his **m**, and in the way of	517
2Ki	3: 2 but not like his father, and like his **m**:	517
	3:13 of thy father, and to the prophets of thy **m**.	517
	4:19 And he said to a lad, Carry him to his **m**.	517
	4:20 brought him to his **m**, he sat on her knees	517
	4:30 the **m** of the child said, *As* the LORD	517
	9:22 long as the whoredoms of thy **m** Jezebel	517
	11: 1 when Athaliah the **m** of Ahaziah saw that	517
	24:12 he, and his **m**, and his servants,	517
	24:15 the king's **m**, and the king's wives, and his	517
1Ch	2:26 name *was* Atarah; she *was* the **m** of Onam.	517
	4: 9 his **m** called his name Jabez, saying,	517
2Ch	15:16 also *concerning* Maachah the **m** of Asa	517
	22: 3 his **m** was his counseller to do wickedly.	517
	22:10 when Athaliah the **m** of Ahaziah saw that	517
Est	2: 7 for she had neither father nor **m**,	517
	2: 7 when her father and **m** were dead,	517
Job	17:14 the worm, *Thou art* my **m**, and my sister.	517
Ps	27:10 When my father and my **m** forsake me,	517
	35:14 as one that mourneth for his **m**:	517
	51: 5 and in sin did my **m** conceive me.	517
	109:14 and let not the sin of his **m** be blotted out.	517
	113: 9 to keep house, *to be* a joyful **m** of children.	517
	131: 2 as a child that is weaned of his **m**:	517
Pr	1: 8 father, and forsake not the law of thy **m**:	517
	4: 3 and only *beloved* in the sight of my **m**.	517
	6:20 and forsake not the law of thy **m**:	517
	10: 1 but a foolish son *is* the heaviness of his **m**.	517
	15:20 but a foolish man despiseth his **m**.	517
	19:26 *his* father, *and* chaseth away *his* **m**,	517
	20:20 Whoso curseth his father or his **m**, his	517
	23:22 and despise not thy **m** when she is old.	517
	23:25 Thy father and thy **m** shall be glad,	517
	28:24 Whoso robbeth his father or his **m**, and	517
	29:15 a child left *to himself* bringeth his **m** to	517
	30:11 their father, and doth not bless their **m**.	517
	30:17 at *his* father, and despiseth to obey *his* **m**,	517
	31: 1 the prophecy that his **m** taught him.	517
SS	3:11 crowned him in the day of his espousals,	517
	6: 9 she *is* the *only* one of her **m**, she *is*	517
	8: 1 brother, that sucked the breasts of my **m**!	517
	8: 5 there thy **m** brought thee forth: there she	517
Isa	8: 4 My father, and my **m**, the riches of	517
	49: 1 from the bowels of my **m** hath he made	517
	50: 1 for your transgressions *is* your **m** put away.	517
	66:13 As one whom his **m** comforteth, so will I	517
Jer	15: 8 I have brought upon them against the **m** of	517
	15:10 Woe is me, my **m**, that thou hast borne me	517
	16: 7 to drink for their father or for their **m**.	517
	20:14 let not the day wherein my **m** bare me be	517
	20:17 or that my **m** might have been my grave,	517
	22:26 thy **m** that bare thee, into another country,	517
	50:12 Your **m** shall be sore confounded; she that	517
Eze	16: 3 father *was* an Amorite, and thy **m** a Hittite.	517
	16:44 saying, As *is* the **m**, *so is* her daughter.	517
	16:45 your **m** *was* a Hittite, and your father an	517
	19: 2 What *is* thy **m**? A lioness: she lay down	517
	19:10 Thy **m** *is* like a vine in thy blood, planted	517
	22: 7 thee have they set light by father and **m**:	517
	23: 2 two women, the daughters of one **m**:	517
	44:25 or for **m**, or for son, or for daughter,	517
Hos	2: 2 Plead with your **m**, plead: for she *is* not	517
	2: 5 For their **m** hath played the harlot: she	517
	4: 5 thee *in* the night, and I will destroy thy **m**.	517
	10:14 the **m** was dashed in pieces upon *her*	517
Mic	7: 6 the daughter riseth up against her **m**,	517
	7: 6 the daughter in law against her **m** in law;	2545
Zec	13: 3 his **m** that begat him shall say unto him,	517
	13: 3 his **m** that begat him shall thrust him	517
Mt	1:18 When as his **m** Mary was espoused to	3384
	2:11 saw the young child with Mary his **m**,	3384
	2:13 and take the young child and his **m**,	3384
	2:14 took the young child and his **m** by night,	3384
	2:20 and take the young child and his **m**,	3384
	2:21 and took the young child and his **m**,	3384
	8:14 he saw his **wife's m** laid, and sick of a	3994
	10:35 and the daughter against her **m**,	3384
	10:35 the daughter in law against her **m** in law.	3994
	10:37 or **m** more than me is not worthy of me:	3384
	12:46 *his* **m** and his brethren stood without,	3384
	12:47 thy **m** and thy brethren stand without,	3384
	12:48 unto him that told him, Who is my **m**?	3384
	12:49 and said, Behold my **m** and my brethren.	3384
	12:50 same is my brother, and sister, and **m**.	3384
	13:55 not his **m** called Mary? and his brethren,	3384
	14: 8 being before instructed of her **m**, said,	3384
	14:11 the damsel: and she brought *it* to her **m**.	3384
	15: 4 saying, Honour thy father and **m**:	3384
	15: 4 He that curseth father or **m**, let him die	3384
	15: 5 Whosoever shall say to *his* father or *his* **m**,	3384
	15: 6 honour not his father or his **m**, *he shall*	3384
	19: 5 this cause shall a man leave father and **m**,	3384
	19:19 Honour thy father and *thy* **m**: and,	3384
	19:29 father, or **m**, or wife, or children, or lands,	3384
	20:20 Then came to him the **m** of Zebedee's	3384
	27:56 and Mary the **m** of James and Joses,	3384
	27:56 Joses, and the **m** of Zebedee's children.	3384
Mk	1:30 But Simon's **wife's m** lay sick of a fever,	3994
	3:31 There came then *his* brethren and his **m**,	3384
	3:32 thy **m** and thy brethren without seek for	3384
	3:33 saying, Who is my **m**, or my brethren?	3384
	3:34 and said, Behold my **m** and my brethren.	3384
	3:35 same is my brother, and my sister, and **m**.	3384

Mk	5:40 taketh the father and the **m** of the damsel,	3384
	6:24 and said unto her **m**, What shall I ask?	3384
	6:28 and the damsel gave it to her **m**.	3384
	7:10 Moses said, Honour thy father and thy **m**;	3384
	7:10 Whoso curseth father or **m**, let him die	3384
	7:11 say, If a man shall say to *his* father or **m**,	3384
	7:12 more to do ought for his father or his **m**;	3384
	10: 7 cause shall a man leave his father and **m**,	3384
	10:19 Defraud not, Honour thy father and **m**.	3384
	10:29 or **m**, or wife, or children, or lands,	3384
	15:40 and Mary the **m** of James the less and	3384
	15:47 Mary the **m** of Joses beheld where he was	NIG
	16: 1 and Mary the **m** of James, and Salome,	NIG
Lk	1:43 the **m** of my Lord should come to me?	3384
	1:60 And his **m** answered and said, Not *so;*	3384
	2:33 his **m** marvelled at those *things* which	3384
	2:34 and said unto Mary his **m**, Behold,	3384
	2:43 and Joseph and his **m** knew not *of it*.	3384
	2:48 and his **m** said unto him, Son, why hast	3384
	2:51 his **m** kept all these sayings in her heart.	3384
	4:38 And Simon's **wife's m** was taken with a	3994
	7:12 the only son of his **m**, and she was a	3384
	7:15 to speak. And he delivered him to his **m**.	3384
	8:19 came to him *his* **m** and his brethren,	3384
	8:20 Thy **m** and thy brethren stand without,	3384
	8:21 My **m** and my brethren are these which	3384
	8:51 and the father and the **m** of the maiden.	3384
	12:53 the **m** against the daughter,	3384
	12:53 and the daughter against the **m**;	3384
	12:53 the **m** in law against her daughter in law,	3994
	12:53 the daughter in law against her **m** in law.	3994
	14:26 and **m**, and wife, and children,	3384
	18:20 witness, Honour thy father and thy **m**.	3384
	24:10 Mary the **m** of James, and other *women*	NIG
Jn	2: 1 of Galilee; and the **m** of Jesus was there:	3384
	2: 3 the **m** of Jesus saith unto him, They have	3384
	2: 5 His **m** saith unto the servants,	3384
	2:12 he, and his **m**, and his brethren,	3384
	6:42 of Joseph, whose father and **m** we know?	3384
	19:25 there stood by the cross of Jesus his **m**,	3384
	19:26 When Jesus therefore saw *his* **m**,	3384
	19:26 he saith unto his **m**, Woman, behold thy	3384
	19:27 saith he to the disciple, Behold thy **m**.	3384
Ac	1:14 and Mary the **m** of Jesus, and with his	3384
	12:12 came to the house of Mary the **m** of John,	3384
Ro	16:13 chosen in the Lord, and his **m** and mine.	3384
Gal	4:26 is above is free, which is the **m** of us all.	3384
Eph	5:31 cause shall a man leave his father and **m**,	3384
2Ti	1: 5 thy grandmother Lois, and thy **m** Eunice;	3384
Heb	7: 3 Without father, **without m**, without	282
Rev	17: 5 THE **M** OF HARLOTS AND	3384

MOTHER'S (75) [MOTHER]

Ge	24:28 told *them of* her **m** house these things.	517
	24:67 Isaac was comforted after his **m** *death*.	517
	27:29 and let thy **m** sons bow down to thee:	517
	28: 2 to the house of Bethuel thy **m** father;	517
	28: 2 of the daughters of Laban thy **m** brother.	517
	29:10 the daughter of Laban his **m** brother,	517
	29:10 sheep of Laban his **m** brother, that Jacob	517
	29:10 watered the flock of Laban his **m** brother.	517
	43:29 his brother Benjamin, his **m** son, and said,	517
Ex	23:19 Thou shalt not seethe a kid in his **m** milk.	517
	34:26 Thou shalt not seethe a kid in his **m** milk.	517
Lev	18:13 not uncover the nakedness of thy **m** sister:	517
	18:13 for she *is* thy **m** near kinswoman.	517
	20:17 or his **m** daughter, and see her nakedness,	517
	20:19 not uncover the nakedness of thy **m** sister,	517
	24:11 (and his **m** name *was* Shelomith,	517
Nu	12:12 when he cometh out of his **m** womb.	517
Dt	14:21 Thou shalt not seethe a kid in his **m** milk.	517
Jdg	9: 1 went to Shechem unto his **m** brethren,	517
	9: 1 with all the family of the house of his **m**	517
	9: 3 his **m** brethren spake of him in the ears of	517
	16:17 a Nazarite unto God from my **m** womb:	517
Ru	1: 8 in law, Go, return each to her **m** house:	517
1Sa	20:30 unto the confusion of thy **m** nakedness?	517
1Ki	11:26 whose **m** name *was* Zeruah, a widow	517
	14:21 his **m** name *was* Naamah an Ammonitess.	517
	14:31 his **m** name *was* Naamah an Ammonitess.	517
	15: 2 his **m** name *was* Maachah, the daughter of	517
	15:10 his **m** name *was* Maachah, the daughter of	517
	22:42 his **m** name *was* Azubah the daughter of	517
2Ki	8:26 his **m** name *was* Athaliah, the daughter of	517
	12: 1 And his **m** name *was* Zibiah of Beer-sheba.	517
	14: 2 his **m** name *was* Jehoaddan of Jerusalem.	517
	15: 2 his **m** name *was* Jecholiah of Jerusalem.	517
	15:33 his **m** name *was* Jerusha, the daughter of	517
	18: 2 His **m** name also *was* Abi, the daughter of	517
	21: 1 And his **m** name *was* Hephzi-bah.	517
	21:19 his **m** name *was* Meshullemeth, the	517
	22: 1 his **m** name *was* Jedidah, the daughter of	517
	23:31 his **m** name *was* Hamutal, the daughter of	517
	23:36 his **m** name *was* Zebudah, the daughter of	517
	24: 8 his **m** name *was* Nehushta, the daughter of	517
	24:18 his **m** name *was* Hamutal, the daughter of	517
2Ch	12:13 his **m** name *was* Naamah an Ammonitess.	517
	13: 2 His **m** name also *was* Michaiah the	517
	20:31 his **m** name *was* Azubah the daughter of	517
	22: 2 his **m** name also *was* Athaliah the daughter	517
	24: 1 His **m** name also *was* Zibiah of Beer-sheba.	517
	25: 1 His **m** name also *was* Jehoaddan of Jerusalem.	517
	26: 3 His **m** name also *was* Jecoliah of Jerusalem.	517
	27: 1 his **m** name also *was* Jerusha, the	517

2Ch	29: 1 his **m** name *was* Abijah, the daughter of	517
Job	1:21 Naked came I out of my **m** womb,	517
	3:10 Because it shut not up the doors of my **m**	NIH
	31:18 and I have guided her from my **m** womb;)	517
Ps	22: 9 me hope *when I was* upon my **m** breasts.	517
	22:10 thou *art* my God from my **m** belly.	517
	50:20 thou slanderest thine own **m** son.	517
	69: 8 and an alien unto my **m** children.	517
	71: 6 thou art he that took me out of my **m**	517
	139:13 thou hast covered me in my **m** womb.	517
Ecc	5:15 As he came forth of his **m** womb,	517
SS	1: 6 my **m** children were angry with me;	517
	3: 4 until I had brought him into my **m** house,	517
	8: 2 thee, *and* bring thee into my **m** house,	517
Isa	50: 1 Where *is* the bill of your **m** divorcement,	517
Jer	52: 1 his **m** name *was* Hamutal the daughter of	517
Eze	16:45 Thou *art* thy **m** daughter, that lotheth her	517
Mt	19:12 which were so born from *their* **m** womb:	3384
Lk	1:15 the Holy Ghost, even from his **m** womb.	3384
Jn	3: 4 can he enter the second time into his **m**	3384
	19:25 and his **m** sister, Mary the **wife** of	3384
Ac	3: 2 a certain man lame from his **m** womb	3384
	14: 8 feet, being a cripple from his **m** womb,	3384
Gal	1:15 who separated me from my **m** womb,	3384

MOTHERS (7) [MOTHER]

Isa	49:23 and their queens thy **nursing m**:	3243
Jer	16: 3 concerning their **m** that bare them,	517
La	2:12 They say to their **m**, Where *is* corn and	517
	5: 3 and fatherless, our **m** *are* as widows.	517
Mk	10:30 sisters, and **m**, and children, and lands,	3384
1Ti	1: 9 of fathers and **murderers of m**,	3389
	5: 2 The elder *women* as **m**; the younger as	3384

MOTHERS' (1) [MOTHER]

La	2:12 their soul was poured out into their **m**	517

MOTHS See MOTHEATEN

MOTIONS (1) [MOVE]

Ro	7: 5 the **m** of sins, which were by the law,	3804

MOULDY (2)

Jos	9: 5 bread of their provision was dry *and* **m**.	5350
	9:12 but now, behold, it is dry, and it is **m**:	5350

MOUND; MOUNDS See EMINENT

MOUNT (263) [MOUNTAIN, MOUNTED, MOUNTING, MOUNTS]

Ge	10:30 thou goest unto Sephar, a **m** of the east.	2022
	14: 6 the Horites in their **m** Seir, unto El-paran,	2042
	22:14 In the **m** of the LORD it shall be seen.	2022
	31:21 and set his face *toward* the **m** Gilead.	2022
	31:23 and they overtook him in the **m** Gilead.	2022
	31:25 Now Jacob had pitched his tent in the **m**:	2022
	31:25 Laban with his brethren pitched in the **m**	2022
	31:54 Jacob offered sacrifice upon the **m**,	2022
	31:54 eat bread, and tarried all night in the **m**.	2022
	36: 8 dwelt Esau in **m** Seir: Esau *is* Edom.	2022
	36: 9 the father of the Edomites in **m** Seir:	2022
Ex	4:27 him in the **m** of God, and kissed him.	2022
	18: 5 where he encamped *at* the **m** of God:	2022
	19: 2 and there Israel camped before the **m**.	2022
	19:11 the sight of all the people upon the **m** Sinai.	2022
	19:12 *that ye go not* up into the **m**, or touch	2022
	19:12 whosoever toucheth the **m** shall be surely	2022
	19:13 long, they shall come up to the **m**.	2022
	19:14 Moses went down from the **m** unto	2022
	19:16 a thick cloud upon the **m**, and the voice	2022
	19:17 they stood at the nether part of the **m**.	2022
	19:18 in Sinai was altogether on a smoke,	2022
	19:18 furnace, and the whole **m** quaked greatly.	2022
	19:20 the LORD came down upon the **m** Sinai,	2022
	19:20 upon mount Sinai, on the top of the **m**:	2022
	19:20 called Moses *up* to the top of the **m**;	2022
	19:23 The people cannot come up to the **m** Sinai:	2022
	19:23 Set bounds about the **m**, and sanctify it.	2022
	24:12 Come up to me into the **m**, and be there:	2022
	24:13 and Moses went up into the **m** of God.	2022
	24:15 Moses went up into the **m**, and a cloud	2022
	24:15 the mount, and a cloud covered the **m**.	2022
	24:16 the glory of the LORD abode upon **m**	2022
	24:17 the **m** in the eyes of the children of Israel.	2022
	24:18 of the cloud, and gat him up into the **m**:	2022
	24:18 Moses was in the **m** forty days and	2022
	25:40 which was shewed thee in the **m**.	2022
	26:30 thereof which was shewed thee in the **m**.	2022
	27: 8 as it was shewed thee in the **m**,	2022
	31:18 of communing with him upon **m** Sinai,	2022
	32: 1 delayed to come down out of the **m**,	2022
	32:15 went down from the **m**, and the two	2022
	32:19 hands, and brake them beneath the **m**.	2022
	33: 6 of their ornaments by the **m** Horeb.	2022
	34: 2 come up in the morning unto **m** Sinai,	2022
	34: 2 thyself there to me in the top of the **m**.	2022
	34: 3 let any man be seen throughout all the **m**;	2022
	34: 3 the flocks nor herds feed before that **m**.	2022
	34: 4 the morning, and went up unto **m** Sinai,	2022
	34:29 Moses came down from Sinai with	2022
	34:29 when he came down from the **m**,	2022
	34:32 LORD had spoken with him in the **m** Sinai.	2022
Lev	7:38 the LORD commanded Moses in **m** Sinai,	2022
	25: 1 the LORD spake unto Moses in **m** Sinai,	2022
	26:46 the children of Israel in **m** Sinai by	2022
	27:34 for the children of Israel in **m** Sinai.	2022

M

Nu 3: 1 the LORD spake with Moses in **m** Sinai. 2022
10:33 they departed from the **m** of the LORD 2022
20:22 from Kadesh, and came *unto* **m** Hor. 2022
20:23 spake unto Moses and Aaron in **m** Hor, 2022
20:25 his son, and bring them up *unto* **m** Hor: 2022
20:27 went up into **m** Hor in the sight of all 2022
20:28 and Aaron died there in the top of the **m**: 2022
20:28 and Eleazar came down from the **m**. 2022
21: 4 they journeyed from **m** Hor *by* the way of 2022
27:12 Get thee up into this **m** Abarim, and see 2022
28: 6 was ordained in **m** Sinai for a sweet 2022
33:23 and pitched in **m** Shapher. 2022
33:24 they removed from **m** Shapher, 2022
33:37 pitched in **m** Hor, in the edge of the land 2022
33:38 Aaron the priest went up into **m** Hor at 2022
33:39 three years old when he died in **m** Hor. 2022
33:41 they departed from Hor, and pitched 2022
34: 7 sea you shall point out for you **m** Hor: 2022
34: 8 From **m** Hor ye shall point out *your* 2022
Dt 1: 2 the way of **m** Seir unto Kadesh-barnea.) 2022
1: 6 Ye have dwelt long enough in this **m** 2022
1: 7 go *to* the **m** of the Amorites, and unto all 2022
2: 1 and we compassed **m** Seir many days. 2022
2: 5 I have given **m** Seir unto Esau *for a* 2022
3: 8 from the river of Arnon unto **m** Hermon; 2022
3:12 half **m** Gilead, and the cities thereof, 2022
4:48 even unto **m** Sion, which *is* Hermon, 2022
5: 4 face in the **m** out of the midst of the fire, 2022
5: 5 of the fire, and went not up into the **m**;) 2022
5:22 in the **m** out of the midst of the fire, 2022
9: 9 I was gone up into the **m** to receive 2022
9: 9 I abode in the **m** forty days and 2022
9:10 which the LORD spake with you in the **m** 2022
9:15 So I turned and came down from the **m**, 2022
9:15 the mount, and the **m** burned with fire: 2022
9:21 the brook that descended out of the **m**. 2022
10: 1 come up unto me into the **m**, and make 2022
10: 3 went up into the **m**, having the two 2022
10: 4 which the LORD spake unto you in the **m** 2022
10: 5 myself and came down from the **m**, 2022
10:10 I stayed in the **m**, according to the first 2022
11:29 that thou shalt put the blessing upon **m** 2022
11:29 Gerizim, and the curse upon **m** Ebal. 2022
27: 4 in **m** Ebal, and thou shalt plaister them 2022
27:12 shall stand upon **m** Gerizzim to bless 2022
27:13 these shall stand upon **m** Ebal to curse; 2022
32:49 **m** Nebo, which *is* in the land of Moab, 2022
32:50 die in the **m** whither thou goest up, 2022
32:50 as Aaron thy brother died in **m** Hor, 2022
33: 2 he shined forth from **m** Paran, and he 2022
Jos 8:30 unto the LORD God of Israel in **m** Ebal, 2022
8:33 half of them over against **m** Gerizim, 2022
8:33 and half of them over against **m** Ebal; 2022
11:17 *Even* from the **m** Halak, that goeth up *to* 2022
11:17 the valley of Lebanon under **m** Hermon: 2022
12: 1 from the river Arnon unto **m** Hermon, 2022
12: 5 reigned in **m** Hermon, and in Salcah, 2022
12: 7 valley of Lebanon even unto the **m** Halak, 2022
13: 5 from Baal-gad under **m** Hermon unto 2022
13:11 **m** Hermon, and all Bashan unto Salcah; 2022
13:19 and Zareth-shahar in the **m** of the valley, 2022
15: 9 and went out to the cities of **m** Ephron; 2022
15:10 from Baalah westward unto **m** Seir, 2022
15:10 passed along unto the side of **m** Jearim, 2022
15:11 passed along *to* **m** Baalah, and went out 2022
16: 1 up from Jericho throughout **m** Beth-el, 2022
17:15 if **m** Ephraim be too narrow for thee. 2022
19:50 *even* Timnath-serah in **m** Ephraim. 2022
20: 7 they appointed Kedesh in Galilee in **m** 2022
20: 7 Shechem in **m** Ephraim, and Kirjath-arba, 2022
21:21 Shechem with her suburbs in **m** Ephraim, 2022
24: 4 I gave unto Esau **m** Seir, to possess it; 2022
24:30 *is* in **m** Ephraim, on the north side of 2022
24:33 which was given him in **m** Ephraim. 2022
Jdg 1:35 the Amorites would dwell in **m** Heres in 2022
2: 9 in the **m** of Ephraim, on the north side of 2022
3: 3 and the Hivites that dwelt in **m** Lebanon, 2022
3: 3 from **m** Baal-hermon unto the entering in 2022
3:27 Israel went down with him from the **m**, 2022
4: 5 Ramah and Beth-el in **m** Ephraim: 2022
4: 6 *saying,* Go and draw toward **m** Tabor, 2022
4:12 son of Abinoam was gone up *to* **m** Tabor. 2022
4:14 So Barak went down from **m** Tabor, 2022
7: 3 return and depart early from **m** Gilead. 2022
7:24 Gideon sent messengers throughout all **m** 2022
9: 7 went and stood in the top of **m** Gerizim, 2022
9:48 Abimelech gat him up *to* **m** Zalmon, 2022
10: 1 and he dwelt in Shamir in **m** Ephraim. 2022
12:15 of Ephraim, in the **m** of the Amalekites. 2022
17: 1 there was a man of **m** Ephraim, whose 2022
17: 8 he came *to* **m** Ephraim to the house of 2022
18: 2 who when they came *to* **m** Ephraim, 2022
18:13 they passed thence *unto* **m** Ephraim, 2022
19: 1 sojourning on the side of **m** Ephraim, 2022
19:16 at even, which *was* also of **m** Ephraim; 2022
19:18 toward the side of **m** Ephraim; 2022
1Sa 1: 1 **m** Ephraim, and his name *was* Elkanah, 2022
9: 4 he passed through **m** Ephraim, 2022
13: 2 with Saul in Michmash and in **m** Beth-el, 2022
14:22 which had hid themselves in **m** Ephraim, 2022
31: 1 and fell down slain in **m** Gilboa. 2022
31: 8 and his three sons fallen in **m** Gilboa. 2022
2Sa 1: 6 As I happened by chance upon **m** Gilboa, 2022
15:30 David went up by the ascent of *m* Olivet, NIH
15:32 top *of* the **m**, where he worshipped God, NIH

2Sa 20:21 a man of **m** Ephraim, Sheba the son of 2022
1Ki 4: 8 names: The son of Hur, in **m** Ephraim: 2022
12:25 Jeroboam built Shechem in **m** Ephraim, 2022
18:19 gather to me all Israel unto **m** Carmel, 2022
18:20 gathered the prophets together unto **m** 2022
19: 8 forty nights unto Horeb the **m** of God. 2022
19:11 and stand upon the **m** before the LORD. 2022
2Ki 2:25 he went from thence to **m** Carmel, 2022
4:25 came unto the man of God to **m** Carmel. 2022
5:22 even now there be come to me from **m** 2022
19:31 and they that escape out of **m** Zion: 2022
23:13 which *were* on the right hand of the **m** of 2022
23:16 the sepulchres that *were* there in the **m**, 2022
1Ch 4:42 five hundred men, went to **m** Seir, 2022
5:23 and Senir, and *unto* **m** Hermon. 2022
6:67 Shechem in **m** Ephraim with her suburbs; 2022
10: 1 and fell down slain in Gilboa. 2022
10: 8 Saul and his sons fallen in **m** Gilboa. 2022
2Ch 3: 1 of the LORD at Jerusalem in **m** Moriah, 2022
13: 4 Abijah stood up upon **m** Zemaraim, 2022
13: 4 *is* in **m** Ephraim, and said, Hear me, 2022
15: 8 of the cities which he had taken from **m** 2022
19: 4 the people from Beer-sheba to **m** Ephraim, 2022
20:10 children of Ammon and Moab and **m** Seir, 2022
20:22 Moab, and **m** Seir, which were come 2022
20:23 stood up against the inhabitants of **m** 2022
33:15 all the altars that he had built in the **m** of 2022
Ne 8:15 Go forth *unto* the **m**, and fetch olive 2022
9:13 Thou camest down also upon **m** Sinai, 2022
Job 26: 6 Though his excellency **m up** to 5927
39:27 Doth the eagle **m up** at thy command, 1361
Ps 48: 2 in **m** Zion, *on* the sides of the north, the city 2022
48:11 Let **m** Zion rejoice, let the daughters of 2022
74: 2 this **m** Zion, wherein thou hast dwelt. 2022
78:68 *of* Judah, the **m** Zion which he loved. 2022
107:26 They **m up** *to* the heaven, they go down 5927
125: 1 They that trust in the LORD *shall be* as **m** 2022
SS 4: 1 flock of goats, that appear from **m** Gilead. 2022
Isa 4: 5 upon every dwelling place of **m** Zion, 2022
8:18 of hosts, which dwelleth in **m** Zion. 2022
9:18 shall **m up** *like* the lifting up of smoke. 55
10:12 performed his whole work upon **m** Zion 2022
10:32 he shall shake his hand *against* the **m** of 2022
14:13 I will sit also upon the **m** of 2022
16: 1 unto the **m** of the daughter of Zion. 2022
18: 7 name of the LORD of hosts, the **m** Zion. 2022
24:23 when the LORD of hosts shall reign in **m** 2022
27:13 shall worship the LORD in the holy **m** at 2022
28:21 For the LORD shall rise up as *in* **m** 2022
29: 3 will lay siege against thee *with* a **m**, 4674
29: 8 the nations be, that fight against **m** Zion. 2022
31: 4 of hosts come down to fight for **m** Zion, 2022
37:32 and they that escape out of the **m** Zion: 2022
40:31 they shall **m up** *with* wings as eagles; 5927
Jer 4:15 publisheth affliction from **m** Ephraim. 2022
6: 6 trees, and cast a **m** against Jerusalem: 5550
31: 6 *that* the watchmen upon the **m** Ephraim 2022
50:19 soul shall be satisfied upon **m** Ephraim 2022
51:53 Though Babylon should **m up** *to* heaven, 5927
Eze 4: 2 a fort against it, and cast a **m** against it; 5550
10:16 lift up their wings to **m up** from the earth, 7311
21:22 the gates, to cast a **m**, *and* to build a fort. 5550
26: 8 cast a **m** against thee, and lift up 5550
35: 2 set thy face against **m** Seir, 2022
35: 3 Behold, O **m** Seir, I *am* against thee, 2022
35: 7 Thus will I make **m** Seir most desolate, 2022
35: 15 O **m** Seir, and all Idumea, *even* all of it: 2022
Da 11:15 cast up a **m**, and take the most fenced 5550
Joel 2:32 for in **m** Zion and in Jerusalem shall be 2022
Ob 1: 8 and understanding out of the **m** of Esau? 2022
1: 9 the end that every one of the **m** of Esau 2022
1:17 upon **m** Zion shall be deliverance, 2022
1:19 *they* of the south shall possess the **m** of 2022
1:21 shall come up on **m** Zion to judge 2022
1:21 on mount Zion to judge the **m** of Esau; 2022
Mic 4: 7 the LORD shall reign over them in **m** 2022
Hab 3: 3 and the Holy One from **m** Paran. 2022
Zec 14: 4 feet shall stand in that day upon the **m** 2022
14: 4 the **m** of Olives shall cleave in the midst 2022
Mt 21: 1 unto the **m** of Olives, then sent Jesus two 3735
24: 3 And as he sat upon the **m** of Olives, 3735
26:30 they went out into the **m** of Olives. 3735
Mk 11: 1 and Bethany, at the **m** of Olives, 3735
13: 3 And as he sat upon the **m** of Olives over 3735
14:26 they went out into the **m** of Olives. 3735
Lk 19:29 at the **m** called *the mount* of Olives, 3735
19:29 at the mount called the **m** of Olives, NIG
19:37 now at the descent of the **m** of Olives, 3735
21:37 abode in the **m** that is called *the mount* of 3735
21:37 abode in the mount that is called *the m* of NIG
22:39 went, as he was wont, to the **m** of Olives; 3735
Jn 8: 1 Jesus went unto the **m** of Olives. 3735
Ac 1:12 unto Jerusalem from the **m** called Olivet, 3735
7:30 **m** Sina an angel of the Lord in a flame of 3735
7:38 angel which spake to him in the **m** Sina, 3735
Gal 4:24 one from the **m** Sinai, which gendereth 3735
4:25 For *this* Agar is **m** Sinai in Arabia, 3735
Heb 8: 5 to the pattern shewed to thee in the **m**. 3735
12:18 ye are not come unto the **m** that might 3735
12:22 But ye are come unto **m** Sion, and unto 3735
2Pe 1:18 when we were with him in the holy **m**. 3735
Rev 14: 1 and lo, a Lamb stood on the **m** Sion, 3735

MOUNTAIN (137) [MOUNT, MOUNTAINS]
Ge 12: 8 he removed from thence unto a **m** on 2022

Ge 14:10 and they that remained fled to the **m**. 2022
19:17 escape to the **m**, lest thou be consumed. 2022
19:19 I cannot escape to the **m**, lest *some* evil 2022
19:30 dwelt in the **m**, and his two daughters 2022
Ex 3: 1 came to the **m** of God, *even* to Horeb. 2022
3:12 of Egypt, ye shall serve God upon this **m**. 2022
15:17 plant them in the **m** of thine inheritance, 2022
19: 3 the LORD called unto him out of the **m**, 2022
20:18 of the trumpet, and the **m** smoking: 2022
Nu 13:17 *way* southward, and go up into the **m**: 2022
14:40 gat them up into the top of the **m**, saying, 2022
Dt 1:19 which you saw *by* the way of the **m** of 2022
1:20 Ye are come unto the **m** of the Amorites, 2022
1:24 they turned and went up into the **m**, 2022
1:44 the Amorites, which dwelt in that **m**, 2022
2: 3 Ye have compassed this **m** long enough: 2022
3:25 that goodly **m**, and Lebanon. 2022
4:11 ye came near and stood under the **m**, 2022
4:11 the **m** burnt with fire unto the midst of 2022
5:23 darkness, (for the **m** did burn with fire,) 2022
32:49 Get thee up into this **m** Abarim, *unto* 2022
33:19 They shall call the people *unto* the **m**; 2022
34: 1 the plains of Moab unto the **m** of Nebo, 2022
Jos 2:16 she said unto them, Get you to the **m**, 2022
2:22 came unto the **m**, and abode there three 2022
2:23 descended from the **m**, and passed over, 2022
11:16 **m** of Israel, and the valley of the same; 2022
14:12 Now therefore give me this **m**, whereof 2022
15: 8 border went up to the top of the **m** that 2022
17:18 the **m** shall be thine; for it *is* a wood, 2022
18:16 border came down to the end of the **m** 2022
20: 7 which *is* Hebron, in the **m** of Judah. 2022
Jdg 1: 9 that dwelt in the **m**, and in the south, 2022
1:19 he drave out *the inhabitants of* the **m**; 2022
1:34 forced the children of Dan into the **m**: 2022
3:27 he blew a trumpet in the **m** of Ephraim, 2022
1Sa 17: 3 the Philistines stood on a **m** on the one 2022
17: 3 Israel stood on a **m** on the other side: 2022
23:14 in a **m** in the wilderness of Ziph. 2022
23:26 Saul went on this side of the **m**, and 2022
23:26 David and his men on that side of the **m**: 2022
2Ki 16:19 him upon some **m**, or into some valley. 2022
6:17 **m** was full *of* horses and chariots of fire 2022
2Ch 2:18 fourscore thousand to hew in the **m**, 2022
2:18 thousand *to be* hewers in the **m**, 2022
Job 14:18 surely the **m** falling cometh to nought, 2022
Ps 11: 1 ye to my soul, Flee *as* a bird *to* your **m**? 2022
30: 7 by thy favour thou hast made my **m** to 2042
48: 1 city of our God, *in* the **m** of his holiness. 2022
78:54 *even* to this **m**, *which* his right hand had 2022
SS 4: 6 I will get me to the **m** of myrrh, and to 2022
Isa 2: 2 that the **m** of the LORD's house shall be 2022
2: 3 and let us go up to the **m** of the LORD, 2022
11: 9 not hurt nor destroy in all my holy **m**: 2022
13: 2 Lift ye up a banner upon the high **m**, 2022
25: 6 in this **m** shall the LORD of hosts make 2022
25: 7 he will destroy in this **m** the face of 2022
25:10 For in this **m** shall the hand of the LORD 2022
30:17 be left as a beacon upon the top of a **m**, 2022
30:25 there shall be upon every high **m**, 2022
30:29 a pipe to come into the **m** of the LORD, 2022
40: 4 and every **m** and hill shall be made low: 2022
40: 9 good tidings, get thee up into the high **m**; 2022
56: 7 Even them will I bring to my holy **m**, 2022
57: 7 a lofty and high **m** hast thou set thy bed: 2022
57:13 the land, and shall inherit my holy **m**; 2022
65:11 that forget my holy **m**, that prepare a table 2022
65:25 not hurt nor destroy in all my holy **m**, 2022
66:20 to my holy **m** Jerusalem, saith the LORD, 2022
Jer 3: 6 she is gone up upon every high **m** and 2022
16:16 and they shall hunt them from every **m**, 2022
17: 3 O my **m** in the field, I will give thy 2042
26:18 the **m** of the house as the high places of 2022
31:23 O habitation of justice, *and* **m** of holiness. 2022
50: 6 they have gone from **m** to hill, they have 2022
51:25 I *am* against thee, O destroying **m**, 2022
51:25 the rocks, and will make thee a burnt **m**. 2022
La 5:18 Because of the **m** of Zion, which is 2022
Eze 11:23 stood upon the **m** which *is* on the east 2022
17:22 will plant *it* upon a high **m** and eminent: 2022
17:23 In the **m** of the height of Israel will I 2022
20:40 For in mine holy **m**, in the mountain of 2022
20:40 in the **m** of the height of Israel, saith 2022
28:14 *so:* thou wast upon the holy **m** of God; 2022
28:16 I will cast thee as profane out of the **m** of 2022
40: 2 set me upon a very high **m**, by which 2022
43:12 Upon the top of the **m** the whole limit 2022
Da 2:35 that smote the image became a great **m**, 2906
2:45 was cut out of the **m** without hands, 2906
9:16 from thy city Jerusalem, thy holy **m**: 2022
9:20 LORD my God for the holy **m** of my God; 2022
11:45 between the seas in the glorious holy **m**; 2022
Joel 2: 1 Zion, and sound an alarm in my holy **m**; 2022
3:17 your God dwelling in Zion, my holy **m**: 2022
Am 4: 1 of Bashan, that *are* in the **m** of Samaria, 2022
6: 1 in Zion, and trust in the **m** of Samaria, 2022
Ob 1:16 For as ye have drunk upon my holy **m**, 2022
Mic 3:12 the **m** of the house as the high places of 2022
4: 1 *that* the **m** of the house of the LORD shall 2022
4: 2 let us go up to the **m** of the LORD, 2022
7:12 from sea to sea, and *from* **m** to mountain. 2022
7:12 from sea to sea, and *from* mountain to **m**. 2022
Zep 3:11 more be haughty because of my holy **m**. 2022
Hag 1: 8 Go up *to* the **m**, and bring wood, 2022
Zec 4: 7 Who *art* thou, O great **m**? 2022

M

Zec	8: 3 the **m** of the LORD of hosts the holy	2022
	8: 3 of the LORD of hosts the holy **m**.	2022
	14: 4 half of the **m** shall remove toward	2022
Mt	4: 8 taketh him *up* into an exceeding high **m**,	3735
	5: 1 the multitudes, he went up into a **m**:	3735
	8: 1 When he was come down from the **m**,	3735
	14:23 he went up into a **m** apart to pray:	3735
	15:29 went up into a **m**, and sat down there.	3735
	17: 1 bringeth them up into a high **m** apart,	3735
	17: 9 as they came down from the **m**, Jesus	3735
	17:20 ye shall say unto this **m**, Remove hence	3735
	21:21 also if ye shall say unto this **m**, Be thou	3735
	28:16 into a **m** where Jesus had appointed them.	3735
Mk	3:13 he goeth up into a **m**, and calleth unto	3735
	6:46 them away, he departed into a **m** to pray.	3735
	9: 2 leadeth them up into a high **m** apart by	3735
	9: 9 And as they came down from the **m**,	3735
	11:23 That whosoever shall say unto this **m**,	3735
Lk	3: 5 every **m** and hill shall be brought low;	3735
	4: 5 the devil, taking him up into a high **m**,	3735
	6:12 *that* he went out into a **m** to pray,	3735
	8:32 a herd of many swine feeding on the **m**:	3735
	9:28 James, and went up into a **m** to pray.	3735
Jn	4:20 Our fathers worshipped in this **m**;	3735
	4:21 when ye shall neither in this **m**,	3735
	6: 3 And Jesus went up into a **m**, and there	3735
	6:15 he departed again into a **m** himself alone.	3735
Heb	12:20 And if *so much as* a beast touch the **m**,	3735
Rev	6:14 every **m** and island were moved out of	3735
	8: 8 *it were* a great **m** burning with fire was	3735
	21:10 away in the spirit to a great and high **m**,	3735

MOUNTAIN GOAT See HIND

MOUNTAIN SHEEP See CHAMOIS

MOUNTAINS (177) [MOUNTAIN]

Ge	7:20 waters prevail; and the **m** were covered.	2022
	8: 4 day of the month, upon the **m** of Ararat.	2022
	8: 5 the month, were the tops of the **m** seen.	2022
	22: 2 upon one of the **m** which I will tell thee	2022
Ex	32:12 to slay them in the **m**, and to consume	2022
Nu	13:29 and the Amorites, dwell in the **m**:	2022
	23: 7 out of the **m** of the east, *saying*, Come,	2042
	33:47 pitched in the **m** of Abarim, before Nebo.	2022
	33:48 they departed from the **m** of Abarim,	2022
Dt	2:37 river Jabbok, *unto* the cities in the **m**,	2022
	12: 2 upon the high **m**, and upon the hills,	2022
	32:22 and set on fire the foundations of the **m**.	2022
	33:15 for the chief things of the ancient **m**,	2042
Jos	10: 6 in the **m** are gathered together against us.	2022
	11: 2 the kings that *were* on the north of the **m**,	2022
	11: 3 the Jebusite in the **m**, and *to* the Hivite	2022
	11:21 cut off the Anakims from the **m**,	2022
	11:21 from all the **m** of Judah, and from all	2022
	11:21 of Judah, and from all the **m** of Israel:	2022
	12: 8 In the **m**, and in the valleys, and in	2022
	15:48 in the **m**, Shamir, and Jattir, and Socoh,	2022
	18:12 and went up through the **m** westward;	2022
Jdg	5: 5 The **m** melted from before the LORD,	2022
	6: 2 made them the dens which *are* in the **m**,	2022
	9:25 liers in wait for him in the top of the **m**,	2022
	9:36 people down from the top of the **m**.	2022
	9:36 Thou seest the shadow of the **m** as *if they*	2022
	11:37 that I may go up and down upon the **m**,	2022
	11:38 and bewailed her virginity upon the **m**.	2022
1Sa	26:20 when *one* doth hunt a partridge in the **m**.	2022
2Sa	1:21 of Gilboa, *let there be* no dew,	2022
1Ki	5:15 and fourscore thousand hewers in the **m**;	2022
	19:11 a great and strong wind rent the **m**,	2022
2Ki	19:23 I am come up *to* the height of the **m**,	2022
1Ch	12: 8 and *were* as swift as the roes upon the **m**:	2022
2Ch	18:16 I did see all Israel scattered upon the **m**,	2022
	21:11 Moreover he made high places in the **m**	2022
	26:10 and vinedressers in the **m**,	2022
	27: 4 he built cities in the **m** of Judah,	2022
Job	9: 5 removeth the **m**, and they know not:	2022
	24: 8 They are wet with the showers of the **m**,	2022
	28: 9 rock; he overturneth the **m** by the roots.	2022
	39: 8 The range of the **m** *is* his pasture,	2022
	40:20 Surely the **m** bring him forth food,	2022
Ps	36: 6 Thy righteousness *is* like the great **m**;	2042
	46: 2 though the **m** be carried into the midst of	2022
	46: 3 *though* the **m** shake with the swelling	2022
	50:11 I know all the fowls of the **m**: and the	2022
	65: 6 Which by his strength setteth fast the **m**;	2022
	72: 3 The **m** shall bring peace to the people,	2022
	72:16 corn in the earth upon the top of the **m**;	2022
	76: 4 and excellent than the **m** of prey.	2042
	83:14 and as the flame setteth the **m** on fire;	2022
	87: 1 His foundation *is* in the holy **m**.	2022
	90: 2 Before the **m** were brought forth,	2022
	104: 6 a garment: the waters stood above the **m**.	2022
	104: 8 They go up *by* the **m**; they go down *by*	2022
	114: 4 The **m** skipped like rams, *and* the little	2022
	114: 6 Ye **m**, *that* ye skipped like rams;	2022
	125: 2 *As* the **m** *are* round about Jerusalem,	2022
	133: 3 *the dew* that descended upon the **m** of	2042
	144: 5 touch the **m**, and they shall smoke.	2022
	147: 8 who maketh grass to grow *upon* the **m**,	2022
	148: 9 **M**, and all hills; fruitful trees,	2022
Pr	8:25 Before the **m** were settled, before the hills	2022
	27:25 and herbs of the **m** are gathered.	2022
SS	2: 8 behold, he cometh leaping upon the **m**,	2022
	2:17 roe or a young hart upon the **m** of Bether.	2022

SS	4: 8 lions' dens, from the **m** of the leopards.	2022
	8:14 or to a young hart upon the **m** of spices.	2022
Isa	2: 2 shall be established in the top of the **m**,	2022
	2:14 all the high **m**, and upon all the hills	2022
	13: 4 The noise of a multitude in the **m**, like as	2022
	14:25 and upon my **m** tread him under foot:	2022
	17:13 be chased as the chaff of the **m** before	2022
	18: 3 when *he* lifteth up an ensign *on* the **m**;	2022
	18: 6 be left together unto the fowls of the **m**,	2022
	22: 5 down the walls, and of crying to the **m**.	2022
	34: 3 the **m** shall be melted with their blood.	2022
	37:24 am I come up *to* the height of the **m**,	2022
	40:12 weighed the **m** in scales, and the hills in	2022
	41:15 thou shalt thresh the **m**, and beat *them*	2022
	42:11 let them shout from the top of the **m**.	2022
	42:15 I will make waste **m** and hills, and dry up	2022
	44:23 ye, O forest, and every tree therein:	2022
	49:11 I will make all my **m** a way,	2022
	49:13 earth; and break forth *into* singing, O **m**:	2022
	52: 7 How beautiful upon the **m** are the feet of	2022
	54:10 For the **m** shall depart, and the hills shall	2022
	55:12 the **m** and the hills shall break forth	2022
	64: 1 that the **m** might flow down at thy	2022
	64: 3 the **m** flowed down at thy presence.	2022
	65: 7 which have burnt incense upon the **m**,	2022
	65: 9 and out of Judah an inheritor of my **m**:	2022
Jer	3:23 the hills, *and from* the multitude of the **m**:	2022
	4:24 I beheld the **m**, and lo, they trembled,	2022
	9:10 For the **m** will I take up a weeping and	2022
	13:16 your feet stumble upon the dark **m**,	2022
	17:26 and from the **m**, and from the south,	2022
	31: 5 Thou shalt yet plant vines upon the **m** of	2022
	32:44 in the cities of the **m**, and in the cities of	2022
	33:13 In the cities of the **m**, in the cities of	2022
	46:18 Surely as Tabor *is* among the **m**,	2022
	50: 6 they have turned them away *on* the **m**:	2022
La	4:19 they pursued us upon the **m**, they laid	2022
Eze	6: 2 set thy face towards the **m** of Israel,	2022
	6: 3 say, Ye **m** of Israel, hear the word of	2022
	6: 3 Thus saith the Lord GOD to the **m**,	2022
	6:13 in all the tops of the **m**, and under every	2022
	7: 7 and not the sounding again of the **m**.	2022
	7:16 be on the **m** like doves of the valleys,	2022
	18: 6 *And* hath not eaten upon the **m**,	2022
	18:11 but even hath eaten upon the **m**,	2022
	18:15 *That* hath not eaten upon the **m**,	2022
	19: 9 no more be heard upon the **m** of Israel.	2022
	22: 9 in thee they eat upon the **m**: in the midst	2022
	31:12 upon the **m** and in all the valleys his	2022
	32: 5 I will lay thy flesh upon the **m**, and fill	2022
	32: 6 wherein thou swimmest, *even* to the **m**;	2022
	33:28 the **m** of Israel shall be desolate, that	2022
	34: 6 My sheep wandered through all the **m**,	2022
	34:13 feed them upon the **m** of Israel by	2022
	34:14 upon the **m** of Israel shall their fold	2022
	34:14 a fat pasture shall they feed upon the **m**.	2022
	35: 8 I will fill his **m** *with* his slain *men*: in thy	2022
	35:12 thou hast spoken against the **m** of Israel,	2022
	36: 1 prophesy unto the **m** of Israel, and say,	2022
	36: 1 say, Ye **m** of Israel, hear the word of	2022
	36: 4 Therefore, ye **m** of Israel, hear the word	2022
	36: 4 Thus saith the Lord GOD to the **m**,	2022
	36: 6 say unto the **m**, and to the hills,	2022
	36: 8 O **m** of Israel, ye shall shoot forth your	2022
	37:22 nation in the land upon the **m** of Israel;	2022
	38: 8 against the **m** of Israel, which have been	2022
	38:20 the **m** shall be thrown down, and the	2022
	38:21 sword against him throughout all my **m**,	2022
	39: 2 and will bring thee upon the **m** of Israel:	2022
	39: 4 Thou shalt fall upon the **m** of Israel, thou,	2022
	39:17 a great sacrifice upon the **m** of Israel,	2022
Hos	4:13 They sacrifice upon the tops of the **m**,	2022
	10: 8 they shall say to the **m**, Cover us; and to	2022
Joel	2: 2 as the morning spread upon the **m**:	2022
	2: 5 the noise of chariots on the tops of **m**	2022
	3:18 *that* the **m** shall drop down new wine,	2022
Am	3: 9 Assemble yourselves upon the **m** of	2022
	4:13 he that formeth the **m**, and createth	2022
	9:13 the **m** shall drop sweet wine, and all	2022
Jnh	2: 6 I went down to the bottoms of the **m**;	2022
Mic	1: 4 the **m** shall be molten under him,	2022
	4: 1 shall be established in the top of the **m**,	2022
	6: 1 contend thou before the **m**, and let the	2022
	6: 2 Hear ye, O **m**, the LORD's controversy,	2022
Na	1: 5 The **m** quake at him, and the hills melt,	3996
	1:15 Behold upon the **m** the feet of him that	2022
	3:18 *dust:* thy people is scattered upon the **m**,	2022
Hab	3: 6 the everlasting **m** were scattered,	2042
	3:10 The **m** saw thee, *and* they trembled:	2022
Hag	1:11 upon the **m**, and upon the corn,	2022
Zec	6: 1 four chariots out from between two **m**;	2022
	6: 1 and the **m** *were* mountains of brass.	2022
	6: 1 and the mountains *were* **m** of brass.	2022
	14: 5 ye shall flee *to* the valley of the **m**;	2022
	14: 5 for the valley of the **m** shall reach unto	2022
Mal	1: 3 laid his **m** and his heritage waste for	2022
Mt	18:12 and goeth into the **m**, and seeketh that	3735
	24:16 them which be in Judea flee into the **m**:	3735
Mk	5: 5 day, he was in the **m**, and in the tombs,	3735
	5:11 Now there was there nigh unto the **m** a	3735
	13:14 let them that be in Judea flee to the **m**:	3735
Lk	21:21 them which are in Judea flee to the **m**;	3735
	23:30 Then shall they begin to say to the **m**,	3735
1Co	13: 2 so that *I* could remove **m**, and have no	3735
Heb	11:38 and *in* **m**, and *in* dens and caves of	3735

Rev	6:15 in the dens and in the rocks of the **m**;	3735
	6:16 And said to the **m** and rocks, Fall on us,	3735
	16:20 fled *away*, and the **m** were not found.	3735
	17: 9 The seven heads are seven **m**, on which	3735

MOUNTED (1) [MOUNT]

| Eze | 10:19 and **m** up from the earth in my sight: | 7426 |

MOUNTING (1) [MOUNT]

| Isa | 15: 5 for *by* the **m** up of Luhith with weeping | 4608 |

MOUNTS (3) [MOUNT]

Jer	32:24 Behold the **m**, they are come *unto* the	5550
	33: 4 which are thrown down by the **m**,	5550
Eze	17:17 by casting up **m**, and building forts, to cut	5550

MOURN (45) [MOURNED, MOURNER, MOURNERS, MOURNETH, MOURNFULLY, MOURNING]

Ge	23: 2 Abraham came to **m** for Sarah, and to	5594
1Sa	16: 1 Samuel, How long wilt thou **m** for Saul,	56
2Sa	3:31 you with sackcloth, and **m** before Abner.	5594
1Ki	13:29 came to the city, to **m** and to bury him.	5594
	14:13 all Israel shall **m** for him, and bury him:	5594
Ne	8: 9 the LORD your God; **m** not, nor weep.	56
Job	2:11 together to come to **m** with him	5110
	5:11 that those which **m** may be exalted *to*	6937
	14:22 pain, and his soul within him shall **m**.	56
Ps	55: 2 I **m** in my complaint, and make a noise;	7300
Pr	5:11 thou **m** at the last, when thy flesh and	5098
	29: 2 the wicked beareth rule, the people **m**.	584
Ecc	3: 4 laugh; a time to **m**, and a time to dance;	5594
Isa	3:26 her gates shall lament and, and she	56
	16: 7 foundations of Kir-hareseth shall ye **m**;	1897
	19: 8 The fishers also shall **m**, and all they that	578
	38:14 I did **m** as a dove: mine eyes fail *with*	1897
	59:11 like bears, and **m** sore like doves;	1897+1897
	61: 2 of our God; to comfort all that **m**;	57
	61: 3 To appoint unto them that **m** in Zion,	57
	66:10 for joy with her, all ye that **m** for her:	56
Jer	4:28 For this shall the earth **m**, and the heavens	56
	12: 4 How long shall the land **m**, and the herbs	1897
	48:31 *mine heart* shall **m** for the men of	1897
La	1: 4 The ways of Zion do **m**, because none	57
Eze	7:12 let not the buyer rejoice, nor the seller **m**:	56
	7:27 The king shall **m**, and the prince shall be	56
	24:16 yet neither shalt thou **m** nor weep,	5594
	24:23 ye shall not **m** nor weep; but ye shall pine	5594
	24:23 iniquities, and **m** one towards another.	5098
	31:15 I *caused* Lebanon to **m** for him, and all	6937
Hos	4: 3 Therefore shall the land **m**, and every one	56
	10: 5 for the people thereof shall **m** over it,	56
Joel	1: 9 the priests, the LORD's ministers, **m**.	56
Am	1: 2 the habitations of the shepherds shall **m**,	56
	8: 8 and every one **m** that dwelleth therein?	56
	9: 5 melt, and all that dwell therein shall **m**:	56
Zec	12:10 they shall **m** for him, as one mourneth for	5594
	12:12 the land shall **m**, every family apart;	5594
Mt	5: 4 Blessed *are* they that **m**: for they shall be	3996
	9:15 Can the children of the bridechamber **m**,	3996
	24:30 and then shall all the tribes of the earth **m**,	2875
Lk	6:25 that laugh now: for ye shall **m** and weep.	3996
Jas	4: 9 Be afflicted, and **m**, and weep: let your	3996
Rev	18:11 of the earth *shall* weep and **m** over her;	3996

MOURNED (22) [MOURN]

Ge	37:34 his loins, and **m** for his son many days.	56
	50: 3 the Egyptians **m** for him threescore and	1058
	50:10 there they **m** with a great and very sore	5594
Ex	33: 4 the people heard these evil tidings, they **m**:	56
Nu	14:39 children of Israel: and the people **m** greatly.	56
	20:29 they **m** for Aaron thirty days, *even* all	1058
1Sa	15:35 nevertheless Samuel **m** for Saul:	56
2Sa	1:12 they **m**, and wept, and fasted until even,	5594
	11:26 was dead, she **m** for her husband.	5594
	13:37 And *David* **m** for his son every day.	56
	14: 2 be as a woman *that had* a long time **m** for	56
1Ki	13:30 **m** over him, *saying*, Alas, my brother.	5594
	14:18 Israel **m** for him, according to the word	5594
1Ch	7:22 And Ephraim their father **m** many days,	56
2Ch	35:24 And all Judah and Jerusalem **m** for Josiah.	56
Ezr	10: 6 he **m** because of the transgression of them	56
Ne	1: 4 **m** *certain* days, and fasted, and prayed	56
Zec	7: 5 When ye fasted and **m** in the fifth and	5594
Mt	11:17 we have **m** unto you, and ye have not	2354
Mk	16:10 had been with him, as they **m** and wept.	3996
Lk	7:32 we have **m** to you, and ye have not wept.	2354
1Co	5: 2 ye are puffed up, and have not rather **m**,	3996

MOURNER (1) [MOURN]

| 2Sa | 14: 2 feign thyself **to** be a **m**, and put on now | 56 |

MOURNERS (4) [MOURN]

Job	29:25 in the army, as *one* that comforteth the **m**.	57
Ecc	12: 5 home, and the **m** go about the streets:	5594
Isa	57:18 restore comforts unto him and to his **m**.	57
Hos	9: 4 *shall be* unto them as the bread of **m**;	205

MOURNETH (11) [MOURN]

2Sa	19: 1 the king weepeth and **m** for Absalom.	56
Ps	35:14 down heavily, as one that **m** for his mother.	57
	88: 9 Mine eye **m** by reason of affliction:	1669
Isa	24: 4 The earth **m** *and* fadeth away, the world	56
	24: 7 The new wine **m**, the vine languisheth,	56
	33: 9 The earth **m** *and* languisheth: Lebanon is	56
Jer	12:11 desolate, *and being* desolate it **m** unto me;	56

M

M

Jer 14: 2 Judah **m**, and the gates thereof languish; 56
 23:10 for because of swearing the land **m**; 56
Joel 1:10 The field is wasted, the land **m**; for the corn 56
Zec 12:10 as one **m** for *his* only *son,* and shall be in 4553

MOURNFULLY (1) [MOURN]

Mal 3:14 that we have walked **m** before the Lᴏʀᴅ 6941

MOURNING (51) [MOURN]

Ge 27:41 The days of **m** for my father are at hand; 60
 37:35 will go down into the grave unto my son **m**. 57
 50: 4 when the days of his **m** were past, 1068
 50:10 and he made a **m** for his father seven days. 60
 50:11 saw the **m** in the floor of Atad, they said, 60
 50:11 This *is* a grievous **m** to the Egyptians: 60
Dt 26:14 I have eaten thereof in my **m**, 205
 34: 8 of weeping *and* **m** for Moses were ended. 60
2Sa 11:27 when the **m** was past, David sent and fet 60
 14: 2 put on now **m** apparel, and anoint not 60
 19: 2 the victory that day was *turned* into **m** unto 60
Est 4: 3 *there was* great **m** among the Jews, 60
 6:12 Haman hasted to his house **m**, and having 57
 9:22 sorrow to joy, and from **m** into a good day: 60
Job 3: 8 the day, who are ready to raise up their **m**. 3882
 30:28 I went in without the sun: I stood up, 6937
 30:31 My harp also is *turned* to **m**, and my organ 60
Ps 30:11 Thou hast turned for me my **m** into 4553
 38: 6 down greatly; I go **m** all the day long. 6937
 42: 9 why go I because of the oppression of 6937
 43: 2 why go I because of the oppression of 6937
Ecc 7: 2 *It is* better to go to the house of **m**, than to 60
 7: 4 The heart of the wise *is* in the house of **m**; 60
Isa 22:12 to **m**, and to baldness, and to girding with 4553
 51:11 and joy; *and* sorrow and **m** shall flee away. 585
 60:20 and the days of thy **m** shall be ended. 60
 61: 3 them beauty for ashes, the oil of joy for **m**, 60
Jer 6:26 make thee, *as* for an only *son,* most 60
 9:17 for the **m** *women,* that they may come; 6969
 16: 5 the Lᴏʀᴅ, Enter not *into* the house of **m**, 4798
 16: 7 shall *men* tear *themselves* for them in **m**, 60
 31:13 for I will turn their **m** into joy, 60
La 2: 5 increased in the daughter of Judah **m** 8386
 5:15 is ceased; our dance is turned into **m**. 60
Eze 2:10 therein lamentations, and **m**, and woe. 1899
 7:16 all of them, every one for his iniquity. 1993
 24:17 Forbear to cry, make no **m** *for* the dead, 56
 31:15 he went down to the grave I **caused a m**: 56
Da 10: 2 those days I Daniel was **m** three full weeks. 56
Joel 2:12 and with weeping, and with **m**: 4553
Am 5:16 and they shall call the husbandman to **m**, 60
 8:10 I will turn your feasts into **m**, and all your 60
 8:10 I will make it as the **m** of an only *son,* and 60
Mic 1: 8 like the dragons, and **m** as the owls. 60
 1:11 came not forth *in* the **m** of Beth-ezel; 4553
Zec 12:11 In that day shall there be a great **m** in 4553
 12:11 as the **m** of Hadadrimmon in the valley of 4553
Mt 2:18 lamentation, and weeping, and great **m**, 3602
2Co 7: 7 your **m**, your fervent mind toward me; 3602
Jas 4: 9 let your laughter be turned to **m**, 3997
Rev 18: 8 in one day, death, and **m**, and famine; 3997

MOUSE (2) [MICE]

Lev 11:29 and the **m**, and the tortoise after his kind, 5909
Isa 66:17 and the abomination, and the **m**, 5909

MOUTH (424) [MOUTHS]

Ge 4:11 which hath opened her **m** to receive thy 6310
 8:11 lo, in her **m** *was* an olive leaf pluckt off: 6310
 24:57 we will call the damsel, and inquire at her **m**. 6310
 29: 2 and a great stone *was* upon the well's **m**. 6310
 29: 3 they rolled the stone from the well's **m**, 6310
 29: 3 put the stone again upon the well's **m** in 6310
 29: 8 *till* they roll the stone from the well's **m**; 6310
 29:10 rolled the stone from the well's **m**, 6310
 42:27 for behold, it *was* in his sack's **m**. 6310
 43:12 money that was brought again in the **m** 6310
 43:21 every man's money *was* in the **m** of his 6310
 44: 1 put every man's money in his sack's **m**. 6310
 44: 2 in the sack's **m** of the youngest, 6310
 45:12 that *it is* my **m** that speaketh unto you. 6310
Ex 4:11 said unto him, Who hath made man's **m**? 6310
 4:12 therefore go, and I will be with thy **m**, 6310
 4:15 speak unto him, and put words in his **m**: 6310
 4:15 I will be with thy **m**, and with his mouth, 6310
 4:15 with his **m**, and will teach you what ye 6310
 4:16 *even* he shall be to thee instead of a **m**, 6310
 13: 9 that the Lᴏʀᴅ's law may be in thy **m**: 6310
 23:13 neither let it be heard out of thy **m**. 6310
Nu 12: 8 With him will I speak **m** to mouth, 6310
 12: 8 With him will I speak mouth to **m**, 6310
 16:30 earth open her **m**, and swallow them up, 6310
 16:32 the earth opened her **m**, 6310
 22:28 the Lᴏʀᴅ opened the **m** of the ass, 6310
 22:38 the word that God putteth in my **m**, that 6310
 23: 5 And the Lᴏʀᴅ put a word in Balaam's **m**, 6310
 23:12 that which the Lᴏʀᴅ hath put in my **m**? 6310
 23:16 put a word in his **m**, and said, Go again 6310
 26:10 the earth opened her **m**, 6310
 30: 2 to all that proceedeth out of his **m**. 6310
 32:24 that which proceeded out of your **m**. 6310
 35:30 murderer shall be put to death by the **m** 6310
Dt 8: 3 every *word* that proceedeth out of the **m** 6310
 11: 6 how the earth opened her **m**, 6310
 17: 6 At the **m** of two witnesses, 6310
 17: 6 at the **m** of one witness he shall not be 6310

Dt 18:18 thee, and will put my words in his **m**; 6310
 19:15 at the **m** of two witnesses, or at the 6310
 19:15 or at the **m** of three witnesses, shall 6310
 23:23 which thou hast promised with thy **m**; 6310
 30:14 in thy **m**, and in thy heart, that *thou* 6310
 32: 1 and hear, O earth, the words of my **m**. 6310
Jos 1: 8 of the law shall not depart out of thy **m**; 6310
 6:10 shall *any* word proceed out of your **m**, 6310
 9:14 asked not *counsel* at the **m** of the Lᴏʀᴅ. 6310
 10:18 Roll great stones upon the **m** of the cave, 6310
 10:22 Open the **m** of the cave, and bring out 6310
 10:27 laid great stones in the cave's **m**, 6310
Jdg 7: 6 putting their hand to their **m**, were three 6310
 9:38 Where *is* now thy **m**, wherewith thou 6310
 11:35 for I have opened my **m** unto the Lᴏʀᴅ, 6310
 11:36 *if* thou hast opened thy **m** unto the Lᴏʀᴅ, 6310
 11:36 that which hath proceeded out of thy **m**; 6310
 18:19 lay thine hand upon thy **m**, and go with 6310
1Sa 1:12 before the Lᴏʀᴅ, that Eli marked her **m**. 6310
 2: 1 my **m** is enlarged over mine enemies; 6310
 2: 3 let *not* arrogancy come out of your **m**: 6310
 14:26 but no man put his hand to his **m**: 6310
 14:27 a honeycomb, and put his hand to his **m**; 6310
 17:35 smote him, and delivered *it* out of his **m**: 6310
2Sa 1:16 thy **m** hath testified against thee, 6310
 14: 3 him. So Joab put the words in her **m**. 6310
 14:19 he put all these words in the **m** of thine 6310
 17:19 and spread a covering over the well's **m**, 6440
 18:25 If he *be* alone, *there is* tidings in his **m**. 6310
 22: 9 nostrils, and fire out of his **m** devoured: 6310
1Ki 7:31 the **m** of it within the chapiter and 6310
 7:31 the **m** thereof *was* round after the work 6310
 7:31 also upon the **m** of it *were* gravings with 6310
 8:15 which spake with his **m** unto David my 6310
 8:24 thou spakest also with thy **m**, 6310
 13:21 Forasmuch as thou hast disobeyed the **m** 6310
 17:24 *that* the word of the Lᴏʀᴅ in thy **m** *is* 6310
 19:18 and every **m** which hath not kissed him. 6310
 22:13 *declare* good unto the king *with* one **m**: 6310
 22:22 I will be a lying spirit in the **m** of all his 6310
 22:23 the Lᴏʀᴅ hath put a lying spirit in the **m** 6310
2Ki 4:34 put his **m** upon his mouth, and his eyes 6310
 4:34 put his mouth upon his **m**, and his eyes 6310
1Ch 16:12 his wonders, and the judgments of his **m**; 6310
2Ch 6: 4 he spake with his **m** to my father David, 6310
 6:15 spakest with thy **m**, and hast fulfilled *it* 6310
 18:21 a lying spirit in the **m** of all his prophets. 6310
 18:22 the Lᴏʀᴅ hath put a lying spirit in the **m** 6310
 35:22 the words of Necho from the **m** of God, 6310
 36:12 *speaking* from the **m** of the Lᴏʀᴅ. 6310
 36:21 To fulfil the word of the Lᴏʀᴅ by the **m** 6310
 36:22 **m** of Jeremiah might be accomplished, 6310
Ezr 1: 1 that the word of the Lᴏʀᴅ by the **m** of 6310
Ne 9:20 withheldest not thy manna from their **m**, 6310
Est 4: 8 the word went out of the king's **m**, 6310
Job 3: 1 After this opened Job his **m**, and cursed 6310
 5:15 from their **m**, and from the hand of 6310
 5:16 hath hope, and iniquity stoppeth her **m**. 6310
 7:11 Therefore I will not refrain my **m**; I will 6310
 8: 2 *how long shall* the words of thy **m** *be* like 6310
 8:21 Till he fill thy **m** *with* laughing, 6310
 9:20 mine own **m** shall condemn me: 6310
 12:11 ear try words? and the **m** taste his meat? 2441
 15: 5 For thy **m** uttereth thine iniquity, 6310
 15: 6 Thine own **m** condemneth thee, and not 6310
 15:13 and lettest *such* words go out of thy **m**? 6310
 15:30 by the breath of his **m** shall he go away. 6310
 16: 5 *But* I would strengthen you with my **m**, 6310
 16:10 They have gaped upon me with their **m**; 6310
 19:16 no answer; I intreated him with my **m**. 6310
 20:12 Though wickedness be sweet in his **m**, 6310
 20:13 it not; but keep it still within his **m**: 2441
 21: 5 and lay *your* hand upon your **m**. 6310
 22:22 the law from his **m**, and lay up his words 6310
 23: 4 him, and fill my **m** *with* arguments. 6310
 23:12 I have esteemed the words of his **m** more 6310
 29: 9 and laid *their* hand on their **m**. 6310
 29:10 tongue cleaved to the roof of their **m**. 2441
 29:23 they opened their **m** wide *as* for the latter 6310
 31:27 or my **m** hath kissed my hand: 6310
 31:30 (Neither have I suffered my **m** to sin by 2441
 32: 5 no answer in the **m** of *these* three men, 6310
 33: 2 Behold now I have opened my **m**, 6310
 33: 2 my tongue hath spoken in my **m**. 2441
 34: 3 ear trieth words, as the **m** tasteth meat. 2441
 35:16 Therefore doth Job open his **m** in vain; 6310
 37: 2 and the sound *that* goeth out of his **m**. 6310
 40: 4 I will lay my hand upon my **m**. 6310
 40:23 that he can draw up Jordan into his **m**. 6310
 41:19 Out of his **m** go burning lamps, 6310
 41:21 and a flame goeth out of his **m**. 6310
Ps 5: 9 For *there is* no faithfulness in their **m**; 6310
 8: 2 Out of the **m** of babes and sucklings hast 6310
 10: 7 His **m** is full *of* cursing and deceit and 6310
 17: 3 I am purposed *that* my **m** shall not 6310
 17:10 own fat: *with* their **m** they speak proudly. 6310
 18: 8 nostrils, and fire out of his **m** devoured: 6310
 19:14 the words of my **m**, and the meditation 6310
 22:21 Save me from the lion's **m**: for thou hast 6310
 32: 9 whose **m** must be held in with bit and 5716
 33: 6 the host of them by the breath of his **m**. 6310
 34: 1 his praise *shall* continually *be* in my **m**. 6310
 35:21 they opened their **m** wide against me, 6310
 36: 3 words of his **m** *are* iniquity and deceit: 6310
 37:30 The **m** of the righteous speaketh wisdom, 6310

Ps 38:13 as a dumb *man that* openeth not his **m**. 6310
 38:14 and in whose **m** *are* no reproofs. 6310
 39: 1 I will keep my **m** with a bridle, while 6310
 39: 9 I was dumb, I opened not my **m**; because 6310
 40: 3 he hath put a new song in my **m**, 6310
 49: 3 My **m** shall speak of wisdom; 6310
 50:16 shouldest take my covenant in thy **m**? 6310
 50:19 Thou givest thy **m** to evil, and thy tongue 6310
 51:15 and my **m** shall shew forth thy praise. 6310
 54: 2 O God; give ear to the words of my **m**. 6310
 55:21 *The words of* his **m** were smoother than 6310
 58: 6 Break their teeth, O God, in their **m**: 6310
 59: 7 Behold, they belch out with their **m**: 6310
 59:12 *For* the sin of their **m** *and* the words of 6310
 62: 4 they bless with their **m**, but they curse 6310
 63: 5 my **m** shall praise *thee* with joyful lips: 6310
 63:11 the **m** of them that speak lies shall be 6310
 66:14 hath spoken, when I was in trouble. 6310
 66:17 I cried unto him *with* my **m**, and *he was* 6310
 69:15 and let not the pit shut her **m** upon me. 6310
 71: 8 Let my **m** be filled *with* thy praise 6310
 71:15 My **m** shall shew forth thy righteousness 6310
 73: 9 They set their **m** against the heavens, 6310
 78: 1 incline your ears to the words of my **m**. 6310
 78: 2 I will open my **m** in a parable: I will utter 6310
 78:36 they did flatter him with their **m**, 6310
 81:10 Egypt: open thy **m** wide, and I will fill it. 6310
 89: 1 with my **m** will I make known thy 6310
 103: 5 Who satisfieth thy **m** with good *things;* 5716
 105: 5 his wonders, and the judgments of his **m**; 6310
 107:42 rejoice: and all iniquity shall stop her **m**. 6310
 109: 2 For the **m** of the wicked and the mouth 6310
 109: 2 the **m** of the deceitful are opened against 6310
 109:30 will greatly praise the Lᴏʀᴅ with my **m**; 6310
 119:13 I declared all the judgments of thy **m**. 6310
 119:43 not the word of truth utterly out of my **m**; 6310
 119:72 The law of thy **m** *is* better unto me than 6310
 119:88 so shall I keep the testimony of thy **m**. 6310
 119:103 taste! yea, *sweeter* than honey to my **m**! 6310
 119:108 the freewill offerings of my **m**, O Lᴏʀᴅ, 6310
 119:131 I opened my **m**, and panted: for I longed 6310
 126: 2 was our **m** filled *with* laughter, 6310
 137: 6 my tongue cleave to the roof of my **m**; 2441
 138: 4 when they hear the words of thy **m**. 6310
 141: 3 Set a watch, O Lᴏʀᴅ, before my **m**; 6310
 141: 7 Our bones are scattered at the grave's **m**, 6310
 144: 8 Whose **m** speaketh vanity, and their right 6310
 144:11 whose **m** speaketh vanity, and their right 6310
 145:21 My **m** shall speak the praise of the Lᴏʀᴅ: 6310
 149: 6 *Let* the high *praises* of God *be* in their **m**, 1627
Pr 2: 6 out of his **m** *cometh* knowledge and 6310
 4: 5 neither decline from the words of my **m**. 6310
 4:24 Put away from thee a froward **m**, 6310
 5: 3 and her **m** *is* smoother than oil: 2441
 5: 7 and depart not from the words of my **m**. 6310
 6: 2 Thou art snared with the words of thy **m**, 6310
 6: 2 thou art taken with the words of thy **m**, 6310
 6:12 wicked man, walketh *with* a froward **m**. 6310
 7:24 and attend to the words of my **m**. 6310
 8: 7 For my **m** shall speak truth; 2441
 8: 8 All the words of my **m** *are* in 6310
 8:13 evil way, and the froward **m**, do I hate. 6310
 10: 6 violence covereth the **m** of the wicked. 6310
 10:11 The **m** of a righteous *man is* a well of life: 6310
 10:11 violence covereth the **m** of the wicked. 6310
 10:14 the **m** of the foolish *is* near destruction. 6310
 10:31 The **m** of the just bringeth forth wisdom: 6310
 10:32 the **m** of the wicked *speaketh* frowardness. 6310
 11: 9 A hypocrite with *his* **m** destroyeth his 6310
 11:11 it is overthrown by the **m** of the wicked. 6310
 12: 6 the **m** of the upright shall deliver them. 6310
 12:14 satisfied *with* good by the fruit of *his* **m**: 6310
 13: 2 man shall eat good by the fruit of *his* **m**: 6310
 13: 3 He that keepeth his **m** keepeth his life: 6310
 14: 3 In the **m** of the foolish *is* a rod of pride: 6310
 15: 2 the **m** of fools poureth out foolishness. 6310
 15:14 but the **m** of fools feedeth on foolishness. 6310
 15:23 A man hath joy by the answer of his **m**. 6310
 15:28 the **m** of the wicked poureth out evil 6310
 16:10 his **m** transgresseth not in judgment. 6310
 16:23 The heart of the wise teacheth his **m**, 6310
 16:26 for himself; for his **m** craveth it of him. 6310
 18: 4 The words of a man's **m** *are as* deep 6310
 18: 6 and his **m** calleth for strokes. 6310
 18: 7 A fool's **m** *is* his destruction, and his lips 6310
 18:20 shall be satisfied with the fruit of his **m**; 6310
 19:24 not so much as bring it to his **m** again. 6310
 19:28 the **m** of the wicked devoureth iniquity. 6310
 20:17 his **m** shall be filled *with* gravel. 6310
 21:23 Whoso keepeth his **m** and his tongue 6310
 22:14 The **m** of strange *women is* a deep pit: 6310
 24: 7 a fool: he openeth not his **m** in the gate. 6310
 26: 7 equal: so *is* a parable in the **m** of fools. 6310
 26: 9 so *is* a parable in the **m** of fools. 6310
 26:15 it grieveth him to bring it again to his **m**. 6310
 26:28 by it; and a flattering **m** worketh ruin. 6310
 27: 2 *man* praise thee, and not thine own **m**; 6310
 30:20 she eateth, and wipeth her **m**, and saith, 6310
 30:32 thought evil, *lay* thine hand upon thy **m**. 6310
 31: 8 Open thy **m** for the dumb in the cause of 6310
 31: 9 Open thy **m**, judge righteously, 6310
 31:26 She openeth her **m** with wisdom; and in 6310
Ecc 5: 2 Be not rash with thy **m**, and let not thine 6310
 5: 6 Suffer not thy **m** to cause thy flesh to sin; 6310
 6: 7 All the labour of man *is* for his **m**, 6310

Ecc	10:12 words of a wise *man's* **m** *are* gracious;	6310
	10:13 The beginning of the words of his **m** *is*	6310
SS	1: 2 Let him kiss me with the kisses of his **m**:	6310
	5:16 His **m** *is* most sweet: yea, he *is* altogether	2441
	7: 9 the roof of thy **m** like the best wine,	2441
Isa	1:20 for the **m** of the LORD hath spoken *it.*	6310
	5:14 and opened her **m** without measure:	6310
	6: 7 he laid *it* upon my **m**, and said,	6310
	9:12 they shall devour Israel with open **m**.	6310
	9:17 an evildoer, and every **m** speaketh folly.	6310
	10:14 the wing, or opened the **m**, or peeped.	6310
	11: 4 smite the earth with the rod of his **m**,	6310
	19: 7 by the **m** of the brooks, and every thing	6310
	29:13 this people draw near *me* with their **m**,	6310
	30: 2 *into* Egypt, and have not asked *at* my **m**;	6310
	34:16 my **m** it hath commanded, and his spirit	6310
	40: 5 for the **m** of the LORD hath spoken *it.*	6310
	45:23 the word is gone out of my **m** in	6310
	48: 3 went forth out of my **m**, and I shewed	6310
	49: 2 he hath made my **m** like a sharp sword;	6310
	51:16 I have put my words in thy **m**,	6310
	53: 7 he was afflicted, yet he opened not his **m**:	6310
	53: 7 is dumb, so he openeth not his **m**.	6310
	53: 9 neither *was any* deceit in his **m**.	6310
	55:11 my word be that goeth forth out of my **m**:	6310
	57: 4 against whom make ye a wide **m**,	6310
	58:14 for the **m** of the LORD hath spoken *it.*	6310
	59:21 and my words which I have put in thy **m**,	6310
	59:21 shall not depart out of thy **m**, nor out of	6310
	59:21 thy mouth, nor out of the **m** of thy seed,	6310
	59:21 nor out of the **m** of thy seed's seed,	6310
	62: 2 which the **m** of the LORD shall name.	6310
Jer	1: 9 put forth his hand, and touched my **m**.	6310
	1: 9 Behold, I have put my words in thy **m**.	6310
	5:14 I will make my words in thy **m** fire,	6310
	7:28 is perished, and is cut off from their **m**.	6310
	9: 8 peaceably to his neighbour with his **m**,	6310
	9:12 *who is* he to whom the **m** of the LORD	6310
	9:20 let your ear receive the word of his **m**,	6310
	12: 2 thou *art* near in their **m**, and far from	6310
	15:19 from the vile, thou shalt be as my **m**:	6310
	23:16 *and* not out of the **m** of the LORD.	6310
	32: 4 shall speak with him **m** to mouth,	6310
	32: 4 shall speak with him mouth to **m**,	6310
	34: 3 he shall speak with thee **m** to mouth,	6310
	34: 3 he shall speak with thee mouth to **m**,	6310
	36: 4 Baruch wrote from the **m** of Jeremiah all	6310
	36: 6 which thou hast written from my **m**,	6310
	36:17 didst thou write all these words at his **m**?	6310
	36:18 all these words unto me with his **m**,	6310
	36:27 the words which Baruch wrote at the **m**	6310
	36:32 wrote therein from the **m** of Jeremiah	6310
	44:17 thing goeth forth out of our own **m**,	6310
	44:26 of any man of Judah in all the land of	6310
	45: 1 words in a book at the **m** of Jeremiah,	6310
	48:28 her nest in the sides of the hole's **m**.	6310
	51:44 I will bring forth out of his **m** that which	6310
La	2:16 All thine enemies have opened their **m**	6310
	3:29 He putteth his **m** in the dust; if so be	6310
	3:38 Out of the **m** of the most High proceedeth	6310
	4: 4 cleaveth to the roof of his **m** for thirst:	2441
Eze	2: 8 open thy **m**, and eat that I give thee.	6310
	3: 2 I opened my **m**, and he caused me to eat	6310
	3: 3 it was in my **m** as honey for sweetness.	6310
	3:17 therefore hear the word at my **m**,	6310
	3:26 thy tongue cleave to the roof of thy **m**,	2441
	3:27 I will open thy **m**, and thou shalt say unto	6310
	4:14 came there abominable flesh into my **m**.	6310
	16:56 by thy **m** in the day of thy pride,	6310
	16:63 never open thy **m** any more, because of	6310
	21:22 to open the **m** in the slaughter,	6310
	24:27 In that day shall thy **m** be opened to him	6310
	29:21 I will give thee the opening of the **m** in	6310
	33: 7 thou shalt hear the word at my **m**,	6310
	33:22 had opened my **m**, until *he* came to me	6310
	33:22 my **m** was opened, and I was no more	6310
	33:31 for with their **m** they shew much love,	6310
	34:10 for I will deliver my flock from their **m**,	6310
	35:13 Thus with your **m** ye have boasted	6310
Da	3:26 Nebuchadnezzar came near to the **m** of	8651
	4:31 While the word *was* in the king's **m**,	6433
	6:17 and laid upon the **m** of the den;	6433
	7: 5 *it had* three ribs in the **m** of it between	6433
	7: 8 of man, and a **m** speaking great *things.*	6433
	7:20 a **m** that spake very great *things*, whose	6433
	10: 3 neither came flesh nor wine in my **m**,	6310
	10:16 I opened my **m**, and spake, and said unto	6310
Hos	2:17 away the names of Baalim out of her **m**,	6310
	6: 5 I have slain them by the words of my **m**:	6310
	8: 1 *Set* the trumpet to thy **m**. He shall come	2441
Joel	1: 5 new wine, for it is cut off from your **m**.	6310
Am	3:12 As the shepherd taketh out of the **m** of	6310
Mic	4: 4 for the **m** of the LORD of hosts hath	6310
	6:12 and their tongue *is* deceitful in their **m**.	6310
	7: 5 keep the doors of thy **m** from her that	6310
	7:16 they shall lay *their* hand upon *their* **m**,	6310
Na	3:12 shall even fall into the **m** of the eater.	6310
Zep	3:13 a deceitful tongue be found in their **m**:	6310
Zec	5: 8 he cast the weight of lead upon the **m**	6310
	8: 9 these words by the **m** of the prophets,	6310
	9: 7 I will take away his blood out of his **m**,	6310
	14:12 tongue shall consume away in their **m**.	6310
Mal	2: 6 The law of truth was in his **m**,	6310
	2: 7 and they should seek the law at his **m**:	6310
Mt	4: 4 every word that proceedeth out of the **m**	4750

Mt	5: 2 And he opened his **m**, and taught them,	4750
	12:34 abundance of the heart the **m** speaketh.	4750
	13:35 saying, I will open my **m** in parables;	4750
	15: 8 draweth nigh unto me with their **m**,	4750
	15:11 Not that which goeth into the **m** defileth	4750
	15:11 but that which cometh out of the **m**,	4750
	15:17 whatsoever entereth in at the **m** goeth	4750
	15:18 out of the **m** come forth from the heart;	4750
	17:27 and when thou hast opened his **m**,	4750
	18:16 that in the **m** of two or three witnesses	4750
	21:16 Out of the **m** of babes and sucklings thou	4750
Lk	1:64 And his **m** was opened immediately,	4750
	1:70 he spake by the **m** of his holy prophets,	4750
	4:22 words which proceeded out of his **m**.	4750
	6:45 for of the abundance of the heart his **m**	4750
	11:54 seeking to catch something out of his **m**,	4750
	19:22 Out of thine own **m** will I judge thee,	4750
	21:15 For I will give you a **m** and wisdom,	4750
	22:71 we ourselves have heard of his own **m**.	4750
Jn	19:29 put *it* upon hyssop, and put *it* to his **m**.	4750
Ac	1:16 which the Holy Ghost by the **m** of David	4750
	3:18 had shewed by the **m** of all his prophets,	4750
	3:21 of all his holy prophets since the world	4750
	4:25 Who by the **m** of thy servant David hast	4750
	8:32 his shearer, so opened he not his **m**:	4750
	8:35 Then Philip opened his **m**,	4750
	10:34 Then Peter opened *his* **m**, and said, Of a	4750
	11: 8 hath at any time entered into my **m**.	4750
	15: 7 that the Gentiles by my **m** should hear	4750
	15:27 shall also tell *you* the same *things* by **m**.	3056
	18:14 Paul was *now* about to open *his* **m**,	4750
	22:14 and shouldest hear the voice of his **m**.	4750
	23: 2 that stood by him to smite him on the **m**.	4750
Ro	3:14 Whose **m** is full of cursing and bitterness:	4750
	3:19 that every **m** may be stopped, and all	4750
	10: 8 thee, *even* in thy **m**, and in thy heart:	4750
	10: 9 That if thou shalt confess with thy **m**	4750
	10:10 with the **m** confession is made unto	4750
	15: 6 with one mind *and* one **m** glorify God,	4750
1Co	9: 9 Thou shalt not muzzle the **m** of the ox	NIG
2Co	6:11 ye Corinthians, our **m** is open unto you,	4750
	13: 1 In the **m** of two or three witnesses shall	4750
Eph	4:29 communication proceed out of your **m**,	4750
	6:19 unto me, that *I* may open my **m** boldly,	4750
Col	3: 8 filthy communication out of your **m**.	4750
2Th	2: 8 shall consume with the spirit of his **m**,	4750
2Ti	4:17 I was delivered out of the **m** of the lion.	4750
Jas	3:10 Out of the same **m** proceedeth blessing	4750
1Pe	2:22 no sin, neither was guile found in his **m**:	4750
Jude	1:16 their **m** speaketh great swelling *words*,	4750
Rev	1:16 of his **m** went a sharp twoedged sword:	4750
	2:16 against them with the sword of my **m**.	4750
	3:16 nor hot, I will spue thee out of my **m**.	4750
	9:19 For their power is in their **m**, and in their	4750
	10: 9 but it shall be in thy **m** sweet as honey.	4750
	10:10 it up; and it was in my **m** sweet as honey:	4750
	11: 5 fire proceedeth out of their **m**,	4750
	12:15 the serpent cast out of his **m** water as a	4750
	12:16 and the earth opened her **m**,	4750
	12:16 flood which the dragon cast out of his **m**.	4750
	13: 2 a bear, and his **m** as the mouth of a lion:	4750
	13: 2 a bear, and his mouth as the **m** of a lion:	4750
	13: 5 And there was given unto him a **m**	4750
	13: 6 he opened his **m** in blasphemy against	4750
	14: 5 in their **m** was found no guile: for they	4750
	16:13 frogs *come* out of the **m** of the dragon,	4750
	16:13 and out of the **m** of the beast, and out of	4750
	16:13 and out of the **m** of the false prophet.	4750
	19:15 And out of his **m** goeth a sharp sword,	4750
	19:21 which *sword* proceeded out of his **m**:	4750

MOUTHS (18) [MOUTH]

Ge	44: 8 which we found in our sacks' **m**,	6310
Dt	31:19 put it in their **m**, that this song may be a	6310
	31:21 it shall not be forgotten out of the **m** of	6310
Ps	22:13 They gaped upon me *with* their **m**, *as a*	6310
	78:30 But while their meat *was* yet in their **m**,	6310
	115: 5 They have a **m**, but they speak not: eyes	6310
	135:16 They have a **m**, but they speak not: eyes	6310
	135:17 neither is there *any* breath in their **m**.	6310
Isa	52:15 the kings shall shut their **m** at him:	6310
Jer	44:25 wives have both spoken with your **m**,	6310
La	3:46 All our enemies have opened their **m**	6310
Da	6:22 hath shut the lions' **m**, that they have not	6433
Mic	3: 5 that putteth not into their **m**, they even	6310
Tit	1:11 Whose **m** must be stopped, who subvert	1993
Heb	11:33 obtained promises, stopped the **m** of lions,	4750
Jas	3: 3 Behold, we put bits in the horses' **m**,	4750
Rev	9:17 and out of their **m** issued fire and smoke	4750
	9:18 brimstone, which issued out of their **m**.	4750

MOVE (13) [MOTIONS, MOVEABLE, MOVED, MOVEDST, MOVER, MOVETH, MOVING, UNMOVEABLE]

Ex	11: 7 of Israel shall not a dog **m** his tongue,	2782
Lev	11:10 all that in the waters, and of any living	8318
Dt	23:25 thou shalt not **m** a sickle unto thy	5130
	32:21 I will **m** them to jealousy with *those*	7065
Jdg	13:25 to **m** him at *times* in the camp of Dan,	6470
2Sa	7:10 in a place of their own, and **m** no more;	7264
2Ki	21: 8 Neither will I **make** the feet of Israel **m**	5110
	23:18 Let him alone; let no man **m** his bones.	5128
Jer	10: 4 nails and with hammers, that it **m** not.	6328
Mic	7:17 they shall **m** out of their holes like worms	7264
Mt	23: 4 they *themselves* will not **m** them with	2795

Ac	17:28 him we live, and **m**, and have our being;	2795
	20:24 But none of these *things* **m** me,	4160

MOVEABLE (1) [MOVE]

Pr	5: 6 her ways are **m**, *that* thou canst not know	5128

MOVED (75) [MOVE]

Ge	1: 2 the Spirit of God **m** upon the face of	7363
	7:21 all flesh died that **m** upon the earth, *both*	7430
Dt	32:21 They have **m** me to jealousy with *that*	7065
Jos	10:21 none **m** his tongue against any of	2782
	15:18 as she came *unto him*, that she **m** him to	5496
Jdg	1:14 when she came *to him*, that she **m** him to	5496
Ru	1:19 that all the city was **m** about them,	1949
1Sa	1:13 only her lips **m**, but her voice was not	5128
2Sa	18:33 the king was **much m**, and went up to	7264
	22: 8 the foundations of heaven and **m** and shook,	7264
	24: 1 he **m** David against them to say,	5496
1Ch	16:30 also shall be stable, that it be not **m**;	4131
	17: 9 in their place, and shall be **m** no more;	7264
2Ch	18:31 and God **m** them *to depart* from him.	5496
Ezr	4:15 that they have **m** sedition within the same	5648
Est	5: 9 that he stood not up, nor **m** for him, he	2111
Job	37: 1 heart trembleth, and is **m** out of his place.	5425
	41:23 are firm in themselves; they cannot be **m**.	4131
Ps	10: 6 He hath said in his heart, I shall not be **m**:	4131
	13: 4 that trouble me rejoice when I am **m**.	4131
	15: 5 that doeth these *things* shall never be **m**.	4131
	16: 8 *he is* at my right hand, I shall not be **m**.	4131
	18: 7 the foundations also of the hills **m** and	7264
	21: 7 of the most High he shall not be **m**.	4131
	30: 6 my prosperity I said, I shall never be **m**.	4131
	46: 5 *is* in the midst of her; she shall not be **m**:	4131
	46: 6 heathen raged, the kingdoms were **m**:	4131
	55:22 shall never suffer the righteous to be **m**.	4131
	62: 2 *is* my defence; I shall not be greatly **m**.	4131
	62: 6 *he is* my defence; I shall not be **m**.	4131
	66: 9 in life, and suffereth not our feet to be **m**.	4132
	68: 8 *even* Sinai itself was *m* at the presence of	NIH
	78:58 **m** him to jealousy with their graven	7065
	93: 1 also is stablished, *that* it cannot be **m**.	4131
	96:10 shall be established *that* it shall not be **m**:	4131
	99: 1 the cherubims; let the earth be **m**.	5120
	112: 6 Surely he shall not be **m** for ever:	4131
	121: 3 He will not suffer thy foot to be **m**: he	4132
Pr	12: 3 the root of the righteous shall not be **m**.	4131
SS	5: 4 *the door*, and my bowels were **m** for him.	1993
Isa	6: 4 the posts of the door **m** at the voice of	5128
	7: 2 his heart was **m**, and the heart of his	5128
	7: 2 as the trees of the wood are **m** with	5128
	10:14 there was none that **m** the wing,	5074
	14: 9 Hell from beneath is **m** for thee to meet	7264
	19: 1 the idols of Egypt shall be **m** at his	5128
	24:19 the earth is **exceedingly.**	4131+4131
	40:20 a graven image, *that* shall not be **m**.	4131
	41: 7 it with nails, *that* it should not be **m**.	4131
Jer	4:24 they trembled, and all the hills **m** lightly.	7043
	25:16 be **m**, and be mad, because of the sword	1607
	46: 7 a flood, whose waters are **m** as the rivers?	1607
	46: 8 and *his* waters are **m** like the rivers;	1607
	49:21 The earth is **m** at the noise of their fall,	7493
	50:46 of the taking of Babylon the earth is **m**,	7493
Da	8: 7 he was **m** with choler against him,	4843
	11:11 king of the south shall be **m with choler**,	4843
Mt	9:36 he was **m with compassion** on them,	4697
	14:14 was **m with compassion** toward them,	4697
	18:27 of that servant was **m with compassion**,	4697
	20:24 **m with indignation** against the two	23
	21:10 all the city was **m**, saying, Who is this?	4579
Mk	1:41 Jesus, **m with compassion**, put forth	4697
	6:34 was **m with compassion** toward them,	4697
	15:11 But the chief priests **m** the people, that he	383
Ac	2:25 on my right hand, that I should not be **m**:	4531
	7: 9 And the patriarchs, **m with envy**,	2206
	17: 5 Jews which believed not, **m with envy**,	2206
	21:30 all the city was **m**, and the people ran	2795
	21:30 not **away** from the hope of the gospel,	3334
Col	1:23 not **away** from the hope of the gospel,	3334
1Th	3: 3 That no *man* should be **m** by these	4525
Heb	11: 7 **m with fear**, prepared an ark to the	2125
	12:28 receiving a kingdom which **cannot be m**,	761
2Pe	1:21 holy men of God spake *as they were* **m** by	5342
Rev	6:14 and island were **m** out of their places.	2795

MOVEDST (1) [MOVE]

Job	2: 3 thou **m** me against him, to destroy	5496

MOVER (1) [MOVE]

Ac	24: 5 a **m** of sedition among all the Jews	2795

MOVETH (8) [MOVE]

Ge	1:21 and every living creature that **m**,	7430
	1:28 over every living thing that **m** upon	7430
	9: 2 upon all that **m** *upon* the earth, and upon	7430
Lev	11:46 of every living creature that **m** in	7430
Job	40:17 He **m** his tail like a cedar: the sinews of	2654
Ps	69:34 the seas, and every *thing* that **m** therein.	7430
Pr	23:31 colour in the cup, *when* it **m** itself aright.	1980
Eze	47: 9 *that* every thing that liveth, which **m**,	8317

MOVING (5) [MOVE]

Ge	1:20 abundantly the **m creature** that hath life,	5315
	9: 3 Every **m thing** that liveth shall be meat	7431
Job	16: 5 the **m** of my lips should asswage *your*	5205
Pr	16:30 **m** his lips he bringeth evil to pass.	7169
Jn	5: 3 withered, waiting for the **m** of the water.	2796

M

MOWER (1) [MOWINGS, MOWN]

Ps 129: 7 Wherewith the **m** filleth not his hand; 7114

MOWINGS (1) [MOWER]

Am 7: 1 *was* the latter growth after the king's **m**. 1488

MOWN (1) [MOWER]

Ps 72: 6 come down like rain upon the **m grass**; 1488

MOZA (5)

1Ch 2:46 bare Haran, and **M**, and Gazez; 4162
 8:36 and Zimri; and Zimri begat **M**, 4162
 8:37 **M** begat Binea: Rapha *was* his son, 4162
 9:42 and Zimri; and Zimri begat **M**, 4162
 9:43 **M** begat Binea; and Rephaiah his son, 4162

MOZAH (1)

Jos 18:26 And Mizpeh, and Chephirah, and **M**, 4681

MUCH (287) [FORASMUCH, FORSOMUCH, INASMUCH, INSOMUCH, MORE, MOST, OVERMUCH]

Ge 23: 9 **for as m** money **as** it is worth he shall 871.1
 26:16 from us; for thou art **m** mightier than we. 3966
 30:43 had **m** cattle, and maidservants, 7227
 34:12 **Ask** me **never so m** dowry and 3966+7235
 41:49 the sea, very **m**, until he left numbering; 7235
 43:34 five times **so m** as any of theirs. 4480+7235
 44: 1 **as m as** they can carry, 834+3509.1
 50:20 as *it is* this day, to save **m** people alive. 7227
Ex 12:38 and flocks, and herds, *even* very **m** cattle. 3515
 12:42 It *is* a night to be **m observed** unto 8107
 14:28 there remained not **so m as** one of them. 5704
 16: 5 be twice **as m as** they gather daily. 834+5921
 16:18 he that **gathered m** had nothing over, 7235
 16:22 day they gathered **twice as m** bread, 4932
 30:23 and of sweet cinnamon **half so m**, 4276
 36: 5 The people bring **m more** than enough 7235
 36: 7 for all the work to make it, and too **m** 3498
Lev 7:10 sons of Aaron have, one *as* **m** as another. NIH
 13: 7 if the scab **spread m abroad** in 6581+6581
 13:22 if it **spread m abroad** in the skin, 6581+6581
 13:27 *and* if it be **spread m abroad** in 6581+6581
 13:35 if the scall **spread m** in the skin 6581+6581
 14:21 cannot get **so m**; then he shall take one NIH
Nu 16: 3 said unto them, *Ye* take too **m** upon you, 7227
 16: 7 *ye* take **too m** upon you, ye sons of Levi. 7227
 20:20 came out against him with **m** people, 3515
 21: 4 soul of the people was **m** discouraged NIH
 21: 6 the people; and **m** people of Israel died. 7227
Dt 2: 5 land, no, not **so m** as a foot breadth; 5704
 3:19 (*for* I know that ye have **m** cattle,) 7227
 28:38 Thou shalt carry **m** seed out *into* the field, 7227
 31:27 and **how m more** after my death? 637+3588
Jos 11: 4 and all their hosts with them, **m** people, 7227
 13: 1 there remaineth *yet* very **m** land to be 7235
 19: 9 children of Judah was **too m** for them: 7227
 22: 8 Return with **m** riches unto your tents, 7227
 22: 8 with very **m** cattle, with silver, 7227
 22: 8 and with iron, and with very **m** raiment: 7235
Ru 1:13 for it grieveth me **m** for your sakes that 3966
1Sa 2:16 *then* take *as* **m** as thy soul desireth; NIH
 14:30 **How m more**, if haply the people 637+3588
 14:30 for had there not been now a **m greater** 7235
 18:30 of Saul; so that his name was **m** set by. 3966
 19: 2 Saul's son delighted **m** in David: 3966
 20:13 **L**ord do so and **m** more to Jonathan: 3541
 23: 3 **how m more** then if we come *to* Keilah 637
 26:24 as thy life was **m set by** this day in mine 1431
 26:24 let my life be **m set by** in the eyes of 1431
2Sa 4:11 **How m more**, when wicked men have 637
 8: 8 king David took exceeding **m** brass. 7235
 13:34 came **m** people by the way of the hill 7227
 14:25 so **m** praised as Absalom for his beauty: 3966
 16:11 How **m** more now *may this* 637+3588
 17:12 him there shall not be left **so m** as one. 1571
 18:33 the king was **m moved**, and went up to 7264
1Ki 4:29 and understanding exceeding **m**, 7235
 8:27 **how m less** this house that I have 637+3588
 10: 2 and very **m** gold, and precious stones: 7227
 12:28 *It is* too **m** for you to go up to Jerusalem: 7227
2Ki 5:13 not have done *it?* **how m rather** then, 637
 10:18 Baal a little; *but* Jehu shall serve him **m**. 7235
 12:10 they saw that *there was* **m** money in 7227
 21: 6 he wrought **m** wickedness in the sight of 7235
 21:16 Manasseh shed innocent blood very **m**, 7235
1Ch 18: 8 Hadarezer, brought David very **m** brass, 7227
 20: 2 he brought also exceeding **m** spoil *out of* 7235
 22: 4 they of Tyre brought **m** cedar wood to 7230
 22: 8 thou hast shed **m** blood upon the earth in 7227
2Ch 2:16 **as m** as thou shalt need: 3605+3509.1
 6:18 **how m less** this house which I have 637+3588
 14:13 and they carried away very **m** spoil. 7235
 14:14 there was *exceeding* **m** spoil in them. 7227
 17:13 he had **m** business in the cities of Judah: 7227
 20:25 in gathering of the spoil, it was so **m**. 7227
 24:11 when they saw that *there was* **m** money, 7227
 25:13 thousand of them, and took **m** spoil. 7227
 26:10 for he had **m** cattle, both in the low 7227
 27: 3 on the wall of Ophel he built **m**. 7230+3807.1
 27: 5 **So** did the children of Ammon pay 2063
 28: 8 took also away **m** spoil from them, 7227
 30:13 there assembled *at* Jerusalem **m** people to 7227
 32: 4 So there was gathered **m** people together, 7227

2Ch 32: 4 kings of Assyria come, and find **m** water? 7227
 32:15 **how m less** shall your God 637+3588+3808
 32:27 Hezekiah had exceeding **m** riches and 7235
 32:29 for God had given him substance very **m**. 7227
 33: 6 he wrought **m** evil in the sight of 7235
 36:14 **transgressed** very **m** after all 4603+4604
Ezr 7:22 oil, and salt without prescribing *how* **m**. NIH
 10:13 *is* a time of **m rain**, and *we are* not able 1653
Ne 4:10 is decayed, and *there is* **m** rubbish; NIH
 6:16 they were **m** cast down in their own eyes: 3966
 9:37 it yieldeth **m** increase unto the kings 7235
Est 1:18 Thus *shall there arise* too **m** contempt 1767
Job 4:19 How **m** less **in** them that dwell in houses 637
 9:14 **How m less** shall I answer him, 637+3588
 15:10 very aged men, **m** elder than thy father. 3524
 15:16 **How m more** abominable and filthy 637+3588
 25: 6 **How m less** man, *that is* a worm? 637+3588
 31:25 and because mine hand had gotten **m**; 3524
 34:19 *How* **m less** *to him* that accepteth not NIH
 42:10 Job twice **as m** as he had before. 834+3605
Ps 19:10 *are they* than gold, yea, than **m** fine gold: 7227
 33:16 a mighty *man* is not delivered by **m** 7230
 35:18 I will praise thee among **m** people. 6099
 119:14 of thy testimonies, as *m as* in all riches. NIH
 119:107 I am afflicted **very m**: quicken me, 3966+5704
Pr 7:21 With her **m** fair speech she caused him to 7230
 11:31 the wicked and the sinner. 637+3588
 13:23 **M** food *is in* the tillage of the poor; 7230
 14: 4 **m** increase *is* by the strength of the ox. 7230
 15: 6 the house of the righteous *is* **m** treasure: 7227
 15:11 **how m more** then the hearts of 637+3588
 16:16 **How m** better *is* it to get wisdom than 4100
 17: 7 a fool: **m less** do lying lips a prince. 637+3588
 19: 7 **how m more** do his friends go far 637+3588
 19:10 **m less for** a servant to have rule 637+3588
 19:24 **and** will not **so m as** bring it to his 1571
 21:27 **how m more**, when he bringeth it 637+3588
 25:16 eat **so m as** is **sufficient** for thee, lest 1767
 25:27 *It is* not good to eat **m** honey: so *for men* 7235
Ecc 1:18 In **m** wisdom *is* much grief: and he that 7230
 1:18 in much wisdom *is* much grief: and he that 7230
 5:12 *man* is sweet, whether he eat little or **m**: 7235
 5:17 he hath **m** sorrow and wrath with his 7235
 5:20 For he shall not **m** remember the days of 7235
 7:16 Be not righteous **over m**; neither make 7235
 7:17 Be not **over m** wicked, neither be thou 7235
 9:18 of war: but one sinner destroyeth **m** good. 7235
 10:18 By **m slothfulness** the building decayeth; 6103
 12:12 and **m** study *is* a weariness of the flesh. 7235
SS 4:10 **how m** better is thy love than wine! and 4100
Isa 7:13 and he hearkened diligently **with m** heed: 7227
 30:33 the pile thereof *is* fire and **m** wood; 7235
 56:12 be as this day, *and* **m** more abundant. 3966
Jer 2:22 take thee with nitre, and **take** thee **m** sope, 7235
 2:36 thou about **so m** to change thy way? 3966
 40:12 gathered wine and summer fruits very **m**. 7235
Eze 14:21 **How m more** when I send my four 637+3588
 15: 5 **how m less** shall it be meet yet for 637+3588
 17:15 *they* might give him horses and **m** people. 7227
 22: 5 which *art* infamous *and* **m** vexed. 7227
 23:32 and had in derision; *it* containeth **m**. 4767
 26: 7 and companies, and **m** people. 7227
 33:31 for with their mouth they shew **m love**, 5690
Da 4:12 the fruit thereof **m**, and in it *was* meat for 7690
 4:21 the fruit thereof **m**, and in it *was* meat for 7690
 7: 5 said thus unto it, Arise, devour **m** flesh. 7690
 7:28 my cogitations **m** troubled me, 7690
 11:13 with a great army and with **m** riches. 7227
Joel 2: 6 their face the people shall be **pained**: 2342
Jnh 4:11 and their left hand; and *also* **m** cattle? 7235
Na 2:10 **m** pain *is* in all loins, and the faces of 2479
Hag 1: 6 Ye have sown **m**, and bring in little; 7235
 1: 9 *Ye* looked for **m**, and lo, *it* came to little; 7235
Mal 3:13 What have we spoken **so m** against thee? NIH
Mt 6: 7 they shall be heard for their **m speaking**. 4180
 6:26 Are ye not **m** better than they? 3123
 6:30 *shall* he not **m** more **clothe** you, O ye of 4183
 7:11 **how m** more **shall** your Father which is 4214
 10:25 **how m** more **shall they call** them of his 4214
 12:12 **How m** then is a man better than a 4214
 13: 5 places, where they had not **m** earth: 4183
 15:33 we have **so m** bread in the wilderness, 5118
 26: 9 ointment might have been sold for **m**, 4183
Mk 1:45 and began to publish *it* **m**, and to blaze 4183
 2: 2 *them*, no, not **so m as** about the door: 3366
 3:20 so that they could not **so m as** eat bread. 3383
 4: 5 stony ground, where it had not **m** earth; 4183
 5:10 he besought him **m** that he would not 4183
 5:21 other side, **m** people gathered unto him: 4183
 5:24 and **m** people followed him, 4183
 6:31 and they had **no** leisure **so m as** to 2532+3761
 6:34 saw **m** people, and was moved with 4183
 7:36 the **more** a great deal they published 3123
 10:14 when Jesus saw *it*, he was **m displeased**, 23
 10:41 began to be **m displeased** with James 23
 12:41 and many *that were* rich cast in **m**. 4183
Lk 5:15 **m** the more went there a fame abroad of NIH
 6: 3 ye not read **so m** as this, what David NIG
 6:34 to sinners, to receive **as m** again. 2470+3588
 7:11 disciples went with him, and **m** people. 4183
 7:12 and **m** people of the city was with her. 2425
 7:26 unto you, and **more than** a prophet. 4054
 7:47 are many, are forgiven; for she loved **m**: 4183
 8: 4 And when **m** people were gathered 4183
 9:37 down from the hill, **m** people met him. 4183

Lk 10:40 Martha was cumbered about **m** serving, 4183
 11:13 **how m** more shall *your* heavenly Father 4214
 12:19 thou hast **m** goods laid up for many years; 4183
 12:24 **how m** more are ye better than the fowls? 4214
 12:28 **how m** more *will* he **clothe** you, O ye of 4214
 12:48 of **stripes**. For, unto whomsoever **m** is given, 4183
 12:48 much is given, of him shall be **m** required: 4183
 12:48 and to whom **men** have committed **m**, 4183
 16: 5 first, **How m** owest thou unto my lord? 4214
 16: 7 he to another, And **how m** owest thou? 4214
 16:10 in *that which* is least is faithful also in **m**: 4183
 16:10 is unjust in the least is unjust also in **m**. 4183
 18:13 would not lift up **so m as** *his* eyes unto 3761
 18:39 but he cried *so* **m** the more, *Thou* Son of 4183
 19:15 he might know **how m** every *man* had 5101
 24: 4 as they were **m** perplexed thereabout, NIG
Jn 3:23 Salim, because there was **m** water there: 4183
 6:10 Now there was **m** grass in the place. 4183
 6:11 likewise of the fishes **as m as** they would. 3745
 7:12 And there was **m** murmuring among 4183
 12: 9 **M** people of the Jews therefore knew that 4183
 12:12 On the next day **m** people that were come 4183
 12:24 but if it die, it bringeth forth **m** fruit. 4183
 14:30 Hereafter I will not talk **m** with you: 4183
 15: 5 I in him, the same bringeth forth **m** fruit: 4183
 15: 8 my Father glorified, that ye bear **m** fruit; 4183
Ac 5: 8 me whether ye sold the land for **so m**? 5118
 5: 8 so much? And she said, Yea, for **so m**. 5118
 5:37 and drew away **m** people after him: 2425
 7: 5 in it, **no**, not **so m** as to set his foot on: 3761
 9:13 how **m** evil he hath done to thy saints at 3745
 10: 2 which gave **m** alms to the people, 4183
 11:24 and **m** people was added unto the Lord. 2425
 11:26 taught **m** people, and the disciples were 2425
 14:22 that we must through **m** tribulation enter 4183
 15: 7 And when there had been **m** disputing, 4183
 16:16 which brought her masters **m** gain by 4183
 18:10 hurt thee: for I have **m** people in this city. 4183
 18:27 helped them **m** which had believed 4183
 19: 2 We have **not so m** as heard whether 235+3761
 19:26 persuaded and turned away **m** people, 2425
 20: 2 had given them **m** exhortation, he came 4183
 26:24 **m** learning doth make thee mad. 4183
 27: 9 Now when **m** time was spent, 2425
 27:10 voyage will be with hurt and **m** damage, 4183
 27:16 had **m** work to come by the boat: 2480+3433
Ro 1:15 So, **as m** as in me is, I am ready to preach 2596
 3: 2 **M** every way: chiefly, because that unto 4183
 5: 9 **M** more then, being now justified by his 4183
 5:10 **m** more, being reconciled, we shall be 4183
 5:15 **m** more the grace of God, and the gift by 4183
 5:17 **m** more they which receive abundance of 4183
 5:20 sin abounded, grace did **m more abound**: 5248
 9:22 endured with **m** longsuffering the vessels 4183
 11:12 the Gentiles; how **m** more their fulness? 4214
 11:24 **how m** more shall these, which be 4214
 12:18 If *it be* possible, **as m as lieth in** you, 1537
 15:22 For which cause also I have been **m** 4183
 16: 6 Mary, who bestowed **m** labour on us. 4183
 16:12 which laboured **m** in the Lord. 4183
1Co 2: 3 and in fear, and in **m** trembling. 4183
 5: 1 such fornication as **not so m** as named 3761
 6: 3 **how m more** things that pertain to *this*? 3386
 12:22 Nay, **m** more those members of the body, 4183
 16:19 and Priscilla salute you **m** in the Lord, 4183
2Co 2: 4 out of **m** affliction and anguish of heart 4183
 3: 9 **m** more doth the ministration of 4183
 3:11 **m** more that which remaineth *is* glorious. 4183
 6: 4 in patience, in afflictions, in necessities, 4183
 8: 4 Praying us with **m** intreaty that we would 4183
 8:15 He that had **gathered m** had nothing over; 4183
 8:22 in many *things*, but now **m** more diligent, 4183
Php 1:14 **m more** bold to speak the word without 4056
 2:12 but now **m** more in my absence, 4183
1Th 1: 5 in the Holy Ghost, and in **m** assurance; 4183
 1: 6 having received the word in **m** affliction, 4183
 2: 2 the gospel of God with **m** contention. 4183
1Ti 3: 8 not doubletongued, not given to **m** wine, 4183
2Ti 4:14 Alexander the coppersmith did me **m** evil: 4183
Tit 2: 3 not false accusers, not given to **m** wine, 4183
Phm 1: 8 though I might be **m** bold in Christ to 4214
 1:16 to me, but **how m** more unto thee, 4214
Heb 1: 4 Being made so **m** better than the angels, 5118
 7:22 **so m** was Jesus made a surety of a better 5118
 8: 6 by **how m** also he is the mediator of a 3745
 9:14 **How m** more shall the blood of Christ, 4214
 10:25 *one another:* and **so m** the more, 5118
 10:29 Of **how m** sorer punishment, suppose ye, 4214
 12: 9 shall we not **m** rather be in subjection 4183
 12:20 if *so an as* a beast touch the mountain, NIV
 12:25 **m** more *shall not we* escape, if we turn 4183
Jas 5:16 prayer of a righteous *man* availeth **m**. 4183
1Pe 1: 7 *being* **m** more precious than of gold that 4183
2Pe 2:18 lusts of the flesh, through **m** wantonness, NIG
Rev 5: 4 I wept **m**, because no *man* was found 4183
 8: 3 and there was given unto him **m** incense, 4183
 18: 7 **How m** she hath glorified herself, 3745
 18: 7 **so m** torment and sorrow give her: 5118
 19: 1 a great voice of **m** people in heaven, 4183

MUDDY See FOUL

MUFFLERS (1)

Isa 3:19 The chains, and the bracelets, and the **m**, 7479

MULBERRY (4)
2Sa 5:23 upon them over against the **m** trees. 1057
 5:24 of a going in the tops of the **m** trees, 1057
1Ch 14:14 upon them over against the **m** trees. 1057
 14:15 sound of going in the tops of the **m** trees, 1057

MULE (9) [MULES, MULES']
2Sa 13:29 man gat him up upon his **m**, and fled. 6505
 18: 9 Absalom rode upon a **m**, and the mule 6505
 18: 9 the **m** went under the thick boughs of a 6505
 18: 9 the **m** that *was* under him went away. 6505
1Ki 1:33 my son to ride upon mine own **m**, 6506
 1:38 Solomon to ride upon king David's **m**, 6506
 1:44 caused him to ride upon the king's **m**: 6506
Ps 32: 9 Be ye not as the horse, *or* as the **m**, 6505
Zec 14:15 of the **m**, of the camel, and of the ass, 6505

MULES (11) [MULE]
Ge 36:24 this *was that* Anah that found the **m** in 3222
1Ki 10:25 and armour, and spices, horses, and **m**, 6505
 18: 5 find grass to save the horses and **m** alive, 6505
1Ch 12:40 on **m**, and on oxen, *and* meat, meal, 6505
2Ch 9:24 harness, and spices, horses, and **m**, 6505
Ezr 2:66 six; their **m**, two hundred forty and five; 6505
Ne 7:68 six; their **m**, two hundred forty and five; 6505
Est 8:10 *and* riders on **m**, camels, 7409
 8:14 So the posts that rode upon **m** *and* 7409
Isa 66:20 and upon **m**, and upon swift beasts, 6505
Eze 27:14 fairs with horses and horsemen and **m**. 6505

MULES' (1) [MULE]
2Ki 5:17 be given to thy servant two **m** burden of 6505

MULTIPLIED (44) [MULTIPLY]
Ge 47:27 and grew, and **m** exceedingly. 7235
Ex 1: 7 and **m**, and waxed exceeding mighty; 7235
 1:12 them, the more they **m** and grew. 7235
 1:20 the people **m**, and waxed very mighty. 7235
 11: 9 that my wonders may be **m** in the land of 7235
Dt 1:10 The LORD your God hath **m** you, 7235
 8:13 thy silver and thy gold is **m**, and all that 7235
 8:13 is multiplied, and all that thou hast is **m**; 7235
 11:21 That your days may be **m**, and the days 7235
Jos 24: 3 and his seed, and gave him Isaac. 7235
1Ch 5: 9 their cattle were **m** in the land of Gilead. 7235
Job 27:14 If his children be **m**, *it is* for the sword: 7235
 35: 6 or *if* thy transgressions be **m**, what doest 7231
Ps 16: 4 Their sorrows shall be **m** *that* hasten 7235
 38:19 they that hate me wrongfully are **m**. 7231
 107:38 them also, so that they are **m** greatly; 7235
Pr 9:11 For by me thy days shall be **m**, 7235
 29:16 When the wicked are **m**, 7235
Isa 9: 3 hast **m** the nation, *and* not increased 7235
 59:12 For our transgressions are **m** before thee, 7231
Jer 3:16 when ye be **m** and increased in the land, 7235
Eze 5: 7 Because ye **m** more than the nations that 1995
 11: 6 Ye have **m** your slain in this city, 7235
 16:25 that passed by, and **m** thy whoredoms. 7235
 16:29 Thou hast moreover **m** thy fornication in 7235
 16:51 thou hast **m** thine abominations more 7235
 21:15 heart may faint, and *their* ruins be **m**: 7235
 23:19 Yet she **m** her whoredoms, in calling to 7235
 31: 5 his boughs were **m**, and his branches 7235
 35:13 and have **m** your words against me. 6280
Da 4: 1 in all the earth; Peace be **m** unto you. 7680
 6:25 in all the earth; Peace be **m** unto you. 7680
Hos 2: 8 and oil, and **m** her silver and gold, 7235
 8:14 and Judah hath **m** fenced cities; 7235
 12:10 I have **m** visions, and used similitudes by 7235
Na 3:16 hast **m** thy merchants above the stars 7235
Ac 6: 1 when the number of the disciples was **m**, 4129
 6: 7 number of the disciples **m** in Jerusalem 4129
 7:17 the people grew and **m** in Egypt, 4129
 9:31 the comfort of the Holy Ghost, were **m**. 4129
 12:24 But the word of God grew and **m**. 4129
1Pe 1: 2 Grace unto you, and peace, be **m**. 4129
2Pe 1: 2 peace be **m** unto you through 4129
Jude 1: 2 unto you, and peace, and love, be **m**. 4129

MULTIPLIEDST (1) [MULTIPLY]
Ne 9:23 Their children also **m** thou as the stars of 7235

MULTIPLIETH (3) [MULTIPLY]
Job 9:17 and **m** my wounds without cause. 7235
 34:37 and **m** his words against God. 7235
 35:16 in vain; he **m** words without knowledge. 3527

MULTIPLY (46) [MULTIPLIED, MULTIPLIEDST, MULTIPLIETH, MULTIPLYING]
Ge 1:22 **m**, and fill the waters in the seas, and let 7235
 1:22 in the seas, and let fowl **m** in the earth. 7235
 1:28 **m**, and replenish the earth, and subdue it; 7235
 3:16 I will **greatly m** thy sorrow and 7235+7235
 6: 1 when men began to **m** on the face of 7231
 8:17 and be fruitful, and **m** upon the earth. 7235
 9: 1 fruitful, and **m**, and replenish the earth. 7235
 9: 7 you, be ye fruitful, and **m**; bring forth 7235
 9: 7 abundantly in the earth, and **m** therein. 7235
 16:10 I will **m** thy seed **exceedingly**, 7235+7235
 17: 2 and thee, and will **m** thee exceedingly. 7235
 17:20 him fruitful, and will **m** him exceedingly; 7235
 22:17 multiplying I will **m** thy seed as the stars 7235
 26: 4 I will **make** thy seed to **m** as the stars of 7235
 26:24 **m** thy seed for my servant Abraham's 7235
 28: 3 and make thee fruitful, and **m** thee, 7235

Ge 35:11 fruitful and **m**; a nation and a company 7235
 48: 4 thee, and I will make of thee a 7235
Ex 1:10 lest they **m**, and it come to pass, that, 7235
 7: 3 **m** my signs and my wonders in the land 7235
 23:29 and the beast of the field **m** against thee. 7227
 32:13 I will **m** your seed as the stars of heaven, 7235
Lev 26: 9 you, and establish my covenant with 7235
Dt 7:13 love thee, and bless thee, and **m** thee: 7235
 8: 1 **m**, and go in and possess the land which 7235
 8:13 *when* thy herds and thy flocks **m**, and 7235
 13:17 have compassion upon thee, and **m** thee, 7235
 17:16 shall not **m** horses to himself, nor cause 7235
 17:16 to the end that he should **m** horses: 7235
 17:17 Neither shall he **m** wives to himself, 7235
 17:17 neither shall he greatly **m** to himself silver 7235
 28:63 over you to do you good, and to **m** you; 7235
 30: 5 thee good, and **m** thee above thy fathers. 7235
 30:16 judgments, that thou mayest live and **m**: 7235
1Ch 4:27 neither did all their family **m**, like to 7235
Job 29:18 nest, and I shall **m** my days as the sand. 7235
Jer 30:19 I will **m** them, and they shall not be few; 7235
 33:22 so will I **m** the seed of David my servant, 7235
Eze 16: 7 I have caused thee to **m** as the bud of 7233
 36:10 I will **m** men upon you, all the house of 7235
 36:11 I will **m** upon you man and beast; 7235
 36:30 I will **m** the fruit of the tree, 7235
 37:26 **m** them, and will set my sanctuary in 7235
Am 4: 4 *at* Gilgal **m** transgression; and bring your 7235
2Co 9:10 and **m** your seed sown, and increase 4129
Heb 6:14 bless thee, and multiplying I will **m** thee. 4129

MULTIPLYING (2) [MULTIPLY]
Ge 22:17 in **m** I will multiply thy seed as the stars 7235
Heb 6:14 bless thee, and **m** I will multiply thee. 4129

MULTITUDE (243) [MULTITUDES]
Ge 16:10 that it shall not be numbered for **m**. 7230
 28: 3 that thou mayest be a **m** of people; 6951
 30:30 I came, and it is *now* increased unto a **m**; 7230
 32:12 sea, which cannot be numbered for **m**. 7230
 48: 4 and I will make of thee a **m** of people; 6951
 48:16 let them grow into a **m** in the midst of 7230
 48:19 and his seed shall become a **m** of nations. 4393
Ex 12:38 a mixed **m** went up also with them; 7227
 23: 2 Thou shalt not follow a **m** to do *evil*; 7227
Lev 25:16 According to the **m** of years thou shalt 7230
Nu 11: 4 the **mixt m** that *was* among them fell a 628
 32: 1 the children of Gad had a very great **m** of 7227
Dt 1:10 *are this* day as the stars of heaven for **m**. 7230
 10:22 made thee as the stars of heaven for **m**. 7230
 28:62 ye were as the stars of heaven for **m**; 7230
Jos 11: 4 the sand that *is* upon the sea shore in **m**, 7230
Jdg 7: 1 Jabin's army, with his chariots and his **m**; 1995
 6: 5 and they came as grasshoppers for **m**; 7230
 7:12 in the valley like grasshoppers for **m**; 7230
 7:12 as the sand by the sea side for **m**. 7230
1Sa 13: 5 the sand which *is* on the sea shore in **m**; 1995
 14:16 the **m** melted away, and they went on 1995
 6:19 among the whole **m** of Israel, as well 7230
2Sa 6:19 as the sand that *is* by the sea for **m**. 7230
1Ki 3: 8 cannot be numbered nor counted for **m**. 7230
 4:20 as the sand which *is* by the sea in **m**, 7230
 8: 5 could not be told nor numbered for **m**. 7230
 20:13 Hast thou seen all this great **m**? 1995
 20:28 will I deliver all this great **m** into thine 1995
2Ki 7:13 they *are* as all the **m** of Israel that are left 1995
 7:13 *I say*, they *are even* as all the **m** of 1995
 19:23 With the **m** of my chariots I am come up 7230
 25:11 of Babylon, with the remnant of the **m**, 1995
2Ch 1: 9 a people like the dust of the earth in **m**. 7227
 5: 6 could not be told nor numbered for **m**. 7230
 13: 8 ye *be* a great **m**, and *there are* with you 1995
 14:11 and in thy name we go against this **m**. 1995
 20: 2 There cometh a great **m** against thee from 1995
 20:15 nor dismayed by reason of this great **m**; 1995
 20:24 they looked unto the **m**, and behold, 1995
 28: 5 carried away a **great m** of them captives, 1419
 30:18 For a **m** of the people, *even many* of 4768
 32: 7 nor for all the **m** that *is* with him: 1995
Ne 13: 3 separated from Israel all the **mixed m**. 6154
Est 5:11 the **m** of his children, and all the *things* 7230
 10: 3 and accepted of the **m** of his brethren, 7230
Job 11: 2 Should not the **m** of words be answered? 7230
 31:34 Did I fear a great **m**, or did the contempt 1995
 32: 7 and **m** of years should teach wisdom. 7230
 33:19 and the **m** of his bones with strong *pain*: 7379
 35: 9 by reason of the **m** of oppressions they 1995
 39: 7 He scorneth the **m** of the city, 1995
Ps 5: 7 I will come *into* thy house in the **m** of thy 7230
 5:10 cast them out in the **m** of their 7230
 33:16 There is no king saved by the **m** of a host: 7230
 42: 4 I had gone with the **m**, I went with them 5519
 42: 4 and praise, *with* a **m** that kept holyday. 1995
 49: 6 boast themselves in the **m** of their riches; 7230
 51: 1 unto the **m** of thy tender mercies 7230
 68:30 the **m** of the bulls, with the calves of 5712
 69:13 O God, in the **m** of thy mercy hear me, 7230
 69:16 turn unto me according to the **m** of thy 7230
 74:19 *of the wicked*: forget not 2416
 94:19 In the **m** of my thoughts within me thy 7230
 97: 1 let the **m** of isles be glad *thereof*. 7230
 106: 7 remembered not the **m** of thy mercies; 7230
 106:45 according to the **m** of his mercies. 7230
 109:30 yea, I will praise him among the **m**. 7227
Pr 10:19 In the **m** of words there wanteth not sin: 7230

Pr 11:14 but in the **m** of counsellers *there is* safety. 7230
 14:28 In the **m** of people *is* the king's honour: 7230
 15:22 the **m** of counsellers *they* are established. 7230
 20:15 There is gold, and a **m** of rubies: 7230
 24: 6 and in **m** of counsellers *there is* safety. 7230
Ecc 5: 3 For a dream cometh through the **m** of 7230
 5: 3 a fool's voice *is known* by **m** of words. 7230
 5: 7 For in the **m** of dreams and many words 7230
Isa 1:11 what purpose *is* the **m** of your sacrifices 7230
 5:13 and their **m** dried up with thirst. 1995
 5:14 their **m**, and their pomp, and he that 1995
 13: 4 The noise of a **m** in the mountains, like as 1995
 16:14 shall be contemned, with all *that* great **m**; 1995
 17:12 Woe to the **m** of many people, *which* 1995
 29: 5 Moreover the **m** of thy strangers shall be 1995
 29: 5 the **m** of the terrible ones *shall be* as chaff 1995
 29: 7 the **m** of all the nations that fight against 1995
 29: 8 so shall the **m** of all the nations be, 1995
 31: 4 when a **m** of shepherds is called forth 4393
 32:14 the **m** of the city shall be left; the forts 1995
 37:24 By the **m** of my chariots am I come up *to* 7230
 47: 9 their perfection for the **m** of thy sorceries, 7230
 47:12 and with the **m** of thy sorceries, 7230
 47:13 art wearied in the **m** of thy counsels. 7230
 60: 6 The **m** of camels shall cover thee, 8229
 63: 7 to the **m** of his lovingkindnesses. 1995
Jer 3:23 the hills, *and from* the **m** of mountains: 1995
 10:13 *there is* a **m** of waters in the heavens, 1995
 12: 6 yea, they have called a **m** after thee: 4392
 30:14 of a cruel one, for the **m** of thine iniquity; 7230
 30:15 thy sorrow is incurable for the **m** of thine 7230
 44:15 all the women that stood *by*, a great **m**, 6951
 46:25 I will punish the **m** of No, and Pharaoh, 527
 49:32 a booty, and the **m** of their cattle a spoil: 1995
 51:16 *there is* a **m** of waters in the heavens; 1995
 51:42 she is covered with the **m** of the waves 1995
 52:15 the king of Babylon, and the rest of the **m**. 527
La 1: 5 for the LORD hath afflicted her for the **m** 7230
 3:32 according to the **m** of his mercies. 7230
Eze 7:11 none of them *shall remain*, nor of their **m**, 1995
 7:12 for wrath *is* upon all the **m** thereof. 1995
 7:13 for the vision *is* touching the whole **m** 1995
 7:14 for my wrath *is* upon all the **m** thereof. 1995
 14: 4 cometh according to the **m** of his idols; 7230
 19:11 she appeared in her height with the **m** of 7230
 23:42 a voice of a **m** being at ease *was* with her: 1995
 27:12 by reason of the **m** of all *kind of* riches; 7230
 27:16 *was* thy merchant by reason of the **m** 7230
 27:18 Damascus *was* thy merchant in the **m** of 7230
 27:18 of thy making, for the **m** of all riches; 7230
 27:33 of the earth with the **m** of thy riches 7230
 28:16 By the **m** of thy merchandise they have 7230
 28:18 hast defiled thy sanctuaries by the **m** 7230
 28:19 he shall take her **m**, and take her spoil, 1995
 30: 4 they shall take *away* her **m**, 1995
 30:10 I will also make the **m** of Egypt to cease 1995
 30:15 of Egypt; and I will cut off the **m** of No. 1995
 31: 2 unto Pharaoh king of Egypt, and to his **m**; 1995
 31: 5 became long because of the **m** of waters, 7227
 31: 9 I have made him fair by the **m** of his 7230
 31:18 This *is* Pharaoh and all his **m**, saith 1995
 32:12 of the mighty will I cause thy **m** to fall, 1995
 32:12 and all the **m** thereof shall be destroyed. 1995
 32:16 *even* for Egypt, and for all her **m**, saith 1995
 32:18 wail for the **m** of Egypt, and cast them 1995
 32:24 and all her **m** round about her grave, 1995
 32:25 in the midst of the slain with all her **m**: 1995
 32:26 There *is* Meshech, Tubal, and all her **m**: 1995
 32:31 shall be comforted over all his **m**, 1995
 32:32 Pharaoh and all his **m**, saith the Lord 1995
 39:11 there shall they bury Gog and all his **m**: 1995
 47: 9 there shall be a very **great m** of fish, 7227
Da 10: 6 voice of his words like the voice of a **m**. 1995
 11:10 and shall assemble a **m** of great forces: 1995
 11:11 he shall set forth a great **m**; 1995
 11:11 but the **m** shall be given into his hand. 1995
 11:12 *And* when he hath taken away the **m**, 1995
 11:13 set forth a **m** greater than the former, 1995
Hos 9: 7 for the **m** of thine iniquity, and great 7230
 10: 1 according to the **m** of his fruit he hath 7230
 10:13 in thy way, in the **m** of thy mighty men. 7230
Mic 2:12 great noise by reason of the **m** of men. NIH
Na 3: 3 *there is* a **m** of slain, and a great number 7230
 3: 4 Because of the **m** of the whoredoms of 7230
Zec 2: 4 as towns without walls for the **m** of men 7230
Mt 12: 2 sat; and the whole **m** stood on the shore. 3793
 13:34 All these *things* spake Jesus unto the **m** in 3793
 13:36 Jesus sent the **m** away, and went into 3793
 14: 5 feared the **m**, because they counted him 3793
 14:14 and saw a great **m**, and was moved with 3793
 14:15 send the **m** away, that they may go into 3793
 14:19 And he commanded the **m** to sit down on 3793
 14:19 to *his* disciples, and the disciples to the **m**, 3793
 15:10 And he called the **m**, and said unto them, 3793
 15:31 Insomuch that the **m** wondered, when 3793
 15:32 and said, I have compassion on the **m**, 3793
 15:33 in the wilderness, as to fill so great a **m**? 3793
 15:35 he commanded the **m** to sit down on 3793
 15:36 his disciples, and the disciples to the **m**. 3793
 15:39 And he sent away the **m**, and took ship, 3793
 17:14 And when they were come to the **m**, 3793
 20:29 from Jericho, a great **m** followed him. 3793
 20:31 And the **m** rebuked them, because 3793
 21: 8 And a very great **m** spread their garments 3793
 21:11 the **m** said, This is Jesus the prophet of 3793

M

Mt	21:46 they feared the **m**, because they took him	3793
	22:33 And when the **m** heard *this*, they were	3793
	23: 1 Then spake Jesus to the **m**, and to his	3793
	26:47 and with him a great **m** with swords and	3793
	27:20 persuaded the **m** that they should ask	3793
	27:24 washed *his* hands before the **m**, saying,	3793
Mk	2:13 and all the **m** resorted unto him,	3793
	3: 7 and a great **m** from Galilee followed him,	4128
	3: 8 they about Tyre and Sidon, a great **m**,	4128
	3: 9 should wait on him because of the **m**,	3793
	3:20 And *the* **m** cometh together again,	3793
	3:32 And *the* **m** sat about him, and they said	3793
	4: 1 there was gathered unto him a great **m**,	3793
	4: 1 the whole **m** was by the sea on the land.	3793
	4:36 And when they had sent away the **m**,	3793
	5:31 Thou seest the **m** thronging thee,	3793
	7:33 And he took him aside from the **m**,	3793
	8: 1 In those days the **m** being very great,	3793
	8: 2 I have compassion on the **m**, because	3793
	9:14 he saw a great **m** about them,	3793
	9:17 And one of the **m** answered and said,	3793
	14:43 with him a great **m** with swords and	3793
	15: 8 And the **m** crying aloud began to desire	3793
Lk	1:10 And the whole **m** of the people were	4128
	2:13 suddenly there was with the angel a **m**	4128
	3: 7 said he to the **m** that came forth to be	3793
	5: 6 done, they inclosed a great **m** of fishes:	4128
	5:19 might bring him in because of the **m**,	3793
	6:17 a great **m** of people out of all Judea and	4128
	6:19 And the whole **m** sought to touch him:	3793
	8:37 Then the whole **m** of the country of	4128
	8:45 the **m** throng thee and press *thee*, and	3793
	9:12 and said unto him, Send the **m** away,	3793
	9:16 gave to the disciples to set before the **m**.	3793
	12: 1 together an **innumerable m** of people,	3461
	18:36 hearing the **m** pass by, he asked what	3793
	19:37 the whole **m** of the disciples began to	4128
	19:39 Pharisees from among the **m** said unto	3793
	22: 6 him unto them in the absence of the **m**.	3793
	22:47 behold a **m**, and he that was called Judas,	3793
	23: 1 And the whole **m** of them arose,	4128
Jn	5: 3 In these lay a great **m** of impotent *folk*, of	4128
	5:13 himself away, a **m** being in *that* place.	3793
	6: 2 And a great **m** followed him, because	3793
	6: 5 they were not able to draw it for the **m**	4128
Ac	2: 6 **m** came together, and were confounded,	4128
	4:32 And the **m** of them that believed were of	4128
	5:16 came also a **m** *out* of the cities round	4128
	6: 2 Then the twelve called the **m** of	4128
	6: 5 And the saying pleased the whole **m**:	4128
	14: 1 a great **m** both of the Jews and *also* of	4128
	14: 4 But the **m** of the city was divided:	4128
	15:12 Then all the **m** kept silence,	4128
	15:30 when they had gathered the **m** together,	4128
	16:22 And the **m** rose up together against them:	3793
	17: 4 and of the devout Greeks a great **m**,	4128
	19: 9 but spake evil of *that* way before the **m**,	4128
	19:33 And they drew Alexander out of the **m**,	3793
	21:22 the **m** must needs come together: for they	4128
	21:34 one *thing*, some another, among the **m**:	3793
	21:36 For the **m** of the people followed *after*,	4128
	23: 7 the Sadducees: and the **m** was divided.	4128
	24:18 temple, neither with **m**, nor with tumult.	3793
	25:24 ye see this *man*, about whom all the **m** of	4128
Heb	11:12 *so many* as the stars of the sky in **m**,	4128
Jas	5:20 from death, and shall hide a **m** of sins.	4128
1Pe	4: 8 for charity shall cover the **m** of sins.	4128
Rev	7: 9 After this I beheld, and lo, a great **m**,	3793
	19: 6 I heard as *it were* the voice of a great **m**,	3793

MULTITUDES (24) [MULTITUDE]

Eze	32:20 *to* the sword: draw her and all her **m**.	1995
Joel	3:14 **M**, multitudes in the valley of decision:	1995
	3:14 Multitudes, **m** in the valley of decision:	1995
Mt	4:25 there followed him great **m** of people	3793
	5: 1 And seeing the **m**, he went up into a	3793
	8: 1 the mountain, great **m** followed him.	3793
	8:18 Now when Jesus saw great **m** about him,	3793
	9: 8 But when the **m** saw *it*, they marvelled,	3793
	9:33 and the **m** marvelled, saying, It was never	3793
	9:36 But when he saw the **m**, he was moved	3793
	11: 7 Jesus began to say unto the **m** concerning	3793
	12:15 and great **m** followed him, and he healed	3793
	13: 2 And great **m** were gathered together unto	3793
	14:22 the other side, while he sent the **m** away.	3793
	14:23 when he had sent the **m** away, he went	3793
	15:30 And great **m** came unto him, having with	3793
	19: 2 And great **m** followed him; and he healed	3793
	21: 9 And the **m** that went before,	3793
	26:55 In that *same* hour said Jesus to the **m**,	3793
Lk	5:15 and great **m** came together to hear,	3793
	14:25 And there went great **m** with him:	3793
Ac	5:14 to the Lord, **m** both of men and women.)	4128
	13:45 But when the Jews saw the **m**, they were	3793
Rev	17:15 and **m**, and nations, and tongues.	3793

MUNITION (2) [MUNITIONS]

Isa	29: 7 even all that fight against her and her **m**,	4685
Na	2: 1 keep the **m**, watch the way, make *thy*	4694

MUNITIONS (1) [MUNITION]

Isa	33:16 his place of defence *shall be* the **m** of	4679

MUPPIM (1)

Ge	46:21 Ehi, and Rosh, **M**, and Huppim, and Ard.	4649

MURDER (9) [MURDERER, MURDERERS, MURDERS]

Ps	10: 8 the secret places doth he **m** the innocent:	2026
	94: 6 and the stranger, and **m** the fatherless.	7523
Jer	7: 9 **m**, and commit adultery, and swear	7523
Hos	6: 9 the company of priests **m** *in* the way by	7523
Mt	19:18 Jesus said, Thou shalt do no **m**, Thou	5407
Mk	15: 7 who had committed **m** in the insurrection.	5408
Lk	23:19 the city, and *for* **m**, was cast into prison.)	5408
	23:25 for sedition and **m** was cast into prison,	5408
Ro	1:29 full of envy, **m**, debate, deceit, malignity;	5408

MURDERER (20) [MURDER]

Nu	35:16 of iron, so that he die, he *is a* **m**:	7523
	35:16 the **m** shall surely be put to death.	7523
	35:17 he may die, and he die, he *is a* **m**:	7523
	35:17 the **m** shall surely be put to death.	7523
	35:18 he may die, and he die, he *is a* **m**:	7523
	35:18 the **m** shall surely be put to death.	7523
	35:19 of blood himself shall slay the **m**:	7523
	35:21 shall surely be put to death; *for he is a* **m**:	7523
	35:21 the revenger of blood shall slay the **m**,	7523
	35:30 the **m** shall be put to death by the mouth	7523
	35:31 take no satisfaction for the life of a **m**,	7523
2Ki	6:32 See ye how this son of a **m** hath sent to	7523
Job	24:14 The **m** rising with the light killeth the	7523
Hos	9:13 *shall* bring forth his children to the **m**.	2026
Jn	8:44 He was a **m** from the beginning,	443
Ac	3:14 desired a **m** to be granted unto you;	435+5406
	28: 4 No doubt this man is a **m**, whom,	5406
1Pe	4:15 But let none of you suffer as a **m**, or *as a*	5406
1Jn	3:15 Whosoever hateth his brother is a **m**:	443
	3:15 know that no **m** hath eternal life abiding	443

MURDERERS (10) [MURDER]

2Ki	14: 6 the children of the **m** he slew not:	5221
Isa	1:21 Righteousness lodged in it; but now **m**.	7523
Jer	4:31 for my soul is wearied because of **m**.	2026
Mt	22: 7 destroyed those **m**, and burnt up their	5406
Ac	7:52 ye have been now the betrayers and **m**:	5406
	21:38 four thousand men that were **m**?	4607
1Ti	1: 9 **m** of fathers and murderers of mothers,	3964
	1: 9 murderers of fathers and **m** of mothers,	3389
Rev	21: 8 and **m**, and whoremongers, and sorcerers,	5406
	22:15 **m**, and idolaters, and whosoever loveth	5406

MURDERS (4) [MURDER]

Mt	15:19 **m**, adulteries, fornications, thefts,	5408
Mk	7:21 evil thoughts, adulteries, fornications, **m**,	5408
Gal	5:21 Envyings, **m**, drunkenness, revellings,	5408
Rev	9:21 Neither repented they of their **m**, nor of	5408

MURMUR (9) [MURMURED, MURMURERS, MURMURING, MURMURINGS]

Ex	16: 7 and what *are* we, that ye **m** against us?	3885
	16: 8 murmurings which ye **m** against him:	3885
Nu	14:27 evil congregation, which **m** against me?	3885
	14:27 of Israel, which they **m** against me.	3885
	14:36 made all the congregation to **m** against	3885
	16:11 what *is* Aaron, that ye **m** against him?	3885
	17: 5 of Israel, whereby they **m** against you.	3885
Jn	6:43 said unto them, **M** not among yourselves.	1111
1Co	10:10 Neither **m** ye, as some of them also	1111

MURMURED (19) [MURMUR]

Ex	15:24 the people **m** against Moses, saying,	3885
	16: 2 of the children of Israel **m** against Moses	3885
	17: 3 the people **m** against Moses, and said,	3885
Nu	14: 2 all the children of Israel **m** against Moses	3885
	14:29 and upward, which have **m** against me,	3885
	16:41 of the children of Israel **m** against Moses	3885
Dt	1:27 ye **m** in your tents, and said, Because	7279
Jos	9:18 the congregation **m** against the princes.	3885
Ps	106:25 **m** in their tents, *and* hearkened not unto	7279
Isa	29:24 and they that **m** shall learn doctrine.	7279
Mt	20:11 And when they had received *it*, they **m**	1111
Mk	14: 5 to the poor. And they **m** against her.	1690
Lk	5:30 and Pharisees **m** against his disciples,	1111
	15: 2 And the Pharisees and scribes **m**, saying,	1234
	19: 7 And when they saw *it*, they all **m**, saying,	1234
Jn	6:41 The Jews then **m** at him, because he said,	1111
	6:61 knew in himself that his disciples **m** at it,	1111
	7:32 Pharisees heard that the people **m** such	1111
1Co	10:10 as some of them also **m**,	1111

MURMURERS (1) [MURMUR]

Jude	1:16 These are **m**, complainers, walking after	1113

MURMURING (2) [MURMUR]

Jn	7:12 And there was much **m** among the people	1112
Ac	6: 1 there arose a **m** of the Grecians against	1112

MURMURINGS (9) [MURMUR]

Ex	16: 7 that he heareth your **m** against	8519
	16: 8 for that the LORD heareth your **m** which	8519
	16: 8 your **m** *are* not against us, but against	8519
	16: 9 to the LORD: for he hath heard your **m**.	8519
	16:12 have heard the **m** of the children of Israel:	8519
Nu	14:27 have heard the **m** of the children of Israel,	8519
	17: 5 I will make to cease from me the **m** of	8519
	17:10 quite take away their **m** from me,	8519
Php	2:14 Do all *things* without **m** and disputings;	1112

MURRAIN (1)

Ex	9: 3 sheep: there *shall be* a very grievous **m**.	1698

MUSE (1) [MUSED, MUSING]

Ps	143: 5 thy works; I **m** on the work of thy hands.	7878

MUSED (1) [MUSE]

Lk	3:15 and all *men* **m** in their hearts of John,	1260

MUSHI (8) [MUSHITES]

Ex	6:19 the sons of Merari; Mahali and **M**:	4187
Nu	3:20 Merari by their families; Mahli, and **M**.	4187
1Ch	6:19 The sons of Merari; Mahli, and **M**.	4187
	6:47 the son of **M**, the son of Merari, the son	4187
	23:21 The sons of Merari; Mahli, and **M**.	4187
	23:23 The sons of **M**; Mahli, and Eder,	4187
	24:26 The sons of Merari *were* Mahli and **M**:	4187
	24:30 The sons also of **M**; Mahli, and Eder,	4187

MUSHITES (2) [MUSHI]

Nu	3:33 of the Mahlites, and the family of the **M**:	4188
	26:58 of the Mahlites, the family of the **M**,	4188

MUSICAL (3) [MUSICK]

1Ch	16:42 with a sound, and with instruments of God.	7892
Ne	12:36 with the **m** instruments of David the man	7892
Ecc	2: 8 **m** instruments, and	
	that of **all sorts**.	7705+7705

MUSICIAN (55) [MUSICK]

Ps	4: T To the **chief M** on Neginoth, A Psalm of	5329
	5: T To the **chief M** upon Nehiloth, A Psalm	5329
	6: T To the **chief M** on Neginoth upon	5329
	8: T To the **chief M** upon Gittith, A Psalm of	5329
	9: T To the **chief M** upon Muth-labben,	5329
	11: T To the **chief M**, *A Psalm of* David.	5329
	12: T To the **chief M** upon Sheminith, A Psalm	5329
	13: T To the **chief M**, A Psalm of David.	5329
	14: T To the **chief M**, *A Psalm of* David.	5329
	18: T To the **chief M**, *A Psalm of* David.	5329
	19: T To the **chief M**, A Psalm of David.	5329
	20: T To the **chief M**, A Psalm of David.	5329
	21: T To the **chief M**, A Psalm of David.	5329
	22: T To the **chief M** upon Aijeleth Shahar,	5329
	31: T To the **chief M**, A Psalm of David	5329
	36: T To the **chief M**, *A Psalm* of David	5329
	39: T To the **chief M**, *even* to Jeduthun,	5329
	40: T To the **chief M**, A Psalm of David.	5329
	41: T To the **chief M**, A Psalm of David.	5329
	42: T To the **chief M**, Maschil, for the sons of	5329
	44: T To the **chief M** for the sons of Korah,	5329
	45: T To the **chief M** upon Shoshannim,	5329
	46: T To the **chief M** for the sons of Korah,	5329
	47: T To the **chief M**, A Psalm for the sons of	5329
	49: T To the **chief M**, A Psalm for the sons of	5329
	51: T To the **chief M**, A Psalm of David,	5329
	52: T To the **chief M**, Maschil, *A Psalm* of	5329
	53: T To the **chief M** upon Mahalath, Maschil,	5329
	54: T To the **chief M** on Neginoth, Maschil,	5329
	55: T To the **chief M** on Neginoth, Maschil,	5329
	56: T To the **chief M** upon	5329
	57: T To the **chief M**, Al-taschith, Michtam of	5329
	58: T To the **chief M**, Al-taschith, Michtam of	5329
	59: T To the **chief M**, Al-taschith, Michtam of	5329
	60: T To the **chief M** upon Shushan-eduth,	5329
	61: T To the **chief M** upon Neginah, *A Psalm*	5329
	62: T To the **chief M**, to Jeduthun, *A Psalm*	5329
	64: T To the **chief M**, A Psalm of David.	5329
	65: T To the **chief M**, A Psalm *and* Song of	5329
	66: T To the **chief M**, A Song of Praise.	5329
	67: T To the **chief M** on Neginoth, A Psalm *or*	5329
	68: T To the **chief M**, A Psalm *or* Song of	5329
	69: T To the **chief M** upon Shoshannim,	5329
	70: T To the **chief M**, *A Psalm* of David, to	5329
	75: T To the **chief M**, Al-taschith, A Psalm *or*	5329
	76: T To the **chief M** on Neginoth, A Psalm *or*	5329
	77: T To the **chief M**, to Jeduthun, A Psalm of	5329
	80: T To the **chief M** upon Shoshannim-Eduth,	5329
	81: T To the **chief M** upon Gittith, *A Psalm* of	5329
	84: T To the **chief M** upon Gittith, A Psalm for	5329
	85: T To the **chief M**, A Psalm for the sons of	5329
	88: T To the **chief M** upon Mahalath Leannoth	5329
	109: T To the **chief M**, *A Psalm of* David.	5329
	139: T To the **chief M**, A Psalm of David.	5329
	140: T To the **chief M**, A Psalm of David.	5329

MUSICIANS (1) [MUSICK]

Rev	18:22 and **m**, and of pipers, and trumpeters,	3451

MUSICK (16) [MUSICAL, MUSICIAN, MUSICIANS]

1Sa	18: 6 with joy, and with **instruments of m**.	7991
1Ch	15:16 *to be* the singers with instruments of **m**,	7892
2Ch	5:13 and cymbals and instruments of **m**,	7892
	7: 6 the Levites also with instruments of **m**,	7892
	23:13 also the singers with instruments of **m**,	7892
	34:12 all that could skill of instruments of **m**,	7892
Ecc	12: 4 the daughters of **m** shall be brought low;	7892
La	3:63 and their rising up, I *am* their **m**.	4485
	5:14 the gate, the young men from their **m**.	5058
Da	3: 5 psaltery, dulcimer, and all kinds of **m**,	2170
	3: 7 sackbut, psaltery, and all kinds of **m**,	2170
	3:10 and dulcimer, and all kinds of **m**,	2170
	3:15 and dulcimer, and all kinds of **m**,	2170
	6:18 neither were **instruments of m** brought	1761
Am	6: 5 invent to themselves instruments of **m**,	7892
Lk	15:25 to the house, he heard **m** and dancing.	4858

MUSING (1) [MUSE]
Ps 39: 3 within me, while I was **m** the fire burned: 1901

MUST (132)
Ge 17:13 **m** needs be circumcised: 4135+4135
 24: 5 **m** I needs bring thy son **again** 7725+7725
 29:26 Thou **m** not be so done in our country, NIH
 30:16 and said, Thou **m** come in unto me; NIH
 43:11 unto them, If *it* **m** *be* so now, do this; NIH
 47:29 the time drew nigh that Israel **m** die: 3807.1
Ex 10: 9 for we **m** hold a feast unto the LORD. NIH
 10:25 Thou **m** give us also sacrifices and NIH
 10:26 for thereof **m** we take to serve the LORD NIH
 10:26 we know not with what **m** we serve NIH
 12:16 save *that* which every man **m** eat, that NIH
 18:20 shalt shew them the way *wherein* they **m** NIH
 18:20 must walk, and the work that they **m** do. NIH
Lev 11:32 it **m** be put into water, and it shall be NIH
 23: 6 seven days ye **m** eat unleavened bread. NIH
Nu 6:21 so he **m** do after the law of his separation. NIH
 18:22 Neither **m** the children of Israel NIH
 20:10 **m** we fetch you water out of this rock? NIH
 23:12 **M** I not take heed to speak that which NIH
 23:26 All that the LORD speaketh, that I **m** do? NIH
Dt 1:22 bring us word again by what way we **m** go NIH
 4:22 I **m** die in this land, I *must* not go over NIH
 4:22 die in this land, I *m* not go over Jordan: NIH
 12:18 thou **m** eat them before the LORD thy God NIH
 31: 7 thou **m** go with this people unto the land NIH
 31:14 thy days approach that *thou* **m** die: NIH
Jos 3: 4 that ye may know the way by which ye **m** NIH
 22:18 ye **m** turn away this day from following NIH
Jdg 13:16 thou **m** offer it unto the LORD. NIH
 21:17 *There* **m** be an inheritance for them that NIH
Ru 4: 5 thou **m** buy *it* also of Ruth the Moabitess, NIH
1Sa 14:43 that *was* in mine hand, *and* lo, I **m** die. NIH
2Sa 14:14 For we **m** needs die, and *are* as 4191+4191
 23: 3 He that ruleth over men *m* *be* just, ruling NIH
 23: 7 man *that* shall touch them **m** be fenced NIH
1Ki 18:27 he sleepeth, and **m** be awaked. NIH
1Ch 17:11 thy days be expired that *thou* **m** go *to* NIH
 22: 5 for the LORD *m* be exceeding magnifical, NIH
Ezr 10:12 loud voice, As thou hast said, so **m** we do. NIH
Ps 32: 9 whose mouth **m** be held in with bit and NIH
Pr 18:24 A man that hath friends **m** shew himself NIH
 19:19 for if thou deliver *him,* yet thou **m** do *it* NIH
Ecc 10:10 the edge, then **m** he put to more strength: NIH
SS 8:12 **m** have a thousand, and those that keep NIH
Isa 28:10 For precept **m** be upon precept, NIH
Jer 10: 5 they **m** needs be borne, because 5375+5375
 10:19 I said, Truly this *is* a grief, and I **m** bear it. NIH
Eze 34:18 **m** tread down with your feet the residue NIH
 34:18 but ye **m** foul the residue with your feet? NIH
Mt 16:21 how that he **m** go unto Jerusalem, 1163
 17:10 say the scribes that Elias **m** first come? 1163
 18: 7 for it **m** needs be that offences come; 318
 24: 6 for all *these things* **m** come to pass, 1163
 26:54 scriptures be fulfilled, that thus it **m** be? 1163
Mk 2:22 but new wine **m** be put into new bottles. NIG
 8:31 the Son of man **m** suffer many *things,* 1163
 9:11 Why say the scribes that Elias **m** first 1163
 9:12 he **m** suffer many *things,* and be set at NIG
 13: 7 for *such things* **m** needs be; but the end 1163
 13:10 the gospel **m** first be published among 1163
 14:49 me not: but the scriptures **m** be fulfilled. 2443
Lk 2:49 wist ye not that I **m** be about my Father's 1163
 4:43 I **m** preach the kingdom of God to other 1163
 5:38 But new wine **m** be put into new bottles; 902
 9:22 The Son of man **m** suffer many *things,* 1163
 13:33 Nevertheless I **m** walk to day, 1163
 14:18 of ground, and I **m** needs go and see it: 2192
 17:25 But first **m** he suffer many *things,* and 1163
 19: 5 for to day I **m** abide at thy house. 1163
 21: 9 for these *things* **m** first come to pass; 1163
 22: 7 when the passover **m** be killed. 1163
 22:37 that this that is written **m** yet be 1163
 23:17 (For of necessity he **m** release one unto 2192
 24: 7 The Son of man **m** be delivered into 1163
 24:44 yet with you, that all *things* **m** be fulfilled, 1163
Jn 3: 7 I said unto thee, Ye **m** be born again. 1163
 3:14 *even* so **m** the Son of man be lifted up: 1163
 3:30 He **m** increase, but I *must* decrease. 1163
 3:30 He must increase, but I **m** decrease. NIG
 4: 4 And he **m** needs go through Samaria. 1163
 4:24 they that worship him **m** worship *him* in NIH
 9: 4 I **m** work the works of him that sent me, 1163
 10:16 also I **m** bring, and they shall hear my 1163
 12:34 sayest thou, The Son of man **m** be lift up? 1163
 20: 9 that he **m** rise again from the dead. 1163
Ac 1:16 this scripture **m** needs have been fulfilled, 1163
 1:22 **m** one be ordained *to be* a witness with us 1163
 3:21 the heaven **m** receive until the times 1163
 4:12 among men, whereby we **m** be saved. 1163
 9: 6 and it shall be told thee what thou **m** do. 1163
 9:16 I will shew him how great *things* he **m** 1163
 14:22 that we **m** through much tribulation enter 1163
 15:24 *Ye* **m** be circumcised, and keep the law: NIG
 16:30 and said, Sirs, what **m** I do to be saved? 1163
 17: 3 that Christ **m** needs have suffered, 1163
 18:21 I **m** by all means keep *this* feast that 1163
 19:21 I have been there, I **m** also see Rome. 1163
 21:22 the multitude **m** needs come 1163+3843
 23:11 so **m** thou bear witness also at Rome. 1163
 27:24 Paul; thou **m** be brought before Cesar: 1163
 27:26 Howbeit we **m** be cast upon a certain 1163

Ro 13: 5 Wherefore *ye* **m** needs be subject, not 318
1Co 5:10 for then **m** ye needs go out of the world. 3784
 11:19 For there **m** be also heresies among you, 1163
 15:25 he **m** reign, till he hath put all enemies 1163
 15:53 this corruptible **m** put on incorruption, 1163
 15:53 and this mortal **m** put on immortality. NIG
2Co 5:10 For we **m** all appear before the judgment 1163
 11:30 If I **m** needs glory, I will glory of the 1163
1Ti 3: 2 A bishop then **m** be blameless, the 1163
 3: 7 he **m** have a good report of them 1163
 3: 8 Likewise **m** the deacons *be* grave, 1163
 3:11 Even so *m* *their* wives *be* grave, NIG
2Ti 2: 6 husbandman that laboureth **m** be first 1163
 2:24 And the servant of the Lord **m** not strive; 1163
Tit 1: 7 For a bishop **m** be blameless, 1163
 1:11 mouths **m** be stopped, who subvert 1163
Heb 4: 6 it remaineth that some *m* enter therein, NIG
 9:16 where a testament *is,* there **m** also of NIG
 9:26 he often have suffered since 1163
 11: 6 that cometh to God **m** believe that he is, 1163
 13:17 as they that **m** give account, that they NIG
1Pe 4:17 the time *is come* that judgment **m** begin 1163
2Pe 1:14 Knowing that shortly *I* **m** put off *this* my 1510
Rev 1: 1 shew unto his servants *things* which **m** 1163
 4: 1 I will shew thee *things* which **m** be 1163
 10:11 Thou **m** prophesy again before many 1163
 11: 5 hurt them, he **m** in this manner be killed. 1163
 13:10 that killeth with the sword **m** be killed 1163
 17:10 he cometh, he **m** continue a short *space.* 1163
 20: 3 after that he **m** be loosed a little season. 1163
 22: 6 *the things* which **m** shortly be done. 1163

MUSTARD (5)
Mt 13:31 of heaven is like unto a grain of **m** seed, 4615
 17:20 If ye have faith as a grain of **m** seed, 4615
Mk 4:31 *It is* like a grain of **m** seed, which, when 4615
Lk 13:19 It is like a grain of **m** seed, which a man 4615
 17: 6 If ye had faith as a grain of **m** seed, 4615

MUSTERED (2) [MUSTERETH]
2Ki 25:19 which **m** the people of the land, 6633
Jer 52:25 the host, who **m** the people of the land; 6633

MUSTERETH (1) [MUSTERED]
Isa 13: 4 the LORD of hosts **m** the host of 6485

MUTE See DUMB

MUTH-LABBEN
Ps 9: T Musician upon **M** 1121+4192+1886.1+3807.1

MUTILATORS OF THE FLESH See CONCISION

MUTTER (1) [MUTTERED]
Isa 8:19 and unto wizards that peep, and that **m**: 1897

MUTTERED (1) [MUTTER]
Isa 59: 3 your tongue hath **m** perverseness. 1897

MUTUAL (1)
Ro 1:12 with you by the **m** faith both of you 240

MUZZLE (3)
Dt 25: 4 shalt not **m** the ox when he treadeth 2629
1Co 9: 9 shalt not **m** the mouth of the ox that 5392
1Ti 5:18 shalt not **m** the ox that treadeth out 5392

MY (4370) [I] See Index of Articles, Etc.

MYRA (1)
Ac 27: 5 of Cilicia and Pamphylia, we came to **M**, 3460

MYRRH (17)
Ge 37:25 camels bearing spicery and balm and **m**, 3910
 43:11 spices, and **m**, nuts, and almonds; 3910
Ex 30:23 of pure **m** five hundred *shekels,* and 4753
Est 2:12 *to wit,* six months with oil of **m**, 4753
Ps 45: 8 All thy garments *smell of* **m**, and aloes, 4753
Pr 7:17 I have perfumed my bed *with* **m**, aloes, 4753
SS 1:13 A bundle of **m** *is* my well-beloved unto 4753
 3: 6 perfumed *with* **m** and frankincense, with 4753
 4: 6 I will get me to the mountain of **m**, 4753
 4:14 **m** and aloes, with all the chief spices: 4753
 5: 1 I have gathered my **m** with my spice; 4753
 5: 5 hands dropped *with* **m**, and my fingers 4753
 5: 5 my fingers *with* sweet smelling **m**, 4753
 5:13 lips *like* lilies, dropping sweet smelling **m**. 4753
Mt 2:11 him gifts; gold, and frankincense, and **m**. 4666
Mk 15:23 gave him to drink wine **mingled** with **m**: 4669
Jn 19:39 and brought a mixture of **m** and aloes, 4666

MYRTLE (6)
Ne 8:15 **m** branches, and palm branches, 1918
Isa 41:19 shittah tree, and the **m**, and the oil tree; 1918
 55:13 of the brier shall come up the **m** tree: 1918
Zec 1: 8 he stood among the **m** trees that *were* in 1918
 1:10 the man that stood among the **m** trees 1918
 1:11 the LORD that stood among the **m** trees, 1918

MYSELF (118) [I]
Ge 3:10 because I *was* naked; and I hid **m**. NIH
 22:16 said, By **m** have I sworn, saith 2967.1
Ex 19: 4 eagles' wings, and brought you unto **m**. 2967.1
Nu 8:17 land of Egypt, I sanctified them for **m**. 2967.1
 12: 6 I the LORD will make **m** known unto him NIH
Dt 1: 9 I am not able to bear you **m** alone: 2967.1
 1:12 can I **m** alone bear your cumbrance, 2967.1

Dt 10: 5 I turned **m** and came down from the NIH
Jdg 16:20 as at other times *before,* and shake **m**. NIH
Ru 4: 6 kinsman said, I cannot redeem *it* for **m**, 2967.1
1Sa 13:12 I forced **m** therefore, and offered a burnt NIH
 20: 5 that I may hide **m** in the fields unto the NIH
 25:33 *from* avenging **m** with mine own hand. 2967.1
2Sa 18: 2 I will surely go forth with you **m** also. 589
 22:24 and have kept **m** from mine iniquity. NIH
1Ki 18:15 I will surely shew unto him to day. NIH
 22:30 I will disguise **m**, and enter into the battle; NIH
2Ki 5:18 and I bow **m** in the house of Rimmon: NIH
 5:18 when I bow down **m** *in* the house of NIH
2Ch 7:12 have chosen this place to **m** for a house 2967.1
 18:29 will disguise **m**, and will go to the battle; NIH
Ne 5: 7 consulted with **m**, and I rebuked 3820+2967.1
Est 5:12 banquet that she had prepared but **m**; 2967.1
 6: 6 delight to do honour more than to **m**? 5204.1
Job 6:10 yea, I would harden **m** in sorrow; let him NIH
 7:20 thee, so that I am a burden to **m**? 2967.1
 9:20 If I justify **m**, mine own mouth shall NIH
 9:27 leave off my heaviness, and comfort **m**: NIH
 9:30 If I wash **m** with snow water, and make NIH
 10: 1 I will leave my complaint upon **m**; 2967.1
 13:20 me: then will I not hide **m** from thee. NIH
 19: 4 erred, mine error remaineth with **m**. 2967.1
 19:27 Whom I shall see for **m**, and mine eyes 2967.1
 31:17 Or have eaten my morsel **m** alone, 905+2967.1
 31:29 or lift up **m** when evil found him: NIH
 42: 6 Wherefore I abhor **m**, and repent in dust NIH
Ps 18:23 and I kept **m** from mine iniquity. NIH
 35:14 I behaved as though *he had been* my NIH
 55:12 then I would have hid **m** from him: NIH
 57: 8 and harp: I *m* will awake early. NIH
 101: 2 I will behave **m** wisely in a perfect way. NIH
 108: 2 and harp: I *m* will awake early. NIH
 109: 4 my adversaries: but I *give m* unto prayer. NIH
 119:16 I will delight **m** in thy statutes: I will not NIH
 119:47 I will delight **m** in thy commandments, NIH
 119:52 of old, O LORD; and have comforted **m**. NIH
 131: 1 neither do I exercise **m** in great *matters,* NIH
 131: 2 I have behaved and quieted **m**, 5315+2967.1
Ecc 2: 3 I sought in mine heart to give **m** 1320+2967.1
 2:12 turned **m** to behold wisdom, and madness, NIH
 2:14 I **m** perceived also that one event 589
 2:19 where*in* I have shewed **m** wise under NIH
Isa 33:10 now will I be exalted; now will I lift up **m**. NIH
 42:14 I have been still, *and* refrained **m**. NIH
 43:21 This people have I formed for **m**; 2967.1
 44:24 that spreadeth abroad the earth by **m**; 2967.1
 45:23 I have sworn by **m**, the word is gone 2967.1
Jer 8:18 I would comfort **m** against sorrow, 2967.1
 21: 5 I **m** will fight against you with an 589
 22: 5 I swear by **m**, saith the LORD, 2967.1
 49:13 For I have sworn by **m**, saith the LORD, 2967.1
Eze 14: 7 the LORD will answer him by **m**: 2967.1
 20: 5 made **m** known unto them in the land of NIH
 20: 9 whose sight I made **m** known unto them, NIH
 29: 3 *is* mine own, and I have made *it for* **m**. 5204.1
 35:11 I will make **m** known amongst them, NIH
 38:23 will I magnify **m**, and sanctify myself; NIH
 38:23 will I magnify myself, and sanctify **m**; NIH
Da 10: 3 neither did I anoint **m** at all, till three NIH
Mic 6: 6 and bow **m** before the high God? NIH
Hab 3:16 into my bones, and I trembled in **m**, 2967.1
Zec 7: 3 separating **m**, as I have done these so NIH
Lk 7: 7 Wherefore neither thought I **m** worthy to 1683
 24:39 my hands and my feet, that it is I **m**: 846
Jn 5:31 If I bear witness of **m**, my witness is not 1683
 7:17 it be of God, or *whether* I speak of **m**. 1683
 7:28 and I am not come of **m**, but he that sent 1683
 8:14 unto them, Though I bear record of **m**, 1683
 8:18 I am *one* that bear witness of **m**, 1683
 8:28 that I am *he,* and *that* I do nothing of **m**; 1683
 8:42 and came from God; neither came I of **m**, 1683
 8:54 answered, If I honour **m**, my honour 1683
 10:18 taketh it from me, but I lay it down of **m**. 1683
 12:49 I have not spoken of **m**; but the Father 1683
 14: 3 will come again, and receive you unto **m**; 1683
 14:10 that I speak unto you, I speak not of **m**: 1683
 14:21 will love him, and will manifest **m** to him. 1683
 17:19 And for their sakes I sanctify **m**, that they 1683
Ac 10:26 saying, Stand up; I **m** also am a man. 1683
 20:24 neither count I my life dear unto **m**, 1683
 24:10 I do the more cheerfully answer for **m**: 1683
 24:16 herein do I exercise **m**, to have always a 846
 25:22 unto Festus, I would also hear the man **m**. 846
 26: 2 I think **m** happy, king Agrippa, because 1683
 26: 2 I shall answer for **m** this day before thee NIG
 26: 9 I verily thought with **m**, that *I* ought to do 1683
Ro 7:25 with the mind I **m** serve the law of God; 846
 9: 3 I could wish that **m** were accursed from 846
 11: 4 I have reserved to **m** seven thousand men, 1683
 15:14 And I also am persuaded of you, 846
 16: 2 a succourer of many, and of **m** also. 846+1473
1Co 4: 4 For I know nothing by **m**; yet am I not 1683
 4: 6 I have in a figure transferred to **m** and 1683
 7: 7 For I would that all men were even as I **m**. 1683
 9:19 *men,* yet have I made **m** servant unto all, 1683
 9:27 to others, I **m** should be a castaway. 846
2Co 2: 1 But I determined this with **m**, that *I* would 1683
 11: 1 I Paul beseech you by the meekness 846
 11: 7 Have I committed an offence in abasing **m** 1683
 11: 9 in all *things* I have kept **m** from being 1683
 11: 9 burdensome to you, and *so* will I keep **m**. NIG
 11:16 receive me, that I may boast **m** a little. NIG

M

2Co	12: 5 yet of *m* I will not glory, but in mine	*1683*
	12:13 except *it be* that I *m* was not burdensome	*846*
Gal	2:18 I destroyed, I make a transgressor.	*1683*
Php	2:24 But I trust in the Lord that I also *m* shall	*846*
	3:13 I count not *m* to have apprehended:	*1683*
Phm	1:17 therefore a partner, receive him as *m*.	*1473*

MYSIA (2)

Ac	16: 7 After they were come to **M**, they assayed	*3465*
	16: 8 And they passing by **M** came down to	*3465*

MYSTERIES (5) [MYSTERY]

Mt	13:11 it is given unto you to know the **m**	*3466*
Lk	8:10 Unto you it is given to know the **m** of	*3466*
1Co	4: 1 of Christ, and stewards of the **m** of God.	*3466*
	13: 2 and understand all **m**, and all knowledge;	*3466*
	14: 2 *him;* howbeit in the spirit he speaketh **m**.	*3466*

MYSTERY (22) [MYSTERIES]

Mk	4:11 Unto you it is given to know the **m** of	*3466*
Ro	11:25 that ye should be ignorant of this **m**,	*3466*
	16:25 according to the revelation of the **m**,	*3466*
1Co	2: 7 But we speak the wisdom of God in a **m**,	*3466*
	15:51 Behold, I shew you a **m**; We shall not all	*3466*
Eph	1: 9 Having made known unto us the **m** of his	*3466*
	3: 3 he made known unto me the **m**;	*3466*
	3: 4 may understand my knowledge in the **m**	*3466*
	3: 9 *men* see what *is* the fellowship of the **m**,	*3466*
	5:32 This is a great: but I speak concerning	*3466*
	6:19 to make known the **m** of the gospel,	*3466*
Col	1:26 the **m** which hath been hid from ages	*3466*
	1:27 the glory of this **m** among the Gentiles;	*3466*
	2: 2 to the acknowledgement of the **m** of God	*3466*
	4: 3 to speak the **m** of Christ, for which I am	*3466*
2Th	2: 7 For the **m** of iniquity doth already work:	*3466*
1Ti	3: 9 Holding the **m** of the faith in a pure	*3466*
	3:16 And without controversy great is the **m** of	*3466*
Rev	1:20 The **m** of the seven stars which thou	*3466*
	10: 7 sound, the **m** of God should be finished,	*3466*
	17: 5 **M**, BABYLON THE GREAT,	*3466*
	17: 7 I will tell thee the **m** of the woman,	*3466*

MYTHS See FABLES

N

NAAM (1)

1Ch	4:15 the son of Jephunneh; Iru, Elah, and **N**:	*5277*

NAAMAH (5)

Ge	4:22 iron: and the sister of Tubal-cain *was* **N**.	*5279*
Jos	15:41 Beth-dagon, and **N**, and Makkedah;	*5279*
1Ki	14:21 mother's name *was* **N** an Ammonitess.	*5279*
	14:31 mother's name *was* **N** an Ammonitess.	*5279*
2Ch	12:13 mother's name *was* **N** an Ammonitess.	*5279*

NAAMAN (16) [NAAMAN'S, NAAMITES]

Ge	46:21 and Ashbel, Gera, and **N**, Ehi, and Rosh,	*5283*
Nu	26:40 the sons of Bela were Ard and **N**: *of Ard,*	*5283*
	26:40 *and* of **N**, the family of the Naamites.	*5283*
2Ki	5: 1 Now **N**, captain of the host of the king of	*5283*
	5: 6 I have *therewith* sent **N** my servant to	*5283*
	5: 9 So **N** came with his horses and with his	*5283*
	5:11 **N** was wroth, and went away, and said,	*5283*
	5:17 **N** said, Shall there not then, I pray thee,	*5283*
	5:20 my master hath spared this **N** this Syrian,	*5283*
	5:21 So Gehazi followed after **N**. And when	*5283*
	5:21 when **N** saw *him* running after him,	*5283*
	5:23 **N** said, Be content, take two talents.	*5283*
	5:27 therefore of **N** shall cleave unto thee,	*5283*
1Ch	8: 4 And Abishua, and **N**, and Ahoah,	*5283*
	8: 7 **N**, and Ahiah, and Gera, he removed	*5283*
Lk	4:27 them was cleansed, saving **N** the Syrian.	*3497*

NAAMAN'S (1) [NAAMAN]

2Ki	5: 2 a little maid; and she waited on **N** wife.	*5283*

NAAMATHITE (4)

Job	2:11 Bildad the Shuhite, and Zophar the **N**:	*5284*
	11: 1 Then answered Zophar the **N**, and said,	*5284*
	20: 1 Then answered Zophar the **N**, and said,	*5284*
	42: 9 the Shuhite *and* Zophar the **N** went,	*5284*

NAAMITES (1) [NAAMAN]

Nu	26:40 *and* of Naaman, the family of the **N**.	*5280*

NAARAH (3)

1Ch	4: 5 of Tekoa had two wives, Helah and **N**.	*5292*
	4: 6 **N** bare him Ahuzam, and Hepher, and	*5292*
	4: 6 Haahashtari. These *were* the sons of **N**.	*5292*

NAARAI (1)

1Ch	11:37 Hezro the Carmelite, **N** the son of Ezbai,	*5293*

NAARAN (1)

1Ch	7:28 and eastward **N**, and westward Gezer,	*5295*

NAARATH (1)

Jos	16: 7 to **N**, and came to Jericho, and went out	*5292*

NAASHON (1)

Ex	6:23 of Amminadab, sister of **N**, to wife;	*5177*

NAASSON (3)

Mt	1: 4 Aminadab begat **N**; and Naasson begat	*3476*
	1: 4 begat Naasson; and **N** begat Salmon;	*3476*
Lk	3:32 *son* of Salmon, which was *the son* of **N**,	*3476*

NABAL (18) [NABAL'S]

1Sa	25: 3 Now the name of the man *was* **N**;	*5037*
	25: 4 David heard in the wilderness that **N** did	*5037*
	25: 5 go to **N**, and greet him in my name:	*5037*
	25: 9 they spake to **N** according to all those	*5037*
	25:10 answered David's servants, and said,	*5037*
	25:19 But she told not her husband **N**.	*5037*
	25:25 regard this man of Belial, even **N**:	*5037*
	25:25 he; **N** *is* his name, and folly *is* with him:	*5037*
	25:26 they that seek evil to my lord, be as **N**.	*5037*
	25:34 surely there had not been left unto **N** by	*5037*
	25:36 Abigail came to **N**; and, behold, he held a	*5037*
	25:37 when the wine was gone out of **N**,	*5037*
	25:38 ten days *after,* that the LORD smote **N**,	*5037*
	25:39 when David heard that **N** was dead, he	*5037*
	25:39 cause of my reproach from the hand of **N**,	*5037*
	25:39 the wickedness of **N** upon his own head.	*5037*
	30: 5 and Abigail the wife of **N** the Carmelite,	*5037*
2Sa	2: 3 of Abigail the wife of **N** the Carmelite;	*5037*

NABAL'S (4) [NABAL]

1Sa	25:14 men told Abigail, **N** wife, saying, Behold,	*5037*
	25:36 **N** heart *was* merry within him, for he *was*	*5037*
	27: 3 and Abigail the Carmelitess, **N** wife.	*5037*
2Sa	2: 2 and Abigail **N** wife the Carmelite.	*5037*

NABOTH (22) [NACHON'S]

1Ki	21: 1 *that* **N** the Jezreelite had a vineyard,	*5022*
	21: 2 Ahab spake unto **N**, saying, Give me thy	*5022*
	21: 3 **N** said to Ahab, The LORD forbid it me,	*5022*
	21: 4 of the word which **N** the Jezreelite had	*5022*
	21: 6 Because I spake unto **N** the Jezreelite,	*5022*
	21: 7 I will give thee the vineyard of **N**	*5022*
	21: 8 that *were* in his city, dwelling with **N**.	*5022*
	21: 9 fast, and set **N** on high among the people:	*5022*
	21:12 fast, and set **N** on high among the people.	*5022*
	21:13 *even* against **N**, in the presence of	*5022*
	21:13 **N** did blaspheme God and the king.	*5022*
	21:14 Jezebel, saying, **N** is stoned, and is dead.	*5022*
	21:15 when Jezebel heard that **N** was stoned,	*5022*
	21:15 take possession of the vineyard of **N**	*5022*
	21:15 for money: for **N** is not alive, but dead.	*5022*
	21:16 pass, when Ahab heard that **N** was dead,	*5022*
	21:16 down to the vineyard of **N** the Jezreelite,	*5022*
	21:18 behold, *he is* in the vineyard of **N**,	*5022*
	21:19 the blood of **N** shall dogs lick thy blood,	*5022*
2Ki	9:21 met him in the portion of **N** the Jezreelite.	*5022*
	9:25 cast him in the portion of the field of **N**;	*5022*
	9:26 I have seen yesterday the blood of **N**,	*5022*

NACHON'S (1) [NABOTH]

2Sa	6: 6 when they came to **N** threshingfloor,	*5225*

NACHOR (2) [NAHOR]

Jos	24: 2 father of Abraham, and the father of **N**:	*5152*
Lk	3:34 *son* of Thara, which was *the son* of **N**,	*3493*

NACON See NACHON'S

NADAB (20)

Ex	6:23 she bare him **N**, and Abihu, Eleazar,	*5070*
	24: 1 **N**, and Abihu, and seventy of the elders	*5070*
	24: 9 **N**, and Abihu, and seventy of the elders	*5070*
	28: 1 **N** and Abihu, Eleazar and Ithamar,	*5070*
Lev	10: 1 **N** and Abihu, the sons of Aaron, took	*5070*
Nu	3: 2 **N** the firstborn, and Abihu, Eleazar,	*5070*
	3: 4 **N** and Abihu died before the LORD,	*5070*
	26:60 unto Aaron was born **N**, and Abihu,	*5070*
	26:61 **N** and Abihu died, when they offered	*5070*
1Ki	14:20 and **N** his son reigned in his stead.	*5070*
	15:25 **N** the son of Jeroboam *began* to reign	*5070*
	15:27 **N** and all Israel laid siege to Gibbethon.	*5070*
	15:31 Now the rest of the acts of **N**, and all that	*5070*
1Ch	2:28 the sons of Shammai; **N**, and Abishur.	*5070*
	2:30 the sons of **N**; Seled, and Appaim:	*5070*
	6: 3 **N**, and Abihu, Eleazar, and Ithamar.	*5070*
	8:30 and Zur, and Kish, and Baal, and **N**,	*5070*
	9:36 Zur, and Kish, and Baal, and Ner, and **N**,	*5070*
	24: 1 **N**, and Abihu, Eleazar, and Ithamar.	*5070*
	24: 2 **N** and Abihu died before their father,	*5070*

NAGGAI See NAGGE

NAGGE (1)

Lk	3:25 *the son* of Esli, which was *the son* of **N**,	*3477*

NAHALAL (1)

Jos	21:35 with her suburbs, **N** with her suburbs;	*5096*

NAHALIEL (2)

Nu	21:19 from Mattanah *to* **N**: and from Nahaliel	*5160*
	21:19 *to* Nahaliel: and from **N** *to* Bamoth:	*5160*

NAHALLAL (1)

Jos	19:15 **N**, and Shimron, and Idalah,	*5096*

NAHALOL (1)

Jdg	1:30 of Kitron, nor the inhabitants of **N**;	*5096*

NAHAM (1)

1Ch	4:19 sons of *his* wife Hodiah the sister of **N**,	*5163*

NAHAMANI (1)

Ne	7: 7 Azariah, Raamiah, **N**, Mordecai, Bilshan,	*5167*

NAHARAI (2)

2Sa	23:37 Zelek the Ammonite, **N** the Beerothite,	*5171*
1Ch	11:39 Zelek the Ammonite, **N** the Berothite,	*5171*

NAHASH (9)

1Sa	11: 1 **N** the Ammonite came up,	*5176*
	11: 1 all the men of Jabesh said unto **N**, Make	*5176*
	11: 2 **N** the Ammonite answered them, On this	*5176*
	12:12 ye saw that **N** the king of the children	*5176*
2Sa	10: 2 shew kindness unto Hanun the son of **N**,	*5176*
	17:25 that went in to Abigail the daughter of **N**,	*5176*
	17:27 that Shobi the son of **N** of Rabbah of	*5176*
1Ch	19: 1 that **N** the king of the children of Ammon	*5176*
	19: 2 shew kindness unto Hanun the son of **N**,	*5176*

NAHATH (5)

Ge	36:13 **N**, and Zerah, Shammah, and Mizzah:	*5184*
	36:17 duke **N**, duke Zerah, duke Shammah,	*5184*
1Ch	1:37 Reuel; **N**, Zerah, Shammah, and Mizzah.	*5184*
	6:26 of Elkanah; Zophai his son, and **N** his son,	*5184*
2Ch	31:13 **N**, and Asahel, and Jerimoth, and Jozabad,	*5184*

NAHBI (1)

Nu	13:14 the tribe of Naphtali, **N** the son of Vophsi.	*5147*

NAHOR (15) [NACHOR, NAHOR'S]

Ge	11:22 And Serug lived thirty years, and begat **N**:	*5152*
	11:23 Serug lived after he begat **N** two hundred	*5152*
	11:24 **N** lived nine and twenty years,	*5152*
	11:25 **N** lived after he begat Terah an hundred	*5152*
	11:26 and begat Abram, **N**, and Haran.	*5152*
	11:27 Terah begat Abram, **N**, and Haran;	*5152*
	11:29 Abram and **N** took them wives: the name	*5152*
	22:20 also born children unto thy brother **N**;	*5152*
	22:23 these eight Milcah did bear to **N**,	*5152*
	24:10 went to Mesopotamia, unto the city of **N**.	*5152*
	24:15 son of Milcah, the wife of **N**,	*5152*
	24:24 the son of Milcah, which she bare unto **N**.	*5152*
	29: 5 unto them, Know ye Laban the son of **N**?	*5152*
	31:53 The God of Abraham, and the God of **N**,	*5152*
1Ch	1:26 Serug, **N**, Terah,	*5152*

NAHOR'S (2) [NAHOR]

Ge	11:29 the name of **N** wife, Milcah, the daughter	*5152*
	24:47 she said, The daughter of Bethuel, **N** son,	*5152*

NAHSHON (9)

Nu	1: 7 Of Judah; **N** the son of Amminadab.	*5177*
	2: 3 **N** the son of Amminadab *shall be* captain	*5177*
	7:12 first day was **N** the son of Amminadab,	*5177*
	7:17 this *was* the offering of **N** the son of	*5177*
	10:14 his host *was* **N** the son of Amminadab.	*5177*
Ru	4:20 Amminadab begat **N**, and Nahshon begat	*5177*
	4:20 begat Nahshon, and **N** begat Salmon,	*5177*
1Ch	2:10 Amminadab begat **N**, prince of the	*5177*
	2:11 **N** begat Salma, and Salma begat Boaz,	*5177*

NAHUM (1)

Na	1: 1 The book of the vision of **N** the Elkoshite.	*5151*

NAIL (8) [NAILING, NAILS]

Jdg	4:21 Jael Heber's wife took a **n** of the tent,	*3489*
	4:21 smote the **n** into his temples, and fastened	*3489*
	4:21 lay dead, and the **n** *was* in his temples.	*3489*
	5:26 She put her hand to the **n**, and her right	*3489*
Ezr	9: 8 and to give us a **n** in his holy place,	*3489*
Isa	22:23 I will fasten him *as* a **n** in a sure place;	*3489*
	22:25 the **n** that is fastened in the sure place	*3489*
Zec	10: 4 of him the **n**, out of him the battle bow,	*3489*

NAILING (1) [NAIL]

Col	2:14 took it out of the way, **n** it to *his* cross;	*4338*

NAILS (10) [NAIL]

Dt	21:12 she shall shave her head, and pare her **n**;	*6856*
1Ch	22: 3 prepared iron in abundance for the **n**	*4548*
2Ch	3: 9 the weight of the **n** *was* fifty shekels of	*4548*
Ecc	12:11 as **n** fastened *by* the masters of assemblies,	*4930*
Isa	41: 7 he fastened it with **n**, *that* it should not be	*4548*
Jer	10: 4 they fasten it with **n** and with hammers,	*4548*
Da	4:33 and his **n** like birds' *claws*.	*2953*
	7:19 teeth *were of* iron, and his **n** *of* brass;	*2953*
Jn	20:25 I shall see in his hands the print of the **n**,	*2247*
	20:25 and put my finger into the print of the **n**,	*2247*

NAIN (1)

Lk	7:11 day after, *that* he went into a city called **N**;	*3484*

NAIOTH (6)

1Sa	19:18 And he and Samuel went and dwelt in **N**.	*5121*
	19:19 Behold, David *is* at **N** in Ramah.	*5121*
	19:22 *one* said, Behold, *they be* at **N** in Ramah.	*5121*
	19:23 he went thither to **N** in Ramah:	*5121*
	19:23 prophesied, until he came to **N** in Ramah.	*5121*
	20: 1 David fled from **N** in Ramah, and came	*5121*

NAKED (47) [NAKEDNESS]

Ge	2:25	they were both **n**, the man and his wife,	6174
	3: 7	and they knew that they *were* **n**;	5903
	3:10	and I was afraid, because I *was* **n**;	5903
	3:11	he said, Who told thee that thou *wast* **n**?	5903
Ex	32:25	when Moses saw that the people *were* **n**;	6544
	32:25	(for Aaron had **made** them **n** unto *their*	6544
1Sa	19:24	lay down **n** all that day and all *that* night.	6174
2Ch	28:15	with the spoil clothed all *that were* **n**	4636
	28:19	for he **made** Judah **n**, and transgressed	6544
Job	1:21	**N** came I out of my mother's womb,	6174
	1:21	womb, and **n** shall I return thither:	6174
	22: 6	and stripped the **n** of their clothing.	6174
	24: 7	cause the **n** to lodge without clothing,	6174
	24:10	They cause *him* to go **n** without clothing,	6174
	26: 6	Hell *is* **n** before him, and destruction hath	6174
Ecc	5:15	shall he return to go as he came,	6174
Isa	20: 2	And he did so, walking **n** and barefoot.	6174
	20: 3	Like as my servant Isaiah hath walked **n**	6174
	20: 4	young and old, **n** and barefoot,	6174
	58: 7	thou seest the **n**, that thou cover him;	6174
La	4:21	be drunken, and shalt **make** thyself **n**.	6168
Eze	16: 7	is grown, whereas thou *wast* **n** and bare.	5903
	16:22	when thou wast **n** and bare,	5903
	16:39	thy fair jewels, and leave thee **n** and bare.	5903
	18: 7	and hath covered the **n** with a garment,	5903
	18:16	and hath covered the **n** with a garment,	5903
	23:29	labour, and shall leave thee **n** and bare:	5903
Hos	2: 3	Lest I strip her **n**, and set her as *in* the day	6174
Am	2:16	the mighty shall flee away in that day,	6174
Mic	1: 8	I will wail and howl, I will go stript and **n**:	6174
	1:11	inhabitant of Saphir, having *thy* shame **n**:	6181
Hab	3: 9	Thy bow was **made quite n**,	5783+6181
Mt	25:36	**N**, and ye clothed me: I was sick,	1131
	25:38	and took *thee* in? or **n**, and clothed *thee*?	1131
	25:43	**n**, and ye clothed me not: sick,	1131
	25:44	or **n**, or sick, or in prison, and did not	1131
Mk	14:51	having a linen cloth cast about *his* **n** *body*;	1131
	14:52	left the linen cloth, and fled from them **n**.	1131
Jn	21: 7	*his* fisher's coat *unto him*, (for he was **n**,)	1131
Ac	19:16	so that *they* fled out of that house **n** and	1131
1Co	4:11	and are **n**, and are buffeted, and have no	1130
2Co	5: 3	being clothed we shall not be found **n**.	1131
Heb	4:13	but all *things are* **n** and opened unto	1131
Jas	2:15	If a brother or sister be **n**, and destitute of	1131
Rev	3:17	and miserable, and poor, and blind, and **n**:	1131
	16:15	lest he walk **n**, and they see his shame.	1131
	17:16	and shall make her desolate and **n**,	1131

NAKEDNESS (57) [NAKED]

Ge	9:22	saw the **n** of his father, and told his two	6172
	9:23	and covered the **n** of their father;	6172
	9:23	and they saw not their father's **n**.	6172
	42: 9	to see the **n** of the land you are come.	6172
	42:12	but to see the **n** of the land you are come.	6172
Ex	20:26	that thy **n** be not discovered thereon.	6172
	28:42	linen breeches to cover *their* **n**;	1320+6172
Lev	18: 6	is near of kin to him, to uncover *their* **n**.	6172
	18: 7	The **n** of thy father, or the nakedness of	6172
	18: 7	or the **n** of thy mother, shalt thou not	6172
	18: 7	thy mother; thou shalt not uncover her **n**.	6172
	18: 8	The **n** of thy father's wife shalt thou not	6172
	18: 8	thou not uncover: it *is* thy father's **n**.	6172
	18: 9	The **n** of thy sister, the daughter of thy	6172
	18: 9	*even* their **n** thou shalt not uncover.	6172
	18:10	The **n** of thy son's daughter, or of thy	6172
	18:10	*even* their **n** thou shalt not uncover:	6172
	18:10	not uncover: for theirs *is* thine own **n**.	6172
	18:11	The **n** of thy father's wife's daughter,	6172
	18:11	*is* thy sister, thou shalt not uncover her **n**.	6172
	18:12	Thou shalt not uncover the **n** of thy	6172
	18:13	Thou shalt not uncover the **n** of thy	6172
	18:14	Thou shalt not uncover the **n** of thy	6172
	18:15	Thou shalt not uncover the **n** of thy	6172
	18:15	son's wife; thou shalt not uncover her **n**.	6172
	18:16	Thou shalt not uncover the **n** of thy	6172
	18:16	of thy brother's wife: it *is* thy brother's **n**.	6172
	18:17	Thou shalt not uncover the **n** of a woman	6172
	18:17	daughter's daughter, to uncover her **n**;	6172
	18:18	to vex *her*, to uncover her **n**, besides	6172
	18:19	approach unto a woman to uncover her **n**,	6172
	20:11	father's wife hath uncovered his father's **n**:	6172
	20:17	and see her **n**, and she see his nakedness;	6172
	20:17	and see her nakedness, and she see his **n**;	6172
	20:17	he hath uncovered his sister's **n**; he shall	6172
	20:18	her sickness, and shall uncover her **n**;	6172
	20:19	thou shalt not uncover the **n** of thy	6172
	20:20	he hath uncovered his uncle's **n**:	6172
	20:21	he hath uncovered his brother's **n**:	6172
Dt	28:48	in **n**, and in want of all *things*: and he	5903
1Sa	20:30	and unto the confusion of thy mother's **n**?	6172
Isa	47: 3	Thy **n** shall be uncovered, yea, thy shame	6172
La	1: 8	her, because they have seen her **n**:	6172
Eze	16: 8	my skirt over thee, and covered thy **n**:	6172
	16:36	thy **n** discovered through thy whoredoms	6172
	16:37	will discover thy **n** unto them, that they	6172
	16:37	unto them, that they may see all thy **n**.	6172
	22:10	thee have they discovered their father's **n**:	6172
	23:10	These discovered her **n**: they took her	6172
	23:18	her whoredoms, and discovered her **n**:	6172
	23:29	the **n** of thy whoredoms shall be	6172
Hos	2: 9	wool and my flax *given* to cover her **n**.	6172
Na	3: 5	I will shew the nations thy **n**,	4626
Hab	2:15	that thou mayest look on their **n**!	4589
Ro	8:35	or famine, or **n**, or peril, or sword?	1132

2Co	11:27	and thirst, in fastings often, in cold and **n**.	1132
Rev	3:18	and *that* the shame of thy **n** do not appear;	1132

NAME (928) [NAME'S, NAMED, NAMELY, NAMES, NAMETH]

Ge	2:11	The **n** of the first *is* Pison: that *is it* which	8034
	2:13	the **n** of the second river *is* Gihon: the	8034
	2:14	the **n** of the third river *is* Hiddekel: that	8034
	2:19	living creature, that *was* the **n** thereof.	8034
	3:20	Adam called his wife's **n** Eve; because	8034
	4:17	builded a city, and called the **n** of the city,	8034
	4:17	of the city, after the **n** of his son, Enoch.	8034
	4:19	the **n** of the one *was* Adah, and the name	8034
	4:19	*was* Adah, and the **n** of the other Zillah.	8034
	4:21	brother's **n** *was* Jubal: he was the father	8034
	4:25	she bare a son, and called his **n** Seth:	8034
	4:26	he called his **n** Enos; then began *men* to	8034
	4:26	began *men* to call upon the **n** of	8034
	5: 2	blessed them, and called their **n** Adam,	8034
	5: 3	after his image; and called his **n** Seth:	8034
	5:29	he called his **n** Noah, saying, This *same*	8034
	10:25	the **n** of one *was* Peleg; for in his days	8034
	10:25	and his brother's **n** *was* Joktan.	8034
	11: 4	let us make us a **n**, lest we be scattered	8034
	11: 9	Therefore is the **n** of it called Babel;	8034
	11:29	the **n** of Abram's wife *was* Sarai;	8034
	11:29	the **n** of Nahor's wife, Milcah, the	8034
	12: 2	I will bless thee, and make thy **n** great;	8034
	12: 8	and called upon the **n** of the LORD.	8034
	13: 4	there Abram called on the **n** of the LORD.	8034
	16: 1	an Egyptian, whose **n** *was* Hagar.	8034
	16:11	bear a son, and shalt call his **n** Ishmael;	8034
	16:13	she called the **n** of the LORD that spake	8034
	16:15	Abram called his son's **n**, which Hagar	8034
	17: 5	Neither shall thy **n** any more be called	8034
	17: 5	Abram, but thy **n** shall be Abraham;	8034
	17:15	thou shalt not call her **n** Sarai,	8034
	17:15	her name Sarai, but Sarah *shall* her **n** be.	8034
	17:19	indeed; and thou shalt call his **n** Isaac:	8034
	19:22	the **n** of the city was called Zoar.	8034
	19:37	bare a son, and called his **n** Moab:	8034
	19:38	bare a son, and called his **n** Ben-ammi:	8034
	21: 3	Abraham called the **n** of his son that was	8034
	21:33	called there on the **n** of the LORD,	8034
	22:14	Abraham called the **n** of that place	8034
	22:24	his concubine, whose **n** *was* Reumah,	8034
	24:29	had a brother, and his **n** *was* Laban:	8034
	25: 1	took a wife, and her **n** *was* Keturah.	8034
	25:25	hairy garment; and they called his **n** Esau.	8034
	25:26	Esau's heel; and his **n** was called Jacob:	8034
	25:30	faint: therefore was his **n** called Edom.	8034
	26:20	he called the **n** of the well Esek; because	8034
	26:21	that also: and he called the **n** of it Sitnah.	8034
	26:22	called the **n** of it Rehoboth; and he said,	8034
	26:25	called upon the **n** of the LORD,	8034
	26:33	the **n** of the city *is* Beer-sheba unto this	8034
	28:19	he called the **n** of that place Beth-el:	8034
	28:19	the **n** of *that* city *was called* Luz at the	8034
	29:16	the **n** of the elder *was* Leah, and the	8034
	29:16	and the **n** of the younger *was* Rachel.	8034
	29:32	bare a son, and she called his **n** Reuben:	8034
	29:33	this *son* also: and she called his **n** Simeon.	8034
	29:34	sons: therefore was his **n** called Levi.	8034
	29:35	therefore she called his **n** Judah;	8034
	30: 6	me a son: therefore called she his **n** Dan.	8034
	30: 8	and she called his **n** Naphtali.	8034
	30:11	A troop cometh: and she called his **n** Gad.	8034
	30:13	me blessed: and she called his **n** Asher.	8034
	30:18	husband: and she called his **n** Issachar.	8034
	30:20	six sons: and she called his **n** Zebulun.	8034
	30:21	bare a daughter, and called her **n** Dinah.	8034
	30:24	she called his **n** Joseph; and said,	8034
	31:48	Therefore was the **n** of it called Galeed;	8034
	32: 2	he called the **n** of that place Mahanaim.	8034
	32:27	he said unto him, What *is* thy **n**? And he	8034
	32:28	Thy **n** shall be called no more Jacob,	8034
	32:29	and said, Tell *me*, I pray thee, thy **n**.	8034
	32:29	is it *that* thou dost ask after my **n**?	8034
	32:30	Jacob called the **n** of the place Peniel: for	8034
	33:17	the **n** of the place is called Succoth.	8034
	35: 8	and the **n** of it was called Allon-bachuth.	8034
	35:10	God said unto him, Thy **n** *is* Jacob:	8034
	35:10	thy **n** shall not be called any more Jacob,	8034
	35:10	any more Jacob, but Israel shall be thy **n**:	8034
	35:10	be thy name: and he called his **n** Israel.	8034
	35:15	Jacob called the **n** of the place where God	8034
	35:18	she died) that she called his **n** Ben-oni:	8034
	36:32	and the **n** of his city *was* Dinhabah.	8034
	36:35	his stead: and the **n** of his city *was* Avith.	8034
	36:39	the **n** of his city *was* Pau; and his wife's	8034
	36:39	his wife's **n** *was* Mehetabel, the daughter	8034
	38: 1	a certain Adullamite, whose **n** *was* Hirah.	8034
	38: 2	a certain Canaanite, whose **n** *was* Shuah;	8034
	38: 3	and bare a son; and he called his **n** Er.	8034
	38: 4	bare a son; and she called his **n** Onan.	8034
	38: 5	bare a son; and called his **n** Shelah:	8034
	38: 6	for Er his firstborn, whose **n** *was* Tamar.	8034
	38:29	therefore his **n** was called Pharez.	8034
	38:30	his hand: and his **n** was called Zarah.	8034
	41:45	Pharaoh called Joseph's **n**	8034
	41:51	Joseph called the **n** of the firstborn	8034
	41:52	the **n** of the second called he Ephraim:	8034
	48: 6	be called after the **n** of their brethren	8034
	48:16	my **n** be named on them, and the name	8034
	48:16	the **n** of my fathers Abraham and Isaac;	8034

Ge	50:11	wherefore the **n** of it was called	8034
Ex	1:15	of which the **n** of the one *was* Shiphrah,	8034
	1:15	Shiphrah, and the **n** of the other Puah:	8034
	2:10	she called his **n** Moses: and she said,	8034
	2:22	*him* a son, and he called his **n** Gershom:	8034
	3:13	and they shall say to me, What *is* his **n**?	8034
	3:15	this *is* my **n** for ever, and this *is* my	8034
	5:23	since I came to Pharaoh to speak in thy **n**,	8034
	6: 3	by the **n** of God Almighty, but *by* my	NIH
	6: 3	*by* my **n** JEHOVAH was I not known to	8034
	9:16	that my **n** may be declared throughout all	8034
	15: 3	is a man of war: the LORD *is* his **n**.	8034
	15:23	the **n** of it was called Marah.	8034
	16:31	the house of Israel called the **n** thereof	8034
	17: 7	he called the **n** of the place Massah,	8034
	17:15	and called the **n** of it Jehovah-nissi:	8034
	18: 3	of which the **n** of the one *was* Gershom;	8034
	18: 4	the **n** of the other *was* Eliezer; for the God	8034
	20: 7	Thou shalt not take the **n** of the LORD thy	8034
	20: 7	him guiltless that taketh his **n** in vain.	8034
	20:24	in all places where I record my **n** I will	8034
	23:13	make no mention of the **n** of other gods,	8034
	23:21	your transgressions: for my **n** *is* in him.	8034
	28:21	every one with his **n** shall they be	8034
	31: 2	I have called by **n** Bezaleel the son of Uri,	8034
	33:12	I know thee by **n**, and thou hast also	8034
	33:17	grace in my sight, and I know thee by **n**.	8034
	33:19	I will proclaim the **n** of the LORD before	8034
	34: 5	and proclaimed the **n** of the LORD.	8034
	34:14	for the LORD, whose **n** *is* Jealous, *is* a	8034
	35:30	the LORD hath called by **n** Bezaleel	8034
	39:14	every one with his **n**, according to	8034
Lev	18:21	shalt thou profane the **n** of thy God:	8034
	19:12	ye shall not swear by my **n** falsely,	8034
	19:12	shalt thou profane the **n** of thy God:	8034
	20: 3	my sanctuary, and to profane my holy **n**.	8034
	21: 6	not profane the **n** of their God:	8034
	22: 2	that they profane not my holy **n** in *those*	8034
	22:32	Neither shall ye profane my holy **n**;	8034
	24:11	son blasphemed the **n** *of the LORD*,	8034
	24:11	(and his mother's **n** *was* Shelomith,	8034
	24:16	he that blasphemeth the **n** of the LORD,	8034
	24:16	when he blasphemeth the **n** *of the LORD*,	8034
Nu	4:32	by **n** ye shall reckon the instruments of	8034
	6:27	they shall put my **n** upon the children of	8034
	11: 3	he called the **n** of the place Taberah:	8034
	11:26	the **n** of the one *was* Eldad, and the name	8034
	11:26	*was* Eldad, and the **n** of the other Medad:	8034
	11:34	he called the **n** of that place	8034
	17: 2	write thou every man's **n** upon his rod.	8034
	17: 3	thou shalt write Aaron's **n** upon the rod	8034
	21: 3	and he called the **n** of the place Hormah.	8034
	25:14	Now the **n** of the Israelite that was slain,	8034
	25:15	the **n** of the Midianitish woman that was	8034
	26:46	the **n** of the daughter of Asher *was* Sarah.	8034
	26:59	the **n** of Amram's wife *was* Jochebed,	8034
	27: 4	Why should the **n** of our father be done	8034
	32:42	and called it Nobah, after his own **n**.	8034
Dt	3:14	called them after his own **n**,	8034
	5:11	Thou shalt not take the **n** of the LORD thy	8034
	5:11	*him* guiltless that taketh his **n** in vain.	8034
	6:13	and serve him, and shalt swear by his **n**.	8034
	7:24	thou shalt destroy their **n** from under	8034
	9:14	and blot out their **n** from under heaven:	8034
	10: 8	and to bless in his **n**, unto this day.	8034
	10:20	shalt thou cleave, and swear by his **n**.	8034
	12: 5	out of all your tribes to put his **n** there,	8034
	12:11	shall choose to cause his **n** to dwell there;	8034
	12:21	to put his **n** there be too far from thee,	8034
	14:23	he shall choose to place his **n** there,	8034
	14:24	thy God shall choose to set his **n** there,	8034
	16: 2	LORD shall choose to place his **n** there.	8034
	16: 6	**n** *in*, there thou shalt sacrifice the	8034
	16:11	thy God hath chosen to place his **n** there.	8034
	18: 5	to stand to minister in the **n** of the LORD,	8034
	18: 7	he shall minister in the **n** of the LORD his	8034
	18:19	my words which he shall speak in my **n**,	8034
	18:20	shall presume to speak a word in my **n**,	8034
	18:20	or that shall speak in the **n** of other gods,	8034
	18:22	When a prophet speaketh in the **n** of	8034
	21: 5	and to bless in the **n** of the LORD;	8034
	22:14	bring up an evil **n** upon her, and say,	8034
	22:19	hath brought up an evil **n** upon a virgin	8034
	25: 6	in the **n** of his brother which is dead,	8034
	25: 6	is dead, that his **n** be not put out of Israel.	8034
	25: 7	to raise up unto his brother a **n** in Israel,	8034
	25:10	his **n** shall be called in Israel, The house	8034
	26: 2	thy God shall choose to place his **n** there.	8034
	26:19	in praise, and in **n**, and in honour;	8034
	28:10	that thou art called by the **n** of the LORD;	8034
	28:58	mayest fear this glorious and fearful **n**,	8034
	29:20	the LORD shall blot out his **n** from under	8034
	32: 3	Because I will publish the **n** of the LORD:	8034
Jos	5: 9	Wherefore the **n** of the place is called	8034
	7: 9	round, and cut off our **n** from the earth:	8034
	7: 9	and what wilt thou do unto thy great **n**?	8034
	7:26	Wherefore the **n** of that place was called,	8034
	9: 9	because of the **n** of the LORD thy God:	8034
	14:15	the **n** of Hebron before *was* Kirjath-arba;	8034
	15:15	the **n** of Debir before *was* Kirjath-sepher.	8034
	19:47	Dan, after the **n** of Dan their father.	8034
	21: 9	cities which are *here* mentioned by **n**,	8034
	23: 7	neither make mention of the **n** of their	8034
Jdg	1:10	(now the **n** of Hebron before *was*	8034
	1:11	the **n** of Debir before *was* Kirjath-sepher.	8034

N

N

Jdg
1:17 and the n of the city was called Hormah. 8034
1:23 (Now the n of the city before was Luz.) 8034
1:26 built a city, and called the n thereof Luz: 8034
1:26 which is the n thereof unto this day. 8034
2: 5 they called the n of that place Bochim: 8034
8:31 him a son, whose n he called Abimelech. 8034
13: 2 of the Danites, whose n was Manoah: 8034
13: 6 whence he was, neither told he me his n: 8034
13:17 the angel of the Lord, What is thy n, 8034
13:18 Why askest thou thus after my n, seeing 8034
13:24 bare a son, and called his n Samson: 8034
15:19 wherefore he called the n thereof 8034
16: 4 the valley of Sorek, whose n was Delilah. 8034
17: 1 of mount Ephraim, whose n was Micah. 8034
18:29 they called the n of the city Dan, after 8034
18:29 after the n of Dan their father, who was 8034
18:29 howbeit the n of the city was Laish at 8034

Ru
1: 2 the n of the man was Elimelech, 8034
1: 2 the n of his wife Naomi, and the name of 8034
1: 2 the n of his two sons Mahlon and Chilion, 8034
1: 4 the n of the one was Orpah, and the 8034
1: 4 was Orpah, and the n of the other Ruth: 8034
2: 1 family of Elimelech; and his n was Boaz. 8034
2:19 man's n with whom I wrought to day 8034
4: 5 to raise up the n of the dead upon his 8034
4:10 to raise up the n of the dead upon his 8034
4:10 that the n of the dead be not cut off from 8034
4:14 that his n may be famous in Israel. 8034
4:17 the women her neighbours gave it a n, 8034
4:17 to Naomi; and they called his n Obed: 8034

1Sa
1: 1 mount Ephraim, and his n was Elkanah, 8034
1: 2 the n of the one was Hannah, and the 8034
1: 2 and the n of the other Peninnah: 8034
1:20 she bare a son, and called his n Samuel, 8034
7:12 Shen, and called the n of it Eben-ezer, 8034
8: 2 Now the n of his firstborn was Joel; 8034
8: 2 was Joel; and the n of his second, Abiah: 8034
9: 1 whose n was Kish, the son of Abiel, 8034
9: 2 he had a son, whose n was Saul, a choice 8034
14: 4 the n of the one was Bozez, and the name 8034
14: 4 was Bozez, and the n of the other Seneh. 8034
14:49 were these; the n of the firstborn Merab, 8034
14:49 and the n of the younger Michal: 8034
14:50 the n of Saul's wife was Ahinoam, 8034
14:50 the n of the captain of his host was Abner, 8034
16: 3 thou shalt anoint unto me him whom I n 559
17:12 of Beth-lehem-judah, whose n was Jesse; 8034
17:23 the Philistine of Gath, Goliath by n, 8034
17:45 I come to thee in the n of the Lord of 8034
18:30 of Saul; so that his n was much set by. 8034
20:42 sworn both of us in the n of the Lord, 8034
21: 7 his n was Doeg, an Edomite, the chiefest 8034
24:21 that thou wilt not destroy my n out of my 8034
25: 3 Now the n of the man was Nabal; 8034
25: 3 was Nabal; and the n of his wife Abigail: 8034
25: 5 go to Nabal, and greet him in my n: 8034
25: 9 to all those words in the n of David, 8034
25:25 for as his n is, so is he; Nabal is his name, 8034
25:25 Nabal is his n, and folly is with him: 8034
28: 8 him up, whom I shall n unto thee. 559

2Sa
3: 7 was Rizpah, the daughter of Aiah: 8034
4: 2 the n of the one was Baanah, and the 8034
4: 2 Baanah, and the n of the other Rechab, 8034
4: 4 And his n was Mephibosheth. 8034
5:20 Therefore he called the n of that place 8034
6: 2 whose n is called by the name of 8034
6: 2 whose name is called by the n of 8034
6: 8 he called the n of the place Perez-uzzah to NIH
6:18 he blessed the people in the n of 8034
7: 9 thy sight, and have made thee a great n, 8034
7: 9 unto the n of the great men that are in 8034
7:13 He shall build a house for my n, and I 8034
7:23 to make him a n, and to do for you great 8034
7:26 let thy n be magnified for ever, saying, 8034
8:13 David gat him a n when he returned 8034
9: 2 of Saul a servant whose n was Ziba. 8034
9:12 had a young son, whose n was Micha. 8034
12:24 bare a son, and he called his n Solomon: 8034
12:25 he called his n Jedidah, because of 8034
12:28 I take the city, and it be called after my n. 8034
13: 1 had a fair sister, whose n was Tamar; 8034
13: 3 had a friend, whose n was Jonadab, 8034
14: 7 not leave to my husband neither n nor 8034
14:27 and one daughter, whose n was Tamar: 8034
15: 5 whose n was Shimei, the son of Gera: 8034
17:25 man's son, whose n was Ithra an Israelite, 8034
18:18 I have no son to keep my n in 8034
18:18 he called the pillar after his own n: and it 8034
20: 1 whose n was Sheba, the son of Bichri, 8034
20:21 Sheba the son of Bichri by n, 8034
22:50 and I will sing praises unto thy n. 8034
23:18 slew them, and had the n among three. 8034
23:22 and had the n among three mighty men. 8034

1Ki
1:47 God make the n of Solomon better than 8034
1:47 the name of Solomon better than thy n, 8034
3: 2 there was no house built unto the n of 8034
5: 3 n of the Lord his God for the wars 8034
5: 5 I purpose to build a house unto the n of 8034
5: 5 room, I will build a house unto my n. 8034
7:21 pillar, and called the n thereof Jachin: 8034
7:21 left pillar, and called the n thereof Boaz. 8034
8:16 a house, that my n might be therein; 8034
8:17 for the n of the Lord God of Israel. 8034
8:18 thine heart to build a house unto my n, 8034
8:19 he shall build the house unto my n. 8034

1Ki
8:20 have built a house for the n of the Lord 8034
8:29 thou hast said, My n shall be there: 8034
8:33 confess thy n, and pray, 8034
8:35 confess thy n, and turn from their sin, 8034
8:42 (For they shall hear of thy great n, and of 8034
8:43 all people of the earth may know thy n, 8034
8:43 which I have builded, is called by thy n. 8034
8:44 the house that I have built for thy n: 8034
8:48 the house which I have built for thy n: 8034
9: 3 hast built, to put my n there for ever; 8034
9: 7 which I have hallowed for my n, 8034
10: 1 Solomon concerning the n of the Lord, 8034
11:26 whose mother's n was Zeruah, a widow 8034
11:36 I have chosen me to put my n there. 8034
13: 2 unto the house of David, Josiah by n; 8034
14:21 all the tribes of Israel, to put his n there. 8034
14:21 his mother's n was Naamah an 8034
14:31 his mother's n was Naamah an 8034
15: 2 mother's n was Maachah, the daughter 8034
15:10 mother's n was Maachah, the daughter 8034
16:24 called the n of the city which he built, 8034
16:24 after the n of Shemer, owner of the hill, 8034
18:24 call ye on the n of your gods, and I will 8034
18:24 and I will call on the n of the Lord: 8034
18:25 call on the n of your gods, but put no fire 8034
18:26 called on the n of Baal from morning 8034
18:31 Lord came, saying, Israel shall be thy n: 8034
18:32 the stones he built an altar in the n of 8034
21: 8 So she wrote letters in Ahab's n, 8034
22:16 that which is true in the n of the Lord? 8034
22:42 his mother's n was Azubah the daughter 8034

2Ki
2:24 and cursed them in the n of the Lord. 8034
5:11 call on the n of the Lord his God, 8034
8:26 his mother's n was Athaliah, the daughter 8034
12: 1 his mother's n was Zibiah of Beer-sheba. 8034
14: 2 his mother's n was Jehoaddan of 8034
14: 7 called the n of it Joktheel unto this day. 8034
14:27 blot out the n of Israel from under heaven 8034
15: 2 his mother's n was Jecholiah of Jerusalem. 8034
15:33 his mother's n was Jerusha, the daughter 8034
18: 2 his mother's n also was Abi, the daughter 8034
21: 1 And his mother's n was Hephzi-bah. 8034
21: 4 Lord said, In Jerusalem will I put my n. 8034
21: 7 tribes of Israel, will I put my n for ever: 8034
21:19 his mother's n was Meshullemeth, 8034
22: 1 his mother's n was Jedidah, the daughter 8034
23:27 of which I said, My n shall be there. 8034
23:31 his mother's n was Hamutal, the daughter 8034
23:34 turned his n to Jehoiakim, and took 8034
23:36 mother's n was Zebudah, the daughter 8034
24: 8 mother's n was Nehushta, the daughter 8034
24:17 his stead, and changed his n to Zedekiah. 8034
24:18 mother's n was Hamutal, the daughter 8034

1Ch
1:19 the n of the one was Peleg; because in his 8034
1:19 and his brother's n was Joktan. 8034
1:43 and the n of his city was Dinhabah. 8034
1:46 his stead: and the n of his city was Avith. 8034
1:50 the n of his city was Pai; and his wife's 8034
1:50 his wife's n was Mehetabel, the daughter 8034
2:26 also another wife, whose n was Atarah; 8034
2:29 the n of the wife of Abishur was Abihail, 8034
2:34 servant, an Egyptian, whose n was Jarha. 8034
4: 3 and the n of their sister was Hazelelponi: 8034
4: 9 his mother called his n Jabez, saying, 8034
4:41 these written by n came in the days of 8034
7:15 whose sister's n was Maachah;) 8034
7:15 and the n of the second was Zelophehad: 8034
7:16 bare a son, and she called his n Peresh; 8034
7:16 the n of his brother was Sheresh; 8034
7:23 called his n Beriah, because it went evil 8034
8:29 of Gibeon; whose wife's n was Maachah: 8034
9:35 Jehiel, whose wife's n was Maachah: 8034
11:20 slew them, and had a n among the three. 8034
11:24 and had the n among the three mighties. 8034
12:31 which were expressed by n, to come and 8034
13: 6 the cherubims, whose n is called on it. 8034
14:11 they called the n of that place 8034
16: 2 he blessed the people in the n of 8034
16: 8 thanks unto the Lord, call upon his n, 8034
16:10 Glory ye in his holy n: let the heart of 8034
16:29 unto the Lord the glory due unto his n: 8034
16:35 that we may give thanks to thy holy n, 8034
16:41 were chosen, who were expressed by n, 8034
17: 8 have made thee a n like the name of 8034
17: 8 have made thee a name like the n of 8034
17:21 to make thee a n of greatness and 8034
17:24 that thy n may be magnified for ever, 8034
21:19 which he spake in the n of the Lord. 8034
22: 7 a house unto the n of the Lord my God: 8034
22: 8 thou shalt not build a house unto my n, 8034
22: 9 for his n shall be Solomon, and I will give 8034
22:10 He shall build a house for my n; 8034
22:19 the house that is to be built to the n of 8034
23:13 unto him, and to bless in his n for ever. 8034
28: 3 Thou shalt not build a house for my n, 8034
29:13 we thank thee, and praise thy glorious n. 8034
29:16 for thine holy n cometh of thine hand, 8034

2Ch
2: 1 to build a house for the n of the Lord, 8034
2: 4 I build a house to the n of the Lord my 8034
3:17 called the n of that on the right hand 8034
3:17 and the n of that on the left Boaz. 8034
6: 5 a house in, that my n might be there; 8034
6: 6 that my n might be there; 8034
6: 7 for the n of the Lord God of Israel. 8034
6: 8 in thine heart to build a house for my n, 8034

2Ch
6: 9 loins, he shall build the house for my n. 8034
6:10 have built the house for the n of 8034
6:20 said that thou wouldest put thy n there; 8034
6:24 shall return and confess thy n, and pray 8034
6:26 confess thy n, and turn from their sin, 8034
6:33 all people of the earth may know thy n, 8034
6:33 which I have built is called by thy n. 8034
6:34 the house which I have built for thy n; 8034
6:38 the house which I have built for thy n: 8034
7:14 If my people, which are called by my n, 8034
7:16 house, that my n may be there for ever: 8034
7:20 which I have sanctified for my n, 8034
12:13 all the tribes of Israel, to put his n there. 8034
12:13 his mother's n was Naamah an 8034
13: 2 His mother's n also was Michaiah 8034
14:11 and in thy n we go against this multitude. 8034
18:15 but the truth to me in the n of the Lord? 8034
20: 8 built thee a sanctuary therein for thy n, 8034
20: 9 thy presence, (for thy n is in this house,) 8034
20:26 the n of the same place was called, 8034
20:31 his mother's n was Azubah the daughter 8034
22: 2 His mother's n also was Athaliah 8034
24: 1 His mother's n also was Zibiah of 8034
25: 1 His mother's n was Jehoaddan of 8034
26: 3 His mother's n also was Jecoliah of 8034
26: 8 his n spread abroad even to the entering 8034
26:15 his n spread far abroad; for he was 8034
27: 1 His mother's n also was Jerushah, 8034
28: 9 the Lord was there, whose n was Oded: 8034
28:15 the men which were expressed by n rose 8034
29: 1 his mother's n was Abijah, the daughter 8034
31:19 the men that were expressed by n, 8034
33: 4 In Jerusalem shall my n be for ever. 8034
33: 7 tribes of Israel, will I put my n for ever: 8034
33:18 him in the n of the Lord God of Israel, 8034
36: 4 Jerusalem, and turned his n to Jehoiakim. 8034

Ezr
2:61 the Gileadite, and was called after their n: 8034
5: 1 Jerusalem in the n of the God of Israel, 8036
5:14 were delivered unto one, whose n was 8036
6:12 the God that hath caused his n to dwell 8036
8:20 all of them were expressed by n. 8034

Ne
1: 9 that I have chosen to set my n there. 8034
1:11 of thy servants, who desire to fear thy n: 8034
7:63 to wife, and was called after their n. 8034
9: 5 blessed be thy glorious n, which is exalted 8034
9: 7 and gavest him the n of Abraham; 8034
9:10 So didst thou get thee a n, as it is this day. 8034

Est
2: 5 whose n was Mordecai, the son of Jair, 8034
2:14 in her, and that she were called by n. 8034
2:22 certified the king thereof in Mordecai's n. 8034
3:12 in the n of king Ahasuerus was it written, 8034
8: 8 in the king's n, and seal it with the king's 8034
8: 8 writing which is written in the king's n, 8034
8:10 And he wrote in the king Ahasuerus' n, 8034
9:26 called these days Purim after the n of Pur. 8034

Job
1: 1 man in the land of Uz, whose n was Job; 8034
1:21 away; blessed be the n of the Lord. 8034
18:17 and he shall have no n in the street. 8034
42:14 he called the n of the first, Jemima; 8034
42:14 the n of the second, Kezia; and the name 8034
42:14 and the n of the third, Keren-happuch. 8034

Ps
5:11 let them also that love thy n be joyful in 8034
7:17 will sing praise to the n of the Lord 8034
8: 1 how excellent is thy n in all the earth! 8034
8: 9 how excellent is thy n in all the earth! 8034
9: 2 I will sing praise to thy n, O thou most 8034
9: 5 hast put out their n for ever and ever. 8034
9:10 that know thy n will put their trust in 8034
18:49 the heathen, and sing praises unto thy n. 8034
20: 1 the n of the God of Jacob defend thee; 8034
20: 5 in the n of our God we will set up our 8034
20: 7 we will remember the n of the Lord our 8034
22:22 I will declare thy n unto my brethren: 8034
29: 2 unto the Lord the glory due unto his n; 8034
33:21 because we have trusted in his holy n. 8034
34: 3 with me, and let us exalt his n together. 8034
41: 5 me, When shall he die, and his n perish? 8034
44: 5 through thy n will we tread them under 8034
44: 8 all the day long, and praise thy n for ever. 8034
44:20 If we have forgotten the n of our God, 8034
45:17 I will make thy n to be remembered in all 8034
48:10 According to thy n, O God, so is thy 8034
52: 9 hast done it: and I will wait on thy n; 8034
54: 1 by thy n, and judge me by thy strength. 8034
54: 6 I will praise thy n, O Lord; for it is 8034
61: 5 me the heritage of those that fear thy n. 8034
61: 8 So will I sing praise unto thy n for ever, 8034
63: 4 I live: I will lift up my hands in thy n. 8034
66: 2 Sing forth the honour of his n: make his 8034
66: 4 sing unto thee; they shall sing to thy n. 8034
68: 4 sing unto God, sing praises unto his n: 8034
68: 4 rideth upon the heavens by his n JAH, 8034
69:30 I will praise the n of God with a song, 8034
69:36 they that love his n shall dwell therein. 8034
72:17 His n shall endure for ever: his name shall 8034
72:17 his n shall be continued as long as the sun 8034
72:19 blessed be his glorious n for ever: 8034
74: 7 the dwelling place of thy n to the ground. 8034
74:10 shall the enemy blaspheme thy n for ever? 8034
74:18 the foolish people have blasphemed thy n. 8034
74:21 let the poor and needy praise thy n. 8034
75: 1 for that thy n is near thy wondrous works 8034
76: 1 is God known: his n is great in Israel. 8034
79: 6 kingdoms that have not called upon thy n. 8034
79: 9 of our salvation, for the glory of thy n: 8034

Ps 80:18 quicken us, and we will call upon thy **n**.	8034
83: 4 that the **n** of Israel may be no more in	8034
83:16 that they may seek thy **n**, O Lord.	8034
83:18 that thou, whose **n** alone *is* JEHOVAH,	8034
86: 9 thee, O Lord; and shall glorify thy **n**.	8034
86:11 in thy truth: unite my heart to fear thy **n**.	8034
86:12 and I will glorify thy **n** for evermore.	8034
89:12 Tabor and Hermon shall rejoice in thy **n**.	8034
89:16 In thy **n** shall they rejoice all the day:	8034
89:24 and in my **n** shall his horn be exalted.	8034
91:14 on high, because he hath known my **n**.	8034
92: 1 to sing *praises* unto thy **n**, O most High:	8034
96: 2 Sing unto the Lord, bless his **n**;	8034
96: 8 unto the Lord the glory due unto his **n**:	8034
99: 3 Let them praise thy great and terrible **n**;	8034
99: 6 Samuel among them that call upon his **n**;	8034
100: 4 be thankful unto him, *and* bless his **n**.	8034
102:15 So the heathen shall fear the **n** of	8034
102:21 To declare the **n** of the Lord in Zion,	8034
103: 1 and all that is within me, *bless* his holy **n**.	8034
105: 1 thanks unto the Lord; call upon his **n**:	8034
105: 3 Glory ye in his holy **n**: let the heart of	8034
106:47 to give thanks unto thy holy **n**,	8034
109:13 in the generation following let their **n** be	8034
111: 9 for ever: holy and reverend *is* his **n**.	8034
113: 1 of the Lord, praise the **n** of the Lord.	8034
113: 2 Blessed be the **n** of the Lord from this	8034
113: 3 the same the Lord's **n** *is* to be praised.	8034
115: 1 not unto us, but unto thy **n** give glory,	8034
116: 4 called I upon the **n** of the Lord;	8034
116:13 and call upon the **n** of the Lord.	8034
116:17 and will call upon the **n** of the Lord.	8034
118:10 in the **n** of the Lord will I destroy them.	8034
118:11 in the **n** of the Lord I will destroy them.	8034
118:12 for in the **n** of the Lord I will destroy	8034
118:26 Blessed *be* he that cometh in the **n** of	8034
119:55 I have remembered thy **n**, O Lord,	8034
119:132 usest to do unto those that love thy **n**.	8034
122: 4 to give thanks unto the **n** of the Lord.	8034
124: 8 Our help *is* in the **n** of the Lord,	8034
129: 8 we bless you in the **n** of the Lord.	8034
135: 1 Praise ye the **n** of the Lord; praise *him*,	8034
135: 3 sing *praises* unto his **n**; for *it is* pleasant.	8034
135:13 Thy **n**, O Lord, *endureth* for ever;	8034
138: 2 praise thy **n** for thy lovingkindness and	8034
138: 2 hast magnified thy word above all thy **n**.	8034
139:20 *and* thine enemies take *thy n* in vain.	NIH
140:13 righteous shall give thanks unto thy **n**:	8034
142: 7 soul out of prison, that *I* may praise thy **n**:	8034
145: 1 and I will bless thy **n** for ever and ever.	8034
145: 2 and I will praise thy **n** for ever and ever.	8034
145:21 let all flesh bless his holy **n** for ever and	8034
148: 5 Let them praise the **n** of the Lord: for he	8034
148:13 Let them praise the **n** of the Lord:	8034
148:13 for his **n** alone *is* excellent; his glory *is*	8034
149: 3 Let them praise his **n** in the dance: let	8034
Pr 10: 7 blessed: but the **n** of the wicked shall rot.	8034
18:10 The **n** of the Lord *is* a strong tower:	8034
21:24 Proud *and* haughty scorner *is* his **n**,	8034
22: 1 A *good* **n** is rather to be chosen than	8034
30: 4 what *is* his **n**, and what *is* his son's **n**,	8034
30: 4 and what *is* his son's **n**, if thou canst tell?	8034
30: 9 steal, and take the **n** of my God in vain.	8034
Ecc 6: 4 and his **n** shall be covered with darkness.	8034
7: 1 A *good* **n** is better than precious ointment	8034
SS 1: 3 ointments thy **n** *is* as ointment poured	8034
Isa 4: 1 let us be called by thy **n**, to take away	8034
7:14 bear a Son, and shall call his **n** Immanuel.	8034
8: 3 to me, Call his **n** Maher-shalal-hash-baz.	8034
9: 6 his **n** shall be called Wonderful,	8034
12: 4 ye say, Praise the Lord, call upon his **n**,	8034
12: 4 make mention that his **n** *is* exalted.	8034
14:22 cut off from Babylon the **n**, and remnant,	8034
18: 7 to the place of the **n** of the Lord of	8034
24:15 *even* the **n** of the Lord God of Israel in	8034
25: 1 I will exalt thee, I will praise thy **n**;	8034
26: 8 the desire of *our* soul *is* to thy **n**, and to	8034
26:13 thee only will we make mention of thy **n**.	8034
29:23 they shall sanctify my **n**, and sanctify	8034
30:27 the **n** of the Lord cometh from far,	8034
41:25 rising of the sun shall he call upon my **n**:	8034
42: 8 that *is* my **n**: and my glory will I not give	8034
43: 1 thee, I have called *thee* by thy **n**,	8034
43: 7 *Even* every one that is called by my **n**: for	8034
44: 5 shall call *himself* by the **n** of Jacob;	8034
44: 5 and surname *himself* by the **n** of Israel.	8034
45: 3 the Lord, which call *thee* by thy **n**,	8034
45: 4 I have even called thee by thy **n**:	8034
47: 4 our redeemer, the Lord of hosts *is* his **n**,	8034
48: 1 which are called by the **n** of Israel,	8034
48: 1 which swear by the **n** of the Lord,	8034
48: 2 of Israel; The Lord of hosts *is* his **n**.	8034
48:11 will I do *it*: for how should *my n* be	NIH
48:19 his **n** should not have been cut off nor	8034
49: 1 mother hath he made mention of my **n**.	8034
50:10 let him trust in the **n** of the Lord,	8034
51:15 The Lord of hosts *is* his **n**.	8034
52: 5 **n** continually every day *is* blasphemed.	8034
52: 6 Therefore my people shall know my **n**:	8034
54: 5 the Lord of hosts *is* his **n**;	8034
55:13 it shall be to the Lord for a **n**,	8034
56: 5 a **n** better than *of* sons and *of* daughters:	8034
56: 5 I will give them an everlasting **n**, that	8034
56: 6 serve him, and to love the **n** of the Lord,	8034
57:15 that inhabiteth eternity, whose **n** *is* Holy;	8034

Isa 59:19 So shall they fear the **n** of the Lord from	8034
60: 9 unto the **n** of the Lord thy God,	8034
62: 2 thou shalt be called by a new **n**, which	8034
62: 2 which the mouth of the Lord shall **n**.	5344
63:12 to make himself an everlasting **n**?	8034
63:14 thy people, to make thyself a glorious **n**.	8034
63:16 our redeemer; thy **n** *is* from everlasting.	8034
63:19 over them; they were not called by thy **n**.	8034
64: 2 make thy **n** known to thine adversaries,	8034
64: 7 *there is* none that calleth upon thy **n**,	8034
65: 1 a nation *that* was not called by my **n**.	8034
65:15 ye shall leave your **n** for a curse unto my	8034
65:15 and call his servants by another **n**:	8034
66:22 so shall your seed and your **n** remain.	8034
Jer 3:17 to the **n** of the Lord, to Jerusalem:	8034
7:10 which is called by my **n**, and say,	8034
7:11 Is this house, which is called by my **n**,	8034
7:12 where I set my **n** at the first, and see what	8034
7:14 which is called by my **n**, wherein ye trust,	8034
7:30 in the house which is called by my **n**,	8034
10: 6 thou *art* great, and thy **n** *is* great in might.	8034
10:16 The Lord of hosts *is* his **n**.	8034
10:25 upon the families that call not on thy **n**:	8034
11:16 The Lord called thy **n**, A Green olive	8034
11:19 that his **n** may be no more remembered.	8034
11:21 Prophesy not in the **n** of the Lord,	8034
12:16 to swear by my **n**, The Lord liveth;	8034
13:11 for a **n**, and for a praise, and for a glory:	8034
14: 9 midst of us, and we are called by thy **n**;	8034
14:14 The prophets prophesy lies in my **n**:	8034
14:15 the prophets that prophesy in my **n**,	8034
15:16 for I am called by thy **n**, O Lord God of	8034
16:21 they shall know that my **n** *is* The Lord.	8034
20: 3 The Lord hath not called thy **n** Pashur,	8034
20: 9 of him, nor speak any more in his **n**.	8034
23: 6 this *is his* **n** whereby he shall be called,	8034
23:25 that prophesy lies in my **n**, saying, I have	8034
23:27 **n** by their dreams which they tell every	8034
23:27 as their fathers have forgotten my **n** for	8034
25:29 evil on the city which is called by my **n**,	8034
26: 9 Why hast thou prophesied in the **n** of	8034
26:16 for he hath spoken to us in the **n** of	8034
26:20 that prophesied in the **n** of the Lord,	8034
27:15 yet they prophesy a lie in my **n**;	8034
29: 9 they prophesy falsely unto you in my **n**:	8034
29:21 which prophesy a lie unto you in my **n**;	8034
29:23 have spoken lying words in my **n**, which I	8034
29:25 Because thou hast sent letters in thy **n**	8034
31:35 thereof roar; The Lord of hosts *is* his **n**:	8034
32:18 Mighty God, the Lord of hosts, *is* his **n**,	8034
32:20 and hast made thee a **n**, as *at* this day;	8034
32:34 which is called by my **n**, to defile it.	8034
33: 2 to establish it; the Lord *is* his **n**;	8034
33: 9 it shall be to me a **n** of joy, a praise and	8034
33:16 *is the* **n** wherewith she shall be called,	NIH
34:15 me in the house which is called by my **n**,	8034
34:16 ye turned and polluted my **n**,	8034
37:13 whose **n** *was* Irijah, the son of Shelemiah,	8034
44:16 hast spoken unto us in the **n** of the Lord,	8034
44:26 Behold, I have sworn by my great **n**,	8034
44:26 that my **n** shall no more be named in	8034
46:18 the King, whose **n** *is* the Lord of hosts,	8034
48:15 the King, whose **n** *is* the Lord of hosts.	8034
48:17 all ye that know His **n**, say, How is	8034
50:34 *is* strong; the Lord of hosts *is* his **n**:	8034
51:19 the Lord of hosts *is* his **n**.	8034
51:57 the King, whose **n** *is* the Lord of hosts.	8034
52: 1 his mother's **n** *was* Hamutal the daughter	8034
La 3:55 I called upon thy **n**, O Lord, out of	8034
Eze 20:29 **n** thereof is called Bamah unto this day.	8034
20:39 pollute ye my holy **n** no more with your	8034
24: 2 Son of man, write thee the **n** of the day,	8034
36:20 they went, they profaned my holy **n**,	8034
36:21 I had pity for mine holy **n**, which the	8034
36:23 I will sanctify my great **n**, which was	8034
39: 7 So will I make my holy **n** known in	8034
39: 7 I will not let *them* pollute my holy **n** any	8034
39:16 also the **n** of the city *shall be* Hamonah.	8034
39:25 Israel, and will be jealous for my holy **n**;	8034
43: 7 my holy **n**, shall the house of Israel no	8034
43: 8 they have even defiled my holy **n** by their	8034
48:35 the **n** of the city from *that day shall be*,	NIH
Da 1: 7 for he gave unto Daniel the **n** of	NIH
2:20 Blessed be the **n** of God for ever and ever:	8036
2:26 said to Daniel, whose **n** *was* Belteshazzar,	8036
4: 8 whose **n** *was* Belteshazzar, according to	8036
4: 8 according to the **n** of my god, and in	8036
4:19 Daniel, whose **n** *was* Belteshazzar,	8036
9: 6 which spake in thy **n** to our kings,	8034
9:18 and the city which is called by thy **n**:	8034
9:19 city and thy people are called by thy **n**.	8034
10: 1 whose **n** was called Belteshazzar;	8034
Hos 1: 4 Lord said unto him, Call his **n** Jezreel;	8034
1: 6 said unto him, Call her **n** Lo-ruhamah:	8034
1: 9 said *God*, Call his **n** Lo-ammi: for ye *are*	8034
2:17 and no more be remembered by their **n**.	8034
Joel 2:26 and praise the **n** of the Lord your God,	8034
2:32 *that* whosoever shall call on the **n** of	8034
Am 2: 7 the *same* maid, to profane my holy **n**:	8034
4:13 The Lord, The God of hosts, *is* his **n**.	8034
5: 8 the face of the earth: The Lord *is* his **n**:	8034
5:27 the Lord, whose **n** *is* The God of hosts.	8034
6:10 for *we may* not make mention of the **n** of	8034
9: 6 the face of the earth: The Lord *is* his **n**.	8034
9:12 all the heathen, which are called by my **n**,	8034

Mic 4: 5 all people will walk every one in the **n**	8034
4: 5 we will walk in the **n** of the Lord our	8034
5: 4 in the majesty of the **n** of the Lord his	8034
6: 9 and *the man of* wisdom shall see thy **n**:	8034
Na 1:14 *that* no more of thy **n** be sown:	8034
Zep 1: 4 the **n** of the Chemarims with the priests;	8034
3: 9 that they may all call upon the **n** of	8034
3:12 and they shall trust in the **n** of the Lord.	8034
3:20 I will make you a **n** and a praise among	8034
Zec 5: 4 of him that sweareth falsely by my **n**:	8034
6:12 the man whose **n** *is* The BRANCH;	8034
10:12 they shall walk up and down in his **n**,	8034
13: 3 for thou speakest lies in the **n** of	8034
13: 9 they shall call on my **n**, and I will hear	8034
14: 9 shall there be one Lord, and his **n** one.	8034
Mal 1: 6 unto you, O priests, that despise my **n**.	8034
1: 6 ye say, Wherein have we despised thy **n**?	8034
1:11 my **n** *shall* be great among the Gentiles;	8034
1:11 place incense *shall* be offered unto my **n**,	8034
1:11 my **n** *shall* be great among the heathen,	8034
1:14 and my **n** *is* dreadful among the heathen.	8034
2: 2 to give glory unto my **n**, saith the Lord	8034
2: 5 he feared me, and was afraid before my **n**.	8034
3:16 the Lord, and that thought upon his **n**.	8034
4: 2 unto you that fear my **n** shall the Sun of	8034
Mt 1:21 a son, and thou shalt call his **n** JESUS:	3686
1:23 a son, and they shall call his **n** Emmanuel,	3686
1:25 firstborn son: and *he* called his **n** JESUS.	3686
6: 9 which art in heaven, Hallowed be thy **n**.	3686
7:22 Lord, have we not prophesied in thy **n**?	3686
7:22 and in thy **n** have cast out devils?	3686
7:22 in thy **n** done many wonderful works?	3686
10:41 He that receiveth a prophet in the **n** of a	3686
10:41 he that receiveth a righteous *man* in the **n**	3686
10:42 of cold *water* only in the **n** of a disciple,	3686
12:21 And in his **n** shall the Gentiles trust.	3686
18: 5 such little child in my **n** receiveth me.	3686
18:20 or three are gathered together in my **n**,	3686
21: 9 Blessed *is* he that cometh in the **n** of	3686
23:39 Blessed is he that cometh in the **n** of	3686
24: 5 many shall come in my **n**, saying, I am	3686
27:32 they found a man of Cyrene, Simon by **n**:	3686
28:19 baptizing them in the **n** of the Father,	3686
Mk 5: 9 And he asked him, What *is* thy **n**? And he	3686
5: 9 And he answered, saying, My **n** *is* Legion:	3686
5:22 of the rulers of the synagogue, Jairus by **n**;	3686
6:14 And king Herod heard *of him*; (for his **n**	3686
9:37 receive one of such children in my **n**,	3686
9:38 we saw one casting out devils in thy **n**,	3686
9:39 no *man* which shall do a miracle in my **n**,	3686
9:41 give you a cup of water to drink in my **n**,	3686
11: 9 Blessed *is* he that cometh in the **n** of	3686
11:10 that cometh in the **n** of the Lord:	3686
13: 6 many shall come in my **n**, saying, I am	3686
16:17 In my **n** shall they cast out devils;	3686
Lk 1: 5 of Aaron, and her **n** *was* Elisabeth.	3686
1:13 thee a son, and thou shalt call his **n** John.	3686
1:27 a virgin espoused to a man whose **n** was	3686
1:27 of David; and the virgin's **n** *was* Mary.	3686
1:31 forth a son, and shalt call his **n** JESUS.	3686
1:49 done to me great things; and holy *is* his **n**.	3686
1:59 him Zacharias, after the **n** of his father.	3686
1:61 of thy kindred that is called by this **n**.	3686
1:63 and wrote, saying, His **n** is John.	3686
2:21 his **n** was called JESUS, which was *so*	3686
2:25 a man in Jerusalem, whose **n** *was* Simeon;	3686
6:22 reproach *you*, and cast out your **n** as evil,	3686
8:30 Jesus asked him, saying, What *is* thy **n**?	3686
9:48 Whosoever shall receive this child in my **n**	3686
9:49 we saw one casting out devils in thy **n**;	3686
10:17 devils are subject unto us through thy **n**.	3686
11: 2 which art in heaven, Hallowed be thy **n**.	3686
13:35 Blessed *is* he that cometh in the **n** of	3686
19:38 Blessed *be* the King that cometh in the **n**	3686
21: 8 for many shall come in my **n**, saying, I am	3686
24:18 And the one of *them*, whose **n** *was*	3686
24:47 be preached in his **n** among all nations,	3686
Jn 1: 6 a man sent from God, whose **n** *was* John.	3686
1:12 God, *even* to them that believe on his **n**:	3686
2:23 in the feast *day*, many believed in his **n**,	3686
3:18 he hath not believed in the **n** of the only	3686
5:43 I am come in my Father's **n**, and ye	3686
5:43 if another shall come in his own **n**, him ye	3686
10: 3 and he calleth his own sheep by **n**,	3686
10:25 the works that I do in my Father's **n**,	3686
12:13 of Israel that cometh in the **n** of the Lord.	3686
12:28 Father, glorify thy **n**. Then came there a	3686
14:13 And whatsoever ye shall ask in my **n**,	3686
14:14 If ye shall ask any *thing* in my **n**, I will do	3686
14:26 whom the Father will send in my **n**,	3686
15:16 ye shall ask of the Father in my **n**,	3686
16:23 ye shall ask the Father in my **n**,	3686
16:24 Hitherto have ye asked nothing in my **n**:	3686
16:26 At that day ye shall ask in my **n**: and I say	3686
17: 6 I have manifested thy **n** unto the men	3686
17:11 keep through thine own **n** those whom	3686
17:12 them in the world, I kept them in thy **n**:	3686
17:26 have I declared unto them thy **n**,	3686
18:10 right ear. The servant's **n** was Malchus.	3686
20:31 believing ye might have life through his **n**.	3686
Ac 2:21 *that* whosoever shall call on the **n** of	3686
2:38 be baptized every one of you in the **n** of	3686
3: 6 In the of Jesus Christ of Nazareth rise	3686
3:16 And his **n** through faith in his name hath	3686
3:16 And his name through faith in his **n** hath	3686

N

Ac 4: 7 they asked, By what power, or by what **n**, *3686*
4:10 that by the **n** of Jesus Christ of Nazareth, *3686*
4:12 for there is none other **n** under heaven *3686*
4:17 speak henceforth to no man in this **n**. *3686*
4:18 to speak at all nor teach in the **n** of Jesus. *3686*
4:30 wonders may be done by the **n** of thy holy *3686*
5:28 you that *you* should not teach in this **n**? *3686*
5:40 *they* should not speak in the **n** of Jesus, *3686*
5:41 counted worthy to suffer shame for his **n**. *3686*
7:58 at a young man's feet, whose **n** was Saul. *2564*
8:12 and the **n** of Jesus Christ, they were *3686*
8:16 only they were baptized in the **n** *3686*
9:14 chief priests to bind all that call on thy **n**. *3686*
9:15 bear my **n** before the Gentiles, and kings, *3686*
9:21 them which called on this **n** in Jerusalem, *3686*
9:27 boldly at Damascus in the **n** of Jesus. *3686*
9:29 And he spake boldly in the **n** of the Lord *3686*
10:43 that through his **n** whosoever believeth in *3686*
10:48 them to be baptized in the **n** of the Lord. *3686*
13: 6 a Jew, whose **n** *was* Bar-jesus: *3686*
13: 8 sorcerer (for so is his **n** by interpretation) *3686*
15:14 to take out of them a people for his **n**. *3686*
15:17 upon whom my **n** is called, saith the Lord, *3686*
15:26 that have hazarded their lives for the **n** *3686*
16:18 I command thee in the **n** of Jesus Christ *3686*
19: 5 were baptized in the **n** of the Lord Jesus. *3686*
19:13 had evil spirits in the **n** of the Lord Jesus, *3686*
19:17 the **n** of the Lord Jesus was magnified. *3686*
21:13 also to die at Jerusalem for the **n** of *3686*
22:16 thy sins, calling on the **n** of the Lord. *3686*
26: 9 contrary to the **n** of Jesus of Nazareth. *3686*
28: 7 man of the island, whose **n** was Publius: *3686*
Ro 1: 5 to the faith among all nations, for his **n**: *3686*
2:24 For the **n** of God is blasphemed among *3686*
9:17 that my **n** might be declared throughout *3686*
10:13 For whosoever shall call upon the **n** of *3686*
15: 9 among the Gentiles, and sing unto thy **n**. *3686*
1Co 1: 2 with all that in every place call upon the **n** *3686*
1:10 by the **n** of our Lord Jesus Christ, *3686*
1:13 or were ye baptized in the **n** of Paul? *3686*
1:15 say that I had baptized in mine own **n**. *3686*
5: 4 In the **n** of our Lord Jesus Christ, when *3686*
6:11 ye are justified in the **n** of the Lord Jesus, *3686*
Eph 1:21 and dominion, and every **n** that is named, *3686*
5:20 Father in the **n** of our Lord Jesus Christ; *3686*
Php 2: 9 him a **n** which is above every name: *3686*
2: 9 him a name which is above every **n**: *3686*
2:10 That at the **n** of Jesus every knee should *3686*
Col 3:17 or deed, *do* all in the **n** of the Lord Jesus, *3686*
2Th 1:12 the **n** of our Lord Jesus Christ may be *3686*
3: 6 in the **n** of our Lord Jesus Christ, *3686*
1Ti 6: 1 that the **n** of God and *his* doctrine be not *3686*
2Ti 2:19 Let every one that nameth the **n** of Christ *3686*
Heb 1: 4 obtained a more excellent **n** than they. *3686*
2:12 I will declare thy **n** unto my brethren, *3686*
6:10 which ye have shewed toward his **n**, *3686*
13:15 the fruit of *our* lips giving thanks to his **n**. *3686*
Jas 2: 7 Do not they blaspheme that worthy **n** by *3686*
5:10 who have spoken in the **n** of the Lord, *3686*
5:14 him with oil in the **n** of the Lord: *3686*
1Pe 4:14 If ye be reproached for the **n** of Christ, *3686*
1Jn 3:23 That we should believe on the **n** of his Son *3686*
5:13 that believe on the **n** of the Son of God; *3686*
5:13 that ye may believe on the **n** of the Son of *3686*
3Jn 1:14 friends salute thee. Greet the friends by **n**. *3686*
Rev 2:13 Satan's seat *is*: and thou holdest fast my **n**, *3686*
2:17 and in the stone a new **n** written, *3686*
3: 1 that thou hast a **n** that thou livest, *3686*
3: 5 I will not blot out his **n** out of the book of *3686*
3: 5 but I will confess his **n** before my Father, *3686*
3: 8 kept my word, and hast not denied my **n**. *3686*
3:12 I will write upon him the **n** of my God, *3686*
3:12 the **n** of the city of my God, *which is* *3686*
3:12 *and I will write upon him* my new **n**. *3686*
6: 8 and his **n** that sat on him *was* Death, *3686*
8:11 the **n** of the star is called Wormwood: *3686*
9:11 **n** in the Hebrew tongue *is* Abaddon, *3686*
9:11 in the Greek *tongue* hath his **n** Apollyon, *3686*
11:18 and them that fear thy **n**, small and great; *3686*
13: 1 and upon his heads the **n** of blasphemy. *3686*
13: 6 to blaspheme his **n**, and his tabernacle, *3686*
13:17 or the **n** of the beast, or the number of his *3686*
14: 1 the number of the beast, or the number of his **n**. *3686*
14: 1 having his Father's **n** written in their *3686*
14:11 whosoever receiveth the mark of his **n**. *3686*
15: 2 his mark, *and* over the number of his **n**, *3686*
15: 4 not fear thee, O Lord, and glorify thy **n**? *3686*
16: 9 blasphemed the **n** of God, which hath *3686*
17: 5 And upon her forehead *was* a **n** written, *3686*
19:12 he had a **n** written, that no *man* knew, *3686*
19:13 and his **n** is called The Word of God. *3686*
19:16 *his* vesture and on his thigh a **n** written, *3686*
22: 4 and his **n** *shall be* in their foreheads. *3686*

NAME'S (30) [NAME]

1Sa 12:22 not forsake his people for his great **n** sake: 8034
1Ki 8:41 cometh out of a far country for thy **n** sake; 8034
2Ch 6:32 is come from a far country for thy great **n** sake. 8034
Ps 23: 3 the paths of righteousness for his **n** sake. 8034
25:11 For thy **n** sake, O Lord, pardon mine 8034
31: 3 therefore for thy **n** sake lead me, 8034
79: 9 and purge away our sins, for thy **n** sake. 8034
106: 8 he saved them for his **n** sake, 8034
109:21 for me, O God the Lord, for thy **n** sake: 8034
143:11 Quicken me, O Lord, for thy **n** sake: 8034

Isa 48: 9 For my **n** sake will I defer mine anger, 8034
66: 5 that cast you out for my **n** sake, said, 8034
Jer 14: 7 against us, do thou *it* for thy **n** sake: 8034
14:21 Do not abhor *us*, for thy **n** sake, do not 8034
Eze 20: 9 I wrought for my **n** sake, that *it* should 8034
20:14 I wrought for my **n** sake, that *it* should 8034
20:22 mine hand, and wrought for my **n** sake, 8034
20:44 when I have wrought with you for my **n** 8034
36:22 house of Israel, but for mine holy **n** sake, 8034
Mt 10:22 And ye shall be hated of all *men* for my **n** *3686*
19:29 wife, or children, or lands, for my **n** sake, *3686*
24: 9 ye shall be hated of all nations for my **n** *3686*
Mk 13:13 And ye shall be hated of all *men* for my **n** *3686*
Lk 21:12 before kings and rulers for my **n** sake. *3686*
21:17 And ye shall be hated of all *men* for my **n** *3686*
Jn 15:21 will they do unto you for my **n** sake, *3686*
Ac 9:16 great *things* he must suffer for my **n** sake. *3686*
1Jn 2:12 *your* sins are forgiven you for his **n** sake. *3686*
3Jn 1: 7 Because that for his **n** sake they went *3686*
Rev 2: 3 and for my **n** sake hast laboured, *3686*

NAMED (57) [NAME]

Ge 23:16 he had **n** in the audience of the sons 1696
27:36 he said, Is not he rightly **n** Jacob? 7121+8034
48:16 let my name be **n** on them, and the name 7121
Jos 2: 1 harlot's house, **n** Rahab, and lodged there. 8034
1Sa 4:21 she **n** the child Ichabod, saying, The glory 7121
17: 4 **n** Goliath, of Gath, whose height was six 8034
22:20 **n** Abiathar, escaped, and fled after David. 8034
2Ki 17:34 of Jacob, whom he **n** Israel; 7760+8034
1Ch 23:14 God, his sons were **n** of the tribe of Levi. 8034
Ecc 6:10 That which hath been is **n** already, 7121+8034
Isa 61: 6 ye shall be **n** the Priests of the Lord: 7121
Jer 44:26 that my name shall no more be **n** in 7121
Da 5:12 whom the king **n** Belteshazzar: 7761+8036
Am 6: 1 which *are* **n** chief of the nations, 5344
Mic 2: 7 O thou that *art* **n** the house of Jacob, 559
Mt 9: 9 he saw a man, **n** Matthew, sitting at 3004
27:57 came a rich man of Arimathea, **n** Joseph, 5122
Mk 14:32 And they came to a place which was **n** 3004
15: 7 And there was one **n** Barabbas, *which lay* 3004
Lk 1: 5 king of Judea, a certain priest **n** Zacharias, *3686*
1:26 God unto a city of Galilee, **n** Nazareth. *3686*
2:21 **n** of the angel before he was conceived in *2564*
5:27 and saw a publican, **n** Levi, sitting at *3686*
6:13 he chose twelve, whom also he **n** apostles; *3687*
6:14 Simon, (whom he also **n** Peter,) and *3686*
8:41 there came a man **n** Jairus, and he was a *3686*
10:38 a certain woman **n** Martha received him *3686*
16:20 And there was a certain beggar **n** Lazarus, *3686*
19: 2 And behold, *there was* a man **n** Zaccheus, *3686*
23:50 And behold, *there was* a man **n** Joseph, *3686*
Jn 3: 1 Nicodemus, a ruler of the Jews, *3686*
11: 1 Lazarus, of Bethany, the town of Mary NIG
11:49 And one of them, **n** Caiaphas, being NIG
Ac 5: 1 a certain man **n** Ananias, with Sapphira *3686*
5:34 a Pharisee, **n** Gamaliel, a doctor of law, *3686*
9:10 a certain disciple at Damascus, **n** Ananias; *3686*
9:12 hath seen in a vision a man **n** Ananias *3686*
9:33 And there he found a certain man **n** *3686*
9:36 there was at Joppa a certain disciple **n** *3686*
11:28 And there stood up one of them **n** Agabus, *3686*
12:13 a damsel came to hearken, **n** Rhoda. *3686*
16: 1 **n** Timotheus, the son of a certain woman, *3686*
16:14 And a certain woman **n** Lydia, a seller of *3686*
17:34 and a woman **n** Damaris, and others with *3686*
18: 2 And found a certain Jew **n** Aquila, born in *3686*
18: 7 **n** Justus, one that worshipped God, *3686*
18:24 And a certain Jew **n** Apollos, born at *3686*
19:24 For a certain man **n** Demetrius, *3686*
20: 9 window a certain young man **n** Eutychus, *3686*
21:10 from Judea a certain prophet, **n** Agabus, *3686*
24: 1 and *with* a certain orator **n** Tertullus, NIG
27: 1 certain other prisoners unto one **n** Julius, *3686*
Ro 15:20 the gospel, not where Christ was **n**, *3687*
1Co 5: 1 is not so much as **n** amongst the Gentiles, *3687*
Eph 1:21 and dominion, and every name that is **n**, *3687*
3:15 whole family in heaven and earth is **n**, *3687*
5: 3 let it not be once **n** amongst you, *3687*

NAMELY (23) [NAME]

Lev 1:10 **n**, of the sheep, or of the goats, for a burnt NIH
Nu 1:32 **n**, of the children of Ephraim, *by* their NIH
9:15 tabernacle, **n**, the tent of the Testimony: NIH
13:11 **n**, of the tribe of Manasseh, Gaddi the son NIH
31: 8 **n**, Evi, and Rekem, and Zur, and Hur, NIH
Dt 4:43 **N**, Bezer in the wilderness, in the plain NIH
13: 7 **N**, of the gods of the people which *are* NIH
20:17 **n**, the Hittites, and the Amorites, NIH
Jdg 3: 3 **N**, five lords of the Philistines, and all NIH
8:35 to the house of Jerubbaal, **n**, Gideon, NIH
1Ch 6:57 **n**, Hebron, *the city* of refuge, and Libnah NIH
6:61 **n**, out of the half *tribe* of Manasseh, by lot, NIH
9:23 **n**, the house of the tabernacle, by wards. NIH
23: 6 of Levi, **n**, Gershon, Kohath, and Merari. NIH
Ezr 10:18 **n**, of the sons of Jeshua the son of Jozadak, NIH
Ne 12:35 **n**, Zechariah the son of Jonathan, the son NIH
Est 8:12 **n**, upon the thirteenth *day* of the twelfth NIH
Ecc 5:13 **n**, riches kept for the owners thereof to NIH
Isa 7:20 **n**, by them beyond the river, by the king NIH
Jer 32: 9 **n**, Elnathan the son of Achbor, NIH
Mk 12:31 And the second *is* like, **n** this, Thou shalt NIG
Ac 15:22 **n**, Judas surnamed Barsabas, and Silas, NIG
Ro 13: 9 **n**, Thou shalt love thy neighbour as *1722+3588*

NAMES (97) [NAME]

Ge 2:20 Adam gave **n** to all cattle, and to the fowl 8034
25:13 the **n** of the sons of Ishmael, 8034
25:13 by their **n**, according to their generations: 8034
25:16 these *are* their **n**, by their towns, 8034
26:18 he called their **n** after the names by which 8034
26:18 he called their names after the **n** by which 8034
36:10 These *are* the **n** of Esau's sons; Eliphaz 8034
36:40 these *are* the **n** of the dukes *that came* of 8034
36:40 their families, after their places, by their **n**; 8034
46: 8 these *are* the **n** of the children of Israel, 8034
Ex 1: 1 Now these *are* the **n** of the sons of Levi 8034
6:16 these *are* the **n** of the sons of Levi 8034
28: 9 grave on them the **n** of the children 8034
28:10 Six of their **n** on one stone, and the *other* 8034
28:10 the *other* six **n** of the rest on the other 8034
28:11 stones with the **n** of the children of Israel: 8034
28:12 Aaron shall bear their **n** before the Lord 8034
28:21 the stones shall be with the **n** of 8034
28:21 twelve, according to their **n**, *like* 8034
28:29 Aaron shall bear the **n** of the children of 8034
39: 6 with the **n** of the children of Israel. 8034
39:14 the stones *were* according to the **n** of 8034
39:14 twelve, according to their **n**, *like* 8034
Nu 1: 2 with the number of *their* **n**, every male by 8034
1: 5 these *are* the **n** of the men that shall stand 8034
1:17 these men which are expressed by *their* **n**: 8034
1:18 according to the number of the **n**, 8034
1:20 according to the number of the **n**, by their 8034
1:22 according to the number of the **n**, by their 8034
1:24 according to the number of the **n**, 8034
1:26 according to the number of the **n**, 8034
1:28 according to the number of the **n**, 8034
1:30 according to the number of the **n**, 8034
1:32 according to the number of the **n**, 8034
1:34 according to the number of the **n**, 8034
1:36 according to the number of the **n**, 8034
1:38 according to the number of the **n**, 8034
1:40 according to the number of the **n**, 8034
1:42 according to the number of the **n**, 8034
3: 2 these *are* the **n** of the sons of Aaron; 8034
3: 3 These *are* the **n** of the sons of Aaron, 8034
3:17 these were the sons of Levi by their **n**; 8034
3:18 these *are* the **n** of the sons of Gershon by 8034
3:40 upward, and take the number of their **n**. 8034
3:43 all the firstborn males by the number of **n**, 8034
13: 4 these *were* their **n**: of the tribe of Reuben, 8034
13:16 These *are* the **n** of the men which Moses 8034
26:33 the **n** of the daughters of Zelophehad 8034
26:53 inheritance according to the number of **n**. 8034
26:55 according to the **n** of the tribes of their 8034
27: 1 these *are* the **n** of his daughters; Mahlah, 8034
32:38 and Baal-meon, (*their* **n** being changed,) 8034
32:38 gave *other* **n** unto the cities which 8034+8034
34:17 These *are* the **n** of the men which shall 8034
34:19 the **n** of the men are these: Of the tribe of 8034
Dt 12: 3 destroy the **n** of them out of that place. 8034
Jos 17: 3 these *are* the **n** of his daughters; Mahlah, 8034
1Sa 14:49 the **n** of his two daughters *were these*; 8034
17:13 the **n** of his three sons that went to 8034
2Sa 5:14 these *be* the **n** of those that were born 8034
23: 8 These *be* the **n** of the mighty *men* whom 8034
1Ki 4: 8 *are* their **n**: The son of Hur, in mount 8034
1Ch 4:38 These mentioned by *their* **n** *were* princes 8034
6:17 these *be* the **n** of the sons of Gershom; 8034
6:65 these cities, which are called by *their* **n**. 8034
8:38 whose **n** *are* these, Azrikam, Bocheru, 8034
9:44 whose **n** *are* these, Azrikam, Bocheru, 8034
14: 4 Now these *are* the **n** of *his* children which 8034
23:24 as they were counted by number of **n** by 8034
Ezr 5: 4 What *are* the **n** of the men that make this 8036
5:10 We asked their **n** also, to certify thee, 8036
5:10 that we might write the **n** of the men that 8036
8:13 whose **n** *are* these, Eliphelet, Jeiel, 8034
10:16 all of them by *their* **n**, were separated, 8034
Ps 16: 4 not offer, nor take up their **n** into my lips. 8034
49:11 they call *their* lands after their own **n**. 8034
147: 4 of the stars; he calleth them all by *their* **n**. 8034
Isa 40:26 he calleth them all by **n** by the greatness 8034
23: 4 Thus *were* their **n**; Samaria *is* Aholah, 8034
48: 1 Now these *are* the **n** of the tribes. From 8034
48:31 the gates of the city *shall be* after the **n** of 8034
Da 1: 7 whom the prince of the eunuchs gave **n**: 8034
Hos 2:17 For I will take away the **n** of Baalim out of 8034
Zec 13: 2 that I will cut off the **n** of the idols out of 8034
Mt 10: 2 the **n** of the twelve apostles are these; *3686*
Lk 10:20 because your **n** are written in heaven. *3686*
Ac 1:15 (the number of **n** together were about an *3686*
18:15 But if it be a question of words and **n**, *3686*
Php 4: 3 whose **n** *are* in the book of life. *3686*
Rev 3: 4 Thou hast a few **n** even in Sardis, *3686*
3: 8 whose **n** are not written in the book of life *3686*
17: 3 full of **n** of blasphemy, having seven heads *3686*
17: 8 **n** were not written in the book of life *3686*
21:12 twelve angels, and **n** written *there*on, *3686*
21:12 which are the **n** of the twelve tribes of NIG
21:14 in them the **n** of the twelve apostles of *3686*

NAMETH (1) [NAME]

2Ti 2:19 Let every one that **n** the name of Christ *3687*

NAOMI (20) [NAOMI'S]

Ru 1: 2 the name of his wife **N**, and the name of 5281
1: 8 **N** said unto her two daughters in law, 5281

Ru	1:11 **N** said, Turn again, my daughters: why	5281
	1:19 about them, and they said, *Is* this **N**?	5281
	1:20 unto them, Call me not **N**, call me Mara:	5281
	1:21 why *then* call ye me **N**, seeing the LORD	5281
	1:22 So **N** returned, and Ruth the Moabitess,	5281
	2: 1 **N** had a kinsman of her husband's,	5281
	2: 2 Ruth the Moabitess said unto **N**, Let me	5281
	2: 6 back with **N** out of the country of Moab;	5281
	2:20 **N** said unto her daughter in law, Blessed	5281
	2:20 said unto her, The man *is* near of kin	5281
	2:22 **N** said unto Ruth her daughter in law, *It*	5281
	3: 1 **N** her mother in law said unto her,	5281
	4: 3 he said unto the kinsman, **N**, that is come	5281
	4: 5 thou buyest the field of the hand of **N**,	5281
	4: 9 and Mahlon's, of the hand of **N**.	5281
	4:14 the women said unto **N**, Blessed *be*	5281
	4:16 **N** took the child, and laid it in her bosom,	5281
	4:17 a name, saying, There is a son born to **N**;	5281

NAOMI'S (1) [NAOMI]
Ru	1: 3 Elimelech **N** husband died; and she was	5281

NAPHISH (2)
Ge	25:15 Hadar, and Tema, Jetur, **N**, and Kedemah:	5305
1Ch	1:31 **N**, and Kedemah. These *are* the sons	5305

NAPHTALI (50) [KEDESH-NAPHTALI, NEPHTHALIM]
Ge	30: 8 prevailed: and she called his name **N**.	5321
	35:25 Bilhah, Rachel's handmaid; Dan, and **N**:	5321
	46:24 sons of **N**; Jahzeel, and Guni, and Jezer,	5321
	49:21 **N** *is* a hind let loose: he giveth goodly	5321
Ex	1: 4 Dan, and **N**, Gad, and Asher.	5321
Nu	1:15 Of **N**; Ahira the son of Enan.	5321
	1:42 *Of* the children of **N**, *throughout* their	5321
	1:43 *even* of the tribe of **N**, *were* fifty and	5321
	2:29 the tribe of **N**: and the captain of	5321
	2:29 the captain of the children of **N** *shall be*	5321
	7:78 prince of the children of **N**, *offered*:	5321
	10:27 children of **N** *was* Ahira the son of Enan.	5321
	13:14 the tribe of **N**, Nahbi the son of Vophsi.	5321
	26:48 *Of* the sons of **N** after their families:	5321
	26:50 These *are* the families of **N** according to	5321
	34:28 prince of the tribe of the children of **N**,	5321
Dt	27:13 and Asher, and Zebulun, Dan, and **N**.	5321
	33:23 of **N** he said, O Naphtali, satisfied with	5321
	33:23 O **N**, satisfied with favour, and full *with*	5321
	34: 2 all **N**, and the land of Ephraim,	5321
Jos	19:32 sixth lot came out to the children of **N**,	5321
	19:32 *even* for the children of **N** according to	5321
	19:39 children of **N** according to their families,	5321
	20: 7 appointed Kedesh in Galilee in mount **N**,	5321
	21: 6 out of the tribe of **N**, and out of the half	5321
	21:32 out of the tribe of **N**, Kedesh in Galilee	5321
Jdg	1:33 Neither did **N** drive out the inhabitants of	5321
	4: 6 ten thousand men of the children of **N**	5321
	4:10 Barak called Zebulun and **N** to Kedesh;	5321
	5:18 **N** *were* a people *that* jeoparded their lives	5321
	6:35 Asher, and unto Zebulun, and unto **N**;	5321
	7:23 gathered themselves together out of **N**,	5321
1Ki	4:15 Ahimaaz *was* in **N**, he also took Basmath	5321
	7:14 He *was* a widow's son of the tribe of **N**,	5321
	15:20 and all Cinneroth, with all the land of **N**.	5321
2Ki	15:29 all the land of **N**, and carried them captive	5321
1Ch	2: 2 Joseph, and Benjamin, **N**, Gad, and Asher.	5321
	6:62 out of the tribe of **N**, and out of the tribe	5321
	6:76 out of the tribe of **N**; Kedesh in Galilee	5321
	7:13 The sons of **N**; Jahziel, and Guni,	5321
	12:34 of **N** a thousand captains, and with them	5321
	12:40 *even* unto Issachar and Zebulun and **N**,	5321
	27:19 of **N**, Jerimoth the son of Azriel:	5321
2Ch	16: 4 and all the store cities of **N**.	5321
	34: 6 and Ephraim, and Simeon, even unto **N**,	5321
Ps	68:27 princes of Zebulun, *and* the princes of **N**.	5321
Isa	9: 1 the land of Zebulun and the land of **N**,	5321
Eze	48: 3 even unto the west side, a *portion for* **N**.	5321
	48: 4 by the border of **N**, from the east side	5321
	48:34 of Gad, one gate of Asher, one gate of **N**.	5321

NAPHTUHIM (2)
Ge	10:13 and Anamim, and Lehabim, and **N**,	5320
1Ch	1:11 and Anamim, and Lehabim, and **N**,	5320

NAPHTUHITES See NAPHTUHIM

NAPKIN (3)
Lk	19:20 pound, which I have kept laid up in a **n**:	4676
Jn	11:44 and his face was bound about with a **n**.	4676
	20: 7 And the **n**, that was about his head,	4676

NARCISSUS (1)
Ro	16:11 Greet them that be of the *household* of **N**,	3488

NARD See SPIKENARD

NARROW (9) [NARROWED, NARROWER, NARROWLY]
Nu	22:26 went further, and stood in a **n** place,	6862
Jos	17:15 if mount Ephraim be too **n** for thee.	213
1Ki	6: 4 the house he made windows of **n** lights.	331
Pr	23:27 ditch; and a strange *woman is* a **n** pit.	6862
Isa	49:19 shall even now be too **n** by reason of	3334
Eze	40:16 *were* **n** windows to the little chambers,	331
	41:16 the **n** windows, and the galleries round	331
	41:26 *there were* **n** windows and palm trees on	331
Mt	7:14 and **n** *is* the way, which leadeth unto life,	2346

NARROWED (1) [NARROW]
1Ki	6: 6 the house he made **n** rests round about,	4052

NARROWER (1) [NARROW]
Isa	28:20 the covering **n** than that *he* can wrap	6887

NARROWLY (2) [NARROW]
Job	13:27 stocks, and **lookest n** unto all my paths;	8104
Isa	14:16 They that see thee shall **n look** upon thee,	7688

NATHAN (43)
2Sa	5:14 and Shobab, and **N**, and Solomon,	5416
	7: 2 That the king said unto **N** the prophet,	5416
	7: 3 **N** said to the king, Go, do all that *is* in	5416
	7: 4 that the word of the LORD came unto **N**,	5416
	7:17 all this vision, so did **N** speak unto David.	5416
	12: 1 the LORD sent **N** unto David. And he	5416
	12: 5 he said to **N**, *As* the LORD liveth, the man	5416
	12: 7 **N** said to David, Thou *art* the man.	5416
	12:13 David said unto **N**, I have sinned against	5416
	12:13 **N** said unto David, The LORD also hath	5416
	12:15 **N** departed unto his house.	5416
	12:25 he sent by the hand of **N** the prophet;	5416
	23:36 Igal the son of **N** of Zobah, Bani	5416
1Ki	1: 8 **N** the prophet, and Shimei, and Rei,	5416
	1:10 **N** the prophet, and Benaiah, and the	5416
	1:11 Wherefore **N** spake unto Bath-sheba	5416
	1:22 the king, **N** the prophet also came in.	5416
	1:23 the king, saying, Behold **N** the prophet.	5416
	1:24 **N** said, My lord O king, hast thou said,	5416
	1:32 **N** the prophet, and Benaiah the son of	5416
	1:34 **N** the prophet anoint him there king over	5416
	1:38 **N** the prophet, and Benaiah the son of	5416
	1:44 **N** the prophet, and Benaiah the son of	5416
	1:45 **N** the prophet have anointed him king in	5416
	4: 5 Azariah the son of **N** *was* over the officers	5416
	4: 5 Zabud the son of **N** *was* principal officer,	5416
1Ch	2:36 Attai begat **N**, and Nathan begat Zabad,	5416
	2:36 Attai begat Nathan, and **N** begat Zabad,	5416
	3: 5 and Shobab, and **N**, and Solomon, four,	5416
	11:38 Joel the brother of **N**, Mibhar the son of	5416
	14: 4 Shammua, and Shobab, **N**, and Solomon,	5416
	17: 1 that David said to **N** the prophet,	5416
	17: 2 **N** said unto David, Do all that *is* in thine	5416
	17: 3 that the word of God came to **N**, saying,	5416
	17:15 all this vision, so did **N** speak unto David.	5416
	29:29 in the book of **N** the prophet, and in	5416
2Ch	9:29 *are* they not written in the book of **N**	5416
	29:25 of Gad the king's seer, and **N** the prophet:	5416
Ezr	8:16 for **N**, and for Zechariah,	5416
	10:39 And Shelemiah, and **N**, and Adaiah,	5416
Ps	51: T when **N** the prophet came unto him,	5416
Zec	12:12 the family of the house of **N** apart,	5416
Lk	3:31 was *the son* of **N**, which was *the son*	3481

NATHANAEL (6)
Jn	1:45 Philip findeth **N**, and saith unto him,	3482
	1:46 And **N** said unto him, Can there any good	3482
	1:47 Jesus saw **N** coming to him, and saith of	3482
	1:48 **N** saith unto him, Whence knowest thou	3482
	1:49 **N** answered and saith unto him, Rabbi,	3482
	21: 2 and **N** of Cana in Galilee, and the *sons* of	3482

NATHAN-MELECH (1)
2Ki	23:11 by the chamber of **N** the chamberlain,	5419

NATION (145) [NATIONS]
Ge	12: 2 I will make of thee a great **n**, and I will	1471
	15:14 also that **n**, whom they shall serve, will I	1471
	17:20 he beget, and I will make him a great **n**.	1471
	18:18 shall surely become a great and mighty **n**,	1471
	20: 4 Lord, wilt thou slay also a righteous **n**?	1471
	21:13 son of the bondwoman will I make a **n**,	1471
	21:18 thine hand; for I will make him a great **n**.	1471
	35:11 a **n** and a company of nations shall be of	1471
	46: 3 for I will there make of thee a great **n**:	1471
Ex	9:24 all the land of Egypt since it became a **n**.	1471
	19: 6 me a kingdom of priests, and a holy **n**.	1471
	21: 8 sell her unto a strange *n* he shall have no	5971
	32:10 and I will make of thee a great **n**.	1471
	33:13 and consider that this **n** *is* thy people.	1471
	34:10 been done in all the earth, nor in any **n**:	1471
Lev	18:26 *neither* any of **your own n**, nor any	249
	20:23 ye shall not walk in the manners of the **n**,	1471
Nu	14:12 wilt make of thee a greater **n** and	1471
Dt	4: 6 Surely this great **n** *is* a wise and	1471
	4: 7 what **n** *is there so* great, who hath God	1471
	4: 8 what **n** *is there so* great, that hath statutes	1471
	4:34 take him a **n** from the midst of *another*	1471
	4:34 nation a **n** from the midst of *another* **n**,	1471
	9:14 I will make of thee a **n** mightier	1471
	26: 5 became there a **n**, great, mighty,	1471
	28:33 shall a **n** which thou knowest not eat up;	5971
	28:36 unto a **n** which neither thou nor thy	1471
	28:49 The LORD shall bring a **n** against thee	1471
	28:49 a **n** whose tongue thou shalt not	1471
	28:50 A **n** of fierce countenance, which shall not	1471
	32:21 provoke them to anger with a foolish **n**.	1471
	32:28 they *are* a **n** void of counsel, neither *is*	1471
2Sa	7:23 what one **n** in the earth *is* like thy people,	1471
1Ki	18:10 thy God liveth, there is no **n** or kingdom,	1471
	18:10 he took an oath of the kingdom and **n**,	1471
2Ki	17:29 Howbeit **every n** made gods of	1471+1471
	17:29 **every n** in their cities wherein they	1471+1471
1Ch	16:20 when they went from **n** to **n**,	1471

1Ch	16:20 *when* they went from nation to **n**,	1471
	17:21 what one **n** in the earth *is* like thy people	1471
2Ch	15: 6 **n** was destroyed of nation, and city of city:	1471
	15: 6 nation was destroyed of **n**, and city of city:	1471
	32:15 no god of any **n** or kingdom was able to	1471
Job	34:29 whether *it be* done against a **n**, or against	1471
Ps	33:12 Blessed *is* the **n** whose God is the LORD;	1471
	43: 1 and plead my cause against an ungodly **n**:	1471
	83: 4 and let us cut them off from *being* a **n**;	1471
	105:13 When they went from one to another,	1471
	106: 5 that *I* may rejoice in the gladness of thy **n**,	1471
	147:20 He hath not dealt so with any **n**: and *as*	1471
Pr	14:34 Righteousness exalteth a **n**: but sin *is* a	1471
Isa	1: 4 Ah sinful **n**, a people laden with iniquity,	1471
	2: 4 **n** shall not lift up sword against nation,	1471
	2: 4 nation shall not lift up sword against **n**,	1471
	9: 3 Thou hast multiplied the **n**,	1471
	10: 6 I will send him against a hypocritical **n**,	1471
	14:32 then answer the messengers of the **n**?	1471
	18: 2 to a **n** scattered and peeled,	1471
	18: 2 a **n** meted out and trodden down,	1471
	18: 7 a **n** meted out and trodden under foot,	1471
	26: 2 the righteous **n** which keepeth the truth	1471
	26:15 Thou hast increased the **n**, O LORD,	1471
	26:15 O LORD, thou hast increased the **n**:	1471
	49: 7 him whom the **n** abhorreth, to a servant	1471
	51: 4 my people; and give ear unto me, O my **n**:	3816
	55: 5 thou shalt call a **n** *that* thou knowest not,	1471
	58: 2 as a **n** that did righteousness,	1471
	60:12 For the **n** and kingdom that will not serve	1471
	60:22 a thousand, and a small one a strong **n**:	1471
	65: 1 unto a **n** *that* was not called by my name.	1471
	66: 8 shall a **n** be born at once? for as soon as	1471
Jer	2:11 Hath a **n** changed *their* gods, which *are*	1471
	5: 9 not my soul be avenged on such a **n** as	1471
	5:15 Lo, I will bring a **n** upon you from far,	1471
	5:15 it *is* a mighty **n**, it *is* an ancient nation,	1471
	5:15 it *is* a mighty nation, it *is* an ancient **n**,	1471
	5:15 a **n** whose language thou knowest not,	1471
	5:29 not my soul be avenged on such a **n** as	1471
	6:22 a great **n** shall be raised from the sides of	1471
	7:28 This *is* a **n** that obeyeth not the voice of	1471
	9: 9 not my soul be avenged on such a **n** as	1471
	12:17 I will utterly pluck up and destroy that **n**,	1471
	18: 7 *what* instant I shall speak concerning a **n**,	1471
	18: 8 that **n**, against whom I have pronounced,	1471
	18: 9 *what* instant I shall speak concerning a **n**,	1471
	25:12 that **n**, saith the LORD, for their iniquity,	1471
	25:32 evil *shall* go forth from **n** to nation,	1471
	25:32 evil *shall* go forth from nation to **n**,	1471
	27: 8 that the **n** and kingdom which will not	1471
	27: 8 that **n** will I punish, saith the LORD,	1471
	27:13 as the LORD hath spoken against the **n**	1471
	31:36 cease from being a **n** before me for ever.	1471
	33:24 that *they* should be no more a **n** before	1471
	48: 2 come, and let us cut it off from *being* a **n**.	1471
	49:31 Arise, get you up unto the wealthy **n**,	1471
	49:36 there shall be no **n** whither the outcasts	1471
	50: 3 For out of the north there cometh up a **n**	1471
	50:41 great **n**, and many kings shall be raised up	1471
La	4:17 in our watching we have watched for a **n**	1471
Eze	2: 3 to a rebellious **n** that hath rebelled against	1471
	37:22 I will make them one **n** in the land upon	1471
Da	3:29 That every people, and language,	524
	8:22 four kingdoms shall stand up out of the **n**,	1471
	12: 1 such as never was since there was a **n**	1471
Joel	1: 6 For a **n** is come up upon my land, strong,	1471
Am	6:14 behold, I *will* raise up against you a **n**,	1471
Mic	4: 3 **n** shall not lift up a sword against nation,	1471
	4: 3 nation shall not lift up a sword against **n**,	1471
	4: 7 and her that was cast far off a strong **n**:	1471
Hab	1: 6 up the Chaldeans, *that* bitter and hasty **n**,	1471
Zep	2: 1 yea, gather together, O **n** not desired;	1471
	2: 5 of the sea coast, the **n** of the Cherethites!	1471
Hag	2:14 so *is* this people, and so *is* this **n** before me,	1471
Mal	3: 9 for ye *have* robbed me, *even* this whole **n**.	1471
Mt	21:43 given to a **n** bringing forth the fruits	1484
	24: 7 For **n** shall rise against nation,	1484
	24: 7 For nation shall rise against **n**,	1484
Mk	7:26 was a Greek, a Syrophenician by **n**;	1085
	13: 8 For **n** shall rise against nation,	1484
	13: 8 For nation shall rise against **n**,	1484
Lk	7: 5 he loveth our **n**, and he hath built us a	1484
	21:10 **N** shall rise against nation,	1484
	21:10 Nation shall rise against **n**,	1484
	23: 2 We found this *fellow* perverting the **n**,	1484
Jn	11:48 and take away both our place and **n**.	1484
	11:50 people, and *that* the whole **n** perish not.	1484
	11:51 prophesied that Jesus should die for *that* **n**;	1484
	11:52 And not for *that* only, but that also he	1484
	18:35 Thine own **n** and the chief priests have	1484
Ac	2: 5 devout men, out of every **n** under heaven.	1484
	7: 7 And the **n** to whom they shall be in	1484
	10:22 of good report among all the **n** of the Jews,	1484
	10:28 or come unto **one of another** n;	246
	10:35 But in every **n** he that feareth him,	1484
	24: 2 very worthy deeds are done unto this **n**	1484
	24:10 been of many years a judge unto this **n**,	1484
	24:17 many years I came to bring alms to my **n**,	1484
	26: 4 was at the first among mine own **n** at	1484
	28:19 not that I had ought to accuse my **n** of.	1484
Ro	10:19 *and* by a foolish **n** I will anger you.	1484
Gal	1:14 above many *my* equals in mine own **n**,	1085
Php	2:15 in the midst of a crooked and perverse **n**,	1074
1Pe	2: 9 a holy **n**, a peculiar people;	1484

N

Rev 5: 9 and tongue, and people, and n; *1484*
 14: 6 and to every n, and kindred, and tongue, *1484*

NATIONS (336) [NATION]

Ge 10: 5 his tongue, after their families, in their n. 1471
 10:20 in their countries, *and* in their n. 1471
 10:31 their tongues, in their lands, after their n. 1471
 10:32 Noah, after their generations, in their n: 1471
 10:32 by these were the n divided in the earth 1471
 14: 1 king of Elam, and Tidal king of n; 1471
 14: 9 with Tidal king of n, and Amraphel king 1471
 17: 4 and thou shalt be a father of many n. 1471
 17: 5 for a father of many n have I made thee. 1471
 17: 6 I will make n of thee, and kings shall 1471
 17:16 bless her, and she shall be a *mother* of n; 1471
 18:18 all the n of the earth shall be blessed in 1471
 22:18 in thy seed shall all the n of the earth be 1471
 25:16 twelve princes according to their n. 523
 25:23 Two n *are* in thy womb, and two manner 1471
 26: 4 in thy seed shall all the n of the earth be 1471
 27:29 serve thee, and n bow down to thee: 3816
 35:11 and a company of n shall be of thee, 1471
 48:19 his seed shall become a multitude of n. 1471
Ex 34:24 For I will cast out the n before thee, 1471
Lev 18:24 n are defiled which I cast out before you: 1471
 18:28 it spued out the n that *were* before you. 1471
Nu 14:15 the n which have heard the fame of thee 1471
 23: 9 and shall not be reckoned among the n. 1471
 24: 8 he shall eat up the n his enemies, 1471
 24:20 and said, Amalek *was* the first of the n; 1471
Dt 2:25 the fear of thee upon the n *that are* under 5971
 4: 6 your understanding in the sight of the n, 5971
 4:19 unto all n under the whole heaven. 5971
 4:27 the LORD shall scatter you among the n, 5971
 4:38 To drive out n from before thee greater 1471
 7: 1 hath cast out many n before thee, 1471
 7: 1 seven n greater and mightier than thou; 1471
 7:17 in thine heart, These n *are* moe than I; 1471
 7:22 the LORD thy God will put out those n 1471
 8:20 As the n which the LORD destroyeth 1471
 9: 1 to go in to possess n greater and 1471
 9: 4 for the wickedness of these n the LORD 1471
 9: 5 for the wickedness of these n the LORD 1471
 11:23 will the LORD drive out all these n from 1471
 11:23 ye shall possess greater n and mightier 1471
 12: 2 wherein the n which ye shall possess 1471
 12:29 God shall cut off the n from before thee, 1471
 12:30 How did these n serve their gods? 1471
 14: 2 above all the n that *are* upon the earth. 5971
 15: 6 thou shalt lend unto many n, but thou 1471
 15: 6 thou shalt reign over many n, but they 1471
 17:14 me, like as all the n that *are* about me; 1471
 18: 9 to do after the abominations of those n. 1471
 18:14 For these n, which thou shalt possess, 1471
 19: 1 the LORD thy God hath cut off the n, 1471
 20:15 which are not of the cities of these n. 1471
 26:19 to make thee high above all n which he 1471
 28: 1 set thee on high above all n of the earth: 1471
 28:12 thou shalt lend unto many n, and thou 1471
 28:37 among all n whither the LORD shall lead 5971
 28:65 among these n shalt thou find no ease, 1471
 29:16 how we came through the n which ye 1471
 29:18 to go *and* serve the gods of these n; 1471
 29:24 Even all n shall say, Wherefore hath 1471
 30: 1 shalt call *them* to mind among all the n, 1471
 30: 3 will return and gather thee from all the n, 5971
 31: 3 he will destroy these n from before thee, 1471
 32: 8 the most High divided to the nations 1471
 32:43 Rejoice, O ye n, *with* his people: for he 1471
Jos 12:23 one; the king of the n of Gilgal, one; 1471
 23: 3 your God hath done unto all these n 1471
 23: 4 I have divided unto you *by lot* these n that 1471
 23: 4 with all the n that I have cut off, 1471
 23: 7 That *ye* come not among these n, these 1471
 23: 9 hath driven out from before you great n 1471
 23:12 cleave unto the remnant of these n, 1471
 23:13 drive out *any of* these n from before you; 1471
Jdg 2:21 of the n which Joshua left when he died: 1471
 2:23 Therefore the LORD left those n, without 1471
 3: 1 Now these *are* the n which the LORD left, 1471
1Sa 8: 5 make us a king to judge us like all the n. 1471
 8:20 That we also may be like all the n; 1471
 27: 8 for those n *were* of old the inhabitants of NIH
2Sa 7:23 from Egypt, *from* the n and their gods? 1471
 8:11 gold that he had dedicated of all which 1471
1Ki 4:31 and his fame was in all n round about. 1471
 11: 2 Of the n *concerning* which the LORD said 1471
 14:24 which the LORD cast out before 1471
2Ki 17:26 The n which thou hast removed, 1471
 17:33 after the manner of the n whom they 1471
 17:41 So these n feared the LORD, and served 1471
 18:33 Hath any of the gods of the n delivered at 1471
 19:12 Have the gods of the n delivered them 1471
 19:17 the kings of Assyria have destroyed the n 1471
 21: 9 n whom the LORD destroyed before 1471
1Ch 14:17 LORD brought the fear of him upon all n. 1471
 16:24 his marvellous works among all the n, 5971
 16:31 let *men* say among the n, The LORD 1471
 17:21 by driving out n from before thy people, 1471
 18:11 the gold that he brought from all *these* n; 1471
2Ch 7:20 be a proverb and a byword among all n. 5971
 13: 9 after the manner of the n of *other* lands? 5971
 32:13 were the gods of the n of *those* lands any 1471
 32:14 those n that my fathers utterly destroyed, 1471
 32:17 As the gods of the n of *other* lands have 1471

2Ch 32:23 that he was magnified in the sight of all n 1471
Ezr 4:10 the rest of the n whom the great and 524
Ne 1: 8 I will scatter you abroad among the n: 5971
 9:22 thou gavest them kingdoms and n, 5971
 13:26 many n was there no king like him, 1471
Job 12:23 He increaseth the n, and destroyeth them: 1471
 12:23 he enlargeth the n, and straiteneth them 1471
Ps 9:17 into hell, *and* all the n that forget God. 1471
 9:20 that the n may know themselves *to be* 1471
 22:27 all the kindreds of the n shall worship 1471
 22:28 and *he is* the governor among the n. 1471
 47: 3 under us, and the n under our feet. 3816
 57: 9 I will sing unto thee among the n. 3816
 66: 7 his power for ever; his eyes behold the n: 1471
 67: 2 earth, thy saving health among all n. 1471
 67: 4 O let the n be glad and sing for joy: 3816
 67: 4 and govern the n upon earth. 3816
 72:11 down before him: all n shall serve him. 1471
 72:17 blessed in him: all n shall call him blessed. 1471
 82: 8 the earth: for thou shalt inherit all n. 1471
 86: 9 All n whom thou hast made shall come 1471
 96: 5 For all the gods of the n *are* idols: 5971
 106:27 overthrow their seed also among the n, 1471
 106:34 They did not destroy the n, 5971
 108: 3 I will sing *praises* unto thee among the n. 3816
 113: 4 The LORD *is* high above all n, 1471
 117: 1 O praise the LORD, all ye n: praise him, 1471
 118:10 All n compassed me about: but in the 1471
 135:10 smote great n, and slew mighty kings; 1471
Pr 24:24 shall the people curse, n shall abhor him: 3816
Isa 2: 2 the hills; and all n shall flow unto it. 1471
 2: 4 he shall judge among the n, 1471
 5:26 he will lift up an ensign to the n from far, 1471
 9: 1 sea, beyond Jordan, in Galilee of the n. 1471
 10: 7 heart to destroy and cut off n not a few. 1471
 11:12 he shall set up an ensign for the n, 1471
 13: 4 a tumultuous noise of the kingdoms of n 1471
 14: 6 he that ruled the n in anger, *is* persecuted, 1471
 14: 9 from thy thrones all the kings of the n. 1471
 14:12 to the ground, which didst weaken the n! 1471
 14:18 All the kings of the n, *even* all of them, 1471
 14:26 hand that is stretched out upon all the n. 1471
 17:12 to the rushing of n, *that* make a rushing 3816
 17:13 The n shall rush like the rushing of many 3816
 23: 3 *is her* revenue; and she is a mart of n. 1471
 25: 3 the city of the terrible n shall fear thee. 1471
 25: 7 and the vail that is spread over all n. 1471
 29: 7 the multitude of all the n that fight against 1471
 29: 8 so shall the multitude of all the n be, 1471
 30:28 to sift the n with the sieve of vanity: 1471
 33: 3 at the lifting up of thyself the n were 1471
 34: 1 Come near, ye n, to hear; and hearken, 1471
 34: 2 the indignation of the LORD *is* upon all n, 1471
 36:18 Hath any of the gods of the n delivered his 1471
 37:12 Have the gods of the n delivered them 1471
 37:18 kings of Assyria have laid waste all the n, 776
 40:15 the n *are* as a drop of a bucket, 1471
 40:17 All n before him *are* as nothing; 1471
 41: 2 gave the n before him, and made *him* rule 1471
 43: 9 Let all the n be gathered together, 1471
 45: 1 I have holden, to subdue n before him; 1471
 45:20 together, ye *that are* escaped of the n: 1471
 52:10 bare his holy arm in the eyes of all the n; 1471
 52:15 shall he sprinkle many n; the kings shall 1471
 55: 5 that knew not thee shall run unto thee 1471
 60:12 yea, *those* n shall be utterly wasted. 1471
 61:11 and praise to spring forth before all the n. 1471
 64: 2 *that* the n may tremble at thy presence. 1471
 66:18 that *I* will gather all n and tongues; 1471
 66:19 those that escape of them unto the n, 1471
 66:20 unto the LORD out of all n upon horses, 1471
Jer 1: 5 *and* I ordained thee a prophet unto the n. 1471
 1:10 I have this day set thee over the n and 1471
 3:17 all the n shall be gathered unto it, 1471
 3:19 a goodly heritage of the hosts of n? 1471
 4: 2 and the n shall bless themselves in him, 1471
 4:16 Make ye mention to the n; behold, 1471
 6:18 Therefore hear, ye n, and know, 1471
 9:26 for all these n *are* uncircumcised, 1471
 10: 7 Who would not fear thee, O King of n? 1471
 10: 7 as among all the wise *men* of the n, 1471
 10:10 the n shall not be able to abide his 1471
 22: 8 many n shall pass by this city, 1471
 25: 9 against all these n round about, 1471
 25:11 these n shall serve the king of Babylon 1471
 25:13 Jeremiah hath prophesied against all the n. 1471
 25:14 For many n and great kings shall serve 1471
 25:15 cause all the n, to whom I send thee, 1471
 25:17 made all the n to drink, unto whom 1471
 25:31 the LORD hath a controversy with the n, 1471
 26: 6 will make this city a curse to all the n 1471
 27: 7 all n shall serve him, and his son, and his 1471
 27: 7 *then* many n and great kings shall serve 1471
 27:11 the n that bring their neck under the yoke 1471
 28:11 of all within the space of two full years. 1471
 28:14 yoke of iron upon the neck of all these n, 1471
 29:14 I will gather you from all the n, 1471
 29:18 among all the n whither I have driven 1471
 30:11 though I make a full end of all n whither 1471
 31: 7 and shout among the chief of the n: 1471
 31:10 O ye n, and declare *it* in the isles afar off, 1471
 33: 9 an honour before all the n of the earth, 1471
 36: 2 against Judah, and against all the n, 1471
 43: 5 that were returned from all n, whither 1471
 44: 8 a reproach among all the n of the earth? 1471

Jer 46:12 The n have heard *of* thy shame, and thy 1471
 46:28 for I will make a full end of all the n 1471
 50: 2 Declare ye among the n, and publish, 1471
 50: 9 assembly of great n from the north 1471
 50:12 the hindermost of the n *shall be* a 1471
 50:23 become a desolation among the n! 1471
 50:46 moved, and the cry is heard among the n. 1471
 51: 7 the n have drunken of her wine; therefore 1471
 51: 7 of her wine; therefore the n are mad. 1471
 51:20 for with thee will I break in pieces the n, 1471
 51:27 blow the trumpet among the n, prepare 1471
 51:27 the nations, prepare the n against her, 1471
 51:28 Prepare against her the n with the kings 1471
 51:41 become an astonishment among the n! 1471
 51:44 the n shall not flow *together* any more 1471
La 1: 1 she *that* was great among the n, 1471
Eze 5: 5 I have set it in the midst of the n and 1471
 5: 6 into wickedness more than the n, 1471
 5: 7 Because ye multiplied more than the n 1471
 5: 7 of the n that *are* round about you; 1471
 5: 8 in the midst of thee in the sight of the n. 1471
 5:14 a reproach among the n that *are* round 1471
 5:15 astonishment unto the n that *are* round 1471
 6: 8 that shall escape the sword among the n, 1471
 6: 9 whither they shall be carried captives, 1471
 12:15 when I shall scatter them among the n, 1471
 19: 4 The n also heard of him; he was taken in 1471
 19: 8 the n set against him on every side from 1471
 25:10 may not be remembered among the n. 1471
 26: 3 cause many n to come up against thee, 1471
 26: 5 and it shall become a spoil to the n. 1471
 28: 7 strangers upon thee, the terrible of the n: 1471
 29:12 I will scatter the Egyptians among the n, 1471
 29:15 shall it exalt itself any more above the n: 1471
 29:15 that *they* shall no more rule over the n. 1471
 30:11 his people with him, the terrible of the n, 1471
 30:23 I will scatter the Egyptians among the n, 1471
 30:26 I will scatter the Egyptians among the n, 1471
 31: 6 and under his shadow dwelt all great n. 1471
 31:12 the terrible of the n, have cut him 1471
 31:16 I made the n to shake at the sound of his 1471
 32: 2 Thou art like a young lion of the n, 1471
 32: 9 I shall bring destruction among the n, 1471
 32:12 to fall, the terrible of the n, all of them: 1471
 32:16 the daughters of the n shall lament her: 1471
 32:18 and the daughters of the famous n, 1471
 35:10 These two n and these two countries shall 1471
 36:13 up men, and hast bereaved thy n, 1471
 36:14 neither bereave thy n any more, saith 1471
 36:15 neither shalt thou cause thy n to fall any 1471
 37:22 they shall be no more two n, neither shall 1471
 38: 8 it is brought forth out of the n, 5971
 38:12 the people *that are* gathered out of the n, 1471
 38:23 I will be known in the eyes of many n, 1471
 39:27 sanctified in them in the sight of many n; 1471
Da 3: 4 commanded, O people, n, and languages, 524
 3: 7 the n, and the languages, fell down and 524
 4: 1 all people, n, and languages, that dwell 524
 5:19 n, and languages, trembled and feared 524
 6:25 n, and languages, that dwell in all the 524
 7:14 kingdom, that all people, n, and languages, 524
Hos 8:10 Yea, though they have hired among the n, 1471
 9:17 and they shall be wanderers among the n. 1471
Joel 3: 2 I will also gather all n, and will bring 1471
 3: 2 whom they have scattered among the n, 1471
Am 6: 1 Samaria, *which are* named chief of the n, 1471
 9: 9 I will sift the house of Israel among all n, 1471
Mic 4: 2 many n shall come, and say, Come, 1471
 4: 3 many people, and rebuke strong n afar off; 1471
 4:11 also many n are gathered against thee, 1471
 7:16 The n shall see and be confounded at all 1471
Na 3: 4 that selleth n through her whoredoms, 1471
 3: 5 I will shew the n thy nakedness, 1471
Hab 1:17 and not spare continually to slay the n? 1471
 2: 5 gathereth unto him all n, and heapeth 1471
 2: 8 Because thou hast spoiled many n, 1471
 3: 6 he beheld, and drove asunder the n; 1471
Zep 2:14 in the midst of her, all the beasts of the n: 1471
 3: 6 I have cut off *the* n: their towers are 1471
 3: 8 for my determination *is* to gather the n, 1471
Hag 2: 7 I will shake all n, and the desire of all 1471
 2: 7 and the desire of all n shall come: 1471
Zec 2: 8 After the glory hath he sent me unto the n 1471
 2:11 many n shall be joined to the LORD in 1471
 7:14 among all the n whom they knew not: 1471
 8:22 strong n shall come to seek the LORD of 1471
 8:23 take hold out of all languages of the n, 1471
 12: 9 *that* I will seek to destroy all the n that 1471
 14: 2 For I will gather all n against Jerusalem to 1471
 14: 3 LORD go forth, and fight against those n, 1471
 14:19 every one that is left of all the n which 1471
Mal 3:12 all n shall call you blessed: for ye shall be 1471
Mt 24: 9 ye shall be hated of all n for my name's *1484*
 24:14 in all the world for a witness unto all n; *1484*
 25:32 And before him shall be gathered all n: *1484*
 28:19 Go ye therefore, and teach all n, *1484*
Mk 11:17 My house shall be called of all n the *1484*
 13:10 gospel must first be published among all n. *1484*
Lk 12:30 For all these *things* do the n of the world *1484*
 21:24 and shall be led away captive into all n: *1484*
 21:25 and upon the earth distress of n, *1484*
 24:47 be preached in his name among all n, *1484*
Ac 13:19 And when he had destroyed seven n in *1484*
 14:16 Who in times past suffered all n to walk in *1484*

Ac	17:26 And hath made of one blood all **n** of men	1484
Ro	1: 5 for obedience to the faith among all **n**,	1484
	4:17 I have made thee a father of many **n**,)	1484
	4:18 he might become the father of many **n**;	1484
	16:26 made known to all **n** for the obedience of	1484
Gal	3: 8 *saying*, In thee shall all **n** be blessed.	1484
Rev	2:26 to him will I give power over the **n**:	1484
	7: 9 of all **n**, and kindreds, and people,	1484
	10:11 and **n**, and tongues, and kings.	1484
	11: 9 **n** shall see their dead bodies three days	1484
	11:18 And the **n** were angry, and thy wrath is	1484
	12: 5 who was to rule all **n** with a rod of iron:	1484
	13: 7 him over all kindreds, and tongues, and **n**.	1484
	14: 8 she made all **n** drink of the wine of	1484
	15: 4 for all **n** shall come and worship before	1484
	16:19 into three parts, and the cities of the **n** fell:	1484
	17:15 and multitudes, and **n**, and tongues.	1484
	18: 3 For all **n** have drunk of the wine of	1484
	18:23 for by thy sorceries were all **n** deceived.	1484
	19:15 that with it he should smite the **n**:	1484
	20: 3 that he should deceive the **n** no more,	1484
	20: 8 And shall go out to deceive the **n** which	1484
	21:24 And the **n** of them which are saved shall	1484
	21:26 bring the glory and honour of the **n** into it.	1484
	22: 2 of the tree *were* for the healing of the **n**.	1484

NATIVE (1)

Jer	22:10 return no more, nor see his **n** country.	4138

NATIVITY (7)

Ge	11:28 his father Terah in the land of his **n**,	4138
Ru	2:11 the land of thy **n**, and art come unto a	4138
Jer	46:16 to the land of our **n**, from the oppressing	4138
Eze	16: 3 and thy **n** *is* of the land of Canaan;	4138
	16: 4 *as for* thy **n**, in the day thou wast born	4138
	21:30 thou wast created, in the land of thy **n**.	4351
	23:15 of Chaldea, the land of their **n**:	4138

NATURAL (13) [NATURE]

Dt	34: 7 eye was not dim, nor his **n** force abated.	3893
Ro	1:26 even their women did change the **n** use	5446
	1:27 the men, leaving the **n** use of the woman,	5446
	1:31 **without n affection**, implacable,	794
	11:21 if God spared not the **n** branches,	2596+5449
	11:24 which be the **n** *branches*, be graffed	2596+5449
1Co	2:14 But the **n** man receiveth not the *things* of	5591
	15:44 It is sown a **n** body; it is raised a spiritual	5591
	15:44 There is a **n** body, and there is a spiritual	5591
	15:46 first *which is* spiritual, but *that which is* **n**;	5591
2Ti	3: 3 **Without n affection**, trucebreakers,	794
Jas	1:23 he is like unto a man beholding his **n** face	1078
2Pe	2:12 But these, as **n** brute beasts, made to be	5446

NATURALLY (2) [NATURE]

Php	2:20 who will **n** care for your state.	1104
Jude	1:10 but what they know **n**, as brute beasts,	5447

NATURE (12) [NATURAL, NATURALLY]

Ro	1:26 natural use into that which is against **n**;	5449
	2:14 do by **n** the *things* contained in the law,	5449
	2:27 shall not uncircumcision which is by **n**,	5449
	11:24 out of the olive tree which is wild by **n**,	5449
	11:24 graffed contrary to **n** into a good olive	5449
1Co	11:14 Doth not even **n** itself teach you, that, if a	5449
Gal	2:15 We *who are* Jews by **n**, and not sinners of	5449
	4: 8 ye did service unto them which by **n** are	5449
Eph	2: 3 and were by **n** the children of wrath,	5449
Heb	2:16 For verily he took not on *him* the **n** of	NIG
Jas	3: 6 and setteth on fire the course of **n**,	1078
2Pe	1: 4 you might be partakers of the divine **n**,	5449

NAUGHT (3) [NOUGHT]

2Ki	2:19 the water *is* **n**, and the ground barren;	7451
Pr	20:14 *It is* **n**, *it is* naught, saith the buyer:	7451
	20:14 *it is* naught, *it is* **n**, saith the buyer:	7451

NAUGHTINESS (3) [NAUGHTY]

1Sa	17:28 know thy pride, and the **n** of thine heart;	7455
Pr	11: 6 shall be taken in their own **n**.	1942
Jas	1:21 lay apart all filthiness and superfluity of **n**,	2549

NAUGHTY (3) [NAUGHTINESS]

Pr	6:12 A **n** person, a wicked man, walketh *with*	1100
	17: 4 *and* a liar giveth ear to a **n** tongue.	1942
Jer	24: 2 the other basket *had* very **n** figs,	7451

NAUM (1)

Lk	3:25 was *the son* of **N**, which was *the son*	3486

NAVEL (4)

Job	40:16 and his force *is* in the **n** of his belly.	8306
Pr	3: 8 It shall be health to thy **n**, and marrow to	8270
SS	7: 2 Thy **n** *is* like a round goblet, which	8326
Eze	16: 4 the day thou wast born thy **n** was not cut,	8270

NAVES (1)

1Ki	7:33 their **n**, and their felloes, and their spokes,	1354

NAVY (6)

1Ki	9:26 king Solomon made a **n** *of ships* in	590
	9:27 Hiram sent in the **n** his servants,	590
	10:11 the **n** also of Hiram, that brought gold from	590
	10:22 the king had at sea a **n** of Tharshish with	590
	10:22 a navy of Tharshish with the **n** of Hiram:	590
	10:22 in three years came the **n** of Tharshish,	590

NAY (55)

Ge	18:15 And he said, **N**; but thou didst laugh.	3808
	19: 2 said, **N**; but we will abide in the street	3808
	23:11 **N**, my lord, hear me: the field give I thee,	3808
	33:10 Jacob said, **N**, I pray thee, if now I have	408
	42:10 **N**, my lord, but to buy food are thy	3808
	42:12 **N**, but to see the nakedness of the land	3808
Nu	22:30 wont to do so unto thee? And he said, **N**.	3808
Jos	5:14 he said, **N**; but *as* captain of the host of	3808
	24:21 the people said unto Joshua, **N**; but we	3808
Jdg	12: 5 *Art* thou an Ephraimite? If he said, **N**;	3808
	19:23 said unto them, **N**, my brethren, *nay*,	408
	19:23 **n**, I pray you, do not *so* wickedly;	NIH
Ru	1:13 **N**, my daughters; for it grieveth me much	408
1Sa	2:16 **N**; but thou shalt give *it* me now:	NIH
	2:24 **N**, my sons; for *it is* no good report that I	3808
	8:19 **N**; but we will have a king over us;	3808
	10:19 said unto him, **N**, but set a king over us;	NIH
	12:12 came against you, ye said unto me, **N**;	3808
2Sa	13:12 **N**, my brother, do not force me;	408
	13:25 **N**, my son, let us not all now go,	408
	16:18 Hushai said unto Absalom, **N**;	3808
	24:24 the king said unto Araunah, **N**; but I will	3808
1Ki	2:17 king, (for he will not **say** thee **n**,)	6440+7725
	2:20 of thee, I *pray thee*, **say** thee not **n**.	6440+7725
	2:20 mother: for I will not **say** thee **n**.	6440+7725
	2:30 he said, **N**; but I will die here.	3808
	3:22 the other woman said, **N**; but the living *is*	3808
	3:23 the other saith, **N**; but thy son *is* the dead,	3808
2Ki	3:13 the king of Israel said unto him, **N**:	408
	4:16 she said, **N**, my lord, thou man of God,	408
	4:18 but let the shadow return backward	3808
1Ch	21:24 king David said to Ornan, **N**; but I will	3808
Jer	6:15 **n**, they were not at all ashamed, neither	1571
	8:12 **n**, they were not at all ashamed, neither	1571
Mt	5:37 your communication be, Yea, yea; **N**, nay:	3756
	5:37 your communication be, Yea, yea; Nay, **n**:	3756
	13:29 But he said, **N**; lest while ye gather up	3756
Lk	12:51 on earth? I tell you, **N**; but rather division:	3780
	13: 3 I tell you, **N**: but, except ye repent, ye	3780
	13: 5 I tell you, **N**: but except ye repent, ye	3780
	16:30 he said, **N**, father Abraham: but if one	3780
Jn	7:12 He is a good *man*: others said, **N**;	3756
Ac	16:37 **n** verily; but let them come themselves	3780
Ro	3:27 of works? **N**: but by the law of faith.	3780
	7: 7 **N**, I had not known sin, but by the law:	235
	8:37 **N**, in all these *things* we are more than	235
	9:20 **N** but, O man, who art thou that repliest	3304
1Co	6: 8 **N**, you do wrong, and defraud, and that	235
	12:22 **N**, much more those members of the	235
2Co	1:17 me there should be yea yea, and **n** nay?	3756
	1:17 me there should be yea yea, and nay **n**?	3756
	1:18 our word toward you was not yea and **n**.	3756
	1:19 was not yea and **n**, but in him was yea.	3756
Jas	5:12 but let your yea be yea; and *your* **n**, nay;	3756
	5:12 but let your yea be yea; and *your* nay, **n**;	3756

NAZARENE (1) [NAZARETH]

Mt	2:23 by the prophets, He shall be called a **N**.	3480

NAZARENES (1) [NAZARETH]

Ac	24: 5 and a ringleader of the sect of the **N**:	3480

NAZARETH (29) [NAZARENE, NAZARENES]

Mt	2:23 And he came and dwelt in a city called **N**:	3478
	4:13 And leaving **N**, he came and dwelt in	3478
	21:11 This is Jesus the prophet of **N** of Galilee.	3478
	26:71 This *fellow* was also with Jesus of **N**.	3480
Mk	1: 9 *that* Jesus came from **N** of Galilee,	3478
	1:24 have we to do with thee, *thou* Jesus of **N**?	3479
	10:47 when he heard that it was Jesus **of N**,	3480
	14:67 said, *And* thou also wast with Jesus of **N**.	3479
	16: 6 Ye seek Jesus of **N**, which was crucified:	3479
Lk	1:26 God unto a city of Galilee, named **N**,	3478
	2: 4 out of the city of **N**, into Judea, unto	3478
	2:39 returned into Galilee, to their own city **N**.	3478
	2:51 came to **N**, and was subject unto them	3478
	4:16 And he came to **N**, where he had been	3478
	4:34 have we to do with thee, *thou* Jesus of **N**?	3479
	18:37 they told him, that Jesus **of N** passeth by.	3480
	24:19 Concerning Jesus of **N**, which was a	3480
Jn	1:45 and the prophets, did write, Jesus of **N**,	3478
	1:46 Can there any good *thing* come out of **N**?	3478
	18: 5 They answered him, Jesus of **N**. Jesus	3480
	18: 7 Whom seek ye? And they said, Jesus of **N**.	3480
	19:19 JESUS **OF N** THE KING OF THE JEWS.	3480
Ac	2:22 Jesus of **N**, a man approved of God	3478
	3: 6 In the name of Jesus Christ **of N** rise up	3480
	4:10 that by the name of Jesus Christ **of N**,	3480
	6:14 this Jesus **of N** shall destroy this place,	3478
	10:38 How God anointed Jesus **of N** with	3478
	22: 8 And he said unto me, I am Jesus of **N**,	3480
	26: 9 *things* contrary to the name of Jesus of **N**.	3480

NAZARITE (9) [NAZARITES]

Nu	6: 2 separate *themselves* to vow a vow of a **N**,	5139
	6:13 this *is* the law of the **N**, when the days of	5139
	6:18 **N** shall shave the head of his separation	5139
	6:19 shall put *them* upon the hands of the **N**,	5139
	6:20 and after that the **N** may drink wine.	5139
	6:21 This *is* the law of the **N** who hath vowed,	5139
Jdg	13: 5 for the child shall be a **N** unto God from	5139
	13: 7 **N** to God from the womb to the day of	5139
	16:17 for I *have* been a **N** unto God from my	5139

NAZARITES (3) [NAZARITE]

La	4: 7 Her **N** were purer than snow, they were	5139
Am	2:11 prophets, and of your young men for **N**.	5139
	2:12 ye gave the **N** wine to drink;	5139

NAZIRITE See NAZARITE

NEAH (1)

Jos	19:13 and goeth out to Remmon-methoar to **N**;	5269

NEAPOLIS (1)

Ac	16:11 to Samothracia, and the next *day* to **N**;	3496

NEAR (211) [NEARER]

Ge	12:11 when he was **come n** to enter into Egypt,	7126
	18:23 Abraham **drew n**, and said, Wilt thou	5066
	19: 9 *even* Lot, and **came n** to break the door.	5066
	19:20 this city *is* **n** to flee unto, and it *is* a little	7138
	20: 4 Abimelech had not **come n** her:	7126
	27:21 Come **n**, I pray thee, that I may feel thee,	5066
	27:22 Jacob **went n** unto Isaac his father;	5066
	27:25 **Bring** *it* **n** to me, and I will eat of my	5066
	27:25 he **brought** *it* **n** to him, and he did eat:	5066
	27:26 **Come n** now, and kiss me, my son.	5066
	27:27 he **came n**, and kissed him: and he	5066
	29:10 that Jacob **went n**, and rolled the stone	5066
	33: 3 times, until he **came n** to his brother.	5066
	33: 6 the handmaidens **came n**, they and	5066
	33: 7 Leah also with her children **came n**,	5066
	33: 7 after **came** Joseph **n** and Rachel,	5066
	37:18 off, even before he **came n** unto them,	7126
	43:19 they **came n** to the steward of Joseph's	5066
	44:18 Judah **came n** unto him, and said, O my	5066
	45: 4 his brethren, **Come n** to me, I pray you.	5066
	45: 4 they **came n**. And he said, I *am* Joseph	5066
	45:10 thou shalt be **n** unto me, thou,	7138
	48:10 he **brought** them **n** unto him; and he	5066
	48:13 hand, and **brought** *them* **n** unto him.	5066
Ex	12:48 and then let him **come n** and keep it;	7126
	13:17 of the Philistines, although that *was* **n**;	7138
	14:10 that the one **came n**t the other all	7126
	16: 9 of Israel, **Come n** before the LORD:	7126
	19:22 which **come n** to the LORD,	5066
	20:21 Moses **drew n** unto the thick darkness	5066
	24: 2 Moses alone shall **come n** the LORD:	5066
	28:43 they **come n** unto the altar to minister	5066
	30:20 they **come n** to the altar to minister,	5066
	40:32 when they **came n** unto the altar,	7126
Lev	9: 5 all the congregation **drew n** and	7126
	10: 4 of Aaron, and said unto them, **Come n**,	7126
	10: 5 So they **went n**, and carried them in their	5066
	18: 6 of you shall approach to any that is **n**	7607
	18:12 she *is* thy father's **n kinswoman**.	7607
	18:13 for she *is* thy mother's **n kinswoman**.	7607
	18:17 *for* they *are* her **n kinswomen**.	7608
	20:19 he uncovereth his **n kin**: they shall bear	7607
	21: 2 for his kin, that is **n** unto him, *that is*, for	7138
Nu	3: 6 **Bring** the tribe of Levi **n**, and present	7126
	5:16 the priest shall **bring** her **n**, and set her	7126
	16: 5 and will **cause** *him* to **come n** unto him:	7126
	16: 5 will he **cause** to **come n** unto him.	7126
	16: 9 to **bring** you **n** to himself to do the	7126
	16:10 he hath **brought** thee **n** to *him*, and all	7126
	16:40 **come n** to offer incense before the LORD;	7126
	17:13 Whosoever **cometh** any thing **n**	7131+7131
	26: 3 in the plains of Moab by Jordan *n* Jericho,	NIH
	26:63 in the plains of Moab by Jordan *n* Jericho.	NIH
	31:12 of Moab, which *are* by Jordan *n* Jericho.	NIH
	31:48 of hundreds, **came n** unto Moses:	7126
	32:16 they **came n** unto him, and said, We will	5066
	33:48 pitched in the plains of Moab by Jordan *n*	NIH
	33:50 in the plains of Moab by Jordan *n* Jericho,	NIH
	34:15 on *this* side Jordan *n* Jericho eastward,	NIH
	35: 1 in the plains of Moab by Jordan *n* Jericho,	NIH
	36: 1 **came n**, and spake before Moses,	7126
	36:13 in the plains of Moab by Jordan *n* Jericho.	NIH
Dt	1:22 ye **came n** unto me every one of you,	7126
	4:11 ye **came n** and stood under the mountain;	7126
	5:23 ye **came n** unto me, *even* all the heads	7126
	5:27 **Go** thou **n**, and hear all that the LORD our	7126
	16:21 **n** unto the altar of the LORD thy God,	681
	21: 5 the priests the sons of Levi shall **come n**;	5066
	25:11 wife of the one **draweth n** for to deliver	7126
Jos	3: 4 **come** not **n** unto it, that ye may know	7126
	10:24 **Come n**, put your feet upon the necks of	7126
	10:24 they **came n**, and put their feet upon	7126
	15:46 *lay* **n** Ashdod, and their villages;	3027+5921
	17: 4 they **came n** before Eleazar the priest,	7126
	18:13 in the hill that *lieth* on the south side of	5921
	21: 1 **came n** the heads of the fathers of	5066
Jdg	18:22 the men that *were* in the houses **n** to	5973
	19:13 let us **draw n** to one of *these* places to	7126
	20:24 the children of Israel **came n** against	7126
	20:34 but they knew not that evil *was* **n** them.	5060
Ru	2:20 The man *is* **n** of kin unto us, one of our	7138
	3: 9 handmaid; for thou *art* a **kinsman**.	1350
	3:12 now it is true that I *am* thy **n** kinsman:	1350
1Sa	4:19 was with child, **n** to be delivered:	NIH
	7:10 the Philistines **drew n** to battle against	5066
	9:18 Saul **drew n** to Samuel in the gate,	5066
	10:20 **caused** all the tribes of Israel to **come n**,	7126
	10:21 **caused** the tribe of Benjamin to **come n**	7126
	14:36 priest, Let us **draw n** hither unto God.	7126
	14:38 Saul said, **Draw** ye **n** hither, all the chief	5066
	17:16 Philistine **drew n** morning and evening,	5066

N

1Sa	17:40	his hand: and he **drew n** to the Philistine.	5066
	17:41	came on and **drew n** unto David;	7131
	30:21	when David **came n** to the people,	5066
2Sa	1:15	and said, **Go n**, *and* fall upon him.	5066
	14:30	Joab's field *is* n mine, and he hath	413+3027
	18:25	And he came apace, and **drew n.**	7131
	19:42	Israel, Because the king *is* n **of kin** to us:	7138
	20:16	I pray you, unto Joab, **Come n** hither,	7126
	20:17	he was **come n** unto her, the woman	7126
1Ki	8:46	unto the land of the enemy, far or n;	7138
	18:30	unto all the people, **Come n** unto me.	5066
	18:30	all the people **came n** unto him. And he	5066
	18:36	that Elijah the prophet **came n**, and said,	5066
	21: 2	of herbs, because it *is* n unto my house,	7138
	22:24	Zedekiah the son of Chenaanah **went n**,	5066
2Ki	4:27	Gehazi **came n** to thrust her away.	5066
	5:13	his servants **came n**, and spake unto him,	5066
2Ch	6:36	away captives unto a land far off or n;	7138
	18:23	Zedekiah the son of Chenaanah **came n**,	5066
	21:16	that *were* n the Ethiopians	3027+5921
	29:31	**come n** and bring sacrifices and	5066
Est	5: 2	So Esther **drew n**, and touched the top of	7126
	9: 1	his decree **drew n** to be put in execution,	5060
Job	31:37	as a prince would I **go n** unto him.	7126
	33:22	his soul **draweth n** unto the grave,	7126
	41:16	One is so n to another, that no air can	5066
Ps	22:11	Be not far from me; for trouble *is* n;	7138
	32: 9	and bridle, lest *they* **come n** unto thee.	7126
	73:28	*it is* good for me to **draw n** to God: I have	7132
	75: 1	*that* thy name *is* n thy wondrous works	7138
	107:18	and they **draw n** unto the gates of death.	5060
	119:151	Thou *art* n, O Lord; and all thy	7138
	119:169	Let my cry **come n** before thee, O Lord:	7126
	148:14	children of Israel, a people n unto him.	7138
Pr	7: 8	Passing through the street n her corner;	681
	10:14	the mouth of the foolish *is* n destruction.	7138
	27:10	*for* better *is* a neighbour *that is* n than a	7138
Isa	13:22	her time *is* n to come, and her days shall	7138
	26:17	*that* **draweth n the time** of her delivery,	7126
	29:13	Forasmuch as this people **draw n** *me* with	5066
	33:13	and ye *that are* n, acknowledge my might.	7138
	34: 1	**Come n**, ye nations, to hear; and hearken,	7126
	41: 1	let them **come n**; then let them speak:	5066
	41: 1	let us **come n** together to judgment.	7126
	41: 5	the earth were afraid, **drew n**, and came.	5066
	45:20	**draw n** together, ye *that are* escaped of	5066
	45:21	Tell ye, and **bring** *them* n; yea, let them	5066
	46:13	I **bring n** my righteousness; it shall not be	7126
	48:16	**Come ye** n unto me, hear ye this; I have	7126
	50: 8	*is* n that justifieth; who will contend	7138
	50: 8	*is* mine adversary? let him **come n** to me.	7126
	51: 5	righteousness *is* n; my salvation is gone	7138
	54:14	from terror; for it shall not **come n** thee.	7126
	55: 6	be found, call ye upon him while he is n:	7138
	56: 1	for my salvation *is* n to come,	7138
	57: 3	**draw n** hither, ye sons of the sorceress,	7126
	57:19	and to *him that is* n, saith the Lord;	7138
	65: 5	Stand by thyself, **come** not n to me;	5066
Jer	12: 2	thou *art* n in their mouth, and far from	7138
	25:26	far and n, one with another, and all	7138
	30:21	I will **cause** him to **draw n**, and he shall	5066
	42: 1	the least even **unto** the greatest, came n,	5704
	46: 3	and shield, and **draw n** to battle.	5066
	48:16	The calamity of Moab *is* n to come,	7138
	48:24	all the cities of the land of Moab, far or n.	7138
	52:25	seven men of them that were n the king's	7200
La	3:57	Thou **drewest n** in the day *that* I called	7126
	4:18	our end is n, our days are fulfilled; for our	7126
Eze	6:12	*he* that *is* n shall fall by the sword;	7138
	7: 7	the day of trouble *is* n, and not	7138
	7:12	The time is come, the day **draweth n:**	5060
	9: 1	**Cause** them that have charge over the city **to draw n,**	7126
	9: 6	**come** not n any man upon whom *is*	5066
	11: 3	Which say, *It is* not n; *let us* build	7138+871.1
	18: 6	neither hath **come n** to a menstruous	7126
	22: 4	thou hast **caused** thy days to **draw n,**	7126
	22: 5	*Those* that be n, and *those that* be far	7138
	30: 3	For the day *is* n, even the day of	7138
	30: 3	even the day of the Lord *is* n, a cloudy	7138
	40:46	which **come n** to the Lord to minister	7131
	44:13	they shall not **come n** unto me, to do	5066
	44:13	nor to **come n** to any of my holy *things,*	5066
	44:15	they shall **come n** to me to minister unto	7126
	44:16	they shall **come n** to my table, to minister	7126
	45: 4	which shall **come n** to minister unto	7131
Da	3: 8	at that time certain Chaldeans **came n,**	7127
	3:26	Nebuchadnezzar **came n** to the mouth of	7127
	6:12	they **came n**, and spake before the king	7127
	7:13	and they **brought** him n before him.	7127
	7:16	I **came n** unto one of them that stood *by,*	7127
	8:17	So he came n where I stood: and when he	681
	9: 7	all Israel, *that are* n, and *that are* far off,	7138
Joel	3: 9	**men**, let all the men of war **draw n;**	5066
	3:14	for the day of the Lord *is* n in the valley	7138
Am	6: 3	**cause** the seat of violence to **come n;**	5066
Ob	1:15	For the day of the Lord *is* n upon all	7138
Zep	1:14	The great day of the Lord *is* n, *it is* near,	7138
	1:14	Lord *is* near, *it is* n, and hasteth greatly,	7138
	3: 2	in the Lord; she **drew** not n to her God.	7126
Mal	3: 5	and I will **come n** to you to judgment;	7126
Mt	21:34	And when the time of the fruit **drew n,**	1448
	24:33	see all these *things,* know that it is n,	1451
Mk	13:28	forth leaves, ye know that summer is n:	1451
Lk	15: 1	Then **drew n** unto him all the publicans	1448

Lk	18:40	and when he was **come n**, he asked him,	1448
	19:41	And when he was **come n**, he beheld	1448
	21: 8	I am *Christ;* and the time **draweth n:**	1448
	22:47	and **drew n** unto Jesus to kiss him.	1448
	24:15	Jesus himself **drew n**, and went with	1448
Jn	3:23	John also was baptizing in Aenon n to	1451
	4: 5	n to the parcel of ground *that* Jacob gave	4139
	11:54	went thence unto a country n to	1451
Ac	7:31	as he **drew n** to behold *it,* the voice of	4334
	8:29	**Go n**, and join thyself to this chariot.	4334
	9: 3	as *he* journeyed, he **came n** Damascus:	1448
	10:24	called together his kinsmen and n friends.	316
	21:33	Then the chief captain **came n,**	1448
	23:15	we, or ever he **come n**, are ready to kill	1448
	27:27	that they **drew n** to some country;	4317
Heb	10:22	Let us **draw n** with a true heart in full	4334

NEARER (2) [NEAR]

Ru	3:12	howbeit there is a kinsman n than I.	7138
Ro	13:11	for now *is* our salvation n than when we	1452

NEARIAH (3)

1Ch	3:22	and Bariah, and N, and Shaphat, six.	5294
	3:23	and the sons of N; Elioenai, and Hezekiah,	5294
	4:42	N, and Rephaiah, and Uzziel, the sons of	5294

NEBAI (1)

Ne	10:19	Hariph, Anathoth, N,	5109

NEBAIOTH See NEBAJOTH

NEBAJOTH (5)

Ge	25:13	the firstborn of Ishmael, N; and Kedar,	5032
	28: 9	the sister of N, to be his wife.	5032
	36: 3	Ishmael's daughter, sister of N.	5032
1Ch	1:29	The firstborn of Ishmael, N; then Kedar,	5032
Isa	60: 7	the rams of N shall minister unto thee:	5032

NEBALLAT (1)

Ne	11:34	Hadid, Zeboim, N,	5041

NEBAT (25)

1Ki	11:26	Jeroboam the son of N, an Ephrathite of	5028
	12: 2	to pass, when Jeroboam the son of N,	5028
	12:15	Shilonite unto Jeroboam the son of N.	5028
	15: 1	the son of N reigned Abijam over Judah.	5028
	16: 3	like the house of Jeroboam the son of N.	5028
	16:26	in all the way of Jeroboam the son of N,	5028
	16:31	in the sins of Jeroboam the son of N,	5028
	21:22	like the house of Jeroboam the son of N,	5028
	22:52	in the way of Jeroboam the son of N,	5028
2Ki	3: 3	unto the sins of Jeroboam the son of N,	5028
	9: 9	like the house of Jeroboam the son of N,	5028
	10:29	*from* the sins of Jeroboam the son of N,	5028
	13: 2	the sins of Jeroboam the son of N,	5028
	13:11	all the sins of Jeroboam the son of N,	5028
	14:24	all the sins of Jeroboam the son of N,	5028
	15: 9	from the sins of Jeroboam the son of N,	5028
	15:18	from the sins of Jeroboam the son of N,	5028
	15:24	from the sins of Jeroboam the son of N,	5028
	15:28	from the sins of Jeroboam the son of N,	5028
	17:21	they made Jeroboam the son of N king:	5028
	23:15	high place which Jeroboam the son of N,	5028
2Ch	9:29	the seer against Jeroboam the son of N?	5028
	10: 2	when Jeroboam the son of N, who *was* in	5028
	10:15	the Shilonite to Jeroboam the son of N,	5028
	13: 6	Yet Jeroboam the son of N, the servant of	5028

NEBO (13)

Nu	32: 3	Elealeh, and Shebam, and N, and Beon,	5015
	32:38	N, and Baal-meon, (*their* names being	5015
	33:47	in the mountains of Abarim, before N.	5015
Dt	32:49	*unto* mount N, which *is* in the land of	5015
	34: 1	plains of Moab unto the mountain of N,	5015
1Ch	5: 8	in Aroer, even unto N and Baal-meon:	5015
Ezr	2:29	The children of N, fifty and two.	5015
	10:43	Of the sons of N; Jeiel, Mattithiah, Zabad,	5015
Ne	7:33	The men of the other N, fifty and two.	5015
Isa	15: 2	shall howl over N, and over Medeba:	5015
	46: 1	Bel boweth down, N stoopeth, their idols	5015
Jer	48: 1	of hosts, the God of Israel; Woe unto N!	5015
	48:22	and upon N, and upon Beth-diblathaim,	5015

NEBO-SARSEKIM See SARSECHIM

NEBUCHADNEZZAR (60) [NEBUCHADREZZAR]

2Ki	24: 1	In his days N king of Babylon came up,	5019
	24:10	At that time the servants of N king of	5019
	24:11	N king of Babylon came against the city,	5019
	25: 1	*that* N king of Babylon came, he,	5019
	25: 8	*is* the nineteenth year of king N king	5019
	25:22	whom N king of Babylon had left,	5019
1Ch	6:15	and Jerusalem by the hand of N.	5019
2Ch	36: 6	Against him came up N king of Babylon,	5019
	36: 7	N also carried of the vessels of the house	5019
	36:10	king N sent, and brought him to Babylon,	5019
	36:13	he also rebelled against king N, who had	5019
Ezr	1: 7	which N had brought forth out of	5019
	2: 1	whom N the king of Babylon had carried	5019
	5:12	he gave them into the hand of N the king	5020
	5:14	which N took out of the temple that *was*	5020
	6: 5	which N took forth out of the temple	5020
Ne	7: 6	whom N the king of Babylon had carried	5019
Est	2: 6	whom N the king of Babylon had carried	5019
Jer	27: 6	into the hand of N the king of Babylon,	5019
	27: 8	which will not serve the same N	5019

Jer	27:20	Which N king of Babylon took not,	5019
	28: 3	that N king of Babylon took away from	5019
	28:11	will I break the yoke of N king of Babylon	5019
	28:14	that *they* may serve N king of Babylon;	5019
	29: 1	all the people whom N had carried away	5019
	29: 3	sent unto Babylon to N king of Babylon,	5019
	34: 1	when N king of Babylon, and all his army,	5019
	39: 5	they brought him up to N king of Babylon	5019
Da	1: 1	came N king of Babylon *unto* Jerusalem,	5019
	1:18	of the eunuchs brought them in before N.	5019
	2: 1	in the second year of the reign of N,	5019
	2: 1	N dreamed dreams, wherewith his spirit	5019
	2:28	maketh known to the king N what shall	5020
	2:46	the king N fell upon his face,	5020
	3: 1	N the king made an image of gold,	5020
	3: 2	N the king sent to gather together	5020
	3: 2	of the image which N the king had set up.	5020
	3: 3	of the image that N the king had set up	5020
	3: 3	they stood before the image that N had set	5020
	3: 5	worship the golden image that N the king	5020
	3: 7	worshipped the golden image that N	5020
	3: 9	spake and said to the king N, O king,	5020
	3:13	N in *his* rage and fury commanded to	5020
	3:14	N spake and said unto them, *Is it* true,	5020
	3:16	answered and said to the king, O N,	5020
	3:19	was N full *of* fury, and the form of his	5020
	3:24	N the king was astonied, and rose up in	5020
	3:26	N came near to the mouth of the burning	5020
	3:28	*Then* N spake, and said, Blessed *be*	5020
	4: 1	N the king, unto all people, nations,	5020
	4: 4	I N was at rest in mine house,	5020
	4:18	This dream I king N have seen.	5020
	4:28	All this came upon the king N.	5020
	4:31	*saying,* O king N, to thee it is spoken;	5020
	4:33	same hour was the thing fulfilled upon N:	5020
	4:34	the end of the days I N lift up mine eyes	5020
	4:37	Now I N praise and extol and honour	5020
	5: 2	silver vessels which his father N had taken	5020
	5:11	whom the king N thy father, the king,	5020
	5:18	the most high God gave N thy father a	5020

NEBUCHADREZZAR (31) [NEBUCHADNEZZAR]

Jer	21: 2	for N king of Babylon maketh war against	5019
	21: 7	into the hand of N king of Babylon,	5019
	22:25	even into the hand of N king of Babylon,	5019
	24: 1	after that N king of Babylon had carried	5019
	25: 1	that *was* the first year of N king of	5019
	25: 9	and N the king of Babylon, my servant,	5019
	29:21	will deliver them into the hand of N king	5019
	32: 1	which *was* the eighteenth year of N.	5019
	32:28	into the hand of N king of Babylon,	5019
	35:11	when N king of Babylon came up into	5019
	37: 1	whom N king of Babylon made king in	5019
	39: 1	came N king of Babylon and all his army	5019
	39:11	Now N king of Babylon gave charge	5019
	43:10	*will* send and take N the king of Babylon,	5019
	44:30	Judah into the hand of N king of Babylon,	5019
	46: 2	which N king of Babylon smote in	5019
	46:13	how N king of Babylon should come	5019
	46:26	into the hand of N king of Babylon,	5019
	49:28	which N king of Babylon shall smite,	5019
	49:30	for N king of Babylon hath taken counsel	5019
	50:17	last this N king of Babylon hath broken	5019
	51:34	The king of Babylon hath devoured me,	5019
	52: 4	*that* N king of Babylon came, he and all	5019
	52:12	which *was* the nineteenth year of N king	5019
	52:28	This *is* the people whom N carried away	5019
	52:29	In the eighteenth year of N he carried	5019
	52:30	twentieth year of N Nebuzar-adan	5019
Eze	26: 7	I *will* bring upon Tyrus N king of Babylon,	5019
	29:18	king of Babylon caused his army to	5019
	29:19	I will give the land of Egypt unto N king	5019
	30:10	cease by the hand of N king of Babylon.	5019

NEBUSHASBAN (1)

Jer	39:13	N, Rab-saris, and Nergal-sharezer,	5021

NEBUSHAZBAN See NEBUSHASBAN

NEBUZAR-ADAN (15)

2Ki	25: 8	came N, captain of the guard, a servant of	5018
	25:11	did N the captain of the guard carry away.	5018
	25:20	N captain of the guard took these,	5018
Jer	39: 9	N the captain of the guard carried away	5018
	39:10	N the captain of the guard left of the poor	5018
	39:11	Jeremiah to N the captain of the guard,	5018
	39:13	So N the captain of the guard sent,	5018
	40: 1	after that N the captain of the guard had	5018
	41:10	whom N the captain of the guard had	5018
	43: 6	person that N the captain of the guard	5018
	52:12	N, captain of the guard, *which* served	5018
	52:15	N the captain of the guard carried away	5018
	52:16	N the captain of the guard left *certain* of	5018
	52:26	So N the captain of the guard took them,	5018
	52:30	twentieth year of Nebuchadrezzar N	5018

NECESSARY (9) [NECESSITY]

Job	23:12	words of his mouth more than my n *food.*	2706
Ac	13:46	It was n that the word of God should first	316
	15:28	no greater burden than these n *things;*	1876
	15:28	they laded *us* with such *things* as were n.	5532
1Co	12:22	which seem to be more feeble, are n:	316
2Co	9: 5	Therefore I thought it n to exhort	316
Php	2:25	Yet I supposed it n to send to you	316
Tit	3:14	learn to maintain good works for n uses,	316

Heb 9:23 **n** that the patterns of *things* in the heavens 318

NECESSITIES (3) [NECESSITY]
Ac 20:34 these hands have ministered unto my **n**, 5532
2Co 6: 4 in afflictions, in **n**, in distresses, 318
 12:10 in reproaches, in **n**, in persecutions, 318

NECESSITY (10) [NECESSARY, NECESSITIES]
Lk 23:17 (For of **n** he must release one unto them at 318
Ro 12:13 Distributing to the **n** of saints; given to 5532
1Co 7:37 having no **n**, but hath power over his own 318
 9:16 for **n** is laid upon me; yea, woe is unto me, 318
2Co 9: 7 *so let him give*; not grudgingly, or of **n**: 318
Php 4:16 ye sent once and again unto my **n**. 5532
Phm 1:14 thy benefit should not be as *it were* of **n**, 318
Heb 7:12 is made of **n** a change also of the law. 318
 8: 3 wherefore *it is* of **n** that this *man* have 316
 9:16 must also of **n** be the death of the testator. 318

NECHO (3)
2Ch 35:20 **N** king of Egypt came up to fight against 5224
 35:22 hearkened not unto the words of **N** from 5224
 36: 4 **N** took Jehoahaz his brother, 5224

NECK (62) [NECKS, STIFFNECKED]
Ge 27:16 his hands, and upon the smooth of his **n**: 6677
 27:40 thou shalt break his yoke from off thy **n**. 6677
 33: 4 and fell on his **n**, and kissed him: 6677
 41:42 linen, and put a gold chain about his **n**; 6677
 45:14 he fell upon his brother Benjamin's **n**, 6677
 45:14 wept; and Benjamin wept upon his **n**. 6677
 46:29 he fell on his **n**, and wept on his neck a 6677
 46:29 his neck, and wept on his **n** a good while. 6677
 49: 8 hand *shall be* in the **n** of thine enemies; 6203
Ex 13:13 redeem *it*, then thou shalt **break** his **n** 6202
 34:20 him not, then shalt thou **break** his **n**. 6202
Lev 5: 8 wring off his head from his **n**, but shall 6203
Dt 21: 4 shall **strike off** the heifer's **n** there in 6202
 28:48 he shall put a yoke of iron upon thy **n**, 6677
 31:27 For I know thy rebellion, and thy stiff **n**: 6203
1Sa 4:18 of the gate, and his **n** brake, and he died: 4665
2Ki 17:14 their necks, like to the **n** of their fathers, 6203
2Ch 36:13 he stiffened his **n**, and hardened his heart 6203
Ne 9:29 hardened their **n**, and would not hear. 6203
Job 15:26 He runneth upon him, *even* on his **n**, 6677
 16:12 he hath also taken *me* by my **n**, 6203
 39:19 hast thou clothed his **n** with thunder? 6677
 41:22 In his **n** remaineth strength, and sorrow 6677
Ps 75: 5 horn on high: speak *not* with a stiff **n**. 6677
Pr 1: 9 unto thy head, and chains about thy **n**. 1621
 3: 3 bind them about thy **n**; write them upon 1621
 3:22 be life unto thy soul, and grace to thy **n**. 1621
 6:21 thine heart, *and* tie them about thy **n**. 1621
 29: 1 being often reproved hardeneth *his* **n**, 6203
SS 1:10 rows *of jewels*, thy **n** with chains *of gold*. 6677
 4: 4 Thy **n** *is* like the tower of David builded 6677
 4: 9 one of thine eyes, with one chain of thy **n**. 6677
 7: 4 Thy **n** *is* as a tower of ivory; thine eyes 6677
Isa 8: 8 and go over, he shall reach *even* to the **n**; 6677
 10:27 his yoke from off thy **n**, and the yoke shall 6677
 30:28 shall reach to the midst of the **n**, 6677
 48: 4 **n** *is* an iron sinew, and thy brow brass: 6203
 52: 2 loose thyself from the bands of thy **n**, 6677
 66: 3 a lamb, *as if* he **cut off** a dog's **n**; 6202
Jer 7:26 inclined their ear, but hardened their **n**: 6203
 17:23 their **n** stiff, that *they* might not hear, 6203
 27: 2 and yokes, and put them upon thy **n**, 6677
 27: 8 that will not put their **n** under the yoke of 6677
 27:11 nations that bring their **n** under the yoke 6677
 28:10 yoke from off the prophet Jeremiah's **n**, 6677
 28:11 of all nations within the space of two 6677
 28:12 from off the **n** of the prophet Jeremiah, 6677
 28:14 I have put a yoke of iron upon the **n** of all 6677
 30: 8 *that* I will break his yoke from off thy **n**, 6677
La 1:14 are wreathed, *and* come up upon my **n**: 6677
Eze 16:11 upon thine hands, and a chain on thy **n**. 1627
Da 5: 7 have a chain of gold about his **n**, 6676
 5:16 have a chain of gold about thy **n**, 6676
 5:29 *put* a chain of gold about his **n**, and made 6676
Hos 10:11 *corn*; but I passed over upon her fair **n**: 6677
Hab 3:13 by discovering the foundation unto the **n**. 6677
Mt 18: 6 that a millstone were hanged about his **n**, 5137
Mk 9:42 that a millstone were hanged about his **n**, 5137
Lk 15:20 and ran, and fell on his **n**, and kissed him. 5137
 17: 2 that a millstone were hanged about his **n**, 5137
Ac 15:10 to put a yoke upon the **n** of the disciples, 5137
 20:37 and fell on Paul's **n**, and kissed him, 5137

NECKLACES See TIRES

NECKS (18) [NECK]
Jos 10:24 put your feet upon the **n** of these kings. 6677
 10:24 and put their feet upon the **n** of them. 6677
Jdg 5:30 *meet* for the **n** of *them that take* the spoil? 6677
 8:21 ornaments that *were* on their camels' **n**. 6677
 8:26 chains that *were* about their camels' **n**. 6677
2Sa 22:41 Thou hast also given me the **n** of mine 6203
2Ki 17:14 hardened their **n**, like to the neck of their 6203
Ne 3: 5 their nobles put not their **n** to the work of 6677
 9:16 hardened their **n**, and hearkened not to 6203
 9:17 hardened their **n**, and in their rebellion 6203
Ps 18:40 Thou hast also given me the **n** of mine 1627
Isa 3:16 walk with stretched forth **n** and 6203
Jer 19:15 because they have hardened their **n**, 6203
 27:12 Bring your **n** under the yoke of the king 6677
La 5: 5 Our **n** *are* under persecution: we labour, 6677

Eze 21:29 to bring thee upon the **n** of *them that are* 6677
Mic 2: 3 from which ye shall not remove your **n**; 6677
Ro 16: 4 have for my life laid down their own **n**: 5137

NECO See NECHO

NECROMANCER (1)
Dt 18:11 or a wizard, or a **n**. 413+1875+1886.1+4191

NEDABIAH (1)
1Ch 3:18 Shenazar, Jecamiah, Hoshama, and **N**. 5072

NEED (49) [NEEDED, NEEDEST, NEEDETH,
NEEDFUL, NEEDS, NEEDY]
Dt 15: 8 shalt surely lend him sufficient for his **n**, 4270
1Sa 21:15 *Have* I **n** of mad men, that ye have 2638
2Ch 2:16 out of Lebanon, as much as thou shalt **n**: 6878
 20:17 Ye shall not **n** to fight in this *battle*: set NIH
Ezr 6: 9 that which *they* **have n** of, both young 2818
Pr 31:11 in her, so that he shall **have** no **n** of spoil. 2637
Mt 3:14 I have **n** to be baptized of thee, 5532
 6: 8 Father knoweth what *things* ye have **n** of, 5532
 6:32 knoweth that ye **have n** of all these 5535
 9:12 They that be whole **n** not a 2192+5532
 14:16 said unto them, They **n** not depart; 2192+5532
 21: 3 ye shall say, The Lord hath **n** of them; 5532
 26:65 what further **n** have we of witnesses? 5532
Mk 2:17 They that are whole have no **n** of 5532
 2:25 when he had **n**, and was a hungred, he, 5532
 11: 3 say ye that the Lord hath **n** of him; 5532
 14:63 What **n** we any further witnesses? 2192+5532
Lk 5:31 that are whole **n** not a physician; 2192+5532
 9:11 and healed them that had **n** of healing. 5532
 12:30 your Father knoweth that ye **have n** of 5535
 15: 7 *persons* which **n** no repentance. 2192+5532
 19:31 him, Because the Lord hath **n** of him. 5532
 19:34 And they said, The Lord hath **n** of him. 5532
 22:71 What **n** we any further witness? 2192+5532
Jn 13:29 Buy *those things* that we have **n** of against 5532
Ac 2:45 them to all *men*, as every *man* had **n**. 5532
 4:35 unto every man according as he had **n**. 5532
Ro 16: 2 in whatsoever business she hath **n** of you: 5535
1Co 7:36 and so require, let him do what he will, 3784
 12:21 say unto the hand, I have no **n** of thee: 5532
 12:21 the head to the feet, I have no **n** of you. 5532
 12:24 For our comely *parts* have no **n**: 5532
2Co 3: 1 or **n** we, as some *others*, epistles of 5535
Php 4:12 hungry, both to abound and to **suffer n**. 5302
 4:19 But my God shall supply all your **n** 5532
1Th 1: 8 that we **n** not to speak any *thing*, 2192+5532
 4: 9 But as touching brotherly love ye **n** 2192+5532
 5: 1 ye have no **n** that I write unto you. 5532
Heb 4:16 and find grace to help in **time of n**. 2121
 5:12 ye have **n** that *one* teach you again which 5532
 5:12 and are become such as have **n** of milk, 5532
 7:11 further **n** *was there* that another priest 5532
 10:36 For ye have **n** of patience, that, after ye 5532
1Pe 1: 6 though now for a season, if **n** be, 1163
1Jn 2:27 ye **n** not that any *man* teach you: 2192+5532
 3:17 and seeth his brother have **n**, 5532
Rev 3:17 with goods, and have **n** of nothing; 5532
 21:23 And the city had no **n** of the sun, neither 2192+5532
 22: 5 they **n** no candle, neither light of 2192+5532

NEEDED (2) [NEED]
Jn 2:25 And **n** not that any should testify of 2192+5532
Ac 17:25 as though he **n** any *thing*, seeing he giveth 4326

NEEDEST (1) [NEED]
Jn 16:30 **n** not that any *man* should ask 2192+5532

NEEDETH (6) [NEED]
Ge 33:15 he said, What **n** it? let me find grace in NIH
Lk 11: 8 will rise and give him as many as he **n**. 5535
Jn 13:10 He that is washed **n** not save to 2192+5532
Eph 4:28 he may have to give to him that **n**. 2192+5532
2Ti 2:15 a workman that **n not to be ashamed**, 422
Heb 7:27 **n** not daily, as *those* high priests, 318+2250

NEEDFUL (6) [NEED]
Ezr 7:20 whatsoever more *shall be* **n** for the house 2819
Lk 10:42 But one *thing* is **n**: and Mary hath chosen 5532
Ac 15: 5 That it was **n** to circumcise them, 1163
Php 1:24 to abide in the flesh *is* more **n** 316
Jas 2:16 not those *things* which *are* **n** to the body; 2006
Jude 1: 3 it was **n** for me to write unto you, 318+2192

NEEDLE (2) [NEEDLE'S, NEEDLEWORK]
Mt 19:24 for a camel to go through the eye of a **n**, 4476
Mk 10:25 for a camel to go through the eye of a **n**, 4476

NEEDLE'S (1) [NEEDLE]
Lk 18:25 it is easier for a camel to go through a **n** 4476

NEEDLEWORK (9) [NEEDLE, WORK]
Ex 26:36 fine twined linen, **wrought with n**. 4639+7551
 27:16 fine twined linen, wrought with **n**. 7551
 28:39 thou shalt make the girdle *of* **n**. 4639+7551
 36:37 scarlet, and fine twined linen, *of* **n**; 4639+7551
 38:18 for the gate of the court *was* **n**, 4639+7551
 39:29 blue, and purple, and scarlet, *of* **n**; 4639+7551
Jdg 5:30 a prey of divers colours of **n**, 7553
 5:30 of divers colours of **n** on both sides, 7553
Ps 45:14 brought unto the king in **raiment of n**: 7553

NEEDS (16) [NEED]
Ge 17:13 money, **must n** be circumcised: 4135+4135
 19: 9 sojourn, and he will **n** be a judge: 8199+8199
 24: 5 must I **n** bring thy son **again** unto 7725+7725
 31:30 *though* thou wouldest **n** be gone, 1980+1980
2Sa 14:14 we **must n** die, and *are* as water 4191+4191
Jer 10: 5 they **must n** be borne, because 5375+5375
Mt 18: 7 for it **must n** be that offences come; 318
Mk 13: 7 *such things* **must n** be; but the end *shall* 1163
Lk 14:18 piece of ground, and I must **n** go and see it: 318
Jn 4: 4 And he **must n** go through Samaria. 1163
Ac 1:16 this scripture **must n** have been fulfilled, 1163
 17: 3 that Christ **must n** have suffered, 1163
 21:22 multitude **must n** come together: 1163+3843
Ro 13: 5 Wherefore *ye* **must n** be subject, not only 318
1Co 5:10 for then **must** ye **n** go out of the world. 3784
2Co 11:30 If I **must n** glory, I will glory of the *things* 1163

NEEDY (38) [NEED]
Dt 15:11 to thy poor, and to thy **n**, in thy land. 34
 24:14 oppress a hired servant *that is* poor and **n**, 34
Job 24: 4 They turn the **n** out of the way: the poor of 34
 24:14 rising with the light killeth the poor and **n**, 34
Ps 9:18 For the **n** shall not alway be forgotten: 34
 12: 5 for the sighing of the, now will I arise, 34
 35:10 and the **n** from him that spoileth him? 34
 37:14 to cast down the poor and **n**, *and* to slay 34
 40:17 I *am* poor and **n**; *yet* the Lord thinketh 34
 70: 5 I *am* poor and **n**: make haste unto me, 34
 72: 4 he shall save the children of the **n**, 34
 72:12 For he shall deliver the **n** when he crieth; 34
 72:13 He shall spare the poor and **n**, and shall save 34
 72:13 and needy, and shall save the souls of the **n**. 34
 74:21 let the poor and **n** praise thy name. 34
 82: 3 fatherless: do justice to the afflicted and **n**. 7326
 82: 4 Deliver the poor and **n**: rid *them* out of 34
 86: 1 O Lord, hear me: for I *am* poor and **n**. 34
 109:16 persecuted the poor and **n** man, that *he* 34
 109:22 I *am* poor and **n**, and my heart is wounded 34
 113: 7 dust, *and* lifteth the **n** out of the dunghill; 34
Pr 30:14 off the earth, and the **n** from *among* men. 34
 31: 9 and plead the cause of the poor and **n**. 34
 31:20 yea, she reacheth forth her hands to the **n**. 34
Isa 10: 2 To turn aside the **n** from judgment, 1800
 14:30 feed, and the **n** shall lie down in safety: 34
 25: 4 a strength to the **n** in his distress, a refuge 34
 26: 6 feet of the poor, *and* the steps of the **n**. 1800
 32: 7 words, even when the **n** speaketh right. 34
 41:17 *When* the poor and **n** seek water, and 34
Jer 5:28 and the right of the **n** do they not judge. 34
 22:16 He judged the cause of the poor and **n**; 34
Eze 16:49 she strengthen the hand of the poor and **n**. 34
 18:12 Hath oppressed the poor and **n**, hath spoiled 34
 22:29 and have vexed the poor and **n**: 34
Am 4: 1 which oppress the poor, which crush the **n**, 34
 8: 4 Hear this, O ye that swallow up the **n**, even 34
 8: 6 poor for silver, and the **n** for a pair of shoes; 34

NEESED (1) [NEESINGS]
2Ki 4:35 the child **n** seven times, and the child 2237

NEESINGS (1) [NEESED]
Job 41:18 *By* his **n** a light doth shine, and his eyes 5846

NEGINAH (1)
Ps 61: T To the chief Musician upon **N**, *A Psalm* of 5058

NEGINOTH (6)
Ps 4: T To the chief Musician on **N**, *A Psalm* of 5058
 6: T To the chief Musician on **N** upon 5058
 54: T To the chief Musician on **N**, Maschil, 5058
 55: T To the chief Musician on **N**, Maschil, 5058
 67: T To the chief Musician on **N**, *A Psalm or* 5058
 76: T To the chief Musician on **N**, *A Psalm or* 5058

NEGLECT (4) [NEGLECTED, NEGLECTING,
NEGLIGENT]
Mt 18:17 if he shall **n to hear** them, tell *it* unto 3878
 18:17 but if he **n to hear** the church, let him be 3878
1Ti 4:14 **N** not the gift that is in thee, which was 272
Heb 2: 3 shall we escape, if we **n** so great salvation; 272

NEGLECTED (1) [NEGLECT]
Ac 6: 1 their widows were **n** in the daily 3865

NEGLECTING (1) [NEGLECT]
Col 2:23 humility, and **n** of the body, not in any 857

NEGLIGENT (2) [NEGLECT]
2Ch 29:11 My sons, be not now **n**: for the Lord 7952
2Pe 1:12 I will not be **n** to put you always 272

NEHELAMITE (3)
Jer 29:24 shalt also speak to Shemaiah the **N**, 5161
 29:31 the Lord concerning Shemaiah the **N**; 5161
 29:32 punish Shemaiah the **N**, and his seed: 5161

NEHEMIAH (8)
Ezr 2: 2 Jeshua, **N**, Seraiah, Reelaiah, Mordecai, 5166
Ne 1: 1 The words of **N** the son of Hachaliah. 5166
 3:16 After him repaired **N** the son of Azbuk, 5166
 7: 7 Jeshua, **N**, Azariah, Raamiah, Nahamani, 5166
 8: 9 **N**, which *is* the Tirshatha, and Ezra 5166
 10: 1 Now those that sealed *were*, **N**, 5166
 12:26 in the days of **N** the governor, and of Ezra 5166
 12:47 in the days of **N**, gave the portions of 5166

N

NEHILOTH (1)

Ps 5: T To the chief Musician upon **N**, A Psalm of 5155

NEHUM (1)

Ne 7: 7 Bilshan, Mispereth, Bigvai, **N**, Baanah. 5149

NEHUSHTA (1)

2Ki 24: 8 his mother's name *was* **N**, the daughter of 5179

NEHUSHTAN (1)

2Ki 18: 4 did burn incense to it: and he called it **N**. 5180

NEIEL (1)

Jos 19:27 **N**, and goeth out to Cabul on the left 5272

NEIGHBOUR (106) [NEIGHBOUR'S, NEIGHBOURS, NEIGHBOURS']

Ex	3:22 every woman shall borrow of her **n**,	7453
	2: 2 let every man borrow of his **n**,	7453
	11: 2 every woman of her **n**, jewels of silver,	7468
	12: 4 his **n** next unto his house take *it*	7934
	20:16 shalt not bear false witness against thy **n**.	7453
	21:14 a man come presumptuously upon his **n**,	7453
	22: 7 If a man shall deliver unto his **n** money or	7453
	22: 9 he shall pay double unto his **n**,	7453
	22:10 If a man deliver unto his **n** an ass, or an	7453
	22:14 if a man borrow *ought* of his **n**, and it be	7453
	32:27 man his companion, and every man his **n**.	7138
Lev	6: 2 lie unto his **n** in that which was delivered	5997
	6: 2 away by violence, or hath deceived his **n**;	5997
	19:13 Thou shalt not defraud thy **n**, neither rob	7453
	19:15 in righteousness shalt thou judge thy **n**.	5997
	19:16 thou stand against the blood of thy **n**:	7453
	19:17 thou shalt in any wise rebuke thy **n**,	5997
	19:18 but thou shalt love thy **n** as thyself:	7453
	24:19 if a man cause a blemish in his **n**; as he	5997
	25:14 if thou sell ought unto thy **n**,	5997
	25:15 after the jubile thou shalt buy of thy **n**,	5997
Dt	4:42 which should kill his **n** unawares,	7453
	5:20 shalt thou bear false witness against thy **n**.	7453
	15: 2 creditor that lendeth *ought* unto his **n**	7453
	15: 2 release *it*; he shall not exact *it* of his **n**,	7453
	19: 4 Whoso killeth his **n** ignorantly, whom he	7453
	19: 5 into the wood with his **n** to hew wood,	7453
	19: 5 and lighteth upon his **n**, that he die;	7453
	19:11 if any man hate his **n**, and lie in wait for	7453
	22:26 for as when a man riseth against his **n**,	7453
	27:24 Cursed *be* he that smiteth his **n** secretly.	7453
Jos	20: 5 because he smote his **n** unwittingly,	7453
Ru	4: 7 plucked off his shoe, and gave *it* to his **n**:	7453
1Sa	15:28 hath given it to a **n** of thine, *that is* better	7453
	28:17 and given it to thy **n**, *even* to David:	7453
2Sa	12:11 give *them* unto thy **n**, and he shall lie	7453
1Ki	8:31 If any man trespass against his **n**,	7453
	20:35 said unto his **n** in the word of the LORD,	7453
2Ch	6:22 If a man sin against his **n**, and an oath be	7453
Job	12: 4 I am *as* one mocked of his **n**, who calleth	7453
	16:21 with God, as a man *pleadeth* for his **n**.	7453
Ps	12: 2 They speak vanity every one with his **n**:	7453
	15: 3 with his tongue, nor doeth evil to his **n**,	7453
	15: 3 nor taketh up a reproach against his **n**.	7138
	101: 5 Whoso privily slandereth his **n**, him will I	7453
Pr	3:28 Say not unto thy **n**, Go, and come again,	7453
	3:29 Devise not evil against thy **n**, seeing he	7453
	11: 9 with *his* mouth destroyeth his **n**:	7453
	11:12 He that is void of wisdom despiseth his **n**:	7453
	12:26 righteous *is* more excellent than his **n**:	7453
	14:20 The poor is hated even of his own **n**:	7453
	14:21 He that despiseth his **n** sinneth: but he	7453
	16:29 A violent man enticeth his **n**,	7453
	18:17 but his **n** cometh and searcheth him.	7453
	19: 4 but the poor is separated from his **n**.	7453
	21:10 his **n** findeth no favour in his eyes.	7453
	24:28 Be not a witness against thy **n** without	7453
	25: 8 when thy **n** hath put thee to shame.	7453
	25: 9 Debate thy cause with thy **n** *himself*; and	7453
	25:18 false witness against his **n** *is* a maul,	7453
	26:19 So *is* the man *that* deceiveth his **n**,	7453
	27:10 better *is* a **n** *that is* near than a brother	7934
	29: 5 man that flattereth his **n** spreadeth a net	7453
Ecc	4: 4 that for this a man is envied of his **n**.	7453
Isa	3: 5 one by another, and every one by his **n**:	7453
	19: 2 his brother, and every one against his **n**;	7453
	41: 6 They helped every one his **n**; and *every*	7453
Jer	6:21 the **n** and his friend shall perish.	7934
	7: 5 judgment between a man and his **n**;	7453
	9: 4 Take ye heed every one of his **n**, and trust	7453
	9: 4 every **n** will walk *with* slanders.	7453
	9: 5 they will deceive every one his **n**,	7453
	9: 8 *one* speaketh peaceably to his **n** with his	7453
	9:20 and every one her **n** lamentation.	7468
	22: 8 and they shall say every man to his **n**,	7453
	23:27 which they tell every man to his **n**,	7453
	23:30 that steal my words every one from his **n**.	7453
	23:35 Thus shall ye say every one to his **n**,	7453
	31:34 they shall teach no more every man his **n**,	7453
	34:15 in proclaiming liberty every man to his **n**,	7453
	34:17 to his brother, and every man to his **n**:	7453
	49:18 and Gomorrah and the **n** *cities* thereof,	7934
	50:40 and Gomorrah and the **n** *cities* thereof,	7934
Hab	2:15 Woe unto him that giveth his **n** drink,	7453
Zec	3:10 shall ye call every man his **n**, under	7453
	8:10 for I set all men every one against his **n**.	7453
	8:16 Speak ye every man the truth to his **n**;	7453
	8:17 imagine evil in your hearts against his **n**;	7453

Zec	14:13 lay hold every one on the hand of his **n**,	7453
	14:13 shall rise up against the hand of his **n**.	7453
Mt	5:43 Thou shalt love thy **n**, and hate thine	4139
	19:19 and, Thou shalt love thy **n** as thyself:	4139
	22:39 unto it, Thou shalt love thy **n** as thyself.	4139
Mk	12:31 Thou shalt love thy **n** as thyself.	4139
	12:33 the strength, and to love *his* **n** as himself,	4139
Lk	10:27 with all thy mind; and thy **n** as thyself.	4139
	10:29 said unto Jesus, And who is my **n**?	4139
	10:36 **n** unto him that fell among the thieves?	4139
Ac	7:27 But he that did his **n** wrong thrust him	4139
Ro	13: 9 namely, Thou shalt love thy **n** as thyself.	4139
	13:10 Love worketh no ill to his **n**: therefore	4139
	15: 2 Let every one of us please his **n** for *his*	4139
Gal	5:14 *even* in *this*; Thou shalt love thy **n** as	4139
Eph	4:25 speak every man truth with his **n**:	4139
Heb	8:11 they shall not teach every man his **n**,	4139
Jas	2: 8 shalt love thy **n** as thyself, ye do well:	4139

NEIGHBOUR'S (29) [NEIGHBOUR]

Ex	20:17 Thou shalt not covet thy **n** house, thou	7453
	20:17 thou shalt not covet thy **n** wife, nor his	7453
	20:17 thy **n** ass, nor any thing that *is* thy **n**.	7453
	22: 8 he have put his hand unto his **n** goods.	7453
	22:11 that he hath not put his hand unto his **n**	7453
	22:26 If thou at all take thy **n** raiment to pledge,	7453
Lev	18:20 thou shalt not lie carnally with thy **n** wife,	5997
	20:10 *he* that committeth adultery with his **n**	5997
	25:14 buyest *ought* of thy **n** hand, ye shall not	5997
Dt	5:21 Neither shalt thou desire thy **n** wife,	7453
	5:21 neither shalt thou covet thy **n** house,	7453
	5:21 his ass, or any *thing* that *is* thy **n**.	7453+3807.1
	19:14 Thou shalt not remove thy **n** landmark,	7453
	22:24 because he hath humbled his **n** wife:	7453
	23:24 When thou comest into thy **n** vineyard,	7453
	23:25 comest into the standing corn of thy **n**,	7453
	23:25 thou shalt not move a sickle unto thy **n**	7453
	27:17 *be* he that removeth his **n** landmark.	7453
Job	31: 9 or *if* I have laid wait at my **n** door;	7453
Pr	6:29 So he that goeth in to his **n** wife;	7453
	25:17 Withdraw thy foot from thy **n** house;	7453
Jer	5: 8 every one neighed after his **n** wife.	7453
	22:13 *that* useth his **n** service without wages,	7453
Eze	18: 6 neither hath defiled his **n** wife, neither	7453
	18:11 the mountains, and defiled his **n** wife,	7453
	18:15 of Israel, hath not defiled his **n** wife,	7453
	22:11 hath committed abomination with his **n**	7453
	33:26 and defile every one his **n** wife:	7453
Zec	11: 6 I *will* deliver the men every one into his **n**	7453

NEIGHBOURS (21) [NEIGHBOUR]

Jos	9:16 that they heard that they *were* their **n**,	7138
Ru	4:17 the women her **n** gave it a name, saying,	7934
2Ki	4: 3 borrow thee vessels abroad of all thy **n**,	7934
Ps	28: 3 which speak peace to their **n**,	7453
	31:11 especially among my **n**, and a fear to mine	7934
	44:13 makest us a reproach to our **n**, a scorn	7934
	79: 4 are become a reproach to our **n**, a scorn	7934
	79:12 render unto our **n** sevenfold into their	7934
	80: 6 Thou makest us a strife unto our **n**:	7934
	89:41 way spoil him: he is a reproach to his **n**.	7934
Jer	12:14 saith the LORD against all mine evil **n**,	7934
	49:10 and his brethren, and his **n**, and he *is* not.	7934
Eze	16:26 fornication with the Egyptians thy **n**,	7934
	22:12 thou hast greedily gained of thy **n** by	7453
	23: 5 on her lovers, on the Assyrians *her* **n**,	7138
	23:12 She doted upon the Assyrians her **n**,	7138
Lk	1:58 And her **n** and her cousins heard how	4040
	14:12 neither thy kinsmen, nor thy rich **n**;	1069
	15: 6 he calleth together *his* friends and **n**,	1069
	15: 9 she calleth *her* friends and *her* **n** together,	1069
Jn	9: 8 The **n** therefore, and they which before	1069

NEIGHBOURS' (1) [NEIGHBOUR]

Jer 29:23 have committed adultery with their **n** 7453

NEIGHED (1) [NEIGHING]

Jer 5: 8 every one **n** after his neighbour's wife. 6670

NEIGHING (1) [NEIGHED, NEIGHINGS]

Jer 8:16 at the sound of the **n** of his strong ones; 4684

NEIGHINGS (1) [NEIGHING]

Jer 13:27 I have seen thine adulteries, and thy **n**, 4684

NEITHER (879)

Ge	3: 3 **n** shall ye touch it, lest ye die.	3808
	8:21 **n** will I again smite any more	3808+2050.1
	9:11 **n** shall all flesh be cut off any more	3808+2050.1
	9:11 **n** shall there any more be a flood	3808+2050.1
	17: 5 **N** shall thy name any more be	3808+2050.1
	19:17 stay thou in all the plain;	408+2050.1
	21:26 **n** didst thou tell me,	1571+3808+2050.1
	21:26 **n** yet heard I *of it*, but to	1571+3808+2050.1
	22:12 **n** do thou any thing unto him:	408+2050.1
	24:16 **n** had any man known her:	3808+2050.1
	29: 7 **n** *is it* time that the cattle should be	3808
	39: 9 greater in this house than I; **n**	3808+2050.1
	45: 6 *in the which* there shall **n** be earing nor	369
Ex	4: 8 **n** hearken to the voice of the first	3808+2050.1
	4: 9 **n** hearken unto thy voice,	3808+2050.1
	4:10 Lord, I *am* not eloquent, **n** heretofore,	1571
	5: 2 **n** will I let Israel go.	1571+3808+2050.1
	5:23 hast thou delivered thy people	3808+2050.1
	7:22 **n** did he hearken unto them;	3808+2050.1

Ex	7:23 **n** did he set his heart to this also.	3808+2050.1
	8:32 **n** would he let the people go.	3808+2050.1
	9:29 **n** shall there be any more hail;	3808+2050.1
	9:35 **n** would he let the children of	3808+2050.1
	10: 6 **n** thy fathers, nor thy fathers' fathers	3808
	10:14 they, **n** after them shall be such.	3808+2050.1
	10:23 **n** rose any from his place for	3808+2050.1
	12:39 **n** had they prepared for	1571+3808+2050.1
	12:46 **n** shall ye break a bone thereof.	3808+2050.1
	13: 7 **n** shall there be leaven seen with	3808+2050.1
	16:24 **n** was there any worm therein.	3808+2050.1
	20:23 **n** shall ye make unto you gods of	3808+2050.1
	20:26 **N** shalt thou go up by steps unto	3808+2050.1
	22:21 Thou shalt **n** vex a stranger,	3808+2050.1
	22:25 usurer, **n** shalt thou lay upon him usury.	3808
	22:31 **n** shall ye eat *any* flesh that is	3808+2050.1
	23: 2 **n** shalt thou speak in a cause to	3808+2050.1
	23: 3 **N** shalt thou countenance a poor	3808+2050.1
	23:13 **n** let it be heard out of thy mouth.	3808
	23:18 **n** shall the fat of my sacrifice	3808+2050.1
	24: 2 **n** shall the people go up with	3808+2050.1
	30: 9 **n** shall ye pour drink offering	3808+2050.1
	30:32 **n** shall ye make *any other* like it,	3808+2050.1
	32:18 **n** *is it* the voice of *them that* cry	369+2050.1
	34: 3 let any man be seen	408+1571+2050.1
	34: 3 let the flocks nor herds feed before	408+1571
	34:24 **n** shall any man desire thy land,	3808+2050.1
	34:25 **n** shall the sacrifice of the feast of	3808+2050.1
	34:28 he did **n** eat bread, nor drink water.	3808
	36: 6 **n** man nor woman make any more work	408
Lev	2:13 **n** shalt thou suffer the salt of	3808+2050.1
	3:17 dwellings, *that* ye eat **n** fat nor blood.	3808
	5:11 **n** shall he put *any* frankincense	3808+2050.1
	7:18 **n** shall it be imputed unto him that	3808
	10: 6 your heads, **n** rend your clothes;	3808+2050.1
	11:43 **n** shall ye make yourselves	3808+2050.1
	11:44 **n** shall ye defile yourselves with	3808+2050.1
	17:12 No soul of you shall eat blood, **n**	3808+2050.1
	18: 3 **n** shall ye walk in their	3808
	18:17 **n** shalt thou take her son's daughter,	3808
	18:18 **N** shalt thou take a wife to her	3808+2050.1
	18:21 **n** shalt thou profane the name of	3808+2050.1
	18:23 **N** shalt thou lie with any beast to	3808+2050.1
	18:23 **n** shall any woman stand before a	3808+2050.1
	18:26 **n** any of your own nation, nor any	NIH
	19: 9 **n** shalt thou gather the gleanings	3808+2050.1
	19:10 **n** shalt thou gather *every* grape of	3808+2050.1
	19:11 Ye shall **n** steal, **n** deal falsely,	3808+2050.1
	19:11 deal falsely, **n** lie one to another.	3808+2050.1
	19:12 **n** shalt thou profane the name of thy	2050.1
	19:13 **n** rob *him*: the wages of him that	3808
	19:16 **n** shalt thou stand against the blood of	3808
	19:19 **n** shall a garment mingled of	3808+2050.1
	19:26 **n** shall ye use enchantment, nor observe	3808+2050.1
	19:27 **n** shalt thou mar the corners of	3808+2050.1
	19:31 **n** seek after wizards, to be defiled	408+2050.1
	21: 5 **n** shall they shave off the corner	3808+2050.1
	21: 7 **n** shall they take a woman put	3808+2050.1
	21:11 **N** shall he go in to any dead	3808+2050.1
	21:12 **N** shall he go out of the	3808+2050.1
	21:15 **N** shall he profane his seed	3808+2050.1
	22:24 **n** shall you make *any* offering	3808+2050.1
	22:25 **N** from a stranger's hand shall ye	3808+2050.1
	22:32 **N** shall ye profane my holy name;	3808+2050.1
	23:14 ye shall eat **n** bread, nor parched *corn*,	3808
	23:22 **n** shalt thou gather *any* gleaning	3808+2050.1
	25: 4 thou shalt **n** sow thy field, nor prune thy	3808
	25: 5 **n** gather the grapes of thy vine	3808+2050.1
	25:11 ye reap that which groweth of	3808+2050.1
	26: 1 **n** rear you up a standing image,	2050.1
	26: 1 **n** shall ye set up *any* image of	3808+2050.1
	26: 6 **n** shall the sword go through	3808+2050.1
	26:20 shall not yield her increase, **n**	3808+2050.1
	26:44 **n** will I abhor them, to destroy	3808+2050.1
	27:33 or bad, **n** shall he change it:	3808+2050.1
Nu	1:49 **n** take the sum of them among	3808+2050.1
	5:13 she be taken *with the manner*;	3808+2050.1
	6: 3 **n** shall he drink any liquor of	3808+2050.1
	11:19 nor two days, nor five days, **n** ten	3808+2050.1
	14: 9 **n** fear ye the people of the land;	408+2050.1
	14:23 **n** shall any of them that provoked	3808+2050.1
	16:15 **n** have I hurt one of them.	3808+2050.1
	18: 3 the sanctuary and the altar, that **n** they,	3808
	18:20 **n** shalt thou have any part among	3808+2050.1
	18:22 **N** must the children of Israel	3808+2050.1
	18:32 shalt ye pollute the holy *things*	3808+2050.1
	20: 5 *is there any* water to drink.	369+2050.1
	20:17 **n** will we drink *of* the water of	3808+2050.1
	21: 5 *there is* no bread, **n** *is there any*	369+2050.1
	23:19 the son of man, that he should repent:	2050.1
	23:21 **n** hath he seen perverseness in	3808+2050.1
	23:23 **n** *is there* any divination against	3808+2050.1
	23:25 Balak said unto Balaam, **N** curse	1571+3808
	35:23 his enemy, **n** sought his harm:	3808
	36: 9 **N** shall the inheritance remove	3808+2050.1
Dt	1:21 fear not, **n** be discouraged.	408+2050.1
	1:29 Dread not, **n** be afraid of them.	408+2050.1
	1:42 unto them, Go not up, **n** fight;	3808+2050.1
	2: 9 **n** contend with them in battle:	408+2050.1
	2:27 I will **n** turn *unto* the right hand nor *to*	3808
	4: 2 **n** shall you diminish *ought* from	3808+2050.1
	4:28 wood and stone, which **n** see, nor hear,	3808
	4:31 will not forsake thee, **n** destroy	3808+2050.1
	5:18 **N** shalt thou commit adultery.	2050.1
	5:19 **N** shalt thou steal.	3808+2050.1

Dt	5:20 N shalt thou bear false witness 3808+2050.1
	5:21 N shalt thou desire thy 3808+2050.1
	5:21 n shalt thou covet thy 3808+2050.1
	7: 3 N shalt thou make marriages 3808+2050.1
	7:16 n shalt thou serve their gods; 3808+2050.1
	7:26 N shalt thou bring an 3808+2050.1
	8: 3 n did thy fathers know; 3808+2050.1
	8: 4 n did thy foot swell, these forty 3808+2050.1
	9: 9 n did I eat bread nor drink water: 3808
	9:18 did n eat bread, nor drink water, 3808+2050.1
	13: 8 n shall thine eye pity him, 3808+2050.1
	13: 8 n shall thou spare, neither shalt 3808+2050.1
	13: 8 n shall thou conceal him: 3808+2050.1
	16: 4 n shall there any thing of the 3808+2050.1
	16:19 not respect persons, n take a gift: 3808+2050.1
	16:22 N shall thou set thee up any 3808+2050.1
	17:17 N shall he multiply wives to 3808+2050.1
	17:17 n shall he greatly multiply to 3808+2050.1
	18:16 n let me see this great fire any 3808+2050.1
	20: 3 n be ye terrified, because of them; 408+2050.1
	21: 4 is n eared nor sown, and shall strike 3808
	21: 7 blood, n have our eyes seen it. 3808+2050.1
	22: 5 n shall a man put on a woman's 3808+2050.1
	24: 5 n shall he be charged with any 3808+2050.1
	24:15 n shall the sun go down upon it; 3808+2050.1
	24:16 n shall the children be put to 3808+2050.1
	26:13 n have I forgotten them: 3808+2050.1
	26:14 n have I taken away ought 3808+2050.1
	28:36 a nation which n thou nor thy fathers 3808
	28:39 dress them, but shalt n drink of the wine, 3808
	28:64 which n thou nor thy fathers have known, 3808
	28:65 n shall the sole of thy foot have 3808+2050.1
	29: 6 n have you drunk wine or 3808+2050.1
	29:14 N with you only do I make this 3808+2050.1
	30:11 hidden from thee, n is it far off. 3808+2050.1
	30:13 N is it beyond the sea, that thou 3808+2050.1
	31: 8 will not fail thee, n forsake thee: 3808+2050.1
	31: 8 fear not, n be dismayed. 3808+2050.1
	32:28 n is there any understanding in 369+2050.1
	32:39 n is there any that can deliver out 369+2050.1
	33: 9 n did he acknowledge his 3808+2050.1
Jos	1: 9 be not afraid, n be thou dismayed: 408+2050.1
	2:11 n did there remain any more 3808+2050.1
	5: 1 n was there spirit in them any 3808+2050.1
	5:12 n had the children of Israel 3808+2050.1
	6:10 n shall any word proceed out of 3808+2050.1
	7:12 n will I be with you any more, except ye 3808
	8: 1 Fear not, n be thou dismayed: 408+2050.1
	11:14 them, n left they any to breathe. 3808
	23: 7 n make mention of the name of 3808+2050.1
	23: 7 nor cause to swear by them, n 3808+2050.1
Jdg	1:27 N did Manasseh drive out 3808+2050.1
	1:29 N did Ephraim drive out 3808+2050.1
	1:30 N did Zebulun drive out the inhabitants 3808
	1:31 N did Asher drive out the inhabitants of 3808
	1:33 N did Naphtali drive out the inhabitants 3808
	2:23 n delivered he them into the 3808+2050.1
	6: 4 for Israel, n sheep, nor ox, nor ass. 2050.1
	8:23 n shall my son rule over you: 3808+2050.1
	8:35 N shewed they kindness to 3808+2050.1
	11:34 beside her he had n son nor daughter. 369
	13: 6 asked him not whence he was, n 3808+2050.1
	13: 7 n eat any unclean thing: for the 408+2050.1
	13:14 n let her drink wine or strong 408+2050.1
	13:14 n would he have shewed us all 3808
	20: 8 n will we any of us turn into his 3808+2050.1
Ru	2: 8 n go from hence, 1571+3808+2050.1
1Sa	1:15 I have drunk n wine nor strong drink, 2050.1
	2: 2 n is there any rock like our God. 369+2050.1
	3: 7 n was the word of the LORD yet 2962+2050.1
	4:20 answered not, n did she regard it. 3808+2050.1
	5: 5 Therefore n the priests of Dagon, nor any 3808
	12: 4 n hast thou taken ought of any 3808+2050.1
	13:22 that there was n sword nor spear 3808+2050.1
	16: 8 N hath the LORD chosen this. 1571+3808
	16: 9 N hath the LORD chosen this. 1571+3808
	20:27 of Jesse to meat, n yesterday, nor to day? 1571
	21: 8 for I have n brought my sword nor my 1571
	24:11 see that there is n evil nor transgression in 369
	25: 7 n was there ought missing unto 3808+2050.1
	25:15 not hurt, n missed we any thing, 3808+2050.1
	26:12 saw it, nor knew it, n awaked: 369+2050.1
	27: 9 left n man nor woman alive, and took 3808
	27:11 David saved n man nor woman alive, 3808
	28: 6 n by dreams, nor by Urim, nor by 1571
	28:15 no more, n by prophets, nor by dreams: 1571
	30:15 unto me by God, that thou wilt n kill me, 518
	30:19 n small nor great, neither sons nor 4480
	30:19 n sons nor daughters, neither spoil, 2050.1
	30:19 neither sons nor daughters, n spoil, 2050.1
2Sa	1:21 let there be no dew, n let there be 408+2050.1
	2:28 pursued after Israel no more, n 3808+2050.1
	7:10 n shall the children of 3808+2050.1
	7:22 n is there any God beside thee, 369+2050.1
	12:17 n did he eat bread with them. 3808+2050.1
	13:22 Absalom spake unto his brother Amnon n NIH
	14: 7 shall not leave to my husband n name nor NIH
	14:14 n doth God respect any person: 3808+2050.1
	18: 3 n if half of us die, will they care 3808+2050.1
	19: 6 that thou regardest n princes nor servants: 369
	19:19 n do thou remember that which 408+2050.1
	19:24 had n dressed his feet, nor trimmed his 3808
	20: 1 n have we inheritance in the son 3808+2050.1
	21: 4 of his house; n for us shalt thou 369+2050.1
	21:10 suffered n the birds of the air to rest on 3808

2Sa	24:24 n will I offer burnt offerings unto 3808+2050.1
1Ki	3:11 n hast asked riches for thyself, 3808+2050.1
	3:12 n after thee shall any arise like 3808+2050.1
	3:26 Let it be n mine nor thine, but divide it. 1571
	5: 4 there is n adversary nor evil occurrent. 369
	6: 7 that there was n hammer nor axe nor any NIH
	7:47 n was the weight of the brass found out. 3808
	11: 2 n shall they come in unto you: 3808+2050.1
	12:16 n have we inheritance in the son 3808+2050.1
	13: 8 n will I eat bread nor drink water 3808+2050.1
	13:16 n will I eat bread nor drink water 3808+2050.1
	16:11 of his kinsfolks, nor of his friends. 2050.1
	17:14 n shall the cruse of oil fail, 3808+2050.1
	17:16 n did the cruse of oil fail, 3808+2050.1
	18:29 that there was n voice, nor any to 369+2050.1
	22:31 saying, Fight n with small nor great, 3808
2Ki	3:17 not see wind, n shall ye see rain; 3808+2050.1
	4:23 it is n new moon, nor sabbath. And she 3808
	4:31 child; but there was n voice, nor hearing. 369
	5:17 thy servant will henceforth offer n burnt 3808
	6:19 is not the way, n is this the city: 3808+2050.1
	7:10 n voice of man, but horses tied, and 2050.1
	10:14 forty men; n left he any of them. 3808+2050.1
	12: 8 n to repair the breaches of 1115+2050.1
	13: 7 N did he leave of the people to 3588+3808
	13:23 n cast he them from his presence 3808+2050.1
	17:34 they fear not the LORD, n do they 369+2050.1
	17:38 n shall ye fear other gods. 3808+2050.1
	18:30 N let Hezekiah make you trust in 408+2050.1
	21: 8 N will I make the feet of Israel 3808+2050.1
	23:25 n after him arose there any like 3808+2050.1
1Ch	4:27 n did all their family multiply, 3808+2050.1
	17: 9 n shall the children of wickedness 3808+2050.1
	17:20 n is there any God besides thee, 369+2050.1
	19:19 n would the Syrians help 3808+2050.1
	27:24 n was the number put in 3808+2050.1
2Ch	1:11 n yet hast asked long life; 3808+2050.1
	1:12 n shall there any after thee have 3808+2050.1
	6: 5 that my name might be there; n 3808+2050.1
	9: 9 n was there any such spice as 3808+2050.1
	13:20 N did Jeroboam recover strength 3808+2050.1
	20:12 n know we what to do: 3808+2050.1
	25: 4 shall not die for the children, n 3808+2050.1
	26:18 n shall it be for thine honour 3808+2050.1
	30: 3 n had the people gathered 3808+2050.1
	32:15 this manner, n yet believe him: 408+2050.1
	33: 8 N will I any more remove the 3808+2050.1
	34: 2 N to the right hand, nor to the left. 3808
	34:28 n shall thine eyes see all the evil 3808+2050.1
	35:18 n did all the kings of Israel keep 3808+2050.1
Ezr	9:12 n take their daughters unto your 408+2050.1
	10:13 n is this a work of one day or 3808+2050.1
Ne	2:12 n told I any man what my God 3808+2050.1
	2:12 n was there any beast with me, 369+2050.1
	2:16 n had I as yet told it to the Jews, 3808+2050.1
	4:11 They shall not know, n see, 3808+2050.1
	4:23 n I, nor my brethren, nor my servants, 369
	5: 5 n is it in our power to redeem 369+2050.1
	5:16 this wall, n bought we any land: 3808+2050.1
	8:10 n be ye sorry; for the 408+2050.1
	8:11 the day is holy; n be ye grieved. 408+2050.1
	9:17 n were mindful of thy wonders 3808+2050.1
	9:19 the pillar of fire by night, to shew 2050.1
	9:34 N have our kings, our princes, 2050.1
	9:35 n turned they from their wicked 369
Est	2: 7 for she had n father nor mother, 369
	3: 8 n keep they the king's laws: 369+2050.1
	4:16 n eat nor drink three days, night or day; 408
Job	3: 4 let the light shine upon it. 408+2050.1
	3: 9 n let it see the dawning of the day: 408+2050.1
	3:26 I was not in safety, n had I rest, 3808+2050.1
	3:26 neither had I rest, n was I quiet; 3808+2050.1
	5: 4 n is there any to deliver them. 369+2050.1
	5: 6 n doth trouble spring out of 3808+2050.1
	5:21 n shalt thou be afraid of 3808+2050.1
	5:22 n shalt thou be afraid of the beasts 408+2050.1
	7:10 n shall his place know him any 3808+2050.1
	8:20 man, n will he help the evil doers: 3808+2050.1
	9:33 N is there any daysman betwixt us, 3863
	15:29 n shall his substance continue, 3808+2050.1
	15:29 n shall he prolong the perfection 3808+2050.1
	18:19 He shall n have son nor nephew among 3808
	20: 9 n shall his place any more behold 3808+2050.1
	21: 9 n is the rod of God upon them. 3808+2050.1
	23:12 N have I gone back from 3808+2050.1
	23:17 n hath he covered the darkness from my NIH
	28:13 n is it found in the land of 3808+2050.1
	28:15 n shall silver be weighed for 3808+2050.1
	28:19 n shall it be valued with pure gold. 3808
	31:30 (N have I suffered my mouth to 3808+2050.1
	32: 9 n do the aged understand judgment. 2050.1
	32:14 n will I answer him with your 3808+2050.1
	32:21 n let me give flattering titles unto 3808+2050.1
	33: 7 n shall my hand be heavy upon 3808+2050.1
	33: 9 n is there iniquity in me. 3808+2050.1
	34:12 n will the Almighty pervert 3808+2050.1
	35:13 n will the Almighty regard it. 3808+2050.1
	36:26 n can the number of his years be 3808+2050.1
	39: 7 n regardeth he the crying of the driver. 3808
	39:17 n hath he imparted to her 3808+2050.1
	39:22 n turneth he back from 3808+2050.1
	39:24 n believeth he that it is the sound 3808+2050.1
Ps	4 wickedness: neither shall evil dwell with thee. 3808
	6: 1 chasten me in thy hot 408+2050.1
	16:10 n wilt thou suffer thine Holy One to see 3808

Ps	18:37 n did I turn again till they were 3808+2050.1
	22:24 n hath he hid his face from him; 3808+2050.1
	26: 4 n will I go in with dissemblers. 3808+2050.1
	27: 9 me not, n forsake me, O God 408+2050.1
	33:17 n shall he deliver any by his great 3808+2050.1
	35:19 n let them wink with the eye that hate me NIH
	37: 1 be thou envious against the workers of 408
	38: 1 n chasten me in thy hot displeasure. 2050.1
	38: 3 n is there any rest in my bones because 369
	44: 3 n did their own arm save them: 3808+2050.1
	44: 6 n shall my sword save me. 3808+2050.1
	44:17 n have we dealt falsely in thy 3808+2050.1
	44:18 n have our steps declined from thy way; 2050.1
	55:12 have borne it: n was it he that hated 3808
	69:15 n let the deep swallow me up, 408+2050.1
	73: 5 n are they plagued like other 3808+2050.1
	74: 9 n is there among us any that 3808+2050.1
	75: 6 For promotion cometh n from the east, 3808
	78:37 n were they stedfast in his 3808+2050.1
	81: 9 n shall thou worship any strange 3808+2050.1
	82: 5 They know not, n will they 3808+2050.1
	86: 8 n are there any works like unto 369+2050.1
	91:10 n shall any plague come nigh thy 3808+2050.1
	92: 6 n doth a fool understand this. 3808+2050.1
	94: 7 n shall the God of Jacob regard 3808+2050.1
	94:14 n will he forsake his inheritance. 3808+2050.1
	103: 9 n will he keep his anger for ever. 3808+2050.1
	109:12 n let there be any to favour his 408+2050.1
	115: 7 not: n speak they through their throat. 3808
	115:17 n any that go down into silence. 3808+2050.1
	121: 4 he that keepeth Israel shall n slumber nor 3808
	129: 8 N do they which go by say, 3808+2050.1
	131: 1 n do I exercise myself in great 3808+2050.1
	135:17 they hear not; n is there any breath 369+637
Pr	2:19 n take they hold of the paths of 3808+2050.1
	3:11 n be weary of his correction: 408+2050.1
	3:25 n of the desolation of the wicked, 2050.1
	4: 5 n decline from the words of my 408+2050.1
	6:25 n let her take thee with her 408+2050.1
	6:35 n will he rest content, though 3808+2050.1
	15:12 him: n will he go unto the wise. 3808
	22:22 n oppress the afflicted in the gate: 408+2050.1
	23: 6 n desire thou his dainty meats: 408+2050.1
	24: 1 evil men, n desire to be with them. 408+2050.1
	24:19 evil men, n be thou envious at the wicked; 408
	27:10 n go into thy brother's house in 408+2050.1
	30: 3 I learned wisdom, nor have 3808+2050.1
	30: 8 give me n poverty nor riches; feed me 408
Ecc	1:11 n shall there be any 1571+3808+2050.1
	4: 8 a second; yea, he hath n child nor brother: 369
	4: 8 his eye satisfied with riches; 1571+3808
	4: 8 saith he, For whom do I labour, 2050.1
	5: 6 n say thou before the angel, that it 408+2050.1
	6:10 n may he contend with him that 3808+2050.1
	7:16 not righteous over much; n make 408+2050.1
	7:17 much wicked, n be thou foolish: 408+2050.1
	8: 8 n hath he power in the day of 369+2050.1
	8: 8 shall wickedness deliver those 3808+2050.1
	8:13 n shall he prolong his days, 3808+2050.1
	8:16 (for also there is that n day nor night seeth 369
	9: 5 have they any more a reward; 369+2050.1
	9: 6 n have they any more a portion for 369+2050.1
	9:11 strong, n yet bread to the wise, 3808+2050.1
SS	8: 7 n can the floods drown it: 3808+2050.1
Isa	1: 6 have not been closed, n bound 3808+2050.1
	1: 6 n mollified with ointment. 3808+2050.1
	1:23 n doth the cause of the widow 3808+2050.1
	2: 4 lift up sword against nation, n 3808+2050.1
	2: 7 n is there any end of their 369+2050.1
	2: 7 n is there any end of their chariots: 369+2050.1
	3: 7 in my house is n bread nor clothing: 369
	5:12 n consider the operation of his 3808+2050.1
	5:27 n shall the girdle of their loins be 3808+2050.1
	7: 4 n be fainthearted for the two tails 408+2050.1
	7: 7 not stand, n shall it come to pass. 3808+2050.1
	7:12 not ask, n will I tempt the LORD. 3808+2050.1
	8:12 n fear ye their fear, nor be afraid. 408+2050.1
	9:13 n do they seek the LORD of 3808+2050.1
	9:17 shall have mercy on their 3808+2050.1
	10: 7 not so, n doth his heart think so; 3808+2050.1
	11: 3 n reprove after the hearing of his 3808+2050.1
	13:20 n shall it be dwelt in from 3808+2050.1
	13:20 n shall the Arabian pitch tent 3808+2050.1
	13:20 n shall the shepherds make their 3808+2050.1
	16:10 be no singing, n shall there be shouting: 3808
	17: 8 n shall respect that which his 3808+2050.1
	19:15 N shall there be any work for 3808+2050.1
	22:11 n had respect unto him that 3808+2050.1
	23: 4 do I nourish up young men, 3808+2050.1
	26:18 n have the inhabitants of the 1077+2050.1
	28:27 n is a cart wheel turned about upon 2050.1
	29:22 n shall his face now wax pale. 3808+2050.1
	31: 1 One of Israel, n seek the LORD. 3808+2050.1
	33:20 thereof shall ever be removed, n 1077+2050.1
	33:21 n shall gallant ship pass thereby. 3808+2050.1
	36:15 N let Hezekiah make you trust in 408+2050.1
	40:28 earth, fainteth not, n is weary? 3808+2050.1
	42: 8 another, n my praise to graven images. 2050.1
	42:24 n were they obedient unto his 3808+2050.1
	43: 2 n shall the flame kindle upon 3808+2050.1
	43:10 n shall there be after me. 3808+2050.1
	43:18 n consider the things of old. 3808+2050.1
	43:23 n hast thou honoured me with 3808+2050.1
	43:24 n hast thou filled me with the fat 3808+2050.1
	44: 8 Fear ye not, n be afraid: have not 408+2050.1

N

Isa
44:19 **n** *is there* knowledge nor 3808+2050.1
47: 7 **n** didst remember the latter end of it. 3808
47: 8 **n** shall I know the loss of 3808+2050.1
49:10 shall not hunger nor thirst; **n** 3808+2050.1
50: 5 I was not rebellious, **n** turned away back. 3808
51: 7 **n** be ye afraid of their revilings. 408+2050.1
51:18 **n** *is there any* that taketh her by 369+2050.1
53: 9 **n** *was any* deceit in his mouth. 3808+2050.1
54: 4 **n** be thou confounded; for thou 408+2050.1
54:10 **n** shall the covenant of my peace 3808+2050.1
55: 8 **n** *are* your ways my ways, saith 3808+2050.1
56: 3 **N** let the son of the stranger, 408+2050.1
56: 3 **n** let the eunuch say, Behold, I *am* 408+2050.1
57:16 For I will not contend for ever, **n** 3808+2050.1
59: 1 *it* cannot save; **n** his ear heavy, 3808+2050.1
59: 6 **n** shall they cover themselves 3808+2050.1
59: 9 **n** doth justice overtake us: 3808+2050.1
60:19 be no more thy light by day; **n** 3808+2050.1
60:20 **n** shall thy moon withdraw itself: 3808+2050.1
62: 4 **n** shall thy land any more be 3808+2050.1
64: 4 **n** hath the eye seen, O God, besides thee, 3808
64: 9 **n** remember iniquity for ever: 408+2050.1
66:19 my fame, **n** have seen my glory; 3808+2050.1
66:24 **n** shall their fire be quenched; 3808+2050.1

Jer
2: 6 **N** said they, Where *is* the Lᴏʀᴅ 3808+2050.1
3:16 **n** shall it come to mind: 3808+2050.1
3:16 **n** shall they remember it; 3808+2050.1
3:16 **n** shall they visit *it;* neither shall 3808+2050.1
3:16 neither shall they visit *it;* **n** shall 3808+2050.1
3:17 **n** shall they walk any more after 3808+2050.1
4:28 **n** will I turn back from it. 3808+2050.1
5:12 not he; **n** shall evil come upon us; 3808+2050.1
5:12 **n** shall we see sword nor famine: 3808+2050.1
5:15 **n** understandest what they say. 3808+2050.1
5:24 **N** say they in their heart, Let us 3808+2050.1
6:15 at all ashamed, **n** could they blush: 1571+3808
7: 6 **n** walk after other gods to your 3808+2050.1
7:16 pray not thou for this people, **n** 408+2050.1
7:16 them, **n** make intercession to me: 408+2050.1
7:31 which I commanded *them* not, **n** 3808+2050.1
8:12 all ashamed, **n** could they blush: 3808+2050.1
9:10 none can pass through *them;* **n** 3808+2050.1
9:13 my voice, **n** walked therein; 3808+2050.1
9:16 **n** they nor their fathers have known: 3808
9:23 **n** let the mighty *man* glory in his 408+2050.1
10: 5 **n** also *is it* in them to do good. 369+2050.1
11:14 pray not thou for this people, **n** 408+2050.1
14:13 sword, **n** shall ye have famine; 3808+2050.1
14:14 I sent them not, **n** have I 3808+2050.1
14:14 **n** spake unto them: 3808+2050.1
15:10 I have **n** lent on usury, nor *men* have 3808
16: 2 **n** shalt thou have sons nor 3808+2050.1
16: 4 **n** shall they be buried; 3808+2050.1
16: 5 **n** go to lament nor bemoan them: 408+2050.1
16: 6 **n** shall *men* lament for them, 3808+2050.1
16: 7 **N** shall *men* tear *themselves* for 3808+2050.1
16: 7 **n** shall *men* give them the cup of 3808+2050.1
16:13 that ye know not, **n** ye nor your fathers; NIH
16:17 they are not hid from my face, **n** 3808+2050.1
17: 8 **n** shall cease from yielding fruit. 3808+2050.1
17:16 have I desired the woeful day; 3808+2050.1
17:22 **N** carry forth a burden out of 3808+2050.1
17:22 **n** do ye any work, but hallow ye 3808+2050.1
17:23 **n** inclined their ear, but made 3808+2050.1
18:23 **n** blot out their sin from thy sight, 408+2050.1
19: 4 **n** they nor their fathers have known, 3808
19: 5 spake *it,* **n** came *it* into my mind: 3808+2050.1
21: 7 **n** have pity, nor have mercy. 3808+2050.1
22: 3 **n** shed innocent blood in this 408+2050.1
22:10 ye not for the dead, **n** bemoan 408+2050.1
23: 4 nor be dismayed, **n** shall they be 408+2050.1
25:33 gathered, nor buried; 3808+2050.1
29: 8 **n** hearken to your dreams which 408+2050.1
29:32 to dwell among this people; **n** 3808+2050.1
30:10 be dismayed, O Israel: 408+2050.1
32:23 thy voice, **n** walked in thy law; 3808+2050.1
32:35 not, **n** came it into my mind, 3808+2050.1
33:18 **N** shall the priests the Levites 3808+2050.1
33:22 the sand of the sea measured: 2050.1
34:14 not unto me, **n** inclined their ear. 3808+2050.1
35: 6 no wine, *n* ye, nor your sons for ever: NIH
35: 7 **N** shall ye build house, nor sow 3808+2050.1
35: 9 we have vineyard, nor field, nor seed: 2050.1
36:24 nor rent their garments, the king, NIH
37: 2 **n** he, nor his servants, nor the people of 3808
38:16 I will not put thee to death, **n** will I NIH
42:13 **n** obey the voice of the Lᴏʀᴅ your God, 1115
44: 3 knew not, **n** they, you, nor your fathers. NIH
44:10 have they feared, nor walked in 3808+2050.1
48:11 **n** hath he gone into captivity: 3808+2050.1
49:18 **n** shall a son of man dwell in it. 3808+2050.1
49:31 the Lᴏʀᴅ, which have **n** gates nor bars, 3808
50:39 **n** shall it be dwelt in from 3808+2050.1
50:40 **n** shall *any* son of man dwell 3808+2050.1
51:43 **n** doth *any* son of man pass 3808+2050.1
51:62 **n** man nor beast, but that it shall 4480+3807.1

Eze
2: 6 be afraid of their words, 408+2050.1
3: 9 fear them not, **n** be dismayed at 3808+2050.1
4:14 **n** came there abominable flesh 3808+2050.1
5: 7 **n** have kept my judgments, 3808+2050.1
5: 7 **n** have done according to 3808+2050.1
5:11 will I also diminish *thee;* **n** shall 3808+2050.1
5:11 eye spare, **n** will I have any pity. 3808+2050.1
7: 4 not spare thee, **n** will I have pity: 3808+2050.1
7: 9 shall not spare, **n** will I have pity: 3808+2050.1

Eze
7:11 **n** *shall there be* wailing for them. 3808+2050.1
7:13 **n** shall any strengthen himself in 3808+2050.1
7:19 their souls, **n** fill their bowels: 3808+2050.1
8:18 mine eye shall not spare, **n** will I 3808+2050.1
9: 5 not your eye spare, **n** have ye pity: 408+2050.1
9:10 **n** will I have pity, but I will 3808+2050.1
11:11 **n** shall ye be the flesh in the midst 2050.1
11:12 **n** executed my judgments, 3808+2050.1
13: 5 **n** made up the hedge for the house of 2050.1
13: 9 **n** shall they be written in 3808+2050.1
13: 9 **n** shall they enter into the land of 3808+2050.1
13:15 *is* no *more,* **n** they that daubed it; 369+2050.1
14:11 **n** be polluted any more with all 3808+2050.1
14:16 they shall deliver **n** sons nor daughters; 518
14:18 they shall deliver **n** sons nor daughters, 3808
14:20 they shall deliver **n** son nor daughter; 518
16: 4 **n** wast thou washed in water to 3808+2050.1
16:16 *the like things shall* not come, **n** 3808+2050.1
16:49 **n** did she strengthen the hand of 3808+2050.1
16:51 **N** hath Samaria committed half 3808+2050.1
17:17 **N** shall Pharaoh with *his* mighty 3808+2050.1
18: 6 **n** hath lift up his eyes to the idols 3808+2050.1
18: 6 **n** hath defiled his neighbour's 3808+2050.1
18: 6 **n** hath come near to a 3808+2050.1
18: 8 **n** hath taken any increase, 3808+2050.1
18:15 **n** hath lift up his eyes to the idols 3808+2050.1
18:16 **N** hath oppressed any, hath not 3808+2050.1
18:16 **n** hath spoiled by violence, 3808+2050.1
18:20 shall the father bear the 3808+2050.1
20: 8 **n** did they forsake the idols of 3808+2050.1
20:17 **n** did I make an end of them in 3808+2050.1
20:18 **n** observe their judgments, 408+2050.1
20:21 **n** kept my judgments to do them, 3808+2050.1
22:26 have they shewed *difference* 3808+2050.1
23: 8 **N** left she her whoredoms 3808+2050.1
24:14 **n** will I spare, neither will I 3808+2050.1
24:14 will I spare, **n** will I repent; 3808+2050.1
24:16 **n** shalt thou mourn nor 3808+2050.1
24:16 **n** shall thy tears run down. 3808+2050.1
29:11 **n** shall it be inhabited forty years. 3808+2050.1
29:15 shall it exalt itself any more 3808+2050.1
31:14 **n** shoot up their top among 3808+2050.1
31:14 **n** their trees stand up in their 3808+2050.1
32:13 **n** shall the foot of man trouble 3808+2050.1
33:12 shall the righteous be able to 3808+2050.1
34: 4 **n** have ye healed that which was 3808+2050.1
34: 4 **n** have ye bound up that which 3808+2050.1
34: 4 **n** have ye brought again that 3808+2050.1
34: 4 **n** have ye sought that which was 3808+2050.1
34: 8 **n** did my shepherds search for 3808+2050.1
34:10 shall the shepherds feed 3808+2050.1
34:28 shall the beast of the land 3808+2050.1
34:29 **n** bear the shame of the heathen 3808+2050.1
36:14 bereave thy nations any more, 3808+2050.1
36:15 **N** will I cause *men* to hear in 3808+2050.1
36:15 **n** shalt thou bear the reproach of 3808+2050.1
36:15 **n** shalt thou cause thy nations to 3808+2050.1
37:22 **n** shall they be divided into two 3808+2050.1
37:23 **N** shall they defile themselves 3808+2050.1
38:11 walls, and having **n** bars nor gates, 369
39:10 **n** cut down *any* out of the forests 3808+2050.1
39:29 **N** will I hide my face any more 3808+2050.1
43: 7 *n* they, nor their kings, by their whoredom NIH
44:20 **N** shall they shave their heads, 3808+2050.1
44:21 **N** shall any priest drink wine, 3808+2050.1
44:22 **N** shall they take for their wives 3808+2050.1
47:12 **n** shall the fruit thereof be 3808+2050.1
48:14 shall not sell of it, **n** exchange, 3808+2050.1

Da
3:27 **n** were their coats changed, 3809+2050.3
6: 4 **n** was there any error or fault 3809+2050.3
6:18 **n** were instruments of musick 3809+2050.3
8: 4 **n** *was there any* that could deliver 369+2050.1
9: 6 **N** have we hearkened unto thy 3808+2050.1
9:10 **N** have we obeyed the voice of 3808+2050.1
10: 3 **n** came flesh nor wine in my 3808+2050.1
10: 3 **n** did I anoint myself at all, till 3808+2050.1
10:17 me, **n** is there breath left in me. 3808+2050.1
11: 6 **n** shall he stand, nor his arm: 3808+2050.1
11:15 not withstand, **n** his chosen people, 2050.1
11:15 *n* *shall there be any* strength to 369+2050.1
11:17 shall not stand *on his side,* **n** be 3808+2050.1
11:20 **n** in anger, nor in battle. 3808+2050.1
11:37 **N** shall he regard the God of his 5921+2050.1

Hos
2: 2 for she *is* not my wife, **n** *am* I her 3808+2050.1
4:15 go ye up to Beth-aven, nor 408+2050.1
9: 4 shall they be pleasing unto him: 3808+2050.1
14: 3 **n** will we say any more to the 3808+2050.1

Joel
2: 2 **n** shall be any more after it, 3808+2050.2
2: 8 **N** shall one thrust another; 3808+2050.1

Am
2:14 shall the mighty deliver himself 3808+2050.1
2:15 **N** shall he stand that handleth 3808+2050.1
2:15 shall he that rideth the horse 3808+2050.1
5:22 I will not accept *them:* **n** will I 3808+2050.1
7:14 *n* *was* I a prophet's son; 3808+2050.1

Ob
1:12 shouldest thou have rejoiced 408+2050.1
1:12 shouldest thou have spoken 408+2050.1
1:14 **N** shouldest thou have stood in 408+2050.1
1:14 shouldest thou have delivered 408+2050.1

Jnh
3: 7 his nobles, saying, Let **n** man nor beast, 408
4:10 not laboured, **n** madest it grow; 3808+2050.1

Mic
2: 3 shall ye go haughtily: 3808+2050.1
4: 3 shall they learn war any more. 3808+2050.1
4:12 **n** understand they his counsel: 3808+2050.1

Hab
2: 5 a proud man, **n** keepeth at home, 3808+2050.1
3:17 **n** *shall* fruit *be* in the vines; 369+2050.1

Zep
1:12 not do good, **n** will he do evil. 3808+2050.1
1:18 **N** their silver nor their gold shall 1571+3808
3:13 **N** shall a deceitful tongue be 3808+2050.1

Zec
8:10 **n** *was there any* peace to him that 369+2050.1
11:16 shall seek the young one, nor heal that 3808
13: 4 **n** shall they wear a rough 3808+2050.1

Mal
1:10 **n** do ye kindle *fire* on mine altar 3761
1:10 **n** will I accept an offering at your 3808+2050.1
3:11 **n** shall your vine cast her fruit 3808+2050.1
4: 1 it shall leave them **n** root nor branch. 3808

Mt
5:15 **N** do men light a candle, and put it under 3761
5:34 unto you, Swear not at all; **n** by heaven; 3383
5:35 **n** by Jerusalem; for it is the city of the 3383
5:36 **N** shalt thou swear by thy head, because 3383
6:15 **n** will your Father forgive your trespasses. 3761
6:20 where **n** moth nor rust doth corrupt, 3777
6:26 they sow not, **n** do they reap, nor gather 3761
6:28 they grow; they toil not, **n** do they spin: 3761
7: 6 **n** cast ye your pearls before swine, lest 3366
7:18 **n** can a corrupt tree bring forth good fruit. 3761
9:17 **n** do *men* put new wine into old bottles: 3761
10: 9 Provide **n** gold, nor silver, nor brass in 3361
10:10 **n** two coats, neither shoes, nor yet staves: 3366
10:10 neither two coats, **n** shoes, nor yet staves: 3366
11:18 For John came **n** eating nor drinking, 3383
11:27 **n** knoweth any *man* the Father, save 3761
12: 4 **n** for them which were with him, but 3761
12:19 **n** shall any *man* hear his voice in 3761
12:32 shall not be forgiven him, **n** in this world, 3777
12:32 in this world, **n** in the *world* to come. 3777
13:13 they hear not, **n** do they understand. 3761
16: 9 **n** remember the five loaves of the five 3761
16:10 **N** the seven loaves of the four thousand, 3761
21:27 **N** tell I you by what authority I do 3761
22:16 **n** carest thou for any *man:* for thou 2532+3756
22:30 For in the resurrection they **n** marry, 3777
22:46 **n** durst any *man* from that day forth ask 3761
23:10 **N** be ye called masters: for one is your 3366
23:13 for ye **n** go in yourselves, neither suffer ye 3756
23:13 **n** suffer ye them that are entering to go in. 3761
24:18 **N** let him which is in the field 2532+3361
24:20 not in the winter, **n** on the sabbath day: 3366
25:13 ye know **n** the day nor the hour wherein 3756

Mk
4:22 **n** was *any thing* kept secret, but that it 3761
5: 4 in pieces: **n** could any *man* tame him. 2532
8:14 had they in the ship with them 2532+3756
8:17 perceive ye not yet, **n** understand? have 3761
8:26 **N** go into the town, nor tell *it* to any 3366
11:26 **n** will your Father which is in heaven 3761
11:33 **N** do I tell you by what authority I do 3761
12:21 took her, and died, **n** left he *any* seed: 3761
12:24 not the scriptures, **n** the power of God? 3366
12:25 they **n** marry, nor are given in marriage; 3777
13:11 what ye shall speak, **n** do ye premeditate: 3366
13:15 **n** enter *therein,* to take any thing out of 3366
13:19 created unto this time, **n** shall be. 2532+3364
13:32 are in heaven, **n** the Son, but the Father. 3761
14:40 **n** wist they what to answer him. 2532+3756
14:59 But **n** so did their witness agree together. 3761
16: 8 **n** said they *any thing* to any *man;* 2532+3762
16:13 *it* unto the residue: **n** believed they them. 3761

Lk
1:15 and shall drink **n** wine nor strong drink; 3364
3:14 violence to no man, **n** accuse *any* falsely; 3366
6:43 **n** doth a corrupt tree bring forth good 3761
7: 7 Wherefore **n** thought I myself worthy to 3761
7:33 For John the Baptist came **n** eating bread 3383
8:17 **n** *any thing* hid, that shall not be known 3761
8:27 **n** abode in *any* house, but in 2532+3756
8:43 **n** could be healed of *any,* 3756+3762
9: 3 **n** staves, nor scrip, neither bread, 3383
9: 3 **n** neither staves, nor scrip, **n** bread, 3383
9: 3 nor scrip, neither bread, **n** money; 3383
9: 3 neither money; **n** have two coats apiece. 3383
10: 4 Carry **n** purse, nor scrip, nor shoes: 3361
11:33 **n** under a bushel, but on a candlestick, 3761
12: 2 revealed; **n** hid, that shall not be known. 2532
12:22 **n** for the body, what ye shall put on. 3366
12:24 they **n** sow nor reap; which neither have 3756
12:24 have storehouse nor barn; and God 3756
12:29 drink, **n** be ye of doubtful mind. 2532+3361
12:33 no thief approacheth, **n** moth corrupteth. 3761
12:47 prepared not *himself,* **n** did according to 3366
14:12 nor thy brethren, **n** thy kinsmen, 3366
14:35 It is **n** fit for the land, nor yet for 3777
15:29 **n** transgressed I *at any time* thy 2532+3763
16:26 **n** can they pass to us, that *would come* 3366
16:31 the prophets, **n** will they be persuaded, 3761
17:21 Nor shall they say, Lo here: or, lo there: 3761
18: 2 feared not God, **n** regarded man: 2532+3361
18:34 knew they *the things* which were 2532+3756
20: 8 **N** tell I you by what authority I do these 3761
20:21 **n** acceptest thou the person *of any,* 2532+3756
20:35 **n** marry, nor are given in marriage: 3777
20:36 **N** can they die any more: for they are 3777

Jn
1:25 not *that* Christ, nor Elias, **n** *that* prophet? 3761
3:20 **n** cometh to the light, lest his 2532+3756
4:15 that I thirst not, **n** come hither to draw. 3366
4:21 when ye shall **n** in this mountain, 3777
5:37 Ye have **n** heard his voice at any time, 3777
6:24 **n** his disciples, they also took shipping, 3777
7: 5 For **n** did his brethren believe in him. 3761
8:11 Jesus said unto her, **N** do I condemn thee: 3761
8:19 Ye **n** know me, nor my Father: 3777
8:42 and came from God; **n** came I of myself, 3761

Jn	9: 3	N hath this *man* sinned, nor his parents:	3777
	10:28	n shall any *man* pluck them out of	2532+3756
	13:16	n he that is sent greater than he that sent	3761
	14:17	because it seeth him not, n knoweth him:	3761
	14:27	your heart be troubled, n let it be afraid.	3366
	17:20	N pray I for these alone, but for	1161+3756
Ac	2:27	n wilt thou suffer thine Holy One to see	3761
	2:31	left in hell, n his flesh did see corruption.	3761
	4:12	N is there salvation in any other:	2532+3756
	4:32	said any *of them* that ought of	2532+3756
	4:34	N was there any among them that lacked:	3761
	8:21	Thou hast n part nor lot in this matter:	3756
	9: 9	without sight, and n did eat nor drink.	3756
	15:10	which n our fathers nor we were able to	3777
	16:21	us to receive, n to observe, being Romans.	3761
	17:25	N is worshipped with men's hands,	3761
	19:37	which *are* n robbers of churches, nor yet	3777
	20:24	n count I my life dear unto myself, so that	3761
	21:21	children, n to walk after the customs.	3366
	23: 8	there is no resurrection, n angel nor spirit:	3366
	23:12	saying that *they* would n eat nor drink till	3383
	23:21	that *they* will n eat nor drink till they have	3383
	24:12	And they n found me in the temple	3777
	24:12	with any *man*, n raising up the people,	2228
	24:12	n in the synagogues, nor in the city:	3777
	24:13	N can they prove *the things* whereof they	3777
	24:18	n with multitude, nor with tumult.	3756
	25: 8	N against the law of the Jews,	3777
	25: 8	n against the temple, nor *yet* against Cesar	3777
	27:20	And when n sun nor stars in many days	3383
	28:21	We n received letters out of Judea	3777
	28:21	n any of the brethren that came shewed	3777
Ro	1:21	glorified *him* as not as God, n were thankful;	2228
	2:28	n *is that* circumcision, which is outward	3761
	4:19	n *yet* the deadness of Sara's womb:	2532
	6:13	N yield ye your members as instruments	3366
	8: 7	to the law of God, n indeed can be.	3761
	8:38	that n death, nor life, nor angels,	3777
	9: 7	N, because they are not seed of Abraham,	3761
	9:11	yet born, n having done any good or evil,	3366
	14:21	*It is* good n to eat flesh, nor to drink wine,	3361
1Co	2: 9	n have entered into the heart of	2532+3756
	2:14	n can he know *them*, because	2532+3756
	3: 2	for hitherto ye were not able to bear it, n	3777
	3: 7	n is he that planteth any *thing*, neither he	3777
	3: 7	neither is he that planteth any *thing*, n he	3366
	5: 8	n with the leaven of malice and	3366
	6: 9	fornicators, nor idolaters, nor adulterers,	3777
	8: 8	for n, if we eat, are we the better; neither,	3777
	8: 8	n, if we eat not, are we the worse.	3777
	9:15	n have I written *these things*, that	1161+3756
	10: 7	N be ye idolaters, as *were* some of them;	3366
	10: 8	N let us commit fornication, as some of	3366
	10: 9	N let us tempt Christ, as some of them	3366
	10:10	N murmur ye, as some of them also	3366
	10:32	Give none offence, n to the Jews, nor to	2532
	11: 9	N was the man created for	2532+3756
	11:11	Nevertheless n *is* the man without	3777
	11:11	the woman without the man, in the	3777
	11:16	no such custom, n the churches of God.	3761
	15:50	n doth corruption inherit incorruption.	3761
Gal	1: 1	n by man, but by Jesus Christ, and God	3761
	1:12	For I received it of man, neither was I	3777
	1:12	n was I taught *it*, but by the revelation of	3777
	1:17	N went I up to Jerusalem to them which	3761
	2: 3	But n Titus, who was with me, being a	3761
	3:28	There is n Jew nor Greek, there is neither	3756
	3:28	Jew nor Greek, there is n bond nor free,	3756
	3:28	bond nor free, there is n male nor female:	3756
	5: 6	in Jesus Christ n circumcision availeth	3777
	6:13	n they themselves who are circumcised	3761
	6:15	For in Christ Jesus n circumcision availeth	3777
Eph	4:27	N give place to the devil.	3383
	5: 4	N filthiness, nor foolish talking, nor	2532
	6: 9	n is there respect of persons with	2532+3756
Php	2:16	I have not run in vain, n laboured in vain.	3761
Col	3:11	Where there is n Greek nor Jew,	3756
1Th	2: 5	n at any time used we flattering words,	3777
	2: 6	we glory, n of you, nor *yet* of others,	3777
2Th	2: 2	be troubled, n by spirit, nor by word,	3383
	3: 8	N did we eat any *man's* bread for nought;	3761
	3:10	if any would not work, n should he eat.	3366
1Ti	1: 4	give heed to fables and	3366
	1: 7	understanding n what they say, nor	3383
	5:22	Lay hands suddenly on no *man*, n be	3366
Heb	4:13	N is there any creature *that is* not	2532+3756
	7: 3	having n beginning of days, nor end of life	3383
	9:12	N by the blood of goats and calves,	3761
	9:18	Whereupon n the first *testament* was	3761
	9:18	n hadst pleasure *therein:* which are	3761
Jas	1:13	with evil, n tempteth he any *man:*	1161+3762
	1:17	is no variableness, n shadow of turning.	2228
	5:12	swear not, n by heaven, neither by	3383
	5:12	neither by heaven, n by the earth,	3383
	5:12	neither by the earth, n by any other oath:	3383
1Pe	2:22	no sin, n was guile found in his mouth:	3761
	3:14	be not afraid of their terror, n be troubled;	3366
	5: 3	N as being lords over *God's* heritage,	3366
2Pe	1: 8	they make *you that ye shall* n be barren	3756
1Jn	2:15	world, n the *things* that are in the world.	3366
	3: 6	sinneth hath n seen him, n known him.	3761
	3:10	of God, n he that loveth not his brother.	2532
	3:18	let us not love in word, n in tongue;	3366
2Jn	1:10	*your* house, n bid him God speed:	2532+3361
3Jn	1:10	n doth himself receive the brethren,	3777

Rev	3:15	thy works, that thou art n cold nor hot:	3777
	3:16	thou art lukewarm, and n cold nor hot,	3777
	5: 3	in heaven, nor in earth, n under the earth,	3761
	5: 3	able to open the book, n to look thereon.	3761
	5: 4	and to read the book, n to look thereon.	3777
	7: 1	not the earth, n the sea, nor the trees,	3383
	7:16	shall hunger no more, n thirst any more;	3761
	7:16	n shall the sun light on them, nor any	3761
	9: 4	n any green *thing*, neither any tree;	3761
	9: 4	neither any green *thing*, n any tree;	3761
	9:20	which n can see, nor hear, nor walk:	3777
	9:21	N repented they of their murders,	2532+3756
	12: 8	n was their place found any more in	3777
	20: 4	not worshipped the beast, n his image,	3777
	20: 4	n had received *his* mark upon their	2532+3756
	21: 4	be no more death, n sorrow, nor crying,	3777
	21: 4	nor crying, n shall there be any more pain:	3777
	21:23	of the sun, n of the moon, to shine in it:	3761
	21:27	n *whatsoever* worketh abomination,	2532
	22: 5	they need no candle, n light of the sun;	2532

NEKEB (1)

Jos	19:33	and Adami, N, and Jabneel, unto Lakum;	5346

NEKODA (4)

Ezr	2:48	The children of Rezin, the children of N,	5353
	2:60	the children of N, six hundred fifty and	5353
Ne	7:50	the children of Rezin, the children of N,	5353
	7:62	the children of N, six hundred forty and	5353

NEMUEL (3) [NEMUELITES]

Nu	26: 9	sons of Eliab; N, and Dathan, and Abiram.	5241
	26:12	of N, the family of the Nemuelites:	5241
1Ch	4:24	The sons of Simeon *were*, N, and Jamin,	5241

NEMUELITE See NEMUELITES

NEMUELITES (1) [NEMUEL]

Nu	26:12	of Nemuel, the family of the N: of Jamin,	5242

NEPHEG (4)

Ex	6:21	sons of Izhar; Korah, and N, and Zichri.	5298
2Sa	5:15	Ibhar also, and Elishua, and N, and Japhia,	5298
1Ch	3: 7	And Nogah, and N, and Japhia,	5298
	14: 6	And Nogah, and N, and Japhia,	5298

NEPHEW (2) [NEPHEWS]

Job	18:19	He shall neither have son nor n among	5220
Isa	14:22	remnant, and son, and n, saith the LORD.	5220

NEPHEWS (2) [NEPHEW]

Jdg	12:14	he had forty sons and thirty n, that	1121+1121
1Ti	5: 4	But if any widow have children or n,	1549

NEPHISH (1)

1Ch	5:19	with Jetur, and N, and Nodab.	5305

NEPHISHESIM (1) [NEPHUSIM]

Ne	7:52	children of Meunim, the children of N,	5300

NEPHTHALIM (3) [NAPHTALI]

Mt	4:13	coasts, in the borders of Zabulon and N:	3508
	4:15	The land of Zabulon, and the land of N,	3508
Rev	7: 6	Of the tribe of N *were* sealed twelve	3508

NEPHTOAH (2)

Jos	15: 9	hill unto the fountain of the water of N,	5318
	18:15	and went out to the well of waters of N:	5318

NEPHUSIM (1) [NEPHISHESIM]

Ezr	2:50	children of Mehunim, the children of N,	5300

NEPHUSSIM See NEPHISHESIM; NEPHUSIM

NER (16)

1Sa	14:50	*was* Abner, the son of N, Saul's uncle.	5369
	14:51	The father of Abner *was* the son of	5369
	26: 5	Abner the son of N, the captain of his	5369
	26:14	to Abner the son of N, saying, Answerest	5369
2Sa	2: 8	Abner the son of N, captain of Saul's host,	5369
	2:12	Abner the son of N, and the servants of	5369
	3:23	Abner the son of N came to the king,	5369
	3:25	Thou knowest Abner the son of N, that	5369
	3:28	from the blood of Abner the son of N:	5369
	3:37	not of the king to slay Abner the son of N.	5369
1Ki	2: 5	unto Abner the son of N, and unto Amasa	5369
	2:32	*thereof, to wit*, Abner the son of N,	5369
1Ch	8:33	begat Kish, and Kish begat Saul,	5369
	9:36	and Kish, and Baal, and N, and Nadab,	5369
	9:39	N begat Kish; and Kish begat Saul;	5369
	26:28	the son of N, and Joab the son of	5369

NEREUS (1)

Ro	16:15	N, and his sister, and Olympas, and all	3517

NERGAL (1)

2Ki	17:30	the men of Cuth made N, and the men of	5370

NERGAL-SHAREZER (3)

Jer	39: 3	*even* N, Samgar-nebo, Sarsechim,	5371
	39: 3	Sarsechim, Rab-saris, N, Rab-mag,	5371
	39:13	N, Rab-mag, and all the king of Babylon's	5371

NERI (1)

Lk	3:27	*son* of Salathiel, which was *the son* of N,	3518

NERIAH (10)

Jer	32:12	of the purchase unto Baruch the son of N,	5374
	32:16	of the purchase unto Baruch the son of N,	5374
	36: 4	Jeremiah called Baruch the son of N:	5374
	36: 8	Baruch the son of N did according to all	5374
	36:14	So Baruch the son of N took the roll in his	5374
	36:32	gave it to Baruch the scribe, the son of N;	5374
	43: 3	Baruch the son of N setteth thee on	5374
	43: 6	the prophet, and Baruch the son of N.	5374
	45: 1	prophet spake unto Baruch the son of N,	5374
	51:59	prophet commanded Seraiah the son of N,	5374

NERO (1)

2Ti	4: S	when Paul was brought before N	3505

NEST (15) [NESTS]

Nu	24:21	and thou puttest thy n in a rock.	7064
Dt	22: 6	If a bird's n chance to be before thee in	7064
	32:11	As an eagle stirreth up her n, fluttereth	7064
Job	29:18	shall die in my n, and I shall multiply *my*	7064
	39:27	thy command, and make her n on high?	7064
Ps	84: 3	the swallow a n for herself, where she	7064
Pr	27: 8	As a bird that wandereth from her n, so *is*	7064
Isa	10:14	my hand hath found as a n the riches of	7064
	16: 2	as a wandering bird cast out of the n,	7064
	34:15	There shall the great owl make her n,	7077
Jer	22:23	that *makest* thy n in the cedars,	7077
	48:28	be like the dove *that* maketh her n in	7077
	49:16	though thou shouldest make thy n as	7064
Ob	1: 4	though *thou* set thy n among the stars,	7064
Hab	2: 9	he may set his n on high, that *he* may	7064

NESTS (4) [NEST]

Ps	104:17	Where the birds make their n: *as for*	7077
Eze	31: 6	All the fowls of heaven made their n in	7077
Mt	8:20	holes, and the birds of the air *have* n;	2682
Lk	9:58	have holes, and the birds of the air *have* n;	2682

NET (39) [NETS, NETWORK, NETWORKS]

Ex	27: 4	upon the n shalt thou make four brasen	7568
	27: 5	that it may be even to the midst of	7568
Job	18: 8	For he is cast into a n by his own feet,	7568
	19: 6	and hath compassed me with his n.	4686
Ps	9:15	in the n which they hid is their own foot	7568
	10: 9	poor, when he draweth him into his n.	7568
	25:15	for he shall pluck my feet out of the n.	7568
	31: 4	Pull me out of the n that they have laid	7568
	35: 7	have they hid for me their n in a pit,	7568
	35: 8	let his n that he hath hid catch himself:	7568
	57: 6	They have prepared a n for my steps;	7568
	66:11	Thou broughtest us into the n; thou laidst	4686
	140: 5	they have spread a n by the way side;	7568
Pr	1:17	Surely in vain the n *is* spread in the sight	7568
	12:12	The wicked desireth the n of evil *men:*	4685
	29: 5	his neighbour spreadeth a n for his feet.	7568
Ecc	9:12	as the fishes that are taken in an evil n;	4685
Isa	51:20	of all the streets, as a wild bull *in* a n:	4364
La	1:13	he hath spread a n for my feet, he hath	7568
Eze	12:13	My n also will I spread upon him,	7568
	17:20	And I will spread my n upon him, and he shall	7568
	19: 8	provinces, and spread their n over him:	7568
	32: 3	spread out my n over thee with a	7568
	32: 3	and they shall bring thee up in my n.	2764
Hos	5: 1	on Mizpah, and a n spread upon Tabor.	7568
	7:12	shall go, I will spread my n upon them;	7568
Mic	7: 2	they hunt every man his brother *with* a n.	2764
Hab	1:15	Catch them in their n, and gather them	2764
	1:16	Therefore they sacrifice unto their n,	2764
	1:17	Shall they therefore empty their n,	2764
Mt	4:18	Andrew his brother, casting a n into the	293
	13:47	the kingdom of heaven is like unto a n,	4522
Mk	1:16	Andrew his brother casting a n into the	293
Lk	5: 5	at thy word I will let down the n.	1350
	5: 6	multitude of fishes: and their n brake.	1350
Jn	21: 6	Cast the n on the right side of the ship,	1350
	21: 8	cubits,) dragging the n with fishes.	1350
	21:11	and drew the n to land full of great fishes,	1350
	21:11	so many, *yet* was not the n broken.	1350

NETHANEEL (14)

Nu	1: 8	Of Issachar; N the son of Zuar.	5417
	2: 5	N the son of Zuar *shall be* captain of	5417
	7:18	On the second day N the son of Zuar,	5417
	7:23	this *was* the offering of N the son of Zuar.	5417
	10:15	of Issachar *was* N the son of Zuar.	5417
1Ch	2:14	N the fourth, Raddai the fifth,	5417
	15:24	N, and Amasai, and Zechariah,	5417
	24: 6	Shemaiah the son of N the scribe, *one* of	5417
	26: 4	and Sacar the fourth, and N the fifth,	5417
2Ch	17: 7	to Zechariah, and to N, and to Michaiah,	5417
	35: 9	Shemaiah and N, his brethren,	5417
Ezr	10:22	Ishmael, N, Jozabad, and Elasah.	5417
Ne	12:21	Of Hilkiah, Hashabiah; of Jedaiah, N.	5417
	12:36	Gilalai, Maai, N, and Judah, Hanani,	5417

NETHANEL See NETHANEEL

NETHANIAH (20)

2Ki	25:23	even Ishmael the son of N, and Johanan	5418
	25:25	*that* Ishmael the son of N, the son of	5418
1Ch	25: 2	Zaccur, and Joseph, and N, and Asarelah,	5418
	25:12	The fifth *to* N, *he*, his sons,	5418
2Ch	17: 8	N, and Zebadiah, and Asahel.	5418
Jer	36:14	all the princes sent Jehudi the son of N,	5418
	40: 8	even Ishmael the son of N, and Johanan	5418

N

Jer	40:14 sent Ishmael the son of **N** to slay thee?	5418
	40:15 I will slay Ishmael the son of **N**,	5418
	41: 1 *that* Ishmael the son of **N** the son of	5418
	41: 2 arose Ishmael the son of **N**, and the ten	5418
	41: 6 Ishmael the son of **N** went forth from	5418
	41: 7 that Ishmael the son of **N** slew them,	5418
	41: 9 Ishmael the son of **N** filled it *with them*	5418
	41:10 Ishmael the son of **N** carried them away	5418
	41:11 evil that Ishmael the son of **N** had done,	5418
	41:12 went to fight with Ishmael the son of **N**,	5418
	41:15 Ishmael the son of **N** escaped from	5418
	41:16 had recovered from Ishmael the son of **N**,	5418
	41:18 Ishmael the son of **N** had slain Gedaliah	5418

NETHER (15) [NETHERMOST]

Ex	19:17 they stood at the **n part** of the mount.	8482
Dt	24: 6 No *man* shall take the **n** or the upper	7347
Jos	15:19 her the upper springs, and the **n** springs.	8482
	16: 3 unto the coast of Beth-horon the **n**,	8481
	18:13 on the south side of the **n** Beth-horon.	8481
Jdg	1:15 her the upper springs and the **n** springs.	8482
1Ki	9:17 built Gezer, and Beth-horon the **n**,	8481
1Ch	7:24 built Beth-horon the **n**, and the upper,	8481
2Ch	8: 5 Beth-horon the **n**, fenced cities, *with*	8481
Job	41:24 yea, as hard as a piece of the **n** *millstone*.	8482
Eze	31:14 the **n parts** of the earth, in the midst of	8482
	31:16 shall be comforted in the **n parts** of	8482
	31:18 of Eden unto the **n parts** of the earth:	8482
	32:18 unto the **n parts** of the earth, with them	8482
	32:24 into the **n parts** of the earth,	8482

NETHERMOST (1) [NETHER]

1Ki	6: 6 The **n** chamber *was* five cubits broad,	8481

NETHINIMS (18)

1Ch	9: 2 the priests, Levites, and the **N**.	5411
Ezr	2:43 The **N**: the children of Ziha, the children	5411
	2:58 All the **N**, and the children of Solomon's	5411
	2:70 the singers, and the porters, and the **N**,	5411
	7: 7 the singers, and the porters, and the **N**,	5411
	7:24 **N**, or ministers of this house of God,	5412
	8:17 *and to* his brethren the **N**, at the place	5411
	8:20 of the Levites, whom David and the princes	5411
	8:20 the Levites, two hundred and twenty **N**:	5411
Ne	3:26 Moreover the **N** dwelt in Ophel, unto	5411
	3:31 goldsmith's son unto the place of the **N**,	5411
	7:46 The **N**: the children of Ziha, the children	5411
	7:60 All the **N**, and the children of Solomon's	5411
	7:73 of the people, and the **N**, and all Israel,	5411
	10:28 the **N**, and all they that had separated	5411
	11: 3 the **N**, and the children of Solomon's	5411
	11:21 the **N** dwelt in Ophel: and Ziha and	5411
	11:21 and Ziha and Gispa *were* over the **N**.	5411

NETOPHAH (2)

Ezr	2:22 The men of **N**, fifty and six.	5199
Ne	7:26 men of Beth-lehem and **N**, an hundred	5199

NETOPHATHI (1)

Ne	12:28 and from the villages of **N**;	5200

NETOPHATHITE (8)

2Sa	23:28 Zalmon the Ahohite, Maharai the **N**,	5200
	23:29 Heleb the son of Baanah, a **N**, Ittai the	5200
2Ki	25:23 Seraiah the son of Tanhumeth the **N**,	5200
1Ch	11:30 Maharai the **N**, Heled the son of Baanah	5200
	11:30 Heled the son of Baanah the **N**,	5200
	27:13 for the tenth month *was* Maharai the **N**,	5200
	27:15 for the twelfth month *was* Heldai the **N**,	5200
Jer	40: 8 the sons of Ephai the **N**, and Jezaniah	5200

NETOPHATHITES (2)

1Ch	2:54 Beth-lehem, and the **N**, Ataroth, the	5200
	9:16 that dwelt in the villages of the **N**.	5200

NETS (13) [NET]

1Ki	7:17 And **n** of checker work, *and* wreaths of	7639
Ps	141:10 Let the wicked fall into their own **n**,	4364
Ecc	7:26 whose heart *is* snares and **n**, *and* her	2764
Isa	19: 8 they that spread **n** upon the waters shall	4365
Eze	26: 5 It shall be *a place for* the spreading of **n** in	2764
	26:14 thou shalt be *a place* to spread **n** upon;	2764
	47:10 they shall be a place to spread forth **n**;	2764
Mt	4:20 And they straightway left *their* **n**,	1350
	4:21 Zebedee their father, mending their **n**;	1350
Mk	1:18 And straightway they forsook their **n**,	1350
	1:19 also *were* in the ship mending *their* **n**.	1350
Lk	5: 2 out of them, and were washing *their* **n**.	1350
	5: 4 deep, and let down your **n** for a draught.	1350

NETTLES (5)

Job	30: 7 under the **n** they were gathered together.	2738
Pr	24:31 *and* **n** had covered the face thereof,	2738
Isa	34:13 **n** and brambles in the fortresses thereof:	7057
Hos	9: 6 for their silver, **n** shall possess them:	7057
Zep	2: 9 *even* the breeding of **n**, and saltpits,	2738

NETWORK (7) [NET, WORK]

Ex	27: 4 thou shalt make for it a grate of **n**	4639+7568
	38: 4 **n** under the compass thereof	4639+7568
1Ki	7:18 two rows round about upon the one **n**,	7639
	7:20 against the belly which *was* by the **n**:	7639
	7:42 two rows of pomegranates for one **n**,	7639
Jer	52:22 with **n** and pomegranates upon	7639
	52:23 all the pomegranates upon the **n** *were* an	7639

NETWORKS (3) [NET, WORK]

1Ki	7:41 the two **n**, to cover the two bowls of	7639
	7:42 four hundred pomegranates for the two **n**,	7639
Isa	19: 9 they that weave **n**, shall be confounded.	2355

NEVER (86)

Ge	34:12 **Ask** me so much dowry and gift,	3966+7235
	41:19 such as I **n** saw in all the land of Egypt for	3808
Lev	6:13 burning upon the altar; it shall **n** go out.	3808
Nu	19: 2 blemish, *and* upon which **n** came yoke:	3808
Dt	15:11 For the poor shall **n** cease out of the land:	3808
Jdg	2: 1 I break my covenant with	3808+5769+3807.1
	14: 3 *Is there* **n** a woman among the daughters	369
	16: 7 with seven green withs that were **n** dried,	3808
	16:11 If they bind me fast with new ropes that **n**	3808
2Sa	12:10 **n** depart from thine house,	3808+5704+5769
2Ch	18: 7 for he **n** prophesied good unto me,	369
	21:17 so that there was **n** a son left him,	3808
Job	3:16 not been; as infants *which* **n** saw light.	3808
	9:30 **make** my hands **n** so clean	1253+2141+871.1
	21:25 of his soul, and **n** eateth with pleasure.	3808
Ps	10: 6 **n** *be* in adversity.	1755+1755+3808+2050.1
	10:11 his face; he will **n** see *it*.	1077+5331+3807.1
	15: 5 *things* shall **n** be moved.	3808+5769+3807.1
	30: 6 I said, I shall **n** be moved.	1097+5769+3807.1
	31: 1 let me **n** be ashamed.	408+5769+3807.1
	49:19 they shall **n** see light.	3808+5331+5704
	55:22 **n** suffer the righteous to be	3808+5769+3807.1
	58: 5 voice of charmers, charming *n* so wisely.	NIH
	71: 1 me **n** be put to confusion.	408+5769+3807.1
	119:93 will **n** forget thy precepts:	3808+5769+3807.1
Pr	10:30 The righteous shall **n** be	1077+5769+3807.1
	27:20 Hell and destruction are **n** full; so the eyes	3808
	27:20 so the eyes of man are **n** satisfied.	3808
	30:15 There are three *things that are* **n** satisfied,	3808
Isa	13:20 It shall **n** be inhabited,	3808+5331+3807.1
	14:20 shall **n** be renowned.	3808+5769+3807.1
	25: 2 no city; it shall **n** be built.	3808+5769+3807.1
	56:11 *they are* greedy dogs *which* can **n** have	3808
	62: 6 which shall **n** hold their peace day	3808+8548
	63:19 We are *thine*: thou **n** barest	3808+4480+5769
Jer	20:11 *their* everlasting confusion shall **n** be	3808
	33:17 David shall **n** want a man to sit upon	3808
Eze	16:63 mayest open thy mouth any more, because of	3808
	26:21 yet shalt thou **n** be found	3808+5769+3807.1
	27:36 shalt be a terror, and **n** *shalt* be any more.	369
	28:19 be a terror, and **n** *shalt* thou be any more.	369
Da	2:44 shall **n** be destroyed:	3809+5957+3807.2
	12: 1 as **n** was since there was a nation *even*	3808
Joel	2:26 shall **n** be ashamed.	3808+5769+3807.1
	2:27 shall **n** be ashamed.	3808+5769+3807.1
Am	8: 7 **Surely** I will **n** forget any of	518+5331+3807.1
	8:14 they shall fall, and **n** rise up **again**.	3808+5750
Hab	1: 4 judgment doth **n** go forth:	3808+5331+3807.1
Mt	7:23 will I profess unto them, I **n** knew you:	3763
	9:33 saying, It was **n** so seen in Israel.	3763
	21:16 ye **n** read, Out of the mouth of babes	3763
	21:42 them, Did ye **n** read in the scriptures,	3763
	26:33 because of thee, *yet* will I **n** be offended.	3763
	27:14 And he answered him to **n** a word;	3761
Mk	2:12 saying, We **n** saw *it* on this fashion.	3763
	2:25 Have ye **n** read what David did, when he	3763
	3:29 hath **n** forgiveness,	165+1519+3588+3756
	9:43 into the fire that **n** shall **be quenched**:	762
	9:45 into the fire that **n** shall **be quenched**:	762
	11: 2 find a colt tied, whereon **n** man sat;	3762+3768
	14:21 good were it for that man if he had **n** been	3756
Lk	15:29 yet thou **n** gavest me a kid, that I might	3763
	19:30 a colt tied, whereon **yet n** man sat;	3762+4455
	23:29 and the wombs that **n** bare, and the paps	3756
	23:29 and the paps which **n** gave suck.	3756
	23:53 wherein **n** man **before** was laid.	3756+3764
Jn	4:14 him shall **n** thirst;	165+1487+1519+3588+3756
	6:35 he that cometh to me shall **n** hunger;	3364
	6:35 on me shall **n** thirst.	3361+3756+4455
	7:15 man letters, having **n** learned?	3361
	7:46 **n** man spake like this man.	3763
	8:33 in bondage to any *man*: how sayest	4455
	8:51 shall **n** see death.	165+1519+3361+3588+3756
	8:52 **n** taste of death.	165+1519+3361+3588+3756
	10:28 and they shall **n**	165+1519+3361+3588+3756
	11:26 in me shall **n** die.	165+1519+3361+3588+3756
	13: 8 thou shalt **n** wash my feet.	165+1519+3361+3588+3756
	19:41 sepulchre, wherein was **n** man **yet** laid.	3764
Ac	10:14 I have **n** eaten any *thing that is* common	3763
	14: 8 his mother's womb, who **n** had walked:	3763
1Co	13: 8 Charity **n** faileth:	3763
2Ti	3: 7 **n** able to come to the knowledge of	3368
Heb	10: 1 can **n** with those sacrifices which they	3763
	10:11 which can **n** take away sins:	3763
	13: 5 for he hath said, I will **n** leave thee,	3364
2Pe	1:10 these *things*, ye shall **n** fall:	3361+3756+4218

NEVERTHELESS (97)

Ex	32:34 **n** in the day when I visit, I will visit	2050.1
Lev	11: 4 These shall ye not eat of them that chew	389
	11:36 **N** a fountain or pit, *wherein there* is plenty	389
Nu	13:28 **N** the people *be* strong that dwell in	657+3588
	14:44 in the ark of the covenant of the LORD,	2050.1
	18:15 the firstborn of man shalt thou surely	389
	24:22 **N** the Kenite shall be wasted,	518+3588
	31:23 **n** it shall be purified with the water of	389
Dt	14: 7 **N** these ye shall not eat of them that chew	389
	23: 5 **N** the LORD thy God would not	2050.1
Jos	13:13 (**N** the children of Israel expelled not	2050.1

Jos	14: 8 **N** my brethren that went up with me	2050.1
Jdg	1:33 in the inhabitants of Beth-shemesh and	2050.1
	2:16 **N** the LORD raised up judges,	2050.1
1Sa	8:19 **N** the people refused to obey the voice	2050.1
	15:35 **n** Samuel mourned for Saul:	3588
	20:26 **N** Saul spake not any thing that day:	2050.1
	29: 6 this day: **n** the lords favour thee not.	2050.1
2Sa	5: 7 **N** David took the strong hold of Zion:	2050.1
	17:18 **N** a lad saw them, and told Absalom:	2050.1
	23:16 **n** he would not drink thereof,	3808+2050.1
1Ki	8:19 **N** thou shalt not build the house; but thy	7535
	15: **N** for David's sake did the LORD his God	3588
	15:14 Asa's heart was perfect with the LORD	7535
	15:23 **N** in the time of his old age he was	7535
	22:43 **n** the high places were not taken away;	389
2Ki	2:10 **n**, if thou see me *when I am* taken from	NIH
	3: 3 **N** he cleaved unto the sins of Jeroboam	7535
	3: 6 **N** they departed not from the sins of	389
	23: 9 **N** the priests of the high places came not	389
1Ch	11: 5 **N** David took the castle of Zion, which	2050.1
	21: 4 **N** the king's word prevailed against	2050.1
2Ch	12: 8 **N** they shall be his servants; that they	3588
	15:17 the heart of Asa was perfect all his days.	7535
	19: 3 **N** there are good things found in thee, in	61
	30:11 **N** divers of Asher and Manasseh and	389
	33:17 **N** the people did sacrifice still in the high	61
	35:22 **N** Josiah would not turn his face from	3588
Ne	4: 9 **N** we made our prayer unto our God,	2050.1
	9:26 **N** they were disobedient,	2050.1
	9:31 **N** for thy great mercies' sake thou didst	2050.1
	13:26 *n* even him did outlandish women cause	NIH
Est	5:10 **N** Haman refrained himself: and when	2050.1
Ps	31:22 **N** thou heardest the voice of my	403
	49:12 **N** man *being* in honour abideth not: he	2050.1
	73:23 **N** I *am* continually with thee: thou hast	2050.1
	78:36 **N** they did flatter him with their mouth,	2050.1
	89:33 **N** my lovingkindness will I not utterly	2050.1
	106: 8 **N** he saved them for his name's sake,	2050.1
	106:44 **N** he regarded their affliction, when he	2050.1
Pr	19:21 **N** the counsel of the LORD, that shall	2050.1
Ecc	9:16 the poor *man's* wisdom *is* despised,	2050.1
Isa	9: 1 **N** the dimness *shall* not *be* such as *was* in	3588
Jer	5:18 **N** in those days, saith the LORD,	1571+2050.1
	26:24 **N** the hand of Ahikam the son of Shaphan	389
	28: 7 **N** hear thou now this word that I speak in	389
	36:25 **N** Elnathan and Delaiah and	1571+2050.1
Eze	3:21 **N** if thou warn the righteous *man*, that	2050.1
	16:60 **N** I will remember my covenant with	2050.1
	20:17 mine eye spared them from	2050.1
	20:22 **N** I withdrew mine hand, and wrought	2050.1
	33: 9 **N**, if thou warn the wicked of his way to	2050.1
Da	4:15 **N** leave the stump of his roots in the	1297
Jnh	1:13 **N** the men rowed hard to bring *it* to	2050.1
Mt	14: 9 **n** for the oaths' sake, and them which sat	1161
	26:39 from me: **n** not as I will, but as thou *wilt*.	4133
	26:64 I say unto you, Hereafter shall ye see	4133
Mk	14:36 **n** not that I will, but what thou *wilt*.	235
Lk	5: 5 at thy word I will let down the net.	1161
	13:33 **N** I must walk to day, and to morrow,	4133
	18: 8 **N** when the Son of man cometh, shall he	4133
	22:42 me: **n** not my will, but thine, be done.	4133
Jn	11:15 ye may believe; **n** let us go unto him.	1161
	12:42 **N** among the *chief* rulers also many	3305+3676
	16: 7 **N** I tell you the truth; It is expedient for	235
Ac	14:17 he left not himself without witness,	2544
	27:11 **N** the centurion believed the master and	1161
Ro	5:14 **N** death reigned from Adam to Moses,	1161
	15:15 **N**, brethren, I have written the more	1161
1Co	7: 2 **N**, to avoid fornication, let every man	1161
	7:28 **N** such shall have trouble in the flesh:	1161
	7:37 **N** he that standeth stedfast in *his* heart,	1161
	9:12 **N** we have not used this power; but suffer	235
	11:11 **N** neither is the man without the woman,	4133
2Co	3:16 **N** when *it* shall turn to the Lord, the vail	1161
	7: 6 **N** God, that comforteth *those that are* cast	235
	12:16 **n**, being crafty, I caught you with guile.	235
Gal	2:20 I live; yet not I, but Christ liveth in me:	1161
	4:30 **N** what saith the scripture? Cast out	235
Eph	5:33 **N** let every one of you in particular	2532+4133
Php	1:24 **N** to abide in the flesh *is* more needful for	1161
	3:16 **N**, whereto we have *already* attained, *let*	4133
2Ti	1:12 suffer these *things*: **n** I am not ashamed:	235
	2:19 **N** the foundation of God standeth sure,	3305
Heb	12:11 **N** afterward it yieldeth the peaceable fruit	1161
2Pe	3:13 **N** we, according to his promise, look for	1161
Rev	2: 4 **N** I have *somewhat* against thee, because	235

NEW (150) [NEWBORN, NEWLY, NEWNESS]

Ex	1: 8 Now there arose up a **n** king over Egypt,	2319
Lev	23:16 ye shall offer a **n** meat offering unto	2319
	26:10 bring forth the old because of the **n**.	2319
Nu	16:30 if the LORD make a **n** thing,	1278
	28:26 when ye bring a **n** meat offering unto	2319
Dt	20: 5 man *is there* that hath built a **n** house,	2319
	22: 8 When thou buildest a **n** house, then	2319
	24: 5 When a man hath taken a **n** wife, he shall	2319
	32:17 knew not, *to* **n** gods *that* came newly up,	2319
Jos	9:13 bottles of wine, which we filled, *were* **n**;	2319
Jdg	5: 8 They chose **n** gods; then *was* war in	2319
	15:13 they bound him with two **n** cords,	2319
	15:15 he found a **n** jawbone of an ass,	2961
	16:11 If they bind me fast with **n** ropes that	2319
	16:12 Delilah therefore took **n** ropes,	2319
1Sa	6: 7 therefore make a **n** cart, and take two	2319
	20: 5 to morrow *is* the **n** moon, and I should	2320

1Sa	20:18 said to *David*, To morrow *is* the **n** moon:	2320
	20:24 when the **n** moon was come, the king sat	2320
2Sa	6: 3 they set the ark of God upon a **n** cart,	2319
	6: 3 the sons of Abinadab, drave the **n** cart.	2319
	21:16 he being girded *with a* **n** *sword*, thought	2319
1Ki	11:29 he had clad himself with a **n** garment;	2319
	11:30 Ahijah caught the **n** garment that *was* on	2319
2Ki	2:20 Bring me a **n** cruse, and put salt therein.	2319
	4:23 *it is* neither **n** moon, nor sabbath.	2320
1Ch	13: 7 they carried the ark of God in a **n** cart out	2319
	23:31 in the **n** moons, and on the set feasts,	2320
2Ch	2: 4 the **n** moons, and on the solemn feasts	2320
	8:13 the **n** moons, and on the solemn feasts	2320
	20: 5 house of the LORD, before the **n** court,	2319
	31: 3 for the **n** moons, and for the set feasts,	2320
Ezr	3: 5 both of the **n** moons, and of all the set	2320
	6: 4 great stones, and a row of **n** timber:	2323
Ne	10:33 the sabbaths, of the **n** moons, for the set	2320
	10:39 of the **n** wine, and the oil, unto	8492
	13: 5 of the corn, the **n** wine, and the oil,	8492
	13:12 **n** wine and the oil unto the treasuries.	8492
Job	32:19 no vent; it is ready to burst like **n** bottles.	2319
Ps	33: 3 Sing unto him a **n** song; play skilfully	2319
	40: 3 he hath put a **n** song in my mouth,	2320
	81: 3 Blow up the trumpet in the **n** moon,	2320
	96: 1 O sing unto the LORD a **n** song: sing unto	2319
	98: 1 O sing unto the LORD a **n** song; for he	2319
	144: 9 I will sing a **n** song unto thee, O God:	2319
	149: 1 Sing unto the LORD a **n** song,	2319
Pr	3:10 thy presses shall burst out with **n** wine.	8492
Ecc	1: 9 and *there is* no **n** *thing* under the sun.	2319
	1:10 whereof it may be said, See, this *is* **n**?	2319
SS	7:13 gates *are* all *manner of* pleasant *fruits*, **n**	2319
Isa	1:13 the **n** moons and sabbaths, the calling of	2320
	1:14 Your **n** moons and your appointed feasts	2320
	24: 7 **n** wine mourneth, the vine languisheth,	8492
	41:15 I will make thee a **n** sharp threshing	2319
	42: 9 come to pass, and *new things* do I declare:	2319
	42:10 Sing unto the LORD a **n** song,	2319
	43:19 I will do a **n** *thing*; now it shall spring	2319
	48: 6 not ye declare *it*? I have shewed thee **n**	2319
	62: 2 thou shalt be called by a **n** name, which	2319
	65: 8 As the **n** wine is found in the cluster,	8492
	65:17 I create **n** heavens and a new earth:	2319
	65:17 I create new heavens and a **n** earth:	2319
	66:22 For as the **n** heavens and the new earth,	2319
	66:22 For as the new heavens and the **n** earth,	2319
	66:23 *that* from one **n** moon to another,	2320
Jer	26:10 sat down in the entry of the **n** gate of	2319
	31:22 for the LORD hath created a **n** *thing* in	2319
	31:31 that I will make a **n** covenant with	2319
	36:10 the higher court *at* the entry of the **n** gate	2319
La	3:23 *They are* every morning: great *is* thy	2319
Eze	11:19 and I will put a **n** spirit within you;	2319
	18:31 and make you a **n** heart and a new spirit:	2319
	18:31 and make you a new heart and a **n** spirit:	2319
	36:26 A **n** heart also will I give you, and a new	2319
	36:26 and a **n** spirit will I put within you:	2319
	45:17 in the **n** moons, and in the sabbaths in all	2320
	46: 1 the day of the **n** moon it shall be opened.	2320
	46: 3 in the sabbaths and in the **n** moons.	2320
	46: 6 in the day of the **n** moon *it shall be* a	2320
	47:12 it shall **bring forth n fruit** according to	1069
Hos	2:11 her feast *days*, her **n** moons,	2320
	4:11 wine and **n** wine take *away* the heart.	8492
	9: 2 them, and the **n** wine shall fail in her.	8492
Joel	1: 5 drinkers of wine, because of the **n** wine,	6071
	1:10 **n** wine is dried up, the oil languisheth.	8492
	3:18 the mountains shall drop down **n** wine,	6071
Am	8: 5 Saying, When will the **n** moon be gone,	2320
Hag	1:11 upon the **n** wine, and upon the oil,	8492
Zec	9:17 men cheerful, and **n** wine the maids.	8492
Mt	9:16 No *man* putteth a piece of **n** cloth unto	46
	9:17 do *men* put **n** wine into old bottles:	3501
	9:17 but they put **n** wine into new bottles,	3501
	9:17 but they put new wine into **n** bottles,	2537
	13:52 bringeth forth out of his treasure *things* **n**	2537
	26:28 For this is my blood of the **n** testament,	2537
	26:29 until that day when I drink it **n** with you	2537
	27:60 And laid it in his own **n** tomb, which he	2537
Mk	1:27 what a doctrine *is* this? for with authority	2537
	2:21 No *man* also seweth a piece of **n** cloth on	46
	2:21 the **n** piece that filled it up taketh away	2537
	2:22 no *man* putteth **n** wine into old bottles:	3501
	2:22 else the **n** wine doth burst the bottles,	3501
	2:22 but **n** wine must be put into new bottles.	3501
	2:22 but new wine must be put into **n** bottles.	2537
	14:24 This is my blood of the **n** testament,	2537
	14:25 until that day that I drink it **n** in	2537
	16:17 devils; they shall speak with **n** tongues;	2537
Lk	5:36 No *man* putteth a piece of a **n** garment	2537
	5:36 both the **n** maketh a rent, and the piece	2537
	5:36 the piece that was *taken* out of the **n**	2537
	5:37 no *man* putteth **n** wine into old bottles;	3501
	5:37 else the **n** wine will burst the bottles,	3501
	5:38 But **n** wine must be put into new bottles;	3501
	5:38 But new wine must be put into **n** bottles;	2537
	5:39 drunk old *wine* straightway desireth **n**:	3501
	22:20 This *cup is* the **n** testament in my blood,	2537
Jn	13:34 A **n** commandment I give unto you, That	2537
	19:41 and in the garden a **n** sepulchre,	2537
Ac	2:13 These *men* are full of **n** wine.	1098
	17:19 May we know what this **n** doctrine,	2537
	17:21 *either* to tell, or to hear some **n** *thing*.)	2537
1Co	5: 7 the old leaven, that ye may be a **n** lump,	3501

1Co	11:25 This cup is the **n** testament in my blood:	2537
2Co	3: 6 able ministers of the **n** testament;	2537
	5:17 any *man* be in Christ, he *is* a **n** creature:	2537
	5:17 away; behold, all *things* are become **n**.	2537
Gal	6:15 nor uncircumcision, but a **n** creature.	2537
Eph	2:15 to make of twain one **n** man,	2537
	4:24 that ye put on the **n** man, which after	2537
Col	2:16 or of the **n** moon, or of the sabbath days:	3561
	3:10 And have put on the **n** *man*, which is	3501
Heb	8: 8 when I will make a **n** covenant with	2537
	8:13 A *covenant*, he hath made the first old.	3501
	9:15 he is the mediator of the **n** testament,	2537
	10:20 *By* a **n** and living way, which he hath	4372
	12:24 And to Jesus the mediator of the **n**	3501
2Pe	3:13 look for **n** heavens and a new earth,	2537
	3:13 look for new heavens and a **n** earth,	2537
1Jn	2: 7 I write no **n** commandment unto you,	2537
	2: 8 a **n** commandment I write unto you,	2537
2Jn	1: 5 not as though I wrote a **n** commandment	2537
Rev	2:17 and in the stone a **n** name written,	2537
	3:12 the city of my God, *which is* **n** Jerusalem,	2537
	3:12 *and I will write upon him* my **n** name.	2537
	5: 9 And they sung a **n** song, saying, Thou art	2537
	14: 3 And they sung as *it were* a **n** song before	2537
	21: 1 And I saw a **n** heaven and a new earth:	2537
	21: 1 And I saw a new heaven and a **n** earth:	2537
	21: 2 And I John saw the holy city, **n** Jerusalem,	2537
	21: 5 throne said, Behold, I make all *things* **n**.	2537

NEWBORN (1) [BEAR, NEW]

1Pe	2: 2 As **n** babes, desire the sincere milk of	738

NEWLY (2) [NEW]

Dt	32:17 to new *gods that* came **n** up,	4480+7138
Jdg	7:19 *and* they had but **n** set the watch:	6965+6965

NEWNESS (2) [NEW]

Ro	6: 4 *even* so we also should walk in **n** of life.	2538
	7: 6 that we should serve in **n** of spirit,	2538

NEWS (1)

Pr	25:25 so *is* good **n** from a far country.	8052

NEXT (60)

Ge	17:21 unto thee at this set time in the **n** year.	312
Ex	12: 4 his neighbour **n** unto his house take *it*	7138
Nu	2: 5 those that do pitch **n** unto him *shall be*	5921
	11:32 the **n** day, and they gathered the quails:	4283
	27:11 his kinsman that is **n** to him of his family,	7138
Dt	21: 3 the city which *is* **n** unto the slain *man*,	7138
	21: 6 *that are* **n** unto the slain *man*, shall wash	7138
Ru	2:20 of kin unto us, one of our **n** *kinsmen*.	1350
1Sa	17:13 unto him Abinadab, and the third	4932
	23:17 over Israel, and I shall be **n** unto thee;	4932
	23:17 even unto the evening of the **n** day:	4283
2Ki	6:29 I said unto her on the **n** day, Give thy son,	312
1Ch	5:12 Shapham the **n**, and Jaanai, and Shaphat	4932
	16: 5 to him Zechariah, Jeiel,	4932
2Ch	11:19 him *was* Jehohanan the	3027+5921
	17:16 **n** him *was* Amasiah the son of	3027+5921
	17:18 **n** him *was* Jehozabad, and with	3027+5921
	28: 7 and Elkanah *that was* **n** to the king.	4932
	31:12 and Shimei his brother *was* the **n**.	4932
	31:15 him *were* Eden, and Miniamin,	4932
Ne	3: 2 **n** unto him builded the men of	3027+5921
	3: 2 to them builded Zaccur the son	3027+5921
	3: 4 **n** unto them repaired Meremoth	3027+5921
	3: 4 **n** unto them repaired Meshullam	3027+5921
	3: 4 **n** unto them repaired Zadok the	3027+5921
	3: 5 **n** unto them the Tekoites repaired;	3027+5921
	3: 7 **n** unto them repaired Melatiah	3027+5921
	3: 8 **N** unto him repaired Uzziel the son	3027+5921
	3: 8 **N** unto him also repaired Hananiah	3027+5921
	3: 9 **n** unto them repaired Rephaiah	3027+5921
	3:10 **n** unto them repaired Jedaiah the	3027+5921
	3:10 **n** unto him repaired Hattush the	3027+5921
	3:12 **n** unto him repaired Shallum the	3027+5921
	3:17 **N** unto him repaired Hashabiah,	3027+5921
	3:19 **n** to him repaired Ezer the son of	3027+5921
	3:13 **n** to them *was* Hanan the son of	3027+5921
Est	1:14 **n** unto him *was* Carshena, Shethar,	7138
	10: 3 For Mordecai the Jew *was* **n** unto king	4932
Jnh	4: 7 worm when the morning rose the **n** day,	4283
Mt	27:62 Now the **n** day, that followed the *day of*	1887
Mk	1:38 unto them, Let us go into the **n** towns,	2192
Lk	9:37 And it came to pass, *that* on the **n** day,	1836
Jn	1:29 The **n** day John seeth Jesus coming unto	1887
	1:35 Again the **n** day *after* John stood,	1887
	12:12 On the **n** day much people that were	1887
Ac	4: 3 and put *them* in hold unto the **n** day:	839
	7:26 And the **n** day he shewed himself unto	1966
	13:42 might be preached to them the **n** sabbath.	3342
	13:44 And the **n** sabbath day came almost	2064
	14:20 the **n** day he departed with Barnabas to	1887
	16:11 Samothracia, and the **n** *day* to Neapolis,	1966
	20:15 and came the **n** *day* over against Chios;	1966
	20:15 and the **n** *day* we arrived at Samos,	2087
	21: 8 And the **n** *day* we that were of Paul's	1887
	21:26 the **n** day purifying himself with them	2192
	25: 6 the **n** day sitting in the judgment seat,	1887
	27: 3 And the **n** *day* we touched at Sidon.	2087
	27:18 the **n** *day* they lightened the ship;	1836
	28:13 and we came the **n** *day* to Puteoli:	1206

NEZIAH (2)

Ezr	2:54 children of **N**, the children of Hatipha.	5335
Ne	7:56 children of **N**, the children of Hatipha.	5335

NEZIB (1)

Jos	15:43 And Jiphtah, and Ashnah, and **N**,	5334

NIBHAZ (1)

2Ki	17:31 the Avites made **N** and Tartak,	5026

NIBSHAN (1)

Jos	15:62 **N**, and the city of salt, and En-gedi;	5044

NICANOR (1)

Ac	6: 5 and **N**, and Timon, and Parmenas,	3527

NICODEMUS (5)

Jn	3: 1 Pharisees, named **N**, a ruler of the Jews:	3530
	3: 4 **N** saith unto him, How can a man be born	3530
	3: 9 **N** answered and said unto him, How can	3530
	7:50 **N** saith unto them, (he that came to *Jesus*	3530
	19:39 And there came also **N**, which at the first	3530

NICOLAITANS (2)

Rev	2: 6 that thou hatest the deeds of the **N**, I	3531
	2:15 also them that hold the doctrine of the **N**,	3531

NICOLAS (1)

Ac	6: 5 Parmenas, and **N** a proselyte of Antioch:	3532

NICOPOLIS (2)

Tit	3:12 be diligent to come unto me to **N**:	3533
	3: S of the Cretians, from **N** of Macedonia.	3533

NIGER (1)

Ac	13: 1 and Simeon that was called **N**,	3526

NIGH (100)

Ge	47:29 the time **drew n** that Israel must die:	7126
Ex	3: 5 he said, **Draw** not **n** hither: put off thy	7126
	14:10 when Pharaoh **drew n**, the children of	7126
	24: 2 they shall not **come n**; neither shall	5066
	32:19 as soon as he **came n** unto the camp,	7126
	34:30 and they were afraid to **come n** him.	5066
	34:32 all the children of Israel **came n**:	5066
Lev	10: 3 be sanctified in them that **come n** me,	7138
	21: 3 for his sister a virgin, that is **n** unto him,	7138
	21:21 shall **come n** to offer the offerings of	5066
	21:21 shall not **come n** to offer the bread of his	5066
	21:23 nor **come n** unto the altar, because he	5066
	25:49 that is **n** of kin unto him of his family	7607
Nu	1:51 the stranger that **cometh n** shall be put to	7131
	3:10 the stranger that **cometh n** shall be put to	7131
	3:38 the stranger that **cometh n** shall be put to	7131
	8:19 when the children of Israel **come n** unto	5066
	18: 3 only they shall not **come n** the vessels of	7126
	18: 4 and a stranger shall not **come n** unto you.	7126
	18: 7 the stranger that **cometh n** shall be put to	7131
	18:22 **come n** the tabernacle of the	7126
	24:17 I shall behold him, but not **n**: there shall	7138
Dt	1: 7 all *the places* **n** thereunto, in the plain,	7934
	2:19 when thou **comest n** over against	7126
	4: 7 *so* great, who hath God so **n** unto them,	7138
	13: 7 you, **n** unto thee, or far off from thee,	7126
	20: 2 when ye are **come n** unto the battle,	7126
	20:10 When thou **comest n** unto a city to fight	7126
	22: 2 if thy brother *be* not **n** unto thee, or *if*	7138
	30:14 word *is* very **n** unto thee, in thy mouth,	7138
Jos	8:11 **drew n**, and came before the city,	5066
1Sa	17:48 came and **drew n** to meet David,	7126
2Sa	10:13 Joab **drew n**, and the people that *were*	5066
	11:20 Wherefore **approached** ye so **n** unto	5066
	11:21 why **went** ye **n** the wall?	5066
	15: 5 that when any man **came n** *to him* to do	7126
1Ki	2: 1 Now the days of David **drew n** that *he*	7126
	8:59 be **n** unto the LORD our God day and	7138
1Ch	12:40 Moreover they *that were* **n** them, *even*	5066
	19:14 the people that *were* with him **drew n**	5066
Est	9:20 of the king Ahasuerus, *both* **n** and far,	7138
Ps	32: 6 waters they shall not **come n** unto him.	5060
	34:18 The LORD *is* **n** unto them that are of a	7138
	69:18 **Draw n** unto my soul, *and* redeem it:	7138
	73: 2 my steps had **well n** slipt.	369+3509.1
	85: 9 his salvation *is* **n** them that fear him;	7138
	88: 3 and my life **draweth n** unto the grave.	5060
	91: 7 right hand; *but* it shall not **come n** thee.	5066
	91:10 neither shall *any* plague **come n** thy	7126
	119:150 They **draw n** that follow after mischief:	7126
	145:18 The LORD *is* **n** unto all them that call	7138
Pr	5: 8 and **come** not **n** the door of her house:	7126
Ecc	12: 1 the years **draw n**, when thou shalt say,	5060
Isa	5:19 counsel of the Holy One of Israel **draw n**	7126
Joel	2: 1 of the LORD cometh, for *it is* **n at hand**;	7138
Mt	15: 8 This people **draweth n** unto me with	1448
	15:29 and came **n** unto the sea of Galilee;	3844
	21: 1 And when they **drew n** unto Jerusalem,	1448
	24:32 forth leaves, ye know that summer *is* **n**:	1451
Mk	2: 4 when they could not **come n** unto him	4331
	5:11 there was there **n** unto the mountains	4314
	5:21 unto him: and he was **n** unto the sea.	3844
	11: 1 And when they **drew n** to Jerusalem,	1448
	13:29 pass, know that it is **n**, *even* at the doors.	1451
Lk	7:12 Now when he **came n** to the gate of	1448
	10: 9 The kingdom of God is **come n** unto you.	1448
	10:11 that the kingdom of God is **come n** unto	1448

N

N

Lk 15:25 and as he came and **drew n** to the house, 1448
18:35 pass, *that* as he was **come n** unto Jericho, 1448
19:11 because he was **n** to Jerusalem, 1451
19:29 when he was **come n** to Bethphage and 1448
19:37 And when he was **come n**, *even* now at 1448
21:20 **know that** the desolation thereof is **n**. 1448
21:28 for your redemption **draweth n**. 1448
21:30 selves that summer is now **n at hand**. 1451
21:31 ye that the kingdom of God is **n at hand**. 1451
22: 1 the feast of unleavened bread **drew n**, 1448
24:28 And they **drew n** unto the village, 1448
Jn 6: 4 a passover, a feast of the Jews, was **n**. 1451
6:19 on the sea, and drawing **n** unto the ship: 1451
6:23 **n** unto the place where they did eat bread, 1451
11:18 Now Bethany was **n** unto Jerusalem, 1451
11:55 And the Jews' passover was **n at hand**: 1451
19:20 Jesus was crucified was **n to** the city: 1451
19:42 *day*; for the sepulchre was **n at hand**. 1451
Ac 7:17 when the time of the promise **drew n**, 1448
9:38 And forasmuch as Lydda was **n** to Joppa, 1451
10: 9 their journey, and **drew n** unto the city, 1448
22: 6 was **come n** unto Damascus about noon, 1448
27: 8 **n** whereunto was the city *of* Lasea. 1451
Ro 10: 8 The word is **n**, *even* in thy mouth, 1451
Eph 2:13 far off are made **n** by the blood of Christ. 1451
2:17 were afar off, and to them that were **n**, 1451
Php 2:27 For indeed he was sick **n unto** death: 3897
2:30 Because for the work of Christ he was **n** 1448
Heb 6: 8 briers *is* rejected, and *is* **n** unto cursing; 1451
7:19 *did*; by the which we **draw n** unto God. 1448
Jas 4: 8 **Draw n** to God, and he will draw nigh to 1448
4: 8 nigh to God, and he will **draw n** to you. 1448
5: 8 for the coming of the Lord **draweth n**. 1448

NIGHT (307) [MIDNIGHT, NIGHTS, YESTERNIGHT]

Ge 1: 5 light Day, and the darkness he called **N**. 3915
1:14 the heaven to divide the day from the **n**; 3915
1:16 the day, and the lesser light to rule the **n**: 3915
1:18 to rule over the day and over the **n**, 3915
8:22 and winter, and day and **n** shall not cease. 3915
14:15 by **n**, and smote them, and pursued them 3915
19: 2 **tarry all n**, and wash your feet, 3915
19: 2 Nay; but we will **abide** in the street **all n**. 3885
19: 5 *are* the men which came in to thee this **n**? 3915
19:33 they made their father drink wine that **n**: 3915
19:34 let us make him drink wine this **n** also; 3915
19:35 they made their father drink wine that **n** 3915
20: 3 God came to Abimelech in a dream by **n**, 3915
24:54 that *were* with him, and **tarried all n**; 3885
26:24 the LORD appeared unto him the same **n**, 3915
28:11 **tarried** there all **n**, because the sun was 3885
30:15 to **n** for thy son's mandrakes. 3915+1886.1
30:16 And he lay with her that **n**. 3915
31:24 came to Laban the Syrian in a dream by **n**, 3915
31:39 *whether* stolen by day, or stolen by **n**. 3915
31:40 drought consumed me, and the frost by **n**; 3915
31:54 eat bread, and **tarried all n** in the mount. 3885
32:13 he lodged there that *same* **n**; and took of 3915
32:21 and himself lodged that **n** in the company. 3915
32:22 he rose up that **n**, and took his two wives, 3915
40: 5 of them, each man his dream in one **n**, 3915
41:11 we dreamed a dream in one **n**, I and he; 3915
46: 2 spake unto Israel in the visions of the **n**, 3915
49:27 prey, and at **n** he shall divide the spoil. 6153
Ex 10:13 upon the land all that day, and all that **n**; 3915
12: 8 they shall eat the flesh in that **n**, roast 3915
12:12 will pass through the land of Egypt this **n**, 3915
12:30 Pharaoh rose up in the **n**, he, and all his 3915
12:31 he called for Moses and Aaron by **n**, 3915
12:42 It *is* a be to be much observed unto 3915
12:42 this *is* that **n** of the LORD to be observed 3915
13:21 by **n** in a pillar of fire, to give them light; 3915
13:21 to give them light; to go by day and by 3915
13:22 nor the pillar of fire by **n**, *from* before 3915
14:20 to them, but it gave light by **n** *to* these: 3915
14:20 the one came not near the other all the **n**. 3915
14:21 go *back* by a strong east wind all that **n**, 3915
40:38 fire was on it by **n**, in the sight of all 3915
Lev 6: 9 of the burning upon the altar all **n** unto 3915
6:20 of it in the morning, and half thereof at **n**. 6153
8:35 of the congregation day and **n** seven days, 3915
11:16 the **n hawk**, and the cuckow, and the 8464
11:19 **abide** with thee **all n** until the morning. 3885
Nu 9:16 it *by* day, and the appearance of fire by **n**. 3915
9:21 day or by **n** that the cloud was taken up, 3915
11: 9 the dew fell upon the camp in the **n**, 3915
11:32 all that **n**, and all the next day, 3915
14: 1 and cried; and the people wept that **n**. 3915
14:14 of a cloud, and in a pillar of fire by **n**. 3915
22:19 I pray you, tarry ye also here this **n**, 3915
22:20 God came unto Balaam at **n**, and said 3915
Dt 1:33 a place to pitch your tents *in*, in fire by **n**, 3915
14:15 the **n hawk**, and the cuckow, and the 8464
16: 1 God brought thee forth out of Egypt by **n**. 3915
16: 4 at even, **remain all n** until the morning. 3885
21:23 His body shall not **remain all n** upon 3885
23:10 of *uncleanness* that chanceth him by **n**, 3915
28:66 thou shalt fear day and **n**, and shalt have 3915
Jos 1: 8 thou shalt meditate therein day and **n**, 3915
2: 2 there came men in hither to **n** of 3915
4: 3 place, where you shall lodge *this* **n**. 3915
8: 3 *men* of valour, and sent them away by **n**. 3915
8: 9 Joshua lodged that **n** among the people. 3915
8:13 Joshua went that **n** into the midst of 3915

Jos 10: 9 *and* went up from Gilgal all **n**. 3915
Jdg 6:25 it came to pass the same **n**, that the LORD 3915
6:27 could not do *it* by day, that he did *it* by **n**. 3915
6:40 God did so that **n**: for it was dry upon 3915
7: 9 it came to pass the same **n**, that the LORD 3915
9:32 therefore up by **n**, thou and the people 3915
9:34 by **n**, and they laid wait against Shechem 3915
16: 2 laid wait for him all **n** in the gate of 3915
16: 2 quiet all the **n**, saying, In the morning, 3915
19: 6 **tarry all n**, and let thine heart be merry. 3885
19: 9 towards evening, I pray you **tarry all n**. 3885
19:10 the man would not **tarry** that **n**, but he 3885
19:13 near to one of *these* places to **lodge all n**, 3885
19:25 abused her all the **n** until the morning: 3915
20: 5 the house round about upon me by **n**, 3915
Ru 1:12 should have a husband also **to n**, 3915+1886.1
2: 2 he winnoweth barley **to n** in 3915+1886.1
3:13 Tarry this **n**, and it shall be in the 3915
1Sa 14:34 every man his ox with him *that* **n**, 3915
14:36 Let us go down after the Philistines by **n**, 3915
15:11 and he cried unto the LORD all **n**. 3915
15:16 what the LORD hath said to me *this* **n**. 3915
19:10 and David fled, and escaped that **n**. 3915
19:11 If thou save not thy life **to n**, 3915+1886.1
19:24 lay down naked all that day and all *that* **n**. 3915
25:16 They were a wall unto us both by **n** and 3915
26: 7 and Abishai came to the people by **n**: 3915
28: 8 and they came to the woman by **n**: 3915
28:20 eaten no bread all the day, nor all the **n**. 3915
28:25 they arose up, and went away that **n**. 3915
31:12 went all **n**, and took the body of Saul and 3915
2Sa 2:29 men walked all that **n** through the plain, 3915
2:32 Joab and his men went all **n**, and they 3915
4: 7 gat them away through the plain all **n**. 3915
7: 4 it came to pass that **n**, that the word of 3915
12:16 and went in, and lay **all n** upon the earth. 3885
17: 1 I will arise and pursue after David *this* **n**: 3915
17:16 Lodge not *this* **n** in the plains of 3915
19: 7 there will not tarry one with thee *this* **n**: 3915
21:10 by day, nor the beasts of the field by **n**. 3915
1Ki 3: 5 appeared to Solomon in a dream by **n**: 3915
3:19 this woman's child died in the **n**; because 3915
8:29 eyes may be open toward this house **n** 3915
8:59 nigh unto the LORD our God day and **n**, 3915
2Ki 6:14 they came by **n**, and compassed the city 3915
7:12 the king arose in the **n**, and said unto his 3915
8:21 he rose by **n**, and smote the Edomites 3915
19:35 it came to pass that **n**, that the angel of 3915
25: 4 all the men of war *fled* by **n** by the way 3915
1Ch 9:33 were employed in *that* work day and **n**. 3915
17: 3 it came to pass the same **n**, that the word 3915
2Ch 1: 7 In that **n** did God appear unto Solomon, 3915
6:20 may be open upon this house day and **n**, 3915
7:12 the LORD appeared to Solomon by **n**, 3915
21: 9 he rose up by **n**, and smote the Edomites 3915
35:14 of burnt offerings and the fat until **n**; 3915
Ne 1: 6 which I pray before thee now, day and **n**, 3915
2:12 I arose in the **n**, I and *some* few men with 3915
2:13 I went out by **n** by the gate of the valley, 3915
2:15 went I up in the **n** by the brook, and 3915
4: 9 set a watch against them day and **n**, 3915
4:22 that in the **n** they may be a guard to us, 3915
6:10 yea, in the **n** will they come to slay thee. 3915
9:12 in the **n** by a pillar of fire, to give them 3915
9:19 neither the pillar of fire by **n**, to shew 3915
Est 4:16 neither eat nor drink three days, **n** or day; 3915
1: 1 On that **n** could not the king sleep, 3915
Job 3: 3 the **n** *in which it was* said, There is a man 3915
3: 6 *As for* that **n**, let darkness seize upon it; 3915
3: 7 let that **n** be solitary, let no joyful voice 3915
4:13 In thoughts from the visions of the **n**, 3915
5:14 and grope in the noonday as in the **n**. 3915
7: 4 When shall I arise, and the **n** be gone? 6153
17:12 They change the **n** into day: the light *is* 3915
20: 8 shall be chased away as a vision of the **n**. 3915
24:14 and needy, and in the **n** is as a thief. 3915
26:10 until the day and **n** come to an end. 2822
27:20 a tempest stealeth him away in the **n**. 3915
29:19 and the dew lay **all n** upon my branch. 3885
30:17 bones are pierced in me in the **n season**: 3915
33:15 In a dream, *in* a vision of the **n**, when 3915
34:25 overturneth *them* in the **n**, so that they 3915
35:10 my Maker, who giveth songs in the **n**; 3915
36:20 Desire not the **n**, when people are cut off 3915
Ps 1: 2 in his law doth he meditate day and **n**. 3915
6: 6 all the **n** make I my bed to swim; 3915
16: 7 reins also instruct me *in* the **n seasons**. 3915
17: 3 hast visited *me* in the **n**; thou hast tried 3915
19: 2 and **n** unto night sheweth knowledge. 3915
19: 2 and night unto **n** sheweth knowledge. 3915
22: 2 and in the **n season**, and am not silent. 3915
30: 5 weeping may endure for a **n**, 6153
32: 4 and **n** thy hand was heavy upon me: 3915
42: 3 My tears have been my meat day and **n**, 3915
42: 8 in the **n** his song *shall be* with me, 3915
55:10 they go about it upon the walls thereof: 3915
63: 6 and meditate on thee in the **n** watches. NIH
74:16 The day *is* thine, the **n** also *is* thine: 3915
77: 2 my sore ran in the **n**, and ceased not: 3915
77: 6 I call to remembrance my song in the **n**: 3915
78:14 a cloud, and all the **n** with a light of fire. 3915
88: 1 I have cried day *and* **n** before thee: 3915
90: 4 when it is past, and *as* a watch in the **n**. 3915
91: 5 shalt not be afraid for the terror by **n**; 3915
92: 2 morning, and thy faithfulness every **n**, 3915

Ps 104:20 Thou makest darkness, and it is **n**: 3915
105:39 a covering; and fire to give light in the **n**. 3915
119:55 O LORD, in the **n**, and have kept thy law. 3915
119:148 Mine eyes prevent the **n** watches, that *I* NIH
121: 6 not smite thee by day, nor the moon by **n**. 3915
134: 1 which by **n** stand in the house of 3915
136: 9 The moon and stars to rule by **n**: for his 3915
139:11 even the **n** *shall be* light about me. 3915
139:12 from thee; but the **n** shineth as the day: 3915
Pr 7: 9 in the evening, in the black and dark **n**: 3915
31:15 She riseth also while *it is* yet **n**, 3915
31:18 *is* good: her candle goeth not out by **n**. 3915
Ecc 2:23 yea, his heart taketh not rest in the **n**. 3915
8:16 (for also *there is that* neither day nor **n** 3885
SS 1:13 he shall **lie all n** betwixt my breasts. 3885
3: 1 By **n** on my bed I sought *him* whom my 3915
3: 8 upon his thigh because of fear in the **n**. 3915
5: 2 *and* my locks *with* the drops of the **n**. 3915
Isa 4: 5 and the shining of a flaming fire by **n**: 3915
5:11 that continue until **n**, *till* wine inflame 5399
15: 1 Because in the Ar of Moab is laid waste, 3915
15: 1 because in the **n** Kir of Moab is laid waste, 3915
16: 3 make thy shadow as the **n** in the midst of 3915
21: 4 the **n** of my pleasure hath he turned into 5399
21:11 me out of Seir, Watchman, what of the **n**? 3915
21:11 of the night? Watchman, what of the **n**? 3915
21:12 The morning cometh, and also the **n**: 3915
26: 9 *With* my soul have I desired thee in the **n**; 3915
27: 3 lest *any* hurt it, I will keep it **n** and day. 3915
28:19 shall it pass over, by day and by **n**: 3915
29: 7 that be as a dream of a **n** vision. 3915
30:29 as *in* the **n** when a holy solemnity is kept; 3915
34:10 It shall not be quenched **n** nor day; 3915
38:12 from day *even* to **n** wilt thou make an end 3915
38:13 from day *even* to **n** wilt thou make an end 3915
59:10 we stumble at noonday as in the **n**; we 5399
60:11 they shall not be shut day nor **n**; 3915
62: 6 shall never hold their peace day nor **n**: 3915
Jer 6: 5 let us go by **n**, and let us destroy her 3915
9: 1 **n** for the slain of the daughter of my 3915
14: 8 man *that* turneth aside to **tarry for a n**? 3885
14:17 Let mine eyes run down *with* tears **n** and 3915
16:13 there shall ye serve other gods day and **n**; 3915
31:35 the moon and the stars for a light by **n**, 3915
33:20 my covenant of the **n**, and that there 3915
33:20 should not be day and **n** in their season; 3915
33:25 If my covenant *be* not with day and **n**, 3915
36:30 day to the heat, and in the **n** to the frost. 3915
39: 4 and went forth out of the city by **n**, 3915
49: 9 if thieves by **n**, they will destroy till they 3915
52: 7 went forth out of the city by **n** *by* the way 3915
La 1: 2 She weepeth sore in the **n**, and her tears 3915
2:18 let tears run down like a river day and **n**: 3915
2:19 Arise, cry out in the **n**: in the beginning of 3915
Da 2:19 *was* the secret revealed unto Daniel in a **n** 3916
5:30 In that **n** *was* Belshazzar the king of 3916
6:18 to his palace, and **passed the n** fasting: 956
7: 2 said, I saw in my vision by **n**, and behold, 3916
7: 7 After this I saw in the **n** visions, 3916
7:13 I saw in the **n** visions, and behold, *one* 3916
Hos 4: 5 prophet also shall fall with thee *in* the **n**, 3915
7: 6 their baker sleepeth all the **n**; 3915
Joel 1:13 come, **lie all n** in sackcloth, ye ministers 3885
Am 5: 8 and maketh the day dark *with* **n**: 3915
Ob 1: 5 if robbers by **n**, (how art thou cut off!) 3915
Jnh 4:10 which came up in a **n**, 1121+3915
4:10 up in a night, and perished in a **n**: 1121+3915
Mic 3: 6 Therefore **n** *shall be* unto you, that *ye* 3915
Zec 1: 8 I saw by **n**, and behold a man riding upon 3915
14: 7 be known to the LORD, not day, nor **n**: 3915
Mt 2:14 took the young child and his mother by **n**, 3571
14:25 in the fourth watch of the **n** Jesus went 3571
26:31 ye shall be offended because of me this **n**: 3571
26:34 That this **n**, before *the* cock crow, 3571
27:64 lest his disciples come by **n**, and steal him 3571
28:13 His disciples came by **n**, and stole him 3571
Mk 4:27 and rise **n** and day, and the seed should 3571
5: 5 And always, **n** and day, he was in 3571
6:48 about the fourth watch of the **n** he cometh 3571
14:27 ye shall be offended because of me this **n**: 3571
14:30 unto thee, That this day, *even* in this **n**, 3571
Lk 2: 8 keeping watch over their flock by **n**. 3571
2:37 *God* with fastings and prayers **n** and day. 3571
5: 5 we have toiled all the **n**, and have taken 3571
6:12 and continued **all n** in prayer to God. 1273
12:20 this **n** thy soul shall be required of thee: 3571
17:34 in that **n** there shall be two *men* in one 3571
18: 7 which cry day and **n** unto him, though he 3571
21:37 and at **n** he went out, and abode in 3571
Jn 3: 2 The same to Jesus by **n**, and said 3571
7:50 (he that came to *Jesus* by **n**, being one of 3571
9: 4 the **n** cometh, when no *man* can work. 3571
11:10 But if a man walk in the **n**, he stumbleth, 3571
13:30 sop went immediately out: and it was **n**. 3571
19:39 which at the first came to Jesus by **n**, 3571
21: 3 and that **n** they caught nothing. 3571
Ac 5:19 But the angel of the Lord by **n** opened 3571
9:24 watched the gates day and **n** to kill him. 3571
9:25 Then the disciples took him by **n**, 3571
12: 6 the same Peter was sleeping between 3571
16: 9 And a vision appeared to Paul in the **n**; 3571
16:33 And he took them the same hour of the **n**, 3571
17:10 sent away Paul and Silas by **n** unto Berea: 3571
18: 9 Then spake the Lord to Paul in the **n** by a 3571
20:31 years I ceased not to warn every one **n** 3571

Ac 23:11 the **n** following the Lord stood by him, 3571
23:23 two hundred, at the third hour of the **n**; 3571
23:31 and brought *him* by **n** to Antipatris. 3571
26: 7 instantly serving *God* day and **n**, hope to 3571
27:23 For there stood by me this **n** *the* angel of 3571
27:27 But when the fourteenth **n** was come, 3571
Ro 13:12 The **n** is far spent, the day is at hand: let 3571
1Co 11:23 That the Lord Jesus the *same* **n** in which 3571
2Co 11:25 **a n and a day** I have been in the deep; 3574
1Th 2: 9 labouring **n** and day, because *we* would 3571
3:10 **N** and day praying exceedingly that *we* 3571
5: 2 of the Lord so cometh as a thief in the **n**. 3571
5: 5 we are not of the **n**, nor of darkness. 3571
5: 7 For they that sleep sleep in the **n**; 3571
5: 7 that be drunken are drunken in the **n**. 3571
2Th 3: 8 with labour and travail **n** and day, 3571
1Ti 5: 5 in supplications and prayers **n** and day. 3571
2Ti 1: 3 remembrance of thee in my prayers **n** 3571
2Pe 3:10 of the Lord will come as a thief in the **n**; 3571
Rev 4: 8 and they rest not day and **n**, saying, Holy, 3571
7:15 and serve him day and **n** in his temple: 3571
8:12 for a third *part* of it, and the **n** likewise. 3571
12:10 accused them before our God day and **n**. 3571
14:11 and they have no rest day nor **n**, 3571
20:10 be tormented day and **n** for ever and ever. 3571
21:25 at all by day: for there shall be no **n** there. 3571
22: 5 And there shall be no **n** there; 3571

NIGHTS (18) [NIGHT]

Ge 7: 4 rain upon the earth forty days and forty **n**; 3915
7:12 was upon the earth forty days and forty **n**. 3915
Ex 24:18 was in the mount forty days and forty **n**. 3915
34:28 with the LORD forty days and forty **n**; 3915
Dt 9: 9 abode in the mount forty days and forty **n**, 3915
9:11 pass at the end of forty days and forty **n**, 3915
9:18 as at the first, forty days and forty **n**: 3915
9:25 before the LORD forty days and forty **n**; 3915
10:10 to the first time, forty days and forty **n**; 3915
1Sa 30:12 drunk *any* water, three days and three **n**. 3915
1Ki 19: 8 and forty **n** unto Horeb the mount of God. 3915
Job 2:13 upon the ground seven days and seven **n**, 3915
7: 3 and wearisome **n** are appointed to me. 3915
Isa 21: 8 and I *am* set in my ward whole **n**: 3915
Jnh 1:17 belly of the fish three days and three **n**. 3915
Mt 4: 2 when he had fasted forty days and forty **n**, 3571
12:40 days and three **n** in the whale's belly; 3571
12:40 and three **n** in the heart of the earth. 3571

NIMRAH (1) [BETH-NIMRAH]

Nu 32: 3 **N**, and Heshbon, and Elealeh, and 5247

NIMRIM (2)

Isa 15: 6 For the waters of **N** shall be desolate: 5249
Jer 48:34 for the waters also of **N** shall be desolate. 5249

NIMROD (4)

Ge 10: 8 Cush begat **N**: he began to be a mighty 5248
10: 9 *Even* as **N** the mighty hunter before 5248
1Ch 1:10 Cush begat **N**: he began to be mighty 5248
Mic 5: 6 the land of **N** in the entrances thereof: 5248

NIMSHI (5)

1Ki 19:16 Jehu the son of **N** shalt thou anoint to be 5250
2Ki 9: 2 Jehu the son of Jehoshaphat the son of **N**, 5250
9:14 the son of **N** conspired against Joram. 5250
9:20 *is* like the driving of Jehu the son of **N**; 5250
2Ch 22: 7 with Jehoram against Jehu the son of **N**, 5250

NINE (50) [NINTH]

Ge 5: 5 all the days that Adam lived were **n** 8672
5: 8 all the days of Seth were **n** hundred 8672
5:11 all the days of Enos were **n** hundred 8672
5:14 all the days of Cainan were **n** hundred 8672
5:20 all the days of Jared were **n** hundred sixty 8672
5:27 the days of Methuselah were **n** hundred 8672
5:27 were nine hundred sixty and **n** years: 8672
9:29 all the days of Noah were **n** hundred and 8672
11:19 he begat Reu two hundred and **n** years, 8672
11:24 Nahor lived **n** and twenty years, 8672
17: 1 when Abram was ninety years old and **n**, 8672
17:24 Abraham *was* ninety years old and **n**, 8672
Ex 38:24 was twenty and **n** talents, 8672
Lev 25: 8 years shall be unto thee forty and **n** years. 8672
Nu 1:23 *were* fifty and **n** thousand and 8672
2:13 *were* fifty and **n** thousand and 8672
29:26 on the fifth day **n** bullocks, two rams, 8672
34:13 commanded to give unto the **n** tribes, 8672
Dt 3:11 **n** cubits *was* the length thereof, 8672
Jos 13: 7 land for an inheritance unto the **n** tribes, 8672
14: 2 for the **n** tribes, and *for* the half tribe. 8672
15:32 all the cities *are* twenty and **n**, with their 8672
15:44 and Mareshah; **n** cities with their villages. 8672
15:54 and Zior; **n** cities with their villages. 8672
21:16 suburbs; **n** cities out of those two tribes. 8672
Jdg 4: 3 for he had **n** hundred chariots of iron; 8672
4:13 *even* **n** hundred chariots of iron, and all 8672
2Sa 24: 8 they came *to* Jerusalem at the end of **n** 8672
2Ki 14: 2 reigned twenty and **n** years in Jerusalem. 8672
15:13 the son of Jabesh *began* to reign in the **n** 8672
15:17 In the **n** and thirtieth year of Azariah king 8672
17: 1 to reign in Samaria over Israel **n** years. 8672
18: 2 reigned twenty and **n** years in Jerusalem. 8672
1Ch 3: 8 Elishama, and Eliada, and Eliphelet, **n**. 8672
9: 9 **n** hundred and fifty and six. 8672
2Ch 25: 1 reigned twenty and **n** years in Jerusalem. 8672

2Ch 29: 1 reigned **n** and twenty years in Jerusalem. 8672
Ezr 1: 9 chargers of silver, **n** and twenty knives, 8672
2: 8 of Zattu, **n** hundred forty and five. 8672
2:36 of Jeshua, **n** hundred seventy and three. 8672
2:42 of Shobai, *in* all an hundred thirty and **n**. 8672
Ne 7:38 three thousand **n** hundred and thirty. 8672
7:39 of Jeshua, **n** hundred seventy and three. 8672
11: 1 and **n** parts *to dwell in other* cities. 8672
11: 8 Sallai, **n** hundred twenty and eight. 8672
Mt 18:12 doth he not leave the ninety and **n**, 1767
18:13 the ninety and **n** which went not astray. 1767
Lk 15: 4 leave the ninety and **n** in the wilderness, 1767
15: 7 *persons* which need no repentance. 1767
17:17 not ten cleansed? but where *are* the **n**? 1767

NINETEEN (3) [NINETEENTH]

Ge 11:25 Terah an hundred and **n** years, 6240+8672
Jos 19:38 **n** cities with their villages. 6240+8672
2Sa 2:30 there lacked of David's servants **n** 6240+8672

NINETEENTH (4) [NINETEEN]

2Ki 25: 8 which *is* the **n** year of king 6240+8672
1Ch 24:16 The **n** to Pethahiah, the twentieth 6240+8672
25:26 The **n** to Mallothi, *he*, his sons, 6240+8672
Jer 52:12 which *was* the **n** year of 6240+8672

NINETY (24)

Ge 5: 9 And Enos lived **n** years, and begat Cainan: 8673
5:17 days of Mahalaleel were eight hundred **n** 8673
5:30 lived after he begat Noah five hundred **n** 8673
17: 1 when Abram was **n** years old and nine, 8673
17:17 and shall Sarah, that is **n** years old, bear? 8673
17:24 Abraham *was* **n** years old and nine, 8673
1Sa 4:15 Now Eli *was* **n** and eight years old; 8673
1Ch 9: 6 and their brethren, six hundred and **n**. 8673
Ezr 2:16 The children of Ater of Hezekiah, **n** and eight. 8673
2:20 The children of Gibbar, **n** and five. 8673
2:58 *were* three hundred **n** and two. 8673
8:35 and six rams, seventy and seven lambs, 8673
Ne 7:21 children of Ater of Hezekiah, **n** and eight. 8673
7:25 The children of Gibeon, **n** and five. 8673
7:60 *were* three hundred **n** and two. 8673
Jer 52:23 there were **n** and six pomegranates on a 8673
Eze 4: 5 of the days, three hundred and **n** days: 8673
4: 9 and **n** days shalt thou eat thereof. 8673
41:12 and the length thereof **n** cubits. 8673
Da 12:11 *be* a thousand two hundred and **n** days. 8673
Mt 18:12 doth he not leave the **n** and nine, 1768
18:13 rejoiceth more of that *sheep*, than of the **n** 1768
Lk 15: 4 doth not leave the **n** and nine in 1768
15: 7 *more* than over **n** and nine just *persons* 1768

NINEVEH (19) [NINEVITES]

Ge 10:11 builded **N**, and the city Rehoboth, 5210
10:12 Resen between **N** and Calah: the same *is* 5210
2Ki 19:36 and went and returned, and dwelt at **N**. 5210
Isa 37:37 and went and returned, and dwelt at **N**. 5210
Jnh 1: 2 Arise, go to **N**, *that* great city, 5210
3: 2 Arise, go unto **N**, *that* great city, 5210
3: 3 So Jonah arose, and went unto **N**, 5210
3: 3 **N** was an exceeding great city of three 5210
3: 4 forty days, and **N** *shall* be overthrown. 5210
3: 5 So the people of **N** believed God, 5210
3: 6 For word came unto the king of **N**, 5210
3: 7 published through **N** by the decree of 5210
4:11 should not I spare **N**, *that* great city, 5210
Na 1: 1 The burden of **N**. The book of the vision 5210
2: 8 **N** *is* of old like a pool of water: yet they 5210
3: 7 flee from thee, and say, **N** is laid waste: 5210
Zep 2:13 will make **N** a desolation, *and* dry like a 5210
Mt 12:41 men of **N** shall rise in judgment with 3536
Lk 11:32 men of **N** shall rise up in the judgment 3535

NINEVITES (1) [NINEVEH]

Lk 11:30 For as Jonas was a sign unto the **N**, 3536

NINTH (34) [NINE]

Lev 23:32 In *day* of the month at even, 8672
25:22 and eat *yet* of old fruit until the **n** year; 8672
Nu 7:60 On the **n** day Abidan the son of Gideoni, 8671
2Ki 17: 6 In the **n** year of Hoshea, the king of 8671
18:10 that *is* the **n** year of Hoshea king of Israel, 8671
25: 1 it came to pass in the **n** year of his reign, 8671
25: 3 the **n** *day* of the *fourth* month the famine 8671
1Ch 12:12 Johanan the eighth, Elzabad the **n**, 8671
24:11 The **n** to Jeshua, the tenth to Shecaniah, 8671
25:16 The **n** *to* Mattaniah, *he*, his sons, 8671
27:12 The **n** *captain* for the ninth month 8671
27:12 The ninth *captain* for the **n** month *was* 8671
2Ch 16:12 **n** year of his reign was diseased in his 8671
Ezr 10: 9 It *was* the **n** month, on the twentieth *day* 8671
Jer 36: 9 the **n** month, *that* they proclaimed a fast 8671
36:22 sat *in* the winterhouse in the **n** month: 8671
39: 1 In the **n** year of Zedekiah king of Judah, 8672
39: 2 the fourth month, the **n** *day* of the month, 8672
52: 4 it came to pass in the **n** year of his reign, 8671
52: 6 fourth month, in the **n** *day* of the month, 8672
Eze 24: 1 Again in the **n** year, in the tenth month, 8671
Hag 2:10 twentieth *day* of the **n** *month*, in the 8671
2:18 twentieth *day* of the **n** *month*, *even* from 8671
Zec 7: 1 in the fourth *day* of the **n** *month*,
Mt 20: 5 he went out about the sixth and **n** hour, 1766
27:45 darkness over all the land unto the **n** hour. 1766
27:46 And about the **n** hour Jesus cried with a 1766
Mk 15:33 over the whole land until the **n** hour. 1766

Mk 15:34 And at the **n** hour Jesus cried with a loud 1766
Lk 23:44 over all the earth until the **n** hour. 1766
Ac 3: 1 at the hour of prayer, *being* the **n** *hour*. 1766
10: 3 about the **n** hour of the day, 1766
10:30 and at the **n** hour I prayed in my house, 1766
Rev 21:20 eighth, beryl; the **n**, a topaz; the tenth, 1766

NISAN (2)

Ne 2: 1 it came to pass in the month **N**, 5212
Est 3: 7 In the first month, that *is*, the month **N**, 5212

NISROCH (2)

2Ki 19:37 as he was worshipping *in* the house of **N** 5268
Isa 37:38 as he was worshipping *in* the house of **N** 5268

NITRE (2)

Pr 25:20 *as* vinegar upon **n**, so *is* he that singeth 5427
Jer 2:22 For though thou wash thee with **n**, 5427

NO (1393) [NONE, NOR, NOT]

Ge 8: 9 the dove found **n** rest for the sole of her 3808
9:15 the waters shall **n** more become a flood to 3808
11:30 But Sarai was barren; she had **n** child. 369
13: 8 Let there be **n** strife, I pray thee, between 408
15: 3 Behold, to me thou hast given **n** seed: 3808
16: 1 Now Sarai Abram's wife bare him **n** 3808
26:29 thou wilt do us **n** hurt, as we have not 518
30: 1 when Rachel saw that she bare Jacob **n** 3808
31:50 beside my daughters, **n** man *is* with us; 369
32:28 Thy name shall be called **n** more Jacob, 3808
37:22 Shed **n** blood, *but* cast him into this pit 408
37:22 lay **n** hand upon him, that he might rid 408
37:24 pit *was* empty, *there was* **n** water in it. 369
37:32 now whether it *be* thy son's coat or **n**. 3808
38:21 said, There was **n** harlot in this *place*. 3808
38:22 *that* there was **n** harlot in this *place*. 3808
38:26 my son. And he knew her again **n** more. 3808
40: 8 a dream, and *there is* **n** interpreter of it. 369
41:44 without thee shall **n** man lift up his hand 3808
42:11 we *are* true *men*, thy servants are **n** spies. 3808
42:31 him, We *are* true *men*; we are **n** spies: 3808
42:34 shall I know that ye *are* **n** spies, but *that* 3808
44:23 with you, ye shall see my face **n** more. 3808
45: 1 there stood **n** man with him, while Joseph 3808
47: 4 for thy servants have **n** pasture for their 369
47:13 *there was* **n** bread in all the land; 369
Ex 2:12 and when he saw that *there was* **n** man, 3808
3:19 not let you go, **n**, not by a mighty hand. NIH
5: 7 Ye shall **n** more give the people straw to 3808
5:16 *There is* **n** straw given unto thy servants, 369
5:18 for there shall **n** straw be given you, 3808
8:22 that **n** swarms *of flies* shall be there; 1115
9:26 children of Israel *were*, was there **n** hail. 3808
9:28 that there be **n** *more* mighty thunderings 4480
9:28 will let you go, and ye shall stay **n** longer. 3808
10:14 them there were **n** such locusts as they, 3808
10:28 take heed to thyself, see my face **n** more; 408
10:29 I will see thy face again **n** more. 3808
12:16 **n** *manner of* work shall be done in 3605+3808
12:19 Seven days shall there be **n** leaven found 3808
12:43 There shall **n** stranger eat thereof: 3605+3808
12:48 for **n** uncircumcised person shall eat 3605+3808
13: 3 there shall **n** leavened bread be eaten. 3808
13: 7 there shall **n** leavened bread be seen with 3808
14:11 *there were* **n** graves in Egypt, 369+1097
14:13 ye shall see them **n** more for ever. 3808
15:22 in the wilderness, and found **n** water. 3808
16: 4 whether they will walk in my law, or **n**. 3808
16:18 and he that gathered little had **n** lack; 3808
16:19 Let **n** man leave of it till the morning. 408
16:29 **n** man go out of his place on the seventh 408
17: 1 *there was* **n** water for the people to drink. 369
20: 3 Thou shalt have **n** other gods before me. 3808
21: 8 a strange nation he shall have **n** power, 3808
21:22 *from her*, and yet **n** mischief follow: 3808
22: 2 die, *there shall* **n** blood *be shed* for him. 369
22:10 be hurt, or driven away, **n** man seeing *it*: 369
23: 8 thou shalt take **n** gift: for the gift blindeth 3808
23:13 mention of the name of other gods, 3808
23:32 Thou shalt make **n** covenant with them, 3808
30: 9 Ye shall offer **n** strange incense thereon, 3808
30:12 that there be **n** plague amongst them, 3808
33: 4 and **n** man did put on him his ornaments. 3808
33:20 for there shall **n** man see me, and live. 3808
34: 3 **n** man shall come up with thee, neither 3808
34: 7 *that* will by **n** means* clear *the guilty*; 3808
34:14 For thou shalt worship **n** other god: 3808
34:17 Thou shalt make thee **n** molten gods. 3808
35: 3 Ye shall kindle **n** fire throughout your 3808
Lev 2:11 **N** meat offering, which ye shall 3605+3808
2:11 for ye shall burn **n** leaven, nor any 3605+3808
5:11 he shall put **n** oil upon it, neither shall he 3808
6:30 sin offering, whereof *any* of 3808
7:23 Ye shall eat **n** *manner* fat, of ox, 3605+3808
7:24 but ye shall in **n** wise eat* of it. 398+398+3808
7:26 Moreover ye shall eat **n** *manner of* 3605+3808
11:12 Whatsoever hath **n** fins nor scales in 369
12: 4 shall touch **n** hallowed *thing*, nor 3605+3808
13:21 *there be* **n** white hairs therein, and *if* it 369
13:26 *there be* **n** white hair in the bright spot, 369
13:26 it *be* **n** lower than the *other* skin, but *be* 3808
13:31 the skin, and *that there is* **n** black hair in it; 369
13:32 the scall in it **n** yellow hair, and the scall 3808
16:17 shall be **n** man in the tabernacle 3605+3808
16:29 do **n** work at all, whether it be one 3605+3808

Lev 17: 7 they shall **n** more offer their sacrifices | 3808
17:12 I said unto the children of Israel, **N** | 3605+3808
17:14 eat the blood of **n** *manner of* flesh: | 3605+3808
19:15 shall do **n** unrighteousness in judgment: | 3808
19:35 shall do **n** unrighteousness in judgment, | 3808
20:14 that there be **n** wickedness among you. | 3808
21: 3 unto him, which hath had **n** husband, | 3808
21:21 **N** man that hath a blemish, | 3605+3808
22:10 shall **n** stranger eat of the holy | 3605+3808
22:13 have **n** child, and is returned unto her | 369
22:13 there shall **n** stranger eat thereof. | 3605+3808
22:21 there shall be **n** blemish therein. | 3605+3808
23: 3 ye shall do **n** work *therein*: it *is* | 3605+3808
23: 7 ye shall do **n** servile work *therein*. | 3605+3808
23: 8 ye shall do **n** servile work *therein*. | 3605+3808
23:21 ye shall do **n** servile work *therein*. | 3605+3808
23:25 Ye shall do **n** servile work *therein:* | 3605+3808
23:28 shall do **n** work in that same day: | 3605+3808
23:31 Ye shall do **n** *manner of* work: | 3605+3808
23:35 ye shall do **n** servile work *therein*. | 3605+3808
23:36 ye shall do **n** servile work *therein*. | 3605+3808
25:31 houses of the villages which have **n** wall | 369
25:36 Take thou **n** usury of him, or increase: | 408
26: 1 Ye shall make you **n** idols nor graven | 3808
26:37 ye shall have **n** power to stand before | 3808
27:26 LORD's firstling, **n** man shall sanctify it; | 3808
27:28 Notwithstanding **n** devoted thing, | 3605+3808
Nu 1:53 there be **n** wrath upon the congregation | 3808
3: 4 of Sinai, and they had **n** children: | 3808
5: 8 if the man have **n** kinsman to recompense | 369
5:13 and *there be* **n** witness against her, | 369
5:15 he shall pour **n** oil upon it, nor put | 3808
5:19 If **n** man have lain with thee, and if thou | 3808
6: 3 *and* shall drink **n** vinegar of wine, | NIH
6: 5 there shall **n** rasor come upon his head: | 3808
6: 6 the LORD he shall come at **n** dead body. | 3808
8:19 that there be **n** plague among the children | 3808
8:25 service *thereof*, and shall serve **n** more: | 3808
8:26 keep the charge, and shall do **n** service. | 3808
14:18 **by n means** clearing *the guilty*, visiting | 3808
16:40 that **n** stranger, which *is* not of the seed | 3808
18: 5 that there be **n** wrath any more upon | 3808
18:20 shalt have **n** inheritance in their land, | 3808
18:23 children of Israel they have **n** inheritance. | 3808
18:24 of Israel they shall have **n** inheritance. | 3808
18:32 ye shall bear **n** sin by reason of it, when ye | 3808
19: 2 wherein *is* **n** blemish, *and* upon which | 369
19:15 which hath **n** covering bound upon it, | 369
20: 2 there was **n** water for the congregation: | 3808
20: 5 it *is n* place of seed, or of figs, or vines, | 3808
21: 5 for *there is* **n** bread, neither *is there any* | 369
22:26 *was* **n** way to turn *either* to the right | 369
23:23 Surely *there is* **n** enchantment against | 3808
26:33 Zelophehad the son of Hepher had **n** sons, | 3808
26:62 was **n** inheritance given them among | 3808
27: 3 but died in his own sin, and had **n** sons. | 3808
27: 4 among his family, because he hath **n** son? | 369
27: 8 have **n** son, then ye shall cause his | 369
27: 9 if he have **n** daughter, then ye shall give his | 369
27:10 if he have **n** brethren, then ye shall give his | 369
27:11 if his father have **n** brethren, then ye shall | 369
27:17 be not as sheep which have **n** shepherd. | 369
28:18 shall do **n** *manner of* servile work | 3605+3808
28:25 ye shall do **n** servile work. | 3605+3808
28:26 ye shall do **n** servile work: | 3605+3808
29: 1 ye shall do **n** servile work: | 3605+3808
29:12 ye shall do **n** servile work, | 3605+3808
29:35 ye shall do **n** servile work *therein*: | 3605+3808
33:14 was **n** water for the people to drink. | 3808
35:31 Moreover ye shall take **n** satisfaction for | 3808
35:32 ye shall take **n** satisfaction for him that is | 3808
Dt 1:39 which *in that* day had **n** knowledge | 3808
2: 5 land, **n**, not so much as a foot breadth; | NIH
3:26 speak **n** more unto me of this matter. | 408
4:12 voice of the words, but saw **n** similitude; | 369
4:15 ye saw **n** *manner of* similitude on | 3605+3808
5:22 he added **n** more. And he wrote them in | 3808
7: 2 thou shalt make **n** covenant with them, | 3808
7:16 thine eye shall have **n** pity upon them: | 3808
7:24 there shall **n** man *be able to* stand before | 3808
8: 2 wouldest keep his commandments, or **n**. | 3808
8:15 and drought, where *there was* **n** water; | 369
10: 9 Wherefore Levi hath **n** part nor | 3808
10:16 of your heart, and be **n** more stiffnecked. | 3808
11:17 there be **n** rain, and *that* the land yield | 3808
11:25 There shall **n** man *be able to* stand before | 3808
12:12 as he hath **n** part nor inheritance | 369
13:11 shall do **n** more any such wickedness as | 3808
14:27 he hath **n** part nor inheritance with thee. | 369
14:29 he hath **n** part nor inheritance with thee,) | 369
15: 4 Save when there shall be **n** poor among | 3808
15:19 thou shalt do **n** work with the firstling of | 3808
16: 3 Thou shalt eat **n** leavened bread with it; | 3808
16: 4 there shall be **n** leavened bread seen with | 3808
16: 8 thy God: thou shalt do **n** work *therein*. | 3808
17:13 and fear, and do **n** more presumptuously. | 3808
17:16 shall henceforth return **n** more that way. | 3808
18: 1 shall have **n** part nor inheritance with | 3808
18: 2 Therefore shall they have **n** inheritance | 3808
19:20 shall henceforth commit **n** more any such | 3808
20:12 if it will make **n** peace with thee, | 3808
21:14 if thou have **n** delight in her, then thou | 3808
22:26 *is* in the damsel **n** sin *worthy* of death: | 369
23:14 that he see **n** unclean thing in thee, | 3808
23:17 There shall be **n** whore of the daughters | 3808

Dt 23:22 forbear to vow, it shall be **n** sin in thee. | 3808
24: 1 come to pass that she find **n** favour in his | 3808
24: 6 **N** *man* shall take the nether or the upper | 3808
25: 5 and one of them die, and have **n** child, | 369
28:26 earth, and **n** *man* shall fray *them* away. | 369
28:29 and **n** *man* shall save *thee*. | 369
28:32 and *there shall be* **n** might in thine hand. | 369
28:65 these nations shalt thou find **n** ease, | 3808
28:68 unto thee, Thou shalt see it **n** more again: | 3808
28:68 bondwomen, and **n** *man* shall buy *you*. | 369
31: 2 *this* day; I can **n** more go out and come in: | 3808
32:12 and *there was* **n** strange god with him. | 369
32:20 children in whom *is* **n** faith. | 3808
32:39 I, *am* he, and *there is* **n** god with me: | 369
34: 6 **n** man knoweth of his sepulchre unto this | 3808
Jos 8:20 they had **n** power to flee this way or | 3808
8:31 over which **n** *man* hath lift up *any* iron: | 3808
10:14 there was **n** day like that before it or | 3808
11:20 that they might have **n** favour, | 1115+3807.1
14: 4 they gave **n** part unto the Levites in | 3808
17: 3 of Manasseh, had **n** sons, but daughters: | 3808
18: 7 the Levites have **n** part among you; | 369
22:25 of Gad; ye have **n** part in the LORD: | 369
22:27 time to come, Ye have **n** part in the LORD. | 369
23: 9 **n** man hath *been able to* stand before you | 3808
23:13 **n** more drive out *any of* these nations | 3808
Jdg 2: 2 shall make **n** league with the inhabitants | 3808
4:20 any man here? that thou shalt say, **N**. | 369
5:19 of Megiddo; they took **n** gain of money. | 3808
6: 4 left **n** sustenance for Israel, neither sheep, | 3808
8:28 so that they lifted up their heads **n** more. | 3808
10:13 wherefore I will deliver you **n** more. | 3808
11:39 she knew **n** man. And it was a custom in | 3808
13: 5 a son; and **n** rasor shall come on his head: | 3808
13: 7 now drink **n** wine nor strong drink, | 408
13:21 the angel of the LORD did **n** more appear | 3808
15:13 they spake unto him, saying, **N**; but we | 3808
17: 6 In those days *there was* **n** king in Israel, | 369
18: 1 In those days *there was* **n** king in Israel: | 369
18: 7 *was* **n** magistrate in the land, that might | 369
18: 7 and had **n** business with *any* man. | 369
18:10 a place where *there is* **n** want of any thing | 369
18:28 *there was* **n** deliverer, because it *was* far | 369
18:28 and they had **n** business with *any* man; | 369
19: 1 days, when *there was* **n** king in Israel, | 369
19:15 for *there was* **n** man that took them into | 369
19:18 there *is* **n** man that receiveth me to house. | 369
19:19 thy servants: there *is* **n** want of any thing. | 369
19:30 There was **n** such *deed* done nor seen | 3808
21:12 that had known **n** man by lying with *any* | 3808
21:25 In those days *there was* **n** king in Israel: | 369
1Sa 1: 2 had children, but Hannah had **n** children. | 369
1:11 there shall **n** rasor come upon his head. | 3808
1:15 Hannah answered and said, **N**, my lord, | 3808
1:18 and her countenance was **n** more *sad*. | 3808
2: 3 Talk **n** more *so* exceeding proudly; let *not* | 408
2: 9 for by strength shall **n** man prevail. | 3808
2:24 sons; for *it is* **n** good report that I hear: | 3808
3: 1 in those days; *there was* **n** open vision. | 369
6: 7 on which there hath come **n** yoke, | 3808
7:13 they came **n** more into the coast of Israel: | 3808
10:14 when we saw that *they were* **n** where, | 369
10:27 despised him, and brought him **n** presents. | 3808
11: 3 if *there be* **n** man to save us, we will | 369
13:19 Now there was **n** smith found throughout | 3808
14: 6 for *there is* **n** restraint to the LORD to save | 369
14:26 but **n** man put his hand to his mouth: | 369
15:35 Samuel came **n** more to see Saul until | 3808
17:32 Let **n** man's heart fail because of him; | 408
17:50 *there was* **n** sword in the hand of David. | 369
18: 2 would let him go **n** more home *to* his | 3808
20:15 **n**, not when the LORD hath cut off | NIH
20:21 for *there is* **n** peace to thee, and **n** hurt; | 369
20:34 eat **n** meat the second day of the month: | 3808
21: 1 Why *art* thou alone, and **n** man with thee? | 369
21: 2 Let **n** man know any thing of the business | 408
21: 4 is **n** common bread under mine hand, | 369
21: 6 hallowed *bread:* for there was **n** bread | 3808
21: 9 take *it:* for *there is* **n** other save that here. | 369
25:31 That this shall be **n** grief unto thee, | 3808
26:12 **n** man *saw it*, nor knew *it*, neither | 369
26:21 for I will **n** more do thee harm, because | 3808
27: 4 and he sought **n** more again for him. | 3808
28:10 there shall **n** punishment happen to thee | 518
28:15 me **n** more, neither by prophets, | 3808
28:20 there was **n** strength in him; for he had | 369
28:20 for he had eaten **n** bread all the day, nor | 3808
29: 3 I have found **n** *fault* in him since he | 3808+3972
30: 4 until they had **n** more power to weep. | 369
30:12 for he had eaten **n** bread, nor drunk *any* | 3808
2Sa 1:21 mountains of Gilboa, *let there be* **n** dew, | 408
2:28 still, and pursued after Israel **n** more, | 3808
6:23 had **n** child unto the day of her death. | 3808
7:10 in a place of their own, and move **n** more; | 3808
12: 6 did this thing, and because he had **n** pity. | 369
13:12 **n** such thing ought to be done in Israel: | 3808
13:16 said unto him, There *is* **n** cause: this evil | 408
14:25 of his head there was **n** blemish in him. | 369
15: 3 is **n** man *deputed* of the king to hear | 369
15:26 if he thus say, I have **n** delight in thee; | 2656
18:13 for there is **n** matter hid from | 3605+3808
18:18 I have **n** son to keep my name in | 369
18:20 this day thou shalt bear **n** tidings, because | 3808
18:22 seeing that thou hast **n** tidings ready? | 3808
20: 1 and said, We have **n** part in David, | 369

2Sa 20:10 Amasa took **n** heed to the sword that *was* | 3808
21: 4 We will have **n** silver nor gold of Saul, | 369
21:17 shalt go **n** more out with us to battle, | 3808
1Ki 1: 1 him with clothes, but he gat **n** heat. | 3808
3: 2 there was **n** house built unto the name of | 3808
3:18 *there was* **n** stranger with us in the house, | 369
3:22 this said, **N**; but the dead *is* thy son, | 3808
3:26 her the living child, and in **n** wise slay it. | 408
3:27 her the living child, and in **n** wise slay it: | 3808
6:18 all *was* cedar; there was **n** stone seen. | 369
8:16 I chose **n** city out of all the tribes of Israel | 3808
8:23 there is **n** God like thee, in heaven above, | 369
8:35 there is **n** rain, because they have sinned | 3808
8:46 (for *there is* **n** man that sinneth not,) | 369
9:22 of Israel did Solomon make **n** bondman: | 3808
10: 5 the LORD; there was **n** more spirit in her. | 3808
10:10 there came **n** more such abundance of | 3808
10:12 there came **n** such almug trees, nor were | 3808
13: 9 Eat **n** bread, nor drink water, | 3808
13:17 Thou shalt eat **n** bread nor drink water | 3808
13:22 to thee, Eat **n** bread, and drink **n** water; | 408
13:22 to thee, Eat no bread, and drink **n** water; | 408
17: 7 because there had been **n** rain in the land. | 3808
17:17 sore, that there was **n** breath left in him. | 3808
18:10 God liveth, there is **n** nation or kingdom, | 518
18:23 put **n** fire *under:* and I will dress the other | 3808
18:23 and lay *it* on wood, and put **n** fire *under:* | 3808
18:25 name of your gods, but put **n** fire *under.* | 3808
18:26 *there was* **n** voice, nor any that answered. | 369
21: 4 away his face, and would eat **n** bread. | 3808
21: 5 thy spirit so sad, that thou eatest **n** bread? | 369
22:17 the LORD said, These have **n** master: | 369
22:18 I not tell thee that he would prophesy **n** | 3808
22:47 There was then **n** king in Edom: a deputy | 369
2Ki 1:16 there is **n** God in Israel to inquire of his | 369
1:17 king of Judah; because he had **n** son. | 3808
2:12 he saw him **n** more: and he took hold of | 3808
3: 9 there was **n** water for the host, and for | 3808
4:14 Verily she hath **n** child, and her husband | 369
4:41 And there was **n** harm in the pot. | 1697+3808
5:15 now I know that *there is* **n** God in all | 369
5:25 And he said, Thy servant went **n** whither. | 3808
6:23 So the bands of Syria came **n** more into | 369
7: 5 of Syria, behold, *there was* **n** man there. | 369
7:10 *there was* **n** man there, neither voice | 369
9:35 they found **n** more of her than the skull, | 3808
10:31 Jehu took **n** heed to walk in the law of | 3808
12: 7 **n** more money of your acquaintance, | 408
12: 8 the priests consented to receive **n** more | 1115
17: 4 brought **n** present to the king of Assyria, | 3808
19:18 for they were **n** gods, but the work of | 3808
22: 7 Howbeit there was **n** reckoning made | 3808
23:10 that **n** man might make his son or his | 1115
23:18 Let him alone; let **n** man move his bones. | 408
23:25 unto him was there **n** king before him, | 3808
25: 3 there was **n** bread for the people of | 3808
1Ch 2:34 Now Sheshan had **n** sons, but daughters. | 3808
12:17 seeing *there is* **n** wrong in mine hands, | 3808
16:21 He suffered **n** man to do them wrong; | 3808
16:22 anointed, and do my prophets **n** harm. | 408
17: 9 their place, and shall be moved **n** more; | 3808
22:16 the brass, and the iron, *there is* **n** number. | 369
23:22 and had **n** sons, but daughters: | 3808
23:26 *they* shall **n** more carry the tabernacle, | 369
24: 2 before their father, and had **n** children: | 3808
24:28 Of Mahli *came* Eleazar, who had **n** sons. | 3808
2Ch 6: 5 in city among all the tribes of Israel to | 3808
6:14 *there is* **n** God like thee in the heaven, | 369
6:26 there is **n** rain, because they have sinned | 3808
6:36 (for *there is* **n** man which sinneth not,) | 369
7:13 If I shut up heaven that there be **n** rain, | 3808
8: 9 Solomon make **n** servants for his work; | 3808
9: 4 the LORD; there was **n** more spirit in her. | 3808
13: 9 *same* way be a priest of *them that are* **n** | 3808
14: 6 had rest, and he had **n** war in those years; | 369
14:11 many, *or* with *them that have* **n** power: | 369
15: 5 those times *there was* **n** peace to him that | 369
15:19 there was **n** *more* war unto the five and | 3808
17:10 they made **n** war against Jehoshaphat. | 3808
18:16 as sheep that have **n** shepherd: | 369
18:16 the LORD said, These have **n** master; | 369
19: 7 do *it:* for *there is* **n** iniquity with the LORD | 369
20:12 for we have **n** might against this great | 3808
21:19 his people made **n** burning for him, like | 3808
22: 9 So the house of Ahaziah had **n** power to | 3808
32:15 for **n** god of any nation or | 3605+3808
35:18 there was **n** passover like to that, kept in | 3808
36:16 against his people, till *there was* **n** remedy. | 369
36:17 had **n** compassion upon young man or | 3808
Ezr 4: 6 by this means thou shalt have **n** portion | 3809
9:14 *there should be* **n** remnant nor escaping? | 369
10: 6 he did eat **n** bread, nor drink water: | 3808
Ne 2:14 *there was* **n** place for the beast *that was* | 369
2:17 Jerusalem, that we be **n** more a reproach. | 3808
2:20 have **n** portion, nor right, nor memorial, | 369
6: 1 and *that* there was **n** breach left therein; | 3808
6: 8 There are **n** such things *done* as thou | 369
13:19 there should **n** burden be brought in on | 3808
13:21 From that time forth came they **n** more | 3808
13:26 many nations was there **n** king like him, | 3808
Est 1:19 That Vashti come **n** more before king | 3808
2:14 she came in unto the king **n** more, | 3808
5:12 Esther the queen did let **n** *man* come in | 3808
8: 8 with the king's ring, may **n** man reverse. | 369
9: 2 **n** man could withstand them; for the fear | 3808

Job
3: 7 be solitary, let **n** joyful voice therein. 408
4:18 Behold, he put **n** trust in his servants; 3808
5:19 yea, in seven there shall **n** evil touch thee. 3808
7: 7 is wind: mine eye shall **n** more see good. 3808
7: 8 see me **n** more: thine eyes are upon me, 3808
7: 9 down to the grave shall come up **n** more. 3808
7:10 He shall return **n** more to his house, 3808
9:25 a post: they flee away, they see **n** good. 3808
10:18 up the ghost, and **n** eye had seen me! 3808
11: 3 shall **n** man make thee ashamed? 369
12: 2 **N** doubt but ye are the people, 551
12:14 up a man, and there can be **n** opening. 3808
12:24 in a wilderness where there is **n** way. 3808
13: 4 of lies, ye are all physicians **of n** value. 457
14:12 till the heavens be **n** more, they shall not 1115
15: 3 with speeches wherewith he can do **n** 3808
15:15 Behold, he putteth **n** trust in his saints; 3808
15:19 and a stranger passed among them. 3808
15:28 and in houses which **n** man inhabiteth, 3808
16:18 my blood, and let my cry have **n** place. 408
18:17 and he shall have **n** name in the street. 3808
19: 7 I cry aloud, but there is **n** judgment. 369
19:16 my servant, and he gave me **n** answer; 3808
20: 9 also which saw him shall see him **n** more; 3808
20:21 therefore shall **n** man look for his goods. 3808
23: 6 **N**; but he would put strength in me. 3808
24: 7 that they have **n** covering in the cold. 369
24:15 the twilight, saying, **N** eye shall see me: 3808
24:20 he shall be **n** more remembered; 3808
24:22 he riseth up, and **n** man is sure of life. 3808
26: 2 how savest thou the arm that hath **n** 3808
26: 3 hast thou counselled him that hath **n** 369
26: 6 him, and destruction hath **n** covering. 3808
28: 7 There is a path which **n** fowl knoweth, 3808
28:18 **N** mention shall be made of coral, 3808
30:13 forward my calamity, they have **n** helper. 3808
30:17 night season: and my sinews take **n** rest. 3808
32: 3 because they had found **n** answer, 3808
32: 5 When Elihu saw that there was **n** answer 3808
32:15 were amazed, they answered **n** more: 3808
32:16 but stood still, and answered **n** more:) 3808
32:19 my belly is as wine which hath **n** vent; 3808
34:22 There is **n** darkness, nor shadow of death, 369
34:32 if I have done iniquity, I will do **n** more. 3808
36:16 a broad place, where there is **n** straitness; 3808
36:19 **n**, not gold, nor all the forces of strength. NIH
38:11 Hitherto shalt thou come, but **n** further: 3808
38:26 where **n** man is; on the wilderness, 3808
38:26 the wilderness, wherein there is **n** man; 3808
40: 5 yea, twice; but I will proceed **n** further. 3808
41: 8 him, remember the battle, do **n** more. 408
41:16 that **n** air can come between them. 3808
42: 2 **n** thought can be withholden from thee. 3808
42:15 in all the land were **n** women found so 3808

Ps
3: 2 my soul, There is **n** help for him in God. 369
5: 9 For there is **n** faithfulness in their mouth; 369
5: 9 in death there is **n** remembrance of thee: 369
10:18 that the man of the earth may **n** more 1077
14: 1 fool hath said in his heart, There is **n** God. 369
14: 3 there is none that doeth good, **n**, not one. 369
14: 4 Have all the workers of iniquity **n** 3808
19: 3 There is **n** speech nor language, where 369
22: 6 I am a worm, and **n** man; a reproach of 3808
23: 4 of the shadow of death, I will fear **n** evil: 3808
32: 2 and in whose spirit there is **n** guile. 369
32: 9 as the mule, which have **n** understanding: 369
33:16 There is **n** king saved by the multitude of 369
34: 9 for there is **n** want to them that fear him. 369
36: 1 that there is **n** fear of God before his eyes. 369
38: 3 There is **n** soundness in my flesh because 369
38: 7 and there is **n** soundness in my flesh. 369
38:14 and in whose mouth are **n** reproofs. 369
39:13 before I go hence, and be **n** more. 369
40:17 my deliverer; make **n** tarrying, O my God. 408
41: 8 now that he shall rise up **n** more. 3808
50: 9 I will take **n** bullock out of thy house, 3808
53: 1 fool hath said in his heart, There is **n** God. 369
53: 3 there is none that doeth good, **n**, not one. 369
53: 4 the workers of iniquity **n** knowledge? 3808
53: 5 were they in great fear, where **n** fear was: 3808
55:19 Because they have **n** changes, therefore 369
63: 1 a dry and thirsty land, where **n** water is; 1097
69: 2 in deep mire, where there is **n** standing: 369
70: 5 my deliverer; O LORD, make **n** tarrying. 408
72:12 the poor also, and him that hath **n** helper. 369
73: 4 For there are **n** bands in their death: 369
74: 9 there is **n** more any prophet: neither is 3808
77: 7 and will he be favourable **n** more? 3808
78:64 and their widows made **n** lamentation. 3808
81: 9 There shall **n** strange god be in thee; 3808
83: 4 that the name of Israel may be **n** more in 3808
84:11 **n** good thing will he withhold from them 3808
88: 4 the pit: I am as a man that hath **n** strength: 369
88: 5 grave, whom thou rememberest **n** more: 3808
91:10 There shall **n** evil befall thee, neither shall 3808
92:15 and there is **n** unrighteousness in him. 3808
101: 3 will set **n** wicked thing before mine eyes: 3808
102:27 the same, and thy years shall have **n** end. 3808
103:16 the place thereof shall know it **n** more. 3808
104:35 the earth, and let the wicked be **n** more. 369
105:14 He suffered **n** man to do them wrong: yea, 3808
105:15 anointed, and do my prophets **n** harm. 408
107: 4 solitary way; they found **n** city to dwell in. 3808
107:40 in the wilderness, where there is **n** way. 3808
119: 3 They also do **n** iniquity: they walk in his 3808

Ps 142: 4 there was **n** man that would know me: 369
142: 4 refuge failed me; **n** man cared for my soul. 369
143: 2 for in thy sight shall **n** man living 3605+3808
144:14 that there be **n** breaking in, nor going out; 369
144:14 that there be **n** complaining in our streets. 369
146: 3 the son of man, in whom there is **n** help. 369

Pr
1:24 out my hand, and **n** man regarded; 369
3:30 cause, if he have done thee **n** harm. 3808
6: 7 Which having **n** guide, overseer, or ruler, 369
8:24 When there were **n** depths, I was brought 369
8:24 there were **n** fountains abounding with 369
10:22 and he addeth **n** sorrow with it. 3808
10:25 so is the wicked **n** more: but the righteous 369
11:14 Where **n** counsel is, the people fall: 369
12:21 shall **n** evil happen to the just: 3605+3808
12:28 in the pathway thereof there is **n** death. 408
14: 4 Where **n** oxen are, the crib is clean: 369
17:16 get wisdom, seeing he hath **n** heart to it? 369
17:20 He that hath a froward heart findeth **n** 3808
17:21 and the father of a fool hath **n** joy. 3808
18: 2 A fool hath **n** delight in understanding, 3808
21:10 his neighbour findeth **n** favour in his eyes. 3808
21:30 There is **n** wisdom nor understanding nor 369
22:24 Make **n** friendship with an angry man; 408
24:20 there shall be **n** reward to the evil man; 3808
25:28 He that hath **n** rule over his own spirit is 369
26:20 Where **n** wood is, there the fire goeth out: 657
26:20 so where there is **n** talebearer, the strife 369
28: 1 The wicked flee when **n** man pursueth: 369
28: 3 like a sweeping rain which leaveth **n** food. 369
28:17 shall flee to the pit; let **n** man stay him. 408
28:24 his mother, and saith, It is **n** transgression; 369
29: 9 whether he rage or laugh, there is **n** rest. 369
29:18 Where there is **n** vision, the people perish: 3808
30:20 and saith, I have done **n** wickedness. 369
30:27 The locusts have **n** king, yet go they forth 369
30:31 a king, against whom there is **n** rising up. 510
31: 7 and remember his misery **n** more. 3808
31:11 her, so that he shall have **n** need of spoil. 3808

Ecc
1: 9 there is **n** new thing under the sun. 369+3605
1:11 There is **n** remembrance of former things; 369
2:11 and there was **n** profit under the sun. 369
2:16 For there is **n** remembrance of the wise 369
3:11 **n** man can find out the work that God 369
3:12 I know that there is **n** good in them, but 369
3:19 that a man hath **n** preeminence above a 369
4: 1 were oppressed, and they had **n** comforter; 369
4: 1 was power; but they had **n** comforter. 369
4: 8 yet is there **n** end of all his labour; neither 3808
4:13 who will **n** more be admonished. 3808
4:16 There is **n** end of all the people, even of all 369
5: 4 to pay it; for he hath **n** pleasure in fools: 369
5: 3 with good, and also that he have **n** burial; 3808
6: 6 years twice told, yet hath he seen **n** good: 3808
7:21 Also take **n** heed unto all words that are 408
8: 5 the commandment shall feel **n** evil thing: 3808
8: 7 For he **n** man that hath power over 369
8: 8 there is **n** discharge in that war; neither 369
8:15 a man hath **n** better thing under the sun, 369
9: 1 **n** man knoweth either love or hatred by all 369
9: 8 and let thy head lack **n** ointment. 408
9:10 for there is **n** work, nor device, 369
9:15 yet **n** man remembered that same poor 3808
10:11 and a babbler is **n** better. 369
10:20 Curse not the king, **n** not in thy thought; 1571
12: 1 thou shalt say, I have **n** pleasure in them; 369
12:12 of making many books there is **n** end; 369

SS
4: 7 art all fair, my love; there is **n** spot in thee. 369
5: 6 I called him, but he gave me **n** answer. 3808
8: 8 have a little sister, and she hath **n** breasts: 369

Isa
1: 6 unto the head there is **n** soundness in it; 369
1:13 Bring **n** more vain oblations; incense is an 3808
1:30 and as a garden that hath **n** water. 369
5: 6 the clouds that they rain **n** rain upon it. 4480
5: 8 that lay field to field, till there be **n** place, 657
5:13 because they have **n** knowledge: 1097
8:20 it is because there is **n** light in them. 369
9: 7 and peace there shall be **n** end, 3808
9:17 Therefore the Lord shall have **n** joy in 3808
9:19 of the fire: **n** man shall spare his brother. 3808
10:15 should lift up itself, as if it were **n** wood. 3808
10:20 shall **n** more again stay upon him that 3808
13:14 and as a sheep that **n** man taketh up: 369
13:18 they shall have **n** pity on the fruit of 3808
14: 1 laid down, **n** feller is come up against us. 3808
15: 6 the grass faileth, there is **n** green thing. 3808
16:10 in the vineyards there shall be **n** singing, 3808
16:10 the treaders shall tread out **n** wine in their 3808
19: 7 wither, be driven away, and be **n** more. 369
23: 1 so that there is **n** house, no entering in: 4480
23: 1 so that there is **n** house, no entering in: 4480
23:10 of Tarshish: there is **n** more strength. 369
23:12 he said, Thou shalt **n** more rejoice, O 3808
23:12 Chittim; there also shalt thou have **n** rest. 3808
24:10 is shut up, that **n** man may come in. 4480
25: 2 a palace of strangers to be **n** city; it shall 4480
26:21 blood, and shall **n** more cover her slain. 3808
27:11 for it is a people of **n** understanding: 3808
27:11 he that formed them will shew them **n** 3808
28: 8 filthiness, so that there is **n** place clean. 1097
29:16 that framed it, He had **n** understanding? 3808
30: 7 shall help in vain, and to **n** purpose: 7385
30:16 ye said, **N**; for we will flee upon horses; 3808
30:19 thou shalt weep **n** more: he will be very 3808
32: 5 The vile person shall be **n** more called 3808

Isa 33: 8 despised the cities, he regardeth **n** man. 3808
33:21 wherein shall go **n** galley with oars, 1077
34:16 one of these shall fail, none shall want 3808
35: 9 lion shall be there, nor any ravenous 3808
37:19 for they were **n** gods, but the work of 3808
38:11 I shall behold man **n** more with 3808
40:20 impoverished that he hath **n** oblation NIH
40:28 there is **n** searching of his understanding. 369
40:29 to them that have **n** might he increaseth 369
41:28 For I beheld, and there was **n** man; 369
41:28 and there was **n** counsellor, that, 369
43:10 before me there was **n** God formed, 3808
43:11 and beside me there is **n** saviour. 369
43:12 there was **n** strange god among you: 369
43:24 Thou hast bought me **n** sweet cane with 3808
44: 6 the last; and besides me there is **n** God. 369
44: 8 yea, there is **n** God; I know not any. 369
44:12 he drinketh **n** water, and is faint. 3808
45: 5 is none else, there is **n** God besides me: 369
45: 9 or thy work, He hath **n** hands? 369
45:14 and there is none else, there is **n** God. 657
45:20 they have **n** knowledge that set up 3808
45:21 there is **n** God else beside me; a just God 369
47: 1 there is **n** throne, O daughter of 369
47: 1 for thou shalt **n** more be called tender 3808
47: 5 for thou shalt **n** more be called, The lady 3808
47: 6 thou didst shew them **n** mercy; upon 3808
48:22 There is **n** peace, saith the LORD, unto 369
50: 2 when I came, was there **n** man? 369
50: 2 have I **n** power to deliver? behold, at my 369
50: 2 there is **n** water, and dieth for thirst. 369
50:10 that walketh in darkness, and hath **n** light? 369
51:22 my fury; thou shalt **n** more drink it again: 3808
52: 1 for henceforth there shall **n** more come 3808
52:11 touch **n** unclean thing; go ye out of the 408
53: 2 he hath **n** form nor comeliness; 3808
53: 2 in beauty that we should desire him. 3808
53: 9 because he had done **n** violence, 3808
54: 9 of Noah should **n** more go over the earth; 4480
54:17 **N** weapon that is formed against 3605+3808
55: 1 to the waters, and he that hath **n** money; 369
57: 1 and **n** man layeth it to heart: 369
57:10 yet saidst thou not, There is **n** hope. 2976
57:21 There is **n** peace, saith my God, 369
58: 3 our soul, and thou takest **n** knowledge? 3808
59: 8 is **n** judgment in their goings: 369
59:10 blind, and we grope as if we had **n** eyes: 369
59:15 displeased him that there was **n** judgment. 369
59:16 he saw that there was **n** man, 369
59:16 wondered that there was **n** intercessor: 369
60:15 that **n** man went through thee, I will 3808
60:18 Violence shall **n** more be heard in thy 3808
60:19 The sun shall be **n** more thy light by day; 3808
60:20 Thy sun shall **n** more go down; 3808
62: 4 Thou shalt **n** more be termed Forsaken; 3808
62: 7 give him **n** rest, till he establish, and till he 408
62: 8 **Surely** I will **n** more give thy corn to be 518
65:19 voice of weeping shall be **n** more heard 3808
65:20 There shall be **n** more thence an infant of 3808

Jer
2: 6 a land that **n** man passed through, 3808
2: 6 passed through, and where **n** man dwelt? 3808
2:11 changed their gods, which are yet **n** gods? 3808
2:13 broken cisterns, that can hold **n** water. 3808
2:25 saidst, There is **n** hope: no; for I have 2976
2:25 **n**; for I have loved strangers, and after 3808
2:30 your children; they received **n** correction: 3808
2:31 lords; we will come **n** more unto thee? 3808
3: 3 and there hath been **n** latter rain; 3808
3:16 saith the LORD, they shall say **n** more, 3808
4:22 but to do good they have **n** knowledge. 3808
4:23 and the heavens, and they had **n** light. 369
4:25 lo, there was **n** man, and all the birds of 369
5: 7 and sworn by them that are **n** gods: 3808
6:10 a reproach; they have **n** delight in it. 3808
6:14 Peace, peace; when there is **n** peace. 369
6:23 spear; they are cruel, and have **n** mercy; 3808
7:32 that it shall **n** more be called Tophet, 369
7:32 shall bury in Tophet, till there be **n** place. 369
8: 6 **n** man repented him of his wickedness, 3808
8:11 Peace, peace; when there is **n** peace. 369
8:13 shall be **n** grapes on the vine, nor figs 369
8:15 in good came; and for a time of health, 369
8:22 Is there **n** balm in Gilead; is there **n** 369
8:22 balm in Gilead; is there **n** physician there? 369
10:14 falsehood, and there is **n** breath in them. 3808
11:19 his name may be **n** more remembered. 3808
11:23 there shall be **n** remnant of them: for 3808
12:11 because **n** man layeth it to heart. 369
12:12 **n** flesh shall have peace. 369+3605+3807.1
14: 3 they came to the pits, and found **n** water; 3808
14: 4 for there was **n** rain in the earth, 3808
14: 5 and forsook it, because there was **n** grass. 3808
14: 6 eyes did fail, because there was **n** grass. 369
14:19 smitten us, and there is **n** healing for us? 369
14:19 we looked for peace, and there is **n** good; 369
16:14 the LORD, that it shall **n** more be said, 3808
16:19 and things wherein there is **n** profit. 369
16:20 gods unto himself, and they are **n** gods? 3808
17:21 bear **n** burden on the sabbath day, 408
17:24 to bring in **n** burden through the gates of 1115
17:24 sabbath day, to do **n** work therein; 1115+3605
18:12 they said, There is **n** hope: but we will 2976
19: 6 that this place shall **n** more be called 3808
19:11 in Tophet, till there be **n** place to bury. 369
22: 3 do **n** wrong, do no violence, to the 408

N

Jer 22: 3 no wrong, do **n** violence, to the stranger, 408
22:10 for he shall **n** return no more, nor see his 3808
22:12 captive, and shall see this land **n** more. 3808
22:28 *is he* a vessel wherein *is* **n** pleasure? 369
22:30 for **n** man of his seed shall prosper, 3808
23: 4 they shall fear **n** more, nor be dismayed, 3808
23: 7 the LORD, that they shall **n** more say, 3808
23:17 own heart, N evil shall come upon you. 3808
23:36 of the LORD shall ye mention **n** more: 3808
25: 6 of your hands; and I will do you **n** hurt. 3808
25:27 spue, and fall, and rise **n** more, because 3808
25:35 the shepherds shall **have n** way to flee, 6+4480
30: 8 strangers shall **n** more serve themselves of 3808
30:13 bound up: thou hast **n** healing medicines. 369
30:17 This *is* Zion, whom **n** man seeketh after. 369
31:29 In those days they shall say **n** more, 3808
31:34 they shall teach **n** more every man his 3808
31:34 and I will remember their sin **n** more. 3808
33:24 *they* should be **n** more a nation before 4480
35: 6 they said, We will drink **n** wine: 3808
35: 6 saying, Ye shall drink **n** wine, *neither* ye, 3808
35: 8 drink **n** wine all our days, we, our wives, 1115
36:19 Jeremiah; and let **n** man know where ye 408
38: 6 the dungeon *there was* **n** water, but mire: 369
38: 9 he is: for *there is* **n** more bread in the city. 369
38:24 Let **n** man know of these words, 408
39:12 well to him, and do him **n** harm; 408+3972
40:15 **n** man shall know *it:* wherefore should 3808
41: 4 had slain Gedaliah, and **n** man knew *it,* 3808
42:14 Saying, No; but we will go *into* the land of 3808
42:14 land of Egypt, where we shall see **n** war, 3808
42:18 and ye shall see this place **n** more. 3808
44: 2 a desolation, and **n man** dwelleth therein, 369
44: 5 to burn **n** incense unto other gods. 1115
44:17 of victuals, and were well, and saw **n** evil. 3808
44:22 So that the LORD could **n** longer bear, 3808
44:26 that my name shall **n** more be named in 518
45: 3 I fainted in my sighing, and I find **n** rest. 3808
46:25 I will punish the multitude of N, 4996
48: 2 *There shall be* **n** more praise of Moab: 369
48: 8 upon every city, and **n** city shall escape: 3808
48:33 *their* shouting *shall be* **n** shouting. 3808
48:38 Moab like a vessel wherein *is* **n** pleasure, 369
49: 1 thus saith the LORD; Hath Israel **n** sons? 369
49: 1 Hath he **n** heir? why *then* doth their king 369
49: 7 of hosts; *Is* wisdom **n** more in Teman? 369
49:18 saith the LORD, **n** man shall abide there, 3808
49:33 shall **n** man abide there, nor *any* son 3808
49:36 shall be **n** nation whither the outcasts 408
50:14 the bow, shoot at her, spare **n** arrows: 408
50:39 it shall be **n** more inhabited for ever; 3808
50:40 shall **n** man abide there, neither shall any 3808
51:17 falsehood, and *there is* **n** breath in them. 3808
51:43 a land wherein **n** man dwelleth, 3605+3808
52: 6 that there was **n** bread for the people of 3808

La 1: 3 among the heathen, she findeth **n** rest: 3808
1: 6 are become like harts *that* find **n** pasture, 3808
1: 9 she had **n** comforter. O LORD, behold my 369
2: 9 law *is* **n** *more;* her prophets also find no 369
2: 9 law *is* no *more;* her prophets also find **n** 3808
2:18 give thyself **n** rest; let not the apple of 408
4: 4 bread, and **n man** breaketh *it* unto them. 369
6: 6 in a moment, and **n** hands stayed on her. 3808
4:15 They shall **n** more sojourn *there.* 3808
4:16 them; he will **n** more regard them: 3808
4:22 he will **n** more carry thee away into 3808
5: 5 we labour, *and* have **n** rest. 3808

Eze 12:23 they shall **n** more use it as a proverb in 3808
12:24 For there shall be **n** more any vain vision 3808
12:25 to pass; it shall be **n** more prolonged: 3808
13:10 *was* **n** peace; and one built up a wall, 369
13:15 The wall *is* **n** *more,* neither they that 369
13:16 and *there is* **n** peace, saith the Lord GOD. 369
13:21 they shall be **n** more in your hand to be 3808
13:23 Therefore ye shall see **n** more vanity, 3808
14:11 That the house of Israel may go **n** more 3808
14:15 that **n man** may pass through because of 1097
15: 5 it was whole, it was meet for **n** work: 3808
16:34 reward is given unto thee, therefore 3808
16:41 and thou also shalt give **n** hire any more. 3808
16:42 I will be quiet, and will be **n** more angry. 3808
18:32 For I have **n** pleasure in the death of him 3808
19: 9 his voice should **n** more be heard upon 3808
19:14 she hath **n** strong rod *to be* a sceptre to 3808
20:39 pollute ye my holy name **n** more with 3808
21:13 it shall be **n** *more,* saith the Lord GOD. 3808
21:27 it shall be **n** *more,* until he come whose 3808
21:32 land; thou shalt be **n** *more* remembered: 3808
22:26 have put **n** difference between the holy 3808
24: 6 it out piece by piece; let **n** lot fall upon it. 3808
24:17 to cry, make **n** mourning *for* the dead, 3808
24:27 thou shalt speak, and be **n** more dumb: 3808
26:13 the sound of thy harps shall be **n** more 3808
26:14 nets upon thee; thou shalt be built **n** more: 3808
26:21 *shalt be* **n** *more:* though thou be sought 369
28: 3 *there is* **n** secret *that* they can hide 3605+3808
28: 9 *shalt be* a man, and **n** God, in the hand 3808
28:24 there shall be **n** more a pricking brier unto 3808
29:11 N foot of man shall pass through it, 3808
29:15 **that** *they* shall **n more** rule over 1115+3807.1
29:16 it shall be **n** more the confidence of 3808
29:18 yet had he **n** wages, nor his army, 3808
30:13 shall be **n** more a prince of the land of 3808
30:14 in Zoan, and will execute judgments in N. 4996
30:15 and I will cut off the multitude of N. 4996

Eze 30:16 N shall be rent asunder, and Noph *shall* 4996
33:11 **n** pleasure in the death of the wicked; 518
33:22 was opened, and I was **n** more dumb. 3808
34: 5 scattered, because *there is* **n** shepherd: 1097
34: 8 because *there was* **n** shepherd, neither 369
34:22 my flock, and they shall **n** more be a prey; 3808
34:28 shall **n** more be a prey to the heathen, 3808
34:29 shall be **n** more consumed with hunger 3808
36:12 shalt **n** more henceforth bereave them 3808
36:14 Therefore thou shalt devour men **n** more, 3808
36:29 increase it, and lay **n** famine upon you. 3808
36:30 that ye shall receive **n** more reproach of 3808
37: 8 above: but *there was* **n** breath in them. 369
37:22 they shall be **n** more two nations, 3808
39:10 So that they shall take **n** wood out of 3808
43: 7 shall the house of Israel **n** more defile, 3808
44: 2 opened, and **n** man shall enter in by it; 3808
44: 9 Thus saith the Lord GOD; N 3605+3808
44:17 wool shall come upon them, whiles 3808
44:25 they shall come at **n** dead person to defile 3808
44:25 or for sister that hath had **n** husband, 3808
44:28 ye shall give them **n** possession in Israel: 3808
45: 8 my princes shall **n** more oppress my 3808

Da 1: 4 Children in whom *was* **n** blemish, 369+3605
2:10 therefore *there is* **n** king, lord, 3606+3809
2:35 that **n** place was found for them: 3606+3809
3:25 midst of the fire, and they have **n** hurt; 3809
3:27 upon whose bodies the fire had **n** power, 3809
3:29 there is **n** other God that can deliver after 3809
4: 9 in thee, and **n** secret troubleth thee, 3606+3809
6: 2 and the king should have **n** damage. 3809
6:15 Persians *is,* That *no* decree nor statute 3606
6:22 before thee, O king, have I done **n** hurt. 3809
6:23 manner of hurt was found upon him, 3809
8: 4 so that **n** beasts might stand before 3605+3808
8: 7 there was **n** power in the ram to stand 3808
10: 3 I ate **n** pleasant bread, neither came flesh 3808
10: 8 and there remained **n** strength in me: 3808
10: 8 into corruption, and I retained **n** strength. 3808
10:16 upon me, and I have retained **n** strength. 3808
10:17 straightway there remained **n** strength in 3808

Hos 1: 6 for I will **n** more have mercy upon 3808
2:16 *me* Ishi; and shalt call me **n** more Baali. 3808
2:17 they shall **n** more be remembered by their 3808
4: 1 because *there is* **n** truth, nor mercy, 369
4: 4 Yet let **n** man strive, nor reprove another: 408
4: 6 thee, that *thou* shalt be **n** priest to me: NIH
8: 7 it hath **n** stalk: the bud shall yield no meal: 369
8: 7 the bud shall yield **n** meal: if so be it yield, 1097
8: 8 Gentiles as a vessel wherein *is* **n** pleasure. 3808
9:15 of mine house, I will love them **n** more: 3808
9:16 root is dried up, they shall bear **n** fruit: 1077
10: 3 We have **n** king, because we feared not 369
13: 4 and thou shalt know **n** god but me: 3808
13: 4 but me: for *there is* **n** saviour beside me. 3808

Joel 1:18 perplexed, because they have **n** pasture; 369
2:19 I will **n** more make you a reproach 3808
3:17 there shall **n** strangers pass through her 3808

Am 3: 4 roar in the forest, when he hath **n** prey? 369
3: 5 upon the earth, where **n** gin *is* for him? 369
5: 2 of Israel is fallen; she shall **n** more rise: 3808
5:20 even very dark, and **n** brightness in it? 3808
6:10 he shall say, N. Then shall he say, Hold 657
7:14 and said to Amaziah, I *was* **n** prophet, 3808
9:15 they shall **n** more be pulled up out of their 3808

Mic 3: 7 their lips; for *there is* **n** answer of God. 369
4: 9 *is there* **n** king in thee? is thy counsellor 369
5:12 and thou shalt have **n** *more* soothsayers: 3808
5:13 thou shalt **n** more worship the work of 3808
7: 1 *there is* **n** cluster to eat: my soul desired 369

Na 1:12 afflicted thee, I will afflict thee **n** more. 3808
1:14 *that* **n** more of thy name be sown: 3808
1:15 for the wicked shall **n** more pass through 3808
2:13 the voice of thy messengers shall **n** more 3808
3: 8 Art thou better than populous N, that was 4996
3:18 mountains, and **n** man gathereth *them.* 3808
3:19 *is* **n** healing of thy bruise; thy wound 369

Hab 2: 6 *that* have **n** ruler over them? 3808
2:19 *there is* **n** breath at all in the midst of it. 369
3:17 shall fail, and the fields shall yield **n** meat; 3808
3:17 and *there shall be* **n** herd in the stalls: 369

Zep 2: 5 that there shall be **n** inhabitant. 369+4480
3: 5 but the unjust knoweth **n** shame. 3808
3: 6 destroyed, so that there is **n** man, 1097+4480
3:11 thou shalt **n** more be haughty because 3808

Hag 2:12 And the priests answered and said, N. 3808

Zec 1:21 so that **n** man did lift up his head: 3808
4: 5 what these *be?* And I said, N, my lord. 3808
4:13 what these *be?* And I said, N, my lord. 3808
7:14 **that n** man passed through nor returned: 4480
8:10 For before these days there was **n** hire for 3808
8:17 his neighbour; and love **n** false oath: 408
9: 8 oppressor shall pass through them any 3808
9:11 prisoners out of the pit wherein *is* **n** water. 369
10: 2 because *there was* **n** shepherd. 369
11: 6 For I will **n** more pity the inhabitants of 3808
13: 2 and they shall **n** more be remembered: 3808
13: 5 he shall say, I *am* **n** prophet, I *am* a 3808
14:11 there shall be **n** more utter destruction; 3808
14:17 of hosts, even upon them shall be **n** rain. 3808
14:18 that *have* **n** rain; there shall be the plague, 3808
14:21 in that day there shall be **n** more 3808

Mal 1:10 I have **n** pleasure in you, saith the LORD of 369

Mt 5:18 tittle shall **in n wise** pass from the law, 3364
5:20 ye shall **in n case** enter into the kingdom 3364

Mt 5:26 Thou shalt **by n means** come out thence, 3364
6: 1 ye have **n** reward of your Father 3756
6:24 N **man** can serve two masters: for either 3762
6:25 Take **n** thought for your life, what ye shall 3361
6:31 Therefore take **n** thought, saying, 3361
6:34 Take therefore **n** thought for the morrow: 3361
8: 4 See thou tell **n** man; but go thy way, 3361
8:10 not found so great faith, **n** not in Israel. NIG
8:28 so that **n** man might pass by that way. 3361
9:16 N **man** putteth a piece of new cloth unto 3762
9:30 saying, See that **n** man know *it.* 3367
9:36 as sheep having **n** shepherd. 3361
10:19 **n** thought how or what ye shall speak: 3361
10:42 he shall **in n wise** lose his reward. 3364
11:27 **n** man knoweth the Son, but the Father; 3762
12:39 and there shall **n** sign be given to it, 3756
13: 5 because *they* had **n** deepness of earth: 3361
16: 4 and there shall **n** sign be given unto it, 3756
16: 7 *It is* because we have taken **n** bread. 3756
16: 8 because ye have brought **n** bread? 3756
16:20 tell **n** man that he was Jesus the Christ. 3367
17: 8 eyes, they saw **n** man, save Jesus only. 3762
17: 9 Tell the vision to **n** man, until the Son of 3367
19: 6 Wherefore they are **n** more twain, 3765
19:18 Jesus said, Thou shalt do **n** murder, 3756
20: 7 unto him, Because **n** man hath hired us. 3762
20:13 and said, Friend, I do thee **n** wrong: 3756
21:19 Let **n** fruit grow on thee **henceforward** 3371
22:23 which say that there is **n** resurrection, 3361
22:24 said, If a man die, having **n** children, 3361
22:25 and, having issue, left his wife unto his 3361
22:46 And **n** man was able to answer him a 3762
23: 9 call **n man** your father upon the earth: 3361
24: 4 Take heed that **n** man deceive you. 3361
24:21 world to this time, **n**, nor ever shall be. 3761
24:22 there should **n** flesh be saved: 3756+3956
24:36 of that day and hour knoweth **n** man, no, 3762
24:36 of that day and hour knoweth no *man*, **n**, NIG
25: 3 their lamps, and took **n** oil with them: 3756
25:42 I was a hungred, and ye gave me **n** meat: 3756
25:42 I was thirsty, and ye gave me **n** drink: 3756
26:55 in the temple, and ye laid **n** hold on me. 3756

Mk 1:45 that *Jesus* could **n more** openly 3371
2: 2 that there was **n** room to receive 3371
2: 2 there was no room to receive *them,* **n,** NIG
2:17 They that are whole have **n** need of 3756
2:21 N **man** also seweth a piece of new cloth 3762
2:22 And **n** man putteth new wine into old 3762
3:27 N **man** can enter into a strong *man's* 3762
4: 5 up, because it had **n** depth of earth: 3361
4: 6 because *it* had **n** root, it withered away. 3361
4: 7 and choked it, and it yielded **n** fruit. 3756
4:17 And have **n** root in themselves, and so 3756
4:40 so fearful? how *is it that* you have **n** faith? 3756
5: 3 and **n** man could bind him, no, not with 3762
5: 3 *man* could bind him, no, not with chains: NIG
5:37 And he suffered **n** man to follow him, 3762
5:43 And he charged them straitly that **n** man 3367
6: 5 And he could there do **n** mighty work, 3762
6: 8 in scrip, no bread, no money in *their* 3361
6: 8 scrip, **n** bread, no money in *their* 3361
6: 8 scrip, no bread, **n** money in *their* purse: 3361
6:31 **and** they had **n** leisure
 so much as to 2532+3761
7:12 And ye suffer him **n more** to do ought for 3765
7:24 and would have **n** man know *it:* but 3762
7:36 he charged them that they should tell **n** 3367
8:12 There shall **n** sign be given unto this 1487
8:16 saying, *It is* because we have **n** bread. 3756
8:17 Why reason ye, because ye have **n** bread? 3756
8:30 he charged them that they should tell **n** 3367
9: 3 so as **n** fuller on earth can white *them.* 3756
9: 8 they saw **n** man any more, save Jesus only 3762
9: 9 charged them that they should tell **n** man 3367
9:25 out of him, and enter **n more** into him. 3371
9:39 there is **n man** which shall do a miracle 3762
10: 8 so then they are **n more** twain, 3765
10:29 There is **n man** that hath left house, 3762
11:14 N **man** eat fruit of thee hereafter for ever. 3367
12:14 carest for **n** man: for thou regardest not 3762
12:18 which say there is **n** resurrection, 3361
12:19 *his* wife *behind him,* and leave **n** children, 3361
12:20 the first took a wife, and dying left **n** seed. 3756
12:22 And the seven had her, and left **n** seed: 3756
12:34 And **n** man after that durst ask him any 3762
13:11 take **n** thought beforehand what ye shall 3361
13:20 *those* days, **n** flesh should be saved: 3756+3956
13:32 day and *that* hour knoweth **n** man, no, 3762
13:32 day and *that* hour knoweth no *man,* **n,** NIG
14:25 I will drink **n** more of the fruit of the vine, 3364

Lk 1: 7 And they had **n** child, because 3756
1:33 and of his kingdom there shall be **n** end. 3756
2: 7 there was **n** room for them in the inn. 3756
3:13 Exact **n** more than that which is appointed 3367
3:14 he said unto them, Do violence to **n** man, 3367
4:24 N prophet is accepted in his own country. 3762
5:14 And he charged him to tell **n** man; but go, 3367
5:36 N **man** putteth a piece of a new garment 3762
5:37 And **n** man putteth new wine into old 3762
5:39 N **man** also having drunk old *wine* 3762
7: 9 I have not found so great faith, **n**, not in NIG
7:44 thou gavest me **n** water for my feet: 3756
7:45 Thou gavest me **n** kiss: but this *woman* 3756
8:13 and these have **n** root, which for a while 3756
8:14 of *this* life, and bring **n** fruit to perfection. 3756

Lk
8:16 N man, when he hath lighted a candle,	3762
8:27 and ware n clothes, neither abide in any	3756
8:51 he suffered n man to go in, save Peter,	3762
8:56 charged them that they should tell n man	3367
9:13 We have n more but five loaves and	3756
9:21 them to tell n man that thing;	3367
9:36 told n man in those days any of those	3762
9:62 N man having put his hand to the plough,	3762
10: 4 nor shoes: and salute n man by the way.	3367
10:22 and n man knoweth who the Son is,	3762
11:20 n doubt the kingdom of God is come	686
11:29 and there shall n sign be given it,	3756
11:33 N man, when he hath lighted a candle,	3762
11:36 be full of light, having n part dark,	3361+5100
12: 4 after that have n more that they can do.	3361
12:11 take ye n thought how or what thing ye	3361
12:17 I have n room where to bestow my fruits?	3756
12:22 Take n thought for your life, what ye shall	3361
12:33 where n thief approacheth, neither moth	3756
13:11 n in wise lift up	1519+3361+3588+3838
15: 7 just persons which need n repentance.	3756
15:16 swine did eat: and n man gave unto him.	3762
15:19 And am n more worthy to be called thy	3765
15:21 am n more worthy to be called thy son.	3765
16: 2 for thou mayest be n longer steward.	3756
16:13 N servant can serve two masters: for	3762
18:17 as a little child shall n in wise enter	3364
18:29 There is n man that hath left house,	3762
20:22 for us to give tribute unto Cesar, or n?	3756
20:31 and they left n children, and died.	3756
22:36 and he that hath n sword, let him sell his	3361
22:53 ye stretched forth n hands against me:	3756
23: 4 to the people, I find n fault in this man.	3762
23:14 have found n fault in this man touching	3762
23:15 N, nor yet Herod: for I sent you to him;	235
23:22 I have found n cause of death in him:	3762

Jn
1:18 N man hath seen God at any time; the	3762
1:21 thou that prophet? And he answered, N.	3756
1:47 an Israelite indeed, in whom is n guile.	3756
2: 3 Jesus saith unto him, They have n wine.	3756
3: 2 for n man can do these miracles that thou	3762
3:13 And n man hath ascended up to heaven,	3762
3:32 and n man receiveth his testimony.	3762
4: 9 For the Jews have n dealings with	3756
4:17 and said, I have n husband.	3756
4:17 Thou hast well said, I have n husband:	3756
4:27 yet n man said, What seekest thou?	3762
4:38 reap that whereon ye bestowed n labour:	3756
4:44 that a prophet hath n honour in his own	3756
5: 7 Sir, I have n man, when the water is	3756
5:14 sin n more, lest a worse thing come unto	3371
5:22 For the Father judgeth n man, but	3762
6:37 that cometh to me I will in n wise cast	3364
6:44 N man can come to me, except the Father	3762
6:53 and drink his blood, ye have n life in you.	3756
6:65 I unto you, that n man can come unto me,	3762
6:66 went back, and walked n more with him.	3765
7: 4 For there is n man that doeth any thing in	3762
7:13 Howbeit n man spake openly of him for	3762
7:18 is true, and n unrighteousness is in him.	3756
7:27 no man knoweth whence he is.	3762
7:30 but n man laid hands on him, because	3762
7:44 taken him; but n man laid hands on him.	3762
7:52 look: for out of Galilee ariseth n prophet.	3756
8:10 hath n man condemned thee?	3762
8:11 She said, N man, Lord. And Jesus said	3762
8:11 do I condemn thee: go, and sin n more.	3371
8:15 Ye judge after the flesh; I judge n man.	3762
8:20 and n man laid hands on him; for his hour	3762
8:37 because my word hath n place in you.	3756
8:44 the truth, because there is n truth in him.	3756
9: 4 the night cometh, when n man can work.	3762
9:25 Whether he be a sinner or n, I know not:	NIG
9:41 If ye were blind, ye should have n sin:	3756
10:18 N man taketh it from me, but I lay it	3762
10:29 n man is able to pluck them out of my	3762
10:41 unto him, and said, John did n miracle:	3762
11:10 because there is n light in him.	3756
11:54 walked n more openly among the Jews;	3765
13: 8 wash thee not, thou hast n part with me.	3756
13:28 Now n man at the table knew for what	3762
14: 6 n man cometh unto the Father, but by	3762
14:19 and the world seeth me n more;	3765
15: 4 n more can ye, except ye abide in me.	3761
15:13 Greater love hath n man than this, that a	3762
15:22 but now they have n cloke for their sin.	3756
16:10 I go to my Father, and ye see me n more;	3765
16:21 she remembereth n more the anguish,	3765
16:22 and your joy n man taketh from you.	3762
16:25 when I shall n more speak unto you in	3765
16:29 thou plainly, and speakest n proverb.	3762
17:11 And now I am n more in the world,	3765
18:38 unto them, I find in him n fault at all.	3762
19: 4 ye may know that I find n fault in him.	3762
19: 6 and crucify him: for I find n fault in him.	3762
19: 9 art thou? But Jesus gave him n answer.	3756
19:11 Thou couldest have n power at all against	3756
19:15 We have n king but Cesar.	3756
21: 5 ye any meat? They answered him, N.	3756

Ac
1:20 be desolate, and let n man dwell therein:	3361
4:17 But that it spread n further among	3361
4:17 they speak henceforth to n man in this	3367
5:13 of the rest durst n man join himself to	3762
5:23 we had opened, we found n man within.	3762
7: 5 n, not so much as to set his foot on:	3761
7: 5 after him, when as yet he had n child.	3756
7:11 and our fathers found n sustenance.	3756
8:39 that the eunuch saw him n more:	3765
9: 7 hearing a voice, but seeing n man.	3367
9: 8 he saw n man: but they led him by	3762
10:34 a truth I perceive that God is n respecter	3756
12:18 there was n small stir among the soldiers,	3756
13:28 though they found n cause of death in	3367
13:34 n more to return to corruption, he said	3371
13:37 God raised again, saw n corruption.	3756
13:41 work which you shall in n wise believe,	3364
15: 2 and Barnabas had n small dissension and	3756
15: 9 put n difference between us and them,	3762
15:24 whom we gave n such commandment:	3756
15:28 to lay upon you n greater burden than	3367
16:28 a loud voice, saying, Do thyself n harm:	3367
18:10 and n man shall set on thee to hurt thee:	3762
18:15 look ye to it; for I will be n judge of such	3756
19:23 And the same time there arose n small stir	3756
19:24 brought n small gain unto the craftsmen;	3756
19:26 much people, saying that they be n gods,	3756
19:40 there being n cause whereby we may give	3367
20:25 of God, shall see my face n more.	3765
20:33 I have coveted n man's silver, or gold,	3762
20:38 that they should see his face n more.	3765
21:25 concluded that they observe n such thing,	3367
21:39 a city in Cilicia, a citizen of n mean city:	3756
23: 8 For the Sadducees say that there is n	3361
23: 9 strove, saying, We find n evil in this man:	3762
23:22 charged him, See thou tell n man that	3367
25:10 to the Jews have I done n wrong, as thou	3762
25:11 n man may deliver me unto them.	3762
26:22 Of whom I have n certain prophecy to write	3756
27:20 n small tempest lay on us, all hope that	3756
27:22 for there shall be n loss of any man's life	3756
28: 2 the barbarous people shewed us n little	3756
28: 4 N doubt this man is a murderer, whom,	3843
28: 5 off the beast into the fire, and felt n harm.	3762
28: 6 saw n harm come to him, they changed	3367
28:18 because there was n cause of death in me.	3367
28:31 all confidence, n man forbidding him.	209

Ro
2:11 there is n respect of persons with God.	3756
3: 9 are we better than they? N, in no wise:	3756
3: 9 are we better than they? No, in no wise:	3843
3:10 There is none righteous, n, not one:	NIG
3:12 that doeth good, n, not one.	1520+2193+3756
3:18 There is n fear of God before their eyes.	3756
3:20 shall n flesh be justified in his sight:	3756+3956
3:22 that believe: for there is n difference:	3756
4:15 for where n law is, there is no	3756
4:15 where no law is, there is n transgression.	3761
5:13 sin is not imputed when there is n law.	3361
6: 9 being raised from the dead dieth n more;	3765
6: 9 death hath n more dominion over him.	3765
7: 3 so that she is n adulteress, though she be	3361
7:17 Now then it is n more I that do it,	3765
7:18 dwelleth n good thing: for to will is	3756
7:20 it is n more I that do it, but sin that	3765
8: 1 now n condemnation to them which are	3762
10:12 For there is n difference between the Jew	3756
10:19 you to jealousy by them that are n people,	3756
11: 6 if by grace, then is it n more of works:	3765
11: 6 otherwise grace is n more grace. But if it	3765
11: 6 if it be of works, then is it n more grace:	3765
11: 6 otherwise work is n more work.	3765
12:17 Recompense to n man evil for evil.	3367
13: 1 there is n power but of God: the powers	3756
13: 8 Owe n man any thing, but to love one	3367
13:10 Love worketh n ill to his neighbour.	3756
14: 7 To himself, and n man dieth to himself.	3762
14:13 that n man put a stumblingblock or	3361
15:23 But now having n more place in these	3371

1Co
1: 7 So that ye come behind in n gift;	3367
1:10 and that there be n divisions among you;	3361
1:29 That n flesh should glory in his	3361+3956
2:11 so the things of God knoweth n man, but	3762
2:15 things, yet he himself is judged of n man.	3762
3:11 For other foundation can n man lay than	3762
3:18 Let n man deceive himself. If any man	3367
3:21 Therefore let n man glory in men. For all	3361
4: 6 that n one of you be puffed up for one	3762
4:11 and have n certain dwelling place;	790
5:11 extortioner; with such a one n not to eat.	3366
6: 5 n, not one that shall be able to judge	NIG
7:25 Now concerning virgins I have n	3364
7:37 having n necessity, but hath power over	3361
8:13 I will eat n flesh while the world standeth,	3364
9:10 For our sakes, n doubt, this is written:	1063
10:13 There hath n temptation taken you but	3756
10:24 Let n man seek his own, but every man	3367
10:25 asking n question for conscience sake:	3367
10:27 eat, asking n question for conscience sake.	3367
11:16 we have n such custom, neither	3756
12: 3 that n man speaking by the Spirit of God	3762
12: 3 that n man can say that Jesus is the Lord,	3762
12:21 say unto the hand, I have n need of thee:	3756
12:21 the head to the feet, I have n need of you.	3756
12:24 For our comely parts have n need:	3756
12:25 there should be n schism in the body;	3361
13: 2 and have n charity, I am nothing.	3361
13: 5 is not easily provoked, thinketh n evil;	3756
14: 2 for n man understandeth him; howbeit	3762
14:28 But if there be n interpreter, let him keep	3361
15:12 how say some among you that there is n	3756
15:13 But if there be n resurrection of the dead,	3756

1Co
16: 2 that there be n gatherings when I come.	3361
16:11 Let n man therefore despise him:	3361

2Co
2:13 I had n rest in my spirit, because I found	3756
3:10 made glorious had n glory in this respect,	3761
5:16 Wherefore henceforth know we n man	3762
5:16 now henceforth know we him n more.	3765
5:21 him to be sin for us, who knew n sin;	3361
6: 3 Giving n offence in any thing; that	3367
7: 2 we have wronged n man, we have	3762
7: 2 n man, we have defrauded no man.	3762
7: 2 no man, we have defrauded n man.	3762
7: 5 flesh had n rest, but we were troubled	3762
8:15 he that had gathered little had n lack.	3756
8:20 that n man should blame us in this	3361
11: 9 I was chargeable to n man: for that which	3762
11:10 n man shall stop me of this boasting in	3756
11:14 And no marvel; for Satan himself is	3756
11:15 it is n great thing if his ministers	3756
11:16 I say again, Let n man think me a fool;	3361
13: 7 Now I pray to God that ye do n evil;	3367

Gal
2: 5 place by subjection, n, not for an hour;	NIG
2: 6 they were, it maketh n matter to me:	3762
2: 6 God accepteth n man's person:) for they	3756
2:16 by the works of the law shall n flesh be	3756
3:11 But that n man is justified by the law in	3762
3:15 n man disannulleth, or addeth thereto.	3762
3:18 be of the law, it is n more of promise:	3765
3:25 we are n longer under a schoolmaster.	3765
4: 7 Wherefore thou art n more a servant,	3765
4: 8 unto them which by nature are n gods.	3361
5: 4 Christ is become of n effect unto you,	2673
5:23 against such there is n law.	3756
6:17 From henceforth let n man trouble me:	3367

Eph
2:12 having n hope, and without God in	3361
2:19 Now therefore ye are n more strangers	3765
4:14 That we henceforth be n more children,	3371
4:28 Let him that stole steal n more:	3371
4:29 Let n corrupt communication	3361+3956
5: 5 For this ye know, that n whoremonger,	3756
5: 6 Let n man deceive you with vain words:	3367
5:11 And have n fellowship with the unfruitful	3756
5:29 For n man ever yet hated his own flesh;	3762

Php
2: 7 But made himself of n reputation,	2758
2:20 For I have n man likeminded, who will	3762
3: 3 and have n confidence in the flesh.	3756
4:15 n church communicated with me as	3762

Col
2:16 Let n man therefore judge you in meat,	3361
2:18 Let n man beguile you of your reward in	3367
3:25 done: and there is n respect of persons.	3756

1Th
3: 1 Wherefore when we could n longer	3371
3: 3 That n man should be moved by these	3367
3: 5 cause, when I could n longer forbear,	3371
4: 6 That n man go beyond and defraud his	3361
4:13 even as others which have n hope.	3361
5: 1 ye have n need that I write unto you.	3756

2Th
2: 3 Let n man deceive you by any means:	3361
3:14 that man, and have n company with him,	3361

1Ti
1: 3 some that they teach n other doctrine,	3361
3: 3 Not given to wine, n striker, not greedy	3361
4:12 Let n man despise thy youth; but be thou	3367
5:22 Lay hands suddenly on n man, neither be	3367
5:23 Drink n longer water, but use a little	3371
6:16 light which n man can approach unto;	676
6:16 whom n man hath seen, nor can see:	3762

2Ti
2: 4 N man that warreth entangleth himself	3762
2:14 they strive not about words to n profit,	3762
3: 9 But they shall proceed n further: for their	3756
4:16 At my first answer n man stood with me,	3762

Tit
1: 7 soon angry, not given to wine, n striker,	3361
2: 8 having n evil thing to say of you.	3367
2:15 with all authority. Let n man despise thee.	3367
3: 2 To speak evil of n man, to be no brawlers,	3367
3: 2 speak evil of no man, to be n brawlers,	269

Heb
5: 4 n man taketh this honour unto himself,	3756
6:13 because he could swear by n greater,	3762
7:13 of which n man gave attendance at	3762
8: 7 should n place have been sought for	3756
8:12 their iniquities will I remember n more.	3364
9:17 otherwise it is of n strength at all whilst	3379
9:22 without shedding of blood is n remission.	2089+3367
10: 2 had n more conscience of sins.	2089+3367
10: 6 sacrifices for sin thou hast had n pleasure.	3756
10:17 and iniquities will I remember n more.	3364
10:18 these is, there is n more offering for sin.	3765
10:26 there remaineth n more sacrifice for sins,	3765
10:38 my soul shall have n pleasure in him.	3756
12:11 Now n chastening for the present	3756+3956
12:14 without which n man shall see the Lord:	3762
12:17 for he found n place of repentance,	3756
13:10 whereof they have n right to eat which	3756
13:14 For here have we n continuing city,	3756

Jas
1:11 the sun is n sooner risen with a burning	NIG
1:13 Let n man say when he is tempted, I am	3367
1:17 with whom is n variableness,	3756
2:11 if thou commit n adultery, yet if thou	3756
2:13 mercy, that hath shewed n mercy;	3361
3: 8 But the tongue can n man tame; it is an	3762
3:12 so can n fountain both yield salt water	3762

1Pe
2:22 Who did n sin, neither was guile found in	3756
3:10 and his lips that they speak n guile:	3361
4: 2 That he n longer should live the rest of	3371

2Pe
1:20 that n prophecy of the scripture is of	3756+3956

1Jn
1: 5 God is light, and in him is n darkness at	3756
1: 8 If we say that we have n sin, we deceive	3756
2: 7 I write n new commandment unto you,	3756

N

1Jn	2:19	would *n* doubt have continued with us:	NIG
	2:21	and that *n* lie is of the truth.	3756+3956
	2:27	is *n* lie, and even as it hath taught you,	3756
	3: 5	to take away our sins; and in him is *n* sin.	3756
	3: 7	Little children, let *n man* deceive you:	3367
	3:15	know that *n* murderer hath eternal	3756+3956
	4:12	No *man* hath seen God at any time. If we	3762
	4:18	There is *n* fear in love; but perfect love	3756
3Jn	1: 4	I have *n* greater joy than to hear that my	3756
Rev	2:17	which *n man* knoweth saving he that	3762
	3: 7	he that openeth, and *n man* shutteth;	3762
	3: 7	and shutteth, and *n man* openeth;	3762
	3: 8	an open door, and *n man* can shut it:	3762
	3:11	thou hast, that *n man* take thy crown.	3367
	3:12	of my God, and he shall go *n* more out:	3364
	5: 3	And *n man* in heaven, nor in earth,	3762
	5: 4	*n man* was found worthy to open and	3762
	7: 9	*n man* could number, of all nations,	3762
	7:16	They shall hunger *n* more, neither thirst	3756
	10: 6	that there should be time *n* longer:	3756
	13:17	that *n man* might buy or sell, save he	3361
	14: 3	and *n man* could learn *that* song but	3762
	14: 5	And in their mouth was found *n* guile:	3756
	14:11	and they have *n* rest day nor night,	3756
	15: 8	*n man* was able to enter into the temple,	3762
	17:12	which have received *n* kingdom *as yet;*	3768
	18: 7	am widow, and shall see *n* sorrow.	3756
	18: 7	am *n* widow, and shall see *n* sorrow.	3364
	18:11	for *n man* buyeth their merchandise any	3762
	18:14	find them *n* more at all.	3361+3756+3765
	18:21	and shall be found *n* more at all.	3364
	18:22	shall be heard *n* more at all in thee;	3364
	18:22	*n* craftsman, of whatsoever craft *he be,*	3364
	18:22	shall be heard *n* more at all in thee;	3364
	18:23	a candle shall shine *n* more at all in	3364
	18:23	the bride shall be heard *n* more at all in	3364
	19:12	that *n man* knew, but he himself.	3762
	20: 3	he should deceive the nations *n* more,	3361
	20: 6	on such the second death hath *n* power,	3756
	20:11	and there was found *n* place for them.	3756
	21: 1	passed away; and there was *n* more sea.	3756
	21: 4	and there shall be *n* more death,	3756
	21:22	And I saw *n* temple therein: for the Lord	3756
	21:23	And the city had *n* need of the sun,	3756
	21:25	all by day: for there shall be *n* night there.	3756
	21:27	And there shall in *n* wise enter into it	3364
	22: 3	And there shall be *n* more curse:	3756
	22: 5	And there shall be *n* night there;	3756
	22: 5	and they need *n* candle, neither light of	3756

NOADIAH (2)

Ezr	8:33	Jeshua, and **N** the son of Binnui, Levites;	5129
Ne	6:14	on the prophetess **N**, and the rest of	5129

NOAH (51) [NOAH'S, NOE]

Ge	5:29	he called his name **N**, saying, This *same*	5146
	5:30	Lamech lived after he begat **N** five	5146
	5:32	**N** was five hundred years old:	5146
	5:32	and **N** begat Shem, Ham, and Japheth.	5146
	6: 8	**N** found grace in the eyes of the Lord.	5146
	6: 9	These *are* the generations of **N**: Noah was	5146
	6: 9	**N** was a just man *and* perfect in his	5146
	6: 9	his generations, *and* **N** walked with God.	5146
	6:10	**N** begat three sons, Shem, Ham,	5146
	6:13	God said unto **N**, The end of all flesh is	5146
	6:22	Thus did **N**; according to all that God	5146
	7: 1	the Lord said unto **N**, Come thou and	5146
	7: 5	**N** did according to all that the Lord	5146
	7: 6	**N** *was* six hundred years old when	5146
	7: 7	**N** went in, and his sons, and his wife,	5146
	7: 9	went in two and two unto **N** into the ark,	5146
	7: 9	the female, as God had commanded **N**.	5146
	7:13	In the selfsame day entered **N**, and Shem,	5146
	7:13	the sons of **N**, and Noah's wife,	5146
	7:15	they went in unto **N** into the ark, two and	5146
	7:23	**N** only remained *alive,* and *they* that *were*	5146
	8: 1	God remembered **N**, and every living	5146
	8: 6	**N** opened the window of the ark which	5146
	8:11	**N** knew that the waters were abated from	5146
	8:13	**N** removed the covering of the ark,	5146
	8:15	And God spake unto **N**, saying,	5146
	8:18	**N** went forth, and his sons, and his wife,	5146
	8:20	**N** builded an altar unto the Lord;	5146
	9: 1	God blessed **N** and his sons, and said unto	5146
	9: 8	God spake unto **N**, and to his sons with	5146
	9:17	God said unto **N**, This *is* the token of	5146
	9:18	the sons of **N**, that went forth of the ark,	5146
	9:19	These *are* the three sons of **N**: and of	5146
	9:20	**N** began *to be* a husbandman,	5146
	9:24	**N** awoke from his wine, and knew what	5146
	9:28	**N** lived after the flood three hundred and	5146
	9:29	all the days of **N** were nine hundred and	5146
	10: 1	these *are* the generations of the sons of **N**,	5146
	10:32	These *are* the families of the sons of **N**,	5146
Nu	26:33	and **N**, Hoglah, Milcah, and Tirzah.	5270
	27: 1	**N**, and Hoglah, and Milcah, and Tirzah.	5270
	36:11	Tirzah, and Hoglah, and Milcah, and **N**,	5270
Jos	17: 3	and **N**, Hoglah, Milcah, and Tirzah.	5270
1Ch	1: 4	**N**, Shem, Ham, and Japheth.	5146
Isa	54: 9	For this *is as* the waters of **N** unto me:	5146
	54: 9	for *as* I have sworn that the waters of **N**	5146
Eze	14:14	**N**, Daniel, and Job, were in it, they should	5146
	14:20	Though **N**, Daniel, and Job, were in it, *as*	5146
Heb	11: 7	By faith **N**, being warned of God of *things*	3575
1Pe	3:20	of God waited in the days of **N**,	3575

NOAH'S (2) [NOAH]

Ge	7:11	In the six hundredth year of **N** life,	5146
	7:13	**N** wife, and the three wives of his sons	5146

NOB (6)

1Sa	21: 1	came David to **N** to Ahimelech the priest:	5011
	22: 9	said, I saw the son of Jesse coming to **N**,	5011
	22:11	father's house, the priests that *were* in **N**:	5011
	22:19	**N**, the city of the priests, smote he with	5011
Ne	11:32	*And at* Anathoth, **N**, Ananiah,	5011
Isa	10:32	As yet shall *he* remain at **N** *that* day:	5011

NOBAH (3)

Nu	32:42	**N** went and took Kenath, and the villages	5025
	32:42	and called it **N**, after his own name.	5025
Jdg	8:11	them that dwelt in tents on the east of **N**	5025

NOBLE (7) [NOBLEMAN, NOBLES]

Ezr	4:10	the great and *n* Asnappar brought over,	3358
Est	6: 9	hand of one of the king's **most** *n* princes,	6579
Jer	2:21	Yet I had planted thee a *n* vine, wholly a	8321
Ac	17:11	These were **more** *n* than those in	2104
	24: 3	*it* always, and in all places, **most** *n* Felix,	2903
	26:25	But he said, I am not mad, **most** *n* Festus,	2903
1Co	1:26	not many mighty, not many *n, are called:*	2104

NOBLEMAN (3) [MAN, NOBLE]

Lk	19:12	A certain *n* went into a far country to	444+2104
Jn	4:46	And there was a certain *n*, whose son was	937
	4:49	The *n* saith unto him, Sir, come down ere	937

NOBLES (30) [NOBLE]

Ex	24:11	upon the *n* of the children of Israel he laid	678
Nu	21:18	the well, the *n* of the people digged it,	5081
Jdg	5:13	dominion over the *n* among the people:	117
1Ki	21: 8	elders and to the *n* that *were* in his city,	2715
	21:11	the *n* who *were* the inhabitants in his city,	2715
2Ch	23:20	the *n*, and the governors of the people,	117
Ne	2:16	the priests, nor to the *n*, nor to the rulers,	2715
	3: 5	their *n* put not their necks to the work of	117
	4:14	said unto the *n*, and to the rulers, and to	2715
	4:19	I said unto the *n*, and to the rulers,	2715
	5: 7	I rebuked the *n*, and the rulers,	2715
	6:17	in those days the *n* of Judah sent	2715
	7: 5	into mine heart to gather together the *n*,	2715
	10:29	their *n*, and entered into a curse, and into	117
	13:17	I contended with the *n* of Judah,	2715
Est	1: 3	Media, the *n* and princes of the provinces,	6579
Job	29:10	The *n* held their peace, and their tongue	5057
Ps	83:11	Make their *n* like Oreb, and like Zeeb:	5081
	149: 8	chains, and their *n* with fetters of iron;	3513
Pr	8:16	By me princes rule, and *n, even* all	5081
Ecc	10:17	when thy king *is* the son of *n*,	2715
Isa	13: 2	that they may go *into* the gates of the *n*.	5081
	34:12	They shall call the *n* thereof to	2715
	43:14	have brought down all their *n*,	1281
Jer	14: 3	their *n* have sent their little ones to	117
	27:20	and all the *n* of Judah and Jerusalem;	2715
	30:21	their *n* shall be of themselves,	117
	39: 6	also the king of Babylon slew all the *n* of	2715
Jnh	3: 7	by the decree of the king and his *n*,	1419
Na	3:18	thy *n* shall dwell *in the dust:* thy people	117

NOD (1)

Ge	4:16	in the land of **N**, on the east of Eden.	5113

NODAB (1)

1Ch	5:19	with Jetur, and Nephish, and **N**.	5114

NOE (5) [NOAH]

Mt	24:37	But as the days of **N** *were,* so shall also	3575
	24:38	until the day that **N** entered into the ark,	3575
Lk	3:36	*the* son of Sem, which was *the* son of **N**,	3575
	17:26	as it was in the days of **N**, so shall it be	3575
	17:27	until the day that **N** entered into the ark,	3575

NOGAH (2)

1Ch	3: 7	And **N**, and Nepheg, and Japhia,	5052
	14: 6	And **N**, and Nepheg, and Japhia,	5052

NOHAH (1)

1Ch	8: 2	**N** the fourth, and Rapha the fifth.	5119

NOISE (88) [NOISED]

Ex	20:18	the *n* of the trumpet, and the mountain	6963
	32:17	when Joshua heard the *n* of the people as	6963
	32:17	There is a *n* of war in the camp.	6963
	32:18	*but* the *n* of *them that* sing do I hear.	6963
Jos	6:10	shout, nor **make** any *n* with your voice,	8085
Jdg	5:11	*They* that are delivered from the *n* of	6963
1Sa	4: 6	when the Philistines heard the *n* of	6963
	4: 6	What *meaneth* the *n* of this great shout	6963
	4:14	Eli heard the *n* of the crying, he said,	6963
	4:14	said, What *meaneth* the *n* of this tumult?	6963
	14:19	that the *n* that *was* in the host of	1995
1Ki	1:41	Wherefore *is this n* of the city being in an	6963
	1:45	This *is* the *n* that ye have heard.	6963
2Ki	7: 6	host of the Syrians to hear a *n* of chariots,	6963
	7: 6	a *n* of horses, *even* the noise of a great	6963
	7: 6	a noise of horses, *even* the *n* of a great	6963
	11:13	when Athaliah heard the *n* of the guard	6963
1Ch	15:28	**making** a *n* with psalteries and harps.	8085
2Ch	23:12	Now when Athaliah heard the *n* of	6963
Ezr	3:13	that the people could not discern the *n*	6963

2Pe	2: 5	saved **N** the eighth *person,* a preacher of	3575

Ezr	3:13	from the *n* of the weeping of the people:	6963
	3:13	loud shout, and the *n* was heard afar off.	6963
Job	36:29	of the clouds, *or* the *n* of his tabernacle?	8663
	36:33	The *n* thereof sheweth concerning it,	7452
	37: 2	Hear attentively the *n* of his voice,	7267
Ps	33: 3	a new song; play skilfully with a **loud** *n*.	8643
	42: 7	Deep calleth unto deep at the *n* of thy	6963
	55: 2	I mourn in my complaint, and **make a** *n;*	1949
	59: 6	they **make a** *n* like a dog, and go round	1993
	59:14	*and* let them **make a** *n* like a dog,	1993
	65: 7	Which stilleth the *n* of the seas, the noise	7588
	65: 7	the *n* of their waves, and the tumult of	7588
	66: 1	**Make a joyful** *n* unto God, all ye lands:	7321
	81: 1	**make a joyful** *n* unto the God of Jacob.	7321
	93: 4	The Lord on high *is* mightier than the *n*	6963
	95: 1	let us **make a joyful** *n* to the rock of our	7321
	95: 2	**make a joyful** *n* unto him with psalms.	7321
	98: 4	**Make a joyful** *n* unto the Lord,	7321
	98: 4	**make a loud** *n*, and rejoice,	6476
	98: 6	sound of cornet **make a joyful** *n* before	7321
	100: 1	**Make a joyful** *n* unto the Lord, all ye	7321
Isa	9: 5	battle of the warrior *is* with **confused** *n*,	7494
	13: 4	The *n* of a multitude in the mountains,	6963
	13: 4	a tumultuous *n* of the kingdoms of nations	6963
	14:11	down to the grave, *and* the *n* of thy viols:	1998
	17:12	**make a** *n* like the noise of the seas;	1993
	17:12	*which* **make** a noise like the *n* of the seas;	1993
	24: 8	of them that rejoice endeth, the joy	7588
	24:18	*that* he who fleeth from the *n* of the fear	6963
	25: 5	Thou shalt bring down the *n* of strangers,	7588
	29: 6	great *n*, *with* storm and tempest,	1995
	31: 4	nor abase himself for the *n* of them:	1995
	33: 3	At the *n* of the tumult the people fled;	6963
	66: 6	A voice of *n* from the city, a voice from	7588
Jer	4:19	my heart **maketh** a *n* in me; I cannot	1993
	4:29	The whole city shall flee for the *n* of	6963
	10:22	the *n* of the bruit is come, and a great	6963
	11:16	the *n* of a great tumult he hath kindled	6963
	25:31	A *n* shall come *even* to the ends of	7588
	46:17	there, Pharaoh king of Egypt *is but* a *n;*	7588
	47: 3	At the *n* of the stamping of the hoofs	6963
	49:21	The earth is moved at the *n* of their fall,	6963
	49:21	the *n* thereof was heard in the Red sea.	6963
	50:46	At the *n* of the taking of Babylon the	6963
	51:55	great waters, a *n* of their voice is uttered:	7588
La	2: 7	they have made a *n* in the house of	6963
Eze	1:24	they went, I heard the *n* of their wings,	6963
	1:24	like the *n* of great waters, as the voice of	6963
	1:24	the voice of speech, as the *n* of a host:	6963
	3:13	*heard* also the *n* of the wings of the living	6963
	3:13	the *n* of the wheels over against them,	6963
	3:13	against them, and a *n* of a great rushing.	6963
	19: 7	fulness thereof, by the *n* of his roaring.	6963
	26:10	thy walls shall shake at the *n* of	6963
	26:13	I will cause the *n* of thy songs to cease;	1995
	37: 7	there was a *n*, and, behold a shaking,	6963
	43: 2	his voice *was* like a *n* of many waters:	6963
Joel	2: 5	Like the *n* of chariots on the tops of	6963
	2: 5	like the *n* of a flame of fire that devoureth	6963
Am	5:23	Take thou away from me the *n* of thy	1995
Mic	2:12	they shall **make great** *n* by reason of	1949
Na	3: 2	The *n* of a whip, and the noise of	6963
	3: 2	the *n* of the rattling of the wheels,	6963
Zep	1:10	that there shall be the *n* of a cry from	6963
Zec	9:15	drink, *and* **make a** *n* as *through* wine;	1993
Mt	9:23	the minstrels and the people **making** a *n*,	2350
2Pe	3:10	heavens shall pass away with a **great** *n*,	4500
Rev	6: 1	and I heard, as *it were* the *n* of thunder,	5456

NOISED (4) [NOISE]

Jos	6:27	his fame was *n* throughout all the country.	NIH
Mk	2: 1	it was *n* that he was in the house.	191
Lk	1:65	all these sayings were *n* **abroad**	1255
Ac	2: 6	when this **was** *n* abroad,	1096+3588+5456

NOISOME (4)

Ps	91: 3	of the fowler, *and* from the *n* pestilence.	1942
Eze	14:15	I cause *n* beasts to pass through the land,	7451
	14:21	and the beast, and the pestilence,	7451
Rev	16: 2	and there fell a *n* and grievous sore upon	2556

NOISY See CONCOURSE

NON (1)

1Ch	7:27	**N** his son, Jehoshua his son.	5126

NON-GREEKS See BARBARIANS

NONE (358) [NO]

Ge	23: 6	of us shall withhold from thee his	376+3808
	28:17	this *is n* other but the house of God,	369
	39: 9	*There* is *n* greater in this house than I;	369
	39:11	there was *n* of the men of the house there	369
	41: 8	there was *n* that could interpret them unto	369
	41:15	dream, and *there* is *n* that can interpret it:	369
	41:24	but *there* was *n* that could declare *it* to me.	369
	41:39	*there* is *n* so discreet and wise as thou *art:*	369
Ex	8:10	that thou mayest know that *there* is *n* like	369
	9:14	thou mayest know that *there* is *n* like me	369
	9:24	such as there was *n* like it in all the land	369
	11: 6	such as there was *n* like it, nor shall be	3808
	12:22	of you shall go out at the door of	376+3808
	15:26	put *n* of *these* diseases upon thee,	3605+3808
	16:26	in the sabbath, in it there shall be *n*.	3808
	16:27	day for to gather, and they found *n*.	3808
	23:15	and *n* shall appear before me empty:	3808

Ex	34:20	and **n** shall appear before me empty. 3808
Lev	18: 6	**N** of you shall approach to any 376+376+3808
	21: 1	There shall **n** be defiled for the dead 3808
	22:30	ye shall leave **n** of it until the morrow: 3808
	25:26	if the man have **n** to redeem *it*, 3808+2050.2
	26: 6	lie down, and **n** shall make *you* afraid: 369
	26:17	and ye shall flee when **n** pursueth you. 369
	26:36	sword; and they shall fall when **n** pursueth. 369
	26:37	it were before a sword, when **n** pursueth; 369
	27:29	**N** devoted, which shall be devoted 3605+3808
Nu	7: 9	unto the sons of Kohath he gave **n**: 3808
	9:12	They shall leave it unto the morning, 3808
	21:35	people, until there was **n** left him alive: 1115
	30: 8	she bound her soul, of **n effect**: 6565
	32:11	**Surely** if the men that came up out of 518
Dt	2:34	of every city, we left **n** to remain: 3808
	3: 3	we smote him until **n** was left to him 1115
	4:35	he is God; *there is* **n** else besides him. 369
	4:39	upon the earth beneath: *there is* **n** else. 369
	5: 7	Thou shalt have **n** other gods before me. 3808
	7:15	will put **n** of the evil diseases of 3605+3808
	22:27	damsel cried, and *there was* **n** to save her. 369
	28:31	and thou shalt have **n** to rescue *them*. 369
	28:66	and shalt have **n** assurance of thy life: 3808
	32:36	is gone, and *there is* **n** shut up, or left. 657
	33:26	*There is* **n** like unto the God of Jeshurun, 369
Jos	6: 1	of Israel: **n** went out, and none came in. 369
	6: 1	of Israel: none went out, and **n** came in. 369
	8:22	that *they* let **n** of them remain or escape. 1115
	9:23	there shall **n** of you be freed from being 3808
	10:21	moved his tongue against 376+3808+3807.1
	10:28	souls that *were* therein; he let **n** remain: 3808
	10:30	he let **n** remain in it; but did unto the king 3808
	10:33	until *he* had left him **n** remaining. 1115
	10:37	he left **n** remaining, according to all that 3808
	10:39	that *were* therein; he left **n** remaining: 3808
	10:40	he left **n** remaining, but utterly destroyed 3808
	11: 8	until *they* left them **n** remaining. 1115
	11:13	burned **n** of them, save Hazor only; 3605+3808
	11:22	was **n** of the Anakims left in the land 3808
	13:14	Only unto the tribe of Levi he gave **n** 3808
	14: 3	unto the Levites he gave **n** inheritance 3808
Jdg	19:28	**n** answered. Then the man took her *up* 369
	21: 8	there came **n** to the camp from 376+3808
	21: 9	*there were* **n** of the inhabitants of 369+376
Ru	4: 4	for *there is* **n** to redeem *it* besides thee; 369
1Sa	2: 2	*There is* **n** holy as the LORD: for *there is* 369
	2: 2	*there is* **n** beside thee: neither *is there any* 369
	3:19	let **n** of his words fall to the ground. 3605+3808
	10:24	*there is* **n** like him among all the people? 369
	14:24	So **n** of the people tasted *any* food. 3605+3808
	21: 9	David said, *There is* **n** like that; give it me. 369
	22: 8	*there is* **n** that sheweth me that my son 369
	22: 8	*there is* **n** of you that is sorry for me, 369
2Sa	7:22	*there is* **n** like thee, neither *is there any* 369
	14: 6	*was* **n** to part them, but the one smote 369
	14:19	**n** can turn to the right hand or to the left 518
	14:25	in all Israel there was **n** to be so 376+3808
	18:12	Beware that **n** *touch* the young man 4310
	22:42	They looked, but *there was* **n** to save; 369
1Ki	3:12	so that there was **n** like thee before thee, 3808
	8:60	the LORD *is* God, *and that there is* **n** else. 369
	10:21	**n** *were of* silver: it was nothing accounted 369
	12:20	there was **n** that followed the house of 3808
	15:22	throughout all Judah; **n** *was* exempted: 369
	21:25	(But there was **n** like unto Ahab, which 3808
2Ki	5:16	before whom I stand, I will receive **n**. 518
	6:12	of his servants said, **N**, my lord, O king: 3808
	9:10	*there shall be* **n** to bury her. And he 369
	9:15	let **n** go forth *nor* escape out of the city to 408
	10:11	his priests, until he left him **n** remaining. 1115
	10:19	and all his priests; let **n** be wanting: 376+408
	10:23	look that there be here with you **n** of 6435
	10:25	in, *and* slay them; let **n** come forth. 376+408
	17:18	was **n** left but the tribe of Judah only. 3808
	18: 5	that after him was **n** like him among all 3808
	24:14	**n** remained, save the poorest sort of 3808
1Ch	15: 2	**N** ought to carry the ark of God but 3808
	17:20	O LORD, *there is* **n** like thee, neither *is* 369
	23:17	Eliezer had **n** other sons; but the sons of 369
	29:15	*are* as a shadow, and *there is* **n** abiding. 369
2Ch	1:12	such as **n** of the kings have had that 834+3808
	9:11	there were **n** such seen before in the land 3808
	9:20	**n** *were of* silver; it was *not* any thing 369
	10:16	we have **n** inheritance in the son of Jesse: 3808
	16: 1	to the intent that *he* might let **n** go out or 1115
	20: 6	might, so that **n** is able to withstand thee? 369
	20:24	bodies fallen to the earth, and **n** escaped. 369
	23: 6	But let **n** come *into* the house of the LORD, 408
	23:19	that **n** *which was* unclean in any thing 3808
Ezr	8:15	found there **n** of the sons of Levi. 3808+4480
Ne	4:23	followed me, **n** of us put off our clothes, 369
Est	1: 8	*was* according to the law; **n** did compel: 369
	4: 2	for **n** might enter into the king's gate 369
Job	1: 8	*there is* **n** like him in the earth, a perfect 369
	2: 3	*there is* **n** like him in the earth, a perfect 369
	2:13	nights, and **n** spake a word unto him: 369
	3: 9	let it look for light, but *have* **n**; neither let 369
	10: 7	*is* **n** that can deliver out of thine hand. 369
	11:19	lie down, and **n** shall make *thee* afraid; 369
	18:15	in his tabernacle, because *it is* **n** of his: 1097
	20:21	*There shall* **n** of his meat be left; therefore 369
	29:12	and him that had **n** to help him. 3808
	32:12	*there was* **n** of you that convinced Job, 369
	35:10	**n** saith, Where is God my Maker, 3808

Job	35:12	**n** giveth answer, because of the pride of 3808
	41:10	**N** *is so* fierce that dare stir him up: 3808
Ps	7: 2	*it* in pieces, while *there is* **n** to deliver. 369
	10:15	seek out his wickedness *till* thou find **n**. 1077
	14: 1	*there is* **n** that doeth good. 369
	14: 3	*there is* **n** that doeth good, no, not one. 369
	18:41	*there was* **n** to save *them: even* unto 369
	22:11	for trouble *is* near; for *there is* **n** to help. 369
	22:29	and **n** can keep alive his own soul. 3808
	25: 3	Yea, let them that wait on thee be 3605+3808
	33:10	**maketh** the devices of the people of **n** effect. 5106
	34:22	of them that trust in him shall be 3605+3808
	37:31	*is* in his heart; **n** of his steps shall slide. 3808
	49: 7	**N** of them can by any means redeem 376+3808
	50:22	*you* in pieces, and *there be* **n** to deliver. 369
	53: 1	*there is* **n** that doeth good. 369
	53: 3	*there is* **n** that doeth good, no, not one. 369
	69:20	for some to take pity, but *there was* **n**; 369
	69:20	and for comforters, but I found **n**. 3808
	69:25	be desolate; *and* let **n** dwell in their tents. 408
	71:11	and take him; for *there is* **n** to deliver *him*. 369
	73:25	*there is* **n** upon earth *that* I desire beside 3808
	76: 5	**n** of the men of might have found 3605+3808
	79: 3	and *there was* **n** to bury *them*. 369
	81:11	to my voice; and Israel would **n** of me. 3808
	86: 8	Among the gods *there is* **n** like unto thee, 369
	107:12	they fell down, and *there was* **n** to help. 369
	109:12	Let there be **n** to extend mercy unto him: 408
	139:16	when *as yet there was* **n** of them. 259+3808
Pr	1:25	my counsel, and would **n** of my reproof: 3808
	1:30	They would **n** of my counsel: they 3808
	2:19	**N** that go *unto* her return *again*, 3605+3808
	3:31	choose **n** of his ways. 408+3605+871.1
SS	4: 2	twins, and **n** *is* barren among them. 369
Isa	1:31	burn together, and **n** shall quench *them*. 369
	5:27	**N** shall be weary nor stumble amongst 369
	5:27	**n** shall slumber nor sleep; neither shall 3808
	5:29	carry *it* away safe, and **n** shall deliver *it*. 369
	10:14	there was **n** that moved the wing, 3808
	14: 6	in anger, *is* persecuted, *and* **n** hindereth. 1097
	14:31	and **n** *shall be* alone in his appointed times. 369
	17: 2	lie down, and **n** shall make *them* afraid. 369
	22:22	so he shall open, and **n** shall shut; 369
	22:22	and he shall shut, and **n** shall open. 369
	34:10	**n** shall pass through it for ever and ever. 369
	34:12	**n** *shall be* there, and all her princes shall 369
	34:16	shall fail, nˢ shall want her mate: 802+3808
	41:17	is **n**, *and* their tongue faileth for thirst, 369
	41:26	yea, *there is* **n** that sheweth, yea, *there is* 369
	41:26	yea, *there is* **n** that declareth, yea, 369
	41:26	yea, *there is* **n** that heareth your words. 369
	42:22	they are for a prey, and **n** delivereth; *for a* 369
	42:22	*for a* spoil, and **n** saith, Restore. 369
	43:13	*there is* **n** that can deliver out of my hand: 369
	44:19	**n** considereth in his heart, neither *is there* 3808
	45: 5	*I am* the LORD, and *there is* **n** else, *there is* 369
	45: 6	from the west, that *there is* **n** besides me. 657
	45: 6	*I am* the LORD, and *there is* **n** else. 369
	45:14	thee; and *there is* **n** else, *there is* no God. 369
	45:18	*I am* the LORD; and *there is* **n** else. 369
	45:21	God and a saviour; *there is* **n** beside me. 369
	45:22	earth: for *I am* God, and *there is* **n** else. 369
	46: 9	*I am* God, and *there is* **n** else; *I am* God, 369
	46: 9	else; *I am* God, and *there is* **n** like me, 657
	47: 8	thine heart, *I am*, and **n** else besides me; 657
	47:10	thou hast said, **N** seeth me. Thy wisdom 369
	47:10	thine heart, *I am*, and **n** else besides me. 657
	47:15	every one to his quarter; **n** shall save thee. 369
	50: 2	when I called, *was there* **n** to answer? 369
	51:18	*There is* **n** to guide her among all the sons 369
	57: 1	**n** considering that the righteous is taken 369
	59: 4	**N** calleth for justice, nor any pleadeth for 369
	59:11	we look for judgment, but *there is* **n**; 369
	63: 3	of the people *there was* **n** with me: 369+376
	63: 5	I looked, and *there was* **n** to help; 369
	63: 5	I wondered that *there was* **n** to uphold: 369
	64: 7	*there is* **n** that calleth upon thy name, 369
	66: 4	because when I called, **n** did answer; 369
Jer	4: 4	burn that **n** can quench *it*, because of the 369
	4:22	and they have **n** understanding. 3808
	7:33	of the earth; and **n** shall fray *them* away. 369
	9:10	that **n** can pass through *them*; 376+1097
	9:12	wilderness, that **n** passeth through? 1097+4480
	9:22	the harvestman, and **n** shall gather *them*. 369
	10: 6	Forasmuch as *there is* **n** like unto thee, 369
	10: 7	*there is* **n** like unto thee. 369+4480
	10:20	is **n** to stretch forth my tent any more, 369
	13:19	**n** shall open *them*: Judah shall be carried 369
	14:16	they *shall* have **n** to bury them, 369
	21:12	burn that **n** can quench *it*, because of the 369
	23:14	**n** doth return from his wickedness: 376+1115
	30: 7	for that day *is* great, so that **n** *is* like it: 369
	30:10	and be quiet, and **n** shall make *him* afraid. 369
	30:13	*There is* **n** to plead thy cause, that thou 369
	34: 9	that **n** should serve himself of them, 376+1115
	34:10	that **n** should serve themselves of them 1115
	35:14	for unto this day they drink **n**, 3808
	36:30	He shall have **n** to sit upon the throne of 3808
	42:17	in Judah; that **n** shall remain or escape from 3808
	44: 7	out of Judah, to leave you **n** to remain; 1115
	44:14	So that **n** of the remnant of Judah, 3808
	44:14	**n** shall return but such as shall escape. 3808
	46:27	and at ease, and **n** shall make *him* afraid. 369
	48:33	**n** shall tread *with* shouting; *their* shouting 3808

Jer	49: 5	**n** shall gather up him that wandereth. 369
	50: 3	land desolate, and **n** shall dwell therein: 3808
	50: 9	mighty expert *man;* **n** shall return in vain. 3808
	50:20	shall be sought for, and *there shall be* **n**; 369
	50:29	against it round about; let **n** thereof escape: 408
	50:32	and fall, and **n** shall raise him up: 369
	51:62	to cut it off, that **n** shall remain in it, 1115
La	1: 2	among all her lovers she hath **n** to comfort 369
	1: 4	because **n** come to the solemn feasts: 1097
	1: 7	the hand of the enemy, and **n** did help her: 369
	1:17	her hands, *and there is* **n** to comfort her: 369
	1:21	heard that I sigh; *there is* **n** to comfort me: 369
	2: 2	that in the day of the LORD's anger **n** 3808
	5: 8	*there is* **n** that doth deliver *us* out of their 369
Eze	7:11	of them *shall* remain, nor of their 3808
	7:14	to make all ready; but **n** goeth to the battle: 369
	7:25	they shall seek peace, and *there shall be* **n**. 369
	12:28	There shall **n** of my words be 3605+3808
	16: 5	**N** eye pitied thee, to do any of these unto 369
	16:34	whereas **n** followeth thee to commit 3808
	18: 7	hath spoiled by violence, hath given his 3808
	22:30	that *I* should not destroy it: but I found **n**. 3808
	31:14	To the end that **n** of all the trees by 3808
	33:16	Of his sins that he hath 3605+3808
	33:28	shall be desolate, that **n** shall pass through. 369
	34: 6	and **n** did search or seek *after them*. 369
	34:28	dwell safely, and **n** shall make *them* afraid. 369
	39:26	in their land, and **n** made them afraid. 369
	39:28	and have left **n** of them any more there. 3808
Da	1:19	among them all was found **n** like Daniel, 369
	2:11	there is **n** other that can shew it before 3809
	4:35	**n** can stay his hand, or say 383+1768+3809
	6: 4	could find **n** occasion nor fault; 3606+3809
	8: 7	was **n** that could deliver the ram out 3808
	8:27	astonished at the vision, but **n** understood 369
	10:21	*is* **n** that holdeth with me in these 259+369
	11:16	his own will, and **n** shall stand before him: 369
	11:45	come to his end, and **n** shall help him. 369
	12:10	**n** of the wicked shall understand; 3605+3808
Hos	2:10	**n** shall deliver her out of mine hand, 376+3808
	5:14	I will take away, and **n** shall rescue *him*. 369
	7: 5	**n** among them that calleth unto me. 369
	11: 7	the most High, **n** would at all exalt *him*. 3808
	12: 8	all my labours they shall find **n** iniquity 3808
Joel	2:27	that I am the LORD your God, and **n** else: 369
Am	5: 2	upon her land; *there is* **n** to raise her up. 369
	5: 6	and *there be* **n** to quench *it* in Beth-el. 369
Ob	1: 7	thee: *there is* **n** understanding in him. 369
Mic	2: 5	Therefore thou shalt have **n** that shall cast 3808
	3:11	among us? **n** evil can come upon us. 3808
	4: 4	his fig tree; and **n** shall make *them* afraid: 369
	5: 8	and teareth in pieces, and **n** can deliver. 369
	7: 2	*there is* **n** upright among men: they all lie 369
Na	2: 8	stand, *shall they cry;* but **n** shall look back. 369
	2: 9	for *there is* **n** end of the store *and* glory out 369
	2:11	the lion's whelp, and **n** made *them* afraid? 369
	3: 3	and *there is* **n** end of *their* corpses; 369
Zep	2:15	her heart, I *am*, and *there is* **n** beside me: 657
	3: 6	streets waste, that **n** passeth by: 1097+4480
	3: 6	is no man, that there is **n** inhabitant. 369+4480
	3:13	lie down, and **n** shall make *them* afraid. 369
Hag	1: 6	ye clothe you, but **there is** **n** warm; 369
Zec	7:10	let **n** of you imagine evil against his 376+408
	8:17	let **n** of you imagine evil in your hearts 376+408
Mal	2:15	let **n** deal treacherously against the wife of 408
Mt	12:43	dry places, seeking rest, and findeth **n**. 3756
	15: 6	made the commandment of God of **n** effect 208
	19:17	*there is* **n** good but one, *that is*, God: 3762
	26:60	But found **n**: yea, though many false 3756
	26:60	false witnesses came, *yet* found they **n**. 3756
Mk	7:13	Making the word of God of **n** effect through 208
	10:18	*there is* **n** good but one, *that is*, God. 3762
	12:31	There is **n** other commandment greater 3756
	12:32	is one God; and there is **n** other but he: 3756
	14:55	Jesus to put him to death; and found **n**. 3756
Lk	1:61	There is **n** of thy kindred that is called by 3762
	3:11	let him impart to him that hath **n**; 3361
	4:26	But unto **n** of them was Elias sent, 3762
	4:27	and **n** of them was cleansed, 3762
	11:24	and finding **n**, he saith, I will return unto 3361
	13: 6	and sought fruit thereon, and found **n**. 3756
	13: 7	seeking fruit on this fig tree, and find **n**: 3756
	14:24	That **n** of those men which were bidden 3762
	18:19	good? **n** *is* good, save one, *that is*, God. 3762
	18:34	And they understood **n** of these *things*: 3762
Jn	6:22	sea saw that there was **n** other boat there, 3756
	7:19	the law, and *yet* **n** of you keepeth the law? 3762
	8:10	lift up *himself*, and saw **n** but the woman, 3367
	15:24	them the works which **n** other *man* did, 3762
	16: 5	and **n** of you asketh me, Whither goest 3762
	17:12	and **n** of them is lost, but the son of 3762
	18: 9	them which thou gavest me have I lost **n**. 3762
	21:12	And **n** of the disciples durst ask him, 3762
Ac	3: 6	Then Peter said, Silver and gold have I **n**; 3756
	4:12	for there is **n** other name under heaven 3777
	7: 5	And he gave **n** inheritance in it, no, 3756
	8:16	(For as yet he was fallen upon **n** of them: 3762
	8:24	**n** of *these things* which ye have spoken 3367
	11:19	the word to **n** but unto the Jews 3367
	18:17	And Gallio cared for **n** of those *things*. 3367
	20:24	But **n** of these *things* move me, 3056+3762
	24:23	he should forbid **n** of his acquaintance 3367
	25:11	if there be **n** of these *things* whereof these 3762

N

| Ac | 25:18 | **n** accusation of *such things* as I supposed: | 3762 |

Ac 25:18 **n** accusation of *such things* as I supposed: 3762
26:22 saying **n** other *things* than those which 3762
26:26 for I am persuaded that **n** of these *things* 3762
Ro 3:10 written, There is **n** righteous, no, not one: 3756
3:11 is **n** that understandeth, there is none 3756
3:11 there is **n** that seeketh after God. 3756
3:12 there is **n** that doeth good, no, not one. 3756
4:14 and the promise made of **n** effect: 2673
8: 9 not the Spirit of Christ, he is **n** of his. 3756
9: 6 the word of God hath taken **n** effect. 1601
14: 7 For **n** of us liveth to himself, and no *man* 3762
1Co 1:14 I thank God that I baptized **n** of you, 3762
1:17 of Christ should be made of **n** effect. 2758
2: 8 **n** of the princes of this world knew: 3762
7:29 than wives as though they had **n**; 3361
8: 4 and that *there is* **n** other God but one. 3762
9:15 But I have used of these *things:* 3756+3762
10:32 Give **n** offence, neither to the Jews, nor to 677
14:10 and in **n** of them *is* without signification. 3762
2Co 1:13 For we write **n** other *things* unto you, 3756
Gal 1:19 But other of the apostles saw I **n**, 3756
3:17 *it* should make the promise of **n** effect, 2673
5:10 that you will be **n** otherwise minded: 3762
1Th 5:15 See that **n** render evil for evil unto 3361+5100
1Ti 5:14 give **n** occasion to the adversary to speak 3367
1Pe 4:15 let **n** of you suffer as a murderer, 3361+5100
1Jn 2:10 there is **n** occasion of stumbling in him. 3756
Rev 2:10 Fear **n** *of those things* which thou shalt 3367
2:24 I will put upon you **n** other burden. 3756

NOON (13) [NOONDAY, NOONDAYS, NOONTIDE]

Ge 43:16 for *these* men shall dine with me at **n**. 6672
43:25 the present against Joseph came at **n**: 6672
2Sa 4: 5 of Ish-bosheth, who lay on a bed at **n**. 6672
1Ki 18:26 name of Baal from morning even until **n**, 6672
18:27 it came to pass at **n**, that Elijah mocked 6672
20:16 they went out at **n**. But Ben-hadad *was* 6672
2Ki 4:20 he sat on her knees till **n**, and *then* died. 6672
Ps 55:17 and morning, and at **n**, will I pray, 6672
SS 1: 7 where thou makest *thy flock* to rest at **n**: 6672
Jer 6: 4 against her; arise, and let us go up at **n**. 6672
Am 8: 9 that I will cause the sun to go down at **n**, 6672
Zep 2: 4 they shall drive out Ashdod at the **n day**, 6672
Ac 22: 6 was come nigh unto Damascus about **n**, 3314

NOONDAY (8) [DAY, NOON]

Job 5:14 and grope in the **n** as in the night. 6672
11:17 *thine* age shall be clearer than the **n**; 6672
Ps 37: 6 as the light, and thy judgment as the **n**. 6672
91: 6 *nor* for the destruction *that* wasteth at **n**. 6672
Isa 16: 3 shadow as the night in the midst of the **n**; 6672
58:10 in obscurity, and thy darkness *be* as the **n**: 6672
59:10 we stumble at **n** as *in* the night; *we are* in 6672
Jer 15: 8 mother of the young men a spoiler at **n**: 6672

NOONDAYS (1) [DAY, NOON]

Dt 28:29 thou shalt grope at **n**, as the blind gropeth 6672

NOONTIDE (1) [NOON]

Jer 20:16 the morning, and the shouting at **n**; 6256+6672

NOPH (7)

Isa 19:13 the princes of **N** are deceived; 5297
Jer 2:16 the children of **N** and Tahapanes have 5297
44: 1 at **N**, and in the country of Pathros, 5297
46:14 and publish in **N** and in Tahpanhes: 5297
46:19 for **N** shall be waste and desolate without 5297
Eze 30:13 will cause *their* images to cease out of **N**; 5297
30:16 and **N** shall have distresses daily. 5297

NOPHAH (1)

Nu 21:30 we have laid *them* waste even unto **N**, 5302

NOR (758) [NO]

Ge 19:33 when she lay down, **n** when she arose. 2050.1
19:35 when she lay down, **n** when she arose. 2050.1
21:23 **n** with my son, nor with my son's son: 2050.1
21:23 nor with my son, **n** with my son's son: 2050.1
45: 5 **n** angry with yourselves, 408+2050.1
45: 6 *there shall* neither **n** be earing in harvest. 2050.1
49:10 **n** a lawgiver from between his feet, 2050.1
Ex 4: 1 **n** hearken unto my voice: 3808+2050.1
4:10 since thou hast spoken unto thy servant: 1571
10: 6 thy fathers' fathers have seen, 2050.1
11: 6 like it, **n** shall be like it any more. 3808+2050.1
12: 9 **n** sodden at all with water, but roast 2050.1
13:22 the pillar of fire by night, *from* before 2050.1
20: 5 thyself to them, **n** serve them: 3808+2050.1
20:10 thou, **n** thy son, nor thy daughter, 2050.1
20:10 thou, nor thy son, **n** thy daughter, 2050.1
20:10 **n** thy maidservant, nor thy cattle, 2050.1
20:10 nor thy maidservant, **n** thy cattle, 2050.1
20:10 **n** thy stranger that *is* within thy gates: 2050.1
20:17 **n** his manservant, nor his maidservant, 2050.1
20:17 his maidservant, **n** his ox, nor his ass, 2050.1
20:17 his maidservant, **n** his ox, nor his ass, 2050.1
20:17 **n** any thing that *is* thy neighbour's. 2050.1
22:21 vex a stranger, **n** oppress him: 3808+2050.1
22:28 **n** curse the ruler of thy people. 3808+2050.1
23:24 **n** serve them, nor do after their 3808+2050.1
23:24 them, **n** do after their works: 3808+2050.1
23:26 their young, **n** be barren, in thy land: 2050.1
23:32 covenant with them, **n** with their gods. 2050.1

Ex 30: 9 **n** burnt sacrifice, nor meat offering; 2050.1
30: 9 nor burnt sacrifice, **n** meat offering; 2050.1
34: 3 neither let the flocks **n** herds feed before 2050.1
34:10 done in all the earth, **n** in any nation: 2050.1
34:28 neither eat bread, **n** drink water. 3808+2050.1
36: 6 neither man **n** woman make any more 2050.1
Lev 2:11 ye shall burn no leaven, **n** any honey, 2050.1
3:17 *that* ye eat neither fat **n** blood. 3605+2050.1
10: 9 Do not drink wine **n** strong drink, thou, 2050.1
10: 9 strong drink, thou, **n** thy sons with thee, 2050.1
11:10 all that have not fins **n** scales in the seas, 2050.1
11:12 Whatsoever hath no fins **n** scales in 2050.1
11:26 *is* not clovenfooted, **n** cheweth 369+2050.1
12: 4 *thing*, **n** come into the sanctuary, 3808+2050.1
13:34 *be* in sight deeper than the skin; 369+2050.1
17:16 if he wash *them* not, **n** bathe his 3808+2050.1
18:26 **n** any stranger that sojourneth among 2050.1
19: 4 **n** make to yourselves molten 3808+2050.1
19:14 **n** put a stumblingblock before 3808+2050.1
19:15 **n** honour the person of the 3808+2050.1
19:18 **n** bear any grudge against 3808+2050.1
19:20 all redeemed, **n** freedom given her; 176+3808
19:26 **n** observe times. 3808+2050.1
19:28 **n** print any marks upon you: 3808+2050.1
20:19 mother's sister, **n** thy father's sister: 2050.1
21: 5 **n** make any cuttings in their flesh. 3808+2050.1
21:10 his head, **n** rend his clothes; 3808+2050.1
21:11 **n** defile himself for his father, or for his 3808
21:12 **n** profane the sanctuary of his 3808+2050.1
21:23 **n** come nigh unto the altar, 3808+2050.1
22:22 make an offering for the **n** 3808+2050.1
23:14 **n** parched *corn*, nor green ears, 2050.1
23:14 nor parched *corn*, **n** green ears, 2050.1
25: 4 thy field, **n** prune thy vineyard. 3808+2050.1
25:11 **n** gather *the grapes* in it of thy 3808+2050.1
25:20 not sow, **n** gather in our increase: 3808+2050.1
25:37 **n** lend him thy victuals for 3808+2050.1
26: 1 Ye shall make you no idols **n** 3808+2050.1
27:10 **n** change it, a good for a bad, 3808+2050.1
Nu 5:15 **n** put frankincense thereon; 3808+2050.1
6: 3 **n** eat moist grapes, or dried. 3808+2050.1
9:12 **n** break any bone of it: 3808+2050.1
11:19 two days, nor five days, 2050.1
11:19 nor two days, **n** five days, 2050.1
11:19 neither ten days, **n** twenty days; 2050.1
18: 3 altar, that neither **n** you also, die. 1571
20:17 we will not turn *to* the right hand **n** to 2050.1
23:25 them at all, **n** bless them at all. 1571+3808
Dt 1:45 your voice, **n** give ear unto you. 3808+2050.1
2:19 them not, **n** meddle with them: 408+2050.1
2:27 neither turn *unto* the right hand **n** to 2050.1
2:37 **n** *unto* any place of the river Jabbok, NIH
2:37 **n** *unto* the cities in the mountains, 2050.1
2:37 *unto* whatsoever the Lord our God 2050.1
4:28 **n** hear, nor eat, nor smell. 3808+2050.1
4:28 hear, **n** eat, nor smell. 3808+2050.1
4:28 nor hear, nor eat, **n** smell. 3808+2050.1
4:31 **n** forget the covenant of thy 3808+2050.1
5: 9 thyself unto them, **n** serve them: 3808+2050.1
5:14 thy son, nor thy daughter, nor thy 2050.1
5:14 thy son, **n** thy daughter, nor thy 2050.1
5:14 nor thy daughter, **n** thy manservant, 2050.1
5:14 **n** thy maidservant, nor thine ox, nor 2050.1
5:14 maidservant, **n** thine ox, nor thine ass, 2050.1
5:14 maidservant, nor thine ox, **n** thine ass, 2050.1
5:14 ox, nor thine ass, **n** any of thy cattle, 2050.1
5:14 **n** thy stranger that *is* within thy gates; 2050.1
7: 2 **n** shew mercy unto them: 3808+2050.1
7: 3 **n** his daughter shalt thou take 3808+2050.1
7: 7 **n** choose you, because ye were more in 2050.1
7:25 gold *that is* on them, **n** take *it* unto thee, 2050.1
9: 9 did eat bread **n** drink water: 3808+2050.1
9:18 **n** drink water, because of all your sins 3808
9:23 not, **n** hearkened to his voice. 3808+2050.1
9:27 **n** to their wickedness, nor to their sin: 2050.1
9:27 nor to their wickedness, **n** to their sin: 2050.1
10: 9 Wherefore Levi hath no part **n** 2050.1
10:17 not persons, **n** taketh reward: 3808+2050.1
12:12 forasmuch as he hath no part **n** 2050.1
12:17 **n** any of thy vows which thou vowest, 2050.1
12:17 thy freewill offerings, or heave 2050.1
12:32 add thereto, **n** diminish from it. 3808+2050.1
13: 6 hast not known, thou, **n** thy fathers; 2050.1
13: 8 unto him, **n** hearken unto him; 3808+2050.1
14: 1 **n** make *any* baldness between 3808+2050.1
14: 8 **n** touch their dead carcase. 2050.1
14:27 hath no part **n** inheritance with thee. 2050.1
14:29 hath no part **n** inheritance with thee,) 2050.1
15: 7 **n** shut thine hand from thy poor 3808+2050.1
15:19 **n** shear the firstling of thy sheep. 3808+2050.1
17:11 thee, *to* the right hand, **n** *to* the left. 2050.1
17:16 **n** cause the people to return to 3808+2050.1
18: 1 have no part **n** inheritance with Israel: 2050.1
18:22 if the thing follow not, **n** come to 3808+2050.1
21: 4 which is neither eared **n** sown, 3808+2050.1
22:30 **n** discover his father's skirt. 2050.1
23: 6 Thou shalt not seek their peace **n** their 2050.1
23:17 **n** a sodomite of the sons of Israel. 3808+2050.1
24:17 of the stranger, **n** of the fatherless; NIH
24:17 **n** take a widow's raiment to 2050.1
26:14 **n** given *ought* thereof for the 3808+2050.1
28:36 unto a nation which neither thou **n** thy 2050.1
28:39 **n** gather *the grapes*; for the 3808+2050.1
28:50 **n** shew favour to the young: 3808+2050.1
28:64 which neither thou **n** thy fathers have 2050.1

Dt 29:23 *that* it is not sown, **n** beareth, 3808+2050.1
29:23 **n** any grass groweth therein, 3808+2050.1
31: 6 fear not, **n** be afraid of them: 408+2050.1
31: 6 will not fail thee, **n** forsake thee. 3808+2050.1
33: 9 knew his own children; 3808+2050.1
34: 7 dim, **n** his natural force abated. 3808+2050.1
Jos 1: 5 fail thee, **n** forsake thee. 3808+2050.1
6:10 make any noise with your 3808+2050.1
10:25 Fear not, **n** be dismayed, be strong 408+2050.1
13:13 the Geshurites, **n** the Maachathites: 2050.1
22:19 the Lord, **n** rebel against us, 408+2050.1
22:26 for burnt offering, **n** for sacrifice: 2050.1
22:28 burnt offerings, **n** for sacrifices; 2050.1
23: 7 **n** cause to swear *by them*, 3808+2050.1
23: 7 **n** bow yourselves unto them. 3808+2050.1
24:12 with thy sword, **n** with thy bow. 2050.1
24:19 will not forgive your transgressions **n** 2050.1
Jdg 1:27 her towns, **n** Taanach and her towns, 2050.1
1:27 the inhabitants of Dor and her towns, 2050.1
1:27 the inhabitants of Ibleam and her 2050.1
1:27 the inhabitants of Megiddo and her 2050.1
1:30 of Kitron, **n** the inhabitants of Nahalol; 2050.1
1:31 the inhabitants of Zidon, nor of 2050.1
1:31 of Ahlab, **n** of Achzib, nor of 2050.1
1:31 of Ahlab, nor of Achzib, **n** of Helbah, 2050.1
1:31 of Helbah, **n** of Aphik, nor of 2050.1
1:31 of Helbah, nor of Aphik, **n** of Rehob: 2050.1
1:31 of Helbah, **n** of Aphik, nor of Rehob: 2050.1
1:33 the inhabitants of Beth-anath; 2050.1
2:10 **n** yet the works which he had done for 2050.1
2:19 own doings, **n** from their stubborn way. 2050.1
6: 4 for Israel, neither sheep, **n** ox, nor ass. 2050.1
6: 4 for Israel, neither sheep, nor ox, **n** ass. 2050.1
11:15 the land of the children of Ammon: 2050.1
11:34 her he had neither son **n** daughter. 176
13: 4 drink not wine **n** strong drink, 2050.1
13: 7 now drink no wine **n** strong drink, 2050.1
13:14 **n** eat any unclean *thing*: all that I 408+2050.1
13:23 **n** would as *at this* time have told us 2050.1
14:16 have not told *it* my father **n** my mother, 2050.1
19:30 There was no such *deed* done **n** 3808+2050.1
1Sa 1:15 have drunk neither wine **n** strong 3808+2050.1
3:14 purged with sacrifice **n** offering for ever. 2050.1
5: 5 **n** any that come *into* Dagon's house, 2050.1
12: 4 not defrauded us, **n** oppressed us, 3808+2050.1
12:21 which cannot profit **n** deliver; 3808+2050.1
13:22 that there was neither sword **n** spear 2050.1
15:29 of Israel will not lie **n** repent: 3808+2050.1
20:27 to meat, neither yesterday, **n** to day? 1571
20:31 shalt not be stablished, **n** thy kingdom. 2050.1
21: 8 **n** my weapons with me, 1571+3808+2050.1
22:15 servant, **n** to all the house of my father: NIH
24:11 see that *there is* neither evil **n** 2050.1
25:31 offence of heart unto my lord, 2050.1
26:12 saw *it*, **n** knew *it*, neither awaked: 369+2050.1
27: 9 left neither man **n** woman alive, 2050.1
27:11 saved neither man **n** woman alive, 2050.1
28: 6 by dreams, **n** by Urim, nor by prophets. 1571
28: 6 by dreams, nor by Urim, **n** by prophets. 1571
28:15 more, neither by prophets, **n** by dreams; 1571
28:18 executedst his fierce wrath 3808+2050.1
28:20 no bread all the day, **n** all the night. 2050.1
30:12 drunk *any* water, three days 3808+2050.1
30:15 deliver me into the hands of my 518+2050.1
30:19 neither small **n** great, neither sons nor 2050.1
30:19 neither sons **n** daughters, neither spoil, 2050.1
30:19 **n** any *thing* that they had taken to 2050.1
2Sa 1:21 *be* rain upon you, **n** fields of offerings: 2050.1
2: 9 going he turned not to the right hand **n** 2050.1
3:34 thy feet put into fetters: 3808+2050.1
13:22 good **n** bad: 4480+5704+2050.1+3807.1
14: 7 name **n** remainder upon the earth. 2050.1
19: 6 that thou regardest neither princes **n** 2050.1
19:24 he trimmed his beard, nor washed 3808+2050.1
19:24 his beard, **n** washed his clothes, 3808+2050.1
21: 4 We will have no silver **n** gold of Saul, 2050.1
21: 4 silver nor gold of Saul, **n** of his house; 2050.1
21:10 day, **n** the beasts of the field by night. 2050.1
1Ki 3: 8 cannot be numbered **n** counted 3808+2050.1
3:11 hast asked the life of thine 3808+2050.1
3:26 Let it be neither mine **n** thine, 1571+3808
5: 4 *there is* neither adversary **n** evil 369+2050.1
6: 7 that there was neither hammer **n** 3808+2050.1
6: 7 there was neither hammer nor axe **n** NIH
8: 5 could not be told **n** numbered 3808+2050.1
8:57 let him not leave us, **n** forsake us: 408+2050.1
10:12 were seen unto this day. 3808+2050.1
12:24 **n** fight against your brethren 3808+2050.1
13: 8 neither will I eat bread **n** drink 3808+2050.1
13: 9 Eat no bread, **n** drink water, 3808+2050.1
13: 9 **n** turn again by the *same* way 3808+2050.1
13:16 return with thee, **n** go in with thee: 2050.1
13:16 neither will I eat bread **n** drink 3808+2050.1
13:17 Thou shalt eat no bread **n** drink 3808+2050.1
13:17 **n** turn again to go by the way that thou 3808
13:28 lion had not eaten the carcase, **n** 3808+2050.1
16:11 neither *of* his kinsfolks, **n** *of* his friends. 2050.1
17: 1 shall not be dew **n** rain these years, 2050.1
18:26 *was* no voice, **n** any that answered. 2050.1
18:29 **n** any to answer, nor any that 2050.1
18:29 to answer, **n** any, that regarded. 369+2050.1
20: 8 not *unto him*, **n** consent. 3808+2050.1
22:31 Fight neither with small **n** great, 2050.1
2Ki 3:14 not look toward thee, **n** see thee. 518+2050.1
4:23 *is* neither new moon, **n** sabbath. 3808+2050.1

2Ki 4:31 *there was* neither voice, **n** hearing. 369+2050.1
5:17 offering **n** sacrifice unto other gods, 2050.1
6:10 himself there, not once **n** twice. 3808+2050.1
9:15 let none go forth **n** escape out of the city NIH
14: 6 put to death for the children, **n** 3808+2050.1
14:26 *there was* not any shut up, **n any** 657+2050.1
14:26 any left, **n any** helper for Israel. 369+2050.1
17:35 **n** bow yourselves to them, 3808+2050.1
17:35 **n** serve them, nor sacrifice to 3808+2050.1
17:35 nor serve them, **n** sacrifice to 3808+2050.1
18: 5 of Judah, **n** *any* that were before him. 2050.1
18:12 would not hear *them*, **n** do *them*. 3808+2050.1
19:32 **n** shoot an arrow there, nor come 3808+2050.1
19:32 **n** come before it *with* shield, 3808+2050.1
19:32 **n** cast a bank against it. 3808+2050.1
20:13 in his house, **n** in all his dominion, 2050.1
23:22 **n** *in* all the days of the kings of Israel, 2050.1
23:22 kings of Israel, **n** of the kings of Judah; 2050.1
1Ch 21:24 **n** offer burnt offerings without cost. 2050.1
22:13 dread not, **n** be dismayed. 408+2050.1
23:26 **n** any vessels of it for the service 2050.1
28:20 and do *it:* fear not, **n** be dismayed: 408+2050.1
28:20 will not fail thee, **n** forsake thee, 3808+2050.1
2Ch 1:11 or honour, **n** the life of thine enemies, 2050.1
5: 6 which could not be told **n** 3808+2050.1
6:14 like thee in the heaven, **n** in the earth; 2050.1
11: 4 fight against your brethren: 3808+2050.1
15: 5 **n** to him that came in, but great 2050.1
19: 7 **n** respect of persons, nor taking of gifts. 2050.1
19: 7 nor respect of persons, **n** taking of gifts. 2050.1
20:15 not afraid **n** dismayed by reason 408+2050.1
20:17 fear not, **n** be dismayed: 408+2050.1
21:12 **n** in the ways of Asa king of Judah, 2050.1
29: 7 have not burnt incense **n** offered 3808+2050.1
32: 7 be not afraid **n** dismayed for 408+2050.1
32: 7 **n** for all the multitude that *is* with him: 2050.1
32:15 **n** persuade you on this *manner*, 408+2050.1
34: 2 neither *to* the right hand, **n** *to* the left. 2050.1
Ezr 9:12 **n** seek their peace or their wealth 3808+2050.1
9:14 that *there should be* no remnant **n** 2050.1
10: 6 did eat no bread, **n** drink water: 3808+2050.1
Ne 1: 7 **n** the statutes, nor the judgments, 2050.1
1: 7 nor the statutes, **n** the judgments, 2050.1
2:16 to the priests, nor to the nobles, nor 2050.1
2:16 to the nobles, nor to the rulers, 2050.1
2:16 nor to the rulers, **n** the rest that did the work. 2050.1
2:16 rulers, **n** to the rest that did the work. 2050.1
2:20 **n** right, nor memorial, in Jerusalem. 2050.1
2:20 nor right, **n** memorial, in Jerusalem. 2050.1
4:23 So neither I, **n** my brethren, nor my 2050.1
4:23 I, nor my brethren, **n** my servants, 2050.1
4:23 **n** the men of the guard which followed 2050.1
7:61 their seed, whether they *were* of 2050.1
8: 9 your God; mourn not, **n** weep. 408+2050.1
9:31 consume them, **n** forsake them; 3808+2050.1
9:34 our priests, **n** our fathers, 3808+2050.1
9:34 **n** hearkened unto thy 2050.1
10:30 **n** take their daughters for our 3808+2050.1
13:25 **n** take their daughters unto your 518+2050.1
Est 2: 7 for she had neither father **n** mother, 2050.1
2:10 Esther had not shewed her people **n** her 2050.1
2:20 Esther had not *yet* shewed her kindred **n** 2050.1
3: 2 bowed not, **n** did *him* reverence. 3808+2050.1
3: 5 **n** did him reverence, *then* was Haman 2050.1
4:16 neither eat **n** drink three days, 408+2050.1
5: 9 that he stood not up, **n** moved for 3808+2050.1
9:28 **n** the memorial of them perish 3808+2050.1
Job 1:22 **n** charged God foolishly. 3808+2050.1
3:10 **n** hid sorrow from mine eyes. 3808
7:19 let me alone till I swallow down my 3808
14:12 **n** be raised out of their sleep. 3808+2050.1
18:19 He shall neither have son **n** 3808+2050.1
18:19 **n** *any* remaining in his dwellings. 369+2050.1
24:13 **n** abide in the paths thereof. 3808+2050.1
27: 4 **n** my tongue utter deceit. 518+2050.1
28: 8 trodden it, **n** the fierce lion passed by it. 3808
34:19 **n** regardeth the rich more than 3808+2050.1
34:22 *There is* no darkness, **n** shadow of 369+2050.1
36:19 no, not gold, **n** all the forces of strength. 2050.1
41:12 **n** *his* power, nor his comely proportion. 2050.1
41:12 nor *his* power, **n** his comely proportion. 2050.1
41:26 the spear, the dart, **n** the habergeon. 2050.1
Ps 1: 1 **n** standeth in the way of sinners, 3808+2050.1
1: 1 **n** sitteth in the seat of the 3808+2050.1
1: 5 **n** sinners in the congregation of 2050.1
15: 3 his tongue, **n** doeth evil to his neighbour, 3808
15: 3 **n** taketh up a reproach against 3808+2050.1
15: 5 **n** taketh reward against 3808+2050.1
16: 4 **n** take up their names into my 1077+2050.1
19: 3 *There is* no speech **n** language, 369+2050.1
22:24 For he hath not despised **n** 3808+2050.1
24: 4 unto vanity, **n** sworn deceitfully. 3808+2050.1
25: 7 sins of my youth, **n** my transgressions: 2050.1
26: 9 sinners, **n** my life with bloody men: 2050.1
28: 5 the operation of his hands, he shall 2050.1
37:25 **n** his seed begging bread. 2050.1
37:33 **n** condemn him when he is 3808+2050.1
40: 4 the proud, **n** such as turn aside to lies. 2050.1
49: 7 **n** give to God a ransom for him: 3808
50: 9 of thy house, **n** he goats out of thy folds. NIH
59: 3 **n** *for* my sin, O LORD. 2050.1
66:20 away my prayer, **n** his mercy from me. 2050.1
75: 6 **n** from the west, nor from the south. 2050.1
75: 6 from the west, **n** from the south. 3808+2050.1
78:42 **n** the day when he delivered them from NIH

Ps 89:22 **n** the son of wickedness afflict 3808+2050.1
89:33 I not utterly take from him, **n** 3808+2050.1
89:34 **n** alter the thing that is gone out 3808+2050.1
91: 5 by night; **n** for the arrow *that* flieth by day; NIH
91: 6 *N* for the pestilence *that* walketh in NIH
91: 6 **n** for the destruction *that* wasteth at NIH
103:10 **n** rewarded us according to our 3808+2050.1
121: 4 shall neither slumber **n** sleep. 3808+2050.1
121: 6 smite thee by day, **n** the moon by night. 2050.1
129: 7 **n** he that bindeth sheaves his bosom. 2050.1
131: 1 is not haughty, **n** mine eyes lofty: 3808+2050.1
132: 3 of my house, **n** go up into my bed; 518
144:14 *be* no breaking in, **n** going out; 369+2050.1
146: 3 **n** in the son of man, in whom *there is* no NIH
Pr 4:27 Turn not *to* the right hand **n** *to* the left: 2050.1
5:13 inclined mine ear to them that 3808+2050.1
6: 4 thine eyes, **n** slumber to thine eyelids. 2050.1
8:26 he had not made the earth, **n** the fields, 2050.1
8:26 **n** the highest part of the dust of the 2050.1
17:26 *is* not good, **n** to strike princes for equity. NIH
21:30 *is* no wisdom **n** understanding 369+2050.1
21:30 **n** counsel against the LORD. 369+2050.1
30: 3 **n** have the knowledge of the holy. 2050.1
30: 8 give me neither poverty **n** riches; feed 2050.1
31: 3 **n** thy ways to *that which* destroyeth 2050.1
31: 4 to drink wine; **n** for princes strong drink: 176
Ecc 1: 8 eye is not satisfied with seeing, **n** 3808+2050.1
3:14 to it, **n any** thing taken from it: 369+2050.1
4: 8 yea, he hath neither child **n** brother: 2050.1
5:10 **n** he that loveth abundance *with* 3808+2050.1
6: 5 known *any thing:* this hath 3808+2050.1
8:16 also *there is that* neither day **n** night 2050.1
9:10 device, nor knowledge, nor wisdom, 2050.1
9:10 nor device, **n** knowledge, nor wisdom, 2050.1
9:10 nor knowledge, **n** wisdom, in the grave, 2050.1
9:11 **n** the battle to the strong, 3808+2050.1
9:11 **n** yet riches to men of 3808+2050.1
9:11 **n** yet favour to men of skill: 3808+2050.1
11: 5 **n** how the bones *do grow* in the womb of NIH
12: 1 in the years draw nigh, when thou shalt 2050.1
12: 2 **n** the clouds return after the rain: 2050.1
SS 2: 7 **n** awake *my* love, till he please. 518+2050.1
3: 5 **n** awake *my* love, till he please. 518+2050.1
8: 4 **n** awake *my* love, until he please. 4100+2050.1
Isa 3: 7 house *is* neither bread **n** clothing: 369+2050.1
5: 6 it shall not be pruned, **n** digged; 3808+2050.1
5:27 None *shall be* weary **n** stumble 369+2050.1
5:27 none shall slumber **n** sleep; 3808+2050.1
5:27 the latchet of their shoes be 3808+2050.1
8:12 fear ye their fear, **n** be afraid. 2050.1
11: 9 shall not hurt **n** destroy in all 3808+2050.1
14:21 they do not rise, **n** possess the land, 2050.1
14:21 **n** fill the face of the world *with* cities. 2050.1
22: 2 *are* not slain with the sword, **n** 3808+2050.1
23: 4 travail not, **n** bring forth children, 2050.1
23: 4 nourish up young men, **n** bring up virgins. NIH
23:18 **n** be treasured **n** laid up; 3808+2050.1
28:28 break it *with* the wheel of his cart, 2050.1
28:28 **n** bruise it *with* his horsemen. 3808+2050.1
30: 5 **n** be a help nor profit, but a shame, 3808
30: 5 be a help **n** profit, but a shame, 3808+2050.1
31: 4 **n** abase himself for the noise of 3808+2050.1
32: 5 shall be no more called liberal, **n** 2050.1
34:10 It shall not be quenched night **n** day; 2050.1
35: 9 No lion shall be there, **n** *any* 1077+2050.1
37:33 **n** shoot an arrow there, nor 3808+2050.1
37:33 **n** come before it *with* shields, 3808+2050.1
37:33 **n** cast a bank against it. 3808+2050.1
39: 2 in his house, **n** in all his dominion, 2050.1
40:16 *is* not sufficient to burn, **n** 369+2050.1
42: 2 He shall not cry, **n** lift up, 3808+2050.1
42: 2 **n** cause his voice to be heard in 3808+2050.1
42: 4 shall not fail **n** be discouraged, 3808+2050.1
42:23 thee to serve with an offering, **n** 3808+2050.1
44: 9 they see not, **n** know; that they 1077+2050.1
44:18 They have not known **n** 3808+2050.1
44:19 neither *is there* knowledge **n** 3808+2050.1
44:20 that he cannot deliver his soul, **n** 3808+2050.1
45:13 not for price **n** reward, saith 3808+2050.1
45:17 ye shall not be ashamed **n** 3808+2050.1
46: 7 not answer, **n** save him out of his trouble. 3808
47:14 *be* a coal to warm at, **n** fire to sit before it. NIH
48: 1 not in truth, **n** in righteousness. 3808+2050.1
48:19 off **n** destroyed from before me. 3808+2050.1
49:10 They shall not hunger **n** thirst; 3808+2050.1
49:10 neither shall the heat **n** sun smite them: 2050.1
51:14 he should not die in the pit, **n** 3808+2050.1
52:12 go out with haste, **n** go by flight: 3808+2050.1
53: 2 he hath no form **n** comeliness; 3808+2050.1
54: 9 wroth with thee, **n** rebuke thee. 4480+2050.1
57:11 remembered me, **n** laid *it* to thy heart? 3808
58:13 own ways, **n** finding thine own pleasure, 4480
58:13 **n** speaking *thine own* words: 2050.1
59: 2 justice, **n** *any* pleadeth for truth: 369+2050.1
59:21 **n** out of the mouth of thy seed, 2050.1
59:21 **n** out of the mouth of thy seed's seed, 2050.1
60:11 they shall not be shut day **n** night; 2050.1
60:18 destruction within thy borders; 2050.1
62: 6 shall never hold their peace day **n** 2050.1
64: 4 **n** perceived by the ear, neither hath the 3808
65:17 shall not be remembered, **n** 3808+2050.1
65:19 heard in her, the voice of crying. 2050.1
65:20 an old man that hath not filled his 2050.1
65:23 in vain, **n** bring forth for trouble; 3808+2050.1
65:25 They shall not hurt **n** destroy in 2050.1

Jer 4:11 people, not to fan, **n** to cleanse, 3808+2050.1
5: 4 of the LORD, **n** the judgment of their God. NIH
5:12 neither shall we see sword **n** famine; 2050.1
6:19 my words, **n** *to* my law, but rejected it. 2050.1
6:20 your sacrifices sweet unto me. 3808+2050.1
6:25 forth *into* the field, **n** walk by the way; 2050.1
7:16 neither lift up cry **n** prayer for them, 2050.1
7:22 **n** commanded them in the day 3808+2050.1
7:24 inclined their ear, but walked 2050.1
7:26 inclined their ear, 3808+2050.1
7:28 their God, **n** receiveth correction: 3808+2050.1
7:32 **n** the valley of the son of Hinnom, 2050.1
8: 2 they shall not be gathered, **n** be 3808+2050.1
8:13 **n** figs on the fig tree, and the leaf 369+2050.1
9:16 whom neither they **n** their fathers have 2050.1
11: 8 inclined their ear, 3808+2050.1
13:14 I will not pity, **n** spare, nor have 3808+2050.1
13:14 have mercy, but destroy them. 2050.1
14:16 them, their wives, **n** their sons, nor 2050.1
14:16 nor their sons, **n** their daughters: 2050.1
15:10 neither lent on usury, **n** men 3808+2050.1
15:17 assembly of the mockers, **n** rejoiced; 2050.1
16: 2 shalt thou have sons **n** daughters 2050.1
16: 5 go to lament **n** bemoan them: 2050.1
16: 6 for them, **n** cut themselves, 3808+2050.1
16: 6 make themselves bald for 3808+2050.1
16:13 ye know not, *neither* ye **n** your fathers; 2050.1
17:21 bring *it* in by the gates of Jerusalem; 2050.1
17:23 **n** receive instruction. 1115+2050.1+3807.1
18:18 **n** counsel from the wise, nor the word 2050.1
18:18 the wise, **n** the word from the prophet. 2050.1
19: 4 whom neither they **n** their fathers have 2050.1
19: 4 **n** the kings of Judah, and have filled this 2050.1
19: 5 **n** spake *it*, neither came *it* into 3808+2050.1
19: 6 **n** The valley of the son of Hinnom, 2050.1
20: 9 **n** speak any more in his name. 3808+2050.1
21: 7 neither have pity, **n** have mercy. 3808+2050.1
22: 3 stranger, the fatherless, **n** the widow, 2050.1
22:10 no more, **n** see his native country. 2050.1
23: 4 fear no more, **n** be dismayed, 2050.1
23:32 them not, **n** commanded them: 2050.1
25: 4 **n** inclined your ear to hear. 2050.1
25:33 neither gathered, **n** buried; 3808+2050.1
25:35 the principal of the flock to 4480+2050.1
27: 9 to your diviners, nor to your dreamers 2050.1
27: 9 nor to your diviners, **n** to your dreamers 2050.1
27: 9 to your enchanters, nor to your 2050.1
27: 9 to your sorcerers, which speak unto 2050.1
31:40 **n** thrown down any more 3808+2050.1
35: 6 wine, *neither* ye, **n** your sons for ever: 2050.1
35: 7 **n** sow seed, nor plant vineyard, 3808+2050.1
35: 7 **n** plant vineyard, nor have *any:* 3808+2050.1
35: 7 have *any:* but all your days ye 3808+2050.1
35: 8 our wives, our sons, **n** our daughters; 2050.1
35: 9 **N** to build houses for us 1115+2050.1+3807.1
35: 9 we vineyard, **n** field, nor seed: 3808+2050.1
35: 9 we vineyard, nor field, **n** seed: 3808+2050.1
35:15 your ear, **n** hearkened unto me. 3808+2050.1
36:24 Yet they were not afraid, **n** rent 3808+2050.1
36:24 **n** any of his servants that heard all 2050.1
37: 2 he, **n** his servants, nor the people 2050.1
37: 2 his servants, **n** the people of the land, 2050.1
37:19 come against you, **n** against this land? 2050.1
42:14 **n** hear the sound of the trumpet, 3808+2050.1
42:14 **n** have hunger of bread; 3808+2050.1
42:21 any *thing* for the which he hath sent 2050.1
44: 3 *neither* they, you, **n** your fathers. 2050.1
44: 5 **n** inclined their ear to turn from 3808+2050.1
44:10 walked in my law, nor in my 3808+2050.1
44:10 in my statutes, that I set before you 2050.1
44:23 walked in his law, nor in his statutes, 2050.1
44:23 nor walked in his law, **n** in his statutes, 2050.1
44:23 his statutes, **n** in his testimonies; 3808+2050.1
46: 6 away, **n** the mighty *man* escape; 408+2050.1
49:31 which have neither gates **n** bars, 2050.1
49:33 **n** *any* son of man dwell in it. 3808+2050.1
51: 5 **n** Judah of his God, of the LORD of 2050.1
51:26 for a corner, **n** a stone for foundations; 2050.1
51:62 neither man **n** beast, but that it 5704+2050.1
La 2:22 anger none escaped **n** remained: 2050.1
3:33 For he doth not afflict willingly **n** grieve 2050.1
Eze 2: 6 be dismayed at their looks, 408+2050.1
3:18 speakest to warn the wicked 3808+2050.1
3:19 from this wicked way, he shall die in 2050.1
7:11 none of them *shall remain*, **n** of 3808+2050.1
7:11 multitude, **n** of any of theirs: 3808+2050.1
7:12 not the buyer rejoice, **n** the seller 408+2050.1
12:24 flattering divination within the house 2050.1
13:23 more vanity, **n** divine divinations: 3808+2050.1
14:16 deliver neither sons **n** daughters; 518+2050.1
14:18 they shall deliver neither sons **n** 2050.1
14:20 they shall deliver neither son **n** daughter; 518
16: 4 salted at all, **n** swaddled at all. 3808+2050.1
16:47 done after their abominations: 2050.1
16:48 she **n** her daughters, as thou hast done, 2050.1
18:17 *that* hath not received usury **n** 2050.1
20:18 **n** defile yourselves with their idols: 408+2050.1
20:44 according to your corrupt doings, 2050.1
22:24 **n** rained upon in the day of indignation. 3808
23:27 remember Egypt any more. 3808
24:16 yet neither shalt thou mourn **n** 3808+2050.1
24:22 *your* lips, **n** eat the bread of men. 3808+2050.1
24:23 ye shall not mourn **n** weep; 3808+2050.1
28:24 **n** *any* grieving thorn of all *that are* 2050.1
29: 5 be brought together, **n** gathered: 3808+2050.1

N

Eze	29:11	n foot of beast shall pass through 3808+2050.1
	29:18	yet had he no wages, n his army, 2050.1
	31: 8	n any tree in the garden of God was like 3808
	32:13	n the hoofs of beasts trouble 3808+2050.1
	37:23	n with their detestable things, nor with 2050.1
	37:23	n with any of their transgressions: 2050.1
	38:11	and having neither bars n gates, 2050.1
	43: 7	neither they, n their kings, by their 2050.1
	43: 7	n by the carcases of their kings in their 2050.1
	44: 9	in heart, uncircumcised in flesh, 2050.1
	44:13	n to come near to any of my holy 2050.1
	44:20	n suffer their locks to grow long; 3808+2050.1
	44:22	a widow, n her that is put away: 2050.1
	48:14	n alienate the firstfruits of the 3808+2050.1
Da	1: 8	n with the wine which he drank: 2050.1
	2:10	therefore there is no king, lord, n ruler, 2050.3
	3:12	n worship the golden image 3809+2050.3
	3:14	n worship the golden image 3809+2050.3
	3:18	n worship the golden image which thou 3809
	3:27	n was a hair of their head singed, 3809+2050.3
	3:27	n the smell of fire had passed on 3809+2050.3
	3:28	they might not serve n worship 3809+2050.3
	5: 8	n make known to the king 2050.3
	5:10	n let thy countenance be changed. 409+2050.3
	5:23	stone, which see not, n hear, nor know: 3809
	5:23	which see not, nor hear, n know: 3809+2050.3
	6: 4	they could find none occasion n fault; 2050.3
	6:13	n the decree that thou hast 5922+2050.3
	6:15	Persians is, That no decree n 3809+2050.3
	10: 3	neither came flesh n wine in my mouth, 2050.1
	11: 4	not to his posterity, n according 3808+2050.1
	11: 6	arm; neither shall he stand, n his arm: 2050.1
	11:20	neither in anger, n in battle. 3808+2050.1
	11:24	have not done, n his fathers' fathers; 2050.1
	11:37	n the desire of women, nor 3808+2050.1
	11:37	of women, n regard any god: 3808+2050.1
Hos	1: 7	by sword, nor by battle, by horses, 2050.1
	1: 7	by sword, n by battle, by horses, 2050.1
	1: 7	by battle, by horses, n by horsemen. 2050.1
	1:10	be measured n numbered; 3808+2050.1
	4: 1	because there is no truth, n mercy, 369+2050.1
	4: 1	n knowledge of God in the land. 369+2050.1
	4: 4	Yet let no man strive, n reprove 408+2050.1
	4:14	n your spouses when they commit 2050.1
	4:15	n swear, The Lord liveth. 408+2050.1
	5:13	yet could he not heal you n cure 3808+2050.1
	7:10	their God, n seek him for all this. 3808+2050.1
Am	5: 5	enter into Gilgal, and pass not 3808+2050.1
	8:11	n a thirst for water, but of 3808+2050.1
	9:10	The evil shall not overtake n prevent us. 2050.1
Ob	1:13	n have laid hands on their 408+2050.1
Jnh	3: 7	saying, Let neither man n beast, 2050.1
	3: 7	nor beast, herd n flock, taste any thing: 2050.1
	3: 7	let them not feed, n drink water: 408+2050.1
Mic	5: 7	n waiteth for the sons of men. 3808+2050.1
Zep	1: 6	that have not sought the Lord, n 3808+2050.1
	1:18	Neither their silver n their gold shall be 1571
	3:13	shall not do iniquity, n speak lies; 3808+2050.1
Zec	1: 4	they did not hear, n hearken unto 3808+2050.1
	4: 6	Not by might, n by power, but by 3808+2050.1
	7:10	n the fatherless, the stranger, 2050.1
	7:10	the fatherless, the stranger, n the poor; 2050.1
	7:14	man passed through n returned: 4480+2050.1
	8:10	hire for man, n any hire for beast; 369+2050.1
	11:16	n heal that that is broken, nor 3808+2050.1
	11:16	is broken, n feed that that standeth still: 3808
	14: 6	that the light shall not be clear, n dark: NIH
	14: 7	to the Lord, not day, n night: 3808+2050.1
Mal	4: 1	that it shall leave them neither root n 2050.1
Mt	5:35	N by the earth; for it is his footstool: 3383
	6:20	where neither moth n rust doth corrupt, 3777
	6:20	thieves do not break through n steal: 3777
	6:25	n yet for your body, what ye shall put on. 3366
	6:26	neither do they reap, n gather into barns; 3761
	10: 9	Provide neither gold, n silver, nor brass in 3366
	10: 9	nor silver, n brass in your purses; 3366
	10:10	N scrip for your journey, neither two coats 3361
	10:10	two coats, neither shoes, n yet staves: 3366
	10:14	n hear your words, when ye depart out of 3366
	10:24	his master, n the servant above his lord. 3761
	11:18	For John came neither eating n drinking, 3366
	12:19	shall not strive, n cry; neither shall any 3761
	22:29	the scriptures, n the power of God. 3366
	22:30	neither marry, n are given in marriage, 3777
	24:21	world to this time, no, n ever shall be. 3364
	25:13	for ye know neither the day n the hour 3761
Mk	6:11	n hear you, when ye depart thence, 3366
	8:26	the town, n tell it to any in the town. 3366
	12:25	neither marry, n are given in marriage; 3777
Lk	1:15	shall drink neither wine n strong drink; 2532
	6:44	n of a bramble bush gather they grapes. 3761
	7:33	neither eating bread n drinking wine; 3383
	9: 3	neither staves, n scrip, neither bread, 3383
	10: 4	Carry neither purse, n scrip, nor shoes: 3361
	10: 4	Carry neither purse, nor scrip, n shoes. 3366
	12:24	they neither sow n reap; which neither 3761
	12:24	which neither have storehouse n barn; 3366
	14:12	call not thy friends, n thy brethren, 3366
	14:12	thy kinsmen, n thy rich neighbours; 3366
	14:35	fit for the land, n yet for the dunghill; 3777
	17:23	there: go not after them, n follow them. 3366
	18: 4	I fear not God, n regard man; 2532+3756
	20:35	neither marry, n are given in marriage: 3777
	21:15	shall not be able to gainsay n resist. 3761
	22:68	you will not answer me, n let me go. 2228

Lk	23:15	No, n yet Herod: for I sent you to him; 3761
Jn	1:13	not of blood, n of the will of the flesh, 3761
	1:13	flesh, n of the will of man, but of God. 3761
	1:25	that Christ, n Elias, neither that prophet? 3777
	4:21	n yet at Jerusalem, worship the Father. 3777
	5:37	his voice at any time, n seen his shape. 3777
	8:19	Ye neither know me, n my Father: 3777
	9: 3	hath this man sinned, n his parents: 3777
	11:50	N consider that it is expedient for us, 3761
	12:40	n understand with their heart, 2532
	16: 3	they have not known the Father, n me. 3761
Ac	4:18	commanded them not to speak at all n 3366
	8:21	hast neither part n lot in this matter: 3761
	9: 9	without sight, and neither did eat n drink. 3761
	13:27	n yet the voices of the prophets which are 2532
	15:10	neither our fathers n we were able to 3777
	19:37	n yet blasphemers of your goddess. 3777
	23: 8	is no resurrection, neither angel n spirit: 3383
	23:12	saying that they would neither eat n drink 3383
	23:21	that they will neither eat n drink till they 3383
	24:12	neither in the synagogues, n in the city: 3777
	24:18	neither with multitude, n with tumult. 3761
	25: 8	against the temple, n yet against Cesar, 3777
	27:20	when neither sun n stars in many days 3383
Ro	8:38	n life, nor angels, nor principalities, 3777
	8:38	nor life, n angels, nor principalities, 3777
	8:38	nor life, nor angels, n principalities, 3777
	8:38	nor angels, nor principalities, n powers, 3777
	8:38	nor powers, n things present, 3777
	8:38	nor things present, n things to come, 3777
	8:39	N height, nor depth, nor any other 3777
	8:39	height, n depth, nor any other creature, 3777
	8:39	height, nor depth, n any other creature, 3777
	9:16	n of him that runneth, but of God that 3761
	14:21	good neither to eat flesh, n to drink wine, 3366
	14:21	n any thing whereby thy brother 3366
1Co	2: 6	n of the princes of this world, that come 3761
	2: 9	Eye hath not seen, n ear heard, 2532+3756
	6: 9	nor idolaters, nor adulterers, nor effeminate, 3777
	6: 9	idolaters, nor adulterers, nor effeminate, 3777
	6: 9	nor idolaters, nor adulterers, n effeminate, 3777
	6: 9	nor idolaters, n adulterers, nor effeminate, 3777
	6: 9	n abusers of themselves with mankind, 3777
	6:10	N thieves, nor covetous, nor drunkards, 3777
	6:10	Nor thieves, n covetous, nor drunkards, 3777
	6:10	nor covetous, n drunkards, nor revilers, 3756
	6:10	nor covetous, nor drunkards, n revilers, 3756
	6:10	drunkards, nor revilers, n extortioners, 3756
	10:32	neither to the Jews, n to the Gentiles, 2532
	10:32	to the Gentiles, n to the church of God: 2532
	12:21	n again the head to the feet, I have no 2228
2Co	4: 2	n handling the word of God deceitfully; 3366
	7:12	n for his cause that suffered wrong, 3761
Gal	3:28	There is neither Jew n Greek, there is 3761
	3:28	nor Greek, there is neither bond n free, 3761
	3:28	nor free, there is neither male n female: 2532
	4:14	in my flesh ye despised not, n rejected; 3761
	5: 6	availeth any thing, n uncircumcision; 3777
	6:15	availeth any thing, n uncircumcision, 3777
Eph	5: 4	foolish talking, nor jesting, 2532
	5: 4	nor foolish talking, n jesting, 2228
	5: 5	unclean person, nor covetous man who 2228
	5: 5	nor unclean person, n covetous man who 2228
Col	3:11	Where there is neither Greek n Jew, 2532
	3:11	circumcision n uncircumcision, barbarian, 2532
	3:11	barbarian, Scythian, bond n free: NIG
1Th	2: 3	of deceit, n of uncleanness, nor in guile: 3761
	2: 3	of deceit, nor of uncleanness, n in guile: 3777
	2: 5	as ye know, n a cloke of covetousness; 3777
	2: 6	N of men sought we glory, neither of you, 3777
	2: 6	we glory, neither of you, n yet of others, 3761
	5: 5	we are not of the night, n of darkness. 3761
2Th	2: 2	be troubled, neither by spirit, n by word, 3383
	2: 2	nor by word, n by letter as from us, 3383
1Ti	1: 7	what they say, n whereof they affirm. 3383
	2:12	n to usurp authority over the man, but to 3761
	6:16	whom no man hath seen, n can see: 3761
	6:17	n trust in uncertain riches, but in the 3366
2Ti	1: 8	of our Lord, n of me his prisoner: 3366
Heb	7: 3	neither beginning of days, n end of life; 3383
	9:25	N yet that he should offer himself often, 3761
	12: 5	nor faint when thou art rebuked of him: 3366
	12:18	with fire, n unto blackness, and darkness, 2532
	13: 5	I will never leave thee, n forsake thee. 3761
2Pe	1: 8	unfruitful in the knowledge of our Lord 3761
Rev	3:15	works, that thou art neither cold n hot: 3777
	3:16	art lukewarm, and neither cold n hot, 3777
	5: 3	n in earth, neither under the earth, 3761
	7: 1	the earth, n on the sea, nor on any tree. 3383
	7: 1	the earth, nor on the sea, n on any tree. 3383
	7: 3	the earth, nor the sea, n the trees, 3383
	7:16	shall the sun light on them, n any heat. 3761
	9:20	which neither can see, n hear, nor walk: 3777
	9:20	which neither can see, nor hear, n walk: 3777
	9:21	n of their sorceries, nor of their 3777
	9:21	n of their fornication, nor of their thefts. 3777
	9:21	nor of their fornication, n of their thefts. 3777
	14:11	and they have no rest day n night, 2532
	21: 4	no more death, neither sorrow, n crying, 3777

NORTH (132) [NORTHERN, NORTHWARD, NORTHWARDS]

Ge	28:14	the east, and to the n, and to the south: 6828
Ex	26:20	the n side there shall be twenty boards: 6828
	26:35	and thou shalt put the table on the n side. 6828
	27:11	likewise for the n side in length there 6828

Ex	36:25	which is toward the n corner, he made 6828
	38:11	for the n side the hangings were an 6828
Nu	2:25	shall be on the n side by their armies: 6828
	34: 7	this shall be your n border: from the great 6828
	34: 9	at Hazar-enan: this shall be your n border. 6828
	35: 5	and on the n side two thousand cubits; 6828
Jos	8:11	the city, and pitched on the n side of Ai, 6828
	8:13	even all the host that was on the n of 6828
	11: 2	to the kings that were on the n of 6828
	15: 5	their border in the n quarter was 6828+1886.5
	15: 6	and passed along by the n of Beth-arabah; 6828
	15:10	n side, and went down to 6828+1886.5
	16: 6	the sea to Michmethah on the n side; 6828
	17: 9	also was on the n side of the river, 6828
	17:10	they met together in Asher on the n, 6828
	18: 5	Joseph shall abide in their coasts on the n. 6828
	18:12	border on the n side was from Jordan; 6828
	18:12	up to the side of Jericho on the n side, 6828
	18:16	is in the valley of the giants on the n, 6828
	18:17	was drawn from the n, and went forth to 6828
	18:19	the outgoings of the border were at the n 6828
	19:14	the border compasseth it on the n side to 6828
	19:27	toward the n side of Beth-emek, 6828
	24:30	on the n side of the hill of Gaash. 6828
Jdg	2: 9	Ephraim, on the n side of the hill Gaash. 6828
	7: 1	Midianites were on the n side of them, 6828
	21:19	which is on the n side of Beth-el, 4480+6828
1Ki	7:25	three looking toward the n, 6828
2Ki	16:14	put it on the n side of the altar. 6828+1886.5
1Ch	9:24	toward the east, west, n, and south. 6828
2Ch	4: 4	three looking toward the n, 6828
Job	26: 7	He stretcheth out the n over the empty 6828
	37: 9	the whirlwind: and cold out of the n. 4215
	37:22	Fair weather cometh out of the n: with 6828
Ps	48: 2	is mount Zion, on the sides of the n, 6828
	89:12	The n and the south thou hast created 6828
	107: 3	the west, from the n, and from the south. 6828
Pr	25:23	The n wind driveth away rain: so doth an 6828
Ecc	1: 6	the south, and turneth about unto the n; 6828
	11: 3	fall toward the south, or toward the n, 6828
SS	4:16	Awake, O n wind; and come thou south; 6828
Isa	14:13	of the congregation, in the sides of the n: 6828
	14:31	for there shall come from the n a smoke, 6828
	41:25	I have raised up one from the n, 6828
	43: 6	I will say to the n, Give up; and to 6828
	49:12	lo, these from the n and from the west; 6828
Jer	1:13	the face thereof is towards the n. 6828+1886.5
	1:14	Out of the n an evil shall break forth 6828
	1:15	families of the kingdoms of the n, 6828+1886.5
	3:12	and proclaim these words toward the n, 6828
	3:18	n to the land that I have given for an 6828
	4: 6	I will bring evil from the n, and a great 6828
	6: 1	for evil appeareth out of the n, 6828
	6:22	a people cometh from the n country, 6828
	10:22	a great commotion out of the n country, 6828
	13:20	and behold them that come from the n: 6828
	16:15	children of Israel from the land of the n, 6828
	23: 8	of Israel out of the n country, 6828+1886.5
	25: 9	send and take all the families of the n, 6828
	25:26	all the kings of the n, far and near, one 6828
	31: 8	I will bring them from the n country, 6828
	46: 6	fall toward the n by the river Euphrates. 6828
	46:10	in the n country by the river Euphrates. 6828
	46:20	cometh; it cometh out of the n. 6828
	46:24	into the hand of the people of the n. 6828
	47: 2	waters rise up out of the n, and shall be 6828
	50: 3	For out of the n there cometh up a nation 6828
	50: 9	of great nations from the n country: 6828
	50:41	people shall come from the n, and a great 6828
	51:48	spoilers shall come unto her from the n, 6828
Eze	1: 4	behold, a whirlwind came out of the n, 6828
	8: 3	the inner gate that looketh toward the n; 6828
	8: 5	thine eyes now the way towards the n. 6828
	8: 5	I lift up mine eyes the way toward the n, 6828
	8:14	Lord's house which was towards the n; 6828
	9: 2	which lieth toward the n, and every man 6828
	20:47	all faces from the south to the n shall be 6828
	21: 4	against all flesh from the south to the n: 6828
	26: 7	the n, with horses, and with chariots, 6828
	32:30	There be the princes of the n, all of them, 6828
	38: 6	the house of Togarmah of the n quarters, 6828
	38:15	shalt come from thy place out of the n 6828
	39: 2	cause thee to come up from the n parts, 6828
	40:20	outward court that looked toward the n, 6828
	40:23	was over against the gate toward the n; 6828
	40:35	he brought me to the n gate, 6828
	40:40	goeth up to the entry of the n 6828+1886.5
	40:44	which was at the side of the n gate; 6828
	40:44	gate having the prospect toward the n. 6828
	40:46	chamber whose prospect is toward the n 6828
	41:11	one door toward the n, and another door 6828
	42: 1	the utter court, the way toward the n: 6828
	42: 1	was before the building toward the n. 6828
	42: 2	of an hundred cubits was the n door, 6828
	42: 4	one cubit; and their doors toward the n, 6828
	42:11	the chambers which were toward the n, 6828
	42:13	The n chambers and the south chambers, 6828
	42:17	measured the n side, five hundred reeds, 6828
	44: 4	brought he me the way of the n gate 6828
	46: 9	that entereth in by the way of the n gate 6828
	46: 9	forth by the way of the n gate: 6828+1886.5
	46:19	which looked toward the n: 6828
	47:15	of the land toward the n side, 6828+1886.5
	47:17	n northward, and the border of Hamath. 6828
	47:17	border of Hamath. And this is the n side. 6828

N

Eze	48: 1	From the **n** end to the coast of 6828+1886.5
	48:10	toward the **n** five and twenty thousand *in* 6828
	48:16	the **n** side four thousand and five hundred, 6828
	48:17	suburbs of the city shall be toward the **n** 6828
	48:30	on the **n** side, four thousand and 6828
Da	11: 6	the king of the **n** to make an agreement: 6828
	11: 7	enter into the fortress of the king of the **n**, 6828
	11: 8	*more* years than the king of the **n**. 6828
	11:11	with him, *even* with the king of the **n:** 6828
	11:13	For the king of the **n** shall return, 6828
	11:15	the king of the **n** shall come, and cast up 6828
	11:40	the king of the **n** shall come against him 6828
	11:44	east and out of the **n** shall trouble him: 6828
Am	8:12	from the **n** even to the east, they shall run 6828
Zep	2:13	he will stretch out his hand against the **n**, 6828
Zec	2: 6	*forth*, and flee from the land of the **n**, 6828
	6: 6	*are* therein go forth into the **n** country; 6828
	6: 8	these that go toward the **n** country have 6828
	6: 8	have quieted my spirit in the **n** country. 6828
	14: 4	the mountain shall remove toward the **n**, 6828
Lk	13:29	and from the **n**, and *from* the south, 1005
Ac	27:12	lieth toward the south west and **n west**. 5566
Rev	21:13	the east three gates; on the **n** three gates; 1005

NORTHEASTER See EUROCLYDON

NORTHERN (2) [NORTH]

| Jer | 15:12 | Shall iron break the **n** iron and 4480+6828 |
| Joel | 2:20 | will remove far off from you the **n** *army*, 6830 |

NORTHWARD (23) [NORTH]

Ge	13:14	from the place where thou *art* **n**, 6828+1886.5
Ex	40:22	the side of the tabernacle **n**, 6828+1886.5
Lev	1:11	of the altar **n** before the LORD: 6828+1886.5
Dt	2: 3	long enough: turn you **n**. 6828+1886.5
	3:27	**n**, and southward, and eastward, 6828+1886.5
Jos	3: 1	unto the borders of Ekron **n**, 6828+1886.5
	15: 7	**n**, looking toward Gilgal, that *is* 6828+1886.5
	15: 8	end of the valley of the giants **n:** 6828+1886.5
	15:11	out unto the side of Ekron **n**, 6828+1886.5
	17:10	**n** *it was* Manasseh's, and the sea 6828+1886.5
	18:18	the side over against Arabah **n**, 6828+1886.5
	18:19	to the side of Beth-hoglah **n:** 6828+1886.5
Jdg	12: 1	went **n**, and said unto Jephthah, 6828+1886.5
1Sa	14: 5	situate **n** over against Michmash, 4480+6828
1Ch	26:14	cast lots; and his lot came out **n**. 6828+1886.5
	26:17	**n** four a day, southward four a 6828+1886.5
Eze	8: 5	**n** at the gate of the altar this 4480+6828
	40:19	an hundred cubits east*ward* and **n**. 6828
	47: 2	me out *of* the way of the gate **n**, 6828+1886.5
	47:17	north **n**, and the border of 6828+1886.5
	48: 1	the border of Damascus **n**, 6828+1886.5
	48:31	gates **n**; one gate of Reuben, 6828+1886.5
Da	8: 4	and **n**, and southward; 6828+1886.5

NORTHWARDS (1) [NORTH]

| Nu | 3:35 | on the side of the tabernacle **n**. 6828+1886.5 |

NOSE (12) [NOSES]

Lev	21:18	or he that hath a **flat n**, or any thing, 2763
2Ki	19:28	therefore I will put my hook in thy **n**, 639
Job	40:24	his eyes: *his* **n** pierceth through snares. 639
	41: 2	Canst thou put a hook into his **n**? or bore 639
Pr	30:33	the wringing of the **n** bringeth forth blood; 639
SS	7: 4	thy **n** *is* as the tower of Lebanon which 639
	7: 8	vine, and the smell of thy **n** like apples; 639
Isa	3:21	The rings, and **n** jewels, 639
	37:29	therefore will I put my hook in thy **n**, 639
	65: 5	These *are* a smoke in my **n**, a fire that 639
Eze	8:17	and lo, they put the branch to their **n**. 639
	23:25	they shall take away thy **n** and thine ears; 639

NOSES (2) [NOSE]

| Ps | 115: 6 | hear not: **n** have they, but they smell not: 639 |
| Eze | 39:11 | and it *shall* stop the **n** *of the* passengers: NIH |

NOSTRILS (15)

Ge	2: 7	and breathed into his **n** the breath of life; 639
	7:22	All in whose **n** *was* the breath of life, of all 639
Ex	15: 8	with the blast of thy **n** the waters were 639
Nu	11:20	until it come out at your **n**, and it be 639
2Sa	22: 9	There went up a smoke out of his **n**, 639
	22:16	at the blast of the breath of his **n**. 639
Job	4: 9	by the breath of his **n** are they consumed. 639
	27: 3	*is* in me, and the spirit of God *is* in my **n**; 5170
	39:20	grasshopper? the glory of his **n** is terrible. 639
	41:20	Out of his **n** goeth smoke, as *out of a* 5156
Ps	18: 8	There went up a smoke out of his **n**, 639
	18:15	O LORD, at the blast of the breath of thy **n**. 639
Isa	2:22	ye from man, whose breath *is* in his **n**: 639
La	4:20	The breath of our **n**, the anointed of 639
Am	4:10	of your camps to come up unto your **n**: 639

NOT (6596) [NO] See Index of Articles, Etc.

NOTABLE (5) [NOTE]

Da	8: 5	the goat *had* a **n** horn between his eyes. 2380
	8: 8	for it came up four **n** ones toward the 2380
Mt	27:16	And they had then a **n** prisoner, 1978
Ac	2:20	*that* great and **n** day of the Lord come: 2016
	4:16	that indeed a **n** miracle hath been done 1110

NOTE (3) [NOTABLE, NOTED]

Isa	30: 8	before them in a table, and **n** it in a book, 2710
Ro	16: 7	who are of **n** among the apostles, 1978
2Th	3:14	**n** that *man*, and have no company with 4593

NOTED (1) [NOTE]

| Da | 10:21 | I will shew thee that which is **n** in 7559 |

NOTHING (225) [THING]

Ge	11: 6	will be restrained from them, 3605+3808
	19: 8	only unto these men do **n**; 408+1697
	26:29	as we have done unto thee **n** *but* good, 7535
	40:15	here also have I done **n** that they 3808+3972
Ex	9: 4	when shall **n** die of all *that is* 1697+3808
	12:10	shall let **n** of it remain until the morning; 3808
	12:20	Ye shall eat **n** leavened; in all your 3605+3808
	16:18	he that gathered much had **n** over, 3808
	21: 2	in the seventh he shall go out free **for n**. 2600
	22: 3	if he have **n**, then he shall be sold for his 369
	23:26	There shall **n** cast their young, nor be 3808
Nu	6: 4	eat **n** that is made of the vine tree, 3605+3808
	11: 6	*there is* **n** at all, beside *this* manna, 369
	16:26	wicked men, and touch **n** of theirs, 408+3605
	22:16	Let **n**, I pray thee, hinder thee from 408
Dt	2: 7	hast been with thee; thou hast lacked **n**. 1697+3808
	20:16	shalt save alive **n** that breatheth: 3605+3808
	22:26	unto the damsel thou shalt do **n**; 1697+3808
	28:55	because he hath **n** left him in 1097+3605
Jos	11:15	he left **n** undone of all that 1697+3808
Jdg	3: 2	the least such as before knew **n** thereof: 3808
	7:14	This *is* **n** else save the sword of 369+1115
	14: 6	rent a kid, and *he had* **n** in his hand: 369+3972
1Sa	3:18	told him every whit, and hid **n** from him. 3808
	20: 2	my father will do **n** *either* great or 1697+3808
	22:15	for thy servant knew **n** of all this, 1697+3808
	25:21	that **n** was missed of all that 3808+3972
	25:36	wherefore she told him **n**, less or 1697+3808
	27: 1	*there is* **n** better for me than that I should 369
	30:19	there was **n** lacking to them, neither small 3808
2Sa	12: 3	the poor *man* had **n**, save one little 369+3605
	24:24	my God of that which doth **cost** me **n**. 2600
1Ki	4:27	*man in* his month: they lacked **n**. 1697+3808
	8: 9	There was **n** in the ark save the two tables 369
	10:21	it was **n** accounted of in the days of 3808+3972
	11:22	he answered, **N**: howbeit let me go in any 3808
	18:43	and looked, and said, There is **n**. 369+3972
	22:16	shall I adjure thee that thou tell me **n** 3808
2Ki	10:10	unto the earth **n** of the word of the LORD, 3808
	20:13	there was in his house, nor in all 1697+3808
	20:15	there is **n** among my treasures that I 1697+3808
	20:17	**n** shall be left, saith the LORD. 1697+3808
2Ch	5:10	*There was* **n** in the ark save the two tables 369
	9: 2	was **n** hid from Solomon which 1697+3808
	14:11	said, LORD, *it is* **n** with thee to help, 369
	18:15	times shall I adjure thee that thou say **n** 3808
Ezr	4: 3	You have **n** to do with us to build a house 3808
Ne	2: 2	this *is* **n** *else* but sorrow of heart. 369
	5: 8	peace, and found **n** to answer. 1697+3808
	5:12	restore *them*, and will require **n** of them; 3808
	8:10	send portions unto *them* for whom **n** is 369
	9:21	in the wilderness, *so that* they lacked **n**. 3808
Est	2:15	she required **n** but what Hegai 1697+3808
	5:13	Yet all this availeth me **n**, so long as I see 369
	6: 3	unto him, There is **n** done for him. 1697+3808
	6:10	let **n** fail of all that thou hast spoken. 408+1697
Job	6:18	turned aside; they go to **n**, and perish. 8414
	6:21	now ye are **n**; ye see *my* casting down, 3808
	8: 9	know **n**, because our days upon earth *are* 3808
	24:25	me a liar, and make my speech **n** worth? 408
	26: 7	and hangeth the earth upon **n**. 1097+4100
	34: 9	It profiteth a man **n** that he should delight 3808
Ps	17: 3	thou hast tried me, *and* shalt find **n**; 1077
	19: 6	and there is **n** hid from the heat thereof. 369
	39: 5	and mine age *is* as **n** before thee: 369
	49:17	he dieth he shall carry **n** 3605+3808+1886.1
	119:165	love thy law: and **n** *shall* offend them. 369
Pr	8: 8	*there is* **n** froward or perverse in them. 369
	9:13	she *is* simple, and knoweth **n**. 1077+4100
	10: 2	Treasures of wickedness profit **n**: 3808
	13: 4	soul of the sluggard desireth, and *hath* **n**: 369
	13: 7	that maketh himself rich, yet *hath* **n**: 369+3605
	20: 4	shall he beg in harvest, and have **n**. 369
	22:27	If thou hast **n** to pay, why should he take 369
Ecc	2:24	*There is* **n** better for a man, *than* that he 369
	3:14	**n** can be put to it, nor any thing taken from 369
	3:22	Wherefore I perceive that *there is* **n** better, 369
	5:14	a son, and *there is* **n** in his hand. 369+3972
	5:15	shall take **n** of his labour, which he 3808+3972
	6: 2	he wanteth **n** for his soul of all that he 369
	7:14	that man should find **n** after him. 3808+3972
Isa	34:12	*be* there, and all her princes shall be **n**. 657
	39: 2	there was in his house, nor in all 1697+3808
	39: 4	there is **n** among my treasures 1697+3808
	39: 6	**n** shall be left, saith the LORD. 1697+3808
	40:17	All nations before him *are* as **n**; and they 369
	40:17	and they are counted to him less than **n**, 657
	40:23	That bringeth the princes to **n**; he maketh 369
	41:11	they shall be as **n**; and they that strive 369
	41:12	they that war against thee shall be as **n**, 369
	41:24	ye *are* of **n**, and your work of nought: 369
	41:29	they *are* all vanity; their works *are* **n**: 657
	44:10	a graven image *that* is profitable for **n**? 1115
Jer	10:24	in thine anger, lest thou **bring me to n**. 4591
	13: 7	it was profitable for **n**. 3605+3808+1886.1
	13:10	which is good for **n**. 3605+3808+1886.1
	32:17	there is **n** too hard for thee: 1697+3605+3808
	32:23	they have done **n** of all that thou 3808
	38:14	ask thee a thing; hide **n** from me. 408+1697
	39:10	which had **n**, in the land of Judah, 369+3972
	42: 4	I will keep **n** back from you. 1697+3808

Jer	50:26	destroy her utterly: let **n** of her be left. 408
La	1:12	*Is it* **n** to you, all ye that pass by? behold, 3808
Eze	13: 3	follow their own spirit, and have seen **n**! 1115
Da	4:35	inhabitants of the earth *are* reputed as **n**: 3809
Joel	2: 3	yea, and **n** shall escape them. 3808
Am	3: 4	lion cry out of his den, if he have taken **n**? 1115
	3: 5	from the earth, and have taken **n** at all? 3808
	3: 7	Surely the Lord GOD will do **n**, 3808+3972
Hag	2: 3	not in your eyes in comparison of it as **n**? 369
Mt	5:13	it is thenceforth good for **n**, but to be cast 3762
	10:26	for there is **n** covered, that shall not be 3762
	15:32	now three days, and have **n** to eat: 3756+5101
	17:20	and **n** shall be unpossible unto you. 3762
	21:19	he came to it, and found **n** thereon, 3762
	23:16	shall swear by the temple, it is **n**; 3762
	23:18	Whosoever shall swear by the altar, it is **n**; 3762
	26:62	and said unto him, Answerest thou **n**? 3762
	27:12	chief priests and elders, he answered **n**. 3762
	27:19	Have thou **n** to do with that just *man:* for 3367
	27:24	When Pilate saw that he could prevail **n**, 3762
Mk	1:44	thou say **n** to any *man:* but go thy way, 3367
	4:22	For there is **n** hid, which shall not be 3756
	5:26	was **n** bettered, but rather grew worse, 3367
	6: 8	that they should take **n** for *their* journey, 3367
	6:36	for they have **n** to eat. 3756+5101
	7:15	There is **n** from without a man, 3762
	8: 1	having **n** to eat, Jesus called his 3361+5101
	8: 2	me three days, and have **n** to eat: 3756+5101
	9:29	This kind can come forth by **n**, but by 3762
	11:13	he came to it, he found **n** but leaves; 3762
	14:60	asked Jesus, saying, Answerest thou **n**? 3762
	14:61	But he held his peace, and answered **n**. 3762
	15: 3	him of many *things:* but he answered **n**. 3762
	15: 4	him again, saying, Answerest thou **n**? 3762
	15: 5	But Jesus yet answered **n**; so that Pilate 3762
Lk	1:37	For with God **n** shall be 3756+3956+4487
	4: 2	And in those days he did eat **n**: 3762
	5: 5	toiled all the night, and have taken **n**: 3762
	6:35	do good, and lend, hoping for **n** again; 3367
	7:42	And when they had **n** to pay, he frankly 3361
	8:17	For **n** is secret, that shall not be made 3756
	9: 3	Take **n** for *your* journey, neither staves, 3367
	10:19	and **n** shall by any means hurt you. 3762
	11: 6	me, and I have **n** to set before him: 3739+3756
	12: 2	For there is **n** covered, that shall not be 3762
	22:35	lacked ye any *thing?* And they said, **N**. 3762
	23: 9	in many words; but he answered him **n**. 3762
	23:15	lo, **n** worthy of death is done unto him. 3762
	23:41	deeds: but this *man* hath done **n** amiss. 3762
Jn	3:27	and said, A man can receive **n**, 3762
	4:11	thou hast **n** to draw with, and the well 3777
	5:19	The Son can do **n** of himself, but what he 3762
	5:30	I can of mine own self do **n**: as I hear, 3762
	6:12	that remain, that **n** be lost. 3361+5100
	6:39	given me I should lose **n**, 846+1537+3361
	6:63	that quickeneth; the flesh profiteth **n**: 3762
	7:26	speaketh boldly, and they say **n** unto him. 3762
	8:28	that I am *he*, and *that* I do **n** of myself; 3762
	8:54	If I honour myself, my honour is **n**: 3762
	9:33	this *man* were not of God, he could do **n**. 3762
	11:49	said unto them, Ye know **n** at all, 3756+3762
	12:19	Perceive ye how ye prevail **n**? 3762
	14:30	of this world cometh, and hath **n** in me. 3762
	15: 5	much fruit: for without me ye can do **n**. 3762
	16:23	And in that day ye shall ask me **n**. Verily, 3762
	16:24	Hitherto have ye asked **n** in my name: 3762
	18:20	always resort; and in secret have I said **n**. 3762
	21: 3	and that night they caught **n**. 3762
Ac	4:14	with them, they could say **n** against *it*. 3762
	4:21	finding **n** how they might punish them, 3367
	10:20	down, and go with them, doubting **n**: 3367
	11: 8	**n** common or unclean hath
		at any time 3763+3956
	11:12	Spirit bade me go with them, **n** doubting. 3367
	17:21	were there spent their time in **n** else, 3762
	19:36	ye ought to be quiet, and to do **n** rashly. 3367
	20:20	*And* how I kept back **n** that was profitable 3762
	21:24	were informed concerning thee, are **n**; 3762
	23:14	*we* will eat **n** until we have slain Paul. 3367
	23:29	have **n** laid to his charge worthy of death 3367
	25:25	when I found that he had committed **n** 3367
	26:31	This man doeth **n** worthy of death or 3762
	27:33	and continued fasting, having taken **n**. 3367
	28:17	though I have committed **n** against 3762
Ro	14:14	Jesus, that *there is* **n** unclean of itself: 3762
1Co	1:19	will **bring to n** the understanding of 114
	4: 4	For I know **n** by myself; yet am I not 3762
	4: 5	Therefore judge **n** before the 3361+5100
	7:19	Circumcision is **n**, and uncircumcision is 3762
	7:19	uncircumcision is **n**, but the keeping of 3762
	8: 2	he knoweth **n** yet as he ought to know. 3762
	8: 4	we know that an idol *is* **n** in the world, 3762
	9:16	I preach the gospel, I have **n** to glory of: 3756
	13: 2	and have no charity, I am **n**. 3762
	13: 3	and have not charity, it profiteth me **n**. 3762
2Co	6:10	as having **n**, and *yet* possessing all *things*. 3367
	7: 9	that ye might receive damage by us in **n**. 3367
	8:15	He that *had* gathered much had **n** over; 3756
	12:11	for *in* **n** am I behind the very chiefest 3762
	12:11	the very chiefest apostles, though I be **n**. 3762
	13: 8	For we can do **n** against the truth, 3756+5100
Gal	2: 6	*somewhat* in conference added **n** to me: 3762
	4: 1	as he is a child, differeth **n** from a servant, 3762
	5: 2	be circumcised, Christ shall profit you **n**. 3762
	6: 3	when he is **n**, he deceiveth himself. 3367

N

Php	1:20	that in **n** I shall be ashamed, but *that* with	3762
	1:28	And in **n** terrified by *your* adversaries:	3367
	2: 3	*Let* **n** be done through strife or vainglory;	3367
	4: 6	Be careful for **n**; but in every *thing* by	3367
1Th	4:12	and *that* ye may have lack of **n**.	3367
1Ti	4: 4	Of God *is* good, and **n** to be refused,	3762
	5:21	one before another, doing **n** by partiality.	3367
	6: 4	knowing **n**, but doting about questions	3367
	6: 7	we brought **n** into *this* world, *and it is*	3762
	6: 7	*and it is* certain we can carry **n** out.	3761+5100
Tit	1:15	that are defiled and unbelieving *is* **n** pure;	3762
	3:13	that **n** be wanting unto them.	3367
Phm	1:14	without thy mind would I do **n**; that thy	3762
Heb	2: 8	he left **n** *that is* not put under him.	3762
	7:14	of which tribe Moses spake **n** concerning	3762
	7:19	For the law made **n** perfect,	3762
Jas	1: 4	ye may be perfect and entire, wanting **n**.	3367
	1: 6	let him ask in faith, **n** wavering: for he	3367
3Jn	1: 7	they went forth, taking **n** of the Gentiles.	3367
Rev	3:17	increased with goods, and have need of **n**;	3762

NOTICE (2)

2Sa	3:36	all the people **took n** *of it*, and it pleased	5234
2Co	9: 5	whereof *ye* **had n before**, that the same	4293

NOTWITHSTANDING (36)

Ex	16:20	**N** they hearkened not unto Moses;	2050.1
	21:21	**N**, if he continue a day or two, he shall not	389
Lev	25:32	the cities of the Levites, *and the*	2050.1
	27:28	**N** no devoted thing, that a man shall	389
Nu	26:11	**N** the children of Korah died not.	2050.1
	26:55	**N** the land shall be divided by lot:	389
Dt	1:26	**N** ye would not go up,	2050.1
	12:15	**N** thou mayest kill and eat flesh in all thy	7535
Jos	22:19	**N**, if the land of your possession	389+2050.1
Jdg	4: 9	the journey that thou takest shall	657+3588
	9: 5	**n yet** Jotham the youngest son of	2050.1
1Sa	2:25	**N** they hearkened not unto	3808+2050.1
	20: 8	**n**, if there be in me iniquity, slay me	2050.1
	29: 9	**n** the princes of the Philistines have said,	389
2Sa	24: 4	**N** the king's word prevailed against	2050.1
1Ki	2:17	**N** in thy days I will not do it for David	389
2Ki	17:14	**N** they would not hear, but hardened	2050.1
	23:26	the LORD turned not from the fierceness	389
2Ch	6: 9	**N** thou shalt not build the house;	7535
	32:26	**N** Hezekiah humbled himself for	2050.1
Jer	35:14	**n** I have spoken unto you, rising early	2050.1
Eze	20:21	**N** the children rebelled against me:	2050.1
Mic	7:13	**N** the land shall be desolate because	2050.1
Mt	2:22	**n**, being warned of God in a dream,	1161
	11:11	**n** he that is least in the kingdom of	1161
	17:27	**N**, lest we should offend them, go thou to	1161
Lk	10:11	**n** be ye sure of this, that the kingdom of	4133
	10:20	**N** in this rejoice not, that the spirits are	4133
Ac	15:34	**N** it pleased Silas to abide there *still*.	1161
	24: 4	**N**, that I be not further tedious unto thee,	1161
Php	1:18	**n**, every way, whether in pretence,	4133
	4:14	**N** ye have well done, that ye did	4133
1Ti	2:15	**N** she shall be saved in childbearing, if	1161
2Ti	4:17	**N** the Lord stood with me,	1161
Jas	2:16	**n** ye give them not those *things* which	1161
Rev	2:20	**N** I have a few *things* against thee,	235

NOUGHT (36) [NAUGHT]

Ge	29:15	shouldest thou therefore serve me **for n**?	2600
Dt	13:17	there shall cleave **n** of the cursed	3808+3972
	15: 9	thy poor brother, and thou givest him **n**;	3808
	28:63	to destroy you, and to **bring you** to **n**;	8045
Ne	4:15	God had **brought** their counsel **to n**,	6565
Job	1: 9	and said, Doth Job fear God **for n**?	2600
	8:22	place of the wicked shall **come to n**.	369
	14:18	surely the mountain falling **cometh to n**,	5034
	22: 6	taken a pledge from thy brother **for n**,	2600
Ps	33:10	**bringeth** the counsel of the heathen **to n**,	6331
	44:12	Thou sellest thy people **for n**,	1952+3808
Pr	1:25	ye have **set at n** all my counsel,	6544
Isa	8:10	counsel together, and it shall **come to n**,	6565
	29:20	For the **terrible one** is brought **to n**,	6184
	29:21	and turn aside the just for a **thing of n**.	8414
	41:12	shall be as nothing, and as a **thing of n**.	657
	41:24	*ye are* of nothing, and your work of **n**:	659
	49: 4	I have spent my strength **for n**, and in vain:	8414
	52: 3	the LORD, Ye have sold yourselves **for n**;	2600
	52: 5	that my people is taken away **for n**?	2600
Jer	14:14	a **thing** of **n**, and the deceit of their heart.	457
Am	5: 5	into captivity, and Beth-el shall come to **n**.	205
	6:13	which rejoice in a thing of **n**, which say,	3808
Mal	1:10	that would shut the doors **for n**?	NIH
	1:10	do ye kindle *fire* on mine altar **for n**.	2600
Mk	9:12	**must suffer many** *things*, and be **set at n**.	1847
Lk	23:11	Herod with his men of war **set** him **at n**,	1848
Ac	4:11	This is the stone which was **set at n** of	1848
	5:36	were scattered, and brought to **n**.	3762
	5:38	or this work be of men, it will **come to n**:	2647
	19:27	this our craft is in danger to be **set at n**;	557
Ro	14:10	or why dost thou **set at n** thy brother?	1848
1Co	1:28	are not, to **bring to n** *things* that are:	2673
	2: 6	the princes of this world, that **come to n**:	2673
2Th	3: 8	Neither did we eat any *man's* bread **for n**;	1432
Rev	18:17	in one hour so great riches is **come to n**.	2049

NOURISH (5) [NOURISHED, NOURISHER, NOURISHETH, NOURISHING, NOURISHMENT]

Ge	45:11	there will I **n** thee; for yet *there are* five	3557
	50:21	I will **n** you and your little ones. And he	3557

Isa	7:21	*that* a man shall **n** a young cow,	2421
	23: 4	neither do I **n up** young men, *nor* bring	1431
	44:14	he planteth an ash, and the rain doth **n** *it*.	1431

NOURISHED (10) [NOURISH]

Ge	47:12	Joseph his father, and his brethren,	3557
2Sa	12: 3	lamb, which he had bought and **n up**:	2421
Isa	1: 2	I have **n** and brought up children,	1431
Eze	19: 2	she **n** her whelps among young lions.	7235
Ac	7:20	**n up** in his father's house three months:	397
	7:21	took him up, and **n** for her own son.	397
	12:20	their country was **n** by the king's *country*.	5142
1Ti	4: 6	**n up** in the words of faith and of good	1789
Jas	5: 5	ye have **n** your hearts, as in a day of	5142
Rev	12:14	where she is **n** for a time, and times,	5142

NOURISHER (1) [NOURISH]

Ru	4:15	of *thy* life, and a **n** of thine old age:	3557

NOURISHETH (1) [NOURISH]

Eph	5:29	but **n** and cherisheth it, even as the Lord	1625

NOURISHING (1) [NOURISH]

Da	1: 5	so **n** them three years, that at the end	1431

NOURISHMENT (1) [NOURISH]

Col	2:19	by joints and bands having **n ministered**,	2023

NOVICE (1)

1Ti	3: 6	Not a **n**, lest being lifted up with pride he	3504

NOW (1356)

Ge	2:23	This *is* **n** bone of my bones, and flesh of	6471
	3: 1	**N** the serpent was more subtil than any	2050.1
	3:22	**n**, lest he put forth his hand, and take also	6258
	4:11	**n** *art* thou cursed from the earth, which	6258
	10: 1	**N** these *are* the generations of the sons	2050.1
	11: 6	**n** nothing will be restrained from them,	6258
	11:27	**N** these *are* the generations of Terah:	2050.1
	12: 1	**N** the LORD had said unto Abram,	2050.1
	12:11	that he said unto Sarai his wife, Behold **n**,	4994
	12:19	**n** therefore behold thy wife, take *her*, and	6258
	13:14	Lift up **n** thine eyes, and look from	4994
	15: 5	Look **n** towards heaven, and tell the stars,	4994
	16: 1	**N** Sarai Abram's wife bare him no	4994
	16: 2	Sarai said unto Abram, Behold **n**,	4994
	18: 3	if **n** I have found favour in thy sight,	4994
	18:11	**N** Abraham and Sarah *were* old *and*	2050.1
	18:21	I will go down **n**, and see whether they	4994
	18:27	Abraham answered and said, Behold **n**,	4994
	18:31	he said, Behold **n**, I have taken upon me	4994
	19: 2	Behold **n**, my lords, turn in, I pray you,	4994
	19: 8	Behold **n**, I have two daughters which	4994
	19:10	**n** will we deal worse with thee, than with	6258
	19:19	Behold **n**, thy servant hath found grace in	4994
	19:20	Behold **n**, this city *is* near to flee unto,	4994
	20: 7	**n** therefore restore the man *his* wife; for	6258
	21:23	**N** therefore swear unto me here by God	6258
	22: 2	he said, Take **n** thy son, thine only *son*	4994
	22:12	for **n** I know that thou fearest God,	6258
	24:42	if **n** thou do prosper my way which I go:	4994
	24:49	**n** if ye will deal kindly and truly with my	6258
	25:12	**N** these *are* the generations of Ishmael,	2050.1
	26:22	For **n** the LORD hath made room for us,	6258
	26:28	said, Let there be **n** an oath betwixt us,	4994
	26:29	thou *art* **n** the blessed of the LORD.	6258
	27: 2	he said, Behold **n**, I am old, I know not	4994
	27: 3	**N** therefore take, I pray thee, thy	6258
	27: 8	**N** therefore, my son, obey my voice	6258
	27: 9	**Go n** to the flock, and fetch me from	4994
	27:26	Come near **n**, and kiss me, my son.	4994
	27:36	he hath taken away my blessing.	6258
	27:37	and what shall I do **n** unto thee, my son?	645
	27:43	**N** therefore, my son, obey my voice;	6258
	29:32	**n** therefore my husband will love me.	6258
	29:34	**N** *this* time will my husband be joined	6258
	29:35	she said, **N** will I praise	6471+1886.1
	30:20	**n** will my husband dwell with me,	6471
	30:30	and it is **n** increased unto a multitude;	NIH
	30:30	**n** when shall I provide for mine own	6258
	31:12	he said, Lift up **n** thine eyes, and see,	4994
	31:13	**n** arise, get thee out from this land,	6258
	31:16	**n** then, whatsoever God hath said unto	6258
	31:25	**N** Jacob had pitched his tent in	2050.1
	31:28	thou hast **n** done foolishly in *so* doing.	6258
	31:30	**n**, *though* thou wouldest needs be gone,	6258
	31:34	**N** Rachel had taken the images,	2050.1
	31:42	surely thou hadst sent me away **n** empty.	6258
	31:44	**N** therefore come thou, let us make a	2050.1
	32: 4	with Laban, and stayed *there* until **n**:	6258
	32:10	Jordan; and I am become two bands.	6258
	33:10	if **n** I have found grace in thy sight, then	4994
	33:15	Let me **n** leave with thee *some* of the folk	4994
	34: 5	**n** his sons were with his cattle in	2050.1
	35:22	Israel heard *it*. **N** the sons of Jacob were	2050.1
	36: 1	**N** these *are* the generations of Esau,	2050.1
	37: 3	**N** Israel loved Joseph more than all his	2050.1
	37:20	Come **n** therefore, and let us slay him,	6258
	37:32	know **n** whether it *be* thy son's coat or	4994
	41:33	**N** therefore let Pharaoh look out a man	6258
	42: 1	**N when** Jacob saw that there was corn	2050.1
	43:10	we had returned this second time.	6258
	43:11	said unto them, If *it must be* so **n**, do this;	645
	44:10	**N** also *let* it *be* according unto your	6258
	44:30	**N** therefore when I come to thy servant	6258

Ge	44:33	**N** therefore, I pray thee, let thy servant	6258
	45: 5	**N** therefore be not grieved, nor angry	6258
	45: 8	So **n** *it was* not you *that* sent me hither,	6258
	45:19	**N** thou art commanded, this do ye;	2050.1
	46:30	Israel said unto Joseph, **N** let me	6471+1886.1
	46:34	about cattle from our youth even until **n**,	6258
	47: 4	**n** therefore, we pray thee, let thy servants	6258
	47:29	If **n** I have found grace in thy sight, put,	4994
	48: 5	thy two sons, Ephraim and Manasseh,	6258
	48:10	**N** the eyes of Israel were dim for age,	2050.1
	50: 4	If **n** I have found grace in your eyes,	4994
	50: 5	**N** therefore let me go up, I pray thee,	6258
	50:17	Forgive, I pray thee **n**, the trespass of thy	4994
	50:17	**n**, we pray thee, forgive the trespass of	6258
	50:21	**N** therefore fear ye not: I will nourish you	6258
Ex	1: 1	**N** these *are* the names of the children	2050.1
	1: 8	**N** there arose up a new king over Egypt,	2050.1
	2:15	**N when** Pharaoh heard this thing,	2050.1
	2:16	the priest of Midian had seven	2050.1
	3: 1	**N** Moses kept the flock of Jethro his	2050.1
	3: 3	I will **n** turn aside, and see this great sight,	4994
	3: 9	**N** therefore, behold, the cry of the	6258
	3:10	Come **n** therefore, and I will send thee	6258
	3:18	**n** let us go, we beseech thee, three days'	6258
	4: 6	him, Put **n** thine hand into thy bosom.	4994
	4:12	**n** therefore go, and I will be with thy	6258
	5: 5	the people of the land *are* **n** many,	6258
	5:18	Go therefore **n**, *and* work; for there shall	6258
	6: 1	**N** shalt thou see what I will do to	6258
	7:11	the magicians of Egypt, they also did	2050.1
	9:15	**n** I will stretch out my hand, that I may	6258
	9:18	since the foundation thereof even until **n**.	6258
	9:19	Send therefore **n**, *and* gather thy cattle,	6258
	10:11	go ye *that are* men, and serve	4994
	10:17	**N** therefore forgive, I pray thee, my sin	4994
	11: 2	Speak **n** in the ears of the people,	4994
	12:40	the sojourning of the children of	2050.1
	16:36	**N** an omer *is* the tenth *part* of an ephah	2050.1
	18:11	**N** I know that the LORD *is* greater than	6258
	18:19	Hearken **n** unto my voice, I will give thee	6258
	19: 5	**N** therefore, if ye will obey my voice	6258
	21: 1	**N** these *are* the judgments which thou	2050.1
	29:38	**N** this *is that* which thou shalt offer	2050.1
	32:10	**N** therefore let me alone, that my wrath	6258
	32:30	**n** I will go up unto the LORD;	6258
	32:32	Yet **n**, if thou wilt forgive their sin;	6258
	32:34	Therefore **n** go, lead the people unto	6258
	33: 5	**n** put off thy ornaments from thee,	6258
	33:13	**N** therefore, I pray thee, if I have found	6258
	33:13	shew me **n** thy way, that I may know	4994
	34: 9	If **n** I have found grace in thy sight,	4994
Nu	11: 6	**n** our soul *is* dried away: *there is* nothing	6258
	11:23	thou shalt see **n** whether my word shall	6258
	12: 3	(**N** the man Moses was very meek,	2050.1
	12: 6	he said, Hear **n** my words: If there be a	4994
	12:13	Heal her **n**, O God, I beseech thee.	4994
	13:20	**N** the time *was* the time of the first ripe	2050.1
	13:22	*were*. (**N** Hebron was built seven years	2050.1
	14:15	**N** *if* thou shalt kill *all* this people as one	2050.1
	14:17	**n**, I beseech thee, let the power of my	6258
	14:19	this people, from Egypt even until **n**.	2008
	14:22	have tempted me **n** these ten times,	NIH
	14:25	(**N** the Amalekites and the Canaanites	2050.1
	14:41	Wherefore **n** do ye transgress	2088
	16: 1	**N** Korah, the son of Izhar, the son of	2050.1
	16:49	**n** they that died in the plague were	2050.1
	20:10	and he said unto them, Hear **n**, ye rebels;	4994
	22: 4	**N** this company lick up all *that are*	6258
	22: 6	Come **n** therefore, I pray thee, curse me	6258
	22:11	come **n**, curse me them; peradventure I	6258
	22:19	**N** therefore, I pray you, tarry ye also here	6258
	22:22	**N** he was riding upon his ass, and his	2050.1
	22:29	in mine hand, for **n** would I kill thee.	6258
	22:33	**n** also I had slain thee, and saved her	6258
	22:34	**n** therefore, if it displease thee, I will get	6258
	22:38	I **n** any power at all to say any thing?	6258
	24:11	Therefore **n** flee thou to thy place:	6258
	24:14	**n** behold, I go unto my people: come	6258
	24:17	I shall see him, but not **n**: I shall behold	6258
	25:14	**N** the name of the Israelite that was	2050.1
	31:17	**N** therefore kill every male among the	6258
	31:43	(**N** the half that pertained unto	2050.1
	32: 1	**N** the children of Reuben and the	2050.1
Dt	2:13	**N** rise up, *said I*, and get you over	6258
	4: 1	**N** therefore hearken, O Israel, unto	6258
	4:32	For ask **n** of the days that are past,	4994
	5:25	**N** therefore why should we die? for this	6258
	6: 1	**N** these *are* the commandments,	2050.1
	10:12	**n**, Israel, what doth the LORD thy God	6258
	10:22	**n** the LORD thy God hath made thee as	6258
	26:10	**n**, behold, I have brought the firstfruits of	6258
	31:19	**N** therefore write ye this song for you,	6258
	31:21	which they go about, *even* **n**,	3117+1886.1
	32:39	See **n** that I, *even* I, *am* he, and *there is*	6258
Jos	1: 1	**N** after the death of Moses the servant	2050.1
	1: 2	**n** therefore arise, go over this Jordan,	6258
	2:12	**N** therefore, I pray you, swear unto me	6258
	3:12	**N** therefore take ye twelve men out of	6258
	5: 5	**N** all the people that came out were	3588
	5:14	*as* captain of the host of the LORD am I **n**	628
	6: 1	**N** Jericho was straitly shut up because	2050.1
	7:19	tell me **n** what thou hast done; hide *it* not	4994
	8:11	*n there was* a valley between them and	2050.1
	9: 6	**n** therefore make ye a league with us.	2050.1
	9:11	therefore **n** make ye a league with us.	2050.1

Jos
9:12 but **n**, behold, it is dry, and it is mouldy: 6258
9:17 **N** their cities were Gibeon, 2050.1
9:19 **n** therefore we may not touch them. 2050.1
9:23 **N** therefore ye are cursed, and there 2050.1
9:25 **n**, behold, we are in thine hand: as it 6258
10: 1 **N** it came to pass, when Adoni-zedek 2050.1
12: 1 **N** these are the kings of the land, 2050.1
13: 1 **N** Joshua was old and stricken in years; 2050.1
13: 7 **N** therefore divide this land for an 2050.1
14:10 **n** behold, the LORD hath kept me alive, 6258
14:10 **n** lo, I am this day fourscore and five years 6258
14:11 even so is my strength **n**, for war, both to 6258
14:12 **N** therefore give me this mountain, 6258
17: 8 **N** Manasseh had the land of Tappuah: NIH
18:21 **N** the cities of the tribe of the children 2050.1
22: 4 **n** the LORD your God hath given rest 6258
22: 4 therefore **n** return ye, and get ye unto 6258
22: 7 **N** to the one half of the tribe of 2050.1
22:26 Let us **n** prepare to build us an altar, 4994
22:31 **n** ye have delivered the children of Israel 227
24:14 **N** therefore fear the LORD, and serve him 6258
24:23 **N** therefore put away, said he, the strange 4994

Jdg
1: 1 **N** after the death of Joshua it came to 2050.1
1: 8 **N** the children of Judah had fought 2050.1
1:10 (**n** the name of Hebron before was 2050.1
1:23 **N** the name of the city before was Luz. 2050.1
3: 1 **N** these are the nations which the LORD 2050.1
4:11 **N** Heber the Kenite, which was of 2050.1
6:13 **n** the LORD hath forsaken us, 6258
6:17 If **n** I have found grace in thy sight, then 4994
6:39 let it **n** be dry only upon the fleece, 4994
7: 3 **N** therefore go to, proclaim in the ears of 6258
8: 2 have I done **n** in comparison of you? 6258
8: 6 of Zebah and Zalmunna **n** in thine hand, 6258
8:10 **N** Zebah and Zalmunna were in Karkor, 2050.1
8:15 of Zebah and Zalmunna **n** in thine hand, 6258
9:16 **N** therefore, if ye have done truly and 6258
9:32 **N** therefore up by night, thou and 6258
9:38 Where is **n** thy mouth, wherewith thou 645
9:38 go out, I pray **n**, and fight with them. 4994
11: 1 **N** Jephthah the Gileadite was a mighty 2050.1
11: 7 why are ye come unto me **n** when ye are 6258
11: 8 Therefore we turn again to thee **n**, that 6258
11:13 **n** therefore restore those lands again 6258
11:23 So **n** the LORD God of Israel hath 6258
11:25 **n** art thou any thing better than Balak 6258
12: 6 said they unto him, Say **n** Shibboleth: 4994
13: 3 said unto her, Behold **n**, thou art barren, 4994
13: 4 **N** therefore beware, I pray thee, 6258
13: 7 **n** drink no wine nor strong drink, 6258
13:12 said, **N** let thy words come to pass. 6258
14: 2 **n** therefore get her for me to wife. 6258
14:12 I will **n** put forth a riddle unto you: 4994
15: 3 **N** shall I be more blameless than 6471
15:18 **n** shall I die for thirst, and fall into the 6258
16: 9 **N** there were men lying in wait, 2050.1
16:10 **n** tell me, I pray thee, wherewith thou 6258
16:27 **N** the house was full of men and 2050.1
17: 3 **n** therefore I will restore it unto thee. 6258
17:13 **N** know I that the LORD will do me good, 6258
18:14 **n** therefore consider what ye have to do. 6258
19: 9 damsel's father, said unto him, Behold **n**, 4994
19:18 I am **n** going to the house of the LORD; NIH
19:22 **N** as they were making their hearts merry, NIH
19:24 them I will bring out **n**, and humble ye 4994
20: 3 **N** the children of Benjamin heard that 2050.1
20: 9 **n** this shall be the thing which we will do 6258
20:13 **N** therefore deliver us the men, the 6258
20:38 **N** there was an appointed sign between 2050.1
21: 1 **N** the men of Israel had sworn in 2050.1

Ru
1: 1 **N** it came to pass in the days when 2050.1
2: 2 Let me **n** go to the field, and glean ears of 4994
2: 7 continued even from the morning until **n**, 6258
3: 2 **n** is not Boaz our kindred, with whose 6258
3:11 **n**, my daughter, fear not; I will do to thee 6258
3:12 **n** it is true that I am thy near 3588+6258
4: 7 **N** this was the manner in former time 2050.1
4:18 **N** these are the generations of Pharez: 2050.1

1Sa
1: 1 **N** there was a certain man of 2050.1
1: 9 **N** Eli the priest sat upon a seat by a post 2050.1
1:13 **N** Hannah, she spake in her heart; 2050.1
2:12 **N** the sons of Eli were sons of Belial; 2050.1
2:16 Nay; but thou shalt give it me **n**: 6258
2:22 **N** Eli was very old, and heard all that 2050.1
2:30 **n** the LORD saith, Be it far from me; 2050.1
3: 7 **N** Samuel did not yet know the LORD, 2050.1
4: 1 **N** Israel went out against the Philistines 2050.1
4:15 **N** Eli was ninety and eight years old; 2050.1
6: 7 **N** therefore make a new cart, and take 6258
8: 2 **N** the name of his firstborn was Joel; 2050.1
8: 5 **n** make us a king to judge us like all 6258
8: 9 **N** therefore hearken unto their voice: 6258
9: 1 **N** there was a man of Benjamin, whose 2050.1
9: 3 Take **n** one of the servants with thee, 4994
9: 6 he said unto him, Behold **n**, there is in 4994
9: 6 **n** let us go thither; peradventure he can 6258
9: 9 for he that is **n** called a Prophet was 3117
9:12 make haste **n**, for he came to day to 6258
9:13 **N** therefore get you up; for about this 6258
9:15 **N** the LORD had told Samuel in his ear 2050.1
10:19 **N** therefore present yourselves before 6258
12: 2 **n** behold, the king walketh before you: 6258
12: 7 **N** therefore stand still, that I may reason 6258
12:10 **n** deliver us out of the hand of our 6258
12:13 **N** therefore behold the king whom ye 6258

12:16 **N** therefore stand and see this great thing, 6258
13:12 The Philistines will come down **n** upon 6258
13:13 for **n** would the LORD have established 6258
13:14 **n** thy kingdom shall not continue: 6258
13:19 **N** there was no smith found throughout 2050.1
14: 1 **N** it came to pass upon a day, 2050.1
14:17 Number **n**, and see who is gone from us. 4994
14:30 for had there not been a much greater 6258
14:49 **N** the sons of Saul were Jonathan, 2050.1
15: 1 **n** therefore hearken thou unto the voice 6258
15: 3 **N** go and smite Amalek, and utterly 6258
15:25 **N** therefore, I pray thee, pardon my sin, 6258
15:30 yet honour me **n**, I pray thee, before 6258
16:12 **N** he was ruddy, and withal of a 2050.1
16:15 Saul's servants said unto him, Behold **n**, 4994
16:16 Let our lord **n** command thy servants 4994
16:17 Provide me **n** a man that can play well, 4994
17: 1 **N** the Philistines gathered together their 2050.1
17:12 **N** David was the son of that Ephrathite 2050.1
17:17 Take **n** for thy brethren an ephah of this 4994
17:19 **N** Saul, and they, and all the men of 2050.1
17:29 David said, What have I **n** done? Is there 6258
18:22 **n** therefore be the king's son in law. 6258
19: 2 **n** therefore, I pray thee, take heed to 6258
20:29 hath commanded me to be there: and **n**, 6258
20:31 Wherefore **n** send and fetch him unto me, 6258
20:36 Run, find out **n** the arrows which I shoot. 4994
21: 3 **N** therefore what is under thine hand? 6258
21: 7 **N** a certain man of the servants of Saul 2050.1
22: 6 (**n** Saul abode in Gibeah under a tree in 2050.1
22: 7 stood about him, Hear **n**, ye Benjamites; 4994
22:12 Saul said, Hear **n**, thou son of Ahitub. 4994
23:20 **N** therefore, O king, come down 6258
24:20 **n** behold, I know well that thou shalt 6258
24:21 Swear **n** therefore unto me by the LORD, 6258
25: 3 **N** the name of the man was Nabal; 2050.1
25: 7 **n** I have heard that thou hast shearers: 6258
25: 7 **n** thy shepherds which were with us, 6258
25:10 there be many servants **n a days** 3117+1886.1
25:17 **N** therefore know and consider what thou 6258
25:21 **N** David had said, Surely in vain have I 2050.1
25:26 **N** therefore, my lord, as the LORD liveth, 6258
25:26 **n** let thine enemies, and they that seek 6258
25:27 **n** this blessing which thine handmaid 6258
26: 8 **n** therefore let me smite him, I pray thee, 6258
26:11 take thou **n** the spear that is at his bolster, 4994
26:16 **n** see where the king's spear is, and 6258
26:19 **N** therefore, I pray thee, let my lord 6258
26:20 **N** therefore, let not my blood fall to 6258
27: 1 I shall **n** perish one day by the hand of 6258
27: 5 If I have **n** found grace in thine eyes, 4994
28: 3 **N** Samuel was dead, and all Israel had 2050.1
28:22 **N** therefore, I pray thee, hearken thou 6258
29: 1 **N** the Philistines gathered together all 2050.1
29: 7 Wherefore **n** return, and go in peace, 6258
29:10 Wherefore **n** rise up early in the morning 6258
31: 1 **N** the Philistines fought against Israel: 2050.1

2Sa
1: 1 **N** it came to pass after the death of Saul, 2050.1
2: 6 **n** the LORD shew kindness and truth unto 6258
2: 7 **n** let your hands be strengthened, 6258
2:14 Let the young men **n** arise, and play 4994
3: 1 **N** there was long war between the 2050.1
3:18 **N** then do it: for the LORD hath spoken of 6258
4:11 **n** require his blood of your hand, 4994
7: 2 See **n**, I dwell in a house of cedar, 4994
7: 8 **N** therefore so shalt thou say unto my 6258
7:25 **n**, O LORD God, the word that thou hast 6258
7:28 **n**, O Lord GOD, thou art that God, 6258
7:29 Therefore **n** let it please thee to bless 6258
9: 6 **N** when Mephibosheth, the son of 2050.1
9:10 **N** Ziba had fifteen sons and 2050.1
12:10 **N** therefore the sword shall never depart 6258
12:23 **n** he is dead, wherefore should I fast? 6258
12:28 **N** therefore gather the rest of the people 6258
13: 7 Go **n** to thy brother Amnon's house, 4994
13:13 **N** therefore, I pray thee, speak unto 6258
13:17 Put **n** this woman out from me, and bolt 4994
13:20 hold **n** thy peace, my sister: he is thy 6258
13:24 said, Behold **n**, thy servant hath 4994
13:25 Nay, my son, let us not all **n** go, 4994
13:28 **N** Absalom had commanded his 2050.1
13:28 Mark ye **n** when Amnon's heart is merry 4994
13:33 **N** therefore let not my lord the king take 6258
14: 1 **N** Joab the son of Zeruiah perceived that 2050.1
14: 2 put on **n** mourning apparel, and anoint 4994
14:15 **N** therefore that I am come to speak of 6258
14:15 said, I will **n** speak unto the king; 4994
14:17 The word of my lord the king shall **n** be 4994
14:18 said, Let my lord the king **n** speak. 4994
14:21 Joab, Behold **n**, I have done this thing: 4994
14:32 **N** therefore let me see the king's face; 6258
15:34 so will I **n** also be thy servant: 6258
16:11 how much more **n** may this Benjamite do 6258
17: 1 me **n** choose out twelve thousand men, 4994
17: 5 Call **n** Hushai the Archite also, and let us 4994
17: 9 he is hid **n** in some pit, or in some other 6258
17:16 **N** therefore send quickly, and tell David, 6258
17:17 **N** Jonathan and Ahimaaz stayed by 2050.1
18: 3 **n** thou art worth ten thousand of us: 6258
18: 3 **n** it is better that thou succour us out of 6258
18:18 **N** Absalom in his lifetime had taken 2050.1
18:19 Let me **n** run, and bear the king tidings, 4994
19: 7 **N** therefore arise, go forth, 6258
19: 7 that befell thee from thy youth until **n**. 6258
19: 9 **n** he is fled out of the land for Absalom. 6258

19:10 **N** therefore why speak ye not a word of 6258
19:32 **N** Barzillai was a very aged man, 2050.1
20: 6 **N** shall Sheba the son of Bichri do us 6258
20:23 **N** Joab was over all the host of Israel: 2050.1
21: 2 (**n** the Gibeonites were not of the 2050.1
23: 1 **N** these be the last words of David. 2050.1
24: 2 Go **n** through all the tribes of Israel, 4994
24: 3 **N** the LORD thy God add unto 2050.1
24:10 **n**, I beseech thee, O LORD, take away 6258
24:13 **n** advise, and see what answer I shall 6258
24:14 let us fall **n** into the hand of the LORD; 4994
24:16 stay **n** thine hand. And the angel of 6258

1Ki
1: 1 **N** king David was old and stricken in 2050.1
1:12 **N** therefore come, let me, I pray thee, 6258
1:18 **n** behold, Adonijah reigneth; and now, 6258
1:18 **n**, my lord the king, thou knowest it not: 6258
2: 1 **N** the days of David drew nigh that he 2050.1
2: 9 **N** therefore hold him not guiltless: for 6258
2:16 **N** I ask one petition of thee, deny me not. 6258
2:24 **N** therefore, as the LORD liveth, 6258
3: 7 **n**, O LORD my God, thou hast made thy 6258
5: 4 **n** the LORD my God hath given me rest 6258
5: 6 **N** therefore command thou that they hew 6258
8:25 Therefore **n**, LORD God of Israel, 6258
8:26 **n**, O God of Israel, let thy word, I pray 6258
9:11 (**N** Hiram the king of Tyre had furnished NIH
10:14 **N** the weight of gold that came to 2050.1
12: 4 **n** therefore make thou the grievous 6258
12:11 **n** whereas my father did lade you with a 6258
12:16 **n** see to thine own house, David. 6258
12:26 **N** shall the kingdom return to the house 6258
13: 6 Intreat **n** the face of the LORD thy God, 4994
13:11 **N** there dwelt an old prophet in Beth-el; 2050.1
14:14 of Jeroboam that day: but what? even **n**. 6258
14:29 **N** the rest of the acts of Rehoboam, 2050.1
15: 1 **N** in the eighteenth year of king 2050.1
15: 7 **N** the rest of the acts of Abijam, 2050.1
15:31 **N** the rest of the acts of Nadab, 2050.1
16: 5 **N** the rest of the acts of Baasha, 2050.1
16:14 **N** the rest of the acts of Elah, and all 2050.1
16:20 **N** the rest of the acts of Zimri, 2050.1
16:27 **N** the rest of the acts of Omri which he 2050.1
17:24 **N** by this I know that thou art a man of 6258
18: 3 (**N** Obadiah feared the LORD greatly: 2050.1
18:11 **n** thou sayest, Go, tell thy lord, Behold, 6258
18:14 **n** thou sayest, Go, tell thy lord, Behold, 6258
18:19 **N** therefore send, and gather to me all 6258
18:43 his servant, Go up **n**, look toward the sea. 4994
19: 4 is enough; **n**, O LORD, take away my life; 6258
20:31 his servants said unto him, Behold **n**, 4994
20:33 **N** the men did diligently observe 2050.1
21: 7 thou **n** govern the kingdom of Israel? 6258
22:13 spake unto him, saying, Behold **n**, 4994
22:23 **N** therefore behold, the LORD hath put a 6258
22:39 **N** the rest of the acts of Ahab, and all 2050.1
22:45 **N** the rest of the acts of Jehoshaphat, 2050.1

2Ki
1: 4 **N** therefore thus saith the LORD, 2050.1
1: 5 unto them, Why are ye **n** turned back? 2088
1:14 let my life **n** be precious in thy sight. 6258
1:18 **N** the rest of the acts of Ahaziah which 2050.1
2:16 they said unto him, Behold **n**, there be 4994
3: 1 **N** Jehoram the son of Ahab began to 2050.1
3:15 **n** bring me a minstrel. And it came to 6258
3:23 **n** therefore, Moab, to the spoil. 6258
4: 1 **N** there cried a certain woman of 2050.1
4: 9 she said unto her husband, Behold **n**, 4994
4:13 he said unto him, Say **n** unto her, Behold, 4994
4:26 Run **n**, I pray thee, to meet her, 6258
5: 1 **N** Naaman, captain of the host of the 2050.1
5: 6 **N** when this letter is come unto thee, 6258
5: 8 let him come **n** to me, and he shall know 4994
5:15 **n** I know that there is no God in all 4994
5:15 **n** therefore, I pray thee, take a blessing of 6258
5:22 even **n** there be come to me from 2088+6258
6: 1 of the prophets said unto Elisha, Behold **n**, 6258
7: 4 **N** therefore come, and let us fall unto 6258
7: 9 **n** therefore come, that we may go and 6258
7:12 I will **n** shew you what the Syrians have 4994
7:19 the man of God, and said, **N** behold, 2050.1
8: 6 day that she left the land, even until **n**. 6258
9:12 they said, It is false; tell us **n**. And he said, 4994
9:14 (**N** Joram had kept Ramoth-gilead, he 2050.1
9:26 **N** therefore take and cast him into the 6258
9:34 see **n** this cursed woman, and bury her: 4994
10: 2 **N** as soon as this letter cometh to you, 6258
10: 6 **N** the king's sons, being seventy 2050.1
10:10 Know **n** that there shall fall unto the earth 645
10:19 **N** therefore call unto me all the prophets 6258
10:34 **N** the rest of the acts of Jehu, and all 2050.1
12: 7 **N** therefore receive no more money of 6258
13: 8 **N** the rest of the acts of Jehoahaz, 2050.1
13:14 **N** Elisha was fallen sick of his sickness 2050.1
13:19 it: whereas **n** thou shalt smite Syria 6258
14:15 **N** the rest of the acts of Jehoash which 2050.1
14:19 **N** they made a conspiracy against him 2050.1
14:28 **N** the rest of the acts of Jeroboam, 2050.1
15:36 **N** the rest of the acts of Jotham, 2050.1
16:19 **N** the rest of the acts of Ahaz which he 2050.1
18: 1 **N** it came to pass in the third year of 2050.1
18:13 **N** in the fourteenth year of king 2050.1
18:19 Speak **n** to Hezekiah, Thus saith 4994
18:20 **N** on whom dost thou trust, that thou 6258
18:21 **N** behold, thou trustest upon the staff of 6258
18:23 **N** therefore, I pray thee, give pledges to 6258
18:25 Am I **n** come up without the LORD 6258

N

N

```
2Ki 19:19  N therefore, O Lord our God, I beseech        6258
    19:25  n have I brought it to pass, that thou        6258
    20: 3  remember n how I have walked before          4994
    21:17  N the rest of the acts of Manasseh,           2050.1
    21:25  N the rest of the acts of Amon which          2050.1
    22:14  (n she dwelt in Jerusalem in the              2050.1
    23:28  N the rest of the acts of Josiah,             2050.1
    24: 5  N the rest of the acts of Jehoiakim,          2050.1
    25: 4  (n the Chaldees were against the city         2050.1
    25:11  N the rest of the people that were left       2050.1
1Ch  1:32  N the sons of Keturah,                        2050.1
     1:43  N these are the kings that reigned in         2050.1
     2:34  N Sheshan had no sons, but daughters.         2050.1
     2:42  N the sons of Caleb the brother of            2050.1
     3: 1  N these were the sons of David,               2050.1
     5: 1  N the sons of Reuben the firstborn of         2050.1
     6:54  N these are their dwelling places             2050.1
     7: 1  N the sons of Issachar were, Tola,            2050.1
     8: 1  N Benjamin begat Bela his firstborn,          2050.1
     9: 2  N the first inhabitants that dwelt in         2050.1
    10: 1  N the Philistines fought against Israel;      2050.1
    11:15  N three of the thirty captains went           2050.1
    12: 1  N these are they that came to David to        2050.1
    14: 1  N Hiram king of Tyre sent messengers          2050.1
    14: 4  N these are the names of his children         2050.1
    17: 1  N it came to pass, as David sat in his        2050.1
    17: 7  N therefore thus shalt thou say unto my       6258
    17:23  Therefore n, Lord, let the thing that thou    6258
    17:26  n, Lord, thou art God,                        6258
    17:27  N therefore let it please thee to bless       6258
    18: 1  N after this it came to pass, that David      2050.1
    18: 9  N when Tou king of Hamath heard               2050.1
    19: 1  N it came to pass after this, that Nahash     2050.1
    19:10  N when Joab saw that the battle was           2050.1
    21: 8  n, I beseech thee, do away the iniquity of    6258
    21:12  N therefore advise thyself what word I        6258
    21:13  let me fall n into the hand of the Lord;      4994
    21:15  It is enough, stay n thine hand.              6258
    21:20  N Ornan was threshing wheat.                  2050.1
    22: 5  I will therefore n make preparation for it.   4994
    22:11  N, my son, the Lord be with thee;             6258
    22:14  N behold, in my trouble I have prepared       2050.1
    22:19  N set your heart and your soul to seek        6258
    23: 3  N the Levites were numbered from              2050.1
    23:14  N concerning Moses the man of God,            2050.1
    24: 1  N these are the divisions of the sons of      2050.1
    24: 7  N the first lot came forth to Jehoiarib,      2050.1
    25: 9  N the first lot came forth for Asaph to       2050.1
    27: 1  N the children of Israel after their          2050.1
    28: 8  N therefore in the sight of all Israel        6258
    28:10  Take heed n; for the Lord hath chosen         6258
    29: 2  N I have prepared with all my might for       2050.1
    29:13  N therefore, our God, we thank thee,          6258
    29:17  and n have I seen with joy thy people,        6258
    29:20  N bless the Lord your God.                    4994
    29:29  N the acts of David the king, first and       2050.1
2Ch  1: 9  N, O Lord God, let thy promise unto           6258
     1:10  Give me n wisdom and knowledge, that          6258
     2: 7  Send me n therefore a man cunning to          6258
     2:13  n I have sent a cunning man, endued           6258
     2:15  N therefore the wheat, and the barley,        6258
     3: 3  N these are the things wherein                2050.1
     6: 7  N it was in the heart of David my father      2050.1
     6:16  N therefore, O Lord God of Israel,            6258
     6:17  N then, O Lord God of Israel, let thy         6258
     6:40  N, my God, let, I beseech thee, thine eyes    6258
     6:41  N therefore arise, O Lord God, into thy       6258
     7: 1  N when Solomon had made an end of             2050.1
     7:15  N mine eyes shall be open, and mine ears      6258
     7:16  For n have I chosen and sanctified this       6258
     8:16  N all the work of Solomon was                 2050.1
     9:13  N the weight of gold that came to             2050.1
     9:29  N the rest of the acts of Solomon, first      2050.1
    10: 4  n therefore ease thou somewhat                6258
    10:16  and n, David, see to thine own house.         6258
    12:15  N the acts of Rehoboam, first and last,       2050.1
    13: 1  N in the eighteenth year of king Jeroboam     NIH
    13: 8  n ye think to withstand the kingdom of        2050.1
    15: 3  N for a long season Israel hath been          2050.1
    18: 1  N Jehoshaphat had riches and honour           2050.1
    18:22  N therefore behold, the Lord hath put a       6258
    18:30  N the king of Syria had commanded             2050.1
    19: 7  Wherefore n let the fear of the Lord be       6258
    20:10  n behold, the children of Ammon and           6258
    20:34  N the rest of the acts of Jehoshaphat,        2050.1
    21: 1  N Jehoshaphat slept with his fathers,         2050.1
    21: 4  N when Jehoram was risen up to                2050.1
    23:12  N when Athaliah heard the noise of            2050.1
    24:11  N it came to pass, that at what time          2050.1
    24:17  N after the death of Jehoiada came            2050.1
    24:27  N concerning his sons, and the                2050.1
    25: 3  N it came to pass, when the kingdom           2050.1
    25:14  N it came to pass, after that Amaziah         2050.1
    25:19  abide n at home; why shouldest thou           6258
    25:26  N the rest of the acts of Amaziah, first      2050.1
    25:27  N after the time that Amaziah did turn        2050.1
    26:22  N the rest of the acts of Uzziah, first       2050.1
    27: 7  N the rest of the acts of Jotham,             2050.1
    28:10  n ye purpose to keep under the children       6258
    28:11  N hear me therefore, and deliver             6258
    28:26  N the rest of his acts and of all his ways,   2050.1
    29: 5  sanctify yourselves, and sanctify             6258
    29:10  N it is in mine heart to make a covenant      6258
    29:11  My sons, be not n negligent:                  6258
    29:17  N they began on the first day of the first    2050.1
```

```
2Ch 29:31  N ye have consecrated yourselves unto         6258
    30: 8  N be ye not stiffnecked, as your fathers      6258
    31: 1  N when all this was finished, all Israel      2050.1
    32:15  N therefore let not Hezekiah deceive you,     6258
    32:32  N the rest of the acts of Hezekiah,           2050.1
    33:14  N after this he built a wall without          2050.1
    33:18  N the rest of the acts of Manasseh,           2050.1
    34: 8  N in the eighteenth year of his reign,        2050.1
    34:22  (n she dwelt in Jerusalem in the              2050.1
    35: 3  serve n the Lord your God, and his            6258
    35:26  N the rest of the acts of Josiah,             2050.1
    36: 8  N the rest of the acts of Jehoiakim,          2050.1
    36:22  N in the first year of Cyrus king of          2050.1
Ezr  1: 1  N in the first year of Cyrus king of          2050.1
     2: 1  N these are the children of the province      2050.1
     3: 8  N in the second year of their coming          2050.1
     4: 1  N when the adversaries of Judah and           2050.1
     4:13  Be it known n unto the king, that, if this    3705
     4:14  N because we have maintenance from            3705
     4:21  Give ye n commandment to cause these          3705
     4:22  Take heed n that ye fail not to do this:      2050.3
     4:23  N when the copy of king Artaxerxes'         116+1768
     5:16  that time even until n hath it been in        3705
     5:17  N therefore, if it seem good to the king,     3705
     6: 6  N therefore, Tatnai, governor beyond          3705
     7: 1  N after these things, in the reign of         2050.1
     7:11  N this is the copy of the letter that         2050.1
     8: 1  These are the chief of their fathers,         2050.1
     8:33  N on the fourth day was the silver and        2050.1
     9: 1  N when these things were done,                2050.1
     9: 8  n for a little space grace hath been          6258
     9:10  n, O our God, what shall we say after         6258
     9:12  N therefore give not your daughters           2050.1
    10: 1  N when Ezra had prayed, and when he           2050.1
    10: 2  n there is hope in Israel concerning this     6258
    10: 3  N therefore let us make a covenant with       6258
    10:11  N therefore make confession unto             6258
    10:14  Let n our rulers of all the congregation      4994
Ne   1: 6  Let thine ear n be attentive, and thine      4994
     1: 6  which I pray before thee n, day and night,    3117
     1:10  N these are thy servants and thy people,      2050.1
     1:11  let n thine ear be attentive to the prayer    4994
     2: 1  N I had not been beforetime sad in his        2050.1
     2: 9  N the king had sent captains of the           2050.1
     4: 3  N Tobiah the Ammonite was by him,             2050.1
     5: 5  Yet n our flesh is as the flesh of our        6258
     5:18  N that which was prepared for me daily        2050.1
     6: 1  N it came to pass, when Sanballat,            2050.1
     6: 7  n shall it be reported to the king            6258
     7: 1  N it came to pass, when the wall was          2050.1
     7: 4  N the city was large and great:               2050.1
     9: 1  N in the twenty and fourth day of this        2050.1
     9:32  N therefore, our God, the great, the          6258
    10: 1  N those that sealed were, Nehemiah,           2050.1
    11: 3  N these are the chief of the province         2050.1
    12: 1  N these are the priests and the Levites       2050.1
    13: 3  N it came to pass, when they had heard        2050.1
Est  1: 1  N it came to pass in the days of              2050.1
     2: 5  N in Shushan the palace there was a           NIH
     2:12  N when every maid's turn was come to          2050.1
     2:15  N when the turn of Esther,                    2050.1
     3: 4  N it came to pass, when they spake            2050.1
     5: 1  N it came to pass on the third day,           2050.1
     6: 4  N Haman was come into the outward             2050.1
     6: 6  N Haman thought in his heart, To              2050.1
     9: 1  N in the twelfth month, that is, the          2050.1
     9:12  n what is thy petition? and it shall be       2050.1
Job  1: 6  N there was a day when the sons of            2050.1
     1:11  put forth thine hand n, and touch all         4994
     2: 5  put forth thine hand n, and touch his         4994
     2:11  N when Job's three friends heard of all       2050.1
     3:13  For n should I have lien still and            6258
     4: 5  n it is come upon thee, and thou faintest;    6258
     4:12  N a thing was secretly brought to me,         2050.1
     5: 1  Call n, if there be any that will answer      4994
     6: 3  For n it would be heavier than the sand       6258
     6:21  For n ye are nothing; ye see my casting       6258
     6:28  N be content, look upon me;                   6258
     7:21  n shall I sleep in the dust; and thou shalt   6258
     8: 6  surely he would awake for thee,               6258
     9:25  N my days are swifter than a post:            2050.1
    12: 7  ask n the beasts, and they shall teach        4994
    13: 6  Hear n my reasoning, and hearken to           4994
    13:18  Behold n, I have ordered my cause;            4994
    13:19  for n, if I hold my tongue, I shall give up   6258
    14:16  For n thou numberest my steps: dost thou      6258
    16: 7  n he hath made me weary: thou hast            6258
    16:19  Also n, behold my witness is in heaven,       6258
    17: 3  Lay down n, put me in a surety with thee;     4994
    17:10  as for you all, do you return; and come n:    4994
    17:15  where is n my hope? as for my hope,           645
    19: 6  Know n that God hath overthrown me,           645
    19:23  O that my words were n written! O that        645
    22:21  Acquaint n thyself with him, and be at        4994
    24:25  if it be not so n, who will make me a liar,   645
    30: 1  n they that are younger than I have me in     6258
    30: 9  n am I their song, yea, I am their byword.    6258
    30:16  n my soul is poured out upon me; the          6258
    32: 4  N Elihu had waited till Job had spoken,       2050.1
    32:14  N he hath not directed his words              2050.1
    33: 2  Behold n I have opened my mouth,              4994
    34:16  If n thou hast understanding, hear this:      2050.1
    35:15  n, because it is not so, he hath visited      6258
```

```
Job 37:21  n men see not the bright light which is in    6258
    38: 3  Gird up n thy loins like a man; for I will    4994
    40: 7  Gird up thy loins like a man: I will          4994
    40:10  Deck thyself n with majesty and               4994
    40:15  Behold n behemoth, which I made with          4994
    40:16  Lo n, his strength is in his loins,           4994
    42: 5  of the ear: but n mine eye seeth thee.        6258
    42: 8  Therefore take unto you n seven bullocks      6258
Ps   2:10  Be wise n therefore, O ye kings:              6258
    12: 5  the needy, n will I arise, saith the Lord;    6258
    17:11  They have n compassed us in our steps:        6258
    20: 6  N know I that the Lord saveth his             6258
    27: 6  n shall mine head be lifted up above          6258
    37:25  I have been young, and n am old; yet          NIH
    39: 7  n, Lord, what wait I for? my hope is in       6258
    41: 8  n that he lieth he shall rise up no more.     NIH
    50:22  N consider this, ye that forget God, lest I   4994
    71:18  N also when I am old and grayheaded,          2050.1
    74: 6  n they break down the carved work            6258
   115: 2  the heathen say, Where is n their God?        4994
   116:14  I will pay my vows unto the Lord n in         4994
   116:18  I will pay my vows unto the Lord n in         4994
   118: 2  Let Israel n say, that his mercy endureth     4994
   118: 3  Let the house of Aaron n say, that his        4994
   118: 4  Let them n that fear the Lord say,            4994
   118:25  Save n, I beseech thee, O Lord:               4994
   118:25  I beseech thee, send n prosperity.            4994
   119:67  I went astray: but n have I kept thy word.    6258
   122: 8  and companions' sakes, I will n say,          4994
   124: 1  who was on our side, n may Israel say;        4994
   129: 1  me from my youth, may Israel n say:           4994
Pr   5: 7  Hear me n therefore, O ye children,           6258
     6: 3  Do this n, my son, and deliver thyself,       645
     7:12  N is she without, now in the streets,         6471
     7:12  n in the streets, and lieth in wait at every  6471
     7:24  Hearken unto me n therefore, O ye             6258
     8:32  N therefore hearken unto me, O ye             6258
Ecc  2: 1  I said in mine heart, Go to n, I will prove   4994
     2:16  seeing that which n is, in the days to        3528
     3:15  That which hath been, is n; and that          3528
     9: 6  hatred, and their envy, is perished;          3528
     9: 7  for God n accepteth thy works.                3528
     9:15  N there was found in it a poor wise           2050.1
    12: 1  Remember n thy Creator in the days of         2050.1
SS   3: 2  I will rise n, and go about the city in       4994
     7: 8  n also thy breasts shall be as clusters of    2050.1
Isa  1:18  Come n, and let us reason together,           4994
     1:21  lodged in it; but n murderers.                6258
     5: 1  N will I sing to my wellbeloved a song of     4994
     5: 3  n, O inhabitants of Jerusalem, and men        6258
     5: 5  n go to, I will tell you what I will do to    6258
     7: 3  Go forth n to meet Ahaz, thou,                4994
     7:13  he said, Hear ye n, O house of David;         4994
     8: 7  N therefore behold, the Lord bringeth         2050.1
    16:14  n the Lord hath spoken, saying,               6258
    19:12  thy wise men? and let them tell thee n,       4994
    22: 1  What aileth thee n, that thou art wholly      645
    28:22  N therefore be ye not mockers, lest your      6258
    29:22  of Jacob, Jacob shall not n be ashamed,       6258
    29:22  neither shall his face n wax pale.            6258
    30: 8  N go, write it before them in a table,        4994
    31: 3  N the Egyptians are men, and not God;         2050.1
    33:10  N will I rise, saith the Lord; now will I     6258
    33:10  I rise, saith the Lord; n will I be exalted;  6258
    33:10  will I be exalted; n will I lift up myself.   6258
    36: 1  N it came to pass in the fourteenth year      2050.1
    36: 4  Say ye n to Hezekiah, Thus saith the          4994
    36: 5  n on whom dost thou trust, that thou          4994
    36: 8  N therefore give pledges, I pray thee,        6258
    36:10  am I n come up without the Lord               6258
    37:20  N therefore, O Lord our God, save us          6258
    37:26  n have I brought it to pass, that thou        6258
    38: 3  said, Remember n, O Lord, I beseech           577
    42:14  n will I cry like a travailing woman; I will  NIH
    43: 1  n thus saith the Lord that created thee,      6258
    43:19  do a new thing; n it shall spring forth;      6258
    44: 1  Yet n hear, O Jacob my servant; and           6258
    47: 8  Therefore hear n this, thou that art given    6258
    47:12  Stand n with thine enchantments,             4994
    47:13  Let n the astrologers, the stargazers,        4994
    48: 7  They are created n, and not from              6258
    48:16  n the Lord God, and his Spirit, hath sent     6258
    49: 5  n, saith the Lord that formed me from         6258
    49:19  shall even n be too narrow by reason of       6258
    51:21  Therefore hear n this, thou afflicted,        4994
    52: 5  N therefore, what have I here, saith          6258
    64: 8  n, O Lord, thou art our father; we are        6258
Jer  2:18  n what hast thou to do in the way of          6258
     4:12  n also will I give sentence against them.     6258
     4:31  her hands, saying, Woe is me n!               4994
     5: 1  see n, and know, and seek in the broad        4994
     5:21  Hear n this, O foolish people,                4994
     5:24  Let us n fear the Lord our God,               4994
     7:12  go ye n unto my place which was in            4994
     7:13  n, because ye have done all these works,      6258
    14:10  he will n remember their iniquity,            6258
    17:15  is the word of the Lord? let it come n.       4994
    18:11  N therefore go to, speak to the men of        6258
    18:11  return ye n every one from his evil way,      4994
    18:13  Ask ye n among the heathen, who hath          4994
    20: 1  N Pashur the son of Immer the priest,         2050.1
    25: 5  Turn ye again n every one from his evil       4994
    26: 8  N it came to pass, when Jeremiah had          2050.1
    26:13  Therefore n amend your ways and               6258
    27: 6  n have I given all these lands into the       6258
```

Jer
27:16 the vessels of the LORD's house *shall* **n** — 6258
27:18 let them **n** make intercession to the LORD — 4994
28: 7 Nevertheless hear thou **n** this word that I — 4994
28:15 Hananiah the prophet, Hear **n**, Hananiah, — 4994
29: 1 **N** these *are* the words of the letter that — 2050.1
29:27 **N** therefore why hast thou not reproved — 2050.1
30: 6 Ask ye **n**, and see whether a man doth — 4994
32:16 **N** when I had delivered the evidence of — 2050.1
32:36 **n** therefore thus saith the LORD, the God — 6258
34:10 *N* when all the princes, and all the people, — NIH
34:15 ye were **n** turned, and had done — 3117+1886.1
35:15 Return ye **n** every man from his evil way, — 4994
36:15 Sit down **n**, and read it in our ears. — 4994
36:16 **N** it came to pass when they had heard — 2050.1
36:17 they asked Baruch, saying, Tell us **n**, — 4994
36:22 **N** the king sat *in* the winterhouse in — 2050.1
37: 3 Pray **n** unto the LORD our God for us. — 4994
37: 4 **N** Jeremiah came in and went out — 2050.1
37:19 Where *are* **n** your prophets which — 4994
37:20 Therefore hear **n**, I pray thee, O my lord — 1288
38: 7 **N when** Ebed-melech the Ethiopian, — 2050.1
38:12 Put **n** *these* old cast clouts and rotten rags — 4994
38:25 Declare unto us **n** what thou hast said — 4994
39:11 **N** Nebuchadrezzar king of Babylon gave — 2050.1
39:15 **N** the word of the LORD came unto — 2050.1
40: 3 **N** the LORD hath brought *it*, and — 2050.1
40: 4 **n** behold, I loose thee *this* day from — 6258
40: 5 **N** while he was not yet gone back, — 2050.1
40: 7 *N* when all the captains of the forces — NIH
41: 1 **N** it came to pass in the seventh month, — 2050.1
41: 9 **N** the pit wherein Ishmael had cast all — 2050.1
41:13 **N** it came to pass, *that* when all — 2050.1
42:15 **n** therefore hear the word of the LORD, — 6258
42:21 And *n* I have *this* day declared *it* to you; — NIH
42:22 **N** therefore know certainly that ye shall — 6258
44: 7 Therefore **n** thus saith the LORD, the God — 6258
45: 3 Thou didst say, Woe is me **n**! for — 4994
52: 7 (**n** the Chaldeans *were* by the city round — 2050.1
52:12 **N** in the fifth month, in the tenth *day* — 2050.1

Eze
1: 1 **N** it came to pass in the thirtieth year, — 2050.1
1:15 **N** *as* I beheld the living creatures, — 2050.1
4:14 for from my youth up even till **n** have I — 6258
7: 3 **N** *is* the end *come* upon thee, and I will — 6258
7: 8 **N** will I shortly pour out my fury upon — 6258
8: 5 lift up thine eyes **n** the way towards — 4994
8: 8 unto me, Son of man, dig **n** in the wall: — 4994
10: 3 **N** the cherubims stood on the right side — 2050.1
16: 8 **N when** I passed by thee, — 2050.1
17:12 Say **n** to the rebellious house, Know ye — 4994
18:14 **N** lo, *if* he beget a son, that seeth all his — 2050.1
18:25 Hear **n**, O house of Israel; Is not my way — 4994
19: 5 **N when** she saw that she had waited, — 2050.1
19:13 **n** she *is* planted in the wilderness, in a — 6258
22: 2 **N**, thou son of man, wilt thou judge, — 6258
23:43 Will they **n** commit whoredoms with her, — 6258
26: 2 I shall be replenished, *n* she is laid waste: — NIH
26:18 **N** shall the isles tremble *in* the day of thy — 6258
27: 2 **N**, thou son of man, take up a — 2050.1
33:22 **N** the hand of the LORD was upon me — 2050.1
38:12 the desolate places that *are* **n** inhabited, — NIH
39:25 **N** will I bring again the captivity of Jacob, — 6258
41:12 **N** the building that *was* before — 2050.1
42: 5 **N** the upper chambers *were* shorter: — 2050.1
42:15 **N when** he had made an end of — 2050.1
43: 9 **N** let them put away their whoredom, — 6258
46:12 **N** when the prince shall prepare a — 2050.1
47: 7 **N** when I had returned, behold, — 2050.1
48: 1 **N** these *are* the names of the tribes. — 2050.1

Da
1: 6 **N** among these were of the children of — 2050.1
1: 9 **N** God had brought Daniel into favour — 2050.1
1:18 **N** at the end of the days that the king — 2050.1
2:23 hast made known unto me **n** what we — 3705
2:23 for thou hast *n* made known unto us — NIH
3:15 **N** if ye be ready that at what time ye hear — 3705
4:18 **N** thou, O Belteshazzar, declare — 2050.3
4:37 **N** I Nebuchadnezzar praise and extol and — 3705
5:10 *N* the queen, by reason of the words of — NIH
5:12 **n** let Daniel be called, and he will shew — 3705
5:15 **N** the wise *men*, the astrologers, have — 3705
5:16 **n** if thou canst read the writing, — 3705
6: 8 **N**, O king, establish the decree, — 3705
6:10 **N** when Daniel knew that the writing — 2050.3
6:16 *N* the king spake and said unto Daniel, — NIH
8:18 **N** as he was speaking with me, I was in — 2050.1
8:22 **N** that being broken, whereas four — 2050.1
9:15 **n**, O Lord our God, that hast brought thy — 6258
9:17 **N** therefore, O our God, hear the prayer — 6258
9:22 I am **n** come forth to give thee skill and — 6258
10:11 unto thee am I **n** sent. And when he had — 6258
10:14 **N** I am come to make thee understand — 2050.1
10:20 **n** will I return to fight with the prince of — 6258
11: 2 **n** will I shew thee the truth. Behold, — 6258
11:34 **N** when they shall fall, they shall be — 2050.1

Hos
1: 8 **N when** she had weaned Lo-ruhamah, — 2050.1
2: 7 for then *was* it better with me than **n**. — 6258
2:10 **n** will I discover her lewdness in the sight — 6258
4:16 **n** the LORD will feed them as a lamb in a — 6258
5: 3 for **n**, O Ephraim, thou committest — 6258
5: 7 **n** shall a month devour them with their — 6258
7: 2 **n** their own doings have beset them — 6258
8: 8 **n** shall they be among the Gentiles as a — 6258
8:10 **n** will I gather them, and they shall — 6258
8:13 **n** will he remember their iniquity, — 6258
10: 2 is divided; **n** shall they be found faulty: — 6258
10: 3 For **n** they shall say, We have no king, — 6258

Hos
13: 2 **n** they sin more and more, and have — 6258
13:12 Therefore also **n**, saith the LORD, turn ye — 6258

Joel
2:12 Therefore also **n**, saith the LORD, turn ye — 6258

Am
6: 7 Therefore **n** shall they go captive with — 6258
7:16 Therefore hear thou the word of — 6258

Jnh
1: 1 **N** the word of the LORD came unto — 2050.1
1:17 **N** the LORD had prepared a great fish to — 2050.1
3: 3 **N** Nineveh was an exceeding great city — 2050.1
4: 3 Therefore **n**, O LORD, take, I beseech — 6258

Mic
4: 9 **N** why dost thou cry aloud? *is there* — 6258
4:10 for **n** shalt thou go forth out of the city, — 6258
4:11 **N** also many nations are gathered against — 6258
5: 1 **N** gather thyself in troops, O daughter of — 6258
5: 4 for **n** shall he be great unto the ends of — 6258
6: 1 Hear ye **n** what the LORD saith; Arise, — 4994
6: 5 remember **n** what Balak king of Moab — 4994
7: 4 **n** shall be their perplexity. — 6258
7:10 **n** shall she be trodden down as the mire — 6258

Na
1:13 For **n** will I break his yoke from off thee, — 6258

Hag
1: 5 **N** therefore thus saith the LORD of hosts; — 6258
2: 2 Speak **n** to Zerubbabel the son of — 4994
2: 3 how do ye see it **n**? *is it* not in your eyes — 6258
2: 4 Yet *be* strong, O Zerubbabel, saith — 4994
2:11 Ask **n** the priests *concerning* the law, — 4994
2:15 **n**, I pray you, consider from this day and — 6258
2:18 Consider **n** from this day and upward, — 4994

Zec
1: 4 Turn ye **n** from your evil ways, — 4994
3: 3 **N** Joshua was clothed with filthy — 2050.1
3: 8 Hear **n**, O Joshua the high priest, thou, — 4994
5: 5 Lift up **n** thine eyes, and see what *is* this — 4994
8:11 **n** I *will* not *be* unto the residue of this — 6258
9: 8 more: for **n** have I seen with mine eyes. — 6258

Mal
1: 8 offer it **n** unto thy governor; will he be — 4994
1: 9 **n**, I pray you, beseech God that he will be — 6258
2: 1 **n**, O ye priests, this commandment *is* for — 6258
3:10 prove me **n** herewith, saith the LORD of — 4994
3:15 **n** we call the proud happy; yea, they that — 6258

Mt
1:18 **N** the birth of Jesus Christ was on this — 1161
1:22 **N** all this was done, that it might be — 1161
2: 1 **N** when Jesus was born in Bethlehem of — 1161
3:10 And **n** also the axe is laid unto the root of — 2235
3:15 said unto him, Suffer *it to be so* **n**: — 737
4:12 **N** when Jesus heard that John was — 1161
8:18 **N** when Jesus saw great multitudes about — 1161
9:18 saying, My daughter is *even* **n** dead: — 737
10: 2 **N** the names of the twelve apostles are — 1161
11: 2 **N** when John had heard in the prison — 1161
11:12 from the days of John the Baptist until **n** — 737
14:15 is a desert place, and the time is **n** past; — 2235
14:24 the ship was **n** in the midst of the sea, — 2235
15:32 they continue with me **n** three days, — 2235
21:18 **N** in the morning as he returned into — 1161
22:25 **N** there were with us seven brethren: — 1161
24:32 **N** learn a parable of the fig tree; When his — 1161
26: 6 **N** when Jesus was in Bethany, in the — 1161
26:17 **N** the first *day* of the *feast* of unleavened — 1161
26:20 **N** when the even was come, he sat down — 1161
26:45 Sleep on **n**, and take your rest: — 3062+3588
26:48 **N** he that betrayed him gave them a sign, — 1161
26:53 Thinkest thou that I cannot **n** pray to my — NIG
26:59 **N** the chief priests, and elders, and all — 1161
26:65 behold, **n** ye have heard his blasphemy. — 3568
26:69 **N** Peter sat without in the palace: — 1161
27:15 **N** at *that* feast the governor was wont to — 1161
27:42 let him **n** come down from the cross, — 3568
27:43 let him deliver him **n**, if he will have him: — 3568
27:45 **N** from the sixth hour there was darkness — 1161
27:54 **N** when the centurion, and they that were — 1161
27:62 **N** the next day, that followed the *day* of — 1161
28:11 **N** when they were going, behold, some of — 1161

Mk
1:14 **N** after that John was put in prison, Jesus — 1161
1:16 **N** as he walked by the sea of Galilee, — 1161
4:37 beat into the ship, so that it was **n** full. — 2235
5:11 **N** there was there nigh unto the — 1161
6:35 **N** when the day was **n** far spent, — 2235
6:35 desert place, and **n** the time *is* far passed: — 2235
8: 2 they have **n** been with me three days, — 2532
8:14 **N** the *disciples* had forgotten to take — 2532
10:30 But he shall receive an hundredfold **n** — 3568
11:11 all *things*, and **n** the eventide was come, — 2235
12:20 **N** there were seven brethren: and the — NIG
13:12 **N** the brother shall betray the brother to — 1161
13:28 **N** learn a parable of the fig tree; When **n** — 1161
14:41 Sleep on **n**, and take your rest: — 3062+3588
15: 6 **N** at *that* feast he released unto them one — 1161
15:32 Let Christ the King of Israel descend **n** — 3568
15:42 **N** when the even was come, because — 2235
16: 9 **N** when *Jesus* was risen early the first *day* — 1161

Lk
1: 7 they both were **n** well stricken in years. — NIG
1:57 **N** Elisabeth's full time came that she — 1161
2:15 Let us **n** go *even* unto Bethlehem, — 1211
2:29 **n** lettest thou thy servant depart in peace, — 3568
2:41 his parents went to Jerusalem every — 2532
3: 1 **N** in the fifteenth year of the reign of — 1161
3: 9 And **n** also the axe is laid unto the root of — 2235
3:21 **N** when all the people were baptized, — 1161
4:40 **N** when the sun was setting, all they that — 1161
5: 4 **N** when he had left speaking, he said unto — 1161
6:21 Blessed *are* ye that hunger **n**: for ye shall — 3568
6:21 Blessed *are* ye that weep **n**: for ye shall — 3568
6:25 Woe unto you that laugh **n**! for ye shall — 3568
7: 1 **N** when he had ended all his sayings in — 1161
7: 6 when he was **n** not far from the house, — 2235
7:12 **N** when he came nigh to the gate of — 1161
7:39 **N** when the Pharisee which had bidden — 1161
8:11 **N** the parable is this: The seed is the word — 1161

Lk
8:22 **N** it came to pass on a certain day, that he — 1161
8:38 **N** the man out of whom the devils were — 1161
9: 7 **N** Herod the tetrarch heard of all that was — 1161
10:36 Which **n** of these three, thinkest thou, — 3767
10:38 **N** it came to pass, as they went, that he — 1161
11: 7 door is **n** shut, and my children are with — 2235
11:39 **N** do ye Pharisees make clean the outside — 3568
14:17 Come; for all *things* are **n** ready. — 2235
15:25 **N** his elder son was in the field: and as he — 1161
16:25 Lazarus *evil things*: but **n** he is comforted, — 3568
18:22 **N** when Jesus heard these *things*, he said — 1161
19:37 *even* **n** at the descent of the mount of — 2235
19:42 but **n** they are hid from thine eyes. — 3568
20:37 **N** that the dead are raised, even Moses — 1161
21:30 When they **n** shoot forth, ye see and — 2235
21:30 of your own selves that summer is **n** — 2235
22: 1 **N** the feast of unleavened bread drew — 1161
22:36 **n**, he that hath a purse, let him take *it*, — 3568
23:47 **N** when the centurion saw what was — 1161
24: 1 **N** upon the first *day* of the week, very — 1161

Jn
1:44 **N** Philip was of Bethsaida, the city of — 1161
2: 8 Draw out **n**, and bear unto the governor — 3568
2:10 *but* thou hast kept the good wine until **n**. — 737
2:23 **N** when he was in Jerusalem at — 1161
4: 6 **N** Jacob's well was there. Jesus therefore, — 1161
4:18 he whom thou **n** hast is not thy husband: — 3568
4:23 But the hour cometh, and **n** is, when — 3568
4:42 **N** we believe, not because of thy saying: — NIG
4:43 **N** after two days he departed thence, — 1161
4:51 And as he was **n** going down, his servants — 2235
5: 2 **N** there is at Jerusalem by the sheep — 1161
5: 6 knew that he had been **n** a long time *in* — 2235
5:25 unto you, The hour is coming, and **n** is, — 3568
6:10 **N** there was much grass in the place. — 1161
6:16 And when even was **n** come, his disciples — NIG
6:17 it was **n** dark, and Jesus was not come — 2235
7: 2 **N** the Jews' feast of tabernacles was at — 1161
7:14 **N** *about* the midst of the feast — 1161+2235
8: 5 **N** Moses in the law commanded us, — 1161
8:40 But ye seek to kill me, a man that hath — 3568
8:52 him, **N** we know that thou hast a devil. — 3568
9:19 was born blind? how then doth he **n** see? — 737
9:21 But by what means he **n** seeth, we know — 3568
9:25 I know, that, whereas I was blind, **n** I see. — 737
9:31 **N** we know that God heareth no sinners: — 1161
9:41 but **n** ye say, We see; therefore your sin — 3568
11: 1 **N** a certain *man* was sick, *named* Lazarus, — 1161
11: 5 **N** Jesus loved Martha, and her sister, — 1161
11:18 **N** Bethany was nigh unto Jerusalem, — 1161
11:22 But I know, that even **n**, whatsoever thou — 3568
11:30 **N** Jesus was not yet come into the town, — 1161
11:57 **N** both the chief priests and the Pharisees — 1161
12:27 **N** is my soul troubled; and what shall I — 1161
12:31 **N** is the judgment of this world: now shall — 3568
12:31 now shall the prince of this world be cast out — 3568
13: 1 **N** before the feast of the passover, — 1161
13: 2 the devil having **n** put into the heart of — 1161
13: 7 unto him, What I do thou knowest not **n**; — 737
13:19 **N** I tell you before it come, that, — 575+737
13:23 **N** there was leaning on Jesus' bosom one — 1161
13:28 **N** no *man* at the table knew for what — 1161
13:31 **N** is the Son of man glorified, and God is — 3568
13:33 I go, ye cannot come; so **n** I say to you. — 737
13:36 Whither I go, thou canst not follow me **n**; — 3568
13:37 him, Lord, why cannot I follow thee **n**? — 737
14:29 And **n** I have told you before it come to — 3568
15: 3 **N** ye are clean through the word which I — 2235
15:22 but **n** they have no cloke for their sin. — 3568
15:24 but **n** have they both seen and hated both — 3568
16: 5 But **n** I go my way to him that sent me; — 3568
16:12 say unto you, but ye cannot bear *them* **n**. — 737
16:19 **N** Jesus knew that they were desirous to — 3767
16:22 And ye **n** therefore have sorrow: but I will — 3568
16:29 Lo, **n** speakest thou plainly, — 3568
16:30 **N** are we sure that thou knowest all — 3568
16:31 Jesus answered them, Do ye **n** believe? — 737
16:32 Behold, the hour cometh, yea, is **n** come, — 3568
17: 5 **n**, O Father, glorify thou me with thine — 3568
17: 7 **N** they have known that all *things* — 3568
17:11 And *n* I am no more in the world, — 1161
17:13 And **n** come I to thee; and these *things* I — 3568
18:14 **N** Caiaphas was he, which gave counsel — 1161
18:24 **N** Annas had sent him bound unto — 3767
18:36 but **n** is my kingdom not from hence. — 3568
18:40 but Barabbas. **N** Barabbas was a robber. — 1161
19:23 in the coat was without seam, woven from — 1161
19:25 **N** there stood by the cross of Jesus his — 1161
19:28 Jesus knowing that all *things* were **n** — 2235
19:29 **N** there was set a vessel full of vinegar: — 3767
19:41 **N** in the place where he was crucified — 1161
21: 4 But when the morning was **n** come, — 2235
21: 6 **n** they were **not** able to draw it for — 3765
21: 7 **N** when Simon Peter heard that it was — 3767
21:10 Bring of the fish which ye have **n** caught. — 3568
21:14 This *is* **n** the third time *that* Jesus shewed — 2235

Ac
1:18 **N** this *man* purchased a field with — 3767
2: 6 **N** when this was noised abroad, — 1161
2:33 shed forth this, which ye **n** see and hear. — 3568
2:37 **N** when they heard *this*, they were — 1161
3: 1 **N** Peter and John went up together into — 1161
3:17 And **n**, brethren, I wot that through — 3568
4: 3 unto the next day: for it was **n** eventide. — 2235
4:13 **N** when they saw the boldness of Peter — 3568
4:29 And **n**, Lord, behold their threatenings: — 3569
5:24 **N** when the *high* priest and the captain of — 1161

N

Ac
5:38 And n I say unto you, Refrain from these — 3569
7: 4 him into this land, wherein ye n dwell. — 3568
7:11 N there came a dearth over all the land of — 1161
7:34 And come, I will send thee into Egypt. — 3568
7:52 whom we have been n the betrayers and — 3568
8:14 N when the apostles which were at — 1161
9:36 N there was at Joppa a certain disciple — 1161
10: 5 And n send men to Joppa, and call for — 3568
10:17 when Peter doubted in himself what — 1161
10:33 N therefore are we all here present before — 3568
11:19 N they which were scattered abroad upon — 3767
12: 1 N about that time Herod the king — 1161
12:11 said, N I know of a surety, that the Lord — 3568
12:18 N as soon as it was day, there was no — 1161
13: 1 N there were in the church that was at — 1161
13:11 N behold, the hand of the Lord is upon — 3568
13:13 N when Paul and his company loosed — 1161
13:34 n no more to return to corruption, he said — NIG
13:43 N when the congregation was broken up, — 1161
15:10 N therefore why tempt ye God, to put a — 3568
16: 6 N when they had gone throughout — 1161
16:36 go: n therefore depart, and go in peace. — 3568
16:37 and n do they thrust us out privily? — 3568
17: 1 N when they had passed through — 1161
17:16 N while Paul waited for them at Athens, — 1161
17:30 n commandeth all men every where to — 3569
18:14 And when Paul was n about to open his — NIG
20:22 N behold, I go bound in the spirit unto — 3568
20:25 And n behold, I know that ye all, — 3568
20:32 And n, brethren, I commend you to God, — 3569
21: 3 N when we had discovered Cyprus, we — 1161
22: 1 hear ye my defence which I make n unto — 3568
22:16 And n why tarriest thou? arise, — 3568
23:15 N therefore ye with the council signify to — 3568
23:21 n are they ready, looking for a promise — 3568
24:13 the things whereof they n accuse me. — 3568
24:17 N after many years I came to bring alms — 1161
25: 1 N when Festus was come into the — 3767
26: 6 And n I stand and am judged for the hope — 3568
26:17 the Gentiles, unto whom N I send thee, — 3568
27: 9 N when much time was spent, — 1161
27: 9 when sailing was n dangerous, because — 2235
27: 9 because the fast was n already past, Paul — 2235
27:22 And n I exhort you to be of good cheer: — 3569

Ro
1:10 if by any means n at length I might have a — 2235
1:13 N I would not have you ignorant, — 1161
3:19 N we know that what things soever the — 1161
3:21 But N the righteousness of God without — 3570
4: 4 N to him that worketh is the reward not — 1161
4:19 he considered not his own body n dead, — 2235
4:23 N it was not written for his sake alone, — 1161
5: 9 more then, being n justified by his blood, — 3568
5:11 by whom we have n received — 3568
6: 8 N if we be dead with Christ, we believe — 1161
6:19 n yield your members servants to — 3568
6:21 those things whereof ye are n ashamed? — 3568
6:22 But n being made free from sin, — 3570
7: 6 But n we are delivered from the law, — 3570
7:17 N then it is no more I that do it, but sin — 3570
7:20 N if I do that I would not, it is no more I — 1161
8: 1 n no condemnation to them which are in — 3568
8: 9 N if any man have not the Spirit of Christ, — 1161
8:22 and travaileth in pain together until n. — 3568
11:12 N if the fall of them be the riches of — 1161
11:30 yet have ye n obtained mercy through their — 3568
11:31 Even so have these also n not believed, — 3568
13:11 n it is **high time** to awake out of — 2235+5610
13:11 for n is our salvation nearer than when — 1161
14:15 thy meat, n walkest thou not charitably. — 3765
15: 5 N the God of patience and consolation — 1161
15: 8 N I say that Jesus Christ was a minister of — 1161
15:13 N the God of hope fill you with all joy and — 1161
15:23 But n having no more place in these parts, — 3570
15:25 But n I go unto Jerusalem to minister unto — 3570
15:30 N I beseech you, brethren, for the Lord — 1161
15:33 N the God of peace be with you all. — 1161
16:17 N I beseech you, brethren, mark them — 1161
16:25 N to him that is of power to stablish you — 1161
16:26 But n is made manifest, and by — 3568

1Co
1:10 N I beseech you, brethren, by the name — 1161
1:12 N this I say, that every one of you saith, — 1161
2:12 N we have received, not the spirit of — 1161
3: 2 to bear it, neither yet n are ye able. — 2089+3568
3: 8 N he that planteth and he that watereth — 1161
3:12 N if any man build upon this foundation — 1161
4: 7 n if thou didst receive it, why dost thou — 1161
4: 8 N ye are full, now ye are rich, ye have — 2235
4: 8 Now ye are full, n ye are rich, ye have — 2235
4:18 N some are puffed up, as though I would — 1161
5:11 But n I have written unto you not to keep — 3570
6: 7 N therefore there is utterly a fault among — 2235
6:13 N the body is not for fornication, — 1161
7: 1 N concerning the things whereof ye — 1161
7:14 children unclean; but n are they holy. — 3568
7:25 N concerning virgins I have no — 1161
8: 1 N as touching things offered unto idols, — 1161
9:25 N they do it to obtain a corruptible crown — 3767
10: 6 N these things were our examples, — 1161
10:11 N all these things happened unto them for — 1161
12: 1 N concerning spiritual gifts, brethren, — 1161
12: 4 N there are diversities of gifts, but the — 1161
12:18 n hath God set the members every one — 3570
12:20 But n are they many members, yet but — 3568

1Co
12:27 N ye are the body of Christ, — 1161
13:12 For n we see through a glass, darkly; — 737
13:12 n I know in part; but then shall I know — 737
13:13 And n abideth faith, hope, charity, — 3570
14: 6 N, brethren, if I come unto you speaking — 1161
15:12 N if Christ be preached that he rose from — 1161
15:20 But n is Christ risen from the dead, — 3570
15:50 N this I say, brethren, that flesh and — 1161
16: 1 N concerning the collection for the saints, — 1161
16: 5 N I will come unto you, when I shall pass — 1161
16: 7 For I will not see you n by the way; but I — 737
16:10 N if Timotheus come, see that he may be — 1161

2Co
1:21 N he which stablisheth us with you in — 1161
2:14 N thanks be unto God, which always — 1161
3:17 N the Lord is that Spirit: and where — 1161
5: 5 N he that hath wrought us for the — 1161
5:16 yet n henceforth know we him no more. — 3568
5:20 N then we are ambassadors for Christ, — NIG
6: 2 behold, n is the accepted time; behold, — 3568
6: 2 behold, n is the day of salvation.) — 3568
6:13 N for a recompence in the same, (I speak — 1161
7: 9 N I rejoice, not that ye were made sorry, — 3568
8:11 N therefore perform the doing of it; that — 3570
8:14 n at this time your abundance may be a — 3568
8:22 many things, but n much more diligent, — 3570
9:10 N he that ministereth seed to the sower — 1161
10: 1 N I Paul myself beseech you by — 1161
12: 6 n I forbear, lest any man should think of — NIG
13: 2 being absent n I write to them which — 3568
13: 7 N I pray to God that ye do no evil; not — 1161

Gal
1: 1 As we said before, so say I n again, If any — 737
1:10 For do I n persuade men, or God? or do I — 737
1:20 N the things which I write unto you, — 1161
1:23 he which persecuted us in times past n — 3568
2:20 the life which I n live in the flesh I live — 3568
3: 3 are ye n made perfect by the flesh? — 3568
3:16 N to Abraham and his seed were — 1161
3:20 N a mediator is not a mediator of one, — 1161
4: 1 N I say, That the heir, as long as he is a — 1161
4: 9 But n, after that ye have known God, — 3568
4:20 I desire to be present with you n, — 737
4:25 and answereth to Jerusalem which n is, — 3568
4:28 N we, brethren, as Isaac was, — 1161
4:29 was born after the Spirit, even so it is n. — 3568
5:19 N the works of the flesh are manifest, — 1161

Eph
2: 2 the spirit that n worketh in the children — 3568
2:13 But n in Christ Jesus ye who sometimes — 3570
2:19 N therefore ye are no more strangers and — 686
3: 5 as it is n revealed unto his holy apostles — 3568
3:10 the intent that n unto the principalities — 3568
3:20 N unto him that is able to do exceeding — 1161
4: 9 (N that he ascended, what is it but that — 1161
5: 8 but n are ye light in the Lord: — 3568

Php
1: 5 in the gospel from the first day until n; — 3568
1:20 n also Christ shall be magnified in my — 3568
1:30 ye saw in me, and hear to be in me. — 3568
2:12 but n much more in my absence, — 3568
3:18 you often, and n tell you even weeping, — 3568
4:10 n at the last your care of me hath — 2235
4:15 N ye Philippians know also, that in — 1161
4:20 N unto God and our Father be glory for — 1161

Col
1:21 wicked works, yet n hath he reconciled — 3570
1:24 Who n rejoice in my sufferings for you, — 3568
1:26 but n is made manifest to his saints: — 3570
3: 8 But n you also put off all these; anger, — 3570

1Th
3: 6 But n when Timotheus came from you — 737
3: 8 For n we live, if ye stand fast in the Lord. — 3568
3:11 N God himself and our Father, — 1161
5:14 N we exhort you, brethren, warn them — 1161

2Th
2: 1 N we beseech you, brethren, by the — 1161
2: 6 And ye know what withholdeth that he — 3568
2: 7 only he who n letteth will let, until he be — 737
2:16 N our Lord Jesus Christ himself, and God, — 1161
3: 6 N we command you, brethren, in the — 1161
3:12 N them that are such we command and — 1161
3:16 N the Lord of peace himself give you — 1161

1Ti
1: 5 N the end of the commandment is charity — 1161
1:17 N unto the King eternal, immortal, — 1161
4: 1 N the Spirit speaketh expressly, that in — 1161
4: 8 having promise of the life that n is, — 3568
5: 5 N she that is a widow indeed, and — 1161

2Ti
1:10 But is n made manifest by the appearing — 3568
3: 8 N as Jannes and Jambres withstood Moses — 1161
4: 6 For I am n ready to be offered, — 2235

Phm
1: 9 and n also a prisoner of Jesus Christ. — 3570
1:11 but n profitable to thee and to me: — 3570
1:16 Not n as a servant, but above a servant, — 3765

Heb
2: 8 But n we see not yet all things put under — 3568
7: 4 N consider how great this man was, unto — 1161
8: 1 N of the things which we have spoken — 1161
8: 6 But n hath he obtained a more excellent — 3568
8:13 N that which decayeth and waxeth old is — 1161
9: 5 of which we cannot n speak particularly. — 3568
9: 6 N when these things were thus ordained, — 1161
9:24 n to appear in the presence of God for us: — 3568
9:26 n once in the end of the world hath he — 1161
10:18 N where remission of these is, there is no — 1161
10:38 N the just shall live by faith: but if any — 1161
11: 1 N faith is the substance of things hoped — 1161
11:16 But n they desire a better country, that is, — 3570
12:11 N no chastening for the present seemeth — 1161
12:26 but n he hath promised, saying, Yet once — 1161
13:20 N the God of peace, that brought again — 1161

Jas
2:11 N if thou commit no adultery, yet if thou — 1161
4:13 Go to n, ye that say, To day or to morrow — 3568

Jas
4:16 But n ye rejoice in your boastings: all such — 3568

1Pe
1: 1 Go to n, ye rich men, weep and howl for — 3568
1: 6 though n for a season, if need be, — 737
1: 8 in whom, though n ye see him not, — 737
1:12 which are reported unto you by them — 3568
2:10 not a people, but are n the people of God: — 3568
2:10 but n have obtained mercy. — 3568
2:25 but are n returned unto the Shepherd and — 3568
3:21 n save us (not the putting away of the filth — 3568

2Pe
2: 3 whose judgment n of a long time lingereth — NIG
3: 1 epistle, beloved, I n write unto you; — 2235
3: 7 the heavens and the earth, which are n, — 3568
3:18 To him be glory both n and for ever. — 3568

1Jn
2: 8 is past, and the true light n shineth. — 2235
2: 9 his brother, is in darkness even until n. — 737
2:18 even n are there many antichrists; — 3568
2:28 And n, little children, abide in him; that, — 3568
3: 2 n are we the sons of God, and it doth not — 3568
4: 3 and even n already is it in the world. — 3568

2Jn
1: 5 And n I beseech thee, lady, not as though — 3568

Jude
1:24 N unto him that is able to keep you from — 1161
1:25 dominion and power, both n and ever. — 3568

Rev
12:10 N is come salvation, and strength, — 737

NULLIFIES See VOID

NULLIFY See NOUGHT; VOID

NUMBER (178) [NUMBERED, NUMBEREST, NUMBERING, NUMBERS]

Ge
13:16 that if a man can n the dust of the earth, — 4487
15: 5 tell the stars, if thou be able to n them: — 5608
34:30 I being few in n, they shall gather — 4557
41:49 he left numbering; for it was without n. — 4557

Ex
12: 4 take it according to the n of the souls; — 4373
16:16 according to the n of your persons; — 4557
23:26 in thy land: the n of thy days I will fulfil. — 4557
30:12 sum of the children of Israel after their n, — 6485

Lev
15:13 he shall n to himself seven days for his — 5608
15:28 she shall n to herself seven days, — 5608
23:16 the seventh sabbath shall ye n fifty days; — 5608
25: 8 thou shalt n seven sabbaths of years unto — 5608
25:15 According to the n of years after the jubile — 4557
25:15 according unto the n of years of the fruits — 4557
25:16 according for to the n of the years of — 4557
25:50 shall be according to the n of years, — 4557
26:22 your cattle, and **make** you **few in n**; — 4591

Nu
1: 2 with the n of their names, every male by — 4557
1: 3 and Aaron shall n them by their armies. — 6485
1:18 according to the n of the names, — 4557
1:20 according to the n of the names, by their — 4557
1:22 according to the n of the names, by their — 4557
1:24 according to the n of the names, — 4557
1:26 according to the n of the names, — 4557
1:28 according to the n of the names, — 4557
1:30 according to the n of the names, — 4557
1:32 according to the n of the names, — 4557
1:34 according to the n of the names, — 4557
1:36 according to the n of the names, — 4557
1:38 according to the n of the names, — 4557
1:40 according to the n of the names, — 4557
1:42 according to the n of the names, — 4557
1:49 Only thou shalt not n the tribe of Levi, — 6485
3:15 N the children of Levi after the house of — 6485
3:15 month old and upward shalt thou n them. — 6485
3:22 according to the n of all the males, — 4557
3:28 In the n of all the males, from a month — 4557
3:34 according to the n of all the males, from — 4557
3:40 N all the firstborn of the males of — 6485
3:40 upward, and take the n of their names. — 4557
3:43 all the firstborn males by the n of names, — 4557
3:48 wherewith the **odd n** of them is to be — 5736
4:23 upward until fifty years old shalt thou n — 6485
4:29 thou shalt n them after their families, — 6485
4:30 upward fifty years old shalt thou n them, — 6485
4:37 Aaron did n according to — 6485
4:41 Aaron did n according to — 6485
14:29 according to your whole n, from twenty — 4557
14:34 After the n of the days in which ye — 4557
15:12 According to the n that ye shall prepare, — 4557
15:12 ye do to every one according to their n. — 4557
23:10 and the n of the fourth part of Israel? — 4557
26:53 inheritance according to the n of names. — 4557
29:18 the lambs, shall be according to their n, — 4557
29:21 the lambs, shall be according to their n, — 4557
29:24 the lambs, shall be according to their n, — 4557
29:27 the lambs, shall be according to their n, — 4557
29:30 the lambs, shall be according to their n, — 4557
29:33 the lambs, shall be according to their n, — 4557
29:37 the lambs, shall be according to their n, — 4557
31:36 in n three hundred thousand and seven — 4557

Dt
4:27 shall be left few in n among the heathen, — 4557
7: 7 ye were moe in n than any people; — 7230
16: 9 Seven weeks shalt thou n unto thee: — 5608
16: 9 begin to n the seven weeks from such — 5608
25: 2 according to his fault, by a certain n. — 4557
28:62 ye shall be left few in n, whereas ye were — 4962
32: 8 to the n of the children of Israel. — 4557

Jos
4: 5 according unto the n of the tribes of — 4557
4: 8 according to the n of the tribes of — 4557

Jdg
6: 5 they and their camels were without n: — 4557
7: 6 the n of them that lapped, putting their — 4557
7:12 their camels were without n, as the sand — 4557

N

Jdg 21:23 took *them* wives, according to their **n**, 4557
1Sa 6: 4 *according to* the **n** of the lords of 4557
 6:18 *according to* the **n** of all the cities of 4557
 14:17 **N** now, and see who is gone from us. 6485
2Sa 2:15 and went over by **n** twelve of Benjamin, 4557
 21:20 every foot six toes, four and twenty *in* **n**; 4557
 24: 1 them to say, Go, **n** Israel and Judah. 4487
 24: 2 even to Beer-sheba, and **n** ye the people, 6485
 24: 2 that I may know the **n** of the people. 4557
 24: 4 of the king, to **n** the people *of* Israel. 6485
 24: 9 Joab gave *up* the sum of the **n** of the 4662
1Ki 18:31 *according to* the **n** of the tribes of David two 4557
 20:25 **n** thee an army, like the army that thou 4487
1Ch 7: 2 whose **n** *was* in the days of David 4557
 7: 9 the **n** of them, **after** their **genealogy** by 3187
 7:40 the **n** throughout the genealogy of them 4557
 11:11 this *is* the **n** of the mighty *men* whom 4557
 21: 1 and provoked David to **n** Israel. 4487
 21: 2 Go, **n** Israel from Beer-sheba even to Dan; 5608
 21: 2 bring the **n** of them to me, that I may 4557
 21: 5 Joab gave the sum of the **n** of the people 4662
 22:16 and the brass, and the iron, *there* is no **n**. 4557
 23: 3 their **n** by their polls, man by man, 4557
 23:24 as they were counted by **n** of names by 4557
 23:31 new moons, and on the set feasts, by **n**, 4557
 25: 1 the **n** of the workmen according to their 4557
 25: 7 So the **n** of them, with their brethren *that* 4557
 27: 1 Now the children of Israel after their **n**, 4557
 27:23 David took not the **n** of them from twenty 4557
 27:24 Joab the son of Zeruiah began to **n**, 4487
 27:24 neither was the **n** put in the account of 4557
2Ch 12: 3 the people *were* without **n** that came with 4557
 26:11 according to the **n** of their account by 4557
 26:12 The whole **n** of the chief of the fathers of 4557
 29:32 the **n** of the burnt offerings, which 4557
 30:24 **great n** of priests sanctified 7230+3807.1
 35: 7 to the **n** of thirty thousand, 4557
Ezr 1: 9 this *is* the **n** of them: thirty chargers of 4557
 2: 2 The **n** of the men of the people of Israel: 4557
 3: 4 and *offered* the daily burnt offerings by **n**, 4557
 6:17 according to the **n** of the tribes of Israel. 4510
 8:34 By **n** *and* by weight of every one: 4557
Ne 7: 7 The **n**, *I say*, of the men of the people 4557
Est 9:11 On that day the **n** of those that were slain 4557
Job 1: 5 offered burnt offerings *according to* the **n** 4557
 3: 6 let it not come into the **n** of the months. 4557
 5: 9 marvellous *things* without **n**: 4557
 9:10 finding out; yea, and wonders without **n**. 4557
 14: 5 the **n** of his months *are* with thee, 4557
 15:20 the **n** of years is hidden to the oppressor. 4557
 21:21 when the **n** of his months is cut off in 4557
 25: 3 Is there *any* **n** of his armies? 4557
 31:37 declare unto him the **n** of my steps; 4557
 34:24 break in pieces mighty *men* without **n**, 2714
 36:26 neither can the **n** of his years be searched 4557
 38:21 or *because* the **n** of thy days *is* great? 4557
 38:37 Who can **n** the clouds in wisdom? 4557
 39: 2 Canst thou **n** the months *that* they fulfil? 5608
Ps 90:12 So teach *us* to **n** our days, that we may 4487
 105:12 When they were *but a few* men in **n**; yea, 4557
 105:34 and caterpillars, and that without **n**, 4557
 139:18 they are moe in **n** than the sand: 7235
 147: 4 He telleth the **n** of the stars; he calleth 4557
SS 6: 8 and virgins without **n**. 4557
Isa 21:17 the residue of the **n** of archers, the mighty 4557
 40:26 *things*, that bringeth out their host by **n**: 4557
 65:11 that furnish the drink offering unto *that* **n**. 4507
 65:12 Therefore will I **n** you to the sword, 4487
Jer 2:28 for *according to* the **n** of thy cities are thy 4557
 2:32 people have forgotten me days without **n**. 4557
 11:13 *according to* the **n** of thy cities were thy 4557
 11:13 *according to* the **n** of the streets of 4557
 44:28 Yet a small **n** that escape the sword shall 4557
Eze 4: 4 *according to* the **n** of the days that thou 4557
 4: 5 according to the **n** of the days, 4557
 4: 9 *according to* the **n** of the days that thou 4557
 5: 3 Thou shalt also take thereof a few in **n**, 4557
Da 9: 2 understood by books the **n** of the years, 4557
Hos 1:10 Yet the **n** of the children of Israel shall be 4557
Joel 1: 6 strong, and without **n**, whose teeth *are* 4557
Na 1: 3 of slain, and a **great n** of carcases; 3514
Mk 10:46 with his disciples and a **great n** of people, 2425
Lk 22: 3 being of the **n** of the twelve. 706
Jn 6:10 men sat down, in **n** about five thousand. 706
Ac 1:15 (the **n** of names together were about an 3793
 4: 4 the **n** of the men was about five thousand. 706
 5:36 to whom a **n** of men, about four hundred, 706
 6: 1 the **n** of the disciples was multiplied, NIG
 6: 7 the **n** of the disciples multiplied in 706
 11:21 and a great **n** believed, and turned unto 706
 16: 5 in the faith, and increased in **n** daily. 706
Ro 9:27 Though the **n** of the children of Israel be 706
2Co 10:12 For we dare not **make** *ourselves* **of the n**, 1469
1Ti 5: 9 not a widow **taken into the n** under 2639
Rev 5:11 the **n** of them was ten thousand times ten 706
 7: 4 And I heard the **n** of them which were 705
 7: 9 which no *man* could **n**, of all nations, 706
 9:16 the **n** of the army of the horsemen *were* 706
 9:16 and I heard the **n** of them. 706
 13:17 the name of the beast, or the **n** of his name. 706
 13:18 him that hath understanding count the **n** 706
 13:18 for it is the **n** of a man; and his number *is* 706
 13:18 and his **n** *is* Six hundred threescore *and* six. 706
 15: 2 over his mark, *and* over the **n** of his name, 706
 20: 8 the **n** of whom *is* as the sand of the sea. 706

NUMBERED (128) [NUMBER]

Ge 13:16 of the earth, *then* shall thy seed also be **n**. 4487
 16:10 that it shall not be **n** for multitude. 5608
 32:12 the sea, which cannot be **n** for multitude. 5608
Ex 30:13 one that passeth among them that are **n**, 6485
 30:14 one that passeth among them that are **n**, 6485
 38:25 the silver of them that were **n** of 6485
 38:26 for every one that went to be **n**, 6485
Nu 1:19 so he **n** them in the wilderness of Sinai. 6485
 1:21 that were **n** of them, *even* of the tribe 6485
 1:22 their fathers, those that were **n** of them, 6485
 1:23 that were **n** of them, *even* of the tribe 6485
 1:25 that were **n** of them, *even* of the tribe 6485
 1:27 that were **n** of them, *even* of the tribe 6485
 1:29 that were **n** of them, *even* of the tribe 6485
 1:31 that were **n** of them, *even* of the tribe 6485
 1:33 that were **n** of them, *even* of the tribe 6485
 1:35 that were **n** of them, *even* of the tribe 6485
 1:37 that were **n** of them, *even* of the tribe 6485
 1:39 that were **n** of them, *even* of the tribe 6485
 1:41 that were **n** of them, *even* of the tribe 6485
 1:43 that were **n** of them, *even* of the tribe 6485
 1:44 *are* those that were **n**, which Moses 6485
 1:44 Moses and Aaron **n**, and the princes 6485
 1:45 So were all those that were **n** of 6485
 1:46 all they that were **n** were six hundred 6485
 1:47 of their fathers were not **n** among them. 6485
 2: 4 his host, and those that were **n** of them, 6485
 2: 6 those that were **n** thereof, *were* fifty and 6485
 2: 8 those that were **n** thereof, *were* fifty and 6485
 2: 9 All that were **n** in the camp of Judah *were* 6485
 2:11 those that were **n** thereof, *were* forty and 6485
 2:13 those that were **n** of them, *were* fifty and 6485
 2:15 those that were **n** of them, *were* forty and 6485
 2:16 All that were **n** in the camp of Reuben 6485
 2:19 his host, and those that were **n** of them, 6485
 2:21 that were **n** of them, *were* thirty and 6485
 2:23 that were **n** of them, *were* thirty and 6485
 2:24 All that were **n** of the camp of Ephraim 6485
 2:26 his host, and those that were **n** of them, 6485
 2:28 those that were **n** of them, *were* forty and 6485
 2:30 those that were **n** of them, *were* fifty and 6485
 2:31 All that were **n** in the camp of Dan 6485
 2:32 These *are* those which were **n** of 6485
 2:32 all those that were **n** of the camps 6485
 2:33 Levites were not **n** among the children 6485
 3:16 Moses **n** them according to the word of 6485
 3:22 Those that were **n** of them, according to 6485
 3:22 those that were **n** of them *were* seven 6485
 3:34 those that were **n** of them, according to 6485
 3:39 All that were **n** of the Levites, which 6485
 3:39 Aaron **n** at the commandment of 6485
 3:42 Moses **n**, as the Lᴏʀᴅ commanded him, 6485
 3:43 upward, of those that were **n** of them, 6485
 4:34 chief of the congregation **n** the sons of 6485
 4:36 that were **n** of them by their families 6485
 4:37 *were* they that were **n** of the families 6485
 4:38 those that were **n** of the sons of Gershon, 6485
 4:40 Even those that were **n** of them, 6485
 4:41 These *are* they that were **n** of the families 6485
 4:42 that were **n** of the families of the sons 6485
 4:44 Even those that were **n** of them after their 6485
 4:45 These *be* those that were **n** of the families 6485
 4:45 Aaron **n** according to the word of 6485
 4:46 All those that were **n** of the Levites, 6485
 4:46 and Aaron and the chief of Israel **n**, 6485
 4:48 those that were **n** of them, were eight 6485
 4:49 Lᴏʀᴅ they were **n** by the hand of Moses, 6485
 4:49 thus *were they* **n** of him, as the Lᴏʀᴅ 6485
 7: 2 and were over them that were **n**, offered: 6485
 14:29 all that were **n** of you, according to your 6485
 26: 7 they that were **n** of them were forty and 6485
 26:18 according to those that were **n** of them, 6485
 26:22 according to those that were **n** of them, 6485
 26:25 according to those that were **n** of them, 6485
 26:27 according to those that were **n** of them, 6485
 26:34 those that were **n** of them, fifty and 6485
 26:37 according to those that were **n** of them, 6485
 26:41 they that were **n** of them *were* forty and 6485
 26:43 according to those that were **n** of them, 6485
 26:47 according to those that were **n** of them, 6485
 26:50 they that were **n** of them *were* forty and 6485
 26:51 These *were* the **n** of the children of Israel, 6485
 26:54 according to those that were **n** of him. 6485
 26:57 these *are* they that were **n** of the Levites 6485
 26:62 those that were **n** of them were twenty 6485
 26:62 for they were not **n** among the children 6485
 26:63 These *are* they that were **n** by Moses and 6485
 26:63 who **n** the children of Israel in the plains 6485
 26:64 whom Moses and Aaron the priest **n**, 6485
 26:64 when they **n** the children of Israel in 6485
Jos 8:10 the people, and went up, he and the 6485
Jdg 20:15 the children of Benjamin were **n** at that 6485
 20:15 were **n** seven hundred chosen men. 6485
 20:17 were **n** four hundred thousand men that 6485
 21: 9 For the people were **n**, and behold, 6485
1Sa 11: 8 when he **n** them in Bezek, the children 6485
 13:15 Saul **n** the people that were present with 6485
 14:17 when they had **n**, behold Jonathan and 6485
 15: 4 **n** them in Telaim, two hundred thousand 6485
2Sa 18: 1 David **n** the people *that were* with him, 6485
 24:10 heart smote him after that he had **n** 5608
1Ki 3: 8 cannot be **n** nor counted for multitude. 4487
 8: 5 could not be told nor **n** for multitude. 4487

1Ki 20:15 he **n** the young men of the princes of 6485
 20:15 after them he **n** all the people, *even* all 6485
 20:26 Ben-hadad **n** the Syrians, and went up 6485
 20:27 the children of Israel were **n**, and were all 6485
2Ki 3: 6 of Samaria the same time, and **n** all Israel. 6485
1Ch 21:17 not I *that* commanded the people to be **n**? 4487
 23: 3 Now the Levites were **n** from the age of 5608
 23:27 the Levites *were* **n** from twenty years old 4557
2Ch 2:17 Solomon **n** all the strangers that *were* in 5608
 2:17 where*with* David his father had **n** them; 5608
 5: 6 could not be told nor **n** for multitude. 4487
 25: 5 **n** them from twenty years old and 6485
Ezr 1: 8 **n** them unto Sheshbazzar, the prince of 5608
Ps 40: 5 *if* them, they are moe than can be **n**. 6186
Ecc 1:15 and that which is wanting cannot be **n**. 4487
Isa 22:10 And ye have **n** the houses of Jerusalem, 5608
 53:12 he was **n** with the transgressors; 4487
Jer 33:22 As the host of heaven cannot be **n**, 5608
Da 5:26 God hath **n** thy kingdom, and finished it. 4483
Hos 1:10 sea, which cannot be measured nor **n**; 5608
Mt 10:30 But the very hairs of your head are all **n**. 705
Mk 15:28 And he was **n** with the transgressors. 3049
Lk 12: 7 even the *very* hairs of your head are all **n**. 705
Ac 1:17 he was **n** with us, and had obtained part 2674
 1:26 and he was **n** with the eleven apostles. 4785

NUMBEREST (3) [NUMBER]

Ex 30:12 soul unto the Lᴏʀᴅ, when *thou* **n** them; 6485
 30:12 plague amongst them, when *thou* **n** them. 6485
Job 14:16 For now thou **n** my steps: dost thou not 5608

NUMBERING (2) [NUMBER]

Ge 41:49 sand of the sea, very much, until he left **n**; 5608
2Ch 2:17 after the **n** where*with* David his father 5610

NUMBERS (3) [NUMBER]

1Ch 12:23 *are* the **n** of the bands that were ready 4557
2Ch 17:14 these *are* the **n** of them according to 6486
Ps 71:15 all the day; for I know not the **n** *thereof*. 5615

NUMEROUS See POPULOUS

NUN (29)

Ex 33:11 Joshua, the son of **N**, a young man, 5126
Nu 11:28 Joshua the son of **N**, the servant of Moses 5126
 13: 8 the tribe of Ephraim, Oshea the son of **N**. 5126
 13:16 called Oshea the son of **N**, Jehoshua. 5126
 14: 6 Joshua the son of **N**, and Caleb the son 5126
 14:30 of Jephunneh, and Joshua the son of **N**. 5126
 14:38 Joshua the son of **N**, and Caleb the son 5126
 26:65 of Jephunneh, and Joshua the son of **N**. 5126
 27:18 Take thee Joshua the son of **N**, a man in 5126
 32:12 the Kenezite, and Joshua the son of **N**: 5126
 32:28 Joshua the son of **N**, and the chief fathers 5126
 34:17 the priest, and Joshua the son of **N**. 5126
Dt 1:38 *But* Joshua the son of **N**, which standeth 5126
 31:23 he gave Joshua the son of **N** a charge, 5126
 32:44 the people, he and Hoshea the son of **N**. 5126
 34: 9 Joshua the son of **N** was full *of* the spirit 5126
Jos 1: 1 Lᴏʀᴅ spake unto Joshua the son of **N**, 5126
 2: 1 Joshua the son of **N** sent out of Shittim 5126
 2:23 came to Joshua the son of **N**, and told 5126
 6: 6 Joshua the son of **N** called the priests, 5126
 14: 1 Joshua the son of **N**, and the heads of 5126
 17: 4 before Joshua the son of **N**, and before 5126
 19:49 to Joshua the son of **N** among them: 5126
 19:51 Joshua the son of **N**, and the heads of 5126
 21: 1 unto Joshua the son of **N**, and unto 5126
 24:29 that Joshua the son of **N**, the servant of 5126
Jdg 2: 8 Joshua the son of **N**, the servant of 5126
1Ki 16:34 which he spake by Joshua the son of **N**. 5126
Ne 8:17 for since the days of Jeshua the son of **N** 5126

NURSE (10) [NURSED, NURSING]

Ge 24:59 **n**, and Abrabah's servant, and his men. 3243
 35: 8 Deborah Rebekah's **n** died, and she was 3243
Ex 2: 7 call to thee a **n** of the Hebrew women, 3243
 2: 7 that she may **n** the child for thee? 3243
 2: 9 **n** it for me, and I will give *thee* thy 3243
Ru 4: 4 laid it in her bosom, and became **n** unto it. 539
2Sa 4: 4 of Jezreel, and his **n** took him up, and fled: 539
2Ki 11: 2 they hid him, *even* him and his **n**, 3243
2Ch 22:11 and put him and his **n** in a bedchamber. 3243
1Th 2: 7 *even* as a **n** cherisheth her children: 5162

NURSED (2) [NURSE]

Ex 2: 9 And the woman took the child, and **n** it. 5134
Isa 60: 4 and thy daughters shall be **n** at *thy* side. 539

NURSING (3) [NURSE]

Nu 11:12 as a **n father** beareth the sucking child, 539
Isa 49:23 kings shall be thy **n fathers**, 539
 49:23 and their queens thy **n mothers**: 3243

NURTURE (1)

Eph 6: 4 but bring them up in the **n** and 3809

NUTS (2)

Ge 43:11 spices, and myrrh, **n**, and almonds, 992
SS 6:11 I went down into the garden of **n** to see 93

NYMPHA See NYMPHAS

NYMPHAS (1)

Col 4:15 and **N**, and the church which is in his 3564

O

O (1086) [OH] See Index of Articles, Etc.

OAK (15) [OAKS]
Ge 35: 4 Jacob hid them under the **o** which *was* by 424
 35: 8 she was buried beneath Beth-el under an **o**: 437
Jos 24:26 great stone, and set it up there under an **o**, 427
Jdg 6:11 sat under an **o** which *was* in Ophrah, 424
 6:19 and brought *it* out unto him under the **o**, 424
2Sa 18: 9 went under the thick boughs of a great **o**, 424
 18: 9 his head caught hold of the **o**, and he was 424
 18:10 Behold, I saw Absalom hanged in an **o**. 424
 18:14 he *was* yet alive in the midst of the **o**. 424
1Ki 13:14 of God, and found him sitting under an **o**: 424
1Ch 10:12 buried their bones under the **o** in Jabesh, 424
Isa 1:30 For ye shall be as an **o** whose leaf fadeth, 424
 6:13 as a teil tree, and as an **o**, whose substance 437
 44:14 and taketh the cypress and the **o**, 437
Eze 6:13 every green tree, and under every thick **o**, 424

OAKS (6) [OAK]
Isa 1:29 For they shall be ashamed of the **o** which 352
 2:13 and lifted up, and upon all the **o** of Bashan, 437
Eze 27: 6 *Of* the **o** of Bashan have they made thine 437
Hos 4:13 under **o** and poplars and elms, because 437
Am 2: 9 of the cedars, and he *was* strong as the **o**; 437
Zec 11: 2 howl, O ye **o** of Bashan; for the forest of 437

OAR (1) [OARS]
Eze 27:29 all that handle the **o**, the mariners, 4880

OARS (2) [OAR]
Isa 33:21 wherein shall go no galley with **o**, 7885
Eze 27: 6 oaks of Bashan have they made thine **o**; 4880

OARSMEN See ROWERS

OATH (59) [OATHS, OATHS']
Ge 24: 8 then thou shalt be clear from this my **o**: 7621
 24:41 shalt thou be clear from *this* my **o**, 423
 24:41 I thee shalt be clear from my **o**. 423
 26: 3 I will perform the **o** which I sware unto 7621
 26:28 said, Let there be now an **o** betwixt us, 423
 50:25 Joseph **took an o** of the children of Israel, 7650
Ex 22:11 *Then* shall an **o** of the Lord be between 7621
Lev 5: 4 *be* that a man shall pronounce with an **o**, 7621
Nu 5:19 the priest shall **charge** her **by an o**, 7650
 5:21 **charge** the woman
 with an o 7621+7650+871.1
 5:21 thee a curse and an **o** among thy people, 7621
 30: 2 swear an **o** to bind his soul with a bond; 7621
 30:10 or bound her soul by a bond with an **o**; 7621
 30:13 and every binding **o** to afflict the soul, 7621
Dt 7: 8 he would keep the **o** which he had sworn 7621
 29:12 into his **o**, which the Lord thy God 423
 29:14 only do I make this covenant and this **o**; 423
Jos 2:17 We *will be* blameless of this thine **o** which 7621
 2:20 we will be quit of thine **o** which thou hast 7621
 9:20 of the **o** which we sware unto them. 7621
Jdg 21: 5 For *they* had made a great **o** concerning 7621
1Sa 14:26 to his mouth: for the people feared the **o**. 7621
 14:27 his father **charged** the people **with the o**: 7650
 14:28 **straitly charged** the people
 with an o, 7650+7650
2Sa 21: 7 of the Lord's **o** that *was* between them, 7621
1Ki 2:43 hast thou not kept the **o** of the Lord, 7621
 8:31 o be laid upon him to cause him to swear, 423
 8:31 the **o** come before thine altar in this house: 423
 18:10 *He is* not *there*; he **took an o** of 7650
2Ki 11: 4 **took an o** of them in the house of 7650
1Ch 16:16 with Abraham, and of his **o** unto Isaac; 7621
2Ch 6:22 an **o** be laid upon him to make him swear, 423
 6:22 the **o** come before thine altar in this house; 423
 15:15 all Judah rejoiced at the **o**: for they had 7621
Ne 5:12 called the priests, and **took an o** of them, 7650
 10:29 and entered into a curse, and into an **o**, 7621
Ps 105: 9 with Abraham, and his **o** unto Isaac; 7621
Ecc 8: 2 and *that* in regard of the **o** of God. 7621
 9: 2 he that sweareth, as he that feareth an **o**. 7621
Jer 11: 5 That *I* may perform the **o** which I have 7621
Eze 16:59 which hast despised the **o** in breaking 423
 17:13 with him, and hath taken an **o** of him: 423
 17:16 whose **o** he despised, and whose covenant 423
 17:18 Seeing he despised the **o** by breaking 423
 17:19 surely mine **o** that he hath despised, 423
Da 9:11 the **o** that *is* written in the law of Moses 7621
Zec 8:17 against his neighbour; and love no false **o**: 7621
Mt 14: 7 Whereupon he promised with an **o** to give 3727
 26:72 And again he denied with an **o**, I do not 3727
Lk 1:73 The **o** which he sware to our father 3727
Ac 2:30 knowing that God had sworn with an **o** to 3727
 23:21 which have **bound** themselves **with an o**, 332
Heb 6:16 an **o** for confirmation *is* to them an end of 3727
 6:17 of his counsel, confirmed *it* by an **o**: 3728
 7:20 inasmuch as not without an **o** *he was* 3728
 7:21 those priests were made without an **o**; 3728
 7:21 this with an **o** by him that said unto him, 3728

OATHS (3) [OATH]
Eze 21:23 in their sight, to them that have sworn **o**: 7621
Hab 3: 9 *according to* the **o** of the tribes, *even thy* 7621
Mt 5:33 but shalt perform unto the Lord thine **o**: 3727

OATHS' (2) [OATH]
Mt 14: 9 nevertheless for the **o** sake, and them 3727
Mk 6:26 *yet* for his **o** sake, and for their sakes 3727

OBADIAH (20)
1Ki 18: 3 Ahab called **O**, which *was* the governor of 5662
 18: 3 (Now **O** feared the Lord greatly: 5662
 18: 4 that **O** took an hundred prophets, 5662
 18: 5 Ahab said unto **O**, Go into the land, unto 5662
 18: 6 **O** went another way by himself. 5662
 18: 7 as **O** was in the way, behold Elijah met 5662
 18:16 So **O** went to meet Ahab, and told him: 5662
1Ch 3:21 the sons of Arnan, the sons of **O**, 5662
 7: 3 Michael, and **O**, and Joel, Ishiah, five: 5662
 8:38 Ishmael, and Sheariah, and **O**, and Hanan. 5662
 9:16 the son of Shemaiah, the son of Galal, 5662
 9:44 Ishmael, and Sheariah, and **O**, and Hanan: 5662
 12: 9 the first, **O** the second, Eliab the third, 5662
 27:19 Of Zebulun, Ishmaiah the son of **O**: 5662
2Ch 17: 7 to **O**, and to Zechariah, and to Nethaneel, 5662
 34:12 the overseers of them *were* Jahath and **O**, 5662
Ezr 8: 9 the son of Jehiel, and with him two 5662
Ne 10: 5 Harim, Meremoth, **O**, 5662
 12:25 Mattaniah, and Bakbukiah, **O**, Meshullam, 5662
Ob 1: 1 The vision of **O**. Thus saith the Lord God 5662

OBAL (1)
Ge 10:28 And **O**, and Abimael, and Sheba, 5745

OBED (13)
Ru 4:17 to Naomi; and they called his name **O**: 5744
 4:21 Salmon begat Boaz, and Boaz begat **O**, 5744
 4:22 And **O** begat Jesse, and Jesse begat David. 5744
1Ch 2:12 And Boaz begat **O**, and Obed begat Jesse, 5744
 2:12 And Boaz begat Obed, and **O** begat Jesse, 5744
 2:37 Zabad begat Ephlal, and Ephlal begat **O**, 5744
 2:38 **O** begat Jehu, and Jehu begat Azariah, 5744
 11:47 Eliel, and **O**, and Jasiel the Mesobaite. 5744
 26: 7 Othni, and Rephael, and **O**, Elzabad, 5744
2Ch 23: 1 Azariah the son of **O**, and Maaseiah the 5744
Mt 1: 5 Booz begat **O** of Ruth; and Obed begat 5601
 1: 5 begat Obed of Ruth; and **O** begat Jesse; 5601
Lk 3:32 was *the son* of **O**, which was *the son* 5601

OBED-EDOM (20)
2Sa 6:10 David carried it aside *into* the house of **O** 5654
 6:11 the house of **O** the Gittite three months: 5654
 6:11 the Lord blessed **O**, and all his 5654
 6:12 The Lord hath blessed the house of **O**, 5654
 6:12 of **O** *into* the city of David with gladness. 5654
1Ch 13:13 carried it aside into the house of **O** 5654
 13:14 the family of **O** in his house three months. 5654
 13:14 the Lord blessed the house of **O**, 5654
 15:18 Elipheleh, and Mikneiah, and **O**, and Jeiel, 5654
 15:21 Mikneiah, and **O**, and Jeiel, and Azaziah, 5654
 15:24 **O** and Jehiah *were* doorkeepers for the 5654
 15:25 the house **O** out of the house of **O** with joy. 5654
 16: 5 and Eliab, and Benaiah, and **O**: 5654
 16:38 **O** with their brethren, threescore and 5654
 16:38 also the son of Jeduthun and Hosah to 5654
 26: 4 Moreover the sons of **O** *were*, Shemaiah 5654
 26: 8 All these of the sons of **O**: they and 5654
 26: 8 service, *were* threescore and two of **O**. 5654
 26:15 To **O** southward; and to his sons the 5654
2Ch 25:24 were found in the house of God with **O**, 5654

OBEDIENCE (12) [OBEY]
Ro 1: 5 for **o** to the faith among all nations, 5218
 5:19 by the **o** of one shall many be made 5218
 6:16 unto death, or of **o** unto righteousness? 5218
 16:19 For your **o** is come abroad unto all *men*. I 5218
 16:26 made known to all nations for the **o** of 5218
1Co 14:34 but *they are commanded* to be **under o**, 5293
2Co 7:15 whilst he remembereth the **o** of you all, 5218
 10: 5 captivity every thought to the **o** of Christ; 5218
 10: 6 all disobedience, when your **o** is fulfilled. 5218
Phm 1:21 Having confidence in thy **o** I wrote unto 5218
Heb 5: 8 *yet* learned he **o** by *the things* which he 5218
1Pe 1: 2 unto **o** and sprinkling of the blood of Jesus 5218

OBEDIENT (16) [OBEY]
Ex 24: 7 the Lord hath said will we do, and be **o**. 8085
Nu 27:20 of the children of Israel may be **o**. 8085
Dt 4:30 thy God, and shalt be **o** unto his voice; 8085
 8:20 ye would not be **o** unto the voice of 8085
2Sa 22:45 as they hear, they shall be **o** unto me. 8085
Pr 25:12 *so is* a wise reprover upon an **o** ear. 8085
Isa 1:19 If ye be willing and **o**, ye shall eat the 8085
 42:24 ways, neither were they **o** unto his law. 8085
Ac 6: 7 a great company of the priests were **o** to 5219
Ro 15:18 make the Gentiles **o**, by word and deed, 5218
2Co 2: 9 of you, whether ye be **o** in all *things*. 5255
Eph 6: 5 be **o** to them *that are* your masters 5219
Php 2: 8 himself, and became **o** unto death, 5255
Tit 2: 5 at home, good, **o** to their own husbands, 5293
 2: 9 *Exhort* servants to be **o** unto their own 5293
1Pe 1:14 As **o** children, not fashioning yourselves 5218

OBEISANCE (9) [OBEY]
Ge 37: 7 round about, and **made o** to my sheaf. 7812
 37: 9 and the eleven stars **made o** to me. 7812
 43:28 bowed down their heads, and **made o**. 7812
Ex 18: 7 father in law, and **did o**, and kissed him; 7812
2Sa 1: 2 David, that he fell to the earth, and did **o**. 7812
 14: 4 and did **o**, and said, Help, O king. 7812
 15: 5 any man came nigh *to him* to do him **o**, 7812
1Ki 1:16 bowed, and **did o** unto the king. 7812
2Ch 24:17 princes of Judah, and **made o** to the king. 7812

OBEY (69) [OBEDIENCE, OBEDIENT, OBEISANCE, OBEYED, OBEYEDST, OBEYETH, OBEYING]
Ge 27: 8 **o** my voice according to *that* 8085+871.1
 27:13 **o** my voice, and go fetch me *them* 8085+871.1
 27:43 therefore, my son, **o** my voice; 8085+871.1
Ex 5: 2 should **o** his voice to let Israel go? 8085
 19: 5 ye will **o** my voice **indeed**, 8085+8085+871.1
 23:21 Beware of him, and **o** his voice, 8085+871.1
 23:22 if thou shalt **indeed o** his voice, 8085+8085
Dt 11:27 if ye **o** the commandments of the Lord 8085
 11:28 If ye will not **o** the commandments of 8085
 13: 4 **o** his voice, and you shall serve him, 8085
 21:18 which will not **o** the voice of his 8085+871.1
 21:20 rebellious, he will not **o** our voice; 8085+871.1
 27:10 **o** the voice of the Lord thy God, 8085+871.1
 28:62 thou wouldest not **o** the voice of 8085+871.1
 30: 2 shalt **o** his voice according to all 8085+871.1
 30: 8 and **o** the voice of the Lord, 8085+871.1
 30:20 and that thou mayest **o** his voice, 8085+871.1
Jos 24:24 will we serve, and his voice will we **o**. 8085
1Sa 8:19 the people refused to **o** 8085+871.1
 12:14 **o** his voice, and not rebel against 8085+871.1
 12:15 if ye will not **o** the voice of 8085+871.1
 15:19 thou not **o** the voice of the Lord, 8085+871.1
 15:22 to **o** *is* better than sacrifice, *and* to 8085
Ne 9:17 refused to **o**, neither were mindful of thy 8085
Job 36:11 If they **o** and serve *him*, they shall spend 8085
 36:12 If they **o** not, they shall perish by the 8085
Ps 18:44 As soon as they hear *of me*, they shall **o** 8085
Pr 30:17 *his* father, and despiseth to **o** *his* mother, 3349
Isa 11:14 and the children of Ammon shall **o** them. 4928
Jer 7:23 **O** my voice, and I will be your 8085+871.1
 11: 4 **O** my voice, and do them, 8085+871.1
 11: 7 protesting, saying, **O** my voice. 8085
 12:17 if they will not **o**, I will utterly pluck up 8085
 18:10 that *it* **o** not my voice, then I will 8085+871.1
 26:13 **o** the voice of the Lord your God; 8085+871.1
 35:14 but **o** their father's commandment: 8085
 38:20 They shall not deliver *thee*. **O**, 8085+871.1
 42: 6 **o** the voice of the Lord our God, 8085+871.1
 42: 6 when we **o** the voice of the Lord 8085+871.1
 42:13 neither **o** the voice of the Lord 8085+871.1
Da 7:27 and all dominions shall serve and **o** him. 8086
 9:11 that *they* might not **o** thy voice; 8085+871.1
Zec 6:15 if ye will **diligently o** the voice of 8085+8085
Mt 8:27 that even the winds and the sea **o** him? 5219
Mk 1:27 the unclean spirits, and they do **o** him. 5219
 4:41 that even the wind and the sea **o** him? 5219
Lk 8:25 the winds and water, and they **o** him. 5219
 17: 6 planted in the sea; and it should **o** you. 5219
Ac 5:29 said, We ought to **o** God rather than men. 3980
 5:32 God hath given to them that **o** him. 3980
 7:39 To whom our fathers would not **o**, 1096+5255
Ro 2: 8 and do **not o** the truth, 544
 2: 8 but **o** unrighteousness, indignation and 3982
 6:12 that *ye* should **o** it in the lusts thereof. 5219
 6:16 to whom ye yield yourselves servants to **o**, 5219
 6:16 to obey, *his* servants ye are to whom ye **o**; 5219
Gal 3: 1 that you should not **o** 3982
 5: 7 who did hinder you that *ye* should not **o** 3982
Eph 6: 1 Children, **o** your parents in the Lord: 5219
Col 3:20 **o** *your* parents in all *things*: for this is well 5219
 3:22 **o** in all *things your* masters according to 5219
2Th 1: 8 that know not the gospel of our Lord Jesus 5219
 3:14 And if any *man* **o** not our word by this 5219
Tit 3: 1 and powers, to **o magistrates**, 3980
Heb 5: 9 eternal salvation unto all them that **o** him; 5219
 13:17 **O** them that have the rule over you, 3982
Jas 3: 3 in the horses' mouths, that they may **o** us; 3982
1Pe 3: 1 that, if any **o not** the word, they also may 544
 4:17 what *shall* the end *be* of them that **o not** 544

OBEYED (41) [OBEY]
Ge 22:18 because thou hast **o** my voice. 8085+871.1
 26: 5 Because that Abraham **o** my voice, 8085+871.1
 28: 7 that Jacob **o** his father and his mother, 8085
Jos 5: 6 they **o** not the voice of the Lord: 8085+871.1
 22: 2 have **o** my voice in all that I commanded 8085
Jdg 2: 2 ye have not **o** my voice: why have ye 8085
 6:10 but ye have not **o** my voice. 8085+871.1
1Sa 15:20 I have **o** the voice of the Lord, 8085+871.1
 15:24 the people, and **o** their voice. 8085+871.1
 28:21 thine handmaid hath **o** thy voice, 8085+871.1
1Ki 20:36 Because thou hast not **o** the voice 8085+871.1
2Ki 18:12 Because they **o** not the voice of 8085+871.1
1Ch 29:23 and prospered; and all Israel **o** him. 8085
2Ch 11: 4 they **o** the words of the Lord, 8085
Pr 5:13 not **o** the voice of my teachers, 8085
Jer 3:13 ye have not **o** my voice, saith the Lord. 8085
 3:25 have not **o** the voice of the Lord 8085+871.1
 9:13 not **o** my voice, neither walked 8085
 11: 8 Yet they **o** not, nor inclined their ear, 8085
 17:23 they **o** not, neither inclined their ear, 8085
 32:23 **o** not thy voice, neither walked 8085+871.1

Jer	34:10 any more, then they **o**, and let *them* go.	8085
	35: 8 Thus have we **o** the voice of	8085+871.1
	35:10 have **o**, and done according to all that	8085
	35:18 Because ye have **o** the commandment of	8085
	40: 3 have not **o** his voice, therefore this	8085+871.1
	42:21 ye have not **o** the voice of	8085+871.1
	43: 4 the people, **o** not the voice of the LORD,	8085
	43: 7 for they **o** not the voice of	8085+871.1
	44:23 have not **o** the voice of the LORD,	8085+871.1
Da	9:10 Neither have we **o** the voice of	8085+871.1
	9:14 he doeth: for we **o** not his voice.	8085+871.1
Zep	3: 2 She **o** not the voice; she received not	8085
Hag	1:12 **o** the voice of the LORD their God,	8085
Ac	5:36 and all, as many as **o** him, were scattered,	3982
	5:37 and all, *even* as many as **o** him,	3982
Ro	6:17 ye have **o** from the heart *that* form of	5219
	10:16 But they have not all **o** the gospel.	5219
Php	2:12 my beloved, as ye have always **o**,	5219
Heb	11: 8 should after receive for an inheritance, **o**;	5219
1Pe	3: 6 *Even* as Sara **o** Abraham, calling him lord:	5219

OBEYEDST (2) [OBEY]

1Sa	28:18 Because thou **o** not the voice of	8085+871.1
Jer	22:21 youth, that thou **o** not my voice.	8085+871.1

OBEYETH (3) [OBEY]

Isa	50:10 that **o** the voice of his servant,	8085+871.1
Jer	7:28 This *is* a nation that **o** not the	8085+871.1
	11: 3 Cursed *be* the man that **o** not the words	8085

OBEYING (3) [OBEY]

Jdg	2:17 **o** the commandments of the LORD,	8085
1Sa	15:22 as in **o** the voice of the LORD?	8085+871.1
1Pe	1:22 Seeing ye have purified your souls in **o**	5218

OBIL (1)

1Ch	27:30 Over the camels also *was* **O** the Ishmaelite.	179

OBJECT (1)

Ac	24:19 and **o**, if they had ought against me.	2723

OBLATION (35) [OBLATIONS]

Lev	2: 4 if thou bring an **o** of a meat offering baken	7133
	2: 5 if thy **o** *be* a meat offering *baken* in a pan,	7133
	2: 7 if thy **o** *be* a meat offering *baken* in	7133
	2:12 *As for* the **o** of the firstfruits, ye shall offer	7133
	2:13 every **o** of thy meat offering shalt thou	7133
	3: 1 if his **o** *be* a sacrifice of peace offering,	7133
	7:14 of it he shall offer one out of the whole **o**	7133
	7:29 **o** unto the LORD of the sacrifice of his	7133
	22:18 that will offer his **o** for all his vows,	7133
Nu	18: 9 every **o** of theirs, every meat offering of	7133
	31:50 therefore brought an **o** for the LORD,	7133
Isa	19:21 in that day, and shall do sacrifice and **o**;	4503
	40:20 impoverished that he hath no **o** chooseth	8641
	66: 3 he that offereth an **o**, *as if* he *offered*	4503
Jer	14:12 when they offer burnt offering and an **o**,	4503
Eze	44:30 firstfruits of all *things*, and every **o** of all,	8641
	45: 1 ye shall offer an **o** unto the LORD, a holy	8641
	45: 6 over against the **o** of the holy *portion*: it	8641
	45: 7 on the other side of the **o** of the holy	8641
	45: 7 before the **o** of the holy *portion*, and the	8641
	45:13 This *is* the **o** that ye shall offer; the sixth	8641
	45:16 All the people of the land shall give this **o**	8641
	48: 9 The **o** that ye shall offer unto the LORD	8641
	48:10 *even* for the priests, shall be this holy **o**;	8641
	48:12 *this* **o** of the land that is offered shall be	8642
	48:18 the residue in length over against the **o** of	8641
	48:18 it shall be over against the **o** of the holy	8641
	48:20 the **o** *shall be* five and twenty thousand	8641
	48:20 ye shall offer the holy **o** foursquare,	8641
	48:21 one side and on the other of the holy **o**,	8641
	48:21 twenty thousand of the **o** toward the east	8641
	48:21 it shall be the holy **o**; and the sanctuary of	8641
Da	2:46 commanded that *they* should offer an **o**	4504
	9:21 me about the time of the evening **o**.	4503
	9:27 cause the sacrifice and the **o** to cease,	4503

OBLATIONS (5) [OBLATION]

Lev	7:38 of Israel to offer their **o** unto the LORD,	7133
2Ch	31:14 to distribute the **o** of the LORD,	8641
Isa	1:13 Bring no more vain **o**; incense *is* an	4503
Eze	20:40 the firstfruits of your **o**, with all your holy	4864
	44:30 every *sort* of your **o**, shall be the priests':	8641

OBOTH (4)

Nu	21:10 of Israel set forward, and pitched in **O**.	88
	21:11 they journeyed from **O**, and pitched at	88
	33:43 departed from Punon, and pitched in **O**.	88
	33:44 they departed from **O**, and pitched in	88

OBSCURE (1) [OBSCURITY]

Pr	20:20 his lamp shall be put out in **o** darkness.	380

OBSCURITY (3) [OBSCURE]

Isa	29:18 the eyes of the blind shall see out of **o**,	652
	58:10 shall thy light rise in **o**, and thy darkness	2822
	59: 9 we wait for light, but behold **o**;	2822

OBSERVATION (1) [OBSERVE]

Lk	17:20 The kingdom of God cometh not with **o**:	3907

OBSERVE (55) [OBSERVATION, OBSERVED, OBSERVER, OBSERVERS, OBSERVEST, OBSERVETH]

Ex	12:17 ye shall **o** the *feast of* unleavened bread;	8104

Ex	12:17 shall ye **o** this day in your generations by	8104
	12:24 ye shall **o** this thing for an ordinance to	8104
	31:16 to **o** the sabbath throughout their	6213
	34:11 **O** thou that which I command thee *this*	8104
	34:22 thou shalt **o** the feast of weeks,	6213
Lev	19:26 shall ye use enchantment, nor **o** times.	6049
	19:37 Therefore shall ye **o** all my statutes, and	8104
Nu	28: 2 shall ye **o** to offer unto me in their due	8104
Dt	5:32 Ye shall **o** to do therefore as the LORD	8104
	6: 3 **o** to do *it*; that it may be well with thee,	8104
	6:25 if we **o** to do all these commandments	8104
	8: 1 I command thee *this* day shall ye **o** to do,	8104
	11:32 ye shall **o** to do all the statutes and	8104
	12: 1 which ye shall **o** to do in the land,	8104
	12:28 **O** and hear all these words which I	8104
	12:32 thing soever I command you, **o** to do it:	8104
	15: 5 to **o** to do all these commandments which	8104
	16: 1 **O** the month of Abib, and keep	8104
	16:12 and thou shalt **o** and do these statutes.	8104
	16:13 Thou shalt **o** the feast of tabernacles seven	6213
	17:10 thou shalt **o** to do according to all that	8104
	24: 8 that *thou* **o** diligently, and do according to	8104
	24: 8 as I commanded them, *so* ye shall **o** to do.	8104
	28: 1 to **o** *and* to do all his commandments	8104
	28:13 thee *this* day, to **o** and to do *them*:	8104
	28:15 to **o** to do all his commandments and	8104
	28:58 If thou wilt not **o** to do all the words of	8104
	31:12 and **o** to do all the words of this law:	8104
	32:46 ye shall command your children to **o**	8104
Jos	1: 7 that *thou* mayest **o** to do according to all	8104
	1: 8 that thou mayest **o** to do according to all	8104
	23:14 *thing*: all that I commanded her let her **o**.	8104
1Ki	20:33 the men did **diligently o** whether *any*	5172
2Ki	17:37 for you, ye shall **o** to do for evermore;	8104
	21: 8 only if they will **o** to do according to all	8104
2Ch	7:17 shalt **o** my statutes and my judgments;	8104
Ne	1: 5 that love him and **o** his commandments	8104
	10:29 to **o** and do all the commandments of	8104
Ps	105:45 That they might **o** his statutes, and keep	8104
	107:43 will **o** these *things*, even they shall	8104
	119:34 yea, I shall **o** it with *my* whole heart.	8104
Pr	23:26 thine heart, and let thine eyes **o** my ways.	5341
Jer	8: 7 the swallow **o** the time of their coming;	8104
Eze	20:18 neither **o** their judgments, nor defile	8104
	37:24 and **o** my statutes, and do them.	8104
Hos	13: 7 as a leopard by the way will I **o** *them*:	7789
Jnh	2: 8 They that **o** lying vanities forsake their	8104
Mt	23:3 All therefore whatsoever they bid you **o**,	5083
	23: 3 they bid you observe, *that* **o** and do;	5083
	28:20 Teaching them to **o** all *things* whatsoever	5083
Ac	16:21 to receive, neither to **o**, being Romans.	4160
	21:25 concluded that they **o** no such *thing*, save	5083
Gal	4:10 Ye **o** days, and months, and times,	3906
1Ti	5:21 thou **o** these *things* without preferring	5442

OBSERVED (11) [OBSERVE]

Ge	37:11 envied him; but his father **o** the saying.	8104
Ex	12:42 It *is* a night to be **much o** unto the LORD	8107
	12:42 this *is* that night of the LORD to be **o** of	8107
Nu	15:22 and not **o** all these commandments,	6213
Dt	33: 9 for they have **o** thy word, and kept thy	8104
2Sa	11:16 it came to pass, when Joab **o** the city,	8104
2Ki	21: 6 **o** times, and used enchantments,	6049
2Ch	33: 6 also he **o** times, and used enchantments,	6049
Hos	14: 8 I have heard *him*, and **o** him: I *am* like a	7789
Mk	6:20 he *was* a just man and a holy, and **o** him;	4933
	10:20 Master, all these have I **o** from my youth.	5442

OBSERVER (1) [OBSERVE]

Dt	18:10 *or* an **o** of times, or an enchanter,	6049

OBSERVERS (1) [OBSERVE]

Dt	18:14 hearkened unto **o** of times,	6049

OBSERVEST (1) [OBSERVE]

Isa	42:20 Seeing many *things*, but thou **o** not;	8104

OBSERVETH (1) [OBSERVE]

Ecc	11: 4 He that **o** the wind shall not sow;	8104

OBSTINATE (2)

Dt	2:30 **made** his heart **o**, that he might deliver	553
Isa	48: 4 Because I knew that thou *art* **o**,	7186

OBTAIN (15) [OBTAINED, OBTAINETH, OBTAINING]

Ge	16: 2 it may be that I may **o children** by her.	1129
Pr	8:35 and shall **o** favour of the LORD.	6329
Isa	35:10 they shall **o** joy and gladness, and sorrow	5381
	51:11 they shall **o** gladness and joy; *and* sorrow	5381
Da	11:21 and **o** the kingdom by flatteries.	2388
Mt	5: 7 are the merciful: for they shall **o mercy**.	1653
Lk	20:35 be accounted worthy to **o** that world,	5177
Ro	11:31 your mercy they also may **o mercy**.	1653
1Co	9:24 receiveth the prize? So run, that ye may **o**.	2638
	9:25 Now they *do it* to **o** a corruptible crown;	2983
1Th	5: 9 to **o** salvation by our Lord Jesus Christ,	4047
2Ti	2:10 that they may also **o** the salvation which	5177
Heb	4:16 that we may **o** mercy, and find grace to	2983
	11:35 that they might **o** a better resurrection:	5177
Jas	4: 2 ye kill, and desire to **have**, and cannot **o**:	2013

OBTAINED (28) [OBTAIN]

Ne	13: 6 after certain days **o** I *leave* of the king:	7592
Est	2: 9 pleased him, and she **o** kindness of him;	5375
	2:15 Esther **o** favour in the sight of all them	5375

Est	2:17 she **o** grace and favour in his sight more	5375
	5: 2 in the court, *that* she **o** favour in his sight:	5375
Hos	2:23 mercy upon her that had not **o mercy**;	7355
Ac	1:17 with us, and had **o** part of this ministry.	2975
	22:28 With a great sum **o** I this freedom.	2932
	26:22 Having therefore **o** help of God, I continue	5177
	27:13 supposing that *they* had **o** *their* purpose,	2902
Ro	11: 7 Israel hath not **o** that which he seeketh	2013
	11: 7 the election hath **o** *it*, and the rest were	2013
	11:30 yet have now **o mercy** through their	1653
1Co	7:25 as one that hath **o mercy** of the Lord to	1653
Eph	1:11 In whom also we have **o an inheritance**,	2820
1Ti	1:13 I **o** mercy, because I did *it* ignorantly in	1653
	1:16 Howbeit for this cause I **o mercy**, that in	1653
Heb	1: 4 as he hath by **inheritance o** a more	2816
	6:15 had patiently endured, he **o** the promise.	2013
	8: 6 But now hath he **o** a more excellent	5177
	9:12 *place*, having **o** eternal redemption *for us*.	2147
	11: 2 For by it the elders **o a good report**.	3140
	11: 4 by which he **o witness** that he was	3140
	11:33 wrought righteousness, **o** promises,	2013
	11:39 having **o a good report** through faith,	3140
1Pe	2:10 which had not **o mercy**, but now have	1653
	2:10 obtained mercy, but now have **o mercy**.	1653
2Pe	1: 1 them that have **o** a like precious faith with	2975

OBTAINETH (2) [OBTAIN]

Pr	12: 2 A good *man* **o** favour of the LORD:	6329
	18:22 a good *thing*, and **o** favour of the LORD.	6329

OBTAINING (1) [OBTAIN]

2Th	2:14 to the **o** of the glory of our Lord Jesus	4047

OCCASION (21) [OCCASIONED, OCCASIONS]

Ge	43:18 he may **seek o** against us, and fall upon	1556
Jdg	9:33 thou do to them as thou shalt **find o**.	4672
	14: 4 that he sought an **o** against the Philistines;	8385
1Sa	10: 7 *that* thou do as **o** serve thee;	3027+4672
2Sa	12:14 **given** great **o** to the enemies of	5006+5006
	the LORD **to blaspheme**,	
Ezr	7:20 which thou shalt have **o** to bestow,	5308
Jer	2:24 in her **o** who can turn her away?	8385
Eze	18: 3 ye shall not have **o** any more to use this	NIH
Da	6: 4 princes sought to find **o** against Daniel	5931
	6: 4 they could find none **o** nor fault;	5931
	6: 5 shall not find any **o** against this Daniel,	5931
Ro	7: 8 But sin, taking **o** by the commandment,	874
	7:11 For sin, taking **o** by the commandment,	874
	14:13 or an **o** to **fall** in *his* brother's way.	4625
2Co	5:12 but give you **o** to glory on our behalf,	874
	8: 8 but **by o** of the forwardness of others,	1223
	11:12 I may cut off **o** from them which desire	874
	11:12 cut off occasion **o** from them which desire **o**;	874
Gal	5:13 only *use* not liberty for an **o** to the flesh,	874
1Ti	5:14 give none **o** to the adversary to speak	874
1Jn	2:10 and there is none **o** of **stumbling** in him.	4625

OCCASIONED (1) [OCCASION]

1Sa	22:22 I have **o** *the death* of all the persons of thy	5437

OCCASIONS (3) [OCCASION]

Dt	22:14 give **o** of speech against her, and bring up	5949
	22:17 he hath given **o** of speech *against her*,	5949
Job	33:10 Behold, he findeth **o** against me,	8569

OCCUPATION (5) [OCCUPY]

Ge	46:33 call you, and shall say, What *is* your **o**?	4639
	47: 3 said unto his brethren, What *is* your **o**?	4639
Jnh	1: 8 this evil *is* upon us; What *is* thine **o**?	4399
Ac	18: 3 for *by* their **o** they were tentmakers.	5078
	19:25 together with the workmen of **like o**,	5108

OCCUPIED (7) [OCCUPY]

Ex	38:24 All the gold that was **o** for the work in all	6213
Jdg	16:11 with new ropes that never were **o**,	4399+6213
Eze	27:16 they **o** in thy fairs with emeralds, purple,	5414
	27:19 and Javan going to and fro **o** in thy fairs:	5414
	27:21 **o** with thee in lambs, and rams,	3027+5503
	27:22 they **o** in thy fairs with chief of all spices,	5414
Heb	13: 9 profited them that have been **o therein**.	4043

OCCUPIERS (1) [OCCUPY]

Eze	27:27 the **o** of thy merchandise, and all thy men	6148

OCCUPIETH (1) [OCCUPY]

1Co	14:16 how shall he that **o** the room of	378

OCCUPY (2) [OCCUPATION, OCCUPIED, OCCUPIERS, OCCUPIETH, UNOCCUPIED]

Eze	27: 9 were in thee to **o** thy merchandise.	6148
Lk	19:13 and said unto them, **O** till I come.	4231

OCCURRENT (1)

1Ki	5: 4 *that there is* neither adversary nor evil **o**.	6294

OCRAN (5)

Nu	1:13 Of Asher; Pagiel the son of **O**.	5918
	2:27 Of Asher *shall be* Pagiel the son of **O**.	5918
	7:72 On the eleventh day Pagiel the son of **O**,	5918
	7:77 *was* the offering of Pagiel the son of **O**.	5918
	10:26 children of Asher *was* Pagiel the son of **O**.	5918

ODD (1)

Nu	3:48 wherewith the **o number** of them is to	5736

O

ODED (3)

2Ch 15:	1 of God came upon Azariah the son of O:	5752
15:	8 the prophecy of O the prophet, he took	5752
28:	9 the LORD was there, whose name was O:	5752

ODIOUS (2) [ODOUR]

1Ch 19:	6 they had made themselves o to David,	887
Pr 30:23	For an o woman when she is married;	8130

ODOUR (2) [ODIOUS, ODOURS]

Jn 12:	3 the house was filled with the o of	3744
Php 4:18	an o of a sweet smell, a sacrifice	3744

ODOURS (7) [ODOUR]

Lev 26:31	will not smell the savour of your sweet o.	5207
2Ch 16:14	in the bed which was filled with sweet o	1314
Est 2:12	six months with sweet o, and with other	1314
Jer 34:	5 before thee, so shall they burn o for thee;	NIH
Da 2:46	offer an oblation and sweet o unto him.	5208
Rev 5:	8 and golden vials full of o, which are	2368
18:13	and o, and ointments, and frankincense,	2368

OF (34750) [HEREOF, THEREOF, WHEREOF] See Index of Articles, Etc.

OFF (507)

Ge 7:	4 will I destroy from o the face of the earth.	5921
8:	3 the waters returned from o the earth	5921
8:	7 until the waters were dried up from o	5921
8:	8 to see if the waters were abated from o	5921
8:11	in her mouth was an olive leaf pluckt o:	2965
8:11	the waters were abated from o the earth.	5921
8:13	waters were dried up from o the earth;	5921
9:11	neither shall all flesh be cut o any more	3772
11:	8 the earth: and they left o to build the city.	2308
17:14	that soul shall be cut o from his people;	3772
17:22	he left o talking with him, and God went	3615
21:16	down over against him a good way o,	7368
22:	4 his eyes, and saw the place afar o.	4480+7350
24:64	saw Isaac, she lighted o the camel.	4480+5921
27:40	that thou shalt break his yoke from o thy	5921
37:18	when they saw him afar o, even	4480+7350
38:14	she put her widow's garments o from her,	5493
40:19	shall Pharaoh lift up thy head from o thee,	5921
40:19	the birds shall eat thy flesh from o thee.	5921
41:42	Pharaoh took o his ring from his hand,	5493
44:	4 and not yet far o, Joseph said unto his	7368
Ex 2:	4 his sister stood afar o, to wit what	4480+7350
3:	5 put o thy shoes from off thy feet;	5394
3:	5 put off thy shoes from o thy feet,	5921
4:25	cut o the foreskin of her son, and cast it	3772
9:15	and thou shalt be cut o from the earth.	3582
12:15	that soul shall be cut o from Israel.	3772
12:19	even that soul shall be cut o from	3772
14:25	took o their chariot wheels, that they	5493
20:18	it, they removed, and stood afar o.	4480+7350
20:21	the people stood afar o,	4480+7350
23:23	and the Jebusites: and I will cut them o.	3582
24:	1 of Israel; and worship ye afar o.	4480+7350
30:33	shall even be cut o from his people.	3772
30:38	shall even be cut o from his people.	3772
31:14	that soul shall be cut o from amongst his	3772
32:	2 unto them, Break o the golden earrings,	6561
32:	3 all the people brake o the golden earrings	6561
32:24	hath any gold, let them break it o.	6561
33:	5 now put o thy ornaments from thee,	3381
33:	7 afar o from the camp, and called it	7368
34:34	he took the vail o, until he came out.	5493
Lev 1:15	wring o his head, and burn it on the altar	4454
3:	9 it shall take o hard by the back bone;	5493
4:	8 he shall take o from it all the fat of	7311
4:10	As it was taken o from the bullock of	7311
4:31	the fat is taken away from o the sacrifice	5921
5:	8 wring o his head from his neck,	4454
6:11	he shall put o his garments, and put on	6584
7:20	even that soul shall be cut o from his	3772
7:21	even that soul shall be cut o from his	3772
7:25	even the soul that eateth it shall be cut o	3772
7:27	even that soul shall be cut o from his	3772
7:34	from o the sacrifices of their peace	4480
8:28	Moses took them from o their hands,	5921
13:40	the man whose hair is fallen o his head,	4803
13:41	that hath his hair fallen o from the part	4803
14:	8 shave o all his hair, and wash himself in	1548
14:	9 that he shall shave all his hair o his head	1548
14:	9 even all his hair he shall shave o:	1548
14:41	scrape o without the city into an unclean	7096
16:12	of fire from o the altar before the LORD,	5921
16:23	shall put o the linen garments, which he	6584
17:	4 that man shall be cut o from among his	3772
17:	9 even that man shall be cut o from among	3772
17:10	will I cut him o from among his people.	3772
17:14	whosoever eateth it shall be cut o.	3772
18:29	shall be cut o from among their people.	3772
19:	8 that soul shall be cut o from among his	3772
20:	3 will cut him o from among his people;	3772
20:	5 will cut him o, and all that go a whoring	3772
20:	6 will cut him o from among his people.	3772
20:17	they shall be cut o in the sight of their	3772
20:18	both of them shall be cut o from among	3772
21:	5 neither shall they shave o the corner of	1548
22:	3 that soul shall be cut o from my presence:	3772
23:29	he shall be cut o from among his people.	3772
Nu 2:	2 far o about the tabernacle of	4480+5048
4:18	Cut ye not o the tribe of the families of	3772
Nu 7:89	o the mercy seat that was upon the ark of	5921
9:10	or be in a journey afar o, yet he shall keep	7350
9:13	even the same soul shall be cut o from	3772
10:11	that the cloud was taken up from o	5921
12:10	the cloud departed from o the tabernacle;	5921
15:30	that soul shall be cut o from among his	3772
15:31	that soul shall utterly be cut o;	3772+3772
16:46	put fire therein from o the altar, and put	5921
19:13	and that soul shall be cut o from Israel:	3772
19:20	that soul shall be cut o from among	3772
Dt 4:26	that ye shall soon utterly perish from o	5921
6:15	destroy thee from o the face of the earth.	5921
11:17	ye perish quickly from o the good land	5921
12:29	When the LORD thy God shall cut o	3772
13:	7 nigh unto thee, or far o from thee,	7350
19:	1 When the LORD thy God hath cut o	3772
20:15	the cities which are very far o from thee,	7350
21:	4 shall strike o the heifer's neck there in	6202
21:13	the raiment of her captivity from her,	5921
23:	1 stones, or hath his privy member cut o,	3772
25:	9 loose his shoe from o his foot, and spit in	5921
25:12	thou shalt cut o her hand, thine eye shall	7112
28:21	until he have consumed thee from o	5921
28:63	shall be plucked from o the land whither	5921
30:11	not hidden from thee, neither is it far o.	7350
Jos 3:13	that the waters of Jordan shall be cut o	3772
3:16	even the salt sea, failed, and were cut o:	3772
4:	7 the waters of Jordan were cut o before	3772
4:	7 the waters of Jordan were cut o:	3772
5:	9 away the reproach of Egypt from o you.	5921
5:15	Loose thy shoe from o thy foot;	5921
7:	9 and cut o our name from the earth:	3772
10:27	they took them down o the trees,	4480+5921
11:21	cut o the Anakims from the mountains,	3772
15:18	she lighted o her ass;	4480+5921+6795
23:	4 with all the nations that I have cut o,	3772
23:13	until ye perish from o this good land	5921
23:15	until he have destroyed you from o this	5921
23:16	ye shall perish quickly from o the good	5921
Jdg 1:	6 and cut o his thumbs and his great toes.	7112
1:	7 their thumbs and their great toes cut o,	7112
1:14	she lighted from o her ass; and Caleb said	5921
4:15	so that Sisera lighted down o his	4480+5921
5:26	she smote o his head, when she had	4277
13:20	went up toward heaven from o the altar,	5921
15:14	and his bands loosed from o his hands.	5921
16:12	he brake them from o his arms like a	5921
16:19	caused him to shave o the seven locks	1548
21:	6 There is one tribe cut o from Israel this	1438
Ru 2:20	who hath not left o his kindness to	5800
4:	7 a man plucked o his shoe, and gave it to	8025
4:	8 Buy it for thee. So he drew o his shoe.	8025
4:10	the name of the dead be not cut o from	3772
1Sa 2:31	that I will cut o thine arm, and the arm	1438
2:33	whom I shall not cut o from mine altar,	3772
4:18	that he fell from o the seat backward by	5921
5:	4 both the palms of his hands were cut o	3772
5:	5 he will lighten his hand from o you,	5921
6:	5 from o your gods, and from off your land.	5921
6:	5 from off your gods, and from o your land.	5921
17:39	proved them. And David put them o him.	5493
17:51	slew him, and cut o his head therewith.	3772
19:24	he stript o his clothes also,	6584
20:15	thou shalt not cut o thy kindness from	3772
20:15	not when the LORD hath cut o	3772
24:	4 and cut o the skirt of Saul's robe privily.	3772
24:	5 because he had cut o Saul's skirt.	3772
24:11	for in that I cut o the skirt of thy robe,	3772
24:21	that thou wilt not cut o my seed after me,	3772
25:23	lighted o the ass, and fell before	4480+5921
26:13	stood on the top of a hill afar o;	4480+7350
28:	9 how he hath cut o those that have familiar	3772
31:	9 they cut o his head, and stripped off his	3772
31:	9 stripped o his armour, and sent into	6584
2Sa 4:12	cut o their hands and their feet,	7112
7:	9 have cut o all thine enemies out of thy	3772
10:	4 shaved o the one half of their beards,	1548
10:	4 cut o their garments in the middle, even	3772
11:	2 that David arose from o his bed,	5921
11:24	the shooters shot from o the wall upon	5921
12:30	took their king's crown from o his head,	5921
15:17	and tarried in a place that was far o.	4801
16:	9 go over, I pray thee, and take o his head.	5493
20:22	they cut o the head of Sheba the son of	3772
1Ki 9:	7 will I cut o Israel out of the land which I	3772
11:16	until he had cut o every male in Edom:	3772
13:34	even to cut it o, and to destroy it from off	3582
13:34	to destroy it from o the face of the earth.	5921
14:10	will cut o from Jeroboam him that pisseth	3772
14:14	who shall cut o the house of Jeroboam	3772
15:21	when Baasha heard thereof, that he left o	2308
18:	4 when Jezebel cut o the prophets of	3772
20:11	boast himself as he that putteth o his	6605
21:21	will cut o from Ahab him that pisseth	3772
2Ki 1:16	thou shalt not come down o that bed on	4480
2:	7 and stood to view afar o:	4480
4:25	the man of God saw her afar o,	4480+5048
9:	8 I will cut o from Ahab him that pisseth	3772
16:17	king Ahaz cut o the borders of the bases,	7112
16:17	and removed the laver from o them;	5921
16:17	took down the sea from o the brasen oxen	5921
18:16	At that time did Hezekiah cut o the gold	7112
19:21	wilt cast o this city Jerusalem which I	3988
1Ch 17:	8 have cut o all thine enemies from before	3772
19:	4 cut o their garments in the midst hard by	3772
1Ch 20:	2 David took the crown of their king from o	5921
28:	9 forsake him, he will cast thee o for ever.	2186
2Ch 6:36	them away captives unto a land far o	7350
11:14	his sons had cast them o from executing	2186
16:	5 when Baasha heard it, that he left o	2308
20:25	which they strip o for themselves,	5337
22:	7 whom the LORD had anointed to cut o	3772
26:21	for he was cut o from the house of	1504
32:21	which cut o all the mighty men of valour,	1504
Ezr 3:13	was heard afar o.	4480+5704+7350+3807.1
9:	3 pluckt o the hair of my head and of my	4803
Ne 4:23	followed me, none of us put o our clothes,	6584
4:23	saving that every one put them o for	7973
5:10	I pray you, let us leave o this usury.	5800
12:43	Jerusalem was heard even afar o.	4480+7350
13:25	pluckt o their hair, and made them swear	4803
Est 8:	2 the king took o his ring, which he had	5493
Job 2:12	when they lift up their eyes afar o,	4480+7350
4:	7 or where were the righteous cut o?	3582
6:	9 would let loose his hand, and cut me o!	1214
8:14	Whose hope shall be cut o, and whose	6990
9:27	I will leave o my heaviness,	5800
11:10	If he cut o, and shut up, or gather	2498
15:	4 thou castest o fear, and restrainest prayer	6565
15:33	He shall shake o his unripe grape as	2554
15:33	and shall cast o his flower as the olive.	7993
17:11	days are past, my purposes are broken o,	5423
18:16	above shall his branch be cut o.	5243
21:21	of his months is cut o in the midst?	2686
23:17	Because I was not cut o before	6789
24:24	and cut o as the tops of the ears of corn.	5243
32:15	no more: they left o speaking.	4480+6275
36:20	when people are cut o in their place.	5927
36:25	see it; man may behold it afar o.	4480+7350
39:25	he smelleth the battle afar o,	4480+7350
39:29	prey, and her eyes behold afar o.	4480+7350
Ps 10:	1 Why standest thou afar o,	7350+871.1
12:	3 The LORD shall cut o all flattering lips,	3772
30:11	thou hast put o my sackcloth,	6605
31:22	I am cut o from before thine eyes:	1629
34:16	to cut o the remembrance of them from	3772
36:	3 he hath left o to be wise, and to do good.	2308
37:	9 For evildoers shall be cut o: but those that	3772
37:22	they that be cursed of him shall be cut o.	3772
37:28	but the seed of the wicked shall be cut o.	3772
37:34	when the wicked are cut o, thou shalt see	3772
37:38	the end of the wicked shall be cut o.	3772
38:11	and my kinsmen stand afar o.	4480+7350
43:	2 why dost thou cast me o? why go I	2186
44:	9 thou hast cast o, and put us to shame;	2186
44:23	O Lord? arise, cast us not o for ever.	2186
54:	5 mine enemies: cut them o in thy truth.	6789
55:	7 Lo, then would I wander far o,	7368
60:	1 O God, thou hast cast us o, thou hast	2186
60:10	not thou, O God, which hadst cast us o?	2186
65:	5 and of them that are afar o upon the sea:	7350
71:	9 Cast me not o in the time of old age;	7993
74:	1 O God, why hast thou cast us o for ever?	2186
75:10	the horns of the wicked also will I cut o;	1438
76:12	He shall cut o the spirit of princes: he is	1219
77:	7 Will the Lord cast o for ever? and will he	2186
83:	4 let us cut them o from being a nation;	3582
88:	5 and they are cut o from thy hand.	1504
88:14	LORD, why castest thou o my soul?	2186
88:16	goeth over me; thy terrors have cut me o.	6789
89:38	thou hast cast o and abhorred, thou hast	2186
90:10	for it is soon cut o, and we fly away.	1468
94:14	For the LORD will not cast o his people,	5203
94:23	cut them o in their own wickedness;	6789
94:23	yea, the LORD our God shall cut them o.	6789
101:	5 his neighbour, him will I cut o:	6789
101:	8 that I may cut o all wicked doers from	3772
108:11	not thou, O God, who hast cast us o?	2186
109:13	Let his posterity be cut o; and in	3772
109:15	that he may cut o the memory of them	3772
138:	6 but the proud he knoweth afar o.	4480+4801
139:	2 understandest my thought afar o.	4480+7350
143:12	of thy mercy cut o mine enemies,	6789
Pr 2:22	the wicked shall be cut o from the earth,	3772
17:14	therefore leave o contention, before it be	5203
23:18	and thine expectation shall not be cut o.	3772
24:14	and thy expectation shall not be cut o.	3772
26:	6 by the hand of a fool cutteth o the feet,	7096
27:10	that is near than a brother far o.	7350
30:14	to devour the poor from o the earth,	4480
Ecc 7:24	That which is far o, and exceeding deep,	4480
SS 5:	3 have put o my coat; how shall I put it on?	6584
Isa 6:	6 he had taken with the tongs from o	5921
9:14	Therefore the LORD will cut o from	3772
10:	7 to destroy and cut o nations not a few.	3772
10:27	his burden shall be taken away from o	5921
10:27	his yoke from o thy neck, and the yoke	5921
11:13	the adversaries of Judah shall be cut o:	3772
14:22	cut o from Babylon the name, and	3772
14:25	shall his yoke depart from o them,	5921
14:25	his burden depart from o their shoulders.	5921
15:	2 shall be baldness, and every beard cut o.	1438
17:13	they shall flee far o, and shall be chased	4480+4801
18:	5 shall both cut o the sprigs with pruning	3772
20:	2 and loose the sackcloth from o thy loins,	5921
20:	2 loins, and put o thy shoe from thy foot.	2502
22:25	burden that was upon it shall be cut o:	3772
23:	7 own feet shall carry her afar o to	4480+7350
25:	8 will wipe away tears from o all faces;	5921
25:	8 shall he take away o all the earth:	5921

Isa
27:11 are withered, they shall be **broken o**: 7665
27:12 that the LORD shall **beat o** from 2251
29:20 and all that watch for iniquity are **cut o**: 3772
33: 9 Bashan and Carmel **shake o** their fruits. 5287
33:13 Hear, ye that are **far o**, what I have done; 7350
33:17 shall behold the land that is **very far o**. 4801
34: 4 as the leaf **falleth o** from the vine, and as 5034
38:10 I said, in the **cutting o** of my days, I shall 1824
38:12 I have **cut o** like a weaver my life: he will 7088
38:12 he will **cut me o** with pining sickness: 1214
46:13 it shall not be **far o**, and my salvation shall 7368
47:11 thee; thou shalt not be able to **put it o** 3722
48: 9 I refrain for thee, that I **cut** thee not o. 3772
48:19 his name should not have been **cut o** nor 3772
50: 6 cheeks to them that **plucked o** the **hair**: 4803
53: 8 for he was **cut o** out of the land of 1504
55:13 an everlasting sign that shall not be **cut o**. 3772
56: 5 everlasting name, that shall not be **cut o**. 3772
57: 9 didst send thy messengers **far o**, 4480+7350
57:19 peace to him that is **far o**, and to him 7350
59:11 for salvation, but it is **far o** from us. 7368
59:14 and justice standeth **afar o**: 4480+7350
66: 3 a lamb, as if he **cut o** a dog's **neck**; 6202
66:19 to Tubal, and Javan, to the isles **afar o**, 7350

Jer
7:28 perished, and is **cut o** from their mouth. 3772
7:29 **Cut o** thine hair, O Jerusalem, and cast it 1494
9:21 to **cut o** the children from without, 3772
11:19 us **cut him o** from the land of the living, 3772
23:23 the LORD, and not a God **afar o**? 4480+7350
24:10 they be consumed from o the land that I 5921
28:10 the prophet took the yoke from o 5921
28:12 from o the neck of the prophet Jeremiah, 5921
28:16 will cast thee from o the face of the earth: 5921
30: 8 that I will break his yoke from o thy neck, 5921
31:10 declare it in the isles **afar o**, and 4480+4801
31:37 I will also **cast o** all the seed of Israel for 3988
33:24 hath chosen, he hath even **cast them o**? 3988
38:27 So they **left o speaking** with him; 2790
44: 7 to **cut o** from you man and woman, child 3772
44: 8 ye might **cut** yourselves **o**, and that ye 3772
44:11 you for evil, and to **cut o** all Judah. 3772
44:18 we **left o** to burn incense to the queen 2308
46:27 I will save thee from **afar o**, and thy seed 7350
47: 4 and to **cut o** from Tyrus and Zidon every 3772
47: 5 Ashkelon is **cut o** with the remnant of 1820
48: 2 and let us **cut it o** from being a nation. 3772
48:25 The horn of Moab is **cut o**, and his arm is 1438
49:26 all the men of war shall be **cut o** in that 1826
49:30 Flee, get you **far o**, dwell deep, O ye 3966
50:16 **Cut o** the sower from Babylon, 3772
50:30 all her men of war shall be **cut o** in that 1826
51: 6 be not **cut o** in her iniquity; for this is 1826
51:50 remember the LORD **afar o**, 4480+7350
51:62 to **cut it o**, that none shall remain in it, 3772

La
2: 3 He hath **cut o** in his fierce anger all 1438
2: 7 The Lord hath **cast o** his altar, he hath 2186
3:17 Thou hast **removed** my soul **far o** from 2186
3:31 For the Lord will not **cast o** for ever: 2186
3:53 They have **cut o** my life in the dungeon, 6789
3:54 over mine head; then I said, I am **cut o**. 1504

Eze
6:12 He that is **far o** shall die of the pestilence; 7350
8: 6 that I should go **far o** from my sanctuary? 7368
10:18 the glory of the LORD departed from o 5921
11:16 Although I have **cast** them **far o** among 7368
12:27 he prophesieth of the times that are far o. 7350
14: 8 I will **cut him o** from the midst of my 3772
14:13 and will **cut o** man and beast from it: 3772
14:17 so that I **cut o** man and beast from it: 3772
14:19 in blood, to **cut o** from it man and beast: 3772
14:21 to **cut o** from it man and beast? 3772
17: 4 He **cropt o** the top of his young twigs, 6998
17: 9 and **cut o** the fruit thereof, that it wither? 7082
17:17 and building forts, to **cut o** many persons: 3772
17:22 set it; I will **crop o** from the top of his 7725
18:17 hath **taken o** his hand from the poor, 7725
21: 3 will **cut o** from thee the righteous and 3772
21: 4 that I will **cut o** from thee the righteous 3772
21:26 the diadem, and **take o** the crown: 7311
23:34 and **pluck o** thine own breasts: 5423
25: 7 I will **cut** thee **o** from the people, and I 3772
25:13 and will **cut o** man and beast from it, 3772
25:16 I will **cut o** the Cherethims, and destroy 3772
26:16 and **put o** their broidered garments; 6584
29: 8 and **cut o** man and beast out of thee. 3772
30:15 and I will **cut o** the multitude of No. 3772
31:12 have **cut him o**, and have left him: 3772
35: 7 **cut o** from it him that passeth out and 3772
37:11 hope is lost: we are **cut o** for our parts. 1504
44:19 they shall **put o** their garments wherein 6584

Da
4:14 down the tree, and **cut o** his branches, 7113
4:14 **shake o** his leaves, and scatter his fruit: 5426
4:27 **break o** thy sins by righteousness, 6562
9: 7 Israel, that are near, and that are **far o**, 7350
9:26 and two weeks shall Messiah be **cut o**, 3772

Hos
4:10 thy have **left o** to take heed to the LORD. 5800
8: 3 Israel hath **cast o** the thing that is good: 2186
8: 4 made them idols, that they may be **cut o**. 3772
8: 5 Thy calf, O Samaria, hath **cast thee o**; 2186
10: 7 her king is **cut o** as the foam upon 1820
10:15 the king of Israel **utterly** be **cut o**. 1820+1820
11: 4 was to them as they that **take o** the yoke 7311

Joel
1: 5 wine, for it is **cut o** from your mouth. 3772
1: 9 The drink offering is **cut o** from the house 3772
1:16 Is not the meat **cut o** before our eyes, 3772
2:20 will **remove far o** from you the northern 7368

Joel
3: 8 them to the Sabeans, to a people **far o**: 7350
Am
1: 5 **cut o** the inhabitant from the plain of 3772
1: 8 I will **cut o** the inhabitant from Ashdod, 3772
1:11 did **cast o** all pity, and his anger did tear 7843
2: 3 I will **cut o** the judge from the midst 3772
3:14 and the horns of the altar shall be **cut o**, 1438
5: 7 and **leave o** righteousness in the earth, 3240
9: 8 will destroy it from o the face of the earth; 5921

Ob
1: 5 if robbers by night, (how art thou **cut o**!) 1820
1: 9 mount of Esau may be **cut o** by slaughter. 3772
1:10 thee, and thou shalt be **cut o** for ever. 3772
1:14 to **cut o** those of his that did escape; 3772

Mic
2: 8 ye pull o the robe with the garment 4136+4480
3: 2 who **pluck o** their skin from off them, 1497
3: 2 who pluck off their skin from o them, 5921
3: 2 them, and their flesh from o their bones; 5921
3: 3 people, and flay their skin from o them; 5921
4: 7 her that was **cast far o** a strong nation: 1972
5: 9 and all thine enemies shall be **cut o**. 3772
5:10 I will **cut o** thy horses out of the midst 3772
5:11 I will **cut o** the cities of thy land, 3772
5:12 I will **cut o** witchcrafts out of thine hand; 3772
5:13 Thy graven images also will I **cut o**, 3772

Na
1:13 For now will I break his yoke from o thee, 5921
1:14 out of the house of thy gods will I **cut o** 3772
1:15 pass through thee; he is utterly **cut o**. 3772
2:13 and I will **cut o** thy prey from the earth, 3772
3:15 the sword shall **cut thee o**, it shall eat thee 3772

Hab
2:10 to thy house by **cutting o** many people, 7096
3:17 the flock shall be **cut o** from the fold, 1504

Zep
1: 2 all things **from o** the land, 4480+5921+6440
1: 3 I will **cut o** man from off the land, saith 3772
1: 3 I will **cut off** man **from o** 4480+5921+6440
1: 4 I will **cut o** the remnant of Baal from this 3772
1:11 down; all they that bear silver are **cut o**. 3772
3: 6 I have **cut o** the nations: their towers are 3772
3: 7 so their dwelling should not be **cut o**, 3772

Zec
5: 3 every one that stealeth shall be **cut o** as 5352
5: 3 every one that sweareth shall be **cut o** as 5352
6:15 they that are **far o** shall come and build 7350
9: 6 I will **cut o** the pride of the Philistines. 3772
9:10 I will **cut o** the chariot from Ephraim, 3772
9:10 and the battle bow shall be **cut o**: 3772
10: 6 shall be as though I had not **cast** them o: 2186
11: 8 Three shepherds also I **cut o** in one 3582
11: 9 that that is to be **cut o**, let it be cut off; 3582
11: 9 that that is to be **cut o**, let it be **cut o**; 3582
11:16 which shall not visit those that be **cut o**, 3582
13: 2 I will **cut o** the names of the idols out 3772
13: 8 two parts therein shall be **cut o** and die; 3772
14: 2 residue of the people shall not be **cut o**. 3772

Mal
2:12 The LORD will **cut o** the man that doth 3772

Mt
5:30 thee, **cut it o**, and cast it from thee: 1581
8:30 there was a **good way o** from them 3112
10:14 or city, **shake** the dust of your feet. 1621
18: 8 **cut** them **o**, and cast them from thee: 1581
26:51 of the high priest's, and **smote o** his ear. 851
26:58 Peter followed him **afar o** unto the high 575
27:31 they **took** the robe **from** him, and put 1562
27:55 many women were there beholding **afar o**, 575

Mk
6: 8 But when he saw Jesus **afar o**, he ran and 575
6:11 **shake o** the dust under your feet for a 1621
9:43 And if thy hand **offend thee**, cut it o: 609
9:45 And if thy foot **offend thee**, cut it o: it is 609
11: 8 and others **cut** down branches **o** the trees, 1537
11:13 And seeing a fig tree **afar o** having leaves, 3113
14:47 servant of the high priest, and **cut o** his ear. 851
14:54 And Peter followed him **afar o**, even into 575
15:20 they **took** the purple **from** him, 1562
15:40 There were also women looking on **afar o**: 575

Lk
9: 5 **shake o** the very dust from your feet for a 660
10:11 cleaveth on us, we do **wipe o against** you: 631
14:32 while the other is yet a **great way o**, 4206
15:20 But when he was yet a **great way o**, 568
16:23 and seeth Abraham **afar o**, 575+3113
17:12 men that were lepers, which stood **afar o**: 4207
18:13 standing **afar o**, would not lift up so 3113
22:50 of the high priest, and **cut o** his right ear. 851
22:54 priest's house. And Peter followed **afar o**. 3113
23:49 stood **afar o**, beholding these things. 575+3113

Jn
11:18 unto Jerusalem, about fifteen furlongs o: 575
18:10 priest's servant, and **cut o** his right ear. 609
18:26 being his kinsman whose ear Peter **cut o**, 609

Ac
2:39 and to all that are **afar o**, 1519+3112
7:33 to him, **Put o** thy shoes from thy feet: 3089
12: 7 And his chains **fell o** from his hands. 1601
13:51 But they **shook o** the dust of their feet 1621
16:22 and the magistrates **rent o** their clothes, 4048
22:23 cast o their clothes, and threw dust into NIG
27:32 the soldiers **cut o** the ropes of the boat, 609
27:32 off the ropes of the boat, and let her **fall o**. 1601
28: 5 And he **shook o** the beast into the fire, 660

Ro
11:17 And if some of the branches be **broken o**, 1575
11:19 say then, The branches were **broken o**, 1575
11:20 because of unbelief they were **broken o**, 1575
11:22 otherwise thou also shalt be **cut o**. 1581
13:12 therefore **cast o** the works of darkness, 659

2Co
11:12 I may **cut o** occasion **from** them which 609

Gal
5:12 they were even **cut o** which trouble 609

Eph
2:13 **far o** are made nigh by the blood of 3112
2:17 preached peace to you which were **afar o**, 3112
4:22 That ye **put o** concerning the former 659

Col
2:11 in **putting o** the body of the sins of the 555
3: 8 But now you also **put o** all these; anger, 659

Col
3: 9 seeing that ye have **put o** the old man with 554
1Ti
5:12 because they have **cast o** their first faith. 114
Heb
11:13 but having seen them **afar o**, and hath 4207
2Pe
1: 9 and **cannot see far o**, and hath forgotten 3467
1:14 Knowing that shortly I must **put o** this my 595
Rev
18:14 Standing **afar o** for the fear of her 575+3113
18:15 shall stand **afar o** for the fear of her 575+3113
18:17 many as trade by sea, stood **afar o**, 575+3113

OFFENCE (19) [OFFEND]

1Sa 25:31 unto thee, nor o of heart unto my lord, 4383
Isa 8:14 for a rock of o to both the houses of Israel, 4383
Hos 5:15 till they **acknowledge** their o, and seek 816
Mt 16:23 thou art an o unto me: for thou savourest 4625
18: 7 woe to that man by whom o cometh. 4625
Ac 24:16 to have always a conscience **void of** o, 677
Ro 5:15 But not as the o, so also is the free gift. 3900
5:15 For if through the o of one many be dead, 3900
5:17 if by one man's o death reigned by one; 3900
5:18 Therefore as by the o of one judgment 3900
5:20 the law entered, that the o might abound. 3900
9:33 in Sion a stumblingstone and rock of o: 4625
14:20 it is evil for that man who eateth with o. 4348
1Co 10:32 Give none o, neither to the Jews, nor to 677
2Co 6: 3 Giving no o in any thing, that the ministry 4349
11: 7 Have I committed an o in abasing myself 266
Gal 5:11 then is the o of the cross ceased. 4625
Php 1:10 and **without o** till the day of Christ; 677
1Pe 2: 8 And a stone of stumbling, and a rock of o, 4625

OFFENCES (7) [OFFEND]

Ecc 10: 4 thy place; for yielding pacifieth great o. 2399
Mt 18: 7 Woe unto the world because of o: for it 4625
18: 7 it must needs be that o come; but woe to 4625
Lk 17: 1 It is impossible but that o will come: 4625
Ro 4:25 Who was delivered for our o, 3900
5:16 free gift is of many o unto justification. 3900
16:17 o contrary to the doctrine which ye have 4625

OFFEND (25) [OFFENCE, OFFENCES, OFFENDED, OFFENDER, OFFENDERS]

Job 34:31 borne chastisement, I will not o any 2254
Ps 73:15 I should o against the generation of thy 898
119:165 love thy law: and nothing shall o them. 4383
Jer 2: 3 all that devour him shall o; evil shall come 816
50: 7 We o not, because they have sinned 816
Hos 4:15 Israel, play the harlot, yet let not Judah o; 816
Hab 1:11 change, and he shall pass over, and o, 816
Mt 5:29 And if thy right eye o thee, pluck it out, 4624
5:30 And if thy right hand o thee, cut it off, 4624
13:41 out of his kingdom all things that o, 4625
17:27 Notwithstanding, lest we should o them, 4624
18: 6 But whoso shall o one of these little ones 4624
18: 8 Wherefore if thy hand or thy foot o thee, 4624
18: 9 And if thine eye o thee, pluck it out, 4624
Mk 9:42 And whosoever shall o one of these little 4624
9:43 if thy hand o thee, cut it off: it is better 4624
9:45 if thy foot o thee, cut it off: it is better 4624
9:47 And if thine eye o thee, pluck it out: it is 4624
Lk 17: 2 than that he should o one of these little 4624
Jn 6:61 at it, he said unto them, Doth this o you? 4624
1Co 8:13 if meat **make** my brother to o, 4624
8:13 lest I **make** my brother to o. 4624
Jas 2:10 and yet o in one point, he is guilty of all. 4417
3: 2 For in many things we o all. If any man 4417
3: 2 If any man o not in word, the same is a 4417

OFFENDED (25) [OFFEND]

Ge 20: 9 have I o thee, that thou hast brought 2398
40: 1 baker had o their lord the king of Egypt. 2398
2Ki 18:14 of Assyria to Lachish, saying, I have o; 2398
2Ch 28:13 for whereas we have o against the LORD 819
Pr 18:19 A brother o is harder to be won than a 6586
Jer 37:18 What have I o against thee, or against thy 2398
Eze 25:12 hath **greatly** o, and revenged himself 816+816
Hos 13: 1 in Israel; but when he o in Baal, he died. 816
Mt 11: 6 blessed is he, whosoever shall not be o 4624
13:21 because of the word, by and by he is o. 4624
13:57 And they were o in him. But Jesus said 4624
15:12 Knowest thou that the Pharisees were o, 4624
24:10 then shall many be o, and shall betray 4624
26:31 All ye shall be o because of me this night: 4624
26:33 all men shall be o because of thee, 4624
26:33 because of thee, yet will I never be o. 4624
Mk 4:17 the word's sake, immediately they are o. 4624
6: 3 here with us? And they were o at him. 4624
14:27 All ye shall be o because of me this night: 4624
14:29 Although all shall be o, yet will not I. 4624
Lk 7:23 blessed is he, whosoever shall not be o 4624
Jn 16: 1 spoken unto you, that ye should not be o. 4624
Ac 25: 8 yet against Cesar, have I o any thing at all. 264
Ro 14:21 stumbleth, or is o, or is made weak. 4624
2Co 11:29 I am not weak? who is o, and I burn not? 4624

OFFENDER (2) [OFFEND]

Isa 29:21 That **make** a man an o for a word, 2398
Ac 25:11 if I be an o, or have committed any thing 91

OFFENDERS (1) [OFFEND]

1Ki 1:21 and my son Solomon shall be **counted** o. 2400

OFFER (236) [OFFERED, OFFERETH, OFFERING, OFFERINGS]

Ge 22: 2 o him there for a burnt offering upon one 5927
Ex 22:29 Thou shalt not delay to o the first of thy NIH

Ex
23:18 Thou shalt not o the blood of my sacrifice 2076
29:36 thou shalt o every day a bullock *for* a sin 6213
29:38 Now this *is that* which thou shalt o upon 6213
29:39 one lamb thou shalt o in the morning; 6213
29:39 and the other lamb thou shalt o at even: 6213
29:41 the other lamb thou shalt o at even, 6213
30: 9 Ye shall o no strange incense thereon, 5927
34:25 Thou shalt not o the blood of my sacrifice 7819
35:24 Every one that did o an offering of silver 7311

Lev
1: 3 herd, let him o a male without blemish: 7126
1: 3 he shall o it of his own voluntary will at 7126
1: 1 when any will o a meat offering unto 7126
2:12 ye shall o them unto the Lord: 7126
2:13 with all thine offerings thou shalt o salt. 7126
2:14 if thou o a meat offering of *thy* firstfruits 7126
2:14 thou shalt o for the meat offering of thy 7126
3: 1 of peace offering, if he o *it* of the herd; 7126
3: 1 he shall o it without blemish before 7126
3: 3 he shall o of the sacrifice of the peace 7126
3: 6 or female, he shall o it without blemish. 7126
3: 7 If he o a lamb for his offering, then shall 7126
3: 7 then shall he o it before the Lord. 7126
3: 9 he shall o of the sacrifice of the peace 7126
3:12 a goat, then he shall o it before the Lord. 7126
3:14 he shall o thereof his offering, *even* an 7126
4:14 the congregation shall o a young bullock 7126
5: 8 who shall o *that* which *is* for the sin 7126
5:10 he shall o the second *for* a burnt offering, 6213
6:14 the sons of Aaron shall o it before 7126
6:20 which they shall o unto the Lord in 7126
6:21 thou o *for* a sweet savour unto the Lord: 6213
6:22 sons that is anointed in his stead shall o it: 6213
7: 3 shall o of it all the fat thereof; the rump, 7126
7:11 which he shall o unto the Lord. 7126
7:12 If he o it for a thanksgiving, then he shall 7126
7:12 shall o with the sacrifice of thanksgiving 7126
7:13 he shall o *for* his offering leavened bread 7126
7:14 of it he shall o one out of the whole 7126
7:25 of which *men* o an offering made by fire 7126
7:38 Israel to o their oblations unto the Lord, 7126
9: 2 and o *them* before the Lord. 7126
9: 7 o thy sin offering, and thy burnt offering, 6213
9: 7 o the offering of the people, and make an 6213
12: 7 Who shall o it before the Lord, 7126
14:12 o him for a trespass offering, and the log 7126
14:19 the priest shall o the sin offering, 6213
14:20 And the priest shall o the burnt offering 5927
14:30 And he shall o the one of the turtledoves, 6213
15:15 the priest shall o them, the one *for* a sin 6213
15:30 priest shall o the one *for* a sin offering, 6213
16: 6 Aaron shall o *his* bullock of the sin 7126
16: 9 lot fell, and o *him* for a sin offering. 6213
16:24 o his burnt offering, and the burnt offering 7126
17: 4 to o an offering unto the Lord before 7126
17: 5 which they o in the open field, even that 2076
17: 5 o them *for* peace offerings unto 2076
17: 7 they shall no more o their sacrifices unto 2076
17: 9 the congregation, to o it unto the Lord; 6213
19: 5 ye o **a sacrifice** of peace offerings 2076+2077
19: 5 the Lord, ye shall o it at your own will. 2076
19: 6 It shall be eaten the same day ye o it, 2077
21: 6 *and* the bread of their God, they do o: 7126
21:17 let him not approach to o the bread of his 7126
21:21 shall come nigh to o the offerings of 7126
21:21 he shall not come nigh to o the bread of 7126
22:15 of Israel, which they o unto the Lord; 7311
22:18 that will o his oblation for all his vows, 7126
22:18 which they will o unto the Lord for a 7126
22:19 *Ye shall o* at your own will a male without NIH
22:20 hath a blemish, *that* shall ye not o: 7126
22:22 ye shall not o these unto the Lord, 7126
22:23 That mayest thou o *for* a freewill offering; 6213
22:24 Ye shall not o unto the Lord that which 7126
22:25 Neither from a stranger's hand shall ye o 7126
22:29 when ye will o a sacrifice of thanksgiving 2076
22:29 unto the Lord, o *it* at your own will. 2076
23: 8 ye shall o an offering made by fire unto 7126
23:12 shall o that day when ye wave the sheaf 6213
23:16 ye shall o a new meat offering unto 7126
23:18 ye shall o with the bread seven lambs 7126
23:25 ye shall o an offering made by fire unto 7126
23:27 o an offering made by fire unto 7126
23:36 Seven days ye shall o an offering made by 7126
23:36 ye shall o an offering made by fire unto 7126
23:37 to o an offering made by fire unto 7126
27:11 of which they do not o a sacrifice unto 7126

Nu
5:25 before the Lord, and o it upon the altar: 7126
6:11 the priest shall o the one for a sin offering, 6213
6:14 he shall o his offering unto the Lord, 6213
6:16 shall o his sin offering, and his burnt 6213
6:17 he shall o the ram *for* a sacrifice of peace 6213
6:17 the priest shall o also his meat offering, 6213
7:11 They shall o their offering, each prince on 7126
7:18 the son of Zuar, prince of Issachar, did o: 7126
7:24 prince of the children of Zebulun, *did o.* NIH
7:30 prince of the children of Reuben, *did o.* NIH
7:36 prince of the children of Simeon, *did o.* NIH
8:11 Aaron shall o the Levites before 5130
8:12 thou shalt o the one *for* a sin offering, 6213
8:13 o them *for* an offering unto the Lord. 5130
8:15 cleanse them, and o them *for* an offering, 5130
9: 7 that *we* may not o an offering of 7126
15: 7 for a drink offering thou shalt o the third 7126
15:14 will o an offering made by fire, of a sweet 6213
15:19 ye shall o **up** a heave offering unto 7311

Nu
15:20 Ye shall o **up** a cake *of* the first of your 7311
15:24 all the congregation shall o one young 6213
16:40 come near to o incense before the Lord; 6999
18:12 the firstfruits of them which they shall o 5414
18:19 the children of Israel o unto the Lord, 7311
18:24 which they o *as* a heave offering unto 7311
18:26 ye shall o **up** a heave offering of it for 7311
18:28 you also shall o a heave offering unto 7311
18:29 Out of all your gifts ye shall o every heave 7311
28: 2 shall ye observe to o unto me in their due 7126
28: 3 by fire which ye shall o unto the Lord; 7126
28: 4 The one lamb shalt thou o in the morning, 6213
28: 4 and the other lamb shalt thou o at even; 6213
28: 8 the other lamb shalt thou o at even: 6213
28: 8 thou shalt o *it,* a sacrifice made by fire, 6213
28:11 the beginnings of your months ye shall o 7126
28:19 ye shall o a sacrifice made by fire *for a* 7126
28:20 three tenth deals shall ye o for a bullock, 6213
28:21 A several tenth deal shalt thou o for every 6213
28:23 Ye shall o these beside the burnt offering 6213
28:24 After this manner ye shall o daily, 6213
28:27 ye shall o the burnt offering for a sweet 7126
28:31 Ye shall o *them* besides the continual 6213
29: 2 ye shall o a burnt offering for a sweet 6213
29: 8 ye shall o a burnt offering unto the Lord 7126
29:13 ye shall o a burnt offering, a sacrifice 7126
29:17 the second day *ye shall o* twelve young NIH
29:36 shall o a burnt offering, a sacrifice made 7126

Dt
12:13 Take heed to thyself that thou o not thy 5927
12:14 there thou shalt o thy burnt offerings, 5927
12:27 thou shalt o thy burnt offerings, the flesh 6213
18: 3 from them that o a sacrifice, whether *it* 2076
27: 6 thou shalt o burnt offerings thereon unto 5927
27: 7 thou shalt o peace offerings, and shalt eat 2076
33:19 there they shall o sacrifices of 2076

Jos
22:23 or if to o thereon burnt offering or 5927
22:23 or if to o peace offerings thereon, 6213

Jdg
3:18 he had made an end to o the present, 7126
6:26 o a burnt sacrifice with the wood of 7126
11:31 and I will o it **up** *for* a burnt offering. 5927
13:16 if thou wilt o a burnt offering, thou must 6213
13:16 thou must o it unto the Lord. 5927
16:23 o a great sacrifice unto Dagon their god, 2076

1Sa
1:21 went up to o unto the Lord the yearly 2076
2:19 when she came up with her husband to o 2076
2:28 to o upon mine altar, to burn incense, 5927
10: 8 to o burnt offerings, *and* to sacrifice 5927

2Sa
24:12 I o thee three *things;* choose thee one of 5190
24:22 and o **up** what seemeth good unto him: 5927
24:24 neither will I o burnt offerings unto 5927

1Ki
3: 4 burnt offerings did Solomon o **up** 5927
9:25 three times in a year did Solomon o burnt 5927
13: 2 upon thee shall he o the priests of the 2076

2Ki
5:17 for thy servant will henceforth o neither 6213
10:24 when they went in to o sacrifices and 6213

1Ch
16:40 To o burnt offerings unto the Lord upon 5927
21:10 I o thee three *things:* choose thee one of 5186
21:24 nor o burnt offerings without cost. 5927
23:31 to o all burnt sacrifices unto the Lord in 5927
29:14 that we should be able to o *so* **willingly** 5068
29:17 present here, to o **willingly** unto thee. 5068

2Ch
23:18 to o the burnt offerings of David, as it 5927
24:14 *withal,* and spoons, and vessels of gold 5927
29:21 Aaron to o *them* on the altar of the Lord. 5927
29:27 Hezekiah commanded to o the burnt 5927
35:12 to o unto the Lord, as it is written in 7126
35:16 to o burnt offerings upon the altar of 5927

Ezr
3: 2 God of Israel, to o burnt offerings thereon, 5927
3: 6 they to o burnt offerings unto the Lord. 5927
6:10 they may o sacrifices of sweet savours 1934
7:17 o them upon the altar of the house of your 7127

Job
42: 8 and o **up** for yourselves a burnt offering; 5927

Ps
4: 5 O the sacrifices of righteousness, 2076
16: 4 their drink offerings of blood will I not o, 5258
27: 6 will I o in his tabernacle sacrifices of joy; 2076
50:14 O unto God thanksgiving; and pay thy 2076
51:19 shall they o bullocks upon thine altar. 5927
66:15 I will o unto thee burnt sacrifices of 5927
66:15 of rams; I will o bullocks with goats. 6213
72:10 the kings of Sheba and Seba shall o gifts. 7126
116:17 I will o to thee the sacrifice of 2076

Isa
57: 7 thither wentest thou up to o sacrifice. 2076

Jer
11:12 the gods unto whom they o **incense:** 6999
14:12 they o burnt offering and an oblation, 5927
33:18 a man before me to o burnt offerings, 5927

Eze
20:31 For when ye o your gifts, when *ye* make 5375
43:18 o burnt offerings thereon, and to sprinkle 5927
43:22 on the second day thou shalt o a kid of 7126
43:23 shalt o a young bullock without blemish, 7126
43:24 thou shalt o them before the Lord, 7126
43:24 they shall o them **up** *for* a burnt offering 5927
44: 7 ye o my bread, the fat and the blood, 7126
44:15 they shall stand before me to o unto me 7126
44:27 he shall o his sin offering, saith the Lord 7126
45: 1 ye shall o an oblation unto the Lord, 7311
45:13 This *is* the oblation that ye shall o; 7311
45:14 *ye shall o* the tenth part of a bath out of NIH
46: 4 The burnt offering that the prince shall o 7126
48: 8 shall be the offering which ye shall o *of* 7311
48: 9 The oblation that ye shall o unto 7311
48:20 ye shall o the holy oblation foursquare, 7311

Da
2:46 that *they* should o an oblation 5260

Hos
9: 4 They shall not o wine *offerings* to 5258

Am
4: 5 o a sacrifice of thanksgiving with leaven, 6999

Am
5:22 Though ye o me burnt offerings and 5927
Hag
2:14 and *that* which they o there *is* unclean. 7126
Mal
1: 7 *Ye* o polluted bread upon mine altar; 5066
1: 8 if ye o the blind for sacrifice, *is it* not evil? 5066
1: 8 if ye o the lame and sick, *is it* not evil? 5066
1: 8 o it now unto thy governor; will he be 7126
3: 3 that they may o unto the Lord an 5066
Mt
5:24 thy brother, and then come and o thy gift. 4374
Mk
1:44 o for thy cleansing *those things* which 4374
Lk
2:24 to o a sacrifice according to that which 1325
5:14 to the priest, and o for thy cleansing, 4374
6:29 thee on *the one* cheek o also the other; 3930
11:12 shall ask an egg, will he o him a scorpion? 1929
Heb
5: 1 that he may o both gifts and sacrifices for 4374
5: 3 people, so also for himself, to o for sins. 4374
7:27 as *those* high priests, to o **up** sacrifice, 399
8: 3 For every high priest is ordained to o gifts 4374
8: 3 that this *man* have somewhat also to o. 4374
8: 4 seeing that there are priests that o gifts 4374
9:25 Nor yet that he should o himself often, 4374
13:15 let us o the sacrifice of praise to God 399
1Pe
2: 5 priesthood, to o **up** spiritual sacrifices, 399
Rev
8: 3 that he should o *it* with the prayers of all 1325

OFFERED (143) [OFFER]

Ge
8:20 and o burnt offerings on the altar. 5927
22:13 o him **up** for a burnt offering in the stead 5927
31:54 Jacob o sacrifice upon the mount, 2076
46: 1 sacrifices unto the God of his father 2076
Ex
24: 5 which o burnt offerings, 5927
32: 6 o burnt offerings, and brought peace 5927
35:22 every man that o *offered* an offering of 5130
35:22 man that offered o an offering of gold NIH
40:29 o upon it the burnt offering and the meat 5927
Lev
7: 8 of the burnt offering which he hath o. 7126
7:15 shall be eaten the same day that it is o; 7133
9:15 and slew it, and o it **for sin,** as the first. 2398
9:16 and o it according to the manner. 6213
10: 1 o strange fire before the Lord, 7126
10:19 *this* day have they o their sin offering and 7126
16: 1 when they o before the Lord, and died; 7126
Nu
3: 4 when they o strange fire before 7126
3: 4 were over them that were numbered, o: 7126
7:10 the princes o *for* dedicating of the altar in 7126
7:10 even the princes o their offering before 7126
7:12 he that o his offering the first day was 7126
7:19 He o *for* his offering one silver charger, 7126
7:42 of Deuel, prince of the children of Gad, o. NIH
7:48 prince of the children of Ephraim, o. NIH
7:54 On the eighth day o Gamaliel the son of NIH
7:60 prince of the children of Benjamin, o. NIH
7:66 prince of the children of Dan, o. NIH
7:72 prince of the children of Asher, o. NIH
7:78 prince of the children of Naphtali, o. NIH
8:21 Aaron o them *as* an offering before 5130
16:35 hundred and fifty men that o incense. 7126
16:38 for they o them before the Lord, 7126
16:39 wherewith they that were burnt had o; 7126
22:40 Balak o oxen and sheep, and sent to 2076
23: 2 and Balaam o *on every* altar a bullock and 5927
23: 4 I have o upon *every* altar a bullock and 5927
23:14 and o a bullock and a ram on *every* altar. 5927
23:30 and o a bullock and a ram on *every* altar. 5927
26:61 when they o strange fire before 7126
28:15 a sin offering unto the Lord shall be o, 6213
28:24 it shall be o beside the continual burnt 6213
31:52 all the gold of the offering that they o **up** 7311
Jos
8:31 they o thereon burnt offerings unto 5927
Jdg
5: 2 when the people **willingly** o themselves. 5068
5: 9 that o themselves **willingly** among 5068
6:28 the second bullock was o upon the altar 5927
13:19 and o *it* upon a rock unto the Lord: 5927
20:26 o burnt offerings and peace offerings 5927
21: 4 and o burnt offerings and peace offerings. 5927
1Sa
1: 4 when the time was that Elkanah o, he 2076
2:13 *was,* that when any man o sacrifice, 2076
6:14 o the kine a burnt offering unto 5927
6:15 men of Beth-shemesh o burnt offerings 5927
7: 9 it *for* a burnt offering wholly unto 5927
13: 9 And he o the burnt offering. 5927
13:12 myself therefore, and o a burnt offering. 5927
2Sa
6:17 David o burnt offerings and peace 5927
15:12 even from Giloh, while he o sacrifices. 2076
24:25 and o burnt offerings and peace offerings. 5927
1Ki
3:15 o **up** burnt offerings, and offered peace 5927
3:15 o peace offerings, and made a feast to all 6213
8:62 with him, o sacrifice before the Lord. 2076
8:63 Solomon o a sacrifice of peace offerings, 2076
8:63 which he o unto the Lord, two and 2076
8:64 for there he o burnt offerings, and meat 6213
12:32 he o upon the altar (so did he in Beth-el,) 5927
12:33 he o upon the altar which he had made 5927
12:33 he o upon the altar, and burnt incense. 5927
22:43 *for* the people o and burnt incense yet in 2076
2Ki
3:20 the meat offering was o, that behold, 5927
3:27 o him for a burnt offering upon the wall. 5927
16:12 approached to the altar, and o thereon. 5927
1Ch
6:49 his sons o upon the altar of the burnt 6999
15:26 they o seven bullocks and seven rams. 2076
16: 1 they o burnt sacrifices and peace offerings 7126
21:26 o burnt offerings and peace offerings, 5927
29: 6 rulers over the king's work, o **willingly** 5068
29: 9 for that they o **willingly,** because 5068
29: 9 with perfect heart they o **willingly** to 5068

1Ch 29:17 heart I have **willingly** o all these *things:*	5068
29:21 o burnt offerings unto the LORD,	5927
2Ch 1: 6 and o a thousand burnt offerings upon it.	5927
4: 6 such **things** as they o for the burnt	4639
7: 4 all the people o sacrifices before	2076
7: 5 king Solomon o a sacrifice of twenty and	2076
7: 7 there he o burnt offerings, and the fat of	6213
8:12 Solomon o burnt offerings unto the LORD	5927
15:11 they o unto the LORD the same time,	2076
17:16 who **willingly** o himself unto the LORD;	5068
24:14 they o burnt offerings in the house of	5927
29: 7 not burnt incense nor o burnt offerings	5927
Ezr 1: 6 beside all *that* was **willingly** o.	5068
2:68 o **freely** for the house of God to set it up	5068
3: 3 they o burnt offerings thereon unto	5927
3: 4 and *o* the daily burnt offerings by number,	NIH
3: 5 afterward *o* the continual burnt offering,	NIH
3: 5 of every one that **willingly** o a freewill	5068
6: 3 the place where they o sacrifices,	1684
6:17 o at the dedication of this house of God	7127
7:15 counsellers have **freely** o unto the God	5069
8:25 lords, and all Israel *there* present, had o:	7311
8:35 o burnt offerings unto the God of Israel,	7126
10:19 *they* o a ram of the flock for their trespass.	NIH
Ne 11: 2 that **willingly** o themselves to dwell at	5068
12:43 Also that day they o great sacrifices,	2076
Job 1: 5 o burnt offerings *according to* the number	5927
Isa 57: 6 o drink offering, thou hast o a meat offering.	5927
66: 3 an oblation, *as if he* o swine's blood;	NIH
Jer 32:29 whose roofs they have o **incense** unto	6999
Eze 20:28 they o there their sacrifices, and there	2076
48:12 *this* oblation of the land that is o shall be	8641
Da 11:18 cause the reproach *by* him to cease;	3807.1
Am 5:25 Have ye o unto me sacrifices and	5066
Jnh 1:16 o a sacrifice unto the LORD,	2076
Mal 1:11 in every place incense *shall be* o unto my	5066
Ac 7:41 o sacrifice unto the idol, and rejoiced in	321
7:42 have ye o to me slain beasts and	4374
8:18 Holy Ghost was given, he o them money,	4374
15:29 That *ye* abstain from **meats** o to idols,	1494
21:25 keep themselves from **things** o to idols,	1494
21:26 until that an offering should be o for every	4374
1Co 8: 1 Now as touching **things** o unto idols,	1494
8: 4 **things** that are o in sacrifice unto idols,	1494
8: 7 this hour, eat *it* as a **thing** o unto an idol;	1494
8:10 to eat those **things** which are o to idols,	1494
10:19 that which is o **in sacrifice to idols** is any	1494
10:28 you, This is o **in sacrifice unto idols**,	1494
Php 2:17 and if I be o upon the sacrifice and	4689
2Ti 4: 6 For I am now ready to be o, and the time	4689
Heb 5: 7 when he had o **up** prayers and	4374
7:27 this he did once, when he o **up** himself.	399
9: 7 he o for himself, and *for* the errors of	4374
9: 9 in which were o both gifts and sacrifices,	4374
9:14 who through the eternal Spirit o himself	4374
9:28 So Christ was once o to bear the sins of	4374
10: 1 never with those sacrifices which they o	4374
10: 2 then would they not have ceased to be o?	4374
10: 8 hadst pleasure *therein:* which are o	4374
10:12 But this *man*, after he had o one sacrifice	4374
11: 4 By faith Abel o unto God a more excellent	4374
11:17 when he was tried, o **up** Isaac:	4374
11:17 that had received the promises o **up** *his*	4374
Jas 2:21 he had o Isaac his son upon the altar?	399

OFFERETH (15) [OFFER]

Lev 6:26 The priest that o *it* **for sin** shall eat it:	2398
7: 8 the priest that o *any* man's burnt offering,	7126
7: 9 in the pan, shall be the priest's that o it.	7126
7:16 shall be eaten the *same* day that he o his	7126
7:18 shall it be imputed unto him that o	7126
7:29 He that o the sacrifice of his peace	7126
7:33 that o the blood of the peace offerings,	7126
17: 8 that o a burnt offering or sacrifice,	5927
21: 8 for he o the bread of thy God:	7126
22:21 whosoever o a sacrifice of peace offerings	7126
Nu 15: 4 shall he that o his offering unto the LORD	7126
Ps 50:23 Whoso o praise glorifieth me: and to him	2076
Isa 66: 3 he that o an oblation, *as if he offered*	5927
Jer 48:35 him that o *in* the high places, and him	5927
Mal 2:12 him that o an offering unto the LORD of	5066

OFFERING (724) [OFFER]

Ge 4: 3 fruit of the ground an o unto the LORD.	4503
4: 4 LORD had respect unto Abel and to his o:	4503
4: 5 unto Cain and to his o he had not respect.	4503
22: 2 offer him there for a **burnt** o upon one of	5930
22: 3 clave the wood for the **burnt** o,	5930
22: 6 Abraham took the wood of the **burnt** o,	5930
22: 7 but where *is* the lamb for a **burnt** o?	5930
22: 8 will provide himself a lamb for a **burnt** o:	5930
22:13 offered him up for a **burnt** o in the stead	5930
35:14 poured a **drink** o thereon, and he poured	5262
Ex 18:12 took a **burnt** o and sacrifices for God:	5930
25: 2 children of Israel, that they bring me an o:	8641
25: 2 willingly with his heart ye shall take my o.	8641
25: 3 this *is* the o which ye shall take of them:	8641
29:14 with fire without the camp: it *is* a **sin** o.	2403
29:18 it *is* a **burnt** o unto the LORD: it *is* a	5930
29:18 an o **made by fire** unto the LORD.	801
29:24 shalt wave them *for* a **wave** o before	8573
29:25 burn *them* upon the altar for a **burnt** o,	5930
29:25 it *is* an o **made by fire** unto the LORD.	801
29:26 wave it *for* a **wave** o before the LORD:	8573
29:27 shalt sanctify the breast of the **wave** o,	8573

Ex 29:27 the shoulder of the **heave** o, which is	8641
29:28 for it *is* a **heave** o: and it shall be a heave	8641
29:28 it shall be a **heave** o from the children of	8641
29:28 *even their* **heave** o unto the LORD.	8641
29:36 day a bullock *for* a **sin** o for atonement:	2403
29:40 fourth *part* of a hin of wine *for* a **drink** o.	5262
29:41 shalt do thereto according to the **meat** o	4503
29:41 according to the **drink** o thereof, for a	5262
29:41 an o **made by fire** unto the LORD.	801
29:42 *This shall be* a continual burnt o	5930
30: 9 nor burnt sacrifice, nor **meat** o;	4503
30: 9 neither shall ye pour **drink** o thereon.	5262
30:10 with the blood of the **sin** o of atonements:	2403
30:13 a half shekel *shall be* the o of the LORD.	8641
30:14 above, shall give an o unto the LORD.	8641
30:15 when *they* give an o unto the LORD,	8641
30:20 to burn o **made by fire** unto the LORD:	801
30:28 the altar of **burnt** o with all his vessels,	5930
31: 9 the altar of **burnt** o with all his furniture,	5930
35: 5 Take ye from amongst you an o unto	8641
35: 5 let him bring it, an o of the LORD;	8641
35:16 The altar of **burnt** o with his brasen grate,	5930
35:21 they brought the LORD's o to the work of	8641
35:22 man that offered *offered* an o of gold	8573
35:24 Every one that did offer an o of silver and	8641
35:24 of silver and brass brought the LORD's o:	8641
35:29 The children of Israel brought a **willing** o	5071
36: 3 they received of Moses all the o, which	8641
36: 6 any more work for the o of the sanctuary.	8641
38: 1 he made the altar of **burnt** o *of* shittim	5930
38:24 of the holy *place*, even the gold of the o,	8573
38:29 the brass of the o *was* seventy talents,	8573
40: 6 shalt set the altar of the **burnt** o before	5930
40:10 thou shalt anoint the altar of the **burnt** o	5930
40:29 he put the altar of **burnt** o *by* the door of	5930
40:29 offered upon it the **burnt** o and the meat	5930
40:29 upon it the burnt offering and the **meat** o;	4503
Lev 1: 2 If *any* man of you bring an o unto	7133
1: 2 ye shall bring your o of the cattle, *even* of	7133
1: 3 If his o *be* a **burnt** sacrifice of the herd,	7133
1: 4 his hand upon the head of the **burnt** o,	5930
1: 6 he shall flay the **burnt** o, and cut it into	5930
1: 9 *to be* a burnt sacrifice, an o **made by fire,**	801
1:10 If his o *be* of the flocks, namely, of	7133
1:13 it *is* a burnt sacrifice, an o **made by fire,**	801
1:14 if the burnt sacrifice for his o to	7133
1:14 he shall bring his o of turtledoves,	7133
1:17 it *is* a burnt sacrifice, an o **made by fire,**	801
2: 1 when any will offer a **meat** o unto	4503
2: 1 the LORD, his o shall be *of* fine flour;	7133
2: 2 be an o **made by fire,** of a sweet savour	801
2: 3 remnant of the **meat** o *shall be* Aaron's	4503
2: 4 thou bring an oblation of a **meat** o baken	4503
2: 5 thy oblation *be* a **meat** o baken in a pan,	4503
2: 6 and pour oil thereon: it *is* a **meat** o.	4503
2: 7 if thy oblation *be* a **meat** o baken in	4503
2: 8 shalt bring the **meat** o that is made of	4503
2: 9 the priest shall take from the **meat** o a	4503
2: 9 *it is* an o **made by fire,** of a sweet savour	801
2:10 that which is left of the **meat** o *shall be*	4503
2:11 No **meat** o, which ye shall bring unto	4503
2:11 *in* any of the LORD **made by fire.**	801
2:13 every oblation of thy **meat** o shalt thou	4503
2:13 of thy God to be lacking from thy **meat** o:	4503
2:14 thou offer a **meat** o of *thy* firstfruits unto	4503
2:14 thou shalt offer for the **meat** o of thy	4503
2:15 lay frankincense thereon: it *is* a **meat** o.	4503
2:16 *it is* an o **made by fire** unto the LORD.	801
3: 1 If his oblation *be* a sacrifice of **peace** o,	8002
3: 2 shall lay his hand upon the head of his o,	7133
3: 3 shall offer of the sacrifice of the **peace** o	8002
3: 3 offering an o **made by fire** unto the LORD;	801
3: 5 *it is* an o **made by fire,** of a sweet savour	801
3: 6 if his o *be* for a sacrifice of **peace** offering	7133
3: 6 if his offering for a sacrifice of **peace** o	8002
3: 7 If he offer a lamb for his o, then shall he	7133
3: 8 shall lay his hand upon the head of his o,	7133
3: 9 shall offer of the sacrifice of the **peace** o	8002
3: 9 offering an o **made by fire** unto the LORD;	801
3:11 *it is* the food of the o **made by fire** unto	801
3:12 if his o *be* a goat, then he shall offer it	7133
3:14 shall offer thereof his o, *even* an offering	7133
3:14 *even* an o **made by fire** unto the LORD;	801
3:16 *it is* the food of the o **made by fire** for a	801
4: 3 a blemish unto the LORD for a **sin** o.	2403
4: 7 at the bottom of the altar of the **burnt** o,	5930
4: 8 all the fat of the bullock *for the* **sin** o;	2403
4:10 burn them upon the altar of the **burnt** o.	5930
4:18 at the bottom of the altar of the **burnt** o,	5930
4:20 as he did with the bullock for a **sin** o,	2403
4:21 it *is* a **sin** o for the congregation.	2403
4:23 shall bring his o, a kid of the goats,	7133
4:24 they kill the **burnt** o before the LORD:	5930
4:24 offering before the LORD: it *is* a **sin** o.	2403
4:25 of the blood of the **sin** o with his finger,	2403
4:25 *it* upon the horns of the altar of **burnt** o,	5930
4:25 at the bottom of the altar of **burnt** o.	5930
4:28 he shall bring his o, a kid of the goats,	7133
4:29 lay his hand upon the head of the **sin** o,	2403
4:29 slay the **sin** o in the place of the burnt	2403
4:29 slay the sin o in the place of the **burnt**	5930
4:30 *it* upon the horns of the altar of **burnt** o,	5930
4:32 he bring a lamb for a **sin** o, he shall bring	2403
4:33 lay his hand upon the head of the **sin** o,	2403
4:33 slay it for a **sin** o in the place where they	2403

Lev 4:33 in the place where they kill the **burnt** o.	5930
4:34 of the blood of the **sin** o with his finger,	2403
4:34 upon the horns of the altar of **burnt** o,	5930
5: 6 he shall bring his **trespass** o unto	817
5: 6 a lamb or a kid of the goats, for a **sin** o;	2403
5: 7 one for a **sin** o, and the other for a burnt	5930
5: 7 a sin offering, and the other for a **burnt** o.	5930
5: 8 who shall offer *that* which *is* for the **sin** o	2403
5: 9 he shall sprinkle of the blood of the **sin** o	2403
5: 9 out at the bottom of the altar: it *is* a **sin** o.	2403
5:10 he shall offer the second *for* a **burnt** o,	5930
5:11 that sinned shall bring for his o the tenth	7133
5:11 *part* of an ephah of fine flour for a **sin** o;	2403
5:11 *any* frankincense thereon: for it *is* a **sin** o.	2403
5:12 made by fire unto the LORD: it *is* a **sin** o.	2403
5:13 *remnant* shall be the priest's, as a **meat** o.	4503
5:15 shekel of the sanctuary, for a **trespass** o,	817
5:16 for him with the ram of the **trespass** o,	817
5:18 for a **trespass** o, unto the priest:	817
5:19 It *is* a **trespass** o: he hath certainly	817
6: 5 appertaineth, in the day of his **trespass** o.	819
6: 6 he shall bring his **trespass** o unto	817
6: 6 for a **trespass** o, unto the priest:	817
6: 9 saying, This *is* the law of the **burnt** o:	5930
6: 9 It *is* the **burnt** o, because of the burning	5930
6:10 consumed with the **burnt** o on the altar,	5930
6:12 lay the **burnt** o in order upon it;	5930
6:14 this *is* the law of the **meat** o: the sons of	4503
6:15 of the flour of the **meat** o, and of the oil	4503
6:15 frankincense which *is* upon the **meat** o,	4503
6:17 *is* the **sin** o, and as the trespass offering.	2403
6:17 *is* the sin offering, and as the **trespass** o.	817
6:20 This *is* the o of Aaron and his sons,	7133
6:20 of fine flour *for* a **meat** o perpetual,	4503
6:21 the baken pieces of the **meat** o shalt thou	4503
6:23 For every **meat** o for the priest shall be	4503
6:25 saying, This *is* the law of the **sin** o:	2403
6:25 In the place where the **burnt** o is killed	5930
6:25 shall the **sin** o be killed before the LORD:	2403
6:30 no **sin** o, whereof *any* of the blood is	2403
7: 1 Likewise this *is* the law of the **trespass** o:	817
7: 2 In the place where they kill the **burnt** o	5930
7: 2 offering shall they kill the **trespass** o:	817
7: 5 for an o **made by fire** unto the LORD:	801
7: 5 by fire unto the LORD: it *is* a **trespass** o:	817
7: 7 As the **sin** o *is*, so *is* the trespass offering:	2403
7: 7 As the sin offering *is*, so *is* the **trespass** o:	817
7: 8 the priest that offereth *any* man's **burnt** o,	5930
7: 8 skin of the **burnt** o which he hath offered.	5930
7: 9 all the **meat** o that is baken in the oven,	4503
7:10 every **meat** o, mingled with oil, and dry,	4503
7:13 he shall offer *for* his o leavened bread	7133
7:14 oblation *for* a **heave** o unto the LORD,	8641
7:16 if the sacrifice of his o *be* a vow,	7133
7:16 his offering *be* a vow, or a **voluntary** o,	5071
7:25 which *men* offer an o **made by fire** unto	801
7:30 the breast may be waved *for* a **wave** o	8573
7:32 **heave** o of the sacrifices of your peace	8641
7:37 *is* the law of the **burnt** o, of the meat	5930
7:37 of the **meat** o, and of the sin offering,	4503
7:37 of the **sin** o, and of the trespass offering,	2403
7:37 the **trespass** o, and of the consecrations,	817
8: 2 a bullock *for* the **sin** o, and two rams,	2403
8:14 he brought the bullock *for the* **sin** o.	2403
8:14 the head of the bullock *for the* **sin** o.	2403
8:18 he brought the ram for the **burnt** o:	5930
8:21 *and* an o **made by fire** unto the LORD;	801
8:27 waved *them for* a **wave** o before	8573
8:28 burnt *them* on the altar upon the **burnt** o:	5930
8:28 It *is* an o **made by fire** unto the LORD.	801
8:29 waved it *for* a **wave** o before the LORD:	8573
9: 2 Take thee a young calf for a **sin** o,	2403
9: 2 a ram for a **burnt** o, without blemish,	5930
9: 3 Take ye a kid of the goats for a **sin** o;	2403
9: 3 first year, without blemish, for a **burnt** o:	5930
9: 4 and a **meat** o mingled with oil:	4503
9: 7 offer thy **sin** o, and thy burnt offering,	2403
9: 7 thy **burnt** o, and make an atonement for	5930
9: 7 offer the o of the people, and make an	7133
9: 8 the altar, and slew the calf of the **sin** o,	2403
9:10 and the caul above the liver of the **sin** o,	2403
9:12 he slew the **burnt** o; and Aaron's sons	5930
9:13 they presented the **burnt** o unto him,	5930
9:14 burnt *them* upon the **burnt** o on the altar.	5930
9:15 he brought the people's o, and took	7133
9:15 which *was* the **sin** o for the people,	2403
9:16 he brought the **burnt** o, and offered it	5930
9:17 brought the **meat** o, and took a handful	4503
9:21 waved *for* a **wave** o before the LORD;	8573
9:22 came down from o of the sin offering,	6213
9:22 came down from offering of the **sin** o,	2403
9:22 and the **burnt** o, and peace offerings.	5930
9:24 consumed upon the altar the **burnt** o and	5930
10:12 Take the **meat** o that remaineth	4503
10:15 to wave *it for* a **wave** o before the LORD;	8573
10:16 diligently sought the goat of the **sin** o,	2403
10:17 Wherefore have ye not eaten the **sin** o in	2403
10:19 *this* day have they offered their **sin** o	2403
10:19 and their **burnt** o before the LORD;	5930
10:19 *if* I had eaten the sin o to day, should it	2403
12: 6 a lamb of the first year for a **burnt** o,	5930
12: 6 young pigeon, or a turtledove, for a **sin** o,	2403
12: 8 the one for the **burnt** o, and the other for	5930
12: 8 burnt offering, and the other for a **sin** o:	2403
14:10 tenth deals of fine flour *for* a **meat** o,	4503

O

O

Ref	Text	Strong's
Lev	14:12 him for a **trespass o**, and the log of oil,	817
	14:12 wave them *for a* **wave o** before	8573
	14:13 in the place where he shall kill the **sin o**	2403
	14:13 shall kill the **sin o** ffering and the **burnt o**,	5930
	14:13 for as the **sin o** *is* the priest's, *so is*	2403
	14:13 *is* the priest's, *so is* the **trespass o**:	817
	14:14 take *some* of the blood of the **trespass o**,	817
	14:17 foot, upon the blood of the **trespass o**:	817
	14:19 the priest shall offer the **sin o**, and make	2403
	14:19 and afterward he shall kill the **burnt o**:	5930
	14:20 the priest shall offer the **burnt o** and	5930
	14:20 and the **meat o** upon the altar:	4503
	14:21 shall take one lamb *for a* **trespass o** to be	817
	14:21 fine flour mingled with oil for a **meat o**,	4503
	14:22 the one shall be a **sin o**, and the other a	2403
	14:22 be a sin offering, and the other a **burnt o**.	5930
	14:24 shall take the lamb of the **trespass o**,	817
	14:24 the priest shall wave them *for a* **wave o**	8573
	14:25 he shall kill the lamb of the **trespass o**:	817
	14:25 take *some* of the blood of the **trespass o**,	817
	14:28 the place of the blood of the **trespass o**:	817
	14:31 one *for a* **sin o**, and the other *for a* burnt	2403
	14:31 the other *for a* **burnt o**, with the meat	5930
	14:31 a burnt offering, with the **meat o**:	4503
	15:15 one *for a* **sin o**, and the other *for a* burnt	2403
	15:15 a sin offering, and the other *for a* **burnt o**;	5930
	15:30 the priest shall offer the one *for a* **sin o**,	2403
	15:30 a sin offering, and the other *for a* **burnt o**,	5930
	16: 3 *place:* with a young bullock for a **sin o**,	2403
	16: 3 for a sin offering, and a ram for a **burnt o**.	5930
	16: 5 of Israel two kids of the goats for a **sin o**,	2403
	16: 5 a sin offering, and one ram for a **burnt o**.	5930
	16: 6 Aaron shall offer *his* bullock of the **sin o**,	2403
	16: 9 **Lord**'s lot fell, and offer him *for a* **sin o**.	2403
	16:11 Aaron shall bring the bullock of the **sin o**,	2403
	16:11 shall kill the bullock of the **sin o** which *is*	2403
	16:15 he kill the goat of the **sin o**, that *is* for	2403
	16:24 offer his **burnt o**, and the burnt offering	5930
	16:24 the **burnt o** of the people, and make an	5930
	16:25 the fat of the **sin o** shall he burn upon	2403
	16:27 the bullock for the **sin o**, and the goat for	2403
	16:27 sin offering, and the goat for the **sin o**,	2403
	17: 4 to offer an **o** unto the **Lord** before	7133
	17: 8 that offereth a **burnt o** or sacrifice,	5930
	19:21 he shall bring his **trespass o** unto	817
	19:21 *even* a ram for a **trespass o**.	817
	19:22 **trespass o** before the **Lord** for his sin	817
	22:12 she may not eat of an o of the holy *things*.	8641
	22:18 will offer unto the **Lord** for a **burnt o**;	5930
	22:21 or a **freewill o** in beeves or sheep, it shall	5071
	22:22 make an **o by fire** of them upon the altar	801
	22:23 that mayest thou offer *for a* **freewill o**,	5071
	22:24 neither shall you make any o *thereof*in	NIH
	22:27 an **o made by fire** unto the **Lord**.	801+7133
	23: 8 ye shall offer an **o made by fire** unto	801
	23:12 first year for a **burnt o** unto the **Lord**.	5930
	23:13 the **meat o** thereof *shall be* two tenth	4503
	23:13 an **o made by fire** unto the **Lord** *for a*	801
	23:13 the **drink o** thereof *shall be* of wine,	5262
	23:14 that ye have brought an **o** unto your God:	7133
	23:15 that ye brought the sheaf of the **wave o**,	8573
	23:16 ye shall offer a new **meat o** unto	4503
	23:18 they shall be *for a* **burnt o** unto	5930
	23:18 their **meat o**, and their drink offerings,	4503
	23:18 drink offerings, *even* an **o made by fire**,	801
	23:19 sacrifice one kid of the goats for a **sin o**,	2403
	23:20 firstfruits *for a* **wave o** before the **Lord**,	8573
	23:25 ye shall offer an **o made by fire** unto	801
	23:27 offer an **o made by fire** unto the **Lord**.	801
	23:36 days ye shall offer an **o made by fire**	801
	23:36 ye shall offer an **o made by fire** unto	801
	23:37 to offer an **o made by fire** unto the **Lord**,	801
	23:37 a **burnt o**, and a meat offering, a sacrifice,	5930
	23:37 a **meat o**, a sacrifice, and drink offerings,	4503
	24: 7 *even* an **o made by fire** unto the **Lord**.	801
	27: 9 whereof *men* bring an **o** unto the **Lord**,	7133
Nu	4:16 the daily **meat o**, and the anointing oil,	4503
	5: 9 every **o** of all the holy *things* of the	8641
	5:15 he shall bring her **o** for her, the tenth *part*	7133
	5:15 for it *is* an **o** of jealousy, an offering of	4503
	5:15 an offering of jealousy, an **o** of memorial,	4503
	5:18 and put the **o** of memorial in her hands,	4503
	5:18 in her hands, which *is* the jealousy **o**:	4503
	5:25 the priest shall take the jealousy **o** out of	4503
	5:25 shall wave the **o** before the **Lord**,	4503
	5:26 the priest shall take a handful of the **o**,	4503
	6:11 the priest shall offer the one for a **sin o**,	2403
	6:11 the other for a **burnt o**, and make an	5930
	6:12 a lamb of the first year for a **trespass o**:	817
	6:14 he shall offer his **o** unto the **Lord**, one he	7133
	6:14 first year without blemish for a **burnt o**,	5930
	6:14 the first year without blemish for a **sin o**,	2403
	6:15 their **meat o**, and their drink offerings.	4503
	6:16 offer his **sin o**, and his burnt offering:	2403
	6:16 offer his sin offering, and his **burnt o**:	5930
	6:17 the priest shall offer also his **meat o**,	4503
	6:17 also his meat offering, and his **drink o**.	5262
	6:20 the priest shall wave them *for a* **wave o**	8573
	6:21 *of* his **o** unto the **Lord** for his separation,	7133
	7: 3 they brought their **o** before the **Lord**,	7133
	7:10 even the princes offered *for* **o** before the	7133
	7:11 They shall offer their **o**, each prince on	7133
	7:12 he that offered his **o** the first day was	7133
	7:13 his **o** *was* one silver charger, the weight	7133
	7:13 fine flour mingled with oil for a **meat o**:	4503

Ref	Text	Strong's
Nu	7:15 one lamb of the first year, for a **burnt o**:	5930
	7:16 One kid of the goats for a **sin o**:	2403
	7:17 this *was* the **o** of Nahshon the son of	7133
	7:19 He offered *for* his **o** one silver charger,	7133
	7:19 fine flour mingled with oil for a **meat o**,	4503
	7:21 one lamb of the first year, for a **burnt o**:	5930
	7:22 One kid of the goats for a **sin o**:	2403
	7:23 *was* the **o** of Nethaneel the son of Zuar.	7133
	7:25 His **o** *was* one silver charger, the weight	7133
	7:25 fine flour mingled with oil for a **meat o**,	4503
	7:27 one lamb of the first year, for a **burnt o**:	5930
	7:28 One kid of the goats for a **sin o**:	2403
	7:29 this *was* the **o** of Eliab the son of Helon.	7133
	7:31 His **o** *was* one silver charger of the weight	7133
	7:31 fine flour mingled with oil for a **meat o**:	4503
	7:33 one lamb of the first year, for a **burnt o**:	5930
	7:34 One kid of the goats for a **sin o**:	2403
	7:35 *was* the **o** of Elizur the son of Shedeur.	7133
	7:37 His **o** *was* one silver charger, the weight	7133
	7:37 fine flour mingled with oil for a **meat o**:	4503
	7:39 one lamb of the first year, for a **burnt o**:	5930
	7:40 One kid of the goats for a **sin o**:	2403
	7:41 this *was* the **o** of Shelumiel the son of	7133
	7:43 His **o** *was* one silver charger of the weight	7133
	7:43 fine flour mingled with oil for a **meat o**:	4503
	7:45 one lamb of the first year, for a **burnt o**:	5930
	7:46 One kid of the goats for a **sin o**:	2403
	7:47 *was* the **o** of Eliasaph the son of Deuel.	7133
	7:49 His **o** *was* one silver charger, the weight	7133
	7:49 fine flour mingled with oil for a **meat o**:	4503
	7:51 one lamb of the first year, for a **burnt o**:	5930
	7:52 One kid of the goats for a **sin o**:	2403
	7:53 this *was* the **o** of Elishama the son of	7133
	7:55 His **o** *was* one silver charger of the weight	7133
	7:55 fine flour mingled with oil for a **meat o**:	4503
	7:57 one lamb of the first year, for a **burnt o**:	5930
	7:58 One kid of the goats for a **sin o**:	2403
	7:59 this *was* the **o** of Gamaliel the son of	7133
	7:61 His **o** *was* one silver charger, the weight	7133
	7:61 fine flour mingled with oil for a **meat o**:	4503
	7:63 one lamb of the first year, for a **burnt o**:	5930
	7:64 One kid of the goats for a **sin o**:	2403
	7:65 this *was* the **o** of Abidan the son of	7133
	7:67 His **o** *was* one silver charger, the weight	7133
	7:67 fine flour mingled with oil for a **meat o**:	4503
	7:69 one lamb of the first year, for a **burnt o**:	5930
	7:70 One kid of the goats for a **sin o**:	2403
	7:71 this *was* the **o** of Ahiezer the son of	7133
	7:73 His **o** *was* one silver charger, the weight	7133
	7:73 fine flour mingled with oil for a **meat o**:	4503
	7:75 one lamb of the first year, for a **burnt o**:	5930
	7:76 One kid of the goats for a **sin o**:	2403
	7:77 this *was* the **o** of Pagiel the son of Ocran.	7133
	7:79 His **o** *was* one silver charger, the weight	7133
	7:79 fine flour mingled with oil for a **meat o**:	4503
	7:81 one lamb of the first year, for a **burnt o**:	5930
	7:82 One kid of the goats for a **sin o**:	2403
	7:83 this *was* the **o** of Ahira the son of Enan.	7133
	7:87 All the oxen for the **burnt o** were twelve	5930
	7:87 the first year twelve, with their **meat o**:	4503
	7:87 the kids for **sin o** twelve.	2403
	8: 8 take a young bullock with his **meat o**,	4503
	8: 8 young bullock shalt thou take for a **sin o**.	2403
	8:11 **Lord** *for* an **o** of the children of Israel,	8573
	8:12 thou shalt offer the one *for a* **sin o**,	2403
	8:12 the other *for a* **burnt o**, unto the **Lord**,	5930
	8:13 and offer them *for* an **o** unto the **Lord**.	8573
	8:15 cleanse them, and offer them *for* an **o**.	8573
	8:21 Aaron offered them *as* an **o** before	8573
	9: 7 that *we* may not offer an **o** of the **Lord**	7133
	9:13 he brought not the **o** of the **Lord** in his	7133
	15: 3 will make an **o by fire** unto the **Lord**,	801
	15: 3 a **burnt o**, or a sacrifice in performing a	5930
	15: 3 in a **freewill o**, or in your solemn feasts,	5071
	15: 4 shall he that offereth his **o** unto the **Lord**	7133
	15: 4 **meat o** of a tenth deal *of* flour mingled	4503
	15: 5 **drink o** shalt thou prepare with the burnt	5262
	15: 5 shalt thou prepare with the **burnt o**	5930
	15: 6 shalt prepare *for a* **meat o** two tenth	4503
	15: 7 a **drink o** thou shalt offer the third *part*	5262
	15: 8 thou preparest a bullock *for a* **burnt o**,	5930
	15: 9 shall he bring with a bullock a **meat o** of	4503
	15:10 thou shalt bring for a **drink o** half a hin	5262
	15:10 *for* an **o made by fire**, of a sweet savour	801
	15:13 in *an* offering made by fire, of a sweet	7126
	15:13 in offering an **o made by fire**, of a sweet	801
	15:14 will offer an **o made by fire**, of a sweet	801
	15:19 ye shall offer up a **heave o** unto	8641
	15:20 *of* the first of your dough *for a* **heave o**:	8641
	15:20 *ye do* the **heave o** of the threshingfloor,	8641
	15:21 the **Lord** a **heave o** in your generations.	8641
	15:24 offer one young bullock for a **burnt o**,	5930
	15:24 with his **meat o**, and his drink offering,	4503
	15:24 with his meat offering, and his **drink o**,	5262
	15:24 and one kid of the goats for a **sin o**.	2403
	15:25 they shall bring their **o**, a sacrifice made	7133
	15:25 their **sin o** before the **Lord**, for their	2403
	15:27 a she goat of the first year for a **sin o**.	2403
	16:15 unto the **Lord**, Respect not thou their **o**:	4503
	18: 9 every **meat o** of theirs, and every sin	4503
	18: 9 every **sin o** of theirs, and every trespass	2403
	18: 9 of theirs, and every **trespass o** of theirs,	817
	18:11 the **heave o** of their gift, with all the	8641
	18:17 shalt burn their fat *for* an **o made by fire**,	801
	18:24 which they offer *as* a **heave o** unto	8641

Ref	Text	Strong's
Nu	18:26 ye shall offer up a **heave o** of it for	8641
	18:27 your **heave o** shall be reckoned unto	8641
	18:28 Thus you also shall offer a **heave o** unto	8641
	18:28 ye shall give thereof the **Lord**'s **heave o**	8641
	18:29 ye shall offer every **heave o** of the **Lord**,	8641
	23: 3 Stand by thy **burnt o**, and I will go:	5930
	23:15 unto Balak, Stand here by thy **burnt o**,	5930
	23:17 he stood by his **burnt o**, and the princes	5930
	28: 2 My **o**, *and* my bread for my sacrifices	7133
	28: 3 This *is* the **o made by fire** which ye shall	801
	28: 3 spot day by day, *for a* continual **burnt o**.	5930
	28: 5 *part* of an ephah *of* flour for a **meat o**,	4503
	28: 6 *It is* a continual **burnt o**, which was	5930
	28: 7 the **drink o** thereof *shall be* the fourth	5262
	28: 7 be poured unto the **Lord** *for a* **drink o**.	5262
	28: 8 as the **meat o** of the morning, and as	4503
	28: 8 the morning, and as the **drink o** thereof,	5262
	28: 9 two tenth deals *of* flour *for a* **meat o**,	4503
	28: 9 with oil, and the **drink o** thereof:	5262
	28:10 *is* the **burnt o** of every sabbath, beside	5930
	28:10 beside the continual **burnt o**, and his	5930
	28:10 continual burnt offering, and his **drink o**.	5262
	28:11 ye shall offer a **burnt o** unto the **Lord**;	5930
	28:12 three tenth deals *of* flour *for a* **meat o**,	4503
	28:12 two tenth deals *of* flour *for a* **meat o**,	4503
	28:13 with oil *for a* **meat o** unto one lamb;	4503
	28:13 a **burnt o** *of* a sweet savour, a sacrifice	5930
	28:14 this *is* the **burnt o** of every month	5930
	28:15 one kid of the goats for a **sin o** unto	2403
	28:15 the continual **burnt o**, and his drink	5930
	28:15 continual burnt offering, and his **drink o**.	5262
	28:19 by fire *for a* **burnt o** unto the **Lord**;	5930
	28:20 their **meat o** *shall be* of flour mingled	4503
	28:22 goat for a **sin o**, to make an atonement	2403
	28:23 Ye shall offer these beside the **burnt o** in	5930
	28:23 which *is* for a continual **burnt o**.	5930
	28:24 be offered beside the continual **burnt o**,	5930
	28:24 continual burnt offering, and his **drink o**.	5262
	28:26 when ye bring a new **meat o** unto	4503
	28:27 ye shall offer the **burnt o** for a sweet	5930
	28:28 their **meat o** *of* flour mingled with oil,	4503
	28:31 offer *them* besides the continual **burnt o**,	5930
	28:31 his **meat o**, (they shall be unto you	4503
	29: 2 ye shall offer a **burnt o** for a sweet savour	5930
	29: 3 their **meat o** *shall be* of flour mingled	4503
	29: 5 kid of the goats for a **sin o**, to make an	2403
	29: 6 Beside the **burnt o** of the month,	5930
	29: 6 his **meat o**, and the daily burnt offering,	4503
	29: 6 the daily **burnt o**, and his meat offering,	5930
	29: 6 and his **meat o**, and their drink offerings,	4503
	29: 8 ye shall offer a **burnt o** unto the **Lord**	5930
	29: 9 their **meat o** *shall be* of flour mingled	4503
	29:11 One kid of the goats *for a* **sin o**; beside	2403
	29:11 beside the **sin o** of atonement,	2403
	29:11 the continual **burnt o**, and the meat	5930
	29:11 the **meat o** of it, and their drink offerings.	4503
	29:13 ye shall offer a **burnt o**, a sacrifice made	5930
	29:14 their **meat o** *shall be* of flour mingled	4503
	29:16 one kid of the goats *for a* **sin o**; beside	2403
	29:16 beside the continual **burnt o**, his meat	5930
	29:16 his **meat o**, and his drink offering.	4503
	29:16 his meat offering, and his **drink o**.	5262
	29:18 their **meat o** and their drink offerings for	4503
	29:19 one kid of the goats *for a* **sin o**; beside	2403
	29:19 the continual **burnt o**, and the meat	5930
	29:19 the **meat o** thereof, and their drink	4503
	29:21 their **meat o** and their drink offerings for	4503
	29:22 one goat for a **sin o**; beside the continual	2403
	29:22 the continual **burnt o**, and his meat	5930
	29:22 and his **meat o**, and his drink offering.	4503
	29:22 and his meat offering, and his **drink o**.	5262
	29:24 Their **meat o** and their drink offerings for	4503
	29:25 one kid of the goats *for a* **sin o**; beside	2403
	29:25 beside the continual **burnt o**, his meat	5930
	29:25 his **meat o**, and his drink offering.	4503
	29:25 his meat offering, and his **drink o**.	5262
	29:27 their **meat o** and their drink offerings for	4503
	29:28 one goat for a **sin o**; beside the continual	2403
	29:28 the continual **burnt o**, and his meat	5930
	29:28 and his **meat o**, and his drink offering.	4503
	29:28 and his meat offering, and his **drink o**.	5262
	29:30 their **meat o** and their drink offerings for	4503
	29:31 one goat for a **sin o**; beside the continual	2403
	29:31 beside the continual **burnt o**, his meat	5930
	29:31 his **meat o**, and his drink offering.	4503
	29:31 his meat offering, and his **drink o**.	5262
	29:33 their **meat o** and their drink offerings for	4503
	29:34 one goat for a **sin o**; beside the continual	2403
	29:34 beside the continual **burnt o**, his meat	5930
	29:34 his **meat o**, and his drink offering.	4503
	29:34 his meat offering, and his **drink o**.	5262
	29:36 ye shall offer a **burnt o**, a sacrifice made	5930
	29:37 Their **meat o** and their drink offerings for	4503
	29:38 one goat for a **sin o**; beside the continual	2403
	29:38 the continual **burnt o**, and his meat	5930
	29:38 and his **meat o**, and his drink offering.	4503
	29:38 and his meat offering, and his **drink o**.	5262
	31:29 the priest, *for a* **heave o** of the **Lord**.	8641
	31:41 *which* was the **Lord**'s **heave o**,	8641
	31:52 all the gold of the **o** that they offered up	8641
Dt	12:11 the **heave o** of your hand, and all your	8641
	12:17 offerings, or **heave o** of thine hand,	8641
	16:10 a tribute of a **freewill o** of thine hand,	5071
	23:23 a **freewill o**, according as thou hast	5071
Jos	22:23 or if to offer thereon **burnt o** or	5930

Jos	22:23 to offer thereon burnt offering or **meat o**,	4503
	22:26 an altar, not for **burnt o**, nor for sacrifice:	5930
Jdg	11:31 and I will offer it up for a **burnt o**.	5930
	13:16 thou wilt offer a **burnt o**, thou must offer	5930
	13:19 So Manoah took a kid with a **meat o**,	4503
	13:23 would not have received a **burnt o** and	5930
	13:23 burnt offering and a **meat o** at our hands,	4503
1Sa	2:17 for men abhorred the **o** of the LORD.	4503
	2:29 kick ye at my sacrifice and at mine **o**,	4503
	3:14 be purged with sacrifice nor **o** for ever.	4503
	6: 3 but in any wise return him a **trespass o**:	817
	6: 4 What *shall be* the **trespass o** which we	817
	6: 8 which ye return him for a **trespass o**,	817
	6:14 offered the kine a **burnt o** unto	5930
	6:17 returned for a **trespass o** unto the LORD;	817
	7: 9 offered it for a **burnt o** wholly unto	5930
	7:10 as Samuel was a **o** up the burnt offering,	5927
	7:10 as Samuel was offering up the **burnt o**,	5930
	13: 9 Bring hither a **burnt o** to me, and peace	5930
	13: 9 And he offered the **burnt o**.	5930
	13:10 that as soon as he had made an end of **o**	5927
	13:10 had made an end of offering the **burnt o**,	5930
	13:12 myself therefore, and offered a **burnt o**.	5930
	26:19 thee up against me, let him accept an **o**:	4503
2Sa	6:18 as soon as David had made an end of **o**	5927
1Ki	18:29 they prophesied until *the time* of the **o** of	5927
	18:36 it came to pass at *the time* of the **o** of	5927
2Ki	3:20 the **meat o** was offered, that behold,	4503
	3:27 offered him for a **burnt o** upon the wall.	5930
	5:17 **burnt o** nor sacrifice unto other gods,	5930
	10:25 as soon as he had made an end of **o**	6213
	10:25 had made an end of offering the **burnt o**,	5930
	16:13 burnt his **burnt o** and his meat offering,	5930
	16:13 burnt his burnt offering and his **meat o**,	4503
	16:13 his **drink o**, and sprinkled the blood	5262
	16:15 great altar burn the morning **burnt o**,	5930
	16:15 the evening **meat o**, and the king's burnt	4503
	16:15 king's burnt sacrifice, and his **meat o**,	4503
	16:15 with the **burnt o** of all the people of	5930
	16:15 their **meat o**, and their drink offerings;	4503
	16:15 upon it all the blood of the **burnt o**,	5930
1Ch	6:49 sons offered upon the altar of the **burnt o**,	5930
	16: 2 David had made an end of the **burnt**	5927
	16:29 bring an **o**, and come before him:	4503
	16:40 altar of the **burnt o** continually morning	5930
	21:23 for wood, and the wheat for the **meat o**;	4503
	21:26 heaven by fire upon the altar of **burnt o**.	5930
	21:29 wilderness, and the altar of the **burnt o**,	5930
	22: 1 this *is* the altar of the **burnt o** for Israel.	5930
	23:29 for the fine flour for **meat o**, and for	4503
2Ch	4: 6 things as they offered for the **burnt o**	5930
	7: 1 consumed the **burnt o** and the sacrifices;	5930
	8:13 according to the commandment of	5927
	29:18 the altar of **burnt o**, with all the vessels	5930
	29:21 for a **sin o** for the kingdom, and for	2403
	29:23 brought forth the he goats for the **sin o**	2403
	29:24 the king commanded *that* the **burnt o**	5930
	29:24 the **sin o** *should be made* for all Israel.	2403
	29:27 commanded to offer the **burnt o**	5930
	29:27 when the **burnt o** began, the song of	5930
	29:28 all *this* continued until the **burnt o** was	5930
	29:29 *they* had made an end of **o**, the king	5927
	29:32 all these *were* for a **burnt o** to the LORD.	5930
	29:35 and the drink offerings for *every* **burnt o**.	5930
	30:22 **o** peace offerings, and making confession	2076
	35:14 Aaron *were busied* in **o** of burnt offerings	5927
Ezr	1: 4 the **freewill o** for the house of God	5071
	3: 5 afterward *offered* the continual **burnt o**,	5930
	3: 5 offered a **freewill o** unto the LORD.	5071
	6:17 for a **sin o** for all Israel, twelve he goats,	2409
	7:16 with the **freewill o** of the people, and of	5069
	7:16 **o** willingly for the house of their God	5069
	8:25 *even* the **o** of the house of our God,	8641
	8:28 the gold *are* a **freewill o** unto the LORD	5071
	8:35 seven lambs, twelve he goats for a **sin o**:	2403
	8:35 all this *was* a **burnt o** unto the LORD.	5930
Ne	10:33 for the continual **meat o**, and for	4503
	10:33 for the continual **burnt o**, of the sabbaths,	5930
	10:34 Levites, and the people, for the wood	7133
	10:39 the children of Levi shall bring the **o** of	8641
	13: 9 with the **meat o** and the frankincense.	4503
	13:31 for the wood **o**, at times appointed,	7133
Job	42: 8 and offer up for yourselves a **burnt o**;	5930
Ps	40: 6 Sacrifice and **o** thou didst not desire; mine	4503
	40: 6 **burnt o** and sin offering hast thou not	5930
	40: 6 **sin o** hast thou not required.	2401
	51:16 I give *it*: thou delightest not in **burnt o**.	5930
	51:19 with **burnt o** and whole *burnt offering*:	5930
	51:19 with burnt offering and whole **burnt o**:	NIH
	96: 8 bring an **o**, and come into his courts.	4503
Isa	40:16 the beasts thereof sufficient for a **burnt o**.	4503
	43:23 I have not caused thee to serve with an **o**,	4503
	53:10 thou shalt make his soul an **o** for sin,	817
	57: 6 to them hast thou poured a **drink o**,	5262
	57: 6 offering, thou hast offered a **meat o**.	4503
	61: 8 judgment, I hate robbery for **burnt o**;	5930
	65:11 furnish the **drink o** unto *that* number.	4469
	66:20 they shall bring all your brethren for an **o**	4503
	66:20 as the children of Israel bring an **o** in a	4503
Jer	11:17 me to anger in a **incense** unto Baal.	6999
	14:12 when they offer **burnt o** and an oblation,	5930
Eze	20:28 they presented the provocation of their **o**:	7133
	40:38 gates, where they washed the **burnt o**.	5930
	40:39 to slay thereon the **burnt o** and the sin	5930
	40:39 and the **sin o** and the trespass offering.	2403

Eze	40:39 and the sin offering and the **trespass o**.	817
	40:42 *were* of hewn stone for the **burnt o**,	5930
	40:42 wherewith they slew the **burnt o**	5930
	40:43 upon the tables *was* the flesh of the **o**	7133
	42:13 the most holy *things*, and the **meat o**,	4503
	42:13 and the **sin o**, and the trespass offering,	2403
	42:13 and the sin offering, and the **trespass o**;	817
	43:19 Lord GOD, a young bullock for a **sin o**.	2403
	43:21 shalt take the bullock also of the **sin o**,	2403
	43:22 of the goats without blemish for a **sin o**;	2403
	43:24 shall offer them up for a **burnt o** unto	5930
	43:25 thou prepare every day a goat for a **sin o**:	2403
	44:11 shall slay the **burnt o** and the sacrifice	5930
	44:27 he shall offer his **sin o**, saith the Lord	2403
	44:29 They shall eat the **meat o**, and the sin	4503
	44:29 and the **sin o**, and the trespass offering,	2403
	44:29 and the sin offering, and the **trespass o**;	817
	45:15 for a **meat o**, and for a burnt offering,	4503
	45:15 and for a **burnt o**, and for peace offerings,	5930
	45:17 he shall prepare the **sin o**, and the meat	2403
	45:17 the **meat o**, and the burnt offering,	4503
	45:17 and the **sin o**, and the peace offerings,	2403
	45:19 priest shall take of the blood of the **sin o**,	2403
	45:22 people of the land a bullock for a **sin o**.	2403
	45:23 he shall prepare a **burnt o** to the LORD,	5930
	45:23 and a kid of the goats daily for a **sin o**.	2403
	45:24 he shall prepare a **meat o** of an ephah for	4503
	45:25 according to the **sin o**, according to	2403
	45:25 according to the **burnt o**, and according	5930
	45:25 according to the **meat o**, and according to	4503
	46: 2 the priests shall prepare his **burnt o** and	5930
	46: 4 the **burnt o** that the prince shall offer	5930
	46: 5 the **meat o** *shall be* an ephah for a ram,	4503
	46: 5 the **meat o** for the lambs as he shall be	4503
	46: 7 he shall prepare a **meat o**, an ephah for a	4503
	46:11 in the solemnities the **meat o** shall be an	4503
	46:12 prince shall prepare a voluntary **burnt o**	5930
	46:12 shall prepare his **burnt o** and his peace	5930
	46:13 Thou shalt daily prepare a **burnt o** unto	5930
	46:14 thou shalt prepare a **meat o** for it every	4503
	46:14 a **meat o** continually *by* a perpetual	4503
	46:15 the lamb, and the **meat o**, and the oil,	4503
	46:15 every morning for a continual **burnt o**.	5930
	46:20 the priests shall boil the **trespass o**	817
	46:20 boil the trespass offering and the **sin o**,	2403
	46:20 where they shall bake the **meat o**;	4503
	48: 8 shall be the **o** which ye shall offer of five	8641
Joel	1: 9 The **meat o** and the drink offering is cut	4503
	1: 9 **drink o** is cut off from the house of	5262
	1:13 for the **meat o** and the drink offering is	4503
	1:13 the **drink o** is withholden from the house	5262
	2:14 *even* a **meat o** and a drink offering unto	4503
	2:14 and a **drink o** unto the LORD your God?	5262
Zep	3:10 of my dispersed, shall bring mine **o**.	4503
Mal	1:10 neither will I accept an **o** at your hand.	4503
	1:11 *be* offered unto my name, and a pure **o**:	4503
	1:13 and the sick; thus ye brought an **o**:	4503
	2:12 him that offereth an **o** unto the LORD of	4503
	2:13 insomuch that *he* regardeth not the **o** any	4503
	3: 3 that they may offer unto the LORD an **o** in	4503
	3: 4 shall the **o** of Judah and Jerusalem be	4503
Lk	23:36 coming to *him*, and **o** him vinegar,	*4374*
Ac	21:26 until that an **o** should be offered for every	*4376*
Ro	15:16 that the **o** up of the Gentiles might be	*4376*
Eph	5: 2 and hath given himself for us an **o** and	*4376*
Heb	10: 5 Sacrifice and **o** thou wouldest not,	*4376*
	10: 8 Sacrifice and **o** and burnt offerings and	*4376*
	10: 8 and **o** for sin thou wouldest not,	NIG
	10:10 **o** of the body of Jesus Christ once for all.	*4376*
	10:11 and **o** oftentimes the same sacrifices,	*4374*
	10:14 For by one **o** he hath perfected for ever	*4376*
	10:18 of these *is, there is* no more **o** for sin.	*4376*

OFFERINGS (265) [OFFER]

Ge	8:20 and offered **burnt o** on the altar.	5930
Ex	10:25 must give us also sacrifices and **burnt o**,	5930
	20:24 shalt sacrifice thereon thy **burnt o**, and	5930
	20:24 thy **peace o**, thy sheep, and thine oxen:	8002
	24: 5 which offered **burnt o**,	5930
	24: 5 sacrificed peace **o** of oxen unto	2077
	29:28 of Israel of the sacrifice of their **peace o**,	8002
	32: 6 offered **burnt o**, and brought peace	5930
	32: 6 burnt offerings, and brought **peace o**.	8002
	36: 3 yet unto him **free** every morning.	5071
Lev	2: 3 holy of the **o** of the LORD **made by fire**.	801
	2:10 holy of the **o** of the LORD **made by fire**.	801
	2:13 with all thine **o** thou shalt offer salt.	7133
	4:10 the bullock of the sacrifice of **peace o**:	8002
	4:26 as the fat of the sacrifice of **peace o**:	8002
	4:31 away from off the sacrifice of **peace o**;	8002
	4:35 away from the sacrifice of the **peace o**,	8002
	4:35 according to the **o made by fire** unto	801
	5:12 according to the **o made by fire** unto	801
	6:12 shall burn thereon the fat of the **peace o**.	8002
	6:17 for their portion of my **o made by fire**;	801
	6:18 the **o** of the LORD **made by fire**:	801
	7:11 this *is* the law of the sacrifice of **peace o**,	8002
	7:13 sacrifice of thanksgiving of his **peace o**.	8002
	7:14 that sprinkleth the blood of the **peace o**,	8002
	7:15 flesh of the sacrifice of his **peace o** for	8002
	7:18 **peace o** be eaten at all on the third day,	8002
	7:20 of the flesh of the sacrifice of **peace o**,	8002
	7:21 of the flesh of the sacrifice of **peace o**	8002
	7:29 that offereth the sacrifice of his **peace o**	8002
	7:29 the LORD of the sacrifice of his **peace o**.	8002

Lev	7:30 bring the **o** of the LORD **made by fire**,	801
	7:32 offering of the sacrifices of your **peace o**.	8002
	7:33 that offereth the blood of the **peace o**,	8002
	7:34 from off the sacrifices of their **peace o**,	8002
	7:35 out of the **o** of the LORD **made by fire**,	801
	7:37 and of the sacrifice of **peace o**;	8002
	9: 4 Also a bullock and a ram for **peace o**,	8002
	9:18 and the ram *for* a sacrifice of **peace o**,	8002
	9:22 and the burnt offering, and **peace o**.	8002
	10:12 of the **o** of the LORD **made by fire**,	801
	10:14 of **peace o** of the children of Israel.	8002
	10:15 bring with the **o made by fire** of the fat,	801
	17: 5 offer them for **peace o** unto the LORD.	2077
	19: 5 if ye offer a sacrifice of **peace o** unto	8002
	21: 6 for the **o** of the LORD **made by fire**,	801
	21:21 to offer the **o** of the LORD **made by fire**:	801
	22:18 all his vows, and for all his **freewill o**	5071
	22:21 whosoever offereth a sacrifice of **peace o**	8002
	23:18 their meat offering, and their **drink o**,	5262
	23:19 of the first year for a sacrifice of **peace o**.	8002
	23:37 a meat offering, a sacrifice, and **drink o**,	5262
	23:38 vows, and beside all your **freewill o**	5071
	24: 9 him of the **o** of the LORD **made by fire**,	801
Nu	6:14 one ram without blemish for **peace o**,	8002
	6:15 meat offering, and their **drink o**.	5262
	6:17 for a sacrifice of **peace o** unto the LORD,	8002
	6:18 *is* under the sacrifice of the **peace o**.	8002
	7:17 for a sacrifice of **peace o**, two oxen,	8002
	7:23 for a sacrifice of **peace o**, two oxen,	8002
	7:29 for a sacrifice of **peace o**, two oxen,	8002
	7:35 for a sacrifice of **peace o**, two oxen,	8002
	7:41 for a sacrifice of **peace o**, two oxen,	8002
	7:47 for a sacrifice of **peace o**, two oxen,	8002
	7:53 for a sacrifice of **peace o**, two oxen,	8002
	7:59 for a sacrifice of **peace o**, two oxen,	8002
	7:65 for a sacrifice of **peace o**, two oxen,	8002
	7:71 for a sacrifice of **peace o**, two oxen,	8002
	7:77 for a sacrifice of **peace o**, two oxen,	8002
	7:83 for a sacrifice of **peace o**, two oxen,	8002
	7:88 the oxen for the sacrifice of the **peace o**	8002
	10:10 with the trumpets over your **burnt o**,	5930
	10:10 and over the sacrifices of your **peace o**;	8002
	15: 8 a vow, or **peace o** unto the LORD:	8002
	18: 8 **heave o** of all the hallowed *things* of	8641
	18:11 all the **wave o** of the children of Israel:	8573
	18:19 All the **heave o** of the holy *things*, which	8641
	28:14 their **drink o** shall be half a hin of wine	5262
	28:31 you without blemish) and their **drink o**,	5262
	29: 6 and his meat offering, and their **drink o**,	5262
	29:11 the meat offering of it, and their **drink o**,	5262
	29:18 and their **drink o** for the bullocks,	5262
	29:19 meat offering thereof, and their **drink o**,	5262
	29:21 and their **drink o** for the bullocks,	5262
	29:24 and their **drink o** for the bullocks,	5262
	29:27 and their **drink o** for the bullocks,	5262
	29:30 and their **drink o** for the bullocks,	5262
	29:33 and their **drink o** for the bullocks,	5262
	29:37 and their **drink o** for the bullocks,	5262
	29:39 besides your vows, and your **freewill o**,	5071
	29:39 for your **burnt o**, and for your meat	5930
	29:39 for your **meat o**, and for your drink	4503
	29:39 for your **drink o**, and for your peace	5262
	29:39 drink offerings, and for your **peace o**.	8002
Dt	12: 6 thither ye shall bring your **burnt o**,	5930
	12: 6 **heave o** of your hand, and your vows,	8641
	12: 6 your **freewill o**, and the firstlings of your	5071
	12:11 your **burnt o**, and your sacrifices,	5930
	12:13 **burnt o** in every place that thou seest:	5930
	12:14 there thou shalt offer thy **burnt o**,	5930
	12:17 nor thy **freewill o**, or heave offering of	5071
	12:27 thou shalt offer thy **burnt o**, the flesh and	5930
	18: 1 shall eat the **o** of the LORD **made by fire**,	801
	27: 6 thou shalt offer **burnt o** thereon unto	5930
	27: 7 thou shalt offer **peace o**, and shalt eat	8002
	32:38 *and* drank the wine of their **drink o**?	5257
Jos	8:31 they offered thereon **burnt o** unto	5930
	8:31 unto the LORD, and sacrificed **peace o**.	8002
	22:23 or if to offer **peace o** thereon,	2077
	22:27 the LORD before him with our **burnt o**,	5930
	22:27 our sacrifices, and with our **peace o**;	8002
	22:28 not for **burnt o**, nor for sacrifices:	5930
	22:29 to build an altar for **burnt o**, for meat	5930
	22:29 for **meat o**, or for sacrifices,	4503
Jdg	20:26 offered **burnt o** and peace offerings	5930
	20:26 and **peace o** before the LORD.	8002
	21: 4 and offered **burnt o** and peace offerings.	5930
	21: 4 and offered burnt offerings and **peace o**.	8002
1Sa	2:28 **made by fire** of the children of Israel?	801
	2:29 chiefest of all the **o** of Israel my people?	4503
	6:15 the men of Beth-shemesh offered **burnt o**	5930
	10: 8 to offer **burnt o**, *and* to sacrifice sacrifices	5930
	10: 8 *and* to sacrifice sacrifices of **peace o**:	8002
	11:15 there they sacrificed sacrifices of **peace o**	8002
	13: 9 a burnt offering to me, and **peace o**.	8002
	15:22 the LORD *as great delight as* **burnt**	5930
2Sa	1:21 *there be* rain upon you, nor fields of **o**:	8641
	6:17 David offered **burnt o** and peace offerings	5930
	6:17 and **peace o** before the LORD.	8002
	6:18 had made an end of offering **burnt o**	5930
	6:18 of offering burnt offerings and **peace o**,	8002
	24:24 neither will I offer **burnt o** unto	5930
	24:25 and offered **burnt o** and peace offerings.	5930
	24:25 and offered burnt offerings and **peace o**.	8002
1Ki	3: 4 a thousand **burnt o** did Solomon offer up	5930
	3:15 offered up **burnt o**, and offered peace	5930

1Ki	3:15 offered **peace** o, and made a feast to all	8002
	8:63 Solomon offered a sacrifice of **peace** o,	8002
	8:64 for there he offered **burnt** o, and meat	5930
	8:64 **meat** o, and the fat of the peace offerings:	4503
	8:64 meat offerings, and the fat of the **peace** o:	8002
	8:64 *was* too little to receive the **burnt** o,	5930
	8:64 **meat** o, and the fat of the peace offerings.	4503
	8:64 meat offerings, and the fat of the **peace** o:	8002
	9:25 times in a year did Solomon offer **burnt** o	5930
	9:25 **peace** o upon the altar which he built	8002
2Ki	10:24 went in to offer sacrifices and **burnt** o,	5930
	16:13 sprinkled the blood of his **peace** o, upon	8002
	16:15 their meat offering, and their **drink** o;	5262
1Ch	16: 1 burnt sacrifices and **peace** o before God.	8002
	16: 2 had made an end of offering the **burnt** o	5930
	16: 2 the burnt offerings and the **peace** o,	8002
	16:40 To offer **burnt** o unto the Lord upon	5930
	21:23 lo, I give *thee* the oxen *also* to offer **burnt** o	5930
	21:24 the Lord, nor offer **burnt** o without cost.	5930
	21:26 offered **burnt** and peace offerings,	5930
	21:26 offered burnt offerings and **peace** o,	8002
	29:21 offered **burnt** o unto the Lord,	5930
	29:21 with their **drink** o, and sacrifices in	5262
2Ch	1: 6 and offered a thousand **burnt** o upon it.	5930
	2: 4 *for the* **burnt** o morning and evening,	5930
	7: 7 there he offered **burnt** o, and the fat of	5930
	7: 7 the fat of the **peace** o, because the brasen	8002
	7: 7 made was not able to receive the **burnt** o,	5930
	7: 7 offerings, and the **meat** o, and the fat.	4503
	8:12 Solomon offered **burnt** o unto the Lord	5930
	23:18 to offer the **burnt** o of the Lord, as it is	5930
	24:14 they offered **burnt** o in the house of	5930
	29: 7 not burnt incense nor offered **burnt** o	5930
	29:31 and **thank** o into the house of the Lord.	8426
	29:31 brought in sacrifices and **thank** o;	8426
	29:31 as many as were of a free heart **burnt** o	5930
	29:32 the number of the **burnt** o, which	5930
	29:34 so that they could not flay all the **burnt** o:	5930
	29:35 also the **burnt** o *were* in abundance,	5930
	29:35 with the fat of the **peace** o, and the drink	8002
	29:35 and the **drink** o for *every* burnt offering.	5262
	30:15 brought in the **burnt** o *into* the house of	5930
	30:22 offering peace o, and making confession	2077
	31: 2 the priests and Levites for **burnt** o and	5930
	31: 2 for burnt offerings and for **peace** o,	8002
	31: 3 portion of his substance for **burnt** o,	5930
	31: 3 for the morning and evening **burnt** o,	5930
	31: 3 the **burnt** o for the sabbaths, and for	5930
	31:10 Since *the* people began to bring the o	8641
	31:12 brought in the o and the tithes and	8641
	31:14 the east, *was* over the **freewill** o of God,	5071
	33:16 sacrificed thereon peace o and **thank**	2077
	33:16 thereon peace offerings and **thank** o,	8426
	35: 7 all for the passover o, for all that were	NIH
	35: 8 gave unto the priests for the passover o	NIH
	35: 9 gave unto the Levites for passover o five	NIH
	35:12 removed the **burnt** o, that they might	5930
	35:13 the *other* holy o sod their in pots,	NIH
	35:14 Aaron *were busied* in offering of **burnt** o	5930
	35:16 to offer **burnt** o upon the altar of	5930
Ezr	3: 2 God of Israel, to offer **burnt** o thereon,	5930
	3: 3 they offered **burnt** o thereon unto	5930
	3: 3 *even* **burnt** o morning and evening.	5930
	3: 4 and offered the daily **burnt** o by number,	5930
	3: 6 they to offer **burnt** o unto the Lord.	5930
	6: 9 for the **burnt** o of the God of heaven,	5928
	7:17 their **meat** o and their drink offerings,	4504
	7:17 their meat offerings and their **drink** o,	5261
	8:35 offered **burnt** o unto the God of Israel,	5930
Ne	10:33 for the **sin** o to make an atonement for	2403
	10:37 our o, and the fruit of all *manner of* trees,	8641
	12:44 for the o, for the firstfruits, and for	8641
	13: 5 where aforetime they laid the **meat** o,	4503
	13: 5 and the porters; and the o of the priests.	8641
Job	1: 5 offered **burnt** o *according to* the number	5930
Ps	16: 4 their **drink** o of blood will I not offer,	5262
	20: 3 Remember all thy o, and accept thy burnt	4503
	50: 8 thee for thy sacrifices or thy **burnt** o,	5930
	66:13 I will go *into* thy house with **burnt** o:	5930
	119:108 the **freewill** o of my mouth, O Lord,	5071
Pr	7:14 *I have* peace with me; *this* day have I	2077
Isa	1:11 I am full *of the* **burnt** o of rams, and the	5930
	43:23 me the small cattle of thy **burnt** o:	5930
	56: 7 their **burnt** o and their sacrifices *shall be*	5930
Jer	6:20 your **burnt** o *are* not acceptable, nor your	5930
	7:18 to pour out **drink** o unto other gods, that	5262
	7:21 Put your **burnt** o unto your sacrifices,	5930
	7:22 of Egypt, concerning **burnt** o or sacrifices:	5930
	17:26 bringing **burnt** o, and sacrifices,	5930
	17:26 **meat** o, and incense,	4503
	19: 5 burn their sons with fire *for* **burnt** o unto	5930
	19:13 have poured out **drink** o unto other gods.	5262
	32:29 poured out **drink** o unto other gods,	5262
	33:18 want a man before me to offer **burnt** o,	5930
	33:18 to kindle **meat** o, and to do sacrifice	4503
	41: 5 with o and incense in their hand,	4503
	44:17 to pour out **drink** o unto her, as we have	5262
	44:18 to pour out **drink** o unto her, we have	5262
	44:19 poured out **drink** o unto her, did we	5262
	44:19 pour out **drink** o unto her, without our	5262
	44:25 and to pour out **drink** o unto her:	5262
Eze	20:28 and poured out there their **drink** o.	5262
	20:40 there will I require your o,	8641
	43:18 to offer **burnt** o thereon, and to sprinkle	5930
	43:27 the priests shall make your **burnt** o upon	5930

Eze	43:27 upon the altar, and your **peace** o;	8002
	45:15 and for a burnt offering, and for **peace** o,	8002
	45:17 shall be the prince's part *to give* **burnt** o,	5930
	45:17 **meat** o, and drink offerings, in the feasts,	4503
	45:17 **drink** o, in the feasts, and in the new	5262
	45:17 and the burnt offering, and the **peace** o,	8002
	46: 2 his burnt offering and his **peace** o,	8002
	46:12 or **peace** o voluntarily unto the Lord,	8002
	46:12 his burnt offering and his **peace** o,	8002
Hos	6: 6 knowledge of God more than **burnt** o.	5930
	8:13 sacrifice flesh *for* the sacrifices of mine o,	1890
	9: 4 They shall not offer wine *o* to the Lord,	NIH
Am	4: 5 and proclaim *and* publish the **free** o;	5071
	5:22 Though ye offer me **burnt** o and your	5930
	5:22 offer me burnt offerings and your **meat** o,	4503
	5:22 I regard the **peace** o of your fat beasts.	8002
	5:25 and o in the wilderness forty years,	4503
Mic	6: 6 shall I come before him with **burnt** o,	5930
Mal	3: 8 have we robbed thee? *In* tithes and o.	8641
Mk	12:33 is more than all **whole burnt** o and	3646
Lk	21: 4 abundance cast in unto the o of God:	*1435*
Ac	24:17 I came to bring alms to my nation, and o.	4376
Heb	10: 6 In **burnt** o and *sacrifices* for sin thou hast	3646
	10: 8 Sacrifice and offering and **burnt** o and	3646

OFFICE (46) [OFFICER, OFFICERS, OFFICES]

Ge	41:13 me he restored unto mine o, and him he	3653
Ex	1:16 When ye **do the o of a midwife** to	3205
	28: 1 may **minister** unto me **in the priest's o,**	3547
	28: 3 may **minister** unto me **in the priest's o.**	3547
	28: 4 may **minister** unto me **in the priest's o.**	3547
	28:41 may **minister** unto me **in the priest's o:**	3547
	29: 1 to **minister** unto me **in the priest's o:**	3547
	29: 9 the **priest's o** shall be theirs for a	3550
	29:44 to **minister** to me **in the priest's o.**	3547
	30:30 may **minister** unto me **in the priest's o.**	3547
	31:10 of his sons, **to minister in the priest's o,**	3547
	35:19 of his sons, **to minister in the priest's o.**	3547
	39:41 to **minister in the priest's o.**	3547
	40:13 may **minister** unto me **in the priest's o;**	3547
	40:15 may **minister** unto me **in the priest's o:**	3547
Lev	7:35 **minister** unto the Lord **in the priest's o;**	3547
	16:32 **minister in the priest's o** in his father's	3547
Nu	3: 3 consecrated to **minister in the priest's o.**	3547
	3: 4 Ithamar **ministered in the priest's o** in	3547
	3:10 and they shall wait on their **priest's o:**	3550
	4:16 to the o of Eleazar the son of Aaron	6486
	18: 7 your **priest's o** for every thing of the altar,	3550
	18: 7 I have given your **priest's o** *unto* you as a	3550
Dt	10: 6 **ministered in the priest's o** in his stead.	3547
1Ch	6:10 he it is that **executed the priest's o** in	3547
	6:32 they waited on their o according to their	5656
	9:22 Samuel the seer did ordain in their **set o.**	530
	9:26 were in their **set o,** and were over	530
	9:31 the **set o** over the things that were made	530
	23:28 Because their o *was* to wait on the sons of	4612
	24: 2 and Ithamar **executed the priest's o.**	3547
2Ch	11:14 **executing the priest's o** unto the Lord:	3547
	24:11 the king's o by the hand of the Levites,	6486
	31:15 in the cities of the priests, in *their* **set o,**	530
	31:18 in their **set o:** they sanctified themselves	530
Ne	13:13 o *was* to distribute unto their brethren.	5921
Ps	109: 8 days be few; *and* let another take his o.	6486
Eze	44:13 to **do the o of a priest** unto me,	3547
Lk	1: 8 *that* while he **executed the priest's o**	2407
	1: 9 According to the custom of the **priest's o,**	2405
Ro	11:13 apostle of the Gentiles, I magnify mine o:	1248
	12: 4 and all members have not the same o:	4234
1Ti	3: 1 If a man desire the o of a **bishop,**	1984
	3:10 then let them **use the o of a deacon,**	1247
	3:13 they that have **used the o of a deacon**	1247
Heb	7: 5 of the **priesthood** have a	2405

OFFICER (12) [OFFICE]

Ge	37:36 o of Pharaoh's, *and* captain of the guard.	5631
	39: 1 Potiphar, an o of Pharaoh, captain of	5631
Jdg	9:28 Zebul his o? serve the men of Hamor	6496
1Ki	4: 5 Zabud the son of Nathan *was* **principal** o,	3548
	4:19 *he was* the only o which *was* in the land.	5333
	22: 9 the king of Israel called an o, and said,	5631
2Ki	8: 6 the king appointed unto her a certain o,	5631
	25:19 out of the city he took an o that was set	5631
2Ch	24:11 and the high priest's o came and	6496
Mt	5:25 and the judge deliver thee to the o,	*5257*
Lk	12:58 and the judge deliver thee to the o,	*4233*
	12:58 officer, and the o cast thee into prison.	*4233*

OFFICERS (58) [OFFICE]

Ge	40: 2 Pharaoh was wroth against two *of* his o,	5631
	40: 7 he asked Pharaoh's o that *were* with him	5631
	41:34 this, and let him appoint o over the land,	6496
Ex	5: 6 of the people, and their o, saying,	7860
	5:10 their o, and they spake to the people,	7860
	5:14 the o of the children of Israel,	7860
	5:15 the o of the children of Israel came and	7860
	5:19 the o of the children of Israel did see *that*	7860
Nu	11:16 the elders of the people, and o over them;	7860
	31:14 Moses was wroth with the o of the host,	6485
	31:48 the o which *were* over thousands of	6485
Dt	1:15 over tens, and o among your tribes.	7860
	16:18 o shalt thou make thee in all thy gates,	7860
	20: 5 the o shall speak unto the people, saying,	7860
	20: 8 the o shall speak further unto the people,	7860
	20: 9 the o have made an end of speaking	7860
	29:10 your elders, and your o, *with* all the men	7860

Dt	31:28 your o, that I may speak these words in	7860
Jos	1:10 Joshua commanded the o of the people,	7860
	3: 2 days, that the o went through the host;	7860
	8:33 and their elders, and o, and their judges,	7860
	23: 2 for their o, and said unto them, I am old	7860
	24: 1 and for their judges, and for their o;	7860
1Sa	8:15 and give to his o, and to his servants.	5631
1Ki	4: 5 Azariah the son of Nathan *was* over the o:	5324
	4: 7 Solomon had twelve o over all Israel,	5324
	4:27 those o provided victual for king Solomon,	5324
	4:28 they unto the place where *the o* were,	NIH
	5:16 Besides the chief of Solomon's o which	5324
	9:23 These *were* the chief of the o that *were*	5324
2Ki	11:15 the o of the host, and said unto them,	6485
	11:18 the priest appointed o over the house of	6485
	24:12 his servants, and his princes, and his o:	5631
	24:15 and his o, and the mighty of the land,	5631
1Ch	23: 4 and six thousand *were* o and judges.	7860
	26:29 business over Israel, for o and judges.	7860
	26:30 *were* o among them of Israel on *this* side	6486
	27: 1 their o that served the king in any matter	7860
	28: 1 with the o, and *with* the mighty *men,* and	5631
2Ch	8:10 these *were* the chief of king Solomon's o,	5324
	18: 8 the king of Israel called for one *of his* o,	5631
	19:11 also the Levites *shall be* o before you.	7860
	34:13 *there were* scribes, and o, and porters.	7860
Est	1: 8 the king had appointed to all the o of his	7227
	2: 3 let the king appoint o in all the provinces	6496
	9: 3 and of the o, helped the Jews;	4399+6213+1886.1
Isa	60:17 I will also make thy o peace,	6486
Jer	29:26 that *ye* should be in the house of	6496
Jn	7:32 and the chief priests sent to take him.	5257
	7:45 Then came the o to the chief priests and	5257
	7:46 The o answered, Never man spake like	5257
	18: 3 and from the chief priests and Pharisees,	5257
	18:12 the captain and o of the Jews took Jesus,	5257
	18:18 stood *there,* who had made a fire of	5257
	18:22 one of the o which stood by struck Jesus	5257
	19: 6 the chief priests therefore and o saw him,	5257
Ac	5:22 when the o came, and found them not	5257
	5:26 Then went the captain with the o,	5257

OFFICES (5) [OFFICE]

1Sa	2:36 I pray thee, into one of the **priests'** o,	3550
1Ch	24: 3 according to their o in their service.	6486
2Ch	7: 6 the priests waited on their o: the Levites	4931
	23:18 Jehoiada appointed the o of the house	6486
Ne	13:14 house of my God, and for the o thereof.	4929

OFFSCOURING (2)

La	3:45 Thou hast made us *as the* o and refuse in	5501
1Co	4:13 *and are the* o of all *things* unto this day.	4067

OFFSPRING (12)

Job	5:25 and thine o *as* the grass of the earth.	6631
	21: 8 with them, and their o before their eyes.	6631
	27:14 and his o shall not be satisfied *with* bread.	6631
	31: 8 another eat; yea, let my o be rooted out.	6631
Isa	22:24 the o and the issue, all vessels of small	6631
	44: 3 thy seed, and my blessing upon thine o:	6631
	48:19 the o of thy bowels like the gravel thereof;	6631
	61: 9 Gentiles, and their o among the people:	6631
	65:23 of the Lord, and their o with them.	6631
Ac	17:28 own poets have said, For we are also his o.	1085
	17:29 Forasmuch then as we are the o of God,	1085
Rev	22:16 I am the root and the o of David,	*1085*

OFT (13) [OFTEN]

2Ki	4: 8 *so* it was, *that* **as o as** he passed by,	1767+4480
Job	21:17 **How** is the candle of the	4100+3509.1
	21:17 how o cometh their destruction upon	NIH
Ps	78:40 **How** o did they provoke him in	4100+3509.1
Mt	9:14 Why do we and the Pharisees fast o,	4183
	17:15 falleth into the fire, and o into the water.	4178
	18:21 **how** o shall my brother sin against me,	4212
Mk	7: 3 except they wash *their* hands o, eat not,	4435
Ac	26:11 I punished them o in every synagogue,	4178
1Co	11:25 **as o as** ye drink *it,* in remembrance	302+3740
2Co	11:23 in prisons more frequent, in deaths o.	4178
2Ti	1:16 for o refreshed me, and was not ashamed	4178
Heb	6: 7 *in* the rain that cometh o upon it,	4178

OFTEN (15) [OFT, OFTENER, OFTENTIMES, OFTTIMES]

Pr	29: 1 that being o reproved hardeneth *his* neck,	NIH
Mal	3:16 they that feared the Lord spake o one to	NIH
Mt	23:37 **how** o would I have gathered thy children	4212
Mk	5: 4 Because that he had been o bound with	4178
Lk	5:33 Why do the disciples of John fast o,	4437
	13:34 **how** o would I have gathered thy children	4212
1Co	11:26 For **as o as** ye eat this bread,	302+3740
2Co	11:26 *In* journeyings o, *in* perils of waters,	4178
	11:27 in watchings o, in hunger and thirst,	4178
	11:27 in hunger and thirst, in fastings o, in cold	4178
Php	3:18 of whom I have told you o, and now tell	4178
1Ti	5:23 thy stomach's sake and thine o infirmities.	4437
Heb	9:25 Nor yet that he should offer himself o,	4178
	9:26 must he o have suffered since	4178
Rev	11: 6 with all plagues, **as o as** they will.	1437+3740

OFTENER (1) [OFTEN]

Ac	24:26 wherefore he sent for him the o,	4437

OFTENTIMES (6) [OFTEN, TIME]

Job	33:29 *things* worketh God o with man,	6471+7969

Ecc	7:22 For **o** also thine own heart knoweth	6471+7227
Lk	8:29 For it had caught him: and he	4183+5550
Ro	1:13 that I purposed to come unto you, (but	*4178*
2Co	8:22 whom we have **o** proved diligent in many	*4178*
Heb	10:11 and offering **o** the same sacrifices,	*4178*

OFTTIMES (3) [OFTEN, TIME]

Mt	17:15 for **o** he falleth into the fire, and oft into	*4178*
Mk	9:22 And **o** it hath cast him into the fire,	*4178*
Jn	18: 2 for Jesus **o** resorted thither with his	*4178*

OG (22)

Nu	21:33 **O** the king of Bashan went out against	5747
	32:33 kingdom of **O** king of Bashan, the land,	5747
Dt	1: 4 in Heshbon, and **O** the king of Bashan,	5747
	3: 1 **O** the king of Bashan came out against us,	5747
	3: 3 our God delivered into our hands **O** also,	5747
	3: 4 of Argob, the kingdom of **O** in Bashan.	5747
	3:10 cities of the kingdom of **O** in Bashan.	5747
	3:11 For only **O** king of Bashan remained of	5747
	3:13 and all Bashan, *being* the kingdom of **O**,	5747
	4:47 land of **O** king of Bashan, two kings of	5747
	29: 7 of Heshbon, and **O** the king of Bashan,	5747
	31: 4 unto them as he did to Sihon and to **O**,	5747
Jos	2:10 and **O**, whom ye utterly destroyed.	5747
	9:10 to **O** king of Bashan, which *was* at	5747
	12: 4 the coast of **O** king of Bashan, *which was*	5747
	13:12 All the kingdom of **O** in Bashan,	5747
	13:30 all the kingdom of **O** king of Bashan,	5747
	13:31 cities of the kingdom of **O** in Bashan,	5747
1Ki	4:19 of the Amorites, and of **O** king of Bashan;	5747
Ne	9:22 and the land of **O** king of Bashan.	5747
Ps	135:11 **O** king of Bashan, and all the kingdoms of	5747
	136:20 **O** the king of Bashan: for his mercy	5747

OH (17) [O]

Ge	18:30 he said *unto him,* **O** let not the Lord be	4994
	18:32 **O** let not the Lord be angry, and I will	4994
	19:18 Lot said unto them, **O**, not so, my Lord:	4994
	19:20 **O**, let me escape thither, (*is* it not a little	4994
Ex	32:31 **O**, this people have sinned a great sin,	577
2Sa	15: 4 **O that** I were made judge in the land,	4310
	23:15 **O that** one would give me drink of	4310
1Ch	4:10 **O that** thou wouldest bless me indeed,	518
	11:17 **O that** one would give me drink of	4310
Job	6: 2 **O that** my grief were throughly weighed,	3863
	10:18 **O** *that* I had given up the ghost, and no	NIH
Ps	107: 8 **O** that *men* would praise the LORD *for* his	NIH
	107:15 **O** that *men* would praise the LORD *for* his	NIH
	107:21 **O** that *men* would praise the LORD *for* his	NIH
	107:31 **O** that *men* would praise the LORD *for* his	NIH
	116:16 **O** LORD, truly I *am* thy servant; I *am* thy	577
Jer	44: 4 rising early and sending *them,* saying, **O**,	4994

OHAD (2)

Ge	46:10 **O**, and Jachin, and Zohar, and Shaul the	161
Ex	6:15 **O**, and Jachin, and Zohar, and Shaul the	161

OHEL (1)

1Ch	3:20 **O**, and Berechiah, and Hasadiah,	169

OHOLAH See AHOLAH

OHOLIAB See AHOLIAB

OHOLIBAH See AHOLIBAH

OHOLIBAMAH See AHOLIBAMAH

OIL (202) [OILED]

Ge	28:18 a pillar, and poured **o** upon the top of it.	8081
	35:14 thereon, and he poured **o** thereon.	8081
Ex	25: 6 **O** for the light, spices for anointing oil,	8081
	25: 6 spices for anointing **o**, and for sweet	8081
	27:20 they bring thee pure **o** olive beaten for	8081
	29: 2 cakes unleavened tempered with **o**,	8081
	29: 2 and wafers unleavened anointed with **o**:	8081
	29: 7 thou take the anointing **o**, and pour *it*	8081
	29:21 of the anointing **o**, and sprinkle *it* upon	8081
	29:40 with the fourth part of a hin of beaten **o**;	8081
	30:24 of the sanctuary, and of **o** olive a hin:	8081
	30:25 thou shalt make it an **o** of holy ointment,	8081
	30:25 it shall be a holy anointing **o**.	8081
	30:31 This shall be a holy anointing **o** unto me	8081
	31:11 the anointing **o**, and sweet incense for	8081
	35: 8 **o** for the light, and spices for anointing oil,	8081
	35: 8 spices for anointing **o**, and for the sweet	8081
	35:14 and his lamps, with the **o** for the light,	8081
	35:15 the anointing **o**, and the sweet incense,	8081
	35:28 for the light, and for the anointing oil,	8081
	35:28 for the anointing **o**, and for the sweet	8081
	37:29 made the holy anointing **o**, and the pure	8081
	39:37 all the vessels thereof, and the **o** for light,	8081
	39:38 the anointing **o**, and the sweet incense,	8081
	40: 9 thou shalt take the anointing **o**,	8081
Lev	2: 1 he shall pour **o** upon it,	8081
	2: 2 of the thereof, with all the frankincense	8081
	2: 4 cakes of fine flour mingled with **o**,	8081
	2: 4 or unleavened wafers anointed with **o**.	8081
	2: 5 *of* fine flour unleavened, mingled with **o**.	8081
	2: 6 shalt part it in pieces, and pour **o** thereon:	8081
	2: 7 it shall be made *of* fine flour with **o**.	8081
	2:15 thou shalt put **o** upon it,	8081
	2:16 corn thereof, and *part* of the **o** thereof,	8081
	5:11 he shall put no **o** upon it, neither shall he	8081
	6:15 of the **o** thereof, and all the frankincense	8081

Lev	6:21 In a pan it shall be made with **o**;	8081
	7:10 meat offering, mingled with **o**, and dry,	8081
	7:12 unleavened cakes mingled with **o**,	8081
	7:12 and unleavened wafers anointed with **o**,	8081
	7:12 cakes mingled with **o**, of fine flour, fried.	8081
	8: 2 the anointing **o**, and a bullock *for* the sin	8081
	8:10 Moses took the anointing **o**,	8081
	8:12 poured of the anointing **o** upon Aaron's	8081
	8:30 Moses took of the anointing **o**, and of	8081
	9: 4 and a meat offering mingled with **o**:	8081
	10: 7 for the anointing **o** of the LORD *is* upon	8081
	14:10 mingled with **o**, and one log of oil.	8081
	14:10 mingled with oil, and one log of **o**.	8081
	14:12 the log of **o**, and wave them *for* a wave	8081
	14:15 the priest shall take of the log of **o**,	8081
	14:16 priest shall dip his right finger in the **o**	8081
	14:16 sprinkle of the **o** with his finger seven	8081
	14:17 the rest of the **o** that *is* in his hand shall	8081
	14:18 remnant of the **o** that *is* in the priest's	8081
	14:21 tenth deal of fine flour mingled with **o**,	8081
	14:21 oil for a meat offering, and a log of **o**;	8081
	14:24 log of **o**, and the priest shall wave them	8081
	14:26 priest shall pour of the **o** into the palm	8081
	14:27 **o** that *is* in his left hand seven times	8081
	14:28 the priest shall put of the **o** that *is* in his	8081
	14:29 rest of the **o** that *is* in the priest's hand	8081
	21:10 upon whose head the anointing **o** was	8081
	21:12 the crown of the anointing **o** of his God	8081
	23:13 tenth deals *of* fine flour mingled with **o**,	8081
	24: 2 that they bring unto thee pure **o** olive	8081
Nu	4: 9 and all the **o** vessels thereof,	8081
	4:16 the priest *pertaineth* the **o** for the light,	8081
	4:16 the anointing **o**, *and* the oversight of all	8081
	5:15 he shall pour no **o** upon it, nor put	8081
	6:15 cakes *of* fine flour mingled with **o**,	8081
	6:15 of unleavened bread anointed with **o**,	8081
	7:13 flour mingled with **o** for a meat offering:	8081
	7:19 flour mingled with **o** for a meat offering:	8081
	7:25 flour mingled with **o** for a meat offering:	8081
	7:31 flour mingled with **o** for a meat offering:	8081
	7:37 flour mingled with **o** for a meat offering:	8081
	7:43 flour mingled with **o** for a meat offering:	8081
	7:49 flour mingled with **o** for a meat offering:	8081
	7:55 flour mingled with **o** for a meat offering:	8081
	7:61 flour mingled with **o** for a meat offering:	8081
	7:67 flour mingled with **o** for a meat offering:	8081
	7:73 flour mingled with **o** for a meat offering:	8081
	7:79 flour mingled with **o** for a meat offering:	8081
	8: 8 *even* fine flour mingled with **o**,	8081
	11: 8 the taste of it was as the taste of fresh **o**.	8081
	15: 4 with the fourth *part* of a hin of **o**.	8081
	15: 6 mingled with the third *part* of a hin of **o**.	8081
	15: 9 *of* flour mingled with half a hin of **o**.	8081
	18:12 All the best of the **o**, and all the best of	3323
	28: 5 with the fourth *part* of a hin of beaten **o**.	8081
	28: 9 mingled with **o**, and the drink offering	8081
	28:12 mingled with **o**, for one bullock;	8081
	28:12 offering, mingled with **o**, for one ram;	8081
	28:13 several tenth deal of flour mingled with **o**	8081
	28:20 offering *shall be of* flour mingled with **o**:	8081
	28:28 meat offering *of* flour mingled with **o**,	8081
	29: 3 offering *shall be of* flour mingled with **o**,	8081
	29: 9 offering *shall be of* flour mingled with **o**,	8081
	29:14 offering *shall be of* flour mingled with **o**,	8081
	35:25 which was anointed with the holy **o**.	8081
Dt	7:13 thy corn, and thy wine, and thine **o**,	3323
	8: 8 a land of **o** olive, and honey;	8081
	11:14 in thy corn, and thy wine, and thine **o**.	3323
	12:17 of thy **o**, or the firstlings of thy herds or	3323
	14:23 of thine **o**, and the firstlings of thy herds	3323
	18: 4 of thy **o**, and the first of the fleece of thy	3323
	28:40 thou shalt not anoint *thyself* with the **o**;	8081
	28:51 or **o**, *or* the increase of thy kine,	3323
	32:13 of the rock, and **o** out of the flinty rock;	8081
	33:24 his brethren, and let him dip his foot in **o**.	8081
1Sa	10: 1 Samuel took a vial of **o**, and poured *it*	8081
	16: 1 fill thine horn with **o**, and go, I will send	8081
	16:13 Samuel took the horn of **o**,	8081
2Sa	1:21 *though* he had not *been* anointed with **o**.	8081
	14: 2 anoint not *thyself* with **o**, but be as a	8081
1Ki	1:39 Zadok the priest took a horn of **o** out of	8081
	5:11 and twenty measures of pure **o**:	8081
	17:12 meal in a barrel, and a little **o** in a cruse:	8081
	17:14 waste, neither shall the cruse of **o** fail,	8081
	17:16 not, neither did the cruse of **o** fail,	8081
2Ki	4: 2 any thing in the house, save a pot of **o**.	8081
	4: 6 *is* not a vessel more. And the **o** stayed.	8081
	4: 7 sell the **o**, and pay thy debt, and live	8081
	9: 1 take this box of **o** in thine hand, and go	8081
	9: 3 take the box of **o**, and pour *it* on his head,	8081
	9: 6 he poured the **o** on his head, and said	8081
	18:32 vineyards, a land of **o** olive and of honey,	3323
1Ch	9:29 **o**, and the frankincense, and the spices.	8081
	12:40 and **o**, and oxen, and sheep abundantly:	8081
	27:28 and over the cellars of **o** was Joash:	8081
2Ch	2:10 of wine, and twenty thousand baths of **o**.	8081
	2:15 and the barley, the **o**, and the wine,	8081
	11:11 and store of victual, and of **o** and wine.	8081
	31: 5 **o**, and honey, and of all the increase of	3323
	32:28 for the increase of corn, and wine, and **o**;	3323
Ezr	3: 7 and drink, and **o**, unto them of Zidon,	8081
	6: 9 God of heaven, wheat, salt, wine, and **o**,	4887
	7:22 an hundred baths *of* **o**, and salt without	4887
Ne	5:11 *of* the corn, the wine, and the **o**, that ye	3323
	10:37 trees, of wine, and of **o**, unto the priests,	3323

Ne	10:39 of the new wine, and the **o**, unto	3323
	13: 5 of the corn, the new wine, and the **o**,	3323
	13:12 new wine and the **o** unto the treasuries.	3323
Est	2:12 *to wit*, six months with **o** of myrrh,	8081
Job	24:11 Which **make o** within their walls,	6671
	29: 6 and the rock poured me out rivers of **o**;	8081
Ps	23: 5 thou anointest my head with **o**; my cup	8081
	45: 7 hath anointed thee *with* the **o** of gladness	8081
	55:21 his words were softer than **o**, yet *were*	8081
	89:20 with my holy **o** have I anointed him:	8081
	92:10 unicorn: I shall be anointed with fresh **o**.	8081
	104:15 *and* **o** to make *his* face to shine,	8081
	109:18 like water, and like **o** into his bones.	8081
	141: 5 *it shall be* an excellent **o**, *which* shall not	8081
Pr	5: 3 and her mouth *is* smoother than **o**:	8081
	21:17 that loveth wine and **o** shall not be rich.	8081
	21:20 and **o** in the dwelling of the wise;	8081
Isa	41:19 tree, and the myrtle, and the **o** tree;	8081
	61: 3 for ashes, the **o** of joy for mourning,	8081
Jer	31:12 for **o**, and for the young of the flock and	3323
	40:10 **o**, and put *them* in your vessels,	8081
	41: 8 of barley, and *of* **o**, and *of* honey.	8081
Eze	16: 9 from thee, and I anointed thee with **o**.	8081
	16:13 didst eat fine flour, and honey, and **o**:	8081
	16:18 thou hast set mine **o** and mine incense	8081
	16:19 fine flour, and **o**, and honey, *wherewith* I	8081
	23:41 thou hast set mine incense and mine **o**.	8081
	27:17 and Pannag, and honey, and **o**, and balm.	8081
	32:14 cause their rivers to run like **o**, saith	8081
	45:14 Concerning the ordinance of **o**, the bath	8081
	45:14 the ordinance of oil, the bath *of* **o**,	8081
	45:24 for a ram, and a hin of **o** for an ephah.	8081
	45:25 the meat offering, and according to the **o**.	8081
	46: 5 be able to give, and a hin of **o** to an ephah.	8081
	46: 7 attain unto, and a hin of **o** to an ephah.	8081
	46:11 is able to give, and a hin of **o** to an ephah.	8081
	46:14 an ephah, and the third *part* of a hin of **o**,	8081
	46:15 lamb, and the meat offering, and the **o**.	8081
Hos	2: 5 and my flax, mine **o** and my drink.	8081
	2: 8 and **o**, and multiplied her silver and gold,	3323
	2:22 hear the corn, and the wine, and the **o**;	3323
	12: 1 the Assyrians, and **o** is carried into Egypt.	8081
Joel	1:10 new wine is dried up, the **o** languisheth.	3323
	2:19 and **o**, and ye shall be satisfied therewith:	3323
	2:24 the fats shall overflow *with* wine and **o**.	3323
Mic	6: 7 *or* with ten thousands of rivers of **o**?	8081
	6:15 but thou shalt not anoint *thee* with **o**;	8081
Hag	1:11 the **o**, and upon *that* which the ground	3323
	2:12 or pottage, or wine, or **o**, or any meat,	8081
Zec	4:12 empty the golden **o** out of themselves?	NIH
Mt	25: 3 their lamps, and took no **o** with them:	1637
	25: 4 But the wise took **o** in their vessels with	1637
	25: 8 said unto the wise, Give us of your **o**;	1637
Mk	6:13 and anointed with **o** many *that* were sick,	1637
Lk	7:46 Mine head with **o** thou didst not anoint:	1637
	10:34 pouring in **o** and wine, and set him on his	1637
	16: 6 And he said, An hundred measures of **o**.	1637
Heb	1: 9 hath anointed thee *with* the **o** of gladness	1637
Jas	5:14 anointing him with **o** in the name of	1637
Rev	6: 6 and *see* thou hurt not the **o** and the wine.	1637
	18:13 and **o**, and fine flour, and wheat,	1637

OILED (2) [OIL]

Ex	29:23 one cake of **o** bread, and one wafer out	8081
Lev	8:26 a cake of **o** bread, and one wafer,	8081

OINTMENT (27) [OINTMENTS]

Ex	30:25 thou shalt make it an oil of holy **o**,	4888
	30:25 an **o** compound *after* the art of	7545
2Ki	20:13 the precious **o**, and all the house of his	8081
1Ch	9:30 of the sons of the priests made the **o**	4842
Job	41:31 a pot: he maketh the sea like a **pot of o**.	4841
Ps	133: 2 *It* is like the precious **o** upon the head,	8081
Pr	27: 9 **O** and perfume rejoice the heart:	8081
	27:16 the wind, and the **o** of his right hand,	8081
Ecc	7: 1 A *good* name *is* better than precious **o**;	8081
	9: 8 always white; and let thy head lack no **o**.	8081
	10: 1 Dead flies cause the **o** of the apothecary	8081
SS	1: 3 ointments thy name *is as* **o** poured forth,	8081
Isa	1: 6 bound up, neither mollified with **o**.	8081
	39: 2 the precious **o**, and all the house of his	8081
	57: 9 thou wentest to the king with **o**,	8081
Mt	26: 7 an alabaster box of very precious **o**,	3464
	26: 9 For this **o** might have been sold for much,	3464
	26:12 For in that she hath poured this **o** on my	3464
Mk	14: 3 box of **o** of spikenard very precious;	3464
	14: 4 said, Why was this waste of the **o** made?	3464
Lk	7:37 brought an alabaster box of **o**,	3464
	7:38 his feet, and anointed *them* with the **o**.	3464
	7:46 this *woman* hath anointed my feet with **o**.	3464
Jn	11: 2 Mary which anointed the Lord with **o**,	3464
	12: 3 took Mary a pound of **o** of spikenard,	3464
	12: 3 house was filled with the odour of the **o**.	3464
	12: 5 Why was not this **o** sold for three hundred	3464

OINTMENTS (5) [OINTMENT]

SS	1: 3 Because of the savour of thy good **o** thy	8081
	4:10 and the smell of thine **o** than all spices!	8081
Am	6: 6 and anoint themselves *with* the chief of **o**:	8081
Lk	23:56 they returned, and prepared spices and **o**;	3464
Rev	18:13 and frankincense, and wine, and oil,	3464

OLD (380) [ELDER, ELDERS, ELDEST, OLDNESS]

Ge	5:32 Noah was five hundred years **o**:	1121
	6: 4 *became* mighty *men* which *were* of **o**,	5769

O

Ge
7: 6 Noah *was* six hundred years **o** when — 1121
11:10 Shem *was* an hundred years **o**, — 1121
12: 4 years **o** when he departed out of Haran. — 1121
15: 9 Take me a heifer of **three years o**, — 8027
15: 9 a she goat of **three years o**, and a ram of — 8027
15: 9 a ram of **three years o**, and a turtle-dove, — 8027
15:15 thou shalt be buried in a good **o age**. — 7872
16:16 Abram *was* fourscore and six years **o**, — 1121
17: 1 when Abram was ninety years **o** and nine, — 1121
17:12 that is eight days **o** shall be circumcised — 1121
17:17 unto him that is an hundred years **o**? — 1121
17:17 shall Sarah, that is ninety years **o**, bear? — 1323
17:24 Abraham *was* ninety years **o** and nine, — 1121
17:25 Ishmael his son *was* thirteen years **o**, — 1121
18:11 Now Abraham and Sarah *were* **o** *and* — 2205
18:12 After I am **waxed o** shall I have pleasure, — 1086
18:12 I have pleasure, my lord being **o** also? — 2204
18:13 I of a surety bear *a child*, which am **o**? — 2204
19: 4 the house round, both **o** and young, — 2205
19:31 Our father *is* **o**, and *there is* not a man in — 2204
21: 2 and bare Abraham a son in his **o age**, — 2208
21: 4 his son Isaac being eight days **o**, — 1121
21: 5 Abraham *was* an hundred years **o**, when — 1121
21: 7 for I have born *him* a son in his **o age**. — 2208
23: 1 hundred and seven and twenty **years o**: — 8141
24: 1 Abraham was **o**, *and* well stricken in age: — 2204
24:36 bare a son to my master when she was **o**: — 2209
25: 8 died in a good **age**, an old man, — 7872
25: 8 an **o man**, and full *of years*; and — 2205
25:20 Isaac *was* forty years **o** when he took — 1121
25:26 Isaac *was* threescore years **o** when she — 1121
26:34 Esau *was* forty years **o** when he took to — 1121
27: 1 that when Isaac was **o**, and his eyes were — 2204
27: 2 he said, Behold now, I am **o**, I know not — 2204
35:29 unto his people, *being* **o** and full of days: — 2205
37: 2 Joseph, *being* seventeen years **o**, — 1121
37: 3 because he *was* the son of his **o age**: — 2208
41:46 Joseph *was* thirty years **o** when he stood — 1121
43:27 well, the **o man** of whom ye spake? — 2205
44:20 an **o man**, and a child of *his* old age, — 2205
44:20 and a child of *his* **o age**, a little one; — 2208
47: 8 unto Jacob, How **o** *art* thou? — 2416+3117+8141
49: 9 he couched as a lion, and as an **o lion**; — 3833
50:26 *being* an hundred and ten years **o**. — 1121

Ex
7: 7 Moses *was* fourscore years **o**, — 1121
7: 7 Aaron fourscore and three years **o**, — 1121
10: 9 will go with our young and with our **o**, — 2205
30:14 from twenty years **o** and above, shall give — 1121
38:26 from twenty years **o** and upward, for six — 1121

Lev
13:11 It *is* an **o** leprosy in the skin of his flesh, — 3462
19:32 honour the face of the **o man**, and fear — 2205
25:22 and eat *yet* of **o** fruit until the ninth year; — 3465
25:22 her fruits come in ye shall eat *of* the **o**. — 3465
26:10 ye shall eat **o store**, and bring forth — 3462+3465
26:10 bring forth the **o** because of the new. — 3465
27: 3 of the male from twenty years **o** even unto — 1121
27: 3 twenty years old even unto sixty years **o**, — 1121
27: 5 if *it be* from five years **o** even unto twenty — 1121
27: 5 five years old even unto twenty years **o**, — 1121
27: 6 *it be* from a month **o** even unto five years — 1121
27: 6 from a month old even unto five years **o**, — 1121
27: 7 if *it be* from sixty years **o** and above; if — 1121

Nu
1: 3 From twenty years **o** and upward, all that — 1121
1:18 from twenty years **o** and upward, by their — 1121
1:20 every male from twenty years **o** and — 1121
1:22 every male from twenty years **o** and — 1121
1:24 from twenty years **o** and upward, all that — 1121
1:26 from twenty years **o** and upward, all that — 1121
1:28 from twenty years **o** and upward, all that — 1121
1:30 from twenty years **o** and upward, all that — 1121
1:32 from twenty years **o** and upward, all that — 1121
1:34 from twenty years **o** and upward, all that — 1121
1:36 from twenty years **o** and upward, all that — 1121
1:38 from twenty years **o** and upward, all that — 1121
1:40 from twenty years **o** and upward, all that — 1121
1:42 from twenty years **o** and upward, all that — 1121
1:45 from twenty years **o** and upward, — 1121
3:15 every male from a month **o** and — 1121
3:22 the males, from a month **o** and upward, — 1121
3:28 from a month **o** and upward, *were* eight — 1121
3:34 from a month **o** and upward, *were* six — 1121
3:39 the males from a month **o** and upward, — 1121
3:40 of the children of Israel from a month **o** — 1121
3:43 a month **o** and upward, of those that — 1121
4: 3 thirty years **o** and upward even until — 1121
4: 3 and upward even until fifty years **o**, — 1121
4:23 thirty years **o** and upward until fifty — 1121
4:23 upward until fifty years **o** shalt thou — 1121
4:30 thirty years **o** and upward even unto — 1121
4:30 upward even unto fifty years **o** shalt thou — 1121
4:35 thirty years **o** and upward even unto — 1121
4:35 and upward even unto fifty years **o**, — 1121
4:39 thirty years **o** and upward even unto — 1121
4:39 and upward even unto fifty years **o**, — 1121
4:43 thirty years **o** and upward even unto — 1121
4:43 and upward even unto fifty years **o**, — 1121
4:47 thirty years **o** and upward even unto — 1121
4:47 and upward even unto fifty years **o**, — 1121
8:24 from twenty and five years **o** and — 1121
14:29 from twenty years **o** and upward, — 1121
18:16 from a month **o** shalt thou redeem, — 1121
26: 2 from twenty years **o** and upward, — 1121
26: 4 sum *of the people*, from twenty years **o** — 1121
26:62 all males from a month **o** and upward: — 1121
32:11 twenty years **o** and upward, shall see — 1121
33:39 three years **o** when he died in mount Hor. — 1121

Dt
2:20 giants dwelt therein **in o time**; — 6440+3807.1
8: 4 Thy raiment **waxed** not **o** upon thee, — 1086
19:14 which they of **o time** have set in thine — 7223
28:50 shall not regard the person of the **o**, — 2205
29: 5 your clothes are not **waxen o** upon you, — 1086
29: 5 thy shoe is not **waxen o** upon thy foot. — 1086
31: 2 an hundred and twenty years **o** *this* day; — 1121
32: 7 Remember the days of **o**, consider the — 5769
34: 7 and twenty years **o** when he died: — 1121

Jos
5:11 they did eat of the **o corn** of the land on — 5669
5:12 they had eaten of the **o corn** of the land; — 5669
6:21 and **o**, and ox, and sheep, and ass, — 2205
9: 4 took **o** sacks upon their asses, — 1087
9: 4 wine bottles, **o**, and rent, and bound up; — 1087
9: 5 **o** shoes and clouted upon their feet, — 1087
9: 5 their feet, and **o** garments upon them; — 1087
9:13 our shoes are **become o** by reason of — 1086
13: 1 Now Joshua was **o** *and* stricken in years; — 2204
13: 1 Thou art **o** *and* stricken in years, — 2204
14: 7 Forty years **o** *was* I when Moses the — 1121
14:10 I *am this* day fourscore and five years **o**. — 1121
23: 1 that Joshua **waxed o** *and* stricken in age. — 2204
23: 2 unto them, I am **o** *and* stricken in age: — 2204
24: 2 on the *other* side of the flood in **o time**, — 5769
24:29 died, *being* an hundred and ten years **o**. — 1121

Jdg
2: 8 died, *being* an hundred and ten years **o**. — 1121
6:25 the second bullock of seven **years o**, — 8141
8:32 the son of Joash died in a good **o age**, — 7872
19:16 there came an **o** man from his work out — 2205
19:17 the **o** man said, Whither goest thou? — 2205
19:20 the **o** man said, Peace *be* with thee; — 2205
19:22 master of the house, the **o man**, saying, — 2205

Ru
1:12 go *your way*; for I am too **o** to have a — 2204
4:15 of *thy* life, and a nourisher of thine **o age**: — 7872

1Sa
2:22 Now Eli was very **o**, and heard all that his — 2204
2:31 that there shall not be an **o man** in thine — 2205
2:32 shall not be an **o man** in thine house — 2205
4:15 Now Eli *was* ninety and eight years **o**; — 1121
4:18 for he was an **o** man, and heavy. And he — 2204
8: 1 it came to pass, when Samuel was **o**, that — 2204
8: 5 thou art **o**, and thy sons walk not in thy — 2204
12: 2 I am **o** and grayheaded; and behold, — 2204
17:12 man went among men *for* an **o man** in — 2204
27: 8 those *nations were* of **o** the inhabitants — 5769
28:14 she said, An **o** man cometh up; and he *is* — 2205

2Sa
2:10 Ish-bosheth Saul's son *was* forty years **o** — 1121
4: 4 was five years **o** when the tidings came of — 1121
5: 4 David *was* thirty years **o** when he *began* — 1121
19:32 a very aged man, *even* fourscore years **o**: — 1121
19:35 I *am this* day fourscore years **o**: *and* can I — 1121
20:18 They were wont to speak in **o time**, — 7223

1Ki
1: 1 Now king David was **o** *and* stricken in — 2204
1:15 the king was very **o**; and Abishag — 2204
11: 4 it came to pass, when Solomon was **o**, — 2209
12: 6 Rehoboam consulted with the **o men**, — 2205
12: 8 he forsook the counsel of the **o men**, — 2205
12:13 forsook the **o men's** counsel that they — 2205
13:11 Now there dwelt an **o** prophet in Beth-el; — 2205
13:25 in the city where the **o** prophet dwelt. — 2205
13:29 the **o** prophet came to the city, to mourn — 2205
14:21 and one years **o** when he *began* to reign, — 1121
15:23 Nevertheless in the time of his **o age** he — 2209
22:42 and five years **o** when he *began* to reign; — 1121

2Ki
4:14 she hath no child, and her husband is **o**. — 2204
8:17 years **o** was he when he *began* to reign; — 1121
8:26 twenty years **o** *was* Ahaziah when he — 1121
11:21 Seven years **o** *was* Jehoash when he — 1121
14: 2 and five years **o** when he *began* to reign, — 1121
14:21 which *was* sixteen years **o**, and made him — 1121
15: 2 Sixteen years **o** *was* he when he *began* — 1121
15:33 twenty years **o** was he when he *began* to — 1121
16: 2 Twenty years **o** *was* Ahaz when he *began* — 1121
18: 2 years **o** was he when he *began* to reign; — 1121
21: 1 Manasseh *was* twelve years **o** when he — 1121
21:19 and two years **o** when he *began* to reign, — 1121
22: 1 Josiah *was* eight years **o** when he *began* — 1121
23:31 and three years **o** when he *began* to reign; — 1121
23:36 and five year **o** when he *began* to reign; — 1121
24: 8 Jehoiachin *was* eighteen years **o** when he — 1121
24:18 and one years **o** when he *began* to reign, — 1121

1Ch
1: 1 married when he *was* threescore years **o** — 1121
4:40 of Ham had dwelt there of **o**. — 6440+3807.1
23: 1 So when David was **o** and full *of* days, — 2204
23:27 *were* numbered from twenty years **o** — 1121
27:23 the number of them from twenty years **o** — 1121
29:28 died in a good **o age**, full of days, riches, — 7872

2Ch
10: 6 Rehoboam took counsel with the **o men** — 2205
10: 8 he forsook the counsel which the **o men** — 2205
10:13 forsook the counsel of the **o men**, — 2205
12:13 and forty years **o** when he *began* to reign, — 1121
20:31 and five years **o** when he *began* to reign, — 1121
21: 5 and two years **o** when he *began* to reign, — 1121
21:20 and two years **o** when he *began* to reign, — 1121
22: 2 two years **o** *was* Ahaziah when he *began* — 1121
24: 1 Joash *was* seven years **o** when he *began* — 1121
24:15 Jehoiada **waxed o**, and was full *of* days — 2204
24:15 and thirty years **o** was *he* when he died. — 1121
25: 1 and five years **o** *when* he *began* to reign, — 1121
25: 5 he numbered them from twenty years **o** — 1121
26: 1 who *was* sixteen years **o**, and made him — 1121
26: 3 Sixteen years **o** *was* Uzziah when he — 1121
27: 1 and five years **o** when he *began* to reign, — 1121
27: 8 twenty years **o** when he *began* to reign, — 1121
28: 1 Ahaz *was* twenty years **o** when he *began* — 1121
29: 1 *when* he *was* five and twenty years **o**, — 1121
31:16 of males, from three years **o** and upward, — 1121
31:17 the Levites from twenty years **o** and — 1121
33: 1 Manasseh *was* twelve years **o** when he — 1121
33:21 twenty years **o** when he *began* to reign, — 1121
34: 1 Josiah *was* eight years **o** when he *began* — 1121
36: 2 three years **o** when he *began* to reign, — 1121
36: 5 and five years **o** when he *began* to reign, — 1121
36: 9 Jehoiachin *was* eight years **o** when he — 1121
36:11 twenty years **o** when he *began* to reign, — 1121
36:17 **o man**, or him that stooped for age: — 2205

Ezr
3: 8 appointed the Levites from twenty years **o** — 1121
4:15 moved sedition within the same of **o** time: — 5957
4:19 found that this city of **o** time *hath* made — 5957

Ne
3: 6 Moreover the **o** gate repaired Jehoiada — 3465
9:21 their clothes **waxed** not **o**, and their feet — 1086
12:39 above the **o** gate, and above the fish gate, — 3465
12:46 Asaph of **o** *there were* chief of the singers — 6924

Est
3:13 all Jews, both young and **o**, little children — 2205

Job
4:11 The **o lion** perisheth for lack of prey, — 3918
14: 8 the root thereof **wax o** in the earth, — 2204
20: 4 Knowest thou *not* this of **o**, since man — 5703
21: 7 **become o**, yea, are mighty *in* power? — 6275
22:15 thou marked the **o** way which wicked — 5769
30: 2 profit me, in whom **o age** was perished? — 3624
32: 6 and said, I *am* young, and ye *are* **very o**; — 3453
42:17 So Job died, *being* **o** and full of days. — 2205

Ps
6: 7 it **waxeth o** because of all mine enemies. — 6275
25: 6 for they have been **ever of o**. — 4480+5769
32: 3 my bones **waxed o** through my roaring — 1086
37:25 I have been young, and *now* am **o**; yet — 2204
44: 1 thou didst in their days, in the times of **o**. — 6924
55:19 afflict them, even he that abideth of **o**. — 6924
68:33 the heavens of heavens, *which were* of **o**; — 6924
71: 9 Cast me not off in the time of **o age**; — 2209
71:18 Now also when I am **o** and grayheaded, — 2209
74: 2 *which* thou hast purchased **of o**; — 6924
74:12 God *is* my King of **o**, working salvation — 6924
77: 5 I have considered the days of **o**, the years — 6924
77:11 surely I will remember thy wonders of **o**. — 6924
78: 2 in a parable: I will utter dark sayings of **o**: — 6924
92:14 They shall still bring forth fruit in **o age**; — 7872
93: 2 Thy throne is established of **o**: thou *art* — 227
102:25 **Of o** hast thou laid the — 6440+3807.1
102:26 all of them shall **wax o** like a garment; — 1086
119:52 I remembered thy judgments of **o**, — 5769
119:152 I have known **of o** that thou hast founded — 6924
143: 5 I remember the days of **o**; I meditate on — 6924
148:12 and maidens; **o men**, and children: — 2205

Pr
8:22 of his way, before his works of **o**. — 227
17: 6 children *are* the crown of **o men**; — 2205
20:29 the beauty of **o men** *is* the gray head. — 2205
22: 6 when he is **o**, he will not depart from it. — 2204
23:10 Remove not the **o** landmark; and enter — 5769
23:22 despise not thy mother when she is **o**. — 2204

Ecc
1:10 it hath been already of **o o** time, — 5769+3807.1
4:13 a wise child than an **o** and foolish king, — 2205

SS
7:13 all *manner of* pleasant *fruits*, new and **o**, — 3465

Isa
15: 5 *flee* unto Zoar, a heifer of **three years o** — 7992
20: 4 young and **o**, naked and barefoot, — 2205
22:11 the two walls for the water of the **o** pool: — 3465
25: 1 counsels of **o** *are* faithfulness *and* truth. — 7350
30: 6 from whence *come* the young and **o lion**, — 3918
30:33 Tophet is ordained of **o**; yea, for the king — 5769
43:18 *things*, neither consider the *things* of **o**. — 6931
46: 4 even to *your* **o age** I *am* he; and *even* to — 2209
46: 9 Remember the former *things* of **o**: for I — 5769
50: 9 lo, they all shall **wax o** as a garment; — 1086
51: 6 the earth shall **wax o** like a garment, — 1086
51: 9 the ancient days, *in* the generations of **o**. — 5769
57:11 have not I held my peace even of **o**, — 5769
58:12 *that shall be* of thee shall build the **o** — 5769
61: 4 they shall build the **o** wastes, they shall — 5769
63: 9 and carried them all the days of **o**. — 5769
63:11 he remembered the days of **o**, Moses, — 5769
65:20 an **o man** that hath not filled his days: — 2205
65:20 for the child shall die an hundred years **o**; — 1121
65:20 the sinner *being* an hundred years **o** shall — 1121

Jer
2:20 For **of o time** I have broken thy — 4480+5769
6:16 ways, and see, and ask for the **o** paths, — 5769
28: 8 before thee and of **o** prophesied both against — 5769
31: 3 The Lord hath appeared of **o** unto me, — 7350
31:13 dance, both young men and **o** together; — 2205
38:11 took thence **o** cast clouts and old rotten — 1094
38:11 thence old cast clouts and **o** rotten rags, — 1094
38:12 Put now these **o** cast clouts and rotten — 1094
46:26 as *in* the days of **o**, saith the Lord. — 6924
48:34 *as* a heifer of **three years o**: — 7992
51:22 with thee will I break in pieces **o** and — 5769
52: 1 twenty year **o** when he *began* to reign, — 1121

La
1: 7 *things* that she had in the days of **o**, — 6924
2:17 that he had commanded in the days **of o**: — 6924
2:21 and the **o** lie on the ground in the streets: — 2205
3: 4 My flesh and my skin hath he **made o**, — 1086
3: 6 in dark places, as *they* that be dead of **o**. — 5769
5:21 shall be turned; renew our days as of **o**. — 6924

Eze
9: 6 Slay utterly *and* young, both maids, — 2205
23:43 said I unto *her that was* **o** in adulteries, — 1087
25:15 to destroy *it for* the **o** hatred; — 5769
26:20 with the people of **o time**, and shall set — 5769
26:20 in places desolate of **o**, with them that go — 5769
36:11 I will settle you after your **o estates**, — 6927
38:17 *Art* thou he of whom I have spoken in **o** — 6931

Da
5:31 *being* about threescore and two year **o**. — 1247

Joel
1: 2 Hear this, ye **o men**, and give ear, all ye — 2205

Joel	2:28	your **o** men shall dream dreams,	2205
Am	9:11	and I will build it as *in* the days of **o**:	5769
Mic	5: 2	whose goings forth *have been* from of **o**,	6924
	6: 6	burnt offerings, with calves of a year **o**?	1121
	7:14	*in* Bashan and Gilead, as *in* the days of **o**.	5769
	7:20	sworn unto our fathers from the days of **o**.	6924
Na	2: 8	Nineveh *is* of a like a pool of water:	3117
	2:11	*even* the **o** lion, walked, *and* the lion's	3833
Zec	8: 4	There shall yet **o** men and old women	2205
	8: 4	**o** women dwell in the streets of	2205
Mal	3: 4	as *in* the days of **o**, and as *in* former years.	5769
Mt	2:16	thereof, from **two years o** and under,	1332
	5:21	heard that it was said by them **of o time**,	744
	5:27	heard that it was said by them **of o time**,	744
	5:33	that it hath been said by them **of o time**,	744
	9:16	a piece of new cloth unto an **o** garment;	3820
	9:17	Neither do *men* put new wine into **o**	3820
	13:52	forth out of his treasure *things* new and **o**.	3820
Mk	2:21	a piece of new cloth on an **o** garment:	3820
	2:21	that filled it up taketh away *from* the **o**,	3820
	2:22	And no *man* putteth new wine into **o**	3820
Lk	1:18	for I am an **o** man, and my wife well	4246
	1:36	hath also conceived a son in her **o age**:	1094
	2:42	And when he was twelve **years o**,	2094
	5:36	a piece of a new garment upon an **o**;	3820
	5:36	out of the new agreeth not with the **o**.	3820
	5:37	And no *man* putteth new wine into **o**	3820
	5:39	No *man* also having drunk **o wine**	3820
	5:39	desireth new: for he saith, The **o** is better.	3820
	9: 8	that one of the **o** prophets was risen again.	744
	9:19	*say*, that one of the **o** prophets is risen	744
	12:33	provide yourselves bags which **wax not o**,	3822
Jn	3: 4	How can a man be born when he is **o**?	1088
	8:57	art not yet fifty **years o**, and hast thou	2094
	21:18	when thou shalt be **o**, thou shalt stretch	1095
Ac	2:17	and your **o** men shall dream dreams:	4245
	4:22	For the man was above forty **years o**,	2094
	7:23	when he was full forty years **o**, it came	5550
	15:21	Moses of **o** time hath in every city them	744
	21:16	an **o** disciple, with whom we should lodge.	744
Ro	4:19	when he was about an **hundred year o**,	1541
	6: 6	that our **o** man is crucified with *him*, that	3820
1Co	5: 7	Purge out therefore the **o** leaven, that ye	3820
	5: 8	let us keep the feast, not with **o** leaven,	3820
2Co	3:14	away in the reading of the **o** testament;	3820
	5:17	**o** *things* are past away; behold, all *things*	744
Eph	4:22	the former conversation the **o** man,	3820
Col	3: 9	seeing that ye have put off the **o** man with	3820
1Ti	4: 7	But refuse profane and **o wives'** fables,	1126
	5: 9	the number under threescore **years o**,	2094
Heb	1:11	they all shall **wax o** as *doth* a garment;	3822
	8:13	new *covenant*, he hath **made** the first **o**.	3822
	8:13	and **waxeth o** *is* ready to vanish away.	1095
1Pe	3: 5	after this manner in the **o time** the holy	4218
2Pe	1: 9	that *he* was purged from his **o** sins.	3819
	1:21	For the prophecy came not **in o time** by	4218
	2: 5	spared not the **o** world, but saved Noah	744
	3: 5	the word of God the heavens were of **o**,	1597
1Jn	2: 7	an **o** commandment which ye had from	3820
	2: 7	The commandment is the word which	3820
Jude	1: 4	who were before **of o** ordained to this	3819
Rev	12: 9	And the great dragon was cast *out*, that **o**	744
	20: 2	serpent, which is the devil, and Satan,	744

OLDNESS (1) [OLD]

Ro	7: 6	of spirit, and not *in* the **o** of the letter.	3821

OLIVE (38) [OLIVES, OLIVET, OLIVEYARD, OLIVEYARDS]

Ge	8:11	lo, in her mouth *was* an **o** leaf pluckt off:	2132
Ex	27:20	that they bring thee pure oil **o** beaten for	2132
	30:24	shekel of the sanctuary, and of oil **o** a hin:	2132
Lev	24: 2	they bring unto thee pure oil **o** beaten	2132
Dt	6:11	thou diggedst not, vineyards and **o trees**,	2132
	8: 8	pomegranates; a land of oil **o**, and honey;	2132
	24:20	When thou beatest thine **o tree**, thou	2132
	28:40	Thou shalt have **o trees** throughout all	2132
	28:40	*with* the oil; for thine **o** shall cast *his fruit*.	2132
Jdg	9: 8	they said unto the **o tree**, Reign thou over	2132
	9: 9	the **o tree** said unto them, Should I leave	2132
1Ki	6:23	oracle he made two cherubims **o**fo tree:	8081
	6:31	of the oracle he made doors of **o** tree:	8081
	6:32	The two doors also *were* of **o** tree;	8081
	6:33	for the door of the temple posts of **o** tree,	8081
2Ki	18:32	vineyards, a land of oil **o** and of honey,	2132
1Ch	27:28	over the **o trees** and the sycomore trees	2132
Ne	8:15	fetch **o** branches, and pine branches,	2132
Job	15:33	and shall cast off his flower as the **o**.	2132
Ps	52: 8	I am like a green **o tree** in the house of	2132
	128: 3	thy children like **o** plants round about thy	2132
Isa	17: 6	as the shaking of an **o tree, two** *or*	2132
	24:13	*there* shall *be* as the shaking of an **o tree**,	2132
Jer	11:16	A green **o tree**, fair, *and* of goodly fruit:	2132
Hos	14: 6	his beauty shall be as the **o tree**, and his	2132
Am	4: 9	your fig trees and your **o trees** increased,	2132
Hab	3:17	the labour of the **o** shall fail, and the fields	2132
Hag	2:19	and the pomegranate, and the **o** tree,	2132
Zec	4: 3	**two o trees** by it, one upon the right *side*	2132
	4:11	What *are* these two **o trees** upon the	2132
	4:12	*are these* two **o** branches which	2132
Ro	11:17	thou, being a **wild o tree**, wert graffed in	65
	11:17	of the root and fatness of the **o tree**;	1636
	11:24	out of the **o tree which is wild** by nature,	65
	11:24	contrary to nature into a **good o tree**:	2505
	11:24	be graffed into their own **o tree**?	1636

Jas	3:12	the fig tree, my brethren, bear **o berries**?	1636
Rev	11: 4	These are the two **o trees**, and the two	1636

OLIVE GROVES See OLIVEYARD

OLIVES (15) [OLIVE]

Jdg	15: 5	standing corn, with the vineyards *and* **o**.	2132
Mic	6:15	thou shalt tread the **o**, but thou shalt not	2132
Zec	14: 4	stand in that day upon the mount of **O**,	2132
	14: 4	the mount of **O** shall cleave in the midst	2132
Mt	21: 1	unto the mount of **O**, then sent Jesus two	1636
	24: 3	And as he sat upon the mount of **O**,	1636
	26:30	hymn, they went out into the mount of **O**.	1636
Mk	11: 1	and Bethany, at the mount of **O**,	1636
	13: 3	And as he sat upon the mount of **O** over	1636
	14:26	hymn, they went out into the mount of **O**.	1636
Lk	19:29	at the mount called *the mount* of **O**,	1636
	19:37	now at the descent of *the* mount of **O**.	1636
	21:37	the mount that is called *the mount* of **O**.	1636
	22:39	went, as he was wont, to the mount of **O**;	1636
Jn	8: 1	Jesus went unto the mount of **O**.	1636

OLIVET (2) [OLIVE]

2Sa	15:30	David went up by the ascent of *mount* **O**,	2132
Ac	1:12	unto Jerusalem from the mount called **O**,	1638

OLIVEYARD (1) [OLIVE]

Ex	23:11	deal with thy vineyard, *and* with thy **o**.	2132

OLIVEYARDS (5) [OLIVE]

Jos	24:13	and **o** which ye planted not do ye eat.	2132
1Sa	8:14	your vineyards, and your **o**, *even* the best	2132
2Ki	5:26	**o**, and vineyards, and sheep, and oxen,	2132
Ne	5:11	their vineyards, their **o**, and their houses,	2132
	9:25	and **o**, and fruit trees in abundance:	2132

OLYMPAS (1)

Ro	16:15	and **O**, and all the saints which are with	3652

OMAR (3)

Ge	36:11	**O**, Zepho, and Gatam, and Kenaz.	201
	36:15	duke **O**, duke Zepho, duke Kenaz,	201
1Ch	1:36	**O**, Zephi, and Gatam, Kenaz, and Timna,	201

OMEGA (4)

Rev	1: 8	I am Alpha and **O**, the beginning and	5598
	1:11	Saying, I am Alpha and **O**, the first and	5598
	21: 6	I am Alpha and **O**, the beginning and	5598
	22:13	I am Alpha and **O**, the beginning and	5598

OMER (5) [OMERS]

Ex	16:16	an **o** for every man, *according to*	6016
	16:18	when they did mete *it* with an **o**, he that	6016
	16:32	Fill an **o** of it to be kept for your	6016
	16:33	an **o** full of manna therein, and lay it up	6016
	16:36	Now an **o** *is* the tenth *part* of an ephah.	6016

OMERS (1) [OMER]

Ex	16:22	two **o** for one *man:* and all the rulers of	6016

OMITTED (1)

Mt	23:23	have **o** the weightier *matters* of the law,	863

OMNIPOTENT (1)

Rev	19: 6	Alleluia: for the Lord God **O** reigneth.	3841

OMRI (18)

1Ki	16:16	wherefore all Israel made **O**, the captain	6018
	16:17	**O** went up from Gibbethon, and all Israel	6018
	16:21	to make him king; and half followed **O**.	6018
	16:22	the people that followed **O** prevailed	6018
	16:22	of Ginath: so Tibni died, and **O** reigned.	6018
	16:23	first year of Asa king of Judah *began* **O** to	6018
	16:25	**O** wrought evil in the eyes of the LORD,	6018
	16:27	the rest of the acts of **O** which he did,	6018
	16:28	slept with his fathers, and was buried	6018
	16:29	Ahab the son of **O** to reign over Israel:	6018
	16:29	Ahab the son of **O** reigned over Israel in	6018
	16:30	Ahab the son of **O** did evil in the sight of	6018
2Ki	8:26	the daughter of **O** king of Israel.	6018
1Ch	7: 8	**O**, and Jerimoth, and Abiah, and	6018
	9: 4	the son of **O**, the son of Imri, the son of	6018
	27:18	of Issachar, **O** the son of Michael:	6018
2Ch	22: 2	also *was* Athaliah the daughter of **O**.	6018
Mic	6:16	For the statutes of **O** are kept, and all	6018

ON (2016) [THEREON, WHEREON]

Ge	2: 2	**o** the seventh day God ended his work	871.1
	2: 2	he rested **o** the seventh day from all his	871.1
	4:15	vengeance shall be taken **o** him sevenfold.	NIH
	4:16	in the land of Nod, **o** the east of Eden.	NIH
	6: 1	when men began to multiply **o** the face of	5921
	6: 6	LORD that he had made man **o** the earth,	871.1
	8: 4	**o** the seventeenth day of the month,	871.1
	8: 5	in the tenth *month*, **o** the first *day* of	871.1
	8: 9	for the waters *were* **o** the face of the	5921
	8:14	the seven and twentieth day of	871.1
	8:20	and offered burnt offerings **o** the altar.	871.1
	12: 8	removed from thence unto a mountain **o**	4480
	12: 8	*having* Beth-el **o** the west, and Hai on	4480
	12: 8	Beth-el on the west, and Hai **o** the east:	4480
	12: 9	*going* **o** still toward the south.	1980
	13: 3	he went **o** his journeys from the south	3807.1
	13: 4	there Abram called **o** the name of	871.1
	14:15	which *is* **o** the left hand of Damascus.	4480
	17: 3	Abram fell **o** his face: and God talked with	5921

Ge	18: 5	ye your hearts; after *that* you shall **pass o**:	5674
	18:16	went with them to **bring** them **o the way**.	7971
	19: 2	shall rise up early, and go **o** your ways.	3807.1
	19:34	it came to pass **o** the morrow, that	4480
	20: 9	that thou hast brought **o** me and on my	5921
	20: 9	on me and **o** my kingdom a great sin?	5921
	21:14	putting *it* **o** her shoulder, and the child,	5921
	21:33	called there **o** the name of the LORD,	871.1
	22: 4	**o** the third day Abraham lift up his eyes,	871.1
	22: 9	and laid him **o** the altar upon the wood.	5921
	24:33	told mine errand. And he said, **Speak o**.	1696
	24:45	Rebekah came forth with her pitcher **o** her	5921
	25:26	and his hand took hold **o** Esau's heel;	871.1
	28:12	behold a ladder set up **o** the earth,	1886.5
	28:12	of God ascending and descending **o** it.	871.1
	28:20	me bread to eat, and raiment to **put o**,	3847
	29: 1	Jacob **went o** his **journey**,	5375+7272
	31:22	was told Laban **o** the third day that Jacob	871.1
	32: 1	Jacob went **o** his way, and the angels of	3807.1
	32:19	**O** this manner shall you speak unto	3509.1
	33: 4	and fell **o** his neck, and kissed him:	5921
	33:14	I will **lead o** softly, according as the cattle	5095
	33:16	Esau returned that day **o** his way unto	3807.1
	34:25	came to pass **o** the third day, when they	871.1
	37:23	*his* coat of many colours that *was* **o** him;	5921
	38: 9	that he spilled *it* **o** the ground,	1886.5
	39: 4	**put o** the garments of her widowhood.	3847
	40:14	**think o** me when it shall be well with	2142
	40:16	I *had* three white baskets **o** my head:	5925
	40:19	from off thee, and shall hang thee **o** a tree;	5921
	41:45	the daughter of Poti-pherah priest of **O**.	204
	41:50	of Poti-pherah priest of **O** bare unto him.	204
	43:31	refrained himself, and said, **Set o** bread.	7760
	43:32	they **set o** for him by himself, and for	7760
	44:14	and they fell before him **o** the ground.	1886.5
	44:34	I see the evil that shall **come o** my father.	4672
	46:20	of Poti-pherah priest of **O** bare unto him.	204
	46:29	he fell **o** his neck, and wept on his neck a	5921
	46:29	neck, and wept **o** his neck a good while.	5921
	48:16	let my name be named **o** them,	871.1
	49:26	they shall be **o** the head of Joseph,	3807.1
	49:26	**o** the crown of the head of him *that was*	3807.1
Ex	1:10	**Come o**, let us deal wisely with them;	3051
	2: 6	she had compassion **o** him, and said, This	5921
	2:11	his brethren, and looked **o** their burdens:	871.1
	4: 3	he said, Cast it **o** the ground. And he	1886.5
	4: 3	he cast it **o** the ground, and it became a	1886.5
	6:28	it came to pass **o** the day *when* the LORD	871.1
	8: 4	the frogs shall come up *both* **o** thee,	871.1
	9: 6	the LORD did that thing **o** the morrow,	4480
	12: 7	strike *it* **o** the two side posts and on	5921
	12: 7	and **o** the upper door post of the houses,	5921
	12:11	your shoes **o** your feet, and your staff in	871.1
	12:18	In the first *month*, **o** the fourteenth day	871.1
	12:23	**o** the two side posts, the LORD will pass	5921
	12:29	the firstborn of Pharaoh that sat **o** his	5921
	12:37	about six hundred thousand **o foot** *that*	7273
	14:16	children of Israel shall go **o** dry *ground*	871.1
	14:22	the waters *were* a wall unto them **o** their	4480
	14:22	them **o** their right hand, and **o** their left.	4480
	14:29	the waters *were* a wall unto them **o** their	4480
	14:29	them **o** their right hand, and **o** their left.	4480
	15:14	sorrow shall take hold **o** the inhabitants	871.1
	15:19	the children of Israel went **o** dry *land* in	871.1
	16: 1	**o** the fifteenth day of the second month	871.1
	16: 5	that **o** the sixth day they shall prepare	871.1
	16:14	*as* small as the hoar frost **o** the ground.	5921
	16:22	*that* **o** the sixth day they gathered twice	871.1
	16:26	**o** the seventh day, which *is* the sabbath,	871.1
	16:27	*that* there went out *some* of the people **o**	871.1
	16:29	he giveth you **o** the sixth day the bread	871.1
	16:29	let no man go out of his place **o**	871.1
	16:30	So the people rested **o** the seventh day.	871.1
	17: 5	**Go o** before the people, and take with	5674
	17: 9	to morrow I will stand **o** the top of the	5921
	17:12	the one **o** the one side, and the other **o**	4480
	17:12	one side, and the other **o** the other side;	4480
	18:13	it came to pass **o** the morrow, that Moses	4480
	19: 4	*how* I bare you **o** eagles' wings,	5921
	19:16	it came to pass **o** the third day in	871.1
	19:18	mount Sinai was altogether **o** a smoke,	NIH
	19:20	upon mount Sinai, **o** the top of the mount:	413
	21:30	If there be laid **o** him a sum of money,	5921
	22:30	**o** the eighth day thou shalt give it me.	871.1
	23:12	and **o** the seventh day thou shalt rest:	871.1
	24: 6	half of the blood he sprinkled **o** the altar.	5921
	24: 8	and sprinkled *it* **o** the people, and said,	5921
	24:17	**o** the top of the mount in the eyes of	871.1
	25:19	make one cherub **o** the one end,	4480
	25:19	and the other cherub **o** the other end:	4480
	25:19	the cherubims **o** the two ends thereof.	5921
	25:20	forth *their* wings **o high**,	4605+1886.5+3807.1
	25:26	the rings in the four corners that *are* **o**	3807.1
	26:10	thou shalt make fifty loops **o** the edge of	5921
	26:13	a cubit **o** the one side, and a cubit **o**	4480
	26:13	a cubit **o** the other side of that which	4480
	26:13	over the sides of the tabernacle **o** this side	4480
	26:13	the tabernacle on this side and *on* that side,	4480
	26:18	twenty boards **o** the south side	3807.1
	26:20	for the second side of the tabernacle **o**	3807.1
	26:35	the candlestick over against the table **o**	5921
	26:35	thou shalt put the table **o** the north side.	5921
	27:12	*for* the breadth of the court **o** the west	3807.1
	27:13	the breadth of the court **o** the east side	1886.5
	27:15	**o** the other side *shall be* hangings,	3807.1

O

Ex
27:21 **o the behalf of** the children of Israel 854+4480
28: 9 grave **o** them the names of the children of 5921
28:10 Six of their names **o** one stone, 5921
28:10 the *other* six names of the rest **o** the other 5921
28:23 shalt put the two rings **o** the two ends of 5921
28:24 which *are* **o** the two sides of the breastplate. 413
28:25 *them* **o** the shoulderpieces of the ephod 5921
28:27 put them **o** the two sides of the ephod 5921
28:37 thou shalt put it **o** a blue lace, that it may 5921
29: 9 his sons, and put the bonnets **o** them: 3807.1
29:30 in his stead shall **put** them **o** seven days, 3847
31:17 in the seventh day he rested, 871.1
32: 6 they rose up early **o** the morrow, 4480
32:15 the tables *were* written **o** both their sides; 4480
32:15 the one side and on the other *were* they 4480
32:15 side and **o** the other *were* they written. 4480
32:22 the people, that they *are set* **o** mischief. 871.1
32:26 and said, Who *is* **o** the LORD's **side**? 3807.1
32:30 it came to pass **o** the morrow, that Moses 4480
33: 4 and no man did put **o** him his ornaments. 5921
33:19 shew mercy **o** whom I will shew mercy. NIH
34:21 but **o** the seventh day thou shalt rest: 871.1
34:33 with them, he put a vail **o** his face. 5921
35: 2 **o** the seventh day there shall be to you a 871.1
36:11 he made loops of blue **o** the edge of one 5921
37: 7 them, **o** the two ends of the mercy seat; 4480
37: 8 One cherub **o** the one end on this side, 4480
37: 8 One cherub on the end **o** this side, 4480
37: 8 cherub **o** the *other* end on that side: 4480
37: 8 cherub on the *other* end **o** that side: 4480
37: 8 he the cherubims **o** the two ends thereof. 4480
37: 9 out *their* wings **o high**, 4605+1886.5+3807.1
38: 2 he made the horns thereof **o** the four 5921
38: 7 he put the staves into the rings **o** the sides 5921
38: 9 **o** the south side southward the hangings 3807.1
38:15 **o** this hand and that hand, *were* hangings 4480
39: 7 he put them **o** the shoulders of the ephod, 5921
39:17 the two rings **o** the ends of the breastplate, 4480
39:18 them **o** the shoulderpieces of the ephod, 5921
39:19 *them* **o** the two ends of the breastplate, 5921
39:19 which *was* **o** the side of the ephod inward. 413
39:20 put them **o** the two sides of the ephod 5921
39:31 **o high** upon 4480+4605+1886.5+3807.1
40: 2 **O** the first day of the first month shalt 871.1
40:17 **o** the first *day* of the month, *that* 871.1
40:20 set the staves **o** the ark, and put the 5921
40:24 **o** the side of the tabernacle southward. 4480
40:38 fire was **o** it by night, in the sight of all 871.1

Lev
1: 8 in order upon the wood that *is* **o** the fire 5921
1: 9 the priest shall burn all **o** the altar, *to be* 1886.5
1:11 he shall kill it **o** the side of the altar 5921
1:12 the priest shall lay them in order **o** 5921
1:12 that *is* **o** the fire which *is* upon the altar: 5921
1:15 off his head, and burn *it* **o** the altar; 1886.5
1:16 cast it beside the altar **o** the east part, 1886.5
2:12 they shall not be burnt **o** the altar for a 413
3: 4 two kidneys, and the fat that *is* **o** them, 5921
3: 5 Aaron's sons shall burn it **o** the altar 1886.5
3: 5 which *is* upon the wood that *is* **o** the fire: 5921
4:12 and burn him **o** the wood with fire: 5921
5:12 thereof, and burn *it* **o** the altar, 1886.5
6:10 the priest shall **put o** his linen garment, 3847
6:10 with the burnt offering **o** the altar, 5921
6:11 **put o** other garments, and carry forth 3847
6:12 the priest shall burn wood **o** it every 5921
7: 4 two kidneys, and the fat that *is* **o** them, 5921
7:16 **o** the morrow also the remainder of it 4480
7:17 remainder of the flesh of the sacrifice **o** 871.1
7:18 offerings be eaten at all **o** the third day, 871.1
8:26 put *them* **o** the fat, and upon the right 5921
8:28 burnt *them* **o** the altar upon the burnt 1886.5
9: 1 it came to pass **o** the eighth day, *that* 871.1
9:14 burnt *them* upon the burnt offering **o** 1886.5
9:24 they shouted, and fell **o** their faces. 5921
11: 2 among all the beasts that *are* **o** the earth. 5921
11:27 among all *manner of* beasts that go **o** *all* 5921
11:34 *that* **o** which such water cometh shall be 5921
13: 3 the priest shall look **o** the plague in the NIH
13: 3 the priest shall look **o** him, NIH
13: 5 priest shall look **o** him the seventh day: 871.1
13: 6 the priest shall look **o** him again 871.1
13:21 if the priest look **o** it, and behold, *there be* NIH
13:26 if the priest look **o** it, and behold, *there be* NIH
13:31 if the priest look **o** the plague of the scall, NIH
13:32 in the seventh day the priest shall look **o** NIH
13:34 in the seventh day the priest shall look **o** NIH
13:36 the priest shall look **o** him: and behold, NIH
13:51 he shall look **o** the plague on the seventh NIH
13:51 he shall look on the plague **o** the seventh 871.1
13:55 the priest shall look **o** the plague, after NIH
14: 9 it shall be **o** the seventh day, that he shall 871.1
14:10 **o** the eighth day he shall take two he 871.1
14:23 he shall bring them **o** the eighth day for 871.1
14:37 he shall look **o** the plague, and behold, NIH
15: 6 he that sitteth **o** *any* thing whereon he sat 5921
15:14 **o** the eighth day he shall take to him two 871.1
15:23 if it *be* **o** *her* bed, or on *any* thing whereon 5921
15:23 or **o** *any* thing whereon she sitteth, when 5921
15:29 **o** the eighth day she shall take unto her 871.1
16: 4 He shall **put o** the holy linen coat, 3847
16: 4 and *so* **put** them **o**. 3847
16:10 **o** which the lot fell to be the scapegoat, NIH
16:23 he **put o** when he went into the holy 3847
16:24 **put o** his garments, and come forth, 3847
16:29 **o** the tenth *day* of the month, ye shall 871.1

Lev
16:30 For **o** that day shall *the priest* make an 871.1
16:32 shall **put o** the linen clothes, *even the* 3847
19: 6 *same* day ye offer it, and **o** the morrow: 4480
19: 7 if it be eaten at all **o** the third day, it is 871.1
20:25 of *living thing* that creepeth **o** the ground, NIH
21:10 that is consecrated to **put o** the garments, 3847
22:30 **O** the same day it shall be eaten up; 871.1
23: 6 **o** the fifteenth day of the same month *is* 871.1
23:11 **o** the morrow after the sabbath the priest 4480
23:21 ye shall proclaim **o** the selfsame day, 871.1
23:27 **O** the tenth day of this seventh month 871.1
23:35 **O** the first day *shall be* a holy 871.1
23:36 **o** the eighth day *shall be* a holy 871.1
23:39 **o** the first day *shall be* a sabbath, 871.1
23:39 and **o** the eighth day *shall be* a sabbath. 871.1
23:40 shall take you **o** the first day the boughs 871.1
24: 6 shalt set them in two rows, six **o** a row, NIH
24: 7 it may be **o** the bread for a memorial, 3807.1
25: 9 **o** the tenth *day* of the seventh month, 871.1

Nu
1: 1 **o** the first *day* of the second month, 871.1
1:18 **o** the first *day* of the second month, 871.1
2: 3 **o** the east side toward the rising of 1886.5
2:10 **O** the south side *shall be* the standard 1886.5
2:18 **O** the west side *shall be* the standard of 1886.5
2:25 **O** the north side by their armies: 1886.5
3:10 and they shall **wait o** their priest's office: 8104
3:13 *for* **o** the day that I smote all the firstborn 871.1
3:29 **o** the side of the tabernacle southward. 5921
3:35 shall pitch **o** the side of the tabernacle 5921
4:12 badgers' skins, and shall put *them* **o** a bar: 5921
6: 9 **o** the seventh day shall he shave it. 871.1
6:10 **o** the eighth day he shall bring two 871.1
6:23 **O this wise** ye shall bless the children of 3541
7: 1 it came to pass **o** the day that Moses had 871.1
7:11 each prince **o** *his* day, for the dedicating 3807.1
7:18 **O** the second day Nethaneel the son of 871.1
7:24 **O** the third day Eliab the son of Helon, 871.1
7:30 **O** the fourth day Elizur the son of 871.1
7:36 **O** the fifth day Shelumiel the son of 871.1
7:42 **O** the sixth day Eliasaph the son of Deuel 871.1
7:48 **O** the seventh day Elishama the son of 871.1
7:54 **O** the eighth day *offered* Gamaliel the 871.1
7:60 **O** the ninth day Abidan the son of 871.1
7:66 **O** the tenth day Ahiezer the son of 871.1
7:72 **O** the eleventh day Pagiel the son of 871.1
7:78 **O** the twelfth day Ahira the son of Enan, 871.1
8:17 **o** the day that I smote every firstborn in 871.1
9: 5 kept the passover **o** the fourteenth day 871.1
9: 6 they could not keep the passover **o** that 871.1
9: 6 Moses and before Aaron **o** that day: 871.1
9:15 **o** the day that the tabernacle was reared 871.1
10: 5 camps that lie **o** the east parts shall go 1886.5
10: 6 the camps that lie **o** the south side shall 1886.5
10:11 it came to pass **o** the twentieth *day* of 871.1
11:31 as it were a day's journey **o this side**, 3541
11:31 it were a day's journey **o the other side**, 3541
14: 5 Aaron fell **o** their faces before all 5921
16: 1 **O**, the son of Peleth, sons of Reuben, 203
16:27 Dathan, and Abiram, **o** every side: 4480
16:41 **o** the morrow all the congregation of 4480
16:46 **put o** incense, and go quickly unto 7760
16:47 he **put o** incense, and made an atonement 5414
17: 8 that **o** the morrow Moses went into 4480
19:12 He shall purify himself with it **o** the third 871.1
19:12 and **o** the seventh day he shall be clean: 871.1
19:19 upon the unclean **o** the third day, 871.1
19:19 on the third day, and **o** the seventh day: 871.1
19:19 **o** the seventh day he shall purify him*self*, 871.1
20:19 *doing any* thing *else*, go through **o** 871.1
21:13 and pitched **o** the *other* side of Arnon, 4480
22: 1 pitched in the plains of Moab **o** *this* side 4480
22:24 wall *being* **o** *this* side, and a wall on that 4480
22:24 *being* on this side, and a wall **o** that **side**: 4480
22:31 down his head, and fell flat **o** his face. 3807.1
22:41 it came to pass **o** the morrow, that Balak 4480
23: 2 Balaam offered **o** *every* altar a bullock 871.1
23:14 offered a bullock and a ram **o** *every* altar. 871.1
23:30 offered a bullock and a ram **o** *every* altar. 871.1
24:20 when he looked **o** Amalek, he took up NIH
24:21 he looked **o** the Kenites, and took up his NIH
28: 9 **o** the sabbath day two lambs of the first 871.1
28:25 **o** the seventh day ye shall have a holy 871.1
29: 1 **o** the first *day* of the month, 871.1
29: 7 ye shall have **o** the tenth *day of* this 871.1
29:12 **o** the fifteenth day of the seventh month 871.1
29:17 **o** the second day *ye shall offer* twelve 871.1
29:20 **o** the third day eleven bullocks, 871.1
29:23 **o** the fourth day ten bullocks, two rams, 871.1
29:26 **o** the fifth day nine bullocks, two rams, 871.1
29:29 **o** the sixth day eight bullocks, two rams, 871.1
29:32 **o** the seventh day seven bullocks, 871.1
29:35 **O** the eighth day ye shall have a solemn 871.1
30: 8 if her husband disallow her **o** the day 871.1
30:12 them void **o** the day he heard *them;* 871.1
31:19 and your captives **o** the third day, 871.1
31:19 on the third day, and **o** the seventh day. 871.1
31:24 ye shall wash your clothes **o** the seventh 871.1
32:19 we will not inherit with them **o** *yonder* 4480
32:19 our inheritance is fallen to us **o** *this* side 4480
32:32 the possession of our inheritance **o** *this* 4480
33: 3 **o** the fifteenth day of the first month; 871.1
33: 3 **o** the morrow after the passover 4480
34: 4 ascent of Akrabbim, and **pass o** to Zin: 5674
34: 4 shall **go o** *to* Hazar-addar, and pass on to 3318
34: 4 on *to* Hazar-addar, and **pass o** to Azmon: 5674

Nu
34: 9 the border shall **go o** to Ziphron, 3318
34:11 Shepham to Riblah, **o** the east side of Ain; 4480
34:15 **o** *this* side Jordan *near* Jericho eastward, 4480
35: 5 ye shall measure from without the city **o** NIH
35: 5 **o** the south side two thousand cubits, NIH
35: 5 and **o** the west side two thousand cubits, NIH
35: 5 on the north side two thousand cubits; NIH
35:14 shall give three cities **o** *this* side Jordan, 4480

Dt
1: 1 Israel **o** *this* side Jordan in the wilderness, 871.1
1: 3 **o** the first *day* of the month, 871.1
1: 5 **O** *this* side Jordan, in the land of Moab, 871.1
1:41 when ye had **girded o** every man his 2296
2:28 only I will pass through **o** my feet; 871.1
3: 8 the land that *was* **o** *this* side Jordan, 871.1
4:15 for ye saw no *manner of* similitude **o** 871.1
4:17 The likeness of any beast *that is* **o** 871.1
4:18 The likeness of any *thing* that creepeth **o** 871.1
4:41 Moses severed three cities **o** *this* side 871.1
4:46 **O** *this* side Jordan, in the valley over 871.1
4:47 which *were* **o** *this* side Jordan *toward* 871.1
4:49 all the plain **o** *this* side Jordan eastward, NIH
6: 9 the posts of thy house, and **o** thy gates. 871.1
7:25 desire the silver or gold *that is* **o** them, 5921
9:10 **o** them *was* written according to all 5921
10: 2 I will write **o** the tables the words that 5921
10: 4 wrote **o** the tables, according to the first 5921
11:30 *Are* they not **o** the *other* side Jordan, 871.1
16: 8 **o** the seventh day *shall be* a solemn 871.1
21:19 his father and his mother lay hold **o** him, 871.1
21:22 *put* to death, and thou hang him **o** a tree: 5921
22: 5 neither shall a man **put o** a woman's 3847
22: 6 or **o** the ground, *whether they be* young 5921
22:28 **lay hold o** her, and lie with her, and they 8610
23:11 it shall be, when evening **cometh o**, 6437
26: 7 looked **o** our affliction, and our labour, NIH
27: 2 it shall be **o** the day when you shall pass 871.1
28: 1 thee **o high** above all nations of the earth: 5945
28: 2 all these blessings shall come **o** thee, 5921
30: 7 **o** them that hate thee, which persecuted 5921
32:11 taketh them, beareth **o** her wings: 5921
32:13 He made him ride **o** the high places of 5921
32:22 **set o fire** the foundations of the 3857
32:41 and mine hand take hold **o** judgment; 871.1
33:26 thy help, and in his excellency **o** the sky. NIH

Jos
1:14 which Moses gave you **o** *this* side Jordan; 871.1
1:15 **o** *this* side Jordan *toward* the sunrising. 871.1
2:10 that *were* **o** the *other* side Jordan, Sihon 871.1
2:19 his blood *shall be* **o** our head, if *any man* 871.1
3:17 firm **o** dry *ground* in the midst of Jordan, 871.1
3:17 the Israelites passed over **o** dry *ground*, 871.1
4:14 **O** that day the LORD magnified Joshua 871.1
4:19 the people came up out of Jordan **o** 871.1
4:22 Israel came over this Jordan **o** dry *land.* 871.1
5: 1 *were* **o** the side of Jordan westward, 871.1
5:10 kept the passover **o** the fourteenth day of 871.1
5:11 they did eat of the old corn of the land **o** 4480
5:12 the manna ceased **o** the morrow after 4480
5:14 Joshua fell **o** his face to the earth, 413
6: 7 **Pass o**, and compass the city, and let him 5674
6: 7 him that is armed **pass o** before the ark 5674
6: 8 rams' horns **passed o** before the LORD, 5674
6: 9 the priests **going o**, and blowing with 1980
6:13 of the LORD **went o continually**, 1980+1980
6:13 the priests **going o**, and blowing with 1980
6:15 it came to pass **o** the seventh day, that 871.1
6:15 only **o** that day they compassed the city 871.1
7: 2 **o** the east side of Beth-el, and spake unto 4480
7: 7 and dwelt **o** the *other* side Jordan! 871.1
8: 8 the city, *that* ye shall set the city **o** fire: 871.1
8: 9 and Ai, **o** the west side of Ai: 4480
8:11 city, and pitched **o** the north side of Ai: 4480
8:12 and Ai, **o** the west side of the city. 4480
8:13 even all the host that *was* **o** the north of 4480
8:13 their liers in wait **o** the west of the city, 4480
8:19 took it, and hasted and set the city **o** fire. 871.1
8:22 some **o** *this* **side**, and some on that side: 4480
8:22 some on this side, and some **o** that **side**: 4480
8:24 *when* they were all fallen **o** the edge of 3807.1
8:29 the king of Ai he hanged **o** a tree until 5921
8:33 stood **o** *this* **side** the ark and on that side 4480
8:33 **o** that side before the priests the Levites, 4480
9: 1 all the kings which *were* **o** *this* side 4480
9:12 **o** the day we came forth to go unto you; 871.1
9:17 came unto their cities **o** the third day. 871.1
10:26 slew them, and hanged them **o** five trees: 5921
10:32 which took it **o** the second day, 871.1
10:35 they took it **o** that day, and smote it with 4480
11: 2 to the kings that *were* **o** the north of 4480
11: 2 and in the borders of Dor **o** the west, 4480
11: 3 *And* to the Canaanite **o** the east and on 4480
11: 3 the Canaanite on the east and **o** the west, 4480
12: 1 their land **o** the *other* side Jordan 871.1
12: 1 and all the plain **o** the east: 1886.5
12: 3 *from* the plain to the sea of Cinneroth **o** 1886.5
12: 3 of the plain, *even* the salt sea **o** the east, 1886.5
12: 7 the children of Israel smote **o** *this* side 871.1
12: 7 smote on *this* side Jordan **o** the west, 1886.5
13:16 that *is* **o** the bank of the river Arnon, 5921
13:27 unto the edge of the sea of Cinnereth **o** NIH
13:32 **o** the *other* side Jordan, *by* Jericho, 4480
14: 3 and a half tribe **o** the *other* side Jordan: 4480
14: 9 Moses sware **o** that day, saying, Surely 871.1
15: 4 ascended up **o** the south side unto 4480
15: 7 which *is* **o** the south side of the river: 871.1
15:10 **o** the north side, and went down *to* 4480

Jos
15:10 Beth-shemesh, and **passed** o to Timnah: 5674
16: 1 unto the water of Jericho o the east, 1886.5
16: 5 o the east side was Ataroth-addar, 1886.5
16: 6 the sea to Michmethah o the north side; 4480
16: 6 and passed by it o the east to Janohah; 4480
17: 5 which were o the other side Jordan; 4480
17: 7 the border went along o the right hand 413
17: 8 Tappuah o the border of Manasseh 413
17:10 coast of Manasseh also was o the north 4480
17:10 they met together in Asher o the north, 4480
17:10 on the north, and in Issachar o the east. 4480
18: 5 shall abide in their coast o the south, 4480
18: 5 shall abide in their coasts o the north. 4480
18: 7 inheritance beyond Jordan o the east, 1886.5
18:12 their border o the north side was from 3807.1
18:12 border went up to the side of Jericho o 4480
18:13 near the hill that lieth o the south side of 4480
18:15 the border went out o the west, 1886.5
18:16 which is in the valley of the giants o 1886.5
18:16 to the side of Jebusi o the south, 1886.5
18:20 was the border of it o the east side 3807.1
19:13 thence **passeth** o along on the east to 5674
19:13 thence passeth on along o the east to 1886.5
19:14 the border compasseth it o the north side 4480
19:27 and goeth out to Cabul o the left hand, 4480
19:34 reacheth to Zebulun o the south side, 4480
19:34 reacheth to Asher o the west side, 4480
20: 8 o the other side Jordan by Jericho 4480
22: 4 LORD gave you o the other side Jordan. 871.1
22: 7 brethren o this side Jordan westward. 871.1
22:20 wrath fell o all the congregation of Israel? 5921
24: 2 Your fathers dwelt o the other side of 871.1
24: 8 which dwelt o the other side Jordan; 871.1
24:14 served o the other side of the flood, 871.1
24:15 that were o the other side of the flood, 871.1
24:30 o the north side of the hill of Gaash. 4480

Jdg
1: 8 edge of the sword, and set the city o fire. 871.1
2: 9 o the north side of the hill Gaash. 4480
3:25 lord was fallen down dead o the earth. 1886.5
4:15 off his chariot, and fled away o his feet. 4480
4:17 Howbeit Sisera fled away o his feet to 871.1
4:23 God subdued o that day Jabin the king 871.1
5: 1 Barak the son of Abinoam o that day, 871.1
5:10 ye that **ride** o white asses, ye that sit 7392
5:15 he was sent o foot into the valley. 871.1
5:17 Asher continued o the sea shore, 3807.1
5:30 of divers colours of needlework o both NIH
6:32 Therefore o that day he called him 871.1
6:37 and if the dew be o the fleece only, 5921
6:38 for he rose up early o the morrow, 4480
6:40 and there was dew o all the ground. 5921
7: 1 that the host of the Midianites were o 4480
7:17 unto them, Look o me, and do likewise: 4480
7:18 blow ye the trumpets also o **every side** 5439
7:25 Zeeb to Gideon o the other side Jordan. 4480
8:11 that dwelt in tents o the east of Nobah 4480
8:21 away the ornaments that were o their 871.1
8:26 purple raiment that was o the kings of 5921
8:34 of all their enemies o **every side**: 4480+5439
9: 8 The trees **went forth** o a time to 1980+1980
9:42 it came to pass o the morrow, that 4480
9:48 laid it o his shoulder, and said unto 5921
9:49 hold, and set the hold o fire upon them; 871.1
10: 4 he had thirty sons that rode o thirty ass 5921
10: 8 all the children of Israel that were o 871.1
11:18 pitched o the other side of Arnon, 871.1
12:14 that rode o threescore and ten ass colts: 5921
13: 5 a son; and no rasor shall come o his head: 5921
13:19 and Manoah and his wife **looked** o. 7200
13:20 Manoah and his wife **looked** o it, and 7200
13:20 on it, and fell o their faces to the ground. 5921
14: 9 **went** o eating, and came to his 1980+1980
14:15 it came to pass o the seventh day, that 871.1
14:17 it came to pass o the seventh day, that he 871.1
14:18 the men of the city said unto him o 871.1
15: 5 when he had set the brands o fire, he let 871.1
15:18 and called o the LORD, and said, 413
16:29 o which it was borne up, of the one with 5921
19: 1 there was a certain Levite sojourning o 871.1
19: 5 it came to pass o the fourth day, when 871.1
19: 8 he arose early in the morning o the fifth 871.1
19: 9 to morrow get you early o your way, 3807.1
19:14 they **passed** o and went their way; and 5674
19:29 laid hold o his concubine, and divided 871.1
20:30 the children of Benjamin o the third day, 871.1
20:48 also they set o fire all the cities that they 871.1
21: 4 it came to pass o the morrow, that 871.1
21:19 which is o the north side of Beth-el, 1886.5
21:19 o the east side of the highway that 1886.5
21:19 to Shechem, and o the south of Lebonah. 4480

Ru
1: 7 went o the way to return unto the land 871.1
2: 3 her hap was to **light** o a part of the field 7136
2: 9 Let thine eyes be o the field that they do 871.1
2:10 she fell o her face, and bowed herself to 5921
3:15 six measures of barley, and laid it o her: 5921

1Sa
1:11 if thou wilt indeed look o the affliction of 871.1
2:26 child Samuel grew o, and was in favour 1980
2:34 thy two sons, o Hophni and Phinehas; 413
5: 3 when they of Ashdod arose early o 4480
5: 4 when they arose early o the morrow 4480
5: 5 tread o the threshold of Dagon in Ashdod 5921
6: 4 for one plague was o you all, and on 3807.1
6: 4 plague was on you all, and o your lords. 3807.1
6: 7 o which there hath come no yoke, 5921
6:15 were, and put them o the great stone: 413

1Sa
7: 6 and fasted o that day, and said there, 871.1
7:10 thunder o that day upon the Philistines, 871.1
9:20 days ago, set not thy mind o them; 3807.1
9:20 o whom is all the desire of Israel? Is it 3807.1
9:20 Is it not o thee, and on all thy father's 3807.1
9:20 on thee, and o all thy father's house? 3807.1
9:27 Bid the servant **pass** o before us, (and 5674
9:27 pass on before us, (and he **passed** o,) 5674
10: 3 shalt thou **go** o forward from thence, 2498
11: 2 O this condition will I make a covenant 871.1
11: 7 the fear of the LORD fell o the people, 5921
11:11 it was so o the morrow, that Saul put 4480
12:11 of the hand of your enemies o every side, 4480
13: 5 as the sand which is o the sea shore 5921
14: 1 garrison, that is o the other side. 4480
14: 4 there was a sharp rock o the one side, 4480
14: 4 side, and a sharp rock o the other side: 4480
14:16 they **went** o beating down one another. 1980
14:19 the host of the Philistines went o 1980+1980
14:24 that I may be avenged o mine enemies. 4480
14:32 calves, and slew them o the ground: 1886.5
14:40 Be ye o one side, and I and Jonathan my 3807.1
14:40 my son will be o the other side. 3807.1
14:47 against all his enemies o **every side**, 5439
15:12 and passed o, and gone down to Gilgal. 5674
15:16 this night. And he said unto him, **Say** o. 1696
15:18 the LORD sent thee o a journey, and said, 871.1
16: 6 come, that he looked o Eliab, and said, NIH
16: 7 Look not o his countenance, or on the 413
16: 7 o or o the height of his stature; 413
16: 7 for man looketh o the outward 3807.1
16: 7 but the LORD looketh o the heart. 3807.1
16:16 a man, who is a cunning player o a harp: 871.1
17: 3 the Philistines stood o a mountain on the 413
17: 3 the Philistines stood on a mountain o 4480
17: 3 Israel stood o a mountain on the other 413
17: 3 Israel stood on a mountain on the other 4480
17:41 Philistine **came** o and drew near 1980+1980
18:10 came to pass o the morrow, that the evil 871.1
18:24 saying, O this manner spake David. 3509.1
19:23 he **went** o, and prophesied, until 1980+1980
20:20 I will shoot three arrows o the side 1886.5
20:21 the arrows are o **this side** of thee, 2008
20:27 it came to pass o the morrow, which was 4480
20:41 fell o his face to the ground, 3807.1
21:13 scrabled o the doors of the gate, and let 5921
22:18 slew o that day fourscore and five 871.1
23:19 which is o the south of Jeshimon? 4480
23:21 the LORD; for ye have compassion o me. 5921
23:24 in the plain o the south of Jeshimon. 413
23:26 Saul went o this side of the mountain, 4480
23:26 and his men o that side of the mountain: 4480
24: 7 up out of the cave, and went o his way. 871.1
25:13 men, **Gird** you o every man his sword. 2296
25:13 they **girded** o every man his sword; 2296
25:13 and David also **girded** o his sword: 2296
25:14 salute our master; and he railed o them. 871.1
25:18 cakes of figs, and laid them o asses. 5921
25:19 said unto her servants, **Go** o before me; 5674
25:20 it was so, as she rode o the ass, that she 5921
25:23 fell before David o her face, 5921
25:41 bowed herself o her face to the earth, NIH
26:13 and stood o the top of a hill afar off; 5921
26:25 So David went o his way, 3807.1
27:11 saying, Lest they should tell o us, saying, 5921
28: 8 **put** o other raiment, and he went, 3847
28:20 fell straightway all along o the earth, 1886.5
28:22 strength, when thou goest o thy way. 871.1
29: 2 the lords of the Philistines **passed** o by 5674
29: 2 his men **passed** o in the rereward with 5674
30: 1 his men were come to Ziklag o the third 871.1
30: 2 them away, and went o their way. 3807.1
31: 7 when the men of Israel that were o 871.1
31: 7 they that were o the other side Jordan, 871.1
31: 8 it came to pass o the morrow, when 4480

2Sa
1: 2 It came even to pass o the third day, that 871.1
1:10 the bracelet that was o his arm, 5921
1:11 David took hold o his clothes, 871.1
1:24 who put o ornaments of gold upon your 5927
2:13 the one o the one side of the pool, 5921
2:13 and the other o the other side of the pool. 5921
2:21 lay thee **hold** o one of the young men, 270
2:25 one troop, and stood o the top of a hill. 5921
3:12 sent messengers to David o his **behalf**, 8478
3:29 Let it rest o the head of Joab, and on all 5921
3:29 head of Joab, and o all his father's house; 413
3:29 or that leaneth o a staff, or that falleth on 871.1
3:29 that falleth o the sword, or that lacketh 871.1
4: 5 who lay o a bed at noon. 4904+7901
4: 7 he lay o his bed in his bedchamber, 5921
5: 8 David said o that day, Whosoever getteth 871.1
5:10 David **went** o, and grew great, 1980+1980
6: 5 o all manner of instruments made of fir 871.1
6: 5 even o harps, and on psalteries, 871.1
6: 5 o psalteries, and on timbrels, 871.1
6: 5 o timbrels, and on cornets, 871.1
6: 5 and o cornets, and on cymbals. 871.1
6: 5 and o cornets, and on cymbals. 871.1
8: 7 David took the shields of gold that were o 413
9: 3 hath yet a son, which is lame o his feet. NIH
9: 6 he fell o his face, and did reverence. 5921
9:13 king's table; and was lame o both his feet. NIH
11:13 at even he went out to lie o his bed with 871.1
12:18 it came to pass o the seventh day, that 871.1
12:30 it was set o David's head. And he brought 5921

2Sa
13: 5 Lay thee down o thy bed, and make 5921
13:19 Tamar put ashes o her head, and rent her 5921
13:19 garment of divers colours that was o her, 5921
13:19 laid her hand o her head, and went on 5921
13:19 on her head, and **went** o crying. 1980+1980
13:31 tare his garments, and lay o the earth; 1886.5
14: 2 put o now mourning apparel, 3847
14: 3 and speak o this manner unto him. 3509.1
14: 4 she fell o her face to the ground, 5921
14: 9 the iniquity be o me, and on my father's 5921
14: 9 be on me, and o my father's house: 5921
14:12 my lord the king. And he said, **Say** o. 1696
14:14 and are as water spilt o the ground, 1886.5
14:22 Joab fell to the ground o his face, 413
14:26 because the hair was heavy o him, 5921
14:30 he hath barley there; go and set it o fire. 871.1
14:30 Absalom's servants set the field o fire. 871.1
14:31 have thy servants set my field o 871.1
14:33 bowed himself o his face to the ground 5921
15: 6 o this manner did Absalom to all Israel 3509.1
15:18 all his servants **passed** o beside him; 5674
15:18 him from Gath, **passed** o before the king. 5674
15:33 If thou **passest** o with me, then thou 5674
16: 2 be for the king's household to **ride** o; 7392
16: 6 all the mighty men were o his right hand 4480
16: 6 were on his right hand and o his left. 4480
16:12 It may be that the LORD will look o mine 413
16:13 Shimei went along o the hill's side over 871.1
17:12 will light upon him as the dew falleth o 5921
19:40 the king **went** o to Gilgal, 5674
19:40 Gilgal, and Chimham **went** o with him: 5674
20: 8 Joab's garment that he had put o was 3830
20:13 the people **went** o after Joab, to pursue 5674
21:10 neither the birds of the air to rest o 5921
21:20 that had o every hand six fingers, NIH
21:20 o every foot six toes, four and twenty in NIH
22: 4 I will **call** o the LORD, who is worthy to 7121
22:49 thou also hast **lifted** me up o **high** above 7311
23: 1 and the man who was raised up o **high**, 5920
24: 5 o the right side of the city that lieth in NIH
24:20 and his servants **coming** o toward him: 5674
24:20 bowed himself before the king o his face NIH

1Ki
1:20 thou shouldest tell them who shall sit o 5921
1:27 who should sit o the throne of my lord 5921
1:46 also Solomon sitteth o the throne of 5921
1:48 which hath given one to sit o my throne 5921
1:50 and caught hold o the horns of the altar. 871.1
1:51 hath caught hold o the horns of the altar, 871.1
2: 4 a man o the throne of Israel. 4480+5921
2: 5 and in his shoes that were o his feet. 871.1
2:14 to say unto thee. And she said, **Say** o. 1696
2:15 that all Israel set their faces o me, that I 5921
2:16 me not. And she said unto him, **Say** o. 1696
2:19 sat down o his throne, and caused a seat 5921
2:19 and she sat o his right hand. 3807.1
2:20 king said unto her, **Ask** o, my mother: 7592
2:24 set me o the throne of David my father, 5921
2:28 and caught hold o the horns of the altar. 871.1
2:37 that o the day thou goest out, 871.1
2:42 o the day thou goest out, 871.1
3: 4 offerings did Solomon offer up o that altar. 5921
3: 6 that thou hast given him a son to sit o his 5921
4:24 For he had dominion over all the region o NIH
4:24 over all the kings o this side the river: NIH
4:24 he had peace o all sides round about him. 4480
4:29 even as the sand that is o the sea shore. 5921
5: 3 which were **about** him o **every side**, 5437
5: 4 my God hath given me rest o every side, 4480
6:10 rested o the house with timber of cedar. NIH
6:15 he covered them o the inside with wood, 4480
6:16 he built twenty cubits o the sides of 4480
7: 3 lay o forty five pillars, fifteen in a row. 5921
7: 9 so o the outside toward the great court. 4480
7:28 the work of the bases was o this manner: NIH
7:29 o the borders that were between the 5921
7:35 o the top of the base the ledges thereof 5921
7:36 For o the plates of the ledges thereof, 5921
7:36 o the borders thereof, he graved 5921
7:39 he put five bases o the right side of 5921
7:39 and five o the left side of the house: 5921
7:39 he set the sea o the right side of the house 4480
7:41 the two bowls of the chapiters that were o 5921
7:43 the ten bases, and ten lavers o the bases; 5921
7:49 five o the right side, and five on the left, 4480
7:49 five o the left, before the oracle, with 4480
8:20 sit o the throne of Israel, as the LORD 5921
8:23 in heaven above, or o earth beneath, 5921
8:25 in my sight to sit o the throne of Israel; 5921
8:27 will God indeed dwell o the earth? 5921
8:50 that they may have compassion o them: NIH
8:54 from kneeling o his knees with his hands 5921
8:66 O the eighth day he sent the people away 871.1
9:26 o the shore of the Red sea, in the land of 5921
10: 9 in thee, to set thee o the throne of Israel: 5921
10:19 o either side on 2088+2088+4480+4480+2050.1
10:19 there were stays on either side o the place 413
10:20 twelve lions stood there o the one side 4480
10:20 side and o the other upon the six steps: 4480
11:30 caught the new garment that was o 5921
12:32 the fifteenth day of the month, like 871.1
13: 4 from the altar, saying, **Lay hold** o him. 8610
14:23 o every high hill, and under every green 5921
16:11 to reign, as soon as he sat o his throne, 5921
16:24 built o the hill, and called the name of NIH

O

O

1Ki	18: 7 he knew him, and fell o his face, and said,	5921
	18:23 lay it o wood, and put no fire under: and	5921
	18:23 lay it o wood, and put no fire under:	5921
	18:24 call ye o the name of your gods, and I	871.1
	18:24 and I will call o the name of the LORD:	871.1
	18:25 call o the name of your gods, but put no	871.1
	18:26 called o the name of Baal from morning	871.1
	18:33 and laid him o the wood, and said,	5921
	18:33 pour it o the burnt sacrifice, and on	5921
	18:33 it on the burnt sacrifice, and on the wood.	5921
	18:39 all the people saw it, they fell o their	5921
	18:46 the hand of the LORD was o Elijah;	413
	19: 6 there was a cake baken o the coals,	7529
	19:15 return o thy way to the wilderness of	3807.1
	20:11 Tell him, Let not him that girdeth o his	2296
	20:20 Ben-hadad the king of Syria escaped o a	5921
	20:31 put sackcloth o our loins, and ropes upon	871.1
	20:32 So they girded sackcloth o their loins,	871.1
	20:32 put ropes o their heads, and came to	871.1
	21: 9 and set Naboth o high among the people:	871.1
	21:12 and set Naboth o high among the people.	871.1
	22: 2 it came to pass o the third year, that	5921
	22:10 Jehoshaphat the king of Judah sat each o	5921
	22:10 on his throne, having put o their robes,	3847
	22:19 I saw the LORD sitting o his throne,	5921
	22:19 the host of heaven standing by him o his	4480
	22:19 by him on his right hand o his left.	4480
	22:20 one said o this manner, and another said	871.1
	22:20 and another said o that manner.	871.1
	22:24 and smote Micaiah o the cheek, and said,	5921
	22:30 into the battle; but put thou o thy robes.	3847
2Ki	1: 4 shalt not come down from that bed o	8033
	1: 6 shalt not come down from that bed o	8033
	1: 9 behold, he sat o the top of a hill. And he	5921
	1:13 came and fell o his knees before Elijah,	5921
	1:16 thou shalt not come down off that bed o	8033
	2: 6 will not leave thee. And they two went o.	1980
	2: 8 that they two went over o dry ground.	871.1
	2:11 as they still went o, and talked,	1980+1980
	2:15 The spirit of Elijah doth rest o Elisha.	5921
	2:24 looked o them, and cursed them in the	NIH
	3:11 which poured water o the hands of Elijah.	5921
	3:21 all that were able to put o armour,	2290+2296
	3:22 o the other side as red as blood:	4480+5048
	3:25 o every good piece of land cast every man	NIH
	4: 8 it fell o a day, that Elisha passed to	1961
	4:10 a little chamber, I pray thee, o the wall;	NIH
	4:11 it fell o a day, that he came thither,	1961
	4:18 when the child was grown, it fell o a day,	1961
	4:20 sat o her knees till noon, and then died.	5921
	4:21 laid him o the bed of the man of God,	5921
	4:31 Gehazi passed o before them, and laid	5674
	4:38 Set o the great pot, and seethe pottage for	8239
	5: 2 waited o Naaman's wife.	1961+6440+3807.1
	5:11 call o the name of the LORD his God,	871.1
	5:18 leaneth o my hand, and I bow myself in	5921
	6:29 I said unto her o the next day, Give thy	871.1
	6:31 son of Shaphat shall stand o him this day.	5921
	7: 2 a lord o whose hand the king leaned	5921
	7:17 the king appointed the lord o whose hand	5921
	8:12 their strong holds wilt thou set o fire,	871.1
	8:15 it came to pass o the morrow, that he took	4480
	8:15 and spread o his face, so that he died:	5921
	9: 3 pour it o his head, and say, Thus saith	5921
	9: 6 he poured the oil o his head, and said unto	413
	9:13 put it under him o the top of the stairs,	413
	9:17 there stood a watchman o the tower in	5921
	9:18 So there went one o horseback to	5483+7392
	9:19 he sent out a second o horseback,	5483+7392
	9:32 the window, and said, Who is o my side?	854
	9:33 of her blood was sprinkled o the wall,	413
	9:33 sprinkled on the wall, and o the horses:	413
	10: 3 set him o his father's throne, and fight for	5921
	10:15 he lighted o Jehonadab the son of Rechab	4672
	10:30 generation shall sit o the throne of Israel.	5921
	11: 5 A third part of you that enter in o	NIH
	11: 7 two parts of all you that go forth o	NIH
	11: 9 men that were to come in o the sabbath,	NIH
	11: 9 them that should go out o the sabbath,	NIH
	11:16 they laid hands o her; and she went by	3807.1
	11:19 And he sat o the throne of the kings.	5921
	12: 9 o the right side as one cometh into	4480
	12:15 the money to be bestowed o workmen:	3807.1
	13:21 he revived, and stood up o his feet.	5921
	13:23 had compassion o them, and had respect	NIH
	14: 4 and burnt incense o the high places.	871.1
	14:20 they brought him o horses: and he was	5921
	15: 4 and burnt incense still o the high places.	871.1
	15:12 Thy sons shall sit o the throne of Israel	5921
	16: 4 o the hills, and under every green tree.	5921
	16:14 and put it o the north side of the altar.	5921
	18:14 that which thou puttest o me will I bear.	5921
	18:20 Now o whom dost thou trust, that thou	5921
	18:21 even upon Egypt, o which if a man lean,	NIH
	18:21 king of Egypt unto all that trust o him.	5921
	18:23 if thou be able o thy part to set riders	3807.1
	18:24 put thy trust o Egypt for chariots and	5921
	18:26 the ears of the people that are o the wall.	5921
	18:27 he not sent me to the men which sit o	5921
	19:22 thy voice, and lift up thine eyes o high?	4791
	19:26 as the grass on the housetops, and as corn	NIH
	20: 5 the third day thou shalt go up unto	871.1
	20: 7 they took and laid it o the boil,	5921
	23: 8 were o a man's left hand at the gate	5921
	23:12 altars that were o the top of the upper	5921

2Ki	23:13 were o the right hand of the mount	4480
	25: 3 the ninth day of the fourth month	871.1
	25: 8 o the seventh day of the month,	871.1
	25:27 o the seven and twentieth day of	871.1
1Ch	4:10 Jabez called o the God of Israel, saying,	3807.1
	6:32 they waited o their office according to	5921
	6:39 Asaph, who stood o his right hand,	5921
	6:44 their brethren the sons of Merari stood o	5921
	6:49 o the altar of incense, and were	5921
	6:78 o the other side Jordan by Jericho,	4480
	6:78 by Jericho, o the east side of Jordan,	3807.1
	10: 5 he fell likewise o the sword, and died.	5921
	10: 8 it came to pass o the morrow, when	4480
	12:18 and o thy side, thou son of Jesse:	5973
	12:37 on the other side of Jordan,	4480
	12:40 brought bread o asses, and on camels,	871.1
	12:40 o camels, and on mules, and on oxen,	871.1
	12:40 o mules, and on oxen, and meat, meal,	871.1
	12:40 on mules, and on oxen, and meat, meal,	871.1
	13: 6 the cherubims, whose name is called o it.	NIH
	14: 2 was lift up o high,	4605+1886.5+3807.1
	15:20 and Benaiah, with psalteries o Alamoth;	5921
	15:21 with harps o the Sheminith to excel.	5921
	16: 7 o that day David delivered first this	871.1
	18: 7 David took the shields of gold that were o	5921
	20: 6 six on each hand, and six o each foot:	NIH
	20: 6 six on each hand, and six o each foot:	NIH
	21:17 be o me, and on my father's house;	871.1
	21:17 be on me, and o my father's house;	871.1
	21:17 not o thy people, that they should be	871.1
	22:18 he not given you rest o every side?	4480+5439
	23:28 their office was to wait o the sons	3027
	23:31 and o the set feasts, by number,	3807.1
	26:30 were officers among them of Israel o this	4480
	29:15 our days o the earth are as a shadow,	5921
	29:21 the morrow after that day, even a	3807.1
	29:22 drink before the LORD o that day with	871.1
	29:23 Solomon sat o the throne of the LORD as	5921
	29:25 not been o any king before him in Israel.	5921
2Ch	2: 4 the sabbaths, and on the new moons,	3807.1
	2: 4 o the new moons, and on the solemn	3807.1
	2: 4 o the solemn feasts of the LORD our	3807.1
	3: 7 and graved cherubims o the walls.	5921
	3:13 they stood o their feet, and their faces	5921
	3:15 the chapiter that was o the top of each of	5921
	3:16 and put them o the heads of the pillars;	871.1
	3:16 and put them o the chains.	871.1
	3:17 one o the right hand, and the other on	4480
	3:17 on the right hand, and the other o the left;	4480
	3:17 called the name of that o the right hand	NIH
	3:17 and the name of that o the left Boaz.	NIH
	4: 6 put five o the right hand, and five on	4480
	4: 6 and five o the left, to wash in them:	4480
	4: 7 five o the right hand, and five on the left.	4480
	4: 7 five on the right hand, and five o the left.	4480
	4: 8 five o the right side, and five on the left.	4480
	4: 8 five on the right side, and five o the left.	4480
	4:10 he set the sea o the right side of the east	4480
	4:12 the chapiters which were o the top of	5921
	4:12 which were o the top of the pillars;	5921
	4:13 four hundred pomegranates o the two	3807.1
	4:13 rows of pomegranates o each wreath,	3807.1
	6:10 am set o the throne of Israel, as the LORD	5921
	6:18 will God in very deed dwell with men o	5921
	7: 6 the priests waited o their offices:	5975
	7:10 the three and twentieth day of	871.1
	7:22 laid hold o other gods,	871.1
	8:12 unto the LORD o the altar of the LORD,	5921
	8:13 the sabbaths, and on the new moons,	3807.1
	8:13 o the new moons, and on the solemn	3807.1
	8:13 new moons, and o the solemn feasts,	3807.1
	8: 9 which delighted in thee to set thee o his	5921
	9:18 o each side	2088+2088+4480+4480+2050.1
	9:19 twelve lions stood there o the one side	5921
	9:19 side and o the other upon the six steps.	4480
	10:12 all the people came to Rehoboam o.	871.1
	10:12 Come again to me o the third day.	871.1
	11:12 having Judah and Benjamin o his side.	3807.1
	14: 7 he hath given us rest o every side.	4480+5439
	14:11 for we rest o thee, and in thy name we go	5921
	16: 7 Because thou hast relied o the king of	5921
	16: 7 not relied o the LORD thy God, therefore	5921
	16: 8 yet, because thou didst rely o the LORD,	5921
	17:19 These waited o the king, besides those	8334
	18: 9 of Judah sat either of them o his throne,	5921
	18:18 all the host of heaven standing o his right	5921
	18:18 standing on his right hand and o his left.	NIH
	18:24 thou shalt see o that day when thou shalt	871.1
	18:29 go to the battle; but put thou o thy robes.	3847
	20: 2 thee from beyond the sea o this side Syria;	4480
	20:19 a loud voice o high.	4605+1886.5+3807.1
	20:26 o the fourth day they assembled	871.1
	20:29 the fear of God was o all the kingdoms of	5921
	23: 4 A third part of you entering o the sabbath,	NIH
	23: 8 men that were to come in o the sabbath,	NIH
	23: 8 them that were to go out o the sabbath:	NIH
	23:15 So they laid hands o her; and when she	3807.1
	24:25 and slew him o his bed, and he died:	5921
	26:15 invented by cunning men, to be o	5921
	27: 3 and o the wall of Ophel he built much.	871.1
	28: 4 o the hills, and under every green tree.	5921
	29:17 they began o the first day of the first	3807.1
	29:17 the eighth day of the month came they	871.1
	29:21 to offer them o the altar of the LORD.	5921
	29:22 the blood, and sprinkled it o the altar:	1886.5

2Ch	30:15 they killed the passover o the fourteenth	871.1
	32:15 nor persuade you o this manner, neither	3509.1
	32:17 He wrote also letters to rail o the LORD	3807.1
	32:18 people of Jerusalem that were o the wall,	5921
	32:22 and guided them o every side,	4480+5439
	33:14 o the west side of Gihon, in the valley,	1886.5
	34: 4 o high above them,	4605+1886.5+3807.1
	35: 1 they killed the passover o the fourteenth	871.1
	36:15 because he had compassion o his people,	5921
	36:15 on his people, and o his dwelling place:	5921
Ezr	4:10 and the rest that are o this side the river,	NIH
	4:11 Thy servants the men o this side the river,	NIH
	4:16 this means thou shalt have no portion o	871.2
	5: 3 governor o this side the river,	NIH
	5: 6 governor o this side the river,	NIH
	5: 6 which were o this side the river, sent	871.2
	5: 8 this work goeth fast o, and prospereth in	5648
	6:13 Tatnai, governor o this side the river,	NIH
	6:15 this house was finished the third day of	5705
	7: 9 o the first day of the fifth month came he	871.1
	8:31 we departed from the river of Ahava o	871.1
	8:33 Now o the fourth day was the silver and	871.1
	8:36 and to the governors o this side the river:	NIH
	10: 9 o the twentieth day of the month;	871.1
Ne	2:14 I went o to the gate of the fountain,	5674
	3: 7 unto the throne of the governor o this side	NIH
	3:13 thousand cubits o the wall unto the dung	871.1
	4:13 behind the wall, and o the higher places,	871.1
	4:17 They which builded o the wall,	871.1
	4:22 be a guard to us, and o labour in the day.	NIH
	6:14 the prophetess Noadiah, and the rest	3807.1
	8: 4 Hilkiah, and Maaseiah, o his right hand;	5921
	8: 4 o his left hand, Pedaiah, and Mishael,	4480
	8:13 o the second day were gathered together	871.1
	8:18 o the eighth day was a solemn assembly,	871.1
	9:10 o all his servants, and on all the people of	871.1
	9:10 and o all the people of his land:	871.1
	9:11 the midst of the sea o the dry land;	871.1
	9:32 o our kings, on our princes, and on our	3807.1
	9:32 o our princes, and on our priests,	3807.1
	9:32 our priests, and on our prophets,	3807.1
	9:32 o our prophets, and on our fathers,	3807.1
	9:32 and o our fathers, and on all thy people,	3807.1
	9:32 and on our fathers, and o all thy people,	3807.1
	10:31 or any victuals o the sabbath day to sell,	871.1
	10:31 that we would not buy it of them o	871.1
	10:31 them on the sabbath, or o the holy day:	871.1
	12:31 whereof one went o the right hand	3807.1
	13: 1 O that day they read in the book of	871.1
	13:15 treading wine presses o the sabbath,	871.1
	13:15 which they brought into Jerusalem o	871.1
	13:16 sold o the sabbath unto the children of	871.1
	13:19 there should no burden be brought in o	871.1
	13:21 if ye do so again, I will lay hands o you.	871.1
	13:21 that time forth came they no more o	871.1
Est	1: 2 the king Ahasuerus sat o the throne	5921
	1:10 O the seventh day, when the heart of	871.1
	1:11 her beauty: for she was fair to look o.	4758
	2:14 o the morrow she returned into the	871.1
	2:21 sought to lay hand o the king Ahasuerus.	871.1
	2:23 therefore they were both hanged o a tree:	5921
	3: 6 he thought scorn to lay hands o Mordecai	871.1
	3:12 were the king's scribes called o	871.1
	4: 1 put o sackcloth with ashes, and went out	3847
	5: 1 Now it came to pass o the third day,	871.1
	5: 1 that Esther put o her royal apparel, and	3847
	6: 1 O that night could not the king sleep,	871.1
	6: 2 who sought to lay hand o the king	871.1
	6: 9 speak unto the king to hang Mordecai	5921
	6: 9 bring him o horseback through the street	5921
	6:11 brought him o horseback through	7392
	7: 2 the king said again unto Esther o	871.1
	7:10 So they hanged Haman o the gallows that	5921
	8: 1 O that day did the king Ahasuerus give	871.1
	8: 9 o the three and twentieth day thereof;	871.1
	8:10 sent letters by posts o horseback,	871.1
	8:10 and riders o mules, camels,	NIH
	8:13 to avenge themselves o their enemies.	4480
	8:14 pressed o by the king's commandment,	1765
	9: 1 o the thirteenth day of the same,	871.1
	9: 2 to lay hand o such as sought their hurt:	871.1
	9:10 but o the spoil laid they not their hand.	871.1
	9:11 O that day the number of those that	871.1
	9:15 o the fourteenth day also of the month	871.1
	9:15 but o the prey they laid not their hand.	871.1
	9:16 but they laid not their hands o the prey,	871.1
	9:17 O the thirteenth day of the month Adar;	871.1
	9:17 o the fourteenth day of the same rested	871.1
	9:18 together o the thirteenth day thereof,	871.1
	9:18 day thereof, and o the fourteenth thereof;	871.1
	9:18 o the fifteenth day of the same they	871.1
	9:25 his sons should be hanged o the gallows.	5921
Job	1:10 all that he hath o every side?	4480+5439
	4:13 the night, when deep sleep falleth o men.	5921
	5:11 To set up o high those that be low;	3807.1
	9:11 he passeth o also, but I perceive him not.	2498
	13:13 may speak, and let come o me what will.	5921
	15:26 He runneth upon him, even o his neck,	5921
	15:27 and maketh collops of fat o his flanks.	5921
	16:16 mine eyelids is the shadow of death;	5921
	16:19 is in heaven, and my record is o high.	871.1
	17: 9 The righteous also shall hold o his way,	270
	18:11 shall make him afraid o every side,	5439
	19:10 He hath destroyed me o every side,	5439
	21: 3 and after that I have spoken, mock o.	NIH

Job	21: 6 and trembling **taketh hold o** my flesh.	270
	23: 9 **O** the left hand, where he doth work,	NIH
	23: 9 I cannot behold *him*: he hideth *himself o*	NIH
	24:20 the worm shall **feed sweetly o** him;	4988
	27:17 may prepare *it*, but the just shall **put** *it* **o**,	3847
	27:20 Terrors **take hold o** him as waters,	5381
	29: 9 and laid *their* hand **o** their mouth.	3807.1
	29:14 I **put o** righteousness, and it clothed me:	3847
	29:24 *If* I laughed **o** them, they believed *it* not;	413
	31: 2 inheritance of the Almighty from **o high**?	4791
	36: 2 that *I have* yet to speak **o** God's **behalf**.	3807.1
	36: 7 with kings *are* they **o** the throne; yea,	3807.1
	36:16 **that which** should **be set o** thy table	5183
	36:17 judgment and justice **take hold o** thee.	8551
	37: 6 he saith to the snow, Be thou **o** the earth;	NIH
	38:26 To cause it to rain **o** the earth, *where* no	5921
	38:26 *where* no man *is*; **o** the wilderness,	NIH
	39:18 What time she lifteth up herself **o** high,	871.1
	39:21 He **goeth o** to meet the armed men.	3318
	39:27 command, and **make** her nest **o high**?	7311
	39:28 She dwelleth and abideth **o** the rock,	NIH
	40:12 Look **o** every one *that is* proud,	3807.1
Ps	4: T To the chief Musician **o** Neginoth,	871.1
	6: T To the chief Musician **o** Neginoth upon	871.1
	7: 7 their sakes therefore return thou **o** high.	3807.1
	12: 8 The wicked walk **o** every side, when	5439
	21: 3 thou settest a crown of pure gold **o** his	3807.1
	22: 8 He trusted **o** the Lord *that* he would	413
	25: 3 let none that **wait o** thee be ashamed:	6960
	25: 5 my salvation; **o** thee do I **wait** all the day.	NIH
	25:21 preserve me; for I **wait o** thee.	6960
	27:14 **Wait o** the Lord: be of good courage,	413
	27:14 thine heart: **wait**, I say, **o** the Lord.	413
	31:13 fear *was* **o every side**: while they	4480+5439
	35:17 Lord, how long wilt thou look **o**? rescue	NIH
	37:34 **Wait o** the Lord, and keep his way,	413
	48: 2 *is* mount Zion, **o** the sides of the north,	NIH
	49:14 death shall feed **o** them; and the upright	NIH
	52: 9 hast done *it*: and I will **wait o** thy name;	6960
	54: T To the chief Musician **o** Neginoth	871.1
	55: T To the chief Musician **o** Neginoth	871.1
	57: 4 lie *even among* them that are **set o fire**,	3857
	63: 6 meditate **o** thee in the *night* watches.	871.1
	65:12 and the little hills rejoice **o** every side.	2296
	66: 6 *land*: they went through the flood **o** foot:	871.1
	67: T To the chief Musician **o** Neginoth.	871.1
	68:18 Thou hast ascended **o** high, thou hast	3807.1
	68:21 a one as **goeth o** still in his trespasses.	1980
	68:25 **players o instruments** *followed* after;	5059
	69: 6 Let not them that **wait o** thee, O Lord	6960
	69:29 thy salvation, O God, **set** me **up o high**.	7682
	71:21 greatness, and comfort me **o** every side.	5437
	75: 5 Lift not up your horn **o** high: speak *not*	3807.1
	76: T To the chief Musician **o** Neginoth,	871.1
	78:53 he **led** them **o** safely, so that they feared	5148
	79: 1 they have laid Jerusalem **o** heaps.	3807.1
	81: 3 time appointed, **o** our solemn feast day.	3807.1
	82: 5 understand; they **walk o** in darkness:	1980
	83:14 the flame **setteth** the mountains **o** fire;	3857
	87: 7 **players o instruments** *shall be* there:	2490
	91:14 I will **set** him **o** high, because he hath	7682
	92:11 Mine eye also shall see *my desire* **o** mine	871.1
	93: 4 The Lord **o** high *is*	4791+871.1+1886.1
	104:32 He looketh **o** the earth, and it trembleth:	3807.1
	107:41 Yet **setteth** he the poor **o** high from	7682
	113: 5 the Lord our God, who dwelleth **o** high,	1361
	118: 6 The Lord *is* **o** my **side**; I will not fear:	3807.1
	119:59 I **thought o** my ways, and turned my feet	2803
	119:84 when wilt thou execute judgment **o** them	871.1
	119:143 and anguish have **taken hold o** me:	4672
	124: 1 not *been* the Lord who was **o** our **side**,	3807.1
	124: 2 not *been* the Lord who was **o** our **side**,	3807.1
	142: 4 I looked **o** *my* right hand, and beheld,	NIH
	143: 5 days of old; I meditate **o** all thy works;	871.1
	143: 5 works; I muse **o** the work of thy hands.	871.1
Pr	4:25 Let thine eyes look **right o**,	5227+3807.1
	5: 5 down *to* death; her steps take hold **o** hell.	NIH
	9:14 **o** a seat in the high places of the city,	5921
	9:15 To call passengers who go **right o** their	NIH
	14:21 he that hath mercy **o** the poor, happy *is* he.	NIH
	14:31 he that honoureth him hath mercy **o**	NIH
	15:14 the mouth of fools **feedeth o** foolishness.	7462
	20:22 *but* wait **o** the Lord, and he shall save	3807.1
	22: 3 but the simple **pass o**, and are punished.	5674
	27:12 *but* the simple **pass o**, *and* are punished.	5674
	27:18 he that **waiteth o** his master shall be	8104
Ecc	2: 3 to lay hold **o** folly, till I might see what	871.1
	2:11 I looked **o** all the works that my hands	871.1
	2:11 **o** the labour that I had laboured to do:	871.1
	4: 1 **o** the side of their oppressors *there was*	4480
SS	2:12 The flowers appear **o** the earth; the time	871.1
	3: 1 By night **o** my bed I sought *him* whom	5921
	5: 3 have put off my coat; how shall I **put** it **o**?	3847
Isa	7:25 **o** all hills that shall be digged with	NIH
	9:17 neither shall have mercy **o** their fatherless	NIH
	9:20 he shall snatch **o** the right hand,	5921
	9:20 he shall eat **o** the left hand, and they shall	5921
	10:12 work upon mount Zion and **o** Jerusalem,	871.1
	11: 8 the sucking child shall play **o** the hole of	5921
	11: 8 the weaned child shall put his hand **o**	5921
	13:18 they shall have no pity **o** the fruit of	5921
	14: 1 For the Lord will have mercy **o** Jacob,	NIH
	15: 2 **o** all their heads *shall be* baldness,	871.1
	15: 3 **o** the tops of their houses, and in their	5921
	16:12 when it is seen that Moab is weary **o**	5921

Isa	18: 3 world, and dwellers **o** the earth, see ye,	NIH
	18: 3 when *he* lifteth up an ensign **o**	NIH
	22:16 that heweth him out a sepulchre **o** high,	4791
	24:18 for the windows from **o high** are open,	4791
	24:21 the host of the high ones *that are* **o** high,	871.1
	25: 6 a feast of **wines o the lees**, of fat things	8105
	25: 6 of **wines o the lees** well refined.	8105
	26: 3 *whose* mind *is* stayed **o** thee: because	NIH
	26: 5 bringeth down them that dwell **o high**;	4791
	27:11 the women come, *and* **set** them **o fire**:	215
	27:11 he that made them will not have mercy **o**	NIH
	28: 1 which *are* **o** the head of the fat valleys of	5921
	28: 4 which *is* **o** the head of the fat valley,	5921
	28:20 than that *a man* can stretch himself **o** *it*:	NIH
	30:17 of a mountain, and as an ensign **o** a hill.	5921
	31: 1 stay **o** horses, and trust in chariots,	NIH
	31: 4 and the young lion roaring **o** his prey,	5921
	32:15 the spirit be poured upon us from **o** high,	4791
	32:19 it shall hail, coming down **o** the forest;	NIH
	33: 5 Lord *is* exalted; for he dwelleth **o** high:	4791
	33:16 He shall dwell **o high**: his place of	4791
	36: 5 now **o** whom dost thou trust, that thou	5921
	36: 6 in the staff of this broken reed, **o** Egypt;	5921
	36: 8 if thou be able **o** thy **part** to set riders	3807.1
	36: 9 put thy trust **o** Egypt for chariots and	5921
	36:11 the ears of the people that *are* **o** the wall.	5921
	37:23 *thy* voice, and lifted up thine eyes **o** high?	4791
	37:27 *as* the grass **o** the housetops, and *as* corn	NIH
	40:26 Lift up your eyes **o** high, and behold who	4791
	42:25 it hath **set** him **o fire** round about, yet he	3857
	44:20 He **feedeth o** ashes: a deceived heart	7462
	47: 1 daughter of Babylon, sit **o** the ground:	3807.1
	48:14 he will do his pleasure **o** Babylon,	871.1
	48:14 and his arm *shall be* **o** the Chaldeans.	NIH
	49:10 for he that hath mercy **o** them shall lead	NIH
	49:15 that *she* should not have compassion **o**	NIH
	49:18 and bind them **o** thee, as a bride *doth*.	NIH
	51: 5 upon me, and mine arm shall they trust.	413
	51: 9 Awake, awake, **put o** strength, O arm of	3847
	52: 1 awake; **put o** thy strength, O Zion;	3847
	52: 1 **put o** thy beautiful garments,	3847
	53: 6 the Lord hath laid **o** him the iniquity of	871.1
	54: 3 For thou shalt break forth **o** the right hand	NIH
	54: 3 forth *on* the right hand and **o** the left;	NIH
	54: 8 kindness will I have mercy **o** thee,	NIH
	54:10 saith the Lord that hath mercy **o** thee.	NIH
	56: 2 and the son of man *that* layeth hold **o** it;	871.1
	57:17 he **went o** frowardly in the way of his	1980
	58: 4 to make your voice to be heard **o** high.	871.1
	58:13 *from* doing thy pleasure **o** my holy day;	871.1
	59:17 For he **put o** righteousness as a breastplate,	3847
	59:17 **put o** the garments of vengeance	
	for *clothing*,	3847+8516
	60: 7 shall come up with acceptance **o** mine	NIH
	60:10 but in my favour have I had mercy **o** thee.	NIH
	63: 7 to all that the Lord hath **bestowed o** us,	1580
	63: 7 he hath **bestowed o** them according	1580
Jer	4: 7 destroyer of the Gentiles is **o** his **way**;	5265
	5: 9 shall not my soul be avenged **o** such a	871.1
	5:29 shall not my soul be avenged **o** such a	871.1
	6:23 They shall **lay hold o** bow and spear;	2388
	6:25 enemy *and* fear *is* **o every side**.	4480+5439
	7:29 and take up a lamentation **o** high places;	5921
	8:13 *shall be* no grapes **o** the vine, nor figs	871.1
	8:13 nor figs **o** the fig tree, and the leaf shall	2050.1
	8:21 astonishment hath **taken hold o** me.	2388
	9: 9 shall not my soul be avenged **o** such a	871.1
	10:25 the families that call not **o** thy name:	871.1
	11:20 heart, let me see thy vengeance **o** them:	4480
	12:15 have compassion **o** them, and will bring	NIH
	13: 2 word of the Lord, and put *it* **o** my loins.	5921
	13:27 abominations **o** the hills in the fields.	NIH
	15:10 have neither **lent o usury**, nor *men* have	5383
	15:10 usury, nor *men* have **lent** to me **o usury**;	5383
	17:11 *As* the partridge sitteth **o** eggs, and	NIH
	17:21 bear no burden **o** the sabbath day,	871.1
	17:22 out of your houses **o** the sabbath day,	871.1
	17:24 the gates of this city **o** the sabbath day,	871.1
	17:25 riding in chariots and **o** horses, they,	871.1
	17:27 entering in at the gates of Jerusalem **o**	871.1
	18: 3 behold, he wrought a work **o** the wheels.	5921
	20: 3 it came to pass **o** the morrow, that Pashur	4480
	20:10 of many, fear **o every side**.	4480+5439
	20:10 and we shall take our revenge **o** him.	4480
	20:12 heart, let me see thy vengeance **o** them:	4480
	22: 4 riding in chariots and **o** horses, he,	871.1
	23:12 they shall be **driven o**, and fall therein:	1760
	25:29 I begin to bring evil **o** the city which is	871.1
	25:30 The Lord shall roar from **o** high,	4791
	30: 6 see every man *with* his hands **o** his loins,	5921
	30:18 and have mercy **o** his dwelling places;	NIH
	31:29 and the children's teeth are **set o edge**.	6949
	31:30 sour grape, his teeth shall be **set o edge**.	6949
	32:29 shall come and **set fire o** this city,	3341
	33:26 to return, and have mercy **o** them.	NIH
	36:22 *there was a fire* **o** the hearth burning	NIH
	36:23 cast *it* into the fire that *was* **o** the hearth,	413
	36:23 in the fire that *was* **o** the hearth.	5921
	38:22 Thy friends have **set** thee **o**,	5496
	43: 3 Baruch the son of Neriah **setteth** thee **o**	5496
	43:12 as a shepherd **putteth o** his garment;	5844
	46: 4 the spears, *and* **put o** the brigandines.	3847
	48:11 he hath **settled o** his lees, and hath not	413
	49:23 *is* sorrow **o** the sea; it cannot be quiet.	871.1
	49:24 fear hath seized **o** *her*: anguish and	NIH

Jer	49:29 unto them, Fear *is* **o** every side.	4480+5439
	50: 6 they have turned them away **o**	NIH
	50:19 and he shall feed **o** Carmel and Bashan,	NIH
	52:23 and six pomegranates **o** a side;	1886.5
La	1: 2 the night, and her tears *are* **o** her cheeks:	5921
	2:21 the old lie **o** the ground in the streets:	3807.1
	4: 6 in a moment, and no hands stayed **o** her.	871.1
Eze	1: 8 man under their wings **o** their four sides;	5921
	1:10 and the face of a lion, **o** the right side:	413
	1:10 they four had the face of an ox **o** the left	4480
	1:23 covered **o** this *side*, and every one	3807.1
	1:23 covered **o** that *side*, their bodies.	3807.1
	3:23 by the river of Chebar: and I fell **o** my face.	5921
	4: 6 lie again **o** thy right side, and thou shalt	5921
	7:16 shall be **o** the mountains like doves of	413
	10: 3 Now the cherubims stood **o** the right side	4480
	11:23 upon the mountain which *is* **o** the east	4480
	16:11 upon thine hands, and a chain **o** thy neck.	5921
	16:12 I put a jewel **o** thy forehead, and earrings	5921
	16:15 pouredst out thy fornications **o** every one	5921
	16:33 **o** every side for thy whoredom.	4480+5439
	18: 2 and the children's teeth are **set o edge**?	6949
	19: 8 the nations set against him **o** every side	5439
	21:16 *either* **o the right hand**, *or* on the left,	3231
	21:16 *either* on the right hand, *or* **o the left**,	8041
	23: 5 she doted **o** her lovers, on the Assyrians	5921
	23: 7 her lovers, on the Assyrians *her* neighbours,	413
	23: 7 Assyria, and with all **o** whom she doted:	NIH
	23:22 them against thee **o** every side,	4480+5439
	24: 3 **Set** a pot, set *it* on, and also pour water	8239
	24: 3 a pot, **set** *it* **o**, and also pour water into it:	8239
	24:10 Heap **o** wood, kindle the fire, consume	7760
	24:17 **put o** thy shoes upon thy feet,	7760
	25: 9 from his cities *which are* **o** his frontiers,	4480
	26:17 which cause their terror *to be* **o** all that	3807.1
	28:23 the sword upon her **o** every side;	4480+5439
	31: 4 deep **set** him **up o high** with her rivers	7311
	33:32 and can **play** well **o** an instrument:	5059
	36: 3 swallowed you up **o** every side,	4480+5439
	37:21 will gather them **o** every side,	4480+5439
	39: 6 I will send a fire **o** Magog,	871.1
	39: 9 shall **set o fire** and burn the weapons,	1197
	39:11 the valley of the passengers **o** the east of	NIH
	39:17 gather yourselves **o** every side to	4480+5439
	40: 2 by which *was* as the frame of a city **o**	4480
	40: 5 behold a wall **o** the outside of the house	4480
	40:10 the gate eastward *were* three **o** this side,	4480
	40:10 three on this side, and three **o** that side;	4480
	40:10 the posts had one measure **o** this side and	4480
	40:10 one measure on this side and **o** that side.	4480
	40:12 little chambers *was* one cubit **o** this *side*,	NIH
	40:12 and the space *was* one cubit **o** that side:	4480
	40:12 the little chambers *were* six cubits **o** this	4480
	40:12 on this side, and six cubits **o** that side.	4480
	40:21 little chambers thereof *were* three **o** this	4480
	40:21 three on this side and three **o** that side:	4480
	40:26 one **o** this side, and another on that side,	4480
	40:26 one on this side, and another **o** that side,	4480
	40:34 thereof, **o** this side, and on that side:	4480
	40:34 thereof, on this side, and **o** that side:	4480
	40:37 thereof, **o** this side, and on that side:	4480
	40:37 thereof, on this side, and **o** that side:	4480
	40:39 in the porch of the gate *were* two tables **o**	4480
	40:39 two tables **o** that side, to slay thereon	4480
	40:40 the other side, which *was* at the porch	413
	40:41 Four tables *were* **o** this side, and four	4480
	40:41 four tables **o** that side, by the side of	4480
	40:48 five cubits **o** this side, and five cubits on	4480
	40:48 on this side, and five cubits **o** that side:	4480
	40:48 breadth of the gate *was* three cubits **o**	4480
	40:48 on this side, and three cubits **o** that side.	4480
	40:49 one **o** this side, and another on that side.	4480
	40:49 one on this side, and another **o** that side.	4480
	41: 1 six cubits broad **o** the one side,	4480
	41: 1 and six cubits broad **o** the other side,	4480
	41: 2 the sides of the door *were* five cubits **o**	4480
	41: 2 one side, and five cubits **o** the other side:	4480
	41: 5 round about the house **o** every side.	5439
	41:10 about the house **o** every side,	5439+5439
	41:15 the galleries thereof **o** the one side and	4480
	41:15 on the one side and **o** the other side,	4480
	41:16 the galleries round about **o** their three	3807.1
	41:19 *was* toward the palm tree **o** the one side,	4480
	41:19 toward the palm tree **o** the other side:	4480
	41:20 trees made, and **o** the wall of the temple.	NIH
	41:25 *there were* made **o** them, on the doors of	413
	41:25 **o** the doors of the temple, cherubims and	413
	41:26 palm trees **o** the one side and on the	4480
	41:26 trees on the one side and **o** the other side,	4480
	41:26 **o** the sides of the porch, and *upon* the side	413
	42: 7 towards the utter court **o** the forepart of	413
	42: 9 under these chambers *was* the entry **o**	4480
	42:14 shall **put o** other garments,	3847
	43:20 put *it* **o** the four horns of it, and on the	5921
	43:20 **o** the four corners of the settle, and	413
	43:22 the second day thou shalt offer a kid **o**	871.1
	44:19 and they shall **put o** other garments;	3847
	45: 7 *a portion shall be* for the prince **o** the one	4480
	45: 7 **o** the other side of the oblation of the holy	4480
	46: 1 **o** the sabbath it shall be opened, and in	871.1
	46:12 as he did **o** the sabbath day:	871.1
	46:19 *was* a place **o** the two sides westward.	871.1
	47: 2 there ran out waters **o** the right side.	4480
	47: 7 river *were* very many trees **o** the one side	4480
	47: 7 trees on the one side and **o** the other.	4480

O

Eze	47:12	o this side and on that side, shall grow all	4480
	47:12	on this side and o that side, shall grow all	4480
	48:16	o the east side four thousand and	4480
	48:21	o the one side and on the other of the	4480
	48:21	and o the other of the holy oblation,	4480
	48:30	o the north side, four thousand and	4480
Da	3:27	nor the smell of fire had passed o them,	871.2
	6:14	set his heart o Daniel to deliver him:	5922
	7: 5	it raised up itself o one side, and it had	3807.2
	8: 5	a he goat came from the west o the face	5921
	8:18	I was in a deep sleep o my face toward	5921
	10: 9	was I in a deep sleep o my face,	5921
	11:17	she shall not stand o his side, neither be	NIH
	11:31	arms shall stand o his part, and they shall	4480
	12: 5	the one o this side of the bank of	3807.1
	12: 5	the other o that side of the bank of	3807.1
Hos	4: 8	and they set their heart o their iniquity.	413
	5: 1	because ye have been a snare o Mizpah,	3807.1
	6: 3	if we follow o to know the LORD:	NIH
	10: 5	the priests thereof that rejoiced o it,	5921
	10: 8	the thistle shall come up o their altars;	5921
	10: 8	Cover us; and to the hills, Fall o us.	5921
	11: 4	they that take off the yoke o their jaws,	5921
	11: 6	the sword shall abide o his cities,	871.1
	12: 1	Ephraim feedeth o wind,	7462
	12: 6	judgment, and wait o thy God continually.	413
Joel	2: 5	Like the noise of chariots o the tops of	5921
	2: 7	they shall march every one o his ways,	871.1
	2:32	that whosoever shall call o the name of	871.1
Am	1: 7	I will send a fire o the wall of Gaza,	871.1
	1:10	I will send a fire o the wall of Tyrus,	871.1
	2: 7	That pant after the dust of the earth o	871.1
	5:19	leaned his hand o the wall, and a serpent	5921
Ob	1:11	In the day that thou stoodest o the other	4480
	1:12	thou shouldest not have looked o the day	NIH
	1:13	thou shouldest not have looked o their	NIH
	1:13	nor have laid hands o their substance in	871.1
	1:21	saviours shall come up o mount Zion to	871.1
Jnh	3: 5	proclaimed a fast, and put o sackcloth,	3847
	4: 5	sat o the east side of the city,	4480
	4:10	Thou hast had pity o the gourd,	5921
Mic	2:13	and the LORD on the head of them.	871.1
Na	1: 2	the LORD will take vengeance o his	3807.1
Hab	1:13	behold evil, and canst not look o iniquity:	413
	2: 9	that he may set his nest o high, that he	871.1
	2:15	that thou mayest look o their nakedness!	5921
	2:16	and shameful spuing shall be o thy glory.	5921
	3:10	his voice, and lift up his hands o high.	7315
	3:19	To the chief singer o my stringed	871.1
Zep	1: 9	punish all those that leap o the threshold,	5921
	1:12	the men that are settled o their lees:	5921
Zec	1:12	how long wilt thou not have mercy o	NIH
	1:12	on Jerusalem and o the cities of Judah,	NIH
	5: 3	be cut off as o this side according to it;	4480
	5: 3	one that sweareth shall be cut off as o	4480
	10: 5	the riders o horses shall be confounded.	NIH
	12: 6	o the right hand and on the left:	5921
	12: 6	on the right hand and o the left:	5921
	13: 9	they shall call o my name, and I will hear	871.1
	14: 4	which is before Jerusalem o the east,	4480
	14:13	they shall lay hold every one o the hand	NIH
Mal	1:10	do ye kindle fire o mine altar for nought.	NIH
Mt	1:18	the birth of Jesus Christ was o this wise:	3779
	1:20	But while he thought o these things,	1760
	4: 5	setteth him o a pinnacle of the temple,	1909
	4:21	going o from thence, he saw other two	4260
	5:14	A city that is set o a hill cannot be hid.	1883
	5:15	put it under a bushel, but o a candlestick;	1909
	5:28	whosoever looketh o a woman to lust	991
	5:39	whosoever shall smite thee o thy right	1909
	5:45	he maketh his sun to rise o the evil and	1909
	5:45	sun to rise on the evil and o the good,	NIG
	5:45	and sendeth rain o the just and on	1909
	5:45	sendeth rain on the just and o the unjust.	NIG
	6:25	yet for your body, what ye shall put o.	1746
	9: 2	him a man sick of the palsy, lying o a bed:	1909
	9: 6	of man hath power o earth to forgive sins,	1909
	9:27	Thou Son of David, have mercy o us.	NIG
	9:36	he was moved with compassion o them,	4012
	10:29	one of them shall not fall o the ground	1909
	10:34	Think not that I am come to send peace o	1909
	12: 1	At that time Jesus went o the sabbath day	NIG
	12: 5	how that o the sabbath days the priests in	NIG
	12:10	Is it lawful to heal o the sabbath days?	NIG
	12:11	and if it fall into a pit o the sabbath day;	NIG
	12:11	will he not lay hold o it, and lift it out?	2902
	12:12	Wherefore it is lawful to do well o	NIG
	13: 2	the whole multitude stood o the shore.	1909
	14: 3	For Herod had laid hold o John,	2902
	14:13	they followed him o foot out of the cities.	3979
	14:19	the multitude to sit down o the grass,	1909
	14:25	Jesus went unto them, walking o the sea.	1909
	14:26	when the disciples saw him walking o	1909
	14:28	thou, bid me come unto thee o the water.	1909
	14:29	he walked o the water, to go to Jesus.	1909
	15:22	saying, Have mercy o me, O Lord,	NIG
	15:32	said, I have compassion o the multitude,	1909
	15:35	the multitude to sit down o the ground.	1909
	16:19	whatsoever thou shalt bind o earth shall	1909
	16:19	whatsoever thou shalt loose o earth shall	1909
	17: 6	when the disciples heard it, they fell o	1909
	17:15	Lord, have mercy o my son: for he is	NIG
	18:18	Whatsoever ye shall bind o earth shall be	1909
	18:18	whatsoever ye shall loose o earth shall be	1909
	18:19	That if two of you shall agree o earth as	1909

Mt	18:28	he laid hands o him, and took him by	2902
	18:33	have had compassion o thy fellowservant,	NIG
	18:33	fellowservant, even as I had pity o thee?	NIG
	19:15	And he laid his hands o them,	2007
	20:21	the one o thy right hand, and the other	1537
	20:21	the other o the left, in thy kingdom.	1537
	20:23	baptized with: but to sit o my right hand,	1537
	20:23	and o my left, is not mine to give,	1537
	20:30	out, saying, Have mercy o us, O Lord,	NIG
	20:31	Have mercy o us, O Lord, thou Son	NIG
	20:34	So Jesus had compassion o them, and	NIG
	21: 7	and the colt, and put o them their clothes,	1883
	21:19	Let no fruit grow o thee henceforward for	1537
	21:38	kill him, and let us seize o his inheritance.	NIG
	21:44	And whosoever shall fall o this stone shall	1909
	21:44	o whomsoever it shall fall, it will grind	1909
	21:46	whom they sought to lay hands o him,	2902
	22:11	he saw there a man which had not o a	1746
	22:40	O these two commandments hang all	1722
	22:44	unto my Lord, Sit thou o my right hand,	1537
	23: 4	and lay them o men's shoulders;	2007
	24:17	Let him which is on the housetop not come	1909
	24:20	in the winter, neither o the sabbath day:	1722
	25:33	he shall set the sheep o his right hand,	1537
	25:33	on his right hand, but the goats o the left.	1537
	25:34	Then shall the King say unto them o his	1537
	25:41	Then shall he say also unto them o the left	1537
	26: 5	Not o the feast day, lest there be an uproar	1722
	26: 7	poured it o his head, as he sat at meat.	1909
	26:12	in that she hath poured this ointment o	1909
	26:39	and fell o his face, and prayed, saying,	1909
	26:45	them, Sleep o now, and take your rest:	NIG
	26:50	and laid hands o Jesus, and took him.	1909
	26:55	in the temple, and ye laid no hold o me.	NIG
	26:57	And they that had laid hold o Jesus led	1909
	26:64	of man sitting o the right hand of power,	1537
	27:19	he was set down o the judgment seat,	1909
	27:25	His blood be o us, and on our children.	1909
	27:25	His blood be on us, and o our children.	1909
	27:28	him, and put o him a scarlet robe.	4060
	27:30	took the reed, and smote him o the head.	1519
	27:31	and put his own raiment o him,	1746
	27:38	one o the right hand, and another on	1537
	27:38	on the right hand, and another o the left.	1537
	27:48	put it o a reed, and gave him to drink.	4060
Mk	1:21	straightway o the sabbath day he entered	NIG
	2:10	of man hath power o earth to forgive sins,	1909
	2:12	saying, We never saw it o this fashion.	3779
	2:21	man also seweth a piece of new cloth o	1909
	2:23	that he went through the corn fields o	1722
	2:24	why do they o the sabbath day that which	1722
	3: 2	whether he would heal him o the sabbath	NIG
	3: 4	Is it lawful to do good o the sabbath days,	NIG
	3: 5	And when he had looked round about o	NIG
	3: 9	a small ship should wait o him because	4342
	3:21	of it, they went out to lay hold o him:	2902
	3:34	he looked round about o them which	NIG
	4: 1	the whole multitude was by the sea o	1909
	4: 5	some fell o stony ground, where it had	1909
	4: 8	other fell o good ground, and did yield	1519
	4:16	likewise which are sown o stony ground;	1909
	4:20	these are they which are sown o good	1909
	4:21	and not to be set o a candlestick?	1909
	4:38	hinder part of the ship, asleep o a pillow:	1909
	5:19	for thee, and hath had compassion o thee.	NIG
	5:23	I pray thee, come and lay thy hands o her,	2007
	6: 9	with sandals; and not put o two coats.	1746
	6:21	that Herod o his birthday made a supper	NIG
	6:47	midst of the sea, and he alone o the land.	1909
	8: 2	I have compassion o the multitude,	1909
	8: 6	the people to sit down o the ground:	1909
	8:23	when he had spit o his eyes, and put his	1519
	8:33	turned about and looked o his disciples,	1492
	9: 3	so as no fuller o earth can white them.	1909
	9:20	and he fell o the ground,	1909
	9:22	canst do any thing, have compassion o us,	1909
	9:40	For he that is not against us is o our part.	5228
	10:37	one o thy right hand, and the other on thy	1537
	10:37	and the other o thy left hand, in thy glory.	1537
	10:40	But to sit o my right hand and on my left	1537
	10:40	and o my left hand is not mine to give;	1537
	10:47	thou Son of David, have mercy o me.	NIG
	10:48	Thou Son of David, have mercy o me.	NIG
	11: 7	to Jesus, and cast their garments o him;	1911
	11:12	o the morrow, when they were come	1887
	12:12	And they sought to lay hold o him,	2902
	12:36	said to my Lord, Sit thou o my right hand,	1537
	13:15	And let him that is o the housetop not go	1909
	14: 2	Not o the feast day, lest there be an uproar	1722
	14: 3	brake the box, and poured it o his head.	2596
	14: 6	she hath wrought a good work o me.	1519
	14:35	fell o the ground, and prayed that, if it	1909
	14:41	them, Sleep o now, and take your rest:	NIG
	14:46	And they laid their hands o him,	1909
	14:51	and the young men laid hold o him:	2902
	14:62	ye shall see the Son of man sitting o	1537
	14:65	some began to spit o him, and to cover	1716
	15:19	they smote him o the head with a reed,	NIG
	15:20	put his own clothes o him, and led him	1746
	15:27	the one o his right hand, and the other on	1537
	15:27	on his right hand, and the other o his left.	1537
	15:29	And they that passed by railed o him,	987
	15:36	put it o a reed, and gave him to drink,	4060
	15:40	were also women looking o afar off:	2334

Mk	16: 5	they saw a young man sitting o the right	1722
	16:18	They shall lay hands o the sick,	1909
	16:19	and sat o the right hand of God.	1537
Lk	1:11	o the right side of the altar of incense.	1537
	1:25	looked o, to take away my reproach	1896
	1:50	his mercy is o them that fear him from	NIG
	1:59	that o the eighth day they came to	1722
	1:65	fear came o all that dwelt round about	1909
	1:78	whereby the dayspring from o high hath	5311
	2:14	o earth peace, good will towards men.	1909
	4: 9	and set him o a pinnacle of the temple,	1909
	4:16	he went into the synagogue o the sabbath	1722
	4:20	in the synagogue were fastened o him.	NIG
	4:31	and taught them o the sabbath days.	1722
	4:40	he laid his hands o every one of them,	2007
	5:12	who seeing Jesus fell o his face,	1909
	5:17	And it came to pass o a certain day, as he	1722
	6: 1	And it came to pass o the second sabbath	1722
	6: 2	do ye that which is not lawful to do o	1722
	6: 6	it came to pass also o another sabbath,	1722
	6: 7	whether he would heal o the sabbath day;	1722
	6: 9	I will ask you one thing; Is it lawful o	NIG
	6:20	And he lifted up his eyes o his disciples,	1519
	6:29	And unto him that smiteth thee o the one	1909
	6:48	and laid the foundation o a rock:	1909
	7:13	had compassion o her, and said unto her,	1909
	7:16	And there came a fear o all:	NIG
	7:40	And he saith, Master, say o.	NIG
	8: 8	And other fell o good ground,	1909
	8:13	They o the rock are they, which, when	1909
	8:15	But that o the good ground are they,	1722
	8:16	but setteth it o a candlestick,	2007
	8:22	it came to pass o a certain day, that he	1722
	8:23	there came down a storm of wind o	1519
	8:32	of many swine feeding o the mountain:	1722
	9:37	And it came to pass, that o the next day,	1722
	10:11	which cleaveth o us, we do wipe off	2853
	10:19	I give unto you power to tread o serpents	1883
	10:31	saw him, he passed by o the other side.	492
	10:32	came and looked o him, and passed by on	NIG
	10:32	on him, and passed by o the other side.	492
	10:33	he saw him, he had compassion o him,	NIG
	10:34	and set him o his own beast,	1913
	10:35	And o the morrow when he departed,	1909
	10:37	he said, He that shewed mercy o him.	3326
	11:33	under a bushel, but o a candlestick,	1909
	12:22	neither for the body, what ye shall put o.	1746
	12:49	I am come to send fire o the earth;	1519
	12:51	ye that I am come to give peace o	1722
	13: 7	three years I come seeking fruit o this	1722
	13:10	in one of the synagogues o the sabbath.	1722
	13:13	And he laid his hands o her:	2007
	13:14	that Jesus had healed o the sabbath day,	NIG
	13:14	be healed, and not o the sabbath day.	NIG
	13:15	not each one of you o the sabbath loose	NIG
	13:16	loosed from this bond o the sabbath day?	NIG
	14: 1	Pharisees to eat bread o the sabbath day,	NIG
	14: 3	Is it lawful to heal o the sabbath day?	NIG
	14: 5	will not straightway pull him out o	1722
	15: 5	And when he hath found it, he layeth it o	1909
	15:20	ran, and fell o his neck, and kissed him.	1909
	15:22	forth the best robe, and put it o him;	1746
	15:22	put it on him; and put a ring o his hand,	1519
	15:22	a ring on his hand, and shoes o his feet:	1519
	16:24	have mercy o me, and send Lazarus,	NIG
	17:13	and said, Jesus, Master, have mercy o us.	NIG
	17:16	And fell down o his face at his feet,	1909
	18: 8	cometh, shall he find faith o the earth?	1909
	18:32	and spitefully entreated, and spitted o:	1716
	18:38	thou Son of David, have mercy o me.	NIG
	18:39	Thou Son of David, have mercy o me.	NIG
	19:43	round, and keep thee in o every side,	3840
	20: 1	it came to pass, that o one of those days,	1722
	20:18	o whomsoever it shall fall, it will grind	1909
	20:19	hour sought to lay hands o him;	1911
	20:42	to my Lord, Sit thou o my right hand,	1537
	21:12	they shall lay their hands o you,	1911
	21:26	things which are coming o the earth:	1904
	21:35	For as a snare shall it come o all	1904
	21:35	that dwell o the face of the whole earth.	1909
	22:21	that betrayeth me is with me o the table.	1909
	22:30	sit o thrones judging the twelve tribes of	1909
	22:64	they stroke him o the face, and asked him,	NIG
	22:69	Hereafter shall the Son of man sit o	1537
	23:26	country, and o him they laid the cross,	2007
	23:30	begin to say to the mountains, Fall o us;	1909
	23:33	one o the right hand, and the other on	1537
	23:33	on the right hand, and the other o the left.	1537
	23:39	which were hanged railed o him,	NIG
	23:54	the preparation, and the sabbath drew o.	2020
	24:49	ye be endued with power from o high.	5311
Jn	1:12	even to them that believe o his name:	1519
	1:33	Spirit descending, and remaining o him,	1909
	2:11	his glory; and his disciples believed o him.	1519
	3:18	that believeth o him is not condemned:	1519
	3:36	that believeth o the Son hath everlasting	1519
	3:36	but the wrath of God abideth o him.	1909
	4: 6	with his journey, sat thus o the well:	1909
	4:35	Lift up your eyes, and look o the fields;	2300
	4:39	o him for the saying of the woman,	1519
	5: 9	and on the same day was the sabbath.	1722
	5:16	had done these things o the sabbath day.	1722
	5:24	and believeth o him that sent me,	NIG
	6: 2	saw his miracles which he did o them	1909
	6:19	they see Jesus walking o the sea,	1909

O

Jn	6:22 **o the other side** of the sea saw that	4008
	6:25 found him **o the other side** of the sea,	4008
	6:29 that ye believe **o** him whom he hath sent.	1519
	6:35 he that believeth **o me** shall never thirst.	1519
	6:40 believeth **o** him, may have everlasting.	1519
	6:47 that believeth **o** me hath everlasting life.	1519
	7:22 ye **o** the sabbath day circumcise a man.	1722
	7:23 If a man **o** the sabbath day receive	1722
	7:23 I have made a man every whit whole **o**	1722
	7:30 but no *man* laid hands **o** him, because	1909
	7:31 And many of the people believed **o** him,	1519
	7:38 that believeth **o** me, as the scripture hath	1519
	7:39 which they that believe **o** him should	1519
	7:44 taken him; but no *man* laid hands **o** him.	1909
	7:48 or of the Pharisees believed **o** him?	1519
	8: 6 and with *his* finger wrote **o** the ground,	1519
	8: 8 stooped down, and wrote **o** the ground.	1519
	8:20 no *man* laid hands **o** him; for his hour	4084
	8:30 As he spake these *words*, many believed **o**	1519
	8:31 Jesus to those Jews which believed **o** him,	NIG
	9: 6 he spat **o the ground**, and made clay of	5476
	9:35 Dost thou believe **o the Son of God?**	1519
	9:36 is he, Lord, that I might believe **o** him?	1519
	10:42 And many believed **o** him there.	1519
	11:45 *things* which Jesus did, believed **o** him.	1519
	11:48 thus alone, all *men* will believe **o** him:	1519
	12:11 the Jews went away, and believed **o** Jesus.	1519
	12:12 O the next day much people that were	NIG
	12:15 thy King cometh, sitting **o** an ass's colt.	1909
	12:37 before them, *yet* they believed not **o** him:	1519
	12:42 the *chief* rulers also many believed **o** him;	1519
	12:44 and said, He that believeth **o me**,	1519
	12:44 believeth not on me, but on him that sent	1519
	12:44 believeth not on me, but **o** him that sent	1519
	12:46 that whosoever believeth **o** me should not	1519
	13:22 Then the disciples looked one **o** another,	1519
	13:23 Now there was leaning **o** Jesus' bosom	1722
	13:25 then lying **o** Jesus' breast saith unto him,	1909
	14:12 I say unto you, He that believeth **o** me,	1519
	16: 9 Of sin, because they believe not **o** me;	1519
	17: 4 I have glorified thee **o** the earth: I have	1909
	17:20 for them also which shall believe **o** me	1519
	19: 2 **put** *it* **o** his head, and they put on him a	2007
	19: 2 head, and they **put o** him a purple robe,	4016
	19:18 him, **o either side one**,	1782+1782+2532
	19:19 Pilate wrote a title, and put *it* **o** the cross.	1909
	19:31 remain upon the cross **o** the sabbath day,	1722
	19:37 They shall look **o** *him* whom they pierced.	1519
	20:22 **breathed** *o* them, and saith unto them,	1720
	21: 1 and **o this wise** shewed he *himself.*	3779
	21: 4 was now come, Jesus stood **o** the shore:	1519
	21: 6 Cast the net **o** the right side of the ship,	1909
	21:20 which also leaned **o** his breast at supper,	1909
Ac	2:18 And **o** my servants and on my	1909
	2:18 **o** my handmaidens I will pour out in those	1909
	2:21 *that* whosoever shall **call o** the name of	1941
	2:25 for he is **o** my right hand, that I should not	1537
	2:30 would raise up Christ to sit **o** his throne;	1909
	2:34 unto my Lord, Sit thou **o** my right hand,	1537
	3: 4 eyes upon him with John, said, Look **o** us.	1519
	3:12 why look ye *so* earnestly **o** us, as though	NIG
	4: 3 they **laid** hands **o** them, and put *them*	1911
	4: 5 And it came to pass **o** the morrow,	1909
	4:22 **o** whom this miracle of healing was	1909
	5: 5 great fear came **o** all them that heard these	1909
	5:15 and laid *them* **o** beds and couches,	1909
	5:18 And laid their hands **o** the apostles,	1909
	5:30 whom ye slew and hanged **o** a tree.	1909
	6: 6 had prayed, they **laid** *their* hands **o** them.	2007
	6:15 in the council, looking stedfastly **o** him,	1519
	7: 5 In it, no, not so much as to **set** his foot **o**:	968
	7: 6 And God spake **o this wise**, That his seed	3779
	7:54 and they gnashed **o** him *with their* teeth.	1909
	7:55 Jesus standing **o** the right hand of God,	1537
	7:56 the Son of man standing **o** the right hand	1537
	8:17 Then **laid** they *their* hands **o** them,	2007
	8:18 when Simon saw that through **laying o**	1936
	8:19 power, that **o** whomsoever I **lay** hands,	2007
	8:36 And as they went **o** *their* way, they came	2596
	8:39 no more: and he went **o** his way rejoicing.	NIG
	9:12 and **putting** *his* hand **o** him, that he might	2007
	9:14 priests to bind all that **call o** thy name.	1941
	9:17 and **putting** his hands **o** him said,	2007
	9:21 which **called o** this name in Jerusalem,	1941
	10: 4 And when he looked **o** him, he was afraid,	NIG
	10: 7 of them that **waited o** him **continually**;	4342
	10: 9 **O the morrow**, as they went on their	1887
	10: 9 as they **went o** their **journey**,	3596
	10:19 Peter thought **o** the vision, the Spirit	4012
	10:23 lodged *them.* And **o** the **morrow** Peter	1887
	10:39 whom they slew and hanged **o** a tree:	1909
	10:44 the Holy Ghost **fell o** all them which	1968
	10:45 that the Gentiles also was poured out	1909
	11:15 to speak, the Holy Ghost **fell o** them,	1968
	11:15 fell on them, as **o** us at the beginning.	1909
	11:17 who believed **o** the Lord Jesus Christ;	1909
	12: 7 and he smote Peter **o** the side,	NIG
	12: 8 Gird thyself, and **bind o** thy sandals.	5265
	12:10 out, and **passed o** through one street;	4281
	13: 3 and prayed, and **laid** *their* hands **o** them,	2007
	13: 9 with the Holy Ghost, set his eyes **o** him,	1519
	13:11 And immediately there **fell o** him a	1968
	13:14 into the synagogue **o** the sabbath day,	NIG
	13:15 word of exhortation for the people, say **o**.	NIG
	13:34 return to corruption, he said **o this wise**,	3779

Ac	13:36 **fell o** sleep, and was laid unto his fathers,	2837
	14:10 a loud voice, Stand upright **o** thy feet.	1909
	14:23 them to the Lord, **o** whom they believed.	1519
	15: 3 And being **brought o** their **way** by	4311
	16:13 And **o** the sabbath we went out of the city	1909
	16:31 Believe **o** the Lord Jesus Christ,	1909
	17: 5 and **set** all the city **o an uproar**,	2350
	17:26 for to dwell **o** all the face of the earth,	1909
	18: 8 believed **o** the Lord with all his house;	NIG
	18:10 and no *man* shall **set o** thee to hurt thee:	2007
	19: 4 that they should believe **o** him which	1519
	19: 4 come after him, that is, **o** Christ Jesus.	1519
	19: 6 upon them, the Holy Ghost came **o** them;	1909
	19:16 the evil spirit was **leapt o** them,	2177
	19:17 and fear **fell o** them all, and the name	1968
	20: 7 unto them, ready to depart **o** the **morrow**;	1887
	20:10 and **fell o** him, and embracing *him* said,	1968
	20:37 and fell **o** Paul's neck, and kissed him,	1909
	21: 3 we left it **o** the left hand, and sailed into	NIG
	21: 5 and *they* all **brought** us **o** our way,	4311
	21: 5 and we kneeled down **o** the shore,	1909
	21:23 We have four men which have a vow **o**	1909
	21:27 up all the people, and laid hands **o** him,	1909
	21:40 Paul stood **o** the stairs, and beckoned with	1909
	22:16 thy sins, **calling o** the name of the Lord.	1941
	22:19 synagogue them that believed **o** thee:	1909
	22:30 **O the morrow**, because he would have	1887
	23: 2 stood by him to smite him **o** the mouth.	NIG
	23:24 that they may **set** Paul **o**, and bring *him*	1913
	23:32 **O the morrow** they left the horsemen to	1887
	25:17 **o** the **morrow** I sat on the judgment seat,	1836
	25:17 on the morrow I sat **o** the judgment seat,	1909
	25:23 And **o** the **morrow**, when Agrippa was	1887
	27:20 no small tempest **lay o** us, all hope that	1945
	27:33 And while the day was **coming o**, Paul	3195
	27:44 some **o** boards, and some on broken	1909
	27:44 and some **o** broken pieces of the ship.	1909
	28: 3 laid *them* **o** the fire, there came a viper	1909
	28: 3 out of the heat, and fastened **o** his hand.	NIG
	28: 4 saw the *venomous* beast hang **o** his hand,	1537
	28: 8 **laid** *his* hands **o** him, and healed him.	2007
Ro	4: 5 believeth **o** him that justifieth the ungodly,	1909
	4:24 if we believe **o** him that raised up Jesus	1909
	9:15 I will have mercy **o** whom I will have	NIG
	9:15 I will have compassion **o** whom I will	NIG
	9:18 Therefore hath he mercy **o** whom he will	NIG
	9:23 riches of his glory **o** the vessels of mercy,	1909
	9:33 whosoever believeth **o** him shall not be	1909
	10: 6 which is of faith speaketh **o this wise**,	3779
	10:11 Whosoever believeth **o** him shall not be	1909
	10:14 shall they **call o** *him* in whom they have	1941
	11:22 **o** them which fell, severity; but toward	1909
	12: 7 Or ministry, *let us wait* **o** *our* ministering.	1722
	12: 7 he that teacheth, **o** teaching;	1722
	12: 8 Or he that exhorteth, **o** exhortation: he	1722
	12:20 doing thou shalt heap coals of fire **o** his	1909
	13:12 and let us **put o** the armour of light.	1746
	13:14 But **put** ye **o** the Lord Jesus Christ,	1746
	15: 3 of them that reproached thee fell **o** me.	1909
	15:24 to be **brought o** my **way** thitherward by	4311
	16: 2 who bestowed much labour **o** us.	1519
	16:19 *men.* I am glad therefore **o** your **behalf:**	1909
1Co	1: 4 I thank my God always **o** your **behalf**,	4012
	11:10 the woman to have power **o** *her* head	1909
	14:25 falling down **o** *his* face he will worship	1909
	15:53 For this corruptible must **put o**	1746
	15:53 and this mortal *must* **put o** immortality.	1746
	15:54 So when this corruptible shall have **put o**	1746
	15:54 this mortal shall have **put o** immortality,	1746
	16: 2 that ye may **bring** me **o** my **journey**	4311
	16:17 for that which was lacking **o** your **part**	4771
2Co	1:11 may be given by many **o** our **behalf.**	5228
	1:16 of you to be **brought o** *my* **way** toward	4311
	4: 8 *We are* troubled **o** every **side**, yet not	1722
	5:12 give you occasion to glory **o** our **behalf**,	5228
	6: 7 by the armour of righteousness **o** the right	NIG
	6: 7 on the right hand and **o** the left,	NIG
	7: 5 *we were* troubled **o** every **side**; without	1722
	8: 1 bestowed **o** the churches of Macedonia;	1722
	8:24 and of our boasting **o** your **behalf.**	5228
	10: 7 Do ye **look o** *things* after the outward	991
	11:20 himself, if a man smite you **o** the face.	1519
Gal	3:13 Cursed *is* every one that hangeth **o** a tree:	1909
	3:14 come **o** the Gentiles through Jesus Christ;	1519
	3:27 baptized into Christ have **put o** Christ.	1746
	6:16 to this rule, peace *be* **o** them, and mercy,	1909
Eph	1:10 are in heaven, and which are **o** earth;	1519
	4: 8 *he* saith, When he ascended up **o** high,	1519
	4:24 that ye **put o** the new man, which after	1746
	6: 3 and thou mayest live long **o** the earth.	1909
	6:11 **Put o** the whole armour of God, that ye	1746
	6:14 **having o** the breastplate of righteousness;	1746
Php	1:29 not only to believe **o** him, but also to	1519
	2: 4 Look not every man **o** his own *things*, but	NIG
	2: 4 but every man also **o** the *things* of others.	NIG
	2:27 God had mercy **o** him; and not on him	NIG
	2:27 and not on him only, but on me also, lest I	NIG
	2:27 and not on him only, but **o** me also, lest I	NIG
	4: 8 *there be* any praise, think **o** these *things.*	NIG
Col	3: 1 where Christ sitteth **o** the right hand of	1722
	3: 2 **Set** your **affection o** *things* above, not on	5426
	3: 2 *things* above, not **o** *things* on the earth.	NIG
	3: 2 *things* above, not on *things* on the earth.	1909
	3: 6 cometh **o** the children of disobedience:	1909
	3:10 And have **put o** the new *man*, which is	1746

Col	3:12 **Put o** therefore, as the elect of God, holy	1746
	3:14 And above all these *things* **put o** charity,	1909
1Th	5: 8 **putting o** the breastplate of faith and love;	1746
2Th	1: 8 taking vengeance **o** them that know not	NIG
1Ti	1:16 hereafter believe **o** him to life everlasting.	1909
	1:18 the prophecies which went before **o** thee,	1909
	3:16 believed **o** in the world, received up into	NIG
	4:14 with the **laying o** of the hands of	1936
	5:22 **Lay** hands suddenly **o** no *man*, neither be	2007
	6:12 good fight of faith, **lay hold o** eternal life,	1949
	6:19 that they may **lay hold o** eternal life.	1949
2Ti	1: 6 which is in thee by the **putting o** of my	1936
	2:22 with them that **call o** the Lord out of a	1941
Tit	3: 6 Which he shed **o** us abundantly through	1909
	3:13 **Bring** Zenas the lawyer and Apollos	
	o their **journey**	4311
Phm	1:18 *thee* ought, **put** that **o** mine **account**;	1677
Heb	1: 3 sat down **o** the right hand of the Majesty	1722
	1: 3 down **o** the right hand of the Majesty **o**	1722
	1:13 Sit **o** my right hand, until I make thine	1537
	2:16 verily he **took** not **o** *him* the nature of	1949
	2:16 but he **took o** the seed of Abraham.	1949
	4: 4 place of the seventh *day* **o this wise**,	3779
	5: 2 Who can have compassion **o** the ignorant,	NIG
	5: 2 and **o** them that are out of the way;	NIG
	6: 1 of Christ, let us **go o** unto perfection;	5342
	6: 2 and of **laying o** of hands,	1936
	8: 1 who is set **o** the right hand of the throne	1722
	8: 4 For if he were **o** earth, he should not be a	1909
	9:10 imposed **o** *them* until the time of	NIG
	10:12 ever, sat down **o** the right hand of God;	1722
	11:13 were strangers and pilgrims **o** the earth.	1909
	12:25 not who refused him that spake **o** earth,	1909
Jas	3: 6 and **setteth o fire** the course of nature;	5394
	3: 6 of nature; and it is **set o fire** of hell.	5394
	4:14 know not what *shall be* **o** the **morrow**:	839
	5: 5 Ye have lived in pleasure **o** the earth,	1909
	5:17 it rained not **o** the earth *by the space of*	1909
1Pe	1:17 And if ye **call o** the Father, who without	1941
	2: 6 he that believeth **o** him shall not be	1909
	2:24 bare our sins in his own body **o** the tree,	1909
	3: 3 of gold, or of **putting o** of apparel;	1745
	3:22 heaven, and is **o** the right hand of God;	1722
	4:14 their **part** he is evil spoken of,	2596
	4:14 spoken of, but **o** your **part** he is glorified.	2596
	4:16 but let him glorify God **o** this behalf.	1722
2Pe	3:12 wherein the heavens being **o fire** shall be	4448
1Jn	3:23 That we should believe **o** the name of his	NIG
	5:10 He that believeth **o** the Son of God hath	1519
	5:13 that believe **o** the name of the Son of God;	1519
	5:13 that ye may believe **o** the name of the Son	1519
3Jn	1: 6 **bring forward o** their **journey** after a	4311
	1:20 building up yourselves **o** your most holy	NIG
Jude	1:10 I was in the spirit **o** the Lord's day,	1722
Rev	3: 3 I will come **o** thee as a thief, and thou	1909
	4: 2 set in heaven, and one sat **o** the throne.	1909
	4: 4 they had **o** their heads crowns of gold.	1909
	4: 9 and thanks to him that sat **o** the throne,	1909
	4:10 fall down before him that sat **o** the throne,	1909
	5: 1 that sat **o** the throne a book written	1909
	5: 1 book written within and **o the backside**,	3693
	5:10 priests: and we shall reign **o** the earth.	1909
	5:13 and **o** the earth, and under the earth,	1722
	6: 2 and he that sat **o** him had a bow;	1909
	6: 5 he that sat **o** him had a pair of balances in	1909
	6: 8 and his name that sat **o** him *was* Death,	1883
	6:10 avenge our blood **o** them that dwell on	575
	6:10 avenge our blood **o** them that dwell **o**	1909
	6:16 **Fall o** us, and hide us from the face of him	1909
	6:16 hide us from the face of him that sitteth **o**	1909
	7: 1 standing **o** the four corners of the earth,	1909
	7: 1 the wind should not blow **o** the earth,	1909
	7: 1 the earth, nor **o** the sea, nor on any tree.	1909
	7: 1 the earth, nor on the sea, nor **o** any tree.	1909
	7:11 and fell before the throne **o** their faces,	1909
	7:15 he that sitteth **o** the throne shall dwell	1909
	7:16 neither shall the sun light **o** them, nor any	1909
	9: 7 **o** their heads *were* as *it were* crowns like	1909
	9:17 and them that sat **o** them,	1909
	10: 2 upon the sea, and *his* left *foot* **o** the earth,	1909
	11:10 tormented them that dwelt **o** the earth.	1909
	11:16 which sat before God **o** their seats,	1909
	13:13 heaven **o** the earth in the sight of men,	1519
	13:14 deceiveth them that dwell **o** the earth	1909
	13:14 saying to them that dwell **o** the earth,	1909
	14: 1 and lo, a Lamb stood **o** the mount Sion,	1909
	14: 6 preach unto them that dwell **o** the earth,	1909
	14:14 having **o** his head a golden crown,	1909
	14:15 crying with a loud voice to him that sat **o**	1909
	14:16 And he that sat **o** the cloud thrust in his	1909
	14:16 the cloud thrust in his sickle **o** the earth;	1909
	15: 2 stand **o** the sea of glass, having *the* harps	1909
	17: 8 they that dwell **o** the earth shall wonder,	1909
	17: 9 **o** which the woman sitteth.	1909
	18:19 they cast dust **o** their heads, and cried,	1909
	18:20 for God hath avenged you **o** her.	1537
	19: 4 worshipped God that sat **o** the throne,	1909
	19:12 of fire, and **o** his head *were* many crowns;	1909
	19:16 he hath **o** *his* vesture and on his thigh a	1909
	19:16 vesture and **o** his thigh a name written,	1909
	19:18 of them that sit **o** them, and the flesh of	1909
	19:19 make war against him that sat **o** the horse,	1909
	20: 2 And he **laid hold o** the dragon, *that old*	2902
	20: 6 **o** such the second death hath no power,	1909
	20: 9 And they went up **o** the breadth of	1909

O

Rev 20:11 and him that sat **o** it, from whose face	*1909*
21:13 **O** the east three gates; on the north three	*575*
21:13 east three gates; **O** the north three gates;	*575*
21:13 **o** the south three gates; and on the west	*575*
21:13 three gates; and **o** the west three gates.	*575*

ONAM (4)

Ge 36:23 and Manahath, and Ebal, Shepho, and **O**.	*208*
1Ch 1:40 and Manahath, and Ebal, Shephi, and **O**.	*208*
2:26 *was* Atarah; she *was* the mother of **O**.	*208*
2:28 the sons of **O** were, Shammai, and Jada.	*208*

ONAN (8)

Ge 38: 4 and bare a son; and she called his name **O**.	*209*
38: 8 Judah said unto **O**, Go in unto thy	*209*
38: 9 **O** knew that the seed should not be his;	*209*
46:12 Er, and **O**, and Shelah, and Pharez,	*209*
46:12 Er and **O** died in the land of Canaan.	*209*
Nu 26:19 The sons of Judah *were* Er and **O**: and Er	*209*
26:19 and Er and **O** died in the land of Canaan.	*209*
1Ch 2: 3 The sons of Judah; Er, and **O**, and Shelah.	*209*

ONCE (59) [ONE]

Ge 18:32 be angry, and I will speak yet but *this* **o**:	*6471*
Ex 10:17 my sin only *this* **o**, and intreat the LORD	*6471*
30:10 **o** in a year with the blood of the sin	*259*
30:10 **o** in the year shall he make atonement	*259*
Lev 16:34 children of Israel for all their sins **o** a year.	*259*
Nu 13:30 Let us **go up** at **o**, and possess it;	*5927+5927*
Dt 7:22 thou mayest not consume them **at o**,	*4118*
Jos 6: 3 war, *and* go round about the city **o**,	*259+6471*
6:11 compassed the city, going about *it* **o**:	*259+6471*
6:14 day they compassed the city **o**,	*259+6471*
Jdg 6:39 against me, and I will speak but *this* **o**:	*6471*
6:39 I pray thee, but *this* **o** with the fleece;	*6471*
16:18 Come up *this* **o**, for he hath shewed	*6471*
16:28 I pray thee, only *this* **o**, O God,	*6471*
16:28 I may be **at o** avenged of the Philistines	*259*
1Sa 26: 8 with the spear even to the earth **at o**,	*259+6471*
1Ki 10:22 **o** in three years came the navy of	*259*
2Ki 6:10 and saved himself there, not **o** nor twice.	*259*
2Ch 9:21 every three years **o** came the ships of	*259*
Ne 5:18 and **o** in ten days store of all *sorts of* wine:	*996*
13:20 *kind of* ware lodged without Jerusalem **o**	*6471*
Job 33:14 For God speaketh **o**, yea twice,	*259+871.1*
40: 5 **O** have I spoken; but I will not answer:	*259*
Ps 62:11 God hath spoken **o**; twice have I heard	*259*
74: 6 the carved work thereof **at o** with axes	*3162*
76: 7 who may stand in thy sight **when o**	*227+4480*
89:35 **O** have I sworn by my holiness that I will	*259*
Pr 28:18 that is perverse in *his* ways shall fall **at o**.	*3162*
Isa 42:14 I will destroy and devour **at o**.	*3162*
66: 8 *or* shall a nation be born **at o**? for as	*259+6471*
Jer 10:18 out the inhabitants of the land at this **o**,	*6471*
13:27 not be made clean? when shall it **o** be?	*5750*
16:21 this **o** cause them to know,	*6471+871.1+1886.1*
Hag 2: 6 Yet **o**, it *is* a little while, and I *will* shake	*259*
Lk 13:25 **o** the master of the house	*302+575+3739*
23:18 And they cried out **all at o**, saying,	*3826*
Ro 6:10 For in that he died, he died unto sin **o**:	*2178*
7: 9 For I was alive without the law **o**:	*4218*
1Co 15: 6 seen of above five hundred brethren **at o**;	*2178*
2Co 11:25 **o** was I stoned, thrice I suffered shipwrack,	*530*
Gal 1:23 preacheth the faith which **o** he destroyed.	*4218*
Eph 5: 3 let it **not** be **o** named amongst you,	*3366*
Php 4:16 For even in Thessalonica ye sent **o** and	*530*
1Th 2:18 come unto you, even I Paul, **o** and again;	*530*
Heb 6: 4 For *it is* impossible for those who were **o**	*2178*
7:27 for this he did, **o**, when he offered up	*2178*
9: 7 *went* the high priest alone **o** every year,	*530*
9:12 by his own blood he entered in **o** into	*2178*
9:26 now **o** in the end of the world hath he	*530*
9:27 And as it is appointed unto men **o** to die,	*530*
9:28 So Christ was **o** offered to bear the sins of	*530*
10: 2 that the worshippers **o** purged should have	*530*
10:10 of the body of Jesus Christ **o for all**.	*2178*
12:26 Yet **o** *more* I shake not the earth only,	*530*
12:27 And this *word*, Yet **o** *more*, signifieth	*530*
1Pe 3:18 For Christ also hath **o** suffered for sins,	*530*
3:20 when **o** the longsuffering of God waited in	*530*
Jude 1: 3 faith which was **o** delivered unto the saints.	*530*
1: 5 though ye **o** knew this, how that the Lord,	*530*

ONE (1967) [ONCE, ONE'S, ONES]

Ge 1: 9 heaven be gathered together unto **o** place,	*259*
2:21 took **o** of his ribs, and closed up the flesh	*259*
2:24 unto his wife: and they shall be **o** flesh.	*259*
3: 6 a tree to be desired to make *o* wise, she	NIH
3:22 Behold, the man is become as **o** of us,	*259*
4:14 **every o** that findeth me shall slay me.	*3605*
4:19 name of the **o** *was* Adah, and the name of	*259*
10: 5 **every o** after his tongue, after their	*376*
10: 8 he began to be a mighty *o* in the earth.	NIH
10:25 the name of **o** *was* Peleg; for in his days	*259*
11: 1 And the whole earth was *of* **o** language,	*259*
11: 1 was *of* one language, and *of* **o** speech.	*259*
11: 3 They said **o** to another, Go to, let us make	*376*
11: 6 the people *is* **o**, and they have all one	*259*
11: 6 *is* one, and they have all **o** language;	*259*
11: 7 that they may not understand **o** another's	*376*
13:11 they separated themselves the **o** from	*376*
14:13 there came **o** that had escaped,	NIH
15: 3 and lo, **o** **born** in my house is mine heir.	*1121*
15:10 and laid each piece **o**'s against another:	*2050.2*
19: 9 they said *again*, This **o** *fellow* came in to	*259*

Ge 19:14 seemed as **o** that mocked unto his sons in	NIH
19:20 city *is* near to flee unto, and it *is* a **little** **o**:	*4705*
19:20 let me escape thither, (*is it* not a **little o**?)	*4705*
21:15 she cast the child under **o** of the shrubs.	*259*
22: 2 him there for a burnt offering upon **o** of	*259*
24:41 if they give not thee **o**, thou shalt be clear	NIH
25:23 the **o** people shall be stronger than the	NIH
26:10 **o** of the people might lightly have lien	*259*
26:26 Ahuzzath **o** of his friends, and Phichol	NIH
26:31 in the morning, and sware **o** to another;	*376*
27:29 cursed *be* every **o** that curseth thee,	NIH
27:38 Hast thou but **o** blessing, my father?	*259*
27:45 I be deprived also of you both **in o** day?	*259*
30:33 **every o** that *is* not speckled and	*3605*
30:35 *and* **every o** that had *some* white in it,	*3605*
31:49 when we are absent **o** from another.	*376*
32: 8 If Esau come to the **o** company, and smite	*259*
33:13 if *men* should overdrive them **o** day,	*259*
34:14 give our sister to **o** that is uncircumcised;	*376*
34:16 with you, and we will become **o** people.	*259*
34:22 to be **o** people, if every male among us be	*259*
37:19 said **o** to another, Behold, this dreamer	*376*
38:28 she travailed, that the **o** *put* out *his* hand:	NIH
40: 5 of them, each man his dream in **o** night,	*259*
41: 5 seven ears of corn came up upon **o** stalk,	*259*
41:11 we dreamed a dream in **o** night, I and he;	*259*
41:22 ears came up in **o** stalk, full and good:	*259*
41:25 unto Pharaoh, The dream of Pharaoh *is* **o**:	*259*
41:26 good ears *are* seven years: the dream *is* **o**.	*259*
41:38 Can we find *such a* **o** as this *is*, a man in	NIH
42: 1 his sons, Why do ye look **o** upon another?	NIH
42:11 We are all **o** man's sons; *we are* true *men*,	*259*
42:13 the sons of **o** man in the land of Canaan;	*259*
42:13 *is* this day with our father, and **o** *is* not.	*259*
42:16 Send **o** of you, and let him fetch your	*259*
42:19 If ye be true *men*, let **o** of your brethren be	*259*
42:21 they said **o** to another, We *are* verily guilty	*376*
42:27 as **o** *of them* opened his sack to give his ass	*259*
42:28 and they were afraid, saying **o** to another,	*376*
42:32 **o** *is* not, and the youngest *is* this day with	*259*
42:33 leave **o** of your brethren *here* with me,	*259*
43:33 and the men marvelled **o** at another.	*376*
44:20 and a child of *his* old age, a **little** **o**;	*6996*
44:28 the **o** went out from me, and I said, Surely	NIH
47:21 he removed them to cities from **o** end of	NIH
48: 1 that **o** told Joseph, Behold, thy father is	NIH
48: 2 **o** told Jacob, and said, Behold, thy son	NIH
48:22 Moreover I have given to thee **o** portion	NIH
49:16 judge his people, as **o** of the tribes of Israel.	*259*
49:28 **every o** according to his blessing he	*376*
Ex 1:15 of which the name of the **o** *was* Shiphrah,	*259*
2: 6 said, This *is* **o** of the Hebrews' children.	NIH
2:11 smiting a Hebrew, **o** of his brethren.	NIH
6:25 Eleazar Aaron's son took him **o** of	NIH
8:31 and from his people; there remained not **o**.	*259*
9: 6 cattle of the children of Israel died not **o**.	*259*
9: 7 was not **o** of the cattle of the Israelites	NIH
10: 5 that **o** cannot be able to see the earth:	NIH
10:19 remained not **o** locust in all the coasts	*259*
10:23 They saw not **o** another, neither rose any	*376*
11: 1 Yet will I bring **o** plague *more* upon	*259*
12:18 until the **o** and twentieth day of the month	*259*
12:30 not a house where *there was* not **o** dead.	NIH
12:46 In **o** house shall it be eaten; thou shalt not	*259*
12:48 he shall be as **o** that is born in the land:	NIH
12:49 **O** law shall be to him that is homeborn,	*259*
14: 7 and captains over **every o** of them.	*3605*
14:20 that the **o** came not near the other all	*2088*
14:28 there remained not so much as **o** of them.	*259*
16:15 of Israel saw *it*, they said **o** to another,	*376*
16:22 two omers for **o** *man:* and all the rulers of	*259*
17:12 the **o** on the one side, and the other on	*259*
17:12 the one on the **o** side, and the other	*2088*
18: 3 of which the name of the **o** *was* Gershom;	*259*
18:16 I judge between **o** and another, and I do	*376*
18:18 **o** smite another with a stone, or with *his*	*376*
21:35 if **o** **man's** ox hurt another's, that he die;	*376*
23:29 drive them out from before thee in **o** year;	*259*
24: 3 all the people answered with **o** voice,	*259*
25:12 and two rings shall be in the **o** side of it,	*259*
25:19 make a cherub on the one end, and	*259*
25:19 make one cherub on the **o** end,	*2088*
25:20 their faces *shall look* **o** to another;	*376*
25:32 branches of the candlestick out of the **o**	*259*
25:33 *with* a knop and a flower in **o** branch;	*259*
25:36 all it *shall* be **o** beaten work of pure gold.	*259*
26: 2 The length of **o** curtain shall be eight and	*259*
26: 2 the breadth of **o** curtain four cubits:	*1886.1*
26: 2 every **o** of the curtains shall have one	*259*
26: 2 every **o** of the curtains shall have **o**	*259*
26: 3 five curtains shall be coupled together **o**	*802*
26: 3 *other* five curtains *shall be* coupled **o o**	*802*
26: 4 curtain from the selvedge in the	*259*
26: 5 loops shalt thou make in the **o** curtain,	*259*
26: 5 that the loops may take hold of another.	*802*
26: 6 the taches: and it shall be **o** tabernacle.	*259*
26: 8 length of **o** curtain *shall be* thirty cubits,	*259*
26: 8 and the breadth of **o** curtain four cubits:	*259*
26: 8 eleven curtains *shall be* all of **o** measure.	*259*
26:10 curtain that *is* outmost in the coupling,	*259*
26:11 couple the tent together, that it may be **o**.	*259*
26:13 a cubit on the **o** side, and a cubit on	*2088*
26:16 and a half *shall be* the breadth of **o** board.	*259*
26:17 Two tenons *shall there be* in **o** board, set	*259*
26:17 one board, set in order **o** against	*802*

Ex 26:19 two sockets under **o** board for his two	*259*
26:21 two sockets under **o** board, and two	*259*
26:24 together above the head of it unto **o** ring:	*259*
26:25 two sockets under **o** board, and two	*259*
26:26 five for the boards of the **o** side of	*259*
27: 9 linen of an hundred cubits long for **o** side:	*259*
27:14 The hangings of **o** side *of the gate shall*	NIH
28:10 Six of their names on **o** stone, and the	*259*
28:21 **every o** with his name shall they be	*376*
29: 1 Take **o** young bullock, and two rams	*259*
29: 3 thou shalt put them into **o** basket,	*259*
29:15 Thou shalt also take **o** ram; and Aaron and	*259*
29:23 **o** loaf of bread, and one cake of oiled	*259*
29:23 **o** cake of oiled bread, and one wafer out	*259*
29:23 **o** wafer out of the basket of the	*259*
29:39 **o** lamb thou shalt offer in the morning;	*259*
29:40 the **o** lamb a tenth deal of flour mingled	*259*
30:13 **every o** that passeth among them that are	*3605*
30:14 **Every o** that passeth among them that are	*3605*
31:14 *every* **o** that defileth it shall surely be put	NIH
32:15 on the **o** side and on the other were they	*2088*
33: 7 *that* **every o** which sought the LORD went	*3605*
34:15 **o** call thee, and thou eat of his sacrifice;	NIH
35:21 every **o** whose heart stirred him up,	*376*
35:21 **o** whom his spirit made willing,	*3605*
35:24 **Every o** that did offer an offering of silver	*3605*
36: 2 *even* **every o** whose heart stirred him up	*3605*
36: 9 The length of **o** curtain *was* twenty and	*259*
36: 9 The breadth of **o** curtain four cubits:	*259*
36: 9 four cubits: the curtains *were* all of **o** size.	*259*
36:10 coupled the five curtains **o** unto another:	*259*
36:10 *the other* five curtains he coupled **o** unto	*259*
36:11 he made loops of blue on the edge of **o**	*259*
36:12 Fifty loops made he in **o** curtain,	*259*
36:12 the loops held **o** *curtain* to another.	*259*
36:13 coupled the curtains **o** unto another with	*259*
36:13 with the taches: so it became **o** tabernacle.	*259*
36:15 The length of **o** curtain *was* thirty cubits,	*259*
36:15 four cubits *was* the breadth of **o** curtain:	*259*
36:15 the eleven curtains *were* of **o** size.	*259*
36:18 couple the tent together, that *it* might be **o**.	*259*
36:21 the breadth of a board **o** cubit and a half.	*259*
36:22 **O** board had two tenons, equally distant	*259*
36:22 tenons, equally distant **o** from another:	*259*
36:24 two sockets under **o** board for his two	*259*
36:26 sockets under **o** board, and two sockets	*259*
36:29 together at the head thereof, to **o** ring:	*259*
36:31 five for the boards of the **o** side of	*259*
36:33 the boards from **the** **o** end to the other.	*1886.1*
37: 3 even two rings upon the **o** side of it,	*259*
37: 6 and a cubit and a half the breadth thereof.	*259*
37: 7 **beaten** out of **o** piece made he them,	*4749*
37: 8 **O** cherub on the end on this side,	*259*
37: 9 mercy seat, with their faces **o** to another;	*376*
37:18 branches of the candlestick out of the **o**	*259*
37:19 after the fashion of almonds in **o** branch,	*259*
37:22 all of it *was* **o** beaten work *of* pure gold.	*259*
38:14 The hangings of **o** side *of the gate*	NIH
38:26 for **every o** that went to be numbered,	*3605*
39:14 **every o** with his name, according to	*259*
Lev 4:27 if any **o** of the common people sin through	*5315*
5: 4 of *it*, then he shall be guilty in **o** of these,	*259*
5: 5 he shall be guilty in **o** of these *things*,	*259*
5: 7 **o** for a sin offering, and the other for a	*259*
5:13 his sin that he hath sinned in **o** of these,	*259*
6:18 **every o** that toucheth them shall be holy.	*3605*
7: 7 *there is* **o** law for them: the priest that	*259*
7:10 sons of Aaron have, **o** *as much* as another.	*376*
7:14 of it he shall offer **o** out of the whole	*259*
8:26 he took **o** unleavened cake, and a cake of	*259*
8:26 wafer, and put *them* on the fat,	*259*
11:26 **every o** that toucheth them shall be	*3605*
12: 8 the **o** for the burnt offering, and the other	*259*
13: 2 the priest, or unto **o** of his sons the priests:	*259*
14: 5 the priest shall command that **o** of the birds	*259*
14:10 ewe lamb of the first year without	*259*
14:10 mingled with oil, and **o** log of oil.	*259*
14:12 priest shall take **o** he lamb, and offer him	*259*
14:21 he shall take **o** lamb *for a* trespass offering	*259*
14:21 **o** **tenth deal** of fine flour mingled	*259+6241*
14:22 the **o** shall be a sin offering, and the other	*259*
14:30 And he shall offer the **o** of the turtledoves,	*259*
14:31 the **o** *for a* sin offering, and the other *for a*	*259*
14:50 he shall kill the **o** of the birds in an earthen	*259*
15:15 the **o** *for a* sin offering, and the other *for a*	*259*
15:30 the priest shall offer the **o** *for a* sin offering,	*259*
16: 5 sin offering, and **o** ram for a burnt offering.	*259*
16: 8 lot for the LORD, and the other lot for	*259*
16:27 shall *o* carry forth without the camp;	NIH
16:29 no work at all, *whether it be* **o** of your	*1886.1*
17:15 *whether it be* **o** of your **own country**,	*1886.1*
18:30 that ye commit not *any* **o** of these	NIH
19: 8 Therefore *every* **o** that eateth it shall bear	NIH
19:11 neither deal falsely, neither lie **o** to another.	*376*
19:34 shall be unto you as **o** **born amongst** you,	*249*
20: 9 For **every o** that curseth his father or	*376+376*
22:28 not kill it and her young both in **o** day.	*259*
23:18 and **o** young bullock, and two rams:	*259*
23:19 ye shall sacrifice **o** kid of the goats for a sin	*259*
24: 5 two tenth deals shall be in **o** cake.	*259*
24:22 Ye shall have **o** **manner** of law, as well for	*259*
24:22 stranger, as for **o** of your **own country**:	*249*
25:14 ye shall not oppress **o** another:	*376*
25:17 Ye shall not therefore oppress **o** another;	*376*
25:46 shall not rule **o** over another with rigour.	*376*

O

Lev 25:48 o of his brethren may redeem him: 259
26:26 women shall bake your bread in o oven, 259
26:37 they shall fall o upon another, as it were 376
Nu 1: 4 every o head of the house of his fathers. 376
1:41 forty and o thousand and five hundred. 259
1:44 each o was for the house of his fathers. 259
2:16 fifty and o thousand and four hundred and 259
2:28 forty and o thousand and five hundred. 259
2:34 set forward, **every** o after their families, 376
4:19 appoint them **every** o to his service 376+376
4:30 **every** o that entereth into the service, 3605
4:35 **every** o that entereth into the service, 3605
4:39 **every** o that entereth into the service, 3605
4:43 **every** o that entereth into the service, 3605
4:47 **every** o that came to do the service of 3605
4:49 **every** o according to his service, 376+376
5: o **every** o that hath an issue, 3605
6:11 the priest shall offer the o for a sin offering, 259
6:14 he lamb of the first year without blemish 259
6:14 o ewe lamb of the first year without 259
6:14 o ram without blemish for peace offerings, 259
6:19 and o unleavened cake out of the basket, 259
6:19 o unleavened wafer, and shall put *them* 259
7: 3 two of the princes, and for *each* o an ox: 259
7:13 offering *was* o silver charger, the weight 259
7:13 thirty *shekels,* o silver bowl of seventy 259
7:14 o spoon of gold, full *of* 259
7:15 O young bullock, one ram, one lamb of 259
7:15 One young bullock, o ram, one lamb of 259
7:15 one ram, o lamb of the first year, 259
7:16 O kid of the goats for a sin offering: 259
7:19 He offered *for* his offering o silver charger, 259
7:19 thirty *shekels,* o silver bowl of seventy 259
7:20 O spoon of gold of ten *shekels,* full *of* 259
7:21 O young bullock, one ram, one lamb of 259
7:21 One young bullock, o ram, one lamb of 259
7:21 one ram, o lamb of the first year, 259
7:22 O kid of the goats for a sin offering: 259
7:25 offering *was* o silver charger, the weight 259
7:25 thirty *shekels,* o silver bowl of seventy 259
7:26 O golden spoon of ten *shekels,* full *of* 259
7:27 O young bullock, one ram, one lamb of 259
7:27 One young bullock, o ram, one lamb of 259
7:27 one ram, o lamb of the first year, 259
7:28 O kid of the goats for a sin offering: 259
7:31 His offering *was* o silver charger of 259
7:31 thirty *shekels,* o silver bowl of seventy 259
7:32 O golden spoon of ten *shekels,* full *of* 259
7:33 O young bullock, one ram, one lamb of 259
7:33 One young bullock, o ram, one lamb of 259
7:33 one ram, o lamb of the first year, 259
7:34 O kid of the goats for a sin offering: 259
7:37 offering *was* o silver charger, the weight 259
7:37 thirty *shekels,* o silver bowl of seventy 259
7:38 O golden spoon of ten *shekels,* full *of* 259
7:39 O young bullock, one ram, one lamb of 259
7:39 One young bullock, o ram, one lamb of 259
7:39 one ram, o lamb of the first year, 259
7:40 O kid of the goats for a sin offering: 259
7:43 His offering *was* o silver charger of 259
7:44 O golden spoon of ten *shekels,* full *of* 259
7:45 O young bullock, one ram, one lamb of 259
7:45 One young bullock, o ram, one lamb of 259
7:45 one ram, o lamb of the first year, 259
7:46 O kid of the goats for a sin offering: 259
7:49 offering *was* o silver charger, the weight 259
7:49 thirty *shekels,* o silver bowl of seventy 259
7:50 O golden spoon of ten *shekels,* full *of* 259
7:51 O young bullock, one ram, one lamb of 259
7:51 One young bullock, o ram, one lamb of 259
7:51 one ram, o lamb of the first year, 259
7:52 O kid of the goats for a sin offering: 259
7:55 His offering *was* o silver charger of 259
7:55 thirty *shekels,* o silver bowl of seventy 259
7:56 O golden spoon of ten *shekels,* full *of* 259
7:57 O young bullock, one ram, one lamb of 259
7:57 One young bullock, o ram, one lamb of 259
7:57 one ram, o lamb of the first year, 259
7:58 O kid of the goats for a sin offering: 259
7:61 offering *was* o silver charger, the weight 259
7:61 thirty *shekels,* o silver bowl of seventy 259
7:62 O golden spoon of ten *shekels,* full *of* 259
7:63 O young bullock, one ram, one lamb of 259
7:63 One young bullock, o ram, one lamb of 259
7:63 one ram, o lamb of the first year, 259
7:64 O kid of the goats for a sin offering: 259
7:67 offering *was* o silver charger, the weight 259
7:67 thirty *shekels,* o silver bowl of seventy 259
7:68 O golden spoon of ten *shekels,* full *of* 259
7:69 O young bullock, one ram, one lamb of 259
7:69 One young bullock, o ram, one lamb of 259
7:69 one ram, o lamb of the first year, 259
7:70 O kid of the goats for a sin offering: 259
7:73 offering *was* o silver charger, the weight 259
7:73 thirty *shekels,* o silver bowl of seventy 259
7:74 O golden spoon of ten *shekels,* full *of* 259
7:75 O young bullock, one ram, one lamb of 259
7:75 One young bullock, o ram, one lamb of 259
7:75 one ram, o lamb of the first year, 259
7:76 O kid of the goats for a sin offering: 259
7:79 offering *was* o silver charger, the weight 259
7:79 thirty *shekels,* o silver bowl of seventy 259
7:80 O golden spoon of ten *shekels,* full *of* 259
7:81 O young bullock, one ram, one lamb of 259
7:81 One young bullock, o ram, one lamb of 259

Nu 7:81 one ram, o lamb of the first year, 259
7:82 O kid of the goats for a sin offering: 259
7:89 he heard the voice of o speaking unto him NIH
8:12 thou shalt offer the o for a sin offering, 259
9:14 ye shall have o ordinance, both for 259
10: 4 *but* with o *trumpet,* then the princes, 259
11:19 Ye shall not eat o day, nor two days, nor 259
11:26 name of the o *was* Eldad, and the name 259
11:28 o of his young men, answered and said, NIH
12:12 Let her not be as o dead, of whom 1886.1
13: 2 send a man, **every** o a ruler among them. 3605
13:23 cut down from thence a branch with o 259
14: 4 said o to another, Let us make a captain, 376
14:15 Now *if* thou shalt kill *all* this people as o 259
15: 5 the burnt offering or sacrifice, for o lamb. 259
15:11 Thus shall it be done for o bullock, 259
15:11 or for o ram, or for a lamb, or a kid. 259
15:12 shall ye do to *every* o according to their 259
15:15 O ordinance *shall be* both for you of 259
15:16 O law and one manner shall be for you, 259
15:16 One law and o manner shall be for you, 259
15:24 all the congregation shall offer o young 259
15:24 and o kid of the goats for a sin offering. 259
15:29 You shall have o law for him that sinneth 259
16: 3 **every** o of them, that the Lord *is* among 3605
16:15 I have not taken o ass from them, 259
16:15 from them, neither have I hurt o of them. 259
16:22 shall o man sin, and wilt thou be wroth 259
17: 2 take of every o of them a rod according to NIH
17: 3 for o rod *shall be* for the head of the house 259
17: 6 **every** o of their princes gave him a rod 3605
17: 6 each prince o, according to their fathers' 259
18:11 **every** o *that is* clean in thy house shall eat 3605
18:13 **every** o *that is* clean in thine house shall 3605
19: 3 and o shall slay her before his face: NIH
19: 5 o shall burn the heifer in his sight; her NIH
19:16 whosoever toucheth o that is slain with 1886.1
19:18 bone, or o slain, or one dead, or a grave: 1886.1
19:18 bone, or one slain, or o dead, or a grave: 1886.1
21: 8 come to pass, that **every** o that is bitten, 3605
25: 5 Slay ye **every** o his men that were joined 376
25: 6 of the children of Israel came and 376
26:54 *to* **every** o shall his inheritance be given 259
28: 4 The o lamb shalt thou offer in the morning, 259
28: 7 *be* the fourth *part* of a hin for the o lamb: 259
28:11 young bullocks, and o ram, seven lambs 259
28:12 mingled with oil, for o bullock; 259
28:12 meat offering, mingled with oil, for o ram; 259
28:13 with oil *for* a meat offering unto o lamb; 259
28:15 o kid of the goats for a sin offering unto 259
28:19 o ram, and seven lambs of the first year: 259
28:22 o goat for a sin offering, to make an 259
28:27 two young bullocks, o ram, seven lambs of 259
28:28 three tenth deals unto o bullock, two tenth 259
28:28 one bullock, two tenth deals unto o ram, 259
28:29 several tenth deal unto o lamb, throughout 259
28:30 *And* o kid of the goats, to make an 259
29: 2 o young bullock, one ram, *and* seven lambs 259
29: 2 o ram, *and* seven lambs of the first year 259
29: 4 o tenth deal for one lamb, throughout 259
29: 4 one tenth deal for o lamb, throughout 259
29: 5 o kid of the goats for a sin offering, to make 259
29: 8 o young bullock, one ram, *and* seven lambs 259
29: 8 o ram, *and* seven lambs of the first year; 259
29: 9 to a bullock, *and* two tenth deals to o ram, 259
29:10 A several tenth deal for o lamb, throughout 259
29:11 O kid of the goats *for* a sin offering; beside 259
29:16 o kid of the goats *for* a sin offering; beside 259
29:19 o kid of the goats *for* a sin offering; beside 259
29:22 o goat for a sin offering; beside the 259
29:25 o kid of the goats for a sin offering; beside 259
29:28 o goat for a sin offering; beside the 259
29:31 o goat for a sin offering; beside the 259
29:34 o goat for a sin offering; beside the 259
29:36 o bullock, one ram, seven lambs of the first 259
29:36 one bullock, o ram, seven lambs of the first 259
29:38 o goat for a sin offering; beside the 259
31:28 o soul of five hundred, *both* of the persons, 259
31:30 thou shalt take o portion of fifty, 259
31:34 And threescore and o thousand asses, 259
31:39 *was* threescore and o. 259+8346+2050.1
31:47 Moses took o portion of fifty, *both* of man 259
31:49 and there lacketh not o **man** of us. 376
34:18 ye shall take o prince of every tribe, 376
35: 8 **every** o shall give of his cities unto 259
35:15 that **every** o that killeth *any* person 3605
35:30 o witness shall not testify against *any* 259
36: 7 for **every** o of the children of Israel shall 376
36: 8 be wife unto o of the family of the tribe 259
36: 9 shall the inheritance remove from o NIH
36: 9 **every** o of the tribes of the children of 376
Dt 1:22 ye came near unto me **every** o of you, 3605
1:23 I took twelve men of you, o of a tribe: 259
1:35 Surely there shall not o of these men of 376
2:36 there was not o city too strong for us: NIH
4: 4 God *are* alive **every** o of you *this* day. 3605
4:32 *ask* from the o side of heaven unto NIH
4:42 that fleeing unto o of these cities he might 259
6: 4 O Israel: The Lord our God *is* o Lord: 259
12:14 the Lord shall choose in o of thy tribes, 259
13: 7 from the o end of the earth even unto NIH
13:12 If thou shalt hear *say* in o of thy cities, 259
15: 7 be among you a poor man of o of thy 259
17: 6 at the mouth of o witness he shall not be 259
17:15 o from among thy brethren shalt thou set NIH

Dt 18:10 There shall not be found among you *any* o NIH
19: 5 shall flee unto o of those cities, and live: 259
19:11 he die, and fleeth into o of these cities, 259
19:15 O witness shall not rise up against a man 259
21: 1 If *o* be found slain in the land which NIH
21:15 o beloved, and another hated, and they 259
23:16 in *that* place which he shall choose in o of 259
24: 5 *but* he shall be free at home o year, 259
25: 5 and o of them die, and have no child, 259
25:11 When men strive together o with another, 376
25:11 wife of the o draweth near for to deliver 259
28: 7 they shall come out against thee o way, 259
28:25 thou shalt go out o way against them, 259
28:57 towards her **young** o that cometh out 7988
28:64 from the o end of the earth even unto NIH
32:30 How should o chase a thousand, and two 259
33: 3 thy feet; *every* o shall receive of thy words. NIH
33: 8 and thy Urim *be* with thy holy o, 376
Jos 9: 2 with Joshua and with Israel, *with* o accord. 259
10: 2 as o of the royal cities, and because it *was* 259
10:42 and their land did Joshua take *at* o time, 259
12: 9 The king of Jericho, o; the king of Ai, 259
12: 9 the king of Ai, which *is* beside Beth-el, o; 259
12:10 The king of Jerusalem, o; the king of 259
12:10 of Jerusalem, one; the king of Hebron, o; 259
12:11 The king of Jarmuth, o; the king of Lachish, 259
12:11 of Jarmuth, one; the king of Lachish, o; 259
12:12 The king of Eglon, o; the king of Gezer, 259
12:12 king of Eglon, one; the king of Gezer, o; 259
12:13 The king of Debir, o; the king of Geder, 259
12:13 king of Debir, one; the king of Geder, o; 259
12:14 The king of Hormah, o; the king of Arad, 259
12:14 king of Hormah, one; the king of Arad, o; 259
12:15 king of Libnah, o; the king of Adullam, 259
12:15 of Libnah, one; the king of Adullam, o; 259
12:16 The king of Makkedah, o; the king of 259
12:16 of Makkedah, one; the king of Beth-el, o; 259
12:17 king of Tappuah, o; the king of Hepher, 259
12:17 of Tappuah, one; the king of Hepher, o; 259
12:18 king of Aphek, o; the king of Lasharon, 259
12:18 of Aphek, one; the king of Lasharon, o; 259
12:19 The king of Madon, o; the king of Hazor, 259
12:19 king of Madon, one; the king of Hazor, o; 259
12:20 The king of Shimron-meron, o; the king of 259
12:20 one; the king of Achshaph, o; 259
12:21 The king of Taanach, o; the king of 259
12:21 of Taanach, one; the king of Megiddo, o; 259
12:22 king of Kedesh, o; the king of Jokneam 259
12:22 one; the king of Jokneam of Carmel, o; 259
12:23 The king of Dor in the coast of Dor, o; 259
12:23 one; the king of the nations of Gilgal, o; 259
12:24 The king of Tirzah, o: all the kings thirty 259
12:24 of Tirzah, one: all the kings thirty and o. 259
13:31 to the o **half** of the children of Machir 2677
17:14 me *but* o lot and one portion to inherit, 259
17:14 me *but* one lot and o portion to inherit, 259
17:17 power: thou shalt not have o lot *only:* 259
20: 4 he that doth flee unto o of those cities 259
21:42 These **cities** were **every** o with 5892+5892
22: 7 Now to the o half of the tribe of Manasseh NIH
22:14 **each** o *was* a head of the house of their 376
23:10 O man of you shall chase a thousand: 259
23:14 that not o thing hath failed of all the good 259
23:14 you, *and* not o thing hath failed thereof. 259
Jdg 6:16 thou shalt smite the Midianites as o man. 259
6:29 they said o to another, Who hath done 376
6:31 because o hath cast down his altar. NIH
7: 5 **Every** o that lappeth of the water with 3605
7: 5 likewise **every** o that boweth down upon 3605
8:18 *each* o resembled the children of a king. 259
9: 2 reign over you, or that o reign over you? 259
9: 5 and ten persons, upon o stone: 259
9:18 upon o stone, and have made Abimelech, 259
10:18 *and* princes of Gilead said o to another, 376
11:35 and thou art o of them that trouble me: NIH
12: 7 and was buried in *o* of the cities of Gilead. NIH
16: 5 we will give thee **every** o *of us* eleven 376
16:29 the o with his right hand, and of the other 259
17: 5 teraphim, and consecrated o of his sons, 259
17:11 the young man was unto him as o of his 259
18:19 to be a priest unto the house of o man, 259
19:13 us draw near to o of *these* places to lodge 259
20: 1 congregation was gathered together as o 259
20: 8 all the people arose as o man, saying, 259
20:11 against the city, knit together as o man. 259
20:16 every o could sling stones at a hair 2088
20:31 *of* which o goeth up *to* the house of God, 259
21: 3 that there should be to day o tribe lacking 259
21: 6 There is o tribe cut off from Israel *this* day. 259
21: 8 What *is there* o of the tribes of Israel that 259
Ru 1: 4 name of the o *was* Orpah, and the name 259
2:13 though I be not like unto o of thy 259
2:20 of kin unto us, o of our next kinsmen. 4480
3:14 she rose up before o could know another. 376
4: 1 **such** a o, turn aside, sit down here. 492+6423
1Sa 1: 2 name of the o *was* Hannah, and the name 259
1:24 ephah of flour, and a bottle of wine, 259
2:25 If o **man** sin against another, the judge 376
2:34 in o day they shall die both of them. 259
2:36 that **every** o that is left in thine house 3605
2:36 I pray thee, into o of the priests' offices, 259
3:11 *at* which both the ears of **every** o that 3605
6: 4 for o plague *was* on you all, and on your 259
6:17 for Ashdod o, for Gaza one, for Askelon 259
6:17 for Ashdod one, for Gaza o, for Askelon 259

1Sa
6:17 for Gaza one, for Askelon o, for Gath one, 259
6:17 for Askelon one, for Gath o, for Ekron one; 259
6:17 for Askelon one, for Gath o, for Ekron o; 259
9: 3 Take now o of the servants with thee, 259
10: 3 o carrying three kids, and another carrying 259
10:11 then the people said o to another, 376
10:12 o of the same place answered and said, 376
11: 7 and they came out with o consent. 259
13: 1 Saul reigned o year; and when he had 1121
13:17 o company turned unto the way that 259
14: 4 there was a sharp rock on the o side, 2088
14: 4 the name of the o was Bozez, and the 259
14: 5 The forefront of the o was situate 259
14:16 they went on beating down o another. NIH
14:28 answered o of the people, and said, 376
14:40 Be ye on o side, and I and Jonathan my 259
14:45 there shall not o hair of his head fall to 4480
16:18 answered o of the servants, and said, 259
17: 3 stood on a mountain on the o side, 2088
17: 7 and o bearing a shield went before him. NIH
17:36 this uncircumcised Philistine shall be as o 259
18: 7 The women answered o another as they NIH
18:21 be my son in law in the o of the twain. NIH
19:22 o said, Behold, they be at Naioth in NIH
20:15 David every o from the face of the earth. 376
20:41 they kissed o another, and wept one with 376
20:41 wept o with another, until David exceeded. 376
21:11 did they not sing o to another of him in NIH
22: 2 every o that was in distress, and every one 376
22: 2 every o that was in debt, and every one 376
22: 2 debt, and every o that was discontented, 376
22: 7 will the son of Jesse give every o of you 3605
22:20 o of the sons of Ahimelech the son of 259
25:14 o of the young men told Abigail, 259
26:15 there came o of the people in to destroy 259
26:20 as when o doth hunt a partridge in NIH
26:22 let o of the young men come over and 259
27: 1 shall now perish o day by the hand of Saul; 259
29: 5 of whom they sang o to another in dances, NIH

2Sa
1:15 David called o of the young men, and said, 259
2:13 the o on the one side of the pool, 428
2:13 the one on the o side of the pool, 2088+4480
2:16 caught every o his fellow by the head, 376
2:21 and lay thee hold on o of the young men, 259
2:25 became o troop, and stood on the top of a 259
2:27 up every o from following his brother. 376
3:13 o thing I require of thee, that is, Thou shalt 259
3:29 let there not fail from the house of Joab o NIH
4: 2 the name of the o was Baanah, and the 259
4:10 When o told me, saying, Behold, Saul is 1886.1
6:19 to every o a cake of bread, and a good 376
6:19 the people departed every o to his house. 376
6:20 as o of the vain fellows shamelessly 259
7:23 o nation in the earth is like thy people, 259
8: 2 and with o full line to keep alive. 1886.1
9:11 eat at my table, as o of the king's sons. 259
10: 4 shaved off the o half of their beards, NIH
11: 3 o said, Is not this Bath-sheba, the daughter NIH
11:25 for the sword devoureth o as well as 2090
12: 1 unto him, There were two men in o city; 259
12: 1 in one city; the o rich, and the other poor. 259
12: 3 save o little ewe lamb, which he had 259
13:13 thou shalt be as o of the fools in Israel. 259
13:30 king's sons, and there is not o of them left. NIH
14: 6 but the o smote the other, and slew him. 259
14:11 there shall not o hair of thy son fall to 4480
14:12 speak o word unto my lord the king. NIH
14:13 the king doth speak this thing as o which NIH
14:27 and o daughter, whose name was Tamar: 259
15: 2 Thy servant is of o of the tribes of Israel. NIH
15:31 o told David, saying, Ahithophel is among NIH
17:12 him there shall not be left so much as o. 259
17:13 there be not o small stone found there. NIH
17:22 by the morning light there lacked not o of 259
18:17 and all Israel fled every o to his tent. 376
19: 7 there will not tarry o with thee this night: 376
19:14 men of Judah, even as the heart of o man; 259
20:11 o of Joab's men stood by him, and said, 376
20:12 he saw that every o that came by him 3605
20:19 I am o of them that are peaceable and NIH
23: 8 eight hundred, whom he slew at o time. 259
23: 9 o of the three mighty men with David, NIH
23:15 that o would give me drink of the water NIH
23:24 Asahel the brother of Joab was o of 871.1
24:12 I offer thee three things; choose thee o of 259

1Ki
1:48 which hath given o to sit on my throne NIH
2:16 now I ask o petition of thee, deny me not. 259
2:20 she said, I desire o small petition of thee; 259
3:17 the o woman said, O my lord, I and 259
3:17 lord, I and this woman dwell in o house; 259
3:23 said the king, The o saith, This is my son 2063
3:25 give half to the o, and half to the other. 259
4:22 Solomon's provision for o day was thirty 259
6:24 five cubits was the o wing of the cherub, 259
6:24 from the uttermost part of the o wing 2050.2
6:25 both the cherubims were of o measure 259
6:25 cherubims were of one measure and o size. 259
6:26 The height of the o cherub was ten cubits, 259
6:27 the wing of the o touched the one wall, 259
6:27 the wing of the one touched the o wall, 259
6:27 wings touched o another 413+3671+3671
6:34 the two leaves of the o door were folding, 259
7: 1 it was covered with cedar from o side of 4480
7:16 the height of the o chapter was five cubits, 259
7:17 seven for the o chapter, and seven for 259

1Ki
7:18 rows round about upon the o network, 259
7:23 ten cubits from the o^S brim to the other: 2050.2
7:27 four cubits was the length of o base, 259
7:34 undersetters to the four corners of o base: 259
7:36 according to the proportion of every o, 376
7:37 all of them had o casting, one measure, 259
7:37 had one casting, o measure, and one size. 259
7:37 had one casting, one measure, and o size. 259
7:38 o laver contained forty baths: 259
7:38 upon every o of the ten bases one laver. 259
7:38 upon every one of the ten bases o laver. 259
7:42 even two rows of pomegranates for o 259
7:44 And o sea, and twelve oxen under the sea; 259
8:56 there hath not failed o word of all his good 259
9: 8 every o that passeth by it shall be 3605
10:14 in o year was six hundred threescore 259
10:16 hundred shekels of gold went to o target. 259
10:17 three pound of gold went to o shield: 259
10:20 twelve lions stood there on the o side 2088
11:13 will give o tribe to thy son for David my 259
11:32 (But he shall have o tribe for my servant 259
11:36 unto his son will I give o tribe, that David 259
12:29 he set the o in Beth-el, and the other put 259
12:30 the people went to worship before the o, 259
13:33 he became o of the priests of the high NIH
14:21 and o years old when he began to reign, 259
15:10 and o years reigned he in Jerusalem. 259
16:11 left him not o that pisseth against a wall, NIH
18: 6 Ahab went o way by himself, 259
18:23 let them choose o bullock for themselves, 259
18:25 Choose you o bullock for yourselves, 259
18:40 prophets of Baal; let not o of them escape. 376
19: 2 if I make not thy life as the life of o of 259
20:20 slew every o his man: and the Syrians 376
20:29 pitched o over against the other seven 428
20:29 an hundred thousand footmen in o day. 259
22: 8 There is yet o man, Micaiah the son of 259
22:13 declare good unto the king with o mouth: 259
22:13 be like the word of o of them, and speak 259
22:20 o said on this manner, and another said 2088
22:28 said, Hearken, O people, every o of you. 3605
22:38 o washed the chariot in the pool of NIH

2Ki
3:11 o of the king of Israel's servants answered 259
3:23 and they have smitten o another: 376
4:22 o of the young men, and one of the asses, 259
4:22 one of the young men, and o of the asses, 259
4:39 went out into the field to gather herbs, 259
5: 4 went in, and told his lord, saying, Thus NIH
6: 3 o said, Be content, I pray thee, and go with 259
6: 5 as o was felling a beam, the axe head fell 259
6:12 o of his servants said, None, my lord, 259
7: 3 said o to another, Why sit we here until 376
7: 6 said o to another, Lo, the king of Israel 376
7: 8 went into o tent, and did eat and drink, 259
7: 9 they said o to another, We do not well: 376
7:13 of his servants answered and said, 376
8:26 reign; and he reigned o year in Jerusalem. 259
9: 1 Elisha the prophet called o of the children 259
9:11 o said unto him, Is all well? wherefore NIH
9:18 there went o on horseback to meet him, NIH
10:21 the house of Baal was full from o end to 6310
12: 4 even the money of every o that passeth 376
12: 9 the right side as o cometh into the house 259
14: 8 Come, let us look o another in the face. NIH
14:11 Amaziah king of Judah looked o another NIH
14:23 in Samaria, and reigned forty and o years. 259
17:27 Carry thither o of the priests whom ye 259
17:28 o of the priests whom they had carried 259
18:24 wilt thou turn away the face of o captain 259
18:31 every o of his fig tree, and drink ye every 376
18:31 drink ye every o the waters of his cistern: 376
19:22 even against the Holy O of Israel. 6918
21:16 till he had filled Jerusalem from o end to 6310
22: 1 he reigned thirty and o years in Jerusalem. 259
23:35 of every o according to his taxation, to 376
24:18 and o years old when he began to reign, 259
25:16 o sea, and the bases which Solomon had 259
25:17 The height of the o pillar was eighteen 259

1Ch
1:19 name of the o was Peleg; because in his 259
9:31 Mattithiah, o of the Levites, who was NIH
10:13 also for asking counsel of o that had a NIH
11:11 three hundred slain by him at o time. NIH
11:12 who was o of the three mighties. NIH
11:17 that o would give me drink of the water NIH
12:14 o of the least was over an hundred, 259
11:25 the war, seven thousand and o hundred. 3967
12:38 all the rest also of Israel were of o heart to NIH
16: 3 he dealt to every o of Israel, both man and 376
16: 3 to every o a loaf of bread, and a good 259
16:20 and from o kingdom to another people; NIH
17: 5 to tent, and from o tabernacle to another. 259
17:21 o nation in the earth is like thy people 259
21:10 I offer thee three things; choose thee o of 259
23:11 therefore they were in o reckoning, 259
24: 5 they divided by lot, o sort with another; 428
24: 6 o of the Levites, wrote them before NIH
24: 6 principal household being taken for 259
24: 6 taken for Eleazar, and o taken for Ithamar. 259
24:17 The o and twentieth to Jachin, the two 259
25:28 The o and twentieth to Hothir, the his 259
26:12 men, having wards o against another, NIH
27:18 Judah, Elihu, o of the brethren of David: NIH
29: 7 and o hundred thousand talents of iron. 3967

2Ch
3:11 o wing of the one cherub was five cubits, NIH
3:11 one wing of the o cherub was five cubits, 259

2Ch
3:12 o wing of the other cherub was five cubits, NIH
3:17 o on the right hand, and the other on the 259
4:15 O sea, and twelve oxen under it. 259
5:13 as the trumpeters and singers were as o, 259
5:13 to make o sound to be heard in praising 259
6:29 when every o shall know his own sore 376
7:21 shall be an astonishment to every o that 3605
9: 6 the o half of the greatness of thy wisdom NIH
9:13 to Solomon in o year was six hundred 259
9:15 hundred shekels of beaten gold went to o 259
9:16 three hundred shekels of gold went to o 259
9:19 lions stood there on the o side 2088+4480
12:13 for Rehoboam was o and forty years old 259
16:13 died in the o and fortieth year of his reign. 259
18: 7 There is yet o man, by whom we may 259
18: 8 the king of Israel called for o of his officers, 259
18:12 declare good to the king with o assent; 259
18:12 be like o of theirs, and speak thou good. 259
18:19 o spake saying after this manner, 2088
20:23 of Seir, every o helped to destroy another. 376
22: 2 reign, and he reigned o year in Jerusalem. 259
25:17 Come, let us see o another in the face. NIH
25:21 they saw o another in the face, both he NIH
26:11 hand of Hananiah, o of the king's captains. NIH
28: 6 an hundred and twenty thousand in o day, 259
30:12 o heart to do the commandment of the 259
30:17 passovers for every o that was not clean, 3605
30:18 The good LORD pardon every o 3605
31:16 even unto every o that entereth into 3605
32:12 Ye shall worship before o altar, 259
34: 1 he reigned in Jerusalem o and thirty years. 259
35:24 was buried in o of the sepulchres of his NIH
36:11 Zedekiah was o and twenty years old 259

Ezr
1 and Judah, every o unto his city; 376
2:26 and Gaba, six hundred twenty and o. 259
2:69 threescore and o thousand
505+7239+8337+2050.1
2:69 silver, and o hundred priests' garments. 3967
3: 1 people gathered themselves together as o 259
3: 5 of every o that willingly offered a freewill 3605
5:14 they were delivered unto o, whose name NIH
6: 5 every o to his place, and place them in NIH
8:34 By number and by weight of every o: 3605
9: 4 were assembled unto me every o that 3605
9:11 which have filled it from o end to another NIH
10: 2 o of the sons of Elam, answered and 259
10:13 neither is this a work of o day or two: 259

Ne
1: 2 o of my brethren, came, he and certain 259
3: 8 Hananiah the son of o of the apothecaries, NIH
3:28 the priests, every o over against his house. 376
4:15 of us to the wall, every o unto his work. 376
4:17 every o with one of his hands wrought in NIH
4:17 every one with o of his hands wrought in 259
4:18 every o had his sword girded by his side, 376
4:19 upon the wall, o far from another. 376
4:22 Let every o with his servant lodge within 376
4:23 saving that every o put them off for 259
5: 7 You exact usury, every o of his brother. 376
5:18 was prepared for me daily was o ox 259
6: 2 let us meet together in some o of NIH
7: 3 every o in his watch, and every one to be 376
7: 3 and every o to be over against his house. 376
7: 6 and to Judah, every o unto his city; 259
7:30 and Geba, six hundred twenty and o. 259
7:37 and Ono, seven hundred twenty and o. 259
7:63 which took o of the daughters of Barzillai NIH
8: 1 o man into the street that was before 259
8:16 every o upon the roof of his house, 376
9: 3 LORD their God o fourth part of the day; NIH
10:28 every o having knowledge, 3605
11: 1 to bring o of ten to dwell in Jerusalem 259
11: 3 in the cities of Judah dwelt every o in his 376
11:14 was Zabdiel, the son of o of the great men. NIH
11:20 cities of Judah, every o in his inheritance. 376
12:31 whereof o went on the right hand upon NIH
13:10 the work, were fled every o to his field. 376
13:28 of the sons of Joiada, the son of Eliashib NIH
13:30 and the Levites, every o in his business; 376

Est
1: 7 vessels being diverse o from another,) 3627
3:13 old, little children and women, in o day, 259
4: 5 for Hatach, o of the king's chamberlains, NIH
4:11 there is o law of his to put him to death, 259
6: 9 horse be delivered to the hand of o of 376
7: 9 Harbonah, o of the chamberlains, said 259
8:12 Upon o day in all the provinces of king 259
9:19 and of sending portions o to another, 376
9:22 of sending portions o to another, and gifts 376

Job
1: 1 o that feared God, and eschewed evil. 3373
1: 4 feasted in their houses, every o his day; NIH
1: 8 o that feareth God, and escheweth evil? 3373
2: 3 o that feareth God, and escheweth evil? 3373
2:10 Thou speakest as o of the foolish women 259
2:11 they came every o from his own place; 376
2:12 they rent every o his mantle, 376
5: 2 foolish man, and envy slayeth the silly o. 6601
6:10 not concealed the words of the Holy O. 6918
6:26 the speeches of o that is desperate, NIH
9: 3 he cannot answer him o of a thousand. 259
9:22 This is o thing, therefore I said it, He 259
12: 4 I am as o mocked of his neighbour, 7814
13: 9 or as o man mocketh another, do ye so NIH
14: 3 dost thou open thine eyes upon such a o, 2088
14: 4 a clean thing out of an unclean? not o. 259
16:21 O that o might plead for a man with God, NIH
17:10 for I cannot find o wise man among you. NIH

Job
19:11 he counteth me unto him as **o** of his NIH
21:23 O dieth in his full strength, *being* wholly 2088
23:13 he *is* in a *mind,* and who can turn him? 259
24: 6 They reap *every* **o** his corn in the field: NIH
24:17 if *I* know *them, they are in* the terrors of 259
29:25 army, as **o** *that* comforteth the mourners. NIH
31:15 and did not **o** fashion us in the womb? 259
31:35 that **o** would hear me! behold, my desire 259
33:23 an interpreter, **o** among a thousand, 259
40:11 behold *every* **o** *that is* proud, 3605
40:12 Look on *every* **o** *that is* proud, 3605
41: 9 *not* **o** be cast down even at the sight of NIH
41:16 **O** is so near to another, that no air can 259
41:17 They are joined **o** to another, they stick 376
41:32 **o** would think the deep to be hoary. NIH
42:11 of money, and *every* **o** an earring of gold. 376

Ps
12: 2 They speak vanity *every* **o** with his 376
14: 3 *there is* none that doeth good, no, not **o**. 259
16:10 wilt thou suffer thine **Holy O** to see 2623
27: 4 **O** *thing* I have desired of the Lord, that 259
29: 9 in his temple doth *every* **o** speak of *his* 2050.2
32: 6 For this shall *every* **o** *that is* godly pray 3605
34:20 all his bones: not **o** of them is broken. 259
35:14 as **o** that mourneth for his mother. NIH
49:16 Be not thou afraid when **o** is made rich, 376
50:21 that I was altogether *such a* **o** as thyself: NIH
53: 3 *Every* **o** of them is gone back, they are 3605
53: 3 *there is* none that doeth good, no, not **o**. 259
58: 8 let *every* **o** of them pass away: NIH
63:11 *every* **o** that sweareth by him shall glory: 3605
64: 6 the inward *thought* of *every* **o** *of them,* 376
68:21 the hairy scalp of such a **o** as goeth on still NIH
68:30 *till every* **o** submit himself with pieces of 3605
71:18 thy power to *every* **o** *that is* to come. 3605
71:22 with the harp, **O** thou **Holy O** of Israel. 6918
73:20 As a dream when **o** awaketh; *so,* O Lord, NIH
75: 7 putteth down **o**, and setteth up another. 2088
78:41 and limited the **Holy O** of Israel. 6918
78:65 Then the Lord awaked as **o** out of sleep, NIH
82: 7 die like men, and fall like **o** of the princes. 259
83: 5 For they have consulted together *with* **o** NIH
84: 7 *every* **o** *of them* in Zion appeareth before NIH
89:10 broken Rahab in pieces, as **o** that is slain; NIH
89:18 and the **Holy O** of Israel *is* our king. 6918
89:19 thou spakest in vision to thy **holy o,** 2623
89:19 I have laid help upon **o** *that is* mighty; NIH
89:19 I have exalted **o** chosen out of the people. NIH
105:13 they went from **o** nation to another, NIH
105:13 from **o** kingdom to another people; NIH
105:37 there was not **o** feeble *person* among NIH
106:11 enemies: there was not **o** of them left. 259
115: 8 *so is* *every* **o** that trusteth in them. 3605
119:160 *every* **o** of thy righteous judgments 3605
119:162 at thy word, as **o** that findeth great spoil. NIH
128: 1 Blessed *is* *every* **o** that feareth the Lord;
135:18 *so is* *every* **o** that trusteth in them. 3605
137: 3 *saying,* Sing us **o** of the songs of Zion. NIH
141: 7 as when **o** cutteth and cleaveth *wood* NIH
145: 4 **O** generation shall praise thy works to NIH

Pr
1:14 thy lot among us; let us all have **o** purse: 259
1:19 So *are* the ways of *every* **o** that is greedy 3605
1:18 and happy is *every* **o** that retaineth her. NIH
6:11 So shall thy poverty come as **o** that NIH
6:28 Can **o** go upon hot coals, and his feet not 376
8:30 *as* **o** **brought up** *with him:* and I was daily 525
15:12 A scorner loveth not **o** that reproveth him: NIH
16: 5 *Every* **o** *that is* proud in heart is an 3605
17:14 beginning of strife *is* as when **o** letteth NIH
19:25 reprove **o** that hath understanding, NIH
20: 6 Most men will proclaim *every* **o** his own 376
21: 5 but *of* *every* **o** that is hasty only to want. 3605
22:26 Be not thou **o** of them that strike hands, NIH
24:34 So shall thy poverty come as **o** that NIH
26:17 *is like* **o** that taketh a dog by the ears. NIH

Ecc
1: 4 **O** generation passeth away, NIH
2:14 I myself perceived also that **o** event 259
3:19 even **o** *thing* befalleth them: 259
3:19 as **the o** dieth, so dieth the other; yea, 2088
3:19 yea, they have all **o** breath; so that a man 259
3:20 All go unto **o** place, all *are* of the dust, 259
4: 8 There is **o** *alone,* and *there is* not a second; 259
4: 9 Two *are* better than **o**; because they have 259
4:10 For if they fall, the **o** will lift up his fellow: 259
4:11 have heat: but how can **o** be warm *alone?* 259
4:12 prevail against him, two shall withstand 259
5:18 good and comely *for* **o** to eat and to drink, NIH
6: 6 he see two places: do not all go to **o** place? 259
7:14 God also hath set the **o** over against 2088
7:27 saith the Preacher, *counting* **o** by one, 259
7:27 saith the Preacher, *counting* one by **o**, 259
7:28 **o** man among a thousand have I found; 259
8: 9 *there is* a time wherein **o** man ruleth 1886.1
9: 2 *there is* **o** event to the righteous, and to 259
9: 3 the sun, that *there is* **o** event unto all; 259
9:18 war: but **o** sinner destroyeth much good. 259
10: 3 and he saith to *every* **o** *that he is* a fool. 259
10:15 The foolish wearieth *every* **o** of them, 5105.2
12:11 which are given from **o** shepherd. 259

SS
1: 7 why should I be as **o** that turneth aside NIH
2:10 my love, my **fair o,** and come away. 3303
2:13 Arise, my love, my **fair o,** and come away. 3303
4: 2 whereof *every* **o** beareth twins, and none 3605
4: 9 hast ravished my heart with **o** of thine 259
4: 9 of thine eyes, with **o** chain of thy neck. 259
6: 6 whereof *every* **o** beareth twins, and 3605

SS
6: 6 and *there is* not **o** barren among them. NIH
6: 9 My dove, my undefiled *is but* **o**; she *is* 259
6: 9 she *is* the *only* **o** of her mother, she *is* 259
6: 9 she *is* the choice **o** of her that bare her. NIH
8:10 was I in his eyes as **o** that found favour. NIH
8:11 *every* **o** for the fruit thereof was to bring a 376

Isa
1: 4 they have provoked the **Holy O** of Israel 6918
1:23 *every* **o** loveth gifts, and followeth after 3605
1:24 Lord of hosts, the **mighty O** of Israel, 46
2:12 hosts *shall be* upon *every* **o** *that is* proud 3605
2:12 lofty, and upon *every* **o** that is lifted up; 3605
2:20 which they made *each* **o** for himself to NIH
3: 5 *every* **o** by another, and every one by his 376
3: 5 by another, and *every* **o** by his neighbour: 376
4: 1 that day seven women shall take hold of **o** 259
4: 3 *even every* **o** that is written among 3605
5:10 ten acres of vineyard shall yield **o** bath, 259
5:19 the counsel of the **Holy O** of Israel draw 6918
5:24 despised the word of the **Holy O** of Israel. 6918
5:30 if **o** look unto the land, behold darkness NIH
6: 2 *each* **o** had six wings; with twain he 259
6: 3 **o** cried unto another, and said, Holy, 2088
6: 6 flew **o** of the seraphims unto me, having 259
7:22 honey shall *every* **o** eat that is left in 3605
9:14 and tail, branch and rush, *in* **o** day. 259
9:17 for *every* **o** *is* a hypocrite and an evildoer, 3605
10:14 as **o** gathereth eggs *that are* left, have I NIH
10:17 be for a fire, and his **Holy O** for a flame: 6918
10:17 devour his thorns and his briers in **o** day; 259
10:20 the Lord, the **Holy O** of Israel, in truth. 6918
10:34 and Lebanon shall fall by a **mighty o**. 117
12: 6 for great *is* the **Holy O** of Israel in 6918
13: 8 they shall be amazed **o** at another; their 376
13:14 and flee *every* **o** into his own land. 376
13:15 *Every* **o** that is found shall be thrust 3605
13:15 *every* **o** that is joined *unto them* shall fall 3605
14:18 lie in glory, *every* **o** in his own house. 376
14:32 What shall **o** then answer the messengers NIH
15: 3 in their streets, *every* **o** shall howl, 1886.4
16: 7 howl for Moab, every **o** shall howl: 1886.4
17: 7 eyes shall have respect to the **Holy O** of 6918
19: 2 they shall fight *every* **o** against his brother, 376
19: 2 and *every* **o** against his neighbour; 376
19:17 *every* **o** that maketh mention thereof 3605
19:18 **o** shall be called, The city of destruction. 259
19:20 and a *great* **o**, and he shall deliver them. 7227
23:15 according to the days of **o** king: 259
27:12 shall be gathered **o** by one, O ye children 259
27:12 be gathered one by **o**, O ye children 259
28: 2 the Lord hath a mighty and strong **o**, NIH
29: 4 as of **o** that hath a familiar spirit, out of NIH
29:11 which *men* deliver to **o** that is learned, NIH
29:19 men shall rejoice in the **Holy O** of Israel. 6918
29:20 For the **terrible o** is brought **to nought**, 6184
29:23 sanctify the **Holy O** of Jacob, and shall 6918
30:11 cause the **Holy O** of Israel to cease from 6918
30:12 Wherefore thus saith the **Holy O** of Israel, 6918
30:15 saith the Lord God, the **Holy O** of Israel; 6918
30:17 **O** thousand *shall flee* at the rebuke of one; 259
30:17 One thousand *shall flee* at the rebuke of **o**; 259
30:29 as when **o** goeth with a pipe to come 1886.1
30:29 of the Lord, to the **mighty O** of Israel. 6697
31: 1 they look not unto the **Holy O** of Israel, 6918
33:20 not **o** of the stakes thereof shall ever be NIH
34:15 also be gathered, *every* **o** with her mate. 802
34:16 no **o** of these shall fail, none shall want her 259
36: 9 wilt thou turn away the face of **o** captain 259
36:16 eat ye *every* **o** of his vine, and every one 376
36:16 *every* **o** of his fig tree, and drink ye every 376
36:16 drink ye *every* **o** the waters of his own 376
37:23 *even* against the **Holy O** of Israel. 6918
40:25 or shall I be equal? saith the **Holy O**. 6918
40:26 that *he is* strong in power; not **o** faileth. 376
41: 6 They helped *every* **o** his neighbour; 376
41: 6 *every* **o** said to his brother, Be of good NIH
41:14 and thy redeemer, the **Holy O** of Israel. 6918
41:16 *and* shalt glory in the **Holy O** of Israel. 6918
41:20 and the **Holy O** of Israel hath created it. 6918
41:25 I have raised up **o** from the north, NIH
41:27 I will give to Jerusalem **o** that bringeth NIH
43: 3 God, the **Holy O** of Israel, thy Saviour: 6918
43: 7 *Even* *every* **o** that is called by my name: 3605
43:14 your redeemer, the **Holy O** of Israel; 6918
43:15 I *am* the Lord, your **Holy O**, the creator 6918
44: 5 **O** shall say, I *am* the Lord's; 2088
45:11 the **Holy O** of Israel, and his maker, 6918
45:24 Surely, shall *one* say, in the Lord have I NIH
46: 7 yea, **o** shall cry unto him, yet can he not 259
47: 4 of hosts *is* his name, the **Holy O** of Israel. 6918
47: 9 shall come to thee *in* a moment in **o** day, 259
47:15 they shall wander *every* **o** to his quarter; 376
48:17 thy redeemer, the **Holy O** of Israel; 6918
49: 7 the redeemer of Israel, *and* his **Holy O**,
49: 7 *and* the **Holy O** of Israel, and he shall 6918
49:26 and thy redeemer, the **mighty O** of Jacob. 46
53: 6 we have turned *every* **o** to his own way; 376
54: 5 and thy redeemer the **Holy O** of Israel; 6918
55: 1 Ho, *every* **o** that thirsteth, come ye to 3605
55: 5 thy God, and for the **Holy O** of Israel; 6918
56: 2 *every* **o** that keepeth the sabbath from 3605
56:11 *every* **o** for his gain, from his quarter. 376
57: 2 *each* **o** walking in his uprightness. NIH
57:15 high and lofty **O** that inhabiteth eternity, NIH
60: 9 to the **Holy O** of Israel, because he hath 6918
60:14 The Zion of the **Holy O** of Israel. 6918

Isa
60:16 and thy redeemer, the **mighty O** of Jacob. 46
60:22 A *little* **o** shall become a thousand, 6996
60:22 thousand, and a **small o** a strong nation: 6810
65: 8 in the cluster, and **o** saith, Destroy it not; NIH
66: 8 the earth be made to bring forth in **o** day? 259
66:13 As **o** whom his mother comforteth, so will 376
66:17 purify themselves in the gardens behind **o** 376
66:23 to another, and from **o** sabbath to another, NIH

Jer
1:15 they shall set *every* **o** his throne *at* 376
3:14 I will take you **o** of a city, and two of a 259
5: 6 *every* **o** that goeth out thence shall be 3605
5: 8 *every* **o** neighed after his neighbour's 376
6: 3 they shall feed *every* **o** *in* his place. 376
6:13 them *every* **o** *is* given to covetousness; 3605
6:13 unto the priest *every* **o** dealeth falsely. 2050.2
8: 6 *every* **o** turned to his course, as the 3605
8:10 *every* **o** from the least even unto 3605
8:10 unto the priest *every* **o** dealeth falsely. 376
9: 4 Take ye heed *every* **o** of his neighbour, 376
9: 5 they will deceive *every* **o** his neighbour, 376
9: 8 **o** speaketh peaceably to his neighbour NIH
9:20 and *every* **o** her neighbour lamentation. 802
10: 3 for **o** cutteth a tree out of the forest, NIH
11: 8 walked *every* **o** in the imagination of their 376
12:12 **o** end of the land even to the *other* end of 376
13:14 I will dash them **o** against another, even 259
15:10 *yet* *every* **o** of them doth curse me. 3605
16:12 ye walk *every* **o** after the imagination of 376
18:11 return ye now *every* **o** from his evil way, 376
18:12 we will *every* **o** do the imagination of his 376
18:16 *every* **o** that passeth thereby shall be 3605
19: 8 *every* **o** that passeth thereby shall be 3605
19: 9 shall eat *every* **o** the flesh of his friend 376
19:11 this city, as **o** breaketh a potter's vessel, NIH
20: 7 in derision daily, every **o** mocketh me. 1886.4
20:11 Lord *is* with me as a mighty **terrible o**: 6184
22: 7 against thee, *every* **o** with his weapons: 376
23:17 they say *unto* every **o** that walketh after 3605
23:30 that steal my words *every* **o** from his 376
23:35 Thus shall ye say *every* **o** to his neighbour, 376
23:35 *every* **o** to his brother, What hath 376
24: 2 **O** basket *had* very good figs, *even* like 259
25: 5 Turn ye again now *every* **o** from his evil 376
25:26 **o** with another, and all the kingdoms of 376
25:33 **o** end of the earth even unto the *other* end 376
30:14 *with* the chastisement of a **cruel o**, 394
30:16 all thine adversaries, *every* **o** of them, 3605
31:30 *every* **o** shall die for his own iniquity: 376
32:19 to give *every* **o** according to his ways, 376
32:39 I will give them **o** heart, and one way, 259
32:39 **o** way, that *they* may fear me for ever, 259
34:10 that *every* **o** should let his manservant, 376
34:10 and *every* **o** his maidservant, go free, 376
34:17 *every* **o** to his brother, and every man to 376
35: 2 into **o** of the chambers, and give them 259
36: 7 and will return *every* **o** from his evil way: 376
36:16 they were afraid both **o** and other, 376
38: 7 **o** of the eunuchs which *was* in the king's 376
46:16 many to fall, yea, **o** fell upon another: 376
49:17 *every* **o** that goeth by it shall be 3605
50:13 *every* **o** that goeth by Babylon shall be 3605
50:16 they shall turn *every* **o** to his people, 376
50:16 they shall flee *every* **o** to his own land. 376
50:29 the Lord, against the **Holy O** of Israel. 6918
50:42 *every* **o** put in array, like a man to the NIH
51: 5 *with* sin against the **Holy O** of Israel. 6918
51: 9 let us go *every* **o** into his own country: 376
51:31 **O** post shall run to meet another, NIH
51:31 and **o** messenger to meet another, NIH
51:31 of Babylon that his city is taken at **o** end, NIH
51:46 a rumour shall both come **o** year, NIH
51:56 are taken, *every* **o** of their bows is broken: NIH
52: 1 Zedekiah *was* **o** and twenty year old when 259
52:20 **o** sea, and twelve brasen bulls that *were* 259
52:21 the height of **o** pillar *was* eighteen cubits; 259
52:22 the height of **o** chapiter *was* five cubits, 259

Eze
1: 6 *every* **o** had four faces, and every one had 259
1: 6 four faces, and *every* **o** had four wings. 259
1: 9 Their wings *were* joined **o** to another; 802
1: 9 they went *every* **o** straight forward. 376
1:11 two *wings* of *every* **o** *were* joined one to 259
1:11 two *wings* of every one *were* joined **o** to 259
1:12 they went *every* **o** straight forward: 376
1:15 **o** wheel upon the earth by the living 259
1:16 they four had **o** likeness: 259
1:23 wings straight, the **o** toward the other: 802
1:23 *every* **o** had two, which covered on this 376
1:23 covered on this *side,* and *every* **o** had two, 376
1:28 face, and I heard a voice of **o** that spake. NIH
3:13 living creatures that touched **o** another; 802
4: 8 thou shalt not turn thee from **o** side to NIH
4: 9 put them in **o** vessel, and make thee bread 259
4:17 be astonied **o** with another, 259
7:16 them mourning, *every* **o** for his iniquity. 376
9: 2 **o** man among them *was* clothed *with* linen 259
10: 7 cherub stretched forth his hand from NIH
10: 9 one wheel by **o** cherub, and another wheel 259
10: 9 one wheel by **o** cherub, and another wheel 259
10:10 their appearances, they four had **o** likeness, 259
10:14 *every* **o** had four faces: the first face *was* 259
10:19 *every* **o** stood *at* the door of the east gate of NIH
10:21 *Every* **o** had four faces apiece, and every 259
10:21 four faces apiece, and *every* **o** four wings; 259
10:22 they went *every* **o** straight forward. 376

O

O

Eze
11: 5 come into your mind, *every* o *of* them. NIH
11:19 I will give them one heart, and I will put a 259
13:10 o built up a wall, and, lo, others daubed it 1931
14: 7 For **every** o of the house of Israel, 376+376
15: 7 they shall go out from o fire, and *another* NIH
16:15 pouredst out thy fornications on **every** o 3605
16:25 opened thy feet to **every** o that passed 3605
16:44 **every** o that useth proverbs shall use *this* 3605
17:22 the top of his young twigs a **tender** o, 7390
18:10 doeth the like to *any* o of these *things*, 259
18:30 of Israel, **every** o according to his ways, 259
19: 3 she brought up o of her whelps: it became 259
20:39 serve ye **every** o his idols, 376
21:16 Go thee o **way or other**, *either* on the 258
21:19 both twain shall come forth out of o land: 259
22: 6 **every** o were in thee to their power to 376
22:11 o hath committed abomination with his 376
23: 2 two women, the daughters of o mother: 259
23:13 she was defiled, *that* they took both o way, 259
24:23 and mourn o towards another. 376
31:11 him into the hand of the **mighty** o 410
33:20 I will judge you **every** o after his ways. 376
33:21 *that* o that had **escaped** out of Jerusalem 6412
33:24 Abraham was o, and he inherited the land: 259
33:26 and ye defile **every** o his neighbour's wife: 2297
33:30 speak o to another, every one to his 376
33:30 **every** o to his brother, saying, Come, I 376
33:32 lovely song *of* o that hath a pleasant voice, NIH
34:23 And I will set up o shepherd over them, 259
37:16 take thee o stick, and write upon it, 259
37:17 join them o to another into one stick; 259
37:17 join them one to another into o stick; 259
37:17 and they shall become o in thine hand. 259
37:19 make them o stick, and they shall be one 259
37:19 stick, and they shall be o in mine hand. 259
37:22 I will make them o nation in the land 259
37:22 and o king shall be king to them all: 259
37:24 and they all shall have o shepherd. 259
39: 7 that I *am* the Lord, the **Holy O** in Israel. 6918
40: 5 the breadth of the building, o reed; 259
40: 5 one reed; and the height, o reed. 259
40: 6 of the gate, *which was* o reed broad; 259
40: 6 other threshold *of the gate, which was* o 259
40: 7 *every* little chamber *was* o reed long, 259
40: 7 *was* one reed long, and o reed broad; 259
40: 7 by the porch of the gate within *was* o reed. 259
40: 8 also the porch of the gate within, o reed. 259
40:10 on that side; they three *were* of o measure: 259
40:10 the posts had o measure on this side and 259
40:12 little chambers *was* o cubit *on this side,* 259
40:12 and the space *was* o cubit on that side: 259
40:13 the gate from the roof of o little chamber NIH
40:26 o on this side, and another on that side, 259
40:40 as o goeth up to the entry of the north 1886.1
40:42 a cubit and a half broad, and o cubit high: 259
40:44 o at the side of the east gate *having* 259
40:49 on this side, and another on that side. 259
41: 1 six cubits broad on the o **side**, 6311
41: 2 the door *were* five cubits on the o **side**, 6311
41: 6 o's over another, and thirty *in* order; 6763
41:11 o door toward the north, and another door 259
41:15 the galleries thereof on the o **side** and 6311
41:19 *was* toward the palm tree on the o **side**, 6311
41:21 the appearance of the o as the appearance NIH
41:24 two *leaves* for the o door, and two leaves 259
41:26 palm trees on the o **side** and on the other 6311
42: 4 ten cubits breadth inward, a way of o cubit: 259
42: 9 o goeth into them from the utter court. 2050.2
42:12 toward the east, as o entereth into them. NIH
43:14 *be* two cubits, and the breadth o cubit; 259
43:14 *be* four cubits, and the breadth o cubit. NIH
45: 7 for the prince on the o **side** 2088
45: 7 the length *shall be* over against o of 259
45:11 and the bath shall be of o measure, 259
45:15 a lamb out of the flock, out of two hundred 259
45:20 *day* of the month for **every** o that erreth, 376
46:12 o shall then open him the gate that NIH
46:12 after his going forth o shall shut the gate. NIH
46:17 if he give a gift of his inheritance to o of 259
46:22 these four corners *were* of o measure. NIH
47: 7 river *were* very many trees on the o **side** 2088
47:14 ye shall inherit it, o as well as another: 376
48: 1 as o goeth to Hamath, Hazar-enan, NIH
48: 8 and *in* length as o of the *other* parts, 259
48:21 on the o **side** and on the other of the 2088
48:31 o gate of Reuben, one gate of Judah, 259
48:31 Reuben, one gate of Judah, one gate of Levi. 259
48:31 Reuben, one gate of Judah, o gate of Levi. 259
48:32 o gate of Joseph, one gate of Benjamin, 259
48:32 o gate of Benjamin, one gate of Dan. 259
48:32 one gate of Benjamin, o gate of Dan. 259
48:33 o gate of Simeon, one gate of Issachar, 259
48:33 one gate of Simeon, o gate of Issachar, 259
48:33 one gate of Issachar, o gate of Zebulun. 259
48:34 o gate of Gad, one gate of Asher, one gate 259
48:34 one gate of Gad, o gate of Asher, one gate 259
48:34 one gate of Asher, o gate of Naphtali. 259

Da
2: 9 the dream, *there is but* o decree for you: 2298
2:43 they shall not cleave o to another, even 1836
3:19 o seven *times* more than *it was* wont to 2298
4:13 and a **holy** o came down from heaven; 6922
4:19 was astonied for o hour, and his thoughts 2298
4:23 and a **holy** o coming down from heaven, 6922
5: 6 and his knees smote o against another. 1668
7: 3 up from the sea, diverse o from another. 1668

Da
7: 5 raised up itself up on o side, and *it had* three 2298
7:13 o like the Son of man came with the NIH
7:16 I came near unto o of them that stood *by,* 2298
8: 3 o *was* higher than the other, and the 259
8: 9 out of o of them came forth a little horn, 259
8:13 I heard o saint speaking, and another saint 259
9:27 the covenant with many for o week: 259
10:13 of the kingdom of Persia withstood me o 259
10:13 Michael, o of the chief princes, came to 259
10:16 o like the similitude of the sons of men NIH
10:18 me o like the appearance of a man, 259
11: 5 south shall be strong, and o of his princes; NIH
11: 7 of a branch of her roots shall o stand up NIH
11:10 o shall certainly come, and overflow, NIH
11:27 and they shall speak lies at o table; 259
12: 1 **every** o that *shall* be found written in 3605
12: 5 the o on this side of the bank of the river, 259
12: 6 o said to the man clothed in linen, NIH

Hos
1:11 appoint themselves o head, and they shall 259
4: 3 **every** o that dwelleth therein shall 3605
11: 9 not man; the **Holy O** in the midst of thee: 6918

Joel
2: 7 they shall march **every** o on his ways, 376
2: 8 Neither shall o thrust another; they shall 376
2: 8 they shall walk **every** o in his path: 1397

Am
3: 3 shall o take up a snare from the earth, NIH
4: 7 I caused it to rain upon o city, and caused 259
4: 7 o piece was rained upon, and the piece 259
4: 8 two or three cities wandered unto o city, 259
6: 9 if there remain ten men in o house, that 259
6:12 will o plow *there* with oxen? for ye have NIH
8: 8 **every** o mourn that dwelleth therein? 3605

Ob
1: 9 to the end that **every** o of the mount of 376
1:11 even thou *wast* as o of them. 259

Jnh
1: 7 they said **every** o to his fellow, Come, 376
1: 7 let them turn **every** o from his evil way, 376

Mic
2: 4 In that day shall o take up a parable NIH
4: 5 all people will walk **every** o in the name 376

Na
1:11 is o come out of thee, that imagineth NIH
2: 4 they shall justle o against another in NIH

Hab
1:12 O Lord my God, mine **Holy O**? 6918
3: 3 and the **Holy O** from mount Paran. 6918

Zep
2:11 shall worship him, **every** o from his place, 376
2:15 **every** o that passeth by her shall hiss, 3605
3: 9 of the Lord, to serve him with o consent. 259

Hag
2: 1 In the seventh *month,* in the o and 259
2:12 If o bear holy flesh in the skirt of his 376
2:13 If o *that* is unclean *by* a dead body touch NIH
2:16 o came to a heap of twenty *measures,* NIH
2:16 o came to the pressfat for to draw out NIH
2:22 **every** o by the sword of his brother. 376

Zec
3: 9 upon o stone *shall be* seven eyes: NIH
3: 9 I will remove the iniquity of that land in o 259
4: 3 o upon the right *side* of the bowl, 259
5: 3 **every** o that stealeth shall be cut off *as* 3605
5: 3 **every** o that sweareth shall be cut off *as* 3605
8:10 for I set all men **every** o against his 376
8:21 inhabitants of o *city* shall go to another, 259
10: 1 of rain, to **every** o grass in the field. 376
11: 6 I *will* deliver the men **every** o into his 376
11: 7 the o I called Beauty, and the other I called 259
11: 8 Three shepherds also I cut off in o month; 259
11: 9 the rest eat **every** o the flesh of another. 802
11:16 neither shall seek the **young** o, nor heal 5289
12:10 as o mourneth for *his* only *son,* and shall NIH
12:10 as o that is in bitterness for *his* firstborn. NIH
13: 4 the prophets shall be ashamed **every** o 376
13: 6 o shall say unto him, What *are* these NIH
14: 7 it shall be o day which shall be known to 259
14: 9 in that day shall there be o Lord, 259
14: 9 *that* day shall there be one Lord, and his name o. 259
14:13 they shall lay hold **every** o on the hand of 376
14:16 *that* **every** o that is left of all the nations 3605

Mal
2: 3 and o shall take you away with it. NIH
2:10 we not all o father? hath not one God 259
2:10 hath not o God created us? why do we 259
2:15 did not he make o? Yet had he the residue 259
2:15 wherefore o? That he might seek a godly 259
2:16 for o covereth violence with his garment, NIH
2:17 **Every** o that doeth evil *is* good in the 3605
3:16 they that feared the Lord spake often o to 376

Mt
3: 3 The voice of o crying in the wilderness, NIG
5:18 o jot or one tittle shall in no wise pass 1520
5:18 o tittle shall in no wise pass from the law, 1520
5:19 break o of these least commandments, 1520
5:29 for it is profitable for thee that o of thy 1520
5:30 for it is profitable for thee that o of thy 1520
5:36 canst not make o hair white or black. 1520
6:24 for either he will hate the o, and love 1520
6:24 or else he will hold to the o, and despise 1520
6:27 of you by taking thought can add o 1520
6:29 his glory was not arrayed like o of these. 1520
7: 8 For **every** o that asketh receiveth; 3956
7:21 Not **every** o that saith unto me, Lord, 3956
7:26 And **every** o that heareth these sayings of 3956
7:29 For he taught them as o having authority, NIG
10:29 o of them shall not fall on the ground 1520
10:42 And whosoever shall give to drink unto o 1520
12: 6 That in this place is o greater than NIG
12:11 that shall have o sheep, and if it fall into 1520
12:22 unto him o **possessed with a devil,** 1139
12:29 else how can o enter into a strong *man's* 5100
12:47 Then said unto him, Behold, thy 5100
13:19 When **any** o heareth the word of 3956
13:19 then cometh the **wicked o,** 4190
13:38 tares are the children of the **wicked o;** 4190

Mt
13:46 when he had found o pearl of great price, 1520
16:14 and others, Jeremias, or o of the prophets. 1520
17: 4 o for thee, and one for Moses, and one for 1520
17: 4 o for Moses, and one for Elias. 1520
17: 4 and one for Moses, and o for Elias. 1520
18: 5 whoso shall receive o such little child 1520
18: 6 But whoso shall offend o of these little 1520
18: 9 for thee to enter into life with o eye, 3442
18:10 Take heed that ye despise not o of these 1520
18:12 and o of them be gone astray, doth he not 1520
18:14 that o of these little ones should perish. 1520
18:16 *then* take with thee o or two more, 1520
18:24 to reckon, o was brought unto him, 1520
18:28 out, and found o of his fellowservants, 1520
18:35 if ye from your hearts forgive not **every** o 1538
19: 5 his wife: and they twain shall be o flesh? 1520
19: 6 they are no more twain, but o flesh. 1520
19:16 And behold, o came and said unto him, 1520
19:17 *there is* none good but o, *that is,* God: 1520
19:29 And **every** o that hath forsaken houses, 3956
20:12 These last have wrought *but* o hour, 1520
20:13 But he answered o of them, and said, 1520
20:21 the o on thy right hand, and the other on 1520
21:24 unto them, I also will ask you o thing, 1520
21:35 took his servants, and beat o, 3739
22: 5 of *it,* and went their ways, o to his farm, 3739
22:35 Then o of them, *which was* a lawyer, 1520
23: 4 *themselves* will not move them with o NIG
23: 8 for o is your Master, *even* Christ; 1520
23: 9 for o is your Father, which is in heaven. 1520
23:10 for o is your Master, *even* Christ. 1520
23:15 compass sea and land to make o proselyte, 1520
24: 2 There shall not be left here o stone upon NIG
24:10 and shall betray o **another,** and shall hate 240
24:10 one another, and shall hate o **another.** 240
24:31 from o end of heaven to the other. NIG
24:40 *the* o shall be taken, and *the* other left. 1520
24:41 *the* o shall be taken, and *the* other left. 1520
25:15 unto o he gave five talents, to another 3739
25:15 to another two, and to another o; 1520
25:18 But he that had received o went and 1520
25:24 Then he which had received the o talent 1520
25:29 For unto **every** o that hath shall be given, 3956
25:32 he shall separate them o from **another,** 240
25:40 Inasmuch as ye have done *it* unto o of 1520
25:45 Inasmuch as ye did *it* not to o of the least 1520
26:14 Then o of the twelve, called Judas Iscariot, 1520
26:21 unto you, that o of you shall betray me. 1520
26:22 began **every** o of them to say unto him, 1538
26:40 could ye not watch with me o hour? 1520
26:47 o of the twelve, came, and with him a 1520
26:51 o of them which were with Jesus 1520
26:73 to Peter, Surely thou also art o of them; NIG
27:38 o on the right hand, and another on the 1520
27:48 And straightway o of them ran, and took 1520

Mk
1: 3 The voice of o crying in the wilderness, NIG
1: 7 There cometh o mightier than I after me, 3588
1:22 he taught them as o that had authority, NIG
1:24 thee who thou art, the **Holy O** of God. 40
2: 3 bringing o **sick of the palsy,** *which was* 3885
4:41 said o to **another,** What *manner of* man 240
5:22 there cometh o of the rulers of 1520
6:15 it is a prophet, or as o of the prophets. 1520
7:14 Hearken unto me **every** o of you, 3956
7:32 And they bring unto him o *that was* deaf, NIG
8:14 in the ship with them more than o loaf. 1520
8:28 *say,* Elias; and others, O of the prophets. 1520
9: 5 for thee, and one for Moses, and one 1520
9: 5 and o for Moses, and one for Elias. 1520
9: 5 and one for Moses, and o for Elias. 1520
9:10 questioning o with *another* what the NIG
9:17 o of the multitude answered and said, 1520
9:26 came out of *him:* and he was as o **dead;** 3498
9:37 Whosoever shall receive o of such 1520
9:38 we saw o casting out devils in thy name, 5100
9:42 whosoever shall offend o of *these* little 1520
9:47 into the kingdom of God with o eye, 3442
9:49 For **every** o shall be salted with fire, 3956
9:50 and have peace o with **another.** 240
10: 8 And they twain shall be o flesh: so then 1520
10: 8 then they are no more twain, but o flesh. 1520
10:17 came o running, and kneeled to him, 1520
10:18 *there is* none good but o, *that is,* God. 1520
10:21 and said unto him, O *thing* thou lackest: 1520
10:37 o on thy right hand, and the other on thy 1520
11:29 I will also ask of you o question, 1520
12: 6 Having yet therefore o son, 1520
12:28 And one of the scribes came, 1520
12:29 O Israel; The Lord our God is o Lord: 1520
13: 1 o of his disciples saith unto him, Master, 1520
13: 2 shall **not** be left o stone upon another, 3364
14:10 And Judas Iscariot, o of the twelve, 1520
14:18 O of you which eateth with me shall 1520
14:19 and to say unto him o **by one,** *Is* it I? 1527
14:19 and to say unto him one **by o,** *Is* it I? 1527
14:20 and said unto them, *It is* o of the twelve, 1520
14:37 couldest not thou watch o hour? 1520
14:43 o of the twelve, and with him a great 1520
14:47 And o of them that stood by drew 1520+5100
14:66 there cometh o of the maids of the high NIG
14:69 o that stood by, This is o of them. NIG
14:70 again to Peter, Surely thou art o of them: NIG
15: 6 Now at *that* feast he released unto them o 1520
15: 7 And there was o named Barabbas, NIG

Mk	
15:21 And they compel o Simon a Cyrenian,	5100
15:27 the o on *his* right hand, and the other on	1520
15:36 And o ran and filled a spunge *full of*	1520
Lk	
2: 3 to be taxed, every o into his own city.	1538
2:15 the shepherds said o to another, Let us	240
2:36 And there was o Anna, a prophetess,	NIG
3: 4 The voice of o crying in the wilderness,	NIG
3:16 o mightier than I cometh, the latchet of	3588
4:34 who thou art, the **Holy O** of God.	40
4:40 and he laid *his* hands on every o of them,	1520
5: 3 And he entered into o of the ships,	1520
6: 9 I will ask you o thing; Is it lawful on	5101
6:11 communed o with **another** what they	240
6:29 *And* unto him that smiteth thee on the o	NIG
6:40 every o that is perfect shall be as his	3956
7: 8 and I say unto o, Go, and he goeth;	3778
7:32 and calling o to **another**, and saying,	240
7:36 And o of the Pharisees desired him that	5100
7:41 the o ought five hundred pence,	1520
8:25 saying o to **another**, What *manner* of	240
8:42 he had **only** daughter, about twelve	3439
8:49 there cometh o from the ruler of	5100
9: 8 that o of the old prophets is risen again.	1520
9:19 others *say*, that o of the old prophets is	5100
9:33 o for thee, and one for Moses, and one for	1520
9:33 and o for Moses, and one for Elias:	1520
9:33 and one for Moses, and o for Elias:	1520
9:43 But while they wondered **every** o at all	3956
9:49 we saw o casting out devils in thy name;	5100
10:42 But o *thing* is needful: and Mary hath	1520
11: 1 o of his disciples said unto him, Lord,	5100
11: 4 we also forgive **every** o *that is* indebted	3956
11:10 For **every** o that asketh receiveth;	3956
11:45 Then answered o of the lawyers,	5100
11:46 yourselves touch not the burdens with o	1520
12: 1 insomuch that *they* trode o upon **another**,	240
12: 6 not o of them is forgotten before God?	1520
12:13 And o of the company said unto him,	5100
12:25 thought can add to his stature o cubit?	1520
12:27 his glory was not arrayed like o of these.	1520
12:52 from henceforth there shall be five in o	1520
13:10 And he was teaching in o of	1520
13:15 not **each** o of you on the sabbath loose	1538
13:23 Then said o unto him, Lord, are there few	5100
14: 1 as he went into the house of o of the chief	5100
14:15 And when o of them that sat at meat with	5100
14:18 they all with o **consent** began to make	1520
15: 4 if he lose o of them, doth not leave	1520
15: 7 likewise joy shall be in heaven over o	1520
15: 8 she lose o piece, doth not light a candle,	1520
15:10 of God over o sinner that repenteth.	1520
15:19 make me as o of thy hired *servants*.	1520
15:26 And he called o of the servants,	1520
16: 5 So he called every o of his lord's debtors	1520
16:13 for either he will hate the o, and love	1520
16:13 or else he will hold to the o, and despise	1520
16:17 to pass, than o tittle of the law to fail.	1520
16:30 but if o went unto them from the dead,	5100
16:31 persuaded, though o rose from the dead.	1520
17: 2 than that he should offend o of these little	1520
17:15 And o of them, when he saw that he was	1520
17:22 when ye shall desire to see o of the days	1520
17:24 that lighteneth out of the o *part* under	3588
17:34 in that night there shall be two *men* in o	1520
17:34 the o shall be taken, and the other shall	1520
17:35 the o shall be taken, and the other left.	1520
17:36 the o shall be taken, and the other left.	1520
18:10 the o a Pharisee, and the other a publican.	1520
18:14 for **every** o that exalteth himself shall be	3956
18:19 for good, save o, *that is*, God.	1520
18:22 Yet lackest thou o *thing*: sell all that thou	1520
19:26 That unto **every** o which hath shall be	3956
19:44 they shall not leave in thee o stone upon	NIG
20: 1 it came to pass, *that* on o of those days,	1520
20: 3 unto them, I will also ask you o thing;	1520
21: 6 the which there shall not be left o stone	NIG
22:36 let him sell his garment, and buy o.	NIG
22:47 o of the twelve, went before them,	1520
22:50 And o of them smote the servant	1520+5100
22:59 about the space of o hour after another	1520
23:14 unto me, as o that perverteth the people:	NIG
23:17 (For of necessity he must release o unto	1520
23:26 they laid hold upon o Simon, a Cyrenian,	5100
23:33 o on the right hand, and the other on	3739
23:39 And o of the malefactors which were	1520
24:17 *are* these that ye have o to **another**,	240
24:18 And the o *of them*, whose name *was*	1520
24:32 And they said o to **another**, Did not our	240
Jn	
1:23 the voice of o crying in the wilderness,	NIG
1:26 but there standeth o among you, whom	NIG
1:40 O of the two which heard John speak,	1520
3: 8 so is **every** o that is born of the Spirit.	3956
3:20 **every** o that doeth evil hateth the light,	3956
4:33 Therefore said the disciples o to **another**,	240
4:37 And herein is that saying true, **O** soweth,	243
5:44 which receive honour o of **another**,	240
5:45 there is o that accuseth you, *even* Moses,	NIG
6: 7 that **every** o of them may take a little.	1538
6: 8 **O** of his disciples, Andrew, Simon Peter's	1520
6:22 save that o whereinto his disciples were	1520
6:40 that **every** o which seeth the Son,	3956
6:70 you twelve, and o of you is a devil?	1520
6:71 should betray him, being o of the twelve.	1520
7:21 I have done o work, and ye all marvel.	1520
7:50 came to *Jesus* by night, being o of them,)	1520

Jn	
8: 9 out o **by one**, beginning at the eldest,	1527
8: 9 **one by o**, beginning at the eldest,	1527
8:18 I am o that bear witness of myself,	NIG
8:41 fornication; we have o Father, *even* God.	1520
8:50 there is o that seeketh and judgeth.	NIG
9:25 o *thing* I know, that, whereas I was blind,	1520
9:32 opened the eyes of o that was born blind.	NIG
10:16 there shall be o fold, *and* one shepherd.	1520
10:16 there shall be one fold, *and* o shepherd.	1520
10:30 I and *my* Father are o.	1520
11:49 And o of them, *named* Caiaphas, being	1520
11:50 that o man should die for the people,	1520
11:52 that also he should gather together in o	1520
12: 2 Lazarus was o of them that sat at the table	1520
12: 4 Then saith o of his disciples, Judas Iscariot,	1520
12:48 not my words, hath o that judgeth him:	NIG
13:14 ye also ought to wash o **another's** feet.	240
13:21 unto you, that o of you shall betray me.	1520
13:22 Then the disciples looked o on **another**,	240
13:23 there was leaning on Jesus' bosom o	1520
13:34 I give unto you, That ye love o **another**;	240
13:34 loved you, that ye also love o **another**.	240
13:35 my disciples, if ye have love o to **another**.	240
15:12 ye love o **another**, as I have loved you.	240
15:17 I command you, that ye love o **another**.	240
17:11 given me, that they may be o, as we *are*.	1520
17:21 That they all may be o; as thou, Father,	1520
17:21 in thee, that they also may be o in us:	1520
17:22 that they may be o, even as we are one:	1520
17:22 that they may be one, even as we are o:	1520
17:23 me, that they may be made perfect in o;	1520
18:14 it was expedient that o man should die	1520
18:17 Art not thou also o of this man's disciples?	NIG
18:22 o of the officers which stood by stroke	1520
18:25 Art not thou also o of his disciples?	NIG
18:26 O of the servants of the high priest,	1520
18:37 **Every** o that is of the truth heareth my	3956
18:39 that I should release unto you o at	1520
19:18 with him, **on either side o**,	1782+1782+2532
19:34 But o of the soldiers with a spear pierced	1520
20:12 the o at the head, and the other at the feet,	1520
20:24 But Thomas, o of the twelve,	1520
21:25 if they should be written every o,	1520
Ac	
1:14 These all continued **with o** accord in	3661
1:22 must o be ordained *to be* a witness with	1520
2: 1 they were all **with o** accord in one place.	3661
2: 1 with one accord in o place.	840+1909+3588
2: 7 marvelled, saying o to **another**, Behold,	240
2:12 and were in doubt, saying o to another,	243
2:27 wilt thou suffer thine **Holy O** to see	3741
2:38 be baptized **every** o of you in the name	1538
2:46 continuing daily **with o** accord in	3661
3:14 But ye denied the **Holy O** and the Just,	40
3:26 in turning away **every** o of you from *his*	1538
4:24 lift up their voice to God **with o** accord,	3661
4:32 of them that believed were of o heart	1520
4:32 believed were of one heart and of o soul:	NIG
5:12 were all **with o** accord in Solomon's	3661
5:16 and they were healed **every** o.	537
5:25 Then came o and told them, saying,	5100
5:34 Then stood there up o in the council,	5100
7:24 And seeing o *of them* suffer wrong,	5100
7:26 **set them at o** again, saying,	1515+1519+4900
7:26 why do ye wrong o to **another**?	240
7:52 before of the coming of the **Just O**;	1342
7:57 ears, and ran upon him **with o** accord,	3661
8: 6 And the people **with o** accord gave heed	3661
8: 9 giving out that himself was some great o:	3173
9:11 inquire in the house of Judas for o called	NIG
9:43 that he tarried many days in Joppa with o	5100
10: 2 and o that feared God with all his house,	NIG
10: 5 and call for o Simon, whose surname is	5100
10: 6 He lodgeth with o Simon a tanner,	5100
10:22 that feareth God, and of good report	NIG
10:28 or come unto o of **another nation**;	246
10:32 he is lodged in the house of o Simon a	NIG
11:28 And there stood up o of them named	1520
12:10 went out, and passed on through o street;	1520
12:20 but they came **with o** accord to him,	3661
13:25 But behold, there cometh o after me,	NIG
13:35 not suffer thine **Holy O** to see corruption.	3741
15:25 unto us, being assembled **with o** accord,	3661
15:39 they departed asunder o from the other:	240
17: 7 saying that there is another king, o Jesus.	NIG
17:26 And hath made of o blood all nations of	1520
17:27 him, though he be not far from every o	1520
18: 7 named Justus, o that worshipped God,	1520
18:12 Jews made insurrection with o accord	3661
19: 9 daily in the school of o Tyrannus.	5100
19:14 And there were seven sons of o Sceva,	NIG
19:29 rushed **with o** accord into the theatre.	3661
19:32 Some therefore cried o *thing*, and	5100
19:34 all with o voice about the space of two	1520
19:38 are deputies: let them implead o **another**.	240
20:31 years I ceased not to warn every o night	1520
21: 6 we had taken our leave o of **another**,	240
21: 7 The brethren, and abode with them o day.	1520
21: 8 the evangelist, which was o of the seven;	NIG
21:16 brought *with them* o Mnason of Cyprus,	1520
21:26 should be offered for every o of them.	1520
22:34 And some cried o *thing*, some another,	5100
22:12 **O** Ananias, a devout man according to	1342
22:14 and see *that* **Just O**, and shouldest hear	1342
23: 6 But when Paul perceived that the o part	1520
23:17 Then Paul called o of the centurions unto	1520

Ac	
24:21 Except *it be* for this o voice, that I cried	1520
25:19 of o Jesus, *which was* dead, whom Paul	5100
27: 1 other prisoners unto o named Julius,	NIG
27: 2 o Aristarchus, a Macedonian of	NIG
28: 2 and received us **every** o, because of	3956
28:13 and after o day the south wind blew,	1520
28:25 after that Paul had spoken o word,	1520
Ro	
1:16 unto salvation to **every** o that believeth;	3956
1:27 burned in their lust o towards **another**;	240
2:15 accusing or else excusing o another;)	240
2:28 For he is not a Jew, which is o outwardly;	NIG
2:29 But he *is* a Jew, which is o inwardly;	NIG
3:10 There is none righteous, no, not o:	1520
3:12 that doeth good, **no, not o**.	1520+2193+3756
3:30 Seeing *it is* o God, which shall justify	1520
5: 7 scarcely for a righteous *man* will o die:	5100
5:12 as by o man sin entered into the world,	1520
5:15 For if through the offence of o be many	1520
5:15 by grace, which is by o man, Jesus Christ,	1520
5:16 And not as *it was* by o that sinned, *so is*	1520
5:16 for the judgment *was* by o to	1520
5:17 For if by o man's offence death reigned by	1520
5:17 by one man's offence death reigned by o;	1520
5:17 of righteousness shall reign in life by o,	1520
5:18 Therefore as by the offence of o *judgment*	1520
5:18 the righteousness of o *the free gift* came	1520
5:19 as by o man's disobedience many were	1520
5:19 by the obedience of o shall many be made	1520
9:10 when Rebecca also had conceived by o,	1520
9:21 of the same lump to make o vessel unto	3739
10: 4 righteousness to **every** o that believeth.	3956
12: 4 For as we have many members in o *body*,	1520
12: 5 are o body in Christ, and every one	1520
12: 5 and every o members one of another.	1520
12: 5 and every one members o of **another**.	240
12:10 Be kindly affectioned o to **another** with	240
12:10 in honour preferring o **another**;	240
12:16 Be of the same mind o towards **another**.	240
13: 8 no *man* any *thing*, but to love o **another**:	240
14: 2 For o believeth that *he* may eat all *things*:	3739
14: 5 **O** man esteemeth one day above another:	3739
14: 5 One man esteemeth o day above another:	NIG
14:12 **every** o of us shall give account of himself	1538
14:13 not therefore judge o **another** any more:	240
14:19 *things* wherewith o may edify **another**.	240
15: 2 Let **every** o of us please *his* neighbour for	1538
15: 5 o towards **another** according to Christ	240
15: 6 That ye may with o **mind** *and* one mouth	3661
15: 6 with one mind and o mouth glorify God,	1520
15: 7 Wherefore receive ye o **another**, as Christ	240
15:14 able also to admonish o **another**.	240
16:16 Salute o **another** with a holy kiss.	240
1Co	
1:12 that **every** o of you saith, I am of Paul;	1538
3: 4 For while o saith, I am of Paul;	5100
3: 8 that planteth and he that watereth are o:	1520
4: 6 that no o of you be puffed up for one	1520
4: 6 that no one of you be puffed up for o	1520
5: 1 that o should have *his* father's wife.	5108
5: 5 To deliver **such a** o unto Satan for	5108
5:11 extortioner; with **such a** o no not to eat.	5108
6: 5 that shall be able to judge between	1520
6: 7 because ye go to law o with **another**	1438
6:16 he which is joined to a harlot is o body?	1520
6:16 for two, saith *he*, shall be o flesh.	1520
6:17 But he that is joined unto the Lord is o	1520
7: 5 Defraud ye not o **the other**, except *it be*	240
7: 7 gift of God, o after this manner,	3303+3739
7:17 as the Lord hath called **every** o, so let him	1538
7:25 as so that hath obtained mercy of the Lord	5100
8: 4 and that *there is* none other God but o.	1520
8: 6 But to us *there is* o God, the Father,	1520
8: 6 and o Lord Jesus Christ, by whom *are* all	1520
9:24 in a race run all, but o receiveth the prize?	1520
9:26 so fight I, not as o that beateth the air:	NIG
10: 8 fell in o day three and twenty thousand.	1520
10:17 For we being many are o bread,	1520
10:17 being many are one bread, *and* o body:	1520
10:17 for we are all partakers of that o bread.	1520
11: 5 **even all o as if** she	846+1520+2532+3588
11:20 therefore **into o place**,	846+1909+3588
11:21 For in eating **every** o taketh before *other*	1538
11:21 and o is hungry, and another is drunken.	3739
11:33 come together to eat, tarry o for **another**.	240
12: 8 For to o is given by the Spirit the word of	3739
12:11 But all these worketh that o and	1520
12:12 For as the body is o, and hath many	1520
12:12 and all the members of that o body,	1520
12:12 of *that* one body, being many, are o body:	1520
12:13 by o Spirit are we all baptized into one	1520
12:13 by one Spirit are we all baptized into o	1520
12:13 have been all made to drink into o Spirit.	1520
12:14 For the body is not o member, but many.	1520
12:18 now hath God set the members every o	1520
12:19 if they were all o member, where were	1520
12:20 *are they* many members, yet *but* o body.	1520
12:25 should have the same care o for **another**.	240
12:26 And whether o member suffer,	1520
12:26 suffer with *it*; or o member be honoured,	1520
14:23 come together **into o place**,	846+1909+3588
14:24 and there come in o that believeth not,	5100
14:24 or unlearned, he is convinced of all, he is	1520
14:26 **every** o of you hath a psalm, hath a	1538
14:27 and that by course; and let o interpret.	1520
14:31 For ye may all prophesy o **by one**,	1520+2596
14:31 For ye may all prophesy **one by o**,	1520+2596

O

1Co 15: 8 of me also, as of o born out of due time. 3588
15:39 but *there is* a *kind of* flesh of men, 243
15:40 but the glory of the celestial *is* o, 2087
15:41 *There is* o glory of the sun, 243
15:41 for o star differeth from *another* star in NIG
16: 2 Upon the first *day* of the week let **every** o 1538
16:16 and to **every** o that helpeth with **us,** and 3956
16:20 Greet ye o **another** with a holy kiss. 240

2Co 2: 7 comfort **him,** lest perhaps **such a** o should 5108
2:16 To the o **we are** the savour of death unto 3739
5:10 that **every** o may receive the *things done* 1538
5:14 that if o died for all, then were all dead: 1520
10:11 Let **such a** o think this, that, such as we 5108
11: 2 for I have espoused you to o **husband,** 1520
11:24 five times received I forty *stripes* save o. 1520
12: 2 **such a** o caught up to the third heaven. 5108
12: 5 Of **such a** o will I glory: yet of myself I 5108
13:11 good comfort, be of o mind, live in peace; 846
13:12 Greet o **another** with a holy kiss. 240

Gal 3:10 Cursed *is* **every** o that continueth not in 3956
3:13 Cursed *is* **every** o that hangeth on a tree: 3956
3:16 but as of o, And to thy seed, which is 1520
3:20 Now a mediator is not a *mediator* of o, 1520
3:20 is not a *mediator* of one, but God is o. 1520
3:28 nor female: for ye are all o in Christ Jesus. 1520
4:22 the o by a bondmaid, the other by a 1520
4:24 the o from the mount Sinai, 1520
5:13 to the flesh, but by love serve o **another.** 240
5:14 For all the law is fulfilled in o word, 1520
5:15 But if ye bite and devour o **another,** 240
5:15 heed ye be not consumed o of **another.** 240
5:17 and these are contrary the o to the other: 240
5:26 provoking o **another,** envying one another. 240
5:26 provoking one another, envying o **another.** 240

6: 1 restore **such a** o in the spirit of meekness; 5108
6: 2 Bear ye o **another's** burdens, and so 240

Eph 1:10 **gather together in** o all *things* in Christ, 346
2:14 who hath made both o, and hath broken 1520
2:15 to make in himself of twain o new man, 1520
2:16 both unto God in o **body** by the cross, 1520
2:18 through him we both have access by o 1520
4: 2 forbearing o **another** in love; 240
4: 4 *There is* o body, and one Spirit, even as ye 1520
4: 4 *There is* one body, and o Spirit, and ye 1520
4: 4 even as ye are called in o hope of your 1520
4: 5 O Lord, one faith, one baptism, 1520
4: 5 One Lord, one faith, o baptism, 1520
4: 5 One Lord, o faith, one baptism, 1520
4: 6 O God and Father of all, who *is* above all, 1520
4: 7 But unto **every** o of us is given grace 1520
4:25 for we are members o of **another.** 240
4:32 be ye kind o to **another,** tenderhearted, 240
4:32 tenderhearted, forgiving o **another,** 1438
5:21 Submitting yourselves o to **another** in 240
5:31 his wife, and they two shall be o flesh. 1520
5:33 Nevertheless let **every** o of you in 1520

Php 1:16 The o preach Christ of contention, 3303
1:27 your affairs, that ye stand fast in o spirit, 1520
1:27 with o mind striving together for the faith 1520
2: 2 love, *being* of o **accord,** of one mind. 4861
2: 2 love, *being* of one accord, of o mind. 1520
3:13 *this* o *thing* I do, forgetting those *things* 1520

Col 3: 9 Lie not to o **another,** seeing that ye have 240
3:13 Forbearing o **another,** and forgiving one 240
3:13 one another, and forgiving o **another,** 1438
3:15 to the which also ye are called in o **body;** 1520
3:16 admonishing o **another** in psalms and 1438
4: 9 and beloved **brother,** who is o of you. NIG
4:12 Epaphras, who is o of you, a servant of NIG

1Th 3: 2 comforted and charged **every** o of you, 1520
3:12 and abound in love o towards **another,** 240
4: 4 That **every** o of you should know how to 1538
4: 9 are taught of God to love o **another.** 240
4:18 Wherefore comfort o **another** with these 240
5:11 o **another,** even as also ye 1520+1520+3588

2Th 1: 3 the charity of **every** o of you all towards 1520

1Ti 2: 5 For *there is* o God, and one mediator 1520
2: 5 and o mediator between God and men, 1520
3: 2 the husband of o **wife,** vigilant, sober, 1520
3: 4 O that ruleth well his own house, having NIG
3:12 Let the deacons be the husbands of o **wife,** 1520
5: 9 years old, having been the wife of o **man,** 1520
5:21 o *before another,* doing nothing by NIG

2Ti 2:19 Let **every** o that nameth the name of 3956

Tit 1: 6 If any be blameless, the husband of o **wife,** 1520
1:12 Of themselves, *even* a prophet of their 5100
3: 3 and envy, hateful, *and* hating o **another.** 240

Phm 1: 9 **thee,** being **such a** o as Paul the aged, 5108

Heb 2: 6 But o in a certain place testified, saying, 5100
2:11 and they who are sanctified *are* all of o: 1520
3:13 But exhort o **another** daily, while it is 1438
5:12 ye have need that o teach you again NIG
5:13 For **every** o that useth milk *is* unskilful in 3956
6:11 we desire that **every** o of you do shew 1538
10:12 But this **man,** after he had offered o 1520
10:14 For by o offering he hath perfected for 1520
10:24 And let us consider o **another** to provoke 240
10:25 but exhorting o **another:** and so much NIG
11:12 Therefore sprang there even of o, 1520
12:16 who for o morsel of meat sold his 1520
13:14 continuing city, but we seek o to come. 3588

Jas 2:10 *yet* offend in o *point,* he is guilty of all. 1520
2:16 And o of you say unto them, Depart in 5100
2:19 Thou believest that there is o **God;** 1520
4:11 Speak not evil o of **another,** brethren. 240

Jas 4:12 There is o lawgiver, who is able to save 1520
5: 9 Grudge not o against **another,** brethren, 240
5:16 Confess *your* faults o to **another,** 240
5:16 and pray o for **another,** that ye may be 240
5:19 do err from the truth, and o convert him; 5100

1Pe 1:22 *that* ye love o **another** with a pure heart 240
3: 8 Finally, *be* ye all of o **mind,** 3675
3: 8 having **compassion** o of **another,** love 4835
4: 9 Use hospitality o to **another** without 240
4:10 *even* so minister the same o to **another,** 1438
5: 5 all *of you* be subject o to **another,** 240
5:14 Greet ye o **another** with a kiss of charity. 240

2Pe 3: 8 not ignorant of this o *thing,* that one day 1520
3: 8 not ignorant of this one *thing,* that o day 1520
3: 8 and a thousand years as o day. 1520

1Jn 1: 7 we have fellowship o with **another,** 240
2:13 you have overcome the **wicked** o. 4190
2:14 and ye have overcome the **wicked** o. 4190
2:20 But ye have an unction from the **Holy O,** 40
2:29 ye know that **every** o which doeth 3956
3:11 that we should love o **another.** 240
3:12 *who* was of that **wicked** o, and slew his 4190
3:23 and love o **another,** as he gave us 240
4: 7 Beloved, let us love o **another:** for love is 240
4: 7 and **every** o that loveth is born of God, 3956
4:11 loved us, we ought also to love o **another.** 240
4:12 If we love o **another,** God dwelleth in us, 240
5: 1 **every** o that loveth him that begat loveth 3956
5: 7 and the Holy Ghost: and these three are o. 1520
5: 8 and the blood: and *these* three agree in o. 1520
5:18 and that **wicked** o toucheth him not. 4190

2Jn 1: 5 the beginning, that we love o **another.** 240

Rev 1:13 in the midst of the seven candlesticks o NIG
2:23 I will give unto **every** o of you according 1538
4: 2 set in heaven, and o sat on the throne. NIG
5: 4 And o of the elders saith unto me, 1520
5: 8 having **every** o of them harps, 1538
6: 1 And I saw when the Lamb opened o of 1520
6: 1 o of the four beasts saying, Come and see. 1538
6: 4 and that they should kill o **another:** 240
6:11 And white robes were given unto **every** o 1538
7:13 And o of the elders answered, saying unto 1520
9:12 O woe is past; *and* behold, there come 1520
11:10 and shall send gifts o to **another;** 240
13: 3 And I saw o of his heads as *it were* NIG
14:14 upon the cloud o sat like unto the Son of NIG
15: 7 And o of the four beasts gave unto 1520
17: 1 And there came o of the seven angels 1520
17:10 and is, *and* the other is not yet come; 1520
17:12 receive power as kings o hour with 1520
17:13 These have o mind, and shall their 1520
18: 8 Therefore shall her plagues come in o day, 1520
18:10 For in o hour is thy judgment come. 1520
18:17 For in o hour so great riches is come to 1520
18:19 for in o hour is she made desolate. 1520
21: 9 And there came unto me o of the seven 1520
21:21 every several gate was o of o pearl: 1520

ONE'S (2) [ONE]
Ecc 7: 1 the day of death than the day of o birth. 2050.2
Ac 16:26 and **every** o bands were loosed. 3956

ONES (77) [ONE]
Ge 34:29 all their **little** o, and their wives took 2945
43: 8 both we, and thou, *and* also our **little** o. 2945
45:19 out of the land of Egypt for your **little** o, 2945
46: 5 and their **little** o, and their wives, 2945
47:24 and for food for your **little** o. 2945
50: 8 only their **little** o, and their flocks, 2945
50:21 I will nourish you and your **little** o. 2945
Ex 10:10 as I will let you go, and your **little** o: 2945
10:24 let your **little** o also go with you. 2945
Nu 14:31 your **little** o, which ye said should be a 2945
31: 9 their **little** o, and took the spoil of all 2945
31:17 kill every male among the **little** o, 2945
32:16 for our cattle, and cities for our **little** o: 2945
32:17 **little** o shall dwell in the fenced cities 2945
32:24 Build ye cities for your **little** o, 2945
32:26 Our **little** o, our wives, our flocks, 2945
Dt 1:39 Moreover your **little** o, which ye said 2945
2:34 women, and the **little** o, of every city, 2945
3:19 and your **little** o, and your cattle, 2945
20:14 the **little** o, and the cattle, and all that is 2945
2: 6 whether they be **young** o, or eggs, 667
29:11 Your **little** o, your wives, and thy stranger 2945
Jos 1:14 Your wives, your **little** o, and your cattle, 2945
8:35 the **little** o, and the strangers that were 2945
Jdg 5:22 the pransings of their **mighty** o. NIH
18:21 put the **little** o and the cattle and 2945
2Sa 15:22 and all the **little** o that *were* with him. 2945
1Ch 16:13 ye children of Jacob, his chosen o. NIH
2Ch 20:13 with their **little** o, their wives, 2945
31:18 to the genealogy of all their **little** o, 2945
Ezr 8:21 for our **little** o, and for all our substance. 2945
Est 8:11 *both* **little** o and women, and *to take* 2945
Job 21:11 They send forth their **little** o like a flock, 5759
38:41 when his **young** o cry unto God, 3206
39: 3 they bring forth their **young** o, 3206
39: 4 Their **young** o are in good liking, 1121
39:16 She is hardened against her **young** o, 1121
39:30 Her **young** o also suck up blood: and 667
Ps 10:10 that the poor may fall by his strong o. NIH
83: 3 and consulted against thy **hidden** o. 6845
137: 9 dasheth thy **little** o against the stones. 5768
Pr 1:22 How long, ye **simple** o, will ye love 6612

Pr 7: 7 beheld among the **simple** o, I discerned 6612
Isa 5:17 waste places of the **fat** o shall strangers 4220
10:16 of hosts, send among his **fat** o leanness; 4924
10:33 **high** o of stature *shall* be hewn down, 7311
11: 7 their **young** o shall lie down together: 3206
13: 3 I have commanded my **sanctified** o, 6942
13: 3 I have also called my **mighty** o for mine 1368
14: 9 for thee, *even* all the **chief** o of the earth; 6260
24:21 the host of the **high** o *that are* on high, 4791
25: 4 when the blast of the **terrible** o *is* as a 6184
25: 5 the branch of the **terrible** o shall be 6184
29: 5 the multitude of the **terrible** o *shall be* as 6184
32:11 that are at ease; be troubled, ye careless o: NIH
33: 7 Behold, their **valiant** o shall cry without: 691
57:15 and to revive the heart of the **contrite** o. 1792
Jer 2:33 hast thou also taught the **wicked** o thy 7451
8:16 the sound of the neighing of his **strong** o; 47
14: 3 their nobles have sent their **little** o to 6810
46: 5 their **mighty** o are beaten down, 1368
48: 4 her **little** o have caused a cry to be heard. 6810
48:45 crown of the head of the tumultuous o. 1121
La 4: 3 breast, they give suck to their **young** o: 1482
Da 4:17 the demand *by* the word of the **holy** o: 6922
8: 8 for it came up four **notable** o toward 2380
11:17 whole kingdom, and **upright** o with him; 3477
Joel 3:11 cause thy **mighty** o to come down, 1368
Zec 4:14 said he, These *are* the two anointed o, 1121
13: 7 I will turn mine hand upon the **little** o. 6819
Mt 10:42 **little** o a cup of cold *water* only in the 3398
18: 6 whoso shall offend one of these **little** o 3398
18:10 that ye despise not one of these **little** o; 3398
18:14 that one of these **little** o should perish. 3398
Mk 9:42 one of *these* **little** o that believe in me, 3398
10:42 **great** o exercise authority upon them. 3173
Lk 17: 2 that he should offend one of these **little** o. 3398

ONESIMUS (4)
Col 4: 9 With **O,** a faithful and beloved brother, 3682
4: 9 S to the Colossians by Tychicus and **O.** 3682
Phm 1:10 beseech thee for my son **O,** whom I have 3682
1: S from Rome to Philemon, by **O** a servant. 3682

ONESIPHORUS (2)
2Ti 1:16 The Lord give mercy unto the house of **O;** 3683
4:19 and Aquila, and the household of **O.** 3683

ONIONS (1)
Nu 11: 5 and the leeks, and the **o,** and the garlick: 1211

ONLY (253)
Ge 6: 5 of his heart *was* o evil continually. 7535
7:23 Noah o remained *alive,* and *they* that 389
14:24 Save o that which the young men have 7535
19: 8 o unto these men do nothing; for 7535
22: 2 Take now thy son, thine o *son* Isaac, 3173
22:12 withheld thy son, thine o *son* from me. 3173
22:16 hast not withheld thy son, thine o *son:* 3173
24: 8 oath: o bring not my son thither again. 7535
27:13 obey my voice, and go fetch them o to me. 389
34:22 O herein will the men consent unto us for 389
34:23 o let us consent unto them, and they will 389
41:40 o *in* the throne will I be greater than thou. 7535
47:22 O the land of the priests bought he not; 7535
47:26 except the land of the priests o, 905+3807.1
50: 8 o their little ones, and their flocks, 7535
Ex 8: 9 *that* they may remain in the river o? 7535
8:11 people; they shall remain in the river o. 7535
8:28 o ye shall not go very far away: 7535
9:26 O in the land of Goshen, where the 7535
10:17 my sin o *this* once, and intreat the LORD 389
10:17 he may take away from me this death o. 7535
10:24 o let your flocks and your herds be stayed: 7535
12:16 eat, that o may be done of you. 905+3807.1
21:19 o he shall pay *for* the loss of his time, 7535
22:20 Save unto the LORD o, he shall be 905+3807.1
22:27 For that *is* his covering o, it *is* his 905+3807.1
23: O he shall not go in unto the vail, nor 389
Lev 21:23 O he shall not go in unto the vail, nor 389
27:26 the firstling of the beasts, which should 389
Nu 1:49 O thou shalt not number the tribe of Levi, 389
12: 2 Hath the LORD **indeed** spoken o by 389+7535
14: 9 O rebel not ye against the LORD, 389
18: 3 o they shall not come nigh the vessels of 389
20:19 I will o, without *doing any* thing *else,* go 7535
22:35 o the word that I shall speak unto thee, 657
31:22 O the gold, and the silver, the brass, 389
36: 6 o to the family of the tribe of their father 389
Dt 2:28 o I will pass through on my feet; 7535
2:35 O the cattle we took for a prey unto 7535
2:37 O unto the land of the children of 7535
3:11 For Og king of Bashan remained o of 7535
4: 9 O take heed to thyself, and keep thy soul 7535
4:12 but saw no similitude; o *ye heard* a voice. 2108
8: 3 that man doth not live by bread o, 905+3807.1
10:15 the LORD had a delight in thy fathers 7535
12:16 O ye shall not eat the blood; ye shall pour 7535
12:23 Be sure that thou eat not the blood: 7535
12:26 O thy holy *things* which thou hast, 7535
15: 5 O if thou carefully hearken unto the voice 7535
15:23 o thou shalt not eat the blood thereof; 7535
20:20 O the trees which thou knowest that they 7535
22:25 man o that lay with her shall die: 905+3807.1
28:13 thou shalt be above o, and thou shalt not 7535
28:29 thou shalt be o oppressed and 389
28:33 thou shalt be o oppressed and 7535
29:14 Neither with you o do I make this 905+3807.1

Jos	1: 7 O be thou strong and very courageous,	7535
	1:17 to the LORD thy God be with thee, as he	7535
	1:18 death: o be strong and of a good courage.	7535
	6:15 o on that day they compassed the city	7535
	6:17 o Rahab the harlot shall live, she and	7535
	6:24 o the silver, and the gold, and the vessels	7535
	8: 2 o the spoil thereof, and the cattle thereof,	7535
	8:27 O the cattle and the spoil of that city	7535
	11:13 none of them, save Hazor o;	905+3807.1
	11:22 o in Gaza, in Gath, and in Ashdod,	7535
	13: 6 o divide thou it by lot unto the Israelites	7535
	13:14 O unto the tribe of Levi he gave none	7535
	17:17 power: thou shalt not have one lot o:	NIH
Jdg	3: 2 O that the generations of the children of	7535
	6:37 and if the dew be on the fleece o,	905+3807.1
	6:39 let it now be dry o upon the fleece,	905+3807.1
	6:40 for it was dry upon the fleece o,	905+3807.1
	10:15 deliver us o, we pray thee, this day.	389
	11:34 she was his o child; beside her he had	7535
	16:28 I pray thee, o this once, O God,	389
	19:20 lie upon me; o lodge not in the street.	7535
1Sa	1:13 o her lips moved, but her voice was not	7535
	1:23 o the LORD establish his word.	389
	5: 4 o the stump of Dagon was left to him.	7535
	7: 3 unto the LORD, and serve him o	905+3807.1
	7: 4 and served the LORD o.	905+3807.1
	12:24 O fear the LORD, and serve him in truth	389
	18:17 o be thou valiant for me, and fight	389
	20:14 thou shalt not o while yet I live shew me	518
	20:39 Jonathan and David knew the matter.	389
2Sa	13:32 king's sons; for Amnon o is dead:	905+3807.1
	13:33 sons are dead: for Amnon is dead.	905+3807.1
	17: 2 and I will smite the king o:	905+3807.1
	20:21 deliver him o, and I will depart	905+3807.1
	23:10 the people returned after him o to spoil.	389
1Ki	3: 2 O the people sacrificed in high places,	7535
	3: 3 o he sacrificed and burnt incense in high	7535
	4:19 was the o officer which was in the land.	259
	8:39 (for thou, even thou o, knowest	905+3807.1
	12:20 of David, but the tribe of Judah o.	905+3807.1
	14: 8 do that o which was right in mine eyes;	7535
	14:13 for he o of Jeroboam shall come to	905+3807.1
	15: 5 save o in the matter of Uriah the Hittite.	7535
	18:22 I, even I o, remain a prophet of	905+3807.1
	19:10 I, even I o, am left; and they seek	905+3807.1
	19:14 I, even I o, am left; and they seek	905+3807.1
	22:31 save o with the king of Israel.	905+3807.1
2Ki	3:25 o in Kir-haraseth left they the stones	5704
	10:23 but the worshippers of Baal o.	905+3807.1
	17:18 none left but the tribe of Judah o.	905+3807.1
	19:19 art the LORD God, even thou o.	905+3807.1
	21: 8 o if they will observe to do according to	7535
1Ch	22:12 O the LORD give thee wisdom and	389
2Ch	2: 6 save o to burn sacrifice before him?	518+3588
	6:30 (for thou o knowest the hearts of	905+3807.1
	18:30 save o with the king of Israel.	905+3807.1
	33:17 yet unto the LORD their God o.	7535
Ezr	10:15 O Jonathan the son of Asahel and	389
Est	1:16 hath not done wrong to the king o,	905+3807.1
Job	1:12 o upon himself put not forth thine hand.	7535
	1:15 and I o am escaped alone to tell thee.	7535
	1:16 and I o am escaped alone to tell thee.	7535
	1:17 and I o am escaped alone to tell thee.	7535
	1:19 and I o am escaped alone to tell thee.	7535
	13:20 O do not two things unto me: then will I	389
	34:29 done against a nation, or against a man o:	3162
Ps	4: 8 o makest me dwell in safety.	910+3807.1
	51: 4 Against thee, thee o, have I sinned,	905+3807.1
	62: 2 He o is my rock and my salvation;	389
	62: 4 They o consult to cast him down from his	389
	62: 5 My soul, wait thou o upon God; for my	389
	62: 6 He o is my rock and my salvation: he is	389
	71:16 thy righteousness, even of thine o.	905+3807.1
	72:18 who o doeth wondrous things.	905+3807.1
	91: 8 O with thine eyes shalt thou behold and	7535
Pr	4: 3 and o beloved in the sight of my mother.	3173
	5:17 Let them be o thine own,	905+3807.1
	11:23 The desire of the righteous is o good:	389
	13:10 O by pride cometh contention: but with	7535
	14:23 the talk of the lips tendeth o to penury.	389
	17:11 An evil man seeketh o rebellion: therefore	389
	21: 5 The thoughts of the diligent tend o to	389
	21: 5 but of every one that is hasty o to want.	389
Ecc	7:29 Lo, this o have I found, that God	905+3807.1
SS	6: 9 she is the o one of her mother, she is	NIH
Isa	4: 1 o let us be called by thy name, to take	7535
	26:13 by thee o will we make mention of	905+3807.1
	28:19 it shall be a vexation o to understand	7535
	37:20 thou art the LORD, even thou o.	905+3807.1
Jer	3:13 O acknowledge thine iniquity, that thou	389
	6:26 as for an o son, most bitter lamentation:	3173
	32:30 children of Judah have o done evil before	389
	32:30 for the children of Israel have o provoked	389
Eze	7: 5 An evil, an o evil, behold, is come.	259
	14:16 they o shall be delivered,	905+3807.1
	14:18 they o shall be delivered	905+3807.1
	44:20 they shall o poll their heads.	3697+3697
Am	3: 2 You o have I known of all the families of	7535
	8:10 will make it as the mourning of an o son,	3173
Zec	12:10 as one mourneth for his o son, and shall	3173
Mt	4:10 Lord thy God, and him o shalt thou serve.	3441
	5:47 And if ye salute your brethren o, what do	3440
	8: 8 speak the word o, and my servant shall	3440
	10:42 of cold water o in the name of a disciple,	3440
	12: 4 were with him, but o for the priests?	3441

Mt	14:36 besought him that they might o touch	3440
	17: 8 eyes, they saw no man, save Jesus o.	3441
	21:19 but leaves o, and said unto it,	3440
	21:21 ye shall not o do this which is done to	3440
	24:36 not the angels of heaven, but my Father o.	3441
Mk	2: 7 who can forgive sins but God o?	1520
	5:36 of the synagogue, Be not afraid, o believe.	3440
	6: 8 nothing for their journey, save a staff o;	3440
	8: 9 any more, save Jesus o with themselves.	3441
Lk	4: 8 Lord thy God, and him o shalt thou serve.	3441
	7:12 the o son of his mother, and she was a	3439
	8:42 For he had one o daughter, about twelve	3439
	8:50 believe o, and she shall be made whole.	3440
	9:38 look upon my son: for he is mine o child.	3439
	24:18 Art thou o a stranger in Jerusalem,	3441
Jn	1:14 the glory as of the o begotten	3439
	1:18 o begotten Son, which is in the bosom	3439
	3:16 world, that he gave his o begotten Son,	3439
	3:18 the name of the o begotten Son of God.	3439
	5:18 because he not o had broken the sabbath,	3440
	5:44 not the honour that cometh from God o?	3441
	11:52 And not for that nation o, but that also he	3440
	12: 9 and they came not for Jesus' sake o,	3440
	13: 9 not my feet o, but also my hands and	3440
	17: 3 they might know thee the o true God,	3441
Ac	8:16 o they were baptized in the name of	3440
	11:19 the word to none but unto the Jews o.	3440
	18:25 the Lord, knowing o the baptism of John.	3440
	19:27 So that not o this our craft is in danger to	3440
	21:13 For I am ready not to be bound o,	3440
	21:25 save o from keeping themselves from	1508
	26:29 not o thou, but also all that hear me this	3440
	27:10 not o of the lading and ship, but also of	3440
Ro	1:32 not o do the same, but have pleasure in	3440
	3:29 Is he the God of the Jews o? is he not also	3440
	4: 9 then upon the circumcision o,	NIG
	4:12 them who are not of the circumcision o,	3440
	4:16 not to that o which is of the law, but to	3440
	5: 3 And not o so, but we glory in tribulations	3440
	5:11 And not o so, but we also joy in God	3440
	8:23 And not o they, but ourselves also,	3440
	9:10 And not o this; but when Rebecca also	3440
	9:24 not of the Jews o, but also of the Gentiles?	3440
	13: 5 not for wrath, but also for conscience	3440
	16: 4 unto whom not o I give thanks, but also	3441
	16:27 To God o wise, be glory through Jesus	3441
1Co	7:39 married to whom she will; o in the Lord.	3440
	9: 6 Or I o and Barnabas, have not we power	3441
	14:36 God out from you? or came it unto you o?	3441
	15:19 If in this life o we have hope in Christ,	3440
2Co	7: 7 And not by his coming o, but by	3440
	8:10 not to do, but also to be forward a year	3440
	8:19 And not that o, but who was also chosen	3440
	8:21 Providing for honest things, not o in	3440
	9:12 the administration of this service not o	3440
Gal	1:23 But they had heard o, That he which	3440
	2:10 O they would that we should remember	3440
	3: 2 This o would I learn of you, Received ye	3440
	4:18 and not o when I am present with you.	3440
	5:13 use not liberty for an occasion to	3440
	6:12 o lest they should suffer persecution for	3440
Eph	1:21 not o in this world, but also in that which	3440
Php	1:27 O let your conversation be as it becometh	3440
	1:29 not o to believe on him, but also to suffer	3440
	2:12 not as in my presence o, but now much	3440
	2:27 and not on him o, but on me also, lest I	3440
	4:15 concerning giving and receiving, but ye o.	3441
Col	4:11 These o are my fellowworkers unto	3441
1Th	1: 5 our gospel came not unto you in word o,	3440
	1: 8 the word of the Lord not o in Macedonia	3440
	2: 8 the gospel of God o, but also our own	3440
2Th	2: 7 o he who now letteth will let, until he be	3440
1Ti	1:17 immortal, invisible, the o wise God,	3441
	5:13 and not o idle, but tattlers also and	3441
	6:15 who is the blessed and o Potentate,	3441
	6:16 Who o hath immortality, dwelling in	3441
2Ti	2:20 in a great house there are not o vessels	3440
	4: 8 not to me o, but unto all them also that	3440
	4:11 O Luke is with me. Take Mark,	3441
Heb	9:10 Which stood o in meats and drinks,	3440
	11:17 promises offered up his o begotten son,	3439
	12:26 Yet once more I shake not the earth o,	3440
Jas	1:22 and not hearers o, deceiving your own	3440
	2:24 a man is justified, and not by faith o.	3440
1Pe	2:18 not o to the good and gentle, but also to	3440
1Jn	2: 2 and not for ours o, but also for the sins of	3440
	4: 9 that God sent his o begotten Son into	3439
	5: 6 not by water o, but by water and blood.	3440
2Jn	1: 1 and not I o, but also all they that have	3441
Jude	1: 4 denying the o Lord God, and our Lord	3441
	1:25 To the o wise God our Saviour, be glory	3441
Rev	9: 4 o those men which have not the seal of	3441
	15: 4 for thou o art holy: for all nations shall	3441

ONO (5)

1Ch	8:12 and Shamed, who built O, and Lod,	207
Ezr	2:33 The children of Lod, Hadid, and O,	207
Ne	6: 2 some one of the villages in the plain of O.	207
	7:37 The children of Lod, Hadid, and O,	207
	11:35 Lod, and O, the valley of craftsmen.	207

ONWARD (1)

Ex	40:36 the children of Israel went o in all their	5265

ONYCHA (1)

Ex	30:34 sweet spices, stacte, and o, and galbanum;	7827

ONYX (11)

Ge	2:12 is good: there is bdellium and the o stone.	7718
Ex	25: 7 O stones, and stones to be set in	7718
	28: 9 thou shalt take two o stones, and grave	7718
	28:20 fourth row a beryl, and an o, and a jasper:	7718
	35: 9 o stones, and stones to be set for the	7718
	35:27 rulers brought o stones, and stones to be	7718
	39: 6 they wrought o stones inclosed in ouches	7718
	39:13 the fourth row, a beryl, an o, and a jasper:	7718
1Ch	29: 2 o stones, and stones to be set,	7718
Job	28:16 with the precious o, or the sapphire.	7718
Eze	28:13 the beryl, the o, and the jasper,	7718

OPEN (124) [OPENED, OPENEST, OPENETH,
OPENING, OPENINGS, OPENLY]

Ge	1:20 fowl that may fly above the earth in the o	6440
	38:14 and sat in an o place,	5869+6607
Ex	21:33 if a man shall o a pit, or if a man shall dig	6605
Lev	14: 7 shall let the living bird loose into the o	6440
	14:53 living bird out of the city into the o fields,	6440
	17: 5 which they offer in the o field, even that	6440
Nu	8:16 instead of such as o every womb,	6363
	16:30 the earth o her mouth, and swallow them	6475
	19:15 every o vessel, which hath no covering	6605
	19:16 that is slain with a sword in the o fields,	6440
	24: 3 and the man whose eyes are o hath said:	8365
	24: 4 into a trance, but having his eyes o:	1540
	24:15 and the man whose eyes are o hath said:	8365
	24:16 into a trance, but having his eyes o:	1540
Dt	15: 8 thou shalt o thine hand wide unto	6605+6605
	15:11 Thou shalt o thine hand wide unto	6605+6605
	20:11 peace, and o unto thee, then it shall be,	6605
	28:12 The LORD shall o unto thee his good	6605
Jos	8:17 left the city o, and pursued after Israel.	6605
	10:22 O the mouth of the cave, and bring out	6605
1Sa	3: 1 in those days; there was no o vision.	6555
2Sa	11:11 of my lord, are encamped in the o fields;	6440
1Ki	6:18 was carved with knops and o flowers;	6358
	6:29 cherubims and palm trees and o flowers,	6358
	6:32 cherubims and palm trees and o flowers,	6358
	6:35 and palm trees and o flowers:	6358
	8:29 That thine eyes may be o toward this	6605
	8:52 That thine eyes may be o unto	6605
2Ki	6:17 said, LORD, I pray thee, o his eyes,	6491
	6:20 the eyes of these men, that they may	6605
	9: 3 Then o the door, and flee, and tarry not.	6605
	13:17 he said, O the window eastward. And he	6605
	19:16 o, LORD, thine eyes, and see:	6491
2Ch	6:20 That thine eyes may be o upon this house	6605
	6:40 eyes be o, and let thine ears be attent	6605
	7:15 Now mine eyes shall be o, and mine ears	6605
Ne	1: 6 ear now be attentive, and thine eyes o,	6605
	6: 5 the fifth time with an o letter in his hand;	6605
Job	11: 5 would speak, and o his lips against thee;	6605
	14: 3 dost thou o thine eyes upon such a one,	6491
	32:20 be refreshed: I will o my lips and answer.	6605
	34:26 He striketh them as wicked men in the o	4725
	35:16 Therefore doth Job o his mouth in vain;	6475
	41:14 Who can o the doors of his face? his teeth	6605
Ps	5: 9 their throat is an o sepulchre; they flatter	6605
	34:15 and his ears are o unto their cry.	NIH
	49: 4 I will o my dark saying upon the harp.	6605
	51:15 O Lord, o thou my lips; and my mouth	6605
	78: 2 I will o my mouth in a parable: I will utter	6605
	81:10 o thy mouth wide, and I will fill it.	7337
	118:19 O to me the gates of righteousness: I will	6605
	119:18 O thou mine eyes, that I may behold	1540
Pr	13:16 but a fool layeth o his folly.	6566
	20:13 o thine eyes, and thou shalt be satisfied	6491
	27: 5 O rebuke is better than secret love.	1540
	31: 8 O thy mouth for the dumb in the cause	6605
	31: 9 O thy mouth, judge righteously,	6605
SS	5: 2 beloved that knocketh saying, O to me,	6605
	5: 5 I rose up to o to my beloved; and my	6605
Isa	9:12 they shall devour Israel with o mouth.	3605
	22:22 so he shall o, and none shall shut;	6605
	22:22 and he shall shut, and none shall o.	6605
	24:18 for the windows from on high are o,	6605
	26: 2 O ye the gates, that the righteous nation	6605
	28:24 doth he o and break the clods of his	6605
	37:17 and hear; o thine eyes, O LORD, and see:	6491
	41:18 I will o rivers in high places,	6605
	42: 7 To o the blind eyes, to bring out	6491
	45: 1 to o before him the two leaved gates;	6605
	45: 8 let the earth o, and let them bring forth	6605
	60:11 Therefore thy gates shall be o continually;	6605
Jer	5:16 Their quiver is as an o sepulchre, they	6605
	9:22 of men shall fall as dung upon the o field,	6440
	13:19 none shall o them: Judah shall be carried	6605
	32:11 law and custom, and that which was o:	1540
	32:14 is sealed, and this evidence which is o;	1540
	32:19 for thine eyes are o upon all the ways of	6491
	50:26 the utmost border, o her storehouses:	6605
Eze	2: 8 o thy mouth, and eat that I give thee.	6475
	3:27 I will o thy mouth, and thou shalt say	6605
	16: 5 thou wast cast out in the o field,	6440
	16:63 never o thy mouth any more, because of	6610
	21:22 to o the mouth in the slaughter,	6605
	25: 9 I will o the side of Moab from the cities,	6605
	29: 5 thou shalt fall upon the o fields; thou shalt	6440
	32: 4 I will cast thee forth upon the o field,	6440
	33:27 him that is in the o field will I give to	6440

O

Eze	37: 2 *there* were very many in the **o** valley;	6440
	37:12 I *will* **o** your graves, and cause you to	6605
	39: 5 Thou shalt fall upon the **o** field: for I have	6440
	46:12 **o** him the gate that looketh *toward* the	6605
Da	6:10 windows being **o** in his chamber toward	6606
	9:18 **o** thine eyes, and behold our desolations,	6491
Na	3:13 the gates of thy land shall be set wide **o**	6605
Zec	11: 1 **O** thy doors, O Lebanon, that the fire	6605
	12: 4 will **o** mine eyes upon the house of Judah,	6491
Mal	3:10 if I will not **o** you the windows of heaven,	6605
Mt	11:35 saying, I will **o** my mouth in parables;	455
	25:11 other virgins, saying, Lord, Lord, **o** to us.	455
Lk	12:36 they may **o** unto him immediately.	455
	13:25 at the door, saying, Lord, Lord, **o** unto us;	455
Jn	1:51 Hereafter ye shall see heaven **o**,	455
	10:21 a devil. Can a devil **o** the eyes of the blind?	455
Ac	16:27 and seeing the prison doors **o**, he drew out	455
	18:14 And when Paul was now about to **o** his	455
	19:38 a matter against any *man*, the law is **o**,	71
	26:18 To **o** their eyes, *and* to turn *them* from	455
Ro	3:13 Their throat *is* an **o** sepulchre; with their	455
2Co	3:18 **o** face beholding as in a glass the glory	343
	6:11 O *ye* Corinthians, our mouth is **o** unto you,	455
Eph	6:19 unto me, that *I* may **o** my mouth boldly,	457
Col	4: 3 that God would **o** unto us a door of	455
1Ti	5:24 Some men's sins are **o** beforehand,	4271
Heb	6: 6 God afresh, and *put him* to an **o** shame.	3856
1Pe	3:12 and his ears *are* **o** unto their prayers:	NIG
Rev	3: 8 I have set before thee an **o** door, and no	455
	3:20 and **o** the door, I will come in to him,	455
	5: 2 Who is worthy to **o** the book, and to loose	455
	5: 3 under the earth, was able to **o** the book,	455
	5: 4 because no *man* was found worthy to **o**	455
	5: 5 hath prevailed to **o** the book, and to loose	455
	5: 9 to take the book, and to **o** the seals thereof:	455
	10: 2 And he had in his hand a little book **o**:	455
	10: 8 take the little book which is **o** in the hand	455

OPENED (137) [OPEN]

Ge	3: 5 your eyes shall be **o**, and ye shall be as	6491
	3: 7 the eyes of them both were **o**,	6491
	4:11 which hath **o** her mouth to receive thy	6475
	7:11 and the windows of heaven were **o**.	6605
	8: 6 Noah **o** the window of the ark which he	6605
	21:19 God **o** her eyes, and she saw a well of	6491
	29:31 saw that Leah *was* hated, he **o** her womb:	6605
	30:22 God hearkened to her, and **o** her womb.	6605
	41:56 Joseph **o** all the storehouses, and sold	6605
	42:27 as one *of them* **o** his sack to give his ass	6605
	43:21 to the inn, that we **o** our sacks,	6605
	44:11 to the ground, and **o** every man his sack.	6605
Ex	2: 6 when she had **o** *it*, she saw the child:	6605
Nu	16:32 the earth **o** her mouth, and swallowed	6605
	22:28 the LORD **o** the mouth of the ass,	6605
	22:31 Then the LORD **o** the eyes of Balaam,	1540
	26:10 the earth **o** her mouth, and swallowed	6605
Dt	11: 6 how the earth **o** her mouth,	6475
Jdg	3:25 behold, he **o** not the doors of the parlour,	6605
	3:25 they took a key, and **o** *them*: and behold,	6605
	4:19 **o** a bottle of milk, and gave him drink,	6605
	11:35 for I have **o** my mouth unto the LORD,	6475
	11:36 *if* thou hast **o** thy mouth unto the LORD,	6475
	19:27 **o** the doors of the house, and went out to	6605
1Sa	3:15 and **o** the doors of the house of the LORD.	6605
2Ki	4:35 seven times, and the child **o** his eyes.	6491
	6:17 the LORD **o** the eyes of the young man;	6491
	6:20 And the LORD **o** their eyes, and they saw;	6491
	9:10 *shall be* none to bury *her*. And he **o**	6605
	13:17 he **o** *it*. Then Elisha said, Shoot. And he	6605
	15:16 because they **o** not *to him*, therefore	6605
2Ch	29: 3 **o** the doors of the house of the LORD,	6605
Ne	7: 3 Let not the gates of Jerusalem be **o** until	6605
	8: 5 Ezra **o** the book in the sight of all	6605
	8: 5 when he **o** *it*, all the people stood *up*:	6605
	13:19 charged that they should not be **o** till after	6605
Job	3: 1 After this **o** Job his mouth, and cursed his	6605
	29:23 they **o** their mouth **wide** *as* for the latter	6473
	31:32 street: *but* I **o** my doors to the traveller.	6605
	33: 2 now I have **o** my mouth, my tongue	6605
	38:17 Have the gates of death been **o** unto thee?	1540
Ps	35:21 they **o** their mouth **wide** against me,	7337
	39: 9 I was dumb, I **o** not my mouth; because	6605
	40: 6 didst not desire; mine ears hast thou **o**:	3738
	78:23 from above, and **o** the doors of heaven,	6605
	105:41 He **o** the rock, and the waters gushed out;	6605
	106:17 The earth **o** and swallowed up Dathan,	6605
	109: 2 mouth of the deceitful are **o** against me:	6605
	119:131 I **o** my mouth, and panted: for I longed	6473
SS	5: 6 I **o** to my beloved; but my beloved had	6605
Isa	5:14 and **o** her mouth without measure:	6473
	10:14 moved the wing, or **o** the mouth, or	6475
	14:17 *that* **o** not the house of his prisoners?	6605
	35: 5 the eyes of the blind shall be **o**, and the	6491
	48: 8 from that time *that* thine ear was not **o**:	6605
	50: 5 The Lord GOD hath **o** mine ear, and I was	6605
	53: 7 he was afflicted, yet he **o** not his mouth:	6605
Jer	20:12 on them: for unto thee have I **o** my cause.	1540
	50:25 The LORD hath **o** his armoury,	6605
La	2:16 All thine enemies have **o** their mouth	6475
	3:46 All our enemies have **o** their mouths	6475
Eze	1: 1 the heavens were **o**, and I saw visions	6605
	3: 2 I **o** my mouth, and he caused me to eat	6605
	16:25 **o** thy feet to every one that passed by,	6589
	24:27 In that day shall thy mouth be **o** to him	6605
	33:22 had **o** my mouth, until *he* came to me in	6605

Eze	33:22 mouth was **o**, and I was no more dumb.	6605
	37:13 when I have **o** your graves, O my people,	6605
	44: 2 shall not be **o**, and no man shall enter in	6605
	46: 1 on the sabbath it shall be **o**, and in the	6605
	46: 1 in the day of the new moon it shall be **o**.	6605
Da	7:10 judgment was set, and the books were **o**.	6606
	10:16 I **o** my mouth, and spake, and said unto	6605
Na	2: 6 The gates of the rivers shall be **o**,	6605
Zec	13: 1 In that day there shall be a fountain **o** to	6605
Mt	2:11 and when they had **o** their treasures,	455
	3:16 and lo, the heavens were **o** unto him,	455
	5: 2 he **o** his mouth, and taught them,	455
	7: 7 find; knock, and it shall be **o** unto you:	455
	7: 8 and to him that knocketh it shall be **o**.	455
	9:30 And their eyes were **o**; and Jesus straitly	455
	17:27 when thou hast **o** his mouth, thou shalt	455
	20:33 unto him, Lord, that our eyes may be **o**.	455
	27:52 the graves were **o**; and many bodies of	455
Mk	1:10 he saw the heavens **o**, and the Spirit like a	4977
	7:34 unto him, EPHPHATHA, that is, Be **o**.	1272
	7:35 straightway his ears were **o**,	455
Lk	1:64 And his mouth was **o** immediately,	455
	3:21 and praying, the heaven was **o**,	455
	4:17 And when he had **o** the book, he found	380
	11: 9 find; knock, and it shall be **o** unto you.	455
	11:10 and to him that knocketh it shall be **o**.	455
	24:31 their eyes were **o**, and they knew him;	1272
	24:32 and while he **o** to us the scriptures?	1272
	24:45 Then he **o** their understanding, that *they*	1272
Jn	9:10 they said unto him, How were thine eyes **o**?	455
	9:14 when Jesus made the clay, and **o** his eyes.	455
	9:17 thou of him, that he hath **o** thine eyes?	455
	9:21 or who hath **o** his eyes, we know not:	455
	9:26 What did he to thee? how **o** he thine eyes?	455
	9:30 whence he is, and *yet* he hath **o** mine eyes.	455
	9:32 *man* **o** the eyes of one that was born blind.	455
	11:37 Could not this *man*, which **o** the eyes of	455
Ac	5:19 But *the* angel of the Lord by night **o**	455
	5:23 when we had **o**, we found no *man* within.	455
	7:56 And said, Behold, I see the heavens **o**,	455
	8:32 before his shearer, so **o** he not his mouth:	455
	8:35 Then Philip **o** his mouth, and began at	455
	9: 8 and when his eyes were **o**, he saw no *man*:	455
	9:40 she **o** her eyes: and when she saw Peter,	455
	10:11 And saw heaven **o**, and a certain vessel	455
	10:34 Peter **o** *his* mouth, and said, Of a truth	455
	12:10 city; which **o** to them of his own accord:	455
	12:14 she **o** not the gate for gladness, but ran in,	455
	12:16 when they had **o** *the door*, and saw him,	455
	14:27 how he had **o** *the* door of faith unto	455
	16:14 heard *us:* whose heart the Lord **o**,	1272
	16:26 and immediately all the doors were **o**,	455
1Co	16: 9 For a great door and effectual is **o** unto me,	455
2Co	2:12 and a door was **o** unto me of the Lord,	455
Heb	4:13 **o** unto the eyes of him with whom we	5136
Rev	4: 1 and behold, a door *was* **o** in heaven:	455
	6: 1 I saw when the Lamb **o** one of the seals,	455
	6: 3 when he had **o** the second seal, I heard	455
	6: 5 And when he had **o** the third seal, I heard	455
	6: 7 when he had **o** the fourth seal, I heard	455
	6: 9 And when he had **o** the fifth seal, I saw	455
	6:12 I beheld when he had **o** the sixth seal,	455
	8: 1 And when he had **o** the seventh seal,	455
	9: 2 he **o** the bottomless pit; and there arose	455
	11:19 And the temple of God was **o** in heaven,	455
	12:16 the earth **o** her mouth, and swallowed up	455
	13: 6 And he **o** his mouth in blasphemy against	455
	15: 5 of the testimony in heaven was **o**:	455
	19:11 And I saw heaven **o**, and behold a white	455
	20:12 stand before God; and the books were **o**:	455
	20:12 another book was **o**, which is *the book*	455

OPENEST (2) [OPEN]

| Ps | 104:28 thou **o** thine hand, they are filled *with* | 6605 |
| | 145:16 Thou **o** thine hand, and satisfiest the | 6605 |

OPENETH (21) [OPEN]

Ex	13: 2 **o** the womb among the children	6363
	13:12 apart unto the LORD all that **o** the matrix,	6363
	13:15 I sacrifice to the LORD all that **o**	6363
	34:19 All that **o** the matrix *is* mine;	6363
Nu	3:12 **o** the matrix among the children of Israel:	6363
	18:15 Every thing *that* **o** the matrix in all flesh,	6363
Job	27:19 be gathered: he **o** his eyes, and he *is* not.	6491
	33:16 he **o** the ears of men, and sealeth their	1540
	36:10 He **o** also their ear to discipline,	1540
	36:15 affliction, and **o** their ears in oppression.	1540
Ps	38:13 *was* as a dumb *man that* **o** not his mouth.	6605
	146: 8 The LORD **o** *the eyes of* the blind:	6491
Pr	13: 3 he that **o** **wide** his lips shall have	6589
	24: 7 a fool: he **o** not his mouth in the gate.	6605
	31:26 She **o** her mouth with wisdom; and in	6605
Isa	53: 7 shearers is dumb, so he **o** not his mouth.	6605
Eze	20:26 pass through *the fire* all that **o** the womb,	6363
Lk	2:23 Every male that **o** the womb shall be	1272
Jn	10: 3 him the porter **o**; and the sheep hear his	455
Rev	3: 7 of David, he that **o**, and no *man* shutteth;	455
	3: 7 *man* shutteth; and shutteth, and no *man* **o**;	455

OPENING (7) [OPEN]

1Ch	9:27 the **o** *thereof* every morning pertained to	4668
Job	12:14 shutteth up a man, and there can be no **o**.	6605
Pr	8: 6 and the of my lips *shall be* right things.	4669
Isa	42:20 **o** the ears, but he heareth not.	6491
	61: 1 the **o of the prison** to *them that are*	6495

| Eze | 29:21 I will give thee the **o** of the mouth in | 6610 |
| Ac | 17: 3 **O** and alleging, that Christ must needs | 1272 |

OPENINGS (1) [OPEN]

| Pr | 1:21 place of concourse, in the **o** of the gates: | 6607 |

OPENLY (15) [OPEN]

Ge	38:21 *was* **o** by the way side?	5869+871.1+1886.1
Ps	98: 2 righteousness hath he **o** shewed in	1540
Mt	6: 4 secret himself shall reward thee **o**.	1722+5318
	6: 6 seeth in secret shall reward thee **o**.	1722+5318
	6:18 seeth in secret, shall reward thee **o**.	1722+5318
Mk	1:45 that *Jesus* could no more **o** enter	5320
	8:32 And he spake *that* saying **o**. And Peter	3954
Jn	7: 4 he himself seeketh to be **known o**.	1722+3954
	7:10 the feast, not **o**, but as it were in secret.	5320
	7:13 Howbeit no *man* spake of him for fear	3954
	11:54 walked no more **o** among the Jews;	3954
	18:20 answered him, I spake **o** to the world;	3954
Ac	10:40 up the third day, and shewed him **o**;	1717
	16:37 They have beaten us **o** uncondemned,	1219
Col	2:15 he made a shew of *them* **o**,	1722+3954

OPERATION (3) [OPERATIONS]

Ps	28: 5 nor the **o** of his hands, he shall destroy	4639
Isa	5:12 neither consider the **o** of his hands.	4639
Col	2:12 *him* through the faith of the **o** of God,	1753

OPERATIONS (1) [OPERATION]

| 1Co | 12: 6 And there are diversities of **o**, but it is | 1755 |

OPHEL (5)

2Ch	27: 3 and on the wall of **O** he built much.	6077
	33:14 compassed about **O**, and raised it up a	6077
Ne	3:26 Moreover the Nethinims dwelt in **O**,	6077
	3:27 that lieth out, even unto the wall of **O**.	6077
	11:21 the Nethinims dwelt in **O**: and Ziha and	6077

OPHIR (13)

Ge	10:29 **O**, and Havilah, and Jobab: all these *were*	211
1Ki	9:28 they came to **O**, and fet from thence gold,	211
	10:11 also of Hiram, that brought gold from **O**,	211
	10:11 brought in from **O** great plenty of almug	211
	22:48 ships of Tharshish to go to **O** for gold:	211
1Ch	1:23 **O**, and Havilah, and Jobab. All these *were*	211
	29: 4 the gold of **O**, and seven thousand talents	211
2Ch	8:18 went with the servants of Solomon to **O**,	211
	9:10 brought gold from **O**, brought algum	211
Job	22:24 *the gold of* **O** as the stones of the brooks.	211
	28:16 It cannot be valued with the gold of **O**,	211
Ps	45: 9 hand did stand the queen in gold of **O**.	211
Isa	13:12 even a man than the golden wedge of **O**.	211

OPHNI (1)

| Jos | 18:24 and **O**, and Gaba; | 6078 |

OPHRAH (8)

Jos	18:23 And Avim, and Parah, and **O**,	6084
Jdg	6:11 sat under an oak which *was* in **O**,	6084
	6:24 unto this day it *is* yet in **O** of	6084
	8:27 and put it in his city, *even* in **O**:	6084
	8:32 Joash his father, in **O** of the Abi-ezrites.	6084
	9: 5 he went unto his father's house at **O**,	6084
1Sa	13:17 turned unto the way that leadeth to **O**,	6084
1Ch	4:14 Meonothai begat **O**: and Seraiah begat	6084

OPINION (3) [OPINIONS]

Job	32: 6 afraid, and durst not shew you mine **o**.	1843
	32:10 Hearken to me; I also will shew mine **o**.	1843
	32:17 also my part, I also will shew mine **o**.	1843

OPINIONS (1) [OPINION]

| 1Ki | 18:21 said, How long halt ye between two **o**? | 5587 |

OPPORTUNITY (5)

Mt	26:16 And from that time he sought to betray	2120
Lk	22: 6 sought **o** to betray him unto them in	2120
Gal	6:10 As we have therefore **o**, let us do good	2540
Php	4:10 ye were also careful, but ye **lacked o**.	170
Heb	11:15 they might have had **o** to have returned.	2540

OPPOSE (1) [OPPOSED, OPPOSEST, OPPOSETH, OPPOSITIONS]

| 2Ti | 2:25 instructing those that **o** themselves; | 475 |

OPPOSED (1) [OPPOSE]

| Ac | 18: 6 And when they **o** themselves, | 498 |

OPPOSEST (1) [OPPOSE]

| Job | 30:21 thy strong hand thou **o** thyself against | 7852 |

OPPOSETH (1) [OPPOSE]

| 2Th | 2: 4 Who **o** and exalteth himself above all that | 480 |

OPPOSITIONS (1) [OPPOSE]

| 1Ti | 6:20 and **o** of science falsely so called: | 477 |

OPPRESS (23) [OPPRESSED, OPPRESSETH, OPPRESSING, OPPRESSION, OPPRESSIONS, OPPRESSOR, OPPRESSORS]

Ex	3: 9 wherewith the Egyptians **o** them.	3905
	22:21 shalt neither vex a stranger, nor **o** him:	3905
	23: 9 Also thou shalt not **o** a stranger: for ye	3905
Lev	25:14 ye shall not **o** one another:	3238
	25:17 Ye shall not therefore **o** one another;	3238
Dt	23:16 it liketh him best: thou shalt not **o** him.	3238

Dt 24:14 Thou shalt not **o** a hired servant *that is* 6231
Jdg 10:12 and the Maonites, did **o** you; 3905
Job 10: 3 *Is it* good unto thee that thou shouldest **o**, 6231
Ps 10:18 that the man of the earth may no more **o**. 6206
 17: 9 From the wicked that **o** me, *from* my 7703
 119:122 servant for good: let not the proud **o** me. 6231
Pr 22:22 *is* poor: neither **o** the afflicted in the gate: 1792
Isa 49:26 I will feed them that **o** thee with their 3238
Jer 7: 6 *If* ye **o** not the stranger, the fatherless, 6231
 30:20 me, and I will punish all that **o** them. 3905
Eze 45: 8 my princes shall no more **o** my people; 3238
Hos 12: 7 of deceit *are* in his hand: he loveth to **o**. 6231
Am 4: 1 which **o** the poor, which crush the needy, 6231
Mic 2: 2 they **o** a man and his house, even a man 6231
Zec 7:10 **o** not the widow, nor the fatherless, 6231
Mal 3: 5 against those that **o** the hireling in *his* 6231
Jas 2: 6 Do not rich *men* **o** you, and draw you 2616

OPPRESSED (38) [OPPRESS]

Dt 28:29 shalt be only **o** and spoiled evermore, 6231
 28:33 thou shalt be only **o** and crushed alway: 6231
Jdg 2:18 their groanings by reason of them that **o** 3905
 4: 3 twenty years he mightily **o** the children of 3905
 6: 9 out of the hand of all that **o** you, 3905
 10: 8 they vexed and **o** the children of Israel: 7533
1Sa 10:18 of all kingdoms, *and* of them that **o** you: 3905
 12: 3 whom have I **o**? or of whose hand have I 7533
 12: 4 Thou hast not defrauded us, nor **o** us, 7533
2Ki 13: 4 of Israel, because the king of Syria **o** them. 3905
 13:22 Hazael king of Syria **o** Israel all the days of 3905
2Ch 16:10 this *thing*. And Asa **o** *some* of the people 7533
Job 20:19 Because he hath **o** *and* hath forsaken 7533
 35: 9 of oppressions they make the **o** to cry: NIH
Ps 9: 9 The LORD also will be a refuge for the **o**, 1790
 10:18 To judge the fatherless and the **o**, that 1790
 74:21 let not the **o** return ashamed: let the poor 1790
 103: 6 and judgment for all that are **o**. 6231
 106:42 Their enemies also **o** them, and they were 3905
 146: 7 Which executeth judgment for the **o**: 6231
Ecc 4: 1 tears of such as were **o**, and they had no 6231
Isa 1:17 seek judgment, relieve the **o**, judge 2541
 3: 5 people shall be **o**, every one by another, 5065
 23:12 O thou **o** virgin, daughter of Zidon: 6231
 38:14 LORD, I am **o**; undertake for me. 6234
 52: 4 and the Assyrian **o** them without cause. 6231
 53: 7 He was **o**, and he was afflicted, yet he 5065
 58: 6 let the **o** go free, and *that* ye break every 7533
Jer 50:33 the children of Judah *were* **o** together: 6231
Eze 18: 7 hath not **o** any, *but* hath restored *to* 3238
 18:12 Hath **o** the poor and needy, hath spoiled 3238
 18:16 Neither hath **o** any, hath not withholden 3238
 18:18 his father, because he **cruelly o**, 6231+6233
 22:29 they have **o** the stranger wrongfully. 6231
Hos 5:11 Ephraim *is* **o** and broken in judgment, 6231
Am 3: 9 and the **o** in the midst thereof. 6217
Ac 7:24 *him*, and avenged him that was **o**, 2669
 10:38 and healing all that were **o** of the devil; 2616

OPPRESSETH (5) [OPPRESS]

Nu 10: 9 your land against the enemy that **o** you, 6887
Ps 56: 1 swallow me up; he fighting daily **o** me. 3905
Pr 14:31 He that **o** the poor reproacheth his Maker: 6231
 22:16 He that **o** the poor to increase his *riches*, 6231
 28: 3 A poor man that **o** the poor *is like* a 6231

OPPRESSING (3) [OPPRESS]

Jer 46:16 the land of our nativity, from the **o** sword. 3238
 50:16 fear of the **o** sword they shall turn every 3238
Zep 3: 1 that is filthy and polluted, to the **o** city! 3238

OPPRESSION (24) [OPPRESS]

Ex 3: 9 I have also seen the **o** wherewith 3906
Dt 26: 7 our affliction, and our labour, and our **o**: 3906
2Ki 13: 4 he saw the **o** of Israel, because the king 3906
Job 36:15 his affliction, and openeth their ears in **o**. 3906
Ps 12: 5 For the **o** of the poor, for the sighing of 7701
 42: 9 mourning because of the **o** of the enemy? 3906
 43: 2 mourning because of the **o** of the enemy? 3906
 44:24 *and* forgettest our affliction and our **o**? 3906
 55: 3 enemy, because of the **o** of the wicked: 6125
 62:10 Trust not in **o**, and become not vain in 6233
 73: 8 and speak wickedly *concerning* **o**: 6233
 107:39 are minished and brought low through **o**, 6115
 119:134 Deliver me from the **o** of man: so will I 6233
Ecc 5: 8 If thou seest the **o** of the poor, 6233
 7: 7 Surely **o** maketh a wise *man* mad; and a 6233
Isa 5: 7 he looked for judgment, but behold **o**; 4939
 30:12 trust in **o** and perverseness, 6233
 54:14 thou shalt be far from **o**; for thou shalt 6233
 59:13 speaking **o** and revolt, conceiving and 6233
Jer 6: 6 she *is* wholly **o** in the midst of her. 6233
 22:17 and for **o**, and for violence, to do *it*. 6233
Eze 22: 7 in the midst of thee have they dealt by **o** 6233
 22:29 people of the land have **used o**, 6231+6233
 46:18 **o** to thrust them out of their possession; 3238

OPPRESSIONS (3) [OPPRESS]

Job 35: 9 By reason of the multitude of **o** they 6217
Ecc 4: 1 considered all the **o** that *are* done under 6217
Isa 33:15 that despiseth the gain of **o**, that shaketh 4642

OPPRESSOR (14) [OPPRESS]

Job 3:18 they hear not the voice of the **o**. 5065
 15:20 the number of years is hidden to the **o**. 6184
Ps 72: 4 the needy, and shall break in pieces the **o**. 6231

Pr 3:31 Envy thou not the **o**, and choose 376+2555
 28:16 wanteth understanding *is* also a great **o**: 4642
Isa 9: 4 the rod of his **o**, as *in* the day of Midian. 5065
 14: 4 and say, How hath the **o** ceased! 5065
 51:13 every day because of the fury of the **o**, 6693
 51:13 to destroy? and where *is* the fury of the **o**? 6693
Jer 21:12 *that is* spoiled out of the hand of the **o**, 6231
 22: 3 the spoiled out of the hand of the **o**; 6216
 25:38 because of the fierceness of the **o**, 3238
Zec 9: 8 no **o** shall pass through them any more: 5065
 10: 4 battle bow, out of him every **o** together. 5065

OPPRESSORS (8) [OPPRESS]

Job 27:13 the heritage of **o**, *which* they shall receive 6184
Ps 54: 3 up against me, and **o** seek after my soul: 6184
 119:121 and justice: leave me not to mine **o**. 6231
Ecc 4: 1 on the side of their **o** *there was* power; 6231
Isa 3:12 children *are* their **o**, and women rule over 5065
 14: 2 they were; and they shall rule over their **o**. 5065
 16: 4 the **o** are consumed out of the land. 7429
 19:20 shall cry unto the LORD because of the **o**, 3905

OR (1130)

Ge 13: 9 **o** if *thou* depart *to* the right hand, then 2050.1
 17:12 **o** bought with money of any stranger, 2050.1
 24:21 had made his journey prosperous **o** not. 518
 24:49 I may turn to the right hand, **o** to the left. 176
 24:50 we cannot speak unto thee bad **o** good. 176
 26:11 He that toucheth this man **o** his wife 2050.1
 27:21 whether thou *be* my very son Esau **o** not. 518
 30: 1 Give me children, **o** else I die. 518+2050.1
 31:14 *Is there* yet any portion **o** inheritance 2050.1
 31:24 thou speak not to Jacob either good **o** bad. 5704
 31:29 thou speak not to Jacob either good **o** bad. 5704
 31:39 stolen by day, **o** stolen by night. 2050.1
 31:43 **o** unto their children which they have 176
 31:50 **o** if thou shalt take *other* wives beside 2050.1
 37: 8 **o** shalt thou indeed have dominion over 518
 37:32 now **whether** it *be* thy son's coat **o** no. 518
 39:10 unto her, to lie by her, **o** to be with her. NIH
 41:44 his hand **o** foot in all the land of Egypt. 2050.1
 42:16 **o** else by the life of Pharaoh surely ye 2050.1
 44: 8 steal out of thy lord's house silver **o** gold? 176
 44:16 how shall we clear ourselves? God 2050.1
 44:19 Have ye a father, **o** a brother? 176
Ex 4:11 **o** who maketh the dumb, or deaf, 176
 4:11 dumb, **o** deaf, or the seeing, or the blind? 176
 4:11 dumb, or deaf, **o** the seeing, or the blind? 176
 4:11 dumb, or deaf, or the seeing, **o** the blind? 176
 5: 3 upon us with pestilence, **o** with the sword. 176
 10:15 **o** in the herbs of the field, through all 2050.1
 11: 7 move his tongue, against man **o** beast: 2050.1
 12: 5 it out from the sheep, **o** from the goats: 2050.1
 12:19 he be a stranger, **o** born in the land. 2050.1
 16: 4 whether they will walk in my law, **o** no. 518
 17: 7 Is the LORD amongst us, **o** not? 518
 19:12 into the mount, **o** touch the border of it: 2050.1
 19:13 he shall surely be stoned, **o** shot through; 176
 19:13 whether *it be* beast **o** man, it shall not live: 518
 20: 4 **o** any likeness *of any thing* that *is* in 2050.1
 20: 4 **o** that is in the earth beneath, or that *is* 2050.1
 20: 4 **o** that *is* in the water under the earth: 2050.1
 21: 4 and she have born him sons **o** daughters; 176
 21: 6 him to the door, **o** unto the door post; 176
 21:15 his mother, shall be surely put to 2050.1
 21:16 him, **o** if he be found in his hand, 2050.1
 21:17 his mother, shall surely be put to 2050.1
 21:18 **o** with *his* fist, and he die not, 176
 21:20 his maid, with a rod, and he die under 176
 21:21 if he continue a day **o** two, 176
 21:26 the eye of his maid, that it perish; 176
 21:27 **o** his maidservant's tooth; 176
 21:28 If an ox gore a man **o** a woman, that they 176
 21:29 but that he hath killed a man **o** a woman; 176
 21:31 have gored a son, **o** have gored a daughter, 176
 21:32 shall push a manservant **o** a maidservant; 176
 21:33 if a man shall dig a pit, and not cover it, 176
 21:33 not cover it, and an ox **o** an ass fall therein; 176
 21:36 O *if* it be known that the ox *hath* used to 176
 22: 1 steal an ox, **o** a sheep, and kill it, or sell it; 176
 22: 1 steal an ox, or a sheep, and kill it, **o** sell it; 176
 22: 4 whether it be ox, **o** ass, or sheep; 5704
 22: 4 whether it be ox, or ass, **o** sheep; 5704
 22: 5 shall cause a field **o** vineyard to be eaten, 176
 22: 6 of corn, **o** the standing corn, or the field, 176
 22: 6 of corn, or the standing corn, **o** the field, 176
 22: 7 unto his neighbour money **o** stuff to keep, 176
 22: 9 *o* for any manner of lost *thing*, which NIH
 22:10 **o** an ox, or a sheep, or any beast, to keep; 176
 22:10 or an ox, **o** a sheep, or any beast, to keep; 176
 22:10 or an ox, or a sheep, **o** any beast, to keep; 2050.1
 22:10 it die, **o** be hurt, or driven away, no man 176
 22:10 it die, or be hurt, **o** driven away, no man 176
 22:14 it be hurt, **o** die, the owner thereof *being* 176
 22:22 not afflict any widow, **o** fatherless child. 2050.1
 23: 4 thine enemy's ox **o** his ass going astray, 176
 28:43 **o** when they come near unto the altar to 176
 29:34 **o** of the bread, remain unto the 2050.1
 30:20 when they come near to the altar 176
 30:33 whosoever putteth *any* of it upon a 2050.1
 34:19 *whether* ox **o** sheep, *that is* male. 2050.1
Lev 1:10 **o** of the goats, for a burnt sacrifice; 176
 1:14 of turtledoves, **o** of young pigeons. 176

Lev 2: 4 **o** unleavened wafers anointed with oil. 2050.1
 3: 1 *it be* a male **o** female, he shall offer 518
 3: 6 male **o** female, he shall offer it without 176
 4:23 O if his sin, wherein he hath sinned, come 176
 4:28 O if his sin, which he hath sinned, come 176
 5: 1 he hath seen **o** known *of it;* if he do 176
 5: 2 O if a soul touch any unclean thing, 176
 5: 2 a carcase of unclean cattle, or the carcase 176
 5: 2 the carcase of unclean creeping things, 176
 5: 3 O if he touch the uncleanness of man, 176
 5: 4 O if a soul swear, pronouncing with *his* 176
 5: 4 with *his* lips to do evil, **o** to do good, 176
 5: 6 a lamb **o** a kid of the goats, for a sin 176
 5: 7 two turtledoves, **o** two young pigeons, 176
 5:11 **o** two young pigeons, then he that sinned 176
 6: 2 in fellowship, **o** in a thing taken away 176
 6: 2 in a thing taken away by violence, 176
 6: 2 violence, **o** hath deceived his neighbour; 176
 6: 3 O have found that which was lost, 176
 6: 4 **o** the thing which he hath deceitfully 176
 6: 4 **o** that which was delivered him to keep, 176
 6: 4 to keep, **o** the lost *thing* which he found, 176
 6: 5 O *all that* about which he hath sworn 176
 7:16 offering *be* a vow, **o** a voluntary offering, 176
 7:21 **o** *any* unclean beast, or any abominable 176
 7:21 **o** any abominable unclean *thing*, and eat 176
 7:23 fat, of ox, **o** of sheep, or of goat. 2050.1
 7:23 fat, of ox, or of sheep, **o** of goat. 2050.1
 7:26 *it be* of fowl **o** of beast, in any of 2050.1
 11: 4 the cud, **o** of them that divide the hoof: 2050.1
 11:32 vessel of wood, **o** raiment, or skin, or sack, 176
 11:32 vessel of wood, or raiment, **o** skin, or sack, 176
 11:32 vessel of wood, or raiment, or skin, **o** sack, 176
 11:35 *whether it be* oven, **o** ranges for pots, 2050.1
 11:36 Nevertheless a fountain **o** pit, 2050.1
 11:42 **o** whatsoever hath more feet among all 5704
 12: 6 are fulfilled, for a son, **o** for a daughter, 176
 12: 6 a young pigeon, **o** a turtledove, for a sin 176
 12: 7 for her that hath born a male **o** a female. 176
 12: 8 bring two turtles, **o** two young pigeons; 176
 13: 2 **o** bright spot, and it be in the skin of his 176
 13: 2 priest, **o** unto one of his sons the priests: 176
 13:16 O if the raw flesh turn again, and be 176
 13:19 **o** a bright spot, white, 176
 13:24 O if there be *any* flesh, in the skin 176
 13:24 bright spot, somewhat reddish, **o** white; 176
 13:29 If a man **o** woman hath a plague upon 176
 13:29 hath a plague upon the head **o** the beard; 176
 13:30 *even* a leprosy upon the head **o** beard. 176
 13:38 If a man also **o** a woman have in the skin 176
 13:42 bald forehead, a white reddish sore; 176
 13:42 up in his bald head, **o** his bald forehead. 176
 13:43 **o** in his bald forehead, as the leprosy 176
 13:47 *it be* a woollen garment, **o** a linen garment; 176
 13:48 Whether *it be* in the warp, **o** woof; of linen, 176
 13:48 warp, or woof; of linen, **o** of woollen; 2050.1
 13:48 in a skin, **o** in any thing made of skin; 176
 13:49 be greenish **o** reddish in the garment, 176
 13:49 in the skin, either in the warp, or in 176
 13:49 or in the woof, or in any thing of skin; 176
 13:49 or in the woof, **o** in any thing of skin; 176
 13:51 **o** in the woof, or in a skin, **o** in any work 176
 13:51 in a skin, *or* in any work that is made of 176
 13:51 a skin, **o** in any work that is made of skin; NIH
 13:52 warp **o** woof, in woollen or in linen, 176
 13:52 in woollen **o** in linen, or any thing of skin, 176
 13:52 in woollen or in linen, **o** any thing of skin, 176
 13:53 in the woof, or in any thing of skin; 176
 13:53 or in the woof, **o** in any thing of skin; 176
 13:55 *whether* it *be* bare within **o** without. 176
 13:56 **o** out of the skin, or out of the warp, 176
 13:56 **o** out of the warp, or out of the woof: 176
 13:56 or out of the warp, **o** out of the woof: 176
 13:57 **o** in the woof, or in any thing of skin; 176
 13:57 or in the woof, **o** in any thing of skin; 176
 13:58 **o** woof, or whatsoever thing of skin *it be*, 176
 13:58 **o** whatsoever thing of skin *it be*, which 176
 13:59 of leprosy in a garment of woollen **o** linen, 176
 13:59 *in* the warp, **o** woof, or any thing of skins, 176
 13:59 *in* the warp, or woof, **o** any thing of skins, 176
 13:59 it clean, **o** to pronounce it unclean. 176
 14:22 two turtledoves, **o** two young pigeons, 176
 14:30 **o** of the young pigeons, such as he can get; 176
 14:37 greenish **o** reddish, which in sight *are* 176
 15: 3 **o** his flesh be stopped from his issue, it *is* 176
 15:14 **o** two young pigeons, and come before 176
 15:23 **o** on *any* thing whereon she sitteth, when 176
 15:25 **o** if it run beyond the time of her 176
 15:29 **o** two young pigeons, and bring them unto 176
 16:29 **o** a stranger that sojourneth among you: 2050.1
 17: 3 lamb, **o** goat, in the camp, or that killeth 176
 17: 3 lamb, or goat, in the camp, **o** that killeth 176
 17: 3 the camp, **o** that killeth *it* out of the camp, 176
 17: 8 **o** of the strangers which sojourn among 2050.1
 17: 8 that offereth a burnt offering **o** sacrifice, 176
 17:10 **o** of the strangers that sojourn among 2050.1
 17:13 **o** of the strangers that sojourn among 2050.1
 17:13 which hunteth and catcheth *any* beast **o** 176
 17:15 **o** that which was torn *with beasts*, 2050.1
 17:15 **o** a stranger, he shall both wash his 176
 18: 7 **o** the nakedness of thy mother, shalt 2050.1
 18: 9 thy father, **o** daughter of thy mother, 176
 18: 9 *she be* born at home, **o** born abroad, 176
 18:10 daughter, **o** of thy daughter's daughter, 176
 18:17 **o** her daughter's daughter, to uncover 2050.1

O

Lev 19:35 in meteyard, in weight, **o** in measure.	2050.1
20: 2 **o** of the strangers that sojourn in Israel,	2050.1
20: 9 every one that curseth his father **o** his	2050.1
20: 9 he hath cursed his father **o** his mother;	2050.1
20:17 **o** his mother's daughter, and see her	176
20:25 **o** by fowl, or by any *manner of living*	2050.1
20:25 **o** any *manner of living thing* that	2050.1
20:27 A man also **o** woman that hath a familiar	176
20:27 **o** that is a wizard, shall surely be put to	176
21: 7 take a wife *that is* a whore, **o** profane;	2050.1
21:11 himself for his father, **o** for his mother;	2050.1
21:14 **o** a divorced *woman*, **o** profane,	2050.1
21:14 or a divorced *woman*, **o** profane,	2050.1
21:14 a divorced *woman*, or profane, **o** a harlot,	NIH
21:18 **o** a lame, or he that hath a flat nose,	176
21:18 **o** he that hath a flat nose, or any thing	176
21:18 hath a flat nose, **o** any thing superfluous,	176
21:19 **O** a man that is brokenfooted,	176
21:19 man that is brokenfooted, **o** brokenhanded,	176
21:20 **O** crookbackt, or a dwarf, or that hath a	176
21:20 **o** a dwarf, or that hath a blemish in his eye,	176
21:20 **o** that hath a blemish in his eye,	176
21:20 **o** be scurvy, or scabbed, or hath his stones	176
21:20 **o** scabbed, or hath his stones broken;	176
21:20 or scabbed, **o** hath his stones broken;	176
22: 4 of Aaron *is* a leper, **o** hath a running issue;	176
22: 4 a man whose seed goeth from him;	176
22: 5 **O** whosoever toucheth any creeping thing,	176
22: 5 a man of whom he may take uncleanness	176
22: 8 **o** is torn *with beasts*, he shall not eat to	2050.1
22:10 **o** a hired servant, shall not eat *of* the	2050.1
22:13 divorced, and have no child,	2050.1
22:16 **O** suffer them to bear the iniquity of	2050.1
22:18 of Israel, **o** of the strangers in Israel,	2050.1
22:19 the beeves, of the sheep, **o** of the goats.	2050.1
22:21 **o** a freewill offering in beeves or sheep,	176
22:21 or a freewill offering in beeves **o** sheep,	176
22:22 **o** broken, or maimed, or having a wen,	176
22:22 **o** maimed, or having a wen, or scurvy,	176
22:22 having a wen, or scurvy, or scabbed,	176
22:22 or having a wen, **o** scurvy, or scabbed,	176
22:22 or having a wen, **o** scurvy, or scabbed,	176
22:23 Either a bullock **o** a lamb that hath any	2050.1
22:23 thing superfluous **o** lacking in his parts,	2050.1
22:24 is bruised, **o** crushed, or broken, or cut;	2050.1
22:24 is bruised, or crushed, **o** broken, or cut;	2050.1
22:24 is bruised, or crushed, or broken, **o** cut;	2050.1
22:27 **o** a sheep, or a goat, is brought forth, then	176
22:27 or a sheep, **o** a goat, is brought forth, then	176
22:28 *whether it be* cow **o** ewe, ye shall not kill	176
25:14 **o** buyest *ought* of thy neighbour's hand,	176
25:35 yea, *though he be* a stranger, **o**	2050.1
25:36 Take thou no usury of him, **o** increase:	2050.1
25:47 if a sojourner **o** stranger wax rich by	2050.1
25:47 unto the stranger **o** sojourner by thee,	NIH
25:47 **o** to the stock of the stranger's family:	176
25:49 Either his uncle, **o** his uncle's son,	176
25:49 **o** any that is nigh of kin unto him of his	176
25:49 **o** if he be able, he may redeem himself.	176
26:15 **o** if your soul abhor my judgments,	2050.1
27:10 a good for a bad, **o** a bad for a good:	2050.1
27:12 shall value it, whether it be good **o** bad:	2050.1
27:14 estimate it, whether it be good **o** bad:	2050.1
27:20 **o** if he have sold the field to another	2050.1
27:26 shall sanctify it; whether *it be* ox, **o** sheep:	518
27:27 **o** if it be not redeemed, then it shall be	2050.1
27:28 possession, shall be sold **o** redeemed:	2050.1
27:30 **o** of the fruit of the tree, *is* the LORD's:	NIH
27:32 the tithe of the herd, **o** of the flock,	2050.1
27:33 shall not search whether it be good **o** bad,	NIH
Nu 5: 6 When a man **o** woman shall commit any	176
5:14 **o** if the spirit of jealousy come upon him,	176
5:30 **O** when the spirit of jealousy cometh upon	176
6: 2 When either man **o** woman shall separate	176
6: 3 of wine, **o** vinegar of strong drink,	2050.1
6: 3 of grapes, nor eat moist grapes, **o** dried.	2050.1
6: 7 for his mother, for his brother, or for	2050.1
6: 7 for his sister, when they die:	2050.1
6:10 **o** two young pigeons, to the priest,	176
9:10 If any man of you **o** of your posterity shall	176
9:10 **o** *be* in a journey afar off, yet he shall keep	176
9:21 whether *it was* by day **o** by night that	2050.1
9:22 **O** *whether it were* two days, or a month,	176
9:22 *it were* two days, **o** a month, or a year,	176
9:22 *it were* two days, or a month, **o** a year,	176
11: 8 **o** beat *it* in a mortar, and baked *it* in pans,	176
11:22 shall all the fish of the sea be gathered	518
11:23 word shall come to pass unto thee **o** not.	518
13:18 whether they *be* strong **o** weak,	1886.2
13:18 they *be* strong or weak, few **o** many;	518
13:19 they dwell in, whether it *be* good **o** bad;	518
13:19 in, whether in tents, **o** in strong holds;	518
13:20 what the land *is*, whether it *be* fat **o** lean,	518
13:20 whether there be wood therein, **o** not.	518
14: 2 **o** would God we had died in this	176
15: 3 **o** a sacrifice in performing a vow, or in a	176
15: 3 **o** in a freewill offering, or in your solemn	176
15: 3 a freewill offering, **o** in your solemn feasts,	176
15: 3 unto the LORD, of the herd, or of the flock:	176
15: 5 prepare with the burnt offering **o** sacrifice,	176
15: 6 **O** for a ram, thou shalt prepare *for* a meat	176
15: 8 **o** *for* a sacrifice in performing a vow,	176
15: 8 a vow, **o** peace offerings unto the LORD:	176
15:11 **o** for one ram, or for a lamb, or a kid.	176
15:11 or for one ram, or for a lamb, **o** a kid.	176

Nu 15:11 or for one ram, or for a lamb, **o** a kid.	176
15:14 whosoever *be* among you in your	176
15:30 *he be* born in the land, **o** a stranger,	2050.1
16:14 given us inheritance of fields and	2050.1
16:29 if they be visited after the visitation of	2050.1
18:15 *whether it be* of men **o** beasts, shall be	2050.1
18:17 the firstling of a sheep, or the firstling of	176
18:17 **o** the firstling of a goat, thou shalt not	176
19:16 **o** a dead *body*, or a bone of a man, or a	176
19:16 or a dead *body*, **o** a bone of a man, or a	176
19:16 dead *body*, or a bone of a man, **o** a grave,	176
19:18 bone, **o** one slain, or one dead, or a grave:	176
19:18 bone, or one slain, **o** one dead, or a grave:	176
19:18 bone, or one slain, or one dead, **o** a grave:	176
20: 5 **o** of figs, or vines, or of pomegranates;	2050.1
20: 5 or of figs, **o** vines, or of pomegranates;	2050.1
20: 5 or of figs, or vines, **o** of pomegranates;	2050.1
20:17 the fields, **o** through the vineyards,	2050.1
21:22 into the fields, **o** into the vineyards;	2050.1
22:18 of the LORD my God, to do less **o** more.	2050.1
22:26 *either* to the right hand **o** to the left.	2050.1
23: 8 how shall I defy, *whom* the LORD	2050.1
23:19 shall he not do *it?* **o** hath he spoken,	2050.1
24:13 do *either* good **o** bad of mine own mind;	176
30: 2 swear an oath to bind his soul with a	176
30: 5 **o** of her bonds wherewith she hath	2050.1
30: 6 vowed, **o** uttered ought out of her lips,	176
30:10 **o** bound her soul by a bond with an oath;	176
30:12 concerning the bond of her soul,	2050.1
30:13 **o** her husband may make it void.	176
30:14 **o** all her bonds, which *are* upon her:	176
32:19 them on *yonder* side Jordan, **o** forward;	2050.1
35:18 **O** *if* he smite him with a hand weapon of	176
35:20 **o** hurl at him by laying of wait, that he die;	176
35:21 In enmity smite him with his hand,	176
35:22 have cast upon him any thing without	176
35:23 **O** with any stone, wherewith *a man* may	176
Dt 3:24 for what God *is there* in heaven **o**	2050.1
4:16 any figure, the likeness of male **o** female,	176
4:23 **o** the likeness of any *thing*, which	NIH
4:25 **o** the likeness of any *thing*, and shall do	NIH
4:32 great thing *is*, **o** hath been heard like it?	176
4:34 **O** hath God assayed to go *and* take him a	176
5: 8 **o** any likeness *of any thing* that *is* in	NIH
5: 8 **o** that *is* in the earth beneath, or that *is*	2050.1
5: 8 **o** that *is* in the waters beneath the	2050.1
5:21 **o** his manservant, or his maidservant,	2050.1
5:21 **o** his maidservant, his ox, or his ass,	2050.1
5:21 **o** his ass, or any *thing* that *is* thy	2050.1
5:21 **o** any *thing* that *is* thy neighbour's.	2050.1
5:32 aside *to* the right hand **o** *to* the left.	2050.1
7:14 there shall not be male **o** female barren	2050.1
7:14 barren among you, **o** among your cattle.	2050.1
7:25 desire the silver **o** gold *that is* on them,	2050.1
8: 2 wouldest keep his commandments, **o** no.	518
9: 5 **o** for the uprightness of thine heart,	2050.1
12:17 of thy wine, or of thy oil,	2050.1
12:17 of thy oil, or of the firstlings of thy herds	2050.1
12:17 the firstlings of thy herds or of thy	2050.1
12:17 the firstlings of thy herds **o** of thy flock,	2050.1
12:17 **o** heave offering of thine hand:	2050.1
13: 1 **o** a dreamer of dreams, and giveth thee a	176
13: 1 and giveth thee a sign **o** a wonder,	176
13: 2 the sign **o** the wonder come to pass,	176
13: 3 of that prophet, **o** that dreamer of dreams:	176
13: 5 That prophet, **o** that dreamer of dreams,	176
13: 6 **o** thy son, or thy daughter, or the wife of	176
13: 6 **o** thy daughter, or the wife of thy bosom,	176
13: 6 the wife of thy bosom, or thy friend,	176
13: 6 or the wife of thy bosom, **o** thy friend,	176
13: 7 nigh unto thee, **o** far off from thee,	176
14: 7 **o** of them that divide the cloven hoof:	2050.1
14:21 eat it; **o** thou mayest sell *it* unto an alien:	176
14:24 **o** if the place be too far from thee, which	NIH
14:26 **o** for sheep, or for wine, or for strong	2050.1
14:26 for wine, **o** for strong drink,	2050.1
14:26 **o** for strong drink, or for whatsoever thy	2050.1
14:26 **o** for whatsoever thy soul desireth:	2050.1
15: 2 *it* of his neighbour, **o** of his brother;	2050.1
15:12 Hebrew man, **o** a Hebrew woman, be sold	176
15:21 be lame, **o** blind, *or have* any ill blemish,	176
15:21 be lame, or blind, **o** have any ill blemish,	NIH
17: 1 *o* sheep, wherein is blemish, *or* any evil	2050.1
17: 1 is blemish, **o** any evil favouredness:	NIH
17: 2 LORD thy God giveth thee, man **o** woman,	176
17: 3 **o** moon, or any of the host of heaven,	176
17: 3 or moon, **o** any of the host of heaven,	176
17: 5 thou bring forth that man **o** that woman,	176
17: 5 *that* man **o** *that* woman, and shalt stone	176
17: 6 mouth of two witnesses, **o** three witnesses,	176
17:12 unto the judge, even that man shall die:	176
17:20 *to* the right hand, **o** *to* the left:	176
18: 3 offer a sacrifice, whether *it be* ox **o** sheep;	518
18:10 his daughter to pass through the fire,	2050.1
18:10 **o** that useth divination, *or* an observer of	NIH
18:10 **o** an observer of times, or an enchanter,	NIH
18:10 of times, **o** an enchanter, or a witch,	2050.1
18:10 of times, or an enchanter, **o** a witch,	2050.1
18:11 **O** a charmer, or a consulter with	2050.1
18:11 **o** a consulter with familiar spirits,	2050.1
18:11 **o** a wizard, or a necromancer.	2050.1
18:11 or a wizard, **o** a necromancer.	2050.1
18:20 that shall speak in the name of other	176
19:15 **o** for any sin, in any sin that he sinneth:	2050.1
19:15 **o** at the mouth of three witnesses, shall	176

Dt 21:18 **o** the voice of his mother, and *that,*	2050.1
22: 1 see thy brother's ox **o** his sheep go astray,	176
22: 2 **o** *if* thou know him not, then thou shalt	2050.1
22: 4 ass **o** his ox fall down by the way,	176
22: 6 **o** on the ground, *whether they be* young	176
22: 6 **o** eggs, and the dam sitting upon the	176
22: 6 sitting upon the young, **o** upon the eggs,	176
23: 1 **o** hath *his* privy member cut off,	2050.1
23: 3 Ammonite **o** Moabite shall not enter	2050.1
23:18 hire of a whore, **o** the price of a dog,	2050.1
24: 3 **o** if the latter husband die, which took her	176
24: 6 No *man* shall take the nether **o** the	2050.1
24: 7 merchandise of him, **o** selleth him;	2050.1
24:14 **o** of thy strangers that *are* in thy land	176
27:15 maketh *any* graven **o** molten image,	2050.1
27:16 setteth light by his father **o** his mother.	176
27:22 his father, **o** the daughter of his mother.	176
28:14 the right hand, **o** to the left, to go after	2050.1
28:51 oil, *or* the increase of thy kine,	2050.1
28:51 **o** the increase of thy kine, or flocks of thy	NIH
28:51 of thy kine, **o** flocks of thy sheep,	2050.1
29: 6 have you drunk wine **o** strong drink:	2050.1
29:18 you man, **o** woman, or family, or tribe,	176
29:18 you man, or woman, **o** family, or tribe,	176
29:18 you man, or woman, or family, **o** tribe,	176
32:36 gone, and *there is* none shut up, **o** left.	2050.1
Jos 1: 7 from it *to* the right hand **o** *to* the left,	2050.1
5:13 *Art* thou for us, **o** for our adversaries?	518
7: 3 let about two **o** three thousand men go up	176
8:17 there was not a man left in Ai **o** Beth-el,	2050.1
8:20 no power to flee this way **o** that way:	2050.1
8:22 *they* let none of them remain **o** escape.	2050.1
10:14 was no day like that before it **o** after it,	2050.1
19: 2 **o** Sheba, and Moladah,	2050.1
22:22 **o** if in transgression against the LORD,	2050.1
22:23 **o** if to offer thereon burnt offering or	2050.1
22:23 thereon burnt offering **o** meat offering,	2050.1
22:23 **o** if to offer peace offerings thereon,	2050.1
22:28 when they should *so* say to us **o** to our	2050.1
22:29 for meat offerings, **o** for sacrifices,	2050.1
23: 6 therefrom *to* the right hand **o** *to* the left;	2050.1
24:15 **o** the gods of the Amorites, in	518+2050.1
Jdg 2:22 as their fathers did keep *it,* **o** not.	518
5: 8 was there a shield **o** spear seen among	2050.1
5:30 the prey; to every man a damsel **o** two;	NIH
9: 2 over you, **o** that one reign over you?	176
11:25 **o** did he ever fight against them,	518
13:14 let her drink wine **o** strong drink,	2050.1
14: 3 of thy brethren, **o** among all my people,	2050.1
14: 6 told not his father **o** his mother what	2050.1
18:19 **o** that thou be a priest unto a tribe and	176
19:13 to lodge all night, in Gibeah, **o** in Ramah.	176
20:28 of Benjamin my brother, **o** shall I cease?	518
21:22 when their fathers **o** their brethren come	176
Ru 1:16 **o** to return from following after thee:	NIH
3:10 young men, whether poor **o** rich.	518+2050.1
1Sa 2:14 *it* into the pan, **o** kettle, or caldron, or pot;	176
2:14 *it* into the pan, or kettle, **o** caldron, or pot;	176
2:14 *it* into the pan, or kettle, **o** caldron, or pot;	176
6:12 not aside *to* the right hand **o** *to* the left;	2050.1
12: 3 **o** whose ass have I taken? or whom	2050.1
12: 3 **o** whom have I defrauded? whom have	2050.1
12: 3 **o** of whose hand have I received *any*	2050.1
13:19 the Hebrews make *them* swords **o** spears:	176
14: 6 to the LORD to save by many **o** by few.	176
14:52 **o** any valiant man, he took him unto	2050.1
16: 7 **o** on the height of his stature;	2050.1
18:18 *is* my life, *or* my father's family in Israel,	NIH
20: 2 father will do nothing *either* great **o** small,	176
20:10 **o** what *if* thy father answer thee roughly?	176
20:12 the third *day,* and behold, *if there be*	NIH
21: 3 in mine hand, **o** what there is present.	176
21: 8 not here under thine hand spear **o** sword?	176
22: 8 sheweth unto me that my son hath	2050.1
22:15 knew nothing of all this, less **o** more.	2050.1
25:31 **o** that my lord hath avenged himself:	2050.1
25:36 **o** more, until the morning light.	2050.1
26:10 **o** his day shall come to die; or he shall	176
26:10 **o** he shall descend into battle, and perish.	176
26:18 I done? **o** what evil *is* in mine hand?	2050.1
29: 3 **o** these years, and I have found no *fault* in	176
30: 2 either great **o** small,	5704+2050.1
2Sa 2:21 thee aside to thy right hand **o** to thy left,	176
3:29 **o** that is a leper, or that leaneth on	2050.1
3:29 **o** that leaneth on a staff, or that falleth	2050.1
3:29 **o** that falleth on the sword, or that	2050.1
3:29 on the sword, that lacketh bread.	2050.1
3:35 more also, if I taste bread, **o** ought else,	176
14:19 none can turn to the right hand **o** to	2050.1
15: 4 *any* suit **o** cause might come unto me,	2050.1
15:21 whether in death **o** life, even there *also*	518
17: 9 now in some pit, **o** in some *other* place:	176
19:35 servant taste what I eat **o** what I drink?	2050.1
19:42 king's *cost?* **o** hath he given us *any* gift?	518
20:20 that I should swallow up **o** destroy.	518+2050.1
24:13 wilt thou flee three months before thine	518
24:13 **o** that there be three days' pestilence in	2050.1
1Ki 3: 7 I know not *how* to go out **o** come in.	2050.1
8:23 in heaven above, **o** on earth beneath,	2050.1
8:37 mildew, locust, **o** if there be caterpiller;	NIH
8:38 by any man, **o** by all thy people Israel,	NIH
8:46 unto the land of the enemy, far **o** near;	176
9: 0 you your children, and will not keep	2050.1
15:17 go out **o** come in to Asa king of Judah.	2050.1
18:10 liveth, there is no nation **o** kingdom,	2050.1

1Ki
18:27 either he is talking, **o** he is 3588+2050.1
18:27 or he is pursuing, **o** he is in a 3588+2050.1
18:27 **o** peradventure he sleepeth, and must be NIH
20:18 **o** whether they be come out for war, 2050.1
20:39 **o** else thou shalt pay a talent of silver. 176
21: 2 **o**, if it seem good to thee, I will give thee NIH
21: 6 **o** else, if it please thee, I will give thee 176
22: 6 Ramoth-gilead to battle, **o** shall I forbear? 518
22:15 Ramoth-gilead to battle, **o** shall we forbear 518

2Ki
2:16 upon some mountain, **o** into some valley. 176
2:21 thence any more death **o** barren land. 2050.1
4:13 to the king, **o** to the captain of the host? 176
6:27 of the barnfloor, **o** out of the winepress? NIH
9:32 looked out to him two **o** three eunuchs. NIH
12:13 any vessels of gold, **o** vessels of silver, 2050.1
13:19 shouldest have smitten five **o** six times; 176
17:34 **o** after their ordinances, or after the law 2050.1
17:34 **o** after the law and commandment 2050.1
20: 9 ten degrees, **o** go back ten degrees? 518
22: 2 not aside *to the* right hand **o** *to the* left. 2050.1
23:10 that no man might make his son **o** his 2050.1

1Ch
21:12 **o** three months to be destroyed 518+2050.1
21:12 **o** else three days the sword of 518+2050.1

2Ch
1:11 not asked riches, wealth, **o** honour, 2050.1
6:28 of mildew, locusts, **o** caterpillars; 2050.1
6:28 or mildew, locusts, **o** caterpillars; 2050.1
6:28 whatsoever sore **o** whatsoever sickness 2050.1
6:29 *Then* what prayer **o** what supplication NIH
6:29 **o** of all thy people Israel, when every 2050.1
6:36 away captives unto a land far off **o** near; 176
7:13 **o** if I command the locusts to devour 2050.1
7:13 **o** if I send pestilence among my people; 2050.1
8:15 any matter, **o** concerning the treasures. 2050.1
14:11 many, **o** with *them that have* no power: NIH
15:13 whether small **o** great, 5704+2050.1
15:13 or great, whether man **o** woman. 5704+2050.1
16: 1 go out **o** come in to Asa king of Judah. 2050.1
18: 5 Ramoth-gilead to battle, **o** shall I forbear? 518
18:14 Ramoth-gilead to battle, **o** shall I forbear? 518
18:30 saying, Fight ye not with small **o** great, NIH
20: 9 judgment, **o** pestilence, or famine, 2050.1
20: 9 judgment, or pestilence, **o** famine, 2050.1
32:15 for no god of any nation **o** kingdom was 2050.1
36:17 compassion upon young man **o** maiden, 2050.1
36:17 old man, **o** him that stooped for age: 2050.1

Ezr
7:24 **o** ministers of this house of God, 2050.3
7:24 toll, tribute, **o** custom, upon them. 2050.3
7:26 **o** to banishment, or to confiscation of 2006
7:26 **o** to confiscation of goods, 2006
7:26 of goods, **o** to imprisonment. 2050.3
9:12 their peace **o** their wealth for ever: 2050.1
10:13 *is this* a work of one day **o** two: 2050.1

Ne
2:16 not whither I went, **o** what I did; 2050.1
5: 8 shall they be sold unto us? Then held 2050.1
10:31 **o** any victuals on the sabbath day to sell 2050.1
10:31 them on the sabbath, **o** on the holy day: 2050.1
13:20 lodged without Jerusalem once **o** twice. 2050.1
13:25 unto your sons, **o** for yourselves. 2050.1

Est
4:11 whosoever, *whether* man **o** woman, 2050.1
4:16 eat nor drink three days, night **o** day; 2050.1
8: 6 how can I endure to see the 2050.1
9:12 **o** what *is* thy request further? 2050.1

Job
3:12 **o** why the breasts that I should suck? 2050.1
3:15 O with princes that had gold, who filled 176
3:16 O as a hidden untimely birth I had not 176
4: 7 **o** where were the righteous cut off? 2050.1
6: 5 **o** loweth the ox over his fodder? 518
6: 6 **o** is there *any* taste in the white of an egg? 518
6:12 strength of stones? **o** *is* my flesh of brass? 518
6:22 **o**, Give a reward for me of your 2050.1
6:23 O, Deliver me from the enemy's hand? 2050.1
6:23 **o**, Redeem me from the hand of 2050.1
7:12 *Am* I a sea, **o** a whale, that thou settest a 518
8: 3 **o** doth the Almighty pervert 518+2050.1
10: 4 eyes of flesh? **o** seest thou as man seeth? 518
11:10 **o** gather together, then who can hinder 2050.1
12: 8 O speak to the earth, and it shall teach 176
13: 9 **o** as *one* man mocketh another, do ye *so* 518
13:22 **o** let me speak, and answer thou me. 176
15: 3 **o** *with* speeches wherewith he can do 2050.1
15: 7 **o** wast thou made before the hills? 2050.1
16: 3 **o** what emboldeneth thee that thou 176
22: 3 **o** *is it* gain *to him,* that thou makest thy 2050.1
22:11 O darkness, *that* thou canst not see; 176
25: 4 **o** how can he be clean *that is* born of a 2050.1
28:16 with the precious onyx, **o** the sapphire. 2050.1
28:18 shall be made of coral, **o** of pearls: 2050.1
31: 5 **o** *if* my foot hath hasted to deceit; 2050.1
31: 9 **o** *if* I have laid wait at my neighbour's 2050.1
31:13 of my manservant **o** of my maidservant, 2050.1
31:16 **o** have caused the eyes of the widow to 2050.1
31:17 O have eaten my morsel myself alone, 2050.1
31:19 clothing, **o** *any* poor without covering; 2050.1
31:24 **o** have said to the fine gold, *Thou art* 2050.1
31:26 the moon walking *in* brightness; 2050.1
31:27 **o** my mouth hath kissed my hand: 2050.1
31:29 **o** lift up myself when evil found him: 2050.1
31:34 **o** did the contempt of families terrify 2050.1
31:38 **o** the furrows likewise thereof 2050.1
31:39 **o** have caused the owners thereof to 2050.1
32:12 Job, **o** that answered his words: NIH
34:13 **o** who hath disposed the whole world? 2050.1
34:29 against a nation, **o** against a man only: NIH
34:33 thou refuse, **o** whether thou choose; NIH
35: 6 **o** *if* thy transgressions be multiplied, 2050.1

Job
35: 7 **o** what receiveth he of thine hand? 176
36:23 **o** who can say, Thou hast wrought 2050.1
36:29 the clouds, **o** the noise of his tabernacle? NIH
37:13 for correction, **o** for his land, or for mercy. 518
37:13 for correction, or for his land, **o** for mercy. 518
38: 5 **o** who hath stretched the line upon it? 176
38: 6 **o** who laid the corner stone thereof; 176
38: 8 O who shut up the sea with doors, 2050.1
38:16 **o** hast thou walked in the search of 2050.1
38:17 **o** hast thou seen the doors of the 2050.1
38:21 **o** because the number of thy days *is* 2050.1
38:22 **o** hast thou seen the treasures of the 2050.1
38:25 **o** a way for the lightning of thunder; 2050.1
38:28 **o** who hath begotten the drops of dew? 176
38:31 of Pleiades, **o** loose the bands of Orion? 176
38:32 **o** canst thou guide Arcturus with his 2050.1
38:36 **o** who hath given understanding to the 176
38:37 **o** who can stay the bottles of heaven, 2050.1
38:39 **o** fill the appetite of the young lions, 2050.1
39: 1 **o** canst thou mark when the hinds do 2050.1
39: 2 **o** knowest thou the time when they 2050.1
39: 5 **o** who hath loosed the bands of the 2050.1
39: 9 willing to serve thee, **o** abide by thy crib? 518
39:10 **o** will he harrow the valleys after thee? 518
39:11 **o** wilt thou leave thy labour to him? 2050.1
39:13 wings and feathers *unto* the ostrich? 518
39:15 **o** *that* the wild beast may break them. 2050.1
40: 9 **o**, canst thou thunder with a voice like 2050.1
41: 1 **o** his tongue with a cord *which* thou 2050.1
41: 2 **o** bore his jaw through with a thorn? 2050.1
41: 5 **o** wilt thou bind him for thy maidens? 2050.1
41: 7 **o** his head with fish spears? 2050.1
41:13 **o** who can come *to him* with his double NIH
41:20 as *out of a* seething pot **o** caldron. 2050.1

Ps
18:31 **o** who *is* a rock save our God? 2050.1
32: 9 Be ye not as the horse, **o** as the mule, NIH
35:14 though *he had been* my friend **o** brother: 2050.1
44:20 **o** stretched out our hands to a strange 2050.1
50: 8 for thy sacrifices **o** thy burnt offerings, 2050.1
50:13 of bulls, **o** drink the blood of goats? 2050.1
50:16 **o** *that* thou shouldest take my covenant 2050.1
66: T To the chief Musician, A Song **o** Psalm. NIH
67: T Musician on Neginoth, A Psalm **o** Song. NIH
68: T chief Musician, A Psalm **o** Song of David. NIH
69:31 ox **o** bullock that hath horns *and* hoofs. NIH
75: T Al-taschith, A Psalm **o** Song of Asaph. NIH
76: T on Neginoth, A Psalm **o** Song of Asaph. NIH
83: T A Song **o** Psalm of Asaph. NIH
87: T A Psalm **o** Song for the sons of Korah. NIH
88: T A Song **o** Psalm for the sons of Korah. NIH
88:11 grave? **o** thy faithfulness in destruction? NIH
89: 8 **o** *to* thy faithfulness round about thee? 2050.1
90: 2 **o** ever thou hadst formed the earth and 2050.1
92: T A Psalm **o** Song for the sabbath day. NIH
94:16 **o** who will stand up for me against NIH
108: T A Song **o** Psalm of David. NIH
120: 3 **o** what shall be done unto thee, thou 2050.1
131: 1 *matters,* **o** in *things* too high for me. 2050.1
132: 4 to mine eyes, **o** slumber to mine eyelids, 2050.1
139: 7 **o** whither shall I flee from thy presence? 2050.1
144: 3 **o** the son of man, that thou makest NIH

Pr
6: 7 having no guide, overseer, **o** ruler, 2050.1
7:22 **o** as a fool to the correction of the 2050.1
8: 8 *is* nothing froward **o** perverse in them. 2050.1
8:23 beginning, **o** ever the earth **was.** 4480+6924
20:20 Whoso curseth his father **o** his mother, 2050.1
22:26 **o** of them that are sureties for debts. NIH
23:34 **o** as he that lieth upon the top of a mast. 2050.1
28:24 Whoso robbeth his father **o** his mother, 2050.1
29: 9 he rage **o** laugh, *there is* no rest. 2050.1
30: 4 ascended up *into* heaven, **o** descended? 2050.1
30: 9 **o** lest I be poor, and steal, and take 2050.1
30:32 **o** if thou hast thought evil, *lay thine* 2050.1

Ecc
2:19 whether he shall be a wise *man* **o** a fool? 176
2:25 **o** who else can hasten *hereunto,* more 2050.1
5:12 *is* sweet, whether he eat little **o** much: 2050.1
9: 1 no man knoweth either love **o** hatred *by* 1571
11: 3 toward the south, **o** toward the north, 2050.1
11: 6 either this **o** that, or whether they both 176
11: 6 **o** whether they both *shall* be alike good 2050.1
12: 2 of the light, or the moon, or the stars, 2050.1
12: 2 or the light, **o** the moon, or the stars, 2050.1
12: 2 or the light, or the moon, **o** the stars, 2050.1
12: 6 O ever the silver cord be 834+3808+5704
12: 6 **o** the golden bowl be broken, 2050.1
12: 6 **o** the pitcher be broken at the fountain, 2050.1
12: 6 **o** the wheel broken at the cistern. 2050.1
12:14 *it be* good, **o** whether *it be* evil. 2050.1

SS
2: 9 My beloved *is* like a roe **o** a young hart: 176
2:17 be thou like a roe **o** a young hart upon 176
6:12 O ever I was aware, my soul made me 3808
8:14 thou like to a roe **o** to a young hart upon 176

Isa
1:11 of bullocks, **o** of lambs, or of he goats. 2050.1
1:11 of bullocks, or of lambs, **o** of he goats. 2050.1
7:11 either in the depth, **o** in the height above. 176
10:14 wing, **o** opened the mouth, or peeped. 2050.1
10:14 wing, or opened the mouth, **o** peeped. 2050.1
10:15 **o** shall the saw magnify itself against him NIH
10:15 **o** as if the staff should lift up *itself, as if it* NIH
17: 6 two **o** three berries in the top of NIH
17: 6 four **o** five in the outmost fruitful branches NIH
17: 8 either the groves, **o** the images. 2050.1
19:15 which the head **o** tail, branch or rush, 2050.1
19:15 which the head or tail, branch **o** rush, 2050.1
27: 5 O let him take hold of my strength, *that* 176

Isa
27: 7 **o** is he slain according to the slaughter of NIH
29: 8 **o** as when a thirsty *man* dreameth, 2050.1
29:16 **o** shall the thing framed say of him that 2050.1
30:14 **o** to take water *withal* out of the pit. 2050.1
38:14 Like a crane **o** a swallow, so did I chatter: NIH
40:13 **o** *being* his counseller hath taught him? 2050.1
40:18 **o** what likeness will ye compare unto 2050.1
40:25 then will ye liken me, **o** shall I be equal? 2050.1
41:22 of them; **o** declare us *things* for to come. 176
41:23 yea, do good, **o** do evil, that we may be 2050.1
42:19 **o** deaf, as my messenger *that* I sent? 2050.1
43: 9 **o** let them hear, and say, It is truth. 2050.1
44:10 **o** molten a graven image *that is* 2050.1
45: 9 **o** thy work, He hath no hands? 2050.1
45:10 **o** to the woman, What hast thou 2050.1
49:24 **o** the lawful captive delivered? 518+2050.1
50: 1 **o** which of my creditors *is it* to whom I 176
50: 2 **o** have I no power to deliver? 518+2050.1
57:11 of whom hast thou been afraid **o** feared, 2050.1
66: 8 **o** shall a nation be born at once? for as NIH

Jer
2:18 **o** what hast thou to do in the way of 2050.1
2:32 forget her ornaments, **o** a bride her attire? NIH
7:22 concerning burnt offerings **o** sacrifices: 2050.1
11:14 neither lift up a cry **o** prayer for them: 2050.1
11:19 I *was* like a lamb **o** an ox *that is* brought NIH
13:23 change his skin, **o** the leopard his spots? NIH
14:22 **o** can the heavens give showers? *art* not 2050.1
15: 5 **o** who shall bemoan thee? or who shall 2050.1
15: 5 **o** who shall go aside to ask how thou 2050.1
16: 7 drink for their father **o** for their mother. 2050.1
16:10 **o** what *is* our iniquity? or what *is* our 2050.1
16:10 **o** what *is* our sin that we have 2050.1
18:14 **o** shall the cold flowing waters that come NIH
20:17 **o** that my mother might have been my 2050.1
21:13 **o** who shall enter into our habitations? 2050.1
22:18 **o**, Ah sister! they shall not lament for 2050.1
22:18 him, *saying,* Ah lord! **o**, Ah his glory. 2050.1
23:33 the prophet, or a priest, shall ask thee, 176
23:33 or the prophet, **o** a priest, shall ask thee, 176
32:43 say, *It is* desolate without man **o** beast: 2050.1
34: 9 *being* a Hebrew **o** a Hebrewess, go free; 2050.1
36:23 Jehudi had read three **o** four leaves, 2050.1
37:18 **o** against thy servants, or against this 2050.1
37:18 thy servants, **o** against this people, 2050.1
40: 5 **o** go wheresoever it seemeth convenient 176
42: 6 *it be* good, **o** whether *it be* evil, 2050.1
42:17 none of them shall remain, **o** escape 2050.1
44:14 shall escape **o** remain, that *they* should 2050.1
44:28 whose words shall stand, mine, **o** theirs. 2050.1
48:24 cities of the land of Moab, far **o** near. 2050.1

Eze
2: 5 will hear, **o** whether they will forbear, 2050.1
2: 7 will hear, **o** whether they will forbear: 2050.1
3:11 will hear, **o** whether they will forbear. 2050.1
4:14 which dieth of itself, **o** is torn in pieces; 2050.1
14: 7 **o** of the stranger that sojourneth in 2050.1
14:17 O *if* I bring a sword upon that land, and 176
14:19 O *if* I send a pestilence into that land, 176
15: 2 **o** *than* a branch which is among the trees NIH
15: 3 **o** will *men* take a pin of it to hang any 518
17: 9 without great power **o** many people 2050.1
17:15 **o** shall he break the covenant, 2050.1
21:16 **Go thou one way o other,** *either* on 258
21:16 *either* on the right hand, **o** on the left, NIH
22:14 endure, **o** can thine hands be strong, 518
34: 6 and none did search **o** seek *after* them. 2050.1
44:22 **o** a widow that had a priest before. 2050.1
44:25 **o** for mother, or for son, or for daughter, 2050.1
44:25 or for mother, **o** for son, or for daughter, 2050.1
44:25 or for mother, or for son, **o** for daughter, 2050.1
44:25 or for sister that hath no husband, 2050.1
44:31 **o** torn, whether it be fowl or beast. 2050.1
44:31 or torn, whether it be fowl **o** beast. 2050.1
46:12 peace offerings voluntarily unto 176

Da
2:10 any magician, **o** astrologer, or Chaldean. 2050.3
2:10 any magician, or astrologer, **o** Chaldean. 2050.3
4:19 **o** the interpretation thereof, trouble 2050.3
4:35 **o** say unto him, What doest thou? 2050.3
6: 4 there any error **o** fault found in him. 2050.3
6: 7 of any God **o** man for thirty days, 2050.3
6:12 of any God **o** man within thirty days, 2050.3
6:24 brake all their bones in pieces **o** ever they 5705
11:29 not be as the former, **o** as the latter. 2050.1

Joel
1: 2 even in the days of your fathers? 2050.1

Am
3:12 of the lion two legs, **o** a piece of an ear; 176
4: 8 So two **o** three cities wandered unto one NIH
5:19 **o** went *into* the house, and leaned his 2050.1
6: 2 **o** their border greater than your border? 518

Mic
6: 7 **o** with ten thousands of rivers of oil? NIH

Hag
2:12 **o** pottage, or wine, or oil, or any meat, 2050.1
2:12 **o** pottage, or wine, or oil, or any meat, 2050.1
2:12 or pottage, **o** wine, or oil, or any meat, 2050.1
2:12 or pottage, or wine, or oil, **o** any meat, 2050.1
2:12 or pottage, or wine, **o** oil, or any meat, 2050.1

Zec
8:10 **o** came in because of the affliction; 2050.1

Mal
1: 8 pleased with thee, **o** accept thy person? 176
2:13 **o** receiveth *it* with good will at your 2050.1
2:17 in them; **o**, Where *is* the God of judgment? 176

Mt
5:17 come to destroy the law, **o** the prophets: 2228
5:18 one jot **o** one tittle shall in no wise pass 2228
5:36 canst not make one hair white **o** black. 2228
6:24 he will hold to the one, 2228
6:25 what ye shall eat, **o** what ye shall drink; 2532
6:31 **o**, What shall we drink? or, 2228
6:31 **o**, Wherewithal shall we be clothed? 2228
7: 4 O how wilt thou say to thy brother, Let 2228
7: 9 O what man is there of you, whom if his 2228

O

Mt
7:10 **O** if he ask a fish, will he give him a — 2532
7:16 gather grapes of thorns, **o** figs of thistles? — 2228
9: 5 forgiven thee; **o** to say, Arise, and walk? — 2228
10:11 whatsoever city **o** town ye shall enter, — 2228
10:14 when ye depart out of that house **o** city, — 2228
10:19 no thought how **o** what ye shall speak: — 2228
10:37 He that loveth father **o** mother more than — 2228
10:37 he that loveth son **o** daughter more than — 2228
11: 3 should come, **o** do we look for another? — 2228
12: 5 **O** have ye not read in the law, how that — 2228
12:25 every city **o** house divided against itself — 2228
12:29 **o else** how can one enter into a strong — 2228
12:33 **o else** make the tree corrupt, and his fruit — 2228
13:21 **o** persecution ariseth because of the word, — 2228
15: 4 and, He that curseth father **o** mother, — 2228
15: 5 shall say to *his* father **o** *his* mother, — 2228
15: 6 And honour not his father **o** his mother, — 2228
16:14 others, Jeremias, **o** one of the prophets. — 2228
16:26 **o** what shall a man give in exchange for — 2228
17:25 kings of the earth take custom **o** tribute? — 2228
17:25 of their own children, **o** of strangers? — 2228
18: 8 if thy hand **o** thy foot offend thee, — 2228
18: 8 far than to enter into life halt **o** maimed, — 2228
18: 8 rather than having two hands **o** two feet — 2228
18:16 *then* take with thee one **o** two more, — 2228
18:16 in the mouth of two **o** three witnesses — 2228
18:20 where two **o** three are gathered together — 2228
19:29 **o** brethren, or sisters, or father, or mother, — 2228
19:29 **o** sisters, or father, or mother, or wife, — 2228
19:29 **o** father, or mother, or wife, or children, — 2228
19:29 **o** mother, or wife, or children, or lands, — 2228
19:29 **o** mother, or wife, or children, or lands, — 2228
19:29 **o** mother, or wife, or children, or lands, — 2228
21:25 from heaven, **o** of men? And they — 2228
22:17 lawful to give tribute unto Cesar, **o** not? — 2228
23:17 unto the temple that sanctifieth the gold? — 2228
23:19 gift, **o** the altar that sanctifieth the gift? — 2228
24:23 say unto you, Lo, here *is* Christ, **o** there; — 2228
25:37 and fed *thee?* **o** thirsty, and gave *thee* — 2228
25:38 took *thee* in? **o** naked, and clothed *thee?* — 2228
25:39 **O** when saw we thee sick, — 1161
25:39 sick, **o** in prison, and came unto thee? — 2228
25:44 **o** athirst, or a stranger, or naked, or sick, — 2228
25:44 **o** a stranger, or naked, or sick, or in — 2228
25:44 **o** naked, or sick, or in prison, and did not — 2228
25:44 sick, or in prison, and did not minister — 2228
25:44 **o** in prison, and did not minister unto — 2228
27:17 Barabbas, **o** Jesus which is called Christ? — 2228

Mk
2: 9 **o** to say, Arise, and take up thy bed, — 2228
3: 4 do good on the sabbath days, **o** to do evil? — 2228
3: 4 to save life, **o** to kill? But they held their — 2228
3:33 Who is my mother, **o** my brethren? — 2228
4:17 when affliction **o** persecution ariseth for — 2228
4:21 to be put under a bushel, **o** under a bed? — 2228
4:30 **o** with what comparison shall we — 2228
6:15 it is a prophet, **o** as one of the prophets. — 2228
6:56 into villages, **o** cities, or country, — 2228
6:56 into villages, or cities, **o** country, — 2228
7:10 and, Whoso curseth father **o** mother, — 2228
7:11 If a man shall say to *his* father **o** mother, — 2228
7:12 to do ought for his father **o** his mother; — 2228
8:37 **O** what shall a man give in exchange for — 2228
10:29 **o** brethren, or sisters, or father, or mother — 2228
10:29 **o** sisters, or father, or mother, or wife, — 2228
10:29 **o** father, or mother, or wife, or children, — 2228
10:29 **o** mother, or wife, or children, or lands, — 2228
10:29 **o** mother, or wife, or children, or lands, — 2228
10:29 **o** mother, or wife, or children, or lands, — 2228
11:30 of John, was *it* from heaven, **o** of men? — 2228
12:14 Is it lawful to give tribute to Cesar, **o** not? — 2228
12:15 Shall we give, **o** shall we not give? But — 2228
13:21 you, Lo, here *is* Christ; **o** lo, *he is* there; — 2228
13:35 **o** at midnight, or at the cockcrowing, — 2228
13:35 **o** at the cockcrowing, or in the morning: — 2228
13:35 or at the cockcrowing, **o** in the morning: — 2228

Lk
2:24 pair of turtledoves, **o** two young pigeons. — 2228
3:15 John, **whether** he were the Christ, **o** not; — 3379
5:23 forgiven thee; **o** to say, Rise up and walk? — 2228
6: 9 the sabbath days to do good, **o** to do evil? — 2228
6: 9 or to do evil? to save life, **o** to destroy *it?* — 2228
7:19 that should come? **o** look we for another? — 2228
7:20 that should come? **o** look we for another? — 2228
8:16 it with a vessel, **o** putteth *it* under a bed; — 2228
9:25 and lose himself, **o** be cast away? — 2228
11:11 **o** if *he* ask a fish, will he for a fish give — 2532
11:12 Or if he shall ask an egg, will he offer him — 2228
12:11 take ye no thought how **o** what *thing* ye — 2228
12:11 *thing* ye shall answer, **o** what ye shall say: — 2228
12:14 made me a judge **o** a divider over you? — 2228
12:29 **o** what ye shall drink, neither be ye of — 2228
12:38 **o** come in the third watch, and find *them* — 2532
12:41 thou this parable unto us, **o** even to all? — 2228
13: 4 **O** those eighteen, upon whom the tower — 2228
13:15 loose his ox **o** *his* ass from the stall, — 2228
14: 5 shall have an ass **o** an ox fallen into a pit, — 2228
14:12 When thou makest a dinner **o** a supper, — 2228
14:31 What king, going to make war against — 2228
14:32 **O else**, while the other is yet a great way — 1490
16:13 **o else** he will hold to the one, — 2228
17: 7 having a servant plowing **o** feeding cattle, — 2228
17:21 **o**, lo there: for behold, the kingdom of — 2228
17:23 shall say to you, See here; **o**, see there: — 2228
18:11 unjust, adulterers, **o** even as this publican. — 2228

Lk
18:29 **o** parents, or brethren, or wife, or — 2228
18:29 parents, **o** brethren, or wife, or children, — 2228
18:29 parents, **o** brethren, or wife, or children, — 2228
18:29 parents, **o** brethren, or wife, or children, — 2228
20: 2 **o** who is he that gave thee this authority? — 2228
20: 4 of John, was it from heaven, **o** of men? — 2228
20:22 for us to give tribute unto Cesar, **o** no? — 2228
22:27 he that sitteth at meat, **o** he that serveth? — 2228

Jn
2: 6 containing two **o** three firkins apiece. — 2228
4:27 thou? **o**, Why talkest thou with her? — 2228
6:19 about five and twenty **o** thirty furlongs, — 2228
7:17 it be of God, **o** whether I speak of myself. — 2228
7:48 Have any of the rulers **o** of the Pharisees — 2228
9: 2 who did sin, this *man,* **o** his parents, — 2228
9:21 **o** who hath opened his eyes, we know — 2228
9:25 Whether he be a sinner **o** *no,* I know not: — NIG
13:29 **o** that he should give something to the — 2228
14:11 **o else** believe me for the very works' — 1490
18:34 of thyself, **o** did others tell *it* thee of me? — 2228

Ac
1: 7 for you to know *the* times **o** *the* seasons, — 2228
3:12 why look ye *so* earnestly on us, as — 2228
3:12 as though by our own power **o** holiness — 2228
4: 7 By what power, **o** by what name, — 2228
4:34 possessors of lands **o** houses sold them, — 2228
5:38 for if this counsel **o** this work be of men, — 2228
7:49 the Lord: **o** what *is* the place of my rest? — 2228
8:34 of himself, **o** of some other *man?* — 2228
9: 2 way, whether they were men **o** women, — 2532
10:14 any *thing that is* common **o** unclean. — 2228
10:28 **o** come unto one of another nation; — 2228
10:28 not call any man common **o** unclean. — 2228
11: 8 nothing common **o** unclean hath at any — 2228
17:21 *either* to tell, **o** to hear some new *thing.)* — 2532
17:29 **o** silver, or stone, graven by art and — 2228
17:29 **o** silver, or stone, graven by art and — 2228
18:14 a matter of wrong **o** wicked lewdness, — 2228
19:12 unto the sick handkerchiefs **o** aprons, — 2228
20:33 no *man's* silver, **o** gold, or apparel. — 2228
20:33 no *man's* silver, or gold, **o** apparel. — 2228
23: 9 but if a spirit **o** an angel hath spoken to — 2228
23:15 we, **o** ever he come near, are ready to — NIG
23:29 to his charge worthy of death **o** of bonds. — 2228
24:20 **O else** let these same *here* say, if they — 2228
24:23 acquaintance to minister **o** come unto — 2228
25:11 **o** have committed any *thing* worthy of — 2532
26:31 nothing worthy of death **o** of bonds. — 2228
28: 6 swollen, **o** fallen down dead suddenly: — 2228
28:17 the people, **o** customs of our fathers, — 2228
28:21 came shewed **o** spake any harm of thee. — 2228

Ro
2: 4 **O** despisest thou the riches of his — 2228
2:15 **o else** excusing one another;) — 2228
3: 1 **o** what profit *is there* of circumcision? — 2228
4: 9 then upon the circumcision *only,* **o** — 2228
4:10 in circumcision, **o** in uncircumcision? — 2228
4:13 **o** to his seed, through the law, — 2228
6:16 **o** of obedience unto righteousness? — 2228
8:35 **o** distress, or persecution, or famine, — 2228
8:35 **o** persecution, or famine, or nakedness, — 2228
8:35 **o** famine, or nakedness, or peril, or — 2228
8:35 **o** famine, or nakedness, or peril, or sword? — 2228
8:35 **o** famine, or nakedness, or peril, or sword? — 2228
8:35 **o** famine, or nakedness, or peril, or sword? — 2228
9:11 neither having done any good **o** evil, — 2228
10: 7 **O,** Who shall descend into the deep? — 2228
11:34 Lord? **o** who hath been his counsellor? — 2228
11:35 **O** who hath first given to him, and it — 2228
12: 7 ministry, *let us wait on our* ministering: — 1535
12: 7 **o** he that teacheth, on teaching; — 1535
12: 8 **O** he that exhorteth, on exhortation: he — 1535
14: 4 to his own master he standeth **o** falleth. — 2228
14: 8 **o** die, we are the Lord's. — 1437+5037
14:10 **o** why dost thou set at nought thy brother? — 2228
14:13 that no *man* put a stumblingblock **o** — 2228
14:21 is offended, or is *made* weak. — 2228
14:21 or is offended, **o** is *made* weak. — 2228

1Co
1:13 were ye baptized in the name of Paul? — 2228
2: 1 with excellency of speech **o** of wisdom, — 2228
3:22 **o** Apollos, or Cephas, or the world, or life, — 1535
3:22 **o** Cephas, or the world, or life, or death, — 1535
3:22 **o** the world, or life, or death, — 1535
3:22 **o** life, or death, or *things* present, — 1535
3:22 **o** death, or *things* present, or *things* to — 1535
3:22 **o** *things* present, or *things* to come; — 1535
3:22 or *things* present, **o** *things* to come; — 1535
4: 3 be judged of you, **o** of man's judgment: — 2228
4:21 **o** in love, and *in* the spirit of meekness? — 2228
5:10 **o** with the covetous, or extortioners, — 2228
5:10 **o** extortioners, or with idolaters; — 2228
5:10 or extortioners, or with idolaters; — 2228
5:11 **o** covetous, or an idolater, or a railer, — 2228
5:11 **o** an idolater, or a railer, or a drunkard, — 2228
5:11 **o** a railer, or a drunkard, or an extortioner — 2228
5:11 a railer, **o** a drunkard, or an extortioner; — 2228
5:11 a railer, or a drunkard, **o** an extortioner; — 2228
7:11 **o** be reconciled to *her* husband: — 2228
7:15 A brother **o** a sister is not under bondage — 2228
7:16 **o** how knowest thou, O man, whether — 2228
8: 5 whether in heaven **o** in earth, (as there — 1535
9: 6 **O** I only and Barnabas, have not we — 2228
9: 7 **o** who feedeth a flock, and eateth not of — 2228
9: 8 a man? **o** saith not the law the same also? — 2228
9:10 **O** saith he *it* altogether for our sakes? — 2228
10:19 that the idol is any *thing,* **o** that which is — 2228
10:31 ye eat, **o** drink, or whatsoever ye do, — 1535
10:31 ye eat, or drink, **o** whatsoever ye do, — 1535

1Co
11: 4 Every man praying **o** prophesying, — 2228
11: 5 But every woman that prayeth **o** — 2228
11: 6 shame for a woman to be shorn **o** shaven, — 2228
11:22 ye not houses to eat and to drink *in?* **o** — 2228
12:13 whether *we be* Jews **o** Gentiles, whether — 1535
12:13 or Gentiles, whether *we be* bond **o** free; — 1535
12:26 suffer with *it;* **o** one member be honoured, — 1535
13: 1 *as* sounding brass, **o** a tinkling cymbal. — 2228
14: 6 **o** by knowledge, or by prophesying, — 2228
14: 6 **o** by prophesying, or by doctrine? — 2228
14: 6 **o** by prophesying, **o** by doctrine? — 2228
14: 7 life giving sound, whether pipe **o** harp, — 1535
14: 7 shall it be known what is piped **o** harped? — 2228
14:23 **o** unbelievers, will they not say that ye — 2228
14:24 **o** *one* unlearned, he is convinced of all, — 2228
14:27 **o** at the most by three, and that by course; — 2228
14:29 Let the prophets speak two **o** three, — 2228
14:36 out from you? **o** came it unto you only? — 2228
14:37 think himself to be a prophet, **o** spiritual, — 2228
15:11 Therefore whether *it were* I **o** they, — 1535
15:37 chance of wheat, **o** of some other *grain:* — 2228

2Co
1: 6 **o whether** we be comforted, *it is* for your — 1535
1:13 than what you read **o** acknowledge; — 2228
1:17 **o** *the* things that I purpose, do I purpose — 2228
3: 1 need we, as some *others,* epistles of — 2228
3: 1 *letters* of commendation from you? — 2228
5: 9 labour, that, whether present **o** absent, — 1535
5:10 he hath done, whether *it be* good **o** bad. — 1535
5:13 **o whether** we be sober, *it is* for your — 1535
6:15 what part hath he that believeth with — 2228
8:23 **o** our brethren *be inquired of, they are* — 2228
9: 7 *him give;* not grudgingly, **o** of necessity: — 2228
10:12 compare ourselves with some that — 2228
11: 4 **o** *if* ye receive another spirit, which ye — 2228
11: 4 ye have not received, **o** another gospel, — 2228
12: 2 **o whether** out of the body, I cannot tell: — 1535
12: 3 the body, or out of the body, I cannot tell: — 1535
12: 6 seeth me *to be,* **o** that he heareth of me. — 2228
13: 1 In the mouth of two **o** three witnesses — 2532

Gal
1: 8 But though we, **o** an angel from heaven, — 2228
1:10 For do I now persuade men, **o** God? — 2228
1:10 do I seek to please men? for if I yet — 2228
2: 2 means I should run, **o** had run, in vain. — 2228
3: 2 of the law, **o** by the hearing of faith? — 2228
3: 5 of the law, **o** by the hearing of faith? — 2228
3:15 no *man* disannulleth, **o** added thereto. — 2228
4: 9 rather are known of God, how turn ye — 1161

Eph
3:20 abundantly above all that we ask **o** think, — 2228
5: 3 and all uncleanness, **o** covetousness, — 2228
5:27 **o** wrinkle, or any such *thing;* but that it — 2228
5:27 **o** any such *thing;* but that it should be — 2228
6: 8 of the Lord, whether *he be* bond **o** free. — 1535

Php
1:18 in pretence, **o** in truth, Christ is preached; — 1535
1:20 body, whether *it be* by life, **o** by death. — 1535
1:27 I come and see you, **o** *else* be absent, — 1535
2: 3 *be done* through strife **o** vainglory; — 2228

Col
1:16 **o** dominions, or principalities, or powers: — 1535
1:16 or dominions, or principalities, or powers: — 1535
1:16 or dominions, or principalities, **o** powers: — 1535
1:20 *be things* in earth, **o** *things* in heaven. — 1535
2:16 **o** in drink, or in respect of a holyday, — 2228
2:16 **o** in respect of a holyday, or of the new — 2228
2:16 **o** of the new moon, or of the sabbath — 2228
2:16 of the new moon, **o** of the sabbath days: — 2228
3:17 And whatsoever ye do in word **o** deed, — 2228

1Th
2:19 *is* our hope, **o** joy, or crown of rejoicing? — 2228
2:19 *is* our hope, or joy, **o** crown of rejoicing? — 2228
5:10 for us, that, whether we wake **o** sleep, — 1535

2Th
2: 2 be troubled, neither by spirit, nor by — 3366
2: 4 that is called God, **o** that is worshipped; — 2228
2:15 whether by word, **o** by our epistle. — 1535

1Ti
2: 9 **o** gold, or pearls, or costly array; — 2532
2: 9 or gold, **o** pearls, or costly array; — 2228
2: 9 or gold, or pearls, **o** costly array; — 2228
5: 4 if any widow have children **o** nephews, — 2228
5:16 If any man **o** woman that believeth have — 2228
5:19 but before two **o** three witnesses. — 2228

Tit
1: 6 children not accused of riot **o** unruly. — 2228
3:12 shall send Artemas unto thee, **o** Tychicus, — 2228

Phm
1:18 hath wronged thee, **o** oweth *thee* ought, — 2228

Heb
2: 6 the son of man, that thou visitest him? — 2228
10:28 mercy under two **o** three witnesses: — 2228
12:16 any fornicator, **o** profane *person,* as Esau, — 2228
12:20 be stoned, **o** thrust through with a dart: — 2228

Jas
2: 3 thou there, **o** sit here under my footstool: — 2228
2:15 If a brother **o** sister be naked, — 2228
4:13 To day **o** to morrow we will go into such — 2532
4:15 will, we shall live, and do this, **o** that. — 2228

1Pe
1:11 **o** what manner of time the Spirit of — 2228
2:14 **O** unto governors, as unto them that are — 1535
3: 3 of gold, **o** of putting on of apparel; — 2228
3: 9 evil for evil, **o** railing for railing: — 2228
4:15 *as* a thief, or *as* an evildoer, or as a — 2228
4:15 *as* an evildoer, or as a busybody in — 2228
4:15 as a busybody in other men's matters. — 2228

Rev
2: 5 **o else** I *will* come unto thee quickly, — 1490
2:16 **o else** I *will* come unto thee quickly, — 1490
3:15 nor hot: I would thou wert cold **o** hot. — 2228
13:16 in their right hand, **o** in their foreheads: — 2228
13:17 that no *man* might buy **o** sell, save he — 2228
13:17 **o** the name of the beast, or the number of — 2228
13:17 of the beast, **o** the number of his name. — 2228
14: 9 *his* mark in his forehead, **o** in his hand, — 2228
20: 4 upon their foreheads, **o** in their hands; — 2532
21:27 worketh abomination, **o** *maketh* a lie: — 2532

O

ORACLE (17) [ORACLES]

2Sa	16:23 *was* as if a man had inquired at the o of	1697
1Ki	6: 5 both of the temple and the o	1687
	6:16 *even* for the o, *even* for the most holy	1687
	6:19 the o he prepared in the house within,	1687
	6:20 the o in the forepart *was* twenty cubits in	1687
	6:21 by the chains of gold before the o;	1687
	6:22 also the whole altar that *was* by the o he	1687
	6:23 within the o he made two cherubims *of*	1687
	6:31 for the entering of the o he made doors of	1687
	7:49 five on the left, before the o, with	1687
	8: 6 into the o of the house, to the most holy	1687
	8: 8 seen out in the holy *place* before the o,	1687
2Ch	3:16 *as* in the o, and put *them* on the heads of	1687
	4:20 burn after the manner before the o,	1687
	5: 7 to the o of the house, into the most holy	1687
	5: 9 were seen from the ark before the o;	1687
Ps	28: 2 I lift up my hands toward thy holy o.	1687

ORACLES (4) [ORACLE]

Ac	7:38 who received *the* lively o to give unto us:	3051
Ro	3: 2 that unto them were committed the o of	3051
Heb	5:12 *be* the first principles of the o of God;	3051
1Pe	4:11 *man* speak, *let* him speak as the o of God;	3051

ORATION (1) [ORATOR]

Ac	12:21 his throne, and made an o unto them.	1215

ORATOR (2) [ORATION]

Isa	3: 3 the cunning artificer, and the eloquent o.	3908
Ac	24: 1 and *with* a certain o *named* Tertullus,	4489

ORCHARD (1) [ORCHARDS]

SS	4:13 Thy plants *are* an o of pomegranates,	6508

ORCHARDS (1) [ORCHARD]

Ecc	2: 5 I made me gardens and o, and I planted	6508

ORDAIN (5) [FOREORDAINED, ORDAINED, ORDAINETH]

1Ch	9:22 Samuel the seer did in their set office.	3245
	17: 9 Also I will o a place for my people Israel,	7760
Isa	26:12 LORD, thou wilt o peace for us: for thou	8239
1Co	7:17 let him walk. And so o I in all churches.	1299
Tit	1: 5 and o elders in every city, as I had	2525

ORDAINED (37) [ORDAIN]

Nu	28: 6 which was o in mount Sinai for a sweet	6213
1Ki	12:32 Jeroboam o a feast in the eighth month,	6213
	12:33 and o a feast unto the children of Israel:	6213
2Ki	23: 5 whom the kings of Judah had o to burn	5414
2Ch	11:15 he o him priests for the high places,	5975
	23:18 with singing, **as** it was o **by** David.	3027+5921
	29:27 the instruments o **by** David king	3027+5921
Est	9:27 The Jews o, and took upon them,	6965
Ps	8: 2 sucklings hast thou o strength because	3245
	8: 3 moon and the stars, which thou hast o;	3559
	81: 5 This he o in Joseph *for* a testimony,	7760
	132:17 to bud: I have o a lamp for mine anointed.	6186
Isa	30:33 Tophet *is* o of old; yea, for the king it is	6186
Jer	1: 5 *and* I o thee a prophet unto the nations.	5414
Da	2:24 whom the king had o to destroy the wise	4483
Hab	1:12 O LORD, thou hast o them for judgment;	7760
Mk	3:14 he o twelve, that they should be with	4160
Jn	15:16 and o you, that you should go and	5087
Ac	1:22 must one be o *to be* a witness with us of	1096
	10:42 to testify that it is he which was o of God	3724
	13:48 as many as were o to eternal life believed.	5021
	14:23 when they had o them elders in every	5500
	16: 4 that were o of the apostles and elders	2919
	17:31 by *that* man whom he hath o;	3724
Ro	7:10 the commandment, which was o to life,	NIG
	13: 1 of God: the powers that be are o of God.	5021
1Co	2: 7 *even* the hidden *wisdom,* which God o	4309
	9:14 hath the Lord o that they which preach	1299
Gal	3:19 *it was* o by angels in the hand of a	1299
Eph	2:10 which God hath **before** o that we should	4282
1Ti	2: 7 Whereunto I am o a preacher,	5087
2Ti	4: 5 o the first bishop of the church of	5500
Tit	3: 5 o the first bishop of the church of	5500
Heb	5: 1 is o for men *in* things pertaining to God,	2525
	8: 3 For every high priest is o to offer gifts and	2525
	9: 6 Now when these *things* were thus o,	2680
Jude	1: 4 who were **before** of old o to this	4270

ORDAINETH (1) [ORDAIN]

Ps	7:13 he o his arrows against the persecutors.	6466

ORDER (61) [ORDERED, ORDERETH, ORDERINGS, ORDERLY]

Ge	22: 9 **laid** the wood **in** o, and bound Isaac his	6186
Ex	26:17 one board, **set in** o one against another:	7947
	27:21 sons shall o it from evening to morning	6186
	39:37 *even with* the lamps to be **set in** o, and	4634
	40: 4 **set in** o the things that are to be set in	6186
	40: 4 in order the things that are to be **set in** o	6187
	40:23 set the bread **in** o upon it before	6186+6187
Lev	1: 7 and **lay** the wood **in** o upon the fire:	6186
	1: 8 **lay** the parts, the head, and the fat, **in** o	6186
	1:12 priest shall **lay** them **in** o on the wood	6186
	6:12 **lay** the burnt offering **in** o upon it;	6186
	24: 3 shall Aaron o it from the evening unto	6186
	24: 4 He shall o the lamps upon the pure	6186
	24: 8 Every sabbath he shall **set it in** o before	6186
Jos	2: 6 which she had **laid in** o upon the roof.	6186

Jdg	13:12 How shall we o the child,	1961+4941
2Sa	17:23 **put** his household in o,	6680
1Ki	18:33 he **put** the wood **in** o, and cut the bullock	6186
	20:14 he said, Who shall o the battle? And he	631
2Ki	1: 1 saith the LORD, **Set** thine house in o:	6680
	23: 4 priest, and the priests of the **second** o;	4932
1Ch	6:32 on their office according to their o.	4941
	15:13 that we sought him not after the **due** o.	4941
	23:31 to the o **commanded** unto them,	4941
	25: 2 which prophesied according to the o of	3027
	25: 6 according to the king's o to Asaph,	3027
2Ch	8:14 according to the o of David his father,	4941
	13:11 the *shew*bread also *set* they **in** o upon	4635
	29:35 of the house of the LORD was **set in** o.	3559
Job	10:22 without any o, and *where* the light is as	5468
	23: 4 I would o *my* cause before him, and fill	6186
	33: 5 **set** thy words **in** o before me, stand up.	6186
	37:19 *for* we cannot o *our* speech by reason of	6186
Ps	40: 5 they cannot be **reckoned up in** o unto	6186
	50:21 and **set** *them* **in** o before thine eyes.	6186
	110: 4 Thou *art* a priest for ever after the o	1700
	119:133 O my steps in thy word: and let not any	3559
Ecc	12: 9 sought out, *and* **set in** o many proverbs.	8626
Isa	9: 7 to o it, and to stablish it with judgment	3559
	38: 1 saith the LORD, **Set** thine house in o:	6680
	44: 7 and shall declare it, and **set** it **in** o for me,	6186
Jer	46: 3 O ye the buckler and shield, and draw	6186
Eze	41: 6 one over another, and thirty *in* o;	6471
Lk	1: 1 set **forth in** o a declaration of those things	392
	1: 3 to write unto these **in** o, most excellent	2517
	1: 8 office before God in the o of his course,	5010
Ac	11: 4 expounded *it* **by** o unto them, saying,	2517
	18:23 the country of Galatia and Phrygia **in** o,	2517
1Co	11:34 And the rest will I **set in** o when I come.	1299
	14:40 Let all *things* be done decently and in o.	5010
	15:23 But every man in his own o: *Christ*	5001
	16: 1 as I have **given** o to the churches of	1299
Col	2: 5 joying and beholding your o,	5010
Tit	1: 5 that thou shouldest **set in** o the *things*	1930
Heb	5: 6 priest for ever after the o of Melchisedec.	5010
	5:10 Called of God a high priest after the o of	5010
	6:20 made a high priest for ever after the o of	5010
	7:11 should rise after the o of Melchisedec,	5010
	7:11 and not be called after the o of Aaron?	5010
	7:17 Thou *art* a priest for ever after the o of	5010
	7:21 Thou *art* a priest for ever after the o of	5010

ORDERED (4) [ORDER]

Jdg	6:26 in the o **place**, and take the second	4634
2Sa	23: 5 o in all *things,* and sure:	6186
Job	13:18 Behold now, I have o *my* cause; I know	6186
Ps	37:23 The steps of a *good* man are o by	3559

ORDERETH (1) [ORDER]

Ps	50:23 to him that o *his* conversation *aright* will	7760

ORDERINGS (1) [ORDER]

1Ch	24:19 These *were* the o of them in their service	6486

ORDERLY (1) [ORDER]

Ac	21:24 but *that* thou thyself also **walkest** o,	4748

ORDINANCE (30) [ORDINANCES]

Ex	12:14 you shall keep it a feast by an o for ever.	2708
	12:17 day in your generations by an o for ever.	2708
	12:24 ye shall observe this thing for an o to thee	2706
	12:43 and Aaron, This *is* the o of the passover:	2708
	13:10 this o in his season from year to year.	2708
	15:25 he made for them a statute and an o,	4941
Lev	18:30 Therefore ye shall keep mine o, that ye	4931
	22: 9 They shall therefore keep mine o, lest	4931
Nu	9:14 according to the o of the passover,	2708
	9:14 ye shall have one o, both for the stranger,	2708
	10: 8 they shall be to you for an o for ever	2708
	15:15 One o *shall be* both for you *of*	2708
	15:15 *you,* an o for ever in your generations:	2708
	18: 8 and to thy sons, by an o for ever.	2706
	19: 2 This *is* the o of the law which the LORD	2708
	31:21 This *is* the o of the law which the LORD	2708
Jos	24:25 set them a statute and an o in Shechem.	4941
1Sa	30:25 a statute and an o for Israel unto this day.	4941
2Ch	2: 4 our God. This *is* an o for ever to Israel.	NIH
	35:13 the passover with fire according to the o:	4941
	35:25 to *this* day, and made them an o in Israel:	2706
Ezr	3:10 after the o of David king of Israel.	3027
Ps	99: 7 and the o *that* he gave them.	2706
Isa	24: 5 transgressed the laws, changed the o,	2706
	58: 2 and forsook not the o of their God:	4941
Eze	45:14 Concerning the o of oil, the bath *of* oil,	2706
	46:14 meat offering continually *by* a perpetual o	2708
Mal	3:14 what profit *is it* that we have kept his o,	4931
Ro	13: 2 resisteth the power, resisteth the o of God:	1296
1Pe	2:13 Submit yourselves to every o of man for	2937

ORDINANCES (27) [ORDINANCE]

Ex	18:20 thou shalt teach them o and laws,	2706
Lev	18: 3 not do: neither shall ye walk in their o.	2708
	18: 4 and keep mine o, to walk therein:	2708
Nu	9:12 according to all the o of the passover they	2708
2Ki	17:34 or after their o, or after the law and	4941
	17:37 o, and the law, and the commandment,	4941
2Ch	33: 8 statutes and the o by the hand of Moses.	4941
Ne	10:32 we made o for us, to charge ourselves	4687
Job	38:33 Knowest thou the o of heaven? canst	2708
Ps	119:91 continue *this* day according to thine o:	4941

Isa	58: 2 they ask of me the o of justice; they take	4941
Jer	31:35 the o of the moon and of the stars for a	2708
	31:36 If those o depart from before me, saith	2706
	33:25 *if* I have not appointed the o of heaven	2708
Eze	11:20 statutes, and keep mine o, and do them:	4941
	43:11 all the o thereof, and all the forms thereof,	2708
	43:11 and all the o thereof, and do them.	2708
	43:18 These *are* the o of the altar in the day	2708
	44: 5 all the o of the house of the LORD,	2708
Mal	3: 7 fathers ye are gone away from mine o,	2706
Lk	1: 6 and o of the Lord blameless.	1345
1Co	11: 2 me in all *things,* and keep the o,	3862
Eph	2:15 law of commandments **contained** in o;	1378
Col	2:14 Blotting out the handwriting of o that	1378
	2:20 living in the world, are ye **subject to** o,	1379
Heb	9: 1 verily the first *covenant* had also o of	1345
	9:10 drinks, and divers washings, and carnal o,	1345

ORDINARY (1)

Eze	16:27 have diminished thine o *food,* and	2706

OREB (7)

Jdg	7:25 princes of the Midianites, O and Zeeb;	6159
	7:25 slew O upon the rock Oreb, and Zeeb	6159
	7:25 slew Oreb upon the rock O, and Zeeb	6159
	7:25 the heads of O and Zeeb to Gideon	6159
	8: 3 the princes of Midian, O and Zeeb:	6159
Ps	83:11 Make their nobles like O, and like Zeeb:	6159
Isa	10:26 to the slaughter of Midian at the rock O:	6159

OREN (1)

1Ch	2:25 Bunah, and O, and Ozem, *and* Ahijah.	767

ORGAN (3) [ORGANS]

Ge	4:21 of all such as handle the harp and o.	5748
Job	21:12 harp, and rejoice at the sound of the o.	5748
	30:31 my o into the voice of them that weep.	5748

ORGANS (1) [ORGAN]

Ps	150: 4 him with stringed instruments and o.	5748

ORION (3)

Job	9: 9 O, and Pleiades, and the chambers of	3685
	38:31 of Pleiades, or loose the bands of O?	3685
Am	5: 8 *him* that maketh the seven stars and O,	3685

ORNAMENT (7) [ORNAMENTS]

Pr	1: 9 For they *shall be* an o of grace unto thy	3880
	4: 9 She shall give to thine head an o of grace:	3880
	25:12 an o of fine gold, *so is* a wise reprover	2481
Isa	30:22 and the o of thy molten images of gold:	642
	49:18 as with an o, and bind them on *thee,* as a	5716
Eze	7:20 As for the beauty of his o, he set it in	5716
1Pe	3: 4 *even the* o of a meek and quiet spirit,	NIG

ORNAMENTS (14) [ORNAMENT]

Ex	33: 4 and no man did put on him his o.	5716
	33: 5 therefore now put off thy o from thee,	5716
	33: 6 of their o by the mount Horeb.	5716
Jdg	8:21 took away the o that *were* on their	7720
	8:26 beside o, and collars, and purple raiment	7720
2Sa	1:24 who put on o of gold upon your apparel.	5716
Isa	3:18 of *their* **tinkling** o *about their feet,*	5914
	3:20 the o of the legs, and the headbands,	6807
	61:10 as a bridegroom decketh *himself* with o,	6287
Jer	2:32 Can a maid forget her o, *or* a bride her	5716
	4:30 though thou deckest thee with o of gold,	5716
Eze	16: 7 and thou art come to **excellent** o:	5716+5921
	16:11 I decked thee also *with* o, and I put	5716
	23:40 and **deckedst** thyself **with** o,	5710+5716

ORNAN (12) [ARAUNAH]

1Ch	21:15 by the threshingfloor of O the Jebusite.	771
	21:18 in the threshingfloor of O the Jebusite.	771
	21:20 O turned back, and saw the angel;	771
	21:20 Now O was threshing wheat.	771
	21:21 And as David came to O, Ornan looked	771
	21:21 O looked and saw David, and went out of	771
	21:22 David said to O, Grant me the place of *this*	771
	21:23 And O said unto David, Take *it* to thee,	771
	21:24 king David said to O, Nay; but I will verily	771
	21:25 So David gave to O for the place six	771
	21:28 him in the threshingfloor of O the Jebusite,	771
2Ch	3: 1 in the threshingfloor of O the Jebusite.	771

ORPAH (2)

Ru	1: 4 the name of the one *was* O, and the name	6204
	1:14 O kissed her mother in law; but Ruth	6204

ORPHANS (1)

La	5: 3 We are o and fatherless, our mothers *are*	3490

OSEE (1) [HOSEA]

Ro	9:25 As he saith also in O, I will call *them* my	5617

OSHEA (2) [JOSHUA]

Nu	13: 8 of the tribe of Ephraim, O the son of Nun.	1954
	13:16 Moses called O the son of Nun, Jehoshua.	1954

OSPRAY (2)

Lev	11:13 the eagle, and the ossifrage, and the o,	5822
Dt	14:12 the eagle, and the ossifrage, and the o,	5822

OSPREY See GIER

OSSIFRAGE (2)

Lev	11:13 the eagle, and the o, and the ospray,	6538

Dt 14:12 the eagle, and the **o**, and the ospray, 6538

OSTRICH (1) [OSTRICHES]
Job 39:13 or wings and feathers *unto* the **o**? 2624

OSTRICHES (1) [OSTRICH]
La 4: 3 cruel, like the **o** in the wilderness. 3283

OTHER (465) [OTHER'S, OTHERS, OTHERWISE]
Ge 4:19 *was* Adah, and the name of the **o** Zillah. 8145
 8:10 he stayed yet **o** seven days; and again he 312
 8:12 he stayed yet **o** seven days; and sent forth 312
 13:11 separated themselves the one from the **o**s. 251
 20:16 and with all **o**: thus she was reproved. NIH
 25:23 *one* people shall be stronger than *the* **o** NIH
 28:17 this *is* **none** *o* but the house of God, 369
 29:27 thou shalt serve with me yet seven **o** years. 312
 29:30 and served with him yet seven **o** years. 312
 31:50 if thou shalt take **o** wives beside my NIH
 32: 8 the **o** company which is left shall escape. NIH
 41: 3 seven **o** kine came up after them out of 312
 41: 3 stood by the **o** kine upon the brink of NIH
 41:19 seven **o** kine came up after them, poor and 312
 43:14 that he may send away your **o** brother, 312
 43:22 **o** money have we brought down in our 312
 47:21 of Egypt even to the **o** end thereof. NIH
Ex 1:15 Shiphrah, and the name of the **o** Puah: 8145
 4: 7 behold, it was turned again as his **o** flesh. NIH
 14:20 that the one came not near the **o** all 2088
 17:12 the one side, and the **o** on the other side; 259
 17:12 the one side, and the other on the **o side**; 2088
 18: 4 the name of the **o** *was* Eliezer; for the God 259
 18: 7 and they asked each **o**s of *their* welfare; 7453
 20: 3 Thou shalt have no **o** gods before me. 312
 23:13 make no mention of the name of **o** gods, 312
 25:12 side of it, and two rings in the **o** side of it. 8145
 25:19 end, and the **o** cherub on the other end: 259
 25:19 and the other cherub on the **o** end: 2088
 25:32 of the candlestick out of the **o** side: 8145
 25:33 three bowls made like almonds in the **o** 259
 26: 3 *o* five curtains *shall be* coupled one to NIH
 26:13 a cubit on the **o side** of that which 2088
 26:27 five bars for the boards of the **o** side of 8145
 27:15 on the **o** side *shall be* hangings, 8145
 28:10 the **o** six names of the rest on the other NIH
 28:10 *other* six names of the rest on the **o** 8145
 28:25 *the* **o** two ends of the two wreathen NIH
 28:27 two **o** rings of gold thou shalt make, NIH
 28:27 over against *the* **o** coupling thereof, NIH
 29:19 thou shalt take the **o** ram; and Aaron and 8145
 29:39 and the **o** lamb thou shalt offer at even; 8145
 29:41 the **o** lamb thou shalt offer at even, 8145
 30:32 neither shall ye make *any* **o** like it, after NIH
 32:15 one side and on **the o** *were* they written. 2088
 34:14 For thou shalt worship no **o** god: 312
 36:10 *the* **o** five curtains he coupled one unto NIH
 36:25 for the **o** side of the tabernacle, *which is* 8145
 36:32 five bars for the boards of the **o** side of 8145
 36:33 the boards from the one end to the **o**s. 7097
 37: 3 of it, and two rings upon the **o** side of it. 8145
 37: 8 another cherub on the **o** end on that side: NIH
 37:18 the candlestick out of the **o** side thereof: 8145
 38:15 for the **o** side of the court gate, on this 8145
 39:20 made two **o** golden rings, and put them NIH
 39:20 of it, over against *the* **o** coupling thereof, NIH
Lev 5: 7 sin offering, and the **o** for a burnt offering. 259
 6:11 put on **o** garments, and carry forth the 312
 7:24 *with beasts,* may be used in any **o** use: NIH
 8:22 he brought the **o** ram, the ram of 8145
 11:23 all **o** flying creeping things, which have NIH
 12: 8 burnt offering, and the **o** for a sin offering; 259
 13:26 it *be* no lower than the **o** skin, but *be* NIH
 14:22 a sin offering, and the **o** a burnt offering. 259
 14:31 the **o** *for* a burnt offering, with the meat 259
 14:42 they shall take **o** stones, and put *them* in 312
 14:42 he shall take **o** morter, and shall plaister 312
 15:15 sin offering, and the **o** *for* a burnt offering; 259
 15:30 sin offering, and the **o** *for* a burnt offering; 259
 16: 8 the LORD, and the **o** lot for the scapegoat. 259
 18:18 besides the **o** in her life *time*. 1886.3
 20:24 which have separated you from **o** people. NIH
 20:26 have severed you from **o** people, that ye NIH
 25:53 *the* **o** shall not rule with rigour over him NIH
Nu 6:11 the **o** for a burnt offering, and make an 259
 8:12 the **o** for a burnt offering, unto the LORD, 259
 10:21 *the* **o** did set up the tabernacle against NIH
 11:26 was Eldad, and the name of the **o** Medad: 8145
 11:31 as it were a day's journey **on the o side**, 3541
 21:13 and pitched on the **o** side of Arnon, NIH
 24: 1 he went not, as **at o times**, 6471+6471+871.1
 28: 4 and the **o** lamb shalt thou offer at even; 8145
 28: 8 the **o** lamb shalt thou offer at even: 8145
 32:38 gave **o names** unto the cities 8034+8034
 36: 3 be married to any of the sons of the **o** NIH
Dt 4:32 the one side of heaven unto the **o**s, 7097+8064
 5: 7 Thou shalt have none **o** gods before me. 312
 6:14 Ye shall not go after **o** gods, of the gods of 312
 7: 4 following me, that they may serve **o** gods: 312
 8:19 walk after **o** gods, and serve them, 312
 11:16 and serve **o** gods, and worship them; 312
 11:28 go after **o** gods, which ye have not known. 312
 11:30 *Are* they not on the **o** side Jordan, NIH
 13: 2 saying, Let us go after **o** gods, which thou 312
 13: 6 saying, Let us go and serve **o** gods, 312
 13: 7 the earth even unto the **o** end of the earth; NIH

Dt 13:13 saying, Let us go and serve **o** gods, which 312
 17: 3 hath gone and served **o** gods, 312
 18:20 or that shall speak in the name of **o** gods, 312
 28:14 to the left, to go after **o** gods to serve them. 312
 28:36 and there shalt thou serve **o** gods, wood 312
 28:64 the *one* end of the earth even unto the **o**s; 7097
 28:64 there thou shalt serve **o** gods, which 312
 29:26 For they went and served **o** gods, 312
 30:17 and worship **o** gods, and serve them; 312
 31:18 in that they are turned unto **o** gods. 312
 31:20 they turn unto **o** gods, and serve them, 312
Jos 2:10 that *were* on the **o** side Jordan, Sihon and NIH
 7: 4 and dwelt on the **o** side Jordan! NIH
 8:22 he issued out of the city against them; 428
 11:19 of Gibeon: all **o** they took in battle. NIH
 12: 1 possessed their land on the **o** side Jordan NIH
 13:27 Cinnereth on the **o** side Jordan eastward. NIH
 13:32 on the **o** side Jordan, *by* Jericho, eastward. NIH
 14: 3 and a half tribe on the **o** side Jordan: NIH
 17: 5 which *were* on the **o** side Jordan; NIH
 20: 8 on the **o** side Jordan *by* Jericho eastward, NIH
 21:27 out of the **o** half tribe of Manasseh *they* NIH
 22: 4 the LORD gave you on the **o** side Jordan: NIH
 22: 7 unto the **o** half thereof gave Joshua among NIH
 23:16 have gone and served **o** gods, 312
 24: 2 fathers dwelt on the **o** side of the flood NIH
 24: 2 father of Nachor: and they served **o** gods. 312
 24: 3 took your father Abraham from the **o** side NIH
 24: 8 which dwelt on the **o** side Jordan; NIH
 24:14 fathers served on the **o** side of the flood, NIH
 24:15 served that *were* on the **o** side of the flood, NIH
 24:16 should forsake the LORD, to serve **o** gods; 312
Jdg 2:12 of the land of Egypt, and followed **o** gods, 312
 2:17 they went a whoring after **o** gods, 312
 2:19 in following **o** gods to serve them, 312
 7: 1 let all the **o** people go every man unto his NIH
 7:25 and Zeeb to Gideon on the **o** side Jordan. NIH
 9:44 the two **o** companies ran upon all NIH
 10: 8 the children of Israel that *were* on the **o** NIH
 10:13 ye have forsaken me, and served **o** gods: 312
 11:18 pitched on the **o** side of Arnon, NIH
 13:10 unto me, that came unto me the **o** day. NIH
 16:17 become weak, and be like any **o** man. NIH
 16:20 I will go out as **at o times**, 6471+6471+871.1
 16:29 his right hand, and of the **o** with his left. 259
Ru 20:30 Gibeah, as **at o times**. 6471+6471+871.1
 20:31 **at o times**, in the highways 6471+6471+871.1
 20:31 the **o** to Gibeah in the field, about thirty 259
Ru 1: 4 *was* Orpah, and the name of the **o** Ruth: 8145
 2:22 that they meet thee not in *any* **o** field. 312
1Sa 1: 2 and the name of the **o** Peninnah: 8145
 3:10 and called as **at o times**, 6471+6471+871.1
 8: 8 served **o** gods, so do they also unto thee. 312
 14: 1 Philistines' garrison, that *is* on the **o** side. 1975
 14: 4 one side, and a sharp rock on the **o** side: 2088
 14: 4 *was* Bozez, and the name of the **o** Seneh. 259
 14: 5 and the southward over against Gibeah. 259
 14:40 and Jonathan my son will be on the **o** side. 259
 17: 3 Israel stood on a mountain on the **o** side 2088
 18:10 his hand, as **at o times**: 3117+3117+871.1
 19:21 sent **o** messengers, and they prophesied 312
 20:25 at **o times**, upon a 6471+6471+871.1
 21: 9 take *it:* for *there is* no **o** save that here. 312
 26:13 David went over to the **o** side, and stood 5676
 26:19 of the LORD, saying, Go, serve **o** gods. 312
 28: 8 put on **o** raiment, and he went, and two NIH
 30:20 *which* they drave before those **o** cattle, NIH
2Sa 31: 7 when the men of Israel that *were* on the **o** NIH
 31: 7 that *were* on the **o** side Jordan, saw that NIH
 1:24 who clothed you in scarlet, with **o** delights, NIH
 2:13 and the **o** on the other side of the pool. NIH
 2:13 The other on the **o side** of the pool. 2088+4480
 4: 2 Baanah, and the name of the **o** Rechab, 8145
 12: 1 in one city; the one rich, and the **o** poor. 259
 13:16 greater than the **o** that thou didst unto me. 312
 14: 6 but the one smote the **o**, and slew him. 259
 17: 9 is hid now in some pit, or in some **o** place: NIH
 24:22 and *instruments* of the oxen for wood. NIH
1Ki 3:22 the **o** woman said, Nay; but the living *is* 312
 3:23 the **o** saith, Nay; but thy son *is* the dead, 2063
 3:25 and give half to the one, and half to the **o**. 259
 3:26 the **o** said, Let it be neither mine nor 2088
 6:24 and five cubits the **o** wing of the cherub: 8145
 6:24 uttermost part of the **o**s *were* ten cubits. 3671
 6:25 the **o** cherub *was* ten cubits: both 8145
 6:26 ten cubits, and so *was it* of the **o** cherub. 8145
 6:27 wing of the **o** cherub touched the other 8145
 6:27 wing of the other cherub touched the **o** 8145
 6:34 the two leaves of the **o** door were folding. 8145
 7: 6 the **o** pillars and the thick beam *were* NIH
 7: 7 cedar from one side of the floor to the **o**s. 7172
 7:16 height of the **o** chapiter *was* five cubits: 8145
 7:17 one chapiter, and seven for the **o** chapiter. 8145
 7:18 and so did he for the **o** chapiter. NIH
 7:20 *in* rows round about upon the **o** chapiter. 8145
 7:23 ten cubits from the one brim to the **o**: 8193
 9: 6 go and serve **o** gods, and worship them: 312
 9: 9 have taken hold upon **o** gods, 312
 10:20 one side and on **the o** upon the six steps: 2088
 11: 4 *that* his wives turned away his heart after **o** 312
 11:10 thing, that *he* should not go after **o** gods: 312
 12:29 one in Beth-el, and the **o** put he in Dan. 259
 14: 9 for thou hast gone and made thee **o** gods, 312
 18:23 fire *under:* and I will dress the **o** bullock, 259
 20:29 they pitched one over against the **o** seven 428

2Ki 3:22 water **on the o side** *as* red as 4480+5048
 5:17 burnt offering nor sacrifice unto **o** gods, 312
 12: 7 the **o** priests, and said unto them, NIH
 17: 7 king of Egypt, and had feared **o** gods, 312
 17:35 saying, Ye shall not fear **o** gods, 312
 17:37 for evermore; and ye shall not fear **o** gods. 312
 17:38 not forget; neither shall ye fear **o** gods. 312
 22:17 and have burnt incense unto **o** gods, 312
1Ch 6:78 on the **o** side Jordan *by* Jericho, on the east NIH
 9:32 **o** of their brethren, of the sons of NIH
 12:37 on the **o** side of Jordan, of the Reubenites, NIH
 23:17 Eliezer had none **o** sons; but the sons of 312
2Ch 3:11 the **o** wing *was likewise* five cubits, 312
 3:11 reaching to the wing of the **o** cherub. 312
 3:12 *one* wing of the **o** cherub *was* five cubits, 259
 3:12 the **o** wing *was* five cubits *also*, joining to 312
 3:12 *also*, joining to the wing of the **o** cherub. 259
 3:17 on the right hand, and the **o** on the left; 259
 7:19 go and serve **o** gods, and worship them; 312
 7:22 laid hold on **o** gods, and worshipped them, 312
 9:19 one side and on **the o** upon the six steps: 2088
 13: 9 after the manner of the nations of **o** lands? NIH
 20: 1 and with them **o** beside the Ammonites, NIH
 25:12 **o** ten thousand *left* alive did the children NIH
 28:25 high places to burn incense unto **o** gods, 312
 29:34 the **o** priests had sanctified themselves: NIH
 30:23 whole assembly took counsel to keep **o** 312
 30:23 and they kept **o** seven days *with* gladness. NIH
 32:13 have done unto all the people of **o** lands? NIH
 32:17 As the gods of the nations of **o** lands have NIH
 32:22 from the hand of all **o**, and guided them NIH
 34:12 of **o** the Levites, all that could skill of NIH
 34:25 and have burned incense unto **o** gods, 312
 35:13 the **o** holy *offerings* sod they in pots, NIH
Ezr 1:10 and ten, *and* **o** vessels a thousand. 312
 2:31 The children of **o** Elam, a thousand 312
Ne 3:11 repaired the **o** piece, and the tower of 8145
 3:20 of Zabbai earnestly repaired the **o** piece, 8145
 4:16 the **o** half of them held both the spears, NIH
 4:17 and with the **o** hand held a weapon. 259
 5: 5 redeem them; for **o men** have our lands 312
 7:33 The men of the **o** Nebo, fifty and two. 312
 7:34 The children of **o** Elam, a thousand 312
 11: 1 city, and nine parts *to dwell* in **o** cities. NIH
 12:38 the **o** *company* of them that gave thanks 8145
Est 2:12 with **o** things for the purifying of NIH
 9:16 the **o** Jews that *were* in the king's 7605
Job 8:12 cut down, it withereth before any **o** herb. NIH
 24:24 they are taken out of the way as all **o**, NIH
Ps 73: 5 They are not in trouble *as o* men; neither NIH
 73: 5 neither are they plagued like **o** men. 312
 85:10 and peace have kissed *each* **o**. NIH
Ecc 3:19 as the one dieth, so dieth the **o**; yea, 2088
 6: 5 *any thing:* this hath more rest than **the o**. 2088
 7:14 also hath set the one over against the **o**, 2088
Isa 26:13 **o** lords besides thee have had dominion NIH
 49:20 after thou hast lost the **o**, shall say again NIH
Jer 1:16 have burnt incense unto **o** gods, 312
 7: 6 neither walk after **o** gods to your hurt: 312
 7: 9 and walk after **o** gods whom ye know not; 312
 7:18 to pour out drink offerings unto **o** gods, 312
 11:10 and they went after **o** gods to serve them: 312
 12:12 of the land even to the **o** end of the land: NIH
 13:10 walk after **o** gods, to serve them, 312
 16:11 have walked after **o** gods, and have served 312
 16:13 there shall ye serve **o** gods day and night; 312
 19: 4 and have burnt incense in it unto **o** gods, 312
 19:13 poured out drink offerings unto **o** gods, 312
 22: 9 and worshipped **o** gods, and served them. 312
 24: 2 the **o** basket *had* very naughty figs, 259
 25: 6 go not after **o** gods to serve them, 312
 25:33 the earth even unto the **o** end of the earth: NIH
 32:20 day, and in Israel, and amongst **o** men; NIH
 32:29 poured out drink offerings unto **o** gods, 312
 35:15 go not after **o** gods to serve them, 312
 36:16 they were afraid both one and **o**s, 7453
 44: 3 to serve **o** gods, whom they knew not, 312
 44: 5 to burn no incense unto **o** gods. 312
 44: 8 burning incense unto **o** gods in the land of 312
 44:15 their wives had burnt incense unto **o** gods, 312
Eze 1:23 their wings straight, the one toward the **o**s: 269
 16:34 the contrary is in thee from **o** women in NIH
 21:16 Go thee **one way or o**, *either* on the right 258
 40: 6 the **o** threshold *of the gate, which was* one 259
 40:40 on the **o** side, which *was* at the porch of NIH
 41: 1 side, and six cubits broad on the **o side**, 6311
 41: 2 one side, and five cubits on the **o side**: 6311
 41:15 on the one side and on the **o side**, 6311
 41:19 lion toward the palm tree on the **o side**; 6311
 41:21 of the one as the appearance of *the* **o**. NIH
 41:24 one door, and two leaves for the **o** door. 312
 41:26 trees on the one side and on the **o side**, 6311
 42:14 put on **o** garments, and shall approach 312
 44:19 and they shall put on **o** garments; 312
 45: 7 on the **o side** of the oblation of the holy 2088
 47: 7 many trees on the one side and on **the o**. 2088
 48: 8 and *in* length as one of the **o** parts, NIH
 48:21 side and on **the o** of the holy oblation, 2088
Da 2:11 there is none **o** that can shew it before 321
 2:44 the kingdom shall not be left to **o** people, 321
 3:21 their **o** garments, and were cast into NIH
 3:29 there is no **o** God that can deliver after 321
 7:20 *of* the **o** which came up, and before 317
 8: 3 one *was* higher than the **o**, and the higher 8145
 12: 5 and behold, there stood **o** two, 312

Da	12: 5 the **o** on that side of the bank of the river.	259
Hos	3: 1 who look to **o** gods, and love flagons of	312
	9: 1 Rejoice not, O Israel, for joy, as **o** people:	NIH
	13:10 where *is any* **o** that may save thee in all	NIH
Ob	1:11 the day that thou stoodest on the **o** side,	5048
Zec	4: 3 and the **o** upon the left *side* thereof.	259
	11: 7 I called Beauty, and the **o** I called Bands;	259
	11:14 I cut asunder mine **o** staff, *even* Bands,	8145
Mt	4:21 he saw **o** two brethren, James the *son of*	243
	5:39 on thy right cheek, turn to him the **o** also.	243
	6:24 he will hate the one, and love the **o**;	2087
	6:24 will hold to the one, and despise the **o** side.	2087
	8:18 commandment to depart unto the **o** side	4008
	8:28 when he was come to the **o** side into	4008
	12:13 and it was restored whole, *like* as the **o**.	243
	12:45 taketh with himself seven **o** spirits more	2087
	13: 8 But **o** fell into good ground,	243
	14:22 and to go before him unto the **o** side,	4008
	16: 5 his disciples were come to the **o** side,	4008
	20:21 and the **o**^s on the left, in thy kingdom.	1520
	21:36 he sent **o** servants moe than the first:	243
	21:41 let out *his* vineyard unto **o** husbandmen,	243
	22: 4 Again, he sent forth **o** servants, saying,	243
	23:23 done, **and** not to leave the **o** undone.	2548
	24:31 from one end of heaven to the **o**^s.	206
	24:40 the one shall be taken, and the **o**^s left.	1520
	24:41 *the one* shall be taken, and the **o**^s left.	1520
	25:11 Afterward came also the **o** virgins, saying,	3062
	25:16 the same, and made them **o** five talents.	243
	25:17 *had received* two, he also gained **o** two.	243
	25:20 talents came and brought **o** five talents,	243
	25:22 I have gained two **o** talents besides them:	243
	27:61 was Mary Magdalene, and the **o** Mary,	243
	28: 1 and the **o** Mary to see the sepulchre.	243
Mk	3: 5 and his hand was restored whole as the **o**.	243
	4: 8 And **o** fell on good ground, and did yield	243
	4:19 and the lusts of **o** *things* entering in,	3062
	4:35 them, Let us pass over unto the **o** side.	4008
	4:36 there were also with him **o** little ships.	243
	5: 1 And they came over unto the **o** side of	4008
	5:21 passed over again by ship unto the **o** side,	4008
	6:45 to go to the **o** side before unto Bethsaida,	4008
	7: 4 And many **o** things there be, which they	243
	7: 8 cups: and many **o** such like *things* ye do.	243
	8:13 into the ship again departed to the **o** side.	4008
	10:37 and the **o** on thy left hand, in thy glory.	1520
	12:31 There is none **o** commandment greater	243
	12:32 is one God; and there is none **o** but he:	243
	15:27 on *his* right hand, and the **o** on his left.	1520
	15:41 many **o** *women* which came up with him	243
Lk	3:18 And many **o** *things* in his exhortation	2087
	4:43 I must preach the kingdom of God to **o**	2087
	5: 7 which were in the **o** ship, that *they*	2087
	6:10 and his hand was restored whole as the **o**.	243
	6:29 thee on the *one* cheek offer also the **o**;	243
	7:41 ought five hundred pence, and the **o** fifty.	2087
	8: 6 fell on good ground, and sprang up,	2087
	8:22 Let us go over unto the **o** side of the lake.	4008
	10: 1 After these *things* the Lord appointed **o**	2087
	10:31 he saw him, he **passed by on the o** side.	492
	10:32 on him, and **passed by on the o** side.	492
	11:16 And **o**, tempting *him*, sought of him a sign	2087
	11:26 taketh to *him* seven **o** spirits more wicked	2087
	11:42 done, **and** not to leave the **o** undone.	2548
	14:32 else, while the **o**^s is yet a great way off,	846
	16:13 he will hate the one, and love the **o**;	2087
	16:13 will hold to the one, and despise the **o**.	2087
	17:24 shineth unto the **o** *part* under heaven;	3588
	17:34 one shall be taken, and the **o** shall be left.	2087
	17:35 the one shall be taken, and the **o** left.	2087
	17:36 the one shall be taken, and the **o** left.	2087
	18: 9 that they were righteous, and despised **o**:	3062
	18:10 the one a Pharisee, and the **o** a publican.	2087
	18:11 that I am not as **o** men *are*, extortioners,	3062
	18:14 to his house justified *rather* than the **o**^s:	1565
	22:65 And many **o** *things* blasphemously spake	2087
	23:32 And there were also two **o**, malefactors,	2087
	23:33 on the right hand, and the **o** on the left.	3739
	23:40 But the **o** answering rebuked him, saying,	2087
	24:10 and **o** *women that were* with them,	3062
Jn	4:38 **o** *men* laboured, and ye are entered into	243
	6:22 the people which stood on the **o** side	4008
	6:22 sea saw that there was none **o** boat there,	243
	6:23 (Howbeit there came **o** boats from Tiberias	243
	6:25 had found him **on the o** side of the sea,	4008
	10: 1 but climbeth up **some o** way, the same is	237
	10:16 And **o** sheep I have, which are not of this	243
	15:24 them the works which none **o** *man* did,	243
	18:16 Then went out *that* **o** disciple, which was	243
	19:18 and two **o** with him, on either side one,	243
	19:32 of the **o** which was crucified with him.	243
	20: 2 and to the **o** disciple, whom Jesus loved,	243
	20: 3 and *that* **o** disciple, and came to	243
	20: 4 and the **o** disciple did outrun Peter,	243
	20: 8 Then went in also *that* **o** disciple,	243
	20:12 one at the head, and the **o**^s at the feet,	1520
	20:25 The **o** disciples therefore said unto him,	243
	20:30 And many **o** signs truly did Jesus in	243
	21: 2 of Zebedee, and two **o** of his disciples.	243
	21: 8 And the **o** disciples came in a little ship;	243
	21:25 And there are also many **o** *things* which	243
Ac	2: 4 and began to speak with **o** tongues,	2087
	2:40 with many **o** words did he testify and	243
	4:12 Neither is there salvation in any **o**: for	243
	4:12 for there is none **o** name under heaven	2087

Ac	5:29 and the **o** apostles answered and said,	NIG
	8:34 of himself, or of some **o** man?	2087
	15: 2 and Barnabas, and certain **o** of them,	243
	15:39 they departed asunder **one** from the **o**:	240
	17: 9 of Jason, and *of* the **o**, they let them go.	3062
	17:18 **o** *some*, He seemeth to be a setter	1161+3588
	19:39 But if ye inquire any *thing* concerning **o**	2087
	23: 6 and the **o** Pharisees, he cried out in	2087
	26:22 saying none **o** *things* than those which	1622
	27: 1 certain **o** prisoners unto *one* named Julius,	2087
Ro	1:13 you also, even as among **o** Gentiles.	3062
	8:39 height, nor depth, nor any **o** creature,	2087
	13: 9 if *there be* any **o** commandment, it is	2087
1Co	1:16 I know not whether I baptized any **o**.	243
	3:11 For **o** foundation can no *man* lay than that	243
	7: 5 Defraud you not **one** the **o**, except *it be*	240
	8: 4 and that *there* is none **o** God but one.	2087
	9: 5 as well as **o** apostles, and *as* the brethren	3062
	11:21 For in eating every one taketh before **o** his	NIG
	14:17 givest thanks well, but the **o** is not edified,	2087
	14:21 With *men* of **o** tongues and other lips	2084
	14:21 and **o** lips will I speak unto this people;	2087
	14:29 speak two or three, and let the **o** judge.	243
	15:37 may chance of wheat, or of some **o** *grain*:	3062
2Co	1:13 For we write none **o** *things* unto you,	243
	2:16 and to the **o** the savour of life unto life.	3739
	8:13 For *I mean* not that **o** men be eased,	243
	10:15 *our* measure, that *is*, of **o** men's labours;	245
	11: 8 robbed **o** churches, taking wages *of them*,	243
	12:13 what is it wherein ye were inferior to **o**	3062
	13: 2 to all **o**, that, if I come again, I will not	3062
Gal	1: 8 preach **any** **o** gospel unto you **than** *that*	3844
	1: 9 **any** **o** gospel unto you **than** that ye have	3844
	1:19 But **o** of the apostles saw I none,	2087
	2:13 And the **o** Jews dissembled likewise with	3062
	4:22 by a bondmaid, the **o**^s by a freewoman.	1520
	5:17 and these are contrary the **one** to the **o**:	240
Eph	3: 5 Which in **o** ages was not made known	2087
	4:17 that ye henceforth walk not as **o** Gentiles	3062
Php	1:13 in all the palace, and *in* all **o** *places*;	3062
	1:17 But the **o** of love, knowing that I am set	3588
	2: 3 lowliness of mind *let* **each** esteem **o** better	240
	3: 4 if any **o** *man* thinketh that *he* hath	243
	4: 3 and *with* **o** my fellowlabourers,	3062
2Th	1: 3 one of you all towards **each** **o** aboundeth;	240
1Ti	1: 3 some that *they* **teach** no **o** doctrine,	2085
	1:10 if *there be* any **o** *thing* that is contrary to	2087
	5:22 *man*, neither be partaker of **o** men's sins:	245
Jas	5:12 neither by the earth, neither by any **o** oath:	243
1Pe	4:15 or as a **busybody** in **o** men's matters.	244
2Pe	3:16 as *they* do also the **o** scriptures,	3062
Rev	2:24 I will put upon you none **o** burden.	243
	8:13 **o** voices of the trumpet of the three angels	3062
	17:10 and one is, *and* the **o** is not yet come;	243

OTHER'S (1) [OTHER]

1Co	10:29 I say, not thine own, but of the **o**:	2087

OTHERS (67) [OTHER]

Job	8:19 his way, and out of the earth shall **o** grow.	312
	31:10 another, and let **o** bow down upon her.	312
	34:24 without number, and set **o** in their stead.	312
	34:26 as wicked *men* in the open sight of **o**;	NIH
Ps	49:10 person perish, and leave their wealth to **o**.	312
Pr	5: 9 Lest thou give thine honour unto **o**,	312
Ecc	7:22 that thou thyself likewise hast cursed **o**.	312
Isa	56: 8 Yet will I gather **o** to him, besides those	NIH
Jer	6:12 houses shall be turned unto **o**, *with their*	312
	8:10 Therefore will I give their wives unto **o**,	312
Eze	5: 6 the **o** he said in mine hearing, Go ye	428
	13: 6 they have made **o** to hope that *they* would	NIH
	13:10 **o** daubed it *with* untempered *morter*:	3961.1
Da	7:19 which was diverse from all the **o**,	2006.2
	11: 4 be pluckt up, even for **o** besides those.	312
Mt	5:47 what do ye more *than* **o** do not even	NIG
	15:30 many **o**, and cast them *down* at Jesus'	2087
	16:14 and **o**, Jeremias, or one of the prophets.	2087
	20: 3 saw **o** standing idle in the marketplace,	243
	20: 6 and found **o** standing idle, and saith unto	243
	21: 8 **o** cut down branches from the trees,	243
	26:67 **o** smote *him* with the palms of their	3588
	27:42 He saved **o**; himself he cannot save. If he	243
Mk	6:15 **O** said, That it is Elias. And others said,	243
	6:15 And **o** said, That it is a prophet, or as one	243
	8:28 say, Elias; and **o**, One of the prophets.	243
	11: 8 and **o** cut down branches from the trees,	243
	12: 5 and him they killed, and many **o**;	243
	12: 9 and will give the vineyard unto **o**.	243
	15:31 themselves with the scribes, He saved **o**;	243
Lk	5:29 and of **o** that sat down with them.	243
	8: 3 and Susanna, and many **o**,	2087
	8:10 to **o** in parables; that seeing they might	3062
	9: 8 and *of* **o**, that one of the old prophets was	243
	9:19 *say*, that one of the old prophets is risen	243
	20:16 and shall give the vineyard to **o**.	243
	23:35 them derided *him*, saying, He saved **o**;	243
	24: 1 had prepared, and certain **o** with them.	NIG
Jn	7:12 some said, He is a good *man*: **o** said, Nay,	243
	7:41 **O** said, This is the Christ. But some said,	243
	9: 9 **o** *said*, He is like him: *but* he said, I am *he*.	243
	9:16 **O** said, How can a man *that* is a sinner do	243
	10:21 **O** said, These are not the words of him	243
	12:29 thundered: **o** said, An angel spake to him.	243
	18:34 *thing* of thyself, or did **o** tell *it* thee of me?	243
Ac	2:13 **O** mocking said, These men are full of	2087

Ac	15:35 the word of the Lord, with many **o** also.	2087
	17:32 and **o** said, We will hear thee again of this	3588
	17:34 woman named Damaris, and **o** with them.	2087
1Co	9: 2 If I be not an apostle unto **o**, yet doubtless	243
	9:12 If ye be partakers of *this* power over you,	243
	9:27 by any means, when I have preached to **o**,	243
	14:19 that *by my voice* I might teach **o** also,	243
2Co	3: 1 as some **o**, epistles of commendation to	NIG
	8: 8 but by occasion of the forwardness of **o**,	2087
Eph	2: 3 nature the children of wrath, even as **o**.	3062
Php	2: 4 but every man also on the *things* of **o**.	2087
1Th	2: 6 we glory, neither of you, nor *yet* of **o**,	243
	4:13 not, even as **o** which have no hope.	3062
	5: 6 Therefore let us not sleep, as *do* **o**;	3062
1Ti	5:20 rebuke before all, that **o** also may fear.	3062
2Ti	2: 2 who shall be able to teach **o** also.	243
Heb	9:25 the holy *place* every year with blood of **o**;	245
	11:35 and **o** were tortured, not accepting	243
	11:36 And **o** had trial of *cruel* mockings and	2087
Jude	1:23 And **o** save with fear, pulling *them* out of	3739

OTHERWISE (15) [OTHER]

2Sa	18:13 **O** I should have wrought falsehood	176
1Ki	1:21 **O** it shall come to pass, when my lord	2050.1
2Ch	30:18 **o** than it was written.	3808+871.1+3509.1
Ps	38:16 lest *o* they should rejoice over me:	NIH
Mt	6: 1 **o** ye have no reward of your Father which	1490
Lk	5:36 if **o**, *then* both the new maketh a rent,	1490
Ro	11: 6 **o** grace is no more grace. But if *it be* of	1893
	11: 6 it no more grace: **o** work is no more work.	1893
	11:22 *his* goodness: **o** thou also shalt be cut off.	1893
2Co	11:16 if **o**, yet as a fool receive me, that I may	1490
Gal	5:10 the Lord, that you will be none **o** minded:	243
Php	3:15 and if in any *thing* ye be **o** minded,	2088
1Ti	5:25 and they that are **o** cannot be hid.	247
	6: 3 If any *man* **teach** **o**, and consent not to	2085
Heb	9:17 **o** it is of no strength at all whilst	1893

OTHNI (1)

1Ch	26: 7 **O**, and Rephael, and Obed, Elzabad,	6273

OTHNIEL (7)

Jos	15:17 **O** the son of Kenaz, the brother of Caleb,	6274
Jdg	1:13 **O** the son of Kenaz, Caleb's younger	6274
	3: 9 delivered them, *even* **O** the son of Kenaz,	6274
	3:11 forty years. And **O** the son of Kenaz died.	6274
1Ch	4:13 And the sons of Kenaz; **O**, and Seraiah:	6274
	4:13 and Seraiah: and the sons of **O**; Hathath.	6274
	27:15 *was* Heldai the Netophathite, of **O**:	6274

OUCHES (8)

Ex	28:11 shalt make them to be set in **o** *of* gold.	4865
	28:13 And thou shalt make **o** *of* gold;	4865
	28:14 and fasten the wreathen chains to the **o**.	4865
	28:25 *chains* thou shalt fasten in the two **o**,	4865
	39: 6 they wrought onyx stones inclosed in **o**	4865
	39:13 they were inclosed in **o** *of* gold in their	4865
	39:16 they made two **o** *of* gold, and two gold	4865
	39:18 *chains* they fastened in the two **o**,	4865

OUGHT (100) [OUGHTEST]

Ge	20: 9 thou hast done deeds unto me that **o** not	NIH
	34: 7 which thing **o** not to be done.	NIH
	39: 6 he knew not **o** he had, save the bread	3972
	47:18 there is not **o** left in the sight of my lord,	NIH
Ex	5: 8 them; you shall not diminish **o** thereof:	NIH
	5:11 not **o** of your work *shall be* diminished.	1697
	5:19 Ye shall not minish **o** from your bricks of	NIH
	12:46 thou shalt not carry forth **o** of the flesh	NIH
	22:14 if a man borrow **o** of his neighbour,	NIH
	29:34 And if *o* of the flesh of the consecrations,	NIH
Lev	4: 2 *things* which **o** not to be done),	NIH
	4:27 *things* which **o** not to be done,	NIH
	11:25 whosoever beareth **o** of the carcase of	NIH
	19: 6 if **o** remain until the third day, it shall be	NIH
	25:14 if thou **sell o** unto thy neighbour,	4376+4465
	25:14 or buyest **o** of thy neighbour's hand,	NIH
	27:31 if a man will at all redeem **o** of his tithes,	NIH
Nu	15:24 if **o** be committed by ignorance without	NIH
	15:30 the soul that doeth **o** presumptuously,	NIH
	30: 6 she vowed, or **uttered o** out of her lips,	4008
Dt	4: 2 neither shall you diminish **o** from it,	NIH
	15: 2 Every creditor that lendeth **o** unto his	NIH
	26:14 neither have I taken away **o** thereof for	NIH
	26:14 *use*, nor given **o** thereof for the dead.	NIH
Jos	21:45 There failed not **o** of any good thing	1697
Ru	1:17 also, *if* **o** but death part thee and me.	NIH
1Sa	12: 4 neither hast thou taken **o** of any man's	3972
	12: 5 that ye have not found **o** in my hand.	3972
	25: 7 neither was there **o** missing unto them,	3972
	30:22 we will not give them **o** of the spoil that	NIH
2Sa	3:35 also, if I taste bread, or **o** else,	3605+3972
	13:12 for no such thing **o** to be done in Israel:	NIH
	14:10 Whosoever saith **o** unto thee, bring him to	NIH
	14:19 the left from **o** that my lord the king hath	3605
1Ch	12:32 of the times, to know what Israel **o** to do;	NIH
	15: 2 None **o** to carry the ark of God but	NIH
2Ch	13: 5 **O** you not to know that the LORD God of	NIH
Ne	5: 9 **o** ye not to walk in the fear of our God	NIH
Ps	76:11 presents unto him that **o** to be feared.	NIH
Mt	18:23 there rememberest that thy brother hath **o**	5100
	18:24 him, which **o** him ten thousand talents.	3781
	18:28 which **o** him an hundred pence:	3784
	21: 3 And if any *man* say **o** unto you, ye shall	5100

Mt 23:23 these **o** *ye* **to have** done, and not to leave 1163
Mk 7:12 And ye suffer him no more to do **o** for his 3762
8:23 upon him, he asked him if he saw **o**. 5100
11:25 forgive, if ye have **o** against any: 5100
13:14 the prophet, standing where it **o** not, 1163
Lk 7:41 one **o** five hundred pence, and the other 3784
11:42 these **o** *ye* **to** have done, and not to leave 1163
12:12 you in the same hour what ye **o** to say. 1163
13:14 are six days in which *men* **o** to work: 1163
13:16 **o** not this *woman*, being a daughter of 1163
18: 1 *to* this end, that *men* **o** always to pray, 1163
24:26 **O** not Christ **to** have suffered these *things*, 1163
Jn 4:20 is the place where *men* **o** to worship. 1163
4:33 Hath any *man* brought him **o** to eat? NIG
13:14 ye also **o** to wash one another's feet. 3784
19: 7 and by our law he **o** to die, because 3784
Ac 4:32 said any *of them* that **o** of the things 5100
5:29 said, We **o** to obey God rather than men. 1163
17:29 we **o** not to think that the Godhead is like 3784
19:36 ye **o** to be quiet, and to do nothing rashly. 1163
20:35 so labouring **o** to support the weak, 1163
21:21 saying that they **o** not to circumcise *their* 1163
24:19 Who **o** to have been here before thee, 1163
24:19 and object, if they had **o** against me. 1536
25:10 judgment seat, where I **o** to be judged: 1163
25:24 crying that he **o** not to live any longer. 1163
26: 9 that *I* **o** to do many *things* contrary to 1163
28:19 not that I had **o** to accuse my nation of. 5100
Ro 8:26 not what we should pray for as we **o**: 1163
12: 3 *of himself* more highly than he **o** to think; 1163
15: 1 that are strong **o** to bear the infirmities of 3784
1Co 8: 2 he knoweth nothing yet as he **o** to know. 1163
11: 7 For a man indeed **o** not to cover *his* head, 3784
11:10 this cause **o** the woman to have power 3784
2Co 2: 3 sorrow from *them of* whom I **o** to rejoice; 1163
2: 7 So that contrariwise ye **o** rather to forgive NIG
12:11 for I **o** to have been commended of you: 3784
12:14 for the children **o** not to lay up for 3784
Eph 5:28 So **o** men to love their wives as their own 3784
6:20 I may speak boldly, as I **o** to speak. 1163
Col 4: 4 I make it manifest, as I **o** to speak. 1163
4: 6 that *you* may know how ye **o** to answer 1163
1Th 4: 1 as ye have received of us how ye **o** to 1163
2Th 3: 7 For yourselves know how *ye* **o** to follow 1163
1Ti 5:13 speaking *things* which they **o** not. 1163
Tit 1:11 teaching *things* which *they* **o** not, for 1163
Phm 1:18 he hath wronged thee, or oweth *thee* **o**, 5100
Heb 2: 1 Therefore we **o** to give the more earnest 1163
5: 3 And by reason hereof he **o**, as for 3784
5:12 when for the time ye **o** to be teachers, 3784
Jas 3:10 My brethren, these *things* **o** not so to be. 5534
4:15 For that ye **o** to say, If the Lord will, NIG
2Pe 3:11 what manner *of persons* **o** ye to be in all 3784
1Jn 2: 6 He that saith *he* abideth in him **o** himself 3784
3:16 **o** to lay down *our* lives for the brethren. 3784
4:11 loved us, we **o** also to love one another. 3784
3Jn 1: 8 We therefore **o** to receive such, that we 3784

OUGHTEST (4) [OUGHT]

1Ki 2: 9 and knowest what thou **o** to do unto him; NIH
Mt 25:27 Thou **o** therefore **to have** put my money 1163
Ac 10: 6 he shall tell thee what thou **o** to do. 1163
1Ti 3:15 that thou mayest know how *thou* **o** to 1163

OUR (1165) [WE] See Index of Articles, Etc.

OURS (12) [WE]

Ge 26:20 saying, The water *is* **o**: 3807.1+5105.1
31:16 that *is* **o**, and our children's: 3807.1+5105.1
34:23 and every beast of theirs **o**? 3807.1+5105.1
Nu 32:32 on *this* side Jordan *may be* **o**. 5105.1
1Ki 22: 3 ye that Ramoth in Gilead *is* **o**, 3807.1+5105.1
Eze 36: 2 the ancient high places are **o** 3807.1+5105.1
Mk 12: 7 kill him, and the inheritance shall be **o**. 1473
Lk 20:14 kill him, that the inheritance may be **o**. 1473
1Co 1: 2 Jesus Christ our Lord, both theirs and **o**: 1473
2Co 1: 14 as ye also *are* **o** in the day of the Lord 1473
Tit 3:14 let **o** also learn to maintain good works 2251
1Jn 2: 2 not for **o** only, but also for *the sins of* 2251

OURSELVES (51) [WE]

Ge 37:10 brethren indeed come to bow down **o** to NIH
44:16 how shall we clear **o**? God hath found out NIH
Nu 32:17 **we o** will go ready armed before the 587
Dt 2:35 the cattle we took for a prey unto **o**, 5105.1
3: 7 of the cities, we took for a prey to **o**. 5105.1
1Sa 14: 8 and we will discover **o** unto them. NIH
1Ch 19:13 let us behave **o** valiantly for our people, NIH
Ezr 4: 3 **we o** together will build unto the LORD 587
8:21 that *we* might afflict **o** before our God, NIH
Ne 10:32 to charge **o** yearly with the third *part* of 5105.1
Job 34: 4 let us know among **o** what *is* good. NIH
Ps 83:12 Let us take to **o** the houses of God in 5105.1
100: 3 *it is* he *that* hath made us, and not we **o**; 587
Pr 7:18 the morning: let us solace **o** with loves. NIH
Isa 28:15 and under falsehood have we hid **o**: NIH
56:12 and we will fill **o** with strong drink; NIH
Jer 50: 5 let us join **o** to the LORD *in* a perpetual NIH
Lk 22:71 for **o** have heard of his own mouth. 846
Jn 4:42 we have heard *him* **o**, and know that this 846
Ac 6: 4 But we will give **o** continually to prayer, NIG
23:14 We have bound **o** under a great curse, 1438
Ro 8:23 And not only *they*, but **o** also, which have 846
8:23 even we **o** groan within ourselves, 846
8:23 even we ourselves groan within **o**, 1438

Ro 15: 1 of the weak, and not to please **o**. 1438
1Co 11:31 For if we would judge **o**, we should not 1438
2Co 1: 4 by the comfort wherewith we **o** are 846
1: 9 But we had the sentence of death in **o**, 1438
1: 9 that we should not trust in **o**, but in God 1438
3: 1 Do we begin again to commend **o**? 1438
3: 5 Not that we are sufficient of **o** to think 1438
3: 5 of ourselves to think any *thing* as of **o**; 1438
4: 2 manifestation of the truth commending **o** 1438
4: 5 For we preach not **o**, but Christ Jesus 1438
4: 5 and **o** your servants for Jesus' sake. 1438
5:12 For we commend not **o** again unto you, 1438
5:13 whether we be **besides o**, *it is* to God: 1839
6: 4 But in all *things* approving **o** as 1438
7: 1 let us cleanse **o** from all filthiness of 1438
10:12 For we dare not make **o** of the number, NIG
10:12 compare **o** with some that commend 1438
10:14 we stretch not **o** beyond *our* measure, 1438
12:19 think you that we **excuse o** unto you? 626
Gal 2:17 we **o** also are found sinners, *is* therefore 846
1Th 2:10 unblameably we behaved **o** among you NIG
2Th 1: 4 that we **o** glory in you in the churches of 846
3: 7 we behaved not **o** disorderly among you; NIG
3: 9 make **o** an ensample unto you to follow 1438
Tit 3: 3 For we **o** also were sometimes foolish, 1473
Heb 10:25 forsaking the assembling of **o** together, 1438
1Jn 1: 8 we deceive **o**, and the truth is not in us. 1438

OUT (2777) [OUTER, OUTMOST, THEREOUT, WITHOUT] See Index of Articles, Etc.

OUTCAST (1) [CAST, OUTCASTS]

Jer 30:17 because they called thee an **O**, *saying*, 5080

OUTCASTS (7) [CAST, OUTCAST]

Ps 147: 2 he gathereth together the **o** of Israel. 1760
Isa 11:12 shall assemble the **o** of Israel, 1760
16: 3 hide the **o**; bewray not him that 5080
16: 4 Let mine **o** dwell with thee, Moab; be 5080
27:13 the **o** in the land of Egypt, 5080
56: 8 The Lord GOD which gathereth the **o** of 1760
Jer 49:36 there shall be no nation whither the **o** of 5080

OUTER (3) [OUT]

Mt 8:12 kingdom shall be cast out into **o** darkness: 1857
22:13 him away, and cast *him* into **o** darkness; 1857
25:30 cast ye the unprofitable servant into **o** 1857

OUTGOINGS (8) [GO]

Jos 17: 9 the river, and the **o** of it were at the sea: 8444
17:18 the **o** of it shall be thine: for thou shalt 8444
18:19 the **o** of the border were at the north bay 8444
19:14 the **o** thereof are *in* the valley of 8444
19:22 and the **o** of their border were *at* Jordan: 8444
19:29 the **o** thereof are at the sea from the coast 8444
19:33 and the **o** thereof were *at* Jordan: 8444
Ps 65: 8 thou makest the **o** of the morning and 4161

OUTLANDISH (1)

Ne 13:26 *nevertheless* even him did **o** women 5237

OUTLIVED (1) [LIVE]

Jdg 2: 7 all the days of the elders that **o** 310+748+3117

OUTMOST (4) [OUT]

Ex 26:10 the one curtain *that is* **o** in the coupling, 7020
Nu 34: 3 the **o** coast of the salt sea eastward: 4480+7097
Dt 30: 4 driven out unto the **o** *parts* of heaven, 7097
Isa 17: 6 *or* five **in** the **o** fruitful branches thereof, 871.1

OUTRAGEOUS (1)

Pr 27: 4 Wrath *is* cruel, and anger *is* **o**; but who is 7858

OUTRUN (1) [RUN]

Jn 20: 4 and the other disciple did **o** Peter, 4390+5030

OUTSIDE (8)

Jdg 7:11 **o** of the armed *men* that *were* in the host. 7097
7:17 when I come to the **o** of the camp, 7097
7:19 came unto the **o** of the camp *in* 7097
1Ki 7: 9 and *so* on the **o** toward the great court. 2351
Eze 40: 5 behold a wall on the **o** of the house round 2351
Mt 23:25 for ye make clean the **o** of the cup and 1855
23:26 that the **o** of them may be clean also. 1622
Lk 11:39 Now do ye Pharisees make clean the **o** of 1855

OUTSTRETCHED (3) [STRETCH]

Dt 26: 8 an **o** arm, and with great terribleness, 5186
Jer 21: 5 I myself will fight against you with an **o** 5186
27: 5 by my great power and by my **o** arm, 5186

OUTWARD (14) [OUTWARDLY]

Nu 35: 4 **o** a thousand cubits round about. 2351+1886.5
1Sa 16: 7 for man looketh on the **o** **appearance**, 5869
1Ch 26:29 sons *were* for the **o** business of Israel, 2435
Ne 11:16 had the oversight of the **o** business of 2435
Est 6: 4 Now Haman was come into the **o** court 2435
Eze 40:17 brought he me into the **o** court, and lo, 2435
40:20 the gate of the **o** court that looked toward 2435
40:34 arches thereof *were* toward the **o** court; 2435
44: 1 **o** sanctuary which looketh *toward* the 2435
Mt 23:27 which indeed appear beautiful **o**, 1855
Ro 2:28 which is **o** in the flesh: 1722+3588+5318
2Co 4:16 though our **o** man perish, yet the inward 1854
10: 7 ye look on *things* after the **o** **appearance**? 4383
1Pe 3: 3 Whose adorning let it not be that **o** 1855

OUTWARDLY (2) [OUTWARD]

Mt 23:28 so ye also **o** appear righteous unto men, 1855
Ro 2:28 is not a Jew, which is one **o**; 1722+3588+5318

OUTWENT (1) [GO]

Mk 6:33 and **o** them, and came together unto him. 4281

OVEN (12) [OVENS]

Lev 2: 4 oblation of a meat offering baken in the **o**, 8574
7: 9 the meat offering that is baken in the **o**, 8574
11:35 whether it be **o**, or ranges for pots, 8574
26:26 women shall bake your bread in one **o**, 8574
Ps 21: 9 Thou shalt make them as a fiery **o** in 8574
La 5:10 Our skin was black like an **o** because of 8574
Hos 7: 4 all adulterers, as an **o** heated by the baker, 8574
7: 6 have made ready their heart like an **o**, 8574
7: 7 are all hot as an **o**, and have devoured 8574
Mal 4: 1 the day cometh, that *shall* burn as an **o**; 8574
Mt 6:30 is, and to morrow is cast into the **o**, 2823
Lk 12:28 field, and to morrow is cast into the **o**; 2823

OVENS (1) [OVEN]

Ex 8: 3 thine **o**, and into thy kneadingtroughs; 8574

OVER (1009)

Ge 1:18 to rule **o** the day and over the night, 871.1
1:18 to rule over the day and **o** the night, 871.1
1:26 let them have dominion **o** the fish of 871.1
1:26 **o** the fowl of the air, and over the cattle, 871.1
1:26 the cattle, and over all the earth, 871.1
1:26 **o** all the earth, and over every creeping 871.1
1:26 **o** every creeping thing that creepeth 871.1
1:28 have dominion **o** the fish of the sea, 871.1
1:28 **o** the fowl of the air, and over every 871.1
1:28 **o** every living thing that moveth upon 871.1
3:16 to thy husband, and he shall rule **o** thee. 871.1
4: 7 *be* his desire, and thou shalt rule **o** him. 871.1
8: 1 God made a wind to pass **o** the earth, 5921
9:14 to pass, when I bring a cloud **o** the earth, 5921
21:16 her down **o** against *him* a good way off, 4480
21:16 sat **o** against *him*, and lift up her voice, 4480
24: 2 of his house that ruled **o** all that he had, 871.1
25:25 came out red, **all o** like a hairy garment; 3605
27:29 be lord **o** thy brethren, and let thy 3807.1
31:21 **passed o** the river, and set his face 5674
31:52 that I will not **pass o** this heap to thee, 5674
31:52 that thou shalt not **pass o** this heap and 5674
32:10 for with my staff I **passed o** this Jordan; 5674
32:16 **Pass o** before me, and put a space betwixt 5674
32:21 So **went** the present **o** before him: 5674
32:22 eleven sons, and **passed o** the ford 5674
32:23 sent them **o** the brook, and sent over that 5674
32:23 over the brook, and **sent o** that he had, 5674
32:31 as he **passed o** Penuel the sun rose upon 5674
33: 3 he **passed o** before them, 5674
33:14 I pray thee, **pass o** before his servant: 5674
36:31 before there reigned *any* king **o** 3807.1
37: 8 said to him, Shalt thou indeed reign **o** us? 5921
37: 8 or shalt thou indeed have dominion **o** us? 871.1
39: 4 he made him overseer **o** his house, 5921
39: 5 **o** all that he had, that the LORD blessed 5921
41:33 and wise, and set him **o** the land of Egypt. 5921
41:34 and let him appoint officers **o** the land, 5921
41:40 Thou shalt be **o** my house, 5921
41:41 See, I have set thee **o** all the land of Egypt. 5921
41:43 he made him *ruler* **o** all the land of Egypt. 5921
41:45 Joseph went out **o** all the land of Egypt. 5921
41:56 the famine was **o** all the face of the earth: 5921
42: 6 Joseph *was* the governor **o** the land, 5921
45:26 and he *is* governor **o** all the land of Egypt. 871.1
47: 6 then make them rulers **o** my cattle. 5921
47:20 because the famine prevailed **o** them: 5921
47:26 Joseph made it a law **o** the land of Egypt 5921
49:22 by a well; *whose* branches run **o** the wall. 5921
Ex 1: 8 Now there arose up a new king **o** Egypt, 5921
1:11 Therefore they did set **o** them taskmasters 5921
2:14 Who made thee a prince and a judge **o** us? 5921
5:14 which Pharaoh's taskmasters had set **o** 5921
8: 5 Stretch forth thine hand with thy rod **o** 5921
8: 5 **o** the rivers, and over the ponds, 5921
8: 5 **o** the ponds, and cause frogs to come up 5921
8: 6 Aaron stretched out his hand **o** the waters 5921
8: 9 Moses said unto Pharaoh, Glory **o** me: 5921
10:12 Stretch out thine hand **o** the land of Egypt 5921
10:13 Moses stretched forth his rod **o** the land 5921
10:14 locusts went up **o** all the land of Egypt, 5921
10:21 that there may be darkness **o** the land of 5921
12:13 I will **pass o** you, and the plague shall not 6452
12:23 the LORD will **pass o** the door, 6452
12:27 who **passed o** the houses of the children 6452
14: 2 and the sea, **o** against Baal-zephon: 6440
14: 7 Egypt, and captains **o** every one of them. 5921
14:16 stretch out thine hand **o** the sea, 5921
14:21 Moses stretched out his hand **o** the sea; 5921
14:26 Stretch out thine hand **o** the sea, 5921
14:27 Moses stretched forth his hand **o** the sea, 5921
15:16 till thy people **pass o**, O LORD, till 5674
15:16 pass over, O LORD, till the people **pass o**, 5674
16:18 he that gathered much **had** nothing **o**, 5736
16:23 that which **remaineth o** lay up for you to 5736
18:21 place *such* **o** them, *to be* rulers of 5921
18:25 made them heads **o** the people, rulers of 5921
25:27 **O** against the border shall the rings be 3807.1
25:37 that they may give light **o** against it. 5921
26:12 hang **o** the backside of the tabernacle. 5921

Ex	26:13 it shall hang **o** the sides of the tabernacle	5921
	26:35 the candlestick **o against** the table on	5227
	28:27 the forepart thereof, **o against**	5980+3807.1
	30: 6 before the mercy seat that *is* **o**	5921
	36:14 *of* goats' *hair* for the tent **o** the tabernacle:	5921
	37: 9 covered with their wings **o** the mercy seat,	5921
	37:14 **O against** the border were	5980+3807.1
	39:20 it, **o against** the *other* coupling thereof,	3807.1
	40:19 spread abroad the tent **o** the tabernacle,	5921
	40:24 **o against** the table, on the side of	5227
	40:36 when the cloud was taken up from **o**	5921
Lev	14: 5 in an earthen vessel **o** running water:	5921
	14: 6 bird *that was* killed **o** the running water:	5921
	14:50 in an earthen vessel **o** running water:	5921
	16:21 confess **o** him all the iniquities of	5921
	25:43 Thou shalt not rule **o** him with rigour;	871.1
	25:46 *o* your brethren the children of Israel,	871.1
	25:46 shall not rule one **o** another with rigour.	871.1
	25:53 *other* shall not **rule** with rigour **o** him in	7287
	26:16 I will even appoint **o** you terror,	5921
	26:17 they that hate you shall reign **o** you;	871.1
Nu	1:50 thou shalt appoint the Levites **o**	5921
	1:50 **o** all the vessels thereof, and over all	5921
	1:50 and **o** all *things* that *belong* to it:	5921
	3:32 *shall be* **chief o** the chief of the Levites,	5387
	3:49 of them that were **o and above**	5736+5921
	4: 6 shall spread **o** it a	4480+4605+1886.5+3807.1
	5:30 he be jealous **o** his wife, and shall set	NIH
	7: 2 were **o** them that were numbered,	5921+5975
	8: 2 **o against** the candlestick.	413+4136+6440
	8: 3 **o against** the candlestick,	413+4136+6440
	10:10 ye shall blow with the trumpets **o** your	5921
	10:10 the sacrifices of your peace offerings;	5921
	10:14 **o** his host *was* Nahshon the son of	5921
	10:15 **o** the host of the tribe of the children of	5921
	10:16 **o** the host of the tribe of the children of	5921
	10:18 **o** his host *was* Elizur the son of Shedeur.	5921
	10:19 **o** the host of the tribe of the children of	5921
	10:20 **o** the host of the tribe of the children of	5921
	10:22 **o** his host *was* Elishama the son of	5921
	10:23 **o** the host of the tribe of the children of	5921
	10:24 **o** the host of the tribe of the children of	5921
	10:25 **o** his host *was* Ahiezer the son of	5921
	10:26 **o** the host of the tribe of the children of	5921
	10:27 **o** the host of the tribe of the children of	5921
	11:16 elders of the people, and officers **o** them;	NIH
	14:14 *that* thy cloud standeth **o** them,	5921
	16:13 make thyself altogether a prince **o** us?	5921
	22: 5 and they abide **o against** me:	4136+4480
	25:15 *was* head **o** a people, *and* of a chief house	NIH
	27:16 of all flesh, set a man **o** the congregation,	5921
	31:14 *with* the captains **o** thousands,	NIH
	31:14 captains **o** hundreds, which came from	NIH
	31:48 the officers which *were* **o** thousands of	3807.1
	32: 5 a possession, *and* **bring** us not **o** Jordan.	5674
	32: 7 **going o** into the land which the LORD	5674
	32:21 will **go** all of you armed **o** Jordan before	5674
	32:27 thy servants will **pass o**, every man armed	5674
	32:29 children of Reuben will **pass** with you **o**	5674
	32:30 if they will not **pass o** with you armed,	5674
	32:32 We will **pass o** armed before the LORD	5674
	33:51 When ye are **passed o** Jordan into the	5674
	35:10 When ye be **come o** Jordan into the land	5674
Dt	1: 1 in the plain **o against** the Red *sea*,	5921
	1:13 and I will make them rulers **o** you.	871.1
	1:15 and known, and made them heads **o** you,	5921
	1:15 captains **o** thousands, and captains over	NIH
	1:15 captains **o** hundreds, and captains over	NIH
	1:15 captains **o** fifties, and captains over tens,	NIH
	1:15 captains **o** tens, and officers among your	NIH
	2:13 *said I*, and **get** you **o** the brook Zered.	5674
	2:13 And we **went o** the brook Zered.	5674
	2:14 until we were **passed o** the brook Zered,	5674
	2:18 Thou art to **pass o** *through* Ar, the coast	5674
	2:19 when thou comest nigh **o against**	4136
	2:24 your journey, and **pass o** the river Arnon:	5674
	2:29 until I shall **pass o** Jordan into the land	5674
	3:18 ye shall **pass o** armed before your	5674
	3:25 let me **go o**, and see the good land that *is*	5674
	3:27 for thou shalt not **go o** this Jordan.	5674
	3:28 for he shall **go o** before this people,	5674
	3:29 So we abode in the valley **o against**	4136
	4:14 in the land whither ye **go o** to possess it.	5674
	4:21 sware that I should not **go o** Jordan,	5674
	4:22 die in this land, I *must* not **go o** Jordan:	5674
	4:22 ye *shall* **go o**, and possess that good land.	5674
	4:26 whereunto ye **go o** Jordan to possess it;	5674
	4:46 in the valley **o against** Beth-peor,	4136
	9: 1 Thou art to **pass o** Jordan *this* day, to go	5674
	9: 3 thy God *is* he which **goeth o** before thee;	5674
	11:30 which dwell in the champaign **o against**	4136
	11:31 For ye shall **pass o** Jordan to go in to	5674
	12:10 ye **go o** Jordan and dwell in the land	5674
	15: 6 thou shalt reign **o** many nations,	871.1
	15: 6 but they shall not reign **o** thee.	871.1
	17:14 shalt say, I will set a king **o** me,	5921
	17:15 shalt in any wise set *him* king **o** thee,	5921
	17:15 thy brethren shalt thou set king **o** thee:	5921
	17:15 mayest not set a stranger **o** thee,	5921
	21: 6 **o** the heifer that is beheaded in the valley:	5921
	24:20 thou shalt not **go o** the **boughs** again,	6286
	27: 2 shall be on the day when you shall **pass o**	5674
	27: 3 of this law, when thou art **passed o**,	5674
	27: 4 Therefore it shall be when ye be **gone o**	5674
	27:12 the people, when ye are **come o** Jordan;	5674

Dt	28:23 heaven that *is* **o** thy head shall be brass,	5921	
	28:36 and thy king which thou shalt set **o** thee,	5921	
	28:63 *that* as the LORD rejoiced **o** you to do you	5921	
	28:63 the LORD will rejoice **o** you to destroy	5921	
	30: 9 for the LORD will again rejoice **o** thee for	5921	
	30: 9 thee for good, as he rejoiced **o** thy fathers:	5921	
	30:13 Who shall go **o** the sea for us, and bring it	5676	
	30:18 whither thou **passest o** Jordan to go to	5674	
	31: 2 unto me, Thou shalt not **go o** this Jordan.	5674	
	31: 3 he will **go o** before thee, *and* he will	5674	
	31: 3 and Joshua, he shall **go o** before thee.	5674	
	31:13 long as ye live in the land whither ye **go o**	5674	
	31:15 the pillar of the cloud stood **o** the door of	5921	
	32:11 fluttereth **o** her young, spreadeth abroad	5921	
	32:47 whither ye **go o** Jordan to possess it.	5674	
	32:49 of Moab, that *is* **against** Jericho;	5921+6440	
	34: 1 of Pisgah, that *is* **against** Jericho,	5921+6440	
	34: 4 thine eyes, but thou shalt not **go o** thither.	5674	
	34: 6 in the land of Moab, **o against** Beth-peor:	4136	
Jos	1: 2 **go o** this Jordan, thou, and all this people,	5674	
	1:11 for within three days ye shall **pass o** this	5674	
	2:23 **passed o**, and came to Joshua the son of	5674	
	3: 1 and lodged there before they **passed o**.	5674	
	3: 6 covenant, and **pass o** before the people.	5674	
	3:11 *even* the Lord of all the earth **passeth o**	5674	
	3:14 to **pass o** Jordan, and the priests bearing	5674	
	3:16 the people **passed o** right against Jericho.	5674	
	3:17 all the Israelites **passed o** on dry *ground*,	5674	
	3:17 the people were **passed** clean **o** Jordan.	5674	
	4: 1 when all the people were clean **passed o**	5674	
	4: 3 ye shall **carry** them **o** with you,	5674	
	4: 5 **Pass o** before the ark of the LORD your	5674	
	4: 7 when it **passed o** Jordan, the waters of	5674	
	4: 8 **carried** them **o** with them unto the place	5674	
	4:10 and the people hasted and **passed o**.	5674	
	4:11 all the people were clean **passed o**,	5674	
	4:11 that the ark of the LORD **passed o**,	5674	
	4:12 **passed o** armed before the children of	5674	
	4:13 **passed o** before the LORD unto battle,	5674	
	4:18 flowed **o** all his banks, as *they did* before.	5674	
	4:22 Israel **came o** this Jordan on dry *land*.	5674	
	4:23 until ye were **passed o**, as the LORD your	5674	
	4:23 up from before us, until we were **gone o**:	5674	
	5: 1 until we were **passed o**, that their heart	5674	
	5:13 there stood a man **o against** him	5048+4480	
	7: 7 **at all brought** this people **o** Jordan,	5674+5674	
	7:26 they raised **o** him a great heap of stones	5921	
	8:31 **o** which no *man* hath lift up *any* iron:	5921	
	8:33 half of them **o against** mount	413+4136	
	8:33 and half of them **o** against mount Ebal;	413	
	9: 1 in all the coasts of the great sea **o** against	413	
	18:13 border **went o** from thence toward Luz,	5674	
	18:17 which *is* **o** against the going up of	5227	
	18:18 passed along toward the side **o against**	4136	
	22:11 built an altar **o** against the land of Canaan,	413	
	22:19 **pass** ye **o** unto the land of the possession	5674	
	24:11 ye **went o** Jordan, and came unto Jericho:	5674	
Jdg	3:28 and suffered not a man to **pass o**.	5674	
	5:13 **made** him that remaineth		
		have dominion **o**	7287
	5:13 the LORD **made** me **have dominion o**	7287	
	6:33 **went o**, and pitched in the valley of	5674	
	8: 4 and **passed o**, he and the three hundred	5674	
	8:22 Rule thou **o** us, both thou, and thy son,	871.1	
	8:23 said unto them, I will not rule **o** you,	871.1	
	8:23 you, neither shall my son rule **o** you:	871.1	
	8:23 rule over you: the LORD shall rule **o** you.	871.1	
	9: 2 reign **o** you, or that one reign over you?	871.1	
	9: 2 reign over you, or that one reign **o** you?	871.1	
	9: 8 forth on a time to anoint a king **o** them;	5921	
	9: 8 said unto the olive tree, Reign thou **o** us.	5921	
	9: 9 man, and go to be promoted **o** the trees?	5921	
	9:10 the fig tree, Come thou, *and* reign **o** us.	5921	
	9:11 and go to be promoted **o** the trees?	5921	
	9:12 the vine, Come thou, *and* reign **o** us.	5921	
	9:13 man, and go to be promoted **o** the trees?	5921	
	9:14 the bramble, Come thou, *and* reign **o** us.	5921	
	9:15 If in truth ye anoint me king **o** you, *then*	5921	
	9:18 king **o** the men of Shechem, because he *is*	5921	
	9:22 Abimelech had reigned three years **o**	5921	
	9:26 his brethren, and **went o** to Shechem:	5674	
	10: 9 the children of Ammon **passed o**	5674	
	10:18 he shall be head **o** all the inhabitants of	3807.1	
	11: 8 our head **o** all the inhabitants of Gilead.	3807.1	
	11:11 made him head and captain **o** them:	5921	
	11:29 he **passed o** Gilead and Manasseh,	5674	
	11:29 **passed o** Mizpeh of Gilead,	5674	
	11:29 from Mizpeh of Gilead he **passed o** *unto*	5674	
	11:32 Jephthah **passed o** unto the children of	5674	
	12: 1 Wherefore **passedst** thou **o** to fight	5674	
	12: 3 **passed o** against the children of Ammon,	5674	
	12: 5 which were escaped said, Let me **go o**;	5674	
	14: 4 the Philistines had dominion **o** Israel.	4910	
	15:11 not that the Philistines *are* rulers **o** us?	871.1	
	19:10 and departed, and came **o** against Jebus,	5704	
	19:12 of Israel; we will **pass o** to Gibeah.	5704	
	20:43 trode them down with ease **o** against	5704	
Ru	2: 5 said Boaz unto his servant that was set **o**	5921	
	2: 6 the servant that was set **o** the reapers	5921	
	3: 9 therefore thy skirt **o** thine handmaid;	5921	
1Sa	2: 1 my mouth is enlarged **o** mine enemies;	5921	
	8: 1 that he made his sons judges **o** Israel.	3807.1	
	8: 7 me, that *I* should not reign **o** them.	5921	
	8: 9 of the king that shall reign **o** them.	5921	
	8:11 manner of the king that shall reign **o** you:	5921	

1Sa	8:12 he will appoint him captains **o** thousands,	NIH
	8:12 over thousands, and captains **o** fifties;	NIH
	8:19 Nay, but we will have a king **o** us;	5921
	9: 6 thou shalt anoint him to be captain **o** my	5921
	9:17 this *same* shall reign **o** my people.	871.1
	10: 1 thee to be captain **o** his inheritance?	5921
	10:19 said unto him, *Nay*, but set a king **o** us.	5921
	11:12 Who *is* he that said, Shall Saul reign **o** us?	5921
	12: 1 unto me, and have made a king **o** you.	5921
	12:12 unto me, Nay; but a king shall reign **o** us:	5921
	12:13 behold, the LORD hath set a king **o** you.	5921
	12:14 also the king that reigneth **o** you continue	5921
	13: 1 when he had reigned two years **o** Israel,	5921
	13: 7 *some* of the Hebrews **went o** Jordan *to*	5674
	13:14 him to be captain **o** his people,	5921
	14: 1 and let us **go o** to the Philistines' garrison,	5674
	14: 4 *by* which Jonathan sought to **go o** unto	5674
	14: 5 situate northward **o against** Michmash,	4136
	14: 5 the other southward **o against** Gibeah.	4136
	14: 6 let us **go o** to the garrison of these	5674
	14: 8 we will **pass o** unto *these* men, and we	5674
	14:23 the battle **passed o** *unto* Beth-aven.	5674
	14:47 So Saul took the kingdom **o** Israel,	5921
	15: 1 me to anoint thee to be king **o** his people,	5921
	15: 1 thee to be king over his people, **o** Israel:	5921
	15: 7 *to* Shur, that *is* **o against** Egypt.	5921+6440
	15:17 the LORD anointed thee king **o** Israel?	5921
	15:26 rejected thee from being king **o** Israel.	5921
	15:35 that he had made Saul king **o** Israel.	5921
	16: 1 seeing I have rejected him from reigning **o**	5921
	17:50 So David prevailed **o** the Philistine with a	4480
	18: 5 Saul set him **o** the men of war, and he	5921
	18:13 and made him his captain **o** a thousand;	NIH
	19:20 Samuel standing *as* appointed **o** them,	5921
	22: 2 him; and he became a captain **o** them:	5921
	22: 9 which *was* set **o** the servants of Saul,	5921
	23:17 thou shalt be king **o** Israel, and I shall be	5921
	25:30 shall have appointed thee ruler **o** Israel;	5921
	26:13 David **went o** to the *other* side,	5674
	26:22 let one of the young men **come o** and	5674
	27: 2 he **passed o** with the six hundred men	5674
	30:10 faint that they could not **go o** the brook	5674
2Sa	1:17 David lamented with this lamentation **o**	5921
	1:17 over Saul and **o** Jonathan his son:	5921
	1:24 Ye daughters of Israel, weep **o** Saul,	413
	2: 4 there they anointed David king **o** the	5921
	2: 7 of Judah have anointed me king **o** them.	5921
	2: 8 of Saul, and **brought** him **o** *to* Mahanaim;	5674
	2: 9 he made him king **o** Gilead, and over	413
	2: 9 the Ashurites, and over Jezreel,	413
	2: 9 **o** Jezreel, and over Ephraim,	413
	2: 9 **o** Ephraim, and over Benjamin, and over	5921
	2: 9 and **o** Benjamin, and over all Israel.	5921
	2: 9 and over Benjamin, and **o** all Israel.	5921
	2:10 years old when he *began* to reign **o** Israel,	5921
	2:11 the time that David was king in Hebron **o**	5921
	2:15 **went o** by number twelve of Benjamin,	5674
	2:29 **passed o** Jordan, and went *through* all	5674
	3:10 to set up the throne of David **o** Israel and	5921
	3:10 throne of David over Israel and **o** Judah,	5921
	3:17 For David in times past to be king **o** you:	5921
	3:21 thou mayest reign **o** all that thine heart	871.1
	3:33 the king lamented **o** Abner, and said, Died	413
	3:34 And all the people wept again **o** him.	5921
	4:12 hanged *them* up **o** the pool in Hebron.	5921
	5: 2 In time past, when Saul was king **o** us,	5921
	5: 2 and thou shalt be a captain **o** Israel.	5921
	5: 3 and they anointed David king **o** Israel.	5921
	5: 5 In Hebron he reigned **o** Judah seven years	5921
	5: 5 and three years **o** all Israel and Judah.	5921
	5:12 LORD had established him king **o** Israel,	5921
	5:17 they had anointed David king **o** Israel,	5921
	5:23 come upon them **o against**	4136+4480
	6:21 to appoint me ruler **o** the people of	5921
	6:21 over the people of the LORD, **o** Israel:	5921
	7: 8 to be ruler **o** my people, over Israel:	5921
	7: 8 to be ruler over my people, **o** Israel:	5921
	7:11 judges *to be* **o** my people Israel,	5921
	7:26 The LORD of hosts *is* the God **o** Israel:	5921
	8:15 David reigned **o** all Israel; and David	5921
	8:16 Joab the son of Zeruiah *was* **o** the host;	5921
	8:18 Benaiah the son of Jehoiada *was* **o** both	NIH
	10:17 and **passed o** Jordan, and came to Helam.	5674
	12: 7 I anointed thee king **o** Israel,	5921
	15:22 David said to Ittai, Go and **pass o**.	5674
	15:22 Ittai the Gittite **passed o**, and all his men,	5674
	15:23 a loud voice, and all the people **passed o**:	5674
	15:23 the king also *himself* **passed o** the brook	5674
	15:23 all the people **passed o**, toward the way of	5674
	16: 9 let me **go o**, I pray thee, and take off his	5674
	16:13 Shimei went along on the hill's side **o**	3807.1
	17:16 wilderness, but **speedily pass o**;	5674+5674
	17:19 and spread a covering **o** the well's mouth,	5921
	17:20 They be **gone o** the brook of water.	5674
	17:21 Arise, and pass quickly **o** the water:	5674
	17:22 with him, and they **passed o** Jordan:	5674
	17:22 one *of them* that was not **gone o** Jordan.	5674
	17:24 Absalom **passed o** Jordan, he and all	5674
	18: 1 and captains of hundreds **o** them.	5921
	18: 8 the battle was there scattered **o** the face	5921
	18:24 watchman went *up* to the roof **o** the gate	NIH
	18:33 went up to the chamber **o** the gate,	NIH
	19:10 Absalom, whom we anointed **o** us, is dead	5921
	19:15 the king, to **conduct** the king **o** Jordan.	5674
	19:17 and they **went o** Jordan before the king.	6743

2Sa 19:18 there **went** o a ferry boat to carry over 5674
19:18 there went over a ferry boat to **carry** o 5674
19:18 the king, as he was **come** o Jordan; 5674
19:22 do not I know that I am this day king o 5921
19:31 **went** o Jordan with the king, to conduct 5674
19:31 with the king, to conduct him o Jordan. NIH
19:33 **Come** thou o with me, and I will feed 5674
19:36 Thy servant will **go** a little way o Jordan 5674
19:37 let him **go** o with my lord the king; 5674
19:38 Chimham shall **go** o with me, and I will 5674
19:39 all the people **went** o Jordan. 5674
19:39 the king was **come** o, the king kissed 5674
19:41 **brought** the king, and his household,
 and all David's men with him, o 5674
20:21 head shall be thrown to thee o the wall. 1157
20:23 Now Joab was o all the host of Israel: 5921
20:23 Benaiah the son of Jehoiada was o 5921
20:23 over the Cherethites and o the Pelethites: 5921
20:24 Adoram was o the tribute: 5921
22:30 troop: by my God have I **leaped** o a wall. 1801
23: 3 He that ruleth o men must be just, ruling 871.1
23:23 first three. And David set him o his guard. 413
24: 5 **passed** o Jordan, and pitched in Aroer, 5674
1Ki 1:34 the prophet anoint him there king o 5921
1:35 I have appointed him to be ruler o Israel 5921
1:35 him to be ruler over Israel and o Judah. 5921
2:11 the days that David reigned o Israel were 5921
2:35 son of Jehoiada in his room o the host: 5921
2:37 out, and **passest** o the brook Kidron, 5674
4: 1 So king Solomon was king o all Israel. 5921
4: 4 the son of Jehoiada was o the host: 5921
4: 5 Azariah the son of Nathan was o 5921
4: 6 Ahishar was o the household; 5921
4: 6 Adoniram the son of Abda was o 5921
4: 7 Solomon had twelve officers o all Israel, 5921
4:21 Solomon reigned o all kingdoms from 871.1
4:24 For he had dominion o all the region on 871.1
4:24 o all the kings on this side the river: 871.1
5: 7 hath given unto David a wise son o 5921
5:14 at home: and Adoniram was o the levy. 5921
5:16 officers which were o the work, 5921
5:16 which ruled o the people that wrought in 871.1
6: 1 in the fourth year of Solomon's reign o 5921
7:20 o against the belly which was by 4480
7:39 the house eastward o against the south. 4480
8: 7 their two wings o the place of the ark, 413
8:16 I chose David to be o my people Israel. 5921
9:23 the officers that were o Solomon's work, 5921
9:23 which bare rule o the people that 871.1
11:24 unto him, and became captain o a band, NIH
11:25 he abhorred Israel, and reigned o Syria. 5921
11:28 he made him ruler o all the charge of 3807.1
11:37 soul desireth, and shalt be king o Israel. 5921
11:42 in Jerusalem o all Israel was forty years. 5921
12:17 of Judah, Rehoboam reigned o them. 5921
12:18 sent Adoram, who was o the tribute; 5921
12:20 and made him king o all Israel: 5921
13:30 they mourned o him, saying, Alas, 5921
14: 2 which told me that I should be king o this 5921
14: 7 and made thee prince o my people Israel, 5921
14:14 **Lord** shall raise him up a king o Israel, 5921
15: 1 the son of Nebat reigned Abijam o Judah. 5921
15: 9 king of Israel **reigned** Asa o Judah. 4427+4428
15:25 Israel in the second year of Asa king of 5921
15:25 of Judah, and reigned o Israel two years. 5921
15:33 of Ahijah to reign o all Israel in Tirzah, 5921
16: 2 and made thee prince o my people Israel; 5921
16: 8 son of Baasha to reign o Israel in Tirzah, 5921
16:16 host, king o Israel that day in the camp. 5921
16:18 burnt the king's house o him with fire, 5921
16:23 of Judah began Omri to reign o Israel, 5921
16:29 Ahab the son of Omri to reign o Israel: 5921
16:29 Ahab the son of Omri reigned o Israel in 5921
19:15 anoint Hazael to be king o Syria: 5921
19:16 shalt thou anoint to be king o Israel: 5921
20:29 pitched one o against the other seven 5227
22:31 two captains that had rule o his chariots, NIH
22:41 o Judah in the fourth year of Ahab king of 5921
22:51 Ahaziah the son of Ahab began to reign o 5921
22:51 of Judah, and reigned two years o Israel. 5921
2Ki 2: 8 so that they two **went** o on dry ground. 5674
2: 9 it came to pass, when they were **gone** o, 5674
2:14 and thither: and Elisha **went** o. 5674
3: 1 o Israel in Samaria the eighteenth year 5921
5:11 strike his hand o the place, and recover 413
8:13 me that thou shalt be king o Syria. 5921
8:20 of Judah, and made a king o themselves. 5921
8:21 So Joram **went** o to Zair, and all 5674
9: 3 I have anointed thee king o Israel. 413
9: 6 I have anointed thee king o the people of 413
9: 6 over the people of the **Lord**, even o Israel. 413
9:12 I have anointed thee king o Israel. 413
9:29 of Ahab began Ahaziah to reign o Judah. 5921
10: 5 he that was o the house, and he that was 5921
10: 5 he that was o the city, the elders also, 5921
10:22 he said unto him that was o the vestry, 5921
10:36 the time that Jehu reigned o Israel in 5921
11: 3 And Athaliah did reign o the land. 5921
11: 4 sent and fet the rulers o hundreds, NIH
11: 9 captains o the hundreds did according to NIH
11:10 to the captains o hundreds did the priest NIH
11:18 priest appointed officers o the house of 5921
11:19 he took the rulers o hundreds, NIH
13: 1 of Jehu began to reign o Israel in Samaria, 5921
13:10 of Jehoahaz to reign o Israel in Samaria, 5921

2Ki 13:14 wept o his face, and said, O my father, 5921
15: 5 Jotham the king's son o the house, 5921
15: 8 reign o Israel in Samaria six months. 5921
15:17 the son of Gadi to reign o Israel, 5921
15:23 began to reign o Israel in Samaria, 5921
15:27 began to reign o Israel in Samaria, 5921
17: 1 to reign in Samaria o Israel nine years. 5921
18:18 which was o the household, and Shebna 5921
18:37 which was o the household, and Shebna 5921
19: 2 which was o the household, and Shebna 5921
21:13 I will stretch o Jerusalem the line of 5921
25:19 an officer that was set o the men of war, 5921
25:22 even o them he made Gedaliah the son 5921
1Ch 1:43 king reigned o the children of Israel; 3807.1
5:11 children of Gad dwelt o against them, 3807.1
6:31 these are they whom David set o 5921
8:32 brethren in Jerusalem, o against them. 5048
9:19 were o the work of the service, 5921
9:19 being o the host of the **Lord**, 5921
9:20 the son of Eleazar was the ruler o 5921
9:26 were o the chambers and treasuries of 5921
9:31 had the set office o the things that were 5921
9:32 were o the shewbread, to prepare it every 5921
9:38 at Jerusalem, o against their brethren. 5048
11: 2 thou shalt be ruler o my people Israel. 5921
11: 3 they anointed David king o Israel, 5921
11:25 first three: and David set him o his guard. 5921
12: 4 man among the thirty, and o the thirty; 5921
12:14 one of the least o an hundred, 3807.1
12:14 hundred, and the greatest o a thousand. 3807.1
12:15 These are they that **went** o Jordan in 5674
12:38 Hebron, to make David king o all Israel: 5921
14: 2 **Lord** had confirmed him king o Israel, 5921
14: 8 that David was anointed king o all Israel, 5921
14:14 come upon them o **against** 4136+4480
15:25 of Israel, and the captains o thousands, NIH
17: 7 that thou shouldest be ruler o my people 5921
17:10 judges to be o my people Israel. 5921
18:14 David reigned o all Israel, and executed 5921
18:15 Joab the son of Zeruiah was o the host; 5921
18:17 Benaiah the son of Jehoiada was o 5921
19:17 **passed** o Jordan, and came upon them, 5674
21:16 in his hand stretched out o Jerusalem. 5921
22:10 will establish the throne of his kingdom o 5921
23: 1 he made Solomon his son king o Israel. 5921
24:31 These likewise cast lots o against their 3807.1
24:31 even the principal fathers o against their 3807.1
26:20 Ahijah was o the treasures of the house 5921
26:20 o the treasures of the dedicate things. 3807.1
26:22 which were o the treasures of the house 5921
26:26 his brethren were o all the treasures of 5921
26:26 the captains o thousands and hundreds, NIH
26:29 his sons were for the outward business o 5921
26:32 whom king David made rulers o 5921
27: 2 O the first course for the first month was 5921
27: 4 o the course of the second month was 5921
27:16 Furthermore o the tribes of Israel: 5921
27:25 the king's treasures was Azmaveth 5921
27:25 the storehouses in the fields, in the 5921
27:26 them that did the work of the field for 5921
27:27 the vineyards was Shimei the 5921
27:27 the increase of the vineyards for the 5921
27:28 the olive trees and the sycomore trees 5921
27:28 and o the cellars of oil was Joash: 5921
27:29 the herds that fed in Sharon was Shitrai 5921
27:29 the herds that were in the valleys was 5921
27:30 O the camels also was Obil the 5921
27:30 o the asses was Jehdeiah the 5921
27:31 the flocks was Jaziz the Hagerite. 5921
28: 1 the captains o the thousands, NIH
28: 1 captains o the hundreds, and the stewards NIH
28: 1 the stewards o all the substance and NIH
28: 4 of my father to be king o Israel for ever: 5921
28: 4 he liked me to make me king o all Israel: 5921
28: 5 of the kingdom of the **Lord** o Israel. 5921
29: 3 o and above 4480+4605+1886.5+3807.1
29: 6 with the rulers o the king's work, NIH
29:12 come of thee, and thou reignest o all; 871.1
29:26 Thus David the son of Jesse reigned o all 5921
29:27 the time that he reigned o Israel was forty 5921
29:30 times that went o him, and over Israel, 5921
29:30 o Israel, and over all the kingdoms of 5921
29:30 and o all the kingdoms of the countries. 5921
2Ch 1: 9 thou hast made me king o a people like 5921
1:11 people, o whom I have made thee king: 5921
1:13 of the congregation, and reigned o Israel. 5921
2:11 people, he hath made them king o them. 5921
4:10 side of the east end, o against the south. 4480
5: 8 forth their wings o the place of the ark, 5921
6: 5 neither chose I any man to be a ruler o 5921
6: 6 have chosen David to be o my people 5921
6:36 deliver them o before their enemies, NIH
8:10 and fifty, that bare rule o the people. 871.1
9: 8 therefore made he thee king o Israel, 5921
9:26 he reigned o all the kings from the river 871.1
9:30 Solomon reigned in Jerusalem o all Israel 5921
10:17 of Judah, Rehoboam reigned o them. 5921
10:18 king Rehoboam sent Hadoram that was o 5921
13: 1 Jeroboam began Abijah to reign o Judah. 5921
13: 5 the kingdom o Israel to David for ever, 5921
19:11 Amariah the chief priest is o you in all 5921
20: 6 rulest not thou o all the kingdoms of 871.1
20:27 for the **Lord** had made them to rejoice o 4480
20:31 Jehoshaphat reigned o Judah: he was 5921
22:12 years: and Athaliah reigned o the land. 5921

2Ch 23:14 of hundreds that were **set** o the host, 6485
25: 5 made them captains o thousands, NIH
25: 5 over thousands, and captains o hundreds, NIH
26:21 Jotham his son was o the king's house. 5921
31:12 o which Cononiah the Levite was ruler, 5921
31:14 was o the freewill offerings of God, 5921
32: 6 he set captains of war o the people, 5921
32:11 not Hezekiah persuade you to **give** o 5414
34:13 Also they were o the bearers of burdens, 5921
36: 4 made Eliakim his brother king o Judah 5921
36:10 made Zedekiah his brother king o Judah 5921
Ezr 4:10 the great and noble Asnappar **brought** o, 1541
4:20 There have been mighty kings also o 5922
4:20 which have ruled o all countries beyond 871.2
9: 6 iniquities are increased o 4605+1886.5+3807.1
Ne 2: 7 they may **convey** me o till I come into 5674
3:10 of Harumaph, even o **against** his house. 5048
3:16 unto the place o **against** the sepulchres 5048
3:19 piece o **against** the going up 4480+5048
3:23 and Hashub o **against** their house. 5048
3:25 Palal the son of Uzai, o **against** 4480+5048
3:26 unto the place o **against** the water gate 5048
3:27 o **against** the great tower that lieth 4480+5048
3:28 every one o **against** his house. 5048+3807.1
3:29 the son of Immer o **against** his house. 5048
3:30 son of Berechiah o **against** his chamber. 5048
3:31 o against the gate Miphkad, and to 5048
5:15 yea, even their servants bare rule o 5921
7: 2 ruler of the palace, charge o Jerusalem: 5921
7: 2 and every one to be o **against** his house. 5048
9:28 so that they had the dominion o them: 871.1
9:37 unto the kings whom thou hast set o us 5921
9:37 also they have dominion o our bodies, 5921
9:37 o our cattle, at their pleasure, and we are 871.1
11: 9 Judah the son of Senuah was second o 5921
11:21 Ziha and Gispa were o the Nethinims. 5921
11:22 the singers were o the business of 5048+3807.1
12: 8 which was o the thanksgiving, he and 5921
12: 9 brethren, were o **against** them 5048+3807.1
12:24 their brethren o **against** them, 5048+3807.1
12:24 of God, ward o **against** ward, 5980+3807.1
12:37 fountain gate, which was o **against** them, 5048
12:38 that gave thanks went o **against** them, 4136
12:44 at that time were some appointed o 5921
13:13 I made treasurers o the treasuries, 5921
13:26 even God made him king o all Israel: 5921
Est 1: 1 o an hundred and seven and NIH
3:12 to the governors that were o every 5921
5: 1 king's house, o **against** the king's house: 5227
5: 1 o **against** the gate of the house. 5227
8: 2 Esther set Mordecai o the house of 5921
9: 1 of the Jews hoped to have power o them, 871.1
9: 1 Jews had rule o them that hated them;) 871.1
Job 6: 5 hath grass? or loweth the ox o his fodder? 5921
7:12 a whale, that thou settest a watch o me? 5921
14:16 my steps: dost thou not watch o my sin? 5921
16:11 **turned** me o into the hands of the 3399
26: 7 He stretcheth out the north o the empty 5921
34:13 Who hath given him a charge o the earth? 5921
41:34 beholdeth all high things: he is a king o 5921
42:11 comforted him o all the evil that 5921
Ps 8: 6 Thou madest him to have dominion o 871.1
12: 4 our lips are our own: who is lord o us? 3807.1
13: 2 how long shall mine enemy be exalted o 5921
18:29 and by my God have I **leaped** o a wall. 1801
19:13 sins; let them not have dominion o me: 871.1
23: 5 my head with oil; my cup **runneth** o. 7310
25: 2 let not mine enemies triumph o me. 3807.1
27:12 **Deliver** me not o unto the will of mine 5414
30: 1 hast not made my foes to rejoice o me. 3807.1
35:19 mine enemies wrongfully rejoice o me: 3807.1
35:24 and let them not rejoice o me. 3807.1
38: 4 For mine iniquities are gone o mine head: NIH
38:16 lest otherwise they should rejoice o me: 3807.1
41:11 mine enemy doth not triumph o me. 5921
42: 7 thy waves and thy billows are gone o me. 5921
47: 2 terrible; he is a great King o all the earth. 5921
47: 8 God reigneth o the heathen: God sitteth 5921
49:14 the upright shall have dominion o them 871.1
60: 8 Edom will I cast out my shoe: 5921
65:13 the valleys also are **covered** o with corn; 5848
66:12 Thou hast caused men to ride o our 3807.1
68:34 his excellency is o Israel, and his strength 5921
78:50 but **gave** their life o to the pestilence; 5462
78:62 He **gave** his people o also unto the sword; 5462
83:18 art the most High o all the earth. 5921
88:16 Thy fierce wrath goeth o me; thy terrors 5921
91:11 he shall give his angels charge o thee, 3807.1
103:16 For the wind passeth o it, and it is gone; 871.1
103:19 heavens; and his kingdom ruleth o all. 871.1
104: 9 set a bound that they may not **pass** o; 5674
106:41 and they that hated them ruled o them. 871.1
108: 9 o Edom will I cast out my shoe; 5921
108: 9 o out my shoe; Philistia will I triumph. 5921
109: 6 Set thou a wicked man o him: and let 5921
110: 6 shall wound the heads o many countries. 5921
118:18 he hath not **given** me o unto death. 5414
119:133 let not any iniquity have dominion o me. 871.1
124: 1 the stream had **gone** o our soul: 5674
124: 5 the proud waters had **gone** o our soul. 5674
145: 9 his tender mercies are o all his works. 5921
Pr 17: 2 A wise servant shall have rule o a son 871.1
19:10 much less for a servant to have rule o 871.1
19:11 it is his glory to pass o a transgression. 5921
20:26 wicked, and bringeth the wheel o them. 5921

O

Pr
22: 7 The rich ruleth **o** the poor, 871.1
24:31 it was all **grown o** with thorns, 5927
25:28 He that hath no rule **o** his own spirit is 3807.1
28:15 so is a wicked ruler **o** the poor people. 5921

Ecc
1:12 I the Preacher was king **o** Israel in 5921
2:19 yet shall he have rule **o** all my labour 871.1
7:14 also hath set the one **o against** 5980+3807.1
7:16 Be not righteous **o much;** neither make 7235
7:16 over much; neither make thyself **o** wise: 3148
7:17 Be not **o much** wicked, neither be thou 7235
8: 8 There is no man that hath power **o** 871.1
8: 9 there is a time wherein one man ruleth **o** 871.1

SS
2: 4 and his banner **o** me was love. 5921
2:11 the winter is past, the rain is **o** and gone; 2498

Isa
3: 4 princes, and babes shall rule **o** them. 871.1
3:12 oppressors, and women rule **o** them. 871.1
8: 7 and he shall come up **o** all his channels, 5921
8: 7 all his channels, and go **o** all his banks: 5921
8: 8 he shall overflow and go **o,** he shall reach 5674
10:29 They are **gone o** the passage: they have 5674
11:15 wind shall he shake his hand **o** the river, 5921
11:15 and **make** men **go o** dryshod. 1869
14: 2 and they shall rule **o** their oppressors. 871.1
15: 2 Moab shall howl **o** Nebo, 5921
15: 2 shall howl over Nebo, and **o** Medeba: 5921
16: 8 are stretched out, they are **gone o** the sea. 5674
19: 4 the Egyptians will I **give o** into the hand 5534
19: 4 a fierce king shall rule **o** them, saith 871.1
19:16 the LORD of hosts, which he shaketh **o** it. 5921
22:15 which is **o** the house, and say, 5921
23: 2 that **pass o** the sea, have replenished. 5674
23: 6 **Pass** ye **o** to Tarshish; howl, ye 5674
23:11 He stretched out his hand **o** the sea, 5921
23:12 arise, **pass o** to Chittim; there also shalt 5674
25: 7 the face of the covering cast **o** all people, 5921
25: 7 and the vail that is spread **o** all nations. 5921
26:13 besides thee have had **dominion o** us: 1166
28:19 for morning by morning shall it **pass o,** 5674
31: 5 and **passing o** he will preserve it. 6452
31: 9 he shall **pass o** to his strong hold for fear, 5674
35: 8 the unclean shall not **pass o** it; but it 5674
36: 3 which was **o** the house, and Shebna 5921
36:22 that was **o** the household, and Shebna 5921
37: 2 who was **o** the household, and Shebna 5921
40:19 the goldsmith **spreadeth** it **o** with gold, 7554
40:27 my judgment is **passed o** from my God? 5674
41: 2 before him, and **made** him **rule o** kings? 7287
45:14 shall **come o** unto thee, and they shall be 5674
45:14 in chains they shall **come o,** and the 5674
47: 2 leg, uncover the thigh, **pass o** the rivers. 5674
51:10 sea a way for the ransomed to **pass o?** 5674
51:23 thy soul, Bow down, that we may **go o:** 5674
51:23 and as the street, to them that **went o.** 5674
52: 5 that **rule o** them make them to howl, 4910
54: 9 of Noah should no more **go o** the earth; 5921
62: 5 as the bridegroom rejoiceth **o** the bride, 5921
62: 5 the bride, so shall thy God rejoice **o** thee. 5921
63:19 We are thine: thou never barest rule **o** 871.1

Jer
1:10 I have this day set thee **o** the nations and 5921
1:10 over the nations and **o** the kingdoms, 5921
2:10 For **pass o** the isles of Chittim, and see; 5674
5: 6 a leopard shall watch **o** their cities: 5921
5:22 they roar, yet can they not **pass o** it? 5674
6:17 Also I set watchmen **o** you, 5921
13:21 them to be captains, and as chief **o** thee: 5921
15: 3 I will appoint **o** them four kinds, saith 5921
23: 4 I will set up shepherds **o** them which 5921
31:28 like as I have watched **o** them, to pluck 5921
31:28 so will I watch **o** them, to build, 5921
31:39 go forth **o against** it upon the hill Gareb, 5048
32:41 I will rejoice **o** them to do them good, 5921
33:26 seed to be rulers **o** the seed of Abraham, 413
40: 5 hath made governor **o** the cities of Judah, 871.1
40:11 that he had set **o** them Gedaliah the son 5921
41: 2 Babylon had made governor **o** the land. 871.1
41:10 and departed to **go o** to the Ammonites 5674
43:10 he shall spread his royal pavilion **o** them. 5921
44:27 I will watch **o** them for evil, and not for 5921
48:32 thy plants are **gone o** the sea, they reach 5674
48:40 eagle, and shall spread his wings **o** Moab. 413
49:19 is a chosen man, that I may appoint **o** 413
49:22 the eagle, and spread his wings **o** Bozrah: 5921
50:44 is a chosen man, that I may appoint **o** 413

La
2:17 he hath caused thine enemy to rejoice **o** 5921
3:54 Waters flowed **o** mine head; then I said, 5921
5: 8 Servants have ruled **o** us: there is none 871.1

Eze
1:20 were lifted up **o against** them: 5980+3807.1
1:21 were lifted up **o against** them: 5980+3807.1
1:22 stretched forth **o** their heads above. 5921
1:25 the firmament that was **o** their heads, 5921
1:26 the firmament that was **o** their heads 5921
3:13 noise of the wheels **o against** 5980+3807.1
9: 1 Cause them **that have charge o** the city 6486
10: 1 **o** them as it were a sapphire stone, 5921
10: 2 cherubims, and scatter them **o** the city. 5921
10: 4 and **stood o** the threshold of the house; 5921
10:18 of the house, and stood **o** the cherubims. 5921
10:19 the glory of the God of Israel **o** them 5921
11:22 the glory of the God of Israel was **o** them 5921
16: 8 I spread my skirt **o** thee, and covered thy 5921
16:27 I have stretched out my hand **o** thee, 5921
19: 8 the provinces, and spread their net **o** him: 5921
20:33 with fury poured out, will I rule **o** you: 5921
27:32 lament **o** thee, saying, What city is like 5921
29:15 they shall no more rule **o** the nations. 871.1

Eze
32: 3 spread out my net **o** thee with a company 5921
32: 8 lights of heaven will I make dark **o** thee, 5921
32:31 shall be comforted **o** all his multitude, 5921
34:23 I will set up one shepherd **o** them, 5921
37:24 David my servant shall be king **o** them; 5921
40:18 **o against** the length of the gates 5980+3807.1
40:23 the gate of the inner court was **o against** 5048
41: 6 one **o** another, and thirty in order; 413
41:15 **o against** the separate place which 413+6440
41:16 on their inner stories, **o against** the door, 5048
42: 1 that was **o against** the separate place, 5048
42: 3 **O against** the twenty cubits which were 5048
42: 3 **o against** the pavement which was for 5048
42: 7 wall that was without **o against** 5980+3807.1
42:10 **o against** the separate place, and 413+6440
42:10 and **o against** the building. 413+6440
45: 6 **o against** the oblation of the holy 5980+3807.1
45: 7 the length shall be **o against** 5980+3807.1
46: 9 came in, but shall go forth **o against** it. 5226
47: 5 and it was a river that I could not **pass o:** 5674
47: 5 in, a river that could not be **passed o.** 5674
47:20 till a man come **o against** Hamath. 5227
48:13 **o against** the border of the 5980+3807.1
48:15 are left in the breadth **o against** 5921+6440
48:18 the residue in length **o against** 5980+3807.1
48:18 it shall be **o against** the oblation 5980+3807.1
48:21 **o against** the five and 413+6440
48:21 westward **o against** the five and 5921+6440
48:21 **o against** the portions for 5980+3807.1

Da
1:11 the prince of the eunuchs had set **o** 5921
2:38 and hath made thee ruler **o** them all. 871.2
2:39 which shall bear rule **o** all the earth. 871.2
2:48 made him ruler **o** the whole province of 5922
2:48 chief of the governors **o** all the wise men 5922
2:49 the affairs of the province of Babylon: 5922
3:12 set to the affairs of the province of Babylon, 5922
4:16 unto him, and let seven times pass **o** him. 5922
4:17 and setteth up **o** it the basest of men. 5922
4:23 of the field, till seven times pass **o** him; 5922
4:25 and seven times shall pass **o** thee, 5922
4:32 oxen, and seven times shall pass **o** thee, 5922
5: 5 wrote **o against** the candlestick upon 3807.2
5:21 he appointeth **o** it whomsoever he will. 5922
6: 1 It pleased Darius to set **o** the kingdom an 5922
6: 1 which should be **o** the whole kingdom; 871.2
6: 2 **o** these three presidents; of whom 4481+5924
6: 3 the king thought to set him **o** the whole 5922
9: 1 which was made king **o** the realm of 5921
11:39 he shall cause them to **rule o** many, 4910
11:40 and shall overflow and **pass o.** 5674
11:43 he shall have power **o** the treasures of 871.1
11:43 and **o** all the precious things of Egypt: 871.1

Hos
10: 5 for the people thereof shall mourn **o** it, 5921
10:11 corn; but I **passed o** upon her fair neck: 5674
12: 4 he had power **o** the angel, and prevailed: 413

Joel
2:17 that the heathen should **rule o** them: 4910

Ob
1:12 neither shouldest thou have rejoiced **o** 3807.1

Jnh
2: 3 thy billows and thy waves passed **o** me. 5921
4: 6 and made it to come up **o** Jonah, 4480+5921
4: 6 that it might be a shadow **o** his head, 5921

Mic
3: 6 the sun shall go down **o** the prophets, 5921
3: 6 and the day shall be dark **o** them. 5921
4: 7 the LORD shall reign **o** them in mount 5921

Na
3:19 bruit of thee shall clap the hands **o** thee: 5921

Hab
1:11 and he shall **pass o,** and offend, 5674
1:14 things, that have no ruler **o** them? 871.1
2:19 it is **laid o** with gold and silver, and 8610

Zep
3:17 will save, he will rejoice **o** thee with joy; 5921
3:17 his love, he will joy **o** thee with singing. 5921

Hag
1:10 Therefore the heaven **o** you is stayed from 5921

Zec
1:21 lift up their horn **o** the land of Judah 413
5: 3 is the curse that goeth forth **o** the face 5921
9:14 the LORD shall be seen **o** them, 5921
14: 9 the LORD shall be king **o** all the earth: 5921

Mt
2: 9 and stood **o** where the young child was. 1883
9: 1 **passed o,** and came into his own city. 1276
10:23 Ye shall not have **gone o** the cities of 5055
14:34 And when they were **gone o,** they came 1276
20:25 the Gentiles **exercise dominion o** them, 2634
21: 2 Go into the village **o against** you, 561
24:45 whom his lord hath made ruler **o** his 1909
24:47 That he shall make him ruler **o** all his 1909
25:21 thou hast been faithful **o** a few things, 1909
25:21 **o** many things: enter thou into the joy of 1909
25:23 thou hast been faithful **o** a few things, 1909
25:23 **o** many things: enter thou into the joy of 1909
27:37 And set up **o** his head his accusation 1883
27:45 darkness **o** all the land unto the ninth 1909
27:61 Mary, sitting **o against** the sepulchre. 561

Mk
4:35 Let us **pass o** unto the other side. 1330
5: 1 And they came **o** unto the other side of NIG
5:21 And when Jesus was **passed o** again by 1276
6: 7 and gave them **power o** unclean spirits; 1849
6:53 And when they had **passed o,** they came 1276
10:42 **rule o** the Gentiles exercise lordship over 757
10:42 the Gentiles **exercise lordship o** them, 2634
11: 2 Go your way into the village **o against** 2713
12:41 And Jesus sat **o against** the treasury, 2713
13: 3 the mount of Olives **o against** the temple, 2713
15:26 of his accusation was **written o,** 1924
15:33 there was darkness **o** the whole land until 1909
15:39 which stood **o against** him, saw 1537+1727

Lk
1:33 he shall reign **o** the house of Jacob for 1909
2: 8 keeping watch **o** their flock by night. 1909
4:10 He shall give his angels charge **o** thee, 4012

Lk
4:39 he stood **o** her, and rebuked the fever; 1883
6:38 and shaken together, and **running o,** 5240
8:22 Let us **go o** unto the other side of the lake. 1330
8:26 the Gadarenes, which is **o against** Galilee. 495
9: 1 them power and authority **o** all devils, 1909
10:19 and **o** all the power of the enemy: 1909
11:42 **pass o** judgment and the love of God: 3928
11:44 men that walk **o** them are not aware of 1883
12:14 who made me a judge or a divider **o** you? 1909
12:42 whom his lord shall make ruler **o** his 1909
12:44 that he will make him ruler **o** all that he 1909
15: 7 that likewise joy shall be in heaven **o** one 1909
15: 7 more than **o** ninety and nine just persons 1909
15:10 angels of God **o** one sinner that repenteth. 1909
19:14 We will not have this man to reign **o** us. 1909
19:17 very little, have thou authority **o** ten cities. 1883
19:19 likewise to him, Be thou also **o** five cities. 1883
19:27 would not that I should reign **o** them, 1909
19:30 Go ye into the village **o against** you; in 2713
19:41 he beheld the city, and wept **o** it, 1909
22:25 the Gentiles **exercise lordship o** them; 2961
23:38 And a superscription also was written **o** 1909
23:44 there was a darkness **o** all the earth until 1909

Jn
6: 1 After these things Jesus went **o** the sea of 4008
6:13 which remained **o** and above unto them 4052
6:17 and went **o** the sea towards Capernaum. 4008
17: 2 As thou hast given him **power o** all flesh, 1849
18: 1 with his disciples **o** the brook Cedron, 4008

Ac
6: 3 whom we may appoint **o** this business. 1909
7:10 and he made him governor **o** Egypt and 1909
7:11 Now there came a dearth **o** all the land of 1909
7:16 And were **carried o** into Sychem, 3346
7:27 Who made thee a ruler and a judge **o** us? 1909
8: 2 and made great lamentation **o** him. 1909
16: 9 **Come o** into Macedonia, and help us. 1224
18:23 and **went o** all the country of Galatia and 1330
19:13 took upon them to call **o** them which had 1909
20: 2 And when he had **gone o** those parts, 1330
20:15 and came the next day **o against** Chios; 481
20:28 **o** the which the Holy Ghost hath made 1722
21: 2 finding a ship **sailing o** unto Phenicia, 1276
27: 5 And when we had **sailed o** the sea of 1277
27: 7 and scarce were come **o against** Cnidus, 2596
27: 7 sailed under Crete, **o against** Salmone; 2596

Ro
1:28 God **gave** them **o** to a reprobate mind, 3860
5:14 even **o** them that had not sinned after 1909
6: 9 death hath no more **dominion o** him. 2961
6:14 For sin shall not have dominion **o** you: 2961
7: 1 that the law hath **dominion o** a man, 2961
9: 5 the flesh Christ came, who is **o** all, 1909
9:21 Hath not the potter **power o** the clay, 1849
10:12 for the same Lord **o** all is rich unto all that NIG
15:12 he that shall **rise o** the Gentiles; 757

1Co
7:37 but hath power **o** his own will, and hath 4012
9:12 If others be partakers of this **power o** you, 1849

2Co
1:24 Not for that we have **dominion o** your 2961
3:13 not as Moses, which put a vail **o** his face, 1909
8:15 that had gathered much **had** nothing **o;** 4121
11: 2 I am jealous **o** you with godly jealousy: NIG

Eph
1:22 gave him to be the head **o** all things to 5228
4:19 **given** themselves **o** unto lasciviousness, 3860

Col
2:15 of them openly, **triumphing o** them in it. 2358

1Th
3: 7 we were comforted **o** you in all our 1909
5:12 and are **o** you in the Lord, 4291

1Ti
2:12 nor to **usurp authority o** the man, but to 831

Heb
2: 7 didst set him **o** the works of thy hands: 1909
3: 6 But Christ as a Son **o** his own house; 1909
9: 5 **o** it the cherubims of glory shadowing 5231
10:21 And having a high priest **o** the house of 1909
13: 7 Remember them which **have the rule o** 2233
13:17 Obey them that **have the rule o** you, 2233
13:24 Salute all them that **have the rule o** you, 2233

Jas
1: 9 and let them pray **o** him, anointing him 1909

1Pe
3:12 the eyes of the Lord are **o** the righteous, 1909
5: 3 Neither as being **lords o** God's heritage, 2634

Jude
1: 7 **giving** themselves **o** to fornication, 1608

Rev
2:26 to him will I give power **o** the nations: 1909
6: 8 And power was given unto them **o** 1909
9:11 And they had a king **o** them, which is 1909
11: 6 power **o** waters to turn them to blood, 1909
11:10 dwell upon the earth shall rejoice **o** them, 1909
13: 7 and power was given him **o** all kindreds, 1909
14:18 from the altar, which had power **o** fire; 1909
15: 2 that had gotten the victory **o** the beast, 1537
15: 2 and **o** his image, and over his mark, 1537
15: 2 and over his image, and **o** his mark, 1537
15: 2 his mark, and **o** the number of his name, 1537
16: 9 God, which hath power **o** these plagues: 1909
17:18 which reigneth **o** the kings of the earth. 1909
18:11 of the earth shall weep and mourn **o** her; 1909
18:20 Rejoice **o** her, thou heaven, and ye holy 1909

OVERCAME (3) [OVERCOME]
Ac 19:16 and prevailed against them, 2634
Rev 3:21 as I also **o,** and am set down with my 3528
 12:11 they **o** him by the blood of the Lamb, 3528

OVERCAST See LOWRING

OVERCHARGE (1) [CHARGE, OVERCHARGED]
2Co 2: 5 but in part: that I may not **o** you all. 1912

OVERCHARGED (1) [OVERCHARGE]
Lk 21:34 lest at any time your hearts be **o** with 925

OVERCOME (22) [OVERCAME, OVERCOMETH]

Ge	49:19 Gad, a troop shall **o** him: but he shall	1464
	49:19 overcome him: but he shall **o** at the last.	1464
Ex	32:18 *it* the voice of *them that* cry for being **o**:	2476
Nu	13:30 for we are **well able to o** it.	3201+3201
	22:11 peradventure I shall be able to **o** them,	3898
2Ki	16: 5 they besieged Ahaz, but could not **o** *him*.	3898
SS	6: 5 thine eyes from me, for they have **o** me:	7292
Isa	28: 1 fat valleys of them that are **o** with wine.	1986
Jer	23: 9 like a man whom wine hath **o**, because of	5674
Lk	11:22 than he shall come upon *him*, and **o** him,	3528
Jn	16:33 but be of good cheer; I have **o** the world.	3528
Ro	3: 4 and mightest **o** when thou art judged.	3528
	12:21 Be not **o** of evil, but overcome evil with	3528
	12:21 overcome of evil, but **o** evil with good.	3528
2Pe	2:19 for of whom a man is **o**, of the same is he	2274
	2:20 they are again entangled therein, and **o**,	2274
1Jn	2:13 because you have **o** the wicked one.	3528
	2:14 in you, and ye have **o** the wicked one.	3528
	4: 4 of God, little children, and have **o** them:	3528
Rev	11: 7 and shall **o** them, and kill them.	3528
	13: 7 make war with the saints, and to **o** them:	3528
	17:14 the Lamb, and the Lamb shall **o** them:	3528

OVERCOMETH (11) [OVERCOME]

1Jn	5: 4 whatsoever is born of God **o** the world.	3528
	5: 4 and this is the victory that **o** the world,	3528
	5: 5 Who is he that **o** the world, but he that	3528
Rev	2: 7 To him that **o** will I give to eat of the tree	3528
	2:11 He that **o** shall not be hurt of the second	3528
	2:17 To him that **o** will I give to eat of	3528
	2:26 he that **o**, and keepeth my works unto	3528
	3: 5 He that **o**, the same shall be clothed in	3528
	3:12 Him that **o** will I make a pillar in	3528
	3:21 To him that **o** will I grant to sit with me	3528
	21: 7 He that **o** shall inherit all *things*; and I	3528

OVERDRIVE (1) [DRIVE]

Ge	33:13 *men* should **o** them one day, all the flock	1849

OVERFLOW (13) [FLOW, OVERFLOWED, OVERFLOWETH, OVERFLOWING, OVERFLOWN]

Dt	11: 4 he **made** the water of the Red sea to **o**	6687
Ps	69: 2 into deep waters, where the floods **o** me.	7857
	69:15 Let not the waterflood **o** me, neither let	7857
Isa	8: 8 he shall **o** and go over, he shall reach	7857
	10:22 the consumption decreed shall **o** *with*	7857
	28:17 and the waters shall **o** the hiding place.	7857
	43: 2 through the rivers, they shall not **o** thee:	7857
Jer	47: 2 shall **o** the land, and all that is therein;	7857
Da	11:10 certainly come, and **o**, and pass through:	7857
	11:26 shall destroy him, and his army shall **o**	7857
	11:40 the countries, and shall **o** and pass over.	7857
Joel	2:24 and the fats shall **o** *with* wine and oil.	7783
	3:13 you down; for the press is full, the fats **o**;	7783

OVERFLOWED (2) [OVERFLOW]

Ps	78:20 the waters gushed out, and the streams **o**;	7857
2Pe	3: 6 world that then was, being **o** with water,	2626

OVERFLOWETH (1) [OVERFLOW]

Jos	3:15 (for Jordan **o** all his banks all	4390+5921

OVERFLOWING (11) [OVERFLOW]

Job	28:11 He bindeth the floods from **o**; and the	1065
	38:25 a watercourse for the **o of waters**,	7858
Isa	28: 2 as a flood of mighty waters **o**,	7857
	28:15 when the **o** scourge shall pass through,	7857
	28:18 when the **o** scourge shall pass through,	7857
	30:28 his breath, as an **o** stream, shall reach to	7857
Jer	47: 2 shall be an **o** flood, and shall overflow	7857
Eze	13:11 there shall be an **o** shower; and ye,	7857
	13:13 there shall be an **o** shower in mine anger,	7857
	38:22 an **o** rain, and great hailstones, fire,	7857
Hab	3:10 the **o** of the water passed by: the deep	2230

OVERFLOWN (3) [OVERFLOW]

1Ch	12:15 when it had **o** all his banks;	4390+5921
Job	22:16 whose foundation was **o** *with* a flood:	3332
Da	11:22 *with* the arms of a flood shall they be **o**	7857

OVERLAID (35) [OVERLAY]

Ex	26:32 four pillars of shittim *wood* **o** with gold:	6823
	36:34 he **o** the boards with gold, and made	6823
	36:34 for the bars, and the bars with gold.	6823
	36:36 of shittim *wood*, and **o** them with gold:	6823
	36:38 he **o** their chapiters and their fillets with	6823
	37: 2 **o** it with pure gold within and without,	6823
	37: 4 of shittim wood, and **o** them with gold,	6823
	37:11 he **o** it with pure gold, and made	6823
	37:15 and **o** them with gold, to bear the table.	6823
	37:26 he **o** it with pure gold, *both* the top of it,	6823
	37:28 *of* shittim wood, and **o** them with gold.	6823
	38: 2 were of the same: and he **o** it with brass.	6823
	38: 6 of shittim wood, and **o** them with brass.	6823
	38:28 and of their chapiters, and filleted them.	6823
1Ki	3:19 died in the night; because she **o** it.	5921+7901
	6:20 he **o** it with pure gold; and *so* covered	6823
	6:21 So Solomon **o** the house within with pure	6823
	6:21 before the oracle; and he **o** it with gold.	6823
	6:22 the whole house he **o** with gold, until *he*	6823
	6:22 that *was* by the oracle he **o** with gold.	6823
	6:28 And he **o** the cherubims with gold.	6823
	6:30 the floor of the house he **o** with gold,	6823
	6:32 **o** *them* with gold, and spread gold upon	6823

1Ki	10:18 of ivory, and **o** it with the best gold.	6823
2Ki	18:16 which Hezekiah king of Judah had **o**,	6823
2Ch	3: 4 twenty: and he **o** it within with pure gold.	6823
	3: 5 he **o** with fine gold, and set thereon	2645
	3: 7 **o** also the house, the beams, the posts,	2645
	3: 8 he **o** it with fine gold, *amounting* to six	2645
	3: 9 And he **o** the upper chambers with gold.	2645
	3:10 of image work, and **o** them with gold.	6823
	4: 9 and **o** the doors of them with brass.	6823
	9:17 throne of ivory, and **o** it with pure gold.	6823
SS	5:14 belly *is as* bright ivory **o** with sapphires.	5968
Heb	9: 4 ark of the covenant **o** round about with	4028

OVERLAY (13) [LAY, OVERLAID, OVERLAYING]

Ex	25:11 thou shalt **o** it with pure gold, within and	6823
	25:11 within and without shalt thou **o** it,	6823
	25:13 of shittim wood, and **o** them with gold.	6823
	25:24 thou shalt **o** it with pure gold,	6823
	25:28 **o** them with gold, that the table may be	6823
	26:29 thou shalt **o** the boards with gold, and	6823
	26:29 and thou shalt **o** the bars with gold.	6823
	26:37 of shittim *wood*, and **o** them with gold,	6823
	27: 2 the same: and thou shalt **o** it with brass.	6823
	27: 6 of shittim wood, and **o** them with brass.	6823
	30: 3 thou shalt **o** it with pure gold, the top	6823
	30: 5 of shittim wood, and **o** them with gold.	6823
1Ch	29: 4 to **o** the walls of the houses *withal*:	2902

OVERLAYING (2) [OVERLAY]

Ex	38:17 the **o** of their chapiters *of* silver; and all	6826
	38:19 the **o** of their chapiters and their fillets *of*	6826

OVERLIVED (1) [LIVE]

Jos	24:31 all the days of the elders that **o**	310+748+3117

OVERMUCH (1) [MUCH]

2Co	2: 7 should be swallowed up with **o** sorrow.	4055

OVERPASS (1) [OVERPAST]

Jer	5:28 yea, they **o** the deeds of the wicked:	5674

OVERPAST (2) [OVERPASS]

Ps	57: 1 my refuge, until *these* calamities be **o**.	5674
Isa	26:20 little moment, until the indignation be **o**.	5674

OVERPLUS (1)

Lev	25:27 restore the **o** unto the man to whom he	5736

OVERRAN (1) [OVERRUNNING]

2Sa	18:23 ran *by* the way of the plain, and **o** Cushi.	5674

OVERRUNNING (1) [OVERRAN, RUN]

Na	1: 8 with an **o** flood he will make an utter end	5674

OVERSEE (2) [OVERSEER, OVERSEERS, OVERSIGHT, SEE]

1Ch	9:29 *Some* of them also *were* appointed to **o**	5921
2Ch	2: 2 and six hundred to **o** them.	5329+5921

OVERSEER (7) [OVERSEE]

Ge	39: 4 he **made** him **o** over his house, and all	6485
	39: 5 *that* he had **made** him **o** in his house,	6485
Ne	11: 9 Joel the son of Zichri *was* their **o**:	6496
	11:14 their **o** *was* Zabdiel, the son of *one* of	6496
	11:22 The **o** also of the Levites at Jerusalem *was*	6496
	12:42 singers sang loud, with Jezrahiah *their* **o**.	6496
Pr	6: 7 Which having no guide, **o**, or ruler,	7860

OVERSEERS (6) [OVERSEE]

2Ch	2:18 six hundred **o** to set the people a work.	5329
	31:13 *were* under the hand of Cononiah and	6496
	34:12 the **o** of them *were* Jahath and Obadiah,	6485
	34:13 *were* of all that wrought the work in	5329
	34:17 have delivered it into the hand of the **o**,	6485
Ac	20:28 which the Holy Ghost hath made you **o**,	1985

OVERSHADOW (2) [OVERSHADOWED, SHADOW]

Lk	1:35 and the power of the Highest shall **o** thee:	1982
Ac	5:15 of Peter passing by might **o** some of them.	1982

OVERSHADOWED (3) [OVERSHADOW]

Mt	17: 5 yet spake, behold, a bright cloud **o** them:	1982
Mk	9: 7 And there was a cloud that **o** them:	1982
Lk	9:34 spake, there came a cloud, and **o** them:	1982

OVERSIGHT (11) [OVERSEE]

Ge	43:12 in your hand; peradventure it *was* an **o**:	4870
Nu	3:32 *have* the **o** of them that keep the charge	6486
	4:16 *and* the **o** of all the tabernacle, and of all	6486
2Ki	12:11 that *had* the **o** of the house of the LORD:	6485
	22: 5 that have the **o** of the house of the LORD:	6485
	22: 9 have the **o** *of* the house of the LORD,	6485
1Ch	9:23 their children had the **o** of the gates of	5921
2Ch	34:10 that had the **o** of the house of the LORD,	6485
Ne	11:16 had the **o** of the outward business of	5921
	13: 4 having the **o** of the chamber of	5414+871.1
1Pe	5: 2 taking the **o** *thereof*, not by constraint,	1983

OVERSPREAD (1) [SPREAD, OVERSPREADING]

Ge	9:19 and of them was the whole earth **o**.	5310

OVERSPREADING (1) [OVERSPREAD]

Da	9:27 for the **o** of abominations he *shall* make *it*	3671

OVERTAKE (17) [OVERTAKEN, OVERTAKETH, OVERTOOK, TAKE]

Ge	44: 4 when thou dost **o** them, say unto them,	5381
Ex	15: 9 The enemy said, I will pursue, I will **o**,	5381
Dt	19: 6 **o** him, because the way is long,	5381
	28: 2 blessings shall come on thee, and **o** thee,	5381
	28:15 curses shall come upon thee, and **o** thee:	5381
	28:45 shall pursue thee, and **o** thee, till thou be	5381
Jos	2: 5 after them quickly; for ye shall **o** them.	5381
1Sa	30: 8 shall I **o** them? And he answered him,	5381
	30: 8 for thou shalt **surely o** *them*, and	5381+5381
2Sa	15:14 lest he **o** us suddenly, and bring evil upon	5381
Isa	59: 9 far from us, neither doth justice **o** us:	5381
Jer	42:16 shall ye there in the land of Egypt,	5381
Hos	2: 7 after her lovers, but she shall not **o** them;	5381
	10: 9 the children of iniquity did not **o** them.	5381
Am	9:10 The evil shall not **o** nor prevent us.	5066
	9:13 that the plowman shall **o** the reaper,	5066
1Th	5: 4 that *that* day should **o** you as a thief.	2638

OVERTAKEN (2) [OVERTAKE]

Ps	18:37 have pursued mine enemies, and **o** them:	5381
Gal	6: 1 if a man be **o** in a fault, ye which	4301

OVERTAKETH (1) [OVERTAKE]

1Ch	21:12 while that the sword of thine enemies **o**	5381

OVERTHREW (12) [OVERTHROW]

Ge	19:25 he **o** those cities, and all the plain, and all	2015
	19:29 he **o** the cities in the which Lot dwelt.	2015
Ex	14:27 the LORD **o** the Egyptians in the midst of	5287
Dt	29:23 which the LORD **o** in his anger, and in his	2015
Ps	136:15 **o** Pharaoh and his host in the Red sea:	5287
Isa	13:19 shall be as when God **o** Sodom and	4114
Jer	20:16 man be as the cities which the LORD **o**,	2015
	50:40 As God **o** Sodom and Gomorrah and	4114
Am	4:11 as God **o** Sodom and Gomorrah,	4114
Mt	21:12 and the tables of the moneychangers,	2690
Mk	11:15 and the tables of the money-changers,	2690
Jn	2:15 out the changers' money, and **o** the tables;	390

OVERTHROW (19) [OVERTHREW, OVERTHROWETH, OVERTHROWN, THROW]

Ge	19:21 I will not **o** *this* city, for the which thou	2015
	19:29 sent Lot out of the midst of the **o**,	2018
Ex	23:24 thou shalt **utterly o** them,	2040+2040
Dt	12: 3 you shall **o** their altars, and break their	5422
	29:23 like the **o** of Sodom, and Gomorrah,	4114
2Sa	10: 3 the city, and to spy it out, and to **o** it?	2015
	11:25 *more* strong against the city, and **o** it:	2040
1Ch	19: 3 search, and to **o**, and to spy out the land?	2015
Ps	106:26 against them, to **o** them in the wilderness:	5307
	106:27 To **o** their seed also among the nations,	5307
	140: 4 who have purposed to **o** my goings.	1760
	140:11 evil shall hunt the violent man to **o** *him*.	4073
Pr	18: 5 wicked, to **o** the righteous in judgment.	5186
Jer	49:18 As *in* the **o** of Sodom and Gomorrah and	4114
Hag	2:22 I will **o** the throne of kingdoms, and I will	2015
	2:22 I will **o** the chariots, and those that ride in	2015
Ac	5:39 But if it be of God, ye cannot **o** it;	2647
2Ti	2:18 is past already; and **o** the faith of some.	396
2Pe	2: 6 into ashes condemned *them* with an **o**,	2692

OVERTHROWETH (5) [OVERTHROW]

Job	12:19 princes away spoiled, and **o** the mighty.	5557
Pr	13: 6 in the way: but wickedness **o** the sinner.	5557
	21:12 *God* the wicked for *their* wickedness.	5557
	22:12 and he **o** the words of the transgressor.	5557
	29: 4 the land: but he that receiveth gifts **o** it.	2040

OVERTHROWN (16) [OVERTHROW]

Ex	15: 7 hast **o** them that rose up against thee:	2040
Jdg	9:40 him, and many were **o** *and* wounded,	5307
2Sa	17: 9 when *some* of them be **o** at the first,	5307
2Ch	14:13 the Ethiopians were **o**, that they could not	5307
Job	19: 6 Know now that God hath **o** me,	5791
Ps	141: 6 When their judges are **o** in stony places,	8058
Pr	11:11 but it is **o** by the mouth of the wicked.	2040
	12: 7 The wicked *are* **o**, and *are* not:	2015
	14:11 The house of the wicked shall be **o**:	8045
Isa	1: 7 and *it is* desolate, as **o** by strangers.	4114
Jer	18:23 thy sight, but let them be **o** before thee;	3782
La	4: 6 that *was* **o** as in a moment, and no hands	2015
Da	11:41 and many *countries* shall be **o**:	3782
Am	4:11 I have *some* of you, as God overthrew	2015
Jnh	3: 4 Yet forty days, and Nineveh *shall be* **o**.	2015
1Co	10: 5 for they were **o** in the wilderness.	2693

OVERTOOK (10) [OVERTAKE]

Ge	31:23 and they **o** him in the mount Gilead.	1692
	31:25 Laban **o** Jacob. Now Jacob had pitched his	5381
	44: 6 he **o** them, and he spake unto them these	5381
Ex	14: 9 **o** them encamping by the sea,	5381
Jdg	18:22 and the children of Dan.	1692
	20:42 the battle **o** them; and them which *came*	1692
2Ki	25: 5 king, and **o** him in the plains of Jericho:	5381
Jer	39: 5 and **o** Zedekiah in the plains of Jericho.	5381
	52: 8 and **o** Zedekiah in the plains of Jericho;	5381
La	1: 3 her persecutors **o** her between the straits.	4713

OVERTURN (4) [OVERTURNED, OVERTURNETH, TURN]

Job	12:15 sendeth them out, and they **o** the earth.	2015
Eze	21:27 I will **o**, overturn, overturn it: and it shall	5754
	21:27 I will overturn, **o**, overturn it: and it shall	5754

Eze 21:27 I will overturn, overturn, **o** it: and it shall 5754

OVERTURNED (1) [OVERTURN]
Jdg 7:13 it fell, and **o** it, 2015+4605+1886.5+3807.1

OVERTURNETH (3) [OVERTURN]
Job 9: 5 know not: which **o** them in his anger. 2015
 28: 9 rock; he **o** the mountains by the roots. 2015
 34:25 he **o** *them* in the night, so that they are 2015

OVERWHELM (1) [OVERWHELMED]
Job 6:27 ye **o** the fatherless, and you dig 5307+5921

OVERWHELMED (8) [OVERWHELM]
Ps 55: 5 are come upon me, and horror hath **o** me. 3680
 61: 2 will I cry unto thee, when my heart is **o**: 5848
 77: 3 I complained, and my spirit was **o**. Selah. 5848
 78:53 feared not: but the sea **o** their enemies. 3680
 102: T he is **o**, and poureth out his complaint 5848
 124: 4 the waters had **o** us, the stream had gone 7857
 142: 3 When my spirit was **o** within me, then 5848
 143: 4 Therefore is my spirit **o** within me; 5848

OWE (1) [OWEST, OWETH]
Ro 13: 8 O no *man* any *thing*, but to love one *3784*

OWEST (4) [OWE]
Mt 18:28 by the throat, saying, Pay me that thou **o**. *3784*
Lk 16: 5 the first, How much thou unto my lord? *3784*
 16: 7 he to another, And how much thou? *3784*
Phm 1:19 **o** unto me even thine own self **besides**. *4359*

OWETH (2) [OWE]
Ac 21:11 Jerusalem bind the man that **o** this girdle, *1510*
Phm 1:18 If he hath wronged thee, or **o** *thee* ought, *3784*

OWL (10) [OWLS]
Lev 11:16 the **o**, and the night hawk, 1323+3284
 11:17 the **little o**, and the cormorant, 3563
 11:17 and the cormorant, and the **great o**, 3244
Dt 14:15 the **o**, and the night hawk, 1323+3284
 14:16 The **little o**, and the great owl, 3563
 14:16 little owl, and the **great o**, and the swan, 3244
Ps 102: 6 wilderness: I am like an **o** of the desert. 3563
Isa 34:11 the **o** also and the raven shall dwell in it: 3244
 34:14 the **shrich o** also shall rest there, 3917
 34:15 There shall the **great o** make her nest, 7091

OWLS (6) [OWL]
Job 30:29 to dragons, and a companion to **o**. 1323+3284
Isa 13:21 **o** shall dwell there, and satyrs shall 1323+3284
 34:13 of dragons, *and* a court for **o**. 1323+3284
 43:20 honour me, the dragons and the **o**: 1323+3284
Jer 50:39 and the **o** shall dwell therein: 1323+3284
Mic 1: 8 dragons, and mourning as the **o**. 1323+3284

OWN (596) [OWNER, OWNERS, OWNETH]
Ge 1:27 So God created man in **his o** image, 2050.2
 5: 3 and begat a son in **his o** likeness, 2050.2
 14:14 trained *servants*, born in **his o** house, 2050.2
 15: 4 he that shall come forth out of **thine o** 3509.2
 30:25 that I may go unto **mine o** place, 2967.1
 30:30 now when shall I provide for **mine o** 2967.1
 30:40 he put **his o** flocks by 2050.2+3807.1
 47:24 four parts shall be **your o**, for seed of 3641.1
Ex 5:16 the fault *is in* **thine o** people. 3509.2
 18:27 and he went his way into **his o** land. 2050.2
 21:36 and the dead shall be **his o**. 2050.2+3807.1
 22: 5 of the best of **his o** field, and of the best 1930.2
 22: 5 of the best of **his o** vineyard, shall he 2050.2
 32:13 to whom thou swarest by **thine o** self, 3509.2
Lev 1: 3 he shall offer it of **his o** voluntary will at 2050.2
 7:30 **His o** hands shall bring the offerings of 2050.2
 14:15 into the palm of **his o** left hand: 3548+1886.1
 14:26 into the palm of **his o** left hand: 3548+1886.1
 16:29 *whether it be* one of **your o** country, 249
 17:15 *whether it be* one of **your o** country, 249
 18:10 for theirs *is* **thine o** nakedness. 3509.2
 18:26 *neither* any of **your o** nation, nor any 249
 19: 5 ye shall offer it at **your o** will. 3641.1
 21:14 he shall take a virgin of **his o** people to 2050.2
 22:19 Ye shall offer at **your o** will a male 3641.1
 22:29 unto the Lord, offer *it* at **your o** will. 3641.1
 24:22 stranger, as for one of **your o** country: 249
 25: 5 **That which groweth** of it **o** accord of 5599
 25:41 shall return unto **his o** family, 2050.2
Nu 1:52 every man by **his o** camp, and every 1930.2
 1:52 every man by **his o** standard, 2050.2
 2: 2 of Israel shall pitch by **his o** standard, 2050.2
 10:30 I will depart to **mine o** land, and to my 2967.1
 13:33 we were in **our o** sight as grasshoppers, 5105.1
 15:39 that ye seek not after **your o** heart and 3641.1
 15:39 after your own heart and **your o** eyes, 3641.1
 16:28 *I have* not *done them* of **mine o** mind. 2967.1
 16:38 of these sinners against **their o** souls, 3963.1
 24:13 do *either* good or bad of **mine o** mind; 2967.1
 27: 3 but died in **his o** sin, and had no sons. 2050.2
 32:42 and called it Nobah, after **his o** name. 2050.2
 36: 9 shall keep himself to **his o** inheritance. 2050.2
Dt 3:14 called them after **his o** name, 2050.2
 12: 8 every man whatsoever *is* right in **his o** 2050.2
 13: 6 or thy friend, which *is as* **thine o** soul, 3509.2
 22: 2 thou shalt bring it unto **thine o** house, 3509.2
 23:24 mayest eat grapes thy fill at **thine o** 3509.2
 24:13 that he may sleep in **his o** raiment, 2050.2
 24:16 man shall be put to death for **his o** 2050.2

Dt 28:53 thou shalt eat the fruit of **thine o** body, 3509.2
 33: 9 his brethren, nor knew his children: 2050.2
Jos 7:11 have put *it* even amongst **their o** stuff. 1992.1
 20: 6 come unto **his o** city, and unto his own 2050.2
 20: 6 his own city, and unto **his o** house, 2050.2
Jdg 2:19 they ceased not from **their o** doings, 1992.1
 7: 2 saying, Mine **o** hand hath saved me. 2967.1
 8:29 Joash went and dwelt in **his o** house. 2050.2
 17: 6 did *that which was* right in **his o** eyes. 2050.2
 21:25 did *that which was* right in **his o** eyes. 2050.2
Ru 4: 6 myself, lest I mar **mine o** inheritance. 2967.1
1Sa 2:20 And they went unto **their o** home. 2050.2
 5:11 let it go again to **his o** place, that it slay 2050.2
 6: 9 if it goeth up *by* the way of **his o** coast 2050.2
 13:14 sought him a man after **his o** heart, 2050.2
 14:46 the Philistines went to **their o** place. 3963.1
 15:17 When thou *wast* little in **thine o** sight, 3509.2
 18: 1 and Jonathan loved him as **his o** soul. 2050.2
 18: 3 because he loved him as **his o** soul. 2050.2
 20:17 for he loved him as he loved **his o** soul. 2050.2
 20:30 the son of Jesse to **thine o** confusion, 3509.2
 25:26 avenging thyself with **thine o** hand, 3509.2
 25:33 avenging myself with **mine o** hand. 2967.1
 25:39 wickedness of Nabal upon **his o** head. 2050.2
 28: 3 him in Ramah, even in **his o** city. 2050.2
2Sa 4:11 person in **his o** house upon his bed? 2050.2
 6:22 and will be base in **mine o** sight: 2967.1
 7:10 they may dwell in a place of **their o**, 2050.2
 7:21 and according to **thine o** heart, 3509.2
 12: 3 it did eat of **his o** meat, and drank of 2050.2
 12: 3 drank of **his o** cup, and lay in his 2050.2
 12: 4 he spared to take of **his o** flock and of 2050.2
 12: 4 take of his own flock and of **his o** herd, 2050.2
 12:11 evil against thee out of **thine o** house, 3509.2
 12:20 he came to **his o** house; and when he 2050.2
 14:24 Let him turn to **his o** house, and let 2050.2
 14:24 So Absalom returned to **his o** house, and 2050.2
 17:11 *that* thou go to battle in **thine o** person. 3509.2
 18:13 wrought falsehood against **mine o** life: 2967.1
 18:18 he called the pillar after **his o** name: 2050.2
 19:28 them that did eat at **thine o** table. 3509.2
 19:30 come *again* in peace unto **his o** house. 2050.2
 19:37 that I may die in **mine o** city, 2967.1
 19:39 and he returned unto **his o** place. 2050.2
 23:21 and slew him with **his o** spear. 2050.2
1Ki 1:12 that thou mayest save **thine o** life, 3509.3
 1:33 son to ride upon **mine o** mule, 2967.1+3807.1
 2:23 not spoken this word against **his o** life. 2050.2
 2:26 thee *to* Anathoth, unto **thine o** fields; 3509.2
 2:32 shall return **his o** blood upon **his o** head, 2050.2
 2:34 he was buried in **his o** house in 2050.2
 2:37 thy blood shall be upon **thine o** head. 3509.2
 2:44 thy wickedness upon **thine o** head; 3509.2
 3: 1 made an end of building **his o** house, 2050.2
 7: 1 Solomon was building **his o** house 2050.2
 8:38 every man the plague of **his o** heart, 2050.2
 9:15 **his o** house, and Millo, and the wall of 2050.2
 10: 6 a true report that I heard in **mine o** 2967.1
 10:13 she turned and went to **her o** country, 1886.3
 11:19 he gave him *to* wife the sister of **his o** 2050.2
 11:21 that I may go to **mine o** country. 2967.1
 11:22 thou seekest to go to **thine o** country? 3509.2
 12:16 now see to **thine o** house, David. 3509.2
 12:33 which he had devised of **his o** heart; 2050.2
 13:30 he laid his carcase in **his o** grave; 2050.2
 14:12 therefore, get thee to **thine o** house: 3509.3
 17:19 he abode, and laid him upon **his o** bed. 2050.2
 22:36 city, and every man to **his o** country. 2050.2
2Ki 2:12 he took hold of **his o** clothes, 2050.2
 3:27 from him, and returned to **their o** land. NIH
 4:13 I dwell among **mine o** people. 2967.1
 12:18 **his o** hallowed *things*, and all the gold 2050.2
 14: 6 man shall be put to death for **his o** 2050.2
 17:23 was Israel carried away out of **their o** 2050.2
 17:29 every nation made gods of **their o**, 1992.1
 17:33 the Lord, and served **their o** gods, 1992.1
 18:27 *they* may eat **their o** dung, and drink 3963.1
 18:27 and drink **their o** piss with you? 1992.1
 18:31 then eat ye every man of **his o** vine, 2050.2
 18:32 you away to a land like **your o** land, 3641.1
 19: 7 rumour, and shall return to **his o** land; 2050.2
 19: 7 him to fall by the sword in **his o** land. 2050.2
 19:34 for **mine o** sake, and for my servant 2967.1
 20: 6 I will defend this city for **mine o** sake, 2967.1
 21:18 buried in the garden of **his o** house, 2050.2
 21:23 and slew the king in **his o** house. 2050.2
 23:30 and buried him in **his o** sepulchre. 2050.2
1Ch 11:23 and slew him with **his o** spear. 2050.2
 17:19 and according to **thine o** heart, 3509.2
 17:21 to redeem *to be* **his o** people, 2050.2+3807.1
 17:22 make **thine o** people for ever; 3509.2+3807.1
 29: 3 I have of **mine o** proper good, 2967.1+3807.1
 29:14 thee, and of thine **o** have we given thee. 3027
 29:16 of thine hand, and *is* all **thine o**. 3509.2
2Ch 6:23 recompensing his way upon **his o** head; 2050.2
 6:29 when every one shall know **his o** sore 2050.2
 6:29 shall know his own sore and **his o** grief, 2050.2
 7:11 in **his o** house, he prosperously effected. 2050.2
 8: 1 the house of the Lord, and **his o** house, 2050.2
 9: 5 I heard in **mine o** land of thine acts, 2967.1
 9:12 went away to **her o** land, she and 1886.3
 10:16 *and* now, David, see to **thine o** house. 2050.2
 16:14 they buried him in **his o** sepulchres, 2050.2
 24:25 **his o** servants conspired against him for 2050.2
 25: 4 but every man shall die for **his o** sin. 2050.2

2Ch 25:15 which could not deliver **their o** people 3963.1
 31: 1 to his possession, into **their o** cities. 1992.1
 32:21 with shame of face to **his o** land. 2050.2
 32:21 that came forth of **his o** bowels slew 2050.2
 33:20 and they buried him *in* **his o** house: 2050.2
 33:24 him, and slew him in **his o** house. 2050.2
Ezr 7:13 *are* **minded** of their **o** freewill to go 5069
Ne 4: 4 turn their reproach upon **their o** head, 3963.1
 6: 8 feignest them out of **thine o** heart. 3509.2
 6:16 were much cast down in **their o** eyes: 1992.1
Est 1:22 every man should bear rule in **his o** 2050.2
 2: 7 were dead, took for **his o** daughter. 2050.2
 9:25 should return upon **his o** head, and that 2050.2
Job 2:11 they came every one from **his o** place; 2050.2
 5:13 He taketh the wise in **their o** craftiness: 3963.1
 9:20 **mine o** mouth shall condemn me: 2967.1
 9:31 and **mine o** clothes shall abhor me. 2967.1
 13:15 will maintain **mine o** ways before him. 2967.1
 15: 6 **Thine o** mouth condemneth thee, 3509.2
 15: 6 yea, **thine o** lips testify against thee. 3509.2
 18: 7 and **his o** counsel shall cast him down. 1930.2
 18: 8 For he is cast into a net by **his o** feet, 2050.2
 19:17 for the children's *sake* of mine **o** body. NIH
 20: 7 *Yet* he shall perish for ever like **his o** 2050.2
 32: 1 because he *was* righteous in **his o** eyes. 2050.2
 40:14 I also confess unto thee that **thine o** 3509.2
Ps 4: 4 commune with **your o** heart upon your 3641.1
 5:10 God; let them fall by **their o** counsels; 1992.1
 7:16 mischief shall return upon **his o** head, 2050.2
 7:16 shall come down upon **his o** pate. 2050.2
 9:15 the net which they hid in **their o** foot 3963.1
 9:16 wicked is snared in the work of **his o** 2050.2
 12: 4 will we prevail; our lips *are* **our o**: 854
 15: 4 *He that* sweareth to *his* **o** hurt, NIH
 17:10 They are inclosed in **their o** fat: 4123.1
 20: 4 Grant thee according to **thine o** heart, 3509.2
 21:13 thou exalted, Lord, in **thine o** strength: 3509.2
 22:29 and none can keep alive **his o** soul. 2050.2
 33:12 people *whom* he hath chosen for **his o** 2050.2
 35:13 my prayer returned into **mine o** bosom. 2967.1
 36: 2 For he flattereth himself in **his o** eyes, 3963.1
 37:15 sword shall enter into **their o** heart, 3963.1
 41: 9 Yea, **mine o** familiar friend, in whom I 2967.1
 44: 3 land in possession by **their o** sword, 3963.1
 44: 3 neither did **their o** arm save them: 3509.3
 45:10 forget also **thine o** people, 3509.3
 49:11 call *their* lands after **their o** names. 3963.1
 50:20 thou slanderest **thine o** mother's son. 3509.2
 64: 8 So they shall make **their o** tongue to 3963.1
 67: 6 God, *even* **our o** God, shall bless us. 5105.1
 74:22 Arise, O God, plead **thine o** cause: 3509.2
 77: 6 I commune with **mine o** heart: 2967.1
 78:29 for he gave them **their o** desire; 2050.2
 78:52 his **o** people to go forth like sheep, 3963.1
 81:12 So I gave them up unto **their o** heart's 3963.1
 81:12 *and* they walked in **their o** counsels. 1992.1
 94:23 shall bring upon them **their o** iniquity, 3963.1
 94:23 cut them off in **their o** wickedness; 3963.1
 106:39 Thus were they defiled with **their o** 1992.1
 106:39 a whoring with **their o** inventions. 1992.1
 106:40 insomuch that he abhorred **his o** 2050.2
 109:29 let them cover *themselves* with **their o** 3963.1
 138: 8 forsake not the works of **thine o** hands. 3509.2
 140: 9 the mischief of **their o** lips cover them. 4123.1
 141:10 Let the wicked fall into **their o** nets, 2050.2
Pr 1:18 they lay wait for **their o** blood; they 3963.1
 1:18 they lurk privily for **their o** lives. 3963.1
 1:31 shall they eat of the fruit of **their o** way, 3963.1
 1:31 and be filled with **their o** devices. 1992.1
 3: 5 lean not unto **thine o** understanding. 3509.2
 3: 7 Be not wise in **thine o** eyes: fear 3509.2
 5:15 Drink waters out of **thine o** cistern, 3509.2
 5:15 and running waters out of **thine o** well. 3509.2
 5:17 Let them be only **thine o**, 3509.2+3807.1
 5:22 **His o** iniquities shall take the wicked 2050.2
 6:32 he *that* doeth it destroyeth **his o** soul. 1931
 8:36 that sinneth *against* me wrongeth **his o** 2050.2
 11: 5 wicked shall fall by **his o** wickedness. 2050.2
 11: 6 transgressors shall be taken in **their o** NIH
 11:17 The merciful man doeth good to **his o** 2050.2
 11:17 *he that is* cruel troubleth **his o** flesh. 2050.2
 11:19 that pursueth evil *pursueth it* to **his o** 2050.2
 11:29 He that troubleth **his o** house shall 2050.2
 12:15 The way of a fool *is* right in **his o** eyes: 2050.2
 14:10 heart knoweth **his o** bitterness; 5315+2050.2
 14:14 in heart shall be filled with **his o** ways: 2050.2
 14:20 The poor is hated even of **his o** 1930.2
 15:27 that is greedy of gain troubleth **his o** 2050.2
 15:32 instruction despiseth **his o** soul: 2050.2
 16: 2 the ways of a man *are* clean in **his o** 2050.2
 18:11 and as a high wall in **his o** conceit. 2050.2
 18:17 *He that is* first in **his o** cause *seemeth* 2050.2
 19: 8 that getteth wisdom loveth **his o** soul: 2050.2
 19:16 the commandment keepeth **his o** soul; 2050.2
 20: 2 him to anger sinneth *against* **his o** soul. 2050.2
 20: 6 men will proclaim every one **his o** 2050.2
 20:24 can a man then understand **his o** way? 2050.2
 21: 2 way of a man *is* right in **his o** eyes: 2050.2
 23: 4 to be rich: cease from **thine o** wisdom. 3509.2
 25:27 men to search **their o** glory *is not* glory. 3963.1
 25:28 He that *hath* no rule over **his o** spirit *is* 2050.2
 26: 5 folly, lest he be wise in **his o** conceit. 2050.2
 26:12 Seest thou a man wise in **his o** conceit? 2050.2
 26:16 The sluggard *is* wiser in **his o** conceit 2050.2
 27: 2 praise thee, and not **thine o** mouth; 3509.2

Pr 27: 2 a stranger, and not **thine** o lips. 3509.2
27:10 **Thine** o friend, and thy father's friend, 3509.2
28:10 he shall fall himself into **his** o pit: 2050.2
28:11 The rich man *is* wise in **his** o conceit; 2050.2
28:26 He that trusteth in **his** o heart *is* a fool: 2050.2
29:24 is partner with a thief hateth **his** o 2050.2
30:12 generation *that are* pure in **their** o eyes, 2050.2
31:31 let **her** o works praise her in the gates. 1886.3
Ecc 1:16 I communed with **mine** o heart, saying, 2967.1
3:22 than that a man should rejoice in **his** o 2050.2
4: 5 hands together, and eateth **his** o flesh. 2050.2
7:22 oftentimes also **thine** o heart knoweth 3509.2
8: 9 over another to **his** o hurt. 2050.2+3807.1
SS 1: 6 *but* **mine** o vineyard have I not kept. 2967.1
Isa 2: 8 they worship the work of **their** o hands, 2050.2
2: 8 *that* which **their** o fingers have made: 2050.2
4: 1 We will eat **our** o bread, and wear our 5105.1
4: 1 our own bread, and wear our o apparel: 5105.1
5:21 Woe unto *them that are* wise in **their** o 1992.1
5:21 own eyes, and prudent in **their** o sight! 1992.1
9:20 shall eat every man the flesh of **his** o 2050.2
13:14 shall every man turn to **his** o people, 2050.2
13:14 and flee every one into **his** o land. 2050.2
14: 1 and set them in **their** o land: 3963.1
14:18 lie in glory, every one in **his** o house. 2050.2
23: 7 **her** o feet shall carry her afar off to 1886.3
31: 7 which **your** o hands have made unto 3641.1
36:12 they may eat **their** o dung, and drink 3963.1
36:12 and drink **their** o piss with you? 1992.1
36:16 drink ye every one the waters of **his** o 2050.2
36:17 you away to a land like **your** o land, 3641.1
37: 7 a rumour, and return to **his** o land; 2050.2
37: 7 him to fall by the sword in **his** o land. 2050.2
37:35 this city to save it for **mine** o sake, 2967.1
43:25 out thy transgressions for **mine** o sake, 2967.1
44: 9 they *are* witnesses; they see not, 1992.1
48:11 For **mine** o sake, *even* for mine own 2967.1
48:11 mine own sake, *even* for **mine** o 2967.1
49:26 that oppress thee with **their** o flesh; 3963.1
49:26 shall be drunken with **their** o blood, 3963.1
53: 6 we have turned every one to **his** o way; 2050.2
56:11 they all look to **their** o way, every one 3963.1
58: 7 that thou hide not thyself from **thine** o 3509.2
58:13 honour him, not doing **thine** o ways, 3509.2
58:13 own ways, nor finding **thine** o pleasure, 3509.2
58:13 pleasure, nor speaking *thine o* words: NIH
63: 5 **mine** o arm brought salvation unto me; 2967.1
65: 2 was not good, after **their** o thoughts; 1992.1
66: 3 they have chosen **their** o ways, 1992.1
Jer 1:16 worshipped the works of **their** o hands. 1992.1
2:19 **Thine** o wickedness shall correct thee, 3509.3
2:30 **your** o sword hath devoured your 3641.1
7:19 to the confusion of **their** o faces? 1992.1
9:14 after the imagination of **their** o heart, 3963.1
18:12 we will walk after **our** o devices, 5105.1
23: 8 and they shall dwell in **their** o land. 3963.1
23:16 they speak a vision of **their** o heart, 3963.1
23:17 after the imagination of **their** o heart, 2050.2
23:26 *are* prophets of the deceit of **their** o 3963.1
25: 7 the works of your hands to **your** o hurt. 3641.1
25:14 to the works of **their** o hands. 1992.1
27:11 will I let remain still in **their** o land, 2050.2
30:18 city shall be builded upon **her** o heap, 1886.3
31:17 shall come again to **their** o border. 3963.1
31:30 every one shall die for **his** o iniquity: 2050.2
37: 7 shall return to Egypt into **their** o land. 2050.2
42:12 and cause you to return to **your** o land. 3641.1
44: 9 **your** o wickedness, and the wickedness 3641.1
44:17 thing goeth forth out of **our** o mouth, 5105.1
46:16 let us go again to **our** o people, and to 5105.1
50:16 they shall flee every one to **his** o land. 2050.2
51: 9 let us go every one into **his** o country: 2050.2
52:27 carried away captive out of **his** o land. 2050.2
La 4:10 women have sodden **their** o children: 2006.1
Eze 11:21 will recompense their way upon **their** o 3963.1
13: 2 that prophesy out of **their** o hearts, 3963.1
13: 3 that follow **their** o spirit, and have seen 3963.1
14: 5 which prophesy out of **their** o heart; 2006.1
14: 5 take the house of Israel in **their** o heart, 3963.1
14:14 *but* **their** o souls by their righteousness, 3963.1
14:20 **their** o souls by their righteousness. 3963.1
16: 6 and saw thee polluted in **thine** o blood, 3509.3
16:15 thou didst trust in **thine** o beauty, 3509.3
16:52 bear **thine** o shame for thy sins that 3509.3
16:54 That thou mayest bear **thine** o shame, 3509.3
17:19 it will I recompense upon **his** o head. 2050.2
20:26 I polluted them in **their** o gifts, in that 3963.1
20:43 ye shall lothe yourselves in **your** o sight 3641.1
22:31 **their** o way have I recompensed upon 3963.1
23:34 and pluck off **thine** o breasts: 3509.3
29: 3 My river *is* **mine** o, and I have 2967.1+3807.1
32:10 every man for **his** o life, in the day of 2050.2
33: 4 his blood shall be upon **his** o head. 2050.2
33:13 if he trust to **his** o righteousness, 2050.2
34:13 will bring them to **their** o land, 3963.1
36:17 the house of Israel dwelt in **their** o 3963.1
36:17 they defiled it by **their** o way and by 3963.1
36:24 and will bring you into **your** o land. 3641.1
36:31 shall ye remember **your** o evil ways, 3641.1
36:31 shall lothe yourselves in **your** o sight 3641.1
36:32 and confounded for **your** o ways, 3641.1
37:14 and I shall place you in **your** o land: 3641.1
37:21 and bring them into **their** o land: 3963.1
39:28 have gathered them into **their** o land, 3963.1
46:18 inheritance out of **his** o possession: 2050.2

Da 3:28 worship any god, except **their** o God. 1952.1
6:17 the king sealed it with **his** o signet, 1886.8
8:24 shall be mighty, but not by **his** o power: 2050.2
9:19 defer not, for **thine** o sake, O my God: 3509.2
11: 9 and shall return into **his** o land. 2050.2
11:16 him shall do according to **his** o will, 2050.2
11:18 a prince for **his** o behalf shall cause 2050.2
11:18 without **his** o reproach he shall cause 2050.2
11:19 his face towards the fort of **his** o land: 2050.2
11:28 do *exploits*, and return to **his** o land. 2050.2
Hos 7: 2 now **their** o doings have beset them 1992.1
10: 6 shall be ashamed of **his** o counsel. 2050.2
11: 6 *them*, because of **their** o counsels. 1992.1
13: 2 according to **their** o understanding, 3963.1
Joel 3: 4 your recompence upon **your** o head; 3641.1
3: 7 return your recompence upon **your** o 3641.1
Am 6:13 Have we not taken to us horns by **our** o 5105.1
7:11 be led away captive out of **their** o land. 2050.2
Ob 1:15 reward shall return upon **thine** o head. 3509.2
Jnh 2: 8 lying vanities forsake **their** o mercy. 3963.1
Mic 7: 6 a man's enemies *are* the men of **his** o 2050.2
Hag 1: 9 ye run every man unto **his** o house. 2050.2
Zec 5:11 and set there upon **her** o base. 1886.3
11: 5 and **their** o shepherds pity them not. 1992.1
12: 6 shall be inhabited again in **her** o place, 1886.3
Mal 3:17 man spareth **his** o son that serveth him. 2050.2
Mt 2:12 departed into **their** o country another 846
7: 3 not the beam that is in **thine** o 4674
7: 4 and behold, a beam *is* in **thine** o eye? 4771
7: 5 cast out the beam out of **thine** o eye; 4771
9: 1 passed over, and came into **his** o city. 2398
10:36 And a man's foes *shall be* they of **his** o 846
13:54 when he was come into **his** o country, 846
13:57 in **his** o country, and in his own house. 846
13:57 in his own country, and in **his** o house. 846
16:26 gain the whole world, and lose **his** o soul? 846
17:25 of **their** o children, or of strangers? 846
20:15 for me to do what I will with **mine** o? 1699
25:14 who called **his** o servants, 2398
25:27 should have received **mine** o with usury. 1699
27:31 put **his** o raiment on him, and led him 846
27:60 laid it in **his** o new tomb, which he had 846
Mk 6: 1 from thence, and came into **his** o country; 846
6: 4 in **his** o country, and among his own kin, 846
6: 4 among **his** o kin, and in his own house. 846
6: 4 among his own kin, and in **his** o house. 846
7: 9 God, that ye may keep **your** o tradition. 4771
8: 3 And if I send them away fasting to **their** o 846
8:36 gain the whole world, and lose **his** o soul? 846
15:20 and put his o clothes on him, and led him 2398
Lk 1:23 he departed to **his** o house. 846
1:56 three months, and returned to **her** o house. 846
2: 3 to be taxed, every one into **his** o city. 2398
2:35 sword shall pierce through thy o soul also,) 846
2:39 into Galilee, to **their** o city Nazareth. 846
4:24 No prophet is accepted in **his** o country. 846
5:25 departed to **his** o house, glorifying God. 846
5:29 And Levi made him a great feast in **his** o 846
6:41 perceivest not the beam that is in **thine** o 2398
6:42 not the beam that is in **thine** o eye? 4771
6:42 cast out first the beam out of **thine** o eye, 4771
6:44 For every tree is known by **his** o fruit. 2398
8:39 Return to **thine** o house, and shew how 4771
9:26 when he shall come in **his** o glory, and 846
10:34 set him on **his** o beast, and brought him 2398
14:26 and sisters, yea, and **his** o life also, 1438
16:12 who shall give you that which is **your** o? 5212
18: 7 And shall not God avenge **his** o elect, 846
19:22 Out of **thine** o mouth will I judge thee, 4771
19:23 I might have required **mine** o with usury? NIG
21:30 know of **your** o selves that summer is 1438
22:71 we ourselves have heard of **his** o mouth. 846
Jn 1:11 came unto **his** o, and his own received 2398
1:11 his own, and **his** o received him not. 2398
1:41 He first findeth **his** o brother Simon, 2398
4:41 many moe believed because of his o word; NIG
4:44 that a prophet hath no honour in **his** o 2398
5:30 I can of **mine** o self do nothing: as I hear, 1683
5:30 is just; because I seek not **mine** o will, 1699
5:43 if another shall come in **his** o name, him 2398
6:38 not to do **mine** o will, but the will of him 1699
7:18 He that speaketh of himself seeketh **his** o 2398
7:53 And every man went unto **his** o house. 846
8: 9 *it*, being convicted by *their o* conscience, NIG
8:44 he speaketh a lie, he speaketh of **his** o: 2398
8:50 I seek not **mine** o glory: there is *one* 1473
10: 3 and he calleth **his** o sheep by name, 2398
10: 4 And when he putteth forth **his** o sheep, 2398
10:12 the shepherd, whose o the sheep are not, 2398
13: 1 having loved **his** o which were in 2398
15:19 the world, the world would love **his** o: 2398
16:32 every man to **his** o, and shall leave me 2398
17: 5 glorify thou me with **thine** o self with 4572
17:11 keep through **thine** o name those whom 4571
18:35 **Thine** o nation and the chief priests have 4674
19:27 *that* disciple took her unto **his** o *home*. 1438
20:10 went away again unto **their** o home. 1438
Ac 1: 7 the Father hath put in **his** o power. 2398
1:25 that *he* might go to **his** o place. 2398
2: 6 every man heard them speak in **his** o 2398
2: 8 And how hear we every man in **our** o 2398
3:12 as though by **our** o power or holiness we 2398
4:23 they went to **their** o company, and 2398
4:32 the *things* which he possessed was **his** o; 2398
5: 4 Whiles it remained, was it not **thine** o? 4771

Ac 5: 4 it was sold, was it not in **thine** o power? 4674
7:21 him up, and nourished him for **her** o son, 1438
7:41 and rejoiced in the works of **their** o hands. 846
12:10 which opened to them of **his** o accord: 844
13:22 man after **mine** o heart, which shall fulfil 1473
13:36 after he had served **his** o generation by 2398
14:16 all nations to walk in **their** o ways. 846
15:22 send chosen men of **their** o company to 846
17:28 as certain also of **your** o poets have 2596+4771
18: 6 Your blood *be* upon **your** o heads; 4771
20:28 he hath purchased with **his** o blood. 2398
20:30 Also of your **selves** shall men arise, 846
21:11 and bound his o hands and feet, and said, NIG
25:19 against him of **their** o superstition, 2398
26: 4 was at the first among **mine** o nation 1473
27:19 **with** our o hands the tackling of the ship. 849
28:30 And Paul dwelt two whole years in **his** o 2398
Ro 1:24 through the lusts of **their** o hearts, 846
1:24 to dishonour **their** o bodies between 846
4:19 he considered not **his** o body now dead, 1438
8: 3 God sending **his** o Son in the likeness of 1438
8:32 He that spared not **his** o Son, 2398
10: 3 going about to establish **their** o 2398
11:24 be graffed into **their** o olive tree? 2398
11:25 ye should be wise in **your** o conceits; 1438
12:16 estate. Be not wise in **your** o conceits. 1438
14: 4 to his master he standeth or falleth. 2398
14: 5 man be fully persuaded in **his** o mind. 2398
16: 4 Who have for my life laid down **their** o 1438
16:18 our Lord Jesus Christ, but **their** o belly; 1438
1Co 1:15 say that I had baptized in **mine** o name. 1699
3: 8 every man shall receive **his** o reward 2398
3: 8 own reward according to **his** o labour. 2398
3:19 He taketh the wise in **their** o craftiness. 846
4: 3 yea, I judge not **mine** o self. 1683
4:12 And labour, working with **our** o hands: 2398
6:14 and will *also* raise us up by **his** o power. 846
6:18 fornication sinneth against **his** o body. 2398
6:19 ye have of God, and ye are not **your** o? 1438
7: 2 let every man have **his** o wife, and let 1438
7: 2 let every woman have **her** o husband. 2398
7: 4 The wife hath not power of **her** o body, 2398
7: 4 husband hath not power of **his** o body, 2398
7:35 this I speak for your o profit; not that I 846
7:37 hath power over **his** o will, and hath so 2398
9: 7 Who goeth a warfare any time at **his** o 1438
10:24 Let no *man* seek **his** o, but every man 1438
10:29 I say, not **thine** o, but of the other's: 1438
10:33 in all *things*, not seeking **mine** o profit, 1683
11:21 one taketh before *other* **his** o supper: 2398
13: 5 seeketh not **her** o, is not easily provoked, 1438
15:23 But every man in **his** o order: Christ 2398
15:38 him, and to every seed **his** o body. 2398
16:21 The salutation of *me* Paul with **mine** o 1699
2Co 6:12 but ye are straitened in **your** o bowels. 4771
8: 5 but first gave **their** o selves to the Lord, 1438
8:17 of **his** o accord he went unto you. 830
11:26 of robbers, in perils by *my* o countrymen, NIG
13: 5 ye be in the faith; prove **your** o selves. 1438
13: 5 Know ye not **your** o selves, how that 1438
Gal 1:14 above many *my* equals in **mine** o nation, 1473
4:15 ye would have plucked out **your** o eyes, 4771
6: 4 But let every man prove **his** o work, 1438
6: 5 For every man shall bear **his** o burden. 2398
6:11 have written unto you with **mine** o hand. 1699
Eph 1:11 all *things* after the counsel of **his** o will: 846
1:20 set *him* at **his** o right hand in the heavenly 846
5:22 submit yourselves unto **your** o husbands, 2398
5:24 *let* the wives be to **their** o husbands in 2398
5:28 ought men to love their wives as **their** o 1438
5:29 For no *man* ever yet hated **his** o flesh; 1438
Php 2: 4 Look not every man on **his** o *things*, but 1438
2:12 work out **your** o salvation with fear and 1438
2:21 For all seek **their** o, not the *things which* 1438
3: 9 not having **mine** o righteousness, which 1699
3:18 submit yourselves unto **your** o husbands, 2398
2: 8 also **our** o souls, because ye were dear 1438
2:14 like *things* of **your** o countrymen, 2398
2:15 their o prophets, and have persecuted 2398
4:11 and to do **your** o *business*, and to work 2398
4:11 and to work with your o hands, 2398
2Th 3:12 they work, and eat **their** o bread. 1438
3:17 The salutation of Paul with **mine** o hand, 1699
1Ti 1: 2 Unto Timothy, *my* o son in the faith: 1103
3: 4 One that ruleth well **his** o house, having 2398
3: 5 (For if a man know not how to rule **his** o 2398
3:12 *their* children and **their** o houses well. 2398
5: 8 But if any provide not for **his** o, 2398
5: 8 and specially for those of **his** o house, NIG
6: 1 their o masters worthy of all honour, 2398
2Ti 1: 9 but according to **his** o purpose and grace, 2398
3: 2 men shall be lovers of **their** o selves, 5367
4: 3 after **their** o lusts shall they heap to 2398
Tit 1: 4 *mine* o son after the common faith: 1103
1:12 *even* a prophet of **their** o, said, 2398
2: 5 good, obedient to **their** o husbands, 2398
2: 9 servants to be obedient unto **their** o 2398
Phm 1:12 receive him, that is, **mine** o bowels: 1699
1:19 I Paul have written *it* with **mine** o hand, 1699
1:19 owest unto me even **thine** o self besides. 4572
Heb 2: 4 of the Holy Ghost, according to **his** o will? 846
3: 6 But Christ as a Son over **his** o house; 2398
4:10 he also hath ceased from **his** o works, 2398
7:27 first for **his** o sins, *and* then for 2398
9:12 by **his** o blood he entered in once into 2398

Heb	12:10 days chastened *us* after **their o** pleasure;	846
	13:12 he might sanctify the people with **his o**	2398
Jas	1:14 when he is drawn away of **his o** lust,	2398
	1:18 **Of** his **o will** begat he us with the word	1014
	1:22 hearers only, deceiving **your o** selves.	1438
	1:26 not his tongue, but deceiveth **his o** heart,	846
1Pe	2:24 **his o** self bare our sins in his own body	846
	2:24 his own self bare our sins in **his o** body	846
	3: 1 *be* in subjection to **your o** husbands;	2398
	3: 5 in subjection unto **their o** husbands.	2398
2Pe	2:12 shall utterly perish in their **o** corruption;	846
	2:13 themselves with **their o** deceivings	2398
	2:22 The dog *is* turned to **his o** vomit again;	2398
	3: 3 days scoffers, walking after **their o** lusts,	2398
	3:16 scriptures, unto **their o** destruction.	2398
	3:17 the wicked, fall from **your o** stedfastness.	2398
1Jn	3:12 Because **his o** works were evil, and his	846
Jude	1: 6 first estate, but left **their o** habitation,	2398
	1:13 of the sea, foaming out **their o** shame;	1438
	1:16 complainers, walking after **their o** lusts;	846
	1:18 who should walk after **their o** ungodly	1438
Rev	1: 5 washed us from our sins in **his o** blood,	846

OWNER (13) [OWN]

Ex	21:28 be eaten; but the **o** of the ox *shall be* quit.	1167
	21:29 it hath been testified to his **o**, and he hath	1167
	21:29 and his **o** also shall be put to death.	1167
	21:34 The **o** of the pit shall make *it* good,	1167
	21:34 good, *and* give money unto the **o** of them;	1167
	21:36 time past, and his **o** hath not kept him in;	1167
	22:11 the **o** of it shall accept *thereof*, and he	1167
	22:12 shall make restitution unto the **o** thereof.	1167
	22:14 or die, the **o** thereof *being* not with it,	1167
	22:15 *But if* the **o** thereof *be* with it, he shall not	1167
1Ki	16:24 name of Shemer, **o** of the hill, Samaria.	113
Isa	1: 3 The ox knoweth his **o**, and the ass his	7069
Ac	27:11 believed the master and the **o of the ship**,	3490

OWNERS (5) [OWN]

Job	31:39 caused the **o** thereof to lose their life:	1167
Pr	1:19 taketh away the life of the **o** thereof.	1167
Ecc	5:11 what good *is there* to the **o** thereof,	1167
	5:13 *namely*, riches kept for the **o** thereof to	1167
Lk	19:33 the **o** thereof said unto them, Why loose	2962

OWNETH (1) [OWN]

Lev	14:35 he that **o** the house shall come and tell	3807.1

OX (64) [OXEN]

Ex	20:17 his maidservant, nor his **o**, nor his ass,	7794
	21:28 If an **o** gore a man or a woman, that they	7794
	21:28 the **o** shall be surely stoned, and his flesh	7794
	21:28 but the owner of the **o** *shall be* quit.	7794
	21:29 if the **o** *were* wont to push with his horn	7794
	21:29 the **o** shall be stoned, and his owner also	7794
	21:32 If the **o** shall push a manservant or	7794
	21:32 *of* silver, and the **o** shall be stoned.	7794
	21:33 cover it, and an **o** or an ass fall therein;	7794
	21:35 one man's **o** hurt another's, that he die;	7794
	21:35 they shall sell the live **o**, and divide	7794
	21:35 and the dead *o* also they shall divide.	NIH
	21:36 Or *if* it be known that the **o** *hath* used to	7794
	21:36 he shall surely pay **o** for ox; and the dead	7794
	21:36 he shall surely pay ox for **o**; and the dead	7794
	22: 1 If a man shall steal an **o**, or a sheep,	7794
	22: 1 he shall restore five oxen for an **o**,	7794
	22: 4 alive, whether it be **o**, or ass, or sheep;	7794
	22: 9 *whether it be* for **o**, for ass, for sheep,	7794
	22:10 or an **o**, or a sheep, or any beast, to keep;	7794
	23: 4 If thou meet thine enemy's **o** or his ass	7794
	23:12 that thine **o** and thine ass may rest,	7794
	34:19 cattle, *whether* **o** or sheep, *that is* male.	7794
Lev	7:23 *manner* fat, of **o**, or of sheep, or of goat.	7794
	17: 3 that killeth an **o**, or lamb, or goat,	7794
	27:26 shall sanctify it; whether *it be* **o**, or sheep:	7794
Nu	7: 3 two of the princes, and for *each* one an **o**:	7794
	22: 4 as the **o** licketh up the grass of the field.	7794
Dt	5:14 maidservant, nor thine **o**, nor thine ass,	7794
	5:21 his **o**, or his ass, or any *thing* that *is* thy	7794
	14: 4 shall eat: the **o**, the sheep, and the goat,	7794
	14: 5 and the **wild o**, and the chamois,	8377
	18: 3 offer a sacrifice, whether *it be* **o** or sheep;	7794
	22: 1 Thou shalt not see thy brother's **o** or his	7794
	22: 4 ass or his **o** fall down by the way,	7794
	22:10 Thou shalt not plow with an **o** and an ass	7794
	25: 4 Thou shalt not muzzle the **o** when he	7794
	28:31 Thine **o** *shall be* slain before thine eyes,	7794
Jos	6:21 and old, and **o**, and sheep, and ass,	7794
Jdg	3:31 six hundred men with an **o** goad:	1241
	6: 4 for Israel, neither sheep, nor **o**, nor ass.	7794
1Sa	12: 3 whose **o** have I taken? or whose ass have	7794
	14:34 Bring me hither every man his **o**, and	7794
	14:34 the people brought every man his **o** with	7794
	15: 3 and suckling, **o** and sheep, camel and ass.	7794
Ne	5:18 was prepared *for me* daily was one **o**	7794
Job	6: 5 grass? or loweth the **o** over his fodder?	7794
	24: 3 they take the widow's **o** for a pledge.	7794
	40:15 made with thee; he eateth grass as an **o**.	1241
Ps	69:31 shall please the LORD better than an **o**	7794
	106:20 the similitude of an **o** that eateth grass.	7794
Pr	7:22 as an **o** goeth to the slaughter, or as a fool	7794
	14: 4 much increase *is* by the strength of the **o**.	7794
	15:17 than a stalled **o** and hatred therewith.	7794
Isa	1: 3 The **o** knoweth his owner, and the ass his	7794
	11: 7 and the lion shall eat straw like the **o**.	1241

Isa	32:20 send forth *thither* the feet of the **o** and	7794
	66: 3 He that killeth an **o** *is* as *if* he slew a man;	7794
Jer	11:19 or an **o** *that* is brought to the slaughter;	441
Eze	1:10 they four had the face of an **o** on the left	7794
Lk	13:15 one of you on the sabbath loose his **o**	1016
	14: 5 shall have an ass or an **o** fallen into a pit,	1016
1Co	9: 9 Thou shalt not muzzle the mouth of the **o**	1016
1Ti	5:18 Thou shalt not muzzle the **o** that treadeth	1016

OXEN (102) [OX]

Ge	12:16 **o**, and he asses, and menservants,	1241
	20:14 **o**, and menservants, and womenservants,	1241
	21:27 Abraham took sheep and **o**, and gave	1241
	32: 5 I have **o**, and asses, flocks,	7794
	34:28 their **o**, and their asses, and that which	1241
Ex	9: 3 camels, upon the **o**, and upon the sheep:	1241
	20:24 peace offerings, thy sheep, and thine **o**:	1241
	22: 1 he shall restore five **o** for an ox,	1241
	22:30 Likewise shalt thou do with thine **o**,	7794
	24: 5 sacrificed peace offerings *of* **o** unto	6499
Nu	7: 3 six covered wagons, and twelve **o**;	1241
	7: 6 Moses took the wagons and the **o**,	1241
	7: 7 four **o** he gave unto the sons of Gershon,	1241
	7: 8 eight **o** he gave unto the sons of Merari,	1241
	7:17 two **o**, five rams, five he goats, five lambs	1241
	7:23 two **o**, five rams, five he goats, five lambs	1241
	7:29 two **o**, five rams, five he goats, five lambs	1241
	7:35 two **o**, five rams, five he goats, five lambs	1241
	7:41 two **o**, five rams, five he goats, five lambs	1241
	7:47 two **o**, five rams, five he goats, five lambs	1241
	7:53 two **o**, five rams, five he goats, five lambs	1241
	7:59 two **o**, five rams, five he goats, five lambs	1241
	7:65 two **o**, five rams, five he goats, five lambs	1241
	7:71 two **o**, five rams, five he goats, five lambs	1241
	7:77 two **o**, five rams, five he goats, five lambs	1241
	7:83 two **o**, five rams, five he goats, five lambs	1241
	7:87 the **o** for the burnt offering *were* twelve	1241
	7:88 all the **o** for the sacrifice of the peace	1241
	22:40 Balak offered **o** and sheep, and sent to	1241
	23: 1 prepare me here seven **o** and seven rams.	6499
Dt	14:26 for **o**, or for sheep, or for wine,	1241
Jos	7:24 his **o**, and his asses, and his sheep, and	7794
1Sa	11: 7 he took a yoke of **o**, and hewed them in	1241
	11: 7 Samuel, so shall it be done unto his **o**.	1241
	14:14 of land, *which* a yoke of **o** *might plow*.	NIH
	14:32 **o**, and calves, and slew *them* on the	1241
	15: 9 the **o**, and of the fatlings, and the lambs,	1241
	15:14 the lowing of the **o** which I hear?	1241
	15:15 spared the best of the sheep and of the **o**,	1241
	15:21 the people took of the spoil, sheep and **o**,	1241
	22:19 sucklings, and **o**, and asses, and sheep,	7794
	27: 9 the **o**, and the asses, and the camels,	1241
2Sa	6: 6 and took hold of it; for the **o** shook *it*.	1241
	6:13 six paces, he sacrificed **o** and fatlings.	7794
	24:22 *be* **o** for burnt sacrifice, and threshing	1241
	24:22 and *other* instruments of the **o** for wood.	1241
	24:24 and the **o** for fifty shekels of silver.	1241
1Ki	1: 9 Adonijah slew sheep and **o** and fat cattle	1241
	1:19 he hath slain **o** and fat cattle and sheep in	7794
	1:25 hath slain **o** and fat cattle and sheep in	7794
	4:23 Ten fat **o**, and twenty oxen out of	1241
	4:23 twenty **o** out of the pastures,	1241
	7:25 It stood upon twelve **o**, three looking	1241
	7:29 the ledges *were* lions, **o**, and cherubims:	1241
	7:29 **o** *were certain* additions made of thin	1241
	7:44 And one sea, and twelve **o** under the sea;	1241
	8: 5 before the ark, sacrificing sheep and **o**,	1241
	8:63 two and twenty thousand **o**, and an	1241
	19:19 who *was* plowing *with* twelve yoke *of* **o**	NIH
	19:20 left the **o**, and ran after Elijah, and said,	1241
	19:21 took a yoke of **o**, and slew them, and	1241
	19:21 their flesh with the instruments of the **o**,	1241
2Ki	5:26 and menservants, and maidservants?	1241
	16:17 took down the sea from off the brasen **o**	1241
1Ch	12:40 on mules, and on **o**, *and* meat, meal,	1241
	12:40 and oil, and **o**, and sheep abundantly:	1241
	13: 9 hand to hold the ark; for the **o** stumbled.	1241
	21:23 I give *thee* the **o** also for burnt offerings,	1241
2Ch	4: 3 under it *was* the similitude of **o**, which	1241
	4: 3 Two rows of **o** were cast, when it was	1241
	4: 4 It stood upon twelve **o**, three looking	1241
	4:15 One sea, and twelve **o** under it.	1241
	5: 6 sacrificed sheep and **o**, which could not	1241
	7: 5 a sacrifice of twenty and two thousand **o**,	1241
	15:11 hundred and seven thousand sheep.	1241
	18: 2 killed sheep and **o** for him in abundance,	1241
	29:33 consecrated *things were* six hundred **o**	1241
	31: 6 they also brought in the tithe of **o** and	1241
	35: 8 *small cattle*, and three hundred **o**.	1241
	35: 9 *small cattle*, and five hundred **o**.	1241
	35:12 of Moses. And so *did they* with the **o**.	1241
Job	1: 3 five hundred yoke of **o**, and five hundred	1241
	1:14 were plowing, and the asses feeding	1241
	42:12 a thousand yoke of **o**, and a thousand she	1241
Ps	8: 7 All sheep and **o**, yea, and the beasts of	504
	144:14 *That* our **o** *may* be strong to labour;	441
Pr	14: 4 Where no **o** *are*, the crib *is* clean:	504
Isa	7:25 it shall be for the sending forth of **o**,	7794
	22:13 and gladness, slaying **o**, and killing sheep,	1241
	30:24 The **o** likewise and the young asses that	504
Jer	51:23 the husbandman and his **yoke of o**;	6776
Da	4:25 they shall make thee to eat grass as **o**,	8450
	4:32 they shall make thee to eat grass as **o**,	8450
	4:33 did eat grass as **o**, and his body was wet	8450
	5:21 they fed him with grass like **o**, and his	8450

Am	6:12 will *one* plow *there* with **o**? for ye have	1241
Mt	22: 4 my **o** and *my* fatlings *are* killed,	5022
Lk	14:19 I have bought five yoke of **o**, and I go to	1016
Jn	2:14 And found in the temple those that sold **o**,	1016
	2:15 of the temple, and the sheep and the **o**;	1016
Ac	14:13 brought **o** and garlands unto the gates,	5022
1Co	9: 9 out the corn. Doth God take care for **o**?	1016

OXGOAD See GOAD

OZEM (2)

1Ch	2:15 **O** the sixth, David the seventh:	684
	2:25 and Bunah, and Oren, and **O**, *and* Ahijah.	684

OZIAS (2) [AHAZIAH]

Mt	1: 8 Josaphat begat Joram; and Joram begat **O**;	3604
	1: 9 And **O** begat Joatham; and Joatham begat	3604

OZNI (1) [OZNITES]

Nu	26:16 Of **O**, the family of the Oznites: of Eri,	244

OZNITES (1) [OZNI]

Nu	26:16 Of Ozni, the family of the **O**: of Eri,	244

P

PAARAI (1)

2Sa	23:35 Hezrai the Carmelite, **P** the Arbite,	6474

PACATIANA (1)

1Ti	6: S which is the chiefest city of Phrygia **P**.	3818

PACES (1)

2Sa	6:13 ark of the LORD had **gone** six **p**,	6805+6806

PACIFIED (2) [PACIFY]

Est	7:10 Mordecai. Then was the king's wrath **p**.	7918
Eze	16:63 I am **p** toward thee for all that thou	3722

PACIFIETH (2) [PACIFY]

Pr	21:14 A gift in secret **p** anger: and a reward in	3711
Ecc	10: 4 thy place; for yielding **p** great offences.	3240

PACIFY (1) [PACIFIED, PACIFIETH]

Pr	16:14 of death: but a wise man will **p** it.	3722

PADAN (1) [PADAN-ARAM]

Ge	48: 7 as for me, when I came from **P**,	6307

PADAN-ARAM (10) [ARAM, PADAN]

Ge	25:20 the daughter of Bethuel the Syrian of **P**,	6307
	28: 2 Arise, go to **P**, to the house of Bethuel	6307
	28: 5 he went to **P** unto Laban, son of Bethuel	6307
	28: 6 sent him away to **P**, to take him a wife	6307
	28: 7 and his mother, and was gone to **P**;	6307
	31:18 of his getting, which he had gotten in **P**,	6307
	33:18 land of Canaan, when he came from **P**;	6307
	35: 9 when he came out of **P**, and blessed him.	6307
	35:26 of Jacob, which were born to him in **P**.	6307
	46:15 which she bare unto Jacob in **P**, with his	6307

PADDAN See PADAN

PADDAN ARAM See PADAN-ARAM

PADDLE (1)

Dt	23:13 thou shalt have a **p** upon thy weapon;	3489

PADON (2)

Ezr	2:44 the children of Siaha, the children of **P**,	6303
Ne	7:47 the children of Sia, the children of **P**,	6303

PAGAN See CHEMARIMS

PAGANS See PUBLICAN

PAGIEL (5)

Nu	1:13 Of Asher; **P** the son of Ocran.	6295
	2:27 of Asher *shall be* **P** the son of Ocran.	6295
	7:72 On the eleventh day **P** the son of Ocran.	6295
	7:77 *was* the offering of **P** the son of Ocran.	6295
	10:26 children of Asher *was* **P** the son of Ocran.	6295

PAHATH-MOAB (6)

Ezr	2: 6 The children of **P**, of the children of	6355
	8: 4 Of the sons of **P**; Elihoenai the son of	6355
	10:30 of the sons of **P**; Adna, and Chelal,	6355
Ne	3:11 Hashub the son of **P**, repaired the other	6355
	7:11 The children of **P**, of the children of	6355
	10:14 the people; Parosh, **P**, Elam, Zatthu, Bani,	6355

PAI (1)

1Ch	1:50 the name of his city *was* **P**; and his wife's	6464

PAID (4) [PAY]

Ezr	4:20 tribute, and custom, *was* **p** unto them.	3052
Jnh	1: 3 so he **p** the fare thereof, and went down	5414
Mt	5:26 till thou hast **p** the uttermost farthing.	591

Lk 12:59 till thou hast **p** the very last mite. 591

PAIN (25) [PAINED, PAINFUL, PAINFULNESS, PAINS]
Job 14:22 his flesh upon him shall **have** p, 3510
15:20 The wicked *man* **travaileth with** p all his 2342
33:19 He is chastened also with p upon his bed, 4341
33:19 the multitude of his bones *with* strong p: NIH
Ps 25:18 Look upon mine affliction and my p; 5999
48: 6 there, *and* p, as of a woman in travail. 2427
Isa 13: 8 shall be **in** p as a woman that travaileth: 2342
21: 3 Therefore are my loins filled **with** p: 2479
26:17 is in p, *and* crieth out in her pangs; 2342
26:18 have been with child, we have been **in** p, 2342
66: 7 before her p came, she was delivered of a 2256
Jer 6:24 of us, *and* p, as of a woman in travail. 2427
12:13 have **put** themselves **to** p, *but* shall not 2470
15:18 Why is my p perpetual, and my wound 3511
22:23 upon thee, the p as of a woman in travail. 2427
30:23 it shall **fall with** p upon the head of 2342
51: 8 take balm for her p, if so be she may be 4341
Eze 30: 4 **great** p shall be in Ethiopia, when the 2479
30: 9 **great** p shall come upon them, as *in* 2479
30:16 Sin shall **have great** p, and No 2342+2342
Mic 4:10 Be **in** p, and labour to bring forth, 2342
Na 2:10 **much** p *is* in all loins, and the faces 2479
Ro 8:22 and **travaileth in** p together until now. 4944
Rev 16:10 and they gnawed their tongues for p, 4192
21: 4 neither shall there be any more p: 4192

PAINED (5) [PAIN]
Ps 55: 4 My heart is **sore** p within me: 2342
Isa 23: 5 **sorely** p *at* the report of Tyre. 2342
Jer 4:19 I am p *at* my very heart; my heart maketh 2342
Joel 2: 6 their face the people shall be **much** p: 2342
Rev 12: 2 travailing in birth, and p to be delivered. 928

PAINFUL (1) [PAIN]
Ps 73:16 thought to know this, it *was* too p for me; 5999

PAINFULNESS (1) [PAIN]
2Co 11:27 In weariness and p, in watchings often, 3449

PAINS (4) [PAIN]
1Sa 4:19 travailed; for her p came upon her. 6735
Ps 116: 3 the p of hell gat hold upon me: 4712
Ac 2:24 raised up, having loosed the p of death: 5604
Rev 16:11 because of their p and their sores, 4192

PAINTED (2) [PAINTEDST, PAINTING]
2Ki 9:30 and she p her face, 7760+7760+871.1+1886.1
Jer 22:14 cieled with cedar, and p with vermilion. 4886

PAINTEDST (1) [PAINTED]
Eze 23:40 for whom thou didst wash *thyself,* p thy 3583

PAINTING (1) [PAINTED]
Jer 4:30 thou rentest thy face with p, in vain 6320

PAIR (4)
Am 2: 6 for silver, and the poor for a p of shoes; NIH
8: 6 for silver, and the needy for a p of shoes. NIH
Lk 2:24 A p of turtledoves, or two young pigeons. 2201
Rev 6: 5 he that sat on him had a p of balances in 2218

PALACE (48) [PALACES]
1Ki 16:18 he went into the p of the king's house, 759
21: 1 hard by the p of Ahab king of Samaria. 1964
2Ki 15:25 in the p of the king's house, with Argob 759
20:18 shall be eunuchs in the p of the king of 1964
1Ch 29: 1 for the p *is* not for man, but for the LORD 1002
29:19 to do all *these things,* and to build the p, 1002
2Ch 9:11 to the king's p, and harps and psalteries 1004
Ezr 4:14 we have maintenance from *the king's* p, 1965
6: 2 in the p that *is* in the province of 1001
Ne 1: 1 twentieth year, as I was in Shushan the p, 1002
2: 8 of the p which *appertained* to the house, 1002
7: 2 Hananiah the ruler of the p, charge over 1002
Est 2: 2 his kingdom, which *was* in Shushan the p, 1002
1: 5 people that were present in Shushan the p, 1002
1: 5 in the court of the garden of the king's p; 1055
2: 3 the fair young virgins unto Shushan the p, 1002
2: 5 *Now* in Shushan the p there was a certain 1002
2: 8 gathered together unto Shushan the p, 1002
3:15 the decree was given in Shushan the p. 1002
7: 7 wine in his wrath *went* into the p garden: 1055
7: 8 the king returned out of the p garden into 1055
8:14 the decree was given at Shushan the p. 1002
9: 6 in Shushan the p the Jews slew and 1002
9:11 Shushan the p was brought before the 1002
9:12 five hundred men in Shushan the p, 1002
Ps 45:15 they shall enter into the king's p. 1964
144:12 polished *after* the similitude of a p: 1964
SS 8: 9 wall, we will build upon her a p of silver: 2918
Isa 25: 2 a p of strangers to be no city; it shall never 759
39: 7 shall be eunuchs in the p of the king of 1964
Jer 30:18 the p shall remain after the manner 759
Da 1: 4 ability in them to stand in the king's p, 1964
1: 4 in mine house, and flourishing in my p: 1965
4:29 in the p of the kingdom of Babylon. 1965
5: 5 the plaister of the wall of the king's p: 1965
6:18 king went to his p, and passed the night 1965
8: 2 I saw, that I *was* at Shushan *in* the p, 1002
11:45 he shall plant the tabernacles of his p 643
Am 4: 3 ye shall cast *them* into the p, saith 2038
Na 2: 6 be opened, and the p shall be dissolved. 1964

Mt 26: 3 the people, unto the p of the high priest, 833
26:58 him afar off unto the high priest's p, 833
26:69 Peter sat without in the p: and a damsel 833
Mk 14:54 afar off, even into the p of the high priest: 833
14:66 And as Peter was beneath in the p, 833
Lk 11:21 When a strong *man* armed keepeth his p, 833
Jn 18:15 went in with Jesus into the p of the high 833
Php 1:13 bonds in Christ are manifest in all the p, 4232

PALACES (33) [PALACE]
2Ch 36:19 burnt all the p thereof with fire, 759
Ps 45: 8 and aloes, *and* cassia, out of the ivory p, 1964
48: 3 God is known in her p for a refuge. 759
48:13 ye well her bulwarks, consider her p; 759
78:69 he built his sanctuary like high p, like NIH
122: 7 thy walls, *and* prosperity within thy p. 759
Pr 30:28 hold with her hands, and *is* in kings' p. 1964
Isa 13:22 and dragons in *their* pleasant p: 1964
23:13 thereof, they raised up the p thereof; 759
32:14 Because the p shall be forsaken; 759
34:13 thorns shall come up in her p, nettles and 759
Jer 6: 5 let us go by night, and let us destroy her p. 759
9:21 *and* is entered into our p, to cut off 759
17:27 it shall devour the p of Jerusalem, 759
49:27 and it shall consume the p of Ben-hadad. 759
La 2: 5 up Israel, he hath swallowed up all her p: 759
2: 7 the hand of the enemy the walls of her p; 759
Eze 19: 7 knew their **desolate** p, and he laid waste 490
25: 4 they shall set their p in thee, and make 2918
Hos 8:14 cities, and it shall devour the p thereof. 759
Am 1: 4 which shall devour the p of Ben-hadad. 759
1: 7 of Gaza, which shall devour the p thereof: 759
1:10 of Tyrus, which shall devour the p thereof. 759
1:12 which shall devour the p of Bozrah. 759
1:14 it shall devour the p thereof, with shouting 759
2: 2 and it shall devour the p of Kerioth: 759
2: 5 and it shall devour the p of Jerusalem. 759
3: 9 Publish in the p at Ashdod, and in 759
3: 9 and in the p in the land of Egypt, and say, 759
3:10 store up violence and robbery in their p. 759
3:11 from thee, and thy p shall be spoiled. 759
6: 8 the excellency of Jacob, and hate his p: 759
Mic 5: 5 when he shall tread in our p, then shall we 759

PALAL (1)
Ne 3:25 P the son of Uzai, over against the turning 6420

PALE (2) [PALENESS]
Isa 29:22 neither shall his face now **wax** p. 2357
Rev 6: 8 And I looked, and behold a p horse: 5515

PALENESS (1) [PALE]
Jer 30: 6 in travail, and all faces are turned into p? 3420

PALESTINA (3) [PALESTINE]
Ex 15:14 shall take hold on the inhabitants of P. 6429
Isa 14:29 whole P, because the rod of him that 6429
14:31 cry, O city; thou, whole P, *art* dissolved; 6429

PALESTINE (1) [PALESTINA]
Joel 3: 4 Tyre, and Zidon, and all the coasts of P? 6429

PALLU (4) [PALLUITES]
Ex 6:14 Hanoch, and P, Hezron, and Carmi; 6396
Nu 26: 5 of P, the family of the Palluites: 6396
26: 8 And the sons of P; Eliab. 6396
1Ch 5: 3 *were,* Hanoch, and P, Hezron, and Carmi. 6396

PALLUITES (1) [PALLU]
Nu 26: 5 of Pallu, the family of the P: 6384

PALM (37) [PALMS]
Ex 15:27 of water, and threescore and ten p **trees:** 8558
Lev 14:15 pour *it* into the p of his own left **hand:** 3709
14:26 of the oil into the p of his own left **hand:** 3709
23:40 branches of p trees, and the boughs of 8558
Nu 33: 9 of water, and threescore and ten p **trees;** 8558
Dt 34: 3 of Jericho, the city of p trees, unto Zoar. 8558
Jdg 1:16 went up out of the city of p **trees** with 8558
3:13 and possessed the city of p **trees.** 8558
4: 5 she dwelt under the **tree** of Deborah 8560
1Ki 6:29 cherubims and p **trees** and open flowers, 8561
6:32 cherubims and p **trees** and open flowers, 8561
6:32 the cherubims, and upon the p **trees.** 8561
6:35 and p **trees** and open flowers: 8561
7:36 he graved cherubims, lions, and p **trees,** 8561
2Ch 3: 5 and set thereon p **trees** and chains. 8561
28:15 the city of p **trees,** to their brethren: 8558
Ne 8:15 branches, and branches of thick trees, 8558
Ps 92:12 righteous shall flourish like the p **tree:** 8558
SS 7: 7 This thy stature is like to a p **tree,** 8558
7: 8 I said, I will go up to the p **tree,** I will 8558
Jer 10: 5 They *are* upright as the p **tree,** 8560
Eze 40:16 and upon *each* post *were* p **trees.** 8561
40:22 and their arches, and their p **trees,** 8561
40:26 it had p **trees,** one on this side, 8561
40:31 and p **trees** *were* upon the posts thereof; 8561
40:34 p **trees** *were* upon the posts thereof, on 8561
40:37 p **trees** *were* upon the posts thereof, on 8561
41:18 *it was* made with cherubims and p **trees,** 8561
41:18 so that a p **tree** *was* between a cherub 8561
41:19 *was* toward the p **tree** on the one side, 8561
41:19 face of a young lion toward the p **tree,** 8561
41:20 door *were* cherubims and p **trees** made, 8561
41:25 of the temple, cherubims and p **trees,** 8561
41:26 p **trees** on the one side and on the other 8561

Joel 1:12 the p tree also, and the apple tree, 8558
Jn 12:13 Took branches of p **trees,** and went forth 5404
18:22 **stroke** Jesus **with the**
p of his hand, 1325+4475

PALMERWORM (3) [WORM]
Joel 1: 4 That which the p hath left hath the locust 1501
2:25 and the caterpillar, and the p, 1501
Am 4: 9 the p devoured *them:* yet have ye not 1501

PALMS (7) [PALM]
1Sa 5: 4 both the p of his hands *were* cut off upon 3709
2Ki 9:35 and the feet, and the p of *her* hands. 3709
Isa 49:16 graven thee upon the p of *my* **hands,** 3709
Da 10:10 my knees and upon the p of my hands. 3709
Mt 26:67 **smote** him **with the** p of their **hands,** 4474
Mk 14:65 **strike** him **with the**
p of their **hands.** 906+4475
Rev 7: 9 with white robes, and p in their hands; 5404

PALSIES (1) [PALSY]
Ac 8: 7 **with** them: and many **taken with** p, 3886

PALSY (13) [PALSIES]
Mt 4:24 were lunatick, and those that **had the** p; 3885
8: 6 my servant lieth at home **sick of the** p, 3885
9: 2 they brought to him a **man sick of the** p, 3885
9: 2 their faith said unto the **sick of the** p; 3885
9: 6 (then saith he to the **sick of the** p,) 3885
Mk 2: 3 bringing **one sick of the** p, *which was* 3885
2: 4 the bed wherein the **sick of the** p lay. 3885
2: 5 he said unto the **sick of the** p, Son, 3885
2: 9 is it easier to say to the **sick of the** p, 3885
2:10 (he saith to the **sick of the** p,) 3885
Lk 5:18 a bed a man which was **taken with a** p: 3886
5:24 (he said unto the **sick of the** p,) 3886
Ac 9:33 bed eight years, and was **sick of the** p. 3886

PALTI (1)
Nu 13: 9 the tribe of Benjamin, P the son of Raphu. 6406

PALTIEL (1)
Nu 34:26 children of Issachar, P the son of Azzan. 6409

PALTITE (1)
2Sa 23:26 Helez the P, Ira the son of Ikkesh 6407

PAMPHYLIA (5)
Ac 2:10 Phrygia, and P, in Egypt, and in the parts 3828
13:13 from Paphos, they came to Perga in P: 3828
14:24 passed throughout Pisidia, they came to P. 3828
15:38 *them,* who departed from them from P, 3828
27: 5 had sailed over the sea of Cilicia and P, 3828

PAN (7) [FIREPANS, FRYINGPAN, PANS]
Lev 2: 5 oblation *be* a meat offering **baken** in a p, 4227
6:21 In a p it shall be made with oil; *and when* 4227
7: 9 is dressed in the fryingpan, and in the p, 4227
1Sa 2:14 he strooke *it* into the p, or kettle, 3595
2Sa 13: 9 she took a p, and poured *them* out before 4958
1Ch 23:29 for *that which is* baked *in* the p, and for 4227
Eze 4: 3 Moreover take thou unto thee an iron p, 4227

PANELED See CIELED

PANELS See CIELED

PANGS (9)
Isa 13: 8 p and sorrows shall take hold of *them;* 6735
21: 3 p have taken hold upon me, as the pangs 6735
21: 3 as the p of a woman that travaileth: 6735
26:17 is in pain, *and* crieth out in her p; 2256
Jer 22:23 how gracious shalt thou be when p come 2256
48:41 shall be as the heart of a woman **in** her p. 6887
49:22 be as the heart of a woman **in** her p. 6887
50:43 of him, *and* p, as a woman in travail. 2427
Mic 4: 9 p have taken thee as a woman in travail. 2427

PANIC See DISCOMFITED; DISCOMFITURE

PANNAG (1)
Eze 27:17 and P, and honey, and oil, and balm. 6436

PANS (4) [PAN]
Ex 27: 3 thou shalt make his p to receive his ashes, 5518
Nu 11: 8 and baked *it* in p, and made cakes *of it:* 6517
1Ch 9:31 over the things that were made in the p. 2281
2Ch 35:13 in p, and divided *them* speedily among all 6745

PANT (1) [PANTED, PANTETH]
Am 2: 7 That p after the dust of the earth on 7602

PANTED (2) [PANT]
Ps 119:131 I opened my mouth, and p: for I longed 7602
Isa 21: 4 My heart p, fearfulness affrighted me: 8582

PANTETH (3) [PANT]
Ps 38:10 My heart p, my strength faileth me: as for 5503
42: 1 As the hart p after the water brooks, 6165
42: 1 so p my soul after thee, O God. 6165

PAPER (2)
Isa 19: 7 The p reeds by the brooks, by the mouth 6169
2Jn 1:12 you, I would not *write* with p and ink; 5489

PAPHOS (2)
Ac 13: 6 they had gone through the isle unto P, 3974

P

Ac 13:13 Paul and his company loosed from **P,** *3974*

PAPS (4)
Eze 23:21 by the Egyptians for the **p** of thy youth. *7699*
Lk 11:27 and the **p** which thou hast sucked. *3149*
 23:29 and the **p** which never gave suck. *3149*
Rev 1:13 and girt about the **p** with a golden girdle. *3149*

PAPYRUS See BULRUSH; BULRUSHES

PARABLE (49) [PARABLES]
Nu 23: 7 he took up his **p,** and said, Balak the king *4912*
 23:18 he took up his **p,** and said, Rise up, Balak, *4912*
 24: 3 he took up his **p,** and said, Balaam the son *4912*
 24:15 he took up his **p,** and said, Balaam the son *4912*
 24:20 on Amalek, he took up his **p,** and said, *4912*
 24:21 took up his **p,** and said, Strong *is* thy *4912*
 24:23 he took up his **p,** and said, Alas, who shall *4912*
Job 27: 1 Moreover Job continued his **p,** and *4912*
 29: 1 Moreover Job continued his **p,** and said, *4912*
Ps 49: 4 I will incline mine ear to a **p:** I will open *4912*
 78: 2 I will open my mouth in a **p:** I will utter *4912*
Pr 26: 7 not equal: so *is* a **p** in the mouth of fools. *4912*
 26: 9 drunkard, so *is* a **p** in the mouth of fools. *4912*
Eze 17: 2 **speak a p** unto the house of Israel; *4911+4912*
 24: 3 And utter a **p** unto the rebellious house, *4912*
Mic 2: 4 In that day shall *one* take up a **p** against *4912*
Hab 2: 6 Shall not all these take up a **p** against him, *4912*
Mt 13:18 Hear ye therefore the **p** of the sower. *3850*
 13:24 Another **p** put he forth unto them, saying, *3850*
 13:31 Another **p** put he forth unto them, saying, *3850*
 13:33 Another **p** spake he unto them; *3850*
 13:34 and without a **p** spake he not unto them: *3850*
 13:36 Declare unto us the **p** of the tares of *3850*
 15:15 and said unto him, Declare unto us this **p.** *3850*
 21:33 Hear another **p:** There was a certain *3850*
 24:32 Now learn a **p** of the fig tree; When his *3850*
Mk 4:10 him with the twelve asked of him the **p.** *3850*
 4:13 he said unto them, Know ye not this **p?** *3850*
 4:34 But without a **p** spake he not unto them: *3850*
 7:17 his disciples asked him concerning the **p.** *3850*
 12:12 for they knew that he had spoken the **p** *3850*
 13:28 Now learn a **p** of the fig tree; When her *3850*
Lk 5:36 And he spake also a **p** unto them; No *man* *3850*
 6:39 he spake a **p** unto them, Can the blind *3850*
 8: 4 to him out of every city, he spake by a **p:** *3850*
 8: 9 asked him, saying, What might this **p** be? *3850*
 8:11 Now the **p** is this: The seed is the word of *3850*
 12:16 And he spake a **p** unto them, saying, *3850*
 12:41 thou this **p** unto us, or even to all? *3850*
 13: 6 He spake also this **p;** A certain *man* had a *3850*
 14: 7 And he put forth a **p** to those which were *3850*
 15: 3 And he spake this **p** unto them, saying, *3850*
 18: 1 And he spake a **p** unto them *to this end,* *3850*
 18: 9 And he spake this **p** unto certain which *3850*
 19:11 these *things,* he added and spake a **p,** *3850*
 20: 9 began he to speak to the people this **p;** *3850*
 20:19 they perceived that he had spoken this **p** *3850*
 21:29 And he spake to them a **p;** Behold the fig *3850*
Jn 10: 6 This **p** spake Jesus unto them: *3942*

PARABLES (16) [PARABLE]
Eze 20:49 they say of me, Doth he not speak **p?** *4912*
Mt 13: 3 he spake many *things* unto them in **p,** *3850*
 13:10 Why speakest thou unto them in **p?** *3850*
 13:13 Therefore speak I to them in **p:** because *3850*
 13:34 spake Jesus unto the multitude in **p;** *3850*
 13:35 saying, I will open my mouth in **p,** *3850*
 13:53 *that* when Jesus had finished these **p,** *3850*
 21:45 priests and Pharisees had heard his **p,** *3850*
 22: 1 and spake unto them again by **p,** *3850*
Mk 3:23 them unto *him,* and said unto them in **p,** *3850*
 4: 2 And he taught them many *things* by **p,** *3850*
 4:11 without, all *these things* are done in **p:** *3850*
 4:13 and how *then* will ye know all **p?** *3850*
 4:33 And with many such **p** spake he the word *3850*
 12: 1 And he began to speak unto them by **p.** *3850*
Lk 8:10 but to others in **p;** that seeing they might *3850*

PARADISE (3)
Lk 23:43 To day shalt thou be with me in **p.** *3857*
2Co 12: 4 How that he was caught up into **p,** *3857*
Rev 2: 7 which is in the midst of the **p** of God. *3857*

PARAH (1)
Jos 18:23 And Avim, and **P,** and Ophrah, *6511*

PARALYTIC See PALSY

PARALYZED See PALSY

PARAMOURS (1)
Eze 23:20 she doted upon their **p,** whose flesh *is* *6370*

PARAN (11) [EL-PARAN]
Ge 21:21 he dwelt in the wilderness of **P:** *6290*
Nu 10:12 the cloud rested in the wilderness of **P.** *6290*
 12:16 and pitched in the wilderness of **P.** *6290*
 13: 3 sent them from the wilderness of **P:** *6290*
 13:26 unto the wilderness of **P,** to Kadesh; *6290*
Dt 1: 1 over against the Red *sea,* between **P,** *6290*
 33: 2 he shined forth from mount **P,** and he *6290*
1Sa 25: 1 and went down to the wilderness of **P.** *6290*
1Ki 11:18 they arose out of Midian, and came *to* **P:** *6290*
 11:18 they took men with them out of **P,** *6290*
Hab 3: 3 and the Holy One from mount **P.** *6290*

PARAPET See BATTLEMENT

PARBAR (2)
1Ch 26:18 At **P** westward, four at the causeway, *6503*
 26:18 four at the causeway, *and* two at **P.** *6503*

PARCEL (6)
Ge 33:19 he bought a **p** of a field, where he had *2513*
Jos 24:32 in a **p** of ground which Jacob bought of *2513*
Ru 4: 3 selleth a **p** of land, which *was* our brother *2513*
1Ch 11:13 where was a **p** of ground full *of* barley; *2513*
 11:13 they set themselves in the midst of that **p,** *2513*
Jn 4: 5 near to the **p of ground** that Jacob gave to *5564*

PARCHED (9)
Lev 23:14 neither bread, nor **p** *corn,* nor green ears, *7039*
Jos 5:11 and **p** *corn* in the selfsame day. *7033*
Ru 2:14 she reached her **p** *corn,* and she did eat, *7039*
1Sa 17:17 thy brethren an ephah of this **p** *corn,* *7039*
 25:18 five measures of **p** *corn,* and an hundred *7039*
2Sa 17:28 **p** *corn,* and beans, and lentiles, *7039*
 17:28 and beans, and lentiles, and **p** *pulse,* *7039*
Isa 35: 7 And the **p ground** shall become a pool, *8273*
Jer 17: 6 inhabit the **p places** in the wilderness. *2788*

PARCHMENTS (1)
2Ti 4:13 and the books, *but* especially the **p.** *3200*

PARDON (16) [PARDONED, PARDONETH]
Ex 23:21 for he will not **p** your transgressions: *5375*
 34: 9 **p** our iniquity and our sin, and take us for *5545*
Nu 14:19 **P,** I beseech thee, the iniquity of this *5545*
1Sa 15:25 **p** my sin, and turn again with me, *5375*
2Ki 5:18 In this thing the LORD **p** thy servant, *5545*
 5:18 the LORD **p** thy servant in this thing. *5545*
 24: 4 which the LORD would not **p.** *5545*
2Ch 30:18 The good LORD **p** every one *3722*
Ne 9:17 thou *art* a God *ready* to **p,** gracious and *5547*
Job 7:21 why dost thou not **p** my transgression, *5375*
Ps 25:11 name's sake, O LORD, **p** mine iniquity; *5545*
Isa 55: 7 and to our God, for he will abundantly **p.** *5545*
Jer 5: 1 that seeketh the truth; and I will **p** it. *5545*
 5: 7 How shall I **p** thee for this? thy children *5545*
 33: 8 I will **p** all their iniquities, whereby they *5545*
 50:20 found: for I will **p** them whom I reserve. *5545*

PARDONED (3) [PARDON]
Nu 14:20 I have **p** according to thy word: *5545*
Isa 40: 2 is accomplished, that her iniquity is **p:** *7521*
La 3:42 We have rebelled: thou hast not **p.** *5545*

PARDONETH (1) [PARDON]
Mic 7:18 that **p** iniquity, and passeth by *5375*

PARE (1)
Dt 21:12 she shall shave her head, and **p** her nails; *6213*

PARENTS (21)
Mt 10:21 the children shall rise up against *their* **p,** *1118*
Mk 13:12 and children shall rise up against *their* **p,** *1118*
Lk 2:27 when the **p** brought in the child Jesus, *1118*
 2:41 his **p** went to Jerusalem every year at *1118*
 8:56 her **p** were astonished: but he charged *1118*
 18:29 or **p,** or brethren, or wife, or children, *1118*
 21:16 And ye shall be betrayed both by **p,** *1118*
Jn 9: 2 Master, who did sin, this *man,* or his **p,** *1118*
 9: 3 Neither hath this *man* sinned, nor his **p:** *1118*
 9:18 until they called the **p** of him that had *1118*
 9:20 His **p** answered them and said, We know *1118*
 9:22 These *words* spake his **p,** because *1118*
 9:23 Therefore said his **p,** He is of age; ask him. *1118*
Ro 1:30 inventors of evil *things,* disobedient to **p,** *1118*
2Co 12:14 the children ought not to lay up for the **p,** *1118*
 12:14 for the parents, but the **p** for the children. *1118*
Eph 6: 1 Children, obey your **p** in the Lord: for this *1118*
Col 3:20 obey *your* **p** in all *things:* for this is well *1118*
1Ti 5: 4 piety at home, and to requite *their* **p:** *4269*
2Ti 3: 2 disobedient to **p,** unthankful, unholy, *1118*
Heb 11:23 was hid three months of his **p,** because *3962*

PARLOUR (5) [PARLOURS]
Jdg 3:20 he was sitting in a summer **p,** which he *5944*
 3:23 shut the doors of the **p** upon him, *5944*
 3:24 the doors of the **p** *were* locked, they said, *5944*
 3:25 behold, he opened not the doors of the **p;** *5944*
1Sa 9:22 brought them into the **p,** and made them *3957*

PARLOURS (1) [PARLOUR]
1Ch 28:11 of the inner **p** thereof, and of the place of *2315*

PARMASHTA (1)
Est 9: 9 **P,** and Arisai, and Aridai, and Vajezatha, *6534*

PARMENAS (1)
Ac 6: 5 and **P,** and Nicolas a proselyte of Antioch: *3937*

PARNACH (1)
Nu 34:25 of Zebulun, Elizaphan the son of **P.** *6535*

PAROSH (5)
Ezr 2: 3 The children of **P,** two thousand an *6551*
 10:25 of the sons of **P;** Ramiah, and Jeziah, *6551*
Ne 3:25 prison. After him Pedaiah the son of **P.** *6551*
 7: 8 The children of **P,** two thousand an *6551*
 10:14 **P,** Pahath-moab, Elam, Zatthu, Bani, *6551*

PARSHANDATHA (1)
Est 9: 7 And **P,** and Dalphon, and Aspatha, *6577*

PARSIN See UPHARSIN

PART (214) [APART, FOREPART, PARTED, PARTETH, PARTING, PARTITION, PARTLY, PARTS]
Ge 41:34 take up the fifth **p** of the land of Egypt in NIH
 47:24 you shall give the fifth **p** unto Pharaoh, NIH
 47:26 Pharaoh should have the fifth **p;** except NIH
Ex 16:36 Now an omer *is* the tenth **p** of an ephah. NIH
 19:17 they stood at the **nether p** of the mount. *8482*
 29:26 before the LORD: and it shall be thy **p.** *4490*
 29:40 with the **fourth p** of a hin of beaten oil; *7253*
 29:40 the fourth **p** of a hin of wine *for* a drink NIH
Lev 1:16 cast it beside the altar on the **east p,** *6924*
 2: 6 Thou shalt **p** it **in pieces,** *6595+6626*
 2:16 **p** of the beaten corn thereof, and *part* of NIH
 2:16 corn thereof, and **p** of the oil thereof, NIH
 5:11 **p** of an ephah of fine flour for a sin NIH
 5:16 holy *thing,* and shall add the fifth **p** thereto NIH
 6: 5 shall add the fifth **p** more thereto, NIH
 6:20 the tenth **p** of an ephah of fine flour *for* a NIH
 7:33 shall have the right shoulder for his **p.** *4490*
 8:29 the ram of consecration it was Moses' **p;** *4490*
 11:35 every *thing* whereupon *any* **p** of their NIH
 11:37 if *any* **p** of their carcase fall upon any NIH
 11:38 *any* **p** of their carcase fall thereon, it *shall* NIH
 13:41 that hath his hair fallen off from the **p** of *6285*
 22:14 he shall put the fifth **p** thereof unto it, NIH
 23:13 *shall be* of wine, the fourth **p** of a hin. NIH
 27:13 he shall add a fifth **p** thereof unto thy NIH
 27:15 he shall add the fifth **p** of the money of thy NIH
 27:16 LORD *some* **p** of a field of his possession, NIH
 27:19 he shall add the fifth **p** of the money of thy NIH
 27:27 and shall add a fifth **p** of it thereto: NIH
 27:31 he shall add thereto the fifth **p** thereof. NIH
Nu 5: 7 add unto it the fifth **p** thereof, and give *it* NIH
 5:15 the tenth **p** of an ephah of barley meal; NIH
 15: 4 mingled with the fourth **p** of a hin of oil. NIH
 15: 5 the fourth **p** of a hin *of* wine for a drink NIH
 15: 6 mingled with the third **p** of a hin of oil. NIH
 15: 7 shalt offer the third **p** of a hin of wine, NIH
 18:20 shalt thou have any **p** among them: *2506*
 18:20 I *am* thy **p** and thine inheritance among *2506*
 18:26 for the LORD, *even* a tenth **p** of the tithe. NIH
 18:29 *even* the hallowed **p** thereof out of it. NIH
 22:41 that thence he might see the **utmost p** of *7097*
 23:10 and the number *of* the **fourth p** of Israel? *7255*
 23:13 thou shalt see but the **utmost p** of them, *7097*
 28: 5 a tenth **p** of an ephah *of* flour for a meat NIH
 28: 5 mingled with the fourth **p** of a hin of NIH
 28: 7 be the fourth **p** of a hin for the one lamb: NIH
 28:14 the third **p** of a hin unto a ram, and a NIH
 28:14 ram, and a fourth **p** of a hin unto a lamb: NIH
Dt 10: 9 Wherefore Levi hath no **p** nor inheritance *2506*
 12:12 forasmuch as he hath no **p** nor inheritance *2506*
 14:27 he hath no **p** nor inheritance with thee. *2506*
 14:29 he hath no **p** nor inheritance with thee,) *2506*
 18: 1 have no **p** nor inheritance with Israel: *2506*
 33:21 he provided the first **p** for himself, NIH
Jos 14: 4 gave no **p** unto the Levites in the land, *2506*
 15: 1 the **uttermost p** of the south *coast.* *4480+7097*
 15: 5 of the sea at the **uttermost p** of Jordan: *7097*
 15:13 he gave a **p** among the children of Judah, *2506*
 18: 7 the Levites have no **p** among you; *2506*
 19: 9 for the **p** of the children of Judah was too *2506*
 22:25 of Gad; ye have no **p** in the LORD: *2506*
 22:27 time to come, Ye have no **p** in the LORD. *2506*
Ru 1:17 *if ought* but death **p** thee and me. *6504*
 3: 2 her hap was to light on a **p** of the field *2513*
 3:13 **perform** unto thee the **p of a kinsman,** *1350*
 3:13 well; let him **do the kinsman's p:** *1350*
 3:13 if he will not **do the p of a kinsman** to *1350*
 3:13 will I **do the p of a kinsman** to thee, *1350*
1Sa 9: 8 here at hand the **fourth p** of a shekel *7253*
 14: 2 Saul tarried in the **uttermost p** of Gibeah *7097*
 23:20 our **p** *shall be* to deliver him into the NIH
 30:24 as his **p** *is* that goeth down to the battle, *2506*
 30:24 so *shall* his **p** *be* that tarrieth by the stuff: *2506*
 30:24 tarrieth by the stuff: they shall **p** alike. *2505*
2Sa 14: 6 *there* was none to **p** them, but the *996+5337*
 18: 2 David sent forth a **third p** of the people *7992*
 18: 2 a **third p** under the hand of Abishai the *7992*
 18: 2 a **third p** under the hand of Ittai the *7992*
 20: 1 and said, We have no **p** in David, *2506*
1Ki 6:24 from the **uttermost p** of the one wing *7098*
 6:24 **uttermost p** of the other were ten cubits. *7098*
 6:31 *and* side posts *were* a fifth **p** of the wall. NIH
 6:33 posts of olive tree, a fourth **p** of the wall. NIH
2Ki 6:25 the fourth **p** of a kab of dove's dung *7255*
 7: 5 they were come to the **uttermost p** of *7097*
 7: 8 these lepers came to the **uttermost p** *7097*
 11: 5 fifth **p** of you that enter in on the sabbath NIH
 11: 6 And a third **p** *shall* be at the gate of Sur; NIH
 11: 6 and a third **p** at the gate by the guard: NIH
 18:23 if thou be able **on** thy **p** to set riders *3807.1*
1Ch 24: 4 hitherto the **greatest p** of them had kept *4768*
2Ch 23: 4 A third **p** of you entering on the sabbath, NIH
 23: 5 a third **p** *shall* be at the king's house; NIH
 23: 5 a third **p** at the gate of the foundation: NIH
 29:16 the priests went into the **inner p** of *6441*
Ne 1: 9 out unto the **uttermost p** of the heaven, *7097*
 3: 9 of Hur, the ruler of the half **p** of Jerusalem. *6418*

P

Ne 3:12 the ruler of the half **p** of Jerusalem, he and — 6418
3:14 Rechab, the ruler of **p** of Beth-haccerem; — 6418
3:15 of Col-hozeh, the ruler of **p** of Mizpah; — 6418
3:16 the ruler of the half **p** of Beth-zur; — 6418
3:17 ruler of the half **p** of Keilah, in his part. — 6418
3:17 ruler of the half part of Keilah, in his **p.** — 6418
3:18 ruler of the half **p** of Keilah. — 6418
5:11 also the hundredth **p** of the money, — NIH
9: 3 LORD their God one fourth **p** of the day; — NIH
9: 3 another fourth **p** they confessed, — NIH
10:32 charge ourselves yearly with the third **p** — NIH
Job 32:17 *I said,* will answer also my **p,** I also will — 2506
41: 6 shall they **p** him among the merchants? — 2673
Ps 5: 9 their inward **p** is very wickedness; — NIH
22:18 They **p** my garments among them, — 2505
51: 6 in the hidden **p** thou shalt make me to — NIH
118: 7 The LORD **taketh** my **p** with them that — 3807.1
Pr 8:26 the **highest p** of the dust of the world. — 7218
8:31 Rejoicing in the **habitable p** of his earth; — 8398
17: 2 shall **have p** of the inheritance among — 2505
Isa 7:18 in the **uttermost p** of the rivers of Egypt, — 7097
24:16 From the **uttermost p** of the earth have — 3807.1
36: 8 if thou be able **on** thy **p** to set riders — 3807.1
44:16 He burneth **p** thereof in the fire; with part — 2677
44:16 with **p** thereof he eateth flesh; he roasteth — 2677
44:19 to say, I have burnt **p** of it in the fire; — 2677
Eze 4:11 also water by measure, the sixth **p** of a hin: — NIH
5: 1 Thou shalt burn with fire a third **p** in — NIH
5: 2 thou shalt take a third **p,** *and* smite about — NIH
5: 2 a third **p** thou shalt scatter in the wind; — NIH
5:12 A third **p** of thee shall die with — NIH
5:12 third **p** shall fall by the sword round about — NIH
5:12 I will scatter a third **p** into all the winds, — NIH
39: 2 **leave** but the **sixth p** of thee, — 8338
45:11 that the bath may contain the **tenth p** of a — 4643
45:11 and the ephah the tenth **p** of a homer: — NIH
45:13 sixth **p** of an ephah of a homer of wheat, — NIH
45:13 ye shall **give the sixth p** of an ephah of a — 8341
45:14 ye shall **offer** the **tenth p** of an ephah of a — NIH
45:17 it shall be the prince's **p** *to give* burnt — 5921
46:14 the sixth **p** of an ephah, and the third **part** — NIH
46:14 of an ephah, and the third **p** of a hin of oil, — NIH
Da 1: 2 of the vessels of the house of — 4480+7117
2:33 of iron, his feet **p** of iron and part of clay. — 4481
2:33 of iron, his feet part of iron and **p** of clay. — 4481
2:41 toes, **p** of potter's clay, and part of iron, — 4481
2:41 toes, part of potter's clay, and **p** of iron, — 4481
2:42 *as the* toes of the feet *were* **p** of iron, — 4481
2:42 of clay, *so* the kingdom shall be partly — 4481
5: 5 king saw the **p** of the hand that wrote. — 6447
5:24 *was* the **p** of the hand sent from him; — 6447
11:31 arms shall stand **on** his **p,** and they shall — 4480
Joel 2:20 his **hinder p** towards the utmost sea, — 5490
Am 7: 4 the great deep, and did eat up a **p.** — 2506
Zec 13: 9 I will bring the third **p** through the fire, — NIH
Mk 4:38 And he was in the **hinder p** of the **ship,** — 4403
9:40 For he that is not against us is **on** our **p.** — 5228
13:27 from the **uttermost p** of the earth to — 206
13:27 of the earth to the **uttermost p** of heaven. — 206
Lk 10:42 and Mary hath chosen *that* good **p,** — 3310
11:36 therefore *be* full of light, having no **p** dark, — 3313
11:39 but your **inward p** is full of ravening and — 2081
17:24 that lighteneth out of the one **p** under — NIG
17:24 shineth unto the other **p** under heaven; — NIG
Jn 13: 8 I wash thee not, thou hast no **p** with me. — 3313
Ac 1: 8 and unto the **uttermost p** of the earth. — 2078
1:17 and had obtained **p** of this ministry. — 2819
1:25 That *he* may take **p** of this ministry and — 2819
5: 2 And kept back **p** of the price, his wife also — NIG
5: 2 being privy *to it,* and brought a certain **p,** — NIG
5: 3 to keep back **p** of the price of the land? — NIG
8:21 Thou hast neither **p** nor lot in this matter: — 3310
14: 4 and **p** held with the Jews, and part — 3303+3588
14: 4 the Jews, and **p** with the apostles. — 1161+3588
16:12 which is the chief city of that **p** of — 3310
19:32 the **more p** knew not wherefore they — 4183
23: 6 But when Paul perceived that the one **p** — 3313
23: 9 the scribes that were of the Pharisees' — 3313
27:12 the **more p** to depart thence also, — 3313
27:41 **hinder p** was broken with the violence — 4403
Ro 11:25 that blindness in **p** is happened to Israel, — 3313
1Co 12:24 abundant honour to that **p** which lacked: — NIG
13: 9 we know in **p,** and we prophesy in part. — 3313
13: 9 we know in part, and we prophesy in **p.** — 3313
13:10 that which is in **p** shall be done away. — 3313
13:12 now I know in **p;** but then shall I know — 3313
15: 6 of whom the **greater p** remain unto this — 4183
16:17 that which was lacking **on your p** they — 4771
2Co 1:14 As also ye have acknowledged us in **p,** — 3313
2: 5 he hath not grieved me, but in **p:** — 3313
6:15 what **p** hath he that believeth with an — 3310
Eph 4:16 working in the measure of every **p,** — 3313
Tit 2: 8 that he that is of the contrary **p** may be — NIG
Heb 2:14 he also himself likewise **took p** of — 3348
7: 2 To whom also Abraham gave a tenth **p** of — NIG
1Pe 4:14 **on their p** he is evil spoken of, but on — 2596
4:14 spoken of, but **on your p** he is glorified. — 2596
Rev 6: 8 unto them over the fourth **p** of the earth, — NIG
8: 7 the third **p** of trees was burnt up, and all — NIG
8: 8 and the third **p** of the sea became blood; — NIG
8: 9 the third **p** of the creatures which were — NIG
8: 9 the third **p** of the ships were destroyed. — NIG
8:10 and it fell upon the third **p** of the rivers, — NIG
8:11 the third **p** of the waters became — NIG

Rev 8:12 and the third **p** of the sun was smitten, — NIG
8:12 and the third **p** of the moon, and the third — NIG
8:12 of the moon, and the third **p** of the stars; — NIG
8:12 as the third **p** thereof was darkened and — NIG
8:12 and the day shone not for a third **p** of it, — NIG
9:15 and a year, for to slay the third **p** of men. — NIG
9:18 these three was the third **p** of men killed, — NIG
11:13 and the tenth **p** of the city fell, and in — NIG
12: 4 And his tail drew the third **p** of the stars of — NIG
20: 6 holy *is* he that hath **p** in the first — 3313
21: 8 have their **p** in the lake which burneth — 3313
22:19 God shall take away his **p** out of the book — 3313

PARTAKER (9) [PARTAKERS, PARTAKEST]
Ps 50:18 him, and hast been **p** with adulterers. — 2506
1Co 9:10 he that thresheth in hope should be **p** of — 3348
9:23 that I might be **p** thereof **with** *you.* — 4791
10:30 For if I by grace be a **p,** why am I evil — 4791
1Ti 5:22 no **man,** neither be **p** of other **men's** sins: — 2841
2Ti 2: 6 be thou **p** of the **afflictions** of the gospel — 4777
2: 6 that laboureth must be first **p** of the fruits. — 3335
1Pe 5: 1 also a **p** of the glory that shall be revealed: — 2844
2Jn 1:11 For he that biddeth him God speed is **p** of — 2841

PARTAKERS (22) [PARTAKER]
Mt 23:30 we would not have been **p** with them in — 2844
Ro 15:27 For if the Gentiles have been **made p** of — 2841
1Co 9:12 If others be **p** of *this* power over you, — 3348
9:13 they which wait at the altar are **p with** — 4829
10:17 body: for we are all **p** of *that* one bread. — 3348
10:18 not they which eat *of* the sacrifices **p** of — 2844
10:21 ye cannot be **p** of the Lord's table, — 3348
2Co 1: 7 that as you are **p** of the sufferings, — 2844
Eph 3: 6 of his promise in Christ by the gospel: — 4830
5: 7 Be not ye therefore **p with** them. — 4830
Php 1: 7 of the gospel, ye all are **p** of my grace. — 4791
Col 1:12 which hath made us meet to be **p** of — 3310
1Ti 6: 2 are faithful and beloved, **p** of the benefit. — 482
Heb 2:14 then as the children are **p** of flesh and — 2841
3: 1 holy brethren, **p** of the heavenly calling, — 3353
3:14 For we are made **p** of Christ, if we hold — 3353
6: 4 and were made **p** of the Holy Ghost, — 3353
12: 8 whereof all are **p,** then are ye bastards, — 3353
12:10 that *we* might be **p** of his holiness. — 3335
1Pe 4:13 inasmuch as ye are **p** of Christ's sufferings — 2841
2Pe 1: 4 that by these you might be **p** of the divine — 2844
Rev 18: 4 that ye be not **p** of her sins, and that ye — 4790

PARTAKEST (1) [PARTAKER]
Ro 11:17 and with *them* **p** of the root and — 1096+4791

PARTED (12) [PART]
Ge 2:10 from thence it was **p,** and became into — 6504
2Ki 2:11 horses of fire, and **p** them both asunder; — 6504
2:14 the waters, they **p** hither and thither: — 2673
Job 38:24 By what way is the light **p,** *which* — 2505
Joel 3: 2 among the nations, and **p** my land. — 2505
Mt 27:35 and **p** his garments, casting lots: — 1266
27:35 They **p** my garments among them, — 1266
Mk 15:24 they **p** his garments, casting lots upon — 1266
Lk 23:34 And they **p** his raiment, and cast lots. — 1266
24:51 he was **p** from them, and carried up into — 1339
Jn 19:24 They **p** my raiment **among,** — 1266
Ac 2:45 **p** them to all *men,* as every *man* had — 1266

PARTETH (3) [PART]
Lev 11: 3 Whatsoever the hoof, — 6536
Dt 14: 6 every beast that **p** the hoof, — 6536
Pr 18:18 to cease, and **p** between the mighty. — 6504

PARTHIANS (1)
Ac 2: 9 **P,** and Medes, and Elamites, — 3934

PARTIAL (2) [PARTIALITY]
Mal 2: 9 my ways, but have been **p** in the law. — 6440
Jas 2: 4 Are ye not then **p** in yourselves, — 1252

PARTIALITY (2) [PARTIAL]
1Ti 5:21 one before another, doing nothing by **p.** — 4346
Jas 3:17 **without p,** and without hypocrisy. — 87

PARTICIPATION See COMMUNION

PARTICULAR (2) [PARTICULARLY]
1Co 12:27 are the body of Christ, and members in **p.** — 3313
Eph 5:33 Nevertheless let every one of you in **p** so — 2596

PARTICULARLY (2) [PARTICULAR]
Ac 21:19 declared **p** what *things* God — 1520+1538+2596
Heb 9: 5 of which *we* cannot now speak **p.** — 2596+3313

PARTIES (1)
Ex 22: 9 the cause of both **p**s shall come before — 1992.1

PARTING (1) [PART]
Eze 21:21 For the king of Babylon stood at the **p** of — 517

PARTITION (2) [PART]
1Ki 6:21 he **made a p** by the chains of gold before — 5674
Eph 2:14 hath broken down the middle wall of **p** — 5418

PARTLY (5) [PART]
Da 2:42 *so* the kingdom shall be **p** strong, — 4481+7118
2:42 be partly strong, and **p** broken. — 4481
1Co 11:18 among you; and I **p** believe *it.* — 3313+5100
Heb 10:33 **P,** whilst ye were made a — 3303+3778

Heb 10:33 **and p,** whilst ye became — 1161+3778

PARTNER (3) [PARTNERS]
Pr 29:24 Whoso is **p** with a thief hateth his own — 2505
2Co 8:23 *he is* my **p** and fellowhelper concerning — 2844
Phm 1:17 If thou count me therefore a **p,** receive — 2844

PARTNERS (2) [PARTNER]
Lk 5: 7 they beckoned unto *their* **p,** — 3353
5:10 of Zebedee, which were **p** with Simon. — 2844

PARTRIDGE (2)
1Sa 26:20 as when *one* doth hunt a **p,** — 7124
Jer 17:11 As the sitteth *on* eggs, and hatcheth *them* — 7124

PARTS (64) [PART]
Ge 47:24 four **p** shall be your own, for seed of — 3027
Ex 33:23 mine hand, and thou shalt see my **back p:** — 268
Lev 1: 8 shall lay the **p,** the head, and the fat, — 5409
22:23 any thing superfluous or **lacking** in his **p,** — 7038
Nu 10: 5 the camps that lie on the **east p** shall go — 6924
11: 1 *that were* in the **uttermost p** of the camp. — 7097
31:27 **divide** the prey **into two p;** between — 2673
Dt 19: 3 **divide** the coasts . . . , **into three p,** — 8027
30: 4 driven out unto the **outmost p** of heaven, — 7097
Jos 18: 5 they shall divide it into **seven p:** Judah — 2506
18: 6 therefore describe the land **into seven p,** — 2506
18: 9 described it by cities **into seven p** in a — 2506
1Sa 5: 9 and they had emerods in their **secret p.** — 8368
2Sa 19:43 We have ten **p** in the king, and have — 3027
1Ki 6:38 the house finished throughout all the **p** — 1697
7:25 and all their **hinder p** *were* inward. — 268
16:21 the people of Israel divided into **two p:** — 2677
2Ki 7: 2 **two p** of all you that go forth on — 3027
2Ch 4: 4 and all their **hinder p** *were* inward. — 268
Ne 11: 1 and nine **p** *to dwell* in *other* cities. — 3027
Job 26:14 these *are* **p** of his ways: but how little a — 7098
38:36 Who hath put wisdom in the **inward p?** — 2910
41:12 I will not conceal his **p,** nor *his* power, — 907
Ps 2: 8 the **uttermost p** of the earth *for* thy — 657
51: 6 thou desirest truth in the **inward p:** — 2910
63: 9 to destroy *it,* shall go into the **lower p** of — 8482
65: 8 They also that dwell in the **uttermost p** — 7099
78:66 he smote his enemies in the **hinder p:** he — 268
136:13 To him which divided the Red sea **into p:** — 1506
139: 9 and dwell in the **uttermost p** of the sea; — 319
139:15 curiously wrought in the **lowest p** of — 8482
Pr 18: 8 they go down **into** the **innermost p** of — 2315
20:27 searching all the **inward p** of the belly. — 2315
20:30 so *do* stripes the **inward p** of the belly. — 2315
26:22 they go down **into** the **innermost p** of — 2315
Isa 3:17 the LORD will discover their **secret p.** — 6596
16:11 and mine **inward p** for Kir-haresh. — 7130
44:23 done *it:* shout, ye **lower p** of the earth: — 8482
Jer 31:33 I will put my law in their **inward p,** — 7130
34:18 twain, and passed between the **p** thereof, — 1335
34:19 which passed between the **p** of the calf; — 1335
Eze 26:20 shall set thee in the **low p** of the earth, — 8482
31:14 to the **nether p** of the earth, in the midst — 8482
31:16 shall be comforted in the **nether p** of — 8482
31:18 of Eden unto the **nether p** of the earth: — 8482
32:18 unto the **nether p** of the earth, with them — 8482
32:24 into the **nether p** of the earth, — 8482
37:11 hope is lost: we are cut off **for** our **p.** — 3807.1
38:15 come from thy place out of the **north p,** — 3411
39: 2 cause thee to come up from the **north p,** — 3411
48: 8 and **in** length as one of the *other* **p,** — 2506
Zec 13: 8 **two p** therein shall be cut off *and* die; — 6310
Mt 2:22 he turned aside into the **p** of Galilee: — 3313
12:42 for she came from the **uttermost p** of — 4009
Mk 8:10 and came into the **p** of Dalmanutha. — 3313
Lk 11:31 she came from the **utmost p** of the earth — 4009
Jn 19:23 took his garments, and made four **p,** — 3313
Ac 2:10 and in the **p** of Libya about Cyrene, — 3313
20: 2 And when he had gone over those **p,** — 3313
Ro 15:23 But now having no more place in these **p,** — 2824
1Co 12:23 our uncomely **p** have more abundant — NIG
12:24 For our comely **p** have no need: — NIG
Eph 4: 9 He also descended first into the **lower p** — 2737
Rev 16:19 the great city was **divided** into three **p,** — 3313

PARUAH (1)
1Ki 4:17 Jehoshaphat the son of **P,** in Issachar: — 6515

PARVAIM (1)
2Ch 3: 6 for beauty: and the gold *was* gold of **P.** — 6516

PASACH (1)
1Ch 7:33 of Japhlet; **P,** and Bimhal, and Ashvath. — 6457

PAS-DAMMIM (1)
1Ch 11:13 He was with David at **P,** and there — 6450

PASEAH (3) [PHASEAH]
1Ch 4:12 **P,** and Tehinnah the father of Irnahash. — 6454
Ezr 2:49 the children of **P,** the children of Besai, — 6454
Ne 3: 6 old gate repaired Jehoiada the son of **P,** — 6454

PASHUR See PASHUR

PASHUR (14)
1Ch 9:12 the son of **P,** the son of Malchijah, — 6583
Ezr 2:38 children of **P,** a thousand two hundred — 6583
10:22 of the sons of **P;** Elioenai, Maaseiah, — 6583
Ne 7:41 children of **P,** a thousand two hundred — 6583
10: 3 **P,** Amariah, Malchijah, — 6583

P

Ne	11:12 the son of **P**, the son of Malchiah,	6583
Jer	20: 1 Now **P** the son of Immer the priest,	6583
	20: 2 **P** smote Jeremiah the prophet, and put	6583
	20: 3 that **P** brought forth Jeremiah out of	6583
	20: 3 The LORD hath not called thy name **P**,	6583
	20: 6 **P**, and all that dwell in thine house shall	6583
	21: 1 when king Zedekiah sent unto him **P**	6583
	38: 1 Gedaliah the son of **P**, and Jucal the son	6583
	38: 1 of Shelemiah, and **P** the son of Malchiah,	6583

PASS (830) [OVERPASS, PASSAGE, PASSAGES, PASSED, PASSEDST, PASSENGERS, PASSEST, PASSETH, PASSING, PAST]

Ge	4: 3 in process of time it **came to p**, that Cain	1961
	4: 8 it **came to p**, when they were in the field,	1961
	4:14 it shall **come to p**, that every one that	1961
	6: 1 it **came to p**, when men began to	1961
	7:10 it **came to p** after seven days, that	1961
	8: 1 God **made** a wind to **p** over the earth,	5674
	8: 6 it **came to p** at the end of forty days,	1961
	8:13 it **came to p** in the six hundredth and	1961
	9:14 it shall **come to p**, when I bring a cloud	1961
	11: 2 it **came to p**, as they journeyed from	1961
	12:11 it **came to p**, when he was come near to	1961
	12:12 Therefore it shall **come to p**, when	1961
	12:14 it **came to p**, that, when Abram was	1961
	14: 1 it **came to p** in the days of Amraphel king	1961
	15:17 it **came to p**, that, when the sun went	1961
	18: 3 **p** not **away**, I pray thee, from thy servant:	5674
	18: 5 ye your hearts; after that ye shall **p on:**	5674
	19:17 it **came to p**, when they had brought	1961
	19:29 it **came to p**, when God destroyed the	1961
	19:34 it **came to p** on the morrow, that	1961
	21:13 it **came to p**, when God caused me to	1961
	21:22 it **came to p** at that time, that Abimelech	1961
	22: 1 it **came to p** after these things, that God	1961
	22:20 it **came to p** after these things, that it was	1961
	24:14 let it **come to p**, that the damsel to whom	1961
	24:15 it **came to p**, before he had done	1961
	24:22 it **came to p**, as the camels had done	1961
	24:30 it **came to p**, when he saw the earring	1961
	24:43 it shall **come to p**, that when the virgin	1961
	24:52 it **came to p**, that, when Abraham's	1961
	25:11 it **came to p** after the death of Abraham,	1961
	26: 8 it **came to p**, when he had been there a	1961
	26:32 it **came to p** the same day, that Isaac's	1961
	27: 1 it **came to p**, that when Isaac was old,	1961
	27:30 it **came to p**, as soon as Isaac had made	1961
	27:40 it shall **come to p** when thou shalt have	1961
	29:10 it **came to p**, when Jacob saw Rachel	1961
	29:13 it **came to p**, when Laban heard the	1961
	29:23 it **came to p** in the evening, that he took	1961
	29:25 it **came to p**, that in the morning, behold,	1961
	30:25 it **came to p**, when Rachel had born	1961
	30:32 I will **p through** all thy flock to day,	5674
	30:41 it **came to p**, whensoever the stronger	1961
	31:10 it **came to p** at the time that the cattle	1961
	31:52 that I will not **p** over this heap to thee,	5674
	31:52 that thou shalt not **p over** this heap and	5674
	32:16 **P over** before me, and put a space	5674
	33:14 I pray thee, **p over** before thy servant:	5674
	34:25 it **came to p** on the third day, when they	1961
	35:17 it **came to p**, when she was in hard	1961
	35:18 it **came to p**, as her soul was in departing	1961
	35:22 it **came to p**, when Israel dwelt in that	1961
	37:23 it **came to p**, when Joseph was come	1961
	38: 1 it **came to p** at that time, that Judah went	1961
	38: 9 it **came to p**, when he went in unto his	1961
	38:24 it **came to p** about three months after,	1961
	38:27 it **came to p** in the time of her travail,	1961
	38:28 it **came to p**, when she travailed, that	1961
	38:29 it **came to p**, as he drew back his hand,	1961
	39: 5 it **came to p** from the time that he had	1961
	39: 7 it **came to p** after these things, that his	1961
	39:10 it **came to p**, as she spake to Joseph day	1961
	39:11 it **came to p** about this time, that Joseph	1961
	39:13 it **came to p**, when she saw that he had	1961
	39:15 it **came to p**, when he heard that I lifted	1961
	39:18 it **came to p**, as I lift up my voice and	1961
	39:19 it **came to p**, when his master heard	1961
	40: 1 it **came to p** after these things, that	1961
	40:20 it **came to p** the third day, which was	1961
	41: 1 it **came to p** at the end of two full years,	1961
	41: 8 it **came to p** in the morning that his spirit	1961
	41:13 And it **came to p**, as he interpreted to us,	1961
	41:32 God, and God will shortly **bring** it to **p**.	6213
	42:35 it **came to p** as they emptied their sacks,	1961
	43: 2 it **came to p**, when they had eaten up	1961
	43:21 it **came to p**, when we came to the inn,	1961
	44:24 it **came to p** when we came up unto thy	1961
	44:31 It shall **come to p**, when he seeth that	1961
	46:33 it shall **come to p**, when Pharaoh shall	1961
	47:24 it shall **come to p** in the increase, that	1961
	48: 1 it **came to p** after these things, that one	1961
	50:20 unto good, to **bring** to **p**, as it is this day,	6213
Ex	1:10 lest they multiply, and it **come to p**, that,	1961
	1:21 it **came to p**, because the midwives	1961
	2:11 it **came to p** in those days, when Moses	1961
	2:23 it **came to p** in process of time, that	1961
	3:21 it shall **come to p**, that, when ye go,	1961
	4: 8 it shall **come to p**, if they will not believe	1961
	4: 9 it shall **come to p**, if they will not believe	1961
	4:24 it **came to p** by the way in the inn, that	1961
	6:28 it **came to p** on the day when the LORD	1961
	12:12 For I will **p through** the land of Egypt this	5674

Ex	12:13 I will **p over** you, and the plague shall	6452
	12:23 For the LORD will **p through** to smite	5674
	12:23 the LORD will **p over** the door,	6452
	12:25 it shall **come to p**, when ye be come to	1961
	12:26 it shall **come to p**, when your children	1961
	12:29 it **came to p**, that at midnight the LORD	1961
	12:41 it **came to p** at the end of the four	1961
	12:41 even the selfsame day it **came to p**,	1961
	12:51 it **came to p** the selfsame day, that	1961
	13:15 it **came to p**, when Pharaoh would	1961
	13:17 it **came to p**, when Pharaoh had let	1961
	14:24 it **came to p**, that in the morning watch	1961
	15:16 till thy people **p over**, O LORD, till	5674
	15:16 O LORD, till the people **p over**,	5674
	16: 5 it shall **come to p** on the sixth day	1961
	16:10 it **came to p**, as Aaron spake unto	1961
	16:13 it **came to p**, that at even the quails came	1961
	16:22 it **came to p**, that on the sixth day they	1961
	16:27 it **came to p**, that there went out some	1961
	17:11 it **came to p**, when Moses held up his	1961
	18:13 it **came to p** on the morrow, that Moses	1961
	19:16 it **came to p** on the third day in	1961
	22:27 it shall **come to p**, when he crieth unto	1961
	32:19 it **came to p**, as soon as he came nigh	1961
	32:30 it **came to p** on the morrow, that Moses	1961
	33: 7 it **came to p**, that every one which	1961
	33: 8 it **came to p**, when Moses went out unto	1961
	33: 9 it **came to p**, as Moses entered into	1961
	33:19 I will **make** all my goodness **p** before	5674
	33:22 it shall **come to p**, while my glory passeth	1961
	33:22 cover thee with my hand while I **p by:**	5674
	34:29 it **came to p**, when Moses came down	1961
	40:17 it **came to p** in the first month in	1961
Lev	9: 1 it **came to p** on the eighth day, that	1961
	18:21 shalt not let any of thy seed **p through**	5674
Nu	5:27 it shall **come to p**, that, if she be defiled,	1961
	7: 1 it **came to p** on the day that Moses had	1961
	10:11 it **came to p** on the twentieth day of	1961
	10:35 it **came to p**, when the ark set forward,	1961
	11:23 whether my word shall **come to p** unto	7136
	11:25 it **came to p**, that when the spirit rested	1961
	16:31 it **came to p**, as he had made an end of	1961
	16:42 it **came to p**, when the congregation was	1961
	17: 5 it shall **come to p**, that the man's rod,	1961
	17: 8 it **came to p**, that on the morrow Moses	1961
	20:17 Let us **p**, I pray thee, through thy country:	5674
	20:17 we will not **p through** the fields,	5674
	20:18 said unto him, Thou shalt not **p** by me,	5674
	21: 8 it shall **come to p**, that every one that is	1961
	21: 9 put it upon a pole, and it **came to p**, that	1961
	21:22 Let me **p through** thy land: we will not	5674
	21:23 Sihon would not suffer Israel to **p through**	5674
	22:41 it **came to p** on the morrow, that Balak	1961
	26: 1 it **came to p** after the plague, that	1961
	27: 7 **cause** the inheritance of their father to **p**	5674
	27: 8 ye shall **cause** his inheritance **to p** unto	5674
	32:27 servants will **p over**, every man armed	5674
	32:29 of Reuben will **p** with you **over** Jordan,	5674
	32:30 if they will not **p over** with you armed,	5674
	32:32 We will **p over** armed before the LORD	5674
	33:55 it shall **come to p**, that those which ye	1961
	33:56 Moreover it shall **come to p**, that I shall	1961
	34: 4 the ascent of Akrabbim, and **p on** to Zin:	5674
	34: 4 on to Hazar-addar, and **p on** to Azmon:	5674
Dt	1: 3 it **came to p** in the fortieth year,	1961
	2: 4 Ye are to **p through** the coast of your	5674
	2:16 it **came to p**, when all the men of war	1961
	2:18 Thou art to **p over through** Ar, the coast	5674
	2:24 your journey, and **p over** the river Arnon:	5674
	2:27 Let me **p through** thy land: I will go along	5674
	2:28 only I will **p through** on my feet;	5674
	2:29 until I shall **p over** Jordan into the land	5674
	2:30 Sihon king of Heshbon would not let us **p**	5674
	3:18 shall **p over** armed before your brethren	5674
	5:23 it **came to p**, when ye heard the voice	1961
	7:12 it shall **come to p**, if ye hearken	1961
	9: 1 Thou art to **p over** Jordan this day, to go	5674
	9:11 it **came to p** at the end of forty days and	1961
	11:13 it shall **come to p**, if you shall hearken	1961
	11:29 it shall **come to p**, when the LORD thy	1961
	11:31 For ye shall **p over** Jordan to go in to	5674
	13: 2 the sign or the wonder **come to p**,	935
	18:10 **maketh** his son or his daughter	
	to **p through**	5674
	18:19 it shall **come to p**, that whosoever will	1961
	18:22 if the thing follow not, nor **come to p**,	935
	24: 1 it **come to p** that she find no favour in his	1961
	27: 2 be on the day when you shall **p over**	5674
	28: 1 it shall **come to p**, if thou shalt hearken	1961
	28:15 it shall **come to p**, if thou wilt not	1961
	28:63 it shall **come to p**, that as the LORD	1961
	29:19 it **come to p**, when he heareth the words	1961
	30: 1 it shall **come to p**, when all these things	1961
	31:21 it shall **come to p**, when many evils and	1961
	31:24 it **came to p**, when Moses had made an	1961
Jos	1: 1 the servant of the LORD it **came to p**,	1961
	1:11 **P through** the host, and command	5674
	1:11 for within three days ye shall **p over** this	5674
	1:14 ye shall **p** before your brethren armed,	5674
	2: 5 it **came to p about** the time of shutting of	1961
	3: 2 it **came to p** after three days, that	1961
	3: 6 covenant, and **p over** before the people.	5674
	3:13 it shall **come to p**, as soon as the soles of	1961
	3:14 it **came to p**, when the people removed	1961
	3:14 to **p over** Jordan, and the priests bearing	5674

Jos	4: 1 it **came to p**, when all the people were	1961
	4: 5 **P over** before the ark of the LORD your	5674
	4:11 it **came to p**, when all the people were	1961
	4:18 it **came to p**, when the priests that bare	1961
	5: 1 it **came to p**, when all the kings of	1961
	5: 8 it **came to p**, when they had done	1961
	5:13 it **came to p**, when Joshua was by Jericho,	1961
	6: 5 it shall **come to p**, that when they make	1961
	6: 7 **P on**, and compass the city, and let him	5674
	6: 7 let him that is armed **p on** before the ark	5674
	6: 8 it **came to p**, when Joshua had spoken	1961
	6:15 it **came to p** on the seventh day, that	1961
	6:16 it **came to p** at the seventh time, when	1961
	6:20 it **came to p**, when the people heard	1961
	8: 5 it shall **come to p**, when they come out	1961
	8:14 it **came to p**, when the king of Ai saw it,	1961
	8:24 it **came to p**, when Israel had made an	1961
	9: 1 it **came to p**, when all the kings which	1961
	9:16 it **came to p** at the end of three days after	1961
	10: 1 it **came to p**, when Adoni-zedek king	1961
	10:11 it **came to p**, as they fled from before	1961
	10:20 it **came to p**, when Joshua and the	1961
	10:24 it **came to p**, when they brought out	1961
	10:27 it **came to p** at the time of the going	1961
	11: 1 it **came to p**, when Jabin king of Hazor	1961
	15:18 it **came to p**, as she came unto him, that	1961
	17:13 Yet it **came to p**, when the children of	1961
	21:45 unto the house of Israel; all **came to p**.	935
	22:19 ye **over** unto the land of the possession	5674
	23: 1 it **came to p** a long time after that	1961
	23:14 all are **come to p** unto you, and not one	935
	23:15 Therefore it shall **come to p**, that as all	1961
	24:29 it **came to p** after these things, that	1961
Jdg	1: 1 after the death of Joshua it **came to p**,	1961
	1:14 it **came to p**, when she came to him,	1961
	1:28 it **came to p**, when Israel was strong,	1961
	2: 4 it **came to p**, when the angel of the LORD	1961
	2:19 it **came to p**, when the judge was dead,	1961
	3:27 it **came to p**, when he was come, that he	1961
	3:28 and suffered not a man to **p over**.	5674
	6: 7 it **came to p**, when the children of Israel	1961
	6:25 it **came to p** the same night, that	1961
	7: 9 it **came to p** the same night, that	1961
	8:33 it **came to p**, as soon as Gideon was dead,	1961
	9:42 it **came to p** on the morrow, that the	1961
	11: 4 it **came to p** in process of time, that	1961
	11:17 Let me, I pray thee, **p through** thy land:	5674
	11:19 said unto him, Let us **p**, we pray thee,	5674
	11:20 Sihon trusted not Israel to **p through** his	5674
	11:35 it **came to p**, when he saw her, that he	1961
	11:39 it **came to p** at the end of two months,	1961
	13:12 said, Now let thy words **come to p**.	935
	13:17 that when thy sayings **come to p** we may	935
	13:20 it **came to p**, when the flame went up	1961
	14:11 it **came to p**, when they saw him, that	1961
	14:15 it **came to p** on the seventh day, that	1961
	14:17 it **came to p** on the seventh day, that he	1961
	15: 1 it **came to p** within a while after,	1961
	15:17 it **came to p**, when he had made an end	1961
	16: 4 it **came to p** afterward, that he loved a	1961
	16:16 it **came to p**, when she pressed him daily	1961
	16:25 it **came to p**, when their hearts were	1961
	19: 1 it **came to p** in those days, when there	1961
	19: 5 it **came to p** on the fourth day, when	1961
	19:12 of Israel; we will **p over** to Gibeah.	5674
	21: 3 of Israel, why is this **come to p** in Israel,	1961
	21: 4 it **came to p** on the morrow, that the	1961
Ru	1: 1 Now it **came to p** in the days when	1961
	1:19 it **came to p**, when they were come to	1961
	3: 8 it **came to p** at midnight, that the man	1961
1Sa	1:12 it **came to p**, as she continued praying	1961
	1:20 Wherefore it **came to p**, when the time	1961
	2:36 it shall **come to p**, that every one that is	1961
	3: 2 it **came to p** at that time, when Eli was	1961
	4:18 it **came to p**, when he made mention of	1961
	5:10 it **came to p**, as the ark of God came to	1961
	7: 2 it **came to p**, while the ark abode in	1961
	8: 1 it **came to p**, when Samuel was old, that	1961
	9: 6 all that he saith **cometh surely to p:**	935+935
	9:26 it **came to p about** the spring of the day,	1961
	9:27 Bid the servant **p on** before us, (and	5674
	10: 5 it shall **come to p**, when thou art come	1961
	10: 9 and all those signs **came to p** that day.	935
	10:11 it **came to p**, when all that knew him	1961
	11:11 it **came to p**, that they which remained	1961
	13:10 it **came to p**, as soon as he had made	1961
	13:22 So it **came to p** in the day of battle,	1961
	14: 1 it **came to p** upon a day, that Jonathan	1961
	14: 8 we will **p over** unto these men, and we	5674
	14:19 it **came to p**, while Saul talked with	1961
	16: 6 it **came to p**, when they were come, that	1961
	16: 8 and **made** him **p** before Samuel.	5674
	16: 9 Jesse **made** Shammah to **p by**. And he	5674
	16:10 Jesse **made** seven of his sons to **p** before	5674
	16:16 it shall **come to p**, when the evil spirit	1961
	16:23 it **came to p**, when the evil spirit from	1961
	17:48 it **came to p**, when the Philistine arose,	1961
	18: 1 it **came to p**, when he had made an end of	1961
	18: 6 it **came to p** as they came, when David	5674
	18:10 it **came to p** on the morrow, that the evil	1961
	18:19 it **came to p** at the time when Merab	1961
	18:30 it **came to p**, after they went forth,	1961
	20:27 it **came to p** on the morrow, which was	1961
	20:35 it **came to p** in the morning, that	1961
	23: 6 it **came to p**, when Abiathar the son of	1961

P

1Sa
23:23 it shall **come to p**, if he be in the land, 1961
24: 1 it **came to p**, when Saul was returned 1961
24: 5 it **came to p** afterward, that David's heart 1961
24:16 it **came to p**, when David had made an 1961
25:30 it shall **come to p**, when the LORD shall 1961
25:37 it **came to p** in the morning, when the 1961
25:38 it **came to p** about ten days *after,* that 1961
28: 1 it **came to p** in those days, that 1961
30: 1 it **came to p**, when David and his men 1961
31: 8 it **came to p** on the morrow, when 1961

2Sa
1: 1 Now it **came to p** after the death of Saul, 1961
1: 2 it **came** even **to p** on the third day, that 1961
2: 1 it **came to p** after this, that David 1961
2:23 it **came to p**, that as many as came to 1961
3: 6 it **came to p**, while there was war 1961
4: 4 it **came to p**, as she made haste to flee, 1961
7: 1 it **came to p**, when the king sat in his 1961
7: 4 it **came to p** that night, that the word of 1961
8: 1 after this it **came to p**, that David smote 1961
10: 1 it **came to p** after this, that the king of 1961
11: 1 it **came to p**, after the year was expired, 1961
11: 2 it **came to p** in an eveningtide, that David 1961
11:14 it **came to p** in the morning, that David 1961
11:16 it **came to p**, when Joab observed the 1961
12:18 it **came to p** on the seventh day, that 1961
12:31 and **made** them **p** through the brickkiln: 5674
13: 1 it **came to p** after this, that Absalom 1961
13:23 it **came to p** after two full years, 1961
13:30 it **came to p**, while they *were* in the way, 1961
13:36 it **came to p**, as soon as he had made an 1961
15: 1 it **came to p** after this, that Absalom 1961
15: 7 it **came to p** after forty years, that 1961
15:22 David said to Ittai, Go and **p over.** 5674
15:32 it **came to p**, that *when* David was come 1961
16:16 it **came to p**, when Hushai the Archite, 1961
17: 9 it will **come to p**, when *some* of them be 1961
17:16 wilderness, but **speedily p over;** 5674+5674
17:21 it **came to p**, after they were departed, 1961
17:21 Arise, and **p quickly** over the water: 4120
17:27 it **came to p**, when David was come to 1961
19:25 it **came to p**, when he was come *to* 1961
21:18 it **came to p** after this, that there was 1961

1Ki
1:21 it shall **come to p**, when my lord 1961
2:39 it **came to p** at the end of three years, 1961
3:18 it **came to p** the third day after that I was 1961
5: 7 it **came to p**, when Hiram heard the 1961
6: 1 it **came to p** in the four hundred and 1961
8:10 it **came to p**, when the priests were come 1961
9: 1 it **came to p**, when Solomon had finished 1961
9:10 it **came to p** at the end of twenty years, 1961
11: 4 For it **came to p**, when Solomon was old, 1961
11:15 For it **came to p**, when David was in 1961
11:29 it **came to p** at that time when Jeroboam 1961
12: 2 it **came to p**, when Jeroboam the son of 1961
12:20 it **came to p**, when all Israel heard that 1961
13: 4 it **came to p**, when king Jeroboam heard 1961
13:20 it **came to p**, as they sat at the table, 1961
13:23 it **came to p**, after he had eaten bread, 1961
13:31 it **came to p**, after he had buried him, 1961
13:32 Samaria, shall **surely come to p.** 1961+1961
14:25 it **came to p** in the fifth year of king 1961
15:21 it **came to p**, when Baasha heard *thereof,* 1961
15:29 it **came to p**, when he reigned, *that* he 1961
16:11 it **came to p**, when he **began** to reign, 1961
16:18 it **came to p**, when Zimri saw that the 1961
16:31 it **came to p**, as if it had been a light thing 1961
17: 7 it **came to p** after a while, that the brook 1961
17:17 it **came to p** after these things, *that* the 1961
18: 1 it **came to p** *after* many days, that the 1961
18: 6 they divided the land between them to **p** 5674
18:12 it shall **come to p**, as soon as I am gone 1961
18:17 it **came to p**, when Ahab saw Elijah, 1961
18:27 it **came to p** at noon, that Elijah mocked 1961
18:29 it **came to p**, when midday was past, 1961
18:36 it **came to p** at *the time of* the offering of 1961
18:44 it **came to p** at the seventh *time,* that he 1961
18:45 it **came to p** in the mean while, that 1961
19:17 it shall **come to p**, *that* him that escapeth 1961
20:12 it **came to p**, when *Ben-hadad* heard this 1961
20:26 it **came to p** at the return of the year, 1961
21: 1 it **came to p** after these things, *that* 1961
21:15 it **came to p**, when Jezebel heard that 1961
21:16 it **came to p**, when Ahab heard that 1961
21:27 it **came to p**, when Ahab heard those 1961
22: 2 it **came to p** on the third year, that 1961
22:32 it **came to p**, when the captains of 1961
22:33 it **came to p**, when the captains of 1961

2Ki
1: 1 it **came to p**, when the LORD would take 1961
2: 9 it **came to p**, when they were gone over, 1961
2:11 it **came to p**, *as* they still went on, 1961
3: 5 it **came to p**, when Ahab was dead, that 1961
3:15 it **came to p**, when the minstrel played, 1961
3:20 it **came to p** in the morning, when the 1961
4: 6 it **came to p**, when the vessels were full, 1961
4:25 it **came to p**, when the man of God saw 1961
4:40 it **came to p**, as they were eating of 1961
5: 7 it **came to p**, when the king of Israel had 1961
6: 9 Beware that *thou* **p** not such a place; 5674
6:20 it **came to p**, when they were come *into* 1961
6:24 it **came to p** after this, that Ben-hadad 1961
6:30 it **came to p**, when the king heard 1961
7:18 it **came to p** as the man of God had 1961
8: 3 it **came to p** at the seven years' end, 1961
8: 5 it **came to p**, *as* he was telling the king 1961
8:15 it **came to p** on the morrow, that he took 1961

2Ki
9:22 it **came to p**, when Joram saw Jehu, that 1961
10: 7 it **came to p**, when the letter came to 1961
10: 9 it **came to p** in the morning, that he went 1961
10:25 it **came to p**, as soon as he had made an 1961
13:21 it **came to p**, as they were burying a man, 1961
14: 5 it **came to p**, as soon as the kingdom was 1961
15:12 fourth *generation.* And so it **came to** 1961
16: 3 and **made** his son **to p** through the fire, 5674
17:17 **caused** their sons and their daughters **to p** 5674
18: 1 Now it **came to p** in the third year of 1961
18: 9 it **came to p** in the fourth year of David's 1961
19: 1 it **came to p**, when king Hezekiah heard 1961
19:25 now have I **brought** it **to p**, that thou 935
19:35 it **came to p** that night, that the angel of 1961
19:37 it **came to p**, as he was worshipping *in* 1961
20: 4 it **came to p**, afore Isaiah was gone out 1961
21: 6 he **made** his son **p** through the fire, 5674
22: 3 it **came to p** in the eighteenth year of 1961
22:11 it **came to p**, when the king had heard 1961
23:10 might **make** his son or his daughter **to p** 5674
24:20 of the LORD it **came to p** in Jerusalem 1961
25: 1 it **came to p** in the ninth year of his reign, 1961
25:25 it **came to p** in the seventh month, 1961
25:27 it **came to p** in the seven and thirtieth 1961

1Ch
10: 8 it **came to p** on the morrow, when 1961
15:26 it **came to p**, when God helped the 1961
15:29 it **came to p**, *as* the ark of the covenant 1961
17: 1 Now it **came to p**, as David sat in his 1961
17: 3 it **came to p** the same night, that the 1961
17:11 it shall **come to p**, when thy days be 1961
18: 1 Now after this it **came to p**, that David 1961
19: 1 Now it **came to p** after this, that Nahash 1961
20: 1 it **came to p**, that after the year was 1961
20: 4 it **came to p** after this, that there arose 1961

2Ch
5:11 it **came to p**, when the priests were come 1961
5:13 It **came** even **to p**, as the trumpeters and 1961
8: 1 it **came to p** at the end of twenty years, 1961
10: 2 it **came to p**, when Jeroboam the son of 1961
12: 1 it **came to p**, when Rehoboam had 1961
12: 2 it **came to p**, *that* in the fifth year of king 1961
13:15 it **came to p**, that God smote Jeroboam 1961
16: 5 it **came to p**, when Baasha heard *it,* that 1961
18:31 it **came to p**, when the captains of 1961
18:32 it **came to p**, that when the captains of 1961
20: 1 it **came to p** after this also, *that* 1961
21:19 it **came to p**, that in process of time, after 1961
22: 8 it **came to p**, that when Jehu was 1961
24: 4 it **came to p** after this, *that* Joash was 1961
24:11 Now it **came to p**, that at *what* time 1961
24:23 it **came to p** at the end of the year, *that* 1961
25: 3 it **came to p**, when the kingdom was 1961
25:14 it **came to p**, after that Amaziah was 1961
25:16 it **came to p**, as he talked with him, that 1961
33: 6 **caused** his children **to p** through the fire 5674
34:19 it **came to p**, when the king had heard 1961

Ne
1: 1 it **came to p** in the month Chisleu, 1961
1: 4 it **came to p**, when I heard these words, 1961
2: 1 it **came to p** in the month Nisan, 1961
2:14 for the beast *that* was under me to **p** 5674
4: 1 it **came to p**, that when Sanballat heard 1961
4: 7 it **came to p**, *that* when Sanballat, 1961
4:12 it **came to p**, that when the Jews which 1961
4:15 it **came to p**, when our enemies heard 1961
4:16 it **came to p** from that time forth, *that* 1961
6: 1 Now it **came to p**, when Sanballat, 1961
6:16 it **came to p**, that when all our enemies 1961
7: 1 it **came to p**, when the wall was built, 1961
13: 3 Now it **came to p**, when they had heard 1961
13:19 it **came to p**, when the gates of 1961

Est
1: 1 it **came to p** in the days of Ahasuerus, 1961
2: 8 So it **came to p**, when the king's 1961
3: 4 Now it **came to p**, when they spake daily 1961
5: 1 it **came to p** on the third day, 1961

Job
6:15 *and* as the stream of brooks they **p away;** 5674
11:16 *and* remember it as waters *that* **p away:** 5674
14: 5 appointed his bounds that he cannot **p;** 5674
19: 8 hath fenced up my way that I cannot **p,** 5674
34:20 be troubled at midnight, and **p away:** 5674

Ps
37: 5 also in him; and he shall **bring** *it* **to p.** 6213
37: 7 man who **bringeth** wicked devices **to p.** 6213
58: 8 let *every one of them* **p away:** 1980
78:13 the sea, and **caused** them **to p through;** 5674
80:12 that all they which **p** by the way do pluck 5674
89:41 All that **p by** the way spoil him: he is a 5674
104: 9 set a bound that they may not **p over;** 5674
136:14 **made** Israel **to p through** the midst of it: 5674
148: 6 he hath made a decree which shall not **p.** 5674

Pr
4:15 Avoid it, **p** not by it, turn from it, 5674
4:15 pass not by it, turn from it, and **p away.** 5674
8:29 that the waters should not **p** his 5674
16:30 moving his lips he **bringeth** evil **to p.** 3615
19:11 *it is* his glory to **p over** a transgression. 5674
22: 3 but the simple **p on,** and are punished. 5674
27:12 *but* the simple **p on,** *and* are punished. 5674

Isa
2: 2 it shall **come to p** in the last days, that 1961
3:24 it shall **come to p**, that instead of sweet 1961
4: 3 it shall **come to p**, *that* he that is left in 1961
7: 1 it **came to p** in the days of Ahaz the son 1961
7: 7 not stand, neither shall it **come to p.** 1961
7:18 it shall **come to p** in that day, *that* 1961
7:21 it shall **come to p** in that day, *that* a man 1961
7:22 it shall **come to p**, for the abundance of 1961
7:23 it shall **come to p** in that day, *that* every 1961
8: 8 shall **p through** Judah; he shall overflow 2498
8:21 they shall **p through** it, hardly bestead and 5674

Isa
8:21 shall **come to p**, that when they shall be 1961
10:12 Wherefore it shall **come to p**, *that* when 1961
10:20 it shall **come to p** in that day, *that* 1961
10:27 it shall **come to p** in that day, *that* his 1961
11:11 it shall **come to p** in that day, *that* the Lord 1961
14: 3 it shall **come to p** in the day that 1961
14:24 as I have thought, so shall it **come to p;** 1961
16:12 it shall **come to p**, when it is seen that 1961
17: 4 that day it shall **come to p**, *that* the glory 1961
21: 1 As whirlwinds in the south **p through;** 2498
22: 7 shall **come to p**, *that* thy choicest valleys 1961
22:20 it shall **come to p** in that day, that I will 1961
23: 2 that **p over** the sea, have replenished. 5674
23: 6 **P** ye **over** to Tarshish; howl, ye 5674
23:10 **P through** thy land as a river, O daughter 5674
23:12 arise, **p over** to Chittim; there also shalt 5674
23:15 it shall **come to p** in that day, that Tyre 1961
23:17 it shall **come to p** after the end of seventy 1961
24:18 it shall **come to p**, *that* he who fleeth 1961
24:21 it shall **come to p** in that day, *that* 1961
27:12 it shall **come to p** in that day, *that* 1961
27:13 it shall **come to p** in that day, *that* the 1961
28:15 the overflowing scourge shall **p through,** 5674
28:18 the overflowing scourge shall **p through,** 5674
28:19 for morning by morning shall it **p over,** 5674
28:21 and **bring to p** his act, his strange act. 5647
30:32 *place* where the grounded staff shall **p,** 4569
31: 9 he shall **p over** *to* his strong hold for fear, 5674
33:21 neither shall gallant ship **p** thereby. 5674
34:10 none shall **p through** it for ever and ever. 5674
35: 8 the unclean shall not **p over** it; but it 5674
36: 1 it **came to p** in the fourteenth year of 1961
37: 1 it **came to p**, when king Hezekiah heard 1961
37:26 now have I **brought** it **to p**, that thou 935
37:38 it **came to p**, as he was worshipping *in* 1961
42: 9 the former *things* are **come to p,** 935
46:11 I have spoken *it,* I will also **bring** it **to p;** 935
47: 2 uncover the thigh, **p over** the rivers. 5674
48: 3 I did *them* suddenly, and they **came to p.** 935
48: 5 before it **came to p** I shewed *it* thee: 935
51:10 the sea a way for the ransomed to **p over?** 5674
65:24 it shall **come to p**, *that* before they call, 1961
66:23 shall **come to p**, *that* from one new moon 1961

Jer
2:10 For **p over** the isles of Chittim, and see; 5674
3: 9 it **came to p** through the lightness of her 1961
3:16 it shall **come to p**, when ye be multiplied 1961
4: 9 it shall **come to p** at that day, saith 1961
5:19 it shall **come to p**, when ye shall say, 1961
5:22 *by* a perpetual decree, that it cannot **p** it: 5674
5:22 they roar, yet can they not **p over** it? 5674
8:13 given them shall **p away from** them. 5674
9:10 that none can **p through** *them;* neither 5674
12:15 it shall **come to p**, after that I have 1961
12:16 it shall **come to p**, if they will diligently 1961
13: 6 it **came to p** after many days, that 1961
15: 2 it shall **come to p**, if they say unto thee, 1961
15:14 I will **make** *thee* **to p** with thine enemies 5674
16:10 it shall **come to p**, when thou shalt shew 1961
17:24 it shall **come to p**, if ye diligently hearken 1961
20: 3 it **came to p** on the morrow, that Pashur 1961
22: 8 many nations shall **p** by this city, 5674
25:12 it shall **come to p**, when seventy years 1961
26: 8 Now it **came to p**, when Jeremiah had 1961
27: 8 it shall **come to p**, that the nation and 1961
28: 1 it **came to p** the same year, 1961
28: 9 the word of the prophet shall **come to p,** 935
30: 8 For it shall **come to p** in that day, saith 1961
31:28 it shall **come to p**, *that* like as I have 1961
32:24 what thou hast spoken is **come to p;** 1961
32:35 **cause** their sons and their daughters
 to p through 5674
33:13 shall the flocks **p** again under the hands of 5674
35:11 it **came to p**, when Nebuchadrezzar king 1961
36: 1 it **came to p** in the fourth year of 1961
36: 9 it **came to p** in the fifth year of Jehoiakim 1961
36:16 Now it **came to p**, when they had heard 1961
36:23 it **came to p**, *that* when Jehudi had read 1961
37:11 it **came to p**, *that* when the army of 1961
39: 4 it **came to p**, *that* when Zedekiah the 1961
41: 1 Now it **came to p** in the seventh month, 1961
41: 4 it **came to p** the second day after *he* had 1961
41: 6 it **came to p**, as he met them, he said 1961
41:13 it **came to p**, *that* when all the people 1961
42: 4 it **came to p**, *that* whatsoever thing 1961
42: 7 it **came to p** after ten days, that the word 1961
42:16 it shall **come to p**, *that* the sword, which 1961
43: 1 it **came to p**, *that* when Jeremiah had 1961
49:39 it shall **come to p** in the latter days, that I 1961
51:43 neither doth *any* son of man **p** thereby. 5674
52: 3 it **came to p** in Jerusalem 1961
52: 4 it **came to p** in the ninth year of his reign, 1961
52:31 it **came to p** in the seven and thirtieth 1961

La
1:12 *it* nothing to you, all ye that **p by**? 1870+5674
2:15 All that **p** by clap *their* hands at thee; 5674
3:37 Who *is* he *that* saith, and it **cometh to p,** 1961
3:44 that *our* prayer should not **p through.** 5674
4:21 the cup also shall **p through** unto thee: 5674

Eze
1: 1 Now it **came to p** in the thirtieth year, 1961
3:16 it **came to p** at the end of seven days, 1961
5: 1 **cause** *it* **to p** upon thine head and upon 5674
5:14 about thee, in the sight of all that **p by.** 5674
5:17 pestilence and blood shall **p through** thee; 5674
8: 1 it **came to p** in the sixth year, in the sixth 1961
9: 8 it **came to p**, while they were slaying 1961
10: 6 it **came to p**, *that* when he had 1961

Eze 11:13 it **came to p**, when I prophesied,	1961	
12:25 word that I shall speak shall **come to p**;	6213	
14:15 If I **cause** noisome beasts **to p** through	5674	
14:15 that no man may **p through** because of	5674	
16:21 them to **cause** them **to p through**	5674	
16:23 it **came to p** after all thy wickedness,	1961	
20: 1 it **came to p** in the seventh year, in the	1961	
20:26 they **caused** your sons **to p** through	5674	
20:31 when *ye* **make** your sons **to p** through	5674	
20:37 I will **cause** you **to p** under the rod,	5674	
21: 7 it cometh, and shall be **brought to p**	1961	
23:37 **caused** their sons, whom they bare		
unto me, **to p** for them through	5674	
24:14 LORD have spoken it: it shall **come to p**,	935	
26: 1 it **came to p** in the eleventh year,	1961	
29:11 No foot of man shall **p** through it, nor foot	5674	
29:11 nor foot of beast shall **p** through it,	5674	
29:17 it **came to p** in the seven and	1961	
30:20 it **came to p** in the eleventh year,	1961	
31: 1 it **came to p** in the eleventh year,	1961	
32: 1 it **came to p** in the twelfth year,	1961	
32:17 It **came to p** also in the twelfth year,	1961	
32:19 Whom dost thou **p** in beauty? go down,	4480	
33:21 it **came to p** in the twelfth year of our	1961	
33:28 be desolate, that none shall **p through**.	5674	
33:33 when this **cometh to p**, (lo, it will come)	935	
37: 2 **caused** me **to p** by them round about:	5674	
38:10 It shall also **come to p**, *that* at the same	1961	
38:18 it shall **come to p** at the same time when	1961	
39:11 it shall **come to p** in that day, *that* I will	1961	
39:15 the passengers *that* **p through** the land,	5674	
44:17 it shall **come to p**, *that* when they enter	1961	
46:21 **caused** me **to p** by the four corners of	5674	
47: 5 *and it was* a river that I could not **p over**:	5674	
47: 5 it shall **come to p**, *that* every thing that	1961	
47:10 it shall **come to p**, *that* the fishers shall	1961	
47:22 it shall **come to p**, *that* ye shall divide it	1961	
47:23 it shall **come to p**, *that* in what tribe	1961	
Da 2:29 bed, what should **come to p** hereafter:	1934	
2:29 known to thee what shall **come to p**.	1934	
2:45 the king what shall **come to p** hereafter:	1934	
4:16 unto him; and let seven times **p** over him.	2499	
4:23 of the field, till seven times **p** over him;	2499	
4:25 and seven times shall **p** over thee,	2499	
4:32 oxen, and seven times shall **p** over thee,	2499	
7:14 which shall not **p away**, and his kingdom	5709	
8: 2 it **came to p**, when I saw, that I *was* at	1961	
8:15 it **came to p**, when I, *even* I Daniel,	1961	
11:10 and overflow, and **p through**:	5674	
11:40 and shall overflow and **p** through.	5674	
Hos 1: 5 it shall **come to p** at that day, that I will	1961	
1:10 it shall **come to p**, *that* in the place	1961	
2:21 it shall **come to p** in that day, I will hear,	1961	
2:28 it shall **come to p** afterward, that I will	1961	
Joel 2:32 it shall **come to p**, *that* whosoever shall	1961	
3:17 there shall no strangers **p** through her any	5674	
3:18 it shall **come to p** in that day, *that*	1961	
Am 5: 5 enter *into* Gilgal, and **p** not *to* Beer-sheba:	5674	
5:17 for I will **p** through thee, saith the LORD.	5674	
6: 2 **P** ye *unto* Calneh, and see; and from	5674	
6: 9 it shall **come to p**, if there remain ten	1961	
7: 2 it **came to p**, *that* when they had made	1961	
7: 8 I will not again **p** by them any more.	5674	
8: 2 I will not again **p** by them any more.	5674	
8: 9 it shall **come to p** in that day, saith the	1961	
Jnh 4: 8 it **came to p**, when the sun did arise,	1961	
Mic 1:11 **P** ye **away**, thou inhabitant of Saphir,	5674	
2: 8 **p** by securely *as men* averse from war.	5674	
2:13 their king shall **p** before them,	5674	
4: 1 in the last days it shall **come to p**, *that*	1961	
5:10 it shall **come to p** in that day, saith	1961	
Na 1:12 be cut down, when he shall **p through**.	5674	
1:15 for the wicked shall no more **p** through	5674	
3: 7 it shall **come to p**, *that* all they that look	1961	
Hab 1:11 and he shall **p over**, and offend,	5674	
Zep 1: 8 it shall **come to p** in the day of	1961	
1:10 it shall **come to p** in that day, saith	1961	
1:12 it shall **come to p** at that time, *that* I will	1961	
2: 2 bring forth, *before* the day **p** as the chaff,	5674	
Zec 3: 4 I have **caused** thine iniquity **to p** from	5674	
6:15 *this* shall **come to p**, if ye will diligently	1961	
7: 1 it **came to p** in the fourth year of the	1961	
7:13 Therefore it is **come to p**, *that* as he cried	1961	
8:13 shall **come to p**, *that* as ye were a curse	1961	
8:20 *It shall* yet *come to p*, that there shall	NIH	
8:23 In those days *it shall come to p*, that ten	NIH	
9: 8 no oppressor shall **p** through them any	5674	
10:11 he shall **p** through the sea *with* affliction,	5674	
12: 9 it shall **come to p** in that day, *that* I will	1961	
13: 2 it shall **come to p** in that day, saith	1961	
13: 2 **cause** the prophets and the		
unclean spirit **to p**	5674	
13: 3 it shall **come to p**, *that* when any shall	1961	
13: 4 it shall **come to p** in that day, *that*	1961	
13: 8 it shall **come to p**, *that* in all the land,	1961	
14: 6 it shall **come to p** in that day, *that* the	1961	
14: 7 it shall **come to p**, *that* at evening time it	1961	
14:13 it shall **come to p** in that day, *that* a great	1961	
14:16 it shall **come to p**, *that* every one that is	1961	
Mt 5:18 heaven and earth *p*, one jot or one tittle	3928	
5:18 one tittle shall in no wise **p** from the law,	3928	
7:28 And it **came to p**, when Jesus had ended	1096	
8:28 so that no *man* might **p** by that way.	3928	
9:10 And it **came to p**, as Jesus sat at meat in	1096	
11: 1 And it **came to p**, when Jesus had made	1096	

Mt 13:53 And it **came to p**, *that* when Jesus had	1096	
19: 1 And it **came to p**, *that* when Jesus had	1096	
24: 6 for all *these things* must **come to p**,	1096	
24:34 say unto you, This generation shall not **p**,	3928	
24:35 Heaven and earth shall **p away**,	3928	
24:35 away, but my words shall not **p away**.	3928	
26: 1 it **came to p**, when Jesus had finished	1096	
26:39 if it be possible, let this cup **p** from me:	3928	
26:42 this cup may not **p away** from me,	3928	
Mk 1: 9 it **came to p** in those days, *that* Jesus	1096	
2:15 it **came to p**, that as *Jesus* sat at meat	1096	
2:23 And it **came to p**, that he went through	1096	
4: 4 And it **came to p**, as he sowed, some fell	1096	
4:35 Let us **p over** unto the other side.	1330	
11:23 *things* which he saith shall **come to p**;	1096	
13:29 when ye shall see these *things* **come to p**,	1096	
13:30 unto you, that this generation shall not **p**,	3928	
13:31 Heaven and earth shall **p away**:	3928	
13:31 away: but my words shall not **p away**.	3928	
14:35 were possible, the hour might **p** from him.	3928	
Lk 1: 8 it **came** to **p**, *that* while he executed	1096	
1:23 it **came to p**, *that*, as soon as the days	1096	
1:41 And it **came to p**, *that*, when Elisabeth	1096	
1:59 And it **came to p** on the eighth day	1096	
2: 1 it **came to p** in those days, *that* there	1096	
2:15 it **came to p**, as the angels were gone	1096	
2:15 and see this thing which is **come to p**,	1096	
2:46 it **came to p**, *that* after three days they	1096	
3:21 it **came to p**, *that* Jesus also being	1096	
5: 1 And it **came to p**, *that*, as the people	1096	
5:12 it **came to p**, when he was in a certain	1096	
5:17 And it **came to p** on a certain day, as he	1096	
6: 1 it **came to p** on the second sabbath	1096	
6: 6 it **came to p** also on another sabbath,	1096	
6:12 it **came to p** in those days, *that* he	1096	
7:11 it **came to p** the *day* after, *that* he went	1096	
8: 1 it **came to p** afterward, that he went	1096	
8:22 it **came to p** on a certain day, that he	1096	
8:40 And it **came to p**, *that*, when Jesus was	1096	
9:18 it **came to p**, as he was alone praying,	1096	
9:28 it **came to p** about an eight days after	1096	
9:33 And it **came to p**, as they departed from	1096	
9:37 And it **came to p**, *that* on the next day,	1096	
9:51 it **came to p**, when the time was come	1096	
9:57 And it **came to p**, as they went in	1096	
10:38 Now it **came to p**, as they went, that he	1096	
11: 1 it **came to p**, *that*, as he was praying in	1096	
11:14 it **came to p**, when the devil was gone	1096	
11:27 it **came to p**, as he spake these *things*,	1096	
11:42 **p over** judgment and the love of God:	3928	
12:55 There will be heat; and it **cometh to p**.		
14: 1 it **came to p**, as he went into the house	1096	
16:17 it is easier for heaven and earth to **p**,	3928	
16:22 And it **came to p**, that the beggar died,	1096	
16:26 they which would **p** from hence to you	1224	
16:26 neither can they **p** to us, that *would come*	1276	
17:11 it **came to p**, as he went to Jerusalem,	1096	
17:14 And it **came to p**, that, as they went,	1096	
18:35 it **came to p**, *that* as he was come nigh	1279	
18:36 And hearing the multitude **p by**, he asked	1279	
19: 4 tree to see him: for he was to **p** that *way*.	1330	
19:15 And it **came to p**, *that* when he was	1096	
19:29 it **came to p**, when he was come nigh	1096	
20: 1 And it **came to p**, *that* on one of those	1096	
21: 7 be when these *things* shall **come to p**?	1096	
21: 9 for these *things* must first **come to p**;	1096	
21:28 when these *things* begin to **come to p**,	1096	
21:31 when ye see these *things* **come to p**,	1096	
21:32 This generation shall not **p away**, till all	3928	
21:33 Heaven and earth shall **p away**:	3928	
21:33 away: but my words shall not **p away**.	3928	
21:36 all these *things* that shall **come to p**,	1096	
24: 4 it **came to p**, as they were *much*	1096	
24:12 in himself at that which was **come to p**.	1096	
24:15 And it **came to p**, *that* while they	1096	
24:18 which are **come to p** there in these days?	1096	
24:30 And it **came to p**, as he sat at meat with	1096	
24:51 And it **came to p**, while he blessed them,	1096	
Jn 13:19 when it is **come to p**, ye may believe	1096	
14:29 now I have told you before it **come to p**,	1096	
14:29 that; when it is **come to p**, ye might	1096	
15:25 this cometh to **p**, that the word might be	NIG	
Ac 2:17 And it shall **come to p** in the last days,	1510	
2:21 And it shall **come to p**, *that* whosoever	1510	
3:23 And it shall **come to p**, *that* every soul,	1510	
4: 5 it **came to p** on the morrow, their	1096	
9:32 And it **came to p**, as Peter passed	1096	
9:37 And it **came to p** in those days, that she	1096	
9:43 And it **came to p**, that he tarried many days	1096	
11:26 And it **came to p**, that a whole year they	1096	
11:28 which **came to p** in the days of Claudius	1096	
14: 1 it **came to p** in Iconium, that they	1096	
16:16 And it **came to p**, as we went to prayer,	1096	
18:27 And when he was disposed to **p** into	1330	
19: 1 it **came to p**, *that*, while Apollos was at	1096	
21: 1 it **came to p**, *that* after we were gotten	1096	
22: 6 And it **came to p**, that, as I made my	1096	
22:17 And it **came to p**, that, when I was come	1096	
27:44 so it **came to p**, that *they* escaped all	1096	
28: 8 it **came to p**, that the father of Publius	1096	
28:17 it **came to p**, that after three days Paul	1096	
Ro 9:26 And it shall **come to p**, *that* in the place	1510	
1Co 7:36 if she **p** the flower of *her* age,	1510+5230	
15:54 shall be **brought to p** the saying that is	1096	
16: 5 when I shall **p through** Macedonia:	1330	

1Co 16: 5 for I do **p through** Macedonia.	1330	
2Co 1:16 And to **p** by you into Macedonia,	1330	
1Th 3: 4 we **came** to **p**, even ye, and ye know.	1096	
Jas 1:10 as the flower of the grass he shall **p away**.	3928	
1Pe 1:17 **p** the time of your sojourning *here* in fear:	390	
2Pe 3:10 in the which the heavens shall **p away**	3928	
Rev 1: 1 *things* which must shortly **come to p**;	1096	

PASSAGE (4) [PASS]

Nu 20:21 Edom refused to give Israel **p** through	5674	
Jos 22:11 Jordan, at the **p** of the children of Israel.	5676	
1Sa 13:23 went out to the **p** of Michmash.	4569	
Isa 10:29 are gone over the **p**: they have taken	4569	

PASSAGES (5) [PASS]

Jdg 12: 5 the Gileadites took the **p** of Jordan before	4569	
12: 6 him, and slew him at the **p** of Jordan:	4569	
1Sa 14: 4 between the **p**, *by* which Jonathan sought	4569	
Jer 22:20 thy voice in Bashan, and cry from the **p**:	5676	
51:32 that the **p** are stopped, and the reeds they	4569	

PASSED (161) [PASS]

Ge 12: 6 Abram **p** through the land unto the place	5674	
15:17 burning lamp that **p** between those pieces.	5674	
31:21 **p over** the river, and set his face *toward*	5674	
32:10 for with my staff I **p over** this Jordan;	5674	
32:22 eleven sons, and **p over** the ford Jabbok.	5674	
32:31 as he **p over** Penuel the sun rose upon	5674	
33: 3 he **p over** before them, and bowed	5674	
37:28 there **p by** Midianites merchantmen;	5674	
Ex 12:27 who **p over** the houses of the children of	6452	
34: 6 the LORD **p** by before him,	5674	
Nu 14: 7 The land, which we **p** through to search	5674	
20:17 *to* the left, until we have **p** thy borders.	5674	
33: 8 **p through** the midst of the sea into	5674	
33:51 When ye are **p over** Jordan into the land	5674	
Dt 2: 8 when we **p by** from our brethren	5674	
2: 8 **p** *by* the way of the wilderness of Moab.	5674	
27: 3 words of this law, when thou art **p over**,	5674	
29:16 came through the nations which ye **p by**;	5674	
Jos 2:23 **p over**, and came to Joshua the son of	5674	
3: 1 and lodged there before they **p over**.	5674	
3: 4 for ye have not **p** *this* way heretofore.	5674	
3:16 the people **p over** right against Jericho.	5674	
3:17 all the Israelites **p over** on dry *ground*,	5674	
3:17 all the people were **p clean over** Jordan.	5674	
4: 1 when all the people were clean **p over**	5674	
4: 7 it **p over** Jordan, the waters of Jordan	5674	
4:10 and the people hasted and **p over**.	5674	
4:11 when all the people were clean **p over**,	5674	
4:11 that the ark of the LORD **p over**,	5674	
4:12 the power armed before the children of Israel	5674	
4:13 war **p over** before the LORD unto battle,	5674	
4:23 until ye were **p over**, as the LORD your	5674	
5: 1 until we were **p over**, that their heart	5674	
6: 8 of rams' horns **p on** before the LORD,	5674	
10:29 Joshua **p** from Makkedah, and all Israel	5674	
10:31 Joshua **p** from Libnah, and all Israel with	5674	
10:34 from Lachish Joshua **p** unto Eglon,	5674	
15: 3 **p along** to Zin, and ascended up on	5674	
15: 3 **p along** to Hezron, and went up to Adar,	5674	
15: 4 *From thence* it **p** toward Azmon,	5674	
15: 6 and **p along** by the north of Beth-arabah;	5674	
15: 7 the border **p** towards the waters of	5674	
15:10 **p along** unto the side of mount Jearim,	5674	
15:10 *to* Beth-shemesh, and **p on** to Timnah:	5674	
15:11 **p along** to mount Baalah, and went out	5674	
16: 6 and **p by** it on the east *side* to Janohah,	5674	
18: 9 the men went and **p through** the land,	5674	
18:18 **p along** toward the side over against	5674	
18:19 the border **p along** to the side of	5674	
24:17 all the people through whom we **p**:	5674	
Jdg 3:26 **p beyond** the quarries, and escaped unto	5674	
8: 4 **p over**, he, and the three hundred men	5674	
10: 9 Moreover the children of Ammon **p over**	5674	
11:29 he **p over** Gilead and Manasseh,	5674	
11:29 **p over** Mizpeh of Gilead, and from	5674	
11:29 from Mizpeh of Gilead he **p over** *unto*	5674	
11:32 So Jephthah **p over** unto the children of	5674	
12: 3 **p over** against the children of Ammon,	5674	
18:13 they **p** thence *unto* mount Ephraim,	5674	
19:14 they **p on** and went *their way*; and the	5674	
1Sa 9: 4 he **p** through mount Ephraim,	5674	
9: 4 **p** through the land of Shalisha,	5674	
9: 4 they **p** through the land of Shalim,	5674	
9: 4 he **p** through the land of the Benjamites,	5674	
9:27 servant pass on before us, (and he **p on**,)	5674	
14:23 and the battle **p over** *unto* Beth-aven.	5674	
15:12 and **p on**, and gone down *to* Gilgal.	5674	
27: 2 he **p over** with the six hundred men that	5674	
29: 2 the lords of the Philistines **p on** by	5674	
29: 2 men **p on** in the rereward with Achish.	5674	
2Sa 2:29 **p over** Jordan, and went through all	5674	
10:17 **p over** Jordan, and came to Helam.	5674	
15:18 all his servants **p on** beside him; and all	5674	
15:18 him from Gath, **p on** before the king.	5674	
15:22 Ittai the Gittite **p over**, and all his men,	5674	
15:23 a loud voice, and all the people **p over**:	5674	
15:23 the king also *himself* **p over** the brook	5674	
15:23 all the people **p over**, toward the way of	5674	
17:22 *were* with him, and they **p over** Jordan:	5674	
17:24 Absalom **p over** Jordan, he and all the	5674	
24: 5 they **p over** Jordan, and pitched in Aroer,	5674	
1Ki 13:25 men **p by**, and saw the carcase cast in	5674	
19:11 the LORD **p by**, and a great and	5674	

P

1Ki 19:19 Elijah **p** by him, and cast his mantle upon | 5674
 20:39 as the king **p by**, he cried unto the king: | 5674
2Ki 4: 8 it fell on a day, that Elisha **p** to Shunem, | 5674
 4: 8 *so* it was, *that* as oft as he **p by**, he turned | 5674
 4:31 Gehazi **p on** before them, and laid the | 5674
 6:30 he **p by** upon the wall, and the people | 5674
 14: 9 there **p by** a wild beast that *was* in | 5674
1Ch 19:17 **p over** Jordan, and came upon them, | 5674
2Ch 9:22 king Solomon **p** all the kings of | 1431+4480
 25:18 there **p by** a wild beast that *was* in | 5674
 30:10 So the posts **p** from city to city through | 5674
Job 4:15 a spirit **p** before my face; the hair of my | 2498
 9:26 They are **p away** as the swift ships; | 2498
 15:19 given, and no stranger **p** among them. | 5674
 28: 8 not trodden it, nor the fierce lion **p** by it. | 5710
Ps 18:12 *that* was before him his thick clouds **p**, | 5674
 37:36 Yet he **p away**, and, lo, he *was* not: yea, | 5674
 48: 4 were assembled, they **p by** together. | 5674
 90: 9 For all our days are **p away** in thy wrath: | 6437
SS 3: 4 *It was* but a little that I **p** from them, but I | 5674
Isa 10:28 He is come to Aiath, he is **p** to Migron; | 5674
 40:27 my judgment is **p over** from my God? | 5674
 41: 3 He pursued them, *and* **p** safely; *even by* | 5674
Jer 2: 6 through a land that no man **p** through, | 5674
 11:15 and the holy flesh is **p** from thee? | 5674
 34:18 in twain, and **p** between the parts thereof, | 5674
 34:19 which **p** between the parts of the calf; | 5674
 46:17 *but* a noise; he hath **p** the time appointed. | 5674
Eze 16: 6 when I **p** by thee, and saw thee polluted | 5674
 16: 8 Now when I **p** by thee, and looked upon | 5674
 16:15 thy fornications on every one that **p by**; | 5674
 16:25 opened thy feet to every one that **p by**, | 5674
 36:34 lay desolate in the sight of all that **p by**. | 5674
 47: 5 swim in, a river that could not be **p over**. | 5674
Da 3:27 nor the smell of fire had **p** on them. | 5709
 6:18 to his palace, and **p the night** fasting: | 956
Hos 10:11 *corn*; but I **p over** upon her fair neck: | 5674
Jnh 2: 3 all thy billows and thy waves **p** over me. | 5674
Mic 2:13 have **p through** the gate, and are gone | 5674
Na 3:19 upon whom hath not thy wickedness **p** | 5674
Hab 3:10 the overflowing of the water **by**: the | 5674
Zec 7:14 that no man **p through** nor returned: | 5674
Mt 9: 1 and **p over**, and came into his own city. | 1276
 9: 9 as Jesus **p forth** from thence, he saw a | 3855
 20:30 they heard that Jesus **p by**, cried out, | 3855
 27:39 And they that **p by**, reviled him, | 3899
Mk 2:14 And as he **p by**, he saw Levi the *son of* | 3855
 5:21 And when Jesus was **p over** again by ship | 1276
 6:35 a desert place, and now the time *is* **far p**: | 4183
 6:48 upon the sea, and would have **p by** them: | 3928
 6:53 when they had **p over**, they came into | 1276
 9:30 departed thence, and **p through** Galilee; | 3899
 11:20 in the morning, as they **p by**, they saw | 3899
 15:21 who **p by**, coming out of the country, | 3855
 15:29 And they that **p by** railed on him, | 3899
Lk 10:31 he saw him, he **p by** on the other side. | 492
 10:32 on him, and **p by** on the other side. | 492
 17:11 that he **p through** the midst of | 1330
 19: 1 And *Jesus* entered and **p through** Jericho. | 1330
Jn 5:24 but is **p** from death unto life. | 3327
 8:59 through the midst of them, and so **p by**. | 3855
 9: 1 And as *Jesus* **p by**, he saw a man *which* | 3855
Ac 9:32 Peter **p** throughout all *quarters*, he came | 1330
 12:10 went out, and **p on** through one street; | 4281
 14:24 And after they had **p throughout** Pisidia, | 1330
 15: 3 they **p through** Phenice and Samaria, | 1330
 17: 1 when they had **p through** Amphipolis | 1353
 17:23 For as I **p by**, and beheld your devotions, | 1330
 19: 1 Paul having **p through** the upper coasts | 1330
 19:21 when he had **p through** Macedonia and | 1330
Ro 5:12 and so death **p** upon all men, for that all | 1330
1Co 10: 1 the cloud, and all **p** through the sea; | 1330
Eph 2:11 that ye *being* **in time p** Gentiles in | 4218
Heb 4:14 that is **into** the heavens, Jesus the Son | 1330
 11:29 By faith they **p through** the Red sea as by | 1224
1Jn 3:14 We know that we have **p** from death unto | 3327
Rev 21: 1 and the first earth were **p away**; | 3928
 21: 4 pain: for the former *things* are **p away**. | 565

PASSEDST (1) [PASS]
Jdg 12: 1 Wherefore **p** thou **over** to fight against | 5674

PASSENGERS (5) [PASS]
Pr 9:15 call **p** who go right *on* their ways: | 1870+5674
Eze 39:11 the valley of the **p** on the east of the sea: | 5674
 39:11 it *shall* stop the noses of the **p**: | 5674
 39:14 through the land to bury with the **p** | 5674
 39:15 the **p** that pass through the land, when | 5674

PASSEST (5) [PASS]
Dt 3:21 do unto all the kingdoms whither thou **p**. | 5674
 30:18 thou **p over** Jordan to go to possess | 5674
2Sa 15:33 If thou **p on** with me, then thou shalt be | 5674
1Ki 2:37 goest out, and **p over** the brook Kidron, | 5674
Isa 43: 2 thou **p** through the waters, I *will* be | 5674

PASSETH (38) [PASS]
Ex 30:13 every one that **p** among them that are | 5674
 30:14 Every one that **p** among them that are | 5674
 33:22 shall come to pass, while my glory **p by**, | 5674
Lev 27:32 *even of* whatsoever **p** under the rod, | 5674
Jos 3:11 the Lord of all the earth **p over** before | 5674
 16: 2 **p along** unto the borders of Archi *to* | 5674
 19:13 from thence **p on along** the east to | 5674
1Ki 9: 8 every one that **p** by it shall be astonished, | 5674

2Ki 4: 9 man of God, which **p** by us continually. | 5674
 12: 4 *even* the money of every one that **p** | 5674
2Ch 7:21 be an astonishment to every one that **p** | 5674
Job 9:11 he **p** on also, but I perceive him not. | 2498
 14:20 prevailest for ever against him, and he **p**: | 1980
 30:15 and my welfare **p away** as a cloud. | 5674
 37:21 but the wind **p**, and cleanseth them. | 5674
Ps 8: 8 **p** *through* the paths of the seas. | 5674
 78:39 wind that **p away**, and cometh not again. | 1980
 103:16 For the wind **p** over it, and it is gone; | 5674
 144: 4 his days are as a shadow that **p away**. | 5674
Pr 10:25 As the whirlwind **p**, so *is* the wicked no | 5674
 26:17 He that **p by**, *and* meddleth with strife | 5674
Ecc 1: 4 One generation **p away**, | 1980
Isa 29: 5 ones *shall be* as chaff that **p away**: | 5674
Jer 9:12 like a wilderness, that none **p through**? | 5674
 13:24 **p away** by the wind of the wilderness. | 5674
 18:16 every one that **p** thereby shall be | 5674
 19: 8 one that **p** thereby shall be astonished | 5674
Eze 35: 7 cut off from it him that **p out** and him | 5674
Hos 13: 3 and as the early dew that **p away**, | 1980
Mic 7:18 **p by** the transgression of the remnant of | 5674
Zep 2:15 every one that **p by** her shall hiss, | 5674
 3: 6 made their streets waste, that none **p by**: | 5674
Zec 9: 8 because of him that **p by**, and that | 5674
Lk 18:37 told him, that Jesus of Nazareth **p by**. | 3928
1Co 7:31 *it*: for the fashion of this world **p away**. | 3855
Eph 3:19 the love of Christ, which **p** knowledge, | 5235
Php 4: 7 which **p** all understanding, shall keep | 5242
1Jn 2:17 the world **p away**, and the lust thereof: | 3855

PASSING (13) [PASS]
Jdg 19:18 We are **p** from Beth-lehem-judah toward | 5674
2Sa 1:26 was wonderful, **p** the love of women. | 4480
 15:24 until all the people had done **p** out of | 5674
2Ki 6:26 as the king of Israel was **p by** upon | 5674
Ps 84: 6 *Who* **p** through the valley of Baca make it | 5674
Pr 7: 8 **P** through the street near her corner; | 5674
Isa 31: 5 deliver *it*; *and* **p over** he will preserve *it*. | 6452
Eze 39:14 **p through** the land to bury with | 5674
Lk 4:30 But he **p through** the midst of them | 1330
Ac 5:15 that at the least the shadow of Peter **p by** | 2064
 8:40 **p through** he preached in all the cities, | 1330
 16: 8 they **p by** Mysia came down to Troas. | 3928
 27: 8 hardly **p** it, came unto a place *which is* | 3881

PASSION (1) [PASSIONS]
Ac 1: 3 alive after his **p** by many infallible proofs, | 3958

PASSIONS (2) [PASSION]
Ac 14:15 We also are men **of like p with** you, | 3663
Jas 5:17 Elias was a man **subject to like p** as we | 3663

PASSOVER (76) [PASSOVERS]
Ex 12:11 ye shall eat it in haste: it *is* the Lord's **p**. | 6453
 12:21 according to your families, and kill the **p**. | 6453
 12:27 It *is* the sacrifice of the Lord's **p**, | 6453
 12:43 and Aaron, This *is* the ordinance of the **p**: | 6453
 12:48 will keep the **p** to the Lord, let all his | 6453
 34:25 feast of the **p** be left unto the morning. | 6453
Lev 23: 5 the first month at even *is* the Lord's **p**. | 6453
Nu 9: 2 the children of Israel also keep the **p** at | 6453
 9: 4 of Israel, that they should keep the **p**. | 6453
 9: 5 they kept the **p** on the fourteenth day of | 6453
 9: 6 they could not keep the **p** on that day: | 6453
 9:10 yet he shall keep the **p** unto the Lord. | 6453
 9:12 according to all the ordinances of the **p** | 6453
 9:13 a journey, and forbeareth to keep the **p**, | 6453
 9:14 and will keep the **p** unto the Lord; | 6453
 9:14 according to the ordinance of the **p**, | 6453
 28:16 of the first month *is* the **p** of the Lord. | 6453
 33: 3 on the morrow after the **p** the children of | 6453
Dt 16: 1 and keep the **p** unto the Lord thy God: | 6453
 16: 2 sacrifice the **p** unto the Lord thy God, | 6453
 16: 5 mayest not sacrifice the **p** within any | 6453
 16: 6 there thou shalt sacrifice the **p** at even, | 6453
Jos 5:10 kept the **p** on the fourteenth day | 6453
 5:11 of the land on the morrow after the **p**, | 6453
2Ki 23:21 Keep the **p** unto the Lord your God, | 6453
 23:22 there was not holden such a **p** from | 6453
 23:23 wherein this **p** was holden to the Lord in | 6453
2Ch 30: 1 to keep the **p** unto the Lord God of | 6453
 30: 2 to keep the **p** in the second month. | 6453
 30: 5 that *they* should come to keep the **p** | 6453
 30:15 they killed the **p** on the fourteenth *day* | 6453
 30:18 did they eat the **p** otherwise than it was | 6453
 35: 1 Moreover Josiah kept a **p** unto the Lord | 6453
 35: 1 they killed the **p** on the fourteenth *day* | 6453
 35: 6 So kill the **p**, and sanctify yourselves, | 6453
 35: 7 all for the **p** *offerings*, for all that were | 6453
 35: 8 unto the priests for the **p** *offerings* two | 6453
 35: 9 gave unto the Levites for **p** *offerings* five | 6453
 35:11 they killed the **p**, and the priests sprinkled | 6453
 35:13 they roasted the **p** with fire according to | 6453
 35:16 to keep the **p**, and to offer burnt offerings | 6453
 35:17 that were present kept the **p** at that time, | 6453
 35:18 there was no **p** like to that, kept in Israel | 6453
 35:18 of Israel keep such a **p** as Josiah kept, | 6453
 35:19 year of the reign of Josiah was this **p** kept. | 6453
Ezr 6:19 children of the captivity kept the **p** upon | 6453
 6:20 killed the **p** for all the children of | 6453
Eze 45:21 ye shall have the **p**, a feast of seven days: | 6453
Mt 26: 2 that after two days *is* the feast of the **p**, | 3957
 26:17 thou *that* we prepare for thee to eat the **p**? | 3957
 26:18 I will keep the **p** at thy house with my | 3957

Mt 26:19 them; and they made ready the **p**. | 3957
Mk 14: 1 After two days *was the feast* of the **p**, | 3957
 14:12 when they killed the **p**, his disciples said | 3957
 14:12 and prepare that thou mayest eat the **p**? | 3957
 14:14 where I shall eat the **p** with my disciples? | 3957
 14:16 unto them: and they made ready the **p**. | 3957
Lk 2:41 Jerusalem every year at the feast of the **p**. | 3957
 22: 1 bread drew nigh, which is called the **P**. | 3957
 22: 7 when the **p** must be killed. | 3957
 22: 8 John, saying, Go and prepare us the **p**, | 3957
 22:11 where I shall eat the **p** with my disciples? | 3957
 22:13 unto them: and they made ready the **p**. | 3957
 22:15 With desire I have desired to eat this **p** | 3957
Jn 2:13 And the Jews' **p** was at hand, | 3957
 2:23 Now when he was in Jerusalem at the **p**, | 3957
 6: 4 And the **p**, a feast of the Jews, was nigh. | 3957
 11:55 And the Jews' **p** was nigh at hand: | 3957
 11:55 the country up to Jerusalem before the **p**, | 3957
 12: 1 Then Jesus six days before the **p** came to | 3957
 13: 1 Now before the feast of the **p**, when Jesus | 3957
 18:28 be defiled; but that they might eat the **p**. | 3957
 18:39 I should release unto you one at the **p**: | 3957
 19:14 And it was the preparation of the **p**, | 3957
1Co 5: 7 For even Christ our **p** is sacrificed for us: | 3957
Heb 11:28 Through faith he kept the **p**, | 3957

PASSOVERS (1) [PASSOVER]
2Ch 30:17 of the **p** for every one *that was* not clean, | 6453

PAST (51) [PASS]
Ge 50: 4 when the days of his mourning were **p**, | 5674
Ex 21:29 with his horn **in time p**, | 4480+8032+8543
 21:36 *hath* used to push **in time p**, | 4480+8032+8543
Nu 21:22 *high* way, until we be **p** thy borders. | 5674
Dt 2:10 Emims dwelt therein **in times p**, | 6440+3807.1
 4:32 For ask now of the days that are **p**, | 7223
 4:42 hated him not **in times p**; | 4480+8032+8543
 19: 4 he hated not in **time** | 4480+8032+8543
 19: 6 hated him not **in time p**. | 4480+8032+8543
1Sa 15:32 Surely the bitterness of death is **p**. | 5493
 19: 7 was in his presence, as **in times p**. | 865+8032
2Sa 3:17 **in times p** to be king | 1571+1571+8032+8543
 5: 2 Also **in time p**, when Saul | 865+1571+8032
 11:27 when the mourning was **p**, David sent | 5674
 16: 1 when David was a little **p** the top of | 5674
1Ki 18:29 when midday was **p**, and they prophesied | 5674
1Ch 9:20 the ruler over them **in time p**, | 6440+3807.1
 11: 2 moreover **in time p**, even when | 8032+8543
Job 9:10 Which doeth great *things* **p** finding | 369+5704
 14:13 keep me secret, until thy wrath be **p**, | 7725
 17:11 My days are **p**, my purposes are broken | 5674
 29: 2 that I were as **in months p**, as *in* the days | 6924
Ps 90: 4 thy sight *are but* as yesterday when it is **p**, | 5674
Ecc 3:15 and God requireth that which is **p**. | 7291
SS 2:11 lo, the winter is **p**, the rain is over *and* | 5674
Jer 8:20 The harvest is **p**, the summer is ended, | 5674
Mt 14:15 is a desert place, and the time is now **p**; | 3928
Mk 16: 1 And when the sabbath was **p**, | 1230
Lk 9:36 And when the voice was **p**, Jesus was | 1096
Ac 12:10 they were **p** the first and the second | 1330
 14:16 in times **p** suffered all nations to walk | 3944
 27: 9 because the fast was now already **p**, Paul | 3928
Ro 3:25 for the remission of sins that are **p**, | 4266
 11:30 For as ye **in times p** have not believed | 4218
 11:33 judgments, and his ways **p finding out**! | 421
2Co 5:17 old *things* are **p away**; behold, all *things* | 3928
Gal 1:13 **in time p** in the Jews' religion, | 4218
 1:23 That he which persecuted us **in times p** | 4218
 5:21 as I have also **told** *you* **in time p**, | 4302
Eph 2: 2 Wherein **in time p** ye walked according | 4218
 2: 3 **in times p** in the lusts of our flesh, | 4218
 4:19 being **p feeling** have given themselves | 524
2Ti 2:18 saying that the resurrection is **p** already; | 1096
Phm 1:11 **in time p** was to thee unprofitable, | 4218
Heb 1: 1 in *divers* manners spake in time **p** unto | 3819
 11:11 was delivered of a child when *she* was **p** | 3844
1Pe 2:10 Which **in time p** *were* not a people, | 4218
 4: 3 For the time **p** of *our* life may suffice us to | 3928
1Jn 2: 8 the darkness is **p**, and the true light | 3855
Rev 9:12 One woe is **p**; *and* behold, there come | 565
 11:14 The second woe is **p**; *and* behold, the third | 565

PASTOR (1) [PASTORS]
Jer 17:16 I have not hastened from *being* a **p** to | 7462

PASTORS (8) [PASTOR]
Jer 2: 8 the **p** also transgressed against me, | 7462
 3:15 I will give you **p** according to mine heart, | 7462
 10:21 For the **p** are become brutish, and have | 7462
 12:10 Many **p** have destroyed my vineyard, | 7462
 22:22 The wind shall eat up all thy **p**, | 7462
 23: 1 Woe be unto *the* **p** that destroy and | 7462
 23: 2 of Israel against the **p** that feed my people; | 7462
Eph 4:11 evangelists; and some, **p** and teachers; | 4166

PASTURE (20) [PASTURES]
Ge 47: 4 for thy servants have no **p** for their flocks: | 4829
1Ch 4:39 of the valley, to seek **p** for their flocks. | 4829
 4:40 found fat **p** and good, and the land *was* | 4829
 4:41 because *there was* **p** there for their flocks. | 4829
Job 39: 8 The range of the mountains *is* his **p**, | 4829
Ps 74: 1 anger smoke against the sheep of thy **p**? | 4830
 79:13 sheep of thy **p** will give thee thanks for | 4830
 95: 7 we *are* the people of his **p**, and the sheep | 4830
 100: 3 *we are* his people, and the sheep of his **p**. | 4830

Isa 32:14 for ever, a joy of wild asses, a **p** of flocks; 4829
Jer 23: 1 that destroy and scatter the sheep of my **p**! 4830
 25:36 heard: for the LORD *hath* spoiled their **p**. 4830
La 1: 6 are become like harts *that* find no **p**, 4829
Eze 34:14 I will feed them in a good **p**, and upon 4829
 34:14 *in* a fat **p** shall they feed upon 4829
 34:18 unto you to have eaten up the good **p**, 4829
 34:31 the flock of my **p**, *are* men, *and* I am 4829
Hos 13: 6 According to their **p**, so were they filled; 4829
Joel 1:18 are perplexed, because they have no **p**; 4829
Jn 10: 9 and shall go in and out, and find **p**. 3542

PASTURELAND See SUBURBS

PASTURES (11) [PASTURE]
1Ki 4:23 twenty oxen out of the **p**, and an hundred 7471
Ps 23: 2 He maketh me to lie down in green **p**: 4999
 65:12 They drop *upon* the **p** of the wilderness. 4999
 65:13 The **p** are clothed with flocks; the valleys 3733
Isa 30:23 in that day shall thy cattle feed in large **p**. 3733
 49: 9 and their *shall be* in all high places. 4830
Eze 34:18 with your feet the residue of your **p**? 4829
 45:15 of two hundred, out of the **fat p** of Israel; 4945
Joel 1:19 for the fire hath devoured the **p** of 4999
 1:20 the fire hath devoured the **p** of 4999
 2:22 for the **p** of the wilderness do spring, 4999

PATARA (1)
Ac 21: 1 unto Rhodes, and from thence unto **P**: 3959

PATE (1)
Ps 7:16 dealing shall come down upon his own **p**. 6936

PATH (23) [PATHS, PATHWAY]
Ge 49:17 adder in the **p**, that biteth the horse heels, 734
Nu 22:24 the angel of the LORD stood in a **p** of 4934
Job 28: 7 *There is* a **p** which no fowl knoweth, 5410
 30:13 They mar my **p**, they set forward my 5410
 41:32 He maketh a **p** to shine after him; 5410
Ps 16:11 Thou wilt shew me the **p** of life: in thy 734
 27:11 lead me in a plain **p**, because of mine 734
 77:19 thy **p** in the great waters, and thy 7635
 119:35 Make me to go in the **p** of thy 4546
 119:105 lamp unto my feet, and a light unto my **p**. 5410
 139: 3 compassest my **p** and my lying down, 734
 142: 3 within me, then thou knewest my **p**. 5410
Pr 1:15 with them; refrain thy foot from their **p**: 5410
 2: 9 judgment, and equity; *yea*, every good **p**. 4570
 4:14 Enter not into the **p** of the wicked, 734
 4:18 the **p** of the just *is* as the shining light, 734
 4:26 Ponder the **p** of thy feet, and let all thy 4570
 5: 6 Lest thou shouldest ponder the **p** of life, 734
Isa 26: 7 most upright, dost weigh the **p** of the just. 4570
 30:11 ye out of the way, turn aside out of the **p**, 734
 40:14 taught him in the **p** of judgment, 734
 43:16 in the sea, and a **p** in the mighty waters; 5410
Joel 2: 8 they shall walk every one in his **p**: 4546

PATHROS (5)
Isa 11:11 from **P**, and from Cush, and from Elam, 6624
Jer 44: 1 at Noph, and in the country of **P**, saying, 6624
 44:15 of Egypt, in **P**, answered Jeremiah, saying, 6624
Eze 29:14 cause them to return *into* the land of **P**, 6624
 30:14 I will make **P** desolate, and will set fire in 6624

PATHRUSIM (2)
Ge 10:14 **P**, and Casluhim, (out of whom came 6625
1Ch 1:12 **P**, and Casluhim, (of whom came 6625

PATHRUSITES See PATHRUSIM

PATHS (42) [PATH]
Job 6:18 The **p** of their way are turned aside; they 734
 8:13 So *are* the **p** of all that forget God; 734
 13:27 and lookest narrowly unto all my **p**; 734
 19: 8 and he hath set darkness in my **p**. 5410
 24:13 ways thereof, nor abide in the **p** thereof. 5410
 33:11 my feet in the stocks, he marketh all my **p**. 734
 38:20 thou shouldest know the **p** to the house 5410
Ps 8: 8 *whatsoever* passeth *through* the **p** of 734
 17: 4 I have kept me *from* the **p** of the destroyer. 734
 17: 5 Hold up my goings in thy **p**, *that* my 4570
 23: 3 he leadeth me in the **p** of righteousness 4570
 25: 4 me thy ways, O LORD; teach me thy **p**. 734
 25:10 All the **p** of the LORD *are* mercy and 734
 65:11 thy goodness; and thy **p** drop fatness. 4570
Pr 2: 8 He keepeth the **p** of judgment, 734
 2:13 Who leave the **p** of uprightness, to walk 734
 2:15 *are* crooked, and *they* froward in their **p**: 4570
 2:18 unto death, and her **p** unto the dead. 4570
 2:19 neither take they hold of the **p** of life. 734
 2:20 *men*, and keep the **p** of the righteous. 734
 3: 6 him, and he shall direct thy **p**. 5410
 3:17 of pleasantness, and all her **p** *are* peace. 5410
 4:11 way of wisdom; I have led thee in right **p**. 4570
 7:25 to her ways, go not astray in her **p**. 5410
 8: 2 places by the way, *in* the places of the **p**. 734
 8:20 in the midst of the **p** of judgment: 5410
Isa 2: 3 us of his ways, and we will walk in his **p**: 734
 3:12 *thee* to err, and destroy the way of thy **p**. 734
 42:16 I will lead them in **p** *that* they have not 5410
 58:12 the breach, The restorer of **p** to dwell in. 5410
 59: 7 wasting and destruction are in their **p**. 4546
 59: 8 they have made them crooked **p**: 5410
Jer 6:16 the ways, and see, and ask for the old **p**, 5410
 18:15 stumble in their ways *from* the ancient **p**, 7635

Jer 18:15 to walk in **p**, *in* a way not cast up; 5410
La 3: 9 hewn stone, he hath made my **p** crooked. 5410
Hos 2: 6 make a wall, that she shall not find her **p**. 734
Mic 4: 2 us of his ways, and we will walk in his **p**: 734
Mt 3: 3 the way of the Lord, make his **p** straight. 5147
Mk 1: 3 the way of the Lord, make his **p** straight. 5147
Lk 3: 4 the way of the Lord, make his **p** straight. 5147
Heb 12:13 make straight **p** for your feet, lest that 5163

PATHWAY (1) [PATH]
Pr 12:28 and *in* the **p** *thereof there is* no death.1870+5410

PATIENCE (34) [PATIENT, PATIENTLY]
Mt 18:26 **have p** with me, and I will pay thee all. 3114
 18:29 **have p** with me, and I will pay thee all. 3114
Lk 8:15 keep *it*, and bring forth fruit with **p**. 5281
 21:19 In your **p** possess ye your souls. 5281
Ro 5: 3 knowing that tribulation worketh **p**; 5281
 5: 4 And **p**, experience; and experience, hope: 5281
 8:25 we see not, *then* do we with **p** wait for *it*. 5281
 15: 4 that we through **p** and comfort of 5281
 15: 5 Now the God of **p** and consolation grant 5281
2Co 6: 4 in much **p**, in afflictions, in necessities, 5281
 12:12 apostle were wrought among you in all **p**, 5281
Col 1:11 unto all **p** and longsuffering with 5281
1Th 1: 3 and **p** of hope in our Lord Jesus Christ, 5281
2Th 1: 4 in you in the churches of God for your **p** 5281
1Ti 6:11 godliness, faith, love, **p**, meekness. 5281
2Ti 3:10 faith, longsuffering, charity, **p**, 5281
Tit 2: 2 temperate, sound in faith, in charity, in **p**. 5281
Heb 6:12 through faith and **p** inherit the promises. 3115
 10:36 For ye have need of **p**, that, after ye have 5281
 12: 1 let us run with **p** the race that is set before 5281
Jas 1: 3 that the trying of your faith worketh **p**. 5281
 1: 4 But let **p** have *her* perfect work, that ye 5281
 5: 7 and **hath long** for it, until he receive 3114
 5:10 example of suffering affliction, and of **p**. 3115
 5:11 Ye have heard of the **p** of Job, 5281
2Pe 1: 6 and to temperance; and to patience 5281
 1: 6 temperance patience; and to **p** godliness; 5281
Rev 1: 9 and in the kingdom and **p** of Jesus Christ, 5281
 2: 2 and thy **p**, and how thou canst not bear 5281
 2: 3 and hast **p**, and for my name's sake hast 5281
 2:19 and faith, and thy **p**, and thy works; 5281
 3:10 Because thou hast kept the word of my **p**, 5281
 13:10 Here is the **p** and the faith of the saints. 5281
 14:12 Here is the **p** of the saints: here *are* they 5281

PATIENT (9) [PATIENCE]
Ecc 7: 8 the **p** in spirit *is* better than the proud in 750
Ro 2: 7 To them who by **p** continuance in well 5281
 12:12 Rejoicing in hope; **p** in tribulation; 5278
1Th 5:14 support the weak, be **p** toward all *men*. 3114
2Th 3: 5 of God, and into the **p** waiting for Christ. 5281
1Ti 3: 3 but **p**, not a brawler, not covetous; 1933
2Ti 2:24 be gentle unto all *men*, apt to teach, **p**, 420
Jas 5: 7 be therefore, brethren, unto the coming 3114
 5: 8 Be ye also **p**; stablish your hearts: 3114

PATIENTLY (6) [PATIENCE]
Ps 37: 7 Rest in the LORD, and **wait p** for him: 2342
 40: 1 I **waited p for** the LORD; 6960+6960
Ac 26: 3 wherefore I beseech thee to hear me **p**. 3116
Heb 6:15 And so, after he had **p endured**, 3114
1Pe 2:20 buffeted for your faults, ye **take it p**? 5278
 2:20 do well, and suffer *for it*, ye **take it p**, 5278

PATMOS (1)
Rev 1: 9 in the isle that is called **P**, for the word 3963

PATRIARCH (2) [PATRIARCHS]
Ac 2:29 let me freely speak unto you of the **p** 3966
Heb 7: 4 Abraham gave the tenth of the spoils. 3966

PATRIARCHS (2) [PATRIARCH]
Ac 7: 8 begat Jacob; and Jacob *begat* the twelve **p**. 3966
 7: 9 And the **p**, moved with envy, sold Joseph 3966

PATRIMONY (1)
Dt 18: 8 that which cometh of the sale of his **p**. 1

PATROBAS (1)
Ro 16:14 **P**, Hermes, and the brethren which are 3969

PATTERN (14) [PATTERNS]
Ex 25: 9 *after* the **p** of the tabernacle, and the 8403
 25: 9 the **p** of all the instruments thereof, even 8403
 25:40 look that thou make *them* after their **p**, 8403
Nu 8: 4 according unto the **p** which the LORD had 4758
Jos 22:28 that we may say *again*, Behold the **p** 8403
2Ki 16:10 the **p** of it, according to all 8403
1Ch 28:11 David gave to Solomon his son the **p** of 8403
 28:12 the **p** of all that he had by the spirit, 8403
 28:18 gold for the **p** of the chariot of 8403
 28:19 upon me, *even* all the works of *this* **p**. 8403
Eze 43:10 iniquities: and let them measure the **p**. 8508
1Ti 1:16 for a **p** to them which should hereafter 5296
Tit 2: 7 In all *things* shewing thyself a **p** of good 5179
Heb 8: 5 to the **p** shewed to thee in the mount. 5179

PATTERNS (1) [PATTERN]
Heb 9:23 necessary that the **p** of *things* in 5262

PAU (1)
Ge 36:39 the name of his city *was* **P**; and his wife's 6464

PAUL (157) [PAUL'S, SAUL]
Ac 13: 9 Then Saul, (who also *is called* **P**,) 3972
 13:13 when **P** and his company loosed from 3972
 13:16 Then **P** stood up, and beckoning with *his* 3972
 13:43 and religious proselytes followed **P** and 3972
 13:45 those *things* which were spoken by **P**, 3972
 13:46 But **P** and Barnabas waxed bold, and said, 3972
 13:50 and raised persecution against **P** and 3972
 14: 9 The same heard **P** speak: who stedfastly 3972
 14:11 when the people saw what **P** had done, 3972
 14:12 **P**, Mercurius, because he was the chief 3972
 14:14 *Which* when the apostles, Barnabas and **P**, 3972
 14:19 and, having stoned **P**, drew *him* out of 3972
 15: 2 When therefore **P** and Barnabas had no 3972
 15: 2 they determined that **P** and Barnabas, 3972
 15:12 and gave audience to Barnabas and **P**, 3972
 15:22 of their own company to Antioch with **P** 3972
 15:25 you with our beloved Barnabas and **P**, 3972
 15:35 **P** also and Barnabas continued in Antioch, 3972
 15:36 And some days after **P** said unto Barnabas, 3972
 15:38 But **P** thought not good to take him with 3972
 15:40 And **P** chose Silas, and departed, 3972
 16: 3 Him would **P** have to go forth with him; 3972
 16: 9 And a vision appeared to **P** in the night; 3972
 16:14 unto the *things* which were spoken of **P**. 3972
 16:17 The same followed **P** and us, and cried, 3972
 16:18 But **P**, being grieved, turned and said to 3972
 16:19 they caught **P** and Silas, and drew *them* 3972
 16:25 And at midnight **P** and Silas prayed, 3972
 16:28 But **P** cried with a loud voice, saying, 3972
 16:29 and fell down before **P** and Silas, 3972
 16:36 keeper of the prison told this saying to **P**, 3972
 16:37 **P** said unto them, They have beaten us 3972
 17: 2 And **P**, as his manner was, went in unto 3972
 17: 4 and consorted with **P** and Silas; 3972
 17:10 the brethren immediately sent away **P** 3972
 17:13 word of God was preached of **P** at Berea, 3972
 17:14 immediately the brethren sent away **P** to 3972
 17:15 And they that conducted **P** brought him 3972
 17:16 Now while **P** waited for them at Athens, 3972
 17:22 Then **P** stood in the midst of Mars' hill, 3972
 17:33 So **P** departed from among them. 3972
 18: 1 After these *things* **P** departed from Athens 3972
 18: 5 **P** was pressed in spirit, and testified to 3972
 18: 9 Then spake the Lord to **P** in the night by a 3972
 18:12 insurrection made with one accord against **P**, 3972
 18:14 And when **P** was *now* about to open *his* 3972
 18:18 And **P** *after this* tarried *there* yet a good 3972
 19: 1 **P** having passed through the upper coasts 3972
 19: 4 Then said **P**, John verily baptized *with* 3972
 19: 6 when **P** had laid *his* hands upon them, 3972
 19:11 special miracles by the hands of **P**: 3972
 19:13 adjure you by Jesus whom **P** preacheth. 3972
 19:15 and said, Jesus I know, and **P** I know; 3972
 19:21 were ended, **P** purposed in the spirit, 3972
 19:26 this **P** hath persuaded and turned away 3972
 19:30 And when **P** would have entered in unto 3972
 20: 1 **P** called unto *him* the disciples, 3972
 20: 7 **P** preached unto them, ready to depart on 3972
 20: 9 as **P** was long preaching, he sunk down 3972
 20:10 And **P** went down, and fell on him, 3972
 20:13 unto Assos, there intending to take in **P**: 3972
 20:16 For **P** had determined to sail by Ephesus, 3972
 21: 4 who said to **P** through the Spirit, that *he* 3972
 21:13 Then **P** answered, What mean ye to weep 3972
 21:18 And the *day* following **P** went in with us 3972
 21:26 Then **P** took the men, and the next day 3972
 21:29 whom they supposed that **P** had brought 3972
 21:30 and they took **P**, and drew him out of 3972
 21:32 and the soldiers, they left beating of **P**. 3972
 21:37 And as **P** was to be led into the castle, 3972
 21:39 But **P** said, I am a man *which am* a Jew of 3972
 21:40 **P** stood on the stairs, and beckoned with 3972
 22:25 **P** said unto the centurion that stood by, Is 3972
 22:28 And **P** said, But I was *free* born. 3972
 22:30 and brought **P** down, and set *him* before 3972
 23: 1 And **P**, earnestly beholding the council, 3972
 23: 3 said unto him, God shall smite thee, 3972
 23: 5 Then said **P**, I wist not, brethren, that he 3972
 23: 6 But when **P** perceived that the one part 3972
 23:10 fearing lest **P** should have been pulled in 3972
 23:11 by him, and said, **Be of good cheer, P**: 3972
 23:12 neither eat nor drink till they had killed **P**. 3972
 23:14 we will eat nothing until we have slain **P**. 3972
 23:16 and entered into the castle, and told **P**. 3972
 23:17 Then **P** called one of the centurions unto 3972
 23:18 The prisoner called me unto *him*, and 3972
 23:20 bring down **P** to morrow into the council, 3972
 23:24 that they may set **P** on, and bring *him* safe 3972
 23:31 took **P**, and brought *him* by night to 3972
 23:33 the governor, presented **P** also before him. 3972
 24: 1 who informed the governor against **P**. 3972
 24:10 Then **P**, after that the governor had 3972
 24:23 he commanded a centurion to keep **P**, 3972
 24:24 he sent for **P**, and heard him concerning 3972
 24:26 money should have been given him of **P**, 3972
 24:27 to shew the Jews a pleasure, left **P** bound. 3972
 25: 2 chief of the Jews informed him against **P**, 3972
 25: 4 that **P** should be kept at Cesarea, 3972
 25: 6 commanded **P** to be brought. 3972
 25: 7 and grievous complaints against **P**, 3972
 25: 9 answered **P**, and said, Wilt thou go up to 3972
 25:10 Then said **P**, I stand at Cesar's judgment 3972
 25:19 *was* dead, whom **P** affirmed to be alive. 3972

Ac	25:21 But when **P** had appealed to be reserved	3972
	25:23 at Festus' commandment **P** was brought	3972
	26: 1 Then Agrippa said unto **P**, Thou art	3972
	26: 1 Then **P** stretched forth the hand,	3972
	26:24 a loud voice, **P**, thou art beside thyself;	3972
	26:28 Then Agrippa said unto **P**, Almost thou	3972
	26:29 And **P** said, I would to God, that not only	3972
	27: 1 delivered **P** and certain other prisoners	3972
	27: 3 And Julius courteously entreated **P**,	3972
	27: 9 now already past, **P** admonished *them,*	3972
	27:11 those *things* which were spoken by **P**.	3972
	27:21 But after long abstinence **P** stood *forth* in	3972
	27:24 Fear not, **P**; thou must be brought	3972
	27:31 **P** said to the centurion and to the soldiers,	3972
	27:33 **P** besought *them* all to take meat, saying,	3972
	27:43 But the centurion, willing to save **P**,	3972
	28: 3 And when **P** had gathered a bundle of	3972
	28: 8 to whom **P** entered in, and prayed,	3972
	28:15 whom when **P** saw, he thanked God,	3972
	28:16 **P** was suffered to dwell by himself with a	3972
	28:17 that after three days **P** called the chief of	3972
	28:25 after that **P** had spoken one word,	3972
	28:30 And **P** dwelt two whole years in his own	3972
Ro	1: 1 **P**, a servant of Jesus Christ, called *to be*	3972
1Co	1: 1 **P**, called *to be* an apostle of Jesus Christ	3972
	1:12 that every one of you saith, I am of **P**;	3972
	1:13 was **P** crucified for you? or were ye	5547
	1:13 or were ye baptized in the name of **P**?	3972
	3: 4 while one saith, I am of **P**; and another,	3972
	3: 5 Who then is **P**, and who *is* Apollos,	3972
	3:22 Whether **P**, or Apollos, or Cephas,	3972
	16:21 The salutation of *me* **P** with mine own	3972
2Co	1: 1 **P**, an apostle of Jesus Christ by the will of	3972
	10: 1 Now I **P** myself beseech you by	3972
Gal	1: 1 **P**, an apostle, (not of men, neither by man	3972
	5: 2 Behold, I **P** say unto you, that if ye be	3972
Eph	1: 1 **P**, an apostle of Jesus Christ by the will of	3972
	3: 1 For this cause I **P**, the prisoner of Jesus	3972
Php	1: 1 **P** and Timotheus, the servants of Jesus	3972
Col	1: 1 **P**, an apostle of Jesus Christ by the will of	3972
	1:23 whereof I **P** am made a minister;	3972
	4:18 The salutation by the hand of me **P**.	3972
1Th	1: 1 **P**, and Silvanus, and Timotheus, unto	3972
	2:18 come unto you, even I **P**, once and again;	3972
2Th	1: 1 **P**, and Silvanus, and Timotheus, unto	3972
	3:17 The salutation of **P** with mine own hand,	3972
1Ti	1: 1 **P**, an apostle of Jesus Christ by	3972
2Ti	1: 1 **P**, an apostle of Jesus Christ by the will of	3972
	4: S when **P** was brought before Nero	3972
Tit	1: 1 **P**, a servant of God, and an apostle of	3972
Phm	1: 1 **P**, a prisoner of Jesus Christ,	3972
	1: 9 *thee,* being such a one as **P** the aged,	3972
	1:19 I **P** have written *it* with mine own hand,	3972
2Pe	3:15 even as our beloved brother **P** also	3972

PAUL'S (6) [PAUL]

Ac	19:29 of Macedonia, **P** companions in travel,	3972
	20:37 and fell on **P** neck, and kissed him,	3972
	21: 8 And the next day we that were of **P**	3972
	21:11 took **P** girdle, and bound his *own* hands	3972
	23:16 And when **P** sister's son heard of *their*	3972
	25:14 Festus declared **P** cause unto the king,	3972

PAULUS (1)

| Ac | 13: 7 with the deputy *of the country,* Sergius **P**, | 3972 |

PAVED (2) [PAVEMENT]

| Ex | 24:10 *was* under his feet as it were a **p** work | 3840 |
| SS | 3:10 the midst thereof being **p** *with* love, | 7528 |

PAVEMENT (9) [PAVED]

2Ki	16:17 under it, and put it upon a **p** of stones.	4837
2Ch	7: 3 *with their* faces to the ground upon the **p**,	7531
Est	1: 6 upon a **p** of red, and blue, and white,	7531
Eze	40:17 and a **p** made for the court round about:	7531
	40:17 thirty chambers *were* upon the **p**.	7531
	40:18 the **p** by the side of the gates over against	7531
	40:18 the length of the gates *was* the lower **p**.	7531
	42: 3 over against the **p** which *was* for the utter	7531
Jn	19:13 seat in a place that is called the **P**,	3038

PAVILION (4) [PAVILIONS]

Ps	18:11 his **p** round about him *were* dark waters	5521
	5 time of trouble he shall hide me in his **p**:	5520
	31:20 thou shalt keep them secretly in a **p** from	5521
Jer	43:10 he shall spread his **royal p** over them.	8237

PAVILIONS (3) [PAVILION]

2Sa	22:12 he made darkness **p** round about him,	5521
1Ki	20:12 *was* drinking, he and the kings in the **p**,	5521
	20:16 *was* drinking *himself* drunk in the **p**,	5521

PAW (2) [PAWETH, PAWS]

| 1Sa | 17:37 The LORD that delivered me out of the **p** | 3027 |
| | 17:37 out of the **p** of the bear, he will deliver me | 3027 |

PAWETH (1) [PAW]

| Job | 39:21 He **p** in the valley, and rejoiceth in *his* | 2658 |

PAWS (1) [PAW]

| Lev | 11:27 whatsoever goeth upon his **p**, among all | 3709 |

PAY (39) [PAID, PAYED, PAYETH, PAYMENT]

Ex	21:19 only he shall **p** *for* the loss of his time,	5414
	21:22 and he shall **p** as the judges determine.	5414
	21:36 he shall **surely p** ox for ox;	7999+7999

Ex	22: 7 if the thief be found, let him **p** double.	7999
	22: 9 he shall **p** double unto his neighbour.	7999
	22:17 he shall **p** money according to the dowry	8254
Nu	20:19 *of* thy water, then I will **p** for it:	4377+5414
Dt	23:21 thy God, thou shalt not be slack to **p** it:	7999
2Sa	15: 7 I pray thee, let me go and **p** my vow,	7999
1Ki	20:39 or else thou shalt **p** a talent of silver.	8254
2Ki	4: 7 **p** thy debt, and live thou and thy children	7999
2Ch	8: 8 did Solomon **make to p** tribute until	5927
	27: 5 much did the children of Ammon **p** unto	7725
Ezr	4:13 set up *again, then* will they not **p** toll,	5415
Est	3: 9 I will **p** ten thousand talents of silver to	8254
	4: 7 to **p** to the king's treasuries for the Jews,	8254
Job	22:27 hear thee, and thou shalt **p** thy vows.	7999
Ps	22:25 I will **p** my vows before them that fear	7999
	50:14 and **p** thy vows unto the most High:	7999
	66:13 burnt offerings: I will **p** thee my vows,	7999
	76:11 Vow, and **p** unto the LORD your God:	7999
	116:14 I will **p** my vows unto the LORD now in	7999
	116:18 I will **p** my vows unto the LORD now in	7999
Pr	19:17 which he hath given will he **p** him **again**.	7999
	22:27 If thou hast nothing to **p**, why should he	7999
Ecc	5: 4 vowest a vow unto God, defer not to **p** it;	7999
	5: 4 in fools: **p** that which thou hast vowed.	7999
	5: 5 than that thou shouldest vow and not **p**.	7999
Jnh	2: 9 I will **p** *that* I have vowed.	7999
Mt	17:24 and say, Doth not your master **p** tribute?	5055
	18:25 But forasmuch as he had not to **p**, his lord	591
	18:26 patience with me, and I will **p** thee all.	591
	18:28 the throat, saying, **P** me that thou owest.	591
	18:29 patience with me, and I will **p** thee all.	591
	18:30 him into prison, till he should **p** the debt.	591
	18:34 till he should **p** all that was due unto him.	591
	23:42 ye **p tithe** of mint and anise and cummin,	586
Lk	7:42 when they had nothing to **p**, he frankly	591
Ro	13: 6 For this cause **p** you tribute also:	5055

PAYED (2) [PAY]

| Pr | 7:14 with me; *this* day have I **p** my vows. | 7999 |
| Heb | 7: 9 receiveth tithes, **p** tithes in Abraham. | 1183 |

PAYETH (1) [PAY]

| Ps | 37:21 The wicked borroweth, and **p** not **again**: | 7999 |

PAYMENT (1) [PAY]

| Mt | 18:25 and all that he had, and **p** to be **made**. | 591 |

PEACE (429) [PEACEABLE, PEACEABLY, PEACEMAKERS]

Ge	15:15 thou shalt go to thy fathers in **p**; thou	7965
	24:21 man wondering at her **held his p**, to wit	2790
	26:29 but good, and have sent thee away in **p**:	7965
	26:31 and they departed from him in **p**.	7965
	28:21 I come again to my father's house in **p**;	7965
	34: 5 Jacob **held his p** until they were come.	2790
	41:16 God shall give Pharaoh an answer of **p**.	7965
	43:23 he said, **P** *be* to you, fear not: your God,	7965
	44:17 for you, get you up in **p** unto your father.	7965
Ex	4:18 And Jethro said to Moses, Go in **p**.	7965
	14:14 fight for you, and ye shall **hold** your **p**.	2790
	18:23 people shall also go to their place in **p**.	7965
	20:24 **p offerings**, thy sheep, and thine oxen:	8002
	24: 5 sacrificed **p offerings** *of* oxen unto	8002
	29:28 Israel of the sacrifice of their **p offerings**,	8002
	32: 6 burnt offerings, and brought **p offerings**;	8002
Lev	3: 1 if his oblation *be* a sacrifice of **p offering**,	8002
	3: 3 **p offering** an offering made by fire unto	8002
	3: 6 If his offering for a sacrifice of **p offering**	8002
	3: 9 **p offering** an offering made by fire unto	8002
	4:10 the bullock of the sacrifice of **p offerings**:	8002
	4:26 as the fat of the sacrifice of **p offerings**:	8002
	4:31 away from off the sacrifice of **p offerings**,	8002
	4:35 from the sacrifice of the **p offerings**;	8002
	6:12 burn thereon the fat of the **p offerings**.	8002
	7:11 *is* the law of the sacrifice of **p offerings**,	8002
	7:13 thanksgiving of his **p offerings**.	8002
	7:14 sprinkleth the blood of the **p offerings**	8002
	7:15 flesh of the sacrifice of his **p offerings**	8002
	7:18 **p offerings** be eaten at all on the third	8002
	7:20 *of* the flesh of the sacrifice of **p offerings**,	8002
	7:21 of the flesh of the sacrifice of **p offerings**,	8002
	7:29 **p offerings** unto the LORD shall bring his	8002
	7:29 LORD of the sacrifice of his **p offerings**.	8002
	7:32 of the sacrifices of your **p offerings**.	8002
	7:33 that offereth the blood of the **p offerings**,	8002
	7:34 off the sacrifices of their **p offerings**,	8002
	7:37 and of the sacrifice of the **p offerings**;	8002
	9: 4 Also a bullock and a ram for **p offerings**,	8002
	9:18 and the ram *for* a sacrifice of **p offerings**,	8002
	9:22 and the burnt offering, and **p offerings**.	8002
	10: 3 I will be glorified. And Aaron **held his p**.	1826
	10:14 of **p offerings** of the children of Israel.	8002
	17: 5 offer *them for* **p offerings** unto the LORD.	8002
	19: 5 if ye offer a sacrifice of **p offerings** unto	8002
	22:21 **p offerings** unto the LORD to accomplish	8002
	23:19 the first year for a sacrifice of **p offerings**,	8002
	26: 6 I will give **p** in the land, and ye shall lie	7965
Nu	6:14 one ram without blemish for **p offerings**,	8002
	6:17 a sacrifice of **p offerings** unto the LORD,	8002
	6:18 *is* under the sacrifice of the **p offerings**.	8002
	6:26 countenance upon thee, and give thee **p**.	7965
	7:17 for a sacrifice of **p offerings**, two oxen,	8002
	7:23 for a sacrifice of **p offerings**, two oxen,	8002
	7:29 for a sacrifice of **p offerings**, two oxen,	8002
	7:35 for a sacrifice of **p offerings**, two oxen,	8002

Nu	7:41 for a sacrifice of **p offerings**, two oxen,	8002
	7:47 for a sacrifice of **p offerings**, two oxen,	8002
	7:53 for a sacrifice of **p offerings**, two oxen,	8002
	7:59 for a sacrifice of **p offerings**, two oxen,	8002
	7:65 for a sacrifice of **p offerings**, two oxen,	8002
	7:71 for a sacrifice of **p offerings**, two oxen,	8002
	7:77 for a sacrifice of **p offerings**, two oxen,	8002
	7:83 for a sacrifice of the **p offerings**, two oxen,	8002
	7:88 sacrifice of the **p offerings** *were* twenty	8002
	10:10 over the sacrifices of your **p offerings**.	8002
	15: 8 a vow, or **p offerings** unto the LORD:	8002
	25:12 I give unto him my covenant of **p**:	7965
	29:39 drink offerings, and for your **p offerings**.	8002
	30: 4 and her father shall **hold** his **p** at her:	2790
	30: 7 **held** his **p** at her in the day that he heard	2790
	30:11 husband heard *it,* and **held** his **p** at her,	2790
	30:14 her husband **altogether hold** his **p**	2790+2790
	30:14 **held** his **p** at her in the day that he	2790
Dt	2:26 Sihon king of Heshbon *with* words of **p**,	7965
	20:10 to fight against it, then proclaim **p** unto it.	7965
	20:11 it make thee answer of **p**, and open unto	7999
	20:12 if it will **make** no **p** with thee,	7999
	23: 6 Thou shalt not seek their **p** nor their	7965
	27: 7 thou shalt offer **p offerings**, and shalt eat	8002
	29:19 himself in his heart, saying, I shall have **p**,	7965
Jos	8:31 the LORD, and sacrificed **p offerings**.	8002
	9:15 Joshua made **p** with them, and made a	7965
	10: 1 the inhabitants of Gibeon had **made p**	7999
	10: 4 for it hath **made p** with Joshua and with	7999
	10:21 to the camp to Joshua *at* Makkedah in **p**:	7965
	11:19 There was not a city that **made p** with	7999
	22:23 or if it *be* offerings thereon,	8002
	22:27 our sacrifices, and with our **p offerings**;	8002
Jdg	4:17 for *there was* **p** between Jabin the king of	7965
	6:23 the LORD said unto him, **P** *be* to thee;	7965
	8: 9 saying, When I come again in **p**, I will	7965
	11:31 when I return in **p** from the children of	7965
	18: 6 the priest said unto them, Go in **p**:	7965
	18:19 they said unto him, **Hold** thy **p**, lay thine	2790
	19:20 the old man said, **P** *be* with thee;	7965
	20:26 and **p offerings** before the LORD.	8002
	21: 4 offered burnt offerings and **p offerings**.	8002
1Sa	1:17 Eli answered and said, Go in **p**:	7965
	7:14 there was **p** between Israel and	7965
	10: 8 *and* to sacrifice sacrifices of **p offerings**:	8002
	10:27 But he **held** his **p**.	1961+2790+3509.1
	11:15 *of* **p offerings** before the LORD;	8002
	13: 9 a burnt offering to me, and **p offerings**.	8002
	20: 7 thus, *It is* well; thy servant shall have **p**:	7965
	20:13 send thee away, that thou mayest go in **p**:	7965
	20:21 for *there is* **p** to thee, and no hurt;	7965
	20:42 Jonathan said to David, Go in **p**,	7965
	25: 6 liveth in prosperity, **P** *be* both to thee,	7965
	25: 6 *be to* thine house, and peace *be unto*	7965
	25: 6 *be unto* all that thou hast.	7965
	25:35 said unto her, Go up in **p** to thine house;	7965
	29: 7 Wherefore now return, and go in **p**,	7965
2Sa	3:21 David sent Abner away; and he went in **p**.	7965
	3:22 had sent him away, and he was gone in **p**.	7965
	3:23 hath sent him away, and he is gone in **p**.	7965
	6:17 and **p offerings** before the LORD.	8002
	6:18 offering burnt offerings and **p offerings**,	8002
	10:19 **made p** with Israel, and served them.	7999
	13:20 **hold** now thy **p**, my sister: he *is* thy	2790
	15: 9 the king said unto him, Go in **p**. So he	7965
	15:27 return *into* the city in **p**, and your two	7965
	17: 3 all returned: *so* all the people shall be in **p**.	7965
	19:24 departed until the day he came *again* in **p**.	7965
	19:30 is come *again* in **p** unto his own house.	7965
	24:25 offered burnt offerings and **p offerings**.	8002
1Ki	2: 5 shed the blood of war in **p**, and put	7965
	2: 6 his hoar head go down *to* the grave in **p**.	7965
	2:33 shall there be **p** for ever from the LORD.	7965
	3:15 offered **p offerings**, and made a feast to	8002
	4:24 he had **p** on all sides round about him.	7965
	5:12 there was **p** between Hiram and Solomon;	7965
	8:63 offered a sacrifice of **p offerings**,	8002
	8:64 and the fat of the **p offerings**:	8002
	8:64 and the fat of the **p offerings**.	8002
	9:25 **p offerings** upon the altar which he built	8002
	20:18 he said, Whether they be come out for **p**,	7965
	22:17 them return every man to his house in **p**.	7965
	22:27 with water of affliction, until I come in **p**.	7965
	22:28 Micaiah said, If thou return at all in **p**,	7965
	22:44 Jehoshaphat **made p** with the king of	7999
2Ki	2: 3 he said, Yea, I know *it*; **hold** you your **p**.	2814
	2: 5 Yea, I know *it*; **hold** you your **p**.	2814
	5:19 he said unto him, Go in **p**. So he departed	7965
	7: 9 a day of good tidings, and we **hold** our **p**:	2814
	9:17 to meet them, and let him say, *Is it* **p**?	7965
	9:18 and said, Thus saith the king, *Is it* **p**?	7965
	9:18 Jehu said, What hast thou to do with **p**?	7965
	9:19 and said, Thus saith the king, *Is it* **p**?	7965
	9:19 What hast thou to do with **p**?	7965
	9:22 Joram saw Jehu, that he said, *Is it* **p**, Jehu?	7965
	9:22 What **p**, so long as the whoredoms of thy	7965
	9:31 she said, *Had* Zimri **p**, who slew his	7965
	16:13 sprinkled the blood of his **p offerings**,	8002
	18:36 people **held** their **p**, and answered him	2790
	20:19 *it* not *good,* if **p** and truth be in my days?	7965
	20:20 thou shalt be gathered into thy grave in **p**;	7965
1Ch	12:18 **p**, peace *be* unto thee, and peace *be to*	7965
	12:18 **p** *be* unto thee, and peace *be* to thine	7965
	12:18 *be* unto thee, and peace *be* to thine helpers;	7965
	16: 1 and **p offerings** before God.	8002

1Ch 16: 2 the burnt offerings and the **p offerings**, 8002
19:19 they **made p** with David, and became his 7999
21:26 offered burnt offerings and **p offerings**, 8002
22: 9 I will give **p** and quietness unto Israel in 7965
2Ch 7: 7 the fat of the **p offerings**, because 8002
15: 5 in those times *there was* no **p** to him that 7965
18:16 *therefore* every man to his house in **p**. 7965
18:26 water of affliction, until I return in **p**. 7965
18:27 If thou certainly return in **p**, then hath 7965
19: 1 returned to his house in **p** to Jerusalem. 7965
29:35 with the fat of the **p offerings**, 8002
30:22 **p offerings**, 8002
31: 2 for burnt offerings and for **p offerings**, 8002
33:16 sacrificed thereon **p** offerings and 8002
34:28 thou shalt be gathered to thy grave in **p**, 7965
Ezr 4:17 beyond the river; and at such a time. 8001
5: 7 written thus: Unto Darius the king, all **p**. 8001
7:12 of heaven, perfect **p**, and at such a time. NIH
9:12 nor seek their **p** or their wealth for ever: 7965
Ne 5: 8 **held** they their **p**, and found nothing to 2790
8:11 Hold your **p**, for the day *is* holy; 2013
Est 4:14 if thou **altogether holdest** thy **p** 2790+2790
9:30 of Ahasuerus, *with* words of **p** and truth, 7965
10: 3 his people, and speaking **p** to all his seed. 7965
Job 5:23 the beasts of the field shall be **at p** with 7999
5:24 know that thy tabernacle *shall be* in **p**; 7965
11: 3 Should thy lies **make men hold** their **p**? 2790
15: 5 would **altogether hold** your **p**, 2790+2790
13:13 **Hold** your **p**, let me alone, that I may 2790
22:21 now thyself with him, and be **at p**: 7999
25: 2 with him, he maketh **p** in his high places. 7965
29:10 The nobles **held** their **p**, 2244+6963
33:31 unto me: **hold** thy **p**, and I will speak. 2790
33:33 **hold** thy **p**, and I will teach thee wisdom 2790
Ps 4: 8 I will both lay me down in **p**, and sleep; 7965
7: 4 evil *unto* him that was **at p** with me; 7999
28: 3 which speak **p** to their neighbours, 7965
29:11 the LORD will bless his people with **p**. 7965
34:14 and do good; seek **p**, and pursue it. 7965
35:20 For they speak not **p**: but they devise 7965
37:11 delight themselves in the abundance of **p**. 7965
37:37 the upright: for the end of *that man is* **p**. 7965
39: 2 silence, I **held** my **p**, *even* from good; 2814
39:12 unto my cry; **hold** not thy **p** at my tears: 2790
55:18 He hath delivered my soul in **p** from 7965
55:20 hands against such as be **at p** with him: 7965
72: 3 mountains shall bring **p** to the people, 7965
72: 7 abundance of **p** so long as the moon 7965
83: 1 **hold** not thy **p**, and be not still, O God. 2790
85: 8 for he will speak **p** unto his people, 7965
85:10 and **p** have kissed *each other*. 7965
109: 1 **Hold** not thy **p**, O God of my praise; 2790
119:165 Great **p** have they which love thy law: 7965
120: 6 hath long dwelt with him that hateth **p**. 7965
120: 7 I *am for* **p**: but when I speak, they *are* for 7965
122: 6 Pray for the **p** of Jerusalem: they shall 7965
122: 7 **P** be within thy walls, and prosperity 7965
122: 8 I will now say, **P** *be* within thee. 7965
125: 5 of iniquity: *but* **p** *shall be* upon Israel. 7965
128: 6 thy children's children, *and* **p** upon Israel. 7965
147:14 He maketh **p** *in* thy borders, and filleth 7965
Pr 3: 2 For length of days, and long life, and **p**, 7965
3:17 of pleasantness, and all her paths *are* **p**. 7965
7:14 I *have* **p** offerings with me; this day have 8002
11:12 a man of understanding **holdeth** his **p**. 2790
12:20 but to the counsellers of **p** *is* joy. 7965
16: 7 he **maketh** even his enemies **to be at p** 7999
17:28 Even a fool, when he **holdeth** his **p**, 2790
Ecc 3: 8 to hate; a time of war, and a time of **p**. 7965
Isa 9: 6 The everlasting Father, The Prince of **P**. 7965
9: 7 government and of **p** *there shall be* no end, 7965
26: 3 Thou wilt keep *him in* **perfect p**, 7965+7965
26:12 LORD, thou wilt ordain **p** for us: for thou 7965
27: 5 strength, *that* he may make **p** with me; 7965
27: 5 with me; *and* he shall make **p** with me. 7965
32:17 the work of righteousness shall be **p**; 7965
33: 7 the ambassadors of **p** shall weep bitterly. 7965
36:21 they **held** their **p**, and answered him not 2790
38:17 Behold, for **p** I had great bitterness: 7965
39: 8 For there shall be **p** and truth in my days. 7965
42:14 I have long time **holden** my **p**; I have 2814
45: 7 I make **p**, and create evil: I the LORD do 7965
48:18 had thy **p** been as a river, 7965
48:22 *There is* no **p**, saith the LORD, unto 7965
52: 7 bringeth good tidings, that publisheth **p**; 7965
53: 5 the chastisement of our **p** *was* upon him; 7965
54:10 neither shall the covenant of my **p** be 7965
54:13 and great *shall be* the **p** of thy children. 7965
55:12 go out with joy, and be led forth with **p**: 7965
57: 2 He shall enter *into* **p**: they shall rest in 7965
57:11 have not I **held** my **p** even of old, and 7965
57:19 **P**, peace to *him that is* far off, and to *him* 7965
57:19 **p** to *him that is* far off, and to *him that is* 7965
57:21 no **p**, saith my God, to the wicked. 7965
59: 8 The way of **p** they know not; and *there is* 7965
59: 8 goeth therein shall not know **p**. 7965
60:17 I will also make thy officers **p**, 7965
62: 1 For Zion's sake will I not **hold my p**, 2814
62: 6 *which* shall never **hold p** day nor 2814
64:12 wilt thou **hold** thy **p**, and afflict us very 2814
66:12 I will extend **p** to her like a river, 7965
Jer 4:10 Jerusalem, saying, Ye shall have **p**; 7965
4:19 I cannot **hold** my **p**, because thou hast 2790
6:14 *of* my people slightly, saying, **P**, peace; 7965
6:14 *of* my people slightly, saying, Peace, **p**; 7965

Jer 6:14 Peace, peace; when *there is* no **p**. 7965
8:11 of my people slightly, saying, **P**, peace; 7965
8:11 of my people slightly, saying, Peace, **p**; 7965
8:11 Peace, peace; when *there is* no **p**. 7965
8:15 We looked for **p**, but no good *came; and* 7965
12: 5 *if* in the land of **p**, *wherein* thou trustedst, 7965
12:12 end of the land: no flesh *shall* have **p**. 7965
14:13 but I will give you assured **p** in this place. 7965
14:19 we looked for **p**, and *there is* no good; 7965
16: 5 for I have taken away my **p** from this 7965
23:17 The LORD hath said, Ye shall have **p**; 7965
28: 9 The prophet which prophesieth of **p**, 7965
29: 7 seek the **p** of the city whither I have 7965
29: 7 for in the **p** thereof shall ye have peace. 7965
29: 7 for in the peace thereof shall ye have **p**. 7965
29:11 the LORD, thoughts of **p**, and not of evil, 7965
30: 5 a voice of trembling, of fear, and not of **p**. 7965
33: 6 will reveal unto them the abundance of **p** 7965
34: 5 *But* thou shalt die in **p**: and with 7965
43:12 and he shall go forth from thence in **p**. 7965
La 3:17 thou hast removed my soul far off from **p**: 7965
Eze 7:25 they shall seek **p**, and *there shall be* none. 7965
13:10 they have seduced my people, saying, **P**; 7965
13:10 *there was* no **p**; and one built up a wall, 7965
13:16 which see visions of **p** for her, and *there* 7965
13:16 and *there is* no **p**, saith the Lord GOD. 7965
34:25 I will make with them a covenant of **p**, 7965
37:26 I will make a covenant of **p** with 7965
43:27 upon the altar, and your **p offerings**, 8002
45:15 for a burnt offering, and for **p offerings**, 8002
45:17 the burnt offering, and the **p offerings**, 8002
46: 2 his burnt offering and his **p offerings**, 8002
46:12 or **p offerings** voluntarily unto the LORD, 8002
46:12 his burnt offering and his **p offerings**, 8002
Da 4: 1 in all the earth; **P** be multiplied unto you. 8001
6:25 in all the earth; **P** be multiplied unto you. 8001
8:25 in his heart, and by **p** shall destroy many: 7962
10:19 *be* unto thee, be strong, yea, be strong. 7965
Am 5:22 I regard the **p offerings** of your fat beasts. 8002
Ob 1: 7 the men that were at **p** with thee have 7965
Mic 3: 5 that bite with their teeth, and cry, **P**; 7965
5: 5 *man* shall be the **p**, when the Assyrian 7965
Na 1:15 bringeth good tidings, that publisheth **p**. 7965
Zep 1: 7 **Hold** thy **p** at the presence of the Lord 2013
Hag 2: 9 in this place will I give **p**, saith the LORD 7965
Zec 6:13 the counsel of **p** shall be between them 7965
8:10 neither *was there any* **p** to him that went 7965
8:16 the judgment of truth and **p** in your gates: 7965
8:19 therefore love the truth and **p**. 7965
9:10 he shall speak **p** unto the heathen; 7965
Mal 2: 5 My covenant was with him of life and **p**; 7965
2: 6 he walked with me in **p** and equity, 7965
Mt 10:13 house be worthy, let your **p** come upon it: 1515
10:13 it be not worthy, let your **p** return to you. 1515
10:34 Think not that I am come to send **p** on 1515
10:34 earth: I came not to send **p**, but a sword. 1515
20:31 because they should **hold** their **p**: 4623
26:63 But Jesus **held** his **p**. And the high priest 4623
Mk 1:25 saying, **Hold** thy **p**, and come out of him. 5392
3: 4 save life, or to kill? But they **held** their **p**. 4623
4:39 wind, and said unto the sea, **P**, be still. 4623
5:34 go in **p**, and be whole of thy plague. 1515
9:34 But they **held** their **p**: for by the way 4623
9:50 yourselves, and **have p** one with another. 1514
10:48 charged him that he should **hold** his **p**: 4623
14:61 But he **held** his **p**, and answered nothing. 4623
Lk 1:79 to guide our feet into the way of **p**. 1515
2:14 and on earth **p**, good will towards men. 1515
2:29 now lettest thou thy servant depart in **p**, 1515
4:35 saying, **Hold** thy **p**, and come out of him. 5392
7:50 Thy faith hath saved thee; go in **p**. 1515
8:48 thy faith hath made thee whole; go in **p**.) 1515
10: 5 ye enter, first say, **P** *be* to this house. 1515
10: 6 And if the son of **p** be there, your peace 1515
10: 6 peace be there, your **p** shall rest upon it: 1515
11:21 keepeth his palace, his goods are in **p**: 1515
12:51 Suppose ye that I am come to give **p** on 1515
14: 4 And they **held** their **p**. And he took *him*, 2270
14:32 ambassage, and desireth conditions of **p**. 1515
18:39 rebuked him, that he should **hold** his **p**: 4623
19:38 in heaven, and glory in the highest. 1515
19:40 tell you that, if these should **hold** their **p**, 4623
19:42 the *things* which belong unto thy **p**! 1515
20:26 marvelled at his answer, and **held** their **p**. 4601
24:36 and saith unto them, **P** *be* unto you. 1515
Jn 14:27 **P** I leave with you, my peace I give unto 1515
14:27 I leave with you, my **p** I give unto you: 1515
16:33 unto you, that in me ye might have **p**. 1515
20:19 and saith unto them, **P** *be* unto you. 1515
20:21 said Jesus to them again, **P** *be* unto you: 1515
20:26 in the midst, and said, **P** *be* unto you. 1515
Ac 10:36 of Israel, preaching **p** by Jesus Christ: 2270
11:18 heard these *things*, they **held** their **p**, 4601
12:17 unto them with the hand to **hold** their **p**, 4601
12:20 king's chamberlain their friend, desired **p**; 1515
15:13 And after they had **held** their **p**, 4601
15:33 were let go in **p** from the brethren unto 1515
16:36 now go: now therefore depart, and go in **p**. 1515
18: 9 not afraid, but speak, and **hold** not thy **p**: 4623
Ro 1: 7 Grace to you and **p** from God our Father, 1515
2:10 glory, honour, and **p**, to every *man* that 1515
3:17 And the way of **p** have they not known: 1515
5: 1 we have **p** with God through our Lord 1515
8: 6 but to be spiritually minded *is* life and **p**. 1515
10:15 feet of them that preach the gospel of **p**, 1515

Ro 14:17 and **p**, and joy in the Holy Ghost. 1515
14:19 follow *after* the things which make for **p**, 1515
15:13 fill you with all joy and **p** in believing, 1515
15:33 Now the God of **p** *be* with you all. Amen. 1515
16:20 And the God of **p** shall bruise Satan under 1515
1Co 1: 3 Grace *be* unto you, and **p**, from God our 1515
7:15 such *cases*: but God hath called us to **p**. 1515
14:30 that sitteth *by*, let the first **hold** his **p**. 4601
14:33 but of **p**, as in all churches of the saints. 1515
16:11 but conduct him forth in **p**, that he may 1515
2Co 1: 2 *be* to you and **p** from God our Father, 1515
13:11 good comfort, be of one mind, **live in p**; 1514
13:11 the God of love and **p** shall be with you. 1515
Gal 1: 3 Grace *be* to you and **p** from God the 1515
5:22 longsuffering, gentleness, goodness, 1515
6:16 to this rule, **p** *be* on them, and mercy, 1515
Eph 1: 2 Grace *be* to you, and **p**, from our God 1515
2:14 For he is our **p**, who hath made both one, 1515
2:15 of twain one new man, *so* making **p**; 1515
2:17 preached **p** to you which were afar off, 1515
4: 3 the unity of the Spirit in the bond of **p**. 1515
6:15 with the preparation of the gospel of **p**; 1515
6:23 **P** *be* to the brethren, and love with faith, 1515
Php 1: 2 Grace *be* unto you, and **p**, from God our 1515
4: 7 And the **p** of God, which passeth all 1515
4: 9 do: and the God of **p** shall be with you. 1515
Col 1: 2 Grace *be* unto you, and **p**, from God our 1515
1:20 having **made p** through the blood of his 1517
3:15 And let the **p** of God rule in your hearts, 1515
1Th 1: 1 Grace *be* unto you, and **p**, from God our 1515
5: 3 For when they shall say, **P** and safety; 1515
5:13 *And* be at **p** among yourselves. 1514
5:23 the very God of **p** sanctify you wholly; 1515
2Th 1: 2 Grace unto you, and **p**, from God our 1515
3:16 Now the Lord of **p** himself give you peace 1515
3:16 Now the Lord of peace himself give you **p** 1515
1Ti 1: 2 mercy, *and* **p**, from God our Father 1515
2Ti 1: 2 mercy, *and* **p**, from God the Father 1515
2:22 follow righteousness, faith, charity, **p**, 1515
Tit 1: 4 mercy, *and* **p**, from God the Father 1515
Phm 1: 3 Grace to you, and **p**, from God our Father 1515
Heb 7: 2 also King of Salem, which is, King of **p**; 1515
11:31 when she had received the spies with **p**. 1515
12:14 Follow **p** with all *men*, and holiness, 1515
13:20 Now the God of **p**, that brought again 1515
Jas 2:16 Depart in **p**, be you warmed and filled; 1515
3:18 the fruit of righteousness is sown in **p** 1515
3:18 is sown in peace of them that make **p**. 1515
1Pe 1: 2 Grace unto you, and **p**, be multiplied. 1515
3:11 and do good; let him seek **p**, and ensue it. 1515
5:14 **P** *be* with you all that are in Christ Jesus. 1515
2Pe 1: 2 be multiplied unto you through 1515
3:14 diligent that ye may be found of him in **p**, 1515
2Jn 1: 3 Grace *be* with you, mercy, *and* **p**, from 1515
3Jn 1:14 **P** *be* to thee. *Our* friends salute thee. 1515
Jude 1: 2 unto you, and **p**, and love, be multiplied. 1515
Rev 1: 4 Grace *be* unto you, and **p**, from him 1515
6: 4 that sat thereon to take **p** from the earth, 1515

PEACEABLE (8) [PEACE]
Ge 34:21 These men *are* **p** with us; therefore let 8003
2Sa 20:19 I *am* one of them that are **p** *and* faithful 7999
1Ch 4:40 and the land *was* wide, and quiet, and **p**; 7961
Isa 32:18 my people shall dwell in a **p** habitation, 7965
Jer 25:37 the **p** habitations are cut down because of 7965
1Ti 2: 2 and **p** life in all godliness and honesty. 2272
Heb 12:11 afterward it yieldeth the **p** fruit 1516
Jas 3:17 then **p**, gentle, *and* easy to be intreated, 1516

PEACEABLY (12) [PEACE]
Ge 37: 4 him, and could not speak **p** unto him. 7965
Jdg 11:13 restore those *lands* again **p**. 7965+871.1
21:13 rock Rimmon, and to call **p** unto them. 7965
1Sa 16: 4 at his coming, and said, Comest thou **p**? 7965
16: 5 he said, **P**: I am come to sacrifice unto 7965
1Ki 2:13 she said, Comest thou **p**? And he said, 7965
2:13 Comest thou peaceably? And he said, **P**. 7965
1Ch 12:18 be come **p** unto me to help me, 7965+3807.1
Jer 9: 8 *one* speaketh **p** to his neighbour with his 7965
Da 11:21 shall come in **p**, and obtain the kingdom 7962
11:24 He shall enter **p** even upon 7962+871.1
Ro 12:18 much as lieth in you, **live p** with all men. 1514

PEACEMAKERS (1) [PEACE]
Mt 5: 9 Blessed *are* the **p**: for they shall be called 1518

PEACOCKS (3)
1Ki 10:22 and silver, ivory, and apes, and **p**. 8500
2Ch 9:21 and silver, ivory, and apes, and **p**. 8500
Job 39:13 *Gavest* thou the goodly wings unto the **p**? 5965

PEARL (2) [PEARLS]
Mt 13:46 when he had found one **p** of great price, 3135
Rev 21:21 every several gate was of one **p**: 3135

PEARLS (8) [PEARL]
Job 28:18 mention shall be made of coral, or of **p**: 1378
Mt 7: 6 neither cast ye your **p** before swine, 3135
13:45 a merchant man, seeking goodly **p**: 3135
1Ti 2: 9 broided hair, or gold, or **p**, or costly array; 3135
Rev 17: 4 with gold and precious stone and **p**, 3135
18:12 and of **p**, and fine linen, and purple, 3135
18:16 with gold, and precious stones, and **p**! 3135
21:21 And the twelve gates *were* twelve **p**; 3135

P

PECULIAR (7)

Ex	19: 5 ye shall be a **p treasure** unto me above	5459
Dt	14: 2 the LORD hath chosen thee to be a **p**	5459
	26:18 avouched thee *this* day to be his **p** people,	5459
Ps	135: 4 himself, *and* Israel for his **p treasure**.	5459
Ecc	2: 8 the **p treasure** of kings and of	5459
Tit	2:14 and purify unto himself a **p** people,	4041
1Pe	2: 9 a holy nation, a **p** people;	1519+4047

PEDAHEL (1)

Nu	34:28 of Naphtali, **P** the son of Ammihud.	6300

PEDAHZUR (5)

Nu	1:10 of Manasseh; Gamaliel the son of **P**.	6301
	2:20 Manasseh *shall be* Gamaliel the son of **P**.	6301
	7:54 eighth day *offered* Gamaliel the son of **P**,	6301
	7:59 *was* the offering of Gamaliel the son of **P**.	6301
	10:23 of Manasseh *was* Gamaliel the son of **P**.	6301

PEDAIAH (8)

2Ki	23:36 Zebudah, the daughter of **P** of Rumah.	6305
1Ch	3:18 **P**, and Shenazar, Jecamiah, Hoshama,	6305
	3:19 the sons of **P** were, Zerubbabel,	6305
	27:20 half tribe of Manasseh, Joel the son of **P**:	6305
Ne	3:25 the prison. After him **P** the son of Parosh.	6305
	8: 4 **P**, and Mishael, and Malchiah,	6305
	11: 7 the son of Joed, the son of **P**, the son of	6305
	13:13 Zadok the scribe, and of the Levites, **P**:	6305

PEDIGREES (1)

Nu	1:18 they **declared** their **p** after their families,	3205

PEELED (2)

Isa	18: 2 to a nation scattered and **p**,	4178
	18: 7 of hosts *of* a people scattered and **p**,	4178
Eze	29:18 made bald, and every shoulder *was* **p**:	4803

PEEP (1) [PEEPED]

Isa	8:19 and unto wizards that **p**, and that mutter:	6850

PEEPED (1) [PEEP]

Isa	10:14 the wing, or opened the mouth, or **p**.	6850

PEKAH (11)

2Ki	15:25 **P** the son of Remaliah, a captain of his,	6492
	15:27 fiftieth year of Azariah king of Judah **P**	6492
	15:29 In the days of **P** king of Israel came	6492
	15:30 conspiracy against **P** the son of Remaliah,	6492
	15:31 rest of the acts of **P**, and all that he did,	6492
	15:32 the second year of **P** the son of Remaliah	6492
	15:37 king of Syria, and **P** the son of Remaliah.	6492
	16: 1 In the seventeenth year of **P** the son of	6492
	16: 5 **P** son of Remaliah king of Israel came up	6492
2Ch	28: 6 For **P** the son of Remaliah slew in Judah	6492
Isa	7: 1 the son of **P**, king of Israel,	6492

PEKAHIAH (3)

2Ki	15:22 and **P** his son reigned in his stead.	6494
	15:23 **P** the son of Menahem *began* to reign	6494
	15:26 rest of the acts of **P**, and all that he did,	6494

PEKOD (2)

Jer	50:21 against it, and against the inhabitants of **P**:	6489
Eze	23:23 all the Chaldeans, **P**, and Shoa, and Koa,	6489

PELAIAH (3)

1Ch	3:24 **P**, and Akkub, and Johanan, and Dalaiah,	6411
Ne	8: 7 Jozabad, Hanan, **P**, and the Levites,	6411
	10:10 Shebaniah, Hodijah, Kelita, **P**, Hanan,	6411

PELALIAH (1)

Ne	11:12 the son of **P**, the son of Amzi, the son of	6421

PELATIAH (5)

1Ch	3:21 the sons of Hananiah; **P**, and Jesaiah:	6410
	4:42 having for their captains **P**, and Neariah,	6410
Ne	10:22 **P**, Hanan, Anaiah,	6410
Eze	11: 1 **P** the son of Benaiah, princes of the	6410
	11:13 that **P** the son of Benaiah died.	6410

PELEG (7) [PHALEC]

Ge	10:25 the name of one *was* **P**; for in his days	6389
	11:16 lived four and thirty years, and begat **P**:	6389
	11:17 Eber lived after he begat **P** four hundred	6389
	11:18 And **P** lived thirty years, and begat Reu:	6389
	11:19 **P** lived after he begat Reu two hundred	6389
1Ch	1:19 the name of the one *was* **P**; because in	6389
	1:25 Eber, **P**, Rehu,	6389

PELET (2)

1Ch	2:47 Geshan, and **P**, and Ephah, and Shaaph.	6404
	12: 3 Jeziel, and **P**, the sons of Azmaveth;	6404

PELETH (2) [PELETHITES]

Nu	16: 1 On, the son of **P**, sons of Reuben,	6431
1Ch	2:33 the sons of Jonathan; **P**, and Zaza.	6431

PELETHITES (7) [PELETH]

2Sa	8:18 *was over* both the Cherethites and the **P**;	6432
	15:18 and all the **P**, and all the Gittites,	6432
	20: 7 the **P**, and all the mighty *men:* and	6432
	20:23 *was* over the Cherethites and over the **P**:	6432
1Ki	1:38 the **P**, went down, and caused Solomon	6432
	1:44 the **P**, and they have caused him to ride	6432
1Ch	18:17 *was* over the Cherethites and the **P**;	6432

PELICAN (3)

Lev	11:18 the swan, and the **p**, and the gier eagle,	6893
Dt	14:17 the **p**, and the gier eagle,	6893
Ps	102: 6 I am like a **p** of the wilderness: I am like	6893

PELONITE (3)

1Ch	11:27 Shammoth the Harorite, Helez the **P**,	6397
	11:36 Hepher the Mecherathite, Ahijah the **P**,	6397
	27:10 for the seventh month *was* Helez the **P**,	6397

PEN (7)

Jdg	5:14 out of Zebulun they that handle the **p** of	7626
Job	19:24 That they were graven with an iron **p** and	5842
Ps	45: 1 my tongue *is* the **p** of a ready writer.	5842
Isa	8: 1 write in it with a man's **p** concerning	2747
Jer	8: 8 certainly in vain made he *it;* the **p** of	5842
	17: 1 sin of Judah *is* written with a **p** of iron,	5842
3Jn	1:13 I will not with ink and **p** write unto thee:	2563

PENCE (5)

Mt	18:28 which ought him an hundred **p**:	1220
Mk	14: 5 been sold for more than three hundred **p**,	1220
Lk	7:41 one ought five hundred **p**, and the other	1220
	10:35 he took out two **p**, and gave *them* to	1220
Jn	12: 5 this ointment sold for three hundred **p**	1220

PENIEL (1) [PENUEL]

Ge	32:30 Jacob called the name of the place **P**: for I	6439

PENINNAH (3)

1Sa	1: 2 Hannah, and the name of the other **P**:	6444
	1: 2 **P** had children, but Hannah had no	6444
	1: 4 he gave to **P** his wife, and to all her sons	6444

PENKNIFE (1)

Jer	36:23 he cut it with the **p**,	5608+8593+1886.1

PENNY (9) [PENNYWORTH]

Mt	20: 2 agreed with the labourers for a **p** a day,	1220
	20: 9 hour, they received every man a **p**.	1220
	20:10 they likewise received every man a **p**.	1220
	20:13 didst not thou agree with me for a **p**?	1220
	22:19 And they brought unto him a **p**.	1220
Mk	12:15 ye me? bring me a **p**, that I may see *it.*	1220
Lk	20:24 Shew me a **p**. Whose image and	1220
Rev	6: 6 A measure of wheat for a **p**,	1220
	6: 6 and three measures of barley for a **p**;	1220

PENNYWORTH (2) [PENNY]

Mk	6:37 we go and buy two hundred **p** of bread,	1220
Jn	6: 7 Two hundred **p** of bread is not sufficient	1220

PENTECOST (3)

Ac	2: 1 And when the day of **P** was fully come,	4005
	20:16 for him, to be at Jerusalem the day of **P**.	4005
1Co	16: 8 But I will tarry at Ephesus until **P**.	4005

PENUEL (8) [PENIEL]

Ge	32:31 he passed over **P** the sun rose upon him,	6439
Jdg	8: 8 he went up thence *to* **P**, and spake unto	6439
	8: 8 the men of **P** answered him as the men	6439
	8: 9 he spake also unto the men of **P**, saying,	6439
	8:17 he beat down the tower of **P**, and slew	6439
1Ki	12:25 went out from thence, and built **P**.	6439
1Ch	4: 4 **P** the father of Gedor, and Ezer the father	6439
	8:25 Iphedeiah, and **P**, the sons of Shashak;	6439

PENURY (2)

Pr	14:23 but the talk of the lips *tendeth* only to **p**.	4270
Lk	21: 4 she of her **p** hath cast in all the living that	5303

PEOPLE (2139) [PEOPLE'S, PEOPLES]

Ge	11: 6 the **p** *is* one, and they have all one	5971
	14:16 goods, and the women also, and the **p**.	5971
	17:14 that soul shall be cut off from his **p**;	5971
	17:16 of nations; kings of **p** shall be of her.	5971
	19: 4 and young, all the **p** from every quarter:	5971
	23: 7 and bowed himself to the **p** of the land,	5971
	23:11 the presence of the sons of my **p** give I it	5971
	23:12 bowed down himself before the **p** of	5971
	23:13 in the audience of the **p** of the land,	5971
	25: 8 full *of* years; and was gathered to his **p**.	5971
	25:17 and died; and was gathered unto his **p**.	5971
	25:23 two manner of **p** shall be separated from	3816
	25:23 *one* **p** shall be stronger than *the other*	3816
	25:23 people shall be stronger than *the other* **p**;	3816
	26:10 one of the **p** might lightly have lien with	5971
	26:11 Abimelech charged all *his* **p**, saying,	5971
	27:29 Let **p** serve thee, and nations bow down	5971
	28: 3 that thou mayest be a multitude of **p**;	5971
	29: 1 came into the land of the **p** of the east.	1121
	32: 7 and he divided the **p** that *was* with him,	5971
	34:16 with you, and we will become one **p**.	5971
	34:22 to be one **p**, if every male among us be	5971
	35: 6 he and all the **p** that *were* with him.	5971
	35:29 died, and was gathered unto his **p**,	5971
	41:40 according unto thy word shall all my **p** be	5971
	41:55 the **p** cried to Pharaoh for bread:	5971
	42: 6 he *it was* that sold to all the **p** of the land:	5971
	47:21 as for the **p**, he removed them to cities	5971
	47:23 Joseph said unto the **p**, Behold, I have	5971
	48: 4 and I will make of thee a multitude of **p**;	5971
	48:19 I know *it:* he also shall become a **p**,	5971
	49:10 unto him *shall* the gathering of the **p** be.	5971
	49:16 Dan shall judge his **p**, as one of the tribes	5971
	49:29 them, I *am* to be gathered unto my **p**:	5971
	49:33 the ghost, and was gathered unto his **p**.	5971
	50:20 as *it is* this day, to save much **p** alive.	5971
Ex	1: 9 he said unto his **p**, Behold, the people of	5971
	1: 9 the **p** of the children of Israel *are* moe and	5971
	1:20 the **p** multiplied, and waxed very mighty.	5971
	1:22 Pharaoh charged all his **p**, saying,	5971
	3: 7 I have surely seen the affliction of my **p**	5971
	3:10 that thou mayest bring forth my **p**	5971
	3:12 When thou hast brought forth the **p** out	5971
	3:21 I will give this **p** favour in the sight of	5971
	4:16 he shall be thy spokesman unto the **p**:	5971
	4:21 his heart, that he shall not let the **p** go.	5971
	4:30 and did the signs in the sight of the **p**.	5971
	4:31 the **p** believed: and when they heard that	5971
	5: 1 the LORD God of Israel, Let my **p** go,	5971
	5: 4 and Aaron, let the **p** from their works?	5971
	5: 5 the **p** of the land now *are* many,	5971
	5: 6 the same day the taskmasters of the **p**,	5971
	5:10 Ye shall no more give the **p** straw to make	5971
	5:10 the taskmasters of the **p** went out,	5971
	5:10 and they spake to the **p**, saying,	5971
	5:12 the **p** were scattered abroad throughout	5971
	5:16 beaten; but the fault *is* in thine own **p**.	5971
	5:22 hast thou *so* evil entreated this **p**?	5971
	5:23 in thy name, he hath done evil to this **p**;	5971
	5:23 neither hast thou delivered thy **p** at all.	5971
	6: 7 I will take you to me for a **p**, and I will be	5971
	7: 4 *and* my **p** the children of Israel,	5971
	7:14 *is* hardened, he refuseth to let the **p** go.	5971
	7:16 saying, Let my **p** go, that they may serve	5971
	8: 1 Thus saith the LORD, Let my **p** go,	5971
	8: 3 upon thy **p**, and into thine ovens,	5971
	8: 4 upon thy **p**, and upon all thy servants.	5971
	8: 8 away the frogs from me, and from my **p**;	5971
	8: 8 I will let the **p** go, that they may do	5971
	8: 9 thee, and for thy servants, and for thy **p**,	5971
	8:11 and from thy servants, and from thy **p**;	5971
	8:20 Thus saith the LORD, Let my **p** go,	5971
	8:21 Else, if thou wilt not let my **p** go, behold,	5971
	8:21 and upon thy **p**, and into thy houses:	5971
	8:22 in which my **p** dwell, that no swarms *of*	5971
	8:23 I will put a division between my **p** and	5971
	8:23 a division between my people and thy **p**:	5971
	8:29 his servants, and from his **p**, to morrow:	5971
	8:29 letting the **p** go to sacrifice to the LORD.	5971
	8:31 from his servants, and from his **p**;	5971
	8:32 time also, neither would he let the **p** go.	5971
	9: 1 Let my **p** go, that they may serve me.	5971
	9: 7 hardened, and he did not let the **p** go.	5971
	9:13 Let my **p** go, that they may serve me.	5971
	9:14 and upon thy servants, and upon thy **p**;	5971
	9:15 may smite thee and thy **p** with pestilence;	5971
	9:17 As yet exaltest thou thyself against my **p**,	5971
	9:27 *is* righteous, and I and my **p** *are* wicked.	5971
	10: 3 let my **p** go, that they may serve me.	5971
	10: 4 Else, if thou refuse to let my **p** go, behold,	5971
	11: 2 Speak now in the ears of the **p**,	5971
	11: 3 the LORD gave the **p** favour in the sight	5971
	11: 3 and in the sight of the **p**.)	5971
	11: 8 thee out, and all the **p** that follow thee:	5971
	12:27 the **p** bowed the head and worshipped.	5971
	12:31 *and* get you forth from amongst my **p**,	5971
	12:33 the Egyptians were urgent upon the **p**,	5971
	12:34 the **p** took their dough before it was	5971
	12:36 the LORD gave the **p** favour in the sight	5971
	13: 3 Moses said unto the **p**, Remember this	5971
	13:17 to pass, when Pharaoh had let the **p** go,	5971
	13:17 Lest peradventure the **p** repent when they	5971
	13:18 God led the **p** about, *through* the way of	5971
	13:22 pillar of fire by night, *from* before the **p**.	5971
	14: 5 was told the king of Egypt that the **p** fled:	5971
	14: 5 of his servants was turned against the **p**,	5971
	14: 6 his chariot, and took his **p** with him:	5971
	14:13 Moses said unto the **p**, Fear ye not,	5971
	14:31 the **p** feared the LORD, and believed	5971
	15:13 Thou in thy mercy hast led forth the **p**	5971
	15:14 The **p** shall hear, *and* be afraid:	5971
	15:16 till thy **p** pass over, O LORD, till	5971
	15:16 pass over, O LORD, till thy **p** pass over,	5971
	15:24 the **p** murmured against Moses, saying,	5971
	16: 4 the **p** shall go out and gather a certain	5971
	16:27 *that* there went out *some* of the **p** on	5971
	16:30 So the **p** rested on the seventh day.	5971
	17: 1 *there was* no water for the **p** to drink.	5971
	17: 2 Wherefore the **p** did chide with Moses,	5971
	17: 3 the **p** thirsted there for water;	5971
	17: 3 the **p** murmured against Moses, and said,	5971
	17: 4 What shall I do unto this **p**?	5971
	17: 5 Go on before the **p**, and take with thee of	5971
	17: 6 water out of it, that the **p** may drink.	5971
	17:13 and his **p** with the edge of the sword.	5971
	18: 1 for Israel his **p**, *and* that the LORD had	5971
	18:10 who hath delivered the **p** from under	5971
	18:13 morrow, that Moses sat to judge the **p**:	5971
	18:13 the **p** stood by Moses from the morning	5971
	18:14 father in law saw all that he did to the **p**,	5971
	18:14 *is* this thing that thou doest to the **p**?	5971
	18:14 all the **p** stand by thee from morning unto	5971
	18:15 Because the **p** come unto me to inquire of	5971
	18:18 both thou, and this **p** that *is* with thee:	5971
	18:19 be thou for the **p** to God-ward, that thou	5971
	18:21 thou shalt provide out of all the **p**	5971
	18:22 let them judge the **p** at all seasons:	5971
	18:23 all this **p** shall also go to their place in	5971
	18:25 made them heads over the **p**, rulers of	5971

P

Ex		
18:26	they judged the **p** at all seasons: the hard	5971
19: 5	a peculiar treasure unto me above all **p**:	5971
19: 7	and called for the elders of the **p**,	5971
19: 8	all the **p** answered together, and said,	5971
19: 8	Moses returned the words of the **p** unto	5971
19: 9	the **p** may hear when I speak with thee,	5971
19: 9	Moses told the words of the **p** unto	5971
19:10	Go unto the **p**, and sanctify them to day	5971
19:11	in the sight of all the **p** upon mount Sinai.	5971
19:12	thou shalt set bounds unto the **p** round	5971
19:14	went down from the mount unto the **p**,	5971
19:14	unto the people, and sanctified the **p**;	5971
19:15	he said unto the **p**, Be ready against	5971
19:16	all the **p** that was in the camp trembled.	5971
19:17	Moses brought forth the **p** out of the	5971
19:21	said unto Moses, Go down, charge the **p**,	5971
19:23	The **p** cannot come up to mount Sinai:	5971
19:24	thou **p** break through to come up unto	5971
19:25	So Moses went down unto the **p**,	5971
20:18	all the **p** saw the thunderings,	5971
20:18	when the **p** saw it, they removed,	5971
20:20	Moses said unto the **p**, Fear not: for God	5971
20:21	the **p** stood afar off, and Moses drew near	5971
22:25	If thou lend money to any of my **p** that is	5971
22:28	the gods, nor curse the ruler of thy **p**.	5971
23:11	lie still; that the poor of thy **p** may eat:	5971
23:27	will destroy all the **p** to whom thou shalt	5971
24: 2	neither shall the **p** go up with him.	5971
24: 3	and told the **p** all the words of the LORD,	5971
24: 3	all the **p** answered with one voice,	5971
24: 7	and read in the audience of the **p**:	5971
24: 8	and sprinkled it on the **p**, and said,	5971
30:33	stranger, shall even be cut off from his **p**.	5971
30:38	shall even be cut off from his **p**.	5971
31:14	soul shall be cut off from amongst his **p**.	5971
32: 1	when the **p** saw that Moses delayed to	5971
32: 1	the **p** gathered themselves together unto	5971
32: 3	all the **p** brake off the golden earrings	5971
32: 6	the **p** sat down to eat and to drink,	5971
32: 7	for thy **p**, which thou broughtest out of	5971
32: 9	I have seen this **p**, and, behold, it is a	5971
32: 9	and behold, it is a stiffnecked **p**:	5971
32:11	doth thy wrath wax hot against thy **p**,	5971
32:12	and repent of this evil against thy **p**.	5971
32:14	evil which he thought to do unto his **p**.	5971
32:17	when Joshua heard the noise of the **p** as	5971
32:21	What did this **p** unto thee, that thou hast	5971
32:22	thou knowest the **p**, that they are set on	5971
32:25	when Moses saw that the **p** were naked;	5971
32:28	there fell of the **p** that day about three	5971
32:30	Moses said unto the **p**, Ye have sinned	5971
32:31	this **p** have sinned a great sin,	5971
32:34	lead the **p** unto the place of which I have	5971
32:35	the LORD plagued the **p**, because they	5971
33: 1	the **p** which thou hast brought up out of	5971
33: 3	midst of thee; for thou art a stiffnecked **p**:	5971
33: 4	when the **p** heard these evil tidings, they	5971
33: 5	children of Israel, Ye are a stiffnecked **p**:	5971
33: 8	all the **p** rose up, and stood every man	5971
33:10	all the **p** saw the cloudy pillar stand at	5971
33:10	all the **p** rose up and worshipped,	5971
33:12	See, thou sayest unto me, Bring up this **p**:	5971
33:13	and consider that this nation is thy **p**.	5971
33:16	and thy **p** have found grace in thy sight?	5971
33:16	so shall we be separated, I and thy **p**,	5971
33:16	from all the **p** that are upon the face of	5971
34: 9	for it is a stiffnecked **p**; and pardon our	5971
34:10	before all thy **p** I will do marvels, such as	5971
34:10	all the **p** among which thou art shall see	5971
36: 5	The **p** bring much more than enough for	5971
36: 6	So the **p** were restrained from bringing.	5971

Lev		
4: 3	do sin according to the sin of the **p**;	5971
4:27	if any one of the common **p** sin through	5971
7:20	even that soul shall be cut off from his **p**.	5971
7:21	even that soul shall be cut off from his **p**.	5971
7:25	that eateth it shall be cut off from his **p**.	5971
7:27	even that soul shall be cut off from his **p**.	5971
9: 7	an atonement for thyself, and for the **p**:	5971
9: 7	offer the offering of the **p**, and make an	5971
9:15	which was the sin offering for the **p**,	5971
9:18	of peace offerings, which was for the **p**:	5971
9:22	Aaron lift up his hand towards the **p**,	5971
9:23	and came out, and blessed the **p**:	5971
9:23	of the LORD appeared unto all the **p**.	5971
9:24	which when all the **p** saw, they shouted,	5971
10: 3	and before all the **p** I will be glorified.	5971
10: 6	die, and lest wrath come upon all the **p**:	5712
16:15	is for the **p**, and bring his blood within	5971
16:24	the burnt offering of the **p**, and make an	5971
16:24	an atonement for himself, and for the **p**.	5971
16:33	and for all the **p** of the congregation.	5971
17: 4	man shall be cut off from among his **p**:	5971
17: 9	man shall be cut off from among his **p**.	5971
17:10	and will cut him off from among his **p**.	5971
18:29	them shall be cut off from among their **p**.	5971
19: 8	soul shall be cut off from among his **p**.	5971
19:16	man down as a talebearer among thy **p**:	5971
19:18	any grudge against the children of thy **p**,	5971
20: 2	the **p** of the land shall stone him with	5971
20: 3	and will cut him off from among his **p**;	5971
20: 4	if the **p** of the land do any ways hide	5971
20: 5	with Molech, from among their **p**.	5971
20: 6	and will cut him off from among his **p**.	5971
20:17	be cut off in the sight of their **p**:	1121+5971
20:18	them shall be cut off from among their **p**.	5971

Lev		
20:24	which have separated you from other **p**.	5971
20:26	have severed you from other **p**, that ye	5971
21: 1	none be defiled for the dead among his **p**:	5971
21: 4	being a chief man among his **p**, to profane	5971
21:14	he shall take a virgin of his own **p** to wife.	5971
21:15	he shall profane his seed among his **p**.	5971
23:29	he shall be cut off from among his **p**.	5971
23:30	soul will I destroy from among his **p**.	5971
26:12	will be your God, and ye shall be my **p**.	5971

Nu		
5:21	thee a curse and an oath among thy **p**,	5971
5:27	the woman shall be a curse among her **p**.	5971
9:13	soul shall be cut off from among his **p**:	5971
11: 1	when the **p** complained, it displeased	5971
11: 2	the **p** cried unto Moses; and when Moses	5971
11: 8	And the **p** went about, and gathered it,	5971
11:10	Moses heard the **p** weep throughout	5971
11:11	that thou layest the burden of all this **p**	5971
11:12	Have I conceived all this **p**? have I	5971
11:13	should I have flesh to give unto all this **p**?	5971
11:14	I am not able to bear all this **p** alone,	5971
11:16	thou knowest to be the elders of the **p**,	5971
11:17	they shall bear the burden of the **p** with	5971
11:18	say thou unto the **p**, Sanctify yourselves	5971
11:21	Moses said, The **p**, amongst whom I am,	5971
11:24	told the **p** the words of the LORD,	5971
11:24	the seventy men of the elders of the **p**,	5971
11:29	would God that all the LORD's **p** were	5971
11:32	the **p** stood up all that day, and all that	5971
11:33	of the LORD was kindled against the **p**,	5971
11:33	the LORD smote the **p** with a very great	5971
11:34	there they buried the **p** that lusted.	5971
11:35	And the **p** journeyed from	5971
12:15	the **p** journeyed not till Miriam was	5971
12:16	afterward the **p** removed from Hazeroth,	5971
13:18	it is; and the **p** that dwelleth therein,	5971
13:28	Nevertheless the **p** be strong that dwell in	5971
13:30	Caleb stilled the **p** before Moses, and said,	5971
13:31	We be not able to go up against the **p**;	5971
13:32	all the **p** that we saw in it are men of a	5971
14: 1	and cried; and the **p** wept that night.	5971
14: 9	neither fear ye the **p** of the land;	5971
14:11	How long will this **p** provoke me?	5971
14:13	up this **p** in thy might from among them;)	5971
14:14	heard that thou LORD art among this **p**,	5971
14:15	if thou shalt kill all this **p** as one man,	5971
14:16	**p** into the land which he sware unto	5971
14:19	the iniquity of this **p** according unto	5971
14:19	as thou hast forgiven this **p**, from Egypt	5971
14:39	of Israel: and the **p** mourned greatly.	5971
15:26	seeing all the **p** were in ignorance.	5971
15:30	soul shall be cut off from among his **p**.	5971
16:41	saying, Ye have killed the **p** of the LORD.	5971
16:47	the plague was begun among the **p**:	5971
16:47	and made an atonement for the **p**.	5971
20: 1	the **p** abode in Kadesh; and Miriam died	5971
20: 3	the **p** chode with Moses, and spake,	5971
20:20	came out against him with much **p**,	5971
20:24	Aaron shall be gathered unto his **p**: for he	5971
20:26	Aaron shall be gathered unto his **p**,	NIH
21: 2	If thou wilt indeed deliver this **p** into my	5971
21: 4	the soul of the **p** was much discouraged	5971
21: 5	the **p** spake against God,	5971
21: 6	LORD sent fiery serpents among the **p**,	5971
21: 6	among the people, and they bit the **p**;	5971
21: 6	bit the people; and much **p** of Israel died.	5971
21: 7	Therefore the **p** came to Moses, and said,	5971
21: 7	from us. And Moses prayed for the **p**.	5971
21:16	Gather the **p** together, and I will give	5971
21:18	the well, the nobles of the **p** digged it,	5971
21:23	Sihon gathered all his **p** together,	5971
21:29	thou art undone, O **p** of Chemosh: he	5971
21:33	he, and all his **p**, to the battle at Edrei.	5971
21:34	into thy hand, and all his **p**, and his land;	5971
21:35	smote him, and his sons, and all his **p**,	5971
22: 3	Moab was sore afraid of the **p**, because	5971
22: 5	river of the land of the children of his **p**:	5971
22: 5	Behold, there is a **p** come out from Egypt:	5971
22: 6	therefore, I pray thee, curse me this **p**;	5971
22:11	Behold, there is a **p** come out of Egypt,	5971
22:12	go with them; thou shalt not curse the **p**:	5971
22:17	I pray thee, curse me this **p**.	5971
22:41	he might see the utmost part of the **p**.	5971
23: 9	the **p** shall dwell alone, and shall not be	5971
23:24	the **p** shall rise up as a great lion, and lift	5971
24:14	now behold, I go unto my **p**: come	5971
24:14	I will advertise thee what this **p** shall do	5971
24:14	people shall do to thy **p** in the latter days.	5971
25: 1	the **p** begun to commit whoredom with	5971
25: 2	they called the **p** unto the sacrifices of	5971
25: 2	the **p** did eat, and bowed down to their	5971
25: 4	Take all the heads of the **p**, and hang	5971
25:15	he was head over a **p**, and of a chief house	523
26: 4	Take the sum of the **p**, from twenty years	NIH
27:13	thou also shalt be gathered unto thy **p**,	5971
31: 2	shalt thou be gathered unto thy **p**.	5971
31: 3	Moses spake unto the **p**, saying, Arm	5971
32:15	and ye shall destroy all this **p**.	5971
33:14	where was no water for the **p** to drink.	5971

Dt		
1:28	The **p** is greater and taller than we;	5971
2: 4	command thou the **p**, saying, Ye are to	5971
2:10	a **p** great, and many, and tall,	5971
2:16	and dead from among the **p**,	5971
2:21	A **p** great, and many, and tall,	5971
2:32	he and all his **p**, to fight at Jahaz.	5971
2:33	we smote him, and his sons, and all his **p**.	5971

Dt		
3: 1	he and all his **p**, to battle at Edrei.	5971
3: 2	and all his **p**, and his land, into thy hand;	5971
3: 3	Og also, the king of Bashan, and all his **p**	5971
3:28	for he shall go over before this **p**,	5971
4: 6	nation is a wise and understanding **p**.	5971
4:10	Gather me the **p** together, and I will	5971
4:20	to be unto him a **p** of inheritance, as ye	5971
4:33	Did ever **p** hear the voice of God speaking	5971
5:28	heard the voice of the words of this **p**,	5971
6:14	the gods of the **p** which are round about	5971
7: 6	For thou art a holy **p** unto the LORD thy	5971
7: 6	chosen thee to be a special **p** unto himself,	5971
7: 6	above all that are upon the face of	5971
7: 7	ye were moe in number than any **p**;	5971
7: 7	people; for ye were the fewest of all **p**:	5971
7:14	Thou shalt be blessed above all **p**:	5971
7:16	thou shalt consume all the **p** which	5971
7:19	shall the LORD thy God do unto all the **p**	5971
9: 2	A **p** great and tall, the children of	5971
9: 6	for thou art a stiffnecked **p**.	5971
9:12	for thy **p** which thou hast brought forth	5971
9:13	I have seen this **p**, and, behold, it is	5971
9:13	and behold, it is a stiffnecked **p**:	5971
9:26	destroy not thy **p** and thine inheritance,	5971
9:27	look not unto the stubbornness of this **p**,	5971
9:29	Yet they are thy **p** and thine inheritance,	5971
10:11	Arise, take thy journey before the **p**,	5971
10:15	even you above all **p**, as it is this day.	5971
13: 7	Namely, of the gods of the **p** which are	5971
13: 9	and afterwards the hand of all the **p**.	5971
14: 2	For thou art a holy **p** unto the LORD thy	5971
14: 2	chosen thee to be a peculiar **p** unto	5971
14:21	for thou art a holy **p** unto the LORD thy	5971
16:18	they shall judge the **p** with just judgment.	5971
17: 7	and afterward the hands of all the **p**.	5971
17:13	all the **p** shall hear, and fear, and do no	5971
17:16	nor cause the **p** to return to Egypt,	5971
18: 3	this shall be the priest's due from the **p**,	5971
20: 1	and chariots, and a **p** more than thou,	5971
20: 2	shall approach and speak unto the **p**,	5971
20: 8	the officers shall speak unto the **p**, saying,	5971
20: 8	the officers shall speak further unto the **p**,	5971
20: 9	have made an end of speaking unto the **p**,	5971
20: 9	make captains of the armies to lead the **p**.	5971
20:11	that all the **p** that is found therein shall be	5971
20:16	of the cities of these **p**, which the LORD	5971
21: 8	Be merciful, O LORD, unto thy **p** Israel,	5971
21: 8	lay not innocent blood unto thy **p** of	5971
26:15	bless thy **p** Israel, and the land which	5971
26:18	thee this day to be his peculiar **p**,	5971
27: 1	the elders of Israel commanded the **p**,	5971
27: 9	this day thou art become the **p** of	5971
27:11	Moses charged the **p** the same day,	5971
27:12	upon mount Gerizzim to bless the **p**,	5971
27:15	putteth it in a secret place. And all the **p**	5971
27:16	mother. And all the **p** shall say, Amen.	5971
27:17	And all the **p** shall say, Amen.	5971
27:18	the way. And all the **p** shall say, Amen.	5971
27:19	widow. And all the **p** shall say, Amen.	5971
27:20	And all the **p** shall say, Amen.	5971
27:21	of beast. And all the **p** shall say, Amen.	5971
27:22	mother. And all the **p** shall say, Amen.	5971
27:23	in law. And all the **p** shall say, Amen.	5971
27:24	And all the **p** shall say, Amen.	5971
27:25	And all the **p** shall say, Amen.	5971
27:26	do them. And all the **p** shall say, Amen.	5971
28: 9	The LORD shall establish thee a holy **p**	5971
28:10	all **p** of the earth shall see that thou art	5971
28:32	daughters shall be given unto another **p**,	5971
28:64	the LORD shall scatter thee among all **p**,	5971
29:13	That he may establish thee to day for a **p**	5971
31: 7	thou must go with this **p** unto the land	5971
31:12	Gather the **p** together, men, men, and women,	5971
31:16	this **p** will rise up, and go a whoring after	5971
32: 6	the LORD, O foolish **p** and unwise?	5971
32: 8	he set the bounds of the **p** according to	5971
32: 9	For the LORD's portion is his **p**; Jacob is	5971
32:21	to jealousy with those which are not a **p**;	5971
32:36	For the LORD shall judge his **p**,	5971
32:43	Rejoice, O ye nations, with his **p**: for he	5971
32:43	be merciful unto his land, and to his **p**.	5971
32:44	the words of this song in the ears of the **p**,	5971
32:50	goest up, and be gathered unto thy **p**;	5971
32:50	mount Hor, and was gathered unto his **p**:	5971
33: 3	he loved the **p**; all his saints are in thy	5971
33: 5	when the heads of the **p** and the tribes of	5971
33: 7	voice of Judah, and bring him unto his **p**:	5971
33:17	with them he shall push the **p** together to	5971
33:19	They shall call the **p** unto the mountain;	5971
33:21	he came with the heads of the **p**,	5971
33:29	is like unto thee, O **p** saved by the LORD,	5971

Jos		
1: 2	go over this Jordan, thou, and all this **p**,	5971
1: 6	for unto this **p** shalt thou divide for an	5971
1:10	Joshua commanded the officers of the **p**,	5971
1:11	command the **p**, saying, Prepare you	5971
3: 3	they commanded the **p**, saying, When ye	5971
3: 5	Joshua said unto the **p**, Sanctify	5971
3: 6	the covenant, and bare it before the **p**.	5971
3: 6	of the covenant, and went before the **p**.	5971
3:14	when the **p** removed from their tents,	5971
3:14	the ark of the covenant before the **p**;	5971
3:16	the **p** passed over right against Jericho.	5971
3:17	all the **p** were passed clean over Jordan.	1471
4: 1	when all the **p** were clean passed over	1471

P

P

Jos 4: 2 Take you twelve men out of the **p**, out of 5971
4:10 commanded Joshua to speak unto the **p**, 5971
4:10 and the **p** hasted and passed over. 5971
4:11 when all the **p** were clean passed over, 5971
4:11 and the priests, in the presence of the **p**. 5971
4:19 the **p** came up out of Jordan on the tenth 5971
4:24 That all the **p** of the earth might know 5971
5: 4 All the **p** that came out of Egypt, *that* 5971
5: 5 Now all the **p** that came out were 5971
5: 5 all the **p** *that* were born in the wilderness 5971
5: 6 till all the **p** *that* were men of war, 1471
5: 8 they had done circumcising all the **p**, 1471
6: 5 the **p** shall shout *with* a great shout; 5971
6: 5 the **p** shall ascend up every man straight 5971
6: 7 he said unto the **p**, Pass on, 5971
6: 8 when Joshua had spoken unto the **p**, 5971
6:10 Joshua had commanded the **p**, saying, 5971
6:16 trumpets, Joshua said unto the **p**, Shout; 5971
6:20 So the **p** shouted when *the priests* blew 5971
6:20 the **p** heard the sound of the trumpet, 5971
6:20 the **p** shouted *with* a great shout, that 5971
6:20 so that the **p** went up into the city, 5971
7: 3 said unto him, Let not all the **p** go up; 5971
7: 3 *and* make not all the **p** to labour thither; 5971
7: 4 So there went up thither of the **p** about 5971
7: 5 wherefore the hearts of the **p** melted, 5971
7: 7 wherefore hast thou at all brought this **p** 5971
7:13 Up, sanctify the **p**, and say, 5971
8: 1 take all the **p** of war with thee, and arise, 5971
8: 1 of Ai, and his **p**, and his city, and his land: 5971
8: 3 Joshua arose, and all the **p** of war, to go 5971
8: 5 I, and all the **p** that *are* with me, 5971
8: 9 Joshua lodged that night among the **p**. 5971
8:10 numbered the **p**, and went up, he and 5971
8:10 and the elders of Israel, before the **p** *to* Ai. 5971
8:11 all the **p**, *even the people* of war that 5971
8:11 *even the p* of war that *were* with him, NIH
8:13 they had set the **p**, *even* all the host 5971
8:14 he and all his **p**, at a time appointed, 5971
8:16 all the **p** that *were* in Ai were called 5971
8:20 the **p** that fled *to* the wilderness turned 5971
8:33 that they should bless the **p** of Israel. 5971
10: 7 he, and all the **p** of war with him, 5971
10:13 until the **p** had avenged themselves upon 1471
10:21 all the **p** returned to the camp to Joshua 5971
10:33 Joshua smote him and his **p**, until *he* had 5971
11: 4 and all their hosts with them, much **p**, 5971
11: 7 came, and all the **p** of war with them, 5971
14: 8 up with me made the heart of the **p** melt: 5971
17:14 portion to inherit, seeing *I am* a great **p**, 5971
17:15 If thou *be* a great **p**, *then* get thee up to 5971
17:17 Thou *art* a great **p**, and hast great power: 5971
24: 2 Joshua said unto all the **p**, Thus saith 5971
24:16 the **p** answered and said, God forbid that 5971
24:17 all the **p** through whom we passed: 5971
24:18 Lord drave out from before us all the **p**, 5971
24:19 Joshua said unto the **p**, Ye cannot serve 5971
24:21 the **p** said unto Joshua, Nay; but we will 5971
24:22 Joshua said unto the **p**, Ye *are* witnesses 5971
24:24 the **p** said unto Joshua, The Lord our 5971
24:25 Joshua made a covenant with the **p** that 5971
24:27 Joshua said unto all the **p**, Behold, this 5971
24:28 Joshua let the **p** depart, every man unto 5971

Jdg 1:16 and they went and dwelt among the **p**. 5971
2: 4 that the **p** lift up their voice, and wept. 5971
2: 6 Joshua had let the **p** go, the children 5971
2: 7 the **p** served the Lord all the days of 5971
2:12 the gods of the **p** that *were* round about 5971
2:20 Because that this **p** hath transgressed my 1471
3:18 he sent away the **p** that bare the present. 5971
4:13 of iron, and all the **p** that *were* with him, 5971
5: 2 when the **p** willingly offered themselves. 5971
5: 9 offered themselves willingly among the **p**. 5971
5:11 shall the **p** of the Lord go down to 5971
5:13 dominion over the nobles *among* the **p**: 5971
5:14 after thee, Benjamin, among thy **p**; out of 5971
5:18 Naphtali *were* a **p** *that* jeoparded their 5971
7: 1 the **p** that *were* with him, rose up early, 5971
7: 2 The **p** that *are* with thee *are* too many for 5971
7: 3 go to, proclaim in the ears of the **p**, 5971
7: 3 there returned of the **p** twenty and 5971
7: 4 unto Gideon, The **p** *are* yet *too* many; 5971
7: 5 he brought down the **p** unto the water: 5971
7: 6 all the rest of the **p** bowed down upon 5971
7: 7 let all the *other* **p** go every man unto his 5971
7: 8 So the **p** took victuals in their hand, 5971
8: 5 loaves of bread unto the **p** that follow me; 5971
9:29 would to God this **p** were under my hand; 5971
9:32 thou and the **p** that *is* with thee, *and* lie 5971
9:33 the **p** that *is* with him come out against 5971
9:34 all the **p** that were with him, by night, 5971
9:35 the **p** that *were* with him, from lying in 5971
9:36 when Gaal saw the **p**, he said to Zebul, 5971
9:36 there come **p** down from the top of 5971
9:37 See there come **p** down by the middle of 5971
9:38 is not this the **p** that thou hast despised? 5971
9:42 that the **p** went out *into* the field; 5971
9:43 he took the **p**, and divided them into 5971
9:43 the **p** *were* come forth out of the city; 5971
9:44 two *other* companies ran upon all *the p* NIH
9:45 slew the **p** that *was* therein, and beat 5971
9:48 he and all the **p** that *were* with him; 5971
9:48 and said unto the **p** that *were* with him, 5971
9:49 all the **p** likewise cut down every man his 5971
10:18 the **p** *and* princes of Gilead said one to 5971

Jdg 11:11 the **p** made him head and captain over 5971
11:20 Sihon gathered all his **p** together, 5971
11:21 and all his **p** into the hand of Israel, 5971
11:23 the Amorites from before his **p** Israel, 5971
12: 2 my **p** were at great strife with the children 5971
14: 3 of thy brethren, or among all my **p**, 5971
14:16 forth a riddle unto the children of my **p**, 5971
14:17 told the riddle to the children of her **p**. 5971
16:24 the **p** saw him, they praised their god: 5971
16:30 and upon all the **p** that *were* therein. 5971
18: 7 Laish, and saw the **p** that *were* therein, 5971
18:10 ye shall come unto a **p** secure, and to a 5971
18:20 and went in the midst of the **p**. 5971
18:27 unto a **p** *that were* at quiet and secure: 5971
20: 2 the chief of all the **p**, *even* of all the tribes 5971
20: 2 in the assembly of the **p** of God, 5971
20: 8 all the **p** arose as one man, saying, We 5971
20:10 fetch victual for the **p**, that *they* may do, 5971
20:16 Among all this **p** *there were* seven 5971
20:22 the **p** the men of Israel encouraged 5971
20:26 all the **p**, went up, and came *unto* the 5971
20:31 of Benjamin went out against the **p**, 5971
20:31 began to smite of the **p**, *and* kill, as at 5971
21: 2 the **p** came *to* the house of God, 5971
21: 4 that the **p** rose early, and built there an 5971
21: 9 For the **p** were numbered, and, behold, 5971
21:15 the **p** repented them for Benjamin, 5971

Ru 1: 6 had visited his **p** in giving them bread. 5971
1:10 we will return with thee unto thy **p**. 5971
1:15 thy sister in law is gone back unto her **p**, 5971
1:16 thy **p** *shall be* my people, and thy God 5971
1:16 thy **p** *shall be* my **p**, and thy God 5971
2:11 art come unto a **p** which thou knewest 5971
3:11 all the city of my **p** doth know that thou 5971
4: 4 and before the elders of my **p**. 5971
4: 9 *unto* all the **p**, Ye *are* witnesses *this* day, 5971
4:11 all the **p** that *were* in the gate, 5971

1Sa 2:13 the priests' custom with the **p** *was, that* 5971
2:23 I hear of your evil dealings by all this **p**. 5971
2:24 ye make the Lord's **p** to transgress. 5971
2:29 chiefest of all the offerings of Israel my **p**? 5971
4: 3 when the **p** were come into the camp, 5971
4: 4 So the **p** sent to Shiloh, that they might 5971
4:17 been also a great slaughter among the **p**, 5971
5:10 God of Israel to us, to slay us and our **p**. 5971
5:11 own place, that it slay us not, and our **p**: 5971
6: 6 did they not let the **p** go, 3963.1
6:19 even he smote of the **p** fifty thousand 5971
6:19 the **p** lamented, because the Lord had 5971
6:19 the Lord had smitten *many* of the **p** with 5971
8: 7 Hearken unto the voice of the **p** in all that 5971
8:10 unto the **p** that asked of him a king. 5971
8:19 Nevertheless the **p** refused to obey 5971
8:21 Samuel heard all the words of the **p**, 5971
9: 2 upward *he was* higher than any of the **p**. 5971
9:12 for *there is* a sacrifice of the **p** to day in 5971
9:13 for the **p** will not eat until he come, 5971
9:16 anoint him to be captain over my **p** Israel, 5971
9:16 that *he* may save my **p** out of the hand of 5971
9:16 for I have looked upon my **p**, because 5971
9:17 thee of: this *same* shall reign over my **p**. 5971
9:24 for thee since *I* said, I have invited the **p**. 5971
10:11 prophets, then the **p** said one to another, 5971
10:17 Samuel called the **p** together unto 5971
10:23 he stood among the **p**, he was higher 5971
10:23 he was higher than any of the **p** from his 5971
10:24 Samuel said to all the **p**, See ye him 5971
10:24 *there is* none like him among all the **p**? 5971
10:25 Samuel told the **p** the manner of 5971
10:25 Samuel sent all the **p** away, every man to 5971
11: 4 and told the tidings in the ears of the **p**: 5971
11: 4 all the **p** lift up their voices, and wept. 5971
11: 5 said, What aileth the **p** that they weep? 5971
11: 7 the fear of the Lord fell on the **p**, 5971
11:11 that Saul put the **p** *in* three companies; 5971
11:12 the **p** said unto Samuel, Who *is* he that 5971
11:14 said Samuel to the **p**, Come, and let us go 5971
11:15 all the **p** went *to* Gilgal; and there they 5971
12: 6 Samuel said unto the **p**, *It is* the Lord 5971
12:18 all the **p** greatly feared the Lord and 5971
12:19 all the **p** said unto Samuel, Pray for thy 5971
12:20 Samuel said unto the **p**, Fear not: ye have 5971
12:22 For the Lord will not forsake his **p** for 5971
12:22 hath pleased the Lord to make you his **p**. 5971
13: 2 the rest of the **p** he sent every man to his 5971
13: 4 the **p** were called together after Saul *to* 5971
13: 5 **p** as the sand which *is* on the sea shore in 5971
13: 6 in a strait, (for the **p** were distressed,) 5971
13: 6 the **p** did hide themselves in caves, 5971
13: 7 and all the **p** followed him trembling. 5971
13: 8 and the **p** were scattered from him. 5971
13:11 Because I saw that the **p** were scattered 5971
13:14 commanded him to be captain over his **p**, 5971
13:15 Saul numbered the **p** that were present 5971
13:16 and the **p** that were present with them, 5971
13:22 hand of any of the **p** that *were* with Saul 5971
14: 2 the **p** that *were* with him *were* about six 5971
14: 3 the **p** knew not that Jonathan was gone. 5971
14:15 the host, in the field, and among all the **p**: 5971
14:17 said Saul unto the **p** that *were* with him, 5971
14:20 all the **p** that *were* with him assembled 5971
14:24 for Saul had adjured the **p**, saying, 5971
14:24 So none of the **p** tasted *any* food. 5971
14:26 when the **p** were come into the wood, 5971

1Sa 14:26 to his mouth: for the **p** feared the oath. 5971
14:27 his father charged the **p** with the oath: 5971
14:28 answered one of the **p**, and said, Thy 5971
14:28 Thy father straitly charged the **p** with an 5971
14:28 *any* food *this* day. And the **p** were faint. 5971
14:30 if haply the **p** had eaten freely to day of 5971
14:31 to Aijalon: and the **p** were very faint. 5971
14:32 the **p** flew upon the spoil, and took sheep, 5971
14:32 and the **p** did eat *them* with the blood. 5971
14:33 Behold, the **p** sin against the Lord, 5971
14:34 Disperse yourselves among the **p**, 5971
14:34 all the **p** brought every man his ox with 5971
14:38 Draw ye near hither, all the chief of the **p**: 5971
14:39 *there was not a man* among all the **p** *that* 5971
14:40 the **p** said unto Saul, Do what seemeth 5971
14:41 Jonathan were taken: but the **p** escaped. 5971
14:45 the **p** said unto Saul, Shall Jonathan die, 5971
14:45 the **p** rescued Jonathan, that he died not. 5971
15: 1 me to anoint thee to be king over his **p**, 5971
15: 4 Saul gathered the **p** together, 5971
15: 8 utterly destroyed all the **p** with the edge 5971
15: 9 Saul and the **p** spared Agag, and the best 5971
15:15 for the **p** spared the best of the sheep and 5971
15:21 the **p** took of the spoil, sheep and oxen, 5971
15:24 because I feared the **p**, and obeyed their 5971
15:30 the elders of my **p**, and before Israel, 5971
17:27 the **p** answered him after this manner, 5971
17:30 the **p** answered him again after the former 5971
18: 5 he was accepted in the sight of all the **p**, 5971
18:13 he went out and came in before the **p**. 5971
23: 8 Saul called all the **p** together to war, to go 5971
26: 5 and the **p** pitched round about him. 5971
26: 7 and Abishai came to the **p** by night: 5971
26: 7 but Abner and the **p** lay round about him. 5971
26:14 David cried to the **p**, and to Abner the 5971
26:15 for there came one of the **p** in to destroy 5971
27:12 He hath made his **p** Israel utterly to abhor 5971
30: 4 the **p** that *were* with him lift up their 5971
30: 6 for the **p** spake of stoning him, because 5971
30: 6 because the soul of all the **p** was grieved, 5971
30:21 and to meet the **p** that *were* with him: 5971
30:21 David came near to the **p**, he saluted 5971
31: 9 the house of their idols, and among the **p**. 5971

2Sa 1: 4 That the **p** are fled from the battle, 5971
1: 4 many of the **p** also are fallen and dead; 5971
1:12 for the **p** of the Lord, and for the house 5971
2:26 ere thou bid the **p** return from following 5971
2:27 in the morning the **p** had gone up every 5971
2:28 all the **p** stood still, and pursued after 5971
2:30 when he had gathered all the **p** together, 5971
3:18 Israel out of the hand of the Philistines, 5971
3:31 to all the **p** that *were* with him, Rent 5971
3:32 at the grave of Abner; and all the **p** wept. 5971
3:34 And all the **p** wept again over him. 5971
3:35 all the **p** came to cause David to eat 5971
3:36 all the **p** took notice *of it*, and it pleased 5971
3:36 whatsoever the king did, pleased all the **p**. 5971
3:37 all the **p** and all Israel understood that 5971
5: 2 Thou shalt feed my **p** Israel, and thou 5971
5:12 had exalted his kingdom for his **p** 5971
6: 2 went with all the **p** that *were* with him 5971
6:18 he blessed the **p** in the name of the Lord 5971
6:19 he dealt among all the **p**, *even* among 5971
6:19 a flagon *of wine*. So all the **p** departed 5971
6:21 to appoint me ruler over the **p** of 5971
7: 7 whom I commanded to feed my **p** Israel, 5971
7: 8 to be ruler over my **p**, over Israel: 5971
7:10 Moreover I will appoint a place for my **p** 5971
7:11 commanded judges *to be* over my **p** Israel, 5971
7:23 what one nation in the earth *is* like thy **p**, 5971
7:23 whom God went to redeem for a **p** to 5971
7:23 and terrible, for thy land, before thy **p**, 5971
7:24 For thou hast confirmed to thyself thy **p** 5971
7:24 people Israel to be a **p** unto thee for ever; 5971
8:15 and justice unto all his **p**. 5971
10:10 rest of the **p** he delivered into the hand 5971
10:12 let us play the men for our **p**, and for 5971
10:13 drew nigh, and the **p** that *were* with him, 5971
11: 7 \the **p** did, and how the war prospered. 5971
11:17 there fell *some* of the **p** of the servants of 5971
12:28 gather the rest of the **p** together, 5971
12:29 David gathered all the **p** together, 5971
12:31 he brought forth the **p** that *were* therein, 5971
12:31 and all the **p** returned *unto* Jerusalem. 5971
13:34 there came much **p** by the way of the hill 5971
14:13 thou thought such a thing against the **p** 5971
14:15 *it is* because the **p** have made me afraid: 5971
15:12 for the **p** increased continually with 5971
15:17 all the **p** after him, and tarried *in* a place 5971
15:23 a loud voice, and all the **p** passed over: 5971
15:23 all the **p** passed over, toward the way of 5971
15:24 until all the **p** had done passing out of 5971
15:30 all the **p** that *was* with him covered every 5971
16: 6 all the **p** and all the mighty *men* were on 5971
16:14 all the **p** that *were* with him, came weary, 5971
16:15 and all the **p** the men of Israel, 5971
16:18 this **p**, and all the men of Israel, choose, 5971
17: 2 all the **p** that *are* with him shall flee; 5971
17: 3 I will bring back all the **p** unto thee: 5971
17: 3 all returned: *so* all the **p** shall be *in* peace. 5971
17: 8 of war, and will not lodge with the **p**. 5971
17: 9 There is a slaughter among the **p** that 5971
17:16 and all the **p** that *are* with him. 5971
17:22 all the **p** that *were* with him, 5971
17:29 and for the **p** that *were* with him, to eat: 5971

2Sa
17:29 The **p** *is* hungry, and weary, and thirsty, 5971
18: 1 David numbered the **p** that *were* with 5971
18: 2 David sent forth a third part of the **p** 5971
18: 2 the king said unto the **p**, I will surely go 5971
18: 3 he answered, Thou shalt not go forth: 5971
18: 4 all the **p** came out by hundreds and 5971
18: 5 all the **p** heard when the king gave all 5971
18: 6 So the **p** went out *into* the field against 5971
18: 7 Where the **p** of Israel were slain before 5971
18: 8 the wood devoured more **p** that day than 5971
18:16 the **p** returned from pursuing after Israel: 5971
18:16 after Israel: for Joab held back the **p**. 5971
19: 2 was *turned* into mourning unto all the **p**: 5971
19: 2 for the **p** heard say that day *how* the king 5971
19: 3 the **p** gat them by stealth that day *into* 5971
19: 3 as **p** being ashamed steal away when they 5971
19: 8 they told unto all the **p**, saying, Behold, 5971
19: 8 all the **p** came before the king: for Israel 5971
19: 9 all the **p** were at strife throughout all 5971
19:39 all the **p** went over Jordan. And when 5971
19:40 all the **p** of Judah conducted the king, 5971
19:40 the king, and also half the **p** of Israel. 5971
20:12 the man saw that all the **p** stood still, 5971
20:13 all the **p** went on after Joab, to pursue 376
20:15 all the **p** that *were* with Joab battered 5971
20:22 the woman went unto all the **p** in her 5971
22:28 the afflicted **p** thou wilt save: but thine 5971
22:44 delivered me from the strivings of my **p**, 5971
22:44 a **p** *which* I knew not shall serve me. 5971
22:48 and that bringeth down the **p** under me, 5971
23:10 the **p** returned after him only to spoil. 5971
23:11 and the **p** fled from the Philistines. 5971
24: 2 even to Beer-sheba, and number ye the **p**, 5971
24: 2 that I may know the number of the **p**. 5971
24: 3 Now the Lord thy God add unto the **p**, 5971
24: 4 of the king, to number the **p** *of* Israel. 5971
24: 9 sum of the number of the **p** unto the king: 5971
24:10 him after that he had numbered the **p**. 5971
24:15 there died of the **p** from Dan even to 5971
24:16 said to the angel that destroyed the **p**, *It is* 5971
24:17 when he saw the angel that smote the **p**, 5971
24:21 that the plague may be stayed from the **p**. 5971

1Ki
1:39 the **p** said, God save king Solomon. 5971
1:40 all the **p** came up after him, and the 5971
1:40 the **p** piped with pipes, and rejoiced *with* 5971
3: 2 Only the **p** sacrificed in high places, 5971
3: 8 thy servant *is* in the midst of thy **p** which 5971
3: 8 a great **p**, that cannot be numbered nor 5971
3: 9 an understanding heart to judge thy **p**, 5971
3: 9 who is able to judge this thy *so* great a **p**? 5971
4:34 there came of all **p** to hear the wisdom of 5971
5: 7 unto David a wise son over this great **p**. 5971
5:16 which ruled over the **p** that wrought in 5971
6:13 of Israel, and will not forsake my **p** Israel. 5971
8:16 Since the day that I brought forth my **p** 5971
8:16 but I chose David to be over my **p** Israel. 5971
8:30 of thy Israel, when they shall pray 5971
8:33 When thy **p** Israel be smitten down before 5971
8:34 forgive the sin of thy **p** Israel, 5971
8:36 the sin of thy servants, and of thy **p** Israel, 5971
8:36 which thou hast given to thy **p** for an 5971
8:38 *made* by any man, *or* by all thy **p** Israel, 5971
8:41 that *is* not of thy **p** Israel, but cometh out 5971
8:43 all the **p** of the earth may know thy name, 5971
8:43 thy name, to fear thee, as *do* thy **p** Israel; 5971
8:44 If thy **p** go out to battle against their 5971
8:50 forgive thy **p** that have sinned against 5971
8:51 for they *be* thy **p**, and thine inheritance, 5971
8:52 unto the supplication of thy **p** Israel, 5971
8:53 them from among all the **p** of the earth, 5971
8:56 that hath given rest unto his **p** Israel, 5971
8:59 the cause of his **p** Israel at all times, 5971
8:60 That all the **p** of the earth may know that 5971
8:66 On the eighth day he sent the **p** away: 5971
8:66 for David his servant, and for Israel his **p**. 5971
9: 7 be a proverb and a byword among all **p**: 5971
9:20 all the **p** that were left of the Amorites, 5971
9:23 which bare rule over the **p** that wrought 5971
12: 5 come again to me. And the **p** departed. 5971
12: 6 do you advise that *I* may answer this **p**? 5971
12: 7 If thou wilt be a servant unto this **p** *this* 5971
12: 9 give ye that we may answer this **p**, 5971
12:10 Thus shalt thou speak unto this **p** that 5971
12:12 all the **p** came to Rehoboam the third day, 5971
12:13 the king answered the **p** roughly, 5971
12:15 the king hearkened not unto the **p**; 5971
12:16 the **p** answered the king, saying, 5971
12:23 and *to* the remnant of the **p**, saying, 5971
12:27 If this **p** go up to do sacrifice in the house 5971
12:27 shall the heart of this **p** turn again unto 5971
12:30 for the **p** went *to worship* before the one, 5971
12:31 made priests of the lowest of the **p**, 5971
13:33 made again of the lowest of the **p** priests 5971
14: 2 told me that I should be king over this **p**. 5971
14: 7 as I exalted thee from among the **p**, 5971
14: 7 and made thee prince over my **p** Israel, 5971
16: 2 and made thee prince over my **p** Israel; 5971
16: 2 made my **p** Israel to sin, to provoke me 5971
16:15 the **p** were encamped against Gibbethon, 5971
16:16 the **p** *that* were encamped heard say, 5971
16:21 the **p** of Israel divided into two parts: 5971
16:21 half of the **p** followed Tibni the son of 5971
16:22 that followed Omri prevailed against 5971
16:22 **p** that followed Tibni the son of Ginath: 5971
18:21 Elijah came unto all the **p**, and said, 5971

1Ki
18:21 And the **p** answered him not a word. 5971
18:22 said Elijah unto the **p**, I, *even* I only, 5971
18:24 all the **p** answered and said, It is well 5971
18:30 Elijah said unto all the **p**, Come near unto 5971
18:30 all the **p** came near unto him. And he 5971
18:37 that this **p** may know that thou *art* 5971
18:39 when all the **p** saw *it*, they fell on their 5971
19:21 and gave unto the **p**, and they did eat. 5971
20: 8 all the elders and all the **p** said unto him, 5971
20:10 for handfuls for all the **p** that follow me. 5971
20:15 after them he numbered all the **p**, *even* 5971
20:42 go for his life, and thy **p** for his people. 5971
20:42 go for his life, and thy people for his **p**. 5971
21: 9 fast, and set Naboth on high among the **p**: 5971
21:12 fast, and set Naboth on high among the **p**. 5971
21:13 in the presence of the **p**, saying, 5971
22: 4 I *am* as thou *art*, my **p** as thy people, 5971
22: 4 I *am* as thou *art*, my people as thy **p**, 5971
22:28 he said, Hearken, O **p**, every one of you. 5971

2Ki
3: 7 I *am* as thou *art*, my **p** as thy people, 5971
3: 7 I *am* as thou *art*, my people as thy **p**, 5971
4:13 answered, I dwell among mine own **p**. 5971
4:41 he said, Pour out for the **p**, that they may 5971
4:42 said, Give unto the **p**, that they may eat. 5971
4:43 He said again, Give the **p**, that they may 5971
6:18 said, Smite this **p**, I pray thee, 1471
6:30 the wall, and the **p** looked, and behold, 5971
7:16 the **p** went out, and spoiled the tents of 5971
7:17 the **p** trode upon him in the gate, 5971
7:17 the **p** trode upon him in the gate, 5971
7:20 for the **p** trode upon him in the gate, 5971
8:21 chariots: and the **p** fled into their tents. 5971
9: 6 I have anointed thee king over the **p** of 5971
10: 9 stood, and said to all the **p**, Ye *be* 5971
10:18 Jehu gathered all the **p** together, 5971
11:13 heard the noise of the guard *and* of the **p**, 5971
11:13 she came to the **p** *into* the temple of 5971
11:14 all the **p** of the land rejoiced, and blew 5971
11:17 the Lord and the king and the **p**, 5971
11:17 that *they* should be the Lord's **p**; 5971
11:17 between the king also and the **p**. 5971
11:18 all the **p** of the land went *into* the house 5971
11:19 and the guard, and all the **p** of the land; 5971
11:20 all the **p** of the land rejoiced, and the city 5971
12: 3 the **p** still sacrificed and burnt incense in 5971
12: 8 to receive no *more* money of the **p**, 5971
13: 7 Neither did he leave *of* the **p** to Jehoahaz 5971
14: 4 yet the **p** did sacrifice and burnt incense 5971
14:21 all the **p** of Judah took Azariah, which 5971
15: 4 the **p** sacrificed and burnt incense still on 5971
15: 5 over the house, judging the **p** of the land. 5971
15:10 smote him before the **p**, and slew him, 5971
15:35 the **p** sacrificed and burnt incense still in 5971
16: 9 carried the **p** *of* it captive to Kir, and slew NIH
16:15 with the burnt offering of all the **p** of 5971
18:26 in the ears of the **p** that *are* on the wall. 5971
18:36 the **p** held their peace, and answered him 5971
20: 5 and tell Hezekiah the captain of my **p**, 5971
21:24 the **p** of the land slew all them that had 5971
21:24 the **p** of the land made Josiah his son king 5971
22: 4 of the door keepers have gathered of the **p**: 5971
22:13 for me, and for the **p**, and for all Judah, 5971
23: 2 and all the **p**, both small and great: 5971
23: 3 And all the **p** stood to the covenant. 5971
23: 6 upon the graves of the children of the **p**. 5971
23:21 the king commanded all the **p**, saying, 5971
23:30 the **p** of the land took Jehoahaz the son of 5971
23:35 silver and the gold of the **p** of the land, 5971
24:14 save the poorest sort of the **p** of the land. 5971
25: 3 there was no bread for the **p** of the land. 5971
25:11 Now the rest of the **p** that were left in 5971
25:19 which mustered the **p** of the land, 5971
25:19 threescore men of the **p** of the land that 5971
25:22 *as for* the **p** that remained in the land of 5971
25:26 all the **p**, both small and great, 5971

1Ch
5:25 went a whoring after the gods of the **p** of 5971
10: 9 tidings unto their idols, and to the **p**. 5971
11: 2 Thou shalt feed my **p** Israel, and thou 5971
11: 2 and thou shalt be ruler over my **p** Israel. 5971
11:13 and the **p** fled from before the Philistines. 5971
13: 4 thing was right in the eyes of all the **p**. 5971
14: 2 lift up on high, because of his **p** Israel. 5971
16: 2 he blessed the **p** in the name of 5971
16: 8 make known his deeds among the **p**. 5971
16:20 and from *one* kingdom to another **p**; 5971
16:26 For all the gods of the **p** *are* idols: 5971
16:28 unto the Lord, ye kindreds of the **p**, 5971
16:36 all the **p** said, Amen, and praised 5971
16:43 all the **p** departed every man to his house: 5971
17: 6 whom I commanded to feed my **p**, saying, 5971
17: 7 that *thou* shouldest be ruler over my **p** 5971
17: 9 Also I will ordain a place for my **p** Israel, 5971
17:10 commanded judges *to be* over my **p** Israel 5971
17:21 what one nation in the earth *is* like thy **p** 5971
17:21 God went to redeem *to be* his own **p**, 5971
17:21 by driving out nations from before thy **p**, 5971
17:22 thy **p** Israel didst thou make thine own 5971
17:22 didst thou make thine own **p** for ever; 5971
18:14 and justice among all his **p**. 5971
19: 7 and the king of Maachah and his **p**; 5971
19:11 rest of the **p** he delivered unto the hand 5971
19:13 us behave ourselves valiantly for our **p**, 5971
19:14 the **p** that *were* with him drew nigh 5971
20: 3 he brought out the **p** that *were* in it, 5971
20: 3 and all the **p** returned *to* Jerusalem. 5971

1Ch
21: 2 said to Joab and to the rulers of the **p**, 5971
21: 3 The Lord make his **p** an hundred times 5971
21: 5 Joab gave the sum of the number of the **p** 5971
21:17 *Is it* not I *that* commanded the **p** to be 5971
21:17 not on thy **p**, that *they* should be plagued. 5971
21:22 that the plague may be stayed from the **p**. 5971
22:18 before the Lord, and before his **p**. 5971
23:25 God of Israel hath given rest unto his **p**, 5971
28: 2 said, Hear me, my brethren, and my **p**: 5971
28:21 all the **p** *will be* wholly at thy 5971
29: 9 the **p** rejoiced, for that they offered 5971
29:14 who *am* I, and what *is* my **p**, that we 5971
29:17 and now have I seen with joy thy **p**, 5971
29:18 of the thoughts of the heart of thy **p**, 5971

2Ch
1: 9 for thou hast made me king over a **p** like 5971
1:10 I may go out and come in before this **p**: 5971
1:10 for who can judge this thy **p**, *that is so* 5971
1:11 for thyself, that thou mayest judge my **p**, 5971
2:11 Because the Lord loved his **p**, 5971
2:18 six hundred overseers to set the **p** a work. 5971
6: 5 the day that I brought forth my **p** out 5971
6: 5 I any man to be a ruler over my **p** Israel: 5971
6: 6 have chosen David to be over my **p** Israel. 5971
6:21 of thy servant, and of thy **p** Israel, 5971
6:24 if thy **p** Israel be put to the worse before 5971
6:25 forgive the sin of thy **p** Israel, 5971
6:27 the sin of thy servants, and of thy **p** Israel, 5971
6:27 which thou hast given unto thy **p** for an 5971
6:29 of all thy **p** Israel, when every one shall 5971
6:32 which *is* not of thy **p** Israel, but is come 5971
6:33 all of the earth may know thy name, 5971
6:33 as *doth* thy **p** Israel, and may know that 5971
6:34 If thy **p** go out to war against their 5971
6:39 forgive thy **p** which have sinned against 5971
7: 4 all the **p** offered sacrifices before 5971
7: 5 and all the **p** dedicated the house of God. 5971
7:10 month he sent the **p** away into their tents, 5971
7:10 and to Solomon, and to Israel his **p**. 5971
7:13 or if I send pestilence among my **p**; 5971
7:14 If my **p**, which are called by my name, 5971
8: 7 *for* all the **p** that were left of the Hittites, 5971
8:10 and fifty, that bare rule over the **p**. 5971
10: 5 me after three days. And the **p** departed. 5971
10: 6 give ye *me* to return answer to this **p**? 5971
10: 7 If thou be kind to this **p**, and please them, 5971
10: 9 ye that we may return answer to this **p**, 5971
10:10 Thus shalt thou answer the **p** that spake 5971
10:12 all the **p** came to Rehoboam on the third 5971
10:15 So the king hearkened not unto the **p**: 5971
10:16 the **p** answered the king, saying, 5971
12: 3 the **p** were without number that came 5971
13:17 his **p** slew them *with* a great slaughter: 5971
14:13 the **p** that *were* with him pursued them 5971
16:10 oppressed *some* of the **p** the same time. 5971
17: 9 all the cities of Judah, and taught the **p**. 5971
18: 2 for the **p** that *he had* with him, 5971
18: 3 I *am* as thou *art*, and my **p** as thy people; 5971
18: 3 I *am* as thou *art*, and my people as thy **p**; 5971
18:27 by me. And he said, Hearken, all ye **p**. 5971
19: 4 he went out again through the **p** from 5971
20: 7 inhabitants of this land before thy **p** Israel, 5971
20:21 when he had consulted with the **p**, 5971
20:25 his **p** came to take away the spoil of them, 5971
20:33 for as yet the **p** had not prepared their 5971
21:14 a great plague will the Lord smite thy **p**, 5971
21:19 his **p** made no burning for him, like 5971
23: 5 all the **p** *shall be* in the courts of the 5971
23: 6 all the **p** shall keep the watch of 5971
23:10 he set all the **p**, every man having his 5971
23:12 when Athaliah heard the noise of the **p** 5971
23:12 she came to the **p** *into* the house of 5971
23:13 all the **p** of the land rejoiced, 5971
23:16 between all the **p**, and between the king, 5971
23:16 that *they* should be the Lord's **p**. 5971
23:17 all the **p** went *to* the house of Baal, 5971
23:20 governors of the **p**, and all the people of 5971
23:20 all the **p** of the land, and brought down 5971
23:21 all the **p** of the land rejoiced: and the city 5971
24:10 all the princes and all the **p** rejoiced, 5971
24:20 which stood above the **p**, and said unto 5971
24:23 destroyed all the princes of the **p** from 5971
24:23 princes of the people from among the **p**, 5971
25:11 led forth his **p**, and went *to* the valley of 5971
25:15 hast thou sought after the gods of the **p**, 5971
25:15 which could not deliver their own **p** out 5971
26: 1 all the **p** of Judah took Uzziah, who *was* 5971
26:21 king's house, judging the **p** of the land. 5971
27: 2 of the Lord. And the **p** did yet corruptly. 5971
29:36 Hezekiah rejoiced, and all the **p**, that God 5971
29:36 the people, that God had prepared the **p**: 5971
30: 3 neither had the **p** gathered themselves 5971
30:13 there assembled *at* Jerusalem much **p** to 5971
30:18 For a multitude of the **p**, *even* many of 5971
30:20 hearkened to Hezekiah, and healed the **p**. 5971
30:27 the Levites arose and blessed the **p**: 5971
31: 4 Moreover he commanded the **p** that 5971
31: 8 they blessed the Lord, and his **p** Israel. 5971
31:10 Since the **p** began to bring the offerings NIH
31:10 for the Lord hath blessed his **p**; 5971
32: 4 So there was gathered much **p** together, 5971
32: 6 he set captains of war over the **p**, 5971
32: 8 the **p** rested themselves upon the words 5971
32:13 my fathers have done unto all the **p** of 5971
32:14 that could deliver his **p** out of mine hand, 5971
32:15 kingdom was able to deliver his **p** out of 5971

P

P

2Ch 32:17	not delivered their **p** out of mine hand,	5971
32:17	not the God of Hezekiah deliver his **p**	5971
32:18	the **p** of Jerusalem that *were* on the wall,	5971
32:19	as against the gods of the **p** of the earth,	5971
33:10	LORD spake to Manasseh, and to his **p**:	5971
33:17	Nevertheless the **p** did sacrifice still in	5971
33:25	the **p** of the land slew all them that had	5971
33:25	the **p** of the land made Josiah his son king	5971
34:30	the Levites, and all the **p**, great and small:	5971
35: 3	the LORD your God, and his **p** Israel,	5971
35: 5	the fathers of your brethren the **p**,	1121+5971
35: 7	Josiah gave to the **p**, *of* the flock,	1121+5971
35: 8	his princes gave willingly unto the **p**,	5971
35:12	divisions of the families of the **p**,	1121+5971
35:13	*them* speedily among all the **p**.	1121+5971
36: 1	the **p** of the land took Jehoahaz the son of	5971
36:14	all the chief of the priests, and the **p**,	5971
36:15	because he had compassion on his **p**,	5971
36:16	wrath of the LORD arose against his **p**?	5971
36:23	Who *is* there among you of all his **p**?	5971
Ezr 1: 3	Who *is* there among you of all his **p**?	5971
2: 2	The number of the men of the **p** of Israel:	5971
2:70	*some* of the **p**, and the singers,	5971
3: 1	the **p** gathered themselves together as one	5971
3: 3	because of the **p** of *those* countries:	5971
3:11	all the **p** shouted *with* a great shout,	5971
3:13	that the **p** could not discern the noise of	5971
3:13	joy from the noise of the weeping of the **p**:	5971
3:13	for the **p** shouted *with* a loud shout,	5971
4: 4	the **p** of the land weakened the hands of	5971
4: 4	weakened the hands of the **p** of Judah,	5971
5:12	carried the **p** away into Babylon.	5972
6:12	to dwell there destroy all kings and **p**,	5972
7:13	that all they of the **p** of Israel, and *of* his	5972
7:16	with the freewill offering of the **p**,	5972
7:25	which may judge all the **p** that *are* beyond	5972
8:15	I viewed the **p**, and the priests,	5971
8:36	furthered the **p**, and the house of God.	5971
9: 1	The **p** of Israel, and the priests,	5971
9: 1	have not separated themselves from the **p**	5971
9: 2	themselves with the **p** of *those* lands,	5971
9:11	with the filthiness of the **p** of the lands,	5971
9:14	join in affinity with the **p** of these	5971
10: 1	and children: for the **p** wept very sore.	5971
10: 2	have taken strange wives of the **p** of	5971
10: 9	all the **p** sat in the street of the house of	5971
10:11	separate yourselves from the **p** of the land	5971
10:13	the **p** *are* many, and *it is* a time of much	5971
Ne 1:10	Now these *are* thy servants and thy **p**,	5971
4: 6	half thereof: for the **p** had a mind to work.	5971
4:13	I even set the **p** after *their* families with	5971
4:14	and to the rulers, and to the rest of the **p**,	5971
4:19	to the rulers, and to the rest of the **p**,	5971
4:22	at the same time said I unto the **p**,	5971
5: 1	there was a great cry of the **p** and of their	5971
5:13	And the **p** did according to this promise.	5971
5:15	before me were chargeable unto the **p**,	5971
5:15	even their servants bare rule over the **p**:	5971
5:18	the bondage was heavy upon this **p**.	5971
5:19	to all that I have done for this **p**.	5971
7: 4	the **p** *were* few therein, and the houses	5971
7: 5	the rulers, and the **p**, that *they* might be	5971
7: 7	I *say*, of the men of the **p** of Israel *was*	5971
7:72	*that* which the rest of the **p** gave *was*	5971
7:73	*some* of the **p**, and the Nethinims,	5971
8: 1	all the **p** gathered themselves together as	5971
8: 3	the ears of all the **p** *were* attentive unto	5971
8: 5	opened the book in the sight of all the **p**;	5971
8: 5	(for he was above all the **p**;) and when he	5971
8: 5	and when he opened *it*, all the **p** stood *up*:	5971
8: 6	all the **p** answered, Amen, Amen,	5971
8: 7	caused the **p** to understand the law:	5971
8: 7	the law: and the **p** *stood* in their place.	5971
8: 9	the Levites that taught the **p**, said unto all	5971
8: 9	that taught the people, said unto all the **p**,	5971
8: 9	For all the **p** wept, when they heard	5971
8:11	So the Levites stilled all the **p**, saying,	5971
8:12	the **p** went *their way* to eat, and to drink,	5971
8:13	the chief of the fathers of all the **p**,	5971
8:16	So the **p** went forth, and brought *them*,	5971
9:10	his servants, and on all the **p** of his land:	5971
9:24	with their kings, and the **p** of the land,	5971
9:30	gavest thou them into the hand of the **p**	5971
9:32	and on our fathers, and on all thy **p**,	5971
10:14	The chief of the **p**; Parosh, Pahath-moab,	5971
10:28	the rest of the **p**, the priests, the Levites,	5971
10:28	the **p** of the lands unto the law of God,	5971
10:30	give our daughters unto the **p** of the land,	5971
10:31	*if* the **p** of the land bring ware or	5971
10:34	the Levites, and the **p**, for the wood	5971
11: 1	the rulers of the **p** dwelt at Jerusalem:	5971
11: 1	the rest of the **p** also cast lots, to bring one	5971
11: 2	the **p** blessed all the men, that willingly	5971
11:24	hand in all matters concerning the **p**.	5971
12:30	purified the **p**, and the gates, and the wall.	5971
12:38	and the half of the **p** upon the wall,	5971
13: 1	book of Moses in the audience of the **p**;	5971
13:24	to the language of *each* **p**.	5971+5971+2050.1
Est 1: 5	the king made a feast unto all the **p** that	5971
1:11	to shew the **p** and the princes her beauty:	5971
1:16	to all the **p** that *are* in all the provinces of	5971
1:22	to *every* **p** after their	5971+5971+2050.1
1:22	according to the language of every **p**.	5971
2:10	Esther had not shewed her **p** nor her	5971
2:20	not *yet* shewed her kindred nor her **p**;	5971

Est 3: 6	for they had shewed him the **p** of	5971
3: 6	of Ahasuerus, *even* the **p** of Mordecai.	5971
3: 8	There is a certain **p** scattered abroad and	5971
3: 8	dispersed among the **p** in all the provinces	5971
3: 8	their laws *are* diverse from all **p**;	5971
3:11	The silver *is* given to thee, the **p** also,	5971
3:12	to the rulers of *every* **p** of	5971+5971+2050.1
3:12	*every* **p** after their	5971+5971+2050.1
3:14	every province *was* published unto all **p**,	5971
4: 8	and to make request before him for her **p**.	5971
4:11	the **p** of the king's provinces, do know,	5971
4:13	at my petition, and my **p** at my request:	5971
7: 4	I and my **p**, to be destroyed, to be slain,	5971
8: 6	to see the evil that shall come unto my **p**?	5971
8: 9	*unto* *every* **p** after their	5971+5971+2050.1
8:11	all the power of the **p** and province that	5971
8:13	every province *was* published unto all **p**,	5971
8:17	many of the **p** of the land became Jews;	5971
9: 2	for the fear of them fell upon all **p**.	5971
10: 3	seeking the wealth of his **p**,	5971
Job 12: 2	No doubt but ye *are* the **p**,	5971
12:24	the heart of the chief of the **p** of the earth,	5971
17: 6	He hath made me also a byword of the **p**;	5971
18:19	have son nor nephew among his **p**,	5971
34:20	the **p** shall be troubled at midnight,	5971
34:30	reign not, lest the **p** be ensnared.	5971
36:20	night, when **p** are cut off in their place.	5971
36:31	For by them judgeth he the **p**; he giveth	5971
Ps 2: 1	and the **p** imagine a vain *thing*?	3816
3: 6	I will not be afraid of ten thousands of **p**,	5971
3: 8	thy blessing *is* upon thy **p**. Selah.	5971
7: 7	shall the congregation of the **p** compass	3816
7: 8	The LORD shall judge the **p**: judge me,	5971
9: 8	he shall minister judgment to the **p** in	3816
9:11	in Zion: declare among the **p** his doings.	5971
14: 4	who eat up my **p** as they eat bread,	5971
14: 7	bringeth back the captivity of his **p**,	5971
18:27	For thou wilt save the afflicted **p**;	5971
18:43	delivered me from the strivings of the **p**;	5971
18:43	a **p** *whom* I have not known shall serve	5971
18:47	me, and subdueth the **p** under me.	5971
22: 6	a reproach of men, and despised of the **p**.	5971
22:31	declare his righteousness unto a **p** that	5971
28: 9	Save thy **p**, and bless thine inheritance:	5971
29:11	The LORD will give strength unto his **p**;	5971
29:11	the LORD will bless his **p** with peace.	5971
33:10	he maketh the devices of the **p** of none	5971
33:12	the **p** *whom* he hath chosen for his own	5971
35:18	I will praise thee among much **p**.	5971
44: 2	thou didst afflict the **p**, and cast them	3816
44:12	Thou sellest thy **p** for nought, and dost	5971
44:14	a shaking of the head among the **p**.	3816
45: 5	*whereby* the **p** fall under thee.	5971
45:10	forget also thine own **p**, and thy father's	5971
45:12	*even* the rich among the **p** shall intreat	5971
45:17	shall the **p** praise thee for ever and ever.	5971
47: 1	clap *your* hands, all ye **p**; shout unto God	5971
47: 3	He shall subdue the **p** under us,	5971
47: 9	princes of the **p** are gathered together,	5971
47: 9	*even* the **p** of the God of Abraham.	5971
49: 1	Hear this, all ye **p**; give ear, all ye	5971
50: 4	and to the earth, that *he* may judge his **p**.	5971
50: 7	Hear, O my **p**, and I will speak; O Israel,	5971
53: 4	who eat up my **p** *as* they eat bread:	5971
53: 6	God bringeth back the captivity of his **p**,	5971
56: 7	in thine anger cast down the **p**, O God.	5971
57: 9	I will praise thee, O Lord, among the **p**:	5971
59:11	Slay them not, lest my **p** forget:	5971
60: 3	Thou hast shewed thy **p** hard *things*: thou	5971
62: 8	ye **p**, pour out your heart before him:	5971
65: 7	of their waves, and the tumult of the **p**.	3816
66: 8	ye **p**, and make the voice of his praise to	5971
67: 3	Let the **p** praise thee, O God; let all	5971
67: 3	thee, O God; let all the **p** praise thee.	5971
67: 4	for thou shalt judge the **p** righteously,	5971
67: 5	Let the **p** praise thee, O God; let all	5971
67: 5	thee, O God; let all the **p** praise thee.	5971
68: 7	when thou wentest forth before thy **p**,	5971
68:22	I will bring *my* **p** again from the depths of	NIH
68:30	of the bulls, with the calves of the **p**,	5971
68:30	scatter thou the **p** *that* delight in war.	5971
68:35	giveth strength and power unto *his* **p**.	5971
72: 2	He shall judge thy **p** with righteousness,	5971
72: 3	The mountains shall bring peace to the **p**,	5971
72: 4	He shall judge the poor of the **p**, he shall	5971
73:10	Therefore his **p** return hither: and waters	5971
74:14	gavest him *to* *be* meat to the **p** inhabiting	5971
74:18	*that* the foolish **p** have blasphemed thy	5971
77:14	hast declared thy strength among the **p**.	5971
77:15	hast with *thine* arm redeemed thy **p**,	5971
77:20	Thou leddest thy **p** like a flock by the	5971
78: 1	Give ear, O my **p**, to my law: incline your	5971
78:20	bread also? can he provide flesh for his **p**?	5971
78:52	made his own **p** to go forth like sheep,	5971
78:62	He gave his **p** over also unto the sword;	5971
78:71	young he brought him to feed Jacob his **p**,	5971
79:13	So we thy **p** and sheep of thy pasture will	5971
80: 4	thou be angry against the prayer of thy **p**?	5971
81: 8	Hear, O my **p**, and I will testify unto thee:	5971
81:11	my **p** would not hearken to my voice;	5971
81:13	O that my **p** had hearkened unto me,	5971
83: 3	have taken crafty counsel against thy **p**,	5971
85: 2	Thou hast forgiven the iniquity of thy **p**,	5971
85: 6	us again: that thy **p** may rejoice in thee?	5971
85: 8	for he will speak peace unto his **p**,	5971

Ps 87: 6	shall count, when he writeth *up* the **p**,	5971
89:15	Blessed *is* the **p** that know the joyful	5971
89:19	I have exalted *one* chosen out of the **p**.	5971
89:50	bosom the *reproach* of all the mighty **p**;	5971
94: 5	They break in pieces thy **p**, O LORD,	5971
94: 8	Understand, ye brutish among the **p**:	5971
94:14	For the LORD will not cast off his **p**,	5971
95: 7	we *are* the **p** of his pasture, and the sheep	5971
95:10	It *is* a **p** that do err in *their* heart,	5971
96: 3	the heathen, his wonders among all **p**.	5971
96: 7	unto the LORD, O ye kindreds of the **p**,	5971
96:10	moved: he shall judge the **p** righteously.	5971
96:13	righteousness, and the **p** with his truth.	5971
97: 6	and all the **p** see his glory.	5971
98: 9	judge the world, and the **p** with equity.	5971
99: 1	The LORD reigneth; let the **p** tremble:	5971
99: 2	in Zion; and he *is* high above all the **p**.	5971
100: 3	*we* *are* his **p**, and the sheep of his pasture.	5971
102:18	the **p** which *shall* be created shall praise	5971
102:22	When the **p** are gathered together,	5971
105: 1	make known his deeds among the **p**.	5971
105:13	another, from *one* kingdom to another **p**;	5971
105:20	the ruler of the **p**, and let him go free.	5971
105:24	he increased his **p** greatly; and made	5971
105:25	He turned their heart to hate his **p**, to	5971
105:40	*The* **p** asked, and he brought quails,	NIH
105:43	he brought forth his **p** with joy,	5971
105:44	and they inherited the labour of the **p**;	3816
106: 4	the favour *that* thou bearest unto thy **p**:	5971
106:40	wrath of the LORD kindled against his **p**,	5971
106:48	let all the **p** say, Amen. Praise ye	5971
107:32	him also in the congregation of the **p**,	5971
108: 3	I will praise thee, O LORD, among the **p**:	5971
110: 3	Thy **p** *shall* be willing in the day of thy	5971
111: 6	He hath shewed his **p** the power of his	5971
111: 9	He sent redemption unto his **p**: he hath	5971
113: 8	princes, *even* with the princes of his **p**.	5971
114: 1	the house of Jacob from a **p** of strange	5971
116:14	LORD now in the presence of all his **p**.	5971
116:18	LORD now in the presence of all his **p**,	5971
117: 1	all ye nations: praise him, all ye **p**.	523
125: 2	the LORD *is* round about his **p** from	5971
135:12	an heritage, an heritage unto Israel his **p**.	5971
135:14	For the LORD will judge his **p**,	5971
136:16	To him which led his **p** through	5971
144: 2	I trust; who subdueth my **p** under me.	5971
144:15	Happy *is that* **p**, that is in such a case:	5971
144:15	*yea*, happy *is that* **p**, whose God *is*	5971
148:11	Kings of the earth, and all **p**; princes,	3816
148:14	He also exalteth the horn of his **p**,	5971
148:14	the children of Israel, a **p** near unto him.	5971
149: 4	For the LORD taketh pleasure in his **p**:	5971
149: 7	heathen, *and* punishments upon the **p**;	3816
Pr 11:14	Where no counsel *is*, the **p** fall: but in	5971
11:26	withholdeth corn, the **p** shall curse him:	3816
14:28	In the multitude of **p** *is* the king's honour:	5971
14:28	in the want of **p** *is* the destruction of	3816
14:34	a nation: but sin *is* a reproach to any **p**.	3816
24:24	him that saith unto the wicked, Thou *art* righteous; him shall the **p** curse, nations shall abhor	5971
28:15	*so* is a wicked ruler over the poor **p**.	5971
29: 2	righteous are in authority, the **p** rejoice:	5971
29: 2	the wicked beareth rule, the **p** mourn.	5971
29:18	Where *there* *is* no vision, the **p** perish:	5971
30:25	The ants *are* a **p** not strong, yet they	5971
Ecc 4:16	*There* is no end of all the **p**, *even* of all	5971
12: 9	was wise, he still taught the **p** knowledge;	5971
Isa 1: 3	doth not know, my **p** doth not consider.	5971
1: 4	Ah sinful nation, a **p** laden with iniquity,	5971
1:10	the law of our God, ye **p** of Gomorrah.	5971
2: 3	many **p** shall go and say, Come ye,	5971
2: 4	the nations, and shall rebuke many **p**:	5971
2: 6	Therefore thou hast forsaken thy **p**	5971
3: 5	the **p** shall be oppressed, every one by	5971
3: 7	clothing: make me not a ruler of the **p**.	5971
3:12	*As for* my **p**, children *are* their oppressors,	5971
3:12	my **p**, they which lead thee cause *thee* to	5971
3:13	*up* to plead, and standeth to judge the **p**.	5971
3:14	into judgment with the ancients of his **p**,	5971
3:15	mean *ye that* ye beat my **p** to pieces,	5971
5:13	Therefore my **p** are gone into captivity,	5971
5:25	anger of the LORD kindled against his **p**,	5971
6: 5	I dwell in the midst of a **p** of unclean lips:	5971
6: 9	said, Go, and tell this **p**, Hear ye indeed,	5971
6:10	Make the heart of this **p** fat, and make	5971
7: 2	heart was moved, and the heart of his **p**,	5971
7: 8	Ephraim be broken, that *it* *be* not a **p**.	5971
7:17	upon thy **p**, and upon thy father's house,	5971
8: 6	Forsomuch as this **p** refuseth the waters	5971
8: 9	O ye **p**, and ye shall be broken in pieces;	5971
8:11	*I* should not walk in the way of this **p**,	5971
8:12	to all *them* to whom this **p** shall say,	5971
8:19	should not a **p** seek unto their God?	5971
9: 2	The **p** that walked in darkness have seen	5971
9: 9	all the **p** shall know, *even* Ephraim and	5971
9:13	the **p** turneth not unto him that smiteth	5971
9:16	the leaders of this **p** cause *them* to err;	5971
9:19	and the **p** shall be as the fuel of the fire:	5971
10: 2	away the right from the poor of my **p**,	5971
10: 6	against the **p** of my wrath will I give him	5971
10:13	I have removed the bounds of the **p**,	5971
10:14	hath found as a nest the riches of the **p**:	5971
10:22	For though thy *p* Israel be as the sand of	5971
10:24	my **p** that dwellest in Zion, be not afraid	5971
11:10	which shall stand for an ensign of the **p**;	5971
11:11	time to recover the remnant of his **p**,	5971

Isa 11:16 be a highway for the remnant of his **p**,	5971
12: 4 name, declare his doings among the **p**,	5971
13: 4 in the mountains, like as of a great **p**;	5971
13:14 they shall every man turn to his own **p**,	5971
14: 2 the **p** shall take them, and bring them to	5971
14: 6 He who smote the **p** in wrath *with a*	5971
14:20 hast destroyed thy land, *and* slain thy **p**:	5971
14:32 and the poor of his **p** shall trust in it.	5971
17:12 Woe to the multitude of many **p**,	5971
18: 2 to a **p** terrible from their beginning	5971
18: 7 unto the LORD of hosts *of* a **p** scattered	5971
18: 7 from a **p** terrible from their beginning	5971
19:25 Blessed *be* Egypt my **p**, and Assyria	5971
22: 4 of the spoiling of the daughter of my **p**.	5971
23:13 this **p** was not, *till* the Assyrian founded it	5971
24: 2 shall be, as *with* the **p**, so *with* the priest;	5971
24: 4 the haughty **p** of the earth do languish.	5971
24:13 be in the midst of the land among the **p**,	5971
25: 3 Therefore shall the strong **p** glorify thee,	5971
25: 6 hosts make unto all **p** a feast of fat things,	5971
25: 7 the face of the covering cast over all **p**,	5971
25: 8 the rebuke of his **p** shall he take away	5971
26:11 and be ashamed for *their* envy at the **p**;	5971
26:20 my **p**, enter thou into thy chambers,	5971
27:11 it *is* a **p** of no understanding: therefore	5971
28: 5 of beauty, unto the residue of his **p**,	5971
28:11 another tongue will he speak to this **p**.	5971
28:14 that rule this **p** which *is* in Jerusalem.	5971
29:13 Forasmuch as this **p** draw near *me* with	5971
29:14 to do a marvellous work amongst this **p**,	5971
30: 5 were all ashamed of a **p** *that* could not	5971
30: 6 camels, to a **p** *that* shall not profit *them*.	5971
30: 9 That this *is* a rebellious **p**, lying children,	5971
30:19 For the **p** shall dwell in Zion at Jerusalem:	5971
30:26 the LORD bindeth up the breach of his **p**,	5971
30:28 *shall be* a bridle in the jaws of the **p**,	5971
32:13 Upon the land of my **p** shall come up	5971
32:18 my **p** shall dwell in a peaceable habitation,	5971
33: 3 At the noise of the tumult the **p** fled;	5971
33:12 the **p** shall be *as* the burnings of lime:	5971
33:19 Thou shalt not see a fierce **p**, a people of	5971
33:19 a **p** of a deeper speech than *thou* canst	5971
33:24 the **p** that dwell therein *shall be* forgiven	5971
34: 1 ye nations, to hear; and hearken, ye **p**:	3816
34: 5 and upon the **p** of my curse, to judgment.	5971
36:11 in the ears of the **p** that *are* on the wall.	5971
40: 1 Comfort ye, comfort ye my **p**, saith your	5971
40: 7 bloweth upon it: surely the **p** *is* grass.	5971
41: 1 and let the **p** renew *their* strength:	3816
42: 5 he that giveth breath unto the **p** upon it,	5971
42: 6 and give thee for a covenant of the **p**,	5971
42:22 this *is* a **p** robbed and spoiled; *they are* all	5971
43: 4 will I give men for thee, and **p** for thy life.	3816
43: 8 Bring forth the blind **p** that have eyes,	5971
43: 9 and let the **p** be assembled:	3816
43:20 to give drink to my **p**, my chosen.	5971
43:21 This **p** have I formed for myself; they shall	5971
44: 7 for me, since I appointed the ancient **p**?	5971
47: 6 I was wroth with my **p**, I have polluted	5971
49: 1 unto me; and hearken, ye **p**, from afar;	3816
49: 8 and give thee for a covenant of the **p**,	5971
49:13 for the LORD hath comforted his **p**,	5971
49:22 and set up my standard to the **p**:	5971
51: 4 Hearken unto me, my **p**; and give ear	5971
51: 4 my judgment to rest for a light of the **p**.	5971
51: 5 and mine arms shall judge the **p**;	5971
51: 7 the **p** in whose heart *is* my law;	5971
51:16 and say unto Zion, Thou *art* my **p**.	5971
51:22 thy God *that* pleadeth the cause of his **p**,	5971
52: 4 My **p** went down aforetime *into* Egypt to	5971
52: 5 that my **p** is taken away for nought?	5971
52: 6 Therefore my **p** shall know my name:	5971
52: 9 for the LORD hath comforted his **p**,	5971
53: 8 for the transgression of my **p** was he	5971
55: 4 I have given him *for* a witness to the **p**,	3816
55: 4 a leader and commander to the **p**.	3816
56: 3 hath utterly separated me from his **p**:	5971
56: 7 shall be called a house of prayer for all **p**.	5971
57:14 stumblingblock out of the way of my **p**.	5971
58: 1 shew my **p** their transgression,	5971
60: 2 cover the earth, and gross darkness the **p**:	3816
60:21 Thy **p** also *shall be* all righteous: they	5971
61: 9 and their offspring among the **p**:	5971
62:10 prepare you the way of the **p**; cast up,	5971
62:10 the stones; lift up a standard for the **p**.	5971
62:12 they shall call them, The holy **p**,	5971
63: 3 and of the **p** *there was* none with me:	5971
63: 6 I will tread down the **p** in mine anger,	5971
63: 8 For he said, Surely they *are* my **p**,	5971
63:11 the days of old, Moses, *and* his **p**,	5971
63:14 so didst thou lead thy **p**, to make thyself	5971
63:18 The **p** of thy holiness have possessed *it*	5971
64: 9 see, we beseech thee, we *are* all thy **p**.	5971
65: 2 hands all the day unto a rebellious **p**,	5971
65: 3 **p** that provoketh me to anger continually	5971
65:10 down in, for my **p** that have sought me.	5971
65:18 Jerusalem a rejoicing, and her **p** a joy.	5971
65:19 will rejoice in Jerusalem, and joy in my **p**:	5971
65:22 as the days of a tree *are* the days of my **p**,	5971
Jer 1:18 and against the **p** of the land.	5971
2:11 my **p** have changed their glory for *that*	5971
2:13 For my **p** have committed two evils;	5971
2:31 wherefore say my **p**, We are lords; we	5971
2:32 yet my **p** have forgotten me days without	5971
4:10 surely thou hast greatly deceived this **p**	5971

Jer 4:11 At that time shall it be said to this **p** and	5971
4:11 wilderness toward the daughter of my **p**,	5971
4:22 For my **p** *is* foolish, they have not known	5971
5:14 this **p** wood, and it shall devour them.	5971
5:21 O foolish **p**, and without understanding;	5971
5:23 this **p** hath a revolting and a rebellious	5971
5:26 For among my **p** are found wicked *men:*	5971
5:31 their means; and my **p** love *to* have it so:	5971
6:14 the hurt of *the daughter of* my **p** slightly,	5971
6:19 behold, I will bring evil upon this **p**,	5971
6:21 I will lay stumblingblocks before this **p**,	5971
6:22 a **p** cometh from the north country,	5971
6:26 O daughter of my **p**, gird *thee* with	5971
6:27 *for* a tower *and* a fortress among my **p**,	5971
7:12 did to it for the wickedness of my **p** Israel.	5971
7:16 Therefore pray not thou for this **p**, neither	5971
7:23 I will be your God, and ye shall be my **p**:	5971
7:33 the carcases of this **p** shall be meat for	5971
8: 5 is this **p** of Jerusalem slidden back *by* a	5971
8: 7 my **p** know not the judgment of	5971
8:11 the hurt of the daughter of my **p** slightly,	5971
8:19 voice of the cry of the daughter of my **p**	5971
8:21 For the hurt of the daughter of my **p** am I	5971
8:22 is not the health of the daughter of my **p**	5971
9: 1 for the slain of the daughter of my **p**!	5971
9: 2 I might leave my **p**, and go from them!	5971
9: 7 how shall I do for the daughter of my **p**?	5971
9:15 I *will* feed them, *even* this **p**, with	5971
10: 3 the customs of the **p** *are* vain: for *one*	5971
11: 4 so shall ye be my **p**, and I will be your	5971
11:14 Therefore pray not thou for this **p**, neither	5971
12:14 I have caused my **p** Israel to inherit;	5971
12:16 will diligently learn the ways of my **p**,	5971
12:16 as they taught my **p** to swear by Baal;	5971
12:16 shall they be built in the midst of my **p**.	5971
13:10 evil **p**, which refuse to hear my words,	5971
13:11 that *they* might be unto me for a **p**,	5971
14:10 Thus saith the LORD unto this **p**, Thus	5971
14:11 me, Pray not for this **p** for *their* good.	5971
14:16 **p** to whom they prophesy shall be cast	5971
14:17 for the virgin daughter of my **p** is broken	5971
15: 1 *yet* my mind *could* not *be* toward this **p**:	5971
15: 7 *them* of children, I will destroy my **p**,	5971
15:20 make thee unto this **p** a fenced brasen	5971
16: 5 I have taken away my peace from this **p**,	5971
16:10 when thou shalt shew this **p** all these	5971
17:19 stand in the gate of the children of the **p**,	5971
18:15 Because my **p** hath forgotten me, they	5971
19: 1 take of the ancients of the **p**, and of	5971
19:11 Even so will I break this **p** and this city,	5971
19:14 the LORD's house; and said to all the **p**,	5971
21: 7 the **p**, and such as are left in this city	5971
21: 8 unto this **p** thou shalt say, Thus saith	5971
22: 2 and thy **p** that enter in by these gates:	5971
22: 4 on horses, he, and his servants, and his **p**.	5971
23: 2 Israel against the pastors that feed my **p**;	5971
23:13 in Baal, and caused my **p** Israel to err.	5971
23:22 had caused my **p** to hear my words, then	5971
23:27 Which think to cause my **p** to forget my	5971
23:32 cause my **p** to err by their lies, and by	5971
23:32 therefore they shall not profit this **p** at all,	5971
23:33 when this **p**, or the prophet, or a priest,	5971
23:34 and the priest, and the **p**, that shall say,	5971
24: 7 shall be my **p**, and I will be their God:	5971
25: 1 **p** of Judah in the fourth year of Jehoiakim	5971
25: 2 the prophet spake unto all the **p** of Judah,	5971
25:19 his servants, and his princes, and all his **p**;	5971
25:20 all the **mingled p**, and all the kings of	6153
25:24 all the kings of the **mingled p** that dwell	6153
26: 7 all the **p** heard Jeremiah speaking these	5971
26: 8 commanded *him* to speak unto all the **p**,	5971
26: 8 and the prophets and all the **p** took him,	5971
26: 9 all the **p** were gathered against Jeremiah	5971
26:11 prophets unto the princes and to all the **p**,	5971
26:12 unto all the princes and to all the **p**,	5971
26:16 all the **p** unto the priests and to	5971
26:17 spake to all the assembly of the **p**, saying,	5971
26:18 spake to all the **p** of Judah, saying,	5971
26:23 body into the graves of the common **p**.	5971
26:24 the hand of the **p** to put him to death.	5971
27:12 and serve him and his **p**, and live.	5971
27:13 thou and thy **p**, by the sword,	5971
27:16 I spake to the priests and to all this **p**,	5971
28: 1 presence of the priests and of all the **p**,	5971
28: 5 in the presence of all the **p** that stood in	5971
28: 7 in thine ears, and in the ears of all the **p**.	5971
28:11 spake in the presence of all the **p**,	5971
28:15 but thou makest this **p** to trust in a lie.	5971
29: 1 to all the **p** whom Nebuchadnezzar had	5971
29:16 of all the **p** that dwelleth in this city,	5971
29:25 name unto all the **p** that *are* at Jerusalem,	5971
29:32 not have a man to dwell among this **p**;	5971
29:32 behold the good that I will do for my **p**,	5971
30: 3 I will bring again the captivity of my **p**	5971
30:22 ye shall be my **p**, and I will be your God.	5971
31: 1 families of Israel, and they shall be my **p**.	5971
31: 2 The **p** which were left of the sword found	5971
31: 7 praise ye, and say, O LORD, save thy **p**,	5971
31:14 my **p** shall be satisfied with my goodness,	5971
31:33 will be their God, and they shall be my **p**.	5971
32:21 hast brought forth thy **p** Israel out of	5971
32:38 shall be my **p**, and I will be their God:	5971
32:42 brought all this great evil upon this **p**,	5971
33:24 Considerest thou not what this **p** have	5971
33:24 thus they have despised my **p**, that *they*	5971

Jer 34: 1 all the **p**, fought against Jerusalem,	5971
34: 8 with all the **p** which *were* at Jerusalem,	5971
34:10 *Now* when all the princes, and all the **p**,	5971
34:19 and the priests, and all the **p** of the land,	5971
35:16 but this **p** hath not hearkened unto me:	5971
36: 6 **p** *in* the LORD's house upon the fasting	5971
36: 7 The LORD hath pronounced against this **p**.	5971
36: 9 before the LORD *to* all the **p** in Jerusalem,	5971
36: 9 *to* all the **p** that came from the cities of	5971
36:10 LORD's house, in the ears of all the **p**.	5971
36:13 Baruch read the book in the ears of the **p**.	5971
36:14 thou hast read in the ears of the **p**,	5971
37: 2 nor his servants, nor the **p** of the land,	5971
37: 4 came in and went out among the **p**:	5971
37:12 himself thence in the midst of the **p**.	5971
37:18 or against thy servants, or against this **p**,	5971
38: 1 that Jeremiah had spoken unto all the **p**,	5971
38: 1 the hands of all the **p**, in speaking such	5971
38: 4 man seeketh not the welfare of this **p**,	5971
39: 8 the houses of the **p**, with fire, and brake	5971
39: 9 of the **p** that remained in the city,	5971
39: 9 him, with the rest of the **p** that remained.	5971
39:10 of the guard left of the poor of the **p**,	5971
39:14 him home: so he dwelt among the **p**.	5971
40: 5 Judah, and dwell with him among the **p**:	5971
40: 6 with him among the **p** that were left	5971
41:10 the residue of the **p** that *were* in Mizpah,	5971
41:10 and all the **p** that remained in Mizpah,	5971
41:13 *that* when all the **p** which *were* with	5971
41:14 So all the **p** that Ishmael had carried away	5971
41:16 all the remnant of the **p** whom he had	5971
42: 1 all the **p** from the least even unto	5971
42: 8 the **p** from the least even to the greatest,	5971
43: 1 **p** all the words of the LORD their God,	5971
43: 4 the captains of the forces, and all the **p**,	5971
44:15 even all the **p** that dwelt in the land of	5971
44:20 Jeremiah said unto all the **p**, to the men,	5971
44:20 to all the **p** which had given him *that*	5971
44:21 and your princes, and the **p** of the land,	5971
46:16 Moreover Jeremiah said unto all the **p**,	5971
46:16 let us go again to our own **p**, and to	5971
46:24 shall be delivered into the hand of the **p**	5971
48:42 Moab shall be destroyed from *being* a **p**,	5971
48:46 the **p** of Chemosh perisheth: for thy sons	5971
49: 1 inherit Gad, and his **p** dwell in his cities?	5971
50: 6 My **p** hath been lost sheep: their	5971
50:16 sword they shall turn every one to his **p**,	5971
50:37 upon all the mingled **p** that *are* in the	6153
50:41 **p** shall come from the north, and a great	5971
51:45 My **p**, go ye out of the midst of her,	5971
51:58 the **p** shall labour in vain, and the folk in	5971
52: 6 that there was no bread for the **p** of	5971
52:15 away captive *certain* of the poor of the **p**,	5971
52:15 the residue of the **p** that remained in	5971
52:25 the host, who mustered the **p** of the land;	5971
52:25 threescore men of the **p** of the land,	5971
52:28 This *is* the **p** whom Nebuchadrezzar	5971
La 1: 1 the city sit solitary, *that was* full of **p**!	5971
1: 7 her **p** fell into the hand of the enemy,	5971
1:11 All her **p** sigh, they seek bread; they have	5971
1:18 I pray you, all **p**, and behold my sorrow:	5971
2:11 the destruction of the daughter of my **p**;	5971
3:14 was a derision to all my **p**; *and* their song	5971
3:45 and refuse in the midst of the **p**.	5971
3:48 the destruction of the daughter of my **p**.	5971
4: 3 the daughter of my **p** *is* become cruel,	5971
4: 6 **p** is greater than the punishment of the	5971
4:10 the destruction of the daughter of my **p**.	5971
Eze 3: 5 For thou *art* not sent to a **p** of a strange	5971
3: 6 Not to many of a strange speech and of	5971
3:11 unto the children of thy **p**, and speak	5971
7:27 the hands of the **p** of the land shall be	5971
11: 1 the son of Benaiah, princes of the **p**.	5971
11:17 I will even gather you from the **p**,	5971
11:20 shall be my **p**, and I will be their God.	5971
12:19 say unto the **p** of the land, Thus saith	5971
13: 9 shall not be in the assembly of my **p**,	5971
13:10 even because they have seduced my **p**,	5971
13:17 set thy face against the daughters of thy **p**,	5971
13:18 Will ye hunt the souls of my **p**, and will	5971
13:19 will ye pollute me among my **p** for	5971
13:19 by your lying to my **p** that hear *your* lies?	5971
13:21 deliver my **p** out of your hand,	5971
13:23 for I will deliver my **p** out of your hand:	5971
14: 8 I will cut him off from the midst of my **p**;	5971
14: 9 will destroy him from the midst of my **p**	5971
14:11 that they may be my **p**, and I may be	5971
17: 9 many to pluck it up by the roots thereof.	5971
17:15 *they* might give him horses and much **p**.	5971
18:18 did *that* which *is* not good among his **p**,	5971
20:34 I will bring you out from the **p**,	5971
20:35 bring you into the wilderness of the **p**,	5971
20:41 when I bring you out from the **p**,	5971
21:12 for it shall be upon my **p**, it *shall be* upon	5971
21:12 reason of the sword shall be upon my **p**:	5971
22:29 The **p** of the land have used oppression,	5971
23:24 and wheels, and with an assembly of **p**,	5971
24:18 So I spake unto the **p** in the morning:	5971
24:19 the **p** said unto me, Wilt thou not tell us	5971
25: 7 I will cut thee off from the **p**, and I will	5971
25:14 upon Edom by the hand of my **p** Israel:	5971
26: 2 she is broken *that was* the gates of the **p**:	5971
26: 7 and companies, and much **p**.	5971
26:11 he shall slay thy **p** by the sword,	5971
26:20 with the **p** of old time, and shall set thee	5971

Eze 27: 3 which art a merchant of the **p** for many 5971
27:33 forth out of the seas, thou filledst many p; 5971
27:36 the merchants among the **p** shall hiss at 5971
28:19 All they that know thee among the **p** 5971
28:25 the **p** among whom they are scattered: 5971
29:13 from the **p** whither they were scattered: 5971
30: 5 all the **mingled p**, and Chub, and the 6153
30:11 He and his **p** with him, the terrible of 5971
31:12 all the **p** of the earth are gone down from 5971
32: 3 net over thee with a company of many **p**; 5971
32: 9 I will also vex the hearts of many **p**, when 5971
32:10 I will make many **p** amazed at thee, 5971
33: 2 speak to the children of thy **p**, and say 5971
33: 2 if the **p** of the land take a man of their 5971
33: 3 he blow the trumpet, and warn the **p**; 5971
33: 6 the trumpet, and the **p** be not warned; 5971
33:12 of man, say unto the children of thy **p**, 5971
33:17 Yet the children of thy **p** say, The way of 5971
33:30 the children of thy **p** still are talking 5971
33:31 they come unto thee as the **p** cometh, 5971
33:31 sit before thee *as* my **p**, and they hear 5971
34:13 I will bring them out from the **p**, 5971
34:30 of Israel, *are* my **p**, saith the Lord GOD. 5971
36: 3 lips of talkers, and *are* an infamy of the **p**: 5971
36: 8 and yield your fruit to my **p** of Israel; 5971
36:12 men to walk upon you, *even* my **p** Israel; 5971
36:15 shalt thou bear the reproach of the **p** 5971
36:20 These *are* the **p** of the LORD, 5971
36:28 ye shall be my **p**, and I will be your God. 5971
37:12 Behold, O my **p**, I *will* open your graves, 5971
37:13 O my **p**, and brought you up out of your 5971
37:18 the children of thy **p** shall speak unto 5971
37:23 so shall they be my **p**, and I will be their 5971
37:27 be their God, and they shall be my **p**. 5971
38: 6 and all his bands: *and* many **p** with thee. 5971
38: 8 and *is* gathered out of many **p**, against 5971
38: 9 and all thy bands, and many **p** with thee. 5971
38:12 upon the **p** *that are* gathered out of 5971
38:14 In that day when my **p** of Israel dwelleth 5971
38:15 thou, and many **p** with thee, all of them 5971
38:16 thou shalt come up against my **p** of Israel, 5971
38:22 and upon the many **p** that *are* with him, 5971
39: 4 all thy bands, and all the **p** that *is* with thee: 5971
39: 7 name known in the midst of my **p** Israel; 5971
39:13 all the **p** of the land shall bury *them*; and 5971
39:27 I have brought them again from the **p**, 5971
42:14 to *those things* which *are* for the **p**. 5971
44:11 burnt offering and the sacrifice for the **p**, 5971
44:19 *even* into the utter court to the **p**, 5971
44:19 they shall not sanctify the **p** with their 5971
44:23 they shall teach my **p** the *difference* 5971
45: 8 my princes shall no more oppress my **p**; 5971
45: 9 take away your exactions from my **p**, 5971
45:16 the **p** of the land shall give this oblation 5971
45:22 for all the **p** of the land a bullock *for* a sin 5971
46: 3 Likewise the **p** of the land shall worship 5971
46: 9 when the **p** of the land shall come before 5971
46:18 my **p** be not scattered every man from 5971
46:20 out into the utter court, to sanctify the **p**. 5971
46:24 the house shall boil the sacrifice of the **p**. 5971
Da 2:44 the kingdom shall not be left to other **p**, 5972
3: 4 O **p**, nations, and languages, 5972
3: 7 when all the **p** heard the sound of 5972
3: 7 all the **p**, the nations, and the languages, 5972
3:29 That every **p**, nation, and language, 5972
4: 1 unto all **p**, nations, and languages, that 5972
5:19 all **p**, nations, and languages, trembled 5972
6:25 king Darius wrote unto all **p**, nations, 5972
7:14 that all **p**, nations, and languages, 5972
7:27 *shall be* given to the **p** of the saints of 5972
8:24 shall destroy the mighty and the holy **p**. 5971
9: 6 our fathers, and to all the **p** of the land. 5971
9:15 hast brought thy **p** forth out of the land 5971
9:16 thy **p** *are become* a reproach to all *that* 5971
9:19 thy city and thy **p** are called by thy name. 5971
9:20 my sin and the sin of my **p** Israel, 5971
9:24 Seventy weeks are determined upon thy **p** 5971
9:26 the **p** of the prince that *shall* come shall 5971
10:14 what shall befall thy **p** in the latter days: 5971
11:14 also the robbers of thy **p** shall exalt 5971
11:15 shall not withstand, neither his chosen **p**, 5971
11:23 and shall become strong with a small **p**. 1471
11:32 the **p** that do know their God shall be 5971
11:33 they that understand among the **p** shall 5971
12: 1 which standeth for the children of thy **p**: 5971
12: 1 at that time thy **p** shall be delivered, 5971
12: 7 to scatter the power of the holy **p**, 5971
Hos 1: 9 ye *are* not my **p**, and I will not be your 5971
1:10 Ye *are* not my **p**, *there* it shall be said 5971
2:23 I will say to *them* which *were* not my **p**, 5971
2:23 *were* not my **p**, Thou *art* my **p**; 5971
4: 4 for thy **p** *are* as they that strive with 5971
4: 6 My **p** are destroyed for lack of knowledge 5971
4: 8 They eat *up* the sin of my **p**, and they set 5971
4: 9 there shall be, like **p**, like priest: and I will 5971
4:12 My **p** ask *counsel* at their stocks, 5971
4:14 the **p** *that* doth not understand shall fall. 5971
6:11 when I returned the captivity of my **p**, 5971
7: 8 he hath mixed himself among the **p**; 5971
9: 1 Rejoice not, O Israel, for joy, as *other* **p**: 5971
10: 5 for the **p** thereof shall mourn over it, 5971
10:10 the **p** shall be gathered against them, 5971
10:14 shall a tumult arise among thy **p**, 5971
11: 7 my **p** are bent to backsliding from me: 5971
Joel 2: 2 a great **p** and a strong; there hath not 5971

Joel 2: 5 stubble, as a strong **p** set in battle array. 5971
2: 6 Before their face *the* **p** shall be much 5971
2:16 Gather the **p**, sanctify the congregation, 5971
2:17 Spare thy **p**, O LORD, and give not thine 5971
2:17 wherefore should they say among the **p**, 5971
2:18 be jealous for his land, and pity his **p**. 5971
2:19 the LORD will answer and say unto his **p**, 5971
2:26 and my **p** shall never be ashamed. 5971
2:27 and my **p** shall never be ashamed. 5971
Am 3: 2 will plead with them there for my **p** and 5971
3: 3 they have cast lots for my **p**; 5971
3: 8 sell them to the Sabeans, to a **p** far off: 1471
3:16 The LORD *will* be the hope of his **p**, 5971
Am 1: 5 the **p** of Syria shall go into captivity unto 5971
3: 6 blown in the city, and the **p** not be afraid? 5971
7: 8 *will* set a plumbline in the midst of my **p** 5971
7:15 unto me, Go, prophesy unto my **p** Israel. 5971
8: 2 The end is come upon my **p** *of* Israel; 5971
9:10 All the sinners of my **p** shall die by 5971
9:14 I will bring again the captivity of my **p** of 5971
Ob 1:13 gate of my **p** in the day of their calamity: 5971
Jnh 1: 8 *is* thy country? and of what **p** *art* thou? 5971
3: 5 So the **p** of Nineveh believed God, 376
Mic 1: 2 Hear, all ye **p**; hearken, O earth, and all 5971
1: 9 he is come unto the gate of my **p**, *even* to 5971
2: 4 he hath changed the portion of my **p**: 5971
2: 8 of late my **p** is risen up as an enemy: 5971
2: 9 The women of my **p** have ye cast out 5971
2:11 he shall even be the prophet of this **p**. 5971
3: 3 Who also eat the flesh of my **p**, 5971
3: 5 The prophets that make my **p** err, 5971
4: 1 above the hills; and **p** shall flow unto it. 5971
4: 3 he shall judge among many **p**, 5971
4: 5 For all **p** will walk every one in the name 5971
4:13 thou shalt beat in pieces many **p**: and I 5971
5: 7 of many **p** as a dew from the LORD, 5971
5: 8 **p** as a lion among the beasts of the forest, 5971
6: 2 the LORD hath a controversy with his **p**, 5971
6: 3 O my **p**, what have I done unto thee? 5971
6: 5 O my **p**, remember now what Balak king of 5971
6:16 ye shall bear the reproach of my **p**. 5971
7:14 Feed thy **p** with thy rod, the flock of thine 5971
Na 3:13 thy **p** in the midst of thee *are* women: 5971
3:18 thy nobles shall dwell *in the dust*: thy **p** is 5971
Hab 2: 5 all nations, and heapeth unto him all **p**: 5971
2: 8 all the remnant of the **p** shall spoil thee; 5971
2:10 shame to thy house by cutting off many **p**, 5971
2:13 *is* it not of the LORD of hosts that the **p** 5971
2:13 the **p** shall weary themselves for very 3816
3:13 wentest forth for the salvation of thy **p**, 5971
3:16 when *he* cometh up unto the **p**, he will 5971
Zep 1:11 for all the merchant **p** are cut down; 5971
2: 8 whereby they have reproached my **p**, 5971
2: 9 the residue of my **p** shall spoil them, 5971
2: 9 the remnant of my **p** shall possess them. 1471
2:10 magnified *themselves* against the **p** of 5971
3: 9 then will I turn to the **p** a pure language, 5971
3:12 the midst of thee an afflicted and poor **p**, 5971
3:20 and a praise among all of the earth, 5971
Hag 1: 2 This **p** say, The time is not come, 5971
1:12 high priest, with all the remnant of the **p**, 5971
1:12 and the **p** did fear before the LORD. 5971
1:13 in the LORD's message unto the **p**, 5971
1:14 and the spirit of all the remnant of the **p**; 5971
2: 2 the high priest and to the residue of the **p**, 5971
2: 4 be strong, all ye **p** of the land, saith 5971
2:14 So *is* this **p**, and so *is* this nation before 5971
Zec 2:11 the LORD in that day, and shall be my **p**: 5971
7: 5 Speak unto all the **p** of the land, and to 5971
7: 6 of the remnant of this **p** in these days, 5971
8: 7 I *will* save my **p** from the east country, 5971
8: 8 shall be my **p**, and I will be their God, 5971
8:11 I *will* not *be* unto the residue of this **p** 5971
8:12 I will cause the remnant of this **p** to 5971
8:20 yet *come to pass*, that there shall come **p**, 5971
8:22 many **p** and strong nations shall come to 5971
9:16 save them in that day as the flock of his **p**: 5971
10: 9 I will sow them among the **p**: and they 5971
11:10 covenant which I had made with all the **p**. 5971
12: 2 of trembling unto all the **p** round about, 5971
12: 3 Jerusalem a burdensome stone for all **p**: 5971
12: 3 though all the **p** of the earth be gathered 1471
12: 4 will smite every horse of the **p** with 5971
12: 6 they shall devour all the **p** round about, 5971
13: 9 I will say, It *is* my **p**: and they shall say, 5971
14: 2 the residue of the **p** shall not be cut off 5971
14:12 the **p** that have fought against Jerusalem; 5971
Mal 1: 4 **p**, against whom the LORD hath 5971
2: 9 contemptible and base before all the **p**, 5971
Mt 1:21 for he shall save his **p** from their sins. 2992
2: 4 chief priests and scribes of the **p** together, 2992
2: 6 a Governor, that shall rule my **p** Israel. 2992
4:16 The **p** which sat in darkness saw great 2992
4:23 and all *manner* of disease among the **p**. 2992
4:24 they brought unto him all sick **p** 2192+2560
4:25 him great multitudes *of* **p** from Galilee, NIG
7:28 the **p** were astonished at his doctrine: 3793
9:23 the minstrels and the **p** making a noise, 3793
9:25 when the **p** were put forth, he went in, 3793
9:35 and every disease among the **p**. 2992
12:23 all the **p** were amazed, and said, Is this 3793
12:46 While he yet talked to the **p**, behold, 3793
14:13 when the **p** had heard *thereof*, they 3793
15: 8 This **p** draweth nigh unto me with their 2992
21:23 the elders of the **p** came unto him as he 2992

Mt 21:26 But if we shall say, Of men; we fear the **p**; 3793
26: 3 and the scribes, and the elders of the **p**, 2992
26: 5 *day*, lest there be an uproar among the **p**. 2992
26:47 from the chief priests and elders of the **p**. 2992
27: 1 elders of the **p** took counsel against Jesus 2992
27:15 was wont to release unto the **p** a prisoner, 3793
27:25 Then answered all the **p**, and said, 2992
27:64 steal him *away*, and say unto the **p**, 2992
Mk 5:21 other side, much **p** gathered unto him: 3793
5:24 and much **p** followed him, 3793
6:33 And the **p** saw them departing, 3793
6:34 saw much **p**, and was moved with 3793
6:45 unto Bethsaida, while he sent away the **p**. 3793
7: 6 This **p** honoureth me with *their* lips, 2992
7:14 when he had called all the **p** unto *him*, 3793
7:17 was entered into *the* house from the **p**, 3793
8: 6 And he commanded the **p** to sit down on 3793
8: 6 and they did set *them* before the **p**. 3793
8:34 And when he had called the **p** unto *him* 3793
9:15 And straightway all the **p**, when they 3793
9:25 When Jesus saw that the **p** came running 3793
10: 1 the **p** resort unto him again; and, as he 3793
10:46 his disciples and a great number of **p**, 3793
11:18 all the **p** was astonished at his doctrine. 3793
11:32 if we shall say, Of men; they feared the **p**: 2992
12:12 to lay hold on him, but feared the **p**: 3793
12:37 And the common **p** heard him gladly. 3793
12:41 beheld how the **p** cast money into 3793
14: 2 feast *day*, lest there be an uproar of the **p**. 2992
15:11 But the chief priests moved the **p**, that he 3793
15:15 And *so* Pilate, willing to content the **p**, 3793
Lk 1:10 And the whole multitude of the **p** were 2992
1:17 to make ready a **p** prepared for the Lord. 2992
1:21 And the **p** waited for Zacharias, 2992
1:68 for he hath visited and redeemed his **p**, 2992
1:77 To give knowledge of salvation unto his **p** 2992
2:10 tidings of great joy, which shall be to all **p**. 2992
2:31 thou hast prepared before the face of all **p**; 2992
2:32 the Gentiles, and the glory of thy **p** Israel. 2992
3:10 And the **p** asked him, saying, What shall 3793
3:15 And as the **p** were in expectation, 2992
3:18 in his exhortation preached he unto the **p**. 2992
3:21 Now when all the **p** were baptized, it 2992
4:42 the **p** sought him, and came unto him, 3793
5: 1 the **p** pressed upon him to hear the word 3793
5: 3 sat down, and taught the **p** out of the ship. 3793
6:17 a great multitude of **p** out of all Judea and 2992
7: 1 all his sayings in the audience of the **p**, 2992
7: 9 and said unto the **p** that followed him, 3793
7:11 his disciples went with him, and much **p**. 3793
7:12 and much of the city was with her. 3793
7:16 and, That God hath visited his **p**. 2992
7:24 he began to speak unto the **p** concerning 3793
7:29 And all the **p** that heard *him*, and 2992
8: 4 when much **p** were gathered together, 3793
8:40 was returned, the **p** gladly received him: 3793
8:42 (But as he went the **p** thronged him. 3793
8:47 she declared unto him before all the **p** for 2992
9:11 And the **p**, when they knew *it*, followed 3793
9:13 we should go and buy meat for all this **p**. 2992
9:18 saying, Whom say the **p** that I am? 3793
9:37 down from the hill, much **p** met him. 3793
11:14 the dumb spake; and the **p** wondered. 3793
11:29 And when the **p** were gathered thick 3793
12: 1 together an innumerable multitude of **p**, 3793
12:54 And he said also to the **p**, When ye see a 3793
13:14 on the sabbath day, and said unto the **p**, 3793
13:17 all the **p** rejoiced for all the glorious 2992
18:43 all the **p**, when they saw *it*, gave praise 2992
19:47 the chief of the **p** sought to destroy him, 2992
19:48 for all the **p** were very attentive to hear 2992
20: 1 as he taught the **p** in the temple, 2992
20: 6 if we say, Of men; all the **p** will stone us: 2992
20: 9 Then began he to speak to the **p** this 2992
20:19 lay hands on him; and they feared the **p**: 2992
20:26 not take hold of his words before the **p**: 2992
20:45 Then in the audience of all the **p** he said 2992
21:23 in the land, and wrath upon this **p**. 2992
21:38 all the **p** came early in the morning to 2992
22: 2 they might kill him; for they feared the **p**. 2992
22:66 the elders of the **p** and the chief priests 2992
23: 4 Pilate to the chief priests and *to* the **p**, 3793
23: 5 saying, He stirreth up the **p**, 2992
23:13 the chief priests and the rulers and the **p**, 2992
23:14 unto me, as one that perverteth the **p**: 2992
23:27 there followed him a great company of **p**, 2992
23:35 And the **p** stood beholding. And the rulers 2992
23:48 And all the **p** that came together to that 3793
24:19 deed and word before God and all the **p**: 2992
Jn 6:22 the **p** which stood on the other side 3793
6:24 When the **p** therefore saw that Jesus was 3793
7:12 murmuring among the **p** concerning him: 3793
7:12 others said, Nay; but he deceiveth the **p**. 3793
7:20 The **p** answered and said, Thou hast a 3793
7:31 And many of the **p** believed on him, 3793
7:32 The Pharisees heard that the **p** murmured 3793
7:40 Many of the **p** therefore, when they heard 3793
7:43 So there was a division among the **p** 3793
7:49 But this **p** who knoweth not the law are 3793
8: 2 the temple, and all the **p** came unto him; 2992
11:42 of the **p** which stand by I said *it*, that they 3793
11:50 that one man should die for the **p**, 2992
12: 9 Much **p** of the Jews therefore knew that 3793
12:12 On the next day much **p** that were come 3793
12:17 The **p** therefore that was with him when 3793

Jn	12:18 For this cause the **p** also met him, for that	3793
	12:29 Therefore, that stood *by*, and heard	3793
	12:34 The **p** answered him, We have heard out	3793
	18:14 that one man should die for the **p**.	2992
Ac	2:47 and having favour with all the **p**.	2992
	3: 9 And all the **p** saw him walking and	2992
	3:11 all the **p** ran together unto them in	2992
	3:12 Peter saw *it*, he answered unto the **p**,	2992
	3:23 shall be destroyed from among the **p**.	2992
	4: 1 And as they spake unto the **p**, the priests,	2992
	4: 2 Being grieved that they taught the **p**,	2992
	4: 8 Ye rulers of the **p**, and elders of Israel,	2992
	4:10 unto you all, and to all the **p** of Israel,	2992
	4:17 But that it spread no further among the **p**,	2992
	4:21 they might punish them, because of the **p**:	2992
	4:25 and the **p** imagine vain *things*,	2992
	4:27 with the Gentiles, and the **p** of Israel,	2992
	5:12 and wonders wrought among the **p**;	2992
	5:13 to them: but the **p** magnified them.	2992
	5:20 speak in the temple to the **p** all the words	2992
	5:25 in the temple, and teaching the **p**.	2992
	5:26 they feared the **p**, lest they should have	2992
	5:34 had in reputation among all the **p**,	2992
	5:37 and drew away much **p** after him:	2992
	6: 8 great wonders and miracles among the **p**.	2992
	6:12 And they stirred up the **p**, and the elders,	2992
	7:17 the **p** grew and multiplied in Egypt,	2992
	7:34 I have seen the affliction of my **p** which is	2992
	8: 6 the **p** with one accord gave heed unto	3793
	8: 9 bewitched the **p** of Samaria, giving out	1484
	10: 2 which gave much alms to the **p**,	2992
	10:41 Not to all the **p**, but unto witnesses	2992
	10:42 he commanded us to preach unto the **p**,	2992
	11:24 and much **p** was added unto the Lord.	3793
	11:26 taught much **p**, and the disciples were	3793
	12: 4 after Easter to bring him forth to the **p**.	2992
	12:11 *from* all the expectation of the **p** of	2992
	12:22 And the **p** gave a shout, *saying*, It is	1218
	13:15 have *any* word of exhortation for the **p**,	2992
	13:17 The God of this **p** of Israel chose our	2992
	13:17 exalted the **p** when *they* dwelt as	2992
	13:24 of repentance to all the **p** of Israel.	2992
	13:31 who are his witnesses unto the **p**.	2992
	14:11 when the **p** saw what Paul had done,	3793
	14:13 and would have done sacrifice with the **p**.	3793
	14:14 and ran in among the **p**, crying out,	3793
	14:18 sayings scarce restrained they the **p**,	3793
	14:19 and Iconium, who persuaded the **p**, and,	2992
	15:14 to take out of them a **p** for his name.	2992
	17: 5 and sought to bring them out to the **p**.	1218
	17: 8 And they troubled the **p** and the rulers of	3793
	17:13 came thither also, and stirred up the **p**.	3793
	18:10 hurt thee: for I have much **p** in this city.	2992
	19: 4 baptism of repentance, saying unto the **p**,	2992
	19:26 hath persuaded and turned away much **p**,	3793
	19:30 Paul would have entered in unto the **p**,	1218
	19:33 would have made his defence unto the **p**.	1218
	19:35 when the townclerk had appeased the **p**,	3793
	21:27 stirred up all the **p**, and laid hands on him,	3793
	21:28 all *men* every where against the **p**,	2992
	21:30 city was moved, and the **p** ran together:	2992
	21:35 of the soldiers for the violence of the **p**.	3793
	21:36 For the multitude of the **p** followed *after*,	2992
	21:39 thee, suffer me to speak unto the **p**.	2992
	21:40 and beckoned with the hand unto the **p**.	2992
	23: 5 shalt not speak evil of the ruler of thy **p**.	2992
	24:12 with any *man*, neither raising up the **p**,	3793
	26:17 Delivering thee from the **p**, and *from*	2992
	26:23 and should shew light unto the **p**, and to	2992
	28: 2 And the **barbarous p** shewed us no little	915
	28:17 I have committed nothing against the **p**,	2992
	28:26 Saying, Go unto this **p**, and say, Hearing	2992
	28:27 For the heart of this **p** is waxed gross,	2992
Ro	9:25 saith also in Osee, I will call *them* my **p**,	2992
	9:25 *them* my people, which were not my **p**;	2992
	9:26 it was said unto them, Ye *are* not my **p**;	2992
	10:19 you to jealousy by *them that are* no **p**,	1484
	10:21 unto a disobedient and gainsaying **p**.	2992
	11: 1 I say then, Hath God cast away his **p**?	2992
	11: 2 God hath not cast away his **p** which he	2992
	15:10 *he* saith, Rejoice, *ye* Gentiles, with his **p**.	2992
	15:11 all ye Gentiles; and laud him, all ye **p**.	2992
1Co	10: 7 The **p** sat down to eat and drink,	2992
	14:21 and other lips will I speak unto this **p**;	2992
2Co	6:16 will be their God, and they shall be my **p**.	2992
Tit	2:14 and purify unto himself a peculiar **p**,	2992
Heb	2:17 make reconciliation for the sins of the **p**.	2992
	4: 9 therefore a rest to the **p** of God.	2992
	5: 3 as for the **p**, so also for himself, to offer	2992
	7: 5 take tithes of the **p** according to the law,	2992
	7:11 (for under it the **p** received the law,)	2992
	8:10 them a God, and they shall be to me a **p**:	2992
	9: 7 for himself, and *for* the errors of the **p**:	2992
	9:19 precept to all the **p** according to the law,	2992
	9:19 sprinkled both the book, and all the **p**,	2992
	10:30 And again, The Lord shall judge his **p**.	2992
	11:25 to suffer affliction with the **p** of God,	2992
	13:12 that he might sanctify the **p** with his own	2992
1Pe	2: 9 a holy nation, a peculiar **p**;	2992
	2:10 Which in time past *were* not a **p**,	2992
	2:10 not a people, but *are* now the **p** of God:	2992
2Pe	2: 1 were false prophets also among the **p**,	2992
Jude	1: 5 saved the **p** out of the land of Egypt,	2992
Rev	5: 9 and tongue, and **p**, and nation;	2992
	7: 9 and kindreds, and **p**, and tongues,	2992

Rev	11: 9 *they* of the **p** and kindreds and tongues	2992
	14: 6 and kindred, and tongue, and **p**,	2992
	18: 4 saying, Come out of her, my **p**, that ye be	2992
	19: 1 I heard a great voice of much **p** in heaven,	3793
	21: 3 and they shall be his **p**, and God himself	2992

PEOPLE'S (4) [PEOPLE]

Lev	9:15 he brought the **p** offering, and took	5971
Eze	46:18 the prince shall not take of the **p**	5971
Mt	13:15 For this **p** heart is waxed gross, and *their*	2992
Heb	2: 7 first for his own sins, *and* then for the **p**:	2992

PEOPLES (2) [PEOPLE]

Rev	10:11 Thou must prophesy again before many **p**,	2992
	17:15 are **p**, and multitudes, and nations,	2992

PEOR (4) [BAAL-PEOR, BETH-PEOR, PEOR'S]

Nu	23:28 Balak brought Balaam *unto* the top of **P**,	6465
	25:18 they have beguiled you in the matter of **P**,	6465
	31:16 against the Lord in the matter of **P**,	6465
Jos	22:17 *Is* the iniquity of **P** *too* little for us, from	6465

PEOR'S (1) [PEOR]

Nu	25:18 slain in the day of the plague for **P** sake.	6465

PERADVENTURE (32)

Ge	18:24 **P** there be fifty righteous within the city:	194
	18:28 **P** there shall lack five of the fifty righteous:	194
	18:29 said, **P** there shall be forty found there.	194
	18:30 **P** there shall thirty be found there. And he	194
	18:31 **P** there shall be twenty found there.	194
	18:32 **P** ten shall be found there. And he said,	194
	24: 5 The woman will not be willing to follow	194
	24:39 master, **P** the woman will not follow me.	194
	27:12 My father will feel me, and I shall seem	194
	31:31 **P** thou wouldest take by force thy	6435
	32:20 I will see his face; **p** he will accept of me.	194
	38:11 for he said, **Lest** he die also, as his	6435
	42: 4 for he said, **Lest** mischief befall him.	6435
	43:12 again in your hand; it *was* an oversight:	194
	44:34 **lest** I see the evil that shall come on my	6435
	50:15 Joseph will hate us, and will certainly	3863
Ex	13:17 **Lest** *p* the people repent when they see	6435
	32:30 I shall make an atonement for your sin.	194
Nu	22: 6 I shall prevail, *that* we may smite them,	194
	22:11 I shall be able to overcome them,	194
	23: 3 the Lord will come to meet me:	194
	23:27 it will please God that thou mayest curse	194
Jos	9: 7 said unto the Hivites, **P** ye dwell among us;	194
1Sa	6: 5 he will lighten his hand from off you,	194
	6: 9 he can shew us our way that we should	194
1Ki	18: 5 **p** we may find grass to save the horses and	194
	18:27 *or* **p** he sleepeth, and must be awaked.	194
	20:31 to the king of Israel: **p** he will save thy life.	194
2Ki	2:16 **lest p** the spirit of the Lord hath taken	6435
Jer	20:10 *saying*, **P** he will be enticed, and we shall	194
Ro	5: 7 yet **p** for a good *man* some would even	5029
2Ti	2:25 **if** God will give them repentance to	3379

PERAZIM (1) [BAAL-PERAZIM]

Isa	28:21 For the Lord shall rise up as *in* mount **P**,	6559

PERCEIVE (25) [PERCEIVED, PERCEIVEST, PERCEIVETH, PERCEIVING]

Dt	29: 4 the Lord hath not given you a heart to **p**,	3045
Jos	22:31 This day we **p** that the Lord *is* among	3045
1Sa	12:17 ye may **p** and see that your wickedness	3045
2Sa	19: 6 for *this* day I **p**, that if Absalom had lived,	3045
2Ki	4: 9 I **p** that this *is* a holy man of God,	3045
Job	9:11 not: he passeth on also, but I **p** him not.	995
	23: 8 *there*; and backward, but I cannot **p** him:	995
Pr	1: 2 to **p** the words of understanding;	995
Ecc	3:22 Wherefore I **p** that *there is* nothing better,	7200
Isa	6: 9 and see ye indeed, but **p** not.	3045
	33:19 of a deeper speech than *thou* canst **p**;	8085
Mt	13:14 and seeing ye shall see, and shall not **p**:	1492
Mk	4:12 That seeing they may see, and not **p**;	1492
	7:18 Do ye not **p**, that whatsoever *thing* from	3539
	8:17 ye not yet, neither understand? have ye	3539
Lk	8:46 for I **p** that virtue is gone out of me.	1097
Jn	4:19 unto him, Sir, I **p** that thou art a prophet.	2334
	12:19 ye how ye prevail nothing?	2334
Ac	8:23 I **p** that thou art in the gall of bitterness,	3708
	10:34 Of a truth I **p** that God is no respecter of	2638
	17:22 I **p** that in all *things* ye are too	2334
	27:10 I **p** that this voyage will be with hurt and	2334
	28:26 and seeing ye shall see, and not **p**;	1492
2Co	7: 8 I **p** that the same epistle hath made you	991
1Jn	3:16 Hereby **p** we the love *of God*, because	1097

PERCEIVED (35) [PERCEIVE]

Ge	19:33 he **p** not when she lay down, nor when	3045
	19:35 he **p** not when she lay down, nor when	3045
Jdg	6:22 when Gideon **p** that he *was* an angel of	7200
1Sa	3: 8 Eli **p** that the Lord had called the child.	995
	28:14 Saul **p** that it *was* Samuel, and he stooped	3045
2Sa	5:12 David **p** that the Lord had established	3045
	12:19 David **p** that the child was dead:	995
	14: 1 Now Joab the son of Zeruiah **p**	3045
1Ki	22:33 when the captains of the chariots **p** that	7200
1Ch	14: 2 David **p** that the Lord had confirmed	3045
2Ch	18:32 when the captains of the chariots **p** that	7200
Ne	6:12 lo, I **p** that God had not sent him;	5234
	6:16 for they **p** that this work was wrought of	3045
	13:10 I **p** that the portions of the Levites had	3045
Est	4: 1 When Mordecai **p** all that was done,	3045

Job	38:18 Hast thou **p** the breadth of the earth?	995
Ecc	1:17 I **p** that this also *is* vexation of spirit.	3045
	2:14 I myself also **p** that one event happeneth	3045
Isa	64: 4 nor **p** by the ear, neither hath the eye	238
Jer	23:18 and hath **p** and heard his word?	7200
	38:27 with him; for the matter was not **p**.	8085
Mt	16: 8 *Which* when Jesus **p**, he said unto them,	1097
	21:45 his parables, they **p** that he spake of them.	1097
	22:18 But Jesus **p** their wickedness, and said,	1097
Mk	2: 8 when Jesus **p** in his spirit that they so	1921
Lk	1:22 they **p** that he had seen a vision in	1921
	5:22 But when Jesus **p** their thoughts,	1921
	9:45 was hid from them, that they **p** it not:	143
	20:19 for they **p** that he had spoken this parable	1097
	20:23 But he **p** their craftiness, and said unto	2657
Jn	6:15 therefore **p** that they would come and	1097
Ac	4:13 and that they were unlearned and	2638
	23: 6 But when Paul **p** that the one part were	1097
	23:29 Whom I **p** to be accused of questions of	2147
Gal	2: 9 the grace that was given unto me,	1097

PERCEIVEST (2) [PERCEIVE]

Pr	14: 7 when thou **p** not *in* him the lips of	3045
Lk	6:41 **p** not the beam that is in thine own eye?	2657

PERCEIVETH (3) [PERCEIVE]

Job	14:21 are brought low, but he **p** *it* not of them.	995
	33:14 once, yea twice, *yet man* **p** it not.	7789
Pr	31:18 She **p** that her merchandise *is* good:	2938

PERCEIVING (3) [PERCEIVE]

Mk	12:28 and **p** that he had answered them well,	1492
Lk	9:47 And Jesus, **p** the thought of their heart,	1492
Ac	14: 9 and **p** that he had faith to be healed,	1492

PERDITION (8)

Jn	17:12 and none of them is lost, but the son of **p**;	684
Php	1:28 which is to them an evident token of **p**,	684
2Th	2: 3 *that* man of sin be revealed, the son of **p**;	684
1Ti	6: 9 which drown men in destruction and **p**.	684
Heb	10:39 we are not of *them* who draw back unto **p**;	684
2Pe	3: 7 the day of judgment and **p** of ungodly men.	684
Rev	17: 8 out of the bottomless *pit*, and go into **p**:	684
	17:11 and is of the seven, and goeth into **p**.	684

PERES (1)

Da	5:28 **P**; Thy kingdom is divided, and given to	6537

PERESH (1)

1Ch	7:16 bare a son, and she called his name **P**;	6570

PEREZ (3)

1Ch	27: 3 Of the children of **P** *was* the chief of all	6557
Ne	11: 4 son of Mahalaleel, of the children of **P**;	6557
	11: 6 All the sons of **P** that dwelt at Jerusalem	6557

PEREZITE See PHARZITES

PEREZ-UZZA (1) [PEREZ-UZZAH, UZZAH]

1Ch	13:11 that place is called **P** to this day.	6560

PEREZ-UZZAH (1) [PEREZ-UZZA, UZZAH]

2Sa	6: 8 he called *the name* of the place **P** to this	6560

PERFECT (99) [PERFECTED, PERFECTING, PERFECTION, PERFECTLY, PERFECTNESS, UNPERFECT]

Ge	6: 9 was a just man *and* **p** in his generations,	8549
	17: 1 walk before me, and be thou **p**.	8549
Lev	22:21 or sheep, it shall be **p** to be accepted;	8549
Dt	18:13 Thou shalt be **p** with the Lord thy God.	8549
	25:15 *But* thou shalt have a **p** and just weight,	8003
	25:15 a **p** and just measure shalt thou have:	8003
	32: 4 *He is* the Rock, his work *is* **p**: for all his	8549
1Sa	14:41 Give a **p** *lot*. And Saul and Jonathan	8549
2Sa	22:31 *As for* God, his way *is* **p**: the word of	8549
	22:33 *and* power: and he maketh my way **p**.	8549
1Ki	8:61 therefore be **p** with the Lord our God,	8003
	11: 4 his heart was not **p** with the Lord his	8003
	15: 3 his heart was not **p** with the Lord his	8003
	15:14 nevertheless Asa's heart was **p** with	8003
2Ki	20: 3 before thee in truth and with a **p** heart,	8003
1Ch	12:38 rank, came with a **p** heart to Hebron,	8003
	28: 9 serve him with a **p** heart and with a	8003
	29: 9 with **p** heart they offered willingly to	8003
	29:19 give unto Solomon my son a **p** heart,	8003
2Ch	4:21 tongs, *made he of* gold, *and that* **p** gold;	4357
	15:17 nevertheless the heart of Asa was **p** all	8003
	16: 9 of *them* whose heart *is* **p** towards him.	8003
	19: 9 the Lord, faithfully, and with a **p** heart.	8003
	25: 2 sight of the Lord, but not with a **p** heart.	8003
Ezr	7:12 God of heaven, **p** *peace*, and at such a	1585
Job	1: 1 that man was **p** and upright, and one that	8535
	1: 8 a **p** and an upright man, one that feareth	8535
	2: 3 a **p** and an upright man, one that feareth	8535
	8:20 God will not cast away a **p** *man*, neither	8535
	9:20 *if I say*, I am **p**, it shall also prove me	8535
	9:21 *Though* I *were* **p**, yet would I not know	8535
	9:22 therefore I said *it*, He destroyeth the **p**	8535
	22: 3 to him, that thou **makest** thy ways **p**?	8552
	36: 4 he that is **p** in knowledge *is* with thee.	8549
	37:16 the wondrous works of *him which is* **p** in	8549
Ps	18:30 *As for* God, his way *is* **p**: the word of	8549
	18:32 me *with* strength, and maketh my way **p**.	8549
	19: 7 The law of the Lord *is* **p**, converting	8549
	37:37 Mark the **p** *man*, and behold the upright:	8535

Ps 64: 4 That *they* may shoot in secret at the **p**: 8535
101: 2 I will behave myself wisely in a **p** way. 8549
101: 2 will walk within my house with a **p** heart. 8537
101: 6 he that walketh in a **p** way, he shall serve 8549
138: 8 The Lord will **p** that which concerneth 1584
139:22 I hate them with **p** hatred: I count them 8503
Pr 2:21 *in* the land, and the **p** shall remain in it. 8549
4:18 shineth more and more unto the **p** day. 3559
11: 5 The righteousness of the **p** shall direct his 8549
Isa 18: 5 when the bud is **p**, and the sour grape is 8552
26: 3 Thou wilt keep *him* in **p** peace, 7965+7965
38: 3 before thee in truth and with a **p** heart, 8003
42:19 who *is* blind as he that is **p**, and blind as 7999
Eze 16:14 for it *was* **p** through my comeliness, 3632
27: 3 O Tyrus, thou hast said, I *am* of **p** beauty. 3632
27:11 about; they have **made** thy beauty **p**. 3634
28:12 the sum, full *of* wisdom, and **p** in beauty. 3632
28:15 Thou *wast* **p** in thy ways from the day 8549
Mt 5:48 Be ye therefore **p**, even as your Father 5046
5:48 as your Father which is in heaven is **p**. 5046
19:21 If thou wilt be **p**, go *and* sell that thou 5046
Lk 1: 3 having had **p** understanding of all *things* 199
6:40 every one that is **p** shall be as his master. 2675
Jn 17:23 in me, that they may be **made p** in one; 5048
Ac 3:16 **p** soundness in the presence of you all. 3647
22: 3 according to the **p** manner of the law 195
24:22 having **more p** knowledge of *that* way, 197
Ro 12: 2 and acceptable, and **p**, will of God. 5046
1Co 2: 6 we speak wisdom among *them that are* **p**: 5046
13:10 But when *that* which is **p** is come, then 5046
2Co 12: 9 for my strength is **made p** in weakness. 5046
13:11 Be **p**, be of good comfort, be of one mind, 2675
Gal 3: 3 Spirit, are ye now **made p** by the flesh? 2005
Eph 4:13 of the Son of God, unto a **p** man, 5046
Php 3:12 already attained, either were already **p**: 5046
3:15 as many as *be* **p**, be thus minded: 5046
Col 1:28 we may present every man **p** in Christ 5046
4:12 that ye may stand **p** and complete in all 5046
1Th 3:10 **p** that which is lacking in your faith? 2675
2Ti 3:17 That the man of God may be **p**, 739
Heb 2:10 to **make** the captain of their salvation **p** 5048
5: 9 being **made p**, he became the author 5048
7:19 For the law **made** nothing **p**, 5048
9: 9 not **make** him that did the service **p**, 5048
9:11 by a greater and **more p** tabernacle, 5046
10: 1 **make** the comers thereunto **p**. 5048
11:40 they without us should not be **made p**. 5048
12:23 and to the spirits of just *men* **made p**, 5048
13:21 **Make** you in every good work to do his 2675
Jas 1: 4 But let patience have *her* **p** work, that ye 5046
1: 4 that ye may be **p** and entire, 5046
1:17 good gift and every **p** gift is from above, 5046
1:25 whoso looketh into the **p** law of liberty, 5046
2:22 works, and by works was faith **made p**? 5048
3: 2 same *is* a **p** man, *and* able also to bridle 5046
1Pe 5:10 **make** you **p**, stablish, strengthen, 2675
1Jn 4:17 Herein is our love **made p**, that we may 5048
4:18 no fear in love; but **p** love casteth out fear: 5046
4:18 He that feareth is not **made p** in love. 5048
Rev 3: 2 for I have not found thy works **p** before 4137

PERFECTED (8) [PERFECT]

2Ch 8:16 *So* the house of the Lord was **p**. 8003
24:13 the work was **p** by them, and they 724+5927
Eze 27: 4 the seas, thy builders have **p** thy beauty. 3634
Mt 21:16 of babes and sucklings thou hast **p** praise? 2675
Lk 13:32 to morrow, and the third *day* I shall be **p**. 5048
Heb 10:14 by one offering he hath **p** for ever them 5048
1Jn 2: 5 in him verily is the love of God **p**: 5048
4:12 God dwelleth in us, and his love is **p** in us. 5048

PERFECTING (2) [PERFECT]

2Co 7: 1 and spirit, **p** holiness in the fear of God. 2005
Eph 4:12 For the **p** of the saints for the work of 2677

PERFECTION (11) [PERFECT]

Job 11: 7 canst thou find out the Almighty unto **p**? 8503
15:29 neither shall he prolong the **p** thereof 4512
28: 3 searcheth out all **p**, the stones of darkness 8503
Ps 50: 2 Out of Zion, the **p** of beauty, God hath 4359
119:96 I have seen an end of all **p**: 8502
Isa 47: 9 they shall come upon thee in their **p** for 8537
La 2:15 *saying, Is* this the city that *men* call The **p** 3632
Lk 8:14 of *this* life, and **bring** no fruit to **p**. 5052
2Co 13: 9 and this also we wish, *even* your **p**. 2676
Heb 6: 1 the doctrine of Christ, let us go on unto **p**; 5047
7:11 **p** were by the Levitical priesthood, 5050

PERFECTLY (7)

Jer 23:20 the latter days ye shall **consider** it **p**. 995+998
Mt 14:36 as many as touched were **made p** whole. 1295
Ac 18:26 unto him the way of God **more p**. 197
23:15 inquire something **more p** concerning him: 197
23:20 would inquire somewhat of him **more p**. 197
1Co 1:10 *that* ye be **p** joined together in the same 2675
1Th 5: 2 For yourselves know **p** that the day of 199

PERFECTNESS (1) [PERFECT]

Col 3:14 put on charity, which is the bond of **p**. 5047

PERFORM (42) [PERFORMANCE, PERFORMED,
 PERFORMETH, PERFORMING]

Ge 26: 3 the oath which I sware unto 6965
Ex 18:18 thou art not able to **p** it thyself alone. 6213
Nu 4:23 all that enter in to **p** the **service**, 6633+6635

Dt 4:13 which he commanded you to **p**, *even* ten 6213
9: 5 that he may **p** the word which the Lord 6965
23:23 out of thy lips thou shalt keep and **p**; 6213
25: 5 **p** the duty of a husband's **brother** unto 2992
25: 7 **p** the duty of my husband's **brother**. 2992
Ru 3:13 will **p** unto thee **the part of a kinsman**, 1350
1Sa 3:12 In that day I will **p** against Eli all *things* 6965
2Sa 14:15 it may be that the king will **p** the request 6213
1Ki 6:12 will I **p** my word with thee, which I spake 6965
12:15 the Lord, that *he* might **p** his saying, 6965
2Ki 23: 3 to **p** the words of this covenant that were 6965
23:24 that he might **p** the words of the law 6965
2Ch 10:15 of God, that the Lord might **p** his word, 6965
34:31 to **p** the words of the covenant which are 6213
Est 5: 8 to **p** my request, let the king and 6213
Job 5:12 that their hands cannot **p** *their* enterprise. 6213
Ps 21:11 which *they* are not able to **p**. NIH
61: 8 for ever, that I may daily **p** my vows. 7999
119:106 I will **p** *it*, that *I* will keep thy righteous 6965
119:112 have inclined mine heart to **p** thy statutes 6213
Isa 9: 7 The zeal of the Lord of hosts will **p** this. 6213
19:21 shall vow a vow unto the Lord, and **p** *it*. 7999
44:28 my shepherd, and shall **p** all my pleasure: 7999
Jer 1:12 seen: for I will hasten my word to **p** it. 6213
11: 5 That *I* may **p** the oath which I have sworn 6965
28: 6 the Lord **p** thy words which thou hast 6965
29:10 my good word towards you, in causing 6965
33:14 that I will **p** *that* good thing which I have 6965
44:25 We will surely **p** our vows that we have 6965
44:25 vows, and **surely p** your vows. 6213+6213
Eze 12:25 will I say the word, and will **p** it, 6213
Mic 7:20 Thou wilt **p** the truth to Jacob, 5414
Na 1:15 keep thy solemn feasts, **p** thy vows: 7999
Mt 5:33 but shalt **p** unto the Lord thine oaths: 591
Lk 1:72 To **p** the mercy *promised* to our fathers, 4160
Ro 4:21 he had promised, he was able also to **p**. 4160
7:18 how to **p** that which is good I find not. 2716
2Co 8:11 **p** the doing *of it*; that as *there* was a 2005
Php 1: 6 you will **p** *it* until the day of Jesus Christ: 2005

PERFORMANCE (2) [PERFORM]

Lk 1:45 for there shall be a **p** of those *things* 5050
2Co 8:11 may be a **p** also out of that which *you* 2005

PERFORMED (21) [PERFORM]

1Sa 15:11 and hath not **p** my commandments. 6965
15:13 I have **p** the commandment of the Lord. 6965
2Sa 21:14 they **p** all that the king commanded. 6213
1Ki 8:20 the Lord hath **p** his word that he spake, 6965
2Ch 6:10 hath **p** his word that he hath spoken: 6965
Ne 9: 8 *I say*, to his seed, and hast **p** thy words; 6965
Est 1:15 she hath not **p** the commandment of 6213
5: 6 to the half of the kingdom it shall be **p**. 6213
7: 2 it shall be **p**, *even* to the half of 6213
Ps 65: 1 Zion: and unto thee shall the vow be **p**. 7999
Isa 10:12 when the Lord hath **p** his whole work 1214
Jer 23:20 till he have **p** the thoughts of his heart: 6965
30:24 until he have **p** the intents of his heart: 6965
34:18 have not **p** the words of the covenant 6965
35:14 his sons not to drink wine, are **p**; 6965
35:16 have **p** the commandment of their father, 6965
51:29 for every purpose of the Lord shall be **p** 6965
Eze 37:14 have spoken *it*, and **p** *it*, saith the Lord. 6213
Lk 1:20 until the day that these *things* shall be **p**, 1096
2:39 And when they had **p** all *things* according 5055
Ro 15:28 When therefore I have **p** this, 2005

PERFORMETH (4) [PERFORM]

Ne 5:13 from his labour, that **p** not this promise, 6965
Job 23:14 he **p** the thing that is appointed for me: 7999
Ps 57: 2 unto God that **p** *all things* for me. 1584
Isa 44:26 and **p** the counsel of his messengers; 7999

PERFORMING (2) [PERFORM]

Nu 15: 3 or a sacrifice in **p** a vow, or in a freewill 6381
15: 8 or for a sacrifice in **p** a vow, 6381

PERFUME (3) [PERFUMED, PERFUMES]

Ex 30:35 thou shalt make it a **p**, a confection *after* 7004
30:37 *as for* the **p** which thou shalt make, 7004
Pr 27: 9 Ointment and **p** rejoice the heart: 7004

PERFUME-MAKERS See APOTHECARIES

PERFUMED (2) [PERFUME]

Pr 7:17 I have **p** my bed *with* myrrh, aloes, 5130
SS 3: 6 **p** *with* myrrh and frankincense, with all 6999

PERFUMER See APOTHECARY

PERFUMERS See CONFECTIONARIES

PERFUMES (1) [PERFUME]

Isa 57: 9 didst increase thy **p**, and didst send thy 7547

PERGA (3)

Ac 13:13 Paphos, they came to **P** in Pamphylia. 4011
13:14 when they departed from **P**, they came 4011
14:25 when they had preached the word in **P**, 4011

PERGAMOS (2)

Rev 1:11 and unto **P**, and unto Thyatira, 4010
2:12 And to the angel of the church in **P** write; 4010

PERGAMUM See PERGAMOS

PERHAPS (3)

Ac 8:22 if the thought of thine heart may be 686
2Co 2: 7 comfort *him*, **lest** such a one should be 3381
Phm 1:15 For **p** he therefore departed for a season, 5029

PERIDA (1) [PERUDA]

Ne 7:57 children of Sophereth, the children of **P**, 6514

PERIL (2) [PERILOUS, PERILS]

La 5: 9 We gat our bread with *the* **p** of our lives NIH
Ro 8:35 or famine, or nakedness, or **p**, or sword? 2794

PERILOUS (1) [PERIL]

2Ti 3: 1 that in the last days **p** times shall come. 5467

PERILS (8) [PERIL]

2Co 11:26 *in* **p** of waters, *in* perils of robbers, 2794
11:26 in perils of waters, *in* **p** of robbers, 2794
11:26 of robbers, *in* **p** by *my own* countrymen, 2794
11:26 *in* **p** by the heathen, in perils in the city, 2794
11:26 in perils by the heathen, *in* **p** in the city, 2794
11:26 *in* **p** in the wilderness, in perils in the sea, 2794
11:26 in perils in the wilderness, *in* **p** in the sea, 2794
11:26 in the sea, *in* **p** among false brethren; 2794

PERISH (120) [PERISHED, PERISHETH, PERISHING]

Ge 41:36 that the land **p** not through the famine. 3772
Ex 19:21 the Lord to gaze, and many of them **p**. 5307
21:26 servant, or the eye of his maid, that it **p**; 7843
Lev 26:38 shall **p** among the heathen, and the land 6
Nu 17:12 Behold, we die, we **p**, we all perish. 6
17:12 Behold, we die, we perish, we all **p**. 6
24:20 but his latter end *shall* be that he **p** for ever. 8
24:24 shall afflict Eber, and he also shall **p** for ever. 8
Dt 4:26 ye shall soon **utterly p** from off the land 6+6
8:19 against you this day that ye shall **surely p**. 6+6
8:20 destroyeth before your face, so shall ye **p**; 6
11:17 *lest* ye **p** quickly from off the good land 6
26: 5 A Syrian **ready** to **p** *was* my father, 6
28:20 thou be destroyed, and until thou **p** quickly; 6
28:22 and they shall pursue thee until thou **p**. 6
30:18 that ye shall **surely p**, *and that* ye shall 6+6
Jos 23:13 until ye **p** from off this good land which 6
23:16 ye shall **p** quickly from off the good land 6
Jdg 5:31 So let all thine enemies **p**, O Lord: 6
1Sa 26:10 or he shall descend into battle, and **p**. 5595
27: 1 I shall now **p** one day by the hand of Saul: 5595
2Ki 9: 8 the whole house of Ahab shall **p**: and I will 6
Est 3:13 destroy, to kill, and to **cause** to **p**, all Jews, 6
4:16 not according to the law: and if I **p**, I perish. 6
4:16 not according to the law: and if I perish, I **p**. 6
7: 4 to be destroyed, to be slain, and to **p**. 6
8:11 life, to destroy, to slay, and to **cause** to **p**, 6
9:28 the memorial of them **p** from their seed. 5486
Job 3: 3 Let the day **p** wherein I was born, and the 6
4: 9 By the blast of God they **p**, and by the breath 6
4:20 they **p** for ever without *any* regarding *it*. 6
6:18 are turned aside; they go to nothing, and **p**. 6
8:13 forget God; and the hypocrite's hope shall **p**: 6
18:17 His remembrance shall **p** from the earth, 6
20: 7 *Yet* he shall **p** for ever like his own dung: 6
29:13 The blessing of him that was **ready** to **p** 6
31:19 If I have seen *any* **p** for want of clothing, 6
34:15 All flesh shall **p** together, and man shall 1478
36:12 they shall **p** by the sword, and they shall 5674
Ps 1: 6 but the way of the ungodly shall **p**. 6
2:12 lest he be angry, and ye **p** *from* the way, 6
9: 3 they shall fall and **p** at thy presence. 6
9:18 expectation of the poor shall *not* **p** for ever. 6
37:20 the wicked shall **p**, and the enemies of 6
41: 5 of me, When shall he die, and his name **p**? 6
49:10 likewise the fool and the brutish person **p**, 6
49:12 abideth not: he is like the beasts *that* **p**. 1820
49:20 not, is like the beasts *that* **p**. 1820
68: 2 so let the wicked **p** at the presence of God. 6
73:27 For lo, they that are far from thee shall **p**: 6
80:16 they **p** at the rebuke of thy countenance. 6
83:17 yea, let them be put to shame, and **p**: 6
92: 9 O Lord, for lo, thine enemies shall **p**; 6
102:26 They shall **p**, but thou shalt endure: yea, all 6
112:10 melt away: the desire of the wicked shall **p**. 6
146: 4 to his earth; in that *very* day his thoughts **p**. 6
Pr 10:28 but the expectation of the wicked shall **p**. 6
11: 7 a wicked man dieth, *his* expectation shall **p**: 6
11:10 and when the wicked **p**, *there* is shouting. 6
19: 9 and *he that* speaketh lies shall **p**. 6
21:28 A false witness shall **p**: but the man that 6
28:28 but when they **p**, the righteous increase. 6
29:18 Where *there is* no vision, the people **p**: 6544
31: 6 strong drink unto him that is **ready** to **p**, 6
Ecc 5:14 riches by evil travail: and he begetteth 6
Isa 26:14 and **made** all their memory to **p**. 6
27:13 they shall come which were ready to **p** in 6
29:14 for the wisdom of their wise *men* shall **p**, 6
41:11 and they that strive with thee shall **p**. 6
60:12 and kingdom that will not serve thee shall **p**; 6
Jer 4: 9 the heart of the king shall **p**, and the heart 6
6:21 the neighbour and his friend shall **p**. 6
10:11 *even* they shall **p** from the earth, 7
10:15 in the time of their visitation they shall **p**. 6
18:18 for the law shall not **p** from the priest, 6
27:10 that I should drive you out, and ye should **p**. 6
27:15 that ye might **p**, ye, and the prophets that 6
40:15 be scattered, and the remnant in Judah **p**? 6
48: 8 the valley also shall **p**, and the plain shall be 6

Jer	51:18 in the time of their visitation they shall **p**.	6
Eze	7:26 the law shall **p** from the priest,	6
	25: 7 I will **cause** thee **to p** out of the countries:	6
Da	2:18 his fellows should not **p** with the rest of	7
Am	1: 8 the remnant of the Philistines shall **p**, saith	6
	2:14 Therefore the flight shall **p** from the swift,	6
	3:15 the houses of ivory shall **p**, and the great	6
Jnh	1: 6 that God will think upon us, that we **p** not.	6
	1:14 let us not **p** for this man's life, and lay not	6
	3: 9 away from his fierce anger, that we **p** not?	6
Zec	9: 5 the king shall **p** from Gaza, and Ashkelon	6
Mt	5:29 for thee that one of thy members should **p**,	622
	5:30 for thee that one of thy members should **p**,	622
	8:25 awoke him, saying, Lord, save us: we **p**.	622
	9:17 the wine runneth out, and the bottles **p**:	622
	18:14 that one of these little ones should **p**.	622
	26:52 for all they that take the sword shall **p** with	622
Mk	4:38 him, Master, carest thou not that we **p**?	622
Lk	5:37 and be spilled, and the bottles shall **p**.	622
	8:24 awoke him, saying, Master, master, we **p**.	622
	13: 3 except ye repent, ye shall all likewise **p**.	622
	13: 5 except ye repent, ye shall all likewise **p**.	622
	13:33 for it cannot be that a prophet **p** out of	622
	15:17 and to spare, and I **p** with hunger?	622
	21:18 But there shall not a hair of your head **p**.	622
Jn	3:15 whosoever believeth in him should not **p**,	622
	3:16 whosoever believeth in him should not **p**,	622
	10:28 they shall never **p**, neither shall any man	622
	11:50 people, and that the whole nation **p** not.	622
Ac	8:20 Thy money **p** with thee,	684+1510+1519
	13:41 Behold ye despisers, and wonder, and **p**:	853
Ro	2:12 without law shall also **p** without law:	622
1Co	1:18 of the cross is to them that **p** foolishness;	622
	8:11 thy knowledge shall the weak brother **p**,	622
2Co	2:15 in them that are saved, and in them that **p**:	622
	4:16 but though our outward man **p**,	1311
Col	2:22 Which all are to **p** with the using;) after	5356
2Th	2:10 of unrighteousness in them that **p**;	622
Heb	1:11 They shall **p**; but thou remainest;	622
2Pe	2:12 shall **utterly p** in their own corruption;	2704
	3: 9 not willing that any should **p**, but that all	622

PERISHED (26) [PERISH]

Nu	16:33 and they **p** from among the congregation.	6
	21:30 Heshbon is **p** even unto Dibon, and we	6
Jos	22:20 and that man **p** not alone in his iniquity.	1478
2Sa	1:27 mighty fallen, and the weapons of war **p**!	6
Job	4: 7 Remember, I pray thee, who *ever* **p**,	6
	30: 2 hands profit me, in whom old age was **p**?	6
Ps	9: 6 cities; their memorial is **p** *with* them.	6
	10:16 and ever: the heathen are **p** out of his land.	6
	83:10 Which **p** at En-dor: they became *as* dung	8045
	119:92 I should then have **p** in mine affliction.	6
Ecc	9: 6 and their hatred, and their envy, is now **p**;	6
Jer	7:28 truth is **p**, and is cut off from their mouth.	6
	48:36 because the riches he hath gotten are **p**.	6
	49: 7 counsel **p** from the prudent? is their wisdom	6
La	3:18 and my hope is **p** from the Lord:	6
Joel	1:11 barley; because the harvest of the field is **p**.	6
Jnh	4:10 which came up in a night, and **p** in a night:	6
Mic	4: 9 thy counsellor **p**? for pangs have taken thee	6
	7: 2 The good *man* is **p** out of the earth: and	6
Mt	8:32 place into the sea, and **p** in the waters.	599
Lk	11:51 which **p** between the altar and the temple:	622
Ac	5:37 he also **p**; and all, *even* as many as obeyed	622
1Co	15:18 also which are fallen asleep in Christ are **p**.	622
Heb	11:31 By faith the harlot Rahab **p** not **with** them	4881
2Pe	3: 6 then was, being overflowed with water, **p**:	622
Jude	1:11 for reward, and **p** in the gainsaying of Core.	622

PERISHETH (9) [PERISH]

Job	4:11 The old lion **p** for lack of prey, and the stout	6
Pr	11: 7 shall perish: and the hope of unjust *men* **p**.	6
Ecc	7:15 is a just *man* that **p** in his righteousness,	6
Isa	57: 1 The righteous, and no man layeth *it* to	6
Jer	9:12 for what the land **p** *and* is burnt up like a	6
	48:46 the people of Chemosh **p**: for thy sons are	6
Jn	6:27 Labour not for the meat which **p**, but for	622
Jas	1:11 and the grace of the fashion of it **p**:	622
1Pe	1: 7 much more precious than of gold that **p**,	622

PERISHING (1) [PERISH]

Job	33:18 the pit, and his life from **p** by the sword.	5674

PERIZZITE (5) [PERIZZITES]

Ge	13: 7 and the **P** dwelled then in the land.	6522
Ex	33: 2 and the Hivite, and the Jebusite.	6522
	34:11 the **P**, and the Hivite, and the Jebusite.	6522
Jos	9: 1 the **P**, the Hivite, and the Jebusite,	6522
	11: 3 and the Jebusite in the mountains,	6522

PERIZZITES (18) [PERIZZITE]

Ge	15:20 the Hittites, and the Rephaims,	6522
	34:30 land, amongst the Canaanites and the **P**:	6522
Ex	3: 8 the **P**, and the Hivites, and the Jebusites.	6522
	3:17 the **P**, and the Hivites, and the Jebusites,	6522
	23:23 the **P**, and the Canaanites, the Hivites,	6522
Dt	7: 1 the **P**, and the Hivites, and the Jebusites,	6522
	20:17 and the **P**, and the Hivites, and the	6522
Jos	3:10 the **P**, and the Girgashites,	6522
	12: 8 the **P**, the Hivites, and the Jebusites:	6522
	17:15 for thyself in the land of the **P**	6522
	24:11 **P**, and the Canaanites, and the Hittites,	6522
Jdg	1: 4 the Canaanites and the **P** into their hand:	6522
	1: 5 and they slew the Canaanites and the **P**.	6522

Jdg	3: 5 and **P**, and Hivites, and Jebusites:	6522
1Ki	9:20 Hittites, **P**, Hivites, and Jebusites,	6522
2Ch	8: 7 the **P**, and the Hivites, and the Jebusites,	6522
Ezr	9: 1 the Hittites, the **P**, the Jebusites,	6522
Ne	9: 8 the **P**, and the Jebusites,	6522

PERJURED (1)

1Ti	1:10 for **p** *persons*, and if *there be* any other	1965

PERMISSION (1) [PERMIT]

1Co	7: 6 But I speak this by **p**, *and* not of	4774

PERMIT (2) [PERMISSION, PERMITTED]

1Co	16: 7 to tarry a while with you, if the Lord **p**.	2010
Heb	6: 3 And this will we do, if God **p**.	2010

PERMITTED (2) [PERMIT]

Ac	26: 1 unto Paul, Thou art **p** to speak for thyself.	2010
1Co	14:34 for it is not **p** unto them to speak;	2010

PERNICIOUS (1)

2Pe	2: 2 And many shall follow their **p ways**;	684

PERPETUAL (28) [PERPETUALLY]

Ge	9:12 that *is* with you, for **p** generations;	5769
Ex	29: 9 the priest's office shall be theirs for a **p**	5769
	30: 8 a **p** incense before the Lord throughout	8548
	31:16 their generations, *for a* **p** covenant.	5769
Lev	3:17 *It shall be* a **p** statute for your generations	5769
	6:20 ephah of fine flour *for* a meat offering **p**,	8548
	24: 9 of the Lord made by fire, *by* a **p** statute.	5769
	25:34 not be sold; for it *is* their possession.	5769
Nu	19:21 it shall be a **p** statute unto them, that he	5769
Ps	9: 6 destructions are come to a **p** end:	5331+3807.1
	74: 3 Lift up thy feet unto the **p** desolations;	5331
	78:66 hinder parts: he put them to a **p** reproach.	5769
Jer	5:22 *for* the bound of the sea *by a* **p** decree,	5769
	8: 5 Jerusalem slidden back *by a* **p** backsliding?	5329
	15:18 Why is my pain **p**, and my wound	5331
	18:16 make their land desolate, *and* a **p** hissing;	5769
	23:40 a shame, which shall not be forgotten.	5769
	25: 9 and a hissing, and **p** desolations.	5769
	25:12 and will make it **p** desolations.	5769
	49:13 all the cities thereof shall be **p** wastes.	5769
	50: 5 let us join ourselves to the Lord *in a* **p**	5769
	51:39 sleep a **p** sleep, and not wake, saith	5769
	51:57 *men:* and they shall sleep a **p** sleep,	5769
Eze	35: 5 Because thou hast had a **p** hatred,	5769
	35: 9 I will make thee **p** desolations,	5769
	46:14 a meat offering continually by a **p**	5769
Hab	3: 6 were scattered, the **p** hills did bow:	5769
Zep	2: 9 and saltpits, and a **p** desolation.	5704+5769

PERPETUALLY (3) [PERPETUAL]

1Ki	9: 3 heart shall be there **p**.	3117+3605+1886.1
2Ch	7:16 heart shall be there **p**.	3117+3605+1886.1
Am	1:11 his anger did tear **p**, and he kept	5703+3807.1

PERPLEXED (5) [PERPLEXITY]

Est	3:15 to drink; but the city Shushan was **p**.	943
Joel	1:18 the herds of cattle are **p**, because they	943
Lk	9: 7 and he was **p**, because that it was said of	1280
	24: 4 as they were much **p** thereabout, behold,	1280
2Co	4: 8 distressed; *we are* **p**, but not in despair;	639

PERPLEXITY (2) [PERPLEXED]

Isa	22: 5 of **p** by the Lord God of hosts in	3998
Mic	7: 4 vexation cometh; now shall be their **p**.	3998
Lk	21:25 upon the earth distress of nations, with **p**;	640

PERSECUTE (25) [PERSECUTED, PERSECUTEST, PERSECUTING, PERSECUTION, PERSECUTIONS, PERSECUTOR, PERSECUTORS]

Job	19:22 Why do ye **p** me as God, and are not	7291
	19:28 ye should say, Why **p** we him? seeing	7291
Ps	7: 1 save me from all them that **p** me,	7291
	7: 5 Let the enemy **p** my soul, and take *it*; yea,	7291
	10: 2 The wicked in *his* pride doth **p** the poor:	1814
	31:15 mine enemies, and from them that **p** me.	7291
	35: 3 and stop the *way* against them that **p** me:	7291
	35: 6 and let the angel of the Lord **p** them.	7291
	69:26 For they **p** *him* whom thou hast smitten;	7291
	71:11 **p** and take him; for *there is* none to	7291
	83:15 So **p** them with thy tempest,	7291
	119:84 execute judgment on them that **p** me?	7291
	119:86 they **p** me wrongfully; help thou me.	7291
Jer	17:18 Let them be confounded that **p** me,	7291
	29:18 I will **p** them with the sword, with	7291
La	3:66 **Persecute** and destroy them in anger from under	7291
Mt	5:11 and **p** you, and shall say all manner of evil	1377
	5:44 which despitefully use you, and **p** you;	1377
	10:23 But when they **p** you in this city, flee ye	1377
	23:34 and **p** *them* from city to city:	1377
Lk	11:49 and *some* of them they shall slay and **p**:	1559
	21:12 **p** *you*, delivering *you* up to the	1377
Jn	5:16 And therefore did the Jews **p** Jesus,	1377
	15:20 have persecuted me, they will also **p** you;	1377
Ro	12:14 Bless them which **p** you: bless,	1377

PERSECUTED (20) [PERSECUTE]

Dt	30: 7 on them that hate thee, which **p** thee.	7291
Ps	109:16 **p** the poor and needy man, that *he* might	7291
	119:161 Princes have **p** me without a cause:	7291
	143: 3 For the enemy hath **p** my soul; he hath	7291
Isa	14: 6 in anger, *is* **p**, *and* none hindereth:	4783
La	3:43 Thou hast covered with anger, and **p** us:	7291

Mt	5:10 Blessed *are* they which are **p** for	1377
	5:12 **p** they the prophets which were before	1377
Jn	15:20 If they have **p** me, they will also persecute	1377
Ac	7:52 of the prophets have not your fathers **p**?	1377
	22: 4 And I **p** this way unto the death, binding	1377
	26:11 I **p** them even unto strange cities.	1377
1Co	4:12 we bless; being **p**, we suffer *it*:	1377
	15: 9 an apostle, because I **p** the church of God.	1377
2Co	4: 9 **P**, but not forsaken; cast down,	1377
Gal	1:13 how that beyond measure I **p** the church	1377
	1:23 That he which **p** us in times past now	1377
	4:29 he that was born after the flesh **p** him that	1377
1Th	2:15 and their own prophets, and have **p** us;	1559
Rev	12:13 he **p** the woman which brought forth	1377

PERSECUTEST (6) [PERSECUTE]

Ac	9: 4 unto him, Saul, Saul, why **p** thou me?	1377
	9: 5 The Lord said, I am Jesus whom thou **p**	1377
	22: 7 unto me, Saul, Saul, why **p** thou me?	1377
	22: 8 I am Jesus of Nazareth, whom thou **p**.	1377
	26:14 Saul, Saul, why **p** thou me?	1377
	26:15 And he said, I am Jesus whom thou **p**.	1377

PERSECUTING (1) [PERSECUTE]

Php	3: 6 Concerning zeal, **p** the church; touching	1377

PERSECUTION (10) [PERSECUTE]

La	5: 5 Our necks *are* under **p**: we labour,	7291
Mt	13:21 or **p** ariseth because of the word,	1375
Mk	4:17 or **p** ariseth for the word's sake,	1375
Ac	8: 1 at that time there was a great **p** against	1375
	11:19 that arose about Stephen travelled as	2347
	13:50 and raised **p** against Paul and Barnabas,	1375
Ro	8:35 or **p**, or famine, or nakedness, or peril,	1375
Gal	5:11 why do I yet **suffer p**?	1377
	6:12 lest they should **suffer p** for the cross	1377
2Ti	3:12 live godly in Christ Jesus shall **suffer p**.	1377

PERSECUTIONS (5) [PERSECUTE]

Mk	10:30 mothers, and children, and lands, with **p**;	1375
2Co	12:10 in reproaches, in necessities, in **p**,	1375
2Th	1: 4 faith in all your **p** and tribulations that	1375
2Ti	3:11 **p**, afflictions, which came unto me at	1375
	3:11 in Iconium, at Lystra; what I endured:	1375

PERSECUTOR (1) [PERSECUTE]

1Ti	1:13 a blasphemer, and a **p**, and injurious:	1376

PERSECUTORS (8) [PERSECUTE]

Ne	9:11 and their **p** thou threwest into the deeps,	7291
Ps	7:13 he ordaineth his arrows against the **p**.	1814
	119:157 Many *are* my **p** and mine enemies; *yet* do	7291
	142: 6 deliver me from my **p**; for they are	7291
Jer	15:15 and visit me, and revenge me of my **p**;	7291
	20:11 therefore my **p** shall stumble, and they	7291
La	1: 3 all her **p** overtook her between the straits.	7291
	4:19 Our **p** are swifter than the eagles of	7291

PERSEVERANCE (1)

Eph	6:18 and watching thereunto with all **p** and	4343

PERSIA (29) [PERSIAN, PERSIANS]

2Ch	36:20 sons until the reign of the kingdom of **P**:	6539
	36:22 Now in the first year of Cyrus king of **P**,	6539
	36:22 stirred up the spirit of Cyrus king of **P**,	6539
	36:23 Thus saith Cyrus king of **P**,	6539
Ezr	1: 1 Now in the first year of Cyrus king of **P**,	6539
	1: 1 stirred up the spirit of Cyrus king of **P**,	6539
	1: 2 Thus saith Cyrus king of **P**, The Lord	6539
	1: 8 those did Cyrus king of **P** bring forth	6539
	3: 7 grant that they had of Cyrus king of **P**.	6539
	4: 3 as king Cyrus the king of **P** hath	6539
	4: 5 all the days of Cyrus king of **P**,	6539
	4: 5 even until the reign of Darius king of **P**.	6539
	4: 7 unto Artaxerxes king of **P**:	6539
	4:24 year of the reign of Darius king of **P**.	6540
	6:14 and Darius, and Artaxerxes king of **P**.	6540
	7: 1 in the reign of Artaxerxes king of **P**,	6539
	9: 9 unto us in the sight of the kings of **P**,	6539
Est	1: 3 the power of **P** and Media, the nobles	6539
	1:14 the seven princes of **P** and Media,	6539
	1:18 Likewise shall the ladies of **P** and	6539
	10: 2 chronicles of the kings of Media and **P**?	6539
Eze	27:10 They of **P** and of Lud and of Phut were in	6539
	38: 5 **P**, Ethiopia, and Libya with them; all of	6539
Da	8:20 two horns *are* the kings of Media and **P**.	6539
	10: 1 In the third year of Cyrus king of **P** a	6539
	10:13 the prince of the kingdom of **P** withstood	6539
	10:13 and I remained there with the kings of **P**.	6539
	10:20 will I return to fight with the prince of **P**:	6539
	11: 2 there *shall* stand up yet three kings in **P**;	6539

PERSIAN (2) [PERSIA]

Ne	12:22 the priests, to the reign of Darius the **P**.	6542
Da	6:28 of Darius, and in the reign of Cyrus the **P**.	6543

PERSIANS (5) [PERSIA]

Est	1:19 let it be written among the laws of the **P**	6539
Da	5:28 is divided, and given to the Medes and **P**.	6540
	6: 8 according to the law of the Medes and **P**,	6540
	6:12 according to the law of the Medes and **P**,	6540
	6:15 **P** *is*, That no decree nor statute which	6540

PERSIS (1)

Ro	16:12 Salute the beloved **P**, which laboured	4069

P

PERSON (56) [PERSONS]

Ge	39: 6 Joseph was *a* goodly **p**, and well favoured.	NIH
Ex	12:48 for no **uncircumcised p** shall eat thereof.	6189
Lev	19:15 thou shalt not respect the **p** of the poor,	6440
	19:15 the poor, nor honour the **p** of the mighty:	6440
Nu	5: 6 against the LORD, and that **p** be guilty;	5315
	19:17 an unclean **p** they shall take of the ashes	NIH
	19:18 a clean **p** shall take hyssop, and dip *it* in	376
	19:19 clean **p** shall sprinkle upon the unclean	NIH
	19:22 whatsoever the unclean **p** toucheth shall	NIH
	31:19 whosoever hath killed *any* **p**,	5315
	35:11 which killeth *any* **p** at unawares.	5315
	35:15 every one that killeth *any* **p** unawares	5315
	35:30 Whoso killeth *any* **p**, the murderer shall	5315
	35:30 one witness shall not testify against *any* **p**	5315
Dt	15:22 unclean and the clean **p** shall eat *it* alike,	NIH
	27:25 that taketh reward to slay an innocent **p**S.	1818
	28:50 which shall not regard the **p** of the old,	6440
Jos	20: 3 the slayer that killeth *any* **p** unawares	5315
	20: 9 that whosoever killeth *any* **p** at unawares	5315
1Sa	9: 2 the children of Israel a goodlier **p** than he:	376
	16:18 and a comely **p**, and the LORD *is* with him.	376
	25:35 to thy voice, and have accepted thy **p**.	6440
2Sa	4:11 wicked men have slain a righteous **p** in	376
	14:14 up *again*; neither doth God respect *any* **p**:	5315
	17:11 *and that* thou go to battle in thine own **p**.	6440
Job	13: 8 Will ye accept his **p**? will ye contend for	6440
	22:29 and he shall save the **humble p**.	5869+7807
	32:21 me not, I pray you, accept *any* man's **p**,	6440
Ps	15: 4 In whose eyes a vile **p** is contemned; but	NIH
	49:10 likewise the fool and the **brutish p** perish,	1198
	101: 4 from me: I will not know a wicked **p**.	NIH
	105:37 *there was* not *one* feeble **p** among their	NIH
Pr	6:12 A naughty **p**, a wicked man, walketh *with*	120
	18: 5 *It is* not good to accept the **p** of the wicked,	6440
	24: 8 to do evil shall be called a mischievous **p**.	1167
	28:17 to the blood of *any* **p** shall flee to the pit;	5315
Isa	32: 5 The **vile p** shall be no more called liberal,	5036
	32: 6 For the **vile p** will speak villany,	5036
Jer	43: 6 every **p** that Nebuzar-adan the captain of	5315
	52:25 men of them that were near the king's **p**,	6440
Eze	16: 5 to the lothing of thy **p**, in the day that	5315
	33: 6 and take *any* **p** from among them,	5315
	44:25 they shall come at no dead **p** to defile	120
Da	11:21 in his estate shall stand up a **vile p**, to	959
Mal	1: 8 he be pleased with thee, or accept thy **p**?	6440
Mt	22:16 *man*: for thou regardest not the **p** of men.	4383
	27:24 I am innocent of the blood of this just **p**:	NIG
Mk	12:14 *man*: for thou regardest not the **p** of men,	4383
Lk	20:21 neither acceptest thou the **p** *of any*, but	4383
1Co	5:13 from among yourselves *that* wicked **p**.	NIG
2Co	2:10 your sakes *forgave I it* in the **p** of Christ;	4383
Gal	2: 6 God accepteth no man's **p**:) for they who	4383
Eph	5: 5 nor unclean **p**, nor covetous man who is	NIG
Heb	1: 3 and the express image of his **p**,	5287
	12:16 *be* any fornicator, or profane **p**, as Esau,	NIG
2Pe	2: 5 saved Noah the eighth **p**, a preacher of	NIG

PERSONS (56) [PERSON]

Ge	14:21 Give me the **p**, and take the goods to	5315
	36: 6 all the **p** of his house, and his cattle,	5315
Ex	16:16 *according to* the number of your **p**;	5315
Lev	27: 2 the **p** *shall be* for the LORD by thy	5315
Nu	19:18 upon the **p** that were there, and upon	5315
	31:28 *both* of the **p**, and of the beeves, and of	120
	31:30 of the **p**, of the beeves, of the asses,	120
	31:35 thirty and two thousand **p** in all,	120+5315
	31:40 the **p** *were* sixteen thousand;	120+5315
	31:40 the LORD'S tribute *was* thirty and two **p**.	5315
	31:46 And sixteen thousand **p**;)	120+5315
Dt	1:17 Ye shall not respect **p** in judgment;	6440
	10:17 and a terrible, which regardeth not **p**,	6440
	10:22 into Egypt with threescore and ten **p**;	5315
	16:19 shalt not respect **p**, neither take a gift:	6440
Jdg	9: 2 *which are* threescore and ten **p**, reign over	376
	9: 4 Abimelech hired vain and light **p**,	376
	9: 5 threescore and ten **p**, upon one stone:	376
	9:18 threescore and ten **p**, upon one stone,	376
	20:39 *and* kill of the men of Israel about thirty **p**:	376
1Sa	9:22 were bidden, which *were* about thirty **p**.	376
	22:18 and five **p** that did wear a linen ephod.	376
	22:22 I have occasioned the *death* of all the **p** of	5315
2Ki	10: 6 Now the king's sons, *being* seventy **p**,	376
	10: 7 slew seventy **p**, and put their heads in	5315
2Ch	19: 7 nor respect of **p**, nor taking of gifts.	6440
Job	34:19 reprove you, if ye do secretly accept **p**.	6440
	34:19 *to him* that accepteth not the **p** of princes,	6440
Ps	26: 4 I have not sat with vain **p**, neither will I	4962
	82: 2 and accept the **p** of the wicked?	6440
Pr	12:11 he that followeth vain **p** is void of	NIH
	24:23 *It is* not good to have respect of **p** in	6440
	28:19 he that followeth after vain **p** shall have	NIH
	28:21 To have respect of **p** *is* not good: for a	6440
Jer	52:29 Jerusalem eight hundred thirty and two **p**:	5315
	52:30 the Jews seven hundred forty and five **p**:	5315
	52:30 all the **p** *were* four thousand and	5315
La	4:16 they respected not the **p** of the priests,	6440
Eze	17:17 and building forts, to cut off many **p**:	5315
	27:13 they traded the **p** of men and vessels of	5315
Jnh	4:11 are more than sixscore thousand **p**	120
Zep	3: 4 Her prophets *are* light *and* treacherous **p**:	376
Mal	1: 9 will he **regard** your **p**?	4480+5375+6440
Lk	15: 7 nine just **p** which need no repentance.	NIG
Ac	10:34 I perceive that God is no **respecter of p**:	4381
	17:17 and with the devout **p**, and in the market	NIG

Ro	2:11 For there is no **respect of p** with God.	4382
2Co	1:11 **p** thanks may be given by many on our	4383
Eph	6: 9 neither is there **respect of p** with him.	4382
Col	3:25 hath done: and there is no **respect of p**.	4382
1Ti	1:10 for perjured **p**, and if *there* be any other	NIG
Jas	2: 1 *the Lord* of glory, with **respect of p**.	4382
	2: 9 if ye **have respect to p**, ye commit sin,	4380
1Pe	1:17 **without respect of p** judgeth according	678
2Pe	3:11 what manner *of p* ought ye to be in all	NIG
Jude	1:16 words, having **men's p** in admiration	NIG

PERSUADE (9) [PERSUADED, PERSUADEST, PERSUADETH, PERSUADING, PERSUASION]

1Ki	22:20 Who shall **p** Ahab, that he may go up and	6601
	22:21 before the LORD, and said, I will **p** him.	6601
	22:22 said, Thou shalt **p** *him*, and prevail also:	6601
2Ch	32:11 Doth not Hezekiah **p** you to give over	5496
	32:15 nor **p** you on this *manner*, neither yet	5496
Isa	36:18 *Beware* lest Hezekiah **p** you, saying,	5496
Mt	28:14 we will **p** him, and secure you.	3982
2Co	5:11 the terror of the Lord, we **p** men;	3982
Gal	1:10 For do I now **p** men, or God? or do I seek	3982

PERSUADED (20) [PERSUADE]

2Ch	18: 2 **p** him to go up *with him* to Ramoth-gilead	5496
Pr	25:15 by long forbearing is a prince **p**, and a soft	6601
Mt	27:20 elders the multitude that they should	3982
Lk	16:31 and the prophets, neither will they be **p**,	3982
	20: 6 for they be **p** that John was a prophet.	3982
Ac	13:43 **p** them to continue in the grace of God.	3982
	14:19 and Iconium, who **p** the people, and,	3982
	18: 4 and **p** *the* Jews and *the* Greeks.	3982
	19:26 this Paul hath **p** and turned away much	3982
	21:14 And when he would not be **p**, we ceased,	3982
	26:26 for I am **p** that none of these *things* are	3982
Ro	4:21 And being **fully p** that, what he had	4135
	8:38 For I am **p**, that neither death, nor life,	3982
	14: 5 Let every man be **fully p** in his own mind.	4135
	14:14 I know, and am **p** by the Lord Jesus,	3982
	15:14 And I myself also am **p** of you,	3982
2Ti	1: 5 Eunice; and I am **p** that in thee also.	3982
	1:12 I am **p** that he is able to keep that which I	3982
Heb	6: 9 we are **p** better *things* of you,	3982
	11:13 and were **p** of *them*, and embraced *them*,	3982

PERSUADEST (1) [PERSUADE]

Ac	26:28 Almost thou **p** me to be a Christian.	3982

PERSUADETH (2) [PERSUADE]

2Ki	18:32 unto Hezekiah, when he **p** you, saying,	5496
Ac	18:13 This *fellow* **p** men to worship God	374

PERSUADING (2) [PERSUADE]

Ac	19: 8 **p** the things concerning the kingdom of	3982
	28:23 **p** them concerning Jesus, both out of	3982

PERSUASION (1) [PERSUADE]

Gal	5: 8 This **p** *cometh* not of him that calleth you.	3988

PERTAIN (6) [PERTAINED, PERTAINETH, PERTAINING]

Lev	7:20 that **p** unto the LORD, having his	NIH
	7:21 which **p** unto the LORD, even that soul	NIH
1Sa	25:22 I leave of all that **p** to him by the morning	NIH
Ro	15:17 Christ *in those things* which **p** to God.	NIH
1Co	6: 3 how much more *things* that **p** to *this* life?	982
2Pe	1: 3 given unto us all *things* that **p** unto life	NIG

PERTAINED (17) [PERTAIN]

Nu	31:43 the half that **p** unto the congregation	NIH
Jos	24:33 buried him in a hill that **p** to Phinehas	NIH
Jdg	6:11 Ophrah, that **p** unto Joash the Abi-ezrite:	NIH
1Sa	25:21 that nothing was missed of all that **p**	NIH
2Sa	2:15 which **p** to Ish-bosheth the son of Saul,	NIH
	9: 9 have given unto thy master's son all that **p**	1961
	16: 4 thine *are* all that **p** unto Mephibosheth.	NIH
1Ki	4:10 to him *of* Sochoh, and all the land of	NIH
	4:12 *to him* Taanach and Megiddo,	NIH
	4:13 to him **p** the towns of Jair the son of	NIH
	4:13 to him *also* **p** the region of Argob, which *is*	NIH
	7:48 Solomon made all the vessels that **p** unto	NIH
2Ki	24: 7 Euphrates all that **p** to the king of Egypt.	1961
1Ch	9:27 the opening *thereof* every morning **p** to	5921
	11:31 that **p** to the children of Benjamin,	NIH
2Ch	12: 4 took the fenced cities which **p** to Judah,	NIH
	34:33 countries that **p** to the children of Israel,	NIH

PERTAINETH (8) [PERTAIN]

Lev	14:32 hand is not able to get *that which* **p**	NIH
Nu	4:16 of Aaron the priest **p** the oil for the light,	NIH
Dt	22: 5 The woman shall not wear **that which p**	3627
1Sa	27: 1 Ziklag **p** unto the kings of Judah	1961
2Sa	6:12 all that **p** unto him, because of the ark of	NIH
2Ch	26:18 said unto thee, *It* **p** not unto thee, Uzziah,	NIH
Ro	9: 4 to whom **p** the adoption, and the glory,	NIG
Heb	7:13 these *things* are spoken **p** to another tribe,	3348

PERTAINING (8) [PERTAIN]

Jos	13:31 **p** unto the children of Machir the son	NIH
1Ch	26:32 for every matter **p** to God, and affairs of	NIH
Ac	1: 3 speaking of the *things* **p** to the kingdom	4012
Ro	4: 1 our father, **as p** to the flesh, hath found?	2596
1Co	6: 4 ye have judgments *of things* **p** to *this* life,	982
Heb	2:17 and faithful high priest in *things* **p** to God,	4314
	5: 1 is ordained for men *in things* **p** to God,	4314
	9: 9 service perfect, as to the conscience;	2596

PERUDA (1) [PERIDA]

Ezr	2:55 children of Sophereth, the children of P,	6514

PERVERSE (20) [PERVERT]

Nu	22:32 because *thy* way is **p** before me:	3399
Dt	32: 5 *they are* a **p** and crooked generation.	6141
1Sa	20:30 Thou son of the **p** rebellious *woman*, do	5753
Job	6:30 cannot my taste discern **p** things?	1942
	9:20 I *am* perfect, it shall also **prove** me **p**.	6140
Pr	4:24 and **p** lips put far from thee.	3891
	8: 8 *there is* nothing froward or **p** in them.	6141
	12: 8 he that is of a **p** heart shall be despised.	5753
	14: 2 he that is **p** in his ways despiseth him.	3868
	17:20 he that hath a **p** tongue falleth into	2015
	19: 1 than *he that is* **p** in his lips, and *is* a fool.	6141
	23:33 and thine heart shall utter **p** things.	8419
	28: 6 than *he that is* **p** in his ways, though he	6141
	28:18 *he that is* **p** in *his* ways shall fall at once.	6140
Isa	19:14 hath mingled a **p** spirit in	5773
Mt	17:17 and said, O faithless and **p** generation,	1294
Lk	9:41 O faithless and **p** generation,	1294
Ac	20:30 speaking **p** *things*, to draw away disciples	1294
Php	2:15 in the midst of a crooked and **p** nation,	1294
1Ti	6: 5 **P disputings** of men of corrupt minds,	3859

PERVERSELY (3) [PERVERT]

2Sa	19:19 **did p** the day that my lord the king went	5753
1Ki	8:47 We have sinned, and have **done p**,	5753
Ps	119:78 for they **dealt p with** me without a cause:	5791

PERVERSENESS (6) [PERVERT]

Nu	23:21 in Jacob, neither hath he seen **p** in Israel:	5999
Pr	11: 3 the **p** of transgressors shall destroy them.	5558
	15: 4 but **p** therein *is* a breach in the spirit.	5558
Isa	30:12 trust in oppression and **p**, and stay	3868
	59: 3 spoken lies, your tongue hath muttered **p**.	5766
Eze	9: 9 land is full of blood, and the city full of **p**:	4297

PERVERT (10) [PERVERSE, PERVERSELY, PERVERSENESS, PERVERTED, PERVERTETH, PERVERTING]

Dt	16:19 wise, and **p** the words of the righteous.	5557
	24:17 Thou shalt not **p** the judgment of the	5186
Job	8: 3 Doth God **p** judgment? or doth	5791
	8: 3 or doth the Almighty **p** justice?	5791
	34:12 neither will the Almighty **p** judgment.	5791
Pr	17:23 of the bosom to **p** the ways of judgment.	5186
	31: 5 **p** the judgment of any of the afflicted.	8138
Mic	3: 9 that abhor judgment, and **p** all equity.	6140
Ac	13:10 wilt thou not cease to **p** the right ways of	1294
Gal	1: 7 and would **p** the gospel of Christ.	3344

PERVERTED (5) [PERVERT]

1Sa	8: 3 and took bribes, and **p** judgment.	5186
Job	33:27 **p** *that which was* right, and it profited me	5753
Isa	47:10 and thy knowledge, it hath **p** thee;	7725
Jer	3:21 for they have **p** their way, *and* they have	5753
	23:36 for ye have **p** the words of the living God,	2015

PERVERTETH (5) [PERVERT]

Ex	23: 8 wise, and **p** the words of the righteous.	5557
Dt	27:19 Cursed *be* he that **p** the judgment of	5186
Pr	10: 9 but he that **p** his ways shall be known.	6140
	19: 3 The foolishness of a man **p** his way:	5557
Lk	23:14 man unto me, as one that **p** the people:	654

PERVERTING (2) [PERVERT]

Ecc	5: 8 **violent p** of judgment and justice in a	1499
Lk	23: 2 We found this *fellow* **p** the nation,	1294

PESTILENCE (47) [PESTILENCES, PESTILENT]

Ex	5: 3 lest he fall upon us with **p**, or with	1698
	9:15 I may smite thee and thy people with **p**;	1698
Lev	26:25 your cities, I will send the **p** among you;	1698
Nu	14:12 I will smite them with the **p**,	1698
Dt	28:21 The LORD shall make the **p** cleave unto	1698
2Sa	24:13 or that there be three days' **p** in thy land?	1698
	24:15 So the LORD sent a **p** upon Israel from	1698
1Ki	8:37 if there be **p**, blasting, mildew, locust,	1698
1Ch	21:12 even the **p**, in the land, and the angel of	1698
	21:14 So the LORD sent **p** upon Israel:	1698
2Ch	6:28 if there be **p**, if there be blasting,	1698
	7:13 the land, or if I send **p** among my people;	1698
	20: 9 *as* the sword, judgment, or **p**, or famine;	1698
Ps	78:50 death, but gave their life over to the **p**;	1698
	91: 3 of the fowler, *and* from the noisome **p**.	1698
	91: 6 *Nor* for the **p** *that* walketh in darkness;	1698
Jer	14:12 sword, and by the famine, and by the **p**.	1698
	21: 6 and beast: they shall die of a great **p**.	1698
	21: 7 and such as are left in this city from the **p**,	1698
	21: 9 sword, and by the famine, and by the **p**:	1698
	24:10 the famine, and the **p**, among them,	1698
	27: 8 and with the famine, and with the **p**,	1698
	27:13 the sword, by the famine, and by the **p**?	1698
	28: 8 of war, and of evil, and of **p**.	1698
	29:17 the **p**, and will make them like vile figs,	1698
	29:18 with the sword, and I will deliver them to be	1698
	32:24 sword, and *of* the famine, and *of* the **p**:	1698
	32:36 sword, and by the famine, and by the **p**;	1698
	34:17 to the sword, to the **p**, and to the famine;	1698
	38: 2 the sword, by the famine, and by the **p**:	1698
	42:17 the sword, by the famine, and by the **p**:	1698
	42:22 by the famine, and by the **p**, in the place	1698
	44:13 the sword, by the famine, and by the **p**:	1698
Eze	5:12 A third *part* of thee shall die with the **p**,	1698

Eze	5:17 **p** and blood shall pass through thee;	1698
	6:11 the sword, by the famine, and by the **p.**	1698
	6:12 *He* that *is* far off shall die of the **p;**	1698
	7:15 without, and the **p** and the famine	1698
	7:15 in the city, famine and **p** shall devour him:	1698
	12:16 sword, from the famine, and from the **p;**	1698
	14:19 *if* I send a **p** into that land, and pour out	1698
	14:21 and the noisome beast, and the **p,**	1698
	28:23 For I will send into her **p,** and blood into	1698
	33:27 forts and in the caves shall die of the **p.**	1698
	38:22 I will plead against him with **p** and	1698
Am	4:10 I have sent among you the **p** after	1698
Hab	3: 5 Before him went the **p,** and burning coals	1698

PESTILENCES (2) [PESTILENCE]

Mt	24: 7 and **p,** and earthquakes in divers places.	3061
Lk	21:11 be in divers places, and famines, and **p;**	3061

PESTILENT (1) [PESTILENCE]

Ac	24: 5 For we have found this man a **p** *fellow,*	3061

PESTLE (1)

Pr	27:22 a fool in a mortar among wheat with a **p,**	5940

PETER (158) [CEPHAS, PETER'S, SIMON]

Mt	4:18 Simon called **P,** and Andrew his brother,	4074
	10: 2 who is called **P,** and Andrew his brother;	4074
	14:28 **P** answered him and said, Lord, if it be	4074
	14:29 And when **P** was come down out of	4074
	15:15 Then answered **P** and said unto him,	4074
	16:16 Simon **P** answered and said, Thou art	4074
	16:18 That thou art **P,** and upon this rock I will	4074
	16:22 **P** took him, and began to rebuke him,	4074
	16:23 But he turned, and said unto **P,** Get thee	4074
	17: 1 And after six days Jesus taketh **P,** James,	4074
	17: 4 Then answered **P,** and said unto Jesus,	4074
	17:24 that received tribute money came to **P,**	4074
	17:26 **P** saith unto him, Of strangers. Jesus saith	4074
	18:21 Then came **P** to him, and said, Lord,	4074
	19:27 Then answered **P** and said unto him,	4074
	26:33 **P** answered and said unto him, Though	4074
	26:35 **P** said unto him, Though I should die	4074
	26:37 And he took with *him* **P** and the two sons	4074
	26:40 they were asleep, and saith unto **P,** What,	4074
	26:58 But **P** followed him afar off unto the high	4074
	26:69 Now **P** sat without in the palace:	4074
	26:73 *him* they that stood *by,* and said to **P,**	4074
	26:75 And **P** remembered the word of Jesus,	4074
Mk	3:16 And Simon he surnamed **P;**	4074
	5:37 save **P,** and James, and John the brother	4074
	8:29 And **P** answereth and saith unto him,	4074
	8:32 **P** took him, and began to rebuke him.	4074
	8:33 rebuked **P,** saying, Get thee behind me,	4074
	9: 2 after six days Jesus taketh with *him* **P,**	4074
	9: 5 And **P** answered and said to Jesus, Master,	4074
	10:28 **P** began to say unto him, Lo, we have	4074
	11:21 And **P** calling to remembrance saith unto	4074
	13: 3 **P** and James and John and Andrew asked	4074
	14:29 But **P** said unto him, Although all shall be	4074
	14:33 And he taketh with him **P** and James and	4074
	14:37 and saith unto **P,** Simon, sleepest thou?	4074
	14:54 And **P** followed him afar off, even into	4074
	14:66 As as **P** was beneath in the palace,	4074
	14:67 And when she saw **P** warming himself,	4074
	14:70 they that stood by said again to **P,**	4074
	14:72 And **P** called to mind the word that Jesus	4074
	16: 7 that he goeth before you into Galilee:	4074
Lk	5: 8 When Simon **P** saw *it,* he fell down at	4074
	6:14 Simon, (whom he also named **P,**) and	4074
	8:45 And they that were with him said,	4074
	8:51 he suffered no *man* to go in, save **P,**	4074
	9:20 **P** answering said, The Christ of God.	4074
	9:28 took **P** and John and James, and went up	4074
	9:32 But **P** and they that were with him were	4074
	9:33 from him, **P** said unto Jesus, Master,	4074
	12:41 **P** said unto him, Lord, speakest thou	4074
	18:28 Then **P** said, Lo, we have left all,	4074
	22: 8 And he sent **P** and John, saying, Go and	4074
	22:34 And he said, I tell thee, **P,** *the* cock shall	4074
	22:54 priest's house. And **P** followed afar off.	4074
	22:55 down together, **P** sat down among them.	4074
	22:58 also of them. And **P** said, Man, I am not.	4074
	22:60 And **P** said, Man, I know not what thou	4074
	22:61 And the Lord turned, and looked upon **P.**	4074
	22:61 And **P** remembered the word of the Lord,	4074
	22:62 And **P** went out,	4074
	24:12 Then arose **P,** and ran unto the sepulchre;	4074
Jn	1:44 of Bethsaida, the city of Andrew and **P.**	4074
	6:68 Then Simon **P** answered him, Lord,	4074
	13: 6 Then cometh he to Simon **P:**	4074
	13: 6 **P** saith unto him, Lord, dost thou wash	NIG
	13: 8 **P** saith unto him, Thou shalt never wash	4074
	13: 9 Simon **P** saith unto him, Lord, not my feet	4074
	13:24 Simon **P** therefore beckoned to him, that	4074
	13:36 Simon **P** said unto him, Lord, whither	4074
	13:37 **P** said unto him, Lord, why cannot I	4074
	18:10 Then Simon **P** having a sword drew it,	4074
	18:11 Then said Jesus unto **P,** Put up thy sword	4074
	18:15 And Simon **P** followed Jesus, and *so*	4074
	18:16 But **P** stood at the door without. Then	4074
	18:16 her that kept the door, and brought in **P.**	4074
	18:17 the damsel that kept the door unto **P,**	4074
	18:18 and **P** stood with them,	4074
	18:25 And Simon **P** stood and warmed himself.	4074
	18:26 being *his* kinsman whose ear **P** cut off,	4074

Jn	18:27 **P** then denied again: and immediately	4074
	20: 2 and cometh to Simon **P,** and to the other	4074
	20: 3 **P** therefore went forth, and *that* other	4074
	20: 4 and the other disciple did outrun **P,**	4074
	20: 6 Then cometh Simon **P** following him,	4074
	21: 2 There were together Simon **P,**	4074
	21: 3 Simon **P** saith unto them, I go a fishing.	4074
	21: 7 disciple whom Jesus loved saith unto **P,**	4074
	21: 7 Now when Simon **P** heard that it was	4074
	21:11 Simon **P** went up, and drew the net to	4074
	21:15 Jesus saith to Simon **P,** Simon, *son of*	4074
	21:17 **P** was grieved because he said unto him	4074
	21:20 Then **P,** turning about, seeth the disciple	4074
	21:21 **P** seeing him saith to Jesus, Lord,	4074
Ac	1:13 abode both **P,** and James, and John,	4074
	1:15 And in those days **P** stood up in the midst	4074
	2:14 But **P,** standing up with the eleven, lift up	4074
	2:37 and said unto **P** and *to* the rest of	4074
	2:38 Then **P** said unto them, Repent,	4074
	3: 1 Now **P** and John went up together into	4074
	3: 3 Who seeing **P** and John about to go into	4074
	3: 4 And **P,** fastening his eyes upon him with	4074
	3: 6 Then **P** said, Silver and gold have I none;	4074
	3:11 the lame *man* which was healed held **P**	4074
	3:12 And when **P** saw *it,* he answered unto	4074
	4: 8 Then **P,** filled with the Holy Ghost,	4074
	4:13 when they saw the boldness of **P** and	4074
	4:19 But **P** and John answered and said unto	4074
	5: 3 But **P** said, Ananias, why hath Satan filled	4074
	5: 8 **P** answered unto her, Tell me whether	4074
	5: 9 Then **P** said unto her, How *is it* that ye	4074
	5:15 that at the least the shadow of **P** passing	4074
	5:29 Then **P** and the *other* apostles answered	4074
	8:14 of God, they sent unto them **P** and John:	4074
	8:20 But **P** said unto him, Thy money perish	4074
	9:32 as **P** passed throughout all *quarters,* he	4074
	9:34 And **P** said unto him, Aeneas, Jesus Christ	4074
	9:38 the disciples had heard that **P** was there,	4074
	9:39 Then **P** arose and went with them.	4074
	9:40 But **P** put *them* all forth,	4074
	9:40 eyes: and when she saw **P,** she sat up.	4074
	10: 5 call for *one* Simon, whose surname is **P:**	4074
	10: 9 **P** went up upon the house to pray about	4074
	10:13 And there came a voice to him, Rise, **P;**	4074
	10:14 But **P** said, Not so, Lord; for I have never	4074
	10:17 while **P** doubted in himself what this	4074
	10:18 was surnamed **P,** were lodged there.	4074
	10:19 While **P** thought on the vision, the Spirit	4074
	10:21 **P** went down to the men which were	4074
	10:23 lodged *them.* And on the morrow **P** went	4074
	10:25 And as **P** was coming in, Cornelius met	4074
	10:26 But **P** took him up, saying, Stand up:	4074
	10:32 call hither Simon, whose surname is **P;**	4074
	10:34 Then **P** opened *his* mouth, and said, Of a	4074
	10:44 While **P** yet spake these words, the Holy	4074
	10:45 as many as came with **P,** because that on	4074
	10:46 and magnify God. Then answered **P,**	4074
	11: 2 And when **P** was come up to Jerusalem,	4074
	11: 4 But **P** *rehearsed the matter* from	4074
	11: 7 I heard a voice saying unto me, Arise, **P;**	4074
	11:13 and call for Simon, whose surname is **P;**	4074
	12: 3 he proceeded further to take **P** also.	4074
	12: 5 **P** therefore was kept in prison:	4074
	12: 6 the same night **P** was sleeping between	4074
	12: 7 he smote **P** on the side, and raised him	4074
	12:11 when **P** was come to himself, he said,	4074
	12:13 And as **P** knocked at the door of the gate,	4074
	12:14 and told how **P** stood before the gate.	4074
	12:16 **P** continued knocking: and when they	4074
	12:18 the soldiers, what was become of **P.**	4074
	15: 7 **P** rose up, and said unto them, Men *and*	4074
Gal	1:18 years I went up to Jerusalem to see **P,**	4074
	2: 7 *gospel* of the circumcision *was* unto **P;**	4074
	2: 8 (For he that wrought effectually in **P** to	4074
	2:11 But when **P** was come to Antioch,	4074
	2:14 I said unto **P** before *them* all, If thou,	4074
1Pe	1: 1 an apostle of Jesus Christ,	4074
2Pe	1: 1 Simon **P,** a servant and an apostle of Jesus	4074

PETER'S (4) [PETER]

Mt	8:14 when Jesus was come into **P** house,	4074
Jn	1:40 was Andrew, Simon **P** brother.	4074
	6: 8 Andrew, Simon **P** brother, saith unto him,	4074
Ac	12:14 And when she knew **P** voice, she opened	4074

PETHAHIAH (4)

1Ch	24:16 The nineteenth to **P,** the twentieth to	6611
Ezr	10:23 same *is* Kelita,) **P,** Judah, and Eliezer.	6611
Ne	9: 5 *and* **P,** said, Stand up *and* bless the LORD	6611
	11:24 **P** the son of Meshezabeel, of the children	6611

PETHOR (2)

Nu	22: 5 unto Balaam the son of Beor to **P,**	6604
Dt	23: 4 the son of Beor of **P** of Mesopotamia,	6604

PETHUEL (1)

Joel	1: 1 the LORD that came to Joel the son of **P.**	6602

PETITION (13) [PETITIONS]

1Sa	1:17 God of Israel grant *thee* thy **p** that thou	7596
	1:27 the Lord hath given me my **p** which I	7596
1Ki	2:16 now I **ask** one **p** of thee, deny me	7592+7596
	2:20 said, I desire one small **p** of thee; *I pray*	7596
Est	5: 6 at the banquet of wine, What *is* thy **p?**	7596
	5: 7 and said, My **p** and my request *is;*	7596

Est	5: 8 if it please the king to grant my **p,**	7596
	7: 2 of wine, What is *thy* **p,** queen Esther?	7596
	7: 3 let my life be given me at my **p,**	7596
	9:12 now what *is* thy **p?** and it shall be granted	7596
Da	6: 7 that whosoever shall ask a **p** of any God	1159
	6:12 every man that shall ask *a* **p** of any God	NIH
	6:13 **maketh** his **p** three times a day.	1156+1159

PETITIONS (2) [PETITION]

Ps	20: 5 up *our* banners: the LORD fulfil all thy **p.**	4862
1Jn	5:15 know that we have the **p** that we desired	155

PEULLETHAI See PEULTHAI

PEULTHAI (1)

1Ch	26: 5 sixth, Issachar the seventh, **P** the eighth:	6469

PHALEC (1) [PELEG]

Lk	3:35 was *the son* of **P,** which was *the son*	5317

PHALLU (1)

Ge	46: 9 Hanoch, and **P,** and Hezron, and Carmi.	6396

PHALTI (1) [PHALTIEL]

1Sa	25:44 David's wife, to **P** the son of Laish,	6406

PHALTIEL (1) [PHALTI]

2Sa	3:15 husband, *even* from **P** the son of Laish.	6409

PHANUEL (1)

Lk	2:36 prophetess, the daughter of **P,** of the tribe	5323

PHARAOH (225) [PHARAOH'S, PHARAOH-HOPHRA, PHARAOH-NECHO, PHARAOH-NECHOH]

Ge	12:15 The princes also of **P** saw her,	6547
	12:15 saw her, and commended her before **P:**	6547
	12:17 the LORD plagued **P** and his house with	6547
	12:18 **P** called Abram, and said, What *is* this	6547
	12:20 **P** commanded *his* men concerning him:	6547
	39: 1 Potiphar, an officer of **P,** captain of	6547
	40: 2 **P** was wroth against two *of* his officers,	6547
	40:13 Yet within three days shall **P** lift up thine	6547
	40:14 make mention of me unto **P,** and bring	6547
	40:17 *was* of all *manner of* bakemeats for **P;**	6547
	40:19 Yet within three days shall **P** lift up thy	6547
	41: 1 the end of two full years, that **P** dreamed:	6547
	41: 4 well favoured and fat kine. So **P** awoke.	6547
	41: 7 **P** awoke, and, behold, *it was* a dream.	6547
	41: 8 **P** told them his dream; but *there was*	6547
	41: 8 none that could interpret them unto **P.**	6547
	41: 9 spake the chief butler unto **P,** saying, I do	6547
	41:10 **P** was wroth with his servants, and put	6547
	41:14 **P** sent and called Joseph, and they	6547
	41:14 changed his raiment, and came in unto **P.**	6547
	41:15 **P** said unto Joseph, I have dreamed a	6547
	41:16 Joseph answered **P,** saying, It is not in me	6547
	41:16 God shall give **P** an answer of peace.	6547
	41:17 **P** said unto Joseph, In my dream, behold,	6547
	41:25 Joseph said unto **P,** The dream of Pharaoh	6547
	41:25 said unto Pharaoh, The dream of **P** *is* one:	6547
	41:25 God hath shewed **P** what he *is* about to	6547
	41:28 *is* the thing which I have spoken unto **P:**	6547
	41:28 God *is* about to do he sheweth unto **P.**	6547
	41:32 for that the dream was doubled unto **P**	6547
	41:33 let **P** look out a man discreet and wise,	6547
	41:34 Let **P** do *this,* and let him appoint officers	6547
	41:35 lay up corn under the hand of **P,**	6547
	41:37 the thing was good in the eyes of **P,**	6547
	41:38 **P** said unto his servants, Can we find	6547
	41:39 **P** said unto Joseph, Forasmuch as God	6547
	41:41 **P** said unto Joseph, See, I have set thee	6547
	41:42 **P** took off his ring from his hand, and put	6547
	41:44 **P** said unto Joseph, I *am* Pharaoh,	6547
	41:44 I *am* **P,** and without thee shall no man lift	6547
	41:45 **P** called Joseph's name Zaphnath-paaneah;	6547
	41:46 old when he stood before **P** king of Egypt.	6547
	41:46 Joseph went out from the presence of **P,**	6547
	41:55 the people cried to **P** for bread:	6547
	41:55 **P** said unto all the Egyptians, Go unto	6547
	42:15 By the life of **P** ye shall not go forth hence,	6547
	42:16 or else by the life of **P** surely ye *are* spies.	6547
	44:18 against thy servant: for thou *art* even as **P.**	6547
	45: 2 the Egyptians and the house of **P** heard.	6547
	45: 8 he hath made me a father to **P,** and lord	6547
	45:16 and it pleased **P** well, and his servants.	6547
	45:17 **P** said unto Joseph, Say unto thy brethren,	6547
	45:21 according to the commandment of **P,**	6547
	46: 5 in the wagons which **P** had sent to carry	6547
	46:31 will go up, and shew **P,** and say unto him,	6547
	46:33 when **P** shall call you, and shall say,	6547
	47: 1 Joseph came and told **P,** and said,	6547
	47: 2 five men, and presented them unto **P.**	6547
	47: 3 **P** said unto his brethren, What *is* your	6547
	47: 3 they said unto **P,** Thy servants *are*	6547
	47: 4 They said moreover unto **P,** For to	6547
	47: 5 **P** spake unto Joseph, saying, Thy father	6547
	47: 7 in Jacob his father, and set him before **P:**	6547
	47: 7 him before Pharaoh: and Jacob blessed **P.**	6547
	47: 8 And **P** said unto Jacob, How old *art* thou?	6547
	47: 9 Jacob said unto **P,** The days of the years	6547
	47:10 Jacob blessed **P,** and went out from before	6547
	47:10 and went out from before **P.**	6547
	47:11 land of Rameses, as **P** had commanded.	6547
	47:19 we and our land will be servants unto **P:**	6547
	47:20 Joseph bought all the land of Egypt for **P;**	6547

Ge	47:22	priests had a portion assigned them of **P**,	6547
	47:22	did eat their portion which **P** gave them:	6547
	47:23	bought you *this* day and your land for **P**:	6547
	47:24	that you shall give the fifth *part* unto **P**,	6547
	47:26	*that* **P** should have the fifth *part*; except	6547
	50: 4	Joseph spake unto the house of **P**, saying,	6547
	50: 4	speak, I pray you, in the ears of **P**, saying,	6547
	50: 6	**P** said, Go up, and bury thy father,	6547
	50: 7	with him went up all the servants of **P**,	6547
Ex	1:11	they built for **P** treasure cities, Pithom and	6547
	1:19	the midwives said unto **P**, Because	6547
	1:22	**P** charged all his people, saying, Every son	6547
	2: 5	the daughter of **P** came down to wash	6547
	2:15	when **P** heard this thing, he sought to	6547
	2:15	Moses fled from the face of **P**, and dwelt	6547
	3:10	therefore, and I will send thee unto **P**,	6547
	3:11	that I should go unto **P**, and that I should	6547
	4:21	that thou do all *those* wonders before **P**,	6547
	4:22	thou shalt say unto **P**, Thus saith	6547
	5: 1	and Aaron went in, and told **P**,	6547
	5: 2	**P** said, Who *is* the LORD, that I should	6547
	5: 5	**P** said, Behold, the people of the land	6547
	5: 6	**P** commanded the same day	6547
	5:10	spake to the people, saying, Thus saith **P**,	6547
	5:15	children of Israel came and cried unto **P**,	6547
	5:20	in the way, as they came forth from **P**:	6547
	5:21	savour to be abhorred in the eyes of **P**,	6547
	5:23	since I came to **P** to speak in thy name,	6547
	6: 1	Now shalt thou see what I will do to **P**:	6547
	6:11	Go in, speak unto **P** king of Egypt, that he	6547
	6:12	how then shall **P** hear me, who *am* of	6547
	6:13	of Israel, and unto **P** king of Egypt,	6547
	6:27	*These are* they which spake to **P** king of	6547
	6:29	speak thou unto **P** king of Egypt all that I	6547
	6:30	and how shall **P** hearken unto me?	6547
	7: 1	See, I have made thee a god to **P**:	6547
	7: 2	Aaron thy brother shall speak unto **P**,	6547
	7: 4	**P** shall not hearken unto you, that I may	6547
	7: 7	three years old, when they spake unto **P**.	6547
	7: 9	When **P** shall speak unto you, saying,	6547
	7: 9	cast *it* before **P**, *and* it shall become a	6547
	7:10	Moses and Aaron went in unto **P**,	6547
	7:10	Aaron cast down his rod before **P**,	6547
	7:11	**P** also called the wise men and	6547
	7:15	Get thee unto **P** in the morning;	6547
	7:20	in the sight of **P**, and in the sight of his	6547
	7:23	**P** turned and went into his house,	6547
	8: 1	Go unto **P**, and say unto him, Thus saith	6547
	8: 8	**P** called for Moses and Aaron, and said,	6547
	8: 9	Moses said unto **P**, Glory over me: when	6547
	8:12	Moses and Aaron went out from **P**:	6547
	8:12	the frogs which he had brought against **P**.	6547
	8:15	when **P** saw that there was respite,	6547
	8:19	magicians said unto **P**, This *is* the finger	6547
	8:20	early in the morning, and stand before **P**;	6547
	8:24	swarm *of flies* into the house of **P**,	6547
	8:25	**P** called for Moses and for Aaron, and	6547
	8:28	**P** said, I will let you go, that ye may	6547
	8:29	the swarms *of flies* may depart from **P**,	6547
	8:29	let not **P** deal deceitfully any more in not	6547
	8:30	Moses went out from **P**, and intreated	6547
	8:31	he removed the swarms *of flies* from **P**,	6547
	8:32	**P** hardened his heart at this time also,	6547
	9: 1	unto Moses, Go in unto **P**, and tell him,	6547
	9: 7	**P** sent, and behold, there was not one of	6547
	9: 7	the heart of **P** was hardened, and he did	6547
	9: 8	it towards the heaven in the sight of **P**.	6547
	9:10	ashes of the furnace, and stood before **P**;	6547
	9:12	the LORD hardened the heart of **P**,	6547
	9:13	and stand before **P**, and say unto him,	6547
	9:20	the servants of **P** made his servants	6547
	9:27	**P** sent, and called for Moses and Aaron,	6547
	9:33	Moses went out of the city from **P**,	6547
	9:34	when **P** saw that the rain and the hail and	6547
	9:35	the heart of **P** was hardened, neither	6547
	10: 1	the LORD said unto Moses, Go in unto **P**:	6547
	10: 3	Moses and Aaron came in unto **P**,	6547
	10: 6	he turned himself, and went out from **P**.	6547
	10: 8	and Aaron were brought again unto **P**:	6547
	10:16	**P** called for Moses and Aaron in haste;	6547
	10:18	he went out from **P**, and intreated	6547
	10:24	called unto Moses, and said, Go ye,	6547
	10:28	**P** said unto him, Get thee from me,	6547
	11: 1	Yet will I bring one plague *more* upon **P**,	6547
	11: 5	from the firstborn of **P** that sitteth upon	6547
	11: 8	And he went out from **P** in a great anger.	6547
	11: 9	unto Moses, **P** shall not hearken unto you;	6547
	11:10	and Aaron did all these wonders before **P**:	6547
	12:29	from the firstborn of **P** that sat on his	6547
	12:30	**P** rose up in the night, he, and all his	6547
	13:15	to pass, when **P** would hardly let us go,	6547
	13:17	to pass, when **P** had let the people go,	6547
	14: 3	For **P** will say of the children of Israel,	6547
	14: 4	I will be honoured upon **P**, and upon all	6547
	14: 5	the heart of **P** and of his servants was	6547
	14: 8	the LORD hardened the heart of **P** king of	6547
	14: 9	them (all the horses *and* chariots of **P**,	6547
	14:10	**P** drew nigh, the children of Israel lift	6547
	14:17	I will get me honour upon **P**, and upon	6547
	14:18	when I have gotten me honour upon **P**,	6547
	14:28	all the host of **P** that came into the sea	6547
	15:19	the horse of **P** went in with his chariots	6547
	18: 4	and delivered me from the sword of **P**:	6547
	18: 8	in all that the LORD had done unto **P**	6547
	18:10	the Egyptians, out of the hand of **P**,	6547

Dt	6:22	upon **P**, and upon all his household,	6547
	7: 8	from the hand of **P** king of Egypt.	6547
	7:18	what the LORD thy God did unto **P**,	6547
	11: 3	he did in the midst of Egypt unto **P**	6547
	29: 2	your eyes in the land of Egypt unto **P**,	6547
	34:11	sent him to do in the land of Egypt to **P**,	6547
1Sa	6: 6	Egyptians and **P** hardened their hearts?	6547
1Ki	3: 1	Solomon made affinity with **P** king of	6547
	9:16	For **P** king of Egypt had gone up,	6547
	11: 1	together with the daughter of **P**, *women*	6547
	11:18	they came *to* Egypt, unto **P** king of Egypt;	6547
	11:19	found great favour in the sight of **P**,	6547
	11:20	household among the sons of **P**.	6547
	11:21	Hadad said to **P**, Let me depart, that I	6547
	11:22	**P** said unto him, But what *hast* thou	6547
2Ki	17: 7	from under the hand of **P** king of Egypt,	6547
	18:21	*is* **P** king of Egypt unto all that trust on	6547
	23:35	gave the silver and the gold to **P**;	6547
	23:35	according to the commandment of **P**:	6547
2Ch	8:11	Solomon brought up the daughter of **P**	6547
Ne	9: 9	shewedst signs and wonders upon **P**,	6547
Ps	135: 9	Egypt, upon **P**, and upon all his servants.	6547
	136:15	overthrew **P** and his host in the Red sea:	6547
Isa	19:11	the counsel of the wise counsellers of **P** is	6547
	19:11	how say ye unto **P**, I *am* the son of	6547
	30: 2	themselves in the strength of **P**,	6547
	30: 3	Therefore shall the strength of **P** be your	6547
	36: 6	*is* **P** king of Egypt to all that trust in him.	6547
Jer	25:19	**P** king of Egypt, and his servants, and his	6547
	46:17	cry there, **P** king of Egypt *is but* a noise;	6547
	46:25	**P**, and Egypt, with their gods, and their	6547
	46:25	even **P**, and *all* them that trust in him:	6547
	47: 1	the Philistines, before that **P** smote Gaza.	6547
Eze	17:17	Neither shall **P** with *his* mighty army and	6547
	29: 2	set thy face against **P** king of Egypt,	6547
	29: 3	I *am* against thee, **P** king of Egypt,	6547
	30:21	I have broken the arm of **P** king of Egypt;	6547
	30:22	I *am* against **P** king of Egypt,	6547
	30:25	and the arms of **P** shall fall down;	6547
	31: 2	speak unto **P** king of Egypt, and to his	6547
	31:18	This *is* **P** and all his multitude, saith	6547
	32: 2	take up a lamentation for **P** king of Egypt,	6547
	32:31	**P** shall see them, and shall be comforted	6547
	32:31	**P** and all his army slain by the sword,	6547
	32:32	**P** and all his multitude, saith the Lord	6547
Ac	7:10	wisdom in the sight of **P** king of Egypt;	5328
	7:13	kindred was made known unto **P**.	5328
Ro	9:17	the scripture saith unto **P**, Even for this	5328

PHARAOH'S (48) [PHARAOH]

Ge	12:15	and the woman was taken into **P** house.	6547
	37:36	an officer of **P**, *and* captain of the guard.	6547
	40: 7	he asked **P** officers that *were* with him in	6547
	40:11	**P** cup *was* in my hand: and I took	6547
	40:11	pressed them into **P** cup, and I gave the	6547
	40:11	and I gave the cup into **P** hand.	6547
	40:13	thou shalt deliver **P** cup into his hand,	6547
	40:20	pass the third day, *which was* **P** birthday,	6547
	40:21	and he gave the cup into **P** hand:	6547
	45:16	the fame *thereof* was heard *in* **P** house,	6547
	47:14	Joseph brought the money into **P** house.	6547
	47:20	over them: so the land became **P**.	6547+3807.1
	47:25	lord, and we will be **P** servants.	6547+3807.1
	47:26	only, *which* became not **P**.	6547+3807.1
Ex	2: 7	said his sister to **P** daughter, Shall I go	6547
	2: 8	**P** daughter said to her, Go. And the maid	6547
	2: 9	**P** daughter said unto her, Take this child	6547
	2:10	she brought him unto **P** daughter,	6547
	5:14	which **P** taskmasters had set over them,	6547
	7: 3	I will harden **P** heart, and multiply my	6547
	7:13	hardened **P** heart, that he hearkened not	6547
	7:14	**P** heart *is* hardened, he refuseth to let	6547
	7:22	**P** heart was hardened, neither did he	6547
	8:19	**P** heart was hardened, and he hearkened	6547
	9: 7	**P** servants laid upon him, How long shall	6547
	10:11	they were driven out from **P** presence.	6547
	10:20	the LORD hardened **P** heart, so that he	6547
	10:27	the LORD hardened **P** heart,	6547
	11: 3	in the sight of **P** servants, and in the sight	6547
	11:10	the LORD hardened **P** heart, so that he	6547
	14: 4	I will harden **P** heart, that he shall follow	6547
	14:23	*even* all **P** horses, his chariots,	6547
	15: 4	**P** chariots and his host hath he cast into	6547
Dt	6:21	thy son, We were **P** bondmen in Egypt;	6547
1Sa	2:27	when they were in Egypt in **P** house?	6547
1Ki	3: 1	took **P** daughter, and brought her into	6547
	7: 8	made also a house for **P** daughter,	6547
	9:24	**P** daughter came up out of the city of	6547
	11:20	whom Tahpenes weaned in **P** house:	6547
	11:20	Genubath was in **P** household among	6547
SS	1: 9	to a company of horses in **P** chariots.	6547
Jer	37: 5	**P** army was come forth out of Egypt:	6547
	37: 7	Behold, **P** army, which is come forth to	6547
	37:11	up from Jerusalem for fear of **P** army,	6547
	43: 9	which *is* at the entry of **P** house in	6547
Eze	30:24	I will break **P** arms, and he shall groan	6547
Ac	7:21	**P** daughter took him up, and nourished	5328
Heb	11:24	refused to be called the son of **P** daughter;	5328

PHARAOH-HOPHRA (1) [PHARAOH]

Jer	44:30	I *will* give **P** king of Egypt into the hand	6548

PHARAOH-NECHO (1) [PHARAOH]

Jer	46: 2	against the army of **P** king of Egypt,	6549

PHARAOH-NECHOH (4) [PHARAOH]

2Ki	23:29	In his days **P** king of Egypt went up	6549
	23:33	**P** put him in bands at Riblah in the land	6549
	23:34	**P** made Eliakim the son of Josiah king in	6549
	23:35	to his taxation, to give *it* unto **P**.	6549

PHARES (3) [PHAREZ]

Mt	1: 3	And Judas begat **P** and Zara of Thamar;	5329
	1: 3	**P** begat Esrom; and Esrom begat	5329
Lk	3:33	was *the son* of **P**, which was *the son*	5329

PHAREZ (12) [PHARES, PHARZITES]

Ge	38:29	thee: therefore his name was called **P**.	6557
	46:12	and Onan, and Shelah, and Zerah:	6557
	46:12	and the sons of **P** were Hezron and Hamul.	6557
Nu	26:20	of **P**, the family of the Pharzites: of Zerah,	6557
	26:21	the sons of **P** were; of Hezron, the family	6557
Ru	4:12	let thy house be like the house of **P**,	6557
	4:18	Now these *are* the generations of **P**:	6557
	4:18	generations of Pharez: **P** begat Hezron,	6557
1Ch	2: 4	Tamar his daughter in law bare him **P** and	6557
	2: 5	The sons of **P**; Hezron, and Hamul.	6557
	4: 1	**P**, Hezron, and Carmi, and Hur,	6557
	9: 4	of the children of **P** the son of Judah.	6557

PHARISEE (11) [PHARISEE'S, PHARISEES, PHARISEES']

Mt	23:26	Thou blind **P**, cleanse first that *which is*	5330
Lk	7:39	Now when the **P** which had bidden him	5330
	11:37	certain **P** besought him to dine with him:	5330
	11:38	And when the **P** saw *it*, he marvelled that	5330
	18:10	the one a **P**, and the other a publican.	5330
	18:11	**P** stood and prayed thus with himself,	5330
Ac	5:34	a **P**, named Gamaliel, a doctor of law,	5330
	23: 6	Men *and* brethren, I am a **P**, the son of a	5330
	23: 6	brethren, I am a Pharisee, the son of a **P**:	5330
	26: 5	straitest sect of our religion I lived a **P**.	5330
Php	3: 5	of the Hebrews; as touching the law, a **P**;	5330

PHARISEE'S (2) [PHARISEE]

Lk	7:36	And he went into the **P** house,	5330
	7:37	that *Jesus* sat at meat in the **P** house,	5330

PHARISEES (86) [PHARISEE]

Mt	3: 7	But when he saw many of the **P** and	5330
	5:20	the righteousness of the scribes and **P**,	5330
	9:11	when the **P** saw *it*, they said unto his	5330
	9:14	Why do we and the **P** fast oft,	5330
	9:34	But the **P** said, He casteth out the devils	5330
	12: 2	when the **P** saw *it*, they said unto him,	5330
	12:14	Then the **P** went out, and held a council	5330
	12:24	But when the **P** heard *it*, they said,	5330
	12:38	of the scribes and of the **P** answered,	5330
	15: 1	Then came to Jesus scribes and **P**,	5330
	15:12	Knowest thou that the **P** were offended,	5330
	16: 1	The **P** also with the Sadducees came,	5330
	16: 6	and beware of the leaven of the **P** and	5330
	16:11	ye should beware of the leaven of the **P**	5330
	16:12	but of the doctrine of the **P** and *of*	5330
	19: 3	The **P** also came unto him, tempting him,	5330
	21:45	chief priests and **P** had heard his parables,	5330
	22:15	Then went the **P**, and took counsel how	5330
	22:34	But when the **P** had heard that he had put	5330
	22:41	While the **P** were gathered together, Jesus	5330
	23: 2	The scribes and the **P** sit in Moses' seat:	5330
	23:13	woe unto you, scribes and **P**, hypocrites!	5330
	23:14	Woe unto you, scribes and **P**, hypocrites!	5330
	23:15	Woe unto you, scribes and **P**, hypocrites!	5330
	23:23	Woe unto you, scribes and **P**, hypocrites!	5330
	23:25	Woe unto you, scribes and **P**, hypocrites!	5330
	23:27	Woe unto you, scribes and **P**, hypocrites!	5330
	23:29	Woe unto you, scribes and **P**, hypocrites!	5330
	27:62	and **P** came together unto Pilate,	5330
Mk	2:16	and **P** saw him eat with publicans and	5330
	2:18	disciples of John and of the **P** used to fast:	5330
	2:18	do the disciples of John and of the **P** fast,	5330
	2:24	And the **P** said unto him, Behold, why do	5330
	3: 6	the **P** went forth, and straightway took	5330
	7: 1	Then came together unto him the **P**,	5330
	7: 3	For the **P**, and all the Jews, except they	5330
	7: 5	Then the **P** and scribes asked him,	5330
	8:11	And the **P** came forth, and began to	5330
	8:15	beware of the leaven of the **P**, and of	5330
	10: 2	the **P** came to *him*, and asked him, Is it	5330
	12:13	And they send unto him certain of the **P**	5330
Lk	5:17	that there were **P** and doctors of the law	5330
	5:21	the scribes and the **P** began to reason,	5330
	5:30	and **P** murmured against his disciples,	5330
	5:33	and likewise the *disciples* of the **P**;	5330
	6: 2	And certain of the **P** said unto them,	5330
	6: 7	And the scribes and **P** watched him,	5330
	7:30	the **P** and lawyers rejected the counsel	5330
	7:36	one of the **P** desired him that he would	5330
	11:39	Now do ye **P** make clean the outside of	5330
	11:42	woe unto you, **P**! for ye tithe the mint and	5330
	11:43	Woe unto you, **P**! for ye love	5330
	11:44	Woe unto you, scribes and **P**, hypocrites!	5330
	11:53	and the **P** began to urge *him* vehemently,	5330
	12: 1	*of all*, Beware ye of the leaven of the **P**,	5330
	13:31	The same day there came certain of the **P**,	5330
	14: 1	chief **P** to eat bread on the sabbath day,	5330
	14: 3	answering spake unto the lawyers and **P**,	5330
	15: 2	And the **P** and scribes murmured, saying,	5330
	16:14	And the **P** also, who were covetous,	5330
	17:20	And when he was demanded of the **P**,	5330

P

Lk	19:39 And some of the **P** from among	5330
Jn	1:24 And they which were sent were of the **P**.	5330
	3: 1 There was a man of the **P**,	5330
	4: 1 the Lord knew how the **P** had heard that	5330
	7:32 The **P** heard that the people murmured	5330
	7:32 the **P** and the chief priests sent officers	5330
	7:45 the officers to the chief priests and **P**;	5330
	7:47 Then answered them the **P**, Are ye also	5330
	7:48 of the rulers or of the **P** believed on him?	5330
	8: 3 **P** brought unto him a woman taken in	5330
	8:13 The **P** therefore said unto him,	5330
	9:13 They brought to the **P** him that aforetime	5330
	9:15 Then again the **P** also asked him how he	5330
	9:16 Therefore said some of the **P**, This man is	5330
	9:40 And *some* of the **P** which were with him	5330
	11:46 some of them went their ways to the **P**,	5330
	11:47 the chief priests and the **P** a council,	5330
	11:57 and the **P** had given a commandment,	5330
	12:19 The **P** therefore said among themselves,	5330
	12:42 the **P** they did not confess *him,* lest they	5330
	18: 3 and officers from the chief priests and **P**,	5330
Ac	15: 5 certain of the sect of the **P** which believed,	5330
	23: 6 the other **P**, he cried out in the council,	5330
	23: 7 there arose a dissension between the **P**	5330
	23: 8 angel nor spirit: but the **P** confess both.	5330

PHARISEES' (1) [PHARISEE]

Ac	23: 9 the scribes *that were* of the **P** part arose,	5330

PHAROSH (1)

Ezr	8: 3 the sons of Shechaniah, of the sons of **P**;	6551

PHARPAR (1)

2Ki	5:12 *Are* not Abana and **P**, rivers of Damascus,	6554

PHARZITES (1) [PHAREZ]

Nu	26:20 of Pharez, the family of the **P**: of Zerah,	6558

PHASEAH (1) [PASEAH]

Ne	7:51 the children of Uzza, the children of **P**,	6454

PHEBE (2)

Ro	16: 1 I commend unto you **P** our sister, which	5402
	16: S *sent* by **P** servant of the church at	5402

PHENICE (3) [PHENICIA]

Ac	11:19 arose about Stephen travelled as far as **P**,	5403
	15: 3 they passed through **P** and Samaria,	5403
	27:12 if by any means they might attain to **P**,	5405

PHENICIA (1) [PHENICE, SYROPHENICIAN]

Ac	21: 2 And finding a ship sailing over unto **P**,	5403

PHI-BESETH (1)

Eze	30:17 of Aven and of **P** shall fall by the sword:	6364

PHICHOL (3)

Ge	21:22 **P** the chief captain of his host spake unto	6369
	21:32 **P** the chief captain of his host,	6369
	26:26 and **P** the chief captain of his army.	6369

PHICOL See PHICHOL

PHILADELPHIA (2)

Rev	1:11 Sardis, and unto **P**, and unto Laodicea.	5359
	3: 7 And to the angel of the church in **P** write;	5359

PHILEMON (2)

Phm	1: 1 unto **P** our dearly beloved,	5371
	1: S Written from Rome to **P**, by Onesimus a	5371

PHILETUS (1)

2Ti	2:17 a canker: of whom is Hymeneus and **P**;	5372

PHILIP (33) [PHILIP'S]

Mt	10: 3 **P**, and Bartholomew; Thomas,	5376
Mk	3:18 and **P**, and Bartholomew, and Matthew,	5376
Lk	3: 1 and his brother **P** tetrarch of Iturea and	5376
	6:14 and John, **P** and Bartholomew,	5376
Jn	1:43 and findeth **P**, and saith unto him,	5376
	1:44 Now **P** was of Bethsaida, the city of	5376
	1:45 **P** findeth Nathanael, and saith unto him,	5376
	1:46 **P** saith unto him, Come and see.	5376
	1:48 said unto him, Before that **P** called thee,	5376
	6: 5 he saith unto **P**, Whence shall we buy	5376
	6: 7 **P** answered him, Two hundred	5376
	12:21 The same came therefore to **P**, which was	5376
	12:22 **P** cometh and telleth Andrew:	5376
	12:22 and again Andrew and **P** tell Jesus.	5376
	14: 8 **P** saith unto him, Lord, shew us the	5376
	14: 9 and yet hast thou not known me, **P**?	5376
Ac	1:13 and John, and Andrew, **P**, and Thomas,	5376
	6: 5 and **P**, and Prochorus, and Nicanor,	5376
	8: 5 Then **P** went down to the city of Samaria,	5376
	8: 6 heed unto those *things* which **P** spake,	5376
	8:12 But when they believed **P** preaching	5376
	8:13 he continued with **P**, and wondered,	5376
	8:26 And *the* angel of the Lord spake unto **P**,	5376
	8:29 Then the Spirit said unto **P**, Go near,	5376
	8:30 And **P** ran *thither* to *him,* and heard him	5376
	8:31 And he desired **P** that *he* would come up	5376
	8:34 And the eunuch answered **P**, and said,	5376
	8:35 Then **P** opened his mouth,	5376
	8:37 **P** said, If thou believest with all *thine*	5376
	8:38 into the water, both **P** and the eunuch;	5376
	8:39 the Spirit of the Lord caught away **P**,	5376

Ac	8:40 But **P** was found at Azotus:	5376
	21: 8 we entered into the house of **P**	5376

PHILIP'S (3) [PHILIP]

Mt	14: 3 for Herodias' sake, his brother **P** wife.	5376
Mk	6:17 for Herodias' sake, his brother **P** wife:	5376
Lk	3:19 by him for Herodias his brother **P** wife,	5376

PHILIPPI (8) [PHILIPPIANS]

Mt	16:13 Jesus came into the coasts of Cesarea **P**.	5376
Mk	8:27 his disciples, into the towns of Cesarea **P**:	5376
Ac	16:12 And from thence to **P**, which is the chief	5375
	20: 6 And we sailed away from **P** after the days	5375
1Co	15: S was written from **P** by Stephanas,	5375
2Co	13: S to the Corinthians was written from **P**,	5375
Php	1: 1 the saints in Christ Jesus which are at **P**,	5375
1Th	2: 2 shamefully entreated, as ye know, at **P**,	5375

PHILIPPIANS (2) [PHILIPPI]

Php	4:15 ye **P** know also, that in the beginning	5374
	4: S It was written to the **P** from Rome by	5374

PHILISTIA (3) [PHILISTIM, PHILISTIMS, PHILISTINE, PHILISTINES, PHILISTINES']

Ps	60: 8 my shoe: **P**, triumph thou because of me.	6429
	87: 4 behold **P**, and Tyre, with Ethiopia; this	6429
	108: 1 I cast out my shoe; over **P** will I triumph.	6429

PHILISTIM (1) [PHILISTIA]

Ge	10:14 and Casluhim, (out of whom came **P**)	6430

PHILISTIMS (5) [PHILISTIA]

Ge	26: 1 Isaac went unto Abimelech king of the **P**	6430
	26: 8 that Abimelech king of the **P** looked out	6430
	26:14 store of servants: and the **P** envied him.	6430
	26:15 the **P** had stopped them, and filled them	6430
	26:18 the **P** had stopped them after the death	6430

PHILISTINE (33) [PHILISTIA]

1Sa	17: 8 *am* not I a **P**, and you servants to Saul?	6430
	17:10 the **P** said, I defy the armies of Israel this	6430
	17:11 and all Israel heard those words of the **P**,	6430
	17:16 the **P** drew near morning and evening,	6430
	17:23 the **P** of Gath, Goliath by name,	6430
	17:26 be done to the man that killeth this **P**,	6430
	17:26 for who *is* this uncircumcised **P**, that he	6430
	17:32 thy servant will go and fight with this **P**.	6430
	17:33 Thou art not able to go against this **P** to	6430
	17:36 this uncircumcised **P** shall be as one of	6430
	17:37 will deliver me out of the hand of this **P**.	6430
	17:40 in his hand: and he drew near to the **P**.	6430
	17:41 **P** came on and drew near unto David;	6430
	17:42 the **P** looked about, and saw David,	6430
	17:43 the **P** said unto David, *Am* I a dog,	6430
	17:43 And the **P** cursed David by his gods.	6430
	17:44 the **P** said to David, Come to me, and I	6430
	17:45 said David to the **P**, Thou comest to me	6430
	17:48 when the **P** arose, and came and drew	6430
	17:48 and ran *toward* the army to meet the **P**.	6430
	17:49 slang *it,* and smote the **P** in his forehead,	6430
	17:50 David prevailed over the **P** with a sling	6430
	17:50 a stone, and smote the **P**, and slew him;	6430
	17:51 stood upon the **P**, and took his sword,	6430
	17:54 David took the head of the **P**,	6430
	17:55 Saul saw David go forth against the **P**,	6430
	17:57 returned from the slaughter of the **P**,	6430
	17:57 Saul with the head of the **P** in his hand.	6430
	18: 6 was returned from the slaughter of the **P**,	6430
	19: 5 slew the **P**, and the Lord wrought a great	6430
	21: 9 priest said, The sword of Goliath the **P**,	6430
	22:10 and gave him the sword of Goliath the **P**.	6430
2Sa	21:17 and smote the **P**, and killed him.	6430

PHILISTINES (246) [PHILISTIA]

Ge	21:32 and they returned into the land of the **P**.	6430
Ex	13:17 not *through* the way of the land of the **P**,	6430
	23:31 the Red sea even unto the sea of the **P**,	6430
Jos	13: 2 all the borders of the **P**, and all Geshuri,	6430
	13: 3 five lords of the **P**; the Gazathites,	6430
Jdg	3: 3 Namely, five lords of the **P**, and all	6430
	3:31 which slew *of* the **P** six hundred men	6430
	10: 6 the gods of the **P**, and forsook the Lord,	6430
	10: 7 he sold them into the hands of the **P**,	6430
	10:11 the children of Ammon, and from the **P**?	6430
	13: 1 them into the hand of the **P** forty years.	6430
	13: 5 to deliver Israel out of the hand of the **P**.	6430
	14: 1 in Timnath of the daughters of the **P**.	6430
	14: 2 in Timnath of the daughters of the **P**:	6430
	14: 3 to take a wife of the uncircumcised **P**?	6430
	14: 4 that he sought an occasion against the **P**:	6430
	14: 4 for at that time the **P** had dominion over	6430
	15: 3 Now shall I be more blameless than the **P**,	6430
	15: 5 *them* go into the standing corn of the **P**,	6430
	15: 6 the **P** said, Who hath done this? And they	6430
	15: 6 the **P** came up, and burnt her and her	6430
	15: 9 the **P** went up, and pitched in Judah,	6430
	15:11 Knowest thou not that the **P** *are* rulers	6430
	15:12 may deliver thee into the hand of the **P**.	6430
	15:14 unto Lehi, the **P** shouted against him:	6430
	15:20 judged Israel in the days of the **P** twenty	6430
	16: 5 the lords of the **P** came up unto her,	6430
	16: 8 the lords of the **P** brought up to her seven	6430
	16: 9 unto him, The **P** *be* upon thee, Samson.	6430
	16:12 unto him, The **P** *be* upon thee, Samson.	6430
	16:14 unto him, The **P** *be* upon thee, Samson.	6430
	16:18 she sent and called for the lords of the **P**,	6430

Jdg	16:18 the lords of the **P** came up unto her,	6430
	16:20 she said, The **P** *be* upon thee, Samson.	6430
	16:21 the **P** took him, and put out his eyes,	6430
	16:23 the lords of the **P** gathered them together	6430
	16:27 all the lords of the **P** *were* there;	6430
	16:28 that I may be at once avenged of the **P** for	6430
	16:30 Samson said, Let me die with the **P**.	6430
1Sa	4: 1 Israel went out against the **P** to battle,	6430
	4: 1 and the **P** pitched in Aphek.	6430
	4: 2 **P** put *themselves* in array against Israel:	6430
	4: 3 Israel was smitten before the **P**?	6430
	4: 3 the Lord smitten us to day before the **P**?	6430
	4: 6 when the **P** heard the noise of the shout,	6430
	4: 7 the **P** were afraid, for they said, God is	6430
	4: 9 and quit yourselves like men, O ye **P**,	6430
	4:10 the **P** fought, and Israel was smitten,	6430
	4:17 Israel is fled before the **P**, and there hath	6430
	5: 1 The **P** took the ark of God, and brought it	6430
	5: 2 When the **P** took the ark of God, they	6430
	5: 8 gathered all the lords of the **P** unto them,	6430
	5:11 gathered together all the lords of the **P**,	6430
	6: 1 was in the country of the **P** seven months.	6430
	6: 2 **P** called for the priests and the diviners,	6430
	6: 4 to the number the lords of the **P**:	6430
	6:12 the lords of the **P** went after them unto	6430
	6:16 when the five lords of the **P** had seen *it,*	6430
	6:17 *are* the golden emerods which the **P**	6430
	6:18 cities of the **P** *belonging* to the five lords,	6430
	6:21 The **P** have brought again the ark of	6430
	7: 3 will deliver you out of the hand of the **P**.	6430
	7: 7 the **P** heard that the children of Israel	6430
	7: 7 the lords of the **P** went up against Israel.	6430
	7: 7 Israel heard *it,* they were afraid of the **P**.	6430
	7: 8 he will save us out of the hand of the **P**.	6430
	7:10 the **P** drew near to battle against Israel:	6430
	7:10 a great thunder on that day upon the **P**,	6430
	7:11 pursued the **P**, and smote them, until	6430
	7:13 the **P** were subdued, and they came no	6430
	7:13 the hand of the Lord was against the **P**	6430
	7:14 cities which the **P** had taken from Israel	6430
	7:14 Israel deliver out of the hands of the **P**.	6430
	9:16 save my people out of the hand of the **P**.	6430
	10: 5 hill of God, where *is* the garrison of the **P**:	6430
	12: 9 into the hand of the **P**, and into the hand	6430
	13: 3 Jonathan smote the garrison of the **P** that	6430
	13: 3 the **P** heard *of it.* And Saul blew	6430
	13: 4 *that* Saul had smitten a garrison of the **P**,	6430
	13: 4 also was had in abomination with the **P**.	6430
	13: 5 **P** gathered themselves together to fight	6430
	13:11 the **P** gathered themselves together at	6430
	13:12 The **P** will come down now upon me *to*	6430
	13:16 but the **P** encamped in Michmash.	6430
	13:17 spoilers came out of the camp of the **P**	6430
	13:19 the **P** said, Lest the Hebrews make *them*	6430
	13:20 all the Israelites went down *to* the **P**,	6430
	13:23 the garrison of the **P** went out to	6430
	14:11 themselves unto the garrison of the **P**:	6430
	14:11 the **P** said, Behold, the Hebrews come forth	6430
	14:19 the noise that *was* in the host of the **P**	6430
	14:21 the Hebrews *that* were with the **P**	6430
	14:22 *when* they heard that the **P** fled, even	6430
	14:30 a much greater slaughter among the **P**?	6430
	14:31 they smote the **P** that day from Michmash	6430
	14:36 Let us go down after the **P** by night,	6430
	14:37 of God, Shall I go down after the **P**?	6430
	14:46 Saul went up from following the **P**:	6430
	14:46 and the **P** went to their own place.	6430
	14:47 the kings of Zobah, and against the **P**:	6430
	14:52 there was sore war against the **P** all	6430
	17: 1 the **P** gathered together their armies to	6430
	17: 2 and set the battle in array against the **P**.	6430
	17: 3 **P** stood on a mountain on the one side,	6430
	17: 4 out a champion out of the camp of the **P**,	6430
	17:19 in the valley of Elah, fighting with the **P**.	6430
	17:21 and the **P** had put *the battle* in array,	6430
	17:23 out of the armies of the **P**,	6430
	17:46 will give the carcases of the host of the **P**	6430
	17:51 the **P** saw their champion was dead,	6430
	17:52 and shouted, and pursued the **P**,	6430
	17:52 wounded of the **P** fell down by the way	6430
	17:53 Israel returned from chasing after the **P**,	6430
	18:17 but let the hand of the **P** be upon him.	6430
	18:21 that the hand of the **P** may be against him.	6430
	18:25 but an hundred foreskins of the **P**,	6430
	18:25 to make David fall by the hand of the **P**.	6430
	18:27 and slew of the **P** two hundred men;	6430
	18:30 the princes of the **P** went forth: and	6430
	19: 8 fought with the **P**, and slew them *with* a	6430
	23: 1 the **P** fight against Keilah, and they rob	6430
	23: 2 Shall I go and smite these **P**?	6430
	23: 2 Go, and smite the **P**, and save Keilah.	6430
	23: 3 *to* Keilah against the armies of the **P**?	6430
	23: 4 for I will deliver the **P** into thine hand.	6430
	23: 5 fought with the **P**, and brought away their	6430
	23:27 come; for the **P** have invaded the land.	6430
	23:28 after David, and went against the **P**:	6430
	24: 1 Saul was returned from following the **P**,	6430
	27: 1 speedily escape into the land of the **P**;	6430
	27: 7 in the country of the **P** was a full year	6430
	27:11 while he dwelleth in the country of the **P**.	6430
	28: 1 the **P** gathered their armies together for	6430
	28: 4 the **P** gathered themselves together,	6430
	28: 5 when Saul saw the host of the **P**, he was	6430
	28:15 the **P** make war against me, and God is	6430
	28:19 Israel with thee into the hand of the **P**:	6430

P

1Sa 28:19 the host of Israel into the hand of the **P**. 6430
29: 1 Now the **P** gathered together all their 6430
29: 2 the lords of the **P** passed on by hundreds, 6430
29: 3 said the princes of the **P**, What *do* these 6430
29: 3 And Achish said unto the princes of the **P**, 6430
29: 4 the princes of the **P** were wroth with him; 6430
29: 4 the princes of the **P** said unto him, 6430
29: 7 that thou displease not the lords of the **P**, 6430
29:11 to return into the land of the **P**. 6430
29:11 And the **P** went up *to* Jezreel. 6430
30:16 they had taken out of the land of the **P**, 6430
31: 1 Now the **P** fought against Israel: 6430
31: 1 the men of Israel fled from before the **P**, 6430
31: 2 the **P** followed hard upon Saul and upon 6430
31: 2 the **P** slew Jonathan, and Abinadab, 6430
31: 7 fled; and the **P** came and dwelt in them. 6430
31: 8 when the **P** came to strip the slain, that 6430
31: 9 sent into the land of the **P** round about, 6430
31:11 of that which the **P** had done to Saul, 6430
2Sa 1:20 lest the daughters of the **P** rejoice, lest 6430
3:14 to me for an hundred foreskins of the **P**, 6430
3:18 my people Israel out of the hand of the **P**, 6430
5:17 when the **P** heard that they had anointed 6430
5:17 all the **P** came up to seek David; 6430
5:18 The **P** also came and spread themselves in 6430
5:19 to the LORD, saying, Shall I go up to the **P**? 6430
5:19 I will doubtless deliver the **P** into thine 6430
5:22 the **P** came up yet again, 6430
5:24 before thee, to smite the host of the **P**. 6430
5:25 smote the **P** from Geba until thou come 6430
8: 1 David smote the **P**, and subdued them: 6430
8: 1 Metheg-ammah out of the hand of the **P**. 6430
8:12 of the **P**, and of Amalek, and of the spoil 6430
19: 9 he delivered us out of the hand of the **P**; 6430
21:12 where the **P** had hanged them, when 6430
21:12 when the **P** had slain Saul in Gilboa: 6430
21:15 Moreover the **P** had yet war again with 6430
21:15 with him, and fought against the **P**: 6430
21:18 that there was again a battle with the **P** at 6430
21:19 was again a battle in Gob with the **P**, 6430
23: 9 when they defied the **P** *that* were there 6430
23:10 smote the **P** until his hand was weary, 6430
23:11 **P** were gathered together into a troop, 6430
23:11 lentiles: and the people fled from the **P**. 6430
23:12 and defended it, and slew the **P**: 6430
23:13 the troop of the **P** pitched in the valley of 6430
23:14 the garrison of the **P** *was* then 6430
23:16 *men* brake through the host of the **P**, 6430
1Ki 4:21 from the river *unto* the land of the **P**, 6430
15:27 at Gibbethon, which *belongeth* to the **P**; 6430
16:15 which *belonged* to the **P**. 6430
2Ki 8: 2 sojourned in the land of the **P** seven years. 6430
8: 3 woman returned out of the land of the **P**, 6430
18: 8 He smote the **P**, *even* unto Gaza, 6430
1Ch 1:12 and Casluhim, (of whom came the **P**,) 6430
10: 1 Now the **P** fought against Israel; 6430
10: 1 the men of Israel fled from before the **P**, 6430
10: 2 the **P** followed hard after Saul, and after 6430
10: 2 the **P** slew Jonathan, and Abinadab, 6430
10: 7 fled: and the **P** came and dwelt in them. 6430
10: 8 when the **P** came to strip the slain, that 6430
10: 9 sent into the land of the **P** round about, 6430
10:11 when all Jabesh-gilead heard all that the **P** 6430
11:13 the **P** were gathered together to battle, 6430
11:13 and the people fled from before the **P**. 6430
11:14 parcel, and delivered it, and slew the **P**; 6430
11:15 the host of the **P** encamped in the valley 6430
11:18 the three brake through the host of the **P**, 6430
12:19 when he came with the **P** against Saul to 6430
12:19 for the lords of the **P** upon advisement 6430
14: 8 the **P** heard that David was anointed 6430
14: 8 all Israel, all the **P** went up to seek David. 6430
14: 9 the **P** came and spread themselves in 6430
14:10 God, saying, Shall I go up against the **P**? 6430
14:13 the **P** yet again spread themselves abroad 6430
14:15 before thee to smite the host of the **P**. 6430
14:16 they smote the host of the **P** from Gibeon 6430
18: 1 David smote the **P**, and subdued them, 6430
18: 1 and her towns out of the hand of the **P**. 6430
18:11 and from the **P**, and from Amalek. 6430
20: 4 that there arose war at Gezer with the **P**; 6430
20: 5 there was war again with the **P**; 6430
2Ch 9:26 the river even unto the land of the **P**, 6430
17:11 Also *some* of the **P** brought Jehoshaphat 6430
21:16 up against Jehoram the spirit of the **P**, 6430
26: 6 he went forth and warred against the **P**, 6430
26: 6 cities about Ashdod, and among the **P**. 6430
26: 7 God helped him against the **P**, 6430
28:18 The **P** also had invaded the cities of the 6430
Ps 56: T of David, when the **P** took him in Gath. 6429
83: 7 The **P** with the inhabitants of Tyre; 6430
Isa 2: 6 soothsayers like the **P**, and they please 6430
9:12 The Syrians before, and the **P** behind; 6430
11:14 they shall fly upon the shoulders of the **P** 6430
Jer 25:20 all the kings of the land of the **P**, 6430
47: 1 to Jeremiah the prophet against the **P**, 6430
47: 4 of the day that cometh to spoil all the **P**, 6430
47: 4 for the LORD *will* spoil the **P**, 6430
Eze 16:27 daughters of the **P**, which are ashamed 6430
16:57 round about her, the daughters of the **P**, 6430
25:15 Because the **P** have dealt by revenge, 6430
25:16 I *will* stretch out mine hand upon the **P**, 6430
Am 1: 8 the remnant of the **P** shall perish, saith 6430
6: 2 go down *to* Gath of the **P**: *be they* better 6430

Am 9: 7 the **P** from Caphtor, and the Syrians from 6430
Ob 1:19 of Esau; and *they of* the plain the **P**. 6430
Zep 2: 5 O Canaan, the land of the **P**, I will even 6430
Zec 9: 6 and I will cut off the pride of the **P**. 6430

PHILISTINES' (4) [PHILISTIA]

Ge 21:34 Abraham sojourned in the **P** land many 6430
1Sa 14: 1 and let us go over to the **P** garrison, 6430
14: 4 sought to go over unto the **P** garrison, 6430
1Ch 11:16 the **P** garrison *was* then at Beth-lehem. 6430

PHILOLOGUS (1)

Ro 16:15 Salute **P**, and Julia, Nereus, and his sister, 5378

PHILOSOPHERS (1) [PHILOSOPHY]

Ac 17:18 Then certain **p** of the Epicureans, and of 5386

PHILOSOPHY (1) [PHILOSOPHERS]

Col 2: 8 Beware lest any *man* spoil you through **p** 5385

PHINEHAS (24) [PHINEHAS']

Ex 6:25 of Putiel to wife; and she bare him **P**: 6372
Nu 25: 7 when **P**, the son of Eleazar, the son of 6372
25:11 **P**, the son of Eleazar, the son of Aaron 6372
31: 6 them and **P** the son of Eleazar the priest, 6372
Jos 22:13 of Gilead, **P** the son of Eleazar the priest, 6372
22:30 when **P** the priest, and the princes of 6372
22:31 **P** the son of Eleazar the priest said unto 6372
22:32 **P** the son of Eleazar the priest, 6372
24:33 buried him in a hill that pertained to **P** 6372
Jdg 20:28 **P**, the son of Eleazar, the son of Aaron, 6372
1Sa 1: 3 the two sons of Eli, Hophni and **P**, 6372
2:34 upon thy two sons, on Hophni and **P**; 6372
4: 4 the two sons of Eli, Hophni and **P**, 6372
4:11 two sons of Eli, Hophni and **P**, were slain. 6372
4:17 Hophni and **P**, are dead, and the ark of 6372
14: 3 the son of **P**, the son of Eli, 6372
1Ch 6: 4 Eleazar begat **P**, Phinehas begat Abishua, 6372
6: 4 Eleazar begat Phinehas, **P** begat Abishua, 6372
6:50 his son, **P** his son, Abishua his son, 6372
9:20 the son of Eleazar was the ruler over 6372
Ezr 7: 5 the son of **P**, the son of Eleazar, 6372
8: 2 Of the sons of **P**; Gershom: of the sons of 6372
8:33 with him *was* Eleazar the son of **P**; 6372
Ps 106:30 stood up **P**, and executed judgment; 6372

PHINEHAS' (1) [PHINEHAS]

1Sa 4:19 **P** wife, was with child, *near* to be 6372

PHLEGON (1)

Ro 16:14 **P**, Hermas, Patrobas, Hermes, 5393

PHOEBE See PHEBE

PHOENICIA See PHENICE; PHENICIA

PHOENIX See PHENICE

PHRYGIA (4)

Ac 2:10 **P**, and Pamphylia, in Egypt, and in 5435
16: 6 when they had gone throughout **P** and 5435
18:23 *all* the country of Galatia and **P** in order, 5435
1Ti 6: S which is the chiefest city of **P** Pacatiana. 5435

PHURAH (2)

Jdg 7:10 go thou with **P** thy servant down to 6513
7:11 went he down with **P** his servant unto 6513

PHUT (2)

Ge 10: 6 Cush, and Mizraim, and **P**, and Canaan. 6316
Eze 27:10 and of Lud and of **P** were in thine army, 6316

PHUVAH (1) [PUAH]

Ge 46:13 Tola, and **P**, and Job, and Shimron. 6312

PHYGELLUS (1)

2Ti 1:15 me; of whom are **P** and Hermogenes. 5436

PHYGELUS See PHYGELLUS

PHYLACTERIES (1)

Mt 23: 5 they make broad their **p**, and enlarge 5440

PHYSICIAN (5) [PHYSICIANS]

Jer 8:22 no balm in Gilead; *is there* no **p** there? 7495
Mt 9:12 They that be whole need not a **p**, 2395
Mk 2:17 that are whole have no need of *the* **p**, 2395
Lk 4:23 say unto me this proverb, **P**, heal thyself: 2395
5:31 They that are whole need not a **p**; 2395
Col 4:14 Luke, the beloved **p**, and Demas, greet 2395

PHYSICIANS (6) [PHYSICIAN]

Ge 50: 2 Joseph commanded his servants the **p** to 7495
50: 2 his father: and the **p** embalmed Israel. 7495
2Ch 16:12 he sought not *to* the LORD, but to the **p**. 7495
Job 13: 4 are forgers of lies, ye *are* all **p** of no value. 7495
Mk 5:26 And had suffered many *things* of many **p**, 2395
Lk 8:43 which had spent all *her* living upon **p**, 2395

PICK (1)

Pr 30:17 the ravens of the valley shall **p** it **out**, 5365

PICKED TROOPS See WORTHIES

PICTURES (3)

Nu 33:52 destroy all their **p**, and destroy all their 4906
Pr 25:11 spoken *is like* apples of gold in **p** of silver. 4906
Isa 2:16 ships of Tarshish, and upon all pleasant **p**. 7914

PIECE (43) [PIECES, SHOULDERPIECES]

Ge 15:10 and laid each **p** one against another: 1335
Ex 37: 7 beaten out of one **p** made he them, 4749
Nu 10: 2 of a whole **p** thou shalt make them: 4749
Jdg 9:53 a certain woman cast a **p** of a millstone 6400
1Sa 2:36 crouch to him for a **p** of silver and a 95
2:36 offices, that *I* may eat a **p** of bread. 6595
30:12 they gave him a **p** of a cake of figs, and 6400
2Sa 6:19 a good **p** *of* flesh, and a flagon *of* wine. 829
11:21 did not a woman cast a **p** of a millstone 6400
23:11 where was a **p** of ground full *of* lentiles: 2513
2Ki 3:19 mar every good **p** of land with stones. 2513
3:25 *on* every good **p** of land cast every man 2513
1Ch 16: 3 a good **p** *of* flesh, and a flagon *of* wine. 829
Ne 3:11 repaired the other **p**, and the tower of 4060
3:19 another **p** over against the going up to 4060
3:20 of Zabbai earnestly repaired the other **p**, 4060
3:21 son of Urijah the son of Koz another **p**, 4060
3:24 Binnui the son of Henadad another **p**, 4060
3:27 them the Tekoites repaired another **p**, 4060
3:30 Hanun the sixth son of Zalaph, another **p**. 4060
Job 41:24 as hard as a **p** of the nether **millstone**. 6400
42:11 every man also gave him a **p** of money, 7192
Pr 6:26 woman *a man is brought* to a **p** of bread: 3603
28:21 for for a **p** of bread *that* man will 6595
SS 4: 3 thy temples *are* like a **p** of a pomegranate 6400
6: 7 As a **p** of a pomegranate *are* thy temples 6400
Jer 37:21 *they* should give him daily a **p** of bread 3603
Eze 24: 4 even every good **p**, the thigh, 5409
24: 6 bring it out **p** by piece; let no lot fall upon 5409
24: 6 bring it out piece by **p**; let no lot fall upon 5409
Am 3:12 of the lion two legs, or a **p** of an ear; 915
4: 7 one **p** was rained upon, and the piece 2513
4: 7 the **p** whereupon it rained not withered. 2513
Mt 9:16 No man putteth a **p** of new cloth unto an 1915
17:27 his mouth, thou shalt find a **p** of money: 4715
Mk 2:21 No man also seweth a **p** of new cloth on 1915
2:21 else the new **p** that filled it up taketh 4138
Lk 5:36 No man putteth a **p** of a new garment 1915
5:36 the **p** that was *taken* out of the new 1915
14:18 I have bought a **p** of ground, and I must 68
15: 8 if she lose one **p**, doth not light a candle, 1406
15: 9 for I have found the **p** which I had lost. 1406
24:42 And they gave him a **p** of a broiled fish, 3313

PIECES (121) [PIECE]

Ge 15:17 lamp that passed between those **p**. 1506
20:16 I have given thy brother a thousand *p* of 7192
33:19 for an hundred **p** of money. 7192
37:28 Joseph to the Ishmeelites for twenty *p* NIH
37:33 Joseph is without doubt rent in **p**. 2963+2963
44:28 and I said, Surely he is torn in **p**; 2963+2963
45:22 to Benjamin he gave three hundred *p* of NIH
Ex 15: 6 O LORD, hath dashed in **p** the enemy. 7492
22:13 If it be torn in **p**, *then* let him 2963+2963
29:17 thou shalt cut the ram in **p**, and wash 5409
29:17 put *them* unto his **p**, and unto his head. 5409
Lev 1: 6 the burnt offering, and cut it into his **p**. 5409
1:12 he shall cut it into his **p**, with his head 5409
2: 6 Thou shalt **part** it in **p**, and pour 6595+6626
6:21 baken **p** of the meat offering shalt thou 6595
8:20 he cut the ram into **p**; and Moses burnt 5409
8:20 burnt the head, and the **p**, and the fat. 5409
9:13 him, with the **p** thereof, and the head: 5409
Jos 24:32 of Shechem for an hundred **p** of silver: 7192
Jdg 9: 4 ten **p** of silver out of the house of NIH
16: 5 one *of us* eleven hundred **p** of silver. NIH
19:29 into twelve **p**, and sent her into all 5409
20: 6 cut her in **p**, and sent her throughout all 5409
1Sa 2:10 of the LORD shall be broken to **p**; 2865
11: 7 hewed them in **p**, and sent *them* 5408
15:33 Samuel hewed Agag in **p** before 8158
1Ki 11:30 was on him, and rent it in twelve **p**: 7168
11:31 he said to Jeroboam, Take thee ten **p**: 7168
18:23 cut it in **p**, and lay it on wood, and put 5408
18:33 cut the bullock in **p**, and laid *him* on 5408
19:11 brake in **p** the rocks before the LORD; 7665
2Ki 2:12 clothes, and rent them in two **p**. 7167+7168
5: 5 six thousand *p* of gold, and ten changes of NIH
6:25 an ass's head was *sold* for fourscore *p* NIH
6:25 of a kab of dove's dung for five *p* of silver. NIH
11:18 his images brake they in **p** throughly, 7665
18: 4 brake in **p** the brasen serpent that Moses 3807
23:14 he brake in **p** the images, and cut down 7665
24:13 cut in **p** all the vessels of gold which 7112
25:13 did the Chaldees break *in p*, and carried NIH
2Ch 23:17 brake his altars and his images **in p**, 7665
25:12 the rock, that they all were broken in **p**. 1234
28:24 cut in **p** the vessels of the house of God, 7112
31: 1 brake the images *in p*, and cut down NIH
34: 4 he brake *in p*, and made dust of *them*, NIH
Job 16:12 shaken me to **p**, and set me up for his 6327
19: 2 my soul, and break me in **p** with words? 1792
34:24 He shall break in **p** mighty *men* without 7489
40:18 His bones are as strong **p** of brass; his 650
Ps 2: 9 thou shalt dash them in **p** like a potter's 5310
7: 2 rending it in **p**, while *there* is none to 6561
50:22 lest I tear *you* in **p**, and *there be* none to 2963
58: 7 shoot his arrows, let them be as cut in **p**. 4135
68:30 till every one submit himself with **p** of 7518
72: 4 and shall break in **p** the oppressor, 1792
74:14 Thou brakest the heads of leviathan in **p**, 7533
89:10 Thou hast broken Rahab in **p**, as one 1792
94: 5 They break in **p** thy people, O LORD, 1792
SS 8:11 was to bring a thousand *p* of silver. NIH

P

Isa	3:15 mean ye *that* ye **beat** my people **to p**,	1792	
	8: 9 ye people, and ye shall be **broken in p;**	2865	
	8: 9 and ye shall be **broken in p.**	2865	
	8: 9 and ye shall be **broken in p.**	2865	
	13:16 Their children also shall be **dashed to p**	7376	
	13:18 bows also shall **dash** the young men **to p;**	7376	
	30:14 of the potters' vessel that is **broken in p,**	3807	
	45: 2 I will **break in p** the gates of brass,	7665	
Jer	5: 6 that goeth out thence shall be **torn in p**	2963	
	23:29 a hammer *that* **breaketh** the rock in p?	6327	
	50: 2 is confounded, Merodach is **broken in p;**	2865	
	50: 2 her images are **broken in p.**	2865	
	51:20 with thee will I **break in p** the nations,	5310	
	51:21 with thee will I **break in p** the horse and	5310	
	51:21 with thee will I **break in p** the chariot	5310	
	51:22 With thee also will I **break in p** man and	5310	
	51:22 with thee will I **break in p** old and	5310	
	51:22 with thee will I **break in p** the young	5310	
	51:23 I will also **break in p** with thee	5310	
	51:23 with thee will I **break in p** in	5310	
	51:23 with thee will I **break in p** captains and	5310	
La	3:11 aside my ways, and **pulled** me **in p:**	6582	
Eze	4:14 that which dieth of itself, or is **torn in p,**	2966	
	13:19 for handfuls of barley and for **p** of bread,	6595	
	24: 4 Gather the **p** thereof into it, *even* every	5409	
Da	2: 5 ye shall be cut in **p**, and your houses shall	1917	
	2:34 of iron and clay, and **brake** them **in p.**	1855	
	2:35 **broken to p** together, and became like	1855	
	2:40 forasmuch as iron **breaketh in p** and	1855	
	2:40 all these, shall it **break in p** and bruise.	1855	
	2:44 *but* it shall **break in p** and consume all	1855	
	2:45 *that* it **brake in p** the iron, the brass,	1855	
	3:29 shall be cut in **p**, and their houses shall be	1917	
	6:24 **brake** all their bones **in p** or ever they	1855	
	7: 7 it devoured and **brake in p,**	1855	
	7:19 **brake in p**, and stamped the residue with	1855	
	7:23 shall tread it down, and **break** it **in p.**	1855	
Hos	3: 2 I bought her to me for fifteen *p* of silver,	NIH	
	8: 6 the calf of Samaria shall be **broken in p.**	7616	
	10:14 the mother was **dashed in p** upon *her*	7376	
	13:16 their infants shall be **dashed in p,**	7376	
Mic	1: 7 images thereof shall be **beaten to p,**	3807	
	3: 3 **chop** *them* **in p**, as for the pot, and as	6566	
	4:13 thou shalt **beat in p** many people:	1854	
	5: 8 **teareth in p**, and none can deliver.	2963	
Na	2: 1 He that **dasheth in p** is come up before	6327	
	2:12 The lion did **tear in p** enough for his	2963	
	3:10 young children also were **dashed in p**	7376	
Zec	11:12 So they weighed *for* my price thirty *p* of	NIH	
	11:13 I took the thirty *p* of silver, and cast them	NIH	
	11:16 flesh of the fat, and **tear** their claws **in p.**	6561	
	12: 3 with it shall be **cut in p,**	8295+8295	
Mt	26:15 they covenanted with him for thirty **p**	NIG	
	27: 3 brought again the thirty **p** of silver to	NIG	
	27: 5 And he cast down the **p** of silver in	NIG	
	27: 6 And the chief priests took the silver **p,**	NIG	
	27: 9 saying, And they took the thirty **p** of silver,	NIG	
Mk	5: 4 by him, and the fetters **broken in p:**	4937	
Lk	15: Either what woman having ten **p** of silver,	NIG	
Ac	19:19 and found *it* fifty thousand *p* of silver.	NIG	
	23:10 Paul should have been **pulled in p** of	1288	
	27:44 and some on **broken p** of the ship.	5100	

PIERCE (4) [PIERCED, PIERCETH, PIERCING, PIERCINGS]

Nu	24: 8 and **p** *them* **through** with his arrows.	4272
2Ki	18:21 lean, it will go into his hand, and **p** it:	5344
Isa	36: 6 lean, it will go into his hand, and **p** it:	5344
Lk	2:35 a sword shall **p through** thy own soul	1330

PIERCED (8) [PIERCE]

Jdg	5:26 when she had **p** and stricken through his	4272
Job	30:17 My bones are **p** in me in the night season:	5365
Ps	22:16 me: they **p** my hands and my feet.	3738
Zec	12:10 shall look upon me whom they have **p,**	1856
Jn	19:34 But one of the soldiers with a spear **p** his	3572
	19:37 They shall look on *him* whom they **p.**	1574
1Ti	6:10 **p** themselves **through** with many sorrows	4044
Rev	1: 7 shall see him, and they *also* which **p** him:	1574

PIERCETH (1) [PIERCE]

Job	40:24 with his eyes: *his* nose **p** through snares.	5344

PIERCING (2) [PIERCE]

Isa	27: 1 strong sword shall punish leviathan the **p**	1281
Heb	4:12 *even* to the dividing asunder of soul and	1338

PIERCINGS (1) [PIERCE]

Pr	12:18 is that speaketh like the **p** of a sword:	4094

PIETY (1)

1Ti	5: 4 let them learn first to **shew p** at home,	2151

PIG See SWINE

PIGEON (2) [PIGEONS]

Ge	15: 9 old, and a turtle-dove, and a **young p.**	1469
Lev	12: 6 a young **p**, or a turtledove, for a sin	3123

PIGEONS (10) [PIGEON]

Lev	1:14 his offering of turtledoves, or of young **p.**	3123
	5: 7 two turtledoves, or two young **p**, unto	3123
	5:11 two young **p**, then he that sinned shall	3123
	12: 8 shall bring two turtles, or two young **p;**	3123
	14:22 two turtledoves, or two young **p**, such as	3123
	14:30 or of the young **p**, such as he can get;	3123

Lev	15:14 or two young **p**, and come before	3123
	15:29 or two young **p**, and bring them unto	3123
Nu	6:10 two turtles, or two young **p**, to the priest,	3123
Lk	2:24 A pair of turtledoves, or two young **p.**	4058

PI-HAHIROTH (4)

Ex	14: 2 that they turn and encamp before **P,**	6367
	14: 9 by the sea, beside **P**, before Baal-zephon.	6367
Nu	33: 7 turned again unto **P**, which *is* before	6367
	33: 8 they departed from before *P*hahiroth,	6367

PILATE (56)

Mt	27: 2 delivered him to Pontius **P** the governor.	4091
	27:13 Then said **P** unto him, Hearest thou not	4091
	27:17 **P** said unto them, Whom will ye *that* I	4091
	27:22 **P** saith unto them, What shall I do then	4091
	27:24 **P** saw that he could prevail nothing,	4091
	27:58 He went to **P**, and begged the body of	4091
	27:58 Then **P** commanded the body to be	4091
	27:62 and Pharisees came together unto **P,**	4091
	27:65 **P** said unto them, Ye have a watch: go	4091
Mk	15: 1 carried *him* away, and delivered *him* to **P.**	4091
	15: 2 And **P** asked him, Art thou the King of	4091
	15: 4 And **P** asked him again, saying,	4091
	15: 5 yet answered nothing; so that **P** marvelled.	4091
	15: 9 answered them, saying, Will ye *that* I	4091
	15:12 **P** answered and said again unto them,	4091
	15:14 Then **P** said unto them, Why, what evil	4091
	15:15 And so **P**, willing to content the people,	4091
	15:43 and went in boldly unto **P**, and craved	4091
	15:44 And **P** marvelled if he were already dead:	4091
Lk	3: 1 Pontius **P** being governor of Judea,	4091
	13: 1 whose blood **P** had mingled with their	4091
	23: 1 of them arose, and led him unto **P.**	4091
	23: 3 And **P** asked him, saying, Art thou	4091
	23: 4 Then said **P** to the chief priests and *to*	4091
	23: 6 P heard of Galilee, he asked whether	4091
	23:11 a gorgeous robe, and sent him again to **P.**	4091
	23:12 the same day **P** and Herod were made	4091
	23:13 And **P**, when he had called together	4091
	23:20 **P** therefore, willing to release Jesus, spake	4091
	23:24 And **P** gave sentence that it should be as	4091
	23:52 This *man* went unto **P**, and begged	4091
Jn	18:29 **P** then went out unto them, and said,	4091
	18:31 Then said **P** unto them, Take ye him,	4091
	18:33 Then **P** entered into the judgment hall	4091
	18:35 **P** answered, Am I a Jew? Thine own	4091
	18:37 **P** therefore said unto him, Art thou a king	4091
	18:38 **P** saith unto him, What is truth?	4091
	19: 1 Then **P** therefore took Jesus,	4091
	19: 4 **P** therefore went forth again,	4091
	19: 5 And *P* saith unto them, Behold the man.	NIG
	19: 6 Crucify *him*, crucify *him*. **P** saith unto	4091
	19: 8 **P** therefore heard that saying, he was	4091
	19:10 Then saith **P** unto him, Speakest thou not	4091
	19:12 *And* from thenceforth **P** sought to release	4091
	19:13 When **P** therefore heard that saying,	4091
	19:15 **P** saith unto them, Shall I crucify your	4091
	19:19 **P** wrote a title, and put *it* on the cross.	4091
	19:21 said the chief priests of the Jews to **P,**	4091
	19:22 **P** answered, What I have written I have	4091
	19:31 *P* that their legs might be broken,	4091
	19:38 besought **P** that he might take away	4091
	19:38 and **P** gave *him* leave. He came therefore,	4091
Ac	3:13 and denied him in the presence of **P,**	4091
	4:27 both Herod, and Pontius **P**, with	4091
	13:28 *yet* desired they **P** that he should be slain.	4091
1Ti	6:13 who before Pontius **P** witnessed a good	4091

PILDASH (1)

Ge	22:22 Hazo, and **P**, and Jidlaph, and Bethuel.	6394

PILE (2)

Isa	30:33 the **p** thereof *is* fire and much wood;	4071
Eze	24: 9 I will even make the **p for fire** great.	4071

PILE OF RUBBLE See DUNGHILL

PILEHA (1)

Ne	10:24 Hallohesh, **P**, Shobek,	6401

PILGRIMAGE (4) [PILGRIMS]

Ge	47: 9 The days of the years of my **p** *are* an	4033
	47: 9 life of my fathers in the days of their **p.**	4033
Ex	6: 4 the land of their **p**, wherein they were	4033
Ps	119:54 been my songs in the house of my **p.**	4033

PILGRIMS (2) [PILGRIMAGE]

Heb	11:13 they were strangers and **p** on the earth.	3927
1Pe	2:11 I beseech *you* as strangers and **p,**	3927

PILHA See PILEHA

PILLAR (47) [PILLARS]

Ge	19:26 behind him, and she became a **p** of salt.	5333
	28:18 set it up *for* a **p**, and poured oil upon	4676
	28:22 this stone, which I have set for a **p**, shall	4676
	31:13 where thou anointedst the **p,**	4676
	31:45 Jacob took a stone, and set it up *for* a **p.**	4676
	31:51 Behold this heap, and behold *this* **p,**	4676
	31:52 heap *be* witness, and *this* **p** be witness,	4676
	31:52 pass over this heap and this **p** unto me,	4676
	35:14 Jacob set up a **p** in the place where he	4678
	35:14 he talked with him, *even* a **p** of stone:	4678
	35:20 Jacob set a **p** upon her grave: that *is*	4676
	35:20 that *is* the **p** of Rachel's grave unto *this*	4678

Ex	13:21 the Lord went before them by day in a **p**	5982
	13:21 by night in a **p** of fire, to give them light;	5982
	13:22 took not away the **p** of the cloud by day,	5982
	13:22 nor the **p** of fire by night, *from* before	5982
	14:19 the **p** of the cloud went from before their	5982
	14:24 host of the Egyptians through the **p** of fire	5982
	33: 9 the cloudy **p** descended, and stood *at*	5982
	33:10 all the people saw the cloudy **p** stand *at*	5982
Nu	12: 5 the Lord came down in the **p** of	5982
	14:14 by day time in a **p** of a cloud, and in a	5982
	14:14 of a cloud, and in a **p** of fire by night.	5982
Dt	31:15 in the tabernacle in a **p** of a cloud:	5982
	31:15 the **p** of the cloud stood over the door of	5982
Jdg	9: 6 the plain of the **p** that *was* in Shechem.	5324
	20:40 arise up out of the city with a **p** of smoke,	5982
2Sa	18:18 had taken and reared up for himself a **p,**	4678
	18:18 he called the **p** after his own name: and it	4678
1Ki	7: 6 he set up the right **p**, and called the name	5982
	7:21 he set up the left **p**, and called the name	5982
2Ki	11:14 behold, the king stood by a **p,**	5982
	23: 3 king stood by a **p**, and made a covenant	5982
	25:17 The height of the one **p** was eighteen	5982
	25:17 like unto these had the second **p** with	5982
2Ch	23:13 the king stood at his **p** at the entering in,	5982
Ne	9:12 leddest them in the day by a cloudy **p;**	5982
	9:12 in the night by a **p** of fire, to give them	5982
	9:19 the **p** of the cloud departed not from	5982
	9:19 neither the **p** of fire by night, to shew	5982
Ps	99: 7 He spake unto them in the cloudy **p:**	5982
Isa	19:19 and a **p** at the border thereof to the Lord.	4676
Jer	1:18 an iron **p**, and brasen walls against	5982
	52:21 the height of one **p** *was* eighteen cubits;	5982
	52:22 The second *also* and the pomegranates	5982
1Ti	3:15 living God, the **p** and ground of the truth.	4769
Rev	3:12 Him that overcometh will I make a **p** in	4769

PILLARS (89) [PILLAR]

Ex	24: 4 an altar under the hill, and twelve **p,**	4676
	26:32 thou shalt hang it upon four **p** of shittim	5982
	26:37 thou shalt make for the hanging five **p** of	5982
	27:10 the twenty **p** thereof and their twenty	5982
	27:10 the hooks of the **p** and their fillets *shall*	5982
	27:11 his twenty **p** and their twenty sockets *of*	5982
	27:11 hooks of the **p** and their fillets *of* silver.	5982
	27:12 their **p** ten, and their sockets ten.	5982
	27:14 their **p** three, and their sockets three.	5982
	27:15 fifteen *cubits*: their **p** three,	5982
	27:16 their **p** *shall be* four, and their sockets	5982
	27:17 All the **p** round about the court *shall be*	5982
	35:11 his boards, his bars, his **p**, and his sockets,	5982
	35:17 his **p**, and their sockets, and the hanging	5982
	36:36 made thereunto four **p** of shittim *wood*,	5982
	36:38 the five **p** of it with their hooks:	5982
	38:10 Their **p** *were* twenty, and their brasen	5982
	38:10 the hooks of the **p** and their fillets *were*	5982
	38:11 their **p** *were* twenty, and their sockets *of*	5982
	38:11 hooks of the **p** and their fillets *of* silver.	5982
	38:12 their **p** ten, and their sockets ten;	5982
	38:12 hooks of the **p** and their fillets *of* silver.	5982
	38:14 their **p** three, and their sockets three.	5982
	38:15 their **p** three, and their sockets three.	5982
	38:17 the sockets for the **p** *were of* brass;	5982
	38:17 hooks of the **p** and their fillets *of* silver;	5982
	38:17 all the **p** of the court were filleted *with*	5982
	38:19 their **p** *were* four, and their sockets *of* brass	5982
	38:28 five *shekels* he made hooks for the **p,**	5982
	39:33 his bars, and his **p**, and his sockets,	5982
	39:40 his **p**, and his sockets, and the hanging	5982
	40:18 in the bars thereof, and reared up his **p.**	5982
Nu	3:36 the **p** thereof, and the sockets thereof,	5982
	3:37 the **p** of the court round about,	5982
	4:31 and the **p** thereof, and sockets thereof,	5982
	4:32 the **p** of the court round about,	5982
Dt	12: 3 break their **p**, and burn their groves with	4676
Jdg	16:25 sport: and they set him between the **p.**	5982
	16:26 Suffer me that I may feel the **p**	5982
	16:29 Samson took hold of the two middle **p**	5982
1Sa	2: 8 for the **p** of the earth *are* the Lord's,	4690
1Ki	7: 2 thirty cubits, upon four rows of cedar **p,**	5982
	7: 2 pillars, with cedar beams upon the **p.**	5982
	7: 3 that *lay* on forty five **p**, fifteen in a row.	5982
	7: 6 he made a porch of **p**; the length thereof	5982
	7: 6 the *other* **p** and the thick beam *were*	5982
	7:15 For he cast two **p** of brass, of eighteen	5982
	7:16 brass, to set upon the tops of the **p:**	5982
	7:17 which *were* upon the top of the **p;**	5982
	7:18 he made the **p**, and two rows round	5982
	7:19 top of the **p** were of lily work in the	5982
	7:20 the chapiters upon the two **p** had	5982
	7:21 set up the **p** in the porch of the temple:	5982
	7:22 upon the top of the **p** *was* lily work:	5982
	7:22 so was the work of the **p** finished.	5982
	7:41 The two **p**, and the two bowls of	5982
	7:41 that *were* on the top of the *two* **p;**	5982
	7:41 which *were* upon the top of the **p;**	5982
	7:42 of the chapiters that *were* upon the **p;**	5982
	10:12 the king made of the almug trees **p** for	4552
2Ki	18:16 *from* the **p** which Hezekiah king of Judah	547
	25:13 the **p** of brass that *were* in the house of	5982
	25:16 The two **p**, one sea, and the bases which	5982
1Ch	18: 8 and the **p**, and the vessels of brass.	5982
2Ch	3:15 Also he made before the house two **p** of	5982
	3:16 and put *them* on the heads of the **p;**	5982
	3:17 he reared up the **p** before the temple,	5982
	4:12 To wit, the two **p**, and the pommels,	5982

P

2Ch	4:12 *which were* on the top of the two **p,**	5982
	4:12 chapiters which *were* on the top of the **p;**	5982
	4:13 of the chapiters which *were* upon the **p.**	5982
Est	1: 6 and purple to silver rings and **p** of marble:	5982
Job	9: 6 of her place, and the **p** thereof tremble.	5982
	26:11 The **p** of heaven tremble and are	5982
Ps	75: 3 *are* dissolved: I bear up the **p** of it. Selah.	5982
Pr	9: 1 house, she hath hewn out her seven **p:**	5982
SS	3: 6 out of the wilderness like **p** of smoke,	8490
	3:10 He made the **p** thereof *of* silver, the	5982
	5:15 His legs are **p** of marble, set upon	5982
Jer	27:19 saith the Lord of hosts concerning the **p,**	5982
	52:17 the **p** of brass that *were* in the house	5982
	52:20 The two **p,** one sea, and twelve brasen	5982
	52:21 *concerning* the **p,** the height of one pillar	5982
Eze	40:49 *were* **p** by the posts, one on this side,	5982
	42: 6 but had not **p** as the pillars of the courts:	5982
	42: 6 but had not pillars as the **p** of the courts:	5982
Joel	2:30 the earth, blood, and fire, and **p** of smoke.	8490
Gal	2: 9 Cephas, and John, who seemed to be **p,**	4769
Rev	10: 1 as *it were* the sun, and his feet as **p** of fire:	4769

PILLED (2)

Ge	30:37 **p** white strakes in them, and made	6478
	30:38 he set the rods which he had **p** before	6478

PILLOW (3) [PILLOWS]

1Sa	19:13 put a **p** of goats' *hair for* his bolster,	3523
	19:16 with a **p** of goats' *hair for* his bolster.	3523
Mk	4:38 the hinder part of the ship, asleep on a **p:**	4344

PILLOWS (4) [PILLOW]

Ge	28:11 put *them for* his **p,** and lay down in that	4763
	28:18 took the stone that he had put *for* his **p,**	4763
Eze	13:18 Woe to *the* women that sew to all	3704
	13:20 Behold, I *am* against your **p,** where*with*	3704

PILOTS (4)

Eze	27: 8 O Tyrus, *that* were in thee, *were* thy **p.**	2259
	27:27 thy **p,** thy calkers, and the occupiers of	2259
	27:28 shake at the sound of the cry of thy **p,**	2259
	27:29 the mariners, *and* all the **p** of the sea,	2259

PILTAI (1)

Ne	12:17 Zichri; of Miniamin, of Moadiah, **P;**	6408

PIN (3) [PINS]

Jdg	16:14 she fastened *it* with the **p,** and said unto	3489
	16:14 went away with the **p** of the beam,	3489
Eze	15: 3 will *men* take a **p** of it to hang any vessel	3489

PINE (8) [PINETH, PINING]

Lev	26:39 they that are left of you shall **p away** in	4743
	26:39 fathers shall they **p away** with them.	4743
Ne	8:15 **p** branches, and myrtle branches,	8081
Isa	41:19 *and* the **p,** and the box tree together:	8410
	60:13 fir tree, the **p tree,** and the box tree together,	8410
La	4: 9 for these **p away,** stricken through for	2100
Eze	24:23 ye shall **p away** for your iniquities,	4743
	33:10 we **p away** in them, how should we	4743

PINETH (1) [PINE]

Mk	9:18 and gnasheth with his teeth, and **p away:**	3583

PINING (1) [PINE]

Isa	38:12 he will cut me off with **p sickness:**	1803

PINNACLE (2)

Mt	4: 5 and setteth him on a **p** of the temple,	4419
Lk	4: 9 and set him on a **p** of the temple,	4419

PINON (2)

Ge	36:41 Duke Aholibamah, duke Elah, duke **P,**	6373
1Ch	1:52 Duke Aholibamah, duke Elah, duke **P,**	6373

PINS (11) [PIN]

Ex	27:19 all the **p** thereof, and all the pins of	3489
	27:19 all the **p** of the court, *shall be of* brass.	3489
	35:18 The **p** of the tabernacle, and the pins of	3489
	35:18 and the **p** of the court, and their cords,	3489
	38:20 all the **p** of the tabernacle, and of the	3489
	38:31 all the **p** of the tabernacle, and all the	3489
	38:31 and all the **p** of the court round about.	3489
	39:40 his **p,** and all the vessels of the service of	3489
Nu	3:37 their sockets, and their **p,** and their cords.	3489
	4:32 their sockets, and their **p,** and their cords,	3489
Isa	3:22 and the wimples, and the **crisping p,**	2754

PIPE (4) [PIPED, PIPERS, PIPES]

1Sa	10: 5 a tabret, and a **p,** and a harp, before them;	2485
Isa	5:12 and the viol, the tabret, and **p,** and wine,	2485
	30:29 as when one goeth with a **p** to come into	2485
1Co	14: 7 life giving sound, whether **p** or harp,	836

PIPED (4) [PIPE]

1Ki	1:40 the people **p** with pipes, and rejoiced	2490
Mt	11:17 We have **p** unto you, and ye have not	832
Lk	7:32 We have **p** unto you, and ye have not	832
1Co	14: 7 how shall it be known what is **p** or harped?	832

PIPERS (1) [PIPE]

Rev	18:22 and musicians, and of **p,** and trumpeters,	834

PIPES (6) [PIPE]

1Ki	1:40 the people piped with **p,** and rejoiced	2485
Jer	48:36 mine heart shall sound for Moab like **p,**	2485

Jer	48:36 mine heart shall sound like **p** for the men	2485
Eze	28:13 of thy **p** was prepared in thee in the day	5345
Zec	4: 2 and seven **p** to the seven lamps,	4166
	4:12 **p** empty the golden *oil* out of themselves?	6804

PIRAM (1)

Jos	10: 3 unto **P** king of Jarmuth, and unto Japhia	6502

PIRATHON (1) [PIRATHONITE]

Jdg	12:15 was buried in **P** in the land of Ephraim,	6552

PIRATHONITE (5) [PIRATHON]

Jdg	12:13 Abdon the son of Hillel, a **P,** judged Israel.	6553
	12:15 Abdon the son of Hillel the **P** died,	6553
2Sa	23:30 Benaiah the **P,** Hiddai of the brooks of	6553
1Ch	11:31 the children of Benjamin, Benaiah the **P,**	6553
	27:14 the eleventh month *was* Benaiah the **P,**	6553

PISGAH (5)

Nu	21:20 *is* in the country of Moab, *to* the top of **P,**	6449
	23:14 to the top of **P,** and built seven altars,	6449
Dt	3:27 Get thee up *into* the top of **P,** and lift up	6449
	4:49 sea of the plain, under the springs of **P.**	6449
	34: 1 the top of **P,** that *is* over against Jericho.	6449

PISHON See PISON

PISIDIA (2)

Ac	13:14 they came to Antioch in **P,** and went into	4099
	14:24 And after they had passed throughout **P,**	4099

PISON (1)

Ge	2:11 The name of the first *is* **P:** that *is it* which	6376

PISPAH (1)

1Ch	7:38 sons of Jether; Jephunneh, and **P,** and Ara.	6462

PISS (2) [PISSETH]

2Ki	18:27 and drink their own **p** with you?	4325+7272
Isa	36:12 and drink their own **p** with you?	4325+7272

PISSETH (6) [PISS]

1Sa	25:22 morning light *any that* **p** against the wall.	8366
	25:34 morning light *any that* **p** against the wall.	8366
1Ki	14:10 will cut off from Jeroboam *him that* **p**	8366
	16:11 he left him not *one that* **p** against a wall,	8366
	21:21 will cut off from Ahab *him that* **p** against	8366
2Ki	9: 8 will cut off from Ahab *him that* **p** against	8366

PIT (88) [PITS, SALTPITS, SLIMEPITS]

Ge	37:20 and cast him into some **p,** and we will say,	953
	37:22 him into this **p** *that is* in the wilderness,	953
	37:24 they took him, and cast him into a **p:**	953
	37:24 the **p** *was* empty, *there was* no water in it.	953
	37:28 they drew and lift up Joseph out of the **p,**	953
	37:29 Reuben returned unto the **p;** and behold,	953
	37:29 Joseph *was* not in the **p;** and he rent	953
Ex	21:33 a man shall open a **p,** or if a man shall dig	953
	21:33 or if a man shall dig a **p,** and not cover it,	953
	21:34 The owner of the **p** shall make *it* good,	953
Lev	11:36 Nevertheless a fountain or **p,** *wherein*	953
Nu	16:30 and they go down quick into the **p;**	7585
	16:33 went down alive into the **p,** and the earth	7585
2Sa	17: 9 he is hid now in some **p,** or in some	6354
	18:17 and cast him into a great **p** in the wood,	6354
	23:20 slew a lion in the midst of a **p** in time of	953
2Ki	10:14 slew them at the **p** of the shearing house,	953
1Ch	11:22 and slew a lion in a **p** in a snowy day.	953
Job	6:27 and you dig *a* **p** for your friend.	NIH
	7:16 They shall live **p** down *to* the bars of the **p,**	7585
	33:18 He keepeth back his soul from the **p,**	7845
	33:24 Deliver him from going down *to* the **p:**	7845
	33:28 will deliver his soul from going into the **p,**	7845
	33:30 To bring back his soul from the **p,** to be	7845
Ps	7:15 He made a **p,** and digged it, and is fallen	953
	9:15 The heathen are sunk down in the **p** *that*	7845
	28: 1 become like them that go down into the **p.**	953
	30: 3 alive, that I should not go down to the **p.**	953
	30: 9 in my blood, when I go down to the **p?**	7845
	35: 7 have they hid for me their net *in a* **p,**	7845
	40: 2 He brought me up also out of a horrible **p,**	953
	55:23 shalt bring them down into the **p** of	875
	57: 6 they have digged a **p** before me, into	7882
	69:15 and let not the **p** shut her mouth upon me.	875
	88: 4 with them that go down into the **p:**	953
	88: 6 Thou hast laid me in the lowest **p,**	953
	94:13 until the **p** be digged for the wicked.	7845
	143: 7 be like unto them that go down into the **p.**	953
Pr	22:14 whole, as those that go down into the **p:**	953
	22:14 The mouth of strange *women is* a deep **p:**	7745
	23:27 and a strange *woman is* a narrow **p.**	875
	26:27 Whoso diggeth a **p** shall fall therein:	7816
	28:10 he shall fall himself into his own **p:**	7816
	28:17 the blood of *any* person shall flee to the **p;**	953
Ecc	10: 8 He that diggeth a **p** shall fall into it;	1475
Isa	14:15 brought down to hell, to the sides of the **p.**	953
	14:19 sword, that go down to the stones of the **p;**	953
	24:17 Fear, and the **p,** and the snare, *are* upon	6354
	24:18 the noise of the fear shall fall into the **p;**	6354
	24:18 that cometh up out of the midst of the **p**	6354
	24:22 *as* prisoners are gathered in the **p,**	953
	30:14 or to take water *withal* out of the **p.**	1360
	38:17 soul *delivered it* from the **p** of corruption:	7845
	38:18 they that go down into the **p** cannot hope	953
	51: 1 to the hole of the **p** *whence* ye are digged.	953
	51:14 that he should not die in the **p,** nor	7845

Jer	18:20 for they have digged a **p** for my soul.	7745
	18:22 for they have digged a **p** to take me,	7745
	41: 7 *and* cast *them* into the midst of the **p,** he,	953
	41: 9 Now the **p** wherein Ishmael had cast all	953
	48:43 Fear, and the **p,** and the snare, *shall be*	6354
	48:44 fleeth from the fear shall fall into the **p;**	6354
	48:44 that getteth up out of the **p** shall be taken	6354
Eze	19: 4 he was taken in their **p,** and they brought	7845
	19: 8 net over him: he was taken in their **p.**	7845
	26:20 down with them that descend into the **p,**	953
	26:20 of old, with them that go down to the **p,**	953
	28: 8 They shall bring thee down to the **p,**	7845
	31:14 of men, with them that go down to the **p.**	953
	31:16 to hell with them that descend into the **p:**	953
	32:18 earth, with them that go down into the **p.**	953
	32:23 Whose graves are set in the sides of the **p,**	953
	32:24 shame with them that go down to the **p:**	953
	32:25 shame with them that go down to the **p,**	953
	32:29 and with them that go down to the **p.**	953
	32:30 shame with them that go down to the **p.**	953
Zec	9:11 prisoners out of the **p** wherein *is* no water.	953
Mt	12:11 and if it fall into a **p** on the sabbath day,	999
Lk	14: 5 shall have an ox or an ass fallen into a **p,**	5421
Rev	9: 1 him was given the key of the bottomless **p.**	5421
	9: 2 And he opened the bottomless **p;**	5421
	9: 2 and there arose a smoke out of the **p,**	5421
	9: 2 darkened by reason of the smoke of the **p.**	5421
	9:11 *which is* the angel of the bottomless **p,**	NIG
	11: 7 bottomless **p** shall make war against them,	NIG
	17: 8 shall ascend out of the bottomless **p,**	NIG
	20: 1 having the key of the bottomless **p** and	NIG
	20: 3 And cast him into the bottomless **p,**	NIG

PITCH (19) [PITCHED]

Ge	6:14 shalt **p** it within and without with pitch.	3722
	6:14 shalt pitch it within and without with **p.**	3724
Ex	2: 3 daubed it with slime and with **p,**	2203
Nu	1:52 the children of Israel shall **p** their **tents,**	2583
	1:53 the Levites shall **p** round about	2583
	2: 2 Every man of the children of Israel shall **p**	2583
	2: 2 of the congregation shall they **p.**	2583
	2: 3 camp of Judah **p** throughout their armies:	2583
	2: 5 those that do **p** next unto him *shall be*	2583
	2:12 those which **p** by him *shall be* the tribe of	2583
	3:23 The families of the Gershonites shall **p**	2583
	3:29 The families of the sons of Kohath shall **p**	2583
	3:35 *these* shall **p** on the side of the tabernacle	2583
Dt	1:33 search you out a place to **p** your **tents** *in,*	2583
Jos	4:20 took out of Jordan, did Joshua **p** in Gilgal.	6965
Isa	13:20 neither shall the Arabian **p tent** there;	167
	34: 9 the streams thereof shall be turned into **p,**	2203
	34: 9 and the land thereof shall become burning **p.**	2203
Jer	6: 3 they shall **p** *their* tents against her round	8628

PITCHED (82) [PITCH]

Ge	12: 8 **p** his tent, *having* Beth-el on the west,	5186
	13:12 the plain, and **p** his **tent** toward Sodom.	167
	26:17 **p** his **tent** in the valley of Gerar,	2583
	26:25 name of the Lord, and **p** his tent there:	5186
	31:25 Now Jacob had **p** his tent in the mount:	8628
	31:25 Laban with his brethren **p** in the mount	8628
	33:18 and **p** his **tent** before the city.	2583
Ex	17: 1 of the Lord, and **p** in Rephidim:	2583
	19: 2 of Sinai, and had **p** in the wilderness;	2583
	33: 7 **p** it without the camp, afar off from	5186
Nu	1:51 the tabernacle is to be **p,** the Levites	2583
	2:34 they **p** by their standards, and so they set	2583
	9:17 there the children of Israel **p** their **tents:**	2583
	9:18 at the commandment of the Lord they **p:**	2583
	12:16 and **p** in the wilderness of Paran.	2583
	21:10 of Israel set forward, and **p** in Oboth.	2583
	21:11 from Oboth, and **p** at Ije-abarim,	2583
	21:12 removed, and **p** in the valley of Zared.	2583
	21:13 and **p** on the *other* side of Arnon,	2583
	22: 1 **p** in the plains of Moab on *this* side	2583
	33: 5 from Rameses, and **p** in Succoth.	2583
	33: 6 departed from Succoth, and **p** in Etham,	2583
	33: 7 and they **p** before Migdol.	2583
	33: 8 the wilderness of Etham, and **p** in Marah.	2583
	33: 9 and ten palm trees; and they **p** there.	2583
	33:15 and **p** in the wilderness of Sinai.	2583
	33:16 of Sinai, and **p** at Kibroth-hattaavah.	2583
	33:18 from Hazeroth, and **p** in Rithmah.	2583
	33:19 from Rithmah, and **p** at Rimmon-parez.	2583
	33:20 from Rimmon-parez, and **p** in Libnah.	2583
	33:21 removed from Libnah, and **p** at Rissah.	2583
	33:22 from Rissah, and **p** in Kehelathah.	2583
	33:23 Kehelathah, and **p** in mount Shapher.	2583
	33:25 from Haradah, and **p** in Makheloth.	2583
	33:27 departed from Tahath, and **p** at Tarah.	2583
	33:28 removed from Tarah, and **p** in Mithcah.	2583
	33:29 from Mithcah, and **p** in Hashmonah.	2583
	33:31 from Moseroth, and **p** in Bene-jaakan.	2583
	33:33 from Hor-hagidgad, and **p** in Jotbathah.	2583
	33:36 **p** in the wilderness of Zin, which *is*	2583
	33:37 **p** in mount Hor, in the edge of the land	2583
	33:41 from mount Hor, and **p** in Zalmonah.	2583
	33:42 from Zalmonah, and **p** in Punon.	2583
	33:43 departed from Punon, and **p** in Oboth.	2583
	33:44 **p** in Ije-abarim, in the border of Moab.	2583
	33:45 departed from Iim, and **p** in Dibon-gad.	2583
	33:47 **p** in the mountains of Abarim, before	2583
	33:48 **p** in the plains of Moab by Jordan *near*	2583
	33:49 they **p** by Jordan, from Beth-jesimoth	2583
Jos	8:11 the city, and **p** on the north side of Ai:	2583

P

Jos 11: 5 and **p** together at the waters of Merom, 2583
Jdg 4:11 **p** his tent unto the plain of Zaanaim, 5186
 6:33 went over, and **p** in the valley of Jezreel. 2583
 7: 1 up early, and **p** beside the well of Harod: 2583
 11:18 **p** on the *other* side of Arnon, but came 2583
 11:20 and **p** in Jahaz, and fought against Israel. 2583
 15: 9 **p** in Judah, and spread themselves in Lehi 2583
 18:12 up, and **p** in Kirjath-jearim, in Judah: 2583
1Sa 4: 1 to battle, and **p** beside Eben-ezer: 2583
 4: 1 and the Philistines **p** in Aphek. 2583
 13: 5 they came up, and **p** in Michmash, 2583
 17: 1 **p** between Shochoh and Azekah, 2583
 17: 2 **p** by the valley of Elah, and set the battle 2583
 26: 3 Saul **p** in the hill of Hachilah, which *is* 2583
 26: 5 and came to the place where Saul had **p**: 2583
 26: 5 and the people **p** round about him. 2583
 28: 4 and came and **p** in Shunem. 2583
 28: 4 all Israel together, and they **p** in Gilboa. 2583
 29: 1 the Israelites **p** by a fountain which *is* in 2583
2Sa 6:17 of the tabernacle that David had **p** for it: 5186
 17:26 and Absalom **p** *in* the land of Gilead. 2583
 23:13 the troop of the Philistines **p** in the valley 2583
 24: 5 they passed over Jordan, and **p** in Aroer, 2583
1Ki 20:27 the children of Israel **p** before them like 2583
 20:29 they **p** one over against the other seven 2583
2Ki 25: 1 host, against Jerusalem, and **p** against it; 2583
1Ch 15: 1 for the ark of God, and **p** for it a tent. 5186
 16: 1 midst of the tent that David had **p** for it: 5186
 19: 7 who came and **p** before Medeba. 2583
2Ch 1: 4 for he had **p** a tent for it at Jerusalem. 5186
Jer 52: 4 **p** against it, and built forts against it 2583
Heb 8: 2 which the Lord **p**, and not man. 4078

PITCHER (12) [PITCHERS]

Ge 24:14 Let down thy **p**, I pray thee, that I may 3537
 24:15 with her **p** upon her shoulder. 3537
 24:16 to the well, and filled her **p**, and came up. 3537
 24:17 I pray thee, drink a little water of thy **p**. 3537
 24:18 let down her **p** upon her hand, 3537
 24:20 emptied her **p** into the trough, and ran 3537
 24:43 pray thee, a little water of thy **p** to drink; 3537
 24:45 Rebekah came forth with her **p** on her 3537
 24:46 let down her **p** from her *shoulder*, and 3537
Ecc 12: 6 or the **p** be broken at the fountain, 3537
Mk 14:13 there shall meet you a man bearing a **p** of 2765
Lk 22:10 a man meet you, bearing a **p** of water; 2765

PITCHERS (5) [PITCHER]

Jdg 7:16 with empty **p**, and lamps within 3537
 7:16 empty pitchers, and lamps within the **p**. 3537
 7:19 and brake the **p** that *were* in their hands. 3537
 7:20 brake the **p**, and held the lamps in their 3537
La 4: 2 how are they esteemed as earthen **p**, 5035

PITHOM (1)

Ex 1:11 Pharaoh treasure cities, **P** and Raamses. 6619

PITHON (2)

1Ch 8:35 the sons of Micah *were*, **P**, and Melech, 6377
 9:41 the sons of Micah *were*, **P**, and Melech, 6377

PITIED (6) [PITY]

Ps 106:46 made them also to be **p** of all those that 7356
La 2: 2 the habitations of Jacob, and hath not **p**: 2550
 2:17 he hath thrown down, and hath not **p**: 2550
 2:21 thine anger; thou hast killed, *and* not **p**. 2550
 3:43 thou hast slain, thou hast not **p**. 2550
Eze 16: 5 None eye **p** thee, to do any of these unto 2347

PITIETH (3) [PITY]

Ps 103:13 Like as a father **p** his children, 7355
 103:13 *so* the Lord **p** them that fear him. 7355
Eze 24:21 of your eyes, and that which your soul **p**; 4263

PITIFUL (3) [PITY]

La 4:10 The hands of the **p** women have sodden 7362
Jas 5:11 that the Lord is **very p**, and of tender 4184
1Pe 3: 8 love as brethren, *be* **p**, *be* courteous: 2155

PITS (6) [PIT]

1Sa 13: 6 and in rocks, and in high places, and in **p**. 953
Ps 119:85 The proud have digged **p** for me, which 7882
 140:10 into **deep p**, *that* they rise not up again. 4113
Jer 2: 6 through a land of deserts and of **p**, 7745
 14: 3 they came to the **p**, *and* found no water; 1356
La 4:20 was taken in their **p**, *of* whom we said, 7825

PITTANCE See NOUGHT

PITY (30) [PITIED, PITIETH, PITIFUL]

Dt 7:16 thine eye shall have no **p** upon them: 2347
 13: 8 neither shall thine eye **p** him, neither 2347
 19:13 Thine eye shall not **p** him, but thou shalt 2347
 19:21 thine eye shall not **p**; *but* life *shall go* for 2347
 25:12 off her hand, thine eye shall not **p** *her*. 2347
2Sa 12: 6 did this thing, and because he **had** no **p**. 2550
Job 6:14 To him that is afflicted **p** *should be* 2617
 19:21 **Have p** upon me, have pity upon me, 2603
 19:21 **have p** upon me, O ye my friends; 2603
Ps 69:20 I looked *for some* to **take p**, but there 5110
Pr 19:17 He that **hath p** upon the poor lendeth 2603
 28: 8 he shall gather it for him that will **p** 2603
Isa 13:18 they shall **have** no **p** on the fruit of 7355
 63:19 in his love and in his **p** he redeemed 2551
Jer 13:14 I will not **p**, nor spare, nor have mercy, 2550
 15: 5 For who shall **have p** upon thee, 2550

Jer 21: 7 neither **have p**, nor have mercy. 2550
Eze 5:11 mine eye spare, neither will I **have** any **p**. 2550
 7: 4 not spare thee, neither will I **have p**: 2550
 7: 9 eye shall not spare, neither will I **have p**: 2550
 8:18 eye shall not spare, neither will I **have p**. 2550
 9: 5 let not your eye spare, neither **have** ye **p**: 2550
 9:10 will I **have p**, *but* I will recompense 2550
 36:21 I **had p** for mine holy name, which 2550
Joel 2:18 be jealous for his land, and **p** his people. 2550
Am 1:11 did cast off all **p**, and his anger did tear 7356
Jnh 4:10 the Lord, Thou hast **had p** on the gourd, 2347
Zec 11: 5 and their own shepherds **p** them not. 2550
 11: 6 For I will no more **p** the inhabitants of 2550
Mt 18:33 fellowservant, even as I **had p** on thee? *1653*

PLACE (721) [BURYINGPLACE, PLACED, PLACES, THRESHINGPLACE]

Ge 1: 9 heaven be gathered together unto one **p**, 4725
 12: 6 passed through the land unto the **p** 4725
 13: 3 unto the **p** where his tent had been at 4725
 13: 4 Unto the **p** of the altar, which he had 4725
 13:14 from the **p** where thou *art* northward, 4725
 18:24 not spare the **p** for the fifty righteous that 4725
 18:26 then I will spare all the **p** for their sakes. 4725
 18:33 and Abraham returned unto his **p**. 4725
 19:12 hast in the city, bring *them* out of *this* **p**: 4725
 19:13 we will destroy this **p**, because the cry 4725
 19:14 and said, Up, get ye out of this **p**; 4725
 19:27 to the **p** where he stood before the Lord: 4725
 20:11 Surely the fear of God *is* not in this **p**; 4725
 20:13 at every **p** whither we shall come, say of 4725
 21:31 Wherefore he called that **p** Beer-sheba; 4725
 22: 3 went unto the **p** of which God had told 4725
 22: 4 lift up his eyes, and saw the **p** afar off. 4725
 22: 9 they came to the **p** which God had told 4725
 22:14 Abraham called the name of that **p** 4725
 26: 7 the men of the **p** asked *him* of his wife; 4725
 26: 7 *said he*, the men of the **p** should kill me 4725
 28:11 he lighted upon a *certain* **p**, 4725
 28:11 he took of the stones of *that* **p**, 4725
 28:11 pillows, and lay down in that **p** to sleep. 4725
 28:16 and he said, Surely the Lord is in this **p**; 4725
 28:17 and said, How dreadful *is* this **p**! 4725
 28:19 he called the name of that **p** Beth-el: 4725
 29: 3 again upon the well's mouth in his **p**. 4725
 29:22 gathered together all the men of the **p**, 4725
 30:25 that I may go unto mine own **p**, and to 4725
 31:55 Laban departed, and returned unto his **p**. 4725
 32: 2 he called the name of that **p** Mahanaim. 4725
 32:30 Jacob called the name of the **p** Peniel: for 4725
 33:17 the name of the **p** is called Succoth. 4725
 35: 7 there an altar, and called the **p** El-beth-el: 4725
 35:13 God went up from him in the **p** where he 4725
 35:14 Jacob set up a pillar in the **p** where he 4725
 35:15 Jacob called the name of the **p** where God 4725
 38:14 and sat in an **open p**, 5869+6607
 38:21 he asked the men of that **p**, saying, NIH
 38:21 they said, There was no harlot in this **p**. NIH
 38:22 also the men of the **p** said, *that* there was 4725
 38:22 *that* there was no harlot in this **p**. NIH
 39:20 **p** where the king's prisoners *were* bound: 4725
 40: 3 prison, the **p** where Joseph *was* bound. 4725
 40:13 thine head, and restore thee unto thy **p**: 3653
 48: 9 whom God hath given me in this **p**. NIH
 50:19 Fear not: for *am* I in the **p** of God? 8478
Ex 3: 5 for the **p** whereon thou standest *is* holy 4725
 3: 8 unto the **p** of the Canaanites, 4725
 10:23 neither rose any from his **p** for three days: 8478
 13: 3 **p**: there shall no leavened bread be eaten. NIH
 15:17 *in* the **p**, O Lord, *which* thou hast made 4349
 16:29 abide ye every man in his **p**, let no man 8478
 16:29 let no man go out of his **p** on the seventh 4725
 17: 7 he called the name of the **p** Massah, 4725
 18:21 *such* over them, *to be* rulers of 7760
 18:23 all this people shall also go to their **p** in 4725
 21:13 will appoint thee a **p** whither he shall flee. 4725
 23:20 to bring thee into the **p** which I have 4725
 26:33 shall divide unto you between the holy **p** NIH
 26:34 ark of the Testimony in the most holy **p**. NIH
 28:29 when he goeth in unto the holy **p**, for a NIH
 28:35 goeth in unto the holy **p** before the Lord, NIH
 28:43 in the holy **p**; that they bear not iniquity, NIH
 29:30 the congregation to minister in the holy **p**. NIH
 29:31 and seethe his flesh in the holy **p**. 4725
 31:11 sweet incense for the holy **p**: according to NIH
 32:34 lead the people unto the **p** of which I 4725
 33:21 *there is* a **p** by me, and thou shalt stand 4725
 35:19 to do service in the holy **p**, the holy NIH
 38:24 the holy **p**, even the gold of the offering, NIH
 39: 1 to do service in the holy **p**, and made NIH
 39:41 of service to do service in the holy **p**, NIH
Lev 1:16 on the east part, by the **p** of the ashes: NIH
 4:12 forth without the camp unto a clean **p**, 4725
 4:24 kill it in the **p** where they kill the burnt 4725
 4:29 slay the sin offering in the **p** of the burnt 4725
 4:33 slay it for a sin offering in the **p** where 4725
 6:11 ashes without the camp unto a clean **p**. 4725
 6:16 bread shall it be eaten in the holy **p**; 4725
 6:25 In the **p** where the burnt offering is killed 4725
 6:26 in the holy **p** shall it be eaten, in the court 4725
 6:27 whereon it was sprinkled in the holy **p**. 4725
 6:30 *withal* in the **p**, shall be eaten: NIH
 7: 2 In the **p** where they kill the burnt offering 4725
 7: 6 it shall be eaten in the holy **p**: it *is* most 4725
 10:13 ye shall eat it in the holy **p**, because it *is* 4725

Lev 10:14 heave shoulder shall ye eat in a clean **p**; 4725
 10:17 ye not eaten the sin offering in the holy **p**, 4725
 10:18 **p**: ye should indeed have eaten it in the NIH
 10:18 eaten it in the holy **p**, as I commanded. NIH
 13:19 the **p** of the boil there be a white rising, 4725
 13:23 if the bright spot stay in his **p**, 8478
 13:28 if the bright spot stay in his **p**, 8478
 14:13 he shall slay the lamb in the **p** where he 4725
 14:13 and the burnt offering, in the holy **p**: 4725
 14:28 upon the **p** of the blood of the trespass 4725
 14:40 they shall cast them into an unclean **p** 4725
 14:41 off without the city into an unclean **p**: 4725
 14:42 and put *them* in the **p** of *those* stones; 8478
 14:45 forth out of the city into an unclean **p**. 4725
 16: 2 he come not at all times into the holy **p** NIH
 16: 3 Thus shall Aaron come into the holy **p**: NIH
 16:16 shall make an atonement for the holy **p**, NIH
 16:17 atonement in the holy **p**, until he come NIH
 16:20 made an end of reconciling the holy **p**, NIH
 16:23 he put on when he went into the holy **p**, NIH
 16:24 wash his flesh with water in the holy **p**, NIH
 16:27 **p**, shall *one* carry forth without the camp; NIH
 24: 9 sons'; and they shall eat it in the holy **p**: 4725
Nu 2: 17 every man in his **p** by their standards. 3027
 9:17 in the **p** where the cloud abode, there 4725
 10:14 In the first **p** went the standard of the NIH
 10:29 We *are* journeying unto the **p** of which 4725
 10:33 to search out a **resting p** for them. 4496
 11: 3 he called the name of the **p** Taberah: 4725
 11:34 he called the name of that **p** 4725
 13:24 The **p** was called the brook Eshcol, 4725
 14:40 will go up unto the **p** which the Lord 4725
 18:10 In the most holy **p** shalt thou eat it; NIH
 18:31 ye shall eat it in every **p**, ye and 4725
 19: 9 *them* up without the camp in a clean **p**, 4725
 20: 5 of Egypt, to bring us in unto this evil **p**? 4725
 20: 5 it *is* no **p** of seed, or of figs, or vines, 4725
 21: 3 and he called the name of the **p** Hormah. 4725
 22:26 went further, and stood in a narrow **p**, 4725
 23: 3 I will tell thee. And he went to a **high p**. 8205
 23:13 I pray thee, with me unto another **p**, 4725
 23:27 thee, I will bring thee unto another **p**; 4725
 24:11 Therefore now flee thou to thy **p**: 4725
 24:21 Strong *is* thy **dwelling p**, and thou 4186
 24:25 rose up, and went and returned to his **p**: 4725
 28: 7 in the holy **p** shalt thou cause the strong NIH
 32: 1 that behold, the **p** was a place for cattle; 4725
 32: 1 that behold, the place *was* a **p** for cattle; 4725
 32:17 until we have brought them unto their **p**: 4725
 33:54 shall be in the **p** where his lot falleth: 8033
Dt 1:31 that ye went, until ye came into this **p**. 4725
 1:33 to search you out a **p** to pitch your tents 4725
 2:37 *nor* unto any **p** of the river Jabbok, nor 3027
 9: 7 until ye came unto this **p**, ye have been 4725
 11: 5 the wilderness, until ye came into this **p**; 4725
 11:24 Every **p** whereon the soles of your feet 4725
 12: 3 destroy the names of them out of that **p**. 4725
 12: 5 unto the **p** which the Lord your God 4725
 12:11 there shall be a **p** which the Lord your 4725
 12:13 burnt offerings in every **p** that thou seest: 4725
 12:14 in the **p** which the Lord shall choose in 4725
 12:18 **p** which the Lord thy God shall choose, 4725
 12:21 If the **p** which the Lord thy God hath 4725
 12:26 go unto the **p** which the Lord shall 4725
 14:23 in the **p** which he shall choose to place 4725
 14:23 the place which he shall choose to **p** his 7931
 14:24 *or* if the **p** be too far from thee, which 4725
 14:25 shalt go unto the **p** which the Lord thy 4725
 15:20 in the **p** which the Lord shall choose, 4725
 16: 2 in the **p** which the Lord shall choose to 4725
 16: 2 Lord shall choose to **p** his name there. 7931
 16: 6 at the **p** which the Lord thy God shall 4725
 16: 6 **p** his name *in*, there thou shalt sacrifice 7931
 16: 7 eat *it* in the **p** which the Lord thy God 4725
 16:11 in the **p** which the Lord thy God hath 4725
 16:11 thy God hath chosen to **p** his name there. 7931
 16:15 in the **p** which the Lord shall choose: 4725
 16:16 thy God in the **p** which he shall choose; 4725
 17: 8 get thee up into the **p** which the Lord 4725
 17:10 which *they* of that **p** which the Lord 4725
 18: 6 unto the **p** which the Lord shall choose; 4725
 21:19 of his city, and unto the gate of his **p**; 4725
 23:12 shalt have a **p** also without the camp, 3027
 23:16 in *that* **p** which he shall choose in one of 4725
 26: 2 shalt go unto the **p** which the Lord thy 4725
 26: 2 thy God shall choose to **p** his name there. 7931
 26: 9 he hath brought us into this **p**, 4725
 27:15 putteth *it* in *a* secret **p**. And all the people NIH
 29: 7 when ye came unto this **p**, Sihon the king 4725
 31:11 thy God in the **p** which he shall choose, 4725
Jos 1: 3 Every **p** that the sole of your foot shall 4725
 3: 3 ye shall remove from your **p**, and go after 4725
 4: 3 out of the **p** where the priests' feet stood 2088
 4: 3 leave them in the **lodging p**, where you 4411
 4: 8 them unto the **p where** they **lodged**, 4411
 4: 9 in the **p** where the feet of the priests 8478
 4:18 waters of Jordan returned unto their **p**, 4725
 5: 9 Wherefore the name of the **p** is called 4725
 5:15 for the **p** whereon thou standest *is* holy. 4725
 7:26 Wherefore the name of that **p** was called, 4725
 8:19 the ambush arose quickly out of their **p**, 4725
 9:27 this day, in the **p** which he should choose. 4725
 20: 4 give him a **p**, that he may dwell among 4725
Jdg 2: 5 they called the name of that **p** Bochim: 4725
 6:26 in the **ordered p**, and take the second 4634

P

Jdg
7: 7 the *other* people go every man unto his **p.** — 4725
7:21 they stood every man in his p round — 8478
9:55 they departed every man unto his **p.** — 4725
11:19 we pray thee, through thy land into my **p.** — 4725
15:17 his hand, and called that **p** Ramath-lehi. — NIH
15:19 clave a **hollow p** that was in the jaw, — 4388
17: 8 to sojourn where he could find *a p.* — NIH
17: 9 I go to sojourn where I may find *a p.* — NIH
18: 3 what makest thou in this **p**? and what hast — NIH
18:10 a **p** where *there is* no want of any thing — 4725
18:12 they called that **p** Mahaneh-dan — 4725
19:16 but the men of the **p** *were* Benjamites. — 4725
19:28 the man rose up, and gat him unto his **p.** — 4725
20:22 set *their* battle again in array in the **p** — 4725
20:33 the men of Israel rose up out of their **p,** — 4725
20:36 for the men of Israel gave **p** to — 4725
21:19 *a p* which *is* on the north side of Beth-el, — NIH
Ru 1: 7 Wherefore she went forth out of the **p** — 4725
3: 4 that thou shalt mark the **p** where he shall — 4725
4:10 his brethren, and from the gate of his **p:** — 4725
1Sa 3: 2 when Eli *was* laid down in his **p,** — 4725
3: 9 So Samuel went and lay down in his **p.** — 4725
5: 3 took Dagon, and set him in his **p** again. — 4725
5:11 let it go again to his own **p,** that it slay us — 4725
6: 2 us wherewith we shall send it to his **p.** — 4725
9:12 of the people to day in the **high p:** — 1116
9:13 before he go up to the **high p** to eat: — 1116
9:14 against them, for to go up *to* the **high p.** — 1116
9:19 go up before me *unto* the **high p;** for ye — 1116
9:22 made them sit in the chiefest **p** among — 4725
9:25 come down from the **high p** *into* the city, — 1116
10: 5 down from the **high p** with a psaltery, — 1116
10:12 one of **the same p** answered and said, — 8033
10:13 of prophesying, he came *to* the **high p.** — 1116
12: 8 of Egypt, and made them dwell in this **p.** — 4725
14: 9 will stand still in our **p,** and will not go — 8478
14:46 and the Philistines went to their own **p.** — 4725
15:12 he set him up a **p,** and is gone about, — 3027
19: 2 and abide in a **secret p,** and hide thyself: — 5643
20:19 come to the **p** where thou didst hide — 4725
20:25 by Saul's side, and David's **p** was empty. — 4725
20:27 of the month, that David's **p** was empty: — 4725
20:37 when the lad was come to the **p** of — 4725
20:41 David arose out of *a p* toward the south, — NIH
21: 2 *my* servants to such and such a **p.** — 4725
23:22 know and see his **p** where his haunt is, — 4725
23:28 they called that **p** Sela-hammahlekoth. — 4725
26: 5 came to the **p** where Saul had pitched: — 4725
26: 5 David beheld the **p** where Saul lay, — 4725
26:25 on his way, and Saul returned to his **p.** — 4725
27: 5 let them give me a **p** in some town in — 4725
29: 4 return, that he may go again to his **p,** — 4725
2Sa 2:16 wherefore that **p** was called — 4725
2:23 fell down there, and died **in the same p:** — 8478
2:23 as many as came to the **p** where Asahel — 4725
5:20 Therefore he called the name of that **p** — 4725
6: 8 he called the *name* of the **p** Perez-uzzah — 4725
6:17 in the ark of the LORD, and set it in his **p,** — 4725
7:10 Moreover I will appoint a **p** for my people — 4725
7:10 that they may dwell **in a p** of their own, — 8478
11:16 that he assigned Uriah unto a **p** where he — 4725
15:17 him, and tarried in a **p** that was far off. — 1004
15:19 return to thy **p,** and abide with the king: — 4725
15:21 surely in what **p** my lord the king shall be, — 4725
17: 9 hid now in some pit, or in some *other* **p.** — 4725
17:12 So shall we come upon him in some **p** — 4725
18:18 and it is called unto this day, Absalom's **p.** — 3027
19:39 and he returned unto his own **p.** — 4725
22:20 He brought me forth also into a **large p:** — 4800
23: 7 be utterly burnt with fire in the same **p.** — 7675
1Ki 3: 4 for that *was* the great **high p:** — 1116
4:12 *even* unto the **p** *that is* beyond Jokneam: — NIH
4:28 dromedaries brought they unto the **p** — 4725
5: 9 flotes unto the **p** that thou shalt appoint — 4725
6:16 for the oracle, *even* for the most holy **p.** — NIH
7:50 the most holy **p,** *and* for the doors of — NIH
8: 6 of the covenant of the LORD unto his **p,** — NIH
8: 6 to the most holy **p,** even under the wings — NIH
8: 7 *their* two wings over the **p** of the ark, — NIH
8: 8 seen out in the holy **p** before the oracle, — NIH
8:10 **p,** that the cloud filled the house of — NIH
8:13 a **settled p** for thee to abide in for ever. — 4349
8:21 I have set there a **p** for the ark, wherein — 4725
8:29 toward the **p** of which thou hast said, — 4725
8:29 thy servant shall make towards this **p.** — 4725
8:30 when they shall pray towards this **p:** — 4725
8:30 hear thou in heaven thy **dwelling p,** — 4725
8:35 if they pray towards this **p,** and confess — 4725
8:39 hear thou in heaven thy **dwelling p,** — 4349
8:43 Hear thou *in* heaven thy **dwelling p,** — 4349
8:49 supplication *in* heaven thy **dwelling p,** — 4349
10:19 *there were* stays on either side on the **p** — 4725
11: 7 did Solomon build a **high p** for Chemosh, — 1116
13: 8 will I eat bread nor drink water in this **p:** — 4725
13:16 bread nor drink water with thee in this **p:** — 4725
13:22 eaten bread and drunk water in the **p,** — 4725
20:24 every man out of his **p,** and put captains — 4725
21:19 In the **p** where dogs licked the blood of — 4725
22:10 in a **void p** *in* the entrance of the gate of — 1637
2Ki 5:11 strike his hand over the **p,** and recover — 4725
6: 1 the **p** where we dwell with thee is too — 4725
6: 2 let us make us a **p** there, where we may — 4725
6: 6 he shewed him the **p.** And he cut down — 4725
6: 8 In such and such a **p** *shall be* my camp. — 4725
6: 9 Beware that *thou* pass not such a **p;** — 4725

2Ki 6:10 the king of Israel sent to the **p** which — 4725
18:25 the LORD against this **p** to destroy it? — 4725
22:16 I will bring evil upon this **p,** and upon — 4725
22:17 my wrath shall be kindled against this **p,** — 4725
22:19 thou heardest what I spake against this **p,** — 4725
22:20 all the evil which I will bring upon this **p.** — 4725
23:15 the **high p** which Jeroboam the son of — 1116
23:15 that altar and the **high p** he brake down, — 1116
23:15 burnt the **high p,** *and* stampt *it* small to — 1116
1Ch 6:32 they ministered before the **dwelling p** of — 4908
6:49 *were* appointed for all the work of the **p** — 4725
13:11 wherefore that **p** is called Perez-uzza to — 4725
14:11 they called the name of that **p** — 4725
15: 1 prepared a **p** for the ark of God, — 4725
15: 3 bring up the ark of the LORD unto his **p,** — 4725
15:12 Israel unto the **p** *that* I have prepared for — NIH
16:27 strength and gladness *are* in his **p.** — 4725
16:39 LORD in the **high p** that *was* at Gibeon, — 1116
17: 9 I will ordain a **p** for my people Israel, — 4725
17: 9 they shall dwell **in** their **p,** and shall be — 8478
21:22 Grant me the **p** of *this* threshingfloor, — 4725
21:25 So David gave to Ornan for the **p** six — 4725
21:29 at that season in the **high p** at Gibeon. — 1116
23:32 the charge of the holy **p,** and the charge — NIH
28:11 and of the **p** of the mercy seat, — 1004
2Ch 1: 3 went to the **high p** that *was* at Gibeon; — 1116
1: 4 to *the* **p** *which* David had prepared for it: — 4725
1:13 **high p** that *was* at Gibeon to Jerusalem, — 1116
3: 1 in the **p** that David had prepared in — 4725
4:22 inner doors thereof for the most holy **p,** — NIH
5: 7 of the covenant of the LORD unto his **p,** — 4725
5: 7 into the most holy **p,** even under the — 4725
5: 8 forth *their* wings over the **p** of the ark, — 4725
5:11 **p:** (for all the priests that were present — 4725
6: 2 for thee, and a **p** for thy dwelling for ever. — 4349
6:20 upon the **p** whereof thou hast said that — 4725
6:20 which thy servant prayeth towards this **p.** — 4725
6:21 which they shall make towards this **p:** — 4725
6:21 hear thou from thy dwelling **p,** *even* from — 4725
6:26 *yet* if they pray towards this **p,** — 4725
6:30 hear thou from heaven thy **dwelling p,** — 4349
6:33 from thy dwelling **p,** and do according — 4349
6:39 from thy dwelling **p,** their prayer and — 4349
6:40 unto the prayer *that is made* in this **p.** — 4725
6:41 into thy **resting p,** thou, and the ark of — 5118
7:12 have chosen this **p** to myself for a house — 4725
7:15 unto the prayer *that is made* in this **p.** — 4725
9:18 stays on each side of the sitting **p,** — 4725
18: 9 they sat in a **void p** *at* the entering in of — 1637
20:26 the name of the same **p** was called, — 4725
24:11 and took it, and carried it to his **p** again. — 4725
29: 5 carry forth the filthiness out of the holy **p.** — NIH
29: 7 in the holy **p** unto the God of Israel. — 4725
30:16 they stood in their **p** after their manner, — 5977
30:27 prayer came *up* to his holy dwelling **p,** — 4583
34:24 I will bring evil upon this **p,** and upon — 4725
34:25 wrath shall be poured out upon this **p,** — 4725
34:27 thou heardest his words against this **p,** — 4725
34:28 all the evil that I will bring upon this **p,** — 4725
34:31 the king stood in his **p,** and made a — 5977
35: 5 stand in the holy **p** according to — NIH
35:10 priests stood in their **p,** and the Levites — 5977
35:15 singers the sons of Asaph *were* in their **p,** — 4612
35:15 on his people, and on his **dwelling p** — 4583
Ezr 1: 4 whosoever remaineth in any **p** where he — 4725
1: 4 let the men of his **p** help him with silver, — 4725
2:68 for the house of God to set it up in his **p:** — 4349
5:15 let the house of God be builded in his **p.** — 870
6: 3 the **p** where they offered sacrifices, — 870
6: 5 *every* one to his **p,** and place *them* in — 870
6: 5 place, and put *them* in the house of God. — 5182
6: 7 the Jews build this house of God in his **p.** — 870
8:17 unto Iddo the chief at the **p** Casiphia, — 4725
8:17 the Nethinims, at the **p** Casiphia, — 4725
9: 8 and to give us a nail in his holy **p,** — 4725
Ne 1: 9 will bring them unto the **p** that I have — 4725
2: 3 **p** of my fathers' sepulchres, *lieth* waste, — 1004
2:14 *was* no **p** for the beast *that was* under — 4725
3:16 unto *the* **p** over against the sepulchres of — NIH
3:26 unto *the* **p** over against the water gate — NIH
3:31 son unto the **p** of the Nethinims, — 1004
4:20 In what *therefore* ye hear the sound of — 5977
8: 7 the law: and the people *stood* in their **p.** — 5977
9: 3 they stood up in their **p,** and read in — 5977
13:11 them together, and set them in their **p.** — 5977
Est 2: 9 her maids unto the best *p* of the house of — NIH
4:14 arise to the Jews from another **p;** — 4725
7: 8 garden into the **p** of the banquet of wine; — 1004
Job 2:11 they came every one from his own **p;** — 4725
6:17 is hot, they are consumed out of their **p.** — 4725
7:10 neither shall his **p** know him any more. — 4725
8:17 about the heap, *and* seeth the **p** of stones. — 1004
8:18 If he destroy him from his **p,** then *it* shall — 4725
8:22 the **dwelling p** of the wicked shall come — 168
9: 6 Which shaketh the earth out of her **p,** — 4725
14:18 and the rock is removed out of his **p,** — 4725
16:18 thou my blood, and let my cry have no **p.** — 4725
18: 4 shall the rock be removed out of his **p?** — 4725
18:21 *is* the **p** of him that knoweth not God. — 4725
20: 9 neither shall his **p** any more behold him. — 4725
26: 7 out the north over the **empty p,** — 8414
27:21 and as a storm hurleth him out of his **p.** — 4725
27:23 at him, and shall hiss him out of his **p.** — 4725
28: 1 and a **p** for gold *where* they fine *it.* — 4725
28: 6 The stones of it *are* the **p** of sapphires: — 4725

Job 28:12 and where *is* the **p** of understanding? — 4725
28:20 and where *is* the **p** of understanding? — 4725
28:23 thereof, and he knoweth the **p** thereof. — 4725
36:16 thee out of the strait *into* a **broad p,** — 7338
36:20 when people are cut off **in** their **p.** — 8478
37: 1 trembleth, and is moved out of his **p.** — 4725
38:10 brake up for it my decreed **p,** and set bars — NIH
38:12 *and* caused the dayspring to know his **p;** — 4725
38:19 *as for* darkness, where *is* the **p** thereof, — 4725
39:28 the crag of the rock, and the **strong p.** — 4686
40:12 and tread down the wicked in their **p.** — 8478
Ps 18:11 made darkness his **secret p;** his pavilion — 5643
18:19 He brought me forth also into a **large p;** — 4800
24: 3 and who shall stand in his holy **p?** — 4725
26: 8 and the **p** where thine honour dwelleth. — 4725
26:12 My foot standeth in an **even p:** — 4334
32: 7 Thou *art* my **hiding p;** thou shalt preserve — 5643
33:14 From the **p** of his habitation he looketh — 4349
37:10 thou shalt diligently consider his **p,** — 4725
44:19 thou hast sore broken us in the **p** of — 4725
46: 4 the holy **p** of the tabernacles of the most — NIH
52: 5 pluck thee out of *thy* **dwelling p,** — 168
66:12 thou broughtest us out into a wealthy **p.** — NIH
68:17 *is* among them, *as in* Sinai, in the holy **p.** — NIH
74: 7 **dwelling p** of thy name to the ground. — 4908
76: 2 tabernacle, and his **dwelling p** in Zion. — 4585
79: 7 and laid waste his **dwelling p.** — 5116
81: 7 answered thee in the **secret p** of thunder: — 5643
90: 1 thou hast been our **dwelling p** in all — 4583
91: 1 that dwelleth in the **secret p** of the most — 5643
103:16 and the **p** thereof shall know it no more. — 4725
104: 8 they go down *by* the valleys unto the **p** — 4725
118: 5 answered me, *and set me* in a **large p.** — 4800
119:114 Thou *art* my **hiding p** and my shield: — 5643
132: 5 Until I find out a **p** for the LORD, — 4725
Pr 1:21 She crieth in the **chief p** of concourse, — 7218
14:26 and his children shall have a **p of refuge.** — 4268
15: 3 The eyes of the LORD *are* in every **p,** — 4725
24:15 of the righteous; spoil not his **resting p:** — 7258
25: 6 and stand not in the **p** of great *men:* — 4725
27: 8 so *is* a man that wandereth from his **p.** — 4725
Ecc 1: 5 and hasteth to his **p** where he arose. — 4725
1: 7 unto the **p** from whence the rivers come, — 4725
3:16 moreover I saw under the sun the **p** of — 4725
3:16 the **p** of righteousness, *that* iniquity *was* — 4725
3:20 All go unto one **p;** all are of the dust, — 4725
6: 6 he seen no good: do not all go to one **p?** — 4725
8:10 come and gone from the **p** of the holy, — 4725
10: 4 ruler rise up against thee, leave not thy **p;** — 4725
10: 6 in great dignity, and the rich sit in **low p.** — 8216
11: 3 *in* the **p** where the tree falleth, there it — 4725
Isa 4: 5 upon every **dwelling p** of mount Zion, — 4349
4: 6 for a **p of refuge,** and for a covert from — 4268
5: 8 *that* lay field to field, till *there be* no **p,** — 4725
7:23 to pass in that day, *that* every **p** shall be, — 4725
13:13 and the earth shall remove out of her **p,** — 4725
14: 2 shall take them, and bring them to their **p:** — 4725
16:12 is seen that Moab is weary on the **high p,** — 1116
18: 4 I will consider in my **dwelling p** like a — 4349
18: 7 to the name of the LORD of — 4725
22:23 I will fasten him *as* a nail in a sure **p;** — 4725
22:25 shall the nail that is fastened in the sure **p** — 4725
25: 5 noise of strangers, as the heat in a **dry p;** — 6724
26:21 the LORD cometh out of his **p** to punish — 4725
28: 8 *and* filthiness, *so that there is* no **p** *clean.* — 4725
28:17 the waters shall overflow the **hiding p,** — 5643
28:25 appointed barley and the rye in their **p?** — 1367
30:32 *in* every **p** where the grounded staff shall — NIH
32: 2 man shall be as a **hiding p** from the wind, — 4224
32: 2 rivers of water in a **dry p,** as the shadow — 6724
32:19 and the city shall be low in a **low p.** — 8218
33:16 his **p of defence** *shall be* the munitions — 4869
33:21 LORD *will be* unto us a **p** of broad rivers — 4725
34:14 rest there, and find for herself a **p of rest.** — 4494
35: 1 the **solitary p** shall be glad *for* them; — 6723
45:19 spoken in secret, in a dark **p** of the earth: — 4725
46: 7 and set him **in** his **p,** and he standeth; — 8478
46: 7 from his **p** shall he not remove: — 4725
46:13 I will *bring* salvation in Zion for Israel my — 5414
49:20 in thine ears, The **p** *is* too strait for me: — 4725
49:20 for me: **give p** to me that I may dwell. — 5066
54: 2 Enlarge the **p** of thy tent, and let them — 4725
56: 5 within my walls a **p** and a name better — 3027
57:15 holy **p,** with him also *that is* of a contrite — NIH
60:13 to beautify the **p** of my sanctuary; — 4725
60:13 and I will make the **p** of my feet glorious. — 4725
65:10 Achor a **p** for the herds **to lie down in,** — 7258
66: 1 unto me? and where *is* the **p** of my rest? — 4725
Jer 4: 7 he is gone forth from his **p** to make thy — 4725
4:26 lo, the **fruitful p** *was* a wilderness, — 3759
6: 3 they shall feed every one *in* his **p.** — 3027
7: 3 I will cause you to dwell in this **p,** — 4725
7: 6 and shed not innocent blood in this **p,** — 4725
7: 7 I will cause you to dwell in this **p,** — 4725
7:12 ye now unto my **p** which *was* in Shiloh, — 4725
7:14 unto the **p** which I gave to you and to — 4725
7:20 my fury *shall* be poured upon this **p,** — 4725
7:32 shall bury in Tophet, till there be no **p.** — 4725
9: 2 that I had in the wilderness a **lodging p** — 4411
13: 7 took the girdle from the **p** where I had hid — 4725
14:13 but I will give you assured peace in this **p.** — 4725
16: 2 thou shalt have sons nor daughters in this **p.** — 4725
16: 3 the daughters that are born in this **p,** — 4725
16: 9 I will cause to cease out of this **p** in your — 4725
17:12 the beginning *is* the **p** of our sanctuary. — 4725

Jer 18:14 that come from **another p** be forsaken? 2114
19: 3 Behold, I *will* bring evil upon this **p**, 4725
19: 4 have estranged this **p**, and have burnt 4725
19: 4 have filled this **p** with the blood of 4725
19: 6 that this **p** shall no more be called Tophet, 4725
19: 7 counsel of Judah and Jerusalem in this **p**; 4725
19:11 *them* in Tophet, till *there be* no **p** to bury. 4725
19:12 Thus will I do unto this **p**, saith 4725
19:13 shall be defiled as the **p** of Tophet, 4725
22: 3 neither shed innocent blood in this **p**. 4725
22:11 his father, which went forth out of this **p**; 4725
22:12 he shall die in the **p** whither they have led 4725
24: 5 I have sent out of this **p** *into* the land 4725
27:22 bring them up, and restore them to this **p**. 4725
28: 3 **p** all the vessels of the LORD's house, 4725
28: 3 king of Babylon took away from this **p**, 4725
28: 4 I *will* bring again to this **p** Jeconiah the 4725
28: 6 away captive, from Babylon unto this **p**. 4725
29:10 in causing you to return to this **p**. 4725
29:14 I will bring you again into the **p** whence 4725
32:37 I will bring them again unto this **p**, 4725
33:10 Again this be heard in this **p**, 4725
33:12 Again in this **p**, *which is* desolate 4725
38: 9 is like to die for hunger in the **p where** 8478
40: 2 hath pronounced this evil upon this **p**. 4725
42:18 reproach; and ye shall see this **p** no more. 4725
42:22 in the **p** whither ye desire to go *and* 4725
44:29 the LORD, that I will punish you in this **p**, 4725
50: 6 hill, they have forgotten their **resting p**. 7258
51:37 **dwelling p** for dragons, an astonishment, 4583
51:62 O LORD, thou hast spoken against this **p**, 4725
Eze 3:12 *be* the glory of the LORD from his **p**. 4725
6:13 the **p** where they did offer sweet savour NIH
7:22 they shall pollute my secret **p**: 4725
10:11 *to* the **p** whither the head looked they 4725
12: 3 thou shalt remove from thy **p** to another 4725
12: 3 from thy place to another **p** in their sight: 4725
16:24 hast also built unto thee an **eminent p**, 1354
16:24 hast made thee a **high p** in every street. 7413
16:25 Thou hast built thy **high p** at every head 7413
16:31 In that thou buildest thine **eminent p** in 1354
16:31 and makest thine **high p** in every street; 7413
16:39 they shall throw down thine **eminent p**, 1354
17:16 surely in the **p** where the king *dwelleth* 4725
20:29 What *is* the **high p** whereunto ye go? 1116
21:19 choose thou a **p**, choose *it*, at the head of 3027
21:30 will judge thee in the **p** where thou wast 4725
25: 5 the Ammonites a **couching p** for flocks: 4769
26: 5 It shall be a **p** *for* the spreading of nets in NIH
26:14 thou shalt be a **p** to spread nets upon; NIH
37:14 and I shall **p** you in your own land: 3240
37:26 I will **p** them, and multiply them, 5414
38:15 shalt come from thy **p** out of the north 4725
39:11 I will give unto Gog a **p** there of graves 4725
41: 4 he said unto me, This *is* the most holy **p**. NIH
41: 9 *that* which was left *was* the **p** of the 1004
41:11 chambers *were* toward the **p** that *was* left, NIH
41:11 the breadth of the **p** that was left *was* five 4725
41:12 **separate p** *at* the end toward the west 1508
41:13 the **separate p**, and the building, with 1508
41:14 of the **separate p** toward the east, 1508
41:15 against the **separate p** which *was* behind 1508
42: 1 *that was* over against the **separate p**, 1508
42:10 over against the **separate p**, and over 1508
42:13 which *are* before the **separate p**, 1508
42:13 and the trespass offering; for the **p** *is* holy. 4725
42:14 shall they not go out of the holy **p** into NIH
42:20 between the sanctuary and the profane **p**. NIH
43: 7 the **p** of my throne, and the place of 4725
43: 7 and the **p** of the soles of my feet, 4725
43:13 and this *shall be* the **higher p** of the altar. 1354
43:21 he shall burn it in the **appointed p** of 4662
44:13 any of my holy *things*, in the most holy **p**: NIH
45: 3 be the sanctuary *and* the most holy **p**. NIH
45: 4 it shall be a **p** for their houses, and a holy 4725
45: 4 houses, and a **holy p** for the sanctuary. 4720
46:19 there *was* a **p** on the two sides westward 4725
46:20 This *is* the **p** where the priests shall boil 4725
47:10 they shall be a **p** to **spread forth** nets 4894
48:15 *shall be* a profane **p** for the city, NIH
Da 2:35 them away, that no **p** was found for them: 870
8:11 and the **p** of his sanctuary was cast down. 4349
11:31 they shall **p** the abomination that maketh 5414
Hos 1:10 *that in* the **p** where it was said unto them, 4725
4:16 will feed them as a lamb in a **large p**. 4800
5:15 I will go *and* return to my **p**, till they 4725
9:13 as I saw Tyrus, *is* planted in a **pleasant p**: 5116
11:11 I will **p** them in their houses, saith 3427
13:13 for he should not stay long in the **p** of NIH
Joel 3: 7 I *will* raise them out of the **p** whither ye 4725
Am 8: 3 *shall be* many dead bodies in every **p**; 4725
Mic 1: 3 the LORD cometh forth out of his **p**, 4725
1: 4 waters *that are* poured down a **steep p**. 4174
Na 1: 8 will make an utter end of the **p** thereof, 4725
2:11 the **feeding p** of the young lions, where 4829
3:17 and their **p** is not known where they *are*. 4725
Zep 1: 4 cut off the remnant of Baal from this **p**, 4725
2:11 shall worship him, every one from his **p**, 4725
2:15 desolation, a **p** for beasts **to lie down in!** 4769
Hag 2: 9 in this **p** will I give peace, saith the LORD 4725
Zec 6:12 he shall grow up out of his **p**, and he shall 8478
10: 6 and I will **bring** them *again* to **p** them; 3427
10:10 and **p** shall not be found for them. NIH
12: 6 shall be inhabited again **in** her own **p**, 8478
14:10 shall be lifted up, and inhabited **in** her **p**, 8478

Zec 14:10 Benjamin's gate unto the **p** of the first 4725
Mal 1:11 in every **p** incense *shall* be offered unto 4725
Mt 8:32 ran violently down a **steep p** into the sea, 2911
9:24 He said unto them, **Give p**: for the maid 402
12: 6 That **in this p** is one greater than 5602
14:13 thence by ship into a desert **p** apart: 5117
14:15 is a desert **p**, and the time is now past; 5117
14:35 when the men of that **p** had knowledge 5117
17:20 mountain, Remove hence **to yonder p**; 1563
24:15 stand in the holy **p**, (whoso readeth, let 5564
26:36 Then cometh Jesus with them unto a **p** 5564
26:52 Put up again thy sword into his **p**: 5117
27:33 when they were come unto a **p** called 5117
27:33 that is to say, a **p** of a skull, 5117
28: 6 Come, see the **p** where the Lord lay. 5117
Mk 1:35 and departed into a solitary **p**, 5117
5:13 ran violently down a **steep p** into 2911
6:10 **In what p soever** ye enter into a 1437+3699
6:10 there abide till ye depart **from that p**. 1564
6:31 Come ye yourselves apart into a desert **p**, 5117
6:32 And they departed into a desert **p** by ship 5117
6:35 This *is* a desert **p**, and now the time *is* far 5117
11: 4 door without in a **p** where two ways met; NIG
12: 1 about *it*, and digged a **p** *for* the winefat, NIG
14:32 And they came to a **p** which was named 5564
15:22 And they bring him unto the **p** Golgotha, 5117
15:22 being interpreted, The **p** of a skull. 5117
16: 6 here: behold the **p** where they laid him. 5117
Lk 4:17 he found the **p** where it was written, 5117
4:37 the fame of him went out into every **p** 5117
4:42 he departed and went into a desert **p** 5117
8:33 herd ran violently down a **steep p** into 2911
9:10 went aside privately into a desert **p** 5117
9:12 get victuals: for we are here in a desert **p** 5117
10: 1 two before his face into every city and **p**, 5117
10:32 when he was at the **p**, came and looked 5117
11: 1 pass *that*, as he was praying in a certain **p**, 5117
11:33 putteth *it* in a **secret p**, neither under a 2927
14: 9 come and say to thee, Give this *man* **p**; 5117
16:28 lest they also come into this **p** of torment. 5117
19: 5 And when Jesus came to the **p**, he looked 5117
22:40 And when he was at the **p**, he said unto 5117
23: 5 Jewry, beginning from Galilee to **this p**. 5602
23:33 And when they were come to the **p**, 5117
Jn 4:20 in Jerusalem is the **p** where *men* ought 5117
5:13 himself away, a multitude being in that **p**. 5117
6:10 Now there was much grass in the **p**. 5117
6:23 nigh unto the **p** where they did eat bread, 5117
8:37 me, because my word **hath** no **p** in you. 5562
10:40 into the **p** where John at first baptized; 5117
11: 6 abode two days *still* in the same **p** where 5117
11:30 but was in that **p** where Martha met him. 5117
11:41 they took away the stone *from the* **p** NIG
11:48 and take away both our **p** and nation. 5117
14: 2 have told you. I go to prepare a **p** for you. 5117
14: 3 And if I go and prepare a **p** for you, I will 5117
18: 2 which betrayed him, knew the **p**: 5117
19:13 sat down in the judgment seat in a **p** *that* 5117
19:17 he bearing his cross went forth into a **p** 5117
19:17 into a place called *the* **p** of a skull, NIG
19:20 for the **p** where Jesus was crucified was 5117
19:41 Now in the **p** where he was crucified 5117
20: 7 but wrapped together in a **p** by itself. 5117
Ac 1:25 that *he* might go to his own **p**. 5117
2: 1 all with one accord in **one p**. 846+1909+3588
4:31 the **p** was shaken where they were 5117
6:13 blasphemous words against this holy **p**, 5117
6:14 this Jesus of Nazareth shall destroy this **p**, 5117
7: 7 they come forth, and serve me in this **p**. 5117
7:33 for the **p** where thou standest is holy 5117
7:49 saith the Lord: or what *is* the **p** of my rest? 5117
8:32 The **p** of the scripture which he read *was* 4042
12:17 he departed, and went into another **p**. 5117
21:12 they of that **p**, besought him not to go 1786
21:28 the people, and the law, and this **p**: 5117
21:28 the temple, and hath polluted this holy **p**, 5117
25:23 and were entered into the **p of hearing**, 201
27: 8 came unto a **p** *which is* called The fair 5117
27:41 And falling into a **p** where two seas met, 5117
Ro 9:26 *that in* the **p** where it was said unto them, 5117
12:19 but *rather* give **p** unto wrath: 5117
15:23 But now having no more **p** in these parts, 5117
1Co 1: 2 all that in every **p** call upon the name 5117
4:11 and **have no certain dwelling p**; 790
11:20 therefore **into one p**, 846+1909+3588
14:23 be come together into **one p**, 846+1909+3588
2Co 2:14 savour of his knowledge by us in every **p**. 5117
Gal 2: 5 To whom we **gave p** by subjection, 1502
Eph 4:27 Neither give **p** to the devil. 5117
1Th 1: 8 also in every **p** your faith to God-ward is 5117
Heb 4: 4 he spake in a **certain p** of the seventh 4225
4: 4 And *in* this *again*, If they shall enter into NIG
5: 6 As he saith also in another **p**, Thou *art* a NIG
8: 7 should no **p** have been sought for 5117
9:12 **p**, having obtained eternal redemption *for* NIG
9:25 as the high priest entereth into the holy **p** NIG
11: 8 when he was called to go out into a **p** 5117
12:17 he found no **p** of repentance, though he 5117
Jas 2: 3 say unto him, Sit thou **here in** a good **p**; 5602
3:11 Doth a fountain send forth at the same **p** 3692
2Pe 1:19 as unto a light that shineth in a dark **p**, 5117
Rev 2: 5 will remove thy candlestick out of his **p**, 5117
12: 6 where she hath a **p** prepared of God, 5117
12: 8 neither was their **p** found any more in 5117

Rev 12:14 into her **p**, where she is nourished for a 5117
16:16 And he gathered them together into a **p** 5117
20:11 and there was found no **p** for them. 5117

PLACED (14) [PLACE]
Ge 3:24 he **p** at the east of the garden of Eden 7931
47:11 Joseph **p** his father and his brethren, 3427
1Ki 17: 6 **p** them in Beth-el the priests of the high 5975
2Ki 17: 6 **p** them in Halah and in Habor *by* the 3427
17:24 *them* in the cities of Samaria instead of 3427
17:26 *them* and **p** in the cities of Samaria. 3427
2Ch 1:14 which he **p** in the chariot cities, 3240
4: 8 *them* in the temple, five on the right 3240
17: 2 forces in all the fenced cities of Judah, 5414
Job 20: 4 this of old, since man was **p** upon earth, 7760
Ps 78:60 Shiloh, the tent *which* he **p** among men; 7931
Isa 5: 8 that they may be **p** alone in the midst of 3427
Jer 5:22 which have **p** the sand *for* the bound of 7760
Eze 17: 5 he **p** *it* by great waters, *and* set it *as* a 3947

PLACES (220) [PLACE]
Ge 28:15 will keep thee in all **p** whither thou goest, NIH
36:40 families, after their **p**, by their names; 4725
Ex 20:24 in all **p** where I record my name I will 4725
25:27 be for **p** of the staves to bear the table. 1004
26:29 make their rings *of gold for* **p** for the bars: 1004
30: 4 they shall be for **p** for the staves to bear it 1004
36:34 made their rings *of gold to be* **p** for 1004
37:14 the rings for **p** for the staves to bear the table. 1004
37:27 to be **p** for the staves to bear it withal. 1004
38: 5 of the grate of brass, *to be* **p** for the staves. 1004
Lev 26:30 I will destroy your **high p**, and cut down 1116
Nu 21:28 and the lords of the **high p** of Arnon. 1116
22:41 brought him up *into* the **high p** of Baal, 1116
33:52 and quite pluck down all their **high p**: 1116
Dt 7: 5 all *the* **p** nigh thereunto, in the plain, NIH
12: 2 Ye shall utterly destroy all the **p**, 4725
32:13 He made him ride on the **high p** of 1116
33:29 and thou shalt tread upon their **high p**. 1116
Jos 5: 8 that they abode in their **p** in the camp, 8478
Jdg 5:11 **p of drawing** *water*, there shall they 4857
5:18 unto the death in the **high p** of the field. 4791
19:13 us draw near to one of *these* **p** to lodge 4725
20:33 in wait of Israel came forth out of their **p**, 4725
1Sa 7:16 and judged Israel in all those **p**. 4725
13: 6 and in rocks, and in **high p**, and in pits. 6877
23:23 take knowledge of all the **lurking p** 4224
30:31 to all the **p** where David himself and 4725
2Sa 1:19 beauty of Israel *is* slain upon thy **high p**: 1116
1:25 Jonathan, *thou wast* slain in thine **high p**. 1116
7: 7 In all *the* **p** wherein I have walked with NIH
22:34 *feet*: and setteth me upon my **high p**. 1116
22:46 they shall be afraid out of their **close p**. 4526
1Ki 3: 2 Only the people sacrificed in **high p**, 1116
3: 3 he sacrificed and burnt incense in **high p**. 1116
12:31 he made a house of **high p**, 1116
12:32 priests of the **high p** which he had made. 1116
13: 2 the **high p** that burn incense upon thee, 1116
13:32 against all the houses of the **high p** which 1116
13:33 lowest of the people priests of the **high p**: 1116
13:33 became *one of* the priests of the **high p**. 1116
14:23 For they also built them **high p**, 1116
15:14 the **high p** were not removed: 1116
22:43 the **high p** were not taken away; 1116
22:43 and burnt incense yet in the **high p**. 1116
2Ki 12: 3 the **high p** were not taken away: 1116
12: 3 and burnt incense in the **high p**. 1116
14: 4 Howbeit the **high p** were not taken away: 1116
14: 4 and burnt incense on the **high p**. 1116
15: 4 Save that the **high p** were not removed: 1116
15: 4 burnt incense still on the **high p**. 1116
15:35 Howbeit the **high p** were not removed: 1116
15:35 and burnt incense still in the **high p**. 1116
16: 4 and burnt incense in the **high p**, 1116
17: 9 they built them **high p** in all their cities, 1116
17:11 there they burnt incense in all the **high p**, 1116
17:29 put *them* in the houses of the **high p** 1116
17:32 the lowest of them priests of the **high p**, 1116
17:32 for them in the houses of the **high p**. 1116
18: 4 He removed the **high p**, and brake 1116
18:22 whose **high p** and whose altars Hezekiah 1116
19:24 I dried up all the rivers of besieged **p**. NIH
21: 3 For he built *up* again the **high p** which 1116
23: 5 in the **high p** in the cities of Judah, 1116
23: 5 and in the **p** round about Jerusalem; 4524
23: 8 defiled the **high p** where the priests had 1116
23: 8 brake down the **high p** of the gates that 1116
23: 9 Nevertheless the priests of the **high p** 1116
23:13 the **high p** that *were* before Jerusalem, 1116
23:14 and filled their **p** *with* the bones of men. 4725
23:19 all the houses also of the **high p** that 1116
23:20 he slew all the priests of the **high p** that 1116
1Ch 6:54 Now these *are* their **dwelling p** 4186
2Ch 8:11 because *the* **p** *are* holy, whereunto the ark NIH
11:15 he ordained him priests for the **high p**, 1116
14: 3 altars of the strange *gods*, and the **high p**, 1116
14: 5 out of all the cities of Judah the **high p**, 1116
15:17 the **high p** were not taken away out of 1116
17: 6 moreover he took away the **high p** and 1116
20:33 Howbeit the **high p** were not taken away: 1116
21:11 he made **high p** in the mountains 1116
28: 4 and burnt incense in the **high p**, 1116
28:25 **high p** to burn incense unto other gods, 1116
31: 1 threw down the **high p** and the altars out 1116
32:12 the same Hezekiah taken away his **high p** 1116

P

2Ch 33: 3 For he built again the **high p** which 1116
33:17 the people did sacrifice still in the **high p**, 1116
33:19 the **p** wherein he built high places, 4725
33:19 the places wherein he built **high p**, 1116
34: 3 and Jerusalem from the **high p**, 1116
Ne 4:12 From all **p** whence ye shall return unto 4725
4:13 Therefore set I in the lower **p** behind 4725
4:13 behind the wall, *and* on the **higher p**, 6706
12:27 they sought the Levites out of all their **p**, 4725
Job 3:14 which built **desolate p** for themselves; 2723
20:26 All darkness *shall be* hid in his **secret p**. 6845
21:28 where *are* the dwelling **p** of the wicked? 168
25: 2 with him, he maketh peace in his **high p**. 4791
37: 8 beasts go into dens, and remain in their **p**. 4585
Ps 10: 8 He sitteth in the **lurking p** of the villages: 3993
10: 8 in the **secret p** doth he murder 4565
16: 6 The lines are fallen unto me in pleasant *p*, NIH
17:12 it were a young lion lurking in **secret p**. 4565
18:33 *feet*, and setteth me upon my **high p**. 1116
18:45 and be afraid out of their **close p**. 4526
49:11 *and* their **dwelling p** to all generations; 4908
68:35 God, *thou art* terrible out of thy **holy p**: 4720
73:18 Surely thou didst set them in slippery *p*: NIH
74:20 for the **dark p** of the earth are full of 4285
78:58 provoked him to anger with their **high p**, 1116
95: 4 In his hand *are* the **deep p** of the earth: 4278
103:22 all his works in all **p** of his dominion: 4725
105:41 they ran in the dry *p* like a river. NIH
109:10 *their* **bread** also out of their **desolate p**. 2723
110: 6 he shall fill the *p* with the dead bodies; NIH
135: 6 and in earth, in the seas, and all **deep p**. 8415
141: 6 their judges are overthrown in stony **p**, 3027
Pr 8: 2 She standeth in the top of **high p** by 4791
8: 2 places by the way, *in* the **p** of the paths. 1004
9: 3 upon the **highest p** of the city, 1610+4791
9:14 on a seat in the **high p** of the city, 4791
SS 2:14 in the **secret p** of the stairs, let me see 5643
Isa 5:17 the **waste p** of the fat ones shall strangers 2723
15: 2 and *to* Dibon, the **high p**, to weep: 1116
32:18 in sure dwellings, and in quiet **resting p**; 4496
36: 7 whose **high p** and whose altars Hezekiah 1116
37:25 I dried up all the rivers of the besieged *p*. NIH
40: 4 be made straight, and the **rough p** plain: 7406
41:18 I will open rivers in **high p**, 8205
44:26 and I will raise up the **decayed p** thereof: 2723
45: 2 and make the **crooked p** straight; 1921
45: 3 hidden riches of **secret p**, that thou 4565
49: 9 and their pastures *shall be* in all **high p**. 8205
49:19 For thy waste and thy **desolate p**, 8074
51: 3 he will comfort all her **waste p**; and he 2723
52: 9 sing together, ye **waste p** of Jerusalem: 2723
58:12 *be* of thee shall build the old **waste p**: 2723
58:14 I will cause thee to ride upon the **high p** 1116
59:10 night; *we are* in **desolate p** as dead *men*. 820
Jer 3: 2 Lift up thine eyes unto the **high p** 8205
3:21 A voice was heard upon the **high p**, 8205
4:11 dry wind of the **high p** in the wilderness 8205
4:12 *Even* a full wind from those *p* shall come NIH
5: 1 know, and seek in the **broad p** thereof, 7339
7:29 and take up a lamentation on the **high p**; 8205
7:31 they have built the **high p** of Tophet, 1116
8: 3 which remain in all the **p** whither I have 4725
12:12 The spoilers are come upon all **high p** 8205
13:17 my soul shall weep in **secret p** for your 4565
14: 6 the wild asses did stand in the **high p**, 8205
17: 3 *and* thy **high p** for sin, throughout all thy 1116
17: 6 shall inhabit the **parched p** in 2788
17:26 from the **p** about Jerusalem, and from NIH
19: 5 They have built also the **high p** of Baal, 1116
23:10 the **pleasant p** of the wilderness are dried 4999
23:24 Can any hide himself in **secret p** that I 4565
24: 9 curse, in all **p** whither I shall drive them. 4725
26:18 mountain of the house as the **high p** of 1116
29:14 from all the **p** whither I have driven you, 4725
30:18 and have mercy on his **dwelling p**; 4908
32:35 they built the **high p** of Baal, which *are* 1116
32:44 in the **p** about Jerusalem, and in the cities NIH
33:13 in the **p** about Jerusalem, and in the cities NIH
40:12 Even all the Jews returned out of all **p** 4725
45: 5 thee for a prey in all **p** whither thou goest. 4725
48:35 him that offereth in the **high p**, 1116
49:10 I have uncovered his **secret p**, and he 4565
51:30 they have burnt her **dwelling p**; her bars 4908
La 2: 6 he hath destroyed his **p** of the **assembly**. 4150
3: 6 He hath set me in **dark p**, as they that be 4285
3:10 lying in wait, *and as* a lion in **secret p**. 4565
Eze 6: 3 upon you, and I will destroy your **high p**. 1116
6: 6 In all your **dwelling p** the cities shall be 4186
6: 6 waste, and the **high p** shall be desolate: 1116
7:24 to cease; and their **holy p** shall be defiled. 6942
16:16 deckedst thy **high p** with divers colours, 1116
16:39 and shall break down thy **high p**: 7413
21: 2 drop *thy word* toward the **holy p**, 4720
20:20 in **p desolate** of old, with them that go 2723
34:12 will deliver them out of all **p** where they 4725
34:13 and in all the **inhabited p** of the country. 4186
34:26 the **p round** about my hill a blessing; 5439
36: 2 even the ancient **high p** are ours in 1116
36:36 know that I the LORD build the ruined **p**, NIH
37:23 will save them out of all their **dwelling p**, 4186
38:12 to turn thine hand upon the **desolate p** 2723
38:20 the **steep p** shall fall, and every wall shall 4095
43: 7 the carcases of their kings *in* their **high p**. 1116
46:23 *was* made with **boiling p** under the rows 4018
46:24 me, These *are* the **p** of them that boil, 1004

Eze 47:11 the **miry p** thereof and the marishes 1207
11:24 even upon the **fattest p** of the province; 4924
Hos 9: 6 the pleasant *p* for their silver, nettles shall NIH
10: 8 The **high p** also of Aven, the sin of Israel, 1116
Am 4: 6 cities, and want of bread in all your **p**: 4725
4:13 treadeth upon the **high p** of the earth, 1116
7: 9 the **high p** of Isaac shall be desolate, 1116
Mic 1: 3 and tread upon the **high p** of the earth. 1116
1: 5 what *are* the **high p** of Judah? *are* they 1116
3:12 mountain of the house as the **high p** of 1116
Hab 3:19 to possess the **dwelling p** that *are* not 4908
3:19 will make me to walk upon mine **high p**. 1116
Zec 3: 7 I will give thee **p to walk** among these 4108
Mal 1: 4 we will return and build the **desolate p**; 2723
Mt 12:43 he walketh through dry **p**, seeking rest; 5117
13: 5 Some fell upon stony **p**, where they had NIG
13:20 he that received the seed into stony **p**, NIG
24: 7 pestilences, and earthquakes in divers **p**. 5117
Mk 1:45 into the city, but was without in desert **p**: 5117
13: 8 and there shall be earthquakes in divers **p**, 5117
Lk 11:24 he walketh through dry **p**, seeking rest; 5117
21:11 And great earthquakes shall be in divers **p**, 5117
Ac 24: 3 it always, and **in all p**, most noble Felix, 3837
Eph 1: 3 spiritual blessings in heavenly **p** in Christ: NIG
1:20 at his own right hand in the heavenly **p**, NIG
2: 6 sit together in heavenly **p** in Christ NIG
3:10 powers in heavenly **p** might be known by NIG
6:12 against spiritual wickedness in high **p**. NIG
Php 1:13 in all the palace, and *in* all other **p**; NIG
Heb 9:24 For Christ is not entered into the holy **p** NIG
Rev 6:14 and island were moved out of their **p**. 5117

PLAGUE (98) [PLAGUED, PLAGUES]

Ex 11: 1 Yet will I bring one **p** *more* upon Pharaoh, 5061
12:13 **p** shall not be upon you to destroy *you*, 5063
30:12 there be no **p** amongst them, when *thou* 5063
Lev 13: 2 it be in the skin of his flesh like the **p** of 5061
13: 3 the priest shall look on the **p** in the skin 5061
13: 3 *when* the hair in the **p** is turned white, 5061
13: 3 the **p** in sight *be* deeper than the skin of 5061
13: 3 the skin of his flesh, it *is* a **p** of leprosy: 5061
13: 4 priest shall shut up *him that hath* the **p** 5061
13: 5 *if* the **p** in his sight be at a stay, 5061
13: 5 at a stay, *and* the **p** spread not in the skin; 5061
13: 6 *if* the **p** be somewhat dark, and the plague 5061
13: 6 and the **p** spread not in the skin, 5061
13: 9 When the **p** of leprosy is in a man, then 5061
13:12 *hath* the **p** from his head even to his foot, 5061
13:13 pronounce *him* clean *that hath* the **p**: 5061
13:17 behold, *if* the **p** be turned into white; 5061
13:17 pronounce *him* clean *that hath* the **p**: 5061
13:20 it *is* a **p** of leprosy broken out of the boil. 5061
13:22 shall pronounce him unclean: it *is* a **p**. 5061
13:25 him unclean: it *is* the **p** of leprosy. 5061
13:27 him unclean: it *is* the **p** of leprosy. 5061
13:29 a man or woman hath a **p** upon the head 5061
13:30 the priest shall see the **p**: and behold, *if* it 5061
13:31 if the priest look on the **p** of the scall, 5061
13:31 priest shall shut up *him that hath* the **p** 5061
13:32 seventh day the priest shall look on the **p**: 5061
13:44 him utterly unclean, his **p** *is* in his head. 5061
13:45 the leper in whom the **p** *is*, his clothes 5061
13:46 All the days wherein the **p** *shall be* in him 5061
13:47 The garment also that the **p** of leprosy is 5061
13:49 *if* the **p** be greenish or reddish in 5061
13:49 it *is* a **p** of leprosy, and shall be shewed 5061
13:50 priest shall look upon the **p**, and shut up 5061
13:50 and shut up *it that hath* the **p** seven days: 5061
13:51 he shall look on the **p** on the seventh day: 5061
13:51 if the **p** be spread in the garment, either 5061
13:51 the **p** *is* a fretting leprosy; it *is* unclean. 5061
13:52 or any thing of skin, wherein the **p** is: 5061
13:53 the **p** be not spread in the garment, 5061
13:54 that they wash *the thing* wherein the **p** *is*, 5061
13:55 the priest shall look on the **p**, after *that* it 5061
13:55 *if* the **p** have not changed his colour, 5061
13:55 his colour, and the **p** be not spread; 5061
13:56 the **p** *be* somewhat dark after the washing 5061
13:57 it *is* a spreading **p**: thou shalt burn that NIH
13:57 shalt burn that wherein the **p** *is* with fire. 5061
13:58 if the **p** be departed from them, then it 5061
13:59 This *is* the law of the **p** of leprosy in a 5061
14: 3 *if* the **p** of leprosy be healed in the leper; 5061
14:32 This *is* the law *of him* in whom *is* the **p** 5061
14:34 I put the **p** of leprosy in a house of the 5061
14:35 It seemeth to me *there* is as it were a **p** 5061
14:36 before the priest go *into* it to see the **p**, 5061
14:37 he shall look on the **p**, and behold, 5061
14:37 *if* the **p** *be* in the walls of the house with 5061
14:39 the **p** be spread in the walls of the house; 5061
14:40 they take away the stones in which the **p** 5061
14:43 if the **p** come again, and break out in 5061
14:44 behold, *if* the **p** be spread in the house, 5061
14:48 the **p** hath not spread in the house, 5061
14:48 the house clean, because the **p** is healed. 5061
14:54 This *is* the law for all *manner of* **p** of 5061
Nu 8:19 that there be no **p** among the children of 5063
11:33 smote the people with a very great **p**. 4347
14:37 the land, died by the **p** before the LORD. 4046
16:46 gone out from the LORD; the **p** is begun. 5063
16:47 the **p** was begun among the people: 5063
16:48 and the living; and the **p** was stayed. 4046
16:49 they that died in the **p** were fourteen 4046
16:50 the congregation: and the **p** was stayed. 4046
25: 8 So the **p** was stayed from the children of 4046

Nu 25: 9 those that died in the **p** were twenty and 4046
25:18 which was slain in the day of the **p** for 4046
26: 1 it came to pass after the **p**, that the LORD 4046
31:16 there was a **p** among the congregation of 4046
Dt 24: 8 Take heed in the **p** of leprosy, that *thou* 5061
28:61 Also every sickness, and every **p**, which 4347
Jos 22:17 there was a **p** in the congregation 5063
1Sa 6: 4 one **p** *was* on you all, and on your lords. 4046
2Sa 24:21 that the **p** may be stayed from the people. 4046
24:25 land, and the **p** was stayed from Israel. 4046
1Ki 8:37 whatsoever **p**, whatsoever sickness *there* 5061
8:38 which shall know every man the **p** of his 5061
1Ch 21:22 that the **p** may be stayed from the people. 4046
2Ch 21:14 *with* a great **p** will the LORD smite thy 4046
Ps 89:23 before his face, and **p** them that hate him. 5062
91:10 shall any **p** come nigh thy dwelling. 5061
106:29 and the **p** brake in upon them. 4046
106:30 and so the **p** was stayed. 4046
Zec 14:12 this shall be the **p** wherewith the LORD 4046
14:15 shall be the **p** of the horse, of the mule, 4046
14:15 that shall be in these tents, as this **p**. 4046
14:18 that *have no* rain; there shall be the **p**, 4046
Mk 5:29 in *her* body that she was healed of *that* **p**. 3148
5:34 go in peace, and be whole of thy **p**. 3148
Rev 16:21 because of the **p** of the hail; 4127
16:21 for the **p** thereof was exceeding great. 4127

PLAGUED (6) [PLAGUE]

Ge 12:17 the LORD **p** Pharaoh and his house with 5060
Ex 32:35 the LORD **p** the people, because they 5062
Jos 24: 5 sent Moses also and Aaron, and I **p** Egypt, 5062
1Ch 21:17 not on thy people, that *they* should be **p**. 4046
Ps 73: 5 neither are they **p** like *other* men. 5060
73:14 For all the day long have I been **p**, 5060

PLAGUES (24) [PLAGUE]

Ge 12:17 his house with great **p** because of Sarai 5061
Ex 7: 4 For I will at this time send all my **p** upon 4046
Lev 26:21 I will bring seven *times* moe **p** upon you 4347
Dt 28:59 the LORD will make thy **p** wonderful, 4347
28:59 the **p** of thy seed, *even* great plagues, 4347
28:59 *even* great **p**, and of long continuance, 4347
29:22 when they see the **p** of that land, 4347
1Sa 4: 8 Egyptians with all the **p** in the wilderness. 4347
Jer 19: 8 and hiss because of all the **p** thereof. 4347
49:17 and shall hiss at all the **p** thereof. 4347
50:13 shall be astonished, and hiss at all her **p**. 4347
Hos 13:14 O death, I will be thy **p**; O grave, I will be 1698
Mk 3:10 him for to touch him, as many as had **p**. 3148
Lk 7:21 he cured many of *their* infirmities and **p**, 3148
Rev 9:20 yet repented not of the works of their 4127
11: 6 to smite the earth with all **p**, as often as 4127
15: 1 seven angels having the seven last **p**; 4127
15: 6 having the seven **p**, clothed in pure and 4127
15: 8 till the seven **p** of the seven angels were 4127
16: 9 of God, which hath power over these **p**: 4127
18: 4 her sins, and that ye receive not of her **p**. 4127
18: 8 Therefore shall her **p** come in one day, 4127
21: 9 the seven vials full of the seven last **p**, 4127
22:18 him the **p** that are written in this book: 4127

PLAIN (75) [PLAINLY, PLAINNESS, PLAINS]

Ge 11: 2 that they found a **p** in the land of Shinar, 1237
12: 6 the place of Sichem, unto the **p** of Moreh. 436
13:10 his eyes, and beheld all the **p** of Jordan, 3603
13:11 Then Lot chose him all the **p** of Jordan; 3603
13:12 Lot dwelled in the cities of the **p**, 3603
13:18 came and dwelt in the **p** of Mamre, which 436
14:13 he dwelt in the **p** of Mamre the Amorite, 436
19:17 thee, neither stay thou in all the **p**; 3603
19:25 all the **p**, and all the inhabitants of the 3603
19:28 toward all the land of the **p**, and beheld, 3603
19:29 when God destroyed the cities of the **p**, 3603
25:27 Jacob *was* a **p** man, dwelling in tents. 8535
Dt 1: 1 in the **p** over against the Red *sea*, 6160
1: 7 in the **p**, in the hills, and in the vale, 6160
2: 8 through the way of the **p** from Elath, 6160
3:10 All the cities of the **p**, and all Gilead, 4334
3:17 The also, and Jordan, and the coast 6160
3:17 Chinnereth even unto the sea of the **p**, 6160
4:43 in the **p** country, of the Reubenites; 4334
4:49 all the **p** on *this* side Jordan eastward, 6160
4:49 even unto the sea of the **p**, under 6160
34: 3 south, and the **p** of the valley of Jericho, 3603
Jos 3:16 that came down toward the sea of the **p**, 6160
8:14 at a time appointed, before the **p**; 6160
11:16 the **p**, and the mountain of Israel, 6160
12: 1 mount Hermon, and all the **p** on the east: 6160
12: 3 *from* the **p** to the sea of Cinneroth on 6160
12: 3 unto the sea of the **p**, *even* the salt sea on 6160
13: 9 and all the **p** of Medeba unto Dibon, 4334
13:16 of the river, and all the **p** by Medeba; 4334
13:17 and all her cities that *are* in the **p**; 4334
13:21 all the cities of the **p**, and all the kingdom 4334
20: 8 upon the **p** out of the tribe of Reuben, 4334
Jdg 4:11 pitched his tent unto the **p** of Zaanaim, 436
9: 6 by the **p** of the pillar that *was* in Shechem. 436
9:37 another company come along by the **p** of 436
11:33 cities, and unto the **p** of the vineyards, 58
1Sa 10: 3 thou shalt come to the **p** of Tabor, 436
23:24 Maon, in the **p** on the south of Jeshimon. 6160
2Sa 2:29 men walked all that night through the **p**, 6160
4: 7 gat them away through the **p** all night. 6160
15:28 See, I will tarry in the **p** of the wilderness, 6160
18:23 Ahimaaz ran *by* the way of the **p**, 3603

1Ki 7:46 In the **p** of Jordan did the king cast them, 3603
 20:23 let us fight against them in the **p,** 4334
 20:25 we will fight against them in the **p,** 4334
2Ki 14:25 entering of Hamath unto the sea of the **p,** 6160
 25: 4 and *the king* went the way toward the **p,** 6160
2Ch 4:17 In the **p** of Jordan did the king cast them, 3603
Ne 3:22 repaired the priests, the men of the **p,** 3603
 6: 2 *some one of* the villages in the **p** of Ono. 1237
 12:28 both out of the **p** country round about 3603
Ps 27:11 lead me in a **p** path, because of mine 4334
Pr 8: 9 They *are* all **p** to him that understandeth, 5228
 15:19 but the way of the righteous *is* made **p.** 5549
Isa 28:25 When he hath made **p** the face thereof, 7737
 40: 4 be made straight, and the rough places **p:** 1237
Jer 17:26 from the **p,** and from the mountains, 8219
 21:13 *and* rock of the **p,** saith the Lord; 4334
 39: 4 and he went out the way of the **p.** 6160
 48: 8 shall perish, and the **p** shall be destroyed, 4334
 48:21 judgment is come upon the **p** country, 4334
 52: 7 and they went *by* the way of the **p.** 6160
Eze 3:22 go forth into the **p,** and I will there talk 1237
 3:23 I arose, and went forth into the **p:** 1237
 8: 4 according to the vision that I saw in the **p.** 1237
Da 3: 1 set it up in the **p** of Dura, in the province 1236
Am 1: 5 cut off the inhabitant from the **p** of Aven, 1237
Ob 1:19 of Esau; and they of the **p** the Philistines, 8219
Hab 2: 2 the vision, and make *it* **p** upon tables, 874
Zec 4: 7 before Zerubbabel thou shalt become a **p:** 4334
 7: 7 when *men* inhabited the south and the **p?** 8219
 14:10 All the land shall be turned as a **p** from 6160
Mk 7:35 of his tongue was loosed, and he spake **p.** 3723
Lk 6:17 stood in the **p,** and the company 3977+5117

PLAINLY (11) [PLAIN]
Ex 21: 5 If the servant shall **p** say, I love my 559+559
Dt 27: 8 the stones all the words of this law very **p.** 874
1Sa 2:27 Did I **p** appear unto the house of 1540+1540
 10:16 told us **p** that the asses were found. 5046+5046
Ezr 4:18 sent unto us hath been **p** read before me. 6568
Isa 32: 4 the stammerers shall be ready to speak **p.** 6703
Jn 10:24 to doubt? If thou be the Christ, tell us **p.** 3954
 11:14 Then said Jesus unto them **p,** Lazarus is 3954
 16:25 but I shall shew you **p** of the Father. 3954
 16:29 Lo, now speakest thou **p,** 1722+3954
Heb 11:14 For they that say such *things* **declare p** 1718

PLAINNESS (1) [PLAIN]
2Co 3:12 such hope, we use great **p of speech:** 3954

PLAINS (25) [PLAIN]
Ge 18: 1 the Lord appeared unto him in the **p** of 436
Nu 22: 1 pitched in the **p** of Moab on *this* side 6160
 26: 3 the priest spake with them in the **p** 6160
 26:63 in the **p** of Moab by Jordan *near* Jericho. 6160
 31:12 unto the camp at the **p** of Moab, which 6160
 33:48 pitched in the **p** of Moab by Jordan *near* 6160
 33:49 *even* unto Abel-shittim in the **p** of Moab. 6160
 33:50 the Lord spake unto Moses in the **p** of 6160
 35: 1 the Lord spake unto Moses in the **p** of 6160
 36:13 in the **p** of Moab by Jordan *near* Jericho. 6160
Dt 11:30 against Gilgal, beside the **p** of Moreh? 436
 34: 1 Moses went up from the **p** of Moab unto 6160
 34: 8 for Moses in the **p** of Moab thirty days: 6160
Jos 4:13 the Lord unto battle, to the **p** of Jericho. 6160
 5:10 of the month at even in the **p** of Jericho: 6160
 11: 2 of the **p** south of Cinneroth, and in 6160
 12: 8 in the **p,** and in the springs, and in 6160
 13:32 for inheritance in the **p** of Moab, 6160
2Sa 17:16 Lodge not *this* night in the **p** of 6160
2Ki 25: 5 and overtook him in the **p** of Jericho: 6160
1Ch 27:28 sycomore trees that *were* in the **low p** 8219
2Ch 9:27 trees that *are* in the **low p** in abundance. 8219
 26:10 both in the low country, and in the **p:** 4334
Jer 39: 5 and overtook Zedekiah in the **p** of Jericho: 6160
 52: 8 and overtook Zedekiah in the **p** of Jericho: 6160

PLAISTER (7) [PLAISTERED]
Lev 14:42 take other morter, and shall **p** the house. 2902
Dt 27: 2 up great stones, and **p** them with plaister: 7874
 27: 2 up great stones, and plaister them with **p:** 7875
 27: 4 and thou shalt **p** them with plaister. 7874
 27: 4 and thou shalt plaister them with **p:** 7875
Isa 38:21 lay *it* for a **p** upon the boil, and he shall 4799
Da 5: 5 upon the wall of the king's palace: 1528

PLAISTERED (2) [PLAISTER]
Lev 14:43 hath scraped the house, and after it is **p;** 2902
 14:48 in the house, after the house was **p:** 2902

PLAITING (1) [PLATTED]
1Pe 3: 3 be that outward *adorning* of **p** the hair, 1708

PLANE See CHESNUT

PLANES (1)
Isa 44:13 he fitteth it with **p,** and he marketh it out 4741

PLANETS (1)
2Ki 23: 5 to the **p,** and to all the host of heaven. 4208

PLANKS (3)
1Ki 6:15 the floor of the house with **p** of fir. 6763
Eze 41:25 *there were* thick **p** upon the face of 6086
 41:26 side chambers of the house, and **thick p.** 5646

PLANT (42) [PLANTATION, PLANTED, PLANTEDST, PLANTERS, PLANTETH, PLANTING, PLANTINGS, PLANTS]
Ge 2: 5 every **p** of the field before it was in 7880
Ex 15:17 **p** them in the mountain of thine 5193
Dt 16:21 Thou shalt not **p** thee a grove of any trees 5193
 28:30 shalt **p** a vineyard, and shalt not gather 5193
 28:39 Thou shalt **p** vineyards, and dress *them,* 5193
2Sa 7:10 **p** them, that they may dwell in a place 5193
2Ki 19: 9 will **p** them, and eat the fruits thereof. 5193
1Ch 17: 9 will **p** them, and they shall dwell in their 5193
Job 14: 9 will bud, and bring forth boughs like a **p.** 5193
Ps 107:37 sow the fields, and **p** vineyards, which 5193
Ecc 3: 2 a time to **p,** and a time to pluck up *that* 5193
Isa 5: 2 the men of Judah his pleasant **p,** 5194
 17:10 therefore shalt thou **p** pleasant plants, 5193
 17:11 the day shalt thou make thy **p** to grow, 5194
 37:30 and **p** vineyards, and eat the fruit thereof. 5193
 41:19 I will **p** in the wilderness the cedar, 5414
 51:16 that I may **p** the heavens, and lay 5193
 53: 2 shall grow up before him as a **tender p,** 3126
 65:21 inhabit *them;* and they shall **p** vineyards, 5193
 65:22 they shall not **p,** and another eat: 5193
Jer 1:10 to throw down, to build, and to **p.** 5193
 2:21 degenerate **p** of a strange **vine** unto me? 1612
 18: 9 concerning a kingdom, to build and to **p** 5193
 24: 6 and I will **p** them, and not pluck *them* up. 5193
 29: 5 dwell *in them;* and **p** gardens, and eat 5193
 29:28 dwell *in them;* and **p** gardens, and eat 5193
 31: 5 shalt yet **p** vines upon the mountains 5193
 31: 5 the planters shall **p,** and shall eat *them* as 5193
 31:28 to build, and to **p,** saith the Lord. 5193
 32:41 I will **p** them in this land assuredly with 5193
 35: 7 nor **p** vineyard, nor have *any:* but all your 5193
 42:10 and I will **p** you, and not pluck *you* up: 5193
Eze 17:22 will **p** *it* upon a high mountain and 8362
 17:23 of the height of Israel will I **p** it: 8362
 28:26 shall build houses, and **p** vineyards, 5193
 34:29 I will raise up for them a **p** of renown, 4302
 36:36 places, *and* **p** that that was desolate: 5193
Da 11:45 he shall **p** the tabernacles of his palace 5193
Am 9:14 inhabit *them;* and they shall **p** vineyards, 5193
 9:15 I will **p** them upon their land, and they 5193
Zep 1:13 inhabit *them;* and they shall **p** vineyards, 5193
Mt 15:13 But he answered and said, **Every p,** 5451

PLANTATION (1) [PLANT]
Eze 17: 7 *he* might water it by the furrows of her **p.** 4302

PLANTED (39) [PLANT]
Ge 2: 8 the Lord God **p** a garden eastward in 5193
 9:20 *be* a husbandman, and he **p** a vineyard: 5193
 21:33 *Abraham* **p** a grove in Beer-sheba, 5193
Lev 19:23 shall have **p** all *manner of* trees for food, 5193
Nu 24: 6 of lign aloes *which* the Lord hath **p,** 5193
Dt 20: 6 what man *is he* that hath **p** a vineyard, 5193
Jos 24:13 and oliveyards which ye not do ye eat. 5193
Ps 1: 3 he shall be like a tree **p** by the rivers of 8362
 80: 8 thou hast cast out the heathen, and **p** it. 5193
 80:15 vineyard which thy right hand hath **p,** 5193
 92:13 Those that be **p** in the house of the Lord 5193
 94: 9 He that **p** the ear, shall he not hear? 5193
 104:16 the cedars of Lebanon, which he hath **p;** 5193
Ecc 2: 4 I builded me houses; I **p** me vineyards: 5193
 2: 5 and I **p** trees in them of all *kind of* fruits: 5193
 3: 2 and a time to pluck up *that which is* **p;** 5193
Isa 5: 2 **p** it *with* the choicest vine, and built a 5193
 40:24 they shall not be **p;** yea, they shall not 5193
Jer 2:21 Yet I had **p** thee a noble vine, wholly a 5193
 11:17 For the Lord of hosts, that **p** thee, 5193
 12: 2 Thou hast **p** them, yea, they have taken 5193
 17: 8 For he shall be as a tree **p** by the waters, 8362
 45: 4 *that* which I have **p** I *will* pluck up, 5193
Eze 17: 5 of the land, and **p** it in a fruitful field; 5414
 17: 8 It *was* **p** in a good soil by great waters, 8362
 17:10 Yea behold, *being* **p,** shall it prosper? 8362
 19:10 like a vine in thy blood, by the waters: **p** 8362
 19:13 now she *is* **p** in the wilderness, in a dry 8362
Hos 9:13 as I saw Tyrus, *is* **p** in a pleasant place: 8362
Am 5:11 ye have **planted** vineyards, but ye shall 5193
Mt 15:13 which my heavenly Father hath not **p,** 5452
 21:33 which **p** a vineyard, and hedged it round 5452
Mk 12: 1 A *certain* man **p** a vineyard, and set a 5452
Lk 13: 6 A *certain* man had a fig tree **p** in his 5452
 17: 6 up by the root, and be thou **p** in the sea; 5452
 17:28 drank, they bought, they sold, they **p,** 5452
 20: 9 A *certain* man **p** a vineyard, and let it 5452
Ro 6: 5 For if we have been **p together** in 4854
1Co 3: 6 I have **p,** Apollos watered; but God gave 5452

PLANTEDST (2) [PLANT]
Dt 6:11 and olive trees, which thou **p** not; 5193
Ps 44: 2 the heathen *with* thy hand, and **p** them; 5193

PLANTERS (1) [PLANT]
Jer 31: 5 the **p** shall plant, and shall eat *them* as 5193

PLANTETH (5) [PLANT]
Pr 31:16 the fruit of her hands she **p** a vineyard. 5193
Isa 44:14 he **p** an ash, and the rain doth nourish *it.* 5193
1Co 3: 7 neither is he that **p** any *thing,* neither he 5452
 3: 8 he that **p** and he that watereth are one: 5452
 9: 7 who **p** a vineyard, and eateth not of 5452

PLANTING (2) [PLANT]
Isa 60:21 branch of my **p,** the work of my hands, 4302
 61: 3 the **p** of the Lord, that *he* might be 4302

PLANTINGS (1) [PLANT]
Mic 1: 6 a heap of the field, *and as* **p** of a vineyard: 4302

PLANTS (8) [PLANT]
1Ch 4:23 those that dwelt amongst **p** and hedges: 5196
Ps 128: 3 thy children like olive **p** round about thy 8363
 144:12 That our sons *may be* as **p** grown up in 5195
SS 4:13 Thy *are* an orchard of pomegranates, 7973
Isa 16: 8 broken down the **principal p** thereof, 8291
 17:10 therefore shalt thou plant pleasant **p,** 5194
Jer 48:32 thy **p** are gone over the sea, they reach 5189
Eze 31: 4 her rivers running round about his **p,** 4302

PLASTER See MORTER

PLAT (2)
2Ki 9:26 I will requite thee in this **p,** saith 2513
 9:26 cast him into the **p** *of ground,* according 2513

PLATE (3) [BREASTPLATE, BREASTPLATES, PLATES]
Ex 28:36 thou shalt make a **p** of *pure* gold, 6731
 39:30 they made the **p** of the holy crown *of* 6731
Lev 8: 9 did he put the golden **p,** the holy crown; 6731

PLATES (6) [PLATE]
Ex 39: 3 did beat the gold into **thin p,** and cut 6341
Nu 16:38 them make them broad **p** *for* a covering 6341
 16:39 they were made broad **p** *for* a covering of NIH
1Ki 7:30 had four brasen wheels, and **p** of brass: 5633
 7:36 For on the **p** of the ledges thereof, 3871
Jer 10: 9 Silver **spread into p** is brought from 7554

PLATFORM See SCAFFOLD

PLATTED (3) [PLAITING]
Mt 27:29 And when they had **p** a crown of thorns, *4120*
Mk 15:17 and **p** a crown of thorns, and put *it* about *4120*
Jn 19: 2 And the soldiers **p** a crown of thorns, *4120*

PLATTER (3)
Mt 23:25 clean the outside of the cup and of the **p,** *3953*
 23:26 first that *which is* within the cup and **p,** *3953*
Lk 11:39 clean the outside of the cup and the **p;** *4094*

PLAY (17) [PLAYED, PLAYEDST, PLAYER, PLAYERS, PLAYETH, PLAYING]
Ex 32: 6 to eat and to drink, and rose up to **p.** 6711
Dt 22:21 to **p the whore** in her father's house: 2181
1Sa 16:16 that he shall **p** with his hand, and thou 5059
 16:17 Provide me now a man that can **p** well, 5059
 21:15 to **p the mad man** in my presence? 7696
2Sa 2:14 young men now arise, and **p** before us. 7832
 6:21 therefore will I **p** before the Lord. 7832
 10:12 let us **p the men** for our people, and for 2388
Job 40:20 where all the beasts of the field **p?** 7832
 41: 5 Wilt thou **p** with him as *with* a bird? 7832
Ps 33: 3 A new song; **p** skilfully with a loud noise. 5059
 104:26 *whom* thou hast made to **p** therein. 7832
Isa 11: 8 the sucking child shall **p** on the hole of 8173
Eze 33:32 and can **p** well **on an instrument:** 5059
Hos 3: 3 shalt not **p the harlot,** and thou shalt 2181
 4:15 Though thou, Israel, **p the harlot,** *yet* let 2181
1Co 10: 7 down to eat and drink, and rose up to **p.** 3815

PLAYED (18) [PLAY]
Ge 38:24 thy daughter in law hath **p the harlot;** 2181
Jdg 19: 2 his concubine **p the whore** against him, 2181
1Sa 16:23 David took a harp, and **p** with his hand: 5059
 18: 7 women answered *one another* as they **p,** 7832
 18:10 David **p** with his hand, as at other times: 5059
 19: 9 in his hand: and David **p** with *his* hand. 5059
 26:21 I have **p the fool,** and have erred 5528
2Sa 6: 5 all the house of Israel **p** before the Lord 7832
2Ki 3:15 it came to pass, when the minstrel **p,** 5059
1Ch 13: 8 Israel **p** before God with all *their* might, 7832
Jer 3: 1 thou hast **p the harlot** with many lovers; 2181
 3: 6 green tree, and there hath **p the harlot.** 2181
 3: 8 not, but went and **p the harlot** also. 2181
Eze 16:28 Thou hast **p the whore** also with 2181
 16:28 thou hast **p the harlot** with them, 2181
 23: 3 Aholah **p the harlot** when she was mine; 2181
 23:19 wherein she had **p the harlot** in the land 2181
Hos 2: 5 For their mother hath **p the harlot:** she 2181

PLAYEDST (2) [PLAY]
Eze 16:15 **p the harlot** because of thy renown, 2181
 16:16 colours, and **p the harlot** thereupon: 2181

PLAYER (1) [PLAY]
1Sa 16:16 out a man, *who is* a cunning **p** on a harp: 5059

PLAYERS (2) [PLAY]
Ps 68:25 the **p on instruments** *followed* after; 5059
 87: 7 **p on instruments** *shall be there:* all my 2490

PLAYETH (1) [PLAY]
Eze 23:44 go in unto a woman that **p the harlot:** 2181

PLAYING (7) [PLAY]
Lev 21: 9 if she profane herself by **p the whore,** 2181
1Sa 18: 6 *that is* cunning in **p,** and a mighty valiant 5059
1Ch 15:29 a window saw king David dancing and **p:** 7832

P

Ps 68:25 them were the damsels **p** with **timbrels.** 8608
Jer 2:20 green tree thou wanderest, **p the harlot.** 2181
Eze 16:41 cause thee to cease from **p the harlot.** 2181
Zec 8: 5 of boys and girls **p** in the streets thereof. 7832

PLEA (2) [PLEAD]
Dt 17: 8 between **p** and plea, and between stroke 1779
17: 8 between plea and **p**, and between stroke 1779

PLEAD (39) [PLEA, PLEADED, PLEADETH, PLEADINGS]
Jdg 6:31 that stood against him, Will ye **p** for Baal? 7378
6:31 he that will **p** for him, let him be put to 7378
6:31 let him **p** for himself, because one hath 7378
6:32 saying, Let Baal **p** against him, because 7378
1Sa 24:15 **p** my cause, and deliver me out of thine 7378
Job 9:19 judgment, who shall set me a time to **p**? NIH
13:19 Who is he that will **p** with me? for now, 7378
16:21 O that one might **p** for a man with God, 3198
19: 5 me, and **p** against me my reproach: 3198
23: 6 he **p** against me with his great power? 7378
Ps 35: 1 **P** my cause, O Lord, with them that 7378
43: 1 **p** my cause against an ungodly nation: 7378
74:22 Arise, O God, **p** thine own cause: 7378
119:154 **P** my cause, and deliver me: quicken me 7378
Pr 22:23 For the Lord will **p** their cause, 7378
23:11 mighty; he shall **p** their cause with thee. 7378
31: 9 and **p the cause** of the poor and needy. 1777
Isa 1:17 judge the fatherless, **p** for the widow. 7378
3:13 The Lord standeth up to **p**, 7378
43:26 let us **p** together: declare thou, that thou 8199
66:16 by his sword will the Lord **p with** all 8199
Jer 2: 9 Wherefore I will yet **p** with you, saith 7378
2: 9 with your children's children will I **p** 7378
2:29 Wherefore will ye **p** with me? ye all have 7378
2:35 Behold, I will **p with** thee, because 8199
12: 1 art thou, O Lord, when I **p with** thee: 7378
25:31 with the nations, he will **p** with all flesh; 8199
30:13 There is none to **p** thy cause, that thou 1777
50:34 he shall **throughly p** their cause, 7378+3198
51:36 I will **p** thy cause, and take vengeance 7378
Eze 17:20 will **p** with him there for his trespass that 8199
20:35 and there will I **p** with you face to face. 8199
20:36 so will I **p** with you, saith the Lord God. 8199
38:22 I will **p** against him with pestilence and 8199
Hos 2: 2 **P** with your mother, plead: for she is not 7378
2: 2 Plead with your mother, **p**: for she is not 7378
Joel 3: 2 will **p** with them there for my people and 8199
Mic 6: 2 his people, and he will **p** with Israel. 3198
7: 9 he **p** my cause, and execute judgment 7378

PLEADED (3) [PLEAD]
1Sa 25:39 hath **p** the cause of my reproach from 7378
La 3:58 Lord, thou hast **p** the causes of my soul; 7378
Eze 20:36 Like as I **p** with your fathers in 8199

PLEADETH (3) [PLEAD]
Job 16:21 with God, as a man **p** for his neighbour. NIH
Isa 51:22 thy God that **p the cause** of his people, 7378
59: 4 calleth for justice, nor any **p** for truth: 8199

PLEADINGS (1) [PLEAD]
Job 13: 6 and hearken to the **p** of my lips. 7379

PLEASANT (57) [PLEASE]
Ge 2: 9 to grow every tree that is **p** to the sight, 2530
3: 6 that it was **p** to the eyes, and a tree to be 8378
49:15 rest was good, and the land that it was **p**; 5276
2Sa 1:23 Jonathan were lovely and **p** in their lives, 5273
1:26 very **p** hast thou been unto me: thy love 5276
1Ki 20: 6 be, that whatsoever is **p** in thine eyes, 4261
2Ki 2: 19 I pray thee, the situation of this city is **p**, 2896
2Ch 32:27 shields, and for all manner of **p** jewels; 2532
Ps 16: 6 The lines are fallen unto me in **p** places; 5273
81: 2 the timbrel, the **p** harp with the psaltery. 5273
106:24 Yea, they despised the **p** land, 2532
133: 1 how **p** it is for brethren to dwell together 5273
135: 3 sing praises unto his name; for it is **p**. 5273
147: 1 our God; for it is **p**; and praise is comely. 5273
Pr 2:10 and knowledge is **p** unto thy soul; 5276
5:19 Let her be as the loving hind and **p** roe; 2580
9:17 are sweet, and bread eaten in secret is **p**. 5276
15:26 but the words of the pure are **p** words. 5278
16:24 **P** words are as a honeycomb, sweet to 5278
22:18 For it is a **p** thing if thou keep them 5273
24: 4 be filled with all precious and **p** riches. 5273
Ecc 11: 7 **p** thing it is for the eyes to behold the sun 2896
SS 1:16 Behold, thou art fair, my beloved, yea, **p**: 5273
4:13 orchard of pomegranates, with **p** fruits; 4022
4:16 come into his garden, and eat his **p** fruits. 4022
7: 6 How fair and how **p** art thou, O love, 5276
7:13 at our gates are all manner of **p** fruits, 4022
Isa 2:16 ships of Tarshish, and upon all **p** pictures. 2532
5: 7 Israel, and the men of Judah his **p** plant: 8191
13:22 and dragons in their **p** palaces: 6027
17:10 therefore shalt thou plant **p** plants, 5282
32:12 for the **p** fields, for the fruitful vine. 2531
54:12 and all thy borders of **p** stones. 2656
64:11 and all our **p** things are laid waste. 4261
Jer 3:19 the children, and give thee a **p** land, 2532
12:10 they have made my **p** portion a desolate 2532
23:10 **p** places of the wilderness are dried up, 4999
25:34 And ye shall fall like a **p** vessel. 2532
31:20 is he a **p** child? for since I spake against 8191
La 1: 7 of her miseries all her **p** things that she 4262

La 1:10 spread out his hand upon all her **p** things: 4261
1:11 they have given their **p** things for meat to 4261
2: 4 slew all that were **p** to the eye, 4261
Eze 26:12 down thy walls, and destroy thy **p** houses: 2532
33:32 lovely song of one that hath a **p** voice, 3303
Da 8: 9 toward the east, and toward the **p** land. 6643
10: 3 I ate no **p** bread, neither came flesh nor 2532
11:38 and with precious stones, and **p** things. 2532
Hos 9: 6 the **p** places for their silver, nettles shall 4261
9:13 as I saw Tyrus, is planted in a **p** place: 5116
13:15 he shall spoil the treasure of all **p** vessels. 2532
Joel 3: 5 into your temples my goodly **p** things: 4261
Am 5:11 ye have planted **p** vineyards, but ye shall 2531
Mic 2: 9 have ye cast out from their **p** houses; 8588
Na 2: 9 and glory out of all the **p** furniture. 2532
Zec 7:14 for they laid the **p** land desolate. 2532
Mal 1:11 and Jerusalem be **p** unto the Lord, 6149

PLEASANTNESS (1) [PLEASE]
Pr 3:17 Her ways are ways of **p**, and all her paths 5278

PLEASE (39) [MENPLEASERS, PLEASANT, PLEASANTNESS, PLEASED, PLEASETH, PLEASING, PLEASURE, PLEASURES]
Ex 21: 8 If she **p** not her master, 5869+7451+871.1
Nu 23:27 peradventure it will **p** God 3474+5869+871.1
1Sa 20:13 but if it **p** my father to do thee evil, 413+3190
2Sa 7:29 Therefore now let it **p** thee to bless 2974
1Ki 21: 6 or else, if it **p** thee, I will give thee 2655
1Ch 17:27 let it **p** thee to bless the house of thy 2974
2Ch 10: 7 **p** them, and speak good words to them, 7521
Ne 2: 5 If it **p** the king, and if thy servant 2895+5921
2: 7 I said unto the king, If it **p** the king, 2895+5921
Est 1:19 If it **p** the king, let there go a royal 2895
3: 9 If it **p** the king, let it be written that they 2895
5: 8 and if it **p** the king to grant my petition, 2895
7: 3 in thy sight, O king, and if it **p** the king, 2896
8: 5 If it **p** the king, and if I have found favour 2896
9:13 Esther, If it **p** the king, let it be granted 2896
Job 6: 9 Even that it would **p** God to destroy me: 2974
20:10 His children shall seek to **p** the poor, 7521
Ps 69:31 This also shall **p** the Lord better than an 3190
Pr 16: 7 When a man's ways **p** the Lord, 7521
SS 2: 7 stir not up, nor awake my love, till he **p**. 2654
3: 5 stir not up, nor awake my love, till he **p**. 2654
8: 4 stir not up, nor awake my love, until he **p**. 2654
Isa 2: 6 they **p** themselves in the children of 5606
55:11 it shall accomplish that which I **p**, 2654
56: 4 choose the things that **p** me, and take 2654
Jn 8:29 for I do always those things that **p** him. 701
Ro 8: 8 they that are in the flesh cannot **p** God. 700
15: 1 of the weak, and not to **p** ourselves. 700
15: 2 Let every one of us **p** his neighbour for his 700
1Co 7:32 belong to the Lord, how he may **p** the Lord: 700
7:33 are of the world, how he may **p** his wife. 700
7:34 of the world, how she may **p** her husband. 700
10:33 as I **p** all men in all things, not seeking 700
Gal 1:10 or do I seek to **p** men? for if I yet pleased 700
1Th 2:15 and they **p** not God, and are contrary to all 700
4: 1 of us how ye ought to walk and to **p** God, 700
2Ti 2: 4 that he may **p** him who hath chosen him to 700
Tit 2: 9 to **p** them **well** in all things; not 1510+2101
Heb 11: 6 without faith it is impossible to **p** him: 2100

PLEASED (62) [PLEASE]
Ge 28: 8 of Canaan **p not** Isaac 5869+7451+871.1
33:10 face of God, and thou wast **p with** me. 7521
34:18 their words **p** Hamor, 3190+5869+871.1
45:16 **p** Pharaoh **well**, and his 2896+5869+871.1
Nu 24: 1 when Balaam saw that it **p** 2896+5869+871.1
Dt 1:23 the saying **p** me **well**: 3190+5869+871.1
Jos 22:30 Manasseh spake, it **p** them. 3190+5869+871.1
22:33 the thing **p** the children of 3190+5869+871.1
Jdg 13:23 unto him, If the Lord were **p** to kill us, 2654
14: 7 and she **p** Samson **well**. 3474+5869+871.1
1Sa 12:22 it hath **p** the Lord to make you his 2974
18:20 Saul, and the thing **p** him. 3474+5869+871.1
18:26 **p** David **well** to be the 3474+5869+871.1
2Sa 3:36 notice of it, and it **p** them: 3190+5869+871.1
3:36 king did, **p** all the people. 2896+5869+871.1
17: 4 the saying **p** Absalom **well**, 3474+5869+871.1
19: 6 then it had **p** thee **well**. 3477+5869+871.1
1Ki 3:10 the speech **p** the Lord, 3190+5869+871.1
9: 1 Solomon's desire which he was **p** to do, 2654
9:12 and they **p** him not. 3474+5869+871.1
2Ch 30: 4 the thing **p** the king and all 3190+5869+871.1
Ne 2: 6 it **p** the king to send me; 3190+6440+3807.1
Est 1:21 the saying **p** the king and 3190+5869+871.1
2: 4 **p** the king; and he did so. 3190+5869+871.1
2: 9 the maiden **p** him, 3190+5869+871.1
5:14 the thing **p** Haman; and he caused 3190
Ps 40:13 Be **p**, O Lord, to deliver me: O Lord, 7521
51:19 shalt thou be **p** with the sacrifices of 2654
115: 3 heavens: he hath done whatsoever he **p**. 2654
135: 6 Whatsoever the Lord **p**, that did he in 2654
Isa 42:21 The Lord is **well p** for his righteousness' 2654
53:10 Yet it **p** the Lord to bruise him; he hath 2654
Da 6: 1 it **p** Darius to set over the kingdom an 8232
Jnh 1:14 for thou, O Lord, hast done as it **p** thee. 2654
Mic 6: 7 Will the Lord be **p** with thousands of 7521
Mal 1: 8 will he be **p with** thee, or accept thy 7521
Mt 3:17 is my beloved Son, in whom I am **well p**. 2106
12:18 my beloved, in whom my soul is **well p**: 2106
14: 6 danced before them, and **p** Herod. 700
17: 5 is my beloved Son, in whom I am **well p**; 2106

Mk 1:11 my beloved Son, in whom I am **well p**. 2106
6:22 and **p** Herod and them that sat with him, 700
Lk 3:22 art my beloved Son; in thee I am **well p**. 2106
Ac 6: 5 And the saying **p** the whole multitude: 700
12: 3 And because he saw it **p** the Jews, 701+1510
15:22 Then **p** it the apostles and elders, with 1380
15:34 Notwithstanding it **p** Silas to abide there 1380
Ro 15: 3 For even Christ **p** not himself; but, as it is 700
15:26 For it hath **p** them of Macedonia to 2106
15:27 It hath **p** them verily; and their debtors 2106
1Co 1:21 it **p** God by the foolishness of preaching 2106
7:12 she be **p** to dwell with him, let him not 4909
7:13 if he be **p** to dwell with her, let her not 4909
10: 5 with many of them God was not **well p**: 2106
12:18 of them in the body, as it hath **p** him. 2309
15:38 But God giveth it a body as it hath **p** him, 2309
Gal 1:10 if I yet **p** men, I should not be the servant 700
1:15 when it **p** God, who separated me from 2106
Col 1:19 For it **p** the Father that in him should all 2106
Heb 11: 5 he had this testimony, that he **p** God. 2100
13:16 for with such sacrifices God is **well p**. 2100
2Pe 1:17 is my beloved Son, in whom I am **well p**. 2106

PLEASETH (6) [PLEASE]
Ge 16: 6 do to her as it **p** thee. 2896+5869+871.1
20:15 dwell where it **p** thee. 2896+5869+871.1
Jdg 14: 3 Get her for me; for she **p** me **well**. 3474+5869
Est 2: 4 let the maiden which **p** 3190+5869+871.1
Ecc 7:26 whoso **p** God shall escape 2896+6440+3807.1
8: 3 thing; for he doeth whatsoever **p** him. 2654

PLEASING (8) [PLEASE]
Est 8: 5 before the king, and I be **p** in his eyes, 2896
Hos 9: 4 neither shall they be **p** unto him: 6149
Php 4:18 a sacrifice acceptable, **well p** to God. 2101
Col 1:10 might walk worthy of the Lord unto all **p**, 699
3:20 all things: for this is **well p** unto the Lord. 2101
1Th 2: 4 not as to men, but God, which trieth our 700
Heb 13:21 working in you that which is **well p** in 2101
1Jn 3:22 and do those things that are **p** in his sight. 701

PLEASURE (61) [PLEASE]
Ge 18:12 After I am waxed old shall I have **p**, 5730
Dt 23:24 mayest eat grapes thy fill at thine own **p**; 5315
1Ch 29:17 the heart, and hast **p** in uprightness. 7521
Ezr 5:17 let the king send his **p** to us concerning 7470
10:11 Lord God of your fathers, and do his **p**: 7522
Ne 9:37 at their **p**, and we are in great distress. 7522
Est 1: 8 should do according to every man's **p**. 7522
Job 21:21 what **p** hath he in his house after him, 2656
21:25 of his soul, and never eateth with **p**. 2896
22: 3 Is it any **p** to the Almighty, that thou art 2656
Ps 5: 4 For thou art not a God that hath **p** in 2655
35:27 which hath **p** in the prosperity of his 2656
51:18 Do good in thy **good p** unto Zion: 7522
102:14 For thy servants take **p** in her stones, 7521
103:21 hosts; ye ministers of his, that do his **p**. 7522
105:22 bind his princes at his **p**; and teach his 5315
111: 2 out of all them that have **p** therein. 2656
147:10 He **taketh** not **p** in the legs of a man. 7521
147:11 The Lord **taketh p** in them that fear 7521
149: 4 For the Lord **taketh p** in his people: 7521
Pr 21:17 He that loveth **p** shall be a poor man: 8057
Ecc 2: 1 I prove thee with mirth, therefore enjoy **p**: 2896
5: 4 not to pay it; for he hath no **p** in fools: 2656
12: 1 when thou shalt say, I have no **p** in them; 2656
Isa 21: 4 night of my **p** hath he turned into fear 2837
44:28 my shepherd, and shall perform all my **p**: 2656
46:10 shall stand, and I will do all my **p**: 2656
48:14 he will do his **p** on Babylon, and his arm 2656
53:10 the **p** of the Lord shall prosper in his 2656
58: 3 in the day of your fast you find **p**, 2656
58:13 from doing thy **p** on my holy day; 2656
58:13 own ways, nor finding thine own **p**, 2656
Jer 2:24 that snuffeth up the wind at her **p**; 185
22:28 is he a vessel wherein is no **p**? 2656
34:16 whom ye had set at liberty at their **p**, 5315
48:38 Moab like a vessel wherein is no **p**, 2656
Eze 16:37 with whom thou hast **taken p**, and all 6149
18:23 Have I any **p at all** that the wicked 2654+2654
18:32 For I have no **p** in the death of him that 2654
33:11 I have no **p** in the death of the wicked; 2654
Hos 8: 8 the Gentiles as a vessel wherein is no **p**. 2656
Hag 1: 8 I will **take p** in it, and I will be glorified, 7521
Mal 1:10 I have no **p** in you, saith the Lord of 2656
Lk 12:32 for it is your Father's **good p** to give you 2106
Ac 24:27 and Felix, willing to shew the Jews a **p**, 5485
25: 9 But Festus, willing to do the Jews a **p**, 5485
Ro 1:32 same, but have **p** in them that do them. 4909
2Co 12:10 Therefore I **take p** in infirmities, 2106
Eph 1: 5 according to the **good p** of his will, 2107
1: 9 according to his **good p** which he had 2107
Php 2:13 you both to will and to do of his **good p**. 2107
2Th 1:11 and fulfil all the **good p** of his goodness, 2107
2:12 the truth, but had **p** in unrighteousness. 2106
1Ti 5: 6 But she that **liveth in p** is dead while 4684
Heb 10: 6 and sacrifices for sin thou hast **had** no **p**. 2106
10: 8 neither hadst **p** therein: which are offered 2106
10:38 back, my soul shall **have** no **p** in him. 2106
12:10 a few days chastened us after their own **p**; 1380
Jas 5: 5 Ye have **lived in p** on the earth, 5171
2Pe 2:13 as they that count it **p** to riot in the day 2237
Rev 4:11 and for thy **p** they are and were created. 2307

PLEASURES (8) [PLEASE]

Job	36:11 days in prosperity, and their years in **p**.	5273
Ps	16:11 thy right hand *there are* **p** for evermore.	5273
	36: 8 make them drink *of* the river of thy **p**.	5730
Isa	47: 8 *thou that art* **given to p**, that dwellest	5719
Lk	8:14 with cares and riches and **p** of *this life*,	2237
2Ti	3: 4 **lovers of p** more than lovers of God;	5369
Tit	3: 3 deceived, serving divers lusts and **p**,	2237
Heb	11:25 than to enjoy the **p** of sin for a season;	619

PLEDGE (22) [PLEDGES]

Ge	38:17 she said, Wilt thou give *me* a **p**, till thou	6162
	38:18 he said, What **p** shall I give thee? And she	6162
	38:20 to receive *his* **p** from the woman's hand:	6162
Ex	22:26 **at all** take thy neighbour's	
	raiment **to p**,	2254+2254
Dt	24: 6 **take** the nether or the upper	
	millstone **to p**,	2254
	24: 6 pledge: for he **taketh** *a* man's life to **p**.	2254
	24:10 shalt not go into his house to fetch his **p**.	5667
	24:11 shall bring out the **p** abroad unto thee.	5667
	24:12 *be* poor, thou shalt not sleep with his **p**:	5667
	24:13 In any case thou shalt deliver him the **p**	5667
	24:17 nor **take** a widow's raiment **to p**:	2254
1Sa	17:18 how thy brethren fare, and take their **p**.	6161
Job	22: 6 For thou hast **taken** a **p** from thy brother	2254
	24: 3 they **take** the widow's ox **for a p**.	2254
	24: 9 from the breast, and **take** a **p** of the poor.	2254
Pr	20:16 and **take** a **p** of him for a strange *woman*.	2254
	27:13 and **take** a **p** of him for a strange *woman*.	2254
Eze	18: 7 *but* hath restored *to* the debtor his **p**,	2258
	18:12 hath not restored the **p**, and hath lift up	2258
	18:16 hath not **withholden the p**,	2254+2258
	33:15 *If* the wicked restore the **p**, give again	2258
Am	2: 8 upon clothes **laid to p** by every altar,	2254

PLEDGES (2) [PLEDGE]

2Ki	18:23 **give p** to my lord the king of Assyria,	6148
Isa	36: 8 Now therefore **give p**, I pray thee, to my	6148

PLEIADES (2)

Job	9: 9 and **P**, and the chambers of the south.	3598
	38:31 thou bind the sweet influences of **P**,	3598

PLENTEOUS (12) [PLENTY]

Ge	41:34 of the land of Egypt in the seven **p** years.	7647
	41:47 the seven **p** years the earth brought forth	7647
Dt	28:11 the LORD shall **make** thee **p** in goods,	3498
	30: 9 the LORD thy God will **make** thee **p** in	3498
2Ch	1:15 and gold at Jerusalem *as* **p** as stones,	NIH
Ps	86: 5 **p** in mercy unto all them that call upon	7227
	86:15 longsuffering, and **p** in mercy and truth.	7227
	103: 8 gracious, slow to anger, and **p** in mercy.	7227
	130: 7 *is* mercy, and with him *is* **p** redemption.	7235
Isa	30:23 of the earth, and it shall be fat and **p**:	8082
Hab	1:16 their portion *is* fat, and their meat **p**.	1277
Mt	9:37 The harvest truly is **p**, but the labourers	4183

PLENTEOUSNESS (2) [PLENTY]

Ge	41:53 the seven years of **p**, that was in the land	7647
Pr	21: 5 thoughts of the diligent *tend* only to **p**;	4195

PLENTIFUL (4) [PLENTY]

Ps	68: 9 Thou, O God, didst send a **p** rain,	5071
Isa	16:10 is taken away, and joy out of the **p** field;	3759
Jer	2: 7 I brought you into a **p** country, to eat	3759
	48:33 and gladness is taken from the **p** field.	3759

PLENTIFULLY (3) [PLENTY]

Job	26: 3 thou **p** declared the thing as it is?	7230+3807.1
Ps	31:23 and **p** rewardeth the proud doer.	3499
Lk	12:16 of a certain rich man **brought forth p**:	2164

PLENTY (13) [PLENTEOUS, PLENTEOUSNESS, PLENTIFUL, PLENTIFULLY]

Ge	27:28 of the earth, and **p** of corn and wine;	7230
	41:29 there come seven years of great **p**	7647
	41:30 all the **p** shall be forgotten in the land of	7647
	41:31 the **p** shall not be known in the land by	7647
Lev	11:36 or pit, *wherein there is* **p** of water,	4723
1Ki	10:11 brought in from Ophir great **p** of almug	7235
2Ch	31:10 enough to eat, and have **p**:	7230+3807.1
Job	22:25 defence, and thou shalt have **p** of silver.	8443
	37:23 and *in* judgment, and in **p** of justice:	7230
Pr	3:10 So shall thy barns be filled with **p**,	7647
	28:19 He that tilleth his land shall **have p** *of*	7646
Jer	44:17 for *then* **had** we **p** of victuals,	7646
Joel	2:26 ye shall **eat in p**, and be satisfied,	398+398

PLOT See FORECAST

PLOTTETH (1)

Ps	37:12 The wicked **p** against the just,	2161

PLOUGH (1) [PLOW]

Lk	9:62 No *man* having put his hand to the **p**,	723

PLOW (8) [PLOUGH, PLOWED, PLOWERS, PLOWETH, PLOWING, PLOWMAN, PLOWMEN, PLOWSHARES]

Dt	22:10 Thou shalt not **p** with an ox and an ass	2790
1Sa	14:14 of land, *which* a yoke of oxen might **p**.	NIH
Job	4: 8 they that **p** iniquity, and sow wickedness,	2790
Pr	20: 4 The sluggard will not **p** by reason of	2790
Isa	28:24 Doth the plowman **p** all day to sow?	2790
Hos	10:11 Judah shall **p**, *and* Jacob shall break his	2790

Am	6:12 will *one* **p** *there* with oxen? for ye have	2790
1Co	9:10 that he that ploweth should **p** in hope;	722

PLOWED (5) [PLOW]

Jdg	14:18 them, If ye had not **p** with my heifer,	2790
Ps	129: 3 The plowers **p** upon my back: they made	2790
Jer	26:18 Zion shall be **p** *like* a field,	2790
Hos	10:13 Ye have **p** wickedness, ye have reaped	2790
Mic	3:12 Therefore shall Zion for your sake be **p** *as*	2790

PLOWERS (1) [PLOW]

Ps	129: 3 The **p** plowed upon my back: they made	2790

PLOWETH (1) [PLOW]

1Co	9:10 that he that **p** should plow in hope;	722

PLOWING (4) [PLOW]

1Ki	19:19 who *was* **p** with twelve yoke *of* oxen	2790
Job	1:14 The oxen were **p**, and the asses feeding	2790
Pr	21: 4 heart, *and* the **p** of the wicked, *is* sin.	5215
Lk	17: 7 you, having a servant **p** or feeding cattle,	722

PLOWMAN (2) [MAN, PLOW]

Isa	28:24 Doth the **p** plow all day to sow? doth he	2790
Am	9:13 that the **p** shall overtake the reaper,	2790

PLOWMEN (2) [MAN, PLOW]

Isa	61: 5 the sons of the alien *shall be* your **p** and	406
Jer	14: 4 the **p** were ashamed, they covered their	406

PLOWSHARES (3) [PLOW]

Isa	2: 4 they shall beat their swords into **p**,	855
Joel	3:10 Beat your **p** into swords,	855
Mic	4: 3 they shall beat their swords into **p**,	855

PLUCK (30) [PLUCKED, PLUCKETH, PLUCKT]

Lev	1:16 shall **p away** his crop with his feathers,	5493
Nu	33:52 and quite **p down** all their high places:	8045
Dt	23:25 thou mayest **p** the ears with thine hand;	6998
2Ch	7:20 will I **p** them **up by the roots** out of my	5428
Job	24: 9 They **p** the fatherless from the breast,	1497
Ps	25:15 for he shall **p** my feet **out** of the net.	3318
	52: 5 **p** thee out of *thy* dwelling place,	5255
	74:11 thy right hand? **p** *it* out of thy bosom.	3615
	80:12 all they which pass by the way do **p** her?	717
Ecc	3: 2 and a time to **p up** *that which is* planted;	6131
Jer	12:14 I will **p** them out of their land, and pluck	5428
	12:14 **p** out the house of Judah from among	5428
	12:17 I will **utterly p** up and destroy that	5428+5428
	18: 7 to **p up**, and to pull down, and to destroy	5428
	22:24 my right hand, yet would I **p** thee thence;	5423
	24: 6 and I will plant them, and not **p** *them* **up**.	5428
	31:28 to **p up**, and to break down, and to throw	5428
	42:10 and I will plant you, and not **p** *you* **up**:	5428
	45: 4 *that* which I have planted I *will* **p up**,	5428
Eze	17: 9 many people to **p** it **up** by the roots	5375
	23:34 and **p off** thine own breasts:	5423
Mic	3: 2 who **p off** their skin from off them,	1497
	5:14 I will **p up** thy groves out of the midst of	5428
Mt	5:29 offend thee, **p** it **out**, and cast *it* from thee:	1807
	12: 1 began to **p** the ears of corn, and to eat.	5089
	18: 9 offend thee, **p** it **out**, and cast *it* from thee:	1807
Mk	2:23 as they went, to **p** the ears of corn.	5089
	9:47 And if thine eye offend thee, **p** it **out**: it is	1544
Jn	10:28 neither shall any *man* **p** them out of my	726
	10:29 is able to **p** them out of my Father's	726

PLUCKED (14) [PLUCK]

Ex	4: 7 **p** it **out** of his bosom, and behold, it was	3318
Dt	28:63 ye shall be **p** from off the land whither	5255
Ru	4: 7 a man **p off** his shoe, and gave *it* to his	8025
2Sa	23:21 **p** the spear out of the Egyptian's hand,	1497
Isa	50: 6 my cheeks to them that **p off** the hair:	4803
Jer	6:29 in vain: for the wicked are not **p away**.	5423
	12:15 that I have **p** them **out**, I will return,	5428
	31:40 it shall not be **p up**, nor thrown down	5428
Eze	19:12 she was **p up** in fury, she was cast down	5428
Mk	5: 4 the chains had been **p asunder** by him,	1288
Lk	6: 1 and his disciples **p** the ears of corn,	5089
	17: 6 Be thou **p up by the root**, and be thou	1610
Gal	4:15 ye would have **p out** your own eyes,	1846
Jude	1:12 twice dead, **p up by the roots**;	1610

PLUCKETH (1) [PLUCK]

Pr	14: 1 but the foolish **p** it **down** with her hands.	2040

PLUCKT (10) [PLUCK]

Ge	8:11 lo, in her mouth *was* an olive leaf **p off**:	2965
1Ch	11:23 the spear out of the Egyptian's hand,	1497
Ezr	9: 3 **p off** the hair of my head and of my beard	4803
Ne	13:25 **p off** their **hair**, and made them swear by	4803
Job	29:17 wicked, and **p** the spoil out of his teeth.	7993
Da	7: 4 I beheld till the wings thereof were **p**,	4804
	7: 8 of the first horns **p up by the roots**:	6132
	11: 4 for his kingdom shall be **p up**, even for	5428
Am	4:11 were as a firebrand **p out** of the burning:	5337
Zec	3: 2 *is* not this a brand **p out** of the fire?	5337

PLUMBLINE (4) [LINE]

Am	7: 7 the Lord stood upon a wall made by a **p**,	594
	7: 7 made by a plumbline, with a **p** in his hand.	594
	7: 8 I said, A **p**. Then said the Lord, Behold,	594
	7: 8 I *will* set a **p** in the midst of my people	594

PLUMMET (3)

2Ki	21:13 Samaria, and the **p** of the house of Ahab:	4949

Isa	28:17 lay to the line, and righteousness to the **p**:	4949
Zec	4:10 see the **p** in the hand of Zerubbabel	68+913

PLUNDER See BOOTY; PREY; SPOIL

PLUNGE (1)

Job	9:31 Yet shalt thou **p** me in the ditch,	2881

POCHERETH OF ZEBAIM (1) [POCHERETH ZEBAIM]

Ezr	2:57 the children of **P**, the children	6380

POCHERETH ZEBAIM (1) [POCHERETH OF ZEBAIM]

Ne	7:59 of Hattil, the children of **P**,	6380

POETS (1)

Ac	17:28 as certain also of your own **p** have said,	4163

POINT (9) [POINTED, POINTS]

Ge	25:32 Esau said, Behold, I *am* **at the p** to die:	1980
Nu	34: 7 from the great sea ye shall **p out** for you	8376
	34: 8 From mount Hor ye shall **p out** *your*	8376
	34:10 ye shall **p out** your east border from	184
Jer	17: 1 pen of iron, *and* with the **p** of a diamond:	6856
Eze	21:15 I have set the **p** of the sword against all	19
Mk	5:23 daughter **lieth at the p of death**:	2079+2192
Jn	4:47 his son: for he was **at the p of death**.	3195
Jas	2:10 and *yet* offend in one **p**, he is guilty of all.	NIG

POINTED (1) [POINT]

Job	41:30 spreadeth **sharp p** *things* upon the mire.	2742

POINTING See SIGNIFY

POINTS (2) [POINT]

Ecc	5:16 *that* in all **p** as he came, so shall he go:	5980
Heb	4:15 was in all **p** tempted like as *we are*, yet	NIG

POISON (9)

Dt	32:24 with the **p** of serpents of the dust.	2534
	32:33 Their wine *is* the **p** of dragons,	2534
Job	6: 4 the **p** whereof drinketh up my spirit:	2534
	20:16 He shall suck the **p** of asps: the viper's	7219
Ps	58: 4 Their **p** *is* like the poison of a serpent:	2534
	58: 4 Their poison *is* like the **p** of a serpent:	2534
	140: 3 a serpent; adder's **p** *is* under their lips.	2534
Ro	3:13 deceit; the **p** of asps *is* under their lips:	2447
Jas	3: 8 *it is* an unruly evil, full of deadly **p**.	2447

POISONOUS See HEMLOCK

POKERETH HAZZEBAIM See POCHERETH [OF] ZEBAIM

POLE (2)

Nu	21: 8 thee a fiery *serpent*, and set it upon a **p**:	5251
	21: 9 put it upon a **p**, and it came to pass, that	5251

POLES See STAVES

POLICY (1)

Da	8:25 through his **p** also he shall cause craft to	7922

POLISHED (3) [POLISHING]

Ps	144:12 **p** after the similitude of a palace:	2404
Isa	49: 2 hath he hid me, and made me a **p** shaft;	1305
Da	10: 6 and his feet like in colour to **p** brass,	7044

POLISHING (1) [POLISHED]

La	4: 7 body than rubies, their **p** *was* of sapphire:	1508

POLL (3) [POLLED, POLLS]

Nu	3:47 even take five shekels apiece by the **p**,	1538
Eze	44:20 they shall **only p** their heads;	3697+3697
Mic	1:16 and **p** thee for thy delicate children;	1494

POLLED (3) [POLL]

2Sa	14:26 when he **p** his head, (for it was at every	1548
	14:26 for it was at every year's end that he **p** *it*:	1548
	14:26 *hair* was heavy on him, therefore he **p** it:)	1548

POLLS (6) [POLL]

Nu	1: 2 of *their* names, every male by their **p**;	1538
	1:18 twenty years old and upward, by their **p**.	1538
	1:20 by their **p**, every male from twenty years	1538
	1:22 by their **p**, every male from twenty years	1538
1Ch	23: 3 their number by their **p**, man by man,	1538
	23:24 counted by number of names by their **p**,	1538

POLLUTE (11) [POLLUTED, POLLUTING, POLLUTION, POLLUTIONS]

Nu	18:32 neither shall ye **p** the holy *things* of	2490
	35:33 So ye shall not **p** the land wherein ye *are*:	2610
Jer	7:30 which is called by my name, to **p** it.	2930
Eze	7:21 of the earth for a spoil; and they shall **p** it.	2490
	7:22 shall **p** my secret *place*: for the robbers	2490
	13:19 ye **p** me among my people for handfuls	2490
	20:31 ye **p** yourselves with all your idols,	2930
	20:39 ye my holy name no more with your	2490
	39: 7 I will not let *them* **p** my holy name any	2490
	44: 7 in my sanctuary, to **p** it, *even* my house,	2490
Da	11:31 they shall **p** the sanctuary *of* strength,	2490

POLLUTED (40) [POLLUTE]

Ex	20:25 lift up thy tool upon it, thou hast **p** it.	2490
2Ki	23:16 and burnt *them* upon the altar, and **p** it,	2930
2Ch	36:14 **p** the house of the LORD which he had	2930

P

Ezr	2:62 therefore were they, as **p**, put from	1351
Ne	7:64 therefore were they, as **p**, put from	1351
Ps	106:38 Canaan: and the land was **p** with blood.	2610
Isa	47: 6 I have **p** mine inheritance, and given	2490
	48:11 I do *it*: for how should *my name* be **p**?	2490
Jer	2:23 How canst thou say, I am not **p**, I have	2930
	3: 1 shall not that land be **greatly p**?	2610+2610
	3: 2 hast **p** the land with thy whoredoms	2610
	34:16 turned and **p** my name, and caused every	2490
La	2: 2 he hath **p** the kingdom and the princes	2490
	4:14 they have **p** themselves with blood,	1351
Eze	4:14 behold, my soul *hath* not *been* **p**	2930
	14:11 neither be **p** any more with all their	2930
	16: 6 thee, and saw thee **p** in thine own blood,	947
	16:22 and bare, *and* wast **p** in thy blood.	947
	20: 9 *it* should not be **p** before the heathen,	2490
	20:13 in them; and my sabbaths they greatly **p**:	2490
	20:14 *it* should not be **p** before the heathen,	2490
	20:16 not in my statutes, but **p** my sabbaths:	2490
	20:21 even live in them; they **p** my sabbaths:	2490
	20:22 that *it* should not be **p** in the sight of	2490
	20:24 had **p** my sabbaths, and their eyes were	2490
	20:26 I **p** them in their own gifts, in that they	2930
	20:30 Are ye **p** after the manner of your fathers?	2930
	23:17 she was **p** with them, and her mind was	2930
	23:30 *and* because thou art **p** with their idols.	2930
	36:18 for their idols *wherewith* they had **p** it:	2930
Hos	6: 8 that work iniquity, *and is* **p** with blood.	6121
Am	9: 4 mourners; and I will thereof shall be **p**	2930
Mic	7:17 by line; and thou shalt die in a **p** land:	2931
Zep	2:10 because it is **p**, it shall destroy *you*, even	2930
Mal	1: 7 Woe to her that is filthy and **p**,	1351
	1: 7 her priests have **p** the sanctuary, they	2490
	1: 7 and ye say, Wherein have we **p** thee?	1351
	1:12 in that ye say, The table of the LORD *is* **p**;	1351
Ac	21:28 the temple, and hath **p** this holy place.	2840

POLLUTING (2) [POLLUTE]

Isa	56: 2 that keepeth the sabbath from **p** it,	2490
	56: 6 one that keepeth the sabbath from **p**	2490

POLLUTION (1) [POLLUTE]

Eze	22:10 humbled her that was set apart for **p**.	2931

POLLUTIONS (2) [POLLUTE]

Ac	15:20 that they abstain from **p** of idols,	234
2Pe	2:20 For if after they have escaped the **p** of	3393

POLLUX (1)

Ac	28:11 in the isle, *whose* sign *was* **Castor and P**.	1359

POMEGRANATE (10) [POMEGRANATES]

Ex	28:34 A golden bell and a **p**, a golden bell and a	7416
	28:34 and a pomegranate, a golden bell and a **p**,	7416
	39:26 A bell and a **p**, a bell and a pomegranate,	7416
	39:26 A bell and a pomegranate, a bell and a **p**,	7416
1Sa	14: 2 under a **p tree** which *is* in Migron:	7416
SS	4: 3 thy temples *are* like a piece of a **p** within	7416
	6: 7 As a piece of a **p** *are* thy temples within	7416
	8: 2 drink of spiced wine, of the juice of my **p**.	7416
Joel	1:12 **p tree**, the palm tree also, and the apple	7416
Hag	2:19 the fig tree, and the **p**, and the olive tree,	7416

POMEGRANATES (23) [POMEGRANATE]

Ex	28:33 the hem of it thou shalt make **p** of blue,	7416
	39:24 made upon the hems of the robe **p** of	7416
	39:25 put the bells between the **p** upon the hem	7416
	39:25 of the robe, round about between the **p**;	7416
Nu	13:23 *and* they brought of the **p**, and of the figs.	7416
	20: 5 place of seed, or of figs, or vines, or of **p**;	7416
Dt	8: 8 and barley, and vines, and fig trees, and **p**;	7416
1Ki	7:18 chapters that *were* upon the top, with **p**:	7416
	7:20 the chapters upon the two pillars had **p**	NIH
	7:20 the **p** were two hundred in rows round	7416
	7:42 four hundred **p** for the two networks,	7416
	7:42 *even* two rows of **p** for one network,	7416
2Ki	25:17 **p** upon the chapiter round about, all *of*	7416
2Ch	3:16 made an hundred **p**, and put *them* on	7416
	4:13 four hundred **p** on the two wreaths,	7416
	4:13 two rows of **p** on each wreath, to cover	7416
SS	4:13 Thy plants *are* an orchard of **p**,	7416
	6:11 the vine flourished, *and* the **p** budded.	7416
	7:12 tender grape appear, *and* the **p** bud forth:	7416
Jer	52:22 and **p** upon the chapiters round about,	7416
	52:22 pillar also and the **p** *were* like unto these.	7416
	52:23 there were ninety and six **p** on a side;	7416
	52:23 all the **p** upon the network *were* an	7416

POMMELS (3)

2Ch	4:12 the **p**, and the chapiters which *were* on	1543
	4:12 the two wreaths to cover the two **p** of	1543
	4:13 to cover the two **p** of the chapiters which	1543

POMP (7)

Isa	5:14 and their **p**, and he that rejoiceth,	7588
	14:11 Thy **p** is brought down *to* the grave,	1347
Eze	7:24 I will also make the **p** of the strong to	1347
	30:18 the **p** of her strength shall cease in her:	1347
	32:12 they shall spoil the **p** of Egypt, and all	1347
	33:28 the **p** of her strength shall cease;	1347
Ac	25:23 with great **p**, and were entered into	5325

PONDER (2) [PONDERED, PONDERETH]

Pr	4:26 **P** the path of thy feet, and let all thy ways	6424
	5: 6 Lest thou shouldest **p** the path of life,	6424

PONDERED (1) [PONDER]

Lk	2:19 all these things, and **p** *them* in her heart.	4820

PONDERETH (3) [PONDER]

Pr	5:21 eyes of the LORD, and he **p** all his goings.	6424
	21: 2 his own eyes: but the LORD **p** the hearts.	8505
	24:12 doth not he that **p** the heart consider *it*?	8505

PONDS (3)

Ex	7:19 upon their **p**, and upon all their pools of	98
	8: 5 over the **p**, and cause frogs to come up	98
Isa	19:10 all that make sluces *and* **p** for fish.	99

PONTIUS (4)

Mt	27: 2 delivered him to **P** Pilate the governor.	4194
Lk	3: 1 **P** Pilate being governor of Judea,	4194
Ac	4:27 Herod, and **P** Pilate, with the Gentiles,	4194
1Ti	6:13 who before **P** Pilate witnessed a good	4194

PONTUS (3)

Ac	2: 9 in Judea, and Cappadocia, in **P**, and Asia,	4195
	18: 2 born in **P**, lately come from Italy, with	4193
1Pe	1: 1 to the strangers scattered throughout **P**,	4195

POOL (22) [FISHPOOLS, POOLS]

2Sa	2:13 and met together by the **p** of Gibeon:	1295
	2:13 the one on the one side of the **p**,	1295
	2:13 and the other on the other side of the **p**.	1295
	4:12 hanged *them* up over the **p** in Hebron.	1295
1Ki	22:38 washed the chariot in the **p** of Samaria;	1295
2Ki	18:17 and stood by the conduit of the upper **p**,	1295
	20:20 how he made a **p**, and a conduit,	1295
Ne	2:14 gate of the fountain, and to the king's **p**:	1295
	3:15 the wall of the **p** of Siloah by the king's	1295
	3:16 to the **p** that was made, and unto the	1295
Isa	7: 3 at the end of the conduit of the upper **p**	1295
	22: 9 together the waters of the lower **p**.	1295
	22:11 the two walls for the water of the old **p**:	1295
	35: 7 the parched ground shall become a **p**,	98
	36: 2 he stood by the conduit of the upper **p** in	1295
	41:18 I will make the wilderness a **p** of water,	98
Na	2: 8 Nineveh *is* of old like a **p** of water: yet	1295
Jn	5: 2 is at Jerusalem by the sheep *market* a **p**,	2861
	5: 4 went down at a *certain* season into the **p**,	2861
	5: 7 water is troubled, to put me into the **p**:	2861
	9: 7 unto him, Go, wash in the **p** of Siloam,	2861
	9:11 me, Go to the **p** of Siloam, and wash:	2861

POOLS (5) [POOL]

Ex	7:19 their ponds, and upon all their **p** of water,	4723
Ps	84: 6 make it a well; the rain also filleth the **p**.	1295
Ecc	2: 6 I made me **p** of water, to water therewith	1295
Isa	14:23 possession for the bittern, and **p** of water:	98
	42:15 the rivers islands, and I will dry up the **p**.	98

POOR (205) [POVERTY]

Ge	41:19 **p** and very ill favoured and leanfleshed,	1803
Ex	22:25 to *any* of my people that *is* **p** by thee,	6041
	23: 3 Neither shalt thou countenance a **p** *man*	1800
	23: 6 shalt not wrest the judgment of thy **p** in	34
	23:11 lie still; that the **p** of thy people may eat:	34
	30:15 the **p** shall not give less than half a shekel,	1800
Lev	14:21 if he *be* **p**, and cannot get *so much*; then	1800
	19:10 thou shalt leave them for the **p** and	6041
	19:15 thou shalt not respect the person of the **p**,	1800
	23:22 thou shalt leave them unto the **p**, and to	6041
	25:25 If thy brother be **waxen p**, and hath sold	4134
	25:35 if thy brother be **waxen p**, and fallen in	4134
	25:39 *that dwelleth* by thee be **waxen p**,	4134
	25:47 thy brother *that dwelleth* by him **wax p**,	4134
Dt	15: 4 Save when there shall be no **p** among you;	34
	15: 7 If there be among you a **p man** of one of	34
	15: 7 nor shut thine hand from thy **p** brother:	34
	15: 9 thine eye be evil against thy **p** brother,	34
	15:11 For the **p** shall never cease out of the land:	34
	15:11 to thy **p**, and to thy needy, in thy land.	6041
	24:12 if the man *be* **p**, thou shalt not sleep with	6041
	24:14 shalt not oppress a hired servant *that is* **p**	6041
	24:15 for he *is* **p**, and setteth his heart upon it:	6041
Jdg	6:15 my family *is* **p** in Manasseh, and I *am*	1800
Ru	3:10 not young men, whether **p** or rich.	1800
1Sa	2: 7 The LORD **maketh p**, and maketh rich:	3423
	2: 8 He raiseth up the **p** out of the dust,	1800
	18:23 seeing that I *am* a **p** man,	7326
2Sa	12: 1 in one city; the one rich, and the other **p**.	7326
	12: 1 the **p** man had nothing, save one little	7326
	12: 4 took the **p** man's lamb, and dressed it for	7326
2Ki	25:12 the captain of the guard left of the **p** of	1803
Est	9:22 portions one to another, and gifts to the **p**.	34
Job	5:15 he saveth the **p** from the sword, from their	34
	5:16 So the **p** hath hope, and iniquity stoppeth	1800
	20:10 His children shall *seek* to please the **p**,	1800
	20:19 hath oppressed *and* hath forsaken the **p**;	1800
	24: 4 **p** of the earth hide themselves together.	6041
	24: 9 the breast, and take a pledge of the **p**.	6041
	24:14 rising with the light killeth the **p**	6041
	29:12 Because I delivered the **p** that cried,	6041
	29:16 I *was* a father to the **p**: and the cause	34
	30:25 was *not* my soul grieved for the **p**?	34
	31:16 If I have withheld the **p** from *their* desire,	1800
	31:19 of clothing, or *any* **p** without covering;	34
	34:19 nor regardeth the rich more than the **p**?	1800
	34:28 that *they* cause the cry of the **p** to come	1800
	36: 6 of the wicked: but giveth right to the **p**.	6041
	36:15 He delivereth the **p** in his affliction,	6041

Ps	9:18 the expectation of the **p** shall *not* perish	6041
	10: 2 wicked in his pride doth persecute the **p**:	6041
	10: 8 his eyes are privily set against the **p**.	2489
	10: 9 He lieth in wait to catch the **p**: he doth	6041
	10: 9 he doth catch the **p**, when he draweth	2489
	10:10 that the **p** may fall by his strong *ones*.	2489
	10:14 the **p** committeth *himself* unto thee,	2489
	12: 5 For the oppression of the **p**, for the	6041
	14: 6 You have shamed the counsel of the **p**,	6041
	34: 6 This **p** *man* cried, and the LORD heard	6041
	35:10 which deliverest the **p** from him that is	6041
	35:10 **p** and the needy from him that spoileth	6041
	37:14 cast down the **p** and needy, *and* to slay	6041
	40:17 I *am* **p** and needy; *yet* the Lord thinketh	6041
	41: 1 Blessed *is* he that considereth the **p**	1800
	49: 2 Both low and high, rich and **p**, together.	34
	68:10 hast prepared of thy goodness for the **p**.	6041
	69:29 I *am* **p** and sorrowful: let thy salvation,	34
	69:33 For the LORD heareth the **p**, and despiseth	34
	70: 5 I *am* **p** and needy: make haste unto me,	6041
	72: 2 and thy **p** with judgment.	6041
	72: 4 He shall judge the **p** of the people, he	6041
	72:12 the **p** also, and *him* that hath no helper.	6041
	72:13 He shall spare the **p** and needy,	1800
	74:19 not the congregation of thy **p** for ever.	6041
	74:21 let the **p** and needy praise thy name.	6041
	82: 3 Defend the **p** and fatherless: do justice to	1800
	82: 4 Deliver the **p** and needy: rid *them* out of	1800
	86: 1 O LORD, hear me: for I *am* **p** and needy.	6041
	107:41 setteth he the **p** on high from affliction,	34
	109:16 persecuted the **p** and needy man, that *he*	34
	109:22 For I *am* **p** and needy, and my heart is	6041
	109:31 he shall stand at the right hand of the **p**,	34
	112: 9 He hath dispersed, he hath given to the **p**;	34
	113: 7 He raiseth up the **p** out of the dust,	1800
	132:15 provision: I will satisfy her **p** *with* bread.	34
	140:12 of the afflicted, *and* the right of the **p**.	6041
Pr	10: 4 *He becometh* **p** that dealeth *with* a slack	7326
	10:15 the destruction of the **p** *is* their poverty.	1800
	13: 7 *there is* that **maketh** himself **p**, yet *hath*	7326
	13: 8 his riches: but the **p** heareth not rebuke.	1800
	13:23 Much food *is* in the tillage of the **p**:	7326
	14:20 The **p** is hated even of his own neighbour	7326
	14:21 he that hath mercy on the **p**, happy *is* he.	6035
	14:31 He that oppresseth the **p** reproacheth his	1800
	14:31 that honoureth him hath mercy on the **p**.	34
	17: 5 Whoso mocketh the **p** reproacheth his	7326
	18:23 The **p** useth intreaties; but the rich	7326
	19: 1 Better *is* the **p** that walketh in his	7326
	19: 4 but the **p** is separated from his neighbour.	1800
	19: 7 All the brethren of the **p** do hate him:	7326
	19:17 He that hath pity upon the **p** lendeth	1800
	19:22 and a **p** *man is* better than a liar.	7326
	21:13 stoppeth his ears at the cry of the **p**,	1800
	21:17 He that loveth pleasure *shall* be a **p** man:	4270
	22: 2 The rich and **p** meet together: the LORD	7326
	22: 7 The rich ruleth over the **p**, and the	7326
	22: 9 for he giveth of his bread to the **p**.	1800
	22:16 He that oppresseth the **p** to increase his	1800
	22:22 Rob not the **p**, because he *is* **p**:	1800
	22:22 Rob not the poor, because he *is* **p**:	1800
	28: 3 A man that oppresseth the poor *is* like a	7326
	28: 3 A poor man that oppresseth the **p** *is* like a	7326
	28: 6 Better *is* the **p** that walketh in his	7326
	28: 8 shall gather it for him that will pity the **p**.	1800
	28:11 the **p** that hath understanding searcheth	1800
	28:15 *so is* a wicked ruler over the **p** people.	1800
	28:27 He that giveth unto the **p** *shall* not lack:	7326
	29: 7 righteous considereth the cause of the **p**:	1800
	29:13 The **p** and the deceitful man meet	7326
	29:14 The king that faithfully judgeth the **p**,	1800
	30: 9 lest I be **p**, and steal, and take the name	3423
	30:14 to devour the **p** from off the earth,	6041
	31: 9 and plead the cause of the **p** and needy.	6041
	31:20 She stretcheth out her hand to the **p**; yea,	6041
Ecc	4:13 Better *is* a **p** and a wise child than an old	4542
	4:14 *that is* born in his kingdom becometh **p**.	7326
	5: 8 If thou seest the oppression of the **p**,	7326
	6: 8 what hath the **p**, that knoweth to walk	6041
	9:15 Now there was found in it a **p** wise man,	4542
	9:15 no man remembered that *same* **p** man.	4542
	9:16 nevertheless the **p** man's wisdom *is*	4542
Isa	3:14 the spoil of the **p** *is* in your houses.	6041
	3:15 to pieces, and grind the faces of the **p**?	6041
	10: 2 to take away the right from the **p** of my	6041
	10:30 *it* to be heard unto Laish, O **p** Anathoth.	6041
	11: 4 with righteousness shall he judge the **p**,	1800
	14:30 the firstborn of the **p** shall feed,	1800
	14:32 and of his people shall trust in it.	6041
	25: 4 For thou hast been a strength to the **p**,	1800
	26: 6 *even* the feet of the **p**, *and* the steps of	6041
	29:19 the **p** among men shall rejoice in the Holy	34
	32: 7 deviseth wicked devices to destroy the **p**	6041
	41:17 *When* the **p** and needy seek water,	6041
	58: 7 that thou bring the **p** that are cast out to	6041
	66: 2 to *him* that is **p** and of a contrite spirit,	6041
Jer	2:34 the blood of the souls of the **p** innocents:	5355
	5: 4 Therefore I said, Surely these *are* **p**;	1800
	20:13 for he hath delivered the soul of the **p**	34
	22:16 He judged the cause of the **p** and needy;	6041
	39:10 of the guard left of the **p** of the people,	1800
	40: 7 and children, and of the **p** of the land,	1803
	52:15 captive *certain* of the **p** of the people,	1803
	52:16 of the **p** of the land for vinedressers	1803
Eze	16:49 did she strengthen the hand of the **p**	6041

Eze	18:12 Hath oppressed the **p** and needy,	6041
	18:17 *That* hath taken off his hand from the **p**,	6041
	22:29 and have vexed the **p** and needy:	6041
Da	4:27 iniquities by shewing mercy to the **p**;	6033
Am	2: 6 for silver, and the **p** for a pair of shoes;	34
	2: 7 dust of the earth on the head of the **p**,	1800
	4: 1 which oppress the **p**, which crush	1800
	5:11 as your treading *is* upon the **p**,	1800
	5:12 they turn aside the **p** in the gate *from*	34
	8: 4 even to make the **p** of the land to fail,	6041
	8: 6 That *we* may buy the **p** for silver,	1800
Hab	3:14 their rejoicing *was* as to devour the **p**	6041
Zep	3:12 midst of thee an afflicted and **p** people,	1800
Zec	7:10 nor the fatherless, the stranger, nor the **p**;	6041
	11: 7 of slaughter, *even* you, O **p** of the flock.	6041
	11:11 the **p** of the flock that waited upon me	6041
Mt	5: 3 Blessed *are* the **p** in spirit: for theirs is	4434
	11: 5 the **p** have the gospel preached to them.	4434
	19:21 and give to the **p**, and thou shalt have	4434
	26: 9 been sold for much, and given to the **p**.	4434
	26:11 For ye have the **p** always with you;	4434
Mk	10:21 and give to the **p**, and thou shalt have	4434
	12:42 And there came a certain **p** widow,	4434
	12:43 That this **p** widow hath cast more in,	4434
	14: 5 and have been given to the **p**.	4434
	14: 7 For ye have the **p** with you always,	4434
Lk	4:18 me to preach the gospel to the **p**;	4434
	6:20 on his disciples, and said, Blessed *be ye* **p**:	4434
	7:22 are raised, to the **p** the gospel is preached.	4434
	14:13 call the **p**, the maimed, the lame,	4434
	14:21 bring in hither the **p**, and the maimed,	4434
	18:22 and distribute unto the **p**, and thou shalt	4434
	19: 8 Lord, the half of my goods I give to the **p**;	4434
	21: 2 he saw also a certain **p** widow casting	3998
	21: 3 that this **p** widow hath cast in more than	4434
Jn	12: 5 three hundred pence, and given to the **p**?	4434
	12: 6 This he said, not that he cared for the **p**;	4434
	12: 8 For the **p** always ye have with you;	4434
	13:29 or that he should give something to the **p**.	4434
Ro	15:26 for the **p** saints which are at Jerusalem.	4434
1Co	13: 3 I bestow all my goods to feed *the* **p**,	NIG
2Co	6:10 as **p**, yet making many rich; as having	4434
	8: 9 was rich, *yet* for your sakes he became **p**,	4433
	9: 9 dispersed abroad; he hath given to the **p**:	3993
Gal	2:10 *would* that we should remember the **p**;	4434
Jas	2: 2 come in also a **p** *man* in vile raiment;	4434
	2: 3 and say to the **p**, Stand thou there,	4434
	2: 5 Hath not God chosen the **p** of this world	4434
	2: 6 But ye have despised the **p**. Do not rich	4434
Rev	3:17 miserable, and **p**, and blind, and naked:	4434
	13:16 and great, rich and **p**, free and bond,	4434

POORER (1) [POVERTY]

Lev	27: 8 if he be **p** than thy estimation, then he	4134

POOREST (1) [POVERTY]

2Ki	24:14 save the **p** sort of the people of the land.	1803

POPLAR (1) [POPLARS]

Ge	30:37 Jacob took him rods of green **p**, and of	3839

POPLARS (1) [POPLAR]

Hos	4:13 under oaks and **p** and elms, because	3839

POPULOUS (2)

Dt	26: 5 there a nation, great, mighty, and **p**:	7227
Na	3: 8 Art thou better than **p** No, that was situate	527

PORATHA (1)

Est	9: 8 And **P**, and Adalia, and Aridatha,	6334

PORCH (39) [PORCHES]

Jdg	3:23 Ehud went forth through the **p**, and shut	4528
1Ki	6: 3 the **p** before the temple of the house,	197
	7: 6 he made a **p** of pillars; the length thereof	197
	7: 6 **p** *was* before them: and *the other* pillars	197
	7: 7 made a **p** for the throne where he might	197
	7: 7 he might judge, *even* the **p** of judgment:	197
	7: 8 he dwelt *had* another court within the **p**,	197
	7: 8 he had taken *to* wife, like unto this **p**.	197
	7:12 of the LORD, and for the **p** of the house.	197
	7:19 of the pillars were of lily work in the **p**,	197
	7:21 he set up the pillars in the **p** of the temple:	197
1Ch	28:11 to Solomon his son the pattern of the **p**,	197
2Ch	3: 4 the **p** that *was* in the front *of the house*,	197
	8:12 the LORD, which he had built before the **p**,	197
	15: 8 that *was* before the **p** of the LORD.	197
	29: 7 Also they have shut up the doors of the **p**,	197
	29:17 the month came they to the **p** of the LORD:	197
Eze	8:16 between the **p** and the altar, *were* about	197
	40: 7 threshold of the gate by the **p** of the gate	197
	40: 8 He measured also the **p** of the gate within,	197
	40: 9 measured the **p** of the gate, eight cubits;	197
	40: 9 cubits; and the **p** of the gate was inward.	197
	40:15 of the **p** of the inner gate were fifty cubits.	197
	40:39 in the **p** of the gate were two tables on this	197
	40:40 which *was* at the **p** of the gate, were two	197
	40:48 he brought me to the **p** of the house,	197
	40:48 measured *each* post of the **p**, five cubits on	197
	40:49 The length of the **p** *was* twenty cubits,	197
	41:25 planks upon the face of the **p** without.	197
	41:26 on the sides of the **p**, and *upon* the side	197
	44: 3 he shall enter by the way of the **p** of *that*	197
	46: 2 prince shall enter by the way of the **p** of *that*	197
	46: 8 he shall go in *by* the way of the **p** of *that*	197

Joel	2:17 weep between the **p** and the altar,	197
Mt	26:71 And when he was gone out into the **p**,	4440
Mk	14:68 And he went out into the **p**; and *the* cock	4259
Jn	10:23 walked in the temple in Solomon's **p**.	4745
Ac	3:11 them in the **p** that is called Solomon's,	4745
	5:12 were all with one accord in Solomon's **p**.	4745

PORCHES (2) [PORCH]

Eze	41:15 the inner temple, and the **p** of the court;	197
Jn	5: 2 Hebrew tongue Bethesda, having five **p**.	4745

PORCIUS (1)

Ac	24:27 But after two years **P** Festus came into	4201

PORT (1)

Ne	2:13 to the dung **p**, and viewed the walls of	8179

PORTER (6) [PORTERS]

2Sa	18:26 the watchman called unto the **p**, and said,	7778
2Ki	7:10 came and called unto the **p** of the city:	7778
1Ch	9:21 **p** of the door of the tabernacle of	7778
2Ch	31:14 Imnah the Levite, the **p** toward the east,	7778
Mk	13:34 work, and commanded the **p** to watch.	2377
Jn	10: 3 To him the **p** openeth; and the sheep	2377

PORTERS (33) [PORTER]

2Ki	7:11 he called the **p**; and they told *it* to	7778
1Ch	9:17 the **p** were, Shallum, and Akkub,	7778
	9:18 they were **p** in the companies of	7778
	9:22 All these which were chosen to be **p** in	7778
	9:24 four quarters were the **p**, toward the east,	7778
	9:26 these Levites, the four chief **p**, were in	7778
	15:18 and Obed-edom, and Jeiel, the **p**.	7778
	16:38 the son of Jeduthun and Hosah to be **p**:	7778
	16:42 And the sons of Jeduthun were **p**.	8179
	23: 5 Moreover four thousand were **p**;	7778
	26: 1 Concerning the divisions of the **p**:	7778
	26:12 Among these were the divisions of the **p**,	7778
	26:19 These *are* the divisions of the **p** among	7778
2Ch	8:14 the **p** also by their courses at every gate:	7778
	23: 4 of the Levites, *shall be* **p** of the doors;	7778
	23:19 he set the **p** at the gates of the house of	7778
	34:13 there were scribes, and officers, and **p**.	7778
	35:15 seer; and the **p** *waited* at every gate;	7778
Ezr	2:42 The children of the **p**: the children of	7778
	2:70 singers, and the **p**, and the Nethinims,	7778
	7: 7 singers, and the **p**, and the Nethinims,	7778
	7:24 any of the priests and Levites, singers, **p**,	8652
	10:24 of the **p**; Shallum, and Telem, and Uri.	7778
Ne	7: 1 the **p** and the singers and the Levites were	7778
	7:45 The **p**: the children of Shallum,	7778
	7:73 the **p**, and the singers, and *some* of	7778
	10:28 the priests, the Levites, the **p**, the singers,	7778
	10:39 that minister, and the **p**, and the singers:	7778
	11:19 Moreover the **p**, Akkub, Talmon,	7778
	12:25 **p** keeping the ward at the thresholds	7778
	12:45 and the **p** kept the ward of their God,	7778
	12:47 gave the portions of the singers and the **p**,	7778
	13: 5 to the Levites, and the singers, and the **p**;	7778

PORTICO See ARCHES

PORTION (100) [PORTIONS]

Ge	14:24 the **p** of the men which went with me,	2506
	14:24 and Mamre; let them take their **p**.	2506
	31:14 *Is there* yet any **p** or inheritance for us in	2506
	47:22 for the priests had a **p** assigned them of	2706
	47:22 did eat their **p** which Pharaoh gave them:	2706
	48:22 I have given to thee one **p** above	7926
Lev	6:17 I have given it *unto them* for their **p** of	2506
	7:35 This *is the* **p** of the anointing of Aaron,	NIH
Nu	31:30 shalt take one **p** of fifty, of the persons,	270
	31:36 which *was* the **p** of them that went out	2506
	31:47 Moses took one **p** of fifty, *both* of man	270
Dt	21:17 by giving him a double **p** of all that he	6310
	32: 9 For the LORD's **p** *is* his people; Jacob *is*	2506
	33:21 because there, *in a* **p** of the lawgiver,	2513
Jos	17:14 me *but* one lot and one **p** to inherit,	2256
	19: 9 Out of the **p** of the children of Judah *was*	2256
1Sa	1: 5 unto Hannah he gave a worthy **p**; for he	4490
	9:23 Bring the **p** which I gave thee, of which I	4490
1Ki	12:16 king, saying, What **p** have we in David?	2506
2Ki	2: 9 let a double **p** of thy spirit be upon me.	6310
	9:10 The dogs shall eat Jezebel in the **p** of	2506
	9:21 met him in the **p** of Naboth the Jezreelite.	2513
	9:25 cast him in the **p** of the field of Naboth	2513
	9:36 In the **p** of Jezreel shall dogs eat the flesh	2506
	9:37 the face of the field in the **p** of Jezreel;	2506
2Ch	10:16 king, saying, What **p** have we in David?	2506
	28:21 Ahaz **took away a p** *out* of the house	2505
	31: 3 He appointed also the king's **p** of his	4521
	31: 4 in Jerusalem to give the **p** of the priests	4521
	31:16 daily **p** for their service in their charges	1697
Ezr	4:16 by this means thou shalt have no **p** on	2508
Ne	2:20 ye have no **p**, nor right, nor memorial,	2506
	11:23 that a **certain p** *should be* for the singers,	548
	12:47 singers and the porters, every day his **p**	1697
Job	20:29 This *is the* **p** of a wicked man from God,	2506
	24:18 the waters; their **p** is cursed in the earth:	2513
	26:14 how little a **p** is heard of him?	1697
	27:13 This *is the* **p** of a wicked man with God,	2506
	31: 2 For what **p** of God *is there* from above?	2506
Ps	11: 6 *this shall be* the **p** of their cup.	4521
	16: 5 The LORD *is* the **p** of mine inheritance	4490
	17:14 *which have* their **p** in *this* life,	2506
	63:10 by the sword: they shall be a **p** for foxes.	4521

Ps	73:26 strength of my heart, and my **p** for ever.	2506
	119:57 *Thou art* my **p**, O LORD: I have said that	2506
	142: 5 *and* my **p** in the land of the living.	2506
Pr	31:15 her household, and a **p** to her maidens.	2706
Ecc	2:10 this was my **p** of all my labour.	2506
	2:21 laboured therein shall he leave *it for* his **p**.	2506
	3:22 rejoice in his own works; for that *is* his **p**:	2506
	5:18 which God giveth him: for it *is* his **p**.	2506
	5:19 to take his **p**, and to rejoice in his labour;	2506
	9: 6 neither have they any more a **p** for ever	2506
	9: 9 for that *is* thy **p** in *this* life, and in thy	2506
	11: 2 Give a **p** to seven, and also to eight;	2506
Isa	17:14 This *is* the **p** of them that spoil us,	2506
	53:12 Therefore will I divide him *a* **p** with	NIH
	57: 6 the smooth *stones* of the stream *is* thy **p**;	2506
	61: 7 *for* confusion they shall rejoice in their **p**:	2506
Jer	10:16 The **p** of Jacob *is* not like them: for he *is*	2506
	12:10 they have trodden my **p** under foot,	2513
	12:10 they have made my pleasant **p** a desolate	2513
	13:25 *is* thy lot, the **p** of thy measures from me,	4490
	51:19 The **p** of Jacob *is* not like them; for he *is*	2506
	52:34 every day a **p** until the day of his death,	1697
La	3:24 The LORD *is* my **p**, saith my soul;	2506
Eze	45: 1 unto the LORD, a holy **p** of the land:	NIH
	45: 4 The holy **p** of the land shall be for	NIH
	45: 6 over against the oblation of the holy **p**	NIH
	45: 7 a **p** shall be for the prince on the one side	NIH
	45: 7 other side of the oblation of the holy **p**,	NIH
	45: 7 before the oblation of the holy **p**,	NIH
	48: 1 are his sides east *and* west; a **p** for Dan.	NIH
	48: 2 east side unto the west side, a **p** for Asher.	NIH
	48: 3 even unto the west side, a **p** for Naphtali.	NIH
	48: 4 side unto the west side, a **p** for Manasseh.	NIH
	48: 5 side unto the west side, a **p** for Ephraim.	NIH
	48: 6 even unto the west side, a **p** for Reuben.	NIH
	48: 7 east side unto the west side, a **p** for Judah.	NIH
	48:18 the holy **p** shall be ten thousand eastward,	NIH
	48:18 be over against the oblation of the holy **p**,	NIH
	48:23 the west side, Benjamin *shall have* a **p**.	NIH
	48:24 the west side, Simeon *shall have* a **p**.	NIH
	48:25 east side unto the west side, Issachar a **p**.	NIH
	48:26 east side unto the west side, Zebulun a **p**.	NIH
	48:27 the east side unto the west side, Gad a **p**.	NIH
Da	1: 8 himself with the **p** of the king's **meat**,	6598
	1:13 that eat *of* the **p** of the king's **meat**:	6598
	1:15 which did eat the **p** of the king's **meat**.	6598
	1:16 Melzar took away the **p** of their **meat**,	6598
	4:15 *let* his **p** *be* with the beasts in the grass of	2508
	4:23 *let* his **p** *be* with the beasts of the field,	2508
	11:26 they that feed of the **p** of his **meat** shall	6598
Mic	2: 4 he hath changed the **p** of my people:	2506
Hab	1:16 because by them their **p** *is* fat,	2506
Zec	2:12 the LORD shall inherit Judah his **p** in	2506
Mt	24:51 appoint *him* his **p** with the hypocrites:	3313
Lk	12:42 give *them their* **p** of meat in due season?	4620
	12:46 appoint *him* his **p** with the unbelievers.	3313
	15:12 give me the **p** of goods that falleth to *me*.	3313

PORTIONS (16) [PORTION]

Dt	18: 8 They shall have like **p** to eat, beside that	2506
Jos	17: 5 there fell ten **p** to Manasseh, beside	2256
1Sa	1: 4 and to all her sons and her daughters, **p**:	4490
2Ch	31:19 give **p** to all the males among the priests,	4490
Ne	8:10 send **p** unto *them* for whom nothing is	4490
	8:12 to send **p**, and to make great mirth,	4490
	12:44 the cities the **p** of the law for the priests	4521
	12:47 gave the **p** of the singers and the porters,	4521
	13:10 I perceived that the **p** of the Levites had	4521
Est	9:19 day, and *of* sending **p** one to another.	4490
	9:22 of sending **p** one to another, and gifts to	4490
Eze	45: 7 length *shall be* over against one of the **p**,	2506
	47:13 tribes of Israel: Joseph *shall have* two **p**.	2256
	48:21 over against the **p** for the prince:	2506
	48:29 and these *are* their **p**, saith the Lord GOD.	4256
Hos	5: 7 shall a month devour them with their **p**.	2506

POSSESS (106) [POSSESSED, POSSESSEST, POSSESSETH, POSSESSING, POSSESSION, POSSESSIONS, POSSESSOR, POSSESSORS]

Ge	22:17 thy seed shall **p** the gate of his enemies;	3423
	24:60 let thy seed **p** the gate of those which hate	3423
Lev	20:24 land, and I will give it unto you to **p** it,	3423
Nu	13:30 and said, Let us go up at once, and **p** it;	3423
	14:24 he went; and his seed shall **p** it.	3423
	27:11 to him of his family, and he shall **p** it:	3423
	33:53 for I have given you the land to **p** it.	3423
Dt	1: 8 the land which the LORD sware unto	3423
	1:21 **p** *it*, as the LORD God of thy fathers hath	3423
	1:39 them will I give it, and they shall **p** it.	3423
	2:24 begin to **p** *it*, and contend with him *in*	3423
	2:31 begin to **p**, that *thou* mayest inherit his	3423
	3:18 your God hath given you this land to **p** it:	3423
	3:20 *until* they also **p** the land which the LORD	3423
	4: 1 the land which the LORD God of your	3423
	4: 5 so in the land whither ye go to **p** it.	3423
	4:14 in the land whither ye go over to **p** it.	3423
	4:22 but ye *shall* go over, and **p** that good land.	3423
	4:26 whereunto you go over Jordan to **p** it;	3423
	5:31 in the land which I give them to **p** it.	3423
	5:33 *your* days in the land which ye shall **p**.	3423
	6:18 the good land which the LORD sware	3423
	7: 1 into the land whither thou goest to **p** it,	3423
	8: 1 the land which the LORD sware unto	3423
	9: 1 to go in to **p** nations greater and	3423

Dt 9: 4 Lᴏʀᴅ hath brought me in to **p** this land: 3423
 9: 5 thine heart, dost thou go to **p** their land: 3423
 9: 6 good land to **p** it for thy righteousness; 3423
 9:23 and **p** the land which I have given you; 3423
 10:11 that they may go in and **p** the land, 3423
 11: 8 may be strong, and go in and **p** the 3423
 11: 8 possess the land, whither ye go to **p** it; 3423
 11:10 the land, whither thou goest in to **p** it, 3423
 11:11 the land, whither ye go to **p** it, *is* a land 3423
 11:23 shall **p** greater nations and mightier than 3423
 11:29 unto the land whither thou goest to **p** it, 3423
 11:31 For ye shall pass over Jordan to go in to **p** 3423
 11:31 and ye shall **p** it, and dwell therein. 3423
 12: 1 God of thy fathers giveth thee to **p** it, 3423
 12: 2 the nations which ye shall **p** served 3423
 12:29 whither thou goest to **p** them, 3423
 15: 4 God giveth thee *for* an inheritance to **p** it: 3423
 17:14 shalt **p** it, and shalt dwell therein, 3423
 18:14 For these nations, which thou shalt **p,** 3423
 19: 2 which the Lᴏʀᴅ thy God giveth thee to **p** 3423
 19:14 the land the Lᴏʀᴅ thy God giveth thee to **p** it. 3423
 21: 1 the Lᴏʀᴅ thy God giveth thee to **p** it, 3423
 23:20 to in the land whither thou goest to **p** it. 3423
 25:19 God giveth thee *for* an inheritance to **p** it, 3423
 28:21 off the land, whither thou goest to **p** it. 3423
 28:63 off the land whither thou goest to **p** it. 3423
 30: 5 thy fathers possessed, and thou shalt **p** it; 3423
 30:16 thee in the land whither thou goest to **p** it. 3423
 30:18 thou passest over Jordan to go to **p** 3423
 31: 3 from before thee, and thou shalt **p** them: 3423
 31:13 land whither ye go over Jordan to **p** it. 3423
 32:47 land, whither ye go over Jordan to **p** it. 3423
 33:23 the Lᴏʀᴅ: **p** thou the west and the south. 3423
Jos 1:11 over this Jordan, to go in to **p** the land, 3423
 1:11 the Lᴏʀᴅ your God giveth you to **p** it. 3423
 18: 3 long *are* ye slack to go to **p** the land, 3423
 23: 5 ye shall **p** their land, as the Lᴏʀᴅ your 3423
 24: 4 I gave unto Esau mount Seir, to **p** it; 3423
 24: 8 your hand, that ye might **p** their land; 3423
Jdg 2: 6 man unto his inheritance to **p** the land. 3423
 11:23 his people Israel, and shouldest thou **p** it? 3423
 11:24 Wilt not thou **p** that which Chemosh thy 3423
 11:24 Chemosh thy god **giveth** thee to **p?** 3423
 11:24 drive out from before us, them will we **p.** 3423
 18: 9 slothful to go, *and* to enter to **p** the land. 3423
1Ki 21:18 Naboth, whither he is gone down to **p** it. 3423
1Ch 28: 8 that ye may **p** *this* good land, and leave *it* 3423
Ezr 9:11 The land, *unto* which ye go to **p** it, 3423
Ne 9:15 them that *they* should go in to **p** 3423
 9:23 fathers, that *they* should go in to **p** *it.* 3423
Job 7: 3 So am I **made** to **p** months of vanity, 5157
 13:26 **makest** me to **p** the iniquities of my 3423
Isa 14: 2 house of Israel shall **p** them in the land 5157
 14:21 they do not rise, nor **p** the land, nor fill 3423
 34:11 the cormorant and the bittern shall **p** it; 3423
 34:17 they shall **p** it for ever, from generation to 3423
 57:13 the Lᴏʀᴅ that putteth his trust in me shall **p** 5157
 61: 7 in their land they shall **p** the double: 3423
Jer 30: 3 I gave to their fathers, and they shall **p** it. 3423
Eze 7:24 heathen, and they shall **p** their houses: 3423
 33:25 and shed blood: and shall ye **p** the land? 3423
 33:26 neighbour's wife: and shall ye **p** the land? 3423
 35:10 countries shall be mine, and we will **p** it; 3423
 36:12 they shall **p** thee, and thou shalt be their 3423
Da 7:18 **p** the kingdom for ever, even for ever and 2631
Hos 9: 6 for their silver, nettles shall **p** them: 3423
Am 2:10 to **p** the land of the Amorite. 3423
 9:12 That they may **p** the remnant of Edom, 3423
Ob 1:17 the house of Jacob shall **p** their 3423
 1:19 of the south shall **p** the mount of Esau; 3423
 1:19 they shall **p** the fields of Ephraim; 3423
 1:19 of Samaria: and Benjamin *shall* **p** Gilead. NIH
 1:20 of Israel *shall* **p** that of the Canaanites, NIH
 1:20 Sepharad, shall **p** the cities of the south. 3423
Hab 1: 6 **p** the dwelling places *that are* not theirs. 3423
Zep 2: 9 the remnant of my people shall **p** them. 5157
Zec 8:12 **cause** the remnant of this people to **p** 5157
Lk 18:12 in the week, I give tithes of all that I **p.** 2932
 21:19 In your patience ye your souls. 2932
1Th 4: 4 know how to **p** his vessel in sanctification 2932

POSSESSED (39) [POSSESS]

Nu 21:24 **p** his land from Arnon unto Jabbok, 3423
 21:35 none left him alive: and they **p** his land. 3423
Dt 3:12 which we **p** at that time, from Aroer, 3423
 4:47 they **p** his land, and the land of Og king 3423
 30: 5 thee into the land which thy fathers **p,** 3423
Jos 1:15 they also have **p** the land which 3423
 12: 1 **p** their land on the *other* side Jordan 3423
 13: 1 remaineth *yet* very much land to be **p.** 3423
 19:47 in it, and dwelt therein, and called 3423
 21:43 and they **p** it, and dwelt therein. 3423
 22: 9 of their possession, whereof they were **p,** 270
Jdg 3:13 smote Israel, and **p** the city of palm trees. 3423
 11:21 so Israel **p** all the land of the Amorites, 3423
 11:22 they **p** all the coasts of the Amorites, 3423
2Ki 17:24 they **p** Samaria, and dwelt in the cities 3423
Ne 9:22 they **p** the land of Sihon, and the land of 3423
 9:24 So the children went in and **p** the land, 3423
 9:25 a fat land, and **p** houses full of all goods, 3423
Ps 139:13 thou hast **p** my reins: thou hast covered 7069
Pr 8:22 The Lᴏʀᴅ **p** me *in* the beginning of his 7069
Isa 63:18 The people of thy holiness have **p** *it* but 3423
Jer 32:15 vineyards shall be **p** again in this land. 7069
 32:23 came in, and **p** it; but they obeyed not 3423

Da 7:22 the time came that the saints **p** 2631
Mt 4:24 and those which were **p with devils,** 1139
 8:16 unto him many *that were* **p with devils:** 1139
 8:28 there met him two **p with devils,** 1139
 8:33 what was befallen to the **p of the devils.** 1139
 9:32 to him a dumb man **p with a devil.** 1139
 12:22 brought unto him **one p with a devil,** 1139
Mk 1:32 and them that were **p with devils.** 1139
 5:15 and see him that was **p with the devil,** 1139
 5:16 it befell to him that was **p with the devil,** 1139
 5:18 he that had been **p with the devil** prayed 1139
Lk 8:36 he that was **p of the devils** was healed. 1139
Ac 4:32 of the *things* which he **p** was his own; 5225
 8: 7 came out of many that were **p** *with them:* 2192
 16:16 a certain damsel **p with** a spirit of 2192
1Co 7:30 and they that buy, as though they **p** not; 2722

POSSESSEST (1) [POSSESS]

Dt 26: 1 and **p** it, and dwellest therein; 3423

POSSESSETH (2) [POSSESS]

Nu 36: 8 that **p** an inheritance in any tribe of 3423
Lk 12:15 the abundance of the *things* which he **p.** 5225

POSSESSING (1) [POSSESS]

2Co 6:10 as having nothing, and *yet* **p** all *things.* 2722

POSSESSION (105) [POSSESS]

Ge 17: 8 all the land of Canaan, for an everlasting **p;** 272
 23: 4 give me a **p** of a buryingplace with you, 272
 23: 9 me for a **p** of a buryingplace amongst you. 272
 23:18 Unto Abraham for a **p** in the presence of 4736
 23:20 were made sure unto Abraham for a **p** of 272
 26:14 For he had **p** of flocks, and possession of 4735
 26:14 **p** of herds, and great store of servants: 4735
 36:43 to their habitations in the land of their **p:** 272
 47:11 and gave them a **p** in the land of Egypt, 272
 47:27 they **had p** therein, and grew, 270
 48: 4 to thy seed after thee *for* an everlasting **p.** 272
 49:30 Ephron the Hittite for a **p** of a buryingplace. 272
 50:13 Abraham bought with the field for a **p** 272
Lev 14:34 which I give to you for a **p,** and I put 272
 14:34 of leprosy in a house of the land of your **p;** 272
 25:10 and ye shall return every man unto his **p,** 272
 25:13 jubile ye shall return every man unto his **p.** 272
 25:24 in all the land of your **p** ye shall grant a 272
 25:25 hath sold away *some* of his **p,** and *if* any 272
 25:27 he sold it; that he may return unto his **p.** 272
 25:28 shall go out, and he shall return unto his **p.** 272
 25:32 *and* the houses of the cities of their **p,** 272
 25:33 house that was sold, and the city of his **p,** 272
 25:33 *are* their **p** among the children of Israel. 272
 25:34 may not be sold; for it *is* their perpetual **p.** 272
 25:41 unto the **p** of his fathers shall he return. 272
 25:45 in your land: and they shall be your **p.** 272
 25:46 children after you, to inherit *them for* a **p;** 272
 27:16 the Lᴏʀᴅ *some part* of a field of his **p,** 272
 27:21 the **p** thereof shall be the priest's. 272
 27:22 which *is* not of the fields of his **p;** 272
 27:24 *even* to him to whom the **p** of the land *did* 272
 27:28 of man and beast, of the field of his **p,** 272
Nu 24:18 Edom shall be a **p,** Seir also shall be a 3424
 24:18 Seir also shall be a **p** for his enemies; 3424
 26:56 According to the lot shall the **p** thereof be 5159
 27: 4 a **p** among the brethren of our father. 272
 27: 7 thou shalt surely give them a **p** of an 272
 32: 5 land be given unto thy servants for a **p,** 272
 32:22 this land shall be your **p** before the Lᴏʀᴅ. 272
 32:29 shall give them the land of Gilead for a **p:** 272
 32:32 that the **p** of our inheritance on *this* side 272
Dt 2: 5 I have given mount Seir unto Esau *for* a **p.** 3425
 2: 9 I will not give thee of their land *for* a **p;** 3425
 2: 9 given Ar unto the children of Lot *for* a **p.** 3425
 2:12 as Israel did unto the land of his **p,** 3425
 2:19 the land of the children of Ammon *any* **p;** 3425
 2:19 given it unto the children of Lot *for* a **p.** 3425
 3:20 shall ye return every man unto his **p,** 3425
 32:49 I give unto the children of Israel for a **p:** 272
Jos 1:15 ye shall return unto the land of your **p,** 3425
 12: 6 Lᴏʀᴅ gave it *for* a **p** unto the Reubenites, 3425
 12: 7 Israel *for* a **p** according to their divisions; 3425
 13:29 *this was the* **p** of the half tribe of NIH
 21:12 to Caleb the son of Jephunneh for his **p.** 272
 21:41 All the cities of the Levites within the **p** of 272
 22: 4 your tents, and unto the land of your **p,** 272
 22: 7 of Manasseh Moses had given **p** in Bashan: NIH
 22: 9 to the land of their **p,** whereof they were 272
 22:19 if the land of your **p** *be* unclean, *then* pass 272
 22:19 pass ye over unto the land of the **p** of 272
 22:19 tabernacle dwelleth, and **take p** among us: 272
1Ki 21:15 **take p** of the vineyard of Naboth 3423
 21:16 of Naboth the Jezreelite, to **take p** of it. 3423
 21:19 Hast thou killed, and also **taken p?** 3423
1Ch 28: 1 over all the substance and **p** of the king, 4735
2Ch 11:14 the Levites left their suburbs and their **p,** 272
 20:11 us, to come to cast us out of thy **p,** 3425
 31: 1 every man to his **p,** into their own cities. 272
Ne 11: 3 dwelt every one in his **p** in their cities, 272
Ps 2: 8 the uttermost parts of the earth *for* thy **p.** 272
 44: 3 they **got** not the land in **p** by their own 3423
 69:35 they may dwell there, and **have** it in **p.** 3423

Ps 83:12 **take** to ourselves the houses of God **in p.** 3423
Pr 28:10 the upright shall have good *things* in **p.** 5157
Isa 14:23 I will make it a **p** for the bittern, 4180
Eze 11:15 the Lᴏʀᴅ: unto us is this land given in **p.** 4181
 25: 4 deliver thee to the men of the east for a **p,** 4181
 25:10 the Ammonites, and will give them in **p,** 4181
 36: 2 even the ancient high places are ours in **p:** 4181
 36: 3 that ye might be a **p** unto the residue of 4181
 36: 5 have appointed my land into their **p** 4181
 44:28 ye shall give them no **p** in Israel: I *am* their 272
 44:28 them no possession in Israel: I *am* their **p.** 272
 45: 5 themselves, for a **p** *for* twenty chambers. 272
 45: 6 ye shall appoint the **p** of the city five 272
 45: 7 the holy *portion,* and of the **p** of the city, 272
 45: 7 holy *portion,* and before the **p** of the city, 272
 45: 8 In the land shall be his **p** in Israel: 272
 46:16 his sons'; it *shall* be their **p** by inheritance. 272
 46:18 oppression to thrust them out of their **p;** 272
 46:18 give his sons inheritance out of his own **p:** 272
 46:18 be not scattered every man from his **p.** 272
 48:20 oblation foursquare, with the **p** of the city. 272
 48:21 of the **p** of the city, over against the five 272
 48:22 Moreover from the **p** of the Levites, 272
 48:22 of the Levites, *and* from the **p** of the city, 272
Ac 5: 1 with Sapphira his wife, sold a **p,** 2933
 7: 5 that *he* would give it to him for a **p,** 2697
 7:45 in with Jesus into the **p** of the Gentiles, 2697
Eph 1:14 until the redemption of the **purchased p,** 4047

POSSESSIONS (12) [POSSESS]

Ge 34:10 trade you therein, and **get** you **p** therein. 270
Nu 32:30 they shall **have p** among you in the land of 270
1Sa 25: 2 a man in Maon, whose **p** *were* in Carmel; 4639
1Ch 7:28 their **p** and habitations *were,* Beth-el and 272
 9: 2 the first inhabitants that *dwelt* in their **p** 272
2Ch 32:29 and **p** of flocks and herds in abundance: 4735
Ecc 2: 7 also I had great **p** of great and small cattle 4735
Ob 1:17 the house of Jacob shall possess their **p.** 4180
Mk 10:22 went away sorrowful: for he had great **p.** 2933
Ac 2:45 and sold their **p** and goods, 2933
 28: 7 In the same quarters were **p** of the chief 5564

POSSESSOR (2) [POSSESS]

Ge 14:19 the most high God, **p** of heaven and earth; 7069
 14:22 most high God, the **p** of heaven and earth, 7069

POSSESSORS (2) [POSSESS]

Zec 11: 5 Whose **p** slay them, and hold themselves 7069
Ac 4:34 for as many as were **p** of lands or 2935

POSSIBLE (15) [IMPOSSIBLE, UNPOSSIBLE]

Mt 19:26 unpossible; but with God all *things* are **p.** 1415
 24:24 insomuch that, if *it were* **p,** *they shall* 1415
 26:39 prayed, saying, O my Father, if it be **p,** 1415
Mk 9:23 all *things* are **p** to him that believeth. 1415
 10:27 with God: for with God all *things* are **p.** 1415
 13:22 and wonders, to seduce, if *it were* **p,** 1415
 14:35 the ground, and prayed that, if it were **p,** 1415
 14:36 Abba, Father, all *things are* **p** unto thee; 1415
Lk 18:27 *are* unpossible with men are **p** with God. 1415
Ac 2:24 was not **p** that he should be holden of it. 1415
 20:16 he hasted, if it were **p** for him, to be at 1415
 27:39 if it were **p,** to thrust in the ship. 1410
Ro 12:18 If *it be* **p,** as much as lieth in you, 1415
Gal 4:15 I bear you record, that if *it had been* **p,** 1415
Heb 10: 4 For *it is* **not p** that the blood of bulls and 102

POST (11) [POSTS]

Ex 12: 7 and on the **upper door p** of the houses, 4947
 21: 6 him to the door, or unto the **door p;** 4201
1Sa 1: 9 Eli the priest sat upon a seat by a **p** of 4201
Job 9:25 my days are swifter than a **p:** they flee 7323
Jer 51:31 One **p** shall run to meet another, 7323
Eze 40:14 even unto the **p** of the court round about 352
 40:16 and upon *each* **p** were palm trees. 352
 40:48 measured *each* **p** of the porch, five cubits 352
 43: 3 measured the **p** of the door, two cubits; 352
 43: 8 their **p** by my posts, and the wall between 4201
 46: 2 shall stand by the **p** of the gate, 4201

POSTERITY (9)

Ge 45: 7 sent me before you to preserve you a **p** 7611
Nu 9:10 of your **p** shall be unclean by reason of a 1755
1Ki 16: 3 I will take away the **p** of Baasha, 310
 16: 3 posterity of Baasha, and the **p** of his house; 310
 21:21 will take away thy **p,** and will cut off from 310
Ps 49:13 yet their **p** approve their sayings. Selah. 310
 109:13 Let his **p** be cut off; *and* in the generation 319
Da 11: 4 not to his **p,** nor according to his dominion 319
Am 4: 2 with hooks, and your **p** with fishhooks. 319

POSTS (42) [POST]

Ex 12: 7 strike *it* on the two **side p** and on the 4201
 12:22 the two **side p** with the blood that *is* in 4201
 12:23 on the two **side p,** the Lᴏʀᴅ will pass 4201
Dt 6: 9 thou shalt write them upon the **p** of thy 4201
 11:20 thou shalt write them upon the **door p** of 4201
Jdg 16: 3 the two **p,** and went away with them, 4201
1Ki 6:31 *and* side **p** were a fifth *part* of the wall. 4201
 6:33 for the door of the temple of olive tree, 4201
 7: 5 all the doors and **p** were square, *with* 4201
2Ch 3: 7 the **p,** and the walls thereof, and the 5592
 30: 6 the **p** went with the letters from the king 7323
 30:10 So the **p** passed from city to city through 7323

Est 3:13 letters were sent by **p** into all the king's 7323
 3:15 The **p** went out, being hastened by 7323
 8:10 sent letters by **p** on horseback, 7323
 8:14 *So* the **p** that rode upon mules *and* 7323
Pr 8:34 at my gates, waiting at the **p** of my doors. 4201
Isa 6: 4 the **p** of the door moved at the voice of 520
 57: 8 the **p** hast thou set up thy remembrance. 4201
Eze 40: 9 the **p** thereof, two cubits; and the porch of 352
 40:10 the **p** had one measure on this side and 352
 40:14 He made also *of* threescore cubits, 352
 40:16 to their **p** within the gate round about, 352
 40:21 the **p** thereof and the arches thereof were 352
 40:24 he measured the **p** thereof and the arches 352
 40:26 another on that side, and the **p** thereof. 352
 40:29 the **p** thereof, and the arches thereof, 352
 40:31 and palm trees *were* upon the **p** thereof: 352
 40:33 and the **p** thereof, and the arches thereof, 352
 40:34 palm trees *were* upon the **p** thereof, on this 352
 40:36 the **p** thereof, and the arches thereof, 352
 40:37 the **p** thereof *were* toward the utter court; 352
 40:37 palm trees *were* upon the **p** thereof, on this 352
 40:38 entries thereof *were* by the **p** of the gates, 352
 40:49 *were* pillars by the **p**, one on this side, 352
 41: 1 measured the **p**, six cubits broad on the 352
 41:16 The **door p**, and the narrow windows, 5592
 41:21 The **p** of the temple *were* squared, 4201
 43: 8 their post by my **p**, and the wall between 4201
 45:19 put *it* upon the **p** of the house, and upon 4201
 45:19 upon the **p** of the gate of the inner court. 4201
Am 9: 1 lintel of the door, that the **p** may shake: 5592

POT (22) [POTS, POTSHERD, POTSHERDS, POTTER, POTTER'S, POTTERS, POTTERS', WASHPOT, WATERPOT, WATERPOTS]

Ex 16:33 Take a **p**, and put an omer full of manna 6803
Lev 6:28 if it be sodden in a brasen **p**, it shall be 3627
Jdg 6:19 he put the broth in a **p**, and brought *it* out 6517
1Sa 2:14 *it* into the pan, or kettle, or caldron, or **p**; 6517
2Ki 4: 2 not any thing in the house, save a **p** of oil. 610
 4:38 Set on the great **p**, and seethe pottage for 5518
 4:39 and shred *them* into the **p** of pottage: 5518
 4:40 thou man of God, *there is* death in the **p**. 5518
 4:41 he cast *it* into the **p**; and he said, Pour out 5518
 4:41 may eat. And there was no harm in the **p**. 5518
Job 41:20 as *out of* a seething **p** or caldron. 1731
 41:31 He maketh the deep to boil like a **p**: 5518
 41:31 he maketh the sea like a **p of ointment**. 4841
Pr 17: 3 The **fining p** *is* for silver, and the furnace 4715
 27:21 *As* the **fining p** for silver, and the furnace 4715
Ecc 7: 6 For as the crackling of thorns under a **p**, 5518
Jer 1:13 I said, I see a seething **p**; and the face 5518
Eze 24: 3 Set on a **p**, set *it* on, and also pour water 5518
 24: 6 to the **p** whose scum *is* therein, 5518
Mic 3: 3 for the **p**, and as flesh within the caldron. 5518
Zec 14:21 every **p** in Jerusalem and in Judah shall be 5518
Heb 9: 4 *was* the golden **p** that had manna, 4713

POTENTATE (1)

1Ti 6:15 *who is* the blessed and only **P**, the King 1413

POTIPHAR (2)

Ge 37:36 Medanites sold him into Egypt unto **P**, 6318
 39: 1 **P**, an officer of Pharaoh, captain of 6318

POTI-PHERAH (3)

Ge 41:45 Asenath the daughter of **P** priest of On. 6319
 41:50 which Asenath the daughter of **P** priest of 6319
 46:20 which Asenath the daughter of **P** priest of 6319

POTS (15)

Ex 16: 3 when we sat by the flesh **p**, *and* when 5518
 38: 3 the **p**, and the shovels, and the basons, 5518
Lev 11:35 *whether it be* oven, or **ranges for p**, 3600
1Ki 7:45 the **p**, and the shovels, and the basons: 5518
2Ki 25:14 the **p**, and the shovels, and the snuffers, 5518
2Ch 4:11 Huram made the **p**, and the shovels, 5518
 4:16 The **p** also, and the shovels, 5518
 35:13 the *other* holy *offerings* sod they in **p**, 5518
Ps 58: 9 Before your **p** can feel the thorns, he shall 5518
 68:13 Though ye have lien among the **p**, *yet* 8240
 81: 6 his hands were delivered from the **p**. 1731
Jer 35: 5 house of the Rechabites **p** full *of* wine, 1375
Zec 14:20 the **p** in the LORD's house shall be like 5518
Mk 7: 4 and **p**, brasen vessels, and of tables. 3582
 7: 8 of men, *as* the washing of **p** and cups: 3582

POTSHERD (4) [POT]

Job 2: 8 he took him a **p** to scrape himself withal; 2789
Ps 22:15 My strength is dried up like a **p**; 2789
Pr 26:23 a wicked heart *are like* a **p** covered with 2789
Isa 45: 9 *Let* the **p** strive with the potsherds of 2789

POTSHERDS (1) [POT]

Isa 45: 9 *Let* the potsherd *strive* with the **p** of 2789

POTTAGE (7)

Ge 25:29 Jacob sod **p**: and Esau came from the field 5138
 25:30 with that same red **p**; for I *am* faint: NIH
 25:34 Jacob gave Esau bread and **p** of lentiles; 5138
2Ki 4:38 and seethe **p** for the sons of the prophets. 5138
 4:39 came and shred *them* into the pot of **p**: 5138
 4:40 as they were eating of the **p**, that they 5138
Hag 2:12 or **p**, or wine, or oil, or any meat, shall it 5138

POTTER (10) [POT]

Isa 41:25 *upon* morter, and as the **p** treadeth clay. 3335

Isa 64: 8 we *are* the clay, and thou our **p**; and we 3335
Jer 18: 4 of clay was marred in the hand of the **p**: 3335
 18: 4 as seemed good to the **p** to make *it*. 3335
 18: 6 O house of Israel, cannot I do with you as this **p**? 3335
La 4: 2 the work of the hands of the **p**! 3335
Zec 11:13 LORD said unto me, Cast it unto the **p**: 3335
 11:13 cast them to the **p** in the house of 3335
Ro 9:21 Hath not the **p** power over the clay, 2763
Rev 2:27 as the vessels of a **p** shall they be broken 2764

POTTER'S (10) [POT]

Ps 2: 9 thou shalt dash them in pieces like a **p** 3335
Isa 29:16 down shall be esteemed as the **p** clay: 3335
Jer 18: 2 go down *to* the **p** house, and there I will 3335
 18: 3 I went down *to* the **p** house, and, behold, 3335
 18: 6 as the clay *is* in the **p** hand, so *are* ye in 3335
 19: 1 Go and get a **p** earthen bottle, and *take* of 3335
 19:11 this city, as *one* breaketh a **p** vessel, 3335
Da 2:41 and toes, part of **p** clay, and part of iron, 6353
Mt 27: 7 and bought with them the **p** field, to bury 2763
 27:10 And gave them for the **p** field, as the Lord 2763

POTTERS (1) [POT]

1Ch 4:23 These *were* the **p**, and those that dwelt 3335

POTTERS' (1) [POT]

Isa 30:14 he shall break it as the breaking of the **p** 3335

POUND (10) [POUNDS]

1Ki 10:17 three **p** of gold went to one shield: 4488
Ezr 2:69 five thousand **p** of silver, and one 4488
Ne 7:71 thousand and two hundred **p** of silver. 4488
 7:72 two thousand **p** of silver, and threescore 4488
Lk 19:16 Lord, thy **p** hath gained ten pounds. 3414
 19:18 Lord, thy **p** hath gained five pounds. 3414
 19:20 saying, Lord, behold, *here is* thy **p**, 3414
 19:24 Take from him the **p**, and give *it* to him 3414
Jn 12: 3 Then took Mary a **p** of ointment of 3046
 19:39 and aloes, about an hundred **p** *weight*. 3046

POUNDS (5) [POUND]

Lk 19:13 and delivered them ten **p**, and said unto 3414
 19:16 Lord, thy pound hath gained ten **p**. 3414
 19:18 Lord, thy pound hath gained five **p**. 3414
 19:24 and give *it* to him that hath ten **p**. 3414
 19:25 they said unto him, Lord, he hath ten **p**.) 3414

POUR (63) [POURED, POUREDST, POURETH, POURING]

Ex 4: 9 **p** *it* upon the dry *land*: and the water 8210
 29: 7 and **p** *it* upon his head, and anoint him. 3332
 29:12 **p** all the blood beside the bottom of 3332
 30: 9 neither shall ye **p** drink offering thereon. 5258
Lev 2: 1 shall **p** oil upon it, and put frankincense 3332
 2: 6 shalt part it in pieces, and **p** oil thereon: 3332
 4: 7 shall **p** all the blood of the bullock at 8210
 4:18 shall **p** out all the blood at the bottom of 8210
 4:25 shall **p** out his blood at the bottom of 8210
 4:30 shall **p** out all the blood thereof at 8210
 4:34 shall **p** out all the blood thereof at 8210
 14:15 **p** *it* into the palm of his own left hand: 3332
 14:18 **p** upon the head of him that is to be 5414
 14:26 the priest shall **p** of the oil into the palm 3332
 14:41 they shall **p** out the dust that they scrape 8210
 17:13 he shall even **p** out the blood thereof, 8210
Nu 5:15 he shall **p** no oil upon it, nor put 3332
 24: 7 He shall **p** the water out of his buckets, 5140
Dt 12:16 ye shall **p** it upon the earth as water. 8210
 12:24 thou shalt **p** it upon the earth as water. 8210
 15:23 thou shalt **p** it upon the ground as water. 8210
Jdg 6:20 *them* upon this rock, and **p** out the broth. 8210
1Ki 18:33 **p** it on the burnt sacrifice, and on the 3332
2Ki 4: 4 shalt **p** out into all those vessels, 3332
 4:41 said, **P** out for the people, that they may 3332
 9: 3 **p** it on his head, and say, Thus saith 3332
Job 36:27 they **p** down rain according to the 2212
Ps 42: 4 I remember these *things*, I **p** out my 8210
 62: 8 ye people, **p** out your heart before him: 8210
 69:24 **P** out thine indignation upon them, 8210
 79: 6 **P** out thy wrath upon the heathen that 8210
Pr 1:23 behold, I will **p** out my spirit unto you, 5042
Isa 44: 3 I will **p** water upon *him that is* thirsty, 3332
 44: 3 floods upon the dry *ground*: I will **p** my 5140
 45: 8 and let the skies **p** down righteousness: 5140
Jer 6:11 I *will* **p** *it* out upon the children abroad, 8210
 7:18 to **p** out drink offerings unto other gods, 5258
 10:25 **P** out thy fury upon the heathen that 8210
 14:16 for I will **p** their wickedness upon them. 8210
 18:21 **p** out their *blood* by the force of the 5064
 44:17 to **p** out drink offerings unto her, as we 5258
 44:18 to **p** out drink offerings unto her, we 5258
 44:19 **p** out drink offerings unto her, without 5258
 44:25 and to **p** out drink offerings unto her: 5258
La 2:19 **p** out thine heart like water before the 8210
Eze 7: 8 Now will I shortly **p** out my fury upon 8210
 14:19 **p** out my fury upon it in blood, to cut off 8210
 20: 8 I said, *I* will **p** out my fury upon them, 8210
 20:13 *I* would **p** out my fury upon them in 8210
 20:21 I said, *I* would **p** out my fury upon them, 8210
 21:31 I will **p** out mine indignation upon thee, 8210
 24: 3 a pot, set *it* on, and **p** water into it: 3332
 30:15 I will **p** my fury upon Sin, the strength of 8210
Hos 5:10 I will **p** out my wrath upon them like 8210
Joel 2:28 that I will **p** out my spirit upon all flesh; 8210
 2:29 in those days will I **p** out my spirit. 8210

Mic 1: 6 I will **p** down the stones thereof into 5064
Zep 3: 8 to **p** upon them mine indignation, *even* 8210
Zec 12:10 I will **p** upon the house of David, 8210
Mal 3:10 and **p** you out a blessing, 7324
Ac 2:17 I will **p** out of my Spirit upon all flesh: 1632
 2:18 on my handmaidens I will **p** out in those 1632
Rev 16: 1 **p** out the vials of the wrath of God upon 1632

POURED (84) [POUR]

Ge 28:18 up *for* a pillar, and **p** oil upon the top of it. 3332
 35:14 he **p** a drink offering thereon, 5258
 35:14 drink offering thereon, and he **p** oil 3332
Ex 9:33 and the rain was not **p** upon the earth. 5413
 30:32 Upon man's flesh shall it not be **p**, 3251
Lev 4:12 the ashes are **p** out, and burn him on 8211
 4:12 the ashes are **p** out shall he be burnt. 8211
 8:12 he **p** of the anointing oil upon Aaron's 3332
 8:15 **p** the blood at the bottom of the altar, 3332
 9: 9 **p** out the blood at the bottom of the altar: 3332
 21:10 upon whose head the anointing oil was **p**, 3332
Nu 28: 7 **cause** the strong wine **to be p** unto 5258
1Sa 1:15 but have **p** out my soul before the LORD. 8210
 7: 6 **p** *it* out before the LORD, and fasted on 8210
 10: 1 **p** it upon his head, and kissed him, 3332
2Sa 13: 9 took a pan, and **p** *them* out before him; 3332
 23:16 drink thereof, but **p** it out unto the LORD. 5258
1Ki 13: 3 The ashes that are upon it shall be **p** out, 8210
 13: 5 rent, and the ashes **p** out from the altar, 8210
2Ki 3:11 which **p** water on the hands of Elijah. 3332
 4: 5 brought *the vessels* to her; and she **p** out. 3332
 4:40 So they **p** out for the men to eat. And it 3332
 9: 6 **p** the oil on his head, and said unto him, 3332
 16:13 **p** his drink offering, and sprinkled 5258
1Ch 11:18 not drink *of* it, but **p** it out to the LORD, 5258
2Ch 12: 7 my wrath shall not be **p** out upon 5413
 34:21 wrath of the LORD that is **p** out upon us, 5413
 34:25 my wrath shall be **p** out upon this place, 5413
Job 3:24 my roarings are **p** out like the waters. 5413
 10:10 Hast thou not **p** me out as milk, 5413
 29: 6 and the rock **p** me out rivers of oil; 6694
 30:16 now my soul is **p** out upon me; the days 8210
Ps 22:14 I am **p** out like water, and all my bones 8210
 45: 2 grace is **p** into thy lips: therefore God 3332
 77:17 The clouds **p** out water: the skies sent out 2229
 142: 2 I **p** out my complaint before him; 8210
Isa 26:16 they **p** out a prayer *when* thy chastening 6694
 29:10 For the LORD hath **p** out upon you 5258
 32:15 the spirit be **p** upon us from on high, 6168
 42:25 Therefore he hath **p** upon him the fury of 8210
 53:12 he hath **p** out his soul unto death: 6168
 57: 6 to them hast thou **p** a drink offering, 8210
Jer 7:20 my fury *shall* be **p** out upon this place, 5413
 19:13 **p** out drink offerings unto other gods, 5258
 32:29 **p** out drink offerings unto other gods, 5258
 42:18 my fury hath been **p** forth 5413
 42:18 so shall my fury be **p** forth upon you, 5413
 44: 6 my fury and mine anger was **p** forth, 5413
 44:19 **p** out drink offerings unto her, did we 5258
La 2: 4 of Zion: he **p** out his fury like fire. 8210
 2:11 are troubled, my liver is **p** upon the earth, 8210
 2:12 when their soul was **p** out into their 8210
 4: 1 the stones of the sanctuary are **p** out in 8210
 4:11 he hath **p** out his fierce anger, 8210
Eze 16:36 Because thy filthiness was **p** out, 8210
 20:28 and **p** out there their drink offerings. 5258
 20:33 and with fury **p** out, will I rule over you: 8210
 20:34 a stretched out arm, and with fury **p** out. 8210
 22:22 ye shall know that I the LORD have **p** out 8210
 22:31 Therefore have I **p** out mine indignation 8210
 23: 8 and **p** their whoredom upon her. 8210
 24: 7 she **p** it not upon the ground, to cover it 8210
 36:18 Wherefore I **p** my fury upon them for 8210
 39:29 I have **p** out my spirit upon the house of 8210
Da 9:11 therefore the curse is **p** upon us, 5413
 9:27 that determined shall be **p** upon 5413
Mic 1: 4 the waters *that are* **p** down a steep place. 5064
Na 1: 6 his fury is **p** out like fire, and the rocks 5413
Zep 1:17 their blood shall be **p** out as dust, 8210
Mt 26: 7 and **p** *it* on his head, as he sat at meat. 2708
 26:12 in that she hath **p** this ointment on my 906
Mk 14: 3 she brake the box, and **p** *it* on his head. 2708
Jn 2:15 and **p** out the changers' money, 1632
Ac 10:45 on the Gentiles also was **p** out the gift 1632
Rev 14:10 is **p** out without mixture into the cup 2767
 16: 2 and **p** out his vial upon the earth; 1632
 16: 3 And the second angel **p** out his vial upon 1632
 16: 4 And the third angel **p** out his vial upon 1632
 16: 8 And the fourth angel **p** out his vial upon 1632
 16:10 And the fifth angel **p** out his vial upon 1632
 16:12 And the sixth angel **p** out his vial upon 1632
 16:17 And the seventh angel **p** out his vial into 1632

POUREDST (1) [POUR]

Eze 16:15 **p** out thy fornications on every one that 8210

POURETH (11) [POUR]

Job 12:21 He **p** contempt upon princes, 8210
 16:13 he **p** out my gall upon the ground. 8210
 16:20 *but* mine eye **p** out *tears* unto God. 1811
Ps 75: 8 full *of* mixture; and he **p** out of the same: 5064
 102: T and **p** out his complaint before the LORD. 8210
 107:40 He **p** contempt upon princes, 8210
Pr 15: 2 but the mouth of fools **p** out foolishness. 5042

P

Pr 15:28 mouth of the wicked **p out** evil *things.* — 5042
Am 5: 8 **p** them **out** upon the face of the earth: — 8210
 9: 6 **p** them **out** upon the face of the earth: — 8210
Jn 13: 5 **p** water into a bason, and began to wash — 906

POURING (2) [POUR]

Eze 9: 8 in thy **p out** of thy fury upon Jerusalem? — 8210
Lk 10:34 **p in** oil and wine, and set him on his own — 2022

POURTRAY (1) [POURTRAYED]

Eze 4: 1 and **p** upon it *the* city, *even* Jerusalem: — 2710

POURTRAYED (3) [POURTRAY]

Eze 8:10 of Israel, **p** upon the wall round about. — 2707
 23:14 for when she saw men **p** upon the wall, — 2707
 23:14 the images of the Chaldeans **p** with — 2710

POVERTY (15) [IMPOVERISH, IMPOVERISHED, POOR, POORER, POOREST]

Ge 45:11 and all that thou hast, **come to p.** — 3423
Pr 6:11 shall thy **p** come as one that travelleth, — 7389
 10:15 the destruction of the poor *is* their **p.** — 7389
 11:24 more than is meet, but *it tendeth* to **p.** — 4270
 13:18 **P** and shame *shall be* to him that refuseth — 7389
 20:13 lest thou **come to p;** — 3423
 23:21 and the glutton shall **come to p:** — 3423
 24:34 So shall thy **p** come *as* one that travelleth, — 7389
 28:19 after vain *persons* shall have **p** enough. — 7389
 28:22 considereth not that **p** shall come *upon* — 2639
 30: 8 give me neither **p** nor riches; feed me — 7389
 31: 7 forget his **p,** and remember his misery no — 7389
2Co 8: 2 their deep **p** abounded unto the riches of — 4432
 8: 9 that ye through his **p** might be rich. — 4432
Rev 2: 9 and tribulation, and **p,** (but thou art rich) — 4432

POWDER (8) [POWDERS]

Ex 32:20 ground *it* to **p,** and strawed *it* upon — 1854
Dt 28:24 The Lord shall make the rain of thy land **p** — 80
2Ki 23: 6 stampt *it* small to **p,** and cast the powder — 6083
 23: 6 cast the **p** thereof upon the graves of — 6083
 23:15 *and* stampt *it* small to **p,** and burnt — 6083
2Ch 34: 7 had beaten the graven images into **p,** — 1854
Mt 21:44 it shall fall, it will **grind** him **to p.** — 3039
Lk 20:18 it shall fall, it will **grind** him to **p.** — 3039

POWDERS (1) [POWDER]

SS 3: 6 frankincense, with all **p** of the merchant? — 81

POWER (272) [POWERFUL, POWERS]

Ge 31: 6 ye know that with all my **p** I have served — 3581
 31:29 It is in the **p** of my hand to do you hurt: — 410
 32:28 for **as a prince hast** thou **p** with God — 8280
 49: 3 of dignity, and the excellency of **p:** — 5794
Ex 9:16 raised thee up, for to shew in thee my **p;** — 3581
 15: 6 O Lord, is become glorious in **p:** — 3581
 21: 8 unto a strange nation he shall **have** no **p,** — 4910
 32:11 out of the land of Egypt with great **p,** — 3581
Lev 26:19 I will break the pride of your **p;** and I will — 5797
 26:37 ye shall have no **p** to **stand** before your — 8617
Nu 14:17 thee, let the **p** of my Lord be great, — 3581
 22:38 have I now **any p at all** to say any — 3201+3201
Dt 4:37 his sight with his mighty **p** out of Egypt; — 3581
 8:17 My **p** and the might of mine hand hath — 3581
 8:18 *it is* he that giveth thee **p** to get wealth, — 3581
 9:29 thou broughtest out by thy mighty **p** — 3581
 32:36 when he seeth that *their* **p** is gone, — 3027
Jos 8:20 they had no **p** to flee this way or — 3027+871.1
 17:17 Thou *art* a great people, and hast great **p:** — 3581
1Sa 9: 1 Aphiah, a Benjamite, a mighty *man* of **p.** — 2428
 30: 4 wept, until they had no more **p** to weep. — 3581
2Sa 22:33 God *is* my strength *and* **p:** and he maketh — 2428
2Ki 17:36 up out of the land of Egypt with great **p** — 3581
 19:26 their inhabitants *were* of small **p,** — 3027
1Ch 20: 1 *battle,* Joab led forth the **p** of the army, — 2428
 29:11 the **p,** and the glory, and the victory, — 1369
 29:12 in thine hand *is* **p** and might; and in thine — 3581
2Ch 14:11 with many, or with *them that* have no **p:** — 3581
 20: 6 in thine hand *is there not* **p** and might, — 3581
 22: 9 So the house of Ahaziah had no **p** to keep — 3581
 25: 8 for God hath **p** to help, and to cast down. — 3581
 26:13 hundred, that made war with mighty **p,** — 3581
 32: 9 against Lachish, and all his **p** with him,) — 4475
Ezr 4:23 and made them to cease by force and **p.** — 2429
 8:22 his **p** and his wrath *is* against all them — 5797
Ne 1:10 thou hast redeemed by thy great **p,** — 3581
 5: 5 **p** to **redeem** *them;* for other men — 410+3027
Est 1: 3 the **p** of Persia and Media, the nobles and — 2428
 8:11 all the **p** of the people and province that — 2428
 9: 1 of the Jews hoped to **have p** over them, — 7980
 10: 2 all the acts of his **p** and of his might, — 8633
Job 1:12 Behold, all that he hath *is* in thy **p;** — 3027
 5:20 and in war from the **p** of the sword. — 3027
 21: 7 become old, yea, are mighty in **p?** — 2428
 23: 6 he plead against me with *his* great **p?** — 3581
 24:22 He draweth also the mighty with his **p:** — 3581
 26: 2 hast thou helped *him that is* without **p?** — 3581
 26:12 He divideth the sea with his **p,** and by his — 3581
 26:14 the thunder of his **p** who can understand? — 1369
 36:22 Behold, God exalteth by his **p:** — 3581
 37:23 he *is* excellent in **p,** and in judgment, — 3581
 41:12 nor *his* **p,** nor his comely proportion. — 1369
Ps 21:13 *so* will we sing and praise thy **p.** — 1369
 22:20 my darling from the **p** of the dog. — 3027
 37:35 I have seen the wicked in **great p,** — 6184
 49:15 God will redeem my soul from the **p** of — 3027

Ps 59:11 scatter them by thy **p;** and bring them — 2428
 59:16 I will sing of thy **p;** yea, I will sing aloud — 5797
 62:11 I heard this; that **p** *belongeth* unto God. — 5797
 63: 2 To see thy **p** and thy glory, so *as* I have — 5797
 65: 6 fast the mountains; *being* girded with **p:** — 1369
 66: 3 through the greatness of thy **p** shall thine — 5797
 66: 7 He ruleth by his **p** for ever; his eyes — 1369
 68:35 giveth strength and **p** unto *his* people. — 8592
 71:18 *and* thy **p** to every one *that* is to come. — 1369
 78:26 by his **p** he brought in the south wind. — 5797
 79:11 according to the greatness of thy **p;** — 2220
 90:11 Who knoweth the **p** of thine anger? — 5797
 106: 8 that *he* might make his **mighty p** to be — 1369
 110: 3 people *shall* be willing in the day of thy **p,** — 2428
 111: 6 He hath shewed his people the **p** of his — 3581
 145:11 glory of thy kingdom, and talk of thy **p;** — 1369
 147: 5 Great *is* our Lord, and of great **p:** — 3581
 150: 1 praise him in the firmament of his **p.** — 5797
Pr 3:27 when it is in the **p** of thine hand to do *it.* — 410
 18:21 Death and life *are* in the **p** of the tongue: — 3027
Ecc 4: 1 the side of their oppressors *there was* **p;** — 3581
 5:19 hath given him **p** to eat thereof, and to — 7980
 6: 2 yet God **giveth** him not **p** to eat thereof, — 7980
 8: 4 Where the word of a king *is, there is* **p:** — 7983
 8: 8 *is* no man that hath **p** over the spirit — 7989
 8: 8 neither *hath he* **p** in the day of death: — 7983
Isa 37:27 their inhabitants *were* of small **p,** — 3027
 40:26 of *his* might, for that *he* is strong in **p;** — 3581
 40:29 He giveth **p** to the faint; and to *them that* — 3581
 43:17 the chariot and horse, the army and the **p;** — 5808
 47:14 shall not deliver themselves from the **p** — 3027
 50: 2 or have I no **p** to deliver? behold, at my — 3581
Jer 10:12 He hath made the earth by his **p,** he hath — 3581
 27: 5 my great **p** and by my outstretched arm, — 3581
 32:17 the earth by thy great **p** and stretched out — 3581
 51:15 He hath made the earth by his **p,** he hath — 3581
Eze 17: 9 even without great **p** or many people to — 2220
 22: 6 every one were in thee to their **p** to shed — 2220
 30: 6 and the pride of her **p** shall come down: — 5797
Da 2:37 a kingdom, **p,** and strength, and glory. — 2632
 3:27 upon whose bodies the fire had no **p,** — 7981
 4:30 of the kingdom by the might of my **p,** — 2632
 6:27 who hath delivered Daniel from the **p** of — 3028
 8: 6 and ran unto him in the fury of his **p.** — 3581
 8: 7 there was no **p** in the ram to stand before — 3581
 8:22 up out of the nation, but not in his **p.** — 3581
 8:24 his **p** shall be mighty, but not by his own — 3581
 8:24 shall be mighty, but not by his own **p:** — 3581
 11: 6 she shall not retain the **p** of the arm; — 3581
 11:25 he shall stir up his **p** and his courage — 3581
 11:43 he shall **have p** over the treasures of gold — 4910
 12: 7 to scatter the **p** of the holy people, — 3027
Hos 12: 3 and by his strength he **had p** with God: — 8280
 12: 4 he **had p** over the angel, and prevailed: — 7786
 13:14 will ransom them from the **p** of the grave; — 3027
Mic 2: 1 because it is in the **p** of their hand. — 410
 3: 8 truly I am full *of* **p** by the spirit of — 3581
Na 1: 3 great in **p,** and will not at all acquit — 3581
 2: 1 *thy* loins gird, fortify *thy* **p** mightily. — 3581
Hab 1:11 offend, *imputing* this his **p** unto his god. — 3581
 2: 9 he may be delivered from the **p** of evil! — 3709
 3: 4 hand: and there *was* the hiding of his **p.** — 5797
Zec 4: 6 Not by might, nor by **p,** but by my spirit, — 2428
 9: 4 out, and he will smite her **p** in the sea; — 2428
Mt 6:13 and the **p,** and the glory, for ever. — 1411
 9: 6 Son of man hath **p** on earth to forgive sins, — 1849
 9: 8 which had given such **p** unto men. — 1849
 10: 1 he gave them **p** against unclean spirits, — 1849
 22:29 knowing the scriptures, nor the **p** of God. — 1411
 24:30 coming in the clouds of heaven with **p** — 1411
 26:64 Son of man sitting on the right hand of **p,** — 1411
 28:18 All **p** is given unto me in heaven and — 1849
Mk 2:10 Son of man hath **p** on earth to forgive sins, — 1849
 3:15 And to have **p** to heal sicknesses, and to — 1849
 6: 7 and gave them **p over** unclean spirits; — 1849
 9: 1 seen the kingdom of God come with **p.** — 1411
 12:24 not the scriptures, neither the **p** of God? — 1411
 13:26 of man coming in *the* clouds with great **p** — 1411
 14:62 Son of man sitting on the right hand of **p,** — 1849
Lk 1:17 go before him in the spirit and **p** of Elias, — 1411
 1:35 of the Highest shall overshadow thee: — 1411
 4: 6 All this **p** will I give thee, and the glory of — 1849
 4:14 And Jesus returned in the **p** of the Spirit — 1411
 4:32 at his doctrine: for his word was with **p.** — 1849
 4:36 and **p** he commandeth the unclean spirits, — 1411
 5:17 the **p** of the Lord was *present* to heal them. — 1411
 5:24 of man hath **p** upon earth to forgive sins, — 1849
 9: 1 and gave them **p** and authority over all — 1411
 9:43 they were all amazed at the **mighty p** — 3168
 10:19 I give unto you **p** to tread on serpents and — 1849
 10:19 and over all the **p** of the enemy: — 1411
 12: 5 which after *he* hath killed hath **p** to cast — 1849
 20:20 *so they* might deliver him unto the **p** and — 746
 21:27 the Son of man coming in a cloud with **p** — 1411
 22:53 this is your hour, and the **p** of darkness. — 1849
 22:69 man sit on the right hand of the **p** of God. — 1411
 24:49 until ye be endued with **p** from on high. — 1849
Jn 1:12 to them gave he **p** to become the sons of — 1849
 10:18 I have **p** to lay it down, and I have power — 1849
 10:18 lay it down, and I have **p** to take it again. — 1849
 17: 2 As thou hast given him **p over** all flesh, — 1849
 19:10 knowest thou not that I have **p** to crucify — 1849
 19:10 crucify thee, and have **p** to release thee? — 1849
 19:11 Thou couldest have no **p** *at all* against me, — 1849
Ac 1: 7 which the Father hath put in his own **p.** — 1849

Ac 1: 8 But ye shall receive **p,** after that the Holy — 1411
 3:12 as though by our own **p** or holiness we — 1411
 4: 7 they asked, By what **p,** or by what name, — 1411
 4:33 And with great **p** gave the apostles witness — 1411
 5: 4 it was sold, was it not in thine own **p?** — 1849
 6: 8 And Stephen, full of faith and **p,** did great — 1411
 8:10 saying, This *man* is the great **p** of God. — 1411
 8:19 Saying, Give me also this **p,** that on — 1849
 10:38 Nazareth with the Holy Ghost and with **p:** — 1411
 26:18 light, and *from* the **p** of Satan unto God, — 1849
Ro 1: 4 declared *to be* the Son of God with **p,** — 1411
 1:16 for it is the **p** of God unto salvation to — 1411
 1:20 made, *even* his eternal **p** and Godhead; — 1411
 9:17 that I might shew my **p** in thee, and that — 1411
 9:21 Hath not the potter **p over** the clay, — 1849
 9:22 his wrath, and to make his **p** known, — 1415
 13: 1 For there is no **p** but of God: the powers — 1849
 13: 1 Whosoever therefore resisteth the **p,** — 1849
 15:13 in hope, through the **p** of the Holy Ghost. — 1411
 15:19 wonders, by the **p** of the Spirit of God; — 1411
 16:25 Now to him that is of **p** to stablish you — 1410
1Co 1:18 unto us which are saved it is the **p** of God. — 1411
 1:24 Christ the **p** of God, and the wisdom of — 1411
 2: 4 in demonstration of the Spirit and of **p:** — 1411
 2: 5 the wisdom of men, but in the **p** of God. — 1411
 4:19 of them which are puffed up, but the **p.** — 1411
 4:20 kingdom of God *is* not in word, but in **p.** — 1411
 5: 4 with the **p** of our Lord Jesus Christ, — 1411
 6:12 I will not be **brought under** the **p** of any. — 1850
 6:14 and will *also* raise up us by his own **p.** — 1411
 7: 4 The wife **hath** not **p** of her own body, — 1850
 7: 4 likewise also the husband **hath** not **p** of — 1850
 7:37 but hath **p** over his own will, and hath so — 1849
 9: 4 Have we not **p** to eat and to drink? — 1849
 9: 5 we not **p** to lead about a sister, a wife, — 1849
 9: 6 have not we **p** to forbear working? — 1849
 9:12 If others be partakers of *this* **p** over you, — 1849
 9:12 Nevertheless we have not used this **p;** — 1849
 9:18 that *I* abuse not my **p** in the gospel. — 1849
 11:10 this cause ought the woman to have **p** — 1849
 15:24 put down all rule and all authority and **p.** — 1411
 15:43 it is sown in weakness; it is raised in **p:** — 1411
2Co 4: 7 the excellency of the **p** may be of God, — 1411
 6: 7 By the word of truth, by the **p** of God, — 1411
 8: 3 For to *their* **p,** I bear record, *yea,* and — 1411
 8: 3 beyond *their* **p** they were willing of — 1411
 12: 9 that the **p** of Christ may rest upon me. — 1411
 13: 4 yet he liveth by the **p** of God. — 1411
 13: 4 we shall live with him by the **p** of God — 1849
 13:10 according to the **p** which the Lord hath — 1849
Eph 1:19 greatness of his **p** to us-ward who believe, — 1411
 1:19 according to the working of his mighty **p,** — 2479
 1:21 and **p,** and might, and dominion, — 1849
 2: 2 according to the prince of the **p** of the air, — 1849
 3: 7 unto me by the effectual working of his **p.** — 1411
 3:20 according to the **p** that worketh in us, — 1411
 6:10 in the Lord, and in the **p** of his might. — 2904
Php 3:10 and the **p** of his resurrection, — 1411
Col 1:11 according to his glorious **p,** unto all — 2904
 1:13 Who hath delivered us from the **p** of — 1849
 2:10 which is the head of all principality and **p:** — 1849
1Th 1: 5 but also in **p,** and in the Holy Ghost, — 1411
2Th 1: 9 of the Lord, and from the glory of his **p;** — 2479
 1:11 goodness, and the work of faith with **p:** — 1411
 2: 9 is after the working of Satan with all **p** — 1411
 3: 9 Not because we have not **p,** but to make — 1849
1Ti 6:16 to whom *be* honour and **p** everlasting. — 2904
2Ti 1: 7 of **p,** and of love, and of a sound mind. — 1411
 1: 8 of the gospel according to the **p** of God; — 1411
 3: 5 of godliness, but denying the **p** thereof: — 1411
Heb 1: 3 upholding all *things* by the word of his **p,** — 1411
 2:14 might destroy him that had the **p** of death, — 2904
 7:16 but after the **p** of an endless life. — 1411
1Pe 1: 5 are kept by the **p** of God through faith — 1411
2Pe 1: 3 According as his divine **p** hath given unto — 1411
 1:16 when we made known unto you the **p** — 2479
 2:11 which are greater in **p** and might, — 2479
Jude 1:25 *be* glory and majesty, dominion and **p,** — 1849
Rev 2:26 to him will I give **p** over the nations: — 1849
 4:11 Lord, to receive glory and honour and **p:** — 1411
 5:12 is the Lamb that was slain to receive **p,** — 1411
 5:13 Blessing, and honour, and glory, and **p,** — 2904
 6: 4 **p** was given to him that sat thereon to — NIG
 6: 8 **p** was given unto them over the fourth — 1849
 7:12 and honour, and **p,** and might, — 1411
 9: 3 and unto them was given **p,** — 1849
 9: 3 as the scorpions of the earth have **p.** — 1849
 9:10 and their **p** *was* to hurt men five months. — 1849
 9:19 For their **p** is in their mouth, and in their — 1849
 11: 3 And I will give **p** unto my two witnesses, — NIG
 11: 6 These have **p** to shut heaven, that it rain — 1849
 11: 6 have **p** over waters to turn them to blood, — 1849
 11:17 thou hast taken *to thee* thy great **p,** — 1411
 12:10 of our God, and the **p** of his Christ: — 1849
 13: 2 the dragon gave him his **p,** and his seat, — 1411
 13: 4 the dragon which gave **p** unto the beast: — 1849
 13: 5 **p** was given unto him to continue forty — 1849
 13: 7 and **p** was given him over all kindreds, — 1849
 13:12 he exerciseth all the **p** of the first beast — 1849
 13:14 he **had p** to do in the sight of the beast; — 1325
 13:15 he **had p** to give life unto the image of — 1325
 14:18 out from the altar, which had **p** over fire; — 1849
 15: 8 from the glory of God, and from his **p;** — 1411
 16: 8 **p** was given unto him to scorch men with — NIG

Rev 16: 9 of God, which hath **p** over these plagues; *1849*
17:12 **p** as kings one hour with the beast. *1849*
17:13 and shall give their **p** and strength unto *1411*
18: 1 come down from heaven, having great **p**; *1849*
19: 1 Salvation, and glory, and honour, and **p**, *1411*
20: 6 on such the second death hath no **p**, *1849*

POWERFUL (3) [POWER]

Ps 29: 4 The voice of the LORD *is* **p**; the voice of *3581*
2Co 10:10 *his* letters, say they, *are* weighty and **p**; *2478*
Heb 4:12 and **p**, and sharper than any twoedged *1756*

POWERS (14) [POWER]

Mt 24:29 and the **p** of the heavens shall be shaken: *1411*
Mk 13:25 the **p** that are in heaven shall be shaken. *1411*
Lk 12:11 and *unto* magistrates, and **p**, take ye no *1849*
21:26 for the **p** of heaven shall be shaken. *1411*
Ro 8:38 nor angels, nor principalities, nor **p**, *1411*
13: 1 every soul be subject unto the higher **p**. *1849*
13: 1 of God: the **p** that be are ordained of God. *1849*
Eph 3:10 **p** in heavenly *places* might be known by *1849*
6:12 blood, but against principalities, against **p**, *1849*
Col 1:16 or dominions, or principalities, or **p**: *1849*
2:15 *And* having spoiled principalities and **p**, *1849*
Tit 3: 1 mind to be subject to principalities and **p**, *1849*
Heb 6: 5 of God, and the **p** of the world to come, *1411*
1Pe 3:22 and **p** being made subject unto him. *1411*

PRACTICES (1) [PRACTISE]

2Pe 2:14 they have exercised with **covetous p**; *4124*

PRACTISE (4) [PRACTICES, PRACTISED]

Ps 141: 4 to **p** wicked works with men that work *5953*
Isa 32: 6 to **p** hypocrisy, and to utter error against *6213*
Da 8:24 **p**, and shall destroy the mighty and the *6213*
Mic 2: 1 they **p** it, because it is in the power of *6213*

PRACTISED (2) [PRACTISE]

1Sa 23: 9 David knew that Saul **secretly p** mischief *2790*
Da 8:12 to the ground; and it **p**, and prospered. *6213*

PRAISE (248) [PRAISED, PRAISES, PRAISETH, PRAISING]

Ge 29:35 she said, Now will I **p** the LORD: *3034*
49: 8 thou *art he* whom thy brethren shall **p**: *3034*
Lev 19:24 shall be holy to **p** the LORD *withal*. *1974*
Dt 10:21 He *is* thy **p**, and he *is* thy God, that hath *8416*
26:19 in **p**, and in name, and in honour; *8416*
Jdg 5: 2 **P** ye the LORD for the avenging of Israel, *1288*
5: 3 I will sing **p** to the LORD God of Israel. *NIH*
1Ch 4: 4 to thank and to **p** the LORD God of Israel: *1984*
16:35 to thy holy name, *and* glory in thy **p**. *8416*
23: 5 which I made, *said* David, to **p** *therewith*. *1984*
23:30 every morning to thank and to **p** the LORD, *1984*
25: 3 a harp, to give thanks and to **p** the LORD. *1984*
29:13 we thank thee, and **p** thy glorious name. *1984*
2Ch 7: 6 which David the king had made to **p** *3034*
8:14 to **p** and minister before the priests, *1984*
20:19 stood up to **p** the LORD God of Israel *1984*
20:21 that should **p** the beauty of holiness, as *1984*
20:21 before the army, and to say, **P** the LORD; *3034*
20:22 when they began to sing and to **p**, *1984*
23:13 of musick, and such as taught to *sing* **p**. *1984*
29:30 **p** unto the LORD with the words of *1984*
31: 2 to **p** in the gates of the tents of the LORD. *1984*
Ezr 3:10 to **p** the LORD, after the ordinance of *3034*
Ne 9: 5 which *is* exalted above all blessing and **p**. *8416*
12:24 against them, to **p** *and* to give thanks, *1984*
12:46 and songs of **p** and thanksgiving unto God. *8416*
Ps 7:17 I will **p** the LORD according to his *3034*
7:17 will sing **p** to the name of the LORD most *NIH*
9: 1 I will **p** *thee*, O LORD, with my whole *3034*
9: 2 will sing **p** to thy name, O thou most High. *NIH*
9:14 I may shew forth all thy **p** in the gates *8416*
21:13 *so* will we sing and **p** thy power. *2167*
22:22 in the midst of the congregation will I **p** *1984*
22:23 Ye that fear the LORD, **p** him; all ye *1984*
22:25 My **p** *shall be* of thee in the great *8416*
22:26 they shall **p** the LORD that seek him: *1984*
28: 7 and with my song will I **p** him. *3034*
30: 9 Shall the dust **p** thee? shall it declare thy *NIH*
30:12 the end that *my* glory may sing **p** to thee, *1984*
33: 1 *for* **p** is comely for the upright. *8416*
33: 2 **P** the LORD with harp: sing unto him *3034*
34: 1 his **p** *shall* continually *be* in my mouth. *1984*
35:18 I will **p** thee among much people. *1984*
35:28 *and* of thy **p** all the day long. *8416*
40: 3 song in my mouth, *even* **p** unto our God: *8426*
42: 4 with the voice of joy and **p**, *with* a *3034*
42: 5 for I shall yet **p** him *for* the help of his *3034*
42:11 for I shall yet **p** him, *who is* the health of *3034*
43: 4 upon the harp will I **p** thee, O God my *3034*
43: 5 for I shall yet **p** him, *who is* the health of *3034*
43: 5 for I shall yet **p** him, *who is* the health of *3034*
43: 5 all the day long, and **p** thy name for ever. *3034*
45:17 shall the people **p** thee for ever and ever. *3034*
48:10 so *is* thy **p** unto the ends of the earth: *3034*
49:18 *men* will **p** thee, when thou doest well to *3034*
50:23 Whoso offereth **p** glorifieth me: and to *8426*
51:15 and my mouth shall shew forth thy **p**. *8416*
52: 9 I will **p** thee for ever, because thou hast *3034*
54: 6 I will **p** thy name, O LORD; for *it is* good. *3034*
56: 4 In God I will **p** *his* word, in God I have *1984*
56:10 In God will I **p** *his* word: in the LORD *1984*
56:10 *his* word: in the LORD will I **p** *his* word. *1984*
57: 7 my heart is fixed: I will sing and **give p**. *2167*

Ps 57: 9 I will **p** thee, O Lord, among the people: *3034*
61: 8 So will I sing **p** unto thy name for ever, *NIH*
63: 3 *is* better than life, my lips shall **p** thee. *7623*
63: 5 my mouth shall **p** *thee* with joyful lips: *1984*
65: 1 **P** waiteth for thee, O God, in Zion: *8416*
66: 2 honour of his name: make his **p** glorious. *8416*
66: 8 and make the voice of his **p** to be heard: *8416*
67: 3 Let the people **p** thee, O God; let all *3034*
67: 3 O God; let all the people **p** thee. *3034*
67: 5 Let the people **p** thee, O God; let all *3034*
67: 5 O God; let all the people **p** thee. *3034*
69:30 I will **p** the name of God with a song; *1984*
69:34 Let the heaven and earth **p** him, the seas, *1984*
71: 6 my **p** *shall* be continually of thee. *8416*
71: 8 Let my mouth be filled with thy **p** *and* *8416*
71:14 and will yet **p** thee more and more. *8416*
71:22 I will also **p** thee with the psaltery, *even* *3034*
74:21 let the poor and needy **p** thy name. *1984*
76:10 Surely the wrath of man shall **p** thee: *3034*
79:13 will shew forth thy **p** to all generations. *8416*
86:12 I will **p** thee, O LORD my God, with all *3034*
88:10 shall the dead arise *and* **p** thee? Selah. *3034*
89: 5 the heavens shall **p** thy wonders, *3034*
98: 4 a loud noise, and rejoice, and sing **p**. *NIH*
99: 3 Let them **p** thy great and terrible name; *3034*
100: T A Psalm of **p**. *8426*
100: 4 *and* into his courts with **p**: *8416*
102:18 the people which *shall be* created shall **p** *1984*
102:21 the LORD in Zion, and his **p** in Jerusalem; *8416*
104:33 I will sing **p** to my God while I have my *NIH*
104:35 the LORD, O my soul. **P** ye the LORD. *1984*
105:45 and keep his laws. **P** ye the LORD. *1984*
106: 1 **P** ye the LORD: O give thanks unto *1984*
106: 2 the LORD? who can shew forth all his **p**? *8416*
106:12 believed they his words; they sang his **p**. *8416*
106:47 thy holy name, *and* to triumph in thy **p**. *8416*
106:48 all the people say, Amen. **P** ye the LORD. *1984*
107: 8 Oh that *men* would **p** the LORD *for* his *3034*
107:15 Oh that *men* would **p** the LORD *for* his *3034*
107:21 Oh that *men* would **p** the LORD *for* his *3034*
107:31 Oh that *men* would **p** the LORD *for* his *3034*
107:32 and **p** him in the assembly of the elders. *1984*
108: 1 will sing and **give p**, even *with* my glory. *2167*
108: 3 I will **p** thee, O Lord, among the people: *3034*
109: 1 Hold not thy peace, O God of my **p**; *8416*
109:30 I will greatly **p** the LORD with my mouth; *3034*
109:30 yea, I will **p** him among the multitude. *1984*
111: 1 **P** ye the LORD. I will **p**aise the LORD *1984*
111: 1 I will **p** the LORD with *my* whole heart, *3034*
111:10 commandments: his **p** endureth for ever. *8416*
112: 1 **P** ye the LORD. Blessed *is* the man *that* *1984*
113: 1 **P** ye the LORD. Praise, O ye servants of *1984*
113: 1 **P**, O ye servants of the LORD, praise *1984*
113: 1 of the LORD, **p** the name of the LORD. *1984*
113: 9 joyful mother of children. **P** ye the LORD. *1984*
115:17 The dead **p** not the LORD, neither any *1984*
115:18 time forth and for evermore. **P** the LORD. *1984*
116:19 of thee, O Jerusalem. **P** ye the LORD. *1984*
117: 1 O **p** the LORD, all ye nations: praise him, *1984*
117: 1 all ye nations: **p** him, all ye people. *7623*
117: 2 endureth for ever. **P** ye the LORD. *1984*
118:19 will go into them, *and* I will **p** the LORD: *3034*
118:21 I will **p** thee: for thou hast heard me, *3034*
118:28 Thou *art* my God, and I will **p** thee: *thou* *3034*
119: 7 I will **p** thee with uprightness of heart, *3034*
119:164 Seven *times* a day do I **p** thee because *1984*
119:171 My lips shall utter **p**, when thou hast *8416*
119:175 Let my soul live, and it shall **p** thee; *1984*
135: 1 the LORD. Praise ye the name of *1984*
135: 1 **P** ye the name of the LORD; praise *him*, *1984*
135: 1 **p** *him*, O ye servants of the LORD. *1984*
135: 3 **P** the LORD; for the LORD *is* good: *1984*
135:21 dwelleth *at* Jerusalem. **P** ye the LORD. *1984*
138: 1 I will **p** thee with my whole heart: *3034*
138: 1 before the gods will I sing **p** unto thee. *NIH*
138: 2 thy name for thy lovingkindness and *3034*
138: 4 All the kings of the earth shall **p** thee, *3034*
139:14 I will **p** thee; for I am fearfully and *3034*
142: 7 soul out of prison, that *I* may **p** thy name: *3034*
145: T David's *Psalm* of **p**. *8416*
145: 2 and I will **p** thy name for ever and ever. *1984*
145: 4 One generation shall **p** thy works to *7623*
145:10 All thy works shall **p** thee, O LORD; *3034*
145:21 My mouth shall speak the **p** of the LORD: *8416*
146: 1 **P** ye the LORD. Praise the LORD, O my *1984*
146: 1 ye the LORD. **P** the LORD, O my soul. *1984*
146: 2 While I live will I **p** the LORD: I will sing *1984*
146:10 unto all generations. **P** ye the LORD. *1984*
147: 1 **P** ye the LORD: for *it is* good to sing *1984*
147: 1 God; for *it is* pleasant; *and* **p** is comely. *8416*
147: 7 sing **p** upon the harp unto our God: *NIH*
147:12 **P** the LORD, O Jerusalem; praise thy *7623*
147:12 O Jerusalem; **p** thy God, O Zion. *1984*
147:20 have not known them. **P** ye the LORD. *1984*
148: 1 **P** ye the LORD. Praise ye the LORD *1984*
148: 1 **P** ye the LORD from the heavens: *1984*
148: 1 from the heavens: **p** him in the heights. *1984*
148: 2 **P** ye him, all his angels: praise ye him, *1984*
148: 2 all his angels: **p** ye him, all his hosts. *1984*
148: 3 **P** ye him, sun and moon: praise him, all *1984*
148: 3 sun and moon: **p** him, all ye stars of light. *1984*
148: 4 **P** him, ye heavens of heavens, *1984*
148: 5 Let them **p** the name of the LORD: for he *1984*
148: 7 **P** the LORD from the earth, ye dragons, *1984*
148:13 Let them **p** the name of the LORD: for his *1984*

Ps 148:14 horn of his people, the **p** of all his saints; *8416*
148:14 a people near unto him. **P** ye the LORD. *1984*
149: 1 **P** ye the LORD. Sing unto the LORD a *1984*
149: 1 *and* his **p** in the congregation of saints. *8416*
149: 3 Let them **p** his name in the dance: let *1984*
149: 9 have all his saints. **P** ye the LORD. *1984*
150: 1 **P** ye the LORD. Praise God in his *1984*
150: 1 **P** God in his sanctuary: praise him in *1984*
150: 1 **p** him in the firmament of his power. *1984*
150: 2 **P** him for his mighty acts: praise him *1984*
150: 2 **p** him according to his excellent greatness. *1984*
150: 3 **P** him with the sound of the trumpet: *1984*
150: 3 **p** him with the psaltery and harp. *1984*
150: 4 **P** him with the timbrel and dance: *1984*
150: 4 **p** him with stringed instruments and *1984*
150: 5 **P** him upon the loud cymbals: praise him *1984*
150: 5 **p** him upon the high sounding cymbals. *1984*
150: 6 Let every *thing* that hath breath **p** *1984*
150: 6 breath praise the LORD. **P** ye the LORD. *1984*
Pr 27: 2 Let another *man* **p** thee, and not thine *1984*
27:21 the furnace for gold; so *is* a man to his **p**. *4110*
28: 4 They that forsake the law **p** the wicked: *1984*
31:31 and let her own works **p** her in the gates. *1984*
Isa 12: 1 day thou shalt say, O LORD, I will **p** *3034*
12: 1 ye say, **P** the LORD, call upon his name, *3034*
25: 1 I will exalt thee, I will **p** thy name; *3034*
38:18 the grave cannot **p** thee, death can *not* *3034*
38:19 The living, the living, he shall **p** thee, as I *3034*
42: 8 another, neither my **p** to graven images. *8416*
42:10 his **p** from the end of the earth, ye that *8416*
42:12 and declare his **p** in the islands. *8416*
43:21 for myself; they shall shew forth my **p**. *8416*
48: 9 *for* my **p** will I refrain for thee, that *I* cut *8416*
60:18 call thy walls Salvation, and thy gates **P**. *8416*
61: 3 garment of **p** for the spirit of heaviness; *8416*
61:11 **p** to spring forth before all the nations. *8416*
62: 7 till he make Jerusalem a **p** in the earth. *8416*
62: 9 gathered it shall eat it, and **p** the LORD; *1984*
Jer 13:11 for a name, and for a **p**, and for a glory: *8416*
17:14 and I shall be saved: for thou *art* my **p**. *8416*
17:26 incense, and bringing *sacrifices* of **p**, *8426*
20:13 Sing unto the LORD, **p** ye the LORD: *1984*
31: 7 publish ye, **p** ye, and say, O LORD, save *1984*
33: 9 a **p** and an honour before all the nations *8416*
33:11 them that shall say, **P** the LORD of hosts: *3034*
33:11 them that shall bring the **sacrifice** of **p** *8426*
48: 2 *There shall be* no more **p** of Moab: *8416*
49:25 How is the city of **p** not left, the city of *8416*
51:41 *how is* the **p** of the whole earth surprised! *8416*
Da 2:23 I thank thee, and **p** thee, O thou God of *7624*
4:37 Now I Nebuchadnezzar **p** and extol and *7624*
Joel 2:26 and **p** the name of the LORD your God, *1984*
Hab 3: 3 heavens, and the earth was full *of* his **p**. *8416*
Zep 3:19 I will get them **p** and fame in every land *8416*
3:20 and a **p** among all people of the earth, *8416*
Mt 21:16 and sucklings thou hast perfected **p**? *136*
Lk 18:43 when they saw *it*, gave **p** unto God. *136*
19:37 **p** God with a loud voice for all the mighty *134*
Jn 9:24 and said unto him, Give God the **p**: *1391*
12:43 For they loved the **p** of men more than *1391*
12:43 the praise of men more than the **p** of God. *1391*
Ro 2:29 whose **p** *is* not of men, but of God. *1868*
13: 3 good, and thou shalt have **p** of the same: *1868*
15:11 And again, **P** the Lord, all ye Gentiles; *134*
1Co 4: 5 and then shall every man have **p** of God. *1868*
11: 2 Now I **p** you, brethren, that you *1867*
11:17 Now in this that I declare *unto you* I **p** *1867*
11:22 shall I **p** you in this? I praise *you* not. *1867*
11:22 shall I **p**aise you in this? I **p** *you* not. *1867*
2Co 8:18 whose **p** *is* in the gospel throughout all *1868*
Eph 1: 6 To the **p** of the glory of his grace, *1868*
1:12 That we should be to the **p** of his glory, *1868*
1:14 unto the **p** of his glory. *1868*
Php 1:11 Jesus Christ unto the glory and **p** of God. *1868*
4: 8 *there be* any virtue, and *if there be* any **p**, *1868*
Heb 2:12 in the midst of the church will I **sing p** *5214*
13:15 let us offer the sacrifice of **p** to God *133*
1Pe 1: 7 might be found unto **p** and honour and *1868*
2:14 and *for* the **p** of them that do well. *1868*
4:11 to whom be **p** and dominion for ever and *1391*
Rev 19: 5 saying, **P** our God, all ye his servants, *134*

PRAISED (26) [PRAISE]

Jdg 16:24 the people saw him, they **p** their god: *1984*
2Sa 14:25 be so much **p** as Absalom for his beauty: *1984*
22: 4 call on the LORD, who is *worthy* to be **p**: *1984*
1Ch 16:25 great *is* the LORD, and greatly to be **p**: *1984*
16:36 the people said, Amen, and **p** the LORD. *1984*
23: 5 four thousand **p** the LORD with *1984*
2Ch 5:13 and **p** the LORD, *saying*, For he *is* good; *1984*
7: 3 worshipped, and **p** the LORD, *saying*, For *3034*
7: 6 for ever, when David **p** by their ministry; *1984*
30:21 and the priests **p** the LORD day by day, *1984*
Ezr 3:11 when they **p** the LORD, because *1984*
Ne 5:13 Amen, and **p** the LORD. *1984*
Ps 18: 3 upon the LORD, who is *worthy* to be **p**: *1984*
48: 1 and greatly to be **p** in the city of our God, *1984*
72:15 him continually; *and* daily shall he be **p**. *1288*
96: 4 the LORD *is* great, and greatly to be **p**: *1984*
113: 3 of the same the LORD's name *is* to be **p**. *1984*
145: 3 Great *is* the LORD, and greatly to be **p**; *1984*
Ecc 4: 2 that feareth the LORD, he shall be **p**. *1984*
Ecc 4: 2 Wherefore I **p** the dead which are already *7623*
SS 6: 9 and the concubines, and they **p** her. *1984*
Isa 64:11 beautiful house, where our fathers **p** thee, *1984*

Da	4:34 I **p** and honoured him that liveth for ever,	7624
	5: 4 **p** the gods of gold, and of silver, of brass,	7624
	5:23 thou hast the gods of silver, and gold,	7624
Lk	1:64 tongue *loosed,* and he spake, and **p** God.	2127

PRAISES (29) [PRAISE]

Ex	15:11 in holiness, fearful in **p**, doing wonders?	8416
2Sa	22:50 and I will **sing p** unto thy name.	2167
2Ch	29:30 **sang p** with gladness, and they bowed	1984
Ps	9:11 Sing **p** to the Lord, which dwelleth in	NIH
	18:49 the heathen, and sing **p** unto thy name.	NIH
	22: 3 O thou that inhabitest the **p** of Israel.	8416
	27: 6 yea, I will sing **p** unto the Lord.	NIH
	47: 6 Sing **p** to God, sing *praises:* sing *praises*	NIH
	47: 6 sing **p**: sing *praises* unto our King,	NIH
	47: 6 sing *praises:* sing **p** unto our King,	NIH
	47: 6 sing *praises* unto our King, sing **p.**	NIH
	47: 7 all the earth: sing ye **p** with understanding.	NIH
	56:12 O God: I will render **p** unto thee.	8426
	68: 4 Sing unto God, sing **p** to his name:	NIH
	68:32 the earth; O sing **p** unto the Lord; Selah.	NIH
	75: 9 for ever; I will sing **p** to the God of Jacob.	NIH
	78: 4 shewing to the generation to come the **p**	8416
	92: 1 to sing **p** unto thy name, O most High:	NIH
	108: 3 I will sing **p** unto thee among the nations.	NIH
	135: 3 sing **p** unto his name; for *it is* pleasant:	NIH
	144: 9 an instrument of ten strings will I sing **p**	NIH
	146: 2 I will sing **p** unto my God while I have	NIH
	147: 1 for *it is* good to sing **p** unto our God; for *it*	NIH
	149: 3 let them sing **p** unto him with the timbrel	NIH
	149: 6 *Let* the high **p** of God *be* in their mouth,	NIH
Isa	60: 6 they shall shew forth the **p** of the Lord.	8416
	63: 7 of the Lord, *and the* **p** of the Lord,	8416
Ac	16:25 and Silas prayed, and **sang p** unto God:	5214
1Pe	2: 9 that ye should shew forth the **p** of him	703

PRAISETH (1) [PRAISE]

Pr	31:28 blessed; her husband *also,* and he **p** her.	1984

PRAISING (10) [PRAISE]

2Ch	5:13 to make one sound to be heard in **p** and	1984
	23:12 of the people running and **p** the king,	1984
Ezr	3:11 they sung together by course in **p** and	1984
Ps	84: 4 in thy house: they will be still **p** thee.	1984
Lk	2:13 a multitude of the heavenly host **p** God,	134
	2:20 **p** God for all *the things* that they had	134
	24:53 in the temple, **p** and blessing God.	134
Ac	2:47 **P** God, and having favour with all	134
	3: 8 temple, walking, and leaping, and **p** God.	134
	3: 9 all the people saw him walking and **p** God:	134

PRANSING (1) [PRANSINGS]

Na	3: 2 of the **p** horses, and of the jumping	1725

PRANSINGS (2) [PRANSING]

Jdg	5:22 horsehoofs broken by the means of the **p**,	1726
	5:22 the pransings, the **p** of their mighty *ones.*	1726

PRATING (3)

Pr	10: 8 but a **p** fool shall fall.	8193
	10:10 eye causeth sorrow: but a **p** fool shall fall.	8193
3Jn	1:10 **p** against us with malicious words:	5396

PRAY (313) [PRAYED, PRAYER, PRAYERS, PRAYEST, PRAYETH, PRAYING]

Ge	12:13 Say, I **p** thee, thou *art* my sister: that it	4994
	13: 8 I **p** thee, between me and thee,	4994
	13: 9 separate thyself, I **p** thee, from me: if	4994
	16: 2 I **p** thee, go in unto my maid; it may be	4994
	18: 3 pass not away, I **p** thee, from thy servant:	4994
	18: 4 I **p** you, be fetched, and wash your feet,	4994
	19: 2 Behold now, my lords, turn in, I **p** you,	4994
	19: 7 I **p** you, brethren, do not *so* wickedly.	4994
	19: 8 let me, I **p** you, bring them out unto you,	4994
	20: 7 he shall **p** for thee, and thou shalt live:	6419
	23:13 saying, But if thou *wilt* give it, I **p** thee,	3863
	24: 2 Put, I **p** thee, thy hand under my thigh:	4994
	24:12 I **p** thee, send me good speed *this* day,	4994
	24:14 thy pitcher, I **p** thee, that I may drink;	4994
	24:17 to meet her, and said, Let me, I **p** thee,	4994
	24:23 tell me, I **p** thee: is there room *in* thy	4994
	24:43 and I say to her, Give me, I **p** thee,	4994
	24:45 I said unto her, Let me drink, I **p** thee.	4994
	25:30 Esau said to Jacob, Feed me, I **p** thee,	4994
	27: 3 therefore take, I **p** thee, thy weapons,	4994
	27:19 arise, I **p** thee, sit and eat of my venison,	4994
	27:21 Come near, I **p** thee, that I may feel thee	4994
	30:14 Give me, I **p** thee, of thy son's	4994
	30:27 Laban said unto him, I **p** thee, if I have	4994
	32:11 Deliver me, I **p** thee, from the hand of	4994
	32:29 asked *him,* and said, Tell *me,* I **p** thee,	4994
	33:10 Jacob said, Nay, I **p** thee, if now I have	4994
	33:11 Take, I **p** thee, my blessing that is	4994
	33:14 Let my lord, I **p** thee, pass over before	4994
	34: 8 I **p** you give her him to wife.	4994
	37: 6 he said unto them, Hear, I **p** you, this	4994
	37:14 he said to him, Go, I **p** thee, see whether	4994
	37:16 tell me, I **p** thee, where they feed *their*	4994
	38:16 said, Go to, I **p** thee, let me come in unto	4994
	38:25 she said, Discern, I **p** thee, whose *are*	4994
	40: 8 *belong* to God? tell me *them,* I **p** you.	4994
	40:14 I **p** thee, unto me, and make mention of	4994
	44:18 said, O my lord, let thy servant, I **p** thee,	4994
	44:33 Now therefore, I **p** thee, let thy servant	4994
	45: 4 his brethren, Come near to me, I **p** you.	4994

Ge	47: 4 therefore, **we p** thee, let thy servants	4994
	47:29 put, I **p** thee, thy hand under my thigh,	4994
	47:29 with me; bury me not, I **p** thee, in Egypt:	4994
	48: 9 I **p** thee, unto me, and I will bless them.	4994
	50: 4 speak, I **p** you, in the ears of Pharaoh,	4994
	50: 5 I **p** thee, and bury my father, and I will	4994
	50:17 Forgive, I **p** thee now, the trespass of thy	577
	50:17 now, **we p** thee, forgive the trespass of	4994
Ex	4:13 he said, O my Lord, send, I **p** thee,	4994
	4:18 he said, and return unto my brethren	4994
	5: 3 let us go, **we p** thee, three days' journey	4994
	10:17 Now therefore forgive, I **p** thee, my sin	4994
	32:32 if not, blot me, I **p** thee, out of thy book	4994
	33:13 Now therefore, I **p** thee, if I have found	4994
	34: 9 Lord, let my Lord, I **p** thee, go amongst	4994
Nu	10:31 he said, Leave us not, I **p** thee;	4994
	11:15 with me, kill me, I **p** thee, out of hand,	4994
	16: 8 Korah, Hear, I **p** you, ye sons of Levi:	4994
	16:26 Depart, I **p** you, from the tents of	4994
	20:17 Let us pass, I **p** thee, through thy country	4994
	21: 7 **p** unto the Lord, that he take away	6419
	22: 6 Come now therefore, I **p** thee, curse me	4994
	22:16 Let nothing, I **p** thee, hinder thee from	4994
	22:17 come therefore, I **p** thee, curse me this	4994
	22:19 Now therefore, I **p** you, tarry ye also here	4994
	23:13 Balak said unto him, Come, I **p** thee,	4994
	23:27 Balak said to Balaam, Come, I **p** thee,	4994
Dt	3:25 I **p** thee, let me go over, and see the good	4994
Jos	2:12 therefore, I **p** you, swear unto me by	4994
	7:19 said unto Achan, My son, give, I **p** thee,	4994
Jdg	1:24 they said unto him, Shew us, **we p** thee,	4994
	4:19 said unto her, Give me, I **p** thee, a little	4994
	6:18 Depart not hence, I **p** thee, until I come	4994
	6:39 he said, but *this* once with the fleece;	4994
	8: 5 unto the men of Succoth, Give, I **p** you,	4994
	9: 2 Speak, I **p** you, in the ears of all the men	4994
	9:38 go out, I **p** now, and fight with them.	4994
	10:15 deliver us only, **we p** thee, this day.	4994
	11:17 Let me, I **p** thee, pass through thy	4994
	11:19 said unto him, Let us pass, **we p** thee,	4994
	13: 4 I **p** thee, and drink not wine nor strong	4994
	13:15 I **p** thee, let us detain thee, until we shall	4994
	15: 2 take her, I **p** thee, instead of her.	4994
	16: 6 said to Samson, Tell me, I **p** thee,	4994
	16:10 now tell me, I **p** thee, wherewith thou	4994
	16:28 I **p** thee, and strengthen me, I pray thee,	4994
	16:28 I **p** thee, only this once, O God,	4994
	18: 5 him, Ask counsel, **we p** thee, of God,	4994
	19: 6 I **p** thee, and tarry all night, and let thine	4994
	19: 8 father said, Comfort thine heart, I **p** thee.	4994
	19: 9 towards evening, I **p** you tarry all night:	4994
	19:11 the day was, and let us turn in into this city	4994
	19:23 nay, I **p** you, do not *so* wickedly;	4994
Ru	2: 7 I **p** you, let me glean and gather after	4994
1Sa	2:36 of bread, and shall say, Put me, I **p** thee,	4994
	3:17 I **p** thee hide *it* not from me: God do so	4994
	7: 5 and I will **p** for you unto the Lord.	6419
	9:18 said, Tell me, I **p** thee, where the seer's	4994
	10:15 Saul's uncle said, Tell me, I **p** thee,	4994
	12:19 **P** for thy servants unto the Lord thy	6419
	12:23 against the Lord in ceasing to **p** for you:	6419
	14:29 see, I **p** you, how mine eyes have been	4994
	15:25 I **p** thee, pardon my sin, and turn again	4994
	15:30 *yet* honour me now, I **p** thee,	4994
	16:22 saying, Let David, I **p** thee, stand before	4994
	19: 2 now therefore, I **p** thee, take heed to	4994
	20:29 said, Let me go, I **p** thee; for our family	4994
	20:29 get away, I **p** thee, and see my brethren.	4994
	22: 3 I **p** thee, come forth, *and* be with you,	4994
	23:22 Go, I **p** you, prepare yet, and know and	4994
	25: 8 give, I **p** thee, whatsoever cometh to	4994
	25:24 and let thine handmaid, I **p** thee,	4994
	25:25 Let not my lord, I **p** thee, regard this	4994
	25:28 I **p** thee, forgive the trespass of thine	4994
	26: 8 now therefore let me smite him, I **p** thee,	4994
	26:11 I **p** thee, take thou now the spear that	6258
	26:19 Now therefore, I **p** thee, let my lord	4994
	28: 8 he said, I **p** thee, divine unto me by	4994
	28:22 therefore, I **p** thee, hearken thou also	4994
	30: 7 Ahimelech's son, I **p** thee, bring me	4994
2Sa	1: 4 I **p** thee, tell me. And he answered,	4994
	1: 9 Stand, I **p** thee, upon me, and slay me:	4994
	7:27 thy servant found in his heart to **p** this	6419
	13: 5 unto him, I **p** thee, let my sister Tamar	4994
	13: 6 let Tamar my sister come,	4994
	13:13 Now therefore, I **p** thee, speak unto	4994
	13:26 said Absalom, If not, I **p** thee, let my	4994
	14: 2 wise woman, and said unto her, I **p** thee,	4994
	14:11 said she, I **p** thee, let the king remember	4994
	14:12 said, Let thine handmaid, I **p** thee,	4994
	14:18 the woman, Hide not from me, I **p** thee,	4994
	15: 7 the time, let me go and pay my vow,	4994
	15:31 David said, O Lord, I **p** thee, turn	4994
	16: 9 go over, I **p** thee, and take off his head.	4994
	18:22 let me, I **p** thee, also run after	4994
	19:37 thy servant, I **p** thee, turn back again,	4994
	20:16 I **p** you, Come near hither,	4994
	24:17 let thine hand, I **p** thee, be against me,	4994
1Ki	1:12 Now therefore come, let me, I **p** thee,	4994
	2:17 thee, Speak, I **p** thee, unto Solomon	4994
	2:20 petition of thee; *I* **p** thee, say me not nay.	NIH
	8:26 Israel, let thy word, I **p** thee, be verified,	4994
	8:30 when they shall **p** towards this place:	6419
	8:33 **p**, and make supplication unto thee in this	6419
	8:35 if they **p** towards this place, and confess	6419

1Ki	8:42 he shall come and **p** towards this house;	6419
	8:44 shall **p** unto the Lord toward the city	6419
	8:48 and **p** unto thee toward their land,	6419
	13: 6 **p** for me, that my hand may be restored	6419
	14: 2 Arise, I **p** thee, and disguise thyself,	4994
	17:10 to her, and said, Fetch me, I **p** thee,	4994
	17:11 Bring me, I **p** thee, a morsel of bread	4994
	17:21 and said, O Lord my God, I **p** thee,	4994
	19:20 said, Let me, I **p** thee, kiss my father and	4994
	20: 7 I **p** you, and see how this *man* seeketh	4994
	20:31 I **p** thee, put sackcloth on our loins,	4994
	20:32 Ben-hadad saith, I **p** thee, let me live.	4994
	20:35 word of the Lord, Smite me, I **p** thee.	4994
	20:37 man, and said, Smite me, I **p** thee.	4994
	22: 5 Inquire, I **p** thee, at the word of	4994
	22:13 let thy word, I **p** thee, be like the word	4994
2Ki	1:13 I **p** thee, let my life, and the life of these	4994
	2: 2 said unto Elisha, Tarry here, I **p** thee;	4994
	2: 4 unto him, Elisha, tarry here, I **p** thee,	4994
	2: 6 Elijah said unto him, Tarry, I **p** thee,	4994
	2: 9 Elisha said, I **p** thee, let a double portion	4994
	2:16 go, **we p** thee, and seek thy master:	4994
	2:19 I **p** thee, the situation of *this* city *is*	4994
	4:10 a little chamber, I **p** thee, on the wall;	4994
	4:22 Send me, I **p** thee, one of the young	4994
	4:26 Run now, I **p** thee, to meet her,	4994
	5: 7 I **p** you, and see how he seeketh a	4994
	5:15 now therefore, I **p** thee, take a blessing	4994
	5:17 said, Shall there not then, I **p** thee,	4994
	5:22 give them, I **p** thee, a talent of silver,	4994
	6: 2 Let us go, **we p** thee, unto Jordan,	4994
	6: 3 I **p** thee, and go with thy servants.	4994
	6:17 said, Lord, I **p** thee, open his eyes,	4994
	6:18 this people, I **p** thee, with blindness.	4994
	7:13 and said, Let some take, I **p** thee,	4994
	8: 4 saying, Tell me, I **p** thee, all the great	4994
	18:23 Now therefore, I **p** thee, give pledges to	4994
	18:26 Joah, unto Rab-shakeh, Speak, I **p** thee,	4994
1Ch	17:25 thy servant hath found *in his heart* to **p**	6419
	21:17 let thine hand, I **p** thee, O Lord my	6419
2Ch	6:24 **p** and make supplication before thee in	6419
	6:26 *yet* if they **p** towards this place,	6419
	6:32 out arm; if they come and **p** in this house;	6419
	6:34 they **p** unto thee toward this city which	6419
	6:37 **p** unto thee in the land of their captivity,	2603
	6:38 **p** toward their land, which thou gavest	6419
	7:14 **p**, and seek my face, and turn from their	6419
	18: 4 Inquire, I **p** thee, at the word of	4994
	18:12 I **p** thee, be like one of theirs,	4994
Ezr	6:10 **p** for the life of the king, and of his sons.	6739
Ne	1: 6 **p** before thee now, day and night,	6419
	1:11 prosper, I **p** thee, thy servant *this* day,	4994
	5:10 corn: I **p** you, let us leave off this usury.	4994
	5:11 Restore, I **p** you, to them, even this day,	4994
Job	4: 7 Remember, I **p** thee, who *ever* perished,	4994
	6:29 Return, I **p** you, let it not be iniquity;	4994
	8: 8 For inquire, I **p** thee, of the former age,	4994
	21:15 profit should we have, if we **p** unto him?	6293
	22:22 Receive, I **p** thee, the law from his	4994
	32:21 Let me not, I **p** you, accept *any* man's	4994
	33: 1 Wherefore, Job, I **p** thee, hear my	4994
	33:26 He shall **p** unto God, and he will be	6279
	42: 8 and my servant Job shall **p** for you:	6419
Ps	5: 2 and my God: for unto thee will I **p**.	6419
	32: 6 this shall every one that *is* godly **p** unto	6419
	55:17 and at noon, will I **p**, and cry aloud:	7878
	119:76 Let, I **p** thee, thy merciful kindness be	4994
	122: 6 **P** for the peace of Jerusalem: they shall	7592
Isa	5: 3 judge, I **p** you, betwixt me and my	4994
	16:12 that he shall come to his sanctuary to **p**;	6419
	29:11 is learned, saying, Read this, I **p** thee:	4994
	29:12 not learned, saying, Read this, I **p** thee:	4994
	36: 8 Now therefore give pledges, I **p** thee,	4994
	36:11 Joah unto Rabshakeh, Speak, I **p** thee,	4994
	45:20 and **p** unto a god *that* cannot save.	6419
Jer	7:16 Therefore **p** not thou for this people,	6419
	11:14 Therefore **p** not thou for this people,	6419
	14:11 **P** not for this people for *their* good.	6419
	21: 2 Inquire, I **p** thee, of the Lord for us;	6419
	29: 7 and **p** unto the Lord for it:	6419
	29:12 ye shall go and **p** unto me, and I will	6419
	32: 8 said unto me, Buy my field, I **p** thee,	4994
	37: 3 **P** now unto the Lord our God for us.	4994
	37:20 hear now, I **p** thee, O my lord the king:	4994
	37:20 let my supplication, I **p** thee, be accepted	4994
	40:15 I **p** thee, and I will slay Ishmael the son	4994
	42: 2 **p** for us unto the Lord thy God, *even* for	6419
	42: 4 I *will* **p** unto the Lord your God	6419
	42:20 **P** for us unto the Lord our God;	6419
La	1:18 hear, I **p** you, all people, and behold my	4994
Eze	33:30 I **p** you, and hear what *is* the word that	4994
Jnh	1: 8 said they unto him, Tell us, **we p** thee,	4994
	4: 2 said, I **p** thee, O Lord, *was* not this my	577
Mic	3: 1 I said, Hear, I **p** you, O heads of Jacob,	4994
	3: 9 Hear this, I **p** you, ye heads of the house	4994
Hag	2:15 now, I **p** you, consider from this day and	4994
Zec	7: 2 and their men, to **p** before the Lord,	2470
	8:21 Let us go speedily to **p** before the Lord,	2470
	8:22 in Jerusalem, and to **p** before the Lord.	2470
Mal	1: 9 I **p** you, beseech God that he will be	4994
Mt	5:44 **p** for them which despitefully use you,	4336
	6: 5 they love to **p** standing in the synagogues	4336
	6: 6 door, **p** to thy Father which is in secret;	4336
	6: 7 But when ye **p**, use not vain repetitions,	4336
	6: 9 After this manner therefore **p** ye:	4336

P

Mt	9:38	**P** ye therefore the Lord of the harvest,	1189
	14:23	he went up into a mountain apart to **p**	4336
	19:13	he should put *his* hands on them, and **p:**	4336
	24:20	But **p** ye that your flight be not in	4336
	26:36	Sit ye here, while I go and **p** yonder.	4336
	26:41	Watch and **p,** that ye enter not into	4336
	26:53	Thinkest thou that I cannot now **p** to my	3870
Mk	5:17	And they began to **p** him to depart out of	3870
	5:23	I **p** *thee*, come and lay *thy* hands on her,	NIG
	6:46	he departed into a mountain to **p.**	4336
	11:24	when ye **p,** believe that ye receive *them,*	4336
	13:18	And **p** ye that your flight be not in	4336
	13:33	Take ye heed, watch and **p:** for ye know	4336
	14:32	his disciples, Sit ye here, while I shall **p.**	4336
	14:38	Watch ye and **p,** lest ye enter into	4336
Lk	6:12	*that* he went out into a mountain to **p,**	4336
	6:28	**p** for them which despitefully use you.	4336
	9:28	James, and went up into a mountain to **p.**	4336
	10:2	**p** ye therefore the Lord of the harvest,	1189
	11:1	Lord, teach us to **p,** as John also taught	4336
	11:2	And he said unto them, When ye **p,** say,	4336
	14:18	and see it: I **p** thee have me excused.	2065
	14:19	to prove them: I **p** thee have me excused.	2065
	16:27	Then he said, I **p** thee therefore, father,	2065
	18:1	to this end, that *men* ought always to **p,**	4336
	18:10	Two men went up into the temple to **p;**	4336
	21:36	Watch ye therefore, and **p** always, that ye	1189
	22:40	**P** that *ye* enter not into temptation.	4336
	22:46	rise and **p,** lest ye enter into temptation.	4336
Jn	14:16	And I will **p** the Father, and he shall give	2065
	16:26	unto you, that I will **p** the Father for you:	2065
	17:9	I **p** for them: I pray not for the world,	2065
	17:9	I **p** not for the world, but for *them* which	2065
	17:15	I **p** not that thou shouldest take them out	2065
	17:20	Neither **p** I for these alone, but for them	2065
Ac	8:22	of this thy wickedness, and **p** God,	1189
	8:24	and said, **P** ye to the Lord for me,	1189
	8:34	answered Philip, and said, I **p** thee,	1189
	10:9	went up upon the house to **p** about	4336
	24:4	I **p** *thee* that thou wouldest hear us of	3870
	27:34	Wherefore I **p** you to take *some* meat:	3870
Ro	8:26	for we know not what we should **p** for as	4336
1Co	11:13	is it comely that a woman **p** unto God	4336
	14:13	*unknown* tongue **p** that he may interpret.	4336
	14:14	if I **p** in an *unknown* tongue, my spirit	4336
	14:15	I will **p** with the spirit, and will pray with	4336
	14:15	and will **p** with the understanding also:	4336
2Co	5:20	*you* in Christ's stead, be ye reconciled	1189
	13:7	Now I **p** to God that ye do no evil; not	2172
Php	1:9	this I **p,** that your love may abound yet	4336
Col	1:9	the day we heard *it,* do not cease to **p**	4336
1Th	5:17	**P** without ceasing.	
	5:23	*I p* God your whole spirit and soul and	NIG
	5:25	Brethren, **p** for us.	4336
2Th	1:11	Wherefore also we **p** always for you,	4336
	3:1	Finally, brethren, **p** for us, that the word	4336
1Ti	2:8	I will therefore that men **p** every where,	4336
2Ti	4:16	*I p* God that it may not be laid to their	NIG
Heb	13:18	**P** for us: for we trust we have a good	4336
Jas	5:13	let him **p.** Is any merry? let him sing	4336
	5:14	and let them **p** over him, anointing him	4336
	5:16	and **p** one for another, that ye may be	2172
1Jn	5:16	I do not say that he shall **p** for it.	2065

PRAYED (65) [PRAY]

Ge	20:17	Abraham **p** unto God: and God healed	6419
Nu	11:2	when Moses **p** unto the LORD, the fire	6419
	21:7	from us. And Moses **p** for the people.	6419
Dt	9:20	and I **p** for Aaron also the same time.	6419
	9:26	I **p** therefore unto the LORD, and said,	6419
1Sa	1:10	and **p** unto the LORD, and wept sore.	6419
	1:27	For this child I **p;** and the LORD hath	6419
	2:1	Hannah **p,** and said, My heart rejoiceth	6419
	8:6	judge us. And Samuel **p** unto the LORD.	6419
2Ki	4:33	upon them twain, and **p** unto the LORD.	6419
	6:17	Elisha **p,** and said, LORD, I pray thee,	6419
	6:18	Elisha **p** unto the LORD, and said,	6419
	19:15	Hezekiah **p** before the LORD, and said,	6419
	19:20	*That* which thou hast **p** to me against	6419
	20:2	to the wall, and **p** unto the LORD, saying,	6419
2Ch	30:18	Hezekiah **p** for them, saying, The good	6419
	32:20	the son of Amoz, **p** and cried *to* heaven.	6419
	32:24	sick to the death, and **p** unto the LORD:	6419
	33:13	**p** unto him: and he was intreated of him,	6419
Ezr	10:1	Now when Ezra had **p,** and when he had	6419
Ne	1:4	fasted, and **p** before the God of heaven,	6419
	2:4	request? So I **p** to the God of heaven.	6419
Job	42:10	captivity of Job, when he **p** for his friends:	6419
Isa	37:15	And Hezekiah **p** unto the LORD, saying,	6419
	37:21	Whereas thou hast **p** to me against	6419
	38:2	toward the wall, and **p** unto the LORD,	6419
Jer	32:16	son of Neriah, I **p** unto the LORD, saying,	6419
Da	6:10	p, and gave thanks before his God, as he	6739
	9:4	I **p** unto the LORD my God, and made my	6419
Jnh	2:1	Jonah **p** unto the LORD his God out of	6419
	4:2	he **p** unto the LORD, and said, I pray thee,	6419
Mt	26:39	on his face, and **p,** saying, O my Father,	4336
	26:42	second time, and **p,** saying, O my Father,	4336
	26:44	went away again, and **p** the third time,	4336
Mk	1:35	departed into a solitary place, and there **p.**	4336
	5:18	that had been possessed with the devil **p**	3870
	14:35	the ground, and **p** that, if it were possible,	4336
	14:39	and **p,** and spake the same words.	4336
Lk	5:3	**p** him that *he* would thrust out a little	2065
	5:16	himself into the wilderness, and **p.**	4336

Lk	9:29	as he **p,** the fashion of his countenance	4336
	18:11	Pharisee stood and **p** thus with himself,	4336
	22:32	I have **p** for thee, that thy faith fail not:	1189
	22:41	a stone's cast, and kneeled down, and **p,**	4336
	22:44	being in an agony he **p** more earnestly:	4336
Jn	4:31	In the mean while *his* disciples **p** him,	2065
Ac	1:24	And they **p,** and said, Thou, Lord,	4336
	4:31	when they had **p,** the place was shaken	1189
	6:6	when they had **p,** they laid *their* hands	4336
	8:15	when they were come down, **p** for them,	4336
	9:40	*them* all forth, and kneeled down, and **p;**	4336
	10:2	alms to the people, and **p to** God alway.	1189
	10:30	and at the ninth hour I **p** in my house,	4336
	10:48	Then **p** they him to tarry certain days.	2065
	13:3	And when they had fasted and **p,**	4336
	14:23	and had **p** with fasting, they commended	4336
	16:9	and **p** him, saying, Come over into	3870
	16:25	And at midnight Paul and Silas **p,**	4336
	20:36	he kneeled down, and **p** with them all.	4336
	21:5	we kneeled down on the shore, and **p.**	4336
	22:17	even while I **p** in the temple, I was in a	4336
	23:18	**p** *me* to bring this young man unto thee,	2065
	28:8	and **p,** and laid *his* hands on him,	4336
Jas	5:17	**p earnestly** that it might not rain:	4335+4336
	5:18	And he **p** again, and the heaven gave rain.	4336

PRAYER (114) [PRAY]

2Sa	7:27	found in his heart to pray this **p** unto thee.	8605
1Ki	8:28	Yet have thou respect unto the **p** of thy	8605
	8:28	to hearken unto the cry and to the **p,**	8605
	8:29	**p** which thy servant shall **make**	6419+8605
	8:38	What **p** and supplication soever *be made*	8605
	8:45	hear thou in heaven their **p** and their	8605
	8:49	hear thou their **p** and their supplication *in*	8605
	8:54	had made an end of praying all this **p**	8605
	9:3	I have heard thy **p** and thy supplication,	8605
2Ki	19:4	wherefore lift up *thy* **p** for the remnant	8605
	20:5	I have heard thy **p,** I have seen thy tears:	8605
2Ch	6:19	therefore to the **p** of thy servant,	8605
	6:19	the **p** which thy servant prayeth before	8605
	6:20	to hearken unto the **p** which thy servant	8605
	6:29	*Then* what **p** or what supplication soever	8605
	6:35	hear thou from the heavens their **p** and	8605
	6:39	their **p** and their supplications,	8605
	6:40	*let* thine ears *be* attent unto the **p** *that is*	8605
	7:12	I have heard thy **p,** and have chosen this	8605
	7:15	mine ears attent unto the **p** *that is made*	8605
	30:27	their **p** came *up* to his holy dwelling place	8605
	33:18	his **p** unto his God, and the words of	8605
	33:19	His **p** also, and how God was intreated of	8605
Ne	1:6	*thou* mayest hear the **p** of thy servant,	8605
	1:11	now thine ear be attentive to the **p** of thy	8605
	1:11	the **p** of thy servants, who desire to fear	8605
	4:9	we **made** our **p** unto our God,	6419
	11:17	principal to begin the thanksgiving in **p:**	8605
Job	15:4	off fear, and restrainest **p** before God.	7881
	16:17	injustice in mine hands: also my **p** is pure.	8605
	22:27	Thou shalt **make** thy **p** unto him,	6279
Ps	4:1	have mercy upon me, and hear my **p.**	8605
	5:3	the morning will I direct *my* **p** unto thee,	NIH
	6:9	the LORD will receive my **p.**	8605
	17:1	T A **P** of David.	
	17:1	attend unto my cry, give ear unto my **p,**	8605
	35:13	and my **p** returned into mine own bosom.	8605
	39:12	Hear my **p,** O LORD, and give ear unto	8605
	42:8	me, *and my* **p** unto the God of my life.	8605
	54:2	Hear my **p,** O God; give ear to the words	8605
	55:1	Give ear to my **p,** O God; and hide not	8605
	61:1	Hear my cry, O God; attend unto my **p.**	8605
	64:1	Hear my voice, O God, in my **p:**	7879
	65:2	O thou that hearest **p,** unto thee shall all	8605
	66:19	he hath attended to the voice of my **p.**	8605
	66:20	God, which hath not turned away my **p,**	8605
	69:13	*as for* me, my **p** *is* unto thee, O LORD,	8605
	72:15	**p** also shall be **made** for him continually;	6419
	80:4	how long wilt thou be angry against the **p**	8605
	84:8	O LORD God *of* hosts, hear my **p:**	8605
	86:1	T A **P** of David.	
	86:6	Give ear, O LORD, unto my **p;**	8605
	88:2	Let my **p** come before thee: incline thine	8605
	88:13	in the morning shall my **p** prevent thee.	8605
	90:1	T A **P** of Moses the man of God.	
	102:1	T A **P** of the afflicted, when he is	
	102:1	Hear my **p,** O LORD, and let my cry	8605
	102:17	He will regard the **p** of the destitute,	8605
	102:17	of the destitute, and not despise their **p.**	8605
	109:4	my adversaries: but I *give myself unto* **p.**	8605
	109:7	be condemned: and let his **p** become sin.	8605
	141:2	Let my **p** be set forth before thee *as*	8605
	141:5	for yet my **p** also *shall be* in their	8605
	142:1	T of David; A **P** when he was in the cave.	
	143:1	Hear my **p,** O LORD, give ear to my	8605
Pr	15:8	but the **p** of the upright *is* his delight.	8605
	15:29	but he heareth the **p** of the righteous.	8605
	28:9	the law, even his **p** *shall be* abomination.	8605
Isa	26:16	they poured out a **p** *when* thy chastening	3908
	37:4	wherefore lift up *thy* **p** for the remnant	8605
	38:5	I have heard thy **p,** I have seen thy tears:	8605
	56:7	and make them joyful in my house of **p:**	8605
	56:7	mine house shall be called a house of **p**	8605
Jer	7:16	neither lift up cry nor **p** for them:	8605
	11:14	neither lift up a cry or **p** for them:	8605
La	3:8	I cry and shout, he shutteth out my **p.**	8605
	3:44	cloud, that *our* **p** should not pass through.	8605
Da	9:3	seek *by* **p** and supplications, with fasting,	8605

Da	9:13	yet **made** we not our **p** before the LORD.	2470
	9:17	hear the **p** of thy servant,	8605
	9:21	Yea, whiles I *was* speaking in **p,** even	8605
Jnh	2:7	my **p** came in unto thee, into thine holy	8605
Hab	3:1	A **P** of Habakkuk the prophet upon	8605
Mt	17:21	kind goeth not out but by **p** and fasting.	4335
	21:13	My house shall be called the house of **p;**	4335
	21:22	*all things,* whatsoever ye shall ask in **p,**	4335
	23:14	and for a pretence **make** long **p:**	4336
Mk	9:29	forth by nothing, but by **p** and fasting.	4335
	11:17	be called of all nations the house of **p?**	4335
Lk	1:13	for thy **p** is heard; and thy wife Elisabeth	1162
	6:12	pray, and continued all night in **p** to God.	4335
	19:46	It is written, My house is the house of **p:**	4335
	22:45	And when he rose up from **p,**	4335
Ac	1:14	These all continued with one accord in **p**	4335
	3:1	together into the temple at the hour of **p,**	4335
	6:4	we will give ourselves continually to **p,**	4335
	10:31	thy **p** is heard, and thine alms are had in	4335
	12:5	**p** was made without ceasing of the church	4335
	16:13	river side, where **p** was wont to be made;	4335
	16:16	And it came to pass, as we went to **p,**	4335
Ro	10:1	heart's desire and **p** to God for Israel is,	1162
	12:12	in tribulation; continuing instant in **p;**	4335
1Co	7:5	ye may give yourselves to fasting and **p,**	4335
2Co	1:11	You also helping together by **p** for us,	1162
	9:14	And by their **p** for you, which long after	1162
Eph	6:18	Praying always with all **p** and	4335
Php	1:4	Always in every **p** of mine for you all	1162
	1:19	shall turn to my salvation through your **p,**	1162
	4:6	but in every *thing* by **p** and supplication	4335
Col	2:2	Continue in **p,** and watch in the same	4335
1Ti	4:5	it is sanctified by the word of God and **p.**	1783
Jas	5:15	And the **p** of faith shall save the sick,	2171
	5:16	The effectual fervent **p** of a righteous *man*	1162
1Pe	4:7	be ye therefore sober, and watch unto **p.**	4335

PRAYERS (24) [PRAY]

Ps	72:20	The **p** of David the son of Jesse are ended.	8605
Isa	1:15	when ye make many **p,** I will not hear:	8605
Mk	12:40	and for a pretence **make** long **p:**	4336
Lk	2:37	*God* with fastings and **p** night and day.	1162
	5:33	and make **p,** and likewise the *disciples* of	1162
	20:47	and for a shew **make** long **p:**	4336
Ac	2:42	and in breaking of bread, and in **p.**	4335
Ro	1:10	Thy **p** and thine alms are come up for a	4335
	1:9	I make mention of you, always in my **p,**	4335
	15:30	ye strive together with me in your **p** to	4335
Eph	1:16	for you, making mention of you in my **p;**	4335
Col	4:12	always labouring fervently for you in **p,**	4335
1Th	1:2	you all, making mention of you in our **p;**	4335
1Ti	2:1	**p,** intercessions, *and* giving of thanks,	4335
	5:5	in supplications and **p** night and day.	4335
2Ti	1:3	have remembrance of thee in my **p** night	1162
Phm	1:4	making mention of thee always in my **p,**	4335
	1:22	for I trust that through your **p** I shall be	1162
Heb	5:7	when he had offered up **p** and	1162
1Pe	3:7	grace of life; that your **p** be not hindered.	4335
	3:12	and his ears *are* open unto their **p:**	1162
Rev	5:8	full of odours, which are the **p** of saints.	4335
	8:3	that he should offer *it* with the **p** of all	4335
	8:4	*which came* with the **p** of the saints,	4335

PRAYEST (2) [PRAY]

Mt	6:5	And when thou **p,** thou shalt not be as	4336
	6:6	But thou, when thou **p,** enter into thy	4336

PRAYETH (7) [PRAY]

1Ki	8:28	which thy servant **p** before thee to day:	6419
2Ch	6:19	prayer which thy servant **p** before thee:	6419
	6:20	which thy servant **p** towards this place.	6419
Isa	44:17	worshippeth *it,* and **p** unto it, and saith,	6419
Ac	9:11	called Saul, of Tarsus: for behold, he **p,**	4336
1Co	11:5	But every woman that **p** or	4336
	14:14	my spirit **p,** but my understanding is	4336

PRAYING (20) [PRAY]

1Sa	1:12	as she continued **p** before the LORD,	6419
	1:26	that stood by thee here, **p** unto the LORD.	6419
1Ki	8:54	when Solomon had made an end of **p,**	6419
2Ch	7:1	when Solomon had made an end of **p,**	1156
Da	6:11	found Daniel **p** and making supplication	4336
	9:20	and, confessing my sin and the sin of	6419
Mk	11:25	And when ye stand **p,** forgive, if ye have	4336
Lk	1:10	were **p** without at the time of incense.	4336
	3:21	and **p,** the heaven was opened,	4336
	9:18	And it came to pass, as he was alone **p,**	4336
	11:1	And it came to pass *that,* as he was **p** in a	4336
Ac	11:5	was in the city of Joppa **p:** and in a trance	4336
	12:12	where many were gathered together **p.**	4336
1Co	11:4	Every man **p** or prophesying, having *his*	4336
2Co	8:4	**P** us with much intreaty that we would	1189
Eph	6:18	**P** always with all prayer and supplication	4336
Col	1:3	of our Lord Jesus Christ, **p** always for you,	4336
	4:3	Withal **p** also for us, that God would open	4336
1Th	3:10	day **p** exceedingly that *we* might see your	1189
Jude	1:20	your most holy faith, **p** in the Holy Ghost,	4336

PREACH (50) [PREACHED, PREACHER, PREACHEST, PREACHETH, PREACHING]

Ne	6:7	thou hast also appointed prophets to **p** of	7121
Isa	61:1	me to **p** good tidings unto the meek;	1319
Jnh	3:2	**p** unto it the preaching that I bid thee.	7121
Mt	4:17	From that time Jesus began to **p,** and to	2784
	10:7	And as ye go, **p,** saying, The kingdom of	2784

Mt 10:27 in the ear, *that* **p** ye upon the housetops. 2784
11: 1 thence to teach and to **p** in their cities. 2784
Mk 1: 4 **p** the baptism of repentance for 2784
1:38 the next towns, that I may **p** there also: 2784
3:14 and that he might send them forth to **p**, 2784
16:15 and **p** the gospel to every creature. 2784
Lk 4:18 he hath anointed me to **p the gospel** to 2097
4:18 to **p** deliverance to the captives, 2784
4:19 To **p** the acceptable year of the Lord. 2784
4:43 I must **p** the kingdom of God to other 2097
9: 2 he sent them to **p** the kingdom of God, 2784
9:60 but go thou and **p** the kingdom of God. 1229
Ac 5:42 ceased not to teach and **p** Jesus Christ. 2097
10:42 And he commanded us to **p** unto 2784
14:15 **p** unto you that *ye* should turn from these 2097
15:21 time hath in every city them that **p** him, 2784
16: 6 were forbidden of the Holy Ghost to **p** 2980
16:10 called us for to **p the gospel** unto them. 2097
17: 3 this Jesus, whom I **p** unto you, is Christ. 2605
Ro 1:15 I am ready to **p the gospel** to you that are 2097
10: 8 that is, the word of faith, which we **p**; 2784
10:15 how shall they **p**, except they be sent? 2784
10:15 feet of them that **p the gospel** of peace, 2097
15:20 Yea, so have I strived to **p the gospel**, 2097
1Co 1:17 me not to baptize, but to **p the gospel**: 2097
1:23 But we **p** Christ crucified, unto the Jews a 2784
9:14 hath the Lord ordained that they which **p** 2605
9:16 though I **p the gospel**, I have nothing 2097
9:16 woe is unto me, if I **p** not the **gospel**! 2097
9:18 *Verily* that, when I **p the gospel**, I may 2097
15:11 I or they, so we **p**, and so ye believed. 2784
2Co 2:12 I came to Troas to **p** Christ's gospel, NIG
4: 5 For we **p** not ourselves, but Christ Jesus 2784
10:16 To **p the gospel** in the *regions* beyond 2097
Gal 1: 8 **p** any other **gospel** unto you than *that* 2097
1: 9 If any *man* **p** any other **gospel** unto you 2097
1:16 that I might **p** him among the heathen; 2097
2: 2 *that* gospel which I **p** among the Gentiles, 2784
5:11 And I, brethren, if I yet **p** circumcision, 2784
Eph 3: 8 that I should **p** among the Gentiles 2097
Php 1:15 Some indeed **p** Christ even of envy and 2784
1:16 The one **p** Christ of contention, 2605
Col 1:28 Whom we **p**, warning every man, 2605
2Ti 4: 2 **P** the word; be instant in season, out of 2784
Rev 14: 6 having the everlasting gospel to **p** unto 2097

PREACHED (61) [PREACH]

Ps 40: 9 I have **p** righteousness in the great 1319
Mt 11: 5 and the poor have **the gospel p** to them. 2097
24:14 And this gospel of the kingdom shall be **p** 2784
26:13 Wheresoever this gospel shall be **p** in 2784
Mk 1: 7 **p**, saying, There cometh one mightier 2784
1:39 And he **p** in their synagogues throughout 2784
2: 2 the door: and he **p** the word unto them. 2980
6:12 went out, and **p** that *men* should repent. 2784
14: 9 Wheresoever this gospel shall be **p** 2784
16:20 And they went forth, and **p** every where, 2784
Lk 3:18 many other *things* in his exhortation **p** 2097
4:44 And he **p** in the synagogues of Galilee. 2784
7:22 *are raised,* to the poor **the gospel** is **p**. 2097
16:16 since that time the kingdom of God is **p**, 2097
20: 1 and **p the gospel**, the chief priests and 2097
24:47 remission of sins should be **p** in his name 2784
Ac 3:20 Christ, which **before** was **p** unto you: 4296
4: 2 **p** through Jesus the resurrection from 2605
8: 5 city of Samaria, and **p** Christ unto them. 2784
8:25 had testified and **p** the word of the Lord, 2980
8:25 **p the gospel** in many villages of 2097
8:35 the same scripture, and **p** unto him Jesus. 2097
8:40 and passing through he **p** in all the cities, 2097
9:20 And straightway he **p** Christ in 2784
9:27 how he had **p boldly** at Damascus in 3955
10:37 after the baptism which John **p**; 2784
13: 5 they **p** the word of God in the synagogues 2605
13:24 When John had **first p** before his coming 4296
13:38 that through this *man* is **p** unto you 2605
13:42 might be **p** to them the next sabbath. 2980
14: 7 And there they **p the gospel**. 2097
14:21 And when they had **p the gospel** to that 2097
14:25 And when they had **p** the word in Perga, 2980
15:36 where we have **p** the word of the Lord, 2605
17:13 the word of God was **p** of Paul at Berea, 2605
17:18 because he **p** unto them Jesus, 2097
20: 7 Paul **p** unto them, ready to depart on 1256
Ro 15:19 I have fully **p** the gospel of Christ. NIG
1Co 9:27 by any means, when I have **p** to others, 2784
15: 1 I declare unto you the gospel which I **p** 2097
15: 2 if ye keep in memory what I **p** unto you, 2097
15:12 Now if Christ be **p** that he rose from 2784
2Co 1:19 who was **p** among you by us, *even* by me 2784
11: 4 whom we have not **p**, or *if* ye receive 2784
11: 7 I have **p** to you the gospel of God freely? 2097
Gal 1: 8 you than *that* which we have **p** unto you, 2097
1:11 that the gospel which was **p** of me is not 2097
3: 8 **p before the gospel** unto Abraham, 4283
4:13 flesh I **p the gospel** unto you at the first. 2097
Eph 2:17 And **p** peace to you which were afar off, 2097
Php 1:18 in pretence, or in truth, Christ is **p**; 2605
Col 1:23 which was **p** to every creature which is 2784
1Th 2: 9 of you, we **p** unto you the gospel of God. 2784
1Ti 3:16 seen of angels, **p** unto the Gentiles, 2784
Heb 4: 2 For unto us was **the gospel p**, as well as 2097
4: 2 but the word did not profit them, 189
4: 6 they to whom it was first **p** entered not in 2097
1Pe 1:12 **p the gospel** unto you with the Holy 2097

1Pe 1:25 word which by the **gospel** is **p** unto you. 2097
3:19 he went and **p** unto the spirits in prison; 2784
4: 6 for this cause was the **gospel p** also to 2097

PREACHER (11) [PREACH]

Ecc 1: 1 The words of the **P**, the son of David, 6953
1: 2 of vanities, saith the **P**, vanity of vanities; 6953
1:12 I the **P** was king over Israel in Jerusalem. 6953
7:27 Behold, this have I found, saith the **P**, 6953
12: 8 Vanity of vanities, saith the **P**; all *is* vanity 6953
12: 9 moreover, because the **P** was wise, he 6953
12:10 **P** sought to find out acceptable words: 6953
Ro 10:14 and how shall they hear without a **p**? 2784
1Ti 2: 7 Whereunto I am ordained a **p**, 2783
2Ti 1:11 Whereunto I am appointed a **p**, 2783
2Pe 2: 5 saved Noah the eighth *person*, a **p** of 2783

PREACHEST (1) [PREACH]

Ro 2:21 thou that **p** a *man* should not steal, 2784

PREACHETH (3) [PREACH]

Ac 19:13 We adjure you by Jesus whom Paul **p**. 2784
2Co 11: 4 For if he that cometh **p** another Jesus, 2784
Gal 1:23 now **p** the faith which once he destroyed. 2097

PREACHING (27) [PREACH]

Jnh 3: 2 and preach unto it the **p** that I bid thee. 7150
Mt 3: 1 the Baptist, **p** in the wilderness of Judea, 2784
4:23 and **p** the gospel of the kingdom, 2784
9:35 and **p** the gospel of the kingdom, 2784
12:41 because they repented at the **p** of Jonas; 2782
Mk 1:14 **p** the gospel of the kingdom of God, 2784
Lk 3: 3 **p** the baptism of repentance for 2784
8: 1 **p** and shewing the glad tidings of 2784
9: 6 **p** the gospel, and healing every where. 2097
11:32 for they repented at the **p** of Jonas; 2782
Ac 8: 4 abroad went every where **p** the word. 2097
8:12 But when they believed Philip **p** the 2097
10:36 children of Israel, **p** peace by Jesus Christ: 2097
11:19 the word to none but unto the Jews 2980
11:20 unto the Grecians, **p** the Lord Jesus. 2097
15:35 teaching and **p** the word of the Lord, 2097
20: 9 as Paul was long **p**, he sunk down with 1256
20:25 among whom I have gone **p** the kingdom 2784
28:31 **P** the kingdom of God, and teaching those 2784
Ro 16:25 and the **p** of Jesus Christ, according to 2782
1Co 1:18 the **p** of the cross is to them that perish 3056
1:21 it pleased God by the foolishness of **p** to 2782
2: 4 my **p** was not with enticing words of 2782
15:14 then *is* our **p** vain, and your faith *is* also 2782
2Co 10:14 for we are come as far as to you also in **p** NIG
2Ti 4:17 that by me the **p** might be fully known, 2782
Tit 1: 3 due times manifested his word through **p**, 2782

PRECEPT (11) [PRECEPTS]

Isa 28:10 For **p** *must be* upon precept, precept 6673
28:10 For precept *must be* upon **p**, precept 6673
28:10 *must be* upon precept, **p** upon precept; 6673
28:10 *must be* upon precept, precept upon **p**; 6673
28:13 the word of the LORD was unto them **p** 6673
28:13 The LORD was unto them precept upon **p**, 6673
28:13 precept upon precept, **p** upon precept; 6673
28:13 precept upon precept, precept upon **p**; 6673
29:13 their fear towards me is taught *by* the **p** 4687
Mk 10: 5 of your heart he wrote you this **p**. 1785
Heb 9:19 when Moses had spoken every **p** to all 1785

PRECEPTS (24) [PRECEPT]

Ne 9:14 commandedst them **p**, statutes, and laws, 4687
Ps 119: 4 Thou hast commanded *us* to keep thy **p** 6490
119:15 I will meditate in thy **p**, and have respect 6490
119:27 Make me to understand the way of thy **p**: 6490
119:40 Behold, I have longed after thy **p**: 6490
119:45 And I will walk at liberty: for I seek thy **p**. 6490
119:56 This I had, because I kept thy **p**. 6490
119:63 fear thee, and of them that keep thy **p**. 6490
119:69 I will keep thy **p** with *my* whole heart. 6490
119:78 a cause: *but* I will meditate in thy **p**. 6490
119:87 me upon earth; but I forsook not thy **p**. 6490
119:93 I will never forget thy **p**: for with them 6490
119:94 thine, save me; for I have sought thy **p**. 6490
119:100 than the ancients, because I keep thy **p**. 6490
119:104 Through thy **p** I get understanding: 6490
119:110 a snare for me: yet I erred not from thy **p**. 6490
119:128 Therefore I esteem all *thy* **p** concerning 6490
119:134 oppression of man: so will I keep thy **p**. 6490
119:141 and despised: *yet* do not I forget thy **p**. 6490
119:159 Consider how I love thy **p**: quicken me, 6490
119:168 I have kept thy **p** and thy testimonies: 6490
119:173 hand help me; for I have chosen thy **p**. 6490
Jer 35:18 kept all his **p**, and done according unto 4687
Da 9: 5 by departing from thy **p** and from thy 4687

PRECIOUS (76)

Ge 24:53 her brother and to her mother **p** *things*. 4030
Dt 33:13 for the **p** *things* of heaven, for the dew, 4022
33:14 for the **p** fruits brought forth by the sun, 4022
33:14 for the **p** *things* put forth by the moon, 4022
33:15 and for the **p** *things* of the lasting hills, 4022
33:16 for the **p** *things* of the earth and 4022
1Sa 3: 1 the word of the LORD was **p** in those 3368
26:21 my soul was **p** in thine eyes this day: 3365
2Sa 12:30 *was* a talent of gold with the **p** stones: 3368
1Ki 10: 2 and very much gold, and **p** stones: 3368
10:10 of spices very great store, and **p** stones: 3368

1Ki 10:11 great plenty of almug trees, and **p** stones. 3368
2Ki 1:13 these fifty thy servants, be **p** in thy sight. 3365
1:14 therefore let my life now be **p** in thy sight. 3365
20:13 them all the house of his **p things**, 5238
20:13 the **p** ointment, and all the house of his 2896
1Ch 20: 2 of gold, and *there were* **p** stones in it; 3368
29: 2 all *manner of* **p** stones, and marble stones 3368
29: 8 with whom **p** stones were found gave NIH
2Ch 3: 6 he garnished the house with **p** stones for 3368
9: 1 and gold in abundance, and **p** stones: 3368
9: 9 of spices great abundance, and **p** stones: 3368
9:10 brought algum trees, and **p** stones. 3368
20:25 jewels, which they stript off for 2532
21: 3 gold, and of **p** *things*, with fenced cities 4030
32:27 **p** stones, and for spices, and for shields, 3368
Ezr 1: 6 and with beasts, and with **p** *things*, 4030
8:27 and two vessels of fine copper, **p** as gold. 2532
Job 28:16 rocks; and his eye seeth every **p** *thing*. 3366
28:16 Ophir, with the **p** onyx, or the sapphire. 3368
Ps 49: 8 (For the redemption of their soul is **p**, 3365
72:14 and **p** shall their blood be in his sight. 3365
116:15 **P** in the sight of the LORD *is* the death of 3368
126: 6 goeth forth and weepeth, bearing **p** seed, 4901
133: 2 *It is* like the **p** ointment upon the head, 2896
139:17 How **p** also are thy thoughts unto me, 3365
Pr 1:13 We shall find all **p** substance, we shall fill 3368
3:15 *is* more **p** than rubies: and all the things 3368
6:26 and the adulteress will hunt for the **p** life. 3368
12:27 but the substance of a diligent man *is* **p**. 3368
17: 8 A gift *is as a* **p** stone in the eyes of him 2580
20:15 but the lips of knowledge *are* a **p** jewel. 3366
24: 4 shall the chambers be filled *with* all **p** 3368
Ecc 7: 1 A *good* name *is* better than **p** ointment; 2896
Isa 13:12 I will **make** a man more **p** than fine gold; 3365
28:16 a corner *stone*, a sure foundation: 3368
39: 2 shewed them the house of his **p things**, 5238
39: 2 the **p** ointment, and all the house of his 2896
43: 4 Since thou wast **p** in my sight, thou hast 3368
Jer 15:19 if thou take forth the **p** from the vile, 3368
20: 5 all the **p things** thereof, and all 3366
La 4: 2 The **p** sons of Zion, comparable to fine 3368
Eze 22:25 have taken the treasure and **p things**; 3368
27:20 Dedan *was* thy merchant in **p** clothes for 2667
27:22 all spices, and with all **p** stones, and 3368
28:13 every **p** stone *was* thy covering, the, 3368
Da 11: 8 *and* with their **p** vessels *of* silver and 2532
11:38 and with **p** stones, and pleasant things. 3368
11:43 silver, and over all the **p** *things* of Egypt: 2532
Mt 26: 7 an alabaster box of **very p** ointment, 927
Mk 14: 3 box of ointment of spikenard **very p**; 4185
1Co 3:12 silver, **p** stones, wood, hay, stubble; 5093
Jas 5: 7 the husbandman waiteth for the **p** fruit of 5093
1Pe 1: 7 being much **more p** than of gold that 5093
1:19 with the **p** blood of Christ, as of a lamb 5093
2: 4 indeed of men, but chosen of God, *and* **p**, 1784
2: 6 I lay in Sion a chief corner stone, elect, **p**: 1784
2: 7 Unto you therefore which believe *he is* **p**: 5092
2Pe 1: 1 to them that have obtained **like p** faith 2472
1: 4 unto us exceeding great and **p** promises: 5093
Rev 17: 4 decked with gold and **p** stone and pearls, 5093
18:12 and **p** stones, and of pearls, and fine linen, 5093
18:12 and all *manner* vessels of **most p** wood, 5093
18:16 with gold, and **p** stones, and pearls: 5093
21:11 her light *was* like unto a stone **most p**, 5093
21:19 garnished with all *manner* of **p** stones. 5093

PREDESTINATE (2) [PREDESTINATED]

Ro 8:29 also did **p** *to be* conformed to the image 4309
8:30 Moreover whom he did **p**, them he also 4309

PREDESTINATED (1) [PREDESTINATE]

Eph 1: 5 Having **p** us unto the adoption of children 4309
1:11 being **p** according to the purpose of him 4309

PREDESTINED See PREDESTINATE;
PREDESTINATED

PREEMINENCE (3) [EMINENT]

Ecc 3:19 so that a man **hath** no **p** above a beast: 4195
Col 1:18 that in all *things* he might have the **p**. 4409
3Jn 1: 9 who **loveth** to have the **p** among them, 5383

PREFER (1) [PREFERRED, PREFERRING]

Ps 137: 6 if I **p** not Jerusalem above my chief joy. 5927

PREFERRED (5) [PREFER]

Est 2: 9 he **p** her and her maids unto the best 8138
Da 6: 3 this Daniel was **p** above the presidents 5330
Jn 1:15 cometh after me is **p** before me: 1096+1715
1:27 it is, who coming after me is **p** before me, 1096
1:30 a man which is **p** before me: 1096+1715

PREFERRING (2) [PREFER]

Ro 12:10 brotherly love; in honour **p** one another; 4285
1Ti 5:21 that thou observe these *things* without **p** 4299

PREMEDITATE (1)

Mk 13:11 what ye shall speak, neither do ye **p**: 3191

PREPARATION (9) [PREPARE]

1Ch 22: 5 I will *therefore* now **make p** for it. 3559
Na 2: 3 with flaming torches in the day of his **p**, 3559
Mt 27:62 that followed the *day of the* **p**, the chief 3904
Mk 15:42 because it was the **p**, that is, the day 3904
Lk 23:54 And *that* day was the **p**, and the sabbath 3904
Jn 19:14 And it was the **p** of the passover, 3904

Jn 19:31 The Jews therefore, because it was the **p**, 3904
19:42 of the Jews' **p** *day;* for the sepulchre was 3904
Eph 6:15 *your* feet shod with the **p** of the gospel 2091

PREPARATIONS (1) [PREPARE]
Pr 16: 1 The **p** of the heart in man, and the 4633

PREPARE (81) [PREPARATION, PREPARATIONS, PREPARED, PREPAREDST, PREPAREST, PREPARETH, PREPARING, UNPREPARED]
Ex 15: 2 *is* my God, and I will **p** him **a habitation;** 5115
16: 5 that on the sixth day they shall **p** *that* 3559
Nu 15: 5 shalt thou **p** with the burnt offering 6213
15: 6 thou shalt **p** *for* a meat offering two tenth 6213
15:12 According to the number that ye shall **p**, 6213
23: 1 **p** me here seven oxen and seven rams. 3559
23:29 **p** me here seven bullocks and seven rams. 3559
Dt 3: 3 Thou shalt **p** thee a way, and divide 3559
Jos 1:11 the people, saying, **p** you victuals; 3559
22:26 we said, Let us now **p** to build us an altar, 6213
1Sa 7: 3 **p** your hearts unto the LORD, 3559
23:22 yet, and know and see his place where 3559
1Ki 18:44 Ahab, **P** *thy* chariot, and get thee down, 631
1Ch 9:32 over the shewbread, to **p** *it* every sabbath. 3559
29:18 of thy people, and **p** their heart unto thee: 3559
2Ch 2: 9 Even to **p** me timber in abundance: 3559
31:11 Hezekiah commanded to **p** chambers in 3559
35: 4 **p** *yourselves* by the houses of your fathers, 3559
35: 6 sanctify yourselves, and **p** your brethren, 3559
Est 5: 8 Haman come to the banquet that I shall **p** 6213
Job 8: 8 and **p** *thyself* to the search of their fathers: 3559
11:13 If thou **p** thine heart, and stretch out thine 3559
27:16 as the dust, and **p** raiment as the clay; 3559
27:17 He may **p** *it,* but the just shall put *it* on, 3559
Ps 10:17 wilt **p** their heart, thou wilt cause thine 3559
59: 4 and **p** themselves without *my* fault: 3559
61: 7 O **p** mercy and truth, *which* may preserve 4487
107:36 that they may **p** a city for habitation; 3559
Pr 24:27 **P** thy work without, and make it fit for 3559
30:25 yet they **p** their meat in the summer; 3559
Isa 14:21 **P** slaughter for his children for the iniquity 3559
21: 5 **P** the table, watch *in* the watchtower, eat, 6186
40: 3 **P** ye the way of the LORD, 6437
40:20 a cunning workman to **p** a graven image, 3559
57:14 say, Cast ye up, cast ye up, **p** the way, 6437
62:10 **p** you the way of the people; cast up, 6437
65:11 **p** a table for *that* troop, and that furnish 6186
Jer 6: 4 **P** ye war against her; arise, and let us go 6942
12: 3 and **p** them for the day of slaughter. 6942
22: 7 I will **p** destroyers against thee, every one 6942
46:14 Stand fast, and **p** thee; for the sword 3559
51:12 set up the watchmen, **p** the ambushes, 3559
51:27 the nations, **p** the nations against her, 6942
51:28 **P** against her the nations with the kings 6942
Eze 4:15 and thou shalt **p** thy bread therewith. 6213
12: 3 the stuff for removing, and remove by 6213
35: 6 I will **p** thee unto blood, and blood shall 6213
38: 7 **p** for thyself, thou, and all thy company 3559
43:25 Seven days shalt thou **p** every day a goat 6213
43:25 they shall also **p** a young bullock, 6213
45:17 he shall **p** the sin offering, and the meat 6213
45:22 that day shall the prince **p** for himself 6213
45:23 seven days of the feast he shall **p** a burnt 6213
45:24 he shall **p** a meat offering *of* an ephah for 6213
46: 2 the priests shall **p** his burnt offering and 6213
46: 7 he shall **p** a meat offering, an ephah for a 6213
46:12 Now when the prince shall **p** a voluntary 6213
46:12 he shall **p** his burnt offering and his peace 6213
46:13 Thou shalt daily **p** a burnt offering unto 6213
46:13 thou shalt **p** it every morning. 6213
46:14 thou shalt **p** a meat offering for it every 6213
46:15 Thus shall they **p** the lamb, and the meat 6213
Joel 3: 9 **P** war, wake up the mighty *men,* let all 6942
Am 4:12 unto thee, **p** to meet thy God, O Israel. 3559
Mic 3: 5 mouths, they even **p** war against him. 6942
Mal 3: 1 and he shall **p** the way before me: 6437
Mt 3: 3 **P** ye the way of the LORD, make his paths 2090
11:10 *face, which shall* **p** *thy way before thee.* 2680
26:17 Where wilt thou *that* we **p** for thee to eat 2090
Mk 1: 2 face, which shall **p** thy way before thee. 2680
1: 3 **P** ye the way of the Lord, make his paths 2090
14:12 and **p** that thou mayest eat the passover? 2090
Lk 1:76 before the face of the Lord to **p** his ways; 2090
3: 4 **P** ye the way of the Lord, make his paths 2090
7:27 *face, which shall* **p** *thy way before thee.* 2680
22: 8 John, saying, Go and **p** us the passover, 2090
22: 9 unto him, Where wilt thou *that* we **p**? 2090
Jn 14: 2 I have told you. I go to **p** a place for you. 2090
14: 3 And if I go and **p** a place for you, I will 2090
1Co 14: 8 who shall **p** himself to the battle? 3903
Phm 1:22 But withal **p** me also a lodging: for I trust 2090

PREPARED (101) [PREPARE]
Ge 24:31 for I have **p** the house, and room for 6437
27:17 and the bread, which she had **p**, 6213
Ex 12:39 neither had they **p** for themselves *any* 6213
23:20 bring thee into the place which I have **p**. 3559
Nu 21:27 let the city of Sihon be built and **p**: 3559
23: 4 I have **p** seven altars, and I have offered 6186
Jos 4: 4 whom he had **p** of the children of Israel, 3559
4:13 About forty thousand **p** for war passed 2502
2Sa 15: 1 Absalom **p** him chariots and horses, 6213
1Ki 1: 5 he **p** him chariots and horsemen, 6213
5:18 so they **p** timber and stones to build 3559
6:19 the oracle he **p** in the house within, to set 3559

2Ki 6:23 he **p** great provision for them: 3739
1Ch 12:39 for their brethren had **p** for them. 3559
15: 1 **p** a place for the ark of God, 3559
15: 3 unto his place, which he had **p** for it. 3559
15:12 Israel unto *the place that* I have **p** for it. 3559
22: 3 David **p** iron in abundance for the nails 3559
22: 5 So David **p** abundantly before his death. 3559
22:14 in my trouble I have **p** for the house of 3559
22:14 timber also and stone have I **p**; 3559
29: 2 Now I have **p** with all my might for 3559
29: 3 above all *that* I have **p** for the holy house, 3559
29:16 all this store that we have **p** to build thee 3559
2Ch 1: 4 to *the place which* David had **p** for it: 3559
1: 1 in the place that David had **p** in 3559
8:16 Now all the work of Solomon was **p** unto 3559
12:14 he **p** not his heart to seek the LORD. 3559
16:14 divers kinds *of* spices **p** by 7543
17:18 fourscore thousand **ready p** for the war. 2502
19: 3 land, and hast **p** thine heart to seek God. 3559
20:33 as yet the people had not **p** their hearts 3559
26:14 Uzziah **p** for them throughout all the host 3559
27: 6 he **p** his ways before the LORD his God. 3559
29:19 have we **p** and sanctified, and behold, 3559
29:36 all the people, that God had **p** the people: 3559
31:11 the house of the LORD; and they **p** *them,* 3559
35:10 So the service was **p**, and the priests stood 3559
35:14 therefore the Levites **p** for themselves, 3559
35:15 for their brethren the Levites **p** for them. 3559
35:16 So all the service of the LORD was **p** 3559
35:20 all this, when Josiah had **p** the temple, 3559
Ezr 7:10 Ezra had **p** his heart to seek the law of 3559
Ne 5:18 Now *that* which was **p** for me daily *was* 6213
5:18 also fowls were **p** for me, and once in ten 6213
8:10 unto them for whom nothing is **p**: 3559
13: 5 he had **p** for him a great chamber, where 6213
Est 5: 4 unto the banquet that I have **p** for him. 6213
5: 5 came to the banquet that Esther had **p**. 6213
5:12 the king unto the banquet that she had **p** 6213
6: 4 on the gallows that he had **p** for him. 6213
6:14 unto the banquet that Esther had **p**. 6213
7:10 the gallows that he had **p** for Mordecai. 3559
Job 28:27 he **p** it, yea, and searched it out. 3559
29: 7 the city, *when* I **p** my seat in the street; 3559
Ps 7:13 He hath also **p** for him the instruments of 3559
9: 7 he hath **p** his throne for judgment. 3559
57: 6 They have **p** a net for my steps; my soul is 3559
68:10 God, hast **p** of thy goodness for the poor. 3559
74:16 *is* thine: thou hast **p** the light and the sun. 3559
103:19 The LORD hath **p** his throne in 3559
Pr 8:27 When he **p** the heavens, I *was* there: 3559
19:29 Judgments are **p** for scorners, 3559
21:31 The horse *is* **p** against the day of battle: 3559
Isa 30:33 yea, for the king it is **p**; he hath made *it* 3559
64: 4 he hath **p** for him that waiteth for him. 6213
Eze 23:41 a stately bed, and a table **p** before it, 6186
28:13 of thy pipes was **p** in thee in the day that 3559
38: 7 Be thou **p**, and prepare for thyself, thou, 3559
Da 2: 9 for ye have **p** lying and corrupt words to 2164
Hos 2: 8 her silver and gold, *which* they **p** for Baal. 6213
6: 3 his going forth *is* **p** as the morning; 3559
Jnh 1:17 Now the LORD had **p** a great fish to 4487
4: 6 the LORD God **p** a gourd, and made *it* to 4487
4: 7 God **p** a worm when the morning rose 4487
4: 8 arise, that God **p** a vehement east wind; 4487
Na 2: 5 wall thereof, and the defence shall be **p**. 3559
Zep 1: 7 for the LORD hath **p** a sacrifice, he hath 3559
Mt 20:23 *shall be given to them* for whom it is **p** of 2090
22: 4 are bidden, Behold, I have **p** my dinner: 2090
25:34 inherit the kingdom **p** for you from 2090
25:41 **p** for the devil and his angels: 2090
Mk 10:40 *it shall be given to them* for whom it is **p**. 2090
14:15 you a large upper room furnished *and* **p**: 2092
Lk 1:17 to make ready a people **p** for the Lord. 2680
2:31 Which thou hast **p** before the face of all 2090
12:47 **p** not *himself,* neither did according to his 2090
23:56 returned, and **p** spices and ointments; 2090
24: 1 bringing the spices which they had **p**, 2090
Ro 9:23 mercy, which he had **afore p** unto glory, 4282
1Co 2: 9 *the things* which God hath **p** for them 2090
2Ti 2:21 master's use, *and* **p** unto every good work. 2090
Heb 10: 5 wouldest not, but a body hast thou **p** me: 2675
11: 7 an ark to the saving of his house; 2680
11:16 their God: for he hath **p** for them a city. 2090
Rev 8: 6 seven trumpets **p** themselves to sound. 2090
9: 7 locusts *were* like unto horses **p** unto battle 2090
9:15 which were **p** for an hour, and a day, 2090
12: 6 where she hath a place **p** of God, 2090
16:12 way of the kings of the east might be **p**. 2090
21: 2 **p** as a bride adorned for her husband. 2090

PREPAREDST (1) [PREPARE]
Ps 80: 9 Thou **p** *room* before it, and didst cause it 6437

PREPAREST (3) [PREPARE]
Nu 15: 8 thou **p** a bullock *for* a burnt offering, 6213
Ps 23: 5 Thou **p** a table before me in the presence 6186
65: 9 thou **p** them corn, when thou hast so 3559

PREPARETH (3) [PREPARE]
2Ch 30:19 *That* **p** his heart to seek God, the LORD 3559
Job 15:35 bring forth vanity, and their belly **p** deceit. 3559
Ps 147: 8 with clouds, who **p** rain for the earth, 3559

PREPARING (2) [PREPARE]
Ne 13: 7 in **p** him a chamber in the courts of 6213

1Pe 3:20 while the ark was a **p**, wherein few, that 2680

PRESBYTERY (1)
1Ti 4:14 with the laying on of the hands of the **p**. 4244

PRESCRIBED (1) [PRESCRIBING]
Isa 10: 1 write grievousness *which* they have **p**; 3789

PRESCRIBING (1) [PRESCRIBING]
Ezr 7:22 baths *of* oil, and salt without **p** how much. 3792

PRESENCE (116) [PRESENT]
Ge 3: 8 his wife hid themselves from the **p** of 6440
4:16 Cain went out from the **p** of 6440+3807.1
16:12 he shall dwell in the **p** of all his brethren. 6440
23:11 in the **p** of the sons of my people give I it 5869
23:18 Unto Abraham for a possession in the **p** of 5869
25:18 *and* he died in the **p** of all his brethren. 6440
27:30 Jacob was yet scarce gone out from the **p** 6440
41:46 Joseph went out from the **p** of Pharaoh, 6440
45: 3 him; for they were troubled at his **p**. 6440
47:15 for why should we die in thy **p**? 5048
Ex 10:11 they were driven out from Pharaoh's **p**. 6440
33:14 My **p** shall go *with thee,* and I will give 6440
33:15 If thy **p** go not *with me,* carry us not up 6440
35:20 of Israel departed from the **p** of Moses. 6440
Lev 22: 3 that soul shall be cut off from my **p** 6440
Nu 20: 6 Aaron went from the **p** of the assembly 6440
Dt 25: 9 come unto him in the **p** of the elders, 5869
Jos 4:11 and the priests, in the **p** of the people. 6440
8:32 which he wrote in the **p** of the children 6440
1Sa 18:11 *it.* And David avoided out of his **p** twice. 6440
19: 7 and he was in his **p**, as in times past. 6440
19:10 slipt away out of Saul's **p**, and he smote 6440
21:15 this *fellow* to play the mad man in my **p**? 5921
2Sa 16:19 *should I* not *serve* in the **p** of his son? as I 6440
16:19 as I have served in thy father's, so will I 6440
16:19 thy father's presence, so will I be in thy **p**. 6440
24: 4 captains of the host went out from the **p** 6440
1Ki 1:28 she came into the king's **p**, 6440
8:22 in the **p** of all the congregation of Israel, 5048
12: 2 heard *of it,* (for he was fled from the **p** of 6440
21:13 in the **p** of the people, saying, 5048
2Ki 3:14 were it not that I regard the **p** of 6440
5:27 he went out from his **p** a leper *as white* as 6440
13:23 neither cast he them from his **p** as yet. 6440
24:20 until he had cast them out from his **p**, 6440
25:19 of them that were in the king's **p**, 6440+7200
1Ch 16:27 Glory and honour *are* in his **p**; strength 6440
16:33 the trees of the wood sing out at the **p** of 6440
24:31 sons of Aaron in the **p** of David the king, 6440
2Ch 6:12 in the **p** of all the congregation of Israel, 5048
9:23 all the kings of the earth sought the **p** of 6440
10: 2 he had fled from the **p** of Solomon 6440
20: 9 we stand before this house, and in thy **p**, 6440
34: 4 brake down the altars of Baalim in his **p**; 6440
Ne 2: 1 I had not been *beforetime* sad in his **p**. 6440
Est 1:10 seven chamberlains that served **in the p** 6440
8:15 Mordecai went out from the **p** of the king 6440
Job 1:12 So Satan went forth from the **p** of 6440
2: 7 So went Satan forth from the **p** of 6440
23:15 Therefore am I troubled at his **p**: when I 6440
Ps 9: 3 they shall fall and perish at thy **p**. 6440
16:11 in thy **p** *is* fulness of joy; at thy right hand 6440
17: 2 Let my sentence come forth from thy **p**; 6440
23: 5 Thou preparest a table before me **in the p** 5048
31:20 shalt hide them in the secret of thy **p** 6440
51:11 Cast me not away from thy **p**; and take 6440
68: 2 *so* let the wicked perish at the **p** of God. 6440
68: 8 the heavens also dropped at the **p** of God: 6440
68: 8 *even* Sinai itself *was moved* at the **p** of 6440
95: 2 Let us come before his **p** with 6440
97: 5 The hills melted like wax at the **p** of 6440
97: 5 at the **p** of the Lord of the whole earth. 6440
100: 2 come before his **p** with singing. 6440
114: 7 Tremble, thou earth, at the **p** of the Lord, 6440
114: 7 at the **p** of the God of Jacob; 6440+3807.1
116:14 the LORD now in the **p** of all his people. 5048
116:18 the LORD now in the **p** of all his people, 5048
139: 7 or whither shall I flee from thy **p**? 6440
140:13 name: the upright shall dwell in thy **p**. 6440
Pr 14: 7 Go from the **p** of a foolish man, when 5048
17:18 becometh surety in the **p** of his friend. 6440
25: 6 Put not forth thyself in the **p** of the king, 6440
25: 7 of the prince whom thine eyes have 6440
Isa 1: 7 strangers devour it in your **p**, and *it is* 5048
19: 1 idols of Egypt shall be moved at his **p**, 6440
63: 9 and the angel of his **p** saved them: 6440
64: 1 mountains might flow down at thy **p**, 6440
64: 2 *that* the nations may tremble at thy **p**. 6440
64: 3 the mountains flowed down at thy **p**, 6440
Jer 4:26 were broken down at the **p** of the LORD, 6440
5:22 will ye not tremble at my **p**, which have 6440
23:39 your fathers, *and* cast *you* out of my **p**: 6440
28: 1 the **p** of the priests and of all the people, 5869
28: 5 prophet Hananiah in the **p** of the priests, 5869
28: 5 in the **p** of all the people that stood in 5869
28:11 Hananiah spake in the **p** of all the people, 5869
32:12 in the **p** of the witnesses that subscribed 5869
52: 3 till he had cast them out from his **p**, 6440
Eze 38:20 shall shake at my **p**, and the mountains 6440
Da 2:27 Daniel answered **in the p** of the king, 6925
Jnh 1: 3 Tarshish from the **p** of the LORD, 6440+3807.1
1: 3 Tarshish from the **p** of the LORD. 6440+3807.1
1:10 the men knew that he fled from the **p** of 6440

P

Na	1: 5 the earth is burnt at his **p**, yea, the world, 6440
Zep	1: 7 Hold thy peace at the **p** of the Lord GOD: 6440
Lk	1:19 I am Gabriel, that stand in the **p** of God; 1799
	13:26 We have eaten and drunk in thy **p**, 1799
	14:10 shalt thou have worship in the **p** of them 1799
	15:10 there is joy in the **p** of the angels of God 1799
Jn	20:30 truly did Jesus in the **p** of his disciples, 1799
Ac	3:13 and denied him in the **p** of Pilate, 2596+4383
	3:16 this perfect soundness in the **p** of you all. 561
	3:19 shall come from the **p** of the Lord; 4383
	5:41 And they departed from the **p** of 4383
	27:35 and gave thanks to God in the **p** of them all: 1799
1Co	1:29 That no flesh should glory in his **p**. 1799
2Co	10: 1 who in **p** am base among you, 4383
	10:10 but his bodily **p** is weak, and his speech 3952
Php	2:12 not as in my **p** only, but now much more 3952
1Th	2:17 taken from you for a short time in the **p**, 4383
	2:19 Are not even ye in the **p** of our Lord Jesus 1715
2Th	1: 9 destruction from the **p** of the Lord, 4383
Heb	9:24 now to appear in the **p** of God for us: 4383
Jude	1:24 to present you faultless **before the p** of 2714
Rev	14:10 in the **p** of the holy angels, 1799
	14:10 the holy angels, and in the **p** of the Lamb: 1799

PRESENT (106) [PRESENCE, PRESENTED, PRESENTING, PRESENTLY, PRESENTS]

Ge	32:13 took of that which came to his hand a **p** 4503
	32:18 it is a **p** sent unto my lord Esau: 4503
	32:20 I will appease him with the **p** that goeth 4503
	32:21 So went the **p** over before him: 4503
	33:10 thy sight, then receive my **p** at my hand: 4503
	43:11 carry down the man a **p**, a little balm, 4503
	43:15 men took that **p**, and they took double 4503
	43:25 made ready the **p** against Joseph came 4503
	43:26 brought him the **p** which was in their 4503
Ex	34: 2 **p** thyself there to me in the top of 5324
Lev	14:11 the priest that maketh him clean shall **p** 5975
	16: 7 **p** them before the LORD at the door of 5975
	27: 8 he shall **p** himself before the priest, 5975
	27:11 then he shall **p** the beast before the priest: 5975
Nu	3: 6 and **p** them before Aaron the priest, 5975
Dt	31:14 **p** yourselves in the tabernacle of 3320
Jdg	3:15 by him the children of Israel sent a **p** unto 4503
	3:17 brought the **p** unto Eglon king of Moab: 4503
	3:18 when he had made an end to offer the **p**, 4503
	3:18 he sent away the people that bare the **p**, 4503
	6:18 bring forth my **p**, and set it before thee. 4503
1Sa	9: 7 is not a **p** to bring to the man of God: 8670
	10:19 **p** yourselves before the LORD by your 3320
	13:15 Saul numbered the people that were **p** 4672
	13:16 and the people that were **p** with them, 4672
	21: 3 bread in mine hand, or what there is **p**. 4672
	30:26 Behold a **p** for you of the spoil of 1293
2Sa	20: 4 within three days, and be thou here **p**. 5975
1Ki	9:16 given it for a **p** unto his daughter. 7964
	10:25 they brought every man his **p**, vessels of 4503
	15:19 have sent unto thee a **p** of silver and gold; 7810
	20:27 and were all **p**, and went against them: 3557
2Ki	8: 8 Take a **p** in thine hand, and go, meet 4503
	8: 9 went to meet him, and took a **p** with him, 4503
	16: 8 and sent it for a **p** to the king of Assyria. 7810
	17: 4 brought no **p** to the king of Assyria, as he 4503
	18:31 Make an agreement with me by a **p**, 1293
	20:12 sent letters and a **p** unto Hezekiah: 4503
1Ch	29:17 which are here, to offer willingly unto 4672
2Ch	5:11 all the priests that were **p** were sanctified, 4672
	9:24 they brought every man his **p**, vessels of 4503
	29:29 that were **p** with him bowed themselves, 4672
	30:21 the children of Israel that were **p** at 4672
	31: 1 Israel that were **p** went out to the cities 4672
	34:32 he caused all that were **p** in Jerusalem 4672
	34:33 made all that were **p** in Israel to serve, 4672
	35: 7 the passover offerings, for all that were **p**, 4672
	35:17 the children of Israel that were **p** kept 4672
	35:18 all Judah and Israel that were **p**, 4672
Ezr	8:25 lords, and all Israel there **p**, had offered: 4672
Est	5: 5 people that were **p** in Shushan the palace, 4672
	4:16 gather together all the Jews that are **p** in 4672
Job	1: 6 came to **p** themselves before the LORD, 3320
	2: 1 came to **p** themselves before the LORD, 3320
	2: 1 Satan came also among them to **p** himself 3320
Ps	46: 1 and strength, a very **p** help in trouble. 4672
Isa	18: 7 In that time shall the **p** be brought unto 7862
	36:16 Make an agreement with me by a **p**, 1293
	39: 1 sent letters and a **p** to Hezekiah: 4503
Jer	36: 7 It may be they will **p** their supplication 5307
	42: 9 unto whom ye sent me to **p** your 5307
Eze	27:15 they brought for a **p** horns of ivory 814
Da	9:18 for we do not **p** our supplications before 5307
Hos	10: 6 shall be also carried unto Assyria for a **p** 4503
Lk	2:22 him to Jerusalem, to **p** him to the Lord; 3936
	5:17 the power of the Lord was **p** to heal them. NIG
	13: 1 There were at that season some that 3918
	18:30 not receive manifold more in this **p** time, NIG
Jn	14:25 I spoken unto you, being yet **p** with you. 3306
Ac	10:33 therefore are we all **here** before God, 3918
	21:18 us unto James; and all the elders were **p**. 3854
	25:24 and all men which are **here p** with us, 4840
	28: 2 because of the **p** rain, and because of 2186
Ro	7:18 no good thing: for to will is **p** with 3873
	7:21 when I would do good, evil is **p** with me. 3873
	8:18 For I reckon that the sufferings of this **p** 3568
	8:38 principalities, nor powers, nor things **p**, 1764
	11: 5 at this **p** time there is also a remnant 3568
	12: 1 that ye **p** your bodies a living sacrifice, 3936

1Co	3:22 or death, or things **p**, or things to come; 1764
	4:11 Even unto this **p** hour we both hunger, 737
	5: 3 I verily, as absent in body, but **p** in spirit, 3918
	5: 3 have judged already, as though I were **p**, 3918
	7:26 that this is good for the **p** distress, 3918
	15: 6 whom the greater part remain unto this **p**, 737
2Co	4:14 us also by Jesus, and shall **p** us with you. 3936
	5: 6 from the body, and to be **p** with the Lord. 1736
	5: 9 we labour, that, whether **p** or absent, 1736
	10: 2 bold when I am **p** with that confidence, 3918
	10:11 will we be also in deed when we are **p**. 3918
	11: 2 that I may **p** you as a chaste virgin to 3936
	11: 9 And when I was **p** with you, and wanted, 3918
	13: 2 you, as if I were **p**, the second time; 3918
	13:10 lest being **p** I should use sharpness, 3918
Gal	1: 4 that he might deliver us from this **p** evil 1764
	4:18 and not only when I am **p** with you. 3918
	4:20 I desire to be **p** with you now, 3918
Eph	5:27 That he might **p** it to himself a glorious 3936
Col	1:22 to **p** you holy and unblameable and 3936
	1:28 we may **p** every man perfect in Christ 3936
2Ti	4:10 loved this **p** world, and is departed 3568
Tit	2:12 and godly, in this **p** world; 3568
Heb	9: 9 Which was a figure for the time then **p**, 1764
	12:11 Now no chastening for the **p** seemeth to 3918
2Pe	1:12 them, and be stablished in the **p** truth. 3918
Jude	1:24 to **p** you faultless before the presence of 2476

PRESENTED (18) [PRESENT]

Ge	46:29 to Goshen, and **p** himself unto him; 7200
	47: 2 even five men, and **p** them unto Pharaoh. 3322
Lev	2: 8 it is **p** unto the priest, he shall bring it 7126
	7:35 in the day when he **p** them to minister 7126
	9:12 Aaron's sons **p** unto him the blood, 4672
	9:13 they **p** the burnt offering unto him, with 4672
	9:18 Aaron's sons **p** unto him the blood, 4672
	16:10 shall be **p** alive before the LORD, to make 5975
Dt	31:14 **p** themselves in the tabernacle of 3320
Jos	24: 1 and they **p** themselves before God. 3320
Jdg	6:19 it out unto him under the oak, and **p** it. 5066
	20: 2 **p** themselves in the assembly of the 3320
1Sa	17:16 and evening, and **p** himself forty days. 3320
Jer	38:26 I **p** my supplication before the king, 5307
Eze	20:28 there they **p** the provocation of their 5414
Mt	2:11 their treasures, they **p** unto him gifts; 4374
Ac	9:41 called the saints and widows, **p** her alive. 3936
	23:33 to the governor, **p** Paul also **before** him. 3936

PRESENTING (1) [PRESENT]

Da	9:20 **p** my supplication before the LORD my 5307

PRESENTLY (5) [PRESENT]

1Sa	2:16 not fail to burn the fat **p**, 3117+1886.1+3509.1
Pr	12:16 fool's wrath is **p** known: 3117+871.1+1886.1
Mt	21:19 And the fig tree withered away. 3916
	26:53 shall **p** give me more than twelve legions 737
Php	2:23 therefore I hope to send **p**, so soon as 1824

PRESENTS (10) [PRESENT]

1Sa	10:27 they despised him, and brought him no **p**. 4503
1Ki	4:21 they brought **p**, and served Solomon all 4503
2Ki	17: 3 became his servant, and gave him **p**. 4503
2Ch	17: 5 and all Judah brought to Jehoshaphat **p**; 4503
	17:11 of the Philistines brought Jehoshaphat **p**, 4503
	32:23 and **p** to Hezekiah king of Judah: 4030
Ps	68:29 at Jerusalem shall kings bring **p** unto thee. 7862
	72:10 of Tarshish and of the isles shall bring **p**: 4503
	76:11 let all that be round about him bring **p** 7862
Mic	1:14 Therefore shalt thou give **p** to 7964

PRESERVE (30) [PRESERVED, PRESERVER, PRESERVEST, PRESERVETH]

Ge	19:32 him, that we may **p** seed of our father. 2421
	19:34 him, that we may **p** seed of our father. 2421
	45: 5 for God did send me before you to **p** life. 4241
	45: 7 God sent me before you to **p** you a 7760
Dt	6:24 he might **p** us alive, as it is at this day. 2421
Ps	12: 7 thou shalt **p** them from this generation 8104
	16: 1 **P** me, O God: for in thee do I put my 8104
	25:21 Let integrity and uprightness **p** me; for I 5341
	32: 7 place; thou shalt **p** me from trouble; 5341
	40:11 and thy truth continually **p** me. 5341
	41: 2 The LORD will **p** him, and keep him 8104
	61: 7 mercy and truth, which may **p** him. 5341
	64: 1 **p** my life from fear of the enemy. 5341
	79:11 **p** thou those that are appointed to die; 3498
	86: 2 **P** my soul; for I am holy: O thou my God, 8104
	121: 7 The LORD shall **p** thee from all evil: 8104
	121: 7 thee from all evil: he shall **p** thy soul. 8104
	121: 8 The LORD shall **p** thy going out and 8104
	140: 1 the evil man; **p** me from the violent man; 5341
	140: 4 the wicked; **p** me from the violent man; 5341
Pr	2:11 Discretion shall **p** thee, understanding 8104
	4: 6 Forsake her not, and she shall **p** thee: 8104
	14: 3 but the lips of the wise shall **p** them. 8104
	20:28 Mercy and truth **p** the king: and his 5341
	22:12 The eyes of the LORD **p** knowledge, 5341
Isa	31: 5 deliver it; and passing over he will **p** it. 4422
	49: 8 I will **p** thee, and give thee for a covenant 5341
Jer	49:11 fatherless children, I will **p** them **alive**; 2421
Lk	17:33 whosoever shall lose his life shall **p** it. 2225
2Ti	4:18 will **p** me unto his heavenly kingdom: 4982

PRESERVED (16) [PRESERVE]

Ge	32:30 seen God face to face, and my life is **p**. 5337

Jos	24:17 **p** us in all the way wherein we went, 8104
1Sa	30:23 hath **p** us, and delivered the company 8104
2Sa	8: 6 the LORD **p** David whithersoever he 3467
	8:14 the LORD **p** David whithersoever he 3467
1Ch	18: 6 Thus the LORD **p** David whithersoever he 3467
	18:13 Thus the LORD **p** David whithersoever he 3467
Job	10:12 and thy visitation hath **p** my spirit. 8104
	29: 2 as in the days when God **p** me; 8104
Ps	37:28 not his saints; they are **p** for ever: 8104
Isa	49: 6 of Jacob, and to restore the **p** of Israel: 5341
Hos	12:13 out of Egypt, and by a prophet was he **p**. 8104
Mt	9:17 wine into new bottles, and both are 4933
Lk	5:38 be put into new bottles; and both are **p**. 4933
1Th	5:23 body be blameless unto the coming of 5083
Jude	1: 1 and **p** in Jesus Christ, and called: 5083

PRESERVER (1) [PRESERVE]

Job	7:20 shall I do unto thee, O thou **p** of men? 5341

PRESERVEST (2) [PRESERVE]

Ne	9: 6 all that is therein, and thou **p** them all; 2421
Ps	36: 6 O LORD, thou **p** man and beast. 3467

PRESERVETH (8) [PRESERVE]

Job	36: 6 He **p** not the **life** of the wicked: 2421
Ps	31:23 for the LORD **p** the faithful, 5341
	97:10 he **p** the souls of his saints; he delivereth 8104
	116: 6 The LORD **p** the simple: I was brought 8104
	145:20 The LORD **p** all them that love him: 8104
	146: 9 The LORD **p** the strangers; he relieveth 8104
Pr	2: 8 of judgment, and **p** the way of his saints. 8104
	16:17 that keepeth his way **p** his soul. 8104

PRESIDENTS (5)

Da	6: 2 over these three **p**; of whom Daniel was 5632
	6: 3 this Daniel was preferred above the **p** and 5632
	6: 4 the **p** and princes sought to find occasion 5632
	6: 6 these **p** and princes assembled together to 5632
	6: 7 All the **p** of the kingdom, the governors, 5632

PRESS (9) [PRESSED, PRESSES, PRESSETH, PRESSFAT, WINEPRESS, WINEPRESSES]

Joel	3:13 for the **p** is full, the fats overflow; 1660
Hag	2:16 for to draw out fifty vessels out of the **p**, 6333
Mk	2: 4 could not come nigh unto him for the **p**, 3793
	5:27 came in the **p** behind, and touched his 3793
	5:30 turned him about in the **p**, and said, 3793
Lk	8:19 and could not come at him for the **p**. 3793
	8:45 throng thee and **p** thee, and sayest thou, 508
	19: 3 and could not for the **p**, because he was 3793
Php	3:14 I **p** toward the mark for the prize of 1377

PRESS CHARGES See ACCUSE; IMPLEAD

PRESSED (15) [PRESS]

Ge	19: 3 he **p** upon them greatly; and they turned 6484
	19: 9 they **p** sore upon the man, even Lot, 6484
	40:11 **p** them into Pharaoh's cup, and I gave 7818
Jdg	16:16 when she **p** him daily with her words, 6693
2Sa	13:25 he **p** him: howbeit he would not go, 6555
	13:27 Absalom **p** him, that he let Amnon and 6555
Est	8:14 and **p** on by the king's commandment, 1765
Eze	23: 3 there were their breasts **p**, and there they 4600
Am	2:13 Behold, I am **p** under you, as a cart is 5781
	2:13 as a cart is **p** that is full of sheaves. 5781
Mk	3:10 that they **p** upon him for to touch 1968
Lk	5: 1 the people **p** upon him to hear the word 1945
	6:38 **p down**, and shaken together, and 4085
Ac	18: 5 Paul was **p** in spirit, and testified of 4912
2Co	1: 8 that we were **p** out of measure, above 916

PRESSES (4) [PRESS]

Ne	13:15 some treading wine **p** on the sabbath, 1660
Pr	3:10 and thy **p** shall burst out with new wine. 3342
Isa	16:10 shall tread out no wine in their **p**; 3342
Jer	48:33 have caused wine to fail from the **wine p**: 3342

PRESSETH (2) [PRESS]

Ps	38: 2 in me, and thy hand **p** me **sore**. 5181+5921
Lk	16:16 God is preached, and every man **p** into it. 971

PRESSFAT (1) [PRESS]

Hag	2:16 when one came to the **p** to draw out 3342

PRESUME (2) [PRESUMED, PRESUMPTUOUS, PRESUMPTUOUSLY]

Dt	18:20 shall **p** to speak a word in my name, 2102
Est	7: 5 is he, that durst **p** in his heart to do so? 4390

PRESUMED (1) [PRESUME]

Nu	14:44 they **p** to go up unto the hill top: 6075

PRESUMPTUOUS (2) [PRESUME]

Ps	19:13 Keep back thy servant also from **p** sins; 2086
2Pe	2:10 **P** are they, selfwilled, they are not afraid 5113

PRESUMPTUOUSLY (6) [PRESUME]

Ex	21:14 if a man **come p** upon his neighbour, 2102
Nu	15:30 the soul that doeth ought **p**, 3027+7311+871.1
Dt	1:43 of the LORD, and went up **p** into the hill. 2102
	17:12 man that will do **p**, and will not 2087+871.1
	17:13 shall hear, and fear, and do no more **p**. 2102
	18:22 the prophet hath spoken it **p**: 2087+871.1

PRETENCE (3)

Mt	23:14 and for a **p** make long prayer: 4392

Mk	12:40 and for a **p** make long prayers:	4392
Php	1:18 every way, whether in **p**, or in truth,	4392

PRETORIUM (1)

Mk	15:16 led him away into the hall, called **P**;	4232

PREVAIL (29) [PREVAILED, PREVAILEST, PREVAILETH]

Ge	7:20 Fifteen cubits upward did the waters **p**;	1396
Nu	22: 6 peradventure I shall **p**, *that* we may smite	3201
Jdg	16: 5 by what *means* we may **p** against him,	3201
1Sa	2: 9 darkness; for by strength shall no man **p**.	1396
	17: 9 if I **p** against him, and kill him, then	3201
	26:25 great things, and also shalt **still p**.	3201+3201
1Ki	22:22 thou shalt persuade *him*, and **p** also:	6613
2Ch	14:11 art our God; let not man **p** against thee.	6113
	18:21 shalt entice *him*, and thou shalt also **p**:	3201
Est	6:13 thou shalt not **p** against him,	3201
Job	15:24 shall **p** against him, as a king ready to	8630
	18: 9 heel, *and* the robber shall **p** against him.	2388
Ps	9:19 Arise, O Lord; let not man **p**:	5810
	12: 4 have said, With our tongue will we **p**;	1396
	65: 3 Iniquities **p** against me: *as for* our	1396
Ecc	4:12 if one **p** against him, two shall withstand	8630
Isa	7: 1 war against it, but could not **p** against it.	3898
	16:12 his sanctuary to pray; but he shall not **p**.	3201
	42:13 yea, roar; he shall **p** against his enemies.	1396
	47:12 be able to profit, if so be thou mayest **p**.	6206
Jer	1:19 shall not **p** against thee; for I *am* with	3201
	5:22 toss themselves, yet can they not **p**;	3201
	15:20 but they shall not **p** against thee:	3201
	20:10 we shall **p** against him, and we shall take	3201
	20:11 shall stumble, and they shall not **p**:	3201
Da	11: 7 and shall deal against them, and shall **p**:	2388
Mt	16:18 and the gates of hell shall not **p** against it.	2729
	27:24 When Pilate saw that he could **p** nothing,	5623
Jn	12:19 Perceive ye how ye **p** nothing?	5623

PREVAILED (37) [PREVAIL]

Ge	7:18 the waters **p**, and were increased greatly	1396
	7:19 the waters **p** exceedingly upon the earth;	1396
	7:24 the waters **p** upon the earth an hundred	1396
	30: 8 I wrestled with my sister, and I have **p**:	3201
	32:25 when he saw that he **p** not against him,	3201
	32:28 with God and with men, and hast **p**.	3201
	47:20 his field, because the famine **p** over them:	2388
	49:26 The blessings of thy father have **p** above	1396
Ex	17:11 Moses held up his hand, that Israel **p**:	1396
	17:11 he let down his hand, Amalek **p**.	1396
Jdg	1:35 yet the hand of the house of Joseph **p**,	3513
	3:10 his hand **p** against Chushan-rishathaim.	5810
	4:24 **p** against Jabin the king of Canaan,	7186
	6: 2 the hand of Midian **p** against Israel:	5810
1Sa	17:50 David **p** over the Philistine with a sling	2388
2Sa	11:23 \the men **p** against us, and came out	1396
	24: 4 Notwithstanding the king's word **p**	2388
1Ki	16:22 the people that followed Omri **p**	2388
2Ki	25: 3 the *fourth* month the famine **p** in the city,	2388
1Ch	5: 2 Judah **p** above his brethren, and of him	1396
	21: 4 Nevertheless the king's word **p** against	2388
2Ch	8: 3 went *to* Hamath-zobah, and **p** against it.	2388
	13:18 children of Judah **p**, because they relied	553
	27: 5 of the Ammonites, and **p** against them.	2388
Ps	13: 4 mine enemy say, I have **p** against him;	3201
	129: 2 my youth: yet they have not **p** against me.	3201
Jer	20: 7 thou art stronger than I, and hast **p**: I am	3201
	38:22 have set thee on, and have **p** against thee:	3201
La	1:16 are desolate, because the enemy **p**.	1396
Da	7:21 war with the saints, and **p** against them;	3202
Hos	12: 4 Yea, he had power over *the* angel, and **p**:	3201
Ob	1: 7 have deceived thee, *and* **p** against thee;	3201
Lk	23:23 voices of them and of the chief priests **p**.	2729
Ac	19:16 and **p** against them, so that *they* fled out	2480
	19:20 So mightily grew the word of God and **p**.	2480
Rev	5: 5 hath **p** to open the book, and to loose	3528
	12: 8 And **p** not; neither was their place found	2480

PREVAILEST (1) [PREVAIL]

Job	14:20 Thou **p** for ever **against** him,	8630

PREVAILETH (1) [PREVAIL]

La	1:13 fire into my bones, and it **p** against them:	7287

PREVALENT See SUPERFLUITY; SUPERFLUOUS

PREVENT (7) [PREVENTED, PREVENTEST]

Job	3:12 Why did the knees **p** me? or why	6923
Ps	59:10 The God of my mercy shall **p** me:	6923
	79: 8 let thy tender mercies speedily **p** us: for	6923
	88:13 in the morning shall my prayer **p** thee.	6923
	119:148 Mine eyes **p** the *night* watches, that I	6923
Am	9:10 The evil shall not overtake nor **p** us.	6923
1Th	4:15 Lord shall not **p** them which are asleep.	5348

PREVENTED (9) [PREVENT]

2Sa	22: 6 me about; the snares of death **p** me:	6923
	22:19 They **p** me in the day of my calamity:	6923
Job	30:27 rested not: the days of affliction **p** me.	6923
	41:11 Who hath **p** me, that I should repay *him*?	6923
Ps	18: 5 me about: the snares of death **p** me:	6923
	18:18 They **p** me in the day of my calamity:	6923
	119:147 I **p** the dawning of the morning, and	6923
Isa	21:14 they **p** with their bread him that fled.	6923
Mt	17:25 Jesus **p** him, saying, What thinkest thou,	4399

PREVENTEST (1) [PREVENT]

Ps	21: 3 For thou **p** him *with* the blessings of	6923

PREY (73)

Ge	49: 9 from the **p**, my son, thou art gone up:	2964
	49:27 in the morning he shall devour the **p**,	5706
Nu	14: 3 our wives and our children should be a **p**?	957
	14:31 little ones, which ye said should be a **p**,	957
	23:24 he shall not lie down until he eat *of* the **p**,	2964
	31:11 and all the **p**, *both* of men and of beasts.	4455
	31:12 the **p**, and the spoil, unto Moses,	4455
	31:26 Take the sum of the **p** that was taken,	4455
	31:27 divide the **p** into two parts; between	4455
	31:32 the rest of the **p** which the men of war	957
Dt	1:39 which ye said should be a **p**,	957
	2:35 Only the cattle we **took for a p** unto	962
	3: 7 of the cities, we **took for a p** to ourselves.	962
Jos	8: 2 shall ye **take for a p** unto yourselves:	962
	8:27 spoil of that city Israel **took for a p** unto	962
	11:14 the children of Israel **took for a p** unto	962
Jdg	5:30 have they *not* divided the **p**; to every man	7998
	5:30 to Sisera a **p** of divers colours, a prey of	7998
	5:30 a **p** of divers colours of needlework,	7998
	8:24 give me every man the earrings of his **p**.	7998
	8:25 therein every man the earrings of his **p**.	7998
2Ki	21:14 they shall become a **p** and a spoil to all	957
Ne	4: 4 give them for a **p** in the land of captivity:	961
Est	3:13 and *to* take the spoil of them for a **p**.	962
	8:11 and *to* take the spoil of them for a **p**,	962
	9:15 but on the **p** they laid not their hand.	961
	9:16 but they laid not their hands on the **p**,	961
Job	4:11 The old lion perisheth for lack of **p**,	2964
	9:26 ships: as the eagle *that* hasteth to the **p**.	400
	24: 5 forth to their work; rising betimes for a **p**:	2964
	38:39 Wilt thou hunt the **p** for the lion? or fill	2964
	39:29 From thence she seeketh the **p**, *and* her	400
Ps	17:12 Like as a lion *that* is greedy of his **p**,	2963
	76: 4 and excellent than the mountains of **p**.	2964
	104:21 young lions roar after *their* **p**, and seek	2964
	124: 6 hath not given us *as* a **p** to their teeth.	2964
Pr	23:28 She also lieth in wait as *for* a **p**,	2863
Isa	5:29 lay hold of the **p**, and shall carry *it* away	2964
	10: 2 that widows may be their **p**, and *that*	7998
	10: 6 to take the **p**, and to tread them down like	957
	31: 4 and the young lion roaring on his **p**,	2964
	33:23 is the **p** of a great spoil divided; the lame	5706
	33:23 a great spoil divided; the lame take the **p**.	957
	42:22 they are for a **p**, and none delivereth; *for*	957
	49:24 Shall the **p** be taken from the mighty,	4455
	49:25 the **p** of the terrible shall be delivered:	4455
	59:15 departeth from evil **maketh** himself a **p**:	7997
Jer	21: 9 and his life shall be unto him for a **p**.	7998
	30:16 all that **p** upon thee I will give for a prey.	962
	30:16 all that prey upon thee I will give for a **p**,	957
	38: 2 for he shall have his life for a **p**,	7998
	39:18 but thy life shall be for a **p** unto thee:	7998
	45: 5 thy life will I give unto thee for a **p** in all	7998
Eze	7:21 it into the hands of the strangers for a **p**,	957
	19: 3 young lion, and it learned to catch the **p**;	2964
	19: 6 to catch the **p**, *and* devoured men.	2964
	22:25 like a roaring lion ravening the **p**;	2964
	22:27 thereof *are* like wolves ravening the **p**,	2964
	26:12 and make a **p** of thy merchandise:	962
	29:19 and take her spoil, and **take** her **p**;	957+962
	34: 8 surely because my flock became a **p**,	957
	34:22 my flock, and they shall no more be a **p**;	957
	34:28 they shall no more be a **p** to the heathen,	957
	36: 4 became a **p** and a derision to the residue	957
	36: 5 despiteful minds, to cast it out for a **p**	957
	38:12 take a spoil, and to **take a p**; to turn	957+962
	38:13 gathered thy company to **take a p**?	957+962
Da	11:24 shall scatter among them the **p**, and spoil,	961
Am	3: 4 lion roar in the forest, when he hath no **p**?	2964
Na	2:12 filled his holes *with* **p**, and his dens *with*	2964
	2:13 I will cut off thy **p** from the earth,	2964
	3: 1 of lies *and* robbery; the **p** departeth not;	2964
Zep	3: 8 until the day that I rise up to the **p**:	5706

PRICE (33) [PRICES, PRISED]

Lev	25:16 of years thou shalt increase the **p** thereof,	4736
	25:16 of years thou shalt diminish the **p** of it:	4736
	25:50 the **p** of his sale shall be according unto	3701
	25:51 **p** of his **redemption** out of the money	1353
	25:52 give *him* again the **p** of his **redemption**.	1353
Dt	23:18 the hire of a whore, or the **p** of a dog,	4242
2Sa	24:24 Nay; but I will surely buy *it* of thee at a **p**:	4242
1Ki	10:28 merchants received the linen yarn at a **p**.	4242
1Ch	21:22 thou shalt grant it me for the full **p**: that	3701
	21:24 Nay; but I will verily buy *it* for the full **p**:	3701
2Ch	1:16 merchants received the linen yarn at a **p**.	4242
Job	28:13 Man knoweth not the **p** thereof; neither	6187
	28:15 neither shall silver be weighed *for* the **p**	4242
	28:18 for the **p** of wisdom *is* above rubies.	4901
Ps	44:12 dost not increase *thy* wealth by their **p**.	4242
Pr	17:16 *is there* a **p** in the hand of a fool	4242
	27:26 and the goats *are* the **p** of the field.	4377
	31:10 for her **p** *is* far above rubies.	4242
Isa	45:13 not for **p** nor reward, saith the Lord of	4242
	55: 1 and milk without money and without **p**.	4242
Jer	15:13 treasures will I give to the spoil without **p**,	4242
Zec	11:12 them, If ye think good, give *me* my **p**;	7939
	11:12 they weighed *for* my **p** thirty *pieces* of	7939
	11:13 a goodly **p** that I was prised at of them.	3366
Mt	13:46 when he had found one pearl of **great p**,	4186
	27: 6 the treasury, because it is the **p** of blood.	5092

Mt	27: 9 of silver, the **p** of him that was valued,	5092
Ac	5: 2 And kept back *part* of the **p**, his wife also	5092
	5: 3 and to keep back *part* of the **p** of the land?	5092
	19:19 all *men*: and they counted the **p** of them,	5092
1Co	6:20 For ye are bought with a **p**: therefore	5092
	7:23 Ye are bought with a **p**; be not ye	5092
1Pe	3: 4 which is in the sight of God of **great p**.	4185

PRICES (1) [PRICE]

Ac	4:34 brought the **p** of the *things* that were sold,	5092

PRICKED (2) [PRICKING]

Ps	73:21 was grieved, and I was **p** in my reins.	8150
Ac	2:37 when they heard *this*, they were **p** in	2660

PRICKING (1) [PRICKED, PRICKS]

Eze	28:24 there shall be no more a **p** brier unto	3992

PRICKS (3) [PRICKING]

Nu	33:55 remain of them *shall be* **p** in your eyes,	7899
Ac	9: 5 *it is* hard for thee to kick against the **p**.	2759
	26:14 *it is* hard for thee to kick against the **p**.	2759

PRIDE (49) [PROUD, PROUDLY]

Lev	26:19 I will break the **p** of your power; and I	1347
1Sa	17:28 I know thy **p**, and the naughtiness of	2087
2Ch	32:26 humbled himself for the **p** of his heart,	1363
Job	33:17 *from his* purpose, and hide **p** from man.	1466
	35:12 because of the **p** of evil men.	1347
	41:15 *His* **scales** *are his* **p**, shut up *together as*	1346
	41:34 he *is* a king over all the children of **p**.	7830
Ps	10: 2 The wicked in *his* **p** doth persecute	1346
	10: 4 through the **p** of his countenance,	1363
	31:20 secret of thy presence from the **p** of man:	7407
	36:11 Let not the foot of **p** come against me,	1346
	59:12 lips let them even be taken in their **p**:	1347
	73: 6 Therefore **p** compasseth them about as a	1346
Pr	8:13 **p**, and arrogancy, and the evil way,	1344
	11: 2 *When* **p** cometh, then cometh shame:	2087
	13:10 Only by **p** cometh contention: but with	2087
	14: 3 In the mouth of the foolish *is* a rod of **p**:	1346
	16:18 **P** *goeth* before destruction, and a haughty	1347
	29:23 A man's **p** shall bring him low:	1346
Isa	9: 9 that say in the **p** and stoutness of heart,	1346
	16: 6 We have heard of the **p** of Moab; *he is*	1347
	16: 6 his haughtiness, and his **p**, and his wrath:	1347
	23: 9 to stain the **p** of all glory, *and* to bring	1347
	25:11 he shall bring down their **p** together with	1346
	28: 1 Woe to the crown of **p**, to the drunkards	1348
	28: 3 crown of **p**, the drunkards of Ephraim,	1348
Jer	13: 9 this manner will I mar the **p** of Judah,	1347
	13: 9 of Judah, and the great **p** of Jerusalem.	1347
	13:17 shall weep in secret places for *your* **p**;	1466
	48:29 We have heard of the **p** of Moab; *he is*	1347
	48:29 his **p**, and the haughtiness of his heart.	1346
	49:16 deceived thee, *and* the **p** of thine heart,	2087
Eze	7:10 the rod hath blossomed, **p** hath budded.	2087
	16:49 **p**, fulness of bread, and abundance of	1347
	16:56 by thy mouth in the day of thy **p**,	1347
	30: 6 and the **p** of her power shall come down:	1347
Da	4:37 those that walk in **p** he *is* able to abase.	1467
	5:20 lifted up, and his mind hardened in **p**,	2103
Hos	5: 5 the **p** of Israel doth testify to his face:	1347
	7:10 the **p** of Israel testifieth to his face:	1347
Ob	1: 3 The **p** of thine heart hath deceived thee,	2087
Zep	2:10 This shall they have for their **p**, because	1347
	3:11 midst of them that rejoice in thy **p**,	1346
Zec	9: 6 and I will cut off the **p** of the Philistines.	1347
	10:11 the **p** of Assyria shall be brought down,	1347
	11: 3 young lions; for the **p** of Jordan is spoiled.	1347
Mk	7:22 an evil eye, blasphemy, **p**, foolishness:	5243
1Ti	3: 6 lest being **lifted up with p** he fall into	5187
1Jn	2:16 and the lust of the eyes, and the **p** of life,	212

PRIEST (496) [PRIEST'S, PRIESTHOOD, PRIESTS, PRIESTS']

Ge	14:18 and he *was* the **p** of the most high God.	3548
	41:45 the daughter of Poti-pherah **p** of On.	3548
	41:50 of Poti-pherah **p** of On bare unto him.	3548
	46:20 of Poti-pherah **p** of On bare unto him.	3548
Ex	2:16 the **p** of Midian had seven daughters:	3548
	3: 1 Jethro his father in law, the **p** of Midian:	3548
	18: 1 When Jethro, the **p** of Midian,	3548
	29:30 that son that is **p** in his stead shall put	3548
	31:10 the holy garments for Aaron the **p**,	3548
	35:19 *place*, the holy garments for Aaron the **p**,	3548
	38:21 the hand of Ithamar, son to Aaron the **p**.	3548
	39:41 and the holy garments for Aaron the **p**,	3548
Lev	1: 7 the sons of Aaron the **p** shall put fire	3548
	1: 9 the **p** shall burn all on the altar, *to be* a	3548
	1:12 the **p** shall lay them in order on the wood	3548
	1:13 the **p** shall bring it all, and burn *it* upon	3548
	1:15 the **p** shall bring it unto the altar,	3548
	1:17 the **p** shall burn it upon the altar, upon	3548
	2: 2 the **p** shall burn the memorial of it upon	3548
	2: 8 when it is presented unto the **p**, he shall	3548
	2: 9 the **p** shall take from the meat offering a	3548
	2:16 the **p** shall burn the memorial of it, *part of*	3548
	3:11 the **p** shall burn it upon the altar: *it is*	3548
	3:16 the **p** shall burn them upon the altar: *it is*	3548
	4: 3 If the **p** that is anointed do sin according	3548
	4: 5 the **p** that is anointed shall take of	3548
	4: 6 the **p** shall dip his finger in the blood,	3548
	4: 7 the **p** shall put *some* of the blood upon	3548
	4:10 the **p** shall burn them upon the altar of	3548

Lev 4:16 the **p** that is anointed shall bring of	3548
4:17 the **p** shall dip his finger *in some* of	3548
4:20 the **p** shall make an atonement for them,	3548
4:25 the **p** shall take of the blood of the sin	3548
4:26 the **p** shall make an atonement for him as	3548
4:30 the **p** shall take of the blood thereof with	3548
4:31 the **p** shall burn *it* upon the altar for a	3548
4:31 the **p** shall make an atonement for him,	3548
4:34 the **p** shall take of the blood of the sin	3548
4:35 the **p** shall burn them upon the altar,	3548
4:35 the **p** shall make an atonement for his sin	3548
5: 6 the **p** shall make an atonement for him	3548
5: 8 he shall bring them unto the **p**, who shall	3548
5:10 the **p** shall make an atonement for him for	3548
5:12 he bring it to the **p**, and the priest shall	3548
5:12 the **p** shall take his handful of it, *even* a	3548
5:13 the **p** shall make an atonement for him as	3548
5:16 fifth *part* thereto, and give it unto the **p**:	3548
5:16 the **p** shall make an atonement for him	3548
5:18 for a trespass offering, unto the **p**:	3548
5:18 the **p** shall make an atonement for him	3548
6: 6 for a trespass offering, unto the **p**:	3548
6: 7 the **p** shall make an atonement for him	3548
6:10 the **p** shall put on his linen garment,	3548
6:12 **p** shall burn wood on it every morning,	3548
6:22 the **p** of his sons that is anointed in his	3548
6:23 For every meat offering for the **p** shall be	3548
6:26 The **p** that offereth it for sin shall eat it:	3548
7: 5 the **p** shall burn them upon the altar *for*	3548
7: 7 the **p** that maketh atonement therewith	3548
7: 8 the **p** that offereth *any* man's burnt	3548
7: 8 the **p** have to himself the skin of the	3548
7:31 the **p** shall burn the fat upon the altar:	3548
7:32 the right shoulder shall ye give unto the **p**	3548
7:34 have given them unto Aaron the **p** and	3548
12: 6 of the congregation, unto the **p**:	3548
12: 8 the **p** shall make an atonement for her,	3548
13: 2 he shall be brought unto Aaron the **p**,	3548
13: 3 the **p** shall look on the plague in the skin	3548
13: 3 the **p** shall look on him, and pronounce	3548
13: 4 **p** shall shut up *him that hath* the plague	3548
13: 5 the **p** shall look on him the seventh day:	3548
13: 5 the **p** shall shut him up seven days more:	3548
13: 6 the **p** shall look on him again the seventh	3548
13: 6 the skin, the **p** shall pronounce him clean:	3548
13: 7 after that he hath been seen of the **p** for	3548
13: 7 he shall be seen of the **p** again:	3548
13: 8 the **p** see that behold, the scab spreadeth	3548
13: 8 then the **p** shall pronounce him unclean:	3548
13: 9 then he shall be brought unto the **p**;	3548
13:10 **p** shall see *him:* and behold, *if* the rising	3548
13:11 the **p** shall pronounce him unclean,	3548
13:12 to his foot, wheresoever the **p** looketh;	3548
13:13 the **p** shall consider: and behold,	3548
13:15 the **p** shall see the raw flesh,	3548
13:16 unto white, he shall come unto the **p**;	3548
13:17 the **p** shall see him: and behold,	3548
13:17 the **p** shall pronounce *him* clean *that hath*	3548
13:19 and it be shewed to the **p**;	3548
13:20 when the **p** seeth it, behold, it *be* in sight	3548
13:20 the **p** shall pronounce him unclean:	3548
13:21 if the **p** look on it, and behold, *there be*	3548
13:21 then the **p** shall shut him up seven days:	3548
13:22 then the **p** shall pronounce him unclean:	3548
13:23 and the **p** shall pronounce him clean.	3548
13:25 the **p** look upon it: and behold,	3548
13:25 wherefore the **p** shall pronounce him	3548
13:26 if the **p** look on it, and behold, *there be*	3548
13:26 then the **p** shall shut him up seven days:	3548
13:27 **p** shall look upon him the seventh day:	3548
13:27 then the **p** shall pronounce him unclean:	3548
13:28 and the **p** shall pronounce him clean:	3548
13:30 the **p** shall see the plague: and behold,	3548
13:30 then the **p** shall pronounce him unclean:	3548
13:31 if the **p** look on the plague of the scall,	3548
13:31 **p** shall shut up *him that hath* the plague	3548
13:32 in the seventh day the **p** shall look on	3548
13:33 the **p** shall shut up *him that hath* the scall	3548
13:34 in the seventh day the **p** shall look on	3548
13:34 then the **p** shall pronounce him clean:	3548
13:36 the **p** shall look on him: and behold,	3548
13:36 the **p** not seek for yellow hair:	3548
13:37 and the **p** shall pronounce him clean.	3548
13:39 the **p** shall look: and behold, *if* the bright	3548
13:43 the **p** shall look upon it: and behold,	3548
13:44 **p** shall pronounce him utterly unclean;	3548
13:49 leprosy, and shall be shewed unto the **p**:	3548
13:50 the **p** shall look upon the plague	3548
13:53 if the **p** look, and behold, the plague	3548
13:54 the **p** shall command that they wash	3548
13:55 the **p** shall look on the plague, after *that*	3548
13:56 if the **p** look, and behold, the plague *be*	3548
14: 2 He shall be brought unto the **p**:	3548
14: 3 the **p** shall go forth out of the camp;	3548
14: 3 the **p** shall look, and behold, *if* the plague	3548
14: 4 the **p** command to take for him that is	3548
14: 5 the **p** command that one of the birds	3548
14:11 the **p** that maketh *him* clean shall present	3548
14:12 the **p** shall take one he lamb, and offer	3548
14:14 the **p** shall take *some* of the blood of	3548
14:14 the **p** shall put *it* upon the tip of the right	3548
14:15 the **p** shall take *some* of the log of oil,	3548
14:16 the **p** shall dip his right finger in the oil	3548
14:17 **p** put upon the tip of the right ear of him	3548
14:18 the **p** shall make an atonement for him	3548

Lev 14:19 the **p** shall offer the sin offering,	3548
14:20 the **p** shall offer the burnt offering and	3548
14:20 the **p** shall make an atonement for him,	3548
14:23 eighth day for his cleansing unto the **p**,	3548
14:24 the **p** shall take the lamb of the trespass	3548
14:24 the **p** shall wave them *for* a wave offering	3548
14:25 the **p** shall take *some* of the blood of	3548
14:26 the **p** shall pour of the oil into the palm	3548
14:27 the **p** shall sprinkle with his right finger	3548
14:28 the **p** shall put of the oil that *is* in his	3548
14:31 the **p** shall make an atonement for him	3548
14:35 the house shall come and tell the **p**,	3548
14:36 the **p** command that they empty	3548
14:36 before the **p** go *into it* to see the plague,	3548
14:36 the **p** shall go in to see the house:	3548
14:38 the **p** shall go out of the house to the	3548
14:39 the **p** shall come again the seventh day,	3548
14:40 the **p** command that they take away	3548
14:44 the **p** shall come and look, and behold,	3548
14:48 if the **p** shall come in, and look *upon it,*	3548
14:48 the **p** pronounce the house clean,	3548
15:14 congregation, and give them unto the **p**:	3548
15:15 the **p** shall offer them, the one *for* a sin	3548
15:15 the **p** shall make an atonement for him	3548
15:29 pigeons, and bring them unto the **p**,	3548
15:30 the **p** shall offer the one *for* a sin offering,	3548
15:30 the **p** shall make an atonement for her	3548
16:30 For on that day shall *the p* make an	NIH
16:32 the **p**, whom he shall anoint, and whom	3548
17: 5 unto the **p**, and offer them *for* peace	3548
17: 6 **p** shall sprinkle the blood upon the altar	3548
19:22 the **p** shall make an atonement for him	3548
21: 9 the daughter of any **p**, if she profane	3548
21:10 *he that is* the high **p** among his brethren,	3548
21:21 a blemish, of the seed of Aaron the **p**,	3548
22:11 if the **p** buy *any* soul with his money,	3548
22:14 give *it* unto the **p** with the holy *thing.*	3548
23:10 the firstfruits of your harvest unto the **p**:	3548
23:11 the morrow after the sabbath the **p** shall	3548
23:20 the **p** shall wave them with the bread of	3548
23:20 they shall be holy to the LORD for the **p**.	3548
27: 8 he shall present himself before the **p**,	3548
27: 8 the priest, and the **p** shall value him;	3548
27: 8 ability that vowed shall the **p** value him.	3548
27:11 he shall present the beast before the **p**:	3548
27:12 the **p** shall value it, whether it be good or	3548
27:12 valuest it, *who art* the **p**, so shall it be.	3548
27:14 the **p** shall estimate it, whether it be good	3548
27:14 as the **p** shall estimate it, so shall it stand.	3548
27:18 the **p** shall reckon unto him the money	3548
27:23 the **p** shall reckon unto him the worth of	3548
Nu 3: 6 and present them before Aaron the **p**,	3548
3:32 Eleazar the son of Aaron the **p** *shall be*	3548
4:16 Aaron the **p** pertaineth the oil for the	3548
4:28 hand of Ithamar the son of Aaron the **p**.	3548
4:33 hand of Ithamar the son of Aaron the **p**.	3548
5: 8 unto the LORD, *even* to the **p**;	3548
5: 9 which they bring unto the **p**, shall be his.	3548
5:10 whatsoever any man giveth the **p**, it shall	3548
5:15 shall the man bring his wife unto the **p**,	3548
5:16 the **p** shall bring her near, and set her	3548
5:17 the **p** shall take holy water in an earthen	3548
5:17 floor of the tabernacle the **p** shall take,	3548
5:18 the **p** shall set the woman before	3548
5:18 the **p** shall have in his hand the bitter	3548
5:19 the **p** shall charge her by an oath,	3548
5:21 **p** shall charge the woman with an oath	3548
5:21 the **p** shall say unto the woman,	3548
5:23 the **p** shall write these curses in a book,	3548
5:25 the **p** shall take the jealousy offering out	3548
5:26 the **p** shall take a handful of the offering,	3548
5:30 the **p** shall execute upon her all this law.	3548
6:10 turtles, or two young pigeons, to the **p**,	3548
6:11 the **p** shall offer the one for a sin offering,	3548
6:16 the **p** shall bring *them* before the LORD,	3548
6:17 the **p** shall offer also his meat offering,	3548
6:19 the **p** shall take the sodden shoulder of	3548
6:20 the **p** shall wave them *for* a wave offering	3548
6:20 this *is* holy for the **p**, with the wave	3548
7: 8 hand of Ithamar the son of Aaron the **p**.	3548
15:25 the **p** shall make an atonement for all	3548
15:28 the **p** shall make an atonement for the	3548
16:37 unto Eleazar the son of Aaron the **p**,	3548
16:39 Eleazar the **p** took the brasen censers,	3548
18:28 LORD's heave offering to Aaron the **p**.	3548
19: 3 ye shall give her unto Eleazar the **p**, that	3548
19: 4 Eleazar the **p** shall take of her blood with	3548
19: 6 the **p** shall take cedar wood, and hyssop,	3548
19: 7 the **p** shall wash his clothes, and he shall	3548
19: 7 and the **p** shall be unclean until the even.	3548
25: 7 the son of Eleazar, the son of Aaron the **p**,	3548
25:11 the son of Eleazar, the son of Aaron the **p**,	3548
26: 1 and unto Eleazar the son of Aaron the **p**,	3548
26: 3 Eleazar the **p** spake with them in the	3548
26:63 numbered by Moses and Eleazar the **p**,	3548
26:64 whom Moses and Aaron the **p** numbered,	3548
27: 2 before Eleazar the **p**, and before the	3548
27:19 set him before Eleazar the **p**, and before	3548
27:21 he shall stand before Eleazar the **p**,	3548
27:22 set him before Eleazar the **p**, and before	3548
31: 6 and Phinehas the son of Eleazar the **p**,	3548
31:12 Eleazar the **p**, and unto the congregation	3548
31:13 Eleazar the **p**, and all the princes of	3548
31:21 Eleazar the **p** said unto the men of war	3548
31:26 Eleazar the **p**, and the chief fathers of	3548

Nu 31:29 their half, and give *it* unto Eleazar the **p**,	3548
31:31 Eleazar the **p** did as the LORD	3548
31:41 unto Eleazar the **p**, as the LORD	3548
31:51 and Eleazar the **p** took the gold of them,	3548
31:54 Eleazar the **p** took the gold of the captains	3548
32: 2 to Eleazar the **p**, and unto the princes of	3548
32:28 them Moses commanded Eleazar the **p**,	3548
33:38 Aaron the **p** went up into mount Hor at	3548
34:17 Eleazar the **p**, and Joshua the son of Nun.	3548
35:25 abide in it unto the death of the high **p**,	3548
35:28 of his refuge until the death of the high **p**:	3548
35:28 after the death of the high **p** the slayer	3548
35:32 dwell in the land, until the death of the **p**.	3548
Dt 17:12 will not hearken unto the **p** that standeth	3548
18: 3 they shall give unto the **p** the shoulder,	3548
20: 2 that the **p** shall approach and speak unto	3548
26: 3 thou shalt go unto the **p** that shall be in	3548
26: 4 the **p** shall take the basket out of thine	3548
Jos 14: 1 which Eleazar the **p**, and Joshua the son	3548
17: 4 they came near before Eleazar the **p**,	3548
19:51 which Eleazar the **p**, and Joshua the son	3548
20: 6 until the death of the high **p** that shall be	3548
21: 1 fathers of the Levites unto Eleazar the **p**,	3548
21: 4 the children of Aaron the **p**, *which were*	3548
21:13 of Aaron the **p** Hebron with her suburbs,	3548
22:13 Phinehas the son of Eleazar the **p**,	3548
22:30 when Phinehas the **p**, and the princes of	3548
22:31 Phinehas the son of Eleazar the **p** said	3548
22:32 Phinehas the son of Eleazar the **p**,	3548
Jdg 17: 5 one of his sons, who became his **p**.	3548
17:10 be unto me a father and a **p**, and I will	3548
17:12 the young man became his **p**, and was in	3548
17:13 me good, seeing I have a Levite to *my* **p**.	3548
18: 4 me, and hath hired me, and I am his **p**.	3548
18: 6 the **p** said unto them, Go in peace:	3548
18:17 the **p** stood *in* the entering of the gate	3548
18:18 Then said the **p** unto them, What do ye?	3548
18:19 go with us, and be to us a father and a **p**:	3548
18:19 *it* better for thee to be a **p** unto the house	3548
18:19 that thou be a **p** unto a tribe and a family	3548
18:24 I made, and the **p**, and ye are gone away:	3548
18:27 the **p** which he had, and came unto Laish,	3548
1Sa 1: 9 Now Eli the **p** sat upon a seat by a post of	3548
2:11 minister unto the LORD before Eli the **p**.	3548
2:14 that the fleshhook brought up the **p** took	3548
2:15 sacrificed, Give flesh to roast for the **p**;	3548
2:28 out of all the tribes of Israel to be my **p**,	3548
2:35 I will raise me up a faithful **p**, *that* shall	3548
14: 3 the son of Eli, the LORD's **p** in Shiloh,	3548
14:19 to pass, while Saul talked unto the **p**,	3548
14:19 Saul said unto the **p**, Withdraw thine	3548
14:36 said the **p**, Let us draw near hither unto	3548
21: 1 came David to Nob to Ahimelech the **p**:	3548
21: 2 David said unto Ahimelech the **p**, The	3548
21: 4 the **p** answered David, and said, *There is*	3548
21: 5 David answered the **p**, and said unto him,	3548
21: 6 So the **p** gave him hallowed *bread:* for	3548
21: 9 the **p** said, The sword of Goliath	3548
22:11 the king sent to call Ahimelech the **p**,	3548
23: 9 he said to Abiathar the **p**, Bring hither	3548
30: 7 David said to Abiathar the **p**,	3548
2Sa 15:27 The king said also unto Zadok the **p**,	3548
1Ki 1: 7 son of Zeruiah, and with Abiathar the **p**:	3548
1: 8 Zadok the **p**, and Benaiah the son of	3548
1:19 Abiathar the **p**, and Joab the captain of	3548
1:25 captains of the host, and Abiathar the **p**;	3548
1:26 Zadok the **p**, and Benaiah the son of	3548
1:32 Call me Zadok the **p**, and Nathan	3548
1:34 let Zadok the **p** and Nathan the prophet	3548
1:38 So Zadok the **p**, and Nathan the prophet,	3548
1:39 Zadok the **p** took a horn of oil out of	3548
1:42 Jonathan the son of Abiathar the **p** came:	3548
1:44 the king hath sent with him Zadok the **p**,	3548
1:45 Zadok the **p** and Nathan the prophet have	3548
2:22 for Abiathar the **p**, and for Joab the son of	3548
2:26 unto Abiathar the **p** said the king, Get	3548
2:27 Abiathar from being **p** unto the LORD;	3548
2:35 Zadok the **p** did the king put in the room	3548
4: 2 he had; Azariah the son of Zadok the **p**,	3548
2Ki 11: 9 things that Jehoiada the **p** commanded:	3548
11: 9 the sabbath, and came to Jehoiada the **p**,	3548
11:10 the captains over hundreds did the **p** give	3548
11:15 Jehoiada the **p** commanded the captains	3548
11:15 For the **p** had said, Let her not be slain *in*	3548
11:18 Mattan the **p** of Baal before the altars.	3548
11:18 the **p** appointed officers over the house of	3548
12: 2 where*in* Jehoiada the **p** instructed him.	3548
12: 7 king Jehoash called for Jehoiada the **p**,	3548
12: 9 Jehoiada the **p** took a chest, and bored a	3548
12:10 the king's scribe and the high **p** came up,	3548
16:10 king Ahaz sent to Urijah the **p** the fashion	3548
16:11 Urijah the **p** built an altar according to all	3548
16:11 Urijah the **p** made *it* against king Ahaz	3548
16:15 king Ahaz commanded Urijah the **p**,	3548
16:16 Thus did Urijah the **p**, according to all	3548
22: 4 Go up to Hilkiah the high **p**, that he may	3548
22: 8 Hilkiah the high **p** said unto Shaphan	3548
22:10 Hilkiah the **p** hath delivered me a book.	3548
22:12 the king commanded Hilkiah the **p**,	3548
22:14 Hilkiah the **p**, and Ahikam, and Achbor,	3548
23: 4 the king commanded Hilkiah the high **p**,	3548
23:24 the **p** found *in* the house of the LORD.	3548
25:18 of the guard took Seraiah the chief **p**,	3548
25:18 Zephaniah the second **p**, and the three	3548
1Ch 16:39 Zadok the **p**, and his brethren the priests,	3548

1Ch 24: 6	Zadok the **p**, and Ahimelech the son of	3548
27: 5	Benaiah the son of Jehoiada, a chief **p:**	3548
29:22	be the chief governor, and Zadok to be **p.**	3548
2Ch 13: 9	the *same* may be a **p** of *them that are* no	3548
15: 3	without a teaching **p**, and without law.	3548
19:11	Amariah the chief **p** *is* over you in all	3548
22:11	king Jehoram, the wife of Jehoiada the **p**,	3548
23: 8	that Jehoiada the **p** had commanded,	3548
23: 8	for Jehoiada the **p** dismissed not	3548
23: 9	Moreover Jehoiada the **p** delivered to	3548
23:14	Jehoiada the **p** brought out the captains of	3548
23:14	For the **p** said, Slay her not *in* the house	3548
23:17	Mattan the **p** of Baal before the altars.	3548
24: 2	the LORD all the days of Jehoiada the **p**.	3548
24:20	upon Zechariah the son of Jehoiada the **p**,	3548
24:25	the blood of the sons of Jehoiada the **p**,	3548
26:17	Azariah the **p** went in after him,	3548
26:20	Azariah the chief **p**, and all the priests,	3548
31:10	Azariah the chief **p** of the house of Zadok	3548
34: 9	when they came to Hilkiah the high **p**,	3548
34:14	Hilkiah the **p** found a book of the law of	3548
34:18	Hilkiah the **p** hath given me a book.	3548
Ezr 2:63	*things* till there stood *up* a **p** with Urim	3548
7: 5	of Eleazar, the son of Aaron the chief **p:**	3548
7:11	the king Artaxerxes gave unto Ezra the **p**,	3548
7:12	king of kings, unto Ezra the **p**,	3549
7:21	that whatsoever Ezra the **p**, the scribe of	3549
8:33	hand of Meremoth the son of Uriah the **p;**	3548
10:10	Ezra the **p** stood up, and said unto them,	3548
10:16	Ezra the **p**, *with* certain chief of the	3548
Ne 3: 1	Eliashib the high **p** rose up with his	3548
3:20	door of the house of Eliashib the high **p.**	3548
7:65	*things*, till there stood *up* a **p** with Urim	3548
8: 2	Ezra the **p** brought the law before	3548
8: 9	Ezra the **p** the scribe, and the Levites that	3548
10:38	the **p** the son of Aaron shall be with	3548
12:26	governor, and of Ezra the **p**, the scribe.	3548
13: 4	before this, Eliashib the **p**, having	3548
13:13	Shelemiah the **p**, and Zadok the scribe,	3548
13:28	of Joiada, the son of Eliashib the high **p**,	3548
Ps 110: 4	Thou *art* a **p** for ever after the order of	3548
Isa 8: 2	Uriah the **p**, and Zechariah the son of	3548
24: 2	shall be, as *with* the people, so *with* the **p;**	3548
28: 7	the **p** and the prophet have erred through	3548
Jer 6:13	the prophet even unto the **p** every one	3548
8:10	the prophet even unto the **p** every one	3548
14:18	the **p** go about into a land that they know	3548
18:18	for the law shall not perish from the **p**,	3548
20: 1	Now Pashur the son of Immer the **p**,	3548
21: 1	Zephaniah the son of Maaseiah the **p**,	3548
23:11	For both prophet and **p** are profane; yea,	3548
23:33	or the prophet, or a **p**, shall ask thee,	3548
23:34	and the **p**, and the people, that shall say,	3548
29:25	to Zephaniah the son of Maaseiah the **p**,	3548
29:26	The LORD hath made thee **p** in the stead	3548
29:26	thee priest in the stead of Jehoiada the **p**,	3548
29:29	Zephaniah the **p** read this letter in the	3548
37: 3	Zephaniah the son of Maaseiah the **p** to	3548
52:24	of the guard took Seraiah the chief **p**,	3548
52:24	Zephaniah the second **p**, and the three	3548
La 2: 6	of his anger the king and the **p**.	3548
2:20	shall the **p** and the prophet be slain in	3548
Eze 1: 3	LORD came expressly unto Ezekiel the **p**,	3548
7:26	the law shall perish from the **p**,	3548
44:13	unto me, to **do the office of a p** unto me,	3547
44:21	Neither shall any **p** drink wine, when they	3548
44:22	of Israel, or a widow that had a **p** before.	3548
44:30	ye shall also give unto the **p** the first of	3548
45:19	the **p** shall take of the blood of the sin	3548
Hos 4: 4	people *are* as they that strive with the **p**.	3548
4: 6	reject thee, that *thou* shalt be no **p** to me:	3547
4: 9	shall be, like people, like **p:** and I will	3548
Am 7:10	Amaziah the **p** of Beth-el sent to	3548
Hag 1: 1	to Joshua the son of Josedech the high **p**,	3548
1:12	Joshua the son of Josedech the high **p**,	3548
1:14	of Joshua the son of Josedech the high **p**	3548
2: 2	to Joshua the son of Josedech the high **p**	3548
2: 4	O Joshua, son of Josedech, the high **p;**	3548
Zec 3: 1	he shewed me Joshua the high **p** standing	3548
3: 8	Joshua the high **p**, thou, and thy fellows	3548
6:11	of Joshua the son of Josedech the high **p;**	3548
6:13	he shall be a **p** upon his throne:	3548
Mt 8: 4	shew thyself to the **p**, and offer the gift	2409
26: 3	the people, unto the palace of the high **p**,	749
26:57	Jesus led *him* away to Caiaphas the high **p**,	749
26:62	And the high **p** arose, and said unto him,	749
26:63	the high **p** answered and said unto him,	749
26:65	Then the high **p** rent his clothes, saying,	749
Mk 1:44	shew thyself to the **p**, and offer for thy	2409
2:26	of God in the days of Abiathar the high **p**,	749
14:47	and smote a servant of the high **p**,	749
14:53	And they led Jesus away to the high **p:**	749
14:54	afar off, even into the palace of the high **p:**	749
14:60	And the high **p** stood up in the midst,	749
14:61	Again the high **p** asked him, and said unto	749
14:63	Then the high **p** rent his clothes, and saith,	749
14:66	cometh one of the maids of the high **p:**	749
Lk 1: 5	of Judea, a certain **p** named Zacharias,	2409
5:14	man: but go, and shew thyself to the **p**,	2409
10:31	by chance there came down a certain **p**	2409
22:50	of them smote the servant of the high **p**,	749
Jn 11:49	being the high **p** that *same* year, said unto	749
11:51	but being high **p** that year, he prophesied	749
18:13	which was the high **p** that *same* year.	749
18:15	that disciple was known unto the high **p**,	749

Jn 18:15	in with Jesus into the palace of the high **p**.	749
18:16	which was known unto the high **p**,	749
18:19	The high **p** then asked Jesus of his disciples,	749
18:22	saying, Answerest thou the high **p** so?	749
18:24	sent him bound unto Caiaphas the high **p**.	749
18:26	One of the servants of the high **p**, being *his*	749
Ac 4: 6	And Annas the high **p**, and Caiaphas,	749
4: 6	many as were of the kindred of the high **p**,	748
5:17	Then the high **p** rose up, and all they that	749
5:21	But the high **p** came, and they that were	749
5:24	Now when the *high* **p** and the captain of	2409
5:27	the council: and the high **p** asked them,	749
7: 1	Then said the high **p**, Are these *things* so?	749
9: 1	of the Lord, went unto the high **p**,	749
14:13	Then the **p** of Jupiter, which was before	2409
22: 5	As also the high **p** doth bear me witness,	749
23: 2	And the high **p** Ananias commanded them	749
23: 4	stood by said, Revilest thou God's high **p?**	749
23: 5	wist not, brethren, that he was the high **p:**	749
24: 1	And after five days Ananias the high **p**	749
25: 2	Then the high **p** and the chief of the Jews	749
Heb 2:17	faithful high **p** *in* things pertaining to God,	749
3: 1	the Apostle and **High P** of our profession,	749
4:14	Seeing then that we have a great high **p**,	749
4:15	For we have not a high **p** which cannot be	749
5: 1	For every high **p** taken from among men is	749
5: 5	glorified not himself to be made a high **p;**	749
5: 6	**p** for ever after the order of Melchisedec.	2409
5:10	Called of God a high **p** after the order of	749
6:20	made a high **p** for ever after the order of	749
7: 1	king of Salem, **p** of the most high God,	2409
7: 3	the Son of God; abideth a **p** continually.	749
7:11	further need *was there* that another **p**	2409
7:15	of Melchisedec there ariseth another **p**,	2409
7:17	Thou *art* a **p** for ever after the order of	2409
7:20	as not without an oath *he was made* **p:**	NIG
7:21	Thou *art* a **p** for ever after the order of	2409
7:26	For such a high **p** became us, *who is* holy,	749
8: 1	We have such a high **p**, who is set on	749
8: 3	For every high **p** is ordained to offer gifts	749
8: 4	if he were on earth, he should not be a **p**,	2409
9: 7	But into the second *went* the high **p** alone	749
9:11	But Christ being come a high **p** of good	749
9:25	as the high **p** entereth into the holy *place*	749
10:11	every **p** standeth daily ministering and	2409
10:21	And *having* a high **p** over the house of	2409
13:11	into the sanctuary by the high **p** for sin,	749

PRIEST'S (46) [PRIEST]

Ex 28: 1	may **minister** unto me **in the p office**.	3547
28: 3	may **minister** unto me **in the p office**.	3547
28: 4	may **minister** unto me **in the p office**.	3547
28:41	may **minister** unto me **in the p office**.	3547
29: 1	to **minister** unto me **in the p office:**	3547
29: 9	the **p office** shall be theirs for a perpetual	3550
29:44	sons, to **minister** to me **in the p office**.	3547
30:30	may **minister** unto me **in the p office**.	3547
31:10	of his sons, to **minister in the p office**,	3547
35:19	of his sons, to **minister in the p office**,	3547
39:41	garments, to **minister in the p office**,	3547
40:13	may **minister** unto me **in the p office**,	3547
40:15	may **minister** unto me **in the p office:**	3547
Lev 5:13	the *remnant* shall be the **p**, as a 3548+3807.1	
7: 9	in the pan, shall be the **p** that offereth it.	3548
7:14	it shall be the **p** that sprinkleth 3548+3807.1	
7:35	**minister** unto the LORD in the **p office;**	3547
14:13	for as the sin offering *is* the **p**, *so is*	3548
14:18	the remnant of the oil that *is* in the **p** hand	3548
14:29	the rest of the oil that *is* in the **p** hand he	3548
16:32	**minister in the p office** in his father's	3547
22:10	eat of the holy *thing:* a sojourner of the **p**,	3548
22:12	If the **p** daughter also be *married* unto a	3548
22:13	if the **p** daughter be a widow, or divorced,	3548
27:21	the possession thereof shall be the **p**.	3548
Nu 3: 3	consecrated to **minister in the p office**.	3547
3: 4	Ithamar **ministered in the p office** in	3547
3:10	and they shall wait on their **p office:**	3550
18: 7	sons with thee shall keep your **p office**	3550
18: 7	I have given your **p office** *unto you as* a	3550
Dt 10: 6	his son **ministered in the p office**	3547
18: 3	this shall be the **p** due from the people,	3548
Jdg 18:20	the **p** heart was glad, and he took	3548
1Sa 2:13	the **p** servant came, while the flesh was in	3548
2:15	the **p** servant came, and said to the man	3548
1Ch 6:10	(he *it is* that **executed the p office** in	3547
24: 2	and Ithamar **executed the p office**.	3547
2Ch 11:14	**executing the p office** unto the LORD:	3547
24:11	and the high **p** officer came and	3548
Mal 2: 7	For the **p** lips should keep knowledge,	3548
Mt 26:51	and stroke a servant of the high **p**,	749
26:58	him afar off unto the high **p** palace,	749
Lk 1: 8	while he **executed the p office** before	2407
1: 9	According to the custom of the **p office**,	2405
22:54	and brought him into the high **p** house.	749
Jn 18:10	smote the high **p** servant, and cut off his	749

PRIESTHOOD (16) [PRIEST]

Ex 40:15	everlasting **p** throughout their generations.	3550
Nu 16:10	of Levi with thee: and seek ye the **p** also?	3550
18: 1	with thee shall bear the iniquity of your **p**.	3550
25:13	*even* the covenant of an everlasting **p;**	3550
Jos 18: 7	for the **p** of the LORD *is* their inheritance.	3550
Ezr 2:62	were they, as polluted, put from the **p**.	3550
Ne 7:64	were they, as polluted, put from the **p**.	3550
13:29	because they have defiled the **p**,	3550

Ne 13:29	the covenant of the **p**, and of the Levites.	3550
Heb 7: 5	**office of** the **p** have a commandment to	2405
7:11	perfection were by the Levitical **p**,	2420
7:12	For the **p** being changed, there is made of	2420
7:14	tribe Moses spake nothing concerning **p**.	2420
7:24	continueth ever, hath an unchangeable **p**.	2420
1Pe 2: 5	are built *up* a spiritual house, a holy **p**,	2406
2: 9	a royal **p**, a holy nation, a peculiar people;	2406

PRIESTS (392) [PRIEST]

Ge 47:22	Only the land of the **p** bought he not;	3548
47:22	for the **p** had a portion assigned them of	3548
47:26	fifth *part;* except the land of the **p** only,	3548
Ex 19: 6	ye shall be unto me a kingdom of **p**,	3548
19:22	let the **p** also, which come near to	3548
19:24	let not the **p** and the people break through	3548
Lev 1: 5	the **p**, Aaron's sons, shall bring the blood,	3548
1: 8	the **p**, Aaron's sons, shall lay the parts,	3548
1:11	the **p**, Aaron's sons, shall sprinkle his	3548
2: 2	he shall bring it to Aaron's sons the **p:**	3548
3: 2	Aaron's sons the **p** shall sprinkle the blood	3548
6:29	All the males among the **p** shall eat	3548
7: 6	Every male among the **p** shall eat thereof:	3548
13: 2	the priest, or unto one of his sons the **p:**	3548
16:33	he shall make an atonement for the **p**,	3548
21: 1	Speak unto the **p** the sons of Aaron,	3548
Nu 3: 3	of Aaron, the **p** which were anointed,	3548
10: 8	the sons of Aaron, the **p**, shall blow with	3548
Dt 17: 9	thou shalt come unto the **p** the Levites,	3548
17:18	of *that which* is before the **p** the Levites:	3548
18: 1	The **p** the Levites, *and* all the tribe of Levi	3548
19:17	before the **p** and the judges, which shall	3548
21: 5	the **p** the sons of Levi shall come near;	3548
24: 8	do according to all that the **p** the Levites	3548
27: 9	the **p** the Levites spake unto all Israel,	3548
31: 9	delivered it unto the **p** the sons of Levi,	3548
Jos 3: 3	the **p** the Levites bearing it, then ye shall	3548
3: 6	Joshua spake unto the **p**, saying, Take up	3548
3: 8	shalt command the **p** that bear the ark	3548
3:13	as soon as the soles of the feet of the **p**	3548
3:14	the **p** bearing the ark *of* the covenant	3548
3:15	the feet of the **p** that bare the ark were	3548
3:17	the **p** that bare the ark *of* the covenant of	3548
4: 9	in the place where the feet of the **p**	3548
4:10	For the **p** which bare the ark stood in	3548
4:11	and the **p**, in the presence of the people.	3548
4:16	Command the **p** that bear the ark of	3548
4:17	Joshua therefore commanded the **p**,	3548
4:18	the **p** that bare the ark of the covenant	3548
6: 4	seven **p** shall bear before the ark seven	3548
6: 4	and the **p** shall blow with the trumpets.	3548
6: 6	Joshua the son of Nun called the **p**,	3548
6: 6	let seven **p** bear seven trumpets of rams'	3548
6: 8	the seven **p** bearing the seven trumpets	3548
6: 9	armed men went before the **p** that blew	3548
6: 9	*the* **p** going on, and blowing with	NIH
6:12	and the **p** took up the ark of the LORD.	3548
6:13	seven **p** bearing seven trumpets of rams'	3548
6:13	*the* **p** going on, and blowing with	NIH
6:16	the **p** blew with the trumpets, Joshua	3548
6:20	So the people shouted when the **p** blew	NIH
8:33	and on that side before the **p** the Levites,	3548
21:19	the cities of the children of Aaron, the **p**,	3548
Jdg 18:30	his sons were **p** to the tribe of Dan until	3548
1Sa 1: 3	Hophni and Phinehas, the **p** of the LORD,	3548
5: 5	Therefore neither the **p** of Dagon, nor any	3548
6: 2	the Philistines called for the **p** and	3548
22:11	father's house, the **p** that *were* in Nob:	3548
22:17	Turn, and slay the **p** of the LORD;	3548
22:17	their hand to fall upon the **p** of the LORD.	3548
22:18	to Doeg, Turn thou, and fall upon the **p**.	3548
22:18	he fell upon the **p**, and slew on that day	3548
22:19	Nob, the city of the **p**, smote he with	3548
22:21	David that Saul had slain the LORD'S **p**.	3548
2Sa 8:17	the son of Abiathar, *were* the **p;**	3548
15:35	with thee Zadok and Abiathar the **p?**	3548
15:35	shalt tell *it* to Zadok and Abiathar the **p**.	3548
17:15	Hushai unto Zadok and to Abiathar the **p**,	3548
19:11	sent to Zadok and to Abiathar the **p**,	3548
20:25	and Zadok and Abiathar *were* the **p:**	3548
1Ki 4: 4	and Zadok and Abiathar *were* the **p:**	3548
8: 3	of Israel came, and the **p** took up the ark.	3548
8: 4	those did the **p** and the Levites bring	3548
8: 6	the **p** brought in the ark of the covenant	3548
8:10	when the **p** were come out of the holy	3548
8:11	So that the **p** could not stand to minister	3548
12:31	made **p** of the lowest of the people,	3548
12:32	he placed in Beth-el the **p** of the high	3548
13: 2	upon thee shall he offer the **p** of the high	3548
13:33	again of the lowest of the people **p** of	3548
13:33	became *one of* the **p** of the high places.	3548
2Ki 10:11	great men, and his kinsfolks, and his **p**,	3548
10:19	of Baal, all his servants, and all his **p**;	3548
12: 4	Jehoash said to the **p**, All the money of	3548
12: 5	Let the **p** take *it* of them, every man of	3548
12: 6	twentieth year of king Jehoash the **p** had	3548
12: 7	*other* **p**, and said unto them, Why repair	3548
12: 8	the **p** consented to receive no *more*	3548
12: 9	the **p** that kept the door put therein all	3548
17:27	Carry thither one of the **p** whom ye	3548
17:28	one of the **p** whom they had carried away	3548
17:32	of the lowest of them **p** of the high places,	3548
19: 2	Shebna the scribe, and the elders of the **p**,	3548
23: 2	**p**, and the prophets, and all the people,	3548
23: 4	high priest, and the **p** of the second order;	3548

P

2Ki 23: 5 he put down the **idolatrous p**, whom 3649
23: 8 he brought all the **p** out of the cities of 3548
23: 8 defiled the high places where the **p** had 3548
23: 9 Nevertheless the **p** of the high places 3548
23: 20 he slew all the **p** of the high places that 3548
1Ch 9: 2 the **p**, Levites, and the Nethinims. 3548
9:10 the **p**; Jedaiah, and Jehoiarib, and Jachin, 3548
9:30 *some* of the sons of the **p** made 3548
13: 2 with them *also* to the **p** and Levites 3548
15:11 called for Zadok and Abiathar the **p**, 3548
15:14 So the **p** and the Levites santified 3548
15:24 and Benaiah, and Eliezer, the **p**, 3548
16: 6 Jahaziel the **p** with trumpets continually 3548
16:39 Zadok the **p**, and his brethren the **p**, 3548
18:16 the son of Abiathar, *were* the **p**; 3548
23: 2 of Israel, with the **p** and the Levites. 3548
24: 6 *before* the chief of the fathers of the **p** and 3548
24:31 chief of the fathers of the **p** and Levites, 3548
28:13 Also for the courses of the **p** and 3548
28:21 the courses of the **p** and the Levites, 3548
2Ch 4: 6 but the sea was for the **p** to wash in. 3548
4: 9 Furthermore he made the court of the **p**, 3548
5: 5 these did the **p** *and* the Levites bring up. 3548
5: 7 the **p** brought in the ark of the covenant 3548
5:11 when the **p** were come out of the holy 3548
5:11 the **p** that were present were santified, 3548
5:12 and twenty **p** sounding with trumpets:) 3548
5:14 that the **p** could not stand to minister by 3548
6:41 let thy **p**, O LORD God, be clothed *with* 3548
7: 2 the **p** could not enter into the house of 3548
7: 6 the **p** waited on their offices: the Levites 3548
7: 6 the **p** sounded trumpets before them, 3548
8:14 the courses of the **p** to their service, 3548
8:14 to praise and minister before the **p**, 3548
8:15 commandment of the king unto the **p** 3548
11:13 **p** and the Levites that *were* in all Israel 3548
11:15 he ordained him **p** for the high places, 3548
13: 9 Have ye not cast out the **p** of the LORD, 3548
13: 9 have made you a **p** after the manner of 3548
13:10 the **p**, which minister unto the LORD, 3548
13:12 **p** with sounding trumpets to cry alarm 3548
13:14 and the **p** sounded with the trumpets. 3548
17: 8 and with them Elishama and Jehoram, **p**. 3548
19: 8 *of* the **p**, and of the chief of the fathers of 3548
23: 4 the **p** and of the Levites, *shall be* porters 3548
23: 6 save the **p**, and they that minister of 3548
23:18 LORD by the hand of the **p** the Levites. 3548
24: 5 gathered together the **p** and the Levites, 3548
26:17 with him fourscore **p** of the LORD, 3548
26:18 the LORD, but to the **p** the sons of Aaron, 3548
26:19 he was wroth with the **p**, the leprosy 3548
26:19 before the **p** in the house of the LORD, 3548
26:20 all the **p**, looked upon him, and, behold, 3548
29: 4 he brought in the **p** and the Levites, 3548
29:16 the **p** went into the inner part *of* the 3548
29:21 he commanded the **p** the sons of Aaron to 3548
29:22 the **p** received the blood, and sprinkled *it* 3548
29:24 the **p** killed them, and they made 3548
29:26 of David, and the **p** with the trumpets. 3548
29:34 **p** were *too* few, so that they could not 3548
29:34 the *other* **p** had sanctified themselves. 3548
29:34 in heart to santify themselves than the **p**. 3548
30: 3 the **p** had not sanctified themselves 3548
30:15 the **p** and the Levites were ashamed, 3548
30:16 the **p** sprinkled the blood, *which they* 3548
30:21 and the **p** praised the LORD day by day, 3548
30:24 a great number of **p** sanctified themselves. 3548
30:25 with the **p** and the Levites, and all 3548
30:27 the **p** the Levites arose and blessed 3548
31: 2 Hezekiah appointed the courses of the **p** 3548
31: 2 the **p** and Levites for burnt offerings and 3548
31: 4 in Jerusalem to give the portion of the **p** 3548
31: 9 Hezekiah questioned with the **p** and 3548
31:15 and Shecaniah, in the cities of the **p**, 3548
31:17 *to* the genealogy of the **p** by the house 3548
31:19 Also of the sons of Aaron the **p**, 3548
31:19 portions to all the males among the **p**, 3548
34: 5 he burnt the bones of the **p** upon their 3548
34:30 the **p**, and the Levites, and all the people, 3548
35: 2 he set the **p** in their charges, 3548
35: 8 the people, to the **p**, and to the Levites: 3548
35: 8 gave unto the **p** for the passover *offerings* 3548
35:10 the **p** stood in their place, and the Levites 3548
35:11 **p** sprinkled *the blood* from their hands, 3548
35:14 made ready for themselves, and for the **p**: 3548
35:14 the **p** the sons of Aaron were busied in 3548
35:14 and for the the **p** the sons of Aaron. 3548
35:18 the **p**, and the Levites, and all Judah and 3548
36:14 Moreover all the chief of the **p**, 3548
Ezr 1: 5 and Benjamin, and the **p**, and the Levites, 3548
2:36 The **p**: the children of Jedaiah, of the 3548
2:61 of the children of the **p**: the children of 3548
2:70 So the **p**, and the Levites, and *some* of 3548
3: 2 brethren the **p**, and Zerubbabel the son of 3548
3: 8 the remnant of their brethren the **p** and 3548
3:10 they set the **p** in their apparel with 3548
3:12 many of the **p** and Levites and chief of 3548
6: 9 according to the appointment of the **p** 3549
6:16 the **p**, and the Levites, and the rest of 3549
6:18 they set the **p** in their divisions, 3549
6:20 For the **p** and the Levites were purified 3549
6:20 their brethren the **p**, and for themselves, 3548
7: 7 of the **p**, and the Levites, and the singers, 3548
7:13 and *of* his **p** and Levites, in my realm, 3549
7:16 offering of the people, and of the **p**, 3549

Ezr 7:24 that *touching* any of the **p** and Levites, 3549
8:15 the **p**, and found there none of the sons 3548
8:24 I separated twelve of the chief of the **p**, 3548
8:29 ye weigh *them* before the chief of the **p**, 3548
8:30 So took the **p** and the Levites the weight 3548
9: 1 of Israel, and the **p**, and the Levites, 3548
9: 7 iniquities have we, our kings, *and* our **p**, 3548
10: 5 the chief **p**, the Levites, and all Israel, 3548
10:18 among the sons of the **p** there were found 3548
Ne 2:16 nor to the **p**, nor to the nobles, nor to 3548
3: 1 priest rose up with his brethren the **p**, 3548
3:22 after him repaired the **p**, the men of 3548
3:28 From above the horse gate repaired the **p**, 3548
5:12 I called the **p**, and took an oath of them, 3548
7:39 The **p**: the children of Jedaiah, of the 3548
7:63 of the **p**: the children of Habaiah, 3548
7:73 the **p**, and the Levites, and the porters, 3548
8:13 the **p**, and the Levites, unto Ezra the 3548
9:32 on our **p**, and on our prophets, and on 3548
9:34 our princes, our **p**, nor our fathers, kept 3548
9:38 write *it*; and our princes, Levites, *and* **p**, 3548
10: 8 Bilgai, Shemaiah: these *were* the **p**. 3548
10:28 the **p**, the Levites, the porters, the singers, 3548
10:34 we cast the lots *among* the **p**, the Levites, 3548
10:36 unto the **p** that minister in the house of 3548
10:37 of trees, of wine and of oil, unto the **p**, 3548
10:39 the **p** that minister, and the porters, 3548
11: 3 **p**, and the Levites, and the Nethinims, 3548
11:10 the **p**: Jedaiah the son of Joiarib, Jachin, 3548
11:20 residue of Israel, of the **p**, *and* the Levites, 3548
12: 1 Now these *are* the **p** and the Levites that 3548
12: 7 These *were* the chief of the **p** and of their 3548
12:12 in the days of Joiakim were **p**, the chief of 3548
12:22 also the **p**, to the reign of Darius 3548
12:30 the **p** and the Levites purified themselves, 3548
12:41 the **p**; Eliakim, Maaseiah, Miniamin, 3548
12:44 the cities the portions of the law for the **p** 3548
12:44 for Judah rejoiced for the **p** and for 3548
13: 5 and the porters; and the offerings of the **p**. 3548
13:30 appointed the wards of the **p** and 3548
Ps 78:64 Their **p** fell by the sword; and their 3548
99: 6 Moses and Aaron among his **p**, 3548
132: 9 Let thy **p** be clothed *with* righteousness; 3548
132:16 I will also clothe her **p** with salvation: 3548
Isa 37: 2 elders of the **p** covered with sackcloth, 3548
61: 6 But ye shall be named the **P** of the LORD: 3548
66:21 I will also take of them for **p** *and* 3548
Jer 1: 1 the **p** that *were* in Anathoth in the land 3548
1:18 against the **p** thereof, and against 3548
2: 8 The **p** said not, Where *is* the LORD? 3548
2:26 and their **p**, and their prophets, 3548
4: 9 **p** shall be astonished, and the prophets 3548
5:31 and the **p** bear rule by their means; 3548
8: 1 the bones of the **p**, and the bones of 3548
13:13 the **p**, and the prophets, and all 3548
19: 1 the people, and of the ancients of the **p**; 3548
26: 7 the **p** and the prophets and all the people 3548
26: 8 that the **p** and the prophets and all 3548
26:11 spake the **p** and the prophets unto 3548
26:16 all the people unto the **p** and to the 3548
27:16 I spake to the **p** and to all this people, 3548
28: 1 in the presence of the **p** and of all 3548
28: 5 Hananiah in the presence of the **p**, 3548
29: 1 to the **p**, and to the prophets, and to all 3548
29:25 the priest, and to all the **p**, saying, 3548
31:14 will satiate the soul of the **p** with fatness, 3548
32:32 their **p**, and their prophets, and the men 3548
33:18 Neither shall the **p** the Levites want a 3548
33:21 and with the Levites the **p**, my ministers. 3548
34:19 and the **p**, and all the people of the land, 3548
48: 7 shall go forth into captivity with his **p** 3548
49: 3 *and* his **p** and his princes together. 3548
La 1: 4 her **p** sigh: her virgins *are* afflicted, 3548
1:19 my **p** and mine elders gave up the ghost 3548
4:13 her prophets, *and* the iniquities of her **p**, 3548
4:16 they respected not the persons of the **p**, 3548
Eze 22:26 Her **p** have violated my law, 3548
40:45 prospect *is* toward the south, *is* for the **p**, 3548
40:46 prospect *is* toward the north *is* for the **p**, 3548
42:13 where the **p** that approach unto the LORD 3548
42:14 When the **p** enter *therein*, then shall they 3548
43:19 thou shalt give to the **p** the Levites that 3548
43:24 the **p** shall cast salt upon them, 3548
43:27 the **p** shall make your burnt offerings 3548
44:15 the **p** the Levites, the sons of Zadok, 3548
44:31 The **p** shall not eat *of* any thing that is 3548
45: 4 for the **p** the ministers of the sanctuary, 3548
46: 2 the **p** shall prepare his burnt offering and 3548
46:19 into the holy chambers of the **p**, 3548
46:20 This *is* the place where the **p** shall boil 3548
48:10 for them, *even* for the **p**, shall be *this* holy 3548
48:11 *It shall be* for the **p** that are sanctified of 3548
48:13 against the border of the **p**, the Levites 3548
Hos 5: 1 Hear ye this, O **p**; and hearken, ye house 3548
6: 9 the company of **p** murder *in* the way by 3548
10: 5 the **p** thereof *that* rejoiced on it, 3649
Joel 1: 9 the **p**, the LORD's ministers, mourn. 3548
1:13 Gird yourselves, and lament, ye **p**: howl, 3548
2:17 Let the **p**, the ministers of the LORD, 3548
Mic 3:11 the **p** thereof teach for hire, 3548
Zep 1: 4 the name of the Chemarims with the **p**; 3548
3: 4 her **p** have polluted the sanctuary, 3548
Hag 2:11 Ask now the **p** *concerning* the law, 3548
2:12 be holy? And the **p** answered and said, 3548
2:13 the **p** answered and said, It shall be 3548

Zec 7: 3 *And* to speak unto the **p** which *were* in 3548
7: 5 to the **p**, saying, When ye fasted and 3548
Mal 1: 6 unto you, O **p**, that despise my name. 3548
2: 1 O ye **p**, this commandment *is* for you. 3548
Mt 2: 4 And when he had gathered all the **chief p** 749
12: 4 which were with him, but only for the **p**? 2409
12: 5 how that on the sabbath days the **p** in 2409
16:21 the elders and **chief p** and scribes, 749
20:18 of man shall be betrayed unto the **chief p** 749
21:15 And when the **chief p** and scribes saw 749
21:23 the **chief p** and the elders of the people 749
21:45 And when the **chief p** and Pharisees had 749
26: 3 Then assembled together the **chief p**, 749
26:14 Judas Iscariot, went unto the **chief p**, 749
26:47 from the **chief p** and elders of the people. 749
26:59 Now the **chief p**, and elders, and all 749
27: 1 all the **chief p** and elders of the people took 749
27: 3 the thirty pieces of silver to the **chief p** 749
27: 6 And the **chief p** took the silver pieces, 749
27:12 when he was accused of the **chief p** and 749
27:20 But the **chief p** and elders persuaded 749
27:41 Likewise also the **chief p** mocking *him*, 749
27:62 the **chief p** and Pharisees came together 749
28:11 shewed unto the **chief p** all the *things* that 749
Mk 2:26 which is not lawful to eat but for the **p**, 2409
8:31 the elders, and of the **chief p**, and scribes, 749
10:33 of man shall be delivered unto the **chief p**, 749
11:18 And the scribes and **chief p** heard *it*, and 749
11:27 there come to him the **chief p**, 749
14: 1 and the **chief p** and the scribes sought how 749
14:10 one of the twelve, went unto the **chief p** 749
14:43 from the **chief p** and the scribes and 749
14:53 with him were assembled all the **chief p** 749
14:55 And the **chief p** and all the council sought 749
15: 1 straightway in the morning the **chief p** 749
15: 3 the **chief p** accused him of many *things*: 749
15:10 For he knew that the **chief p** had delivered 749
15:11 But the **chief p** moved the people, that he 749
15:31 Likewise also the **chief p** mocking said 749
Lk 3: 2 Annas and Caiaphas being the **high p**, 749
6: 4 it is not lawful to eat but for the **p** alone? 2409
9:22 of the elders and **chief p** and scribes, 749
17:14 them, Go shew yourselves unto the **p**. 2409
19:47 the **chief p** and the scribes and the chief 749
20: 1 the **chief p** and the scribes came upon *him* 749
20:19 And the **chief p** and the scribes the same 749
22: 2 the **chief p** and scribes sought how they 749
22: 4 and communed with the **chief p** and 749
22:52 Then Jesus said unto the **chief p**, 749
22:66 the elders of the people and the **chief p** 749
23: 4 Then said Pilate to the **chief p** and *to* 749
23:10 And the **chief p** and scribes stood and 749
23:13 when he had called together the **chief p** 749
23:23 voices of them and of the **chief p** prevailed. 749
24:20 how the **chief p** and our rulers delivered 749
Jn 1:19 when the Jews sent **p** and Levites from 2409
7:32 and the **chief p** sent officers to take him. 749
7:45 Then came the officers to the **chief p** and 749
11:47 gathered the **chief p** and the Pharisees 749
11:57 both the **chief p** and the Pharisees had 749
12:10 the **chief p** consulted that they might put 749
18: 3 officers from the **chief p** and Pharisees, 749
18:35 the **chief p** have delivered thee unto me: 749
19: 6 When the **chief p** therefore and officers 749
19:15 The **chief p** answered, We have no king 749
19:21 Then said the **chief p** of the Jews to Pilate, 749
Ac 4: 1 the **p**, and the captain of the temple, 2409
4:23 and reported all that the **chief p** and elders 749
5:24 and the **chief p** heard these things, 749
6: 7 a great company of the **p** were obedient to 2409
9:14 here he hath authority from the **chief p** 749
9:21 might bring them bound unto the **chief p**? 749
19:14 a Jew, *and* **chief of the p**, which did so. 749
22:30 and commanded the **chief p** and all their 749
23:14 And they came to the **chief p** and elders, 749
25:15 the **chief p** and the elders of the Jews 749
26:10 having received authority from the **chief p**; 749
26:12 and commission from the **chief p**, 749
Heb 7:21 (For those **p** were made without an oath; 2409
7:23 And they truly were many **p**, because 2409
7:27 as *those* **high p**, to offer up sacrifice, first 749
7:28 the law maketh men **high p** which have 749
8: 4 seeing that there are **p** that offer gifts 2409
9: 6 the **p** went always into the first tabernacle, 2409
Rev 1: 6 us kings and **p** unto God and his Father; 2409
5:10 hast made us unto our God kings and **p**: 2409
20: 6 but they shall be **p** of God and of Christ, 2409

PRIESTS' (10) [PRIEST]

Jos 4: 3 of the place where the **p** feet stood firm, 3548
4:18 the soles of the **p** feet were lift up unto 3548
1Sa 2:13 the **p** custom with the people *was, that* 3548
2:36 I pray thee, into one of the **p** offices, 3550
2Ki 12:16 *into* the house of the LORD: it was the **p**. 3548
Ezr 2:69 of silver, and one hundred **p** garments. 3548
Ne 7:70 five hundred and thirty **p** garments. 3548
7:72 and threescore and seven **p** garments. 3548
12:35 *certain* of the **p** sons with trumpets; 3548
Eze 44:30 of your oblations, shall be the **p**: 3548+3807.1

PRINCE (102) [PRINCE'S, PRINCES, PRINCESS, PRINCESSES]

Ge 23: 6 *art* a mighty **p** among us: in the choice 5387
32:28 for as a **p** hast thou **power** with God 8280
34: 2 **p** of the country, saw her, he took her, 5387

Ex	2:14 Who made thee a **p** and a judge over us?	8269
Nu	7:11 each **p** on *his* day, for the dedicating of	5387
	7:18 the son of Zuar, **p** of Issachar, did offer:	5387
	7:24 **p** of the children of Zebulun, *did offer:*	5387
	7:30 **p** of the children of Reuben, *did offer:*	5387
	7:36 **p** of the children of Simeon, *did offer:*	5387
	7:42 Deuel, **p** of the children of Gad, *offered:*	5387
	7:48 **p** of the children of Ephraim, *offered:*	5387
	7:54 Pedahzur, **p** of the children of Manasseh:	5387
	7:60 **p** of the children of Benjamin, *offered:*	5387
	7:66 **p** of the children of Dan, *offered:*	5387
	7:72 **p** of the children of Asher, *offered:*	5387
	7:78 **p** of the children of Naphtali, *offered:*	5387
	16:13 **make** thyself **altogether a p** over 8323+8323	
	17: 6 for each **p** one, according to their fathers'	5387
	25:14 **p** of a chief house among the Simeonites.	5387
	25:18 the daughter of a **p** of Midian, their sister,	5387
	34:18 shall take one **p** of every tribe, to divide	5387
	34:22 the **p** of the tribe of the children of Dan,	5387
	34:23 The **p** of the tribe of Joseph,	5387
	34:24 the **p** of the tribe of the children of	5387
	34:25 the **p** of the tribe of the children of	5387
	34:26 the **p** of the tribe of the children of	5387
	34:27 the **p** of the tribe of the children of Asher,	5387
	34:28 the **p** of the tribe of the children of	5387
Jos	22:14 of each chief house a **p** throughout all the	1
2Sa	3:38 Know ye not that there is a **p** and a great	8269
1Ki	11:34 I will make him **p** all the days of his life	5387
	14: 7 and made thee **p** over my people Israel,	5057
	16: 2 and made thee **p** over my people Israel;	5057
1Ch	2:10 Nahshon, **p** of the children of Judah;	5387
	5: 6 away captive: he *was* **p** of the Reubenites.	5387
Ezr	1: 8 them unto Sheshbazzar, the **p** of Judah.	5387
Job	21:28 For ye say, Where *is* the house of the **p**?	5081
	31:37 steps; as a **p** would I go near unto him.	5057
Pr	14:28 want of people *is* the destruction of the **p**.	7333
	17: 7 not a fool: much less do lying lips a **p**.	5081
	19: 6 Many will intreat the favour of the **p**:	5081
	25: 7 of the **p** whom thine eyes have seen.	5081
	25:15 By long forbearing is a **p** persuaded,	7101
	28:16 The **p** that wanteth understanding *is* also	5057
Isa	9: 6 The everlasting Father, The **P** of Peace.	8269
Jer	51:59 And *this* Seraiah *was* a quiet **p**.	8269
Eze	7:27 the **p** shall be clothed with desolation,	5387
	12:10 burden *concerneth* the **p** in Jerusalem,	5387
	12:12 the **p** that *is* among them shall bear upon	5387
	21:25 profane wicked **p** of Israel, whose day	5387
	28: 2 Son of man, say unto the **p** of Tyrus,	5057
	30:13 there shall be no more a **p** of the land of	5387
	34:24 and my servant David a **p** among them;	5387
	37:25 servant David *shall be* their **p** for ever.	5387
	38: 2 the chief **p** of Meshech and Tubal,	5387
	38: 3 Gog, the chief **p** of Meshech and Tubal:	5387
	39: 1 Gog, the chief **p** of Meshech and Tubal:	5387
	44: 3 *It is* for the **p**; the prince, he shall sit in it	5387
	44: 3 he, the **p**; he shall sit in it to eat bread before	5387
	45: 7 *portion shall be* for the **p** on the one side	5387
	45:16 shall give this oblation for the **p** in Israel.	5387
	45:22 upon that day shall the **p** prepare for	5387
	46: 2 the **p** shall enter by the way of the porch	5387
	46: 4 the burnt offering that the **p** shall offer	5387
	46: 8 when the **p** shall enter, he shall go in *by*	5387
	46:10 the **p** in the midst of them, when they go	5387
	46:12 when the **p** shall prepare a voluntary	5387
	46:16 If the **p** give a gift unto any of his sons,	5387
	46:17 of liberty; after, it shall return to the **p**:	5387
	46:18 Moreover the **p** shall not take of	5387
	48:21 the residue *shall be* for the **p**, on the one	5387
	48:21 over against the portions for the **p**:	5387
	48:22 the border of Benjamin, shall be for the **p**.	5387
Da	1: 7 Unto whom the **p** of the eunuchs gave	8269
	1: 8 he requested of the **p** of the eunuchs that	8269
	1:10 tender love with the **p** of the eunuchs.	8269
	1:10 the **p** of the eunuchs said unto Daniel,	8269
	1:11 whom the **p** of the eunuchs had set over	8269
	1:18 **p** of the eunuchs brought them in before	8269
	8:11 he magnified *himself even* to the **p** of	8269
	8:25 he shall also stand up against the **P** of	8269
	9:25 build Jerusalem unto the Messiah the **P**	5057
	9:26 the people of the **p** that *shall* come shall	5057
	10:13 the **p** of the kingdom of Persia withstood	8269
	10:20 now will I return to fight with the **p** of	8269
	10:20 gone forth, lo, the **p** of Grecia shall come.	8269
	10:21 me in these *things*, but Michael your **p**.	8269
	11:18 a **p** for his own behalf shall cause	7101
	11:22 broken; yea also, the **p** of the covenant.	5057
	12: 1 great **p** which standeth for the children	8269
Hos	3: 4 without a **p**, and without a sacrifice,	8269
Mic	7: 3 the **p** asketh, and the judge *asketh* for a	8269
Mt	9:34 He casteth out the devils through the **p** of	758
	12:24 but by Beelzebub the **p** of the devils.	758
Mk	3:22 by the **p** of the devils casteth he out devils.	758
Jn	12:31 now shall the **p** of this world be cast out.	758
	14:30 for the **p** of this world cometh,	758
	16:11 because the **p** of this world is judged.	758
Ac	3:15 And killed the **P** of life, whom God hath	747
	5:31 God exalted him with his right hand *to be* a **P**	747
Eph	2: 2 according to the **p** of the power of the air,	758
Rev	1: 5 dead, and the **p** of the kings of the earth.	758

PRINCE'S (3) [PRINCE]

SS	7: 1 are thy feet with shoes, O **p** daughter!	5081
Eze	45:17 shall be the **p** part *to give* burnt offerings,	5387
	48:22 the midst *of that* which is the **p**, 5387+3807.1	

PRINCES (273) [PRINCE]

Ge	12:15 The **p** also of Pharaoh saw her,	8269
	17:20 twelve **p** shall he beget, and I will make	5387
	25:16 twelve **p** according to their nations.	5387
Nu	1:16 **p** of the tribes of their fathers, heads of	5387
	1:44 and Aaron numbered, and the **p** of Israel,	5387
	7: 2 That the **p** of Israel, heads of the house of	5387
	7: 2 *were* the **p** of the tribes, and were over	5387
	7: 3 wagon for two of the **p**, and for *each* one	5387
	7:10 the **p** offered *for* dedicating of the altar in	5387
	7:10 even the **p** offered their offering before	5387
	7:84 when it was anointed, by the **p** of Israel:	5387
	10: 4 blow *but* with one *trumpet*, then the **p**,	5387
	16: 2 two hundred and fifty **p** of the assembly,	5387
	17: 2 all their **p** according to the house of their	5387
	17: 6 one of their **p** gave him a rod apiece,	5387
	21:18 The **p** digged the well, the nobles of	5387
	22: 8 and the **p** of Moab abode with Balaam.	8269
	22:13 unto the **p** of Balak, Get you into your	8269
	22:14 the **p** of Moab rose up, and they went	8269
	22:15 Balak sent yet again **p**, more,	8269
	22:21 his ass, and went with the **p** of Moab.	8269
	22:35 So Balaam went with the **p** of Balak.	8269
	22:40 Balaam, and to the **p** that *were* with him.	8269
	23: 6 burnt sacrifice, he, and all the **p** of Moab.	8269
	23:17 offering, and the **p** of Moab with him.	8269
	27: 2 before the **p** and all the congregation,	5387
	31:13 priest, and all the **p** of the congregation,	5387
	32: 2 unto the **p** of the congregation, saying,	5387
	36: 1 spake before Moses, and before the **p**,	5387
Jos	9:15 the **p** of the congregation sware unto them.	5387
	9:18 the **p** of the congregation had sworn unto	5387
	9:18 congregation murmured against the **p**.	5387
	9:19 all the **p** said unto all the congregation,	5387
	9:21 the **p** said unto them, Let them live;	5387
	9:21 as the **p** had promised them.	5387
	13:21 Moses smote with the **p** of Midian,	5387
	17: 4 the son of Nun, and before the **p**, saying,	5387
	22:14 with him ten **p**, of each chief house a	5387
	22:30 the **p** of the congregation and heads of	5387
	22:32 the **p**, returned from the children of	5387
Jdg	5: 3 give ear, O ye **p**; I, *even* I, will sing unto	7336
	5:15 the **p** of Issachar *were* with Deborah;	8269
	7:25 they took two **p** of the Midianites, Oreb	8269
	8: 3 hath delivered into your hands the **p** of	8269
	8: 6 the **p** of Succoth said, Are the hands of	8269
	8:14 he described unto him the **p** of Succoth,	8269
	10:18 *and* **p** of Gilead said one to another,	8269
1Sa	18:30 to set *them* among **p**, and to make them	5081
	18:30 the **p** of the Philistines went forth:	8269
	29: 3 said the **p** of the Philistines, What *do*	8269
	29: 3 Achish said unto the **p** of the Philistines,	8269
	29: 4 the **p** of the Philistines were wroth with	8269
	29: 4 the **p** of the Philistines said unto him,	8269
	29: 9 notwithstanding the **p** of the Philistines	8269
2Sa	10: 3 the **p** of the children of Ammon said unto	8269
	19: 6 thou regardest neither **p** nor servants:	8269
1Ki	4: 2 these *were* the **p** which he had; Azariah	8269
	9:22 his **p**, and his captains, and rulers of his	8269
	20:14 *Even* by the young men of the **p** of	8269
	20:15 he numbered the young men of the **p** of	8269
	20:17 the young men of the **p** of the provinces	8269
	20:19 So these young men of the **p** of	8269
2Ki	11:14 as the manner *was*, and the **p** and	8269
	24:12 his servants, and his **p**, and his officers:	8269
	24:14 and all the mighty *men* of valour,	8269
1Ch	4:38 These mentioned by *their* names *were* **p**	5387
	7:40 *and* mighty *men* of valour, chief of the **p**,	5387
	19: 3 the **p** of the children of Ammon said to	8269
	22:17 David also commanded all the **p** of Israel	8269
	23: 2 he gathered together all the **p** of Israel,	8269
	24: 6 the **p**, and Zadok the priest,	8269
	27:22 These *were* the **p** of the tribes of Israel.	8269
	28: 1 David assembled all the **p** of Israel,	8269
	28: 1 the **p** of the tribes, and the captains of	8269
	28:21 the **p** and all the people *will be* wholly	8269
	29: 6 of the fathers and **p** of the tribes of Israel,	8269
	29:24 all the **p**, and the mighty *men*, and all	8269
2Ch	12: 5 *to* the **p** of Judah, that were gathered	8269
	12: 6 Whereupon the **p** of Israel and the king	8269
	17: 7 third year of his reign he sent to his **p**,	8269
	21: 4 sword, and *divers* also of the **p** of Israel.	8269
	21: 9 Jehoram went forth with his **p**, and all	8269
	22: 8 found the **p** of Judah, and the sons of	8269
	23:13 and the **p** and the trumpets by the king:	8269
	24:10 all the **p** and all the people rejoiced,	8269
	24:17 after the death of Jehoiada came the **p**	8269
	24:23 destroyed all the **p** of the people from	8269
	28:14 the spoil before the **p** and all	8269
	28:21 of the **p**, and gave *it* unto the king of	8269
	29:30 the **p** commanded the Levites to *sing*	8269
	30: 2 his **p**, and all the congregation in	8269
	30: 6 and his **p** throughout all Israel and Judah,	8269
	30:12 commandment of the king and of the **p**,	8269
	30:24 the **p** gave to the congregation a thousand	8269
	31: 8 and the **p** came and saw the heaps,	8269
	32: 3 took counsel with his **p** and his mighty	8269
	32:31 *of* the ambassadors of the **p** of Babylon,	8269
	35: 8 his **p** gave willingly unto the people,	8269
	36:18 the treasures of the king, and of his **p**;	8269
Ezr	7:28 and before all the king's mighty **p**.	8269
	8:20 the **p** had appointed for the service of	8269
	9: 1 came to me, saying, The people of	8269
	9: 2 the hand of the **p** and rulers hath been	8269

Ezr	10: 8 according to the counsel of the **p** and	8269
Ne	9:32 on our **p**, and on our priests, and on our	8269
	9:34 our **p**, our priests, nor our fathers, kept	8269
	9:38 write *it*; and our **p**, Levites, *and* priests,	8269
	12:31 brought up the **p** of Judah upon the wall,	8269
	12:32 Hoshaiah, and half of the **p** of Judah,	8269
Est	1: 3 he made a feast unto all his **p** and	8269
	1: 3 Media, the nobles and **p** of the provinces,	8269
	1:11 to shew the people and the **p** her beauty:	8269
	1:14 the seven **p** of Persia and Media,	8269
	1:16 answered before the king and the **p**,	8269
	1:16 *also* to all the **p**, and to all the people	8269
	1:18 Media say this day unto all the king's **p**,	8269
	1:21 the saying pleased the king and the **p**;	8269
	2:18 the king made a great feast unto all his **p**	8269
	3: 1 set his seat above all the **p** that *were* with	8269
	5:11 how he had advanced him above the **p**	8269
	6: 9 hand of one of the king's most noble **p**,	8269
Job	3:15 Or with **p** that had gold, who filled their	8269
	12:19 He leadeth **p** away spoiled,	3548
	12:21 He poureth contempt upon **p**,	5081
	29: 9 The **p** refrained talking, and laid *their*	8269
	34:18 *art* wicked? and to **p**, Ye *are* ungodly?	5081
	34:19 *him* that accepteth not the persons of **p**,	8269
Ps	45:16 thou mayest make **p** in all the earth.	8269
	47: 9 The **p** of the people are gathered together,	5081
	68:27 the **p** of Judah *and* their council,	8269
	68:27 the **p** of Zebulun, and the princes of	8269
	68:27 princes of Zebulun, *and* the **p** of Naphtali.	8269
	68:31 **P** shall come out of Egypt; Ethiopia shall	2831
	76:12 shall cut off the spirit of **p**: *he is* terrible	5057
	82: 7 die like men, and fall like one of the **p**.	8269
	83:11 all their **p** as Zebah, and as Zalmunna:	5257
	105:22 To bind his **p** at his pleasure; and teach	8269
	107:40 He poureth contempt upon **p**,	5081
	113: 8 That he may set *him* with **p**, *even* with	5081
	113: 8 princes, *even* with the **p** of his people.	5081
	118: 9 in the LORD than to put confidence in **p**.	5081
	119:23 **P** also did sit *and* speak against me:	8269
	119:161 **P** have persecuted me without a cause:	8269
	146: 3 Put not your trust in **p**, *nor* in the son of	5081
	148:11 all people; **p**, and all judges of the earth:	8269
Pr	8:15 By me kings reign, and **p** decree justice.	7336
	8:16 By me **p** rule, and nobles, *even* all	8269
	17:26 just *is* not good, *nor* to strike **p** for equity.	5081
	19:10 less for a servant to have rule over **p**.	8269
	28: 2 of a land many *are* the **p** thereof:	8269
	31: 4 to drink wine; nor for **p** strong drink:	7336
Ecc	10: 7 and **p** walking as servants upon the earth.	8269
	10:16 *is* a child, and thy **p** eat in the morning.	8269
	10:17 thy **p** eat in due season, for strength,	8269
Isa	1:23 Thy **p** *are* rebellious, and companions of	8269
	3: 4 I will give children *to be* their **p**,	8269
	3:14 ancients of his people, and the **p** thereof:	8269
	10: 8 he saith, *Are* not my **p** altogether kings?	8269
	19:11 the **p** of Zoan *are* fools, the counsel	8269
	19:13 The **p** of Zoan are become fools,	8269
	19:13 fools, the **p** of Noph are deceived;	8269
	21: 5 drink: arise, ye **p**, *and* anoint the shield.	8269
	23: 8 crowning *city*, whose merchants *are* **p**,	8269
	30: 4 For his **p** were at Zoan,	8269
	31: 9 his **p** shall be afraid of the ensign, saith	8269
	32: 1 and **p** shall rule in judgment.	8269
	34:12 *be* there, and all her **p** shall be nothing.	8269
	40:23 bringeth **p** to nothing; he maketh	7336
	41:25 he shall come upon **p** as *upon* morter,	5461
	43:28 Therefore I have profaned the **p** of	8269
	49: 7 shall see and arise, **p** also shall worship,	8269
Jer	1:18 against the **p** thereof, against the priests	8269
	2:26 **p**, and their priests, and their prophets,	8269
	4: 9 king shall perish, and the heart of the **p**;	8269
	8: 1 the bones of his **p**, and the bones of	8269
	17:25 and *p* sitting upon the throne of David,	8269
	17:25 chariots and on horses, they, and their **p**,	8269
	24: 1 the **p** of Judah, with the carpenters and	8269
	24: 8 his **p**, and the residue of Jerusalem,	8269
	25:18 and the kings thereof, *and* the **p** thereof,	8269
	25:19 his servants, and his **p**, and all his people;	8269
	26:10 When the **p** of Judah heard these things,	8269
	26:11 the prophets unto the **p** and to all	8269
	26:12 spake Jeremiah unto all the **p** and to all	8269
	26:16 the **p** and all the people unto the priests	8269
	26:21 with all his mighty *men*, and all the **p**,	8269
	29: 2 the **p** of Judah and Jerusalem,	8269
	32:32 they, their kings, their **p**, their priests,	8269
	34:10 *Now* when all the **p**, and all the people,	8269
	34:19 the **p** of Judah, and the princes of	8269
	34:19 the **p** of Jerusalem, the eunuchs,	8269
	34:21 his **p** will I give into the hand of their	8269
	35: 4 God, which *was* by the chamber of the **p**,	8269
	36:12 lo, all the **p** sat there, *even* Elishama	8269
	36:12 the son of Hananiah,	8269
	36:14 Therefore all the **p** sent Jehudi the son of	8269
	36:19 said the **p** unto Baruch, Go, hide thee,	8269
	36:21 in the ears of all the **p** which stood beside	8269
	37:14 took Jeremiah, and brought him to the **p**.	8269
	37:15 the **p** were wroth with Jeremiah,	8269
	38: 4 Therefore the **p** said unto the king,	8269
	38:17 go forth unto the king of Babylon's **p**,	8269
	38:18 not go forth to the king of Babylon's **p**,	8269
	38:22 brought forth to the king of Babylon's **p**,	8269
	38:25 if the **p** hear that I have talked with thee,	8269
	38:27 came all the **p** unto Jeremiah,	8269
	39: 3 all the **p** of the king of Babylon came in,	8269
	39: 3 with all the residue of the **p** of the king	8269

P

Jer	39:13 Rab-mag, and all the king of Babylon's **p**;	7227
	41: 1 of the seed royal, and the **p** of the king,	7227
	44:17 we, and our fathers, our kings, and our **p**,	8269
	44:21 and your **p**, and the people of the land,	8269
	48: 7 *with* his priests and his **p** together.	8269
	49: 3 *and* his priests and his **p** together.	8269
	49:38 destroy from thence the king and the **p**,	8269
	50:35 and upon her **p**, and upon her wise *men*,	8269
	51:57 make drunk her **p**, and her wise *men*,	8269
	52:10 he slew also all the **p** of Judah in Riblah.	8269
La	1: 6 her **p** are become like harts *that* find no	8269
	2: 2 polluted the kingdom and the **p** thereof.	8269
	2: 9 king and her **p** *are* among the Gentiles:	8269
	5:12 **P** are hanged up by their hand: the faces	8269
Eze	11: 1 the son of Benaiah, **p** of the people.	8269
	17:12 the **p** thereof, and led them with him to	8269
	19: 1 thou up a lamentation for the **p** of Israel,	5387
	21:12 it *shall be* upon all the **p** of Israel:	5387
	22: 6 Behold, the **p** of Israel, every one were in	5387
	22:27 Her **p** in the midst thereof *are* like wolves	8269
	23:15 upon their heads, all of them **p** to look to,	7991
	26:16 all the **p** of the sea shall come down from	5387
	27:21 Arabia, and all the **p** of Kedar,	5387
	32:29 There *is* Edom, her kings, and all her **p**,	5387
	32:30 There *be* the **p** of the north, all of them,	5257
	39:18 drink the blood of the **p** of the earth,	5387
	45: 8 my **p** shall no more oppress my people;	5387
	45: 9 Let it suffice you, O **p** of Israel:	5387
Da	1: 3 and of the king's seed, and of the **p**;	6579
	3: 2 the king sent to gather together the **p**,	324
	3: 3 **p**, the governors and captains, the judges,	324
	3:27 the **p**, governors, and captains,	324
	5: 2 and his **p**, his wives, and his concubines,	7261
	5: 3 the king, and his **p**, his wives,	7261
	6: 1 the kingdom an hundred and twenty **p**,	324
	6: 2 that the **p** might give accounts unto them,	324
	6: 3 was preferred above the presidents and the	324
	6: 4 **p** sought to find occasion against Daniel	324
	6: 6 assembled *together* to the king,	324
	6: 7 the governors, and the **p**, the counsellers	324
	8:25 shall also stand up against the Prince of **p**;	8269
	9: 6 our **p**, and our fathers, and to all the	8269
	9: 8 to our **p**, and to our fathers, because	8269
	10:13 lo, Michael, one of the chief **p**, came to	8269
	11: 5 south shall be strong, and *one* of his **p**;	8269
	11: 8 their **p**, *and* with their precious vessels	5257
Hos	5:10 The **p** of Judah were like them that	8269
	7: 3 wickedness, and the **p** with their lies.	8269
	7: 5 *In* the day of our king the **p** have made	8269
	7:16 their **p** shall fall by the sword for the rage	8269
	8: 4 they have **made p**, and I knew *it* not:	7786
	8:10 a little for the burden of the king of **p**.	8269
	9:15 them no more: all their **p** *are* revolters.	8269
	13:10 thou saidst, Give me a king and **p**?	8269
Am	1:15 he and his **p** together, saith the Lord.	8269
	2: 3 will slay all the **p** thereof with him,	8269
Mic	3: 1 of Jacob, and ye **p** of the house of Israel;	7101
	3: 9 **p** of the house of Israel, that abhor	7101
Hab	1:10 and the **p** shall *be* a scorn unto them:	7336
Zep	1: 8 that I will punish the **p**, and the king's	8269
	3: 3 Her **p** within her *are* roaring lions;	8269
Mt	2: 6 art not the least among the **p** of Juda:	2232
	20:25 Ye know that the **p** of the Gentiles	758
1Co	2: 6 nor of the **p** of this world, that come to	758
	2: 8 Which none of the **p** of this world knew:	758

PRINCESS (1) [PRINCE]

| La | 1: 1 *and* **p** among the provinces, *how* is she | 8282 |

PRINCESSES (1) [PRINCE]

| 1Ki | 11: 3 **p**, and three hundred concubines: | 8282 |

PRINCIPAL (17) [PRINCIPALITIES, PRINCIPALITY]

Ex	30:23 Take thou also unto thee **p** spices, of pure	7218
Lev	6: 5 he shall even restore it in the **p**,	7218
Nu	5: 7 shall recompense his trespass with the **p**	7218
1Ki	4: 5 Zabud the son of Nathan was **p officer**,	3548
2Ki	25:19 in the city, and the **p** scribe of the host,	8269
1Ch	24: 6 one **p** household being taken for Eleazar,	1
	24:31 *even* the **p** fathers over against their	7218
Ne	11:17 *was* the **p** to begin the thanksgiving in	7218
Pr	4: 7 Wisdom *is* the **p thing**; *therefore*	7225
Isa	16: 8 have broken down the **p plants** thereof,	8291
	28:25 cast in the **p** wheat and the appointed	7795
Jer	25:34 wallow yourselves *in the ashes*, ye **p** of	117
	25:35 to flee, nor the **p** of the flock to escape.	117
	25:36 and a howling of the **p** of the flock,	117
	52:25 the **p** scribe of the host, who mustered	8269
Mic	5: 5 him seven shepherds, and **p** men.	5257
Ac	25:23 the chief captains, and **p** men of the city,	1851

PRINCIPALITIES (7) [PRINCIPAL]

Jer	13:18 for your **p** shall come down, *even*	4761
Ro	8:38 nor life, nor angels, nor **p**, nor powers,	746
Eph	3:10 To the intent that now unto the **p** and	746
	6:12 not against flesh and blood, but against **p**,	746
Col	1:16 *be* thrones, or dominions, or **p**, or powers:	746
	2:15 having spoiled **p** and powers, he made a	746
Tit	3: 1 Put them in mind to be subject to **p** and	746

PRINCIPALITY (2) [PRINCIPAL]

| Eph | 1:21 Far above all **p**, and power, and might, | 746 |
| Col | 2:10 him, which is the head of all **p** and power: | 746 |

PRINCIPLES (2)

| Heb | 5:12 which *be* the first **p** of the oracles of God; | 4747 |
| | 6: 1 Therefore leaving the **p** of the doctrine of | 746 |

PRINT (4) [PRINTED]

Lev	19:28 for the dead, nor **p** any marks upon you:	5414
Job	13:27 **settest a p** upon the heels of my feet.	2707
Jn	20:25 Except I shall see in his hands the **p** of	5179
	20:25 and put my finger into the **p** of the nails,	5179

PRINTED (1) [PRINT]

| Job | 19:23 written! O that they were **p** in a book! | 2710 |

PRISCA (1) [PRISCILLA]

| 2Ti | 4:19 Salute **P** and Aquila, and the household of | 4251 |

PRISCILLA (5) [PRISCA]

Ac	18: 2 lately come from Italy, with his wife **P**;	4252
	18:18 into Syria, and with him **P** and Aquila:	4252
	18:26 whom when Aquila and **P** had heard,	4252
Ro	16: 3 Greet **P** and Aquila my helpers in Christ	4252
1Co	16:19 Aquila and **P** salute you much in the Lord	4252

PRISED (1) [PRICE]

| Zec | 11:13 a goodly price that I was **p** at of them. | 3365 |

PRISON (90) [FELLOWPRISONER, FELLOWPRISONERS, IMPRISONED, IMPRISONMENT, IMPRISONMENTS, PRISONER, PRISONERS, PRISONS]

Ge	39:20 and put him into the **p**,	1004+5470+1886.1
	39:20 and he was there in the **p**.	1004+5470+1886.1
	39:21 of the keeper of the **p**.	1004+5470+1886.1
	39:22 the keeper of the **p**	1004+5470+1886.1
	39:22 that *were* in the **p**;	1004+5470+1886.1
	39:23 The keeper of the **p** looked	1004+5470+1886.1
	40: 3 into the **p**, the place where	1004+5470+1886.1
	40: 5 *were* bound in the **p**.	1004+5470+1886.1
	42:16 your brother, and ye shall be **kept in p**,	631
	42:19 brethren be bound in the house of your **p**:	4929
Jdg	16:21 of brass; and he did grind in the **p** house.	631
	16:25 they called for Samson out of the **p** house;	631
1Ki	22:27 Put this *fellow* in the **p**,	1004+3608+1886.1
2Ki	17: 4 shut him up, and bound him in **p**.	1004+3608
	25:27 Jehoiachin king of Judah out of **p**;	1004+3608
	25:29 changed his **p** garments: and he did eat	3608
2Ch	16:10 with the seer, and put him in *a* **p** house;	4115
	18:26 Put this *fellow* in the **p**,	1004+3608+1886.1
Ne	3:25 house, that *was* by the court of the **p**.	4307
	12:39 and they stood still in the **p** gate.	4307
Ps	142: 7 Bring my soul out of **p**, that *I* may praise	4525
Ecc	4:14 For out of **p** he cometh to	631+1004+1886.1
Isa	24:22 shall be shut up in the **p**, and after many	4525
	42: 7 to bring out the prisoners from the **p**,	4525
	42: 7 that sit in darkness out of the **p** house.	3608
	42:22 in holes, and they are hid in **p** houses:	3608
	53: 8 He was taken from **p** and from judgment:	6115
	61: 1 the **opening of the p** to *them* that are	6495
Jer	29:26 that thou shouldest put him in **p**, and in	4115
	32: 2 prophet was shut up in the court of the **p**,	4307
	32: 8 the **p** according to the word of the Lord,	4307
	32:12 all the Jews that sat in the court of the **p**,	4307
	33: 1 he was yet shut up in the court of the **p**,	4307
	37: 4 had not put him *into* **p**.	1004+3608+1886.1
	37:15 put him in **p** *in* the house	612+1004+1886.1
	37:15 they had made the **p**, for the **p**	1004+3608+1886.1
	37:18 that ye have put me in **p**?	1004+3608+1886.1
	37:21 commit Jeremiah into the court of the **p**,	4307
	37:21 Jeremiah remained in the court of the **p**,	4307
	38: 6 that *was* in the court of the **p**:	4307
	38:13 Jeremiah remained in the court of the **p**.	4307
	38:28 So Jeremiah abode in the court of the **p**	4307
	39:14 took Jeremiah out of the court of the **p**,	4307
	39:15 he was shut up in the court of the **p**,	4307
	52:11 **p** till the day of his death.	1004+6486+1886.1
	52:31 brought him out of **p**,	1004+3608+1886.1
	52:33 changed his **p** garments: and he did	3608
Mt	4:12 Jesus had heard that John was **cast into p**,	3860
	5:25 thee to the officer, and thou be **cast into p**.	5438
	11: 2 Now when John had heard in the **p**	1201
	14: 3 and put *him* in **p** for Herodias' sake,	5438
	14:10 And he sent, and beheaded John in the **p**.	5438
	18:30 went and cast him into **p**, till he should	5438
	25:36 I was in **p**, and ye came unto me.	5438
	25:39 thee sick, or in **p**, and came unto thee?	5438
	25:43 sick, and in **p**, and ye visited me not.	5438
	25:44 or in **p**, and did not minister unto thee?	5438
Mk	1:14 Now after that John was **put in p**, Jesus	3860
	6:17 and bound him in **p** for Herodias' sake,	5438
	6:27 and he went and beheaded him in the **p**,	5438
Lk	3:20 this above all, that he shut up John in **p**.	5438
	12:58 the officer, and the officer cast thee into **p**.	5438
	22:33 to go with thee, both into **p**, and to death.	5438
	23:19 the city, and *for* murder, was cast into **p**.)	5438
	23:25 for sedition and murder was cast into **p**,	5438
Jn	3:24 For John was not yet cast into **p**.	5438
Ac	5:18 and put them in the common **p**.	5084
	5:19 of the Lord by night opened the **p** doors,	5438
	5:21 and sent to the **p** to have them brought.	1201
	5:22 found them not in the **p**, they returned,	5438
	5:23 The **p** truly found we shut with all safety,	1201
	5:25 The men whom ye put in **p** are standing	5438
	8: 3 and women committed *them* to **p**.	5438
	12: 4 he put *him* in **p**, and delivered *him* to	5438
	12: 5 Peter therefore was kept in **p**:	5438

Ac	12: 6 *the* keepers before the door kept the **p**.	5438
	12: 7 upon *him*, and a light shined in the **p**:	3612
	12:17 the Lord had brought him out of the **p**.	5438
	16:23 they cast *them* into **p**, charging the jailor	5438
	16:24 thrust them into the inner **p**, and made	5438
	16:26 that the foundations of the **p** were shaken:	1201
	16:27 the **keeper of the p** awaking out of his	1200
	16:27 and seeing the **p** doors open, he drew out	5438
	16:36 the **keeper of the p** told this saying to	1200
	16:37 being Romans, and have cast *us* into **p**;	5438
	16:40 And they went out of the **p**,	5438
	26:10 and many of the saints did I shut up in **p**,	5438
1Pe	3:19 went and preached unto the spirits in **p**;	5438
Rev	2:10 the devil shall cast *some* of you into **p**,	5438
	20: 7 Satan shall be loosed out of his **p**,	5438

PRISONER (13) [PRISON]

Ps	79:11 Let the sighing of the **p** come before thee;	615
	102:20 hear the groaning of the **p**; to loose those	615
Mt	27:15 was wont to release unto the people a **p**,	1198
	27:16 And they had then a notable **p**,	1198
Mk	15: 6 at *that* feast he released unto them one **p**,	1198
Ac	23:18 Paul the **p** called me unto *him*, and	1198
	25:27 seemeth to me unreasonable to send a **p**,	1198
	28:17 *yet* was I delivered **p** from Jerusalem into	1198
Eph	3: 1 the **p** of Jesus Christ for you Gentiles,	1198
	4: 1 I therefore, the **p** of the Lord, beseech you	1198
2Ti	1: 8 the testimony of our Lord, nor of me his **p**:	1198
Phm	1: 1 a **p** of Jesus Christ, and Timothy *our*	1198
	1: 9 the aged, and now also a **p** of Jesus Christ.	1198

PRISONERS (20) [PRISON]

Ge	39:20 a place where the king's **p** *were* bound:	615
	39:22 hand all the **p** that *were* in the prison;	615
Nu	21: 1 and **took** *some* of them **p**.	7617+7628
Job	3:18 *There* the **p** rest together; they hear not	615
Ps	69:33 heareth the poor, and despiseth not his **p**.	615
	146: 7 to the hungry. The Lord looseth the **p**:	631
Isa	10: 4 me they shall bow down under the **p**,	616
	14:17 *that* opened not the house of his **p**?	615
	20: 4 king of Assyria lead away the Egyptians **p**,	7628
	24:22 *as* **p** are gathered in the pit, and shall be	616
	42: 7 to bring out the **p** from the prison,	616
	49: 9 That *thou* mayest say to the **p**, Go forth;	631
La	3:34 crush under his feet all the **p** of the earth,	615
Zec	9:11 thy **p** out of the pit wherein *is* no water.	615
	9:12 Turn ye to the strong hold, ye **p** of hope:	615
Ac	16:25 praises unto God: and the **p** heard them.	1198
	16:27 supposing that the **p** had been fled.	1198
	27: 1 certain other **p** unto *one* named Julius,	1202
	27:42 the soldiers' counsel was to kill the **p**,	1202
	28:16 centurion delivered the **p** to the captain	1198

PRISONS (3) [PRISON]

Lk	21:12 and into **p**, being brought before kings and	5438
Ac	22: 4 binding and delivering into **p** both men	5438
2Co	11:23 in **p** more frequent, in deaths oft.	5438

PRIVATE (1) [PRIVATELY, PRIVILY, PRIVY]

| 2Pe | 1:20 no prophecy of the scripture is of *any* **p** | 2398 |

PRIVATELY (8) [PRIVATE]

Mt	24: 3 the disciples came unto him **p**,	2398+2596
Mk	6:32 into a desert place by ship **p**,	2398+2596
	9:28 his disciples asked him **p**, Why	2398+2596
	13: 3 and John and Andrew asked him **p**,	2398+2596
Lk	9:10 went aside **p** into a desert place	2398+2596
	10:23 him unto *his* disciples, and said **p**,	2398+2596
Ac	23:19 hand, and went *with* him aside **p**,	2398+2596
Gal	2: 2 but **p** to them which were of	2398+2596

PRIVILY (15) [PRIVATE]

Jdg	9:31 messengers unto Abimelech **p**,	8649+871.1
1Sa	24: 4 the skirt of Saul's robe **p**.	3909+871.1+1886.1
Ps	10: 8 his eyes are **p set** against the poor.	6845
	11: 2 *they* may **p** shoot at the upright in	652+1119
	31: 4 \me out of the net that they have **laid p**	2934
	64: 5 commune of **laying snares p**; they say,	2934
	101: 5 Whoso **p** slandereth his neighbour, him	5643
	142: 3 I walked have they **p laid** a snare for me.	2934
Pr	1:11 let us **lurk p** for the innocent without	6845
	1:18 blood; they **lurk p** for their own lives.	6845
Mt	1:19 was minded to put her away **p**.	2977
	2: 7 when he had **p** called the wise men,	2977
Ac	16:37 and now do they thrust us out **p**?	2977
Gal	2: 4 who **came in p** to spy out our liberty	3922
2Pe	2: 1 who **p** shall **bring in** damnable heresies,	3919

PRIVY (4) [PRIVATE]

Dt	23: 1 the stones, or hath *his* **p** member cut off,	8212
1Ki	2:44 the wickedness which thine heart is **p** to,	3045
Eze	21:14 which **entereth into** their **p** chambers.	2314
Ac	5: 2 his wife also being **p** *to it*, and brought a	4894

PRIZE (2)

| 1Co | 9:24 in a race run all, but one receiveth the **p**? | 1017 |
| Php | 3:14 I press toward the mark for the **p** of | 1017 |

PROCEED (15) [PROCEEDED, PROCEEDETH, PROCEEDING]

Ex	25:35 according to the six branches that **p** out	3318
Jos	6:10 shall *any* word **p** out of your mouth,	3318
2Sa	7:12 which shall **p** out of thy bowels, and I	3318
Job	40: 5 yea, twice; but I will **p** no **further**.	3254
Isa	29:14 I will **p** to do a marvellous work amongst	3254
	51: 4 for a law shall **p** from me, and I will make	3318

P

Jer | 9: 3 they **p** from evil to evil, and they know | 3318
30:19 out of them shall **p** thanksgiving and | 3318
30:21 their governor shall **p** from the midst of | 3318
Hab | 1: 7 and their dignity shall **p** of themselves. | 3318
Mt | 15:18 those *things* which **p** out of the mouth | 1607
15:19 For out of the heart **p** evil thoughts, | 1831
Mk | 7:21 **p** evil thoughts, adulteries, fornications, | 1607
Eph | 4:29 Let no corrupt communication **p** out of | 1607
2Ti | 3: 9 But they shall **p** no further: for their folly | 4298

PROCEEDED (9) [PROCEED]

Nu | 30:12 whatsoever **p** out of her lips concerning | 4161
32:24 do that which hath **p** out of your mouth. | 3318
Jdg | 11:36 to me according to that which hath **p** out | 3254
Job | 36: 1 Elihu also **p**, and said, | 3254
Lk | 4:22 gracious words which **p** out of his mouth. | 1607
Jn | 8:42 for I **p** forth and came from God; | 1831
Ac | 12: 3 the Jews, he **p** further to take Peter also. | 4369
Rev | 4: 5 And out of the throne **p** lightnings and | 1607
19:21 horse, which *sword* **p** out of his mouth: | 1607

PROCEEDETH (11) [PROCEED]

Ge | 24:50 and said, The thing **p** from the LORD: | 3318
Nu | 30: 2 he shall do according to all that **p** out of | 3318
Dt | 8: 3 by every *word* **that p out** of the mouth of | 4161
1Sa | 24:13 Wickedness **p** from the wicked: | 3318
Ecc | 10: 5 sun, as an error *which* **p** from the ruler: | 3318
La | 3:38 Out of the mouth of the most High **p** not | 3318
Hab | 1: 4 righteous; therefore wrong judgment **p**. | 3318
Mt | 4: 4 by every *word* that **p** out of the mouth of | 1607
Jn | 15:26 which **p** from the Father, he shall testify | 1607
Jas | 3:10 Out of the same mouth **p** blessing and | 1831
Rev | 11: 5 fire **p** out of their mouth, | 1607

PROCEEDING (1) [PROCEED]

Rev | 22: 1 **p** out of the throne of God and of | 1607

PROCESS (5)

Ge | 4: 3 in p of time it came to pass, that Cain | 7093
38:12 **in p of time** the daughter | 3117+7235+1886.1
Ex | 2:23 pass in **p of time**, | 3117+7227+1886.1
Jdg | 11: 4 it came to pass **in p of time**, that | 3117+4480
2Ch | 21:19 that **in p of time**, | 3117+3117+4480+3807.1

PROCHORUS (1)

Ac | 6: 5 and P, and Nicanor, and Timon, | 4402

PROCLAIM (23) [PROCLAIMED, PROCLAIMETH, PROCLAIMING, PROCLAMATION]

Ex | 33:19 I will **p** the name of the LORD | 7121+871.1
Lev | 23: 2 which ye shall **p** *to be* holy convocations, | 7121
23: 4 which ye shall **p** in their seasons. | 7121
23:21 ye shall **p** on the selfsame day, *that* it may | 7121
23:37 which ye shall **p** *to be* holy convocations, | 7121
25:10 liberty throughout *all* the land unto all | 7121
Dt | 20:10 to fight against it, then **p** peace unto it. | 7121
Jdg | 7: 3 go to, **p** in the ears of the people, | 7121
1Ki | 21: 9 P a fast, and set Naboth on high among | 7121
2Ki | 10:20 Jehu said, P a solemn assembly for Baal. | 6942
Ne | 8:15 and **p** in all their cities, | 5674+6963
Est | 6: 9 the street of the city, and **p** before him, | 7121
Pr | 20: 6 Most men will **p** every one his own | 7121
Isa | 61: 1 to **p** liberty to the captives, and the | 7121
61: 2 To **p** the acceptable year of the LORD, | 7121
Jer | 3:12 Go and **p** these words toward the north, | 7121
7: 2 **p** there this word, and say, Hear the word | 7121
11: 6 P all these words in the cities of Judah, | 7121
19: 2 **p** there the words that I shall tell thee, | 7121
34: 8 at Jerusalem, to **p** liberty unto them; | 7121
34:17 behold, I **p** a liberty for you, saith | 7121
Joel | 3: 9 P ye this among the Gentiles; Prepare | 7121
Am | 4: 5 and **p** *and* publish the free offerings: | 7121

PROCLAIMED (16) [PROCLAIM]

Ex | 34: 5 and **p** the name of the LORD. | 7121+871.1
34: 6 **p**, The LORD, The LORD God, merciful | 7121
36: 6 they **caused** it **to be p** throughout | 5674+6963
1Ki | 21:12 They **p** a fast, and set Naboth on high | 7121
2Ki | 10:20 a solemn assembly for Baal. And they **p** *it*. | 7121
23:16 of the LORD which the man of God **p**, | 7121
23:16 of God proclaimed, who **p** these words. | 7121
23:17 **p** these things that thou hast done against | 7121
2Ch | 20: 3 and **p** a fast throughout all Judah. | 7121
Ezr | 8:21 I **p** a fast there, at the river Ahava, that | 7121
Est | 6:11 the street of the city, and **p** before him, | 8085
Isa | 62:11 the LORD hath **p** unto the end of | 8085
Jer | 36: 9 *that* they **p** a fast before the LORD *to* all | 7121
Jnh | 3: 5 and **p** a fast, and put on sackcloth, | 7121
3: 7 he **caused** *it* to be **p** and published | 2199
Lk | 12: 3 in closets shall be **p** upon the housetops. | 2784

PROCLAIMETH (1) [PROCLAIM]

Pr | 12:23 but the heart of fools **p** foolishness. | 7121

PROCLAIMING (3) [PROCLAIM]

Jer | 34:15 in **p** liberty every man to his neighbour; | 7121
34:17 in **p** liberty, every one to his brother, | 7121
Rev | 5: 2 And I saw a strong angel **p** with a loud | 2784

PROCLAMATION (9) [PROCLAIM]

Ex | 32: 5 Aaron **made p**, and said, To morrow *is* a | 7121
1Ki | 15:22 king Asa **made a p** throughout all Judah; | 8085
22:36 there went a **p** throughout the host about | 7440
2Ch | 24: 9 they made a **p** through Judah and | 6963
30: 5 to **make p** throughout all Israel, | 5674+6963
36:22 he **made a p** throughout all his | 5674+6963

Ezr | 1: 1 he **made a p** throughout all his | 5674+6963
10: 7 they **made p** throughout Judah | 5674+6963
Da | 5:29 his neck, and **made a p** concerning him, | 3745

PROCORUS See PROCHORUS

PROCURE (2) [PROCURED, PROCURETH]

Jer | 26:19 Thus *might* we **p** great evil against our | 6213
33: 9 and for all the prosperity that I **p** unto it. | 6213

PROCURED (2) [PROCURE]

Jer | 2:17 Hast thou not **p** this unto thyself, in that | 6213
4:18 thy doings have **p** these *things* unto thee; | 6213

PROCURETH (1) [PROCURE]

Pr | 11:27 He diligently seeketh good **p** favour: | 1245

PRODUCE (1)

Isa | 41:21 P your cause, saith the LORD; bring forth | 7126

PROFANE (33) [PROFANED, PROFANENESS, PROFANETH, PROFANING]

Lev | 18:21 neither shalt thou **p** the name of thy God: | 2490
19:12 neither shalt thou **p** the name of thy God | 2490
20: 3 my sanctuary, and to **p** my holy name. | 2490
21: 4 chief man among his people, to **p** himself. | 2490
21: 6 God, and not **p** the name of their God: | 2490
21: 7 shall not take a wife *that is* a whore, or **p**; | 2491
21: 9 if she herself by playing the whore, | 2490
21:12 nor **p** the sanctuary of his God; | 2490
21:14 or a divorced *woman*, or **p**, *or* a harlot, | 2491
21:15 Neither shall he **p** his seed among his | 2490
21:23 a blemish; that he **p** not my sanctuaries: | 2490
22: 2 that they **p** not my holy name *in* those | 2490
22: 9 sin for it, and die therefore, if they **p** it: | 2490
22:15 they shall not **p** the holy *things* of | 2490
22:32 Neither shall ye **p** my holy name; but I | 2490
Ne | 13:17 *is* this that ye do, and **p** the sabbath day? | 2490
Jer | 23:11 For both prophet and priest are **p**; yea, | 2610
Eze | 21:25 wicked prince of Israel, whose day | 2491
22:26 no difference between the holy and **p**, | 2455
23:39 the same day into my sanctuary to **p** it; | 2490
24:21 Behold, I *will* **p** my sanctuary, | 2490
28:16 I will **cast** thee **as p** out of the mountain | 2490
42:20 between the sanctuary and the **p** *place*. | 2455
44:23 *the* difference between the holy and **p**, | 2455
48:15 be a **p** *place* for the city, for dwelling, | 2455
Am | 2: 7 unto the *same* maid, to **p** my holy name: | 2490
Mt | 12: 5 the priests in the temple **p** the sabbath, | 953
Ac | 24: 6 Who also hath gone about to **p** the temple: | 953
1Ti | 1: 9 and for sinners, for unholy and **p**, | 952
4: 7 But refuse **p** and old wives' fables, | 952
6:20 avoiding **p** *and* vain babblings, | 952
2Ti | 2:16 But shun **p** *and* vain babblings: for they | 952
Heb | 12:16 *be* any fornicator, or **p** *person*, as Esau, | 952

PROFANED (15) [PROFANE]

Lev | 19: 8 he hath **p** the hallowed *thing* of | 2490
Ps | 89:39 thou hast **p** his crown *by casting it* to | 2490
Isa | 43:28 Therefore I have **p** the princes of | 2490
Eze | 22: 8 mine holy *things*, and hast **p** my sabbaths. | 2490
22:26 have **p** mine holy *things*: they have put | 2490
22:26 my sabbaths, and I am **p** among them. | 2490
23:38 in the same day, and have **p** my sabbaths. | 2490
25: 3 against my sanctuary, when it was **p**; | 2490
36:20 whither they went, they **p** my holy name, | 2490
36:21 which the house of Israel had **p** among | 2490
36:22 which ye have **p** among the heathen, | 2490
36:23 which was **p** among the heathen, | 2490
36:23 which ye have **p** in the midst of them; | 2490
Mal | 1:12 ye *have* **p** it, in that ye say, The table of | 2490
2:11 for Judah hath **p** the holiness of the LORD | 2490

PROFANENESS (1) [PROFANE]

Jer | 23:15 for from the prophets of Jerusalem is **p** | 2613

PROFANETH (1) [PROFANE]

Lev | 21: 9 by playing the whore, she **p** her father: | 2490

PROFANING (2) [PROFANE]

Ne | 13:18 yet ye bring more wrath upon Israel by **p** | 2490
Mal | 2:10 by **p** the covenant of our fathers? | 2490

PROFESS (3) [PROFESSED, PROFESSING, PROFESSION]

Dt | 26: 3 I **p** this day unto the LORD thy God, | 5046
Mt | 7:23 then will I **p** unto them, I never knew | 3670
Tit | 1:16 They **p** that *they* know God; but in works | 3670

PROFESSED (2) [PROFESS]

2Co | 9:13 **p** subjection unto the gospel of Christ, | 3671
1Ti | 6:12 hast **p** a good profession before many | 3670

PROFESSING (3) [PROFESS]

Ro | 1:22 P *themselves* to be wise, they became | 5335
1Ti | 2:10 But (which becometh women **p** godliness) | 1861
6:21 Which some **p** have erred concerning | 1861

PROFESSION (4) [PROFESS]

1Ti | 6:12 hast professed a good **p** before many | 3671
Heb | 3: 1 the Apostle and High Priest of our **p**, | 3671
4:14 the Son of God, let us hold fast *our* **p**. | 3671
10:23 Let us hold fast the **p** of *our* hope without | 3671

PROFIT (45) [PROFITABLE, PROFITED, PROFITETH, PROFITING, UNPROFITABLE]

Ge | 25:32 **what p** shall this birthright do to | 4100+3807.1
37:26 What *is it* if we slay our brother, | 1215
1Sa | 12:21 vain *things*, which cannot **p** nor deliver; | 3276
Est | 3: 8 it *is* not for the king's **p** to suffer them. | 7737
Job | 21:15 **what p** should we have, if we pray unto | 3276
30: 2 *might* the strength of their hands **p** me, | 3807.1
35: 3 and, What **p** shall I have, *if I be cleansed* | 3276
35: 8 thy righteousness *may* **p** the son of man. | NIH
Ps | 30: 9 What **p** *is there* in my blood, when I go | 1215
Pr | 10: 2 Treasures of wickedness **p** nothing: | 3276
11: 4 Riches **p** not in the day of wrath: | 3276
14:23 In all labour there is **p**: but the talk of | 4195
Ecc | 1: 3 What hath a man of all his labour | 3504
2:11 spirit, and *there was* no **p** under the sun. | 3504
3: 9 What **p** *hath* he that worketh in that | 3504
5: 9 Moreover the **p** of the earth *is* for all: | 3504
5:16 what **p** hath he that hath laboured for | 3504
7:11 *by it there is* **p** to them that see the sun. | 3148
Isa | 30: 5 of a people *that* could not **p** them, | 3276
30: 5 nor be a help nor a **p**, but a shame, and also | 3276
30: 6 to a people *that* shall not **p** them. | 3276
44: 9 their delectable *things* shall not **p**; | 3276
47:12 if so be thou shalt be able to **p**, if so be | 3276
48:17 LORD thy God which teacheth thee to **p**, | 3276
57:12 and thy works; for they shall not **p** thee. | 3276
Jer | 2: 8 and walked after *things* that do not **p**. | 3276
2:11 their glory for *that which* doth not **p**. | 3276
7: 8 ye trust in lying words, *that* cannot **p**. | 3276
12:13 put themselves to pain, *but* shall not **p**: | 3276
16:19 vanity, and *things* wherein *there is* no **p**. | 3276
23:32 they shall not **p** this people **at all**, | 3276+3276
Mal | 3:14 *what is it* that we have kept his | 1215
Mk | 8:36 For what shall it **p** a man, if he shall gain | 5623
Ro | 3: 1 or what **p** *is there* of circumcision? | 5622
1Co | 7:35 And this I speak for your own **p**; not that | 4851
10:33 in all *things*, not seeking mine own **p**, | 4851
10:33 the **p** of many, that they may be saved. | NIG
12: 7 Spirit is given to every man to **p** withal. | 4851
14: 6 speaking with tongues, what shall I **p** you, | 5623
Gal | 5: 2 circumcised, Christ shall **p** you nothing. | 5539
2Ti | 2:14 that *they* strive not about words to no **p**, | 5539
Heb | 4: 2 but the word preached did not **p** them, | 5623
12:10 he for *our* **p**, that *we* might be partakers | 4851
Jas | 2:14 What *doth it* **p**, my brethren, though a | 3786
2:16 *are* needful to the body; what *doth it* **p**? | 3786

PROFITABLE (13) [PROFIT]

Job | 22: 2 Can a man be **p** unto God, as he that is | 5532
22: 2 as he that is wise may be **p** unto himself? | 5532
Ecc | 10:10 more strength: but wisdom *is* **p** to direct. | 3504
Isa | 44:10 molten a graven image *that is* **p** for | 3276
Jer | 13: 7 girdle was marred, it was **p** for nothing. | 6743
Mt | 5:29 it is **p** for thee that one of thy members | 4851
5:30 it is **p** for thee that one of thy members | 4851
Ac | 20:20 And how I kept back nothing that was **p** | 4851
1Ti | 4: 8 godliness is **p** unto all *things*, having | 5624
2Ti | 3:16 and *is* **p** for doctrine, for reproof, | 5624
4:11 thee: for he is **p** to me for the ministry. | 2173
Tit | 3: 8 These *things* are good and **p** unto men. | 5624
Phm | 1:11 but now **p** to thee and to me: | 2173

PROFITED (6) [PROFIT]

Job | 33:27 *that which was* right, and it **p** me not; | 7737
Mt | 15: 5 *by* whatsoever thou mightest be **p** by me; | 5623
16:26 For what is a man **p**, if he shall gain | 5623
Mk | 7:11 *by* whatsoever thou mightest be **p** by me; | 5623
Gal | 1:14 and **p** in the Jews' religion above many | 4298
Heb | 13: 9 which have not **p** them that have been | 5623

PROFITETH (6) [PROFIT]

Job | 34: 9 It **p** a man nothing that he should delight | 5532
Hab | 2:18 What **p** the graven image that the maker | 3276
Jn | 6:63 spirit that quickeneth; the flesh **p** nothing: | 5623
Ro | 2:25 For circumcision verily **p**, if thou keep | 5623
1Co | 13: 3 and have not charity, it **p** me nothing. | 5623
1Ti | 4: 8 For bodily exercise **p** little; | 1510+5624

PROFITING (1) [PROFIT]

1Ti | 4:15 to them; that thy **p** may appear to all. | 4297

PROFOUND (1)

Hos | 5: 2 the revolters are **p** to make slaughter, | 6009

PROGENITORS (1)

Ge | 49:26 **p** unto the utmost bound of the | 2029

PROGNOSTICATORS (1)

Isa | 47:13 the monthly **p**, stand *up*, and save thee | 3045

PROJECTIONS See TENONS

PROLONG (14) [PROLONGED, PROLONGETH]

Dt | 4:26 ye shall not **p** *your* days upon it, | 748
4:40 that thou mayest **p** *thy* days upon the earth, | 748
5:33 *that* ye may **p** *your* days in the land which | 748
11: 9 that ye may **p** *your* days in the land, | 748
17:20 to the end that he may **p** *his* days in his | 748
22: 7 with thee, and *that* thou mayest **p** *thy* days. | 748
30:18 *that* ye shall not **p** *your* days upon the land, | 748
32:47 through this thing ye shall **p** *your* days in | 748
Job | 6:11 *what is* mine end, that I should **p** my life? | 748
15:29 neither shall he **p** the perfection thereof | 5186
Ps | 61: 6 wilt **p** the king's *life*: | 3117+3117+3254+5921

P

Pr	28:16 that hateth covetousness shall **p** *his* days.	748
Ecc	8:13 neither shall he **p** *his* days, *which are* as a	748
Isa	53:10 he shall **p** *his* days, and the pleasure of	748

PROLONGED (9) [PROLONG]

Dt	5:16 that thy days may be **p**, and that it may go	748
	6: 2 days of thy life; and that thy days may be **p**.	748
Pr	28: 2 *and* knowledge the state *thereof* shall be **p**.	748
Ecc	8:12 evil an hundred *times*, and *his* days be **p**,	748
Isa	13:22 near to come, and her days shall not be **p**.	4900
Eze	12:22 The days are **p**, and every vision faileth?	748
	12:25 shall come to pass; it shall be no more **p**:	4900
	12:28 There shall none of my words be **p** any	4900
Da	7:12 their lives were **p** for a season and time.	754

PROLONGETH (2) [PROLONG]

Pr	10:27 The fear of the Lᴏʀᴅ **p** days:	3254
Ecc	7:15 there is a wicked *man* that **p** *his* life in his	748

PROMISCUOUS See WHORE; WHORE'S; WHORES

PROMISE (53) [PROMISED, PROMISEDST, PROMISES, PROMISING]

Nu	14:34 and ye shall know my **breach of p**.	8569
1Ki	8:56 hath not failed one word of all his good **p**,	1697
2Ch	1: 9 let thy **p** unto David my father be	1697
Ne	5:12 that they should do according to this **p**.	1697
	5:13 his labour, that performeth not this **p**,	1697
	5:13 And the people did according to this **p**.	1697
Ps	77: 8 for ever? doth *his* **p** fail for evermore?	562
	105:42 For he remembered his holy **p**,	1697
Lk	24:49 I send the **p** of my Father upon you:	1860
Ac	1: 4 but wait for the **p** of the Father, which,	1860
	2:33 having received of the Father the **p** of	1860
	2:39 the **p** is unto you, and to your children,	1860
	7:17 But when the time of the **p** drew nigh,	1860
	13:23 to *his* **p** raised unto Israel a Saviour,	1860
	13:32 how that the **p** which was made unto	1860
	23:21 are they ready, looking for a **p** from thee.	1860
	26: 6 am judged for the hope of the **p** made of	1860
	26: 7 Unto which **p** our twelve tribes,	NIG
Ro	4:13 For the **p**, that he should be the heir of	1860
	4:14 void, and the **p** made of none effect:	1860
	4:16 to the end the **p** might be sure to all	1860
	4:20 He staggered not at the **p** of God through	1860
	9: 8 the children of the **p** are counted for	1860
	9: 9 this *is* the word of **p**, At this time will I	1860
Gal	3:14 that we might receive the **p** of the Spirit	1860
	3:17 that *it* should make the **p** of none effect.	1860
	3:18 *be* of the law, *it is* no more of **p**:	1860
	3:18 but God gave *it* to Abraham by **p**.	1860
	3:19 should come to whom the **p** was **made**;	1861
	3:22 that the **p** by faith of Jesus Christ might	1860
	3:29 and heirs according to the **p**.	1860
	4:23 but he of the freewoman *was* by **p**.	1860
	4:28 as Isaac was, are the children of **p**.	1860
Eph	1:13 ye were sealed with *that* holy Spirit of **p**,	1860
	2:12 and strangers from the covenants of **p**,	1860
	3: 6 partakers of his **p** in Christ by the gospel:	1860
	6: 2 (which is the first commandment with **p**;)	1860
1Ti	4: 8 all *things*, having of the life that now is,	1860
2Ti	1: 1 to the **p** of life which is in Christ	1860
Heb	4: 1 a **p** being left *us* of entering into his rest,	1860
	6:13 For when God **made p** to Abraham,	1861
	6:15 had patiently endured, he obtained the **p**.	1860
	6:17 heirs of **p** the immutability of his counsel,	1860
	9:15 they which are called might receive the **p**	1860
	10:36 the will of God, ye might receive the **p**.	1860
	11: 9 By faith he sojourned in the land of **p**, as	1860
	11: 9 Jacob, the heirs with *him* of the same **p**:	1860
	11:39 report through faith, received not the **p**:	1860
2Pe	2:19 they **p** them liberty, they themselves	1861
	3: 4 And saying, Where is the **p** of his coming?	1860
	3: 9 The Lord is not slack concerning *his* **p**,	1860
	3:13 Nevertheless we, according to his **p**,	1862
1Jn	2:25 this is the **p** that he hath promised us,	1860

PROMISED (48) [PROMISE]

Ex	12:25 according as he hath **p**, that ye shall keep	1696
Nu	14:40 up unto the place which the Lᴏʀᴅ hath **p**:	559
Dt	1:11 ye *are*, and bless you, as he hath **p** you!)	1696
	6: 3 as the Lᴏʀᴅ God of thy fathers hath **p**	1696
	9:28 them into the land which he **p** them,	1696
	10: 9 according as the Lᴏʀᴅ thy God **p** him.	1696
	12:20 as he hath **p** thee, and thou shalt say,	1696
	15: 6 thy God blesseth thee, as he **p** thee:	1696
	19: 8 give thee all the land which he **p** to give	1696
	23:23 God, which thou hast **p** with thy mouth.	1696
	26:18 as he hath **p** thee, and that *thou*	1696
	27: 3 as the Lᴏʀᴅ God of thy fathers hath **p**	1696
Jos	9:21 as the princes had **p** them.	1696
	22: 4 rest unto your brethren, as he **p** them:	1696
	23: 5 as the Lᴏʀᴅ your God hath **p** unto you.	1696
	23:10 *is* that fighteth for you, as he hath **p** you.	1696
	23:15 which the Lᴏʀᴅ your God **p** you;	1696
2Sa	7:28 hast **p** this goodness unto thy servant:	1696
1Ki	2:24 who hath made me a house, as he **p**,	1696
	5:12 gave Solomon wisdom, as he **p** him:	1696
	8:20 as the Lᴏʀᴅ **p**, and have built a house for	1696
	8:56 people Israel, according to all that he **p**:	1696
	8:56 which he **p** by the hand of Moses his	1696
	9: 5 as I **p** to David thy father, saying,	1696
2Ki	8:19 as he **p** him to give to him alway a light,	559
1Ch	17:26 and hast **p** this goodness unto thy servant:	1696

2Ch	6:10 as the Lᴏʀᴅ **p**, and have built the house	1696
	6:15 my father *that* which thou hast **p** him,	1696
	6:16 my father *that* which thou hast **p** him,	1696
	21: 7 as he **p** to give a light to him and to his	559
Ne	9:23 *concerning* which thou hadst **p** to their	559
Est	4: 7 the sum of the money that Haman had **p**	559
Jer	32:42 them all the good that I have **p** them.	1696
	33:14 which I have **p** unto the house of Israel	1696
Mt	14: 7 Whereupon he with an oath to give her	3670
Mk	14:11 they were glad, and **p** to give him money.	1861
Lk	1:72 To perform the mercy **p** to our fathers,	NIG
	22: 6 he **p**, and sought opportunity to betray	1843
Ac	7: 5 yet he **p** that *he* would give it to him for a	1861
Ro	1: 2 (Which he had **p** afore by his prophets in	4279
	4:21 he had **p**, he was able also to perform.	1861
Tit	1: 2 that cannot lie, **p** before the world began;	1861
Heb	10:23 wavering; (for he *is* faithful that **p**;)	1861
	11:11 she judged him faithful who had **p**.	1861
	12:26 but now he hath **p**, saying, Yet once *more*	1861
Jas	1:12 which the Lord hath **p** to them that love	1861
	2: 5 heirs of the kingdom which he hath **p** to	1861
1Jn	2:25 And this is the promise that he hath **p** us,	1861

PROMISEDST (3) [PROMISE]

1Ki	8:24 servant David my father that thou **p** him;	1696
	8:25 servant David my father that thou **p** him,	1696
Ne	9:15 **p** them that *they* should go in to possess	559

PROMISES (13) [PROMISE]

Ro	9: 4 law, and the service *of God*, and the **p**;	1860
	15: 8 to confirm the **p** made unto the fathers:	1860
2Co	1:20 For all the **p** of God in him *are* yea,	1860
	7: 1 Having therefore these **p**, dearly beloved,	1860
Gal	3:16 Abraham and his seed were the **p** made.	1860
	3:21 *Is* the law then against the **p** of God?	1860
Heb	6:12 through faith and patience inherit the **p**.	1860
	7: 6 and blessed him that had the **p**.	1860
	8: 6 which was established upon better **p**.	1860
	11:13 not having received the **p**, but having	1860
	11:17 he that had received the **p** offered up *his*	1860
	11:33 wrought righteousness, obtained **p**,	1860
2Pe	1: 4 unto us exceeding great and precious **p**:	1862

PROMISING (1) [PROMISE]

Eze	13:22 from his wicked way, by **p** him **life**:	2421

PROMOTE (5) [PROMOTED, PROMOTION]

Nu	22:17 **p** thee **unto** very great **honour**,	3513+3513
	22:37 I not able indeed to **p** to **honour**?	3513
	24:11 to **p** thee **unto great honour**;	3513+3513
Est	3: 1 After these things did king Ahasuerus **p**	1431
Pr	4: 8 Exalt her, and she shall **p** thee: she shall	7311

PROMOTED (5) [PROMOTE]

Jdg	9: 9 and man, and go to be **p** over the trees?	5128
	9:11 good fruit, and go to be **p** over the trees?	5128
	9:13 and man, and go to be **p** over the trees?	5128
Est	5:11 the things where*in* the king had **p** him,	1431
Da	3:30 the king **p** Shadrach, Meshach,	6744

PROMOTION (2) [PROMOTE]

Ps	75: 6 For **p** *cometh* neither from the east,	7311
Pr	3:35 but shame shall be the **p** of fools.	7311

PRONOUNCE (23) [PRONOUNCED, PRONOUNCING]

Lev	5: 4 whatsoever *it be* that a man shall **p** with	981
	13: 3 shall look on him, and **p** him **unclean**.	2930
	13: 6 in the skin, the priest shall **p** him **clean**:	2891
	13: 8 then the priest shall **p** him **unclean**:	2930
	13:11 the priest shall **p** him **unclean**:	2930
	13:13 he shall **p** *him* **clean** *that hath* the plague:	2891
	13:15 the raw flesh, and **p** him to be **unclean**:	2930
	13:17 the priest shall **p** *him* **clean** *that hath*	2891
	13:20 the priest shall **p** him **unclean**:	2930
	13:22 then the priest shall **p** him **unclean**:	2930
	13:23 and the priest shall **p** him **clean**.	2891
	13:25 wherefore the priest shall **p** him **unclean**	2930
	13:27 then the priest shall **p** him **unclean**:	2930
	13:28 then the priest shall **p** him **clean**:	2891
	13:30 then the priest shall **p** him **unclean**:	2930
	13:34 skin; then the priest shall **p** him **clean**:	2891
	13:37 *is* clean: and the priest shall **p** him **clean**.	2891
	13:44 priest shall **p** him **utterly unclean**,	2930+2930
	13:59 to **p** it **clean**, or to pronounce it unclean.	2891
	13:59 to pronounce it clean, or to **p** it **unclean**.	2930
	14: 7 shall **p** him **clean**, and shall let the living	2891
	14:48 the priest shall **p** the house **clean**, because	2891
Jdg	12: 6 for he could not frame to **p** *it* right.	1696

PRONOUNCED (14) [PRONOUNCE]

Ne	6:12 but *that* he **p** this prophecy against me:	1696
Jer	11:17 that planted thee, hath **p** evil against thee,	1696
	16:10 Wherefore hath the Lᴏʀᴅ **p** all this great	1696
	18: 8 If that nation, against whom I have **p**,	1696
	19:15 all her towns all the evil that I have **p**	1696
	25:13 all my words which I have **p** against it,	1696
	26:13 him of the evil that he hath **p** against you.	1696
	26:19 of the evil which he had **p** against them?	1696
	34: 5 for I have **p** the word, saith the Lᴏʀᴅ.	1696
	35:17 all the evil that I have **p** against them:	1696
	36: 7 the fury that the Lᴏʀᴅ hath **p** against this	1696
	36:18 He **p** all these words unto me with his	7121
	36:31 all the evil that I have **p** against them;	1696
	40: 2 The Lᴏʀᴅ thy God hath **p** this evil upon	1696

PRONOUNCING (1) [PRONOUNCE]

Lev	5: 4 **p** with *his* lips to do evil, or to do good,	981

PROOF (5) [PROVE]

2Co	2: 9 I write, that I might know the **p** of you,	1382
	8:24 the **p** of your love, and of our boasting on	1732
	13: 3 Since ye seek a **p** of Christ speaking in me,	1382
Php	2:22 But ye know the **p** of him, that, as a son	1382
2Ti	4: 5 an evangelist, **make full p** of thy ministry.	4135

PROOFS (1) [PROVE]

Ac	1: 3 after his passion by many **infallible p**,	5039

PROPER (4)

1Ch	29: 3 I have of mine own **p** good, *of* gold and	5459
Ac	1:19 insomuch as that field is called in their **p**	2398
1Co	7: 7 But every man hath his **p** gift of God,	2398
Heb	11:23 because they saw he was a **p** child;	791

PROPERTY See HABITATION

PROPHECIES (2) [PROPHESY]

1Co	13: 8 but whether *there be* **p**, they shall fail;	4394
1Ti	1:18 according to the **p** which went before on	4394

PROPHECY (21) [PROPHESY]

2Ch	9:29 in the **p** of Ahijah the Shilonite, and in	5016
	15: 8 **p** *of* Oded the prophet, he took courage,	5016
Ne	6:12 but *that* he pronounced *this* **p** against me:	5016
Pr	30: 1 of Agur the son of Jakeh, *even* the **p**:	4853
	31: 1 the **p** that his mother taught him.	4853
Da	9:24 to seal up the vision and **p**, and to anoint	5030
Mt	13:14 And in them is fulfilled the **p** of Esaias,	4394
Ro	12: 6 whether **p**, *let us prophesy* according to	4394
1Co	12:10 to another **p**; to another discerning of	4394
	13: 2 And though I have *the gift of* **p**,	4394
1Ti	4:14 is in thee, which was given thee by **p**,	4394
2Pe	1:19 We have also a more sure word of **p**;	4397
	1:20 that no **p** of the scripture is of *any* private	4394
	1:21 For the **p** came not in old time by the will	4394
Rev	1: 3 and they that hear the words of *this* **p**,	4394
	11: 6 that it rain not in the days of their **p**:	4394
	19:10 for the testimony of Jesus is the spirit of **p**.	4394
	22: 7 keepeth the sayings of the **p** of this book.	4394
	22:10 Seal not the sayings of the **p** of this book:	4394
	22:18 heareth the words of the **p** of this book,	4394
	22:19 from the words of the book of this **p**,	4394

PROPHESIED (50) [PROPHESY]

Nu	11:25 upon them, they **p**, and did not cease.	5012
	11:26 the tabernacle: and they **p** in the camp.	5012
1Sa	10:10 came upon him, and he **p** among them.	5012
	10:11 he **p** among the prophets, then the people	5012
	18:10 and he **p** in the midst of the house:	5012
	19:20 the messengers of Saul, and they also **p**.	5012
	19:21 other messengers, and they **p** likewise.	5012
	19:21 again the third time, and they **p** also.	5012
	19:23 went on, and **p**, until he came to Naioth	5012
	19:24 before Samuel in like manner,	5012
1Ki	18:29 they **p** until *the time* of the offering of	5012
	22:10 and all the prophets **p** before them.	5012
	22:12 all the prophets **p** so, saying, Go up *to*	5012
1Ch	25: 2 according to the order of the king.	5012
	25: 3 who **p** with a harp, to give thanks and	5012
2Ch	18: 7 for he never **p** good unto me,	5012
	18: 9 and all the prophets **p** before them.	5012
	18:11 all the prophets **p** so, saying, Go up *to*	5012
Ezr	5: 1 Eliezer the son of Dodavah of Mareshah **p**	5012
Jer	5: 1 **p** unto the Jews that *were* in Judah and	5013
	2: 8 the prophets **p** by Baal, and walked after	5012
	20: 1 heard *that* Jeremiah **p** these things.	5012
	20: 6 all thy friends, to whom thou hast **p** lies.	5012
	23:13 in Baal, and caused my people Israel	5012
	23:21 I have not spoken to them, yet they **p**.	5012
	25:13 which Jeremiah hath **p** against all	5012
	26: 9 Why hast thou **p** in the name of	5012
	26:11 for he hath **p** against this city, as ye have	5012
	26:18 Micah the Morasthite **p** in the days of	5012
	26:20 there was also a man that **p** in the name	5012
	26:20 against this city and against this land	5012
	28: 6 perform thy words which thou hast **p**,	5012
	28: 8 before thee of old **p** both against many	5012
	29:31 Because that Shemaiah hath **p** unto you,	5012
	37:19 Where *are* now your prophets which **p**	5012
Eze	11:13 it came to pass, when I **p**, that Pelatiah	5012
	37: 7 So I **p** as I was commanded: and as I	5012
	37: 7 as I **p**, there was a noise, and behold a	5012
	37:10 I **p** as he commanded me, and the breath	5012
	38:17 which **p** in those days *many* years, that *I*	5012
Zec	13: 4 every one of his vision, when he hath **p**;	5012
Mt	7:22 Lord, Lord, have we not **p** in thy name?	4395
	11:13 all the prophets and the law **p** until John.	4395
Mk	7: 6 Well hath Esaias **p** of you hypocrites, as it	4395
Lk	1:67 filled with the Holy Ghost, and **p**, saying,	4395
Jn	11:51 he **p** that Jesus should die for *that* nation;	4395
Ac	19: 6 and they spake with tongues, and **p**.	4395
1Co	14: 5 spake with tongues, but rather that ye **p**:	4395
1Pe	1:10 **p** of the grace *that should come* unto	4395
Jude	1:14 from Adam, of these, saying, Behold,	4395

PROPHESIETH (7) [PROPHESY]

Jer	28: 9 The prophet which **p** of peace, when	5012
Eze	12:27 and he **p** of the times that *are* far off.	5012
Zec	13: 3 him shall thrust him through when he **p**,	5012
1Co	11: 5 **p** with *her* head uncovered dishonoureth	4395

P

1Co	14:	3 But he that **p** speaketh unto men *to*	4395
	14:	4 but he that **p** edifieth *the* church.	4395
	14:	5 greater *is* he that **p** than he that speaketh	4395

PROPHESY (90) [PROPHECIES, PROPHECY,
PROPHESIED, PROPHESIETH, PROPHESYING,
PROPHESYINGS, PROPHET, PROPHET'S,
PROPHETESS, PROPHETS]

Nu	11:27	when Eldad and Medad do **p** in the camp.	5012
1Sa	10:	5 and a harp, before them; and they shall **p:**	5012
	10:	6 shalt **p** with them, and shalt be turned	5012
1Ki	22:	8 for he doth not **p** good concerning me,	5012
	22:18	I not tell thee that he would **p** no good	5012
1Ch	25:	1 of Jeduthun, who should **p** with harps,	5012
2Ch	18:17	I not tell thee *that* he would not **p** good	5012
Isa	30:10	**P** not unto us right *things,* speak unto us	2372
	30:10	speak unto us smooth *things,* **p** deceits:	2372
Jer	5:31	prophets **p** falsely, and the priests bear	5012
	11:21	**P** not in the name of the LORD,	5012
	14:14	me, The prophets **p** lies in my name:	5012
	14:14	they **p** unto you a false vision and	5012
	14:15	the prophets that **p** in my name,	5012
	14:16	people to whom they **p** shall be cast out	5012
	19:14	whither the LORD had sent him to **p;**	5012
	23:16	words of the prophets that **p** unto you:	5012
	23:25	that **p** lies in my name, saying, I have	5012
	23:26	be in the heart of the prophets that **p** lies?	5012
	23:32	I *am* against them that **p** false dreams,	5012
	25:30	Therefore **p** thou against them all these	5012
	26:12	The LORD sent me to **p** against this house	5012
	27:10	they **p** a lie unto you, to remove you far	5012
	27:14	king of Babylon: for they **p** a lie unto you.	5012
	27:15	the LORD, yet they **p** a lie in my name;	5012
	27:15	ye, and the prophets that **p** unto you.	5012
	27:16	words of your prophets that **p** unto you,	5012
	27:16	from Babylon: for they **p** a lie to you.	5012
	29:	9 For they **p** falsely unto you in my name:	5012
	29:21	which **p** a lie unto you in my name;	5012
	32:	3 saying, Wherefore dost thou **p,** and say,	5012
Eze	4:	7 *be* uncovered, and thou shalt **p** against it.	5012
	6:	2 mountains of Israel, and **p** against them,	5012
	11:	4 Therefore **p** against them, prophesy,	5012
	11:	4 prophesy against them, **p,** O son of man.	5012
	13:	2 **p** against the prophets of Israel that	5012
	13:	2 against the prophets of Israel that **p,**	5012
	13:	2 thou unto them that **p** out of their own	5030
	13:16	To wit, the prophets of Israel which **p**	5012
	13:17	people, which **p** out of their own heart;	5012
	13:17	their own heart; and **p** thou against them,	5012
	20:46	and **p** against the forest of the south field;	5012
	21:	2 and **p** against the land of Israel,	5012
	21:	9 Son of man, **p,** and say, Thus saith	5012
	21:14	**p,** and smite *thine* hands together,	5012
	21:28	thou, son of man and say, Thus saith	5012
	25:	2 the Ammonites, and **p** against them;	5012
	28:21	thy face against Zidon, and **p** against it,	5012
	29:	2 and **p** against him, and against all Egypt:	5012
	30:	2 of man, and say, Thus saith the Lord	5012
	34:	2 **p** against the shepherds of Israel,	5012
	34:	2 shepherds of Israel, **p,** and say unto them,	5012
	35:	2 face against mount Seir, and **p** against it,	5012
	36:	1 **p** unto the mountains of Israel, and say,	5012
	36:	3 Therefore **p** and say, Thus saith the Lord	5012
	36:	6 **P** therefore concerning the land of Israel,	5012
	37:	4 **P** upon these bones, and say unto them,	5012
	37:	9 **P** unto the wind, prophesy, son of man,	5012
	37:	9 **p,** son of man, and say to the wind,	5012
	37:12	Therefore **p** and say unto them, Thus	5012
	38:	2 of Meshech and Tubal, and **p** against him,	5012
	38:14	son of man, **p** and say unto Gog,	5012
	39:	1 thou son of man, **p** against Gog, and say,	5012
Joel	2:28	your sons and your daughters shall **p,**	5012
Am	2:12	commanded the prophets, saying, **P** not.	5012
	3:	8 Lord GOD hath spoken, who can but **p?**	5012
	7:12	Judah, and there eat bread, and **p** there:	5012
	7:13	**p** not again any more *at* Beth-el: for it *is*	5012
	7:15	unto me, Go, **p** unto my people Israel.	5012
	7:16	**P** not against Israel, and drop not *thy*	5012
Mic	2:	6 **P** ye not, *say* they to them that prophesy:	5197
	2:	6 Prophesy ye not, *say they* to them that **p:**	5197
	2:	6 shall not **p** to them, *that* they shall not	5197
	2:11	*saying,* I will **p** unto thee of wine and	5197
Zec	13:	3 *that* when any shall yet **p,** then his father	5012
Mt	15:	7 well did Esaias **p** of you, saying,	4395
	26:68	Saying, **P** unto us, *thou* Christ, Who is he	4395
Mk	14:65	and to buffet him, and to say unto him, **P:**	4395
Lk	22:64	and asked him, saying, **P,** who is it that	4395
Ac	2:17	and your sons and your daughters shall **p,**	4395
	2:18	those days of my Spirit; and they shall **p:**	4395
	21:	9 had four daughters, virgins, which did **p.**	4395
Ro	12:	6 *us* **p** according to the proportion of faith;	NIG
1Co	13:	9 For we know in part, and we **p** in part.	4395
	13:	1 spiritual *gifts,* but rather that ye may **p.**	4395
	14:24	But if all **p,** and there come in one that	4395
	14:31	For ye may all **p** one by one, that all may	4395
	14:39	covet to **p,** and forbid not to speak with	4395
Rev	10:11	Thou must **p** again before many peoples,	4395
	11:	3 they shall **p** a thousand two hundred *and*	4395

PROPHESYING (6) [PROPHESY]

1Sa	10:13	when he had made an end of **p,** he came	5012
	19:20	they saw the company of the prophets **p,**	5012
Ezr	6:14	they prospered through the **p** of Haggai	5017
1Co	11:	4 Every man praying or **p,** having *his* head	4395
	14:	6 or by knowledge, or by **p,** or by doctrine?	4394

| 1Co | 14:22 | **p** *serveth* not for them that believe not, | 4394 |

PROPHESYINGS (1) [PROPHESY]

| 1Th | 5:20 | Despise not **p.** | 4394 |

PROPHET (242) [PROPHESY]

Ge	20:	7 for he *is* a **p,** and he shall pray for thee,	5030
Ex	7:	1 and Aaron thy brother shall be thy **p.**	5030
Nu	12:	6 If there be a **p** among you, *I* the LORD	5030
Dt	13:	1 there arise among you a **p,** or a dreamer	5030
	13:	3 not hearken unto the words of that **p,**	5030
	13:	5 that **p,** or that dreamer of dreams, shall be	5030
	18:15	up unto thee a **P** from the midst of thee,	5030
	18:18	I will raise them up a **P** from among their	5030
	18:20	**p,** which shall presume to speak a word	5030
	18:20	name of other gods, even that **p** shall die.	5030
	18:22	When a **p** speaketh in the name of	5030
	18:22	the **p** hath spoken it presumptuously:	5030
	34:10	there arose not a **p** since in Israel like	5030
Jdg	6:	8 That the LORD sent a **p** unto the children	5030
1Sa	3:20	*was* established to be a **p** of the LORD.	5030
	9:	9 he that is now *called* a **P** was beforetime	5030
	22:	5 the **p** Gad said unto David, Abide not in	5030
2Sa	7:	2 That the king said unto Nathan the **p,**	5030
	12:25	he sent by the hand of Nathan the **p;**	5030
	24:11	the word of the LORD came unto the **p**	5030
1Ki	1:	8 Nathan the **p,** and Shimei, and Rei,	5030
	1:10	Nathan the **p,** and Benaiah, and the	5030
	1:22	with the king, Nathan the **p** also came in.	5030
	1:23	the king, saying, Behold Nathan the **p.**	5030
	1:32	Nathan the **p,** and Benaiah the son of	5030
	1:34	Nathan the **p** anoint him there king over	5030
	1:38	Nathan the **p,** and Benaiah the son of	5030
	1:44	Nathan the **p,** and Benaiah the son of	5030
	1:45	Nathan the **p** have anointed him king in	5030
	11:29	the Ahijah the Shilonite found him in	5030
	13:11	Now there dwelt an old **p** in Beth-el;	5030
	13:18	I *am* a **p** also as thou *art;* and an angel	5030
	13:20	came unto the **p** that brought him back:	5030
	13:23	*to wit,* for the **p** whom he had brought	5030
	13:25	told *it* in the city where the old **p** dwelt.	5030
	13:26	when the **p** that brought him back from	5030
	13:29	the **p** took up the carcase of the man of	5030
	13:29	the old **p** came to the city, to mourn and	5030
	14:	2 behold, there *is* Ahijah the **p,** which told	5030
	14:18	by the hand of his servant Ahijah the **p,**	5030
	16:	7 also by the hand of the **p** Jehu the son of	5030
	16:12	he spake against Baasha by Jehu the **p,**	5030
	18:22	I, *even* I only, remain a **p** of the LORD;	5030
	18:36	that Elijah the **p** came near, and said,	5030
	19:16	shalt thou anoint to be **p** in thy room.	5030
	20:13	there came a **p** unto Ahab king of Israel,	5030
	20:22	the **p** came to the king of Israel,	5030
	20:38	the **p** departed, and waited for the king	5030
	22:	7 *Is* there not here a **p** of the LORD besides,	5030
2Ki	3:11	*Is* there not here a **p** of the LORD,	5030
	5:	3 Would God my lord *were* with the **p** that	5030
	5:	8 he shall know that there is a **p** in Israel.	5030
	5:13	*if* the **p** had bid thee *do some* great thing,	5030
	6:12	Elisha, the **p** that *is* in Israel, telleth	5030
	9:	1 Elisha the **p** called one of the children of	5030
	9:	4 young man, *even* the young man the **p,**	5030
	14:25	the son of Amittai, the **p,** which *was* of	5030
	19:	2 to Esai the **p** the son of Amoz.	5030
	20:	1 **p** Isaiah the son of Amoz came to him,	5030
	20:11	Isaiah the **p** cried unto the LORD:	5030
	20:14	came Isaiah the **p** unto king Hezekiah,	5030
	23:18	with the bones of the **p** that came out of	5030
1Ch	17:	1 that David said to Nathan the **p,**	5030
	29:29	in the book of Nathan the **p,** and in	5030
2Ch	9:29	not written in the book of Nathan the **p,**	5030
	12:	5 came Shemaiah the **p** to Rehoboam,	5030
	12:15	written in the book of Shemaiah the **p,**	5030
	13:22	*are* written in the story of the **p** Iddo.	5030
	15:	8 the prophecy *of* Oded the **p,** he took	5030
	18:	6 *Is there* not here a **p** of the LORD besides,	5030
	21:12	came a writing to him from Elijah the **p,**	5030
	25:15	sent unto him a **p,** which said unto him,	5030
	25:16	the **p** forbare, and said, I know that God	5030
	26:22	first and last, did Isaiah the **p,** the son of	5030
	28:	9 a **p** of the LORD was there, whose name	5030
	29:25	of Gad the king's seer, and Nathan the **p:**	5030
	32:20	the **p** Isaiah the son of Amoz, prayed and	5030
	32:32	*are* written in the vision of Isaiah the **p,**	5030
	35:18	in Israel from the days of Samuel the **p;**	5030
	36:12	not himself before Jeremiah the **p**	5030
Ezr	5:	1 Haggai the **p,** and Zechariah the son of	5029
	6:14	through the prophesying of Haggai the **P**	5029
Ps	51:	1 when Nathan the **p** came unto him,	5030
	74:	9 *there* is no more any **p:** neither *is there*	5030
Isa	3:	2 the **p,** and the prudent, and the ancient,	5030
	9:15	and the **p** that teacheth lies, he *is* the tail.	5030
	28:	7 the **p** have erred through strong drink,	5030
	37:	2 unto Isaiah the **p** the son of Amoz.	5030
	38:	1 Isaiah the **p** the son of Amoz came unto	5030
	39:	3 came Isaiah the **p** unto king Hezekiah,	5030
Jer	1:	5 *and* I ordained thee a **p** unto the nations.	5030
	6:13	from the **p** even unto the priest every one	5030
	8:10	from the **p** even unto the priest every one	5030
	14:18	both the **p** and the priest go about into a	5030
	18:18	from the wise, nor the word from the **p.**	5030
	20:	2 Pashur smote Jeremiah the **p,** and put	5030
	23:11	For both **p** and priest are profane; yea,	5030
	23:28	The **p** that hath a dream, let him tell a	5030
	23:33	the **p,** or a priest, shall say, saying,	5030

Jer	23:34	*for* the **p,** and the priest, and the people,	5030
	23:37	Thus shalt thou say to the **p,** What hath	5030
	25:	2 The which Jeremiah the **p** spake unto all	5030
	28:	1 *that* Hananiah the son of Azur the **p,**	5030
	28:	5 the **p** Jeremiah said unto the prophet	5030
	28:	5 the prophet Jeremiah said unto the **p**	5030
	28:	6 Even the **p** Jeremiah said, Amen:	5030
	28:	9 The **p** which prophesieth of peace,	5030
	28:	9 the word of the **p** shall come to pass,	5030
	28:	9 *then* shall the **p** be known, that the LORD	5030
	28:10	Hananiah the **p** took the yoke from off	5030
	28:10	the yoke from off the **p** Jeremiah's neck,	5030
	28:11	And the **p** Jeremiah went his way.	5030
	28:12	**p,** after that Hananiah the prophet had	NIH
	28:12	**p** had broken the yoke from off the neck	5030
	28:12	yoke from off the neck of the **p** Jeremiah,	5030
	28:15	said the **p** Jeremiah unto Hananiah	5030
	28:15	prophet Jeremiah unto Hananiah the **p,**	5030
	28:17	So Hananiah the **p** died the same year in	5030
	29:	1 **p** sent from Jerusalem unto the residue of	5030
	29:26	*that is* mad, and **maketh** himself a **p,**	5012
	29:27	which **maketh** himself a **p** to you?	5012
	29:29	this letter in the ears of Jeremiah the **p.**	5030
	32:	2 Jeremiah the **p** was shut up in the court	5030
	34:	6 Jeremiah the **p** spake all these words unto	5030
	36:	8 all that Jeremiah the **p** commanded him,	5030
	36:26	Baruch the scribe and Jeremiah the **p:**	5030
	37:	2 which he spake by the **p** Jeremiah.	5030
	37:	3 of Maaseiah the priest to the **p** Jeremiah,	5030
	37:	6 came the word of the LORD unto the **p**	5030
	37:13	took Jeremiah the **p,** saying, Thou fallest	5030
	38:	9 all that they have done to Jeremiah the **p,**	5030
	38:10	up Jeremiah the **p** out of the dungeon,	5030
	38:14	took Jeremiah the **p** unto him into the	5030
	42:	2 said unto Jeremiah the **p,** Let, we beseech	5030
	42:	4 Jeremiah the **p** said unto them, I have	5030
	43:	6 Jeremiah the **p,** and Baruch the son of	5030
	45:	1 The word that Jeremiah the **p** spake unto	5030
	46:	1 to Jeremiah the **p** against the Gentiles;	5030
	46:13	that the LORD spake to Jeremiah the **p,**	5030
	47:	1 to Jeremiah the **p** against the Philistines,	5030
	49:34	**p** against Elam in the beginning of	5030
	50:	1 land of the Chaldeans by Jeremiah the **p.**	5030
	51:59	The word which Jeremiah the **p**	5030
La	2:20	**p** be slain in the sanctuary of the Lord?	5030
Eze	2:	5 yet shall know that there hath been a **p**	5030
	7:26	shall they seek a vision of the **p;**	5030
	14:	4 before his face, and cometh to the **p;**	5030
	14:	7 cometh to a **p** to inquire of him	5030
	14:	9 if the **p** be deceived when he hath spoken	5030
	14:	9 I the LORD have deceived that **p,**	5030
	14:10	the punishment of the **p** shall be even as	5030
	33:33	they know that a **p** hath been among	5030
Da	9:	2 of the LORD came to Jeremiah the **p,**	5030
Hos	4:	5 the **p** also shall fall with thee *in* the night,	5030
	9:	7 Israel shall know *it:* the **p** *is* a fool,	5030
	9:	8 the **p** *is* a snare of a fowler in all his ways,	5030
	12:13	by a **p** the LORD brought Israel out of	5030
	12:13	of Egypt, and by a **p** was he preserved.	5030
Am	7:14	and said to Amaziah, I *was* no **p,**	5030
Mic	2:11	he shall even be the **p** of this people.	5197
Hab	1:	1 burden which Habakkuk the **p** did see.	5030
	3:	1 A prayer of Habakkuk the **p** upon	5030
Hag	1:	1 **p** unto Zerubbabel the son of Shealtiel,	5030
	1:	3 the word of the LORD by Haggai the **p,**	5030
	1:12	the words of Haggai the **p,** as the LORD	5030
	2:	1 came the word of the LORD by the **p**	5030
	2:10	the word of the LORD by Haggai the **p,**	5030
Zec	1:	1 Berechiah, the son of Iddo the **p,** saying,	5030
	1:	7 Berechiah, the son of Iddo the **p,** saying,	5030
	13:	5 he shall say, I am no **p,** I *am* a	5030
Mal	4:	5 I will send you Elijah the **P** before	5030
Mt	1:22	which was spoken of the Lord by the **p,**	4396
	2:	5 of Judea: for thus it is written by the **p,**	4396
	2:15	spoken of the Lord by the **p,** saying,	4396
	2:17	that which was spoken by Jeremie the **p,**	4396
	3:	3 For this is he that was spoken of by the **p**	4396
	4:14	which was spoken by Esaias the **p,**	4396
	8:17	which was spoken by Esaias the **p,**	4396
	10:41	He that receiveth a **p** in the name of a	4396
	10:41	of a **p** shall receive a prophet's reward;	4396
	11:	9 A **p?** yea, I say unto you, and more than a	4396
	11:	9 yea, I say unto you, and more than a **p.**	4396
	12:17	which was spoken by Esaias the **p,**	4396
	12:39	be given to it, but the sign of the **p** Jonas:	4396
	13:35	be fulfilled which was spoken by the **p,**	4396
	13:57	A **p** is not without honour, save in his	4396
	14:	5 because they counted him as a **p.**	4396
	16:	4 given unto it, but the sign of the **p** Jonas.	4396
	21:	4 be fulfilled which was spoken by the **p,**	4396
	21:11	This is Jesus the **p** of Nazareth of Galilee.	4396
	21:26	fear the people; for all hold John as a **p.**	4396
	21:46	because they took him for a **p.**	4396
	24:15	spoken of by Daniel the **p,** stand in the	4396
	27:	9 that which was spoken by Jeremie the **p,**	4396
	27:35	be fulfilled which was spoken by the **p,**	4396
Mk	6:	4 A **p** is not without honour, but in his	4396
	6:15	That it is a **p,** or as one of the prophets.	4396
	11:32	counted John, that he was a **p** indeed.	4396
	13:14	spoken of by Daniel the **p,** standing	4396
Lk	1:76	child, shalt be called the **p** of the Highest:	4396
	3:	4 in the book of the words of Esaias the **p,**	4396
	4:17	unto him the book of the **p** Esaias.	4396
	4:24	No **p** is accepted in his own country.	4396
	4:27	in Israel in the time of Eliseus the **p;**	4396

P

Lk	7:16 That a great **p** is risen up among us;	4396
	7:26 A **p**? Yea, I say unto you, and much more	4396
	7:26 I say unto you, and much more than a **p**.	4396
	7:28 is not a greater **p** than John the Baptist:	4396
	7:39 saying, This *man*, if he were a **p**,	4396
	11:29 be given it, but the sign of Jonas the **p**.	4396
	13:33 for it cannot be that a **p** perish out of	4396
	20: 6 for they be persuaded that John was a **p**.	4396
	24:19 which was a **p** mighty in deed and	4396
Jn	1:21 Art thou *that* **p**? And he answered,	4396
	1:23 the way of the Lord, as said the **p** Esaias.	4396
	1:25 not *that* Christ, nor Elias, neither *that* **p**?	4396
	4:19 unto him, Sir, I perceive that thou art a **p**.	4396
	4:44 a **p** hath no honour in his own country.	4396
	6:14 This is of a truth *that* **p** that should come	4396
	7:40 *this* saying, said, Of a truth this is the **P**.	4396
	7:52 and look: for out of Galilee ariseth no **p**.	4396
	9:17 opened thine eyes? He said, He is a **p**.	4396
	12:38 That the saying of Esaias the **p** might be	4396
Ac	2:16 this is which was spoken by the **p**	4396
	2:30 Therefore being a **p**, and knowing that	4396
	3:22 A **p** shall the Lord your God raise up unto	4396
	3:23 every soul, which will not hear that **p**,	4396
	7:37 A **p** shall the Lord your God raise up unto	4396
	7:48 temples made with hands; as saith the **p**,	4396
	8:28 sitting in his chariot read Esaias the **p**.	4396
	8:30 to *him*, and heard him read the **p** Esaias	4396
	8:34 I pray thee, of whom speaketh the **p** this?	4396
	13: 6 a **false p**, a Jew, whose name *was*	5578
	13:20 and fifty years, until Samuel the **p**.	4396
	21:10 there came down from Judea a certain **p**,	4396
	28:25 spake the Holy Ghost by Esaias the **p**	4396
1Co	14:37 If any *man* think himself to be a **p**,	4396
Tit	1:12 of themselves, *even* a **p** of their own, said,	4396
2Pe	2:16 man's voice forbad the madness of the **p**.	4396
Rev	16:13 and out of the mouth of the **false p**.	5578
	19:20 him the **false p** that wrought miracles	5578
	20:10 where the beast and the **false p** *are*, and	5578

PROPHET'S (2) [PROPHESY]

Am	7:14 I *was* no prophet, neither *was* I a **p** son;	5030
Mt	10:41 of a prophet shall receive a **p** reward;	4396

PROPHETESS (8) [PROPHESY]

Ex	15:20 Miriam the **p**, the sister of Aaron, took a	5031
Jdg	4: 4 Deborah, a **p**, the wife of Lapidoth,	5031
2Ki	22:14 and Asahiah, went unto Huldah the **p**,	5031
2Ch	34:22 *had appointed*, went to Huldah the **p**,	5031
Ne	6:14 on the **p** Noadiah, and the rest of	5031
Isa	8: 3 I went unto the **p** and she conceived,	5031
Lk	2:36 a **p**, the daughter of Phanuel, of the tribe	4398
Rev	2:20 which calleth herself a **p**, to teach and	4398

PROPHETS (239) [PROPHESY]

Nu	11:29 God that all the Lord's people were **p**,	5030
1Sa	10: 5 that thou shalt meet a company of **p**	5030
	10:10 the hill, behold, a company of **p** met him;	5030
	10:11 prophesied among the **p**, then the people	5030
	10:11 the son of Kish? *Is* Saul also among the **p**?	5030
	10:12 a proverb, *Is* Saul also among the **p**?	5030
	19:20 when they saw the company of the **p**	5030
	19:24 they say, *Is* Saul also among the **p**?	5030
	28: 6 neither by dreams, nor by Urim, nor by **p**.	5030
	28:15 me no more, neither by **p**, nor by dreams:	5030
1Ki	18: 4 when Jezebel cut off the **p** of the Lord,	5030
	18: 4 that Obadiah took an hundred **p**,	5030
	18:13 did when Jezebel slew the **p** of the Lord,	5030
	18:13 men of the Lord's **p** by fifty in a cave,	5030
	18:19 the **p** of Baal four hundred and fifty,	5030
	18:19 and the **p** of the groves four hundred,	5030
	18:20 the **p** together unto mount Carmel.	5030
	18:22 Baal's **p** *are* four hundred and fifty men.	5030
	18:25 Elijah said unto the **p** of Baal, Choose you	5030
	18:40 Elijah said unto them, Take the **p** of Baal;	5030
	19: 1 withal how he had slain all the **p** with	5030
	19:10 altars, and slain thy **p** with the sword;	5030
	19:14 altars, and slain thy **p** with the sword;	5030
	20:35 a certain man of the sons of the **p** said	5030
	20:41 Israel discerned him that he *was* of the **p**.	5030
	22: 6 the king of Israel gathered the **p** together,	5030
	22:10 and all the **p** prophesied before them.	5030
	22:12 all the **p** prophesied so, saying, Go up *to*	5030
	22:13 the words of the **p** *declare* good unto	5030
	22:22 be a lying spirit in the mouth of all his **p**.	5030
	22:23 lying spirit in the mouth of all these thy **p**,	5030
2Ki	2: 3 sons of the **p** that *were* at Beth-el came	5030
	2: 5 sons of the **p** that *were* at Jericho came	5030
	2: 7 fifty men of the sons of the **p** went,	5030
	2:15 the sons of the **p** which *were* to view	5030
	3:13 get thee to the **p** of thy father, and to	5030
	3:13 of thy father, and to the **p** of thy mother.	5030
	4: 1 wives of the sons of the **p** unto Elisha,	5030
	4:38 the sons of the **p** *were* sitting before him:	5030
	4:38 and seethe pottage for the sons of the **p**.	5030
	5:22 two young men of the sons of the **p**:	5030
	6: 1 the sons of the **p** said unto Elisha,	5030
	9: 1 called one of the children of the **p**,	5030
	9: 7 avenge the blood of my servants the **p**,	5030
	10:19 therefore call unto me all the **p** of Baal,	5030
	17:13 by all the **p**, *and* by all the seers, saying,	5030
	17:13 which I sent to you by my servants the **p**.	5030
	17:23 as he had said by all his servants the **p**.	5030
	21:10 the Lord spake by his servants the **p**,	5030
	23: 2 the **p**, and all the people, both small and	5030
	24: 2 which he spake by his servants the **p**.	5030

1Ch	16:22 mine anointed, and do my **p** no harm.	5030
2Ch	18: 5 gathered together *of* **p** four hundred men,	5030
	18: 9 and all the **p** prophesied before them.	5030
	18:11 all the **p** prophesied so, saying, Go up *to*	5030
	18:12 the words of the **p** *declare* good to the	5030
	18:21 be a lying spirit in the mouth of all his **p**.	5030
	18:22 a lying spirit in the mouth of these thy **p**,	5030
	20:20 believe his **p**, so shall ye prosper.	5030
	24:19 he sent **p** to them, to bring them again	5030
	29:25 the commandment of the Lord by his **p**.	5030
	36:16 despised his words, and misused his **p**,	5030
Ezr	5: 1 the **p**, Haggai the prophet,	5029
	5: 2 them *were* the **p** of God helping them.	5029
	9:11 hast commanded by thy servants the **p**,	5030
Ne	6: 7 hast also appointed **p** to preach of thee	5030
	6:14 prophetess Noadiah, and the rest of the **p**,	5030
	9:26 slew thy **p** which testified against them to	5030
	9:30 against them by thy spirit in thy **p**:	5030
	9:32 on our **p**, and on our fathers, and on all	5030
Ps	105:15 not mine anointed, and do my **p** no harm.	5030
Isa	29:10 the **p** and your rulers, the seers hath he	5030
	30:10 the **p**, Prophesy not unto us right *things*,	2374
Jer	2: 8 the **p** prophesied by Baal, and walked	5030
	2:26 princes, and their priests, and their **p**,	5030
	2:30 your own sword hath devoured your **p**,	5030
	4: 9 be astonished, and the **p** shall wonder.	5030
	5:13 the **p** shall become wind, and the word *is*	5030
	5:31 The **p** prophesy falsely, and the priests	5030
	7:25 even sent unto you all my servants the **p**,	5030
	8: 1 the bones of the **p**, and the bones of	5030
	13:13 **p**, and all the inhabitants of Jerusalem,	5030
	14:13 behold, the **p** say unto them, Ye shall not	5030
	14:14 me, The **p** prophesy lies in my name:	5030
	14:15 the **p** that prophesy in my name,	5030
	14:15 and famine shall those **p** be consumed.	5030
	23: 9 within me is broken because of the **p**;	5030
	23:13 I have seen folly in the **p** of Samaria;	5030
	23:14 I have seen also in the **p** of Jerusalem a	5030
	23:15 saith the Lord of hosts concerning the **p**;	5030
	23:15 for from the **p** of Jerusalem is profaneness	5030
	23:16 Hearken not unto the words of the **p** that	5030
	23:21 I have not sent *these* **p**, yet they ran:	5030
	23:25 have heard what the **p** said, that prophesy	5030
	23:26 long shall *this* be in the heart of the **p**	5030
	23:26 *are* **p** of the deceit of their own heart;	5030
	23:30 I *am* against the **p**, saith the Lord,	5030
	23:31 Behold, I *am* against the **p**, saith	5030
	25: 4 hath sent unto you all his servants the **p**,	5030
	26: 5 to the words of my servants the **p**,	5030
	26: 7 So the priests and the **p** and all the people	5030
	26: 8 the priests and the **p** and all the people	5030
	26:11 **p** unto the princes and to all the people,	5030
	26:16 the people unto the priests and to the **p**;	5030
	27: 9 Therefore hearken not ye to your **p**, nor	5030
	27:14 the words of the **p** that speak unto you,	5030
	27:15 ye, and the **p** that prophesy unto you.	5030
	27:16 Hearken not to the words of your **p** that	5030
	27:18 if they *be* **p**, and if the word of the Lord	5030
	28: 8 The **p** that have been before me and	5030
	29: 1 to the **p**, and to all the people whom	5030
	29: 8 Let not your **p** and your diviners, that *be*	5030
	29:15 The Lord hath raised us up **p** in	5030
	29:19 I sent unto them by my servants the **p**,	5030
	32:32 their **p**, and the men of Judah,	5030
	35:15 sent also unto you all my servants the **p**,	5030
	37:19 Where *are* now your **p** which prophesied	5030
	44: 4 I sent unto you all my servants the **p**,	5030
La	2: 9 the law *is* no *more*; her **p** also find no	5030
	2:14 Thy **p** have seen vain and foolish things	5030
	4:13 For the sins of her **p**, *and* the iniquities of	5030
Eze	13: 2 prophesy against the **p** of Israel that	5030
	13: 3 Woe unto the foolish **p**, that follow their	5030
	13: 4 thy **p** are like the foxes in the deserts.	5030
	13: 9 mine hand shall be upon the **p** that see	5030
	13:16 *To wit*, the **p** of Israel which prophesy	5030
	22:25 *is* a conspiracy of her **p** in the midst	5030
	22:28 her **p** have daubed them *with* untempered	5030
	38:17 in old time by my servants the **p** of Israel,	5030
Da	9: 6 we hearkened unto thy servants the **p**,	5030
	9:10 he set before us by his servants the **p**.	5030
Hos	6: 5 Therefore have I hewed *them* by the **p**;	5030
	12:10 I have also spoken by the **p**, and I have	5030
	12:10 used similitudes by the ministry of the **p**.	5030
Am	2:11 I raised up of your sons for **p**, and of your	5030
	2:12 commanded the **p**, saying, Prophesy not.	5030
	3: 7 his secret unto his servants the **p**.	5030
Mic	3: 5 Thus saith the Lord concerning the **p**	5030
	3: 6 the sun shall go down over the **p**,	5030
	3:11 and the **p** thereof divine for money:	5030
Zep	3: 4 Her **p** *are* light *and* treacherous persons:	5030
Zec	1: 4 whom the former **p** have cried, saying,	5030
	1: 5 *are* they? and the **p**, do they live for ever?	5030
	1: 6 which I commanded my servants the **p**,	5030
	7: 3 the **p**, saying, Should I weep in the fifth	5030
	7: 7 the Lord cried by the former **p**,	5030
	7:12 hath sent in his spirit by the former **p**:	5030
	8: 9 days these words by the mouth of the **p**,	5030
	13: 2 I will cause the **p** and the unclean spirit	5030
	13: 4 the **p** shall be ashamed every one of his	5030
Mt	2:23 be fulfilled which was spoken by the **p**,	4396
	5:12 persecuted they the **p** which were before	4396
	5:17 I am come to destroy the law, or the **p**:	4396
	7:12 so to them: for this is the law and the **p**.	4396
	7:15 Beware of **false p**, which come to you in	5578
	11:13 For all the **p** and the law prophesied until	4396

Mt	13:17 That many **p** and righteous *men* have	4396
	16:14 and others, Jeremias, or one of the **p**.	4396
	22:40 hang all the law and the **p**.	4396
	23:29 because ye built the tombs of the **p**,	4396
	23:30 partakers with them in the blood of the **p**.	4396
	23:31 the children of them which killed the **p**.	4396
	23:34 I send unto you **p**, and wise *men*, and	4396
	23:37 *thou* that killest the **p**, and stonest them	4396
	24:11 And many **false p** shall rise,	5578
	24:24 and **false p**, and shall shew great signs	5578
	26:56 that the scriptures of the **p** might be	4396
Mk	1: 2 As it is written in the **p**, Behold, I send my	4396
	6:15 That it is a prophet, or as one of the **p**.	4396
	8:28 some *say*, Elias; and others, One of the **p**.	4396
	13:22 For false Christs and **false p** shall rise,	5578
Lk	1:70 As he spake by the mouth of his holy **p**,	4396
	6:23 like manner did their fathers unto the **p**.	4396
	6:26 for so did their fathers to the **false p**.	5578
	9: 8 that one of the old **p** was risen again.	4396
	9:19 others *say*, that one of the old **p** is risen	4396
	10:24 that many **p** and kings have desired to see	4396
	11:47 for ye build the sepulchres of the **p**,	4396
	11:49 I will send them **p** and apostles,	4396
	11:50 the blood of all the **p**, which was shed	4396
	13:28 and Isaac, and Jacob, and all the **p**,	4396
	13:34 which killest the **p**, and stonest them that	4396
	16:16 The law and the **p** *were* until John:	4396
	16:29 unto him, They have Moses and the **p**;	4396
	16:31 him, If they hear not Moses and the **p**,	4396
	18:31 all *things* that are written by the **p**	4396
	24:25 slow of heart to believe all that the **p** have	4396
	24:27 And beginning at Moses and all the **p**,	4396
	24:44 and *in* the **p**, and *in* the psalms,	4396
Jn	1:45 he did write, Jesus of Nazareth,	4396
	6:45 It is written in the **p**, And they shall be all	4396
	8:52 Abraham is dead, and the **p**;	4396
	8:53 and the **p** are dead: whom makest thou	4396
Ac	3:18 had shewed by the mouth of all his **p**,	4396
	3:21 of all his holy **p** since the world began.	4396
	3:24 and all the **p** from Samuel and those that	4396
	3:25 Ye are the children of the **p**, and of	4396
	7:42 as it is written in the book of the **p**, O *ye*	4396
	7:52 Which of the **p** have not your fathers	4396
	10:43 To him give all the **p** witness, that	4396
	11:27 And in these days came **p** from Jerusalem	4396
	13: 1 the church that was at Antioch certain **p**	4396
	13:15 the rulers of the synagogue sent	4396
	13:27 nor *yet* the voices of the **p** which are read	4396
	13:40 upon you, which is spoken of in the **p**;	4396
	15:15 to this agree the words of the **p**; as it is	4396
	15:32 and Silas, being **p** also themselves,	4396
	24:14 which are written in the law and the **p**:	4396
	26:22 none other *things* than those which the **p**	4396
	26:27 King Agrippa, believest thou the **p**?	4396
	28:23 *out* of the law, from morning till evening.	4396
Ro	1: 2 (Which he had promised afore by his **p** in	4396
	3:21 being witnessed by the law and the **p**;	4396
	11: 3 they have killed thy **p**, and digged down	4396
	16:26 and by the scriptures of the **p**,	4397
1Co	12:28 first apostles, secondarily **p**,	4396
	12:29 *are* all **p**? *are* all teachers? *are* all workers	4396
	14:29 Let the **p** speak two or three, and let	4396
	14:32 And the spirits of the **p** are subject to	4396
	14:32 spirits of the prophets are subject to the **p**:	4396
Eph	2:20 upon the foundation of the apostles and **p**,	4396
	3: 5 unto his holy apostles and **p** by the Spirit;	4396
	4:11 and some, **p**; and some, evangelists;	4396
1Th	2:15 and their own **p**, and have persecuted us;	4396
	11:32 *of* David also, and Samuel, and of the **p**:	4396
Heb	1: 1 in time past unto the fathers by the **p**,	4396
Jas	5:10 my brethren, the **p**, who have spoken	4396
1Pe	1:10 Of which salvation the **p** have inquired	4396
2Pe	2: 1 But there were **false p** also among	5578
	3: 2 which were spoken before by the holy **p**,	4396
1Jn	4: 1 many **false p** are gone out into the world.	5578
Rev	10: 7 as he hath declared to his servants the **p**.	4396
	11:10 two **p** tormented them that dwelt on	4396
	11:18 give reward unto thy servants the **p**,	4396
	16: 6 they have shed the blood of saints and **p**,	4396
	18:20 *thou* heaven, and ye holy apostles and **p**;	4396
	18:24 And in her was found the blood of **p**,	4396
	22: 6 the Lord God of the holy **p** sent his angel	4396
	22: 9 and of thy brethren the **p**, and of them	4396

PROPITIATION (3)

Ro	3:25 God hath set forth *to be* a **p** through	2435
1Jn	2: 2 And he is the **p** for our sins: and not for	2434
	4:10 and sent his Son *to be* the **p** for our sins.	2434

PROPORTION (3)

1Ki	7:36 according to the **p** of every one,	4626
Job	41:12 parts, nor *his* power, nor his comely **p**.	6187
Ro	12: 6 *let us prophesy* according to the **p** of faith;	356

PROPRIETY See SOBRIETY

PROSELYTE (2) [PROSELYTES]

Mt	23:15 ye compass sea and land to make one **p**,	4339
Ac	6: 5 Parmenas, and Nicolas a **p** of Antioch:	4339

PROSELYTES (2) [PROSELYTE]

Ac	2:10 and strangers of Rome, Jews and **p**,	4339
	13:43 and religious **p** followed Paul and	4339

PROSPECT (6)

Eze	40:44 and their **p** *was* toward the south:	6440

Eze 40:44 at the side of the east gate *having* the **p** 6440
40:45 chamber, whose **p** *is* toward the south, 6440
40:46 chamber whose **p** *is* toward the north *is* 6440
42:15 the gate whose **p** *is* toward the east, 6440
43: 4 of the gate whose **p** *is* toward the east. 6440

PROSPER (49) [PROSPERED, PROSPERETH, PROSPERITY, PROSPEROUS, PROSPEROUSLY]
Ge 24:40 send his angel with thee, and **p** thy way; 6743
24:42 if now thou do **p** my way which I go: 6743
39: 3 *that* the LORD **made** all that he did to **p** 6743
39:23 which he did, the LORD **made** *it* to **p**. 6743
Nu 14:41 of the LORD? but it shall not **p**. 6743
Dt 28:29 and thou shalt not **p** in thy ways: 6743
29: 9 do them, that ye may **p** in all that ye do. 7919
Jos 1: 7 that thou mayest **p** whithersoever thou 7919
1Ki 2: 3 that thou mayest **p** *in* all that thou doest, 7919
22:12 saying, Go up to Ramoth-gilead, and **p**: 6743
22:15 he answered him, Go, and **p**: 6743
1Ch 22:11 **p** thou, and build the house of the LORD 6743
22:13 shalt thou **p**, if thou takest heed to fulfil 6743
2Ch 13:12 God of your fathers; for you shall not **p**. 6743
18:11 saying, Go up to Ramoth-gilead, and **p**: 6743
18:14 **p**, and they shall be delivered into your 6743
20:20 believe his prophets, so shall ye **p**. 6743
24:20 of the LORD, that ye cannot **p**? 6743
26: 5 he sought the LORD, God **made** him to **p**. 6743
Ne 1:11 I, pray thee, thy servant *this* day, 6743
2:20 The God of heaven, he will **p** us; 7919
Job 12: 6 The tabernacles of robbers **p**, and they 7951
Ps 1: 3 and whatsoever he doeth shall **p**. 6743
73:12 are the ungodly, who **p** in the world; 7961
122: 6 of Jerusalem: they shall **p** that love thee. 7951
Pr 28:13 He that covereth his sins shall not **p**: 6743
Ecc 11: 6 for thou knowest not whether shall **p**, 3787
Isa 53:10 the pleasure of the LORD shall **p** in his 6743
54:17 *that* is formed against thee shall **p**; 6743
55:11 it shall **p** *in the thing* whereto I sent it. 6743
Jer 2:37 and thou shalt not **p** in them. 6743
5:28 the cause of the fatherless, yet they **p**; 6743
10:21 therefore they shall not **p**; and all their 7919
12: 1 Wherefore doth the way of the wicked **p**? 6743
20:11 for they shall not **p**: *their* everlasting 7919
22:30 a man *that* shall not **p** in his days: 7919
22:30 no man of his seed shall **p**, sitting upon 6743
23: 5 a King shall reign and **p**, and shall execute 7919
32: 5 fight with the Chaldeans, ye shall not **p**? 6743
La 1: 5 adversaries are the chief, her enemies **p**; 7951
Eze 16:13 and thou didst **p** into a kingdom. 6743
17: 9 Thus saith the Lord GOD; Shall it **p**? 6743
17:10 behold, *being* planted, shall it **p**? shall 6743
17:15 Shall he **p**? shall he escape that doeth 6743
Da 8:24 shall **p**, and practise, and shall destroy 6743
8:25 also he shall **cause** craft to **p** in his hand; 6743
11:27 speak lies at one table; but it shall not **p**: 6743
11:36 **p** till the indignation be accomplished. 6743
3Jn 1: 2 wish above all *things* that thou mayest **p** 2137

PROSPERED (13) [PROSPER]
Ge 24:56 me not, seeing the LORD hath **p** my way; 6743
Jdg 4:24 the hand of the children of Israel **p**, 1980
2Sa 11: 7 people did, and **how** the war **p**. 7965+3807.1
2Ki 18: 7 and he **p** whithersoever he went forth: 7919
1Ch 29:23 as king instead of David his father, and **p**; 6743
2Ch 14: 7 us rest on every side. So they built and **p**. 6743
31:21 God, he did *it* with all his heart, and **p**. 6743
32:30 And Hezekiah **p** in all his works. 6743
Ezr 6:14 they **p** through the prophesying of Haggai 6744
Job 9: 4 *himself* against him, and hath **p**? 7999
Da 6:28 So this Daniel **p** in the reign of Darius, 6744
8:12 to the ground; and it practised, and **p**. 6743
1Co 16: 2 as *God* hath **p** him, that there be no 2137

PROSPERETH (4) [PROSPER]
Ezr 5: 8 work goeth fast on, and **p** in their hands. 6744
Ps 37: 7 because of him who **p** *in* his way, 6743
Pr 17: 8 hath it: whithersoever it turneth, it **p**. 7919
3Jn 1: 2 and be in health, even as thy soul **p**. 2137

PROSPERITY (17) [PROSPER]
Dt 23: 6 shalt not seek their peace nor their **p** 2896
1Sa 25: 6 thus shall ye say to him that liveth *in* **p**, NIH
1Ki 10: 7 and **p** exceedeth the fame which I heard. 2896
Job 15:21 in **p** the destroyer shall come *upon* him. 7965
36:11 *him*, they shall spend their days in **p**, 2896
Ps 30: 6 in my **p** I said, I shall never be moved. 7959
35:27 hath pleasure in the **p** of his servant. 7965
73: 3 foolish, *when* I saw the **p** of the wicked. 6743
118:25 O LORD, I beseech thee, **send** now **p**. 7962
122: 7 thy walls, *and* **p** within thy palaces. 7962
Pr 1:32 and the **p** of fools shall destroy them. 7962
Ecc 7:14 In the day of **p** be joyful, but in the day 2896
Jer 22:21 spake unto thee in thy **p**; *but* thou saidst, 7962
33: 9 and for all the **p** that I procure unto it. 7965
La 3:17 my soul far off from peace: I forgat **p**. 2896
Zec 1:17 My cities through **p** shall yet be spread 2896
7: 7 when Jerusalem was inhabited and in **p**, 7961

PROSPEROUS (8) [PROSPER]
Ge 24:21 the LORD had **made** his journey **p** 6743
39: 2 was with Joseph, and he was a **p** man; 6743
Jos 1: 8 for then thou shalt **make** thy way **p**, 6743
Jdg 18: 5 whether our way which we go shall be **p**. 6743
Job 8: 6 **make** the habitation of thy
righteousness **p**. 7999

Isa 48:15 him, and he shall **make** his way **p**. 6743
Zec 8:12 For the seed *shall be* **p**; the vine shall give 7965
Ro 1:10 **have a p journey** by the will of God to 2137

PROSPEROUSLY (2) [PROSPER]
2Ch 7:11 and in his own house, he **p effected**. 6743
Ps 45: 4 *in* thy majesty ride **p** because of truth and 6743

PROSTITUTE (1)
Lev 19:29 Do not **p** thy daughter, to cause her to be 2490

PROSTITUTES See HARLOTS; SODOMITES; WHORE; WHORE'S; WHORES

PROSTITUTION See WHORE; WHORE'S; WHORES; WHOREDOM

PROTECTION (1)
Dt 32:38 rise up and help you, *and* be your **p**. 5643

PROTEST (3) [PROTESTED, PROTESTING]
Ge 43: 3 man did **solemnly p** unto us, 5749+5749
1Sa 8: 9 yet **p solemnly** unto them, 5749+5749
1Co 15:31 I **p** by your rejoicing which I have in 3513

PROTESTED (3) [PROTEST]
1Ki 2:42 unto thee, saying, Know for a certain, 5749
Jer 11: 7 I **earnestly p** unto your fathers 5749+5749
Zec 3: 6 the angel of the LORD **p** unto Joshua, 5749

PROTESTING (1) [PROTEST]
Jer 11: 7 rising early and **p**, saying, Obey my voice. 5749

PROUD (48) [PRIDE]
Job 9:13 anger, the **p** helpers do stoop under him. 7293
26:12 understanding he smiteth through the **p**. 7293
38:11 and here shall thy **p** waves be stayed? 1347
40:11 every one *that is* **p**, and abase him. 1343
40:12 on every one *that is* **p**, and bring him 1343
Ps 12: 3 *and* the tongue that speaketh **p** *things*: 1419
31:23 and plentifully rewardeth the **p** doer. 1346
86:14 respecteth not the **p**, nor such as turn 7295
94: 2 of the earth: render a reward to the **p**. 1343
101: 5 high look and a **p** heart will not I suffer. 7342
119:21 Thou hast rebuked the **p** *that are* cursed, 2086
119:51 The **p** have had me greatly in derision: 2086
119:69 The **p** have forged a lie against me: 2086
119:78 Let the **p** be ashamed; for they dealt 2086
119:85 The **p** have digged pits for me, which *are* 2086
119:122 for good: let not the **p** oppress me. 2086
123: 4 at ease, *and with* the contempt of the **p**. 1349
124: 5 the **p** waters had gone over our soul. 2121
138: 6 the lowly: but the **p** he knoweth afar off. 1364
140: 5 The **p** have hid a snare for me, and cords; 1343
Pr 6:17 A **p** look, a lying tongue, and hands that 7311
15:25 LORD will destroy the house of the **p**: 1343
16: 5 Every one *that is* **p** in heart *is an* 1362
16:19 than to divide the spoil with the **p**. 1343
21: 4 A **p** heart, *and* the plowing of the wicked, 7342
21:24 **P** *and* haughty scorner *is* his name, 2086
21:24 *is* his name, who dealeth in **p** wrath. 2087
28:25 He that is of a **p** heart stirreth up strife: 7342
Ecc 7: 8 the patient in spirit *is* better than the **p** 1362
Isa 2:12 of hosts *shall be* upon every one *that is* **p** 1343
13:11 will cause the arrogancy of the **p** to cease, 2086
16: 6 heard of the pride of Moab; *he is* very **p**: 1341
Jer 13:15 Hear ye, and give ear; be not **p**: 1361
43: 2 all the men, saying unto Jeremiah, 2086
48:29 the pride of Moab; *he is* exceeding **p**: 1343
50:29 for she hath been a **p** against the LORD, 2102
50:31 I *am* against thee, O thou most **p**, 2087
50:32 the **most p** shall stumble and fall, 2087
Hab 2: 5 *he is* a **p** man, neither keepeth at home, 3093
Mal 3:15 now we call the **p** happy; yea, they that 2086
4: 1 all the **p**, yea, and all that do wickedly, 2086
Lk 1:51 he hath scattered the **p** in the imagination 5244
Ro 1:30 haters of God, despiteful, **p**, boasters, 5244
1Ti 6: 4 He is **p**, knowing nothing, but doting 5187
2Ti 3: 2 covetous, boasters, **p**, blasphemers, 5244
Jas 4: 6 God resisteth the **p**, but giveth grace unto 5244
1Pe 5: 5 for God resisteth the **p**, and giveth grace 5244

PROUDLY (9) [PRIDE]
Ex 18:11 for in the thing wherein they **dealt p** *he* 2102
1Sa 2: 3 Talk no more *so* **exceeding p**; 1364+1364
Ne 9:10 thou knewest that they **dealt p** against 2102
9:16 they and our fathers **dealt p**, 2102
9:29 yet they **dealt p**, and hearkened not unto 2102
Ps 17:10 *with* their mouth they speak **p**: 1348+871.1
31:18 which speak grievous things **p** and 1346+871.1
Isa 3: 5 the child shall **behave** himself **p** against 7292
Ob 1:12 neither shouldest thou have spoken **p** in 1431

PROVE (25) [PROOF, PROOFS, PROVED, PROVETH, PROVING]
Ex 16: 4 certain rate every day, that I may **p** them, 5254
20:20 God is come to **p** you, and that his fear 5254
Dt 8: 2 to humble thee, *and* to **p** thee, to know 5254
8:16 humble thee, and that he might **p** thee, 5254
33: 8 whom thou didst **p** at Massah, 5254
Jdg 2:22 That through them I may **p** Israel, 5254
3: 1 with the LORD left, to **p** Israel by them, 5254
3: 4 they were to **p** Israel by them, to know 5254
6:39 let me, I pray thee, but *this* once with 5254
1Ki 10: 1 she came to **p** him with hard questions. 5254

2Ch 9: 1 came to **p** Solomon with hard questions 5254
Job 9:20 I *am* perfect, it shall also **p** me **perverse**. 6140
Ps 26: 2 Examine me, O LORD, and **p** me; try my 5254
Ecc 2: 1 I will **p** thee with mirth, therefore 5254
Da 1:12 **P** thy servants, I beseech thee, ten days; 5254
Mal 3:10 me now herewith, saith the LORD of 974
Lk 14:19 **five yoke of oxen, and I go to p them:** 1381
Jn 6: 6 And this he said to **p** him: for he himself 3985
Ac 24:13 Neither can they **p** *the things* whereof 3936
25: 7 against Paul, which they could not **p**. 584
Ro 12: 2 that ye may **p** what *is that* good, 1381
2Co 8: 8 and to **p** the sincerity of your love. 1381
13: 5 ye be in the faith; **p** your own selves. 1381
Gal 6: 4 let every man **p** his own work, and then 1381
1Th 5:21 **P** all *things*; hold fast *that* which is good. 1381

PROVED (15) [PROVE]
Ge 42:15 Hereby ye shall be **p**: By the life of Pharaoh 974
42:16 kept in prison, that your words may be **p**, 974
Ex 15:25 and an ordinance, and there he **p** them, 5254
1Sa 17:39 for he had not **p** *it*. And David said unto 5254
17:39 I have not **p** *them*. And David put 5254
Ps 17: 3 Thou hast **p** mine heart; thou hast visited 974
66:10 For thou, O God, hast **p** us: thou hast tried 974
81: 7 I **p** thee at the waters of Meribah. Selah. 974
95: 9 fathers tempted me, **p** me, and saw my 974
Ecc 7:23 All this have I **p** by wisdom: I said, I will 5254
Da 1:14 them in this matter, and **p** them ten days. 5254
Ro 3: 9 for we have **before** **p** both Jews and 4256
2Co 8:22 whom we have oftentimes **p** diligent in 1381
1Ti 3:10 And let these also first be **p**; then let them 1381
Heb 3: 9 **p** me, and saw my works forty years. 1381

PROVENDER (7)
Ge 24:25 We have both straw and **p** enough, 4554
24:32 gave straw and **p** for the camels, 4554
42:27 his sack to give his ass **p** in the inn, 4554
43:24 their feet; and he gave their asses **p**. 4554
Jdg 19:19 there is both straw and **p** for our asses; 4554
19:21 into his house, and **gave p** unto the asses: 1101
Isa 30:24 asses that ear the ground shall eat clean **p**, 1098

PROVERB (20) [PROVERBS]
Dt 28:37 an astonishment, a **p**, and a byword, 4912
1Sa 10:12 Therefore it became a **p**, *Is* Saul also 4912
24:13 As saith the **p** of the ancients, 4912
1Ki 9: 7 Israel shall be a **p** and a byword among all 4912
2Ch 7:20 make it to be a **p** and a byword among 4912
Ps 69:11 my garment; and I became a **p** to them. 4912
Pr 1: 6 understand a **p**, and the interpretation; 4912
Isa 14: 4 That thou shalt take up this **p** against 4912
Jer 24: 9 to be a reproach and a **p**, a taunt and a 4912
Eze 12:22 what *is* that *that* ye have in the land of 4912
12:23 I will make this **p** to cease, and they shall 4912
12:23 they shall no more **use** it **as a p** in Israel; 4911
14: 8 make him a sign and a **p**, and I will cut 4912
16:44 proverbs shall **use** *this* **p** against thee, 4911
18: 2 ye **use** this **p** concerning the land 4911+4912
18: 3 any more to **use** this **p** in Israel. 4911+4912
Hab 2: 6 and a taunting **p** against him, and say, 2420
Lk 4:23 **Ye will surely say unto me this p,** 3850
Jn 16:29 speakest thou plainly, and speakest no **p**. 3942
2Pe 2:22 unto them according to the true **p**, 3942

PROVERBS (9) [PROVERB]
Nu 21:27 Wherefore they that **speak in p** say, 4911
1Ki 4:32 he spake three thousand **p**: and his songs 4911
Pr 1: 1 The **p** of Solomon the son of David, king 4912
10: 1 The **p** of Solomon. A wise son maketh a 4912
25: 1 These *are* also **p** of Solomon, which 4912
Ecc 12: 9 and sought out, *and* set in order many **p**. 4911
Eze 16:44 every one that **useth p** shall use *this* 4911
Jn 16:25 These *things* have I spoken unto you in **p**: 3942
16:25 when I shall no more speak unto you in **p**, 3942

PROVETH (1) [PROVE]
Dt 13: 3 for the LORD your God **p** you, to know 5254

PROVIDE (11) [PROVIDED, PROVIDENCE, PROVIDETH, PROVIDING, PROVISION]
Ge 22: 8 God will **p** himself a lamb for a burnt 7200
30:30 now when shall I **p** for mine own house 6213
Ex 18:21 thou shalt **p** out of all the people 2372
1Sa 16:17 **P** me now a man that can play well, 7200
2Ch 2: 7 Jerusalem, whom David my father did **p**. 3559
Ps 78:20 can he **p** flesh for his people? 3559
Mt 10: 9 **P neither gold, nor silver, nor brass in** 2932
Lk 12:33 **p yourselves bags which wax not old,** 4160
Ac 23:24 **p** *them* beasts, that they may set Paul 3936
Ro 12:17 **P** *things* honest in the sight of all men. 4306
1Ti 5: 8 But if any **p** not **for** his own, 4306

PROVIDED (9) [PROVIDE]
Dt 33:21 he **p** the first *part* for himself, because 7200
1Sa 16: 1 for I have **p** me a king among his sons. 7200
2Sa 19:32 he had **p** the king **of sustenance** while 3557
1Ki 4: 7 which **p** victuals for the king and his 3557
4:27 those officers **p** victual for king Solomon, 3557
2Ch 32:29 Moreover he **p** him cities, 6213
Ps 65: 9 them corn, when thou hast so **p** for it. 3559
Lk 12:20 **shall those things be, which thou hast p?** 2090
Heb 11:40 God having **p** some better *thing* for us, 4265

PROVIDENCE (1) [PROVIDE]
Ac 24: 2 deeds are done unto this nation by thy **p**, 4307

P

PROVIDETH (2) [PROVIDE]
Job	38:41 Who **p** for the raven his food? when his	3559
Pr	6: 8 **P** her meat in the summer,	3559

PROVIDING (1) [PROVIDE]
2Co	8:21 **P** *for* honest *things*, not only in the sight	4306

PROVINCE (27) [PROVINCES]
Ezr	2: 1 Now these *are* the children of the **p** that	4082
	5: 8 king, that we went into the **p** of Judea,	4083
	6: 2 the palace that *is* in the **p** of the Medes,	4083
	7:16 gold that thou canst find in all the **p** of	4083
Ne	1: 3 there in the **p** *are* in great affliction	4082
	7: 6 These *are* the children of the **p**, that	4082
	11: 3 these *are* the chief of the **p** that dwelt	4082
Est	1:22 into **every p** according to	4082+4082+2050.1
	3:12 that *were* over **every p**,	4082+4082+2050.1
	3:12 **every p** according to	4082+4082+2050.1
	3:14 **every p** *was* published	3605+4082+4082+2050.1
	4: 3 in **every p**,	3605+4082+4082+2050.1
	8: 9 **every p** according to	4082+4082+2050.1
	8:11 people and **p** that would assault them,	4082
	8:13 **every p** *was*	3605+4082+2050.1
	8:17 in **every p**,	4082+4082+2050.1
	9:28 **every p**, and every city;	4082+4082+2050.1
Ecc	5: 8 perverting of judgment and justice in a **p**,	4082
Da	2:48 made him ruler over the whole **p** of	4083
	2:49 over the affairs of the **p** of Babylon:	4083
	3: 1 in the plain of Dura, in the **p** of Babylon.	4083
	3:12 set over the affairs of the **p** of Babylon,	4083
	3:30 and Abed-nego, in the **p** of Babylon.	4083
	8: 2 *in* the palace, which *is* in the **p** of Elam;	4082
	11:24 even upon the fattest places of the **p**,	4082
Ac	23:34 *the letter*, he asked of what **p** he was:	1885
	25: 1 Now when Festus was come into the **p**,	1885

PROVINCES (30) [PROVINCE]
1Ki	20:14 by the young men of the princes of the **p**.	4082
	20:15 the young men of the princes of the **p**,	4082
	20:17 young men of the princes of the **p** went	4082
	20:19 these young men of the princes of the **p**	4082
Ezr	4:15 hurtful unto kings and **p**, and that they	4082
Est	1: 1 *over* an hundred and seven and twenty **p**:)	4082
	1: 3 Media, the nobles and princes of the **p**,	4082
	1:16 to all the people that *are* in all the **p** of	4082
	1:22 For he sent letters into all the king's **p**,	4082
	2: 3 let the king appoint officers in all the **p** of	4082
	2:18 he made a release to the **p**, and gave gifts,	4082
	3: 8 dispersed among the people in all the king's **p**,	4082
	3:13 were sent by posts into all the king's **p**,	4082
	4:11 the people of the king's **p**, do know,	4082
	8: 5 the Jews which *are* in all the king's **p**:	4082
	8: 9 rulers of the **p** which *are* from India unto	4082
	8: 9 hundred twenty and seven **p**, *unto* every	4082
	8:12 Upon one day in all the **p** of king	4082
	9: 2 all the **p** of the king Ahasuerus,	4082
	9: 3 the rulers of the **p**, and the lieutenants,	4082
	9: 4 his fame went out throughout all the **p**:	4082
	9:12 have they done in the rest of the king's **p**?	4082
	9:16 the other Jews that *were* in the king's **p**	4082
	9:20 *were* in all the **p** of the king Ahasuerus,	4082
	9:30 and seven **p** of the kingdom of Ahasuerus,	4082
Ecc	2: 8 the peculiar treasure of kings and of the **p**:	4082
La	1: 1 *and* princess among the **p**, how is she	4082
Eze	19: 8 set against him on every side from the **p**,	4082
Da	3: 2 the sheriffs, and all the rulers of the **p**,	4083
	3: 3 the sheriffs, and all the rulers of the **p**,	4083

PROVING (2) [PROVE]
Ac	9:22 at Damascus, **p** that this is very Christ.	4822
Eph	5:10 **P** what is acceptable unto the Lord.	1381

PROVISION (11) [PROVIDE]
Ge	42:25 his sack, and to give them **p** for the way:	6720
	45:21 of Pharaoh, and gave them **p** for the way.	6720
Jos	9: 5 all the bread of their **p** was dry *and*	6718
	9:12 our bread we **took** hot for our **p** out of	6679
1Ki	4: 7 each man his month in a year **made p**.	3557
	4:22 Solomon's **p** for one day was thirty	3899
2Ki	6:23 he prepared great **p** for them:	3740
1Ch	29:19 the palace, *for* the which I have **made p**.	3559
Ps	132:15 I will abundantly bless her **p**: I will satisfy	6718
Da	1: 5 the king appointed them a daily **p** of	1697
Ro	13:14 and make not **p** for the flesh, to *fulfil*	4307

PROVOCATION (8) [PROVOKE]
1Ki	15:30 by his **p** where*with* he provoked	3708
	21:22 the **p** wherewith thou hast provoked *me*	3708
Job	17: 2 *doth not* mine eye continue in their **p**?	4784
Ps	95: 8 *in* the **p**, and *as in* the day of temptation	4808
Jer	32:31 hath been to me *as* a **p** of mine **anger**	639
Eze	20:28 they presented the **p** of their offering:	3708
Heb	3: 8 Harden not your hearts, as in the **p**,	3894
	3:15 harden not your hearts, as in the **p**.	3894

PROVOCATIONS (3) [PROVOKE]
2Ki	23:26 of all the **p** that Manasseh had provoked	3708
Ne	9:18 out of Egypt, and had wrought great **p**;	5007
	9:26 them to thee, and they wrought great **p**.	5007

PROVOKE (42) [PROVOCATION,
PROVOCATIONS, PROVOKED, PROVOKEDST,
PROVOKETH, PROVOKING]
Ex	23:21 of him, and obey his voice, **p** him not;	4843
Nu	14:11 How long will this people **p** me?	5006

Dt	4:25 of the Lord thy God, to **p** him **to anger**:	3707
	9:18 the sight of the Lord, to **p** him **to anger**.	3707
	31:20 and **p** me, and break my covenant.	5006
	31:29 to **p** him **to anger** through the work of	3707
	32:21 I will **p** them **to anger** with a foolish	3707
1Ki	14: 9 to **p** me **to anger**, and hast cast me	3707
	16: 2 to sin, to **p** me **to anger** with their sins;	3707
	16:26 to **p** the Lord God of Israel **to anger**	3707
	16:33 **p** the Lord God of Israel **to anger** than	3707
2Ki	17:11 wicked things to **p** the Lord **to anger**:	3707
	17:17 the sight of the Lord, to **p** *him* **to anger**.	3707
	21: 6 the sight of the Lord, to **p** *him* **to anger**.	3707
	22:17 that they might **p** me **to anger** with all	3707
	23:19 Israel had made to *the* Lord **to anger**,	3707
2Ch	33: 6 the sight of the Lord, to **p** him **to anger**:	3707
	34:25 that *they* might **p** me **to anger** with all	3707
Job	12: 6 and they that **p** God are secure;	7264
Ps	78:40 How oft did they **p** him in the wilderness,	4784
Isa	3: 8 the Lord, to **p** the eyes of his glory.	4784
Jer	7:18 other gods, that *they* may **p** me **to anger**.	3707
	7:19 Do they **p** me **to anger**? saith the Lord:	3707
	7:19 *do they* not **p** themselves to the confusion	NIH
	11:17 **p** me in offering incense unto	3707
	25: 6 **p** me not **to anger** with the works of	3707
	25: 7 *ye* might **p** me **to anger** with the works	3707
	32:29 unto other gods, to **p** me **to anger**.	3707
	32:32 which they have done to **p** me **to anger**,	3707
	44: 3 they have committed to **p** me **to anger**,	3707
	44: 8 that *ye* **p** me **unto wrath** with the works	3707
Eze	8:17 *with* violence, and have returned to **p** me	3707
	16:26 thy whoredoms, to **p** me **to anger**.	3707
Lk	11:53 and to **p** him **to speak** of many *things*:	653
Ro	10:19 I will **p** you **to jealousy** by *them that*	3863
	11:11 the Gentiles, for to **p** them **to jealousy**.	3863
	11:14 If by any means I may **p** to emulation	3863
1Co	10:22 Do we **p** the Lord **to jealousy**? are we	3863
Eph	6: 4 ye fathers, **p** not your children **to wrath**:	3949
Col	3:21 **p** not your children *to anger*, lest they be	2042
Heb	3:16 For some, when they had heard, did **p**:	3893
	10:24 let us consider one another to **p** unto	3948

PROVOKED (33) [PROVOKE]
Nu	14:23 neither shall any of them that **p** me see it:	5006
	16:30 shall understand that these men have **p**	5006
Dt	9: 8 Also in Horeb ye **p** the Lord **to wrath**,	7107
	9:22 ye **p** the Lord **to wrath**.	7107
	32:16 **p** him **to jealousy** with strange *gods*,	7065
	32:16 with abominations **p** they him **to anger**.	3707
	32:21 They have **p** me **to anger** with their	3707
Jdg	2:12 unto them, and **p** the Lord **to anger**.	3707
1Sa	1: 6 her adversary also **p** her **sore**, for	3707+3708
	1: 7 to the house of the Lord, so she **p** her;	3707
1Ki	14:22 they **p** him **to jealousy** with their sins	7065
	15:30 he **p** the Lord God of Israel **to anger**.	3707
	21:22 wherewith thou hast **p** *me* **to anger**,	3707
	22:53 and **p** **to anger** the Lord God of Israel,	3707
2Ki	21:15 have **p** me **to anger**, since the day their	3707
	23:26 all the provocations that Manasseh had **p**	3707
1Ch	21: 1 and **p** David to number Israel.	5496
2Ch	28:25 **p** **to anger** the Lord God of his fathers.	3707
Ezr	5:12 had **p** the God of heaven **unto wrath**,	7265
Ne	4: 5 for they have **p** *thee* **to anger** before	3707
Ps	78:56 they tempted and **p** the most high God,	4784
	78:58 For they **p** him **to anger** with their high	3707
	106: 7 but **p** *him* at the sea, *even* at the Red sea.	4784
	106:29 Thus they **p** *him* **to anger** with their	3707
	106:33 Because they **p** his spirit, so that he spake	4784
	106:43 they **p** *him* with their counsel,	4784
Isa	1: 4 **p** the Holy One of Israel **unto anger**,	5006
Jer	8:19 Why have they **p** me **to anger** with their	3707
	32:30 **p** me **to anger** with the work of their	3707
Hos	12:14 Ephraim **p** *him* **to anger** most bitterly:	3707
Zec	8:14 when your fathers **p** me **to wrath**, saith	7107
1Co	13: 5 her own, is not easily **p**, thinketh no evil;	3947
2Co	9: 2 year ago; and your zeal hath **p** very many.	2042

PROVOKEDST (1) [PROVOKE]
Dt	9: 7 how thou **p** the Lord thy God **to wrath**	7107

PROVOKETH (3) [PROVOKE]
Pr	20: 2 *whoso* **p** him **to anger** sinneth *against*	5674
Isa	65: 3 A people that **p** me **to anger** continually	3707
Eze	8: 3 image of jealousy, which **p** to jealousy.	7069

PROVOKING (6) [PROVOKE]
Dt	32:19 because of the **p** of his sons,	3708
1Ki	14:15 made their groves, **p** the Lord **to anger**.	3707
	16: 7 in **p** him **to anger** with the work of his	3707
	16:13 in **p** the Lord God of Israel **to anger**	3707
Ps	78:17 they sinned yet more against him by **p**	4784
Gal	5:26 **p** one another, envying one another.	4292

PRUDENCE (3) [PRUDENT, PRUDENTLY]
2Ch	2:12 endued with **p** and understanding,	7922
Pr	8:12 I wisdom dwell *with* **p**, and find out	6195
Eph	1: 8 abounded toward us in all wisdom and **p**;	5428

PRUDENT (24) [PRUDENCE]
1Sa	16:18 **p** in matters, and a comely person,	995
Pr	12:16 but a **p** man covereth shame.	6175
	12:23 A **p** man concealeth knowledge:	6175
	13:16 Every **p** man dealeth with knowledge:	6175
	14: 8 The wisdom of the **p** *is* to understand his	6175
	14:15 but the **p** man looketh well to his going.	6175
	14:18 but the **p** are crowned *with* knowledge.	6175

Pr	15: 5 but he that regardeth reproof is **p**.	6191
	16:21 The wise in heart shall be called **p**:	995
	18:15 The heart of the **p** getteth knowledge;	995
	19:14 and a **p** wife *is* from the Lord.	7919
	22: 3 A **p** man foreseeth the evil,	6175
	27:12 A **p** man foreseeth the evil,	6175
Isa	3: 2 the prophet, and the **p**, and the ancient,	7080
	5:21 their own eyes, and **p** in their own sight!	995
	10:13 done *it*, and by my wisdom; for I am **p**:	995
	29:14 the understanding of their **p** men shall be	995
Jer	49: 7 is counsel perished from the **p**? is their	995
Hos	14: 9 and he shall understand these *things*? **p**,	995
Am	5:13 Therefore the **p** shall keep silence in that	7919
Mt	11:25 hast hid these *things* from the wise and **p**,	4908
Lk	10:21 hast hid these *things* from the wise and **p**,	4908
Ac	13: 7 *of* the country, Sergius Paulus, a **p** man;	4908
1Co	1:19 to nothing the understanding of the **p**.	4908

PRUDENTLY (1) [PRUDENCE]
Isa	52:13 Behold, my servant shall **deal p**, he shall	7919

PRUNE (2) [PRUNED, PRUNING,
PRUNINGHOOKS]
Lev	25: 3 six years thou shalt **p** thy vineyard,	2168
	25: 4 neither sow thy field, nor **p** thy vineyard.	2168

PRUNED (1) [PRUNE]
Isa	5: 6 it shall not be **p**, nor digged; but there	2168

PRUNING (1) [PRUNE]
Isa	18: 5 both cut off the sprigs with **p hooks**,	4211

PRUNINGHOOKS (3) [HOOK, PRUNE]
Isa	2: 4 into plowshares, and their spears into **p**:	4211
Joel	3:10 into swords, and your **p** into spears:	4211
Mic	4: 3 into plowshares, and their spears into **p**:	4211

PSALM (88) [PSALMIST, PSALMS]
1Ch	16: 7 on that day David delivered first *this* **p** to	NIH
Ps	3: T A **P** of David, when he fled from Absalom	4210
	4: T Musician on Neginoth, A **P** of David.	4210
	5: T Musician upon Nehiloth, A **P** of David.	4210
	6: T Neginoth upon Sheminith, A **P** of David.	4210
	8: T Musician upon Gittith, A **P** of David.	4210
	9: T upon Muth-labben, A **P** of David.	4210
	11: T to the chief Musician, A **P** of David.	NIH
	12: T Musician upon Sheminith, A **P** of David.	4210
	13: T To the chief Musician, A **P** of David.	4210
	14: T To the chief Musician, A **P** of David.	NIH
	15: T A **P** of David.	4210
	18: T To the chief Musician, A **P** of David.	NIH
	19: T To the chief Musician, A **P** of David.	4210
	20: T To the chief Musician, A **P** of David.	4210
	21: T To the chief Musician, A **P** of David.	4210
	22: T upon Aijeleth Shahar, A **P** of David.	4210
	23: T A **P** of David.	4210
	24: T A **P** of David.	4210
	25: T A **P** of David.	NIH
	26: T A **P** of David.	NIH
	27: T A **P** of David.	NIH
	28: T A **P** of David.	NIH
	29: T A **P** of David.	4210
	30: T A **P** *and* Song *at* the dedication of the	4210
	31: T To the chief Musician, A **P** of David.	4210
	32: T A **P** of David, Maschil.	NIH
	34: T A **P** of David, when he changed his	NIH
	35: T A **P** of David.	NIH
	36: T A **P** of David the servant of the Lord.	NIH
	37: T A **P** of David.	NIH
	38: T A **P** of David, to bring to remembrance.	4210
	39: T *even* to Jeduthun, A **P** of David.	4210
	40: T To the chief Musician, A **P** of David.	4210
	41: T To the chief Musician, A **P** of David.	4210
	47: T chief Musician, A **P** for the sons of Korah.	4210
	48: T A Song *and* **P** for the sons of Korah.	4210
	49: T chief Musician, A **P** for the sons of Korah.	4210
	50: T A **P** of Asaph.	4210
	51: T To the chief Musician, A **P** of David,	4210
	52: T chief Musician, Maschil, A **P** of David,	NIH
	53: T upon Mahalath, Maschil, A **P** of David.	NIH
	54: T Maschil, A **P** of David, when the Ziphims	NIH
	55: T on Neginoth, Maschil, A **P** of David.	NIH
	61: T Musician upon Neginah, A **P** of David.	4210
	62: T chief Musician, to Jeduthun, A **P** of David.	4210
	63: T A **P** of David, when he was in	4210
	64: T To the chief Musician, A **P** of David.	4210
	65: T chief Musician, A **P** *and* Song of David.	4210
	66: T To the chief Musician, A Song *or* **P**.	4210
	67: T chief Musician on Neginoth, A **P** *or* Song.	4210
	68: T the chief Musician, A **P** *or* Song of David.	4210
	69: T Musician upon Shoshannim, A **P** of David.	NIH
	70: T To the chief Musician, A **P** of David.	NIH
	72: T A **P** for Solomon.	NIH
	73: T A **P** of Asaph.	4210
	75: T Al-taschith, A **P** *or* Song of Asaph.	4210
	76: T on Neginoth, A **P** *or* Song of Asaph.	4210
	77: T Musician, to Jeduthun, A **P** of Asaph.	4210
	79: T A **P** of Asaph.	4210
	80: T upon Shoshannim-Eduth, A **P** of Asaph.	4210
	81: T Musician upon Gittith, A **P** of Asaph.	NIH
	81: 2 Take a **p**, and bring hither the timbrel,	2172
	82: T A **P** of Asaph.	4210
	83: T A Song *or* **P** of Asaph.	4210
	84: T upon Gittith, A **P** for the sons of Korah.	4210
	85: T Musician, A **P** for the sons of Korah.	4210

Ps 87: T A **P** *or* Song for the sons of Korah. 4210
88: T A Song *or* **P** for the sons of Korah. 4210
92: T A **P** *or* Song for the sabbath day. 4210
98: T A **P**. 4210
98: 5 with the harp, and the voice of a **p**. 2172
100: T A **P** of praise. 4210
101: T A **P** of David. 4210
103: T *A* **P** of David. NIH
108: T A Song *or* **P** of David. 4210
109: T To the chief Musician, A **P** of David. 4210
110: T A **P** of David. 4210
138: T *A* **P** of David. NIH
139: T To the chief Musician, A **P** of David. 4210
140: T To the chief Musician, A **P** of David. 4210
141: T A **P** of David. 4210
143: T A **P** of David. 4210
144: T *A* **P** of David. NIH
145: T David's **P** *of* praise. NIH
Ac 13:33 as it is also written in the second **p**, 5568
13:35 Wherefore he saith also in another **p**, NIG
1Co 14:26 one of you hath a **p**, hath a doctrine, 5568

PSALMIST (1) [PSALM]
2Sa 23: 1 of Jacob, and the sweet **p** of Israel, said, 2158

PSALMS (9) [PSALM]
1Ch 16: 9 Sing unto him, **sing p** unto him, talk you 2167
Ps 95: 2 *and* make a joyful noise unto him with **p**. 2158
105: 2 Sing unto him, **sing p** unto him: talk ye 2167
Lk 20:42 And David himself saith in the book of **P**, 5568
24:44 prophets, and *in* the **p**, concerning me. 5568
Ac 1:20 For it is written in the book of **P**, Let his 5568
Eph 5:19 Speaking to yourselves in **p** and hymns 5568
Col 3:16 and admonishing one another in **p** and 5568
Jas 5:13 him pray. Is any merry? let him **sing p**. 5567

PSALTERIES (14) [PSALTERY]
2Sa 6: 5 on **p**, and on timbrels, and on cornets, 5035
1Ki 10:12 king's house, harps also and **p** for singers: 5035
1Ch 13: 8 with **p**, and with timbrels, 5035
15:16 **p** and harps and cymbals, sounding, 5035
15:20 and Benaiah, with **p** on Alamoth; 5035
15:28 making a noise with **p** and harps. 5035
16: 5 Jeiel with **p** and with harps; 5035
25: 1 with harps, with **p**, and with cymbals: 5035
25: 6 cymbals, **p**, and harps, for the service 5035
2Ch 5:12 having cymbals and **p** and harps, 5035
9:11 king's palace, and harps and **p** for singers: 5035
20:28 they came *to* Jerusalem with **p** and harps 5035
29:25 and **p**, and with harps, according to 5035
Ne 12:27 *with* cymbals, **p**, and with harps. 5035

PSALTERY (13) [PSALTERIES]
1Sa 10: 5 down from the high place with a **p**, 5035
Ps 33: 2 sing unto him with the **p** *and* an 5035
57: 8 Awake up, my glory; awake, **p** and harp: 5035
71:22 I will also praise thee with the **p**, 3627+5035
81: 2 the timbrel, the pleasant harp with the **p**. 5035
92: 3 instrument of ten strings, and upon the **p**; 5035
108: 2 Awake, **p** and harp: I *myself* will awake 5035
144: 9 upon a **p** *and* an instrument of ten strings 5035
150: 3 trumpet: praise him with the **p** and harp. 5035
Da 3: 5 flute, harp, sackbut, **p**, dulcimer, 6460
3: 7 sackbut, **p**, and all kinds of musick, 6460
3:10 **p**, and dulcimer, and all kinds of musick, 6460
3:15 **p**, and dulcimer, and all kinds of musick, 6460

PTOLEMAIS (1)
Ac 21: 7 we came to **P**, and saluted the brethren, 4424

PUA (1) [PUAH]
Nu 26:23 Tolaites: of **P**, the family of the Punites: 6312

PUAH (3) [PHUVAH, PUA, PUNITES]
Ex 1:15 Shiphrah, and the name of the other **P**: 6326
Jdg 10: 1 arose to defend Israel Tola the son of **P**, 6312
1Ch 7: 1 and **P**, Jashub, and Shimron, four. 6312

PUBLIC See OPEN; OPENLY; PUBLICK; PUBLICKLY

PUBLICAN (6) [PUBLICANS]
Mt 10: 3 Thomas, and Matthew the **p**; 5057
18:17 be unto thee as a heathen *man* and a **p**. 5057
Lk 5:27 and saw a **p**, named Levi, sitting at 5057
18:10 the one a Pharisee, and the other a **p**. 5057
18:11 unjust, adulterers, or even as this **p**. 5057
18:13 the **p**, standing afar off, would not lift 5057

PUBLICANS (17) [PUBLICAN]
Mt 5:46 have ye? do not even the **p** the same? 5057
5:47 more *than others?* do not even the **p** so? 5057
9:10 many **p** and sinners came and sat down 5057
9:11 Why eateth your Master with **p** and 5057
11:19 a winebibber, a friend of **p** and sinners. 5057
21:31 That the **p** and the harlots go into 5057
21:32 but the **p** and the harlots believed him: 5057
Mk 2:15 many **p** and sinners sat also together with 5057
2:16 and Pharisees saw him eat with **p** and 5057
2:16 eateth and drinketh with **p** and sinners? 5057
Lk 3:12 Then came also **p** to be baptized, 5057
5:29 and there was a great company of **p** and 5057
5:30 do ye eat and drink with **p** and sinners? 5057
7:29 all the people that heard *him*, and the **p**, 5057
7:34 a winebibber, a friend of **p** and sinners. 5057
15: 1 Then drew near unto him all the **p** and 5057
19: 2 which was the **chief among** the **p**, 754

PUBLICK (1) [PUBLICKLY]
Mt 1:19 not willing to **make** her a **p example**, 3856

PUBLICKLY (2) [PUBLICK]
Ac 18:28 mightily convinced the Jews, *and that* **p**, 1219
20:20 and have taught you **p**, and from house to 1219

PUBLISH (17) [PUBLISHED, PUBLISHETH]
Dt 32: 3 Because I will **p** the name of the LORD: 7121
1Sa 31: 9 to **p** *it in* the house of their idols, 1319
2Sa 1:20 in Gath, **p** *it* not in the streets of Askelon; 1319
Ne 8:15 they should **p** and proclaim in all their 8085
Ps 26: 7 That *I* may **p** with the voice of 8085
Jer 4: 5 Declare ye in Judah, and **p** in Jerusalem; 8085
4:16 **p** against Jerusalem, *that* watchers 8085
5:20 house of Jacob, and **p** it in Judah, saying, 8085
31: 7 ye, praise ye, and say, O LORD, save 8085
46:14 **p** in Migdol, and publish in Noph and 8085
46:14 and **p** in Noph and in Taphanhes: 8085
50: 2 the nations, and **p**, and set up a standard; 8085
50: 2 and set up a standard; **p**, *and* conceal not: 8085
Am 3: 9 **P** in the palaces at Ashdod, and in 8085
4: 5 and proclaim *and* **p** the free offerings: 8085
Mk 1:45 began to **p** *it* much, and to blaze abroad 2784
5:20 began to **p** in Decapolis how great *things* 2784

PUBLISHED (11) [PUBLISH]
Est 1:20 make shall be **p** throughout all his empire, 8085
1:22 that it should be **p** according to 1696
3:14 in every province *was* **p** unto all people, 1540
8:13 in every province *was* **p** unto all people, 1540
Ps 68:11 great *was* the company of those that **p** *it*. 1319
Jnh 3: 7 through Nineveh by the decree of the 559
Mk 7:36 *so* much the more a great deal they **p** *it*; 2784
13:10 And the gospel must first be **p** among all 2784
Lk 8:39 throughout the whole city how great 2784
Ac 10:37 which was **p** throughout all Judea, 1096
13:49 the word of the Lord was **p** throughout 1308

PUBLISHETH (4) [PUBLISH]
Isa 52: 7 that bringeth good tidings, that **p** peace; 8085
52: 7 good tidings of good, that **p** salvation; 8085
Jer 4:15 and **p** affliction from mount Ephraim. 8085
Na 1:15 that bringeth good tidings, that **p** peace. 8085

PUBLIUS (2)
Ac 28: 7 *man* of the island, whose name was **P**; 4196
28: 8 that the father of **P** lay sick of a fever and 4196

PUDENS (1)
2Ti 4:21 and **P**, and Linus, and Claudia, and all 4227

PUFFED (5) [PUFFETH]
1Co 4: 6 no one of you be **p up** for one against 5448
4:18 some are **p up**, as though I would not 5448
4:19 not the speech of them which are **p up**, 5448
5: 2 And ye are **p up**, and have not rather 5448
13: 4 charity vaunteth not itself, is not **p up**, 5448

PUFFETH (3) [PUFFED, PUFT]
Ps 10: 5 *as for* all his enemies, he **p** at them. 6315
12: 5 I will set *him* in safety *from him that* **p** at 6315
1Co 8: 1 Knowledge **p up**, but charity edifieth. 5448

PUFT (1) [PUFFETH]
Col 2:18 not seen, vainly **p up** by his fleshly mind, 5448

PUHITES (1)
1Ch 2:53 the **P**, and the Shumathites, 6336

PUITES See PUNITES

PUL (4) [TIGLATH-PILESER]
2Ki 15:19 And **P** the king of Assyria came against 6322
15:19 Menahem gave **P** a thousand talents of 6322
1Ch 5:26 the God of Israel stirred up the spirit of **P** 6322
Isa 66:19 Tarshish, **P**, and Lud, that draw the bow, 6322

PULL (15) [PULLED, PULLING]
1Ki 13: 4 so that he could not **p** it **in again** to him. 7725
Ps 31: 4 **P** me **out** of the net that they have laid 3318
Isa 22:19 and from thy station shall he **p down**. 2040
Jer 1:10 to **p down**, and to destroy, and to throw 5422
12: 3 **p** them **out** like sheep for the slaughter, 5423
18: 7 and to **p down**, and to destroy *it;* 5422
24: 6 I will build them, and not **p** them **down**; 2040
42:10 not **p** *you* **down**, and I will plant you, 2040
Eze 17: 9 shall he not **p up** the roots thereof, and 5423
Mic 2: 8 ye **p** off the robe with the garment from 6584
Mt 7: 4 Let me **p** out the mote out of thine eye; 1544
Lk 6:42 let me **p out** the mote that is in thine eye, 1544
6:42 thou see clearly to **p out** the mote that 1544
12:18 will **p down** my barns, and build greater; 2507
14: 5 will not straightway **p** him **out** on 385

PULLED (7) [PULL]
Ge 8: 9 her, and **p** her **in** unto him into the ark. 935
19:10 **p** Lot into the house to them, and shut to 935
Ezr 6:11 let timber be **p down** from his house, 5256
La 3:11 aside my ways, and **p** me **in pieces**: 6582
Am 9:15 shall no more be **p up** out of their land 5428
Zec 7:11 **p** away the shoulder, and stopped their 5414
Ac 23:10 Paul should have been **p in pieces** of 1288

PULLING (2) [PULL]
2Co 10: 4 mighty through God to the **p down** of 2506

Jude 1:23 save with fear, **p** them out of the fire; 726

PULPIT (1)
Ne 8: 4 Ezra the scribe stood upon a **p** of wood, 4026

PULSE (3)
2Sa 17:28 and beans, and lentiles, and parched **p**, NIH
Da 1:12 let them give us **p** to eat, and water to 2235
1:16 that they should drink; and gave them **p**. 2235

PUNISH (32) [PUNISHED, PUNISHMENT, PUNISHMENTS, UNPUNISHED]
Lev 26:18 will **p** you seven *times* more for your sins. 3256
26:24 will **p** you yet seven *times* for your sins. 5221
Pr 17:26 to **p** the just *is* not good, *nor* to strike 6064
Isa 10:12 I will **p** the fruit of the stout heart of 6485
13:11 I will **p** the world for *their* evil, 6485
24:21 that the LORD shall **p** the host of the high 6485
26:21 the LORD cometh out of his place to **p** 6485
27: 1 strong sword shall **p** leviathan the 6485
Jer 9:25 I will **p** all *them which are* circumcised 6485
11:22 the LORD of hosts, Behold, I will **p** them: 6485
13:21 What wilt thou say when he shall **p** thee? 6485
21:14 I will **p** you according to the fruit of your 6485
23:34 I will even **p** that man and his house. 6485
25:12 *that* I will **p** the king of Babylon, and that 6485
27: 8 that nation will I **p**, saith the LORD, 6485
29:32 I will **p** Shemaiah the Nehelamite, and 6485
30:20 and I will **p** all that oppress them. 6485
36:31 I will **p** him and his seed and his servants 6485
44:13 For I will **p** them that dwell in the land of 6485
44:29 the LORD, that I will **p** you in this place, 6485
46:25 I will **p** the multitude of No, and Pharaoh, 6485
50:18 I *will* **p** the king of Babylon and his land, 6485
51:44 I will **p** Bel in Babylon, and I will bring 6485
Hos 4: 9 I will **p** them for their ways, 6485
4:14 I will not **p** your daughters when they 6485
12: 2 and *will* **p** Jacob according to his ways; 6485
Am 3: 2 I will **p** you for all your iniquities. 6485
Zep 1: 8 that I will **p** the princes, and the king's 6485
1: 9 In the same day also will I **p** all those that 6485
1:12 the men that are settled on their lees: 6485
Zec 8:14 As I thought to **p** you, when your fathers 7489
Ac 4:21 finding nothing how they might **p** them, 2849

PUNISHED (17) [PUNISH]
Ex 21:20 his hand; he shall be **surely p**. 5358+5358
21:21 continue a day or two, he shall not be **p**: 5358
21:22 he shall be **surely p**, according as 6064+6064
Ezr 9:13 that thou our God hast **p** us less than 2820
Job 31:11 yea, it *is* an iniquity *to be* **p** by the judges. NIH
31:28 This also *were* an iniquity *to be* **p** by NIH
Pr 21:11 When the scorner is **p**, the simple is made 6064
22: 3 but the simple pass on, and are **p**. 6064
27:12 *but* the simple pass on, *and* are **p**. 6064
Jer 44:13 as I have **p** Jerusalem, by the sword, 6485
50:18 his land, as I have **p** the king of Assyria. 6485
Zep 3: 7 not be cut off, howsoever I **p** them: 6485
Zec 10: 3 against the shepherds, and I **p** the goats: 6485
Ac 22: 5 bound unto Jerusalem, for to be **p**. 5097
26:11 And I **p** them oft in every synagogue, 5097
2Th 1: 9 Who shall be **p** *with* everlasting 1349+5099
2Pe 2: 9 unjust unto the day of judgment to be **p**: 2849

PUNISHMENT (27) [PUNISH]
Ge 4:13 My **p** *is* greater than *I* can bear. 5771
Lev 26:41 then accept of the **p** of their **iniquity**: 5771
26:43 shall accept of the **p** of their **iniquity**: 5771
1Sa 28:10 there shall no **p** happen to thee for this 5771
Job 31: 3 a **strange p** to the workers of iniquity? 5235
Pr 19:19 *A man* of great wrath *shall* suffer **p**: for if 6066
La 3:39 complain, a man for the **p** of his *sins*? 2399
4: 6 For the **p** of the **iniquity** of the daughter 5771
4: 6 is greater than the **p** of the **sin** of Sodom, 2403
4:22 The **p** of thine **iniquity** is accomplished, 5771
Eze 14:10 they shall bear the **p** of their **iniquity**: 5771
14:10 the **p** of the prophet shall be even as 5771
14:10 as the **p** of him that seeketh *unto him;* 5771
Am 1: 3 four, I will not turn away the **p** thereof; NIH
1: 6 four, I will not turn away *the* **p** thereof; NIH
1: 9 four, I will not turn away *the* **p** thereof; NIH
1:11 four, I will not turn away *the* **p** thereof; NIH
1:13 four, I will not turn away *the* **p** thereof; NIH
2: 1 four, I will not turn away *the* **p** thereof; NIH
2: 4 four, I will not turn away *the* **p** thereof; NIH
2: 6 four, I will not turn away *the* **p** thereof; NIH
Zec 14:19 This shall be the **p** of Egypt, 2403
14:19 the **p** of all nations that come not up to 2403
Mt 25:46 these shall go away into everlasting **p**: 2851
2Co 2: 6 Sufficient to such *a man is* this **p**, 2009
Heb 10:29 Of how much sorer **p**, suppose ye, shall 5098
1Pe 2:14 unto them that are sent by him for the **p** 1557

PUNISHMENTS (2) [PUNISH]
Job 19:29 for wrath *bringeth* the **p** of the sword, 5771
Ps 149: 7 the heathen, *and* **p** upon the people; 8433

PUNITES (1) [PUAH]
Nu 26:23 the Tolaites: of Pua, the family of the **P**: 6324

PUNON (2)
Nu 33:42 from Zalmonah, and pitched in **P**. 6325
33:43 they departed from **P**, and pitched in 6325

PUR (3) [PURIM]
Est 3: 7 they cast **P**, *that is*, the lot, before Haman 6332

P

Est 9:24 had cast **P**, that *is*, the lot, to consume 6332
 9:26 these days Purim after the name of **P**. 6332

PURAH See PHURAH

PURCHASE (8) [PURCHASED]

Ge 49:32 The **p** of the field and of the cave that *is* 4735
Lev 25:33 if a man **p** of the Levites, then the house 1350
Jer 32:11 So I took the evidence of the **p**, *both* that 4736
 32:12 I gave the evidence of the **p** unto Baruch 4736
 32:12 that subscribed the book of the **p**, 4736
 32:14 evidence of the **p**, both which is sealed, 4736
 32:16 of the **p** unto Baruch the son of Neriah, 4736
1Ti 3:13 well **p** to themselves a good degree, 4046

PURCHASED (9) [PURCHASE]

Ge 25:10 The field which Abraham **p** of the sons of 7069
Ex 15:16 the people pass over, *which* thou hast **p**, 7069
Ru 4:10 wife of Mahlon, have I **p** to be my wife, 7069
Ps 74: 2 congregation, *which* thou hast **p** of old; 7069
 78:54 mountain, *which* his right hand had **p**. 7069
Ac 1:18 Now this *man* **p** a field with the reward 2932
 8:20 the gift of God may be **p** with money. 2932
 20:28 which he hath **p** with his own blood. 4046
Eph 1:14 the redemption of the **p** possession, 4047

PURE (97) [PURIFY]

Ex 25:11 thou shalt overlay it with **p** gold, within 2889
 25:17 thou shalt make a mercy seat *of* **p** gold: 2889
 25:24 thou shalt overlay it with **p** gold, 2889
 25:29 *of* **p** gold shalt thou make them. 2889
 25:31 thou shalt make a candlestick of **p** gold: 2889
 25:36 all it *shall be* one beaten work of **p** gold. 2889
 25:38 snuffdishes thereof, *shall be* of **p** gold. 2889
 25:39 *Of* a talent of **p** gold shall he make it, 2889
 27:20 that they bring thee **p** oil olive beaten for 2134
 28:14 two chains of **p** gold at the ends; 2889
 28:22 at the ends of **p** wreathen work of **p** gold. 2889
 28:36 thou shalt make a plate of **p** gold, 2889
 30: 3 thou shalt overlay it with **p** gold, the top 2889
 30:23 of **p** myrrh five hundred *shekels*, and 1865
 30:34 *these* sweet spices with **p** frankincense: 2134
 30:35 tempered together, **p** *and* holy: 2889
 31: 8 the **p** candlestick with all his furniture, 2889
 37: 2 he overlaid it with **p** gold within 2889
 37: 6 he made the mercy seat *of* **p** gold: 2889
 37:11 he overlaid it with **p** gold, 2889
 37:16 and *his* covers to cover withal, *of* **p** gold. 2889
 37:17 he made the candlestick of **p** gold: 2889
 37:22 all of it *was* one beaten work of **p** gold. 2889
 37:23 his snuffers, and his snuffdishes, *of* **p** gold. 2889
 37:24 *Of* a talent of **p** gold made he it, and all 2889
 37:26 overlaid it with **p** gold, *both* the top of it, 2889
 37:29 and the **p** incense of sweet spices, 2889
 39:15 at the ends, *of* wreathen work *of* **p** gold. 2889
 39:25 they made bells of **p** gold, and put the 2889
 39:30 made the plate of the holy crown *of* **p** 2889
 39:37 The **p** candlestick, *with* the lamps thereof, 2889
Lev 24: 2 they bring unto thee **p** oil olive beaten 2134
 24: 4 He shall order the lamps upon the **p** 2889
 24: 6 a row, upon the **p** table before the LORD. 2889
 24: 7 thou shalt put **p** frankincense upon *each* 2134
Dt 32:14 thou didst drink the **p** blood of the grape. 2561
2Sa 22:27 With the **p** thou wilt shew thyself **p**ure; 1305
 22:27 With the pure thou wilt **shew** thyself **p**; 1305
1Ki 5:11 and twenty measures of **p** oil: 3795
 6:20 he overlaid it with **p** gold: and *so* 5462
 6:21 overlaid the house within with **p** gold: 5462
 7:49 candlesticks *of* **p** gold, five on the right 5462
 7:50 the spoons, and the censers *of* **p** gold; 5462
 10:21 of the forest of Lebanon *were of* **p** gold: 5462
1Ch 28:17 Also **p** gold *for* the fleshhooks, 2889
2Ch 3: 4 and he overlaid it within with **p** gold. 2889
 4:20 the manner before the oracle, *of* **p** gold; 5462
 4:22 the spoons, and the censers, *of* **p** gold: 5462
 9:17 of ivory, and overlaid it with **p** gold: 2889
 9:20 of the forest of Lebanon *were of* **p** gold: 5462
 13:11 also *set they* in order upon the **p** table; 2889
Ezr 6:20 of them *were* **p**, and killed the passover 2889
Job 4:17 shall a man be more **p** than his Maker? 2891
 8: 6 If thou *wert* **p** and upright; surely now he 2134
 11: 4 My doctrine *is* **p**, and I am clean in thine 2134
 16:17 in mine hands: also my prayer is **p**. 2134
 25: 5 yea, the stars are not **p** in his sight. 2141
 28:19 neither shall it be valued with **p** gold. 2889
Ps 12: 6 The words of the LORD *are* **p** words: 2889
 18:26 With the **p** thou wilt shew thyself **p**ure; 1305
 18:26 With the pure thou wilt **shew** thyself **p**; 1305
 19: 8 the commandment of the LORD *is* **p**, 1249
 21: 3 settest a crown of **p** gold on his head. 6337
 24: 4 He that hath clean hands, and a **p** heart; 1249
 119:140 Thy word *is* very **p**: therefore thy servant 6884
Pr 15:26 the *words* of the **p** are pleasant words. 2889
 20: 9 my heart clean, I am **p** from my sin? 2891
 20:11 whether his work *be* **p**, and whether *it* 2134
 21: 8 strange: but *as* for the **p**, his work *is* right. 2134
 30: 5 Every word of God *is* **p**: he *is* a shield 6884
 30:12 *There is* a generation *that are* **p** in their 2889
Da 7: 9 and the hair of his head like the **p** wool: 5343
Mic 6:11 Shall I **count** *them* with the wicked 2135
Zep 3: 9 will I turn to the people a **p** language, 1305
Mal 1:11 offered unto my name, and a **p** offering: 2889
Mt 5: 8 Blessed *are* the **p** in heart: for they shall 2513
Ac 20:26 that I *am* **p** from the blood of all *men*. 2513
Ro 14:20 All *things* indeed *are* **p**; but *it is* evil for 2513

P

Php 4: 8 *things are* just, whatsoever *things are* **p**, 53
1Ti 1: 5 commandment is charity out of a **p** heart, 2513
 3: 9 Holding the mystery of the faith in a **p** 2513
 5:22 of other *men's* sins: keep thyself **p**. 53
2Ti 1: 3 whom I serve from *my* forefathers with **p** 2513
 2:22 them that call on the Lord out of a **p** 2513
Tit 1:15 Unto the **p** all *things* are pure: 2513
 1:15 Unto the pure all *things are* **p**: 2513
 1:15 are defiled and unbelieving *is* nothing **p**; 2513
Heb 10:22 and *our* bodies washed with **p** water. 2513
Jas 1:27 **P** religion and undefiled before God and 2513
 3:17 the wisdom that is from above is first **p**, 53
1Pe 1:22 *that ye* love one another with a **p** heart 2513
1Jn 3: 3 in him purifieth himself, even as he is **p**. 53
Rev 15: 6 clothed in **p** and white linen, 2513
 21:18 and the city *was* **p** gold, like unto clear 2513
 21:21 and the street of the city *was* **p** gold, as *it* 2513
 22: 1 And he shewed me a **p** river of water of 2513

PURELY (1) [PURIFY]

Isa 1:25 **p** purge away thy dross, 1253+1886.1+3509.1

PURENESS (3) [PURIFY]

Job 22:30 it is delivered by the **p** of thine hands. 1252
Pr 22:11 He that loveth **p** of heart, *for* the grace of 2889
2Co 6: 6 By **p**, by knowledge, by longsuffering, 54

PURER (2) [PURIFY]

La 4: 7 Her Nazarites were **p** than snow, they 2141
Hab 1:13 *Thou art* of **p** eyes than to behold evil, 2889

PURGE (15) [PURGED, PURGETH, PURGING]

2Ch 34: 3 in the twelfth year he began to **p** Judah 2891
Ps 51: 7 **P** me with hyssop, and I shall be clean: 2398
 65: 3 transgressions, thou shalt **p** them *away*. 3722
 79: 9 deliver us, and **p** away our sins, for thy 3722
Isa 1:25 purely **p** away thy dross, and take away 6884
Eze 20:38 I will **p** out from among you the rebels, 1305
 43:20 thus shalt thou cleanse and **p** it. 3722
 43:26 Seven days shall they **p** the altar and 3722
Da 11:35 them, and to **p**, and to make *them* white, 1305
Mal 3: 3 of Levi, and **p** them as gold and silver, 2212
Mt 3:12 and he will **throughly p** his floor, 1245
Lk 3:17 and he will **throughly p** his floor, 1245
1Co 5: 7 **P** out therefore the old leaven, that ye 1571
2Ti 2:21 If a man therefore **p** himself from these, 1571
Heb 9:14 **p** your conscience from dead works to 2511

PURGED (14) [PURGE]

1Sa 3:14 the iniquity of Eli's house shall not be **p** 3722
2Ch 34: 8 when he had **p** the land, and the house, 2891
Pr 16: 6 By mercy and truth iniquity is **p**: and by 3722
Isa 4: 4 shall have **p** the blood of Jerusalem from 1740
 6: 7 iniquity is taken away, and thy sin **p**. 3722
 22:14 this iniquity shall not be **p** from you 3722
 27: 9 shall the iniquity of Jacob be **p**; 3722
Eze 24:13 because I have **p** thee, and thou wast not 2891
 24:13 I have purged thee, and thou wast not **p**, 2891
 24:13 thou shalt not be **p** from thy filthiness any 2891
Heb 1: 3 when he had by himself **p** our sins, 2512+4160
 9:22 almost all *things* are by the law **p** with 2511
 10: 2 that the worshippers once **p** should have 2508
2Pe 1: 9 hath forgotten that *he* was **p** from his old 2512

PURGETH (1) [PURGE]

Jn 15: 2 every *branch* that beareth fruit, he **p** it, 2508

PURGING (1) [PURGE]

Mk 7:19 goeth out into the draught, **p** all meats? 2511

PURIFICATION (8) [PURIFY]

Nu 19: 9 for a water of separation: it *is* a **p** for sin, 2403
 19:17 the ashes of the burnt *heifer* of **p** for sin, 2403
2Ch 30:19 according to the **p** of the sanctuary. 2893
Ne 12:45 ward of their God, and the ward of the **p**, 2893
Est 2: 3 and let their **things for p** be given *them*: 8562
 2: 9 he speedily gave her her **things for p**, 8562
Lk 2:22 And when the days of her **p** according to 2512
Ac 21:26 the accomplishment of the days of **p**, 49

PURIFICATIONS (1) [PURIFY]

Est 2:12 so were the days of their **p** accomplished, 4795

PURIFIED (12) [PURIFY]

Lev 8:15 **p** the altar, and poured the blood at 2398
Nu 8:21 the Levites were **p**, and they washed 2398
 31:23 nevertheless it shall be **p** with the water 2398
2Sa 11: 4 for she was **p** from her uncleanness: 6942
Ezr 6:20 priests and the Levites were **p** together, 2891
Ne 12:30 the priests and the Levites **p** themselves, 2891
 12:30 the people, and the gates, and the wall. 2891
Ps 12: 6 tried in a furnace of earth, **p** seven times. 2212
Da 12:10 Many shall be **p**, and made white, 1305
Ac 24:18 Jews from Asia found me **p** in the temple, 48
Heb 9:23 in the heavens should be **p** with these; 2511
1Pe 1:22 Seeing ye have **p** your souls in obeying 48

PURIFIER (1) [PURIFY]

Mal 3: 3 he shall sit *as* a refiner and **p** of silver: 2891

PURIFIETH (2) [PURIFY]

Nu 19:13 not himself, defileth the tabernacle of 2398
1Jn 3: 3 every *man* that hath this hope in him **p** 48

PURIFY (14) [PURE, PURELY, PURENESS, PURER, PURIFICATION, PURIFICATIONS, PURIFIED, PURIFIER, PURIFIETH, PURIFYING, PURITY]

Nu 19:12 shall himself with it on the third day, 2398
 19:12 if he **p** not himself the third day, then 2398
 19:19 on the seventh day he shall **p** him *self*, 2398
 19:20 shall be unclean, and shall not **p** himself, 2398
 31:19 **p** both yourselves and your captives on 2398
 31:20 **p** all *your* raiment, and all that is made of 2398
Job 41:25 by reason of breakings they **p** themselves. 2398
Isa 66:17 **p** themselves in the gardens behind one 2891
Eze 43:26 days shall they purge the altar and **p** it; 2891
Mal 3: 3 shall **p** the sons of Levi, and purge them 2891
Jn 11:55 before the passover, to **p** themselves. 48
Ac 21:24 and **p** thyself with them, and be at charges 48
Tit 2:14 and **p** unto himself a peculiar people, 2511
Jas 4: 8 and **p** *your* hearts, ye double minded. 48

PURIFYING (12) [PURIFY]

Lev 12: 4 continue in the blood of her **p** three and 2893
 12: 4 until the days of her **p** be fulfilled. 2892
 12: 5 she shall continue in the blood of her **p** 2893
 12: 6 when the days of her **p** are fulfilled, for a 2892
Nu 8: 7 Sprinkle water of **p** upon them, 2403
1Ch 23:28 in the **p** of all holy *things*, and the work 2893
Est 2:12 *other* things for the **p** of the women;) 8562
Jn 2: 6 after the manner of the **p** of the Jews, 2512
 3:25 of John's disciples and the Jews about **p**. 2512
Ac 15: 9 and them, **p** their hearts by faith. 2511
 21:26 the next day **p** himself with them entered 48
Heb 9:13 unclean, sanctifieth to the **p** of the flesh: 2514

PURIM (5) [PUR]

Est 9:26 Wherefore they called these days **P** after 6332
 9:28 *that* these days of **P** should not fail from 6332
 9:29 to confirm this second letter of **P**. 6332
 9:31 To confirm these days of **P** in their times 6332
 9:32 of Esther confirmed these matters of **P**; 6332

PURITY (2) [PURIFY]

1Ti 4:12 in charity, in spirit, in faith, in **p**. 47
 5: 2 mothers; the younger as sisters, with all **p**. 47

PURLOINING (1)

Tit 2:10 Not **p**, but shewing all good fidelity; 3557

PURPLE (48)

Ex 25: 4 **p**, and scarlet, and fine linen, 713
 26: 1 twined linen, and blue, and **p**, and scarlet, 713
 26:31 **p**, and scarlet, and fine twined linen *of* 713
 26:36 and **p**, and scarlet, and fine twined linen, 713
 27:16 and **p**, and scarlet, and fine twined linen, 713
 28: 5 and blue, and **p**, and scarlet, and fine linen. 713
 28: 6 blue, and *of* **p**, *of* scarlet, and fine twined 713
 28: 8 and **p**, and scarlet, and fine twined linen. 713
 28:15 **p**, and *of* scarlet, and *of* fine twined linen, 713
 28:33 of **p**, and of scarlet, round about the hem 713
 35: 6 and **p**, and scarlet, and fine linen, 713
 35:23 **p**, and scarlet, and fine linen, and goats' 713
 35:25 and of **p**, *and* of scarlet, and of fine linen. 713
 35:35 blue, and in **p**, in scarlet, and in fine linen, 713
 36: 8 twined linen, and blue, and **p**, and scarlet: 713
 36:35 and **p**, and scarlet, and fine twined linen, 713
 36:37 **p**, and scarlet, and fine twined linen, 713
 38:18 and **p**, and scarlet, and fine twined linen, 713
 38:23 and in **p**, and in scarlet, and in fine linen. 713
 39: 1 of the blue, and **p**, and scarlet, they made 713
 39: 2 and **p**, and scarlet, and fine twined linen, 713
 39: 3 in the **p**, and in the scarlet, and in the fine 713
 39: 5 of the blue, and **p**, and scarlet, and fine 713
 39: 8 and **p**, and scarlet, and fine twined linen, 713
 39:24 blue, and **p**, and scarlet, *and* twined *linen*. 713
 39:29 blue, and **p**, and scarlet, *of* needlework; 713
Nu 4:13 the altar, and spread a **p** cloth thereon: 713
Jdg 8:26 **p** raiment that *was* on the kings of Midian, 713
2Ch 2: 7 in **p**, and crimson, and blue, and that can 710
 2:14 in **p**, in blue, and in fine linen, 713
 3:14 **p**, and crimson, and fine linen, and 713
Est 1: 6 and to silver rings and pillars of marble: 713
 8:15 and *with* a garment of fine linen and **p**: 713
Pr 31:22 of tapestry; her clothing *is* silk and **p**. 713
SS 3:10 thereof *of* gold, the covering of it *of* **p**, 713
 7: 5 and the hair of thine head like **p**; 713
Jer 10: 9 blue and **p** *is* their clothing: they *are* all 713
Eze 27: 7 **p** from the isles of Elishah was that which 713
 27:16 **p**, and broidered work, and fine linen, 713
Mk 15:17 And they clothed him with **p**, and platted 4209
 15:20 they took off the **p** from him, and put his 4209
Lk 16:19 which was clothed in **p** and fine linen, 4209
Jn 19: 2 his head, and they put on him a **p** robe, 4210
 19: 5 the crown of thorns, and the **p** robe. 4210
Ac 16:14 a **seller of p**, of the city of Thyatira, 4211
Rev 17: 4 And the woman was arrayed in **p** and 4209
 18:12 and **p**, and silk, and scarlet, and all thyine 4209
 18:16 and **p**, and scarlet, and decked with gold, 4210

PURPOSE (36) [PURPOSED, PURPOSES, PURPOSETH, PURPOSING]

Ru 2:16 **let fall** also *some* of the
 handfuls of **p** 7997+7997
1Ki 5: 5 I **p** to build a house unto the name of 559
2Ch 28:10 ye **p** to keep under the children of Judah 559
Ezr 4: 5 to frustrate their **p**, all the days of Cyrus 6098
Ne 8: 4 of wood, which they had made for the **p**; 1697
Job 33:17 That *he* may withdraw man *from* his **p**, 4639

Pr	20:18 Every **p** is established by counsel:	4284
Ecc	3: 1 and a time to every **p** under the heaven:	2656
	3:17 for there is a time there for every **p** and	2656
	8: 6 Because to every **p** there is time and	2656
Isa	1:11 To what **p** is the multitude of your	3807.1
	14:26 This is the **p** that is purposed upon	6098
	30: 7 Egyptians shall help in vain, and to no **p**:	7385
Jer	6:20 To what **p** cometh to me incense	2088
	26: 3 which I **p** to do unto them because of	2803
	36: 3 all the evil which I **p** to do unto them;	2803
	49:30 and hath conceived a **p** against you.	4284
	51:29 for every **p** of the LORD shall be	4284
Da	6:17 the **p** might not be changed concerning	6640
Mt	26: 8 saying, To what **p** is this waste?	5101
Ac	11:23 that with **p** of heart they would cleave	4286
	26:16 for I have appeared unto thee for this **p**,	NIG
	27:13 supposing that they had obtained their **p**,	4286
	27:43 to save Paul, kept them from their **p**;	1013
Ro	8:28 who are the called according to his **p**.	4286
	9:11 that the **p** of God according to election	4286
	9:17 for this same **p** have I raised thee up,	NIG
2Co	1:17 or the things that I **p**, do I purpose	1011
	1:17 purpose, do I **p** according to the flesh,	1011
Eph	1:11 being predestinated according to the **p** of	4286
	3:11 According to the eternal **p** which he	4286
	6:22 I have sent unto you for the same **p**,	1519
Col	4: 8 I have sent unto you for the same **p**,	1519
2Ti	1: 9 but according to his own **p** and grace,	4286
	3:10 **p**, faith, longsuffering, charity, patience,	4286
1Jn	3: 8 For this **p** the Son of God was manifested,	NIG

PURPOSED (19) [PURPOSE]

2Ch	32: 2 that he was **p** to fight against Jerusalem,	6440
Ps	17: 3 am **p** that my mouth shall not transgress.	2161
	140: 4 who have **p** to overthrow my goings.	2803
Isa	14:24 to pass; and as I have **p**, so shall it stand:	3289
	14:26 is the purpose that is **p** upon the whole	3289
	14:27 For the LORD of hosts hath **p**,	3289
	19:12 the Lord of hosts hath **p** upon Egypt.	3289
	23: 9 The LORD of hosts hath **p** it, to stain	3289
	46:11 it to pass; I have **p** it, I will also do it.	3335
Jer	4:28 because I have spoken it, I have **p** it, and	2161
	49:20 that he hath **p** against the inhabitants of	2803
	50:45 that he hath **p** against the land of	2803
La	2: 8 The LORD hath **p** to destroy the wall of	2803
Da	1: 8 Daniel **p** in his heart that he would not	7760
Ac	19:21 things were ended, Paul **p** in the spirit,	5087
	20: 3 he **p** to return through Macedonia.	1096+1106
Ro	1:13 that oftentimes I **p** to come unto you,	4388
Eph	1: 9 good pleasure which he had **p** in himself:	4388
	3:11 to the eternal purpose which he **p**	4160

PURPOSES (5) [PURPOSE]

Job	17:11 My days are past, my **p** are broken off,	2154
Pr	15:22 Without counsel **p** are disappointed:	4284
Isa	19:10 they shall be broken in the **p** thereof,	8356
Jer	49:20 his **p**, that he hath purposed against	4284
	50:45 his **p**, that he hath purposed against the	4284

PURPOSETH (1) [PURPOSE]

2Co	9: 7 Every man according as he **p** in his heart,	4255

PURPOSING (1) [PURPOSE]

Ge	27:42 doth comfort himself, **p** to kill thee.	NIH

PURSE (5) [PURSES]

Pr	1:14 in thy lot among us; let us all have one **p**:	3599
Mk	6: 8 no scrip, no bread, no money in their **p**:	2223
Lk	10: 4 Carry neither **p**, nor scrip, nor shoes:	905
	22:35 When I sent you without **p**, and scrip,	905
	22:36 But now, he that hath a **p**, let him take it,	905

PURSES (1) [PURSE]

Mt	10: 9 gold, nor silver, nor brass in your **p**;	2223

PURSUE (29) [PURSUED, PURSUER, PURSUERS, PURSUETH, PURSUING]

Ge	35: 5 and they did not **p** after the sons of Jacob.	7291
Ex	15: 9 The enemy said, I will **p**, I will overtake,	7291
Dt	19: 6 Lest the avenger of the blood **p** the slayer,	7291
	28:22 and they shall **p** thee until thou perish.	7291
	28:45 shall **p** thee, and overtake thee, till thou	7291
Jos	2: 5 **p** after them quickly; for ye shall overtake	7291
	8:16 Ai were called together to **p** after them:	7291
	10:19 but **p** after your enemies, and smite	7291
	20: 5 if the avenger of blood **p** after him, then	7291
1Sa	24:14 after whom dost thou **p**? after a dead dog,	7291
	25:29 Yet a man is risen to **p** thee, and to seek	7291
	26:18 Wherefore doth my lord thus **p** after his	7291
	30: 8 saying, Shall I **p** after this troop?	7291
	30: 8 he answered him, **P**: for thou shalt surely	7291
2Sa	17: 1 I will arise and **p** after David this night:	7291
	20: 6 **p** after him, lest he get him fenced cities,	7291
	20: 7 to **p** after Sheba the son of Bichri.	7291
	20:13 to **p** after Sheba the son of Bichri.	7291
	24:13 before thine enemies, while they **p** thee?	7291
Job	13:25 and fro? and wilt thou **p** the dry stubble?	7291
	30:15 my soul as the wind: and my welfare	7291
Ps	34:14 and do good; seek peace, and **p** it.	7291
Isa	30:16 therefore shall they that **p** you be swift.	7291
Jer	48: 2 O Madmen, the sword shall **p** thee.	310+1980
Eze	35: 6 thee unto blood, and blood shall **p** thee:	7291
	35: 6 not hated blood, even blood shall **p** thee.	7291
Hos	8: 3 thing that is good: the enemy shall **p** him.	7291
Am	1:11 he did **p** his brother with the sword,	7291

Na	1: 8 and darkness shall **p** his enemies.	7291

PURSUED (38) [PURSUE]

Ge	14:14 and pursued them unto Dan.	7291
	14:15 smote them, and **p** them unto Hobah,	7291
	31:23 and **p** after him seven days' journey;	7291
	31:36 sin, that thou hast so **hotly p** after me?	1814
Ex	14: 8 and he **p** after the children of Israel;	7291
	14: 9 the Egyptians **p** after them (all the horses	7291
	14:23 the Egyptians **p**, and went in after them	7291
Dt	11: 4 sea to overflow them as they **p** after you,	7291
Jos	2: 7 The men **p** after them the way to Jordan	7291
	2: 7 as soon as they which **p** after them were	7291
	8:16 **p** after Joshua, and were drawn away	7291
	8:17 they left the city open, and **p** after Israel.	7291
	24: 6 the Egyptians **p** after your fathers with	7291
Jdg	1: 6 they **p** after him, and caught him,	7291
	4:16 Barak **p** after the chariots, and after	7291
	4:22 as Barak **p** Sisera, Jael came out to	7291
	7:23 all Manasseh, and **p** after the Midianites.	7291
	7:25 **p** Midian, and brought the heads of Oreb	7291
	8:12 he **p** after them, and took the two kings	7291
	20:45 **p hard** after them unto Gidom,	1692
1Sa	7:11 **p** the Philistines, and smote them,	7291
	17:52 and shouted, and **p** the Philistines,	7291
	23:25 when Saul heard that, he **p** after David in	7291
	30:10 David **p**, he and four hundred men: for	7291
2Sa	2:19 Asahel **p** after Abner; and in going he	7291
	2:24 Joab also and Abishai **p** after Abner:	7291
	2:28 stood still, and **p** after Israel no more,	7291
	20:10 Abishai his brother **p** after Sheba the son	7291
	22:38 I have **p** mine enemies,	7291
1Ki	20:20 the Syrians fled; and Israel **p** them:	7291
2Ki	25: 5 the army of the Chaldees **p** after the king,	7291
2Ch	13:19 Abijah **p** after Jeroboam, and took cities	7291
	14:13 the people that were with him **p** them	7291
Ps	18:37 I have **p** mine enemies,	7291
Isa	41: 3 He **p** them, and passed safely; even by	7291
Jer	39: 5 the Chaldees' army **p** after them,	7291
	52: 8 army of the Chaldeans **p** after the king,	7291
La	4:19 they **p** us upon the mountains, they laid	1814

PURSUER (1) [PURSUE]

La	1: 6 are gone without strength before the **p**.	7291

PURSUERS (5) [PURSUE]

Jos	2:16 you to the mountain, lest the **p** meet you;	7291
	2:16 there three days, until the **p** be returned:	7291
	2:22 three days, until the **p** were returned:	7291
	2:22 **p** sought them throughout all the way,	7291
	8:20 the wilderness turned back upon the **p**.	7291

PURSUETH (8) [PURSUE]

Lev	26:17 and ye shall flee when none **p** you.	7291
	26:36 a sword; and they shall fall when none **p**.	7291
	26:37 as it were before a sword, when none **p**:	7291
Pr	11:19 that evil pursueth it to his own death.	7291
	11:19 that pursueth evil **p** it to his own death.	NIH
	13:21 Evil **p** sinners: but to the righteous good	7291
	19: 7 he **p** them with words, yet they are	7291
	28: 1 The wicked flee when no man **p**:	7291

PURSUING (8) [PURSUE]

Jdg	8: 4 that were with him, faint, yet **p** them.	7291
	8: 5 I am **p** after Zebah and Zalmunna, kings	7291
1Sa	23:28 Wherefore Saul returned from **p** after	7291
2Sa	3:22 of David and Joab came from **p** a troop,	NIH
	18:16 the people returned from **p** after Israel:	7291
1Ki	18:27 or he is **p**, or he is in a journey,	7873
	22:33 Israel, that they turned back from **p** him.	310
2Ch	18:32 Israel, they turned again from **p** him.	310

PURTENANCE (1)

Ex	12: 9 with his legs, and with the **p** thereof.	7130

PUSH (9) [PUSHING, PUSHT]

Ex	21:29 if the ox were **wont** to **p** with his horn	5056
	21:32 If the ox shall **p** a manservant or	5056
	21:36 it be known that the ox hath **used** to **p**	5056
Dt	33:17 With them he shall **p** the people together	5055
1Ki	22:11 With these thou shalt **p** the Syrians,	5055
2Ch	18:10 With these thou shalt **p** Syria until they	5055
Job	30:12 they **p away** my feet, and they raise up	7971
Ps	44: 5 Through thee will we **p down** our	5055
Da	11:40 end shall the king of the south **p** at him:	5055

PUSHING (1) [PUSH]

Da	8: 4 saw the ram **p** westward, and northward,	5055

PUSHT (1) [PUSH]

Eze	34:21 and **p** all the diseased with your horns,	5055

PUT (911) [PUTTEST, PUTTETH, PUTTING]

Ge	2: 8 he **p** the man whom he had formed.	7760
	2:15 **p** him into the garden of Eden to dress it	3240
	3:15 I will **p** enmity between thee and	7896
	3:22 lest he **p forth** his hand, and take also of	7971
	8: 9 he **p forth** his hand, and took her,	7971
	19:10 men **p forth** their hand, and pulled Lot	7971
	24: 2 **P**, I pray thee, thy hand under my thigh;	7760
	24: 9 the servant **p** his hand under the thigh of	7760
	24:47 I **p** the earring upon her face,	7760
	26:11 wife shall **surely be p to death.**	4191+4191
	27:15 and **p** them **upon** Jacob her younger son:	3847
	27:16 she **p** the skins of the kids of the goats	3847
	28:11 **p** them for his pillows, and lay down in	7760

Ge	28:18 the stone that he had **p** for his pillows,	7760
	28:20 me bread to eat, and raiment to **p on**,	3847
	29: 3 **p** the stone **again** upon the well's mouth	7725
	30:40 he **p** his own flocks by themselves,	7896
	30:40 **p** them not unto Laban's cattle.	7896
	30:42 the cattle were feeble, he **p** them not **in**:	7760
	31:34 **p** them in the camel's furniture,	7760
	32:16 and a space betwixt drove and drove.	7760
	33: 2 he **p** the handmaids and their children	7760
	35: 2 **P away** the strange gods that are among	5493
	37:34 **p** sackcloth upon his loins,	7760
	38:14 she **p** her widow's garments **off** from her,	5493
	38:19 **p on** the garments of her widowhood.	3847
	38:28 travailed, that the one **p out** his hand:	5414
	39: 4 and all that he had he **p** into his hand.	5414
	39:20 took him, and **p** him into the prison,	5414
	40: 3 he **p** them in ward in the house of	5414
	40:15 that they should **p** me into the dungeon,	7760
	41:10 **p** me in ward in the captain of the guard's,	5414
	41:42 **p** it upon Joseph's hand, and arrayed him	5414
	41:42 and **p** a gold chain about his neck;	7760
	42:17 **p** them **all together** into ward three days.	622
	43:22 we cannot tell who **p** our money in our	7760
	44: 1 every man's money in his sack's mouth.	7760
	44: 2 **p** my cup, the silver cup, in the sack's	7760
	46: 4 Joseph shall **p** his hand upon thine eyes.	7896
	47:29 **p**, I pray thee, thy hand under my thigh,	7760
	48:18 **p** thy right hand upon his head.	7760
	50:26 and he was **p** in a coffin in Egypt.	3455
Ex	2: 3 and with pitch, and **p** the child therein;	7760
	3: 5 **p off** thy shoes from off thy feet,	5394
	3:22 ye shall **p** them upon your sons,	7760
	4: 4 **P forth** thine hand, and take it by the tail.	7971
	4: 4 he **p forth** his hand, and caught it,	7971
	4: 6 him, **P** now thine hand into thy bosom.	935
	4: 6 **p** his hand into his bosom: and when	935
	4: 7 said, **P** thine hand into thy bosom **again**.	7725
	4: 7 he **p** his hand into his bosom **again**.	7725
	4:15 unto him, and **p** words in his mouth:	7760
	4:21 which I have **p** in thine hand:	7760
	5:21 to **p** a sword in their hand to slay us.	5414
	8:23 I will **p** a division between my people and	7760
	11: 7 **p** a **difference** between the Egyptians	6395
	12:15 even the first day ye shall **p away** leaven	7673
	15:26 I will **p** none of these diseases upon thee,	7760
	16:33 **p** an omer full of manna therein, and lay	5414
	17:12 and **p** it under him, and he sat thereon;	7760
	17:14 for I will **utterly p** out	4229+4229
	19:12 mount shall be **surely p to death.**	4191+4191
	21:12 he die, shall be **surely p to death.**	4191+4191
	21:15 shall be **surely p to death.**	4191+4191
	21:16 he shall **surely** be **p to death.**	4191+4191
	21:17 shall **surely** be **p to death.**	4191+4191
	21:29 and his owner also shall be **p to death.**	4191
	22: 5 shall **p in** his beast, and shall feed in	7971
	22: 8 to **see** whether he have **p** his hand unto	7971
	22:11 that he hath not **p** his hand unto his	7971
	22:19 a beast shall **surely** be **p to death.**	4191+4191
	23: 1 **p** not thine hand with the wicked to be	7896
	24: 6 took half of the blood, and **p** it in basons;	7760
	25:12 and **p** them in the four corners thereof;	5414
	25:14 thou shalt **p** the staves into the rings by	935
	25:16 thou shalt **p** into the ark the Testimony	5414
	25:21 thou shalt **p** the mercy seat above upon	5414
	25:21 in the ark thou shalt **p** the Testimony	5414
	25:26 **p** the rings in the four corners that are on	5414
	26:11 **p** the taches into the loops, and couple	935
	26:34 thou shalt **p** the mercy seat upon the ark	5414
	26:35 thou shalt **p** the table on the north side.	5414
	27: 5 thou shalt **p** it under the compass of	5414
	27: 7 And the staves shall be **p** into the rings,	935
	28:12 thou shalt **p** the two stones upon	7760
	28:23 shalt **p** the two rings on the two ends of	5414
	28:24 thou shalt **p** the two wreathen chains of	5414
	28:25 **p** them on the shoulderpieces of the	5414
	28:26 thou shalt **p** them upon the two ends of	7760
	28:27 **p** them on the two sides of the ephod	5414
	28:30 shalt **p** in the breastplate of judgment	5414
	28:37 shalt **p** it on a blue lace, that it may be	7760
	28:41 shalt **p** them **upon** Aaron thy brother,	3847
	29: 3 thou shalt **p** them into one basket,	2280
	29: 5 **p upon** Aaron the coat, and the robe of	3847
	29: 6 thou shalt **p** the mitre upon his head,	7760
	29: 6 and **p** the holy crown upon the mitre.	5414
	29: 8 bring his sons, and **p** coats **upon** them.	3847
	29: 9 his sons, and **p** the bonnets on them:	2280
	29:10 sons shall **p** their hands upon the head	5564
	29:12 **p** it upon the horns of the altar with thy	5414
	29:15 sons shall **p** their hands upon the head	5564
	29:17 **p** them unto his pieces, and unto his head	5564
	29:19 his sons shall **p** their hands upon the head	5564
	29:20 **p** it upon the tip of the **right** ear of Aaron,	5414
	29:24 thou shalt **p** all in the hands of Aaron,	7760
	29:30 in his stead shall **p** them on seven days,	3847
	30: 6 thou shalt **p** it before the vail that is by	5414
	30:18 thou shalt **p** it between the tabernacle of	5414
	30:18 the altar, and thou shalt **p** water therein.	5414
	30:36 **p** it before the Testimony in	5414
	31: 6 all that are wise hearted I have **p** wisdom,	5414
	31:14 it shall **surely** be **p to death**:	4191+4191
	31:15 his soul shall **surely** be **p to death.**	4191+4191
	32:27 **P** every man his sword by his side,	7760
	33: 4 and no man did **p** on him his ornaments.	7896
	33: 5 now **p off** thy ornaments from thee,	3381
	33:22 that I will **p** thee in a clift of the rock,	7760

P

Ex	34:33 with them, he **p** a vail on his face.	5414
	34:35 Moses **p** the vail upon his face **again**,	7725
	35: 2 doeth work therein shall be **p to death**.	4191
	35:34 he hath **p** in his heart that *he* may teach,	5414
	36: 1 in whom the LORD wisdom and	5414
	36: 2 in whose heart the LORD had **p** wisdom,	5414
	37: 5 he **p** the staves into the rings by the sides	935
	37:13 **p** the rings upon the four corners that	5414
	38: 7 he **p** the staves into the rings on the sides	935
	39: 7 he **p** them on the shoulders of the ephod,	7760
	39:16 **p** the two rings in the two ends of	5414
	39:17 they **p** the two wreathen *chains of* gold	5414
	39:18 **p** them on the shoulderpieces of the	7760
	39:19 **p** them on the two ends of the	5414
	39:20 **p** them on the two sides of the ephod	5414
	39:25 **p** the bells between the pomegranates	5414
	40: 3 thou shalt **p** therein the ark of	7760
	40: 5 **p** the hanging of the door to the	7760
	40: 7 and the altar, and shalt **p** water therein.	5414
	40:13 shalt **p** upon Aaron the holy garments,	3847
	40:18 **p** in the bars thereof, and reared up his	5414
	40:19 **p** the covering of the tent above upon it;	7760
	40:20 he took and **p** the Testimony into the ark,	5414
	40:20 and the mercy seat above upon the ark:	5414
	40:22 he **p** the table in the tent of	5414
	40:24 he **p** the candlestick in the tent of	7760
	40:26 he **p** the golden altar in the tent of	7760
	40:29 he **p** the altar of burnt offering *by* the door	7760
	40:30 the altar, and **p** water there,	5414
Lev	1: 4 he shall **p** his hand upon the head of	5564
	1: 7 the sons of Aaron the priest shall **p** fire	5414
	2: 1 oil upon it, and **p** frankincense thereon:	5414
	2:15 thou shalt **p** oil upon it,	5414
	4: 7 the priest shall **p** *some* of the blood upon	5414
	4:18 shall **p** *some* of the blood upon the horns	5414
	4:25 **p** *it* upon the horns of the altar of burnt	5414
	4:30 **p** *it* upon the horns of the altar of burnt	5414
	4:34 **p** *it* upon the horns of the altar of burnt	5414
	5:11 he shall **p** no oil upon it, neither shall he	7760
	5:11 shall he **p** *any* frankincense thereon:	5414
	6:10 the priest shall **p on** his linen garment,	3847
	6:10 linen breeches shall he **p** upon his flesh,	3847
	6:10 and he shall **p** them besides the altar.	7760
	6:11 he shall **p off** his garments, and put on	6584
	6:11 **p on** other garments, and carry forth	3847
	6:12 be burning in it; it shall not be **p out**:	3518
	8: 7 he **p** upon him the coat, and girded him	5414
	8: 7 the ephod upon him, and he girded him	5414
	8: 8 the breastplate upon him: also he **p**	7760
	8: 8 also he **p** in the breastplate the Urim and	5414
	8: 9 he **p** the mitre upon his head; also upon	7760
	8: 9 he **p** the golden plate, the holy crown;	7760
	8:13 **p** coats **upon** them, and girded them	3847
	8:13 *with* girdles, and **p** bonnets upon them;	2280
	8:15 **p** *it* upon the horns of the altar round	5414
	8:23 **p** *it* upon the tip of Aaron's right ear,	5414
	8:24 Moses **p** of the blood upon the tip of their	5414
	8:26 **p** *them* on the fat, and upon the right	7760
	8:27 he **p** all upon Aaron's hands, and upon	5414
	9: 9 **p** *it* upon the horns of the altar, and	5414
	9:20 the fat upon the breasts, and he burnt	7760
	10: 1 **p** fire therein, and put incense thereon,	5414
	10: 1 **p** incense thereon, and offered strange fire	7760
	10:10 that ye may **p difference** between holy	914
	11:32 it must be **p** into water, and it shall be	935
	11:38 if *any* water be **p** upon the seed,	5414
	13:45 he shall **p a covering** upon *his* upper lip,	5844
	14:14 priest shall **p** *it* upon the tip of the right	5414
	14:17 **p** upon the tip of the right ear of him that	5414
	14:25 **p** *it* upon the tip of the right ear of him	5414
	14:28 the priest shall **p** of the oil that *is* in his	5414
	14:29 **p** upon the head of him that is to be	5414
	14:34 I **p** the plague of leprosy in a house of	5414
	14:42 and **p** *them* in the place of *those* stones;	935
	15:19 be blood, she shall be **p apart** seven days:	5079
	16: 4 He shall **p on** the holy linen coat,	3847
	16: 4 his flesh in water, and *so* **p** them **on**.	3847
	16:13 he shall **p** the incense upon the fire before	5414
	16:18 **p** *it* upon the horns of the altar round	5414
	16:23 **p off** the linen garments, which he put	6584
	16:23 he **p on** when he went into the holy	3847
	16:24 **p** on his garments, and come forth,	3847
	16:32 **p on** the linen clothes, *even* the holy	3847
	18:19 as long as she is **p apart** for her	5079
	19:14 nor **p** a stumblingblock before the blind,	5414
	19:20 they shall not be **p to death**, because	4191
	20: 2 he shall **surely** be **p to death**:	4191+4191
	20: 9 mother shall be **surely p to death**.	4191+4191
	20:10 shall **surely** be **p to death**.	4191+4191
	20:11 them shall **surely** be **p to death**;	4191+4191
	20:12 them shall **surely** be **p to death**;	4191+4191
	20:13 they shall **surely** be **p to death**;	4191+4191
	20:15 he shall **surely** be **p to death**:	4191+4191
	20:16 they shall **surely** be **p to death**.	4191+4191
	20:25 **p difference** between clean beasts	914
	20:27 wizard, shall **surely** be **p to death**:	4191+4191
	21: 7 neither shall they take a woman **p away**	1644
	21:10 that is consecrated to **p on** the garments,	3847
	22:14 he shall **p** the fifth *part* thereof unto it,	3254
	24: 7 thou shalt **p** pure frankincense upon *each*	5414
	24:12 they **p** him in ward, that the mind of	3240
	24:16 he shall **surely** be **p to death**,	4191+4191
	24:16 name *of* the LORD, shall be **p to death**.	4191
	24:17 man shall **surely** be **p to death**.	4191+4191
	24:21 killeth a man, he shall be **p to death**.	4191

Lev	26: 8 of you shall **p** ten thousand **to flight**:	7291
	27:29 but shall **surely** be **p to death**;	4191+4191
Nu	1:51 that cometh nigh shall be **p to death**.	4191
	3:10 that cometh nigh shall be **p to death**.	4191
	3:38 that cometh nigh shall be **p to death**.	4191
	4: 6 shall **p** thereon the covering of badgers'	5414
	4: 6 of blue, and shall **p** in the staves thereof.	7760
	4: 7 **p** thereon the dishes, and the spoons,	5414
	4: 8 and shall **p** in the staves thereof.	7760
	4:10 they shall **p** it and all the vessels thereof	5414
	4:10 badgers' skins, and shall **p** *it* upon a bar.	5414
	4:11 and shall **p** the staves thereof:	7760
	4:12 **p** *them* in a cloth of blue, and cover them	5414
	4:12 badgers' skins, and shall **p** *them* on a bar:	5414
	4:14 they shall **p** upon it all the vessels thereof,	5414
	4:14 of badgers' skins, and **p** to the staves of it.	7760
	5: 2 that they **p out** of the camp every leper,	7971
	5: 3 Both male and female shall ye **p out**,	7971
	5: 3 out, without the camp shall ye **p** them;	7971
	5: 4 did so, and **p** them **out** without the camp:	7971
	5:15 no oil upon it, nor **p** frankincense thereon;	5414
	5:17 priest shall take, and **p** *it* into the water:	5414
	5:18 **p** the offering of memorial in her hands,	5414
	6:18 **p** *it* in the fire which *is* under the sacrifice	5414
	6:19 shall **p** *them* upon the hands of	5414
	6:27 they shall **p** my name upon the children	7760
	8:10 the children of Israel shall **p** their hands	5564
	11:17 *is* upon thee, and will **p** *it* upon them;	7760
	11:29 that the LORD would **p** his spirit upon	5414
	15:34 they **p** him in ward, because it was not	3240
	15:35 man shall **surely** be **p to death**:	4191+4191
	15:38 that they **p** upon the fringe of the borders	5414
	16: 7 **p** fire therein, and put incense in them	5414
	16: 7 incense in them before the LORD to	7760
	16:14 wilt thou **p out** the eyes of these men?	5365
	16:17 incense in them, and bring ye before	5414
	16:18 **p** fire in them, and laid incense thereon,	5414
	16:46 **p** fire therein from off the altar, and put	5414
	16:46 **p on** incense, and go quickly unto	7760
	16:47 he **p on** incense, and made an atonement	5414
	18: 7 that cometh nigh shall be **p to death**.	4191
	19:17 water shall be **p** thereto in a vessel:	5414
	20:26 and **p** them **upon** Eleazar his son:	3847
	20:28 and **p** them **upon** Eleazar his son;	3847
	21: 9 **p** *it* upon a pole, and it came to pass, that	7760
	23: 5 the LORD **p** a word in Balaam's mouth,	7760
	23:12 which the LORD hath **p** in my mouth?	7760
	23:16 **p** a word in his mouth, and said, Go	7760
	27:20 thou shalt **p** *some* of thine honour upon	5414
	35:16 shall **surely** be **p to death**.	4191+4191
	35:17 shall **surely** be **p to death**.	4191+4191
	35:18 shall **surely** be **p to death**.	4191+4191
	35:21 *him* shall **surely** be **p to death**;	4191+4191
	35:30 the murderer shall be **p to death** by	7523
	35:31 but he shall be **surely p to death**.	4191+4191
	36: 3 shall be **p** to the inheritance of the tribe	3254
	36: 4 shall their inheritance be **p** unto	3254
Dt	2:25 This day will I begin to **p** the dread of	5414
	7:15 will **p** none of the evil diseases of Egypt,	7760
	7:22 the LORD thy God will **p out** those	5394
	10: 2 and thou shalt **p** them in the ark.	7760
	10: 5 **p** the tables in the ark which I had made;	7760
	11:29 thou shalt **p** the blessing upon mount	5414
	12: 5 out of all your tribes to **p** his name there,	7760
	12: 7 rejoice in all that you **p** your hand **unto**,	4916
	12:21 to **p** his name there be too far from thee,	7760
	13: 5 dreamer of dreams, shall be **p to death**;	4191
	13: 5 So shalt thou **p** the evil **away** from	1197
	13: 9 shall be first upon him to **p** him **to death**,	4191
	16: 9 *thou* beginnest to **p** the sickle to the corn.	NIH
	17: 6 he that is *worthy* of death be **p to death**;	4191
	17: 6 one witness he shall not be **p to death**.	4191
	17: 7 be first upon him to **p** him **to death**,	4191
	17: 7 thou shalt **p** the evil **away** from among	1197
	17:12 thou shalt **p away** the evil from Israel.	1197
	18:18 and will **p** my words in his mouth;	5414
	19:13 thou shalt **p away** the *guilt of* innocent	1197
	19:19 thou **p** the evil **away** from among you.	1197
	21: 9 shalt thou **p away** the *guilt of* innocent	1197
	21:13 she shall **p** the raiment of her captivity	5493
	21:21 shalt thou **p** evil **away** from among you;	1197
	21:22 be *to* be **p to death**, and thou hang him	4191
	22: 5 neither shall a man **p on** a woman's	3847
	22:19 he may not **p** her **away** all his days.	7971
	22:21 shalt thou **p** evil **away** from among you.	1197
	22:22 so shalt thou **p away** evil from Israel.	1197
	22:24 thou shalt **p away** evil from among you.	1197
	22:29 he may not **p** her **away** all his days.	7971
	23:24 but thou shalt not **p** *any* in thy vessel.	5414
	24: 7 thou shalt **p** evil **away** from among you.	1197
	24:16 The fathers shall not be **p to death** for	4191
	24:16 neither shall the children be **p to death**	4191
	24:16 man shall be **p to death** for his own	4191
	25: 6 that his name be not **p out** of Israel.	4229
	26: 2 shalt **p** *it* in a basket, and shalt go unto	7760
	28:48 he shall **p** a yoke of iron upon thy neck,	5414
	30: 7 the LORD thy God will **p** all these curses	5414
	31:19 **p** it in their mouths, that this song may	7760
	31:26 **p** it in the side of the ark of the covenant	7760
	32:30 two **p** ten thousand **to flight**, except their	5127
	33:10 they shall **p** incense before thee,	7760
	33:14 for the precious things **p forth** by	1645
Jos	1:18 commandest him, he shall be **p to death**:	4191
	6:24 they **p** *into* the treasury of the house of	5414
	7: 6 of Israel, and **p** dust upon their heads.	5927

Jos	7:11 they have **p** *it* even amongst their own	7760
	10:24 your feet upon the necks of these kings.	7760
	10:24 and **p** their feet upon the necks of them.	7760
	17:13 that they **p** the Canaanites to tribute;	5414
	24: 7 he **p** darkness between you and	7760
	24:14 **p away** the gods which your fathers	5493
	24:23 therefore **p away**, *said he*, the strange	5493
Jdg	1:28 that they **p** the Canaanites to tribute,	7760
	3:21 Ehud **p** his left hand, and took	7971
	5:26 She **p** her hand to the nail, and her right	7971
	6:19 the flesh he **p** in a basket, and he put	7760
	6:19 he **p** the broth in a pot, and brought *it* out	7760
	6:21 the angel of the LORD **p forth** the end of	7971
	6:31 let him be **p to death** whilst *it is* yet	4191
	6:37 I will **p** a fleece of wool in the floor;	3322
	7:16 he **p** a trumpet in every man's hand,	5414
	8:27 and **p** it in his city, *even* in Ophrah:	3322
	9:15 come *and* **p** your **trust** in my shadow:	2620
	9:26 men of Shechem **p** their **confidence** in	982
	9:49 **p** *them* to the hold, and set the hold on	7760
	10:16 they **p away** the strange gods from	5493
	12: 3 I **p** my life in my hands, and passed over	7760
	14:12 I will now **p forth** a riddle unto you:	2330
	14:13 **P forth** thy riddle, that we may hear it.	2330
	14:16 hast **p forth** a riddle unto the children	2330
	15: 4 **p** a firebrand in the midst between two	7760
	15:15 **p forth** his hand, and took it, and slew a	7971
	16: 3 and all, and **p** *them* upon his shoulders,	7760
	16:21 **p out** his eyes, and brought him down to	5365
	18: 7 that might **p** *them* to shame in *any* thing;	3637
	18:21 **p** the little ones and the cattle and	7760
	20:13 we may **p** them **to death**, and put away	4191
	20:13 to death, and **p away** evil from Israel.	1197
	20:20 men of Israel **p** *themselves* **in array**	6186
	20:22 they **p** *themselves* **in array** the first day.	6186
	20:30 **p** *themselves* **in array** against Gibeah,	6186
	20:33 and **p** *themselves* **in array** at Baal-tamar:	6186
	21: 5 He shall **surely** be **p to death**.	4191+4191
Ru	3: 3 **p** thy raiment upon thee, and get thee	7760
1Sa	1:14 be drunken? **p away** thy wine from thee.	5493
	2:36 of bread, and shall say, **P** me, I pray thee,	5596
	4: 2 the Philistines **p** *themselves* **in array**	6186
	6: 8 the jewels of gold, which ye return him	7760
	6:15 gold *were*, and **p** on the great stone:	7760
	7: 3 *then* **p away** the strange gods and	5493
	7: 4 the children of Israel did **p away** Baalim	5493
	8:16 and your asses, and **p** them to his work.	6213
	11:11 that Saul **p** the people *in* three companies;	7760
	11:12 the men, that we may **p** them **to death**.	4191
	11:13 There shall not a man be **p to death** this	4191
	14:26 but no man **p** his hand to his mouth:	5381
	14:27 wherefore he **p forth** the end of the rod	7971
	14:27 honeycomb, and **p** his hand to his mouth;	7725
	17:21 the Philistines had **p** *the battle* **in array**,	6186
	17:38 and he **p** a helmet of brass upon his head;	5414
	17:39 proved *them*. And David **p** them off him.	5493
	17:40 **p** them in a shepherd's bag which he had,	7760
	17:49 David **p** his hand in *his* bag,	7971
	17:54 but he **p** his armour in his tent.	7760
	19: 5 For he did **p** his life in his hand,	7760
	19:13 **p** a pillow of goats' *hair for* his bolster,	7760
	21: 6 **p** hot bread in the day when it was taken	7760
	22:17 servants of the king would not **p forth**	7971
	24:10 I will not **p forth** mine hand against my	7971
	28: 3 Saul had **p away** those that had familiar	5493
	28: 8 **p on** other raiment, and he went,	3847
	28:21 I have **p** my life in my hand,	7760
	31:10 they **p** his armour *in* the house of	7760
2Sa	1:24 who **p on** ornaments of gold upon your	5927
	3:34 not bound, nor thy feet **p** into fetters:	5066
	6: 6 Uzzah **p forth** *his hand* to the ark of God,	7971
	7:15 whom I **p away** before thee.	4480+5493
	8: 2 two lines measured he to **p to death**,	4191
	8: 6 David **p** garrisons in Syria of Damascus:	7760
	8:14 he **p** garrisons in Edom; throughout all	7760
	8:14 throughout all Edom **p** he garrisons,	7760
	10: 8 **p** the battle **in array** *at* the entering in of	6186
	10: 9 and **p** *them* **in array** against the Syrians:	6186
	10:10 that he might **p** *them* **in array** against	6186
	12:13 The LORD also hath **p away** thy sin;	5674
	12:31 **p** *them* under saws, and under harrows	7760
	13:17 **P** now this *woman* out from me,	7971
	13:19 Tamar **p** ashes on her head, and rent her	3947
	14: 2 **p** on now mourning apparel, and anoint	3847
	14: 3 So Joab **p** the words in her mouth.	7760
	14:19 he **p** all these words in the mouth of	7760
	15: 5 he **p forth** his hand, and took him,	7971
	17:23 **p** his household **in order**,	6680
	18:12 would I not **p forth** mine hand against	7971
	19:21 Shall not Shimei be **p to death** for this,	4191
	19:22 there any man be **p to death** *this* day	4191
	20: 3 **p** them *in* ward, and fed them, but went	5414
	20: 8 garment that he had **p on** *was* girded	3830
	21: 9 were **p to death** in the days of harvest,	4191
1Ki	2: 5 **p** the blood of war upon his girdle that	5414
	2: 8 I will not **p** thee **to death** with the sword.	4191
	2:24 Adonijah shall be **p to death** *this* day.	4191
	2:26 I will not at this time **p** thee **to death**,	4191
	2:35 the king Benaiah the son of Jehoiada in	5414
	2:35 Zadok the priest did the king **p** in the	5414
	5: 3 until the LORD **p** them under the soles of	5414
	7:39 he **p** five bases on the right side of	5414
	7:51 did he **p** among the treasures of the house	5414
	8: 9 of stone, which Moses **p** there at Horeb,	3240
	9: 3 hast built, to **p** my name there for ever;	7760

1Ki		
10:17	king **p** them *in* the house of the forest of	5414
10:24	wisdom, which God had **p** in his heart.	5414
11:36	the city which I have chosen me to **p** my	7760
12: 4	heavy yoke which he **p** upon us, lighter,	5414
12: 9	Make the yoke which thy father did **p**	5414
12:29	in Beth-el, and the other **p** he in Dan.	5414
13: 4	that he **p** his hand from the altar,	7971
13: 4	which he **p** forth against him, dried up,	7971
14:21	all the tribes of Israel, to **p** his name there.	7760
18:23	**p** no fire *under:* and I will dress the other	7760
18:23	and lay *it* on wood, and **p** no fire *under:*	7760
18:25	name of your gods, but **p** no fire *under.*	7760
18:33	he **p** the wood **in order,** and cut the	6186
18:42	earth, and **p** his face between his knees,	7760
20: 6	they shall **p** *it* in their hand, and take *it*	7760
20:24	his place, and **p** captains in their rooms:	7760
20:31	**p** sackcloth on our loins, and ropes upon	7760
20:32	**p** ropes on their heads, and came to the	NIH
21:27	**p** sackcloth upon his flesh, and fasted,	7760
22:10	on his throne, having **p** on *their* robes,	3847
22:23	the LORD hath **p** a lying spirit in	5414
22:27	**P** this *fellow in* the prison, and feed him	7760
22:30	into the battle; but **p** thou **on** thy robes.	3847

2Ki		
2:20	Bring me a new cruse, and **p** salt therein.	7760
3: 2	for he **p away** the image of Baal that his	5493
3:21	all that *were able to* **p on** armour,	2290+2296
4:34	**p** his mouth upon his mouth, and his eyes	7760
6: 7	And he **p** out his hand, and took it.	7971
9:13	**p** *it* under him on the top of the stairs,	7760
10: 7	**p** their heads in baskets, and sent him	7760
11:12	the crown upon him, and *gave him*	5414
12: 9	the priests that kept the door **p** therein all	5414
12:10	they **p up** *in* bags, and told the money	6696
13:16	king of Israel, **P** thine hand upon the bow.	7392
13:16	he **p** his hand *upon it:* and Elisha put his	7392
13:16	Elisha **p** his hands upon the king's hands.	7760
14: 6	The fathers shall not be **p to death** for	4191
14: 6	nor the children be **p to death** for	4191
14: 6	man shall be **p to death** for his own	4191
14:12	Judah was **p to the worse** before Israel;	5062
16:14	and **p** it on the north side of the altar.	5414
16:17	and **p** it upon a pavement of stones.	5414
17:29	**p** *them* in the houses of the high places	3240
18:11	**p** them in Halah and in Habor *by the*	5148
18:24	**p** thy **trust** on Egypt for chariots and	982
19:28	therefore I will **p** my hook in thy nose,	7760
21: 4	In Jerusalem will I **p** my name.	7760
21: 7	tribes of Israel, will I **p** my name for ever:	7760
23: 5	he **p down** the idolatrous priests, whom	7673
23:24	and in Jerusalem, did Josiah **p away,**	1197
23:33	Pharaoh-nechoh **p** him in **bands** at Riblah	631
23:33	**p** the land to a tribute of an hundred	5414
25: 7	**p** out the eyes of Zedekiah, and bound	5786

1Ch		
1: 8	Cush, and Mizraim, **P,** and Canaan.	6316
5:20	them; because they **p** their **trust** in him.	982
10:10	they **p** his armour *in* the house of their	7760
11:19	that **have p** their lives **in jeopardy?**	871.1
12:15	they **p to flight** all *them of* the valleys,	1272
13: 9	Uzza **p forth** his hand to hold the ark;	7971
13:10	because he **p** his hand to the ark;	7971
18: 6	David **p garrisons** in Syria-damascus;	7760
18:13	he **p** garrisons in Edom; and all	7760
19: 9	**p** the battle **in array** before the gate of	6186
19:10	and **p** *them* **in array** against the Syrians.	6186
19:16	they were **p to the worse** before Israel,	5062
19:17	So when David had **p** the battle **in array**	6186
19:19	they were **p to the worse** before Israel,	5062
21:27	he **p up** his sword **again** into the sheath	7725
27:24	neither was the number **p** in the account	5927

2Ch		
1: 5	before the tabernacle of the LORD:	7760
2:14	find out every device which shall be **p** to	5414
3:16	and **p** *them* on the heads of the pillars;	5414
3:16	and **p** *them* on the chains.	5414
4: 6	**p** five on the right hand, and five on	5414
5: 1	he among the treasures of the house of	5414
5:10	tables which Moses **p** *therein* at Horeb,	5414
6:11	in it have I **p** the ark, wherein *is*	7760
6:20	said that *thou* wouldest **p** thy name there;	7760
6:24	if thy people Israel be **p to the worse**	5062
9:16	the king **p** them in the house of the forest	5414
9:23	his wisdom, that God had **p** in his heart.	5414
10: 4	his heavy yoke that he **p** upon us,	5414
10: 9	the yoke that thy father did **p** upon us?	5414
10:11	For whereas my father **p** a heavy yoke	6006
10:11	upon you, I will **p more** to your yoke:	3254
11:11	**p** captains in them, and store of victual,	5414
11:12	every several city *he* **p** shields and spears,	NIH
12:13	all the tribes of Israel, to **p** his name there.	7760
15: 8	**p away** the abominable idols out of all	5674
15:13	God of Israel should be **p to death,**	4191
16:10	the seer, and **p** him **in** a prison house;	5414
17:19	besides *those* whom the king **p** in	5414
18:22	the LORD hath **p** a lying spirit in	5414
18:26	**P** this *fellow in* the prison, and feed him	7760
18:29	go to the battle; but **p** thou **on** thy robes.	3847
22:11	and **p** him and his nurse in a bedchamber.	5414
23: 7	into the house, he shall be **p to death:**	4191
23:11	upon him the crown, and *gave him*	5414
25:22	Judah was **p to the worse** before Israel,	5062
29: 7	**p** out the lamps, and have not burnt	3518
33: 7	tribes of Israel, will I **p** my name for ever:	7760
33:14	captains of war in all the fenced cities of	7760
34:10	they **p** *it* in the hand of the workmen that	5414
35: 3	**P** the holy ark in the house which	7760
35:24	**p** him in the second chariot that he had;	7392

2Ch		
36: 3	the king of Egypt **p** him **down** at	5493
36: 7	and **p** them in his temple at Babylon.	5414
36:22	and **p** *it* also in writing, saying,	NIH

Ezr		
1: 1	and **p** *it* also in writing, saying,	NIH
1: 7	and had **p** them in the house of his gods;	5414
2:62	as polluted, **p from** the priesthood.	4480
6:12	that shall **p** to their hand to alter *and*	7972
7:27	which hath **p** *such a thing* as this in	5414
10: 3	with our God to **p away** all the wives,	3318
10:19	that *they* would **p away** their wives;	3318

Ne		
2:12	told I *any* man what my God had **p**	5414
3: 5	their nobles **p** not their necks to the work	935
4:23	followed me, none of us **p off** our clothes,	6584
4:23	*saving that* every one **p** them **off** *for*	7973
6:14	prophets, that would have **p** me **in fear.**	3372
6:19	*And* Tobiah sent letters to **p** me **in fear.**	3372
7: 5	my God **put** into mine heart to gather	5414
7:64	as polluted, **p from** the priesthood.	4480

Est		
4: 1	**p on** sackcloth with ashes, and went out	3847
4:11	*is* one law of his to **p** *him* **to death,**	4191
5: 1	that Esther **p** on *her* royal *apparel,* and	3847
8: 3	besought him with tears to **p away**	5674
8: 5	*I* decree drew near to be **p in execution,**	6213

Job		
1:11	**p forth** thine hand now, and touch all	7971
1:12	only upon himself **p** not **forth** thine hand.	7971
2: 5	**p forth** thine hand now, and touch his	7971
4:18	he **p** no **trust** in his servants; and his	539
11:14	**p** it **far away,** and let not wickedness	7368
13:14	in my teeth, and **p** my life in mine hand?	7760
17: 3	Lay down now, **p** me **in a surety** with	6148
18: 5	the light of the wicked shall be **p** out,	1846
18: 6	and his candle shall be **p** out with him.	1846
19:13	He hath **p** my brethren **far** from me,	7368
21:17	oft is the candle of the wicked **p** out!	1846
22:23	away iniquity **far** from thy tabernacles.	7368
23: 6	No; but he would **p strength** in me.	7760
27:17	may prepare *it,* but the just shall **p** it **on,**	3847
29:14	I **p on** righteousness, and it clothed me:	3847
38:36	Who hath **p** wisdom in the inward parts?	7896
41: 2	Canst thou **p** a hook into his nose?	7760

Ps		
2:12	blessed *are* all they that **p** their **trust** in	2620
4: 5	and **p** your **trust** in the LORD.	982
4: 7	Thou hast **p** gladness in my heart,	5414
5:11	let all those that **p** their **trust** in thee	2620
7: 1	LORD my God, in thee do I **p** my **trust:**	2620
8: 6	thou hast **p** all *things* under his feet:	7896
9: 5	thou hast **p out** their name for ever and	4229
9:10	that know thy name will **p** their **trust** in	982
9:20	**P** them in fear, O LORD: *that* the nations	7896
11: 1	In the LORD **p** I my **trust:** how say ye	2620
16: 1	O God: for in thee do I **p** my **trust.**	2620
17: 7	their **trust** *in thee* from those that rise	2620
18:22	I did not **p away** his statutes from me,	5493
25:20	not be ashamed; for I **p** my **trust** in thee.	2620
27: 9	**p** not thy servant **away** in anger:	5186
30:11	thou hast **p off** my sackcloth,	6605
31: 1	In thee, O LORD, do I **p** my **trust;** let me	2620
31:18	Let the lying lips be **p to silence;**	481
35: 4	and **p to shame** that seek after my soul:	3637
36: 7	the children of men **p** their **trust** under	2620
40: 3	he hath **p** a new song in my mouth,	5414
40:14	and **p to shame** that wish me evil.	3637
44: 7	and hast **p** them **to shame** that hated us.	954
44: 9	thou hast cast off, and **p** us **to shame;**	3637
53: 5	thou hast **p** *them* **to shame,** because	954
55:20	He hath **p forth** his hands against such as	7971
56: 4	praise his word, in God I have **p** my **trust;**	982
56: 8	**p** thou my tears into thy bottle: *are they*	7760
56:11	In God have I **p** my **trust:** I will not be	982
70: 2	and **p to confusion,** that desire my hurt.	3637
71: 1	In thee, O LORD, do I **p** my **trust:** let me	2620
71: 1	my **trust:** let me never be **p to confusion.**	954
73:28	I have **p** my trust in the Lord GOD, that *I*	7896
78:66	he **p** them to a perpetual reproach.	5414
83:17	yea, let them be **p to shame,** and perish:	NIH
88: 8	Thou hast **p away** mine acquaintance **far**	7368
88:18	Lover and friend hast thou **p far** from me,	7368
118: 8	in the LORD than to **p confidence** in man.	982
118: 9	the LORD than to **p confidence** in princes.	982
119:31	O LORD, **p** me not **to shame.**	954
125: 3	lest the righteous **p** forth their hands unto	7971
146: 3	**P** not your **trust** in princes, *nor* in the son	982

Pr		
4:24	**P away** from thee a froward mouth,	5493
4:24	and perverse lips **p far** from thee.	7368
8: 1	and understanding **p forth** her voice?	5414
13: 9	the lamp of the wicked shall be **p** out.	1846
20:20	lamp shall be **p** out in obscure darkness.	1846
23: 2	**p** a knife to thy throat, if thou *be* a man	7760
24:20	the candle of the wicked shall be **p** out.	1846
25: 6	**P** not **forth** thyself in the presence of	1921
25: 7	than that thou shouldest be **p lower** in	8213
25: 8	thy neighbour hath **p** thee **to shame.**	3637
25:10	Lest he that heareth *it* **p** thee **to shame,**	2616
30: 5	*is* a shield unto them that **p** their **trust** in	2620

Ecc		
3:14	nothing can be **p** to it, nor any thing	3254
10:10	edge, then must he **p to more** strength:	1396
11:10	thy heart, and **p away** evil from thy flesh:	5674

SS		
5: 3	have **p off** my coat; how shall I **p** it **on?**	6584
5: 3	have put off my coat; how shall I **p** it **on?**	3847
5: 4	My beloved **p** in his hand by the hole of	7971

Isa		
1:16	**p away** the evil of your doings from	5493
5:20	that **p** darkness for light, and light for	7760
5:20	bitter for sweet, and sweet for bitter!	7760
10:13	I have **p down** the inhabitants like a	3381
11: 8	the weaned child shall **p** his hand on	1911

Isa		
20: 2	loins, and **p off** thy shoe from thy foot.	2502
36: 9	**p** thy **trust** on Egypt for chariots and	982
37:29	therefore will I **p** my hook in thy nose,	7760
42: 1	I have **p** my spirit upon him:	5414
43:26	**P** me **in remembrance:** let us plead	2142
47:11	thee; thou shalt not be able to **p** it **off:**	3722
50: 1	whom I have **p away?**	7971
50: 1	transgressions *is* your mother **p away.**	7971
51: 9	Awake, awake, **p on** strength, O arm of	3847
51:16	I have **p** my words in thy mouth,	7760
51:23	I will **p** it into the hand of them that	7760
52: 1	awake; **p on** thy strength, O Zion;	3847
52: 1	**p on** thy beautiful garments, O Jerusalem,	3847
53:10	to bruise him; he hath **p** *him* **to grief:**	2470
54: 4	for thou shalt not be **p to shame:**	2659
59:17	For he **p on** righteousness as a breastplate,	3847
59:17	**p on** the garments of vengeance *for* clothing,	3847+8516
59:21	my words which I have **p** in thy mouth,	7760
63:11	where *is* he that **p** his holy Spirit within	7760

Jer		
1: 9	the LORD **p forth** his hand,	7971
1: 9	Behold, I have **p** my words in thy mouth.	5414
3: 1	If a man **p away** his wife, and she go	7971
3: 8	committed adultery I had **p** her **away,**	7971
3:19	How shall I **p** thee among the children,	7896
4: 1	if thou wilt **p away** thine abominations	5493
7:21	**P** your burnt offerings unto your sacrifices,	5595
8:14	the LORD our God hath **p us to silence,**	1826
12:13	they have **p** themselves **to pain,**	2470
13: 1	**p** it upon thy loins, and put it not in	7760
13: 1	it upon thy loins, and **p** it not in water.	935
13: 2	word of the LORD, and **p** it on my loins.	7760
18:21	and let their men be **p to death;**	2026+4194
20: 2	**p** him in the stocks that *were* in the high	5414
26:15	ye for certain, that if ye **p** me **to death,**	4191
26:19	all Judah **p** him at all **to death?**	4191+4191
26:21	the king sought to **p** him **to death:**	4191
26:24	the hand of the people to **p** him **to death.**	4191
27: 2	and yokes, and **p** them upon thy neck,	5414
27: 8	will not **p** their neck under the yoke of	5414
28:14	I have **p** a yoke of iron upon the neck of	5414
29:26	that thou shouldest **p** him in prison,	5414
31:33	I will **p** my law in their inward parts,	5414
32: 2	**p** them in an earthen vessel, that they	5414
32:40	I will **p** my fear in their hearts, that *they*	5414
37: 4	for they had not **p** him *into* prison.	5414
37:15	**p** him *in* prison in the house of Jonathan	5414
37:18	this people, that ye have **p** me in prison?	5414
38: 4	beseech thee, let this man be **p to death:**	4191
38: 6	I heard that they had **p** Jeremiah in	5414
38:12	**P** now *these* old cast clouts and rotten	7760
38:15	thou not **surely p** me **to death?**	4191+4191
38:16	us this soul, I will not **p** thee **to death,**	4191
38:25	from us, and we will not **p** thee **to death;**	4191
39: 7	Moreover he **p out** Zedekiah's eyes,	5786
38:18	because thou hast **p** thy **trust** in me, saith	982
40:10	oil, and **p** *them* in your vessels,	7760
43: 3	*they* might **p us to death,** and carry us	4191
46: 4	the spears, *and* **p on** the brigandines.	3847
47: 6	**p** up thyself into thy scabbard, rest,	622
50:14	**P yourselves in array** against Babylon	6186
50:42	*every one* **p in array,** like a man to	6186
52:11	**p out** the eyes of Zedekiah; and the king	5786
52:11	**p** him in prison till the day of his death.	5414
52:27	**p them to death** in Riblah in the land of	4191

Eze		
3:25	shall **p** bands upon thee, and shall bind	5414
4: 9	**p** them in one vessel, and make thee	5414
8: 3	**p forth** the form of a hand, and took me	7971
8:17	and lo, they **p** the branch to their nose.	7971
10: 7	into the hands of *him that was*	5414
11:19	and I will **p** a new spirit within you;	5414
14: 3	**p** the stumblingblock of their iniquity	5414
16:11	I **p** bracelets upon thine hands, and a	5414
16:12	I **p** a jewel on thy forehead, and earrings	5414
16:14	which I had **p** upon thee, saith the Lord	7760
17: 2	**p forth a riddle,** and speak a	2330+2420
19: 9	they **p** him in ward in chains,	5414
22:26	have **p** no **difference** between the holy	914
23:42	which **p** bracelets upon their hands,	5414
24:17	**p on** thy shoes upon thy feet, and cover	7760
26:16	and **p off** their broidered garments;	6584
29: 4	I will **p** hooks in thy jaws, and I will cause	5414
30:13	and I will **p** a fear in the land of Egypt.	5414
30:21	to **p** a roller to bind it, to make it strong to	7760
30:24	of Babylon, and my sword in his hand:	5414
30:25	when I shall **p** my sword into the hand of	5414
32: 7	when I shall **p** thee **out,** I will cover	3518
32:25	he is **p** in the midst of *them that be* slain.	5414
36:26	and a new spirit will I **p** within you:	5414
36:27	I will **p** my spirit within you, and cause	5414
37: 6	and **p** breath in you, and ye shall live;	5414
37:14	shall **p** my spirit in you, and ye shall live,	5414
37:19	will **p** them with him, *even* with the stick	5414
38: 4	**p** hooks into thy jaws, and I will bring	5414
42:14	shall **p on** other garments,	3847
43: 9	**p away** their whoredom, and the carcases of their kings, **far**	7368
43:20	**p** it on the four horns of it, and on the	5414
44:19	shall **p off** their garments wherein they	6584
44:19	and **p on** other garments;	3847
44:22	wives a widow, nor her that is **p away:**	1644
45:19	**p** it upon the posts of the house,	5414

Da		
5:19	set up; and whom he would he **p down.**	8214
5:29	**p** a chain of gold about his neck,	NIH

Hos		
2: 2	**p away** her whoredoms out of her sight,	5493

Joel	3:13 **P** ye in the sickle, for the harvest is ripe: 7971
Am	6: 3 Ye that **p far away** the evil day, 5077
Jnh	3: 5 and proclaimed a fast, and **p on** sackcloth, 3847
Mic	2:12 I will **p** them together as the sheep of 7760
	7: 5 a friend, **p** ye not **confidence** in a guide: 982
Na	3: 9 infinite; **P** and Lubim were thy helpers. 6316
Zep	3:19 in every land where they have been **p** NIH
Hag	1: 6 that earneth wages earneth wages *to p* it NIH
Mt	1:19 was minded to **p** her **away** privily. 630
	5:15 and **p** it under a bushel, but on a 5087
	5:31 said, Whosoever shall **p away** his wife, 630
	5:32 That whosoever shall **p away** his wife, 630
	6:25 nor yet for your body, what ye shall **p on**. 1746
	8: 3 And Jesus **p forth** *his* hand, 1614
	9:16 for that which is **p in to fill** it **up** taketh 4138
	9:17 do **men p** new wine into old bottles: 906
	9:17 but they **p** new wine into new bottles. 906
	9:25 when the people were **p forth**, he went 1544
	10:21 and cause them to be **p to** death. 2289
	12:18 I will **p** my spirit upon him, and he shall 5087
	13:24 Another parable **p** he **forth** unto them, 3908
	13:31 Another parable **p** he **forth** unto them, 3908
	14: 3 and **p** him in prison for Herodias' sake, 5087
	14: 5 when he would have **p** him **to death**, 615
	19: 3 Is it lawful for a man to **p away** his wife 630
	19: 6 joined together, let not man **p asunder**. 5563
	19: 7 of divorcement, and to **p** her **away**? 630
	19: 8 hearts suffered you to **p away** your wives: 630
	19: 9 you, Whosoever shall **p away** his wife, 630
	19: 9 whoso marrieth her which is **p away** doth 630
	19:13 that he should **p** his hands **on** them, 2007
	21: 7 and the colt, and **p on** them their clothes, 2007
	22:34 that he had **p** the Sadducees to **silence**, 5392
	25:27 to have **p** my money to the exchangers, 906
	26:52 **P up again** thy sword into his place: 654
	26:59 witness against Jesus, to **p** him to **death**; 2289
	27: 1 counsel against Jesus to **p** him to **death**: 2289
	27: 6 It is not lawful for to **p** them into 906
	27:28 stripped him, and **p** on him a scarlet robe. 4060
	27:29 they **p** it **upon** his head, and a reed in 2007
	27:31 and **p** his own raiment **on** him, and led 1746
	27:48 and **p** it **on** a reed, and gave him to drink. 4060
Mk	1:14 after that John was **p in prison**, Jesus 3860
	1:41 **p forth** *his* hand, and touched him, 1614
	2:22 but new wine must be **p** into new bottles: 992
	4:21 a candle brought to be **p** under a bushel, 1544
	5:40 when he had **p** them all **out**, he taketh 1544
	6: 9 with sandals; and not **p** on two coats. 1746
	7:32 beseech him to **p** his hand upon him, 2007
	7:33 and **p** his fingers into his ears, and he spit, 906
	8:23 on his eyes, and **p** his hands **upon** him, 2007
	8:25 After that he **p** his hands again upon his 2007
	10: 2 Is it lawful for a man to **p away** his wife? 630
	10: 4 a bill of divorcement, and to **p** her **away**. 630
	10: 9 joined together, let not man **p asunder**. 5563
	10:11 Whosoever shall **p away** his wife, 630
	10:12 if a woman shall **p away** her husband, 630
	10:16 **p** his hands upon them, and blessed them. 5087
	13:12 and shall cause them to be **p to death**. 2289
	14: 1 take him by craft, and **p** him to **death**. 615
	14:55 witness against Jesus to **p** him to **death**; 2289
	15:17 crown of thorns, and **p** it **about** his head, 4060
	15:20 **p** his own clothes **on** him, and led him 1746
	15:36 and **p** it on a reed, and gave him to drink, 4060
Lk	1:52 He hath **p down** the mighty from *their* 2507
	5:13 he **p forth** his hand, and touched him, 1614
	5:38 new wine must be **p** into new bottles; 992
	8:54 And he **p** them all out, and took her by 1544
	9:62 No *man* having **p** his hand to 1911
	12:22 neither for the body, what ye shall **p on**. 1746
	14: 7 And he **p forth** a parable to those which 3004
	15:22 Bring forth the best robe, and **p** it **on** him; 1746
	15:22 **p** it on him; and **p** a ring on his hand, 1325
	16: 4 that, when I am **p out** of the stewardship, 3179
	16:18 marrieth her that is **p away** from 630
	18:33 shall scourge *him*, and **p** him **to death**: 615
	21:16 of you shall they cause to be **p to death**. 2289
	23:32 led with him to be **p to death**. 337
Jn	5: 7 water is troubled, to **p** me into the pool: 906
	9:15 He **p** clay upon mine eyes, and I washed, 2007
	9:22 he should be **p out of the synagogue**. 656
	11:53 counsel together for to **p** him to **death**. 615
	12: 6 had the bag, and bare what was **p** *therein*. 941
	12:10 that they might **p** Lazarus also to **death**; 615
	12:42 they should be **p out of the synagogue**: 656
	13: 2 the devil having now **p** into the heart of 906
	16: 2 They shall **p** you out of the synagogues: 4160
	18:11 unto Peter, **P up** thy sword into the sheath: 906
	18:31 not lawful for us to **p** any *man* to **death**: 615
	19: 2 **p** it **on** his head, and they put on him a 2007
	19: 2 head, and they **p on** him a purple robe, 4016
	19:19 Pilate wrote a title, and **p** it on the cross. 5087
	19:29 and **p** it **upon** hyssop, and put it to his 4060
	19:29 put *it* upon hyssop, and **p** it to his mouth. 4374
	20:25 and **p** my finger into the print of the nails, 906
Ac	1: 7 the Father hath **p** in his own power. 5087
	4: 3 and **p** them in hold unto the next day: 5087
	5:18 and **p** them in the common prison. 5087
	5:25 men whom ye **p** in prison are standing 5087
	5:34 commanded to **p** the apostles forth a little 4160
	7:33 to him, **P off** *thy* shoes **from** thy feet; 3089
	9:40 But Peter **p** them all **forth**, 1544
	12: 4 he **p** him in prison, and delivered *him* to 5087
	12:19 that *they* should be **p to death**. 520
	13:46 but seeing ye **p** it **from** *you*, and 683

Ac	15: 9 **p** no **difference** between us and them, 1252
	15:10 a yoke upon the neck of 2007
	26:10 when they were **p to death**, I gave my 337
	27: 1 sailing into Italy; and he **p** us therein. 1688
Ro	13:12 and let us **p on** the armour of light. 1746
	13:14 But **p ye on** the Lord Jesus Christ, 1746
	14:13 **p** a stumblingblock or an occasion
	to fall in his brother's **way**. 5087
1Co	5:13 Therefore **p away** from among yourselves 1808
	7:11 and let not the husband **p away** *his* wife. 863
	7:12 to dwell with him, let him not **p** her **away**. 863
	13:11 became a man, I **p away** childish *things*. 2673
	15:24 when he shall have **p down** all rule and 2673
	15:25 till he hath **p** all enemies under his feet. 5087
	15:27 For he hath **p** all *things* under his feet. 5293
	15:27 all *things* are **p under** him, it is manifest 5293
	15:27 which did **p** all *things* **under** him. 5293
	15:28 unto him that **p** all *things* under him, 5293
	15:53 this corruptible must **p on** incorruption, 1746
	15:53 and this mortal *must* **p on** immortality, 1746
	15:54 So when this corruptible shall have **p on** 1746
	15:54 this mortal shall have **p on** immortality, 1746
2Co	3:13 not as Moses, *which* **p** a vail over his face, 5087
	8:16 **p** the same earnest care into the heart 1325
Gal	3:27 baptized into Christ have **p on** Christ. 1746
Eph	1:22 And hath **p** all *things* under his feet, 5293
	4:22 That ye **p off** concerning the former 659
	4:24 that ye **p on** the new man, which after 1746
	4:31 and evil speaking, be **p away** from you, 142
	6:11 **P on** the whole armour of God, that ye 1746
Col	3: 8 But now you also **p off** all *these;* anger, 659
	3: 9 seeing that ye have **p off** the old man with 554
	3:10 And have **p on** the new *man*, which is 1746
	3:12 **P on** therefore, as the elect of God, holy 1746
	3:14 And above all these *things* **p on** charity, NIG
1Th	2: 4 of God to be **p in trust** with the gospel, 4100
1Ti	1:19 some having **p away**, concerning faith 683
	4: 6 If thou **p** the brethren **in remembrance** 5294
2Ti	1: 6 Wherefore I **p** thee **in remembrance** that 363
	2:14 these *things* **p** them **in remembrance**, 5279
Tit	3: 1 **P** them **in mind** to be subject to 5279
Phm	1:18 *thee* ought, **p** that **on** mine **account**; 1677
Heb	2: 5 not **p in subjection** the world to come, 5293
	2: 8 Thou hast **p** all *things* in subjection 5293
	2: 8 For in that *he* **p** all in subjection under 5293
	2: 8 he left nothing *that is* not **p under** him. 506
	2: 8 now we see not yet all *things* **p under** 5293
	2:13 And again, I will **p** my **trust** in him. 3982
	6: 6 afresh, and **p** *him* to an **open shame**. 3856
	8:10 I will **p** my laws into their mind, 1325
	9:26 to **p away** sin by the sacrifice of himself. 115
	10:16 I will **p** my laws into their hearts, 1325
Jas	3: 3 Behold, we **p** bits in the horses' mouths, 906
1Pe	2:15 that with well doing *ye* may **p to silence** 5392
	3:18 being **p to death** in the flesh, 2289
2Pe	1:12 **p** you always **in remembrance** of these 5279
	1:14 Knowing that shortly I must **p off** this *my* 595
Jude	1: 5 I will therefore **p** you **in remembrance**, 5279
Rev	2:24 I will **p** upon you none other burden. 906
	11: 9 shall not their dead bodies to be **p** 5087
	17:17 For God hath **p** in their hearts to fulfil his 1325

PUTEOLI (1)
Ac 28:13 blew, and we came the next day to **P**: 4223

PUTHITES See PUHITES

PUTIEL (1)
Ex 6:25 him *one* of the daughters of **P** to wife; 6317

PUTRIFYING (1)
Isa 1: 6 *but* wounds, and bruises, and **p** sores: 2961

PUTTEST (7) [PUT]
Nu 24:21 and thou **p** thy nest in a rock. 7760
Dt 12:18 God in all that thou **p** thine hands **unto**. 4916
 15:10 and in all that thou **p** thine hand **unto**. 4916
2Ki 18:14 *that* which thou **p** on me will I bear. 5414
Job 13:27 Thou **p** my feet also in the stocks, 7760
Ps 119:119 Thou **p away** all the wicked of the earth 7673
Hab 2:15 that **p** thy bottle *to him*, and makest him 5596

PUTTETH (30) [PUT]
Ex 30:33 or whosoever **p** *any* of it upon a stranger, 5414
Nu 22:38 the word that God **p** in my mouth, that 7760
Dt 25:11 **p forth** her hand, and taketh him by 7971
 25:11 *it* in a secret *place.* And all the people 7971
1Ki 20:11 harness boast himself as he that **p** it **off**. 6605
Job 15:15 Behold, he **p** no **trust** in his saints; yea, 539
 28: 9 he **p forth** his hand upon the rock; 7971
 33:11 He **p** my feet in the stocks, he marketh all 7760
Ps 15: 5 *He that* **p** not **out** his money to usury, 5414
 75: 7 he **p down** one, and setteth up another. 8213
Pr 29:25 whoso **p** his **trust** in the Lord shall be 982
SS 2:13 The fig tree **p forth** her green figs, 2590
Isa 57:13 he that **p** his **trust** in me shall possess 2620
Jer 43:12 of Egypt, as a shepherd **p on** his garment; 5844
La 3:29 He **p** his mouth in the dust; if so be there 5414
Eze 14: 4 **p** the stumblingblock of his iniquity before 7760
 14: 7 **p** the stumblingblock of his iniquity before 7760
Mic 3: 5 he that **p** not into their mouths, they even 5414
Mt 9:16 No *man* **p** a piece of new cloth unto an 1911
 24:32 **p forth** leaves, ye know that summer *is* 1631
Mk 2:22 And no *man* **p** new wine into old bottles: 906
 4:29 immediately he **p in** the sickle, because 649

Mk	13:28 **p forth** leaves, ye know that summer is 1631
Lk	5:36 No *man* **p** a piece of a new garment upon 1911
	5:37 And no *man* **p** new wine into old bottles; 906
	5:37 with a vessel, or **p** *it* under a bed; 5087
	11:33 **p** *it* in a secret place, neither under a 5087
	16:18 Whosoever **p away** his wife, 630
Jn	10: 4 And when he **p forth** his own sheep, 1544

PUTTING (17) [PUT]
Ge 21:14 **p** it on her shoulder, and the child, 7760
Lev 16:21 **p** them upon the head of the goat, 5414
Jdg 7: 6 by **p** their hand to their mouth, were three NIH
Isa 58: 9 the **p forth** of the finger, 7971
Mal 2:16 of Israel, saith that he hateth **p away**: 7971
Ac 9:12 and **p** his hand **on** him, that he might 2007
 9:17 and **p** his hands on him, 2007
 19:33 the multitude, the Jews **p** him **forward**. 4261
Ro 15:15 as **p** you in **mind**, because of the grace 1878
Eph 4:25 Wherefore **p away** lying, speak every man 659
Col 2:11 in **p off** the body of the sins of the flesh, 555
1Th 5: 8 **p** on the breastplate of faith and love; 1746
1Ti 1:12 me faithful, **p** *me* into the ministry; 5087
2Ti 1: 6 which is in thee by the **p on** of my hands. 1936
1Pe 3: 3 of wearing of gold, or of **p on** of apparel; 1745
 3:21 us (not the **p away** of the filth of the flesh, 595
2Pe 1:13 to stir you up by **p** *you* **in remembrance**; 5280

PYGARG (1)
Dt 14: 5 the **p**, and the wild ox, and the chamois. 1788

Q

QUAILS (4)
Ex 16:13 that at even the **q** came up, and covered 7958
Nu 11:31 brought **q** from the sea, and let *them* fall 7958
 11:32 all that next day, and they gathered the **q**: 7958
Ps 105:40 he brought **q**, and satisfied them *with* 7958

QUAKE (4) [EARTHQUAKE, EARTHQUAKES, QUAKED, QUAKING]
Joel 2:10 earth shall **q** before them; the heavens 7264
Na 1: 5 mountains **q** at him, and the hills melt, 7493
Mt 27:51 and the earth did **q**, and the rocks rent; 4579
Heb 12:21 Moses said, I exceedingly fear and **q**;) 1790

QUAKED (2) [QUAKE]
Ex 19:18 furnace, and the whole mount **q** greatly. 2729
1Sa 14:15 they also trembled, and the earth **q**: 7264

QUAKING (2) [QUAKE]
Eze 12:18 eat thy bread with **q**, and drink thy water 7494
Da 10: 7 a great **q** fell upon them, so that they fled 2731

QUANTITY (1)
Isa 22:24 and the issue, all vessels of **small q**, 6996

QUARREL (4)
Lev 26:25 shall **avenge the q** of *my* covenant: 5358+5359
2Ki 5: 7 and see how he **seeketh a q** against me. 579
Mk 6:19 Therefore Herodias **had a q against** him, 1758
Col 3:13 if any *man* have a **q** against any: 3437

QUARRIES (2)
Jdg 3:19 he himself turned again from the **q** that 6456
 3:26 passed beyond the **q**, and escaped unto 6456

QUARTER (8) [QUARTERS]
Ge 19: 4 and young, all the people from **every q**: 7097
Nu 34: 3 your south **q** shall be from the wilderness 6285
Jos 15: 5 *their* border in the north **q** *was* 6285+3807.1
 18:14 children of Judah: this *was* the west **q**. 6285
 18:15 the south **q** *was* from the end of 6285
Isa 47:15 they shall wander every one to his **q**; 5676
 56:11 every one for his gain, from his **q**. 7097
Mk 1:45 and they came to him **from every q**. 3836

QUARTERS (9) [QUARTER]
Ex 13: 7 be leaven seen with thee in all thy **q**. 1366
Dt 22:12 fringes upon the four **q** of thy vesture, 3671
1Ch 9:24 In four **q** were the porters, toward the 7307
Jer 49:36 the four winds from the four **q** of heaven, 7098
Eze 38: 6 the house of Togarmah *of the* north **q**, 3411
Ac 9:32 as Peter passed throughout all **q**, he came NIG
 16: 3 of the Jews which were in those **q**: 5117
 28: 7 In the same **q** were possessions of the 5117
Rev 20: 8 which are in the four **q** of the earth, 1137

QUARTUS (1)
Ro 16:23 of the city saluteth you, and **Q** a brother. 2890

QUATERNIONS (1)
Ac 12: 4 delivered *him* to four **q** of soldiers to keep 5069

QUEEN (54) [QUEENS]
1Ki 10: 1 when the **q** of Sheba heard of the fame of 4436
 10: 4 when the **q** of Sheba had seen all 4436

1Ki	10:10	the **q** of Sheba gave to king Solomon.	4436
	10:13	king Solomon gave unto the **q** of Sheba all	4436
	11:19	his own wife, the sister of Tahpenes the **q**.	1377
	15:13	even her he removed from *being* **q**,	1377
2Ki	10:13	of the king and the children of the **q**.	1377
2Ch	9: 1	the **q** of Sheba heard of the fame of	4436
	9: 3	the **q** of Sheba had seen the wisdom	4436
	9: 9	neither was there any such spice as the **q**	4436
	9:12	king Solomon gave to the **q** of Sheba all	4436
	15:16	he removed her from *being* **q**, because	1377
Ne	2: 6	said unto me, (the **q** also sitting by him,)	7694
Est	1: 9	Also Vashti the **q** made a feast for	4436
	1:11	To bring Vashti the **q** before the king with	4436
	1:12	the **q** Vashti refused to come at the king's	4436
	1:15	What shall *we* do unto the **q** Vashti	4436
	1:16	Vashti the **q** hath not done wrong to	4436
	1:17	For *this* deed of the **q** shall come abroad	4436
	1:17	Vashti the **q** to be brought in before him,	4436
	1:18	which have heard of the deed of the **q**	4436
	2: 4	the maiden which pleaseth the king be **q**	4427
	2:17	head, and **made** her **q** instead of Vashti.	4427
	2:22	Mordecai, who told *it* unto Esther the **q**;	4436
	4: 4	was the **q** exceedingly grieved; and she	4436
	5: 2	when the **q** saw Esther the **q** standing	4436
	5: 3	king unto her, What wilt thou, **q** Esther?	4436
	5:12	Esther the **q** did let no *man* come in with	4436
	7: 1	came to banquet with Esther the **q**.	4436
	7: 2	of wine, What *is* thy petition, **q** Esther?	4436
	7: 3	Esther the **q** answered and said, If I have	4436
	7: 5	and said unto Esther the **q**,	4436
	7: 6	was afraid before the king and the **q**.	4436
	7: 7	make request for his life to Esther the **q**;	4436
	7: 8	Will he force the **q** also before me in	4436
	8: 1	the Jews' enemy unto Esther the **q**	4436
	8: 7	king Ahasuerus said unto Esther the **q**,	4436
	9:12	the king said unto Esther the **q**, The Jews	4436
	9:29	Esther the **q**, the daughter of Abihail,	4436
	9:31	and Esther the **q** had enjoined them,	4436
Ps	45: 9	hand did stand the **q** in gold of Ophir.	7694
Jer	7:18	to make cakes to the **q** of heaven,	4446
	13:18	Say unto the king and to the **q**,	1377
	29: 2	the **q**, and the eunuchs, the princes of	1377
	44:17	to burn incense unto the **q** of heaven,	4446
	44:18	we left off to burn incense to the **q** of	4446
	44:19	we burnt incense to the **q** of heaven,	4446
	44:25	to burn incense to the **q** of heaven,	4446
Da	5:10	*Now* the **q**, by reason of the words of	4433
	5:10	and the **q** spake and said, O king, live for	4433
Mt	12:42	The **q** of the south shall rise up in	938
Lk	11:31	The **q** of the south shall rise up in	938
Ac	8:27	under Candace **q** of the Ethiopians,	938
Rev	18: 7	I sit a **q**, and am no widow, and shall see	938

QUEENS (3) [QUEEN]

SS	6: 8	There *are* threescore **q**,	4436
	6: 9	*yea*, the **q** and the concubines,	4436
Isa	49:23	and their **q** thy nursing mothers:	8282

QUENCH (12) [QUENCHED, UNQUENCHABLE]

2Sa	14: 7	*so* they shall **q** my coal which is left,	3518
	21:17	battle, that thou **q** not the light of Israel.	3518
Ps	104:11	of the field: the wild asses **q** their thirst.	7665
SS	8: 7	Many waters cannot **q** love, neither can	3518
Isa	1:31	burn together, and none shall **q** *them*.	3518
	42: 3	and the smoking flax shall he not **q**:	3518
Jer	4: 4	that none can **q** *it*, because of the evil	3518
	21:12	that none can **q** *it*, because of the evil	3518
Am	5: 6	and *there be* none to **q** *it* in Beth-el.	3518
Mt	12:20	break, and smoking flax shall he not **q**,	4570
Eph	6:16	ye shall be able to **q** all the fiery	4570
1Th	5:19	**Q** not the Spirit.	4570

QUENCHED (17) [QUENCH]

Nu	11: 2	prayed unto the LORD, the fire was **q**.	8257
2Ki	22:17	against this place, and shall not be **q**.	3518
2Ch	34:25	out upon this place, and shall not be **q**.	3518
Ps	118:12	like bees; they are *q* as the fire of thorns:	1846
Isa	34:10	It shall not be **q** night nor day; the smoke	3518
	43:17	rise: they are extinct, they are **q** as tow.	3518
	66:24	shall not die, neither shall their fire be **q**;	3518
Jer	7:20	and it shall burn, and shall not be **q**.	3518
	17:27	palaces of Jerusalem, and it shall not be **q**.	3518
Eze	20:47	the flaming flame shall not be **q**,	3518
	20:48	have kindled it: it shall not be **q**.	3518
Mk	9:43	hell, into the fire that **never** shall be **q**:	762
	9:44	their worm dieth not, and the fire is not **q**.	4570
	9:45	hell, into the fire that **never** shall be **q**:	762
	9:46	their worm dieth not, and the fire is not **q**.	4570
	9:48	their worm dieth not, and the fire is not **q**.	4570
Heb	11:34	**Q** the violence of fire, escaped the edge of	4570

QUESTION (14) [QUESTIONED, QUESTIONING, QUESTIONS]

Mt	22:35	asked *him* a **q**, tempting him, and saying,	NIG
Mk	8:11	came forth, and began to **q** with him,	4802
	9:16	asked the scribes, What **q** ye with them?	4802
	11:29	I will also ask of you one **q**,	3056
	12:34	no *man* after that durst ask him *any* **q**.	NIG
Lk	20:40	after that they durst not ask him any **q**	NIG
Jn	3:25	Then there arose a **q** between *some* of	2214
Ac	15: 2	unto the apostles and elders about this **q**.	2213
	18:15	But if it be a **q** of words and names,	1458
	19:40	For we are in danger to be **called in q** for	1458
	23: 6	resurrection of the dead I am **called in q**.	2919
	24:21	the dead I am **called in q** by you this day.	2919

1Co	10:25	*that* eat, **asking** no **q** for conscience sake:	350
	10:27	eat, **asking** no **q** for conscience sake.	350

QUESTIONED (3) [QUESTION]

2Ch	31: 9	Hezekiah **q** with the priests and the	1875
Mk	1:27	insomuch that *they* **q** among themselves,	4802
Lk	23: 9	Then he **q** with him in many words;	1905

QUESTIONING (2) [QUESTION]

Mk	9:10	one **with** *another* what the rising from	4802
	9:14	about them, and the scribes **q** with them.	4802

QUESTIONS (14) [QUESTION]

1Ki	10: 1	she came to prove him with **hard q**.	2420
	10: 3	Solomon told her all her **q**: there was not	1697
2Ch	9: 1	I came to prove Solomon with **hard q** at	2420
	9: 2	Solomon told her all her **q**: and there was	1697
Mt	22:46	from that day forth ask him any moe **q**.	NIG
Lk	2:46	both hearing them, and asking them **q**.	NIG
Ac	23:29	Whom I perceived to be accused of **q** of	2213
	25:19	had certain **q** against him of their own	2213
	25:20	because I doubted of such *manner* of **q**,	2214
	26: 3	customs and **q** which are among the Jews:	2213
1Ti	1: 4	and endless genealogies, which minister **q**,	2214
	6: 4	but doting about **q** and strifes of words,	2214
2Ti	2:23	But foolish and unlearned **q** avoid,	2214
Tit	3: 9	But avoid foolish **q**, and genealogies,	2214

QUICK (10) [QUICKEN, QUICKENED, QUICKENETH, QUICKENING, QUICKLY, QUICKSANDS]

Lev	13:10	*there be* **q** raw flesh in the rising;	2416+4241
	13:24	the **q** *flesh* that burneth have a white	4241
Nu	16:30	them, and they go down **q** into the pit;	2416
Ps	55: 15	*and* let them go down **q** *into* hell:	2416
	124: 3	they had swallowed us up **q**, when their	2416
Isa	11: 3	shall **make** him **of q** understanding in	7306
Ac	10:42	was ordained of God *to be* the Judge of **q**	2198
2Ti	4: 1	who shall judge the **q** and the dead at his	2198
Heb	4:12	For the word of God *is* **q**, and powerful,	2198
1Pe	4: 5	account to him that is ready to judge the **q**	2198

QUICKEN (13) [QUICK]

Ps	71:20	shalt **q** me again, and shalt bring me up	2421
	80:18	**q** us, and we will call upon thy name.	2421
	119:25	dust: **q** thou me according to thy word.	2421
	119:37	*and* **q** thou me in thy way.	2421
	119:40	thy precepts: **q** me in thy righteousness.	2421
	119:88	**Q** me after thy lovingkindness; so shall I	2421
	119:107	**q** me, O LORD, according unto thy word.	2421
	119:149	**q** me according to thy judgment.	2421
	119:154	deliver me: **q** me according to thy word.	2421
	119:156	**q** me according to thy judgments.	2421
	119:159	**q** me, O LORD, according to thy	2421
	143:11	**Q** me, O LORD, for thy name's sake:	2421
Ro	8:11	**q** your mortal bodies by his Spirit that	2227

QUICKENED (7) [QUICK]

Ps	119:50	in my affliction: for thy word hath **q** me.	2421
	119:93	precepts: for with them thou hast **q** me.	2421
1Co	15:36	fool, *that* which thou sowest is not **q**,	2227
Eph	2: 1	And you *hath he* **q**, who were dead in	NIG
	2: 5	hath **q** *us* **together with** Christ, (by grace	4806
Col	2:13	your flesh, hath he **q** **together** with him,	4806
1Pe	3:18	to death in the flesh, but **q** by the Spirit:	2227

QUICKENETH (5) [QUICK]

Jn	5:21	*and* *them*; even so the Son **q**eneth	2227
	5:21	*them*; even so the Son **q** whom he will.	2227
	6:63	It is the spirit that **q**; the flesh profiteth	2227
Ro	4:17	who **q** the dead, and calleth those *things*	2227
1Ti	6:13	who **q** all *things*, and *before* Christ Jesus,	2227

QUICKENING (1) [QUICK]

1Co	15:45	the last Adam *was* made a **q** spirit.	2227

QUICKLY (39) [QUICK]

Ge	18: 6	**Make ready q** three measures of fine	4116
	27:20	How *is it that* thou hast found *it so* **q**,	4116
Ex	32: 8	They have turned aside **q** out of the way	4118
Nu	16:46	go **q** unto the congregation, and make an	4120
Dt	9: 3	thou drive them out, and destroy them **q**,	4118
	9:12	Arise, get thee down **q** from hence;	4118
	9:12	**q** turned aside out of the way which I	4118
	9:16	had turned aside **q** out of the way which	4118
	11:17	*lest* ye perish **q** from off the good land	4120
	28:20	be destroyed, and until thou perish **q**;	4118
Jos	2: 5	pursue after them; for ye shall overtake	4118
	8:19	the ambush arose **q** out of their place,	4120
	10: 6	up to us **q**, and save us, and help us:	4120
	23:16	ye shall perish **q** from off the good land	4120
Jdg	2:17	they turned **q** out of the way which their	4118
1Sa	20:19	then thou shalt go down **q**, and come to	3966
2Sa	17:16	Now therefore send **q**, and tell David,	4120
	17:18	they went both of them away **q**,	4120
	17:21	Arise, and **pass q** over the water:	4120
2Ki	1:11	thus hath the king said, Come down **q**.	4120
2Ch	18: 8	said, **Fetch q** Micaiah the son of Imla.	4120
Ecc	4:12	a threefold cord is not **q** broken.	4120+871.1
Mt	5:25	Agree with thine adversary **q**, whiles thou	5036
	28: 7	And go **q**, and tell his disciples that he is	5036
	28: 8	And they departed **q** from the sepulchre	5036
Mk	16: 8	And they went out **q**, and fled from	5036
Lk	14:21	Go out **q** into the streets and lanes of	5030
	16: 6	thy bill, and sit down **q**, and write fifty.	5030
Jn	11:29	As soon as she heard *that*, she arose **q**,	5030

Jn	13:27	Jesus unto him, That thou doest, do **q**.	5030
Ac	12: 7	raised him up, saying, Arise up **q**.	1722+5034
	22:18	and get *thee* **q** out of Jerusalem:	1722+5034
Rev	2: 5	or else I *will* come unto thee **q**,	5034
	2:16	or else I *will* come unto thee **q**,	5036
	3:11	I come **q**: hold *that* fast which thou	5036
	11:14	past; *and* behold, the third woe cometh **q**.	5036
	22: 7	Behold, I come **q**: blessed *is* he that	5036
	22:12	And behold, I come **q**; and my reward *is*	5036
	22:20	these *things* saith, Surely I come **q**.	5036

QUICKSANDS (1) [QUICK, SAND]

Ac	27:17	and fearing lest they should fall into the **q**,	4950

QUIET (31) [QUIETED, QUIETETH, QUIETLY, QUIETNESS]

Jdg	16: 2	all the night, saying, In the morning,	2790
	18: 7	manner of the Zidonians, **q** and secure;	8252
	18:27	unto a people *that were* at **q** and secure:	8252
2Ki	11:20	the land rejoiced, and the city was in **q**:	8252
1Ch	4:40	the land *was* wide, and **q**, and peaceable;	8252
2Ch	14: 1	In his days the land was **q** ten years.	8252
	14: 5	and the kingdom was **q** before him.	8252
	20:30	So the realm of Jehoshaphat was **q**: for his	8252
	23:21	the city was **q**, after that they had slain	8252
Job	3:13	now should I have lien *still* and been **q**,	8252
	3:26	safety, neither had I rest, neither was I **q**;	5117
	21:23	full strength, being at ease and **q**.	7961
Ps	35:20	against *them that are* **q** in the land.	7282
	107:30	are they glad because they be **q**;	8367
Pr	1:33	and shall be **q** from fear of evil.	7599
Ecc	9:17	The words of wise *men* are heard in **q**,	5183
Isa	7: 4	say unto him, Take heed, and be **q**;	8252
	14: 7	The whole earth is at rest, *and* is **q**:	8252
	32:18	in sure dwellings, and in **q** resting places;	7600
	33:20	thine eyes shall see Jerusalem a **q**	7600
Jer	30:10	and be **q**, and none shall make *him* afraid.	7599
	47: 6	how long *will it* be ere thou be **q**?	8252
	47: 7	How can it be **q**, seeing the LORD hath	8252
	49:23	there is sorrow on the sea; it cannot be **q**.	8252
	51:59	his reign. And *this* Seraiah *was* a **q** prince.	4496
Eze	16:42	I will be **q**, and will be no more angry.	8252
Na	1:12	Though *they be* **q**, and likewise many,	8003
Ac	19:36	ought to be **q**, and to do nothing rashly.	2687
1Th	4:11	And that ye study to be **q**, and to do your	2270
1Ti	2: 2	that we may lead a **q** and peaceable life in	2263
1Pe	3: 4	*even* the ornament of a meek and **q** spirit,	2272

QUIETED (2) [QUIET]

Ps	131: 2	Surely I have behaved and **q** myself, as a	1826
Zec	6: 8	have **q** my spirit in the north country.	5117

QUIETETH (1) [QUIET]

Job	37:17	when he **q** the earth by the south *wind*?	8252

QUIETLY (2) [QUIET]

2Sa	3:27	gate to speak with him **q**,	7987+871.1+1886.1
La	3:26	and **q** wait for the salvation of the LORD.	1748

QUIETNESS (10) [QUIET]

Jdg	8:28	country was **in q** forty years in the days	8252
1Ch	22: 9	give peace and **q** unto Israel in his days.	8253
Job	20:20	Surely he shall not feel **q** in his belly,	7961
	34:29	When he **giveth q**, who then can make	8252
Pr	17: 1	Better *is* a dry morsel, and **q** therewith,	7962
Ecc	4: 6	Better *is* a handful *with* **q**, than both	5183
Isa	30:15	in **q** and in confidence shall be your	8252
	32:17	the effect of righteousness **q** and	8252
Ac	24: 2	Seeing that by thee we enjoy great **q**,	1515
2Th	3:12	that with **q** they work, and eat their own	2271

QUIRINIUS See CYRENIUS

QUIT (6)

Ex	21:19	staff, then shall he that smote *him* be **q**:	5352
	21:28	eaten; but the owner of the ox *shall be* **q**.	5355
Jos	2:20	we will be **q** of thine oath which thou	5355
1Sa	4: 9	Be strong, and **q** yourselves like men,	1961
	4: 9	to you: **q** yourselves like men, and fight.	1961
1Co	16:13	in the faith, **q** you **like men**, be strong.	407

QUITE (6)

Ge	31:15	hath **q** devoured also our money.	398+398
Ex	23:24	and **q** break down their images.	7665+7665
Nu	33:52	thou shalt **take away** their murmurings	3615
	33:52	and **q** pluck down all their high places:	8045
2Sa	3:24	sent him away, and he is **q** gone?	1980+1980
Job	6:13	in me? and is wisdom driven **q** from me?	NIH
Hab	3: 9	Thy bow was **made q** naked,	5783+6181

QUIVER (7)

Ge	27: 3	thy and thy bow, and go out to the field,	8522
Job	39:23	The **q** rattleth against him, the glittering	827
Ps	127: 5	Happy *is* the man that hath his **q** full of	827
Isa	22: 6	Elam bare the **q** with chariots of men *and*	827
	49: 2	a polished shaft; in his **q** hath he hid me;	827
Jer	5:16	Their **q** is as an open sepulchre, they *are*	827
La	3:13	He hath caused the arrows of his **q** to enter	827

QUIVERED (1)

Hab	3:16	my belly trembled; my lips **q** at the voice:	6750

Q

R

RAAMAH (5)
Ge	10: 7 Havilah, and Sabtah, and **R**, and Sabtecha:	7484
	10: 7 and the sons of **R**; Sheba, and Dedan.	7484
1Ch	1: 9 Havilah, and Sabta, and **R**, and Sabtecha.	7484
	1: 9 And the sons of **R**; Sheba, and Dedan.	7484
Eze	27:22 The merchants of Sheba and **R**, they *were*	7484

RAAMIAH (1)
Ne	7: 7 Azariah, **R**, Nahamani, Mordecai, Bilshan,	7485

RAAMSES (1) [RAMESES]
Ex	1:11 for Pharaoh treasure cities, Pithom and **R**.	7486

RABBAH (13) [RABBATH]
Jos	13:25 of Ammon, unto Aroer that *is* before **R**;	7237
	15:60 which *is* Kirjath-jearim, and **R**;	7237
2Sa	11: 1 the children of Ammon, and besieged **R**.	7237
	12:26 Joab fought against **R** of the children of	7237
	12:27 I have fought against **R**, and have taken	7237
	12:29 went to **R**, and fought against it,	7237
	17:27 that Shobi the son of Nahash of **R** of	7237
1Ch	20: 1 of Ammon, and came and besieged **R**.	7237
	20: 1 And Joab smote **R**, and destroyed it.	7237
Jer	49: 2 war to be heard in **R** of the Ammonites;	7237
	49: 3 cry, ye daughters of **R**, gird ye with	7237
Eze	25: 5 I will make **R** a stable for camels,	7237
Am	1:14 I will kindle a fire in the wall of **R**,	7237

RABBATH (2) [RABBAH]
Dt	3:11 *is it* not in **R** of the children of Ammon?	7237
Eze	21:20 that the sword may come to **R** of	7237

RABBI (8) [RABBONI]
Mt	23: 7 and to be called of men, **R**, Rabbi.	4461
	23: 7 and to be called of men, Rabbi, **R**.	4461
	23: 8 But be not ye called **R**: for one is your	4461
Jn	1:38 **R**, (which is to say, being interpreted,	4461
	1:49 answered and saith unto him, **R**,	4461
	3: 2 to Jesus by night, and said unto him, **R**,	4461
	3:26 came unto John, and said unto him, **R**,	4461
	6:25 they said unto him, **R**, when camest thou	4461

RABBIT See HARE

RABBITH (1)
Jos	19:20 And **R**, and Kishion, and Abez,	7245

RABBONI (1) [RABBI]
Jn	20:16 She turned herself, and saith unto him, **R**;	4462

RAB-MAG (2)
Jer	39: 3 Sarsechim, Rab-saris, Nergal-sharezer, **R**,	7248
	39:13 **R**, and all the king of Babylon's princes;	7248

RABSARIS, RAB-SARIS (3) [RABSARIS]
2Ki	18:17 the king of Assyria sent Tartan and **R** and	7249
Jer	39: 3 Samgar-nebo, Sarsechim, **R**,	7249
	39:13 **R**, and Nergal-sharezer, Rab-mag,	7249

RABSHAKEH, RAB-SHAKEH (16) [RAB-SHAKEH]
2Ki	18:17 **R** from Lachish to king Hezekiah with a	7262
	18:19 **R** said unto them, Speak ye now to	7262
	18:26 Shebna, and Joah, unto **R**, Speak, I pray	7262
	18:27 **R** said unto them, Hath my master sent	7262
	18:28 **R** stood and cried with a loud voice in	7262
	18:37 clothes rent, and told him the words of **R**.	7262
	19: 4 thy God will hear all the words of **R**,	7262
	19: 8 So **R** returned, and found the king of	7262
Isa	36: 2 the king of Assyria sent **R** from Lachish to	7262
	36: 4 **R** said unto them, Say ye now to	7262
	36:11 said Eliakim and Shebna and Joah unto **R**,	7262
	36:12 **R** said, Hath my master sent me to thy	7262
	36:13 **R** stood, and cried with a loud voice in	7262
	36:22 clothes rent, and told him the words of **R**.	7262
	37: 4 Lord thy God will hear the words of **R**,	7262
	37: 8 So **R** returned, and found the king of	7262

RACA (1)
Mt	5:22 **R**, shall be in danger of the council:	4469

RACAL See RACHAL

RACE (4)
Ps	19: 5 *and* rejoiceth as a strong *man* to run a **r**.	734
Ecc	9:11 the sun, that the **r** *is* not to the swift,	4793
1Co	9:24 ye that they which run in a **r** run	4712
Heb	12: 1 let us run with patience the **r** that is set	73

RACHAB (1) [RAHAB]
Mt	1: 5 And Salmon begat Booz of **R**;	4477

RACHAL (1)
1Sa	30:29 to *them* which *were* in **R**, and to *them*	7403

RACHEL (42) [RACHEL'S, RAHEL]
Ge	29: 6 his daughter cometh with the sheep.	7354
	29: 9 them, **R** came with her father's sheep:	7354

Ge	29:10 when Jacob saw **R** the daughter of Laban	7354
	29:11 Jacob kissed **R**, and lifted up his voice,	7354
	29:12 Jacob told **R** that he *was* her father's	7354
	29:16 and the name of the younger *was* **R**.	7354
	29:17 but **R** was beautiful and well favoured.	7354
	29:18 Jacob loved **R**; and said, I will serve thee	7354
	29:18 I will serve thee seven years for **R** thy	7354
	29:20 Jacob served seven years for **R**;	7354
	29:25 not I serve with thee for **R**? wherefore	7354
	29:28 he gave him **R** his daughter to wife *also*.	7354
	29:29 Laban gave to **R** his daughter Bilhah his	7354
	29:30 he went in also unto **R**, and he loved also	7354
	29:30 he loved also **R** more than Leah,	7354
	29:31 he opened her womb: but **R** was barren.	7354
	30: 1 when **R** saw that she bare Jacob no	7354
	30: 1 **R** no *children*, **R** envied her sister,	7354
	30: 2 Jacob's anger was kindled against **R**:	7354
	30: 6 **R** said, God hath judged me, and hath	7354
	30: 8 **R** said, With great wrestlings have I	7354
	30:14 **R** said to Leah, Give me, I pray thee, of	7354
	30:15 **R** said, Therefore he shall lie with thee to	7354
	30:22 God remembered **R**, and God hearkened	7354
	30:25 it came to pass, when **R** had born Joseph,	7354
	31: 4 Jacob sent and called **R** and Leah to	7354
	31:14 **R** and Leah answered and said unto him,	7354
	31:19 **R** had stolen the images that *were* her	7354
	31:32 Jacob knew not that **R** had stolen them	7354
	31:34 **R** had taken the images, and put them	7354
	33: 1 unto **R**, and unto the two handmaids.	7354
	33: 2 and **R** and Joseph hindermost.	7354
	33: 7 after came Joseph near and **R**,	7354
	35:16 and **R** travailed, and she had hard labour.	7354
	35:19 **R** died, and was buried in the way to	7354
	35:24 The sons of **R**; Joseph, and Benjamin:	7354
	46:19 The sons of **R** Jacob's wife; Joseph,	7354
	46:22 These *are* the sons of **R**, which were born	7354
	46:25 which Laban gave unto **R** his daughter,	7354
	48: 7 **R** died by me in the land of Canaan in	7354
Ru	4:11 that is come into thine house like **R**	7354
Mt	2:18 **R** weeping for her children, and would	4478

RACHEL'S (5) [RACHEL]
Ge	30: 7 Bilhah **R** maid conceived again,	7354
	31:33 of Leah's tent, and entered into **R** tent.	7354
	35:20 that *is* the pillar of **R** grave unto this day.	7354
	35:25 the sons of Bilhah, **R** handmaid; Dan,	7354
1Sa	10: 2 thou shalt find two men by **R** sepulchre	7354

RADDAI (1)
1Ch	2:14 Nethaneel the fourth, **R** the fifth,	7288

RAFTERS (1)
SS	1:17 of our house *are* cedar, *and* our **r** of fir.	7351

RAGAU (1)
Lk	3:35 was *the* son of **R**, which was *the* son	4466

RAGE (18) [RAGED, RAGETH, RAGING]
2Ki	5:12 So he turned and went away in a **r**.	2534
	19:27 and thy coming in, and thy **r** against me.	7264
	19:28 Because thy **r** against me and thy tumult	7264
2Ch	16:10 for *he was* in a **r** with him because of this	2197
	28: 9 ye have slain *them* in a **r** *that* reacheth up	2197
Job	39:24 the ground with fierceness and **r**:	7267
	40:11 Cast abroad the **r** of thy wrath:	5678
Ps	2: 1 Why do the heathen **r**, and the people	7283
	7: 6 because of the **r** of mine enemies:	5678
Pr	6:34 For jealousy *is* the **r** of a man: therefore	2534
	29: 9 whether he **r** or laugh, *there is* no rest.	7264
Isa	37:28 and thy coming in, and thy **r** against me.	7264
	37:29 Because thy **r** against me, and thy tumult,	7264
Jer	46: 9 **r**, ye chariots; and let the mighty *men*	1984
Da	3:13 Nebuchadnezzar in his **r** and	7266
Hos	7:16 fall by the sword for the **r** of their tongue:	2195
Na	2: 4 The chariots shall **r** in the streets, they	1984
Ac	4:25 Why did the heathen **r**, and the people	5433

RAGED (1) [RAGE]
Ps	46: 6 heathen **r**, the kingdoms were moved:	1993

RAGETH (1) [RAGE]
Pr	14:16 from evil: but the fool **r**, and *is* confident.	5674

RAGGED (1)
Isa	2:21 into the tops of the **r** rocks, for fear of	5553

RAGING (5) [RAGE]
Ps	89: 9 Thou rulest the **r** of the sea: when	1348
Pr	20: 1 Wine *is* a mocker, strong drink *is* **r**:	1993
Jnh	1:15 the sea: and the sea ceased from her **r**.	2197
Lk	8:24 rebuked the wind and the **r** of the water:	2830
Jude	1:13 **R** waves of the sea, foaming out their own	66

RAGS (4)
Pr	23:21 and drowsiness shall clothe *a* man with **r**.	7168
Isa	64: 6 and all our righteousnesses *are* as filthy **r**;	899
Jer	38:11 thence old cast clouts and old **rotten r**,	4418
	38:12 **rotten r** under thine armholes under	4418

RAGUEL (1)
Nu	10:29 the son of **R** the Midianite, Moses' father	7467

RAHAB (10) [RACHAB]
Jos	2: 1 house, named **R**, and lodged there.	7343
	2: 3 the king of Jericho sent unto **R**, saying,	7343
	6:17 only **R** the harlot shall live, she and all	7343

Jos	6:23 brought out **R**, and her father,	7343
	6:25 Joshua saved **R** the harlot alive, and her	7343
Ps	87: 1 I will make mention of **R** and Babylon to	7294
	89:10 Thou hast broken **R** in pieces, as one that	7294
Isa	51: 9 *Art* thou not it that hath cut **R**,	7294
Heb	11:31 By faith the harlot **R** perished not with	4460
Jas	2:25 also was not **R** the harlot justified	4460

RAHAM (1)
1Ch	2:44 Shema begat **R**, the father of Jorkoam:	7357

RAHEL (1) [RACHEL]
Jer	31:15 **R** weeping for her children refused to be	7354

RAIDING See ROVERS

RAIL (1) [RAILED, RAILER, RAILING, RAILINGS]
2Ch	32:17 He wrote also letters to **r** on the Lord	2778

RAILED (3) [RAIL]
1Sa	25:14 to salute our master; and he **r** on them.	5860
Mk	15:29 And they that passed by **r** on him,	987
Lk	23:39 malefactors which were hanged **r** on him,	987

RAILER (1) [RAIL]
1Co	5:11 or a **r**, or a drunkard, or an extortioner;	3060

RAILING (4) [RAIL]
1Pe	3: 9 Not rendering evil for evil, or **r** for railing:	3059
	3: 9 Not rendering evil for evil, or railing for **r**:	3059
2Pe	2:11 bring not **r** accusation against them before	989
Jude	1: 9 durst not bring against *him* a **r** accusation,	988

RAILINGS (1) [RAIL]
1Ti	6: 4 cometh envy, strife, **r**, evil surmisings,	988

RAIMENT (57)
Ge	24:53 of gold, and **r**, and gave *them* to Rebekah:	899
	27:15 Rebekah took goodly **r** of her eldest son	899
	27:27 he smelled the smell of his **r**,	899
	28:20 will give me bread to eat, and **r** to put on,	899
	41:14 he shaved *himself*, and changed his **r**,	8071
	45:22 of them he gave each man changes of **r**;	8071
	45:22 *pieces* of silver, and five changes of **r**.	8071
Ex	3:22 jewels of silver, and jewels of gold, and **r**:	8071
	12:35 jewels of silver, and jewels of gold, and **r**:	8071
	21:10 her **r**, and her duty of marriage, shall he	3682
	22: 9 for **r**, *or* for any manner of lost *thing*,	8008
	22:26 If thou at all take thy neighbour's **r** to	8008
	22:27 *is* his covering only, it *is* his **r** for his skin:	8071
Lev	11:32 any vessel of wood, or **r**, or skin, or sack,	899
Nu	31:20 purify all *your* **r**, and all that is made of	899
Dt	8: 4 Thy **r** waxed not old upon thee, neither	8071
	10:18 the stranger, in giving him food and **r**.	8071
	21:13 she shall put the **r** of her captivity from	8071
	22: 3 shalt thou do with his **r**; and with all lost	8071
	24:13 that he may sleep in his own **r**,	8008
	24:17 nor take a widow's **r** to pledge:	899
Jos	22: 8 and with iron, and with very much **r**:	8008
Jdg	3:16 he did gird it under his **r** upon his right	4055
	8:26 purple **r** that *was* on the kings of Midian,	899
Ru	3: 3 put thy **r** upon thee, and get thee down	8071
1Sa	28: 8 put on other **r**, and he went, and two men	899
2Ki	5: 5 *pieces* of gold, and ten changes of **r**.	899
	7: 8 and went and hid *it*; and came again,	899
2Ch	9:24 **r**, harness, and spices, horses, and mules,	8008
Est	4: 4 she sent **r** to clothe Mordecai, and to take	899
Job	27:16 as the dust, and prepare **r** as the clay;	4403
Ps	45:14 unto the king in **r** of **needlework**:	7553
Isa	14:19 *and as* the **r** of those that are slain,	3830
	63: 3 my garments, and I will stain all my **r**.	4403
Eze	16:13 thy **r** *was* of fine linen, and silk,	4403
Zec	3: 4 and *I will* clothe thee with **change of r**.	4254
Mt	3: 4 And the same John had his **r** of camel's	1742
	6:25 life more than meat, and the body than **r**?	1742
	6:28 And why take ye thought for **r**?	1742
	11: 8 A man clothed in soft **r**? behold, they that	2440
	17: 2 the sun, and his **r** was white as the light.	2440
	27:31 and put his own **r** on him, and led him	2440
	28: 3 like lightning, and his **r** white as snow:	1742
Mk	9: 3 his **r** became shining, exceeding white	2440
Lk	7:25 A man clothed in soft **r**? Behold,	2440
	9:29 and his **r** *was* white and glistering.	2441
	10:30 which **stripped** him of his **r**,	1562
	12:23 than meat, and the body *is* more than **r**.	1742
	23:34 And they parted his **r**, and cast lots.	2440
Jn	19:24 They parted my **r** among them, and for	2440
Ac	18: 6 he shook *his* **r**, and said unto them,	2440
	22:20 and kept the **r** of them that slew him.	2440
1Ti	6: 8 and **r** let us be therewith content.	4629
Jas	2: 2 there come in also a poor *man* in vile **r**;	2066
Rev	3: 5 the same shall be clothed in white **r**;	2440
	3:18 and white **r**, that thou mayest be clothed,	2440
	4: 4 twenty elders sitting, clothed in white **r**;	2440

RAIN (102) [RAINBOW, RAINED, RAINY]
Ge	2: 5 for the Lord God had not **caused** it *to* **r**	4305
	7: 4 cause it *to* **r** upon the earth forty days	4305
	7:12 the **r** was upon the earth forty days and	1653
	8: 2 and the **r** from heaven was restrained;	1653
Ex	9:18 I will **cause** it *to* **r** a very grievous hail,	4305
	9:33 and the **r** was not poured upon the earth.	1653
	9:34 when Pharaoh saw that the **r** and the hail	4306
	16: 4 I will **r** bread from heaven for you;	4305
Lev	26: 4 I will give you **r** in due season, and the	1653
Dt	11:11 *and* drinketh water of the **r** of heaven:	4306

Dt	11:14 That I will give *you* the **r** of your land in	4306
	11:14 the **first r** and the latter rain, that thou	3138
	11:14 the first rain and the **latter r**, that thou	4456
	11:17 that there be no **r**, and *that* the land yield	4306
	28:12 the heaven to give the **r** unto thy land in	4306
	28:24 The LORD shall make the **r** of thy land	4306
	32: 2 My doctrine shall drop as the **r**, my	4306
	32: 2 as the **small r** upon the tender herb,	8164
1Sa	12:17 and he shall send thunder and **r**;	4306
	12:18 the LORD sent thunder and **r** that day:	4306
2Sa	1:21 no dew, neither *let there be* **r** upon you,	4306
	23: 4 out of the earth by clear shining after **r**.	4306
1Ki	8:35 there is no **r**, because they have sinned	4306
	8:36 give **r** upon thy land, which thou hast	4306
	17: 1 there shall not be dew nor **r** these years,	4306
	17: 7 because there had been no **r** in the land.	4306
	17:14 until the day *that* the LORD sendeth **r**	1653
	18: 1 Ahab; and I will send **r** upon the earth.	1653
	18:41 for *there is* a sound of abundance of **r**.	1653
	18:44 get thee down, that the **r** stop thee not.	1653
	18:45 and wind, and there was a great **r**.	1653
2Ki	3:17 shall not see wind, neither shall ye see **r**;	1653
2Ch	6:26 there is no **r**, because they have sinned	4306
	6:27 send **r** upon thy land, which thou hast	4306
	7:13 If I shut up heaven that there be no **r**, or	1653
Ezr	10: 9 of *this* matter, and for the **great r**.	1653
	10:13 is a time of **much r**, and *we are* not able	1653
Job	5:10 Who giveth **r** upon the earth,	4305
	20:23 shall **r** *it* upon him while he is eating,	4305
	28:26 When he made a decree for the **r**,	4306
	29:23 they waited for me as for the **r**;	4306
	29:23 their mouth wide *as* for the **latter r**.	4456
	36:27 they pour down **r** according to the vapour	4306
	37: 6 likewise *to* the small **r**, and *to* the great	1653
	37: 6 rain, and *to* the great **r** of his strength.	1653
	38:26 To **cause** it to **r** on the earth, *where* no	4305
	38:28 Hath the **r** a father? or who hath begotten	4306
Ps	11: 6 Upon the wicked he shall **r** snares, fire	4305
	68: 9 Thou, O God, didst send a plentiful **r**,	1653
	72: 6 He shall come down like **r** upon the	4306
	84: 6 make it a well; the **r** also filleth the pools.	4175
	105:32 He gave them hail for **r**, *and* flaming fire	1653
	135: 7 maketh lightnings for the **r**; he bringeth	4306
	147: 8 clouds, who prepareth **r** for the earth,	4306
Pr	16:15 his favour *is* as a cloud of the **latter r**.	4456
	25:14 gift *is like* clouds and wind without **r**.	1653
	25:23 The north wind driveth away **r**: so *doth*	1653
	26: 1 as **r** in harvest, so honour *is* not seemly	4306
	28: 3 *like* a sweeping **r** which leaveth no food.	4306
Ecc	11: 3 If the clouds be full of **r**, they empty	1653
	12: 2 nor the clouds return after the **r**:	1653
SS	2:11 the winter is past, the **r** is over *and* gone;	1653
Isa	4: 6 and for a covert from storm and from **r**.	4306
	5: 6 will also command the clouds that they **r**	4305
	5: 6 the clouds that they rain no **r** upon it.	4306
	30:23 shall he give the **r** of thy seed, that thou	4306
	44:14 planteth an ash, and the **r** doth nourish *it*.	1653
	55:10 For as the **r** cometh down, and the snow	1653
Jer	3: 3 and there hath been no **latter r**;	4456
	5:24 giveth **r**, both the former and the latter,	1653
	10:13 he maketh lightnings with **r**,	4306
	14: 4 for there was no **r** in the earth,	1653
	14:22 vanities of the Gentiles that can **cause r**?	1652
	51:16 he maketh lightnings with **r**,	4306
Eze	1:28 bow that is in the cloud in the day of **r**,	1653
	38:22 I will **r** upon him, and upon his bands,	4305
	38:22 overflowing **r**, and great hailstones, fire,	1653
Hos	6: 3 shall come unto us as the **r**, as the latter	1653
	6: 3 as the latter *and* **former r** *unto* the earth.	3384
	10:12 he come and **r** righteousness upon you.	3384
Joel	2:23 for he hath given you the **former r**	4175
	2:23 will cause to come down for you the **r**,	1653
	2:23 **former r**, and the latter rain in the first	4175
	2:23 and the **latter r** in the first *month*.	4456
Am	4: 7 also I have withholden the **r** from you,	1653
	4: 7 I **caused** it **to r** upon one city, and caused	4305
	4: 7 and **caused** it not **to r** upon another city:	4305
Zec	10: 1 Ask ye of the LORD **r** in the time of	4306
	10: 1 the LORD rain in the time of the **latter r**,	4456
	10: 1 give them showers of **r**, to every one grass	1653
	14:17 of hosts, even upon them shall be no **r**.	1653
	14:18 that *have no* **r**, there shall be the plague.	NIH
Mt	5:45 sendeth **r** on the just and *on* the unjust.	1026
	7:25 the **r** descended, and the floods came,	1028
	7:27 the **r** descended, and the floods came,	1028
Ac	14:17 and gave us **r** from heaven,	5205
	28: 2 because of the present **r**, and because of	5205
Heb	6: 7 For the earth which drinketh *in* the **r** that	5205
Jas	5: 7 it, until he receive the early and latter **r**.	5205
	5:17 he prayed earnestly that it might not **r**:	1026
	5:18 and the heaven gave **r**, and the earth	5205
Rev	11: 6 **r** not in the days of their prophecy:	1026+5205

RAINBOW (2) [BOW, RAIN]

Rev	4: 3 and *there was* a **r** round about the throne,	2463
	10: 1 a **r** *was* upon *his* head, and his face *was*	2463

RAINED (9) [RAIN]

Ge	19:24 the LORD **r** upon Sodom and	4305
Ex	9:23 the LORD **r** hail upon the land of Egypt.	4305
Ps	78:24 had **r down** manna upon them to eat,	4305
	78:27 He **r** flesh also upon them as dust,	4305
Eze	22:24 nor **r** upon in the day of indignation.	1656
Am	4: 7 one piece was **r** upon, and the piece	4305
	4: 7 the piece whereupon it **r** not withered.	4305

Lk	17:29 day that Lot went out of Sodom it **r** fire	1026
Jas	5:17 it **r** not on the earth *by the space of* three	1026

RAINY (1) [RAIN]

Pr	27:15 A continual dropping in a **very r** day and	5464

RAISE (59) [RAISED, RAISER, RAISETH, RAISING]

Ge	38: 8 marry her, and **r** up seed to thy brother.	6965
Ex	23: 1 Thou shalt not **r** a false report: put not	5375
Dt	18:15 The LORD thy God will **r** up unto thee a	6965
	18:18 I will **r** them **up** a Prophet from among	6965
	25: 7 My husband's brother refuseth to **r** up	6965
Jos	8:29 **r** thereon a great heap of stones,	6965
Ru	4: 5 to **r** up the name of the dead upon his	6965
	4:10 to **r** up the name of the dead upon his	6965
1Sa	2:35 I will **r** me **up** a faithful priest, *that* shall	6965
2Sa	12:11 I will **r** up evil against thee out of thine	6965
	12:17 *went* to him, to **r** him **up** from the earth:	6965
1Ki	14:14 Moreover the LORD shall **r** him **up** a	6965
1Ch	17:11 that I will **r** up thy seed after thee,	6965
Job	3: 8 who are ready to **r** up their mourning.	5782
	19:12 **r** up their way against me,	5549
	30:12 they **r** up against me the ways of their	5549
Ps	41:10 be merciful unto me, and **r** me **up**,	6965
Isa	15: 5 *in* the way of Horonaim they shall **r** up	5782
	29: 3 a mount, and I will **r** forts against thee.	6965
	44:26 I will **r** up the decayed places thereof:	6965
	49: 6 be my servant to **r** up the tribes of Jacob,	6965
	58:12 thou shalt **r** up the foundations of many	6965
	61: 4 they shall **r** up the former desolations,	6965
Jer	23: 5 I will **r** unto David a righteous Branch,	6965
	30: 9 their king, whom I will **r** up unto them.	6965
	50: 9 I *will r* and cause to come up against	5782
	50:32 and fall, and none shall **r** him **up**:	6965
	51: 1 I *will* **r** up against Babylon,	5782
Eze	23:22 I will **r** up thy lovers against thee,	5782
	34:29 I will **r** up for them a plant of renown,	6965
Hos	6: 2 in the third day he will **r** us **up**,	6965
Joel	3: 7 I *will* **r** them out of the place whither ye	5782
Am	5: 2 upon her land; *there* is none to **r** her **up**.	6965
	6:14 I *will* **r** up against you a nation,	6965
	9:11 In that day will I **r** up the tabernacle of	6965
	9:11 I will **r** up his ruins, and I will build it as	6965
Mic	5: 5 shall we **r** against him seven shepherds,	6965
Hab	1: 6 are *that* **r** up strife and contention.	5375
	1: 6 lo, I **r** up the Chaldeans, *that* bitter and	6965
Zec	11:16 For lo, I *will* **r** up a shepherd in the land,	6965
Mt	3: 9 that God is able of these stones to **r** up	1453
	10: 8 the lepers, **r** the dead, cast out devils:	1453
	22:24 his wife, and **r** up seed unto his brother.	450
Mk	12:19 his wife, and **r** up seed unto his brother.	1817
Lk	3: 8 That God is able of these stones to **r** up	1453
	20:28 *his* wife, and **r** up seed unto his brother.	1817
Jn	2:19 temple, and in three days I will **r** it **up**.	1453
	6:39 but should **r** it **up** *again* at the last day.	450
	6:40 and I will **r** him **up** *at* the last day.	450
	6:44 him: and I will **r** him **up** *at* the last day.	450
	6:54 and I will **r** him **up** *at* the last day.	450
Ac	2:30 *he* would **r** up Christ to sit on his throne;	450
	3:22 prophet shall the Lord your God **r** up unto	450
	7:37 prophet shall the Lord your God **r** up unto	450
	26: 8 with you, that God should **r** the dead?	1453
1Co	6:14 and will *also* **r** up us by his own power.	1825
2Co	4:14 the Lord Jesus shall **r** up us also by Jesus,	1453
Heb	11:19 that God *was* able to **r** him **up**,	1453
Jas	5:15 the sick, and the Lord shall **r** him **up**;	1453

RAISED (85) [RAISE]

Ex	9:16 very deed for this cause have I **r** thee **up**,	5975
Jos	5: 7 children, *whom* he **r** up in their stead,	6965
	7:26 they **r** over him a great heap of stones	6965
Jdg	2:16 Nevertheless the LORD **r** up judges,	6965
	2:18 when the LORD **r** them **up** judges, then	6965
	3: 9 the LORD **r** up a deliverer to the children	6965
	3:15 the LORD **r** them **up** a deliverer, Ehud	6965
2Sa	23: 1 and the man *who* was **r** up on high,	6965
1Ki	5:13 king Solomon **r** a levy out of all Israel;	5927
	9:15 reason of the levy which king Solomon **r**;	5927
2Ch	32: 5 **r** *it* **up** to the towers, and another wall	5927
	33:14 **r** it **up** a very **great height**,	1361
Ezr	1: 5 with all *them* whose spirit God had **r**,	5782
Job	14:12 not awake, nor be **r** out of their sleep.	5782
SS	8: 5 I **r** thee **up** under the apple tree: there thy	5782
Isa	14: 9 hath **r** up from their thrones all the kings	6209
	23:13 they **r** up the palaces thereof;	6965
	41: 2 Who **r** up the righteous *man* from the	5782
	41:25 I have **r** up *one* from the north, and he	5782
	45:13 I have **r** him **up** in righteousness, and I	5782
Jer	6:22 a great nation shall be **r** from the sides of	5782
	25:32 a great whirlwind shall be **r** up from	5782
	29:15 The LORD hath **r** us **up** prophets in	6965
	50:41 many kings shall be **r** up from the coasts	5782
	51:11 the LORD hath **r** up the spirit of the kings	5782
Da	7: 5 it **r** up itself on one side, and *it had* three	6966
Am	2:11 I **r** up of your sons for prophets,	6965
Zec	2:13 for he is **r** up out of his holy habitation.	5782
	9:13 thy sons, O Zion, against thy sons,	5782
Mt	1:24 Then Joseph being **r** from sleep did as	1326
	11: 5 the dead are **r up**, and the poor have	1453
	16:21 be killed, and be **r** *again* the third day.	1453
	17:23 the third day he shall be **r** *again*.	1453
Lk	1:69 And hath **r** up a horn of salvation for us in	1453
	7:22 are cleansed, the deaf hear, the dead are **r**,	1453
	9:22 and be slain, and be **r** the third day.	1453
	20:37 Now that the dead are **r**, even Moses	1453

Jn	12: 1 been dead, whom he **r** from the dead.	1453
	12: 9 whom he had **r** from the dead.	1453
	12:17 whom he **r** from the dead, bare record.	1453
Ac	2:24 Whom God hath **r up**, having loosed	450
	2:32 Jesus hath God **r up**, whereof we all are	450
	3:15 of life, whom God hath **r** from the dead;	1453
	3:26 you first God, having **r up** his Son Jesus,	450
	4:10 ye crucified, whom God **r** from the dead,	1453
	5:30 The God of our fathers **r up** Jesus,	1453
	10:40 Him God **r up** the third day,	1453
	12: 7 and **r** him **up**, saying, Arise up quickly.	1453
	13:22 he **r** up unto them David to be their king;	1453
	13:23 of *his* promise **r** unto Israel a Saviour,	1453
	13:30 But God **r** him from the dead:	1453
	13:33 in that he hath **r up** Jesus **again**;	450
	13:34 And as concerning that he **r** him **up** from	450
	13:37 whom God **r** *again*, saw no corruption.	1453
	13:50 and **r** persecution against Paul and	1892
	17:31 men, in that he hath **r** him from the dead.	450
Ro	4:24 if we believe on him that **r up** Jesus our	1453
	4:25 and was **r** *again* for our justification.	1453
	6: 4 that like as Christ was **r** up from the dead	1453
	6: 9 Knowing that Christ being **r** from the dead	1453
	7: 4 even to him who is **r** from the dead,	1453
	8:11 if the Spirit of him that **r up** Jesus from	1453
	8:11 that **r** up Christ from the dead shall also	1453
	9:17 for this same *purpose* have I **r** thee **up**,	1825
	10: 9 believe in thine heart that God hath **r**	1453
1Co	6:14 And God hath both **r** up the Lord,	1453
	15:15 we have testified of God that he **r up**	1453
	15:15 whom he **r** not **up**, if so be that the dead	1453
	15:16 if the dead rise not, then is not Christ **r**:	1453
	15:17 And if Christ be not **r**, your faith *is* vain;	1453
	15:35 *man* will say, How are the dead **r up**?	1453
	15:42 sown in corruption; it is **r** in incorruption:	1453
	15:43 It is sown in dishonour; it is **r** in glory: it	1453
	15:43 it is sown in weakness; it is **r** in power:	1453
	15:44 a natural body; it is **r** a spiritual body.	1453
	15:52 and the dead shall be **r** incorruptible,	1453
2Co	4:14 Knowing that he which **r up** the Lord	1453
Gal	1: 1 the Father, who **r** him from the dead;)	1453
Eph	1:20 when he **r** him from the dead, and set *him*	1453
	2: 6 hath **r** *us* **up together**, and made *us* sit	4891
Col	2:12 of God, who hath **r** him from the dead.	1453
1Th	1:10 whom he **r** from the dead, *even* Jesus,	1453
2Ti	2: 8 **r** from the dead according to my gospel:	1453
Heb	11:35 received their dead **r to life again**;	386+1537
1Pe	1:21 that **r** him **up** from the dead, and gave	1453

RAISER (1) [RAISE]

Da	11:20 shall stand up in his estate a **r** of taxes *in*	5674

RAISETH (8) [RAISE]

1Sa	2: 8 He **r** up the poor out of the dust,	6965
Job	41:25 When he **r** *himself*, the mighty are	7613
Ps	107:25 he commandeth, and **r** the stormy wind,	5975
	113: 7 He **r** up the poor out of the dust,	6965
	145:14 and **r** up all those that be bowed down.	2210
	146: 8 the LORD **r** them that are bowed down:	2210
Jn	5:21 For as the Father **r** up the dead,	1453
2Co	1: 9 ourselves, but in God which **r** the dead:	1453

RAISING (2) [RAISE]

Hos	7: 4 who ceaseth from **r** after *he* hath kneaded	5782
Ac	24:12 any *man*, neither **r up** the people,	1999+4160

RAISINS (4)

1Sa	25:18 corn, and an hundred **clusters of r**,	6778
	30:12 of a cake *of figs*, and two **clusters of r**:	6778
2Sa	16: 1 hundred **bunches of r**, and an hundred	6778
1Ch	12:40 *of figs*, and **bunches of r**, and wine,	6778

RAKEM (1)

1Ch	7:16 and his sons *were* Ulam and **R**.	7552

RAKKATH (1)

Jos	19:35 Zer, and Hammath, **R**, and Chinnereth,	7557

RAKKON (1)

Jos	19:46 Me-jarkon, and **R**, with the border before	7542

RAM (97) [RAM'S, RAMS, RAMS']

Ge	15: 9 a **r** of three years old, and a turtle-dove,	352
	22:13 behind *him* a **r** caught in a thicket by	352
	22:13 Abraham went and took the **r**,	352
Ex	29:15 Thou shalt also take one **r**; and Aaron and	352
	29:15 put their hands upon the head of the **r**.	352
	29:16 thou shalt slay the **r**, and thou shalt take	352
	29:17 thou shalt cut the **r** in pieces, and wash	352
	29:18 thou shalt burn the whole **r** upon the altar:	352
	29:19 thou shalt take the other **r**; and Aaron and	352
	29:19 put their hands upon the head of the **r**.	352
	29:20 shalt thou kill the **r**, and take of his blood,	352
	29:22 Also thou shalt take of the **r** the fat and	352
	29:22 right shoulder; for it *is* a **r** of consecration:	352
	29:26 shalt take the breast of the **r** of Aaron's	352
	29:27 is heaved up, of the **r** of the consecration,	352
	29:31 thou shalt take the **r** of the consecration,	352
	29:32 and his sons shall eat the flesh of the **r**,	352
Lev	5:15 a **r** without blemish out of the flocks,	352
	5:16 for him with the **r** of the trespass offering,	352
	5:18 he shall bring a **r** without blemish out of	352
	6: 6 a **r** without blemish out of the flock, with	352
	8:18 he brought the **r** for the burnt offering:	352
	8:18 laid their hands upon the head of the **r**.	352
	8:20 he cut the **r** into pieces; and Moses burnt	352

Lev	8:21 Moses burnt the whole **r** upon the altar:	352
	8:22 he brought the other **r**, the ram of	352
	8:22 the other ram, the **r** of consecration:	352
	8:22 laid this ram upon the head of the **r**.	352
	8:29 *for* of the **r** of consecration it was Moses'	352
	9: 2 a **r** for a burnt offering, without blemish,	352
	9: 4 Also a bullock and a **r** for peace offerings,	352
	9:18 and the **r** *for* a sacrifice of peace offerings,	352
	9:19 fat of the bullock and of the **r**, the rump,	352
	16: 3 a sin offering, and a **r** for a burnt offering.	352
	16: 5 sin offering, and one **r** for a burnt offering.	352
	19:21 *even* a **r** for a trespass offering.	352
	19:22 **r** of the trespass offering before the LORD	352
Nu	5: 8 beside the **r** of the atonement, whereby an	352
	6:14 one **r** without blemish for peace offerings,	352
	6:17 he shall offer the **r** *for* a sacrifice of peace	352
	6:19 shall take the sodden shoulder of the **r**,	352
	7:15 One young bullock, one **r**, one lamb	352
	7:21 One young bullock, one **r**, one lamb	352
	7:27 One young bullock, one **r**, one lamb	352
	7:33 One young bullock, one **r**, one lamb	352
	7:39 One young bullock, one **r**, one lamb	352
	7:45 One young bullock, one **r**, one lamb	352
	7:51 One young bullock, one **r**, one lamb	352
	7:57 One young bullock, one **r**, one lamb	352
	7:63 One young bullock, one **r**, one lamb	352
	7:69 One young bullock, one **r**, one lamb	352
	7:75 One young bullock, one **r**, one lamb	352
	7:81 One young bullock, one **r**, one lamb	352
	15: 6 Or for a **r**, thou shalt prepare *for* a meat	352
	15:11 or for one **r**, or for a lamb, or a kid.	352
	23: 2 offered on *every* altar a bullock and a **r**.	352
	23: 4 offered upon *every* altar a bullock and a **r**.	352
	23:14 offered a bullock and a **r** on *every* altar.	352
	23:30 offered a bullock and a **r** on *every* altar.	352
	28:11 young bullocks, and one **r**, seven lambs	352
	28:12 a meat offering, mingled with oil, for one **r**;	352
	28:14 the third *part* of a hin unto a **r**, and a fourth	352
	28:19 and one **r**, and seven lambs of the first year:	352
	28:20 for a bullock, and two tenth deals for a **r**;	352
	28:27 two young bullocks, one **r**, seven lambs	352
	28:28 one bullock, two tenth deals unto one **r**,	352
	29: 2 one **r**, *and* seven lambs of the first year	352
	29: 3 for a bullock, *and* two tenth deals for a **r**	352
	29: 8 one **r**, *and* seven lambs of the first year;	352
	29: 9 to a bullock, *and* two tenth deals to one **r**,	352
	29:14 two tenth deals to each **r** of the two rams,	352
	29:36 one bullock, one **r**, seven lambs of the first	352
	29:37 for the **r**, and for the lambs, *shall be*	352
Ru	4:19 Hezron begat **R**, and Ram begat	7410
	4:19 begat Ram, and **R** begat Amminadab,	7410
1Ch	2: 9 him; Jerahmeel, and **R**, and Chelubai.	7410
	2:10 **R** begat Amminadab;	7410
	2:25 **R** the firstborn, and Bunah, and Oren,	7410
	2:27 the sons of **R** the firstborn of Jerahmeel	7410
Ezr	10:19 *they offered* a **r** of the flock for their	352
Job	32: 2 Barachel the Buzite, of the kindred of **R**:	7410
Eze	43:23 and a **r** out of the flock without blemish.	352
	43:25 and a **r** out of the flock, without blemish.	352
	45:24 an ephah for a **r**, and a hin of oil for an	352
	46: 4 without blemish, and a **r** without blemish.	352
	46: 5 the meat offering *shall be* an ephah for a **r**,	352
	46: 6 without blemish, and six lambs, and a **r**.	352
	46: 7 an ephah for a **r**, and for the lambs	352
	46:11 an ephah for a **r**, and to the lambs as he is	352
Da	8: 3 there stood before the river a **r** which had	352
	8: 4 I saw the **r** pushing westward,	352
	8: 6 he came to the **r** that had two horns,	352
	8: 7 I saw him come close unto the **r**, and he	352
	8: 7 and smote the **r**, and brake his two horns:	352
	8: 7 there was no power in the **r** to stand before	352
	8: 7 was none that could deliver the **r** out of	352
	8:20 The **r** which thou sawest having two horns	352

RAM'S (1) [RAM]

Jos	6: 5 when *they* make a long blast with the **r**	3104

RAMA (1) [RAMAH]

Mt	2:18 **R** was there a voice heard, lamentation,	4471

RAMAH (36) [RAMA, RAMATHITE]

Jos	18:25 Gibeon, and **R**, and Beeroth,	7414
	19:29 *then* the coast turneth to **R**, and to	7414
	19:36 And Adamah, and **R**, and Hazor,	7414
Jdg	4: 5 the palm tree of Deborah between **R**	7414
	19:13 to lodge all night, in Gibeah, or in **R**.	7414
1Sa	1:19 returned, and came to their house to **R**:	7414
	2:11 Elkanah went to **R** to his house.	7414
	7:17 his return *was* to **R**; for there *was* his	7414
	8: 4 and came to Samuel unto **R**,	7414
	15:34 Samuel went to **R**; and Saul went up to	7414
	16:13 So Samuel rose up, and went to **R**.	7414
	19:18 came to Samuel to **R**, and told him all	7414
	19:19 Behold, David *is* at Naioth in **R**.	7414
	19:22 he also to **R**, and came to a great well	7414
	19:22 *one* said, Behold, *they be* at Naioth in **R**.	7414
	19:23 he went thither to Naioth in **R**:	7414
	19:23 prophesied, until he came to Naioth in **R**.	7414
	20: 1 David fled from Naioth in **R**, and came	7414
	22: 6 Saul abode in Gibeah under a tree in **R**,	7414
	25: 1 and buried him in his house at **R**.	7414
	28: 3 buried him in **R**, even in his own city.	7414
1Ki	15:17 built **R**, that *he* might not suffer *any* to go	7414
	15:21 *thereof*, that he left off building of **R**,	7414
	15:22 they took away the stones of **R**,	7414

2Ki	8:29 which the Syrians had given him at **R**,	7414
2Ch	16: 1 built **R**, to the intent that *he* might let	7414
	16: 5 heard *it*, that he left off building of **R**,	7414
	16: 6 they carried away the stones of **R**,	7414
	22: 6 the wounds which were given him at **R**,	7414
Ezr	2:26 The children of **R** and Gaba, six hundred	7414
Ne	7:30 The men of **R** and Geba, six hundred	7414
	11:33 Hazor, **R**, Gittaim,	7414
Isa	10:29 at Geba; **R** is afraid; Gibeah of Saul is fled.	7414
Jer	31:15 A voice was heard in **R**, lamentation,	7414
	40: 1 of the guard had let him go from **R**,	7414
Hos	5: 8 cornet in Gibeah, *and* the trumpet in **R**:	7414

RAMATH (1)

Jos	19: 8 cities to Baalath-beer, **R** of the south.	7414

RAMATH MIZPAH See RAMATH-MIZPEH

RAMATHAIM See RAMATHAIM-ZOPHIM

RAMATHAIM-ZOPHIM (1) [ZOPHIM]

1Sa	1: 1 Now there was a certain man of **R**,	7436

RAMATHITE (1) [RAMAH]

1Ch	27:27 over the vineyards *was* Shimei the **R**: over	7435

RAMATH-LEHI (1) [LEHI]

Jdg	15:17 out of his hand, and called that place **R**.	7437

RAMATH-MIZPEH (1) [MIZPEH]

Jos	13:26 from Heshbon unto **R**, and Betonim;	7434

RAMESES (4) [RAAMSES]

Ge	47:11 in the best of the land, in the land of **R**,	7486
Ex	12:37 the children of Israel journeyed from **R** to	7486
Nu	33: 3 they departed from **R** in the first month,	7486
	33: 5 the children of Israel removed from **R**,	7486

RAMIAH (1)

Ezr	10:25 **R**, and Jeziah, and Malchiah, and Miamin,	7422

RAMOTH (8) [RAMOTH-GILEAD]

Dt	4:43 **R** in Gilead, of the Gadites; and Golan in	7216
Jos	20: 8 **R** in Gilead out of the tribe of Gad,	7216
	21:38 of Gad, **R** in Gilead with her suburbs,	7433
1Sa	30:27 to *them* which *were* in south **R**, and to	7418
1Ki	22: 3 Know ye that **R** in Gilead *is* ours,	7433
1Ch	6:73 **R** with her suburbs, and Anem with her	7216
	6:80 **R** in Gilead with her suburbs,	7216
Ezr	10:29 of Adaiah, Jashub, and Sheal, and **R**.	7433

RAMOTH-GILEAD (19) [GILEAD, RAMOTH]

1Ki	4:13 The son of Geber, in **R**; to him *pertained*	1568
	22: 4 Wilt thou go with me to battle to **R**?	7433
	22: 6 Shall I go against **R** to battle, or shall I	7433
	22:12 saying, Go up to **R**, and prosper:	7433
	22:15 shall we go against **R** to battle, or shall we	7433
	22:20 that he may go up and fall at **R**?	7433
	22:29 the king of Judah went up to **R**.	7433
2Ki	8:28 the war against Hazael king of Syria in **R**;	7433
	9: 1 this box of oil in thine hand, and go to **R**:	7433
	9: 4 the young man the prophet, went to **R**.	7433
	9:14 (Now Joram had kept **R**, he and all Israel,	7433
2Ch	18: 2 persuaded him to go up *with him* to **R**.	7433
	18: 3 king of Judah, Wilt thou go with me to **R**?	7433
	18: 5 Shall we go to **R** to battle, or shall I	7433
	18:11 saying, Go up to **R**, and prosper:	7433
	18:14 shall we go against **R** to battle, or shall I	7433
	18:19 of Israel, that he may go up and fall at **R**?	7433
	18:28 the king of Judah went up to **R**:	7433
	22: 5 to war against Hazael king of Syria at **R**:	7433

RAMPART (2)

La	2: 8 therefore he made the **r** and the wall to	2426
Na	3: 8 whose **r** *was* the sea, *and* her wall *was*	2426

RAMS (68) [RAM]

Ge	31:10 the **r** which leaped upon the cattle *were*	6260
	31:12 all the **r** which leap upon the cattle *are*	6260
	31:38 and the **r** of thy flock have I not eaten.	352
	32:14 he goats, two hundred ewes, and twenty **r**,	352
Ex	29: 1 young bullock, and two **r** without blemish,	352
	29: 3 the basket, with the bullock and the two **r**.	352
	35:23 goats' *hair*, and red skins of **r**,	352
Lev	8: 2 two **r**, and a basket of unleavened bread;	352
	23:18 year, and one young bullock, and two **r**:	352
Nu	7:17 two oxen, five **r**, five he goats, five lambs	352
	7:23 two oxen, five **r**, five he goats, five lambs	352
	7:29 two oxen, five **r**, five he goats, five lambs	352
	7:35 two oxen, five **r**, five he goats, five lambs	352
	7:41 two oxen, five **r**, five he goats, five lambs	352
	7:47 two oxen, five **r**, five he goats, five lambs	352
	7:53 two oxen, five **r**, five he goats, five lambs	352
	7:59 two oxen, five **r**, five he goats, five lambs	352
	7:65 two oxen, five **r**, five he goats, five lambs	352
	7:71 two oxen, five **r**, five he goats, five lambs	352
	7:77 two oxen, five **r**, five he goats, five lambs	352
	7:83 two oxen, five **r**, five he goats, five lambs	352
	7:87 the **r** twelve, the lambs of the first year	352
	7:88 *were* twenty and four bullocks, the **r** sixty,	352
	23: 1 prepare me here seven oxen and seven **r**.	352
	23:29 me here seven bullocks and seven **r**.	352
	29:13 two **r**, *and* fourteen lambs of the first year;	352
	29:14 two tenth deals to each ram of the two **r**,	352
	29:17 two **r**, fourteen lambs of the first year	352
	29:18 for the **r**, and for the lambs, *shall be*	352

Nu	29:20 on the third day eleven bullocks, two **r**,	352
	29:21 for the **r**, and for the lambs, *shall be*	352
	29:23 two **r**, *and* fourteen lambs of the first year	352
	29:24 for the **r**, and for the lambs, *shall be*	352
	29:26 two **r**, *and* fourteen lambs of the first year	352
	29:27 for the **r**, and for the lambs, *shall be*	352
	29:29 two **r**, *and* fourteen lambs of the first year	352
	29:30 for the **r**, and for the lambs, *shall be*	352
	29:32 two **r**, *and* fourteen lambs of the first year	352
	29:33 for the **r**, and for the lambs, *shall be*	352
Dt	32:14 and of the breed of Bashan, and goats,	352
1Sa	15:22 *and* to hearken than the fat of **r**.	352
2Ki	3: 4 an hundred thousand **r**, *with* the wool.	352
1Ch	15:26 they offered seven bullocks and seven **r**.	352
	29:21 a thousand **r**, *and* a thousand lambs,	352
2Ch	13: 9 himself with a young bullock and seven **r**,	352
	17:11 seven thousand and seven hundred **r**,	352
	29:21 seven **r**, and seven lambs, and seven he	352
	29:22 likewise, when they had killed the **r**, they	352
	29:32 an hundred **r**, *and* two hundred lambs:	352
Ezr	6: 9 both young bullocks, and **r**, and lambs,	1798
	6:17 two hundred **r**, four hundred lambs;	1798
	7:17 **r**, lambs, with their meat offerings and	1798
	8:35 ninety and six **r**, seventy and seven lambs,	352
Job	42: 8 unto you now seven bullocks and seven **r**,	352
Ps	66:15 sacrifices of fatlings, with the incense of **r**;	352
	114: 4 The mountains skipped like **r**, *and* the	352
	114: 6 Ye mountains, *that* ye skipped like **r**;	352
Isa	1:11 I am full *of* the burnt offerings of **r**,	352
	34: 6 and goats, with the fat of the kidneys of **r**:	352
	60: 7 the **r** of Nebaioth shall minister unto thee:	352
Jer	51:40 bring them down like a lamb... like he goats.	352
Eze	4: 2 and set *battering* **r** against it round about.	3733
	21:22 to appoint *battering* **r** against the gates,	3733
	27:21 with thee in lambs, and **r**, and goats:	352
	34:17 cattle, between the **r** and the he goats.	352
	39:18 of **r**, of lambs, and of goats, of bullocks,	352
	45:23 seven **r** without blemish daily the seven	352
Mic	6: 7 be the LORD pleased with thousands of **r**,	352

RAMS' (9) [RAM]

Ex	25: 5 **r** skins dyed red, and badgers' skins,	352
	26:14 shalt make a covering for the tent *of* **r**	352
	35: 7 **r** skins dyed red, and badgers' skins,	352
	36:19 he made a covering for the tent *of* **r** skins	352
	39:34 the covering of **r** skins dyed red,	352
Jos	6: 4 before the ark seven trumpets of **r** horns:	3104
	6: 6 of **r** horns before the ark of the LORD.	3104
	6: 8 of **r** horns passed on before the LORD,	3104
	6:13 **r** horns before the ark of the LORD went	3104

RAN (61) [RUN]

Ge	18: 2 when he saw *them*, he **r** to meet them	7323
	18: 7 Abraham **r** unto the herd, and fetcht a	7323
	24:17 the servant **r** to meet her, and said, Let	7323
	24:20 again unto the well to draw *water*, and	7323
	24:28 the damsel **r**, and told *them of* her	7323
	24:29 Laban **r** out unto the man, unto the well.	7323
	29:12 and she **r** and told her father.	7323
	29:13 that he **r** to meet him, and embraced him,	7323
	33: 4 Esau **r** to meet him, and embraced him,	7323
Ex	9:23 and the fire **r** along upon the ground,	1980
Nu	11:27 there **r** a young man, and told Moses,	7323
	16:47 and **r** into the midst of the congregation;	7323
Jos	7:22 sent messengers, and they **r** unto the tent;	7323
	8:19 they **r** as soon as *he* had stretched out his	7323
Jdg	7:21 and all the host **r**, and cried, and fled.	7323
	9:21 Jotham **r** away, and fled, and went to	5127
	9:44 the two *other* companies **r** upon all	6584
	13:10 **r**, and shewed her husband, and said unto	7323
1Sa	3: 5 he **r** unto Eli, and said, Here *am* I; for	7323
	4:12 **r** a man of Benjamin out of the army,	7323
	10:23 they **r** and fetched him thence: and when	7323
	17:22 **r** *into* the army, and came and saluted his	7323
	17:48 **r** *toward* the army to meet the Philistine.	7323
	17:51 Therefore David **r**, and stood upon	7323
	20:36 as the lad **r**, he shot an arrow beyond	7323
2Sa	18:21 Cushi bowed himself unto Joab, and **r**.	7323
	18:23 Ahimaaz **r** by the way of the plain,	7323
1Ki	2:39 two of the servants of Shimei **r away**	1272
	18:35 the water **r** round about the altar;	1980
	18:46 **r** before Ahab to the entrance of Jezreel.	7323
	19:20 after Elijah, and said, Let me, I pray	7323
	22:35 the blood **r** out of the wound into the	3332
2Ch	32: 4 the brook that **r** through the midst of	7857
Ps	77: 2 my sore **r** in the night, and ceased not:	5064
	105:41 they **r** in the dry *places like* a river.	1980
	133: 2 that **r** down upon the beard, *even*	3381
Jer	23:21 I have not sent *these* prophets, yet they **r**.	7323
Eze	1:14 the living creatures **r** and returned as	7519
	47: 2 there **r** out waters on the right side.	6379
Da	8: 6 and **r** unto him in the fury of his power.	352
Mt	8:32 the whole herd of swine **r violently** down	3729
	27:48 And straightway one of them **r**, and took a	5143
Mk	5: 6 Jesus afar off, he **r** and worshipped him:	5143
	5:13 the herd **r violently** down a steep place	3729
	6:33 and **r** afoot thither out of all cities,	4936
	6:55 And **r** through that whole region round	4063
	15:36 And one **r** and filled a spunge *full* of	5143
Lk	8:33 the herd **r violently** down a steep place	3729
	15:20 **r**, and fell on his neck, and kissed him.	5143
	19: 4 And he **r** before,	4390
	24:12 arose Peter, and **r** unto the sepulchre;	5143
Jn	20: 4 So they **r** both together: and the other	5143
Ac	3:11 all the people **r together** unto them in	4936

Ac 7:57 ears, and **r** upon him with one accord, *3729*
 8:30 Philip **r** thither to *him*, and heard him *4370*
 12:14 but **r in**, and told how Peter stood before *1532*
 14:14 and **r in** among the people, crying out, *1530*
 21:30 and the people **r together**; *1096+4890*
 21:32 and centurions, and **r down** unto them: *2701*
 27:41 two seas met, they **r** the ship **aground**; *2027*
Jude 1:11 **r greedily after** the error of Balaam for *1632*

RANG (2) [RING]

1Sa 4: 5 a great shout, so that the earth **r again**. *1949*
1Ki 1:45 thence rejoicing, so that the city **r again**. *1949*

RANGE (1) [RANGES, RANGING]

Job 39: 8 The **r** of the mountains *is* his pasture, *3491*

RANGES (4) [RANGE]

Lev 11:35 whether it *be* oven, or **r for pots**, they *3600*
2Ki 1: 8 he that cometh within the **r**, let him be *7713*
 11:15 unto them, Have her forth without the **r**: *7713*
2Ch 23:14 said unto them, Have her forth of the **r**: *7713*

RANGING (1) [RANGE]

Pr 28:15 *As* a roaring lion, and a **r** bear; so *is* a *8264*

RANK (6) [RANKS]

Ge 41: 5 corn came up upon one stalk, **r** and good. *1277*
 41: 7 the seven thin ears devoured the seven **r** *1277*
Nu 2:16 And they shall set forth in the **second r**. *8145*
 2:24 And they shall go forward in the **third r**. *7992*
1Ch 12:33 war, fifty thousand, which could **keep r**: *5737*
 12:38 All these men of war, that could **keep r**, *4634*

RANKS (2) [RANK]

1Ki 7: 4 and light *was* against light *in* three **r**. *6471*
 7: 5 and light *was* against light *in* three **r**. *6471*
Joel 2: 7 his ways, and they shall not break their **r**: *734*
Mk 6:40 they sat down **in r**, by hundreds, *4237+4237*

RANSACKED See RIFLED

RANSOM (13) [RANSOMED]

Ex 21:30 he shall **give r** of his life *6306*
 30:12 shall they give every man a **r** for his soul *3724*
Job 33:24 going down *to* the pit: I have found a **r**. *3724*
 36:18 then a great **r** cannot deliver thee. *3724*
Ps 49: 7 *his* brother, nor give to God a **r** for him: *3724*
Pr 6:35 He will not regard any **r**; neither will he *3724*
 13: 8 The **r** of a man's life *are* his riches: *3724*
 21:18 The wicked *shall be* a **r** for the righteous, *3724*
Isa 43: 3 I gave Egypt *for* thy **r**, Ethiopia and *3724*
Hos 13:14 I will **r** them from the power of the grave; *6299*
Mt 20:28 and to give his life a **r** for many. *3083*
Mk 10:45 and to give his life a **r** for many. *3083*
1Ti 2: 6 Who gave himself a **r** for all, to be testified *487*

RANSOMED (3) [RANSOM]

Isa 35:10 the **r** of the LORD shall return, *6299*
 51:10 of the sea a way for the **r** to pass over? *1350*
Jer 31:11 **r** him from the hand of *him that was* *1350*

RAPHA (2) [BETH-RAPHA]

1Ch 8: 2 Nohah the fourth, and **R** the fifth. *7498*
 8:37 **R** *was* his son, Eleasah his son, Azel his *7498*

RAPHU (1)

Nu 13: 9 the tribe of Benjamin, Palti the son of **R**. *7505*

RARE (1)

Da 2:11 *it is* a **r** thing that the king requireth, *3358*

RASE (2)

Ps 137: 7 **R** *it*, rase *it*, *even* to the foundation *6168*
 137: 7 Rase *it*, **r** *it*, *even* to the foundation *6168*

RASH (2) [RASHLY]

Ecc 5: 2 Be not **r** with thy mouth, and let not thine *926*
Isa 32: 4 The heart also of the **r** shall understand *4116*

RASHLY (1) [RASH]

Ac 19:36 ye ought to be quiet, and to do nothing **r**. *4312*

RASOR (7)

Nu 6: 5 there shall no **r** come upon his head: *8593*
Jdg 13: 5 a son; and no **r** shall come on his head: *4177*
 16:17 There hath not come a **r** upon mine head; *4177*
1Sa 1:11 and there shall no **r** come upon his head. *4177*
Ps 52: 2 like a sharp **r**, working deceitfully. *8593*
Isa 7:20 shall the Lord shave with a **r** that is hired, *8593*
Eze 5: 1 take thee a barber's **r**, and cause *it* to pass *8593*

RAT See MOUSE

RATE (5)

Ex 16: 4 go out and gather a **certain r** every day, *1697*
1Ki 10:25 Horses, and mules, a **r** year by year. *1697*
2Ki 25:30 a daily **r** for every day, all the days of his *1697*
2Ch 8:13 Even after a **certain r** every day, offering *1697*
 9:24 horses, and mules, a **r** year by year. *1697*

RATHER (62)

Jos 22:24 if we have not **r** done it for fear of *this* NIH
2Sa 10: 3 not David **r** sent his servants unto thee, NIH
2Ki 5:13 thou not have done *it?* **how much r** then, 637
Job 7:15 and death **r** than my life. 4480
 32: 2 because he justified himself **r than** God. 4480
 36:21 for this hast thou chosen **r than** affliction. 4480

Ps 52: 3 *and* lying **r than** to speak righteousness. 4480
 84:10 I had **r** be a doorkeeper in the house of 977
Pr 8:10 and knowledge **r than** choice gold. 4480
 16:16 to get understanding, **r** than to be chosen 4480
 17:12 meet a man, **r** than a fool in his folly. 2050.1
 22: 1 A *good* name *is* **r** to be chosen **than** 4480
 22: 1 and loving favour **r** than silver and gold. 4480
Jer 8: 3 death shall be chosen **r** than life by all 4480
Mt 10: 6 But go **r** to the lost sheep of the house of 3123
 10:28 **r** fear him which is able to destroy both 3123
 18: 8 **r than** having two hands or two feet to be 2228
 18: 9 **r than** having two eyes to be cast into hell 2228
 25: 9 but go ye **r** to them that sell, and buy for 3123
 27:24 but *that* a tumult was made, he took 3123
Mk 5:26 was nothing bettered, but **r** grew worse, 3123
 15:11 that he should **r** release Barabbas unto 3123
Lk 10:20 but **r** rejoice, because your names are 3123
 11:28 he said, **Yea r**, blessed *are* they that 3304
 11:41 But **r** give alms *of* such *things* as you 4133
 12:31 But **r** seek ye the kingdom of God; 4133
 12:51 on earth? I tell you, Nay; but **r** division: 2228
 17: 8 And will not **r** say unto him, Make ready NIG
 18:14 man went down to his house justified **r** NIG
Jn 3:19 and men loved darkness **r** than light, 3123
Ac 5:29 said, We ought to obey God **r** than men. 3123
Ro 3: 8 not **r**, (as we be slanderously reported, NIG
 8:34 *It is* Christ that died, yea **r**, that is risen 3123
 11:11 **r** through their fall salvation *is come* unto NIG
 12:19 yourselves, but **r** give place unto wrath: NIG
 14:13 but judge this **r**, that no *man* put a 3123
1Co 5: 2 are puffed up, and have not **r** mourned, 3123
 6: 7 Why do ye not **r** take wrong? why do ye 3123
 6: 7 why do ye not **r** *suffer yourselves* to be 3123
 7:21 but if thou mayest be made free, use *it* **r**. 3123
 9:12 of *this* power over you, *are* not **we r**? 3123
 14: 1 spiritual *gifts*, but **r** that ye may prophesy. 3123
 14: 5 with tongues, but **r** that ye prophesied: 3123
 14:19 Yet in the church I **had r** speak five words 2309
2Co 2: 7 So that contrariwise ye *ought* **r** to forgive 3123
 3: 8 the ministration of the spirit be **r** glorious? 3123
 5: 8 and willing **r** to be absent from the body, 3123
 12: 9 therefore will I **r** glory in my infirmities, 3123
Gal 4: 9 or **r** are known of God, how turn ye again 3123
Eph 4:28 but **r** let him labour, working with *his* 3123
 5: 4 are not convenient: but **r** giving of thanks. 3123
 5:11 works of darkness, but **r** reprove *them*. 3123
Php 1:12 out **r** unto the furtherance of the gospel; 3123
1Ti 1: 4 **r** than godly edifying which is in faith: 3123
 4: 7 and exercise thyself **r** unto godliness. NIG
 6: 2 but **r** do *them* service, because they are 3123
Phm 1: 9 Yet for love's sake I **r** beseech *thee*, being 3123
Heb 11:25 Choosing **r** to suffer affliction with 3123
 12: 9 shall we not much **r** be in subjection unto 3123
 12:13 out of the way; but let it **r** be healed. 3123
 13:19 But I beseech *you* the **r** to do this, that I 4056
2Pe 1:10 Wherefore the **r**, brethren, give diligence 3123

RATS See MICE

RATTLE (1) [RATTLING]

Job 39:23 The quiver **r** against him, the glittering 7439

RATTLING (1) [RATTLETH]

Na 3: 2 the noise of the **r** of the wheels, and of 7494

RAVEN (6) [RAVENS]

Ge 8: 7 he sent forth a **r**, which went forth to and 6158
Lev 11:15 Every **r** after his kind, 6158
Dt 14:14 And every **r** after his kind, 6158
Job 38:41 Who provideth for the **r** his food? 6158
SS 5:11 his locks *are* bushy, *and* black as a **r**. 6158
Isa 34:11 the owl also and the **r** shall dwell in it: 6158

RAVENING (5) [RAVENOUS]

Ps 22:13 their mouths, *as* a **r** and a roaring lion. 2963
Eze 22:25 thereof, like a roaring lion **r** the prey; 2963
 22:27 midst thereof *are* like wolves **r** the prey, 2963
Mt 7:15 but inwardly they are **r** wolves. 727
Lk 11:39 but your inward part is full of **r** and 724

RAVENOUS (3) [RAVENING]

Isa 35: 9 nor *any* **r** beast shall go up thereon, 6530
 46:11 Calling a **r** bird from the east, the man 5861
Eze 39: 4 I will give thee unto the **r** birds of every 5861

RAVENS (5) [RAVEN]

1Ki 17: 4 have commanded the **r** to feed thee there. 6158
 17: 6 the **r** brought him bread and flesh in 6158
Ps 147: 9 his food, *and* to the young **r** which cry. 6158
Pr 30:17 the **r** of the valley shall pick it out, 6158
Lk 12:24 Consider the **r**: for they neither sow nor 2876

RAVIN (2)

Ge 49:27 Benjamin shall **r** *as* a wolf: in the morning 2963
Na 2:12 his holes **with** prey, and his dens **with r**. 2966

RAVINES See BROOKS

RAVISHED (5) [RAVISHT]

SS 4: 9 Thou hast **r** my **heart**, my sister, 3823
 4: 9 thou hast **r** my **heart** with one of thine 3823
Isa 13:16 houses shall be spoiled, and their wives **r**. 7901
La 5:11 They **r** the women in Zion, *and* the maids 6031
Zec 14: 2 and the houses rifled, and the women **r**; 7901

RAVISHT (2) [RAVISHED]

Pr 5:19 be thou **r** always with her love. 7686
 5:20 be **r** with a strange *woman*, and 7686

RAW (7)

Ex 12: 9 Eat not of it **r**, nor sodden at all with 4995
Lev 13:10 *there be* **quick r** flesh in the rising; 2416+4241
 13:14 when **r** flesh appeareth in him, he shall 2416
 13:15 the priest shall see the **r** flesh, 2416
 13:15 *for* the **r** flesh *is* unclean: it *is* a leprosy. 2416
 13:16 if the **r** flesh turn again, and be changed 2416
1Sa 2:15 will not have sodden flesh of thee, but **r**. 2416

RAZOR See RASOR

REACH (15) [REACHED, REACHETH, REACHING]

Ge 11: 4 a tower, whose top *may* **r** unto heaven; NIH
Ex 26:28 of the boards shall **r** from end to end. 1272
 28:42 the loins even unto the thighs they shall **r**: 1961
Lev 26: 5 your threshing shall **r** unto the vintage, 5381
 26: 5 the vintage shall **r** unto the sowing time: 5381
Nu 34:11 shall **r** unto the side of the sea of 4229
 35: 4 shall **r** from the wall of the city and NIH
Job 20: 6 heavens, and his head **r** unto the clouds; 5060
Isa 8: 8 and go over, he shall **r** *even* to the neck; 5060
 30:28 shall **r** to the midst of the neck, 5704
Jer 48:32 the sea, they **r** *even* to the sea of Jazer: 5060
Zec 14: 5 for the valley of the mountains shall **r** unto 5060
Jn 20:27 **R** hither thy finger, and behold my hands; 5342
 20:27 **r** *hither* thy hand, and thrust *it* into my 5342
2Co 10:13 to us, a measure to **r** even unto you. 2185

REACHED (8) [REACH]

Ge 28:12 the earth, and the top of it **r** to heaven: 5060
Jos 19:11 **r** to Dabbasheth, and reached to the river 6293
 19:11 and **r** to the river that *is* before Jokneam; 6293
Ru 2:14 he **r** her parched *corn*, and she did eat, 6642
Da 4:11 the height thereof **r** unto heaven, 4291
 4:20 whose height **r** unto the heaven, 4291
2Co 10:14 measure, as though we **r** not unto you: 2185
Rev 18: 5 For her sins have **r** unto heaven, and God 190

REACHETH (14) [REACH]

Nu 21:30 unto Nophah, which **r** unto Medeba. NIH
Jos 19:22 the coast **r** to Tabor, and Shahazimah, 6293
 19:26 **r** to Carmel westward, 6293
 19:27 **r** to Zebulun, and to the valley of 6293
 19:34 **r** to Zebulun on the south side, 6293
 19:34 **r** to Asher on the west side, and to Judah 5060
2Ch 28: 9 have slain them in a rage *that* **r** up unto 5060
Ps 36: 5 *and* thy faithfulness **r** unto the clouds. NIH
 108: 4 heavens: and thy truth **r** unto the clouds. NIH
Pr 31:20 yea, she **r forth** her hands to the needy. 7971
Jer 4:10 whereas the sword **r** unto the soul;) 5060
 4:18 *it is* bitter, because it **r** unto thine heart. 5060
 51: 9 for her judgment **r** unto heaven, 5060
Da 4:22 **r** unto heaven, and thy dominion to the 4291

REACHING (4) [REACH]

2Ch 3:11 five cubits, **r** to the wall of the house: 5060
 3:11 **r** to the wing of the other cherub. 5060
 3:12 *was* five cubits, **r** to the wall of the house: 5060
Php 3:13 **r** forth unto those *things which are* before 1901

READ (70) [READEST, READETH, READING]

Ex 24: 7 and **r** in the audience of the people: 7121
Dt 17:19 he shall **r** therein all the days of his life: 7121
 31:11 thou shalt **r** this law before all Israel in 7121
Jos 8:34 afterward he **r** all the words of the law, 7121
 8:34 which Joshua **r** not before all 7121
2Ki 5: 7 when the king of Israel had **r** the letter, 7121
 19:14 of the hand of the messengers, and **r** it: 7121
 22: 8 gave the book to Shaphan, and he **r** it. 7121
 22:10 a book. And Shaphan **r** it before the king. 7121
 22:16 the book which the king of Judah hath **r**: 7121
 23: 2 **r** in their ears all the words of the book 7121
2Ch 34:18 a book. And Shaphan **r** it before the king. 7121
 34:24 they have **r** before the king of Judah: 7121
 34:30 **r** in their ears all the words of the book 7121
Ezr 4:18 unto us *hath been* plainly **r** before me. 7123
 4:23 Artaxerxes' letter *was* **r** before Rehum, 7123
Ne 8: 3 he **r** therein before the street that *was* 7121
 8: 8 So they **r** in the book in the law of God 7121
 8:18 day, he **r** in the book of the law of God. 7121
 9: 3 **r** in the book of the law of the LORD their 7121
 13: 1 On that day they **r** in the book of Moses 7121
Est 6: 1 and they were **r** before the king. 7121
Isa 29:11 that is learned, saying, **R** this, I pray thee: 7121
 29:12 is not learned, saying, **R** this, I pray thee: 7121
 34:16 ye out of the book of the LORD, and **r**: 7121
Jer 29:29 Zephaniah the priest **r** this letter in the 7121
 36: 6 Therefore go thou, and **r** in the roll, 7121
 36: 6 also thou shalt **r** them in the ears of all 7121
 36:10 **r** Baruch in the book the words of 7121
 36:13 when Baruch **r** the book in the ears of 7121
 36:14 thou hast **r** in the ears of the people, 7121
 36:15 Sit down now, and **r** it in our ears. 7121
 36:15 it in our ears. So Baruch **r** *it* in their ears. 7121
 36:21 Jehudi **r** it in the ears of the king, and in 7121
 36:23 when Jehudi had **r** three or four leaves, 7121
 51:61 and shalt **r** all these words; 7121
Da 5: 7 Whosoever shall **r** this writing, 7123
 5: 8 men: but they could not **r** the writing, 7123
 5:15 that they should **r** this writing, 7123

R

Da	5:16 now if thou canst **r** the writing,	7123
	5:17 yet I will **r** the writing unto the king,	7123
Mt	12: 3 them, Have ye not **r** what David did,	314
	12: 5 Or have ye not **r** in the law, how that on	314
	19: 4 and said unto them, Have ye not **r**,	314
	21:16 ye never **r**, Out of the mouth of babes	314
	21:42 then, Did ye never **r** in the scriptures,	314
	22:31 have ye not **r** that which was spoken unto	314
Mk	2:25 have ye never **r** what David did, when he	314
	12:10 And have ye not **r** this scripture; The stone	314
	12:26 have ye not **r** in the book of Moses, how	314
Lk	4:16 on the sabbath day, and stood up for to **r**.	314
	6: 3 Have ye not **r** so much as this, what David	314
Jn	19:20 This title then **r** many of the Jews:	314
Ac	8:28 sitting in his chariot **r** Esaias the prophet.	314
	8:30 him, and heard him **r** the prophet Esaias,	314
	8:32 The place of the scripture which he **r** was	314
	13:27 yet the voices of the prophets which are **r**	314
	15:21 **r** in the synagogues every sabbath day.	314
	15:31 Which when they had **r**, they rejoiced for	314
	23:34 And when the governor had **r** the letter,	314
2Co	1:13 you, than what you **r** or acknowledge;	314
	3: 2 in our hearts, known and **r** of all men:	314
	3:15 But even unto this day, when Moses is **r**,	314
Eph	3: 4 Whereby, when ye **r**, ye may understand	314
Col	4:16 And when this epistle is **r** amongst you,	314
	4:16 cause that it be **r** also in the church of	314
	4:16 ye likewise **r** the epistle from Laodicea.	314
1Th	5:27 this epistle be **r** unto all the holy brethren.	314
Rev	5: 4 found worthy to open and to **r** the book,	314

READEST (2) [READ]

Lk	10:26 What is written in the law? how **r** thou?	314
Ac	8:30 and said, Understandest thou what thou **r**?	314

READETH (4) [READ]

Hab	2: 2 upon tables, that he may run that **r** it.	7121
Mt	24:15 holy place, (whoso **r**, let him understand:)	314
Mk	13:14 it ought not, (let him that **r** understand,)	314
Rev	1: 3 Blessed is he that **r**, and they that hear	314

READINESS (3) [READY]

Ac	17:11 received the word with all **r of mind**,	4288
2Co	8:11 the doing of it; that as there was a **r**	4288
	10: 6 And having in a **r** to revenge all	2092

READING (6) [READ]

Ne	8: 8 and caused them to understand the **r**.	4744
Jer	36: 8 **r** in the book the words of the LORD in	7121
	51:63 thou hast made an end of **r** this book,	7121
Ac	13:15 after the **r** of the law and the prophets	320
2Co	3:14 untaken away in the **r** of the old testament;	320
1Ti	4:13 Till I come, give attendance to **r**,	320

READY (100) [ALREADY, READINESS]

Ge	18: 6 Make **r quickly** three measures of fine	4116
	43:16 these men home, and slay, and make **r**;	3559
	43:25 they made **r** the present against Joseph	3559
	46:29 Joseph made **r** his chariot, and went up	631
Ex	14: 6 he made **r** his chariot, and took his	631
	17: 4 this people? they be almost **r** to stone me.	NIH
	19:11 be **r** against the third day: for the third	3559
	19:15 the people, Be **r** against the third day:	3559
	34: 2 be **r** in the morning, and come up in	3559
Nu	32:17 we ourselves will go **r** armed before	2363
Dt	1:41 of war, ye were **r** to go up unto the hill.	1951
	26: 5 A Syrian **r** to perish was my father,	6
Jos	8: 4 not very far from the city, but be ye all **r**:	3559
Jdg	6:19 made **r** a kid, and unleavened cakes of an	6213
	13:15 until we shall have made **r** a kid for thee.	6213
1Sa	25:18 five sheep **r dressed**, and five measures	6213
2Sa	15:15 servants are **r** to do whatsoever my lord	4672
	18:22 son, seeing that thou hast no tidings **r**?	4672
1Ki	6: 7 was built of stone made **r before** it was	8003
2Ki	9:21 Joram said, Make **r**. And his chariot was	631
	9:21 his chariot was made **r**. And Joram king	631
1Ch	12:23 the bands that were **r armed** to the war,	2502
	12:24 and eight hundred, **r armed** to the war.	2502
	28: 2 God, and had made **r** for the building:	3559
2Ch	17:18 thousand **r prepared for** the war.	2502
	35:14 afterward they made **r** for themselves,	3559
Ezr	7: 6 he was a **r** scribe in the law of Moses,	4106
Ne	9:17 thou art a God **r to pardon**, gracious and	5547
Est	3:14 that they should be **r** against that day.	6264
	8:13 that the Jews should be **r** against that day	6264
Job	3: 8 who are **r** to raise up their mourning.	6264
	12: 5 that is **r** to slip with his feet is as a lamp	3559
	15:23 that the day of darkness is **r** at his hand.	3559
	15:24 against him, as a king **r** to the battle.	6264
	15:28 which are **r to become** heaps.	6257
	17: 1 days are extinct, the graves are **r** for me.	NIH
	18:12 and destruction shall be **r** at his side.	3559
	29:13 The blessing of him that was **r to perish**	6
	32:19 no vent; it is **r to burst** like new bottles.	1234
Ps	7:12 he hath bent his bow, and made it **r**.	3559
	11: 2 they make **r** their arrow upon the string,	3559
	21:12 thou shalt make **r** thine arrows upon	3559
	38:17 For I am **r** to halt, and my sorrow is	3559
	45: 1 king: my tongue is the pen of a **r** writer.	4106
	86: 5 For thou, Lord, art good, and **r to forgive**;	5546
	88:15 I am **r to die** from my youth up: while I suffer	1478
Pr	24:11 death, and those that are **r** to be slain;	4131
	31: 6 strong drink unto him that is **r to perish**,	6
Ecc	5: 1 more **r** to hear, than to give the sacrifice	7138
Isa	27:13 they shall come which were **r** to perish in	NIH

Isa	30:13 iniquity shall be to you as a breach **r** to fall	NIH
	32: 4 the tongue of the stammerers shall be **r** to	4116
	38:20 The LORD was **r** to save me: therefore	NIH
	41: 7 the anvil, saying, It is **r** for the sodering:	2896
	51:13 the oppressor, as if he were **r** to destroy?	6263
Eze	7:14 blown the trumpet, even to **make** all **r**;	3559
Da	3:15 Now if ye be **r** that at what time ye hear	6263
Hos	7: 6 For they have **made r** their heart like an	7126
Mt	22: 4 my fatlings are killed, and all things are **r**:	2092
	22: 8 The wedding is **r**, but they which were	2092
	24:44 Therefore be ye also **r**: for in such an hour	2092
	25:10 they that were **r** went in with him to	2092
	26:19 and they **made r** the passover.	2090
Mk	14:15 and prepared: there **make r** for us.	2090
	14:16 unto them: and they **made r** the passover.	2090
	14:38 The spirit truly is **r**, but the flesh is weak.	4289
Lk	1:17 to **make r** a people prepared for the Lord.	2090
	7: 2 was dear unto him, was sick, and **r** to die.	3195
	9:52 of the Samaritans, to **make r** for him.	2090
	12:40 Be ye therefore **r** also: for the Son of man	2092
	14:17 Come; for all things are now **r**.	2092
	17: 8 **Make r** wherewith I may sup,	2090
	22:12 upper room furnished: there **make r**.	2090
	22:13 them: and they **made r** the passover.	2090
	22:33 Lord, I am **r** to go with thee, both into	2092
Jn	7: 6 is not yet come: but your time is alway **r**.	2092
Ac	10:10 while they **made r**, he fell into a trance,	3903
	20: 7 unto them, **r** to depart on the morrow;	3195
	21:13 for I am **r** not to be bound only, but also	2093
	23: 6 or ever he come near, are **r** to kill him.	2092
	23:21 and now are they **r**, looking for a promise	2092
	23:23 **Make r** two hundred soldiers to go to	2090
Ro	1:15 I am **r** to preach the gospel to you that are	4289
2Co	8:19 Lord, and declaration of your **r mind**:	4288
	9: 2 that Achaia was **r** a year ago;	3903
	9: 3 in this behalf; that, as I said, ye may be **r**:	3903
	9: 5 that the same might be **r**, as a matter of	2092
	10:16 line of things **made r** to our hand.	1519+2092
	12:14 the third time I am **r** to come to you;	2093
	6:18 **r to distribute**, willing to communicate;	2130
2Ti	4: 6 I am **now r** to be offered, and the time	2235
Tit	3: 1 to be **r** to every good work,	2092
Heb	8:13 and waxeth old is **r** to vanish away.	1451
1Pe	1: 5 salvation **r** to be revealed in the last time.	2092
	3:15 be **r** always to give an answer to every	2092
	4: 5 Who shall give account to him that is **r** to	2093
	5: 2 not for filthy lucre, but of a **r mind**;	4290
Rev	3: 2 things which remain, that are **r to die**:	3195
	12: 4 the woman which was **r** to be delivered,	3195
	19: 7 come, and his wife hath **made** herself **r**.	2090

REAIA (1)

1Ch	5: 5 Micah his son, **R** his son, Baal his son,	7211

REAIAH (3)

1Ch	4: 2 **R** the son of Shobal begat Jahath;	7211
Ezr	2:47 the children of Gahar, the children of **R**,	7211
Ne	7:50 The children of **R**, the children of Rezin,	7211

REALIZE See WIST

REALLY See SURETY; THROUGHLY

REALM (7)

2Ch	20:30 So the **r** of Jehoshaphat was quiet: for his	4438
Ezr	7:13 and of his priests and Levites, in my **r**,	4437
	7:23 why should there be wrath against the **r**	4437
Da	1:20 and astrologers that were in all his **r**.	4438
	6: 3 king thought to set him over the whole **r**.	4437
	9: 1 which was made king over the **r** of	4438
	11: 2 he shall stir up all against the **r** of Grecia.	4438

REAP (32) [REAPED, REAPER, REAPERS, REAPEST, REAPETH, REAPING]

Lev	19: 9 when ye **r** the harvest of your land,	7114
	19: 9 not **wholly r** the corners	3615+3807.1+7114
	23:10 shall **r** the harvest thereof, then ye shall	7114
	23:22 when ye **r** the harvest of thy land,	7114
	25: 5 accord of thy harvest thou shalt not **r**,	7114
	25:11 neither **r** that which groweth of itself in it,	7114
Ru	2: 9 thine eyes be on the field that they do **r**,	7114
1Sa	8:12 to **r** his harvest, and to make his	7114
2Ki	19:29 **r**, and plant vineyards, and eat the fruits	7114
Job	4: 8 and sow wickedness, **r** the same.	7114
	24: 6 They **r** every one his corn in the field:	7114
Ps	126: 5 They that sow in tears shall **r** in joy.	7114
Pr	22: 8 He that soweth iniquity shall **r** vanity:	7114
Ecc	11: 4 he that regardeth the clouds shall not **r**.	7114
Isa	37:30 **r**, and plant vineyards, and eat the fruit	7114
Jer	12:13 have sown wheat, but shall **r** thorns:	7114
Hos	8: 7 the wind, and they shall **r** the whirlwind:	7114
	10:12 to yourselves in righteousness, **r** in mercy;	7114
Mic	6:15 Thou shalt sow, but thou shalt not **r**;	7114
Mt	6:26 for they sow not, neither do they **r**,	2325
	25:26 thou knewest that I **r** where I sowed not,	2325
Lk	12:24 for they neither sow nor **r**; which neither	2325
Jn	4:38 I sent you to **r** that whereon ye bestowed	2325
1Co	9:11 thing if we shall **r** your carnal things?	2325
2Co	9: 6 soweth sparingly shall **r** also sparingly;	2325
	9: 6 he which soweth bountifully shall **r** also	2325
Gal	6: 7 a man soweth, that shall he also **r**.	2325
	6: 8 his flesh shall of the flesh **r** corruption;	2325
	6: 8 Spirit shall of the Spirit **r** life everlasting.	2325
	6: 9 in due season we shall **r**, if we faint not.	2325
Rev	14:15 on the cloud, Thrust in thy sickle, and **r**:	2325
	14:15 for the time is come for thee to **r**;	2325

REAPED (4) [REAP]

Hos	10:13 plowed wickedness, ye have **r** iniquity;	7114
Jas	5: 4 hire of the labourers which have **r down**	270
	5: 4 cries of them which have **r** are entered	2325
Rev	14:16 sickle on the earth; and the earth was **r**.	2325

REAPER (1) [REAP]

Am	9:13 that the plowman shall overtake the **r**,	7114

REAPERS (9) [REAP]

Ru	2: 3 came, and gleaned in the field after the **r**:	7114
	2: 4 said unto the **r**, The LORD be with you.	7114
	2: 5 unto his servant that was set over the **r**,	7114
	2: 6 servant that was set over the **r** answered	7114
	2: 7 gather after the **r** amongst the sheaves:	7114
	2:14 she sat beside the **r**: and he reached her	7114
2Ki	4:18 that he went out to his father to the **r**.	7114
Mt	13:30 in the time of harvest I will say to the **r**,	2327
	13:39 end of the world; and the **r** are the angels.	2327

REAPEST (2) [REAP]

Lev	23:22 of the corners of thy field when thou **r**,	7114
Lk	19:21 not down, and **r** that thou didst not sow.	2325

REAPETH (4) [REAP]

Isa	17: 5 the corn, and **r** the ears with his arm;	7114
Jn	4:36 And he that **r** receiveth wages,	2325
	4:36 and he that **r** may rejoice together.	2325
	4:37 saying true, One soweth, and another **r**.	2325

REAPING (3) [REAP]

1Sa	6:13 they of Beth-shemesh were **r** their wheat	7114
Mt	25:24 **r** where thou hast not sown,	2325
Lk	19:22 I laid not down, and **r** that I did not sow:	2325

REAR (4) [REARED]

Ex	26:30 thou shalt **r up** the tabernacle according	6965
Lev	26: 1 neither **r** you **up** a standing image,	6965
2Sa	24:18 **r** an altar unto the LORD in	6965
Jn	2:20 and wilt thou **r** it **up** in three days?	1453

REAR GUARD See REREWARD

REARED (10) [REAR]

Ex	40:17 the month, that the tabernacle was **r up**.	6965
	40:18 Moses **r up** the tabernacle, and fastened	6965
	40:18 in the bars thereof, and **r up** his pillars.	6965
	40:33 he **r up** the court round about	6965
Nu	9:15 on the day that the tabernacle was **r up**,	6965
2Sa	18:18 had taken and **r up** for himself a pillar,	5324
1Ki	16:32 he **r up** an altar for Baal in the house of	6965
2Ki	21: 3 he **r up** altars for Baal, and made a grove,	6965
2Ch	3:17 he **r up** the pillars before the temple,	6965
	33: 3 **r up** altars for Baalim, and made groves,	6965

REASON (71) [REASONABLE, REASONED, REASONING, REASONS, UNREASONABLE]

Ge	41:31 land **by r of** that famine following;	4480+6440
	47:13 the land of Canaan fainted **by r of**	4480+6440
Ex	2:23 the children of Israel sighed **by r of**	4480
	2:23 their cry came up unto God **by r of**	4480
	3: 7 have heard their cry **by r of** their	4480+6440
	8:24 the land was corrupted **by r of**	4480+6440
Nu	9:10 your posterity shall be unclean **by r of**	3807.1
	18: 8 unto thee have I given them **by r of**	3807.1
	18:32 ye shall bear no sin **by r of** it, when ye	5921
Dt	5: 5 for ye were afraid **by r of** the fire,	4480+6440
	23:10 that is not clean **by r of uncleanness** that	4480
Jos	9:13 our shoes are become old **by r of** the very	4480
Jdg	2:18 of their groanings **by r of** them that	4480
1Sa	12: 7 that I may **r** with you before the LORD of	8199
1Ki	9:15 this is the **r** of the levy which king	1697
	14: 4 for his eyes were set **by r of** his age.	4480
2Ch	5:14 stand to minister **by r of** the cloud;	4480+6440
	20:15 Be not afraid nor dismayed **by r of**	4480+6440
	21:15 until thy bowels fall out **by r of**	4480
	21:19 his bowels fell out **by r of** his sickness.	5973
Job	6:16 Which are blackish **by r of** the ice,	4480
	9:14 and choose out my words to **r** with him?	NIH
	13: 3 the Almighty, and I desire to **r** with God.	3198
	15: 3 Should he **r with** unprofitable talk?	3198
	17: 7 Mine eye also is dim **by r of** sorrow,	4480
	31:23 **by r of** his highness I could not endure.	4480
	35: 9 **By r of** the multitude of oppressions they	4480
	35: 9 cry out **by r of** the arm of the mighty.	4480
	37:19 order our speech **by r of** darkness.	4480+6440
	41:25 **by r of** breakings they purify themselves.	4480
Ps	38: 8 I have roared **by r of** the disquietness of	4480
	44:16 blasphemeth; **by r of** the enemy	4480+6440
	78:65 like a mighty man that shouteth **by r of**	4480
	88: 9 Mine eye mourneth **by r of** affliction:	4480
	90:10 **by r of** strength they be fourscore years,	871.1
	102: 5 **By r of** the voice of my groaning my	4480
Pr	20: 4 The sluggard will not plow **by r of**	4480
	26:16 than seven men that can render a **r**.	2940
Ecc	7:25 **r of things**, and to know the wickedness	2808
Isa	1:18 Come now, and let us **r together**, saith	3198
	49:19 shall even now be too narrow **by r of**	4480
Eze	19:10 and full of branches **by r of** many waters.	4480
	21:12 terrors **by r of** the sword shall be upon	413
	26:10 **By r of** the abundance of his horses their	4480
	27:12 Tarshish was thy merchant **by r of**	4480
	27:16 Syria was thy merchant **by r of**	4480
	28:17 hast corrupted thy wisdom **by r of** thy	5921
Da	4:36 At the same time my **r** returned unto me;	4486

Da	5:10 by **r** of the words of the king and his lords,	6903
	8:12 the daily *sacrifice* **by r** of transgression,	871.1
Jnh	2: 2 I cried **by r** of mine affliction unto	4480
Mic	2:12 they shall make great noise **by r** of	4480
Mt	16: 8 why **r** ye among yourselves, because	1260
Mk	2: 8 Why **r** ye these *things* in your hearts?	1260
	8:17 Why **r** ye, because ye have no bread?	1260
Lk	5:21 the scribes and the Pharisees began to **r**,	1260
	5:22 said unto them, What **r** ye in your hearts?	1260
Jn	6:18 And the sea arose **by r** of a great wind that	NIG
	12:11 **Because** that **by r** of him many of the	1223
Ac	6: 2 It is not **r** that we should leave the word of	701
	18:14 **r** would that I should bear with you	2596+3056
Ro	8:20 **by r** of him who hath subjected the *same,*	1223
2Co	3:10 respect, **by r** of the glory that excelleth.	1752
Heb	5: 3 And **by r** hereof he ought, as for	1223+3778
	5:14 *even* those who **by r** of use have their	1223
	7:23 suffered to continue **by r** of death:	1223+3588
1Pe	3:15 a **r** of the hope that is in you with	3056
2Pe	2: 2 **by r** of whom the way of truth shall be	1223
Rev	8:13 to the inhabiters of the earth **by r** of	1537
	9: 2 the air were darkened **by r** of the smoke	1537
	18:19 had ships in the sea **by r** of her costliness:	1537

REASONABLE (1) [REASON]

Ro	12: 1 unto God, *which is* your **r** service.	3050

REASONED (12) [REASON]

Mt	16: 7 they **r** among themselves, saying,	1260
	21:25 And they **r** with themselves, saying, If we	1260
Mk	2: 8 his spirit that they so **r** within themselves,	1260
	8:16 And they **r** among themselves, saying,	1260
	11:31 And they **r** with themselves, saying, If we	3049
Lk	20: 5 And they **r** with themselves, saying, If we	4817
	20:14 they **r** among themselves, saying, This is	1260
	24:15 while they communed *together* and **r**,	4802
Ac	17: 2 three sabbath days **r** with them out of	1256
	18: 4 And he **r** in the synagogue every sabbath,	1256
	18:19 into the synagogue, and **r** with the Jews.	1256
	24:25 And as he **r** of righteousness, temperance,	1256

REASONING (5) [REASON]

Job	13: 6 Hear now my **r**, and hearken to	8433
Mk	2: 6 scribes sitting there, and **r** in their hearts,	1260
	12:28 and having heard their **r** **together**,	4802
Lk	9:46 Then there arose a **r** among them, which	1261
Ac	28:29 and had great **r** among themselves.	4803

REASONS (2) [REASON]

Job	32:11 I gave ear to your **r**, whilst you searched	8394
Isa	41:21 bring forth your strong **r**, saith the King of	NIH

REBA (2)

Nu	31: 8 and Rekem, and Zur, and Hur, and **R**,	7254
Jos	13:21 and Rekem, and Zur, and Hur, and **R**,	7254

REBECCA (1) [REBEKAH]

Ro	9:10 but when **R** also had conceived by one,	4479

REBEKAH (28) [REBECCA, REBEKAH'S]

Ge	22:23 Bethuel begat **R**: these eight Milcah did	7259
	24:15 behold, **R** came out, who was born to	7259
	24:29 **R** had a brother, and his name *was* Laban:	7259
	24:30 when he heard the words of **R** his sister,	7259
	24:45 **R** came forth with her pitcher on her	7259
	24:51 Behold, **R** *is* before thee, take *her,* and go,	7259
	24:53 of gold, and raiment, and gave *them* to **R**:	7259
	24:58 they called **R**, and said unto her, Wilt	7259
	24:59 sent away **R** their sister, and her nurse,	7259
	24:60 they blessed **R**, and said unto her, Thou	7259
	24:61 **R** arose, and her damsels, and they rode	7259
	24:61 the servant took **R**, and went his way.	7259
	24:64 **R** lift up her eyes, and when she saw	7259
	24:67 and took **R**, and she became his wife;	7259
	25:20 Isaac was forty years old when he took **R**	7259
	25:21 of him, and **R** his wife conceived.	7259
	25:28 did eat of *his* venison: but **R** loved Jacob.	7259
	26: 7 the men of the place should kill me for **R**;	7259
	26: 8 Isaac *was* sporting with **R** his wife.	7259
	26:35 were a grief of mind unto Isaac and to **R**.	7259
	27: 5 **R** heard when Isaac spake to Esau his son.	7259
	27: 6 **R** spake unto Jacob her son, saying,	7259
	27:11 Jacob said to **R** his mother, Behold,	7259
	27:15 **R** took goodly raiment of her eldest son	7259
	27:42 of Esau her elder son were told to **R**:	7259
	27:46 **R** said to Isaac, I am weary of my life	7259
	28: 5 the brother of **R**, Jacob's and	7259
	49:31 there they buried Isaac and **R** his wife;	7259

REBEKAH'S (2) [REBEKAH]

Ge	29:12 father's brother, and that he *was* **R** son:	7259
	35: 8 Deborah **R** nurse died, and she was	7259

REBEL (14) [REBELLED, REBELLEST, REBELLION, REBELLIOUS, REBELS]

Nu	14: 9 Only **r** not ye against the LORD,	4775
Jos	1:18 Whosoever *he be* that doth **r** against thy	4784
	22:16 that ye might **r** *this* day against the LORD,	4775
	22:18 *seeing* ye turn **r** against the LORD,	4775
	22:19 **r** not against the LORD, nor rebel against	4775
	22:19 not against the LORD, nor **r** against us,	4775
	22:29 God forbid that we should **r** against	4775
1Sa	12:14 not **r** against the commandment of the LORD,	4784
Ne	2:19 that ye do? will ye **r** against the king?	4775
	6: 6 saith *it, that* thou and the Jews mean to **r**:	4775

Job	24:13 They are of those that **r** against the light;	4775
Isa	1:20 if ye refuse and **r**, ye shall be devoured	4784
Hos	7:14 for corn and wine, *and* they **r** against me.	5493

REBELLED (34) [REBEL]

Ge	14: 4 and *in* the thirteenth year they **r**.	4775
Nu	20:24 ye **r** against my word at the water of	4784
	27:14 For ye **r against** my commandment in	4784
Dt	1:26 **r** against the commandment of the LORD	4784
	1:43 **r** against the commandment of the LORD,	4784
	9:23 you **r** against the commandment of	4784
1Ki	12:19 Israel **r** against the house of David unto	6586
2Ki	1: 1 Moab **r** against Israel after the death of	6586
	3: 5 the king of Moab **r** against the king of	6586
	3: 7 The king of Moab hath **r** against me:	6586
	18: 7 he **r** against the king of Assyria,	4775
	24: 1 then he turned and **r** against him.	4775
	24:20 that Zedekiah **r** against the king of	4775
2Ch	10:19 Israel **r** against the house of David unto	6586
	13: 6 is risen up, and hath **r** against his lord.	4775
	36:13 he also **r** against king Nebuchadnezzar,	4775
Ne	9:26 **r** against thee, and cast thy law behind	4784
Ps	5:10 for they have **r** against thee.	4784
	105:28 it dark; and they **r** not against his word.	4784
	107:11 Because they **r** against the words of God,	4784
Isa	1: 2 up children, and they have **r** against me.	6586
	63:10 they **r**, and vexed his holy Spirit:	4784
Jer	52: 3 that Zedekiah **r** against the king of	4775
La	1:18 for I have **r** against his commandment:	4784
	1:20 within me; for I have **grievously r**:	4784+4784
	3:42 We have transgressed and have **r**: thou	4775
Eze	2: 3 to a rebellious nation that hath **r** against	4775
	17:15 he **r** against him in sending his	4775
	20: 8 they **r** against me, and would not hearken	4784
	20:13 the house of Israel **r** against me in	4784
	20:21 Notwithstanding the children **r** against	4784
Da	9: 5 and have done wickedly, and have **r**,	4775
	9: 9 though we have **r** against him;	4775
Hos	13:16 for she hath **r** against her God:	4784

REBELLEST (2) [REBEL]

2Ki	18:20 dost thou trust, that thou **r** against me?	4775
Isa	36: 5 dost thou trust, that thou **r** against me?	4775

REBELLION (9) [REBEL]

Dt	31:27 For I know thy **r**, and thy stiff neck:	4805
Jos	22:22 if *it be* in **r**, or if in transgression against	4777
1Sa	15:23 For **r** *is as* the sin of witchcraft,	4805
Ezr	4:19 **r** and sedition *have* been made therein.	4776
Ne	9:17 in their *r* appointed a captain to return to	4805
Job	34:37 For he addeth **r** unto his sin, he clappeth	6588
Pr	17:11 An evil *man* seeketh only **r**: therefore	4805
Jer	28:16 thou hast taught **r** against the LORD.	5627
	29:32 he hath taught **r** against the LORD.	5627

REBELLIOUS (36) [REBEL]

Dt	9: 7 ye have been **r** against the LORD.	4784
	9:24 You have been **r** against the LORD from	4784
	21:18 If a man have a stubborn and **r** son,	4784
	21:20 our son *is* stubborn and **r**, he will not	4784
	21:20 your son is stubborn and **r**;	4784
	31:27 ye have been **r** against the LORD;	4805
1Sa	20:30 Thou son of the perverse **r** *woman,* do	4780
Ezr	4:12 building the **r** and the bad city, and have	4779
	4:15 know that this city *is a* **r** city,	4779
Ps	66: 7 let not the **r** exalt themselves. Selah.	5637
	68: 6 chains: but the **r** dwell *in* a dry *land.*	5637
	68:18 yea, *for* the **r** also, that the LORD God	5637
	78: 8 their fathers, a stubborn and **r** generation;	4784
Isa	1:23 Thy princes *are* **r**, and companions of	5637
	30: 1 Woe to the **r** children, saith the LORD,	5637
	30: 9 That this *is* a **r** people, lying children,	4805
	50: 5 I was not **r**, neither turned away back.	4784
	65: 2 mine hands all the day unto a **r** people,	5637
Jer	4:17 because she hath been **r** against me,	4784
	5:23 this people hath a revolting and a **r** heart;	4784
Eze	2: 3 a **r** nation that hath rebelled against me:	4775
	2: 5 they will forbear, (for they *are* a **r** house,)	4805
	2: 6 at their looks, though they *be* a **r** house,	4805
	2: 7 they will forbear: for they *are* most **r**.	4805
	2: 8 Be not thou **r** like *that* rebellious house:	4805
	2: 8 Be not thou rebellious like *that* **r** house:	4805
	3: 9 at their looks, though they *be* a **r** house,	4805
	3:26 to them a reprover: for they *are* a **r** house.	4805
	3:27 let him forbear: for they *are* a **r** house.	4805
	12: 2 thou dwellest in the midst of a **r** house,	4805
	12: 2 hear, and hear not: for they *are* a **r** house.	4805
	12: 3 will consider, though they *be* a **r** house.	4805
	12: 9 the **r** house, said unto thee, What doest	4805
	12:25 for in your days, O **r** house, will I say	4805
	17:12 Say now to the **r** house, Know ye not	4805
	24: 3 utter a parable unto the **r** house,	4805
	44: 6 thou shalt say to the **r**, *even* to the house	4805

REBELS (3) [REBEL]

Nu	17:10 to be kept for a token against the **r**;	1121+4805
	20:10 and he said unto them, Hear now, ye **r**;	4784
Eze	20:38 I will purge out from among you the **r**,	4775

REBIRTH See REGENERATION

REBUKE (46) [REBUKED, REBUKER, REBUKES, REBUKETH, REBUKING, UNREBUKEABLE]

Lev	19:17 thou shalt **in any wise r** thy	3198+3198
Dt	28:20 send upon thee cursing, vexation, and **r**,	4045
Ru	2:16 that she may glean *them,* and **r** her not.	1605
2Ki	19: 3 a day of trouble, and of **r**, and blasphemy:	8433

1Ch	12:17 God of our fathers look *thereon,* and **r** *it.*	3198
Ps	6: 1 O LORD, **r** me not in thine anger,	3198
	18:15 of the world were discovered at thy **r**,	1606
	38: 1 O LORD, **r** me not in thy wrath:	3198
	68:30 **R** the company of spearmen, the	1605
	76: 6 At thy **r**, O God of Jacob, both the chariot	1606
	80:16 they perish at the **r** of thy countenance.	1606
	104: 7 At thy **r** they fled; at the voice of thy	1606
Pr	9: 8 a wise *man,* and he will love thee.	3198
	13: 1 but a scorner heareth not **r**.	1606
	13: 8 *are* his riches: but the poor heareth not **r**.	1606
	24:25 to them that **r** *him* shall be delight,	3198
	27: 5 Open *is* better than secret love.	8433
Ecc	7: 5 *It is* better to hear the **r** of the wise, than	1606
Isa	2: 4 the nations, and shall **r** many people:	3198
	17:13 *God* shall **r** them, and they shall flee far	1605
	25: 8 the **r** of his people shall he take away	2781
	30:17 One thousand *shall flee* at the **r** of one;	1606
	30:17 rebuke of one; at the **r** of five shall ye flee:	1606
	37: 3 of trouble, and of **r**, and of blasphemy:	8433
	50: 2 behold, at my **r** I dry up the sea, I make	1606
	51:20 *of* the fury of the LORD, the **r** of thy God.	1606
	54: 9 not be wroth with thee, nor **r** thee.	1605
	66:15 with fury, and his **r** with flames of fire.	1606
Jer	15:15 know that for thy sake I have suffered **r**.	2781
Hos	5: 9 Ephraim shall be desolate in the day of **r**:	8433
Mic	4: 3 many people, and **r** strong nations afar off;	3198
Zec	3: 2 unto Satan, The LORD **r** thee, O Satan;	1605
	3: 2 LORD that hath chosen Jerusalem **r** thee:	1605
Mal	3:11 I will **r** the devourer for your sakes,	1605
Mt	16:22 and began to **r** him, saying, Be it far from	2008
Mk	8:32 And Peter took him, and began to **r** him.	2008
Lk	17: 3 If thy brother trespass against thee, **r** him;	2008
	19:39 said unto him, Master, **r** thy disciples.	2008
Php	2:15 and harmless, the sons of God **without r**,	298
1Ti	5: 1 **R** not an elder, but intreat *him* as a father;	1969
	5:20 Them that sin **r** before all, that others also	1651
2Ti	4: 2 reprove, **r**, exhort with all longsuffering	2008
Tit	1:13 Wherefore **r** them sharply, that they may	1651
	2:15 and exhort, and **r** with all authority.	1651
Jude	1: 9 but said, The Lord **r** thee.	2008
Rev	3:19 As many as I love, I **r** and chasten:	1651

REBUKED (25) [REBUKE]

Ge	31:42 of my hands, and **r** *thee* yesternight.	3198
	37:10 his father **r** him, and said unto him, What	1605
Ne	5: 7 I **r** the nobles, and the rulers, and said	7378
Ps	9: 5 Thou hast **r** the heathen, thou hast	1605
	106: 9 he **r** the Red sea also, and it was dried up:	1605
	119:21 Thou hast **r** the proud *that are* cursed,	1605
Mt	8:26 he arose, and **r** the winds and the sea,	2008
	17:18 And Jesus **r** the devil; and he departed out	2008
	19:13 and pray: and the disciples **r** them.	2008
	20:31 And the multitude **r** them, because	2008
Mk	1:25 And Jesus **r** him, saying, Hold thy peace,	2008
	4:39 and the wind, and said unto the sea,	2008
	8:33 he **r** Peter, saying, Get thee behind me,	2008
	9:25 he **r** the foul spirit, saying unto him,	2008
	10:13 *his* disciples **r** those that brought *them,*	2008
Lk	4:35 And Jesus **r** him, saying, Hold thy peace,	2008
	4:39 And he stood over her, and **r** the fever;	2008
	8:24 the wind and the raging of the water:	2008
	9:42 tare *him.* And Jesus **r** the unclean spirit,	2008
	9:55 But he turned, and **r** them, and said,	2008
	18:15 when *his* disciples saw *it,* they **r** them.	2008
	18:39 they which went before **r** him, that he	2008
	23:40 the other answering **r** him, saying, Dost	2008
Heb	12: 5 faint when thou art **r** of him:	1651
2Pe	2:16 But was **r** for his iniquity: the dumb ass	1649

REBUKER (1) [REBUKE]

Hos	5: 2 though I *have* been a **r** of them all.	4148

REBUKES (3) [REBUKE]

Ps	39:11 When thou with **r** dost correct man for	8433
Eze	5:15 thee in anger and in fury and in furious **r**,	8433
	25:17 vengeance upon them with furious **r**,	8433

REBUKETH (4) [REBUKE]

Pr	9: 7 he that **r** a wicked *man getteth* himself	3198
	28:23 He that **r** a man, afterwards shall find	3198
Am	5:10 They hate him that **r** in the gate,	3198
Na	1: 4 He **r** the sea, and maketh it dry,	1605

REBUKING (2) [REBUKE]

2Sa	22:16 at the **r** of the LORD, at the blast of	1606
Lk	4:41 he **r** *them* suffered them not to speak:	2008

RECAB See RECHAB

RECABITE See RECHABITES

RECAH See RECHAH

RECALL (1)

La	3:21 I **r** to my mind, therefore have I hope.	7725

RECEDED See ABATED

RECEIPT (3) [RECEIVE]

Mt	9: 9 Matthew, sitting at the **r** of custom:	5058
Mk	2:14 *son* of Alpheus sitting at the **r** of custom,	5058
Lk	5:27 named Levi, sitting at the **r** of custom:	5058

RECEIVE (176) [RECEIPT, RECEIVED, RECEIVEDST, RECEIVER, RECEIVETH, RECEIVING]

Ge	4:11 which hath opened her mouth to **r** thy	3947

R

Ge	33:10	thy sight, then **r** my present at my hand:	3947
	38:20	to **r** *his* pledge from the woman's hand:	3947
Ex	27: 3	thou shalt make his pans to **r** his **ashes**,	1878
	29:25	thou shalt **r** them of their hands,	3947
Nu	18:28	which ye of the children of Israel;	3947
Dt	9: 9	When I was gone up into the mount to **r**	3947
	33: 3	at thy feet; *every* one shall **r** of thy words.	5375
1Sa	10: 4	bread; which thou shalt **r** of their hands.	3947
2Sa	18:12	Though I should **r** a thousand *shekels of*	8254
1Ki	5: 9	thou shalt **r** *them:* and thou shalt	5375
	8:64	*was* too little to **r** the burnt offerings,	3557
2Ki	5:16	before whom I stand, I will **r** none.	3947
	5:26	*Is it* a time to **r** money, and to receive	3947
	5:26	to **r** garments, and oliveyards,	3947
	12: 7	**r** no *more* money of your acquaintance,	3947
	12: 8	the priests consented to **r** no *more* money	3947
2Ch	7: 7	was not able to **r** the burnt offerings,	3557
Job	2:10	shall we **r** good at the hand of God,	6901
	2:10	the hand of God, and shall we not **r** evil?	6901
	22:22	**R**, I pray thee, the law from his mouth,	3947
	27:13	*which* they shall **r** of the Almighty.	3947
Ps	6: 9	the LORD will **r** my prayer.	3947
	24: 5	He shall **r** the blessing from the LORD,	5375
	49:15	of the grave: for he shall **r** me. Selah.	3947
	73:24	thy counsel, and afterward **r** me *to* glory.	3947
	75: 2	When I shall **r** the congregation I will	3947
Pr	1: 3	To **r** the instruction of wisdom, justice,	3947
	2: 1	if thou wilt **r** my words, and hide my	3947
	4:10	Hear, O my son, and **r** my sayings;	3947
	8:10	**R** my instruction, and not silver;	3947
	10: 8	The wise in heart will **r** commandments:	3947
	19:20	Hear counsel, and **r** instruction, that thou	6901
Isa	57: 6	offering. Should I **r** **comfort** in these?	5162
Jer	5: 3	*but* they have refused to **r** correction:	3947
	9:20	let your ear **r** the word of his mouth,	3947
	17:23	*they* might not hear, nor **r** instruction.	3947
	32:33	they have not hearkened to **r** instruction.	3947
	35:13	Will ye not **r** instruction to hearken to	3947
Eze	3:10	my words that I shall speak unto thee **r**	3947
	16:61	when thou shalt **r** thy sisters, thine elder	3947
	36:30	ye shall **r** no more reproach of famine	3947
Da	2: 6	ye shall **r** of me gifts and rewards and	6902
Hos	10: 6	Ephraim shall **r** shame, and Israel shall be	3947
	14: 2	away all iniquity, and **r** *us* graciously:	3947
Mic	1:11	Beth-ezel; he shall **r** of you his standing.	3947
Zep	3: 7	thou wilt fear me, thou wilt **r** instruction;	3947
Mal	3:10	*there shall* not be room enough to **r** *it.*	NIH
Mt	10:14	And whosoever shall not **r** you, nor hear	1209
	10:41	of a prophet shall **r** a prophet's reward;	2983
	10:41	*man* shall **r** a righteous *man's* reward.	2983
	11: 5	blind **r** their **sight**, and the lame walk,	308
	11:14	And if ye will **r** *it*, this is Elias, which was	1209
	18: 5	And whoso shall **r** one such little child in	1209
	19:11	unto them, All *men* cannot **r** this saying,	5562
	19:12	He that is able to **r** *it*, let him receive *it.*	5562
	19:12	He that is able to **r** receive *it*, let him **r** *it.*	5562
	19:29	shall **r** an hundredfold, and shall inherit	2983
	20: 7	and whatsoever is right, *that* shall ye **r**.	2983
	21:22	shall ask in prayer, believing, ye shall **r**.	2983
	21:34	that *they* might **r** the fruits of it.	2983
	23:14	ye shall **r** the greater damnation.	2983
Mk	2: 2	that there was no room to **r** *them,*	NIG
	4:16	the word, immediately **r** it with gladness;	2983
	4:20	the word, and **r** *it*, and bring forth fruit,	3858
	6:11	And whosoever shall not **r** you, nor hear	1209
	9:37	Whosoever shall **r** one of such children in	1209
	9:37	and whosoever shall **r** me, receiveth not	1209
	10:15	shall not **r** the kingdom of God	1209
	10:30	But he shall **r** an hundredfold now in this	2983
	10:51	unto him, Lord, that I might **r** my **sight**.	308
	11:24	believe that ye **r** *them*, and ye shall have	2983
	12: 2	that he might **r** from the husbandmen of	2983
	12:40	these shall **r** greater damnation.	2983
Lk	6:34	If ye lend *to them* of whom ye hope to **r**,	618
	6:34	also lend to sinners, to **r** as much **again**.	618
	8:13	when they hear, **r** the word with joy;	1209
	9: 5	whosoever will not **r** you, when ye go	1209
	9:48	Whosoever shall **r** this child in my name	1209
	9:48	whosoever shall **r** me receiveth him that	1209
	9:53	And they did not **r** him, because his face	1209
	10: 8	whatsoever city ye enter, and they **r** you,	1209
	10:10	city ye enter, and they **r** you not,	1209
	16: 4	they may **r** me into their houses.	1209
	16: 9	may **r** you into everlasting habitations.	1209
	18:17	shall not **r** the kingdom of God	1209
	18:30	Who shall not **r** manifold more in this	618
	18:41	And he said, Lord, that I may **r** my **sight**.	308
	18:42	And Jesus said unto him, **R** thy **sight**:	308
	19:12	a far country to **r** for himself a kingdom,	2983
	20:47	the same shall **r** greater damnation.	2983
	23:41	for we **r** the due reward of our deeds:	618
Jn	3:11	we have seen; and ye **r** not our witness.	2983
	3:27	and said, A man can **r** nothing,	2983
	5:34	But I **r** not testimony from man:	2983
	5:41	I **r** not honour from men.	2983
	5:43	in my Father's name, and ye **r** me not:	2983
	5:43	come in his own name, him ye will **r**.	2983
	5:44	which **r** honour one of another,	2983
	7:23	a man on the sabbath day **r** circumcision,	2983
	7:39	which they that believe on him should **r**:	2983
	14: 3	I will come again, and **r** you unto myself;	3880
	14:17	the world cannot **r**, because it seeth	2983
	16:14	for he shall **r** of mine, and shall shew *it,*	2983
	16:24	ask, and ye shall **r**, that your joy may be	2983
	20:22	saith unto them, **R** ye the Holy Ghost:	2983

Ac	1: 8	But ye shall **r** power, after that the Holy	2983
	2:38	and ye shall **r** the gift of the Holy Ghost.	2983
	3: 5	expecting to **r** something of them.	2983
	3:21	Whom the heaven must **r** until the times	1209
	7:59	and saying, Lord Jesus, **r** my spirit.	1209
	8:15	them, that they might **r** the Holy Ghost:	2983
	8:19	I lay hands, he may **r** the Holy Ghost.	2983
	9:12	hand on him, that he might **r** his **sight**.	308
	9:17	thou mightest **r** thy **sight**, and be filled	2983
	10:43	believeth in him shall **r** remission of sins.	2983
	16:21	which are not lawful for us to **r**, neither to	3858
	18:27	exhorting the disciples to **r** him:	588
	20:35	said, It is more blessed to give than to **r**.	2983
	22:13	said unto me, Brother Saul, **r** thy **sight**.	308
	22:18	they will not **r** thy testimony concerning	3858
	26:18	that they may **r** forgiveness of sins,	2983
Ro	5:17	much more they which **r** abundance of	2983
	13: 2	they that resist shall **r** to themselves	2983
	14: 1	Him that is weak in the faith **r** you,	4355
	15: 7	Wherefore **r** ye one another, as Christ also	4355
	16: 2	That ye **r** her in the Lord, as becometh	4327
1Co	3: 8	every man shall **r** his own reward	2983
	3:14	hath built thereupon, he shall **r** a reward.	2983
	4: 7	and what hast thou that thou didst not **r**?	2983
	4: 7	if thou didst **r** *it*, why dost thou glory,	2983
	14: 5	interpret, that the church may **r** edifying.	2983
2Co	5:10	every one may **r** the *things* done in *his*	2865
	6: 1	that ye **r** not the grace of God in vain.	1209
	6:17	not the unclean *thing*; and I will **r** you,	1523
	7: 2	**R** us; we have wronged no *man*, we have	5562
	7: 9	that ye might **r** **damage** by us in nothing.	2210
	8: 4	much intreaty that we would **r** the gift,	1209
	11: 4	if ye **r** another spirit, which ye have not	2983
	11:16	if otherwise, yet as a fool **r** me, that I may	1209
Gal	3:14	that we might **r** the promise of the Spirit	2983
	4: 5	that we might **r** the adoption of sons.	618
Eph	6: 8	the same shall he **r** of the Lord, whether	2865
Php	2:29	**R** him therefore in the Lord with all	4327
Col	3:24	Knowing that of the Lord ye shall **r**	618
	3:25	But he that doeth wrong shall **r** *for*	2865
	4:10	if he come unto you, **r** him;)	1209
1Ti	5:19	Against an elder **r** not an accusation,	3858
Phm	1:12	thou therefore **r** him, that is, mine own	4355
	1:15	season, that thou shouldest **r** him for ever;	568
	1:17	therefore a partner, **r** him as myself.	4355
Heb	5: 5	the office of the priesthood have a	2983
	7: 8	And here men that die **r** tithes; but there	2983
	9:15	they which are called might **r** the promise	2983
	10:36	the will of God, ye might **r** the promise.	2865
	11: 8	he should after **r** for an inheritance,	2983
Jas	1: 7	For let not that man think that he shall **r**	2983
	1:12	he is tried, he shall **r** the crown of life,	2983
	1:21	and **r** with meekness the engrafted word,	1209
	3: 1	knowing that we shall **r** the greater	2983
	4: 3	Ye ask, and **r** not, because ye ask amiss,	2983
	5: 7	for it, until he **r** the early and latter rain.	2983
1Pe	5: 4	ye shall **r** a crown of glory that fadeth not	2865
2Pe	2:13	shall **r** the reward of unrighteousness,	2865
1Jn	3:22	we **r** of him, because we keep his	2983
	5: 9	If we **r** the witness of men, the witness of	2983
2Jn	1: 8	have wrought, but *that* we **r** a full reward.	618
	1:10	this doctrine, **r** him not into *your* house,	2983
3Jn	1: 8	We therefore ought to **r** such, that we	618
	1:10	neither doth he himself **r** the brethren,	1926
Rev	4:11	O Lord, to **r** glory and honour and power:	2983
	5:12	Worthy is the Lamb that was slain to **r**	2983
	13:16	to **r** a mark in their right hand, or in their	1325
	14: 9	and **r** *his* mark in his forehead, or in his	2983
	17:12	**r** power as kings one hour with the beast.	2983
	18: 4	her sins, and that ye **r** not of her plagues.	2983

RECEIVED (160) [RECEIVE]

Ge	26:12	**r** in the same year an hundredfold:	4672
Ex	32: 4	he **r** *them* at their hand, and fashioned it	3947
	36: 3	they **r** of Moses all the offering, which	3947
Nu	12:14	and after *that* let her be **r** in *again.*	622
	23:20	Behold, I have **r** *commandment* to bless:	3947
	34:14	have **r** *their inheritance*; and half the tribe	3947
	34:14	half the tribe of Manasseh have **r** their	3947
	34:15	The half tribe have **r** their inheritance on	3947
	36: 3	of the tribe whereinto they are **r**:	1961+3807.1
	36: 4	of the tribe whereunto they are **r**:	1961+3807.1
Jos	13: 8	and the Gadites have **r** their inheritance,	3947
	18: 2	which had not *yet* **r** their inheritance.	2505
	18: 7	have **r** their inheritance beyond Jordan	3947
Jdg	13:23	he would not have **r** a burnt offering and	3947
1Sa	12: 3	of whose hand have I **r** *any* bribe to blind	3947
	25:35	David **r** of her hand *that* which she had	3947
1Ki	10:28	the king's merchants **r** the linen yarn at a	3947
2Ki	19:14	Hezekiah **r** the letter of the hand of	3947
1Ch	12:18	David **r** them, and made them captains of	6901
2Ch	1:16	the king's merchants **r** the linen yarn at a	3947
	4: 5	and it **r** and held three thousand baths.	2388
	29:22	the priests **r** the blood, and sprinkled *it* on	6901
	30:16	*which they* **r** of the hand of the Levites.	NIH
Est	4: 4	his sackcloth from him: but he **r** *it* not.	6901
Job	4:12	to me, and mine ear **r** a little thereof.	3947
Ps	68:18	thou hast **r** gifts for men; yea,	3947
Pr	24:32	well: I looked upon *it, and* **r** instruction.	3947
Isa	37:14	Hezekiah **r** the letter from the hand of	3947
	40: 2	for she hath **r** of the LORD's hand double	3947
Jer	2:30	your children; they **r** no correction:	3947
Eze	18:17	*that* hath not **r** usury nor increase,	3947
Zep	3: 2	not the voice; she **r** not correction;	3947
Mt	10: 8	out devils: freely ye have **r**, freely give.	2983

Mt	13:19	This is he which **r** **seed** by the way side.	4687
	13:20	But he that **r** the **seed** into stony *places,*	4687
	13:22	He also that **r** **seed** among the thorns is	4687
	13:23	But he that **r** **seed** into the good ground	4687
	17:24	they that **r** tribute money came to Peter,	2983
	20: 9	eleventh hour, they **r** every man a penny.	2983
	20:10	they supposed that they should have **r**	2983
	20:10	and they likewise **r** every man a penny.	2983
	20:11	And when they had **r** *it*, they murmured	2983
	20:34	and immediately their eyes **r** **sight**,	308
	25:16	Then he that had **r** the five talents went	2983
	25:17	And likewise he that had **r** two, he also	NIG
	25:18	But he that had **r** one went and digged in	2983
	25:20	And *so* he that had **r** five talents came	2983
	25:22	He also that had **r** two talents came and	2983
	25:24	Then he which had **r** the one talent came	2983
	25:27	at my coming I should have **r** mine own	2865
Mk	7: 4	which they have **r** to hold, *as* the washing	3880
	10:52	And immediately he **r** his **sight**,	308
	15:23	wine mingled with myrrh: but he **r** it not.	2983
	16:19	was **r** up into heaven, and sat on the right	353
Lk	6:24	are rich: for ye have **r** your consolation.	568
	8:40	Jesus was returned, the people gladly **r**	588
	9:11	and he **r** them, and spake unto them of	1209
	9:51	time was come that he should be **r** up,	354
	10:38	certain woman named Martha **r** him into	5264
	15:27	because he hath **r** him *safe* and sound.	618
	18:43	And immediately he **r** his **sight**,	308
	19: 6	and came down, and **r** him joyfully.	5264
	19:15	**r** the kingdom, then he commanded	2983
Jn	1:11	unto his own, and his own **r** him not.	3880
	1:12	But as many as **r** him, to them gave he	2983
	1:16	And of his fulness have all we **r**,	2983
	3:33	He that hath **r** his testimony hath set to	2983
	4:45	come into Galilee, the Galileans **r** him,	1209
	6:21	Then they willingly **r** him into the ship:	2983
	9:11	and I went and washed, and I **r** **sight**.	308
	9:15	also asked him how he had **r** his **sight**.	308
	9:18	that he had been blind, and had **r** his **sight**,	308
	9:18	the parents of him that had **r** his **sight**.	308
	10:18	commandment have I **r** of my Father.	2983
	13:30	having **r** the sop went immediately out:	2983
	17: 8	and they have **r** *them*, and have known	2983
	18: 3	having **r** a band *of men*, and officers from	2983
	19:30	When Jesus therefore had **r** the vinegar,	2983
Ac	1: 9	and a cloud **r** him out of their sight.	5274
	2:33	having **r** of the Father the promise of	2983
	2:41	Then they that gladly **r** his word were	588
	3: 7	his feet and ankle bones **r** **strength**,	4732
	7:38	who **r** the lively oracles to give unto us:	1209
	7:53	Who have **r** the law by the disposition of	2983
	8:14	that Samaria had **r** the word of God,	1209
	8:17	on them, and they **r** the Holy Ghost.	2983
	9:18	and he **r** **sight** forthwith, and arose,	308
	9:19	And when he had **r** meat, he was	2983
	10:16	the vessel was **r** up again into heaven.	353
	10:47	which have **r** the Holy Ghost as well as	2983
	11: 1	the Gentiles had also **r** the word of God.	1209
	15: 4	they were **r** of the church, and *of*	588
	16:24	Who, having **r** such a charge, thrust them	2983
	17: 7	Whom Jason hath **r**: and these all do	5264
	17:11	in that they **r** the word with all readiness	1209
	19: 2	Have ye **r** the Holy Ghost since ye	2983
	20:24	which I have **r** of the Lord Jesus,	2983
	21:17	to Jerusalem, the brethren **r** us gladly.	1209
	22: 5	from whom also I **r** letters unto	1209
	26:10	having **r** authority from the chief priests;	2983
	28: 2	**r** us every one, because of the present	4355
	28: 7	who **r** us, and lodged *us* three days	324
	28:21	We neither **r** letters out of Judea	1209
	28:30	house, and **r** all that came in unto him,	588
Ro	1: 5	whom we have **r** grace and apostleship,	2983
	4:11	he **r** the sign of circumcision, a seal of	2983
	5:11	by whom we have now **r** the atonement.	2983
	8:15	For ye have not **r** the spirit of bondage	2983
	8:15	but ye have **r** the Spirit of adoption,	2983
	14: 3	him that eateth: for God hath **r** him.	4355
	15: 7	as Christ also **r** us, to the glory of God.	4355
1Co	2:12	we have **r**, not the spirit of the world,	2983
	4: 7	dost thou glory, if thou hadst not **r** *it*?	2983
	11:23	For I have **r** of the Lord *that* which also I	3880
	15: 1	which also you have **r**, and wherein ye	3880
	15: 3	unto you first *of all* that which I also **r**,	3880
2Co	4: 1	as we have **r** **mercy**, we faint not;	1653
	7:15	how with fear and trembling you **r** him.	1209
	11: 4	which ye have not **r**, or another gospel,	2983
	11:24	Of the Jews five times **r** I forty *stripes*	2983
Gal	1: 9	other gospel unto you than that ye have **r**,	3880
	1:12	For I neither **r** it of man, neither was I	3880
	3: 2	**R** ye the Spirit by the works of the law,	2983
	4:14	but **r** me as an angel of God, *even* as	1209
Php	4: 9	and **r**, and heard, and seen in me,	3880
	4:18	having **r** of Epaphroditus the *things which*	1209
Col	2: 6	ye have therefore **r** Christ Jesus the Lord,	3880
	4:10	(touching whom ye **r** commandments:	2983
	4:17	heed to the ministry which thou hast **r**	3880
1Th	1: 6	having **r** the word in much affliction,	1209
	2:13	ye **r** the word of God which *ye* heard	3880
	2:13	ye **r** *it* not as the word of men, but as it	1209
	4: 1	that as ye have **r** of us how ye ought to	3880
2Th	2:10	because they **r** not the love of the truth,	1209
	3: 6	not after the tradition which he **r** of us.	3862
1Ti	3:16	believed on in the world, **r** up into glory.	353
	4: 3	which God hath created to be **r** with	3336
	4: 4	to be refused, if it be **r** with thanksgiving:	2983

Heb	2: 2 disobedience **r** a just recompence of	2983
	7: 6 counted from them **r tithes** of Abraham,	1183
	7:11 [for under it the people **r** the **law**,)	3549
	10:26 For if we sin wilfully after that *we* have **r**	2983
	11:11 Through faith also Sara herself **r** strength	2983
	11:13 not having **r** the promises, but having seen	2983
	11:17 he that had **r** the promises offered up *his*	324
	11:19 from whence also he **r** him in a figure.	2865
	11:31 when she had **r** the spies with peace.	1209
	11:35 Women **r** their dead raised to life again:	2983
	11:39 report through faith, **r** not the promise:	2865
Jas	2:25 when she had **r** the messengers,	5264
1Pe	1:18 **r by tradition from** your **fathers;**	3970
	4:10 As every man hath **r** the **gift**, *even so*	2983
2Pe	1:17 For he **r** from God the Father honour and	2983
1Jn	2:27 But the anointing which ye have **r** of him	2983
2Jn	1: 4 as we have **r** a commandment from	2983
Rev	2:27 to shivers: even as I **r** of my Father.	2983
	3: 3 therefore how thou hast **r** and heard,	2983
	17:12 kings, which have **r** no kingdom as yet;	2983
	19:20 with which he deceived them that had **r**	2983
	20: 4 neither had **r** *his* mark upon their	2983

RECEIVEDST (1) [RECEIVE]

Lk	16:25 remember that thou in thy lifetime **r** thy	618

RECEIVER (1) [RECEIVE]

Isa	33:18 where *is* the **r**? where *is* he that counted	8254

RECEIVETH (37) [RECEIVE]

Jdg	19:18 and there *is* no man that **r** me to house.	622
Job	35: 7 thou him? or what **r** he of thine hand?	3947
Pr	21:11 the wise is instructed, he **r** knowledge.	3947
	29: 4 land: but he that **r** gifts overthroweth it.	NIH
Jer	7:28 of the LORD their God, nor **r** correction:	3947
Mal	2:13 or *it with* good will at your hand.	3947
Mt	7: 8 For every one that asketh **r**; and he that	2983
	10:40 He that **r** you receiveth me, and he that	1209
	10:40 He that receiveth you **r** me, and he that	1209
	10:40 he that **r** me receiveth him that sent me.	1209
	10:40 he that receiveth me **r** him that sent me.	1209
	10:41 He that **r** a prophet in the name of a	1209
	10:41 he that **r** a righteous *man* in the name of a	2983
	13:20 heareth the word, and anon with joy **r** it;	2983
	18: 5 one such little child in my name **r** me.	1209
Mk	9:37 one of such children in my name, **r** me:	1209
	9:37 me, **r** not me, but him that sent me.	1209
Lk	9:48 shall receive this child in my name **r** me:	1209
	9:48 shall receive me **r** him that sent	1209
	11:10 For every one that asketh **r**; and that	2983
	15: 2 This *man* **r** sinners, and eateth with them	4327
Jn	3:32 he testifieth; and no *man* **r** his testimony.	2983
	4:36 And he that reapeth **r** wages,	2983
	12:48 that rejecteth me, and **r** not my words,	2983
	13:20 that **r** whomsoever I send receiveth me;	2983
	13:20 that receiveth whomsoever I send **r** me;	2983
	13:20 he that **r** me receiveth him that sent me.	2983
	13:20 he that receiveth me **r** him that sent me.	2983
1Co	2:14 But the natural man **r** not the *things* of	1209
	9:24 run in a race run all, but one **r** the prize?	2983
Heb	6: 7 whom it is dressed, **r** blessing from God:	3335
	7: 8 there he **r** them, of whom it is witnessed	NIG
	7: 9 as *I* may so say, Levi also, who **r** tithes,	2983
	12: 6 and scourgeth every son whom he **r**.	3858
3Jn	1: 9 the preeminence among them, **r** us not.	1926
Rev	2:17 no *man* knoweth saving he that **r** *it*.	2983
	14:11 and whosoever **r** the mark of his name.	2983

RECEIVING (7) [RECEIVE]

2Ki	5:20 not **r** at his hands *that* which he brought:	3947
Ac	17:15 and a commandment unto Silas and	2983
Ro	1:27 **r** in themselves *that* recompence of their	618
	11:15 what *shall* the **r** *of them be*, but life from	4356
Php	4:15 with me as concerning giving and, **r**,	3028
Heb	12:28 Wherefore we **r** a kingdom which cannot	3880
1Pe	1: 9 **R** the end of your faith, *even* the salvation	2865

RECENT CONVERT See NOVICE

RECHAB (13) [RECHABITES]

2Sa	4: 2 Baanah, and the name of the other **R**,	7394
	4: 5 **R** and Baanah, went, and came about	7394
	4: 6 and **R** and Baanah his brother escaped.	7394
	4: 9 answered **R** and Baanah his brother,	7394
2Ki	10:15 he lighted on Jehonadab the son of **R**	7394
	10:23 Jehu went, and Jehonadab the son of **R**,	7394
1Ch	2:55 of Hemath, the father of the house of **R**.	7394
Ne	3:14 gate repaired Malchiah the son of **R**,	7394
Jer	35: 6 for Jonadab the son of **R** our father	7394
	35: 8 **R** our father in all that he hath charged	7394
	35:14 The words of Jonadab the son of **R**, that	7394
	35:16 Because the sons of Jonadab the son of **R**	7394
	35:19 Jonadab the son of **R** shall not want a	7394

RECHABITES (4) [RECHAB]

Jer	35: 2 Go unto the house of the **R**, and speak	7397
	35: 3 all his sons, and the whole house of the **R**;	7397
	35: 5 I set before the sons of the house of the **R**	7397
	35:18 Jeremiah said unto the house of the **R**,	7397

RECHAH (1)

1Ch	4:12 of Irnahash. These *are* the men of **R**.	7397

RECITE See REHEARSE

RECKON (8) [RECKONED, RECKONETH, RECKONING]

Lev	25:50 he shall **r** with him that bought him from	2803
	27:18 the priest shall **r** unto him the money	2803
	27:23 the priest shall **r** unto him the worth of	2803
Nu	4:32 by name ye shall **r** the instruments of	6485
Eze	44:26 they shall **r** unto him seven days.	5608
Mt	18:24 And when he had begun to **r**, one was	4868
Ro	6:11 Likewise **r** ye also yourselves to be dead	3049
	8:18 For I **r** that the sufferings of *this* present	3049

RECKONED (22) [RECKON]

Nu	18:27 *this* your heave offering shall be **r** unto	2803
	23: 9 and shall not be **r** among the nations.	2803
2Sa	4: 2 (for Beeroth also was **r** to Benjamin:	2803
2Ki	2:5 Moreover they **r** not with the men,	2803
1Ch	5: 1 the **genealogy** is not to be after	3187
	5: 7 the **genealogy** of their generations was **r**,	3187
	5:17 these were **r by genealogies** in the days	3187
	7: 5 **r** in all **by** their **genealogies** fourscore	3187
	7: 7 were **r by** their **genealogies** twenty and	3187
	9: 1 So all Israel were **r by genealogies**;	3187
	9:22 These were **r by** their **genealogies** in their	3187
2Ch	31:19 to all that were **r by genealogies** among	3187
Ezr	2:62 *among* those that were **r by genealogy**,	3187
	8: 3 him were **r by genealogy** of the males	3187
Ne	5: 2 that *they* might be **r by genealogy**.	3187
	7:64 *among* those that were **r by genealogy**,	3187
Ps	40: 5 they cannot be **r up in order** unto thee:	6186
Isa	38:13 I **r** till morning, *that*, as a lion, so will	7737
Lk	22:37 And he was **r** among the transgressors:	3049
Ro	4: 4 that worketh is the reward **r** not of grace,	3049
	4: 9 for we say that faith was **r** to Abraham for	3049
	4:10 How was it then **r**? when he was in	3049

RECKONETH (1) [RECKON]

Mt	25:19 servants cometh, and **r** with them.	3056+4868

RECKONING (2) [RECKON]

2Ki	22: 7 Howbeit there was no **r** made with them	2803
1Ch	23:11 therefore they were in one **r**, according to	6486

RECOMMENDED (2)

Ac	14:26 from whence they had been **r** to the grace	3860
	15:40 being **r** by the brethren unto the grace of	3860

RECOMPENCE (20) [RECOMPENSE]

Dt	32:35 To me *belongeth* vengeance, and **r**;	8005
Job	15:31 trust in vanity: for vanity shall be his **r**.	8545
Pr	12:14 the **r** of a man's hands shall be rendered	1576
Isa	35: 4 come *with* vengeance, *even* God *with* a **r**;	1576
	59:18 fury to his adversaries, **r** to his enemies;	1576
	59:18 his enemies; to the islands he will repay **r**.	1576
	66: 6 a voice of the LORD that rendereth **r** to	1576
Jer	51: 6 he *will* render unto her a **r**.	1576
La	3:64 Render unto them a **r**, O LORD,	1576
Hos	9: 7 are come, the days of **r** are come;	7966
Joel	3: 4 will ye render me a **r**? and if ye	1576
	3: 4 speedily will I return your **r** upon your	1576
	3: 7 will return your **r** upon your own head:	1576
Lk	14:12 also bid thee again, and a **r** be made thee.	468
Ro	1:27 receiving in themselves *that* **r** of their error	489
	11: 9 and a stumblingblock, and a **r** unto them:	468
2Co	6:13 Now for a **r** in the same, (I speak as unto	489
Heb	2: 2 disobedience received a just **r** of reward;	1738
	10:35 which hath great **r** of **reward**.	3405
	11:26 he had respect unto the **r** of the **reward**.	3405

RECOMPENCES (2) [RECOMPENSE]

Isa	34: 8 the year of **r** for the controversy of Zion.	7966
Jer	51:56 for the LORD God of **r** shall surely	1578

RECOMPENSE (26) [RECOMPENCE, RECOMPENCES, RECOMPENSED, RECOMPENSEST, RECOMPENSING]

Nu	5: 7 he shall **r** his trespass with the principal	7725
	5: 8 if the man have no kinsman to **r**	7725
Ru	2:12 The LORD **r** thy work, and a full reward	7999
2Sa	19:36 why should the king **r** it *me* with such a	1580
Job	34:33 he will **r** it, whether thou refuse,	7999
Pr	20:22 Say not thou, I will **r** evil; *but* wait on	7999
Isa	65: 6 I will not keep silence, but will **r**,	7999
	65: 6 recompense, even **r** into their bosom,	7999
Jer	16:18 first I will **r** their iniquity and their sin	7999
	25:14 I will **r** them according to their deeds,	7999
	50:29 **r** her according to her work; according to	7999
Eze	7: 3 will **r** upon thee all thine abominations.	5414
	7: 4 I will **r** thy ways upon thee,	5414
	7: 8 and will **r** thee for all thine abominations.	5414
	7: 9 I will **r** thee according to thy ways and	5414
	9:10 *but* I will **r** their way upon their head.	5414
	11:21 I will **r** their way upon their own heads,	5414
	16:43 I also will **r** thy way upon *thine* head,	5414
	17:19 even it will I **r** upon his own head.	5414
	23:49 they shall **r** your lewdness upon you,	5414
Hos	12: 2 according to his doings will he **r** him.	7725
Joel	3: 4 if ye **r** me, swiftly *and* speedily will I	1580
Lk	14:14 shalt be blessed; for they cannot **r** thee:	467
Ro	12:17 **R** to no *man* evil for evil. Provide *things*	591
2Th	1: 6 Seeing *it is* a righteous *thing* with God to **r**	467
Heb	10:30 *belongeth* unto me, I will **r**, saith the Lord.	467

RECOMPENSED (10) [RECOMPENSE]

Nu	5: 8 *let* the trespass *be* **r** unto the LORD,	7725
2Sa	22:21 the cleanness of my hands hath he **r** me.	7725

2Sa	22:25 Therefore the LORD hath **r** me according	7725
Ps	18:20 the cleanness of my hands hath he **r** me.	7725
	18:24 Therefore hath the LORD **r** me according	7725
Pr	11:31 the righteous shall be **r** in the earth:	7999
Jer	18:20 Shall evil be **r** for good? for they have	7999
Eze	22:31 their own way have I **r** upon their heads,	5414
Lk	14:14 for thou shalt be **r** at the resurrection of	467
Ro	11:35 to him, and it shall be **r** unto him *again*?	467

RECOMPENSEST (1) [RECOMPENSE]

Jer	32:18 the iniquity of the fathers into the bosom	7999

RECOMPENSING (1) [RECOMPENSE]

2Ch	6:23 by **r** his way upon his own head;	5414

RECONCILE (5) [RECONCILED, RECONCILIATION, RECONCILING]

Lev	6:30 **r** *withal* in the holy *place*, shall be eaten:	3722
1Sa	29: 4 for wherewith should he **r** himself unto	7521
Eze	45:20 *him that is* simple: so shall ye **r** the house.	3722
Eph	2:16 And *that* he might **r** both unto God in one	604
Col	1:20 cross, by him to **r** all *things* unto himself;	604

RECONCILED (7) [RECONCILE]

Mt	5:24 first be **r** to thy brother, and then come	1259
Ro	5:10 we were **r** to God by the death of his Son,	2644
	5:10 much more, being **r**, we shall be saved by	2644
1Co	7:11 remain unmarried, or be **r** to *her* husband:	2644
2Co	5:18 who hath **r** us to himself by Jesus Christ,	2644
	5:20 pray *you* in Christ's stead, be ye **r** to God.	2644
Col	1:21 mind by wicked works, yet now hath he **r**	604

RECONCILIATION (8) [RECONCILE]

Lev	8:15 and sanctified it, to **make r** upon it.	3722
2Ch	29:24 they made **r** with their blood upon	2398
Eze	45:15 for peace offerings, to **make r** for them,	3722
	45:17 to **make r** for the house of Israel.	3722
Da	9:24 to **make r** for iniquity, and to bring in	3722
2Co	5:18 and hath given to us the ministry of **r**;	2643
	5:19 hath committed unto us the word of **r**.	2643
Heb	2:17 to **make r** for the sins of the people.	2433

RECONCILING (3) [RECONCILE]

Lev	16:20 when he hath made an end of **r** the holy	3722
Ro	11:15 if the casting away of them *be* the **r** of	2643
2Co	5:19 that God was in Christ **r** the world unto	2644

RECORD (30) [RECORDED, RECORDER, RECORDS]

Ex	20:24 in all places where I **r** my name I will	2142
Dt	30:19 I **call** heaven and earth to **r** *this* day	5749
	31:28 I **call** heaven and earth to **r** against them.	5749
1Ch	16: 4 to **r**, and to thank and praise the LORD	2142
Ezr	6: 2 a roll, and therein *was* a **r** thus written:	1799
Job	16:19 witness *is* in heaven, and my **r** *is* on high.	7717
Isa	8: 2 I took unto me faithful witnesses to **r**,	5749
Jn	1:19 And this is the **r** of John, when the Jews	3141
	1:32 And John bare **r**, saying, I saw the Spirit	3140
	1:34 and **bare r** that this is the Son of God.	3140
	8:13 said unto him, Thou **bearest** of thyself;	3140
	8:13 bearest record of thyself; thy **r** is not true.	3141
	8:14 unto them, Though I **bear r** of myself,	3140
	8:14 I **bear record of myself**, *yet* my **r** is true:	3141
	12:17 and raised him from the dead, **bare r**.	3140
	19:35 he that saw *it* **bare r**, and his record is	3140
	19:35 that saw *it* **bare** record, and his **r** is true:	3141
Ac	20:26 Wherefore I **take** you to **r** this day, that I	3143
Ro	10: 2 For I **bear** them **r** that they have a zeal of	3140
2Co	1:23 Moreover I call God for a **r** upon my soul,	3144
	8: 3 I **bear r**, *yea*, and beyond their power	3140
Gal	4:15 for I **bear** you **r**, that if *it had* been	3140
Php	1: 8 For God is my **r**, how *greatly* I long after	3144
Col	4:13 For I **bear** him **r**, that he hath a great zeal	3140
1Jn	5: 7 For there are three that **bear r** in heaven,	3140
	5:10 he believeth not the **r** that God gave of his	3141
	5:11 this is the **r**, that God hath given to us	3141
3Jn	1:12 and we also **bear r**; and ye know that	3140
	1:12 record; and ye know that our **r** is true.	3141
Rev	1: 2 Who **bare r** of the word of God, and of	3140

RECORDED (1) [RECORD]

Ne	12:22 and Jaddua, *were* **r** chief of the fathers:	3789

RECORDER (9) [RECORD]

2Sa	8:16 and Jehoshaphat the son of Ahilud *was* **r**;	2142
	20:24 and Jehoshaphat the son of Ahilud *was* **r**:	2142
1Ki	4: 3 Jehoshaphat the son of Ahilud, the **r**.	2142
2Ki	18:18 scribe, and Joah the son of Asaph the **r**.	2142
	18:37 scribe, and Joah the son of Asaph the **r**,	2142
1Ch	18:15 and Jehoshaphat the son of Ahilud, **r**.	2142
2Ch	34: 8 the city, and Joah the son of Joahaz the **r**,	2142
Isa	36: 3 the scribe, and Joah, Asaph's son, the **r**,	2142
	36:22 and Joah, the son of Asaph, the **r**,	2142

RECORDS (3) [RECORD]

Ezr	4:15 made in the book of the **r** of thy fathers:	1799
	4:15 so shalt thou find in the book of the **r**,	1799
Est	6: 1 he commanded to bring the book of **r** of	2146

RECOUNT (1)

Na	2: 5 He shall **r** his worthies: they shall stumble	2142

RECOVER (21) [RECOVERED, RECOVERING]

Jdg	11:26 did ye not **r** *them* within that time?	5337
1Sa	30: 8 and **without fail r** *all*.	5337+5337
2Sa	8: 3 as he went to **r** his border at the river	7725

R

2Ki 1: 2 of Ekron whether I shall **r** of this disease. 2421
 5: 3 for he would **r** him of his leprosy. 622
 5: 6 that thou mayest **r** him of his leprosy. 622
 5: 7 this *man* doth send unto me to **r** a man 622
 5:11 his hand over the place, and **r** the leper. 622
 8: 8 by him, saying, Shall I **r** of this disease? 2421
 8: 9 to thee, saying, Shall I **r** of this disease? 2421
 8:10 him, Thou mayest **certainly r:** 2421+2421
 8:14 me *that* thou shouldest **surely r.** 2421+2421
2Ch 13:20 Neither did Jeroboam **r** strength again in 6113
 14:13 that they could not **r** themselves; 4241
Ps 39:13 spare me, that I may **r strength,** before I 1082
Isa 11:11 time to **r** the remnant of his people, 7069
 38:16 so wilt thou **r** me, and make me to live. 2492
 38:21 for a plaister upon the boil, and he shall **r.** 2421
Hos 2: 9 wool and my flax *given* to cover 5337
Mk 16:18 hands on the sick, and they shall **r.** 2192+2573
2Ti 2:26 And *that* they may **r** themselves out of 366

RECOVERED (11) [RECOVER]

1Sa 30:18 David **r** all that the Amalekites had 5337
 30:19 that they had taken to them: David **r** all. 7725
 30:22 them *ought* of the spoil that we have **r,** 5337
2Ki 13:25 Joash beat him, and **r** the cities of Israel. 7725
 14:28 and how he **r** Damascus, and Hamath, 7725
 16: 6 At that time Rezin king of Syria **r** Elath to 7725
 20: 7 they took and laid *it* on the boil, and he **r.** 2421
Isa 38: 9 had been sick, and was **r** of his sickness. 2421
 39: 1 heard that he had been sick, and was **r.** 2388
Jer 8:22 health of the daughter of my people **r?** 5927
 41:16 remnant of the people whom he had **r** 7725

RECOVERING (1) [RECOVER]

Lk 4:18 to the captives, and **r** of sight to the blind, 309

RED (53) [REDDISH, REDNESS]

Ge 25:25 the first came out **r,** all over like a hairy 132
 25:30 with that same *pottage;* for I *am* faint: 122
 49:12 *His* eyes *shall be* **r** with wine, and *his* 2447
Ex 10:19 the locusts, and cast them into the **R** sea, 5488
 13:18 the way of the wilderness of the **R** sea. 5488
 15: 4 captains also are drowned in the **R** sea. 5488
 15:22 So Moses brought Israel from the **R** sea, 5488
 23:31 will set thy bounds from the **R** sea even 5488
 25: 5 rams' skins **dyed r,** and badgers' skins, 119
 26:14 covering for the tent *of* rams' skins **dyed r,** 119
 35: 7 rams' skins **dyed r,** and badgers' skins, 119
 35:23 goats' *hair,* and **r** skins of rams, 119
 36:19 covering for the tent *of* rams' skins **dyed r,** 119
 39:34 And the covering of rams' skins **dyed r,** 119
Nu 14:25 the wilderness *by* the way of the **R** sea. 5488
 19: 2 they bring thee a **r** heifer without spot, 122
 21: 4 from mount Hor *by* the way of the **R** sea, 5488
 21:14 What he did in the **R** sea, and *in* the 5492
 33:10 from Elim, and encamped by the **R** sea. 5488
 33:11 they removed from the **R** sea, 5488
Dt 1: 1 in the plain over against the **R** *sea,* 5489
 1:40 the wilderness *by* the way of the **R** sea. 5488
 2: 1 the wilderness *by* the way of the **R** sea. 5488
 11: 4 how he made the water of the **R** sea to 5488
Jos 2:10 dried up the water of the **R** sea for you, 5488
 4:23 as the LORD your God did to the **R** sea, 5488
 24: 6 chariots and horsemen *unto* the **R** sea. 5488
Jdg 11:16 walked through the wilderness unto the **R** 5488
1Ki 9:26 on the shore of the **R** sea, in the land of 5488
2Ki 3:22 the water on the other side *as* **r** as blood: 122
Ne 9: 9 and heardest their cry by the **R** sea; 5488
Est 1: 6 a pavement of **r,** and blue, and white, 923
Ps 75: 8 LORD *there is* a cup, and the wine is **r;** 2560
 106: 7 *him* at the sea, *even* at the **R** sea. 5488
 106: 9 rebuked the **R** sea also, and it was dried 5488
 106:22 of Ham, *and* terrible *things* by the **R** sea. 5488
 136:13 him which divided the **R** sea into parts: 5488
 136:15 and his host in the **R** sea: 5488
Pr 23:31 Look not thou upon the wine when it is **r,** 119
Isa 1:18 though they be **r** like crimson, they shall 119
 27: 2 sing ye unto her, A vineyard of **r wine.** 2561
 63: 2 Wherefore *art thou* **r** in thine apparel, 122
Jer 49:21 the noise thereof was heard in the **R** sea. 5488
Na 2: 3 The shield of his mighty *men* is **made r,** 119
Zec 1: 8 and behold a man riding upon a **r** horse, 122
 1: 8 behind *him were there* **r** horses, speckled, 122
 6: 2 In the first chariot *were* **r** horses, and in 122
Mt 16: 2 *It will be* fair weather: for the sky is **r.** 4449
 16: 3 for the sky is **r** and lowring. O ye 4449
Ac 7:36 and in the **R** sea, and in the wilderness 2063
Heb 11:29 By faith they passed through the **R** sea as 2063
Rev 6: 4 there went out another horse *that was* **r:** 4450
 12: 3 and behold a great **r** dragon, having seven 4450

REDDISH (6) [RED]

Lev 13:19 *and* **somewhat r,** and it be shewed to 125
 13:24 white bright spot, **somewhat r,** or white; 125
 13:42 bald head, or bald forehead, a white **r** sore; 125
 13:43 the rising of the sore *be* white **r** in his bald 125
 13:49 the plague be greenish or **r** in the garment, 125
 14:37 greenish or **r,** which in sight *are* lower 125

REDEEM (56) [REDEEMED, REDEEMEDST, REDEEMER, REDEEMETH, REDEEMING, REDEMPTION]

Ex 6: 6 I will **r** you with a stretched out arm, 1350
 13:13 every firstling of an ass thou shalt **r** with a 6299
 13:13 if thou wilt not **r** *it,* then thou shalt break 6299
 13:13 of man amongst thy children thou shalt **r.** 6299

Ex 13:15 but all the firstborn of my children I **r.** 6299
 34:20 the firstling of an ass thou shalt **r** with a 6299
 34:20 if thou **r** *him* not, then shalt thou break 6299
 34:20 All the firstborn of thy sons thou shalt **r:** 6299
Lev 25:25 *any of* his kin come to **r** it, then shall he 1350
 25:25 shall he **r** that which his brother sold. 1350
 25:26 if the man have none to **r** *it,* and himself 1350
 25:26 and himself be able to **r** it; 1353+4672
 25:29 may **r** it within a whole year after 1353+1961
 25:29 sold; *within* a full year may he **r** it. 1353+1961
 25:32 may the Levites **r** at any time. 1353
 25:48 one of his brethren may **r** him: 1350
 25:49 may **r** him, or *any* that is nigh of kin unto 1350
 25:49 of kin unto him of his family may **r** him; 1350
 25:49 or if he be able, he may **r** himself. 1350
 27:13 if he will **at all r** it, then he shall 1350+1350
 27:15 if he that sanctified *it* will **r** his house, 1350+1350
 27:19 the field will **in any wise r** it, 1350+1350
 27:20 if he will not **r** the field, or if he have sold 1350
 27:27 he shall **r** *it* according to thine estimation, 6299
 27:31 if a man will **at all r** *ought* of his 1350+1350
Nu 18:15 of man shalt thou **surely r,** 6299+6299
 18:15 firstling of unclean beasts shalt thou **r.** 6299
 18:16 redeemed from a month old shalt thou **r,** 6299
 18:17 or the firstling of a goat, thou shalt not **r;** 6299
Ru 4: 4 If thou wilt **r** *it,* redeem *it:* but if thou wilt 1350
 4: 4 If thou wilt redeem *it,* **r** *it:* but if thou wilt 1350
 4: 4 but if thou wilt not **r** *it,* then tell me, 1350
 4: 4 for *there* is none to **r** *it* besides thee; 1350
 4: 4 I *am* after thee. And he said, I will **r** *it.* 1350
 4: 6 the kinsman said, I cannot **r** *it* for myself, 1350
 4: 6 thou my right to thyself; for I cannot 1350
 4: 6 my right to thyself; for I cannot **r** *it.* 1350
2Sa 7:23 whom God went to **r** for a people to 6299
1Ch 17:21 God went to **r** for a people to be his 6299
Ne 5: 5 **r** *them;* for other men have our lands NIH
Job 5:20 In famine he shall **r** thee from death: 6299
 6:23 or, **R** me from the hand of the mighty? 6299
Ps 25:22 **R** Israel, O God, out of all his troubles. 6299
 26:11 **r** me, and be merciful unto me. 6299
 44:26 our help, and **r** us for thy mercy's sake. 6299
 49: 7 *of them* can **by any means r** 6299+6299
 49:15 God will **r** my soul from the power of 6299
 69:18 Draw nigh unto my soul, *and* **r** it: 1350
 72:14 He shall **r** their soul from deceit and 1350
 130: 8 he shall **r** Israel from all his iniquities. 6299
Isa 50: 2 hand shortened at all, that *it* cannot **r?** 6304
Jer 15:21 will **r** thee out of the hand of the terrible; 6299
Hos 13:14 of the grave; I will **r** them from death: 1350
Mic 4:10 there the LORD shall **r** thee from the hand 1350
Gal 4: 5 To **r** them that were under the law, that 1805
Tit 2:14 that he might **r** us from all iniquity, 3084

REDEEMED (62) [REDEEM]

Ge 48:16 The Angel which **r** me from all evil, 1350
Ex 15:13 led forth the people *which* thou hast **r:** 1350
 21: 8 her to himself, then shall he let her be **r:** 6299
Lev 19:20 not **at all r,** nor freedom given her; 6299+6299
 25:30 if it be not **r** within the space of a full year, 1350
 25:31 they may be **r,** and they shall go 1353+1961
 25:48 *that* he is sold he may be **r** again; 1353+1961
 25:54 If he be not **r** in these *years,* then he shall 1350
 27:20 another man, it shall be **r** any more. 1350
 27:27 or if it be not **r,** then it shall be sold 1350
 27:28 field of his possession, shall be sold or **r:** 1350
 27:29 which shall be devoted of men, shall be **r;** 6299
 27:33 thereof shall be holy; it shall not be **r.** 1350
Nu 3:46 for **those that are** to be **r** of the two 6302
 3:48 the odd number of them is to be **r,** 6302
 3:49 above them that were **r** by the Levites: 6302
 3:51 money of them that were **r** unto Aaron 6302
 18:16 those that are to be **r** from a month old 6299
Dt 7: 8 **r** you out of the house of bondmen, 6299
 9:26 which thou hast **r** through thy greatness, 6299
 13: 5 out of the house of bondage, 6299
 15:15 of Egypt, and the LORD thy God **r** thee: 6299
 21: 8 whom thou hast **r,** and lay not innocent 6299
 24:18 and the LORD thy God **r** thee thence: 6299
2Sa 4: 9 who hath **r** my soul out of all adversity, 6299
1Ki 1:29 that hath **r** my soul out of all distress, 6299
1Ch 17:21 people, whom thou hast **r** out of Egypt? 6299
Ne 1:10 whom thou hast **r** by thy great power, 6299
 5: 8 We after our ability have **r** our brethren 7069
Ps 31: 5 thou hast **r** me, O LORD God of truth. 6299
 71:23 thee; and my soul, which thou hast **r.** 6299
 74: 2 of thine inheritance, *which* thou hast **r;** 1350
 77:15 Thou hast with *thine* arm **r** thy people, 1350
 106:10 **r** them from the hand of the enemy. 1350
 107: 2 Let the **r** of the LORD say *so,* whom he 1350
 107: 2 whom he hath **r** from the hand of 1350
 136:24 hath **r** us from our enemies: for his mercy 6561
Isa 1:27 Zion shall be **r** with judgment, 6299
 29:22 who **r** Abraham, concerning the house of 6299
 35: 9 be found there; but the **r** shall walk *there:* 1350
 43: 1 for I have **r** thee, I have called *thee* by thy 1350
 44:22 thy sins: return unto me; for I have **r** thee. 1350
 44:23 for the LORD hath **r** Jacob, 1350
 48:20 The LORD hath **r** his servant Jacob. 1350
 51:11 Therefore the **r** of the LORD shall return, 6299
 52: 3 and ye shall be **r** without money. 1350
 52: 9 comforted his people, he hath **r** Jerusalem. 1350
 62:12 The holy people, The **r** of the LORD: 1350
 63: 4 mine heart, and the year of my **r** is come. 1350
 63: 9 in his love and in his pity he **r** them; 1350
Jer 31:11 For the LORD hath **r** Jacob, 1350

La 3:58 the causes of my soul; thou hast **r** my life. 1350
Hos 7:13 I have **r** them, yet they have spoken 6299
Mic 6: 4 and **r** thee out of the house of servants; 6299
Zec 10: 8 and gather them; for I have **r** them; 6299
Lk 1:68 for he hath visited and **r** his people, 3085+4160
 24:21 it had been he which should have **r** Israel: 3084
Gal 3:13 Christ hath **r** us from the curse of the law, 1805
1Pe 1:18 Forasmuch as ye know that ye were not **r** 3084
Rev 5: 9 hast **r** us to God by thy blood out of every 59
 14: 3 thousand, which were **r** from the earth. 59
 14: 4 These were **r** from among men, *being* 59

REDEEMEDST (1) [REDEEM]

2Sa 7:23 which thou **r** to thee from Egypt, *from* 6299

REDEEMER (18) [REDEEM]

Job 19:25 For I know *that* my **R** liveth, and *that* he 1350
Ps 19:14 O LORD, my strength, and my **r.** 1350
 78:35 was their rock, and the high God their **r.** 1350
Pr 23:11 For their **R** *is* mighty; he shall plead their 1350
Isa 41:14 will help thee, saith the LORD, and thy **r,** 1350
 43:14 the LORD, your **r,** the Holy One of Israel; 1350
 44: 6 of Israel, and his **r** the LORD of hosts; 1350
 44:24 thy **r,** and he that formed thee from the 1350
 47: 4 *As for* our **r,** the LORD of hosts *is* his 1350
 48:17 the LORD, thy **r,** the Holy One of Israel; 1350
 49: 7 the **r** of Israel, *and* his Holy One, 1350
 49:26 that I the LORD *am* thy Saviour and thy **r,** 1350
 54: 5 name; and thy **r** the Holy One of Israel; 1350
 54: 8 mercy on thee, saith the LORD thy **r.** 1350
 59:20 the **r** shall come to Zion, and unto them 1350
 60:16 that I the LORD *am* thy Saviour and thy **r,** 1350
 63:16 thou, O LORD, *art* our father, our **r;** 1350
Jer 50:34 Their **r** *is* strong; the LORD of hosts *is* his 1350

REDEEMETH (2) [REDEEM]

Ps 34:22 The LORD **r** the soul of his servants: 6299
 103: 4 Who **r** thy life from destruction; 1350

REDEEMING (3) [REDEEM]

Ru 4: 7 in former time in Israel concerning **r** 1353
Eph 5:16 **R** the time, because the days are evil. 1805
Col 4: 5 toward them that are without, **r** the time. 1805

REDEMPTION (20) [REDEEM]

Lev 25:24 possession ye shall grant a **r** for the land. 1353
 25:51 *price* of his **r** out of the money that he 1353
 25:52 shall he give *him* again the *price* of his **r.** 1353
Nu 3:49 Moses took the **r** money of them that 6306
Ps 49: 8 (For the **r** of their soul is precious, 6306
 111: 9 He sent **r** unto his people: he hath 6304
 130: 7 *is* mercy, and with him *is* plenteous **r.** 6304
Jer 32: 7 for the right of **r** *is* thine to buy *it.* 1353
 32: 8 of inheritance *is* thine, and the **r** *is* thine; 1353
Lk 2:38 of him to all them that looked for **r** in 3085
 21:28 lift up your heads; for your **r** draweth nigh. 629
Ro 3:24 grace through the **r** that is in Christ Jesus: 629
 8:23 for the adoption, *to wit,* the **r** of our body. 629
1Co 1:30 righteousness, and sanctification, and **r:** 629
Eph 1: 7 In whom we have **r** through his blood, 629
 1:14 until the **r** of the purchased possession, 629
 4:30 whereby ye are sealed unto the day of **r.** 629
Col 1:14 In whom we have **r** through his blood, 629
Heb 9:12 place, having obtained eternal **r** *for us.* 3085
 9:15 for the **r** of the transgressions that were 629

REDNESS (1) [RED]

Pr 23:29 without cause? who hath **r** of eyes? 2448

REDOUND (1)

2Co 4:15 of many **r** to the glory of God. 4052

REDUCE See MINISH; MINISHED

REED (33) [REEDS]

1Ki 14:15 as a **r** is shaken in the water, and he shall 7070
2Ki 18:21 trustest upon the staff of this bruised **r,** 7070
Job 40:21 trees, in the covert of the **r,** and fens. 7070
Isa 36: 6 thou trustest in the staff of this broken **r,** 7070
 42: 3 A bruised **r** shall he not break, 7070
Eze 29: 6 they have been a staff of **r** to the house of 7070
 40: 3 line of flax in his hand, and a measuring **r;** 7070
 40: 5 in the man's hand a measuring **r** of six 7070
 40: 5 the breadth of the building, one **r;** 7070
 40: 5 one reed; and the height, one **r.** 7070
 40: 6 of the gate, *which was* one **r** broad; 7070
 40: 6 *of* the gate, *which was* one **r** broad. 7070
 40: 7 *every* little chamber *was* one **r** long, 7070
 40: 7 *was* one reed long, and one **r** broad; 7070
 40: 7 by the porch of the gate within *was* one **r.** 7070
 40: 8 also the porch of the gate within, one **r.** 7070
 41: 8 chambers *were* a full **r** of six great cubits. 7070
 42:16 the east side with the measuring **r,** 7070
 42:16 with the measuring **r** round about. 7070
 42:17 with the measuring **r** round about. 7070
 42:18 five hundred reeds, with the measuring **r.** 7070
 42:19 five hundred reeds with the measuring **r.** 7070
Mt 11: 7 to see? A **r** shaken with the wind? 2563
 12:20 A bruised **r** shall he not break, 2563
 27:29 it upon his head, and a **r** in his right hand: 2563
 27:30 took the **r,** and smote him on the head. 2563
 27:48 and put *it* on a **r,** and gave him to drink. 2563
Mk 15:19 And they smote him on the head with a **r,** 2563
 15:36 and put *it* on a **r,** and gave him to drink, 2563
Lk 7:24 for to see? A **r** shaken with the wind? 2563
Rev 11: 1 there was given a **r** like unto a rod: 2563

Rev 21:15 he that talked with me had a golden **r** *2563*
 21:16 and he measured the city with the **r**, *2563*

REEDS (11) [REED]

Isa 19: 6 and dried up: the **r** and flags shall wither. 7070
 19: 7 The **paper r** by the brooks, by the mouth 6169
 35: 7 each lay, *shall be* grass with **r** and rushes. 7070
Jer 51:32 the **r** they have burnt with fire, and the 98
Eze 42:16 five hundred **r**, with the measuring reed 7070
 42:17 measured the north side, five hundred **r**, 7070
 42:18 five hundred **r**, with the measuring reed 7070
 42:19 measured five hundred **r** with 7070
 42:20 five hundred **r** long, and five hundred NIH
 45: 1 twenty thousand **r**, and the breadth *shall* NIH
 48: 8 *of* five and twenty thousand **r** in breadth, NIH

REEL (2)

Ps 107:27 They **r to and fro**, and stagger like a 2287
Isa 24:20 The earth shall **r to and fro** like a *5128+5128*

REELAIAH (1)

Ezr 2: 2 Seraiah, **R**, Mordecai, Bilshan, Mizpar, 7480

REFINE (1) [REFINED, REFINER, REFINER'S]

Zec 13: 9 will **r** them as silver is refined, and will try 6884

REFINED (5) [REFINE]

1Ch 28:18 for the altar of incense **r** gold by weight; 2212
 29: 4 and seven thousand talents of **r** silver, 2212
Isa 25: 6 of marrow, of wines on the lees **well r**. 2212
 48:10 Behold, I have **r** thee, but not with silver; 6884
Zec 13: 9 will refine them as silver is **r**, and will try 6884

REFINER (1) [REFINE]

Mal 3: 3 he shall sit *as* a **r** and purifier of silver: 6884

REFINER'S (1) [REFINE]

Mal 3: 2 for he is like a **r** fire, and like fullers' sope: 6884

REFORMATION (1) [REFORMED]

Heb 9:10 imposed *on them* until the time of **r**. *1357*

REFORMED (1) [REFORMATION]

Lev 26:23 If ye will not be **r** by me by these *things,* 3256

REFRAIN (9) [REFRAINED, REFRAINETH]

Ge 45: 1 Joseph could not **r** himself before all them 662
Job 7:11 Therefore I will not **r** my mouth; I will 2820
Pr 1:15 with them; **r** thy foot from their path: 4513
Ecc 3: 5 and a time to **r** from embracing; 7368
Isa 48: 9 *for* my praise will I **r** for thee, that *I* cut 2413
 64:12 Wilt thou **r** thyself for these *things,* O 662
Jer 31:16 **R** thy voice from weeping, and thine eyes 4513
Ac 5:38 **R** from these men, and let them alone: *868*
1Pe 3:10 let him **r** his tongue from evil, and his lips *3973*

REFRAINED (7) [REFRAIN]

Ge 43:31 went out, and **r** himself, and said, Set on 662
Est 5:10 Nevertheless Haman **r** himself: and when 662
Job 29: 9 The princes **r** talking, and laid *their* hand 6113
Ps 40: 9 lo, I have not **r** my lips, O Lord, 3607
 119:101 I have **r** my feet from every evil way, that 3607
Isa 42:14 my peace; I have been still, *and* **r** myself: 662
Jer 14:10 they have not **r** their feet, therefore 2820

REFRAINETH (1) [REFRAIN]

Pr 10:19 not sin: but he that **r** his lips *is* wise. 2820

REFRESH (3) [REFRESHED, REFRESHETH, REFRESHING]

1Ki 13: 7 **r** *thyself,* and I will give thee a reward. 5582
Ac 27: 3 to go unto *his* friends to **r** himself. *1958+5177*
Phm 1:20 thee in the Lord: **r** my bowels in the Lord. *373*

REFRESHED (10) [REFRESH]

Ex 23:12 thy handmaid, and the stranger, may be **r**. 5314
 31:17 on the seventh day he rested, and was **r**. 5314
1Sa 16:23 so Saul was **r**, and was well, and the evil 7304
2Sa 16:14 came weary, and **r** themselves there. 5314
Job 32:20 I will speak, that I may be **r**: I will open 7304
Ro 15:32 the will of God, and may **with** you be **r**. *4875*
1Co 16:18 For they have **r** my spirit and yours: *373*
2Co 7:13 Titus, because his spirit was **r** by you all. *373*
2Ti 1:16 for he oft **r** me, and was not ashamed of *404*
Phm 1: 7 the bowels of the saints are **r** by thee, *373*

REFRESHETH (1) [REFRESH]

Pr 25:13 send him: for he **r** the soul of his masters. 7725

REFRESHING (2) [REFRESH]

Isa 28:12 cause the weary to rest; and this *is* the **r**: 4774
Ac 3:19 when *the* times of **r** shall come from *403*

REFUGE (47)

Nu 35: 6 the Levites *there shall be* six cities for **r**, 4733
 35:11 ye shall appoint you to be cities of **r** 4733
 35:12 they shall be unto you cities for **r** from 4733
 35:13 ye shall give six cities shall ye have for **r**. 4733
 35:14 land of Canaan, *which* shall be cities of **r**. 4733
 35:15 These six cities shall be a **r**, *both* for 4733
 35:25 shall restore him to the city of his **r**, 4733
 35:26 *without* the border of the city of his **r**, 4733
 35:27 without the borders of the city of his **r**, 4733
 35:28 of his **r** until the death of the high priest: 4733
 35:32 for him that is fled to the city of his **r**, 4733
Dt 33:27 The eternal God *is* thy **r**, and underneath 4585

Jos 20: 2 Appoint out for you cities of **r**, 4733
 20: 3 they shall be your **r** from the avenger of 4733
 21:13 suburbs, *to be* a city of **r** for the slayer; 4733
 21:21 *to be* a city of **r** for the slayer; 4733
 21:27 suburbs, *to be* a city of **r** for the slayer; 4733
 21:32 suburbs, *to be* a city of **r** for the slayer; 4733
 21:38 suburbs, *to be* a city of **r** for the slayer; 4733
2Sa 22: 3 my high tower, and my **r**, my saviour; 4498
1Ch 6:57 *city* of **r**, and Libnah with her suburbs, 4733
 6:67 they gave them, *of* the cities of **r**, 4733
Ps 9: 9 The Lord also will be a **r** 4869
 9: 9 for the oppressed, a **r** in times of trouble. 4869
 46: 1 God *is* our **r** and strength, a very present 4268
 46: 7 is with us; the God of Jacob *is* our **r**. 4869
 46:11 is with us; the God of Jacob *is* our **r**. 4869
 48: 3 God is known in her palaces for a **r**. 4869
 57: 1 shadow of thy wings will I **make** my **r**, 2620
 59:16 defence and **r** in the day of my trouble. 4498
 62: 7 rock of my strength, *and* my **r**, *is* in God. 4268
 62: 8 heart before him: God *is* a **r** for us. Selah. 4268
 71: 7 unto many; but thou *art* my strong **r**. 4268
 91: 2 of the Lord, *He is* my **r** and my fortress: 4268
 91: 9 *which is* my **r**, *even* the most High, 4268
 94:22 and my God *is* the rock of my **r**. 4268
 104:18 The high hills *are* a **r** for the wild goats; 4268
 142: 4 failed me; no man cared for my soul. 4498
 142: 5 Thou *art* my **r** *and* my portion in the land 4268
Pr 14:26 and his children shall have a **place of r**. 4268
Isa 4: 6 for a **place of r**, and for a covert from 4268
 25: 4 a **r** from the storm, a shadow from the 4268
 28:15 for we have made lies our **r**, 4268
 28:17 the hail shall sweep away the **r** of lies, 4268
Jer 16:19 and my **r** in the day of affliction, 4498
Heb 6:18 who have **fled for r** to lay hold upon *2703*

REFUSE (26) [REFUSED, REFUSEDST, REFUSETH]

Ex 4:23 *if* thou **r** to let him go, behold, I will slay 3985
 8: 2 if thou **r** to let *them* go, behold, I will 3986
 9: 2 For if thou **r** to let *them* go, and wilt hold 3986
 10: 3 How long wilt thou **r** to humble thyself 3985
 10: 4 Else, if thou **r** to let my people go, behold, 3986
 16:28 long *r* ye to keep my commandments 3985
 22:17 If her father **utterly r** to give her *3985+3985*
1Sa 15: 9 every thing *that was* vile and **r**, that they 4549
Job 34:33 whether thou **r**, or whether thou choose; 3988
Pr 8:33 instruction, and be wise, and **r** *it* not. 6544
 21: 7 because they **r** to do judgment. 3985
 21:25 killeth him; for his hands **r** to labour. 3985
Isa 1:20 if ye **r** and rebel, ye shall be devoured 3985
 7:15 that he may know to **r** the evil, 3988
 7:16 For before the child shall know to **r** 3988
Jer 8: 5 they hold fast deceit, they **r** to return. 3985
 9: 6 through deceit they **r** to know me, saith 3987
 13:10 evil people, which **r** to hear my words, 3987
 25:28 if they **r** to take the cup at thine hand to 3985
 38:21 if thou **r** to go forth, this *is* the word that 3986
La 3:45 and **r** in the midst of the people. 3973
Am 8: 6 *yea,* and sell the **r** of the wheat? 4651
Ac 25:11 any *thing* worthy of death, I **r** not to die: *3868*
1Ti 4: 7 But **r** profane and old wives' fables, *3868*
 5:11 But the younger widows **r:** for when they *3868*
Heb 12:25 See *that* ye **r** not him that speaketh: for if *3868*

REFUSED (33) [REFUSE]

Ge 37:35 he **r** to be comforted; and he said, For I 3985
 39: 8 he **r**, and said unto his master's wife, 3985
 48:19 his father **r**, and said, I know *it,* my son, 3985
Nu 20:21 Thus Edom **r** to give Israel passage 3985
1Sa 8:19 the people **r** to obey the voice 3985
 16: 7 of his stature; because I have **r** him: 3988
 28:23 he **r**, and said, I will not eat. But his 3985
2Sa 2:23 Howbeit he **r** to turn aside: 3985
 13: 9 *them* out before him; but he **r** to eat. 3985
1Ki 20:35 I pray thee. And the man **r** to smite him. 3985
 21:15 which he **r** to give thee for money; 3985
2Ki 5:16 And he urged him to take *it;* but he **r**. 3985
Ne 9:17 to obey, neither were mindful of thy 3985
Est 1:12 the queen Vashti **r** to come at the king's 3985
Job 6: 7 The things *which* my soul **r** to touch *are as* 3985
Ps 77: 2 ceased not: my soul **r** to be comforted. 3985
 78:10 of God, and **r** to walk in his law; 3985
 78:67 Moreover he **r** the tabernacle of Joseph, 3988
 118:22 The stone *which* the builders **r** is become 3988
Pr 1:24 Because I have called, and ye **r**; I have 3985
Isa 54: 6 youth, when thou wast **r**, saith thy God. 3988
Jer 5: 3 *but* they have **r** to receive correction: 3985
 5: 3 harder than a rock; they have **r** to return. 3985
 11:10 forefathers, which **r** to hear my words; 3985
 31:15 Rahel weeping for her children **r** to be 3985
 50:33 held them fast; they **r** to let them go. 3985
Eze 5: 6 for they have **r** my judgments, 3988
Hos 11: 5 shall be his king, because they **r** to return. 3985
Zec 7:11 they **r** to hearken, and pulled away 3985
Ac 7:35 This Moses whom they **r**, saying, Who *720*
1Ti 4: 4 of God *is* good, and nothing to be **r**, *579*
Heb 11:24 **r** to be called the son of Pharaoh's *720*
 12:25 for if they escaped not who **r** him that *3868*

REFUSEDST (1) [REFUSE]

Jer 3: 3 whore's forehead, thou **r** to be ashamed. 3985

REFUSETH (9) [REFUSE]

Ex 7:14 *is* hardened, he **r** to let the people go. 3985
Nu 22:13 for the Lord **r** to give me leave to go 3985

Nu 22:14 and said, Balaam **r** to come with us. 3985
Dt 25: 7 My husband's brother **r** to raise up unto 3985
Pr 10:17 but he that **r** reproof erreth. 5800
 13:18 shame *shall be* to him that **r** instruction: 6544
 15:32 He that **r** instruction despiseth his own 6544
Isa 8: 6 Forsomuch as this people **r** the waters of 3988
Jer 15:18 wound incurable, *which* **r** to be healed? 3985

REGARD (30) [REGARDED, REGARDEST, REGARDETH, REGARDING]

Ge 45:20 Also **r** not your stuff; for the good *2347+5869*
Ex 5: 9 and let them not **r** vain words. 8159
Lev 19:31 **R** not them that have familiar spirits, *413+6437*
Dt 28:50 which shall not **r** the person of the old, 5375
1Sa 4:20 answered not, neither did she **r** *it.* *3820+7896*
 25:25 I pray thee, **r** this man of Belial, *3820+7760*
2Sa 13:20 he *is* thy brother; **r** not this thing. *3820+7896*
2Ki 3:14 were it not that I **r** the presence of 5375
Job 3: 4 let not God **r** it from above, neither let 1875
 35:13 hear vanity, neither will the Almighty **r** it. 7789
 36:21 Take heed, **r** not iniquity: for this *413+6437*
Ps 28: 5 Because they **r** not the works of the Lord, 995
 31: 6 I have hated them that **r** lying vanities: 8104
 66:18 If I **r** iniquity in my heart, the Lord will 7200
 94: 7 not see, neither shall the God of Jacob **r** it. 995
 102:17 He will **r** the prayer of the destitute, 6437
Pr 5: 2 That *thou* mayest **r** discretion, and *that* 8104
 6:35 He will not **r** any ransom; *5375+6440*
Ecc 8: 2 and *that in* **r** of the oath of God. 1700
Isa 5:12 they **r** not the work of the Lord, 5027
 13:17 against them, which shall not **r** silver; 2803
La 4:16 divided them; he will no more **r** them: 5027
Da 11:37 Neither shall he **r** the God of his fathers, 995
 11:37 nor the desire of women, nor **r** any god: 995
Am 5:22 I will not accept *them:* neither will I **r** 5027
Hab 1: 5 and **r**, and wonder marvellously: 5027
Mal 1: 9 will he **r** your **persons**? *4480+5375+6440*
Lk 18: 4 Though I fear not God, nor **r** man; *1788*
Ac 8:11 And to him they **had r**, because that of *4337*
Ro 14: 6 the Lord he doth not **r** *it.* He that eateth, *5426*

REGARDED (9) [REGARD]

Ex 9:21 he that **r** not the word of the Lord *3820+7760*
1Ki 18:29 nor any to answer, nor any that **r**. 7182
1Ch 17:17 hast *r* me according to the estate of a man 7200
Ps 106:44 Nevertheless he **r** their affliction, when he 7200
Pr 1:24 stretched out my hand, and no man **r**; 7181
Da 3:12 these men, O king, have not **r** thee: *2942+7761*
Lk 1:48 For he hath **r** the low estate of his *1914*
 18: 2 which feared not God, neither **r** man: *1788*
Heb 8: 9 and I **r** them **not**, saith the Lord. *272*

REGARDEST (4) [REGARD]

2Sa 19: 6 that thou **r** neither princes nor servants: *3807.1*
Job 30:20 hear me: I stand *up,* and thou **r** me *not.* 995
Mt 22:16 neither carest thou for any *man:* for thou **r** *991*
Mk 12:14 carest for no *man:* for thou **r** not *991+1519*

REGARDETH (15) [REGARD]

Dt 10:17 and a terrible, which **r** not persons, 5375
Job 34:19 nor **r** the rich more than the poor? 5234
 39: 7 neither **r** he the crying of the driver. 8085
Pr 12:10 A righteous *man* **r** the life of his beast: 3045
 13:18 but he that **r** reproof shall be honoured. 8104
 15: 5 but he that **r** reproof is prudent. 8104
 29: 7 the poor: *but* the wicked **r** not to know *it.* 995
Ecc 5: 8 for *he that is* higher than the highest **r**; 8104
 11: 4 and he that **r** the clouds shall not reap. 7200
Isa 33: 8 he hath despised the cities, he **r** no man. 2803
Da 6:13 **r** not thee, O king, nor the decree that 7761
Mal 2:13 insomuch that *he* **r** not the offering *413+6437*
Ro 14: 6 He that **r** the day, regardeth *it* unto *5426*
 14: 6 that **r** the day, **r** *it* unto the Lord; *5426*
 14: 6 and he that **r** not the day, to the Lord he *5426*

REGARDING (2) [REGARD]

Job 4:20 they perish for ever without *any* **r** *it.* 7760
Php 2:30 not **r** *his* life, to supply your lack of *3851*

REGEM (1)

1Ch 2:47 **R**, and Jotham, and Geshan, and Pelet, 7276

REGEMMELECH (1)

Zec 7: 2 *unto* the house of God Sherezer and **R**, 7278

REGENERATION (2)

Mt 19:28 That ye which have followed me, in the **r**, *3824*
Tit 3: 5 by the washing of **r**, and renewing of *3824*

REGION (15) [REGIONS]

Dt 3: 4 threescore cities, all the **r** of Argob, 2256
 3:13 all the **r** of Argob, with all Bashan, which 2256
1Ki 4:11 The son of Abinadab, *in* all the **r** of Dor; 5299
 4:13 to him *also* pertained the **r** of Argob, 2256
 4:24 For he had dominion over all *the* **r** on NIH
Mt 3: 5 and all the **r** **round about** Jordan, 4066
 4:16 and to them which sat in the **r** and 5561
Mk 1:28 throughout all the **r** **round about** Galilee. 4066
 6:55 ran through that whole **r** **round about**, 4066
Lk 3: 1 of Iturea and of the **r** of Trachonitis, 5561
 4:14 of him through all the **r** **round about**. 4066
 7:17 throughout all the **r** **round about**. 4066
Ac 13:49 Lord was published throughout all the **r**. 5561
 14: 6 and *unto* the **r** that lieth **round about**: 4066
 16: 6 throughout Phrygia and the **r** of Galatia, 5561

R

REGIONS (4) [REGION]
Ac	8: 1 scattered abroad throughout the **r** of Judea	5561
2Co	10:16 To preach the gospel in the **r** beyond you,	NIG
	11:10 stop me of this boasting in the **r** of Achaia.	2824
Gal	1:21 Afterwards I came into the **r** of Syria and	2824

REGISTER (3)
Ezr	2:62 These sought their **r** *among* those that	3791
Ne	7: 5 I found a **r** of the genealogy of them	5612
	7:64 These sought their **r** *among* those that	3791

REGULAR See SERVILE

REHABIAH (5)
1Ch	23:17 the sons of Eliezer *were*, **R** the chief.	7345
	23:17 but the sons of **R** were very many.	7345
	24:21 Concerning **R:** of the sons of Rehabiah,	7345
	24:21 of the sons of **R**, the first *was* Isshiah.	7345
	26:25 **R** his son, and Jeshaiah his son,	7345

REHEARSE (2) [REHEARSED]
Ex	17:14 in a book, and **r** *it* in the ears of Joshua:	7760
Jdg	5:11 they **r** the righteous acts of the LORD,	8567

REHEARSED (4) [REHEARSE]
1Sa	8:21 and he **r** them in the ears of the LORD.	1696
	17:31 David spake, they **r** *them* before Saul:	5046
Ac	11: 4 Peter **r** *the matter* from the beginning,	NIG
	14:27 they had God had done with them,	312

REHOB (10) [BETH-REHOB]
Nu	13:21 land from the wilderness of Zin unto **R**,	7340
Jos	19:28 and **R**, and Hammon, and Kanah,	7340
	19:30 Ummah also, and Aphek, and **R:** twenty	7340
	21:31 her suburbs, and **R** with her suburbs;	7340
Jdg	1:31 nor of Helbah, nor of Aphik, nor of **R:**	7340
2Sa	8: 3 the son of **R**, king of Zobah,	7340
	8:12 of Hadadezer, son of **R**, king of Zobah.	7340
	10: 8 and of **R**, and Ish-tob, and Maacah,	7340
1Ch	6:75 her suburbs, and **R** with her suburbs,	7340
Ne	10:11 Micha, **R**, Hashabiah,	7340

REHOBOAM (50) [ROBOAM]
1Ki	11:43 and **R** his son reigned for in his stead.	7346
	12: 1 **R** went *to* Shechem: for all Israel were	7346
	12: 1 of Israel came to, and spake unto **R**, saying,	7346
	12: 6 king **R** consulted with the old men,	7346
	12:12 all the people came to **R** the third day,	7346
	12:17 the cities of Judah, **R** reigned over them.	7346
	12:18 king **R** sent Adoram, who *was* over	7346
	12:18 Therefore king **R** made speed to get *him*	7346
	12:21 when **R** was come *to* Jerusalem,	7346
	12:21 to bring the kingdom again to **R** the son	7346
	12:23 Speak unto **R**, the son of Solomon, king	7346
	12:27 *even* unto **R** king of Judah, and they shall	7346
	12:27 kill me, and go again to **R** king of Judah.	7346
	14:21 the son of Solomon reigned in Judah.	7346
	14:21 **R** *was* forty and one years old when he	7346
	14:25 it came to pass in the fifth year of king **R**,	7346
	14:27 king **R** made in their stead brasen shields,	7346
	14:29 Now the rest of the acts of **R**, and all that	7346
	14:31 **R** slept with his fathers, and was buried	7346
	15: 6 there was war between **R** and Jeroboam	7346
1Ch	3:10 Solomon's son **R**, Abia his son,	7346
2Ch	9:31 **R** his son reigned in his stead.	7346
	10: 1 **R** went to Shechem: for to Shechem were	7346
	10: 3 and all Israel came and spake to **R**,	7346
	10: 6 king **R** took counsel with the old men	7346
	10:12 all the people came to **R** on the third day,	7346
	10:13 **R** forsook the counsel of the old men,	7346
	10:17 the cities of Judah, **R** reigned over them.	7346
	10:18 king **R** sent Hadoram that *was* over	7346
	10:18 king **R** made speed to get *him* up to *his*	7346
	11: 1 when **R** was come to Jerusalem,	7346
	11: 1 *he* might bring the kingdom again to **R**.	7346
	11: 3 Speak unto **R** the son of Solomon, king of	7346
	11: 5 **R** dwelt in Jerusalem, and built cities for	7346
	11:17 made **R** the son of Solomon strong,	7346
	11:18 **R** took him Mahalath the daughter of	7346
	11:21 **R** loved Maachah the daughter of	7346
	11:22 **R** made Abijah the son of Maachah	7346
	12: 1 when **R** had established the kingdom,	7346
	12: 2 in the fifth year of king **R** Shishak king	7346
	12: 5 came Shemaiah the prophet to **R**, and *to*	7346
	12:10 Instead of which king **R** made shields of	7346
	12:13 So king **R** strengthened himself in	7346
	12:13 **R** *was* one and forty years old when he	7346
	12:15 Now the acts of **R**, first and last, *are* they	7346
	12:15 there *were* wars between **R** and	7346
	12:16 **R** slept with his fathers, and was buried	7346
	13: 7 have strengthened themselves against **R**	7346
	13: 7 when **R** was young and tender hearted,	7346

REHOBOTH (4)
Ge	10:11 Nineveh, and the city **R**, and Calah,	7344
	26:22 he called the name of it **R**; and he said,	7344
	36:37 Saul of **R** *by* the river reigned in his stead.	7344
1Ch	1:48 Shaul of **R** *by* the river reigned in his	7344

REHU (1)
1Ch	1:25 Eber, Peleg, **R**,	7466

REHUM (8)
Ezr	2: 2 Bilshan, Mizpar, Bigvai, **R**, Baanah.	7348
	4: 8 **R** the chancellor and Shimshai the scribe	7348

Ezr	4: 9 wrote **R** the chancellor, and Shimshai	7348
	4:17 Then sent the king an answer unto **R**	7348
	4:23 king Artaxerxes' letter *was* read before **R**,	7348
Ne	3:17 repaired the Levites, **R** the son of Bani.	7348
	10:25 **R**, Hashabnah, Maaseiah,	7348
	12: 3 Shechaniah, **R**, Meremoth,	7348

REI (1)
1Ki	1: 8 **R**, and the mighty *men* which *belonged*	7472

REIGN (168) [REIGNED, REIGNEST, REIGNETH, REIGNING]
Ge	37: 8 him, Shalt thou **indeed r** over us?	4427+4427
Ex	15:18 The LORD shall **r** for ever and ever.	4427
Lev	26:17 they that hate you shall **r** over you;	7287
Dt	15: 6 thou shalt **r** over many nations,	4910
	15: 6 but they shall not **r** over thee.	4910
Jdg	9: 2 **r** over you, or that one reign over you?	4910
	9: 2 reign over you, or that one **r** over you?	4910
	9: 8 said unto the olive tree, **R** thou over us.	4427
	9:10 to the fig tree, Come thou, *and* **r** over us.	4427
	9:12 unto the vine, Come thou, *and* **r** over us.	4427
	9:14 the bramble, Come thou, *and* **r** over us.	4427
1Sa	8: 7 me, that *I* should not **r** over them.	4427
	8: 9 of the king that shall **r** over them.	4427
	8:11 manner of the king that shall **r** over you:	4427
	9:17 thee of: this *same* shall **r** over my people.	6113
	11:12 Who *is* he that said, Shall Saul **r** over us?	4427
	12:12 unto me, Nay; but a king shall **r** over us:	4427
2Sa	2:10 years old when he *began* to **r** over Israel,	4427
	3:21 thou mayest **r** over all that thine heart	4427
	5: 4 *was* thirty years old when he *began* to **r**.	4427
1Ki	1:11 that Adonijah the son of Haggith doth **r**,	4427
	1:13 Assuredly Solomon thy son shall **r** after	4427
	1:13 my throne? why then doth Adonijah **r**?	4427
	1:17 Assuredly Solomon thy son shall **r** after	4427
	1:24 Adonijah shall **r** after me, and he shall sit	4427
	1:30 Assuredly Solomon thy son shall **r** after	4427
	2:15 set their faces on me, that *I* should **r**:	4427
	6: 1 in the fourth year of Solomon's **r** over	4427
	11:37 thou shalt **r** according to all that thy soul	4427
	14:21 and one years old when he *began* to **r**,	4427
	15:25 Nadab the son of Jeroboam *began* to **r**	4427
	15:33 son of Ahijah to **r** over all Israel in Tirzah,	4427
	16: 8 son of Baasha to **r** over Israel in Tirzah,	4427
	16:11 it came to pass, when he *began* to **r**,	4427
	16:15 of Judah did Zimri **r** seven days in Tirzah.	4427
	16:23 king of Judah *began* Omri to **r** over Israel,	4427
	16:29 Ahab the son of Omri to **r** over Israel:	4427
	22:41 Jehoshaphat the son of Asa *began* to **r**	4427
	22:42 and five years old when he *began* to **r**;	4427
	22:51 Ahaziah the son of Ahab *began* to **r** over	4427
2Ki	1: 1 Now Jehoram the son of Ahab *began* to **r**	4427
	8:16 of Jehoshaphat king of Judah *began* to **r**.	4427
	8:17 years old was he when he *began* to **r**;	4427
	8:25 of Jehoram king of Judah *begin* to **r**.	4427
	8:26 old *was* Ahaziah when he *began* to **r**;	4427
	9:29 of Ahab *began* Ahaziah to **r** over Judah.	4427
	11: 3 And Athaliah *did* **r** over the land.	4427
	11:21 old *was* Jehoash when he *began* to **r**;	4427
	12: 1 seventh year of Jehu Jehoash *began* to **r**;	4427
	13: 1 of Jehu *began* to **r** over Israel in Samaria,	4427
	13:10 of Jehoahaz to **r** over Israel in Samaria,	4427
	14: 2 and five years old when he *began* to **r**,	4427
	14:23 Joash king of Israel *began* to **r** in Samaria,	4427
	15: 1 Azariah son of Amaziah king of Judah to **r**,	4427
	15: 2 years old was he when he *began* to **r**,	4427
	15: 8 **r** over Israel in Samaria six months.	4427
	15:13 Shallum the son of Jabesh *began* to **r** in	4427
	15:17 Menahem the son of Gadi to **r** over Israel,	4427
	15:23 *began* to **r** over Israel in Samaria,	4427
	15:27 Remaliah *began* to **r** over Israel in	4427
	15:32 the son of Uzziah king of Judah to **r**.	4427
	15:33 years old was he when he *began* to **r**,	4427
	16: 1 son of Jotham king of Judah *began* to **r**.	4427
	16: 2 years old *was* Ahaz when he *began* to **r**,	4427
	17: 1 Elah to **r** in Samaria over Israel nine years.	4427
	18: 1 the son of Ahaz king of Judah *began* to **r**.	4427
	18: 2 five years old was he when he *began* to **r**;	4427
	21: 1 was twelve years old when he *began* to **r**,	4427
	21:19 and two years old when he *began* to **r**,	4427
	22: 1 *was* eight years old when he *began* to **r**;	4427
	23:31 and three years old when he *began* to **r**;	4427
	23:33 that *he* might not **r** in Jerusalem;	4427
	23:36 and five year old when he *began* to **r**;	4427
	24: 8 eighteen years old when he *began* to **r**,	4427
	24:12 took him in the eighth year of his **r**.	4427
	24:18 and one years old when he *began* to **r**,	4427
	25: 1 it came to pass in the ninth year of his **r**,	4427
	25:27 Babylon, in the year that he *began* to **r**,	4427
1Ch	4:31 *were* their cities unto the **r** of David they	4427
	26:31 In the fortieth year of the **r** of David they	4438
	29:30 With all his **r** and his might, and the	4438
2Ch	1: 8 and hast **made** me to **r** in his stead.	4438
	3: 2 second month, in the fourth year of his **r**.	4438
	12:13 and forty years old when he *began* to **r**;	4427
	13: 1 Jeroboam *began* Abijah to **r** over Judah.	4427
	15:10 in the fifteenth year of the **r** of Asa.	4438
	15:19 the five and thirtieth year of the **r** of Asa.	4438
	16: 1 thirtieth year of the **r** of Asa Baasha king	4438
	16:12 year of his **r** was diseased in his feet,	4438
	16:13 died in the one and fortieth year of his **r**.	4438
	17: 7 Also in the third year of his **r** he sent to	4438
	20:31 and five years old when he *began* to **r**,	4427
	21: 5 and two years old when he *began* to **r**,	4427

2Ch	21:20 years old was he when he *began* to **r**,	4427
	22: 2 old *was* Ahaziah when he *began* to **r**,	4427
	23: 3 unto them, Behold, the king's son shall **r**,	4427
	24: 1 *was* seven years old when he *began* to **r**,	4427
	25: 1 and five years old *when* he *began* to **r**,	4427
	26: 3 years old *was* Uzziah when he *began* to **r**,	4427
	27: 1 and five years old when he *began* to **r**,	4427
	27: 8 and twenty years old when he *began* to **r**,	4427
	28: 1 was twenty years old when he *began* to **r**,	4427
	29: 1 Hezekiah *began* to **r** *when he was* five	4427
	29: 3 He in the first year of his **r**, in the first	4427
	29:19 which king Ahaz in his **r** did cast away in	4438
	33: 1 *was* twelve years old when he *began* to **r**,	4427
	33:21 and twenty years old when he *began* to **r**,	4427
	34: 1 was eight years old when he *began* to **r**,	4427
	34: 3 For in the eighth year of his **r**, while he	4427
	34: 8 Now in the eighteenth year of his **r**,	4427
	35:19 In the eighteenth year of the **r** of Josiah	4438
	36: 2 and three years old when he *began* to **r**,	4427
	36: 5 and five years old when he *began* to **r**,	4427
	36: 9 was eight years old when he *began* to **r**,	4427
	36:11 and twenty years old when he *began* to **r**,	4427
	36:20 his sons until the **r** of the kingdom of	4427
Ezr	4: 5 even until the **r** of Darius king of Persia.	4438
	4: 6 in the **r** of Ahasuerus, in the beginning of	4438
	4: 6 of Ahasuerus, in the beginning of his **r**,	4438
	4:24 So it ceased unto the second year of the **r**	4437
	6:15 which *was in* the sixth year of the **r** of	4437
	7: 1 in the **r** of Artaxerxes king of Persia,	4438
	8: 1 in the **r** of Artaxerxes the king.	4438
Ne	12:22 the priests, to the **r** of Darius the Persian.	4438
Est	1: 3 In the third year of his **r**, he made a feast	4438
	2:16 Tebeth, in the seventh year of his **r**.	4438
Job	34:30 That the hypocrite **r** not, lest the people	4427
Ps	146:10 The LORD shall **r** for ever, *even* thy God,	4427
Pr	8:15 By me kings **r**, and princes decree justice.	4427
Ecc	4:14 For out of prison he cometh to **r**;	4427
Isa	24:23 when the LORD of hosts shall **r** in mount	4427
	32: 1 king shall **r** in righteousness, and princes	4427
Jer	1: 2 of Judah, in the thirteenth year of his **r**.	4427
	22:15 Shalt thou **r**, because thou closest *thyself*	4427
	23: 5 a King shall **r** and prosper,	4427
	26: 1 In the beginning of the **r** of Jehoiakim	4468
	27: 1 In the beginning of the **r** of Jehoiakim	4467
	28: 1 in the beginning of the **r** of Zedekiah king	4467
	33:21 that he should not have a son to **r** upon	4427
	49:34 of the **r** of Zedekiah king of Judah,	4438
	51:59 *into* Babylon in the fourth year of his **r**.	4438
	52: 1 and twenty year old when he *began* to **r**,	4427
	52: 4 it came to pass in the ninth year of his **r**,	4427
	52:31 **r** lifted up the head of Jehoiachin king of	4438
Da	1: 1 In the third year of the **r** of Jehoiakim	4438
	2: 1 In the second year of the **r** of	4438
	6:28 this Daniel prospered in the **r** of Darius,	4437
	6:28 Darius, and in the **r** of Cyrus the Persian.	4437
	8: 1 In the third year of the **r** of king	4438
	9: 1 In the first year of his **r** I Daniel	4438
Mic	4: 7 the LORD shall **r** over them in mount	4427
Mt	2:22 When he heard that Archelaus did **r** in	936
Lk	1:33 And he shall **r** over the house of Jacob for	936
	3: 1 In the fifteenth year of the **r** of	2231
	19:14 We will not have this *man* to **r** over us.	936
	19:27 would not that I should **r** over them,	936
Ro	5:17 of the gift of righteousness shall **r** in life by	936
	5:21 might grace **r** through righteousness unto	936
	6:12 Let not sin therefore **r** in your mortal body,	936
	15:12 he that *shall* rise to **r** over the Gentiles;	757
1Co	4: 8 and I would *to God* ye did **r**, that we also	936
	4: 8 did reign, that we also might **r with** you.	4821
	15:25 For he must **r**, till he hath put all enemies	936
2Ti	2:12 we shall also **r with** him: if we deny *him*,	4821
Rev	5:10 and priests: and we shall **r** on the earth.	936
	11:15 his Christ; and he shall **r** for ever and ever.	936
	20: 6 and **r** with him a thousand years.	936
	22: 5 and they shall **r** for ever and ever.	936

REIGNED (176) [REIGN]
Ge	36:31 these *are* the kings that **r** in the land of	4427
	36:31 before there **r** *any* king over the children	4427
	36:32 Bela the son of Beor **r** in Edom:	4427
	36:33 Jobab the son of Zerah of Bozrah **r** in his	4427
	36:34 Husham of the land of Temani **r** in his	4427
	36:35 Midian in the field of Moab, **r** in his stead	4427
	36:36 and Samlah of Masrekah **r** in his stead.	4427
	36:37 Saul of Rehoboth *by* the river **r** in his	4427
	36:38 Baal-hanan the son of Achbor **r** in his	4427
	36:39 of Achbor died, and Hadar **r** in his stead:	4427
Jos	12: 5 **r** in mount Hermon, and in Salcah,	4910
	13:10 which **r** in Heshbon, unto the border of	4427
	13:12 which **r** in Ashtaroth and in Edrei,	4427
	13:21 of the Amorites, which **r** in Heshbon,	4427
Jdg	4: 2 of Jabin king of Canaan, that **r** in Hazor;	4427
	9:22 When Abimelech had **r** three years over	7786
1Sa	13: 1 Saul **r** one year; and when he had reigned	4427
	13: 1 and when he had **r** two years over Israel,	4427
2Sa	2:10 to reign over Israel, and **r** two years.	4427
	5: 4 he *began* to reign, *and* he **r** forty years.	4427
	5: 5 In Hebron he **r** over Judah seven years	4427
	5: 5 In Jerusalem he **r** thirty and three years	4427
	8:15 David **r** over all Israel; and David	4427
	10: 1 and Hanun his son **r** in his stead.	4427
	16: 8 of Saul, in whose stead thou hast **r**;	4427
1Ki	2:11 days that David **r** over Israel *were* forty	4427
	2:11 seven years **r** he in Hebron, and thirty	4427
	2:11 thirty and three years **r** he in Jerusalem.	4427

1Ki	
4:21 Solomon r over all kingdoms from the	4910
11:24 and dwelt therein, and r in Damascus.	4427
11:25 and he abhorred Israel, and r over Syria.	4427
11:42 the time that Solomon r in Jerusalem over	4427
11:43 and Rehoboam his son r in his stead.	4427
12:17 cities of Judah, Rehoboam r over them.	4427
14:19 Jeroboam, how he warred, and how he r,	4427
14:20 the days which Jeroboam r *were* two and	4427
14:20 and Nadab his son r in his stead.	4427
14:21 Rehoboam the son of Solomon r in Judah.	4427
14:21 and he r seventeen years in Jerusalem.	4427
14:31 And Abijam his son r in his stead.	4427
15: 1 the son of Nebat r Abijam over Judah.	4427
15: 2 Three years r he in Jerusalem. And his	4427
15: 8 of David: and Asa his son r in his stead.	4427
15: 9 king of Israel r Asa over Judah.	4427+4428
15:10 forty and one years r he in Jerusalem.	4427
15:24 and Jehoshaphat his son r in his stead.	4427
15:25 king of Judah, and r over Israel two years.	4427
15:28 did Baasha slay him, and r in his stead.	4427
15:29 to pass, when he r, *that* he smote all	4427
16: 6 in Tirzah: and Elah his son r in his stead.	4427
16:10 of Asa king of Judah, and r in his stead.	4427
16:22 son of Ginath: so Tibni died, and Omri r.	4427
16:23 twelve years: six years r he in Tirzah.	4427
16:28 Samaria: and Ahab his son r in his stead.	4427
16:29 Ahab the son of Omri r over Israel in	4427
22:40 and Ahaziah his son r in his stead.	4427
22:42 he r twenty and five years in Jerusalem.	4427
22:50 and Jehoram his son r in his stead.	4427
22:51 king of Judah, and r two years over Israel.	4427
2Ki	
1:17 Jehoram r in his stead in the second year	4427
3: 1 king of Judah, and r twelve years.	4427
3:27 took his eldest son that should have r in	4427
8:15 so that he died: and Hazael r in his stead.	4427
8:17 reign; and he r eight years in Jerusalem.	4427
8:24 and Ahaziah his son r in his stead.	4427
8:26 to reign; and he r one year in Jerusalem.	4427
10:35 And Jehoahaz his son r in his stead.	4427
10:36 time that Jehu r over Israel in Samaria	4427
12: 1 reign; and forty years r he in Jerusalem.	4427
12:21 and Amaziah his son r in his stead.	4427
13: 1 Israel in Samaria, *and r* seventeen years.	NIH
13: 9 Samaria: and Joash his son r in his stead.	4427
13:10 Israel in Samaria, *and r* sixteen years.	NIH
13:24 and Ben-hadad his son r in his stead.	4427
14: 1 r Amaziah the son of Joash king of Judah.	4427
14: 2 r twenty and nine years in Jerusalem.	4427
14:16 and Jeroboam his son r in his stead.	4427
14:23 in Samaria, *and r* forty and one years.	NIH
14:29 and Zachariah his son r in his stead.	4427
15: 2 and he r two and fifty years in Jerusalem.	4427
15: 7 David: and Jotham his son r in his stead.	4427
15:10 and slew him, and r in his stead.	4427
15:13 Judah; and he r a full month in Samaria.	4427
15:14 and slew him, and r in his stead.	4427
15:17 over Israel, *and r* ten years in Samaria.	NIH
15:22 and Pekahiah his son r in his stead.	4427
15:23 over Israel in Samaria, *and r* two years.	NIH
15:25 he killed him, and r in his room.	4427
15:27 over Israel in Samaria, *and r* twenty years.	NIH
15:30 and slew him, and r in his stead.	4427
15:33 and he r sixteen years in Jerusalem.	4427
15:38 his father: and Ahaz his son r in his stead.	4427
16: 2 r sixteen years in Jerusalem, and did not	4427
16:20 and Hezekiah his son r in his stead.	4427
18: 2 he r twenty and nine years in Jerusalem.	4427
19:37 And Esarhaddon his son r in his stead.	4427
20:21 and Manasseh his son r in his stead.	4427
21: 1 and r fifty and five years in Jerusalem.	4427
21:18 of Uzza: and Amon his son r in his stead.	4427
21:19 to reign, and he r two years in Jerusalem.	4427
21:26 of Uzza: and Josiah his son r in his stead.	4427
22: 1 he r thirty and one years in Jerusalem.	4427
23:31 and he r three months in Jerusalem.	4427
23:36 and he r eleven years in Jerusalem.	4427
24: 6 and Jehoiachin his son r in his stead.	4427
24: 8 and he r in Jerusalem three months.	4427
24:18 and he r eleven years in Jerusalem.	4427
1Ch	
1:43 these *are* the kings that r in the land	4427
1:43 *any* king over the children of Israel;	4427
1:44 Jobab the son of Zerah of Bozrah r in his	4427
1:45 Husham of the land of the Temanites r in	4427
1:46 in the field of Moab, r in his stead.	4427
1:47 Samlah of Masrekah r in his stead.	4427
1:48 Shaul of Rehoboth *by* the river r in his	4427
1:49 Baal-hanan the son of Achbor r in his	4427
1:50 was dead, Hadad r in his stead:	4427
3: 4 there he r seven years and six months:	4427
3: 4 in Jerusalem he r thirty and three years.	4427
18:14 So David r over all Israel, and executed	4427
19: 1 Ammon died, and his son r in his stead.	4427
29:26 Thus David the son of Jesse r over all	4427
29:27 the time that he r over Israel *was* forty	4427
29:27 seven years r he in Hebron, and thirty	4427
29:27 thirty and three *years* r he in Jerusalem.	4427
29:28 and Solomon his son r in his stead.	4427
2Ch	
1:13 of the congregation, and r over Israel.	4427
9:26 he r over all the kings from the river	4910
9:30 Solomon r in Jerusalem over all Israel	4427
9:31 and Rehoboam his son r in his stead.	4427
10:17 cities of Judah, Rehoboam r over them.	4427
12:13 strengthened himself in Jerusalem, and r:	4427
12:13 and he r seventeen years in Jerusalem.	4427
12:16 David: and Abijah his son r in his stead.	4427

2Ch	
13: 2 He r three years in Jerusalem.	4427
14: 1 Asa his son r in his stead. In his days	4427
17: 1 Jehoshaphat his son r in his stead,	4427
20:31 Jehoshaphat r over Judah: *he was* thirty	4427
20:31 he r twenty and five years in Jerusalem.	4427
21: 1 and Jehoram his son r in his stead.	4427
21: 5 reign, and he r eight years in Jerusalem.	4427
21:20 he r in Jerusalem eight years,	4427
22: 1 the son of Jehoram king of Judah r.	4427
22: 2 to reign, and he r one year in Jerusalem.	4427
22:12 six years: and Athaliah r over the land.	4427
24: 1 reign, and he r forty years in Jerusalem.	4427
24:27 And Amaziah his son r in his stead.	4427
25: 1 he r twenty and nine years in Jerusalem.	4427
26: 3 and he r fifty and two years in Jerusalem.	4427
26:23 a leper: and Jotham his son r in his stead.	4427
27: 1 and he r sixteen years in Jerusalem.	4427
27: 8 to reign, and r sixteen years in Jerusalem.	4427
27: 9 of David: and Ahaz his son r in his stead.	4427
28: 1 and he r sixteen years in Jerusalem:	4427
28:27 and Hezekiah his son r in his stead.	4427
29: 1 he r nine and twenty years in Jerusalem.	4427
32:33 And Manasseh his son r in his stead.	4427
33: 1 and he r fifty and five years in Jerusalem.	4427
33:20 and Amon his son r in his stead.	4427
33:21 to reign, and r two years in Jerusalem.	4427
34: 1 in Jerusalem one and thirty years.	4427
36: 2 and he r three months in Jerusalem.	4427
36: 5 and he r eleven years in Jerusalem:	4427
36: 8 and Jehoiachin his son r in his stead.	4427
36: 9 he r three months and ten days in	4427
36:11 to reign, and r eleven years in Jerusalem.	4427
Est	
1: 1 (this *is* Ahasuerus which r, from India	4427
Isa	
37:38 and Esar-haddon his son r in his stead.	4427
Jer	
22:11 which r instead of Josiah his father,	4427
37: 1 Zedekiah the son of Josiah r instead of	4427
52: 1 and he r eleven years in Jerusalem.	4427
Ro	
5:14 Nevertheless death r from Adam to Moses,	936
5:17 For if by one man's offence death r by one;	936
5:21 That as sin hath r unto death, even so	936
1Co	
4: 8 ye are rich, ye have r *as kings* without us:	936
Rev	
11:17 taken to thee thy great power, and hast r.	936
20: 4 and r with Christ a thousand years.	936

REIGNEST (1) [REIGN]
1Ch	29:12 honour *come* of thee, and thou r over all;	4910

REIGNETH (13) [REIGN]
1Sa	12:14 also the king that r over you continue	4427
2Sa	15:10 then ye shall say, Absalom r in Hebron.	4427
1Ki	1:18 behold, Adonijah r; and now, my lord	4427
1Ch	16:31 *men* say among the nations, The LORD r.	4427
Ps	47: 8 God r over the heathen: God sitteth upon	4427
	93: 1 The LORD r, he is clothed with majesty;	4427
	96:10 Say among the heathen *that* the LORD r:	4427
	97: 1 The LORD r; let the earth rejoice;	4427
	99: 1 The LORD r; let the people tremble;	4427
Pr	30:22 For a servant when he r; and a fool when	4427
Isa	52: 7 that saith unto Zion, Thy God r!	4427
Rev	17:18 which r over the kings of the earth.	932+2192
	19: 6 Alleluia: for the Lord God Omnipotent r.	936

REIGNING (1) [REIGN]
1Sa	16: 1 seeing I have rejected him from r over	4427

REINS (15)
Job	16:13 he cleaveth my r asunder, and doth not	3629
	19:27 *though* my r be consumed within me.	3629
Ps	7: 9 the righteous God trieth the hearts and	3629
	16: 7 my r also instruct me *in* the night seasons.	3629
	26: 2 and prove me; try my r and my heart.	3629
	73:21 was grieved, and I was pricked *in* my r.	3629
	139:13 For thou hast possessed my r: thou hast	3629
Pr	23:16 Yea, my r shall rejoice, when thy lips	3629
Isa	11: 5 and faithfulness the girdle of his r.	2504
Jer	11:20 that triest the r and the heart,	3629
	12: 2 near in their mouth, and far from their r.	3629
	17:10 I the LORD search the heart, I *try* the r,	3629
	20:12 righteous, *and* seest the r and the heart,	3629
La	3:13 arrows of his quiver to enter into my r.	3629
Rev	2:23 know that I am he which searcheth the r	3510

REJECT (4) [REJECTED, REJECTETH]
Hos	4: 6 rejected knowledge, I will also r thee,	3988
Mk	6:26 which sat with *him,* he would not r her.	114
	7: 9 Full well ye r the commandment of God,	114
Tit	3:10 after the first and second admonition, r;	3868

REJECTED (29) [REJECT]
1Sa	8: 7 for they have not r thee, but they have	3988
	8: 7 not rejected thee, but they have r me,	3988
	10:19 ye have *this* day r your God, who himself	3988
	15:23 Because thou hast r the word of	3988
	15:23 he hath also r thee from *being* king.	3988
	15:26 for thou hast r the word of the LORD,	3988
	15:26 the LORD hath r thee from being king	3988
	16: 1 seeing I have r him from reigning over	3988
2Ki	17:15 they r his statutes, and his covenant that	3988
	17:20 The LORD r all the seed of Israel,	3988
Isa	53: 3 He is despised and r of men; a man of	2310
Jer	2:37 for the LORD hath r thy confidences,	3988
	6:19 unto my words, nor *to* my law, but r it.	3988
	6:30 call them, because the LORD hath r them.	3988
	7:29 for the LORD hath r and forsaken	3988
	8: 9 lo, they have r the word of the LORD;	3988

Jer	14:19 Hast thou **utterly** r Judah? hath	3988+3988
La	5:22 thou hast **utterly** r us; thou art	3988+3988
Hos	4: 6 because thou hast r knowledge, I will also	3988
Mt	The stone which the builders r,	593
Mk	8:31 suffer many *things,* and be r of the elders,	593
	12:10 The stone which the builders r is become	593
Lk	7:30 lawyers the counsel of God against	114
	9:22 be r of the elders and chief priests and	593
	17:25 many *things,* and be r of this generation.	593
	20:17 is written, The stone which the builders r,	593
Gal	4:14 was in my flesh ye despised not, nor r;	1609
Heb	6: 8 that which beareth thorns and briers *is* r,	96
	12:17 have inherited the blessing, he was r:	593

REJECTETH (1) [REJECT]
Jn	12:48 He that r me, and receiveth not my words,	114

REJOICE (192) [REJOICED, REJOICEST, REJOICETH, REJOICING]
Lev	23:40 ye shall r before the LORD your God	8055
Dt	12: 7 ye shall r in all that you put your hand	8055
	12:12 ye shall r before the LORD your God,	8055
	12:18 thou shalt r before the LORD thy God in	8055
	14:26 thou shalt r, thou and thine household,	8055
	16:11 thou shalt r before the LORD thy God,	8055
	16:14 shalt r in thy feast, thou, and thy son,	8055
	16:15 therefore thou shalt surely r.	1961+8056
	26:11 thou shalt r in every good *thing* which	8055
	27: 7 eat there, and r before the LORD thy God.	8055
	28:63 the LORD will r over you to destroy you,	7797
	30: 9 for the LORD will again r over thee for	7797
	32:43 R, O ye nations, *with* his people: for he	7442
	33:18 he said, R, Zebulun, in thy going out;	8055
Jdg	9:19 *then* r ye in Abimelech, and let him also	8055
	9:19 in Abimelech, and let him also r in you:	8055
	16:23 sacrifice unto Dagon their god, and to r:	8057
1Sa	2: 1 enemies; because I r in thy salvation.	8055
	19: 5 thou sawest *it,* and didst r: wherefore	8055
2Sa	1:20 lest the daughters of the Philistines r,	8055
1Ch	16:10 let the heart of them r that seek	8055
	16:31 the heavens be glad, and let the earth r:	1523
	16:32 let the fields r, and all that *is* therein.	5970
2Ch	6:41 and let thy saints r in goodness.	8055
	20:27 for the LORD had **made** them **to** r over	8055
Ne	12:43 for God had **made** them r *with* great joy:	8055
Job	3:22 Which r **exceedingly,**	413+1524+8056
	20:18 restitution *be,* and he shall not r *therein.*	5965
	21:12 and harp, and r at the sound of the organ.	8055
Ps	2:11 the LORD with fear, and r with trembling.	1523
	5:11 let all those that put their trust in thee r:	8055
	9: 2 I will be glad and r in thee: I will sing	5970
	9:14 daughter of Zion: I will r in thy salvation.	1523
	13: 4 that trouble me r when I am moved.	1523
	13: 5 mercy; my heart shall r in thy salvation.	1523
	14: 7 Jacob shall r, *and* Israel shall be glad.	1523
	20: 5 We will r in thy salvation, and in	7442
	21: 1 in thy salvation how greatly shall he r!	1523
	30: 1 and hast not **made** my foes to r over me.	8055
	31: 7 I will be glad and r in thy mercy: for thou	1523
	32:11 Be glad in the LORD, and r, ye righteous:	8055
	33: 1 R in the LORD, O ye righteous: *for* praise	7442
	33:21 For our heart shall r in him, because	8055
	35: 9 in the LORD: it shall r in his salvation.	7797
	35:19 are mine enemies wrongfully r over me:	8055
	35:24 and let them not r over me.	8055
	35:26 brought to confusion together that r at	8056
	38:16 *me,* lest *otherwise* they should r over	8055
	40:16 Let all those that seek thee r and be glad	7797
	48:11 Let mount Zion r, let the daughters of	8055
	51: 8 the bones *which* thou hast broken may r.	1523
	53: 6 Jacob shall r, *and* Israel shall be glad.	1523
	58:10 The righteous shall r when he seeth	8055
	60: 6 I will r, I will divide Shechem,	5937
	63: 7 in the shadow of thy wings will I r.	7442
	63:11 the king shall r in God; every one that	8055
	65: 8 **makest** the outgoings of the morning and evening to r.	7442
	65:12 and the little hills r on every side.	1524
	66: 6 the flood on foot: there did we r in him.	8055
	68: 3 righteous be glad; let them r before God:	5970
	68: 3 let them **exceedingly** r.	7797+8057+871.1
	68: 4 by his name JAH, and r before him.	5937
	70: 4 Let all those that seek thee r and be glad	7797
	71:23 My lips shall **greatly** r when I sing unto	7442
	85: 6 us again: that thy people may r in thee?	8055
	86: 4 R the soul of thy servant: for unto thee,	8055
	89:12 Tabor and Hermon shall r in thy name.	7442
	89:16 In thy name shall they r all the day:	1523
	89:42 thou hast **made** all his enemies to r.	8055
	90:14 that we may r and be glad all our days.	7442
	96:11 the heavens r, and let the earth be glad;	8055
	96:12 shall all the trees of the wood r	7442
	97: 1 The LORD reigneth; let the earth r;	1523
	97:12 R in the LORD, ye righteous;	8055
	98: 4 make a loud noise, and r, and sing *praise.*	7442
	104:31 for ever: the LORD shall r in his works.	8055
	105: 3 let the heart of them r that seek	8055
	106: 5 that I *may* r in the gladness of thy nation,	8055
	107:42 The righteous shall see *it,* and r:	8055
	108: 7 I will r, I will divide Shechem,	5937
	109:28 them be ashamed; but let thy servant r.	8055
	118:24 hath made; we will r and be glad in it.	1523
	119:162 I r at thy word, as one that findeth great	7797
	149: 2 Let Israel r in him that made him:	8055
Pr	2:14 Who r to do evil, *and* delight in	8056

R

Pr	5:18	and **r** with the wife of thy youth.	8055
	23:15	be wise, my heart shall **r**, even mine.	8055
	23:16	Yea, my reins shall **r**, when thy lips speak	5937
	23:24	of the righteous shall **greatly r**:	1523+1524
	23:25	be glad, and she that bare thee shall **r**.	1523
	24:17	**R** not when thine enemy falleth, and let	8055
	27: 9	Ointment and perfume **r** the heart:	8055
	28:12	When righteous men do **r**, *there is* great	5970
	29: 2	righteous are in authority, the people **r**:	8055
	29: 6	a snare: but the righteous doth sing and **r**.	8056
	31:25	and she shall **r** in time to come.	7832
Ecc	3:12	for *a man* to **r**, and to do good in his life.	8055
	3:22	that a man should **r** in his own works;	8055
	4:16	also that come after shall not **r** in him.	8055
	5:19	to take his portion, and to **r** in his labour;	8055
	11: 8	a man live many years, *and* **r** in them all;	8055
	11: 9	**R**, O young man, in thy youth; and let	8055
SS	1: 4	we will be glad and **r** in thee, we will	8055
Isa	8: 6	and **r** in Rezin and Remaliah's son;	4885
	9: 3	*and as men* **r** when they divide the spoil.	1523
	13: 3	*even* them that **r** in my highness.	5947
	14: 8	the fir trees **r** at thee, *and* the cedars of	8055
	14:29	**R** not thou, whole Palestina, because	8055
	23:12	he said, Thou shalt no more **r**, O thou	5937
	24: 8	the noise of them that **r** endeth, the joy	5947
	25: 9	we will be glad and **r** in his salvation.	8055
	29:19	the poor among men shall **r** in the Holy	1523
	35: 1	desert shall **r**, and blossom as the rose.	1523
	35: 2	**r** even *with* joy and singing:	1523
	41:16	thou shalt **r** in the LORD, *and* shalt glory	1523
	61: 7	*for* confusion they shall **r** in their portion:	7442
	61:10	I will **greatly r** in the LORD,	7797+7797
	62: 5	the bride, *so* shall thy God **r** over thee.	7797
	65:13	my servants shall **r**, but ye shall be	8055
	65:18	and **r** for ever *in that* which I create:	1523
	65:19	will **r** in Jerusalem, and joy in my people:	1523
	66:10	**R** ye with Jerusalem, and be glad with	8055
	66:10	**r** for joy with her, all ye that mourn for	7797
	66:14	when ye see *this*, your heart shall **r**,	7797
Jer	31:13	shall the virgin **r** in the dance, both	8055
	31:13	and **make** them **r** from their sorrow.	8055
	32:41	I will **r** over them to do them good,	7797
	51:39	that they may **r**, and sleep a perpetual	5937
La	2:17	he hath **caused** *thine* enemy to **r** over	8055
	4:21	**R** and be glad, O daughter of Edom,	7797
Eze	7:12	let not the buyer **r**, nor the seller mourn:	8055
	35:15	As thou didst **r** at the inheritance of	8057
Hos	9: 1	**R** not, O Israel, for joy, as *other* people:	8055
Joel	2:21	Fear not, O land; be glad and **r**:	8055
	2:23	of Zion, and **r** in the LORD your God:	1523
Am	6:13	which **r** in a thing of nought, which say,	8056
Mic	7: 8	**R** not against me, O mine enemy: when I	8055
Hab	1:15	their drag: therefore they **r** and are glad.	8055
	3:18	Yet I will **r** in the LORD, I will joy in	5937
Zep	3:11	the midst of thee them that **r** in thy pride,	5947
	3:14	glad and **r** with all the heart, O daughter	5937
	3:17	he will save, he will **r** over thee with joy;	7797
Zec	2:10	Sing and **r**, O daughter of Zion: for lo,	8055
	4:10	the day of small *things?* for they shall **r**,	1523
	9: 9	**R** greatly, O daughter of Zion; shout,	1523
	10: 7	and their heart shall **r** as *through* wine:	8055
	10: 7	be glad; their heart shall **r** in the LORD.	1523
Mt	5:12	**R**, and be exceeding glad: for great *is* your	5463
Lk	1:14	gladness; and many shall **r** at his birth.	5463
	6:23	**R** ye in that day, and leap *for joy:* for	5463
	10:20	Notwithstanding in this **r** not, that	5463
	10:20	but rather **r**, because your names are	5463
	15: 6	saying unto them, **R with** me;	5463
	15: 9	neighbours together, saying, **R with** me;	4796
	19:37	multitude of the disciples began to **r**	5463
Jn	4:36	and he that reapeth may **r** together.	5463
	5:35	were willing for a season to **r** in his light.	21
	14:28	If ye loved me, ye would **r**, because I said,	5463
	16:20	and lament, but the world shall **r**:	5463
	16:22	your heart shall **r**, and your joy no *man*	5463
Ac	2:26	Therefore did my heart **r**, and my tongue	2165
Ro	5: 2	and **r** in hope of the glory of God.	2744
	12:15	**R** with them that do rejoice, and weep	5463
	12:15	Rejoice with them that do **r**, and weep	5463
	15:10	he saith, **R**, ye Gentiles, with his people.	2165
1Co	7:30	they that **r**, as though they rejoiced not;	5463
	12:26	be honoured, all the members **r with** it.	4796
2Co	2: 3	sorrow from *them of* whom I ought to **r**;	5463
	7: 9	Now I **r**, not that ye were made sorry,	5463
	7:16	I **r** therefore that I have confidence in you	5463
Gal	4:27	it is written, **R**, *thou* barren that bearest	2165
Php	1:18	and I therein do **r**, yea, and will rejoice.	5463
	1:18	and I therein do rejoice, yea, and will **r**.	5463
	2:16	I may **r** in the day of Christ, that I have	2745
	2:17	of your faith, I joy, and **r with** you all.	4796
	2:18	*cause* also do ye joy, and **r with** me.	4796
	2:28	ye may **r**, and *that* I may be the less	5463
	3: 1	Finally, my brethren, **r** in the Lord.	5463
	3: 3	and **r** in Christ Jesus, and have no	2744
	4: 4	**R** in the Lord alway: *and* again I say,	5463
	4: 4	in the Lord alway: *and* again I say, **R**.	5463
Col	1:24	Who now **r** in my sufferings for you,	5463
1Th	5:16	**r** evermore.	5463
Jas	1: 9	Let the brother of low degree **r** in that he	2744
	4:16	But now ye **r** in your boastings: all such	2744
1Pe	1: 6	Wherein ye **greatly r**, though now for a	21
	1: 8	ye **r** with joy unspeakable and full of glory:	21
	4:13	But **r**, inasmuch as ye are partakers of	5463
Rev	11:10	And they that dwell upon the earth shall **r**	5463
	12:12	Therefore, **r**, ye heavens, and ye that dwell	2165

Rev	18:20	**R** over her, *thou* heaven, and ye holy	2165
	19: 7	Let us be glad and **r**, and give honour to	21

REJOICED (47) [REJOICE]

Ex	18: 9	Jethro **r** for all the goodness which	2302
Dt	28:63	*that* as the LORD **r** over you to do you	7797
	30: 9	thee for good, as he **r** over thy fathers:	7797
Jdg	19: 3	of the damsel saw him, he **r** to meet him.	8055
1Sa	6:13	eyes, and saw the ark, and **r** to see *it*.	8055
	11:15	and all the men of Israel **r** greatly.	8055
1Ki	1:40	**r** *with* great joy, so that the earth rent	8056
	5: 7	that he **r** greatly, and said, Blessed *be*	8055
2Ki	11:14	all the people of the land **r**, and blew	8056
	11:20	all the people of the land **r**, and the city	8056
1Ch	29: 9	people **r**, for that they offered willingly,	8055
	29: 9	and David the king also **r** *with* great joy.	8055
2Ch	15:15	all Judah **r** at the oath: for they had sworn	8055
	23:13	all the people of the land **r**,	8056
	23:21	all the people of the land **r**: and the city	8055
	24:10	And all the princes and all the people **r**,	8055
	29:36	Hezekiah **r**, and all the people, that God	8055
	30:25	land of Israel, that dwelt in Judah, **r**.	8055
Ne	12:43	day they offered great sacrifices, and **r**:	8055
	12:43	the wives also and the children **r**:	8055
	12:44	for Judah **r** for the priests and for	8057
Est	8:15	and the city of Shushan **r** and was glad.	6670
Job	31:25	If I **r** because my wealth *was* great,	8055
	31:29	If I **r** at the destruction of him that hated	8055
Ps	35:15	in mine adversity they **r**,	8055
	97: 8	the daughters of Judah **r**, because of thy	1523
	119:14	I have **r** in the way of thy testimonies,	7797
	50:11	Because ye were glad, because ye **r**, O ye	8055
Ecc	2:10	any joy; for my heart **r** in all my labour:	8056
Jer	15:17	in the assembly of the mockers, nor **r**;	5937
Eze	25: 6	**r** in heart with all thy despite against	8055
Hos	10: 5	priests thereof *that* **r** on it, for the glory	1523
Ob	1:12	neither shouldest thou have **r** over	8055
Mt	2:10	the star, they **r** with exceeding great joy.	5463
Lk	1:47	And my spirit hath **r** in God my Saviour.	21
	1:58	mercy upon her; and they **r with** her.	4796
	10:21	In that hour Jesus **r** in spirit, and said,	21
	13:17	all the people **r** for all the glorious *things*	5463
Jn	8:56	Your father Abraham **r** to see my day:	21
Ac	7:41	and **r** in the works of their own hands.	2165
	15:31	they had read, they **r** for the consolation.	5463
	16:34	he set meat before *them*, and **r**, believing	21
1Co	7:30	they that rejoice, as though they **r** not;	5463
2Co	7: 7	mind toward me; so that I **r** the more.	5463
Php	4:10	But I **r** in the Lord greatly, that now at	5463
2Jn	1: 4	I **r** greatly that I found of thy children	5463
3Jn	1: 3	For I **r** greatly, when the brethren came	5463

REJOICEST (1) [REJOICE]

Jer	11:15	when thou doest evil, then thou **r**.	5937

REJOICETH (18) [REJOICE]

1Sa	2: 1	and said, My heart **r** in the LORD,	5970
Job	39:21	in the valley, and **r** in *his* strength.	7797
Ps	16: 9	my heart is glad, and my glory **r**:	1523
	19: 5	*and* as a strong *man* to run a race.	7797
	28: 7	therefore my heart **greatly r**; and with	5937
Pr	11:10	goeth well with the righteous, the city **r**:	5970
	13: 9	The light of the righteous **r**: but the lamp	8055
	15:30	The light of the eyes **r** the heart: *and* a	8055
	29: 3	Whoso loveth wisdom **r** his father:	8055
Isa	5:14	and their pomp, and he that **r**,	5938
	62: 5	as the bridegroom **r** over the bride,	4885
	64: 5	Thou meetest him that **r** and	7797
Eze	35:14	When the whole earth **r**, I will make thee	8055
Mt	18:13	**r** more of that *sheep*, than of the ninety	5463
Jn	3:29	**r** greatly because of	5463+5479
1Co	13: 6	**R** not in iniquity, but rejoiceth in the truth	5463
	13: 6	Rejoiceth not in iniquity, but **r** in the truth	4796
Jas	2:13	no mercy; and mercy **r against** judgment.	2620

REJOICING (28) [REJOICE]

1Ki	1:45	they are come up from thence **r**, so that	8056
2Ch	23:18	**r** and with singing, as it was ordained	8057
Job	8:21	mouth *with* laughing, and thy lips *with* **r**.	8643
Ps	19: 8	statutes of the LORD *are* right, **r** the heart:	8055
	45:15	gladness and **r** shall they be brought:	1524
	107:22	and declare his works with **r**.	7440
	118:15	The voice of **r** and salvation *is* in	7440
	119:111	for ever: for they *are* the **r** of my heart.	8342
	126: 6	shall doubtless come again with **r**,	7440
Pr	8:30	daily *his* delight, **r** always before him;	7832
	8:31	**R** in the habitable part of his earth;	7832
Isa	65:18	create Jerusalem a **r**, and her people a joy.	1525
Jer	15:16	was unto me the joy and **r** of mine heart:	8057
Hab	3:14	their **r** *was* as to devour the poor secretly.	5951
Zep	2:15	This *is* the **r** city that dwelt carelessly,	5947
Lk	15: 5	found *it*, he layeth *it* on his shoulders, **r**.	5463
Ac	5:41	**r** that they were counted worthy to suffer	5463
	8:39	him no more: and he went on his way **r**.	5463
Ro	12:12	**R** in hope; patient in tribulation;	5463
1Co	15:31	I protest by your **r** which I have in Christ	2746
2Co	1:12	For our **r** is this, the testimony of our	2746
	1:14	us in part, that we are your **r**,	2745
	6:10	As sorrowful, yet alway **r**; as poor,	5463
Gal	6: 4	and then shall he have **r** in himself alone,	2745
Php	1:26	your **r** may be more abundant in Jesus	2745
1Th	2:19	what *is* our hope, or joy, or crown of **r**?	2746
Heb	3: 6	and the **r** of the hope firm unto the end.	2745
Jas	4:16	rejoice in your boastings: all such **r** is evil.	2746

REKEM (5)

Nu	31: 8	and **R**, and Zur, and Hur, and Reba,	7552
Jos	13:21	Evi, and **R**, and Zur, and Hur, and Reba,	7552
	18:27	And **R**, and Irpeel, and Taralah,	7552
1Ch	2:43	Korah, and Tappuah, and **R**, and Shema.	7552
	2:44	father of Jorkoam: and **R** begat Shammai.	7552

RELATIVES See KINDRED; KINDREDS

RELEASE (21) [RELEASED]

Dt	15: 1	of *every* seven years thou shalt make a **r**.	8059
	15: 2	this *is* the manner of the **r**: Every creditor	8059
	15: 2	**r** *it*; he shall not exact *it* of his neighbour,	8058
	15: 2	because it is called the LORD's **r**.	8059
	15: 3	thine with thy brother thine hand shall **r**;	8058
	15: 9	seventh year, the year of **r**, is at hand;	8059
	31:10	in the solemnity of the year of **r**,	8059
Est	2:18	he made a **r** to the provinces,	2010
Mt	27:15	at *that* feast the governor was wont to **r**	630
	27:17	them, Whom will ye *that* I **r** unto you?	630
	27:21	Whether of the twain will ye *that* I **r** unto	630
Mk	15: 9	Will ye *that* I **r** unto you the King of	630
	15:11	he should rather **r** Barabbas unto them.	630
Lk	23:16	I will therefore chastise him, and **r** *him*.	630
	23:17	(For of necessity he must **r** one unto them	630
	23:18	with this *man*, and **r** unto us Barabbas:	630
	23:20	Pilate therefore, willing to **r** Jesus, spake	630
Jn	18:39	I should **r** unto you one at the passover:	630
	18:39	*that* I **r** unto you the King of the Jews?	630
	19:10	to crucify thee, and have power to **r** thee?	630
	19:12	from thenceforth Pilate sought to **r** him:	630

RELEASED (4) [RELEASE]

Mt	27:26	Then **r** he Barabbas unto them:	630
Mk	15: 6	Now at *that* feast he **r** unto them one	630
	15:15	**r** Barabbas unto them, and delivered Jesus,	630
Lk	23:25	And he **r** unto them him that for sedition	630

RELIED (3) [RELY]

2Ch	13:18	they **r** upon the LORD God of their	8172
	16: 7	Because thou hast **r** on the king of Syria,	8172
	16: 7	not **r** on the LORD thy God, therefore is	8172

RELIEF (1) [RELIEVE, RELIEVED, RELIEVETH]

Ac	11:29	determined to send **r** unto	1248+1519

RELIEVE (7) [RELIEF]

Lev	25:35	in decay with thee; then thou shalt **r** him:	2388
Isa	1:17	seek judgment, **r** the oppressed, judge	833
La	1:11	pleasant things for meat to **r** the soul:	7725
	1:16	the comforter that *should* **r** my soul is far	7725
	1:19	they sought their meat, to **r** their souls.	7725
1Ti	5:16	let them **r** them, and let not the church	1884
	5:16	it may **r** them that are widows indeed.	1884

RELIEVED (1) [RELIEF]

1Ti	5:10	the saints' feet, if she have **r** the afflicted,	1884

RELIEVETH (1) [RELIEF]

Ps	146: 9	he **r** the fatherless and widow:	5749

RELIGION (5) [RELIGIOUS]

Ac	26: 5	that after the most straitest sect of our **r** I	2356
Gal	1:13	conversation in time past in the **Jews' r**,	2454
	1:14	And profited in the **Jews' r** above many	2454
Jas	1:26	his own heart, this *man's* **r** *is* vain.	2356
	1:27	Pure **r** and undefiled before God and	2356

RELIGIOUS (2) [RELIGION]

Ac	13:43	and proselytes followed Paul and	4576
Jas	1:26	If any *man* among you seem to be **r**,	2357

RELY (1) [RELIED]

2Ch	16: 8	yet, because thou didst **r** on the LORD,	8172

REMAIN (79) [REMAINDER, REMAINED, REMAINEST, REMAINETH, REMAINING, REMNANT]

Ge	38:11	**R** a widow *at* thy father's house, till	3427
Ex	8: 9	*that* they may **r** in the river only?	7604
	8:11	thy people; they shall **r** in the river only.	7604
	12:10	ye shall let nothing of it **r** until	3498
	23:18	neither shall the fat of my sacrifice **r** until	3885
	29:34	unto the morning, then thou shalt burn	3498
Lev	19: 6	if ought **r** until the third day, it shall be	3498
	25:28	which is sold shall **r** in the hand of him	1961
	25:52	if there *be* but few years unto the year of	7604
	27:18	the money according to the years that **r**,	3498
Nu	33:55	**come to** pass, *that those* which ye let **r**	3498
Dt	2:34	ones, of every city, we left none to **r**:	8300
	16: 4	at even, **r all night** until the morning.	3885
	19:20	those which **r** shall hear, and fear,	7604
	21:13	shall **r** in thine house, and bewail her	3427
	21:23	body shall not **r all night** upon the tree,	3885
Jos	1:14	shall **r** in the land which Moses gave you	3427
	2:11	neither did there **r** any more courage in	6965
	8:22	so that *they* let none of them **r** or escape.	8300
	10:27	cave's mouth, *which* **r** until this very day.	NIH
	10:28	the souls that *were* therein; he let none **r**	8300
	10:30	he let none **r** in it; but did unto the king	8300
	23: 4	unto you *by lot* these nations that **r**,	7604
	23: 7	these nations, these that **r** amongst you;	7604
	23:12	*even* these that **r** among you,	7604
Jdg	5:17	why did Dan **r** *in* ships? Asher continued	1481
	21: 7	shall we do for wives for them that **r**,	3498
	21:16	shall we do for wives for them that **r**,	3498

1Sa	20:19	*in hand,* and shalt **r** by the stone Ezel.	3427
1Ki	11:16	(For six months did Joab **r** there with all	3427
	18:22	I, *even* I only, **r** a prophet of the LORD;	3498
2Ki	7:13	I pray thee, five of the horses that **r,**	7604
Ezr	9:15	for we **r** escaped, as *it is* this day:	7604
Job	21:32	to the grave, and shall **r** in the tomb.	8245
	27:15	Those that **r** of him shall be buried in	8300
	37: 8	beasts go into dens, and **r** in their places.	7931
Ps	55: 7	I wander far off, *and* **r** in the wilderness.	3885
Pr	2:21	*in* the land, and the perfect shall **r** in it.	3498
	21:16	shall **r** in the congregation of the dead.	5117
Isa	10:32	As yet shall *he* **r** at Nob *that* day: he shall	5975
	32:16	and righteousness **r** in the fruitful field.	3427
	44:13	of a man; that it may **r** *in* the house.	3427
	65: 4	Which **r** among the graves, and lodge in	3427
	66:22	*shall* **r** before me, saith the LORD,	5975
	66:22	so shall your seed and your name **r.**	5975
Jer	8: 3	residue of them that **r** of this evil family,	7604
	8: 3	which **r** in all the places whither I have	7604
	17:25	of Jerusalem: and this city shall **r** for ever.	3427
	24: 8	that **r** in this land, and them that dwell in	7604
	27:11	those will I let **r** **still** in their own land,	3240
	27:19	the residue of the vessels that **r**	3498
	27:21	concerning the vessels that **r** *in* the house	3498
	30:18	palace shall **r** after the manner thereof.	3427
	38: 4	of the men of war that **r** in this city,	7604
	42:17	none of them shall **r** or escape from the	8300
	44: 7	out of Judah, to leave you none to **r;**	7611
	44:14	shall escape or **r,** that *they* should return	8300
	51:62	to cut it off, that none shall **r** in it,	3427
Eze	7:11	them shall *r,* nor of their multitude,	NIH
	17:21	they that **r** shall be scattered towards all	7604
	31:13	ruin shall the fowls of the heaven **r,**	7931
	32: 4	**cause** all the fowls of the heaven to **r**	7931
	39:14	those that **r** upon the face of the earth,	3498
Am	6: 9	if there **r** ten men in one house, that they	3498
Ob	1:14	of his that did **r** in the day of distress.	8300
Zec	5: 4	it shall **r** in the midst of his house,	3885
	12:14	All the families that **r,** every family apart,	7604
Lk	10: 7	And in the same house **r,** eating and	3306
Jn	6:12	Gather up the fragments that **r,** that	4052
	15:11	that my joy might **r** in you, and *that* your	3306
	15:16	forth fruit, and *that* your fruit should **r:**	3306
	19:31	the bodies should not **r** upon the cross	3306
1Co	7:11	let her **r** unmarried, or be reconciled to	3306
	15: 6	of whom the greater part **r** unto this	3306
1Th	4:15	**r** unto the coming of the Lord shall not	4035
	4:17	shall be caught up together with them	4035
Heb	12:27	*things* which cannot be shaken may **r.**	3306
1Jn	2:24	heard from the beginning shall **r** in you,	3306
Rev	3: 2	and strengthen the *things* which **r,**	3062

REMAINDER (6) [REMAIN]

Ex	29:34	then thou shalt burn the **r** with fire:	3498
Lev	6:16	the **r** thereof shall Aaron and his sons eat:	3498
	7:16	on the morrow also the **r** of it shall be	3498
	7:17	the **r** of the flesh of the sacrifice on	3498
2Sa	14: 7	*neither* name nor **r** upon the earth.	7611
Ps	76:10	the **r** of wrath shalt thou restrain.	7611

REMAINED (53) [REMAIN]

Ge	7:23	Noah only **r** *alive,* and *they* that *were*	7604
	14:10	and they that **r** fled to the mountain.	7604
Ex	8:31	and from his people; there **r** not one.	7604
	10:15	there **r** not any green thing in the trees,	3498
	10:19	there **r** not one locust in all the coasts of	7604
	14:28	there **r** not so much as one of them.	7604
Nu	11:26	there **r** two *of* the men in the camp,	7604
	35:28	Because he should have **r** in the city of	3427
	36:12	inheritance **r** in the tribe of the family	1961
Dt	3:11	For only Og king of Bashan **r** of	7604
	4:25	ye shall have **long** in the land,	3462
Jos	10:20	that the rest *which* of them entered into	8277
	11:22	in Gaza, in Gath, and in Ashdod, there **r.**	7604
	13:12	who **r** of the remnant of the giants:	7604
	18: 2	there **r** among the children of Israel seven	7604
	21:20	the Levites which **r** of the children of	3498
	21:26	families of the children of Kohath that **r.**	3498
Jdg	7: 3	two thousand; and there **r** ten thousand.	7604
1Sa	11:11	that they which **r** were scattered,	7604
	23:14	in a mountain in the wilderness of Ziph.	3427
	24: 3	and his men **r** in the sides of the cave.	3427
2Sa	13:20	So Tamar **r** desolate *in* her brother	3427
1Ki	22:46	which **r** in the days of his father Asa,	7604
2Ki	10:11	Jehu slew all that **r** of the house of Ahab	7604
	10:17	he slew all that **r** unto Ahab in Samaria,	7604
	13: 6	there **r** the grove also in Samaria.)	5975
	24:14	none **r,** save the poorest sort of the people	7604
	25:22	*for* the people that **r** in the land of Judah,	7604
1Ch	13:14	the ark of God **r** with the family of	5975
Ecc	2: 9	in Jerusalem: also my wisdom **r** with me.	5975
Jer	34: 7	for these defenced cities **r** of the cities of	7604
	37:10	there **r** *but* wounded men among them,	7604
	37:16	and Jeremiah had **r** there many days;	3427
	37:21	Jeremiah **r** in the court of the prison.	3427
	38:13	and Jeremiah **r** in the court of the prison.	3427
	39: 9	remnant of the people that **r** in the city,	7604
	39: 9	to him, with the rest of the people that **r.**	7604
	41:10	and all the people that **r** in Mizpah,	7604
	48:11	therefore his taste **r** in him, and his sent	5975
	51:30	to fight, they have **r** in *their* holds:	3427
	52:15	residue of the people that **r** in the city,	7604
La	2:22	of the LORD's anger none escaped nor **r:**	8300
Eze	3:15	**r** there astonished among them seven	3427
Da	10: 8	vision, and there **r** no strength in me:	7604

Da	10:13	and I **r** there with the kings of Persia.	3498
	10:17	straightway there **r** no strength in me,	5975
Mt	11:23	in Sodom, it would have **r** until this day.	3306
	14:20	took up of the fragments that **r** twelve	4052
Lk	1:22	beckoned unto them, and **r** speechless.	1265
	9:17	there was taken up of fragments that **r** to	4052
Jn	6:13	which **r** over and above unto them that	4052
Ac	5: 4	Whiles it **r,** was it not thine own?	3306
	27:41	and unmoveable, but the hinder part	3306

REMAINEST (2) [REMAIN]

La	5:19	Thou, O LORD, **r** for ever; thy throne	3427
Heb	1:11	but thou **r;** and they all shall wax old as	1265

REMAINETH (37) [REMAIN]

Ge	8:22	While the earth **r,** seedtime and harvest,	3117
Ex	10: 5	escaped which **r** unto you from the hail,	7604
	12:10	which **r** of it until the morning ye shall	3498
	16:23	which **r** over lay up for you to be kept	5736
	26:12	the remnant that **r** of the curtains of	5736
	26:12	the half curtain that **r,** shall hang over	5736
	26:13	cubit on the other side of that which **r** in	5736
Lev	8:32	that which **r** of the flesh and of the bread	3498
	10:12	Take the meat offering that **r** of	3498
	16:16	that **r** among them in the midst of their	7931
Nu	24:19	and shall destroy him that **r** of the city.	8300
Jos	8:29	great heap of stones, *that* **r** unto this day.	7604
	13: 1	**r** yet very much land to be possessed.	7604
	13: 2	This is the land that yet **r:** all the borders	7604
Jdg	5:13	he made him that **r** have dominion over	8300
1Sa	6:18	which stone **r** unto this day in the field of	NIH
	16:11	There **r** yet the youngest, and behold,	7604
1Ch	17: 1	the ark of the covenant of the LORD **r**	NIH
Ezr	1: 4	whosoever **r** in any place where he	7604
Job	19: 4	I have erred, mine error **r** with myself.	3885
	21:34	seeing *in* your answers there **r** falsehood?	7604
	41:22	In his neck **r** strength, and sorrow is	3885
Isa	4: 3	that **r** in Jerusalem, shall be called holy,	3498
Jer	38: 2	that **r** in this city shall die by the sword,	7604
	47: 4	from Tyrus and Zidon every helper that **r:**	8300
Eze	6:12	he that **r** and is besieged shall die by	7604
Hag	2: 5	out of Egypt, so my spirit **r** among you:	5975
Zec	9: 7	he that **r,** even he, *shall be* for our God,	7604
Jn	9:41	now ye say, We see; therefore your sin **r.**	3306
1Co	7:29	it **r,** that both they that have	1510+3062+3588
2Co	3:11	much more that which **r** *is* glorious.	3306
	3:14	for until this day **r** the same vail untaken	3306
	9: 9	to the poor: his righteousness **r** for ever.	3306
Heb	4: 6	therefore it **r** that some *must* enter therein,	620
	4: 9	therefore a rest to the people of God.	620
	10:26	truth, there **r** no more sacrifice for sins,	620
1Jn	3: 9	not commit sin; for his seed **r** in him:	3306

REMAINING (14) [REMAIN]

Nu	9:22	thereon, the children of Israel abode in	7931
Dt	3: 3	smote him until none was left to him **r.**	8300
Jos	10:33	his people, until *he* had left him none **r.**	8300
	10:37	he left none **r,** according to all that he	8300
	10:39	souls that *were* therein; he left none **r:**	8300
	10:40	he left none **r,** but utterly destroyed all	8300
	11: 8	smote them, until *they* left them none **r.**	8300
	21:40	were **r** of the families of the Levites,	3498
2Sa	21: 5	from **r** in any of the coasts of Israel,	3320
2Ki	10:11	and his priests, until *he* left him none **r.**	8300
1Ch	9:33	who **r** in the chambers *were* free:	NIH
Job	18:19	his people, nor *any* **r** in his dwellings.	8300
Ob	1:18	there shall not be *any* **r** of the house of	8300
Jn	1:33	see the Spirit descending, and **r** on him,	3306

REMALIAH (11) [REMALIAH'S]

2Ki	15:25	Pekah the son of **R,** a captain of his,	7425
	15:27	**R** *began* to reign over Israel in Samaria,	7425
	15:30	a conspiracy against Pekah the son of **R,**	7425
	15:32	In the second year of Pekah the son of **R**	7425
	15:37	the king of Syria, and Pekah the son of **R.**	7425
	16: 1	Ahaz the son of Jotham king of Judah	7425
	16: 5	Pekah son of **R** king of Israel came up *to*	7425
2Ch	28: 6	For Pekah the son of **R** slew in Judah an	7425
Isa	7: 1	and Pekah the son of **R,** king of Israel,	7425
	7: 4	of Rezin with Syria, and of the son of **R.**	7425
	7: 5	Because Syria, Ephraim, and the son of **R,**	7425

REMALIAH'S (2) [REMALIAH]

Isa	7: 9	and the head of Samaria *is* **R** son.	7425
	8: 6	go softly, and rejoice in Rezin and **R** son;	7425

REMEDY (3)

2Ch	36:16	against his people, till *there was* no **r.**	4832
Pr	6:15	suddenly shall he be broken without **r.**	4832
	29: 1	be destroyed, and that without **r.**	4832

REMEMBER (148) [REMEMBERED, REMEMBEREST, REMEMBERETH, REMEMBERING, REMEMBRANCE, REMEMBRANCES]

Ge	9:15	I will **r** my covenant, which *is* between	2142
	9:16	that I may **r** the everlasting covenant	2142
	40:23	Yet did not the chief butler **r** Joseph,	2142
	41: 9	saying, I do **r** my faults this day:	2142
Ex	13: 3	Moses said unto the people, **R** this day,	2142
	20: 8	**R** the sabbath day, to keep it holy.	2142
	32:13	**R** Abraham, Isaac, and Israel, thy servants	2142
Lev	26:42	will I **r** my covenant with Jacob,	2142
	26:42	also my covenant with Abraham will I **r;**	2142
	26:42	will I remember; and I will **r** the land.	2142
	26:45	I will for their sakes **r** the covenant of	2142

Nu	11: 5	We **r** the fish, which we did eat in Egypt	2142
	15:39	**r** all the commandments of the LORD,	2142
	15:40	That ye may **r,** and do all my	2142
Dt	5:15	**r** that thou wast a servant in the land of	2142
	7:18	shalt **well r** what the LORD thy	2142+2142
	8: 2	thou shalt **r** all the way which the LORD	2142
	8:18	thou shalt **r** the LORD thy God: for *it is*	2142
	9: 7	**R,** *and* forget not, how thou provokedst	2142
	9:27	**R** thy servants, Abraham, Isaac, and Jacob	2142
	15:15	thou shalt **r** that thou wast a bondman in	2142
	16: 3	that thou mayest **r** the day when thou	2142
	16:12	thou shalt **r** that thou wast a bondman in	2142
	24: 9	**R** what the LORD thy God did unto	2142
	24:18	thou shalt **r** that thou wast a bondman in	2142
	24:22	thou shalt **r** that thou wast a bondman in	2142
	25:17	**R** what Amalek did unto thee by the way,	2142
	32: 7	**R** the days of old, consider the years of	2142
Jos	1:13	**R** the word which Moses the servant of	2142
Jdg	9: 2	**r** also that I *am* your bone and your flesh.	2142
	16:28	**r** me, I pray thee, and strengthen me,	2142
1Sa	1:11	**r** me, and not forget thine handmaid,	2142
	15: 2	I **r** *that* which Amalek did to Israel,	6485
	25:31	with my lord, then **r** thine handmaid.	2142
2Sa	14:11	let the king **r** the LORD thy God,	2142
	19:19	neither do thou **r** *that* which thy servant	2142
2Ki	9:25	for **r** how that, when I and thou rode	2142
	20: 3	**r** now how I have walked before thee in	2142
1Ch	16:12	**R** his marvellous works that he hath done	2142
2Ch	6:42	**r** the mercies of David thy servant.	2142
Ne	1: 8	**R,** I beseech thee, the word that thou	2142
	4:14	**r** the Lord, *which is* great and terrible,	2142
	13:14	**R** me, O my God, concerning this,	2142
	13:22	**R** me, O my God, *concerning* this also,	2142
	13:29	**R** them, O my God, because they have	2142
	13:31	**R** me, O my God, for good.	2142
Job	4: 7	**R,** I pray thee, who *ever* perished,	2142
	7: 7	**r** that my life *is* wind: mine eye shall no	2142
	10: 9	**R,** I beseech thee, that thou hast made	2142
	11:16	*and* **r** *it* as waters *that* pass away:	2142
	14:13	appoint me a set time, and **r** me.	2142
	21: 6	Even when I **r** I am afraid,	2142
	36:24	**R** that thou magnify his work, which	2142
	41: 8	hand upon him, **r** the battle, do no more.	2142
Ps	20: 3	**R** all thy offerings, and accept thy burnt	2142
	20: 7	we will **r** the name of the LORD our God.	2142
	22:27	All the ends of the world shall **r** and	2142
	25: 6	**R,** O LORD, thy tender mercies and	2142
	25: 7	**R** not the sins of my youth, nor my	2142
	25: 7	according to thy mercy **r** thou me for thy	2142
	42: 4	When I **r** these *things,* I pour out my soul	2142
	42: 6	will I **r** thee from the land of Jordan,	2142
	63: 6	When I **r** thee upon my bed,	2142
	74: 2	**R** thy congregation, *which* thou hast	2142
	74:18	**R** this, *that* the enemy hath reproached,	2142
	74:22	**r** how the foolish *man* reproacheth thee	2142
	77:10	*I will* **r** the years of the right hand of	NIH
	77:11	I will **r** the works of the LORD: surely I	2142
	77:11	surely I will **r** thy wonders of old.	2142
	79: 8	not against us former iniquities: let thy	2142
	89:47	**R** how short my time is: wherefore hast	2142
	89:50	**R,** Lord, the reproach of thy servants;	2142
	103:18	to those that **r** his commandments to do	2142
	105: 5	**R** his marvellous works that he hath done	2142
	106: 4	**R** me, O LORD, with the favour *that thou*	2142
	119:49	**R** the word unto thy servant, upon which	2142
	132: 1	LORD, David, *and* all his afflictions:	2142
	137: 6	If I do not **r** thee, let my tongue cleave to	2142
	137: 7	**R,** O LORD, the children of Edom in	2142
	143: 5	I **r** the days of old; I meditate on all thy	2142
Pr	31: 7	his poverty, and **r** his misery no more.	2142
Ecc	5:20	he shall not much **r** the days of his life;	2142
	11: 8	all; yet let him **r** the days of darkness;	2142
	12: 1	**R** now thy Creator in the days of thy	2142
SS	1: 4	thee, we will **r** thy love more than wine:	2142
Isa	38: 3	said, **R** now, O LORD, I beseech thee,	2142
	43:18	**R** ye not the former *things,* neither	2142
	43:25	mine own sake, and will not **r** thy sins.	2142
	44:21	**R** these, O Jacob and Israel; for thou *art*	2142
	46: 8	**R** this, and shew yourselves men: bring *it*	2142
	46: 9	**R** the former *things* of old: for I *am* God,	2142
	47: 7	*heart,* neither didst **r** the latter end of it.	2142
	54: 4	not **r** the reproach of thy widowhood	2142
	64: 5	*those that* **r** thee in thy ways:	2142
	64: 9	O LORD, neither **r** iniquity for ever:	2142
Jer	2: 2	I **r** thee, the kindness of thy youth, the	2142
	3:16	neither shall they **r** it; neither shall they	2142
	14:10	he will now **r** their iniquity, and visit	2142
	14:21	**r,** break not thy covenant with us.	2142
	15:15	**r** me, and visit me, and revenge me of	2142
	17: 2	Whilst their children **r** their altars and	2142
	18:20	that I stood before thee to speak good	2142
	31:20	to **earnestly** **r** him still:	2142+2142
	31:34	iniquity, and I will **r** their sin no more.	2142
	44:21	did not the LORD **r** them, and came *it not*	2142
	51:50	let the LORD afar off, and let Jerusalem	2142
La	5: 1	**R,** O LORD, what is come upon us:	2142
Eze	6: 9	they that escape of you shall **r** me among	2142
	16:60	I will **r** my covenant with thee	2142
	16:61	thou shalt **r** thy ways, and be ashamed,	2142
	16:63	That thou mayest **r,** and be confounded,	2142
	20:43	there shall ye **r** your ways, and all your	2142
	23:27	eyes unto them, nor **r** Egypt any more.	2142
	36:31	shall ye **r** your own evil ways,	2142
Hos	7: 2	consider not in their hearts *that* I **r** all	2142
	8:13	will he **r** their iniquity, and visit their	2142

Hos	9:	9 therefore he will **r** their iniquity, he will	2142
Mic	6:	5 **r** now what Balak king of Moab	2142
Hab	3:	2 the years make known; in wrath **r** mercy.	2142
Zec	10:	9 they shall **r** me in far countries;	2142
Mal	4:	4 **R** ye the law of Moses my servant, which	2142
Mt	16:	9 neither the five loaves of the five	3421
	27:63	Saying, Sir, we **r** that that deceiver said,	3415
Mk	8:18	having ears, hear ye not? and do ye not **r**?	3421
Lk	1:72	to our fathers, and to **r** his holy covenant.	3415
	16:25	**r** that thou in thy lifetime receivedst thy	3415
	17:32	**R** Lot's wife.	3421
	23:42	**r** me when thou comest into thy kingdom.	3415
	24:	6 how he spake unto you when he was	3415
Jn	15:20	**R** the word that I said unto you,	3421
	16:	4 ye may **r** that I told you of them.	3421
Ac	20:31	Therefore watch, and **r**, that by the space	3421
	20:35	and to **r** the words of the Lord Jesus,	3421
1Co	11:	2 that you **r** me in all things, and keep	3421
Gal	2:10	they would that we should **r** the poor;	3421
Eph	2:11	Wherefore **r**, that ye being in time passed	3421
Col	4:18	**R** my bonds. Grace be with you. Amen.	3421
1Th	2:	9 For ye, brethren, our labour and travail:	3421
2Th	2:	5 **R** ye not, that, when I was yet with you,	3421
2Ti	2:	8 **R** that Jesus Christ of the seed of David	3421
Heb	8:12	and their iniquities will I **r** no more.	3415
	10:17	their sins and iniquities will I **r** no more.	3415
	13:	3 **R** them that are in bonds, as bound with	3403
	13:	7 **R** them which have the rule over you;	3421
3Jn	1:10	I come, I will **r** his deeds which he doeth,	5279
Jude	1:17	**r** ye the words which were spoken before	3415
Rev	2:	5 therefore from whence thou art fallen,	3421
	3:	3 **R** therefore how thou hast received and	3421

REMEMBERED (57) [REMEMBER]

Ge	8:	1 God **r** Noah, and every living thing,	2142
	19:29	that God **r** Abraham, and sent Lot out of	2142
	30:22	God **r** Rachel, and God hearkened to her,	2142
	42:	9 Joseph **r** the dreams which he dreamed of	2142
Ex	2:24	God **r** his covenant with Abraham,	2142
	6:	5 in bondage; and I have **r** my covenant.	2142
Nu	10:	9 ye shall be **r** before the LORD your God,	2142
Jdg	8:34	the children of Israel **r** not the LORD their	2142
1Sa	1:19	Hannah his wife; and the LORD **r** her.	2142
2Ch	24:22	Thus Joash the king **r** not the kindness	2142
Est	2:	1 he **r** Vashti, and what she had done,	2142
	9:28	that these days should be **r** and	2142
Job	24:20	he shall be no more **r**; and wickedness	2142
Ps	45:17	I will **make** thy name to be **r** in all	2142
	77:	3 I **r** God, and was troubled: I complained,	2142
	78:35	they **r** that God was their rock, and the	2142
	78:39	For he **r** that they were but flesh; a wind	2142
	78:42	They **r** not his hand: nor the day when he	2142
	98:	3 He hath **r** his mercy and his truth toward	2142
	105:	8 He hath **r** his covenant for ever, the word	2142
	105:42	For he **r** his holy promise, and Abraham	2142
	106:	7 they **r** not the multitude of thy mercies;	2142
	106:45	he **r** for them his covenant,	2142
	109:14	Let the iniquity of his fathers be **r** with	2142
	109:16	Because that he **r** not to shew mercy,	2142
	111:	4 hath made his wonderful works to be **r**:	2143
	119:52	I **r** thy judgments of old, O LORD;	2142
	119:55	I have **r** thy name, O LORD, in the night,	2142
	136:23	Who **r** us in our low estate: for his mercy	2142
	137:	1 I sat down, yea, we wept, when we **r** Zion.	2142
Ecc	9:15	city; yet no man **r** that same poor man.	2142
Isa	23:16	sing many songs, that thou mayest be **r**.	2142
	57:11	that thou hast lied, and hast not **r** me,	2142
	63:11	**r** the days of old, Moses, and his people,	2142
	65:17	the former shall not be **r**, nor come into	2142
Jer	11:19	living, that his name may be no more **r**.	2142
La	1:	7 Jerusalem **r** in the days of her affliction	2142
	2:	1 **r** not his footstool in the day of his anger!	2142
Eze	3:20	which he hath done shall not be **r**;	2142
	16:22	thy whoredoms thou hast not **r** the days	2142
	16:43	Because thou hast not **r** the days of thy	2142
	21:24	ye have **made** your iniquity to be **r**,	2142
	21:32	of the land; thou shalt be no more:	2142
	25:10	that the Ammonites may not be **r** among	2142
	33:13	all his righteousnesses shall not be **r**;	2142
Hos	2:17	they shall no more be **r** by their name.	2142
Am	1:	9 Edom, and **r** not the brotherly covenant:	2142
Jnh	2:	7 When my soul fainted within me I **r**	2142
Zec	13:	2 of the land, and they shall no more be **r**.	2142
Mt	26:75	And Peter **r** the word of Jesus, which said	3415
Lk	22:61	And Peter **r** the word of the Lord, how he	5279
	24:	8 And they **r** his words,	3415
Jn	2:17	And his disciples **r** that it was written,	3415
	2:22	his disciples **r** that he had said this unto	3415
	12:16	**r** they that these things were written of	3415
Ac	11:16	Then I **r** the word of the Lord, how that	3415
Rev	18:	5 heaven, and God hath **r** her iniquities.	3421

REMEMBEREST (2) [REMEMBER]

Ps	88:	5 lie in the grave, whom thou **r** no more:	2142
Mt	5:23	there **r** that thy brother hath ought against	3415

REMEMBERETH (5) [REMEMBER]

Ps	9:12	maketh inquisition for blood, he **r** them:	2142
	103:14	knoweth our frame; he **r** that we are dust.	2142
La	1:	9 she **r** not her last end; therefore she came	2142
Jn	16:21	of the child, she **r** no more the anguish	3421
2Co	7:15	whilst he **r** the obedience of you all,	363

REMEMBERING (2) [REMEMBER]

La	3:19	**R** mine affliction and my misery,	2142

1Th	1:	3 **R** without ceasing your work of faith,	3421

REMEMBRANCE (53) [REMEMBER]

Ex	17:14	for I will utterly put out the **r** of Amalek	2143
Nu	5:15	of memorial, **bringing** iniquity to **r**.	2142
Dt	25:19	that thou shalt blot out the **r** of Amalek	2143
	32:26	I would make the **r** of them to cease from	2143
2Sa	18:18	I have no son to **keep** my name **in r**:	2142
1Ki	17:18	thou come unto me to call my sin to **r**,	2142
Job	18:17	His **r** shall perish from the earth,	2143
Ps	6:	5 For in death there is no **r** of thee:	2143
	30:	4 and give thanks at the **r** of his holiness.	2143
	34:16	to cut off the **r** of them from the earth.	2143
	38:	T A Psalm of David, to **bring** to **r**.	2142
	70:	T A Psalm of David, to **bring** to **r**.	2142
	77:	6 I call to **r** my song in the night:	2142
	83:	4 the name of Israel may be no more in **r**.	2142
	97:12	and give thanks at the **r** of his holiness.	2143
	102:12	for ever; and thy **r** unto all generations.	2143
	112:	6 the righteous shall be in everlasting **r**.	2143
Ecc	1:11	There is no **r** of former things; neither	2146
	1:11	**r** of things that are to come with those	2146
	2:16	For there is no **r** of the wise more than of	2146
Isa	26:	8 soul is to thy name, and to the **r** of thee.	2143
	43:26	**Put** me in **r**: let us plead together:	2142
	57:	8 and the posts hast thou set up thy **r**:	2146
La	3:20	My soul hath them **still in r**,	2142+2142
Eze	21:23	he will **call** to **r** the iniquity, that they	2142
	21:24	because, I say, that ye are **come to r**,	2142
	23:19	in **calling** to **r** the days of her youth,	2142
	23:21	thou **calledst** to **r** the lewdness of thy	6485
	29:16	which **bringeth** their iniquity to **r**,	2142
Mal	3:16	a book of **r** was written before him for	2146
Mk	11:21	And Peter **calling** to **r** saith unto him,	363
Lk	1:54	his servant Israel, in **r** of his mercy,	3415
	22:19	which is given for you: this do in **r** of	364
Jn	14:26	all things, and **bring** all things to your **r**,	5279
Ac	10:31	alms are had in **r** in the sight of God.	3415
1Co	4:17	who shall **bring** you into **r** of my ways	363
	11:24	which is broken for you: this do in **r** of me.	364
	11:25	this do ye, as oft as ye drink it, in **r** of me.	364
Php	1:	3 I thank my God upon every **r** of you,	3417
1Th	3:	6 and that ye have good **r** of us always,	3417
1Ti	6:	8 If ye **put** the brethren in **r** of these	5294
2Ti	1:	3 that without ceasing I have **r** of thee in	3417
	1:	5 When I call to **r** the unfeigned faith that is	5280
	1:	6 Wherefore I **put** thee in **r** that thou stir up	363
	2:14	Of these things **put** them in **r**,	5279
Heb	10:	3 But in those sacrifices there is a **r** again	364
	10:32	But **call** to **r** the former days, in which,	363
2Pe	1:12	**put** you always in **r** of these things,	5279
	1:13	to stir you up by **putting** you in **r**;	5280
	1:15	decease to have these things always in **r**.	3420
	3:	1 I stir up your pure minds by way of **r**:	5280
Jude	1:	5 I will therefore **put** you in **r**, though ye	5279
Rev	16:19	and great Babylon **came** in **r** before God,	3415

REMEMBRANCES (1) [REMEMBER]

Job	13:12	Your **r** are like unto ashes, your bodies to	2146

REMETH (1)

Jos	19:21	**R**, and En-gannim, and En-haddah,	7432

REMISSION (10) [REMIT]

Mt	26:28	which is shed for many for the **r** of sins.	859
Mk	1:	4 preach the baptism of repentance for the **r**	859
Lk	1:77	unto his people by the **r** of their sins,	859
	3:	3 the baptism of repentance for the **r**	859
	24:47	**r** of sins should be preached in his name	859
Ac	2:38	in the name of Jesus Christ for the **r** of sins,	859
	10:43	believeth in him shall receive **r** of sins.	859
Ro	3:25	declare his righteousness for the **r** of sins	3929
Heb	9:22	and without shedding of blood is no **r**.	859
	10:18	Now where **r** of these is, there is no more	859

REMIT (1) [REMISSION, REMITTED]

Jn	20:23	Whose soever sins ye **r**, they are remitted	863

REMITTED (1) [REMIT]

Jn	20:23	soever sins ye remit, they are **r** unto them;	863

REMMON (1)

Jos	19:	7 Ain, **R**, and Ether, and Ashan; four cities	7417

REMMON-METHOAR (1)

Jos	19:13	goeth out to **R** to Neah;	7417+8388+1886.1

REMNANT (92) [REMAIN]

Ex	26:12	the **r** that remaineth of the curtains of	5629
Lev	2:	3 the **r** of the meat offering shall be Aaron's	3498
	5:13	the **r** shall be the priest's, as a meat	NIH
	14:18	the **r** of the oil that is in the priest's hand	3498
Dt	3:11	king of Bashan remained of the **r** of giants;	3499
	28:54	towards the **r** of his children which he	3499
Jos	12:	4 was of the **r** of the giants, that dwelt	3499
	13:12	who remained of the **r** of the giants:	3499
	23:12	cleave unto the **r** of these nations,	3499
2Sa	21:	2 of Israel, but of the **r** of the Amorites;	3499
1Ki	12:23	and to the **r** of the people, saying,	3499
	14:10	will take away the **r** of the house of	310
	22:46	the **r** of the sodomites, which remained in	3499
2Ki	19:	4 wherefore lift up thy prayer for the **r** that	7611
	19:30	the **r** that is escaped of the house of Judah	7604
	19:31	For out of Jerusalem shall go forth a **r**,	7611
	21:14	I will forsake the **r** of mine inheritance,	7611
	25:11	of Babylon, with the **r** of the multitude,	3499

1Ch	6:70	for the family of the **r** of the sons of	3498
2Ch	30:	6 Israel, and he will return to the **r** of you,	7604
	34:	9 of all the **r** of Israel, and of all Judah and	7611
Ezr	3:	8 the **r** of their brethren the priests and	7605
	9:	8 to leave us a **r** to **escape**, and to give us	6413
	9:14	so that there should be no **r** nor escaping?	7611
Ne	1:	3 The **r** that are left of the captivity there in	7604
Job	22:20	but the **r** of them the fire consumeth.	3499
Isa	1:	9 of hosts had left unto us a very small **r**,	8300
	10:20	of Israel, and such as are escaped	7605
	10:21	The **r** shall return, even the remnant of	7605
	10:21	of Jacob, unto the mighty God.	7605
	10:22	of the sea, yet a **r** of them shall return:	7605
	11:11	second time to recover the **r** of his people,	7605
	11:16	there shall be a highway for the **r** of his	7605
	14:22	and, and son, and nephew, saith the LORD.	7611
	14:30	root with famine, and he shall slay thy **r**.	7611
	15:	9 of Moab, and upon the **r** of the land.	7611
	16:14	the **r** shall be very small and feeble.	7605
	17:	3 from Damascus, and the **r** of Syria:	7605
	37:	4 wherefore lift up thy prayer for the **r** that	7611
	37:31	the **r** that is escaped of the house of Judah	7604
	37:32	For out of Jerusalem shall go forth a **r**,	7611
	46:	3 and all the **r** of the house of Israel,	7611
Jer	6:	9 They shall throughly glean the **r** of Israel	7611
	11:23	there shall be no **r** of them: for I will	7611
	15:11	Verily it shall be well with thy **r**;	8281
	23:	3 I will gather the **r** of my flock out of all	7611
	25:20	and Ekron, and the **r** of Ashdod:	7611
	31:	7 O LORD, save thy people, the **r** of Israel.	7611
	39:	9 of the people that remained in the city,	3499
	40:11	heard that the king of Babylon had left a **r**	7611
	40:15	be scattered, and the **r** in Judah perish?	7611
	41:16	all the **r** of the people whom he had	7611
	42:	2 The LORD thy God, even for all this **r**;	7611
	42:15	the word of the LORD, ye **r** of Judah;	7611
	42:19	hath said concerning you, O ye **r** of Judah;	7611
	43:	5 of the forces, took all the **r** of Judah,	7611
	44:12	I will take the **r** of Judah, that have set	7611
	44:14	So that none of the **r** of Judah, which are	7611
	44:28	all the **r** of Judah, that are gone into	7611
	47:	4 the **r** of the country of Caphtor.	7611
	47:	5 Ashkelon is cut off with the **r** of their	7611
Eze	5:10	the whole **r** of thee will I scatter into all	7611
	6:	8 will I **leave** a **r**, that ye may have some	3498
	11:13	thou make a full end of the **r** of Israel?	7611
	14:22	shall be left a **r** that shall be brought	6413
	23:25	ears; and thy **r** shall fall by the sword:	319
	25:16	and destroy the **r** of the sea coast.	7611
Joel	2:32	and in the **r** whom the LORD shall call.	8300
Am	1:	8 the **r** of the Philistines shall perish, saith	7611
	5:15	will be gracious unto the **r** of Joseph.	7611
	9:12	That they may possess the **r** of Edom,	7611
Mic	2:12	of thee; I will surely gather the **r** of Israel;	7611
	4:	7 I will make her that halted a **r**, and her	7611
	5:	3 the **r** of his brethren shall return unto	3499
	5:	7 the **r** of Jacob shall be in the midst of	7611
	5:	8 the **r** of Jacob shall be among the Gentiles	7611
	7:18	passeth by the transgression of the **r** of his	7611
Hab	2:	8 all the **r** of the people shall spoil thee;	3499
Zep	1:	4 I will cut off the **r** of Baal from this place,	7605
	2:	7 the coast shall be for the **r** of the house of	7611
	2:	9 of my people shall possess them.	3499
	3:13	The **r** of Israel shall not do iniquity,	7611
Hag	1:12	high priest, with all the **r** of the people,	7611
	1:14	and the spirit of all the **r** of the people;	7611
Zec	8:	6 If it be marvellous in the eyes of the **r** of	7611
	8:12	I will cause the **r** of this people to possess	7611
Mt	22:	6 And the **r** took his servants,	3062
Ro	9:27	as the sand of the sea, a **r** shall be saved:	2640
	11:	5 at this present time also there is a **r**	3005
Rev	11:13	the **r** were affrighted, and gave glory to	3062
	12:17	went to make war with the **r** of her seed,	3062
	19:21	the **r** were slain with the sword of him	3062

REMOVE (45) [REMOVED, REMOVETH, REMOVING]

Ge	48:17	to **r** it from Ephraim's head unto	5493
Nu	36:	7 the children of Israel **r** from tribe to tribe:	5437
	36:	9 Neither shall the inheritance **r** from one	5437
Dt	19:14	shalt not **r** thy neighbour's landmark,	5253
Jos	3:	3 ye shall **r** from your place, and go after it.	5265
Jdg	9:29	my hand; then would I **r** Abimelech.	5493
2Sa	6:10	So David would not **r** the ark of	5493
2Ki	23:27	I will **r** Judah also out of my sight,	5493
	24:	3 to **r** them out of his sight, for the sins of	5493
2Ch	33:	8 Neither will I any more **r** the foot of Israel	5493
Job	24:	2 Some **r** the landmarks; they violently take	5381
	27:	5 till I die I will not **r** my integrity from me.	5493
Ps	36:11	and let not the hand of the wicked **r** me.	5110
	39:10	**R** thy stroke away from me: I am	5493
	119:22	**R** from me reproach and contempt; for I	1556
	119:29	**R** from me the way of lying: and grant me	5493
Pr	4:27	hand nor to the left: **r** thy foot from evil.	5493
	5:	8 **R** thy way far from her, and come not	7368
	22:28	**R** not the ancient landmark, which thy	5253
	23:10	**R** not the ancient landmark; and enter not	5253
	30:	8 **R** far from me vanity and lies: give me	7368
Ecc	11:10	Therefore **r** sorrow from thy heart,	5493
Isa	13:13	and the earth shall **r** out of her place,	7493
	46:	7 he standeth: from the place shall he not **r**:	4185
Jer	4:	1 out of my sight, then shalt thou not **r**.	5110
	27:10	lie unto you, to **r** you far from your land;	7368
	32:31	that I should **r** it from before my face,	5493
	50:	3 they shall **r**, they shall depart, both man	5110

Jer 50: 8 **R** out of the midst of Babylon, and go 5110
Eze 12: 3 for removing, and **r** by day in their sight; 1540
12: 3 shalt **r** from thy place to another place 1540
12:11 they shall **r** *and* go into captivity. 1473
21:26 **R** the diadem, and take off the crown: 5493
45: 9 **r** violence and spoil, and execute 5493
Hos 5:10 princes of Judah were like them that **r** 5253
Joel 2:20 will **r** far off from you the northern *army*, 7368
3: 6 *ye* might **r** them **far** from their border, 7368
Mic 2: 3 from which ye shall not **r** your necks; 4185
Zec 3: 9 will **r** the iniquity of that land in one day. 4185
14: 4 half of the mountain shall **r** toward 4185
Mt 17:20 this mountain, **R** hence to yonder place; 3327
17:20 and it shall **r**; and nothing shall be 3327
Lk 22:42 if thou be willing, **r** this cup from me: 3911
1Co 13: 2 so that *I* could **r** mountains, and have no 3179
Rev 2: 5 and will **r** thy candlestick out of his place, 2795

REMOVED (91) [REMOVE]

Ge 8:13 Noah **r** the covering of the ark, and 5493
12: 8 he **r** from thence unto a mountain on 6275
13:18 Abram **r** his **tent**, and came and dwelt in 167
26:22 **r** from thence, and digged another well; 6275
30:35 he **r** that day the he goats that were 5493
47:21 he **r** them to cities from *one* end of 5674
Ex 8:31 the swarms *of flies* from Pharaoh, 5493
14:19 camp of Israel, **r** and went behind them; 5265
20:18 when the people saw *it*, they **r**, 5128
Nu 12:16 afterward the people **r** from Hazeroth, 5265
21:12 From thence they **r**, and pitched in 5265
21:13 From thence they **r**, and pitched on 5265
33: 5 the children of Israel **r** from Rameses, 5265
33: 7 they **r** from Etham, and turned again unto 5265
33: 9 they **r** from Marah, and came unto Elim: 5265
33:10 they **r** from Elim, and encamped by 5265
33:11 they **r** from the Red sea, and encamped in 5265
33:14 they **r** from Alush, and encamped at 5265
33:16 they **r** from the desert of Sinai, 5265
33:21 they **r** from Libnah, and pitched at Rissah. 5265
33:24 they **r** from mount Shapher, 5265
33:25 they **r** from Haradah, and pitched in 5265
33:26 they **r** from Makheloth, and encamped at 5265
33:28 **r** from Tarah, and pitched in Mithcah. 5265
33:32 they **r** from Bene-jaakan, and encamped 5265
33:34 they **r** from Jotbathah, and encamped at 5265
33:36 they **r** from Ezion-gaber, and pitched in 5265
33:37 they **r** from Kadesh, and pitched in 5265
33:46 they **r** from Dibon-gad, and encamped in 5265
33:47 they **r** from Almon-diblathaim, 5265
Dt 28:25 be **r** into all the kingdoms of the earth. 2189
Jos 3: 1 they **r** from Shittim, and came to Jordan, 5265
3:14 when the people **r** from their tents, to 5265
1Sa 6: 3 to you why his hand is not **r** from you. 5493
18:13 Therefore Saul **r** him from him, 5493
2Sa 20:12 he **r** Amasa out of the highway *into* 5437
20:13 When he was **r** out of the highway, 3014
1Ki 15:12 **r** all the idols that his fathers had made. 5493
15:13 even her he **r** from *being* queen, because 5493
15:14 the high places were not **r**: 5493
2Ki 15: 4 Save that the high places were not **r**: 5493
15:35 Howbeit the high places were not **r**: 5493
16:17 the bases, and **r** the laver from off them; 5493
17:18 with Israel, and **r** them out of his sight: 5493
17:23 Until the LORD **r** Israel out of his sight, 5493
17:26 The nations which thou hast **r**, 1540
18: 4 **r** the high places, and brake the images, 5493
23:27 I have **r** Israel, and will cast off this city 5493
1Ch 8: 6 of Geba, and they **r** them to Manahath: 1540
8: 7 he **r** them, and begat Uzza, and Ahihud. 1540
2Ch 15:16 her **r** from *being* queen, because she 5493
35:12 they **r** the burnt offerings, that they might 5493
Job 14:18 nought, and the rock is **r** out of his place. 6275
18: 4 and shall the rock be **r** out of his place? 6275
19:10 and mine hope hath he **r** like a tree. 5265
36:16 would he have **r** thee out of the strait 5496
Ps 46: 2 though the earth be **r**, and though 4171
81: 6 I **r** his shoulder from the burden: his 5493
103:12 *so* far hath he **r** our transgressions from 7368
104: 5 the earth, *that* it should not be **r** for ever. 4131
125: 1 *which* cannot be **r**, *but* abideth for ever. 4131
Pr 10:30 The righteous shall never be **r**: 4131
Isa 6:12 the LORD have **r** men far away, 7368
10:13 I have **r** the bounds of the people, 5493
10:31 Madmenah is **r**; the inhabitants of Gebim 5074
22:25 nail that is fastened in the sure place be **r**, 4185
24:20 a drunkard, and shall be **r** like a cottage; 5110
26:15 thou hadst **r** *it far unto* all the ends of 7368
29:13 have **r** their heart **far** from me, 7368
30:20 shall not thy teachers be **r into a corner** 3670
33:20 one of the stakes thereof shall ever be **r**, 5265
38:12 and is **r** from me as a shepherd's tent: 1540
54:10 mountains shall depart, and the hills be **r**; 4131
54:10 shall the covenant of my peace be **r**, 4131
Jer 15: 4 will cause them to be **r** into all kingdoms 2189
24: 9 I will deliver them to be **r** into all 2189
29:18 will deliver them to be **r** to all 2189
34:17 I will make you to be **r** into all 2189
La 1: 8 hath grievously sinned; therefore she is **r** 5206
3:17 thou hast **r** my soul **far off** from peace: 2186
Eze 7:19 in the streets, and their gold shall be **r**: 5079
23:46 and *will* give them to be **r** and spoiled. 2189
36:17 me as the uncleanness of a **r woman**. 5079
Am 6: 7 them that stretched themselves shall be **r**. 5493
Mic 2: 4 how hath he **r** *it* from me! turning away 4185
7:11 *in* that day shall the decree be **far r**. 7368

Mt 21:21 Be thou **r**, and be thou cast into the sea; 142
Mk 11:23 Be thou **r**, and be thou cast into the sea; 142
Ac 7: 4 he **r** him into this land, wherein ye now 3351
13:22 when he had **r** him, he raised up unto 3179
Gal 1: 6 soon **r** from him that called you into 3346

REMOVETH (5) [REMOVE]

Dt 27:17 Cursed *be* he that **r** his neighbour's 5253
Job 9: 5 Which **r** the mountains, and they know 6275
12:20 He **r** away the speech of the trusty, 5493
Ecc 10: 9 Whoso **r** stones shall be hurt therewith; 5265
Da 2:21 he **r** kings, and setteth up kings: he giveth 5709

REMOVING (5) [REMOVE]

Ge 30:32 **r** from thence all the speckled and 5493
Isa 49:21 am desolate, a captive, and **r to and fro**? 5493
Eze 12: 3 prepare thee stuff for **r**, and remove by 1473
12: 4 stuff by day in their sight, as stuff for **r**: 1473
Heb 12:27 the **r** of those *things* that are shaken, 3331

REMPHAN (1)

Ac 7:43 of Moloch, and the star of your god **R**, 4481

REND (9) [RENDER, RENDERED, RENDEREST, RENDERETH, RENDING, RENDING, RENT, RENTEST]

Ex 39:23 round about the hole, *that* it should not **r**. 7167
Lev 10: 6 not your heads, neither **r** your clothes; 6533
13:56 he shall **r** it out of the garment, or out of 7167
21:10 not uncover his head, nor **r** his clothes; 6533
1Ki 11:11 I will **surely r** the kingdom from 7167+7167
11:12 *but* I will **r** it out of the hand of thy son. 7167
11:13 I will not **r away** all the kingdom; 7167
2Ch 34:27 didst **r** thy clothes, and weep before me; 7167
Isa 64: 1 O that thou wouldest **r** the heavens, 7167

RENDER (33) [REND]

Nu 18: 9 which they shall **r** unto me, *shall be* most 7725
Dt 32:41 I will **r** vengeance to mine enemies, 7725
32:43 and will **r** vengeance to his adversaries, 7725
Jdg 9:57 of Shechem did God **r** upon their heads: 7725
1Sa 26:23 The LORD **r** to every man his 7725
2Ch 6:30 **r** unto every man according unto all his 5414
Job 33:26 for he will **r** unto man his righteousness. 7725
34:11 the work of a man shall he **r** unto him, 7999
Ps 28: 4 of their hands; **r** to them their desert. 7725
38:20 They also that **r** evil for good are mine 7999
56:12 me, O God: I will **r** praises unto thee. 7999
79:12 **r** unto our neighbours sevenfold into their 7725
94: 2 of the earth: **r** a reward to the proud. 7725
116:12 What shall I **r** unto the LORD *for* all his 7725
Pr 24:12 *not* he **r** to *every* man according to his 7725
24:29 I will **r** to the man according to his work. 7725
26:16 than seven *men* that can **r** a reason. 7725
Isa 66:15 to **r** his anger with fury, and his rebuke 7725
Jer 51: 6 he **will r** unto her a recompence. 7999
51:24 I will **r** unto Babylon and to all 7999
La 3:64 **R** unto them a recompence, O LORD, 7725
Hos 14: 2 so will we **r** the calves of our lips. 7999
Joel 3: 4 will *ye* **r** me a recompence? and if ye 7999
Zec 9:12 to day do I declare *that* I will **r** double 7725
Mt 21:41 shall **r** him the fruits in their seasons. 591
22:21 **R** therefore unto Cesar the *things* which 591
Mk 12:17 **R** to Cesar the *things* that are Cesar's, 591
Lk 20:25 **R** therefore unto Cesar the *things* which 591
Ro 2: 6 Who will **r** to every *man* according to his 591
13: 7 **R** therefore to all *their* dues: tribute to 591
1Co 7: 3 Let the husband **r** unto the wife due 591
1Th 3: 9 For what thanks can we **r** to God **again** for 467
5:15 See that none **r** evil for evil unto any *man*; 591

RENDERED (4) [REND]

Jdg 9:56 Thus God **r** the wickedness of Abimelech, 7725
2Ki 3: 4 **r** unto the king of Israel an hundred 7725
2Ch 32:25 Hezekiah **r** not **again** according to 7725
Pr 12:14 recompence of a man's hands shall be **r** 7725

RENDEREST (1) [REND]

Ps 62:12 for thou **r** to *every* man according to his 7999

RENDERETH (1) [REND]

Isa 66: 6 a voice of the LORD that **r** recompence to 7999

RENDERING (1) [REND]

1Pe 3: 9 Not **r** evil for evil, or railing for railing: 591

RENDING (1) [REND]

Ps 7: 2 **r** *it* in pieces, while *there* is none to 6561

RENEW (6) [RENEWED, RENEWEST, RENEWING]

1Sa 11:14 us go *to* Gilgal, and **r** the kingdom there. 2318
Ps 51:10 O God; and **r** a right spirit within me. 2318
Isa 40:31 they that wait upon the LORD shall **r** *their* 2498
41: 1 and let the people **r** *their* strength: 2498
La 5:21 we shall be turned; **r** our days as of old. 2318
Heb 6: 6 fall away, to **r** *them* again unto repentance; 340

RENEWED (6) [RENEW]

2Ch 15: 8 **r** the altar of the LORD, that *was* before 2318
Job 29:20 in me, and my bow is **r** in my hand. 2498
Ps 103: 5 *so that* thy youth is **r** like the eagle's. 2318
2Co 4:16 yet the inward *man* is **r** day by day. 341
Eph 4:23 And be **r** in the spirit of your mind; 365
Col 3:10 have put on the new *man*, which is **r** in 341

RENEWEST (2) [RENEW]

Job 10:17 Thou **r** thy witnesses against me, 2318
Ps 104:30 created: and thou **r** the face of the earth. 2318

RENEWING (2) [RENEW]

Ro 12: 2 be ye transformed by the **r** of your mind, 342
Tit 3: 5 of regeneration, and **r** of the Holy Ghost; 342

RENOUNCED (1)

2Co 4: 2 But have **r** the hidden *things* of dishonesty, 550

RENOWN (7) [RENOWNED]

Ge 6: 4 mighty *men* which *were* of old, men of **r**. 8034
Nu 16: 2 famous in the congregation, men of **r**: 8034
Eze 16:14 thy **r** went forth among the heathen for 8034
16:15 playedst the harlot because of thy **r**, 8034
34:29 I will raise up for them a plant of **r**, 8034
39:13 it shall be to them a **r** the day that I shall 8034
Da 9:15 and hast gotten thee **r**, as *at* this day; 8034

RENOWNED (4) [RENOWN]

Nu 1:16 These *were* the **r** of the congregation, 7121
Isa 14:20 the seed of evildoers shall never be **r**. 7121
Eze 23:23 captains and rulers, great lords and **r**, all 7121
26:17 the **r** city, which wast strong in the sea, 1984

RENT (76) [REND]

Ge 37:29 *was* not in the pit; and he **r** his clothes. 7167
37:33 is **without doubt r in pieces**. 2963+2963
37:34 Jacob **r** his clothes, and put sackcloth 7167
44:13 they **r** their clothes, and laded every man 7167
Ex 28:32 the hole of an habergeon, *that* it be not **r**. 7167
Lev 13:45 whom the plague *is*, his clothes shall be **r**, 6533
Nu 14: 6 that searched the land, **r** their clothes: 7167
Jos 7: 6 Joshua **r** his clothes, and fell to the earth 7167
9: 4 wine bottles, old, and **r**, and bound up; 1234
9:13 filled, *were* new; and behold, they be **r**: 1234
Jdg 11:35 that he **r** his clothes, and said, Alas, 7167
14: 6 he **r** him as he would have rent a kid, 8156
14: 6 he rent him as *he* would have **r** a kid, 8156
1Sa 4:12 *to* Shiloh the same day with his clothes **r**, 7167
15:27 hold upon the skirt of his mantle, and it **r** 7167
15:28 The LORD hath **r** the kingdom of Israel 7167
28:17 for the LORD hath **r** the kingdom out of 7167
2Sa 1: 2 of the camp from Saul with his clothes **r**, 7167
1:11 took hold on his clothes, and **r** them; 7167
3:31 **R** your clothes, and gird you with 7167
13:19 **r** her garment of divers colours that *was* 7167
13:31 his servants stood *by* with their clothes **r**. 7167
15:32 Archite came to meet him with his coat **r**, 7167
1Ki 1:40 that the earth **r** with the sound of them. 1234
11:30 *was* on him, and **r** it in twelve pieces: 7167
11:31 I will **r** the kingdom out of the hand of 7167
13: 3 the altar *shall be* **r**, and the ashes that *are* 7167
13: 5 The altar also was **r**, and the ashes poured 7167
14: 8 the kingdom **away** from the house of 7167
19:11 a great and strong wind **r** the mountains, 6561
21:27 that he **r** his clothes, and put sackcloth 7167
2Ki 2:12 and **r** them **in two pieces**. 7167+7168
5: 7 that he **r** his clothes, and said, *Am* I God, 7167
5: 8 that the king of Israel had **r** his clothes, 7167
5: 8 Wherefore hast thou **r** thy clothes? 7167
6:30 of the woman, that he **r** his clothes; 7167
11:14 Athaliah **r** her clothes, and cried, Treason, 7167
17:21 For he **r** Israel from the house of David; 7167
18:37 to Hezekiah with their clothes **r**, 7167
19: 1 king Hezekiah heard *it*, that he **r** his 7167
22:11 the book of the law, that he **r** his clothes. 7167
22:19 hast **r** thy clothes, and wept before me; 7167
2Ch 23:13 Athaliah **r** her clothes, and said, Treason, 7167
34:19 words of the law, that he **r** his clothes. 7167
Ezr 9: 3 I **r** my garment and my mantle, 7167
9: 5 having **r** my garment and my mantle, I fell 7167
Est 4: 1 Mordecai **r** his clothes, and put on 7167
Job 1:20 **r** his mantle, and shaved his head, 7167
2:12 they **r** every one his mantle, 7167
26: 8 and the cloud is not **r** under them. 1234
Ecc 3: 7 A time to **r**, and a time to sew; a time to 7167
Isa 3:24 instead of a girdle **r**; and instead of well 5364
36:22 to Hezekiah with *their* clothes **r**, 7167
37: 1 king Hezekiah heard *it*, that he **r** his 7167
Jer 36:24 nor **r** their garments, *neither* the king, 7167
41: 5 clothes **r**, and having cut themselves, 7167
Eze 13:11 shall fall; and a stormy wind shall **r** *it*. 1234
13:13 I will even **r** *it* with a stormy wind in my 1234
29: 7 thou didst break, and **r** all their shoulder: 1234
30:16 No shall be **r asunder**, and Noph *shall* 1234
Hos 13: 8 will **r** the caul of their heart, and there 7167
Joel 2:13 **r** your heart, and not your garments, 7167
Mt 7: 6 their feet, and turn *again* and **r** you. 4486
9:16 the garment, and the **r** is made worse. 4978
26:65 Then the high priest **r** his clothes, saying, 1284
27:51 the vail of the temple was **r** in twain from 4977
27:51 and the earth did quake, and the rocks **r**; 4977
Mk 2:21 *from* the old, and the **r** is made worse. 4978
9:26 and **r** him sore, and came out of *him*: and 4682
14:63 the high priest **r** his clothes, and saith, 1284
15:38 And the vail of the temple was **r** in twain 4977
Lk 5:36 *then* both the new **maketh a r**, 4977
23:45 the vail of the temple was **r** in the midst. 4977
Jn 19:24 Let us not **r** it, but cast lots for it, whose it 4977
Ac 14:14 heard *of*, they **r** their clothes, and ran in 1284
16:22 and the magistrates **r** off their clothes, 4048

RENTEST (1) [REND]
Jer 4:30 though thou **r** thy face with painting, 7167

REPAIR (14) [REPAIRED, REPAIRER, REPAIRING]
2Ki 12: 5 let them **r** the breaches of the house, 2388
 12: 7 Why **r** ye not the breaches of the house? 2388
 12: 8 neither to **r** the breaches of the house. 2388
 12:12 stone to **r** the breaches of the house 2388
 12:12 for all that was laid out for the house to **r** 2394
 22: 5 the LORD, to **r** the breaches of the house. 2388
 22: 6 timber and hewn stone to **r** the house. 2388
2Ch 24: 4 *that* Joash was minded to **r** the house of 2318
 24: 5 gather of all Israel money to **r** the house 2388
 24:12 carpenters to **r** the house of the LORD, 2318
 34: 8 to **r** the house of the LORD his God. 2388
 34:10 of the LORD, to **r** and mend the house: 918
Ezr 9: 9 to the desolations thereof, and to give us 5975
Isa 61: 4 shall **r** the waste cities, the desolations 2318

REPAIRED (44) [REPAIR]
Jdg 21:23 and **r** the cities, and dwelt in them. 1129
1Ki 11:27 the breaches of the city of David his 5462
 18:30 he **r** the altar of the LORD that was 7495
2Ki 12: 6 had not **r** the breaches of the house. 2388
 12:14 **r** therewith the house of the LORD. 2388
1Ch 11: 8 about: and Joab **r** the rest of the city. 2421
2Ch 29: 3 of the house of the house, and **r** them. 2388
 32: 5 **r** Millo *in* the city of David, and made 2388
 33:16 he **r** the altar of the LORD, 1129
Ne 3: 4 next unto them **r** Meremoth the son of 2388
 3: 4 next unto them **r** Meshullam the son of 2388
 3: 4 next unto them **r** Zadok the son of Baana. 2388
 3: 5 next unto them the Tekoites **r**; 2388
 3: 6 Moreover the old gate **r** Jehoiada the son 2388
 3: 7 next unto him **r** Melatiah the Gibeonite, 2388
 3: 8 Next unto him **r** Uzziel the son of 2388
 3: 8 Next unto him also **r** Hananiah the son of 2388
 3: 9 next unto him **r** Rephaiah the son of 2388
 3:10 next unto them **r** Jedaiah the son of 2388
 3:10 next unto him **r** Hattush the son of 2388
 3:11 **r** the other piece, and the tower of 2388
 3:12 next unto him **r** Shallum the son of 2388
 3:13 The valley gate **r** Hanun, 2388
 3:14 the dung gate **r** Malchiah the son of 2388
 3:15 the gate of the fountain **r** Shallun the son 2388
 3:16 After him **r** Nehemiah the son of Azbuk, 2388
 3:17 After him **r** the Levites, Rehum the son of 2388
 3:17 Next unto him **r** Hashabiah, the ruler of 2388
 3:18 After him **r** their brethren, Bavai the son 2388
 3:19 next to him **r** Ezer the son of Jeshua, 2388
 3:20 son of Zabbai earnestly **r** the other piece, 2388
 3:21 After him **r** Meremoth the son of Urijah 2388
 3:22 him **r** the priests, the men of the plain. 2388
 3:23 After him **r** Benjamin and Hashub over 2388
 3:23 After him **r** Azariah the son of Maaseiah 2388
 3:24 After him **r** Binnui the son of Henadad 2388
 3:27 After them the Tekoites **r** another piece, 2388
 3:28 From above the horse gate **r** the priests, 2388
 3:29 After them **r** Zadok the son of Immer over 2388
 3:29 After him **r** also Shemaiah the son of 2388
 3:30 After him **r** Hananiah the son of 2388
 3:30 After him **r** Meshullam the son of 2388
 3:31 After him **r** Malchiah the goldsmith's son 2388
 3:32 unto the sheep gate **r** the goldsmiths 2388

REPAIRER (1) [REPAIR]
Isa 58:12 thou shalt be called, The **r** of the breach, 1443

REPAIRING (1) [REPAIR]
2Ch 24:27 upon him, and the **r** of the house of God, 3247

REPAY (8) [REPAYED, REPAYETH]
Dt 7:10 that hateth him, he will **r** him to his face. 7999
Job 21:31 and who shall **r** him *what* he hath done? 7999
 41:11 that I should **r** *him*? whatsoever *is* under 7999
Isa 59:18 accordingly he will **r**, fury to his 7999
 59:18 to the islands he will **r** recompence. 7999
Lk 10:35 when I come again, I will **r** thee. 591
Ro 12:19 Vengeance *is* mine; I will **r**, saith the Lord. 467
Phm 1:19 I will **r** *it*: albeit I do not say to thee how 661

REPAYED (1) [REPAY]
Pr 13:21 but to the righteous good shall be **r**. 7999

REPAYETH (1) [REPAY]
Dt 7:10 them that hate him to their face, 7999

REPAYING See REQUITE; REQUITED; REQUITING

REPEATETH (1) [REPETITIONS]
Pr 17: 9 he that **r** a matter separateth very friends. 8138

REPENT (46) [REPENTANCE, REPENTED, REPENTEST, REPENTETH, REPENTING, REPENTINGS]
Ex 13:17 Lest peradventure the people **r** when they 5162
 32:12 and **r** of *this* evil against thy people. 5162
Nu 23:19 neither the son of man, that he should **r**: 5162
Dt 32:36 his people, and **r** himself for his servants, 5162
1Sa 15:29 the Strength of Israel will not lie nor **r**: 5162
 15:29 for he *is* not a man, that *he* should **r**. 5162
1Ki 8:47 and make supplication unto thee in 7725
Job 42: 6 I abhor *myself*, and **r** in dust and ashes. 5162
Ps 90:13 and let it **r** thee concerning thy servants. 5162
 110: 4 The LORD hath sworn, and will not **r**, 5162
 135:14 he will **r** himself concerning his servants. 5162

Jer 4:28 I have purposed *it*, and will not **r**, 5162
 18: 8 I will **r** of the evil that I thought to do 5162
 18:10 not my voice, then I will **r** of the good, 5162
 26: 3 I may **r** me of the evil, which I purpose 5162
 26:13 the LORD will **r** him of the evil that he 5162
 42:10 I **r** me of the evil that I have done unto 5162
Eze 14: 6 **R**, and turn *yourselves* from your idols; 7725
 18:30 **R**, and turn *yourselves* from all your 7725
 24:14 neither will I spare, neither will I **r**; 5162
Joel 2:14 Who knoweth *if* he will return and **r**, 5162
Jnh 3: 9 Who can tell *if* God will turn and **r**, 5162
Mt 3: 2 And saying, **R** ye: for the kingdom of 3340
 4:17 time Jesus began to preach, and to say, **R**: 3340
Mk 1:15 is at hand: **r** ye, and believe the gospel. 3340
 6:12 out, and preached that *men* should **r**. 3340
Lk 13: 3 but, except ye **r**, ye shall all likewise 3340
 13: 5 except ye **r**, ye shall all likewise perish. 3340
 16:30 unto them from the dead, they will **r**. 3340
 17: 3 rebuke him; and if he **r**, forgive him. 3340
 17: 4 in a day turn again to thee, saying, I **r**; 3340
Ac 2:38 **R**, and be baptized every one of you in 3340
 3:19 **R** ye therefore, and be converted, that 3340
 8:22 **R** therefore of this thy wickedness, 3340
 17:30 commandeth all men every where to **r**: 3340
 26:20 that *they* should **r** and turn to God, 3340
2Co 7: 8 a letter, I do not **r**, though I did repent: 3338
 7: 8 a letter, I do not repent, though I did **r**. 3338
Heb 7:21 unto him, The Lord sware and will not **r**, 3338
Rev 2: 5 art fallen, and **r**, and do the first works; 3340
 2: 5 candlestick out of his place, except thou **r**. 3340
 2:16 **R**; or else I *will* come unto thee quickly, 3340
 2:21 And I gave her space to **r** of her 3340
 2:22 except they **r** of their deeds. 3340
 3: 3 and heard, and hold fast, and **r**. 3340
 3:19 and chasten: be zealous therefore, and **r**. 3340

REPENTANCE (26) [REPENT]
Hos 13:14 **r** shall be hid from mine eyes. 5164
Mt 3: 8 Bring forth therefore fruits meet for **r**: 3341
 3:11 I indeed baptize you with water unto **r**: 3341
 9:13 to call *the* righteous, but sinners to **r**. 3341
Mk 1: 4 preach the baptism of **r** for the remission 3341
 2:17 not to call *the* righteous, but sinners to **r**. 3341
Lk 3: 3 preaching the baptism of **r** for 3341
 3: 8 Bring forth therefore fruits worthy of **r**, 3341
 5:32 not to call *the* righteous, but sinners to **r**. 3341
 15: 7 and nine just *persons* which need no **r**. 3341
 24:47 And that **r** and remission of sins should be 3341
Ac 5:31 for to give **r** to Israel, and forgiveness of 3341
 11:18 also to the Gentiles granted **r** unto life. 3341
 13:24 the baptism of **r** to all the people of Israel. 3341
 19: 4 John verily baptized *with* the baptism of **r**, 3341
 20:21 **r** toward God, and faith toward our Lord 3341
 26:20 and turn to God, and do works meet for **r**. 3341
Ro 2: 4 the goodness of God leadeth thee to **r**? 3341
 11:29 the gifts and calling of God *are* **without r**. 278
2Co 7: 9 made sorry, but that ye sorrowed to **r** 3341
 7:10 For godly sorrow worketh **r** to salvation 3341
2Ti 2:25 if God peradventure will give them **r** to 3341
Heb 6: 1 not laying again the foundation of **r** from 3341
 6: 6 fall away, to renew *them* again unto **r**; 3341
 12:17 for he found no place of **r**, though he 3341
2Pe 3: 9 perish, but that all should come to **r**. 3341

REPENTED (32) [REPENT]
Ge 6: 6 it **r** the LORD that he had made man on 5162
Ex 32:14 the LORD **r** of the evil which he thought 5162
Jdg 2:18 for it **r** the LORD because of their 5162
 21: 6 the children of Israel **r** them for Benjamin 5162
 21:15 the people **r** them for Benjamin, because 5162
1Sa 15:35 the LORD **r** that he had made Saul king 5162
2Sa 24:16 the LORD **r** him of the evil, and said to 5162
1Ch 21:15 he **r** him of the evil, and said to the angel 5162
Ps 106:45 **r** according to the multitude of his 5162
Jer 8: 6 no man **r** him of his wickedness, saying, 5162
 20:16 which the LORD overthrew, and **r** not: 5162
 26:19 the LORD **r** him of the evil which he had 5162
 31:19 Surely after that I was turned, I **r**; 5162
Am 7: 3 The LORD **r** for this: It shall not be, 5162
 7: 6 The LORD **r** for this: This also shall not 5162
Jnh 3:10 God **r** of the evil, that he had said that he 5162
Zec 8:14 saith the LORD of hosts, and I **r** not: 5162
Mt 11:20 works were done, because they **r** not. 3340
 11:21 Sidon they would have **r** long ago in 3340
 12:41 because they **r** at the preaching of Jonas; 3340
 21:29 I will not: but afterward he **r**, and went. 3338
 21:32 ye, when ye had seen *it*, **r** not afterward, 3338
 27: 3 **r** himself, and brought again the thirty 3338
Lk 10:13 they had a great while ago **r**, sitting in 3340
 11:32 for they **r** at the preaching of Jonas; 3340
2Co 7:10 repentance to salvation **not** to be **r** of: 278
 12:21 and have not **r** of the uncleanness and 3340
Rev 2:21 to repent of her fornication; and she **r** not. 3340
 9:20 yet **r** not of the works of their hands, 3340
 9:21 Neither **r** they of their murders, nor of 3340
 16: 9 and they **r** not to give him glory. 3340
 16:11 and their sores, and **r** not of their deeds. 3340

REPENTEST (1) [REPENT]
Jnh 4: 2 of great kindness, and **r** thee of the evil. 5162

REPENTETH (5) [REPENT]
Ge 6: 7 the air; for it **r** me that I have made them. 5162
1Sa 15:11 It **r** me that I have set up Saul to be king: 5162
Joel 2:13 and **r** him of the evil, and of them. 5162

Lk 15: 7 shall be in heaven over one sinner that **r**, 3340
 15:10 the angels of God over one sinner that **r**. 3340

REPENTING (1) [REPENT]
Jer 15: 6 and destroy thee; I am weary with **r**. 5162

REPENTINGS (1) [REPENT]
Hos 11: 8 within me, my **r** are kindled together. 5150

REPETITIONS (1) [REPEATETH]
Mt 6: 7 But when ye pray, **use** not vain **r**, 945

REPHAEL (1)
1Ch 26: 7 Othni, and **R**, and Obed, Elzabad, 7501

REPHAH (1)
1Ch 7:25 **R** *was* his son, also Resheph, and Telah 7506

REPHAIAH (5)
1Ch 3:21 the sons of **R**, the sons of Arnan, the sons 7509
 4:42 Neariah, and **R**, and Uzziel, the sons of 7509
 7: 2 **R**, and Jeriel, and Jahmai, and Jibsam, 7509
 9:43 **R** his son, Eleasah his son, Azel his son. 7509
Ne 3: 9 next unto them repaired **R** the son of Hur, 7509

REPHAIM (6) [REPHAIMS]
2Sa 5:18 and spread themselves in the valley of **R**. 7497
 5:22 and spread themselves in the valley of **R**. 7497
 23:13 the Philistines pitched in the valley of **R**. 7497
1Ch 11:15 Philistines encamped in the valley of **R**. 7497
 14: 9 and spread themselves in the valley of **R**. 7497
Isa 17: 5 as he that gathereth ears in the valley of **R**. 7497

REPHAIMS (2) [REPHAIM]
Ge 14: 5 smote the **R** in Ashteroth Karnaim, 7497
 15:20 the Hittites, and the Perizzites, and the **R**, 7497

REPHAITES See GIANT; REPHAIMS

REPHAN See REMPHAN

REPHIDIM (5)
Ex 17: 1 of the LORD, and pitched in **R**: 7508
 17: 8 came Amalek, and fought with Israel in **R**. 7508
 19: 2 For they were departed from **R**, 7508
Nu 33:14 removed from Alush, and encamped at **R**, 7508
 33:15 they departed from **R**, and pitched in 7508

REPLENISH (2) [REPLENISHED]
Ge 1:28 multiply, and the earth, and subdue it: 4390
 9: 1 Be fruitful, and multiply, and **r** the earth. 4390

REPLENISHED (5) [REPLENISH]
Isa 2: 6 because they be **r** from the east, 4390
 23: 2 of Zidon, that pass over the sea, have **r**. 4390
Jer 31:25 and I have **r** every sorrowful soul. 4390
Eze 26: 2 I shall be **r**, *now* she is laid waste: 4390
 27:25 thou wast **r**, and made very glorious in 4390

REPLIEST (1)
Ro 9:20 O man, who art thou that **r** **against** God? 470

REPORT (30) [REPORTED]
Ge 37: 2 Joseph brought unto his father their evil **r**. 1681
Ex 23: 1 Thou shalt not raise a false **r**: put not 8088
Nu 13:32 they brought up an **evil r** of the land 1681
 14:37 *those* men that did bring up the evil **r** 1681
Dt 2:25 shall hear **r** of thee, and shall tremble, 8088
1Sa 2:24 my sons; for *it is* no good **r** that I hear: 8052
1Ki 10: 6 It was a true **r** that I heard in mine own 1697
2Ch 9: 5 It *was* a true **r** which I heard in mine own 1697
Ne 6:13 *that* they might have **matter** for an evil **r**, 8034
Pr 15:30 *and* a good **r** maketh the bones fat. 8052
Isa 23: 5 As *at* the **r** concerning Egypt, so shall they 8088
 23: 5 be sorely pained *at the* **r** of Tyre. 8088
 28:19 be a vexation only *to* understand the **r**. 8052
 53: 1 Who hath believed our **r**? and to whom is 8052
Jer 20:10 **R**, say they, and we will report it. All my 5046
 20:10 Report, *say they*, and we will **r** it. All my 5046
 50:43 The king of Babylon hath heard the **r** of 8088
Jn 12:38 he spake, Lord, Who hath believed our **r**? 189
Ac 6: 3 out among you seven men **of honest r**, 3140
 10:22 **good r** among all the nation of the Jews, 3140
 22:12 **having a good r** of all the Jews which 3140
Ro 10:16 saith, Lord, who hath believed our **r**? 189
1Co 14:25 and **r** that God is in you of a truth. 518
2Co 6: 8 and dishonour, by **evil r** and good report: 1426
 6: 8 and dishonour, by evil report and good **r**; 2162
Php 4: 8 lovely, whatsoever *things are of* **good r**; 2163
1Ti 3: 7 Moreover he must have a good **r** of them 3141
Heb 11: 2 For by it the elders **obtained a good r**. 3140
 11:39 having **obtained a good r** through faith, 3140
3Jn 1:12 Demetrius **hath good r** of all *men*, and 3140

REPORTED (12) [REPORT]
Ne 6: 6 *It is* **r** among the heathen, 8085
 6: 7 now shall it be **r** to the king according to 8085
 6:19 Also they **r** his good deeds before me, 559
Est 1:17 husbands in their eyes, when it shall be **r**, 559
Eze 9:11 inkhorn by his side, **r** the matter, saying, 7725
Mt 28:15 saying is **commonly r** among the Jews 1310
Ac 4:23 **r** all that the chief priests and elders had 518
 16: 2 Which was **well r** of by the brethren that 3140
Ro 3: 8 And not *rather*, (as we be **slanderously r**, 987
1Co 5: 1 It is **r** *commonly that there is* fornication 191
1Ti 5:10 **Well r** of for good works; if she have 3140
1Pe 1:12 which are now **r** unto you by them that 312

REPRESENTATIVE See DEPUTED

REPROACH (88) [REPROACHED, REPROACHES, REPROACHEST, REPROACHETH, REPROACHFULLY]

Ge	30:23	and said, God hath taken away my **r**:	2781
	34:14	uncircumcised; for that *were* a **r** unto us:	2781
Jos	5: 9	*This* day have I rolled away the **r** of Egypt	2781
Ru	2:15	even among the sheaves, and **r** her not:	3637
1Sa	11: 2	right eyes, and lay it *for* a **r** upon all Israel.	2781
	17:26	and taketh away the **r** from Israel?	2781
	25:39	that hath pleaded the cause of my **r** from	2781
2Ki	19: 4	his master hath sent to **r** the living God;	2778
	19:16	which hath sent him to **r** the living God.	2778
Ne	1: 3	the province *are* in great affliction, and **r**:	2781
	2:17	wall of Jerusalem, that we be no more a **r**.	2781
	4: 4	turn their **r** upon their own head,	2781
	5: 9	of the **r** of the heathen our enemies?	2781
	6:13	for an evil report, that they might **r** me.	2778
Job	15: 5	against me, and plead against me my **r**:	2781
	20: 3	I have heard the check of my **r**,	3639
	27: 6	my heart shall not **r** *me* so long as I live.	2778
Ps	15: 3	nor taketh up a **r** against his neighbour.	2781
	22: 6	a **r** of men, and despised of the people.	2781
	31:11	I was a **r** among all mine enemies,	2781
	39: 8	make me not the **r** of the foolish.	2781
	42:10	a sword in my bones, mine enemies **r** me;	2778
	44:13	Thou makest us a **r** to our neighbours,	2781
	57: 3	save me *from* the **r** of him that would	2778
	69: 7	Because for thy sake I have borne **r**;	2781
	69:10	my soul with fasting, that was to my **r**.	2781
	69:19	Thou hast known my **r**, and my shame,	2781
	69:20	**R** hath broken my heart; and I am full of	2781
	71:13	let them be covered *with* **r** and	2781
	74:10	O God, how long shall the adversary **r**?	2778
	78:66	hinder parts: he put them to a perpetual **r**.	2781
	79: 4	We are become a **r** to our neighbours,	2781
	79:12	sevenfold into their bosom their **r**,	2781
	89:41	way spoil him: he is a **r** to his neighbours.	2781
	89:50	Remember, Lord, the **r** of thy servants;	2781
	89:50	*how* I do bear in my bosom *the* **r** of all	NIH
	102: 8	Mine enemies **r** me all the day;	2778
	109:25	I became also a **r** unto them: *when* they	2781
	119:22	Remove from me **r** and contempt; for I	2781
	119:39	Turn away my **r** which I fear: for thy	2781
Pr	6:33	he get; and his **r** shall not be wiped away.	2781
	14:34	a nation: but sin *is* a **r** to any people.	2617
	18: 3	also contempt, and with ignominy **r**.	2781
	19:26	a son that causeth shame, and **bringeth** **r**.	2659
	22:10	shall go out; yea, strife and **r** shall cease.	7036
Isa	4: 1	be called by thy name, to take away our **r**.	2781
	30: 5	help nor profit, but a shame, and also a **r**.	2781
	37: 4	his master hath sent to **r** the living God,	2778
	37:17	which hath sent to **r** the living God.	2778
	51: 7	fear ye not the **r** of men, neither be ye	2781
	54: 4	not remember the **r** of thy widowhood.	2781
Jer	6:10	the word of the LORD is unto them a **r**;	2781
	20: 8	the word of the LORD was made a **r** unto	2781
	23:40	I will bring an everlasting **r** upon you,	2781
	24: 9	be a **r** and a proverb, a taunt and a curse,	2781
	29:18	an astonishment, and a hissing, and a **r**,	2781
	31:19	because I did bear the **r** of my youth.	2781
	42:18	an astonishment, and a curse, and a **r**;	2781
	44: 8	a **r** among all the nations of the earth?	2781
	44:12	an astonishment, and a curse, and a **r**.	2781
	49:13	a desolation, a **r**, a waste, and a curse;	2781
	51:51	confounded, because we have heard **r**:	2781
La	3:30	that smiteth him: he is filled full with **r**.	2781
	3:61	Thou hast heard their **r**, O LORD,	2781
	5: 1	upon us: consider, and behold our **r**.	2781
Eze	5:14	a **r** among the nations that *are* round	2781
	5:15	it shall be a **r** and a taunt, an instruction	2781
	16:57	as *at* the time of *thy* **r** of the daughters of	2781
	21:28	the Ammonites, and concerning their **r**;	2781
	22: 4	have I made thee a **r** unto the heathen,	2781
	36:15	neither shalt thou bear the **r** of the people	2781
	36:30	that ye shall receive no more **r** of famine	2781
Da	9:16	thy people *are become* a **r** to all *that are*	2781
	11:18	prince for his own behalf shall cause the **r**	2781
	11:18	without his own **r** he shall cause *it* to turn	2781
Hos	12:14	and his **r** shall his Lord return unto him.	2781
Joel	2:17	O LORD, and give not thine heritage to **r**,	2781
	2:19	I will no more make you a **r** among	2781
Mic	6:16	therefore ye shall bear the **r** of my people.	2781
Zep	2: 8	I have heard the **r** of Moab,	2781
	3:18	of thee, *to whom* the **r** of it *was* a burden.	2781
Lk	1:25	on *me*, to take away my **r** among men.	3681
	6:22	and shall **r** you, and cast out your name as	3679
2Co	11:21	I speak as concerning **r**, as though we had	819
1Ti	3: 7	he fall into **r** and the snare of the devil.	3680
	4:10	For therefore we both labour and **suffer** **r**,	3679
Heb	11:26	Esteeming the **r** of Christ greater riches	3680
	13:13	unto him without the camp, bearing his **r**.	3680

REPROACHED (15) [REPROACH]

2Ki	19:22	Whom hast thou **r** and blasphemed?	2778
	19:23	By thy messengers thou hast **r** the Lord,	2778
Job	19: 3	These ten times have ye **r** me: ye are not	3637
Ps	55:12	For *it was* not an enemy *that* **r** me; then	2778
	69: 9	reproaches of them that **r** thee are fallen	2778
	74:18	*that* the enemy hath **r**, O LORD,	2778
	79:12	wherewith they have **r** thee, O Lord.	2778
	89:51	Wherewith thine enemies have **r**,	2778
	89:51	wherewith they have **r** the footsteps of	2778
Isa	37:23	Whom hast thou **r** and blasphemed?	2778

Isa	37:24	By thy servants hast thou **r** the Lord,	2778
Zep	2: 8	whereby they have **r** my people,	2778
	2:10	because they have **r** and	2778
Ro	15: 3	The reproaches of them that **r** thee fell on	3679
1Pe	4:14	If ye be **r** for the name of Christ, happy	3679

REPROACHES (5) [REPROACH]

Ps	69: 9	the **r** of them that reproached thee are	2781
Isa	43:28	given Jacob to the curse, and Israel to **r**.	1421
Ro	15: 3	The **r** of them that reproached thee fell	3680
2Co	12:10	in **r**, in necessities, in persecutions,	5196
Heb	10:33	ye were made a gazingstock both by **r**	3680

REPROACHEST (1) [REPROACH]

Lk	11:45	Master, thus saying thou **r** us also.	5195

REPROACHETH (7) [REPROACH]

Nu	15:30	or a stranger, the same **r** the LORD;	1442
Ps	44:16	For the voice of him that **r** and	2778
	74:22	remember how the foolish *man* **r** thee	2781
	119:42	have wherewith to answer him that **r** me:	2778
Pr	14:31	He that oppresseth the poor **r** his Maker:	2778
	17: 5	Whoso mocketh the poor **r** his Maker:	2778
	27:11	glad, that I may answer him that **r** me.	2778

REPROACHFULLY (2) [REPROACH]

Job	16:10	smitten me upon the cheek **r**;	2781+871.1
1Ti	5:14	occasion to the adversary to **speak** **r**.	3059

REPROBATE (4) [REPROBATES]

Jer	6:30	**R** silver shall *men* call them, because	3988
Ro	1:28	God gave them over to a **r** mind, to do	96
2Ti	3: 8	of corrupt minds, **r** concerning the faith.	96
Tit	1:16	disobedient, and unto every good work **r**.	96

REPROBATES (3) [REPROBATE]

2Co	13: 5	that Jesus Christ is in you, except ye be **r**?	96
	13: 6	I trust that ye shall know that we are not **r**.	96
	13: 7	do *that which* is honest, though we be as **r**.	96

REPROOF (15) [REPROVE]

Job	26:11	tremble and are astonished at his **r**.	1606
Pr	1:23	Turn you at my **r**: behold, I will pour out	8433
	1:25	all my counsel, and would none of my **r**:	8433
	1:30	of my counsel: they despised all my **r**.	8433
	5:12	instruction, and my heart despised **r**;	8433
	10:17	but he that refuseth **r** erreth.	8433
	12: 1	but he that hateth **r** *is* brutish.	8433
	13:18	he that regardeth **r** shall be honoured.	8433
	15: 5	but he that regardeth **r** is prudent.	8433
	15:10	the way: *and* he that hateth **r** shall die.	8433
	15:31	The ear that heareth the **r** of life abideth	8433
	15:32	that heareth **r** getteth understanding.	8433
	17:10	A **r** entereth more into a wise *man* than	1606
	29:15	The rod and **r** give wisdom: but a child	8433
2Ti	3:16	for doctrine, for **r**, for correction,	1650

REPROOFS (2) [REPROVE]

Ps	38:14	not, and in whose mouth *are* no **r**.	8433
Pr	6:23	and **r** of instruction *are* the way of life:	8433

REPROVE (19) [REPROOF, REPROOFS, REPROVED, REPROVER, REPROVETH, UNREPROVEABLE]

2Ki	19: 4	will **r** the words which the LORD thy God	3198
Job	6:25	words! but what doth your arguing **r**?	3198
	6:26	Do ye imagine to **r** words, and the	3198
	13:10	He will **surely** **r** you, if ye do	3198+3198
	22: 4	Will he **r** thee for fear of thee? will he	3198
Ps	50: 8	I will not **r** thee for thy sacrifices or	3198
	50:21	*but* I will **r** thee, and set *them* in order	3198
	141: 5	let him **r** me; *it shall be* an excellent oil,	3198
Pr	9: 8	**R** not a scorner, lest he hate thee: rebuke	3198
	19:25	**r** one that hath understanding, *and* he	3198
	30: 6	lest he **r** thee, and thou be found a liar.	3198
Isa	11: 3	neither **r** after the hearing of his ears:	3198
	11: 4	**r** with equity for the meek of the earth:	3198
	37: 4	will **r** the words which the LORD thy God	3198
Jer	2:19	and thy backslidings shall **r** thee:	3198
Hos	4: 4	Yet let no man strive, nor **r** another: for	3198
Jn	16: 8	he will **r** the world of sin,	1651
Eph	5:11	works of darkness, but rather **r** *them*.	1651
2Ti	4: 2	**r**, rebuke, exhort with all longsuffering	1651

REPROVED (10) [REPROVE]

Ge	20:16	and with all *other:* thus she was **r**.	3198
	21:25	Abraham **r** Abimelech because of a well	3198
1Ch	16:21	wrong: yea, he **r** kings for their sakes,	3198
Ps	105:14	wrong: yea, he **r** kings for their sakes,	3198
Pr	29: 1	He, that being often **r** hardeneth *his* neck,	8433
Jer	29:27	why hast thou not **r** Jeremiah of Anathoth,	1605
Hab	2: 1	and what I shall answer when I am **r**.	8433
Lk	3:19	being **r** by him for Herodias his brother	1651
Jn	3:20	to the light, lest his deeds should be **r**.	1651
Eph	5:13	But all *things* that are **r** are made manifest	1651

REPROVER (2) [REPROVE]

Pr	25:12	*so is* a wise **r** upon an obedient ear.	3198
Eze	3:26	dumb, and shalt not be to them a **r**:	376+3198

REPROVETH (4) [REPROVE]

Job	40: 2	the Almighty instruct *him?* he that **r** God,	3198
Pr	9: 7	He that **r** a scorner getteth to himself	3256
	15:12	A scorner loveth not one that **r** him:	3198
Isa	29:21	lay a snare for him that **r** in the gate,	3198

REPUTATION (5) [REPUTED]

Ecc	10: 1	*doth* a little folly *him that is* in **r** for	3368
Ac	5:34	had in **r** among all the people,	5093
Gal	2: 2	but privately to them which were **of r**,	1380
Php	2: 7	But **made** himself **of no r**, and took *upon*	2758
	2:29	Lord with all gladness; and hold such in **r**:	1784

REPUTED (2) [REPUTATION]

Job	18: 3	as beasts, *and* **r** **vile** in your sight?	2933
Da	4:35	all the inhabitants of the earth *are* **r** as	2804

REQUEST (19) [REQUESTED, REQUESTS]

Jdg	8:24	them, I would **desire** a **r** of you,	7592+7596
2Sa	14:15	it may be that the king will perform the **r**	1697
	14:22	in that the king hath fulfilled the **r** of his	1697
Ezr	7: 6	the king granted him all his **r**, according	1246
Ne	2: 4	unto me, For what dost thou **make r**?	1245
Est	4: 8	and to **make r** before him for her people.	1245
	5: 3	what *is* thy **r**? it shall be even given thee	1246
	5: 6	what *is* thy **r**? even to the half of	1246
	5: 7	and said, My petition and my **r** *is;*	1246
	5: 8	to perform my **r**, let the king and	1246
	7: 2	what *is* thy **r**? and it shall be performed,	1246
	7: 3	me at my petition, and my people at my **r**:	1246
	7: 7	Haman stood *up* to **make r** for his life to	1245
	9:12	or what *is* thy **r** further? and it shall be	1246
Job	6: 8	O that I might have my **r**; and *that* God	7596
Ps	21: 2	and hast not withholden the **r** of his lips.	782
	106:15	he gave them their **r**; but sent leanness	7596
Ro	1:10	**Making r**, if by any means now at length	1189
Php	1: 4	of mine for you all making **r** with joy,	1162

REQUESTED (5) [REQUEST]

Jdg	8:26	weight of the golden earrings that he **r**	7592
1Ki	19: 4	he **r** for himself that he might die;	7592
1Ch	4:10	And God granted *him that* which he **r**.	7592
Da	1: 8	**r** of the prince of the eunuchs that he	1245
	2:49	Daniel **r** of the king, and he set Shadrach,	1156

REQUESTS (1) [REQUEST]

Php	4: 6	supplication with thanksgiving let your **r** be	155

REQUIRE (29) [REQUIRED, REQUIREST, REQUIRETH, REQUIRING]

Ge	9: 5	surely your blood of your lives will I **r**;	1875
	9: 5	at the hand of every beast will I **r** it,	1875
	9: 5	the hand of every man's brother will I **r**	1875
	31:39	of my hand didst thou **r** it, *whether* stolen	1245
	43: 9	for him; of my hand shalt thou **r** him:	1245
Dt	10:12	what doth the LORD thy God **r** of thee,	7592
	18:19	shall speak in my name, I will **r** *it* of him.	1875
	23:21	for the LORD thy God will **surely** **r**	1875+1875
Jos	22:23	let the LORD himself **r** *it*;	1245
1Sa	20:16	saying, Let the LORD even **r** *it* at	1245
2Sa	3:13	one thing I **r** of thee, that is, Thou shalt	7592
	4:11	therefore now **r** his blood of your hand,	1245
	19:38	whatsoever thou shalt **r** of me, *that* will I	977
1Ki	8:59	Israel at all times, **as the matter** shall **r**:	1697
1Ch	21: 3	doth my lord **r** this *thing?* why will he be	1245
2Ch	24:22	he said, The LORD look upon *it*, and **r** *it*.	1875
Ezr	7:21	shall **r** of you, *it* be done speedily,	7593
	8:22	For I was ashamed to **r** of the king a band	7592
Ne	5:12	restore *them*, and will **r** nothing of them;	1245
Ps	10:13	hath said in his heart, Thou wilt not **r** *it*.	1875
Eze	3:18	but his blood will I **r** at thine hand.	1875
	3:20	but his blood will I **r** at thine hand.	1245
	20:40	there will I **r** your offerings,	1875
	33: 6	his blood will I **r** at the watchman's hand.	1875
	33: 8	but his blood will I **r** at thine hand.	1875
	34:10	will I **r** my flock at their hand,	1875
Mic	6: 8	what doth the LORD **r** of thee, but to do	1875
1Co	1:22	For the Jews **r** a sign, and the Greeks seek	154
	7:36	and need so **r**, let him do what he will,	1096

REQUIRED (22) [REQUIRE]

Ge	42:22	therefore, behold, also his blood is **r**.	1875
Ex	12:36	*as they* **r**. And they spoiled the Egyptians.	NIH
1Sa	21: 8	because the king's business **r** haste.	1961
2Sa	12:20	when he **r**, they set bread before him,	7592
1Ch	16:37	ark continually, as every day's **work r**:	1697
2Ch	8:14	the priests, as the **duty** of every day **r**:	1697
	24: 6	Why hast thou not **r** of the Levites to	1875
Ezr	3: 4	to the custom, **as** the duty of every day **r**;	4941
Ne	5:18	yet for *all* this **r** not I the bread of	1245
Est	2:15	she **r** nothing but what Hegai the king's	7592
Ps	40: 6	and sin offering hast thou not **r**.	7592
	137: 3	carried us away captive **r** of us a song;	7592
	137: 3	they that wasted us **r** of us mirth,	NIH
Pr	30: 7	Two *things* have I **r** of thee; deny me	7592
Isa	1:12	who hath **r** this at your hand, to tread my	1245
Lk	11:50	of the world, may be **r** of this generation;	1567
	11:51	unto you, It shall be **r** of this generation.	1567
	12:20	this night thy soul shall be **r** of thee:	523
	12:48	much is given, of him shall be much **r**:	2212
	19:23	at my coming I might have **r** mine own	4238
	23:24	gave sentence that it should be as they **r**.	155
1Co	4: 2	Moreover it is **r** in stewards, that a man	2212

REQUIREST (1) [REQUIRE]

Ru	3:11	fear not; I will do to thee all that thou **r**:	559

REQUIRETH (2) [REQUIRE]

Ecc	3:15	been; and God **r** that which is past.	1245
Da	2:11	*it is* a rare thing that the king **r**, and there	7593

R

REQUIRING (1) [REQUIRE]
Lk 23:23 loud voices, **r** that he might be crucified. 154

REQUITE (9) [REQUITED, REQUITING]
Ge 50:15 will **certainly r** us all the evil 7725+7725
Dt 32: 6 Do ye thus **r** the LORD, O foolish people 1580
2Sa 2: 6 I also will **r** you this kindness, 854+6213
16:12 that the LORD will **r** me good for his 7725
2Ki 9:26 I will **r** thee in this plat, saith the LORD. 7999
Ps 10:14 and spite, to **r** *it* with thy hand: 5414
41:10 and raise me up, that I may **r** them. 7999
Jer 51:56 God of recompences shall **surely r.** 7999+7999
1Ti 5: 4 piety at home, and to **r** *their* parents: 287+591

REQUITED (2) [REQUITE]
Jdg 1: 7 as I have done, so God hath **r** me. 7999
1Sa 25:21 unto him: and he hath **r** me evil for good. 7725

REQUITING (1) [REQUITE]
2Ch 6:23 and judge thy servants, by **r** the wicked, 7725

REREWARD (6)
Nu 10:25 *was* the **r** of all the camps throughout 622
Jos 6: 9 the **r** came after the ark, *the priests* going 622
6:13 the **r** came after the ark of the LORD, 622
1Sa 29: 2 his men passed on in the **r** with Achish. 314
Isa 52:12 and the God of Israel *will be* your **r**. 622
58: 8 the glory of the LORD shall be thy **r**. 622

RESCUE (3) [RESCUED, RESCUETH]
Dt 28:31 and thou shalt have none to **r** *them.* 3467
Ps 35:17 **r** my soul from their destructions, 7725
Hos 5:14 I will take away, and none shall **r** *him.* 5337

RESCUED (3) [RESCUE]
1Sa 14:45 the people **r** Jonathan, that he died not. 6299
30:18 carried away: and David **r** his two wives. 5337
Ac 23:27 then came I with an army, and **r** him, 1807

RESCUETH (1) [RESCUE]
Da 6:27 He delivereth and **r**, and he worketh signs 5338

RESEMBLANCE (1) [RESEMBLE]
Zec 5: 6 This *is* their **r** through all the earth. 5869

RESEMBLE (1) [RESEMBLANCE, RESEMBLED]
Lk 13:18 of God like? and whereunto shall I **r** it? 3666

RESEMBLED (1) [RESEMBLE]
Jdg 8:18 each one **r** the children of a king. 8389+3509.1

RESEN (1)
Ge 10:12 **R** between Nineveh and Calah: the same 7449

RESERVE (3) [RESERVED, RESERVETH]
Jer 3: 5 Will he **r** *his anger* for ever? will he keep 5201
50:20 found: for I will pardon them whom I **r**. 7604
2Pe 2: 9 to **r** the unjust unto the day of judgment 5083

RESERVED (16) [RESERVE]
Ge 27:36 he said, Hast thou not **r** a blessing for me? 680
Nu 18: 9 shall be thine of the most holy *things,* **r** NIH
Jdg 21:22 we **r** not to each man his wife in the war: 3947
Ru 2:18 gave to her that she had **r** after she was 3498
2Sa 8: 4 but **r** of them *for* an hundred chariots. 3498
1Ch 18: 4 but **r** of them an hundred chariots. 3498
Job 21:30 That the wicked is **r** to the day of 2820
38:23 Which I have **r** against the time of trouble 2820
Ac 25:21 But when Paul had appealed to be **r** unto 5083
Ro 11: 4 I have **r** to myself seven thousand men, 2641
1Pe 1: 4 that fadeth not away, **r** in heaven for you, 5083
2Pe 2: 4 chains of darkness, *to be* **r** unto judgment 5083
2:17 to whom the mist of darkness is **r** for ever 5083
3: 7 **r** unto fire against the day of judgment 5083
Jude 1: 6 he hath **r** in everlasting chains under 5083
1:13 to whom is **r** the blackness of darkness 5083

RESERVETH (2) [RESERVE]
Jer 5:24 he **r** unto us the appointed weeks of 8104
Na 1: 2 and he **r** *wrath* for his enemies. 5201

RESHEPH (1)
1Ch 7:25 also **R**, and Telah his son, and Tahan his 7566

RESIDUE (34)
Ex 10: 5 shall eat the **r** of that which is escaped 3499
1Ch 6:66 *the* **r** of the families of the sons of Kohath NIH
Ne 11:20 the **r** of Israel, of the priests, 7605
Isa 21:17 the **r** of the number of archers, the mighty 7605
28: 5 diadem of beauty, unto the **r** of his people, 7605
38:10 I am deprived of the **r** of my years. 3499
44:17 the **r** thereof he maketh a god, *even* his 7611
44:19 shall I make the **r** thereof an abomination? 3499
Jer 8: 3 **r** of them that remain of this evil family, 7611
15: 9 the **r** of them will I deliver to the sword 7611
24: 8 his princes, and the **r** of Jerusalem, 7611
27:19 concerning the **r** of the vessels that remain 3499
29: 1 **r** of the elders which were carried away 3499
39: 3 with all the **r** of the princes of the king of 7611
41:10 Ishmael carried away captive all the **r** of 7611
52:15 the **r** of the people that remained in 3499
Eze 9: 8 *wilt* thou destroy all the **r** of Israel in thy 7611
23:25 and thy **r** shall be devoured by the fire. 319
34:18 ye must tread down with your feet the **r** 3499
34:18 but ye must foul the **r** with your feet? 3498
36: 3 that ye might be a possession unto the **r** 7611

Eze 36: 4 derision to the **r** of the heathen that *are* 7611
36: 5 I spoken against the **r** of the heathen, 7611
48:18 the **r** in length over against the oblation of 3498
48:21 the **r** *shall be* for the prince, on the one 3498

RESIN See BDELLIUM

RESIST (10) [RESISTED, RESISTETH]
Zec 3: 1 Satan standing at his right hand to **r** him. 7853
Mt 5:39 But I say unto you, That ye **r** not evil: 436
Lk 21:15 shall not be able to gainsay nor **r**. 436
Ac 6:10 And they were not able to **r** the wisdom 436
7:51 and ears, ye do always **r** the Holy Ghost: 496
Ro 13: 2 they that **r** shall receive to themselves 436
2Ti 3: 8 so do these also **r** the truth: 436
Jas 4: 7 **R** the devil, and he will flee from you. 436
5: 6 *and* killed the just; *and* he doth not **r** you. 498
1Pe 5: 9 Whom **r** stedfast in the faith, knowing that 436

RESISTED (2) [RESIST]
Ro 9:19 he yet find fault? For who hath **r** his will? 436
Heb 12: 4 Ye have not yet **r** unto blood, 478

RESISTETH (4) [RESIST]
Ro 13: 2 Whosoever therefore **r** the power, 498
13: 2 resisteth the power, **r** the ordinance of God: 436
Jas 4: 6 God **r** the proud, but giveth grace unto 498
1Pe 5: 5 for God **r** the proud, and giveth grace to 498

RESOLVED (1)
Lk 16: 4 I am **r** what to do, that, when I am put 1097

RESORT (4) [RESORTED]
Ne 4:20 sound of the trumpet, **r** ye thither unto us: 6908
Ps 71: 3 whereunto I may continually **r**: 935
Mk 10: 1 the people **r** unto him again; and, as he 4848
Jn 18:20 in the temple, whither the Jews always **r**; 4905

RESORTED (5) [RESORT]
2Ch 11:13 the Levites that *were* in all Israel **r** to him 3320
Mk 2:13 and all the multitude **r** unto him, 2064
Jn 10:41 And many **r** unto him, and said, John did 2064
18: 2 for Jesus ofttimes **r** thither with his 4863
Ac 16:13 spake unto the women which **r** *thither.* 4905

RESPECT (34) [RESPECTED, RESPECTER, RESPECTETH]
Ge 4: 4 the LORD had **r** unto Abel and to his 8159
4: 5 Cain and to his offering he had not **r**. 8159
Ex 2:25 of Israel, and God had **r** unto *them.* 3045
Lev 19:15 thou shalt not **r** the person of the poor, 5375
26: 9 For I will have **r** unto you, and make you 6437
Nu 16:15 unto the LORD, **R** not thou their offering: 6437
Dt 1:17 Ye shall not **r** persons in judgment; 5234
16:19 shalt not **r** persons, neither take a gift: 5234
2Sa 14:14 up *again;* neither doth God **r** *any* person: 5375
1Ki 8:28 Yet **have r** unto the prayer of thy 6437
2Ki 13:23 had **r** unto them, because of his covenant 6437
2Ch 6:19 **Have r** therefore to the prayer of thy 6437
19: 7 nor **r** of persons, nor taking of gifts. 4856
Ps 74:20 **Have r** unto the covenant: for the dark 5027
119: 6 I have **r** unto all thy commandments. 5027
119:15 thy precepts, and **have r** unto thy ways. 5027
119:117 will **have r** unto thy statutes continually. 8159
138: 6 *be* high, yet **hath r** unto the lowly: 7200
Pr 24:23 *It is* not good to **have r** of persons in 5234
28:21 To have **r** of persons *is* not good: for a 5234
Isa 17: 7 his eyes shall have **r** to the Holy One of 7200
17: 8 neither shall **r** *that* which his fingers have 7200
22:11 neither had **r** unto him that fashioned it 7200
Ro 2:11 For there is no **r** of persons with God. 4382
2Co 3:10 was made glorious that had no glory in this, **r** 3313
Eph 6: 9 neither is there **r** of persons with him. 4382
Php 4:11 that I speak **in r** of want: for I have 2596
Col 2:16 or in **r** of a holyday, or of the new moon, 3313
3:25 hath done: and there is no **r** of **persons.** 4382
Heb 11:26 for he had **r** unto the recompence of 578
Jas 2: 1 the *Lord* of glory, with **r** of **persons.** 4382
2: 3 And ye have **r** to him that weareth the gay 1914
2: 9 if ye **have r to persons,** ye commit sin, 4380
1Pe 1:17 **without r of persons** judgeth according 678

RESPECTED (1) [RESPECT]
La 4:16 they **r** not the persons of the priests, 5375

RESPECTER (1) [RESPECT]
Ac 10:34 I perceive that God is no **r of persons**: 4381

RESPECTETH (2) [RESPECT]
Job 37:24 he **r** not any *that are* wise of heart. 7200
Ps 40: 4 **r** not the proud, nor such as turn 413+6437

RESPITE (2)
Ex 8:15 when Pharaoh saw that there was **r**, 7309
1Sa 11: 3 said unto him, Give us seven days' **r**, 7503

RESPONSIBLE See OCCASIONED

REST (275) [RESTED, RESTEST, RESTETH, RESTING, RESTS]
Ge 8: 9 dove found no **r** for the sole of her foot, 4494
18: 4 feet, and **r** yourselves under the tree: 8172
30:36 and Jacob fed the **r** of Laban's flocks. 3498
49:15 he saw that **r** *was* good, and the land that 4496
Ex 5: 5 and you **make** them **r** from their burdens, 7673
16:23 To morrow *is* the **r** of the holy sabbath 7677
23:11 the seventh *year* thou shalt let it **r** and 8058
23:12 and on the seventh day thou shalt **r**: 7673
23:12 that thine ox and thine ass may **r**, 5117
28:10 the *other* six names of the **r** on the other 3498
31:15 in the seventh *is* the sabbath of **r**, holy to 7677
33:14 shall go *with thee,* and I will **give** thee **r.** 5117
34:21 but on the seventh day thou shalt **r**: 7673
34:21 in earing time and in harvest thou shalt **r**. 7673
35: 2 a holy *day,* a sabbath of **r** to the LORD: 7677
Lev 5: 9 the **r** of the blood shall be wrung out at 7604
14:17 of the **r** of the oil that *is* in his hand shall 3499
14:29 the **r** of the oil that *is* in the priest's hand 3498
16:31 It *shall be* a sabbath of **r** unto you, 7677
23: 3 the seventh day *is* the sabbath of **r**, a holy 7677
23:32 It *shall be* unto you a sabbath of **r**, 7677
25: 4 in the seventh year shall be a sabbath of **r** 7677
25: 5 for it *is* a year of **r** unto the land. 7677
26:34 *even* then shall the land **r**, and enjoy her 7673
26:35 As long as it lieth desolate it shall **r**; 7673
26:35 because it did not **r** in your sabbaths, 7673
Nu 31: 8 beside *the* **r** of them that were slain; NIH
31:32 *being* the **r** of the prey which the men of 3499
Dt 3:13 the **r** of Gilead, and all Bashan, *being* 3499
3:20 Until the LORD have **given r** unto your 5117
5:14 thy maidservant may **r** as well as thou. 5117
12: 9 For ye are not as yet come to the **r** and 4496
12:10 when he **giveth** you **r** from all your 5117
25:19 the LORD thy God hath **given** thee **r** 5117
28:65 neither shall the sole of thy foot have **r**: 4494
Jos 1:13 The LORD your God hath **given** you **r**, 5117
1:15 the LORD have **given** your brethren **r**, 5117
3:13 the earth, shall **r** in the waters of Jordan, 5117
10:20 that the **r** *which* remained of them entered 8300
13:27 the **r** of the kingdom of Sihon king of 3499
14:15 Anakims. And the land **had r** from war. 8252
17: 2 There was also a *lot* for the **r** of 3498
17: 6 the **r** of Manasseh's sons had the land of 3498
21: 5 the **r** of the children of Kohath had by lot 3498
21:34 the **r** of the Levites, out of the tribe of 3498
21:44 the LORD **gave** them **r** round about, 5117
22: 4 now the LORD your God hath **given r** 5117
23: 1 **given r** unto Israel from all their enemies. 5117
Jdg 3:11 the land **had r** forty years. And Othniel 8252
3:30 And the land **had r** fourscore years. 8252
5:31 his might. And the land **had r** forty years. 8252
7: 6 **r** of the people bowed down upon 3499
7: 8 he sent all the *r* of Israel every man unto NIH
Ru 1: 9 The LORD grant you that you may find **r**, 4496
3: 1 My daughter, shall I not seek **r** for thee, 4494
3:18 for the man will not be in **r**, until he have 8252
1Sa 13: 2 the **r** of the people he sent every man to 3499
15:15 and the **r** we have utterly destroyed. 3498
2Sa 3:29 Let it **r** on the head of Joab, and on all his 2342
7: 1 the LORD had **given** him **r** round about 5117
7:11 have **caused** thee **to r** from all thine 5117
10:10 the **r** of the people he delivered into 3499
12:28 gather the **r** of the people together, 3499
21:10 suffered neither the birds of the air to **r** on 5117
1Ki 5: 4 now the LORD my God hath **given** me **r** 5117
8:56 that hath given **r** unto his people Israel, 4496
11:41 the **r** of the acts of Solomon, and all that 3499
14:19 the **r** of the acts of Jeroboam, how he 3499
14:29 Now the **r** of the acts of Rehoboam, 3499
15: 7 Now the **r** of the acts of Abijam, and all 3499
15:23 The **r** of all the acts of Asa, and all his 3499
15:31 Now the **r** of the acts of Nadab, and all 3499
16: 5 Now the **r** of the acts of Baasha, 3499
16:14 Now the **r** of the acts of Elah, and all that 3499
16:20 Now the **r** of the acts of Zimri, 3499
16:27 Now the **r** of the acts of Omri which he did, 3499
20:30 the **r** fled to Aphek, into the city; 3498
22:39 Now the **r** of the acts of Ahab, and all that 3499
22:45 Now the **r** of the acts of Jehoshaphat, 3499
2Ki 1:18 Now the **r** of the acts of Ahaziah which 3499
2:15 The spirit of Elijah doth **r** on Elisha. 5117
4: 7 and live thou and thy children of the **r**. 3498
8:23 the **r** of the acts of Joram, and all that he 3499
10:34 Now the **r** of the acts of Jehu, and all that 3499
12:19 the **r** of the acts of Joash, and all that he 3499
13: 8 Now the **r** of the acts of Jehoahaz, 3499
13:12 the **r** of the acts of Joash, and all that he 3499
14:15 Now the **r** of the acts of Jehoash which he 3499
14:18 the **r** of the acts of Amaziah, *are they* not 3499
14:28 Now the **r** of the acts of Jeroboam, 3499
15: 6 the **r** of the acts of Azariah, and all that he 3499
15:11 the **r** of the acts of Zachariah, behold, 3499
15:15 the **r** of the acts of Shallum, 3499
15:21 the **r** of the acts of Menahem, and all that 3499
15:26 the **r** of the acts of Pekahiah, and all that 3499
15:31 the **r** of the acts of Pekah, and all that he 3499
15:36 Now the **r** of the acts of Jotham, and all 3499
16:19 the **r** of the acts of Ahaz which he did, 3499
20:20 the **r** of the acts of Hezekiah, and all his 3499
21:17 Now the **r** of the acts of Manasseh, 3499
21:25 Now the **r** of the acts of Amon which he 3499
23:28 Now the **r** of the acts of Josiah, and all 3499

R

2Ki 24: 5 Now the **r** of the acts of Jehoiakim, 3499
25:11 Now the **r** of the people that were left in 3499
1Ch 4:43 they smote the **r** of the Amalekites that 7611
6:31 of the LORD, after that the ark had **r**. 4494
6:77 Unto the **r** of the children of Merari *were* 3498
11: 8 and Joab repaired the **r** of the city. 7605
12:38 all the **r** also of Israel *were of* one heart to 7611
16:41 Jeduthun, and the **r** that were chosen, 7605
19:11 the **r** of the people he delivered unto 3499
22: 9 *be* born to thee, who shall be a man of **r**; 4496
22: 9 I will give him **r** from all his enemies 5117
22:18 hath he *not* given you **r** on every side? 5117
23:25 The LORD God of Israel hath given **r** 5117
24:20 the **r** of the sons of Levi *were* these: Of 3498
28: 2 **r** for the ark of the covenant of the LORD, 4496
2Ch 9:29 Now the **r** of the acts of Solomon, first 7605
13:22 the **r** of the acts of Abijah, and his ways, 3499
14: 6 for the land had **r**, and he had no war in 8252
14: 6 because the LORD had **given** him **r**. 5117
14: 7 and he hath **given** us **r** on every side. 5117
14:11 for we **r** on thee, and in thy name we go 8172
15:15 and the LORD gave them **r** round about. 5117
20:30 for his God gave **r** round about. 5117
20:34 Now the **r** of the acts of Jehoshaphat, first 3499
24:14 they had finished *it*, they brought the **r** 7605
25:26 Now the **r** of the acts of Amaziah, first 3499
26:22 Now the **r** of the acts of Uzziah, first and 3499
27: 7 Now the **r** of the acts of Jotham, and all 3499
28:26 Now the **r** of his acts and of all his ways, 3499
32:32 Now the **r** of the acts of Hezekiah, 3499
33:18 Now the **r** of the acts of Manasseh, 3499
35:26 Now the **r** of the acts of Josiah, 3499
36: 8 Now the **r** of the acts of Jehoiakim, 3499
Ezr 4: 3 the **r** of the chief of the fathers of Israel, 7605
4: 7 Tabeel, and the **r** of their companions, 7605
4: 9 the scribe, and the **r** of their companions; 7606
4:10 the **r** of the nations whom the great and 7606
4:10 the **r** *that are on this* side the river, 7606
4:17 *to* the **r** of their companions that dwell in 7606
4:17 Samaria, and *unto* the **r** beyond the river: 7606
6:16 and the **r** of the children of the captivity, 7606
7:18 to do with the **r** of the silver and gold, 7606
Ne 2:16 the rulers, nor to the **r** that did the work. 3499
4:14 to the rulers, and to the **r** of the people, 3499
4:19 to the rulers, and to the **r** of the people, 3499
6: 1 the Arabian, and the **r** of our enemies, 3499
6:14 and the **r** of the prophets, 3499
7:72 *that* which the **r** of the people gave *was* 7611
9:28 after they had **r**, they did evil again before 5117
10:28 **r** of the people, the priests, the Levites, 7605
11: 1 the **r** of the people also cast lots, to bring 7605
Est 9:12 what have they done in the **r** of the king's 7605
9:16 had **r** from their enemies, and slew of 5118
Job 3:13 I should have slept: then had I been at **r**, 5117
3:17 troubling; and there the weary be at **r**. 5117
3:18 *There* the prisoners **r** together; they hear 7599
3:26 I was not in safety, neither had I **r**, 8252
11:18 *and* thou shalt take thy **r** in safety. 7901
14: 6 Turn from him, that he may **r**, till he shall 2308
17:16 the pit, when our **r** together *is* in the dust. 5183
30:17 night season: and my sinews **take** no **r**. 7901
Ps 16: 9 my flesh also shall **r** in hope. 7931
17:14 the **r** of their *substance* to their babes. 3499
37: 7 **R** in the LORD, and wait patiently for 1826
38: 3 neither *is there any* **r** in my bones 7965
55: 6 *for then* would I fly away, and be at **r**. 7931
94:13 That *thou* mayest **give** him **r** from the 8252
95:11 that they should not enter into my **r**. 4496
116: 7 Return unto thy **r**, O my soul; 4494
125: 3 For the rod of the wicked shall not **r** upon 5117
132: 8 Arise, O LORD, into thy **r**; thou, 4496
132:14 This *is* my **r** for ever: here will I dwell; 4496
Pr 6:35 neither will he **r** content, though thou 14
29: 9 whether he rage or laugh, *there is* no **r**. 5183
29:17 Correct thy son, and he shall **give** thee **r**; 5117
Ecc 2:23 yea, his heart **taketh** not **r** in the night. 7901
6: 5 nor known *any thing:* this hath more **r** 5183
SS 1: 7 thou **makest** *thy flock to* **r** at noon: 7257
Isa 7:19 shall **r** all of them in the desolate valleys, 5117
10:19 the **r** of the trees of his forest shall be few, 7605
11: 2 the Spirit of the LORD shall **r** upon him, 5117
11:10 Gentiles seek: and his **r** shall be glorious. 4496
14: 3 LORD shall **give** thee **r** from thy sorrow, 5117
14: 7 The whole earth is at **r**, *and* is quiet: 5117
18: 4 I will **take** my **r**, and I will consider in 8252
23:12 Chittim; there also shalt thou have no **r**. 5117
25:10 mountain shall the hand of the LORD **r**, 5117
28:12 This *is the* **r** wherewith ye may **cause** 4496
28:12 wherewith ye may **cause** the weary to **r**; 5117
30:15 In returning and **r** shall ye be saved; 5183
34:14 the shrich owl also shall **r** there, 7280
34:14 there, and find for herself a **place** of **r**. 4494
51: 4 I will **make** my judgment to **r** for a light 7280
57: 2 shall **r** in their beds, *each one* walking 5117
57:20 when it cannot **r**, whose waters cast up 8252
62: 1 and for Jerusalem's sake I will not **r**, 8252
62: 7 give him no **r**, till he establish, and till he 1824
63:14 the Spirit of the LORD **caused** him to **r**: 5117
66: 1 unto me? and where *is* the **place** of my **r**? 4496
Jer 6:16 and ye shall find **r** for your souls. 4771
30:10 shall be in **r**, and be quiet, and none shall 8252
31: 2 Israel when *I* went to **cause** him **r**. 7280
39: 9 with the **r** of the people that remained. 3499
45: 3 I fainted in my sighing, and I find no **r**. 4496
46:27 be in **r** and at ease, and none shall make 8252

Jer 47: 6 thyself into thy scabbard, **r**, and be still. 7280
50:34 that he may **give** **r** to the land, 7280
52:15 of Babylon, and the **r** of the multitude. 3499
La 1: 3 among the heathen, she findeth no **r**: 4494
2:18 give thyself no **r**; let not the apple of thine 6314
5: 5 we labour, *and* have no **r**. 5117
Eze 5:13 I will **cause** my fury **to** **r** upon them, 5117
16:42 will I **make** my fury towards thee **to** **r**, 5117
21:17 and I will **cause** my fury to **r**: 5117
24:13 till I have **caused** my fury to **r** upon thee. 5117
38:11 I will go **to** them that are **at** **r**, that dwell 8252
44:30 that he may **cause** the blessing to **r** in 5117
45: 8 the **r** of the *land* shall they give to the NIH
48:23 As for the **r** of the tribes, from the east 3499
Da 2:18 his fellows should not perish with the **r** of 7606
4: 4 Nebuchadnezzar was at **r** in mine house, 7954
7:12 As concerning the **r** of the beasts, they 7606
12:13 thy way till the end *be:* for thou shalt **r**, 5117
Mic 2:10 Arise ye, and depart; for this *is* not *your* **r**: 4496
Hab 3:16 that I might **r** in the day of trouble: 5117
Zep 3:17 he will **r** in his love, he will joy over thee 2790
Zec 1:11 all the earth sitteth still, and is **at** **r**. 8252
9: 1 and Damascus *shall be* the **r** thereof: 4496
11: 9 the **r** eat every one the flesh of another. 7604
Mt 11:28 are heavy laden, and I will **give** you **r**. 373
11:29 heart: and ye shall find **r** unto your souls. 372
12:43 dry places, seeking **r**, and findeth none. 372
26:45 them, Sleep on now, and **take** *your* **r**: 373
27:49 The **r** said, Let be, let us see whether Elias 3062
Mk 6:31 apart into a desert place, and **r** a while: 373
14:41 them, Sleep on now, and **take** *your* **r**: 373
Lk 10: 6 peace be there, your peace shall **r** upon it: 1879
11:24 he walketh through dry places, seeking **r**; 372
12:26 *is* least, why take ye thought for the **r**? 3062
24: 9 *things* unto the eleven, and **to** all the **r**. 3062
Jn 11:13 he had spoken of **taking** of **r** in sleep. 2838
Ac 2:26 moreover also my flesh shall **r** in hope: 2681
2:37 unto Peter and **to** the **r** of the apostles, 3062
5:13 And of the **r** durst no *man* join himself to 3062
7:49 the Lord: or what *is* the place of my **r**? 2663
9:31 Then had the churches **r** throughout all 1515
27:44 And the **r**, some on boards, and some on 3062
Ro 11: 7 hath obtained *it*, and the **r** were blinded, 3062
1Co 11: 2 But to the **r** speak I, not the Lord: If any 3062
11:34 and the **r** will I set in order when I come. 3062
2Co 2:13 I had no **r** in my spirit, because I found 425
7: 5 our flesh had no **r**, but *we were* troubled 425
12: 9 the power of Christ may **r** upon me. 1981
2Th 1: 7 And to you who are troubled **r** with us, 425
Heb 3:11 my wrath, They shall not enter into my **r**. 2663
3:18 *he* that *they* should not enter into his **r**, 2663
4: 1 promise being left *us* of entering into his **r**, 2663
4: 3 which have believed do enter into **r**, 2663
4: 3 in my wrath, if they shall enter into my **r**: 2663
4: 4 God did **r** the seventh day from all his 2664
4: 5 *place* again, If they shall enter into my **r**. 2663
4: 8 For if Jesus had **given** them **r**, *then* 2664
4: 9 therefore a **r** to the people of God. 4520
4:10 For he that is entered into his **r**, he also 2663
4:11 Let us labour therefore to enter into that **r**, 2663
1Pe 4: 2 That *he* no longer should live the **r** of *his* 1954
Rev 2:24 unto you I say, and unto the **r** in Thyatira, 3062
4: 8 and they **r** not day and night, saying, 372+2192
6:11 that they should **r** yet for a little season, 373
9:20 the **r** of the men which were not killed 3062
14:11 and they have no **r** day nor night, 372
14:13 Spirit, that they may **r** from their labours; 373
20: 5 But the **r** of the dead lived not again until 3062

RESTED (21) [REST]
Ge 2: 2 he **r** on the seventh day from all his work 7673
2: 3 that in it he had **r** from all his work which 7673
8: 4 the ark **r** in the seventh month, 5117
Ex 10:14 of Egypt, and in all the coasts of Egypt: 5117
16:30 So the people **r** on the seventh day. 7673
20:11 all that in them *is*, and **r** the seventh day: 5117
31:17 the seventh day he **r**, and was refreshed. 7673
Nu 9:18 upon the tabernacle they **r** in the **tents**. 2583
9:23 of the LORD they **r** in the **tents**, 2583
10:12 the cloud **r** in the wilderness of Paran. 7931
10:36 when it **r**, he said, Return, O LORD, 5117
11:25 to pass, that when the spirit **r** upon them, 5117
11:26 the spirit **r** upon them; and they were of 5117
Jos 11:23 by their tribes. And the land **r** from war. 8252
1Ki 6:10 they **r** on the house with timber of cedar. 5564
2Ch 32: 8 the people **r** themselves upon the words 5564
Est 9:17 on the fourteenth *day* of the same **r** they, 5118
9:18 on the fifteenth *day* of the same they **r**, 5118
9:22 As the days wherein the Jews from their 5118
Job 30:27 My bowels boiled, and **r** not: the days of 1826
Lk 23:56 the sabbath day according to 2270

RESTEST (1) [REST]
Ro 2:17 and **r** in the law, and makest thy boast of 1879

RESTETH (4) [REST]
Job 24:23 given him *to be* in safety, whereon he **r**; 8172
Pr 14:33 Wisdom **r** in the heart of him that hath 5117
Ecc 7: 9 angry: for anger **r** in the bosom of fools. 5117
1Pe 4:14 the spirit of glory and of God **r** upon you: 373

RESTING (5) [REST]
Nu 10:33 to search out a **r place** for them. 4496
2Ch 6:41 into thy **r place**, thou, and the ark of thy 5118
Pr 24:15 of the righteous; spoil not his **r place**: 7258

Isa 32:18 in sure dwellings, and in quiet **r places**; 4496
Jer 50: 6 to hill, they have forgotten their **r place**. 7258

RESTITUTION (6)
Ex 22: 3 he should **make full r**; if he have 7999+7999
22: 5 best of his own vineyard, shall he **make r**. 7999
22: 6 the fire shall **surely make r**. 7999+7999
22:12 he shall **make r** unto the owner thereof. 7999
Job 20:18 according to *his* substance *shall* the **r** *be*, 8545
Ac 3:21 **r** of all *things*, which God hath spoken by 605

RESTORE (40) [RESTORED, RESTORER, RESTORETH]
Ge 20: 7 Now therefore **r** the man *his* wife; for he 7725
20: 7 if thou **r** *her* not, know thou that thou 7725
40:13 up thine head, and **r** thee unto thy place: 7725
42:25 to **r** every man's money into his sack, 7725
Ex 22: 1 he shall **r** five oxen for an ox, 7999
22: 4 be ox, or ass, or sheep; he shall **r** double. 7999
Lev 6: 4 he shall **r** that which he took violently 7725
6: 5 he shall even **r** it in the principal, 7999
24:21 And he that killeth a beast, he shall **r** it: 7999
25:27 **r** the overplus unto the man to whom he 7725
25:28 be not able to **r** *it* to him, then 7725
Nu 35:25 the congregation shall **r** him to the city of 7725
Dt 22: 2 after it, and thou shalt **r** it to him **again**. 7725
Jdg 11:13 therefore **r** those *lands* **again** peaceably. 7725
17: 3 now therefore I will **r** it unto thee. 7725
1Sa 12: 3 mine eyes therewith? and I will **r** *it* you. 7725
2Sa 9: 7 will **r** thee all the land of Saul thy father; 7725
12: 6 he shall **r** the lamb fourfold, because he 7999
16: 3 To day shall the house of Israel **r** me 7725
1Ki 20:34 my father took from thy father, I will **r**; 7725
2Ki 8: 6 **R** all that *was* hers, and all the fruits of 7725
Ne 5:11 **R**, I pray you, to them, even *this* day, 7725
5:12 We will **r** *them*, and will require nothing 7725
Job 20:10 poor, and his hands shall **r** their goods. 7725
20:18 That which he laboured for shall he **r**, 7725
Ps 51:12 **R** unto me the joy of thy salvation; 7725
Pr 6:31 *if* he be found, he shall **r** sevenfold; 7999
Isa 1:26 I will **r** thy judges as at the first, 7725
42:22 *for* a spoil, and none saith, **R**. 7725
49: 6 of Jacob, and to **r** the preserved of Israel: 7725
57:18 **r** comforts unto him and to his mourners. 7999
Jer 27:22 I bring them up, and **r** them to this place. 7725
30:17 I will **r** health unto thee, and I will heal 5927
Eze 33:15 *If* the wicked the pledge, give again that 7725
Da 9:25 the going forth of the commandment to **r** 7725
Joel 2:25 I will **r** to you the years that the locust 7999
Mt 17:11 Elias truly shall first come, and **r** all *things*. 600
Lk 19: 8 *man* by false accusation, I **r** *him* fourfold. 591
Ac 1: 6 wilt thou at this time **r again** the kingdom 600
Gal 6: 1 **r** such a one in the spirit of meekness; 2675

RESTORED (27) [RESTORE]
Ge 20:14 unto Abraham, and **r** him Sarah his wife. 7725
40:21 the chief butler unto his butlership **again** 7725
41:13 me he **r** unto mine office, and him he 7725
42:28 he said unto his brethren, My money is **r**; 7725
Dt 28:31 before thy face, and shall not be **r** to thee: 7725
Jdg 17: 3 he had **r** the eleven hundred *shekels* 7725
17: 4 Yet he **r** the money unto his mother; 7725
1Sa 7:14 had taken from Israel were **r** to Israel, 7725
1Ki 13: 6 for me, that my hand may be **r** me **again**. 7725
13: 6 the king's hand was **r** him **again**. 7725
2Ki 8: 1 whose son he had **r to life**, saying, Arise, 2421
8: 5 king how he had **r** a dead *body* **to life**, 2421
8: 5 the woman, whose son he had **r to life**, 2421
8: 5 *this is* her son, whom Elisha **r to life**. 2421
14:22 He built Elath, and **r** it to Judah, after that 7725
14:25 He **r** the coast of Israel from the entering 7725
2Ch 8: 2 That the cities which Huram had **r** to 5414
26: 2 He built Eloth, and **r** it to Judah, after that 7725
Ezr 6: 5 be **r**, and brought **again** unto the temple 8421
Ps 69: 4 then I **r** *that* which I took not away. 7725
Eze 18: 7 *but* hath **r** to the debtor his pledge, 7725
18:12 hath not **r** the pledge, and hath lift up his 7725
Mt 12:13 and it was **r** whole, *like* as the other. 600
Mk 3: 5 and his hand was **r** whole as the other. 600
8:25 and he was **r**, and saw every *man* clearly. 600
Lk 6:10 and his hand was **r** whole as the other. 600
Heb 13:19 do this, that I may be **r** to you the sooner. 600

RESTORER (2) [RESTORE]
Ru 4:15 he shall be unto thee a **r** of *thy* life, 7725
Isa 58:12 of the breach, The **r** of paths to dwell in. 7725

RESTORETH (2) [RESTORE]
Ps 23: 3 He **r** my soul: he leadeth me in the paths 7725
Mk 9:12 and **r** all *things; and* how it is written of 600

RESTRAIN (2) [RESTRAINED, RESTRAINEST, RESTRAINT]
Job 15: 8 God? and dost thou **r** wisdom to thyself? 1639
Ps 76:10 the remainder of wrath shalt thou **r**. 2296

RESTRAINED (8) [RESTRAIN]
Ge 8: 2 and the rain from heaven was **r**; 3607
11: 6 now nothing will be **r** from them, 1219
16: 2 the LORD hath **r** me from bearing: 6113
Ex 36: 6 So the people were **r** from bringing. 3607
1Sa 3:13 made themselves vile, and he **r** them not. 3543
Isa 63:15 of thy mercies towards me? are they **r**? 662
Eze 31:15 I **r** the floods thereof, and the great waters 4513
Ac 14:18 And with these sayings scarce **r** they 2664

R

RESTRAINEST (1) [RESTRAIN]
Job 15: 4 castest off fear, and **r** prayer before God. 1639

RESTRAINT (1) [RESTRAIN]
1Sa 14: 6 for *there* is no **r** to the LORD to save by 4622

RESTS (1) [REST]
1Ki 6: 6 house he made **narrowed r** round about, 4052

RESURRECTION (41)
Mt	22:23 say that there is no **r**, and asked him,	386
	22:28 Therefore in the **r** whose wife shall she be	386
	22:30 in the **r** they neither marry, nor are given	386
	22:31 But as touching the **r** of the dead, have ye	386
	27:53 And came out of the graves after his **r**,	1454
Mk	12:18 *the* Sadducees, which say there is no **r**;	386
	12:23 In the **r** therefore, when they shall rise,	386
Lk	14:14 for thou shalt be recompensed at the **r** of	386
	20:27 which deny that there is any **r**;	386
	20:33 Therefore in the **r** whose wife of them is	386
	20:35 and the **r** from the dead, neither marry,	386
	20:36 of God, being the children of the **r**.	386
Jn	5:29 that have done good, unto the **r** of life;	386
	5:29 have done evil, unto the **r** of damnation.	386
	11:24 I know that he shall rise again in the **r** at	386
	11:25 Jesus said unto her, I am the **r**, and the life:	386
Ac	1:22 ordained *to be* a witness with us of his **r**.	386
	2:31 seeing *this* before, spake of the **r** of Christ,	386
	4: 2 through Jesus the **r** from the dead.	386
	4:33 apostles witness of the **r** of the Lord Jesus:	386
	17:18 he preached unto them Jesus, and the **r**.	386
	17:32 And when they heard of the **r** of the dead,	386
	23: 6 and **r** of the dead I am called in question.	386
	23: 8 For the Sadducees say that there is no **r**,	386
	24:15 that there shall be a **r** of the dead, both of	386
	24:21 Touching the **r** of the dead I am called in	386
Ro	1: 4 Spirit of holiness, by the **r** from the dead:	386
	6: 5 we shall be also *in the likeness* of his **r**:	386
1Co	15:12 how say some among you that there is no **r**	386
	15:13 But if there be no **r** of the dead, then	386
	15:21 by man *came* also the **r** of the dead.	386
	15:42 So also *is* the **r** of the dead. It is sown in	386
Php	3:10 and the power of his **r**, and the fellowship	386
	3:11 If by any means I might attain unto the **r**	1815
2Ti	2:18 erred, saying that the **r** is past already;	386
Heb	6: 2 and of **r** of the dead, and of eternal	386
	11:35 that they might obtain a better **r**:	386
1Pe	1: 3 hope by the **r** of Jesus Christ from the dead,	386
	3:21 toward God,) by the **r** of Jesus Christ:	386
Rev	20: 5 years were finished. This *is* the first **r**.	386
	20: 6 and holy *is* he that hath part in the first **r**:	386

RETAIN (7) [RETAINED, RETAINETH]
Job	2: 9 unto him, Dost thou still **r** thine integrity?	2388
Pr	4: 4 said unto me, Let thine heart **r** my words:	8551
	11:16 Honour: and strong *men* **r** riches.	8551
Ecc	8: 8 hath power over the spirit to **r** the spirit;	3607
Da	11: 6 she shall not **r** the power of the arm;	6113
Jn	20:23 *and* whose soever *sins* ye **r**, they are	2902
Ro	1:28 And even as they did not like to **r** God in	2192

RETAINED (6) [RETAIN]
Jdg	7: 8 his tent, and *those* three hundred men:	2388
	19: 4 in law, the damsel's father, **r** him;	2388+871.1
Da	10: 8 in me into corruption, and I **r** no strength.	6113
	10:16 turned upon me, and I have **r** no strength.	6113
Jn	20:23 whose soever *sins* ye retain, they are **r**.	2902
Phm	1:13 Whom I would have **r** with me, that in	2722

RETAINETH (3) [RETAIN]
Pr	3:18 and happy *is* every one that **r** her.	8551
	11:16 A gracious woman **r** honour:	8551
Mic	7:18 he **r** not his anger for ever, because	2388

RETIRE (2) [RETIRED]
2Sa	11:15 **r** ye from him, that he may be smitten,	7725
Jer	4: 6 **r**, stay not: for I will bring evil from	5756

RETIRED (2) [RETIRE]
Jdg	20:39 when the men of Israel **r** in the battle,	2015
2Sa	20:22 **r** from the city, every man to his tent.	6327

RETURN (263) [RETURNED, RETURNETH, RETURNING]
Ge	3:19 eat bread, till thou **r** unto the ground;	7725
	3:19 dust thou *art*, and unto dust shalt thou **r**.	7725
	14:17 his **r** from the slaughter of Chedorlaomer,	7725
	16: 9 **R** to thy mistress, and submit thyself	7725
	18:10 **certainly r** unto thee according	7725+7725
	18:14 At the time appointed I will **r** unto thee,	7725
	31: 3 **R** unto the land of thy fathers, and to thy	7725
	31:13 and **r** unto the land of thy kindred.	7725
	32: 9 **R** unto thy country, and to thy kindred,	7725
Ex	4:18 **r** unto my brethren which *are* in Egypt,	7725
	4:19 unto Moses in Midian, Go, **r** *into* Egypt:	7725
	4:21 When thou goest to **r** into Egypt,	7725
	13:17 when they see war, and they **r** to Egypt:	7725
Lev	25:10 ye shall **r** every man unto his possession,	7725
	25:10 and ye shall **r** every man unto his family.	7725
	25:13 In the year of this jubile ye shall **r** every	7725
	25:27 sold it; that he may **r** unto his possession.	7725
	25:28 go out, and he shall **r** unto his possession.	7725
	25:41 shall **r** unto his own family, and unto	7725
	25:41 the possession of his fathers shall he **r**.	7725
	27:24 In the year of the jubile the field shall **r**	7725

Nu	10:36 when it rested, he said, **R**, O LORD,	7725
	14: 3 were it not better for us to **r** into Egypt?	7725
	14: 4 us make a captain, and let us **r** into Egypt.	7725
	23: 5 **R** unto Balak, and thus thou shalt speak.	7725
	32:18 We will not **r** unto our houses, until	7725
	32:22 afterward ye shall **r**, and be guiltless	7725
	35:28 shall **r** into the land of his possession.	7725
Dt	3:20 shall ye **r** every man unto his possession,	7725
	17:16 nor **cause** the people to **r** to Egypt,	7725
	17:16 Ye shall henceforth **r** no more that way.	7725
	20: 5 let him go and **r** to his house, lest he die	7725
	20: 6 let him *also* go and **r** unto his house, lest	7725
	20: 7 let him go and **r** unto his house, lest he	7725
	20: 8 let him go and **r** unto his house, lest his	7725
	30: 2 shalt **r** unto the LORD thy God,	7725
	30: 3 will **r** and gather thee from all the nations,	7725
	30: 8 thou shalt **r** and obey the voice of	7725
Jos	1:15 shall **r** unto the land of your possession,	7725
	20: 6 shall the slayer **r**, and come unto his own	7725
	22: 4 therefore now **r** ye, and get ye unto your	6437
	22: 8 **R** with much riches unto your tents,	7725
Jdg	7: 3 let him **r** and depart early from mount	7725
	11:31 when I **r** in peace from the children of	7725
Ru	1: 6 she might **r** from the country of Moab:	7725
	1: 7 they went on the way to **r** unto the land	7725
	1: 8 in law, Go, **r** each to her mother's house:	7725
	1:10 we will **r** with thee unto thy people.	7725
	1:15 her gods: **r** thou after thy sister in law.	7725
	1:16 *or* to **r** from following after thee:	7725
1Sa	3: 3 **in any wise r** him a trespass	7725
	6: 4 trespass offering which we shall **r** to him?	7725
	6: 8 which ye **r** him *for* a trespass offering,	7725
	7: 3 If ye do **r** unto the LORD with all your	7725
	7:17 his **r** *was* to Ramah; for there *was* his	8666
	9: 5 that *was* with him, Come, and let us **r**;	7725
	15:26 said unto Saul, I will not **r** with thee:	7725
	26:21 my son David: for I will no more do	7725
	29: 4 **Make** *this* fellow **r**, that he may go again	7725
	29: 7 Wherefore now **r**, and go in peace,	7725
	29:11 to **r** into the land of the Philistines.	7725
2Sa	2:26 ere thou bid the people **r** from following	7725
	3:16 said Abner unto him, Go, **r**. And he	7725
	10: 5 until your beards be grown, and *then* **r**.	7725
	12:23 I shall go to him, but he shall not **r** to me.	7725
	15:19 **r** to thy place, and abide with the king:	7725
	15:20 I may, **r** thou, and take back thy brethren:	7725
	15:27 **r** *into* the city in peace, and your two sons	7725
	15:34 if thou **r** *to* the city, and say unto Absalom	7725
	19:14 the king, **R** thou, and all thy servants.	7725
	24:13 see what answer I shall **r** *to* him that sent	7725
1Ki	2:32 the LORD shall **r** his blood upon his own	7725
	2:33 therefore **r** upon the head of Joab,	7725
	2:44 the LORD shall **r** thy wickedness upon	7725
	8:48 *so* **r** unto thee with all their heart,	7725
	12:24 **r** every man to his house; for this thing is	7725
	12:26 Now shall the kingdom **r** to the house of	7725
	13:16 he said, I may not **r** with thee, nor go in	7725
	19:15 or on thy way to the wilderness of	7725
	20:22 for at the **r** of the year the king of Syria	8666
	20:26 it came to pass at the **r** of the year,	8666
	22:17 them **r** every man to his house in peace.	7725
	22:28 Micaiah said, If thou **r at all** in	7725+7725
2Ki	18:14 I have offended; **r** from me:	7725
	19: 7 a rumour, and shall **r** to his own land;	7725
	19:33 *by the same* shall he **r**, and shall not come	7725
	20:10 let the shadow **r** backward ten degrees.	7725
1Ch	19: 5 until your beards be grown, and *then* **r**.	7725
2Ch	6:24 shall **r** and confess thy name, and pray	7725
	6:38 If they **r** to thee with all their heart and	7725
	10: 6 What counsel give ye me to **r** answer to	7725
	10: 9 advice give ye that we may **r** answer	7725
	11: 4 **r** every man to his house, for this thing is	7725
	18:16 them **r** *therefore* every man to his house	7725
	18:26 with water of affliction, until I **r** in peace.	7725
	18:27 If thou **certainly r** in peace, then	7725+7725
	30: 6 Israel, and he will **r** to the remnant of you,	7725
	30: 9 away *his* face from you, if ye **r** unto him.	7725
Ne	2: 6 when wilt thou **r**? So it pleased the king	7725
	4:12 From all places whence ye shall **r** unto us	7725
	9:17 in their rebellion appointed a captain to **r**	7725
Est	4:15 Esther bade them **r** Mordecai *this answer:*	7725
	9:25 should **r** upon his own head, and that he	7725
Job	1:21 womb, and naked shall I **r** thither:	7725
	6:29 **R**, I pray you, let it not be iniquity; yea,	7725
	6:29 yea, **r** again, my righteousness *is* in it.	7725
	7:10 He shall **r** no more to his house,	7725
	10:21 Before I go whence I shall not **r**, *even* to	7725
	15:22 He believeth not that *he* shall **r** out of	7725
	16:22 I shall go the way *whence* I shall not **r**.	7725
	17:10 *as for* you all, do you **r**, and come now:	7725
	22:23 If thou **r** to the Almighty, thou shalt be	7725
	33:25 he shall **r** to the days of his youth:	7725
	36:10 commandeth that they **r** from iniquity.	7725
	39: 4 they go forth, and **r** not unto them.	7725
Ps	6: 4 **R**, O LORD, deliver my soul: O save me	7725
	6:10 let them **r** *and* be ashamed suddenly.	7725
	7: 7 for their sakes therefore **r** thou on high.	7725
	7:16 His mischief shall **r** upon his own head,	7725
	59: 6 They **r** at evening: they make a noise like	7725
	59:14 at evening let them **r**; *and* let them make	7725
	73:10 Therefore his people **r** hither: and waters	7725
	74:21 O let not the oppressed **r** ashamed:	7725
	80:14 **R**, we beseech thee, O God *of* hosts:	7725
	90: 3 and sayest, **R**, ye children of men.	7725
	90:13 **R**, O LORD, how long? and let it repent	7725

Ps	94:15 judgment shall **r** unto righteousness:	7725	
	104:29 their breath, they die, and **r** to their dust.	7725	
	116: 7 **R** unto thy rest, O my soul; for the LORD	7725	
Pr	2:19 None that go *unto* her **r** again, neither	7725	
	26:27 he that rolleth a stone, it will **r** upon him.	7725	
Ecc	1: 7 rivers come, thither they **r** again.	1980+7725	
	5:15 naked shall he **r** to go as he came,	7725	
	12: 2 nor the clouds **r** after the rain:	7725	
	12: 7 shall the dust **r** to the earth as it was:	7725	
	12: 7 the spirit shall **r** unto God who gave it.	7725	
SS	6:13 **R**, return, O Shulamite; return, return,	7725	
	6:13 Return, O Shulamite; return, return,	7725	
	6:13 **r**, return, that we may look upon thee.	7725	
	6:13 return, that we may look upon thee.	7725	
Isa	6:13 a tenth, and *it* shall **r**, and shall be eaten:	7725	
	10:21 The remnant shall **r**, *even* the remnant of	7725	
	10:22 of the sea, *yet* a remnant of them shall **r**:	7725	
	19:22 and they shall **r** *even* to the LORD,	7725	
	21:12 if ye will inquire, inquire ye: **r**, come.	7725	
	35:10 the ransomed of the LORD shall **r**,	7725	
	37: 7 hear a rumour, and **r** to his own land;	7725	
	37:34 *by the same* shall he **r**, and shall not come	7725	
	44:22 **r** unto me; for I have redeemed thee.	7725	
	45:23 shall not **r**, That unto me every knee shall	7725	
	51:11 the redeemed of the LORD shall **r**,	7725	
	55: 7 let him **r** unto the LORD, and he will have	7725	
	55:11 it shall not **r** unto me void, but it shall	7725	
	63:17 **R** for thy servants' sake, the tribes of thine	7725	
Jer	3: 1 another man's, shall he **r** unto her again?	7725	
	3: 1 yet **r** again to me, saith the LORD,	7725	
	3:12 say, **R**, thou backsliding Israel, saith	7725	
	3:22 **R**, ye backsliding children, *and* I will heal	7725	
	4: 1 If thou wilt **r**, O Israel, saith the LORD,	7725	
	4: 1 O Israel, saith the LORD, **r** unto me:	7725	
	5: 3 harder than a rock; they have refused to **r**.	7725	
	8: 4 not arise? shall he turn away, and not **r**?	7725	
	8: 5 they hold fast deceit, they refuse to **r**.	7725	
	12:15 I will **r**, and have compassion on them,	7725	
	15: 7 people, *sith* they **r** not from their ways.	7725	
	15:19 If thou **r**, then will I bring thee again,	7725	
	15:19 let them **r** unto thee; but return not thou	7725	
	15:19 unto thee; but **r** not thou unto them.	7725	
	18:11 **r** ye now every one from his evil way,	7725	
	22:10 for he shall **r** no more, nor see his native	7725	
	22:11 place; He shall not **r** thither any more:	7725	
	22:27 to the land whereunto they desire to **r**,	7725	
	22:27 desire to return, thither shall they not **r**.	7725	
	23:14 that none doth **r** from his wickedness:	7725	
	23:20 The anger of the LORD shall not **r**,	7725	
	24: 7 for they shall **r** unto me with their whole	7725	
	29:10 in **causing** you to **r** to this place.	7725	
	30: 3 I will **cause** them to **r** to the land that I	7725	
	30:10 Jacob shall **r**, and shall be in rest,	7725	
	30:24 The fierce anger of the LORD shall not **r**,	7725	
	31: 8 a great company shall **r** thither.	7725	
	32:44 for I will **cause** their captivity to **r**,	7725	
	33: 7 **cause** the captivity of Judah and the	7725	
		captivity of Israel to **r**,	7725
	33:11 For I will **cause** to **r** the captivity of	7725	
	33:26 for I will **cause** their captivity to **r**,	7725	
	34:11 **caused** the servants and the handmaids,	7725	
		whom they had let go free, to **r**,	7725
	34:16 **caused** every man his servant, . . . to **r**,	7725	
	34:22 and **cause** them to **r** to this city;	7725	
	35:15 **R** ye now every man from his evil way,	7725	
	36: 3 that they may **r** every man from his evil	7725	
	36: 7 and will **r** every one from his evil way:	7725	
	37: 7 shall **r** to Egypt into their own land.	7725	
	37:20 thou **cause** me not to **r** *to* the house of	7725	
	38:26 that *he* would not **cause** me to **r** to	7725	
	42:12 and **cause** you to **r** to your own land.	7725	
	44:14 that *they* should **r** *into* the land of Judah,	7725	
	44:14 to the which they have a desire to **r** to	7725	
	44:14 for none shall **r** but such as shall escape.	7725	
	44:28 **r** out of the land of Egypt *into* the land of	7725	
	46:27 Jacob shall **r**, and be in rest and at ease,	7725	
	50: 9 mighty expert *man;* none shall **r** in vain.	7725	
Eze	7:13 For the seller shall not **r** to that which is	7725	
	7:13 multitude thereof, *which* shall not **r**;	7725	
	13:22 that *he* should not **r** from his wicked way,	7725	
	16:55 shall **r** to their former estate, and Samaria	7725	
	16:55 daughters shall **r** to their former estate,	7725	
	16:55 daughters shall **r** to your former estate.	7725	
	18:23 *and* not that he should **r** from his ways,	7725	
	21: 5 out of his sheath: it shall not **r** any more.	7725	
	21:30 Shall I **cause** *it* to **r** into his sheath? I will	7725	
	29:14 will **cause** them to **r** *into* the land of	7725	
	35: 9 and thy cities shall not **r**:	7725	
	46: 9 he shall not **r** *by* the way of the gate	7725	
	46:17 of liberty; after, it shall **r** to the prince:	7725	
	47: 6 **caused** me to **r** to the brink of the river.	7725	
Da	10:20 now will I **r** to fight with the prince of	7725	
	11: 9 kingdom, and shall **r** into his own land.	7725	
	11:10 shall he **r**, and be stirred up, *even* to his	7725	
	11:13 For the king of the north shall **r**,	7725	
	11:28 shall he **r** *into* his land with great riches;	7725	
	11:28 shall do **exploits**, and **r** to his own land.	7725	
	11:29 At the time appointed he shall **r**,	7725	
	11:30 **r**, and have indignation against the holy	7725	
	11:30 he shall even **r**, and have intelligence	7725	
Hos	2: 7 say, I will go and **r** to my first husband;	7725	
	2: 9 Therefore will I **r**, and take *away* my corn	7725	
	3: 5 Afterward shall the children of Israel **r**,	7725	
	5:15 I will go *and* **r** to my place, till they	7725	
	6: 1 Come and let us **r** unto the LORD: for he	7725	

Hos 7:10 they do not **r** to the LORD their God,	7725
7:16 They **r**, *but* not *to* the most High: they are	7725
8:13 and visit their sins: they shall **r** to Egypt.	7725
9: 3 Ephraim shall **r** to Egypt, and they shall	7725
11: 5 He shall not **r** into the land of Egypt,	7725
11: 5 be his king, because they refused to **r**.	7725
11: 9 anger, I will not **r** to destroy Ephraim:	7725
12:14 his reproach shall his Lord **r** unto him.	7725
14: 1 O Israel, **r** unto the LORD thy God;	7725
14: 7 They that dwell under his shadow shall **r**;	7725
Joel 2:14 Who knoweth *if* he will **r** and repent,	7725
3: 4 speedily will I **r** your recompence upon	7725
3: 7 will **r** your recompence upon your own head.	7725
Ob 1:15 thy reward shall **r** upon thine own head.	7725
Mic 1: 7 and they shall **r** to the hire of a harlot.	7725
5: 3 the remnant of his brethren shall **r** unto	7725
Mal 1: 4 we will **r** and build the desolate places;	7725
3: 7 have not kept *them*. **R** unto me, and I will	7725
3: 7 I will **r** unto you, saith the LORD of hosts.	7725
3: 7 of hosts. But ye said, Wherein shall we **r**?	7725
3:18 shall ye **r**, and discern between	7725
Mt 2:12 a dream that *they* should not **r** to Herod,	344
10:13 it be not worthy, let your peace **r** to you.	1994
12:44 I will **r** into my house from whence I	1994
24:18 Neither let him which is in the field **r**	1994
Lk 8:39 **R** to thine own house, and shew how	5290
11:24 I will **r** unto my house whence I came	5290
12:36 lord, when he will **r** from the wedding;	360
17:31 in the field, let him likewise not **r** back.	1994
19:12 receive for himself a kingdom, and to **r**.	5290
Ac 13:34 *now* no more to **r** to corruption, he said	5290
15:16 After this I will **r**, and will build again	390
18:21 but I will **r** again unto you, if God will.	344
20: 3 he purposed to **r** through Macedonia.	5290

RETURNED (185) [RETURN]

Ge 8: 3 waters **r** from off the earth continually:	7725
8: 9 unto him into the ark, for the waters	7725
8:12 which **r** not again unto him any more.	7725
14: 7 they **r**, and came to En-mishpat, which *is*	7725
18:33 and Abraham **r** unto his place.	7725
21:32 and they **r** into the land of the Philistines.	7725
22:19 So Abraham **r** unto his young men,	7725
31:55 and Laban departed, and **r** unto his place.	7725
32: 6 the messengers **r** to Jacob, saying,	7725
33:16 So Esau **r** that day on his way unto Seir.	7725
37:29 Reuben **r** unto the pit; and behold,	7725
37:30 he **r** unto his brethren, and said, The	7725
38:22 he **r** to Judah, and said, I cannot find her,	7725
42:24 to them *again*, and communed with	7725
43:10 surely now we had **r** this second time.	7725
43:18 Because of the money that was **r** in our	7725
44:13 laded every man his ass, and **r** to the city.	7725
50:14 Joseph **r** into Egypt, he, and his brethren,	7725
Ex 4:18 and **r** to Jethro his father in law,	7725
4:20 upon an ass, and he **r** to the land of Egypt:	7725
5:22 Moses **r** unto the LORD, and said, Lord,	7725
14:27 sea **r** to his strength when the morning	7725
14:28 the waters **r**, and covered the chariots,	7725
19: 8 Moses **r** the words of the people unto	7725
32:31 Moses **r** unto the LORD, and said,	7725
34:31 all the rulers of the congregation **r** unto	7725
Lev 22:13 no child, and is **r** unto her father's house,	7725
Nu 13:25 they **r** from searching of the land after	7725
14:36 who **r**, and made all the congregation to	7725
16:50 Aaron **r** unto Moses unto the door of	7725
23: 6 he **r** unto him, and lo, *he* stood by his	7725
24:25 rose up, and went and **r** to his place:	7725
Dt 1:45 ye **r** and wept before the LORD;	7725
Jos 2:16 there three days, until the pursuers be **r**:	7725
2:22 three days, until the pursuers were **r**:	7725
2:23 So the two men **r**, and descended from	7725
4:18 the waters of Jordan unto their place,	7725
6:14 the city once, and **r** *into* the camp:	7725
7: 3 they **r** to Joshua, and said unto him, Let	7725
8:24 that all the Israelites **r** *unto* Ai, and smote	7725
10:15 Joshua **r**, and all Israel with him, unto	7725
10:21 all the people **r** to the camp to Joshua *at*	7725
10:38 Joshua **r**, and all Israel with him, to Debir;	7725
10:43 Joshua **r**, and all Israel with him, unto	7725
22: 9 of Gad and the half tribe of Manasseh **r**,	7725
22:32 **r** from the children of Reuben,	7725
Jdg 2:19 *that* they **r**, and corrupted *themselves*	7725
5:29 answered *her*, yea, she **r** answer to herself	7725
7: 3 there **r** of the people twenty and	7725
7:15 into the host of Israel, and said, Arise;	7725
8:13 Gideon the son of Joash **r** from battle	7725
11:39 of two months, that she **r** unto her father,	7725
14: 8 after a time he **r** to take her, and he	7725
21:23 they went and **r** unto their inheritance,	7725
Ru 1:22 So Naomi **r**, and Ruth the Moabitess,	7725
1:22 which **r** out of the country of Moab:	7725
1Sa 1:19 and **r**, and came to their house to Ramah:	7725
6:16 had seen *it*, they **r** to Ekron the same day.	7725
6:17 **r** *for a* trespass offering unto the LORD;	7725
17:15 **r** from Saul to feed his father's sheep *at*	7725
17:53 the children of Israel **r** from chasing after	7725
17:57 as David **r** from the slaughter of	7725
18: 6 when David was **r** from the slaughter of	7725
23:28 Wherefore Saul **r** from pursuing after	7725
24: 1 when Saul was **r** from following	7725
25:39 for the LORD hath **r** the wickedness of	7725
26:25 went on his way, and Saul **r** to his place.	7725
27: 9 the apparel, and **r**, and came to Achish.	7725
2Sa 1: 1 when David was **r** from the slaughter of	7725

2Sa 1:22 and the sword of Saul **r** not empty.	7725
2:30 Joab **r** from following Abner: and when	7725
3:16 Abner unto him, Go, return. And he **r**.	7725
3:27 when Abner was **r** *to* Hebron, Joab took	7725
6:20 David **r** to bless his household.	7725
8:13 David gat *him* a name when he **r** from	7725
10:14 So Joab **r** from the children of Ammon,	7725
11: 4 uncleanness: and she **r** unto her house.	7725
12:31 and all the people *unto* Jerusalem.	7725
14:24 So Absalom **r** to his own house,	5437
16: 8 The LORD hath **r** upon thee all the blood	7725
17: 3 the man whom thou seekest *is* as if all **r**:	7725
17:20 could not find *them*, they **r** to Jerusalem.	7725
18:16 the people **r** from pursuing after Israel:	7725
19:15 So the king **r**, and came to Jordan.	7725
19:39 blessed him; and he **r** unto his own place.	7725
20:22 And Joab **r** *to* Jerusalem unto the king.	7725
23:10 the people **r** after him only to spoil.	7725
1Ki 12:24 to the word of the LORD, and **r** to depart,	7725
13:10 nor by the way that he came to Beth-el.	7725
13:33 After this thing Jeroboam **r** not from his	7725
19:21 he **r** *back* from him, and took a yoke of	7725
2Ki 2:25 and from thence he **r** *to* Samaria.	7725
3:27 from him, and **r** to *their own* land.	7725
4:35 he **r**, and walked in the house to and fro;	7725
5:15 he **r** to the man of God, he and all his	7725
7:15 And the messengers **r**, and told the king.	7725
8: 3 that the woman **r** out of the land of	7725
9:15 king Joram was **r** to be healed in Jezreel	7725
14:14 and hostages, and **r** to Samaria.	7725
19: 8 So Rab-shakeh **r**, and found the king of	7725
19:36 and went and **r**, and dwelt at Nineveh.	7725
23:20 bones upon them, and **r** *to* Jerusalem.	7725
1Ch 16:43 his house: and David **r** to bless his house.	7725
20: 3 and all the people **r** *to* Jerusalem.	5437
2Ch 10: 2 heard *it*, that Jeroboam **r** out of Egypt.	7725
11: 4 and **r** from going against Jeroboam.	7725
14:15 camels in abundance, and **r** *to* Jerusalem.	7725
19: 1 Jehoshaphat the king of Judah **r** to his	7725
19: 8 when they **r** to Jerusalem.	7725
20:27 they **r**, every man of Judah and Jerusalem,	7725
22: 6 he **r** to be healed in Jezreel because of	7725
25:10 and they **r** home in great anger.	7725
25:24 the hostages also, and **r** *to* Samaria.	7725
28:15 to their brethren: then they **r** *to* Samaria.	7725
31: 1 *them* all. Then all the children of Israel **r**,	7725
32:21 he **r** with shame of face to his own land.	7725
34: 7 all the land of Israel, and he **r** *to* Jerusalem.	7725
34: 9 and Benjamin; and they **r** *to* Jerusalem.	7725
Ezr 5: 5 they **r** **answer** by letter concerning this	8421
5:11 thus they **r** us answer, saying, We are	8421
Ne 2:15 entered by the gate of the valley, and so **r**.	7725
4:15 that we **r** all of us to the wall, every one	7725
9:28 yet when they **r**, and cried unto thee,	7725
Est 2:14 the morrow she **r** into the second house	7725
7: 8 the king **r** out of the palace garden into	7725
Ps 35:13 and my prayer **r** into mine own bosom.	7725
60: 1 when Joab **r**, and smote of Edom in	7725
78:34 and they **r** and inquired early after God.	7725
Ecc 4: 1 So I **r**, and considered all the oppressions	7725
4: 7 Then I **r**, and I saw vanity under the sun.	7725
9:11 I **r**, and saw under the sun, that the race	7725
Isa 37: 8 So Rabshakeh **r**, and found the king of	7725
37:37 and went and **r**, and dwelt at Nineveh.	7725
38: 8 the sun **r** ten degrees, by which degrees	7725
Jer 3: 7 she **r** not. And her treacherous sister	7725
14: 3 to water; they **r** *with* their vessels empty:	7725
40:12 Even all the Jews **r** out of all places	7725
41:14 captive from Mizpah cast about and **r**,	7725
43: 5 that were **r** from all nations, whither they	7725
Eze 1:14 **r** as the appearance of a flash of lightning.	7725
8:17 and have **r** to provoke me to anger:	7725
47: 7 Now when I had **r**, behold, at the bank of	7725
Da 4:34 mine understanding **r** unto me,	8421
4:36 At the same time my reason **r** unto me;	8421
4:36 mine honour and brightness **r** unto me;	8421
Hos 6:11 when I **r** the captivity of my people.	7725
Am 4: 6 yet have ye not **r** unto me, saith	7725
4: 8 yet have ye not **r** unto me, saith	7725
4: 9 *them:* yet have ye not **r** unto me,	7725
4:10 yet have ye not **r** unto me, saith	7725
4:11 yet have ye not **r** unto me, saith	7725
Zec 1: 6 they **r** and said, Like as the LORD hath	7725
1:16 I am **r** to Jerusalem with mercies:	7725
7:14 that no man passed through nor **r**:	7725
8: 3 I am **r** unto Zion, and will dwell in	7725
Mt 21:18 Now in the morning as he **r** into the city,	1877
Mk 14:40 And when he **r**, he found them asleep	5290
Lk 1:56 three months, and **r** to her own house.	5290
2:20 And the shepherds **r**, glorifying and	1994
2:39 they **r** into Galilee, to their own city	5290
2:43 they had fulfilled the days, as they **r**,	5290
4: 1 And Jesus being full of the Holy Ghost **r**	5290
4:14 And Jesus **r** in the power of the Spirit into	5290
8:37 went *up* into the ship, and **r** *back again*.	5290
8:40 it came to pass, that, when Jesus was **r**,	5290
9:10 And the apostles, when they were **r**,	5290
10:17 And the seventy **r** *again* with joy, saying,	5290
17:15 There are not found that **r** to give glory to	5290
19:15 And it came to pass, that when he was **r**,	1880
23:48 were done, smote their breasts, and **r**.	5290
23:56 And they **r**, and prepared spices and	5290
24: 9 And **r** from the sepulchre, and told all	5290
24:33 and **r** to Jerusalem, and found the eleven	5290
24:52 and **r** to Jerusalem with great joy:	5290

Ac 1:12 Then **r** they Jerusalem from the	5290
5:22 them not in the prison, they **r**, and told,	390
8:25 **r** to Jerusalem, and preached the gospel in	5290
12:25 And Barnabas and Saul **r** from Jerusalem,	5290
13:13 John departing from them **r** to Jerusalem.	5290
14:21 they **r** again to Lystra, and *to* Iconium,	5290
21: 6 we took ship; and they **r** home *again*.	5290
23:32 to go with him, and **r** to the castle:	5290
Gal 1:17 into Arabia, and **r** again unto Damascus.	5290
Heb 11:15 might have had opportunity to have **r**.	344
1Pe 2:25 but are now **r** unto the Shepherd and	1994

RETURNETH (7) [RETURN]

Ps 146: 4 His breath goeth forth, he **r** to his earth;	7725
Pr 26:11 As a dog **r** to his vomit, *so* a fool	7725
26:11 to his vomit, *so* a fool **r** to his folly.	8138
Ecc 1: 6 the wind **r** *again* according to his circuits.	7725
Isa 55:10 **r** not thither, but watereth the earth,	7725
Eze 35: 7 him that passeth out and him that **r**.	7725
Zec 9: 8 passeth by, and because of him that **r**:	7725

RETURNING (4) [RETURN]

Isa 30:15 In **r** and rest shall ye be saved;	7729
Lk 7:10 And they that were sent, **r** to the house,	5290
Ac 8:28 Was **r**, and sitting in his chariot read	5290
Heb 7: 1 who met Abraham **r** from the slaughter of	5290

REU (4)

Ge 11:18 And Peleg lived thirty years, and begat **R**:	7466
11:19 Peleg lived after he begat **R** two hundred	7466
11:20 **R** lived two and thirty years,	7466
11:21 **R** lived after he begat Serug two hundred	7466

REUBEN (74) [REUBENITE, REUBENITES]

Ge 29:32 bare a son, and she called his name **R**:	7205
30:14 **R** went in the days of wheat harvest,	7205
35:22 **R** went and lay with Bilhah his father's	7205
35:23 **R**, Jacob's firstborn, and Simeon, and Levi,	7205
37:21 **R** heard *it*, and he delivered him out of	7205
37:22 **R** said unto them, Shed no blood,	7205
37:29 **R** returned unto the pit; and behold,	7205
42:22 **R** answered them, saying, Spake I not	7205
42:37 **R** spake unto his father, saying, Slay my	7205
46: 8 Jacob and his sons: **R**, Jacob's firstborn.	7205
46: 9 the sons of **R**; Hanoch, and Phallu,	7205
48: 5 as **R** and Simeon, they shall be mine.	7205
49: 3 **R**, thou *art* my firstborn, my might,	7205
Ex 1: 2 **R**, Simeon, Levi, and Judah,	7205
6:14 The sons of **R** the firstborn of Israel;	7205
6:14 and Carmi: these *be* the families of **R**.	7205
Nu 1: 5 *the tribe of* **R**; Elizur the son of Shedeur.	7205
1:20 the children of **R**, Israel's eldest son,	7205
1:21 *even* of the tribe of **R**, *were* forty and	7205
2:10 the camp of **R** according to their armies:	7205
2:10 the captain of the children of **R** *shall be*	7205
2:16 All that were numbered in the camp of **R**	7205
7:30 prince of the children of **R**, *did offer:*	7205
10:18 the standard of the camp of **R** set forward	7205
13: 4 of the tribe of **R**, Shammua the son of	7205
16: 1 On, the son of Peleth, sons of **R**, took	7205
26: 5 **R**, the eldest son of Israel: the children of	7205
26: 5 the children of **R**; Hanoch, *of whom*	7205
32: 1 Now the children of **R** and the children of	7205
32: 2 children of **R** came and spake unto	7205
32: 6 children of Gad and to the children of **R**,	7205
32:25 and the children of **R** spake unto Moses,	7205
32:29 the children of **R** will pass with you over	7205
32:31 of Gad and the children of **R** answered,	7205
32:33 the children of **R**, and unto half the tribe	7205
32:37 the children of **R** built Heshbon,	7205
34:14 the tribe of the children of **R** according	7206
Dt 11: 6 the sons of Eliab, the son of **R**:	7205
27:13 **R**, Gad, and Asher, and Zebulun, Dan,	7205
33: 6 Let **R** live, and not die; and let *not* his	7205
Jos 4:12 children of **R**, and the children of Gad,	7205
13:15 **R** inheritance according to their families.	7205
13:23 border of the children of **R** was Jordan,	7205
13:23 of the children of **R** after their families,	7205
15: 6 up *to* the stone of Bohan the son of **R**:	7205
18: 7 and **R**, and half the tribe of Manasseh,	7205
18:17 *to* the stone of Bohan the son of **R**,	7205
20: 8 upon the plain out of the tribe of **R**,	7205
21: 7 by their families *had* out of the tribe of **R**,	7205
21:36 out of the tribe of **R**, Bezer with her	7205
22: 9 the children of **R** and the children of Gad	7205
22:10 the children of **R** and the children of	7205
22:11 the children of **R** and the children of Gad	7205
22:13 of Israel sent unto the children of **R**,	7205
22:15 they came unto the children of **R**,	7205
22:21 the children of **R** and the children of Gad	7205
22:25 ye children of **R** and children of Gad;	7205
22:30 heard the words that the children of **R**	7205
22:31 the priest said unto the children of **R**,	7205
22:32 returned from the children of **R**,	7205
22:33 the land wherein the children of **R**	7205
22:34 the children of **R** and the children of Gad	7205
Jdg 5:15 For the divisions of **R** *there were* great	7205
5:16 For the divisions of **R** *there were* great	7205
1Ch 2: 1 **R**, Simeon, Levi, and Judah, Issachar,	7205
5: 1 Now the sons of **R** the firstborn of Israel,	7205
5: 3 *I say*, of **R** the firstborn of Israel *were*,	7205
5:18 The sons of **R**, and the Gadites, and half	7205
6:63 out of the tribe of **R**, and out of the tribe	7205
6:78 *were given* them out of the tribe of **R**,	7205
Eze 48: 6 even unto the west side, a *portion for* **R**.	7205

R

Eze 48: 7 by the border of **R**, from the east side unto 7205
48:31 one gate of **R**, one gate of Judah, one gate 7205
Rev 7: 5 Of the tribe of **R** *were* sealed twelve 4502

REUBENITE (1) [REUBEN]
1Ch 11:42 Adina the son of Shiza the **R**, a captain of 7206

REUBENITES (16) [REUBEN]
Nu 26: 7 These *are* the families of the **R**: 7206
Dt 3:12 gave I unto the **R** and to the Gadites. 7206
3:16 unto the **R** and the Gadites I gave 7206
4:43 in the plain country, of the **R**; 7206
29: 8 gave it for an inheritance unto the **R**, 7206
Jos 1:12 to the **R**, and to the Gadites, and to half 7206
12: 6 Lord gave it *for* a possession unto the **R**, 7206
13: 8 With whom the **R** and the Gadites have 7206
22: 1 Joshua called the **R**, and the Gadites, 7206
2Ki 10:33 the **R**, and the Manassites, from Aroer, 7206
1Ch 5: 6 away captive: he *was* prince of the **R**. 7206
5:26 even the **R**, and the Gadites, and the half 7206
11:42 a captain of the **R**, and thirty with him, 7206
12:37 of the **R**, and the Gadites, and of the half 7206
26:32 whom king David made rulers over the **R**, 7206
27:16 the ruler of the **R** was Eliezer the son of 7206

REUEL (10) [DEUEL]
Ge 36: 4 to Esau Eliphaz; and Bashemath bare **R**; 7467
36:10 **R** the son of Bashemath the wife of Esau. 7467
36:13 *are* the sons of **R**; Nahath, and Zerah, 7467
36:17 these *are* the sons of **R** Esau's son; 7467
36:17 these *are* the dukes *that came* of **R** in 7467
Ex 2:18 when they came to **R** their father, he said, 7467
Nu 2:14 sons of Gad *shall be* Eliasaph the son of **R**. 7467
1Ch 1:35 **R**, and Jeush, and Jaalam, and Korah. 7467
1:37 The sons of **R**; Nahath, Zerah, Shammah, 7467
9: 8 the son of **R**, the son of Ibnijah; 7467

REUMAH (1)
Ge 22:24 concubine, whose name *was* **R**, she bare 7208

REVEAL (7) [REVEALED, REVEALER, REVEALETH, REVELATION, REVELATIONS]
Job 20:27 The heaven shall **r** his iniquity; 1540
Jer 33: 6 will **r** unto them the abundance of peace 1540
Da 2:47 seeing thou couldest **r** this secret. 1541
Mt 11:27 and *he* to whomsoever the Son will **r** *him*. 601
Lk 10:22 Son, and *he* to whom the Son will **r** *him*. 601
Gal 1:16 To **r** his Son in me, that I might preach 601
Php 3:15 God shall **r** even this unto you. 601

REVEALED (38) [REVEAL]
Dt 29:29 *those things* which are **r** belong unto us 1540
1Sa 3: 7 neither was the word of the Lord yet **r** 1540
3:21 for the Lord **r** himself to Samuel in 1540
2Sa 7:27 Israel, hast **r** to thy servant, saying, 241+1540
Isa 22:14 it was **r** in mine ears *by* the Lord of 1540
23: 1 from the land of Chittim it is **r** to them. 1540
40: 5 And the glory of the Lord shall be **r**, 1540
53: 1 and to whom is the arm of the Lord **r**? 1540
56: 1 to come, and my righteousness to be **r**. 1540
Jer 11:20 them: for unto thee have I **r** my cause. 1540
Da 2:19 *was* the secret **r** unto Daniel in a night 1541
2:30 this secret *is not* **r** to me for *any* wisdom 1541
10: 1 king of Persia a thing was **r** unto Daniel, 1540
Mt 10:26 is nothing covered, that shall not be **r**; 601
11:25 and prudent, and hast **r** them unto babes. 601
16:17 for flesh and blood hath not **r** it unto thee, 601
Lk 2:26 And it was **r** unto him by the Holy Ghost, 5537
2:35 that the thoughts of many hearts may be **r**. 601
10:21 and prudent, and hast **r** them unto babes: 601
12: 2 is nothing covered, that shall not be **r**; 601
17:30 it be in the day when the Son of man is **r**. 601
Jn 12:38 to whom hath the arm of the Lord been **r**? 601
Ro 1:17 For therein is the righteousness of God **r** 601
1:18 For the wrath of God is **r** from heaven 601
8:18 with the glory which shall be **r** in us. 601
1Co 2:10 But God hath **r** them unto us by his Spirit: 601
3:13 shall declare *it*, because it shall be **r** by fire; 601
14:30 If *any thing* be **r** to another that sitteth *by*, 601
Gal 3:23 the faith which should afterwards be **r**. 601
Eph 3: 5 as it is now **r** unto his holy apostles and 601
2Th 1: 7 The Lord Jesus shall be **r** from heaven 602
2: 3 and *that* man of sin be **r**, the son of 601
2: 6 withholdeth that he might be **r** in his time. 601
2: 8 And then shall *that* Wicked be **r**, whom 601
1Pe 1: 5 salvation ready to be **r** in the last time. 601
1:12 Unto whom it was **r**, that not unto 601
4:13 that, when his glory shall be **r**, ye may be 602
5: 1 also a partaker of the glory that shall be **r**: 601

REVEALER (1) [REVEAL]
Da 2:47 a Lord of kings, and a **r** of secrets, 1541

REVEALETH (6) [REVEAL]
Pr 11:13 A talebearer **r** secrets: but he that is of a 1540
20:19 He that goeth about *as* a talebearer **r** 1540
Da 2:22 He **r** the deep and secret *things*: he 1541
2:28 there is a God in heaven that **r** secrets, 1541
2:29 he that **r** secrets maketh known to thee 1541
Am 3: 7 he **r** his secret unto his servants 1540

REVELATION (10) [REVEAL]
Ro 2: 5 and **r** of the righteous judgment of God; 602
16:25 according to the **r** of the mystery, 602
1Co 14: 6 except I shall speak to you either by **r**, 602
14:26 hath a doctrine, hath a tongue, hath a **r**, 602

Gal 1:12 was I taught *it*, but by the **r** of Jesus Christ. 602
2: 2 I went up by **r**, and communicated unto 602
Eph 1:17 of wisdom and **r** in the knowledge of him: 602
3: 3 How that by **r** he made known unto me 602
1Pe 1:13 brought unto you at the **r** of Jesus Christ; 602
Rev 1: 1 The **R** of Jesus Christ, which God gave 602

REVELATIONS (2) [REVEAL]
2Co 12: 1 I will come to visions and **r** of the Lord. 602
12: 7 measure through the abundance of the **r**, 602

REVELING See SPORTING

REVELLINGS (2)
Gal 5:21 murders, drunkenness, **r**, and such like: 2970
1Pe 4: 3 **r**, banquetings, and abominable idolatries: 2970

REVENGE (5) [VENGEANCE]
Jer 15:15 and visit me, and **r** me of my persecutors; 5358
20:10 and we shall take our **r** on him. 5360
Eze 25:15 Because the Philistines have dealt by **r**, 5360
2Co 7:11 yea, *what* zeal, yea, *what* **r**! 1557
10: 6 And having in a readiness to **r** all 1556

REVENGED (1) [VENGEANCE]
Eze 25:12 offended, and **r** himself upon them; 5358

REVENGER (7) [VENGEANCE]
Nu 35:19 The **r** of blood himself shall slay 1350
35:21 the **r** of blood shall slay the murderer, 1350
35:24 the **r** of blood according to these 1350
35:25 slayer out of the hand of the **r** of blood, 1350
35:27 of blood find him without the borders 1350
35:27 and the **r** of blood kill the slayer; 1350
Ro 13: 4 a **r** to *execute* wrath upon him that doeth 1558

REVENGERS (1) [VENGEANCE]
2Sa 14:11 thou wouldest not suffer the **r** of blood 1350

REVENGES (1) [VENGEANCE]
Dt 32:42 from the beginning of **r** upon the enemy. 6546

REVENGETH (2) [VENGEANCE]
Na 1: 2 God *is* jealous, and the Lord **r**; 5358
1: 2 the Lord **r**, and *is* furious; 5358

REVENGING (1) [VENGEANCE]
Ps 79:10 **r** of the blood of thy servants which is 5360

REVENUE (2) [REVENUES]
Ezr 4:13 *so* thou shalt endamage the **r** of the kings. 674
Pr 8:19 fine gold; and my **r** than choice silver. 8393
Isa 23: 3 of Sihor, the harvest of the river, *is* her **r**; 8393

REVENUES (3) [REVENUE]
Pr 15: 6 but in the **r** of the wicked *is* trouble. 8393
16: 8 righteousness than great **r** without right. 8393
Jer 12:13 they shall be ashamed of your **r** because 8393

REVERENCE (13) [REVERENCED, REVEREND]
Lev 19:30 keep my sabbaths, and **r** my sanctuary: 3372
26: 2 keep my sabbaths, and **r** my sanctuary: 3372
2Sa 9: 6 unto David, he fell on his face, and did **r**. 7812
1Ki 1:31 did **r** to the king, and said, Let my lord 7812
Est 3: 2 But Mordecai bowed not, nor did *him* **r**. 7812
3: 5 nor did him **r**, *then* was Haman full of 7812
Ps 89: 7 to be had in **r** of all them that are about 3372
Mt 21:37 them his son, saying, They will **r** my son. 1788
Mk 12: 6 unto them, saying, They will **r** my son. 1788
Lk 20:13 it may be they will **r** *him* when they see 1788
Eph 5:33 and the wife *see* that she **r** *her* husband. 5399
Heb 12: 9 which corrected *us*, and we **gave** *them* **r**: 1788
12:28 we may serve God acceptably with **r** 127

REVERENCED (1) [REVERENCE]
Est 3: 2 in the king's gate, bowed, and **r** Haman: 7812

REVEREND (1) [REVERENCE]
Ps 111: 9 covenant for ever: holy and **r** *is* his name. 3372

REVERSE (3)
Nu 23:20 and he hath blessed; and I cannot **r** it. 7725
Est 8: 5 let it be written to **r** the letters devised by 7725
8: 8 sealed with the king's ring, may no man **r**. 7725

REVILE (2) [REVILED, REVILERS, REVILEST, REVILINGS]
Ex 22:28 Thou shalt not **r** the gods, nor curse 7043
Mt 5:11 when *men* shall **r** you, and persecute *you*, 3679

REVILED (6) [REVILE]
Mt 27:39 passed by, **r** him, wagging their heads, 987
Mk 15:32 And they that were crucified with him **r** 3679
Jn 9:28 Then they **r** him, and said, Thou art his 3058
1Co 4:12 being **r**, we bless; being persecuted, 3058
1Pe 2:23 Who, when he was **r**, reviled not again; 3058
2:23 Who, when he was reviled, **r** not **again**; 486

REVILERS (1) [REVILE]
1Co 6:10 nor covetous, nor drunkards, nor **r**, 3060

REVILEST (1) [REVILE]
Ac 23: 4 stood by said, **R** thou God's high priest? 3058

REVILINGS (2) [REVILE]
Isa 51: 7 of men, neither be ye afraid of their **r**. 1421
Zep 2: 8 and the **r** of the children of Ammon, 1421

REVIVE (8) [REVIVED, REVIVING]
Ne 4: 2 will they **r** the stones out of the heaps of 2421
Ps 85: 6 Wilt thou not **r** us again: that thy people 2421
138: 7 in the midst of trouble, thou wilt **r** me: 2421
Isa 57:15 to **r** the spirit of the humble, and to revive 2421
57:15 and to **r** the heart of the contrite ones. 2421
Hos 6: 2 After two days will he **r** us: in the third 2421
14: 7 they shall **r** *as* the corn, and grow as 2421
Hab 3: 2 **r** thy work in the midst of the years, 2421

REVIVED (6) [REVIVE]
Ge 45:27 him, the spirit of Jacob their father **r**: 2421
Jdg 15:19 drunk, his spirit came again, and he **r**: 2421
1Ki 17:22 the child came into him again, and he **r**. 2421
2Ki 13:21 of Elisha, he **r**, and stood up on his feet. 2421
Ro 7: 9 the commandment came, sin **r**, and I died. 326
14: 9 this end Christ both died, and rose, and **r**, 326

REVIVING (2) [REVIVE]
Ezr 9: 8 and give us a little **r** in our bondage. 4241
9: 9 to give us a **r**, to set up the house of our 4241

REVOLT (3) [REVOLTED, REVOLTERS, REVOLTING]
2Ch 21:10 The same time also did Libnah **r** from 6586
Isa 1: 5 ye will **r** more and more: the whole head 5627
59:13 speaking oppression and **r**, conceiving 5627

REVOLTED (7) [REVOLT]
2Ki 8:20 In his days Edom **r** from under the hand 6586
8:22 Yet Edom **r** from under the hand of Judah 6586
8:22 this day. Then Libnah **r** at the same time. 6586
2Ch 21: 8 In his days the Edomites **r** from under 6586
21:10 So the Edomites **r** from under the hand of 6586
Isa 31: 6 whom the children of Israel have deeply **r**. 5627
Jer 5:23 a rebellious heart; they are **r** and are gone. 5493

REVOLTERS (3) [REVOLT]
Jer 6:28 They *are* all grievous **r**, walking with 5637
Hos 5: 2 the **r** are profound to make slaughter, 7846
9:15 love them no more: all their princes *are* **r**. 5637

REVOLTING (1) [REVOLT]
Jer 5:23 this people hath a **r** and a rebellious heart; 5637

REWARD (80) [REWARDED, REWARDER, REWARDETH, REWARDS]
Ge 15: 1 I *am* thy shield, *and* thy exceeding great **r**. 7939
Nu 18:31 for it *is* your **r** for your service in 7939
Dt 10:17 which regardeth not persons, nor taketh **r**: 7810
27:25 Cursed *be* he that taketh **r** to slay an 7810
32:41 and will **r** them that hate me. 7999
Ru 2:12 a full **r** be given thee of the Lord God of 4909
1Sa 24:19 wherefore the Lord **r** thee good for that 7999
2Sa 3:39 the Lord shall **r** the doer of evil 7999
4:10 would have given him a **r** for *his* tidings, 1309
19:36 the king recompense *it* me *with* such a **r**? 1578
1Ki 13: 7 refresh *thyself*, and I will give thee a **r**. 4991
2Ch 20:11 Behold, I say, *how* they **r** us, to come to 1580
Job 6:22 or, **Give a r** for me of your substance? 7809
7: 2 a hireling looketh for the **r** of his **work**: 6467
Ps 15: 5 usury, nor taketh **r** against the innocent. 7810
19:11 *and* in keeping of them *there* is great **r**. 6118
40:15 Let them be desolate for a **r** of their shame 6118
54: 5 He shall **r** evil unto mine enemies: cut 7725
58:11 Verily *there* is a **r** for the righteous: 6529
70: 3 Let them be turned back for a **r** of their 6118
91: 8 thou behold and see the **r** of the wicked. 8011
94: 2 judge of the earth: render a **r** to the proud. 1576
109:20 *Let* this *be* the **r** of mine adversaries from 6468
127: 3 *and* the fruit of the womb *is* his **r**. 7939
Pr 11:18 soweth righteousness *shall be* a sure **r**. 7938
21:14 and a **r** in the bosom strong wrath. 7810
24:14 thou hast found *it*, then there shall be a **r**, 319
24:20 For there shall be no **r** to the evil *man*; 319
25:22 upon his head, and the Lord shall **r** thee. 7999
Ecc 4: 9 they have a good **r** for their labour. 7939
9: 5 any thing, neither have they any more a **r**; 7939
Isa 3:11 *it shall be* ill *with him*: for the **r** of his 1576
5:23 Which justify the wicked for **r**, 7810
40:10 his **r** *is* with him, and his work before 7939
45:13 not for price nor **r**, saith the Lord of 7810
62:11 his **r** *is* with him, and his work before 7939
Jer 40: 5 of the guard gave him victuals and a **r**, 4864
Eze 16:34 in that thou givest a **r**, and no reward is 868
16:34 no **r** is given unto thee, therefore thou art 868
Hos 4: 9 for their ways, and **r** them their doings. 7725
9: 1 thou hast loved a **r** upon every cornfloor. 868
Ob 1:15 thy **r** shall return upon thine own head. 1576
Mic 3:11 The heads thereof judge for **r**, 7810
7: 3 asketh, and the judge *asketh* for a **r** 7966
Mt 5:12 for great *is* your **r** in heaven: for so 3408
5:46 them which love you, what **r** have ye? 3408
6: 1 otherwise ye have no **r** of your Father 3408
6: 2 Verily I say unto you, They have their **r**. 3408
6: 4 seeth in secret himself shall **r** thee openly. 591
6: 5 Verily I say unto you, They have their **r**. 3408
6: 6 Father which seeth in secret shall **r** thee 591
6:16 Verily I say unto you, They have their **r**. 3408
6:18 which seeth in secret, shall **r** thee openly. 591
10:41 of a prophet shall receive a prophet's **r**; 3408
10:41 *man* shall receive a righteous *man's* **r**. 3408
10:42 unto you, he shall in no wise lose his **r**. 3408
16:27 shall **r** every man according to his works. 591
Mk 9:41 I say unto you, he shall not lose his **r**. 3408
Lk 6:23 *joy*: for behold, your **r** *is* great in heaven: 3408

Lk	6:35	and your **r** shall be great, and ye shall be	3408
	23:41	for we receive the **due of r** our deeds:	514
Ac	1:18	this *man* purchased a field with the **r**	3408
Ro	4: 4	Now to him that worketh is the **r** not	3408
1Co	3: 8	every man shall receive his own **r**	3408
	3:14	hath built thereupon, he shall receive a **r**.	3408
	9:17	For if I do this *willingly*, I have a **r**:	3408
	9:18	What is my **r** then? *Verily* that, when I	3408
Col	2:18	Let no *man* **beguile** *you* of your **r** in a	2603
	3:24	ye shall receive the **r** of the inheritance:	469
1Ti	5:18	And, The labourer *is* worthy of his **r**.	3408
2Ti	4:14	the Lord **r** him according to his works:	591
Heb	2: 2	received a just recompence of **r**;	3405
	10:35	which hath great **recompence of r**.	3405
	11:26	respect unto the **recompence of** the **r**.	3405
2Pe	2:13	shall receive the **r** of unrighteousness,	3408
2Jn	1: 8	have wrought, but *that* we receive a full **r**.	3408
Jude	1:11	ran greedily after the error of Balaam for **r**,	3408
Rev	18: 6	*thou* shouldest give **r** unto thy servants	3408
	18: 6	her even as she rewarded **you**,	591
	22:12	and my **r** *is* with me, to give every man	3408

REWARDED (14) [REWARD]

Ge	44: 4	Wherefore have ye **r** evil for good?	7999
1Sa	24:17	for thou hast **r** me good, whereas I have	1580
	24:17	me good, whereas I have **r** thee evil.	1580
2Sa	22:21	The Lord **r** me according to my	1580
2Ch	15: 7	hands be weak: for your work shall be **r**.	7939
Ps	7: 4	If I have **r** evil *unto* him that was at peace	1580
	18:20	The Lord **r** me according to my	1580
	35:12	They **r** me evil for good *to* the spoiling of	7999
	103:10	nor **r** us according to our iniquities.	1580
	109: 5	they have **r** me evil for good, and hatred	7760
Pr	13:13	that feareth the commandment shall be **r**.	7999
Isa	3: 9	for they have **r** evil unto themselves.	1580
Jer	31:16	for thy work shall be **r**, saith the Lord;	7939
Rev	18: 6	Reward her even as she **r** you,	591

REWARDER (1) [REWARD]

Heb	11: 6	*that* he is a **r** of them that diligently seek	3406

REWARDETH (6) [REWARD]

Job	21:19	he **r** him, and he shall know *it*.	7999
Ps	31:23	and plentifully **r** the proud doer.	7999
	137: 8	happy *shall he be*, that **r** thee as thou hast	7999
Pr	17:13	Whoso **r** evil for good, evil shall not	7725
	26:10	great *God* that formed *all* things both **r**	7936
	26:10	**r** the fool, and **r** transgressors.	7936

REWARDS (5) [REWARD]

Nu	22: 7	with the **r of divination** in their hand;	7081
Isa	1:23	one loveth gifts, and followeth after **r**:	8021
Da	2: 6	receive of me gifts and **r** and great honour:	5023
	5:17	be to thyself, and give thy **r** to another;	5023
Hos	2:12	These *are* my **r** that my lovers have given	866

REZEPH (2)

2Ki	19:12	**R**, and the children of Eden which *were*	7530
Isa	37:12	**R**, and the children of Eden which *were*	7530

REZIA (1)

1Ch	7:39	the sons of Ulla; Arah, and Haniel, and **R**.	7525

REZIN (11)

2Ki	15:37	to send against Judah **R** the king of Syria,	7526
	16: 5	**R** king of Syria and Pekah son of Remaliah	7526
	16: 6	At that time **R** king of Syria recovered	7526
	16: 9	*people of* it captive to Kir, and slew **R**.	7526
Ezr	2:48	children of **R**, the children of Nekoda,	7526
Ne	7:50	The children of **R**, the children of Nekoda,	7526
Isa	7: 1	*that* **R** the king of Syria, and Pekah the	7526
	7: 4	for the fierce anger of **R** with Syria,	7526
	7: 8	and the head of Damascus *is* **R**;	7526
	8: 6	and rejoice in **R** and Remaliah's son;	7526
	9:11	set up the adversaries of **R** against him,	7526

REZON (1)

1Ki	11:23	*another* adversary, **R** the son of Eliadah,	7331

RHEGIUM (1)

Ac	28:13	thence we fet a compass, and came to **R**:	4484

RHESA (1)

Lk	3:27	*son* of Joanna, which was *the son* of **R**,	4488

RHODA (1)

Ac	12:13	a damsel came to hearken, named **R**.	4498

RHODES (1)

Ac	21: 1	and the *day* following unto **R**, and from	4499

RIB (5) [RIBS]

Ge	2:22	the **r**, which the Lord God had taken	6763
2Sa	2:23	*hilt* of, that the spear came out behind	NIH
	3:27	smote him there *under* the fifth **r**, that he	NIH
	4: 6	they smote him under the fifth **r**.	NIH
	20:10	so he smote him therewith in the fifth **r**,	NIH

RIBAI (2)

2Sa	23:29	Ittai the son of **R** out of Gibeah of	7380
1Ch	11:31	Ithai the son of **R** of Gibeah, that	7380

RIBBAND (1)

Nu	15:38	upon the fringe of the borders a **r** of blue:	6616

RIBLAH (11)

Nu	34:11	coast shall go down from Shepham to **R**,	7247
2Ki	23:33	Pharaoh-nechoh put him in bands at **R** in	7247
	25: 6	him up to the king of Babylon to **R**;	7247
	25:20	brought them to the king of Babylon to **R**:	7247
	25:21	slew them at **R** in the land of Hamath.	7247
Jer	39: 5	of Babylon to **R** in the land of Hamath,	7247
	39: 6	the sons of Zedekiah in **R** before his eyes:	7247
	52: 9	of Babylon to **R** in the land of Hamath;	7247
	52:10	he slew also all the princes of Judah in **R**.	7247
	52:26	brought them to the king of Babylon to **R**.	7247
	52:27	put them to death in **R** in the land of	7247

RIBS (2) [RIB]

Ge	2:21	took one of his **r**, and closed up the flesh	6763
Da	7: 5	*it had* three **r** in the mouth of it between	5967

RICH (81) [ENRICH, ENRICHED, ENRICHEST, RICHER, RICHES, RICHLY]

Ge	13: 2	Abram *was* very **r** in cattle, in silver,	3513
	14:23	shouldest say, I have **made** Abram **r**:	6238
Ex	30:15	The **r** shall not give more, and the poor	6223
Lev	25:47	or stranger **wax r** by thee,	3027+5381
Ru	3:10	not young men, whether poor or **r**.	6223
1Sa	2: 7	The Lord maketh poor, and **maketh r**:	6238
2Sa	12: 1	in one city; the one **r**, and the other poor.	6223
	12: 2	The **r** *man* had exceeding many flocks	6223
	12: 4	there came a traveller unto the **r** man,	6223
Job	15:29	He shall not be **r**, neither shall his	6223
	27:19	The **r** man shall lie down, but he shall not	6223
	34:19	nor regardeth the **r** more than the poor?	7771
Ps	45:12	*even* the **r** among the people shall intreat	6223
	49: 2	Both low and high, **r** and poor, together.	6223
	49:16	Be not thou afraid when one is **made r**,	6238
Pr	10: 4	but the hand of the diligent **maketh r**.	6223
	10:15	The **r** man's wealth *is* his strong city:	6223
	10:22	it **maketh r**, and he addeth no sorrow	6238
	13: 7	There is that **maketh** himself **r**, yet *hath*	6238
	14:20	but the **r** *hath* many friends.	6223
	18:11	The **r** man's wealth *is* his strong city,	6223
	18:23	but the **r** answereth roughly.	6223
	21:17	he that loveth wine and oil shall not be **r**.	6238
	22: 2	The **r** and poor meet together: the Lord	6223
	22: 7	The **r** ruleth over the poor,	6223
	22:16	his *riches*, *and* he that giveth to the **r**,	6238
	23: 4	Labour not to be **r**: cease from thine own	6238
	28: 6	*is* perverse in *his* ways, though he *be* **r**.	6223
	28:11	The **r** man *is* wise in his own conceit;	6223
	28:20	but he that maketh haste to be **r** shall not be	6238
	28:22	He that hasteth to be **r** *hath* an evil eye,	1952
Ecc	5:12	the abundance of the **r** will not suffer him	6223
	10: 6	in great dignity, and the **r** sit in low place.	6223
	10:20	and curse not the **r** in thy bedchamber:	6223
Isa	53: 9	the wicked, and with the **r** in his death;	6223
Jer	5:27	they are become great, and **waxen r**.	6238
	9:23	let not the **r** *man* glory in his riches:	6223
Eze	27:24	work, and in chests of **r** apparel,	1264
Hos	12: 8	Ephraim said, Yet I am **become r**, I have	6238
Mic	6:12	For the **r men** thereof are full *of* violence,	6223
Zec	11: 5	Blessed *be* the Lord; for I am **r**:	6238
Mt	19:23	That a **r** *man* shall hardly enter into	4145
	19:24	for a **r** *man* to enter into the kingdom	4145
	27:57	there came a **r** man of Arimathea,	4145
Mk	10:25	for a **r** *man* to enter into the kingdom	4145
	12:41	and many *that were* **r** cast in much.	4145
Lk	1:53	and the **r** he hath sent empty away.	4147
	6:24	But woe unto you that are **r**! for ye have	4145
	12:16	The ground of a certain **r** man brought	4145
	12:21	for himself, and is not **r** toward God.	4147
	14:12	thy kinsmen, nor *thy* **r** neighbours;	4145
	16: 1	There was a certain **r** man, which had a	4145
	16:19	There was a certain **r** man, which was	4145
	16:21	crumbs which fell from the **r** *man's* table:	4145
	16:22	the **r** *man* also died, and was buried;	4145
	18:23	he was very sorrowful: for he was very **r**.	4145
	18:25	for a **r** man to enter into the kingdom	4145
	19: 2	chief among the publicans, and he was **r**.	4145
	21: 1	saw the **r** *men* casting their gifts into	4145
Ro	10:12	for the same Lord over all *is* **r** unto all that	4147
1Co	4: 8	Now ye are full, now ye are **r**, ye have	4147
2Co	6:10	as poor, yet **making** many **r**; as having	4148
	8: 9	though he was **r**, *yet* for your sakes he	4145
	8: 9	that ye through his poverty might be **r**.	4147
Eph	2: 4	But God, who is **r** in mercy, for his great	4145
1Ti	6: 9	But they that will be **r** fall into temptation	4147
	6:17	Charge *them* that are **r** in this world,	4145
	6:18	that *they* be **r** in good works, ready to	4147
Jas	1:10	But the **r**, in that he is made low: because	4145
	1:11	shall the **r** man fade away in his ways.	4145
	2: 5	chosen the poor of this world **r** in faith,	4145
	2: 6	Do not **r** men oppress you, and draw you	4145
	5: 1	**r** men, weep and howl for your miseries	4145
Rev	2: 9	tribulation, and poverty, (but thou art **r**)	4145
	3:17	I am **r**, and increased with goods,	4147
	3:18	tried in the fire, that thou mayest be **r**;	4147
	6:15	and the **r** men, and the chief captains,	4145
	13:16	and great, **r** and poor, free and bond,	4145
	18: 3	the merchants of the earth are **waxed r**	4147
	18:15	these *things*, which were **made r** by her,	4147
	18:19	wherein were **made r** all that had ships	4147

RICHER (1) [RICH]

Da	11: 2	fourth shall be far **r** than *they* all:	6238+6239

RICHES (98) [RICH]

Ge	31:16	For all the **r** which God hath taken from	6239
	36: 7	For their **r** were more than that they	7399
Jos	22: 8	Return with much **r** unto your tents,	5233
1Sa	17:25	the king will enrich him *with* great **r**,	6239
1Ki	3:11	neither hast asked for thyself, nor hast	6239
	3:13	thou hast not asked, both **r**, and honour:	6239
	10:23	exceeded all the kings of the earth for **r**	6239
1Ch	29:12	Both **r** and honour *come* of thee,	6239
	29:28	good old age, full of days, **r**, and honour:	6239
2Ch	1:11	thou hast not asked **r**, wealth, or honour,	6239
	1:12	will give thee **r**, and wealth, and honour,	6239
	9:22	passed all the kings of the earth in **r**	6239
	17: 5	and he had **r** and honour in abundance.	6239
	18: 1	Now Jehoshaphat had **r** and honour in	6239
	20:25	abundance both **r** with the dead bodies,	7399
	32:27	Hezekiah had exceeding much **r** and	6239
Est	1: 4	When he shewed the **r** of his glorious	6239
	5:11	Haman told them of the glory of his **r**,	6239
Job	20:15	He hath swallowed down **r**, and he shall	2428
	36:19	Will he esteem thy **r**? *no*, not gold, nor all	7769
Ps	37:16	hath *is* better than the **r** of many wicked.	1995
	39: 6	he heapeth up **r**, and knoweth not who	NIH
	49: 6	themselves in the multitude of their **r**;	6239
	52: 7	trusted in the abundance of his **r**,	6239
	62:10	if **r** increase, set not *your* heart *upon*	2428
	73:12	prosper in the world; they increase *in* **r**.	2428
	104:24	made them all: the earth is full *of* thy **r**.	7075
	112: 3	Wealth and **r** *shall be* in his house:	6239
	119:14	of thy testimonies, *as much as* in all **r**.	1952
Pr	3:16	and in her left hand **r** and honour.	6239
	8:18	**R** and honour *are* with me; *yea*, durable	6239
	8:18	me; *yea*, durable **r** and righteousness.	1952
	11: 4	**R** profit not in the day of wrath:	1952
	11:16	retaineth honour: and strong *men* retain **r**	6239
	11:28	He that trusteth in his **r** shall fall:	6239
	13: 7	that maketh himself poor, yet *hath* great **r**.	1952
	13: 8	The ransom of a man's life *are* his **r**:	6239
	14:24	The crown of the wise *is* their **r**:	6239
	19:14	House and **r** *are* the inheritance of fathers:	1952
	22: 1	name *is* rather to be chosen than great **r**,	6239
	22: 4	*and* the fear of the Lord *are* **r**,	6239
	22:16	that oppresseth the poor to increase his **r**,	NIH
	23: 5	for **r** certainly make themselves wings;	NIH
	24: 4	be filled *with* all precious and pleasant **r**.	1952
	27:24	For **r** *are* not for ever: and doth the crown	2633
	30: 8	give me neither poverty nor **r**; feed me	6239
Ecc	4: 8	neither is his eye satisfied *with* **r**;	6239
	5:13	*namely*, **r** kept for the owners thereof to	6239
	5:14	those **r** perish by evil travail:	6239
	5:19	man also to whom God hath given **r**	6239
	6: 2	man to whom God hath given **r**, wealth,	6239
	9:11	wise, nor yet to men of understanding,	6239
Isa	8: 4	**r** of Damascus and the spoil of Samaria	2428
	10:14	my hand hath found as a nest the **r** of	2428
	30: 6	they will carry their **r** upon the shoulders	2428
	45: 3	**hidden** *r* of secret places, that thou	4301
	61: 6	ye shall eat the **r** of the Gentiles,	2428
Jer	9:23	let not the rich *man* glory in his **r**:	6239
	17:11	*so* he that getteth **r**, and not by right,	6239
	48:36	the **r** *that* he hath gotten are perished.	3502
Eze	26:12	they shall make a spoil of thy **r**, and make	2428
	27:12	by reason of the multitude of all *kind of* **r**;	1952
	27:18	of thy making, for the multitude of all **r**;	1952
	27:27	Thy **r**, and thy fairs, thy merchandise,	1952
	27:33	of the earth with the multitude of thy **r**	1952
	28: 4	understanding thou hast gotten thee **r**,	2428
	28: 5	by thy traffick hast thou increased thy **r**,	2428
	28: 5	thine heart is lifted up because of thy **r**:	2428
Da	11: 2	by his strength through his **r** he shall stir	6239
	11:13	years with a great army and with much **r**.	7399
	11:24	among them the prey, and spoil, and **r**:	7399
	11:28	shall he return *into* his land with great **r**;	7399
Mt	13:22	the deceitfulness of **r**, choke the word,	4149
Mk	4:19	and the deceitfulness of **r**, and the lusts of	4149
	10:23	How hardly shall they that have **r** enter	4149
	10:24	how hard is it for them that trust in **r** to	4149
Lk	8:14	with cares and **r** and pleasures of *this* life,	4149
	16:11	who will commit to your trust the true **r**?	NIG
	18:24	How hardly shall they that have **r** enter	5536
Ro	2: 4	despisest thou the **r** of his goodness and	4149
	9:23	that he might make known the **r** of his	4149
	11:12	Now if the fall of them *be* the **r** of	4149
	11:12	the diminishing of them the **r** of	4149
	11:33	O the depth of the **r** both of the wisdom	4149
2Co	8: 2	their deep poverty abounded unto the **r** of	4149
Eph	1: 7	of sins, according to the **r** of his grace;	4149
	1:18	what the **r** of the glory of his inheritance	4149
	2: 7	**r** of his grace in *his* kindness towards us	4149
	3: 8	the Gentiles the unsearchable **r** of Christ;	4149
	3:16	grant you, according to the **r** of his glory,	4149
Php	4:19	according to his **r** in glory by Christ Jesus.	4149
Col	1:27	**r** of the glory of this mystery among	4149
	2: 2	unto all **r** of the full assurance of	4149
1Ti	6:17	nor trust in uncertain **r**, but in the living	4149
Heb	11:26	Esteeming the reproach of Christ greater **r**	4149
Jas	5: 2	Your **r** are corrupted, and your garments	4149
Rev	5:12	and **r**, and wisdom, and strength,	4149
	18:17	in one hour so great **r** is come to nought.	4149

RICHLY (2) [RICH]

Col	3:16	Let the word of Christ dwell in you **r** in all	4146
1Ti	6:17	who giveth us **r** all *things* to enjoy;	4146

RICHLY ORNAMENTED See DIVERS; DIVERSE

R

RICHLY ORNAMENTED ROBE See COAT OF MANY COLOURS

RID (6) [RIDDANCE]

Ge	37:22 that he might **r** him out of their hands,	5337
Ex	6: 6 I will **r** you out of their bondage, and I	5337
Lev	26: 6 I will **r** evil beasts out of the land,	7673
Ps	82: 4 **r** them out of the hand of the wicked.	5337
	144: 7 **r** me, and deliver me out of great waters,	6475
	144:11 **R** me, and deliver me from the hand of	6475

RIDDANCE (2) [RID]

Lev	23:22 shalt not **make clean r** of the corners	3615
Zep	1:18 for he shall make even a speedy **r** of all	3617

RIDDEN (1) [RIDE]

Nu	22:30 upon which thou hast **r** ever since *I* was	7392

RIDDLE (9)

Jdg	14:12 I will now put forth a **r** unto you:	2420
	14:13 Put forth thy **r**, that we may hear it.	2420
	14:14 could not *in* three days expound the **r**.	2420
	14:15 that he may declare unto us the **r**, lest	2420
	14:16 thou hast put forth a **r** unto the children	2420
	14:17 told the **r** to the children of her people.	2420
	14:18 my heifer, ye had not found out my **r**.	2420
	14:19 unto them which expounded the **r**.	2420
Eze	17: 2 **put forth a r**, and speak a parable	2330+2420

RIDDLES See DARK SAYINGS; DARK SPEECHES; HARD SENTENCES

RIDE (20) [RIDDEN, RIDER, RIDERS, RIDETH, RIDING, RODE]

Ge	41:43 he made him to **r** in the second chariot	7392
Dt	32:13 He made him **r** on the high places of	7392
Jdg	5:10 Speak, ye that **r** on white asses, ye that sit	7392
2Sa	16: 2 asses *be* for the king's household to **r** on;	7392
	19:26 that I may **r** thereon, and go to the king;	7392
1Ki	1:33 **cause** Solomon my son to **r** upon mine	7392
	1:38 **caused** Solomon to **r** upon king David's	7392
	1:44 have **caused** him to **r** upon the king's	7392
2Ki	10:16 So they **made** him **r** in his chariot.	7392
Job	30:22 thou **causest** me to **r** *upon it*, and	7392
Ps	45: 4 *in* thy majesty **r** prosperously because	7392
	66:12 hast **caused** men to **r** over our heads;	7392
Isa	58:16 and, We will **r** upon the swift; therefore	7392
	58:14 will **cause** thee to **r** upon the high places	7392
Jer	6:23 they **r** upon horses, set in array as men for	7392
	50:42 they shall **r** upon horses, *every one* put in	7392
Hos	10:11 I will **make** Ephraim to **r**; Judah shall	7392
	14: 3 we will not **r** upon horses: neither will	7392
Hab	3: 8 that thou didst **r** upon thine horses *and*	7392
Hag	2:22 the chariots, and those that **r** in them;	7392

RIDER (7) [RIDE]

Ge	49:17 so that his **r** shall fall backward.	7392
Ex	15: 1 and his **r** hath he thrown into the sea.	7392
	15:21 and his **r** hath he thrown into the sea.	7392
Job	39:18 on high, she scorneth the horse and his **r**.	7392
Jer	51:21 will I break in pieces the horse and his **r**;	7392
	51:21 will I break in pieces the chariot and his **r**;	7392
Zec	12: 4 astonishment, and his **r** with madness:	7392

RIDERS (5) [RIDE]

2Ki	18:23 if thou be able on thy part to set **r** upon	7392
Est	8:10 *and* **r** on mules, camels,	7392
Isa	36: 8 if thou be able on thy part to set **r** upon	7392
Hag	2:22 the horses and their **r** shall come down,	7392
Zec	10: 5 and the **r** on horses shall be confounded.	7392

RIDETH (7) [RIDE]

Lev	15: 9 what saddle soever he **r** upon that hath	7392
Dt	33:26 who **r** *upon* the heaven in thy help,	7392
Est	6: 8 the horse that the king **r** upon,	7392
Ps	68: 4 extol him that **r** upon the heavens by his	7392
	68:33 him that **r** upon the heavens of heavens,	7392
Isa	19: 1 the LORD **r** upon a swift cloud,	7392
Am	2:15 shall he that **r** the horse deliver himself.	7392

RIDGES (1)

Ps	65:10 *Thou* waterest the **r** thereof abundantly:	8525

RIDICULED See NOUGHT

RIDING (10) [RIDE]

Nu	22:22 Now he was **r** upon his ass, and his two	7392
2Ki	4:24 and go *forward*; slack not *thy* **r** for me,	7392
Jer	17:25 **r** in chariots and on horses, they,	7392
	22: 4 **r** in chariots and on horses, he,	7392
Eze	23: 6 young men, horsemen **r** upon horses.	7392
	23:12 most gorgeously, horsemen **r** upon horses,	7392
	23:23 and renowned, all of them **r** upon horses,	7392
	38:15 of them **r** upon horses, a great company,	7392
Zec	1: 8 behold a man **r** upon a red horse,	7392
	9: 9 **r** upon an ass, and upon a colt the foal of	7392

RIFLED (1)

Zec	14: 2 the houses **r**, and the women ravished;	8155

RIGHT (359) [ARIGHT, BIRTHRIGHT, RIGHTEOUS, RIGHTEOUSLY, RIGHTEOUSNESS, RIGHTEOUSNESS', RIGHTEOUSNESSES, RIGHTLY, UNRIGHTEOUS]

Ge	13: 9 *take* the left hand, then I will **go to the r**;	3231
	13: 9 if *thou depart* to the **r hand**, then I will	3225

Ge	18:25 Shall not the Judge of all the earth do **r**?	4941
	24:48 which had led me in the **r** way to take my	571
	24:49 I may turn to the **r hand**, or to the left.	3225
	48:13 Ephraim in his **r hand** toward Israel's left	3225
	48:13 in his left hand towards Israel's **r**	3225
	48:14 Israel stretched out his **r hand**, and laid	3225
	48:17 when Joseph saw that his father laid his **r**	3225
	48:18 firstborn; put thy **r hand** upon his head.	3225
Ex	14:22 *were* a wall unto them on their **r hand**,	3225
	14:29 *were* a wall unto them on their **r hand**,	3225
	15: 6 Thy **r hand**, O LORD, is become glorious	3225
	15: 6 thy **r hand**, O LORD, hath dashed in	3225
	15:12 stretchedst out thy **r hand**, the earth	3225
	15:26 wilt do that which is **r** in his sight,	3477
	29:20 put *it* upon the tip of the **r** ear of Aaron,	NIH
	29:20 upon the tip of the **r** ear of his sons,	3233
	29:20 upon the thumb of their **r** hand,	3233
	29:20 upon the great toe of their **r** foot,	3233
	29:22 fat *that is* upon them, and the **r** shoulder;	3225
Lev	7:32 the **r** shoulder shall ye give unto the priest	3225
	7:33 shall have the **r** shoulder for *his* part.	3225
	8:23 put *it* upon the tip of Aaron's **r** ear,	3233
	8:23 upon the thumb of his **r** hand, and upon	3233
	8:23 and upon the great toe of his **r** foot.	3233
	8:24 of the blood upon the tip of their **r** ear,	3233
	8:24 upon the thumbs of their **r** hands,	3233
	8:24 and upon the great toes of their **r** feet:	3233
	8:25 and their fat, and the **r** shoulder:	3225
	8:26 *them* on the fat, and upon the **r** shoulder:	3225
	9:21 the **r** shoulder Aaron waved *for* a wave	3225
	14:14 the priest shall put *it* upon the tip of the **r**	3233
	14:14 upon the thumb of his **r** hand, and upon	3233
	14:14 and upon the great toe of his **r** foot:	3233
	14:16 the priest shall dip his **r** finger in the oil	3233
	14:17 of the **r** ear of him that is to be cleansed,	3233
	14:17 upon the thumb of his **r** hand, and upon	3233
	14:17 and upon the great toe of his **r** foot,	3233
	14:25 put *it* upon the tip of the **r** ear of him that	3233
	14:25 upon the thumb of his **r** hand, and upon	3233
	14:25 and upon the great toe of his **r** foot:	3233
	14:27 the priest shall sprinkle with his **r** finger	3233
	14:28 of the **r** ear of him that is to be cleansed,	3233
	14:28 upon the thumb of his **r** hand, and upon	3233
	14:28 and upon the great toe of his **r** foot,	3233
Nu	18: 8 breast and as the **r** shoulder are thine.	3225
	20:17 we will not turn *to* the **r hand** nor *to*	3225
	22:26 *was* no way to turn *either to* the **r hand**	3225
	27: 7 The daughters of Zelophehad speak **r**:	3651
Dt	2:27 I will neither turn *unto* the **r hand** nor *to*	3225
	5:32 ye shall not turn aside *to* the **r hand** or	3225
	6:18 thou shalt do *that which is* **r** and good in	3477
	12: 8 man whatsoever *is* **r** in his own eyes.	3477
	12:25 when thou shalt do *that which is* **r** in	3477
	12:28 and **r** in the sight of the LORD thy God.	3477
	13:18 to do *that which is* **r** in the eyes of	3477
	17:11 shew thee, *to* the **r hand**, nor *to* the left.	3225
	17:20 *to* the **r hand**, or *to* the left:	3225
	21: 9 when thou shalt do *that which is* **r** in	3477
	21:17 his strength; the **r** of the firstborn *is* his.	4941
	28:14 *to* the **r hand**, or *to* the left, to go after	3225
	32: 4 and without iniquity, just and **r** *is* he.	3477
	33: 2 his **r hand** *went* a fiery law for them.	3225
Jos	1: 7 not from it *to* the **r hand** or *to* the left,	3225
	3:16 the people passed over **r against** Jericho.	5048
	9:25 good and **r** unto thee to do unto us,	3477
	17: 7 the border went *along* on the **r hand** unto	3225
	23: 6 ye turn not aside therefrom *to* the **r hand**	3225
Jdg	3:16 he did gird it under his raiment upon his **r**	3225
	3:21 took the dagger from his **r** thigh,	3225
	5:26 her **r hand** to the workmen's hammer;	3225
	7:20 the trumpets in their **r** hands to blow	3225
	12: 6 for he could not frame to pronounce *it* **r**.	3651
	16:29 the one with his **r** hand, and of the other	3225
	17: 6 man did *that which was* **r** in his own	3477
	21:25 man did *that which was* **r** in his own	3477
Ru	4: 6 redeem thou my **r** to thyself; for I cannot	1353
1Sa	6:12 not aside *to* the **r hand** or *to* the left;	3225
	11: 2 that *I* may thrust out all your **r** eyes,	3225
	12:23 I will teach you the good and the **r** way:	3477
2Sa	2:19 in going he turned not to the **r hand** nor	3225
	2:21 Turn thee aside to thy **r hand** or to thy	3225
	14:19 none can **turn to** the **r hand** or to the	3225
	15: 3 unto him, See, thy matters *are* good and **r**;	5228
	16: 6 all the mighty *men were* on his **r hand**	3225
	19:28 What **r** therefore have I yet to cry any	6666
	19:43 and we have also more **r** in David than ye:	NIH
	20: 9 Joab took Amasa by the beard with the **r**	3225
	24: 5 on the **r side** of the city that *lieth* in	3225
1Ki	2:19 king's mother; and she sat on his **r hand**.	3225
	6: 8 chamber *was* in the **r side** of the house:	3233
	7:21 he set up the **r** pillar, and called the name	3233
	7:39 put five bases on the **r side** of the house	3225
	7:39 he set the sea on the **r side** of the house	3233
	7:49 five on the **r side**, and five on the left,	3225
	11:33 to do *that which is* **r** in mine eyes,	3477
	11:38 do that *is* **r** in my sight, to keep my	3477
	14: 8 to do *that only which was* **r** in mine eyes;	3477
	15: 5 Because David did *that which was* **r** in	3477
	15:11 Asa did *that which was* **r** in the eyes of	3477
	22:19 of heaven standing by him on his **r hand**	3225
	22:43 doing *that which was* **r** in the eyes of	3477
2Ki	10:15 and said to him, Is thine heart **r**,	3477
	10:30 in executing *that which is* **r** in mine eyes,	3477
	11:11 from the **r** corner of the temple to the left	3233
	12: 2 Jehoash did *that which was* **r** in the sight	3477

2Ki	12: 9 the **r side** as one cometh *into* the house	3225
	14: 3 he did *that which was* **r** in the sight of	3477
	15: 3 he did *that which was* **r** in the sight of	3477
	15:34 he did *that which was* **r** in the sight of	3477
	16: 2 did not *that which was* **r** in the sight of	3477
	17: 9 *were* not **r** against the LORD their God,	3651
	18: 3 he did *that which was* **r** in the sight of	3477
	22: 2 he did *that which was* **r** in the sight of	3477
	22: 2 turned not aside *to* the **r hand** or *to* the	3225
	23:13 which *were* on the **r hand** of the mount	3225
1Ch	6:39 brother Asaph, who stood on his **r hand**,	3225
	12: 2 could **use** both the **r hand** and the left in	3231
	13: 4 for the thing was **r** in the eyes of all	3474
2Ch	3:17 on the **r hand**, and the other on the left;	3225
	3:17 called the name of *that on* the **r hand**	3233
	4: 6 five on the **r hand**, and five on the left,	3225
	4: 7 five on the **r hand**, and five on the left.	3225
	4: 8 five on the **r side**, and five on the left.	3225
	4:10 set the sea on the **r side** of the east end,	3233
	14: 2 and **r** in the eyes of the LORD his God:	3477
	18:18 the host of heaven standing on his **r hand**	3225
	20:32 doing *that which was* **r** in the sight of	3477
	23:10 the **r side** of the temple to the left side	3233
	24: 2 Joash did *that which was* **r** in the sight of	3477
	25: 2 he did *that which was* **r** in the sight of	3477
	26: 4 he did *that which was* **r** in the sight of	3477
	27: 2 he did *that which was* **r** in the sight of	3477
	28: 1 he did not *that which was* **r** in the sight of	3477
	29: 2 he did *that which was* **r** in the sight of	3477
	31:20 wrought *that* which was good and **r** and	3477
	34: 2 he did *that which was* **r** in the sight of	3477
	34: 2 declined neither *to* the **r hand**, nor *to*	3225
Ezr	8:21 to seek of him a **r** way for us, and for our	3225
Ne	2:20 nor **r**, nor memorial, in Jerusalem.	6666
	8: 4 and Hilkiah, and Maaseiah, on his **r hand**;	3225
	9:13 gavest them **r** judgments, and true laws,	3477
	9:33 for thou hast done **r**, but we have done	571
	12:31 whereof *one* went on the **r hand** upon	3225
Est	8: 5 the thing *seem* **r** before the king, and I	3787
Job	6:25 How forcible are **r** words! but what doth	3476
	23: 9 *him*: he hideth *himself on* the **r hand**,	3225
	30:12 Upon *my* **r hand** rise the youth; they push	3225
	33:27 perverted *that which was* **r**, and it profited	3477
	34: 6 Should I lie against my **r**? my wound *is*	4941
	34:17 Shall even he that hateth **r** govern?	4941
	34:23 he will not lay upon man more *than* **r**,	NIH
	35: 2 Thinkest thou this to be **r**, *that* thou	4941
	36: 6 of the wicked: but giveth **r** to the poor.	4941
	40:14 that thine own **r hand** can save thee.	3225
	42: 7 have not spoken of me *the thing that is* **r**,	3559
	42: 8 not spoken of me *the thing which is* **r**,	3559
Ps	9: 4 For thou hast maintained my **r** and	4941
	4 thou satest in the throne judging **r**.	6664
	16: 8 because *he is* at my **r** hand, I shall not be	3225
	16:11 at thy **r hand** *there are* pleasures for	3225
	17: 1 Hear the **r**, O LORD, attend unto my cry,	6664
	17: 7 O thou that savest by thy **r hand** them	3225
	18:35 thy **r hand** hath holden me up,	3225
	19: 8 The statutes of the LORD *are* **r**,	3477
	20: 6 with the saving strength of his **r hand**.	3225
	21: 8 thy **r hand** shall find out those that hate	3225
	26:10 and their **r hand** is full *of* bribes.	3225
	33: 4 For the word of the LORD *is* **r**; and all his	3477
	44: 3 thy **r hand**, and thine arm, and the light	3225
	45: 4 thy **r hand** shall teach thee terrible *things*.	3225
	45: 6 the sceptre of thy kingdom *is* a **r** sceptre.	4334
	45: 9 **r hand** did stand the queen in gold of	3225
	46: 5 God shall help her, *and that* **r** early.	6437
	48:10 thy **r hand** is full *of* righteousness.	3225
	51:10 O God; and renew a **r** spirit within me.	3559
	60: 5 save *with* thy **r hand**, and hear me.	3225
	63: 8 after thee: thy **r hand** upholdeth me.	3225
	73:23 thou hast holden *me* by my **r hand**.	3225
	74:11 thou thy hand, even thy **r hand**?	3225
	77:10 *I will remember* the years of the **r hand**	3225
	78:37 For their heart was not **r** with him,	3559
	78:54 *which* his **r hand** had purchased.	3225
	80:15 the vineyard which thy **r hand** hath	3225
	80:17 thy hand be upon the man of thy **r hand**,	3225
	89:13 is thy hand, *and* high is thy **r hand**.	3225
	89:25 in the sea, and his **r hand** in the rivers.	3225
	89:42 Thou hast set up the **r hand** of his	3225
	91: 7 thy side, and ten thousand at thy **r hand**;	3225
	98: 1 hath done marvellous *things*: his **r hand**,	3225
	107: 7 he led them forth by the **r** way, that *they*	3477
	108: 6 save *with* thy **r hand**, and answer me.	3225
	109: 6 him: and let Satan stand at his **r hand**.	3225
	109:31 he shall stand at the **r hand** of the poor,	3225
	110: 1 said unto my Lord, Sit thou at my **r hand**,	3225
	110: 5 The Lord at thy **r hand** shall strike	3225
	118:15 the **r hand** of the LORD doeth valiantly.	3225
	118:16 The **r hand** of the LORD is exalted:	3225
	118:16 the **r hand** of the LORD doeth valiantly.	3225
	119:75 that thy judgments *are* **r**, and *that* thou *in*	6664
	119:128 **esteem** all *thy* precepts concerning all *things* **to be r**;	3474
	121: 5 the LORD *is* thy shade upon thy **r** hand.	3225
	137: 5 let my **r hand** forget *her* cunning.	3225
	138: 7 and thy **r hand** shall save me.	3225
	139:10 lead me, and thy **r hand** shall hold me.	3225
	139:14 and *that* my soul knoweth **r** well.	3966
	140:12 of the afflicted, *and* the **r** of the poor.	4941
	142: 4 I looked *on* my **r hand**, and beheld,	3225
	144: 8 their **r hand** *is* a right hand of falsehood.	3225
	144: 8 their right hand *is* a **r hand** of falsehood.	3225

Ps 144:11 their **r** hand *is* a right hand of falsehood: 3225
144:11 their right hand *is* a **r** hand of falsehood: 3225
Pr 3:16 Length of days *is* in her **r** hand; and in 3225
4:11 way of wisdom; I have led thee in **r** paths. 3225
4:25 Let thine eyes look **r** on, 5227+3807.1
4:27 Turn not *to* the **r** hand nor *to* the left: 3225
8: 6 the opening of my lips *shall be* **r** things. 4339
8: 9 and **r** to them that find knowledge. 3477
9:15 call passengers who **go r** on their ways: 3474
12: 5 The thoughts of the righteous *are* **r**: 4941
12:15 The way of a fool *is* **r** in his own eyes: 3477
14:12 There is a way which seemeth **r** unto a 3477
16: 8 than great revenues without **r**. 4941
16:13 kings; and *they* love him that speaketh **r**. 3477
16:25 There is a way that seemeth **r** unto a man, 3477
20:11 his work *be* pure, and whether *it be* **r**. 3477
21: 2 Every way of a man *is* **r** in his own eyes: 3477
21: 8 strange: but *as for* the pure, his work *is* **r**. 3477
23:16 rejoice, when thy lips speak **r** things. 4339
24:26 *man* shall kiss *his* lips that giveth a **r** 5228
27:16 the wind, and the ointment of his **r** hand, 3225
Ecc 4: 4 I considered all travail, and every **r** work, 3788
10: 2 A wise *man's* heart *is* at his **r** hand; 3225
SS 2: 6 head, and his **r** hand doth embrace me. 3225
8: 3 and his **r** hand should embrace me. 3225
Isa 9:20 he shall snatch on the **r** hand, 3225
10: 2 to take away the **r** from the poor of my 4941
30:10 Prophesy not unto us **r** *things,* speak unto 5229
30:21 when ye **turn to the r** hand, and when 541
32: 7 even when the needy speaketh **r**. 4941
41:10 I will uphold thee with the **r** hand of my 3225
41:13 The LORD thy God will hold thy **r** hand, 3225
44:20 nor say, *Is there* not a lie in my **r** hand? 3225
45: 1 to Cyrus, whose **r** hand I have holden, 3225
45:19 I declare **things that are r**. 4339
48:13 and my **r** hand hath spanned the heavens: 3225
54: 3 For thou shalt break forth *on* the **r** hand 3225
62: 8 The LORD hath sworn by his **r** hand, 3225
63:12 That led *them* by the **r** hand of Moses 3225
Jer 2:21 planted thee a noble vine, wholly a **r** seed: 571
5:28 and the **r** of the needy do they not judge. 4941
17:11 *so* he that getteth riches, and not by **r**, 4941
17:16 out of my lips was **r** before thee. 5227+6440
22:24 of Judah were the signet upon my **r** hand, 3225
23:10 course is evil, and their force is not **r**. 3651
32: 7 for the **r** of redemption *is* thine to buy *it.* 4941
32: 8 for the **r** of inheritance *is* thine, 4941
34:15 now turned, and had done **r** in my sight, 4941
49: 5 be driven out every man **r** forth; 6440+3807.1
La 2: 3 he hath drawn back his **r** hand from 3225
2: 4 he stood *with* his **r** hand as an adversary, 3225
3:35 To turn aside the **r** of a man before the 4941
Eze 1:10 man, and the face of a lion, on the **r side**: 3225
4: 6 lie again on thy **r** side, and thou shalt bear 3233
10: 3 the cherubims stood on the **r** side 3225
16:46 that dwelleth at thy **r** hand, *is* Sodom 3225
18: 5 be just, and do that which is lawful and **r**, 6666
18:19 son hath done that which is lawful and **r**, 6666
18:21 do that which is lawful and **r**, he shall 6666
18:27 doeth that which is lawful and **r**, he shall 6666
21:16 *either* **on the r** hand, *or* on the left, 3231
21:22 At his **r** hand was the divination for 3225
21:27 shall be no *more,* until he come whose **r** 4941
33:14 his sin, and do that which is lawful and **r**; 6666
33:16 he hath done that which is lawful and **r**; 6666
33:19 do that which is lawful and **r**, he shall live 6666
39: 3 will cause thine arrows to fall out of thy **r** 3225
47: 1 from under from the **r** side of the house, 3233
47: 2 there ran out waters on the **r** side. 3233
Da 12: 7 when he held up his **r** hand and his left 3225
Hos 14: 9 for the ways of the LORD *are* **r**, 3477
Am 3:10 For they know not to do **r**, saith 5229
5:12 aside the poor in the gate *from their* **r**. NIH
Jnh 4:11 that cannot discern between their **r** hand 3225
Hab 2:16 the cup of the LORD's **r** hand shall be 3225
Zec 3: 1 Satan standing at his **r** hand to resist him. 3225
4: 3 one upon the **r** side of the bowl, 3225
4:11 *are* these two olive trees upon the **r** 3225
11:17 *shall be* upon his arm, and upon his **r** eye: 3225
11:17 and his **r** eye shall be utterly darkened. 3225
12: 6 about, on the **r** hand and on the left: 3225
Mal 3: 5 that turn aside the stranger *from* his **r**, NIH
Mt 5:29 And if thy **r** eye offend thee, pluck it out, 1188
5:30 And if thy **r** hand offend thee, cut it off, 1188
5:39 shall smite thee on thy **r** cheek, 1188
6: 3 not thy left hand know what thy **r** hand 1188
20: 4 and whatsoever is **r** I will give you. 1342
20: 7 and whatsoever is **r**, *that* shall ye receive. 1342
20:21 the one on thy **r** hand, and the other on 1188
20:23 baptized *with:* but to sit on my **r** hand, 1188
22:44 unto my Lord, Sit thou on my **r** hand, 1188
25:33 And he shall set the sheep on his **r** hand, 1188
25:34 the King say unto them on his **r** hand, 1188
26:64 of man sitting on the **r** hand of power, 1188
27:29 *it* upon his head, and a reed in his **r** hand: 1188
27:38 on the **r** hand, and another on the left. 1188
Mk 5:15 sitting, and clothed, and **in** his **r** mind: 4993
10:37 on thy **r** hand, and the other on thy left 1188
10:40 But to sit on my **r** hand and on my left 1188
12:36 said to my Lord, Sit thou on my **r** hand, 1188
14:62 of man sitting on the **r** hand of power, 1188
15:27 one on *his* **r** hand, and the other on his 1188
16: 5 saw a young man sitting on the **r** side, 1188
16:19 heaven, and sat on the **r** hand of God. 1188
Lk 1:11 on the **r** side of the altar of incense. 1188

Lk 6: 6 there was a man whose **r** hand was 1188
8:35 feet of Jesus, clothed, and **in** his **r mind**: 4993
10:28 he said unto him, Thou hast answered **r**: 3723
12:57 even of yourselves judge ye not what *is* **r**? 1342
20:42 said to my Lord, Sit thou on my **r** hand, 1188
22:50 of the high priest, and cut off his **r** ear. 1188
22:69 sit on the **r** hand of the power of God. 1188
23:33 on the **r** hand, and the other on the left. 1188
Jn 18:10 high priest's servant, and cut off his **r** ear. 1188
21: 6 Cast the net on the **r** side of the ship, 1188
Ac 2:25 he is on my **r** hand, that I should not be 1188
2:33 Therefore being by the **r** hand of God 1188
2:34 unto my Lord, Sit thou on my **r hand**, 1188
3: 7 he took him by the **r** hand, and lift *him* 1188
4:19 Whether it be **r** in the sight of God to 1188
5:31 Him hath God exalted with his **r hand** *to* 1188
7:55 and Jesus standing on the **r hand** of God, 1188
7:56 the Son of man standing on the **r hand** of 1188
8:21 for thy heart is not **r** in the sight of God. 2117
13:10 wilt thou not cease to pervert the **r** ways 2117
Ro 8:34 *again,* who is even at the **r hand** of God, 1188
2Co 6: 7 armour of righteousness on the **r** hand 1188
Gal 2: 9 and Barnabas the **r hands** of fellowship: 1188
Eph 1:20 set *him* at his own **r hand** in the heavenly 1188
6: 1 obey your parents in the Lord: for this is **r**. 1342
Col 3: 1 where Christ sitteth on the **r hand** of 1188
Heb 1: 3 sat down on the **r hand** of the Majesty on 1188
1:13 Sit on my **r hand**, until I make thine 1188
8: 1 who is set on the **r hand** of the throne of 1188
10:12 for ever, sat down on the **r hand** of God; 1188
12: 2 is set down at the **r hand** of the throne of 1188
13:10 whereof they have no **r** to eat which serve 1849
1Pe 3:22 into heaven, and is on the **r hand** of God; 1188
2Pe 2:15 Which have forsaken the **r** way, 2117
Rev 1:16 And he had in his **r** hand seven stars: 1188
1:17 And he laid his **r** hand upon me, 1188
1:20 stars which thou sawest in my **r hand,** 1188
2: 1 holdeth the seven stars in his **r hand,** 1188
5: 1 And I saw in the **r hand** of him that sat 1188
5: 7 took the book out of the **r hand** of him 1188
10: 2 and he set his **r** foot upon the sea, 1188
13:16 to receive a mark in their **r** hand, or in 1188
22:14 that they may have **r** to the tree of life, 1849

RIGHTEOUS (238) [RIGHT]

Ge 7: 1 for thee have I seen **r** before me in this 6662
18:23 Wilt thou also destroy the **r** with 6662
18:24 Peradventure there be fifty **r** within 6662
18:24 not spare the place for the fifty **r** that *are* 6662
18:25 manner, to slay the **r** with the wicked: 6662
18:25 that the **r** should be as the wicked, that 6662
18:26 If I find in Sodom fifty **r** within the city, 6662
18:28 there shall lack five of the fifty **r**: 6662
20: 4 Lord, wilt thou slay also a **r** nation? 6662
38:26 and said, She hath been more **r** than I; 6663
Ex 9:27 the LORD is **r**, and I and my people *are* 6662
23: 7 and the innocent and **r** slay thou not: 6662
23: 8 wise, and perverteth the words of the **r**. 6662
Nu 23:10 Let me die the death of the **r**, and let my 3477
Dt 4: 8 and judgments *so* **r** as all this law, 6662
16:19 the wise, and pervert the words of the **r**. 6662
25: 1 they shall justify the **r**, and condemn 6662
Jdg 5:11 they rehearse the **r acts** of the LORD, 6666
5:11 the **r acts** *towards* the inhabitants of 6666
1Sa 12: 7 the LORD of all the **r acts** of the LORD, 6666
24:17 he said to David, Thou *art* more **r** than I: 6662
2Sa 4:11 when wicked men have slain a **r** person 6662
1Ki 2:32 who fell upon two men more **r** and 6662
8:32 justifying the **r**, to give him according to 6662
2Ki 10: 9 stood, and said to all the people, Ye *be* **r**: 6662
2Ch 6:23 by justifying the **r**, by giving him 6662
12: 6 and they said, The LORD *is* **r**. 6662
Ezr 9:15 O LORD God of Israel, thou *art* **r**: for we 6662
Ne 9: 8 hast performed thy words; for thou *art* **r** 6662
Job 4: 7 or where were the **r** cut off? 3477
9:15 Whom, though I were **r**, *yet* would I not 6663
10:15 *if* I be **r**, *yet* will I not lift up my head. 6663
15:14 *is* born of a woman, that he should be **r**? 6663
17: 9 The also shall hold on his way, 6662
22: 3 pleasure to the Almighty, that thou art **r**? 6663
22:19 The **r** see *it,* and are glad: and the 6662
23: 7 There the **r** might dispute with him; 3477
32: 1 because he was **r** in his own eyes. 6662
34: 5 For Job hath said, I am **r**: and God hath 6662
35: 7 If thou be **r**, what givest thou him? 6663
36: 7 He withdraweth not his eyes from the **r**: 6662
36: 7 condemn me, that thou mayest be **r**? 6663
Ps 1: 5 nor sinners in the congregation of the **r**. 6662
1: 6 For the LORD knoweth the way of the **r**: 6662
5:12 For thou, LORD, wilt bless the **r**; 6662
7: 9 for the **r** God trieth the hearts and reins. 6662
7:11 God judgeth the **r**, and God is angry *with* 6662
11: 3 be destroyed, what can the **r** do? 6662
11: 5 The LORD trieth the **r**: but the wicked 6662
11: 7 For the LORD loveth righteousness; 6662
14: 5 for God *is* in the generation of the **r**. 6662
19: 9 of the LORD *are* true *and* **r** altogether. 6663
31:18 and contemptuously against the **r**. 6662
32:11 Be glad in the LORD, and rejoice, ye **r**: 6662
33: 1 Rejoice in the LORD, O ye **r**: *for* praise is 6662
34:15 The eyes of the LORD *are* upon the **r**, 6662
34:17 The **r** cry, and the LORD heareth, NIH
34:19 Many *are* the afflictions of the **r**: 6662
34:21 and they that hate the **r** shall be desolate. 6662
35:27 and be glad, that favour my **r cause**: 6664

Ps 37:16 A little that a **r** man hath *is* better than 6662
37:17 be broken: but the LORD upholdeth the **r**. 6662
37:21 but the **r** sheweth mercy, and giveth. 6662
37:25 yet have I not seen the **r** forsaken, nor his 6662
37:29 The **r** shall inherit the land, 6662
37:30 The mouth of the **r** speaketh wisdom, 6662
37:32 The wicked watcheth the **r**, and seeketh 6662
37:39 the salvation of the **r** *is* of the LORD: 6662
52: 6 The **r** also shall see, and fear, 6662
55:22 he shall never suffer the **r** to be moved. 6662
58:10 The **r** shall rejoice when he seeth 6662
58:11 say, Verily *there is* a reward for the **r**: 6662
64:10 The **r** shall be glad in the LORD, 6662
68: 3 let the **r** be glad; let them rejoice before 6662
69:28 the living, and not be written with the **r**. 6662
72: 7 In his days shall the **r** flourish; 6662
75:10 *but* the horns of the **r** shall be exalted. 6662
92:12 The **r** shall flourish like the palm tree: 6662
94:21 together against the soul of the **r**, 6662
97:11 Light is sown for the **r**, and gladness for 6662
97:12 Rejoice in the LORD, ye **r**; 6662
107:42 The **r** shall see *it,* and rejoice: 3477
112: 4 *is* gracious, and full of compassion, and **r**. 6662
112: 6 the **r** shall be in everlasting remembrance. 6662
116: 5 Gracious *is* the LORD, and **r**; yea, 6662
118:15 salvation *is* in the tabernacles of the **r**: 6662
118:20 of the LORD, into which the **r** shall enter. 6662
119: 7 I shall have learned thy **r** judgments. 6664
119:62 unto thee because of thy **r** judgments. 6664
119:106 I will perform *it,* that *I* will keep thy **r** 6664
119:137 **R** *art* thou, O LORD, and upright *are* thy 6664
119:138 *that* thou hast commanded *are* **r** 6664
119:160 every one of thy **r** judgments *endureth* for 6664
119:164 I praise thee because of thy **r** judgments. 6664
125: 3 wicked shall not rest upon the lot of the **r**; 6662
125: 3 the **r** put forth their hands unto iniquity. 6662
129: 4 The LORD *is* **r**: he hath cut asunder 6662
140:13 Surely the **r** shall give thanks unto thy 6662
141: 5 Let the **r** smite me; *it shall be* a kindness: 6662
142: 7 the **r** shall compass me about; for thou 6662
145:17 The LORD *is* **r** in all his ways, 6662
146: 8 are bowed down: the LORD loveth the **r**: 3477
Pr 2: 7 He layeth up sound wisdom for the **r**: 6662
2:20 of good *men,* and keep the paths of the **r**. 6662
3:32 to the LORD: but his secret *is* with the **r**. 3477
10: 3 The LORD will not suffer the soul of the **r** 6662
10:11 The mouth of a **r** *man* is a well of life: 6662
10:16 The labour of the **r** *tendeth* to life: 6662
10:21 The lips of the **r** feed many: but fools die 6662
10:24 but the desire of the **r** shall be granted. 6662
10:25 but the **r** *is* an everlasting foundation. 6662
10:28 The hope of the **r** *shall be* gladness: 6662
10:30 The **r** shall never be removed: 6662
10:32 The lips of the **r** know what is acceptable: 6662
11: 8 The **r** is delivered out of trouble, 6662
11:10 When it goeth well with the **r**, the city 6662
11:21 but the seed of the **r** shall be delivered. 6662
11:23 The desire of the **r** is only good: 6662
11:28 but the **r** shall flourish as a branch. 6662
11:30 The fruit of the **r** *is* a tree of life; 6662
11:31 the **r** shall be recompensed in the earth: 6662
12: 5 The thoughts of the **r** *are* right: 6662
12: 7 *are* not: but the house of the **r** shall stand. 6662
12:10 A **r** *man* regardeth the life of his beast: 6662
12:12 but the root of the **r** yieldeth *fruit.* 6662
12:26 **r** *is* more excellent than his neighbour: 6662
13: 5 A **r** *man* hateth lying: but a wicked *man* is 6662
13: 9 The light of the **r** rejoiceth: but the lamp 6662
13:21 but to the **r** good shall be repayed. 6662
13:25 The **r** eateth to the satisfying of his soul: 6662
14: 9 at sin: but among the **r** *there is* favour. 3477
14:19 and the wicked at the gates of the **r**. 6662
14:32 but the **r** hath hope in his death. 6662
15: 6 *In* the house of the **r** *is* much treasure: 3477
15:19 but the way of the **r** *is* made plain. 3477
15:28 The heart of the **r** studieth to answer: 6662
15:29 but he heareth the prayer of the **r**. 6662
16:13 **R** lips *are* the delight of kings; 6664
18: 5 wicked, to overthrow the **r** in judgment. 6662
18:10 the **r** runneth into it, and is safe. 6662
21:12 The **r** *man* wisely considereth the house 6662
21:18 The wicked *shall be* a ransom for the **r**, 6662
21:26 day long: but the **r** giveth and spareth not. 6662
23:24 The father of the **r** shall greatly rejoice: 6662
24:15 *man,* against the dwelling of the **r**; 6662
24:24 He that saith unto the wicked, Thou *art* **r**; 6662
25:26 A **r** *man* falling down before the wicked *is* 6662
28: 1 *man* pursueth: but the **r** are bold as a lion. 6662
28:10 Whoso causeth the **r** to go astray in an 3477
28:12 **r** *men* do rejoice, *there is* great glory: 6662
28:28 but when they perish, the **r** increase. 6662
29: 2 When the **r** are in authority, the people 6662
29: 6 *is* a snare: but the **r** doth sing and rejoice. 6662
29: 7 The **r** considereth the cause of the poor: 6662
29:16 but the **r** shall see their fall. 6662
Ecc 3:17 God shall judge the **r** and the wicked: 6662
7:16 Be not **r** over much; neither make thyself 6662
8:14 happeneth according to the work of the **r**: 6662
9: 1 that the **r**, and the wise, and their works, 6662
9: 2 *there is* one event to the **r**, and to 6662
Isa 3:10 Say ye to the **r**, that *it shall be* well with 6662
5:23 take away the righteousness of the **r** from 6662
24:16 have we heard songs, *even* glory to the **r**. 6662
26: 2 that the **r** nation which keepeth the truth 6662

R

Isa	41: 2	Who raised up the r man from the east,	6664
	41:26	beforetime, that we may say, He is r? yea,	6664
	53:11	by his knowledge shall my r servant justify	6662
	57: 1	The r perisheth, and no man layeth it to	6662
	57: 1	none considering that the r is taken away	6662
	60:21	Thy people also shall be all r: they shall	6662
Jer	12: 1	R art thou, O LORD, when I plead with	6662
	20:12	that triest the r, and seest the reins and	6662
	23: 5	that I will raise him unto David a Branch,	6662
La	1:18	The LORD is r; for I have rebelled	6662
Eze	3:20	When a r man doth turn from his	6662
	3:21	Nevertheless if thou warn the r man, that	6662
	3:21	the righteous man, that the r sin not,	6662
	13:22	lies ye have made the heart of the r sad,	6662
	16:52	they are more r than thou: yea, be thou	6663
	18:20	the righteousness of the r shall be upon	6662
	18:24	when the r turneth away from his	6662
	18:26	When a r man turneth away from his	6662
	21: 3	cut off from thee the r and the wicked,	6662
	21: 4	that I will cut off from thee the r and	6662
	23:45	the r men, they shall judge them after	6662
	33:12	The righteousness of the r shall not deliver	6662
	33:12	neither shall the r be able to live for his	6662
	33:13	When I shall say to the r, that he shall	6662
	33:18	the r turneth from his righteousness,	6662
Da	9:14	for the LORD our God is r in all his	6662
Am	2: 6	because they sold the r for silver,	6662
Hab	1: 4	for the wicked doth compass about the r;	6662
	1:13	the man that is more r than he?	6662
Mal	3:18	discern between the r and the wicked,	6662
Mt	9:13	for I am not come to call the r,	1342
	10:41	he that receiveth a r man in the name of a	1342
	10:41	r man shall receive a righteous man's	1342
	10:41	man shall receive a r man's reward.	1342
	13:17	r men have desired to see those things	1342
	13:43	Then shall the r shine forth as the sun in	1342
	23:28	so ye also outwardly appear r unto men,	1342
	23:29	and garnish the sepulchres of the r,	1342
	23:35	That upon you may come all the r blood	1342
	23:35	from the blood of r Abel unto the blood of	1342
	25:37	Then shall the r answer him, saying, Lord,	1342
	25:46	but the r into life eternal.	1342
Mk	2:17	I came not to call the r, but sinners to	1342
Lk	1: 6	And they were both r before God,	1342
	5:32	I came not to call the r, but sinners to	1342
	18: 9	trusted in themselves that they were r,	1342
	23:47	saying, Certainly this was a r man.	1342
Jn	7:24	to the appearance, but judge r judgment.	1342
	17:25	r Father, the world hath not known thee:	1342
Ro	2: 5	and revelation of the r judgment of God;	1341
	3:10	it is written, There is none r, no, not one:	1342
	5: 7	For scarcely for a r man will one die:	1342
	5:19	obedience of one shall many be made r.	1342
2Th	1: 5	Which is a manifest token of the r	1342
	1: 6	Seeing it is a r thing with God to	1342
1Ti	1: 9	that the law is not made for a r man, but	1342
2Ti	4: 8	which the Lord, the r judge, shall give me	1342
Heb	11: 4	which he obtained witness that he was r,	1342
Jas	5:16	The effectual fervent prayer of a r man	1342
1Pe	3:12	For the eyes of the Lord are over the r,	1342
	4:18	And if the r scarcely be saved, where shall	1342
2Pe	2: 8	(For that r man dwelling among them,	1342
	2: 8	vexed his r soul from day to day with	1342
1Jn	2: 1	with the Father, Jesus Christ the r:	1342
	2:29	If ye know that he is r, ye know that every	1342
	3: 7	he that doeth righteousness is r, even as	1342
	3: 7	righteousness is righteous, even as he is r.	1342
	3:12	own works were evil, and his brother's r.	1342
Rev	16: 5	Thou art r, O Lord, which art, and wast,	1342
	16: 7	true and r are thy judgments.	1342
	19: 2	For true and r are his judgments: for he	1342
	22:11	and he that is r, let him be righteous still:	1342
	22:11	and he that is righteous, let him be r still:	1344

RIGHTEOUSLY (8) [RIGHT]

Dt	1:16	judge r between every man and his	6664
Ps	67: 4	for thou shalt judge the people r,	4334
	96:10	he shall judge the people r.	4339+871.1
Pr	31: 9	judge r, and plead the cause of the poor	
Isa	33:15	He that walketh r, and speaketh uprightly;	6666
Jer	11:20	that judgest r, that triest the reins and	6664
Tit	2:12	r, and godly, in this present world;	1346
1Pe	2:23	committed himself to him that judgeth r:	1346

RIGHTEOUSNESS (302) [RIGHT]

Ge	15: 6	the LORD, and he counted it to him for r.	6666
	30:33	So shall my r answer for me in time to	6666
Lev	19:15	but in shalt thou judge thy neighbour.	6664
Dt	6:25	it shall be our r, if we observe to do all	6666
	9: 4	For my r the LORD hath brought me in to	6666
	9: 5	Not for thy r, or for the uprightness of	6666
	9: 6	not this good land to possess it for thy r;	6666
	24:13	it shall be r unto thee before the LORD	6666
	33:19	there they shall offer sacrifices of r:	6664
1Sa	26:23	The LORD render to every man his r and	6666
2Sa	22:21	LORD rewarded me according to my r:	6666
	22:25	hath recompensed me according to my r;	6666
1Ki	3: 6	in r, and in uprightness of heart with thee;	6666
	8:32	to give him according to his r.	6666
2Ch	6:23	by giving him according to his r.	6666
Job	6:29	be iniquity; yea, return again, my r is in it.	6664
	8: 6	make the habitation of thy r prosperous.	6664
	27: 6	My r I hold fast, and will not let it go:	6666
	29:14	put on r, and it clothed me: my judgment	6664
	33:26	joy: for he will render unto man his r.	6666

Job	35: 2	thou saidst, My r is more than God's?	6664
	35: 8	and thy r may profit the son of man.	6664
	36: 3	from afar, and will ascribe r to my Maker.	6664
Ps	4: 1	Hear me when I call, O God of my r:	6664
	4: 5	Offer the sacrifices of r, and put your trust	6664
	5: 8	in thy r because of mine enemies;	6666
	7: 8	according to my r, and according to mine	6664
	7:17	I will praise the LORD according to his r:	6664
	9: 8	he shall judge the world in r, he shall	6664
	11: 7	For the righteous LORD loveth r;	6666
	15: 2	worketh r, and speaketh the truth in his	6666
	17:15	As for me, I will behold thy face in r:	6664
	18:20	LORD rewarded me according to my r;	6666
	18:24	recompensed me according to my r,	6666
	22:31	shall declare his r unto a people that shall	6666
	23: 3	he leadeth me in the paths of r for his	6666
	24: 5	and r from the God of his salvation.	6666
	31: 1	me never be ashamed: deliver me in thy r.	6666
	33: 5	He loveth r and judgment: the earth is full	6666
	35:24	O LORD my God, according to thy r;	6664
	35:28	my tongue shall speak of thy r and of thy	6666
	36: 6	Thy r is like the great mountains;	6666
	36:10	thee; and thy r to the upright in heart.	6666
	37: 6	he shall bring forth thy r as the light,	6664
	40: 9	have preached r in the great congregation:	6664
	40:10	I have not hid thy r within my heart;	6666
	45: 4	of truth and meekness and r;	6664
	45: 7	Thou lovest r, and hatest wickedness:	6664
	48:10	of the earth: thy right hand is full of r.	6666
	50: 6	the heavens shall declare his r: for God is	6664
	51:14	and my tongue shall sing aloud of thy r.	6666
	51:19	thou be pleased with the sacrifices of r,	6664
	52: 3	good; and lying rather than to speak r.	6664
	58: 1	Do ye indeed speak r, O congregation?	6664
	65: 5	terrible things in r wilt thou answer us,	6664
	69:27	and let them not come into thy r.	6666
	71: 2	Deliver me in thy r, and cause me to	6666
	71:15	My mouth shall shew forth thy r and	6666
	71:16	I will make mention of thy r, even of	6666
	71:19	Thy r also, O God, is very high, who hast	6666
	71:24	My tongue also shall talk of thy r all	6666
	72: 1	O God, and thy r unto the king's son.	6666
	72: 2	He shall judge thy people with r,	6664
	72: 3	to the people, and the little hills, by r.	6666
	85:10	r and peace have kissed each other.	6664
	85:11	and r shall look down from heaven.	6664
	85:13	R shall go before him; and shall set us in	6664
	88:12	and thy r in the land of forgetfulness?	6666
	89:16	day: and in thy r shall they be exalted.	6666
	94:15	judgment shall return unto r: and all	6664
	96:13	he shall judge the world with r,	6664
	97: 2	r and judgment are the habitation of his	6664
	97: 6	The heavens declare his r, and all	6664
	98: 2	his r hath he openly shewed in the sight	6666
	98: 9	with r shall he judge the world,	6664
	99: 4	thou executest judgment and r in Jacob.	6666
	103: 6	The LORD executeth r and judgment for	6666
	103:17	him, and his r unto children's children;	6666
	106: 3	and he that doeth r at all times.	6666
	106:31	that was counted unto him for r unto all	6666
	111: 3	and glorious: and his r endureth for ever.	6666
	112: 3	his house: and his r endureth for ever.	6666
	112: 9	given to the poor; his r endureth for ever;	6666
	118:19	Open to me the gates of r: I will go into	6664
	119:40	after thy precepts: quicken me in thy r.	6666
	119:123	thy salvation, and for the word of thy r.	6664
	119:142	Thy r is an everlasting righteousness,	6666
	119:142	Thy righteousness is an everlasting r,	6664
	119:144	The r of thy testimonies is everlasting:	6664
	119:172	word: for all thy commandments are r.	6664
	132: 9	Let thy priests be clothed with r; and let	6664
	143: 1	thy faithfulness answer me, and in thy r.	6666
	145: 7	thy great goodness, and shall sing of thy r.	6666
Pr	2: 9	shalt thou understand r, and judgment,	6664
	8: 8	All the words of my mouth are in r; there	6664
	8:18	are with me; yea, durable riches and r.	6666
	8:20	I lead in the way of r, in the midst of	6666
	10: 2	nothing: but r delivereth from death.	6666
	11: 4	day of wrath: but r delivereth from death.	6666
	11: 5	The r of the perfect direct his way:	6666
	11: 6	The r of the upright shall deliver them:	6666
	11:18	him that soweth r shall be a sure reward.	6666
	11:19	As r tendeth to life: so he that pursueth	6666
	12:17	He that speaketh truth sheweth forth r:	6664
	12:28	In the way of r is life; and in the pathway	6666
	13: 6	R keepeth him that is upright in the way:	6666
	14:34	R exalteth a nation: but sin is a reproach	6666
	15: 9	but he loveth him that followeth after r.	6664
	16: 8	Better is a little with r than great revenues	6666
	16:12	for the throne is established by r.	6664
	16:31	of glory, if it be found in the way of r.	6664
	21:21	that followeth after r and mercy findeth	6664
	21:21	and mercy findeth life, r, and honour.	6666
	25: 5	and his throne shall be established in r.	6664
Ecc	3:16	the place of r, that iniquity was there.	6664
	7:15	there is a just man that perisheth in his r,	6664
Isa	1:21	lodged in it; but now murderers.	6664
	1:26	be called, The city of r, the faithful city.	6664
	1:27	with judgment, and her converts with r.	6664
	5: 7	behold oppression; for r, but behold a cry.	6666
	5:16	God is holy shall be sanctified in r.	6666
	5:23	away the r of the righteous from him.	6666
	10:22	decreed shall overflow with r.	6666
	11: 4	with r shall he judge the poor,	6664
	11: 5	r shall be the girdle of his loins,	6664

Isa	16: 5	and seeking judgment, and hasting r.	6664
	26: 9	the inhabitants of the world will learn r.	6664
	26:10	to the wicked, yet will he not learn r.	6664
	28:17	I lay to the line, and r to the plummet:	6666
	32: 1	a king shall reign in r, and princes shall	6666
	32:16	and r remain in the fruitful field.	6666
	32:17	The work of r shall be peace;	6666
	32:17	the effect of r quietness and assurance for	6666
	33: 5	he hath filled Zion with judgment and r.	6666
	41:10	uphold thee with the right hand of my r.	6664
	42: 6	I the LORD have called thee in r,	6664
	45: 8	above, and let the skies pour down r:	6664
	45: 8	salvation, and let r spring up together;	6666
	45:13	I have raised him up in r, and I will direct	6664
	45:19	I the LORD speak r, I declare things that	6664
	45:23	the word is gone out of my mouth in r,	6666
	45:24	in the LORD have I r and strength:	6666
	46:12	ye stouthearted, that are far from r:	6666
	46:13	I bring near my r; it shall not be far off,	6666
	48: 1	God of Israel, but not in truth, nor in r.	6666
	48:18	a river, and thy r as the waves of the sea:	6666
	51: 1	Hearken to me, ye that follow after r,	6664
	51: 5	My r is near; my salvation is gone forth,	6664
	51: 6	for ever, and my r shall not be abolished.	6666
	51: 7	Hearken unto me, ye that know r,	6666
	51: 8	my r shall be for ever, and my salvation	6666
	54:14	In r shalt thou be established: thou shalt	6666
	54:17	and their r is of me, saith the LORD.	6666
	56: 1	is near to come, and my r to be revealed.	6666
	57:12	I will declare thy r, and thy works; for	6666
	58: 2	as a nation that did r, and forsook not	6666
	58: 8	thy r shall go before thee; the glory of	6664
	59:16	unto him; and his r, it sustained him.	6666
	59:17	For he put on r as a breastplate,	6666
	60:17	thy officers peace, and thine exactors r.	6666
	61: 3	that they might be called trees of r,	6664
	61:10	he hath covered me with the robe of r,	6666
	61:11	so the Lord GOD will cause r and	6666
	62: 1	until the r thereof go forth as brightness,	6664
	62: 2	the Gentiles shall see thy r, and all kings	6664
	63: 1	I that speak in r, mighty to save.	6666
	64: 5	meetest him that rejoiceth and worketh r,	6664
Jer	4: 2	in truth, in judgment, and in r;	6666
	9:24	judgment, and r, in the earth:	6666
	22: 3	Execute ye judgment and r, and deliver	6666
	23: 6	he shall be called, THE LORD OUR R.	6664
	33:15	will I cause the Branch of r to grow up	6666
	33:15	shall execute judgment and r in the land.	6666
	33:16	she shall be called, The LORD our r:	6664
Eze	3:20	a righteous man doth turn from his r,	6664
	3:20	his r which he hath done shall not be	6666
	14:14	but their own souls by their r,	6666
	14:20	but deliver their own souls by their r.	6666
	18:20	the r of the righteous shall be upon him,	6666
	18:22	in his r that he hath done he shall live.	6666
	18:24	the righteous turneth away from his r,	6666
	18:24	All his r that he hath done shall not be	6666
	18:26	a righteous man turneth away from his r,	6666
	33:12	The r of the righteous shall not deliver	6666
	33:12	to live for his r in the day that he sinneth.	NIH
	33:13	if he trust to his own r,	6666
	33:18	When the righteous turneth from his r,	6666
Da	4:27	break off thy sins by r, and thine iniquities	6665
	9: 7	r belongeth unto thee, but unto us	6666
	9:16	O Lord, according to all thy r, I beseech	6666
	9:24	to bring in everlasting r, and to seal up	6664
	12: 3	they that turn many to r as the stars for	6663
Hos	2:19	I will betroth thee unto me in r,	6664
	10:12	Sow to yourselves in r, reap in mercy;	6666
	10:12	till he come and rain r upon you.	6664
Am	5: 7	wormwood, and leave off r in the earth,	6666
	5:24	as waters, and r as a mighty stream.	6666
	6:12	into gall, and the fruit of r into hemlock:	6666
Mic	6: 5	that ye may know the r of the LORD.	6666
	7: 9	forth to the light, and I shall behold his r.	6666
Zep	3: 5	judgment; seek r, seek meekness:	6666
Zec	8: 8	and I will be their God, in truth and in r.	6666
Mal	3: 3	may offer unto the LORD an offering in r.	6666
	4: 2	Sun of r arise with healing in his wings;	6666
Mt	3:15	for thus it becometh us to fulfil all r.	1343
	5: 6	they which do hunger and thirst after r.	1343
	5:20	That except your r shall exceed	1343
	5:20	shall exceed the r of the scribes	NIG
	6:33	ye first the kingdom of God, and his r;	1343
	21:32	For John came unto you in the way of r,	1343
Lk	1:75	In holiness and r before him, all the days	1343
Jn	16: 8	world of sin, and of r, and of judgment:	1343
	16:10	Of r, because I go to my Father, and ye	1343
Ac	10:35	and worketh r, is accepted with him.	1343
	13:10	child of the devil, thou enemy of all r,	1343
	17:31	the which he will judge the world in r by	1343
	24:25	And as he reasoned of r, temperance,	1343
Ro	1:17	For therein is the r of God revealed from	1345
	2:26	Therefore if the uncircumcision keep the r	1343
	3: 5	But if our unrighteousness commend the r	1343
	3:21	But now the r of God without the law is	1343
	3:22	Even the r of God which is by faith of	1343
	3:25	to declare his r for the remission of sins	1343
	3:26	To declare, I say, at this time his r: that he	1343
	4: 3	and it was counted unto him for r.	1343
	4: 5	the ungodly, his faith is counted for r.	1343
	4: 6	whom God imputeth r without works,	1343
	4: 9	that faith was reckoned to Abraham for r.	1343
	4:11	a seal of the r of the faith which he had	1343

Ro	4:11 that **r** might be imputed unto them also:	1343
	4:13 the law, but through the **r** of faith.	1343
	4:22 And therefore it was imputed to him for **r**.	1343
	5:17 of the gift of **r** shall reign in life by one,	1343
	5:18 by the **r** of one *the free gift came* upon all	1345
	5:21 might grace reign through **r** unto eternal	1343
	6:13 your members *as* instruments of **r** unto	1343
	6:16 of sin unto death, or of obedience unto **r**?	1343
	6:18 free from sin, ye became the servants of **r**.	1343
	6:19 yield your members servants to **r** unto	1343
	6:20 the servants of sin, ye were free from **r**.	1343
	8: 4 That the **r** of the law might be fulfilled in	1345
	8:10 of sin; but the Spirit *is* life because of **r**.	1343
	9:28 will finish the work, and cut *it* short in **r**:	1343
	9:30 the Gentiles, which followed not *after* **r**,	1343
	9:30 not *after* righteousness, have attained to **r**,	1343
	9:30 even the **r** which is of faith.	1343
	9:31 which followed *after* the law of **r**,	1343
	9:31 hath not attained to the law of **r**.	1343
	10: 3 For they being ignorant of God's **r**,	1343
	10: 3 and going about to establish their own **r**,	1343
	10: 3 not submitted themselves unto the **r** of	1343
	10: 4 For Christ *is* the end of the law for **r** to	1343
	10: 5 For Moses describeth the **r** which is of	1343
	10: 6 But the **r** which is of faith speaketh on	1343
	10:10 For with the heart *man* believeth unto **r**;	1343
	14:17 **r**, and peace, and joy in the Holy Ghost.	1343
1Co	1:30 and **r**, and sanctification, and redemption:	1343
	15:34 Awake to **r**, and sin not: for some have not	1346
2Co	3: 9 much more doth the ministration of **r**	1343
	5:21 we might be made the **r** of God in him.	1343
	6: 7 by the armour of **r** on the right hand and	1343
	6:14 for what fellowship hath **r** with	1343
	9: 9 to the poor: his **r** remaineth for ever.	1343
	9:10 and increase the fruits of your **r**;)	1343
	11:15 also be transformed as the ministers of **r**;	1343
Gal	2:21 if **r** *come* by the law, then Christ is dead	1343
	3: 6 and it was accounted to him for **r**.	1343
	3:21 verily **r** should have been by the law.	1343
	5: 5 the Spirit wait for the hope of **r** by faith.	1343
Eph	4:24 which after God is created in **r** and	1343
	5: 9 Spirit *is* in all goodness and **r** and truth;)	1343
	6:14 and having on the breastplate of **r**;	1343
Php	1:11 Being filled with the fruits of **r**, which are	1343
	3: 6 touching the **r** which is in the law,	1343
	3: 9 having mine own **r**, which is of the law,	1343
	3: 9 of Christ, the **r** which is of God by faith:	1343
1Ti	6:11 flee these *things*; and follow after **r**,	1343
2Ti	2:22 but follow **r**, faith, charity, peace,	1343
	3:16 for correction, for instruction in **r**:	1343
	4: 8 there is laid up for me a crown of **r**,	1343
Tit	3: 5 Not by works of **r** which we have done,	1343
Heb	1: 8 sceptre of **r** *is* the sceptre of thy kingdom.	2118
	1: 9 Thou hast loved **r**, and hated iniquity;	1343
	5:13 useth milk *is* unskilful in the word of **r**:	1343
	7: 2 first being by interpretation King of **r**,	1343
	11: 7 and became heir of the **r** which is by faith.	1343
	11:33 wrought **r**, obtained promises, stopped	1343
	12:11 **r** unto them which are exercised thereby.	1343
Jas	1:20 For the wrath of man worketh not the **r**	1343
	2:23 and it was imputed unto him for **r**:	1343
	3:18 the fruit of **r** is sown in peace of them	1343
1Pe	2:24 being dead to sins, should live unto **r**:	1343
2Pe	1: 1 faith with us through the **r** of God	1343
	2: 5 Noah the eighth *person*, a preacher of **r**,	1343
	2:21 for them not to have known the way of **r**,	1343
	3:13 and a new earth, wherein dwelleth **r**.	1343
1Jn	2:29 ye know that every one which doeth **r** is	1343
	3: 7 he that doeth **r** is righteous, even as he is	1343
	3:10 whosoever doeth not **r** is not of God,	1343
Rev	19: 8 white: for the fine linen is the **r** of saints.	1345
	19:11 and in **r** he doth judge and make war.	1343

RIGHTEOUSNESS' (4) [RIGHT]

Ps	143:11 thy **r** sake bring my soul out of trouble.	6666
Isa	42:21 The Lord is well pleased for his **r** sake;	6664
Mt	5:10 are they which are persecuted for **r**	1343
1Pe	3:14 But and if ye suffer for **r** sake, happy *are*	1343

RIGHTEOUSNESSES (3) [RIGHT]

Isa	64: 6 and all our **r** *are* as filthy rags;	6666
Eze	33:13 all his **r** shall not be remembered;	6666
Da	9:18 our supplications before thee for our **r**,	6666

RIGHTLY (4) [RIGHT]

Ge	27:36 he said, Is not he **r** named Jacob? for he	3588
Lk	7:43 he said unto him, Thou hast **r** judged.	3723
	20:21 we know that thou sayest and teachest **r**,	3723
2Ti	2:15 ashamed, **r dividing** the word of truth.	3718

RIGOUR (5)

Ex	1:13 the children of Israel to serve with **r**:	6531
	1:14 they made them serve, *was* with **r**.	6531
Lev	25:43 Thou shalt not rule over him with **r**;	6531
	25:46 ye shall not rule one over another with **r**.	6531
	25:53 *the other* shall not rule with **r** over him	6531

RIMMON (14) [GATH-RIMMON, HADADRIMMON, RIMMON-PAREZ]

Jos	15:32 Lebaoth, and Shilhim, and Ain, and **R**:	7417
Jdg	20:45 toward the wilderness unto the rock of **R**:	7417
	20:47 fled to the wilderness unto the rock **R**,	7417
	20:47 and abode in the rock **R** four months.	7417
	21:13 of Benjamin that *were* in the rock **R**,	7417
2Sa	4: 2 the sons of **R** a Beerothite, of the children	7417

2Sa	4: 5 the sons of **R** the Beerothite, Rechab and	7417
	4: 9 the sons of **R** the Beerothite, and said	7417
2Ki	5:18 *into* the house of **R** to worship there,	7417
	5:18 and I bow myself *in* the house of **R**:	7417
	5:18 I bow down myself *in* the house of **R**,	7417
1Ch	4:32 **R**, and Tochen, and Ashan, five cities:	7417
	6:77 **R** with her suburbs, Tabor with her	7417
Zec	14:10 plain from Geba to **R** south of Jerusalem:	7417

RIMMON PEREZ See RIMMON-PAREZ

RIMMON-PAREZ (2) [RIMMON]

Nu	33:19 departed from Rithmah, and pitched at **R**.	7428
	33:20 they departed from **R**, and pitched in	7428

RING (11) [EARRING, EARRINGS, RANG, RINGLEADER, RINGS, RINGSTRAKED]

Ge	41:42 Pharaoh took off his **r** from his hand,	2885
Ex	26:24 together above the head of it unto one **r**:	2885
	36:29 together at the head thereof, to one **r**:	2885
Est	3:10 the king took his **r** from his hand,	2885
	3:12 it written, and sealed with the king's **r**.	2885
	8: 2 the king took off his **r**, which he had	2885
	8: 8 king's name, and seal *it* with the king's **r**:	2885
	8: 8 sealed with the king's **r**, may no man	2885
	8: 8 sealed with the king's **r**, and sent letters	2885
Lk	15:22 put *it* on him; and put a **r** on his hand,	1146
Jas	2: 2 unto your assembly a man **with a gold r**,	5554

RINGLEADER (1) [LEAD, RING]

Ac	24: 5 and a **r** of the sect of the Nazarenes:	4414

RINGS (44) [RING]

Ex	25:12 And thou shalt cast four **r** of gold for it,	2885
	25:12 two **r** *shall be* in the one side of it,	2885
	25:12 of it, and two **r** in the other side of it.	2885
	25:14 thou shalt put the staves into the **r** by	2885
	25:15 The staves shall be in the **r** of the ark:	2885
	25:26 thou shalt make for it four **r** of gold,	2885
	25:26 put the **r** in the four corners that *are on*	2885
	25:27 Over against the border shall the **r** be for	2885
	26:29 their **r** of gold *for* places for the bars:	2885
	27: 4 the net shalt thou make four brasen **r**	2885
	27: 7 the staves shall be put into the **r**,	2885
	28:23 shalt make upon the breastplate two **r**	2885
	28:23 shalt put the two **r** on the two ends of	2885
	28:24 **r** *which are* on the ends of the breastplate	2885
	28:26 thou shalt make two **r** of gold,	2885
	28:27 two *other* **r** of gold thou shalt make,	2885
	28:28 they shall bind the breastplate by the **r**	2885
	28:28 the **r** of the ephod with a lace of blue,	2885
	30: 4 two golden **r** shalt thou make to it under	2885
	35:22 and earrings, and **r**, and tablets,	2885
	36:34 made their **r** *of* gold *to be* places for	2885
	37: 3 he cast for it four **r** of gold, *to be set* by	2885
	37: 3 even two **r** upon the one side of it,	2885
	37: 3 of it, and two **r** upon the other side of it.	2885
	37: 5 he put the staves into the **r** by the sides	2885
	37:13 he cast for it four **r** of gold, and put	2885
	37:13 put the **r** upon the four corners that *were*	2885
	37:14 Over against the border were the **r**,	2885
	37:27 he made two **r** of gold for it under	2885
	38: 5 cast four **r** for the four ends of the grate	2885
	38: 7 he put the staves into the **r** on the sides	2885
	39:16 made two ouches *of* gold, and two gold **r**;	2885
	39:16 put the two **r** in the two ends of	2885
	39:17 the two **r** on the ends of the breastplate.	2885
	39:19 they made two **r** of gold, and put *them* on	2885
	39:20 they made two *other* golden **r**, and put	2885
	39:21 they did bind the breastplate by his **r** unto	2885
	39:21 the **r** of the ephod with a lace of blue,	2885
Nu	31:50 and bracelets, **r**, earrings, and tablets,	2885
Est	1: 6 purple to silver **r** and pillars of marble:	1550
SS	5:14 His hands *are as* gold **r** set with the beryl:	1550
Isa	3:21 The **r**, and nose jewels,	2885
Eze	1:18 As for their **r**, they were so high that they	1354
	1:18 their **r** *were* full of *eyes* round about them	1354

RINGSTRAKED (7) [RING]

Ge	30:35 removed that day the he goats that were **r**	6124
	30:39 brought forth cattle **r**, speckled,	6124
	30:40 set the faces of the flocks toward the **r**,	6124
	31: 8 if he said thus, The **r** shall be thy hire;	6124
	31: 8 shall be thy hire; then bare all the cattle **r**.	6124
	31:10 rams which leaped upon the cattle *were* **r**,	6124
	31:12 the rams which leap upon the cattle are **r**,	6124

RINNAH (1)

1Ch	4:20 and **R**, Ben-hanan, and Tilon.	7441

RINSED (3)

Lev	6:28 it shall be both scoured, and **r** in water.	7857
	15:11 not **r** his hands in water, he shall wash	7857
	15:12 every vessel of wood shall be **r** in water.	7857

RIOT (3) [RIOTING, RIOTOUS]

Tit	1: 6 having faithful children not accused of **r** or	810
1Pe	4: 4 run not with *them* to the same excess of **r**,	810
2Pe	2:13 they count it pleasure to **r** in the day	5172

RIOTING (1) [RIOT]

Ro	13:13 not in **r** and drunkenness, not in	2970

RIOTOUS (3) [RIOT]

Pr	23:20 amongst **r** eaters of flesh:	2151
	28: 7 he that is a companion of **r** *men* shameth	2151

Lk	15:13 there wasted his substance with **r** living.	811

RIP (1) [RIPT]

2Ki	8:12 and **r** up their women with child.	1234

RIPE (8) [FIRSTRIPE, RIPENING, UNRIPE]

Ge	40:10 clusters thereof **brought forth r** grapes:	1310
Ex	22:29 not delay *to offer the first of* thy **r** fruits,	4395
Nu	13:20 Now the time *was* the time of the **first r**	1061
	18:13 *And* whatsoever is **first r** in the land,	1061
Jer	24: 2 figs, *even* like the figs *that are* **first r**:	1073
Joel	3:13 Put ye in the sickle, for the harvest is **r**:	1310
Rev	14:15 to reap; for the harvest of the earth is **r**.	3583
	14:18 of the earth; for her grapes are **fully r**.	187

RIPENING (1) [RIPE]

Isa	18: 5 and the sour grape is **r** in the flower,	1580

RIPHATH (2)

Ge	10: 3 Ashkenaz, and **R**, and Togarmah.	7384
1Ch	1: 6 Ashchenaz, and **R**, and Togarmah.	7384

RIPT (3) [RIP]

2Ki	15:16 therein that were with child he **r up**.	1234
Hos	13:16 and their women with child shall be **r up**.	1234
Am	1:13 they have **r up** the women with child at	1234

RISE (142) [ARISE, ARISETH, ARISING, AROSE, RISEN, RISEST, RISETH, RISING, ROSE, SUNRISING]

Ge	2: ye shall **r up early**, and go on your ways.	7925
	31:35 my lord that I cannot **r** up before thee;	6965
Ex	8:20 **R up early** in the morning,	7925
	9:13 **R up early** in the morning,	7925
	12:31 **R up**, *and* get you forth from amongst my	6965
	21:19 If he **r again**, and walk abroad upon his	6965
Lev	19:32 Thou shalt **r up** before the hoary head,	6965
Nu	10:35 **R up**, Lord, and let thine enemies be	6965
	22:20 to call thee, **r up**, *and* go with them;	6965
	23:18 and said, **R up**, Balak, and hear;	6965
	23:24 the people shall **r up** as a great lion,	6965
	24:17 a Sceptre shall **r** out of Israel,	6965
Dt	2:13 Now **r up**, *said I*, and get you over	6965
	2:24 **R** ye up, take your journey, and pass over	6965
	19:11 **r up** against him, and smite him mortally	6965
	19:15 One witness shall not **r up** against a man	6965
	19:16 If a false witness **r up** against any man to	6965
	28: 7 **r up** against thee *to be* smitten before thy	6965
	29:22 of your children that shall **r up** after you,	6965
	31:16 this people will **r up**, and go a whoring	6965
	32:38 let them **r up** and help you, *and* be your	6965
	33:11 smite through the loins of them that **r**	6965
	33:11 them that hate him, that they **r** not again.	6965
Jos	8: 7 ye shall **r up** from the ambush,	6965
	18: 4 they shall **r**, and go through the land,	6965
Jdg	8:21 Zalmunna said, **R** thou, and fall upon us:	6965
	9:33 thou shalt **r early**, and set upon the city:	7925
	20:38 **make** a great flame with smoke **r up** out	5927
1Sa	22:13 that *he* should **r** against me, to lie in wait,	6965
	24: 7 and suffered them not to **r** against Saul.	6965
	29:10 now **r up early** in the morning	7925
2Sa	12:21 was dead, thou didst **r** and eat bread.	6965
	18:32 all that **r** against thee to do thee hurt, be	6965
2Ki	16: 7 the king of Israel, which **r up** against me.	6965
Ne	2:18 they said, Let us **r up** and build. So they	6965
Job	20:27 and the earth shall **r up** against him.	6965
	30:12 Upon *my* right hand the youth; they	6965
Ps	3: 1 many *are* they that **r up** against me.	6965
	17: 7 from those that **r up** *against them*.	6965
	18:38 them that were not able to **r**:	6965
	18:48 thou liftest me up above those that **r up**	6965
	27: 3 though war should **r** against me, in this	6965
	35:11 False witnesses did **r up**; they laid to my	6965
	36:12 are cast down, and shall not be able to **r**.	6965
	41: 8 *now* that he lieth he shall **r up** no more.	6965
	44: 5 we tread them under that **r up** against us.	6965
	59: 1 me from them that **r up** against me.	6965
	74:23 the tumult of those that **r up** against thee	6965
	92:11 *desire* of the wicked that **r up** against me.	6965
	94:16 Who will **r up** for me against	6965
	119:62 At midnight I will **r** to give thanks unto	6965
	127: 2 It *is* vain for you to **r up** early, to sit up	7925
	139:21 am not I grieved with those that **r up**	8618
	140:10 into deep pits, *that* they **r** not **up again**.	6965
Pr	24:22 For their calamity shall **r** suddenly;	6965
	28:12 but when the wicked **r**, a man is hidden.	6965
	28:28 the wicked **r**, men hide themselves:	6965
Ecc	10: 4 If the spirit of the ruler **r up** against thee,	5927
	12: 4 he shall **r up** at the voice of the bird,	6965
SS	2:10 **R up**, my love, my fair one,	6965
	3: 2 I will **r** now, and go about the city in	6965
Isa	5:11 Woe unto them that **r up early** in	7925
	14:21 that they do not **r**, nor possess the land,	6965
	14:22 For I will **r up** against them, saith	6965
	24:20 upon it; and it shall fall, and not **r again**.	6965
	26:14 live; *they are* deceased, they shall not **r**:	6965
	28:21 For the Lord shall **r up** as *in* mount	6965
	32: 9 **R up**, ye women that are at ease, hear my	6965
	33:10 Now will I **r**, saith the Lord; now will I	6965
	43:17 shall lie down together, they shall not **r**:	6965
	54:17 every tongue *that* shall **r** against thee in	6965
	58:10 shall thy light **r** in obscurity,	2224
Jer	25:27 spue, and fall, and **r** no more, because	6965
	37:10 should they **r up** every man in his tent,	6965
	47: 2 waters **r up** out of the north, and shall be	5927

R

Jer	49:14 come against her, and **r** up to the battle.	6965
	51: 1 in the midst of them that **r** up against me,	6965
	51:64 shall not **r** from the evil that I *will* bring	6965
La	1:14 *from whom* I am not able to **r** up.	6965
Da	7:24 another shall **r** after them; and he shall be	6966
Am	5: 2 of Israel is fallen; she shall no more **r**:	6965
	7: 9 I will **r** against the house of Jeroboam	6965
	8: 8 it shall **r** up wholly as a flood; and it shall	5927
	8:14 even they shall fall, and never **r** up again.	6965
	9: 5 it shall **r** up wholly like a flood;	5927
Ob	1: 1 and let us **r** up against her in battle.	6965
Na	1: 9 affliction shall not **r** up the second time.	6965
Hab	2: 7 Shall they not **r** up suddenly that *shall*	6965
Zep	3: 8 until the day that I **r** up to the prey:	6965
Zec	14:13 his hand shall **r** up against the hand of his	5927
Mt	5:45 for he **maketh** his sun to **r** on the evil and	393
	10:21 the children shall **r** up against *their*	1881
	12:41 *The* men of Nineveh shall **r** in judgment	450
	12:42 *The* queen of the south shall **r** up in	1453
	20:19 and the third day he shall **r** again.	450
	24: 7 For nation shall **r** against nation,	1453
	24:11 And many false prophets shall **r**,	1453
	26:46 **R**, let us be going: behold, he is at hand	1453
	27:63 yet alive, After three days I will **r** *again*.	1453
Mk	3:26 And if Satan **r** up against himself,	450
	4:27 and **r** night and day, and the seed should	1453
	8:31 and be killed, and after three days **r**	450
	9:31 that he is killed, he shall **r** the third day.	450
	10:34 kill him: and the third day he shall **r** again.	450
	10:49 saying unto him, Be of good comfort, **r**;	1453
	12:23 resurrection therefore, when they shall **r**,	450
	12:25 For when they shall **r** from the dead,	450
	12:26 And as touching the dead, that they **r**:	1453
	13: 8 For nation shall **r** against nation,	1453
	13:12 children shall **r** up against *their* parents,	1881
	13:22 For false Christs and false prophets shall **r**,	1453
	14:42 **R** up, let us go; lo, he that betrayeth me is	1453
Lk	5:23 forgiven thee; or to say, **R** up and walk?	1453
	6: 8 **R** up, and stand *forth* in the midst.	1453
	11: 7 with me in bed; I cannot **r** and give thee?	450
	11: 8 Though he will not **r** and give him,	450
	11: 8 because of his importunity he will **r** and	450
	11:31 *The* queen of the south shall **r** up in	1453
	11:32 *The* men of Nineveh shall **r** up in	450
	12:54 When ye see a cloud **r** out of the west,	393
	18:33 death: and the third day he shall **r** again.	450
	21:10 Nation shall **r** against nation,	1453
	22:46 **r** and pray, lest ye enter into temptation.	450
	24: 7 be crucified, and the third day **r** again.	450
	24:46 and to **r** from the dead the third day:	450
Jn	5: 8 unto him, **R**, take up thy bed, and walk.	1453
	11:23 saith unto her, Thy brother shall **r** again.	450
	11:24 I know that he shall **r** again in	450
	20: 9 that he must **r** again from the dead.	450
Ac	3: 6 the name of Jesus Christ of Nazareth **r** up	1453
	10:13 And there came a voice to him, **R**, Peter;	450
	26:16 But **r**, and stand upon thy feet: for I have	450
	26:23 he *should* be the first *that* should **r** from	386
Ro	15:12 he that shall **r** to reign over the Gentiles;	450
1Co	15:15 raised not up, if so be that the dead **r** not.	1453
	15:16 For if the dead **r** not, then is not Christ	1453
	15:29 for the dead, if the dead **r** not at all?	1453
	15:32 what advantageth it me, if the dead **r** not?	1453
1Th	4:16 of God: and the dead in Christ shall **r** first:	450
Heb	7:11 should **r** after the order of Melchisedec,	450
Rev	11: 1 **R**, and measure the temple of God,	1453
	13: 1 and saw a beast **r** up out of the sea,	305

RISEN (51) [RISE]

Ge	19:23 The sun was **r** upon the earth when Lot	3318
Ex	22: 3 If the sun be **r** upon him, *there shall be*	2224
Nu	32:14 ye are **r** up in your fathers' stead,	6965
Jdg	9:18 ye are **r** up against my father's house *this*	6965
Ru	2:15 when she was **r** up to glean, Boaz	6965
1Sa	25:29 Yet a man is **r** to pursue thee, and to seek	6965
2Sa	14: 7 the whole family is **r** against thine	6965
1Ki	8:20 am **r** up in the room of David my father,	6965
2Ki	6:15 the servant of the man of God was **r**	6965
2Ch	6:10 for I am **r** up in the room of David my	6965
	13: 6 is **r** up, and hath rebelled against his lord.	6965
	21: 4 Now when Jehoram was **r** up to	6965
Ps	20: 8 fallen: but we are **r**, and stand upright.	6965
	27:12 for false witnesses are **r** up against me,	6965
	54: 3 For strangers are **r** up against me,	6965
	86:14 the proud are **r** against me,	6965
Isa	60: 1 and the glory of the LORD is **r** upon thee.	2224
Eze	7:11 Violence is **r** up into a rod of wickedness:	6965
	47: 5 for the waters were **r**, waters to swim in,	1342
Mic	2: 8 Even of late my people is **r** up as an	6965
Mt	11:11 hath not **r** a greater than John the Baptist:	1453
	14: 2 he is **r** from the dead; and therefore	1453
	17: 9 the Son of man be **r** again from the dead.	1453
	26:32 But after I am **r** *again*, I will go before you	1453
	27:64 unto the people, He is **r** from the dead:	1453
	28: 6 he is **r**, as he said. Come, see the place	1453
	28: 7 tell his disciples that he is **r** from the dead;	1453
Mk	6:14 That John the Baptist was **r** from the dead,	1453
	6:16 whom I beheaded: he is **r** from the dead.	1453
	9: 9 the Son of man were **r** from the dead.	450
	14:28 But after that I am **r**, I will go before you	1453
	16: 6 he is **r**; he is not here: behold the place	1453
	16: 9 when *Jesus* was **r** early the first *day* of	450
	16:14 them which had seen him after he was **r**.	1453
Lk	7:16 That a great prophet is **r** up among us;	1453
	9: 7 of some, that John was **r** from the	1453

Lk	9: 8 that one of the old prophets was **r** again.	450
	9:19 that one of the old prophets was **r** again.	450
	13:25 once the master of the house is **r** up,	1453
	24: 6 He is not here, but is **r**: remember how he	1453
	24:34 The Lord is **r** indeed, and hath appeared to	1453
Jn	2:22 When therefore he was **r** from the dead,	1453
	21:14 after that he was **r** from the dead.	1453
Ac	17: 3 have suffered, and **r** again from the dead;	450
Ro	8:34 is **r** again, who is even at the right hand	1453
1Co	15:13 of the dead, then is Christ not **r**:	1453
	15:14 And if Christ be not **r**, then *is* our	1453
	15:20 But now is Christ **r** from the dead,	1453
Col	2:12 wherein also you are **r** with *him* through	4891
	3: 1 If ye then be **r** with Christ, seek those	4891
Jas	1:11 For the sun is no sooner **r** with a burning	393

RISEST (2) [RISE]

Dt	6: 7 thou liest down, and when thou **r** up.	6965
	11:19 thou liest down, and when thou **r** up.	6965

RISETH (14) [RISE]

Dt	22:26 as when a man **r** against his neighbour,	6965
Jos	6:26 that **r** up and buildeth this city Jericho:	6965
2Sa	23: 4 *when* the sun **r**, *even* a morning without	2224
Job	9: 7 Which commandeth the sun, and it **r** not;	2224
	14:12 So man lieth down, and **r** not: till	6965
	24:22 he **r** up, and no *man* is sure of life.	6965
	27: 7 that **r** up against me as the unrighteous.	6965
	31:14 What then shall I do when God **r** up?	6965
Pr	24:16 falleth seven *times*, and **r** up *again*: but	6965
	31:15 She **r** also while *it is* yet night,	6965
Isa	47:11 thou shalt not know from whence it **r**:	7837
Jer	46: 8 Egypt **r** up like a flood, and *his* waters are	5927
Mic	7: 6 the daughter **r** up against her mother,	6965
Jn	13: 4 He **r** from supper, and laid aside his	1453

RISING (39) [RISE]

Lev	13: 2 man shall have in the skin of his flesh a **r**,	7613
	13:10 if the **r** be white in the skin, and it have	7613
	13:10 and *there be* quick raw flesh in the **r**;	7613
	13:19 in the place of the boil there be a white **r**,	7613
	13:28 it *is* a **r** of the burning, and the priest shall	7613
	13:43 if the **r** of the sore *be* white reddish in his	7613
	14:56 a **r**, and for a scab, and for a bright spot:	7613
Nu	2: 3 on the east side toward the **r of the sun**	4217
Jos	12: 1 *other* side Jordan toward the **r** of the sun,	4217
2Ch	36:15 messengers, **r** up betimes, and sending;	7925
Ne	4:21 half of them held the spears from the **r** of	5927
Job	16: 8 my leanness **r** up in me beareth witness	6965
	24: 5 forth to their work; **r** betimes for a prey:	7836
	24:14 The murderer **r** with the light killeth	6965
Ps	50: 1 called the earth from the **r** of the sun unto	4217
	113: 3 From the **r** of the sun unto the going	4217
Pr	27:14 **r** early in the morning, it shall be counted	7925
	30:31 a king, against whom *there is* no **r** up.	510
Isa	41:25 from the **r** of the sun shall he call upon	4217
	45: 6 they may know from the **r** of the sun,	4217
	59:19 and his glory from the **r** of the sun.	4217
	60: 3 and kings to the brightness of thy **r**.	2225
Jer	7:13 **r** up early and speaking, but ye heard not	7925
	7:25 daily **r** up early and sending *them*:	7925
	11: 7 **r** early and protesting, saying, Obey my	7925
	25: 3 spoken unto you, **r** early and speaking;	7925
	25: 4 **r** early and sending *them*; but ye have	7925
	26: 5 both **r** up early, and sending *them*, but	7925
	29:19 **r** up early and sending *them*; but ye	7925
	32:33 **r** up early and teaching *them*, yet they	7925
	35:14 spoken unto you, **r** early and speaking;	7925
	35:15 **r** up early and sending *them*, saying,	7925
	44: 4 **r** early and sending *them*, saying,	7925
La	3:63 Behold their sitting down, and their **r** up;	7012
Mal	1:11 For from the **r** of the sun even unto	4217
Mk	1:35 **r** up a great while before day, he went out,	450
	9:10 questioning *one* with *another* what the **r**	450
	16: 2 they came unto the sepulchre at the **r** of	393
Lk	2:34 for the fall and **r** again of many in Israel;	386

RISKED See HAZARDED; JEOPARDED

RISSAH (2)

Nu	33:21 removed from Libnah, and pitched at **R**.	7446
	33:22 they journeyed from **R**, and pitched in	7446

RITES (1)

Nu	9: 3 according to all the **r** of it, and according	2708

RITHMAH (2)

Nu	33:18 departed from Hazeroth, and pitched in **R**.	7575
	33:19 they departed from **R**, and pitched at	7575

RIVAL See VEX; VEXATION; VEXED

RIVER (176) [RIVER'S, RIVERS]

Ge	2:10 a **r** went out of Eden to water the garden;	5104
	2:13 the name of the second **r** *is* Gihon:	5104
	2:14 the name of the third **r** *is* Hiddekel: that	5104
	2:14 of Assyria. And the fourth **r** *is* Euphrates.	5104
	15:18 from the **r** of Egypt unto the great river,	5104
	15:18 from the river of Egypt unto the great **r**,	5104
	15:18 unto the great river, the **r** Euphrates:	5104
	31:21 passed over the **r**, and set his face *toward*	5104
	36:37 Saul of Rehoboth *by* the **r** reigned in his	5104
	41: 1 and behold, he stood by the **r**.	2975
	41: 2 there came up out of the **r** seven well	2975
	41: 3 kine came up after them out of the **r**,	2975
	41: 3 by the *other* kine upon the brink of the **r**.	2975

Ge	41:17 behold, I stood upon the bank of the **r**:	2975
	41:18 there came up out of the **r** seven kine,	2975
Ex	1:22 son that is born ye shall cast into the **r**,	2975
	2: 5 came down to wash *herself* at the **r**;	2975
	4: 9 that thou shalt take of the water of the **r**	2975
	4: 9 the water which thou takest out of the **r**	2975
	7:17 hand upon the waters which *are* in the **r**,	2975
	7:18 the fish that *is* in the **r** shall die,	2975
	7:18 in the river shall die, and the **r** shall stink;	2975
	7:18 shall lothe to drink of the water of the **r**.	2975
	7:20 and smote the waters that *were* in the **r**,	2975
	7:20 the waters that *were* in the **r** were turned	2975
	7:21 fish that *was* in the **r** died; and the river	2975
	7:21 the **r** stunk, and the Egyptians could not	2975
	7:21 could not drink of the water of the **r**;	2975
	7:24 the Egyptians digged round about the **r**	2975
	7:24 could not drink of the water of the **r**.	2975
	7:25 after *that* the LORD had smitten the **r**.	2975
	8: 3 the **r** shall bring forth frogs abundantly,	2975
	8: 9 *that* they may remain in the **r** only?	2975
	8:11 people; they shall remain in the **r** only.	2975
	17: 5 thy rod, wherewith thou smotest the **r**,	2975
	23:31 and from the desert unto the **r**:	5104
Nu	22: 5 which *is* by the **r** of the land of the	5104
	24: 6 spread forth, as gardens by the **r** side,	5104
	34: 5 compass from Azmon unto the **r** of Egypt,	5158
Dt	1: 7 unto Lebanon, unto the great **r**, the river	5104
	1: 7 unto the great river, the **r** Euphrates.	5104
	2:24 your journey, and pass over the **r** Arnon:	5158
	2:36 which *is* by the brink of the **r** of Arnon,	5158
	2:36 *from* the city that *is* by the **r**, even unto	5158
	2:37 nor unto any place of the **r** Jabbok,	5158
	3: 8 from the **r** of Arnon unto mount Hermon,	5158
	3:12 which *is* by the **r** Arnon, and half mount	5158
	3:16 I gave from Gilead even unto the **r** Arnon,	5158
	3:16 and the border, even unto the **r** Jabbok,	5158
	4:48 which *is* by the bank of the **r** Arnon,	5158
	11:24 the wilderness and Lebanon, from the **r**,	5104
	11:24 from the river, the **r** Euphrates,	5104
Jos	1: 4 and this Lebanon even unto the great **r**,	5104
	1: 4 **r** Euphrates, all the land of the Hittites,	5104
	12: 1 from the **r** Arnon unto mount Hermon,	5158
	12: 2 which *is* upon the bank of the **r** of Arnon,	5158
	12: 2 *from* the middle of the **r**, and *from* half	5158
	12: 2 *from* half Gilead, even unto the **r** Jabbok,	5158
	13: 9 that *is* upon the bank of the **r** of Arnon,	5158
	13: 9 and the city that *is* in the midst of the **r**,	5158
	13:16 that *is* on the bank of the **r** Arnon,	5158
	13:16 and the city that *is* in the midst of the **r**,	5158
	15: 4 and went out *unto* the **r** of Egypt;	5158
	15: 7 which *is* on the south side of the **r**:	5158
	15:47 unto the **r** of Egypt, and the great sea,	5158
	16: 8 Tappuah westward *unto* the **r** Kanah:	5158
	17: 9 the coast descended *unto* the **r** Kanah,	5158
	17: 9 *unto* the river Kanah, southward of the **r**:	5158
	17: 9 also *was* on the north side of the **r**,	5158
	19:11 reached to the **r** that *is* before Jokneam;	5158
Jdg	4: 7 I will draw unto thee to the **r** Kishon	5158
	4:13 from Harosheth of the Gentiles unto the **r**	5158
	5:21 The **r** of Kishon swept them away,	5158
	5:21 away, *that* ancient **r**, the river Kishon.	5158
	5:21 away, *that* ancient river, the **r** Kishon.	5158
2Sa	8: 3 as he went to recover his border at the **r**:	5104
	10:16 out the Syrians that *were* beyond the **r**:	5104
	17:13 that city, and we will draw it into the **r**,	5104
	24: 5 city that *lieth* in the midst of the **r** of Gad,	5158
1Ki	4:21 from the **r** *unto* the land of the Philistines,	5104
	4:24 over all *the region* on *this* side the **r**,	5104
	4:24 over all the kings on *this* side the **r**,	5104
	8:65 from the entering in of Hamath unto the **r**	5158
	14:15 shall scatter them beyond the **r**, because	5104
2Ki	10:33 from Aroer, which *is* by the **r** Arnon,	5158
	17: 6 in Halah and in Habor *by* the **r** of Gozan,	5104
	18:11 in Halah and in Habor *by* the **r** of Gozan,	5104
	23:29 the king of Assyria to the **r** Euphrates:	5104
	24: 7 of Egypt unto the river Euphrates all that	5158
	24: 7 Euphrates all that pertained to the king	5104
1Ch	1:48 Shaul of Rehoboth *by* the **r** reigned in his	5104
	5: 9 in of the wilderness from the **r** Euphrates:	5104
	5:26 Habor, and Hara, and to the **r** Gozan,	5104
	18: 3 he went to stablish his dominion by the **r**	5104
	19:16 forth the Syrians that *were* beyond the **r**:	5104
2Ch	7: 8 from the entering in of Hamath unto the **r**	5104
	9:26 he reigned over all the kings from the **r**	5104
Ezr	4:10 the rest *that are* on *this* side the **r**,	5103
	4:11 Thy servants the men *on this* side the **r**,	5103
	4:16 shalt have no portion on *this* side the **r**.	5103
	4:17 Samaria, and unto the rest beyond the **r**,	5103
	4:20 ruled over all *countries* beyond the **r**;	5103
	5: 3 governor on *this* side the **r**,	5103
	5: 6 governor *on this* side the **r**,	5103
	5: 6 which *were* on *this* side the **r**, sent unto	5103
	6: 6 therefore, Tatnai, governor beyond the **r**,	5103
	6: 6 which *are* beyond the **r**, be ye far from	5103
	6: 8 *even* of the tribute beyond the **r**,	5103
	6:13 Tatnai, governor *on this* side the **r**,	5103
	7:21 all the treasurers *on this* side the **r**,	5103
	7:25 judge all the people that *are* beyond the **r**,	5103
	8:15 I gathered them together to the **r** that	5104
	8:21 I proclaimed a fast there, at the **r** Ahava,	5104
	8:31 we departed from the **r** of Ahava on	5104
	8:36 and to the governors on *this* side the **r**,	5104
Ne	2: 7 given me to the governors beyond the **r**,	5104
	2: 9 I came to the governors beyond the **r**,	5104
	3: 7 throne of the governor on *this* side the **r**.	5104

Job	40:23 he drinketh up a **r**, *and* hasteth not:	5104
Ps	36: 8 thou shalt make them drink *of* the **r** of	5158
	46: 4 *There is* a **r**, the streams whereof shall	5104
	65: 9 greatly enrichest it *with* the **r** of God,	6388
	72: 8 and from the **r** unto the ends of the earth.	5104
	80:11 unto the sea, and her branches unto the **r**.	5104
	105:41 they ran in the dry places like a **r**.	5104
Isa	7:20 by them beyond the **r**, by the king	5104
	8: 7 up upon them the waters of the **r**,	5104
	11:15 wind shall he shake over the **r**,	5104
	19: 5 and the **r** shall be wasted and dried up.	5104
	23: 3 the harvest of the **r**, *is* her revenue;	2975
	23:10 Pass through thy land as a **r**, O daughter	2975
	27:12 channel of the **r** unto the stream of Egypt,	5104
	48:18 had thy peace been as a **r**,	5104
	66:12 I will extend peace to her like a **r**,	5104
Jer	2:18 of Assyria, to drink the waters of the **r**?	5104
	17: 8 *that* spreadeth out her roots by the **r**,	3105
	46: 2 which was by the **r** Euphrates,	5104
	46: 6 fall toward the north by the **r** Euphrates.	5104
	46:10 in the north country by the **r** Euphrates.	5104
La	2:18 let tears run down like a **r** day and night:	5158
Eze	1: 1 as I *was* among the captives by the **r** of	5104
	1: 3 in the land of the Chaldeans by the **r**	5104
	3:15 that dwelt by the **r** of Chebar, and I sat	5104
	3:23 as the glory which I saw by the **r** of	5104
	10:15 creature that I saw by the **r** of Chebar.	5104
	10:20 the God of Israel by the **r** of Chebar;	5104
	10:22 faces which I saw by the **r** of Chebar,	5104
	29: 3 My **r** *is* mine own, and I have made *it* for	2975
	29: 9 The **r** *is* mine, and I have made *it*.	2975
	43: 3 like the vision that I saw by the **r** Chebar;	5104
	47: 5 *and it was* a **r** that I could not pass over:	5158
	47: 5 swim in, a **r** that could not be passed over.	5158
	47: 6 caused me to return to the brink of the **r**.	5158
	47: 7 at the bank of the **r** *were* very many trees	5158
	47: 9 thing shall live whither the **r** cometh.	5158
	47:12 by the **r** upon the bank thereof, on this	5158
	47:19 of strife *in* Kadesh, *the* **r** to the great sea.	5159
	48:28 *and to the* **r** toward the great sea.	5159
Da	8: 2 in a vision, and I was by the **r** of Ulai.	180
	8: 3 stood before the **r** a ram which had two	180
	8: 6 which I had seen standing before the **r**,	180
	10: 4 as I was by the side of the great **r**, which	5104
	12: 5 the one on this side of the bank of the **r**,	2975
	12: 5 other on that side of the bank of the **r**.	2975
	12: 6 which *was* upon the waters of the **r**,	2975
	12: 7 which *was* upon the waters of the **r**,	2975
Am	6:14 in of Hemath unto the **r** of the wilderness.	5158
Mic	7:12 from the fortress even to the **r**,	5104
Zec	9:10 from the **r** *even* to the ends of the earth.	5104
	10:11 and all the deeps of the **r** shall dry up:	2975
Mk	1: 5 all baptized of him in the **r** *of* Jordan,	4215
Ac	16:13 we went out of the city by a **r** side,	4215
Rev	9:14 which are bound in the great **r** Euphrates.	4215
	16:12 out his vial upon the great **r** Euphrates.	4215
	22: 1 he shewed me a pure **r** of water of life,	4215
	22: 2 and of either side of the **r**, *was* there	4215

RIVER'S (3) [RIVER]

Ex	2: 3 she laid *it* in the flags by the **r** brink.	2975
	2: 5 her maidens walked along by the **r** side;	2975
	7:15 thou shalt stand by the **r** brink against he	2975

RIVERS (77) [RIVER]

Ex	7:19 upon their, **r** and upon their ponds,	2975
	8: 5 over the **r**, and over the ponds,	2975
Lev	11: 9 the seas, and in the **r**, them shall ye eat.	5158
	11:10 in the **r**, of all that move in the waters,	5158
Dt	10: 7 to Jotbath, a land of **r** of waters.	5158
2Ki	5:12 not Abana and Pharpar, **r** of Damascus,	5104
	19:24 I dried up all the **r** of besieged *places*.	2975
Job	20:17 He shall not see the **r**, the floods,	6390
	28:10 He cutteth out **r** among the rocks;	2975
	29: 6 and the rock poured me out **r** of oil;	6388
Ps	1: 3 he shall be like a tree planted by the **r** of	6388
	74:15 and the flood: thou driedst up mighty **r**.	5104
	78:16 and caused waters to run down like **r**.	5104
	78:44 had turned their **r** into blood;	2975
	89:25 in the sea, and his right hand in the **r**.	5104
	107:33 He turneth **r** into a wilderness,	5104
	119:136 **R** of waters run down mine eyes, because	6388
	137: 1 By the **r** of Babylon, there we sat down,	5104
Pr	5:16 *and* **r** of waters in the streets.	6388
	21: 1 the hand of the LORD, *as the* **r** of water:	6388
Ecc	1: 7 All the **r** run into the sea; yet the sea *is*	5158
	1: 7 unto the place from whence the **r** come,	5158
SS	5:12 His eyes *are as the eyes of* doves by the **r**	650
Isa	7:18 *is* in the uttermost part of the **r** of Egypt,	2975
	18: 1 which *is* beyond the **r** of Ethiopia:	5104
	18: 2 whose land the **r** have spoiled.	5104
	18: 7 foot, whose land the **r** have spoiled,	5104
	19: 6 they shall turn the **r** far away;	5104
	30:25 **r** and streams of waters in the day of	6388
	32: 2 as **r** of water in a dry place, as the shadow	6388
	33:21 LORD *will be* unto us a place of broad **r**	5104
	37:25 I dried up all the **r** of the besieged *places*.	2975
	41:18 I will open **r** in high places,	5104
	42:15 I will make the **r** islands, and I will dry up	5104
	43: 2 through the **r**, they shall not overflow	5104
	43:19 in the wilderness, *and* **r** in the desert.	5104
	43:20 *and* **r** in the desert, to give drink to my	5104
	44:27 the deep, Be dry, and I will dry up thy **r**:	5104
	47: 2 leg, uncover the thigh, pass over the **r**.	5104
	50: 2 dry up the sea, I make the **r** a wilderness:	5104

Jer	31: 9 will cause them to walk by the **r** of waters	5158
	46: 7 a flood, whose waters are moved as the **r**?	5104
	46: 8 and *his* waters are moved like the **r**;	5104
La	3:48 Mine eye runneth down *with* **r** of water	6388
Eze	6: 3 to the hills, to the **r**, and to the valleys;	650
	29: 3 dragon that lieth in the midst of his **r**,	2975
	29: 4 I will cause the fish of thy **r** to stick unto	2975
	29: 4 bring thee up out of the midst of thy **r**,	2975
	29: 4 all the fish of thy **r** shall stick unto thy	2975
	29: 5 thee and all the fish of thy **r**:	2975
	29:10 against thy **r**, and I will make the land of	2975
	30:12 I will make the **r** dry, and sell the land	2975
	31: 4 the deep set him up on high with her **r**	5104
	31: 4 sent out her **little r** unto all the trees of	8585
	31:12 his boughs are broken by all the **r** of	650
	32: 2 thou camest forth with thy **r**,	5104
	32: 2 waters with thy feet, and fouledst their **r**.	5104
	32: 6 mountains; and the **r** shall be full of thee.	650
	32:14 cause their **r** to run like oil, saith the Lord	5104
	34:13 upon the mountains of Israel by the **r**,	650
	35: 8 thy valleys, and in all thy **r**, shall they fall	650
	36: 4 to the hills, to the **r**, and to the valleys,	650
	36: 6 to the hills, to the **r**, and to the valleys,	650
	47: 9 whithersoever the **r** shall come, shall live:	5158
Joel	1:20 the **r** of waters are dried up, and the fire	650
	3:18 all the **r** of Judah shall flow *with* waters,	650
Mic	6: 7 of rams, *or* with ten thousands of **r** of oil?	5158
Na	1: 4 and maketh it dry, and drieth up all the **r**:	5104
	2: 6 The gates of the **r** shall be opened,	5104
	3: 8 No, that was situate among the **r**,	2975
Hab	3: 8 Was the LORD displeased against the **r**?	5104
	3: 8 *was* thine anger against the **r**? *was* thy	5104
	3: 9 Selah. Thou didst cleave the earth with **r**.	5104
Zep	3:10 From beyond the **r** of Ethiopia my	5104
Jn	7:38 out of his belly shall flow **r** of living water.	4215
Rev	8:10 and it fell upon the third *part* of the **r**,	4215
	16: 4 third angel poured out his vial upon the **r**	4215

RIZIA See REZIA

RIZPAH (4)

2Sa	3: 7 whose name *was* **R**, the daughter of Aiah:	7532
	21: 8 the king took the two sons of **R**	7532
	21:10 **R** the daughter of Aiah took sackcloth,	7532
	21:11 it was told David what **R** the daughter of	7532

ROAD (1)

1Sa	27:10 Whither have ye **made a r** to day?	6584

ROAR (23) [ROARED, ROARETH, ROARING, ROARINGS]

1Ch	16:32 Let the sea **r**, and the fulness thereof:	7481
Ps	46: 3 *Though* the waters thereof **r** and	1993
	74: 4 Thine enemies **r** in the midst of thy	7580
	96:11 let the sea **r**, and the fulness thereof.	7481
	98: 7 Let the sea **r**, and the fulness thereof;	7481
	104:21 young lions **r** after *their* prey, and seek	7580
Isa	5:29 like a lion, they shall **r** like young lions:	7580
	5:29 they shall **r**, and lay hold of the prey,	5098
	5:30 in that day they shall **r** against them like	5098
	42:13 he shall cry, yea, **r**; he shall prevail against	6873
	59:11 We **r** all like bears, and mourn sore like	1993
Jer	5:22 they **r**, yet can they not pass over it?	1993
	25:30 The LORD shall **r** from on high,	7580
	25:30 he shall **mightily r** upon his	7580+7580
	31:35 the sea when the waves thereof **r**;	1993
	50:42 their voice shall **r** like the sea,	1993
	51:38 They shall **r** together like lions: they shall	7580
	51:55 when her waves do **r** like great waters,	1993
Hos	11:10 he shall **r** like a lion: when he shall roar,	7580
	11:10 when he shall **r**, then the children shall	7580
Joel	3:16 The LORD also shall **r** out of Zion,	7580
Am	1: 2 The LORD will **r** from Zion, and utter his	7580
	3: 4 Will a lion **r** in the forest, when he hath	7580

ROARED (5) [ROAR]

Jdg	14: 5 behold, a young lion **r** against him.	7580
Ps	38: 8 I have **r** by reason of the disquietness of	7580
Isa	51:15 that divided the sea, whose waves **r**:	1993
Jer	2:15 The young lions **r** upon him, *and* yelled,	7580
Am	3: 8 The lion hath **r**, who will not fear?	7580

ROARETH (3) [ROAR]

Job	37: 4 After it a voice **r**: he thundereth with	7580
Jer	6:23 their voice **r** like the sea; and they ride	1993
Rev	10: 3 cried with a loud voice, as *when* a lion **r**:	3455

ROARING (16) [ROAR]

Job	4:10 The **r** of the lion, and the voice of the	7581
Ps	22: 1 helping me, *and from* the words of my **r**?	7581
	22:13 their mouths, *as* a ravening and a **r** lion.	7580
	32: 3 my bones waxed old through my **r** all	7581
Pr	19:12 The king's wrath *is* as the **r** of a lion;	5099
	20: 2 The fear of a king *is* as the **r** of a lion:	5099
	28:15 As a **r** lion, and a ranging bear; so *is* a	5099
Isa	5:29 Their **r** *shall* be like a lion, they shall roar	7581
	5:30 roar against them like the **r** of the sea:	5100
	31: 4 the lion and the young lion **r** on his prey,	1897
Eze	19: 7 the fulness thereof, by the noise of his **r**.	7581
	22:25 like a **r** lion ravening the prey;	7580
Zep	3: 3 Her princes within her *are* **r** lions;	7580
Zec	11: 3 a voice of the **r** of young lions;	7581
Lk	21:25 with perplexity; the sea and the waves **r**;	2278
1Pe	5: 8 the devil, as a **r** lion, walketh about,	5612

ROARINGS (1) [ROAR]

Job	3:24 and my **r** are poured out like the waters.	7581

ROAST (5) [ROASTED, ROASTETH]

Ex	12: 8 **r** with fire, and unleavened bread;	6748
	12: 9 sodden at all with water, but **r** with fire;	6748
Dt	16: 7 thou shalt **r** and eat *it* in the place which	1310
1Sa	2:15 Give flesh to **r** for the priest;	6740
Isa	44:16 eateth flesh; he roasteth **r**, and is satisfied:	6748

ROASTED (3) [ROAST]

2Ch	35:13 they **r** the passover with fire according to	1310
Isa	44:19 I have **r** flesh, and eaten *it*: and shall I	6740
Jer	29:22 whom the king of Babylon **r** in the fire;	7033

ROASTETH (2) [ROAST]

Pr	12:27 The slothful *man* **r** not that which he	2760
Isa	44:16 he eateth flesh; he **r** roast, and is satisfied:	6740

ROB (8) [ROBBED, ROBBER, ROBBERS, ROBBERY, ROBBETH]

Lev	19:13 neither **r** *him*: the wages of him that is	1497
	26:22 which shall **r** you of your **children**,	7921
1Sa	23: 1 and they **r** the threshingfloors.	8154
Pr	22:22 **R** not the poor, because he *is* poor:	1497
Isa	10: 2 prey, and that they may **r** the fatherless:	962
	17:14 that spoil us, and the lot of them that **r** us.	962
Eze	39:10 **r** those that robbed them, saith the Lord	962
Mal	3: 8 Will a man **r** God? Yet ye *have* robbed me.	6906

ROBBED (13) [ROB]

Jdg	9:25 they **r** all that came along *that* way by	1497
2Sa	17: 8 as a bear **r** of her whelps in the field:	7909
Ps	119:61 The bands of the wicked have **r** me:	5749
Pr	17:12 Let a bear **r** of her whelps meet a man,	7909
Isa	10:13 have **r** their treasures, and I have put	8154
	42:22 this *is* a people **r** and spoiled; *they are* all	962
Jer	50:37 is upon her treasures; and they shall be **r**.	962
Eze	33:15 give again that he had **r**, walk in	1500
	39:10 rob those that **r** them, saith the Lord GOD.	962
Mal	3: 8 ye say, Wherein have we **r** thee? *In* tithes	6906
	3: 8 ye say, Wherein have we **r** thee? In tithes	6906
	3: 9 have **r** me, *even* this whole nation.	6906
2Co	11: 8 I **r** other churches, taking wages *of them*,	4813

ROBBER (5) [ROB]

Job	5: 5 and the **r** swalloweth up their substance.	6782
	18: 9 heel, *and* the **r** shall prevail against him.	6782
Eze	18:10 If he beget a son *that is* a **r**, a shedder of	6530
Jn	10: 1 other way, the same is a thief and a **r**.	3027
	18:40 but Barabbas. Now Barabbas was a **r**.	3027

ROBBERS (11) [ROB]

Job	12: 6 The tabernacles of **r** prosper, and they	7703
Isa	42:24 gave Jacob for a spoil, and Israel to the **r**?	962
Jer	7:11 my name, become a den of **r** in your eyes?	6530
Eze	7:22 shall pollute my secret *place*: for the **r**	6530
Da	11:14 also the **r** of thy people shall exalt	1121+6530
Hos	6: 9 as troops *of* **r** wait for a man,	NIH
	7: 1 *and* the troop *of* **r** spoileth without.	NIH
Ob	1: 5 thee, if **r** by night, (how art thou cut off!)	7703
Jn	10: 8 ever came before me are thieves and **r**:	3027
Ac	19:37 which *are* neither **r** of churches, nor yet	2417
2Co	11:26 *in* perils of waters, *in* perils of **r**,	3027

ROBBERY (7) [ROB]

Ps	62:10 in oppression, and become not vain in **r**:	1498
Pr	21: 7 The **r** of the wicked shall destroy them;	7701
Isa	61: 8 love judgment, I hate **r** for burnt offering;	1498
Eze	22:29 **exercised r**, and have vexed the	1497+1498
Am	3:10 store up violence and **r** in their palaces.	7701
Na	3: 1 *is* all full *of* lies and **r**; the prey departeth	6563
Php	2: 6 thought it not **r** to be equal with God:	725

ROBBETH (1) [ROB]

Pr	28:24 Whoso **r** his father or his mother, and	1497

ROBE (26) [ROBES]

Ex	28: 4 a **r**, and a broidered coat, a mitre,	4598
	28:31 thou shalt make the **r** of the ephod all of	4598
	28:34 upon the hem of the **r** round about.	4598
	29: 5 the **r** of the ephod, and the ephod,	4598
	39:22 made the **r** of the ephod *of* woven work,	4598
	39:23 *there was* a hole in the midst of the **r**,	4598
	39:24 they made upon the hems of the **r**	4598
	39:25 the pomegranates upon the hem of the **r**,	4598
	39:26 round about the hem of the **r** to minister	4598
Lev	8: 7 clothed him with the **r**, and put the ephod	4598
1Sa	18: 4 Jonathan stript himself of the **r** that *was*	4598
	24: 4 and cut off the skirt of Saul's **r** privily.	4598
	24:11 see, yea see the skirt of thy **r** in mine hand:	4598
	24:11 for in that I cut off the skirt of thy **r**,	4598
1Ch	15:27 David *was* clothed with a **r** of fine linen,	4598
Job	29:14 my judgment *was* as a **r** and a diadem.	4598
Isa	22:21 I will clothe him with thy **r**,	3801
	61:10 he hath covered me with the **r** of	4598
Jnh	3: 6 he laid his **r** from him, and covered *him*	155
Mic	2: 8 ye pull off the **r** with the garment from	145
Mt	27:28 stripped him, and put on him a scarlet **r**.	5511
	27:31 they took the **r** off from him, and put his	5511
Lk	15:22 Bring forth the best **r**, and put *it* on him;	4749
	23:11 and arrayed him in a gorgeous **r**,	2066
Jn	19: 2 his head, and they put on him a purple **r**,	2440
	19: 5 the crown of thorns, and the purple **r**.	2440

R

ROBES (11) [ROBE]

2Sa 13:18	for with such **r** were the king's daughters	4598
1Ki 22:10	each on his throne, having put on *their* **r**,	899
22:30	enter into the battle; but put thou on thy **r**.	899
2Ch 18: 9	clothed in *their* **r**, and they sat in a void	899
18:29	will go to the battle; but put thou on thy **r**.	899
Eze 26:16	lay away their **r**, and put off their	4598
Lk 20:46	which desire to walk in long **r**,	4749
Rev 6:11	white **r** were given unto every one of	4749
7: 9	clothed with white **r**, and palms in their	4749
7:13	are these which are arrayed in white **r**?	4749
7:14	and have washed their **r**, and made them	4749

ROBOAM (2) [REHOBOAM]

Mt 1: 7	And Solomon begat **R**; and Roboam begat	4497
1: 7	and **R** begat Abia; and Abia begat Asa;	4497

ROCK (119) [ROCKS]

Ex 17: 6	I will stand before thee there upon the **r**	6697
17: 6	thou shalt smite the **r**, and there shall	6697
33:21	by me, and thou shalt stand upon a **r**:	6697
33:22	that I will put thee in a clift of the **r**,	6697
Nu 20: 8	and speak ye unto the **r** before their eyes;	5553
20: 8	bring forth to them water out of the **r**,	5553
20:10	the congregation together before the **r**,	5553
20:10	must we fetch you water out of this **r**?	5553
20:11	and with his rod he smote the **r** twice:	5553
24:21	and thou puttest thy nest in a **r**.	5553
Dt 8:15	who brought thee forth water out of the **r**	6697
32: 4	*He is* the **R**, his work *is* perfect: for all his	6697
32:13	he made him to suck honey out of the **r**,	6697
32:13	out of the rock, and oil out of the flinty **r**;	6697
32:15	lightly esteemed the **R** of his salvation.	6697
32:18	the **R** *that* begat thee thou art unmindful,	6697
32:30	except their **R** had sold them,	6697
32:31	For their **r** *is* not as our Rock, even our	6697
32:31	For their rock *is* not as our **R**, even our	6697
32:37	their gods, *their* **r** in whom they trusted,	6697
Jdg 1:36	up to Akrabbim, from the **r**, and upward.	5553
6:20	*cakes*, and lay *them* upon this **r**,	5553
6:21	and there rose up fire out of the **r**,	6697
6:26	the LORD thy God upon the top of this **r**,	4581
7:25	slew Oreb upon the **r** Oreb, and Zeeb	6697
13:19	and offered *it* upon a **r** unto the LORD:	6697
15: 8	and dwelt in the top of the **r** Etam.	6697
15:11	of Judah went to the top of the **r** Etam,	5553
15:13	cords, and brought him up from the **r**.	5553
20:45	fled toward the wilderness unto the **r** of	6697
20:47	fled to the wilderness unto the **r** Rimmon,	5553
20:47	and abode in the **r** Rimmon four months.	5553
21:13	of Benjamin that *were* in the **r** Rimmon,	5553
1Sa 2: 2	neither *is there* any **r** like our God.	6697
14: 4	*there was* a sharp **r** on the one side,	5553
14: 4	one side, and a sharp **r** on the other side:	5553
23:25	wherefore he came down *into* a **r**,	5553
2Sa 21:10	and spread it for her upon the **r**,	5553
22: 2	The LORD *is* my **r**, and my fortress,	5553
22: 3	The God of my **r**; in him will I trust: *he is*	6697
22:32	the LORD? and who *is* a **r**, save our God?	6697
22:47	blessed *be* my **r**; and exalted be the God	6697
22:47	be the God of the **r** of my salvation.	6697
23: 3	of Israel said, the **R** of Israel spake to me,	6697
1Ch 11:15	captains went down to the **r** to David,	5553
2Ch 25:12	brought them unto the top of the **r**,	5553
25:12	cast them down from the top of the **r**,	5553
Ne 9:15	forth water for them out of the **r**	5553
Job 14:18	and the **r** is swallowed out of his place.	6697
18: 4	shall the **r** be removed out of his place?	6697
19:24	an iron pen and lead in the **r** for ever!	6697
24: 8	and embrace the **r** for want of a shelter.	6697
28: 9	He putteth forth his hand upon the **r**;	2496
29: 6	and he poured me out rivers of oil;	6697
39: 1	when the wild goats of the **r** bring forth?	5553
39:28	She dwelleth and abideth on the **r**, upon	5553
39:28	the crag of the **r**, and the strong place.	5553
Ps 18: 2	The LORD *is* my **r**, and my fortress,	5553
18:31	the LORD? or who *is* a **r** save our God?	6697
18:46	blessed *be* my **r**; and let the God of my	6697
27: 5	he hide me; he shall set me up upon a **r**.	6697
28: 1	Unto thee will I cry, O LORD, my **r**;	6697
31: 2	thou my strong **r**, for a house of defence	6697
31: 3	thou *art* my **r** and my fortress; therefore	5553
40: 2	set my feet upon a **r**, *and* established my	5553
42: 9	I will say unto God my **r**, Why hast thou	5553
61: 2	lead me to the **r** *that* is higher than I.	6697
62: 2	He only *is* my **r** and my salvation; *he is*	6697
62: 6	He only *is* my **r** and my salvation: *he is*	6697
62: 7	the **r** of my strength, *and* my refuge, *is* in	6697
71: 3	for thou *art* my **r** and my fortress.	6697
78:16	He brought streams also out of the **r**,	5553
78:20	Behold, he smote the **r**, that the waters	6697
78:35	they remembered that God *was* their **r**,	6697
81:16	*with* honey out of the **r** should I have	6697
89:26	my God, and the **r** of my salvation.	6697
92:15	*is* my **r**, and *there is* no unrighteousness	6697
94:22	and my God *is* the **r** of my refuge.	6697
95: 1	let us make a joyful noise to the **r** of our	6697
105:41	He opened the **r**, and the waters gushed	6697
114: 8	Which turned the **r** *into* a standing water,	6697
Pr 30:19	in the air; the way of a serpent upon a **r**;	6697
SS 2:14	O my dove, *that art* in the clefts of the **r**,	5553
Isa 2:10	Enter into the **r**, and hide thee in the dust,	6697
8:14	for a **r** of offence to both the houses of	6697
10:26	to the slaughter of Midian at the **r** Oreb:	6697
17:10	hast not been mindful of the **r** of thy	6697

Isa 22:16	graveth a habitation for himself in a **r**?	5553
32: 2	as the shadow of a great **r** in a weary land.	5553
42:11	let the inhabitants of the **r** sing, let them	5553
48:21	he caused the waters to flow out of the **r**	6697
48:21	he clave the **r** also, and the waters gushed	6697
51: 1	look unto the **r** *whence* ye are hewn,	6697
Jer 5: 3	have made their faces harder than a **r**;	5553
13: 4	and hide it there in a hole of the **r**.	5553
18:14	*which cometh* from the **r** of the field?	6697
21:13	*and* **r** of the plain, saith the LORD;	6697
23:29	a hammer *that* breaketh the **r** in pieces?	5553
48:28	dwell in the **r**, and be like the dove *that*	5553
49:16	O thou that dwellest in the clefts of the **r**,	5553
Eze 24: 7	she set it upon the top of a **r**; she poured	5553
24: 8	I have set her blood upon the top of a **r**,	5553
26: 4	her, and make her like the top of a **r**.	5553
26:14	I will make thee like the top of a **r**:	5553
Am 6:12	horses run upon the **r**? will *one* plow	5553
Ob 1: 3	thou that dwellest in the clefts of the **r**,	5553
Mt 7:24	wise man, which built his house upon a **r**:	4073
7:25	it fell not: for it was founded upon a **r**.	4073
16:18	and upon this **r** I will build my church;	4073
27:60	tomb, which he had hewn out in the **r**:	4073
Mk 15:46	a sepulchre which was hewn out of a **r**,	4073
Lk 6:48	deep, and laid the foundation on a **r**:	4073
6:48	not shake it: for it was founded upon a **r**.	4073
8: 6	And some fell upon a **r**; and as soon as it	4073
8:13	They on the **r** *are they*, which, when they	4073
Ro 9:33	in Sion a stumblingstone and **r** of offence:	4073
1Co 10: 4	for they drank of *that* spiritual **R** that	4073
10: 4	and followed *them*: and *that* **R** was Christ.	4073
1Pe 2: 8	a stone of stumbling, and a **r** of offence,	4073

ROCKS (23) [ROCK]

Nu 23: 9	For from the top of the **r** I see him,	6697
1Sa 13: 6	and in **r**, and in high places, and in pits.	5553
24: 2	and his men upon the **r** of the wild goats.	6697
1Ki 19:11	brake in pieces the **r** before the LORD;	6697
Job 28:10	He cutteth out rivers among the **r**;	6697
30: 6	in caves of the earth, and *in* the **r**.	3710
Ps 78:15	He clave the **r** in the wilderness,	6697
104:18	the wild goats; *and the* **r** for the conies.	5553
Pr 30:26	yet make they their houses in the **r**:	5553
Isa 2:19	they shall go into the holes of the **r**,	6697
2:21	To go into the clifts of the **r**, and into	6697
2:21	into the tops of the **ragged r**, for fear of	5553
7:19	in the holes of the **r**, and in all thorns,	5553
33:16	of defence *shall be* the munitions of **r**:	5553
57: 5	in the valleys under the clifts of the **r**?	5553
Jer 4:29	go into thickets, and climb up upon the **r**:	3710
16:16	every hill, and out of the holes of the **r**.	5553
51:25	roll thee down from the **r**, and will make	5553
Na 1: 6	fire, and the **r** are thrown down by him.	6697
Mt 27:51	and the earth did quake, and the **r** rent;	4073
Ac 27:29	lest we should have fallen upon **r**,	5117+5138
Rev 6:15	in the dens and in the **r** of the mountains;	4073
6:16	said to the mountains and **r**, Fall on us,	4073

ROD (86) [RODS]

Ex 4: 2	*is* that in thine hand? And he said, A **r**.	4294
4: 4	caught it, and it became a **r** in his hand:	4294
4:17	thou shalt take this **r** in thine hand,	4294
4:20	and Moses took the **r** of God in his hand.	4294
7: 9	Take thy **r**, and cast *it* before Pharaoh,	4294
7:10	Aaron cast down his **r** before Pharaoh,	4294
7:12	For they cast down every man his **r**,	4294
7:12	but Aaron's **r** swallowed up their rods.	4294
7:15	the **r** which was turned to a serpent shalt	4294
7:17	will smite with the **r** that *is* in mine hand	4294
7:19	Take thy **r**, and stretch out thine hand	4294
7:20	he lift up the **r**, and smote the waters that	4294
8: 5	Stretch forth thine hand with thy **r** over	4294
8:16	Stretch out thy **r**, and smite the dust of	4294
8:17	Aaron stretched out his hand with his **r**,	4294
9:23	Moses stretched forth his **r** toward	4294
10:13	Moses stretched forth his **r** over the land	4294
14:16	lift thou up thy **r**, and stretch out thine	4294
17: 5	thy **r**, wherewith thou smotest the river,	4294
17: 9	the hill with the **r** of God in mine hand.	4294
21:20	with a **r**, and he die under his hand;	7626
Lev 27:32	*even of* whatsoever passeth under the **r**,	7626
Nu 17: 2	take of every one of them a **r** according to	4294
17: 2	write thou every man's name upon his **r**.	4294
17: 3	thou shalt write Aaron's name upon the **r**	4294
17: 3	one **r** *shall be* for the head of the house	4294
17: 5	*that* the man's **r**, whom I shall choose,	4294
17: 6	every one of their princes gave him a **r**	4294
17: 6	and the **r** of Aaron *was* among their rods.	4294
17: 8	the **r** of Aaron for the house of Levi was	4294
17: 9	they looked, and took every man his **r**.	4294
17:10	Bring Aaron's **r** again before	4294
20: 8	Take the **r**, and gather thou the assembly	4294
20: 9	Moses took the **r** from before the LORD,	4294
20:11	and with his **r** he smote the rock twice:	4294
1Sa 14:27	wherefore he put forth the end of the **r**	4294
14:43	taste a little honey with the end of the **r**	4294
2Sa 7:14	I will chasten him with the **r** of men,	7626
Job 9:34	Let him take his **r** away from me,	7626
21: 9	neither *is* the **r** of God upon them.	7626
Ps 2: 9	Thou shalt break them with a **r** of iron;	7626
23: 4	thy **r** and thy staff they comfort me.	7626
74: 2	the **r** of thine inheritance, *which* thou	7626
89:32	will I visit their transgression with the **r**,	7626
110: 2	The LORD shall send the **r** of thy strength	4294
125: 3	For the **r** of the wicked shall not rest upon	7626

Pr 10:13	a **r** *is* for the back of him that is void of	7626
13:24	He that spareth his **r** hateth his son:	7626
14: 3	In the mouth of the foolish *is* a **r** of pride:	2415
22: 8	vanity: and the **r** of his anger shall fail.	7626
22:15	the **r** of correction shall drive it far from	7626
23:13	for *if* thou beatest him with the **r**, he shall	7626
23:14	Thou shalt beat him with the **r**,	7626
26: 3	for the ass, and a **r** for the fools' back.	7626
29:15	The **r** and reproof give wisdom: but a	7626
Isa 9: 4	the **r** of his oppressor, as *in* the day of	7626
10: 5	The **r** of mine anger, and the staff in their	7626
10:15	as if the **r** should shake *itself against* them	7626
10:24	shall smite thee with a **r**, and shall lift up	7626
10:26	*as* his **r** *was* upon the sea, so shall he lift	4294
11: 1	there shall come forth a **r** out of the stem	2415
11: 4	he shall smite the earth with the **r** of his	7626
14:29	for of him that smote thee is broken:	7626
28:27	with a staff, and the cummin with a **r**.	7626
30:31	be beaten down, *which* smote with a **r**.	7626
Jer 1:11	And I said, I see a **r** of an almond tree.	4731
10:16	and Israel *is* the **r** of his inheritance:	7626
48:17	strong staff broken, *and* the beautiful **r**!	4731
51:19	and *Israel is* the **r** of his inheritance.	7626
La 3: 1	hath seen affliction by the **r** of his wrath.	7626
Eze 7:10	the **r** hath blossomed, pride hath budded.	4294
7:11	Violence is risen up into a **r** of wickedness	4294
19:14	fire is gone out of a **r** of her branches,	4294
19:14	that she hath no strong **r** *to be* a sceptre	4294
20:37	I will cause you to pass under the **r**,	7626
21:10	it contemneth the **r** of my son, *as* every	7626
21:13	what if *the sword* contemn even the **r**?	7626
Mic 5: 1	shall smite the judge of Israel with a **r**	7626
6: 9	hear ye the **r**, and who hath appointed it.	4294
7:14	Feed thy people with thy **r**, the flock of	7626
1Co 4:21	shall I come unto you with a **r**, or in love,	4464
Heb 9: 4	and Aaron's **r** that budded, and the tables	4464
Rev 2:27	And he shall rule them with a **r** of iron;	4464
11: 1	there was given me a reed like unto a **r**:	4464
12: 5	was to rule all nations with a **r** of iron:	4464
19:15	and he shall rule them with a **r** of iron:	4464

RODE (15) [RIDE]

Ge 24:61	they **r** upon the camels, and followed	7392
Jdg 10: 4	had thirty sons that **r** on thirty ass colts,	7392
12:14	that **r** on threescore and ten ass colts:	7392
1Sa 25:20	was so, *as* she **r** on the ass, that she came	7392
25:42	hasted, and rose, and **r** upon an ass,	7392
30:17	men, which **r** upon camels, and fled.	7392
2Sa 18: 9	Absalom **r** upon a mule, and the mule	7392
22:11	he **r** upon a cherub, and did fly: and he	7392
1Ki 13:13	saddled him the ass: and he **r** thereon,	7392
18:45	And Ahab **r**, and went to Jezreel.	7392
2Ki 9:16	Jehu **r** *in a chariot*, and went to Jezreel;	7392
9:25	and thou **r** together after Ahab thy father,	7392
Ne 2:12	with me, save the beast that I **r** upon.	7392
Est 8:14	So the posts that **r** upon mules *and*	7392
Ps 18:10	he **r** upon a cherub, and did fly: yea,	7392

RODENTS See MOLE; MOLES

RODS (15) [ROD]

Ge 30:37	Jacob took him **r** of green poplar,	4731
30:37	the white appear which *was* in the **r**.	4731
30:38	he set the **r** which he had pilled before	4731
30:39	the flocks conceived before the **r**,	4731
30:41	that Jacob laid the **r** before the eyes of	4731
30:41	that they might conceive among the **r**.	4731
Ex 7:12	but Aaron's rod swallowed up their **r**.	4294
Nu 17: 2	to the house of their fathers twelve **r**:	4294
17: 6	to their fathers' houses, *even* twelve **r**:	4294
17: 6	and the rod of Aaron *was* among their **r**.	4294
17: 7	Moses laid up the **r** before the LORD in	4294
17: 9	Moses brought out all the **r** from before	4294
Eze 19:11	she had strong **r** for the sceptres of them	4294
19:12	her strong **r** were broken and withered;	4294
2Co 11:25	Thrice was I **beaten with r**, once was I	4463

ROE (7) [ROEBUCK, ROEBUCKS, ROES]

2Sa 2:18	Asahel was *as* light of foot as a wild **r**.	6643
Pr 5:19	*her be* as the loving hind and pleasant **r**;	3280
6: 5	Deliver thyself as a **r** from the hand *of*	6643
SS 2: 9	My beloved *is* like a **r** or a young hart:	6643
2:17	be thou like a **r** or a young hart upon	6643
8:14	be thou like to a **r** or to a young hart upon	6643
Isa 13:14	it shall be as the chased **r**, and as a sheep	6643

ROEBUCK (4) [ROE]

Dt 12:15	eat thereof, as of the **r**, and as of the hart.	6643
12:22	Even as the **r** and the hart is eaten,	6643
14: 5	the **r**, and the fallow deer, and the wild	6643
15:22	*shall eat it* alike, as the **r**, and as the hart.	6643

ROEBUCKS (1) [ROE]

1Ki 4:23	or **r**, and fallowdeer, and fatted fowl.	6643

ROES (5) [ROE]

1Ch 12: 8	as swift as the **r** upon the mountains:	6643
SS 2: 7	by the **r**, and by the hinds of the field,	6643
3: 5	by the **r**, and by the hinds of the field,	6643
4: 5	Thy two breasts *are* like two young **r** *that*	6646
7: 3	Thy two breasts *are* like two young **r**	6646

ROGELIM (2)

2Sa 17:27	and Barzillai the Gileadite of **R**,	7274
19:31	Barzillai the Gileadite came down from **R**,	7274

R

ROHGAH (1)
1Ch 7:34 Ahi, and **R**, Jehubbah, and Aram. 7303

ROLL (28) [ROLLED, ROLLER, ROLLETH, ROLLING, ROLLS]
Ge 29: 8 they **r** the stone from the well's mouth; 1556
Jos 10:18 **R** great stones upon the mouth of the 1556
1Sa 14:33 **r** a great stone unto me *this* day. 1556
Ezr 6: 2 a **r**, and therein *was* a record thus written: 4040
Isa 8: 1 Take thee a great **r**, and write in it with a 1549
Jer 36: 2 Take thee a **r** of a book, and write therein 4039
36: 4 had spoken unto him, upon a **r** of a book. 4039
36: 6 Therefore go thou, and read in the **r**, 4039
36:14 Take in thine hand the **r** wherein thou 4039
36:14 So Baruch the son of Neriah took the **r** in 4039
36:20 they laid up the **r** in the chamber of 4039
36:21 So the king sent Jehudi to fet the **r**: 4039
36:23 until all the **r** was consumed in the fire 4039
36:25 to the king that *he* would not burn the **r**: 4039
36:27 after that the king had burnt the **r**, 4039
36:28 Take thee again another **r**, and write in it 4039
36:28 the former words that were in the first **r**, 4039
36:29 Thou hast burnt this **r**, saying, Why hast 4039
36:32 took Jeremiah another **r**, and gave it to 4039
51:25 **r** thee **down** from the rocks, and will 1556
Eze 2: 9 and lo, a **r** of a book *was* therein; 4039
3: 1 eat this **r**, and go speak unto the house of 4039
3: 2 mouth, and he caused me to eat that **r**. 4039
3: 3 fill thy bowels with this **r** that I give thee. 4039
Mic 1:10 the house of Aphrah **r** thyself *in* the dust. 6428
Zec 5: 1 and looked, and behold, a flying **r**. 4039
5: 2 I answered, I see a flying **r**; the length 4039
Mk 16: 3 Who shall **r** us **away** the stone from the 617

ROLLED (12) [ROLL]
Ge 29: 3 they **r** the stone from the well's mouth, 1556
29:10 the stone from the well's mouth, 1556
Jos 5: 9 *This* day have I **r away** the reproach of 1556
Job 30:14 desolation they **r** themselves *upon me*. 1556
Isa 9: 5 confused noise, and garments **r** in blood; 1556
34: 4 heavens shall be **r together** as a scroll: 1556
Mt 27:60 he **r** a great stone to the door of 4351
28: 2 came and **r back** the stone from the door, 617
Mk 15:46 **r** a stone unto the door of the sepulchre. 4351
16: 4 they saw that the stone was **r away**: 617
Lk 24: 2 And they found the stone **r away** from 617
Rev 6:14 departed as a scroll when it is **r together**; 1507

ROLLER (1) [ROLL]
Eze 30:21 to put a **r** to bind it, to make it strong to 2848

ROLLETH (1) [ROLL]
Pr 26:27 he that **r** a stone, it will return upon him. 1556

ROLLING (1) [ROLL]
Isa 17:13 and like a **r thing** before the whirlwind. 1534

ROLLS (1) [ROLL]
Ezr 6: 1 search was made in the house of the **r**, 5609

ROMAMTI-EZER (2)
1Ch 25: 4 Hanani, Eliathah, Giddalti, and **R**, 7320
25:31 The four and twentieth to **R**, *he,* his sons, 7320

ROMAN (5) [ROME]
Ac 22:25 for you to scourge a man *that is* a **R**, 4514
22:26 heed what thou doest: for this man is a **R**. 4514
22:27 and said unto him, Tell me, art thou a **R**? 4514
22:29 after he knew that he was a **R**, and 4514
23:27 having understood that he was a **R**. 4514

ROMANS (7) [ROME]
Jn 11:48 and the **R** shall come and take away both 4514
Ac 16:21 to receive, neither to observe, being **R**. 4514
16:37 **R**, and have cast *us* into prison; 444+4514
16:38 when they heard that they were **R**, 4514
25:16 It is not the manner of the **R** to deliver 4514
28:17 from Jerusalem into the hands of the **R**. 4514
Ro 16: S Written to the **R** from Corinthus, 4514

ROME (15) [ROMAN, ROMANS]
Ac 2:10 and strangers of **R**, Jews and proselytes, 4514
18: 2 commanded all Jews to depart from **R**:) 4516
19:21 After I have been there, I must also see **R**. 4516
23:11 so must thou bear witness also at **R**. 4516
28:14 seven days: and so we went toward **R**. 4516
28:16 And when we came to **R**, the centurion 4516
Ro 1: 7 To all that be in **R**, beloved of God, 4516
1:15 preach the gospel to you that are at **R** also. 4516
Gal 6: S Unto the Galatians written from **R**. 4516
Eph 6: S Written from **R** unto the Ephesians by 4516
Php 4: S It was written to the Philippians from **R** 4516
Col 4: S Written from **R** to the Colossians by 4516
2Ti 1:17 But, when he was in **R**, he sought me out 4516
4: S was written from **R**, when Paul was 4516
Phm 1: S Written from **R** to Philemon, by Onesimus 4516

ROOF (20) [ROOFS]
Ge 19: 8 came they under the shadow of my **r**. 6982
Dt 22: 8 thou shalt make a battlement for thy **r**, 1406
Jos 2: 6 brought them up to the **r** of the house, 1406
2: 6 which she had laid in order upon the **r**. 1406
2: 8 she came up unto them upon the **r**; 1406
Jdg 16:27 *were* upon the **r** about three thousand 1406
2Sa 11: 2 walked upon the **r** of the king's house: 1406
11: 2 from the **r** he saw a woman washing 1406

2Sa 18:24 the watchman went *up* to the **r** over 1406
Ne 8:16 every one upon the **r** of his **house**, 1406
Job 29:10 tongue cleaved to the **r** of their **mouth**. 2441
Ps 137: 6 my tongue cleave to the **r** of my **mouth**; 2441
SS 7: 9 the **r** of thy **mouth** like the best wine, 2441
La 4: 4 cleaveth to the **r** of his **mouth** for thirst: 2441
Eze 3:26 thy tongue cleave to the **r** of thy **mouth**, 2441
40:13 the gate from the **r** of *one* little chamber 1406
40:13 of *one* little chamber to the **r** of another: 1406
Mt 8: 8 that thou shouldest come under my **r**: 4721
Mk 2: 4 they uncovered the **r** where he was: 4721
Lk 7: 6 that thou shouldest enter under my **r**: 4721

ROOFS (2) [ROOF]
Jer 19:13 all the houses upon whose **r** they have 1406
32:29 upon whose **r** they have offered incense 1406

ROOM (32) [ROOMS]
Ge 24:23 is there **r** *in* thy father's house for us to 4725
24:25 and provender enough, and **r** to lodge in. 4725
24:31 prepared the house, and **r** for the camels. 4725
26:22 For now the LORD hath **made r** for us, 7337
2Sa 19:13 before me continually in the **r** of Joab. 8478
1Ki 2:35 the son of Jehoiada **in** his **r** over the host: 8478
2:35 Zadok the priest did the king put in the **r** 8478
5: 1 anointed him king **in the r** of his father: 8478
5: 5 whom I will set upon thy throne in thy **r**, 8478
8:20 I am risen up **in the r** of David my father, 8478
19:16 shalt thou anoint to be prophet in thy **r**. 8478
2Ki 15:25 he killed him, and reigned in his **r**. 8478
23:34 of Josiah king **in the r** of Josiah his father, 8478
2Ch 6:10 for I am risen up **in the r** of David my 8478
26: 1 made him king **in the r** of his father 8478
Ps 31: 8 thou hast set my feet in a **large r**. 4800
80: 8 Thou preparedst **r** before it, and didst NIH
Pr 18:16 A man's gift **maketh r** for him, 7337
Mal 3:10 that *there* shall not be **r** enough *to* receive NIH
Mt 2:22 reign in Judea in the **r** of his father Herod, 473
Mk 2: 2 insomuch that there was no **r** to receive 5562
14:15 And he will shew you a large **upper r** 508
Lk 2: 7 there was no **r** for them in the inn. 5117
12:17 I have no **r** where to bestow my fruits? NIG
14: 8 a wedding, sit not down in the **highest r**; 4411
14: 9 begin with shame to take the lowest **r**. 5117
14:10 bidden, go and sit down in the lowest **r**; 5117
14:22 thou hast commanded, and yet there is **r**. 5117
22:12 And he shall shew you a large **upper r** 508
Ac 1:13 went up into an **upper r**, where abode 5253
24:27 Porcius Festus **came into** Felix' **r**: 1240+2983
1Co 14:16 how shall he that occupieth the **r** of 5117

ROOMS (5) [ROOM]
Ge 6:14 **r** shalt thou make *in* the ark, and shalt 7064
1Ki 20:24 of his place, and put captains in their **r**: 8478
1Ch 4:41 utterly unto this day, and dwelt in their **r**. 8478
Mt 23: 6 And love the **uppermost r** at feasts, 4411
Mk 12:39 and the **uppermost r** at feasts; 4411
Lk 14: 7 marked how they chose out the **chief r**; 4411
20:46 the synagogues, and the **chief r** at feasts; 4411

ROOSTER See COCK; COCKCROWING; GREYHOUND

ROOT (44) [ROOTED, ROOTS]
Dt 29:18 lest there should be among you a **r** that 8328
Jdg 5:14 Out of Ephraim *was there* a **r** of them 8328
1Ki 14:15 he shall **r** up Israel out of this good land, 5428
2Ki 19:30 Judah shall yet again take **r** downward, 8328
Job 5: 3 I have seen the foolish **taking r**: 8327
14: 8 the **r** thereof wax old in the earth, 8328
19:28 seeing the **r** of the matter is found in me; 8328
29:19 My **r** *was* spread out by the waters, 8328
31:12 and would **r** out all mine increase. 8327
Ps 52: 5 and **r** thee **out** of the land of the living. 8328
80: 9 didst **cause** it to **take deep r**, 8327+8328
Pr 12: 3 the **r** of the righteous shall not be moved. 8328
12:12 but the **r** of the righteous yieldeth *fruit*. 8328
Isa 5:24 *so* their **r** shall be as rottenness, 8328
11:10 in that day there shall be a **r** of Jesse, 8328
14:29 for out of the serpent's **r** shall come forth 8328
14:30 I will kill thy **r** with famine, and he shall 8328
27: 6 **cause** them that come of Jacob to **take r**: 8327
37:31 of Judah shall again take **r** downward, 8328
40:24 their stock shall not take **r** in the earth: 8327
53: 2 plant, and as a **r** out of a dry ground: 8328
Jer 1:10 **r out**, and to pull down, and to destroy, 5428
12: 2 planted them, yea, they have **taken r**: 8327
Eze 31: 7 branches: for his **r** was by great waters, 8328
Hos 9:16 Ephraim is smitten, their **r** is dried up, 8328
Mal 4: 1 it shall leave them neither **r** nor branch. 8328
Mt 3:10 And now also the axe is laid unto the **r** of 4491
13: 6 because they had not **r**, they withered 4491
13:21 Yet hath he not **r** in himself, but dureth 4491
13:29 tares, ye **r up** also the wheat with them. 1610
Mk 4: 6 because it had no **r**, it withered away. 4491
4:17 have no **r** in themselves, and so endure 4491
Lk 3: 9 And now also the axe is laid unto the **r** of 4491
8:13 and these have no **r**, which for a while 4491
17: 6 Be thou **plucked up by the r**, and be 1610
Ro 11:16 the lump *is* also **holy**: and if the **r** *be* holy, 4491
11:17 and with **them** partakest of the **r** and 4491
11:18 thou bearest not the **r**, but the root thee. 4491
11:18 thou bearest not the root, but the **r** thee. 4491
15:12 There shall be a **r** of Jesse, and he that 4491
1Ti 6:10 For the love of money is the **r** of all evil: 4491

Heb 12:15 lest any **r** of bitterness springing up 4491
Rev 5: 5 Lion of the tribe of Juda, the **r** of David, 4491
22:16 I am the **r** and the offspring of David, 4491

ROOTED (8) [ROOT]
Dt 29:28 the LORD **r** them **out** of their land in 5428
Job 18:14 His confidence shall be **r** out of his 5423
31: 8 eat; yea, let my offspring be **r out**. 8327
Pr 2:22 and the transgressors shall be **r** out of it. 5255
Zep 2: 4 at the noon day, and Ekron shall be **r up**. 6131
Mt 15:13 Father hath not planted, shall be **r up**. 1610
Eph 3:17 that ye, being **r** and grounded in love, 4492
Col 2: 7 **R** and built up in him, and stablished in 4492

ROOTS (20) [ROOT]
2Ch 7:20 will I **pluck** them **up by the r** out of my 5428
Job 8:17 His **r** are wrapped about the heap, 8328
18:16 His **r** shall be dried up beneath, 8328
28: 9 he overturneth the mountains by the **r**. 8328
30: 4 the bushes, and juniper **r** *for their* meat. 8328
Isa 11: 1 and a Branch shall grow out of his **r**: 8328
Jer 17: 8 *that* spreadeth out her **r** by the river, 8328
Eze 17: 6 and the **r** thereof were under him: 8328
17: 7 this vine did bend her **r** toward him, 8328
17: 9 shall he not pull up the **r** thereof, and cut 8328
17: 9 people to pluck it up by the **r** thereof. 8328
Da 4:15 Nevertheless leave the stump of his **r** in 8330
4:23 yet leave the stump of the **r** thereof in 8330
4:26 to leave the stump of the tree **r**; 8330
7: 8 of the first horns **pluckt up by** the **r**: 6132
11: 7 of a branch of her **r** shall *one* stand up 8328
Hos 14: 5 the lily, and cast forth his **r** as Lebanon. 8328
Am 2: 9 fruit from above, and his **r** from beneath. 8328
Mk 11:20 they saw the fig tree dried up from the **r**. 4491
Jude 1:12 twice dead, **plucked up by the r**; 1610

ROPE (1) [ROPES]
Isa 5:18 of vanity, and sin as it were with a cart **r**: 5688

ROPES (6) [ROPE]
Jdg 16:11 If they bind me fast with new **r** that never 5688
16:12 Delilah therefore took new **r**, 5688
2Sa 17:13 shall all Israel bring **r** to that city, 2256
1Ki 20:31 **r** upon our heads, and go out to the king 2256
20:32 **r** on their heads, and came to the king 2256
Ac 27:32 Then the soldiers cut off the **r** of the boat, 4979

ROSE (136) [RISE]
Ge 4: 8 that Cain **r up** against Abel his brother, 6965
18:16 the men **r up** from thence, 6965
19: 1 Lot seeing *them* **r up** to meet them; 6965
20: 8 Therefore Abimelech **r early** in 7925
21:14 Abraham **r up early** in the morning, 6965
21:32 Abimelech **r up**, and Phichol the chief 6965
22: 3 Abraham **r up early** in the morning, 7925
22: 3 **r up**, and went unto the place of which 6965
22:19 **r up** and went together to Beer-sheba; 6965
24:54 they **r up** in the morning, and he said, 6965
25:34 and drink, and **r up**, and went his way: 6965
26:31 they **r up betimes** in the morning, 7925
28:18 Jacob **r up early** in the morning, 7925
31:17 Jacob **r up**, and set his sons and his wives 6965
31:21 he **r up**, and passed over the river, 6965
31:55 **early** in the morning Laban **r up**, 7925
32:22 **r up** that night, and took his two wives, 6965
32:31 as he passed over Penuel the sun **r** upon 2224
37:35 and all his daughters **r up** to comfort him; 6965
43:15 **r up**, and went down to Egypt, 6965
46: 5 Jacob **r up** from Beer-sheba: and the sons 6965
Ex 10:23 neither **r** any from his place for three days: 6965
12:30 Pharaoh **r up** in the night, he, and all his 6965
15: 7 overthrown them that **r up against** thee: 6965
24: 4 Moses **r up** early in the morning, and builded 7925
24:13 Moses **r up**, and his minister Joshua: 6965
32: 6 they **r up early** on the morrow, 7925
32: 6 to eat and to drink, and **r up** to play. 6965
33: 8 *that* all the people **r up**, and stood every 6965
33:10 all the people **r up** and worshipped, 6965
34: 4 Moses **r up early** in the morning, 7925
Nu 14:40 they **r up early** in the morning, 7925
16: 2 they **r up** before Moses, with certain of 6965
16:25 Moses **r up** and went unto Dathan and 6965
22:13 Balaam **r up** in the morning, and said 6965
22:14 the princes of Moab **r up**, and they went 6965
22:21 Balaam **r up** in the morning, 6965
24:25 Balaam **r up**, and went and returned to 6965
25: 7 saw *it*, he **r up** from amongst 6965
Dt 33: 2 from Sinai, and **r up** from Seir unto them; 2224
Jos 3: 1 Joshua **r early** in the morning; 7925
3:16 stood *and* **r up** upon a heap very far, 6965
6:12 Joshua **r early** in the 6965
6:15 that they **r early** about the dawning of 7925
7:16 So Joshua **r up early** in the morning, 7925
8:10 Joshua **r up early** in the morning, 7925
8:14 Ai saw *it*, that they hasted and **r up early**, 7925
Jdg 6:21 and there **r up** fire out of the rock, 5927
6:38 for he **r up early** on the morrow, 7925
7: 1 **r up early**, and pitched beside the well of 7925
9:34 Abimelech **r up**, and all the people that 6965
9:35 Abimelech **r up**, and the people that *were* 6965
9:43 he **r up** against them, and smote them. 6965
19: 5 in the morning, that he **r up** to depart: 6965
19: 7 when the man **r up** to depart, his father 6965
19: 9 when the man **r up** to depart, he, 6965
19:10 he **r up** and departed, and came over 6965

Jdg 19:27 her lord **r** up in the morning, — 6965
19:28 he that **r** up, and gat him unto his place. — 6965
20: 5 the men of Gibeah **r** against me, — 6965
20:19 the children of Israel **r** up in the morning, — 6965
20:33 the men of Israel **r** up out of their place, — 6965
21: 4 that the people **r** early, and built there an — 7925
Ru 3:14 she **r** before one could know another. — 6965
1Sa 1: 9 So Hannah **r** up after *they* had eaten in — 6965
1:19 they **r** up in the morning **early**, — 7925
15:12 when Samuel **r** early to meet Saul in — 7925
16:13 Samuel **r** up, and went to Ramah. — 6965
17:20 David **r** up early in the morning, — 7925
24: 7 Saul **r** up out of the cave, and went on — 6965
24: 8 David also **r** afterward, and went out of — 6965
25:42 Abigail hasted, and, **r**, and rode upon an — 6965
29:11 his men **r** up early to depart in — 7925
2Sa 15: 2 Absalom **r** up early, and stood beside — 7925
18:31 *this* day of all them that **r** up against thee. — 6965
19: 8 the king **r**, and sat in the gate. And they — 6965
22:40 them that **r** up against me hast thou — 6965
22:49 on high above them that **r** up against me: — 6965
1Ki 1:49 and **r** up, and went every man his way. — 6965
2:19 the king **r** up to meet her, — 6965
3:20 she **r** at midnight, and took my son from — 6965
3:21 when I **r** in the morning to give my child — 6965
21:16 Ahab **r** up to go down to the vineyard — 6965
2Ki 3:22 **r** up early in the morning, and the sun — 7925
3:24 Israelites **r** up and smote the Moabites, — 6965
7: 5 they **r** up in the twilight, to go unto — 6965
8:21 he **r** by night, and smote the Edomites — 6965
2Ch 20:20 they **r** early in the morning, and went — 7925
21: 9 he **r** up by night, and smote the Edomites — 6965
26:19 the leprosy even **r** up in his forehead — 2224
28:15 men which were expressed by name **r** up, — 6965
29:20 Hezekiah the king **r** early, and gathered — 7925
Ezr 1: 5 **r** up the chief of the fathers of Judah and — 6965
5: 2 **r** up Zerubbabel the son of Shealtiel, — 6966
10: 6 Ezra **r** from before the house of God, — 6965
Ne 3: 1 Eliashib the high priest **r** up with his — 6965
4:14 **r** up, and said unto the nobles, and to — 6965
Job 1: 5 **r** up early in the morning, — 7925
Ps 18:39 under me those that **r** up against me. — 6965
124: 2 on our side, when men **r** up against us: — 6965
SS 2: 1 I am the **r** of Sharon, *and* the lily of — 2261
5: 5 I **r** up to open to my beloved; — 6965
Isa 35: 1 desert shall rejoice, and blossom as the **r**. — 2261
Jer 26:17 **r** up certain of the elders of the land, — 6965
La 3:62 The lips of those that **r** up against me, — 6965
Da 3:24 **r** up in haste, *and* spake, and said unto — 6966
8:27 afterward I **r** up, and did the king's — 6965
Jnh 1: 3 Jonah **r** up to flee unto Tarshish from — 6965
4: 7 prepared a worm when the morning **r** — 5927
Zep 3: 7 **r** early, *and* corrupted all their doings. — 7925
Mk 10: 1 And he **r** from thence, — 450
10:50 away his garment, **r**, and came to Jesus. — 450
Lk 4:29 And **r** up, and thrust him out of the city, — 450
5:25 And immediately he **r** up before them, — 450
5:28 And he left all, **r** up, and followed him. — 450
8:24 Master, master, we perish. Then he **r**, — 1453
16:31 be persuaded, though one **r** from the dead. — 450
22:45 And when he **r** up from prayer, — 450
24:33 And they **r** up the same hour, — 450
Jn 11:31 that she **r** up hastily and went out, — 450
Ac 5:17 Then the high priest **r** up, and all they that — 450
5:36 For before these days **r** up Theudas, — 450
5:37 After this *man* **r** up Judas of Galilee in — 450
10:41 drink with him after he **r** from the dead. — 450
14:20 him, he **r** up, and came into the city: — 450
15: 5 But there **r** up certain of the sect of — 1817
15: 7 Peter **r** up, and said unto them, Men *and* — 450
16:22 And the multitude **r** up together against — 4911
26:30 spoken, the king **r** up, and the governor, — 450
Ro 14: 9 For to this end Christ both died, and **r**, — 450
1Co 10: 7 down to eat and drink, and **r** up to play. — 450
15: 4 that he **r** again the third day according to — 1453
15:12 Now if Christ be preached that he **r** from — 1453
2Co 5:15 him which died for them, and **r** *again*. — 1453
1Th 4:14 if we believe that Jesus died and **r** **again**, — 450
Rev 19: 3 And her smoke **r** up for ever and ever. — 305

ROSH (1)
Ge 46:21 Ashbel, Gera, and Naaman, Ehi, and, **R**, — 7220

ROT (5) [ROTTEN, ROTTENNESS]
Nu 5:21 when the LORD doth make thy thigh to **r**, — 5307
5:22 *thy* belly to swell, and *thy* thigh to **r**: — 5307
5:27 her belly shall swell, and her thigh shall **r**: — 5307
Pr 10: 7 but the name of the wicked shall **r**. — 7537
Isa 40:20 oblation chooseth a tree *that* will not **r**; — 7537

ROTTEN (5) [ROT]
Job 13:28 he, as a **r** thing, consumeth, as a garment — 7538
41:27 iron as straw, *and* brass as **r** wood. — 7539
Jer 38:11 took thence old cast clouts and old **r rags**, — 4418
38:12 **r** rags under thine armholes under — 4418
Joel 1:17 seed is **r** under their clods, the garners — 5685

ROTTENNESS (5) [ROT]
Pr 12: 4 she that maketh ashamed *is* as **r** in his — 7538
14:30 of the flesh: but envy the **r** of the bones. — 7538
Isa 5:24 their root shall be as **r**, and their blossom — 4716
Hos 5:12 as a moth, and to the house of Judah as **r**. — 7538
Hab 3:16 **r** entered into my bones, and I trembled — 7538

ROUGH (7) [ROUGHLY]
Dt 21: 4 shall bring down the heifer unto a **r** valley, — 386
Isa 27: 8 stayeth his **r** wind in the day of the east — 7186
40: 4 be made straight, and the **r** places plain: — 7406
Jer 51:27 cause the horses to come up as the **r** — 5569
Da 8:21 the **r** goat *is* the king of Grecia: — 8163
Zec 13: 4 neither shall they wear a **r** garment to — 8181
Lk 3: 5 and the **r** ways *shall* be made smooth; — *5138*

ROUGHLY (6) [ROUGH]
Ge 42: 7 unto them, and spake **r** unto them; — 7186
42:30 spake **r** to us, and took us for spies of — 7186
1Sa 20:10 or what *if* thy father answer thee **r**? — 7186
1Ki 12:13 the king answered the people **r**, — 7186
2Ch 10:13 the king answered them **r**; and king — 7186
Pr 18:23 useth intreaties; but the rich answereth **r**. — 5794

ROUND (320)
Ge 19: 4 **compassed** the house **r**, both old and — 5437
23:17 that *were* in all the borders **r about**, — 5439
35: 5 upon the cities that *were* **r about** them, — 5439
37: 7 your sheaves **stood r about**, — 5437
41:48 of the field, which *was* **r about** every city, — 5439
Ex 7:24 all the Egyptians digged **r about** the river — 5439
16:13 in the morning the dew lay **r about** — 5439
16:14 of the wilderness *there lay* a small **r thing**, — 2636
19:12 shalt set bounds unto the people **r about**, — 5439
25:11 make upon it a crown *of* gold **r about**. — 5439
25:24 make thereto a crown *of* gold **r about**. — 5439
25:25 unto it a border of a handbreadth **r about**, — 5439
25:25 crown to the border thereof **r about**. — 5439
27:17 All the pillars **r about** the court shall be — 5439
28:32 of woven work **r about** the hole of it, — 5439
28:33 and of scarlet, **r about** the hem thereof; — 5439
28:33 and bells of gold between them **r about**: — 5439
28:34 upon the hem of the robe **r about**. — 5439
29:16 and sprinkle *it* **r about** upon the altar. — 5439
29:20 sprinkle the blood upon the altar **r about**. — 5439
30: 3 the sides thereof **r about**, and the horns — 5439
30: 3 make unto it a crown *of* gold **r about**. — 5439
37: 2 and made a crown *of* gold to it **r about**, — 5439
37:11 made thereunto a crown *of* gold **r about**. — 5439
37:12 a border of a handbreadth **r about**; — 5439
37:12 of gold for the border thereof **r about**. — 5439
37:26 the sides thereof **r about**, and the horns — 5439
37:26 he made unto it a crown *of* gold **r about**. — 5439
38:16 All the hangings of the court **r about** — 5439
38:20 and of the court **r about**, *were of* brass. — 5439
38:31 the sockets of the court **r about**, — 5439
38:31 and all the pins of the court **r about**. — 5439
39:23 a band **r about** the hole, *that* it should — 5439
39:25 **r about** between the pomegranates; — 5439
39:26 **r about** the hem of the robe to minister — 5439
40: 8 thou shalt set up the court **r about**, — 5439
40:33 he reared up the court **r about** — 5439
Lev 1: 5 sprinkle the blood **r about** upon the altar — 5439
1:11 shall sprinkle his blood **r about** upon — 5439
3: 2 sprinkle the blood upon the altar **r about**. — 5439
3: 8 the blood thereof **r about** upon the altar. — 5439
3:13 the blood thereof upon the altar **r about**. — 5439
7: 2 the blood thereof shall he sprinkle **r about** — 5439
8:15 put *it* upon the horns of the altar **r about**, — 5439
8:19 the blood upon the altar **r about**. — 5439
8:24 the blood upon the altar **r about**. — 5439
9:12 he sprinkled **r about** upon the altar. — 5439
9:18 he sprinkled upon the altar **r about**, — 5439
14:41 the house to be scraped within **r about**, — 5439
16:18 put *it* upon the horns of the altar **r about**. — 5439
19:27 Ye shall not **r** the corners of your heads, — 5362
25:31 **r about** them shall be counted as the — 5439
25:44 *shall be* of the heathen that *are* **r about** — 5439
Nu 1:50 and shall encamp **r about** the tabernacle. — 5439
1:53 the Levites shall pitch **r about** — 5439
3:26 by the altar **r about**, and the cords of it — 5439
3:37 the pillars of the court **r about**, — 5439
4:26 by the tabernacle and by the altar **r about**, — 5439
4:32 the pillars of the court **r about**, — 5439
11:24 and set them **r about** the tabernacle. — 5439
11:31 **r about** the camp, and as it were two — 5439
11:32 abroad for themselves **r about** the camp. — 5439
16:34 all Israel that *were* **r about** them fled at — 5439
22: 4 company lick up all *that are* **r about** us, — 5439
32:33 *even* the cities of the country **r about**, — 5439
34:12 your land with the coasts thereof **r about**. — 5439
35: 2 suburbs for the cities **r about** them. — 5439
35: 4 and outward a thousand cubits **r about**. — 5439
Dt 6:14 the gods of the people which *are* **r about** — 5439
12:10 rest from all your enemies **r about**, — 4480+5439
13: 7 gods of the people which *are* **r about** you, — 5439
21: 2 cities which *are* **r about** him that is slain: — 5439
25:19 rest from all thine enemies **r about**, — 4480+5439
Jos 6: 3 of war, and **go r about** the city once. — 5362
7: 9 shall hear *of it*, and shall **environ** us **r**, — 5362
15:12 Judah **r about** according to their families. — 5439
18:20 by the coasts thereof **r about**, according — 5439
19: 8 all the villages that *were* **r about** these — 5439
21:11 with the suburbs thereof **r about** it. — 5439
21:42 one with their suburbs **r about** them: — 5439
21:44 the LORD gave them rest **r about**, — 5439
23: 1 from all their enemies **r about**, — 4480+5439
Jdg 2:12 the gods of the people that *were* **r about** — 5439
2:14 the hands of their enemies **r about**, — 4480+5439
7:21 they stood every man in his place **r about** — 5439
19:22 **beset** the house **r about**, *and* beat at — 5437
20: 5 **beset** the house **r about** upon me by — 5437

Jdg 20:29 Israel set liers in wait **r about** Gibeah, — 5439
20:43 they inclosed the Benjamites **r about**, — 3803
1Sa 14:21 into the camp *from the country* **r about**, — 5439
23:26 **compassed** David and his men **r about** — 5849
26: 5 and the people pitched **r about** him. — 5439
26: 7 but Abner and the people lay **r about** him. — 5439
31: 9 into the land of the Philistines **r about**, — 5439
2Sa 5: 9 David built **r about** from Millo and — 5439
7: 1 rest **r about** from all his enemies, — 4480+5439
22:12 he made darkness pavilions **r about** him, — 5439
1Ki 3: 1 and the wall of Jerusalem **r about**. — 5439
4:24 had peace on all sides **r about** him. — 4480+5439
4:31 and his fame was in all nations **r about**. — 5439
6: 5 of the house he built chambers **r about**, — 5439
6: 5 *against* the walls of the house **r about**, — 5439
6: 5 oracle: and he made chambers **r about**: — 5439
6: 6 house he made narrowed rests **r about**, — 5439
6:29 carved all the walls of the house **r about** — 4524
7:12 great court **r about** *was* with three rows — 5439
7:18 two rows **r about** upon the one network, — 5439
7:20 *in* rows **r about** upon the other chapiter. — 5439
7:23 *it was* **r** all about, and his height *was* five — 5696
7:23 cubits did **compass** it **r about**. — 5437+5439
7:24 **r about** *there were* — 5437+5439
 knops **compassing** —
7:24 in a cubit, compassing the sea **r about**: — 5439
7:31 the mouth thereof *was* **r** *after* the work of — 5696
7:31 with their borders, foursquare, not **r**. — 5696
7:35 the top of the base *was there* a **r** compass — 5696
7:36 of every one, and additions **r about**. — 5439
10:19 and the top of the throne *was* **r** behind: — 5696
18:35 the water ran **r about** the altar; — 5439
2Ki 6:17 and chariots of fire **r about** Elisha. — 5439
11: 8 ye shall compass the king **r about**, — 5439
11:11 weapons in his hand, **r about** the king, — 5439
17:15 *went* after the heathen that *were* **r about** — 5439
23: 5 and in the **places r about** Jerusalem, — 4524
25: 1 and they built forts against it **r about**. — 5439
25: 4 Chaldees *were* against the city **r about**:) — 5439
25:10 down the walls of Jerusalem **r about**, — 5439
25:17 pomegranates upon the chapiter **r about**, — 5439
1Ch 4:33 all their villages that *were* **r about** the — 5439
6:55 and the suburbs thereof **r about** it. — 5439
9:27 they lodged **r about** the house of God, — 5439
10: 9 into the land of the Philistines **r about**, — 5439
11: 8 he built the city **r about**, even from Millo — 5439
11: 8 **r** round about, even from Millo **r about**: — 5439
22: 9 rest from all his enemies **r about**: — 4480+5439
28:12 of all the chambers **r about**, — 5439
2Ch 4: 2 **r** in compass, and five cubits the height — 5696
4: 2 of thirty cubits did compass it **r about**. — 5439
4: 3 which did compass it **r about**: — 5439+5439
4: 3 in a cubit, compassing the sea **r about**. — 5439
14:14 they smote all the cities **r about** Gerar; — 5439
15:15 the LORD gave them rest **r about**. — 4480+5439
17:10 of the lands that *were* **r about** Judah, — 5439
20:30 for his God gave him rest **r about**. — 4480+5439
23: 7 Levites shall compass the king **r about**, — 5439
23:10 and the temple, by the king **r about**. — 5439
34: 6 Naphtali, with their mattocks **r about**. — 5439
Ne 12:28 both out of the plain country **r about** — 5439
12:29 builded them villages **r about** Jerusalem. — 5439
Job 10: 8 and fashioned me together **r about**; — 5437
16:13 His archers **compass** me **r about**, — 5437
19:12 and encamp **r about** my tabernacle. — 5439
22:10 Therefore snares *are* **r about** thee, — 5439
37:12 it is turned **r about** by his counsels: — 4524
41:14 of his face? his teeth *are* terrible **r about**. — 5439
Ps 3: 6 have set *themselves* against me **r about**. — 5439
18:11 pavilion **r about** him *were* dark waters — 5439
22:12 strong **bulls** of Bashan have **beset** me **r**. — 3803
27: 6 lifted up above mine enemies **r about** me: — 5439
34: 7 encampeth **r about** them that fear him, — 5439
44:13 a derision to them that are **r about** us. — 5439
48:12 Walk about Zion, and **go r about** her: — 5362
50: 3 it shall be very tempestuous **r about** him. — 5439
59: 6 noise like a dog, and **go r about** the city. — 5437
59:14 noise like a dog, and **go r about** the city. — 5437
76:11 let all that be **r about** him bring presents — 5439
78:28 of their camp, **r about** their habitations. — 5439
79: 3 they shed like water **r about** Jerusalem; — 5439
79: 4 and derision to them that are **r about** us. — 5439
88:17 They **came r about** me daily like water; — 5437
89: 8 or *to* thy faithfulness **r about** thee? — 5439
97: 2 Clouds and darkness *are* **r about** him: — 5439
97: 3 and burneth up his enemies **r about**. — 5439
125: 2 *As* the mountains *are* **r about** Jerusalem, — 5439
125: 2 the LORD *is* **r about** his people from — 5439
128: 3 thy children like olive plants **r about** thy — 5439
SS 7: 2 Thy navel *is* like a **r** goblet, *which* — 5469
Isa 3:18 cauls, and *their* **r** tires like the moon, — 7720
15: 8 For the cry is **gone r about** the borders — 5439
29: 3 against thee **r about**, — 1754+1886.1+3509.1
42:25 it hath set him on fire **r about**, — 4480+5439
49:18 Lift up thine eyes **r about**, and behold: — 5439
60: 4 Lift up thine eyes **r about**, and see: all — 5439
Jer 1:15 against all the walls thereof **r about**, — 5439
4:17 a field, are they against her **r about**; — 4480+5439
5: 9 shall pitch *their* tents against her **r about** — 5439
12: 9 the birds **r about** *are* against her; — 5439
21:14 and it shall devour all things **r about** it. — 5439
25: 9 against all these nations **r about**, — 5439
46: 5 fear *was* **r about**, saith the LORD. — 4480+5439
46:14 for the sword shall devour **r about** thee. — 5439
50:14 in array against Babylon **r about**: — 5439

Jer 50:15 Shout against her **r** about: she hath given 5439
 50:29 bend the bow, camp against it **r** about; 5439
 50:32 and it shall devour all **r** about him. 5439
 51: 2 they shall be against her **r** about. 4480+5439
 52: 4 and built forts against it **r** about. 5439
 52: 7 the Chaldeans *were* by the city **r** about:) 5439
 52:14 down all the walls of Jerusalem **r** about. 5439
 52:22 pomegranates upon the chapiters **r** about, 5439
 52:23 the network *were* an hundred **r** about. 5439
La 1:17 his adversaries *should be* **r** about him: 5439
 2: 3 a flaming fire, *which* devoureth **r** about. 5439
 2:22 *in* a solemn day my terrors **r** about, 4480+5439
Eze 1:18 their rings *were* full *of* eyes **r** about them 5439
 1:27 as the appearance of fire **r** about within it, 5439
 1:27 of fire, and it had brightness **r** about. 5439
 1:28 the appearance of the brightness **r** about. 5439
 4: 2 and set *battering* rams against it **r** about. 5439
 5: 5 and countries *that are* **r** about her. 5439
 5: 6 than the countries that *are* **r** about her: 5439
 5: 7 than the nations that *are* **r** about you, 5439
 5: 7 of the nations that *are* **r** about you; 5439
 5:12 a third *part* shall fall by the sword **r** about 5439
 5:14 among the nations that *are* **r** about thee, 5439
 5:15 unto the nations that *are* **r** about thee, 5439
 6: 5 I will scatter your bones **r** about your 5439
 6:13 be among their idols **r** about their altars, 5439
 8:10 pourtrayed upon the wall **r** about. 5439+5439
 10:12 and the wheels, *were* full *of* eyes **r** about, 5439
 11:12 of the heathen that *are* **r** about you. 5439
 16:37 I will even gather them **r** about 4480+5439
 16:57 all *that are* **r** about her, the daughters of 5439
 16:57 which despise thee **r** about. 4480+5439
 23:24 buckler and shield and helmet **r** about: 5439
 27:11 thine army *were* upon thy walls **r** about, 5439
 27:11 their shields upon thy walls **r** about 5439
 28:24 grieving thorn of all *that are* **r** about them, 4480+5439
 28:26 that despise them **r** about them; 5439
 31: 4 with her rivers running **r** about his plants, 5439
 32:23 and her company is **r** about her grave: 5439
 32:24 and all her multitude **r** about her grave, 5439
 32:25 her graves *are* **r** about him: all of them 5439
 32:26 her graves *are* **r** about him: all of them 5439
 34:26 and the places **r** about my hill a blessing; 5439
 36: 4 of the heathen that *are* **r** about 4480+5439
 36:36 the heathen that are left **r** about you shall 5439
 37: 2 caused me to pass by them **r** about: 5439+5439
 40: 5 the outside of the house **r** about, 5439+5439
 40:14 post of the court **r** about the gate. 5439
 40:16 their posts within the gate **r** about, 5439+5439
 40:16 windows *were* **r** about inward: 5439+5439
 40:17 made for the court **r** about: 5439
 40:25 and in the arches thereof **r** about, 5439+5439
 40:29 and in the arches thereof **r** about, 5439+5439
 40:30 the arches **r** about *were* five and 5439+5439
 40:33 in the arches thereof **r** about: 5439+5439
 40:36 and the windows to it **r** about: 5439+5439
 40:43 a hand broad, fastened **r** about: 5439+5439
 41: 5 **r** about the house on every side. 5439+5439
 41: 6 for the side chambers **r** about, 5439+5439
 41: 7 still upward **r** about the house: 5439+5439
 41: 8 the height of the house **r** about: 5439+5439
 41:10 cubits **r** about the house on every side. 5439
 41:11 was left *was* five cubits **r** about, 5439+5439
 41:12 *was* five cubits thick **r** about, 5439+5439
 41:16 the galleries **r** about on their three *stories,* 5439
 41:16 cieled with wood **r** about, 5439+5439
 41:17 by all the wall **r** about within 5439+5439
 41:19 made through all the house **r** about: 5439+5439
 42:15 the east, and measured it **r** about. 5439
 42:16 with the measuring reed **r** about. 5439
 42:17 with the measuring reed **r** about. 5439
 42:20 it had a wall **r** about, five hundred 5439+5439
 43:12 thereof **r** about *shall be* most holy. 5439+5439
 43:13 the edge thereof **r** about *shall be* a span: 5439
 43:20 of the settle, and upon the border **r** about: 5439
 45: 1 be holy in all the borders thereof **r** about. 5439
 45: 2 five hundred *in* breadth, square **r** about; 5439
 45: 2 cubits **r** about *for* the suburbs thereof. 5439
 46:23 *there was* a row of *building* **r** about in 5439
 46:23 **r** about them four, and *it was* made *with* 5439
 46:23 boiling places under the rows **r** about. 5439
 48:35 *It was* **r** about eighteen thousand
Joel 3:11 gather yourselves together **r** about: 4480+5439
 3:12 sit to judge all the heathen **r** about. 4480+5439
Am 3:11 An adversary *There shall be* even **r** about 5439
Jnh 2: 5 the depth **closed** me **r** about, the weeds 5437
Na 3: 8 *that* had the waters **r** about it, 5439
Zec 2: 5 will be unto her a wall of fire **r** about 5439
 7: 7 and the cities thereof **r** about her, 5439
 12: 2 of trembling unto all the people **r** about, 5439
 12: 6 they shall devour all the people **r** about, 5439
 14:14 the wealth of all the heathen **r** about 5439
Mt 3: 5 and all the **region r** about Jordan, 4066
 14:35 sent out into all that **country r** about, 4066
 21:33 and hedged it **r** about, and digged a 4060
Mk 1:28 throughout all the **region r** about Galilee. 4066
 3: 5 when he had **looked r** about on them 4017
 3:34 he **looked r** about on them which sat 2945
 5:32 he **looked r** about to see her that had 4017
 6: 6 he went **r** about the villages, teaching, 2945
 6:36 they may go into the country **r** about, 2945
 6:55 ran through that whole **region r** about, 4066
 9: 8 when they had **looked r** about, 4017
 10:23 Jesus **looked r** about, and saith unto 4017
 11:11 when he had **looked r** about upon all 4017

Lk 1:65 And fear came on all that **dwelt r** about 4039
 2: 9 glory of the Lord **shone r** about them: 4034
 4:14 of him through all the **region r** about. 4066
 4:37 into every place of the **country r** about. 4066
 6:10 **looking r** about upon them all, he said 4017
 7:17 and throughout all the **region r** about. 4066
 8:37 **country** of the Gadarenes **r** about 4066
 9:12 go into the towns and country **r** about, 2945
 19:43 and **compass** thee **r**, and keep thee in on 4033
Jn 10:24 Then **came** the Jews **r** about him, 2944
Ac 5:16 *out* of the cities **r** about unto Jerusalem, 4038
 9: 3 there **shined r** about him a light 4015
 14: 6 and *unto* the **region** that **lieth r** about: 4066
 14:20 as the disciples **stood r** about him, 2944
 22: 6 from heaven a great light **r** about me. 4012
 25: 7 down from Jerusalem **stood r** about, 4026
 26:13 **shining r** about me and them which 4034
Ro 15:19 and **r** about unto Illyricum, 2945
Heb 9: 4 the ark of the covenant overlaid **r** about 3840
Rev 4: 3 *there was* a rainbow **r** about the throne, 2943
 4: 4 And **r** about the throne *were* four and 2943
 4: 6 of the throne, and **r** about the throne, 2945
 5:11 I heard the voice of many angels **r** about 2943
 7:11 all the angels **stood r** about the throne, 2945

ROUSE (1)
Ge 49: 9 and as an old lion; who shall **r** him **up**? 6965

ROUTED See DISCOMFITED; DISCOMFITURE

ROUTING See DISCOMFITED; DISCOMFITURE

ROVERS (1)
1Ch 12:21 helped David against the band *of the* **r.** NIH

ROW (17) [ROWED, ROWERS, ROWING, ROWS]
Ex 28:17 *the first* **r** *shall be* a sardius, a topaz, 2905
 28:17 and a carbuncle: this *shall be* the first **r.** 2905
 28:18 the second **r** *shall be* an emerald, 2905
 28:19 the third **r** a ligure, an agate, 2905
 28:20 the fourth **r** a beryl, and an onyx, 2905
 39:10 *the first* **r** *was* a sardius, a topaz, 2905
 39:10 and a carbuncle: *this was* the first **r.** 2905
 39:11 the second **r**, an emerald, a sapphire, 2905
 39:12 the third **r**, a ligure, an agate, 2905
 39:13 fourth **r**, a beryl, an onyx, and a jasper: 2905
Lev 24: 6 shalt set them *in* two rows, six on a **r**, 4635
 24: 7 shalt put pure frankincense upon *each* **r**, 4635
1Ki 6:36 of hewed stone, and a **r** of cedar beams. 2905
 7: 3 that *lay* upon forty five pillars, fifteen *in* a **r**. 2905
 7:12 a **r** of cedar beams, both for the inner 2905
Ezr 6: 4 of great stones, and a **r** of new timber: 5073
Eze 46:23 *there was* a **r** of *building* round about in 2905

ROWED (2) [ROW]
Jnh 1:13 Nevertheless the men **r** **hard** to bring *it* to 2864
Jn 6:19 So when they had **r** about five and twenty 1643

ROWERS (1) [ROW]
Eze 27:26 Thy **r** have brought thee into great waters: 7751

ROWING (1) [ROW]
Mk 6:48 And he saw them toiling in **r**; for the wind 1643

ROWS (16) [ROW]
Ex 28:17 it settings of stones, *even* four **r** of stones: 2905
 39:10 set in it four **r** of stones: *the first* row 2905
Lev 24: 6 shalt set them *in* two **r**, six on a row, 4634
1Ki 6:36 he built the inner court with three **r** of 2905
 7: 2 thirty cubits, upon four **r** of cedar pillars, 2905
 7: 4 *there were* windows in three **r**, 2905
 7:12 about *was* with three **r** of hewed stones, 2905
 7:18 two **r** round about upon the one network 2905
 7:20 the pomegranates *were* two hundred *in* **r** 2905
 7:24 the knops *were* cast in two **r**, when it 2905
 7:42 even two **r** of pomegranates for one 2905
2Ch 3: 3 Two **r** *of* oxen *were* cast, when it was 2905
 4:13 two **r** of pomegranates on each wreath, 2905
Ezr 6: 4 With three **r** of great stones, and a row of 5073
SS 1:10 Thy cheeks are comely with **r** of jewels, 8447
Eze 46:23 *was* made *with* boiling places under the **r** 2918

ROYAL (29)
Ge 49:20 *shall be* fat, and he shall yield **r** dainties. 4428
Jos 10: 2 as one of the **r** cities, and because it *was* 4467
1Sa 27: 5 for why should thy servant dwell in the **r** city. 4467
2Sa 12:26 children of Ammon, and took the **r** city. 4410
1Ki 10:13 which Solomon gave her of his **r** bounty. 4428
2Ki 11: 1 she arose and destroyed all the seed **r** 4467
 25:25 the seed **r**, came, and ten men with him, 4467
1Ch 29:25 bestowed upon him *such* **r** majesty as had 4438
2Ch 22:10 destroyed all the seed **r** of the house of 4467
Est 1: 7 **r** wine in abundance, according to the 4438
 1: 9 **r** house which *belonged* to king 4438
 1:11 queen before the king with the crown **r**, 4438
 1:19 let there go a **r** commandment from him, 4438
 1:19 the king give her **r** **estate** unto another 4438
 2:16 into his house **r** in the tenth month, 4438
 2:17 so that he set the **r** crown upon her head, 4438
 5: 1 that Esther put on *her* **r** *apparel,* and 4438
 5: 1 the king sat upon his **r** throne in the royal 4438
 5: 1 the king sat upon his royal throne in the **r** 4438
 6: 8 Let the **r** apparel be brought which the 4438
 6: 8 the crown **r** which is set upon his head: 4438
 8:15 presence of the king in **r** apparel of blue 4438
Isa 62: 3 and a **r** diadem in the hand of thy God. 4410

Jer 41: 1 of the seed **r**, and the princes of the king, 4410
 43:10 he shall spread his **r** **pavilion** over them. 8237
Da 6: 7 have consulted together to establish a **r** 4430
Ac 12:21 arrayed in **r** apparel, sat upon his throne, 937
Jas 2: 8 If ye fulfil the **r** law according to 937
1Pe 2: 9 a **r** priesthood, a holy nation, a peculiar 934

RUBBING (1)
Lk 6: 1 corn, and did eat, **r** them in *their* hands. 5597

RUBBISH (2)
Ne 4: 2 out of the heaps of the **r** which are burnt? 6083
 4:10 burdens is decayed, and *there is* much **r**; 6083

RUBIES (6)
Job 28:18 for the price of wisdom *is* above **r**. 6443
Pr 3:15 She *is* more precious than **r**: and all 6443
 8:11 For wisdom *is* better than **r**; and all 6443
 20:15 There is gold, and a multitude of **r**: 6443
 31:10 for her price *is* far above **r**. 6443
La 4: 7 they were more ruddy *in* body than **r**, 6443

RUBY See AGATES; SARDIUS

RUDDER (1)
Ac 27:40 and loosed the **r** bands, and hoised up 4079

RUDDY (4)
1Sa 16:12 Now he *was* **r**, *and* withal of a beautiful 132
 17:42 a youth, and, **r**, and of a fair countenance. 132
SS 5:10 My beloved *is* white and **r**, the chiefest 122
La 4: 7 they were more **r** *in* body than rubies, 119

RUDE (1)
2Co 11: 6 But though *I be* **r** in speech, yet not in 2399

RUDIMENTS (2)
Col 2: 8 after the **r** of the world, and not after 4747
 2:20 dead with Christ from the **r** of the world, 4747

RUE (1)
Lk 11:42 for ye tithe mint and **r** and all *manner of* 4076

RUFUS (2)
Mk 15:21 the father of Alexander and **R**, to bear his 4504
Ro 16:13 Salute **R** chosen in the Lord, 4504

RUHAMAH (1) [LO-RUHAMAH]
Hos 2: 1 Ammi; and to your sisters, **R**. 7355

RUIN (11) [RUINED, RUINOUS, RUINS]
2Ch 28:23 they were the **r** of him, and of all Israel. 3782
Ps 89:40 thou hast brought his strong holds to **r**. 4288
Pr 24:22 and who knoweth the **r** of them both? 6365
 26:28 by it; and a flattering mouth worketh **r**. 4072
Isa 3: 6 ruler, and *let* this **r** *be* under thy hand: 4384
 23:13 palaces thereof; *and* he brought it to **r**. 4654
 25: 2 of a city a heap; *of* a defenced city a **r**: 4654
Eze 18:30 so iniquity shall not be your **r**. 4383
 27:27 the midst of the seas in the day of thy **r**. 4658
 31:13 Upon his **r** shall all the fowls of the 4658
Lk 6:49 it fell; and the **r** of that house was great. 4485

RUINED (3) [RUIN]
Isa 3: 8 For Jerusalem is **r**, and Judah is fallen: 3782
Eze 36:35 and **r** cities are become fenced, 2040
 36:36 know that I the Lord build the **r** places, 2040

RUINOUS (3) [RUIN]
2Ki 19:25 be to lay waste fenced cities *into* **r** heaps. 5327
Isa 17: 1 from *being* a city, and it shall be a **r** heap. 4654
 37:26 to lay waste defenced cities *into* **r** heaps. 5327

RUINS (3) [RUIN]
Eze 21:15 heart may faint, and *their* **r** be multiplied: 4383
Am 9:11 I will raise up his **r**, and I will build it as 2034
Ac 15:16 And I will build again the **r** thereof, 2679

RULE (66) [RULED, RULER, RULER'S, RULERS, RULEST, RULETH, RULING]
Ge 1:16 greater light to **r** the day, and the lesser 4475
 1:16 day, and the lesser light to **r** the night: 4475
 1:18 to **r** over the day and over the night, 4910
 3:16 to thy husband, and he shall **r** over thee. 4910
 4: 7 be his desire, and thou shalt **r** over him. 4910
Lev 25:43 Thou shalt not **r** over him with rigour; 7287
 25:46 shall not **r** one over another with rigour: 7287
 25:53 the *other* shall not **r** with rigour **over** him 7287
Jdg 8:22 **R** thou over us, both thou, and thy son, 4910
 8:23 said unto them, I will not **r** over you, 4910
 8:23 over you, neither shall my son **r** over you: 4910
 8:23 rule over you: the Lord shall **r** over you. 4910
1Ki 9:23 **bare r** over the people that wrought 7287
 22:31 two captains that had **r** over *his* chariots, NIH
2Ch 8:10 that **bare r** over the people. 7287
Ne 5:15 yea, even their servants **bare r** over 7980
Est 1:22 that every man should **bear r** in his own 8323
 9: 1 Jews had **r** over them that hated them;) 7980
Ps 10: 2 **r** thou in the midst of thine enemies. 7287
 136: 8 The sun to **r** by day: for his mercy 4475
 136: 9 The moon and stars to **r** by night: for his 4475
Pr 8:16 By me princes **r**, and nobles, *even* 8323
 12:24 The hand of the diligent shall **bear r**: 4910
 17: 2 A wise servant shall **have r** over a son 4910
 19:10 much less for a servant to **have r** over 4910
 25:28 He that *hath* no **r** over his own spirit *is* 4623

Pr 29: 2 when the wicked **beareth** r, the people — 4910
Ecc 2:19 yet shall he **have** r over all my labour — 7980
Isa 3: 4 their princes, and babes shall r over them. — 4910
 3:12 their oppressors, and women r over them. — 4910
 14: 2 and they shall r over their oppressors. — 7287
 19: 4 a fierce king shall r over them, saith — 4910
 28:14 that r this people which *is* in Jerusalem. — 4910
 32: 1 and princes shall r in judgment. — 8323
 40:10 strong *hand*, and his arm shall r for him: — 4910
 41: 2 before him, and **made** *him* r over kings? — 7287
 44:13 The carpenter stretcheth out *his* r; — 6957
 52: 5 that r **over** them make *them* to howl, — 4910
 63:19 We are *thine*: thou never **barest** r over — 4910
Jer 5:31 and the priests **bear** r by their means; — 7287
Eze 19:11 rods for the sceptres of them that **bare** r, — 4910
 19:14 hath no strong rod *to be* a sceptre to r. — 4910
 20:33 with fury poured out, will I r over you: — 4427
 29:15 *they* shall no more r over the nations. — 7287
Da 2:39 which shall **bear** r over all the earth. — 7981
 4:26 shalt have known that the heavens do r. — 7990
 11: 3 that shall r *with* great dominion, — 4910
 11:39 he shall **cause** them to r over many, — 4910
Joel 2:17 should the heathen should r over them: — 4910
Zec 6:13 and shall sit and r upon his throne: — 4910
Mt 2: 6 a Governor, that shall r my people Israel. — 4165
Mk 10:42 r over the Gentiles exercise lordship over — 757
1Co 15:24 when he shall have put down all r and — 746
2Co 10:13 according to the measure of the r which — 2583
 10:15 by you according to our r abundantly, — 2583
Gal 6:16 And as many as walk according to this r, — 2583
Php 3:16 *let us* walk by the same r, *let us* mind — 2583
Col 3:15 And let the peace of God r in your hearts, — 1018
1Ti 3: 5 (For if a man know not how to r his own — 4291
 5:17 the elders that r well be counted worthy — 4291
Heb 13: 7 Remember them which **have the** r over — 2233
 13:17 Obey them that **have the** r over you, — 2233
 13:24 Salute all them that **have the** r over you, — 2233
Rev 2:27 And he shall r them with a rod of iron; — 4165
 12: 5 was to r all nations with a rod of iron: — 4165
 19:15 and he shall r them with a rod of iron: — 4165

RULED (13) [RULE]

Ge 24: 2 of his house that r over all that he had, — 4910
 41:40 unto thy word shall all my people be r: — 5401
Jos 12: 2 who dwelt in Heshbon, *and* r from Aroer, — 4910
Ru 1: 1 to pass in the days when the judges r, — 8199
1Ki 5:16 which r over the people that wrought in — 7287
1Ch 26: 6 r throughout the house of their father: — 4474
Ezr 4:20 which have r over all *countries* beyond — 7990
Ps 106:41 and they that hated them r over them. — 4910
Isa 14: 6 that r the nations in anger, *is* persecuted, — 7287
La 5: 8 Servants have r over us: *there is* none — 4910
Eze 34: 4 force and with cruelty have ye r them. — 7287
Da 5:21 till he knew that the most high God r in — 7990
 11: 4 according to his dominion which he r: — 4910

RULER (84) [RULE]

Ge 41:43 he made him r over all the land of Egypt. — NIH
 43:16 he said to the r of his house, — 834+5921
 45: 8 and a r throughout all the land of Egypt. — 4910
Ex 22:28 the gods, nor curse the r of thy people. — 5387
Lev 4:22 a r hath sinned, and done somewhat — 5387
Nu 13: 2 send a man, every one a r among them. — 5387
Jdg 9:30 when Zebul the r of the city heard — 8269
1Sa 25:30 shall have appointed thee r over Israel; — 5057
2Sa 6:21 to appoint me r over the people of — 5057
 7: 8 to be r over my people, over Israel: — 5057
 20:26 Ira also the Jairite was a **chief** r about — 3548
1Ki 1:35 I have appointed him to be r over Israel — 5057
 11:28 he **made** him r over all the charge of — 6485
2Ki 25:22 **made** Gedaliah the son of Ahikam, —
 the son of Shaphan, r. — 6485
1Ch 5: 2 brethren, and of him *came* the **chief** r; — 5057
 9:11 son of Ahitub, the r of the house of God; — 5057
 9:20 Phinehas the son of Eleazar was the r — 5057
 11: 2 and thou shalt be r over my people Israel. — 5057
 17: 7 that *thou* shouldest be r over my people — 5057
 26:24 the son of Moses, *was* r of the treasures. — 5057
 27: 4 and *of* his course *was* Mikloth also the r: — 5057
 27:16 the r of the Reubenites *was* Eliezer the — 5057
 28: 4 for he hath chosen Judah to be the r; — 5057
2Ch 6: 5 neither chose I any man to be a r over my — 5057
 7:18 There shall not fail thee a man *to be* r in — 4910
 11:22 the chief, to be r among his brethren: — 5057
 19:11 the r of the house of Judah, for all — 5057
 26:11 of Jeiel the scribe and Maaseiah the r, — 7860
 31:12 over which Cononiah the Levite *was* r, — 5057
 31:13 and Azariah the r of the house of God. — 5057
Ne 3: 9 of Hur, the r of the half part of Jerusalem. — 8269
 3:12 the r of the half part of Jerusalem, he and — 8269
 3:14 of Rechab, the r of part of Beth-haccerem; — 8269
 3:15 son of Col-hozeh, the r of part of Mizpah; — 8269
 3:16 Azbuk, the r of the half part of Beth-zur, — 8269
 3:17 the r of the half part of Keilah, in his part. — 8269
 3:18 Henadad, the r of the half part of Keilah. — 8269
 3:19 Ezer the son of Jeshua, the r of Mizpah, — 8269
 7: 2 Hananiah the r of the palace, charge over — 8269
 11:11 of Ahitub, *was* the r of the house of God. — 5057
Ps 68:27 There *is* little Benjamin *with* their r, — 7287
 105:20 *even* the r of the people, and let him go — 4910
 105:21 of his house, and r of all his substance: — 4910
Pr 6: 7 Which having no guide, overseer, or r, — 4910
 23: 1 When thou sittest to eat with a r, — 4910
 28:15 *so* is a wicked r over the poor people. — 4910
 29:12 If a r hearken to lies, all his servants *are* — 4910

Ecc 10: 4 If the spirit of the r rise up against thee, — 4910
 10:5 as an error *which* proceedeth from the r: — 7989
Isa 3: 6 be thou our r, and *let* this ruin *be* under — 7101
 3: 7 make me not a r of the people. — 7101
 16: 1 Send ye the lamb *to* the r of the land from — 4910
Jer 51:46 and violence in the land, r against ruler. — 4910
 51:46 and violence in the land, ruler against r. — 4910
Da 2:10 therefore *there is* no king, lord, nor r, — 7990
 2:38 and hath **made** thee r over them all. — 7981
 2:48 **made** him r over the whole province of — 7981
 5: 7 and shall be the third r in the kingdom. — 7981
 5:16 and shalt be the third r in the kingdom. — 7981
 5:29 that *he* should be the third r in — 7990
Mic 5: 2 forth unto me *that is* to be r in Israel; — 4910
Hab 1:14 creeping things, *that have* no r over them? — 4910
Mt 9:18 came a *certain* r, and worshipped him, — 758
 24:45 whom his lord hath **made** r over his — 2525
 24:47 That he shall **make** him r over all his — 2525
 25:21 **make** thee r over many *things*: enter — 2525
 25:23 **make** thee r over many *things*: enter — 2525
Mk 5:35 there came from the r **of the synagogue's** — 752
 5:36 he saith unto the r **of the synagogue**, — 752
 5:38 to the house of the r **of the synagogue**, — 752
Lk 8:41 and he was a r of the synagogue: — 758
 8:49 of the **synagogue's** *house*, saying to — 752
 12:42 whom *his* lord shall **make** r over his — 2525
 12:44 that he will **make** him r over all that he — 2525
 13:14 the r **of the synagogue** answered with — 752
 18:18 And a certain r asked him, saying, — 758
Jn 2: 9 the r **of the feast** had tasted the water — 755
 3: 1 named Nicodemus, a r of the Jews: — 758
Ac 7:27 Who made thee a r and a judge over us? — 758
 7:35 saying, Who made thee a r and a judge? — 758
 7:35 the same did God send *to be* a r and — 758
 18: 8 Crispus, the *chief* r **of the synagogue**, — 752
 18:17 the *chief* r **of the synagogue**, and beat — 752
 23: 5 Thou shalt not speak evil of the r of thy — 758

RULER'S (2) [RULE]

Pr 29:26 Many seek the r favour; but *every* man's — 4910
Mt 9:23 And when Jesus came into the r house, — 758

RULERS (78) [RULE]

Ge 47: 6 then make them r over my cattle. — 8269
Ex 16:22 all the r of the congregation came and — 5387
 18:21 *to be* r of thousands, *and* rulers of — 8269
 18:21 *and* r of hundreds, rulers of fifties, — 8269
 18:21 hundreds, r of fifties, and rulers of tens: — 8269
 18:25 r of thousands, rulers of hundreds, rulers — 8269
 18:25 of hundreds, rulers of fifties, and rulers — 8269
 18:25 of hundreds, r of fifties, and rulers of tens. — 8269
 18:25 hundreds, rulers of fifties, and r of tens. — 8269
 34:31 all the r of the congregation returned unto — 5387
 35:27 the r brought onyx stones, and stones to — 5387
Dt 1:13 and I will make them r over you. — 7218
Jdg 15:11 thou not that the Philistines *are* r — 4910
2Sa 8:18 and David's sons were **chief** r. — 3548
1Ki 9:22 and r of his chariots, and his horsemen. — 8269
2Ki 10: 1 unto the r of Jezreel, to the elders, — 8269
 11: 4 Jehoiada sent and fet the r over hundreds, — 8269
 11:19 he took the r over hundreds, — 8269
1Ch 21: 2 said to Joab and to the r of the people, — 8269
 26:32 whom king David **made** r over — 6485
 27:31 All these *were* the r of the substance — 8269
 29: 6 with the r over the king's work, — 8269
2Ch 29:20 gathered the r of the city, and went up *to* — 8269
 35: 8 and Jehiel, r of the house of God, — 5057
Ezr 9: 2 hath been chief in this trespass. — 5461
 10:14 Let now our r of all the congregation — 8269
Ne 2:16 the r knew not whither I went, or what I — 5461
 2:16 the priests, nor to the nobles, nor to the r, — 5461
 4:14 and to the r, and to the rest of the people, — 5461
 4:16 the r *were* behind all the house of Judah. — 8269
 4:19 to the r, and to the rest of the people, — 5461
 5: 7 r, and said unto them, You exact usury, — 5461
 5:17 an hundred and fifty of the Jews and r, — 5461
 7: 5 the r, and the people, that *they* might be — 5461
 11: 1 the r of the people dwelt at Jerusalem: — 8269
 12:40 God, and I, and the half of the r with me: — 5461
 13:11 contended I with the r, and said, Why is — 5461
Est 3:12 to the r of every people of every province — 8269
 8: 9 r of the provinces *which, are* from India — 8269
 9: 3 all the r of the provinces, — 8269
Ps 2: 2 the r take counsel together, against — 7336
Isa 1:10 the word of the LORD, ye r of Sodom; — 7101
 14: 5 of the wicked, *and* the sceptre of the r. — 4910
 22: 3 All thy r are fled together, they are bound — 7101
 29:10 the prophets and your r, the seers hath he — 7218
 49: 7 to a servant of r, Kings shall see and arise, — 4910
Jer 33:26 that *I* will not take *any* of his seed *to be* r — 4910
 51:23 thee will I break in pieces captains and r, — 5461
 51:28 all the r thereof, and all the land of his — 5461
 51:57 her r, and her mighty *men:* and they shall — 5461
Eze 23: 6 *were* clothed with blue, captains and r, — 5461
 23:12 captains and r clothed most gorgeously, — 5461
 23:23 captains and r, great lords and renowned, — 5461
Da 3: 2 the sheriffs, and all the r of the provinces, — 7984
 3: 3 the sheriffs, and all the r of the provinces, — 7984
Hos 4:18 her r *with* shame do love, Give ye. — 4043
Mk 5:22 cometh one of the r **of the synagogue**, — 752
 13: 9 and ye shall be brought before r and — 2232
Lk 21:12 before kings and r for my name's sake. — 2232
 23:13 the chief priests and the r and the people, — 758
 23:35 And the r also with them derided *him*, — 758

Lk 24:20 our r delivered him to be condemned to — 758
Jn 7:26 Do the r know indeed that this is the very — 758
 7:48 Have any of the r or of the Pharisees — 758
Ac 3:17 ignorance ye did *it*, as *did* also your r. — 758
 4: 5 that their r, and elders, and scribes, — 758
 4: 8 Ye r of the people, and elders of Israel, — 758
 4:26 the r were gathered together against — 758
 13:15 the prophets the r **of the synagogue** sent — 752
 13:27 and their r, because they knew him not, — 758
 14: 5 *also of* the Jews with their r, to use them — 758
 16:19 them into the market-place unto the r, — 758
 17: 6 certain brethren unto the r **of the city**, — 4173
 17: 8 troubled the people and the r **of the city**, — 4173
Ro 13: 3 For r are not a terror to good works, — 758
Eph 6:12 against the r of the darkness of this world, — 2888

RULEST (2) [RULE]

2Ch 20: 6 r *not* thou over all the kingdoms of — 4910
Ps 89: 9 Thou r the raging of the sea: when — 4910

RULETH (14) [RULE]

2Sa 23: 3 He that r over men *must be* just, ruling — 4910
Ps 59:13 let them know that God r in Jacob unto — 4910
 66: 7 He r by his power for ever; his eyes — 4910
 103:19 the heavens; and his kingdom r over all. — 4910
Pr 16:32 that r his spirit than he that taketh a city. — 4910
 22: 7 The rich r over the poor, and the — 4910
Ecc 8: 9 *there is* a time wherein one man r over — 7980
 9:17 more than the cry of him that r among — 4910
Da 4:17 the most High r in the kingdom of men, — 7990
 4:25 till thou know that the most High r in — 7990
 4:32 until thou know that the most High r in — 7990
Hos 11:12 Judah yet r with God, and is faithful with — 7300
Ro 12: 8 he that r, with diligence; he that sheweth — 4291
1Ti 3: 4 One that r well his own house, having — 4291

RULING (3) [RULE]

2Sa 23: 3 men *must be* just, r in the fear of God. — 4910
Jer 22:30 throne of David, and r any more in Judah. — 4910
1Ti 3:12 r *their* children and their own houses well — 4291

RUMAH (1)

2Ki 23:36 Zebudah, the daughter of Pedaiah of R. — 7316

RUMBLING (1)

Jer 47: 3 *at* the rushing of his wheels, the fathers shall — 1995

RUMOUR (10) [RUMOURS]

2Ki 19: 7 he shall hear a r, and shall return to his — 8052
Isa 37: 7 he shall hear a r, and return to his own — 8052
Jer 49:14 I have heard a r from the LORD, — 8052
 51:46 ye fear for the r that shall be heard in — 8052
 51:46 a r shall both come *one* year, and after — 8052
 51:46 after that in *another* year *shall come* a r, — 8052
Eze 7:26 mischief, and r shall be upon rumour; — 8052
 7:26 mischief, and rumour shall be upon r; — 8052
Ob 1: 1 We have heard a r from the LORD, — 8052
Lk 7:17 this r of him went forth throughout all — 3056

RUMOURS (2) [RUMOUR]

Mt 24: 6 And ye shall hear of wars and r of wars: — 189
Mk 13: 7 when ye shall hear of wars and r of wars, — 189

RUMP (5)

Ex 29:22 thou shalt take of the ram the fat and the r, — 451
Lev 3: 9 the fat thereof, *and* the whole r, it shall he — 451
 7: 3 the r, and the fat that covereth the inwards — 451
 8:25 the r, and all the fat that *was* upon — 451
 9:19 the r, and that which covereth the *inwards* — 451

RUN (71) [FORERUNNER, OUTRUN, OVERRUNNING, RAN, RUNNEST, RUNNETH, RUNNING]

Ge 49:22 a well; *whose* branches r over the wall. — 6805
Lev 15: 3 *whether* his flesh r with his issue, — 7325
 15:25 if it r beyond the time of her separation; — 2100
Jdg 18:25 lest angry fellows r upon thee, — 6293
1Sa 8:11 and *some* shall r before his chariots. — 7323
 17:17 and r to the camp to thy brethren; — 7323
 20: 6 that he might r to Beth-lehem his city: — 7323
 20:36 he said unto his lad, R, find out now — 7323
2Sa 15: 1 and horses, and fifty men to r before him. — 7323
 18:19 Let me now r, and bear the king tidings, — 7323
 18:22 let me, I pray thee, also r after Cushi. — 7323
 18:22 Joab said, Wherefore wilt thou r, my son, — 7323
 18:23 howsoever, *said he*, let me r. And he said — 7323
 18:23 he said unto him, R. Then Ahimaaz ran — 7323
 22:30 For by thee I have r through a troop; — 7323
1Ki 1: 5 horsemen, and fifty men to r before him. — 7323
2Ki 4:22 that I may r to the man of God, — 7323
 4:26 R now, I pray thee, to meet her, — 7323
 5:20 I will r after him, and take somewhat of — 7323
2Ch 16: 9 For the eyes of the LORD r to and fro — 7751
Ps 18:29 For by thee I have r through a troop; — 7323
 19: 5 and rejoiceth as a strong *man* to r a race. — 7323
 58: 7 away as waters *which* **continually**: — 1980
 59: 4 They r and prepare themselves without — 7323
 78:16 and **caused** waters to r **down** like rivers. — 3381
 104:10 into the valleys, *which* r among the hills. — 1980
 119:32 I will r the way of thy commandments, — 7323
 119:136 Rivers of waters r **down** mine eyes, — 3381
Pr 1:16 For their feet r to evil, and make haste to — 7323
Ecc 1: 7 All the rivers r into the sea; yet the sea *is* — 1980
SS 1: 4 Draw me, we will r after thee: the king — 7323
Isa 33: 4 and fro of locusts shall he r upon them. — 8264

Isa	40:31 they shall **r**, and not be weary;	7323
	55: 5 nations *that* knew not thee shall **r** unto	7323
	59: 7 Their feet **r** to evil, and they make haste	7323
Jer	5: 1 **R** ye **to and fro** through the streets of	7751
	9:18 that our eyes may **r down** *with* tears,	3381
	12: 5 If thou hast **r** with the footmen,	7323
	13:17 **r down** *with* tears, because the LORD'S	3381
	14:17 Let mine eyes **r down** *with* tears night	3381
	49: 3 lament, and **r to and fro** by the hedges;	7751
	49:19 I will suddenly **make** him **r** away from	7323
	50:44 I will **make** them suddenly **r** away from	7323
	51:31 One post shall **r** to meet another,	7323
La	2:18 let tears **r down** like a river day and night;	3381
Eze	24:16 nor weep, neither shall thy tears **r down.**	935
	32:14 **cause** their rivers **to r** like oil, saith	1980
Da	12: 4 many shall **r to and fro**, and knowledge	7751
Joel	2: 4 horses; and as horsemen, so shall they **r.**	7323
	2: 7 They shall **r** like mighty *men;* they shall	7323
	2: 9 They shall **r to and fro** in the city;	8264
	2: 9 they shall **r** upon the wall, they shall	7323
Am	5:24 let judgment **r down** as waters,	1556
	6:12 Shall horses **r** upon the rock? will *one*	7323
	8:12 they shall **r to and fro** to seek the word	7751
Na	2: 4 torches, they shall **r** like the lightnings.	7323
Hab	2: 2 upon tables, that he may **r** that readeth it.	7323
Hag	1: 9 and ye **r** every man unto his own house.	7323
Zec	2: 4 unto him, **R**, speak to this young man,	7323
	4:10 which **r to and fro** through the whole	7751
Mt	28: 8 and did **r** to bring his disciples word.	5143
1Co	9:24 ye not that they which **r** in a race run	5143
	9:24 ye not that they which **r** in a race	5143
	9:24 the prize? So **r**, that ye may obtain.	5143
	9:26 I therefore so **r**, not as uncertainly;	5143
Gal	2: 2 lest by any means I should **r**, or had run,	5143
	2: 2 any means I should run, or had **r**, in vain.	5143
	5: 7 Ye did **r** well; who did hinder you that *ye*	5143
Php	2:16 that I have not **r** in vain, neither laboured	5143
Heb	12: 1 let us **r** with patience the race that is set	5143
1Pe	4: 4 **r** not **with** *them* to the same excess of	4936

RUNNEST (1) [RUN]

Pr	4:12 and when thou **r**, thou shalt not stumble.	7323

RUNNETH (11) [RUN]

Ezr	8:15 gathered them together to the river that **r**	935
Job	15:26 He **r** upon him, *even* on *his* neck, upon	7323
	16:14 upon breach, he **r** upon me like a giant.	7323
Ps	23: 5 my head with oil; my cup **r** over.	7310
	147:15 upon earth: his word **r** very swiftly.	7323
Pr	18:10 the righteous **r** into it, and is safe.	7323
La	1:16 mine eye **r down** with water, because	3381
	3:48 Mine eye **r down** *with* rivers of water for	3381
Mt	9:17 the wine **r out, and the bottles perish;**	1632
Jn	20: 2 Then she **r**, and cometh to Simon Peter,	5143
Ro	9:16 of him that **r**, but of God that sheweth	5143

RUNNING (26) [RUN]

Lev	14: 5 killed in an earthen vessel over **r** water:	2416
	14: 6 the bird *that was* killed over **r** water:	2416
	14:50 birds in an earthen vessel over **r** water:	2416
	14:51 in the **r** water, and sprinkle the house	2416
	14:52 with the **r** water, and with the living bird,	2416
	15: 2 When any man hath a **r issue** out of his	2100
	15:13 bathe his flesh in **r** water, and shall be	2416
	22: 4 of Aaron *is* a leper, or hath a **r issue;**	2100
Nu	19:17 **r** water shall be put thereto in a vessel:	2416
2Sa	18:24 and looked, and behold a man **r** alone.	7323
	18:26 the watchman saw another man **r:**	7323
	18:26 and said, Behold *another* man **r** alone.	7323
	18:27 Me thinketh the **r** of the foremost *is* like	4794
	18:27 *is* like the **r** of Ahimaaz the son of Zadok.	4794
2Ki	5:21 when Naaman saw him **r** after him,	7323
2Ch	23:12 Athaliah heard the noise of the people **r**	7323
Pr	5:15 and **r waters** out of thine own well.	5140
	6:18 feet that be swift in **r** to mischief;	7323
Isa	33: 4 as the **r to and fro** of locusts shall be	4944
Eze	31: 4 with her rivers **r** round about his plants,	1980
Mk	9:15 greatly amazed, and **r to** *him* saluted him.	4370
	9:25 saw that the people **came r together**,	1998
	10:17 there **came** one **r**, and kneeled to him,	4370
Lk	6:38 **shaken together**, and **r over**,	5240
Ac	27:16 And **r under** a certain island *which is*	5295
Rev	9: 9 of chariots of many horses **r** to battle.	5143

RUSE See WILILY

RUSH (4) [BULRUSH, BULRUSHES, RUSHED, RUSHES, RUSHETH, RUSHING]

Job	8:11 Can the **r** grow up without mire?	1573
Isa	9:14 off from Israel head and tail, branch and **r**,	100
	17:13 The nations shall **r** like the rushing of	7582
	19:15 the head or tail, branch or **r**, may do.	100

RUSHED (3) [RUSH]

Jdg	9:44 **r** forward, and stood *in* the entering of	6584
	20:37 liers in wait hasted, and **r** upon Gibeah;	6584
Ac	19:29 they **r** with one accord into the theatre.	3729

RUSHES (1) [RUSH]

Isa	35: 7 each lay, *shall be* grass with reeds and **r**.	1573

RUSHETH (1) [RUSH]

Jer	8: 6 his course, as the horse **r** into the battle.	7857

RUSHING (8) [RUSH]

Isa	17:12 to the **r** of nations, *that* make a rushing	7588

Isa	17:12 *that* **make a r** like the rushing of mighty	7582
	17:12 *that* make a rushing like the **r** of mighty	7588
	17:13 The nations shall rush like the **r** of many	7588
Jer	47: 3 the *noise* of the **r**, at the **r** of his chariots,	7494
Eze	3:12 I heard behind me a voice of a great **r**,	7494
	3:13 against them, and a noise of a great **r**.	7494
Ac	2: 2 sound from heaven as of a **r** mighty wind,	5342

RUST (3)

Mt	6:19 where moth and **r** doth corrupt,	1035
	6:20 where neither moth nor **r** doth corrupt,	1035
Jas	5: 3 the **r** of them shall be a witness against	2447

RUTH (13)

Ru	1: 4 *was* Orpah, and the name of the other **R:**	7327
	1:14 her mother in law; but **R** clave unto her.	7327
	1:16 **R** said, Intreat me not to leave thee,	7327
	1:22 So Naomi returned, and **R** the Moabitess,	7327
	2: 2 **R** the Moabitess said unto Naomi, Let me	7327
	2: 8 said Boaz unto **R**, Hearest thou not,	7327
	2:21 **R** the Moabitess said, He said unto me,	7327
	2:22 Naomi said unto **R** her daughter in law,	7327
	3: 9 she answered, I *am* **R** thine handmaid:	7327
	4: 5 thou must buy *it* also of **R** the Moabitess,	7327
	4:10 Moreover **R** the Moabitess, the wife of	7327
	4:13 So Boaz took **R**, and she was his wife:	7327
Mt	1: 5 Booz begat Obed of **R**; and Obed begat	4503

RUTHLESS See IMPLACABLE

RUTHLESSLY See RIGOUR

RYE (2)

Ex	9:32 the wheat and the **r** were not smitten:	3698
Isa	28:25 appointed barley and the **r** *in* their place?	3698

S

SABACHTHANI (2)

Mt	27:46 a loud voice, saying, ELI, ELI, LAMA **S?**	4518
Mk	15:34 loud voice, saying, ELOI, ELOI, LAMA **S?**	4518

SABAOTH (2)

Ro	9:29 Except the Lord of **s** had left us a seed,	4519
Jas	5: 4 are entered into the ears of the Lord of **s**.	4519

SABBATH (137) [SABBATHS]

Ex	16:23 To morrow *is* the rest of the holy **s** unto	7676
	16:25 to day; for to day *is* a **s** unto the LORD	7676
	16:26 on the seventh day, which *is* the **s**, in it	7676
	16:29 for that the LORD hath given you the **s**,	7676
	20: 8 Remember the **s** day, to keep it holy.	7676
	20:10 the seventh day *is* the **s** of the LORD thy	7676
	20:11 wherefore the LORD blessed the **s** day,	7676
	31:14 Ye shall keep the **s** therefore; for it *is* holy	7676
	31:15 in the seventh *is* the **s** of rest, holy to	7676
	31:15 whosoever doeth *any* work in the **s** day,	7676
	31:16 the children of Israel shall keep the **s**,	7676
	31:16 to observe the **s** throughout their	7676
	35: 2 to you a holy *day*, a **s** of rest to the LORD:	7676
	35: 3 your habitations upon the **s** day.	7676
Lev	16:31 It *shall be* a **s** of rest unto you, and ye	7676
	23: 3 the seventh day *is* the **s** of rest, a holy	7676
	23: 3 ye shall do no work *therein:* it *is* the **s** of	7676
	23:11 on the morrow after the **s** the priest shall	7676
	23:15 unto you from the morrow after the **s**,	7676
	23:16 Even unto the morrow after the seventh **s**	7676
	23:24 *first day* of the month, shall ye have a **s**,	7677
	23:32 It *shall be* unto you a **s** of rest, and ye	7676
	23:32 even, shall ye **celebrate** your **s**.	7673+7676
	23:39 on the first day *shall be* a **s**, and on	7677
	23:39 and on the eighth day *shall be* a **s**.	7677
	24: 8 **Every** he shall set it in order	3117+3117
		+7676+7676+871.1+871.1+1886.1+1886.1
	25: 2 the land **keep a s** unto the LORD.	7673+7676
	25: 4 in the seventh year shall be a **s** of rest	7676
	25: 4 of rest unto the land, a **s** for the LORD:	7676
	25: 6 the **s** of the land shall be meat for you;	7676
Nu	15:32 man that gathered sticks upon the **s** day.	7676
	28: 9 on the **s** day two lambs of the first year	7676
	28:10 burnt offering of **every s**,	7676+7676+871.1
Dt	5:12 Keep the **s** day to sanctify it, as the LORD	7676
	5:14 the seventh day *is* the **s** of the LORD thy	7676
	5:15 God commanded thee to keep the **s** day.	7676
2Ki	4:23 *it is* neither new moon, nor **s**.	7676
	11: 5 A third *part* of you that enter in on the **s**	7676
	11: 7 two parts of all you that go forth on the **s**,	7676
	11: 9 his men that were to come in on the **s**,	7676
	11: 9 with them that should go out on the **s**,	7676
	16:18 the covert for the **s** that they had built in	7676
1Ch	9:32 shewbread, to prepare *it* **every s**.	7676+7676
2Ch	23: 4 A third *part* of you entering on the **s**,	7676
	23: 8 his men that were to come in on the **s**;	7676
	23: 8 with them that were to go out on the **s:**	7676
	36:21 *for* as long as *she* lay desolate she **kept s**,	7673
Ne	9:14 madest known unto them thy holy **s**,	7676

Ne	10:31 or any victuals on the **s** day to sell,	7676
	10:31 we would not buy *it* of them on the **s**,	7676
	13:15 *some* treading wine presses on the **s**,	7676
	13:15 they brought *into* Jerusalem on the **s**	7676
	13:16 sold on the **s** unto the children of Judah,	7676
	13:17 *is* this that ye do, and profane the **s** day?	7676
	13:18 wrath upon Israel by profaning the **s**.	7676
	13:19 Jerusalem began to be dark before the **s**,	7676
	13:19 they should not be opened till after the **s:**	7676
	13:19 no burden be brought in on the **s** day.	7676
	13:21 time forth came they no *more* on the **s**.	7676
	13:22 *and* keep the gates, to sanctify the **s** day.	7676
Ps	92: T A Psalm *or* Song for the **s** day.	7676
Isa	56: 2 that keepeth the **s** from polluting it,	7676
	56: 6 one that keepeth the **s** from polluting	7676
	58:13 If thou turn away thy foot from the **s**,	7676
	58:13 call the **s** a delight, the holy of the LORD,	7676
	66:23 to another, and from one **s** to another,	7676
Jer	17:21 bear no burden on the **s** day,	7676
	17:22 a burden out of your houses on the **s** day,	7676
	17:22 do ye any work, but hallow ye the **s** day,	7676
	17:24 through the gates of this city on the **s** day,	7676
	17:24 hallow the **s** day, to do no work therein;	7676
	17:27 not hearken unto me to hallow the **s** day;	7676
	17:27 in at the gates of Jerusalem on the **s** day;	7676
Eze	46: 1 on the **s** it shall be opened, and in	3117+7676
	46: 4 **s** day shall be six lambs without blemish,	7676
	46:12 his peace offerings, as he did on the **s** day:	7676
Am	8: 5 the **s**, that we may set forth wheat,	7676
Mt	12: 1 At that time Jesus went on the **s** day	4521
	12: 2 which is not lawful to do upon the **s** day.	4521
	12: 5 how that on the **s** days the priests in	4521
	12: 5 the priests in the temple profane the **s**,	4521
	12: 8 For the Son of man is Lord even of the **s**.	4521
	12:10 saying, Is it lawful to heal on the **s** days?	4521
	12:11 and if it fall into a pit on the **s** day, will he	4521
	12:12 Wherefore it is lawful to do well on the **s**	4521
	24:20 be not in the winter, neither on the **s** day:	4521
	28: 1 In the end of the **s**, as it began to dawn	4521
Mk	1:21 straightway on the **s** day he entered into	4521
	2:23 he went through the corn fields on the **s**	4521
	2:24 do they on the **s** day *that* which is not	4521
	2:27 The **s** was made for man, *and* not man for	4521
	2:27 was made for man, *and* not man for the **s:**	4521
	2:28 the Son of man is Lord also of the **s**.	4521
	3: 2 whether he would heal him on the **s** day;	4521
	3: 4 Is it lawful to do good on the **s** days,	4521
	6: 2 And when the **s** day was come, he began	4521
	15:42 that is, the **day before the s**,	4315
	16: 1 when the **s** was past, Mary Magdalene,	4521
Lk	4:16 he went into the synagogue on the **s** day,	4521
	4:31 of Galilee, and taught them on the **s** days.	4521
	6: 1 And it came to pass on the second **s** after	4521
	6: 2 which is not lawful to do on the **s** days?	4521
	6: 5 That the Son of man is Lord also of the **s**.	4521
	6: 6 And it came to pass also on another **s**,	4521
	6: 7 whether he would heal on the **s** day;	4521
	6: 9 Is it lawful on the **s** days to do good,	4521
	13:10 in one of the synagogues on the **s**.	4521
	13:14 that Jesus had healed on the **s** day,	4521
	13:14 and be healed, and not on the **s** day.	4521
	13:15 not each one of you on the **s** loose his	4521
	13:16 be loosed from this bond on the **s** day?	4521
	14: 1 chief Pharisees to eat bread on the **s** day,	4521
	14: 3 saying, Is it lawful to heal on the **s** day?	4521
	14: 5 will not straightway pull him out on the **s**	4521
	23:54 was the preparation, and the **s** drew on.	4521
	23:56 rested the **s** day according to	4521
Jn	5: 9 walked: and on the same day was the **s**.	4521
	5:10 unto him that was cured, It is the **s** day:	4521
	5:16 he had done these *things* on the **s** day.	4521
	5:18 because he not only had broken the **s**,	4521
	7:22 and ye on the **s** day circumcise a man.	4521
	7:23 If a man on the **s** day receive circumcision,	4521
	7:23 a man every whit whole on the **s** day?	4521
	9:14 And it was the **s** day when Jesus made	4521
	9:16 of God, because he keepeth not the **s** day.	4521
	19:31 not remain upon the cross on the **s** day,	4521
	19:31 (for that **s** day was a high day,)	4521
Ac	1:12 Jerusalem a **s day's journey.**	2192+3598+4521
	13:14 and went into the synagogue on the **s** day,	4521
	13:27 the prophets which are read every **s** day,	4521
	13:42 might be preached to them the next **s**.	4521
	13:44 the next **s** day came almost the whole	4521
	15:21 being read in the synagogues every **s** day.	4521
	16:13 And on the **s** we went out of the city by a	4521
	17: 2 three **s** days reasoned with them out of	4521
	18: 4 he reasoned in the synagogue every **s**,	4521
Col	2:16 of the new moon, or of the **s days:**	4521

SABBATHS (35) [SABBATH]

Ex	31:13 Israel, saying, Verily my **s** ye shall keep:	7676
Lev	19: 3 mother, and his father, and keep my **s:**	7676
	19:30 Ye shall keep my **s**, and reverence my	7676
	23:15 wave offering; seven **s** shall be complete:	7676
	23:38 Beside the **s** of the LORD,	7676
	25: 8 thou shalt number seven **s** of years unto	7676
	25: 8 the space of the seven **s** of years shall be	7676
	26: 2 Ye shall keep my **s**, and reverence my	7676
	26:34 the land enjoy her **s**, as long as it lieth	7676
	26:34 then shall the land rest, and enjoy her **s**.	7676
	26:35 because it did not rest in your **s**, when ye	7676
	26:43 shall be left of them, and shall enjoy her **s**,	7676
1Ch	23:31 burnt sacrifices unto the LORD in the **s**,	7676
2Ch	2: 4 on the **s**, and on the new moons, and on	7676

2Ch 8:13 on the **s**, and on the new moons, and on 7676
31: 3 the burnt offerings for the **s**, and for 7676
36:21 until the land had enjoyed her **s**: 7676
Ne 10:33 of the **s**, of the new moons, for the set 7676
Isa 1:13 the new moons and **s**, the calling of 7676
56: 4 LORD unto the eunuchs that keep my **s**, 7676
La 1: 7 saw her, *and* did mock at her **s**. 4868
2: 6 feasts and **s** to be forgotten in Zion, 7676
Eze 20:12 Moreover also I gave them my **s**, to be a 7676
20:13 in them; and my **s** they greatly polluted: 7676
20:16 not in my statutes, but polluted my **s**: 7676
20:20 hallow my **s**; and they shall be a sign 7676
20:21 even live in them; they polluted my **s**: 7676
20:24 had polluted my **s**, and their eyes were 7676
22: 8 mine holy *things*, and hast profaned my **s**. 7676
22:26 have hid their eyes from my **s**, and I am 7676
23:38 in the same day, and have profaned my **s**. 7676
44:24 and they shall hallow my **s**. 7676
45:17 in the **s** in all solemnities of the house of 7676
46: 3 door of this gate before the LORD in the **s** 7676
Hos 2:11 her **s**, and all her solemn feasts. 7676

SABEANS (4)
Job 1:15 **S** fell *upon them*, and took them away; 7614
Isa 45:14 merchandise of Ethiopia and of the **S**, 5436
Eze 23:42 sort *were* brought **S** from the wilderness, 5436
Joel 3: 8 they shall sell them to the **S**, to a people 7615

SABTA (1) [SABTAH]
1Ch 1: 9 and **S**, and Raamah, and Sabtecha 5454

SABTAH (1) [SABTA]
Ge 10: 7 and **S**, and Raamah, and Sabtecha 5454

SABTECA See SABTECHA

SABTECHA (2)
Ge 10: 7 Havilah, and Sabtah, and Raamah, and **S**: 5455
1Ch 1: 9 Havilah, and Sabta, and Raamah, and **S**. 5455

SACAR (2)
1Ch 11:35 Ahiam the son of **S** the Hararite, Eliphal 7940
26: 4 and **S** the fourth, and Nethaneel the fifth, 7940

SACK (9) [SACK'S, SACKBUT, SACKCLOTH, SACKCLOTHES, SACKS, SACKS']
Ge 42:25 to restore every man's money into his **s**, 8242
42:27 as one *of them* opened his **s** to give his 8242
42:28 is restored; and lo, *it is* even in my **s**: 572
42:35 man's bundle of money *was* in his **s**: 8242
43:21 man's money *was* in the mouth of his **s** 572
44:11 they speedily took down every man his **s** 572
44:11 the ground, and opened every man his **s**. 572
44:12 and the cup was found in Benjamin's **s**. 572
Lev 11:32 vessel of wood, or raiment, or skin, or **s**, 8242

SACK'S (3) [SACK]
Ge 42:27 money; for behold, it *was* in his **s** mouth. 572
44: 1 put every man's money in his **s** mouth. 572
44: 2 in the **s** mouth of the youngest, and his 572

SACKBUT (4) [SACK]
Da 3: 5 flute, harp, **s**, psaltery, dulcimer, 5443
3: 7 flute, harp, **s**, psaltery, and all kinds of 5443
3:10 flute, harp, **s**, psaltery, and dulcimer, 5443
3:15 flute, harp, **s**, psaltery, and dulcimer, 5443

SACKCLOTH (46) [CLOTH, SACK]
Ge 37:34 put **s** upon his loins, and mourned for his 8242
2Sa 3:31 gird you with **s**, and mourn before Abner. 8242
21:10 Rizpah the daughter of Aiah took **s**, 8242
1Ki 20:31 put **s** on our loins, and ropes upon our 8242
20:32 So they girded **s** on their loins, 8242
21:27 put **s** upon his flesh, and fasted, and lay 8242
21:27 and fasted, and lay in **s**, and went softly. 8242
2Ki 6:30 behold, *he had* **s** within upon his flesh. 8242
19: 1 covered himself with **s**, and went *into* 8242
19: 2 the elders of the priests, covered with **s**, 8242
1Ch 21:16 elders *of Israel, who were* clothed in **s**, 8242
Est 4: 1 put on **s** with ashes, and went out into 8242
4: 2 enter into the king's gate clothed with **s**. 8242
4: 3 and wailing; *and* many lay in **s** and ashes. 8242
4: 4 and to take away his **s** from him: 8242
Job 16:15 I have sewed **s** upon my skin, 8242
Ps 30:11 thou hast put off my **s**, and girded me 8242
35:13 when they were sick, my clothing *was* **s**: 8242
69:11 I made **s** also my garment; and I became 8242
Isa 3:24 instead of a stomacher a girding of **s**; 8242
15: 3 streets they shall gird themselves with **s**: 8242
20: 2 Go and loose the **s** from off thy loins, 8242
22:12 and to baldness, and to girding with **s**: 8242
32:11 make ye bare, and gird **s** upon *your* loins. NIH
37: 1 covered himself with **s**, and went *into* 8242
37: 2 the elders of the priests covered with **s**, 8242
50: 3 blackness, and I make **s** their covering. 8242
58: 5 to spread a **s** and ashes *under him?* 8242
Jer 4: 8 For this gird you with **s**, lament and howl: 8242
6:26 gird *thee* with **s**, and wallow thyself in 8242
48:37 *shall be* cuttings, and upon the loins **s**. 8242
49: 3 ye daughters of Rabbah, gird ye with **s**; 8242
La 2:10 they have girded themselves with **s**: 8242
Eze 7:18 They shall also gird *themselves* with **s**, 8242
27:31 gird them with **s**, and they shall weep for 8242
Da 9: 3 with fasting, and **s**, and ashes: 8242
Joel 1: 8 Lament like a virgin girded with **s** for 8242
1:13 come, lie all night in **s**, ye ministers of my 8242

Am 8:10 I will bring up **s** upon all loins, 8242
Jnh 3: 5 proclaimed a fast, and put on **s**, 8242
3: 6 and covered *him* with **s**, and sat in ashes. 8242
3: 8 let man and beast be covered with **s**, 8242
Mt 11:21 they would have repented long ago in **s** 4526
Lk 10:13 while ago repented, sitting in **s** and ashes. 4526
Rev 6:12 and the sun became black as **s** of hair, 4526
11: 3 *and* threescore days, clothed in **s**. 4526

SACKCLOTHES (1) [CLOTH, SACK]
Ne 9: 1 and with **s**, and earth upon them. 8242

SACKS (9) [SACK]
Ge 42:25 commanded to fill their **s** *with* corn, 3627
42:35 it came to pass as they emptied their **s**, 8242
43:12 was brought again in the mouth of your **s**, 572
43:18 in our **s** at the first time *are* we brought in; 572
43:21 the inn, that we opened our **s**, and, behold, 572
43:22 cannot tell who put our money in our **s**. 572
43:23 hath given you treasure in your **s**: 572
44: 1 saying, Fill the men's **s** *with* food, as much 572
Jos 9: 4 took old **s** upon their asses, 8242

SACKS' (1) [SACK]
Ge 44: 8 money, which we found in our **s** mouths, 572

SACRED See HALLOW; HALLOWED

SACRIFICE (218) [SACRIFICED, SACRIFICEDST, SACRIFICES, SACRIFICETH, SACRIFICING]
Ge 31:54 Jacob offered **s** upon the mount, 2077
Ex 3:18 that we may **s** to the LORD our God. 2076
5: 3 the desert, and **s** unto the LORD our God; 2076
5: 8 saying, Let us go and **s** to our God. 2076
5:17 ye say, Let us go and **do s** to the LORD. 2076
8: 8 that they may **do s** unto the LORD. 2076
8:25 said, Go ye, **s** to your God in the land. 2076
8:26 for we shall **s** the abomination of 2076
8:26 we **s** the abomination of the Egyptians 2076
8:27 **s** to the LORD our God, as he shall 2076
8:28 that ye may **s** to the LORD your God in 2076
8:29 letting the people go to **s** to the LORD. 2076
10:25 that we may **s** unto the LORD our God. 6213
12:27 It *is* the **s** of the LORD's passover, 2077
13:15 I **s** to the LORD all that openeth 2076
20:24 shalt **s** thereon thy burnt offerings, and 2076
23:18 Thou shalt not offer the blood of my **s** 2077
23:18 neither shall the fat of my **s** remain until 2282
29:28 of Israel of the **s** of their peace offerings, 2077
30: 9 nor **burnt s**, nor meat offering; 5930
34:15 do **s** unto their gods, and *one* call thee, 2076
34:15 and *one* call thee, and thou eat of his **s**; 2077
34:25 Thou shalt not offer the blood of my **s** 2077
34:25 neither shall the **s** of the feast of 2077
Lev 1: 3 If his offering *be* a **burnt s** of the herd, 5930
1: 9 *to be* a **burnt s**, an offering made by fire, 5930
1:10 the sheep, or of the goats, for a **burnt s**; 5930
1:13 it *is* a **burnt s**, an offering made by fire, 5930
1:14 if the **burnt s** for his offering to 5930
1:17 it *is* a **burnt s**, an offering made by fire, 5930
3: 1 if his oblation *be* a **s** of peace offering, 2077
3: 3 shall offer of the **s** of the peace offering 2077
3: 5 burn it on the altar upon the **burnt s**, 5930
3: 6 if his offering for a **s** of peace offering unto 2077
3: 9 he shall offer of the **s** of the peace offering 2077
4:10 the bullock of the **s** of peace offerings: 2077
4:26 as the fat of the **s** of peace offerings: 2077
4:31 as the fat is taken away from off the **s** of 2077
4:35 away from the **s** of the peace offerings; 2077
7:11 this *is* the law of the **s** of peace offerings, 2077
7:12 he shall offer with the **s** of thanksgiving 2077
7:13 the **s** of thanksgiving of his peace offerings. 2077
7:15 the flesh of the **s** of his peace offerings for 2077
7:16 if the **s** of his offering *be* a vow, 2077
7:16 eaten the *same* day that he offereth his **s**: 2077
7:17 the remainder of the flesh of the **s** on 2077
7:18 if *any* of the flesh of the **s** of his peace 2077
7:20 the soul that eateth *of* the flesh of the **s** of 2077
7:21 eat of the flesh of the **s** of peace offerings, 2077
7:29 that offereth the **s** of his peace offerings 2077
7:29 the LORD of the **s** of his peace offerings. 2077
7:37 and of the **s** of the peace offerings; 2077
8:21 it *was* a **burnt s** for a sweet savour, 5930
9: 4 for peace offerings, to **s** before the LORD; 2076
9:17 altar, beside the **burnt s** of the morning. 5930
9:18 and the ram for a **s** of peace offerings, 2077
17: 8 that offereth a burnt offering or **s**, 2077
19: 5 if ye **offer a s** of peace offerings 2076+2077
22:21 whosoever offereth a **s** of peace offerings 2077
22:29 when ye will offer a **s** of thanksgiving 2077
23:19 ye shall **s** one kid of the goats for a sin 6213
23:19 two lambs of the first year for a **s** of peace 2077
23:37 a meat offering, a **s**, and drink offerings, 2077
27:11 of which they do not offer a **s** unto 7133
Nu 6:17 he shall offer the ram for a **s** of peace 2077
6:18 put *it* in the fire which *is* under the **s** of 2077
7:17 for a **s** of peace offerings, two oxen, 2077
7:23 for a **s** of peace offerings, two oxen, 2077
7:29 for a **s** of peace offerings, two oxen, 2077
7:35 for a **s** of peace offerings, two oxen, 2077
7:41 for a **s** of peace offerings, two oxen, 2077
7:47 for a **s** of peace offerings, two oxen, 2077
7:53 for a **s** of peace offerings, two oxen, 2077
7:59 for a **s** of peace offerings, two oxen, 2077
7:65 for a **s** of peace offerings, two oxen, 2077

Nu 7:71 for a **s** of peace offerings, two oxen, 2077
7:77 for a **s** of peace offerings, two oxen, 2077
7:83 for a **s** of peace offerings, two oxen, 2077
7:88 the oxen for the **s** of the peace offerings 2077
15: 3 a **s** in performing a vow, or in a freewill 2077
15: 3 thou prepare with the burnt offering or **s**, 2077
15: 8 or *for* a **s** in performing a vow, 2077
15:25 a **s** made by fire unto the LORD, 801
23: 6 lo, *he* stood by his **burnt s**, he, and all 5930
28: 6 a **s made by fire** unto the LORD. 801
28: 8 thou shalt offer *it*, a **s made by fire**, 801
28:13 a **s made by fire** unto the LORD. 801
28:19 ye shall offer a **s made by fire** for a burnt 801
28:24 days, the meat of the **s made by fire**, 801
29: 6 a **s made by fire** unto the LORD. 801
29:13 offer a burnt offering, a **s made by fire**, 801
29:36 offer a burnt offering, a **s made by fire**, 801
Dt 15:21 thou shalt not **s** it unto the LORD thy 2076
16: 2 **s** the passover unto the LORD thy God, 2076
16: 5 Thou mayest not **s** the passover within 2076
16: 6 there thou shalt **s** the passover at even, 2076
17: 1 Thou shalt not **s** unto the LORD thy God 2076
18: 3 from them that offer a **s**, whether *it be* ox 2077
33:10 and whole **burnt s** upon thine altar. NIH
Jos 22:26 an altar, not for burnt offering, nor for **s**: 2077
Jdg 6:26 offer a **burnt s** with the wood of the 5930
16:23 for to offer a great **s** unto Dagon their god, 2077
1Sa 1: 3 to **s** unto the LORD of hosts in Shiloh. 2076
1:21 up to offer unto the LORD the yearly **s**, 2077
2:13 people *was, that* when any man offered **s**, 2077
2:19 up with her husband to offer the yearly **s**. 2077
2:29 Wherefore kick ye at my **s** and at mine 2077
3:14 not be purged with **s** nor offering for ever. 2077
9:12 for *there is* a **s** of the people to day in 2077
9:13 he come, because he doth bless the **s**; 2077
10: 8 *and* to **s** sacrifices of peace offerings 2076
15:15 of the oxen, to **s** unto the LORD thy God; 2076
15:21 to **s** unto the LORD thy God in Gilgal. 2076
15:22 to obey *is* better than **s**, *and* to hearken 2077
16: 2 say, I am come to **s** to the LORD. 2076
16: 3 call Jesse to the **s**, and I will shew thee 2077
16: 5 I am come to **s** unto the LORD: 2076
16: 5 and come with me to the **s**. 2077
16: 5 and his sons, and called them to the **s**. 2077
20: 6 for *there is* a yearly **s** there for all 2077
20:29 for our family hath a **s** in the city; 2077
2Sa 24:22 *here be* oxen for **burnt s**, and threshing 5930
1Ki 3: 4 the king went to Gibeon to **s** there; for 2076
8:62 with him, offered **s** before the LORD. 2077
8:63 Solomon offered a **s** of peace offerings, 2077
12:27 If this people go up to do **s** in the house 2077
18:29 the time of the offering of the *evening* **s**, 4503
18:33 pour *it* on the **burnt s**, and on the wood. 5930
18:36 *the time of* the offering of the *evening* **s**, 4503
18:38 consumed the **burnt s**, and the wood, 5930
2Ki 5:17 burnt offering nor **s** unto other gods, 2077
10:19 for I have a great **s** *to do* to Baal: 2077
14: 4 as yet the people did **s** and burnt incense 2076
16:15 the king's **burnt s**, and his meat offering, 5930
16:15 burnt offering, and all the blood of the **s**: 2077
17:35 to them, nor serve them, nor **s** to them: 2076
17:36 shall ye worship, and to him shall ye do **s**. 2076
2Ch 2: 6 a house, save only to **burn s** before him? 6999
7: 5 king Solomon offered a **s** of twenty and 2077
7:12 this place to myself for a house of **s**. 2077
11:16 to **s** unto the LORD God of their fathers. 2076
28:23 *therefore* will I **s** to them, that they may 2076
33:17 Nevertheless the people did **s** still in 2076
Ezr 4: 2 we do **s** unto him since the days of 2076
9: 4 and I sat astonied until the evening **s**. 4503
9: 5 at the evening **s** I arose up from my 4503
Ne 4: 2 they **s**? will they make an end in a day? 2076
Ps 20: 3 all thy offerings, and accept thy **burnt s**. 5930
40: 6 **S** and offering thou didst not desire; mine 2077
50: 5 that have made a covenant with me by **s**. 2077
51:16 thou desirest not **s**; else would I give *it*: 2077
54: 6 I will freely **s** unto thee: I will praise thy 2076
107:22 let them **s** the sacrifices of thanksgiving, 2076
116:17 I will offer to thee the **s** of thanksgiving, 2077
118:27 bind the **s** with cords, *even* unto the 2282
141: 2 lifting up of my hands *as* the evening **s**. 4503
Pr 15: 8 The **s** of the wicked *is* an abomination to 2077
21: 3 is more acceptable to the LORD than **s**. 2077
21:27 The **s** of the wicked *is* abomination: 2077
Ecc 5: 1 ready to hear, than to give the **s** of fools: 2077
Isa 19:21 in that day, and shall do a **s** and oblation; 2077
34: 6 for the LORD hath a **s** in Bozrah, 2077
57: 7 even thither wentest thou up to offer **s**. 2077
Jer 33:11 them that shall bring the **s** of praise *into* 8426
33:18 meat offering, and to do **s** continually. 2077
46:10 for the Lord GOD of hosts hath a **s** in 2077
Eze 39:17 gather yourselves on every side to my **s** 2077
39:17 side to my **sacrifice** that I do **s** for you, 2076
39:17 a great **s** upon the mountains of Israel, 2077
39:19 of my **s** which I have sacrificed for you. 2077
40:42 they slew the burnt offering and the **s**. 2077
44:11 burnt offering and the **s** for the people, 2077
46:24 of the house shall boil the **s** of the people. 2077
Da 8:11 by him the daily **s** was taken away, NIH
8:12 a host was given *him* against the daily **s** by NIH
8:13 *shall be* the vision *concerning* the daily **s**, NIH
9:27 the midst of the week he shall cause the **s** 2077
11:31 shall take away the daily **s**, and they shall NIH
12:11 the time *that* the daily **s** shall be taken NIH
Hos 3: 4 without a **s**, and without an image, 2077

Hos 4:13 They **s** upon the tops of the mountains, 2076
 4:14 with whores, and they **s** with harlots: 2076
 6: 6 For I desired mercy, and not **s**; 2077
 8:13 They **s** flesh *for* the sacrifices of mine 2076
 12:11 they **s** bullocks in Gilgal; yea, their altars 2076
 13: 2 them, Let the men that **s** kiss the calves. 2076
Am 4: 5 offer a **s** of **thanksgiving** with leaven, 8426
Jnh 1:16 offered a **s** unto the LORD, 2077
 2: 9 I will **s** unto thee with the voice of 2076
Hab 1:16 Therefore they **s** unto their net, 2076
Zep 1: 7 for the LORD hath prepared a **s**, he hath 2077
 1: 8 come to pass in the day of the LORD'S **s**, 2077
Zec 14:21 they that **s** shall come and take of them, 2076
Mal 1: 8 if ye offer the blind for **s**, *is it* not evil? 2076
Mt 9:13 meaneth, I will have mercy, and not **s**: 2378
 12: 7 meaneth, I will have mercy, and not **s**, 2378
Mk 9:49 and every **s** shall be salted with salt. 2378
Lk 2:24 And to offer a **s** according to that which is 2378
Ac 7:41 and offered **s** unto the idol, and rejoiced in 2378
 14:13 would have done a **s** with the people. 2380
 14:18 that *they* had **done** a **s** unto them. 2380
Ro 12: 1 *ye* present your bodies a living **s**, holy, 2378
1Co 8: 4 **things** that are **offered** in **s** unto idols. 1494
 10:19 that which is **offered** in **s** to idols is any 1494
 10:20 that *the* things which the Gentiles **s**, 2380
 10:20 they **s** to devils, and not to God: 2380
 10:28 unto you, This is **offered** in **s** unto idols, 1494
Eph 5: 2 and a **s** to God for a sweetsmelling savour. 2378
Php 2:17 if I be offered upon the **s** and service of 2378
 4:18 a **s** acceptable, well pleasing to God. 2378
Heb 7:27 as *those* high priests, to offer up **s**, first for 2378
 9:26 to put away sin by the **s** of himself. 2378
 10: 5 **S** and offering thou wouldest not, 2378
 10: 8 **S** and offering and burnt offerings and 2378
 10:12 this *man*, after he had offered one **s** for 2378
 10:26 there remaineth no more **s** for sins, 2378
 11: 4 unto God a more excellent **s** than Cain, 2378
 13:15 let us offer the **s** of praise to God 2378

SACRIFICED (33) [SACRIFICE]

Ex 24: 5 **s** peace offerings *of* oxen unto the LORD. 2076
 32: 8 have **s** thereunto, and said, These *be* thy 2076
Dt 32:17 They **s** unto devils, not *to* God; *to* gods 2076
Jos 8:31 unto the LORD, and **s** peace offerings. 2076
Jdg 2: 5 and they **s** there unto the LORD. 2076
1Sa 2:15 servant came, and said to the man that **s**, 2076
 6:15 **s** sacrifices the same day unto the LORD. 2076
 11:15 there they **s** sacrifices *of* peace offerings 2076
2Sa 6:13 gone six paces, he **s** oxen and fatlings. 2076
1Ki 3: 2 Only the people **s** in high places, because 2076
 3: 3 he **s** and burnt incense in high places. 2076
 11: 8 burnt incense and **s** unto their gods. 2076
2Ki 12: 3 the people still **s** and burnt incense in 2076
 15: 4 the people **s** and burnt incense still on 2076
 15:35 the people **s** and burnt incense still in 2076
 16: 4 he **s** and burnt incense in the high places, 2076
 17:32 which **s** for them in the houses of the high 6213
1Ch 21:28 of Ornan the Jebusite, then he **s** there. 2076
 29:21 they **s** sacrifices unto the LORD, 2076
2Ch 5: 6 **s** sheep and oxen, which could not be 2076
 28: 4 He **s** also and burnt incense in the high 2076
 28:23 For he **s** unto the gods of Damascus, 2076
 33:16 thereon peace offerings and **s** 2076
 33:22 for Amon **s** unto all the carved images 2076
 34: 4 the graves of them that had **s** unto them. 2076
Ps 106:37 they **s** their sons and their daughters unto 2076
 106:38 whom they **s** unto the idols of Canaan: 2076
Eze 16:20 hast thou **s** unto them to be devoured. 2076
 39:19 of my sacrifice which I have **s** for you. 2076
Hos 11: 2 they **s** unto Baalim, and burned incense to 2076
1Co 5: 7 For even Christ our passover is **s** for us: 2380
Rev 2:14 to eat **things s unto idols**, and to commit 1494
 2:20 and to eat **things s unto idols**. 1494

SACRIFICEDST (1) [SACRIFICE]

Dt 16: 4 which thou **s** the first day at even, 2076

SACRIFICES (79) [SACRIFICE]

Ge 46: 1 offered **s** unto the God of his father Isaac. 2077
Ex 10:25 Thou must give us also **s** and 2077
 18:12 law, took a burnt offering and **s** for God: 2077
Lev 7:32 offering of the **s** of your peace offerings. 2077
 7:34 from off the **s** of their peace offerings, 2077
 10:13 of the **s** of the LORD **made by fire**, 801
 10:14 *which* are given out of the **s** of peace 2077
 17: 5 the children of Israel may bring their **s**, 2077
 17: 7 shall no more offer their **s** unto devils, 2077
Nu 10:10 and over the **s** of your peace offerings; 2077
 25: 2 they called the people unto the **s** of their 2077
 28: 2 *and* my bread for my **s made by fire**, 801
Dt 12: 6 **s**, and your tithes, and heave offerings 2077
 12:11 **s**, your tithes, and the heave offering 2077
 12:27 blood of thy **s** shall be poured out upon 2077
 32:38 Which did eat the fat of their **s**, 2077
 33:19 there they shall offer **s** of righteousness 2077
Jos 13:14 **s** of the LORD God of Israel **made by fire** 801
 22:27 with our **s**, and with our peace offerings; 2077
 22:28 not for burnt offerings, nor for **s**, 2077
 22:29 offerings, for meat offerings, or for **s**, 2077
1Sa 1:21 **s** the same day unto the LORD. 2077
 10: 8 *and* to sacrifice **s** of peace offerings: 2077
 11:15 there they sacrificed **s** of peace offerings 2077
 15:22 *as great* delight in burnt offerings and **s**, 2077
2Sa 15:12 *even* from Giloh, while he offered **s**. 2077
2Ki 10:24 when they went in to offer **s** and 2077

1Ch 16: 1 they offered **burnt s** and peace offerings 5930
 23:31 to offer all **burnt s** unto the LORD in 5930
 29:21 they sacrificed **s** unto the LORD, 2077
 29:21 and **s** in abundance for all Israel: 2077
2Ch 7: 1 consumed the burnt offering and the **s**; 2077
 7: 4 all the people offered **s** before the LORD. 2077
 13:11 every evening **burnt s** and sweet incense: 5930
 29:31 come near and bring **s** and thank offerings 2077
 29:31 the congregation brought in **s** and 2077
Ezr 6: 3 the place where they offered **s**, and *let* 1685
 6:10 That they may offer **s** of sweet savours 7127
Ne 12:43 Also that day they offered great **s**, 2077
Ps 4: 5 Offer the **s** of righteousness, and put your 2077
 27: 6 will I offer in his tabernacle **s** of joy; 2077
 50: 8 I will not reprove thee for thy **s** or thy 2077
 51:17 The **s** of God *are* a broken spirit: a broken 2077
 51:19 shalt thou be pleased with the **s** of 2077
 66:15 I will offer unto thee **burnt s** of fatlings, 5930
 106:28 unto Baal-peor, and ate the **s** of the dead. 2077
 107:22 let them sacrifice the **s** of thanksgiving, 2077
Pr 17: 1 than a house full of **s** with strife. 2077
Isa 1:11 what purpose *is* the multitude of your **s** 2077
 29: 1 add ye year to year; let them kill **s**. 2282
 43:23 hast thou honoured me *with* thy **s**. 2077
 43:24 hast thou filled me *with* the fat of thy **s**: 2077
 56: 7 Their **s** *shall be* accepted upon mine altar; 2077
Jer 6:20 not acceptable, nor your **s** sweet unto me. 2077
 7:21 Put your burnt offerings unto your **s**, 2077
 7:22 of Egypt, concerning burnt offerings or **s**: 2077
 17:26 **s**, and meat offerings, and incense, 2077
 17:26 and incense, and bringing **s** *of* praise, NIH
Eze 20:28 they offered there their **s**, and there they 2077
 40:41 eight tables, whereupon they slew *their* **s**. NIH
Hos 4:19 they shall be ashamed because of their **s**. 2077
 8:13 They sacrifice flesh *for* the **s** of mine 2077
 9: 4 their **s** *shall be* unto them as the bread of 2077
Am 4: 4 bring your **s** *every* morning, *and* your 2077
 5:25 Have ye offered unto me **s** and offerings 2077
Mk 12:33 more than all whole burnt offerings and **s**. 2378
Lk 13: 1 blood Pilate had mingled with their **s**. 2378
Ac 7:42 **s** *by the space* of forty years in 2378
1Co 10:18 are not they which eat of the **s** partakers 2378
Heb 8: 3 that he may offer both gifts and **s**: for sins: 2378
 8: 3 high priest is ordained to offer gifts and **s**: 2378
 9: 9 in which were offered both gifts and **s**, 2378
 9:23 themselves with better **s** than these. 2378
 10: 1 can never with those **s** which they offered 2378
 10: 3 In those **s** *there is* a remembrance *again* NIG
 10: 6 and **s** for sin thou hast had no pleasure. NIG
 10:11 and offering oftentimes the same **s**, 2378
 13:16 for with such **s** God is well pleased. 2378
1Pe 2: 5 a holy priesthood, to offer up spiritual **s**, 2378

SACRIFICETH (6) [SACRIFICE]

Ex 22:20 He that **s** unto *any* god, save unto 2076
Ecc 9: 2 to him that **s**, and to him that sacrificeth 2076
 9: 2 that sacrificeth, and to him that **s** not: 2076
Isa 65: 3 that **s** in gardens, and burneth incense 2076
 66: 3 he that **s** a lamb, *as if* he cut off a dog's 2076
Mal 1:14 **s** unto the Lord a corrupt *thing*: for I *am* 2076

SACRIFICING (2) [SACRIFICE]

1Ki 8: 5 him before the ark, **s** sheep and oxen, 2076
 12:32 **s** unto the calves that he had made: 2076

SACRILEGE (1)

Ro 2:22 that abhorrest idols, dost thou **commit s**? 2416

SAD (11) [SADLY, SADNESS]

Ge 40: 6 upon them, and behold, they *were* **s**. 2196
1Sa 1:18 and her countenance was no more **s**. NIH
1Ki 21: 5 said unto him, Why is thy spirit so **s**, 5620
Ne 2: 1 Now I had not been *beforetime* **s** in his 7451
 2: 2 Why *is* thy countenance, seeing thou 7451
 2: 3 why should not my countenance be **s**, 3415
Eze 13:22 have **made** the heart of the righteous **s**, 3512
 13:22 righteous sad, whom I have not **made s**; 3510
Mt 6:16 as the hypocrites, of a **s countenance**: 4659
Mk 10:22 he was **s** at *that* saying, and went away 4768
Lk 24:17 one to another, as ye walk, and are **s**? 4659

SADDLE (4) [SADDLED]

Lev 15: 9 what **s** soever he rideth upon that hath 4817
2Sa 19:26 for thy servant said, I will **s** me an ass, 2280
1Ki 13:13 he said unto his sons, **S** me the ass. 2280
 13:27 spake to his sons, saying, **S** me the ass. 2280

SADDLED (10) [SADDLE]

Ge 22: 3 **s** his ass, and took two of his young men 2280
Nu 22:21 **s** his ass, and went with the princes of 2280
Jdg 19:10 *there were* with him two asses **s**, 2280
2Sa 16: 1 with a couple of asses **s**, and upon them 2280
 17:23 **s** *his* ass, and arose, and gat him *home* 2280
1Ki 2:40 **s** his ass, and went to Gath to Achish to 2280
 13:13 they **s** him the ass: and he rode thereon, 2280
 13:23 he had drunk, that he **s** for him the ass, 2280
 13:27 Saddle me the ass. And they **s** *him*. 2280
2Ki 4:24 she **s** an ass, and said to her servant, 2280

SADDLES See FURNITURE

SADDUCEES (14)

Mt 3: 7 the Pharisees and **S** come to his baptism, 4523
 16: 1 The Pharisees also with the **S** came, 4523
 16: 6 the leaven of the Pharisees and *of the* **S**. 4523
 16:11 the leaven of the Pharisees and *of the* **S**? 4523

Mt 16:12 the doctrine of the Pharisees and *of the* **S**. 4523
 22:23 The same day came to him *the* **S**, which 4523
 22:34 had heard that he had put the **S** to silence, 4523
Mk 12:18 Then come unto him the **S**, which say 4523
Lk 20:27 Then came to *him* certain of the **S**, 4523
Ac 4: 1 the temple, and the **S**, came upon them, 4523
 5:17 with him, (which is the sect of the **S**,) 4523
 23: 6 Paul perceived that the one part were **S**, 4523
 23: 7 between the Pharisees and the **S**: 4523
 23: 8 For the **S** say that there is no resurrection, 4523

SADLY (1) [SAD]

Ge 40: 7 Wherefore look ye *so* **s** to day? 7451

SADNESS (1) [SAD]

Ecc 7: 3 for by the **s** of the countenance the heart 7455

SADOC (2)

Mt 1:14 Azor begat **S**; and Sadoc begat Achim; 4524
 1:14 and **S** begat Achim; and Achim begat 4524

SAFE (13) [SAVE]

1Sa 12:11 enemies on every side, and ye dwelled **s**. 983
2Sa 18:29 king said, Is the young man Absalom **s**? 7965
 18:32 unto Cushi, Is the young man Absalom **s**? 7965
Job 21: 9 Their houses *are* **s** from fear, neither *is* 7965
Ps 119:117 Hold thou me up, and I shall be **s**: 3467
Pr 18:10 the righteous runneth into it, and is **s**. 7682
 29:25 putteth his trust in the LORD shall be **s**. 7682
Isa 5:29 shall **carry away**, and none shall 6403
Eze 34:27 they shall be **s** in their land, and shall 983
Lk 15:27 he hath received him **s and sound**. NIG
Ac 23:24 and **bring** *him* unto Felix the governor. 1295
 27:44 to pass, that *they* **escaped** all **s** to land. 1295
Php 3: 1 indeed *is* not grievous, but for you *it is* **s**. 804

SAFEGUARD (1) [GUARD, SAVE]

1Sa 22:23 thy life: but with me thou *shalt* be **in s**. 4931

SAFELY (21) [SAVE]

Lev 26: 5 the land, and dwell in your land **s**. 983+3807.1
1Ki 4:25 Judah and Israel dwelt **s**, every 983+3807.1
Ps 78:53 led them on **s**, so that they feared 983+3807.1
Pr 1:33 whoso hearkeneth unto me shall dwell **s**, 983
 3:23 shalt thou walk *in* thy way **s**, 983+3807.1
 31:11 The heart of her husband doth **s** trust in NIH
Isa 41: 3 He pursued them, *and* passed **s**; *even* by 7965
Jer 23: 6 be saved, and Israel shall dwell **s**: 983+3807.1
 32:37 I will cause them to dwell **s**: 983+3807.1
 33:16 and Jerusalem shall dwell **s**: 983+3807.1
Eze 28:26 they shall dwell **s** therein, 983+3807.1
 34:25 shall dwell **s** in the wilderness, 983+3807.1
 34:28 they shall dwell **s**, and none shall 983+3807.1
 38: 8 and they shall dwell **s** all of them. 983+3807.1
 38:11 them that are at rest, that dwell **s**, 983+3807.1
 38:14 my people of Israel dwelleth **s**, 983+3807.1
 39:26 when they dwelt **s** in their land, 983+3807.1
Hos 2:18 earth, and will make them to lie down **s**. 983
Zec 14:11 but Jerusalem shall be **s** inhabited. 983
Mk 14:44 same is he; take him, and lead *him* away **s**. 806
Ac 16:23 charging the jailor to keep them **s**: 806

SAFETY (19) [SAVE]

Lev 25:18 them; and ye shall dwell in the land in **s**. 983
 25:19 shall eat *your* fill, and dwell therein in **s**. 983
Dt 12:10 round about, so that ye dwell **in s**; 983
 33:12 The beloved of the LORD shall dwell in **s** 983
 33:28 Israel then shall dwell *in* **s** alone: 983
Job 3:26 I was not in **s**, neither had I rest, 7951
 5: 4 His children are far from **s**, and they are 3468
 5:11 those which mourn may be exalted to **s**. 3468
 11:18 *thee*, *and* thou shalt take thy rest in **s**. 983
 24:23 *Though* it be given him to be in **s**, 983
Ps 4: 8 LORD, only makest me dwell in **s**. 983
 12: 5 I will set *him* in **s** *from* him that puffeth 3468
 33:17 A horse *is* a vain thing for **s**: neither shall 8668
Pr 11:14 in the multitude of counsellers *there is* **s**. 8668
 21:31 the day of battle: but **s** *is* of the LORD. 8668
 24: 6 and in multitude of counsellers *there is* **s**. 8668
Isa 14:30 feed, and the needy shall lie down in **s**: 983
Ac 5:23 The prison truly found we shut with all **s**, 803
1Th 5: 3 For when they shall say, Peace and **s**; then 803

SAFFRON (1)

SS 4:14 Spikenard and **s**; calamus and cinnamon, 3750

SAID (4001) [SAY]

Ge 1: 3 God **s**, Let there be light: and there was 559
 1: 6 God **s**, Let there be a firmament in the 559
 1: 9 God **s**, Let the waters under the heaven be 559
 1:11 God **s**, Let the earth bring forth grass, 559
 1:14 God **s**, Let there be lights in the firmament 559
 1:20 God **s**, Let the waters bring forth 559
 1:24 God **s**, Let the earth bring forth the living 559
 1:26 God **s**, Let us make man in our image, 559
 1:28 God **s** unto them, Be fruitful, and multiply, 559
 1:29 God **s**, Behold, I have given you every herb 559
 2:18 the LORD God **s**, *It is* not good that 559
 2:23 Adam **s**, This *is* now bone of my bones, 559
 3: 1 he **s** unto the woman, Yea, hath God said, 559
 3: 1 he said unto the woman, Yea, hath God **s**, 559
 3: 2 woman **s** unto the serpent, We may eat of 559
 3: 3 God hath **s**, Ye shall not eat of it, 559
 3: 4 the serpent **s** unto the woman, Ye shall not 559
 3: 9 Adam, and **s** unto him, Where *art* thou? 559
 3:10 he **s**, I heard thy voice in the garden, 559

Ge 3:11 he s, Who told thee that thou *wast* naked? 559
3:12 man s, The woman whom thou gavest *to* 559
3:13 the LORD God s unto the woman, What *is* 559
3:13 the woman s, The serpent beguiled me, 559
3:14 the LORD God s unto the serpent, 559
3:16 the woman he s, I will greatly multiply 559
3:17 unto Adam he s, Because thou hast 559
3:22 the LORD God s, Behold, the man is 559
4: 1 she conceived, and bare Cain, and s, 559
4: 6 the LORD s unto Cain, Why art thou 559
4: 9 the LORD s unto Cain, Where *is* Abel thy 559
4: 9 s, I know not: *Am* I my brother's keeper? 559
4:10 he s, What hast thou done? the voice of 559
4:13 Cain s unto the LORD, My punishment *is* 559
4:15 the LORD s unto him, Therefore 559
4:23 Lamech s unto his wives, Adah and Zillah, 559
4:25 s she, hath appointed me another seed NIH
6: 3 the LORD s, My spirit shall not always 559
6: 7 the LORD s, I will destroy man whom I 559
6:13 God s unto Noah, The end of all flesh is 559
7: 1 the LORD s unto Noah, Come thou and 559
8:21 the LORD s in his heart, I will not again 559
9: 1 blessed Noah and his sons, and s unto 559
9:12 God s, This *is* the token of the covenant 559
9:17 God s unto Noah, This *is* the token of 559
9:25 he s, Cursed *be* Canaan; a servant of 559
9:26 he s, Blessed *be* the LORD God of Shem; 559
10: 9 it is s, *Even* as Nimrod the mighty 559
11: 3 they s one to another, Go to, let us make 559
11: 4 they s, Go to, let us build us a city and 559
11: 6 the LORD s, Behold, the people *is* one, 559
12: 1 Now the LORD *had* s unto Abram, 559
12: 7 and s, Unto thy seed will I give this land: 559
12:11 that he s unto Sarai his wife, Behold now, 559
12:18 Pharaoh called Abram, and s, What *is* this 559
13: 8 Abram s unto Lot, Let there be no strife, 559
13:14 the LORD s unto Abram, after that Lot was 559
14:19 he blessed him, and s, Blessed *be* Abram 559
14:21 the king of Sodom s unto Abram, Give me 559
14:22 Abram s to the king of Sodom, I have lift 559
15: 2 Abram s, Lord GOD, what wilt thou give 559
15: 3 Abram s, Behold, to me thou hast given no 559
15: 5 s, Look now towards heaven, and tell 559
15: 5 and he s unto him, So shall thy seed be. 559
15: 7 he s unto him, I *am* the LORD that brought 559
15: 8 he s, Lord GOD, whereby shall I know that 559
15: 9 he s unto him, Take me a heifer of three 559
15:13 he s unto Abram, Know of a surety that thy 559
16: 2 Sarai s unto Abram, Behold now, 559
16: 5 Sarai s unto Abram, My wrong *be* upon 559
16: 6 Abram s unto Sarai, Behold, thy maid *is* in 559
16: 8 he s, Hagar, Sarai's maid, whence camest 559
16: 8 she s, I flee from the face of my mistress 559
16: 9 the angel of the LORD s unto her, 559
16:10 the angel of the LORD s unto her, I will 559
16:11 the angel of the LORD s unto her, Behold, 559
16:13 for she s, Have I also here looked after him 559
17: 1 and s unto him, I *am* the Almighty God; 559
17: 9 God s unto Abraham, Thou shalt keep my 559
17:15 God s unto Abraham, *As for* Sarai thy wife, 559
17:17 his face, and laughed, and s in his heart, 559
17:18 Abraham s unto God, O that Ishmael 559
17:19 God s, Sarah thy wife shall bear thee a son 559
17:23 the selfsame day, as God had s unto him. 1696
18: 3 s, My Lord, if now I have found favour in 559
18: 5 And they s, So do, as thou hast said. 559
18: 5 And they said, So do, as thou hast s. 1696
18: 6 hastened into the tent unto Sarah, and s, 559
18: 9 they s unto him, Where *is* Sarah thy wife? 559
18: 9 thy wife? And he s, Behold, in the tent. 559
18:10 he s, I will certainly return unto thee 559
18:13 the LORD s unto Abraham, Wherefore did 559
18:15 And he s, Nay; but thou didst laugh. 559
18:17 the LORD s, Shall I hide from Abraham 559
18:20 the LORD s, Because the cry of Sodom 559
18:23 Abraham drew near, and s, Wilt thou also 559
18:26 the LORD s, If I find in Sodom fifty 559
18:27 Abraham answered and s, Behold now, 559
18:28 he s, If I find there forty and five, I will not 559
18:29 he spake unto him yet again, and s, 559
18:29 And he s, I will not do *it* for forty's sake. 559
18:30 he s *unto him,* Oh let not the Lord be 559
18:30 he s, I will not do *it,* if I find thirty there. 559
18:31 he s, Behold now, I have taken upon me 559
18:31 he s, I will not destroy it for twenty's sake. 559
18:32 he s, Oh let not the Lord be angry, and I 559
18:32 he s, I will not destroy it for ten's sake. 559
19: 2 he s, Behold now, my lords, turn in, I pray 559
19: 2 they s, Nay; but we will abide in the street 559
19: 5 they called unto Lot, and s unto him, 559
19: 7 s, I pray you, brethren, do not so wickedly. 559
19: 9 they s, Stand back. And they said *again,* 559
19: 9 they s *again,* This one *fellow* came in to 559
19:12 the men s unto Lot, Hast thou here any 559
19:14 and s, Up, get ye out of this place; 559
19:17 forth abroad, that he s, Escape for thy life; 559
19:18 Lot s unto them, Oh, not so, my Lord: 559
19:21 he s unto him, See, I have accepted thee 559
19:31 firstborn s unto the younger, Our father 559
19:34 that the firstborn s unto the younger, 559
20: 2 Abraham s of Sarah his wife, She *is* my 559
20: 3 s to him, Behold, thou *art but* a dead man, 559
20: 4 he s, Lord, wilt thou slay also a righteous 559
20: 5 S he not unto me, She *is* my sister? 559
20: 5 she, even she herself s, He *is* my brother: 559

Ge 20: 6 God s unto him in a dream, Yea, I know 559
20: 9 s unto him, What hast thou done unto us? 559
20:10 Abimelech s unto Abraham, What sawest 559
20:11 Abraham s, Because I thought, Surely 559
20:13 I s unto her, This *is* thy kindness which 559
20:15 Abimelech s, Behold, my land *is* before 559
20:16 unto Sarah he s, Behold, I have given thy 559
21: 1 the LORD visited Sarah as he had s, 559
21: 6 Sarah s, God hath made me to laugh, 559
21: 7 s, Who would have said unto Abraham, 559
21: 7 said, Who would have s unto Abraham, 4448
21:10 Wherefore she s unto Abraham, Cast out 559
21:12 God s unto Abraham, Let it not be 559
21:12 in all that Sarah hath s unto thee, 559
21:16 for she s, Let me not see the death of 559
21:17 and s unto her, What aileth thee, Hagar? 559
21:24 And Abraham s, I will swear. 559
21:26 Abimelech s, I wot not who hath done 559
21:29 Abimelech s unto Abraham, What *mean* 559
21:30 he s, For *these* seven ewe lambs shalt 559
22: 1 Abraham, and s unto him, Abraham: 559
22: 1 Abraham: and he s, Behold, *here* I am. 559
22: 2 he s, Take now thy son, thine only *son* 559
22: 5 Abraham s unto his young men, Abide you 559
22: 7 unto Abraham his father, and s, My father: 559
22: 7 he s, Here *am* I, my son. And he said, 559
22: 7 And he s, Behold the fire and the wood: 559
22: 8 Abraham s, My son, God will provide 559
22:11 out of heaven, and s, Abraham, Abraham: 559
22:11 Abraham, Abraham: and he s, Here *am* I. 559
22:12 he s, Lay not thine hand upon the lad, 559
22:14 as it is s *to this* day, In the mount of 559
22:16 s, By myself have I sworn, saith the LORD, 559
24: 2 Abraham s unto his eldest servant of his 559
24: 5 the servant s unto him, Peradventure 559
24: 6 Abraham s unto him, Beware thou that 559
24:12 he s, O LORD God of my master Abraham, 559
24:17 ran to meet her, and s, Let me, I pray thee, 559
24:18 she s, Drink, my lord: and she hasted, 559
24:19 she s, I will draw *water* for thy camels also, 559
24:23 s, Whose daughter *art* thou? tell me, I pray 559
24:24 she s unto him, I *am* the daughter of 559
24:25 She s moreover unto him, We have both 559
24:27 he s, Blessed *be* the LORD God of my 559
24:31 he s, Come in, thou blessed of the LORD; 559
24:33 he s, I will not eat, until I have told mine 559
24:33 I have told mine errand. And he s, Speak 559
24:34 he s, I *am* Abraham's servant. 559
24:39 I s unto my master, Peradventure the 559
24:40 he s unto me, The LORD, before whom I 559
24:42 I came this day unto the well, and s, 559
24:45 *water:* and I s unto her, Let me drink, 559
24:46 her pitcher from her *shoulder,* and s, 559
24:47 her, and s, Whose daughter *art* thou? 559
24:47 she s, The daughter of Bethuel, Nahor's 559
24:50 Laban and Bethuel answered and s, 559
24:54 they rose up in the morning, and he s, 559
24:55 brother and her mother s, Let the damsel 559
24:56 he s unto them, Hinder me not, seeing 559
24:57 they s, We will call the damsel, 559
24:58 they called Rebekah, and s unto her, Wilt 559
24:58 go with this man? And she s, I will go. 559
24:60 s unto her, Thou *art* our sister, 559
24:65 For she had s unto the servant, What man 559
24:65 servant had s, It *is* my master: therefore 559
25:22 and she s, If *it be* so, why *am* I thus? 559
25:23 the LORD s unto her, Two nations *are* in 559
25:30 Esau s to Jacob, Feed me, I pray thee, 559
25:31 Jacob s, Sell me *this* day thy birthright. 559
25:32 Esau s, Behold, I *am* at the point to die: 559
25:33 Jacob s, Swear to me *this* day; and he 559
26: 2 unto him, and s, Go not down into Egypt; 559
26: 7 *him* of his wife; and he s, She *is* my sister: 559
26: 7 s he, the men of the place should kill me NIH
26: 9 and s, Behold, of a surety she *is* thy wife: 559
26: 9 Isaac s unto him, Because I said, Lest I die 559
26: 9 unto him, Because I s, Lest I die for her. 559
26:10 Abimelech s, What *is* this thou hast done 559
26:16 Abimelech s unto Isaac, Go from us; 559
26:22 he s, For now the LORD hath made room 559
26:24 s, I *am* the God of Abraham thy father: 559
26:27 Isaac s unto them, Wherefore come ye to 559
26:28 they s, We saw certainly that the LORD 559
26:28 we s, Let there be now an oath betwixt us, 559
26:32 and s unto him, We have found water. 559
27: 1 Esau his eldest son, and s unto him, My 559
27: 1 unto him, My son: and he s, Behold, *here* I. 559
27: 2 he s, Behold now, I am old, I know not 559
27:11 Jacob s to Rebekah his mother, Behold, 559
27:13 his mother s unto him, Upon me *be* thy 559
27:18 he came unto his father, and s, My father: 559
27:18 he s, Here *am* I; who *art* thou, my son? 559
27:19 Jacob s unto his father, I *am* Esau thy 559
27:20 Isaac s unto his son, How *is* it *that* thou 559
27:20 he s, Because the LORD thy God brought *it* 559
27:21 Isaac s unto Jacob, Come near, I pray thee, 559
27:22 he felt him, and s, The voice *is* Jacob's 559
27:24 he s, *Art* thou my very son Esau? And he 559
27:24 thou my very son Esau? And he s, I *am.* 559
27:25 he s, Bring *it* near to me, and I will eat of 559
27:26 father Isaac s unto him, Come near now, 559
27:27 his raiment, and blessed him, and s, See, 559
27:31 s unto his father, Let my father arise, 559
27:32 Isaac his father s unto him, Who *art* thou? 559
27:32 And he s, I *am* thy son, thy firstborn Esau. 559

Ge 27:33 trembled very exceedingly, and s, Who? 559
27:34 s unto his father, Bless me, *even* me also, 559
27:35 he s, Thy brother came with subtilty, 559
27:36 he s, Is not he rightly named Jacob? for he 559
27:36 he s, Hast thou not reserved a blessing for 559
27:37 Isaac answered and s unto Esau, Behold, 559
27:38 Esau s unto his father, Hast thou but one 559
27:39 Isaac his father answered and s unto him, 559
27:41 Esau s in his heart, The days of mourning 559
27:42 s unto him, Behold, thy brother Esau, 559
27:46 Rebekah s to Isaac, I am weary of my life 559
28: 1 and charged him, and s unto him, 559
28:13 the LORD stood above it, and s, 559
28:16 and he s, Surely the LORD is in this place; 559
28:17 he was afraid, and s, How dreadful *is* this 559
29: 4 Jacob s unto them, My brethren, whence 559
29: 4 *be* ye? And they s, Of Haran *are* we. 559
29: 5 he s unto them, Know ye Laban the son of 559
29: 5 son of Nahor? And they s, We know *him.* 559
29: 6 he s unto them, *Is* he well? And they said, 559
29: 6 they s, *He is* well: and behold, Rachel his 559
29: 7 he s, Lo, *it is* yet high day, neither *is* it 559
29: 8 they s, We cannot, until all the flocks be 559
29:14 Laban s to him, Surely thou *art* my bone 559
29:15 Laban s unto Jacob, Because thou *art* my 559
29:18 s, I will serve thee seven years for Rachel 559
29:19 Laban s, *It is* better that I give her to thee, 559
29:21 Jacob s to Laban, Give *me* my wife, 559
29:25 he s to Laban, What *is* this thou hast done 559
29:26 Laban s, It must not be so done in our 559
29:32 for she s, Surely the LORD hath looked 559
29:33 s, Because the LORD hath heard that I *was* 559
29:34 s, Now *this* time will my husband be 559
29:35 she s, Now will I praise the LORD: 559
30: 1 s unto Jacob, Give me children, or else I 559
30: 2 he s, *Am* I in God's stead, who hath 559
30: 3 she s, Behold my maid Bilhah, go in unto 559
30: 6 Rachel s, God hath judged me, and hath 559
30: 8 she s, With great wrestlings have I 559
30:11 Leah s, A troop cometh: and she called his 559
30:13 Leah s, Happy am I, for the daughters will 559
30:14 Then Rachel s to Leah, Give me, I pray 559
30:15 she s unto her, *Is it* a small matter that 559
30:15 Rachel s, Therefore he shall lie with thee 559
30:16 Leah went out to meet him, and s, 559
30:18 Leah s, God hath given me my hire, 559
30:20 Leah s, God hath endued me with a good 559
30:23 and s, God hath taken away my reproach: 559
30:24 s, The LORD shall add to me another son. 559
30:25 that Jacob s unto Laban, Send me away, 559
30:27 Laban s unto him, I pray thee, if I have 559
30:28 he s, Appoint me thy wages, and I will give 559
30:29 he s unto him, Thou knowest how I have 559
30:31 he s, What shall I give thee? And Jacob 559
30:31 Jacob s, Thou shalt not give me any thing: 559
30:34 Laban s, Behold, I would it might be 559
31: 3 the LORD s unto Jacob, Return unto 559
31: 5 s unto them, I see your father's 559
31: 8 If he s thus, The speckled shall be thy 559
31: 8 if he s thus, The ringstraked shall be thy 559
31:11 a dream, *saying,* Jacob: And I s, Here *am* I. 559
31:12 he s, Lift up now thine eyes, and see, 559
31:14 and Leah answered and s unto him, 559
31:16 whatsoever God hath s unto thee, 559
31:24 s unto him, Take heed that thou speak not 559
31:26 Laban s to Jacob, What hast thou done, 559
31:31 Jacob answered and s to Laban, Because I 559
31:31 I s, Peradventure thou wouldest take by 559
31:35 she s to her father, Let it not displease my 559
31:36 Jacob answered and s to Laban, What *is* 559
31:43 Laban answered and s unto Jacob, *These* 559
31:46 Jacob s unto his brethren, Gather stones; 559
31:48 Laban s, This heap *is* a witness between 559
31:49 for he s, The LORD watch between me and 559
31:51 And Laban s to Jacob, Behold this heap, 559
32: 2 Jacob saw them, he s, This *is* God's host: 559
32: 8 s, If Esau come to the one company, 559
32: 9 And Jacob s, O God of my father Abraham, 559
32:16 and s unto his servants, Pass over before 559
32:20 he s, I will appease him with the present 559
32:26 he s, Let me go, for the day breaketh. 559
32:26 he s, I will not let thee go, except thou 559
32:27 he s unto him, What *is* thy name? And he 559
32:27 What *is* thy name? And he s, Jacob. 559
32:28 he s, Thy name shall be called no more 559
32:29 asked *him,* and s, Tell *me,* I pray thee, 559
32:29 he s, Wherefore *is* it *that* thou dost ask 559
33: 5 children; and s, Who *are* those with thee? 559
33: 5 he s, The children which God hath 559
33: 8 he s, What meanest thou by all this drove 559
33: 8 he s, *These are* to find grace in the sight of 559
33: 9 Esau s, I have enough, my brother; keep 559
33:10 Jacob s, Nay, I pray thee, if I now I have 559
33:12 he s, Let us take our journey, and let us go, 559
33:13 he s unto him, My lord knoweth that 559
33:15 Esau s, Let me now leave with thee *some* 559
33:15 he s, What needeth it? let me find grace 559
34:11 Shechem s unto her father and unto her 559
34:13 s, because he had defiled Dinah their 1696
34:14 they s unto them, We cannot do this thing, 559
34:30 Jacob s to Simeon and Levi, Ye have 559
34:31 they s, Should he deal with our sister as 559
35: 1 God s unto Jacob, Arise, go up to Beth-el, 559
35: 2 Jacob s unto his household, and to all that 559
35:10 God s unto him, Thy name *is* Jacob: 559

Ge 35:11 God **s** unto him, I *am* God Almighty: 559
35:17 that the midwife **s** unto her, Fear not; 559
37: 6 he **s** unto them, Hear, I pray you, this 559
37: 8 brethren **s** to him, Shalt thou indeed reign 559
37: 9 told it his brethren, and **s**, Behold, I have 559
37:10 his father rebuked him, and **s** unto him, 559
37:13 Israel **s** unto Joseph, Do not thy brethren 559
37:13 unto them. And he **s** to him, Here *am* I. 559
37:14 he **s** to him, Go, I pray thee, see whether it 559
37:16 he **s**, I seek my brethren: tell me, I pray 559
37:17 the man **s**, They are departed hence; for I 559
37:19 they **s** one to another, Behold, this dreamer 559
37:21 of their hands; and **s**, Let us not kill him. 559
37:22 And Reuben **s** unto them, Shed no blood, 559
37:26 Judah **s** unto his brethren, What profit *is it* 559
37:30 unto his brethren, and **s**, The child *is* not; 559
37:32 to their father; and **s**, This have we found: 559
37:33 knew it, and **s**, *It is* my son's coat; an evil 559
37:35 he **s**, For I will go down into the grave 559
38: 8 Judah **s** unto Onan, Go in unto thy 559
38:11 **s** Judah to Tamar his daughter in law, 559
38:11 for he **s**, Lest peradventure he die also, as 559
38:16 **s**, Go to, I pray thee, let me come in unto 559
38:16 she **s**, What wilt thou give me, that thou 559
38:17 he **s**, I will send *thee* a kid from the flock. 559
38:17 she **s**, Wilt thou give *me* a pledge, till thou 559
38:18 he **s**, What pledge shall I give thee? 559
38:18 And she **s**, Thy signet, and thy bracelets, 559
38:21 they **s**, There was no harlot in this *place*. 559
38:22 returned to Judah, and **s**, I cannot find her; 559
38:22 also the men of the place **s**, *that* there was 559
38:23 Judah **s**, Let her take *it* to her, lest we be 559
38:24 Judah **s**, Bring her forth, and let her be 559
38:25 she **s**, Discern, I pray thee, whose *are* 559
38:26 Judah acknowledged *them*, and **s**, She 559
38:29 she **s**, How hast thou broken forth? 559
39: 7 eyes upon Joseph; and she **s**, Lie with me. 559
39: 8 and **s** unto his master's wife, Behold, 559
40: 8 they **s** unto him, We have dreamed a 559
40: 8 Joseph **s** unto them, *Do* not interpretations 559
40: 9 to him, In my dream, behold, a vine *was* 559
40:12 Joseph **s** unto him, This *is* the 559
40:16 he **s** unto Joseph, I also *was* in my dream, 559
40:18 Joseph answered and **s**, This *is* 559
41:15 Pharaoh **s** unto Joseph, I have dreamed a 559
41:17 Pharaoh **s** unto Joseph, In my dream, 1696
41:25 Joseph **s** unto Pharaoh, The dream of 559
41:38 Pharaoh **s** unto his servants, Can we find 559
41:39 Pharaoh **s** unto Joseph, Forasmuch as God 559
41:41 Pharaoh **s** unto Joseph, See, I have set thee 559
41:44 Pharaoh **s** unto Joseph, I *am* Pharaoh, 559
41:51 *s he*, hath made me forget all my toil, NIH
41:54 began to come, according as Joseph had **s**: 559
41:55 Pharaoh **s** unto all the Egyptians, Go unto 559
42: 1 Jacob **s** unto his sons, Why do ye look one 559
42: 2 he **s**, Behold, I have heard that there is 559
42: 4 for he **s**, Lest peradventure mischief befall 559
42: 7 and he **s** unto them, Whence come ye? 559
42: 7 they **s**, From the land of Canaan to buy 559
42: 9 of them, and **s** unto them, Ye *are* spies; 559
42:10 they **s** unto him, Nay, my lord, but to buy 559
42:12 he **s** unto them, Nay, but to see 559
42:13 they **s**, Thy servants *are* twelve brethren, 559
42:14 Joseph **s** unto them, That *is it* that I spake 559
42:18 Joseph **s** unto them the third day, This do, 559
42:21 they **s** one to another, We *are* verily guilty 559
42:28 he **s** to his brethren, My money is 559
42:31 we **s** unto him, We *are* true *men; we are* 559
42:33 the man, the lord of the country, **s** unto us, 559
42:36 Jacob their father **s** unto them, Me have ye 559
42:38 he **s**, My son shall not go down with you; 559
43: 2 their father **s** unto them, Go again, buy us 559
43: 5 for the man **s** unto us, Ye shall not see my 559
43: 6 Israel **s**, Wherefore dealt ye *so* ill with me, 559
43: 7 they **s**, The man asked us straitly of our 559
43: 8 Judah **s** unto Israel his father, Send the lad 559
43:11 their father Israel **s** unto them, If *it must* 559
43:16 he **s** to the ruler of his house, Bring *these* 559
43:18 they **s**, Because of the money that was 559
43:20 **s**, O sir, we came indeed down at the first 559
43:23 he **s**, Peace *be* to you, fear not: your God, 559
43:27 **s**, *Is* your father well, the old man of 559
43:29 brother Benjamin, his mother's son, and **s**, 559
43:29 he **s**, God be gracious unto thee, my son. 559
43:31 and refrained himself, and **s**, Set on bread. 559
44: 4 *yet* far off, Joseph **s** unto his steward, 559
44: 7 they **s** unto him, Wherefore saith my lord 559
44:10 he **s**, Now also *let it be* according unto 559
44:15 Joseph **s** unto them, What deed *is* this that 559
44:16 Judah **s**, What shall we say unto my lord? 559
44:17 And he **s**, God forbid that I should do so: 559
44:18 and **s**, O my lord, let thy servant, I pray 559
44:20 we **s** unto my lord, We have a father, an 559
44:22 we **s** unto my lord, The lad cannot leave 559
44:25 our father **s**, Go again, *and* buy us a little 559
44:26 we **s**, We cannot go down: if our youngest 559
44:27 thy servant my father **s** unto us, Ye know 559
44:28 me, and I **s**, Surely he is torn in pieces; 559
45: 3 Joseph **s** unto his brethren, I *am* Joseph; 559
45: 4 Joseph **s** unto his brethren, Come near to 559
45: 4 he **s**, I *am* Joseph your brother, whom ye 559
45:17 Pharaoh **s** unto Joseph, Say unto thy 559
45:24 he **s** unto them, See that ye fall not out by 1696
45:27 of Joseph, which he had **s** unto them: 1696
45:28 Israel **s**, *It is* enough; Joseph my son *is* yet 559

Ge 46: 2 visions of the night, and **s**, Jacob, Jacob. 559
46: 2 **s**, Jacob, Jacob. And he **s**, Here *am* I. 559
46: 3 he **s**, I *am* God, the God of thy father: 559
46:30 Israel **s** unto Joseph, Now let me die, since 559
46:31 Joseph **s** unto his brethren, and unto his 559
47: 1 **s**, My father and my brethren, 559
47: 3 Pharaoh **s** unto his brethren, What *is* your 559
47: 3 they **s** unto Pharaoh, Thy servants *are* 559
47: 4 They **s** moreover unto Pharaoh, For to 559
47: 7 Pharaoh **s** unto Jacob, How old *art* thou? 559
47: 9 Jacob **s** unto Pharaoh, The days of the 559
47:15 came unto Joseph, and **s**, Give us bread: 559
47:16 Joseph **s**, Give your cattle; and I will give 559
47:18 **s** unto him, We will not hide *it* from my 559
47:23 Joseph **s** unto the people, Behold, I have 559
47:25 they **s**, Thou hast saved our lives: let us 559
47:29 he called his son Joseph, and **s** unto him, 559
47:30 And he **s**, I will do as thou hast said. 559
47:30 And he said, I will do as thou hast **s**. 1697
47:31 he **s**, Swear unto me. And he sware unto 559
48: 2 *one* told Jacob, and **s**, Behold, thy son 559
48: 3 Jacob **s** unto Joseph, God Almighty 559
48: 4 **s** unto me, Behold, I will make thee 559
48: 9 Joseph **s** unto his father, They *are* my sons, 559
48: 9 God hath given me in this *place*. And he **s**, 559
48:11 Israel **s** unto Joseph, I had not thought to 559
48:15 he blessed Joseph, and **s**, God, before 559
48:18 Joseph **s** unto his father, Not so, my father: 559
48:19 his father refused, and **s**, I know *it*, my son, 559
48:21 Israel **s** unto Joseph, Behold, I die: 559
49: 1 his sons, and **s**, Gather yourselves together, 559
49:29 he charged them, and **s** unto them, I *am* 559
50: 6 Pharaoh **s**, Go up, and bury thy father, 559
50:11 the mourning in the floor of Atad, they **s**, 559
50:15 they **s**, Joseph will peradventure hate us, 559
50:18 and they **s**, Behold, we *be* thy servants. 559
50:19 Joseph **s** unto them, Fear not: for *am* I in 559
50:24 Joseph **s** unto his brethren, I die: 559

Ex 1: 9 he **s** unto his people, Behold, the people 559
1:16 he **s**, When ye do the office of a midwife 559
1:18 **s** unto them, Why have ye done this thing, 559
1:19 the midwives **s** unto Pharaoh, Because 559
2: 6 she had compassion on him, and **s**, This *is* 559
2: 7 **s** his sister to Pharaoh's daughter, Shall I go 559
2: 8 Pharaoh's daughter **s** to her, Go. 559
2: 9 Pharaoh's daughter **s** unto her, Take this 559
2:10 she **s**, Because I drew him out of the water. 559
2:13 he **s** to him that did the wrong, Wherefore 559
2:14 he **s**, Who made thee a prince and a judge 559
2:14 Moses feared, and **s**, Surely *this* thing is 559
2:18 he **s**, How *is it that* you are come so soon 559
2:19 they **s**, An Egyptian delivered us out of 559
2:20 he **s** unto his daughters, And where *is* he? 559
2:22 for he **s**, I have been a stranger in a strange 559
3: 3 Moses **s**, I will now turn aside, and see 559
3: 4 midst of the bush, and **s**, Moses, Moses. 559
3: 4 said, Moses, Moses. And he **s**, Here *am* I. 559
3: 5 he **s**, Draw not nigh hither: put off thy 559
3: 6 Moreover he **s**, I *am* the God of thy father, 559
3: 7 the LORD **s**, I have surely seen 559
3:11 Moses **s** unto God, Who *am* I, that I 559
3:12 he **s**, Certainly I will be with thee; 559
3:13 Moses **s** unto God, Behold, *when* I come 559
3:14 And God **s** unto Moses, I AM THAT I AM: 559
3:14 he **s**, Thus shalt thou say unto the children 559
3:15 God **s** moreover unto Moses, Thus shalt 559
3:17 I have **s**, I will bring you up out of the 559
4: 1 Moses answered and **s**, But behold, they 559
4: 2 the LORD **s** unto him, What *is that* in thine 559
4: 2 What *is that* in thine hand? And he **s**, 559
4: 3 he **s**, Cast it on the ground. And he cast it 559
4: 4 the LORD **s** unto Moses, Put forth thine 559
4: 6 the LORD **s** furthermore unto him, Put now 559
4: 7 he **s**, Put thine hand into thy bosom again. 559
4:10 Moses **s** unto the LORD, O my Lord, I *am* 559
4:11 the LORD **s** unto him, Who hath made 559
4:13 he **s**, O my Lord, send, I pray thee, 559
4:14 he **s**, Is not Aaron the Levite thy brother? 559
4:18 **s** unto him, Let me go, I pray thee, 559
4:18 And Jethro **s** to Moses, Go in peace. 559
4:19 the LORD **s** unto Moses in Midian, 559
4:21 the LORD **s** unto Moses, When thou goest 559
4:25 of her son, and cast *it* at his feet, and **s**, 559
4:26 she **s**, A bloody husband *thou art*, because 559
4:27 the LORD **s** to Aaron, Go into 559
5: 2 Pharaoh **s**, Who *is* the LORD, that I should 559
5: 3 they **s**, The God of the Hebrews hath met 559
5: 4 the king of Egypt **s** unto them, Wherefore 559
5: 5 Pharaoh **s**, Behold, the people of the land 559
5:17 he **s**, Ye *are idle, ye are* idle: therefore 559
5:19 *that* they *were* in evil *case*, after it was **s**, 559
5:21 they **s** unto them, The LORD look upon 559
5:22 Lord, wherefore hast thou *so* evil 559
6: 1 the LORD **s** unto Moses, Now shalt thou 559
6: 2 and **s** unto him, I *am* the LORD: 559
6:26 and Moses, to whom the LORD **s**, 559
6:30 Moses **s** before the LORD, Behold, I *am* of 559
7: 1 the LORD **s** unto Moses, See, I have made 559
7:13 not unto them; as the LORD had **s**. 1696
7:14 the LORD **s** unto Moses, Pharaoh's heart *is* 559
7:22 he hearken not unto them; as the LORD had **s**. 1696
8: 8 Pharaoh called for Moses and Aaron, and **s**, 559
8: 9 Moses **s** unto Pharaoh, Glory over me: 559
8:10 he **s**, To morrow. And he said, Be it 559

Ex 8:10 he **s**, *Be it* according to thy word: that thou 559
8:15 not unto them; as the LORD had **s**. 1696
8:16 the LORD **s** unto Moses, Say unto Aaron, 559
8:19 the magicians **s** unto Pharaoh, This *is* 559
8:19 not unto them; as the LORD had **s**. 1696
8:20 the LORD **s** unto Moses, Rise up early in 559
8:25 for Moses and for Aaron, and **s**, Go ye, 559
8:26 Moses **s**, It is not meet so to do; for we 559
8:28 Pharaoh **s**, I will let you go, that ye may 559
8:29 Moses **s**, Behold, I go out from thee, 559
9: 1 the LORD **s** unto Moses, Go in unto 559
9: 8 the LORD **s** unto Moses and unto Aaron, 559
9:13 the LORD **s** unto Moses, Rise up early in 559
9:22 the LORD **s** unto Moses, Stretch forth thine 559
9:27 for Moses and Aaron, and **s** unto them, 559
9:29 Moses **s** unto him, As soon as I am gone 559
10: 1 the LORD **s** unto Moses, Go in unto 559
10: 3 came in unto Pharaoh, and **s** unto him, 559
10: 7 Pharaoh's servants **s** unto him, How long 559
10: 8 he **s** unto them, Go, serve the LORD your 559
10: 9 Moses **s**, We will go with our young and 559
10:10 he **s** unto them, Let the LORD be so 559
10:12 the LORD **s** unto Moses, Stretch out thine 559
10:16 he **s**, I have sinned against the LORD your 559
10:21 the LORD **s** unto Moses, Stretch out thine 559
10:24 unto Moses, and **s**, Go ye, serve the LORD; 559
10:25 Moses **s**, Thou must give us also sacrifices 559
10:28 Pharaoh **s** unto him, Get thee from me, 559
10:29 Moses **s**, Thou hast spoken well, I will see 559
11: 1 (And the LORD **s** unto Moses, Yet will I 559
11: 4 Moses **s**, Thus saith the LORD, 559
11: 9 the LORD **s** unto Moses, Pharaoh shall not 559
12:21 **s** unto them, Draw out and take you a 559
12:31 **s**, Rise up, *and* get you forth from amongst 559
12:31 and go, serve the LORD, as ye have **s**. 1696
12:32 and your herds, as ye have **s**, and be gone; 1696
12:33 in haste; for they **s**, We *be* all dead *men*. 559
12:43 the LORD **s** unto Moses and Aaron, This *is* 559
13: 3 Moses **s** unto the people, Remember this 559
13:17 for God **s**, Lest peradventure the people 559
14: 5 they **s**, Why have we done this, that we 559
14:11 they **s** unto Moses, Because *there were* no 559
14:13 Moses **s** unto the people, Fear ye not, 559
14:15 the LORD **s** unto Moses, Wherefore criest 559
14:25 so that the Egyptians **s**, Let us flee from 559
14:26 the LORD **s** unto Moses, Stretch out thine 559
15: 9 The enemy **s**, I will pursue, I will overtake, 559
15:26 **s**, If thou wilt diligently hearken to the 559
16: 3 the children of Israel **s** unto them, Would 559
16: 4 **s** the LORD unto Moses, Behold, I will rain 559
16: 6 and Aaron **s** unto all the children of Israel, 559
16: 8 Moses **s**, *This shall be*, when the LORD 559
16:15 the children of Israel saw *it*, they **s** one 559
16:15 they wist not what it *was*. And Moses **s** 559
16:19 Moses **s**, Let no man leave of it till 559
16:23 he **s** unto them, This *is that* which 559
16:23 This *is that* which the LORD hath **s**, 1696
16:25 Moses **s**, Eat that to day; for to day *is* a 559
16:28 the LORD **s** unto Moses, How long refuse 559
16:32 Moses **s**, This *is* the thing which the LORD 559
16:33 Moses **s** unto Aaron, Take a pot, and put 559
17: 2 and **s**, Give us water that we may drink. 559
17: 2 Moses **s** unto them, Why chide ye with 559
17: 3 people murmured against Moses, and **s**, 559
17: 5 the LORD **s** unto Moses, Go on before 559
17: 9 Moses **s** unto Joshua, Choose us out men, 559
17:10 So Joshua did as Moses had **s** to him, 559
17:14 the LORD **s** unto Moses, Write this *for* a 559
17:16 For he **s**, Because the LORD hath sworn 559
18: 3 for he **s**, I have been an alien in a strange 559
18: 4 *s he, was* mine help, and delivered me NIH
18: 6 he **s** unto Moses, I thy father in law Jethro 559
18:10 Jethro **s**, Blessed *be* the LORD, who hath 559
18:14 he **s**, What *is* this thing that thou doest to 559
18:15 Moses **s** unto his father in law, Because 559
18:17 Moses' father in law unto him, The thing 559
18:24 his father in law, and did all that he had **s**. 559
19: 8 all the people answered together, and **s**, 559
19: 9 the LORD **s** unto Moses, Lo, I come unto 559
19:10 the LORD **s** unto Moses, Go unto 559
19:15 he **s** unto the people, Be ready against 559
19:21 the LORD **s** unto Moses, Go down, 559
19:23 Moses **s** unto the LORD, The people 559
19:24 the LORD **s** unto him, Away, get thee 559
20:19 they **s** unto Moses, Speak thou with us, 559
20:20 Moses **s** unto the people, Fear not: for God 559
20:22 the LORD **s** unto Moses, Thus thou shalt 559
23:13 in all *things* that I have **s** unto you be 559
24: 1 he **s** unto Moses, Come up unto the LORD, 559
24: 3 people answered *with* one voice, and **s**, 559
24: 3 All the words which the LORD hath **s** will 1696
24: 7 they **s**, All that the LORD hath said will we 559
24: 7 All that the LORD hath **s** will we do, 1696
24: 8 and sprinkled *it* on the people, and **s**, 559
24:12 the LORD **s** unto Moses, Come up to me 559
24:14 he **s** unto the elders, Tarry ye here for us, 559
30:34 the LORD **s** unto Moses, Take unto thee 559
32: 1 **s** unto him, Up, make us gods, which shall 559
32: 2 Aaron **s** unto them, Break off the golden 559
32: 4 they **s**, These *be* thy gods, O Israel, 559
32: 5 Aaron made proclamation, and **s**, To 559
32: 7 the LORD **s** unto Moses, Go, get thee 1696
32: 8 and **s**, These *be* thy gods, O Israel, 559
32: 9 the LORD **s** unto Moses, I have seen this 559
32:11 the LORD his God, and **s**, LORD, 559

S

Ex	32:17 he **s** unto Moses, *There is* a noise of war in	559
	32:18 he **s**, *It is* not the voice of *them that* shout	559
	32:21 Moses **s** unto Aaron, What did this people	559
	32:22 Aaron **s**, Let not the anger of my lord wax	559
	32:23 For they **s** unto me, Make us gods,	559
	32:24 I **s** unto them, Whosoever hath *any* gold,	559
	32:26 and **s**, Who *is* on the LORD's side?	559
	32:27 he **s** unto them, Thus saith the LORD God	559
	32:29 For Moses had **s**, Consecrate yourselves to	559
	32:30 Moses **s** unto the people, Ye have sinned	559
	32:31 **s**, Oh, this people have sinned a great sin,	559
	32:33 the LORD **s** unto Moses, Whosoever hath	559
	33: 1 the LORD **s** unto Moses, Depart,	1696
	33: 5 For the LORD had **s** unto Moses, Say unto	559
	33:12 Moses said unto the LORD, See, thou sayest	559
	33:12 Yet thou hast **s**, I know thee by name,	559
	33:14 he **s**, My presence shall go *with thee*, and	559
	33:15 he **s** unto him, If thy presence go not *with*	559
	33:17 the LORD **s** unto Moses, I will do this	559
	33:18 he **s**, I beseech thee, shew me thy glory.	559
	33:19 he **s**, I will make all my goodness pass	559
	33:20 he **s**, Thou canst not see my face: for there	559
	33:21 the LORD **s**, Behold, *there is* a place by	559
	34: 1 the LORD **s** unto Moses, Hew thee two	559
	34: 9 he **s**, If now I have found grace in thy	559
	34:10 he **s**, Behold, I make a covenant: before all	559
	34:27 the LORD **s** unto Moses, Write thou these	559
	35: 1 **s** unto them, These *are* the words which	559
	35:30 Moses **s** unto the children of Israel, See,	559
Lev	8: 5 Moses **s** unto the congregation, This *is*	559
	8:31 Moses **s** unto Aaron and to his sons, Boil	559
	9: 2 he **s** unto Aaron, Take thee a young calf for	559
	9: 6 Moses **s**, This *is* the thing which the LORD	559
	9: 7 Moses **s** unto Aaron, Go unto the altar,	559
	10: 3 Moses **s** unto Aaron, This *is it* that	559
	10: 4 of Aaron, and **s** unto then, Come near,	559
	10: 5 coats out of the camp; as Moses had **s**.	1696
	10: 6 Moses **s** unto Aaron, and unto Eleazar and	559
	10:19 Aaron **s** unto Moses, Behold, *this* day have	1696
	16: 2 the LORD **s** unto Moses, Speak unto Aaron	559
	17:12 Therefore I **s** unto the children of Israel,	559
	17:14 therefore I **s** unto the children of Israel,	559
	20:24 have **s** unto you, Ye shall inherit their land,	559
	21: 1 the LORD **s** unto Moses, Speak unto	559
Nu	3:40 the LORD **s** unto Moses, Number all	559
	7:11 the LORD **s** unto Moses, They shall offer	559
	9: 7 those men **s** unto him, We *are* defiled by	559
	9: 8 Moses **s** unto them, Stand still, and I will	559
	10:29 Moses **s** unto Hobab, the son of Raguel	559
	10:29 unto the place of which the LORD **s**,	559
	10:30 he **s** unto him, I will not go; but I will	559
	10:31 he **s**, Leave us not, I pray thee; forasmuch	559
	10:35 that Moses **s**, Rise up, LORD, and let thine	559
	10:36 And when it rested, he **s**, Return, O LORD,	559
	11: 4 and **s**, Who shall give us flesh to eat?	559
	11:11 Moses **s** unto the LORD, Wherefore hast	559
	11:16 the LORD **s** unto Moses, Gather unto me	559
	11:21 Moses **s**, The people, amongst whom I *am*,	559
	11:21 thou hast **s**, I will give them flesh, that they	559
	11:23 the LORD **s** unto Moses, Is the LORD's	559
	11:27 **s**, Eldad and Medad do prophesy in	559
	11:28 answered and **s**, My lord Moses,	559
	11:29 Moses **s** unto him, Enviest thou for my	559
	12: 2 they **s**, Hath the LORD indeed spoken only	559
	12: 6 he **s**, Hear now my words: If there be a	559
	12:11 Aaron **s** unto Moses, Alas, my lord,	559
	12:14 the LORD **s** unto Moses, If her father had	559
	13:17 unto them, Get you up this *way*	559
	13:27 told him, and **s**, We came unto the land	559
	13:30 and **s**, Let us go up at once, and possess it;	559
	13:31 men that went up with him **s**, We be not	559
	14: 2 the whole congregation **s** unto them,	559
	14: 4 they **s** one to another, Let us make a	559
	14:11 the LORD **s** unto Moses, How long will	559
	14:13 Moses **s** unto the LORD, Then	559
	14:20 the LORD **s**, I have pardoned according to	559
	14:31 little ones, which ye **s** should be a prey,	559
	14:35 I the LORD have **s**, I will surely do it unto	1696
	14:41 Moses **s**, Wherefore now do ye transgress	559
	15:35 the LORD **s** unto Moses, The man shall be	559
	16: 3 and against Aaron, and **s** unto them,	559
	16: 8 Moses **s** unto Korah, Hear, I pray you,	559
	16:12 of Eliab: which **s**, We will not come up:	559
	16:15 was very wroth, and **s** unto the LORD,	559
	16:16 Moses **s** unto Korah, Be thou and all thy	559
	16:22 they fell upon their faces, and **s**, O God,	559
	16:28 Moses **s**, Hereby ye shall know that	559
	16:34 they **s**, Lest the earth swallow us up *also*.	559
	16:40 as the LORD **s** to him by the hand of	1696
	16:46 And Moses **s** unto Aaron, Take a censer,	559
	17:10 the LORD **s** unto Moses, Bring Aaron's rod	559
	18: 1 the LORD **s** unto Aaron, Thou and thy sons	559
	18:24 therefore I have **s** unto them, Among	559
	20:10 and he **s** unto them, Hear now, ye rebels;	559
	20:18 Edom **s** unto him, Thou shalt not pass by	559
	20:19 the children of Israel **s** unto him, We will	559
	20:20 he **s**, Thou shalt not go through.	559
	21: 2 Israel vowed a vow unto the LORD, and **s**,	559
	21: 7 came to Moses, and **s**, We have sinned,	559
	21: 8 the LORD **s** unto Moses, Make thee a fiery	559
	21:14 Wherefore it is **s** in the book of the wars of	559
	21:34 And the LORD **s** unto Moses, Fear not:	559
	22: 4 Moab **s** unto the elders of Midian, Now	559
	22: 8 he **s** unto them, Lodge here *this* night,	559
	22: 9 God came unto Balaam, and **s**, What men	559

Nu	22:10 Balaam **s** unto God, Balak the son of	559
	22:12 God **s** unto Balaam, Thou shalt not go with	559
	22:13 **s** unto the princes of Balak, Get you into	559
	22:14 they went unto Balak, and **s**,	559
	22:16 they came to Balaam, and **s** to him,	559
	22:18 and **s** unto the servants of Balak,	559
	22:20 and **s** unto him, If the men come to call	559
	22:28 she **s** unto Balaam, What have I done unto	559
	22:29 Balaam **s** unto the ass, Because thou hast	559
	22:30 the ass **s** unto Balaam, *Am* not I thine ass,	559
	22:30 wont to do so unto thee? And he **s**, Nay.	559
	22:32 the angel of the LORD **s** unto him,	559
	22:34 And Balaam **s** unto the angel of the LORD,	559
	22:35 And the angel of the LORD **s** unto Balaam,	559
	22:37 Balak **s** unto Balaam, Did I not earnestly	559
	22:38 Balaam **s** unto Balak, Lo, I am come unto	559
	23: 1 Balaam **s** unto Balak, Build me here seven	559
	23: 3 Balaam **s** unto Balak, Stand by thy burnt	559
	23: 4 he **s** unto him, I have prepared seven	559
	23: 5 **s**, Return unto Balak, and thus thou shalt	559
	23: 7 took up his parable, and **s**, Balak the king	559
	23:11 Balak **s** unto Balaam, What hast thou done	559
	23:12 answered and **s**, Must I not take heed to	559
	23:13 Balak **s** unto him, Come, I pray thee,	559
	23:15 he **s** unto Balak, Stand here by thy burnt	559
	23:16 and **s**, Go again unto Balak, and say thus.	559
	23:17 Balak **s** unto him, What hath the LORD	559
	23:18 parable, and **s**, Rise up, Balak, and hear;	559
	23:19 hath he **s**, and shall he not do *it?* or hath	559
	23:23 according to *this* time it shall be **s** of Jacob	559
	23:25 Balak **s** unto Balaam, Neither curse them	559
	23:26 Balaam answered and **s** unto Balak, Told	559
	23:27 Balak **s** unto Balaam, Come, I pray thee,	559
	23:29 Balaam **s** unto Balak, Build me here seven	559
	23:30 Balak did as Balaam had **s**, and offered a	559
	24: 3 he took up his parable, and **s**, Balaam the	559
	24: 3 Balaam the son of Beor hath **s**, and the	5002
	24: 3 and the man whose eyes are open hath **s**:	5002
	24: 4 He hath **s**, which heard the words of God,	5002
	24:10 Balak **s** unto Balaam, I called thee to curse	559
	24:12 Balaam **s** unto Balak, Spake I not also to	559
	24:15 took up his parable, and **s**, Balaam the son	559
	24:15 Balaam the son of Beor hath **s**, and the	5002
	24:15 and the man whose eyes are open hath **s**:	5002
	24:16 He hath **s**, which heard the words of God,	5002
	24:20 on Amalek, he took up his parable, and **s**,	559
	24:21 took up his parable, and **s**, Strong *is* thy	559
	24:23 he took up his parable, and **s**, Alas,	559
	25: 4 the LORD **s** unto Moses, Take all the heads	559
	25: 5 Moses **s** unto the judges of Israel, Slay ye	559
	26:65 For the LORD had **s** of them, They shall	559
	27:12 the LORD **s** unto Moses, Get thee up into	559
	27:18 the LORD **s** unto Moses, Take thee Joshua	559
	31:15 Moses **s** unto them, Have ye saved all	559
	31:21 Eleazar the priest **s** unto the men of war	559
	31:49 they **s** unto Moses, Thy servants have	559
	32: 5 Wherefore, **s** they, if we have found grace	559
	32: 6 Moses **s** unto the children of Gad and to	559
	32:16 they came near unto him, and **s**, We will	559
	32:20 Moses **s** unto them, If ye will do this thing,	559
	32:29 Moses **s** unto them, If the children of Gad	559
	32:31 As the LORD hath **s** unto thy servants,	1696
	36: 2 they **s**, The LORD commanded my lord to	559
	36: 5 tribe of the sons of Joseph hath **s** well.	1696
Dt	1:14 ye answered me, and **s**, The thing which	559
	1:20 I **s** unto you, Ye are come unto the	559
	1:21 God of thy fathers hath **s** unto thee;	1696
	1:22 **s**, We will send men before us,	559
	1:25 and brought us word again, and **s**,	559
	1:27 and **s**, Because the LORD hated us,	559
	1:29 I **s** unto you, Dread not, neither be afraid	559
	1:39 which ye **s** should be a prey,	559
	1:41 answered and **s** unto me, We have sinned	559
	1:42 the LORD **s** unto me, Say unto them,	559
	2: 9 the LORD **s** unto me, Distress not	559
	2:13 **s** I, and get you over the brook Zered.	NIH
	2:31 the LORD **s** unto me, Behold, I have begun	559
	3: 2 the LORD **s** unto me, Fear him not: for I	559
	3:26 the LORD **s** unto me, Let it suffice thee;	559
	4:10 when the LORD **s** unto me, Gather me	559
	5: 1 unto them, Hear, O Israel, the statutes	559
	5:24 ye **s**, Behold, the LORD our God hath	559
	5:28 the LORD **s** unto me, I have heard	559
	5:28 they have well **s** all that they have spoken.	NIH
	9: 3 as the LORD hath **s** unto thee.	1696
	9:12 the LORD **s** unto me, Arise, get thee down	559
	9:25 the LORD had **s** he would destroy you.	559
	9:26 unto the LORD, and **s**, O Lord GOD,	559
	10: 1 At that time the LORD **s** unto me,	559
	10:11 the LORD **s** unto me, Arise, take thy	559
	11:25 shall tread upon, as he hath **s** unto you.	1696
	17:16 forasmuch as the LORD hath **s** unto you,	559
	18: 2 their inheritance, as he hath **s** unto them.	1696
	18:17 the LORD **s** unto me, They have well	559
	29: 2 called unto all Israel, and **s** unto them,	559
	29:13 hath **s** unto thee, and as he hath sworn	1696
	31: 2 he **s** unto them, I *am* an hundred and	559
	31: 2 also the LORD hath **s** unto me, Thou shalt	559
	31: 3 go over before thee, as the LORD hath **s**.	1696
	31: 7 unto him in the sight of all Israel,	559
	31:14 the LORD **s** unto Moses, Behold, thy days	559
	31:16 the LORD **s** unto Moses, Behold, thou shalt	559
	31:23 **s**, Be strong and of a good courage:	559
	32:20 he **s**, I will hide my face from them, I will	559
	32:26 I **s**, I would scatter them into corners,	559

Dt	32:46 he **s** unto them, Set your hearts unto all	559
	33: 2 And he **s**, The LORD came from Sinai,	559
	33: 7 And he **s**, Hear, LORD, the voice of Judah,	559
	33: 8 of Levi he **s**, *Let* thy Thummim and	559
	33: 9 Who **s** unto his father and to his mother,	559
	33:12 *And* of Benjamin he **s**, The beloved of	559
	33:13 of Joseph he **s**, Blessed of the LORD *be* his	559
	33:18 of Zebulun he **s**, Rejoice, Zebulun, in thy	559
	33:20 of Gad he **s**, Blessed *be* he that enlargeth	559
	33:22 of Dan he **s**, Dan *is* a lion's whelp: he shall	559
	33:23 of Naphtali he **s**, O Naphtali, satisfied with	559
	33:24 of Asher he **s**, *Let* Asher *be* blessed with	559
	34: 4 the LORD **s** unto him, This *is* the land	559
Jos	2: 1 **s**, Go view the land, even Jericho. And	559
	2: 3 have I given unto you, as I **s** unto Moses.	1696
	2: 4 hid them, and **s** thus, There came men	559
	2: 9 she **s** unto the men, I know that the LORD	559
	2:16 she **s** unto them, Get you to the mountain,	559
	2:17 the men **s** unto her, We *will be* blameless	559
	2:21 she **s**, According unto your words, so *be* it.	559
	2:24 they **s** unto Joshua, Truly the LORD hath	559
	3: 5 Joshua **s** unto the people,	559
	3: 7 the LORD **s** unto Joshua, This day will I	559
	3: 9 Joshua **s** unto the children of Israel,	559
	3:10 Joshua **s**, Hereby ye shall know that	559
	4: 5 Joshua **s** unto them, Pass over before the	559
	5: 2 At that time the LORD **s** unto Joshua,	559
	5: 9 the LORD **s** unto Joshua, *This* day have I	559
	5:13 unto him, *Art* thou for us, or for our	559
	5:14 he **s**, Nay; but *as* captain of the host of	559
	5:14 worship, and **s** unto him, What saith my	559
	5:15 the captain of the LORD's host **s** unto	559
	6: 2 the LORD **s** unto Joshua, See, I have given	559
	6: 6 **s** unto them, Take up the ark of the	559
	6: 7 he **s** unto the people, Pass on,	559
	6:16 Joshua **s** unto the people, Shout;	559
	6:22 Joshua had **s** unto the two men that had	559
	7: 3 **s** unto him, Let not all the people go up;	559
	7: 7 Joshua **s**, Alas, O Lord GOD,	559
	7:10 And the LORD **s** unto Joshua, Get thee up;	559
	7:19 Joshua **s** unto Achan, My son, give, I pray	559
	7:20 Achan answered Joshua, and **s**, Indeed I	559
	7:25 Joshua **s**, Why hast thou troubled us?	559
	8: 1 the LORD **s** unto Joshua, Fear not,	559
	8:18 the LORD **s** unto Joshua, Stretch out	559
	9: 6 **s** unto him, and to the men of Israel, We	559
	9: 7 the men of Israel **s** unto the Hivites,	559
	9: 8 they **s** unto Joshua, We *are* thy servants.	559
	9: 8 Joshua **s** unto them, Who *are* ye?	559
	9: 9 they **s** unto him, From a very far country	559
	9:19 all the princes **s** unto all the congregation,	559
	9:21 the princes **s** unto them, Let them live;	559
	9:24 they answered Joshua, and **s**, Because it	559
	10: 8 the LORD **s** unto Joshua, Fear them not:	559
	10:12 he **s** in the sight of Israel, Sun, stand thou	559
	10:18 Joshua **s**, Roll great stones upon the mouth	559
	10:22 Joshua, Open the mouth of the cave,	559
	10:24 **s** unto the captains of the men of war	559
	10:25 Joshua **s** unto them, Fear not, nor be	559
	11: 6 And the LORD **s** unto Joshua, Be not afraid	559
	11:23 according to all that the LORD **s** unto	1696
	13: 1 the LORD **s** unto him, Thou art old *and*	559
	13:14 *are* their inheritance, as he **s** unto them.	1696
	13:33 *was* their inheritance, as the LORD **s**	1696
	14: 6 Caleb the son of Jephunneh the Kenezite **s**	559
	14: 6 Thou knowest the thing that the LORD **s**	1696
	14:10 alive, as he **s**, these forty and five years,	1696
	14:12 *be able to* drive them out, as the LORD **s**.	1696
	15:16 Caleb **s**, He that smiteth Kirjath-sepher,	559
	15:18 Caleb **s** unto her, What wouldest thou?	559
	17:16 the children of Joseph **s**, The hill is not	559
	18: 3 Joshua **s** unto the children of Israel,	559
	22: 2 **s** unto them, Ye have kept all that Moses	559
	22:21 unto the heads of the thousands of	1696
	22:26 Therefore we **s**, Let us now prepare to	559
	22:28 Therefore we **s**, that it shall be, when they	559
	22:31 Phinehas the son of Eleazar the priest **s**	559
	23: 2 **s** unto them, I am old and stricken in age:	559
	24: 2 Joshua **s** unto all the people, Thus saith	559
	24:16 people answered and **s**, God forbid that	559
	24:19 Joshua **s** unto the people, Ye cannot serve	559
	24:21 the people **s** unto Joshua, Nay; but we will	559
	24:22 Joshua **s** unto the people, Ye *are* witnesses	559
	24:22 serve him. And they **s**, We *are* witnesses.	559
	24:23 **s** he, the strange gods which *are* among	NIH
	24:24 the people **s** unto Joshua, The LORD our	559
	24:27 Joshua **s** unto all the people, Behold, this	559
Jdg	1: 2 the LORD **s**, Judah shall go up: behold,	559
	1: 3 Judah **s** unto Simeon his brother, Come up	559
	1: 7 Adoni-bezek **s**, Threescore and ten kings,	559
	1:12 Caleb **s**, He that smiteth Kirjath-sepher,	559
	1:14 and Caleb **s** unto her, What wilt thou?	559
	1:15 she **s** unto him, Give me a blessing: for	559
	1:20 they gave Hebron unto Caleb, as Moses **s**:	1696
	1:24 they **s**, unto him, Shew us, we pray thee,	559
	2: 1 and **s**, I made you to go up out of Egypt,	559
	2: 1 I **s**, I will never break my covenant with	559
	2: 3 Wherefore I also **s**, I will not drive them	559
	2:15 as the LORD had **s**, and as the LORD	1696
	2:20 he **s**, Because that this people hath	559
	3:19 **s**, I have a secret errand unto thee, O king:	559
	3:19 who **s**, Keep silence. And all that stood by	559
	3:20 Ehud **s**, I have a message from God unto	559
	3:24 doors of the parlour *were* locked, they **s**,	559
	3:28 he **s** unto them, Follow after me:	559
	4: 6 **s** unto him, Hath not the LORD God of	559

Jdg	4: 8 Barak **s** unto her, If thou wilt go with me, 559
	4: 9 she **s**, I will surely go with thee: 559
	4:14 Deborah **s** unto Barak, Up; for this *is* the 559
	4:18 unto him, Turn in, my lord, turn in to 559
	4:19 he **s** unto her, Give me, I pray thee, a little 559
	4:20 Again he **s** unto her, Stand *in* the door of 559
	4:22 **s** unto him, Come, and I will shew thee 559
	5:23 Curse ye Meroz, **s** the angel of the LORD, 559
	6: 8 which **s** unto them, Thus saith the LORD 559
	6:10 I **s** unto you, I *am* the LORD your God; 559
	6:12 **s** unto him, The LORD *is* with thee, 559
	6:13 Gideon **s** unto him, O my lord, if the LORD 559
	6:14 **s**, Go in this thy might, and thou shalt save 559
	6:15 he **s** unto him, O my Lord, wherewith 559
	6:16 the LORD **s** unto him, Surely I will be with 559
	6:17 he **s** unto them, If now I have found grace 559
	6:18 he **s**, I will tarry until thou come again. 559
	6:20 angel of God **s** unto him, Take the flesh 559
	6:22 the LORD, Gideon **s**, Alas, O Lord GOD! 559
	6:23 the LORD **s** unto him, Peace *be* unto thee; 559
	6:25 that the LORD **s** unto him, Take thy 559
	6:27 and did as the LORD had **s** unto him: 1696
	6:29 they **s** one to another, Who hath done 559
	6:29 when they inquired and asked, they **s**, 559
	6:30 the men of the city **s** unto Joash, Bring out 559
	6:31 Joash **s** unto all that stood against him, 559
	6:36 Gideon **s** unto God, If thou wilt save Israel 559
	6:36 save Israel by mine hand, as thou hast **s**, 1696
	6:37 save Israel by mine hand, as thou hast **s**. 1696
	6:39 Gideon **s** unto God, Let not thine anger be 559
	7: 2 the LORD **s** unto Gideon, The people that 559
	7: 4 the LORD **s** unto Gideon, The people *are* 559
	7: 5 the LORD **s** unto Gideon, Every one that 559
	7: 7 the LORD **s** unto Gideon, By the three 559
	7: 9 that the LORD **s** unto him, Arise, get thee 559
	7:13 and **s**, Behold, I dreamed a dream, and, lo, 559
	7:14 his fellow answered and **s**, This *is* nothing 559
	7:15 returned into the host of Israel, and **s**, 559
	7:17 he **s** unto them, Look on me, 559
	8: 1 the men of Ephraim **s** unto him, Why hast 559
	8: 2 he **s** unto them, What have I done now in 559
	8: 3 abated toward him, when he had **s** that. 1696
	8: 5 he **s** the men of Succoth, Give, I pray 559
	8: 6 the princes of Succoth **s**, *Are* the hands of 559
	8: 7 Gideon **s**, Therefore when the LORD hath 559
	8:15 **s**, Behold Zebah and Zalmunna, with 559
	8:18 **s** he unto Zebah and Zalmunna, 559
	8:19 he **s**, They *were* my brethren, *even* the 559
	8:20 he **s** unto Jether his firstborn, Up, 559
	8:21 Then Zebah and Zalmunna **s**, Rise thou, 559
	8:22 the men of Israel **s** unto Gideon, Rule thou 559
	8:23 Gideon **s** unto them, I will not rule over 559
	8:24 Gideon **s** unto them, I would desire a 559
	9: 3 for they **s**, He *is* our brother. 559
	9: 7 his voice, and cried, and **s** unto them, 559
	9: 8 they **s** unto the olive tree, Reign thou over 559
	9: 9 the olive tree **s** unto them, Should I leave 559
	9:10 the trees **s** to the fig tree, Come thou, 559
	9:11 the fig tree **s** unto them, Should I forsake 559
	9:12 **s** the trees unto the vine, Come thou, 559
	9:13 the vine **s** unto them, Should I leave my 559
	9:14 **s** all the trees unto the bramble, Come 559
	9:15 the bramble **s** unto the trees, If in truth ye 559
	9:28 Gaal the son of Ebed **s**, Who *is* Abimelech, 559
	9:29 he **s** to Abimelech, Increase thine army, 559
	9:36 Gaal saw the people, he **s** to Zebul, Behold, 559
	9:36 Zebul **s** unto him, Thou seest the shadow 559
	9:37 Gaal spake again and **s**, See there come 559
	9:38 **s** Zebul unto him, Where *is* now thy 559
	9:48 and **s** unto the people that *were* with him, 559
	9:54 **s** unto him, Draw thy sword, and slay me, 559
	10:11 the LORD **s** unto the children of Israel, 559
	10:15 the children of Israel **s** unto the LORD, 559
	10:18 *and* princes of Gilead **s** one to another, 559
	11: 2 they thrust out Jephthah, and **s** unto him, 559
	11: 6 they **s** unto Jephthah, Come, and be our 559
	11: 7 Jephthah **s** unto the elders of Gilead, Did 559
	11: 8 the elders of Gilead **s** unto Jephthah, 559
	11: 9 Jephthah **s** unto the elders of Gilead, If ye 559
	11:10 the elders of Gilead **s** unto Jephthah, 559
	11:15 **s** unto him, Thus saith Jephthah, Israel 559
	11:19 Israel **s** unto him, Let us pass, we pray 559
	11:30 vowed a vow unto the LORD, and **s**, 559
	11:35 rent his clothes, and **s**, Alas, my daughter, 559
	11:36 she **s** unto him, My father, *if* thou hast 559
	11:37 she **s** unto her father, Let this thing be 559
	11:38 he **s**, Go. And he sent her away *for* two 559
	12: 1 and went northward, and **s** unto Jephthah, 559
	12: 2 Jephthah **s** unto them, I and my people 559
	12: 4 of Gilead smote Ephraim, because they **s**, 559
	12: 5 those Ephraimites which were escaped **s**, 559
	12: 5 the men of Gilead **s** unto him, *Art* thou 559
	12: 5 *Art* thou an Ephraimite? If he **s**, Nay; 559
	12: 6 **s** they unto him, Say now Shibboleth: 559
	12: 6 he **s** Sibboleth: for he could not frame to 559
	13: 3 **s** unto her, Behold now, thou *art* barren, 559
	13: 7 he **s** unto me, Behold, thou *shalt* conceive, 559
	13: 8 intreated the LORD, and **s**, O my Lord, 559
	13:10 her husband, and **s** unto him, Behold, 559
	13:11 and came to the man, and **s** unto him, 559
	13:11 spakest unto the woman? And he **s**, I *am*. 559
	13:12 Manoah **s**, Now let thy words come to 559
	13:13 And the angel of the LORD **s** unto Manoah, 559
	13:13 Of all that I **s** unto the woman let her 559
	13:15 And Manoah **s** unto the angel of the LORD, 559

Jdg	13:16 And the angel of the LORD **s** unto Manoah, 559
	13:17 And Manoah **s** unto the angel of the LORD, 559
	13:18 the angel of the LORD **s** unto him, 559
	13:22 Manoah **s** unto his wife, We shall surely 559
	13:23 his wife **s** unto him, If the LORD were 559
	14: 2 and told his father and his mother, and **s**, 559
	14: 3 father and his mother **s** unto him, *Is* there 559
	14: 3 Samson **s** unto his father, Get her for me; 559
	14:12 Samson **s** unto them, I will now put forth 559
	14:13 they **s** unto him, Put forth thy riddle, that 559
	14:14 he **s** unto them, Out of the eater came 559
	14:15 that they **s** unto Samson's wife, Entice thy 559
	14:16 **s**, Thou dost but hate me, and lovest me 559
	14:16 he **s** unto her, Behold, I have not told *it* 559
	14:18 men of the city **s** unto him on the seventh 559
	14:18 he **s** unto them, If ye had not plowed with 559
	15: 1 he **s**, I will go in to my wife into 559
	15: 2 father **s**, I verily thought that thou hadst 559
	15: 3 Samson **s** concerning them, Now shall I be 559
	15: 6 the Philistines **s**, Who hath done this? 559
	15: 7 Samson **s** unto them, Though ye have 559
	15:10 the men of Judah **s**, Why are ye come up 559
	15:11 **s** to Samson, Knowest thou not that 559
	15:11 And he **s** unto them, As they did unto me, 559
	15:12 they **s** unto him, We are come down to 559
	15:12 Samson **s** unto them, Swear unto me, 559
	15:16 Samson **s**, With the jawbone of an ass, 559
	15:18 sore athirst, and called on the LORD, and **s**, 559
	16: 5 **s** unto her, Entice him, and see wherein 559
	16: 6 Delilah **s** to Samson, Tell me, I pray thee, 559
	16: 7 Samson **s** unto her, If they bind me with 559
	16: 9 she **s** unto him, The Philistines *be* upon 559
	16:10 Delilah **s** unto Samson, Behold, thou hast 559
	16:11 he **s** unto her, If they bind me fast with 559
	16:12 and bound him therewith, and **s** unto him, 559
	16:13 Delilah **s** unto Samson, Hitherto thou hast 559
	16:13 he **s** unto her, If thou weavest the seven 559
	16:14 **s** unto him, The Philistines *be* upon thee, 559
	16:15 she **s** unto him, How canst thou say, I love 559
	16:17 he told her all his heart, and **s** unto her, 559
	16:20 she **s**, The Philistines *be* upon thee, 559
	16:20 he awoke out of his sleep, and **s**, I will go 559
	16:23 for they **s**, Our god hath delivered Samson 559
	16:24 for they **s**, Our god hath delivered into our 559
	16:25 that they **s**, Call for Samson, that he may 559
	16:26 Samson **s** unto the lad that held him by 559
	16:28 **s**, O Lord GOD, remember me, I pray thee, 559
	16:30 Samson **s**, Let me die with the Philistines. 559
	17: 2 **s** unto his mother, The eleven hundred 559
	17: 2 his mother **s**, Blessed *be thou* of the LORD, 559
	17: 3 his mother **s**, I had wholly dedicated 559
	17: 9 Micah **s** unto him, Whence comest thou? 559
	17: 9 he **s** unto him, I *am* a Levite of 559
	17:10 Micah **s** unto him, Dwell with me, 559
	17:13 **s** Micah, Now know I that the LORD will 559
	18: 2 and they **s** unto them, Go, search the land: 559
	18: 3 they turned in thither, and **s** unto him, 559
	18: 4 he **s** unto them, Thus and thus dealeth 559
	18: 5 they **s** unto him, Ask *counsel*, we pray 559
	18: 6 the priest **s** unto them, Go in peace: 559
	18: 8 their brethren **s** unto them, What *say* ye? 559
	18: 9 they **s**, Arise, that we may go up against 559
	18:14 **s** unto their brethren, Do ye know that 559
	18:18 Then **s** the priest unto them, What do ye? 559
	18:19 they **s** unto him, Hold thy peace, lay thine 559
	18:23 and **s** unto Micah, What aileth thee, 559
	18:24 he **s**, Ye have taken away my gods which I 559
	18:25 the children of Dan **s** unto him, Let not thy 559
	19: 5 the damsel's father **s** unto his son in law, 559
	19: 6 for the damsel's father had **s** unto the man, 559
	19: 8 the damsel's father **s**, Comfort thine heart, 559
	19: 9 damsel's father, **s** unto him, Behold now, 559
	19:11 servant **s** unto his master, Come, I pray 559
	19:12 master **s** unto him, We will not turn aside 559
	19:13 he **s** unto his servant, Come, and let us 559
	19:17 the old man **s**, Whither goest thou? 559
	19:18 he **s** unto him, We are passing from 559
	19:20 the old man **s**, Peace *be* with thee; 559
	19:23 **s** unto them, Nay, my brethren, *nay*, I pray 559
	19:28 he **s** unto her, Up, and let us be going. 559
	19:30 was so, that all that saw it **s**, There was no 559
	20: 3 the children of Israel, Tell *us*, how was 559
	20: 4 the woman that was slain, answered and **s**, 559
	20:18 of God, and asked *counsel* of God, and **s**, 559
	20:18 And the LORD **s**, Judah *shall go up* first. 559
	20:23 And the LORD **s**, Go up against him.) 559
	20:28 the LORD **s**, Go up; for to morrow I will 559
	20:32 children of Benjamin **s**, They *are* smitten 559
	20:32 the children of Israel **s**, Let us flee, 559
	20:39 for they **s**, Surely they are smitten down 559
	21: 3 **s**, O LORD God of Israel, why is this come 559
	21: 5 children of Israel **s**, Who *is there* among 559
	21: 6 **s**, There is one tribe cut off from Israel *this* 559
	21: 8 they **s**, What one *is there* of the tribes of 559
	21:16 the elders of the congregation **s**, How shall 559
	21:17 they **s**, *There* must be an inheritance for 559
	21:19 they **s**, Behold, *there is* a feast of the LORD 559
Ru	1: 8 Naomi **s** unto her two daughters in law, 559
	1:10 they **s** unto her, Surely we will return with 559
	1:11 Naomi **s**, Turn again, my daughters: 559
	1:15 she **s**, Behold, thy sister in law is gone back 559
	1:16 Ruth **s**, Intreat me not to leave thee, 559
	1:19 about them, and they **s**, *Is* this Naomi? 559
	1:20 she **s** unto them, Call me not Naomi, call 559
	2: 2 Ruth the Moabitess **s** unto Naomi, Let me 559

Ru	2: 2 And she **s** unto her, Go, my daughter. 559
	2: 4 **s** unto the reapers, The LORD *be* with you. 559
	2: 5 **s** Boaz unto his servant that was set over 559
	2: 6 was set over the reapers answered and **s**, 559
	2: 7 she **s**, I pray you, let me glean and 559
	2: 8 **s** Boaz unto Ruth, Hearest thou not, 559
	2:10 herself to the ground, and **s** unto him, 559
	2:11 Boaz answered and **s** unto her, It hath fully 559
	2:13 she **s**, Let me find favour in thy sight, 559
	2:14 Boaz **s** unto her, At mealtime come thou 559
	2:19 her mother in law **s** unto her, Where hast 559
	2:19 **s**, The man's name with whom I wrought 559
	2:20 Naomi **s** unto her daughter in law, 559
	2:20 Naomi **s** unto her, The man *is* near of kin 559
	2:21 Ruth the Moabitess **s**, He said unto me 559
	2:21 Ruth the Moabitess said, He **s** unto me 559
	2:22 Naomi **s** unto Ruth her daughter in law, 559
	3: 1 Naomi her mother in law **s** unto her, 559
	3: 5 she **s** unto her, All that thou sayest unto 559
	3: 9 he **s**, Who *art* thou? And she answered, 559
	3:10 he **s**, Blessed *be* thou of the LORD, 559
	3:14 he **s**, Let it not be known that a woman 559
	3:15 he **s**, Bring the vail that *thou hast* upon 559
	3:16 in law, she **s**, Who *art* thou, my daughter? 559
	3:17 she **s**, These six *measures* of barley gave 559
	3:17 for he **s** to me, Go not empty into thy 559
	3:18 she **s**, Sit still, my daughter, until thou 559
	4: 1 whom he **s**, *Ho*, such a one, turn aside, 559
	4: 2 elders of the city, and **s**, Sit ye down here. 559
	4: 3 he **s** unto the kinsman, Naomi, that is 559
	4: 4 I *am* after thee. And he **s**, I will redeem *it*. 559
	4: 5 **s** Boaz, What day thou buyest the field of 559
	4: 6 kinsman, **s**, I cannot redeem *it* for myself, 559
	4: 8 Therefore the kinsman **s** unto Boaz, Buy *it* 559
	4: 9 Boaz **s** unto the elders, and *unto* all 559
	4:11 gate, and the elders, **s**, *We are* witnesses. 559
	4:14 the women **s** unto Naomi, Blessed *be* 559
1Sa	1: 8 Then **s** Elkanah her husband to her, 559
	1:11 she vowed a vow, and **s**, O LORD of hosts, 559
	1:14 Eli **s** unto her, How long wilt thou be 559
	1:15 Hannah answered and **s**, No, my lord, I 559
	1:17 Eli answered and **s**, Go in peace: 559
	1:18 she **s**, Let thine handmaid find grace in thy 559
	1:22 she **s** unto her husband, *I will not go up* 559
	1:23 Elkanah her husband **s** unto her, Do what 559
	1:26 she **s**, O my lord, *as* thy soul liveth, 559
	2: 1 Hannah prayed, and **s**, My heart rejoiceth 559
	2:15 and **s** to the man that sacrificed, 559
	2:16 *if any* man **s** unto him, Let them not fail to 559
	2:20 Eli blessed Elkanah and his wife, and **s**, 559
	2:23 he **s** unto them, Why do ye such things? 559
	2:27 and **s** unto him, Thus saith the LORD, 559
	2:30 I **s indeed** *that* thy house, and the 559+559
	3: 5 he ran unto Eli, and **s**, Here *am* I; for thou 559
	3: 5 he **s**, I called not; lie down again. And he 559
	3: 6 and went to Eli, and **s**, Here *am* I; 559
	3: 8 he arose and went to Eli, and **s**, Here *am* I; 559
	3: 9 Therefore Eli **s** to Samuel, Go, lie down: 559
	3:11 the LORD **s** to Samuel, Behold, I will do a 559
	3:16 Eli called Samuel, and **s**, Samuel, my son. 559
	3:17 he **s**, What *is* the thing that *the* LORD hath 559
	3:17 What *is* the thing that *the* LORD hath 1696
	3:17 me of all the things that he **s** unto thee. 1696
	3:18 he **s**, *It is* the LORD: let him do what 559
	4: 3 come into the camp, the elders of Israel **s**, 559
	4: 6 heard the noise of the shout, they **s**, 559
	4: 7 for they **s**, God is come into the camp. 559
	4: 7 they **s**, Woe unto us: for there hath not 559
	4:14 **s**, What *meaneth* the noise of this tumult? 559
	4:16 man **s** unto Eli, I *am* he that came out of 559
	4:16 And he **s**, What is there done, my son? 559
	4:17 messenger answered and **s**, Israel is fled 559
	4:20 that stood by her **s** *unto her*, Fear not; 1696
	4:22 she **s**, The glory is departed from Israel: 559
	5: 7 men of Ashdod saw that *it was* so, they **s**, 559
	5: 8 lords of the Philistines unto them, and **s**, 559
	5:11 **s**, Send away the ark of the God of Israel, 559
	6: 3 they **s**, If ye send away the ark of the God 559
	6: 4 **s** they, What *shall be* the trespass offering 559
	6:20 the men of Beth-shemesh **s**, Who is able to 559
	7: 5 Samuel **s**, Gather all Israel to Mizpeh, 559
	7: 6 and fasted on that day, and **s** there, 559
	7: 8 children of Israel **s** to Samuel, Cease not 559
	8: 5 **s** unto him, Behold, thou art old, 559
	8: 6 when they **s**, Give us a king to judge us. 559
	8: 7 the LORD **s** unto Samuel, Hearken unto 559
	8:11 he **s**, This will be the manner of the king 559
	8:19 they **s**, Nay, but we will have a king over 559
	8:22 the LORD **s** to Samuel, Hearken unto their 559
	8:22 Samuel **s** unto the men of Israel, Go ye 559
	9: 3 Kish **s** to Saul his son, Take now one of 559
	9: 5 Saul **s** to his servant that *was* with him, 559
	9: 6 he **s** unto him, Behold now, *there is* in this 559
	9: 7 **s** Saul to his servant, But behold, *if* we go, 559
	9: 8 servant answered Saul again, and **s**, 559
	9:10 Then **s** Saul to his servant, Well said; 559
	9:10 Then said Saul to his servant, Well **s**; 1697
	9:11 and **s** unto them, Is the seer here? 559
	9:12 they answered them, and **s**, He is; behold, 559
	9:17 Samuel saw Saul, the LORD **s** unto him, 6030
	9:18 **s**, Tell me, I pray thee, where the seer's 559
	9:19 Samuel answered Saul, and **s**, I *am* he 559
	9:21 Saul answered and **s**, *Am* not I a 559
	9:23 Samuel **s** unto the cook, Bring the portion 559
	9:23 of which I **s** unto thee, Set it by thee. 559

S

1Sa 9:24 *Samuel* s, Behold that which is left; set *it* 559
9:24 time *hath it* been kept for thee since *I* s, 559
9:27 Samuel s to Saul, Bid the servant pass on 559
10: 1 s, *Is it* not because the LORD hath anointed 559
10:11 then the people s one to another, 559
10:12 one of the same place answered and s, 559
10:14 Saul's uncle s unto him and to his servant, 559
10:14 he s, To seek the asses: and when we saw 559
10:15 Saul's uncle s, Tell me, I pray thee, 559
10:15 I pray thee, what Samuel s unto you. 559
10:16 Saul s unto his uncle, He told us plainly 559
10:18 s unto the children of Israel, Thus saith 559
10:19 ye have s unto him, *Nay*, but set a king 559
10:24 Samuel s to all the people, See ye him 559
10:24 people shouted, and s, God save the king. 559
10:27 children of Belial s, How shall this *man* 559
11: 1 all the men of Jabesh s unto Nahash, Make 559
11: 3 the elders of Jabesh s unto him, Give us 559
11: 5 Saul s, What aileth the people that they 559
11: 9 they s unto the messengers that came, 559
11:10 Therefore the men of Jabesh s, To morrow 559
11:12 the people s unto Samuel, Who *is* he that 559
11:12 Who *is* he that s, Shall Saul reign over us? 559
11:13 Saul s, There shall not a man be put to 559
11:14 Samuel to the people, Come, and let us 559
12: 1 Samuel s unto all Israel, Behold, I have 559
12: 1 unto your voice in all that ye s unto me, 559
12: 4 they s, Thou hast not defrauded us, 559
12: 5 he s unto them, The LORD *is* witness 559
12: 6 Samuel s unto the people, *It is* the LORD 559
12:10 s, We have sinned, because we have 559
12:12 came against you, ye s unto me, Nay; 559
12:19 all the people s unto Samuel, Pray for thy 559
12:20 Samuel s unto the people, Fear not: 559
13: 9 Saul s, Bring hither a burnt offering to me, 559
13:11 Samuel s, What hast thou done? And Saul 559
13:11 Saul s, Because I saw that the people were 559
13:12 Therefore s I, The Philistines will come 559
13:13 Samuel s to Saul, Thou hast done foolishly: 559
13:19 the Philistines s, Lest the Hebrews make 559
14: 1 that Jonathan the son of Saul s unto 559
14: 6 Jonathan s to the young man that bare his 559
14: 7 his armourbearer s unto him, Do all that *is* 559
14: 8 s Jonathan, Behold, we will pass over unto 559
14:11 Philistines s, Behold, the Hebrews come 559
14:12 s, Come up to us, and we will shew you a 559
14:12 Jonathan s unto his armourbearer, Come 559
14:17 s Saul unto the people that *were* with him, 559
14:18 Saul s unto Ahiah, Bring hither the ark of 559
14:19 Saul s unto the priest, Withdraw thine 559
14:28 answered one of the people, and s, 559
14:29 s Jonathan, My father hath troubled the 559
14:33 he s, Ye have transgressed: roll a great 559
14:34 Saul s, Disperse yourselves among 559
14:36 Saul s, Let us go down after the Philistines 559
14:36 they s, Do whatsoever seemeth good unto 559
14:36 the priest, Let us draw near hither unto 559
14:38 Saul s, Draw ye near hither, all the chief 559
14:40 Then s he unto all Israel, Be ye on one 559
14:40 the people s unto Saul, Do what seemeth 559
14:41 Therefore Saul s unto the LORD God of 559
14:42 Saul s, Cast *lots* between me and Jonathan 559
14:43 Saul s to Jonathan, Tell me what thou hast 559
14:43 s, I did but taste a little honey with the end 559
14:45 the people s unto Saul, Shall Jonathan die, 559
15: 1 Samuel also s unto Saul, The LORD sent 559
15: 6 Saul s unto the Kenites, Go, depart, get 559
15:13 Saul s unto him, Blessed *be* thou of 559
15:14 Samuel s, What *meaneth* then this bleating 559
15:15 Saul s, They have brought them from 559
15:16 Samuel s unto Saul, Stay, and I will tell 559
15:16 I will tell thee what the LORD hath s to 1696
15:16 *this* night. And he s unto him, Say on. 559
15:17 Samuel s, When thou *wast* little in thine 559
15:18 s, Go and utterly destroy the sinners 559
15:20 Saul s unto Samuel, Yea, I have obeyed 559
15:22 Samuel s, Hath the LORD *as great* delight 559
15:24 Saul s unto Samuel, I have sinned: for I 559
15:26 Samuel s unto Saul, I will not return with 559
15:28 Samuel s unto him, The LORD hath rent 559
15:30 he s, I have sinned: *yet* honour me now, 559
15:32 s Samuel, Bring you hither to me Agag 559
15:32 Agag s, Surely the bitterness of death is 559
15:33 Samuel s, As thy sword hath made women 559
16: 1 the LORD s unto Samuel, How long wilt 559
16: 2 Samuel s, How can I go? if Saul hear *it*, he 559
16: 2 the LORD s, Take a heifer with thee, 559
16: 4 his coming, and s, Comest thou peaceably? 559
16: 5 he s, Peaceably: I am come to sacrifice 559
16: 6 were come, that he looked on Eliab, and s, 559
16: 7 the LORD s unto Samuel, Look not on his 559
16: 8 he s, Neither hath the LORD chosen this. 559
16: 9 he s, Neither hath the LORD chosen this. 559
16:10 Samuel s unto Jesse, The LORD hath not 559
16:11 Samuel s unto Jesse, Are here all *thy* 559
16:11 he s, There remaineth yet the youngest, 559
16:11 Samuel s unto Jesse, Send and fetch him: 559
16:12 the LORD s, Arise, anoint him: for this *is* 559
16:15 Saul's servants s unto him, Behold now, 559
16:17 Saul s unto his servants, Provide me now 559
16:18 answered one of the servants, and s, 559
16:19 s, Send me David thy son, which *is* with 559
17: 8 unto the armies of Israel, and s unto them, 559
17:10 the Philistine s, I defy the armies of Israel 559
17:17 Jesse s unto David his son, Take now for 559

1Sa 17:25 the men of Israel s, Have ye seen this man 559
17:28 and he s, Why camest thou down hither? 559
17:29 David s, What have I now done? *Is there* 559
17:32 David s to Saul, Let no man's heart fail 559
17:33 Saul s to David, Thou art not able to go 559
17:34 David s unto Saul, Thy servant kept his 559
17:37 David s moreover, The LORD that 559
17:37 Saul s unto David, Go, and the LORD be 559
17:39 for he had not proved *it*. And David s unto 559
17:43 the Philistine s unto David, *Am* I a dog, 559
17:44 the Philistine s to David, Come to me, 559
17:45 s David to the Philistine, Thou comest to 559
17:55 he s unto Abner, the captain of the host, 559
17:55 Abner s, *As* thy soul liveth, O king, I 559
17:56 the king s, Inquire thou whose son 559
17:58 Saul s to him, Whose son *art* thou, *thou* 559
18: 7 s, Saul hath slain his thousands, 559
18: 8 he s, They have ascribed unto David ten 559
18:11 he s, I will smite David even to the wall 559
18:17 Saul s to David, Behold my elder daughter 559
18:17 Saul s, Let not mine hand be upon him, 559
18:18 David s unto Saul, Who *am* I? and what 559
18:21 Saul s, I will give him her, that she may be 559
18:21 Wherefore Saul s to David, Thou shalt *this* 559
18:23 David s, Seemeth it to you a light *thing* to 559
18:25 Saul s, Thus shall ye say to David, The king 559
19: 4 s unto him, Let not the king sin against his 559
19:14 messengers to take David, she s, He *is* sick. 559
19:17 Saul s unto Michal, Why hast thou 559
19:17 answered Saul, He s unto me, Let me go; 559
19:22 he asked and s, Where *are* Samuel and 559
19:22 one s, Behold, *they be* at Naioth in Ramah. 559
20: 1 came and s before Jonathan, What have I 559
20: 2 he s unto him, God forbid; thou shalt not 559
20: 3 David sware moreover, and s, Thy father 559
20: 4 s Jonathan unto David, Whatsoever thy 559
20: 5 David s unto Jonathan, Behold, to morrow 559
20: 9 Jonathan s, Far be it from thee: for if I 559
20:10 s David to Jonathan, Who shall tell me? 559
20:11 Jonathan s unto David, Come, and let us 559
20:12 Jonathan s unto David, O LORD God of 559
20:18 Jonathan s to *David,* To morrow *is* the 559
20:27 Saul s unto Jonathan his son, 559
20:29 he s, Let me go, I pray thee; for our family 559
20:30 against Jonathan, and he s unto him, 559
20:32 s unto him, Wherefore shall he be slain? 559
20:36 he s unto his lad, Run, find out now 559
20:37 Jonathan cried after the lad, and s, *Is* not 559
20:40 s unto him, Go, carry *them* to the city. 559
20:42 Jonathan s to David, Go in peace, 559
21: 1 s unto him, Why *art* thou alone, and no 559
21: 2 David s unto Ahimelech the priest, The 559
21: 2 me a business, and hath s unto me, 559
21: 4 priest answered David, and s, *There is* no 559
21: 5 David answered the priest, and s unto him, 559
21: 8 David s unto Ahimelech, And is there not 559
21: 9 the priest s, The sword of Goliath 559
21: 9 David s, *There is* none like that; give it me. 559
21:11 servants of Achish s unto him, *Is* not this 559
21:14 Achish unto his servants, Lo, you see 559
22: 3 he s unto the king of Moab, Let my father 559
22: 5 the prophet Gad s unto David, Abide not 559
22: 7 Saul s unto his servants that stood about 559
22: 9 s, I saw the son of Jesse coming to Nob, 559
22:12 Saul s, Hear now, thou son of Ahitub. 559
22:13 Saul s unto him, Why have ye conspired 559
22:14 s, And who *is so* faithful among all thy 559
22:16 king s, Thou shalt surely die, Ahimelech, 559
22:17 king s unto the footmen that stood about 559
22:18 king s to Doeg, Turn thou, and fall upon 559
22:22 David s unto Abiathar, I knew *it* that day, 559
23: 2 the LORD s unto David, Go, and smite 559
23: 3 David's men s unto him, Behold, we *be* 559
23: 4 and the LORD answered him and s, Arise, 559
23: 7 Saul s, God hath delivered him into mine 559
23: 9 he s to Abiathar the priest, Bring hither 559
23:10 s David, O LORD God of Israel, 559
23:11 And the LORD s, He will come down. 559
23:12 s David, Will the men of Keilah deliver me 559
23:12 the LORD s, They will deliver thee up. 559
23:17 he s unto him, Fear not: for the hand of 559
23:21 Saul s, Blessed *be* ye of the LORD; for ye 559
24: 4 men of David s unto him, Behold the day 559
24: 4 Behold the day of which the LORD s unto 559
24: 6 he s unto his men, The LORD forbid that I 559
24: 9 David s to Saul, Wherefore hearest thou 559
24:10 I s, I will not put forth mine hand against 559
24:16 that Saul s, *Is* this thy voice, my son David? 559
24:17 he s to David, Thou *art* more righteous 559
25: 5 David s unto the young men, Get you up 559
25:10 David's servants, and s, Who *is* David? 559
25:13 David s unto his men, Gird you on every 559
25:19 she s unto her servants, Go on before me; 559
25:21 David had s, Surely in vain have I kept 559
25:24 fell at his feet, and s, Upon me, my lord, 559
25:32 David s to Abigail, Blessed *be* the LORD 559
25:35 unto her, Go up in peace to thine house; 559
25:39 was dead, he s, Blessed *be* the LORD, 559
25:41 *on her* face to the earth, and s, Behold, 559
26: 6 and s to Ahimelech the Hittite, 559
26: 6 And Abishai s, I will go down with thee. 559
26: 8 Abishai to David, God hath delivered 559
26: 9 David s to Abishai, Destroy him not: 559
26:10 David furthermore, *As* the LORD liveth, 559
26:14 Abner answered and s, Who *art* thou *that* 559

1Sa 26:15 David s to Abner, *Art* thou a *valiant* 559
26:17 and s, *Is* this my voice, my son David? 559
26:17 David s, *It is* my voice, my lord, O king. 559
26:18 he s, Wherefore doth my lord thus pursue 559
26:21 s Saul, I have sinned: return, my son David: 559
26:22 David answered and s, Behold, the king's 559
26:25 Saul s to David, Blessed *be* thou, my son 559
27: 1 David s in his heart, I shall now perish one 559
27: 5 David s unto Achish, If I have now found 559
27:10 Achish s, Whither have ye made a road to 559
27:10 David s, Against the south of Judah, 559
28: 1 Achish s unto David, Know thou assuredly, 559
28: 2 David s to Achish, Surely thou shalt know 559
28: 2 Achish s to David, Therefore will I make 559
28: 7 s Saul unto his servants, Seek me a woman 559
28: 7 his servants s to him, Behold, *there is* a 559
28: 8 he s, I pray thee, divine unto me by 559
28: 9 the woman s unto him, Behold, 559
28:11 the woman, Whom shall I bring up unto 559
28:11 unto thee? And he s, Bring me up Samuel. 559
28:13 the king s unto her, Be not afraid: for what 559
28:13 the woman s unto Saul, I saw gods 559
28:14 he s unto her, What form is he of? And she 559
28:14 she s, An old man cometh up; and he *is* 559
28:15 Samuel s to Saul, Why hast thou disquieted 559
28:16 s Samuel, Wherefore then dost thou ask of 559
28:21 was sore troubled, and s unto him, Behold, 559
28:23 He refused, and s, I will not eat. But his 559
29: 3 s the princes of the Philistines, What *do* 559
29: 3 *do* these Hebrews *here?* And Achish s 559
29: 4 the princes of the Philistines s unto him, 559
29: 6 and s unto him, Surely, *as* the LORD liveth, 559
29: 8 David s unto Achish, But what have I 559
29: 9 Achish answered and s to David, I know 559
29: 9 the princes of the Philistines have s, 559
30: 7 David s to Abiathar the priest, 559
30:13 David s unto him, To whom *belongest* 559
30:13 he s, I *am* a young man of Egypt, servant 559
30:15 David s to him, Canst thou bring me down 559
30:15 he s, Swear unto me by God, that thou 559
30:20 *other* cattle, and s, This *is* David's spoil. 559
30:22 of those that went with David, and s, 559
30:23 s David, Ye shall not do so, my brethren, 559
31: 4 s Saul unto his armourbearer, Draw thy 559
2Sa 1: 3 David s unto him, From whence comest 559
1: 3 s unto him, Out of the camp of Israel 559
1: 4 David s unto him, How went the matter? 559
1: 5 David s unto the young man that told him, 559
1: 6 the young man that told him s, As I 559
1: 8 he s unto me, Who *art* thou? And I 559
1: 9 He s unto me again, Stand, I pray thee, 559
1:13 David s unto the young man that told him, 559
1:14 David s unto him, How wast thou not 559
1:15 and s, Go near, *and* fall upon him. 559
1:16 David s unto him, Thy blood *be* upon thy 559
2: 1 the LORD s unto him, Go up. And David 559
2: 1 David s, Whither shall I go up? And he 559
2: 1 shall I go up? And he s, Unto Hebron. 559
2: 5 s unto them, Blessed *be* ye of the LORD, 559
2:14 Abner s to Joab, Let the young men now 559
2:14 play before us. And Joab s, Let them arise. 559
2:20 behind him, and s, *Art* thou Asahel? 559
2:21 Abner s to him, Turn thee aside to thy 559
2:22 Abner s again to Asahel, Turn thee aside 559
2:26 Abner called to Joab, and s, Shall the 559
2:27 Joab s, *As* God liveth, unless thou hadst 559
3: 7 *Ish-bosheth* s to Abner, Wherefore hast 559
3: 8 of Ish-bosheth, and s, *Am* I a dog's head, 559
3:13 he s, Well; I will make a league with thee: 559
3:16 s Abner unto him, Go, return. And he 559
3:21 Abner s unto David, I will arise and go, 559
3:24 to the king, and s, What hast thou done? 559
3:28 afterward when David heard *it*, he s, I and 559
3:31 David s to Joab, and to all the people that 559
3:33 and s, Died Abner as a fool dieth? 559
3:38 the king s unto his servants, Know ye not 559
4: 8 s to the king, Behold the head of 559
4: 9 and s unto them, *As* the LORD liveth, 559
5: 2 the LORD s to thee, Thou shalt feed my 559
5: 8 David s on that day, Whosoever getteth up 559
5: 8 *be* chief and captain. Wherefore they s, 559
5:19 the LORD s unto David, Go up: for I will 559
5:20 and David smote them there, and s, 559
5:23 of the LORD, he s, Thou shalt not go up; 559
6: 9 s, How shall the ark of the LORD come to 559
6:20 s, How glorious was the king of Israel to 559
6:21 David s unto Michal, *It was* before 559
7: 2 That the king s unto Nathan the prophet, 559
7: 3 Nathan s to the king, Go, do all that *is* in 559
7:18 and he s, Who *am* I, O Lord GOD? 559
7:25 establish *it* for ever, and do as thou hast s. 1696
9: 1 David s, Is there yet *any* that is left of 559
9: 2 the king s unto him, *Art* thou Ziba? 559
9: 2 *Art* thou Ziba? And he s, Thy servant *is* he. 559
9: 3 the king s, *Is there* not yet any of the house 559
9: 3 Ziba s unto the king, Jonathan hath yet a 559
9: 4 the king s unto him, Where *is* he? 559
9: 4 Ziba s unto the king, Behold, he *is* in 559
9: 6 David s, Mephibosheth. And he answered, 559
9: 7 David s unto him, Fear not: for I will 559
9: 8 bowed himself, and s, What *is* thy servant, 559
9: 9 to Ziba, Saul's servant, and s unto him, 559
9:11 s Ziba unto the king, According to all that 559
9:11 s the king, he shall eat at my table, NIH
10: 2 s David, I will shew kindness unto Hanun 559

2Sa 10: 3 princes of the children of Ammon **s** unto	559
10: 5 king **s**, Tarry at Jericho until your beards	559
10:11 he **s**, If the Syrians be too strong for me,	559
11: 3 one **s**, *Is* not this Bath-sheba, the daughter	559
11: 5 and told David, and **s**, I *am* with child.	559
11: 8 David **s** to Uriah, Go down to thy house,	559
11:10 David **s** unto Uriah, Camest thou not from	559
11:11 Uriah **s** unto David, The ark, and Israel,	559
11:12 David **s** to Uriah, Tarry here to day also,	559
11:23 messenger **s** unto David, Surely the men	559
11:25 David **s** unto the messenger, Thus shalt	559
12: 1 he came unto him, and **s** unto him,	559
12: 5 he **s** to Nathan, *As* the LORD liveth,	559
12: 7 Nathan **s** to David, Thou *art* the man.	559
12:13 David **s** unto Nathan, I have sinned against	559
12:13 Nathan **s** unto David, The LORD also hath	559
12:18 for they **s**, Behold, while the child was *yet*	559
12:19 therefore David **s** unto his servants,	559
12:19 Is the child dead? And they **s**, He is dead.	559
12:21 **s** his servants unto him, What thing *is* this	559
12:22 he **s**, While the child *was* yet alive, I fasted	559
12:22 for I **s**, Who can tell *whether* GOD will be	559
12:27 **s**, I have fought against Rabbah,	559
13: 4 he unto him, Why *art* thou, *being*	559
13: 4 Amnon **s** unto him, I love Tamar, my	559
13: 5 Jonadab **s** unto him, Lay *thee* down on thy	559
13: 6 Amnon **s** unto the king, I pray thee,	559
13: 9 Amnon **s**, Have out all men from me.	559
13:10 Amnon **s** unto Tamar, Bring the meat *into*	559
13:11 **s** unto her, Come lie with me, my sister.	559
13:15 And Amnon **s** unto her, Arise, be gone.	559
13:16 she **s** unto him, *There is* no cause: this evil	559
13:17 and **s**, Put now this *woman* out from me,	559
13:20 Absalom her brother **s** unto her, Hath	559
13:24 **s**, Behold now, thy servant hath	559
13:25 the king **s** to Absalom, Nay, my son, let us	559
13:26 **s** Absalom, If not, I pray thee, let my	559
13:26 the king **s** unto him, Why should he go	559
13:32 Shimeah David's brother, answered and **s**,	559
13:35 Jonadab **s** unto the king, Behold, the	559
13:35 king's sons come: as thy servant **s**, so it is.	1697
14: 2 a wise woman, and **s** unto her, I pray thee,	559
14: 4 and did obeisance, and **s**, Help, O king.	559
14: 5 the king **s** unto her, What aileth thee?	559
14: 7 they **s**, Deliver him that smote his brother,	559
14: 8 the king **s** unto the woman, Go to thine	559
14: 9 the woman of Tekoah **s** unto the king,	559
14:10 king **s**, Whosoever saith *ought* unto thee,	559
14:11 **s** she, I pray thee, let the king remember	559
14:11 he **s**, *As* the LORD liveth, there shall not	559
14:12 the woman **s**, Let thine handmaid, I pray	559
14:12 unto my lord the king. And he **s**, Say on.	559
14:13 the woman **s**, Wherefore then hast thou	559
14:15 thy handmaid **s**, I will now speak unto	559
14:17 thine handmaid **s**, The word of my lord	559
14:18 the king answered and **s** unto the woman,	559
14:18 the woman **s**, Let my lord the king now	559
14:19 king **s**, *Is not* the hand of Joab with thee	559
14:19 the woman answered and **s**, *As* thy soul	559
14:21 the king **s** unto Joab, Behold now, I have	559
14:22 Joab **s**, To day thy servant knoweth that I	559
14:24 the king **s**, Let him turn to his own house,	559
14:30 Therefore he **s** unto his servants, See,	559
14:31 Absalom unto *his* house, and **s** unto him,	559
15: 2 unto him, and **s**, Of what city *art* thou?	559
15: 2 he **s**, Thy servant *is* of one of the tribes of	559
15: 3 Absalom **s** unto him, See, thy matters *are*	559
15: 4 Absalom **s** moreover, Oh that I were made	559
15: 7 that Absalom **s** unto the king, I pray thee,	559
15: 9 the king **s** unto him, Go in peace. So he	559
15:14 David **s** unto all his servants that *were*	559
15:15 the king's servants **s** unto the king, Behold,	559
15:19 **s** the king to Ittai the Gittite, Wherefore	559
15:21 **s**, *As* the LORD liveth, and *as* my lord	559
15:22 David **s** to Ittai, Go and pass over.	559
15:25 the king **s** unto Zadok, Carry back the ark	559
15:27 The king **s** also unto Zadok the priest,	559
15:31 David **s**, O LORD, I pray thee, turn	559
15:33 Unto whom David **s**, If thou passest on	559
16: 2 the king unto Ziba, What meanest thou	559
16: 2 Ziba **s**, The asses *be* for the king's	559
16: 3 the king **s**, And where *is* thy master's son?	559
16: 3 Ziba unto the king, Behold, he abideth at	559
16: 3 for he **s**, To day shall the house of Israel	559
16: 4 **s** the king to Ziba, Behold, thine *are* all	559
16: 4 Ziba **s**, I humbly beseech thee *that* I may	559
16: 7 thus **s** Shimei when he cursed, Come out,	559
16: 9 **s** Abishai the son of Zeruiah unto the king,	559
16:10 the king **s**, What have I to do with you,	559
16:10 because the LORD hath **s** unto him,	559
16:11 David **s** to Abishai, and to all his servants,	559
16:16 that Hushai **s** unto Absalom, God save	559
16:17 Absalom **s** to Hushai, *Is* this thy kindness	559
16:18 Hushai **s** unto Absalom, Nay; but whom	559
16:20 **s** Absalom to Ahithophel, Give counsel	559
16:21 Ahithophel **s** unto Absalom, Go in unto	559
17: 1 Moreover Ahithophel **s** unto Absalom,	559
17: 5 **s** Absalom, Call now Hushai the Archite	559
17: 7 Hushai **s** unto Absalom, The counsel that	559
17: 8 For, (**s** Hushai,) thou knowest thy father	559
17:14 Absalom and all the men of Israel **s**,	559
17:15 Hushai unto Zadok and to Abiathar	559
17:20 they **s**, Where *is* Ahimaaz and Jonathan?	559
17:20 the woman **s** unto them, They be gone	559
17:21 **s** unto David, Arise, and pass quickly over	559

2Sa 17:29 they **s**, The people *is* hungry, and weary,	559
18: 2 the king **s** unto the people, I will surely go	559
18: 4 king **s** unto them, What seemeth you best	559
18:10 man saw *it*, and told Joab, and **s**, Behold,	559
18:11 Joab **s** unto the man that told him,	559
18:12 the man **s** unto Joab, Though I should	559
18:14 Joab, I may not tarry thus with thee.	559
18:18 he **s**, I have no son to keep my name in	559
18:19 **s** Ahimaaz the son of Zadok, Let me now	559
18:20 Joab **s** unto him, Thou *shalt* not bear	559
18:21 Joab to Cushi, Go tell the king what thou	559
18:22 **s** Ahimaaz the son of Zadok yet again to	559
18:22 Joab **s**, Wherefore wilt thou run, my son,	559
18:23 howsoever, **s** he, let me run. And he said	NIH
18:23 he **s** unto him, Run. Then Ahimaaz ran *by*	559
18:25 king **s**, If he *be* alone, *there is* tidings in	559
18:26 and **s**, Behold *another* man running alone.	559
18:26 And the king **s**, He also bringeth tidings.	559
18:27 watchman **s**, Me thinketh the running of	559
18:27 the king **s**, He *is* a good man,	559
18:28 and **s** unto the king, All is well.	559
18:28 and **s**, Blessed *be* the LORD thy God,	559
18:29 the king **s**, *Is* the young man Absalom safe?	559
18:30 the king **s** *unto* him, Turn aside,	559
18:31 and Cushi **s**, Tidings, my lord the king:	559
18:32 the king **s** unto Cushi, *Is* the young man	559
18:33 as he went, thus he **s**, O my son Absalom,	559
19: 5 came *into* the house to the king, and **s**,	559
19:19 **s** unto the king, Let not my lord impute	559
19:21 Abishai the son of Zeruiah answered and **s**,	559
19:22 David **s**, What have I to do with you,	559
19:23 Therefore the king **s** unto Shimei, Thou	559
19:25 the king **s** unto him, Wherefore wentest	559
19:26 for thy servant **s**, I will saddle me an ass,	559
19:29 the king **s** unto him, Why speakest thou	559
19:29 I have **s**, Thou and Ziba divide the land.	559
19:30 Mephibosheth **s** unto the king, Yea, let	559
19:33 the king **s** unto Barzillai, Come thou over	559
19:34 Barzillai **s** unto the king, How long have I	559
19:41 came to the king, and **s** unto the king,	559
19:43 **s**, We have ten parts in the king,	559
20: 1 blew a trumpet, and **s**, We have no part in	559
20: 4 **s** the king to Amasa, Assemble me the men	559
20: 6 David **s** to Abishai, Now shall Sheba the	559
20: 9 Joab **s** to Amasa, *Art* thou in health,	559
20:11 **s**, He that favoureth Joab, and he that *is*	559
20:17 near unto her, the woman **s**, *Art* thou Joab?	559
20:17 answered, I *am he*. Then she **s** unto him,	559
20:20 Joab answered and **s**, Far be it, far be it	559
20:21 the woman **s** unto Joab, Behold, his head	559
21: 2 called the Gibeonites, and **s** unto them;	559
21: 3 Wherefore David **s** unto the Gibeonites,	559
21: 4 the Gibeonites **s** unto him, We will have	559
21: 4 he **s**, What you shall say, *that* will I do for	559
21: 6 And the king **s**, I will give *them*.	559
22: 2 he **s**, The LORD *is* my rock,	559
23: 1 David the son of Jesse **s**, and the man	5002
23: 1 Jacob, and the sweet psalmist of Israel, **s**,	5002
23: 3 The God of Israel **s**, the Rock of Israel	559
23:15 David longed, and **s**, Oh that one would	559
23:17 he **s**, Be it far from me, O LORD, that I	559
24: 2 the king **s** to Joab the captain of the host,	559
24: 3 Joab **s** unto the king, Now the LORD thy	559
24:10 David **s** unto the LORD, I have sinned	559
24:13 to David, and told him, and **s** unto him,	559
24:14 David **s** unto Gad, I am in a great strait:	559
24:16 **s** to the angel that destroyed the people,	559
24:17 **s**, Lo, I have sinned, and I have done	559
24:18 that day to David, and **s** unto him, Go up,	559
24:21 Araunah **s**, Wherefore is my lord the king	559
24:21 David **s**, To buy the threshingfloor of thee,	559
24:22 Araunah **s** unto David, Let my lord the	559
24:23 Araunah **s** unto the king, The LORD thy	559
24:24 the king **s** unto Araunah, Nay; but I will	559
1Ki 1: 2 Wherefore his servants **s** unto him, Let	559
1:16 And the king **s**, What wouldest thou?	559
1:17 she **s** unto him, My lord, thou swarest by	559
1:24 Nathan **s**, My lord O king, hast thou said,	559
1:24 Nathan said, My lord O king, hast thou **s**,	559
1:28 king David answered and **s**, Call me	559
1:29 the king sware, and **s**, *As* the LORD liveth,	559
1:31 reverence to the king, and **s**, Let my lord	559
1:32 king David **s**, Call me Zadok the priest,	559
1:33 The king also **s** unto them, Take with you	559
1:36 Jehoiada answered the king, and **s**, Amen:	559
1:39 all the people **s**, God save king Solomon.	559
1:41 Joab heard the sound of the trumpet, he **s**,	559
1:42 Adonijah **s** *unto him*, Come in; for thou *art*	559
1:43 Jonathan answered and **s** to Adonijah,	559
1:48 also thus **s** the king, Blessed *be* the LORD	559
1:52 Solomon **s**, If he will shew himself a	559
1:53 Solomon **s** unto him, Go to thine house.	559
2: 4 all their soul, there shall not fail thee (**s** he)	559
2:13 she **s**, Comest thou peaceably? And he said,	559
2:13 thou peaceably? And he **s**, Peaceably.	559
2:14 He **s** moreover, I have somewhat to say	559
2:14 to say unto thee. And she **s**, Say on.	559
2:15 he **s**, Thou knowest that the kingdom was	559
2:16 deny me not. And she **s** unto him, Say on.	559
2:17 he **s**, Speak, I pray thee, unto Solomon	559
2:18 Bath-sheba **s**, Well; I will speak for thee	559
2:20 she **s**, I desire one small petition of thee;	559
2:20 the king **s** unto her, Ask on, my mother:	559
2:21 she **s**, Let Abishag the Shunammite be	559
2:22 Solomon answered and **s** unto his mother,	559

1Ki 2:26 Abiathar the priest **s** the king, Get thee	559
2:30 **s** unto him, Thus saith the king, Come	559
2:30 he **s**, Nay; but I will die here. And Benaiah	559
2:30 Thus **s** Joab, and thus he answered me.	1696
2:31 the king **s** unto him, Do as he hath said,	559
2:31 Do as he hath **s**, and fall upon him,	1696
2:36 and called for Shimei, and **s** unto him,	559
2:38 Shimei **s** unto the king, The saying *is* good:	559
2:38 as my lord the king hath **s**, so will thy	1696
2:42 and called for Shimei, and **s** unto him,	559
2:44 The king **s** moreover to Shimei,	559
3: 5 and God **s**, Ask what I shall give thee.	559
3: 6 Solomon **s**, Thou hast shewed unto thy	559
3:11 God **s** unto him, Because thou hast asked	559
3:17 the one woman **s**, O my lord, I and	559
3:22 the other woman **s**, Nay; but the living *is*	559
3:22 this **s**, No; but the dead *is* thy son,	559
3:23 **s** the king, The one saith, This *is* my son	559
3:24 the king **s**, Bring me a sword. And they	559
3:25 the king **s**, Divide the living child in two,	559
3:26 she **s**, O my lord, give her the living child,	559
3:26 other **s**, Let it be neither mine nor thine,	559
3:27 king answered and **s**, Give her the living	559
5: 7 that he rejoiced greatly, and **s**, Blessed *be*	559
8:12 The LORD **s** that *he* would dwell in	559
8:15 he **s**, Blessed *be* the LORD God of Israel,	559
8:18 the LORD **s** unto David my father,	559
8:23 he **s**, LORD God of Israel, *there is* no God	559
8:29 toward the place of which thou hast **s**,	559
9: 3 the LORD **s** unto him, I have heard thy	559
9:13 he **s**, What cities *are* these which thou hast	559
10: 6 she **s** to the king, It was a true report that I	559
11: 2 the LORD **s** unto the children of Israel,	559
11:11 Wherefore the LORD **s** unto Solomon,	559
11:21 Hadad **s** to Pharaoh, Let me depart, that I	559
11:22 Pharaoh **s** unto him, But what *hast* thou	559
11:31 he **s** to Jeroboam, Take thee ten pieces:	559
12: 5 he **s** unto them, Depart yet *for* three days,	559
12: 6 **s**, How do you advise that *I* may answer	559
12: 9 he **s** unto them, What counsel give ye that	559
12:26 Jeroboam **s** in his heart, Now shall	559
12:28 made two calves of gold, and **s** unto them,	559
13: 2 and **s**, O altar, altar, thus saith the LORD;	559
13: 6 king answered and **s** unto the man of God,	559
13: 7 the king **s** unto the man of God,	1696
13: 8 the man of God **s** unto the king, If thou	1696
13:12 their father **s** unto them, What way went	1696
13:13 he **s** unto his sons, Saddle me the ass.	559
13:14 he **s** unto him, *Art* thou the man of God	559
13:14 that camest from Judah? And he **s**, I *am*.	559
13:15 he **s** unto him, Come home with me,	559
13:16 he **s**, I may not return with thee, nor go in	559
13:17 For it was **s** to me by the word of	1697
13:18 He **s** unto him, I *am* a prophet also as thou	559
13:26 him back from the way heard *thereof*, he **s**,	559
14: 2 Jeroboam **s** to his wife, Arise, I pray thee,	559
14: 5 the LORD **s** unto Ahijah, Behold, the wife	559
14: 6 that he **s**, Come in, thou wife of Jeroboam;	559
17: 1 **s** unto Ahab, *As* the LORD God of Israel	559
17:10 called to her, and **s**, Fetch me, I pray thee,	559
17:11 **s**, Bring me, I pray thee, a morsel of bread	559
17:12 she **s**, *As* the LORD thy God liveth, I have	559
17:13 Elijah **s** unto her, Fear not; go *and* do as	559
17:13 her, Fear not; go *and* do as thou hast **s**:	1697
17:18 she **s** unto Elijah, What have I to do with	559
17:19 he **s** unto her, Give me thy son.	559
17:20 unto the LORD, and **s**, O LORD my God,	559
17:21 and **s**, O LORD my God, I pray thee,	559
17:23 mother: and Elijah **s**, See, thy son liveth.	559
17:24 the woman **s** to Elijah, Now *by* this I know	559
18: 5 Ahab **s** unto Obadiah, Go into the land,	559
18: 7 he knew him, and fell on his face, and **s**,	559
18: 9 he **s**, What have I sinned, that thou	559
18:10 they **s**, He *is* not *there*; he took an oath	559
18:15 And Elijah **s**, *As* the LORD of hosts liveth,	559
18:17 Ahab saw Elijah, that Ahab **s** unto him,	559
18:21 Elijah came unto all the people, and **s**,	559
18:22 **s** Elijah unto the people, I, *even* I only,	559
18:24 all the people answered and **s**, It is well	559
18:25 Elijah **s** unto the prophets of Baal,	559
18:27 that Elijah mocked them, and **s**, Cry aloud:	559
18:30 Elijah **s** unto all the people, Come near	559
18:33 in pieces, and laid *him* on the wood, and **s**,	559
18:34 he **s**, Do *it* the second time. And they did	559
18:34 he **s**, Do *it* the third time. And they did *it*	559
18:36 **s**, LORD God of Abraham, Isaac,	559
18:39 they **s**, The LORD, he *is* the God;	559
18:40 Elijah **s** unto them, Take the prophets of	559
18:41 Elijah **s** unto Ahab, Get thee up, eat and	559
18:43 **s** to his servant, Go up now, look toward	559
18:43 he went up, and looked, and **s**, *There* is	559
18:43 *is* nothing. And he **s**, Go again seven times.	559
18:44 came to pass at the seventh *time*, that he **s**,	559
18:44 he **s**, Go up, say unto Ahab, Prepare *thy*	559
19: 4 **s**, *It is* enough; now, O LORD, take away	559
19: 5 him, and **s** unto him, Arise *and* eat.	559
19: 7 and touched him, and **s**, Arise *and* eat;	559
19: 9 he **s** unto him, What doest thou here,	559
19:10 he **s**, I have been very jealous for	559
19:11 he **s**, Go forth, and stand upon the mount	559
19:13 and **s**, What doest thou here, Elijah?	559
19:14 he **s**, I have been very jealous for	559
19:15 the LORD **s** unto him, Go, return on thy	559
19:20 and **s**, Let me, I pray thee, kiss my father	559
19:20 he **s** unto him, Go back again: for what	559

S

1Ki 20: 2 and **s** unto him, Thus saith Ben-hadad, 559
20: 4 the king of Israel answered and **s**, My lord, 559
20: 5 **s**, Thus speaketh Ben-hadad, saying, 559
20: 7 **s**, Mark, I pray you, and see how this *man* 559
20: 8 all the elders and all the people **s** unto him, 559
20: 9 Wherefore he **s** unto the messengers of 559
20:10 **s**, The gods do so unto me, and more also, 559
20:11 the king of Israel answered and **s**, Tell *him,* 559
20:12 in the pavilions, that he **s** unto his servants, 559
20:14 Ahab **s**, By whom? And he said, Thus saith 559
20:14 he **s**, Thus saith the LORD, *Even* by 559
20:14 he **s**, Who shall order the battle? And he 559
20:18 he **s**, Whether they be come out for peace, 559
20:22 **s** unto him, Go, strengthen thyself, and 559
20:23 servants of the king of Syria **s** unto him, 559
20:28 king of Israel, and **s**, Thus saith the LORD, 559
20:28 the LORD, Because the Syrians have **s**, 559
20:31 his servants **s** unto him, Behold now, 559
20:32 and came to the king of Israel, and **s**, 559
20:32 And he **s**, *Is* he yet alive? he *is* my brother. 559
20:33 did hastily catch *it:* and they **s**, Thy brother 559
20:33 he **s**, Go ye, bring him. Then Ben-hadad 559
20:34 Ben-*hadad* **s** unto him, The cities, which 559
20:34 **s** Ahab, I will send thee away with *this* NIH
20:35 a certain man of the sons of the prophets **s** 559
20:36 he unto him, Because thou hast not 559
20:37 another man, and **s**, Smite me, I pray thee. 559
20:39 he **s**, Thy servant went out into the midst 559
20:39 a man unto me, and **s**, Keep this man: 559
20:40 the king of Israel **s** unto him, So *shall* thy 559
20:42 he **s** unto him, Thus saith the LORD, 559
21: 3 Naboth **s** to Ahab, The LORD forbid it me, 559
21: 4 for he had **s**, I will not give thee 559
21: 5 **s** unto him, Why is thy spirit so sad, 1696
21: 6 he **s** unto her, Because I spake unto 1696
21: 6 **s** unto him, Give me thy vineyard for 559
21: 7 Jezebel his wife **s** unto him, Dost thou now 559
21:15 and was dead, that Jezebel **s** to Ahab, Arise, 559
21:20 Ahab **s** to Elijah, Hast thou found me, 559
22: 3 the king of Israel **s** unto his servants, Know 559
22: 4 he **s** unto Jehoshaphat, Wilt thou go with 559
22: 4 Jehoshaphat **s** to the king of Israel, I *am* as 559
22: 5 Jehoshaphat **s** unto the king of Israel, 559
22: 6 about four hundred men, and **s** unto them, 559
22: 6 they **s**, Go up; for the Lord shall deliver *it* 559
22: 7 Jehoshaphat **s**, *Is there* not here a prophet 559
22: 8 the king of Israel **s** unto Jehoshaphat, 559
22: 8 And Jehoshaphat **s**, Let not the king say so. 559
22: 9 **s**, Hasten *hither* Micaiah the son of Imlah. 559
22:11 he **s**, Thus saith the LORD, With these 559
22:14 Micaiah **s**, *As* the LORD liveth, what 559
22:15 the king unto him, Micaiah, shall we go 559
22:16 the king **s** unto him, How many times shall 559
22:17 he **s**, I saw all Israel scattered upon the 559
22:17 the LORD, These have no master: 559
22:18 the king of Israel **s** unto Jehoshaphat, Did I 559
22:19 he **s**, Hear thou therefore the word of 559
22:20 the LORD, Who shall persuade Ahab, 559
22:20 one **s** on this manner, and another said on 559
22:20 manner, and another **s** on that manner. 559
22:21 the LORD, and **s**, I will persuade him. 559
22:22 the LORD **s** unto him, Wherewith? And he 559
22:22 he **s**, I will go forth, and I will be a lying 559
22:22 he **s**, Thou shalt persuade *him,* and 559
22:24 and smote Micaiah on the cheek, and **s**, 559
22:25 Micaiah **s**, Behold, thou shalt see in that 559
22:26 the king of Israel **s**, Take Micaiah, 559
22:28 Micaiah **s**, If thou return at all in peace, 559
22:28 he **s**, Hearken, O people, every one of you. 559
22:30 the king of Israel **s** unto Jehoshaphat, I will 559
22:32 that they **s**, Surely it *is* the king of Israel. 559
22:34 to the driver of his chariot, 559
2:49 **s** Ahaziah the son of Ahab unto 559

2Ki 1: 2 he sent messengers, and **s** unto them, 559
1: 3 the angel of the LORD **s** to Elijah 1696
1: 5 he **s** unto them, Why are ye now turned 559
1: 6 they **s** unto him, There came a man up to 559
1: 6 a man up to meet us, and **s** unto us, 559
1: 7 he **s** unto them, What manner of man 1696
1: 8 his loins. And he **s**, It *is* Elijah the Tishbite. 559
1: 9 of God, the king hath **s**, Come down. 1696
1:10 and **s** to the captain of fifty, 1696
1:11 he answered and **s** unto him, O man of 1696
1:11 O man of God, thus hath the king **s**, 559
1:12 Elijah answered and **s** unto them, If I *be* a 1696
1:13 besought him, and **s** unto him, O man of 1696
1:15 the angel of the LORD **s** unto Elijah, 1696
1:16 he **s** unto him, Thus saith the LORD, 1696
2: 2 Elijah **s** unto Elisha, Tarry here, I pray 559
2: 2 Elisha **s** *unto him, As* the LORD liveth, 559
2: 3 came forth to Elisha, and **s** unto him, 559
2: 3 he **s**, Yea, I know *it;* hold you your peace. 559
2: 4 Elijah **s** unto him, Elisha, tarry here, I pray 559
2: 4 he **s**, *As* the LORD liveth, and *as* thy soul 559
2: 5 at Jericho came to Elisha, and **s** unto him, 559
2: 6 Elijah **s** unto him, Tarry, I pray thee, here; 559
2: 6 he **s**, *As* the LORD liveth, and *as* thy soul 559
2: 9 were gone over, that Elijah **s** unto Elisha, 559
2: 9 Elisha, I pray thee, let a double portion of 559
2:10 he **s**, Thou hast asked a hard thing: 559
2:14 smote the waters, and **s**, Where *is* 559
2:15 they **s**, The spirit of Elijah doth rest on 559
2:16 they **s** unto him, Behold now, there be 559
2:16 some valley. And he **s**, Ye shall not send. 559
2:17 urged him till *he* was ashamed, he **s**, Send. 559

2Ki 2:18 he **s** unto them, Did I not say unto you, 559
2:19 the men of the city **s** unto Elisha, Behold, 559
2:20 Bring me a new cruse, and put salt 559
2:21 cast the salt in there, and **s**, Thus saith 559
2:23 mocked him, and **s** unto him, Go up, 559
3: 7 he **s**, I will go up: I *am* as thou *art,* my 559
3: 8 he **s**, Which way shall we go up? And he 559
3:10 the king of Israel **s**, Alas, that the LORD 559
3:11 Jehoshaphat **s**, *Is* there not here a prophet 559
3:11 king of Israel's servants answered and **s**, 559
3:12 Jehoshaphat **s**, The word of the LORD is 559
3:13 Elisha **s** unto the king of Israel, What have 559
3:13 the king of Israel **s** unto him, Nay: 559
3:14 And Elisha **s**, *As* the LORD of hosts liveth, 559
3:16 he **s**, Thus saith the LORD, Make this 559
3:23 they **s**, This *is* blood: the kings are surely 559
4: 2 Elisha **s** unto her, What shall I do for thee? 559
4: 2 she **s**, Thine handmaid hath not any thing 559
4: 3 he **s**, Go, borrow thee vessels abroad of all 559
4: 6 that she **s** unto her son, Bring me yet a 559
4: 6 he **s** unto her, *There is* not a vessel more. 559
4: 7 she **s**, Go, sell the oil, and pay thy debt, 559
4: 9 she **s** unto her husband, Behold now, 559
4:12 he **s** to Gehazi his servant, Call this 559
4:13 he **s** unto him, Say now unto her, Behold, 559
4:14 he **s**, What then *is* to be done for her? 559
4:15 he **s**, Call her. And when he had called 559
4:16 he **s**, About this season, according to 559
4:16 she **s**, Nay, my lord, thou man of God, 559
4:17 bare a son at that season that Elisha had **s** 1696
4:19 he **s** unto his father, My head, my head. 559
4:19 he **s** to a lad, Carry him to his mother. 559
4:22 **s**, Send me, I pray thee, one of the young 559
4:23 **s**, Wherefore wilt thou go to him to day? 559
4:23 nor sabbath. And she **s**, *It shall be* well. 559
4:24 to her servant, Drive, and go *forward;* 559
4:25 that he **s** to Gehazi his servant, Behold, 559
4:27 man of God **s**, Let her alone; for her soul 559
4:28 she **s**, Did I desire a son of my lord? did I 559
4:29 he **s** to Gehazi, Gird up thy loins, 559
4:30 the mother of the child **s**, *As* the LORD 559
4:36 he called Gehazi, and **s**, Call this 559
4:36 come in unto him, he **s**, Take up thy son. 559
4:38 he **s** unto his servant, Set on the great pot, 559
4:40 that they cried out, and **s**, O thou man of 559
4:41 he **s**, Then bring meal. And he cast *it* into 559
4:41 he **s**, Pour out for the people, that they 559
4:42 he **s**, Give unto the people, that they may 559
4:43 servitor **s**, What, should I set this before 559
4:43 He **s** again, Give the people, that they may 559
5: 3 she **s** unto her mistress, Would God my 559
5: 4 **s** the maid that *is* of the land of Israel. 1696
5: 5 king of Syria **s**, Go to, go, and I will send 559
5: 7 and **s**, *Am* I God, to kill and to make alive, 559
5:11 and went away, and **s**, Behold, I thought, 559
5:13 and spake unto him, and **s**, My father, 559
5:15 he **s**, Behold, now I know that *there is* no 559
5:16 he **s**, *As* the LORD liveth, before whom I 559
5:17 Naaman **s**, Shall there not then, I pray 559
5:19 he **s** unto him, Go in peace. So he departed 559
5:20 servant of Elisha the man of God, **s**, 559
5:21 the chariot to meet him, and **s**, *Is* all well? 559
5:22 he **s**, *All is* well. My master hath sent me, 559
5:23 Naaman **s**, Be content, take two talents. 559
5:25 Elisha **s** unto him, Whence *comest thou,* 559
5:25 And he **s**, Thy servant went no whither. 559
5:26 he **s** unto him, Went not mine heart *with* 559
6: 1 the sons of the prophets **s** unto Elisha, 559
6: 3 one **s**, Be content, I pray thee, and go with 559
6: 5 he cried, and **s**, Alas, master, for it *was* 559
6: 6 the man of God **s**, Where fell it? And he 559
6: 7 Therefore **s** he, Take *it* up to thee. And he 559
6:11 he called his servants, and **s** unto them, 559
6:12 one of his servants, None, my lord, 559
6:13 he **s**, Go and spy where he *is,* that I may 559
6:15 his servant **s** unto him, Alas, my master, 559
6:17 **s**, LORD, I pray thee, open his eyes, that he 559
6:18 **s**, Smite this people, I pray thee, 559
6:19 Elisha **s** unto them, This *is* not the way, 559
6:20 come *into* Samaria, that Elisha **s**, LORD, 559
6:21 king of Israel **s** unto Elisha, when he saw 559
6:27 he **s**, *If* the LORD do not help thee, whence 559
6:28 the king **s** unto her, What aileth thee? 559
6:28 This woman **s** unto me, Give thy son, 559
6:29 I **s** unto her on the next day, Give thy son, 559
6:31 he **s**, God do so and more also to me, 559
6:32 messenger came to him, he **s** to the elders, 559
6:33 and he **s**, Behold, this evil *is* of the LORD; 559
7: 1 Elisha **s**, Hear ye the word of the LORD; 559
7: 2 **s**, Behold, if the LORD would make 559
7: 2 he **s**, Behold, thou shalt see *it* with thine 559
7: 3 they **s** one to another, Why sit we here 559
7: 6 they **s** one to another, Lo, the king of Israel 559
7: 9 they **s** one to another, We do not well: 559
7:12 arose in the night, and **s** unto his servants, 559
7:13 one of his servants answered and **s**, Let 559
7:17 and he died, as the man of God had **s**, 1696
7:19 the man of God, and **s**, Now behold, 559
7:19 he **s**, Behold, thou shalt see *it* with thine 559
8: 5 Gehazi **s**, My lord, O king, this *is* 559
8: 8 the king **s** unto Hazael, Take a present in 559
8: 9 and came and stood before him, and **s**, 559
8:10 Elisha **s** unto him, Go, say unto him, 559
8:12 Hazael **s**, Why weepeth my lord? And he 559
8:13 Hazael **s**, But what, *is* thy servant a dog, 559

2Ki 8:14 who **s** to him, What said Elisha to thee? 559
8:14 who said to him, What **s** Elisha to thee? 559
9: 1 **s** unto him, Gird up thy loins, and take this 559
9: 5 he **s**, I have an errand to thee, O captain. 559
9: 5 Jehu **s**, Unto which of all us? And he said, 559
9: 5 of all us? And he **s**, To thee, O captain. 559
9: 6 poured the oil on his head, and **s** unto him, 559
9:11 one **s** unto him, *Is* all well? wherefore 559
9:11 he **s** unto them, Ye know the man, and his 559
9:12 they **s**, *It is* false; tell us now. And he said, 559
9:12 he **s**, Thus and thus spake he to me, 559
9:15 Jehu **s**, If it be your minds, *then* let none 559
9:17 Jehu as he came, and **s**, I see a company. 559
9:17 Joram, Take a horseman, and send to 559
9:18 and **s**, Thus saith the king, *Is it* peace? 559
9:18 Jehu, What hast thou to do with peace? 559
9:19 and **s**, Thus saith the king, *Is it* peace? 559
9:21 Joram **s**, Make ready. And his chariot was 559
9:22 saw Jehu, that he **s**, *Is it* peace, Jehu? 559
9:23 fled, and **s** to Ahaziah, There *is* treachery, 559
9:25 **s** to Bidkar his captain, Take up, 559
9:27 Jehu followed after him, and **s**, Smite him 559
9:31 she **s**, *Had* Zimri peace, who slew his 559
9:32 to the window, and **s**, Who *is* on my side? 559
9:33 he **s**, Throw her down. So they threw her 559
9:34 was come in, he did eat and drink, and **s**, 559
9:36 he **s**, This *is* the word of the LORD, 559
10: 4 **s**, Behold, two kings stood not before him: 559
10: 8 he **s**, Lay ye them *in* two heaps *at* 559
10: 9 stood, and **s** to all the people, Ye *be* 559
10:13 Ahaziah king of Judah, and **s**, Who *are* ye? 559
10:14 he **s**, Take them alive. And they took them 559
10:15 he saluted him, and **s** to him, Is thine heart 559
10:16 he **s**, Come with me, and see my zeal for 559
10:18 and **s** unto them, Ahab served Baal a little; 559
10:20 Jehu **s**, Proclaim a solemn assembly for 559
10:22 he **s** unto *him* that *was* over the vestry, 559
10:23 **s** unto the worshippers of Baal, Search, 559
10:24 appointed fourscore men without, and **s**, 559
10:25 that Jehu **s** to the guard and to the captains, 559
10:30 the LORD **s** unto Jehu, Because thou hast 559
11:12 clapt their hands, and **s**, God save the king. 559
11:15 the officers of the host, and **s** unto them, 559
11:15 For the priest had **s**, Let her not be slain *in* 559
12: 4 Jehoash **s** to the priests, All the money of 559
12: 7 the *other* priests, and **s** unto them, 559
13:14 his face, and **s**, O my father, my father, 559
13:15 Elisha **s** unto him, Take bow and arrows. 559
13:16 he **s** to the king of Israel, Put thine hand 559
13:17 he **s**, Open the window eastward. And he 559
13:17 he opened *it.* Then Elisha **s**, Shoot. And he 559
13:17 he **s**, The arrow of the LORD's 559
13:18 he **s**, Take the arrows. And he took *them.* 559
13:18 he took *them.* And he **s** unto the king of 559
13:19 **s**, *Thou* shouldest have smitten five or 559
14:27 the LORD **s** not that *he* would blot out 1696
17:12 whereof the LORD had **s** unto them, 559
17:23 he had **s** by all his servants the prophets. 1696
18:19 Rab-shakeh **s** unto them, Speak ye now to 559
18:22 and hath **s** to Judah and Jerusalem, 559
18:25 The LORD **s** to me, Go up against this 559
18:26 Eliakim the son of Hilkiah, and Shebna, 559
18:27 Rab-shakeh **s** unto them, Hath my master 559
19: 3 they **s** unto him, Thus saith Hezekiah, 559
19: 6 Isaiah **s** unto them, Thus shall ye say to 559
19:15 **s**, O LORD God of Israel, which dwellest 559
19:23 thou hast reproached the Lord, and hast **s**, 559
20: 1 unto him, Thus saith the LORD, Set thine 559
20: 7 Isaiah **s**, Take a lump of figs. And they took 559
20: 8 Hezekiah **s** unto Isaiah, What *shall* be 559
20: 9 Isaiah **s**, This sign shalt thou have of 559
20:14 and **s** unto him, What said these men? 559
20:14 and said unto him, What **s** these men? 559
20:14 Hezekiah, They are come from a far 559
20:15 he **s**, What have they seen in thine house? 559
20:16 Isaiah unto Hezekiah, Hear the word of 559
20:19 **s** Hezekiah unto Isaiah, Good *is* the word 559
20:19 he **s**, *Is it* not good, if peace and truth be 559
21: 4 of which the LORD **s**, In Jerusalem will I 559
21: 7 of which the LORD **s** to David, 559
22: 8 Hilkiah the high priest **s** unto Shaphan 559
22: 9 and brought the king word again, and **s**, 559
22:15 she **s** unto them, Thus saith the LORD God 559
23:17 he **s**, What title *is* that that I see? 559
23:18 he **s**, Let him alone; let no man move his 559
23:27 the LORD **s**, I will remove Judah also out 559
23:27 the house of which I **s**, My name shall be 559
24:13 of the LORD, as the LORD had **s**. 1696
25:24 them, and to their men, and **s** unto them, 559

1Ch 10: 4 Saul to his armourbearer, Draw thy 559
11: 2 the LORD thy God **s** unto thee, Thou shalt 559
11: 5 the inhabitants of Jebus **s** to David, 559
11: 6 David **s**, Whosoever smiteth the Jebusites 559
11:17 David longed, and **s**, Oh that one would 559
11:19 **s**, My God forbid it me, that *I* should do 559
12:17 them, and answered and **s** unto them, 559
12:18 he **s**, Thine *are we*, David, and on thy NIH
13: 2 David **s** unto all the congregation of Israel, 559
13: 4 the congregation **s** that *they* would do so: 559
14:10 the LORD **s** unto him, Go up; for I will 559
14:11 David **s**, God hath broken in upon mine 559
14:14 God **s** unto him, Go not up after them; 559
15: 2 David **s**, None ought to carry the ark of 559
15:12 **s** unto them, Ye *are* the chief of the fathers 559
16:36 all the people **s**, Amen, and praised 559

1Ch 17: 1 that David **s** to Nathan the prophet,	559	
17: 2 Nathan **s** unto David, Do all that *is* in thine	559	
17:16 **s**, Who *am* I, O Lord God, and what *is*	559	
17:23 established for ever, and do as thou hast **s**.	1696	
19: 2 David **s**, I will shew kindness unto Hanun	559	
19: 3 the princes of the children of Ammon **s** to	559	
19: 5 king **s**, Tarry at Jericho until your beards	559	
19:12 he **s**, If the Syrians be too strong for me,	559	
21: 2 David **s** to Joab and to the rulers of	559	
21: 8 David **s** unto God, I have sinned greatly,	559	
21:11 So Gad came to David, and **s** unto him,	559	
21:13 David **s** unto Gad, I am in a great strait:	559	
21:15 **s** to the angel that destroyed, *It is* enough,	559	
21:17 David **s** unto God, *Is it* not I *that*	559	
21:22 David **s** to Ornan, Grant me the place of	559	
21:23 And Ornan **s** unto David, Take *it* to thee,	559	
21:24 king David **s** to Ornan, Nay; but I will	559	
22: 1 David **s**, This *is* the house of the Lord	559	
22: 5 David **s**, Solomon my son *is* young and	559	
22: 7 David **s** to Solomon, My son, *as for* me,	559	
22:11 the Lord thy God, as he hath **s** of thee.	1696	
23: 5 I made, **s** David, to praise *therewith*.	NIH	
23:25 For David **s**, The Lord God of Israel hath	559	
27:23 the Lord had **s** he would increase Israel	559	
28: 2 **s**, Hear me, my brethren, and my people:	559	
28: 3 God **s** unto me, Thou shalt not build a	559	
28: 6 he **s** unto me, Solomon thy son, he shall	559	
28:19 All *this*, **s** David, the Lord made me	NIH	
28:20 David **s** to Solomon his son, Be strong and	559	
29: 1 Furthermore David the king **s** unto all	559	
29:10 David **s**, Blessed *be* thou, Lord God of	559	
29:20 David **s** to all the congregation, Now bless	559	
2Ch 1: 7 and **s** unto him, Ask what I shall give thee.	559	
1: 8 Solomon **s** unto God, Thou hast shewed	559	
1:11 God **s** to Solomon, Because this was in	559	
2:12 Huram **s** moreover, Blessed *be* the Lord	559	
6: 1 Solomon, The Lord hath said that he	559	
6: 1 The Lord hath **s** that *he* would dwell in	559	
6: 4 he **s**, Blessed *be* the Lord God of Israel,	559	
6: 8 the Lord **s** to David my father,	559	
6:14 **s**, O Lord God of Israel, *there is* no God	559	
6:20 the place whereof thou hast **s** that *thou*	559	
7:12 and **s** unto him, I have heard thy prayer,	559	
8:11 for he **s**, My wife shall not dwell in	559	
9: 5 she **s** to the king, *It was* a true report	559	
10: 5 he **s** unto them, Come again unto me after	559	
10: 9 he **s** unto them, What advice give ye that	559	
12: 5 of Shishak, and **s** unto them,	559	
12: 6 and they **s**, The Lord *is* righteous.	559	
13: 4 **s**, Hear me, *thou* Jeroboam, and all Israel;	559	
14: 7 Therefore he **s** unto Judah, Let us build	559	
14:11 **s**, Lord, *it is* nothing with thee to help,	559	
15: 2 **s** unto him, Hear ye me, Asa, and all Judah	559	
16: 7 **s** unto him, Because thou hast relied on	559	
18: 3 Ahab king of Israel **s** unto Jehoshaphat king	559	
18: 4 Jehoshaphat **s** unto the king of Israel,	559	
18: 5 **s** unto them, Shall we go to Ramoth-gilead	559	
18: 5 they **s**, Go up; for God will deliver *it* into	559	
18: 6 Jehoshaphat **s**, *Is there* not here a prophet	559	
18: 7 the king of Israel **s** unto Jehoshaphat,	559	
18: 7 And Jehoshaphat **s**, Let not the king say so.	559	
18: 8 **s**, Fetch quickly Micaiah the son of Imla.	559	
18:10 **s**, Thus saith the Lord, With these thou	559	
18:13 Micaiah **s**, *As* the Lord liveth, even what	559	
18:14 to the king, the king **s** unto him, Micaiah,	559	
18:14 he **s**, Go ye up, and prosper, and they shall	559	
18:15 the king **s**, I did see all Israel scattered upon	559	
18:16 he **s**, These have no master;	559	
18:17 king of Israel **s** to Jehoshaphat, Did I not	559	
18:18 Again he **s**, Therefore hear the word of	559	
18:19 the Lord **s**, Who shall entice Ahab king of	559	
18:20 before the Lord, and **s**, I will entice him.	559	
18:20 And the Lord **s** unto him, Wherewith?	559	
18:21 he **s**, I will go out, and be a lying spirit in	559	
18:21 the Lord **s**, Thou shalt entice *him*, and	559	
18:23 and smote Micaiah upon the cheek, and **s**,	559	
18:24 Micaiah **s**, Behold, thou shalt see on that	559	
18:25 the king of Israel **s**, Take ye Micaiah,	559	
18:27 Micaiah **s**, If thou certainly return in peace,	559	
18:27 by me. And he **s**, Hearken, all ye people.	559	
18:29 the king of Israel **s** unto Jehoshaphat, I will	559	
18:31 that they **s**, It *is* the king of Israel.	559	
18:33 therefore he **s** to *his* chariot man, Turn	559	
19: 2 **s** to king Jehoshaphat, Shouldest thou help	559	
19: 6 **s** to the judges, Take heed what ye do: for	559	
20: 6 **s**, O Lord God of our fathers, *art* not thou	559	
20:15 he **s**, Hearken ye, all Judah,	559	
20:20 Jehoshaphat stood and **s**, Hear me,	559	
22: 9 Because, **s** they, he *is* the son of	559	
23: 3 he **s** unto them, Behold, the king's son	559	
23: 3 as the Lord hath **s** of the sons of David.	1696	
23:11 anointed him, and **s**, God save the king.	559	
23:13 rent her clothes, and **s**, Treason, Treason.	559	
23:14 **s** unto them, Have her forth of the ranges:	559	
23:14 For the priest **s**, Slay her not *in* the house	559	
24: 5 the priests and the Levites, and **s** to them,	559	
24: 6 for Jehoiada the chief, and **s** unto him,	559	
24:20 people, and **s** unto them, Thus saith God,	559	
24:22 when he died, he **s**, The Lord look upon	559	
25: 9 Amaziah **s** to the man of God, But what	559	
25:15 unto him a prophet, which **s** unto him,	559	
25:16 talked with him, that the *king* **s** unto him,	559	
25:16 prophet forbare, and **s**, I know that God	559	
26:18 **s** unto him, *It pertaineth* not unto thee,	559	

2Ch 26:23 to the kings; for they **s**, He *is* a leper:	559	
28: 9 **s** unto them, Behold, because the Lord	559	
28:13 **s** unto them, Ye shall not bring in	559	
28:23 he **s**, Because the gods of the kings of Syria	559	
29: 5 **s** unto them, Hear me, ye Levites,	559	
29:18 they went in to Hezekiah the king, and **s**,	559	
29:31 Hezekiah answered and **s**, Now ye have	559	
31:10 the house of Zadok answered him, and **s**,	559	
33: 4 whereof the Lord had **s**, In Jerusalem	559	
33: 7 of which God had **s** to David and	559	
34:15 and **s** to Shaphan the scribe,	559	
35: 3 **s** unto the Levites that taught all Israel,	559	
35:23 the king **s** to his servants, Have me away;	559	
Ezr 2:63 Tirshatha **s** unto them, that they should	559	
4: 2 and **s** unto them, Let us build with you:	559	
4: 3 chief of the fathers of Israel, **s** unto them,	559	
5: 3 their companions, and **s** thus unto them,	560	
5: 4 **s** we unto them after this manner, What	560	
5: 9 we those elders, *and* **s** unto them thus,	560	
5:15 unto him, Take these vessels,	560	
8:28 I **s** unto them, Ye *are* holy unto the Lord;	559	
9: 6 **s**, O my God, I am ashamed and blush to	559	
10: 2 sons of Elam, answered and **s** unto Ezra,	559	
10:10 **s** unto them, Ye have transgressed,	559	
10:12 and **s** with a loud voice,	559	
10:12 loud voice, As thou hast **s**, so must we do.	1697	
Ne 1: 3 they **s** unto me, The remnant that are left	559	
1: 5 **s**, I beseech thee, O Lord God of heaven,	559	
2: 2 Wherefore the king **s** unto me, Why *is* thy	559	
2: 3 **s** unto the king, Let the king live for ever:	559	
2: 4 king **s** unto me, For what dost thou make	559	
2: 5 I **s** unto the king, If it please the king,	559	
2: 6 king **s** unto me, (the queen also sitting by	559	
2: 7 Moreover I **s** unto the king, If it please	559	
2:17 I **s** unto them, Ye see the distress that we	559	
2:18 they **s**, Let us rise up and build. So they	559	
2:19 despised us, and **s**, What *is* this thing that	559	
2:20 **s** unto them, The God of heaven, he will	559	
4: 2 brethren and the army of Samaria, and **s**,	559	
4: 3 he **s**, Even *that* which they build, if a fox	559	
4:10 Judah **s**, The strength of the bearers of	559	
4:11 our adversaries **s**, They shall not know,	559	
4:12 by them came, they **s** unto us ten times,	559	
4:14 **s** unto the nobles, and to the rulers,	559	
4:19 I **s** unto the nobles, and to the rulers,	559	
4:22 Likewise at the same time **s** I unto	559	
5: 2 For there were that **s**, We, our sons,	559	
5: 3 *Some* also there were that **s**, We *have*	559	
5: 4 There were also that **s**, We have borrowed	559	
5: 7 rulers, and **s** unto them, You exact usury,	559	
5: 8 I **s** unto them, We after our ability have	559	
5: 9 Also I **s**, It *is* not good that ye do: ought ye	559	
5:12 they, We will restore *them*, and	559	
5:13 Also I shook my lap, and **s**, So God shake	559	
5:13 all the congregation **s**, Amen, and praised	559	
6:10 he **s**, Let us meet together in the house of	559	
6:11 I **s**, Should such a man as I flee? and who	559	
7: 3 I **s** unto them, Let not the gates of	559	
7:65 Tirshatha **s** unto them, that they should	559	
8: 9 taught the people, **s** unto all the people,	559	
8:10 he **s** unto them, Go *your* way, eat the fat,	559	
9: 5 Stand up *and* bless the Lord your God	559	
9:18 they had made them a molten calf, and **s**,	559	
13:11 contended I with the rulers, and **s**, Why is	559	
13:17 **s** unto them, What evil thing *is* this that ye	559	
13:21 I testified against them, and **s** unto them,	559	
Est 1:13 the king **s** to the wise *men*, which knew	559	
2: 2 **s** the king's servants that ministered unto	559	
3: 3 *were* in the king's gate, **s** unto Mordecai,	559	
3: 8 Haman **s** unto king Ahasuerus, There is a	559	
3:11 king **s** unto Haman, The silver *is* given to	559	
5: 3 the king unto her, What wilt thou, queen	559	
5: 5 the king **s**, Cause Haman to make haste,	559	
5: 5 that he may do as Esther hath **s**.	1697	
5: 6 the king **s** unto Esther at the banquet of	559	
5: 7 and **s**, My petition and my request *is*;	559	
5: 8 I will do to morrow as the king hath **s**.	1697	
5:12 Haman moreover, Yea, Esther the queen	559	
5:14 Zeresh his wife and all his friends unto	559	
6: 3 the king, What honour and dignity hath	559	
6: 3 the king's servants that ministered unto	559	
6: 4 the king **s**, Who *is* in the court?	559	
6: 5 the king's servants **s** unto him, Behold,	559	
6: 5 And the king **s**, Let him come in.	559	
6: 6 king **s** unto him, What shall be done unto	559	
6:10 the king **s** to Haman, Make haste,	559	
6:10 thou hast **s**, and do *even* so to Mordecai	1696	
6:13 his wise *men* and Zeresh his wife unto	559	
7: 2 the king again unto Esther on the second	559	
7: 3 Esther the queen answered and **s**, If I have	559	
7: 5 and **s** unto Esther the queen,	559	
7: 6 Esther **s**, The adversary and enemy *is* this	559	
7: 8 bed whereon Esther *was*. Then **s** the king,	559	
7: 9 **s** before the king, Behold also,	559	
7: 9 Then the king **s**, Hang him thereon.	559	
8: 5 **s**, If it please the king, and if I have found	559	
8: 7 king Ahasuerus **s** unto Esther the queen	559	
9:12 king **s** unto Esther the queen, The Jews	559	
9:13 Esther, If it please the king, let it be	559	
Job 1: 5 for Job, It may be that my sons have	559	
1: 7 the Lord unto Satan, Whence comest	559	
1: 7 **s**, From going to and fro in the earth,	559	
1: 8 the Lord **s** unto Satan, Hast thou	559	
1: 9 and **s**, Doth Job fear God for nought?	559	
1:12 the Lord **s** unto Satan, Behold, all that he	559	

Job 1:14 **s**, The oxen were plowing, and the asses	559	
1:16 speaking, there came also another, and **s**,	559	
1:17 speaking, there came also another, and **s**,	559	
1:18 **s**, Thy sons and thy daughters *were* eating	559	
1:21 **s**, Naked came I out of my mother's	559	
2: 2 the Lord **s** unto Satan, From whence	559	
2: 2 **s**, From going to and fro in the earth,	559	
2: 3 the Lord **s** unto Satan, Hast thou	559	
2: 4 the Lord, and **s**, Skin for skin, yea,	559	
2: 6 the Lord **s** unto Satan, Behold, he *is* in	559	
2: 9 his wife unto him, Dost thou still retain	559	
2:10 he **s** unto her, Thou speakest as one of	559	
3: 2 And Job spake, and **s**,	559	
3: 3 night *in which it was* **s**, There is a man	559	
4: 1 Eliphaz the Temanite answered and **s**,	559	
6: 1 But Job answered and **s**,	559	
8: 1 Then answered Bildad the Shuhite, and **s**,	559	
9: 1 Then Job answered and **s**,	559	
9:22 therefore I **s** *it*, He destroyeth the perfect	559	
11: 1 answered Zophar the Naamathite, and **s**,	559	
11: 4 For thou hast **s**, My doctrine *is* pure,	559	
12: 1 And Job answered and **s**,	559	
15: 1 answered Eliphaz the Temanite, and **s**,	559	
16: 1 Then Job answered and **s**,	559	
17:14 have **s** to corruption, Thou *art* my father:	7121	
18: 1 Then answered Bildad the Shuhite, and **s**,	559	
19: 1 Then Job answered and **s**,	559	
20: 1 answered Zophar the Naamathite, and **s**,	559	
21: 1 But Job answered and **s**,	559	
22: 1 Eliphaz the Temanite answered and **s**,	559	
22:17 Which **s** unto God, Depart from us:	559	
23: 1 Then Job answered and **s**,	559	
25: 1 Then answered Bildad the Shuhite, and **s**,	559	
26: 1 But Job answered and **s**,	559	
27: 1 Moreover Job continued his parable, and **s**,	559	
28:28 man he **s**, Behold, the fear of the Lord,	559	
29: 1 Moreover Job continued his parable, and **s**,	559	
29:18 I **s**, I shall die in my nest, and I shall	559	
31:24 or have **s** to the fine gold, *Thou art* my	559	
31:31 If the men of my tabernacle **s** not, O that	559	
32: 6 son of Barachel the Buzite answered and **s**,	559	
32: 7 I **s**, Days should speak, and multitude of	559	
32:10 Therefore I **s**, Hearken to me; I also will	559	
32:17 I **s**, I will answer also my part, I also will	NIH	
34: 1 Furthermore Elihu answered and **s**,	559	
34: 5 Job hath **s**, I am righteous: and God hath	559	
34: 9 he hath **s**, It profiteth a man nothing that	559	
34:31 Surely it is *meet to be* **s** unto God, I have	559	
35: 1 Elihu spake moreover, and **s**,	559	
36: 1 Elihu also proceeded, and **s**,	559	
38: 1 answered Job out of the whirlwind, and **s**,	559	
38:11 **s**, Hitherto shalt thou come, but no further:	559	
40: 1 Moreover the Lord answered Job, and **s**,	559	
40: 3 Then Job answered the Lord, and **s**,	559	
40: 6 unto Job out of the whirlwind, and **s**,	559	
42: 1 Then Job answered the Lord, and **s**,	559	
42: 7 the Lord **s** to Eliphaz the Temanite,	559	
Ps 2: 7 the Lord hath **s** unto me, Thou *art* my	559	
10: 6 hath **s** in his heart, I shall not be moved:	559	
10:11 He hath **s** in his heart, God hath forgotten:	559	
10:13 hath **s** in his heart, Thou wilt not require	559	
12: 4 Who have **s**, With our tongue will we	559	
14: 1 fool hath **s** in his heart, *There is* no God.	559	
16: 2 O my *soul*, thou hast **s** unto the Lord,	559	
18: T and from the hand of Saul: And he **s**,	559	
27: 8 my heart **s** unto thee, Thy face, Lord,	559	
30: 6 my prosperity I **s**, I shall never be moved.	559	
31:14 in thee, O Lord: I **s**, Thou *art* my God.	559	
31:22 I **s** in my haste, I am cut off from before	559	
32: 5 I **s**, I will confess my transgressions unto	559	
35:21 and **s**, Aha, aha, our eye hath seen *it*.	559	
38:16 I **s**, *Hear me*, lest *otherwise* they should	559	
39: 1 I **s**, I will take heed to my ways, that *I* sin	559	
40: 7 s I, Lo, I come: in the volume of the book	559	
41: 4 I **s**, Lord, be merciful unto me: heal my	559	
52: T Edomite came and told Saul, and **s** unto	559	
53: 1 fool hath **s** in his heart, *There is* no God.	559	
54: T when the Ziphims came and **s** to Saul,	559	
55: 6 I **s**, O that I had wings like a dove, *for then*	559	
68:22 The Lord **s**, I will bring again from Bashan,	559	
74: 8 They **s** in their hearts, Let us destroy them	559	
75: 4 I **s** unto the fools, Deal not foolishly:	559	
77:10 I **s**, This *is* my infirmity: *but I will*	559	
78:19 they **s**, Can God furnish a table in	559	
82: 6 I have **s**, Ye *are* gods; and all of you *are*	559	
83: 4 They have **s**, Come, and let us cut them	559	
83:12 Who **s**, Let us take to ourselves the houses	559	
87: 5 of Zion it shall be **s**, This and that man was	559	
89: 2 For I have **s**, Mercy shall be built up for	559	
94:18 When I **s**, My foot slippeth; thy mercy,	559	
95:10 **s**, It *is* a people that do err in *their* heart,	559	
102:24 I **s**, O my God, take me not away in	559	
106:23 Therefore he **s** that *he* would destroy	559	
110: 1 The Lord **s** unto my Lord, Sit thou at my	5002	
116:11 I **s** in my haste, All men *are* liars.	559	
119:57 I have **s** that I would keep thy words.	559	
122: 1 I was glad when they **s** unto me, Let us go	559	
126: 2 **s** they among the heathen, The Lord hath	559	
137: 7 **s**, Rase *it*, rase *it, even* to the foundation	559	
140: 6 I **s** unto the Lord, Thou *art* my God:	559	
142: 5 I **s**, Thou *art* my refuge *and* my portion in	559	
Pr 4: 4 taught me also, and **s** unto me, Let thine	559	
7:13 and with an impudent face **s** unto thee,	559	
25: 7 For better *it is* that it be **s** unto thee,	559	
Ecc 1:10 Is there *any* thing whereof it may be **s**, See,	559	

Ecc 2: 1 I **s** in mine heart, Go to now, I will prove 559
2: 2 I of laughter, *It is* mad: and of mirth, 559
2:15 **s** I in my heart, As it happeneth to the fool, 559
2:15 I **s** in my heart, that this also *is* vanity. 1696
3:17 **s** in mine heart, God shall judge 559
3:18 I **s** in my heart concerning the estate of 559
7:23 I, I will be wise; but it *was* far from me. 559
8:14 of the righteous: I **s** that this also *is* vanity. 559
9:16 **s** I, Wisdom *is* better than strength: 559
SS 2:10 **s** unto me, Rise up, my love, my fair one, 559
3: 3 *to whom I* **s**, Saw ye *him* whom my soul NIH
7: 8 I, I will go up to the palm tree, I will take 559
Isa 5: 9 In mine ears *s* the LORD of hosts, Of a NIH
6: 3 **s**, Holy, holy, holy, *is* the LORD of hosts: 559
6: 5 **s** I, Woe *is* me! for I am undone; because 559
6: 7 and **s**, Lo, this hath touched thy lips; 559
6: 8 go for us? Then I **s**, Here *am* I; send me. 559
6: 9 he **s**, Go, and tell this people, Hear ye 559
6:11 **s** I, Lord, how long? And he answered, 559
7: 3 **s** the LORD unto Isaiah, Go forth now to 559
7:12 Ahaz **s**, I will not ask, neither will I tempt 559
7:13 he **s**, Hear ye now, O house of David; *Is it* 559
8: 1 Moreover the LORD **s** unto me, Take thee 559
8: 3 **s** the LORD to me, Call his name 559
14:13 For thou hast **s** in thine heart, I will ascend 559
18: 4 For so the LORD **s** unto me, I will take my 559
20: 3 the LORD **s**, Like as my servant Isaiah hath 559
21: 6 For thus hath the Lord **s** unto me, Go, set 559
21: 9 he answered and **s**, Babylon is fallen, 559
21:12 The watchman **s**, The morning cometh, 559
21:16 For thus hath the Lord **s** unto me, Within 559
22: 4 Therefore I **s**, Look away from me; I will 559
23:12 he **s**, Thou shalt no more rejoice, O thou 559
24:16 I **s**, My leanness, my leanness, woe unto 559
25: 9 it shall be **s** in that day, Lo, this *is* our God; 559
28:12 whom he **s**, This *is* the rest *wherewith* ye 559
28:15 Because ye have **s**, We have made a 559
29:13 Wherefore the Lord **s**, Forasmuch as this 559
30:16 ye **s**, No; for we will flee upon horses; 559
32: 5 liberal, nor the churl **s** *to be* bountiful. 559
36: 4 Rabshakeh **s**, Say ye now to 559
36: 7 **s** to Judah and to Jerusalem, Ye shall 559
36:10 the LORD **s** unto me, Go up against this 559
36:11 **s** Eliakim and Shebna and Joah unto 559
36:12 Rabshakeh **s**, Hath my master sent me to 559
36:13 **s**, Hear ye the words of the great king, 559
37: 3 Isaiah **s** unto them, Thus shall ye say unto 559
37: 6 Isaiah **s** unto them, Thus shall ye say unto 559
37:24 hast thou reproached the Lord, and hast **s**, 559
38: 1 **s** unto him, Thus saith the LORD, Set thine 559
38: 3 **s**, Remember now, O LORD, I beseech 559
38:10 I **s**, in the cutting off of my days, I shall go 559
38:11 I **s**, I shall not see the LORD, *even* 559
38:21 For Isaiah had **s**, Let them take a lump of 559
38:22 Hezekiah also had **s**, What *is* the sign that 559
39: 3 and **s** unto him, What said these men? 559
39: 3 and said unto him, What **s** these men? 559
39: 3 Hezekiah **s**, They are come from a far 559
39: 4 **s** he, What have they seen in thine house? 559
39: 5 Isaiah to Hezekiah, Hear the word of 559
39: 8 Hezekiah to Isaiah, Good *is* the word of 559
39: 8 He **s** moreover, For there shall be peace 559
40: 6 The voice **s**, Cry. And he said, What shall I 559
40: 6 he **s**, What shall I cry? All flesh *is* grass, 559
41: 6 *every one* **s** to his brother, Be of good 559
41: 9 and **s** unto thee, Thou *art* my servant; 559
45:19 I **s** not unto the seed of Jacob, Seek ye me 559
47:10 thou hast **s**, None seeth me. Thy wisdom 559
47:10 thou hast **s** in thine heart, I *am*, and none 559
49: 3 **s** unto me, Thou *art* my servant, O Israel, 559
49: 4 I **s**, I have laboured in vain, I have spent 559
49: 6 he **s**, It is a light thing that thou shouldest 559
49:14 Zion **s**, The LORD hath forsaken me, 559
51:23 which have **s** to thy soul, Bow down, that 559
63: 8 For he **s**, Surely they *are* my people, 559
65: 1 I **s**, Behold me, behold me, unto a nation 559
66: 5 name's sake, **s**, Let the LORD be glorified: 559
Jer 1: 6 **s** I, Ah, Lord GOD, behold, I cannot speak: 559
1: 7 the LORD **s** unto me, Say not, I *am* a child: 559
1: 9 the LORD **s** unto me, Behold, I have put 559
1:11 And I **s**, I see a rod of an almond tree. 559
1:12 the LORD unto me, Thou hast well seen: 559
1:13 I **s**, I see a seething pot; and the face 559
1:14 the LORD **s** unto me, Out of the north an 559
2: 6 Neither **s** they, Where *is* the LORD that 559
2: 8 The priests **s** not, Where *is* the LORD? 559
3: 6 The LORD also unto me in the days of 559
3: 7 I **s** after she had done all these *things*, Turn 559
3:11 the LORD unto me, The backsliding 559
3:19 I **s**, How shall I put thee among the 559
3:19 I **s**, Thou shalt call me, My father; 559
4:10 (Then **s** I, Ah, Lord GOD! surely thou hast 559
4:11 At that time shall it be **s** to this people and 559
4:27 For thus hath the LORD **s**, The whole land 559
5: 4 Therefore I **s**, Surely these *are* poor; they 559
5:12 have belied the LORD, and **s**, *It is* not he; 559
6: 6 For thus hath the LORD of hosts **s**, Hew ye 559
6:16 But they **s**, We will not walk *therein*. 559
6:17 But they **s**, We will not hearken. 559
10:19 I **s**, Truly this *is* a grief, and I must bear it. 559
11: 5 Then answered I, and **s**, So be it, O LORD. 559
11: 6 the LORD **s** unto me, Proclaim all these 559
11: 9 the LORD **s** unto me, A conspiracy is 559
12: 4 they **s**, He shall not see our last end. 559
13: 6 that the LORD **s** unto me, Arise, go to 559

Jer 14:11 **s** the LORD unto me, Pray not for this 559
14:13 I, Ah Lord GOD! behold, the prophets 559
14:14 the LORD **s** unto me, The prophets 559
15: 1 Then **s** the LORD unto me, Though Moses 559
15:11 The LORD **s**, Verily it shall be well with 559
16:14 saith the LORD, that it shall no more be **s**, 559
17:19 Thus **s** the LORD unto me; Go and stand in 559
18:10 wherewith I **s** *I* would benefit them. 559
18:12 they **s**, There is no hope: but we will walk 559
18:18 they **s**, Come, and let us devise devices 559
19:14 the LORD's house; and **s** to all the people, 559
20: 3 Jeremiah unto him, The LORD hath not 559
20: 9 I **s**, I will not make mention of him, 559
21: 3 **s** unto them, Thus shall ye say to 559
23:17 The LORD hath **s**, Ye shall have peace; 1696
23:25 I have heard what the prophets **s**, 559
24: 3 the LORD unto me, What seest thou, 559
24: 3 I **s**, Figs; the good figs, very good; 559
25: 3 *They* **s**, Turn ye again now every one from 559
26:16 the princes and all the people unto 559
28: 5 the prophet Jeremiah **s** unto the prophet 559
28: 6 Even the prophet Jeremiah **s**, Amen: 559
28:15 the prophet Jeremiah unto Hananiah 559
29:15 Because ye have **s**, The LORD hath raised 559
32: 6 Jeremiah **s**, The word of the LORD came 559
32: 8 **s** unto me, Buy my field, I pray thee, that 559
32:25 thou hast **s** unto me, O Lord GOD, 559
35: 5 cups, and I **s** unto them, Drink ye wine. 559
35: 6 they **s**, We will drink no wine: for Jonadab 559
35:11 we **s**, Come, and let us go *to* Jerusalem 559
35:18 Jeremiah **s** unto the house of the 559
36:15 they **s** unto him, Sit down now, and read 559
36:16 both one and other, and **s** unto Baruch, 559
36:19 the princes unto Baruch, Go, hide thee, 559
37:14 Jeremiah, *It is* false; I fall not away to 559
37:17 and **s**, Is there *any* word from the LORD? 559
37:17 Jeremiah **s**, There is: for, said he, thou 559
37:17 for, **s** he, thou shalt be delivered into 559
37:18 Moreover Jeremiah **s** unto king Zedekiah, 559
38: 4 Therefore the princes **s** unto the king, 559
38: 5 Zedekiah the king **s**, Behold, he *is* in your 559
38:12 the Ethiopian **s** unto Jeremiah, 559
38:14 the king **s** unto Jeremiah, I *will* ask thee a 559
38:15 Jeremiah **s** unto Zedekiah, If I declare *it* 559
38:17 **s** Jeremiah unto Zedekiah, Thus saith 559
38:19 Zedekiah the king **s** unto Jeremiah, I am 559
38:20 Jeremiah **s**, They shall not deliver *thee*. 559
38:24 **s** Zedekiah unto Jeremiah, Let no man 559
38:25 Declare unto us now what thou hast **s** 1696
38:25 to death; also what the king **s** unto thee: 1696
40: 2 the guard took Jeremiah, and **s** unto him, 559
40: 3 *it*, and done according as he hath **s**: 1696
40: 5 **s** he, Go back also to Gedaliah the son of NIH
40:14 **s** unto him, Dost thou certainly know that 559
40:16 Gedaliah the son of Ahikam **s** unto Johanan 559
41: 6 to pass, as he met them, he **s** unto them, 559
41: 8 ten men were found among them that **s** 559
42: 2 **s** unto Jeremiah the prophet, Let, we 559
42: 4 Jeremiah the prophet **s** unto them, I have 559
42: 5 they **s** to Jeremiah, The LORD be a true 559
42: 9 **s** unto them, Thus saith the LORD, the God 559
42:19 The LORD hath **s** concerning you, O ye 1696
44:20 Jeremiah **s** unto all the people, to the men, 559
44:24 Moreover Jeremiah **s** unto all the people, 559
46:16 they **s**, Arise, and let us go again to our 559
50: 7 their adversaries **s**, We offend not, because 559
51:61 Jeremiah **s** to Seraiah, When thou comest 559
La 3:18 I **s**, My strength and my hope is perished 559
3:54 over mine head; *then* I **s**, I am cut off. 559
4:15 they **s** among the heathen, They shall no 559
4:20 was taken in their pits, *of* whom we **s**, 559
Eze 2: 1 he **s** unto me, Son of man, stand upon thy 559
2: 3 he **s** unto me, Son of man, I send thee to 559
3: 1 Moreover he **s** unto me, Son of man, eat 559
3: 3 he **s** unto me, Son of man, cause thy belly 559
3: 4 he **s** unto me, Son of man, go, get thee 559
3:10 Moreover he **s** unto me, Son of man, all 559
3:22 he **s** unto me, Arise, go forth into the plain, 559
3:24 and spake with me, and **s** unto me, 559
4:13 the LORD **s**, Even thus shall the children of 559
4:14 **s** I, Ah Lord GOD, behold, my soul *hath* 559
4:15 he **s** unto me, Lo, I have given thee cow's 559
4:16 Moreover he **s** unto me, Son of man, 559
6:10 I have not **s** in vain that *I* would do this 1696
8: 5 he **s** unto me, Son of man, lift up thine 559
8: 6 He **s** furthermore unto me, Son of man, 559
8: 8 **s** he unto me, Son of man, dig now in 559
8: 9 he **s** unto me, Go in, and behold the 559
8:12 he **s** unto me, Son of man, hast thou seen 559
8:13 He **s** also unto me, Turn thee yet again, 559
8:15 **s** he unto me, Hast thou seen *this*, O son 559
8:17 he **s** unto me, Hast thou seen *this*, O son 559
9: 4 the LORD **s** unto him, Go through 559
9: 5 to the others he **s** in mine hearing, Go ye 559
9: 7 he **s** unto them, Defile the house, and fill 559
9: 8 my face, and cried, and **s**, Ah Lord GOD, 559
9: 9 **s** he unto me, The iniquity of the house of 559
10: 2 **s**, Go in between the wheels, *even* under 559
11: 2 **s** he unto me, Son of man, these *are* the 559
11: 5 LORD fell upon me, and **s** unto me, Speak; 559
11: 5 Thus have ye **s**, O house of Israel: 559
11:13 *with* a loud voice, and **s**, Ah Lord GOD, 559
11:15 whom the inhabitants of Jerusalem have **s**, 559
12: 9 unto thee, What doest thou? 559
13:12 the wall is fallen, shall it not be **s** unto you, 559

Eze 16: 6 **s** unto thee *when thou wast* in thy blood, 559
16: 6 **s** unto thee *when thou wast* in thy blood, 559
20: 7 **s** I unto them, Cast ye away every man 559
20: 8 I **s**, *I* will pour out my fury upon them, 559
20:13 I **s**, *I* would pour out my fury upon them in 559
20:18 I **s** unto their children in the wilderness, 559
20:21 I **s**, *I* would pour out my fury upon them, 559
20:29 I **s** unto them, What *is* the high place 559
20:49 **s** I, Ah Lord GOD, they say of me, Doth he 559
21:17 my fury to rest: I the LORD have **s** *it*. 1696
23:36 The LORD **s** moreover unto me; Son of 559
23:43 **s** I unto *her that was* old *in* adulteries, 559
24:19 the people **s** unto me, Wilt thou not tell us 559
26: 2 that Tyrus hath **s** against Jerusalem, 559
27: 3 Tyrus, thou hast **s**, I *am* of perfect beauty. 559
28: 2 thou hast **s**, I *am* a God, I sit *in* the seat of 559
29: 3 which hath **s**, My river *is* mine own, 559
29: 9 because he hath **s**, The river *is* mine, 559
35:10 Because thou hast **s**, These two nations 559
36: 2 Because the enemy hath **s** against you, 559
36:20 my holy name, when *they* **s** to them, 559
37: 3 he **s** unto me, Son of man, can these bones 559
37: 4 Again he **s** unto me, Prophesy upon these 559
37: 9 **s** he unto me, Prophesy unto the wind, 559
37:11 he **s** unto me, Son of man, these bones *are* 559
40: 4 the man **s** unto me, Son of man, 1696
40:45 he **s** unto me, This chamber, 1696
41: 4 he **s** unto me, This *is* the most holy *place*. 559
41:22 he **s** unto me, This *is* the table that *is* 1696
42:13 he **s** unto me, The north chambers *and* 559
43: 7 he **s** unto me, Son of man, the place of my 559
43:18 he **s** unto me, Son of man, thus saith 559
44: 2 **s** the LORD unto me; This gate shall be 559
44: 5 the LORD **s** unto me, Son of man, 559
46:20 **s** he unto me, This *is* the place where 559
46:24 he **s** unto me, These *are* the places of them 559
47: 6 he **s** unto me, Son of man, hast thou seen 559
47: 8 he **s** unto me, These waters issue out 559
Da 1:10 the prince of the eunuchs **s** unto Daniel, 559
1:11 **s** Daniel to Melzar, whom the prince of 559
1:18 the king had **s** he should bring them in, 559
2: 3 the king **s** unto them, I have dreamed a 559
2: 5 The king answered and **s** to the Chaldeans, 560
2: 7 They answered again and **s**, Let the king 560
2: 8 The king answered and **s**, I know of 560
2:10 answered before the king, and **s**, 560
2:15 and **s** to Arioch the king's captain, 560
2:20 Daniel answered and **s**, Blessed be the 560
2:24 he went and **s** thus unto him; Destroy not 560
2:25 **s** thus unto him, I have found a man of 560
2:26 The king answered and **s** to Daniel, 560
2:27 in the presence of the king, and **s**, 560
2:47 The king answered unto Daniel, and **s**, 560
3: 9 and **s** to the king Nebuchadnezzar, 560
3:14 Nebuchadnezzar spake and **s** unto them, 560
3:16 Abed-nego, answered and **s** to the king, 560
3:24 and spake, and **s** unto his counsellors, 560
3:24 They answered and **s** unto the king, True, 560
3:25 answered and **s**, Lo, I see four men loose, 560
3:26 *and* spake, and **s**, Shadrach, Meshach, 560
3:28 *Then* Nebuchadnezzar spake, and **s**, 560
4:14 He cried aloud, and **s** thus, Hew down 560
4:19 king spake, and **s**, Belteshazzar, let not 560
4:19 Belteshazzar answered and **s**, My lord, 560
4:30 The king spake, and **s**, *Is* not this great 560
5: 7 and **s** to the wise *men* of Babylon, 560
5:10 *and* the queen spake and **s**, O king, live for 560
5:13 *And* the king spake and **s** unto Daniel, 560
5:17 Daniel answered and **s** before the king, 560
6: 5 these men, We shall not find any 560
6: 6 **s** thus unto him, King Darius, live for ever. 560
6:12 king answered and **s**, The thing *is* true, 560
6:13 answered they and **s** before the king, 560
6:15 unto the king, Know, O king, that the 560
6:16 *Now* the king spake and **s** unto Daniel, 560
6:20 *and* the king spake and **s** to Daniel, 560
6:21 **s** Daniel unto the king, O king, live for 4449
7: 2 Daniel spake and **s**, I saw in my vision by 560
7: 5 they **s** thus unto it, Arise, devour much 560
7:23 Thus he **s**, The fourth beast shall be 560
8:13 another saint **s** unto that certain *saint* 559
8:14 he **s** unto me, Unto two thousand and 559
8:16 called, and **s**, Gabriel, make this *man* 559
8:17 he **s** unto me, Understand, O son of man: 559
8:19 he **s**, Behold, I *will* make thee know what 559
9: 4 and **s**, O Lord, the great and dreadful God, 559
9:22 and talked with me, and **s**, O Daniel, 559
10:11 he **s** unto me, O Daniel, a man greatly 559
10:12 he **s** unto me, Fear not, Daniel: for from 559
10:16 and unto him that stood before me, 559
10:19 **s**, O man greatly beloved, fear not: peace 559
10:19 strengthened, and **s**, Let my lord speak; 559
10:20 he **s**, Knowest thou wherefore I come unto 559
12: 6 to the man clothed in linen, which *was* 559
12: 8 I **s**, O my lord, what *shall be* the end of 559
12: 9 he **s**, Go thy way, Daniel: for the words 559
Hos 1: 2 the LORD **s** to Hosea, Go, take unto thee a 559
1: 4 the LORD **s** unto him, Call his name 559
1: 6 *God's* unto him, Call her name 559
1: 9 **s** *God*, Call his name Lo-ammi: for ye *are* 559
1:10 in the place where it was **s** unto them, 559
1:10 my people, *there* it shall be **s** unto them, 559
2: 5 she **s**, I will go after my lovers, that give 559
2:12 and her fig trees, where*of* she hath **s**, 559
3: 1 **s** the LORD unto me, Go yet, love a 559

S

Hos	3: 3 I s unto her, Thou shalt abide for me many	559
	12: 8 Ephraim s, Yet I am become rich, I have	559
Joel	2:32 as the LORD hath s, and in the remnant	559
Am	1: 2 he s, The LORD will roar from Zion,	559
	7: 2 I s, O Lord GOD, forgive, I beseech thee:	559
	7: 5 s, O Lord GOD, cease, I beseech thee:	559
	7: 8 the LORD s unto me, Amos, what seest	559
	7: 8 I s, A plumbline. Then said the Lord,	559
	7: 8 the Lord, Behold, I *will* set a plumbline	559
	7:12 Also Amaziah s unto Amos, O thou seer,	559
	7:14 and s to Amaziah, I *was* no prophet,	559
	7:15 the LORD s unto me, Go, prophesy unto	559
	8: 2 he s, Amos, what seest thou? And I said,	559
	8: 2 I s, A basket of summer fruit. Then said	559
	8: 2 the LORD s unto me, The end is come	559
	9: 1 he s, Smite the lintel of the door, that	559
Jnh	1: 6 s unto him, What meanest thou, O sleeper?	559
	1: 7 they s every one to his fellow, Come,	559
	1: 8 s they unto him, Tell us, we pray thee,	559
	1: 9 he s unto them, I *am* a Hebrew; and I fear	559
	1:10 s unto him, Why hast thou done this?	559
	1:11 s they unto him, What shall we do unto	559
	1:12 he s unto them, Take me up, and cast me	559
	1:14 s, We beseech thee, O LORD, we beseech	559
	2: 2 I, I cried by reason of mine affliction unto	559
	2: 4 I s, I am cast out of thy sight; yet I will	559
	3: 4 he cried, and s, Yet forty days,	559
	3:10 he had s that he would do unto them;	1696
	4: 2 s, I pray thee, O LORD, *was* not this my	559
	4: 4 s the LORD, Doest thou well to be angry?	559
	4: 8 and wished in himself to die, and s,	559
	4: 9 God s to Jonah, Doest thou well to be	559
	4: 9 he s, I do well to be angry, *even* unto	559
	4:10 s the LORD, Thou hast had pity on	559
Mic	3: 1 I s, Hear, I pray you, O heads of Jacob,	559
	7:10 shame shall cover her which s unto me,	559
Hab	2: 2 s, Write the vision, and make *it* plain upon	559
Zep	2:15 that s in her heart, I *am*, and *there is* none	559
	3: 7 I s, Surely thou wilt fear me, thou wilt	559
	3:16 In that day it shall be s to Jerusalem,	559
Hag	2:12 be holy? And the priests answered and s,	559
	2:13 s Haggai, If *one that is* unclean *by* a dead	559
	2:13 the priests answered and s, It shall be	559
	2:14 So *is* this people, and so *is* this nation	559
Zec	1: 6 they returned and s, Like as the LORD of	559
	1: 9 s I, O my lord, what *are* these?	559
	1: 9 the angel that talked with me s unto me,	559
	1:10 among the myrtle trees answered and s,	559
	1:11 s, We have walked to and fro through	559
	1:12 the angel of the LORD answered and s,	559
	1:14 the angel that communed with me s unto	559
	1:19 I s unto the angel that talked with me,	559
	1:21 s I, What come these to do? And he spake,	559
	2: 2 s I, Whither goest thou? And he said unto	559
	2: 2 he s unto me, To measure Jerusalem,	559
	2: 4 s unto him, Run, speak to this young man,	559
	3: 2 the LORD s unto Satan, The LORD	559
	3: 4 unto him he s, Behold, I have caused thine	559
	3: 5 I s, Let them set a fair mitre upon his head.	559
	4: 2 And s unto me, What seest thou? And I	559
	4: 2 s, I have looked, and behold, a candlestick	559
	4: 5 talked with me answered and s unto me,	559
	4: 5 Knowest thou not what these *be?* And I s,	559
	4:11 answered I, and s unto him, What *are*	559
	4:12 I answered again, and s unto him, What	559
	4:13 he answered me and s, Knowest thou not	559
	4:13 Knowest thou not what these *be?* And I s,	559
	4:14 s he, These *are* the two anointed ones,	559
	5: 2 he s unto me, What seest thou? And I	559
	5: 3 s he unto me, This *is* the curse that goeth	559
	5: 5 s unto me, Lift up now thine eyes,	559
	6: 1 s, What *is it?* And he said, This *is* an	559
	5: 6 he s, This *is* an ephah that goeth forth.	559
	5: 6 He s moreover, This *is* their resemblance	559
	5: 8 he s, This *is* wickedness. And he cast it	559
	5:10 s I to the angel that talked with me,	559
	5:11 he s unto me, To build it a house in the	559
	6: 4 and s unto the angel that talked with me,	559
	6: 5 angel answered and s unto me, These *are*	559
	6: 7 he s, Get ye *hence*, walk to and fro through	559
	11: 9 s I, I will not feed you: that that dieth, let it	559
	11:12 I s unto them, If ye think good, give *me* my	559
	11:13 the LORD s unto me, Cast it unto	559
	11:15 the LORD s unto me, Take unto thee yet	559
Mal	1:13 Ye s also, Behold, what a weariness *is it!*	559
	3: 7 But ye s, Wherein shall we return?	559
	3:14 Ye have s, It *is* vain to serve God:	559
Mt	2: 5 And they s unto him, In Bethlehem of	3004
	2: 8 and s, Go and search diligently for	3004
	3: 7 he s unto them, O generation of vipers,	3004
	3:15 And Jesus answering s unto him, Suffer *it*	3004
	4: 3 to him, he s, If thou be the Son of God,	3004
	4: 4 But he answered and s, It is written,	3004
	4: 7 Jesus s unto him, It is written again,	5346
	5:21 Ye have heard that it was s by them of old	3004
	5:27 Ye have heard that it was s by them of old	3004
	5:31 It hath been s, Whosoever shall put away	3004
	5:33 have heard that it hath been s by them of	3004
	5:38 Ye have heard that it hath been s, An eye	3004
	5:43 Ye have heard that it hath been s,	3004
	8: 8 The centurion answered and s, Lord, I am	5346
	8:10 s to them that followed, Verily I say	3004
	8:13 And Jesus s unto the centurion, Go thy	3004
	8:19 scribe came, and s unto him, Master,	3004
	8:21 And another of his disciples s unto him,	3004

Mt	8:22 But Jesus s unto him, Follow me;	3004
	8:32 And he s unto them, Go. And when they	3004
	9: 2 Jesus seeing their faith s unto the sick of	3004
	9: 3 certain of the scribes s within themselves,	3004
	9: 4 And Jesus knowing their thoughts s,	3004
	9:11 when the Pharisees saw *it*, they s unto	3004
	9:12 when Jesus heard *that*, he s unto them,	3004
	9:15 Jesus s unto them, Can the children of	3004
	9:21 For she s within herself, If I may but	3004
	9:22 when he saw her, he s, Daughter, be of	3004
	9:24 He s unto them, Give place: for the maid	3004
	9:28 to do this? They s unto him, Yea, Lord.	3004
	9:34 But the Pharisees s, He casteth out	3004
	11: 3 And s unto him, Art thou he that should	3004
	11: 4 Jesus answered and s unto them, Go and	3004
	11:25 that time Jesus answered and s, I thank	3004
	12: 2 when the Pharisees saw *it*, they s unto	3004
	12: 3 he s unto them, Have ye not read what	3004
	12:11 he s unto them, What man shall there	3004
	12:23 and s, Is this the son of David?	3004
	12:24 But when the Pharisees heard *it*, they s,	3004
	12:25 knew their thoughts, and s unto them,	3004
	12:39 he answered and s to them, An evil and	3004
	12:47 Then one s unto him, Behold, thy mother	3004
	12:48 answered and s unto him that told him,	3004
	12:49 s, Behold my mother and my brethren.	3004
	13:10 And the disciples came, and s unto him,	3004
	13:11 answered and s unto them, Because it is	3004
	13:27 of the householder came and s unto him,	3004
	13:28 s unto them, An enemy hath done this.	5346
	13:28 The servants s unto him, Wilt thou then	3004
	13:29 But he s, Nay; lest while ye gather up	5346
	13:37 He answered and s unto them, He that	3004
	13:52 Then s he unto them, Therefore every	3004
	13:54 s, Whence hath this *man* this wisdom,	3004
	13:57 But Jesus s unto them, A prophet is not	3004
	14: 2 And s unto his servants, This is John	3004
	14: 4 For John s unto him, It is not lawful for	3004
	14: 8 being before instructed of her mother, s,	5346
	14:16 But Jesus s unto them, They need not	3004
	14:18 He s, Bring them hither to me.	3004
	14:28 And Peter answered him and s, Lord, if it	3004
	14:29 And he s, Come. And when Peter was	3004
	14:31 caught him, and s unto him, O thou of	3004
	15: 3 he answered and s unto them, Why do	3004
	15:10 and s unto them, Hear, and understand:	3004
	15:12 Then came his disciples, and s unto him,	3004
	15:13 But he answered and s, Every plant,	3004
	15:15 Then answered Peter and s unto him,	3004
	15:16 And Jesus s, Are ye also yet without	3004
	15:24 But he answered and s, I am not sent but	3004
	15:26 But he answered and s, It is not meet to	3004
	15:27 she s, Truth, Lord: yet the dogs eat of	3004
	15:28 Then Jesus answered and s unto her,	3004
	15:32 Jesus called his disciples unto *him*, and s,	3004
	15:34 And they s, Seven, and a few little fishes.	3004
	16: 2 He answered and s unto them, When it is	3004
	16: 6 Then Jesus s unto them, Take heed and	3004
	16: 8 he s unto them, O ye of little faith,	3004
	16:14 And they s, Some *say that thou art* John	3004
	16:16 Simon Peter answered and s, Thou art	3004
	16:17 And Jesus answered and s unto him,	3004
	16:23 But he turned, and s unto Peter, Get thee	3004
	16:24 s Jesus unto his disciples, If any *man*	3004
	17: 4 answered Peter, and s unto Jesus, Lord,	3004
	17: 5 This is my beloved Son, in whom	3004
	17: 7 and s, Arise, and be not afraid.	3004
	17:11 And Jesus answered and s unto them,	3004
	17:17 Jesus answered and s, O faithless and	3004
	17:19 and s, Why could not we cast him out?	3004
	17:20 And Jesus s unto them, Because of your	3004
	17:22 they abode in Galilee, Jesus s unto them,	3004
	17:24 and s, Doth not your master pay tribute?	3004
	18: 3 And s, Verily I say unto you, Except ye be	3004
	18:21 Then came Peter to him, and s, Lord,	3004
	18:32 s unto him, O *thou* wicked servant,	3004
	19: 4 he answered and s unto them, Have ye	3004
	19: 5 And s, For this cause shall a man leave	3004
	19:11 he s unto them, All *men* cannot receive	3004
	19:14 But Jesus s, Suffer little children,	3004
	19:16 And behold, one came and s unto him,	3004
	19:17 And he s unto him, Why callest thou me	3004
	19:18 s, Thou shalt do no murder,	3004
	19:21 Jesus s unto him; If thou wilt be perfect,	5346
	19:23 s Jesus unto his disciples, Verily I say	3004
	19:26 But Jesus beheld *them,* and s unto them,	3004
	19:27 Then answered Peter and s unto him,	3004
	19:28 And Jesus s unto them, Verily I say unto	3004
	20: 4 And s unto them; Go ye also into	3004
	20:13 them, and s, Friend, I do thee no wrong:	3004
	20:17 apart in the way, and s unto them,	3004
	20:21 And he s unto her, What wilt thou?	3004
	20:22 But Jesus answered and s, Ye know not	3004
	20:25 But Jesus called them unto *him*, and s,	3004
	20:32 Jesus stood still, and called them, and s,	3004
	21:11 And the multitude s, This is Jesus	3004
	21:13 And s unto them, It is written, My house	3004
	21:16 And s unto him, Hearest thou what these	3004
	21:19 but leaves only, and s unto it,	3004
	21:21 Jesus answered and s unto them, Verily I	3004
	21:23 and s, By what authority doest thou these	3004
	21:24 Jesus answered and s unto them, I also	3004
	21:27 answered Jesus, and s, We cannot tell.	3004
	21:27 And he s unto them, Neither tell I you by	5346
	21:28 and he came to the first, and s, Son,	3004

Mt	21:29 He answered and s, I will not:	3004
	21:30 he came to the second, and s likewise.	3004
	21:30 And he answered and s, I go, sir:	3004
	21:38 they s among themselves, This is the heir;	3004
	22: 1 spake unto them again by parables, and s,	3004
	22:13 Then s the king to the servants, Bind him	3004
	22:18 and s, Why tempt ye me, *ye* hypocrites?	3004
	22:24 Saying, Master, Moses s, If a man die,	3004
	22:29 answered and s unto them, Ye do err,	3004
	22:37 Jesus s unto him, Thou shalt love the	3004
	22:44 The LORD s unto my Lord, Sit thou on	3004
	24: 2 Jesus s unto them, See ye not all these	3004
	24: 4 And Jesus answered and s unto them,	3004
	25: 8 the foolish s unto the wise, Give us of	3004
	25:12 But he answered and s, Verily I say unto	3004
	25:21 lord s unto him, Well *done, thou* good	5346
	25:22 that had received two talents came and s,	3004
	25:23 His lord s unto him, Well *done*, good and	5346
	25:24 had received the one talent came and s,	3004
	25:26 His lord answered and s unto him,	3004
	26: 1 all these sayings, he s unto his disciples,	3004
	26: 5 they s, Not on the feast *day*, lest there	3004
	26:10 Jesus understood *it*, he s unto them,	3004
	26:15 And s *unto them*, What will ye give me,	3004
	26:18 And he s, Go into the city to such a man,	3004
	26:21 as they did eat, he s, Verily I say unto	3004
	26:23 he answered and s, He that dippeth *his*	3004
	26:25 answered and s, Master, is it I?	3004
	26:25 is it I? He s unto him, Thou hast said.	3004
	26:25 is it I? He said unto him, Thou hast s.	3004
	26:26 gave *it* to the disciples, and s, Take, eat;	3004
	26:33 Peter answered and s unto him, Though	3004
	26:34 Jesus s unto him, Verily I say unto thee,	5346
	26:35 Peter s unto him, Though I should die	3004
	26:35 Likewise also s all the disciples.	3004
	26:49 he came to Jesus, and s, Hail, master;	3004
	26:50 Jesus s unto him, Friend, wherefore art	3004
	26:52 Then s Jesus unto him, Put up again thy	3004
	26:55 that *same* hour s Jesus to the multitudes,	3004
	26:61 and s, This *fellow* said, I am able to	3004
	26:61 And said, This *fellow* s, I am able to	5346
	26:62 and s unto him, Answerest thou nothing?	3004
	26:63 the high priest answered and s unto him,	3004
	26:64 Jesus saith unto him, Thou hast s:	3004
	26:66 answered and s, He is guilty of death.	3004
	26:71 him, and s unto them that were there,	3004
	26:73 *him* they that stood by, and s to Peter,	3004
	26:75 which s unto him, Before *the* cock crow,	3004
	27: 4 they s, What *is that* to us? see thou to	3004
	27: 6 chief priests took the silver pieces, and s,	3004
	27:11 And Jesus s unto him, Thou sayest.	5346
	27:13 Then s Pilate unto him, Hearest thou not	3004
	27:17 Pilate s unto them, Whom will ye that I	3004
	27:21 The governor answered and s unto them,	3004
	27:21 *that* I release unto you? They s, Barabbas.	3004
	27:23 the governor s, Why, what evil hath he	5346
	27:25 and s, His blood *be* on us, and on our	3004
	27:41 *him*, with the scribes and elders, s,	3004
	27:43 have him: for he s, I am the Son of God.	3004
	27:47 when they heard *that*, s, This man calleth	3004
	27:49 The rest s, Let be, let us see whether Elias	3004
	27:63 Sir, we remember that that deceiver s,	3004
	27:65 Pilate s unto them, Ye have a watch:	5346
	28: 5 angel answered and s unto the women,	3004
	28: 6 he is risen, as he s. Come, see the place	3004
	28:10 Then s Jesus unto them, Be not afraid:	3004
Mk	1:17 And Jesus s unto them, Come ye after me,	3004
	1:37 they s unto him, All *men* seek for thee.	3004
	1:38 he s unto them, Let us go into the next	3004
	2: 5 s unto the sick of the palsy, Son, thy sins	3004
	2: 8 within themselves, he s unto them,	3004
	2:14 of custom, and s unto him, Follow me.	3004
	2:16 and sinners, they s unto his disciples,	3004
	2:19 Jesus s unto them, Can the children of	3004
	2:24 And the Pharisees s unto him, Behold,	3004
	2:25 And he s unto them, Have ye never read	3004
	2:27 he s unto them, The sabbath was made	3004
	3:21 on him: for they s, He is beside himself.	3004
	3:22 which came down from Jerusalem s,	3004
	3:23 unto *him*, and s unto them in parables,	3004
	3:30 Because they s, He hath an unclean spirit.	3004
	3:32 and they s unto him, Behold, thy mother	3004
	3:34 s, Behold my mother and my brethren.	3004
	4: 2 and s unto them in his doctrine,	3004
	4: 9 And he s unto them, He that hath ears to	3004
	4:11 he s unto them, Unto you it is given to	3004
	4:13 And he s unto them, Know ye not this	3004
	4:21 he s unto them, Is a candle brought to	3004
	4:24 And he s unto them, Take heed what you	3004
	4:26 he s, So is the kingdom of God, as if a	3004
	4:30 And he s, Whereunto shall we liken	3004
	4:39 wind, and s unto the sea, Peace, be still.	3004
	4:40 And he s unto them, Why are ye so	3004
	4:41 s one to another, What *manner of* man	3004
	5: 7 s, What have I to do with thee, Jesus,	3004
	5: 8 For he s unto him, Come out of the man,	3004
	5:28 For she s, If I may touch but his clothes,	3004
	5:30 press, and s, Who touched my clothes?	3004
	5:31 And his disciples s unto him, Thou seest	3004
	5:34 he s unto her, Daughter, thy faith hath	3004
	5:35 the synagogue's *house* certain which s,	3004
	5:41 hand, and s unto her, TALITHA CUMI;	3004
	6: 4 But Jesus s unto them, A prophet is not	3004
	6:10 he s unto them, In what place soever	3004
	6:14 and he s, That John the Baptist was risen	3004

S

Mk		
6:15	Others s, That it is Elias. And others said,	3004
6:15	others s, That it is a prophet, or as one	3004
6:16	But when Herod heard thereof, he s, It is	3004
6:18	John had s unto Herod, It is not lawful	3004
6:22	when the daughter of the s Herodias	846
6:22	them that sat with him, the king s unto	3004
6:24	and s unto her mother, What shall I ask?	3004
6:24	And she s, The head of John the Baptist.	3004
6:31	And he s unto them, Come ye yourselves	3004
6:35	and s, This is a desert place, and now	3004
6:37	He answered and s unto them, Give ye	3004
7: 6	He answered and s unto them, Well hath	3004
7: 9	And he s unto them, Full well ye reject	3004
7:10	For Moses s, Honour thy father and	3004
7:14	all the people unto him, he s unto them,	3004
7:20	And he s, That which cometh out of	3004
7:27	But Jesus s unto her, Let the children first	3004
7:28	And she answered and s unto him, Yes,	3004
7:29	And he s unto her, For this saying go thy	3004
8: 5	many loaves have ye? And they s, Seven.	3004
8:20	fragments took ye up? And they s, Seven.	3004
8:21	And he s unto them, How is it that ye do	3004
8:24	and s, I see men as trees, walking.	3004
8:34	s unto them, Whosoever will come after	3004
9: 1	he s unto them, Verily I say unto you,	3004
9: 5	Peter answered and s to Jesus, Master,	3004
9:17	one of the multitude answered and s,	3004
9:21	this came unto him? And he s, Of a child.	3004
9:23	Jesus s unto him, If thou canst believe,	3004
9:24	and s with tears, Lord, I believe;	3004
9:26	insomuch that many s, He is dead.	3004
9:29	And he s unto them, This kind can come	3004
9:31	he taught his disciples, and s unto them,	3004
9:36	taken him in his arms, he s unto them,	3004
9:39	Jesus s, Forbid him not: for there is no	3004
10: 3	And he answered and s unto them,	3004
10: 4	And they s, Moses suffered to write a bill	3004
10: 5	And Jesus answered and s unto them,	3004
10:14	s unto them, Suffer the little children to	3004
10:18	Jesus s unto him, Why callest thou me	3004
10:20	And he answered and s unto him, Master,	3004
10:21	and s unto him, One thing thou lackest:	3004
10:29	And Jesus answered and s, Verily I say	3004
10:36	he s unto them, What would ye that I	3004
10:37	They s unto him, Grant unto us that we	3004
10:38	But Jesus s unto them, Ye know not what	3004
10:39	And they s unto him, We can. And Jesus	3004
10:39	And Jesus s unto them, Ye shall indeed	3004
10:51	And Jesus answered and s unto him,	3004
10:51	The blind man s unto him, Lord, that I	3004
10:52	And Jesus s unto him, Go thy way;	3004
11: 5	certain of them that stood there s unto	3004
11: 6	And they s unto them even as Jesus had	3004
11:14	Jesus answered and s unto it, No man	3004
11:29	Jesus answered and s unto them, I will	3004
11:33	And they answered and s unto Jesus,	3004
12: 7	But those husbandmen s amongst	3004
12:15	s unto them, Why tempt ye me?	3004
12:16	And they s unto him, Cesar's.	3004
12:17	And Jesus answering s unto them,	3004
12:24	And Jesus answering s unto them, Do ye	3004
12:32	And the scribe s unto him, Well, Master,	3004
12:32	Well, Master, thou hast s the truth:	3004
12:34	he s unto him, Thou art not far from	3004
12:35	Jesus answered and s, while he taught	3004
12:36	For David himself s by the Holy Ghost,	3004
12:36	The LORD s to my Lord, Sit thou on my	3004
12:38	And he s unto them in his doctrine,	3004
13: 2	Jesus answering s unto him, Seest thou	3004
14: 2	But they s, Not on the feast day, lest there	3004
14: 4	s, Why was this waste of the ointment	3004
14: 6	Jesus s, Let her alone; why trouble you	3004
14:12	his disciples s unto him, Where wilt thou	3004
14:16	the city, and found as he had s unto them:	3004
14:18	And as they sat and did eat, Jesus s,	3004
14:19	one by one, Is it I? and another s, Is it I?	NIG
14:20	he answered and s unto them, It is one	3004
14:22	and gave to them, and s, Take, eat:	3004
14:24	And he s unto them, This is my blood of	3004
14:29	Peter s unto him, Although all shall be	5346
14:31	thee in any wise. Likewise also s they all.	3004
14:36	And he s, Abba, Father, all things are	3004
14:48	And Jesus answered and s unto them,	3004
14:61	s unto him, Art thou the Christ, the Son	3004
14:62	Jesus s, I am: and ye shall see the Son	3004
14:67	she looked upon him, and s,	3004
14:70	they that stood by s again to Peter,	3004
14:72	to mind the word that Jesus s unto him,	3004
15: 2	he answering s unto him, Thou sayest	3004
15:12	Pilate answered and s again unto them,	3004
15:14	Then Pilate s unto them, Why, what evil	3004
15:31	Likewise also the chief priests mocking s	3004
15:35	when they heard it, s, Behold, he calleth	3004
15:39	so cried out, and gave up the ghost, he s,	3004
16: 3	And they s among themselves, Who shall	3004
16: 7	there shall ye see him, as he s unto you.	3004
16: 8	neither s they any thing to any man; for	3004
16:15	And he s unto them, Go ye into all	3004

Lk		
1:13	But the angel s unto him, Fear not,	3004
1:18	And Zacharias s unto the angel,	3004
1:19	the angel answering s unto him, I am	3004
1:28	and s, Hail, thou that art highly favoured,	3004
1:30	And the angel s unto her, Fear not, Mary:	3004
1:34	s Mary unto the angel, How shall this	3004
1:35	And the angel answered and s unto her,	3004

Lk		
1:38	And Mary s, Behold the handmaid of	3004
1:42	and s, Blessed art thou among women,	3004
1:46	And Mary s, My soul doth magnify	3004
1:60	And his mother answered and s, Not so;	3004
1:61	And they s unto her, There is none of thy	3004
2:10	And the angel s unto them, Fear not:	3004
2:15	the shepherds s one to another, Let us	3004
2:24	to that which is s in the law of the Lord,	3004
2:28	up in his arms, and blessed God, and s,	3004
2:34	and s unto Mary his mother, Behold,	3004
2:48	his mother s unto him, Son, why hast	3004
2:49	And he s unto them, How is it that ye	3004
3: 7	s he to the multitude that came forth	3004
3:12	s unto him, Master, what shall we do?	3004
3:13	And he s unto them, Exact no more than	3004
3:14	And he s unto them, Do violence to no	3004
3:22	which s, Thou art my beloved Son;	3004
4: 3	the devil s unto him, If thou be the Son	3004
4: 6	And the devil s unto him, All this power	3004
4: 8	And Jesus answered and s unto him,	3004
4: 9	s unto him, If thou be the Son of God,	3004
4:12	Jesus answering s unto him, It is said,	3004
4:12	Jesus answering said unto him, It is s,	3004
4:22	And they s, Is not this Joseph's son?	3004
4:23	And he s unto them, Ye will surely say	3004
4:24	he s, Verily I say unto you, No prophet	3004
4:43	And he s unto them, I must preach	3004
5: 4	s unto Simon, Launch out into the deep,	3004
5: 5	Simon answering s unto him, Master,	3004
5:10	And Jesus s unto Simon, Fear not;	3004
5:20	he s unto him, Man, thy sins are forgiven	3004
5:22	answering s unto them, What reason ye	3004
5:24	(he s unto the sick of the palsy,)	3004
5:27	of custom: and he s unto him, Follow me.	3004
5:31	And Jesus answering s unto them,	3004
5:33	they s unto him, Why do the disciples	3004
5:34	And he s unto them, Can ye make	3004
6: 2	And certain of the Pharisees s unto them,	3004
6: 3	And Jesus answering s unto them, Have ye not	3004
6: 5	he s unto them, That the Son of man is	3004
6: 8	s to the man which had the withered	3004
6: 9	s Jesus unto them, I will ask you one	3004
6:10	he s unto the man, Stretch forth thy hand.	3004
6:20	on his disciples, and s, Blessed be ye poor;	3004
7: 9	and s unto the people that followed him,	3004
7:13	on her, and s unto her, Weep not.	3004
7:14	And he s, Young man, I say unto thee,	3004
7:20	they s, John Baptist hath sent us unto	3004
7:22	Jesus answering s unto them, Go your	3004
7:31	And the Lord s, Whereunto then shall I	3004
7:40	And Jesus answering s unto him, Simon,	3004
7:43	Simon answered and s, I suppose that he,	3004
7:43	And he s unto him, Thou hast rightly	3004
7:44	s unto Simon, Seest thou this woman?	5346
7:48	And he s unto her, Thy sins are forgiven.	3004
7:50	And he s to the woman, Thy faith hath	3004
8: 8	And when he s these things, he cried,	3004
8:10	And he s, Unto you it is given to know	3004
8:20	And it was told him by certain which s,	3004
8:21	And he answered and s unto them,	3004
8:22	and he s unto them, Let us go over unto	3004
8:25	And he s unto them, Where is your faith?	3004
8:28	before him, and with a loud voice s,	3004
8:30	And he s, Legion: because many devils	3004
8:45	And Jesus s, Who touched me? When all	3004
8:45	Peter and they that were with him s,	3004
8:46	And Jesus s, Somebody hath touched me:	3004
8:48	And he s unto her, Daughter, be of good	3004
8:52	but he s, Weep not; she is not dead,	3004
9: 3	he s unto them, Take nothing for your	3004
9: 7	because that it was s of some,	3004
9: 9	And Herod s, John have I beheaded:	3004
9:12	then came the twelve, and s unto him,	3004
9:13	But he s unto them, Give ye them to eat.	3004
9:13	And they s, We have no more but	3004
9:14	And he s to his disciples, Make them sit	3004
9:19	They answering s, John the Baptist;	3004
9:20	He s unto them, But whom say ye that I	3004
9:20	Peter answering s, The Christ of God.	3004
9:23	he s to them all, If any man will come	3004
9:33	from him, Peter s unto Jesus, Master,	3004
9:33	and one for Elias: not knowing what he s.	3004
9:41	And Jesus answering s, O faithless and	3004
9:43	which Jesus did, he s unto his disciples,	3004
9:48	s unto them, Whosoever shall receive	3004
9:49	John answered and s, Master, we saw	3004
9:50	And Jesus s unto him, Forbid him not:	3004
9:54	disciples James and John saw this, they s,	3004
9:55	But he turned, and rebuked them, and s,	3004
9:57	a certain man s unto him, Lord, I will	3004
9:58	And Jesus s unto him, Foxes have holes,	3004
9:59	And he s unto another, Follow me.	3004
9:59	But he s, Lord, suffer me first to go and	3004
9:60	Jesus s unto him, Let the dead bury their	3004
9:61	And another also s, Lord, I will follow	3004
9:62	Jesus s unto him, No man having put	3004
10: 2	s he unto them, The harvest truly	3004
10:18	And he s unto them, I beheld Satan as	3004
10:21	and s, I thank thee, O Father, Lord of	3004
10:23	him unto his disciples, and s privately,	3004
10:26	s unto him, What is written in the law?	3004
10:27	And he answering s, Thou shalt love	3004
10:28	And he s unto him, Thou hast answered	3004
10:29	willing to justify himself, s unto Jesus,	3004
10:30	Jesus answering s, A certain man went	3004

Lk		
10:35	host, and s unto him, Take care of him;	3004
10:37	And he s, He that shewed mercy on him.	3004
10:37	Then s Jesus unto him, Go, and do thou	3004
10:40	and came to him, and s, Lord,	3004
10:41	And Jesus answered and s unto her,	3004
11: 1	one of his disciples s unto him, Lord,	3004
11: 2	And he s unto them, When ye pray, say,	3004
11: 5	And he s unto them, Which of you shall	3004
11:15	But some of them s, He casteth out devils	3004
11:17	knowing their thoughts, s unto them,	3004
11:27	and s unto him, Blessed is the womb that	3004
11:28	But he s, Yea rather, blessed are they that	3004
11:39	And the Lord s unto him, Now do ye	3004
11:45	of the lawyers, and s unto him, Master,	3004
11:46	And he s, Woe unto you also, ye lawyers!	3004
11:49	Therefore also s the wisdom of God, I will	3004
11:53	And as he s these things unto them,	3004
12:13	And one of the company s unto him,	3004
12:14	he s unto him, Man, who made me a	3004
12:15	And he s unto them, Take heed,	3004
12:18	And he s, This will I do: I will pull down	3004
12:20	God s unto him, Thou fool, this night	3004
12:22	he s unto his disciples, Therefore I say	3004
12:41	Peter s unto him, Lord, speakest thou	3004
12:42	And the Lord s, Who then is that faithful	3004
12:54	he s also to the people, When ye see a	3004
13: 2	And Jesus answering s unto them,	3004
13: 7	s he to the dresser of his vineyard,	3004
13: 8	And he answering s unto him, Lord, let it	3004
13:12	he called her to him, and s unto her,	3004
13:14	the sabbath day, and s unto the people,	3004
13:15	The Lord then answered him, and s,	3004
13:17	And when he had s these things, all his	3004
13:18	Then s he, Unto what is the kingdom of	3004
13:20	And again he s, Whereunto shall I liken	3004
13:23	Then s one unto him, Lord, are there few	3004
13:23	few that be saved? And he s unto them,	3004
13:32	And he s unto them, Go ye, and tell that	3004
14:12	Then s he also to him that bade him,	3004
14:15	him heard these things, he s unto him,	3004
14:16	s he unto him, A certain man made a	3004
14:18	first s unto him, I have bought a piece	3004
14:19	And another s, I have bought five yoke of	3004
14:20	And another s, I have married a wife,	3004
14:21	of the house being angry s to his servant,	3004
14:22	And the servant s, Lord, it is done as thou	3004
14:23	the lord s unto the servant, Go out into	3004
14:25	him: and he turned, and s unto them,	3004
15:11	And he s, A certain man had two sons:	3004
15:12	And the younger of them s to his father,	3004
15:17	And when he came to himself, he s,	3004
15:21	And the son s unto him, Father, I have	3004
15:22	the father s to his servants, Bring forth	3004
15:27	And he s unto him, Thy brother is come;	3004
15:29	And he answering s to his father,	3004
15:31	he s unto him, Son, thou art ever with	3004
16: 1	he s also unto his disciples, There was	3004
16: 2	he called him, and s unto him, How is	3004
16: 3	Then the steward s within himself,	3004
16: 5	debtors unto him, and s unto the first,	3004
16: 6	And he s, An hundred measures of oil.	3004
16: 6	And he s unto him, Take thy bill,	3004
16: 7	Then s he to another, And how much	3004
16: 7	And he s, An hundred measures of wheat.	3004
16: 7	And he s unto him, Take thy bill,	3004
16:15	And he s unto them, Ye are they which	3004
16:24	And he cried and s, Father Abraham,	3004
16:25	Abraham s, Son, remember that thou in	3004
16:27	Then he s, I pray thee therefore, father,	3004
16:30	And he s, Nay, father Abraham: but if one	3004
16:31	he s unto him, If they hear not Moses	3004
17: 1	Then s he unto the disciples, It is	3004
17: 5	And the apostles s unto the Lord,	3004
17: 6	the Lord s, If ye had faith as a grain of	3004
17:13	and s, Jesus, Master, have mercy on us.	3004
17:14	And when he saw them, he s unto them,	3004
17:17	Jesus answering s, Were there not ten	3004
17:19	he s unto him, Arise, go thy way: thy	3004
17:20	should come, he answered them and s,	3004
17:22	And he s unto the disciples, The days will	3004
17:37	they answered and s unto him, Where,	3004
17:37	he s unto them, Wheresoever the body	3004
18: 4	afterward he s within himself, Though I	3004
18: 6	the Lord s, Hear what the unjust judge	3004
18:16	But Jesus called them unto him, and s,	3004
18:19	Jesus s unto him, Why callest thou me	3004
18:21	And he s, All these have I kept from my	3004
18:22	Now when Jesus heard these things, he s	3004
18:24	saw that he was very sorrowful, he s,	3004
18:26	they that heard it s, Who then can be	3004
18:27	he s, The things which are unpossible	3004
18:28	Then Peter s, Lo, we have left all,	3004
18:29	And he s unto them, Verily I say unto you,	3004
18:31	and s unto them, Behold, we go up to	3004
18:41	and he s, Lord, that I may receive my	3004
18:42	And Jesus s unto him, Receive thy sight:	3004
19: 5	and saw him, and s unto him, Zaccheus,	3004
19: 8	And Zaccheus stood, and s unto the Lord;	3004
19: 9	Jesus s unto him, This day is salvation	3004
19:12	He s therefore, A certain nobleman went	3004
19:13	and s unto them, Occupy till I come.	3004
19:17	And he s unto him, Well, thou good	3004
19:19	he s likewise to him, Be thou also over	3004
19:24	And he s unto them that stood by,	3004
19:25	(And they s unto him, Lord, he hath ten	3004

S

Lk	19:32 and found even as he had **s** unto them.	3004
	19:33 owners thereof **s** unto them, Why loose	3004
	19:34 And they **s**, The Lord hath need of him.	3004
	19:39 from among the multitude **s** unto him,	3004
	19:40 he answered and **s** unto them, I tell	3004
	20: 3 And he answered and **s** unto them, I will	3004
	20: 8 And Jesus **s** unto them, Neither tell I you	3004
	20:13 **s** the lord of the vineyard, What shall	3004
	20:16 when they heard *it*, they **s**, God forbid.	3004
	20:17 and **s**, What is this then that is written,	3004
	20:23 and **s** unto them, Why tempt ye me?	3004
	20:24 hath it? They answered and **s**, Cesar's.	3004
	20:25 And he **s** unto them, Render therefore	3004
	20:34 And Jesus answering **s** unto them,	3004
	20:39 Then certain of the scribes answering **s**,	3004
	20:39 answering said, Master, thou hast well **s**.	3004
	20:41 And he **s** unto them, How say they that	3004
	20:42 The LORD **s** to my Lord, Sit thou on my	3004
	20:45 in the audience of all the people he **s**	3004
	21: 3 he **s**, Of a truth I say unto you, that this	3004
	21: 5 with goodly stones and gifts, he **s**,	3004
	21: 8 And he **s**, Take heed that ye be not	3004
	21:10 Then **s** he unto them, Nation shall rise	3004
	22: 9 they **s** unto him, Where wilt thou *that*	3004
	22:10 he **s** unto them, Behold, when ye are	3004
	22:13 and found as he had **s** unto them:	3004
	22:15 And he **s** unto them, With desire I have	3004
	22:17 and **s**, Take this, and divide *it* among	3004
	22:25 And he **s** unto them, The kings of	3004
	22:31 And the Lord **s**, Simon, Simon, behold,	3004
	22:33 he **s** unto him, Lord, I am ready to go	3004
	22:34 And he **s**, I tell thee, Peter, *the* cock shall	3004
	22:35 And he **s** unto them, When I sent you	3004
	22:35 shoes, lacked ye any *thing?* And they **s**,	3004
	22:36 he **s** unto them, But now, he that hath	3004
	22:38 And they **s**, Lord, behold, here *are* two	3004
	22:38 And he **s** unto them, It is enough.	3004
	22:40 he was at the place, he **s** unto them,	3004
	22:46 And **s** unto them, Why sleep ye? rise and	3004
	22:48 Jesus **s** unto him, Judas, betrayest thou	3004
	22:49 they **s** unto him, Lord, shall we smite with	3004
	22:51 And Jesus answered and **s**, Suffer ye thus	3004
	22:52 Then Jesus **s** unto the chief priests,	3004
	22:56 and earnestly looked upon him, and **s**,	3004
	22:58 saw him, and **s**, Thou art also of them.	5346
	22:58 also of them. And Peter **s**, Man, I am not.	3004
	22:60 And Peter **s**, Man, I know not what thou	3004
	22:61 how he had **s** unto him, Before *the* cock	3004
	22:67 And he **s** unto them, If I tell you, you will	3004
	22:70 Then **s** they all, Art thou then the Son of	3004
	22:70 And he **s** unto them, Ye say that I am.	5346
	22:71 And they **s**, What need we any further	3004
	23: 3 And he answered him and **s**, Thou sayest	5346
	23: 4 Then **s** Pilate to the chief priests and *to*	3004
	23:14 **S** unto them, Ye have brought this man	3004
	23:22 And he **s** unto them the third time, Why,	3004
	23:28 **s**, Daughters of Jerusalem, weep not for	3004
	23:34 **s** Jesus, Father, forgive them; for they	3004
	23:42 And he **s** unto Jesus, Lord, remember me	3004
	23:43 And Jesus **s** unto him, Verily I say unto	3004
	23:46 he **s**, Father, into thy hands I commend	3004
	23:46 and having **s** thus, he gave up the ghost.	3004
	24: 5 *their* faces to the earth, they **s** unto them,	3004
	24:17 And he **s** unto them, What *manner of*	3004
	24:18 answering **s** unto him, Art thou only a	3004
	24:19 And he **s** unto them, What *things?*	3004
	24:19 What *things?* And they **s** unto him,	3004
	24:23 of angels, which **s** that he was alive.	3004
	24:24 and found *it* even so as the women had **s**:	3004
	24:25 he **s** unto them, O fools, and slow of	3004
	24:32 And they **s** one to another, Did not our	3004
	24:38 he **s** unto them, Why are ye troubled?	3004
	24:41 and wondered, he **s** unto them, Have ye	3004
	24:44 he **s** unto them, These *are* the words	3004
	24:46 And **s** unto them, Thus it is written,	3004
Jn	1:22 Then **s** they unto him, Who art thou?	3004
	1:23 He **s**, I *am* the voice of one crying in	5346
	1:23 way of the Lord, as **s** the prophet Esaias.	3004
	1:25 And they asked him, and **s** unto him,	3004
	1:30 This is he of whom I **s**, After me cometh	3004
	1:33 baptize with water, the same **s** unto me,	3004
	1:38 They **s** unto him, Rabbi, (which is to say,	3004
	1:42 when Jesus beheld him, he **s**, Thou art	3004
	1:46 Nathanael **s** unto him, Can there any	3004
	1:48 Jesus answered and **s** unto him, Before	3004
	1:50 Jesus answered and **s** unto him, Because I	3004
	1:50 and said unto him, Because I **s** unto thee,	3004
	2:16 And **s** unto them that sold doves,	3004
	2:18 Then answered the Jews and **s** unto him,	3004
	2:19 Jesus answered and **s** unto them,	3004
	2:20 Then **s** the Jews, Forty and six years was	3004
	2:22 disciples remembered that he had **s** this	3004
	2:22 and the word which Jesus had **s**.	3004
	3: 2 to Jesus by night, and **s** unto him, Rabbi,	3004
	3: 3 Jesus answered and **s** unto him, Verily,	3004
	3: 7 Marvel not that I **s** unto thee, Ye must be	3004
	3: 9 Nicodemus answered and **s** unto him,	3004
	3:10 Jesus answered and **s** unto him, Art thou	3004
	3:26 came unto John, and **s** unto him, Rabbi,	3004
	3:27 John answered and **s**, A man can receive	3004
	3:28 that I **s**, I am not the Christ, but that I am	3004
	4:10 Jesus answered and **s** unto her, If thou	3004
	4:13 Jesus answered and **s** unto her,	3004
	4:17 The woman answered and **s**, I have no	3004
	4:17 Jesus **s** unto her, Thou hast well said, I	3004

Jn	4:17 Thou hast well **s**, I have no husband:	3004
	4:27 yet no *man* **s**, What seekest thou?	3004
	4:32 he **s** unto them, I have meat to eat that	3004
	4:33 Therefore **s** the disciples one to another,	3004
	4:42 And **s** unto the woman, *Now* we believe,	3004
	4:48 **s** Jesus unto him, Except ye see signs	3004
	4:52 And they **s** unto him, Yesterday at	3004
	4:53 in the which Jesus **s** unto him, Thy son	3004
	5:10 therefore **s** unto him that was cured,	3004
	5:11 the same **s** unto me, Take up thy bed,	3004
	5:12 What man is that which **s** unto thee,	3004
	5:14 and **s** unto him, Behold, thou art made	3004
	5:18 but **s** also that God was his Father,	3004
	5:19 Then answered Jesus and **s** unto them,	3004
	6: 6 this he **s** to prove him: for he himself	3004
	6:10 And Jesus **s**, Make the men sit down.	3004
	6:12 they were filled, he **s** unto his disciples,	3004
	6:14 had seen the miracle that Jesus did, **s**,	3004
	6:25 they **s** unto him, Rabbi, when camest	3004
	6:26 Jesus answered them and **s**, Verily, verily,	3004
	6:28 Then **s** they unto him, What shall we do,	3004
	6:29 Jesus answered and **s** unto them, This is	3004
	6:30 They **s** therefore unto him, What sign	3004
	6:32 Then Jesus **s** unto them, Verily, verily,	3004
	6:34 Then **s** they unto him, Lord, evermore	3004
	6:35 And Jesus **s** unto them, I am the bread of	3004
	6:36 But I **s** unto you, That ye also have seen	3004
	6:41 then murmured at him, because he **s**,	3004
	6:42 And they **s**, Is not this Jesus, the son of	3004
	6:43 Jesus therefore answered and **s** unto	3004
	6:53 Then Jesus **s** unto them, Verily, verily,	3004
	6:59 These *things* **s** he in the synagogue, as he	3004
	6:60 his disciples, when they had heard *this*, **s**,	3004
	6:61 he **s** unto them, Doth this offend you?	3004
	6:65 he **s**, Therefore said I unto you, that no	3004
	6:65 he said, Therefore **s** I unto you, that no	3004
	6:67 Then **s** Jesus unto the twelve, Will ye also	3004
	7: 3 His brethren therefore **s** unto him,	3004
	7: 6 Jesus **s** unto them, My time is not yet	3004
	7: 9 When he had **s** these *words* unto them,	3004
	7:11 him at the feast, and **s**, Where is he?	3004
	7:12 *for* some **s**, He is a good *man:* others said,	3004
	7:12 said, He is a good *man:* others **s**, Nay;	3004
	7:16 Jesus answered them, and **s**, My doctrine	3004
	7:20 The people answered and **s**, Thou hast a	3004
	7:21 Jesus answered and **s** unto them, I have	3004
	7:25 Then **s** some of them of Jerusalem, Is not	3004
	7:31 on him, and **s**, When Christ cometh,	3004
	7:33 Then **s** Jesus unto them, Yet a little while	3004
	7:35 Then **s** the Jews among themselves,	3004
	7:36 What *manner of* saying is this that he **s**,	3004
	7:38 believeth on me, as the scripture hath **s**,	3004
	7:40 when they heard *this* saying, **s**, Of a truth	3004
	7:41 Others **s**, This is the Christ. But some said,	3004
	7:41 But some **s**, Shall Christ come out of	3004
	7:42 Hath not the scripture **s**, That Christ	3004
	7:45 and they **s** unto them, Why have ye not	3004
	7:52 They answered and **s** unto him, Art thou	3004
	8: 6 This they **s**, tempting him, that they might	3004
	8: 7 lift up *himself*, and **s** unto them, He that	3004
	8:10 but the woman, he **s** unto her, Woman,	3004
	8:11 She **s**, No *man*, Lord. And Jesus said unto	3004
	8:11 Jesus **s** unto her, Neither do I condemn	3004
	8:13 The Pharisees therefore **s** unto him,	3004
	8:14 Jesus answered and **s** unto them, Though	3004
	8:19 **s** they unto him, Where is thy Father?	3004
	8:21 **s** Jesus again unto them, I go my way,	3004
	8:22 Then **s** the Jews, Will he kill himself?	3004
	8:23 he **s** unto them, Ye are from beneath;	3004
	8:24 I **s** therefore unto you, that ye shall die in	3004
	8:25 Then **s** they unto him, Who art thou?	3004
	8:25 Even the same that I **s** unto you *from*	2980
	8:28 **s** Jesus unto them, When ye have lift	3004
	8:31 Then **s** Jesus to those Jews which believed	3004
	8:39 They answered and **s** unto him, Abraham	3004
	8:41 Then **s** they to him, We be not born of	3004
	8:42 **s** unto them, If God were your Father,	3004
	8:48 Then answered the Jews, and **s** unto him,	3004
	8:52 **s** the Jews unto him, Now we know	3004
	8:57 **s** the Jews unto him, Thou art not yet	3004
	8:58 Jesus **s** unto them, Verily, verily, I say	3004
	9: 7 And **s** unto him, Go, wash in the pool of	3004
	9: 8 **s**, Is not this he that sat and begged?	3004
	9: 9 Some **s**, This is he: others *said*, He is like	3004
	9: 9 others **s**, He is like him: *but* he said, I am	NIG
	9: 9 *said*, He is like him: *but* he **s**, I am *he*.	3004
	9:10 Therefore **s** they unto him, How were	3004
	9:11 He answered and **s**, A man *that is* called	3004
	9:11 and anointed mine eyes, and **s** unto me,)	3004
	9:12 Then **s** they unto him, Where is he?	3004
	9:12 unto him, Where is he? He **s**, I know not.	3004
	9:15 He **s** unto them, He put clay upon mine	3004
	9:16 Therefore **s** some of the Pharisees,	3004
	9:16 Others **s**, How can a man *that is* a sinner	3004
	9:17 opened thine eyes? He **s**, He is a prophet.	3004
	9:20 His parents answered them and **s**, We	3004
	9:23 Therefore **s** his parents, He is of age;	3004
	9:24 and **s** unto him, Give God the praise:	3004
	9:25 answered and **s**, Whether he be a sinner	3004
	9:26 Then **s** they to him again, What did he to	3004
	9:28 reviled him, and **s**, Thou art his disciple;	3004
	9:30 The man answered and **s** unto them,	3004
	9:34 answered and **s** unto him, Thou wast	3004
	9:35 when he had found him, he **s** unto him,	3004
	9:36 He answered and **s**, Who is he, Lord, that	3004

Jn	9:37 Jesus **s** unto him, Thou hast both seen	3004
	9:38 And he **s**, Lord, I believe. And he	5346
	9:39 Jesus **s**, For judgment I am come into	3004
	9:40 him heard these *words*, and **s** unto him,	3004
	9:41 Jesus **s** unto them, If ye were blind,	3004
	10: 7 Then **s** Jesus unto them again, Verily,	3004
	10:20 And many of them **s**, He hath a devil,	3004
	10:21 Others **s**, These are not the words of him	3004
	10:24 Jews round about him, and **s** unto him,	3004
	10:26 ye are not of my sheep, as I **s** unto you.	3004
	10:34 not written in your law, I **s**, Ye are gods?	3004
	10:36 because I **s**, I am the Son of God?	3004
	10:41 unto him, and **s**, John did no miracle:	3004
	11: 4 Jesus heard *that*, he **s**, This sickness	3004
	11:11 These *things* **s** he: and after that he saith	3004
	11:12 Then **s** his disciples, Lord, if he sleep,	3004
	11:14 **s** Jesus unto them plainly, Lazarus is	3004
	11:16 **s** Thomas, which is called Didymus,	3004
	11:21 Then **s** Martha unto Jesus, Lord, if thou	3004
	11:25 Jesus **s** unto her, I am the resurrection,	3004
	11:28 when she had so **s**, she went her way,	3004
	11:34 And **s**, Where have ye laid him? They say	3004
	11:36 Then **s** the Jews, Behold, how he loved	3004
	11:37 And some of them **s**, Could not this *man*,	3004
	11:39 Jesus **s**, Take ye away the stone. Martha,	3004
	11:40 Jesus saith unto her, **S** I not unto thee,	3004
	11:41 And Jesus lift up *his* eyes, and **s**, Father,	3004
	11:42 the people which stand by I **s** *it*, that they	3004
	11:47 Pharisees a council, and **s**, What do we?	3004
	11:49 **s** unto them, Ye know nothing at all,	3004
	12: 6 This he **s**, not that he cared for the poor;	3004
	12: 7 **s** Jesus, Let her alone: against the day	3004
	12:19 therefore **s** among themselves,	3004
	12:29 and heard *it*, **s** that it thundered:	3004
	12:29 others **s**, An angel spake to him.	3004
	12:30 Jesus answered and **s**, This voice came	3004
	12:33 This he **s**, signifying what death he should	3004
	12:35 Jesus **s** unto them, Yet a little while is	3004
	12:39 not believe, because that Esaias **s** again,	3004
	12:41 These *things* **s** Esaias, when he saw his	3004
	12:44 Jesus cried and **s**, He that believeth on	3004
	12:50 even as the Father **s** unto me, so I speak.	3004
	13: 7 Jesus answered and **s** unto him, What I	3004
	13:11 therefore he **s**, Ye are not all clean.	3004
	13:12 and was set down again, he **s** unto them,	3004
	13:21 Jesus had thus **s**, he was troubled in	3004
	13:21 and testified, and **s**, Verily, verily, I say	3004
	13:27 Then **s** Jesus unto him, That thou doest,	3004
	13:29 had the bag, that Jesus had **s** unto him,	3004
	13:31 when he was gone out, Jesus **s**,	3004
	13:33 and as I **s** unto the Jews, Whither I go,	3004
	13:36 Simon Peter **s** unto him, Lord,	3004
	13:37 Peter **s** unto him, Lord, why cannot I	3004
	14:23 Jesus answered and **s** unto him, If a man	3004
	14:26 whatso*ever* I have **s** unto you.	3004
	14:28 have heard how I **s** unto you, I go away,	3004
	14:28 loved me, ye would rejoice, because I **s**,	3004
	15:20 Remember the word that I **s** unto you,	3004
	16: 4 And these *things* I **s** not unto you at	3004
	16: 6 because I have **s** these *things* unto you,	2980
	16:15 therefore **s** I, that he shall take of mine,	3004
	16:17 Then **s** *some* of his disciples among	3004
	16:18 **s** therefore, What is this that he saith,	3004
	16:19 and **s** unto them, Do ye inquire among	3004
	16:19 ye inquire among yourselves of that I **s**,	3004
	16:29 disciples **s** unto him, Lo, now speakest	3004
	17: 1 heaven, and **s**, Father, the hour is come;	3004
	18: 4 went forth, and **s** unto them, Whom seek	3004
	18: 6 As soon then as he had **s** unto them, I am	3004
	18: 7 And they **s**, Jesus of Nazareth.	3004
	18:11 **s** Jesus unto Peter, Put up thy sword	3004
	18:20 and in secret have I **s** nothing.	2980
	18:21 ask them which heard *me*, what I have **s**	2980
	18:21 unto them: behold, they know what I **s**.	3004
	18:25 They **s** therefore unto him, Art not thou	3004
	18:25 disciples? He denied *it*, and **s**, I am not.	3004
	18:29 Pilate then went out unto them, and **s**,	3004
	18:30 They answered and **s** unto him, If he	3004
	18:31 Then **s** Pilate unto them, Take ye him,	3004
	18:31 The Jews therefore **s** unto him, It is not	3004
	18:33 and called Jesus, and **s** unto him, Art thou	3004
	18:37 Pilate therefore **s** unto him, Art thou a	3004
	18:38 when he had **s** this, he went out again	3004
	19: 3 And **s**, Hail, King of the Jews:	3004
	19:21 Then **s** the chief priests of the Jews to	3004
	19:21 but that he **s**, I am King of the Jews.	3004
	19:24 They **s** therefore among themselves, Let	3004
	19:30 received the vinegar, he **s**, It is finished:	3004
	20:14 when she had thus **s**, she turned herself	3004
	20:20 And when he had so **s**, he shewed unto	3004
	20:21 **s** Jesus to them again, Peace *be* unto	3004
	20:22 And when he had **s** this, he breathed on	3004
	20:25 The other disciples therefore **s** unto him,	3004
	20:25 he **s** unto them, Except I shall see in his	3004
	20:26 and stood in the midst, and **s**, Peace *be*	3004
	20:28 And Thomas answered and **s** unto him,	3004
	21: 6 And he **s** unto them, Cast the net on	3004
	21:17 because he **s** unto him the third time,	3004
	21:17 he **s** unto him, Lord, thou knowest all	3004
	21:20 and **s**, Lord, which is he that betrayeth	3004
	21:23 yet Jesus **s** not unto him, He shall not die;	3004
Ac	1: 7 he **s** unto them, It is not for you to	3004
	1:11 Which also **s**, Ye men of Galilee,	3004
	1:15 and **s**, (the number of names together	3004
	1:24 And they prayed, and **s**, Thou, Lord,	3004

S

Ac	2:13 Others mocking **s**, *These men* are full of	3004
	2:14 lift up his voice, and **s** unto them, Ye men	669
	2:34 saith himself, The LORD **s** unto my Lord,	3004
	2:37 and **s** unto Peter and *to* the rest of	3004
	2:38 Then Peter **s** unto them, Repent,	5346
	3: 4 eyes upon him with John, **s**, Look on us.	3004
	3: 6 Then Peter **s**, Silver and gold have I none;	3004
	3:22 For Moses truly **s** unto the fathers,	3004
	4: 8 **s** unto them, Ye rulers of the people,	3004
	4:19 and John answered and **s** unto them,	3004
	4:23 chief priests and elders had **s** unto them.	3004
	4:24 and **s**, Lord, thou *art* God, which hast	3004
	4:25 by the mouth of thy servant David hast **s**,	3004
	4:32 neither **s** any *of them* that ought of	3004
	5: 3 Peter **s**, Ananias, why hath Satan filled	3004
	5: 8 so much? And she **s**, Yea, for so much.	3004
	5: 9 Then Peter **s** unto her, How *is it* that ye	3004
	5:19 doors, and brought them forth, and **s**,	3004
	5:29 and the *other* apostles answered and **s**,	3004
	5:35 And **s** unto them, Ye men of Israel,	3004
	6: 2 of the disciples unto *them*, and **s**,	3004
	6:11 they suborned men, which **s**, We have	3004
	6:13 And set up false witnesses, which **s**,	3004
	7: 1 **s** the high priest, Are these *things* so?	3004
	7: 2 And he **s**, Men, brethren, and fathers,	5346
	7: 3 And **s** unto him, Get thee out of thy	3004
	7: 7 shall be in bondage will I judge, **s** God:	3004
	7:33 Then **s** the Lord to him, Put off *thy* shoes	3004
	7:37 which **s** unto the children of Israel,	3004
	7:56 And **s**, Behold, I see the heavens opened,	3004
	7:60 And when he had **s** this, he fell asleep.	3004
	8:20 But Peter **s** unto him, Thy money perish	3004
	8:24 Then answered Simon, and **s**, Pray ye to	3004
	8:29 Then the Spirit **s** unto Philip, Go near,	3004
	8:30 heard him read the prophet Esaias, and **s**,	3004
	8:31 And he **s**, How can I, except some *man*	3004
	8:34 eunuch answered Philip, and **s**, I pray	3004
	8:36 and the eunuch, See, *here is* water;	5346
	8:37 Philip **s**, If thou believest with all *thine*	3004
	8:37 he answered and **s**, I believe that Jesus	3004
	9: 5 And he **s**, Who art thou, Lord?	3004
	9: 5 And the Lord **s**, I am Jesus whom thou	3004
	9: 6 And he trembling and astonished **s**, Lord	3004
	9: 6 the Lord **s** unto him, Arise, and go into	NIG
	9:10 and to him **s** the Lord in a vision, Ananias.	3004
	9:10 And he **s**, Behold, I *am* here, Lord.	3004
	9:11 the Lord **s** unto him, Arise, and go into	NIG
	9:15 But the Lord **s** unto him, Go *thy way*: for	3004
	9:17 and putting his hands on him **s**,	3004
	9:21 all that heard *him* were amazed, and **s**;	3004
	9:34 Peter **s** unto him, Aeneas, Jesus Christ	3004
	9:40 and turning *him* to the body **s**, Tabitha,	3004
	10: 4 he was afraid, and **s**, What is it, Lord?	3004
	10: 4 And he **s** unto him, Thy prayers and	3004
	10:14 But Peter **s**, Not so, Lord; for I have never	3004
	10:19 the Spirit **s** unto him, Behold, three men	3004
	10:21 and **s**, Behold, I am he whom ye seek:	3004
	10:22 they **s**, Cornelius the centurion, a just	5346
	10:28 he **s** unto them, Ye know how that it is	5346
	10:30 And Cornelius, Four days ago I was	5346
	10:31 and **s**, Cornelius, thy prayer is heard,	5346
	10:34 Then Peter opened *his* mouth, and **s**, Of	3004
	11: 8 I **s**, Not so, Lord: for nothing common	3004
	11:13 which stood and **s** unto him, Send men to	3004
	11:16 how that he **s**, John indeed baptized with	3004
	12: 8 And the angel **s** unto him, Gird thyself,	3004
	12:11 he **s**, Now I know of a surety, that the	3004
	12:15 And they **s** unto her, Thou art mad.	3004
	12:15 was *even* so. Then **s** they, It is his angel.	3004
	12:17 he **s**, *Go* shew these *things* unto James,	3004
	13: 2 fasted, the Holy Ghost **s**, Separate me	3004
	13:10 And **s**, O full of all subtilty and	3004
	13:16 and beckoning with *his* hand **s**, Men of	3004
	13:22 to whom also he gave testimony, and **s**,	3004
	13:25 course, he **s**, Whom think ye that I am?	3004
	13:34 to return to corruption, he **s** on this wise,	3004
	13:46 Paul and Barnabas waxed bold, and **s**,	3004
	14:10 **S** with a loud voice, Stand upright on thy	3004
	15: 1 **s**, Except ye be circumcised after	NIG
	15: 7 and **s** unto them, Men *and* brethren,	3004
	15:36 some days after Paul **s** unto Barnabas,	3004
	16:18 being grieved, turned and **s** to the spirit,	3004
	16:30 And brought them out, and **s**, Sirs,	5346
	16:31 And they **s**, Believe on the Lord Jesus	3004
	16:37 Paul **s** unto them, They have beaten us	5346
	17:18 And some **s**, What will this babbler say?	3004
	17:22 of Mars' hill, and **s**, *Ye* men of Athens,	5346
	17:28 as certain also of your own poets have **s**,	3004
	17:32 and others **s**, We will hear thee again of	3004
	18: 6 he shook *his* raiment, and **s** unto them,	3004
	18:14 Gallio **s** unto the Jews, If it were a matter	3004
	19: 2 He **s** unto them, Have ye received the	3004
	19: 2 And they **s** unto him, We have not so	3004
	19: 3 And he **s** unto them, Unto what then	3004
	19: 3 And they **s**, Unto John's baptism.	3004
	19: 4 Then **s** Paul, John verily baptized *with*	3004
	19:15 And the evil spirit answered and **s**, Jesus I	3004
	19:25 and **s**, Sirs, ye know that by this craft we	3004
	19:35 the people, he **s**, *Ye* men of Ephesus,	5346
	20:10 and fell on him, and embracing *him* **s**,	3004
	20:18 come to him, he **s** unto them, Ye know,	3004
	20:35 he **s**, It is more blessed to give than to	3004
	21: 4 who **s** to Paul through the Spirit, that *he*	3004
	21:11 bound his *own* hands and feet, and **s**,	3004
	21:20 and **s** unto him, Thou seest, brother,	3004

Ac	21:37 the **s** unto the chief captain, May I speak	3004
	21:37 Who **s**, Canst thou speak Greek?	5346
	21:39 Paul **s**, I am a man *which am* a Jew of	3004
	22: 8 he **s** unto me, I am Jesus of Nazareth,	3004
	22:10 And I **s**, What shall I do, Lord?	3004
	22:10 the Lord **s** unto me, Arise, and go into	3004
	22:13 and stood, and **s** unto me, Brother Saul,	3004
	22:14 And he **s**, The God of our fathers hath	3004
	22:19 I **s**, Lord, they know that I imprisoned	3004
	22:21 And he **s** unto me, Depart: for I will send	3004
	22:22 and *then* lift up their voices, and **s**,	3004
	22:25 Paul **s** unto the centurion that stood *by*,	3004
	22:27 **s** unto him, Tell me, art thou a Roman?	3004
	22:27 Tell me, art thou a Roman? He **s**, Yea.	5346
	22:28 And Paul **s**, But I was *free* born.	5346
	23: 1 the council, **s**, Men *and* brethren,	3004
	23: 3 **s** Paul unto him, God shall smite thee,	3004
	23: 4 And they that stood by **s**, Revilest thou	3004
	23: 5 Then **s** Paul, I wist not, brethren, that he	5346
	23: 7 And when he had so **s**, there arose a	2980
	23:11 by him, and **s**, Be of good cheer, Paul:	3004
	23:14 to the chief priests and elders, and **s**,	3004
	23:17 one of the centurions unto *him*, and **s**,	5346
	23:18 brought *him* to the chief captain, and **s**,	5346
	23:20 And he **s**, The Jews have agreed to desire	3004
	23:35 will hear thee, **s** he, when thine accusers	5346
	24:22 he deferred them, and **s**, When Lysias	3004
	25: 5 Let them therefore, **s** he, which among	5346
	25: 9 answered Paul, and **s**, Wilt thou go up to	3004
	25:10 Then **s** Paul, I stand at Cæsar's judgment	5346
	25:22 Then Agrippa **s** unto Festus, I would also	5346
	25:22 To morrow, **s** he, thou shalt hear him.	5346
	25:24 And Festus **s**, King Agrippa, and all men	5346
	26: 1 Then Agrippa **s** unto Paul, Thou art	5346
	26:15 I **s**, Who art thou, Lord? And he said,	3004
	26:15 And he **s**, I am Jesus whom thou	3004
	26:24 Festus **s** with a loud voice, Paul, thou art	5346
	26:25 he **s**, I am not mad, most noble Festus;	5346
	26:28 Then Agrippa **s** unto Paul, Almost thou	5346
	26:29 And Paul **s**, I would to God, that not only	3004
	26:32 Then **s** Agrippa unto Festus, This man	5346
	27:10 And **s** unto them, Sirs, I perceive that *this*	3004
	27:21 **s**, Sirs, *ye* should have hearkened unto	3004
	27:31 Paul **s** to the centurion and to the soldiers,	3004
	28: 4 they **s** among themselves, No doubt this	3004
	28: 6 *their minds*, and **s** that he was a god.	3004
	28:17 he **s** unto them, Men *and* brethren,	3004
	28:21 they **s** unto him, We neither received	3004
	28:29 when he had **s** these *words*, the Jews	3004
Ro	7: 7 the law had **s**, Thou shalt not covet.	3004
	9:12 It was **s** unto her, The elder shall serve	3004
	9:26 in the place where it was **s** unto them,	3004
	9:29 as Esaias **s** before, Except the Lord of	4302
1Co	11:24 thanks, he brake *it*, and **s**, Take, eat:	3004
2Co	6:16 as God hath **s**, I will dwell in them,	3004
	7: 3 to condemn *you*: for I have **s** before,	4302
	9: 3 this behalf; that, as I **s**, ye may be ready:	4280
	12: 9 And he **s** unto me, My grace is sufficient	3004
Gal	1: 9 As we **s** before, so say I now again, If	4280
	2:14 I **s** unto Peter before *them* all, If thou,	3004
Tit	1:12 *even* a prophet of their own, **s**,	3004
Heb	1: 5 For unto which of the angels **s** he at any	3004
	1:13 to which of the angels **s** he at any time,	3004
	3:10 and **s**, They do alway err in *their* heart;	3004
	3:15 Whilst it is **s**, To day if ye will hear his	3004
	4: 3 as *he* **s**, As I have sworn in my wrath,	3004
	4: 7 as it is **s**, To day if ye will hear his voice,	3004
	5: 5 but he that **s** unto him, Thou art my Son,	2980
	7:21 this with an oath by him that **s** unto him,	3004
	10: 7 Then **s** I, Lo, I come (in the volume of	3004
	10: 8 Above when he **s**, Sacrifice and offering	3004
	10: 9 Then **s** he, Lo, I come to do thy will,	3004
	10:15 to us: for after that *he* had **s** before,	4302
	10:30 For we know him that hath **s**,	3004
	11:18 Of whom it was **s**, That in Isaac shall thy	2980
	12:21 *that* Moses **s**, I exceedingly fear and	3004
	13: 5 for he hath **s**, I will never leave thee,	3004
Jas	2:11 For he that **s**, Do not commit adultery,	3004
	2:11 not commit adultery, **s** also, Do not kill.	3004
Jude	1: 9 but **s**, The Lord rebuke thee.	3004
Rev	4: 1 which **s**, Come up hither, and I will shew	3004
	5:14 the four beasts **s**, Amen. And the four	3004
	6:11 it was **s** unto them, that they should rest	3004
	6:16 And **s** to the mountains and rocks, Fall	3004
	7:14 And I **s** unto him, Sir, thou knowest.	3004
	7:14 he **s** to me, These are they which came	3004
	10: 8 and **s**, Go *and* take the little book which	3004
	10: 9 and **s** unto him, Give me the little book.	3004
	10: 9 And he **s** unto me, Take *it*, and eat it up;	3004
	10:11 And he **s** unto me, Thou must prophesy	3004
	17: 7 And the angel **s** unto me, Wherefore didst	3004
	19: 3 And again they **s**, Alleluia. And her smoke	3004
	19:10 he **s** unto me, See *thou do it* not: I am	3004
	21: 5 he that sat upon the throne **s**, Behold,	3004
	21: 5 he **s** unto me, Write: for these words	3004
	21: 6 And he **s** unto me, It is done. I am Alpha	3004
	22: 6 And he **s** unto me, These sayings *are*	3004

SAIDST (22) [SAY]

Ge	12:19 Why **s** thou, She *is* my sister? so I might	559
	26: 9 how **s** thou, She *is* my sister? And Isaac	559
	32: 9 father Isaac, the LORD which **s** unto me,	559
	32:12 thou **s**, I will surely do thee good,	559
	44:21 thou **s** unto thy servants, Bring him down	559
	44:23 thou **s** unto thy servants, Except your	559

Ex	32:13 swarest by thine own self, and **s** unto	1696
Jdg	9:38 wherewith thou **s**, Who *is* Abimelech,	559
1Ki	2:42 thou **s** unto me, The word *that* I have	559
Job	35: 2 Thinkest thou this to be right, *that* thou **s**,	559
	35: 3 For thou **s**, What advantage will it be unto	559
Ps	27: 8 *When thou* **s**, Seek ye my face; my heart	NIH
	89:19 **s**, I have laid help upon *one that* is mighty;	559
Isa	47: 7 thou **s**, I shall be a lady for ever: *so that*	559
	57:10 thy way; *yet* **s** thou not, There is no hope:	559
Jer	2:20 thy bands; and thou **s**, I will not transgress;	559
	2:25 thou **s**, There is no hope: no; for I have	559
	22:21 thy prosperity; *but* thou **s**, I will not hear.	559
La	3:57 *that* I called upon thee: thou **s**, Fear not.	559
Eze	25: 3 Because thou **s**, Aha, against my sanctuary,	559
Hos	13:10 judges *of* whom thou **s**, Give me a king	559
Jn	4:18 is not thy husband: *in* that **s** thou truly.	3004

SAIL (8) [SAILED, SAILERS, SAILING]

Isa	33:23 their mast, they could not spread the **s**:	5251
Eze	27: 7 which thou spreadest forth to be thy **s**;	5251
Ac	20: 3 for him, as he was about to **s** into Syria,	321
	20:16 For Paul had determined to **s** by Ephesus,	3896
	27: 1 when it was determined that we should **s**	321
	27: 2 meaning to **s** by the coasts of Asia;	4126
	27:17 strake **s**, and so were driven.	4632
	27:24 God hath given thee all them that **s** with	4126

SAILED (15) [SAIL]

Lk	8:23 But as they **s** he fell asleep: and there	4126
Ac	13: 4 and from thence they **s** to Cyprus.	636
	14:26 thence **s** to Antioch, from whence they	636
	15:39 Barnabas took Mark, and **s** unto Cyprus;	1602
	18:18 and **s** *thence* into Syria, and with him	1602
	18:21 if God will. And he **s** from Ephesus.	321
	20: 6 we **s** away from Philippi after the days	1602
	20:13 we went before to ship, and **s** unto Assos,	321
	20:15 And we **s** thence, and came the next *day*	636
	21: 3 and **s** into Syria, and landed at Tyre:	4126
	27: 4 we **s** under Cyprus, because the winds	5284
	27: 5 when we had **s** over the sea of Cilicia	1277
	27: 7 And when we had **s** slowly many days,	1020
	27: 7 we **s** under Crete, over against Salmone;	5284
	27:13 loosing *thence*, they **s** close by Crete.	3881

SAILERS (1) [SAIL]

Rev	18:17 and **s**, and as many as trade by sea,	3492

SAILING (3) [SAIL]

Ac	21: 2 And finding a ship **s** over unto Phenicia,	1276
	27: 6 found a ship of Alexandria into Italy;	4126
	27: 9 and when **s** was now dangerous, because	4144

SAILORS See SHIPMEN

SAINT (5) [SAINTS, SAINTS']

Ps	106:16 the camp, *and* Aaron the **s** of the LORD.	6918
Da	8:13 I heard one speaking, and another saint	6918
	8:13 another **s** said unto that certain saint	6918
	8:13 another saint said unto that certain **s**	NIH
Php	4:21 Salute every **s** in Christ Jesus. The brethren	40

SAINTS (95) [SAINT]

Dt	33: 2 and he came with ten thousands of **s**:	6944
	33: 3 loved the people; all his **s** *are* in thy hand:	6918
1Sa	2: 9 He will keep the feet of his **s**,	2623
2Ch	6:41 and let thy **s** rejoice in goodness.	2623
Job	5: 1 and to which of the **s** wilt thou turn?	6918
	15:15 Behold, he putteth no trust in his **s**; yea,	6918
Ps	16: 3 *But* to the **s** that *are* in the earth, and *to*	6918
	30: 4 O ye **s** of his, and give thanks at	2623
	31:23 O love the LORD, all ye his **s**:	2623
	34: 9 O fear the LORD, ye his **s**: for *there is* no	6918
	37:28 loveth judgment, and forsaketh not his **s**;	2623
	50: 5 Gather my **s** together unto me; those that	2623
	52: 9 on thy name; for *it is* good before thy **s**.	2623
	79: 2 the flesh of thy **s** unto the beasts of	2623
	85: 8 speak peace unto his people, and to his **s**:	2623
	89: 5 also in the congregation of the **s**.	6918
	89: 7 to be feared in the assembly of the **s**,	6918
	97:10 he preserveth the souls of his **s**;	2623
	116:15 sight of the LORD *is* the death of his **s**.	2623
	132: 9 and let thy **s** shout for joy.	2623
	132:16 and her **s** shall shout aloud for joy.	2623
	145:10 O LORD; and thy **s** shall bless thee.	2623
	148:14 horn of his people, the praise of all his **s**;	2623
	149: 1 *and* his praise in the congregation of the **s**.	2623
	149: 5 Let the **s** be joyful in glory: let them sing	2623
	149: 9 this honour have all his **s**. Praise ye	2623
Pr	2: 8 and preserveth the way of his **s**.	2623
Da	7:18 the **s** of the most High shall take	6922
	7:21 and the same horn made war with the **s**,	6922
	7:22 judgment *was* given to the **s** of the most	6922
	7:22 the time came that the **s** possessed	6922
	7:25 shall wear out the **s** of the most High,	6922
	7:27 *shall* be given to the people of the **s** of	6922
Hos	11:12 with God, and is faithful with the **s**.	6918
Zec	14: 5 God shall come, *and* all the **s** with thee.	6918
Mt	27:52 and many bodies of **s** which slept arose,	40
Ac	9:13 how much evil he hath done to thy **s** at	40
	9:32 down also to the **s** which dwelt at Lydda,	40
	9:41 when he had called the **s** and widows,	40
	26:10 and many of the **s** did I shut up in prison,	40
Ro	1: 7 in Rome, beloved of God, called *to be* **s**:	40
	8:27 maketh intercession for the **s** according to	40
	12:13 Distributing to the necessity of **s**; given to	40
	15:25 I go unto Jerusalem to minister unto the **s**.	40

S

Ref	Text	Num
Ro 15:26	for the poor **s** which are at Jerusalem.	40
15:31	for Jerusalem may be accepted of the **s**;	40
16: 2	as becometh **s**, and *that* ye assist her in	40
16:15	and all the **s** which are with them.	40
1Co 1: 2	are sanctified in Christ Jesus, called *to be* **s**,	40
6: 1	law before the unjust, and not before the **s**?	40
6: 2	Do ye not know that the **s** shall judge	40
14:33	but of peace, as in all churches of the **s**.	40
16: 1	Now concerning the collection for the **s**,	40
16:15	themselves to the ministry of the **s**,)	40
2Co 1: 1	with all the **s** which are in all Achaia:	40
8: 4	the fellowship of the ministering to the **s**.	40
9: 1	as touching the ministering to the **s**, it is	40
9:12	not only supplieth the want of the **s**,	40
13:13	All the **s** salute you.	40
Eph 1: 1	to the **s** which are at Ephesus, and to	40
1:15	in the Lord Jesus, and love unto all the **s**,	40
1:18	of the glory of his inheritance in the **s**,	40
2:19	but fellowcitizens with the **s**, and of	40
3: 8	Unto me, *who am* less than the least of all **s**,	40
3:18	be able to comprehend with all **s** what *is*	40
4:12	For the perfecting of the **s** for the work of	40
5: 3	once named amongst you, as becometh **s**;	40
6:18	all perseverance and supplication for all **s**;	40
Php 1: 1	to all the **s** in Christ Jesus which are at	40
4:22	All the **s** salute you, chiefly they that are of	40
Col 1: 2	To the **s** and faithful brethren in Christ	40
1: 4	of the love which *ye have* to all the **s**,	40
1:12	partakers of the inheritance of the **s** in light:	40
1:26	but now is made manifest to his **s**:	40
1Th 3:13	of our Lord Jesus Christ with all his **s**.	40
2Th 1:10	When he shall come to be glorified in his **s**,	40
Phm 1: 5	toward the Lord Jesus, and toward all **s**;	40
1: 7	the bowels of the **s** are refreshed by thee,	40
Heb 6:10	in that ye have ministered to the **s**,	40
13:24	that have the rule over you, and all the **s**.	40
Jude 1: 3	faith which was once delivered unto the **s**.	40
1:14	Lord cometh with ten thousands of his **s**,	40
Rev 5: 8	full of odours, which are the prayers of **s**.	40
8: 3	he should offer *it* with the prayers of all **s**	40
8: 4	*which came* with the prayers of the **s**,	40
11:18	and to the **s**, and them that fear thy name,	40
13: 7	was given unto him to make war with the **s**,	40
13:10	Here is the patience and the faith of the **s**.	40
14:12	Here is the patience of the **s**: here *are* they	40
15: 3	just and true *are* thy ways, thou King of **s**.	40
16: 6	For they have shed the blood of **s** and	40
17: 6	woman drunken with the blood of the **s**,	40
18:24	and of **s**, and of all that were slain upon	40
19: 8	for the fine linen is the righteousness of **s**.	40
20: 9	and compassed the camp of the **s** about,	40

SAINTS' (1) [SAINT]

Ref	Text	Num
1Ti 5:10	if she have washed the **s** feet,	40

SAITH (1262) [SAY]

Ref	Text	Num
Ge 22:16	the Lord, for because thou hast done	5002
32: 4	Thy servant Jacob **s** thus, I have sojourned	559
41:55	Go unto Joseph; what he **s** to you,	559
44: 7	Wherefore **s** my lord these words?	1696
45: 9	and say unto him, Thus **s** thy son Joseph,	559
Ex 4:22	Thus **s** the Lord, Israel *is* my son,	559
5: 1	Thus **s** the Lord God of Israel,	559
5:10	to the people, saying, Thus **s** Pharaoh,	559
7:17	Thus **s** the Lord, In this thou shalt know	559
8: 1	and say unto him, Thus **s** the Lord,	559
8:20	say unto him, Thus **s** the Lord, Let my	559
9: 1	Thus **s** the Lord God of the Hebrews,	559
9:13	Thus **s** the Lord God of the Hebrews,	559
10: 3	Thus **s** the Lord God of the Hebrews,	559
11: 4	Moses said, Thus **s** the Lord,	559
32:27	unto them, Thus **s** the Lord God of Israel,	559
Nu 14:28	unto them, *As truly as* I live, **s** the Lord,	5002
20:14	Thus **s** thy brother Israel, Thou knowest	559
22:16	to him, Thus **s** Balak the son of Zippor,	559
24:13	*but* what the Lord **s**, that will I speak?	1696
22:27	before the Lord to battle, as my lord **s**.	1696
Jos 5:14	him, What **s** my lord unto his servant?	1696
7:13	for thus **s** the Lord God of Israel, *There is*	559
22:16	Thus **s** the whole congregation of	559
24: 2	the people, Thus **s** the Lord God of Israel,	559
Jdg 6: 8	unto them, Thus **s** the Lord God of Israel,	559
11:15	said unto him, Thus **s** Jephthah, Israel took	559
1Sa 2:27	and said unto him, Thus **s** the Lord,	559
2:30	Wherefore the Lord God of Israel **s**,	5002
2:30	now the Lord **s**, Be it far from me;	5002
9: 6	all that he **s** cometh surely to pass:	1696
10:18	Thus **s** the Lord God of Israel, I brought	559
15: 2	Thus **s** the Lord of hosts, I remember *that*	559
20: 3	he **s**, Let not Jonathan know this, lest he	559
24:13	As **s** the proverb of the ancients,	559
2Sa 7: 5	tell my servant David, Thus **s** the Lord,	559
7: 8	Thus **s** the Lord of hosts, I took thee from	559
12: 7	Thus **s** the Lord God of Israel, I anointed	559
12:11	Thus **s** the Lord, Behold, I will raise up	559
14:10	Whosoever **s** *ought* unto thee, bring him	1696
17: 5	and let us hear likewise what he **s**. 6310+871.1	
24:12	Go and say unto David, Thus **s** the Lord,	559
1Ki 2:30	unto him, Thus **s** the king, Come forth.	559
3:23	the king, The one **s**, This *is* my son that	559
3:23	the other **s**, Nay; but thy son *is* the dead,	559
11:31	for thus **s** the Lord, the God of Israel,	559
12:24	Thus **s** the Lord, Ye shall not go up,	559
13: 2	and said, O altar, altar, thus **s** the Lord;	559
13:21	from Judah, saying, Thus **s** the Lord,	559

Ref	Text	Num
1Ki 14: 7	Thus **s** the Lord God of Israel,	559
17:14	For thus **s** the Lord God of Israel,	559
20: 2	and said unto him, Thus **s** Ben-hadad,	559
20:13	saying, Thus **s** the Lord, Hast thou seen	559
20:14	he said, Thus **s** the Lord, *Even* by	559
20:28	king of Israel, and said, Thus **s** the Lord,	559
20:32	said, Thy servant Ben-hadad **s**, I pray thee,	559
20:42	he said unto him, Thus **s** the Lord,	559
21:19	saying, Thus **s** the Lord, Hast thou killed,	559
21:19	speak unto him, saying, Thus **s** the Lord,	559
22:11	he said, Thus **s** the Lord, With these shalt	559
22:14	what the Lord **s** unto me, that will I	559
22:27	say, Thus **s** the king, Put this *fellow in*	559
2Ki 1: 4	Now therefore thus **s** the Lord, Thou shalt	559
1: 6	Thus **s** the Lord, *Is it* not because *there is*	559
1:16	he said unto him, Thus **s** the Lord,	559
2:21	salt in there, and said, Thus **s** the Lord,	559
3:16	he said, Thus **s** the Lord, Make this valley	559
3:17	For thus **s** the Lord, Ye shall not see	559
4:43	for thus **s** the Lord, They shall eat,	559
5:13	when he **s** to thee, Wash, and be clean?	559
7: 1	Thus **s** the Lord, To morrow about *this*	559
9: 3	*it* on his head, and say, Thus **s** the Lord,	559
9: 6	unto him, Thus **s** the Lord God of Israel,	559
9:12	spake he to me, saying, Thus **s** the Lord,	559
9:18	and said, Thus **s** the king, *Is it* peace?	559
9:19	and said, Thus **s** the king, *Is it* peace?	559
9:26	and the blood of his sons, **s** the Lord;	5002
9:26	will requite thee in this plat, **s** the Lord.	5002
18:19	Thus **s** the great king, the king of Assyria,	559
18:29	Thus **s** the king, Let not Hezekiah deceive	559
18:31	for thus **s** the king of Assyria, Make *an*	559
19: 3	they said unto him, Thus **s** Hezekiah,	559
19: 6	ye say to your master, Thus **s** the Lord,	559
19:20	Thus **s** the Lord God of Israel,	559
19:32	Therefore thus **s** the Lord concerning	559
19:33	shall not come into this city, **s** the Lord.	5002
20: 1	said unto him, Thus **s** the Lord, Set thine	559
20: 5	Thus **s** the Lord, the God of David thy	559
20:17	nothing shall be left, **s** the Lord.	559
21:12	Therefore thus **s** the Lord God of Israel,	559
22:15	unto them, Thus **s** the Lord God of Israel,	559
22:16	Thus **s** the Lord, Behold, I will bring evil	559
22:18	say to him, Thus **s** the Lord God of Israel,	559
22:19	I also have heard *thee*, **s** the Lord.	5002
1Ch 17: 4	tell David my servant, Thus **s** the Lord,	559
17: 7	Thus **s** the Lord of hosts, I took thee from	559
21:10	and tell David, saying, Thus **s** the Lord,	559
21:11	unto him, Thus **s** the Lord, Choose thee	559
2Ch 11: 4	Thus **s** the Lord, Ye shall not go up,	559
12: 5	and said unto them, Thus **s** the Lord,	559
18:10	said, Thus **s** the Lord, With these thou	559
18:13	even what my God **s**, that will I speak.	559
18:26	say, Thus **s** the king, Put this *fellow in*	559
20:15	Thus **s** the Lord unto you,	559
21:12	Thus **s** the Lord God of David thy father,	559
24:20	people, and said unto them, Thus **s** God,	559
32:10	Thus **s** Sennacherib king of Assyria,	559
34:23	Thus **s** the Lord God of Israel,	559
34:24	Thus **s** the Lord, Behold, I will bring evil	559
34:26	Thus **s** the Lord God of Israel concerning	559
34:27	I have even heard *thee* also, **s** the Lord.	5002
36:23	Thus **s** Cyrus king of Persia,	559
Ezr 1: 2	Thus **s** Cyrus king of Persia, The Lord	559
Ne 6: 6	Gashmu **s** *it, that* thou and the Jews think	559
Job 28:14	The depth **s**, It *is* not in me: and the sea	559
28:14	not in me: and the sea **s**, *It is* not with me.	559
33:24	he is gracious unto him, and **s**, Deliver him	559
35:10	none **s**, Where *is* God my Maker, who	559
37: 6	For he **s** to the snow, Be thou *on the earth*;	559
39:25	He **s** among the trumpets, Ha, ha;	559
Ps 12: 5	of the needy, now will I arise, **s** the Lord;	559
36: 1	The transgression of the wicked **s** within	5002
50:16	unto the wicked God **s**, What hast thou to	559
Pr 9: 4	that wanteth understanding, she **s** to him,	559
9:16	that wanteth understanding, she **s** to him,	559
20:14	*It is* naught, *it is* naught, **s** the buyer:	559
22:13	The slothful *man* **s**, There is a lion without,	559
23: 7	Eat and drink, he **s** to thee; but his heart *is*	559
24:24	He that **s** unto the wicked, Thou *art*	559
26:13	The slothful *man* **s**, There *is* a lion in	559
26:19	his neighbour, and **s**, Am not I in sport?	559
28:24	robbeth his father or his mother, and **s**,	559
30:16	and the fire *that* **s** not, *It is* enough.	559
30:20	she eateth, and wipeth her mouth, and **s**,	559
Ecc 1: 2	vanities, **s** the Preacher, vanity of vanities;	559
4: 8	neither *s* he, For whom do I labour,	NIH
7:27	Behold, this have I found, **s** the Preacher,	559
10: 3	and he **s** to every one *that* he *is* a fool.	559
12: 8	Vanity of vanities, **s** the Preacher; all *is*	559
Isa 1:11	the Lord: I am full *of* the burnt offerings	559
1:18	and let us reason together, **s** the Lord:	559
1:24	Therefore **s** the Lord, the Lord of hosts,	5002
3:15	of the poor? **s** the Lord God of hosts.	5002
3:16	Moreover the Lord **s**, Because	559
7: 7	Thus **s** the Lord God, It shall not stand,	559
10: 8	For he **s**, *Are* not my princes altogether	559
10:13	he **s**, By the strength of my hand I have	559
10:24	Therefore thus **s** the Lord God of hosts,	559
14:22	the Lord of hosts, and cut off from	5002
14:22	and son, and nephew, **s** the Lord.	5002
14:23	of destruction, **s** the Lord of hosts.	5002
17: 3	children of Israel, **s** the Lord of hosts.	5002
17: 6	**s** the Lord God of Israel.	5002
19: 4	over them, **s** the Lord, the Lord of hosts.	5002

Ref	Text	Num
Isa 22:14	you till ye die, **s** the Lord God of hosts.	559
22:15	Thus **s** the Lord God of hosts, Go, get thee	559
22:25	In that day, **s** the Lord of hosts, shall	5002
28:16	Therefore thus **s** the Lord God, Behold,	559
29:11	and he **s**, I cannot; for it *is* sealed:	559
29:12	I pray thee: and he **s**, I am not learned.	559
29:22	Therefore thus **s** the Lord, who redeemed	559
30: 1	**s** the Lord, that take counsel, but not of	5002
30:12	Wherefore thus **s** the Holy One of Israel,	559
30:15	For thus **s** the Lord God, the Holy One of	559
31: 9	**s** the Lord, whose fire *is* in Zion, and his	5002
33:10	Now will I rise, **s** the Lord; now will I	559
36: 4	Thus **s** the great king, the king of Assyria,	559
36:14	Thus **s** the king, Let not Hezekiah deceive	559
36:16	for thus **s** the king of Assyria, Make *an*	559
37: 3	they said unto him, Thus **s** Hezekiah,	559
37: 6	ye say unto your master, Thus **s** the Lord,	559
37:21	Thus **s** the Lord God of Israel,	559
37:33	Therefore thus **s** the Lord concerning	559
37:34	shall not come into this city, **s** the Lord.	5002
38: 1	said unto him, Thus **s** the Lord, Set thine	559
38: 5	Go and say to Hezekiah, Thus **s** the Lord,	559
39: 6	nothing shall be left, **s** the Lord.	559
40: 1	comfort ye my people, **s** your God.	559
40:25	or shall I be equal? **s** the Holy One.	5002
41:14	help thee, **s** the Lord, and thy redeemer,	5002
41:21	Produce your cause, **s** the Lord;	559
41:21	bring forth your strong *reasons*, **s** the King	559
42: 5	Thus **s** God the Lord, he that created	559
42:22	*for* a spoil, and none **s**, Restore.	559
43: 1	But now thus **s** the Lord that created thee,	559
43:10	**s** the Lord, and my servant whom I have	5002
43:12	my witnesses, **s** the Lord, that I *am* God.	5002
43:14	Thus **s** the Lord, your redeemer, the Holy	559
43:16	Thus **s** the Lord, which maketh a way in	559
44: 2	Thus **s** the Lord that made thee,	559
44: 6	Thus **s** the Lord the King of Israel,	559
44:16	**s**, Aha, I am warm, I have seen the fire:	559
44:17	and prayeth unto it, and **s**, Deliver me;	559
44:24	Thus **s** the Lord, thy redeemer,	559
44:26	**s** to Jerusalem, Thou shalt be inhabited;	559
44:27	That **s** to the deep, Be dry, and I will dry	559
44:28	That **s** of Cyrus, *He is* my shepherd,	559
45: 1	Thus **s** the Lord to his anointed, to Cyrus,	559
45:10	Woe unto him that **s** unto *his* father,	559
45:11	Thus **s** the Lord, the Holy One of Israel,	559
45:13	for price nor reward, **s** the Lord of hosts.	559
45:14	Thus **s** the Lord, The labour of Egypt,	559
45:18	For thus **s** the Lord that created	559
48:17	Thus **s** the Lord, thy redeemer, the Holy	559
48:22	*is* no peace, **s** the Lord, unto the wicked.	559
49: 5	**s** the Lord that formed me from	559
49: 7	Thus **s** the Lord, the redeemer of Israel,	559
49: 8	Thus **s** the Lord, In an acceptable time	559
49:18	*As* I live, **s** the Lord, thou shalt surely	5002
49:22	Thus **s** the Lord God, Behold, I will lift up	559
49:25	thus **s** the Lord, Even the captives of	559
50: 1	Thus **s** the Lord, Where *is* the bill of your	559
51:22	Thus **s** thy Lord the Lord, and thy God	559
52: 3	For thus **s** the Lord, Ye have sold	559
52: 4	For thus **s** the Lord God, My people went	559
52: 5	what have I here, **s** the Lord,	5002
52: 5	them make *them* to howl, **s** the Lord;	5002
52: 7	that **s** unto Zion, Thy God reigneth!	559
54: 1	children of the married wife, **s** the Lord.	559
54: 6	youth, when thou wast refused, **s** thy God.	559
54: 8	mercy on thee, **s** the Lord thy redeemer.	559
54:10	**s** the Lord that hath mercy on thee.	5002
54:17	their righteousness *is* of me, **s** the Lord.	5002
55: 8	*are* your ways my ways, **s** the Lord.	5002
56: 1	Thus **s** the Lord, Keep ye judgment,	559
56: 4	For thus **s** the Lord unto the eunuchs that	559
56: 8	which gathereth the outcasts of Israel **s**,	5002
57:15	For thus **s** the high and lofty One that	559
57:19	far off, and to *him that is* near, **s** the Lord;	559
57:21	*is* no peace, **s** my God, to the wicked.	559
59:20	from transgression in Jacob, **s** the Lord.	5002
59:21	*is* my covenant with them, **s** the Lord;	559
59:21	**s** the Lord, from henceforth and for ever.	559
65: 7	of your fathers together, **s** the Lord,	559
65: 8	Thus **s** the Lord, As the new wine is	559
65: 8	in the cluster, and *one* **s**, Destroy it not;	559
65:13	Therefore thus **s** the Lord God, Behold,	559
65:25	in all my holy mountain, **s** the Lord.	559
66: 1	Thus **s** the Lord, The heaven *is* my	559
66: 2	all those *things* have been, **s** the Lord.	5002
66: 9	**s** the Lord: shall I cause to bring forth,	559
66: 9	forth, and shut *the womb?* **s** thy God.	559
66:12	For thus **s** the Lord, Behold, I will extend	559
66:17	shall be consumed together, **s** the Lord.	5002
66:20	my holy mountain Jerusalem, **s** the Lord,	559
66:21	for priests *and* for Levites, **s** the Lord.	559
66:22	**s** the Lord, so shall your seed and	5002
66:23	come to worship before me, **s** the Lord.	559
Jer 1: 8	*am* with thee to deliver thee, **s** the Lord.	5002
1:15	of the kingdoms of the north, **s** the Lord;	5002
1:19	*am* with thee, **s** the Lord, to deliver thee.	5002
2: 2	of Jerusalem, saying, Thus **s** the Lord;	559
2: 3	evil shall come upon them, **s** the Lord.	5002
2: 5	Thus **s** the Lord, What iniquity have your	559
2: 9	**s** the Lord, and with your children's	5002
2:12	be ye very desolate, **s** the Lord.	5002
2:19	*is* not in thee, **s** the Lord God of hosts.	5002
2:22	*is* marked before me, **s** the Lord God.	5002
2:29	transgressed against me, **s** the Lord.	5002

Jer		
3: 1	yet return again to me, **s** the LORD.	5002
3:10	whole heart, but feignedly, **s** the LORD.	5002
3:12	thou backsliding Israel, **s** the LORD;	5002
3:12	**s** the LORD, *and* I will not keep *anger* for	5002
3:13	have not obeyed my voice, **s** the LORD.	5002
3:14	O backsliding children, **s** the LORD;	5002
3:16	in the land, in those days, **s** the LORD,	5002
3:20	with me, O house of Israel, **s** the LORD.	5002
4: 1	O Israel, **s** the LORD, return unto me:	5002
4: 3	For thus **s** the LORD to the men of Judah	559
4: 9	come to pass at that day, **s** the LORD,	5002
4:17	been rebellious against me, **s** the LORD.	5002
5: 9	Shall I not visit for these *things?* **s**	5002
5:11	treacherously against me, **s** the LORD.	5002
5:14	Wherefore thus **s** the LORD God of hosts,	559
5:15	from far, O house of Israel, **s** the LORD:	5002
5:18	Nevertheless in those days, **s** the LORD,	5002
5:22	**s** the LORD: will ye not tremble at my	5002
5:29	Shall I not visit for these *things?* **s**	5002
6: 9	Thus **s** the LORD of hosts, They shall	559
6:12	the inhabitants of the land, **s** the LORD.	5002
6:15	them they shall be cast down, **s** the LORD.	559
6:16	Thus **s** the LORD, Stand ye in the ways,	559
6:21	Therefore thus **s** the LORD, Behold, I will	559
6:22	Thus **s** the LORD, Behold, a people cometh	559
7: 3	Thus **s** the LORD of hosts, the God of	559
7:11	Behold, even I have seen *it*, **s** the LORD.	5002
7:13	**s** the LORD, and I spake unto you,	5002
7:19	**s** the LORD: *do they* not *provoke*	5002
7:20	Therefore thus **s** the LORD GOD; Behold,	559
7:21	Thus **s** the LORD of hosts, the God of	559
7:30	have done evil in my sight, **s** the LORD:	5002
7:32	the days come, **s** the LORD,	5002
8: 1	At that time, **s** the LORD, they shall bring	5002
8: 3	I have driven them, **s** the LORD of hosts.	5002
8: 4	shalt say unto them, Thus **s** the LORD;	559
8:12	they shall be cast down, **s** the LORD.	559
8:13	I will surely consume them, **s** the LORD:	5002
8:17	and they shall bite you, **s** the LORD.	5002
9: 3	and they know not me, **s** the LORD.	5002
9: 6	they refuse to know me, **s** the LORD.	5002
9: 7	Therefore thus **s** the LORD of hosts,	559
9: 9	Shall I not visit them for these *things?* **s**	5002
9:13	the LORD **s**, Because they have forsaken	559
9:15	Therefore thus **s** the LORD of hosts,	559
9:17	Thus **s** the LORD of hosts, Consider ye,	559
9:22	Speak, Thus **s** the LORD, Even	5002
9:23	Thus **s** the LORD, Let not the wise *man*	559
9:24	for in these *things* I delight, **s** the LORD.	5002
9:25	Behold, the days come, **s** the LORD, that I	5002
10: 2	Thus **s** the LORD, Learn not the way of	559
10:18	For thus **s** the LORD, Behold, I will sling	559
11: 3	unto them, Thus **s** the LORD God of Israel;	559
11:11	Therefore thus **s** the LORD, Behold, I *will*	559
11:21	Therefore thus **s** the LORD of the men of	559
11:22	Therefore thus **s** the LORD of hosts,	559
12:14	Thus **s** the LORD against all mine evil	559
12:17	and destroy that nation, **s** the LORD.	5002
13: 1	Thus **s** the LORD unto me, Go and get thee	559
13: 9	Thus **s** the LORD, After this manner will I	559
13:11	the whole house of Judah, **s** the LORD;	5002
13:12	Thus **s** the LORD God of Israel,	559
13:13	say unto them, Thus **s** the LORD, Behold,	559
13:14	and the sons together, **s** the LORD:	5002
13:25	of thy measures from me, **s** the LORD;	5002
14:10	Thus **s** the LORD unto this people, Thus	559
14:15	Therefore thus **s** the LORD concerning	559
15: 2	then thou shalt tell them, Thus **s** the LORD;	559
15: 3	over them four kinds, **s** the LORD:	5002
15: 6	Thou hast forsaken me, **s** the LORD,	5002
15: 9	sword before their enemies, **s** the LORD.	5002
15:19	Therefore thus **s** the LORD, If thou return,	559
15:20	save thee and to deliver thee, **s** the LORD.	5002
16: 3	For thus **s** the LORD concerning the sons	559
16: 5	For thus **s** the LORD, Enter not *into*	559
16: 5	the LORD, *even* lovingkindness and	5002
16: 9	For thus **s** the LORD of hosts, the God of	559
16:11	in me, and have walked after other	5002
16:14	the days come, **s** the LORD,	5002
16:16	**s** the LORD, and they shall fish them;	5002
17: 5	Thus **s** the LORD; Cursed *be* the man that	559
17:21	Thus **s** the LORD; Take heed to yourselves,	559
17:24	diligently hearken unto me, **s** the LORD,	5002
18: 6	**s** the LORD. Behold, as the clay *is* in	5002
18:11	of Jerusalem, saying, Thus **s** the LORD;	559
18:13	Therefore thus **s** the LORD; Ask ye now	559
19: 1	Thus **s** the LORD, Go and get a potter's	559
19: 3	Thus **s** the LORD of hosts, the God of	559
19: 6	the days come, **s** the LORD,	5002
19:11	say unto them, Thus **s** the LORD of hosts;	559
19:12	**s** the LORD, and to the inhabitants	5002
19:15	Thus **s** the LORD of hosts, the God of	559
20: 4	For thus **s** the LORD, Behold, I will make	559
21: 4	Thus **s** the LORD God of Israel; Behold,	559
21: 7	afterward, **s** the LORD, I will deliver	5002
21: 8	people thou shalt say, Thus **s** the LORD;	559
21:10	for evil, and not for good, **s** the LORD:	5002
21:12	O house of David, thus **s** the LORD;	559
21:13	*and* rock of the plain, **s** the LORD;	5002
21:14	to the fruit of your doings, **s** the LORD:	5002
22: 1	Thus **s** the LORD; Go down *to* the house of	559
22: 3	Thus **s** the LORD; Execute ye judgment	559
22: 5	I swear by myself, **s** the LORD,	5002
22: 6	For thus **s** the LORD unto the king's house	559
22:11	For thus **s** the LORD touching Shallum	559

Jer		
22:14	That **s**, I will build me a wide house and	559
22:16	*was* not this to know me? **s** the LORD.	5002
22:18	Therefore thus **s** the LORD concerning	559
22:24	*As* I live, **s** the LORD, though Coniah	5002
22:30	Thus **s** the LORD, Write ye this man	559
23: 1	the sheep of my pasture! **s** the LORD.	5002
23: 2	Therefore thus **s** the LORD God of Israel	559
23: 2	you the evil of your doings, **s** the LORD.	5002
23: 4	neither shall they be lacking, **s** the LORD.	5002
23: 5	Behold, the days come, **s** the LORD, that I	5002
23: 7	the days come, **s** the LORD,	5002
23:11	I found their wickedness, **s** the LORD.	5002
23:12	the year of their visitation, **s** the LORD.	5002
23:15	Therefore thus **s** the LORD of hosts	559
23:16	Thus **s** the LORD of hosts, Hearken not	559
23:23	**s** the LORD, and not a God afar off?	5002
23:24	**s** the LORD. Do not I fill heaven and	5002
23:24	not I fill heaven and earth? **s** the LORD.	5002
23:28	*is* the chaff to the wheat? **s** the LORD.	5002
23:29	**s** the LORD; and like a hammer *that*	5002
23:30	I *am* against the prophets, **s** the LORD,	5002
23:31	**s** the LORD, that use their tongues,	5002
23:31	that use their tongues, and say, He **s**.	5002
23:32	**s** the LORD, and do tell them,	5002
23:32	not profit this people at all, **s** the LORD.	5002
23:33	I will even forsake you, **s** the LORD.	5002
23:38	of the LORD; therefore thus **s** the LORD,	559
24: 5	Thus **s** the LORD, the God of Israel;	559
24: 8	surely thus **s** the LORD, So will I give	559
25: 7	have not hearkened unto me, **s** the LORD;	5002
25: 8	Therefore thus **s** the LORD of hosts;	559
25: 9	**s** the LORD, and Nebuchadrezzar the king	5002
25:12	that nation, **s** the LORD, for their iniquity,	5002
25:15	For thus **s** the LORD God of Israel unto	559
25:27	Thus **s** the LORD of hosts, the God of	559
25:28	say unto them, Thus **s** the LORD of hosts;	559
25:29	of the earth, **s** the LORD of hosts.	5002
25:31	*that are* wicked to the sword, **s** the LORD.	5002
25:32	Thus **s** the LORD of hosts, Behold,	559
26: 2	Thus **s** the LORD; Stand in the court of	559
26: 4	shalt say unto them, Thus **s** the LORD;	559
26:18	saying, Thus **s** the LORD of hosts;	559
27: 2	Thus **s** the LORD to me; Make thee bonds	559
27: 4	Thus **s** the LORD of hosts, the God of	559
27: 8	**s** the LORD, with the sword, and with	5002
27:11	still in their own land, **s** the LORD;	5002
27:15	For I have not sent them, **s** the LORD,	5002
27:16	all this people, saying, Thus **s** the LORD;	559
27:19	For thus **s** the LORD of hosts concerning	559
27:21	Yea, thus **s** the LORD of hosts, the God of	559
27:22	the day that I visit them, **s** the LORD;	5002
28: 4	that went into Babylon, **s** the LORD:	5002
28:11	of all the people, saying, Thus **s** the LORD;	559
28:13	tell Hananiah, saying, Thus **s** the LORD;	559
28:14	For thus **s** the LORD of hosts, the God of	559
28:16	Therefore thus **s** the LORD; Behold, I will	559
29: 4	Thus **s** the LORD of hosts, the God of	559
29: 8	For thus **s** the LORD of hosts, the God of	559
29: 9	I have not sent them, **s** the LORD.	5002
29:10	For thus **s** the LORD, That after seventy	559
29:11	**s** the LORD, thoughts of peace, and not of	5002
29:14	I will be found of you, **s** the LORD:	5002
29:14	whither I have driven you, **s** the LORD;	5002
29:16	*Know* that thus **s** the LORD of the king that	559
29:17	Thus **s** the LORD of hosts; Behold, I will	559
29:19	not hearkened to my words, **s** the LORD,	5002
29:19	but ye would not hear, **s** the LORD.	5002
29:21	Thus **s** the LORD of hosts, the God of	559
29:23	I know, and *am* a witness, **s** the LORD.	5002
29:31	Thus **s** the LORD concerning Shemaiah	559
29:32	Therefore thus **s** the LORD; Behold, I will	559
29:32	that I will do for my people, **s** the LORD;	5002
30: 3	For lo, the days come, **s** the LORD, that I	5002
30: 3	my people Israel and Judah, **s** the LORD:	559
30: 5	For thus **s** the LORD; We have heard a	559
30: 8	to pass in that day, **s** the LORD of hosts,	5002
30:10	O my servant Jacob, **s** the LORD;	5002
30:11	I *am* with thee, **s** the LORD, to save thee:	5002
30:12	For thus **s** the LORD, Thy bruise *is*	559
30:17	will heal thee of thy wounds, **s** the LORD;	5002
30:18	Thus **s** the LORD; Behold, I *will* bring	559
30:21	heart to approach unto me? **s** the LORD.	5002
31: 1	At the same time, **s** the LORD, will I be	5002
31: 2	Thus **s** the LORD, The people which were	559
31: 7	For thus **s** the LORD; Sing with gladness	559
31:14	satisfied with my goodness, **s** the LORD.	5002
31:15	Thus **s** the LORD; A voice was heard in	559
31:16	Thus **s** the LORD; Refrain thy voice from	559
31:16	thy work shall be rewarded, **s** the LORD;	5002
31:17	there is hope in thine end, **s** the LORD,	5002
31:20	surely have mercy upon him, **s** the LORD.	5002
31:23	Thus **s** the LORD of hosts, the God of	559
31:27	Behold, the days come, **s** the LORD, that I	5002
31:28	to build, and to plant, **s** the LORD.	5002
31:31	Behold, the days come, **s** the LORD, that I	5002
31:32	I was a husband unto them, **s** the LORD:	5002
31:33	After those days, **s** the LORD, I will put	5002
31:34	unto the greatest of them, **s** the LORD:	5002
31:35	Thus **s** the LORD, which giveth the sun for	559
31:36	**s** the LORD, *then* the seed of Israel also	5002
31:37	Thus **s** the LORD; If heaven above can be	559
31:37	for all that they have done, **s** the LORD.	5002
31:38	Behold, the days come, **s** the LORD,	5002
32: 3	and say, Thus **s** the LORD, Behold,	559
32: 5	shall he be until I visit him, **s** the LORD:	5002

Jer		
32:14	Thus **s** the LORD of hosts, the God of	559
32:15	For thus **s** the LORD of hosts, the God of	559
32:28	Therefore thus **s** the LORD; Behold, I *will*	559
32:30	with the work of their hands, **s** the LORD.	5002
32:36	now therefore thus **s** the LORD, the God of	559
32:42	For thus **s** the LORD; Like as I have	559
32:44	their captivity to return, **s** the LORD.	5002
33: 2	Thus **s** the LORD the maker thereof,	559
33: 4	For thus **s** the LORD, the God of Israel,	559
33:10	Thus **s** the LORD; Again there shall be	559
33:11	of the land as at the first, **s** the LORD.	559
33:12	Thus **s** the LORD of hosts, Again in this	559
33:13	hands of him that telleth *them*, **s** the LORD.	559
33:14	Behold, the days come, **s** the LORD, that I	5002
33:17	For thus **s** the LORD; David shall never	559
33:20	Thus **s** the LORD; If ye can break my	559
33:25	Thus **s** the LORD; If my covenant *be* not	559
34: 2	Thus **s** the LORD, the God of Israel;	559
34: 2	of Judah, and tell him, Thus **s** the LORD;	559
34: 4	thus **s** the LORD of thee, Thou shalt not	559
34: 5	I have pronounced the word, **s** the LORD.	5002
34:13	Thus **s** the LORD, the God of Israel;	559
34:17	Therefore thus **s** the LORD; Ye have not	559
34:17	**s** the LORD, to the sword,	5002
34:22	**s** the LORD, and cause them to return to	5002
35:13	Thus **s** the LORD of hosts, the God of	559
35:13	to hearken to my words? **s** the LORD.	5002
35:17	Therefore thus **s** the LORD God of hosts,	559
35:18	Thus **s** the LORD of hosts, the God of	559
35:19	Therefore thus **s** the LORD of hosts,	559
36:29	king of Judah, Thus **s** the LORD;	559
36:30	Therefore thus **s** the LORD of Jehoiakim	559
37: 7	Thus **s** the LORD, the God of Israel;	559
37: 9	Thus **s** the LORD; Deceive not yourselves,	559
38: 2	Thus **s** the LORD, He that remaineth in this	559
38: 3	Thus **s** the LORD, This city shall surely be	559
38:17	Thus **s** the LORD, the God of hosts,	559
39:16	saying, Thus **s** the LORD of hosts, the God	559
39:17	will deliver thee in that day, **s** the LORD:	5002
39:18	thou hast put thy trust in me, **s** the LORD.	5002
42: 9	Thus **s** the LORD, the God of Israel,	559
42:11	be not afraid of him, **s** the LORD:	5002
42:15	Thus **s** the LORD of hosts, the God of	559
42:18	For thus **s** the LORD of hosts, the God of	559
43:10	Thus **s** the LORD of hosts, the God of	559
44: 2	Thus **s** the LORD of hosts, the God of	559
44: 7	Therefore now thus **s** the LORD, the God	559
44:11	Therefore thus **s** the LORD of hosts,	559
44:25	Thus **s** the LORD of hosts, the God of	559
44:26	sworn by my great name, **s** the LORD,	559
44:29	this *shall be* a sign unto you, **s** the LORD,	5002
44:30	Thus **s** the LORD; Behold, I *will* give	559
45: 2	Thus **s** the LORD, the God of Israel,	559
45: 4	shalt thou say unto him, The LORD **s** thus;	559
45: 5	*will* bring evil upon all flesh, **s** the LORD:	5002
46: 5	*for* fear *was* round about, **s** the LORD.	5002
46: 8	he **s**, I will go up, *and* will cover the earth;	559
46:18	*As* I live, **s** the King, whose name *is*	5002
46:23	**s** the LORD, though it cannot be searched;	5002
46:25	The LORD of hosts, the God of Israel, **s**;	559
46:26	as *in* the days of old, **s** the LORD.	5002
46:28	O Jacob my servant, **s** the LORD:	5002
47: 2	Thus **s** the LORD; Behold, waters rise up	559
48: 1	Against Moab thus **s** the LORD of hosts,	559
48:12	the days come, **s** the LORD,	5002
48:15	**s** the King, whose name *is* the LORD of	5002
48:25	and his arm is broken, **s** the LORD.	5002
48:30	I know his wrath, **s** the LORD; but *it shall*	5002
48:35	**s** the LORD, him that offereth *in* the high	5002
48:38	wherein *is* no pleasure, **s** the LORD.	5002
48:40	For thus **s** the LORD; Behold, he shall fly	559
48:43	O inhabitant of Moab, **s** the LORD.	5002
48:44	the year of their visitation, **s** the LORD.	5002
48:47	of Moab in the latter days, **s** the LORD.	5002
49: 1	the Ammonites, thus **s** the LORD;	559
49: 2	the days come, **s** the LORD,	5002
49: 2	unto them that were his heirs, **s** the LORD.	559
49: 5	a fear upon thee, **s** the Lord GOD of hosts,	5002
49: 6	of the children of Ammon, **s** the LORD.	5002
49: 7	thus **s** the LORD of hosts;	559
49:12	For thus **s** the LORD; Behold, they whose	559
49:13	For I have sworn by myself, **s** the LORD,	5002
49:16	thee down from thence, **s** the LORD.	5002
49:18	So the LORD, no man shall abide there,	559
49:26	cut off in that day, **s** the LORD of hosts.	5002
49:28	of Babylon shall smite, thus **s** the LORD;	559
49:30	O ye inhabitants of Hazor, **s** the LORD;	5002
49:31	that dwelleth without care, **s** the LORD,	5002
49:32	from all sides thereof, **s** the LORD.	5002
49:35	Thus **s** the LORD of hosts; Behold, I *will*	559
49:37	*even* my fierce anger, **s** the LORD;	5002
49:38	the king and the princes, **s** the LORD.	5002
49:39	again the captivity of Elam, **s** the LORD.	5002
50: 4	those days, and in that time, **s** the LORD,	559
50:10	spoil her shall be satisfied, **s** the LORD.	5002
50:18	Therefore thus **s** the LORD of hosts,	559
50:20	those days, and in that time, **s** the LORD,	5002
50:21	**s** the LORD, and do according to all that I	5002
50:30	shall be cut off in that day, **s** the LORD.	5002
50:31	most proud, **s** the Lord GOD of hosts:	5002
50:33	Thus **s** the LORD of hosts; The children of	559
50:35	**s** the LORD, and upon the inhabitants of	5002
50:40	the neighbour *cities* thereof, **s** the LORD;	5002
51: 1	Thus **s** the LORD; Behold, I *will* raise up	559
51:24	done in Zion in your sight, **s** the LORD.	5002

Jer	51:25 O destroying mountain, **s** the LORD,	5002
	51:26 shalt be desolate for ever, **s** the LORD.	559
	51:33 For thus **s** the LORD of hosts, the God of	559
	51:36 Therefore thus **s** the LORD; Behold, I *will*	559
	51:39 and not wake, **s** the LORD.	5002
	51:48 unto her from the north, **s** the LORD.	5002
	51:52 the days come, **s** the LORD,	5002
	51:53 shall spoilers come unto her, **s** the LORD.	5002
	51:57 perpetual sleep, and not wake, **s** the King,	5002
	51:58 Thus **s** the LORD of hosts; The broad walls	559
La	3:24 The LORD *is* my portion, O my soul;	559
	3:37 Who *is* he *that* **s**, and it cometh to pass,	559
Eze	2: 4 shalt say unto them, Thus **s** the Lord GOD.	559
	3:11 and tell them, Thus **s** the Lord GOD;	559
	3:27 shalt say unto them, Thus **s** the Lord GOD;	559
	5: 5 Thus **s** the Lord GOD; This *is* Jerusalem:	559
	5: 7 Therefore thus **s** the Lord GOD;	559
	5: 8 Therefore thus **s** the Lord GOD; Behold,	559
	5:11 Wherefore, *as* I live, **s** the Lord GOD;	5002
	6: 3 Thus **s** the Lord GOD to the mountains,	559
	6:11 Thus **s** the Lord GOD; Smite with thine	559
	7: 2 thus **s** the Lord GOD unto the land of	559
	7: 5 Thus **s** the Lord GOD; An evil, an only	559
	11: 5 said unto me, Speak; Thus **s** the LORD;	559
	11: 7 Therefore thus **s** the Lord GOD; Your slain	559
	11: 8 bring a sword upon you, **s** the Lord GOD.	5002
	11:16 Therefore say, Thus **s** the Lord GOD;	559
	11:17 Therefore say, Thus **s** the Lord GOD; I will	559
	11:21 upon their own heads, **s** the Lord GOD.	5002
	12:10 Say thou unto them, Thus **s** the Lord GOD;	559
	12:19 Thus **s** the Lord GOD, of the inhabitants of	559
	12:23 Tell them therefore, Thus **s** the Lord GOD;	559
	12:25 and will perform it, **s** the Lord GOD.	5002
	12:28 say unto them, Thus **s** the Lord GOD;	559
	12:28 spoken shall be done, **s** the Lord GOD.	5002
	13: 3 Thus **s** the Lord GOD; Woe unto	559
	13: 6 lying divination, saying, The LORD **s**:	5002
	13: 7 The LORD **s** *it;* albeit I have not spoken?	5002
	13: 8 Therefore thus **s** the Lord GOD;	559
	13: 8 behold, I *am* against you, **s** the Lord GOD.	5002
	13:13 Therefore thus **s** the Lord GOD; I will even	559
	13:16 and *there is* no peace, **s** the Lord GOD.	5002
	13:18 say, Thus **s** the Lord GOD; Woe to	559
	13:20 Wherefore thus **s** the Lord GOD; Behold,	559
	14: 4 and say unto them, Thus **s** the Lord GOD;	559
	14: 6 the house of Israel, Thus **s** the Lord GOD;	559
	14:11 and I may be their God, **s** the Lord GOD.	5002
	14:14 by their righteousness, **s** the Lord GOD.	5002
	14:16 men *were* in it, *as* I live, **s** the Lord GOD,	5002
	14:18 men *were* in it, *as* I live, **s** the Lord GOD,	5002
	14:20 Job, *were* in it, *as* I live, **s** the Lord GOD,	5002
	14:21 For thus **s** the Lord GOD; How much more	559
	14:23 all that I have done in it, **s** the Lord GOD.	5002
	15: 6 Therefore thus **s** the Lord GOD;	559
	15: 8 committed a trespass, **s** the Lord GOD.	5002
	16: 3 Thus **s** the Lord GOD unto Jerusalem;	559
	16: 8 the Lord GOD, and thou becamest mine.	5002
	16:14 I had put upon thee, **s** the Lord GOD.	5002
	16:19 and *thus* it was, **s** the Lord GOD.	5002
	16:23 (woe, woe unto thee! **s** the Lord GOD;)	5002
	16:30 How weak is thine heart, **s** the Lord GOD,	5002
	16:36 Thus **s** the Lord GOD; Because thy	559
	16:43 thy way upon *thine* head, **s** the Lord GOD:	5002
	16:48 *As* I live, **s** the Lord GOD, Sodom thy	5002
	16:58 and thine abominations, **s** the LORD.	5002
	16:59 For thus **s** the Lord GOD; I will even deal	559
	16:63 all that thou hast done, **s** the Lord GOD.	5002
	17: 3 say, Thus **s** the Lord GOD; A great eagle	559
	17: 9 Say thou, Thus **s** the Lord GOD; Shall it	559
	17:16 *As* I live, **s** the Lord GOD, surely in	5002
	17:19 Therefore thus **s** the Lord GOD; *As* I live,	559
	17:22 Thus **s** the Lord GOD; I will also take of	559
	18: 3 *As* I live, **s** the Lord GOD, ye shall not	5002
	18: 9 he shall surely live, **s** the Lord GOD.	5002
	18:23 the Lord GOD: *and* not that he should	5002
	18:29 Yet **s** the house of Israel, The way of	559
	18:30 according to his ways, **s** the Lord GOD.	5002
	18:32 death of him that dieth, **s** the Lord GOD:	5002
	20: 3 and say unto them, Thus **s** the Lord GOD;	559
	20: 3 *As* I live, **s** the Lord GOD, I will not be	5002
	20: 5 And say unto them, Thus **s** the Lord GOD;	559
	20:27 and say unto them, Thus **s** the Lord GOD;	559
	20:30 the house of Israel, Thus **s** the Lord GOD;	559
	20:31 *As* I live, **s** the Lord GOD, I will not be	5002
	20:33 *As* I live, **s** the Lord GOD, surely with a	5002
	20:36 so will I plead with you, **s** the Lord GOD.	5002
	20:39 O house of Israel, thus **s** the Lord GOD;	559
	20:40 the Lord GOD, there shall all the house	5002
	20:44 O ye house of Israel, **s** the Lord GOD.	5002
	20:47 Thus **s** the Lord GOD; Behold, I *will* kindle	559
	21: 3 say to the land of Israel, Thus **s** the LORD;	559
	21: 7 shall be brought to pass, **s** the Lord GOD.	559
	21: 9 prophesy, and say, Thus **s** the LORD;	559
	21:13 it shall be no *more,* **s** the Lord GOD.	5002
	21:24 Therefore thus **s** the Lord GOD;	559
	21:26 Thus **s** the Lord GOD; Remove the diadem,	559
	21:28 Thus **s** the Lord GOD concerning	559
	22: 3 say thou, Thus **s** the Lord GOD, The city	559
	22:12 and hast forgotten me, **s** the Lord GOD.	5002
	22:19 Therefore thus **s** the Lord GOD;	559
	22:28 unto them, saying, Thus **s** the Lord GOD,	559
	22:31 upon their heads, **s** the Lord GOD.	5002
	23:22 O Aholibah, thus **s** the Lord GOD;	559
	23:28 For thus **s** the Lord GOD; Behold, I *will*	559
	23:32 Thus **s** the Lord GOD; Thou shalt drink *of*	559

Eze	23:34 for I have spoken *it,* **s** the Lord GOD.	5002
	23:35 Therefore thus **s** the Lord GOD;	559
	23:46 For thus **s** the Lord GOD; *I will* bring up a	559
	24: 3 and say unto them, Thus **s** the Lord GOD;	559
	24: 6 Wherefore thus **s** the Lord GOD; Woe to	559
	24: 9 Therefore thus **s** the Lord GOD; Woe to	559
	24:14 shall they judge thee, **s** the Lord GOD.	5002
	24:21 the house of Israel, Thus **s** the Lord GOD;	559
	25: 3 Thus **s** the Lord GOD; Because thou saidst,	559
	25: 6 For thus **s** the Lord GOD; Because thou	559
	25: 8 Thus **s** the Lord GOD; Because that Moab	559
	25:12 Thus **s** the Lord GOD; Because that Edom	559
	25:13 Therefore thus **s** the Lord GOD; I will also	559
	25:14 know my vengeance, **s** the Lord GOD.	5002
	25:15 Thus **s** the Lord GOD; Because	559
	25:16 Therefore thus **s** the Lord GOD; Behold,	559
	26: 3 Therefore thus **s** the Lord GOD; Behold,	559
	26: 5 for I have spoken *it,* **s** the Lord GOD:	5002
	26: 7 For thus **s** the Lord GOD; Behold, I *will*	559
	26:14 for I the LORD have spoken *it,* **s** the Lord	5002
	26:15 Thus **s** the Lord GOD to Tyrus; Shall not	559
	26:19 For thus **s** the Lord GOD; When I shall	559
	26:21 never be found again, **s** the Lord GOD.	5002
	27: 3 for many isles, Thus **s** the Lord GOD;	559
	28: 2 the prince of Tyrus, Thus **s** the Lord GOD;	559
	28: 6 Therefore thus **s** the Lord GOD;	559
	28:10 for I have spoken *it,* **s** the Lord GOD.	5002
	28:12 and say unto him, Thus **s** the Lord GOD;	559
	28:22 say, Thus **s** the Lord GOD; Behold, I *am*	559
	28:25 Thus **s** the Lord GOD; When I shall have	559
	29: 3 Speak, and say, Thus **s** the Lord GOD;	559
	29: 8 Therefore thus **s** the Lord GOD; Behold,	559
	29:13 Yet thus **s** the Lord GOD; At the end of	559
	29:19 Therefore thus **s** the Lord GOD; Behold,	559
	29:20 they wrought for me, **s** the Lord GOD.	5002
	30: 2 prophesy and say, Thus **s** the Lord GOD;	559
	30: 6 Thus **s** the LORD; They also that uphold	559
	30: 6 fall in it by the sword, **s** the Lord GOD.	5002
	30:10 Thus **s** the Lord GOD; I will also make	559
	30:13 Thus **s** the Lord GOD; I will also destroy	559
	30:22 Therefore thus **s** the Lord GOD; Behold,	559
	31:10 Therefore thus **s** the Lord GOD;	559
	31:15 Thus **s** the Lord GOD; In the day when he	559
	31:18 and all his multitude, **s** the Lord GOD.	5002
	32: 3 Thus **s** the Lord GOD; I will therefore	559
	32: 8 darkness upon thy land, **s** the Lord GOD.	5002
	32:11 For thus **s** the Lord GOD; The sword of	559
	32:14 rivers to run like oil, **s** the Lord GOD.	5002
	32:16 and for all her multitude, **s** the Lord GOD.	5002
	32:31 army slain by the sword, **s** the Lord GOD.	5002
	32:32 and all his multitude, **s** the Lord GOD.	5002
	33:11 Say unto them, *As* I live, **s** the Lord GOD,	5002
	33:25 say unto them, Thus **s** the Lord GOD;	559
	33:27 thus unto them, Thus **s** the Lord GOD;	559
	34: 2 the Lord GOD unto the shepherds;	559
	34: 8 the Lord GOD, surely because my flock	5002
	34:10 Thus **s** the Lord GOD; Behold, I *am* against	559
	34:11 For thus **s** the Lord GOD; Behold, I, *even* I,	559
	34:15 cause them to lie down, **s** the Lord GOD.	5002
	34:17 *for* you, O my flock, thus **s** the Lord GOD;	559
	34:20 Therefore thus **s** the Lord GOD unto them;	559
	34:30 of Israel, *are* my people, **s** the Lord GOD.	5002
	34:31 and I *am* your God, **s** the Lord GOD.	5002
	35: 3 say unto it, Thus **s** the Lord GOD; Behold,	559
	35: 6 Therefore, *as* I live, **s** the Lord GOD,	5002
	35:11 Therefore, *as* I live, **s** the Lord GOD,	5002
	35:14 Thus **s** the Lord GOD; When the whole	559
	36: 2 Thus **s** the Lord GOD; Because the enemy	559
	36: 3 and say, Thus **s** the Lord GOD;	559
	36: 4 Thus **s** the Lord GOD to the mountains,	559
	36: 5 Therefore thus **s** the Lord GOD; Surely in	559
	36: 6 and to the valleys, Thus **s** the Lord GOD;	559
	36: 7 Therefore thus **s** the Lord GOD; I have	559
	36:13 Thus **s** the Lord GOD; Because they say	559
	36:14 thy nations any more, **s** the Lord GOD.	5002
	36:15 nations to fall any more, **s** the Lord GOD.	5002
	36:22 the house of Israel, Thus **s** the Lord GOD;	559
	36:23 that I *am* the LORD, **s** the Lord GOD,	5002
	36:32 Not for your sakes do I *this,* **s** the Lord	5002
	36:33 Thus **s** the Lord GOD; In the day that I	559
	36:37 Thus **s** the Lord GOD; I will yet *for* this be	559
	37: 5 Thus **s** the Lord GOD unto these bones;	559
	37: 9 and say to the wind, Thus **s** the Lord GOD;	559
	37:12 and say unto them, Thus **s** the Lord GOD;	559
	37:14 spoken *it,* and performed *it,* **s** the LORD.	5002
	37:19 Say unto them, Thus **s** the Lord GOD;	559
	37:21 And say unto them, Thus **s** the Lord GOD;	559
	38: 3 say, Thus **s** the Lord GOD; Behold, I *am*	559
	38:10 Thus **s** the Lord GOD; It shall also come to	559
	38:14 and say unto Gog, Thus **s** the Lord GOD;	559
	38:17 Thus **s** the Lord GOD; *Art* thou he of	559
	38:18 **s** the Lord GOD, *that* my fury shall come	5002
	38:21 all my mountains, **s** the Lord GOD:	5002
	39: 1 and say, Thus **s** the Lord GOD;	559
	39: 5 for I have spoken *it,* **s** the Lord GOD.	5002
	39: 8 it is come, and it is done, **s** the Lord GOD;	5002
	39:10 those that robbed them, **s** the Lord GOD.	5002
	39:13 that I shall be glorified, **s** the Lord GOD.	5002
	39:17 thou son of man, thus **s** the Lord GOD;	559
	39:20 and *with* all men of war, **s** the Lord GOD.	5002
	39:25 Therefore thus **s** the Lord GOD; Now will I	559
	39:29 upon the house of Israel, **s** the Lord GOD.	5002
	43:18 unto me, Son of man, thus **s** the Lord GOD;	559
	43:19 to minister unto me, **s** the Lord GOD,	5002
	43:27 and I will accept you, **s** the Lord GOD.	5002

Eze	44: 6 the house of Israel, Thus **s** the Lord GOD;	559
	44: 9 Thus **s** the Lord GOD; No stranger,	559
	44:12 **s** the Lord GOD, and they shall bear their	5002
	44:15 me the fat and the blood, **s** the Lord GOD:	5002
	44:27 offer his sin offering, **s** the Lord GOD.	5002
	45: 9 Thus **s** the Lord GOD; Let it suffice you,	559
	45: 9 from my people, **s** the Lord GOD.	5002
	45:15 reconciliation for them, **s** the Lord GOD.	5002
	45:18 Thus **s** the Lord GOD; In the first *month,* in	559
	46: 1 Thus **s** the Lord GOD; The gate of the inner	559
	46:16 Thus **s** the Lord GOD; If the prince give a	559
	47:13 Thus **s** the Lord GOD; This *shall be*	559
	47:23 give *him* his inheritance, **s** the Lord GOD.	5002
	48:29 these *are* their portions, **s** the Lord GOD.	5002
Hos	2:13 her lovers, and forgat me, **s** the LORD.	5002
	2:16 it shall be at that day, **s** the LORD,	5002
	2:21 I will hear, **s** the LORD, I will hear	5002
	11:11 place them in their houses, **s** the LORD.	5002
Joel	2:12 Therefore also now, **s** the LORD, turn ye	5002
Am	1: 3 Thus **s** the LORD; For three transgressions	559
	1: 5 go into captivity unto Kir, **s** the LORD.	559
	1: 6 Thus **s** the LORD; For three transgressions	559
	1: 8 Philistines shall perish, **s** the Lord GOD.	559
	1: 9 Thus **s** the LORD; For three transgressions	559
	1:11 Thus **s** the LORD; For three transgressions	559
	1:13 Thus **s** the LORD; For three transgressions	559
	1:15 he and his princes together, **s** the LORD.	559
	2: 1 Thus **s** the LORD; For three transgressions	559
	2: 3 the princes thereof with him, **s** the LORD.	559
	2: 4 Thus **s** the LORD; For three transgressions	559
	2: 6 Thus **s** the LORD; For three transgressions	559
	2:11 O ye children of Israel? **s** the LORD.	5002
	2:16 flee away naked in that day, **s** the LORD.	5002
	3:10 So do, who store up violence and	5002
	3:11 Therefore thus **s** the Lord GOD;	559
	3:12 Thus **s** the LORD; As the shepherd taketh	559
	3:13 **s** the Lord GOD, the God of hosts,	5002
	3:15 houses shall have an end, **s** the LORD.	5002
	4: 3 cast *them* into the palace, **s** the LORD.	5002
	4: 5 O ye children of Israel, **s** the Lord GOD.	5002
	4: 6 ye not returned unto me, **s** the LORD.	5002
	4: 8 ye not returned unto me, **s** the LORD.	5002
	4: 9 ye not returned unto me, **s** the LORD.	5002
	4:10 ye not returned unto me, **s** the LORD.	5002
	4:11 ye not returned unto me, **s** the LORD.	5002
	5: 3 For thus **s** the Lord GOD; The city that	559
	5: 4 For thus **s** the LORD unto the house of	559
	5:16 the God of hosts, the Lord, **s** thus;	559
	5:17 for I will pass through thee, **s** the LORD.	559
	5:27 **s** the LORD, whose name *is* The God of	559
	6: 8 the LORD the God of hosts, I abhor	5002
	6:14 of Israel, **s** the LORD the God of hosts;	5002
	7: 3 for this: It shall not be, **s** the LORD.	559
	7: 6 This also shall not be, **s** the Lord GOD.	559
	7:11 For thus Amos **s**, Jeroboam shall die by	559
	7:17 Therefore thus **s** the LORD; Thy wife shall	559
	8: 3 be howlings in that day, **s** the Lord GOD:	5002
	8: 9 come to pass in that day, **s** the Lord GOD,	5002
	8:11 Behold, the days come, **s** the Lord GOD,	5002
	9: 7 **s** the LORD. Have not I brought up Israel	5002
	9: 8 destroy the house of Jacob, **s** the LORD.	5002
	9:12 by my name, **s** the LORD that doeth this.	5002
	9:13 Behold, the days come, **s** the LORD,	5002
	9:15 I have given them, **s** the LORD thy God.	559
Ob	1: 1 Thus **s** the Lord GOD concerning Edom;	559
	1: 3 **s** in his heart, Who shall bring me down	559
	1: 4 will I bring thee down, **s** the LORD.	5002
	1: 8 Shall I not in that day, **s** the LORD,	5002
Mic	2: 3 Therefore thus **s** the LORD; Behold,	559
	3: 5 Thus **s** the LORD concerning the prophets	559
	4: 6 In that day, **s** the LORD, will I assemble	5002
	5:10 come to pass in that day, **s** the LORD,	5002
	6: 1 Hear ye now what the LORD **s**; Arise,	559
Na	1:12 Thus **s** the LORD; Though *they be* quiet,	559
	2:13 **s** the LORD of hosts, and I will burn her	5002
	3: 5 I *am* against thee, **s** the LORD of hosts;	5002
Hab	2:19 Woe unto him that **s** to the wood, Awake;	559
Zep	1: 2 all *things* from off the land, **s** the LORD.	5002
	1: 3 off man from off the land, **s** the LORD.	5002
	1:10 come to pass in that day, **s** the LORD,	5002
	2: 9 **s** the LORD of hosts, the God of Israel,	5002
	3: 8 Therefore wait ye upon me, **s** the LORD,	5002
	3:20 captivity before your eyes, **s** the LORD.	559
Hag	1: 5 Now therefore thus **s** the LORD of hosts;	559
	1: 7 Thus **s** the LORD of hosts; Consider your	559
	1: 8 in it, and I will be glorified, **s** the LORD.	559
	1: 9 **s** the LORD of hosts. Because of mine	5002
	1:13 I *am* with you, **s** the LORD.	5002
	2: 4 be strong, O Zerubbabel, **s** the LORD;	5002
	2: 4 people of the land, **s** the LORD, and work:	5002
	2: 4 for I *am* with you, **s** the LORD of hosts:	5002
	2: 6 For thus **s** the LORD of hosts; Yet once,	559
	2: 7 this house *with* glory, **s** the LORD of hosts.	5002
	2: 8 and the gold *is* mine, **s** the LORD of hosts.	5002
	2: 9 than of the former, **s** the LORD of hosts:	559
	2: 9 will I give peace, **s** the LORD of hosts.	5002
	2:11 Thus **s** the LORD of hosts; Ask now	559
	2:14 so *is* this nation before me, **s** the LORD;	5002
	2:17 yet ye *turned* not to me, **s** the LORD.	5002
	2:23 In that day, **s** the LORD of hosts, will I	5002
	2:23 **s** the LORD, and will make thee as a	5002
	2:23 I have chosen thee, **s** the LORD of hosts.	5002
Zec	1: 3 thou unto them, Thus **s** the LORD of hosts;	559
	1: 3 **s** the LORD of hosts, and I will turn unto	5002
	1: 3 I will turn unto you, **s** the LORD of hosts.	559

S

Zec	1: 4 saying, Thus **s** the LORD of hosts;	559
	1: 4 nor hearken unto me, **s** the LORD.	5002
	1:14 saying, Thus **s** the LORD of hosts;	559
	1:16 Therefore thus **s** the LORD; I am returned	559
	1:16 **s** the LORD of hosts, and a line shall be	5002
	1:17 Cry yet, saying, Thus **s** the LORD of hosts;	559
	2: 5 For I, **s** the LORD, will be unto her a wall	5002
	2: 6 from the land of the north, **s** the LORD:	5002
	2: 6 the four winds of the heaven, **s** the LORD.	5002
	2: 8 For thus **s** the LORD of hosts; After	559
	2:10 dwell in the midst of thee, **s** the LORD.	5002
	3: 7 Thus **s** the LORD of hosts; If thou wilt	559
	3: 9 **s** the LORD of hosts, and I will remove	5002
	3:10 In that day, **s** the LORD of hosts, shall ye	5002
	4: 6 but by my spirit, **s** the LORD of hosts.	559
	5: 4 **s** the LORD of hosts, and it shall enter	5002
	7:13 and I would not hear, **s** the LORD of hosts:	559
	8: 2 Thus **s** the LORD of hosts; I was jealous	559
	8: 3 Thus **s** the LORD; I am returned unto Zion,	559
	8: 4 Thus **s** the LORD of hosts; There shall yet	559
	8: 6 Thus **s** the LORD of hosts; If it be	559
	8: 6 in my eyes? **s** the LORD of hosts.	559
	8: 7 Thus **s** the LORD of hosts; Behold, I *will*	559
	8: 9 Thus **s** the LORD of hosts; Let your hands	559
	8:11 *in* the former days, **s** the LORD of hosts.	5002
	8:14 For thus **s** the LORD of hosts; As I thought	559
	8:14 **s** the LORD of hosts, and I repented not:	559
	8:17 these *are things* that I hate, **s** the LORD.	5002
	8:19 Thus **s** the LORD of hosts; The fast of	559
	8:20 Thus **s** the LORD of hosts; *It shall* yet	559
	8:23 Thus **s** the LORD of hosts; In those days *it*	559
	10:12 and down in his name, **s** the LORD.	5002
	11: 4 Thus **s** the LORD my God; Feed the flock	559
	11: 6 the inhabitants of the land, **s** the LORD:	5002
	12: 1 **s** the LORD, which stretcheth forth	5002
	12: 4 In that day, **s** the LORD, I will smite	5002
	13: 2 to pass in that day, **s** the LORD of hosts,	5002
	13: 7 *that is* my fellow, **s** the LORD of hosts:	5002
	13: 8 to pass, *that* in all the land, **s** the LORD,	5002
Mal	1: 2 I have loved you, **s** the LORD. Yet ye say,	559
	1: 2 **s** the LORD: yet I loved Jacob,	5002
	1: 4 Whereas Edom **s**, We are impoverished,	559
	1: 4 thus **s** the LORD of hosts, They shall build,	559
	1: 6 **s** the LORD of hosts unto you, O priests,	559
	1: 8 or accept thy person? **s** the LORD of hosts.	559
	1: 9 regard your persons? **s** the LORD of hosts.	559
	1:10 no pleasure in you, **s** the LORD of hosts,	559
	1:11 among the heathen, **s** the LORD of hosts.	559
	1:13 ye have snuffed at it, **s** the LORD of hosts.	559
	1:13 I accept this of your hand? **s** the LORD.	559
	1:14 **s** the LORD of hosts, and my name *is*	559
	2: 2 glory unto my name, **s** the LORD of hosts.	559
	2: 4 might be with Levi, **s** the LORD of hosts.	559
	2: 8 the covenant of Levi, **s** the LORD of hosts.	559
	2:16 God of Israel, **s** that he hateth putting away	559
	2:16 with his garment, **s** the LORD of hosts:	559
	3: 1 he *shall* come, **s** the LORD of hosts.	559
	3: 5 and fear not me, **s** the LORD of hosts.	559
	3: 7 I will return unto you, **s** the LORD of hosts.	559
	3:10 me now herewith, **s** the LORD of hosts,	559
	3:11 the time in the field, **s** the LORD of hosts.	559
	3:12 a delightsome land, **s** the LORD of hosts.	559
	3:13 have been stout against me, **s** the LORD.	559
	3:17 they shall be mine, **s** the LORD of hosts,	559
	4: 1 shall burn them up, **s** the LORD of hosts,	559
	4: 3 that I *shall* do *this*, **s** the LORD of hosts.	559
Mt	4: 6 **s** unto him, If thou be the Son of God,	3004
	4: 9 **s** unto him, All these *things* will I give	3004
	4:10 Then **s** Jesus unto him, Get thee hence,	3004
	4:19 he **s** unto them, Follow me, and I will	3004
	7:21 Not every one that **s** unto me, Lord, Lord,	3004
	8: 4 Jesus **s** unto him, See thou tell no *man;*	3004
	8: 7 And Jesus **s** unto him, I will come and	3004
	8:20 And Jesus **s** unto him, The foxes have	3004
	8:26 And he **s** unto them, Why are ye fearful,	3004
	9: 6 (then **s** he to the sick of the palsy,)	3004
	9: 9 and he **s** unto him, Follow me. And he	3004
	9:28 Jesus **s** unto them, Believe ye that I am	3004
	9:37 Then **s** he unto his disciples, The harvest	3004
	12:13 Then **s** he to the man, Stretch forth thine	3004
	12:44 he **s**, I will return into my house from	3004
	13:14 which **s**, By hearing ye shall hear,	3004
	13:51 Jesus **s** unto them, Have ye understood all	3004
	15:34 And Jesus **s** unto them, How many loaves	3004
	16:15 He **s** unto them, But whom say ye that I	3004
	17:25 He **s**, Yes. And when he was come into	3004
	17:26 Peter **s** unto him, Of strangers. Jesus saith	3004
	17:26 Jesus **s** unto him, Then are the children	5346
	18:22 Jesus **s** unto him, I say not unto thee,	3004
	19: 8 He **s** unto them, Moses because of	3004
	19:18 He **s** unto him, Which? Jesus said,	3004
	19:20 The young man **s** unto him, All these	3004
	20: 6 others standing idle, and **s** unto them,	3004
	20: 7 He **s** unto them, Go ye also into	3004
	20: 8 lord of the vineyard **s** unto his steward,	3004
	20:21 She **s** unto him, Grant that these my two	3004
	20:23 he **s** unto them, Ye shall drink indeed	3004
	21:16 Jesus **s** unto them, Yea; have ye never	3004
	21:31 Jesus **s** unto them, Verily I say unto you,	3004
	21:42 Jesus **s** unto them, Did ye never read in	3004
	22: 8 Then **s** he to his servants, The wedding is	3004
	22:12 And he **s** unto him, Friend, how camest	3004
	22:20 And he **s** unto them, Whose *is* this image	3004
	22:21 Then **s** he unto them, Render therefore	3004
	22:43 He **s** unto them, How then doth David in	3004

Mt	26:18 say unto him, The Master **s**, My time is	3004
	26:31 Then **s** Jesus unto them, All ye shall be	3004
	26:36 **s** unto the disciples, Sit ye here, while I	3004
	26:38 **s** he unto them, My soul is exceeding	3004
	26:40 them asleep, and **s** unto Peter, What,	3004
	26:45 and **s** unto them, Sleep on now,	3004
	26:64 Jesus **s** unto him, Thou hast said:	3004
	27:22 Pilate **s** unto them, What shall I do then	3004
Mk	1:41 and touched him, and **s** unto him, I will;	3004
	1:44 And **s** unto him, See thou say nothing to	3004
	2:10 forgive sins, (he **s** to the sick of the palsy,)	3004
	2:17 When Jesus heard *it*, he **s** unto them,	3004
	3: 3 And he **s** unto the man which had	3004
	3: 4 he **s** unto them, Is it lawful to do good	3004
	3: 5 **s** unto the man, Stretch forth thine hand.	3004
	4:35 when the even was come, he **s** unto them,	3004
	5:19 **s** unto him, Go home to thy *friends*, and	3004
	5:36 **s** unto the ruler of the synagogue, Be not	3004
	5:39 he **s** unto them, Why make ye *this* ado,	3004
	6:38 **s** unto them, How many loaves have ye?	3004
	6:50 and **s** unto them, Be of good cheer:	3004
	7:18 And he **s** unto them, Are ye so	3004
	7:34 he sighed, and **s** unto him, EPHPHATHA,	3004
	8: 1 his disciples unto *him*, and **s** unto them,	3004
	8:12 And he sighed deeply in his spirit, and **s**,	3004
	8:17 And when Jesus knew *it*, he **s** unto them,	3004
	8:29 he **s** unto them, But whom say ye that	3004
	8:29 And Peter answereth and **s** unto him,	3004
	9:19 He answereth him, and **s**, O faithless	3004
	9:35 and called the twelve, and **s** unto them,	3004
	10:11 And he **s** unto them, Whosoever shall put	3004
	10:23 round about, and **s** unto his disciples,	3004
	10:24 again, and **s** unto them, Children,	3004
	10:27 And Jesus looking upon them **s**, With men	3004
	10:42 Jesus called them to *him*, and **s** unto them,	3004
	11: 2 And **s** unto them, Go your way into	3004
	11:21 And Peter calling to remembrance **s** unto	3004
	11:22 And Jesus answering **s** unto them,	3004
	11:23 shall believe that *those things* which he **s**	3004
	11:23 to pass; he shall have whatsoever he **s**.	3004
	11:33 And Jesus answering **s** unto them,	3004
	12:16 And they brought *it*. And he **s** unto them,	3004
	12:43 and **s** unto them, Verily I say unto you,	3004
	13: 1 one of his disciples **s** unto him, Master,	3004
	14:13 and **s** unto them, Go ye into the city,	3004
	14:14 The Master **s**, Where is the guestchamber,	3004
	14:27 And Jesus **s** unto them, All ye shall be	3004
	14:30 And Jesus **s** unto him, Verily I say unto	3004
	14:32 he **s** to his disciples, Sit ye here, while I	3004
	14:34 And **s** unto them, My soul is exceeding	3004
	14:37 and **s** unto Peter, Simon, sleepest thou?	3004
	14:41 and **s** unto them, Sleep on now,	3004
	14:45 straightway to him, and **s**, Master, master;	3004
	14:63 the high priest rent his clothes, and **s**,	3004
	15:28 And the scripture was fulfilled, which **s**,	3004
	16: 6 And he **s** unto them, Be not affrighted:	3004
Lk	3:11 answereth and **s** unto them, He that hath	3004
	5:39 desireth new: for he **s**, The old is better.	3004
	7:40 say unto thee. And he **s**, Master, say *on*.	5346
	11:24 and finding none, he **s**, I will return unto	3004
	16:29 Abraham **s** unto him, They have Moses	3004
	18: 6 Lord said, Hear what the unjust judge **s**.	3004
	19:22 he **s** unto him, Out of thine own mouth	3004
	20:42 David himself **s** in the book of Psalms,	3004
	22:11 The Master **s**, Where is	3004
	24:36 and **s** unto them, Peace *be* unto you.	3004
Jn	1:21 he **s**, I am not. Art thou *that* prophet?	3004
	1:29 and **s**, Behold the Lamb of God,	3004
	1:36 walked, he **s**, Behold the Lamb of God.	3004
	1:38 and **s** unto them, What seek ye?	3004
	1:39 He **s** unto them, Come and see.	3004
	1:41 and **s** unto him, We have found	3004
	1:43 Philip, and **s** unto him, Follow me.	3004
	1:45 and **s** unto him, We have found him,	3004
	1:46 Philip **s** unto him, Come and see.	3004
	1:47 and **s** of him, Behold an Israelite indeed,	3004
	1:48 Nathanael **s** unto him, Whence knowest	3004
	1:49 Nathanael answered and **s** unto him,	3004
	1:51 And he **s** unto him, Verily, verily, I say	3004
	2: 3 the mother of Jesus **s** unto him, They have	3004
	2: 4 Jesus **s** unto her, Woman, what have I to	3004
	2: 5 His mother **s** unto the servants,	3004
	2: 5 Whatsoever he **s** unto you, do *it*.	3004
	2: 7 Jesus **s** unto them, Fill the waterpots with	3004
	2: 8 And he **s** unto them, Draw out now,	3004
	2:10 And **s** unto him, Every man at	3004
	3: 4 Nicodemus **s** unto him, How can a man	3004
	4: 7 Jesus **s** unto her, Give me to drink.	3004
	4: 9 Then **s** the woman of Samaria unto him,	3004
	4:10 and who it is that **s** to thee, Give me to	3004
	4:11 The woman **s** unto him, Sir, thou hast	3004
	4:15 The woman **s** unto him, Sir, give me this	3004
	4:16 Jesus **s** unto her, Go, call thy husband,	3004
	4:19 The woman **s** unto him, Sir, I perceive	3004
	4:21 Jesus **s** unto her, Woman, believe me,	3004
	4:25 The woman **s** unto him, I know that	3004
	4:26 Jesus **s** unto her, I that speak unto thee	3004
	4:28 her way into the city, and **s** to the men,	3004
	4:34 Jesus **s** unto them, My meat is to do the	3004
	4:49 nobleman **s** unto him, Sir, come down	3004
	4:50 Jesus **s** unto him, Go *thy way;* thy son	3004
	5: 6 a long time *in that case*, he **s** unto him,	3004
	5: 8 Jesus **s** unto him, Rise, take up thy bed,	3004
	6: 5 he **s** unto Philip, Whence shall we buy	3004
	6: 8 Simon Peter's brother, **s** unto him,	3004

Jn	6:20 But he **s** unto them, It is I; be not afraid.	3004
	6:42 *is it* then *that* he **s**, I came down from	3004
	7:50 Nicodemus **s** unto them, (he that came to	3004
	8:22 because he **s**, Whither I go, ye cannot	3004
	8:25 Jesus **s** unto them, Even the same that	3004
	8:39 Jesus **s** unto them, If ye were Abraham's	3004
	11: 7 after that **s** he to *his* disciples, Let us	3004
	11:11 and after that he **s** unto them, Our friend	3004
	11:23 Jesus **s** unto her, Thy brother shall rise	3004
	11:24 Martha **s** unto him, I know that he shall	3004
	11:27 She **s** unto him, Yea, Lord: I believe that	3004
	11:39 **s** unto him, Lord, by this time he stinketh:	3004
	11:40 Jesus **s** unto her, Said I not unto thee,	3004
	11:44 Jesus **s** unto them, Loose him, and let	3004
	12: 4 Then **s** one of his disciples, Judas Iscariot,	3004
	13: 6 *Peter*... **s** unto him, Lord, dost thou wash	3004
	13: 8 Peter **s** unto him, Thou shalt never wash	3004
	13: 9 Simon Peter **s** unto him, Lord, not my feet	3004
	13:10 Jesus **s** to him, He that is washed needeth	3004
	13:25 He then lying on Jesus' breast **s** unto him,	3004
	14: 5 Thomas **s** unto him, Lord, we know not	3004
	14: 6 Jesus **s** unto him, I am the way, the truth,	3004
	14: 8 Philip **s** unto him, Lord, shew us the	3004
	14: 9 Jesus **s** unto him, Have I been so long	3004
	14:22 Judas **s** unto him, not Iscariot, Lord, how	3004
	16:17 is this that he **s** unto us, A little while,	3004
	16:18 What is this that he **s**, A little while?	3004
	16:18 A little while? we cannot tell what he **s**.	2980
	18: 5 Jesus **s** unto them, I am *he*. And Judas	3004
	18:17 Then **s** the damsel that kept the door unto	3004
	18:17 of this man's disciples? He **s**, I am not.	3004
	18:26 **s**, Did not I see thee in the garden with	3004
	18:38 Pilate **s** unto him, What is truth?	3004
	18:38 and **s** unto them, I find in him no fault *at*	3004
	19: 4 went forth again, and **s** unto them,	3004
	19: 5 And *Pilate* **s** unto them, Behold the man.	3004
	19: 6 Crucify *him*, crucify *him*. Pilate **s** unto	3004
	19: 9 and **s** unto Jesus, Whence art thou?	3004
	19:10 Then **s** Pilate unto him, Speakest thou not	3004
	19:14 and he **s** unto the Jews, Behold your King.	3004
	19:15 Pilate **s** unto them, Shall I crucify your	3004
	19:24 the scripture might be fulfilled, which **s**,	3004
	19:26 he **s** unto his mother, Woman, behold thy	3004
	19:27 Then **s** he to the disciple, Behold thy	3004
	19:28 the scripture might be fulfilled, **s**, I thirst.	3004
	19:35 he knoweth that he **s** true, that ye might	3004
	19:37 And again another scripture **s**, They shall	3004
	20: 2 whom Jesus loved, and **s** unto them,	3004
	20:13 She **s** unto them, Because they have taken	3004
	20:15 Jesus **s** unto her, Woman, why weepest	3004
	20:15 him to be the gardener, **s** unto him, Sir,	3004
	20:16 Jesus **s** unto her, Mary. She turned herself,	3004
	20:16 turned herself, and **s** unto him, Rabboni;	3004
	20:17 Jesus **s** unto her, Touch me not; for I am	3004
	20:19 and stood in the midst, and **s** unto them,	3004
	20:22 he breathed on *them*, and **s** unto them,	3004
	20:27 Then **s** he to Thomas, Reach hither thy	3004
	20:29 Jesus **s** unto him, Thomas, because	3004
	21: 3 Simon Peter **s** unto them, I go a fishing.	3004
	21: 5 Jesus **s** unto them, Children, have ye	3004
	21: 7 that disciple whom Jesus loved **s**	3004
	21:10 Jesus **s** unto them, Bring of the fish which	3004
	21:12 Jesus **s** unto them, Come *and* dine.	3004
	21:15 Jesus **s** to Simon Peter, Simon, *son of*	3004
	21:15 Jesus **s** unto him, Yea, Lord; thou knowest	3004
	21:15 love thee. He **s** unto him, Feed my lambs.	3004
	21:16 **s** to him again the second time, Simon,	3004
	21:16 He **s** unto him, Yea, Lord; thou knowest	3004
	21:16 love thee. He **s** unto him, Feed my sheep.	3004
	21:17 **s** unto him the third time, Simon, *son of*	3004
	21:17 Jesus **s** unto him, Feed my sheep.	3004
	21:19 spoken this, he **s** unto him, Follow me.	3004
	21:21 Peter seeing him **s** to Jesus, Lord,	3004
	21:22 Jesus **s** unto him, If I will that he tarry till	3004
Ac	1: 4 which, *s* he, ye have heard of me.	NIG
	2:17 shall come to pass in the last days, **s** God,	3004
	2:34 but he himself, The LORD said unto my	3004
	7:48 made with hands; as **s** the prophet,	3004
	7:49 **s** the Lord: or what *is* the place of my	3004
	12: 8 he **s** unto him, Cast thy garment about	3004
	13:35 Wherefore he **s** also in another *psalm*,	3004
	15:17 the Lord, who doeth all these *things*.	3004
	21:11 and feet, and said, Thus **s** the Holy Ghost,	3004
	22: 2 they kept the more silence: and he **s**,)	5346
Ro	3:19 know that what *things* soever the law **s**,	3004
	3:19 it **s** to them who are under the law:	2980
	4: 3 what **s** the scripture? Abraham believed	3004
	9:15 For he **s** to Moses, I will have mercy on	3004
	9:17 For the scripture **s** unto Pharaoh, Even for	3004
	9:25 As he **s** also in Osee, I will call them my	3004
	10: 8 But what **s** it? The word is nigh thee,	3004
	10:11 For the scripture **s**, Whosoever believeth	3004
	10:16 For Esaias **s**, Lord, who hath believed our	3004
	10:19 First Moses **s**, I will provoke you to	3004
	10:20 But Esaias is very bold, and **s**, I was found	3004
	10:21 But to Israel he **s**, All day long have I	3004
	11: 2 Wot ye not what the scripture **s** of Elias?	3004
	11: 4 But what **s** the answer of God unto him?	3004
	11: 9 And David **s**, Let their table be made a	3004
	12:19 *is* mine; I will repay, **s** the Lord.	3004
	14:11 it is written, *As* I live, **s** the Lord, every	3004
	15:10 And again he **s**, Rejoice, ye Gentiles,	3004
	15:12 again Esaias **s**, There shall be a root of	3004
1Co	1:12 that every one of you **s**, I am of Paul;	3004
	3: 4 while one **s**, I am of Paul; and another,	3004

1Co	6:16 for two, **s** *he*, shall be one flesh.	5346
	9: 8 as a man? or **s** not the law the same also?	3004
	9:10 Or **s** he *it* altogether for our sakes?	3004
	14:21 all that they will not hear me, **s** the Lord.	3004
	14:34 to be under obedience, as also **s** the law.	3004
	15:27 when *he* **s**, all *things* are put under *him*,	3004
2Co	6: 2 (For he **s**, I have heard thee in a time	3004
	6:17 the Lord, and touch not the unclean	3004
	6:18 and daughters, **s** the Lord Almighty.	3004
Gal	3:16 *He* **s** not, And to seeds, as of many;	3004
	4:30 Nevertheless what **s** the scripture? Cast	3004
Eph	4: 8 Wherefore *he* **s**, When he ascended up	3004
	5:14 Wherefore *he* **s**, Awake thou that sleepest,	3004
1Ti	5:18 For the scripture **s**, Thou shalt not muzzle	3004
Heb	1: 6 he **s**, And let all the angels of God worship	3004
	1: 7 And of the angels he **s**, Who maketh his	3004
	1: 8 unto the Son he **s**, Thy throne, O God,	NIG
	3: 7 Wherefore, as the Holy Ghost **s**, To day if	3004
	5: 6 As he **s** also in another *place*, Thou *art* a	3004
	8: 5 **s** *he, that* thou make all *things* according	5346
	8: 8 **s**, Behold, the days come, saith the Lord,	3004
	8: 9 saith, Behold, the days come, saith the Lord,	3004
	8: 9 and I regarded them not, **s** the Lord.	3004
	8:10 of Israel after those days, **s** the Lord;	3004
	8:13 In that *he* **s**, A new *covenant*, he hath	3004
	10: 5 he **s**, Sacrifice and offering thou wouldest	3004
	10:16 the Lord, I will put my laws into their	3004
	10:30 unto me, I will recompense, **s** the Lord.	3004
Jas	2:23 And the scripture was fulfilled which **s**,	3004
	4: 5 Do ye think that the scripture **s** in vain,	3004
	4: 6 Wherefore *he* **s**, God resisteth the proud,	3004
1Jn	2: 4 He that **s**, I know him, and keepeth not	3004
	2: 6 He that *he* abideth in him ought himself	3004
	2: 9 He that **s** *he* is in the light, and hateth his	3004
Rev	1: 8 the Lord, which is, and which was,	3004
	2: 1 These *things* **s** he that holdeth the seven	3004
	2: 7 let him hear what the Spirit **s** unto	3004
	2: 8 These *things* **s** the first and the last,	3004
	2:11 let him hear what the Spirit **s** unto	3004
	2:12 These *things* **s** he which hath the sharp	3004
	2:17 let him hear what the Spirit **s** unto	3004
	2:18 These *things* **s** the Son of God, who hath	3004
	2:29 let him hear what the Spirit **s** unto	3004
	3: 1 *things* **s** he that hath the seven spirits	3004
	3: 6 let him hear what the Spirit **s** unto	3004
	3: 7 These *things* **s** he *that* is holy, he *that is*	3004
	3:13 let him hear what the Spirit **s** unto	3004
	3:14 These *things* **s** the Amen, the faithful and	3004
	3:22 let him hear what the Spirit **s** unto	3004
	5: 5 one of the elders **s** unto me, Weep not:	3004
	14:13 Yea, **s** the Spirit, that they may rest from	3004
	17:15 he **s** unto me, The waters which thou	3004
	18: 7 for she **s** in her heart, I sit a queen,	3004
	19: 9 he **s** unto me, Write, Blessed *are* they	3004
	19: 9 And he **s** unto me, These are the true	3004
	22: 9 Then **s** he unto me, See *thou do it* not:	3004
	22:10 And he **s** unto me, Seal not the sayings of	3004
	22:20 He which testifieth these *things* **s**, Surely I	3004

SAKE (145) [SAKES]

Ge	3:17 cursed *is* the ground for thy **s**; in sorrow	5668
	8:21 curse the ground any more for man's **s**;	5668
	12:13 it may be well with me for thy **s**;	5668+871.1
	12:16 he entreated Abram well for her **s**:	5668+871.1
	18:29 he said, I will not do *it* for forty's **s**.	5668+871.1
	18:31 I will not destroy *it* for twenty's **s**.	5668+871.1
	18:32 I will not destroy *it* for ten's **s**.	5668+871.1
	20:11 they will slay me for my wife's **s**.	1697+5921
	26:24 seed for my servant Abraham's **s**.	5668
	30:27 that the Lord hath blessed me for thy **s**.	1558
	39: 5 the Egyptian's house for Joseph's **s**;	1558
Ex	18: 8 and to the Egyptians for Israel's **s**,	182
	21:26 he shall let him go free for his eye's **s**.	8478
	21:27 he shall let him go free for his tooth's **s**.	8478
Nu	11:29 said unto him, Enviest thou for my **s**?	3807.1
	25:11 while he was zealous **for my s** among	2967.1
	25:18 slain in the day of the plague for Peor's **s**.	1697
1Sa	12:22 his people for his great name's **s**:	5668+871.1
	23:10 to destroy the city for my **s**.	5668+871.1
2Sa	5:12 kingdom for his people Israel's **s**.	5668+871.1
	7:21 **For** thy word's **s**, and according to	5668+871.1
	9: 1 him kindness for Jonathan's **s**?	5668+871.1
	9: 7 for Jonathan thy father's **s**,	5668+871.1
	18: 5 gently **for my s** with the young man,	3807.1
1Ki	8:41 of a far country for thy name's **s**;	4616+3807.1
	11:12 not do it for David thy father's **s**:	4616+3807.1
	11:13 thy son for David my servant's **s**,	4616+3807.1
	11:13 for Jerusalem's **s**, which I have	4616+3807.1
	11:32 tribe for my servant David's **s**,	4616+3807.1
	11:32 and **for** Jerusalem's **s**,	4616+3807.1
	11:34 his life for David my servant's **s**,	4616+3807.1
	15: 4 Nevertheless for David's **s** did	4616+3807.1
2Ki	8:19 Judah **for** David his servant's **s**,	4616+3807.1
	19:34 to save it, for mine own **s**, and	4616+3807.1
	19:34 and **for** my servant David's **s**.	4616+3807.1
	20: 6 defend this city for mine own **s**,	4616+3807.1
	20: 6 and **for** my servant David's **s**.	4616+3807.1
1Ch	17:19 O Lord, for thy servant's **s**,	5668+871.1
2Ch	6:32 country for thy great name's **s**,	4616+3807.1
Ne	9:31 Nevertheless for thy great mercies' **s**	871.1
Job	19:17 though I intreated for the children's **s** of	NIH
Ps	6: 4 O save me for thy mercy's **s**.	4616+3807.1
	23: 3 of righteousness for his name's **s**.	4616+3807.1
	25: 7 thou me for thy goodness' **s**,	4616+3807.1
	25:11 **For** thy name's **s**, O Lord,	4616+3807.1

SAKES (31) [SAKE]

Ge	18:26 I will spare all the place for their **s**.	5668+871.1
Lev	26:45 I will for their **s** remember the covenant	3807.1
Dt	1:37 the Lord was angry with me for your **s**,	1558

Ps	31: 3 **for** thy name's **s** lead me,	4616+3807.1
	31:16 thy servant: save me for thy mercy's **s**.	871.1
	44:22 **for** thy **s** are we killed all the day long;	5921
	44:26 and redeem us **for** thy mercy's **s**.	4616+3807.1
	69: 6 God of hosts, be ashamed **for** my **s**:	871.1
	69: 6 that seek thee be confounded **for** my **s**,	871.1
	69: 7 Because **for** thy **s** I have borne reproach;	5921
	79: 9 away our sins, **for** thy name's **s**:	4616+3807.1
	106: 8 he saved them **for** his name's **s**,	4616+3807.1
	109:21 God the Lord, **for** thy name's **s**:	4616+3807.1
	115: 1 for thy mercy, *and* for thy truth's **s**.	5921
	132:10 **For** thy servant David's **s** turn not	5668+871.1
	143:11 O Lord, **for** thy name's **s**:	4616+3807.1
	143:11 for thy righteousness' **s** bring my soul	871.1
Isa	37:35 city to save it **for** mine own **s**,	4616+3807.1
	37:35 and **for** my servant David's **s**.	4616+3807.1
	42:21 pleased **for** his righteousness' **s**;	4616+3807.1
	43:14 Holy One of Israel; **For** your **s**	4616+3807.1
	43:25 transgressions **for** mine own **s**,	4616+3807.1
	45: 4 **For** Jacob my servant's **s**,	4616+3807.1
	48: 9 **For** my name's **s** will I defer	4616+3807.1
	48:11 For mine own **s**, *even* for mine	4616+3807.1
	48:11 own sake, *even* for mine own **s**,	4616+3807.1
	54:15 together against thee shall fall **for** thy **s**.	5921
	62: 1 **For** Zion's **s** will I not hold my	4616+3807.1
	62: 1 **for** Jerusalem's **s** I will not rest,	4616+3807.1
	63:17 Return **for** thy servants' **s**,	4616+3807.1
	66: 5 cast you out **for** my name's **s**,	4616+3807.1
Jer	14: 7 do thou *it* **for** thy name's **s**:	4616+3807.1
	14:21 not abhor *us*, **for** thy name's **s**,	4616+3807.1
	15:15 that **for** thy **s** I have suffered rebuke.	5921
Eze	20: 9 I wrought **for** my name's **s**,	4616+3807.1
	20:14 I wrought **for** my name's **s**,	4616+3807.1
	20:22 and wrought **for** my name's **s**,	4616+3807.1
	20:44 with you **for** my name's **s**,	4616+3807.1
	36:22 of Israel, but **for** mine holy name's **s**,	3807.1
Da	9:17 that is desolate, **for** the Lord's **s**.	4616+3807.1
	9:19 for thine own **s**, O my God:	4616+3807.1
Jnh	1:12 for I know that **for** my **s** this great	7945+871.1
Mic	3:12 Therefore shall Zion **for** your **s** be	1558+871.1
Mt	5:10 which are persecuted **for** righteousness' **s**:	1752
	5:11 of evil against you falsely, **for** my **s**.	1752
	10:18 before governors and kings **for** my **s**,	1752
	10:22 shall be hated of all *men* **for** my name's **s**:	1223
	10:39 he that loseth his life **for** my **s** shall find it.	1752
	14: 3 and put *him* in prison **for** Herodias' **s**,	1223
	14: 9 nevertheless **for** the oaths' **s**,	1223
	16:25 whosoever will lose his life **for** my **s** shall	1752
	19:12 eunuchs **for** the kingdom of heaven's **s**.	1223
	19:29 or children, or lands, **for** my name's **s**,	1752
	24: 9 be hated of all nations **for** my name's **s**.	1223
	24:22 **for** the elect's **s** those days shall be	1223
Mk	4:17 or persecution ariseth **for** the word's **s**,	1223
	6:17 and bound him in prison **for** Herodias' **s**,	1223
	6:26 *yet* **for** his oaths' **s**, and for their sakes	1223
	8:35 but whosoever shall lose his life **for** my **s**	1752
	10:29 or wife, or children, or lands, **for** my **s**,	1752
	13: 9 brought before rulers and kings **for** my **s**,	1752
	13:13 shall be hated of all *men* **for** my name's **s**:	1223
	13:20 **for** the elect's **s**, whom he hath chosen,	1223
Lk	6:22 your name as evil, **for** the Son of man's **s**.	1752
	9:24 but whosoever will lose his life **for** my **s**,	1752
	18:29 or children, **for** the kingdom of God's **s**,	1752
	21:12 before kings and rulers **for** my name's **s**.	1752
	21:17 shall be hated of all *men* **for** my name's **s**.	1223
Jn	12: 9 and they came not **for** Jesus' only,	1223
	13:37 I will lay down my life **for** thy **s**.	5228
	13:38 Wilt thou lay down thy life **for** my **s**?	5228
	14:11 or else believe me **for** the very works' **s**.	1223
	15:21 will they do unto you **for** my name's **s**,	1223
Ac	9:16 *things* he must suffer **for** my name's **s**.	1223
	26: 7 **For** which hope's **s**, king Agrippa, I am	4012
Ro	4:23 Now it was not written **for** his **s** alone,	1223
	8:36 **For** thy **s** we are killed all the day long;	1752
	13: 5 only for wrath, but also **for** conscience **s**.	1223
	15:30 **for** the Lord Jesus Christ's **s**, and for	1223
1Co	4:10 *are* fools **for** Christ's **s**, but ye *are* wise	1223
	9:23 And this I do **for** the gospel's **s**, that I	1223
	10:25 asking no question **for** conscience **s**:	1223
	10:27 eat, asking no question **for** conscience **s**.	1223
	10:28 eat not **for** his **s** that shewed *it*, and	1223
	10:28 *for* conscience **s**: for the earth *is* the Lord's	NIG
2Co	4: 5 and ourselves your servants **for** Jesus' **s**.	1223
	4:11 alway delivered unto death **for** Jesus' **s**,	1223
	12:10 persecutions, in distresses **for** Christ's **s**:	5228
Eph	4:32 even as God **for** Christ's **s** hath forgiven	1722
Php	1:29 on him, but also to suffer **for** his **s**;	5228
Col	1:24 of Christ in my flesh **for** his body's **s**,	5228
	3: 6 **For** which *things*' **s** the wrath of God	1223
1Th	1: 5 of *men* we were among you **for** your **s**.	1223
	5:13 very highly in love **for** their work's **s**.	1223
1Ti	5:23 but use a little wine **for** thy stomach's **s**	1223
Tit	1:11 which *they* ought not, **for** filthy lucre's **s**.	5484
Phm	1: 9 *Yet* **for** love's **s** I rather beseech *thee*,	1223
1Pe	2:13 every ordinance of man **for** the Lord's **s**:	1223
	3:14 But and if ye suffer **for** righteousness' **s**,	1223
1Jn	2:12 sins are forgiven you **for** his name's **s**.	1223
2Jn	1: 2 For the truth's **s**, which dwelleth in us,	1223
3Jn	1: 7 Because that **for** his name's **s** they went	5228
Rev	2: 3 and **for** my name's **s** hast laboured,	1223

Dt	3:26 was wroth with me **for** your **s**,	4616+3807.1
	4:21 the Lord was angry with me for your **s**,	1697
Jdg	21:22 Be favourable unto them for our **s**:	NIH
Ru	1:13 for it grieveth me much **for** your **s** that	4480
1Ch	16:21 yea, he reproved kings **for** their **s**,	5921
Ps	7: 7 for their **s** therefore return thou on high.	5921
	105:14 yea, he reproved kings **for** their **s**;	5921
	106:32 it went ill with Moses **for** their **s**:	5668+871.1
	122: 8 **For** my brethren and	
	companions' **s**,	4616+3807.1
Isa	65: 8 so will I do **for** my servants' **s**,	4616+3807.1
Eze	36:22 **for** your **s** do I *this*, O house	4616+3807.1
	36:32 Not **for** your **s** do I *this*, saith	4616+3807.1
Da	2:30 for *their* **s** that shall make known	1701
Mal	3:11 I will rebuke the devourer **for** your **s**,	3807.1
Mk	6:26 for their **s** which sat with *him*, he would	NIG
Jn	11:15 And I am glad **for** your **s** that I was not	1223
	12:30 came not because of me, but **for** your **s**.	1223
	17:19 And **for** their **s** I sanctify myself, that they	5228
Ro	11:28 the gospel, *they* are enemies **for** your **s**:	1223
	11:28 are beloved **for** the fathers' **s**.	1223
1Co	4: 6 to myself and *to* Apollos **for** your **s**;	1223
	9:10 Or saith he *it* altogether **for** our **s**? For our	1223
	9:10 **For** our **s**, no doubt, *this* is written: that	1223
2Co	2:10 **for** your **s** *forgave* I it in the person of	1223
	4:15 For all *things are* **for** your **s**, that	1223
	8: 9 was rich, *yet* **for** your **s** he became poor,	1223
1Th	3: 9 all the joy wherewith we joy **for** your **s**	1223
2Ti	2:10 I endure all *things* **for** the elects' **s**,	1223

SAKIA See SHACHIA

SALA (1) [SALAH]

Lk	3:35 son of Heber, which was *the son* of **S**,	4527

SALAH (6) [SALA]

Ge	10:24 Arphaxad begat **S**; and Salah begat Eber.	7974
	10:24 Arphaxad begat Salah; and **S** begat Eber.	7974
	11:12 lived five and thirty years, and begat **S**:	7974
	11:13 Arphaxad lived after he begat **S** four	7974
	11:14 And **S** lived thirty years, and begat Eber:	7974
	11:15 **S** lived after he begat Eber four hundred	7974

SALAMIS (1)

Ac	13: 5 And when they were at **S**, they preached	4529

SALATHIEL (4)

1Ch	3:17 And the sons of Jeconiah; Assir, **S** his son,	7597
Mt	1:12 brought to Babylon, Jechonias begat **S**;	4528
	1:12 begat Salathiel; and **S** begat Zorobabel;	4528
Lk	3:27 was the son of **S**, which was *the son*	4528

SALCAH (2) [SALCHAH]

Jos	12: 5 Hermon, and in **S**, and in all Bashan,	5548
	13:11 mount Hermon, and all Bashan unto **S**;	5548

SALCHAH (2) [SALCAH]

Dt	3:10 and all Bashan, unto **S** and Edrei,	5548
1Ch	5:11 them, in the land of Bashan unto **S**:	5548

SALE (3) [SELL]

Lev	25:27 let him count the years of the **s** thereof,	4465
	25:50 the price of his **s** shall be according unto	4465
Dt	18: 8 beside **that which cometh of** the **s** of his	4465

SALECAH See SALCAH; SALCHAH

SALEM (4) [JERUSALEM]

Ge	14:18 Melchizedek king of **S** brought forth	8004
Ps	76: 2 In **S** also is his tabernacle, and his	8004
Heb	7: 1 For this Melchisedec, king of **S**, priest of	4532
	7: 2 and after that also King of **S**, which is,	4532

SALIM (1)

Jn	3:23 also was baptizing in Aenon near to **S**,	4530

SALLAI (2)

Ne	11: 8 **S**, nine hundred twenty and eight.	5543
	12:20 Of **S**, Kallai; of Amok, Eber;	5543

SALLU (3)

1Ch	9: 7 **S** the son of Meshullam, the son of	5543
Ne	11: 7 **S** the son of Meshullam, the son of Joed,	5543
	12: 7 **S**, Amok, Hilkiah, Jedaiah. These *were*	5543

SALMA (4)

1Ch	2:11 Nahshon begat **S**, and Salma begat Boaz,	8007
	2:11 Nahshon begat Salma, and **S** begat Boaz,	8007
	2:51 **S** the father of Beth-lehem, Hareph	8007
	2:54 The sons of **S**; Beth-lehem,	8007

SALMON (6)

Ru	4:20 begat Nahshon, and Nahshon begat **S**,	8009
	4:21 And **S** begat Boaz, and Boaz begat Obed,	8012
Ps	68:14 kings in it, it was *white as* snow in **S**.	6756
Mt	1: 4 begat Naasson; and Naasson begat **S**;	4533
	1: 5 And **S** begat Booz of Rachab;	4533
Lk	3:32 *the son* of Booz, which was *the son* of **S**,	4533

SALMONE (1)

Ac	27: 7 we sailed under Crete, over against **S**;	4534

SALOME (2)

Mk	15:40 of James the less and of Joses, and **S**;	4539
	16: 1 and **S**, had bought *sweet* spices, that they	4539

S

SALT (41) [SALTED, SALTNESS, SALTPITS]

Ge	14: 3	in the vale of Siddim, which *is* the s sea.	4417
	19:26	behind him, and she became a pillar of s.	4417
Lev	2:13	meat offering shalt thou season with s;	4417
	2:13	neither shalt thou suffer the s of	4417
	2:13	with all thine offerings thou shalt offer s.	4417
Nu	18:19	it *is* a covenant of s for ever before	4417
	34: 3	the outmost coast of the s sea eastward:	4417
	34:12	the goings out of it shall be *at* the s sea:	4417
Dt	3:17	*even* the s sea, under Ashdoth-pisgah	4417
	29:23	s, *and* burning, *that* it is not sown,	4417
Jos	3:16	*even* the s sea, failed, *and* were cut off:	4417
	12: 3	of the plain, *even* the s sea on the east,	4417
	15: 2	border was from the shore of the s sea,	4417
	15: 5	the east border *was* the s sea, *even* unto	4417
	15:62	and the city of s, and En-gedi;	4417
	18:19	of the s sea at the south end of Jordan:	4417
Jdg	9:45	beat down the city, and sowed it *with* s.	4417
2Sa	8:13	smiting of the Syrians in the valley of s,	4417
2Ki	2:20	Bring me a new cruse, and put s therein.	4417
	2:21	cast the s in there, and said, Thus saith	4417
	14: 7	He slew *of* Edom in the valley of s ten	4417
1Ch	18:12	in the valley of s eighteen thousand.	4417
2Ch	13: 5	to him and to his sons *by* a covenant of s?	4417
	25:11	went *to* the valley of s, and smote *of*	4417
Ezr	6: 9	God of heaven, wheat, s, wine, and oil,	4416
	7:22	and s without prescribing *how much.*	4416
Job	6: 6	which is unsavoury be eaten without s?	4417
Ps	60: T	smote of Edom in the valley of s twelve	4417
Jer	17: 6	in *a* land and not inhabited.	4420
Eze	43:24	the priests shall cast s upon them,	4417
	47:11	not be healed; they shall be given to s.	4417
Mt	5:13	Ye are the s of the earth: but if the salt	217
	5:13	but if the s have lost his savour,	217
Mk	9:49	and every sacrifice shall be salted with s.	251
	9:50	S *is* good: but if the salt have lost his	217
	9:50	but if the s have lost his saltness,	217
	9:50	Have s in yourselves, and have peace one	217
Lk	14:34	S *is* good: but if the salt have lost his savour	217
	14:34	but if the s have lost his savour,	217
Col	4: 6	*be* alway with grace, seasoned with s,	217
Jas	3:12	so *can* no fountain *both* yield s water and	252

SALTED (4) [SALT]

Eze	16: 4	supple *thee;* thou wast not s **at all,**	4414+4414
Mt	5:13	lost his savour, wherewith shall it be s?	233
Mk	9:49	For every one shall be s with fire,	233
	9:49	and every sacrifice shall be salted with s.	233

SALTNESS (1) [SALT]

Mk	9:50	if the salt have **lost** his s, wherewith will	358

SALTPITS (1) [PIT, SALT]

Zep	2: 9	and s, and a perpetual desolation:	4379+4417

SALU (1)

Nu	25:14	*was* Zimri, the son of **S,** a prince of a chief	5543

SALUTATION (6) [SALUTE]

Lk	1:29	cast in her mind what manner of s this	783
	1:41	*that,* when Elisabeth heard the s of Mary,	783
	1:44	soon as the voice of thy s sounded in mine	783
1Co	16:21	The s of *me* Paul with mine own hand.	783
Col	4:18	The s by the hand of me Paul.	783
2Th	3:17	The s of Paul with mine own hand, which	783

SALUTATIONS (1) [SALUTE]

Mk	12:38	and love s in the marketplaces,	783

SALUTE (39) [SALUTATION, SALUTATIONS, SALUTED, SALUTETH]

1Sa	10: 4	they will s thee,	7592+7965+3807.1
	13:10	out to meet him, that he might s him.	1288
	25:14	out of the wilderness to s our master;	1288
2Sa	8:10	to s him, and to bless him,	7592+7965+3807.1
2Ki	4:29	*thy way:* if thou meet any man, s him not;	1288
	4:29	if any s thee, answer him not *again:* and	1288
	10:13	we go down to s the children of the king	7965
Mt	5:47	And if ye s your brethren only, what do ye	782
	10:12	And when ye come into a house s it.	782
Mk	15:18	And began to s him, Hail, King of the Jews.	782
Lk	10: 4	nor shoes: and s no *man* by the way.	782
Ac	25:13	and Bernice came unto Cesarea to s Festus.	782
Ro	16: 5	S my wellbeloved Epenetus, who is	782
	16: 7	S Andronicus and Junia, my kinsmen,	782
	16: 9	Urban our helper in Christ,	782
	16:10	S Apelles approved in Christ. Salute them	782
	16:10	S them which are of Aristobulus's	782
	16:11	S Herodion my kinsman. Greet them that	782
	16:12	S Tryphena and Tryphosa, who labour in	782
	16:12	S the beloved Persis, which laboured much	782
	16:13	S Rufus chosen in the Lord, and his mother	782
	16:14	S Asyncritus, Phlegon, Hermas, Patrobas,	782
	16:15	S Philologus, and Julia, Nereus,	782
	16:16	S one another with a holy kiss.	782
	16:16	a holy kiss. The churches of Christ s you.	782
	16:21	Jason, and Sosipater, my kinsmen, s you.	782
	16:22	who wrote *this* epistle, s you in the Lord.	782
1Co	16:19	The churches of Asia s you. Aquila and	782
	16:19	Aquila and Priscilla s you much in the Lord,	782
2Co	13:13	All the saints s you.	782
Php	4:21	S every saint in Christ Jesus. The brethren	782
	4:22	All the saints s you, chiefly they that are of	782
Col	4:15	S the brethren which are in Laodicea,	782
2Ti	4:19	S Prisca and Aquila, and the household of	782

SALUTED (9) [SALUTE]

Jdg	18:15	of Micah, and s him.	7592+7965+3807.1
1Sa	17:22	came and s his brethren.	7592+7965+3807.1
	30:21	to the people, he s them.	7592+7965+3807.1
2Ki	10:15	he s him, and said to him, Is thine heart	1288
Mk	9:15	greatly amazed, and running to *him* s him.	782
Lk	1:40	the house of Zacharias, and s Elisabeth.	782
Ac	18:22	gone up, and s the church, he went down	782
	21: 7	s the brethren, and abode with them one	782
	21:19	And when he had s them, he declared	782

SALUTETH (5) [SALUTE]

Ro	16:23	mine host, and of the whole church, s you.	782
	16:23	Erastus the chamberlain of the city s you,	782
Col	4:10	Aristarchus my fellowprisoner s you,	782
	4:12	is *one* of you, a servant of Christ, s you,	782
1Pe	5:13	Babylon, elected together with *you,* s you;	782

SALVATION (164) [SAVE]

Ge	49:18	I have waited for thy s, O Lord.	3444
Ex	14:13	stand still, and see the s of the Lord,	3444
	15: 2	and song, and he is become my s:	3444
Dt	32:15	and lightly esteemed the Rock of his s.	3444
1Sa	2: 1	mine enemies; because I rejoice in thy s.	3444
	11:13	for to day the Lord hath wrought s in	8668
	14:45	who hath wrought this great s in Israel?	3444
	19: 5	the Lord wrought a great s for all Israel:	8668
2Sa	22: 3	The horn of s, my high tower,	3444
	22:36	hast also given me the shield of thy s:	3468
	22:47	exalted be the God of the rock of my s.	3468
	22:51	*He is* the tower of s for his king:	3444
	23: 5	for *this is* all my s, and all *my* desire,	3468
1Ch	16:23	earth; shew forth from day to day his s.	3444
	16:35	O God of our s, and gather us together,	3444
2Ch	6:41	clothed *with* s, and let thy saints rejoice	8668
	20:17	and see the s of the Lord with you,	3444
Job	13:16	He also *shall be* my s: for a hypocrite	3444
Ps	3: 8	S *belongeth* unto the Lord: thy blessing	3444
	9:14	daughter of Zion: I will rejoice in thy s.	3444
	13: 5	thy mercy; my heart shall rejoice in thy s.	3444
	14: 7	O that the s of Israel *were* come out of	3444
	18: 2	and the horn of my s, *and* my high tower.	3468
	18:35	hast also given me the shield of thy s:	3468
	18:46	and let the God of my s be exalted.	3468
	20: 5	We will rejoice in thy s, and in the name	3444
	21: 1	and in thy s how greatly shall he rejoice!	3444
	21: 5	His glory *is* great in thy s: honour and	3444
	24: 5	and righteousness from the God of his s.	3468
	25: 5	for thou *art* the God of my s; on thee do I	3468
	27: 1	The Lord *is* my light and my s; whom	3444
	27: 9	not, neither forsake me, O God of my s.	3468
	35: 3	me: say unto my soul, I *am* thy s.	3444
	35: 9	in the Lord: it shall rejoice in his s.	3444
	37:39	the s of the righteous *is* of the Lord:	8668
	38:22	Make haste to help me, O Lord my s.	8668
	40:10	I have declared thy faithfulness and thy s:	8668
	40:16	let such as love thy s say continually,	8668
	50:23	*aright* will I shew the s of God.	3468
	51:12	Restore unto me the joy of thy s;	3468
	51:14	O God, thou God of my s:	8668
	53: 6	O that the s of Israel *were* come out of	3444
	62: 1	upon God: from him *cometh* my s.	3444
	62: 2	He only *is* my rock and my s; *he is* my	3444
	62: 6	He only *is* my rock and my s: *he is* my	3444
	62: 7	In God *is* my s and my glory: the rock of	3468
	65: 5	wilt thou answer us, O God of our s;	3468
	68:19	us *with* benefits, *even* the God of our s.	3444
	68:20	*He that is* our God *is* the God of s;	4190
	69:13	thy mercy hear me, in the truth of thy s.	3444
	69:29	let thy s, O God, set me up on high.	3444
	70: 4	let such as love thy s say continually,	3444
	71:15	thy righteousness *and* thy s all the day;	8668
	74:12	old, working s in the midst of the earth.	3444
	78:22	not in God, and trusted not in his s:	3444
	79: 9	Help us, O God of our s, for the glory of	3468
	85: 4	O God of our s, and cause thine anger	3468
	85: 7	thy mercy, O Lord, and grant us thy s.	3468
	85: 9	Surely his s *is* nigh them that fear him;	3444
	88: 1	O Lord God of my s, I have cried day	3444
	89:26	my Father, my God, and the rock of my s.	3444
	91:16	life will I satisfy him, and shew him my s.	3444
	95: 1	make a joyful noise to the rock of our s.	3468
	96: 2	name; shew forth his s from day to day.	3444
	98: 2	The Lord hath made known his s:	3444
	98: 3	all the ends of the earth have seen the s	3444
	106: 4	unto thy people: O visit me with thy s;	3444
	116:13	I will take the cup of s, and call upon	3444
	118:14	strength and song, and is become my s.	3444
	118:15	s *is* in the tabernacles of the righteous:	3444
	118:21	thou hast heard me, and art become my s.	3444
	119:41	O Lord, *even* thy s, according to thy	8668
	119:81	My soul fainteth for thy s: *but* I hope in	3444
	119:123	Mine eyes fail for thy s, and for the word	3444
	119:155	S *is* far from the wicked: for they seek not	3444
	119:166	I have hoped for thy s, and done thy	3444
	119:174	I have longed for thy s, O Lord;	3444
	132:16	I will also clothe her priests with s:	3468
	140: 7	O God the Lord, the strength of my s,	3444
	144:10	*It is* he that giveth s unto kings:	8668
Ps	149: 4	he will beautify the meek with s.	3444
Isa	12: 2	Behold, God *is* my s; I will trust, and not	3444
	12: 2	and *my* song; he also is become my s.	3444
	12: 3	shall ye draw water out of the wells of s.	3444
	17:10	thou hast forgotten the God of thy s,	3468
	25: 9	we will be glad and rejoice in his s.	3444
	26: 1	s will *God* appoint *for* walls and bulwarks.	3444
	33: 2	our s also in the time of trouble.	3444
	33: 6	the stability of thy times, *and* strength of s:	3444
	45: 8	them bring forth s, and let righteousness	3468
	45:17	saved in the Lord *with* an everlasting s:	8668
	46:13	not be far off, and my s shall not tarry:	8668
	46:13	I will place s in Zion for Israel my glory.	8668
	49: 6	that *thou* mayest be my s unto the end of	3444
	49: 8	and in a day of s have I helped thee:	3444
	51: 5	my s is gone forth, and mine arms shall	3468
	51: 6	my s shall be for ever,	3444
	51: 8	and my s from generation to generation.	3444
	52: 7	good tidings of good, that publisheth s;	3444
	52:10	all the ends of the earth shall see the s of	3444
	56: 1	for my s is near to come,	3444
	59:11	*is* none; for s, *but* it is far off from us.	3444
	59:16	therefore his arm **brought** s unto him;	3467
	59:17	and a helmet of s upon his head;	3444
	60:18	thou shalt call thy walls S, and thy gates	3444
	61:10	hath clothed me with the garments of s,	3468
	62: 1	and the s thereof as a lamp *that* burneth.	3444
	62:11	daughter of Zion, Behold, thy s cometh;	3468
	63: 5	mine own arm **brought** s unto me;	3467
Jer	3:23	Truly in vain *is* s hoped for from the hills,	NIH
	3:23	truly in the Lord our God *is* the s of	8668
La	3:26	and quietly wait for the s of the Lord.	8668
Jnh	2: 9	*that* that I have vowed. S *is* of the Lord.	3444
Mic	7: 7	I will wait for the God of my s:	3468
Hab	3: 8	upon thine horses *and* thy chariots of s?	3444
	3:13	Thou wentest forth for the s of thy people,	3468
	3:13	people, *even* for s with thine anointed;	3468
	3:18	the Lord, I will joy in the God of my s.	3468
Zec	9: 9	he *is* just, and **having** s; lowly,	3467
Lk	1:69	And hath raised up a horn of s for us in	4991
	1:77	To give knowledge of s unto his people by	4991
	2:30	For mine eyes have seen thy s,	4992
	3: 6	And all flesh shall see the s of God.	4992
	19: 9	him, This day is s come to this house,	4991
Jn	4:22	what we worship: for s is of the Jews.	4991
Ac	4:12	Neither is there s in any other: for there is	4991
	13:26	to you is the word of this s sent.	4991
	13:47	thou shouldest be for s unto the ends of	4991
	16:17	God, which shew unto us the way of s.	4991
	28:28	the s of God is sent unto the Gentiles,	4992
Ro	1:16	for it is the power of God unto s to every	4991
	10:10	the mouth confession is made unto s.	4991
	11:11	*rather* through their fall is *come* unto	4991
	13:11	for now is our s nearer than when we	4991
2Co	1: 6	afflicted, *it is* for your consolation and s,	4991
	1: 6	*it is* for your consolation and s.	4991
	6: 2	and in the day of s have I succoured thee:	4991
	6: 2	behold, now *is* the day of s.)	4991
	7:10	godly sorrow worketh repentance to s	4991
Eph	1:13	the word of truth, the gospel of your s:	4991
	6:17	take the helmet of s, and the sword of	4992
Php	1:19	For I know that this shall turn to my s	4991
	1:28	but to you of s, and that of God.	4991
	2:12	work out your own s with fear and	4991
1Th	5: 8	and love; and for a helmet, the hope of s.	4991
	5: 9	but to obtain s by our Lord Jesus Christ,	4991
2Th	2:13	to s through sanctification of the Spirit	4991
2Ti	2:10	that they may also obtain the s which is	4991
	3:15	which are able to make thee wise unto s	4991
Tit	2:11	For the grace of God that bringeth s hath	4992
Heb	1:14	minister for them who shall be heirs of s?	4991
	2: 3	shall we escape, if we neglect so great s;	4991
	2:10	to make the captain of their s perfect	4991
	5: 9	he became the author of eternal s unto all	4991
	6: 9	and *things* that accompany s, though we	4991
	9:28	the second time without sin unto s.	4991
1Pe	1: 5	s ready to be revealed in the last time.	4991
	1: 9	end of your faith, *even* the s of *your* souls.	4991
	1:10	Of which s the prophets have inquired	4991
2Pe	3:15	*that* the longsuffering of our Lord *is* s;	4991
Jude	1: 3	to write unto you of the common s,	4991
Rev	7:10	S to our God which sitteth upon the	4991
	12:10	Now is come s, and strength,	4991
	19: 1	saying, Alleluia; S, and glory, and honour,	4991

SAMARIA (124) [SAMARITAN, SAMARITANS]

1Ki	13:32	high places which *are* in the cities of S,	8111
	16:24	he bought the hill S of Shemer for two	8111
	16:24	the name of Shemer, owner of the hill, S.	8111
	16:28	with his fathers, and was buried in S:	8111
	16:29	son of Omri reigned over Israel in S	8111
	16:32	house of Baal, which he had built in S.	8111
	18: 2	And *there was* a sore famine in S.	8111
	20: 1	he went up and besieged S,	8111
	20:10	if the dust of S suffice for handfuls	8111
	20:17	saying, There are men come out of S.	8111
	20:34	in Damascus, as my father made in S	8111
	20:43	heavy and displeased, and came to S.	8111
	21: 1	hard by the palace of Ahab king of S.	8111
	21:18	to meet Ahab king of Israel, which *is* in S:	8111
	22:10	void place *in* the entrance of the gate of S;	8111
	22:37	So the king died, and was brought to S;	8111
	22:37	*to* Samaria; and they buried the king in S.	8111
	22:38	*one* washed the chariot in the pool of S;	8111
	22:51	S the seventeenth year of Jehoshaphat	8111

S

2Ki	1: 2 lattice in his upper chamber that *was* in **S**,	8111
	1: 3 to meet the messengers of the king of **S**,	8111
	2:25 and from thence he returned to **S**.	8111
	3: 1 **S** the eighteenth year of Jehoshaphat king	8111
	3: 6 Jehoram went out of **S** the same time,	8111
	5: 3 lord *were* with the prophet that *is* in **S**;	8111
	6:19 whom ye seek. But he led them to **S**.	8111
	6:20 when they were come *into* **S**, that Elisha	8111
	6:20 and behold, *they were* in the midst of **S**.	8111
	6:24 all his host, and went up, and besieged **S**.	8111
	6:25 there was a great famine in **S**: and behold,	8111
	7: 1 of barley for a shekel, in the gate of **S**.	8111
	7:18 morrow about *this* time in the gate of **S**:	8111
	10: 1 Ahab had seventy sons in **S**. And Jehu	8111
	10: 1 Jehu wrote letters, and sent to **S**, unto	8111
	10:12 he arose and departed, and came to **S**.	8111
	10:17 when he came to **S**, he slew all that	8111
	10:17 he slew all that remained unto Ahab in **S**,	8111
	10:35 they buried him in **S**. And Jehoahaz his	8111
	10:36 time that Jehu reigned over Israel in **S**	8111
	13: 1 of Jehu *began* to reign over Israel in **S**,	8111
	13: 6 there remained the grove also in **S**.)	8111
	13: 9 his fathers; and they buried him in **S**:	8111
	13:10 son of Jehoahaz to reign over Israel in **S**,	8111
	13:13 Joash was buried in **S** with the kings of	8111
	14:14 and hostages, and returned to **S**.	8111
	14:16 was buried in **S** with the kings of Israel;	8111
	14:23 of Joash king of Israel *began* to reign in **S**,	8111
	15: 8 Jeroboam reign over Israel in **S** six	8111
	15:13 Judah; and he reigned a full month in **S**.	8111
	15:14 came to **S**, and smote Shallum the son of	8111
	15:14 smote Shallum the son of Jabesh in **S**,	8111
	15:17 over Israel, *and* reigned ten years in **S**.	8111
	15:23 Menahem *began* to reign over Israel in **S**,	8111
	15:25 against him, and smote him in **S**,	8111
	15:27 Remaliah *began* to reign over Israel in **S**,	8111
	17: 1 Elah to reign in **S** over Israel nine years.	8111
	17: 5 went up to **S**, and besieged it three years.	8111
	17: 6 the king of Assyria took **S**,	8111
	17:24 placed *them* in the cities of **S** instead of	8111
	17:24 they possessed **S**, and dwelt in the cities	8111
	17:26 removed, and placed in the cities of **S**,	8111
	17:28 whom they had carried away from **S**	8111
	18: 9 king of Assyria came up against **S**,	8111
	18:10 year of Hoshea king of Israel, **S** was taken.	8111
	18:34 have they delivered **S** out of mine hand?	8111
	21:13 I will stretch over Jerusalem the line of **S**,	8111
	23:18 bones of the prophet that came out of **S**.	8111
	23:19 high places that *were* in the cities of **S**,	8111
2Ch	18: 2 years he went down to Ahab to **S**.	8111
	18: 9 place *at* the entering in of the gate of **S**;	8111
	22: 9 they caught him, (for he *was* hid in **S**,)	8111
	25:13 from **S** even unto Beth-horon,	8111
	25:24 the hostages also, and returned to **S**.	8111
	28: 8 from them, and brought the spoil to **S**.	8111
	28: 9 went out before the host that came to **S**,	8111
	28:15 to their brethren: then they returned to **S**.	8111
Ezr	4:10 set in the cities of **S**, and the rest *that are*	8115
	4:17 rest of their companions that dwell in **S**,	8115
Ne	4: 2 before his brethren and the army of **S**,	8111
Isa	7: 9 the head of Ephraim *is* **S**, and the head of	8111
	7: 9 and the head of **S** *is* Remaliah's son.	8111
	8: 4 the spoil of **S** shall be taken away before	8111
	9: 9 *even* Ephraim and the inhabitant of **S**,	8111
	10: 9 Hamath as Arpad? *is* not **S** as Damascus?	8111
	10:10 did excel *them of* Jerusalem and of **S**;	8111
	10:11 as I have done unto **S** and her idols,	8111
	36:19 have they delivered **S** out of my hand?	8111
Jer	23:13 I have seen folly in the prophets of **S**;	8111
	31: 5 yet plant vines upon the mountains of **S**:	8111
	41: 5 from Shiloh, and from **S**, even fourscore	8111
Eze	16:46 elder sister *is* **S**, she and her daughters	8111
	16:51 Neither hath **S** committed half of thy sins;	8111
	16:53 the captivity of **S** and her daughters, then	8111
	16:55 **S** and her daughters shall return to their	8111
	23: 4 **S** is Aholah, and Jerusalem Aholibah.	8111
	23:33 desolation, *with* the cup of thy sister **S**.	8111
Hos	7: 1 was discovered, and the wickedness of **S**:	8111
	8: 5 Thy calf, O **S**, hath cast *thee* off;	8111
	8: 6 but the calf of **S** shall be broken in pieces.	8111
	10: 5 The inhabitants of **S** shall fear because	8111
	10: 7 *As for* **S**, her king is cut off as the foam	8111
	13:16 **S** shall become desolate; for she hath	8111
Am	3: 9 yourselves upon the mountains of **S**,	8111
	3:12 out that dwell in **S** in the corner of a bed,	8111
	4: 1 of Bashan, that *are* in the mountain of **S**,	8111
	6: 1 in Zion, and trust in the mountain of **S**,	8111
	8:14 They that swear by the sin of **S**, and say,	8111
Ob	1:19 the fields of Ephraim, and the fields of **S**:	8111
Mic	1: 1 he saw concerning **S** and Jerusalem.	8111
	1: 5 *is it* not **S**? and what *are* the high places	8111
	1: 6 Therefore I will make **S** as a heap of	8111
Lk	17:11 that he passed through the midst of **S** and	4540
Jn	4: 4 And he must needs go through **S**.	4540
	4: 5 Then cometh he to a city of **S**, which is	4540
	4: 7 cometh a woman of **S** to draw water:	4540
	4: 9 Then saith the woman of **S** unto him,	4542
	4: 9 drink of me, which am a woman of **S**?	4542
Ac	1: 8 and in **S**, and unto the uttermost part of	4540
	1: 8 throughout all the regions of Judea and **S**,	4540
	8: 5 Then Philip went down to the city of **S**,	4540
	8: 9 and bewitched the people of **S**, giving out	4540
	8:14 that **S** had received the word of God,	4540
	9:31 throughout all Judea and Galilee and **S**,	4540
	15: 3 they passed through Phenice and **S**,	4540

SAMARITAN (3) [SAMARIA]

Lk	10:33 But a certain **S**, as he journeyed,	4541
	17:16 feet, giving him thanks: and he was a **S**.	4541
Jn	8:48 Say we not well that thou art a **S**, and	4541

SAMARITANS (7) [SAMARIA]

2Ki	17:29 of the high places which the **S** had made,	8118
Mt	10: 5 and into *any* city of the **S** enter ye not:	4541
Lk	9:52 and entered into a village of the **S**,	4541
Jn	4: 9 For the Jews have no dealings with the **S**.	4541
	4:39 And many of the **S** of that city believed on	4541
	4:40 So when the **S** were come unto him,	4541
Ac	8:25 the gospel in many villages of the **S**.	4541

SAME (332) [SELFSAME]

Ge	2:13 the **s** *it* is that compasseth the whole land	1931
	5:29 This **s** shall comfort us concerning our	NIH
	6: 4 the **s** *became* mighty *men* which *were* of	1992
	7:11 the **s** day were all the fountains of the	2088
	10:12 and Calah: the **s** *is* a great city.	1931
	14: 8 and the king of Bela (the **s** *is* Zoar);	1931
	15:18 In the **s** day the LORD made a covenant	1931
	19:37 the **s** *is* the father of the Moabites unto	1931
	19:38 the **s** *is* the father of the children of	1931
	21: 8 Abraham made a great feast the **s** day that	NIH
	23: 2 the **s** *is* Hebron in the land of Canaan.	1931
	23:19 the **s** *is* Hebron in the land of Canaan.	1931
	24:14 *let* the **s** be she that thou hast appointed	NIH
	24:44 *let* the **s** be the woman whom the LORD	1931
	25:30 with that **s** red *pottage*; for I *am* faint:	122
	26:12 received in the **s** year an hundredfold:	1931
	26:24 the LORD appeared unto him the **s** night,	1931
	26:32 it came to pass the **s** day, that Isaac's	1931
	32:13 he lodged there that **s** night; and took of	NIH
	41:48 about every city, laid he up in the **s**.	1886.3
	44: 6 and he spake unto them these **s** words.	NIH
	48: 7 the way of Ephrath; the **s** *is* Beth-lehem.	1931
Ex	5: 6 Pharaoh commanded the **s** day	1931
	12: 6 until the fourteenth day of the **s** month:	2088
	19: 1 the **s** day came they *into* the wilderness	2088
	25:31 and his flowers, shall be of the **s**.	5089.1
	25:35 *be* a knop under two branches of the **s**,	5089.1
	25:35 a knop under two branches of the **s**,	5089.1
	25:35 a knop under two branches of the **s**,	5089.1
	25:36 and their branches shall be of the **s**:	5089.1
	27: 2 his horns shall be of the **s**: and thou	2050.2
	28: 8 which *is* upon it, shall be of the **s**,	5105.2
	30: 2 the horns thereof *shall be* of the **s**.	5105.2
	37:17 knops, and his flowers, were of the **s**,	5089.1
	37:21 a knop under two branches of the **s**,	5089.1
	37:21 a knop under two branches of the **s**,	5089.1
	37:21 a knop under two branches of the **s**,	5089.1
	37:22 and their branches were of the **s**:	5089.1
	37:25 of it; the horns thereof were of the **s**.	5105.2
	38: 2 of it; the horns thereof were of the **s**:	5105.2
	39: 5 that *was* upon it, *was* of the **s**, according	1931
Lev	7:15 be eaten the **s** day that it is offered;	NIH
	7:16 it shall be eaten the **s** day that he offereth	NIH
	19: 6 It shall be eaten the **s** day ye offer it,	NIH
	22:30 On the **s** day it shall be eaten up; ye shall	1931
	23: 6 on the fifteenth day of the **s** month *is*	2088
	23:28 ye shall do no work in that **s** day: for it *is*	6106
	23:29 *be* that shall not be afflicted in that **s** day,	6106
	23:30 *it be* that doeth any work in that **s** day,	6106
	23:30 the **s** soul will I destroy from among his	1931
Nu	4: 8 cover the **s** with a covering of badgers'	2050.2
	6:11 and shall hallow his head that **s** day.	NIH
	9:13 even the **s** soul shall be cut off from	1931
	10:32 do unto us, the **s** will we do unto thee.	NIH
	15:30 a stranger, the **s** reproacheth the LORD;	1931
	32:10 the LORD's anger was kindled the **s**	1931
Dt	9:20 and I prayed for Aaron also the **s** time.	1931
	14:28 all the tithe of thine increase the **s** year,	1931
	27:11 Moses charged the people the **s** day,	1931
	31:22 therefore wrote this song the **s** day,	1931
Jos	6:15 compassed the city after the **s** manner	2088
	11:16 of Israel, and the valley of the **s**;	1886.4
	15: 8 side of the Jebusite; the **s** *is* Jerusalem:	1931
Jdg	6:25 it came to pass the **s** night, that the LORD	1931
	7: 4 go with thee, the **s** shall go with thee;	1931
	7: 4 shall not go with thee, the **s** shall not go.	1931
	7: 9 it came to pass the **s** night, that the LORD	1931
1Sa	4:12 came to Shiloh the **s** day with his clothes	1931
	6:15 sacrificed sacrifices the **s** day unto	1931
	6:16 seen *it*, they returned to Ekron the **s** day.	1931
	9:17 thee of: this **s** shall reign over my people.	NIH
	10:12 one of the **s** place answered and said,	8033
	14:35 the **s** was the first altar that he built	2050.2
	17:23 and spake according to the **s** words:	428
	17:30 and spake after the **s** manner:	2088
	31: 6 all his men, that **s** day together.	NIH
2Sa	2:23 fell down there, and died in the **s** place:	8478
	5: 7 hold of Zion; the **s** *is* the city of David.	1931
	23: 7 shall be utterly burnt with fire in the **s**	NIH
	23: 8 the captains; the **s** *was* Adino the Eznite:	1931
1Ki	7:35 and the borders thereof *were* of the **s**.	5089.1
	8:64 The **s** day did the king hallow the middle	1931
	13: 3 he gave a sign the **s** day, saying, This *is*	1931
	13: 9 nor turn again by the **s** way that thou	NIH
2Ki	3: 6 king Jehoram went out of Samaria the **s**	1931
	8:22 Then Libnah revolted at the **s** time.	1931
	19:29 year that which springeth of the **s**,	7823
	19:33 *by* the **s** shall he return, and shall not come	NIH
1Ch	1:27 Abram; the **s** *is* Abraham.	1931
	4:33 their villages that *were* round about the **s**	428

1Ch	16:17 hath confirmed the **s** to Jacob for a law,	1886.3
	17: 3 it came to pass the **s** night, that the word	1931
2Ch	8:13 Also at the **s** time Solomon kept the feast	1931
	13: 9 *the* **s** may be a priest of *them that are* no	NIH
	15:11 they offered unto the LORD the **s** time,	1931
	16:10 oppressed *some* of the people the **s** time.	1931
	18: 7 the **s** *is* Micaiah the son of Imla.	1931
	20:26 the name of the **s** place was called,	1931
	21:10 The **s** time also did Libnah revolt from	1931
	27: 5 children of Ammon gave him the **s** year	1931
	32:12 Hath not the **s** Hezekiah taken away his	1931
	32:30 This **s** Hezekiah also stopped the upper	1931
	34:28 and upon the inhabitants of the **s**.	2050.2
	35:16 of the LORD was prepared the **s** day,	1931
Ezr	4:15 sedition within the **s** of old time:	1459+1886.9
	5: 3 At the **s** time came to them Tatnai,	0.2
	5:13 **s** king Cyrus made a decree to build this	NIH
	5:16 came the **s** Sheshbazzar, *and* laid	1791
	6: 3 In the first year of Cyrus the king the **s**	NIH
	10:23 and Shimei, and Kelaiah, (the **s** *is* Kelita,)	1931
Ne	4:22 Likewise at the **s** time said I unto	1931
	6: 4 and I answered them after the **s** manner.	2088
	10:37 that the **s** Levites *might* have the tithes in	1992
Est	9: 1 on the thirteenth day of the **s**,	2050.2
	9:17 the fourteenth day of the **s** rested they,	2050.2
	9:18 on the fifteenth *day* of the **s** they rested,	2050.2
	9:21 and the fifteenth day of the **s**, yearly,	2050.2
Job	4: 8 and sow wickedness, reap the **s**.	1930.2
	13: 2 What ye know, the **s** do I know also. I *am*	NIH
Ps	68:23 *and* the tongue of thy dogs in the **s**.	1930.2
	75: 8 of mixture; and he poureth out of the **s**:	2088
	102:27 thou *art* the **s**, and thy years shall have no	1931
	105:10 confirmed the **s** unto Jacob for a law,	1886.3
	113: 3 the **s** the LORD's name *is* to be praised.	2050.2
Pr	28:24 the **s** *is* the companion of a destroyer.	1931
Ecc	9:15 yet no man remembered that **s** poor man.	NIH
Isa	7:20 In the **s** day shall the Lord shave with a	1931
	20: 2 At the **s** time spake the LORD by Isaiah	1931
	37:30 year that which springeth of the **s**:	7823
	37:34 *by* the **s** shall he return, and shall not come	NIH
Jer	27: 8 kingdom which will not serve the **s**	2050.2
	28: 1 came to pass the **s** year, in the beginning	1931
	28:17 Hananiah the prophet died the **s** year in	1931
	31: 1 At the **s** time, saith the LORD, will I be	1931
	39:10 them vineyards and fields at the **s** time.	1931
Eze	3:18 the **s** wicked *man* shall die in his iniquity;	1931
	10:16 the **s** wheels also turned not from beside	1992
	10:22 the likeness of their faces *was* the **s** faces	1992
	21:26 shall not *be* the **s**: exalt *him that is* low,	2063
	23:38 they have defiled my sanctuary in the **s**	1931
	23:39 they came the **s** day into my sanctuary to	1931
	24: 2 the name of the day, *even* of this **s** day:	6106
	24: 2 set himself against Jerusalem this **s** day.	6106
	38:10 *that* at the **s** time shall things come into	1931
	38:18 it shall come to pass at the **s** time when	1931
	44: 3 and shall go out by the way of the **s**.	2050.2
Da	3: 6 worshippeth shall the **s** hour be cast into	0.2
	3:15 ye shall be cast the **s** hour into the midst	1886.9
	4:33 The **s** hour was the thing fulfilled upon	1886.9
	4:36 At the **s** time my reason returned unto me;	0.2
	5: 5 In the **s** hour came forth fingers of a	1886.9
	5:12 of doubts, were found in the **s**, Daniel,	1886.8
	7:21 the **s** horn made war with the saints,	1797
	12: 1 there was a nation *even* to that **s** time:	1931
Am	2: 7 and his father will go in unto the **s** maid,	NIH
Zep	1: 9 In the **s** day also will I punish all those	1931
Zec	6:10 come thou the **s** day, and go *into* the	1931
Mal	1:11 the **s** my name *shall be* great among	2050.2
Mt	3: 4 And the **s** John had his raiment of camel's	
	5:19 teach *them*, the **s** shall be called great in	3778
	5:46 have ye? do not even the publicans the **s**?	846
	10:19 it shall be given you in that **s** hour what	NIG
	12:50 the **s** is my brother, and sister, and mother.	846
	13: 1 The **s** day went Jesus out of the house,	1565
	13:20 *places*, the **s** is he that heareth the word,	3778
	15:22 a woman of Canaan came out of the **s**	1565
	18: 1 At the **s** time came the disciples unto	1565
	18: 4 the **s** is greatest in the kingdom of heaven.	3778
	18:28 the **s** servant went out, and found one	1565
	21:42 the **s** is become the head of the corner:	3778
	22:23 The **s** day came to him *the* Sadducees,	1565
	24:13 endure unto the end, the **s** shall be saved.	3778
	25:16 five talents went and traded with the **s**,	846
	26:23 me in the dish, the **s** shall betray me.	3778
	26:44 prayed the third time, saying the **s** words.	846
	26:48 Whomsoever I shall kiss, that **s** is he:	NIG
	26:55 In that **s** hour said Jesus to the multitudes,	NIG
	27:44 crucified with him, cast the **s** in his teeth.	846
Mk	3:35 the **s** is my brother, and my sister,	3778
	4:35 And the **s** day, when the even was come,	1565
	8:35 and the gospel's, the **s** shall save it.	3778
	9:35 *the* **s** shall be last of all, and servant of all.	NIG
	10:10 disciples asked him again of the **s** *matter*.	846
	13:13 endure unto the end, the **s** shall be saved.	3778
	14:39 and prayed, and spake the **s** words.	846
	14:44 Whomsoever I shall kiss, that **s** is he;	846
Lk	2: 8 And there were in the **s** country shepherds	846
	2:25 the **s** man *was* just and devout,	3778
	6:33 have ye? for sinners also do even the **s**.	846
	6:38 with the **s** measure that ye mete withal it	846
	7:21 And in that **s** hour he cured many of *their*	NIG
	7:47 whom little is forgiven, the **s** loveth little.	NIG
	9:24 his life for my sake, the **s** shall save it.	3778
	9:48 is least among you all, the **s** shall be great.	3778
	10: 7 And in the **s** house remain, eating and	846

S

Lk 10:10 go *your ways* out into the streets of **the s,** 846
12:12 For the Holy Ghost shall teach you in **the s** 846
13:31 The **s** day there came certain *of* 846
16: 1 **the s** was accused unto him that he had 3778
17:29 But the *s* day that Lot went out of Sodom NIG
20:17 **the s** is become the head of the corner? 3778
20:19 the scribes the **s** hour sought to lay hands 846
20:47 **the s** shall receive greater damnation. 3778
23:12 and **s** day Pilate and Herod were made 846
23:40 seeing thou art in the **s** condemnation? 846
23:51 (**The s** had not consented to the counsel 3778
24:13 two of them went *that* **s** day to a village 846
24:33 they rose up the **s** hour, and returned to 846
Jn 1: 2 **The s** was in the beginning with God. 3778
1: 7 **The s** came for a witness, to bear witness 3778
1:33 to baptize with water, **the s** said unto me, 1565
1:33 **the s** is he which baptizeth with the Holy 3778
3: 2 **The s** came to Jesus by night, and said 3778
3:26 **the s** baptizeth, and all *men* come to him. 3778
4:53 the father knew that *it was* at **the s** hour, 1565
5: 9 walked: and on the **s** day was the sabbath. 1565
5:11 **the s** said unto me, Take up thy bed, 1565
5:36 the works that I do, bear witness of me, 846
7:18 **the s** is true, and no unrighteousness is in 3778
8:25 Even **the s** that I said unto you *from* 5100
10: 1 other way, **the s** is a thief and a robber. 1565
11: 6 he abode two days *still* in the **s** place NIG
11:49 being the high priest that **s** year, said unto NIG
12:21 **The s** came therefore to Philip, which 3778
12:48 **the s** shall judge him in the last day. 1565
15: 5 I in him, **the s** bringeth forth much fruit: 3778
18:13 which was the high priest that **s** year. 1565
20:19 Then **the s** day at evening, being the first 1565
Ac 1:11 this **s** Jesus, which is taken up from you NIG
1:22 unto *that* **s** day that he was taken up from NIG
2:36 that God hath made **that s** Jesus, whom 3778
2:41 the **s** day there were added *unto them* 1565
7:19 **The s** dealt subtilly with our kindred, 3778
7:35 the **s** did God send *to be* a ruler and 3778
8: 9 beforetime in the **s** city used sorcery, NIG
8:35 and began at the **s** scripture, 1565
12: 6 the **s** night Peter was sleeping between 1565
13:33 God hath fulfilled **the s** unto their 3778
14: 9 **The s** heard Paul speak: who stedfastly 846
15:27 who shall also tell *you* the **s** things by 846
16:17 **The s** followed Paul and us, and cried, 3778
16:18 out of her. And he came out the **s** hour. 846
16:33 And he took them the **s** hour of the night, 1565
18: 3 And because *he* was of the **s** craft, 3673
19:23 And the **s** time there arose no small 1565+2596
21: 9 **the s** *man* had four daughters, virgins, 3778
22:13 And the **s** hour I looked up upon him. 846
24:20 Or else let these **s** *here* say, if they have 846
28: 7 In the **s** quarters were possessions 1565+4012
Ro 1:32 not only do the **s,** but have pleasure in 846
2: 1 for thou that judgest doest the **s** *things.* 846
2: 3 which do such *things,* and doest the **s,** 846
8:20 reason of him who hath subjected the **s,** NIG
9:17 For this **s** *purpose* have I raised thee up, 846
9:21 of the **s** lump to make one vessel unto 846
10:12 for the **s** Lord over all *is* rich unto all that 846
12: 4 and all members have not the **s** office: 846
12:16 *Be* of the **s** mind one towards another. 846
13: 3 *is* good, and thou shalt have praise of the **s:** 846
1Co 1:10 ye all speak the **s** *thing,* and *that* there be 846
1:10 *that* ye be perfectly joined together in the **s** 846
1:10 in the same mind and in the **s** judgment. 846
7:20 Let every man abide in the **s** calling 3588
8: 3 *man* love God, the **s** is known of him. 3778
9: 8 as a man? or saith not the law the **s** also? 3778
10: 3 And did all eat the **s** spiritual meat; 846
10: 4 And did all drink the **s** spiritual drink: 846
11:23 That the Lord Jesus the **s** night in which 1565
11:25 **After the s** manner also *he* took the cup, 5615
12: 4 there are diversities of gifts, but the **s** Spirit. 846
12: 5 of administrations, but the **s** Lord. 846
12: 6 but it is the **s** God which worketh all in all. 846
12: 8 to another the word of knowledge by the **s** 846
12: 9 To another faith by the **s** Spirit; to another 846
12: 9 another the gifts of healing by the **s** Spirit; 846
12:25 the members should have the **s** care one 846
15:39 All flesh *is* not the **s** flesh: but there *is* one 846
2Co 1: 6 which is effectual in the enduring of the **s** 846
2: 2 but the **s** which is made sorry by me? NIG
2: 3 And I wrote this **s** unto you, lest, when I 846
3:14 for until this day remaineth the **s** vail 846
3:18 are changed *into* the **s** image from glory to 846
4:13 We having the **s** spirit of faith, according as 846
6:13 Now for a recompence in the **s,** (I speak as 846
7: 8 for I perceive that the **s** epistle hath made 1565
8: 6 he would also finish in you the **s** grace 3778
8:16 which put the **s** earnest care into the heart 846
8:19 by us to the glory of the **s** Lord, 846
9: 4 should be ashamed in this **s** confident NIG
9: 5 that the **s** might be ready, as *a matter of* 3778
12:18 walked we in the **s** spirit? *walked we* 846
12:18 same spirit? *walked* we not in the **s** steps? 846
Gal 2: 8 the **s** was mighty in me towards NIG
2:10 the **s** which I also was forward to do. 846+3778
3: 7 faith, the **s** are the children of Abraham. 846
Eph 3: 6 and **of the s** body, and partakers of his 4954
4:10 that descended is **the s** also that ascended 846
6: 8 the **s** shall he receive of the Lord, 3778
6: 9 ye masters, do the **s** *things* unto them, 846
6:22 Whom I have sent unto you for the **s** 846

Php 1:30 Having the **s** conflict which ye saw in me, 846
2: 2 having the **s** love, *being* of one accord, 846
2:18 For the **s** cause also do ye joy, 846
3: 1 To write the **s** *things* to you, to me indeed 846
3:16 *let us* walk by the **s** rule, *let us* mind 846
3:16 by the same rule, *let us* mind the **s** *thing.* 846
4: 2 that *they* be of the **s** mind in the Lord. 846
Col 4: 2 and watch in the **s** with thanksgiving; 846
4: 8 Whom I have sent unto you for the **s** 846
2Ti 2: 2 the **s** commit thou to faithful men, 3778
Heb 1:12 but thou art **the s,** and thy years shall not 846
2:14 he also himself likewise took part of the **s;** 846
4:11 lest any *man* fall after the **s** example of 846
6:11 **s** diligence to the full assurance of hope 846
10:11 and offering oftentimes the **s** sacrifices, 846
13: 8 Jesus Christ the **s** yesterday, and to day, 846
Jas 3: 2 the **s** *is* a perfect man, *and* able also to 3778
3:10 Out of the **s** mouth proceedeth blessing 846
3:11 Doth a fountain send forth at the **s** place 846
1Pe 2: 7 the **s** is made the head of the corner, 3778
4: 1 arm yourselves likewise with the **s** mind: 846
4: 4 run not with *them* to the excess of riot, 846
4:10 *even so* minister the **s** one to another, 846
4:19 knowing that the **s** afflictions are 846
2Pe 2:19 of the **s** is he brought in bondage. 3778
3: 7 are now, by the **s** word are kept in store, 846
1Jn 2:23 denieth the Son, the **s** hath not the Father: NIG
2:27 the **s** anointing teacheth you of all *things,* 846
Rev 3: 5 the **s** shall be clothed in white raiment; 3778
11:13 And **the s** hour was there a great 1565
14:10 **The s** shall drink of the wine of the wrath 846

SAMGAR See SAMGAR-NEBO

SAMGAR-NEBO (1)

Jer 39: 3 S, Sarsechim, Rab-saris, Nergal-sharezer, 5562

SAMLAH (4)

Ge 36:36 and **S** of Masrekah reigned in his stead. 8072
36:37 **S** died, and Saul of Rehoboth *by* the river 8072
1Ch 1:47 **S** of Masrekah reigned in his stead. 8072
1:48 when **S** was dead, Shaul of Rehoboth *by* 8072

SAMOS (1)

Ac 20:15 and the next *day* we arrived at **S,** 4544

SAMOTHRACE See SAMOTHRACIA

SAMOTHRACIA (1)

Ac 16:11 we came with a straight course to **S,** 4543

SAMSON (36) [SAMSON'S]

Jdg 13:24 woman bare a son, and called his name **S:** 8123
14: 1 **S** went down *to* Timnath, and saw a 8123
14: 3 **S** said unto his father, Get her for me; 8123
14: 5 went **S** down, and his father and 8123
14: 7 with the woman; and she pleased **S** well. 8123
14:10 **S** made there a feast; for so used the 8123
14:12 **S** said unto them, I will now put forth a 8123
15: 1 that **S** visited his wife with a kid; 8123
15: 3 **S** said concerning them, Now shall I be 8123
15: 4 went **S** and caught three hundred foxes, 8123
15: 6 they answered, **S,** the son in law of 8123
15: 7 **S** said unto them, Though ye have done 8123
15:10 answered, To bind **S** are we come up, 8123
15:11 said to **S,** Knowest thou not that 8123
15:12 said unto **S,** Swear unto me, that ye 8123
15:16 **S** said, With the jawbone of an ass, 8123
16: 1 went **S** to Gaza, and saw there a harlot, 8123
16: 2 *told* the Gazites, saying, **S** is come hither. 8123
16: 3 **S** lay till midnight, and arose at midnight, 8123
16: 6 Delilah said to **S,** Tell me, I pray thee, 8123
16: 7 **S** said unto her, If they bind me with 8123
16: 9 him, The Philistines *be* upon thee, **S.** 8123
16:10 Delilah said unto **S,** Behold, thou hast 8123
16:12 him, The Philistines *be* upon thee, **S.** 8123
16:13 Delilah said unto **S,** Hitherto thou hast 8123
16:14 him, The Philistines *be* upon thee, **S.** 8123
16:20 she said, The Philistines *be* upon thee, **S.** 8123
16:23 Our god hath delivered **S** our enemy into 8123
16:25 they said, Call for **S,** that he may make 8123
16:25 they called for **S** out of the prison house; 8123
16:26 **S** said unto the lad that held him by 8123
16:27 women, that beheld while **S** made sport. 8123
16:28 **S** called unto the Lord, and said, O Lord 8123
16:29 **S** took hold of the two middle pillars 8123
16:30 **S** said, Let me die with the Philistines. 8123
Heb 11:32 and *of* Barak, and *of* **S,** and *of* Jephthae, 4546

SAMSON'S (3) [SAMSON]

Jdg 14:15 that they said unto **S** wife, Entice thy 8123
14:16 **S** wife wept before him, and said, 8123
14:20 **S** wife was *given* to his companion, 8123

SAMUEL (142)

1Sa 1:20 she bare a son, and called his name **S,** 8050
2:18 **S** ministered before the Lord, *being* a 8050
2:21 And the child **S** grew before the Lord. 8050
2:26 the child **S** grew on, and was in favour 8050
3: 1 the child **S** ministered unto the Lord 8050
3: 3 God *was,* and **S** was laid down *to sleep;* 8050
3: 4 That the Lord called **S:** 8050
3: 6 the Lord called yet again, **S.** 8050
3: 7 Now **S** did not yet know the Lord, 8050

1Sa 3: 8 the Lord called **S** again the third time. 8050
3: 9 Therefore Eli said unto **S,** Go, lie down: 8050
3: 9 So **S** went and lay down in his place. 8050
3:10 and called as at other times, **S, S**amuel. 8050
3:10 and called as at other times, Samuel, **S.** 8050
3:10 **S** answered, Speak; for thy servant 8050
3:11 The Lord said to **S,** Behold, I will do a 8050
3:15 **S** lay until the morning, and opened 8050
3:15 And **S** feared to shew Eli the vision. 8050
3:16 Eli called **S,** and said, Samuel, my son. 8050
3:16 Eli called Samuel, and said, **S,** my son. 8050
3:18 told him every whit, and hid nothing 8050
3:19 And **S** grew, and the Lord was with him, 8050
3:20 **S** was established to be a prophet of 8050
3:21 for the Lord revealed himself to **S** in 8050
4: 1 the word of **S** came to all Israel. 8050
7: 3 **S** spake unto all the house of Israel, 8050
7: 5 **S** said, Gather all Israel to Mizpeh, 8050
7: 6 **S** judged the children of Israel in Mizpeh. 8050
7: 8 the children of Israel said to **S,** Cease not 8050
7: 9 **S** took a sucking lamb, and offered it *for* a 8050
7: 9 **S** cried unto the Lord for Israel; 8050
7:10 as **S** was offering up the burnt offering, 8050
7:12 **S** took a stone, and set *it* between Mizpeh 8050
7:13 against the Philistines all the days of **S.** 8050
7:15 And **S** judged Israel all the days of his life. 8050
8: 1 it came to pass, when **S** was old, that he 8050
8: 4 and came to **S** unto Ramah, 8050
8: 6 the thing displeased **S,** when they said, 8050
8: 6 judge us. And **S** prayed unto the Lord. 8050
8: 7 the Lord said unto **S,** Hearken unto 8050
8:10 **S** told all the words of the Lord unto 8050
8:19 the people refused to obey the voice of **S;** 8050
8:21 **S** heard all the words of the people, 8050
8:22 the Lord said to **S,** Hearken unto their 8050
8:22 **S** said unto the men of Israel, Go ye every 8050
9:14 **S** came out against them, for to go up 8050
9:15 Now the Lord had told **S** in his ear a day 8050
9:17 when **S** saw Saul, the Lord said unto 8050
9:18 Saul drew near to **S** in the gate, and said, 8050
9:19 **S** answered Saul, and said, I *am* the seer: 8050
9:22 **S** took Saul and his servant, 8050
9:23 **S** said unto the cook, Bring the portion 8050
9:24 **S** said, Behold that which is left; set *it* NIH
9:24 So Saul did eat with **S** that day. 8050
9:25 **S** communed with Saul upon the top of NIH
9:26 that **S** called Saul to the top of the house, 8050
9:26 went out both of them, he and **S,** abroad. 8050
9:27 **S** said to Saul, Bid the servant pass on 8050
10: 1 **S** took a vial of oil, and poured *it* upon his 8050
10: 9 he had turned his back to go from **S,** 8050
10:14 that *they were* no where, we came to **S.** 8050
10:15 Tell me, I pray thee, what **S** said unto 8050
10:16 whereof **S** spake, he told him not. 8050
10:17 **S** called the people together unto 8050
10:20 when **S** had caused all the tribes of Israel 8050
10:24 said to all the people, See ye him whom 8050
10:25 Then **S** told the people the manner of 8050
10:25 **S** sent all the people away, every man to 8050
11: 7 cometh not forth after Saul and after **S,** 8050
11:12 people said unto **S,** Who *is* he that said, 8050
11:14 said **S** to the people, Come, and let us go 8050
12: 1 **S** said unto all Israel, Behold, I have 8050
12: 6 **S** said unto the people, *It is* the Lord that 8050
12:11 **S,** and delivered you out of the hand of 8050
12:18 So **S** called unto the Lord; 8050
12:18 people greatly feared the Lord and **S.** 8050
12:19 all the people said unto **S,** Pray for thy 8050
12:20 **S** said unto the people, Fear not: ye have 8050
13: 8 according to the set time that **S** had 8050
13: 8 *had* appointed: but **S** came not to Gilgal; 8050
13:10 the burnt offering, behold, **S** came; 8050
13:11 Saul said, What hast thou done? And Saul 8050
13:13 **S** said to Saul, Thou hast done foolishly: 8050
13:15 **S** arose, and gat him up from Gilgal *unto* 8050
15: 1 **S** also said unto Saul, The Lord sent me 8050
15:10 came the word of the Lord unto **S,** 8050
15:11 it grieved **S;** and he cried unto the Lord 8050
15:12 when **S** rose early to meet Saul in 8050
15:12 was told **S,** saying, Saul came to Carmel, 8050
15:13 **S** came to Saul: and Saul said unto him, 8050
15:14 **S** said, What *meaneth* then this bleating 8050
15:16 **S** said unto Saul, Stay, and I will tell thee 8050
15:17 Saul, When thou *wast* little in thine 8050
15:20 Saul said unto **S,** Yea, I have obeyed 8050
15:22 **S** said, Hath the Lord *as great* delight in 8050
15:24 Saul said unto **S,** I have sinned: for I have 8050
15:26 **S** said unto Saul, I will not return with 8050
15:27 **S** turned about to go away, he laid hold 8050
15:28 **S** said unto him, The Lord hath rent 8050
15:31 So **S** turned again after Saul; 8050
15:32 said **S,** Bring you hither to me Agag 8050
15:33 **S** said, As thy sword hath made women 8050
15:33 **S** hewed Agag in pieces before the Lord 8050
15:34 **S** went to Ramah; and Saul went up to 8050
15:35 **S** came no more to see Saul until the day 8050
15:35 nevertheless **S** mourned for Saul: 8050
16: 1 the Lord said unto **S,** How long wilt 8050
16: 2 **S** said, How can I go? if Saul hear *it,* he 8050
16: 4 **S** did *that* which the Lord spake, 8050
16: 6 the Lord which **S,** Look not on his 8050
16: 8 and made him pass before **S.** 8050
16:10 made seven of his sons to pass before **S.** 8050
16:10 **S** said unto Jesse, The Lord hath not 8050
16:11 **S** said unto Jesse, Are here all *thy* 8050

1Sa 16:11	**S** said unto Jesse, Send and fetch him:	8050
16:13	**S** took the horn of oil, and anointed him	8050
16:13	So **S** rose up, and went to Ramah.	8050
19:18	came to **S** to Ramah, and told him all that	8050
19:18	And he and **S** went and dwelt in Naioth.	8050
19:20	**S** standing *as* appointed over them,	8050
19:22	asked and said, Where *are* **S** and David?	8050
19:24	prophesied before **S** in like manner,	8050
25: 1	**S** died; and all the Israelites were gathered	8050
28: 3	Now **S** was dead, and all Israel had	8050
28:11	unto thee? And he said, Bring me up **S**.	8050
28:12	when the woman saw **S**, she cried with a	8050
28:14	Saul perceived that it *was* **S**, and he	8050
28:15	**S** said to Saul, Why hast thou disquieted	8050
28:16	said **S**, Wherefore then dost thou ask of	8050
28:20	sore afraid, because of the words of **S**.	8050
1Ch 6:28	And the sons of **S**; the firstborn Vashni,	8050
9:22	**S** the seer did ordain in their set office.	8050
11: 3	according to the word of the LORD by **S**.	8050
26:28	that **S** the seer, and Saul the son of Kish,	8050
29:29	they *are* written in the book of **S** the seer,	8050
2Ch 35:18	kept in Israel from the days of **S**	8050
Ps 99: 6	**S** among them that call upon his name;	8050
Jer 15: 1	Though Moses and **S** stood before me,	8050
Ac 3:24	all the prophets from **S** and those that	4545
13:20	and fifty years, until **S** the prophet.	4545
Heb 11:32	*of* David also, and **S**, and *of* the prophets:	4545

SANBALLAT (10)

Ne 2:10	When **S** the Horonite, and Tobiah	5571
2:19	when **S** the Horonite, and Tobiah	5571
4: 1	when **S** heard that we builded the wall,	5571
4: 7	when **S**, and Tobiah, and the Arabians,	5571
6: 1	when **S**, and Tobiah, and Geshem	5571
6: 2	That **S** and Geshem sent unto me, saying,	5571
6: 5	sent **S** his servant unto me in like manner	5571
6:12	for Tobiah and **S** had hired him.	5571
6:14	and **S** according to these their works,	5571
13:28	*was* son in law to **S** the Horonite.	5571

SANCTIFICATION (5) [SANCTIFY]

1Co 1:30	and righteousness, and **s**, and redemption:	38
1Th 4: 3	For this is the will of God, *even* your **s**,	38
4: 4	should know how to possess his vessel in **s**	38
2Th 2:13	you to salvation through **s** of the Spirit	38
1Pe 1: 2	through **s** of the Spirit, unto obedience and	38

SANCTIFIED (62) [SANCTIFY]

Ge 2: 3	God blessed the seventh day, and **s** it:	6942
Ex 19:14	mount unto the people, and **s** the people;	6942
29:43	and *the tabernacle* shall be **s** by my glory.	6942
Lev 8:10	and all that *was* therein, and **s** them.	6942
8:15	and **s** it, to make reconciliation upon it.	6942
8:30	**s** Aaron, *and* his garments, and his sons,	6942
10: 3	I will be **s** in them that come nigh me,	6942
27:15	if he that **s** *it* will redeem his house, then	6942
27:19	if he that **s** the field will in any wise	6942
Nu 7: 1	**s** it, and all the instruments thereof,	6942
7: 1	and had anointed them, and **s** them;	6942
8:17	in the land of Egypt, I **s** them for myself.	6942
20:13	with the LORD, and he was **s** in them.	6942
Dt 32:51	ye **s** me not in the midst of the children of	6942
1Sa 7: 1	**s** Eleazar his son to keep the ark of	6942
16: 5	he **s** Jesse and his sons, and called them to	6942
21: 5	though it were a *this* day in the vessel.	6942
1Ch 15:14	Levites **s** themselves to bring up the ark	6942
2Ch 5:11	all the priests that were present were **s**,	6942
7:16	For now have I chosen and **s** this house,	6942
7:20	this house, which I have **s** for my name,	6942
29:15	brethren, and **s** themselves, and came,	6942
29:17	they **s** the house of the LORD in eight	6942
29:19	have we prepared and **s**, and behold,	6942
29:34	until the *other* priests had **s** themselves:	6942
30: 3	the priests had not **s** themselves	6942
30: 8	his sanctuary, which he hath **s** for ever:	6942
30:15	themselves, and brought in the burnt	6942
30:17	in the congregation that were not **s**:	6942
30:24	a great number of priests **s** themselves.	6942
31:18	for in their set office they **s** themselves *in*	6942
Ne 3: 1	they **s** it, and set up the doors of it;	6942
3: 1	even unto the tower of Meah they **s** it,	6942
12:47	they **s** *holy things* unto the Levites;	6942
12:47	the Levites **s** *them* unto the children of	6942
Job 1: 5	Job sent and **s** them, and rose up early	6942
Isa 5:16	that is holy shall be **s** in righteousness.	6942
13: 3	I have commanded my **s ones**, I have also	6942
Jer 1: 5	camest forth out of the womb I **s** thee,	6942
Eze 20:41	and I will be **s** in you before the heathen.	6942
28:22	judgments in her, and shall be **s** in her.	6942
28:25	shall be **s** in them in the sight of	6942
36:23	when I shall be **s** in you before their eyes:	6942
38:16	when I shall be **s** in thee, O Gog,	6942
39:27	**s** in them in the sight of many nations;	6942
48:11	*It shall be* for the priests that are **s** of	6942
Jn 10:36	Say ye *of him*, whom the Father hath **s**,	37
17:19	that they also might be **s** through the truth.	37
Ac 20:32	an inheritance among all them which are **s**.	37
26:18	among them which are **s** by faith	37
Ro 15:16	be acceptable, being **s** by the Holy Ghost.	37
1Co 1: 2	to them that are **s** in Christ Jesus, called	37
6:11	ye are **s**, but ye are justified in the name of	37
7:14	the unbelieving husband is **s** by the wife,	37
7:14	the unbelieving wife is **s** by the husband:	37
1Ti 4: 5	For it is **s** by the word of God and prayer.	37
2Ti 2:21	**s**, and meet for the master's use,	37

Heb 2:11	and they who are **s** *are* all of one:	37
10:10	By the which will we are **s** through	37
10:14	he hath perfected for ever them that are **s**.	37
10:29	wherewith he was **s**, an unholy *thing*, and	37
Jude 1: 1	to them that are **s** by God the Father,	37

SANCTIFIETH (4) [SANCTIFY]

Mt 23:17	the gold, or the temple that **s** the gold?	37
23:19	greater, the gift, or the altar that **s** the gift?	37
Heb 2:11	both he that **s** and they who are sanctified	37
9:13	the unclean, **s** to the purifying of the flesh:	37

SANCTIFY (70) [SANCTIFICATION, SANCTIFIED, SANCTIFIETH]

Ex 13: 2	**S** unto me all the firstborn,	6942
19:10	**s** them to day and to morrow, and let	6942
19:22	come near to the LORD, **s** themselves,	6942
19:23	Set bounds about the mount, and **s** it.	6942
28:41	and consecrate them, and **s** them,	6942
29:27	shalt **s** the breast of the wave offering,	6942
29:33	was made, to consecrate and to **s** them:	6942
29:36	for it, and thou shalt anoint it, to **s** it.	6942
29:37	make an atonement for the altar, and **s** it;	6942
29:44	I will **s** the tabernacle of the congregation,	6942
29:44	I will also **s** both Aaron and his sons,	6942
30:29	thou shalt **s** them, that they may be most	6942
31:13	know that I *am* the LORD that doth **s** you.	6942
40:10	and all his vessels, and **s** the altar:	6942
40:11	anoint the laver and his foot, and **s** it.	6942
40:13	garments, and anoint him, and **s** him;	6942
Lev 8:11	both the laver and his foot, to **s** them.	6942
8:12	head, and anointed him, to **s** him.	6942
11:44	shall therefore **s** yourselves, and ye shall	6942
20: 7	**S** yourselves therefore, and be ye holy:	6942
20: 8	and do them: I *am* the LORD which **s** you.	6942
21: 8	Thou shalt **s** him therefore; for he offereth	6942
21: 8	for I the LORD, which **s** you, *am* holy.	6942
21:15	his people: for I the LORD do **s** him.	6942
21:23	my sanctuaries: for I the LORD do **s** them.	6942
22: 9	if they profane it: I the LORD do **s** them.	6942
22:16	holy *things*: for I the LORD do **s** them.	6942
27:14	when a man shall **s** his house *to be* holy	6942
27:16	if a man shall **s** unto the LORD *some part*	6942
27:17	If he **s** his field from the year of jubile,	6942
27:18	if he **s** his field after the jubile, then	6942
27:22	if *a man* **s** unto the LORD a field which he	6942
27:26	be the LORD'S firstling, no man shall **s** it;	6942
Nu 11:18	**S** yourselves against to morrow,	6942
20:12	**s** me in the eyes of the children of Israel,	6942
20:14	to **s** me at the water before their eyes:	6942
Dt 5:12	Keep the sabbath day to **s** it, as the LORD	6942
15:19	of thy flock thou shalt **s** unto the LORD	6942
Jos 3: 5	Joshua said unto the people, **S** yourselves:	6942
7:13	Up, **s** the people, and say,	6942
7:13	and say, **S** yourselves against to morrow:	6942
1Sa 16: 5	**s** yourselves, and come with me to	6942
1Ch 15:12	**s** yourselves, *both* ye and your brethren	6942
23:13	that he should **s** the most holy *things*, he	6942
2Ch 29: 5	**s** now yourselves, and sanctify the house	6942
29: 5	**s** the house of the LORD God of your	6942
29:17	on the first *day* of the first month to **s**,	6942
29:34	in heart to **s** themselves than the priests.	6942
30:17	*was* not clean, to **s** *them* unto the LORD.	6942
35: 6	yourselves, and prepare your brethren,	6942
Ne 13:22	*and* keep the gates, to **s** the sabbath day.	6942
Isa 8:13	**S** the LORD of hosts himself; and *let him*	6942
29:23	they shall **s** my name, and sanctify the	6942
29:23	**s** the Holy One of Jacob, and shall fear	6942
66:17	They that **s** themselves, and purify	6942
Eze 20:12	know that I *am* the LORD that **s** them.	6942
36:23	I will **s** my great name, which was	6942
37:28	shall know that I the LORD do **s** Israel,	6942
38:23	Thus will I magnify myself, and **s** myself;	6942
44:19	they shall not **s** the people with their	6942
46:20	out into the utter court, to **s** the people.	6942
Joel 1:14	**S** ye a fast, call a solemn assembly,	6942
2:15	in Zion, **s** a fast, call a solemn assembly:	6942
2:16	Gather the people, **s** the congregation,	6942
Jn 17:17	**S** them through thy truth: thy word is truth.	37
17:19	And for their sakes I **s** myself, that they also	37
Eph 5:26	That he might **s** and cleanse *it* with	37
1Th 5:23	And the very God of peace **s** you wholly;	37
Heb 13:12	he might **s** the people with his own blood,	37
1Pe 3:15	But **s** the Lord God in your hearts:	37

SANCTUARIES (5) [SANCTUARY]

Lev 21:23	hath a blemish; that he profane not my **s**:	4720
26:31	bring your **s** unto desolation, and I will	4720
Jer 51:51	for strangers are come into the **s** of	4720
Eze 28:18	Thou hast defiled thy **s** by the multitude	4720
Am 7: 9	and the **s** of Israel shall be laid waste;	4720

SANCTUARY (137) [SANCTUARIES]

Ex 15:17	in the **S**, O Lord, *which* thy hands have	4720
25: 8	let them make me a **s**; that I may dwell	4720
30:13	half a shekel after the shekel of the **s**:	6944
30:24	hundred *shekels*, after the shekel of the **s**,	6944
36: 1	*manner of* work for the service of the **s**,	6944
36: 3	for the work of the service of the **s**,	6944
36: 4	men, that wrought all the work of the **s**,	6944
36: 6	any more work for the offering of the **s**.	6944
38:24	thirty shekels, after the shekel of the **s**.	6944
38:25	fifteen shekels, after the shekel of the **s**:	6944
38:26	*is*, half a shekel, after the shekel of the **s**,	6944
38:27	of silver were cast the sockets of the **s**,	6944

Lev 4: 6	before the LORD, before the vail of the **s**.	6944
5:15	after the shekel of the **s**, for a trespass	6944
10: 4	carry your brethren from before the **s** out	6944
12: 4	no hallowed *thing*, nor come into the **s**,	4720
16:33	shall make an atonement for the holy **s**,	4720
19:30	keep my sabbaths, and reverence my **s**:	4720
20: 3	to defile my **s**, and to profane my holy	4720
21:12	shall he go out of the **s**, nor profane	4720
21:12	sanctuary, nor profane the **s** of his God;	4720
26: 2	keep my sabbaths, and reverence my **s**:	4720
27: 3	shekels of silver, after the shekel of the **s**.	6944
27:25	shall be according to the shekel of the **s**.	6944
Nu 3:28	six hundred, keeping the charge of the **s**.	6944
3:31	the vessels of the **s** wherewith they	6944
3:32	of them that keep the charge of the **s**.	6944
3:38	keeping the charge of the **s** for the charge	4720
3:47	after the shekel of the **s** shalt thou take	6944
3:50	and five *shekels*, after the shekel of the **s**:	6944
4:12	wherewith they minister in the **s**,	6944
4:15	sons have made an end of covering the **s**,	6944
4:15	all the vessels of the **s**, as the camp is to	6944
4:16	of all that therein *is*, in the **s**, and in	6944
7: 9	the service of the **s** belonging unto them	6944
7:13	seventy shekels, after the shekel of the **s**;	6944
7:19	seventy shekels, after the shekel of the **s**;	6944
7:25	seventy shekels, after the shekel of the **s**;	6944
7:31	seventy shekels, after the shekel of the **s**;	6944
7:37	seventy shekels, after the shekel of the **s**;	6944
7:43	seventy shekels, after the shekel of the **s**;	6944
7:49	seventy shekels, after the shekel of the **s**;	6944
7:55	seventy shekels, after the shekel of the **s**;	6944
7:61	seventy shekels, after the shekel of the **s**;	6944
7:67	seventy shekels, after the shekel of the **s**;	6944
7:73	seventy shekels, after the shekel of the **s**;	6944
7:79	seventy shekels, after the shekel of the **s**;	6944
7:85	hundred *shekels*, after the shekel of the **s**:	6944
7:86	*shekels* apiece, after the shekel of the **s**.	6944
8:19	children of Israel come nigh unto the **s**.	6944
10:21	the Kohathites set forward, bearing the **s**:	4720
18: 1	with thee shall bear the iniquity of the **s**:	4720
18: 3	shall not come nigh the vessels of the **s**	6944
18: 5	ye shall keep the charge of the **s**,	6944
18:16	after the shekel of the **s**, which *is* twenty	6944
19:20	he hath defiled the **s** of the LORD:	4720
Jos 24:26	an oak, that *was* by the **s** of the LORD.	4720
1Ch 9:29	all the instruments of the **s**, and the fine	6944
22:19	and build ye the **s** of the LORD God,	4720
24: 5	the governors of the **s**, and governors *of*	6944
28:10	chosen thee to build a house for the **s**:	4720
2Ch 20: 8	have built thee a **s** therein for thy name,	4720
26:18	go out of the **s**; for thou hast trespassed;	4720
29:21	the kingdom, and for the **s**, and for Judah.	4720
30: 8	enter into his **s**, which he hath sanctified	4720
30:19	according to the purification of the **s**.	6944
36:17	with the sword in the house of their **s**,	4720
Ne 10:39	where *are* the vessels of the **s**,	6944
Ps 20: 2	Send thee help from the **s**,	6944
63: 2	thy glory, so *as* I have seen thee in the **s**.	6944
68:24	the goings of my God, my King, in the **s**.	6944
73:17	Until I went into the **s** of God; *then*	4720
74: 3	the enemy hath done wickedly in the **s**.	4720
74: 7	They have cast fire into thy **s**, they have	4720
77:13	Thy way, O God, *is* in the **s**: who *is so*	6944
78:54	he brought them to the border of his **s**,	6944
78:69	he built his **s** like high *palaces*, like	4720
96: 6	him: strength and beauty *are* in his **s**.	6944
102:19	looked down from the height of his **s**;	6944
114: 2	Judah was his **s**, *and* Israel his dominion.	6944
134: 2	Lift up your hands *in* the **s**, and bless	6944
150: 1	Praise God in his **s**: praise him in	6944
Isa 8:14	he shall be for a **s**; but for a stone of	4720
16:12	that he shall come to his **s** to pray;	4720
43:28	I have profaned the princes of the **s**,	6944
60:13	together, to beautify the place of my **s**;	4720
63:18	our adversaries have trodden down thy **s**.	4720
Jer 17:12	from the beginning *is* the place of our **s**.	4720
La 1:10	seen *that* the heathen entered into her **s**,	4720
2: 7	cast off his altar, he hath abhorred his **s**,	4720
2:20	the prophet be slain in the **s** of the Lord?	4720
4: 1	the stones of the **s** are poured out in the	6944
Eze 5:11	thou hast defiled my **s** with all thy	4720
8: 6	that *I* should go far off from my **s**?	4720
9: 6	whom *is* the mark; and begin at my **s**.	4720
11:16	yet will I be to them as a little **s** in	4720
23:38	they have defiled my **s** in the same day,	4720
23:39	they came the same day into my **s** to	4720
24:21	I *will* profane my **s**, the excellency	4720
25: 3	Because thou saidst, Aha, against my **s**,	4720
37:26	will set my **s** in the midst of them for	4720
37:28	when my **s** shall be in the midst of them	4720
41:21	*were* squared, *and* the face of the **s**;	6944
41:23	And the temple and the **s** had two doors.	6944
42:20	to make a separation between the **s** and	6944
43:21	place of the house, without the **s**.	6944
44: 1	outward **s** which looketh *toward* the east;	4720
44: 5	the house, with every going forth of the **s**.	4720
44: 7	that ye have brought *into my* **s** strangers,	NIH
44: 7	be in my **s**, to pollute it, *even* my house,	4720
44: 8	ye have set keepers of my charge in my **s**	4720
44: 9	in flesh, shall enter into my **s**,	4720
44:11	Yet they shall be ministers in my **s**,	4720
44:15	that kept the charge of my **s** when	4720
44:16	They shall enter into my **s**, and they shall	4720
44:27	in the day that he goeth into the **s**, unto	6944
44:27	unto the inner court, to minister in the **s**,	6944

S

Eze	45: 2	this there shall be for the **s** five hundred	6944
	45: 3	shall be the **s** *and* the most holy *place*.	4720
	45: 4	be for the priests the ministers of the **s**,	4720
	45: 4	their houses, and a holy place for the **s**.	4720
	45:18	without blemish, and cleanse the **s**:	4720
	47:12	their waters they issued out of the **s**:	4720
	48: 8	and the **s** shall be in the midst of it.	4720
	48:10	the **s** of the LORD shall be in the midst	4720
	48:21	the **s** of the house *shall be* in the midst	4720
Da	8:11	and the place of his **s** was cast down.	4720
	8:13	give both the **s** and the host to be trodden	6944
	8:14	days; then shall the **s** be cleansed.	6944
	9:17	cause thy face to shine upon thy **s** that is	4720
	9:26	come shall destroy the city and the **s**;	6944
	11:31	they shall pollute the **s** of strength,	6944
Zep	3: 4	her priests have polluted the **s**, they have	6944
Heb	8: 2	minister of the **s**, and of the true tabernacle,	40
	9: 1	of divine service, and a worldly **s**.	40
	9: 2	and the shewbread; which is called the **s**.	40
	13:11	whose blood is brought into the **s** by the	40

SAND (28) [QUICKSANDS]

Ge	22:17	and as the **s** which *is* upon the sea shore;	2344
	32:12	make thy seed as the **s** of the sea,	2344
	41:49	Joseph gathered corn as the **s** of the sea,	2344
Ex	2:12	slew the Egyptian, and hid him in the **s**.	2344
Dt	33:19	of the seas, and *of* treasures hid in the **s**.	2344
Jos	11: 4	as the **s** that *is* upon the sea shore in	2344
Jdg	7:12	as the **s** by the sea side for multitude.	2344
1Sa	13: 5	people as the **s** which *is* on the sea shore	2344
2Sa	17:11	as the **s** that *is* by the sea for multitude;	2344
1Ki	4:20	as the **s** which *is* by the sea in multitude,	2344
	4:29	*even* as the **s** that *is* on the sea shore.	2344
Job	6: 3	now it would be heavier than the **s** of	2344
	29:18	and I shall multiply *my* days as the **s**.	2344
Ps	78:27	feathered fowls like as the **s** of the sea:	2344
	139:18	they are moe in number than the **s**:	2344
Pr	27: 3	A stone *is* heavy, and the **s** weighty;	2344
Isa	10:22	For though thy people Israel be as the **s** of	2344
	48:19	Thy seed also had been as the **s**,	2344
Jer	5:22	which have placed the **s** *for* the bound of	2344
	15: 8	increased to me above the **s** of the seas:	2344
	33:22	neither the **s** of the sea measured:	2344
Hos	1:10	of Israel shall be as the **s** of the sea,	2344
Hab	1: 9	they shall gather the captivity as the **s**.	2344
Mt	7:26	which built his house upon the **s**:	285
Ro	9:27	the children of Israel be as the **s** of the sea,	285
Heb	11:12	as the **s** which is by the sea shore	285
Rev	13: 1	I stood upon the **s** of the sea, and saw a	285
	20: 8	the number of whom *is* as the **s** of the sea.	285

SANDAL See SHOE; SHOE'S; SHOES

SANDALS (2)

Mk	6: 9	But *be* shod with **s**; and not put on two	4547
Ac	12: 8	unto him, Gird thyself, and bind on thy **s**.	4547

SANG (11) [SING]

Ex	15: 1	**s** Moses and the children of Israel this	7891
Nu	21:17	Israel **s** this song, Spring up, O well;	7891
Jdg	5: 1	Deborah and Barak the son of Abinoam	7891
1Sa	29: 5	of whom they **s** one to another in dances,	6030
2Ch	29:28	the singers **s**, and the trumpeters sounded:	7891
	29:30	they **s** praises with gladness,	NIH
Ne	12:42	the singers **s loud**, with Jezrahiah *their*	8085
Job	38: 7	When the morning stars **s** together,	7442
Ps	7: T	of David, which he **s** unto the LORD,	7891
	106:12	believed they his words; they **s** his praise.	7891
Ac	16:25	and Silas prayed, and **s praises** unto God:	5214

SANK (2) [SINK]

Ex	15: 5	they **s** into the bottom as a stone.	3381
	15:10	they **s** as lead in the mighty waters.	6749

SANSANNAH (1)

Jos	15:31	And Ziklag, and Madmannah, and **S**,	5578

SAP (1)

Ps	104:16	The trees of the LORD are full *of* **s**;	NIH

SAPH (1)

2Sa	21:18	Sibbechai the Hushathite slew **S**,	5593

SAPHIR (1)

Mic	1:11	Pass ye away, thou inhabitant of **S**,	8208

SAPPHIRA (1)

Ac	5: 1	with **S** his wife, sold a possession,	4551

SAPPHIRE (9) [SAPPHIRES]

Ex	24:10	feet as it were a paved work of a **s** stone,	5601
	28:18	*shall be* an emerald, a **s**, and a diamond.	5601
	39:11	an emerald, a **s**, and a diamond.	5601
Job	28:16	of Ophir, with the precious onyx, or *of* **s**?	5601
La	4: 7	body than rubies, their polishing *was of* **s**:	5601
Eze	1:26	of a throne, as the appearance of a **s** stone:	5601
	10: 1	appeared over them as it were a **s** stone,	5601
	28:13	the beryl, the onyx, and the jasper, the **s**,	5601
Rev	21:19	the second, **s**; the third, a chalcedony;	4552

SAPPHIRES (3) [SAPPHIRE]

Job	28: 6	The stones of it *are* the place of **s**:	5601
SS	5:14	his belly *is as* bright ivory overlaid *with* **s**.	5601
Isa	54:11	colours, and lay thy foundations with **s**.	5601

SARA (3) [SARAH]

Ro	9: 9	time will I come, and **S** shall have a son.	4564
Heb	11:11	Through faith also **S** herself received	4564
1Pe	3: 6	Even as **S** obeyed Abraham, calling him	4564

SARA'S (1) [SARAH]

Ro	4:19	neither *yet* the deadness of **S** womb:	4564

SARAH (37) [SARA, SARA'S, SARAH'S, SARAI, SARAI'S]

Ge	17:15	her name Sarai, but **S** *shall* her name *be*.	8283
	17:17	and shall **S**, that is ninety years old, bear?	8283
	17:19	**S** thy wife shall bear thee a son indeed;	8283
	17:21	**S** shall bear unto thee at this set time	8283
	18: 6	Abraham hastened into the tent unto **S**,	8283
	18: 9	they said unto him, Where *is* **S** thy wife?	8283
	18:10	of life; and lo, **S** thy wife shall have a son.	8283
	18:10	**S** heard *it* in the tent door, which *was*	8283
	18:11	Now Abraham and **S** *were* old and	8283
	18:11	it ceased to be with **S** after the manner of	8283
	18:12	**S** laughed within herself, saying,	8283
	18:13	Wherefore did **S** laugh, saying,	8283
	18:14	to the time of life, and **S** shall have a son.	8283
	18:15	**S** denied, saying, I laughed not; for she	8283
	20: 2	Abraham said of **S** his wife, She *is* my	8283
	20: 2	Abimelech king of Gerar sent, and took **S**.	8283
	20:14	Abraham, and restored him **S** his wife.	8283
	20:16	unto **S** he said, Behold, I have given thy	8283
	20:18	because of **S** Abraham's wife.	8283
	21: 1	the LORD visited **S** as he had said,	8283
	21: 1	the LORD did unto **S** as he had spoken.	8283
	21: 2	For **S** conceived, and bare Abraham a son	8283
	21: 3	unto him, whom **S** bare to him, Isaac.	8283
	21: 6	**S** said, God hath made me to laugh,	8283
	21: 7	that **S** should have given children suck?	8283
	21: 9	**S** saw the son of Hagar the Egyptian,	8283
	21:12	in all that **S** hath said unto thee,	8283
	23: 1	**S** was an hundred and seven and	8283
	23: 1	*these were* the years of the life of **S**.	8283
	23: 2	**S** died in Kirjath-arba; the same *is* Hebron	8283
	23: 2	Abraham came to mourn for **S**, and to	8283
	23:19	Abraham buried **S** his wife in the cave of	8283
	24:36	my master's wife bare a son to my	8283
	25:10	was Abraham buried, and **S** his wife.	8283
	49:31	they buried Abraham and **S** his wife;	8283
Nu	26:46	the name of the daughter of Asher *was* **S**.	8294
Isa	51: 2	your father, and unto **S** *that* bare you:	8283

SARAH'S (2) [SARAH]

Ge	24:67	Isaac brought her into his mother **S** tent,	8283
	25:12	**S** handmaid, bare unto Abraham:	8283

SARAI (16) [SARAH]

Ge	11:29	the name of Abram's wife *was* **S**;	8297
	11:30	But **S** was barren; she had no child.	8297
	11:31	his daughter in law, his son Abram's	8297
	12: 5	Abram took **S** his wife, and Lot his	8297
	12:11	that he said unto **S** his wife, Behold now,	8297
	12:17	great plagues because of **S** Abram's wife.	8297
	16: 1	**S** Abram's wife bare him no *children*:	8297
	16: 2	**S** said unto Abram, Behold now,	8297
	16: 2	And Abram hearkened to the voice of **S**.	8297
	16: 3	**S** Abram's wife took Hagar her maid	8297
	16: 5	**S** said unto Abram, My wrong *be* upon	8297
	16: 6	Abram said unto **S**, Behold, thy maid *is* in	8297
	16: 6	dealt hardly with her, she fled from	8297
	16: 8	I flee from the face of my mistress **S**.	8297
	17:15	God said unto Abraham, *As for* **S** thy wife	8297
	17:15	thou shalt not call her name **S**,	8297

SARAI'S (1) [SARAH]

Ge	16: 8	he said, Hagar, **S** maid, whence camest	8297

SARAPH (1)

1Ch	4:22	the men of Chozeba, and Joash, and **S**,	8315

SARDINE (1)

Rev	4: 3	to look upon like a jasper and a **s** stone:	4555

SARDIS (3)

Rev	1:11	and unto **S**, and unto Philadelphia,	4554
	3: 1	unto the angel of the church in **S** write;	4554
	3: 4	Thou hast a few names even in **S**,	4554

SARDITES (1)

Nu	26:26	of Sered, the family of the **S**: of Elon,	5625

SARDIUS (4)

Ex	28:17	*the first* row shall be a **s**, a topaz,	124
	39:10	*the first* row *was* a **s**, a topaz,	124
Eze	28:13	the **s**, topaz, and the diamond, the beryl,	124
Rev	21:20	The fifth, sardonyx; the sixth, **s**;	4556

SARDONYX (1)

Rev	21:20	fifth, **s**; the sixth, sardius; the seventh,	4557

SAREPTA (1) [ZAREPHATH]

Lk	4:26	unto **S**, *a city* of Sidon, unto a woman	4558

SARGON (1)

Isa	20: 1	(when **S** the king of Assyria sent him,)	5623

SARID (1)

Jos	19:10	border of their inheritance was unto **S**:	8301
	19:12	turned from **S** eastward *toward*	8301

SARON (1)

Ac	9:35	all that dwelt at Lydda and **S** saw him,	4565

SARSECHIM (1)

Jer	39: 3	Samgar-nebo, **S**, Rab-saris,	8310

SARUCH (1)

Lk	3:35	was *the son* of **S**, which was *the son*	4562

SAT (192) [SIT]

Ge	18: 1	**s** *in* the tent door in the heat of the day;	3427
	19: 1	at even; and Lot **s** in the gate of Sodom:	3427
	21:16	her **down** over against *him* a good way	3427
	21:16	she **s** over against *him*, and lift up her	3427
	31:34	in the camel's furniture, and **s** upon them.	3427
	37:25	they **s** down to eat bread: and they lift up	3427
	38:14	wrapped herself, and **s** in an open place,	3427
	43:33	they **s** before him, the firstborn according	3427
	48: 2	strengthened himself, and **s** upon the bed.	3427
Ex	2:15	land of Midian: and he **s** down by a well.	3427
	12:29	from the firstborn of Pharaoh that **s** on his	3427
	16: 3	when we **s** by the flesh pots, *and* when	3427
	17:12	and put *it* under him, and he **s** thereon;	3427
	18:13	that Moses **s** to judge the people:	3427
	32: 6	the people **s** down to eat and to drink,	3427
Lev	15: 6	he that sitteth on *any* thing whereon he **s**	3427
	15:22	whosoever toucheth any thing that he **s**	3427
Dt	33: 3	they **s** down at thy feet; *every one* shall	8497
Jdg	6:11	**s** under an oak which *was* in Ophrah,	3427
	13: 9	unto the woman as she **s** in the field:	3427
	19: 6	they **s** down, and did eat and drink both	3427
	19:15	he **s** down in a street of the city:	3427
	20:26	**s** there before the LORD, and fasted that	3427
Ru	2:14	she **s** beside the reapers: and he reached	3427
	4: 1	Boaz up *to* the gate, and **s** him **down**	3427
	4: 1	And he turned aside, and **s down**.	3427
	4: 2	said, Sit ye down here. And they **s down**.	3427
1Sa	1: 9	Now Eli the priest **s** upon a seat by a post	3427
	4:13	Eli **s** upon a seat *by* the wayside watching:	3427
	19: 9	as he **s** in his house with his javelin in his	3427
	20:24	the king **s** him **down** to eat meat.	3427
	20:25	the king **s** upon his seat, as at other times,	3427
	20:25	Abner **s** by Saul's side, and David's place	3427
	28:23	arose from the earth, and **s** upon the bed.	3427
2Sa	2:13	they **s down**, the one on the one side of	3427
	7: 1	when the king **s** in his house,	3427
	7:18	**s** before the LORD, and he said, Who *am*	3427
	18:24	David **s** between the two gates:	3427
	19: 8	the king rose, and **s** in the gate. And they	3427
	23: 8	The Tachmonite that **s** in the seat,	3427
1Ki	2:12	Solomon upon the throne of David his	3427
	2:19	**s down** on his throne, and caused a seat	3427
	2:19	mother; and she **s** on his right hand.	3427
	13:20	it came to pass, as they **s** at the table,	3427
	16:11	to reign, as soon as he **s** on his throne,	3427
	19: 4	came and **s down** under a juniper tree:	3427
	21:13	children of Belial, and **s** before him:	3427
	22:10	Jehoshaphat the king of Judah **s** each on	3427
2Ki	1: 9	behold, he **s** on the top of a hill. And he	3427
	4:20	**s** on her knees till noon, and *then* died.	3427
	6:32	Elisha **s** in his house, and the elders sat	3427
	6:32	in his house, and the elders **s** with him;	3427
	11:19	And he **s** on the throne of the kings.	3427
	13:13	and Jeroboam **s** upon his throne:	3427
1Ch	17: 1	it came to pass, as David **s** in his house,	3427
	17:16	the king came and **s** before the LORD,	3427
	29:23	Solomon **s** on the throne of the LORD as	3427
2Ch	18: 9	Jehoshaphat king of Judah **s** either of	3427
	18: 9	they **s** in a void place *at* the entering in of	3427
Ezr	9: 3	and of my beard, and **s down** astonied.	3427
	9: 4	I **s** astonied until the evening sacrifice.	3427
	10: 9	all the people **s** in the street of the house	3427
	10:16	**s down** in the first day of the tenth	3427
Ne	1: 4	*that* I **s down** and wept,	3427
	8:17	made booths, and **s** under the booths:	3427
Est	1: 2	when the king Ahasuerus **s** on the throne	3427
	1:14	*and* which **s** the first in the kingdom;)	3427
	2:19	then Mordecai **s** in the king's gate.	3427
	2:21	while Mordecai **s** in the king's gate,	3427
	3:15	the king and Haman **s down** to drink;	3427
	5: 1	king **s** upon his royal throne in the royal	3427
Job	2: 8	and he **s down** among the ashes.	3427
	2:13	they **s down** with him upon the ground	3427
	29:25	**s** chief, and dwelt as a king in the army,	3427
Ps	26: 4	I have not **s** with vain persons, neither	3427
	137: 1	there we **s down**, yea, we wept,	3427
SS	2: 3	I **s down** under his shadow with great	3427
Jer	3: 2	In the ways hast thou **s** for them,	3427
	15:17	I **s** not in the assembly of the mockers,	3427
	15:17	I **s** alone because of thy hand:	3427
	26:10	**s down** in the entry of the new gate of	3427
	32:12	before all the Jews that **s** in the court of	3427
	36:12	lo, all the princes **s** there, *even* Elishama	3427
	36:22	Now the king **s** in the winterhouse in	3427
	39: 3	**s** in the middle gate, *even* Nergal-sharezer	3427
Eze	3:15	I **s** where they sat, and remained there	3427
	3:15	I sat where they **s**, and remained there	3427
	8: 1	as I **s** in mine house, and the elders of	3427
	8: 1	and the elders of Judah **s** before me,	3427
	8:14	there **s** women weeping for Tammuz.	3427
	14: 1	elders of Israel unto me, and **s** before me.	3427
	20: 1	to inquire of the LORD, and **s** before me.	3427
Da	2:49	but Daniel **s** in the gate of the king.	NIH
Jnh	3: 6	*him* with sackcloth, and **s** in ashes.	3427
	4: 5	**s** on the east side of the city,	3427

S

Jnh 4: 5 a booth, and **s** under it in the shadow, 3427
Mt 4:16 The people which **s** in darkness saw great 2521
4:16 and to them which **s** in the region and 2521
9:10 as Jesus **s at meat** in the house, behold, 345
9:10 and **s down** with him and his disciples. 4873
13: 1 out of the house, and **s** by the sea side. 2521
13: 2 him, so that he went into a ship, and **s**; 2521
13:48 and **s down**, and gathered the good into 2523
14: 9 and them which **s with** him at meat, 4873
15:29 up into a mountain, and **s down** there. 2521
24: 3 And as he **s** upon the mount of Olives, 2521
26: 7 poured *it* on his head, as he **s at meat**. 345
26:20 was come, he **s down** with the twelve. 345
26:55 I **s** daily with you teaching in the temple, 2516
26:58 went in, and **s** with the servants, to see 2521
26:69 Now Peter **s** without in the palace: 2521
28: 2 the stone from the door, and **s** upon it. 2521

Mk 2:15 that as *Jesus* **s at meat** in his house, 2621
2:15 sinners **also together with** Jesus and 4873
3:32 And *the* multitude **s** about him, and they 2521
3:34 round about on them which **s** about him, 2521
4: 1 he entered into a ship, and **s** in the sea; 2521
6:22 them that **s with** *him*, the king said unto 4873
6:26 their sakes which **s with** *him*, he would 4873
6:40 And they **s down** in ranks, by hundreds, 377
9:35 And he **s down**, and called the twelve, 2523
10:46 of Timeus, **s** by the *high*way side begging. 2521
11: 2 a colt tied, wherein never man **s**; 2523
11: 7 garments on him; and he **s** upon him. 2523
12:41 And Jesus **s** over against the treasury, 2523
13: 3 as he **s** upon the mount of Olives over 2521
14: 3 of Simon the leper, as he **s at meat**, 2621
14:18 And as they **s** and did eat, Jesus said, 345
14:54 and he **s** with the servants, 4775
16:14 unto the eleven as they **s at meat**, 345
16:19 heaven, and **s** on the right hand of God. 2523

Lk 4:20 gave *it* again to the minister, and **s down**. 2523
5: 3 he **s down**, and taught the people out 2523
5:29 and of others that **s down** with them. 2621
7:15 And he that was dead **s up**, and began to 339
7:36 Pharisee's house, and **s down to meat**. 347
7:37 when she knew that *Jesus* **s at meat** in 345
7:49 they that **s at meat with** *him* began to 4873
10:39 which also **s** at Jesus' feet, and heard his 3869
11:37 and he went in, and **s down to meat**. 377
14:15 when one of them that **s at meat with** 4873
18:35 a certain blind man **s** by the way side 2521
19:30 find a colt tied, whereon yet never man **s**: 2523
22:14 **s down**, and the twelve apostles with him. 377
22:55 together, Peter **s down** among them. 2521
22:56 But a certain maid beheld him as he **s** by 2521
24:30 as he **s at meat** with them, he took bread, 2625

Jn 4: 6 with *his* journey, **s** thus on the well: 2516
6: 3 and there he **s** with his disciples. 2521
6:10 So the men **s down**, *in* number about five 377
8: 2 him; and he **s down**, and taught them. 2523
9: 8 said, Is not this he that **s** and begged? 2521
11:20 met him: but Mary **s** *still* in the house. 2516
12: 2 of them that **s at the table** with him. 4873
12:14 he had found a young ass, **s** thereon; 2523
19:13 **s down** in the judgment seat in a place 2523

Ac 2: 3 like as of fire, and it **s** upon each of them. 2523
3:10 And they knew that it was he which **s** for 2521
6:15 And all that **s** in the council, 2516
9:40 eyes: and when she saw Peter, she **s up**. 339
12:21 **s** upon his throne, and made an oration 2523
13:14 on the sabbath day, and **s down**. 2523
14: 8 And there **s** a certain man at Lystra, 2521
16:13 we **s down**, and spake unto the women 2523
20: 9 And there **s** in a window a certain young 2521
25:17 on the morrow I **s** on the judgment seat, 2523
26:30 and Bernice, and they that **s with** them: 4775

1Co 10: 7 The people **s down** to eat and drink, 2523

Heb 1: 3 **s down** on the right hand of the Majesty 2523
10:12 **s down** on the right hand of God; 2523

Rev 4: 2 set in heaven, and one **s** on the throne. 2521
4: 3 he that **s** was to look upon like a jasper 2521
4: 9 and thanks to him that **s** on the throne, 2521
4:10 twenty elders fall down before him that **s** 2521
5: 1 I saw in the right hand of him that **s** on 2521
5: 7 right hand of him that **s** upon the throne. 2521
6: 2 and he that **s** on him had a bow; 2521
6: 4 *power* was given to him that **s** thereon to 2521
6: 5 he that **s** on him had a pair of balances in 2521
6: 8 and his name that **s** on him *was* Death, 2521
9:17 them that **s** on them, 2521
11:16 which **s** before God on their seats, 2521
14:14 upon the cloud one **s** like unto the Son of 2521
14:15 crying with a loud voice to him that **s** on 2521
14:16 And he that **s** on the cloud thrust in his 2521
19: 4 and worshipped God that **s** on the throne, 2521
19:11 he that **s** upon him *was* called Faithful 2521
19:19 make war against him that **s** on the horse, 2521
19:21 the sword of him that **s** upon the horse, 2521
20: 4 and they **s** upon them, and judgment was 2523
20:11 and him that **s** on it, from whose face 2521
21: 5 And he that **s** upon the throne said, 2521

SATAN (55) [SATAN'S]
1Ch 21: 1 **S** stood *up* against Israel, 7854
Job 1: 6 the LORD, and **S** came also among them. 7854
1: 7 the LORD said unto **S**, Whence comest 7854
1: 7 **S** answered the LORD, and said, 7854
1: 8 the LORD said unto **S**, Hast thou 7854
1: 9 **S** answered the LORD, and said, Doth Job 7854

Job 1:12 the LORD said unto **S**, Behold, all that he 7854
1:12 So went forth from the presence of 7854
2: 1 **S** came also among them to present 7854
2: 2 the LORD said to **S**, From whence 7854
2: 2 **S** answered the LORD, and said, 7854
2: 3 the LORD said unto **S**, Hast thou 7854
2: 4 **S** answered the LORD, and said, Skin for 7854
2: 6 the LORD said unto **S**, Behold, he *is* in 7854
2: 7 So went **S** forth from the presence of 7854
Ps 109: 6 him: and let **S** stand at his right hand. 7854
Zec 3: 1 **S** standing at his right hand to resist him. 7854
3: 2 the LORD said to **S**, The LORD 7854
3: 2 unto Satan, The LORD rebuke thee, O **S**; 7854
Mt 4:10 saith Jesus unto him, Get thee hence, **S**: 4567
12:26 And if **S** cast out Satan, he is divided 4567
12:26 And if Satan cast out **S**, he is divided 4567
16:23 said unto Peter, Get thee behind me, **S**: 4567
Mk 1:13 the wilderness forty days, tempted of **S**; 4567
3:23 in parables, How can **S** cast out Satan? 4567
3:23 in parables, How can Satan cast out **S**? 4567
3:26 And if **S** rise up against himself, 4567
4:15 **S** cometh immediately, and taketh away 4567
8:33 saying, Get thee behind me, **S**: 4567
Lk 4: 8 said unto him, Get thee behind me, **S**: 4567
10:18 I beheld **S** as lightning fall from heaven. 4567
11:18 If **S** also be divided against himself, 4567
13:16 whom **S** hath bound, lo *these* eighteen 4567
22: 3 Then entered **S** into Judas surnamed 4567
22:31 behold, **S** hath desired *to* have you, 4567
Jn 13:27 And after the sop **S** entered into him. 4567
Ac 5: 3 why hath **S** filled thine heart to lie to 4567
26:18 light, and *from* the power of **S** unto God, 4567
Ro 16:20 the God of peace shall bruise **S** under 4567
1Co 5: 5 To deliver such a one unto **S** for 4567
7: 5 **S** tempt you not for your incontinence. 4567
2Co 2:11 Lest **S** should get an advantage of us: 4567
11:14 for **S** himself is transformed into an angel 4566
12: 7 the messenger of **S** to buffet me, lest I 4566
1Th 2:18 I Paul, once and again; but **S** hindered us. 4567
2Th 2: 9 is after the working of **S** with all power 4567
1Ti 1:20 whom I have delivered unto **S**, that they 4567
5:15 For some are already turned aside after **S**. 4567
Rev 2: 9 and are not, but *are* the synagogue of **S**. 4567
2:13 was slain among you, where **S** dwelleth. 4567
2:24 which have not known the depths of **S**, 4567
3: 9 I *will* make *them* of the synagogue of **S**, 4567
12: 9 called the devil, and **S**, which deceiveth 4567
20: 2 and **S**, and bound him a thousand years, 4567
20: 7 **S** shall be loosed out of his prison, 4567

SATAN'S (1) [SATAN]
Rev 2:13 where **S** seat *is:* and thou holdest fast 4567

SATEST (2) [SIT]
Ps 9: 4 thou **s** in the throne judging right. 3427
Eze 23:41 **s** upon a stately bed, and a table prepared 3427

SATIATE (2) [SATIATED, UNSATIABLE]
Jer 31:14 I will **s** the soul of the priests with fatness, 7301
46:10 it shall be **s** and made drunk with their 7646

SATIATED (1) [SATIATE]
Jer 31:25 For I have **s** the weary soul, and I have 7301

SATISFACTION (2) [SATISFY]
Nu 35:31 Moreover ye shall take no **s** for the life of 3724
35:32 ye shall take no **s** for him that is fled to 3724

SATISFIED (43) [SATISFY]
Ex 15: 9 the spoil; my lust shall be **s** upon them; 4390
Lev 26:26 by weight: and ye shall eat, and not be **s**. 7646
Dt 14:29 shall come, and shall eat and be **s**; 7646
33:23 with favour, and full with the blessing 7649
Job 19:22 me as God, and are not **s** with my flesh? 7646
27:14 his offspring shall not be **s** with bread. 7646
31:31 that we had of his flesh! we cannot be **s**. 7646
Ps 17:15 I shall be **s**, when I *awake*, with thy 7646
22:26 The meek shall eat and be **s**: they shall 7646
36: 8 They shall be **abundantly** **s** with 7301
37:19 and in the days of famine they shall be **s**. 7646
59:15 for meat, and grudge if they be not **s**. 7646
63: 5 My soul shall be as *with* marrow and 7646
65: 4 we shall be **s** with the goodness of thy 7646
81:16 honey out of the rock should I have **s** 7646
104:13 the earth is **s** with the fruit of thy works. 7646
105:40 and **s** them *with* the bread of heaven. 7646
Pr 12:11 He that tilleth his land shall be **s** with 7646
12:14 A man shall be **s** *with* good by the fruit of 7646
14:14 and a good man *shall be* **s** from himself. NIH
18:20 A man's belly shall be **s** with the fruit of 7646
19:23 *he that hath it* shall abide **s**; he shall not 7649
20:13 eyes, *and* thou shalt be **s** with bread. 7646
27:20 never full; so the eyes of man are never **s**. 7646
30:15 There are three *things* that are never **s**, 7646
Ecc 1: 8 man cannot utter *it*: the eye is not **s** with 7646
4: 8 his labour; neither is his eye **s** *with* riches; 7646
5:10 He that loveth silver shall not be **s** *with* 7646
Isa 9:20 on the left hand, and they shall not be **s**: 7646
44:16 he eateth flesh; he roasteth roast, and is **s**: 7646
53:11 of the travail of his soul, *and* shall be **s**: 7646
66:11 be **s** with the breasts of her consolations; 7646
Jer 31:14 my people shall be **s** with my goodness, 7646
50:10 all that spoil her shall be **s**, saith 7646
50:19 his soul shall be **s** upon mount Ephraim 7646
La 5: 6 *and* to the Assyrians, to be **s** *with* bread. 7646

Eze 16:28 with them, and yet couldest not be **s**. 7646
16:29 and yet thou wast not **s** herewith. 7646
Joel 2:19 and oil, and ye shall be **s** therewith: 7646
2:26 be **s**, and praise the name of the LORD 7646
Am 4: 8 to drink water; but they were not **s**: 7646
Mic 6:14 thou shalt eat, but not be **s**; and thy 7646
Hab 2: 5 cannot be **s**, but gathereth unto him all 7646

SATISFIEST (1) [SATISFY]
Ps 145:16 and **s** the desire of every living thing. 7646

SATISFIETH (3) [SATISFY]
Ps 103: 5 Who **s** thy mouth with good *things*; so 7646
107: 9 For he **s** the longing soul, and filleth 7646
Isa 55: 2 your labour for *that which* is not? hearken 7654

SATISFY (10) [SATISFACTION, SATISFIED, SATISFIEST, SATISFIETH, SATISFYING]
Job 38:27 To **s** the desolate and waste *ground;* and 7646
Ps 90:14 O **s** us early *with* thy mercy; that we may 7646
91:16 *With* long life will I **s** him, and shew him 7646
132:15 provision: I will **s** her poor *with* bread. 7646
Pr 5:19 let her breasts **s** thee at all times; 7301
6:30 if he steal to **s** his soul when he is hungry; 4390
Isa 58:10 to the hungry, and **s** the afflicted soul; 7646
58:11 **s** thy soul in drought, and make fat thy 7646
Eze 7:19 they shall not **s** their souls, neither fill 7646
Mk 8: 4 From whence can a man these *men* 5526

SATISFYING (2) [SATISFY]
Pr 13:25 The righteous eateth to the **s** of his soul: 7648
Col 2:23 not in any honour to the **s** of the flesh. 4140

SATRAP See LIEUTENANTS

SATYR (1) [SATYRS]
Isa 34:14 island, and the **s** shall cry to his fellow; 8163

SATYRS (1) [SATYR]
Isa 13:21 shall dwell there, and **s** shall dance there. 8163

SAUL (394) [PAUL, SAUL'S]
Ge 36:37 **S** of Rehoboth *by* the river reigned in his 7586
36:38 **S** died, and Baal-hanan the son of Achbor 7586
1Sa 9: 2 he had a son, whose name *was* **S**, 7586
9: 2 Kish said to **S** his son, Take now one of 7586
9: 5 **S** said to his servant that *was* with him, 7586
9: 7 said **S** to his servant, But behold, *if* we go, 7586
9: 8 the servant answered **S** again, and said, 7586
9:10 said **S** to his servant, Well said; come, 7586
9:15 Samuel in his ear a day before **S** came, 7586
9:17 when Samuel saw **S**, the LORD said unto 7586
9:18 **S** drew near to Samuel in the gate, 7586
9:19 Samuel answered **S**, and said, I *am* the 7586
9:21 **S** answered and said, *Am* not I a 7586
9:22 Samuel took **S** and his servant, 7586
9:24 which *was* upon it, and set *it* before **S**. 7586
9:24 So **S** did eat with Samuel that day. 7586
9:25 Samuel communed with **S** upon the top 7586
9:26 that Samuel called to **S** to the top of 7586
9:26 **S** arose, and they went out both of them, 7586
9:27 Samuel said to **S**, Bid the servant pass on 7586
10:11 son of Kish? *Is* **S** also among the prophets? 7586
10:12 a proverb, *Is* **S** also among the prophets? 7586
10:16 **S** said unto his uncle, He told us plainly 7586
10:21 taken, and **S** the son of Kish was taken: 7586
10:26 **S** also went home to Gibeah; 7586
11: 4 came the messengers to Gibeah of **S**, 7586
11: 5 **S** came after the herd out of the field; 7586
11: 5 **S** said, What aileth the people that they 7586
11: 6 the spirit of God came upon **S** when he 7586
11: 7 Whosoever cometh not forth after **S** and 7586
11:11 that **S** put the people *in* three companies; 7586
11:12 Who *is* he that said, Shall **S** reign over us? 7586
11:13 **S** said, There shall not a man be put to 7586
11:15 there they made **S** king before the LORD 7586
11:15 there **S** and all the men of Israel rejoiced 7586
13: 1 **S** reigned one year; and when he had 7586
13: 2 **S** chose him three thousand *men* of Israel; 7586
13: 2 *whereof* two thousand were with **S** in 7586
13: 3 the Philistines heard *of it.* And **S** blew 7586
13: 4 all Israel heard say that **S** had smitten a 7586
13: 4 the people were called together after **S** to 7586
13: 7 As for **S**, he *was* yet in Gilgal, and all 7586
13: 9 **S** said, Bring hither a burnt offering to me, 7586
13:10 **S** went out to meet him, that he might 7586
13:11 **S** said, Because I saw that the people were 7586
13:13 Samuel said to **S**, Thou hast done foolishly 7586
13:15 **S** numbered the people that were present 7586
13:16 **S**, and Jonathan his son, and the people 7586
13:22 of any of the people that *were* with **S** 7586
13:22 **S** and with Jonathan his son was there 7586
14: 1 that Jonathan the son of **S** said unto 7586
14: 2 **S** tarried in the uttermost part of Gibeah 7586
14:16 the watchmen in **S** in Gibeah of Benjamin 7586
14:17 said **S** unto the people that *were* with 7586
14:18 **S** said unto Ahiah, Bring hither the ark of 7586
14:19 to pass, while **S** talked unto the priest, 7586
14:19 said **S** unto the priest, Withdraw thine 7586
14:20 **S** and all the people that *were* with him 7586
14:21 to be with the Israelites that *were* with **S** 7586
14:24 for **S** had adjured the people, saying, 7586
14:33 they told **S**, saying, Behold, the people sin 7586
14:34 **S** said, Disperse yourselves among 7586
14:35 **S** built an altar unto the LORD: the same 7586
14:36 **S** said, Let us go down after the Philistines 7586

S

Ref	Text	Strong's
1Sa 14:37	S asked *counsel* of God, Shall I go down	7586
14:38	S said, Draw ye near hither, all the chief	7586
14:40	the people said unto S, Do what seemeth	7586
14:41	Therefore S said unto the LORD God of	7586
14:41	Give a perfect *lot*. And S and	7586
14:42	S said, Cast *lots* between me and	7586
14:43	S said to Jonathan, Tell me what thou	7586
14:44	S answered, God do so and more also:	7586
14:45	the people said unto S, Shall Jonathan die,	7586
14:46	S went up from following the Philistines:	7586
14:47	So S took the kingdom over Israel,	7586
14:49	Now the sons of S were Jonathan,	7586
14:51	Kish *was* the father of S; and Ner the	7586
14:52	against the Philistines all the days of S:	7586
14:52	S saw any strong man, or any valiant	7586
15: 1	Samuel also said unto S, The LORD sent	7586
15: 4	S gathered the people together,	7586
15: 5	S came to a city of Amalek, and laid wait	7586
15: 6	S said unto the Kenites, Go, depart, get	7586
15: 7	S smote the Amalekites from Havilah	7586
15: 9	S and the people spared Agag, and the	7586
15:11	It repenteth me that I have set up S to be	7586
15:12	when Samuel rose early to meet S in	7586
15:12	S came to Carmel, and behold,	7586
15:13	Samuel came to S: and Saul said unto him	7586
15:13	S said unto him, Blessed *be* thou of	7586
15:15	S said, They have brought them from	7586
15:16	Samuel said unto S, Stay, and I will tell	7586
15:20	S said unto Samuel, Yea, I have obeyed	7586
15:24	S said unto Samuel, I have sinned: for I	7586
15:26	Samuel said unto S, I will not return with	7586
15:31	So Samuel turned again after S;	7586
15:31	after Saul; and S worshipped the LORD.	7586
15:34	went up to his house to Gibeah of Saul.	7586
15:34	S went up to his house to Gibeah of S.	7586
15:35	Samuel came no more to see S until the	7586
15:35	nevertheless Samuel mourned for S:	7586
15:35	the LORD repented that he had made S	7586
16: 1	How long wilt thou mourn for S,	7586
16: 2	if S hear *it*, he will kill me.	7586
16:14	the spirit of the LORD departed from S,	7586
16:17	S said unto his servants, Provide me now	7586
16:19	Wherefore S sent messengers unto Jesse,	7586
16:20	and sent *them* by David his son unto S.	7586
16:21	David came to S, and stood before him:	7586
16:22	S sent to Jesse, saying, Let David, I pray	7586
16:23	when the *evil* spirit from God was upon S,	7586
16:23	so S was refreshed, and was well,	7586
17: 2	S and the men of Israel were gathered	7586
17: 8	not I a Philistine, and you servants to S?	7586
17:11	When S and all Israel heard those words	7586
17:12	men *for* an old man in the days of S.	7586
17:13	Jesse went and followed S to the battle:	7586
17:14	and the three eldest followed S.	7586
17:15	returned from S to feed his father's sheep	7586
17:19	S, and they, and all the men of Israel,	7586
17:31	spake, they rehearsed *them* before S:	7586
17:32	David said to S, Let no man's heart fail	7586
17:33	S said to David, Thou art not able to go	7586
17:34	David said unto S, Thy servant kept his	7586
17:37	S said unto David, Go, and the LORD be	7586
17:38	S armed David with his armour, and he	7586
17:39	had not proved *it*. And David said unto S,	7586
17:55	when S saw David go forth against	7586
17:57	brought him before S with the head of	7586
17:58	S said to him, Whose son *art* thou, *thou*	7586
18: 1	when he made an end of speaking unto S,	7586
18: 2	S took him that day, and would let him go	7586
18: 5	David went out whithersoever S sent him,	7586
18: 5	S set him over the men of war, and he	7586
18: 6	singing and dancing, to meet king S,	7586
18: 7	S hath slain his thousands, and David his	7586
18: 8	S was very wroth, and the saying	7586
18: 9	S eyed David from that day and forward.	7586
18:10	that the evil spirit from God came upon S,	7586
18:11	S cast the javelin; for he said, I will smite	7586
18:12	S was afraid of David, because the LORD	7586
18:12	was with him, and was departed from S.	7586
18:13	Therefore S removed him from him,	7586
18:15	Wherefore when S saw that he behaved	7586
18:17	S said to David, Behold my elder daughter	7586
18:17	S said, Let not mine hand be upon him,	7586
18:18	David said unto S, Who *am* I? and what	7586
18:20	they told S, and the thing pleased him.	7586
18:21	S said, I will give him her, that she may	7586
18:21	Wherefore S said to David, Thou shalt	7586
18:22	S commanded his servants,	7586
18:24	the servants of S told him, saying, On this	7586
18:25	S said, Thus shall ye say to David,	7586
18:25	thought to make David fall by the hand	7586
18:27	S gave him Michal his daughter to wife.	7586
18:28	S saw and knew that the LORD *was* with	7586
18:29	S was yet the more afraid of David;	7586
18:29	and S became David's enemy continually.	7586
18:30	more wisely than all the servants of S;	7586
19: 1	S spake to Jonathan his son, and to all his	7586
19: 2	S my father seeketh to kill thee:	7586
19: 4	Jonathan spake good of David unto S his	7586
19: 6	S hearkened unto the voice of Jonathan:	7586
19: 6	S sware, *As* the LORD liveth, he shall not	7586
19: 7	Jonathan brought David to S, and he was	7586
19: 9	the evil spirit from the LORD was upon S,	7586
19:10	S sought to smite David even to the wall	7586
19:11	S also sent messengers unto David's	7586
19:14	when S sent messengers to take David,	7586

Ref	Text	Strong's
1Sa 19:15	S sent the messengers *again* to see David,	7586
19:17	S said unto Michal, Why hast thou	7586
19:17	Michal answered S, He said unto me,	7586
19:18	and told him all that S had done to him.	7586
19:19	it was told S, saying, Behold, David *is* at	7586
19:20	S sent messengers to take David:	7586
19:20	of God was upon the messengers of S,	7586
19:21	when it was told S, he sent other	7586
19:21	S sent messengers again the third time,	7586
19:24	they say, *Is* S also among the prophets?	7586
20:26	Nevertheless S spake not any thing that	7586
20:27	S said unto Jonathan his son,	7586
20:28	Jonathan answered S, David earnestly	7586
20:32	Jonathan answered S his father,	7586
20:33	S cast a javelin at him to smite him:	7586
21: 7	a *certain* man of the servants of S *was*	7586
21: 7	of the herdmen that *belonged* to S.	7586
21:10	fled that day for fear of S, and went to	7586
21:11	S hath slain his thousands, and David his	7586
22: 6	When S heard that David was discovered,	7586
22: 6	(now S abode in Gibeah under a tree in	7586
22: 7	S said unto his servants that stood about	7586
22: 9	which *was* set over the servants of S,	7586
22:12	S said, Hear now, thou son of Ahitub.	7586
22:13	S said unto him, Why have ye conspired	7586
22:21	Abiathar shewed David that S had slain	7586
22:22	*was* there, that he would surely tell S:	7586
23: 7	it was told S that David was come *to*	7586
23: 7	S said, God hath delivered him into mine	7586
23: 8	S called all the people together to war,	7586
23: 9	David knew that S secretly practised	7586
23:10	thy servant hath certainly heard that S	7586
23:11	Will S come down, as thy servant hath	7586
23:12	me and my men into the hand of S?	7586
23:13	it was told S that David was escaped from	7586
23:14	S sought him every day, but God	7586
23:15	David saw that S was come out to seek	7586
23:17	for the hand of S my father shall not find	7586
23:17	and that also S my father knoweth.	7586
23:19	came up the Ziphites to S to Gibeah,	7586
23:21	S said, Blessed *be* ye of the LORD; for ye	7586
23:24	they arose, and went to Ziph before S:	7586
23:25	S also and his men went to seek *him*.	7586
23:25	S heard *that*, he pursued after David	7586
23:26	S went on this side of the mountain,	7586
23:26	made haste to get away for fear of S;	7586
23:26	for S and his men compassed David and	7586
23:27	there came a messenger unto S, saying,	7586
23:28	Wherefore S returned from pursuing after	7586
24: 1	when S was returned from following	7586
24: 2	S took three thousand chosen men out of	7586
24: 3	a cave; and S went in to cover his feet:	7586
24: 7	and suffered them not to rise against S.	7586
24: 7	S rose up out of the cave, and went on	7586
24: 8	and cried after S, saying, My lord the king.	7586
24: 8	S looked behind him, David stooped	7586
24: 9	David said to S, Wherefore hearest thou	7586
24:16	an end of speaking these words unto S,	7586
24:16	S said, *Is* this thy voice, my son David?	7586
24:16	And S lift up his voice, and wept.	7586
24:22	David sware unto S. And Saul went	7586
24:22	S went home; but David and his men gat	7586
25:44	had given Michal his daughter,	7586
26: 1	the Ziphites came unto S to Gibeah,	7586
26: 2	S arose, and went down to the wilderness	7586
26: 3	S pitched in the hill of Hachilah, which *is*	7586
26: 3	he saw that S came after him into	7586
26: 4	understood that S was come in very deed.	7586
26: 5	came to the place where S had pitched:	7586
26: 5	David beheld the place where S lay,	7586
26: 5	S lay in the trench, and the people	7586
26: 6	Who will go down with me to S to	7586
26: 7	S lay sleeping within the trench,	7586
26:17	S knew David's voice, and said, *Is* this thy	7586
26:21	I, have sinned: return, my son David:	7586
26:25	S said to David, Blessed *be* thou, my son	7586
26:25	on his way, and S returned to his place.	7586
27: 1	now perish one day by the hand of S:	7586
27: 1	I shall despair of me, to seek me any	7586
27: 4	it was told S that David was fled *to* Gath:	7586
28: 3	S had put away those that had familiar	7586
28: 4	S gathered all Israel together,	7586
28: 5	when S saw the host of the Philistines,	7586
28: 6	when S inquired of the LORD,	7586
28: 7	said S unto his servants, Seek me a	7586
28: 8	S disguised himself, and put on other	7586
28: 9	Behold, thou knowest what S hath done,	7586
28:10	S sware to her by the LORD, saying,	7586
28:12	the woman spake to S, saying, Why hast	7586
28:12	hast thou deceived me? for thou *art* S.	7586
28:13	the woman said unto S, I saw gods	7586
28:14	S perceived that it *was* Samuel,	7586
28:15	Samuel said to S, Why hast thou	7586
28:15	S answered, I am sore distressed;	7586
28:20	S fell straightway all along on the earth,	7586
28:21	the woman came unto S, and saw that he	7586
28:25	she brought *it* before S, and before his	7586
29: 3	the servant of S the king of Israel,	7586
29: 5	S slew his thousands, and David his ten	7586
31: 2	the Philistines followed hard upon S and	7586
31: 3	the battle went sore against S,	7586
31: 4	said S unto his armourbearer,	7586
31: 4	therefore S took a sword, and fell upon it.	7586
31: 5	when his armourbearer saw that S was	7586
31: 6	So S died, and his three sons,	7586

Ref	Text	Strong's
1Sa 31: 7	S and his sons were dead, they forsook	7586
31: 8	they found S and his three sons fallen	7586
31:11	that which the Philistines had done to S,	7586
31:12	took the body of S and the bodies of his	7586
2Sa 1: 1	Now it came to pass after the death of S,	7586
1: 2	a man came out of the camp from S with	7586
1: 4	and S and Jonathan his son are dead also.	7586
1: 5	How knowest thou that S and Jonathan	7586
1: 6	behold, S leaned upon his spear;	7586
1:12	for S, and for Jonathan his son, and for	7586
1:17	lamented with this lamentation over S	7586
1:21	the shield of S, *as though he had* not	7586
1:22	and the sword of S returned not empty.	7586
1:23	S and Jonathan *were* lovely and pleasant	7586
1:24	Ye daughters of Israel, weep over S,	7586
2: 4	of Jabesh-gilead *were they* that buried S.	7586
2: 5	*even* unto S, and have buried him.	7586
2: 7	for your master S is dead, and also	7586
2: 8	took Ish-bosheth the son of S,	7586
2:12	the servants of Ish-bosheth the son of S,	7586
2:15	pertained to Ish-bosheth the son of S,	7586
3: 1	was long war between the house of S	7586
3: 1	the house of S waxed weaker and weaker.	7586
3: 6	there was war between the house of S	7586
3: 6	made himself strong for the house of S	7586
3: 7	S had a concubine, whose name *was*	7586
3: 8	*this* day unto the house of S thy father,	7586
3:10	the kingdom from the house of S,	7586
4: 4	five years old when the tidings came of S	7586
4: 8	the head of Ish-bosheth the son of S	7586
4: 8	avenged my lord the king this day of S,	7586
4:10	one told me, saying, Behold, S is dead,	7586
5: 2	in time past, when S was king over us,	7586
6:20	Michal the daughter of S came out to	7586
6:23	Therefore Michal the daughter of S had no	7586
7:15	as I took *it* from S, whom I put away	7586
9: 1	there yet *any* that is left of the house of S,	7586
9: 2	*there was* of the house of S a servant	7586
9: 3	*Is there* not yet any of the house of S,	7586
9: 6	son of Jonathan, the son of S, was come	7586
9: 7	restore thee all the land of S thy father;	7586
9: 9	thy master's son all that pertained to S	7586
12: 7	and I delivered thee out of the hand of S;	7586
16: 5	out a man of the family of the house of S	7586
16: 8	upon thee all the blood of the house of S,	7586
19:17	Ziba the servant of the house of S,	7586
19:24	Mephibosheth the son of S came down to	7586
21: 1	*It is* for S, and for *his* bloody house,	7586
21: 2	S sought to slay them in his zeal to	7586
21: 4	We will have no silver nor gold of S, nor	7586
21: 6	them up unto the LORD in Gibeah of S,	7586
21: 7	the son of Jonathan the son of S, because	7586
21: 7	between David and Jonathan the son of S.	7586
21: 8	whom she bare unto S, Armoni and	7586
21: 8	the five sons of Michal the daughter of S,	7586
21:11	of Aiah, the concubine of S, had done.	7586
21:12	David went and took the bones of S and	7586
21:12	when the Philistines had slain S in Gilboa:	7586
21:13	he brought up from thence the bones of S	7586
21:14	bones of S and Jonathan his son buried	7586
22: 1	his enemies, and out of the hand of S:	7586
1Ch 5:10	in the days of S they made war with	7586
8:33	Kish begat S, and Saul begat Jonathan,	7586
8:33	S begat Jonathan, and Malchishua,	7586
9:39	Kish begat S; and Saul begat Jonathan,	7586
9:39	S begat Jonathan, and Malchishua,	7586
10: 2	the Philistines followed hard after S,	7586
10: 2	and Malchishua, the sons of S.	7586
10: 3	the battle went sore against S,	7586
10: 4	said S to his armourbearer, Draw thy	7586
10: 4	So S took a sword, and fell upon it.	7586
10: 5	when his armourbearer saw that S was	7586
10: 6	So S died, and his three sons, and all his	7586
10: 7	that S and his sons were dead, then	7586
10: 8	that they found S and his sons fallen in	7586
10:11	all that the Philistines had done to S,	7586
10:12	away the body of S, and the bodies of	7586
10:13	So S died for his transgression which he	7586
11: 2	in time past, even when S was king,	7586
12: 1	himself close because of S the son of Kish:	7586
12:19	he came with the Philistines against S	7586
12:19	will fall to his master S to *the jeopardy*	7586
12:23	Hebron, to turn the kingdom of S to him,	7586
12:29	the kindred of S, three thousand:	7586
12:29	them had kept the ward of the house of S.	7586
13: 3	for we inquired not *at* it in the days of S.	7586
15:29	that Michal the daughter of S looking out	7586
26:28	S the son of Kish, and Abner the son of	7586
Ps 18: T	all his enemies, and from the hand of S:	7586
52: T	when Doeg the Edomite came and told S	7586
54: T	when the Ziphims came and said to S,	7586
57: T	David, when he fled from S in the cave.	7586
59: T	when S sent, and they watcht the house	7586
Isa 10:29	Ramah is afraid; Gibeah of S is fled.	7586
Ac 7:58	a young man's feet, whose name was S.	4569
8: 1	And S was consenting unto his death.	4569
8: 3	As for S, he made havock of the church,	4569
9: 4	and yet breathing out threatenings and	4569
9: 4	S, Saul, why persecutest thou me?	4540
9: 4	Saul, S, why persecutest thou me?	4540
9: 8	And S arose from the earth; and when his	4569
9:11	in the house of Judas for *one* called S,	4569
9:17	him said, Brother S, the Lord, *even* Jesus,	4549
9:19	Then was S certain days with the disciples	4569
9:22	But S increased the more in strength,	4569

Ac
9:24 But their laying await was known of **S**. 4569
9:26 And when **S** was come to Jerusalem, 4569
11:25 departed Barnabas to Tarsus, for to seek **S**: 4569
11:30 the elders by the hands of Barnabas and **S**. 4569
12:25 and **S** returned from Jerusalem, 4569
13: 1 up with Herod the tetrarch, and **S**. 4569
13: 2 **S** for the work whereunto I have called 4569
13: 7 who called for Barnabas and **S**, 4569
13: 9 Then **S**, (who also is called Paul,) 4569
13:21 and God gave unto them **S** the son of Cis, 4549
22: 7 me, **S**, Saul, why persecutest thou me? 4549
22: 7 me, Saul, **S**, why persecutest thou me? 4549
22:13 and stood, and said unto me, Brother **S**, 4549
26:14 **S**, Saul, why persecutest thou me? 4549
26:14 Saul, **S**, why persecutest thou me? 4549

SAUL'S (31) [SAUL]
1Sa 9: 3 the asses of Kish **S** father were lost. 7586
10:14 **S** uncle said unto him and to his servant, 7586
10:15 **S** uncle said, Tell me, I pray thee, 7586
14:50 the name of **S** wife was Ahinoam, 7586
14:50 host was Abner, the son of Ner, **S** uncle. 7586
16:15 **S** servants said unto him, Behold now, 7586
18: 5 and also in the sight of **S** servants. 7586
18:10 and there was a javelin in **S** hand. 7586
18:19 it came to pass at the time when Merab **S** 7586
18:20 Michal **S** daughter loved David: 7586
18:23 **S** servants spake those words in the ears 7586
18:28 and that Michal **S** daughter loved him. 7586
19: 2 Jonathan **S** son delighted much in David: 7586
19:10 he slipt away out of **S** presence, 7586
20:25 Abner sat by **S** side, and David's place 7586
20:30 **S** anger was kindled against Jonathan, 7586
23:16 Jonathan **S** son arose, and went to David 7586
24: 4 cut off the skirt of **S** robe privily. 7586+3807.1
24: 5 because he had cut off **S** skirt. 7586+3807.1
26:12 and the cruse of water from **S** bolster; 7586
31: 2 and Abinadab, and Malchishua, **S** sons. 7586
2Sa 2: 8 the son of Ner, captain of **S** host, 7586+3807.1
2:10 Ish-bosheth **S** son was forty years old 7586
3:13 except thou first bring Michal **S** daughter, 7586
3:14 David sent messengers to Ish-bosheth **S** 7586
4: 1 when **S** son heard that Abner was dead in 7586
4: 2 **S** son had two men that were captains of 7586
4: 4 Jonathan, **S** son, had a son that was lame 7586
6:16 Michal **S** daughter looked through a 7586
9: 9 to Ziba, **S** servant, and said unto him, 7586
1Ch 12: 2 of a bow, even of **S** brethren of Benjamin. 7586

SAVE (233) [SAFE, SAFEGUARD, SAFELY, SAFETY, SALVATION, SAVED, SAVEST, SAVETH, SAVING, SAVIOUR, SAVIOURS]
Ge 12:12 will kill me, but they will s thee **alive**. 2421
14:24 S only that which the young men have 1107
39: 6 had, s the bread which he did eat. 518+3588
45: 7 and to s your **lives** by a great deliverance. 2421
50:20 as it is this day, to s much people **alive**. 2421
Ex 1:22 and every daughter ye shall s **alive**. 2421
12:16 s that which every man must eat, that 389
22:20 s unto the Lord only, he shall be utterly 1115
Nu 14:30 s Caleb the son of Jephunneh, 518+3588
26:65 s Caleb the son of Jephunneh, 518+3588
32:12 S Caleb the son of Jephunneh the 1115
Dt 1:36 S Caleb the son of Jephunneh, he shall 2108
15: 4 S when there shall be no poor among you; 657
20: 4 for you against your enemies, to s you. 3467
20:16 thou shalt s **alive** nothing that breatheth: 2421
22:27 cried, and there was none to s her. 3467
28:29 evermore, and no man shall s thee. 3467
Jos 2:13 that ye will s **alive** my father, 2421
10: 6 up to us quickly, and s us, and help us: 3467
11:13 Israel burned none of them, s Hazor only; 2108
11:19 s the Hivites the inhabitants of Gibeon. 1115
14: 4 s cities to dwell in, with their 518+3588
22:22 against the Lord, (s us not this day,) 3467
Jdg 6:14 thou shalt s Israel from the hand of 3467
6:15 O my Lord, wherewith shall I s Israel? 3467
6:31 will ye s him? he that will plead for him, 3467
6:36 If thou wilt s Israel by mine hand, as thou 3467
6:37 I know that thou wilt s Israel by mine 3467
7: 7 hundred men that lapped will I s you, 3467
7:14 This is nothing else s the sword of Gideon 518
1Sa 4: 3 may s us out of the hand of our enemies. 3467
7: 8 that he will s us out of the hand of 3467
9:16 he may s my people out of the hand of 3467
10:24 people shouted, and said, God s the king. 2421
10:27 of Belial said, How shall this man s us? 3467
11: 3 then, if there be no man to s us, we will 3467
14: 6 for there is no restraint to the Lord to s 3467
19:11 saying, If thou s not thy life to night, 4422
21: 9 take it: for there is no other s that here. 2108
23: 2 and smite the Philistines, and s Keilah. 3467
30:17 S four hundred young men, 518+3588
30:22 s to every man his wife and his 518+3588
2Sa 3:18 By the hand of my servant David I will s 3467
12: 3 s one little ewe lamb, which he had 518+3588
16:16 God s the king, God save the king. 2421
16:16 God save the king, God s the king. 2421
22:28 the afflicted people thou wilt s: 3467
22:32 For who is God, s the Lord? 1107+4480
22:32 and who is a rock, s our God? 1107+4480
22:42 They looked, but there was none to s; 3467
1Ki 1:12 that thou mayest s thine own life, 4422
1:25 him, and say, God s king Adonijah. 2421
1:34 trumpet, and say, God s king Solomon. 2421

1Ki 1:39 all the people said, God s king Solomon. 2421
3:18 us in the house, s we two in the house. 2108
8: 9 There was nothing in the ark s the two 7535
15: 5 s only in the matter of Uriah the Hittite. 7535
18: 5 find grass to s the horses and mules **alive**, 2421
20:31 of Israel: peradventure he will s thy life. 2421
22:31 s only with the king of Israel. 518+3588
2Ki 4: 2 any thing in the house, s a pot of oil. 518+3588
7: 4 if they s us **alive**, we shall live; and if 2421
11:12 their hands, and said, God s the king. 2421
15: 4 S that the high places were not removed: 7535
16: 7 s me out of the hand of the king of Syria, 3467
19:19 I beseech thee, s thou us out of his hand, 3467
19:34 to s it, for mine own sake, and for my 3467
24:14 s the poorest sort of the people of the 2108
1Ch 16:35 say ye, S us, O God of our salvation, 3467
2Ch 2: 6 only to burn sacrifice before him? 518+3588
5:10 There was nothing in the ark s the two 7535
18:30 great, s only with the king of Israel. 518+3588
21:17 s Jehoahaz, the youngest of his sons. 518+3588
23: 6 s the priests, and they that minister 518+3588
23:11 anointed him, and said, God s the king. 2421
Ne 2:12 me, s the beast that I rode upon. 518+3588
6:11 would go into the temple to s his **life**? 2421
Job 2: 6 Behold, he is in thine hand; but s his life. 8104
20:20 he shall not s of that which he desired. 4422
22:29 and he shall s the humble person. 3467
40:14 that thine own right hand can s thee. 3467
Ps 3: 7 Arise, O Lord; s me, O my God: 3467
6: 4 my soul: O s me for thy mercy's sake. 3467
7: 1 s me from all them that persecute me, 3467
18:27 For thou wilt s the afflicted people; 3467
18:31 For who is God s the Lord? 1107+4480
18:31 the Lord? or who is a rock s our God? 2108
18:41 there was none to s them: even unto 3467
20: 9 S, Lord: let the king hear us when we 3467
22:21 S me from the lion's mouth: for thou hast 3467
28: 9 S thy people, and bless thine inheritance: 3467
31: 2 rock, for a house of defence to s me. 3467
31:16 thy servant: s me for thy mercy's sake. 3467
37:40 and s them, because they trust in him. 3467
44: 3 neither did their own arm s them: 3467
44: 6 in my bow, neither shall my sword s me. 3467
54: 1 S me, O God, by thy name, and judge me 3467
55:16 call upon God; and the Lord shall s me. 3467
57: 3 s me from the reproach of him that would 3467
59: 2 of iniquity, and s me from bloody men. 3467
60: 5 s with thy right hand, and hear me. 3467
69: 1 S me, O God; for the waters are come in 3467
69:35 For God will s Zion, and will build 3467
71: 2 incline thine ear unto me, and s me. 3467
71: 3 thou hast given commandment to s me; 3467
72: 4 he shall s the children of the needy, 3467
72:13 needy, and shall s the souls of the needy. 3467
76: 9 judgment, to s all the meek of the earth. 3467
80: 2 stir up thy strength, and come and s us. 3444
86: 2 God, s thy servant that trusteth in thee. 3467
86:16 and s the son of thine handmaid. 3467
106:47 S us, O Lord our God, and gather us 3467
108: 6 s with thy right hand, and answer me. 3467
109:26 my God: O s me according to thy mercy; 3467
109:31 s him from those that condemn his soul. 3467
118:25 S now, I beseech thee, O Lord: 3467
119:94 I am thine, s me; for I have sought thy 3467
119:146 s me, and I shall keep thy testimonies. 3467
138: 7 and thy right hand shall s me. 3467
145:19 also will hear their cry, and will s them. 3467
Pr 20:22 but wait on the Lord, and he shall s thee. 3467
Isa 25: 9 we have waited for him, and he will s us: 3467
33:22 the Lord is our king; he will s us. 3467
35: 4 a recompence; he will come and s you. 3467
37:20 O Lord our God, s us from his hand, 3467
37:35 For I will defend this city to s it for mine 3467
38:20 The Lord was ready to s me: therefore 3467
45:20 and pray unto a god that cannot s. 3467
46: 7 not answer, nor s him out of his trouble. 3467
47:13 s thee from these things that shall come 3467
47:15 one to his quarter; none shall s thee. 3467
49:25 with thee, and I will s thy children. 3467
59: 1 hand is not shortened, that it cannot s; 3467
63: 1 I that speak in righteousness, mighty to s. 3467
Jer 2:27 trouble they will say, Arise, and s us. 3467
2:28 they can s thee in the time of thy trouble? 3467
11:12 they shall not s them **at all** in 3467+3467
14: 9 as a mighty man that cannot s? 3467
15:20 for I am with thee to s thee and to deliver 3467
17:14 shall be healed; s me, and I shall be saved: 3467
30:10 I will s thee from afar, and thy seed from 3467
30:11 I am with thee, saith the Lord, to s thee: 3467
31: 7 praise ye, and say, O Lord, s thy people, 3467
42:11 for I am with you, to s you, and to deliver 3467
46:27 I will s thee from afar off, and thy seed 3467
48: 6 s your lives, and be like the heath in 4422
La 4:17 watched for a nation that could not s us. 3467
Eze 3:18 wicked from his wicked way, to s his life; 2421
13:18 will ye s the souls **alive** that come unto 2421
13:19 to s the souls **alive** that should not live, 2421
18:27 lawful and right, he shall s his soul **alive**. 2421
34:22 Therefore will I s my flock, and they shall 3467
36:29 I will also s you from all your 3467
37:23 I will s them out of all their dwelling 3467
Da 6: 7 or man for thirty days, s of thee, O king, 3861
6:12 or man within thirty days, s of thee, 3861
Hos 1: 7 will s them by the Lord their God, 3467
1: 7 will not s them by bow, nor by sword, 3467

Hos 13:10 is any other that may s thee in all thy 3467
14: 3 Asshur shall not s us: we will not ride 3467
Hab 1: 2 thee of violence, and thou wilt not s? 3467
Zep 3:17 will s, he will rejoice over thee with joy; 3467
3:19 will s her that halteth, and gather her that 3467
Zec 8: 7 I will s my people from the east country, 3467
8:13 so will I s you, and ye shall be a blessing: 3467
9:16 the Lord their God shall s them in that 3467
10: 6 I will s the house of Joseph, and I will 3467
12: 7 The Lord also shall s the tents of Judah 3467
Mt 1:21 he shall s his people from their sins. 4982
8:25 to him, and awoke him, saying, Lord, s us: 4982
11:27 s the Son, and he to whomsoever the Son 1508
13:57 s in his own country, and in his own 1508
14:30 to sink, he cried, saying, Lord, s me. 4982
16:25 For whosoever will s his life shall lose it: 4982
17: 8 their eyes, they saw no **man**, s Jesus only. 4982
18:11 the Son of man is come to s that which 4982
19:11 this saying, s they to whom it is given. 235
27:40 and buildest it in three days, s thyself. 4982
27:42 He saved others; himself he cannot s. 4982
27:49 see whether Elias will come to s him. 4982
Mk 3: 4 to s life, or to kill? But they held their 4982
5:37 s Peter, and James, and John the brother 1508
6: 5 s that he laid his hands upon a few sick 1508
6: 8 nothing for their journey, s a staff only; 1508
8:35 For whosoever will s his life shall lose it; 4982
8:35 and the gospel's, the same shall s it. 4982
9: 8 any more, s Jesus only with themselves. 235
15:30 S thyself, and come down from the cross. 4982
15:31 He saved others; himself he cannot s. 4982
Lk 4:26 s unto Sarepta, a city of Sidon, unto a 1508
6: 9 or to do evil? to s life, or to destroy it? 4982
8:51 he suffered no **man** to go in, s Peter, 1508
9:24 For whosoever will s his life shall lose it: 4982
9:24 his life for my sake, the same shall s it. 4982
9:56 to destroy men's lives, but to s them. 4982
17:18 to give glory to God, s this stranger. 1508
17:33 shall seek to s his life shall lose 4982
18:19 good? none is good, s one, that is, God. 1508
19:10 to seek and to s that which was lost. 4982
23:35 let him s himself, if he be Christ, 4982
23:37 If thou be the King of the Jews, s thyself. 4982
23:39 saying, If thou be Christ, s thyself and us. 4982
Jn 6:22 s that one whereinto his disciples were 1508
6:46 s he which is of God, he hath seen 4982
12:27 Father, s me from this hour: but for this 4982
12:47 to judge the world, but to s the world. 4982
13:10 He that is washed needeth not s to wash 2228
Ac 2:40 S yourselves from this untoward 4133
20:23 S that the Holy Ghost witnesseth in every 4133
21:25 s only that they keep themselves from 1508
27:43 But the centurion, willing to s Paul, 1295
Ro 11:14 are my flesh, and might s some of them. 4982
1Co 1:21 of preaching to s them that believe. 4982
2: 2 s Jesus Christ, and him crucified. 1508
2:11 man, the spirit of man which is in him? 1508
7:16 wife, whether thou shalt s thy husband? 4982
7:16 O man, whether thou shalt s thy wife? 4982
9:22 all men, that I might by all means s some. 4982
2Co 11:24 five times received I forty stripes s one. 3844
Gal 1:19 saw I none, s James the Lord's brother. 1508
6:14 s in the cross of our Lord Jesus Christ, 1508
1Ti 1:15 that Christ Jesus came into the world to s 4982
4:16 for in doing this thou shalt both s thyself, 4982
Heb 5: 7 tears unto him that was able to s him 4982
7:25 Wherefore he is able also to s them to 4982
Jas 1:21 which is able to s your souls. 4982
2:14 and have not works? can faith s him? 4982
4:12 who is able to s and to destroy: 4982
5:15 And the prayer of faith shall s the sick, 4982
5:20 error of his way shall s a soul from death, 4982
1Pe 3:21 s us (not the putting away of the filth of 4982
Jude 1:23 others with fear, pulling them out of 4982
Rev 13:17 s he that had the mark, or the name of 1508

SAVED (104) [SAVE]
Ge 47:25 said, Thou hast s our **lives**: let us find 2421
Ex 1:17 but s the men children **alive**. 2421
1:18 and have s the men children **alive**? 2421
14:30 Thus the Lord s Israel that day out of 3467
Nu 10: 9 and ye shall be s from your enemies. 3467
22:33 also I had slain thee, and s her **alive**. 2421
31:15 them, Have ye s all the women **alive**? 2421
Dt 33:29 is like unto thee, O people s by the Lord, 3467
Jos 6:25 Joshua s Rahab the harlot **alive**, and her 2421
Jdg 7: 2 saying, Mine own hand hath s me. 3467
8:19 if ye had s them **alive**, I would not slay 2421
21:14 s **alive** of the women of Jabesh-gilead. 2421
1Sa 10:19 who himself s you out of all your 3467
14:23 So the Lord s Israel that day: 3467
23: 5 So David s the inhabitants of Keilah. 3467
27:11 David s neither man nor woman **alive**, 2421
2Sa 19: 5 this day have s thy life, and the lives 4422
19: 9 The king s us out of the hand of our 5337
22: 4 so shall I be s from mine enemies. 3467
2Ki 6:10 and warned him of, and s himself there, 8104
14:27 he s them by the hand of Jeroboam 3467
1Ch 11:14 the Lord s them by a great deliverance. 3467
2Ch 32:22 Thus the Lord s Hezekiah and 3467
Ne 9:27 who s them out of the hand of their 3467
Ps 18: 3 so shall I be s from mine enemies. 3467
33:16 There is no king s by the multitude of a 3467
34: 6 and s him out of all his troubles. 3467
44: 7 thou hast s us from our enemies, 3467

S

Ref	Text	Strong's
Ps 80: 3	cause thy face to shine; and we shall be **s**.	3467
80: 7	cause thy face to shine; and we shall be **s**.	3467
80:19	cause thy face to shine; and we shall be **s**.	3467
106: 8	Nevertheless he **s** them for his name's	3467
106:10	**s** them from the hand of him that hated	3467
107:13	*and* he **s** them out of their distresses.	3467
Pr 28:18	Whoso walketh uprightly shall be **s**;	
Isa 30:15	In returning and rest shall ye be **s**;	
43:12	and have **s**, and I have shewed,	
45:17	*But* Israel shall be **s** in the Lord *with* an	
45:22	Look unto me, and be ye **s**, all the ends	
49:26	those is continuance, and we shall be **s**.	
63: 9	and the angel of his presence **s** them:	
64: 5	those is continuance, and we shall be **s**.	
Jer 4:14	from wickedness, that thou mayest be **s**.	
8:20	the summer is ended, and we are not **s**.	
17:14	be healed; save me, and I shall be **s**:	
23: 6	In his days Judah shall be **s**, and Israel	
30: 7	Jacob's trouble; but he shall be **s** out of it.	
33:16	In those days shall Judah be **s**,	
Mt 10:22	but he that endureth to the end shall be **s**.	4982
19:25	saying, Who then can be **s**?	4982
24:13	endure unto the end, the same shall be **s**.	4982
24:22	be shortened, there should no flesh be **s**:	4982
27:42	He **s** others; himself he cannot save. If he	4982
Mk 10:26	among themselves, Who then can be **s**?	4982
13:13	endure unto the end, the same shall be **s**.	4982
13:20	*those* days, no flesh should be **s**:	4982
15:31	themselves with the scribes, He **s** others;	4982
16:16	that believeth and is baptized shall be **s**;	4982
Lk 1:71	That *we* should be **s** from our enemies,	4991
7:50	said to the woman, Thy faith hath **s** thee;	4982
8:12	lest they should believe and be **s**.	4982
13:23	unto him, Lord, are there few that be **s**?	4982
18:26	that heard *it* said, Who then can be **s**?	4982
18:42	Receive thy sight: thy faith hath **s** thee.	4982
23:35	them derided *him*, saying, He **s** others;	4982
Jn 3:17	that the world through him might be **s**.	4982
5:34	these *things* I say, that ye might be **s**.	4982
10: 9	he shall be **s**, and shall go in and out,	4982
Ac 2:21	call on the name of the Lord shall be **s**.	4982
2:47	to the church daily such as should be **s**.	4982
4:12	among men, whereby we must be **s**.	4982
11:14	whereby thou and all thy house shall be **s**.	4982
15: 1	the manner of Moses, ye cannot be **s**.	4982
15:11	of the Lord Jesus Christ we shall be **s**,	4982
16:30	and said, Sirs, what must I do to be **s**?	4982
16:31	and thou shalt be **s**, and thy house.	4982
27:20	on *us*, all hope that we should be **s** was	4982
27:31	these abide in the ship, ye cannot be **s**.	4982
Ro 5: 9	we shall be **s** from wrath through him.	4982
5:10	being reconciled, we shall be **s** by his life.	4982
8:24	we are **s** by hope: but hope that is seen	4982
9:27	the sand of the sea, a remnant shall be **s**:	4982
10: 1	to God for Israel is, that *they* might be **s**.	4991
10: 9	raised him from the dead, thou shalt be **s**.	4982
10:13	call upon the name of the Lord shall be **s**.	4982
11:26	And so all Israel shall be **s**: as it is written,	4982
1Co 1:18	us which are **s** it is the power of God.	4982
3:15	but he himself shall be **s**; yet so as by fire.	4982
5: 5	that the spirit may be **s** in the day of	4982
10:33	the *profit* of many, that they may be **s**.	4982
15: 2	By which also ye are **s**, if ye keep in	4982
2Co 2:15	them that are **s**, and in them that perish:	4982
Eph 2: 5	together with Christ, (by grace ye are **s**;)	4982
2: 8	For by grace are ye **s** through faith;	4982
1Th 2:16	speak to the Gentiles that they might be **s**,	4982
2Th 2:10	the love of the truth, that they might be **s**.	4982
1Ti 2: 4	will have all men to be **s**, and to come	4982
2:15	Notwithstanding she shall be **s** in	4982
2Ti 1: 9	Who hath **s** us, and called *us* with a holy	4982
Tit 3: 5	but according to his mercy he **s** us,	4982
1Pe 3:20	that is, eight souls were **s** by water.	1295
4:18	And if the righteous scarcely be **s**,	4982
2Pe 2: 5	**s** Noah the eighth *person*, a preacher of	5442
Jude 1: 5	having **s** the people out of the land of	
Rev 21:24	And the nations of them which are **s** shall	4982

SAVEST (3) [SAVE]

Ref	Text	Strong's
2Sa 22: 3	my saviour; thou **s** me from violence.	3467
Job 26: 2	is thou the arm *that hath* no strength?	
Ps 17: 7	O thou that **s** by thy right hand them	3467

SAVETH (7) [SAVE]

Ref	Text	Strong's
1Sa 14:39	For, *as* the Lord liveth, which **s** Israel,	3467
17:47	know that the Lord **s** not with sword	3467
Job 5:15	he **s** the poor from the sword, from their	3467
Ps 7:10	*is* of God, which **s** the upright in heart.	3467
20: 6	Now know I that the Lord **s** his	3467
34:18	and **s** such as be of a contrite spirit.	3467
107:19	he **s** them out of their distresses.	3467

SAVING (12) [SAVE]

Ref	Text	Strong's
Ge 19:19	which thou hast shewed unto me in **s** my	2421
Ne 4:23	**s** that every one put them off *for* washing.	NIH
Ps 20: 6	with the strength of his right hand.	3468
28: 8	and he *is* the **s** strength of his anointed.	3444
67: 2	earth, thy **s** health among all nations.	3444
Ecc 5:11	**s** the beholding of *them* with their	518+3588
Am 9: 8	that I will not utterly destroy the house	657
Mt 5:32	**s** for the cause of fornication, causeth her	3924
Lk 4:27	them was cleansed, **s** Naaman the Syrian.	1508
Heb 10:39	of *them* that believe to the **s** of the soul.	4047
11: 7	prepared an ark to the **s** of his house;	4991
Rev 2:17	no *man* knoweth **s** he that receiveth	1508

SAVIOUR (37) [SAVE]

Ref	Text	Strong's
2Sa 22: 3	my high tower, and my refuge, my **s**;	3467
2Ki 13: 5	(And the Lord gave Israel a **s**,	3467
Ps 106:21	They forgat God their **s**, which had done	3467
Isa 19:20	he shall send them a **s**, and a great one,	3467
43: 3	thy God, the Holy One of Israel, thy **S**:	3467
43:11	the Lord; and beside me *there* is no **s**.	3467
45:15	that hidest thyself, O God of Israel, the **s**.	3467
45:21	a just God and a **s**; *there is* none beside	3467
49:26	shall know that I the Lord *am* thy **S**	3467
60:16	thou shalt know that I the Lord *am* thy **S**	3467
63: 8	*that* will not lie: so he was their **S**.	3467
Jer 14: 8	of Israel, the **s** thereof in time of trouble,	3467
Hos 13: 4	no god but me: for *there* is no **s** beside	3467
Lk 1:47	And my spirit hath rejoiced in God my **S**.	4990
2:11	is born this day in the city of David a **S**,	4990
Jn 4:42	is indeed the Christ, the **S** of the world.	4990
Ac 5:31	with his right hand *to be* a Prince and a **S**,	4990
13:23	to *his* promise raised unto Israel a **S**,	4990
Eph 5:23	of the church: and he is the **s** of the body.	4990
Php 3:20	from whence also we look for the **S**,	4990
1Ti 1: 1	by the commandment of God our **S**,	4990
2: 3	and acceptable in the sight of God our **S**;	4990
4:10	in the living God, who is the **S** of all men,	4990
2Ti 1:10	by the appearing of our **S** Jesus Christ,	4990
Tit 1: 3	to the commandment of God our **S**;	4990
1: 4	Father and the Lord Jesus Christ our **S**.	4990
2:10	the doctrine of God our **S** in all *things*.	4990
2:13	of the great God and our **S** Jesus Christ;	4990
3: 4	love of God our **S** toward man appeared,	4990
3: 6	us abundantly through Jesus Christ our **S**;	4990
2Pe 1: 1	of God and our **S** Jesus Christ:	4990
1:11	kingdom of our Lord and **S** Jesus Christ.	4990
2:20	knowledge of the Lord and **S** Jesus Christ,	4990
3: 2	of us the apostles of the Lord and **S**:	4990
3:18	knowledge of our Lord and **S** Jesus Christ.	4990
1Jn 4:14	sent the Son *to be* the **S** of the world.	4990
Jude 1:25	To the only wise God our **S**, *be* glory and	4990

SAVIOURS (2) [SAVE]

Ref	Text	Strong's
Ne 9:27	thy manifold mercies thou gavest them **s**,	3467
Ob 1:21	**s** shall come up on mount Zion to judge	3467

SAVOUR (54) [SAVOUREST, SAVOURS, SAVOURY, UNSAVOURY]

Ref	Text	Strong's
Ge 8:21	the Lord smelled a sweet **s**;	7381
Ex 5:21	you have made our **s** to be abhorred in	7381
29:18	it *is* a sweet **s**, an offering made by fire	7381
29:25	for a sweet **s** before the Lord:	7381
29:41	the drink offering thereof, for a sweet **s**,	7381
Lev 1: 9	made by fire, of a sweet **s** unto the Lord.	7381
1:13	made by fire, of a sweet **s** unto the Lord.	7381
1:17	made by fire, a sweet **s** unto the Lord.	7381
2: 2	made by fire, of a sweet **s** unto the Lord.	7381
2: 9	made by fire, of a sweet **s** unto the Lord.	7381
2:12	not be burnt on the altar for a sweet **s**.	7381
3: 5	made by fire, of a sweet **s** unto the Lord.	7381
3:16	of the offering made by fire for a sweet **s**:	7381
4:31	the altar for a sweet **s** unto the Lord;	7381
6:15	shall burn *it* upon the altar *for* a sweet **s**,	7381
6:21	thou offer *for* a sweet **s** unto the Lord.	7381
8:21	it *was* a burnt sacrifice for a sweet **s**,	7381
8:28	they *were* consecrations for a sweet **s**:	7381
17: 6	burn the fat for a sweet **s** unto the Lord.	7381
23:13	made by fire unto the Lord *for* a sweet **s**;	7381
23:18	made by fire, of sweet **s** unto the Lord.	7381
26:31	will not smell the **s** of your sweet odours.	7381
Nu 15: 3	make a sweet **s** unto the Lord,	7381
15: 7	hin *of* wine, for a sweet **s** unto the Lord.	7381
15:10	made by fire, of a sweet **s** unto the Lord.	7381
15:13	made by fire, of a sweet **s** unto the Lord.	7381
15:14	made by fire, of a sweet **s** unto the Lord;	7381
15:24	for a sweet **s** unto the Lord, with his	7381
18:17	by fire, for a sweet **s** unto the Lord.	7381
28: 2	made by fire, *for* a sweet **s** unto me,	7381
28: 6	ordained in mount Sinai for a sweet **s**,	7381
28: 8	made by fire, *of* a sweet **s** unto the Lord.	7381
28:13	a burnt offering *of* a sweet **s**, a sacrifice	7381
28:24	made by fire, *of* a sweet **s** unto the Lord:	7381
28:27	offering for a sweet **s** unto the Lord;	7381
29: 2	shall offer a burnt offering for a sweet **s**	7381
29: 6	unto their manner, for a sweet **s**,	7381
29: 8	offering unto the Lord *for* a sweet **s**;	7381
29:13	made by fire, *of* a sweet **s** unto the Lord:	7381
29:36	made by fire, *of* a sweet **s** unto the Lord:	7381
Ecc 10: 1	the apothecary to send forth a **stinking s**:	887
SS 1: 3	Because of the **s** of thy good ointments	7381
Eze 6:13	place where they did offer sweet **s** to all	7381
16:19	hast even set it before them for a sweet **s**:	7381
20:28	there also they made their sweet **s**,	7381
20:41	I will accept you with *your* sweet **s**, when	7381
Joel 2:20	his **ill s** shall come up, because he hath	6709
Mt 5:13	but if the salt have lost his **s**,	3471
Lk 14:34	but if the salt have lost his **s**,	3471
2Co 2:14	maketh manifest the **s** of his knowledge	3744
2:15	For we are unto God a **sweet s** of Christ,	2175
2:16	the one *we are* the **s** of death unto death;	3744
2:16	and to the other the **s** of life unto life.	3744
Eph 5: 2	a sacrifice to God for a sweetsmelling **s**.	3744

SAVOUREST (2) [SAVOUR]

Ref	Text	Strong's
Mt 16:23	for thou **s** not the *things* that be of God,	5426
Mk 8:33	for thou **s** not the *things* that be of God,	5426

SAVOURS (1) [SAVOUR]

Ref	Text	Strong's
Ezr 6:10	That they may offer sacrifices of **sweet s**	5208

SAVOURY (6) [SAVOUR]

Ref	Text	Strong's
Ge 27: 4	make me **s meat**, such as I love,	4303
27: 7	make me **s meat**, that I may eat,	4303
27: 9	I will make them **s meat** for thy father,	4303
27:14	mother made **s meat**, such as his father	4303
27:17	she gave the **s meat** and the bread,	4303
27:31	he also had made **s meat**, and brought *it*	4303

SAW (548) [SEE, SAWED, SAWN, SAWS]

Ref	Text	Strong's
Ge 1: 4	God **s** the light, that *it was* good:	7200
1:10	he Seas: and God **s** that *it was* good.	7200
1:12	after his kind: and God **s** that *it was* good.	7200
1:18	the darkness: and God **s** that *it was* good.	7200
1:21	after his kind: and God **s** that *it was* good.	7200
1:25	after his kind: and God **s** that *it was* good.	7200
1:31	God **s** every thing that he had made,	7200
3: 6	the woman **s** that the tree *was* good	7200
6: 2	That the sons of God **s** the daughters of	7200
6: 5	God **s** that the wickedness of man *was*	7200
9:22	**s** the nakedness of his father, and told his	7200
9:23	and they **s** not their father's nakedness.	7200
12:15	The princes also of Pharaoh **s** her,	7200
16: 4	when she **s** that she had conceived,	7200
16: 5	when she **s** that she had conceived, I was	7200
18: 2	when he **s** *them*, he ran to meet them	7200
21: 9	Sarah **s** the son of Hagar the Egyptian,	7200
21:19	her eyes, and she **s** a well of water;	7200
22: 4	lift up his eyes, and **s** the place afar off.	7200
24:30	when he **s** the earring and bracelets upon	7200
24:63	he lift up his eyes, and **s**, and behold,	7200
24:64	she **s** Isaac, she lighted off the camel.	7200
26: 8	**s**, and behold, Isaac *was* sporting with	7200
26:28	We **s** **certainly** that the Lord was	7200+7200
28: 6	When Esau **s** that Isaac had blessed Jacob,	7200
29:10	Jacob **s** Rachel the daughter of Laban	7200
29:31	when the Lord **s** that Leah *was* hated,	7200
30: 1	when Rachel **s** that she bare Jacob no	7200
30: 9	When Leah **s** that she had left bearing,	7200
31:10	mine eyes, and **s** in a dream, and behold,	7200
32: 2	when Jacob **s** them, he said, This *is* God's	7200
32:25	he **s** that he prevailed not against him,	7200
33: 5	eyes, and he **s** the women and the children;	7200
34: 2	**s** her, he took her, and lay with her,	7200
37: 4	his brethren **s** that their father loved	7200
37:18	when they **s** him afar off, even before he	7200
38: 2	Judah **s** there a daughter of a certain	7200
38:14	for she **s** that Shelah was grown,	7200
38:15	When Judah **s** her, he thought her to be a	7200
39: 3	his master **s** that the Lord *was* with him,	7200
39:13	she **s** that he had left his garment in	7200
40:16	When the chief baker **s** that	7200
41:19	such as I never **s** in all the land of Egypt	7200
41:22	**s** in my dream, and behold, seven ears	7200
42: 1	Now when Jacob **s** that there was corn in	7200
42: 7	Joseph **s** his brethren, and he knew them,	7200
42:21	in that we **s** the anguish of his soul,	7200
42:35	and their father **s** the bundles of money,	7200
43:16	Joseph **s** Benjamin with them, he said	7200
43:29	his brother Benjamin, his mother's son,	7200
44:28	he is torn in pieces; and I **s** him not since:	7200
45:27	when he **s** the wagons which Joseph had	7200
48:17	when Joseph **s** that his father laid his right	7200
49:15	he **s** that rest *was* good, and the land that	7200
50:11	the mourning in the floor of Atad, they	7200
50:15	when Joseph's brethren **s** that their father	7200
50:23	Joseph **s** Ephraim's children of the third	7200
Ex 2: 2	she **s** him that he *was* a goodly *child*,	7200
2: 5	when she **s** the ark among the flags,	7200
2: 6	when she had opened *it*, she **s** the child:	7200
2:12	and when he **s** that *there was* no man,	7200
3: 4	when the Lord **s** that he turned aside to	7200
8:15	when Pharaoh **s** that there was respite,	7200
9:34	when Pharaoh **s** that the rain and the hail	7200
10:23	They **s** not one another, neither rose any	7200
14:30	Israel **s** the Egyptians dead upon the sea	7200
14:31	Israel **s** *that* great work which the Lord	7200
16:15	when the children of Israel **s** *it*, they said	7200
18:14	Moses' father in law **s** all that he did	7200
20:18	all the people **s** the thunderings,	7200
20:18	when the people **s** *it*, they removed,	7200
24:10	they **s** the God of Israel: and *there* was	7200
24:11	also they **s** God, and did eat and drink.	2372
32: 1	when the people **s** that Moses delayed to	7200
32: 5	Aaron **s** *it*, he built an altar before it;	7200
32:19	that he **s** the calf, and the dancing:	7200
32:25	Moses **s** that the people *were* naked;	7200
33:10	all the people **s** the cloudy pillar stand *at*	7200
34:30	and all the children of Israel **s** Moses,	7200
34:35	the children of Israel **s** the face of Moses,	7200
Lev 9:24	when all the people **s**, they shouted,	7200
Nu 13:28	we **s** the children of Anak there.	7200
13:32	all the people that we **s** in it *are* men of a	7200
13:33	there we **s** the giants, the sons of Anak,	7200
20:29	all the congregation **s** that Aaron was	7200
22: 2	Balak the son of Zippor **s** all that Israel	7200
22:23	the ass **s** the angel of the Lord standing	7200
22:25	when the ass **s** the angel of the Lord,	7200
22:27	when the ass **s** the angel of the Lord,	7200
22:31	he **s** the angel of the Lord standing in	7200
22:33	the ass **s** me, and turned from me these	7200
24: 1	when Balaam **s** that it pleased the Lord	7200
24: 2	he **s** Israel abiding *in* his tents according	7200

Nu 24: 4 which **s** the vision of the Almighty, 2372
24:16 *which* **s** the vision of the Almighty, 2372
25: 7 **s** *it*, he rose up from amongst 7200
32: 1 they **s** the land of Jazer, and the land 7200
32: 9 unto the valley of Eshcol, and **s** the land, 7200
Dt 1:19 which you **s** *by* the way of the mountain 7200
4:12 voice of the words, but **s** no similitude; 7200
4:15 ye **s** no *manner of* similitude on the day 7200
7:19 The great temptations which thine eyes **s**, 7200
32:19 when the LORD **s** *it*, he abhorred *them*, 7200
Jos 7:21 When I **s** among the spoils a goodly 7200
8:14 when the king of Ai **s** *it*, that they hasted 7200
8:20 they **s**, and behold, the smoke of the city 7200
8:21 all Israel **s** that the ambush had taken 7200
Jdg 1:24 spies **s** a man come forth out of the city, 7200
3:24 when they **s** that behold, the doors of 7200
9:36 when Gaal **s** the people, he said to Zebul, 7200
9:55 when the men of Israel **s** that Abimelech 7200
11:35 it came to pass, when he **s** her, that he 7200
12: 3 I **s** that ye delivered *me* not, I put my 7200
14: 1 **s** a woman in Timnath of the daughters 7200
14:11 it came to pass, when they **s** him, that 7200
16: 1 **s** there a harlot, and went in unto her. 7200
16:18 Delilah **s** that he had told her all his 7200
16:24 when they **s** him, they praised their 7200
18: 7 Laish, and **s** the people that *were* therein, 7200
18:26 when Micah **s** that they *were* too strong 7200
19: 3 when the father of the damsel **s** him, 7200
19:17 he **s** a wayfaring man in the street of 7200
19:30 it was so, that all that **s** it said, There was 7200
20:36 So the children of Benjamin **s** that they 7200
20:41 for they **s** that evil was come upon them. 7200
Ru 1:18 she **s** that she *was* stedfastly minded 7200
2:18 mother in law **s** what she had gleaned: 7200
1Sa 5: 7 when the men of Ashdod **s** that *it was* so, 7200
6:13 and **s** the ark, and rejoiced to see it. 7200
9:17 when Samuel **s** Saul, the LORD said unto 7200
10:11 when all that knew him beforetime **s** that 7200
10:14 when we **s** that *they were* no where, 7200
12:12 when ye **s** that Nahash the king of 7200
13: 6 When the men of Israel **s** that they were 7200
13:11 Because I **s** that the people were scattered 7200
14:52 Saul **s** any strong man, or any valiant 7200
17:24 when they **s** the man, fled from him, 7200
17:42 and **s** David, he disdained him: 7200
17:51 when the Philistines **s** their champion 7200
17:55 when Saul **s** David go forth against 7200
18:15 Wherefore when Saul **s** that he behaved 7200
18:28 Saul **s** and knew that the LORD *was* with 7200
19:20 when they **s** the company of the prophets 7200
22: 9 said, I **s** the son of Jesse coming to Nob, 7200
23:15 David **s** that Saul was come out to seek 7200
25:23 when Abigail **s** David, she hasted, 7200
25:25 I thine handmaid **s** not the young men of 7200
26: 3 he **s** that Saul came after him into 7200
26:12 no man **s** *it*, nor knew *it*, neither awaked: 7200
28: 5 when Saul **s** the host of the Philistines, 7200
28:12 when the woman **s** Samuel, she cried with 7200
28:13 I **s** gods ascending out of the earth. 7200
28:21 **s** that he was sore troubled, and said unto 7200
31: 5 when his armourbearer **s** that Saul was 7200
31: 7 **s** that the men of Israel fled, and that Saul 7200
2Sa 1: 7 behind him, he **s** me, and called unto me. 7200
6:16 **s** king David leaping and dancing before 7200
10: 6 when the children of Ammon **s** that they 7200
10: 9 When Joab **s** that the front of the battle 7200
10:14 when the children of Ammon **s** that 7200
10:15 when the Syrians **s** that they were smitten 7200
10:19 **s** that they were smitten before Israel, 7200
11: 2 from the roof he **s** a woman washing 7200
12:19 David **s** that his servants whispered, 7200
14:24 his own house, and **s** not the king's face. 7200
14:28 in Jerusalem, and **s** not the king's face. 7200
17:18 Nevertheless a lad **s** them, 7200
17:23 Ahithophel **s** that his counsel was not 7200
18:10 a certain man **s** *it*, and told Joab, and said, 7200
18:10 Behold, I **s** Absalom hanged in an oak. 7200
18:26 the watchman **s** another man running: 7200
18:29 I **s** a great tumult, but I knew not what *it* 7200
20:12 when the man **s** that all the people stood 7200
20:12 when he **s** that every one that came by 7200
24:17 David spake unto the LORD when he **s** 7200
24:20 **s** the king and his servants coming on 7200
1Ki 3:28 for they **s** that the wisdom of God *was* in 7200
12:16 when all Israel **s** that the king hearkened 7200
13:25 **s** the carcase cast in the way, and the lion 7200
16:18 when Zimri **s** that the city was taken, 7200
18:17 it came to pass, when Ahab **s** Elijah, 7200
18:39 when all the people **s** *it*, they fell on their 7200
19: 3 when he **s** *that*, he arose, and went for his 7200
22:17 I **s** all Israel scattered upon the hills, 7200
22:19 **s** the LORD sitting on his throne, 7200
22:32 when the captains of the chariots **s** 7200
2Ki 2:12 Elisha **s** *it*, and he cried, My father, 7200
2:12 **s** him no more: and he took hold of his 7200
2:15 which *were* to view at Jericho **s** him, 7200
3:22 Moabites **s** the water on the other side 7200
3:26 the king of Moab **s** that the battle was 7200
4:25 when the man of God **s** her afar off, 7200
5:21 when Naaman **s** *him* running after him, 7200
6:17 the eyes of the young man; and he **s**: 7200
6:20 the LORD opened their eyes, and they **s**; 7200
6:21 unto Elisha, when he **s** them, My father, 7200
9: 2 Joram **s** Jehu, that he said, Is it peace, 7200
9:27 when Ahaziah the king of Judah **s** *this*, he 7200

2Ki 11: 1 Athaliah the mother of Ahaziah **s** that 7200
12:10 they **s** that *there was* much money in 7200
13: 4 for he **s** the oppression of Israel, because 7200
14:26 For the LORD **s** the affliction of Israel, 7200
16:10 and **s** an altar that *was* at Damascus: 7200
16:12 come from Damascus, the king **s** the altar: 7200
1Ch 10: 5 when his armourbearer **s** that Saul was 7200
10: 7 that *were* in the valley **s** that they fled, 7200
15:29 out at a window **s** king David dancing 7200
19:10 Now when Joab **s** that the battle was set 7200
19:15 when the children of Ammon **s** that they 7200
19:16 when the Syrians **s** that they were put to 7200
19:19 the servants of Hadarezer **s** that they 7200
21:16 the angel of the LORD stand between 7200
21:20 Ornan turned back, and **s** the angel; 7200
21:21 Ornan looked and **s** David, and went out 7200
21:28 At that time when David **s** that the LORD 7200
2Ch 7: 3 when all the children of Israel **s** how 7200
10:16 when all Israel **s** that the king would not 7200
12: 7 when the LORD **s** that they humbled 7200
15: 9 when they **s** that the LORD his God *was* 7200
18:18 **s** the LORD sitting upon his throne, 7200
18:31 when the captains of the chariots **s** 7200
22:10 Athaliah the mother of Ahaziah **s** that 7200
24:11 when they **s** that *there was* much money, 7200
25:21 they **s** one another *in* the face, *both* he 7200
31: 8 and the princes came and **s** the heaps, 7200
32: 2 when Hezekiah **s** that Sennacherib was 7200
Ne 6:16 all the heathen that *were* about us **s** *these* 7200
13:15 In those days **s** I in Judah some treading 7200
13:23 those days also **s** I Jews *that* had married 7200
Est 1:14 which **s** the king's face, and which sat 7200
3: 5 when Haman **s** that Mordecai bowed not, 7200
5: 2 the king **s** Esther the queen standing 7200
5: 9 Haman **s** Mordecai in the king's gate, 7200
7: 7 for he **s** that there was evil determined 7200
Job 2:13 for they **s** that *his* grief was very great. 7200
3:16 not been; as infants *which* never **s** light. 7200
20: 9 The eye also which **s** him shall *see him* 7805
29: 8 The young men **s** me, and hid themselves: 7200
29:11 when the eye **s** *me*, it gave witness to me: 7200
31:21 fatherless, when I **s** my help in the gate: 7200
32: 5 When Elihu **s** that *there was* no answer in 7200
42:16 and **s** his sons, and his sons' sons, 7200
Ps 48: 5 They **s** *it, and* so they marvelled; they 7200
73: 3 when I **s** the prosperity of the wicked. 7200
77:16 The waters **s** thee, O God, the waters 7200
77:16 saw thee, O God, the waters **s** thee; 7200
95: 9 tempted me, proved me, and **s** my work. 7200
97: 4 the world: the earth **s**, and trembled. 7200
114: 3 The sea **s** *it*, and fled: Jordan was driven 7200
Pr 24:32 I **s**, *and* considered it well: I looked upon 2372
Ecc 2:13 I **s** that wisdom excelleth folly, as far as 7200
2:24 This also I **s**, that it *was* from the hand of 7200
3:16 moreover I **s** under the sun the place of 7200
4: 7 I returned, and I **s** vanity under the sun. 7200
8:10 so I **s** the wicked buried, who had come 7200
9:11 and **s** under the sun, that the race 7200
SS 3: 3 *to whom I said,* S ye *him* whom my soul 7200
6: 9 The daughters **s** her, and blessed her; 7200
Isa 1: 1 which he **s** concerning Judah and 2372
2: 1 The word that Isaiah the son of Amoz **s** 2372
6: 1 In the year that king Uzziah died I **s** also 7200
10:15 shall the magnify itself against him that 4883
21: 7 he **s** a chariot *with* a couple of horsemen, 7200
41: 5 The isles **s** *it*, and feared; the ends of 7200
59:15 the LORD **s** *it*, and it displeased him that 7200
59:16 he **s** that *there was* no man, 7200
Jer 3: 7 And her treacherous sister Judah **s** *it.* 7200
8: 1 **s**, when for all the causes whereby 7200
39: 4 *that* when Zedekiah the king of Judah **s** 7200
41:13 Ishmael **s** Johanan the son of Kareah, 7200
44:17 of victuals, and were well, and **s** no evil. 7200
La 1: 7 the adversaries **s** her, *and* did mock at 7200
Eze 1: 1 were opened, and I **s** visions of God. 7200
1:27 I **s** as the colour of amber, 7200
1:27 I **s** as it were the appearance of fire, 7200
1:28 I **s** *it*, I fell upon my face, and I heard 7200
3:23 as the glory which I **s** by the river of 7200
8: 4 to the vision that I **s** in the plain. 7200
8:10 I went in and **s**; and behold every form 7200
10:15 This *is* the living creature that I **s** by 7200
10:20 This *is* the living creature that I **s** under 7200
10:22 faces which I **s** by the river of Chebar, 7200
11: 1 whom I **s** Jaazaniah the son of Azur, 7200
16: 6 and **s** thee polluted in thine own blood, 7200
16:50 therefore I took them away as I **s** *good.* 7200
19: 5 Now when she **s** that she had waited, 7200
20:28 they **s** every high hill, and all the thick 7200
23:11 when her sister Aholibah **s** *this*, she was 7200
23:13 I **s** that she was defiled, *that* they took 7200
23:14 for when she **s** men pourtrayed upon 7200
23:16 as soon as she **s** them with her eyes, 4758
41: 8 I **s** also the height of the house round 7200
43: 3 to the appearance of the vision which I **s**, 7200
43: 3 according to the vision that I **s** when I 7200
43: 3 the visions which I **s** when that I **s** by 7200
Da 3:27 being gathered together, **s** these men, 2370
4: 5 I **s** a dream which made me afraid, 2370
4:10 I **s**, and behold, a tree in the midst of 2370
4:13 I **s** in the visions of my head upon my 2370
4:23 whereas the king **s** a watcher and a holy 2370
5: 5 the king **s** the part of the hand that wrote. 2370
7: 2 I **s** in my vision by night, and behold, 2370

Da 7: 7 After this I **s** in the night visions, 2370
7:13 I **s** in the night visions, and behold, *one* 2370
8: 2 I **s** in a vision; and it came to pass, when 7200
8: 2 it came to pass, when I **s**, that I was at 7200
8: 2 I **s** in a vision, and I was by the river of 7200
8: 3 I lifted up mine eyes, and **s**, and behold, 7200
8: 4 I **s** the ram pushing westward, 7200
8: 7 I **s** him come close unto the ram, 7200
10: 7 I Daniel alone **s** the vision: for the men 7200
10: 7 for the men that were with me **s** not 7200
10: 8 **s** this great vision, and there remained no 7200
Hos 5:13 When Ephraim **s** his sickness, 7200
5:13 Judah **s** his wound, then went Ephraim to NIH
9:10 I **s** your fathers as the firstripe in the fig 7200
9:13 Ephraim, as I **s** Tyrus, *is* planted in a 7200
Am 1: 1 which he **s** concerning Israel in the days 2372
9: 1 I **s** the Lord standing upon the altar: 7200
Jnh 3:10 God **s** their works, that they turned from 7200
Mic 1: 1 which he **s** concerning Samaria and 2372
Hab 3: 7 I **s** the tents of Cushan in affliction: 7200
3:10 The mountains **s** thee, *and* they trembled: 7200
Hag 2: 3 Who *is* left among you that **s** this house 7200
Zec 1: 8 I **s** by night, and behold a man riding 7200
1:18 mine eyes, and **s**, and behold four horns. 7200
Mt 2: 9 and lo, the star, which they **s** in the east, 1492
2:10 When they **s** the star, they rejoiced *with* 1492
2:11 they **s** the young child with Mary his 1492
2:16 he **s** that he was mocked of the wise 1492
3: 7 But when he **s** many of the Pharisees and 1492
3:16 he **s** the Spirit of God descending like a 1492
4:16 The people which sat in darkness **s** great 1492
4:18 **s** two brethren, Simon called Peter, 1492
4:21 he **s** other two brethren, James the *son of* 1492
8:14 he **s** his wife's mother laid, and sick of a 1492
8:18 Now when Jesus **s** great multitudes about 1492
8:34 and when they **s** him, they besought *him* 1492
9: 8 But when the multitudes **s** *it*, they 1492
9: 9 he **s** a man, named Matthew, sitting at 1492
9:11 when the Pharisees **s** *it*, they said unto 1492
9:22 when he **s** her, he said, Daughter, be of 1492
9:23 and **s** the minstrels and the people making 1492
9:36 But when he **s** the multitudes, he was 1492
12: 2 But when the Pharisees **s** *it*, they said unto 1492
12:22 that the blind and dumb both spake and **s**, 991
14:14 and **s** a great multitude, and was moved 1492
14:26 And when the disciples **s** him walking on 1492
14:30 But when he **s** the wind boysterous, he 991
15:31 they **s** the dumb to speak, the maimed 991
17: 8 their eyes, they **s** no *man*, save Jesus only. 1492
18:31 So when his fellowservants **s** what was 1492
20: 3 **s** others standing idle in the marketplace, 1492
21:15 scribes **s** the wonderful *things* that he did, 1492
21:19 And when he **s** a fig tree in the way, 1492
21:20 when the disciples **s** *it*, they marvelled, 1492
21:38 But when the husbandmen **s** the son, 1492
22:11 he **s** there a man which had not on a 1492
25:37 when **s** we thee a hungred, and fed *thee?* 1492
25:38 When **s** we thee a stranger, and took *thee* 1492
25:39 Or when **s** we thee sick, 1492
25:44 when **s** we thee a hungred, or athirst, 1492
26: 8 But when his disciples **s** *it*, they had 1492
26:71 another maid **s** him, and said unto them 1492
27: 3 when he **s** that he was condemned, 1492
27:24 Pilate **s** that he could prevail nothing, 1492
27:54 the earthquake, and *those things* that 1492
28:17 And when they **s** him, they worshipped 1492
Mk 1:10 **s** the heavens opened, and the Spirit 1492
1:16 he **s** Simon and Andrew his brother 1492
1:19 he **s** James the son of Zebedee, 1492
2: 5 When Jesus **s** their faith, he said unto 1492
2:12 saying, We never **s** *it* on this fashion. 1492
2:14 he **s** Levi the *son of* Alpheus sitting at 1492
2:16 Pharisees **s** him eat with publicans and 1492
3:11 And unclean spirits, when they **s** him, 2334
5: 6 But when he **s** Jesus afar off, he ran and 1492
5:16 they that **s** *it* told them how it befell to 1492
5:22 and when he **s** him, he fell at his feet, 1492
6:33 And the people **s** them departing, 1492
6:34 **s** much people, and was moved with 1492
6:48 And he **s** them toiling in rowing; 1492
6:49 And when they **s** him walking upon the sea, 1492
6:50 For they all **s** him, and were troubled. 1492
7: 2 And when they **s** some of his disciples eat 1492
8:23 upon him, he asked him if he **s** ought. 991
8:25 he was restored, and **s** every *man* clearly. 1689
9: 8 they **s** no *man* any more, save Jesus only 1492
9:14 he **s** a great multitude about them, 1492
9:20 and when he **s** him, straightway the spirit 1492
9:25 Jesus **s** that the people came running 1492
9:38 we **s** one casting out devils in thy name, 1492
10:14 But when Jesus **s** *it*, he was much 1492
11:20 they **s** the fig tree dried from the roots. 1492
12:34 And when Jesus **s** that he answered 1492
14:67 And when she **s** Peter warming himself, 1492
14:69 And a maid **s** him again, and began to say 1492
15:39 **s** that he so cried out, and gave up 1492
16: 4 they **s** that the stone was rolled away: 2334
16: 5 they **s** a young man sitting on the right 1492
Lk 1:12 And when Zacharias **s** *him*, he was 1492
1:29 And when she **s** *him*, she was troubled at 1492
2:48 when they **s** him, they were amazed: 1492
5: 2 And **s** two ships standing by the lake: 1492
5: 8 When Simon Peter **s** *it*, he fell down at 1492
5:20 when he **s** their faith, he said unto him, 1492
5:27 and **s** a publican, named Levi, sitting at 2300

S

Lk
7:13 And when the Lord **s** her, he had — 1492
7:39 bidden him **s** *it*, he spake within himself, — 1492
8:28 When he **s** Jesus, he cried out, — 1492
8:34 they that fed *them* **s** what was done, — 1492
8:36 They also which **s** *it* told them by what — 1492
8:47 And when the woman **s** that she was not — 1492
9:32 they **s** his glory, and the two men that — 1492
9:49 we **s** one casting out devils in thy name; — 1492
9:54 disciples James and John **s** *this*, they said, — 1492
10:31 and when he **s** him, he passed by on — 1492
10:33 when he **s** him, he had compassion *on* — 1492
11:38 And when the Pharisee **s** *it*, he marvelled — 1492
13:12 when Jesus **s** her, he called *her* to *him*, — 1492
15:20 his father **s** him, and had compassion, — 1492
17:14 And when he **s** *them*, he said unto them, — 1492
17:15 he **s** that he was healed, turned back, — 1492
18:15 *his* disciples **s** *it*, they rebuked them. — 1492
18:24 And when Jesus **s** that he was very — 1492
18:43 when they **s** *it*, gave praise unto God. — 1492
19: 5 and **s** him, and said unto him, Zaccheus, — 1492
19: 7 And when they **s** *it*, they all murmured, — 1492
20:14 But when the husbandmen **s** him, — 1492
21: 1 **s** the rich *men* casting their gifts into — 1492
21: 2 he **s** also a certain poor widow casting — 1492
22:49 When they which were about him **s** what — 1492
22:58 And after a little while another **s** him, — 1492
23: 8 when Herod **s** Jesus, he was exceeding — 1492
23:47 when the centurion **s** what was done, — 1492
24:24 the women had said: but him they **s** not. — 1492
Jn
1:32 the Spirit descending from heaven like — 2300
1:34 I **s**, and bare record that this is the Son — 3708
1:38 **s** them following, and saith unto them, — 2300
1:39 They came and **s** where he dwelt, — 1492
1:47 Jesus **s** Nathanael coming to him, — 1492
1:48 thou wast under the fig tree, I **s** thee. — 1492
1:50 I **s** thee under the fig tree, believest thou? — 1492
2:23 when they **s** the miracles which he did. — 2334
5: 6 When Jesus **s** him lie, and knew that he — 1492
6: 2 they **s** his miracles which he did on them — 3708
6: 5 and **s** a great company come unto him, — 2300
6:22 **s** that there was none other boat there, — 1492
6:24 therefore **s** that Jesus was not there, — 1492
8:10 up *himself*, and **s** none but the woman, — 2300
8:56 to see my day: and he **s** *it*, and was glad. — 1492
9: 1 **s** a man *which was* blind from *his* birth. — 1492
11:31 and comforted her, when they **s** Mary, — 1492
11:32 and **s** him, she fell down at his feet, — 1492
11:33 When Jesus therefore **s** her weeping, — 1492
12:41 when he **s** his glory, and spake of him. — 1492
19: 6 chief priests therefore and officers **s** him, — 1492
19:26 When Jesus therefore **s** *his* mother, — 1492
19:33 that he was dead already, they brake — 1492
19:35 he that **s** *it* bare record, and his record — 3708
20: 5 and looking in, **s** the linen clothes lying; — 991
20: 8 to the sepulchre, and he **s**, and believed. — 1492
20:14 and **s** Jesus standing, and knew not that **it** — 2334
20:20 the disciples glad, when they **s** the Lord. — 1492
21: 9 they **s** a fire of coals there, and fish laid — 991
Ac
3: 9 And all the people **s** him walking and — 1492
3:12 And when Peter **s** *it*, he answered unto — 1492
4:13 Now when they **s** the boldness of Peter — 2334
6:15 **s** his face as it had been the face of an — 1492
7:31 Moses **s** *it*, he wondered at the sight: — 1492
7:55 and **s** the glory of God, and Jesus standing — 1492
8:18 And when Simon **s** that through laying on — 2300
8:39 that the eunuch **s** him no more: — 1492
9: 8 **s** no *man*: but they led him by the hand, — 991
9:35 all that dwelt at Lydda and Saron **s** him, — 1492
9:40 eyes: and when she **s** Peter, she sat up. — 1492
10: 3 He **s** in a vision evidently, about the ninth — 1492
10:11 **s** heaven opened, and a certain vessel — 2334
11: 5 in a trance I **s** a vision, A certain vessel — 1492
11: 6 and **s** fourfooted beasts of the earth, — 1492
12: 3 And because he **s** it pleased the Jews, — 1492
12: 9 by the angel; but thought he **s** a vision. — 991
12:16 they had opened the *door*, and **s** him, — 1492
13:12 when he **s** what was done, believed, — 1492
13:36 laid unto his fathers, and **s** corruption: — 1492
13:37 whom God raised *again*, **s** no corruption. — 1492
13:45 But when the Jews **s** the multitudes, — 1492
14:11 when the people **s** what Paul had done, — 2300
16:19 And when her masters **s** that the hope of — 1492
17:16 he **s** the city wholly given to idolatry. — 2334
21:27 when they **s** him in the temple, stirred up — 2300
21:32 and when they **s** the chief captain and — 1492
22: 9 And they that were with me **s** indeed — 2300
22:18 And **s** him saying unto me, Make haste, — 1492
26:13 O king, I **s** in the way a light from heaven, — 1492
28: 4 And when the barbarians **s** the *venomous* — 1492
28: 6 and **s** no harm come to him, they changed — 2334
28:15 whom when Paul **s**, he thanked God, — 1492
Gal
1:19 But other of the apostles **s** I none, — 3708
2: 7 when they **s** that the gospel of — 1492
2:14 when I **s** that they walked not uprightly — 1492
Php
1:30 the same conflict which ye **s** in me, — 1492
Heb
9: 7 proved me, and **s** my works forty years. — 1492
11:23 because they **s** *he was* a proper child; — 1492
Rev
1: 2 of Jesus Christ, and of all *things* that he **s**. — 1492
1:12 turned, I **s** seven golden candlesticks; — 1492
1:17 when I **s** him, I fell at his feet as dead. — 1492
4: 4 and upon the seats I **s** four and — 1492
5: 1 I **s** in the right hand of him that sat on — 1492
5: 2 And I **s** a strong angel proclaiming with a — 1492
6: 1 And I **s** when the Lamb opened one of — 1492

Rev
6: 2 And I **s**, and behold a white horse: — 1492
6: 9 I **s** under the altar the souls of them that — 1492
7: 1 And after these *things* I **s** four angels — 1492
7: 2 And I **s** another angel ascending from — 1492
8: 2 And I **s** the seven angels which stood — 1492
9: 1 I **s** a star fall from heaven unto the earth: — 1492
9:17 And thus I **s** the horses in the vision, — 1492
10: 1 And I **s** another mighty angel come down — 1492
10: 5 the angel which I **s** stand upon the sea — 1492
11:11 great fear fell upon them which **s** them. — 2334
12:13 And when the dragon **s** that he was cast — 1492
13: 1 and **s** a beast rise up out of the sea, — 1492
13: 2 And the beast which I **s** was like unto a — 1492
13: 3 And I **s** one of his heads as *it were* — 1492
14: 6 And I **s** another angel fly in the midst of — 1492
15: 1 And I **s** another sign in heaven, great and — 1492
15: 2 And I **s** as *it were* a sea of glass mingled — 1492
16:13 And I **s** three unclean spirits like frogs — 1492
17: 3 I **s** a woman sit upon a scarlet coloured — 1492
17: 6 I **s** the woman drunken with the blood — 1492
17: 6 and when I **s** her, I wondered *with* great — 1492
18: 1 And after these *things* I **s** another angel — 1492
18:18 And cried when they **s** the smoke of her — 3708
19:11 **s** heaven opened, and behold a white — 1492
19:17 And I **s** an angel standing in the sun; — 1492
19:19 And I **s** the beast, and the kings of — 1492
20: 1 I **s** an angel come down from heaven, — 1492
20: 4 And I **s** thrones, and they sat upon them, — 1492
20: 4 I **s** the souls of them that were beheaded — NIG
20:11 And I **s** a great white throne, and him that — 1492
20:12 And I **s** the dead, small and great, stand — 1492
21: 1 And I **s** a new heaven and a new earth: — 1492
21: 2 And I John **s** the holy city, new Jerusalem, — 1492
21:22 I **s** no temple therein: for the Lord God — 1492
22: 8 And I John **s** these *things*, and heard *them*. — 991

SAWED (1) [SAW]
1Ki
7: 9 **s** with saws, within and without, even — 1641

SAWEST (21) [SEE]
Ge
20:10 What **s** thou, that thou hast done this — 7200
1Sa
19: 5 thou **s** *it*, and didst rejoice: wherefore — 7200
28:13 what **s** thou? And the woman said unto — 7200
2Sa
18:11 thou **s** *him*, and why didst thou not smite — 7200
Ps
50:18 thou **s** a thief, then thou consentedst — 7200
Isa
57: 8 thou lovedst their bed where thou **s** *it*. — 2372
Da
2:31 O king, **s**, and behold a great image. — 2370
2:34 Thou **s** till that a stone was cut out — 2370
2:41 whereas thou **s** the feet and toes, part of — 2370
2:41 forasmuch as thou **s** the iron mixed with — 2370
2:43 whereas thou **s** iron mixt with miry clay, — 2370
2:45 Forasmuch as thou **s** that the stone was — 2370
4:20 The tree that thou **s**, which grew, — 2370
8:20 The ram which thou **s** having two horns — 7200
Rev
1:20 mystery of the seven stars which thou **s** — 1492
1:20 the seven candlesticks which thou **s** are — 1492
17: 8 The beast that thou **s** was, and is not; — 1492
17:12 And the ten horns which thou **s** are ten — 1492
17:15 saith unto me, The waters which thou **s**, — 1492
17:16 And the ten horns which thou **s** upon — 1492
17:18 And the woman which thou **s** is *that* great — 1492

SAWN (1) [SAW]
Heb
11:37 they were **s** asunder, were tempted, — 4249

SAWS (3) [SAW]
2Sa
12:31 put *them* under **s**, and under harrows of — 4050
1Ki
7: 9 sawed with **s**, within and without, even — 4050
1Ch
20: 3 cut *them* with **s**, and with harrows of — 4050

SAY (1057) [GAINSAY, SAID, SAIDST, SAITH, SAYEST, SAYING, SAYINGS]
Ge
12:12 see thee, that they shall **s**, This *is* his wife: — 559
12:13 **S**, I pray thee, thou *art* my sister: that it — 559
14:23 lest thou shouldest **s**, I have made Abram — 559
20:13 we shall come, **s** of me, He *is* my brother. — 559
24:14 the damsel to whom I shall **s**, Let down — 559
24:14 she shall **s**, Drink, and I will give thy — 559
24:43 cometh forth to draw *water*, and I **s** to her, — 559
24:44 she **s** to me, Both drink thou, and I will — 559
26: 7 for he feared to **s**, *She is* my wife; lest, — 559
32:18 thou shalt **s**, *They be* thy servant Jacob's; — 559
32:20 ye moreover, Behold, thy servant Jacob *is* — 559
34:11 and what ye shall **s** unto me I will give. — 559
34:12 I will give according as ye shall **s** unto me: — 559
37:17 for I heard *them* **s**, Let us go to Dothan. — 559
37:20 and cast him into some pit, and we will **s**, — 559
41:15 I have heard **s** of thee, *that* thou canst — 559
43: 7 could we certainly know that he would **s**, — 559
44: 4 thou dost overtake them, **s** unto them, — 559
44:16 Judah said, What shall we **s** unto my lord? — 559
45: 9 and go up to my father, and **s** unto him, — 559
45:17 Joseph, **S** unto thy brethren, This do ye; — 559
46:31 **s** unto him, My brethren, and my father's — 559
46:33 and shall **s**, What *is* your occupation? — 559
46:34 That ye shall **s**, Thy servants' trade hath — 559
50:17 So shall ye **s** unto Joseph, Forgive, I pray — 559
Ex
3:13 children of Israel, and shall **s** unto them, — 559
3:13 and they shall **s** to me, What *is* his name? — 559
3:13 *is* his name? what shall I **s** unto them? — 559
3:14 shalt thou **s** unto the children of Israel, — 559
3:15 shalt thou **s** unto the children of Israel, — 559
3:16 **s** unto them, The LORD God of your — 559
3:18 king of Egypt, and you shall **s** unto him, — 559
4: 1 for they will **s**, The LORD hath not — 559

Ex
4:12 mouth, and teach thee what thou shalt **s**. — 1696
4:22 thou shalt **s** unto Pharaoh, Thus saith — 559
4:23 I **s** unto thee, Let my son go, that he may — 559
5:16 thy servants, and they **s** to us, Make brick: — 559
5:17 therefore ye **s**, Let us go *and* do sacrifice to — 559
6: 6 Wherefore **s** unto the children of Israel, — 559
6:29 Pharaoh king of Egypt all that I **s** unto — 1696
7: 9 thou shalt **s** unto Aaron, Take thy rod, — 559
7:16 thou shalt **s** unto him, The LORD God of — 559
7:19 **S** unto Aaron, Take thy rod, and stretch — 559
8: 1 Go unto Pharaoh, and **s** unto him, Thus — 559
8: 5 LORD spake unto Moses, **S** unto Aaron, — 559
8:16 **S** unto Aaron, Stretch out thy rod, — 559
8:20 **s** unto him, Thus saith the LORD, Let my — 559
9:13 and stand before Pharaoh, and **s** unto him, — 559
12:26 pass, when your children shall **s** unto you, — 559
12:27 That ye shall **s**, It *is* the sacrifice of — 559
13:14 that thou shalt **s** unto him, By strength of — 559
14: 3 For Pharaoh will **s** of the children of Israel, — 559
16: 9 **S** unto all the congregation of the children — 559
19: 3 Thus shalt thou **s** to the house of Jacob, — 559
20:22 thou shalt **s** unto the children of Israel, — 559
21: 5 if the servant shall **plainly s**, I love — 559+559
32:12 **s**, For mischief did he bring them out, — 559
33: 5 **S** unto the children of Israel, Ye *are* a — 559
Lev
1: 2 the children of Israel, and **s** unto them, — 559
15: 2 the children of Israel, and **s** unto them, — 559
17: 2 all the children of Israel, and **s** unto them; — 559
17: 8 thou shalt **s** unto them, Whatsoever man — 559
18: 2 and **s** unto them, I *am* the LORD your God. — 559
19: 2 of Israel, and **s** unto them, Ye shall be holy: — 559
20: 2 Again, thou shalt **s** to the children of Israel, — 559
21: 1 priests the sons of Aaron, and **s** unto them, — 559
22: 3 **S** unto them, Whosoever *he be* of all your — 559
22:18 all the children of Israel, and **s** unto them, — 559
23: 2 the children of Israel, and **s** unto them, — 559
23:10 the children of Israel, and **s** unto them, — 559
25: 2 the children of Israel, and **s** unto them, — 559
25:20 if ye shall **s**, What shall we eat the seventh — 559
27: 2 the children of Israel, and **s** unto them, — 559
Nu
5:12 **s** unto them, If any man's wife go aside, — 559
5:19 **s** unto the woman, If no man have lain — 559
5:21 the priest shall **s** unto the woman, — 559
5:22 And the woman shall **s**, Amen, amen. — 559
6: 2 **s** unto them, When either man or — 559
6:23 Speak unto Aaron, and **s** unto him, — 559
11:12 that thou shouldest **s** unto me, — 559
11:18 **s** unto the people, Sanctify yourselves — 559
14:28 **S** unto them, *As truly as* I live, saith — 559
15: 2 the children of Israel, and **s** unto them, — 559
15:18 the children of Israel, and **s** unto them, — 559
18:26 speak unto the Levites, and **s** unto them, — 559
18:30 Therefore thou shalt **s** unto them, When — 559
21:27 Wherefore they that speak in proverbs **s**, — 559
22:19 that I may know what the LORD will **s** — 1696
22:20 yet the word which I shall **s** unto thee, — 1696
22:38 I now any power at all to **s** any thing? — 1696
23:16 said, Go again unto Balak, and **s** thus. — 1696
25:12 Wherefore **s**, Behold, I give unto him my — 559
28: 2 **s** unto them, My offering, *and* my bread — 559
28: 3 thou shalt **s** unto them, This *is* the offering — 559
33:51 the children of Israel, and **s** unto them, — 559
34: 2 the children of Israel, and **s** unto them, — 559
35:10 the children of Israel, and **s** unto them, — 559
Dt
1:42 **S** unto them, Go not up, neither fight; — 559
4: 6 **s**, Surely this great nation *is* a wise and — 559
5:27 and hear all that the LORD our God shall **s**: — 559
5:30 **s** to them, Get you into your tents again. — 559
6:21 shalt **s** unto thy son, We were Pharaoh's — 559
7:17 If thou shalt **s** in thine heart, These nations — 559
8:17 thou **s** in thine heart, My power and — 559
9: 2 *whom* thou hast heard **s**, Who can stand — NIH
9:28 the land whence thou broughtest us out **s**, — 559
12:20 shalt **s**, I will eat flesh, because thy soul — 559
13:12 If thou shalt hear **s** in one of thy cities, — NIH
15:16 it shall be, if he **s** unto thee, I will not go — 559
17:14 and shalt dwell therein, and shalt **s**, — 559
18:21 if thou **s** in thine heart, How shall we — 559
20: 3 shall **s** unto them, Hear, O Israel, — 559
20: 8 shall **s**, What man *is there that is* fearful — 559
21: 7 shall answer and **s**, Our hands have not — 559
21:20 they shall **s** unto the elders of his city, — 559
22:14 **s**, I took this woman, and when I came to — 559
22:16 the damsel's father shall **s** unto the elders, — 559
25: 7 go up to the gate unto the elders, and **s**, — 559
25: 8 he stand *to it*, and **s**, I like not to take her; — 559
25: 9 and spit in his face, and shall answer and **s**, — 559
26: 3 unto him, I profess *this* day unto — 559
26: 5 and **s** before the LORD thy God, — 559
26:13 thou shalt **s** before the LORD thy God, — 559
27:14 **s** unto all the men of Israel *with* a loud — 559
27:15 And all the people shall answer and **s**, — 559
27:16 And all the people shall **s**, Amen. — 559
27:17 And all the people shall **s**, Amen. — 559
27:18 And all the people shall **s**, Amen. — 559
27:19 And all the people shall **s**, Amen. — 559
27:20 And all the people shall **s**, Amen. — 559
27:21 And all the people shall **s**, Amen. — 559
27:22 And all the people shall **s**, Amen. — 559
27:23 And all the people shall **s**, Amen. — 559
27:24 And all the people shall **s**, Amen. — 559
27:25 And all the people shall **s**, Amen. — 559
27:26 And all the people shall **s**, Amen. — 559
28:67 In the morning thou shalt **s**, Would God it — 559
28:67 at even thou shalt **s**, Would God it were — 559

Dt	29:22 shall **s**, when they see the plagues of that 559
	29:24 Even all nations shall **s**, Wherefore hath 559
	29:25 *men* shall **s**, Because they have forsaken 559
	30:12 It *is* not in heaven, that *thou* shouldest **s**, 559
	30:13 *is* it beyond the sea, that *thou* shouldest **s**, 559
	31:17 that they will **s** in that day, Are not these 559
	32:27 *and* lest they should **s**, Our hand is high, 559
	32:37 he shall **s**, Where *are* their gods, *their* rock 559
	32:40 my hand to heaven, and **s**, I live for ever. 559
	33:27 before thee; and shall **s**, Destroy *them*. 559
Jos	7: 8 O Lord, what shall I **s**, when Israel turneth 559
	7:13 Up, sanctify the people, and **s**, 559
	8: 6 for they will **s**, *They* flee before us, as at 559
	9:11 to meet them, and **s** unto them, We are 559
	22:11 the children of Israel heard **s**, Behold, 559
	22:27 your children may not **s** Sunto our children 559
	22:28 when they should so **s** to us or to our 559
	22:28 that we may **s** *again*, Behold the pattern of 559
Jdg	4:20 man doth come and inquire of thee, and **s**, 559
	4:20 Is there any man here? that thou shalt **s**, 559
	7: 4 it shall be, *that* of whom I **s** unto thee, 559
	7: 4 whomsoever I **s** unto thee, This shall not 559
	7:11 thou shalt hear what they **s**; 1696
	7:18 **s**, *The sword* of the Lord, and of Gideon. 559
	9:54 and slay me, that *men* **s** not of me, 559
	12: 6 said they unto him, **S** now Shibboleth: 559
	16:15 unto him, How canst thou **s**, I love thee, 559
	18: 8 their brethren said unto them, What **s** ye? NIH
	18:24 what *is* this *that* ye **s** unto me, What aileth 559
	21:22 we will **s** unto them, Be favourable unto 559
Ru	1:12 If I should **s**, I have hope, *if* I should have 559
1Sa	2:36 of bread, and shall **s**, Put me, I pray thee, 559
	3: 9 call thee, that thou shalt **s**, Speak, Lord; 559
	8: 7 of the people in all that they **s** unto thee: 559
	10: 2 they will **s** unto thee, The asses which thou 559
	11: 9 Thus shall ye **s** unto the men of 559
	13: 4 all Israel heard **s** *that* Saul had smitten a 559
	14: 9 If they **s** thus unto us, Tarry until we come 559
	14:10 if they **s** thus, Come up unto us; then we 559
	14:34 **s** unto them, Bring me hither every man 559
	15:16 *this* night. And he said unto him, **S** on. 1696
	16: 2 Lord said, Take a heifer with thee, and **s**, 559
	18:22 **s**, Behold, the king hath delight in thee, 559
	18:25 said, Thus shall ye **s** to David, The king 559
	19:24 Wherefore they **s**, *Is* Saul also among 559
	20: 6 If thy father at all miss me, then **s**, 559
	20: 7 If he **s** thus, *It is* well; thy servant shall 559
	20:21 If I **expressly s** unto the lad, Behold, 559+559
	20:22 if I **s** thus unto the young man, Behold, 559
	25: 6 thus shall ye **s** to him that liveth *in* 559
2Sa	7: 8 so shalt thou **s** unto my servant David, 559
	7:20 what can David **s** more unto thee? 1696
	11:20 he **s** unto thee, Wherefore approached ye 559
	11:21 **s** thou, Thy servant Uriah the Hittite is 559
	11:25 Thus shalt thou **s** unto Joab, Let not this 559
	13: 5 **s** unto him, I pray thee, let my sister 559
	13:28 and when I **s** unto you, Smite Amnon; 559
	14:12 unto my lord the king. And he said, **S** on. 1696
	14:32 That I may send thee to the king, to **s**, 559
	15:10 ye shall **s**, Absalom reigneth in Hebron. 559
	15:26 if he thus **s**, I have no delight in thee; 559
	15:34 **s** unto Absalom, I will be thy servant, 559
	16:10 Who shall then **s**, Wherefore hast thou 559
	17: 9 the first, that whosoever heareth *it* will **s**, 559
	19: 2 the people heard **s** that day *how* the king 559
	19:13 **s** ye to Amasa, *Art* thou not *of* my bone, 559
	20:16 **s**, I pray you, unto Joab, Come near hither, 559
	21: 4 he said, What you shall **s**, *that* will I do for 559
	24: 1 he moved David against them to **s**, 559
	24:12 Go and **s** unto David, Thus saith 1696
1Ki	1:13 **s** unto him, Didst not thou, my lord 559
	1:25 they eat and drink before him, and **s**, 559
	1:34 trumpet, and **s**, God save king Solomon. 559
	1:36 the Lord God of my lord the king **s** so 559
	2:14 I have **somewhat to s** unto thee. 1697
	2:14 to say unto thee. And she said, **S** on. 1696
	2:16 And she said unto him, **S** on. 1696
	2:17 king, (for he will not **s** thee **nay**,) 6440+7725
	2:20 of thee; *I pray thee*, **s** me not **nay**. 6440+7725
	2:20 mother: for I will not **s** thee **nay**. 6440+7725
	9: 8 they shall **s**, Why hath the Lord done thus 559
	12:10 shalt thou **s** unto them, My little *finger* 1696
	13:22 of the which *the Lord* did **s** to thee, 1696
	14: 5 thus and thus shalt thou **s** unto her: for it 1696
	16:16 the people that *were* encamped heard **s**, 559
	18:44 he said, Go up, **s** unto Ahab, Prepare *thy* 559
	22: 8 Jehoshaphat said, Let not the king **s** so. 559
	22:27 **s**, Thus saith the king, Put this *fellow in* 559
2Ki	1: 3 unto them, *Is it* not because *there is* not 1696
	1: 6 unto him, Thus saith the Lord, *Is it* not 1696
	2:18 unto them, Did I not **s** unto you, Go not? 559
	4:13 he said unto him, **S** now unto her, Behold, 559
	4:26 I pray thee, to meet her, and **s** unto her, 559
	4:28 of my lord? did I not **s**, Do not deceive me? 559
	7: 4 If we **s**, We will enter *into* the city, then 559
	7:13 *I* **s**, they *are* even as all the multitude of NIH
	8:10 Elisha said unto him, Go, **s** unto him, 559
	9: 3 pour *it* on his head, and **s**, Thus saith 559
	9:17 to meet them, and let him **s**, *Is it* peace? 559
	9:37 *so* that they shall **s**, This *is* Jezebel. 559
	18:22 if ye **s** unto me, We trust in the Lord our 559
	19: 6 Thus shall ye **s** to your master, Thus saith 559
	19: 9 when he heard **s** of Tirhakah king of 559
	22:18 thus shall ye **s** to him, Thus saith the Lord 559
1Ch	5: 3 *I* **s**, of Reuben the firstborn of Israel *were*, NIH

1Ch	16:31 let *men* **s** among the nations, The Lord 559
	16:35 **s** ye, Save us, O God of our salvation, 559
	17: 7 thus shalt thou **s** unto my servant David, 559
	21:18 the Lord commanded Gad to **s** to David, 559
2Ch	7:21 so that he shall **s**, Why hath the Lord 559
	10:10 shalt thou **s** unto them, My little *finger* 1696
	18: 7 Jehoshaphat said, Let not the king **s** so. 559
	18:15 shall I adjure thee that thou **s** nothing 1696
	18:26 **s**, Thus saith the king, Put this *fellow in* 559
	20:11 I **s**, *how* they reward us, to come to NIH
	20:21 the army, and to **s**, Praise the Lord; 559
	34:26 of the Lord, so shall ye **s** unto him, 559
Ezr	8:17 I told them what they should **s** unto Iddo, 1696
	9:10 O our God, what shall we **s** after this? 559
Ne	7: 7 *I* **s**, of the men of the people of Israel *was* NIH
	9: 8 to give *it*, *I* **s**, to his seed, NIH
Est	1:18 Media **s** this day unto all the king's 559
Job	6:22 Did I **s**, Bring unto me? or, Give a reward 559
	7: 4 When I lie down, I **s**, When shall I arise, 559
	7:13 When I **s**, My bed shall comfort me, 559
	9:12 who will **s** unto him, What doest thou? 559
	9:20 *if* I **s**, I *am* perfect, it shall also prove me NIH
	9:27 If I **s**, I will forget my complaint, I will 559
	10: 2 I will **s** unto God, Do not condemn me; 559
	19:28 ye should **s**, Why persecute we him? 559
	20: 7 they which have seen him shall **s**, Where 559
	21:14 Therefore they **s** unto God, Depart from us; 559
	21:28 For ye **s**, Where *is* the house of the prince? 559
	22:29 then thou shalt **s**, *There is* lifting up; 559
	23: 5 and understand what he would **s** unto me. 559
	28:22 Destruction and death **s**, We have heard 559
	32:11 whilst you searched out **what to s**. 4405
	32:13 Lest ye should **s**, We have found out 559
	33:27 *if any* **s**, I have sinned, and perverted *that* 559
	33:32 If *thou* hast **any thing to s**, answer me: 4405
	34:18 *Is it fit* to **s** to a king, *Thou art* wicked? 559
	36:23 or who can **s**, Thou hast wrought iniquity? 559
	37:19 Teach us what we shall **s** unto him; *for* we 559
	38:35 may go, and **s** unto thee, Here we *are*? 559
Ps	3: 2 *there be* which **s** of my soul, *There is* 559
	4: 6 *There be* many that **s**, Who will shew us 559
	11: 1 how **s** ye to my soul, Flee *as a bird to* your 559
	13: 4 Lest mine enemy **s**, I have prevailed 559
	27:14 thine heart: wait, I **s**, on the Lord. NIH
	35: 3 **s** unto my soul, I *am* thy salvation. 559
	35:10 All my bones shall **s**, Lord, who *is* like 559
	35:25 Let them not **s** in their hearts, 559
	35:25 them not **s**, We have swallowed him up. 559
	35:27 yea, let them **s** continually, Let the Lord 559
	40:15 a reward of their shame that **s** unto me, 559
	40:16 such as love thy salvation **s** continually, 559
	41: 8 disease, *s they*, cleaveth fast unto him: NIH
	42: 3 night, while *they* continually **s** unto me, 559
	42: 9 I will **s** unto God my rock, Why hast thou 559
	42:10 while they **s** daily unto me, Where *is* thy 559
	58:11 So that a man shall **s**, Verily *there is* a 559
	59: 7 in their lips: for who, *s they*, doth hear? NIH
	64: 5 snares privily; they **s**, Who shall see them? 559
	66: 3 **S** unto God, How terrible *art thou* in thy 559
	70: 3 back for a reward of their shame that **s**, 559
	70: 4 let such as love thy salvation **s** continually, 559
	73:11 they **s**, How doth God know? and is there 559
	73:15 If I **s**, I will speak thus; behold, I should 559
	79:10 Wherefore should the heathen **s**, Where *is* 559
	91: 2 I will **s** of the Lord, *He is* my refuge and 559
	94: 7 Yet they **s**, The Lord shall not see, 559
	96:10 **S** among the heathen *that* the Lord 559
	106:48 let all the people **s**, Amen. Praise ye 559
	107: 2 Let the redeemed of the Lord **s** *so*, 559
	115: 2 Wherefore should the heathen **s**, Where *is* 559
	118: 2 Let Israel now **s**, that his mercy *endureth* 559
	118: 3 Let the house of Aaron now **s**, that his 559
	118: 4 Let them now that fear the Lord **s**, 559
	122: 8 and companions' sakes, I will now **s**, 1696
	124: 1 who was on our side, now may Israel **s**; 559
	129: 1 me from my youth, may Israel now **s**: 559
	129: 8 Neither do they which go by **s**, The 559
	130: 6 *I* **s**, *more than* they that watch for NIH
	139:11 If I **s**, Surely the darkness shall cover me 559
Pr	1:11 If they **s**, Come with us, let us lay wait for 559
	3:28 **S** not unto thy neighbour, Go, 559
	5:12 **s**, How have I hated instruction, 559
	7: 4 **S** unto wisdom, Thou *art* my sister; 559
	20: 9 Who can **s**, I have made my heart clean, 559
	20:22 **S** not thou, I will recompense evil; 559
	23:35 *shalt thou* **s**, *and* I was not sick; NIH
	24:29 **S** not, I will do so to him as he hath done 559
	30: 9 Lest I be full, and deny *thee*, and **s**, Who *is* 559
	30:15 *yea*, four *things* **s** not, *It is* enough: 559
Ecc	5: 6 neither **s** thou before the angel, that it *was* 559
	6: 3 I **s**, *that* an untimely birth *is* better than he. 559
	7:10 **S** not thou, What is *the cause* that the 559
	8: 4 who may **s** unto him, What doest thou? 559
	12: 1 the years draw nigh, when thou shalt **s**, 559
Isa	2: 3 many people shall go and **s**, Come ye, 559
	3:10 **S** ye *to* the righteous, that *it shall be* well 559
	5:19 That **s**, Let him make speed, *and* hasten 559
	7: 4 **s** unto him, Take heed, and be quiet; 559
	8:12 **S** ye not, A confederacy, to all *them* to 559
	8:12 to all *them* to whom this people shall **s**, 559
	8:19 they shall **s** unto you, Seek unto them 559
	9: 9 that **s** in the pride and stoutness of heart, 559
	12: 1 in that day thou shalt **s**, O Lord, I will 559
	12: 4 in that day shall ye **s**, Praise the Lord, 559
	14: 4 and **s**, How hath the oppressor ceased!

Isa	14:10 All they shall speak and **s** unto thee, Art 559
	19:11 how **s** ye unto Pharaoh, I *am* the son of 559
	20: 6 inhabitant of this isle shall **s** in that day, 559
	22:15 which *is* over the house, *and* **s**, NIH
	29:15 are in the dark, and they **s**, Who seeth us? 559
	29:16 for shall the work **s** of him that made it, 559
	29:16 shall the thing framed **s** of him that framed 559
	30:10 Which **s** to the seers, See not; and to 559
	30:22 thou shalt **s** unto it, Get thee hence. 559
	33:24 the inhabitant shall not **s**, I am sick: 559
	35: 4 **S** to them that are of a fearful heart, 559
	36: 4 **S** ye now to Hezekiah, Thus saith the great 559
	36: 5 I **s**, *sayest thou*, (but *they are but* vain 559
	36: 7 if thou **s** to me, We trust in the Lord our 559
	37: 6 Thus shall ye **s** unto your master, Thus 559
	37: 9 he heard **s** concerning Tirhakah king of 559
	38: 5 Go and **s** to Hezekiah, Thus saith 559
	38:15 What shall I **s**? he hath both spoken unto 1696
	40: 9 **s** unto the cities of Judah, Behold your 559
	41:26 that we may **s**, *He is* righteous? 559
	41:27 The first *shall* **s** to Zion, Behold, NIH
	42:17 **s** to the molten images, Ye *are* our gods. 559
	43: 6 I will **s** to the north, Give *up*; and to 559
	43: 9 or let them hear, and **s**, *It is* truth. 559
	44: 5 One shall **s**, I *am* the Lord's; 559
	44:19 *is there* knowledge nor understanding to **s**, 559
	44:20 that he cannot deliver his soul, nor **s**, 559
	45: 9 Shall the clay **s** to him that fashioneth it, 559
	45:24 Surely, shall *one* **s**, in the Lord have I 559
	48: 5 lest thou shouldest **s**, Mine idol hath done 559
	48: 7 thou shouldest **s**, Behold, I knew them. 559
	48:20 **s** ye, The Lord hath redeemed his servant 559
	49: 9 That *thou* mayest **s** to the prisoners, 559
	49:20 lost the other, shall **s** again in thine ears, 559
	49:21 shalt thou **s** in thine heart, Who hath 559
	51:16 and **s** unto Zion, Thou *art* my people. 559
	56: 3 neither let the eunuch **s**, Behold, I *am* a dry 559
	56:12 **s** they, I will fetch wine, and we will fill NIH
	57:14 shall **s**, Cast ye up, cast ye up, prepare 559
	58: 3 have we fasted, *s they*, and thou seest not? NIH
	58: 9 thou shalt cry, and he shall **s**, Here I *am*. 559
	62:11 **S** ye to the daughter of Zion, Behold, 559
	65: 5 Which **s**, Stand by thyself, come not near 559
Jer	1: 7 Lord said unto me, **S** not, I *am* a child: 559
	2:23 How canst thou **s**, I am not polluted, I 559
	2:27 in the time of their trouble they will **s**, 559
	2:31 wherefore **s** my people, We are lords; 559
	3: 1 They **s**, If a man put away his wife, 559
	3:12 **s**, Return, thou backsliding Israel, saith 559
	3:16 saith the Lord, they shall **s** no more, 559
	4: 5 and **s**, Blow ye the trumpet in the land: 559
	4: 5 cry, gather together, and **s**, 559
	5: 2 though they **s**, The Lord liveth; surely 559
	5:15 neither understand what they **s**. 1696
	5:19 it shall come to pass, when ye shall **s**, 559
	5:24 Neither **s** they in their heart, Let us now 559
	7: 2 proclaim there this word, and **s**, Hear 559
	7:10 which is called by my name, and **s**, 559
	7:28 thou shalt **s** unto them, This *is* a nation 559
	8: 4 Moreover thou shalt **s** unto them, Thus 559
	8: 8 How do ye **s**, We *are* wise, and the law of 559
	10:11 Thus shall ye **s** unto them, The gods that 560
	11: 3 thou unto them, Thus saith the Lord 559
	13:12 they shall **s** unto thee, Do we not certainly 559
	13:13 shalt thou **s** unto them, Thus saith 559
	13:18 **S** unto the king and to the queen, 559
	13:21 wilt thou **s** when he shall punish thee? 559
	13:22 if thou **s** in thine heart, Wherefore come 559
	14:13 behold, the prophets **s** unto them, Ye shall 559
	14:15 yet they **s**, Sword and famine shall not be 559
	14:17 Therefore thou shalt **s** this word unto 559
	15: 2 it shall come to pass, if they **s** unto thee, 559
	16:10 all these words, and they shall **s** unto thee, 559
	16:11 thou **s** unto them, Because your fathers 559
	16:19 **s**, Surely our fathers have inherited lies, 559
	17:15 Behold, they **s** unto me, Where *is* the word 559
	17:20 **s** unto them, Hear ye the word of 559
	19: 3 **s**, Hear ye the word of the Lord, O kings 559
	19:11 shalt **s** unto them, Thus saith the Lord of 559
	20:10 Report, *s they*, and we will report it. All NIH
	21: 3 unto them, Thus shall ye **s** to Zedekiah: 559
	21: 8 unto this people thou shalt **s**, Thus saith 559
	21:11 **s**, Hear ye the word of the Lord. NIH
	21:13 which **s**, Who shall come down against us? 559
	22: 2 **s**, Hear the word of the Lord, O king of 559
	22: 8 they shall **s** every man to his neighbour, 559
	23: 7 saith the Lord, that they shall no more **s**, 559
	23:17 They **still** *s* unto them that despise 559+559
	23:17 they **s** *unto* every one that walketh after 559
	23:31 that use their tongues, and **s**, He saith. 5001
	23:33 thou shalt then **s** unto them, What burden? 559
	23:34 and the priest, and the people, that shall **s**, 559
	23:35 Thus shall ye **s** every one to his neighbour, 559
	23:37 Thus shalt thou **s** to the prophet, What 559
	23:38 sith ye **s**, The burden of the Lord; 559
	23:38 Because you **s** this word, The burden of 559
	23:38 have sent unto you, saying, Ye shall not **s**, 559
	25:27 Therefore thou shalt **s** unto them, Thus 559
	25:28 shalt thou **s** unto them, Thus saith 559
	25:30 unto them, The Lord shall roar from on 559
	26: 4 thou shalt **s** unto them, Thus saith 559
	27: 4 command them to **s** unto their masters, 559
	27: 4 of Israel; Thus shall ye **s** unto your masters; 559
	31: 7 publish ye, praise ye, and **s**, O Lord, save 559
	31:10 and declare *it* in the isles afar off, and **s**, 559

Jer	31:29 In those days they shall **s** no more,	559
	32: 3 and **s**, Thus saith the Lord, Behold,	559
	32:36 of Israel, concerning this city, whereof ye **s**,	559
	32:43 whereof ye **s**, *It is* desolate without man or	559
	33:10 which ye **s** *shall be* desolate without man	559
	33:11 of the bride, the voice of them that shall **s**,	559
	36:29 thou shalt **s** to Jehoiakim king of Judah,	559
	37: 7 Thus shall ye **s** to the king of Judah, that	559
	38:22 those *women shall* **s**, Thy friends have set	559
	38:25 and they come unto thee, and **s** unto thee,	559
	38:26 thou shalt **s** unto them, I presented my	559
	39:12 do unto him even as he shall **s** unto thee.	1696
	42:13 if ye **s**, We will not dwell in this land,	559
	42:20 unto all that the Lord our God shall **s**,	559
	43: 2 the Lord our God hath not sent thee to **s**,	559
	43:10 **s** unto them, Thus saith the Lord of hosts,	559
	45: 3 Thou didst **s**, Woe is me now! for	559
	45: 4 Thus shalt thou **s** unto him, The Lord	559
	46:14 **s** ye, Stand fast, and prepare thee;	559
	48:14 How **s** ye, We *are* mighty and strong men	559
	48:17 all ye that know his name, **s**, How is	559
	48:19 her that escapeth, *and* **s**, What is done?	559
	50: 2 **s**, Babylon is taken, Bel is confounded,	559
	51:35 Babylon, shall the inhabitant of Zion **s**;	559
	51:35 inhabitants of Chaldea, shall Jerusalem **s**.	559
	51:62 shalt thou, O Lord, thou hast spoken	559
	51:64 thou shalt **s**, Thus shall Babylon sink,	559
La	2:12 They **s** to their mothers, Where *is* corn	559
	2:16 they **s**, We have swallowed *her* up:	559
Eze	2: 4 thou shalt **s** unto them, Thus saith the Lord	559
	2: 8 son of man, hear what I **s** unto thee;	1696
	3:18 When I **s** unto the wicked, Thou shalt	559
	3:27 thy mouth, and thou shalt **s** unto them,	559
	6: 3 **s**, Ye mountains of Israel, hear the word of	559
	6:11 thine hand, and stamp with thy foot, and **s**,	559
	8:12 for they **s**, The Lord seeth us not:	559
	9: 9 for they **s**, The Lord hath forsaken	559
	11: 3 Which **s**, *It is* not near; *let us* build houses:	559
	11:16 Therefore **s**, Thus saith the Lord God;	559
	11:17 Therefore **s**, Thus saith the Lord God;	559
	12:10 **S** thou unto them, Thus saith the Lord	559
	12:11 **S**, I *am* your sign: like as I have done,	559
	12:19 **s** unto the people of the land, Thus saith	559
	12:23 unto them, The days are at hand,	1696
	12:25 will I **s** the word, and will perform it,	1696
	12:27 man, behold, *they of* the house of Israel **s**,	559
	12:28 Therefore **s** unto them, Thus saith the Lord	559
	13: 2 **s** thou unto them that prophesy out of their	559
	13: 7 spoken a lying divination, whereas ye **s**,	559
	13:11 **S** unto them which daub *it* with	559
	13:15 untempered *morter*, and will **s** unto you,	559
	13:18 **s**, Thus saith the Lord God; Woe to	559
	14: 4 speak unto them, and **s** unto them,	559
	14: 6 Therefore **s** unto the house of Israel,	559
	14:17 land, and **s**, Sword, go through the land;	559
	16: 3 **s**, Thus saith the Lord God	559
	17: 3 **s**, Thus saith the Lord God; A great eagle	559
	17: 9 **s** thou, Thus saith the Lord God; Shall it	559
	17:12 **S** now to the rebellious house, Know ye not	559
	18:19 Yet **s** ye, Why? doth not the son bear	559
	18:25 Yet ye **s**, The way of the Lord is not equal.	559
	19: 2 **s**, What *is* thy mother? A lioness: she lay	559
	20: 3 and **s** unto them, Thus saith the Lord God;	559
	20: 5 **s** unto them, Thus saith the Lord God;	559
	20:27 and **s** unto them, Thus saith the Lord God;	559
	20:30 Wherefore **s** unto the house of Israel,	559
	20:32 that ye **s**, We will be as the heathen,	559
	20:47 **s** to the forest of the south, Hear the word	559
	20:49 said I, Ah Lord God, they **s** of me, Doth	559
	21: 3 **s** to the land of Israel, Thus saith	559
	21: 7 shall be, when they **s** unto thee, Wherefore	559
	21: 9 Son of man, prophesy, and **s**, Thus saith	559
	21: 9 **S**, A sword, a sword is sharpened,	559
	21:24 *I* **s**, that ye are come to remembrance,	NIH
	21:28 son of man, prophesy, and **s**, Thus saith	559
	21:28 **s** thou, The sword, the sword *is* drawn:	559
	22: 3 **s** thou, Thus saith the Lord God, The city	559
	22:24 Son of man, **s** unto her, Thou *art* the land	559
	24: 3 and **s** unto them, Thus saith the Lord God;	559
	25: 3 **s** unto the Ammonites, Hear the word of	559
	25: 8 Because that Moab and Seir do **s**, Behold,	559
	26:17 **s** to thee, How art thou destroyed, *that*	559
	27: 3 **s** unto Tyrus, O thou that art situate at	559
	28: 2 Son of man, **s** unto the prince of Tyrus,	559
	28: 9 thou **yet s** before him that slayeth	559+559
	28:12 and **s** unto him, Thus saith the Lord God;	559
	28:22 **s**, Thus saith the Lord God; Behold, I *am*	559
	29: 3 Speak, and **s**, Thus saith the Lord God;	559
	30: 2 Son of man, prophesy and **s**, Thus saith	559
	32: 2 unto him, Thou art like a young lion of	559
	33: 2 children of thy people, and **s** unto them,	559
	33: 8 When I **s** unto the wicked, O wicked *man,*	559
	33:11 **S** unto them, *As* I live, saith the Lord God,	559
	33:12 of man, **s** unto the children of thy people,	559
	33:13 When I shall **s** to the righteous, *that* he	559
	33:14 when I **s** unto the wicked, Thou shalt	559
	33:17 Yet the children of thy people **s**, The way	559
	33:20 Yet ye **s**, The way of the Lord is not equal.	559
	33:25 Wherefore **s** unto them, Thus saith the	559
	33:27 **S** thus unto them, Thus saith the Lord	559
	34: 2 of Israel, prophesy, and **s** unto them,	559
	35: 3 **s** unto it, Thus saith the Lord God;	559
	36: 1 **s**, Ye mountains of Israel, hear the word of	559
	36: 3 Therefore prophesy and **s**, Thus saith	559
	36: 6 **s** unto the mountains, and to the hills,	559

Eze	36:13 Because they **s** unto you, Thou *land*	559
	36:22 Therefore **s** unto the house of Israel,	559
	36:35 they shall **s**, This land that was desolate is	559
	37: 4 and **s** unto them, O ye dry bones,	559
	37: 9 prophesy, son of man, and **s** to the wind,	559
	37:11 behold, they **s**, Our bones are dried,	559
	37:12 Therefore prophesy and **s** unto them,	559
	37:19 **S** unto them, Thus saith the Lord God;	1696
	37:21 **s** unto them, Thus saith the Lord God;	1696
	38: 3 **s**, Thus saith the Lord God; Behold, I *am*	559
	38:11 thou shalt **s**, I will go up to the land of	559
	38:13 shall **s** unto thee, Art thou come to take a	559
	38:14 son of man, prophesy and **s** unto Gog,	559
	39: 1 son of man, prophesy against Gog, and **s**,	559
	44: 5 hear with thine ears all that I **s** unto thee	1696
	44: 6 thou shalt **s** to the rebellious, *even* to	559
Da	4:35 his hand, or **s** unto him, What doest thou?	560
	5:11 the king, *I* **s**, thy father, made master of	NIH
Hos	2: 1 **S**ye unto your brethren, Ammi; and to	559
	2: 7 not find *them*: then shall she **s**, I will go	559
	2:23 I will **s** to them which were not my people,	559
	2:23 and they shall **s**, *Thou art* my God.	559
	10: 3 For now they shall **s**, We have no king,	559
	10: 8 they shall **s** to the mountains, Cover us;	559
	13: 2 they **s** of them, Let the men that sacrifice	559
	14: 2 **s** unto him, Take away all iniquity,	559
	14: 3 neither will we **s** any more to the work of	559
	14: 8 Ephraim *shall* **s**, What have I to do any	NIH
Joel	2:17 the porch and the altar, and let them **s**,	559
	2:17 wherefore should they **s** among the people,	559
	2:19 Lord will answer and **s** unto his people,	559
	3:10 into spears: let the weak **s**, I *am* strong.	559
Am	3: 9 in the palaces in the land of Egypt, and **s**,	559
	4: 1 which **s** to their masters, Bring, and let us	559
	5:16 and they shall **s** in all the highways, Alas!	559
	6:10 shall **s** unto *him* that *is* by the sides of	559
	6:10 he shall **s**, No. Then shall he say, Hold thy	559
	6:10 shall he **s**, Hold thy tongue: for *we may* not	559
	6:13 rejoice in a thing of nought, which **s**,	559
	8:14 of Samaria, and **s**, Thy god, O Dan, liveth;	559
	9:10 which **s**, The evil shall not overtake nor	559
Mic	2: 4 and **s**, We be utterly spoiled:	559
	2: 6 ye not, **s** *they* to *them that* prophesy:	NIH
	3:11 and **s**, *Is* not the Lord among us?	559
	4: 2 **s**, Come, and let us go up to the mountain	559
	4:11 that **s**, Let her be defiled, and let our eye	559
Na	3: 7 from thee, and **s**, Nineveh is laid waste:	559
Hab	2: 1 will watch to see what he will **s** unto me,	1696
	2: 6 and a taunting proverb against him, and **s**,	559
Zep	1:12 that *is* in their heart, The Lord will not do	559
Hag	1: 2 This people **s**, The time is not come,	559
Zec	1: 3 Therefore **s** thou unto them, Thus saith	559
	11: 5 they that sell them **s**, Blessed *be* the Lord;	559
	12: 5 governors of Judah shall **s** in their heart,	559
	13: 3 his mother that begat him shall **s** unto him,	559
	13: 5 he shall **s**, I *am* no prophet, I *am* a	559
	13: 6 shall **s** unto him, What *are* these wounds	559
	13: 9 I will **s**, It *is* my people: and they shall **s**,	559
	13: 9 and they shall **s**, The Lord *is* my God.	559
Mal	1: 2 Yet ye **s**, Wherein hast thou loved us?	559
	1: 5 your eyes shall see, and ye shall **s**,	559
	1: 6 ye **s**, Wherein have we despised thy name?	559
	1: 7 and ye **s**, Wherein have we polluted thee?	559
	1: 7 In that ye **s**, The table of the Lord *is*	559
	1:12 *have* profaned it, in that ye **s**, The table of	559
	2:14 Yet ye **s**, Wherefore? Because the Lord	559
	2:17 Yet ye **s**, Wherein have we wearied *him*?	559
	2:17 have we wearied *him*? When ye **s**,	559
	3: 8 ye **s**, Wherein have we robbed thee?	559
	3:13 Yet ye **s**, What have we spoken so	559
Mt	3: 9 And think not to **s** within yourselves,	3004
	3: 9 for I **s** unto you, that God is able of these	3004
	4:17 Jesus began to preach, and to **s**, Repent:	3004
	5:11 shall **s** all manner of evil against you	3004
	5:18 For verily I **s** unto you, Till heaven and	3004
	5:20 For I **s** unto you, That except your	3004
	5:22 I **s** unto you, That whosoever is angry	3004
	5:22 whosoever shall **s** to his brother, Raca,	3004
	5:22 but whosoever shall **s**, *Thou* fool, shall be	3004
	5:26 Verily I **s** unto thee, Thou shalt by no	3004
	5:28 But I **s** unto you, That whosoever looketh	3004
	5:32 But I **s** unto you, That whosoever	3004
	5:34 But I **s** unto you, Swear not at all;	3004
	5:39 But I **s** unto you, That ye resist not evil:	3004
	5:44 But I **s** unto you, Love your enemies,	3004
	6: 2 Verily I **s** unto you, They have their	3004
	6: 5 Verily I **s** unto you, They have their	3004
	6:16 Verily I **s** unto you, They have their	3004
	6:25 Therefore I **s** unto you, Take no thought	3004
	6:29 yet I **s** unto you, That even Solomon in	3004
	7: 4 how wilt thou **s** to thy brother, Let me	3004
	7:22 Many will **s** to me in that day, Lord, Lord,	3004
	8: 9 and I **s** to this *man*, Go, and he goeth;	3004
	8:10 Verily I **s** unto you, I have not found so	3004
	8:11 And I **s** unto you, That many shall come	3004
	9: 5 For whether is easier, to **s**, *Thy* sins be	3004
	9: 5 be forgiven thee; or to **s**, Arise, and walk?	3004
	10:15 Verily I **s** unto you, It shall be more	3004
	10:23 for verily I **s** unto you, Ye shall not have	3004
	10:42 verily I **s** unto you, he shall in no wise	3004
	11: 7 Jesus began to **s** unto the multitudes	3004
	11: 9 I **s** unto you, and more than a prophet.	3004
	11:11 Verily I **s** unto you, Among *them that are*	3004
	11:18 nor drinking, and they **s**, He hath a devil.	3004
	11:19 came eating and drinking, and they **s**,	3004

Mt	11:22 I **s** unto you, It shall be more tolerable	3004
	11:24 But I **s** unto you, that it shall be more	3004
	12: 6 But I **s** unto you, That in this place is *one*	3004
	12:31 Wherefore I **s** unto you, All *manner of* sin	3004
	12:36 I **s** unto you, That every idle word that	3004
	13:17 verily I **s** unto you, That many prophets	3004
	13:30 the time of harvest I will **s** to the reapers,	3004
	13:51 all these *things*? They **s** unto him,	3004
	14:17 They **s** unto him, We have here but five	3004
	15: 5 ye **s**, Whosoever shall say to *his* father	3004
	15: 5 Whosoever shall **s** to *his* father or	3004
	15:33 And his disciples **s** unto him,	3004
	16: 2 unto them, When it is evening, ye **s**,	3004
	16:13 do men **s** that I the Son of man am?	3004
	16:14 Some **s** that thou *art* John the Baptist:	NIG
	16:15 unto them, But whom **s** ye that I am?	3004
	16:18 I also **s** unto thee, That thou art Peter,	3004
	16:28 Verily I **s** unto you, There be some	3004
	17:10 **s** the scribes that Elias must first come?	3004
	17:12 But I **s** unto you, That Elias is come	3004
	17:20 verily I **s** unto you, If ye have faith as a	3004
	17:20 ye shall **s** unto this mountain,	3004
	18: 3 said, Verily I **s** unto you, Except ye be	3004
	18:10 I **s** unto you, That in heaven their angels	3004
	18:13 so be that he find it, verily I **s** unto you,	3004
	18:18 Verily I **s** unto you, Whatsoever ye shall	3004
	18:19 I **s** unto you, That if two of you shall	3004
	18:22 I **s** not unto thee, Until seven times:	3004
	19: 7 They **s** unto him, Why did Moses then	3004
	19: 9 And I **s** unto you, Whosoever shall put	3004
	19:10 His disciples **s** unto him, If the case of	3004
	19:23 unto his disciples, Verily I **s** unto you,	3004
	19:24 And again I **s** unto you, It is easier for a	3004
	19:28 Jesus said unto them, Verily I **s** unto you,	3004
	20: 7 They **s** unto him, Because no *man* hath	3004
	20:22 that I am baptized *with*? They **s** unto him,	3004
	20:33 They **s** unto him, Lord, that our eyes may	3004
	21: 3 And if any *man* **s** ought unto you, ye shall	3004
	21: 3 ye shall **s**, The Lord hath need of them;	3004
	21:16 said unto them, Hearest thou what these **s**?	3004
	21:21 and said unto them, Verily I **s** unto you,	3004
	21:21 but also if ye shall **s** unto this mountain,	3004
	21:25 saying, If we shall **s**, From heaven;	3004
	21:25 he will **s** unto us, Why did ye not then	3004
	21:26 But if we shall **s**, Of men; we fear	3004
	21:31 They **s** unto him, The first. Jesus saith	3004
	21:31 Verily I **s** unto you, That the publicans	3004
	21:41 They **s** unto him, He will miserably	3004
	21:43 Therefore **s** I unto you, The kingdom of	3004
	22:21 They **s** unto him, Cæsar's. Then saith he	3004
	22:23 which **s** that there is no resurrection,	3004
	22:42 They **s** unto him, *The Son* of David.	3004
	23: 3 after their works: for they **s**, and do not.	3004
	23:16 Woe unto you, *ye* blind guides, which **s**,	3004
	23:30 And **s**, If we had been in the days of our	3004
	23:36 Verily I **s** unto you, All these *things* shall	3004
	23:39 For I **s** unto you, Ye shall not see me	3004
	23:39 shall not see me henceforth, till ye shall **s**,	3004
	24: 2 See ye not all these *things*? verily I **s** unto	3004
	24:23 Then if any *man* shall **s** unto you,	3004
	24:26 Wherefore if they shall **s** unto you,	3004
	24:34 Verily I **s** unto you, This generation shall	3004
	24:47 Verily I **s** unto you, That he shall make	3004
	24:48 *and* if that evil servant shall **s** in his heart,	3004
	25:12 he answered and said, Verily I **s** unto you,	3004
	25:34 Then shall the King **s** unto them on his	3004
	25:40 the King shall answer and **s** unto them,	3004
	25:40 and say unto them, Verily I **s** unto you,	3004
	25:41 Then shall he **s** also unto them on the left	3004
	25:45 answer them, saying, Verily I **s** unto you,	3004
	26:13 Verily I **s** unto you, Wheresoever this	3004
	26:18 unto him, The Master saith, My time	3004
	26:21 they did eat, he said, Verily I **s** unto you,	3004
	26:22 began every one of them to **s** unto him,	3004
	26:29 I **s** unto you, I will not drink henceforth	3004
	26:34 Verily I **s** unto thee, That this night,	3004
	26:64 nevertheless I **s** unto you, Hereafter shall	3004
	27:22 *They* all **s** unto him, Let him be crucified.	3004
	27:33 that is to **s**, a place of a skull,	3004
	27:46 that is to **s**, My God, my God, why hast	NIG
	27:64 steal him *away*, and **s** unto the people,	3004
	28:13 Saying, **S** ye, His disciples came by night,	3004
Mk	1:44 See thou **s** nothing to any *man*: but go	3004
	2: 9 Whether is it easier to **s** to the sick of	3004
	2: 9 or to **s**, Arise, and take up thy bed,	3004
	2:11 I **s** unto thee, Arise, and take up thy bed,	3004
	2:18 and they come and **s** unto him, Why do	3004
	3:28 Verily I **s** unto you, All sins shall be	3004
	4:38 they awake him, and **s** unto him, Master,	3004
	5:41 being interpreted, Damsel (I **s** unto thee)	3004
	6:11 Verily I **s** unto you, It shall be more	3004
	6:37 And they **s** unto him, Shall we go and	3004
	6:38 they knew, they **s**, Five, and two fishes.	3004
	7: 2 that is to **s**, with unwashen, hands,	NIH
	7:11 ye **s**, If a man shall say to *his* father or	3004
	7:11 If a man shall **s** to *his* father or mother,	3004
	7:11 or mother, *It is* Corban, that is to **s**, a gift,	NIG
	8:12 verily I **s** unto you, There shall no sign be	3004
	8:19 took ye up? They **s** unto him, Twelve.	3004
	8:27 unto them, Whom do men **s** that I am?	3004
	8:28 but some **s**, Elias; and others, One of	NIG
	8:29 unto them, But whom **s** ye that I am?	3004
	9: 1 he said unto them, Verily I **s** unto you,	3004
	9: 6 For he wist not what to **s**; for they were	2980
	9:11 Why **s** the scribes that Elias must first	3004

Mk		
9:13	I **s** unto you, That Elias is indeed come,	3004
9:41	ye belong to Christ, verily I **s** unto you,	3004
10:15	Verily I **s** unto you, Whosoever shall not	3004
10:28	Then Peter began to **s** unto him,	3004
10:29	and said, Verily I **s** unto you,	3004
10:47	and **s**, Jesus, *thou* Son of David,	3004
11: 3	And if any *man* **s** unto you, Why do ye	3004
11: 3	ye that the Lord hath need of him;	3004
11:23	For verily I **s** unto you, That whosoever	3004
11:23	whosoever shall **s** unto this mountain,	3004
11:24	I **s** unto you, What *things* soever	3004
11:28	And **s** unto him, By what authority doest	3004
11:31	saying, If we shall **s**, From heaven;	3004
11:31	he will **s**, Why then did ye not believe	3004
11:32	But if we shall **s**, Of men; they feared	3004
12:14	they **s** unto him, Master, we know that	3004
12:18	which **s** there is no resurrection;	3004
12:35	How **s** the scribes that Christ is the Son	3004
12:43	and saith unto them, Verily I **s** unto you,	3004
13: 5	And Jesus answering them began to **s**,	3004
13:21	And then if any *man* shall **s** to you,	3004
13:30	Verily I **s** unto you, that this generation	3004
13:37	And what I **s** unto you I say unto all,	3004
13:37	And what I say unto you I **s** unto all,	3004
14: 9	Verily I **s** unto you, Wheresoever this	3004
14:14	ye to the goodman of the house,	3004
14:18	did eat, Jesus said, Verily I **s** unto you,	3004
14:19	and to **s** unto him one by one, *Is* it I?	3004
14:25	Verily I **s** unto you, I will drink no more	3004
14:30	Verily I **s** unto thee, That this day, *even* in	3004
14:58	We heard him **s**, I will destroy this temple	3004
14:65	buffet him, and to **s** unto him, Prophesy:	3004
14:69	and began to **s** to them that stood by,	3004
Lk		
3: 8	and begin not to **s** within yourselves,	3004
3: 8	for I **s** unto you, That God is able of these	3004
4:21	And he began to **s** unto them, This day is	3004
4:23	Ye will surely **s** unto me this proverb,	3004
4:24	And he said, Verily I **s** unto you,	3004
5:23	Whether is easier, to **s**, Thy sins be	3004
5:23	forgiven thee; or to **s**, Rise up and walk?	3004
5:24	I **s** unto thee, Arise, and take up thy	3004
6:27	But I **s** unto you which hear, Love your	3004
6:42	Either how canst thou **s** to thy brother,	3004
6:46	Lord, and do not the *things* which I **s**?	3004
7: 7	but **s** in a word, and my servant shall be	3004
7: 8	and I **s** unto one, Go, and he goeth;	3004
7: 9	I **s** unto you, I have not found so great	3004
7:14	he said, Young man, I **s** unto thee, Arise.	3004
7:26	I **s** unto you, and much more than a	3004
7:28	I **s** unto you, Among *those that are* born	3004
7:33	drinking wine; and ye **s**, He hath a devil.	3004
7:34	and ye **s**, Behold a gluttonous man,	3004
7:40	Simon, I have somewhat to **s** unto thee.	3004
7:40	say unto thee. And he saith, Master, **s** *on.*	3004
7:47	Wherefore I **s** unto thee, Her sins,	3004
7:49	with *him* began to **s** within themselves,	3004
9:18	saying, Whom **s** the people that I am?	3004
9:19	some **s**, Elias; and others *say,* that one of	NIG
9:19	others **s**, that one of the old prophets is	NIG
9:20	unto them, But whom **s** ye that I am?	3004
10: 5	ye enter, first **s**, Peace *be* to this house.	3004
10: 9	the sick that are therein, and **s** unto them,	3004
10:10	out into the streets of the same, and **s**,	3004
10:12	But I **s** unto you, that it shall be more	3004
11: 2	And he said unto them, When ye pray, **s**,	3004
11: 5	and **s** unto him, Friend, lend me three	3004
11: 7	And he from within shall answer and **s**,	3004
11: 8	I **s** unto you, Though he will not rise and	3004
11: 9	I **s** unto you, Ask, and it shall be given	3004
11:18	ye **s** that I cast out devils through	3004
11:29	he began to **s**, This is an evil generation:	3004
11:51	verily I **s** unto you, It shall be required of	3004
12: 1	he began to **s** unto his disciples first *of all,*	3004
12: 4	And I **s** unto you my friends, Be not afraid	3004
12: 5	cast into hell; yea, I **s** unto you, Fear him.	3004
12: 8	I **s** unto you, Whosoever shall confess	3004
12:11	*thing* ye shall answer, or what ye shall **s**:	3004
12:12	you in the same hour what ye ought to **s**.	3004
12:19	And I will **s** to my soul, Soul, thou hast	3004
12:22	Therefore I **s** unto you, Take no thought	3004
12:27	yet I **s** unto you, *that* Solomon in all his	3004
12:37	verily I **s** unto you, that he shall gird	3004
12:44	Of a truth I **s** unto you, that he will make	3004
12:45	But and if that servant **s** in his heart,	3004
12:54	straightway ye **s**, There cometh a shower;	3004
12:55	south wind blow, ye **s**, There will be heat;	3004
13:24	many, I **s** unto you, will seek to enter in,	3004
13:25	he shall answer and **s** unto you, I know	3004
13:26	Then shall ye begin to **s**, We have eaten	3004
13:27	But he shall **s**, I tell you, I know you not	3004
13:35	and verily I **s** unto you, Ye shall not see	3004
13:35	until *the time* come when ye shall **s**,	3004
14: 9	bade thee and him come and **s** to thee,	3004
14:10	he may **s** unto thee, Friend, go up higher:	3004
14:17	And sent his servant at supper time to **s** to	3004
14:24	For I **s** unto you, That none of those men	3004
15: 7	I **s** unto you, that likewise joy shall be in	3004
15:10	Likewise, I **s** unto you, there is joy in	3004
15:18	to my father, and will **s** unto him, Father,	3004
16: 9	And I **s** unto you, Make to yourselves	3004
17: 6	ye might **s** unto this sycamine tree, Be	3004
17: 7	feeding cattle, will **s** *unto him* by and by,	3004
17: 8	will not *rather* **s** unto him, Make ready	3004
17:10	**s**, We are unprofitable servants:	3004
17:21	Neither shall they **s**, Lo here: or, lo there:	3004

Lk		
17:23	And they shall **s** to you, See here;	3004
18:17	Verily I **s** unto you, Whosoever shall not	3004
18:29	he said unto them, Verily I **s** unto you,	3004
19:26	For I **s** unto you, That unto every one	3004
19:31	Why do ye loose *him?* thus shall ye **s** unto	3004
20: 5	saying, If we shall **s**, From heaven;	3004
20: 5	he will **s**, Why then believed ye him not?	3004
20: 6	But *and* if we **s**, Of men; all the people	3004
20:41	How **s** they that Christ is David's son?	3004
21: 3	And he said, Of a truth I **s** unto you,	3004
21:32	Verily I **s** unto you, This generation shall	3004
22:11	And ye shall **s** to the goodman of	3004
22:16	For I **s** unto you, I will not any more eat	3004
22:18	I **s** unto you, I will not drink of the fruit	3004
22:37	For I **s** unto you, that this that is written	3004
22:70	And he said unto them, Ye **s** that I am.	3004
23:29	are coming, in the which they shall **s**,	3004
23:30	shall they begin to **s** to the mountains,	3004
23:43	Jesus said unto him, Verily I **s** unto thee,	3004
Jn		
1:38	Rabbi, (which is to **s**, being interpreted,	3004
1:51	unto him, Verily, verily, I **s** unto you,	3004
3: 3	said unto him, Verily, verily, I **s** unto thee,	3004
3: 5	Verily, verily, I **s** unto thee,	3004
3:11	Verily, verily, I **s** unto thee, We speak that	3004
4:20	and ye **s**, that in Jerusalem is the place	3004
4:35	**S** not ye, There are yet four months,	3004
4:35	behold, I **s** unto you, Lift up your eyes,	3004
5:19	unto them, Verily, verily, I **s** unto you,	3004
5:24	Verily, verily, I **s** unto you, He that	3004
5:25	Verily, verily, I **s** unto you, The hour is	3004
5:34	these *things* I **s**, that ye might be saved.	3004
6:26	and said, Verily, verily, I **s** unto you,	3004
6:32	unto them, Verily, verily, I **s** unto you,	3004
6:47	Verily, verily, I **s** unto you, He that	3004
6:53	unto them, Verily, verily, I **s** unto you,	3004
7:26	and they **s** nothing unto him.	3004
8: 4	They **s** unto him, Master, this woman	3004
8:26	I have many *things* to **s** and to judge of	2980
8:34	them, Verily, verily, I **s** unto you,	3004
8:46	if I **s** the truth, why do ye not believe	3004
8:48	**S** we not well that thou art a Samaritan,	3004
8:51	Verily, verily, I **s** unto you, If a man keep	3004
8:54	of whom ye **s**, that he is your God:	3004
8:55	if I should **s**, I know him not, I shall be	3004
8:58	unto them, Verily, verily, I **s** unto you,	3004
9:17	They **s** unto the blind man again,	3004
9:19	Is this your son, who ye **s** was born blind?	3004
9:41	but now ye **s**, We see; therefore your sin	3004
10: 1	Verily, verily, I **s** unto you, He that	3004
10: 7	Verily, verily, I **s** unto you, I am the door	3004
10:36	**S** ye *of him,* whom the Father hath	3004
11: 8	His disciples **s** unto him, Master, the Jews	3004
11:34	They **s** unto him, Lord, come and see.	3004
12:24	Verily, verily, I **s** unto you, Except a corn	3004
12:27	is my soul troubled; and what shall I **s**?	3004
12:49	what I should **s**, and what I should speak.	3004
13:13	and Lord: and ye **s** well; for *so* I am.	3004
13:16	Verily, verily, I **s** unto you, The servant is	3004
13:20	Verily, verily, I **s** unto you, He that	3004
13:21	and said, Verily, verily, I **s** unto you,	3004
13:33	I go, ye cannot come; so now I **s** to you.	3004
13:38	Verily, verily, I **s** unto thee, *The* cock shall	3004
14:12	Verily, verily, I **s** unto you, He that	3004
16:12	I have yet many *things* to **s** unto you,	3004
16:20	Verily, verily, I **s** unto you, That ye shall	3004
16:23	Verily, verily, I **s** unto you, Whatsoever ye	3004
16:26	and I **s** not unto you, that I will pray	3004
20:13	they **s** unto her, Woman, why weepest	3004
20:16	unto him, Rabboni; which is to **s**, Master.	3004
20:17	but go to my brethren, and **s** unto them,	3004
21: 3	They **s** unto him, We also go with thee.	3004
21:18	Verily, verily, I **s** unto thee, When thou	3004
Ac		
1:19	Aceldama, that is to **s**, The field of blood.	NIG
3:22	all *things* whatsoever he shall **s** unto you.	2980
4:14	them, they could **s** nothing **against** *it.*	471
5:38	And now I **s** unto you, Refrain from these	3004
6:14	we have heard him **s**, that this Jesus of	3004
10:37	*That* word, *I* **s**, you know, which was	NIG
13:15	word of exhortation for the people, **s** *on.*	3004
17:18	And some said, What will this babbler **s**?	3004
17:21	Do therefore this that we **s** to thee: We	3004
23: 8	For the Sadducees **s** that there is no	3004
23:18	who hath something to **s** unto thee,	2980
23:30	to **s** before thee what *they had* against	3004
24:20	Or else let these same *here* **s**, if they have	3004
26:22	prophets and Moses did **s** should come:	2980
28:26	Saying, Go unto this people, and **s**,	3004
Ro		
3: 5	righteousness of God, what shall we **s**?	3004
3: 8	and as some affirm that we **s**,)	3004
3:26	I **s**, at this time his righteousness:	NIG
4: 1	What shall we **s** then that Abraham our	3004
4: 9	for we **s** that faith was reckoned to	3004
6: 1	What shall we **s** then? Shall we continue	3004
7: 7	What shall we **s** then? *Is* the law sin?	3004
8:31	then **s** to these things? If God *be* for us,	3004
9: 1	**s** the truth in Christ, I lie not,	3004
9:14	What shall we **s** then? *Is there*	3004
9:19	Thou wilt **s** then unto me, Why doth he	3004
9:20	the thing formed **s** to him that formed	3004
9:30	What shall we **s** then? That the Gentiles,	3004
10: 6	**S** not in thine heart, Who shall ascend	3004
10:18	But I **s**, Have they not heard? Yes verily,	3004
10:19	But I **s**, Did not Israel know? First Moses	3004
11: 1	I **s** then, Hath God cast away his people?	3004
11:11	I **s** then, Have they stumbled that they	3004

Ro		
11:19	Thou wilt **s** then, The branches were	3004
12: 3	For I **s**, through the grace given unto me,	3004
15: 8	Now I **s** that Jesus Christ was a minister	3004
1Co		
1:12	Now this I **s**, that every one of you saith,	3004
1:15	Lest any should **s** that I had baptized in	3004
7: 8	I **s** therefore to the unmarried and	3004
7:26	I **s**, that *it is* good for a man so to be.	NIG
7:29	But this I **s**, brethren, the time *is* short:	5346
9: 8	**S** I these *things* as a man? or saith not	2980
10:15	I speak as to wise *men;* judge ye what I **s**.	5346
10:19	What **s** I then? that the idol is any *thing,*	5346
10:20	I **s**, that the *things* which the Gentiles	NIG
10:28	But if any *man* **s** unto you, This is offered	3004
10:29	Conscience, I **s**, not thine own, but of	3004
11:22	What shall I **s** to you? shall I praise you in	3004
12: 3	*that* no *man* can **s** that Jesus is the Lord,	3004
12:15	If the foot shall **s**, Because I am not	3004
12:16	And if the ear shall **s**, Because I am not	3004
12:21	the eye cannot **s** unto the hand, I have	3004
14:16	unlearned **s** Amen at thy giving of thanks,	3004
14:23	will they not **s** that ye are mad?	3004
15:12	now **s** some among you that there is no	3004
15:35	But some *man* will **s**, How are the dead	3004
15:50	Now this I **s**, brethren, that flesh and	5346
2Co		
5: 8	I **s**, and willing rather to be absent from	NIG
9: 4	you unprepared, we (that we **s** not, you)	3004
9: 6	But this I **s**, He which soweth sparingly	NIG
10:10	**s** they, *are* weighty and powerful;	5346
11:16	I **s** again, Let no man think me a fool;	3004
12: 6	I shall not be a fool; for I will **s** the truth:	3004
Gal		
1: 9	As we said before, so **s** I now again, If any	3004
3:17	And this I **s**, *that* the covenant, that was	3004
4: 1	Now I **s**, *That* the heir, as long as he is a	3004
5: 2	Behold, I Paul **s** unto you, that if ye be	3004
5:16	*This* I **s** then, Walk in the Spirit,	3004
Eph		
4:17	This I **s** therefore, and testify in the Lord,	3004
Php		
4: 4	in the Lord alway: *and* again I **s**, Rejoice.	3004
Col		
1:20	I **s**, whether *they be* things in earth,	NIG
2: 4	And this I **s**, lest any *man* should beguile	3004
4:17	And **s** to Archippus, Take heed to	3004
1Th		
4:15	For this we **s** unto you by the word of	3004
5: 3	For when they shall **s**, Peace and safety;	3004
1Ti		
1: 7	understanding neither what they **s**,	3004
2Ti		
2: 7	Consider what I **s**; and the Lord give thee	3004
Tit		
2: 8	having no evil *thing* to **s** of you.	3004
Phm		
1:19	I will repay *it:* albeit I do not **s** to thee	3004
1:21	that thou wilt also do more than I **s**.	3004
Heb		
5:11	Of whom we have many things to **s**,	3056
7: 9	as *I* may so **s**, Levi also, who receiveth	3004
9:11	hands, that is to **s**, not of this building,	NIG
10:20	through the vail, that is to **s**, his flesh;	NIG
11:14	they that such *things* declare plainly	3004
11:32	And what shall I more **s**? for the time	3004
13: 6	So that we may boldly **s**, The Lord *is* my	3004
Jas		
1:13	Let no *man* **s** when he is tempted, I am	3004
2: 3	and **s** unto him, Sit thou here in a good	3004
2: 3	and **s** to the poor, Stand thou there,	3004
2:14	though a man **s** *he* hath faith, and have	3004
2:16	And one of you **s** unto them, Depart in	3004
2:18	Yea, a man may **s**, Thou hast faith, and I	3004
4:13	ye that **s**, To day or to morrow we will go	3004
4:15	For that ye *ought* to **s**, If the Lord will,	3004
1Jn		
1: 6	If we **s** that we have fellowship with him,	3004
1: 8	If we **s** that we have no sin, we deceive	3004
1:10	If we **s** that we have not sinned, we make	3004
4:20	If a man **s**, I love God, and hateth his	3004
5:16	I do not **s** that he shall pray for it.	3004
Rev		
2: 2	thou hast tried them which **s** *they* are	5335
2: 9	the blasphemy of them which **s** they	3004
2:24	But unto you I **s**, and unto the rest in	3004
3: 9	which **s** they are Jews, and are not,	3004
6: 3	I heard the second beast **s**, Come and see.	3004
6: 5	I heard the third beast **s**, Come and see.	3004
6: 6	a voice in the midst of the four beasts **s**,	3004
6: 7	I heard the voice of the fourth beast **s**,	3004
16: 5	And I heard the angel of the waters **s**,	3004
16: 7	And I heard another out of the altar **s**,	3004
22:17	And the Spirit and the bride **s**, Come.	3004
22:17	And let him that heareth **s**, Come.	3004

SAYEST (40) [SAY]

Ex	33:12 See, thou **s** unto me, Bring up this people:	559
Nu	22:17 I will do whatsoever thou **s** unto me:	559
Ru	3: 5 unto her, All that thou **s** unto me I will do.	559
1Ki	18:11 now thou **s**, Go, tell thy lord, Behold,	559
	18:14 now thou **s**, Go, tell thy lord, Behold,	559
2Ki	18:20 Thou **s**, (but *they are but* vain words,)	559
2Ch	25:19 **s**, Lo, thou hast smitten the Edomites;	559
Ne	5:12 nothing of them; so will we do as thou **s**.	559
	6: 8 There are no such things *done* as thou **s**,	559
Job	22:13 thou **s**, How doth God know? can he judge	559
	35:14 Although thou **s** thou shalt not see him,	559
Ps	90: 3 and **s**, Return, ye children of men.	559
Pr	24:12 If thou **s**, Behold, we knew it not; doth not	559
Isa	36: 5 I say, **s** *thou,* (but *they are but* vain words)	NIH
	40:27 Why **s** thou, O Jacob, and speakest	559
	47: 8 that *is* thine heart, I *am,* and none else	559
Jer	2:35 Yet thou **s**, Because I am innocent, surely	559
	2:35 these, because thou **s**, I have not sinned.	559
Am	7:16 Thou **s**, Prophesy not against Israel,	559
Mt	26:70 *them* all, saying, I know not what thou **s**.	3004
	27:11 And Jesus said unto him, Thou **s**.	3004
Mk	5:31 and **s** thou, Who touched me?	3004
	14:68 not, neither understand I what thou **s**.	3004
	15: 2 he answering said unto him, Thou **s** *it.*	3004

S

Lk 8:45 throng thee and press *thee*, and **s** thou, 3004
20:21 we know that thou **s** and teachest rightly, 3004
22:60 Peter said, Man, I know not what thou **s**. 3004
23: 3 And he answered him and said, Thou **s** *it*. 3004
Jn 1:22 them that sent us. What **s** thou of thyself? 3004
8: 5 such should be stoned: but what **s** thou? 3004
8:33 were never in bondage to any *man:* how **s** 3004
8:52 and thou **s**, If a man keep my saying, 3004
9:17 What **s** thou of him, that he hath opened 3004
12:34 and how **s** thou, The Son of man must be 3004
14: 9 and how **s** thou *then*, Shew us the Father? 3004
18:34 answered him, **S** thou this *thing* of thyself, 3004
18:37 Jesus answered, Thou **s** that I am a king. 3004
Ro 2:22 Thou that **s** *a man* should not commit 3004
1Co 14:16 seeing he understandeth not what thou **s**? 3004
Rev 3:17 Because thou **s**, I am rich, 3004

SAYING (1445) [SAY]

Ge 1:22 **s**, Be fruitful, and multiply, and fill 559
2:16 the Lord God commanded the man, **s**, 559
3:17 commanded thee, Thou shalt not eat of 559
5:29 he called his name Noah, **s**, This *same* 559
8:15 And God spake unto Noah, **s**, 559
9: 8 unto Noah, and to his sons with him, **s**, 559
15: 1 Abram in a vision, **s**, Fear not, Abram: 559
15: 4 unto him, **s**, This shall not be thine heir: 559
15:18 **s**, Unto thy seed have I given this land, 559
17: 3 on his face: and God talked with him, **s**, 559
18:12 Therefore Sarah laughed within herself, **s**, 559
18:13 Wherefore did Sarah laugh, **s**, 559
18:15 Sarah denied, **s**, I laughed not; for she was 559
19:15 **s**, Arise, take thy wife, and thy two 559
21:22 **s**, God *is* with thee in all that thou doest: 559
22:20 it was told Abraham, **s**, Behold, Milcah, 559
23: 3 dead, and spake unto the sons of Heth, **s**, 559
23: 5 of Heth answered Abraham, **s** unto him, 559
23: 8 he communed with them, **s**, If it be your 559
23:10 of all that went in *at* the gate of his city, **s**, 559
23:13 **s**, But if thou *wilt give it,* I pray thee, 559
23:14 Ephron answered Abraham, **s** unto him, 559
24: 7 spake unto me, and that sware unto me, **s**, 559
24:30 his sister, **s**, Thus spake the man unto me; 559
24:37 my master made me swear, **s**, Thou shalt 559
26:11 **s**, He that toucheth this man or his wife 559
26:20 with Isaac's herdmen, **s**, The water *is* ours: 559
27: 6 spake unto Jacob her son, **s**, Behold, 559
27: 6 thy father speak unto Esau thy brother, **s**, 559
28: 6 as he blessed him he gave him a charge, **s**, 559
28:20 **s**, If God will be with me, and will keep me 559
31: 1 he heard the words of Laban's sons, **s**, 559
31:11 God spake unto me in a dream, **s**, Jacob: NIH
31:29 your father spake unto me yesternight, **s**, 559
32: 4 commanded them, **s**, Thus shall ye speak 559
32: 6 **s**, We came to thy brother Esau, and also 559
32:17 commanded the foremost, **s**, When Esau 559
32:17 and asketh thee, **s**, Whose *art* thou? 559
32:19 third, and all that followed the droves, **s**, 559
34: 4 Hamor, **s**, Get me this damsel to wife. 559
34: 8 Hamor communed with them, **s**, The soul 559
34:20 communed with the men of their city, **s**, 559
37:11 envied him; but his father observed the **s**. 1697
37:15 the man asked him, **s**, What seekest thou? 559
38:13 it was told Tamar, **s**, Behold thy father in 559
38:21 **s**, Where *is* the harlot, that *was* openly by 559
38:24 months after, that it was told Judah, **s**, 559
38:25 sent to her father in law, **s**, By the man, 559
38:28 a scarlet thread, **s**, This came out first. 559
39:12 caught him by his garment, **s**, Lie with me: 559
39:14 of her house, and spake unto them, **s**, See, 559
39:17 **s**, The Hebrew servant, which thou hast 559
39:19 which she spake unto him, **s**, After this 559
40: 7 **s**, Wherefore look ye *so* sadly to day? 559
41: 9 **s**, I do remember my faults *this* day: 559
41:16 Joseph answered Pharaoh, **s**, *It is* not in 559
42:14 *is it* that I spake unto you, **s**, Ye *are* spies: 559
42:22 **s**, Spake I not unto you, saying, Do not sin 559
42:22 saying, Spake I not unto you, **s**, Do not sin 559
42:28 and they were afraid, **s** one to another, 559
42:29 and told him all that befell unto them; **s**, 559
42:37 **s**, Slay my two sons, if I bring him not to 559
43: 3 Judah spake unto him, **s**, The man did 559
43: 3 Ye shall not see my face, except your 559
43: 7 of our kindred, **s**, *Is* your father yet alive? 559
44: 1 **s**, Fill the men's sacks *with* food, as much 559
44:19 **s**, Have ye a father, or a brother? 559
44:32 **s**, If I bring him not unto thee, then I shall 559
45:16 **s**, Joseph's brethren are come: 559
45:26 told him, **s**, Joseph *is* yet alive, and he *is* 559
47: 5 **s**, Thy father and thy brethren are come 559
48:20 **s**, In thee shall Israel bless, saying, 559
48:20 saying, In thee shall Israel bless, **s**, 559
50: 4 **s**, If now I have found grace in your eyes, 559
50: 4 **s**, speak, I pray you, in the ears of Pharaoh, **s**, 559
50: 5 My father made me swear, **s**, Lo, I die: 559
50:16 they sent a messenger unto Joseph, **s**, 559
50:16 Thy father did command before he died, **s**, 559
50:25 **s**, God will surely visit you, and ye shall 559
Ex 1:22 Pharaoh charged all his people, **s**, Every son 559
3:16 of Isaac, and of Jacob, appeared unto me, **s**, 559
5: 6 of the people, and their officers, **s**, 559
5: 8 therefore they cry, **s**, Let us go *and* 559
5:10 spake to the people, **s**, Thus saith Pharaoh, 559
5:13 the taskmasters hasted *them*, **s**, Fulfil your 559
5:15 of Israel came and cried unto Pharaoh, **s**, 559
6:10 And the Lord spake unto Moses, **s**, 559

Ex 6:12 Moses spake before the Lord, **s**, Behold, 559
6:29 spake unto Moses, **s**, I *am* the Lord: 559
7: 8 spake unto Moses and unto Aaron, **s**, 559
7: 9 speak unto you, **s**, Shew a miracle for you: 559
7:16 **s**, Let my people go, that they may serve 559
9: 5 the Lord appointed a set time, **s**, 559
11: 8 **s**, Get thee out, and all the people that 559
12: 1 and Aaron in the land of Egypt, **s**, 559
12: 3 ye unto all the congregation of Israel, **s**, 559
13: 1 And the Lord spake unto Moses, **s**, 559
13: 8 **s**, *This is* done because of that *which* 559
13:14 thee in time to come, **s**, What *is* this? 559
13:19 of Israel, **s**, God will surely visit you; 559
14: 1 And the Lord spake unto Moses, **s**, 559
14:12 **s**, Let us alone, that we may serve 559
15: 1 spake, **s**, I will sing unto the Lord, for he 559
15:24 against Moses, **s**, What shall we drink? 559
16:11 And the Lord spake unto Moses, **s**, 559
16:12 speak unto them, **s**, At even ye shall eat 559
17: 4 **s**, What shall I do unto this people? 559
17: 7 because they tempted the Lord, **s**, 559
19: 3 **s**, Thus shalt thou say to the house of 559
19:12 **s**, Take heed to yourselves, *that ye* go *not* 559
19:23 for thou chargedst us, **s**, Set bounds about 559
20: 1 And God spake all these words, **s**, 559
25: 1 And the Lord spake unto Moses, **s**, 559
30:11 And the Lord spake unto Moses, **s**, 559
30:17 And the Lord spake unto Moses, **s**, 559
30:22 Moreover the Lord spake unto Moses, **s**, 559
30:31 shalt speak unto the children of Israel, **s**, 559
31: 1 And the Lord spake unto Moses, **s**, 559
31:12 And the Lord spake unto Moses, **s**, 559
31:13 **s**, Verily my sabbaths ye shall keep: 559
33: 1 Isaac, and to Jacob, **s**, Unto thy seed will I 559
35: 4 **s**, This *is* the thing which the Lord 559
35: 4 the thing which the Lord commanded, **s**, 559
36: 5 spake unto Moses, **s**, The people bring 559
36: 6 to be proclaimed throughout the camp, **s**, 559
40: 1 And the Lord spake unto Moses, **s**, 559
Lev 1: 1 of the tabernacle of the congregation, **s**, 559
4: 1 And the Lord spake unto Moses, **s**, 559
4: 2 Speak unto the children of Israel, **s**, If a 559
5:14 And the Lord spake unto Moses, **s**, 559
6: 1 And the Lord spake unto Moses, **s**, 559
6: 8 And the Lord spake unto Moses, **s**, 559
6: 9 Command Aaron and his sons, **s**, This *is* 559
6:19 And the Lord spake unto Moses, **s**, 559
6:24 And the Lord spake unto Moses, **s**, 559
6:25 Speak unto Aaron and to his sons, **s**, This 559
7:22 And the Lord spake unto Moses, **s**, 559
7:23 **s**, Ye shall eat no *manner* fat, of ox, 559
7:28 And the Lord spake unto Moses, **s**, 559
7:29 Speak unto the children of Israel, **s**, He 559
8: 1 And the Lord spake unto Moses, **s**, 559
8:31 **s**, Aaron and his sons shall eat it. 559
9: 3 **s**, Take ye a kid of the goats for a sin 559
10: 3 This *is it* that the Lord spake, **s**, 559
10: 8 And the Lord spake unto Aaron, **s**, 559
10:16 the sons of Aaron which were left *alive*, **s**, 559
11: 1 unto Moses and to Aaron, **s** unto them, 559
11: 2 Speak unto the children of Israel, **s**, 559
12: 1 And the Lord spake unto Moses, **s**, 559
12: 2 **s**, If a woman have conceived seed, 559
13: 1 the Lord spake unto Moses and Aaron, **s**, 559
14: 1 And the Lord spake unto Moses, **s**, 559
14:33 spake unto Moses and unto Aaron, **s**, 559
14:35 the house shall come and tell the priest, **s**, 559
15: 1 Lord spake unto Moses and to Aaron, **s**, 559
17: 1 And the Lord spake unto Moses, **s**, 559
17: 2 thing which the Lord hath commanded, **s**, 559
18: 1 And the Lord spake unto Moses, **s**, 559
19: 1 And the Lord spake unto Moses, **s**, 559
20: 1 And the Lord spake unto Moses, **s**, 559
21:16 And the Lord spake unto Moses, **s**, 559
21:17 Speak unto Aaron, **s**, Whosoever *he be* of 559
22: 1 And the Lord spake unto Moses, **s**, 559
22:17 And the Lord spake unto Moses, **s**, 559
22:26 And the Lord spake unto Moses, **s**, 559
23: 1 And the Lord spake unto Moses, **s**, 559
23: 9 And the Lord spake unto Moses, **s**, 559
23:23 And the Lord spake unto Moses, **s**, 559
23:24 **s**, In the seventh month, in the first *day* of 559
23:26 And the Lord spake unto Moses, **s**, 559
23:33 And the Lord spake unto Moses, **s**, 559
23:34 Speak unto the children of Israel, **s**, 559
24: 1 And the Lord spake unto Moses, **s**, 559
24:13 And the Lord spake unto Moses, **s**, 559
24:15 **s**, Whosoever curseth his God shall bear 559
25: 1 Lord spake unto Moses in mount Sinai, **s**, 559
27: 1 And the Lord spake unto Moses, **s**, 559
Nu 1: 1 they were come out of the land of Egypt, **s**, 559
1:48 For the Lord had spoken unto Moses, **s**, 559
2: 1 spake unto Moses and unto Aaron, **s**, 559
3: 5 And the Lord spake unto Moses, **s**, 559
3:11 And the Lord spake unto Moses, **s**, 559
3:14 unto Moses in the wilderness of Sinai, **s**, 559
3:44 And the Lord spake unto Moses, **s**, 559
4: 1 spake unto Moses and unto Aaron, **s**, 559
4:17 spake unto Moses and unto Aaron, **s**, 559
4:21 And the Lord spake unto Moses, **s**, 559
5: 1 And the Lord spake unto Moses, **s**, 559
5: 5 And the Lord spake unto Moses, **s**, 559
5:11 And the Lord spake unto Moses, **s**, 559
6: 1 And the Lord spake unto Moses, **s**, 559
6:22 And the Lord spake unto Moses, **s**, 559

Nu 6:23 Speak unto Aaron and unto his sons, **s**, 559
6:23 bless the children of Israel, **s** unto them, 559
7: 4 And the Lord spake unto Moses, **s**, 559
8: 1 And the Lord spake unto Moses, **s**, 559
8: 5 And the Lord spake unto Moses, **s**, 559
8:23 And the Lord spake unto Moses, **s**, 559
9: 1 they were come out of the land of Egypt, **s**, 559
9: 9 And the Lord spake unto Moses, **s**, 559
9:10 **s**, If any man of you or of your posterity 559
10: 1 And the Lord spake unto Moses, **s**, 559
11:13 unto me, **s**, Give us flesh, that we may eat. 559
11:18 **s**, Who shall give us flesh to eat? 559
11:20 wept before him, **s**, Why came we forth 559
12:13 **s**, Heal her now, O God, I beseech thee. 559
13: 1 And the Lord spake unto Moses, **s**, 559
13:32 **s**, The land, through which we have gone 559
14: 7 **s**, The land, which we passed through to 559
14:15 have heard the fame of thee will speak, **s**, 559
14:17 be great, according as thou hast spoken, **s**, 559
14:26 spake unto Moses and unto Aaron, **s**, 559
14:40 **s**, Lo, we *be here*, and will go up unto 559
15: 1 And the Lord spake unto Moses, **s**, 559
15:17 And the Lord spake unto Moses, **s**, 559
15:37 And the Lord spake unto Moses, **s**, 559
16: 5 unto Korah and unto all his company, **s**, 559
16:20 spake unto Moses and unto Aaron, **s**, 559
16:23 And the Lord spake unto Moses, **s**, 559
16:24 Speak unto the congregation, **s**, Get you 559
16:26 **s**, Depart, I pray you, from the tents of 559
16:36 And the Lord spake unto Moses, **s**, 559
16:41 against Moses and against Aaron, **s**, 559
16:44 And the Lord spake unto Moses, **s**, 559
17: 1 And the Lord spake unto Moses, **s**, 559
17:12 **s**, Behold, we die, we perish, we all perish. 559
18:25 And the Lord spake unto Moses, **s**, 559
19: 1 spake unto Moses and unto Aaron, **s**, 559
19: 2 **s**, Speak unto the children of Israel, that 559
20: 3 the people chode with Moses, and spake, **s** 559
20: 7 And the Lord spake unto Moses, **s**, 559
20:23 by the coast of the land of Edom, **s**, 559
21:21 unto Sihon king of the Amorites, **s**, 559
22: 5 call him, **s**, Behold, there is a people come 559
22:10 king of Moab, hath sent unto me, **s**, NIH
23: 7 **s**, Come, curse me Jacob, and come, NIH
23:26 and said unto Balak, Told not I thee, **s**, 559
24:12 messengers which thou sentest unto me, **s**, 559
25:10 And the Lord spake unto Moses, **s**, 559
25:16 And the Lord spake unto Moses, **s**, 559
26: 1 unto Eleazar the son of Aaron the priest, **s**, 559
26: 3 plains of Moab by Jordan *near* Jericho, **s**, 559
26:52 And the Lord spake unto Moses, **s**, 559
27: 6 And the Lord spake unto Moses, **s**, 559
27: 8 **s**, If a man die, and have no son, then 559
27:15 And Moses spake unto the Lord, **s**, 559
28: 1 And the Lord spake unto Moses, **s**, 559
30: 1 **s**, This *is* the thing which the Lord hath 559
31: 1 And the Lord spake unto Moses, **s**, 559
31: 3 Moses spake unto the people, **s**, Arm some 559
31:25 And the Lord spake unto Moses, **s**, 559
32: 2 and unto the princes of the congregation, **s**, 559
32:10 kindled the same time, and he sware, **s**, 559
32:25 children of Reuben spake unto Moses, **s**, 559
32:31 and the children of Reuben answered, **s**, 559
33:50 plains of Moab by Jordan *near* Jericho, **s**, 559
34: 1 And the Lord spake unto Moses, **s**, 559
34:13 **s**, This *is* the land which ye shall inherit 559
34:16 And the Lord spake unto Moses, **s**, 559
35: 1 plains of Moab by Jordan *near* Jericho, **s**, 559
35: 9 And the Lord spake unto Moses, **s**, 559
36: 5 **s**, The tribe of the sons of Joseph hath said 559
36: 6 **s**, Let them marry to whom they think 559
Dt 1: 5 Moab, began Moses to declare this law, **s**, 559
1: 6 Ye have dwelt long enough in this 559
1: 9 I spake unto you at that time, **s**, I am not 559
1:16 I charged your judges at that time, **s**, 559
1:23 the **s** pleased me well: and I took twelve 1697
1:28 **s**, The people *is* greater and taller than we; 559
1:34 your words, and was wroth, and sware, **s**, 559
1:37 **s**, Thou also shalt not go in thither. 559
2: 2 And the Lord spake unto me, **s**, 559
2: 4 command thou the people, **s**, Ye are to 559
2:17 That the Lord spake unto me, **s**, 559
2:26 king of Heshbon *with* words of peace, **s**, 559
3:18 I commanded you at that time, **s**, 559
3:21 I commanded Joshua at that time, **s**, 559
3:23 And I besought the Lord at that time, **s**, 559
5: 5 fire, and went not up into the mount;) **s**, 559
6:20 **s**, What *mean* the testimonies, 559
9: 4 hath cast them out from before thee, **s**, 559
9:13 **s**, I have seen this people, and, behold, it *is* 559
9:23 **s**, Go up and possess the land which I have 559
12:30 that thou inquire not after their gods, **s**, 559
13: 2 **s**, Let us go after other gods, which thou 559
13: 6 **s**, Let us go and serve other gods, 559
13:12 thy God hath given thee to dwell there, **s**, 559
13:13 **s**, Let us go *and* serve other gods, which *ye* 559
15: 9 **s**, The seventh year, the year of release, is 559
15:11 therefore I command thee, **s**, Thou shalt 559
18:16 **s**, Let me not hear again the voice of 559
19: 7 Wherefore I command thee, **s**, Thou shalt 559
20: 5 the officers shall speak unto the people, **s**, 559
22:17 given occasions of speech *against her*, **s**, 559
27: 1 elders of Israel commanded the people, **s**, 559
27: 9 **s**, Take heed, and hearken, O Israel; 559

Dt 27:11 Moses charged the people the same day, **s,** 559
29:19 himself in his heart, **s,** I shall have peace, 559
31:10 Moses commanded them, **s,** At the end of 559
31:25 the ark of the covenant of the LORD, **s,** 559
32:48 spake unto Moses that selfsame day, **s,** 559
34: 4 unto Isaac, and unto Jacob, **s,** I will give it 559

Jos 1: 1 Joshua the son of Nun, Moses' minister, **s,** 559
1:10 commanded the officers of the people, **s,** 559
1:11 the people, Prepare you victuals; 559
1:12 half the tribe of Manasseh, spake Joshua, **s,** 559
1:13 **s,** The LORD your God hath given you 559
1:16 they answered Joshua, **s,** All that thou 559
2: 1 **s,** Go view the land, even Jericho. 559
2: 2 it was told the king of Jericho, **s,** Behold, 559
2: 3 the king of Jericho sent unto Rahab, **s,** 559
3: 3 they commanded the people, When ye 559
3: 6 **s,** Take up the ark of the covenant, 559
3: 8 **s,** When ye are come to the brink of 559
4: 1 that the LORD spake unto Joshua, **s,** 559
4: 3 command you them, **s,** Take you hence 559
4: 6 come, **s,** What mean you by these stones? 559
4:15 And the LORD spake unto Joshua, **s,** 559
4:17 Joshua therefore commanded the priests, **s,** 559
4:21 he spake unto the children of Israel, **s,** 559
4:21 time to come, **s,** What *mean* these stones? 559
4:22 ye shall let your children know, **s,** 559
6:10 **s,** Ye shall not shout, nor make any noise 559
6:26 Joshua adjured *them* at that time, **s,** 559
7: 2 unto them, **s,** Go up and view the country. 559
8: 4 commanded them, **s,** Behold, ye shall lie 559
9:11 **s,** Take victuals with you for the journey, 559
9:22 for them, and he spake unto them, **s,** 559
9:22 beguiled us, **s,** We *are* very far from you; 559
10: 3 Lachish, and unto Debir king of Eglon, **s,** 559
10: 6 **s,** Slack not thy hand from thy servants; 559
10:17 it was told Joshua, **s,** The five kings are 559
14: 9 Moses sware on that day, **s,** Surely the land 559
17: 4 the son of Nun, and before the princes, **s,** 559
17:14 Why hast thou given me *but* one lot and 559
17:17 *even* to Ephraim and to Manasseh, **s,** 559
18: 8 **s,** Go and walk through the land, 559
20: 1 The LORD also spake unto Joshua, **s,** 559
20: 2 Speak to the children of Israel, **s,** 559
21: 2 them at Shiloh in the land of Canaan, **s,** 559
22: 8 he spake unto them, **s,** Return with much 559
22:15 of Gilead, and they spake with them, **s,** 559
22:24 not *rather* done it for fear of *this* thing, **s,** 559
22:24 **s,** What have you to do with the LORD 559

Jdg 1: 1 the children of Israel asked the LORD, **s,** 559
4: 6 **s,** Go and draw toward mount Tabor, NIH
5: 1 Barak the son of Abinoam on that day, **s,** 559
6:13 **s,** Did not the LORD bring us up from 559
6:32 **s,** Let Baal plead against him, because 559
7: 2 **s,** Mine own hand hath saved me. 559
7: 3 **s,** Whosoever *is* fearful and afraid, let him 559
7:24 **s,** Come down against the Midianites, 559
8: 9 **s,** When I come again in peace, I will break 559
8:15 **s,** *Are* the hands of Zebah and 559
9: 1 of the house of his mother's father, **s,** 559
9:31 **s,** Behold, Gaal the son of Ebed and 559
10:10 **s,** We have sinned against thee, both 559
11:12 **s,** What hast thou to do with me, that thou 559
11:17 **s,** Let me, I pray thee, pass through thy 559
13: 6 the woman came and told her husband, **s,** 559
15:13 they spake unto him, **s,** No; but we will 559
16: 2 *told* the Gazites, **s,** Samson is come hither. 559
16: 2 **s,** In the morning, when it is day, we shall 559
16:18 **s,** Come up *this* once, for he hath shewed 559
19:22 to the master of the house, the old man, **s,** 559
20: 8 **s,** We will not any *of us* go to his tent, 559
20:12 **s,** What wickedness *is* this that is done 559
20:23 and asked *counsel* of the LORD, **s,** 559
20:28 **s,** Shall I yet again go out to battle against 559
21: 1 the men of Israel had sworn in Mizpeh, **s,** 559
21: 5 Mizpeh, **s,** He shall surely be put to death. 559
21:10 **s,** Go and smite the inhabitants of 559
21:18 for the children of Israel have sworn, **s,** 559
21:20 **s,** Go and lie in wait in the vineyards; 559

Ru 2:15 Boaz commanded his young men, **s,** 559
4: 4 **s,** Buy *it* before the inhabitants, 559
4:17 it a name, **s,** There is a son born to Naomi; 559

1Sa 1:20 **s,** Because I have asked him of the LORD. NIH
4:21 **s,** The glory is departed from Israel: 559
5:10 *to* Ekron, that the Ekronites cried out, **s,** 559
6: 2 called for the priests and the diviners, **s,** 559
6:21 **s,** The Philistines have brought again the 559
7: 3 spake unto all the house of Israel, **s,** 559
7:12 and called the name of it Eben-ezer, **s,** 559
9:15 in his ear a day before Saul came, **s,** 559
9:26 house, **s,** Up, that I may send thee away. 559
10: 2 sorroweth for you, **s,** What shall I do for 559
11: 7 **s,** Whosoever cometh not forth after Saul 559
13: 3 all the land, **s,** Let the Hebrews hear. 559
14:24 Saul had adjured the people, **s,** Cursed *be* 559
14:28 **s,** Cursed *be* the man that eateth *any* food 559
14:33 they told Saul, **s,** Behold, the people sin 559
15:10 the word of the LORD unto Samuel, **s,** 559
15:12 was told Samuel, **s,** Saul came to Carmel, 559
16:22 **s,** Let David, I pray thee, stand before me; 559
17:26 spake to the men that stood by him, **s,** 559
17:27 **s,** So shall it be done to the man that 559
18: 8 was very wroth, and the **s** displeased him; 1697
18:22 **s,** Commune with David secretly, and say, NIH
18:24 told him, **s,** On this manner spake David. 559
19: 2 Jonathan told David, **s,** Saul my father 559

1Sa 19:11 Michal David's wife told him, **s,** If thou 559
19:15 **s,** Bring him up to me in the bed, that I 559
19:19 it was told Saul, **s,** Behold, David *is* at 559
20:16 **s,** Let the LORD even require *it* at NIH
20:21 behold, I will send a lad, **s,** Go, find out NIH
20:42 **s,** The LORD be between me and thee, 559
21:11 **s,** Saul hath slain his thousands, 559
23: 1 they told David, **s,** Behold, the Philistines 559
23: 2 **s,** Shall I go and smite these Philistines? 559
23:19 came up the Ziphites to Saul to Gibeah, **s,** 559
23:27 unto Saul, **s,** Haste thee, and come; 559
24: 1 that it was told him, **s,** Behold, David *is* in 559
24: 8 and cried after Saul, **s,** My lord the king. 559
24: 9 **s,** Behold, David seeketh thy hurt? 559
25:14 men told Abigail, Nabal's wife, **s,** David 559
25:40 they spake unto her, **s,** David sent us unto 559
26: 1 the Ziphites came unto Saul to Gibeah, **s,** 559
26: 6 the son of Zeruiah, brother to Joab, **s,** 559
26:14 son of Ner, **s,** Answerest thou not, Abner? 559
26:19 of the LORD, **s,** Go, serve other gods. 559
27:11 bring *tidings to* Gath, **s,** Lest they should 559
27:11 **s,** So did David, and so *will be* his manner 559
27:12 Achish believed David, **s,** He hath made 559
28:10 her by the LORD, **s,** *As* the LORD liveth, 559
28:12 the woman spake to Saul, **s,** Why hast thou 559
29: 5 **s,** Saul slew his thousands, and David his 559
30: 8 **s,** Shall I pursue after this troop? 559
30:26 the elders of Judah, *even* to his friends, **s,** 559

2Sa 1:16 **s,** I have slain the LORD'S anointed. 559
2: 1 that David inquired of the LORD, **s,** 559
2: 4 they told David, **s,** *That* the men of 559
3:12 David on his behalf, **s,** Whose *is* the land? 559
3:12 *also,* Make thy league with me, 559
3:14 Saul's son, **s,** Deliver *me* my wife Michal, 559
3:17 **s,** Ye sought for David in times past to be 559
3:18 *it:* for the LORD hath spoken of David, **s,** 559
3:23 told Joab, **s,** Abner the son of Ner came 559
3:35 David sware, **s,** So do God to me, and 559
4:10 When one told me, **s,** Behold, Saul is dead, 559
5: 1 spake, **s,** Behold, we *are* thy bone and 559
5: 6 spake unto David, **s,** Except thou take 559
5:19 **s,** Shall I go up to the Philistines? 559
6:12 it was told king David, **s,** The LORD hath 559
7: 4 word of the LORD came unto Nathan, **s,** 559
7: 7 **s,** Why build ye not me a house of cedar? 559
7:26 let thy name be magnified for ever, **s,** 559
7:27 to thy servant, **s,** I will build thee a house: 559
11: 6 sent to Joab, **s,** Send me Uriah the Hittite. NIH
11:10 when they had told David, **s,** Uriah went 559
11:15 he wrote in the letter, **s,** Set ye Uriah in 559
11:19 charged the messenger, **s,** When thou hast 559
13: 7 David sent home to Tamar, **s,** Go now *to* 559
13:28 Absalom had commanded his servants, **s,** 559
13:30 in the way, that tidings came to David, **s,** 559
14:32 Behold, I sent unto thee, **s,** Come hither, 559
15: 8 **s,** If the LORD shall bring me again indeed 559
15:10 **s,** As soon as ye hear the sound of 559
15:13 there came a messenger to David, **s,** 559
15:31 *one* told David, **s,** Ahithophel *is* among 559
17: 4 the **s** pleased Absalom well, and all 1697
17: 6 to Absalom, Absalom spake unto him, **s,** 559
17: 6 shall we do *after* his **s?** if not; speak thou. 1697
17:16 therefore send quickly, and tell David, **s,** 559
18: 5 commanded Joab and Abishai and Ittai, **s,** 559
18:12 king charged thee and Abishai and Ittai, **s,** 559
19: 8 **s,** Behold, the king doth sit in the gate. 559
19: 9 **s,** The king saved us out of the hand of our 559
19:11 to Zadok and to Abiathar the priests, **s,** 559
19:11 Speak unto the elders of Judah, **s,** 559
20:18 she spake, **s,** They were wont to speak in 559
20:18 They were wont to speak in old time, **s,** 559
21:17 the men of David sware unto him, **s,** 559
24:11 unto the prophet Gad, David's seer, **s,** 559
24:19 David, according to the **s** of Gad, went up 1697

1Ki 1: 5 Adonijah exalted himself, **s,** I will be king: 559
1: 6 had not displeased him at any time in **s,** 559
1:11 **s,** Hast thou not heard that Adonijah the 559
1:13 O king, swear unto thine handmaid, **s,** 559
1:17 **s,** Assuredly Solomon thy son shall reign NIH
1:23 they told the king, **s,** Behold Nathan 559
1:30 **s,** Assuredly Solomon thy son shall reign 559
1:47 **s,** God make the name of Solomon better 559
1:51 it was told Solomon, **s,** Behold, 559
1:51 caught hold on the horns of the altar, **s,** 559
2: 1 and he charged Solomon his son, **s,** 559
2: 4 **s,** If thy children take heed to their way, 559
2: 8 and I sware to him by the LORD, **s,** 559
2:23 **s,** God do so to me, and more also, 559
2:29 the son of Jehoiada, **s,** Go, fall upon him. 559
2:30 **s,** Thus said Joab, and thus he answered 559
2:38 Shimei said unto the king, The **s** *is* good: 1697
2:39 they told Shimei, **s,** Behold, thy servants 559
2:42 protested unto thee, **s,** Know for a certain, 559
5: 2 And Solomon sent to Hiram, **s,** 559
5: 5 spake unto David my father, **s,** Thy son, 559
5: 8 Hiram sent to Solomon, **s,** I have 559
6:11 the word of the LORD came to Solomon, **s,** 559
8:15 and hath with his hand fulfilled *it,* **s,** 559
8:25 my father that thou promisedst him, **s,** 559
8:47 **s,** We have sinned, and have done 559
8:55 congregation of Israel *with* a loud voice, **s,** 559
9: 5 as I promised to David thy father, **s,** 559
12: 3 Israel came, and spake unto Rehoboam, **s,** 559
12: 7 they spake unto him, **s,** If thou wilt be a 559
12: 9 this people, who have spoken to me, **s,** 559

1Ki 12:10 **s,** Thus shalt thou speak unto this people 559
12:10 **s,** Thy father made our yoke heavy, 559
12:12 as the king had appointed, **s,** Come to me 559
12:14 **s,** My father made your yoke heavy, 559
12:15 the LORD, that *he* might perform his **s,** 1697
12:16 the people answered the king, **s,** 559
12:22 came unto Shemaiah the man of God, **s,** 559
12:23 and *to* the remnant of the people, **s,** 559
13: 3 he gave a sign the same day, **s,** This *is* 559
13: 4 king Jeroboam heard the **s** of the man 1697
13: 4 hand from the altar, **s,** Lay hold on him. 559
13: 9 the LORD, **s,** Eat no bread, nor drink water, 559
13:18 **s,** Bring him back with thee into thine 559
13:21 came from Judah, **s,** Thus saith the LORD, 559
13:27 he spake to his sons, **s,** Saddle me the ass. 559
13:30 mourned over him, **s,** Alas, my brother. NIH
13:31 **s,** When I am dead, then bury me in 559
13:32 For the **s** which he cried by the word of 1697
15:18 king of Syria, that dwelt at Damascus, **s,** 1697
15:29 according unto the **s** of the LORD, 1697
16: 1 Jehu the son of Hanani against Baasha, **s,** 559
17: 2 the word of the LORD came unto him, **s,** 559
17: 8 the word of the LORD came unto him, **s,** 559
17:15 and did according to the **s** of Elijah: 1697
18: 1 third year, **s,** Go, shew thyself unto Ahab; 559
18:26 even until noon, **s,** O Baal, hear us. 559
18:31 LORD came, **s,** Israel shall be thy name: 559
19: 2 So let the gods do *to* me, and more also, 559
20: 4 said, My lord, O king, according to thy **s,** 1697
20: 5 said, Thus speaketh Ben-hadad, **s,** 559
20: 5 Although I have sent unto thee, **s,** 559
20:13 **s,** Thus saith the LORD, Hast thou seen all 559
20:17 Ben-hadad sent out, and they told him, **s,** 559
21: 2 unto Naboth, **s,** Give me thy vineyard, 559
21: 9 **s,** Proclaim a fast, and set Naboth on high 559
21:10 **s,** Thou didst blaspheme God and the king. 559
21:13 Naboth did blaspheme God and the king. 559
21:14 to Jezebel, **s,** Naboth is stoned, and is dead. 559
21:17 of the LORD came to Elijah the Tishbite, **s,** 559
21:19 **s,** Thus saith the LORD, Hast thou killed, 559
21:19 speak unto him, **s,** Thus saith the LORD, 559
21:23 of Jezebel also spake the LORD, **s,** 559
21:28 of the LORD came to Elijah the Tishbite, **s,** 559
22:12 **s,** Go up *to* Ramoth-gilead, and prosper: 559
22:13 Micaiah spake unto him, **s,** Behold now, 559
22:31 **s,** Fight neither with small nor great, 559
22:36 **s,** Every man to his city, and every man to 559

2Ki 2:22 according to the **s** of Elisha which he 1697
3: 7 sent to Jehoshaphat the king of Judah, **s,** 559
4: 1 **s,** Thy servant my husband is dead; 559
4:31 and told him, **s,** The child is not awaked. 559
5: 4 **s,** Thus and thus said the maid that *is* of 559
5: 6 **s,** Now when this letter is come unto thee, 559
5: 8 that he sent to the king, **s,** Wherefore hast 559
5:10 **s,** Go and wash in Jordan seven times, 559
5:14 according to the **s** of the man of God: 1697
5:22 My master hath sent me, **s,** Behold, 559
6: 8 **s,** In such and such a place *shall be* my 559
6: 9 **s,** Beware that *thou* pass not such a place; 559
6:13 it was told him, **s,** Behold, *he is* in Dothan. 559
6:26 a woman unto him, **s,** Help, my lord, 559
7:10 they told them, **s,** We came to the camp 559
7:12 **s,** When they come out of the city, we 559
7:14 after the host of the Syrians, **s,** Go and see. 559
7:18 **s,** Two measures of barley for a shekel, 559
8: 1 **s,** Arise, and go thou and thine household, 559
8: 2 and did after the **s** of the man of God: 1697
8: 4 **s,** Tell me, I pray thee, all the great *things* 559
8: 6 **s,** Restore all that *was* hers, and all the 559
8: 7 it was told him, **s,** The man of God is come 559
8: 8 of God, and inquire of the LORD by him, **s,** 559
8: 9 to thee, **s,** Shall I recover of this disease? 559
9:12 he said, Thus and thus spake he to me, **s,** 559
9:13 and blew with trumpets, **s,** Jehu is king. 559
9:18 the watchman told, **s,** The messenger came 559
9:20 the watchman told, **s,** He came even unto 559
9:36 spake by his servant Elijah the Tishbite, **s,** 559
10: 1 them that brought up Ahab's *children,* **s,** 559
10: 5 **s,** We *are* thy servants, and will do all that 559
10: 6 **s,** If ye *be* mine, and *if* ye will hearken 559
10: 8 there came a messenger, and told him, **s,** 559
10:17 according to the **s** of the LORD, which he 1697
11: 5 he commanded them, **s,** This *is* the thing 559
14: 6 where *in* the LORD commanded, **s,** 559
14: 8 son of Jehu, king of Israel, **s,** Come, 559
14: 9 of Israel sent to Amaziah king of Judah, **s,** 559
14: 9 **s,** Give thy daughter to my son to wife: 559
15:12 of the LORD which he spake unto Jehu, **s,** 559
16: 7 of Assyria, **s,** I *am* thy servant and thy son: 559
16:15 king Ahaz commanded Urijah the priest, **s,** 559
17:13 by all the prophets, *and by* all the seers, **s,** 559
17:26 **s,** The nations which thou hast removed, 559
17:27 the king of Assyria commanded, **s,** 559
17:35 charged them, **s,** Ye shall not fear other 559
18:14 of Assyria to Lachish, **s,** I have offended; 559
18:28 spake, **s,** Hear the word of the great king, 559
18:30 **s,** The LORD will surely deliver us, 559
18:32 Hezekiah, when he persuadeth you, **s,** 559
18:36 commandment was, **s,** Answer him not. 559
19: 7 sent messengers again unto Hezekiah, **s,** 559
19:10 ye speak to Hezekiah king of Judah, **s,** 559
19:10 in whom thou trustest deceive thee, **s,** 559
19:20 **s,** Thus saith the LORD God of Israel, 559
20: 2 to the wall, and prayed unto the LORD, **s,** 559
20: 4 that the word of the LORD came to him, **s,** 559

S

2Ki
21:10 spake by his servants the prophets, s, 559
22: 3 the scribe, *to* the house of the Lord, s, 559
22:10 Shaphan the scribe shewed the king, s, 559
22:12 and Asahiah a servant of the king's, s, 559
23:21 the king commanded all the people, s, 559

1Ch
4: 9 s, Because I bare *him* with sorrow. 559
4:10 Jabez called on the God of Israel, s, 559
11: 1 s, Behold, we *are* thy bone and thy flesh. 559
12:19 s, He will fall to his master Saul to 559
13:12 David was afraid of God that day, s, 559
14:10 David inquired of God, s, Shall I go up 559
16:18 S, Unto thee will I give the land of Canaan, 559
16:22 S, Touch not mine anointed, and do my NIH
17: 3 that the word of God came to Nathan, s, 559
17: 6 whom I commanded to feed my people, s, 559
17:24 thy name may be magnified for ever, s, 559
21: 9 the Lord spake unto Gad, David's seer, s, 559
21:10 Go and tell David, s, Thus saith the Lord, 559
21:19 David went up at the s of Gad, which he 1697
22: 8 s, Thou hast shed blood abundantly, 559
22:17 of Israel to help Solomon his son, s, NIH

2Ch
2: 3 s, As thou didst deal with David my father, 559
5:13 and praised the Lord, s, For *he is* good; NIH
6: 4 with his mouth to my father David, s, 559
6:16 s, There shall not fail thee a man in my 559
6:37 s, We have sinned, we have done amiss, 559
7: 3 and praised the Lord, s, For *he is* good; NIH
7:18 s, There shall not fail thee a man *to be* 559
10: 3 all Israel spake and spake to Rehoboam, s, 559
10: 6 s, What counsel give ye *me* to return 559
10: 7 they spake unto him, s, If thou be kind to 559
10: 9 have spoken to me, s, Ease somewhat 559
10:10 s, Thus shalt thou answer the people that 559
10:10 s, Thy father made our yoke heavy, 559
10:12 as the king bade, s, Come again to me on 559
10:14 s, My father made your yoke heavy, 559
10:16 the people answered the king, s, 559
11: 2 came to Shemaiah the man of God, s, 559
11: 3 and to all Israel in Judah and Benjamin, s, 559
12: 5 s, They have humbled themselves; 559
16: 2 king of Syria, that dwelt at Damascus, s, 559
18:11 s, Go up *to* Ramoth-gilead, and prosper: 559
18:12 went to call Micaiah spake to him, s, 559
18:19 one spake s after this manner, 559
18:19 manner, and another s after that manner. 559
18:30 s, Fight ye not with small or great, save 559
19: 9 he charged them, s, Thus shall ye do in 559
20: 2 there came *some* that told Jehoshaphat, s, 559
20: 8 thee a sanctuary therein for thy name, s, 559
20:37 s, Because thou hast joined thyself with 559
21:12 s, Thus saith the Lord God of David thy 559
25: 4 where the Lord commanded, s, 559
25: 7 came a man of God to him, s, O king, 559
25:17 the son of Jehu, king of Israel, s, Come, 559
25:18 of Israel sent to Amaziah king of Judah, s, 559
25:18 S, Give thy daughter to my son to wife: 559
30: 6 of the king, s, Ye children of Israel, 559
30:18 Hezekiah prayed for them, s, The good 559
32: 4 s, Why should the kings of Assyria come, 559
32: 6 the city, and spake comfortably to them, s, 559
32: 9 unto all Judah that *were* at Jerusalem, s, 559
32:11 to die by famine and by thirst, s, 559
32:12 commanded Judah and Jerusalem, s, 559
32:17 God of Israel, and to speak against him, s, 559
34:16 brought the king word back again, s, All 559
34:18 Shaphan the scribe told the king, s, 559
34:20 and Asaiah a servant of the king's, s, 559
35:21 s, What have I to do with thee, thou king 559
36:22 his kingdom, and *put it* also in writing, s, 559

Ezr
1: 1 his kingdom, and *put it* also in writing, s, 559
5:11 thus they returned us answer, s, We are 560
8:22 because we had spoken unto the king, s, 559
9: 1 s, The people of Israel, and the priests, 559
9:11 s, The land, *unto* which ye go to possess it, 559

Ne
1: 8 s, *If* ye transgress, I will scatter you abroad 559
6: 2 and Geshem sent unto me, s, Come, 559
6: 3 s, I *am* doing a great work, so that I cannot 559
6: 7 at Jerusalem, s, *There is* a king in Judah: 559
6: 8 I sent unto him, s, There are no such 559
6: 9 For they all made us afraid, s, Their hands 559
8:11 s, Hold your peace, for the day *is* holy; 559
8:15 in Jerusalem, s, Go forth *unto* the mount, 559
13:25 s, Ye shall not give your daughters unto NIH

Est
1:21 the s pleased the king and the princes; 1697

Job
4:16 *there was* silence, and I heard a voice, s, NIH
8:18 *it* shall deny him, s, I have not seen thee. NIH
15:23 s, Where *is it?* he knoweth that the day of NIH
24:15 for the twilight, s, No eye shall see me: NIH
33: 8 I have heard the voice of *thy* words, s, NIH

Ps
2: 2 the Lord, and against his anointed, s, NIH
22: 7 shoot out the lip, they shake the head, s, 2420
49: 4 I will open my **dark** s upon the harp. 2420
71:11 S, God hath forsaken him: persecute and 559
105:11 S, Unto thee will I give the land of Canaan 559
105:15 S, Touch not mine anointed, and do my NIH
119:82 Mine eyes fail for thy word, s, When wilt 559
137: 3 s, Sing us *one* of the songs of Zion. NIH

Pr
1:21 in the city she uttereth her words, s, NIH

Ecc
1:16 s, Lo, I am come to great estate, 559

SS
5: 2 my beloved that knocketh, s, Open to me, NIH

Isa
3: 6 s, Thou hast clothing, be thou our ruler, NIH
3: 7 shall he swear, s, I will not be a healer; 559
4: 1 s, We will eat our own bread, and wear 559
6: 8 s, Whom shall I send, and who will go for 559
7: 2 s, Syria is confederate with Ephraim. 559

Isa
7: 5 have taken evil counsel against thee, s, 559
7:10 the Lord spake again unto Ahaz, s, 559
8: 5 The Lord spake also unto me again, s, 559
8:11 not walk in the way of this people, s, 559
14: 8 of Lebanon, s, Since thou art laid down, NIH
14:16 s, *Is* this the man that made the earth to NIH
14:24 s, Surely as I have thought, so shall it 559
16:14 s, Within three years, as the years of a 559
18: 2 s, Go, ye swift messengers, to a nation NIH
19:25 s, Blessed *be* Egypt my people, 559
20: 2 s, Go and loose the sackcloth from off thy 559
23: 4 s, I travail not, nor bring forth children, 559
29:11 that is learned, s, Read this, I pray thee: 559
29:12 that is not learned, Read this, I pray thee: 559
30:21 s, This *is* the way, walk ye in it, when ye 559
36:15 s, The Lord will surely deliver us: 559
36:18 persuade you, s, The Lord will deliver us. 559
36:21 commandment was, s, Answer him not. 559
37: 9 he sent messengers to Hezekiah, s, 559
37:10 s, Let not thy God, in whom thou trustest, 559
37:10 in whom thou trustest, deceive thee, s, 559
37:15 And Hezekiah prayed unto the Lord, s, 559
37:21 s, Thus saith the Lord God of Israel, 559
38: 4 came the word of the Lord to Isaiah, s, 559
41: 7 the anvil, s, It *is* ready for the sodering: 559
41:13 hold thy right hand, s unto thee, Fear not; 559
44:28 even s to Jerusalem, Thou shalt be built; 559
45:14 unto thee, s, Surely God *is* in thee; NIH
46:10 s, My counsel shall stand, and I will do all 559
56: 3 hath joined himself to the Lord, speak, s, 559
63:11 s, Where *is* he that brought them up out NIH

Jer
1: 4 the word of the Lord came unto me, s, 559
1:11 unto me, s, Jeremiah, what seest thou? 559
1:13 me the second time, s, What seest thou? 559
2: 1 the word of the Lord came to me, s, 559
2: 2 ears of Jerusalem, s, Thus saith the Lord; 559
2:27 S to a stock, Thou *art* my father; and to a 559
4:10 deceived this people and Jerusalem, s, 559
4:31 spreadeth her hands, s, Woe *is* me now! NIH
5:20 house of Jacob, and publish it in Judah, s, 559
6:14 of my people slightly, s, Peace, peace; 559
6:17 s, Hearken to the sound of the trumpet. NIH
7: 1 that came to Jeremiah from the Lord, s, 559
7: 4 s, The temple of the Lord, The temple of 559
7:23 s, Obey my voice, and I will be your God, 559
8: 6 of his wickedness, s, What have I done? 559
8:11 of my people slightly, s, Peace, peace; 559
11: 1 that came to Jeremiah from the Lord, s, 559
11: 4 furnace, s, Obey my voice, and do them, 559
11: 6 in the streets of Jerusalem, s, Hear ye 559
11: 7 rising early and protesting, s, Obey my 559
11:19 s, Let us destroy the tree with the fruit NIH
11:21 that seek thy life, s, Prophesy not in 559
13: 3 Came unto me the second time, s, 559
13: 8 the word of the Lord came unto me, s, 559
16: 1 word of the Lord came also unto me, s, 559
18: 1 which came to Jeremiah from the Lord, s, 559
18: 5 Then the word of the Lord came to me, s, 559
18:11 of Jerusalem, s, Thus saith the Lord; 559
20:10 s, Peradventure he will be enticed, NIH
20:15 father, s, A man child is born unto thee; 559
21: 1 the son of Maaseiah the priest, s, 559
22:18 not lament for him, s, Ah my brother! NIH
22:18 they shall not lament for him, s, Ah lord! NIH
23:25 s, I have dreamed, I have dreamed. 559
23:33 the prophet, or a priest, shall ask thee, s, 559
23:38 I have sent unto you, s, Ye shall not say, 559
24: 4 the word of the Lord came unto me, s, 559
25: 2 and to all the inhabitants of Jerusalem, s, 559
26: 1 of Judah came this word from the Lord, s, 559
26: 8 people took him, s, Thou shalt surely die. 559
26: 9 s, This house shall be like Shiloh, and this 559
26:11 unto the princes and to all the people, s, 559
26:12 all the princes and to all the people, s, 559
26:17 spake to all the assembly of the people, s, 559
26:18 of Judah, s, Thus saith the Lord of hosts; 559
27: 1 this word unto Jeremiah from the Lord, s, 559
27: 9 your sorcerers, which speak unto you, s, 559
27:12 s, Bring your necks under the yoke of 559
27:14 s, Ye shall not serve the king of Babylon: 559
27:16 to the priests and to all this people, s, 559
27:16 prophets that prophesy unto you, s, 559
28: 1 of the priests and of all the people, s, 559
28: 2 the Lord of hosts, the God of Israel, s, 559
28:11 of all the people, s, Thus saith the Lord; 559
28:12 off the neck of the prophet Jeremiah, s, 559
28:13 Go and tell Hananiah, s, Thus saith 559
29: 3 to Nebuchadnezzar king of Babylon, s, 559
29:22 s, The Lord make thee like Zedekiah and 559
29:24 also speak to Shemaiah the Nehelamite, s, 559
29:25 the Lord of hosts, the God of Israel, s, 559
29:25 the priest, and to all the priests, s, 559
29:28 us in Babylon, s, This *captivity is* long: 559
29:30 the word of the Lord came unto Jeremiah, s, 559
29:31 Send to all them of the captivity, s, 559
30: 1 that came to Jeremiah from the Lord, s, 559
30: 2 Thus speaketh the Lord God of Israel, s, 559
30:17 called thee an Outcast, s, This is Zion, NIH
31: 3 s, Yea, I have loved thee *with* an 559
31:34 every man his brother, s, Know the Lord: 559
32: 3 s, Wherefore dost thou prophesy, and say, 559
32: 6 The word of the Lord came unto me, s, 559
32: 7 s, Buy thee my field that *is* in Anathoth: 559
32:13 And I charged Baruch before them, s, 559
32:16 son of Neriah, I prayed unto the Lord, s, 559

Jer
32:26 the word of the Lord unto Jeremiah, s, 559
33: 1 yet shut up in the court of the prison, s, 559
33:19 word of the Lord came unto Jeremiah, s, 559
33:23 the word of the Lord came to Jeremiah, s, 559
33:24 s, The two families which the Lord hath 559
34: 1 and against all the cities thereof, s, 559
34: 5 and they will lament thee, s, Ah lord! NIH
34:12 came to Jeremiah from the Lord, s, 559
34:13 of Egypt, out of the house of bondmen, s, 559
35: 1 the son of Josiah king of Judah, s, 559
35: 6 s, Ye shall drink no wine, *neither* ye 559
35:12 the word of the Lord unto Jeremiah, s, 559
35:15 rising up early and sending *them,* s, 559
36: 1 came unto Jeremiah from the Lord, s, 559
36: 5 commanded Baruch, s, I *am* shut up; 559
36:14 the son of Cushi, unto Baruch, s, 559
36:17 they asked Baruch, s, Tell us now, 559
36:27 Baruch wrote at the mouth of Jeremiah, s, 559
36:29 Thou hast burnt this roll, s, Why hast thou 559
36:29 saying, Why hast thou written therein, s, 559
37: 3 s, Pray now unto the Lord our God for us. 559
37: 6 of the Lord unto the prophet Jeremiah, s, 559
37: 9 Deceive not yourselves, s, The Chaldeans 559
37:13 took Jeremiah the prophet, s, Thou fallest 559
37:19 s, The king of Babylon shall not come 559
38: 1 Jeremiah had spoken unto all the people, s, 559
38: 8 the king's house, and spake to the king, s, 559
38:10 s, Take from hence thirty men with thee, 559
38:16 s, *As* the Lord liveth, that made us this 559
39:11 Nebuzar-adan the captain of the guard, s, 559
39:15 was shut up in the court of the prison, s, 559
39:16 s, Thus saith the Lord of hosts, the God 559
40: 9 sware unto them and to their men, s, 559
40:15 s, Let me go, I pray thee, and I will slay 559
42:14 S, No; but we will go *into* the land of 559
42:20 s, Pray for us unto the Lord our God; 559
43: 2 all the proud men, s unto Jeremiah, 559
43: 8 the Lord unto Jeremiah in Tahpanhes, s, 559
44: 1 at Noph, and in the country of Pathros, s, 559
44: 4 rising early and sending *them,* s, Oh, do 559
44:15 of Egypt, in Pathros, answered Jeremiah, s, 559
44:20 which had given him *that* answer, s, 559
44:25 the Lord of hosts, the God of Israel, s; 559
44:25 mouths, and fulfilled with your hand, s, 559
44:26 the land of Egypt, s, The Lord God liveth. 559
45: 1 the son of Josiah king of Judah, s, 559
48:39 shall howl, s, How is it broken down! NIH
49: 4 her treasures, s, Who shall come unto me? NIH
49:14 s, Gather ye together, and come against NIH
49:34 of the reign of Zedekiah king of Judah, s, NIH
50: 5 s, Come, and let us join ourselves to NIH
51:14 s, Surely I will fill thee *with* men, as *with* NIH

La
2:15 s, *Is* this the city that *men* call The NIH

Eze
3:12 s, Blessed *be* the glory of the Lord from NIH
3:16 the word of the Lord came unto me, s, 559
6: 1 the word of the Lord came unto me, s, 559
7: 1 the word of the Lord came unto me, s, 559
9: 1 also in mine ears *with* a loud voice, s, 559
9:11 inkhorn by his side, reported the matter, s, 559
10: 6 s, Take fire from between the wheels, 559
11:14 the word of the Lord came unto me, s, 559
12: 1 word of the Lord also came unto me, s, 559
12: 8 came the word of the Lord unto me, s, 559
12:17 the word of the Lord came to me, s, 559
12:21 the word of the Lord came unto me, s, 559
12:22 s, The days are prolonged, and every vision 559
12:26 the word of the Lord came to me, s, 559
13: 1 the word of the Lord came unto me, s, 559
13: 6 have seen vanity and lying divination, s, 559
13:10 they have seduced my people, s, Peace; 559
14:12 word of the Lord came again to me, s, 559
15: 1 the word of the Lord came unto me, s, 559
16: 1 the word of the Lord came unto me, s, 559
16:44 s, As *is* the mother, *so is* her daughter. 559
17: 1 the word of the Lord came unto me, s, 559
17:11 the word of the Lord came unto me again, s, 559
18: 1 word of the Lord came unto me again, s, 559
18: 2 s, The fathers have eaten sour grapes, 559
20: 2 came the word of the Lord unto me, s, 559
20: 5 unto them, s, I *am* the Lord your God; 559
20:45 the word of the Lord came unto me, s, 559
21: 1 the word of the Lord came unto me, s, 559
21: 8 the word of the Lord came unto me, s, 559
21:18 word of the Lord came unto me again, s, 559
22: 1 word of the Lord came unto me, s, 559
22:17 the word of the Lord came unto me, s, 559
22:23 the word of the Lord came unto me, s, 559
22:28 divining lies unto them, s, Thus saith 559
23: 1 word of the Lord came again unto me, s, 559
24: 1 the word of the Lord came unto me, s, 559
24:15 the word of the Lord came unto me, s, 559
24:20 The word of the Lord came unto me, s, 559
25: 1 word of the Lord came again unto me, s, 559
26: 1 the word of the Lord came unto me, s, 559
27:32 over thee, s, What *city is* like Tyrus, NIH
28: 1 word of the Lord came again unto me, s, 559
28:11 the word of the Lord came unto me, s, 559
28:20 the word of the Lord came unto me, s, 559
29: 1 the word of the Lord came unto me, s, 559
29:17 the word of the Lord came unto me, s, 559
30: 1 word of the Lord came again unto me, s, 559
30:20 the word of the Lord came unto me, s, 559
31: 1 the word of the Lord came unto me, s, 559

S

Eze	32: 1 the word of the LORD came unto me, **s**,	559
	32:17 the word of the LORD came unto me, **s**,	559
	33: 1 the word of the LORD came unto me, **s**,	559
	33:10 Thus ye speak, **s**, If our transgressions and	559
	33:21 came unto me, **s**, The city is smitten.	559
	33:23 the word of the LORD came unto me, **s**,	559
	33:24 **s**, Abraham was one, and he inherited	559
	33:30 **s**, Come, I pray you, and hear what *is*	559
	34: 1 the word of the LORD came unto me, **s**,	559
	35: 1 the word of the LORD came unto me, **s**,	559
	35:12 **s**, They are laid desolate, they are given us	559
	36:16 the word of the LORD came unto me, **s**,	559
	37:15 word of the LORD came again unto me, **s**,	559
	37:18 **s**, Wilt thou not shew us what thou	559
	38: 1 the word of the LORD came unto me, **s**,	559
Da	4: 8 and before him I told the dream, *s*,	NIH
	4:23 **s**, Hew the tree down, and destroy it;	560
	4:31 **s**, O king Nebuchadnezzar, to thee it is	NIH
Am	2:12 commanded the prophets, **s**, Prophesy not.	559
	3: 1 I brought up from the land of Egypt, **s**,	559
	7:10 of Beth-el sent to Jeroboam king of Israel, **s**,	559
	8: 5 **S**, When will the new moon be gone, that	559
Jnh	1: 1 came unto Jonah the son of Amittai, **s**,	559
	3: 1 LORD came unto Jonah the second time, **s**,	559
	3: 7 by the decree of the king and his nobles, **s**,	559
	4: 2 I pray thee, O LORD, *was* not this my **s**,	1697
Mic	2:11 **s**, I will prophesy unto thee of wine and	NIH
Hag	1: 1 the son of Josedech the high priest, **s**,	559
	1: 2 **s**, This people say, The time is not come,	559
	1: 3 of the LORD by Haggai the prophet, **s**,	559
	1:13 **s**, I *am* with you, saith the LORD.	
	2: 1 of the LORD by the prophet Haggai, **s**,	559
	2: 2 and to the residue of the people, **s**,	559
	2:10 of the LORD by Haggai the prophet, **s**,	559
	2:11 Ask now the priests *concerning* the law, **s**,	559
	2:20 four and twentieth *day* of the month, **s**,	559
	2:21 Speak to Zerubbabel, governor of Judah, **s**,	559
Zec	1: 1 Berechiah, the son of Iddo the prophet, **s**,	559
	1: 4 **s**, Thus saith the LORD of hosts;	559
	1: 7 Berechiah, the son of Iddo the prophet, **s**,	559
	1:14 Cry thou, **s**, Thus saith the LORD of hosts:	559
	1:17 Cry yet, **s**, Thus saith the LORD of hosts;	559
	1:21 he spake, **s**, These *are* the horns which	559
	2: 4 unto him, Run, speak to this young man, **s**,	559
	3: 4 spake unto those that stood before him, **s**,	559
	3: 6 of the LORD protested unto Joshua, **s**,	559
	4: 4 with me, **s**, What *are* these, my lord?	559
	4: 6 he answered and spake unto me, **s**, This *is*	559
	4: 6 **s**, Not by might, nor by power, but by my	559
	4: 8 the word of the LORD came unto me, **s**,	559
	6: 8 upon me, and spake unto me, **s**, Behold,	559
	6: 9 the word of the LORD came unto me, **s**,	559
	6:12 speak unto him, **s**, Thus speaketh	559
	6:12 Thus speaketh the LORD of hosts, **s**,	559
	7: 3 the prophets, **s**, Should I weep in the fifth	559
	7: 4 the word of the LORD of hosts unto me, **s**,	559
	7: 5 to the priests, **s**, When ye fasted and	559
	7: 8 word of the LORD came unto Zechariah, **s**,	559
	7: 9 **s**, Execute true judgment, and shew mercy	559
	8: 1 word of the LORD of hosts came *to me,* **s**,	559
	8:18 of the LORD of hosts came unto me, **s**,	559
	8:21 **s**, Let us go speedily to pray before	559
	8:23 him that is a Jew, **s**, We will go with you:	559
Mt	1:20 **s**, Joseph, *thou* son of David, fear not to	3004
	1:22 was spoken of the Lord by the prophet, **s**,	3004
	2: 2 **S**, Where is he that is born King of	3004
	2:13 **s**, Arise, and take the young child and	3004
	2:15 **s**, Out of Egypt have I called my son.	3004
	2:17 was spoken by Jeremie the prophet, **s**,	3004
	2:20 **S**, Arise, and take the young child and	3004
	3: 2 and **s**, Repent ye: for the kingdom of	3004
	3: 3 **s**, The voice of one crying in	3004
	3:14 But John forbad him, **s**, I have need to be	3004
	3:17 **s**, This is my beloved Son, in whom I am	3004
	4:14 was spoken by Esaias the prophet, **s**,	3004
	5: 2 he opened his mouth, and taught them, **s**,	3004
	6:31 take no thought, **s**, What shall we eat?	3004
	8: 2 and worshipped him, **s**, Lord, if thou wilt,	3004
	8: 3 forth *his* hand, and touched him, **s**, I will:	3004
	8: 6 **s**, Lord, my servant lieth at home sick	3004
	8:17 **s**, Himself took our infirmities, and bare	3004
	8:25 to *him,* and awoke him, **s**, Lord, save us:	3004
	8:27 But the men marvelled, **s**, What manner	3004
	8:29 And behold, they cried out, **s**, What have	3004
	8:31 devils besought him, **s**, If thou cast us out,	3004
	9:14 **s**, Why do we and the Pharisees fast oft,	3004
	9:18 a *certain* ruler, and worshipped him, **s**,	3004
	9:27 crying, and **s**, *Thou* Son of David,	3004
	9:29 touched he their eyes, **s**, According to	3004
	9:30 charged them, **s**, See *that* no *man* know	3004
	9:33 **s**, It was never so seen in Israel.	3004
	10: 5 Jesus sent forth, and commanded them, **s**,	3004
	10: 7 And as ye go, preach, **s**, The kingdom of	3004
	11:17 And **s**, We have piped unto you,	3004
	12:10 And they asked him, **s**, Is it lawful to heal	3004
	12:17 was spoken by Esaias the prophet, **s**,	3004
	12:38 and of the Pharisees answered, **s**, Master,	3004
	13: 3 **s**, Behold, a sower went forth to sow;	3004
	13:24 parable put he forth unto them, **s**,	3004
	13:31 parable put he forth unto them, **s**,	3004
	13:35 I will open my mouth in parables;	3004
	13:36 and his disciples came unto him, **s**,	3004
	14:15 *This* is a desert place, and the time is	3004
	14:26 sea, they were troubled, **s**, It is a spirit;	3004
	14:27 spake unto them, **s**, Be of good cheer;	3004

Mt	14:30 to sink, he cried, **s**, Lord, save me.	3004
	14:33 in the ship came and worshipped him, **s**,	3004
	15: 1 Pharisees, which were of Jerusalem, **s**,	3004
	15: 4 **s**, Honour thy father and mother:	3004
	15: 7 well did Esaias prophesy of you, **s**,	3004
	15:12 were offended, after they heard *this* **s**?	3056
	15:22 cried unto him, **s**, Have mercy on me,	3004
	15:23 his disciples came and besought him, **s**,	3004
	15:25 and worshipped him, **s**, Lord, help me.	3004
	16: 7 **s**, *It is* because we have taken no bread.	3004
	16:13 asked his disciples, **s**, Whom do men say	3004
	16:22 rebuke him, **s**, Be it far from thee, Lord:	3004
	17: 9 the mountain, Jesus charged them, **s**,	3004
	17:10 **s**, Why then say the scribes that Elias	3004
	17:14 man, kneeling down to him, and **s**,	3004
	17:25 **s**, What thinkest thou, Simon?	3004
	18: 1 **s**, Who is the greatest in the kingdom of	3004
	18:26 fell down, and worshipped him, **s**, Lord,	3004
	18:28 on him, and took *him* by the throat, **s**,	3004
	18:29 and besought him, **s**, Have patience with	3004
	19: 3 unto him, tempting him, and **s** unto him,	3004
	19:11 unto them, All *men* cannot receive this **s**,	3056
	19:22 But when the young man heard *that* **s**,	3056
	19:25 **s**, Who then can be saved?	3004
	20:12 **S**, These last have wrought *but* one hour,	3004
	20:30 cried out, **s**, Have mercy on us, O Lord,	3004
	20:31 **s**, Have mercy on us, O Lord, *thou* Son of	3004
	21: 2 **S** unto them, Go into the village over	3004
	21: 4 which was spoken by the prophet, **s**,	3004
	21: 9 and that followed, cried, **s**, Hosanna to	3004
	21:10 all the city was moved, **s**, Who is this?	3004
	21:15 and **s**, Hosanna to the Son of David;	3004
	21:20 **s**, How soon is the fig tree withered away!	3004
	21:25 **s**, If we shall say, From heaven;	3004
	21:37 his son, **s**, They will reverence my son.	3004
	22: 4 Again, he sent forth other servants, **s**,	3004
	22:16 Master, we know that thou art true,	3004
	22:24 **s**, Master, Moses said, If a man die,	3004
	22:31 which was spoken unto you by God, **s**,	3004
	22:35 him a question, tempting him, and **s**,	3004
	22:42 **S**, What think ye of Christ? whose son is	3004
	22:43 then doth David in spirit call him Lord, **s**,	3004
	23: 2 **S**, The scribes and the Pharisees sit in	3004
	24: 3 **s**, Tell us, when shall these *things* be?	3004
	24: 5 shall come in my name, **s**, I am Christ;	3004
	25: 9 *Not so;* lest there be not enough for us	3004
	25:11 other virgins, **s**, Lord, Lord, open to us.	3004
	25:20 and brought other five talents, **s**, Lord,	3004
	25:37 **s**, Lord, when saw we thee a hungred,	3004
	25:44 **s**, Lord, when saw we thee a hungred,	3004
	25:45 he answer them, **s**, Verily I say unto you,	3004
	26: 8 **s**, To what purpose *is* this waste?	3004
	26:17 **s** unto him, Where wilt thou *that* we	3004
	26:27 and gave thanks, and gave *it* to them, **s**,	3004
	26:39 on his face, and prayed, **s**, O my Father,	3004
	26:42 second time, and prayed, **s**, O my Father,	3004
	26:44 prayed the third time, **s** the same words.	3004
	26:48 **s**, Whomsoever I shall kiss, *that same* is	3004
	26:65 his clothes, **s**, He hath spoken blasphemy;	3004
	26:68 **s**, Prophesy unto us, *thou* Christ, Who is	3004
	26:69 and a damsel came unto him, **s**, Thou also	3004
	26:70 *them* all, **s**, I know not what thou sayest.	3004
	26:74 and to swear, **s**, I know not the man.	NIG
	27: 4 **S**, I have sinned in that I have betrayed	3004
	27: 9 and, And they took the thirty pieces of silver,	3004
	27:11 and the governor asked him, **s**, Art thou	3004
	27:19 judgment seat, his wife sent unto him, **s**,	3004
	27:23 out the more, **s**, Let him be crucified.	3004
	27:24 washed *his* hands before the multitude, **s**,	3004
	27:29 mocked him, **s**, Hail, King of the Jews!	3004
	27:40 And **s**, *Thou* that destroyest the temple,	3004
	27:46 **s**, ELI, ELI, LAMA SABACHTHANI?	3004
	27:54 that were done, they feared greatly, **s**,	3004
	27:63 **S**, Sir, we remember that that deceiver	3004
	28: 9 behold, Jesus met them, **s**, All hail.	3004
	28:13 Say ye, His disciples came by night,	3004
	28:15 this **s** is commonly reported among	3056
	28:18 And Jesus came and spake unto them, **s**,	3004
Mk	1: 7 And preached, **s**, There cometh one	3004
	1:11 **s**, Thou art my beloved Son, in whom I	NIG
	1:15 And **s**, The time is fulfilled;	3004
	1:24 **S**, Let *us* alone; what have we to do with	3004
	1:25 **s**, Hold thy peace, and come out of him.	3004
	1:27 among themselves, **s**, What *thing* is this?	3004
	1:40 to him, and **s** unto him, If thou wilt,	3004
	2:12 and glorified God, **s**, We never saw *it* on	3004
	3:11 fell down before him, and cried, **s**,	3004
	3:33 **s**, Who is my mother, or my brethren?	3004
	5: 9 And he answered, **s**, My name *is* Legion:	3004
	5:12 **s**, Send us into the swine, that we may	3004
	5:23 And besought him greatly, **s**, My little	3004
	6: 2 many hearing *him* were astonished, **s**,	3004
	6:25 and asked, **s**, I will that thou give me by	3004
	7:29 he said unto her, For this **s** go thy way;	3056
	7:37 **s**, He hath done all *things* well:	3004
	8:15 And he charged them, **s**, Take heed,	3004
	8:16 **s**, *It is* because we have no bread.	3004
	8:26 **s**, Neither go into the town, nor tell *it* to	3004
	8:27 **s** unto them, Whom do men say that I	3004
	8:32 he spake *that* **s** openly. And Peter took	3056
	8:33 he rebuked Peter, **s**, Get thee behind me,	3004
	9: 7 of the cloud, **s**, This is my beloved Son:	3004
	9:10 And they kept *that* **s** with themselves,	3056
	9:11 they asked him, **s**, Why say the scribes	3004
	9:25 **s** unto him, *Thou* dumb and deaf spirit,	3004

Mk	9:32 But they understood not *that* **s**,	4487
	9:38 John answered him, **s**, Master, we saw	3004
	10:22 And he was sad at *that* **s**, and went away	3056
	10:26 **s** among themselves, Who then can be	3004
	10:33 **S**, Behold, we go up to Jerusalem;	NIG
	10:35 of Zebedee, come unto him, **s**, Master,	3004
	10:49 **s** unto him, Be of good comfort, rise;	3004
	11: 9 and they that followed, cried, **s**, Hosanna;	3004
	11:17 And he taught, **s** unto them, Is it not	3004
	11:31 **s**, If we shall say, From heaven;	3004
	12: 6 unto them, **s**, They will reverence my son.	3004
	12:18 is no resurrection; and they asked him, **s**,	3004
	12:26 **s**, I am the God of Abraham, and the God	3004
	13: 6 **s**, I am *Christ;* and shall deceive many.	3004
	14:44 **s**, Whomsoever I shall kiss, *that* same is	3004
	14:57 and bare false witness against him, **s**,	3004
	14:60 and asked Jesus, **s**, Answerest thou	3004
	14:68 But he denied, **s**, I know not, neither	3004
	14:71 **s**, I know not this man of whom ye speak.	NIG
	15: 4 again, **s**, Answerest thou nothing?	3004
	15: 9 But Pilate answered them, **s**, Will ye *that*	3004
	15:29 wagging their heads, and **s**, Ah, *thou* that	3004
	15:34 **s**, ELOI, ELOI, LAMA SABACHTHANI?	3004
	15:36 reed, and gave him to drink, **s**, Let alone;	3004
Lk	1:24 and hid herself five months, **s**,	3004
	1:29 she saw *him*, she was troubled at his **s**,	3056
	1:63 and wrote, **s**, His name is John.	3004
	1:66 **s**, What *manner of* child shall this be!	3004
	1:67 with the Holy Ghost, and prophesied, **s**,	3004
	2:13 of the heavenly host praising God, and **s**,	3004
	2:17 which was told them concerning this	4487
	2:50 And they understood not the **s** which he	4487
	3: 4 **s**, The voice of one crying in	3004
	3:10 asked him, **s**, What shall we do then?	3004
	3:14 of him, **s**, And what shall we do?	3004
	3:16 John answered, **s** unto them all, I indeed	3004
	4: 4 And Jesus answered him, **s**, It is written,	3004
	4:34 **S**, Let *us* alone; what have we to do with	3004
	4:35 **s**, Hold thy peace, and come out of him.	3004
	4:36 among themselves, **s**, What a word *is* this!	3004
	4:41 crying out, and **s**, Thou art Christ the Son	3004
	5: 8 down at Jesus' knees, **s**, Depart from me;	3004
	5:12 and besought him, **s**, Lord, if thou wilt,	3004
	5:13 forth *his* hand, and touched him, **s**, I will:	3004
	5:21 and the Pharisees began to reason, **s**,	3004
	5:26 glorified God, and were filled with fear, **s**,	3004
	5:30 **s**, Why do ye eat and drink with publicans	3004
	7: 4 to Jesus, they besought him instantly, **s**,	3004
	7: 6 **s** unto him, Lord, trouble not thyself:	3004
	7:16 and they glorified God, **s**, That a great	3004
	7:19 to Jesus, **s**, Art thou he that should come?	3004
	7:20 thee, **s**, Art thou he that should come?	3004
	7:32 calling one to another, and **s**, We have	3004
	7:39 **s**, This *man*, if he were a prophet,	3004
	8: 9 asked him, **s**, What might this parable be?	3004
	8:24 awoke him, **s**, Master, master, we perish.	3004
	8:25 one to another, What *manner of man* is	3004
	8:30 Jesus asked him, **s**, What is thy name?	3004
	8:38 be with him: but Jesus sent him away, **s**,	3004
	8:49 ruler of the synagogue's *house*, **s** to him,	3004
	8:50 heard *it*, he answered him, **s**, Fear not:	3004
	8:54 her by the hand, and called, **s**, Maid, arise.	3004
	9:18 he asked them, **s**, Whom say the people	3004
	9:22 **S**, The Son of man must suffer many	3004
	9:35 of the cloud, **s**, This is my beloved Son:	3004
	9:38 **s**, Master, I beseech thee, look upon my	3004
	9:45 But they understood not this **s**, and it was	4487
	9:45 it not: and they feared to ask him of that **s**.	4487
	10:17 seventy returned *again* with joy, **s**, Lord,	3004
	10:25 stood up, and tempted him, **s**, Master,	3004
	11:45 Master, thus **s** thou reproachest us also.	3004
	12:16 And he spake a parable unto them, **s**,	3004
	12:17 **s**, What shall I do, because I have no room	3004
	13:25 at the door, **s**, Lord, Lord, open unto us;	3004
	13:31 **s** unto him, Get *thee* out, and depart	3004
	14: 3 spake unto the lawyers and Pharisees, **s**,	3004
	14: 5 answered them, **s**, Which of you shall	3004
	14: 7 chose out the chief comers; **s** unto them,	3004
	14:30 **S**, This man began to build, and was not	3004
	15: 2 the Pharisees and scribes murmured, **s**,	3004
	15: 3 And he spake this parable unto them, **s**,	3004
	15: 6 his friends and neighbours, **s** unto them,	3004
	15: 9 neighbours together, **s**, Rejoice with me;	3004
	17: 4 in a day turn again to thee, **s**, I repent;	3004
	18: 2 **S**, There was in a city a judge, which	3004
	18: 3 and she came unto him, **s**, Avenge me of	3004
	18:13 heaven, but smote upon his breast, **s**,	3004
	18:18 a certain ruler asked him, **s**, Good Master,	3004
	18:34 *things*: and this **s** was hid from them,	4487
	18:38 And he cried, **s**, Jesus, *thou* Son of David,	3004
	18:41 **s**, What wilt thou *that* I shall do unto	3004
	19: 7 when they saw *it*, they all murmured, **s**,	3004
	19:14 him, and sent a message after him, **s**,	3004
	19:16 came the first, **s**, Lord, thy pound hath	3004
	19:18 And the second came, **s**, Lord, thy pound	3004
	19:20 **s**, Lord, behold, *here is* thy pound,	3004
	19:30 **S**, Go ye into the village over against *you;*	3004
	19:38 Blessed *be* the King that cometh in	3004
	19:42 **S**, If thou hadst known, even thou, at least	3004
	19:46 **S** unto them, It is written, My house is	3004
	20: 2 And spake unto him, **s**, Tell us, by what	3004
	20: 5 **s**, If we shall say, From heaven;	3004
	20:14 among themselves, **s**, This is the heir:	3004
	20:21 And they asked him, **s**, Master, we know	3004
	20:28 **S**, Master, Moses wrote unto us, If any	3004

S

Lk	21: 7 And they asked him, **s**, Master,	3004
	21: 8 **s**, I am *Christ; and the time draweth near:*	3004
	22: 8 John, *and,* Go and prepare us the passover,	3004
	22:19 and brake *it*, and gave unto them, **s**,	3004
	22:20 Likewise also the cup after supper, **s**,	3004
	22:42 **S**, Father, if thou be willing, remove this	3004
	22:57 denied him, **s**, Woman, I know him not.	3004
	22:59 **s**, Of a truth this *fellow* also was with	3004
	22:64 and asked him, **s**, Prophesy, who is it that	3004
	22:66 and led him into their council, **s**,	3004
	23: 2 they began to accuse him, **s**, We found	3004
	23: 2 Cesar, **s** that he himself is Christ a King	3004
	23: 3 Pilate asked him, **s**, Art thou the King	3004
	23: 5 **s**, He stirreth up the people,	3004
	23:18 **s**, Away with this *man*, and release unto	3004
	23:21 they cried, **s**, Crucify *him*, crucify him.	3004
	23:35 the rulers also with them derided *him*, **s**,	3004
	23:37 And **s**, If thou be the King of the Jews,	3004
	23:39 **s**, If thou be Christ, save thyself and us.	3004
	23:40 rebuked him, **s**, Dost not thou fear God,	3004
	23:47 he glorified God, **s**, Certainly this was a	3004
	24: 7 **S**, The Son of man must be delivered into	3004
	24:23 they found not his body, they came, **s**,	3004
	24:29 they constrained him, **s**, Abide with us:	3004
	24:34 **S**, The Lord is risen indeed,	3004
Jn	1:15 John bare witness of him, and cried, **s**,	3004
	1:26 answered them, **s**, I baptize with water:	3004
	1:32 And John bare record, **s**, I saw the Spirit	3004
	4:31 *his* disciples prayed him, **s**, Master, eat.	3004
	4:37 And herein is *that* **s** true, One soweth,	3056
	4:39 believed on him for the **s** of the woman,	3056
	4:42 *Now* we believe, not because of thy **s**:	2981
	4:51 met him, and told *him*, **s**, Thy son liveth.	3004
	6:52 therefore strove amongst themselves, **s**,	3004
	6:60 they had heard *this*, said, This is a hard **s**;	3056
	7:15 And the Jews marvelled, **s**, How knoweth	3004
	7:28 **s**, Ye both know me, and ye know	3004
	7:36 What *manner of* **s** is this that he said,	3056
	7:37 Jesus stood and cried, **s**, If any *man* thirst,	3004
	7:40 they heard *this* **s**, said, Of a truth this	3056
	8:12 unto them, **s**, I am the light of the world:	3004
	8:51 verily, I say unto you, If a man keep my **s**,	3056
	8:52 and thou sayest, If a man keep my **s**,	3056
	8:55 unto you: but I know him, and keep his **s**.	3056
	9: 2 asked him, **s**, Master, who did sin, this *man*, or	3004
	9:19 And they asked them, **s**, Is this your son,	3004
	10:33 The Jews answered him, **s**, For a good	3004
	11: 3 **s**, Lord, behold, he whom thou lovest is	3004
	11:28 **s**, The Master is come, and calleth for	3004
	11:31 up hastily and went out, followed her, **s**,	3004
	11:32 **s** unto him, Lord, if thou hadst been here,	3004
	12:21 desired him, **s**, Sir, we would see Jesus.	3004
	12:23 answered them, **s**, The hour is come,	3004
	12:28 **s**, I have both glorified *it*, and will glorify	NIG
	12:38 That the **s** of Esaias the prophet might be	3056
	15:20 if they have kept my **s**, they will keep	3056
	18: 9 That the **s** might be fulfilled, which he	3056
	18:22 Answerest thou the high priest so?	3004
	18:32 That the **s** of Jesus might be fulfilled,	3056
	18:40 all again, **s**, Not this *man*, but Barabbas.	3004
	19: 6 and officers saw him, they cried out, **s**,	3004
	19: 8 Pilate therefore heard that **s**, he was	3056
	19:12 but the Jews cried out, **s**, If thou let this	3004
	19:13 When Pilate therefore heard that **s**,	3056
	21:23 Then went this **s** abroad among	3056
Ac	1: 6 come together, they asked of him, **s**, Lord,	3004
	2: 7 and marvelled, **s** one to another, Behold,	3004
	2:12 and were in doubt, **s** one to another,	3004
	2:40 other words did he testify and exhort, **s**,	3004
	3:25 made with our fathers, **s** unto Abraham,	3004
	4:16 **S**, What shall we do to these men?	3004
	5:23 **S**, The prison truly found we shut with all	3004
	5:25 Then came one and told them, **s**, Behold,	3004
	5:28 **S**, Did not we straitly command you that	3004
	6: 5 And the **s** pleased the whole multitude:	3056
	7:26 and would have set them at one *again*, **s**,	3004
	7:27 Who made thee a ruler and a judge	3004
	7:29 Then fled Moses at this **s**, and was a	3056
	7:32 **S**, I *am* the God of thy fathers, the God of	NIG
	7:35 Who made thee a ruler and a judge?	3004
	7:40 **S** unto Aaron, Make us gods to go before	3004
	7:59 calling upon *God*, and **s**, Lord Jesus,	3004
	8:10 heed, from the least to the greatest, **s**,	3004
	8:19 **S**, Give me also this power, that on	3004
	8:26 **s**, Arise, and go toward the south unto	3004
	9: 4 and heard a voice **s** unto him, Saul, Saul,	3004
	10: 3 in to him, and **s** unto him, Cornelius,	3004
	10:26 Peter took him up, **s**, Stand up; I myself	3004
	11: 3 **S**, Thou wentest in to men uncircumcised,	3004
	11: 4 *and* expounded *it* by order unto them, **s**,	3004
	11: 7 I heard a voice **s** unto me, Arise, Peter;	3004
	11:18 held their peace, and glorified God, **s**,	3004
	12: 7 and raised him up, **s**, Arise up quickly.	3004
	12:22 **s**, *It is* the voice of a god, and not of a	NIG
	13:15 **s**, Ye men *and* brethren, if ye have *any*	3004
	13:47 **s**, I have set thee to be a light of	NIG
	14:11 their voices, **s** in the speech of Lycaonia,	3004
	14:15 And **s**, Sirs, why do ye these *things?* We	3004
	15: 5 **s**, That it was needful to circumcise them,	3004
	15:13 James answered, **s**, Men *and* brethren,	3004
	15:24 subverting your souls, **s**, Ye must **s**,	3004
	16: 9 and prayed him, **s**, Come over into	3004
	16:15 and her household, she besought *us*, **s**,	3004
	16:17 same followed Paul and us, and cried, **s**,	3004
	16:20 **s**, These men, being Jews, do exceedingly	3004

Ac	16:28 with a loud voice, **s**, Do thyself no harm:	3004
	16:35 sent the sergeants, **s**, Let those men go	3004
	16:36 And the keeper of the prison told this **s** to	3056
	17: 7 **s** that there is another king, *one* Jesus.	3004
	17:19 and brought him unto Areopagus, **s**,	3004
	18:13 **S**, This *fellow* persuadeth men to worship	3004
	18:21 But bade them farewell, **s**, I must by all	3004
	19: 4 baptism of repentance, **s** unto the people,	3004
	19:13 **s**, We adjure you by Jesus whom Paul	3004
	19:21 and Achaia, to go to Jerusalem, **s**,	3004
	19:26 much people, **s** that they be no gods,	3004
	19:28 and cried out, **s**, Great *is* Diana of	3004
	20:23 **s** that bonds and afflictions abide me.	3004
	21:14 ceased, **s**, The will of the Lord be done.	3004
	21:21 **s** that they *ought* not to circumcise *their*	3004
	21:40 spake unto *them* in the Hebrew tongue, **s**,	3004
	22: 7 and heard a voice **s** unto me, Saul, Saul,	3004
	22:18 And saw him **s** unto me, Make haste,	3004
	22:26 *that*, he went and told the chief captain, **s**,	3004
	23: 9 and strove, **s**, We find no evil in this man:	3004
	23:12 **s** that *they* would neither eat nor drink till	3004
	23:23 And he called unto *him* two centurions, **s**,	3004
	24: 2 *forth*, Tertullus began to accuse *him*, **s**,	3004
	24: 9 also assented, **s** that these *things* were so.	5335
	25:14 declared Paul's cause unto the king, **s**,	3004
	26:14 and **s** in the Hebrew tongue, Saul, Saul,	3004
	26:22 none other *things* than those which	3004
	26:31 they talked between themselves, **s**,	3004
	27:24 **S**, Fear not, Paul; thou must be brought	3004
	27:33 Paul besought *them* all to take meat, **s**,	3004
	28:26 **S**, Go unto this people, and say, Hearing	3004
Ro	4: 7 **S**, Blessed *are they* whose iniquities are	NIG
	11: 2 intercession to God against Israel, **s**,	3004
	13: 9 is briefly comprehended in this **s**, namely,	3056
1Co	11:25 *he* had supped, **s**, This cup is the new	3004
	15:54 be brought to pass the **s** that is written,	3056
Gal	3: 8 **s**, In thee shall all nations be blessed.	NIG
1Ti	1:15 *This is* a faithful **s**, and worthy of all	3056
	3: 1 *This is* a true **s**, If a man desire the office	3056
	4: 9 *This is* a faithful **s** and worthy of all	3056
2Ti	2:11 *It is* a faithful **s**: For if we be dead with	3056
	2:18 **s** that the resurrection is past already;	3004
Tit	3: 8 *This is* a faithful **s**, and these *things* I will	3056
Heb	2: 6 **s**, What is man, that thou art mindful of	3004
	2:12 **S**, I will declare thy name unto my	3004
	4: 7 **s** in David, To day, after so long a time;	3004
	6:14 **S**, Surely blessing I will bless thee,	3004
	8:11 every man his brother, **s**, Know the Lord:	3004
	9:20 **S**, This *is* the blood of the testament	3004
	12:26 but now he hath promised, **s**, Yet once	3004
2Pe	3: 4 **s**, Where is the promise of his coming?	3004
Jude	1:14 from Adam, prophesied of these, **s**,	3004
Rev	1:11 **S**, I am Alpha and Omega, the first and	3004
	1:17 right hand upon me, **s** unto me, Fear not;	3004
	4: 8 rest not day and night, **s**, Holy, holy, holy,	3004
	4:10 and cast their crowns before the throne, **s**,	3004
	5: 9 And they sung a new song, **s**, Thou art	3004
	5:12 **S** with a loud voice, Worthy is the Lamb	3004
	5:13 heard I **s**, Blessing, and honour, and glory,	3004
	6: 1 one of the four beasts **s**, Come and see.	3004
	6:10 **s**, How long, O Lord, holy and true,	3004
	7: 3 **S**, Hurt not the earth, neither the sea,	3004
	7:10 cried with a loud voice, **s**, Salvation to	3004
	7:12 **S**, Amen: Blessing, and glory, and	3004
	9:14 **S** to the sixth angel which had the	3004
	10: 4 I heard a voice from heaven **s** unto me,	3004
	11: 1 **s**, Rise, and measure the temple of God,	3004
	11:12 they heard a great voice from heaven **s**	3004
	11:15 and there were great voices in heaven, **s**,	3004
	11:17 **s**, We give thee thanks, O Lord God	3004
	12:10 And I heard a loud voice **s** in heaven,	3004
	13: 4 and they worshipped the beast, **s**, Who *is*	3004
	13:14 **s** to them that dwell on the earth, that	3004
	14: 7 **S** with a loud voice, Fear God,	3004
	14: 8 **s**, Babylon is fallen, is fallen, *that* great	3004
	14: 9 **s** with a loud voice, If any *man* worship	3004
	14:13 I heard a voice from heaven **s** unto me,	3004
	14:18 **s**, Thrust in thy sharp sickle, and gather	3004
	15: 3 **s**, Great and marvellous *are* thy works,	3004
	16: 1 out of the temple **s** to the seven angels,	3004
	16:17 of heaven, from the throne, **s**, It is done.	3004
	17: 1 talked with me, **s** unto me, Come hither;	3004
	18: 2 **s**, Babylon the great is fallen, is fallen,	3004
	18: 4 **s**, Come out of her, my people, that ye be	3004
	18:10 **s**, Alas, alas, *that* great city Babylon,	3004
	18:16 And **s**, Alas, alas, *that* great city, that was	3004
	18:18 **s**, What *city is* like unto *this* great city?	3004
	18:19 cried, weeping and wailing, **s**, Alas, alas,	3004
	18:21 great millstone, and cast *it* into the sea, **s**,	3004
	19: 1 of much people in heaven, **s**, Alleluia;	3004
	19: 4 God that sat on the throne, **s**, Amen;	3004
	19: 5 **s**, Praise our God, all ye his servants,	3004
	19: 6 voice of mighty thunderings, **s**, Alleluia:	3004
	19:17 **s** to all the fowls that fly in the midst of	3004
	21: 3 And I heard a great voice out of heaven **s**,	3004
	21: 9 and talked with me, **s**, Come hither, I will	3004

SAYINGS (31) [SAY]

Nu	14:39 Moses told these **s** unto all the children	1697
Jdg	13:17 that when thy **s** come to pass we may do	1697
1Sa	25:12 and came and told him all those **s**.	1697
2Ch	13:22 the acts of Abijah, and his ways, and his **s**,	1697
	33:19 they *are* written among the **s** of the seers.	1697

Ps	49:13 yet their posterity approve their **s**. Selah.	6310
	78: 2 in a parable: I will utter **dark s** of old:	2420
Pr	1: 6 the words of the wise, and their **dark s**.	2420
	4:10 Hear, O my son, and receive my **s**;	561
	4:20 to my words; incline thine ear unto my **s**.	561
Mt	7:24 Therefore whosoever heareth these **s** of	3056
	7:26 every one that heareth these **s** of mine,	3056
	7:28 to pass, when Jesus had ended these **s**,	3056
	19: 1 *that* when Jesus had finished these **s**,	3056
	26: 1 pass, when Jesus had finished all these **s**,	3056
Lk	1:65 all these **s** were noised abroad throughout	4487
	2:51 his mother kept all these **s** in her heart.	4487
	6:47 me, and heareth my **s**, and doeth them,	3056
	7: 1 Now when he had ended all his **s** in	4487
	9:28 to pass about an eight days after these **s**,	3056
	9:44 Let these **s** sink down into your ears:	3056
Jn	10:19 again among the Jews for these **s**.	3056
	14:24 He that loveth me not keepeth not my **s**:	3056
Ac	14:18 And with these **s** scarce restrained they	3004
	19:28 when they heard *these* **s**, they were full	NIG
Ro	3: 4 That thou mightest be justified in thy **s**,	3056
Rev	19: 9 unto me, These are the true **s** of God.	3056
	22: 6 unto me, These **s** *are* faithful and true:	3056
	22: 7 blessed *is* he that keepeth the **s** of	3056
	22: 9 of them which keep the **s** of this book:	3056
	22:10 Seal not the **s** of the prophecy of this	3056

SCAB (7) [SCABBED]

Lev	13: 2 a **s**, or bright spot, and it be in the skin of	5597
	13: 6 it *is but* a **s**: and he shall wash his clothes,	4556
	13: 7 if the **s** spread much abroad in the skin,	4556
	13: 8 the **s** spreadeth in the skin, then the priest	4556
	14:56 a rising, and for a **s**, and for a bright spot:	5597
Dt	28:27 and with the **s**, and with the itch,	1618
Isa	3:17 Therefore the Lord will **smite with a s**	5596

SCABBARD (1)

Jer	47: 6 put up thyself into thy **s**, rest, and be still.	8593

SCABBED (2) [SCAB]

Lev	21:20 be scurvy, or **s**, or hath his stones broken;	3217
	22:22 maimed, or having a wen, or scurvy, or **s**,	3217

SCAFFOLD (1)

2Ch	6:13 For Solomon had made a brasen **s**, of five	3595

SCALE ARMOR See MAIL

SCALES (10)

Lev	11: 9 whatsoever hath fins and **s** in the waters,	7193
	11:10 all that have not fins nor **s** in the seas,	7193
	11:12 hath no fins nor **s** in the waters,	7193
Dt	14: 9 all that have fins and **s** shall ye eat:	7193
	14:10 hath not fins and **s** ye may not eat;	7193
Job	41:15 His **s** *are his* pride, shut up *together*	650+4043
Isa	40:12 weighed the mountains in **s**, and the hills	6425
Eze	29: 4 the fish of thy rivers to stick unto thy **s**,	7193
	29: 4 the fish of thy rivers shall stick unto thy **s**.	7193
Ac	9:18 there fell from his eyes as it had been **s**:	3013

SCALETH (1)

Pr	21:22 A wise *man* **s** the city of the mighty,	5927

SCALL (14)

Lev	13:30 *is* a **dry s**, *even* a leprosy upon the head	5424
	13:31 if the priest look on the plague of the **s**,	5424
	13:31 *that hath* the plague of the **s** seven days:	5424
	13:32 *if* the **s** spread not, and there be in it no	5424
	13:32 the **s** be not in sight deeper than the skin;	5424
	13:33 be shaven, but the **s** shall he not shave;	5424
	13:33 priest shall shut up *him that hath* the **s**	5424
	13:34 seventh day the priest shall look on the **s**:	5424
	13:34 behold, *if* the **s** be not spread in the skin,	5424
	13:35 if the **s** spread much in the skin after his	5424
	13:36 behold, *if* the **s** be spread in the skin,	5424
	13:37 if the **s** be in his sight at a stay,	5424
	13:37 up therein; the **s** is healed, he *is* clean:	5424
	14:54 for all *manner of* plague of leprosy, and **s**,	5424

SCALP (1)

Ps	68:21 the hairy **s** of such a one as goeth on still	6936

SCANT (1)

Mic	6:10 and the **s** measure *that is* abominable?	7332

SCAPEGOAT (4) [GOAT]

Lev	16: 8 for the Lord, and the other lot for the **s**.	5799
	16:10 the goat, on which the lot fell to be the **s**,	5799
	16:10 to let him go for a **s** into the wilderness.	5799
	16:26 he that let go the goat for the **s** shall wash	5799

SCARCE (3) [SCARCELY, SCARCENESS, SCAREST]

Ge	27:30 Jacob was yet **s** gone out from	3318+3318
Ac	14:18 And with these sayings **s** restrained they	3433
	27: 7 and **s** were come over against Cnidus,	3433

SCARCELY (2) [SCARCE]

Ro	5: 7 For **s** for a righteous *man* will one die:	3433
1Pe	4:18 And if the righteous **s** be saved, where	3433

SCARCENESS (1) [SCARCE]

Dt	8: 9 wherein thou shalt eat bread without **s**,	4544

SCAREST (1) [SCARCE]

Job	7:14 thou **s** me with dreams, and terrifiest me	2865

S

SCARLET (52)
Ge 38:28 and bound upon his hand a **s thread**, 8144
38:30 that had the **s thread** upon his hand: 8144
Ex 25: 4 **s**, and fine linen, and goats' hair, 8144+8438
26: 1 and blue, and purple, and **s**. 8144+8438
26:31 and fine twined linen *of* cunning 8144+8438
26:36 and **s**, and fine twined linen, 8144+8438
27:16 and **s**, and fine twined linen, 8144+8438
28: 5 and purple, and **s**, and fine linen. 8144+8438
28: 6 purple, *of* **s**, and fine twined linen, 8144+8438
28: 8 and **s**, and fine twined linen, 8144+8438
28:15 *of* **s**, and *of* fine twined linen, 8144+8438
28:33 of purple, and of **s**, round about 8144+8438
35: 6 **s**, and fine linen, and goats' *hair,* 8144+8438
35:23 and **s**, and fine twined linen. 8144+8438
35:25 purple, *and of* **s**, and of fine linen. 8144+8438
35:35 and in fine linen, and of 8144+8438
36: 8 and blue, and purple, and **s**: 8144+8438
36:37 and **s**, and fine twined linen, 8144+8438
38:18 and **s**, and fine twined linen, 8144+8438
38:23 and in **s**, and fine linen. 8144+8438+1886.1
39: 1 blue, and purple, and **s**, 8144+8438+1886.1
39: 2 and **s**, and fine twined linen. 8144+8438
39: 3 and in the **s**, and in the fine linen, 8144+8438
39: 5 and **s**, and fine twined linen, 8144+8438
39: 8 and **s**, and fine twined linen, 8144+8438
39:24 purple, and **s**, and twined *linen.* 8144+8438
39:29 and purple, and **s**, *of* needlework; 8144+8438
Lev 14: 4 cedar wood, and **s**, and hyssop: 8144+8438
14: 6 **s**, and the hyssop, and shall dip 8144+8438
14:49 cedar wood, and **s**, and hyssop: 8144+8438
14:51 the **s**, and the living bird, 8144+8438
14:52 with the hyssop, and with the **s**: 8144+8438
Nu 4: 8 spread upon them a cloth of **s**, 8144+8438
19: 6 **s**, and cast *it* into the midst of 8144+8438
Jos 2:18 thou shalt bind this line of **s** thread in 8144
2:21 and she bound the **s** line in the window. 8144
2Sa 1:24 weep over Saul, who clothed you in **s**, 8144
Pr 31:21 for all her household *are* clothed with **s**. 8144
SS 4: 3 Thy lips *are* like a thread of **s**, 8144
Isa 1:18 though your sins be as **s**, they shall be as 8144
La 4: 5 they that were brought up in **s** embrace 8438
Da 5: 7 shall be clothed with **s**, and *have a* chain 711
5:16 thou shalt be clothed with **s**, and *have a* 711
5:29 clothed Daniel with **s**, and *put a* chain 711
Na 2: 3 *is* made red, the valiant men *are* in **s**: 8529
Mt 27:28 stripped him, and put on him a **s** robe. 2847
Heb 9:19 and **s** wool, and hyssop, and sprinkled 2847
Rev 17: 3 a woman sit upon a **s coloured** beast, 2847
17: 4 was arrayed in purple and **s colour**, 2847
18:12 **s**, and all thyine wood, and all *manner* 2847
18:16 and **s**, and decked with gold, 2847

SCATTER (38) [SCATTERED, SCATTERETH, SCATTERING]
Ge 11: 9 from thence did the LORD **s** them **abroad** 6327
49: 7 them in Jacob, and **s** them in Israel. 6327
Lev 26:33 I will **s** you among the heathen, 2219
Nu 16:37 the burning, and **s** thou the fire yonder; 2219
Dt 4:27 the LORD shall **s** you among the nations, 6327
28:64 the LORD shall **s** thee among all people, 6327
32:26 I said, I would **s** them **into corners**, 6284
1Ki 14:15 shall **s** them beyond the river, because 2219
Ne 1: 8 I will **s** you **abroad** among the nations: 6327
Ps 59:11 **s** them by thy power; and bring them 5128
68:30 **s** thou the people *that* delight in war. 967
106:27 the nations, and to **s** them in the lands. 2219
144: 6 Cast forth lightning, and **s** them: shoot 6327
Isa 28:25 the cummin, and cast in the principal 2236
41:16 away, and the whirlwind shall **s** them: 6327
Jer 9:16 I will **s** them also among the heathen, 6327
13:24 Therefore will I **s** them as the stubble that 6327
18:17 I will **s** them as *with* an east wind before 6327
23: 1 destroy and **s** the sheep of my pasture! 6327
49:32 I will **s** into all winds *that are* in 2219
49:36 and will **s** them towards all those winds; 2219
Eze 5: 2 a third *part* thou shalt **s** in the wind; 2219
5:10 the whole remnant of thee will I **s** into all 2219
5:12 I will **s** a third *part* into all the winds, 2219
6: 5 will **s** your bones round about your altars. 2219
10: 2 the cherubims, and **s** *them* over the city. 2236
12:14 I will **s** toward every wind all that *are* 2219
12:15 when I shall **s** them among the nations, 6327
20:23 that *I* would **s** them among the heathen, 6327
22:15 I will **s** thee among the heathen, 6327
29:12 I will **s** the Egyptians among the nations, 6327
30:23 I will **s** the Egyptians among the nations, 6327
30:26 I will **s** the Egyptians among the nations, 6327
Da 4:14 shake off his leaves, and **s** his fruit: 921
11:24 he shall **s** among them the prey, and spoil, 967
12: 7 when he shall have accomplished to **s** 5310
Hab 3:14 they came out as a whirlwind to **s** me: 6327
Zec 1:21 *their* horn over the land of Judah to **s** it. 2219

SCATTERED (71) [SCATTER]
Ge 11: 4 lest we be **s abroad** upon the face of 6327
11: 8 So the LORD **s** them **abroad** from thence 6327
Ex 5:12 So the people were **s abroad** throughout 6327
Nu 10:35 LORD, and let thine enemies be **s**; 6327
Dt 30: 3 whither the LORD thy God hath **s** thee. 6327
1Sa 11:11 that they which remained were **s**, 6327
13: 8 Gilgal; and the people were **s** from him. 6327
13:11 I saw that the people were **s** from 5310
2Sa 18: 8 For the battle was there over the face of 6327

2Sa 22:15 he sent out arrows, and **s** them; lightning, 6327
1Ki 22:17 he said, I saw all Israel **s** upon the hills, 6327
2Ki 25: 5 and all his army were **s** from him. 6327
2Ch 18:16 I did see all Israel **s** upon the mountains, 6327
Est 3: 8 There is a certain people **s abroad** and 6340
Job 4:11 and the stout lion's whelps are **s abroad**. 6504
18:15 brimstone shall be **s** upon his habitation. 2219
Ps 18:14 he sent out his arrows, and **s** them; 6327
44:11 meat; and hast **s** us among the heathen, 2219
53: 5 for God hath **s** the bones of him that 6555
68: 1 God, thou hast cast us off, thou hast **s** us, 6555
68: 1 God arise, let his enemies be: let them 6327
68:14 When the Almighty **s** kings in it, it was 6566
89:10 thou hast **s** thine enemies with thy strong 6340
92: 9 all the workers of iniquity shall be **s**. 6504
141: 7 Our bones are **s** at the grave's mouth, 6340
Isa 18: 2 messengers, to a nation **s** and peeled, 4900
18: 7 unto the LORD of hosts *of* a people **s** 4900
33: 3 lifting up of thyself the nations were **s**. 5310
Jer 3:13 hast **s** thy ways to the strangers under 6327
10:21 not prosper; and all their flocks shall be **s**. 6327
23: 2 have **s** my flock, and driven them away, 6327
30:11 end of all nations whither I have **s** thee, 6327
31:10 He that **s** Israel will gather him, 2219
40:15 are gathered unto thee should be **s**, 6327
50:17 Israel *is* a **s** sheep; the lions have driven 6340
52: 8 and all his army was **s** from him. 6327
Eze 6: 8 when ye shall be **s** through the countries. 2219
11:16 although I have **s** them among 6327
11:17 of the countries where ye have been **s**, 6327
17:21 they that remain shall be **s** towards all 6566
20:34 you out of the countries wherein ye are **s**, 6327
20:41 of the countries wherein ye have been **s**, 6327
28:25 from the people among whom they are **s**, 6327
29:13 from the people whither they were **s**: 6327
34: 5 were **s**, because *there is* no shepherd: 6327
34: 5 the beasts of the field, when they were **s**. 6327
34: 6 my flock was **s** upon all the face of 6327
34:12 day that he is among his sheep *that are* **s**; 6567
34:12 places where they have been **s** in the 6327
34:21 your horns, till ye have **s** them abroad; 6327
36:19 I **s** them among the heathen, and they 6327
46:18 my people be not **s** every man from his 6327
Joel 3: 2 whom they have **s** among the nations, 6340
Na 3:18 *dust:* thy people is **s** upon the mountains, 6335
Hab 3: 6 the everlasting mountains were **s**, 6327
Zec 1:19 These *are* the horns which have **s** Judah, 2219
1:21 These *are* the horns which have **s** Judah, 2219
7:14 I **s** them **with a whirlwind** among all 5590
13: 7 the shepherd, and the sheep shall be **s**: 6327
Mt 9:36 because they fainted, and were **s abroad**, 4496
26:31 the sheep of the flock shall be **s abroad**. 1287
Mk 14:27 the shepherd, and the sheep shall be **s**. 1287
Lk 1:51 he hath **s** the proud in the imagination of 1287
Jn 11:52 the children of God that were **s abroad**. 1287
16:32 yea, is now come, that ye shall be **s**, 4650
Ac 5:36 him, were **s**, and brought to nought. 1262
8: 1 they were all **s abroad** throughout 1289
8: 4 Therefore they that were **s abroad** went 1289
11:19 Now they which were **s abroad** upon 1289
Jas 1: 1 tribes which are **s abroad**, 1290+1722+3588
1Pe 1: 1 to the strangers **throughout** Pontus, 1290

SCATTERETH (10) [SCATTER]
Job 37:11 the thick cloud: he **s** his bright cloud: 6327
38:24 *which* **s** the east wind upon the earth? 6327
Ps 147:16 like wool: he **s** the hoarfrost like ashes. 6340
Pr 11:24 There is that **s**, and yet increaseth; 6340
20: 8 of judgment **s** *away* all evil with his eyes. 2219
20:26 A wise king **s** the wicked, and bringeth 2219
Isa 24: 1 and **s abroad** the inhabitants thereof. 6327
Mt 12:30 he that gathereth not with me **s abroad**. 4650
Lk 11:23 and he that gathereth not with me **s**. 4650
Jn 10:12 the wolf catcheth them, and **s** the sheep. 4650

SCATTERING (1) [SCATTER]
Isa 30:30 *with* **s**, and tempest, and hailstones. 5311

SCENT See SENT (Job 14:9; Jer 48:11; Hos 14:7)

SCEPTRE (15) [SCEPTRES]
Ge 49:10 The **s** shall not depart from Judah, nor a 7626
Nu 24:17 a S shall rise out of Israel, and shall smite 7626
Est 4:11 the king shall hold out the golden **s**, 8275
5: 2 king held out to Esther the golden **s** that 8275
5: 2 drew near, and touched the top of the **s**. 8275
8: 4 the king held out the golden **s** toward 8275
Ps 45: 6 the **s** of thy kingdom *is* a right sceptre. 7626
45: 6 the sceptre of thy kingdom *is* a right **s**. 7626
Isa 14: 5 of the wicked, *and* the **s** of the rulers. 7626
Eze 19:14 she hath no strong rod *to be* a **s** to rule. 7626
Am 1: 5 him that holdeth the **s** from the house of 7626
1: 8 him that holdeth the **s** from Ashkelon, 7626
Zec 10:11 and the **s** of Egypt shall depart away. 7626
Heb 1: 8 a **s** of righteousness *is* the sceptre of thy 4464
1: 8 a sceptre of righteousness *is* the **s** of thy 4464

SCEPTRES (1) [SCEPTRE]
Eze 19:11 she had strong rods for the **s** of them that 7626

SCEVA (1)
Ac 19:14 there were seven sons of *one* **S**, a Jew, 4630

SCHEMES See MISCHIEF; MISCHIEFS

SCHEMING See SLEIGHT

SCHISM (1)
1Co 12:25 That there should be no **s** in the body; 4978

SCHOLAR (2)
1Ch 25: 8 the small as the great, the teacher as the **s**. 8527
Mal 2:12 master and the **s**, out of the tabernacles 6030

SCHOOL (1) [SCHOOLMASTER]
Ac 19: 9 disputing daily in the **s** of one Tyrannus. 4981

SCHOOLMASTER (2) [MASTER, SCHOOL]
Gal 3:24 Wherefore the law was our **s** *to bring us* 3807
3:25 faith is come, we are no longer under a **s**. 3807

SCIENCE (2)
Da 1: 4 understanding **s**, and such as *had* ability 4093
1Ti 6:20 and oppositions of **s** falsely so called: 1108

SCOFF (1) [SCOFFERS]
Hab 1:10 they shall **s** at the kings, and the princes 7046

SCOFFERS (1) [SCOFF]
2Pe 3: 3 that there shall come in the last days **s**, 1703

SCORCH (1) [SCORCHED]
Rev 16: 8 *power* was given unto him to **s** men with 2739

SCORCHED (3) [SCORCH]
Mt 13: 6 And when the sun was up, they were **s**; 2739
Mk 4: 6 But when the sun was up, it was **s**; 2739
Rev 16: 9 And men were **s** *with* great heat, 2739

SCORCHING See VEHEMENT

SCORN (16) [SCORNER, SCORNERS, SCORNEST, SCORNETH, SCORNFUL, SCORNING]
2Ki 19:21 despised thee, *and* **laughed** thee **to s**; 3932
2Ch 30:10 **laughed** them **to s**, and mocked them. 7832
Ne 2:19 heard *it*, they **laughed** us **to s**, 3932
Est 3: 6 thought **s** to lay hands on Mordecai alone; 959
Job 12: 4 the just upright *man* is **laughed to s**. 7814
16:20 My friends **s** me: *but* mine eye poureth 3887
22:19 glad: and the innocent **laugh** them **to s**. 3932
Ps 22: 7 All they that see me **laugh** me **to s**: 3932
44:13 a **s** and a derision to them that are round 3933
79: 4 a **s** and derision to them that are round 3933
Isa 37:22 despised thee, *and* **laughed** thee **to s**; 3932
Eze 23:32 thou shalt be **laughed to s** and had in 6712
Hab 1:10 and the princes *shall be* a **s** unto them: 4890
Mt 9:24 And they **laughed** him **to s**. 2606
Mk 5:40 And they **laughed** him **to s**. But when 2606
Lk 8:53 And they **laughed** him **to s**, knowing 2606

SCORNER (11) [SCORN]
Pr 9: 7 He that reproveth a **s** getteth to himself 3887
9: 8 Reprove not a **s**, lest he hate thee: rebuke 3887
13: 1 but a **s** heareth not rebuke. 3887
14: 6 A **s** seeketh wisdom, and *findeth it* not: 3887
15:12 A **s** loveth not one that reproveth him: 3887
19:25 Smite a **s**, and the simple will beware: 3887
21:11 When the **s** is punished, the simple is 3887
21:24 Proud and haughty **s** *is* his name, 3887
22:10 Cast out the **s**, and contention shall go 3887
24: 9 and the **s** *is* an abomination to men. 3887
Isa 29:20 the **s** is consumed, and all that watch for 3887

SCORNERS (4) [SCORN]
Pr 1:22 the **s** delight in their scorning, 3887
3:34 Surely he scorneth the **s**: but he giveth 3887
19:29 Judgments are prepared for **s**, 3887
Hos 7: 5 wine; he stretched out his hand with **s**. 3945

SCORNEST (2) [SCORN]
Pr 9:12 but *if* thou **s**, thou alone shalt bear *it*. 3887
Eze 16:31 not been as a harlot, in that *thou* **s** hire; 7046

SCORNETH (4) [SCORN]
Job 39: 7 He **s** the multitude of the city, 7832
39:18 on high, she **s** the horse and his rider. 7832
Pr 3:34 Surely he **s** the scorners: but he giveth 3887
19:28 An ungodly witness **s** judgment: 3887

SCORNFUL (3) [SCORN]
Ps 1: 1 of sinners, nor sitteth in the seat of the **s**. 3887
Pr 29: 8 S men bring a city into a snare: 3944
Isa 28:14 hear the word of the LORD, ye **s** men, 3944

SCORNING (3) [SCORN]
Job 34: 7 is like Job, *who* drinketh up **s** like water? 3933
Ps 123: 4 Our soul is exceedingly filled *with* the **s** 3933
Pr 1:22 the scorners delight in their **s**, 3944

SCORPION (2) [SCORPIONS]
Lk 11:12 he shall ask an egg, will he offer him a **s**? 4651
Rev 9: 5 their torment *was* as the torment of a **s**, 4651

SCORPION PASS See MAALEH-ACRABBIM

SCORPIONS (9) [SCORPION]
Dt 8:15 and drought, where *there was* no 6137
1Ki 12:11 with whips, but I will chastise you with **s**. 6137
12:14 with whips, but I *will* chastise you with **s**. 6137
2Ch 10:11 with whips, but I will chastise you with **s**. 6137
10:14 with whips, but I *will* chastise you with **s**. 6137
Eze 2: 6 with them, and thou dost dwell among **s**: 6137
Lk 10:19 you power to tread on serpents and **s**, 4651
Rev 9: 3 as the **s** of the earth have power. 4651

S

Rev 9:10 And they had tails like unto **s**, *4651*

SCOUNDREL See NAUGHTINESS; NAUGHTY

SCOURED (1)
Lev 6:28 it shall be both **s**, and rinsed in water. 4838

SCOURGE (12) [SCOURGED, SCOURGES, SCOURGETH, SCOURGING, SCOURGINGS]
Job 5:21 shalt be hid from the **s** of the tongue: 7752
 9:23 If the **s** slay suddenly, he will laugh at 7752
Isa 10:26 the Lord of hosts shall stir up a **s** for him 7752
 28:15 the overflowing **s** shall pass through, 7752
 28:18 the overflowing **s** shall pass through, 7752
Mt 10:17 and they will **s** you in their synagogues; 3146
 20:19 to **s**, and to crucify *him:* and the third 3146
 23:34 some of them ye shall **s** in your 3146
Mk 10:34 and shall **s** him, and shall spit upon him, 3146
Lk 18:33 they shall **s** *him,* and put him to death: 3146
Jn 2:15 when he had made a **s** of small cords, 5416
Ac 22:25 lawful for you to **s** a man *that is* a Roman, 3147

SCOURGED (4) [SCOURGE]
Lev 19:20 she shall be **s**, they shall not be put to 1244
Mt 27:26 when he had **s** Jesus, he delivered *him* 5417
Mk 15:15 when he had **s** *him,* to be crucified. 5417
Jn 19:1 therefore took Jesus, and **s** *him.* 3146

SCOURGES (1) [SCOURGE]
Jos 23:13 **s** in your sides, and thorns in your eyes, 7850

SCOURGETH (1) [SCOURGE]
Heb 12:6 and **s** every son whom he receiveth. 3146

SCOURGING (1) [SCOURGE]
Ac 22:24 bade that he should be examined by **s**; 3148

SCOURGINGS (1) [SCOURGE]
Heb 11:36 others had trial of *cruel* mockings and **s**, 3148

SCRABLED (1)
1Sa 21:13 **s** on the doors of the gate, and let his 8427

SCRAPE (3) [SCRAPED]
Lev 14:41 shall pour out the dust that they **s off** 7096
Job 2:8 took him a potsherd to **s** himself withal; 1623
Eze 26:4 I will also **s** her dust from her, 5500

SCRAPED (2) [SCRAPE]
Lev 14:41 he shall **cause** the house **to be s** within 7106
 14:43 after he hath **s** the house, and after it is 7096

SCRIBE (52) [SCRIBE'S, SCRIBES]
2Sa 8:17 *were* the priests; and Seraiah *was* the **s**; 5608
 20:25 Sheva *was* **s**: and Zadok and Abiathar 5608
2Ki 12:10 that the king's **s** and the high priest came 5608
 18:18 Shebna the **s**, and Joah the son of Asaph 5608
 18:37 Shebna the **s**, and Joah the son of Asaph 5608
 19:2 Shebna the **s**, and the elders of the priests 5608
 22:3 son of Meshullam, the **s**, *to* the house of 5608
 22:8 high priest said unto Shaphan the **s**, 5608
 22:9 Shaphan the **s** came to the king, 5608
 22:10 Shaphan the **s** shewed the king, saying, 5608
 22:12 Shaphan the **s**, and Asahiah a servant of 5608
 25:19 in the city, and the principal **s** of the host, 5608
1Ch 18:16 *were* the priests; and Shavsha *was* **s**; 5608
 24:6 Shemaiah the son of Nethaneel the **s**, 5608
 27:32 *was* a counsellor, a wise man, and a **s**: 5608
2Ch 24:11 the king's **s** and the high priest's officer 5608
 26:11 of their account by the hand of Jeiel the **s** 5608
 34:15 and said to Shaphan the **s**, 5608
 34:18 Shaphan the **s** told the king, saying, 5608
 34:20 Shaphan the **s**, and Asaiah a servant of 5608
Ezr 4:8 Shimshai the **s** wrote a letter against 5613
 4:9 Shimshai the **s**, and the rest of their 5613
 4:17 *to* Shimshai the **s**, and *to* the rest of their 5613
 4:23 Shimshai the **s**, and their companions, 5613
 7:6 he *was* a ready **s** in the law of Moses, 5608
 7:11 the **s**, *even* a scribe of the words of 5608
 7:11 *even* a **s** of the words of 5608
 7:12 a **s** of the law of the God of heaven, 5613
 7:21 the **s** of the law of the God of heaven, 5613
Ne 8:1 spake unto Ezra the **s** to bring the book 5608
 8:4 Ezra the **s** stood upon a pulpit of wood, 5608
 8:9 Ezra the priest the **s**, and the Levites that 5608
 8:13 priests, and the Levites, unto Ezra the **s**, 5608
 12:26 governor, and of Ezra the priest, the **s**. 5608
 12:36 man of God, and Ezra the **s** before them. 5608
 13:13 Zadok the **s**, and of the Levites, Pedaiah: 5608
Isa 33:18 Where *is* the **s**? where *is* the receiver? 5608
Jer 36:3 Shebna the **s**, and Joah, Asaph's son, 5608
 36:22 Shebna the **s**, and Joah, the son of Asaph, 5608
 37:2 Shebna the **s**, and the elders of the priests 5608
Jer 36:10 of Gemariah the son of Shaphan the **s**, 5608
 36:12 Elishama the **s**, and Delaiah the son of 5608
 36:20 the roll in the chamber of Elishama the **s**, 5608
 36:26 to take Baruch the **s** and Jeremiah 5608
 36:32 gave it to Baruch the **s**, the son of Neriah; 5608
 37:15 *in* prison *in* the house of Jonathan the **s**: 5608
 37:20 to return *to* the house of Jonathan the **s**, 5608
 52:25 the principal **s** of the host, who mustered 5608
Mt 8:19 And a certain **s** came, and said unto him, 1122
 13:52 Therefore every **s** *which is* instructed 1122
Mk 12:32 And the **s** said unto him, Well, Master, 1122
1Co 1:20 where *is* the **s**? where *is* the disputer of 1122

SCRIBE'S (2) [SCRIBE]
Jer 36:12 *into* the king's house, into the **s** chamber: 5608
 36:21 he took it out of Elishama the **s** chamber. 5608

SCRIBES (68) [SCRIBE]
1Ki 4:3 and Ahiah, the sons of Shisha, **s**; 5608
1Ch 2:55 families of the **s** which dwelt at Jabez; 5608
2Ch 34:13 of the Levites *there were* **s**, and officers, 5608
Est 3:12 were the king's **s** called on the thirteenth 5608
 8:9 were the king's **s** called at that time in 5608
Jer 8:8 in vain made he *it;* the pen of the **s** 5608
Mt 2:4 chief priests and **s** of the people together, 1122
 5:20 shall exceed *the righteousness* of the **s** 1122
 7:29 as *one* having authority, and not as the **s**. 1122
 9:3 certain of the **s** said within themselves, 1122
 12:38 Then certain of the **s** and of the Pharisees 1122
 15:1 Then came to Jesus and Pharisees, 1122
 16:21 of the elders and chief priests and **s**, 1122
 17:10 then say the **s** that Elias must first come? 1122
 20:18 unto the chief priests and *unto* the **s**, 1122
 21:15 saw the wonderful *things* that he did, 1122
 23:2 The **s** and the Pharisees sit in Moses' seat: 1122
 23:13 woe unto you, **s** and Pharisees, hypocrites 1122
 23:14 Woe unto you, **s** and Pharisees, hypocrites 1122
 23:15 Woe unto you, **s** and Pharisees, hypocrites 1122
 23:23 Woe unto you, **s** and Pharisees, hypocrites 1122
 23:25 Woe unto you, **s** and Pharisees, hypocrites 1122
 23:27 Woe unto you, **s** and Pharisees, hypocrites 1122
 23:29 Woe unto you, **s** and Pharisees, hypocrites 1122
 23:34 unto you prophets, and wise *men*, and **s**: 1122
 26:3 and the **s**, and the elders of the people, 1122
 26:57 the **s** and the elders were assembled. 1122
 27:41 the chief priests mocking *him*, with the **s** 1122
Mk 1:22 *one* that had authority, and not as the **s**. 1122
 2:6 there were certain of the **s** sitting there, 1122
 2:16 when the **s** and Pharisees saw him eat 1122
 3:22 And the **s** which came down from 1122
 7:1 and certain of the **s**, which came from 1122
 7:5 Then the Pharisees and **s** asked him, 1122
 8:31 the elders, and *of* the chief priests, and **s**, 1122
 9:11 Why say the **s** that Elias must first come? 1122
 9:14 and *the* **s** questioning with them. 1122
 9:16 he asked the **s**, What question ye with 1122
 10:33 unto the chief priests, and unto the **s**; 1122
 11:18 And the **s** and chief priests heard *it*, and 1122
 11:27 chief priests, and the **s**, and the elders, 1122
 12:28 And one of the **s** came, and having heard 1122
 12:35 How say the **s** that Christ is the Son of 1122
 12:38 Beware of the **s**, which love to go in long 1122
 14:1 the **s** sought how they might take him by 1122
 14:43 the chief priests and the **s** and the elders. 1122
 14:53 the chief priests and the elders and the **s**. 1122
 15:1 the elders and **s** and the whole council, 1122
 15:31 said among themselves with the **s**, 1122
Lk 5:21 And the **s** and the Pharisees began to 1122
 5:30 their **s** and Pharisees murmured against 1122
 6:7 And the **s** and Pharisees watched him, 1122
 9:22 of the elders and chief priests and **s**, 1122
 11:44 Woe unto you, **s** and Pharisees, hypocrites 1122
 11:53 the **s** and the Pharisees began to urge *him* 1122
 15:2 the Pharisees and **s** murmured, saying, 1122
 19:47 the chief priests and the **s** and the chief 1122
 20:1 and the **s** came upon *him* with the elders, 1122
 20:19 the **s** the same hour sought to lay hands 1122
 20:39 Then certain of the **s** answering said, 1122
 20:46 Beware of the **s**, which desire to walk in 1122
 22:2 and **s** sought how they might kill him; 1122
 22:66 the chief priests and the **s** came together, 1122
 23:10 And the chief priests and **s** stood and 1122
Jn 8:3 the **s** and Pharisees brought unto him a 1122
Ac 4:5 that their rulers, and elders, and **s**, 1122
 6:12 and the **s**, and came upon *him*, and 1122
 23:9 **s** *that were* of the Pharisees' part arose, 1122

SCRIP (7)
1Sa 17:40 shepherd's bag which he had, even in a **s**; 3219
Mt 10:10 Nor **s** for *your* journey, neither two coats, 4082
Mk 6:8 no **s**, no bread, no money in *their* purse: 4082
Lk 9:3 neither staves, nor **s**, neither bread, 4082
 10:4 Carry neither purse, nor **s**, nor shoes: 4082
 22:35 sent you without purse, and **s**, and shoes, 4082
 22:36 purse, let him take *it*, and likewise *his* **s**: 4082

SCRIPTURE (32) [SCRIPTURES]
Da 10:21 shew thee that which is noted in the **s** 3791
Mk 12:10 And have ye not read this **s**; The stone 1124
 15:28 And the **s** was fulfilled, which saith, 1124
Lk 4:21 This day is this **s** fulfilled in your ears. 1124
Jn 2:22 they believed the **s**, and the word which 1124
 7:38 that believeth on me, as the **s** hath said, 1124
 7:42 Hath not the **s** said, That Christ cometh 1124
 10:35 of God came, and the **s** cannot be broken; 1124
 13:18 but that the **s** may be fulfilled, He that 1124
 17:12 of perdition; that the **s** might be fulfilled. 1124
 19:24 that the **s** might be fulfilled, which saith, 1124
 19:28 that the **s** might be fulfilled, saith, I thirst. 1124
 19:36 were done, that the **s** should be fulfilled, 1124
 19:37 And again another **s** saith, They shall look 1124
 20:9 as yet they knew not the **s**, that he must 1124
Ac 1:16 this **s** must needs have been fulfilled, 1124
 8:32 The place of the **s** which he read was this, 1124
 8:35 began at the same **s**, and preached unto 1124
Ro 4:3 For what saith the **s**? Abraham believed 1124
 9:17 For the **s** saith unto Pharaoh, Even for this 1124
 10:11 For the **s** saith, Whosoever believeth on 1124

Ro 11:2 Wot ye not what the **s** saith of Elias? 1124
Gal 3:8 And the **s**, foreseeing that God would 1124
 3:22 But the **s** hath concluded all under sin, 1124
 4:30 Nevertheless what saith the **s**? Cast out 1124
1Ti 5:18 For the **s** saith, Thou shalt not muzzle 1124
2Ti 3:16 All *is* given by inspiration of God, 1124
Jas 2:8 If ye fulfil the royal law according to the **s**, 1124
 2:23 And the **s** was fulfilled which saith, 1124
 4:5 Do ye think that the **s** saith in vain, 1124
1Pe 2:6 Wherefore also it is contained in the **s**, 1124
2Pe 1:20 that no prophecy of the **s** is of *any* private 1124

SCRIPTURES (21) [SCRIPTURE]
Mt 21:42 unto them, Did ye never read in the **s**, 1124
 22:29 unto them, Ye do err, not knowing the **s**, 1124
 26:54 But how then shall the **s** be fulfilled, 1124
 26:56 the **s** of the prophets might be fulfilled. 1124
Mk 12:24 therefore err, because ye know not the **s**, 1124
 14:49 took me not: but the **s** must be fulfilled. 1124
Lk 24:27 he expounded unto them in all the **s** 1124
 24:32 the way, and while he opened to us the **s**? 1124
 24:45 that *they* might understand the **s**, 1124
Jn 5:39 Search the **S**; for in them ye think ye have 1124
Ac 17:2 days reasoned with them out of the **s**, 1124
 17:11 and searched the **s** daily, whether those 1124
 18:24 an eloquent man, *and* mighty in the **s**, 1124
 18:28 shewing by the **s** that Jesus was Christ. 1124
Ro 1:2 afore by his prophets in the holy **s**,) 1124
 15:4 and comfort of the **s** might have hope. 1124
 16:26 and by the **s** of the prophets, 1124
1Co 15:3 Christ died for our sins according to the **s**; 1124
 15:4 *again* the third day according to the **s**: 1124
2Ti 3:15 from a child thou hast known the holy **s**, 1121
2Pe 3:16 wrest, as *they do* also the other **s**, 1124

SCROLE (2)
Isa 34:4 The heavens shall be rolled together as a **s**: 5612
Rev 6:14 And the heaven departed as a **s** when it is 975

SCROLL See BOOK; SCROLE; VOLUME

SCUM (5)
Eze 24:6 to the pot whose **s** *is* therein, 2457
 24:6 therein, and whose **s** is not gone out of it! 2457
 24:11 in it, *that* the **s** of it may be consumed. 2457
 24:12 and her great **s** went not forth out of her: 2457
 24:12 forth out of her: her **s** *shall be* in the fire. 2457

SCURVY (2)
Lev 21:20 or be **s**, or scabbed, or hath his stones 1618
 22:22 or having a wen, or **s**, or scabbed, 1618

SCYTHIAN (1)
Col 3:11 barbarian, **S**, bond *nor* free: 4658

SEA (400) [SEAFARING, SEAS]
Ge 1:26 have dominion over the fish of the **s**, 3220
 1:28 have dominion over the fish of the **s**, 3220
 9:2 the earth, and upon all the fishes of the **s**; 3220
 14:3 in the vale of Siddim, which *is* the salt **s**. 3220
 22:17 as the sand which *is* upon the **s** shore; 3220
 32:12 make thy seed as the sand of the **s**, 3220
 41:49 Joseph gathered corn as the sand of the **s**, 3220
 49:13 Zebulun shall dwell at the haven of the **s**; 3220
Ex 10:19 the locusts, and cast them into the Red **s**: 3220
 13:18 the way of the wilderness of the Red **s**: 3220
 14:2 between Migdol and the **s**, over against 3220
 14:2 before it shall ye encamp by the **s**. 3220
 14:9 overtook them encamping by the **s**, 3220
 14:16 stretch out thine hand over the **s**, 3220
 14:16 dry *ground* through the midst of the **s**, 3220
 14:21 Moses stretched out his hand over the **s**; 3220
 14:21 the Lord caused the **s** to go *back* by a 3220
 14:21 made the **s** dry *land*, and the waters were 3220
 14:22 the midst of the **s** upon the dry *ground:* 3220
 14:23 went in after them to the midst of the **s**, 3220
 14:26 Stretch out thine hand over the **s**, 3220
 14:27 stretched forth his hand over the **s**, 3220
 14:27 **s** returned to his strength when 3220
 14:27 the Egyptians in the midst of the **s**. 3220
 14:28 the host of Pharaoh that came into the **s**; 3220
 14:29 upon dry *land* in the midst of the **s**; 3220
 14:30 Israel saw the Egyptians dead upon the **s** 3220
 15:1 and his rider hath he thrown into the **s**. 3220
 15:4 and his host hath he cast into the **s**: 3220
 15:4 captains also are drowned in the Red **s**. 3220
 15:8 were congealed in the heart of the **s**. 3220
 15:10 blow with thy wind, the **s** covered them: 3220
 15:19 and with his horsemen into the **s**, 3220
 15:19 again the waters of the **s** upon them; 3220
 15:19 went on dry *land* in the midst of the **s**. 3220
 15:21 and his rider hath he thrown into the **s**. 3220
 15:22 So Moses brought Israel from the Red **s**, 3220
 20:11 the **s**, and all that in them *is*, and rested 3220
 23:31 I will set thy bounds from the Red **s** even 3220
 23:31 Red sea even unto the **s** of the Philistines, 3220
Nu 11:22 shall all the fish of the **s** be gathered 3220
 11:31 brought quails from the **s**, and let *them* 3220
 13:29 the Canaanites dwell by the **s**, and by 3220
 14:25 the wilderness *by* the way of the Red **s**. 3220
 21:4 from mount Hor *by* the way of the Red **s**, 3220
 21:14 What he did in the **Red s**, and *in* the 5492
 33:8 passed through the midst of the **s** into 3220
 33:10 from Elim, and encamped by the Red **s**. 3220
 33:11 they removed from the Red **s**, 3220
 34:3 the outmost coast of the salt **s** eastward: 3220

S

Ref	Text	Strong
Nu 34: 5	and the goings out of it shall be at the **s**.	3220
34: 6	shall even have the great **s** for a border:	3220
34: 7	from the great **s** you shall point out for	3220
34:11	shall reach unto the side of the **s** of	3220
34:12	the goings out of it shall be *at* the salt **s**:	3220
Dt 1: 1	in the plain over against the Red **s**,	NIH
1: 7	vale, and in the south, and by the **s** side,	3220
1:40	the wilderness *by* the way of the Red **s**.	3220
2: 1	the wilderness *by* the way of the Red **s**,	3220
3:17	Chinnereth even unto the **s** of the plain,	3220
3:17	*even* the salt **s**, under Ashdoth-pisgah	3220
4:49	even unto the **s** of the plain, under	3220
11: 4	how he made the water of the Red **s** to	3220
11:24	even unto the uttermost **s** shall your coast	3220
30:13	Neither *is* it beyond the **s**, that *thou*	3220
30:13	Who shall go over the **s** for us, and bring	3220
34: 2	all the land of Judah, unto the utmost **s**,	3220
Jos 1: 4	unto the great **s** *toward* the going down	3220
2:10	dried up the water of the Red **s** for you,	3220
3:16	those that came down toward the **s** of	3220
3:16	even the salt **s**, failed, *and* were cut off:	3220
4:23	as the LORD your God did to the Red **s**,	3220
5: 1	of the Canaanites, which *were* by the **s**,	3220
9: 1	in all the coasts of the great **s** over against	3220
11: 4	as the sand that *is* upon the **s** shore in	3220
12: 3	*from* the plain to the **s** of Cinneroth on	3220
12: 3	unto the **s** of the plain, *even* the salt sea	3220
12: 3	of the plain, *even* the salt **s** on the east,	3220
13:27	unto the edge of the **s** of Cinneroth on	3220
15: 2	border was from the shore of the salt **s**,	3220
15: 4	the goings out of that coast were at the **s**:	3220
15: 5	the east border *was* the salt **s**, *even* unto	3220
15: 5	of the **s** at the uttermost part of Jordan:	3220
15:11	goings out of the border were at the **s**.	3220
15:12	the west border *was* to the great **s**,	3220
15:46	From Ekron even unto the **s**, all *that lay*	3220
15:47	and the great **s**, and the border *thereof*.	3220
16: 3	and the goings out thereof are at the **s**.	3220
16: 6	the border went out toward the **s** *to*	3220
16: 8	and the goings out thereof were at the **s**.	3220
17: 9	and the outgoings of it were at the **s**:	3220
17:10	*was* Manasseh's, and the **s** is his border;	3220
18:14	compassed the corner of the **s** southward,	3220
18:19	of the salt **s** at the south end of Jordan:	3220
19:11	their border went up toward the **s**,	3220
19:29	the outgoings thereof are at the **s** from	3220
23: 4	cut off, even *unto* the great **s** westward.	3220
24: 6	you came unto the **s**; and the Egyptians	3220
24: 6	chariots and horsemen *unto* the Red **s**.	3220
24: 7	brought the **s** upon them,	3220
Jdg 5:17	Asher continued on the **s** shore,	3220
7:12	as the sand by the **s** side for multitude.	3220
11:16	through the wilderness unto the Red **s**,	3220
1Sa 13: 5	as the sand which *is* on the **s** shore	3220
2Sa 17:11	as the sand that *is* by the **s** for multitude;	3220
22:16	the channels of the **s** appeared;	3220
1Ki 4:20	the sand which *is* by the **s** in multitude,	3220
4:29	*even* as the sand that *is* on the **s** shore.	3220
5: 9	*them* down from Lebanon unto the **s**:	3220
5: 9	I will convey them by **s** in flotes unto	3220
7:23	he made a molten **s**, ten cubits from the	3220
7:24	in a cubit, compassing the **s** round about:	3220
7:25	the **s** *was set* above upon them, and all	3220
7:39	he set the **s** on the right side of the house	3220
7:44	one **s**, and twelve oxen under the sea;	3220
7:44	one sea, and twelve oxen under the **s**;	3220
9:26	on the shore of the Red **s**, in the land of	3220
9:27	shipmen that had knowledge of the **s**,	3220
10:22	For the king had at **s** a navy of Tharshish	3220
18:43	servant, Go up now, look toward the **s**.	3220
18:44	there ariseth a little cloud out of the **s**,	3220
2Ki 14:25	of Hamath unto the **s** of the plain,	3220
16:17	took down the **s** from off the brasen oxen	3220
25:13	the brasen **s** that *was* in the house of	3220
25:16	one **s**, and the bases which Solomon had	3220
1Ch 16:32	Let the **s** roar, and the fulness thereof:	3220
18: 8	wherewith Solomon made the brasen **s**,	3220
2Ch 2:16	we will bring it to thee *in* flotes by **s** *to*	3220
4: 2	he made a molten **s** of ten cubits from	3220
4: 3	in a cubit, compassing the **s** round about.	3220
4: 4	the **s** *was set* above upon them, and all	3220
4: 6	but the **s** *was* for the priests to wash in.	3220
4:10	set the **s** on the right side of the east end,	3220
4:15	One **s**, and twelve oxen under it.	3220
8:17	Eloth, at the **s** side in the land of Edom.	3220
8:18	servants that had knowledge of the **s**;	3220
20: 2	thee from beyond the **s** on this side Syria;	3220
Ezr 3: 7	bring cedar trees from Lebanon to the **s**	3220
Ne 9: 9	and heardest their cry by the Red **s**;	3220
9:11	thou didst divide the **s** before them,	3220
9:11	that they went through the midst of the **s**	3220
Est 10: 1	the land, and *upon* the isles of the **s**.	3220
Job 6: 3	would be heavier than the sand of the **s**:	3220
7:12	*Am* I a **s**, or a whale, that thou settest a	3220
9: 8	and treadeth upon the waves of the **s**.	3220
11: 9	than the earth, and broader than the **s**.	3220
12: 8	the fishes of the **s** shall declare unto thee.	3220
14:11	the waters fail from the **s**, and the flood	3220
26:12	He divideth the **s** with his power,	3220
28:14	in me: and the **s** saith, *It is* not with me.	3220
36:30	and covereth the bottom of the **s**.	3220
38: 8	Or *who* shut up the **s** with doors, when it	3220
38:16	thou entered into the springs of the **s**?	3220
41:31	he maketh the **s** like a pot of ointment.	3220
Ps 8: 8	the fish of the **s**, *and* whatsoever passeth	3220

Ref	Text	Strong
Ps 33: 7	He gathereth the waters of the **s** together	3220
46: 2	be carried into the midst of the **s**;	3220
65: 5	and of them that are afar off *upon* the **s**:	3220
66: 6	He turned the **s** into dry *land*: they went	3220
68:22	*people* again from the depths of the **s**:	3220
72: 8	shall have dominion also from **s** to sea,	3220
72: 8	shall have dominion also from sea to **s**,	3220
74:13	Thou didst divide the **s** by thy strength:	3220
77:19	Thy way *is* in the **s**, and thy path in	3220
78:13	He divided the **s**, and caused them	3220
78:27	feathered fowls like as the sand of the **s**:	3220
78:53	but the **s** overwhelmed their enemies.	3220
80:11	She sent out her boughs unto the **s**,	3220
89: 9	Thou rulest the raging of the **s**: when	3220
89:25	I will set his hand also in the **s**,	3220
93: 4	*yea, than* the mighty waves of the **s**.	3220
95: 5	The **s** *is* his, and he made it: and his	3220
96:11	let the **s** roar, and the fulness thereof;	3220
98: 7	Let the **s** roar, and the fulness thereof;	3220
104:25	*So is* this great and wide **s**, wherein *are*	3220
106: 7	*him* at the sea, *even* at the Red **s**.	3220
106: 7	*him* at the sea, *even* at the Red **s**.	3220
106: 9	rebuked the Red **s** also, and it was dried	3220
106:22	of Ham, *and* terrible *things* by the Red **s**.	3220
107:23	They that go down to the **s** in ships, that	3220
114: 3	The **s** saw *it*, and fled: Jordan was driven	3220
114: 5	What ailed thee, O thou **s**, that thou	3220
136:13	him which divided the Red **s** into parts:	3220
136:15	and his host in the Red **s**:	3220
139: 9	*and* dwell in the uttermost parts of the **s**;	3220
146: 6	and earth, the **s**, and all that therein is:	3220
Pr 8:29	When he gave to the **s** his decree, that	3220
23:34	he that lieth down in the midst of the **s**,	3220
30:19	the way of a ship in the midst of the **s**;	3220
Ecc 1: 7	All the rivers run into the **s**; yet the sea *is*	3220
1: 7	run into the sea; yet the **s** *is* not full;	3220
Isa 5:30	against them like the roaring of the **s**:	3220
9: 1	grievously afflict *her by* the way of the **s**,	3220
10:22	thy people Israel be as the sand of the **s**,	3220
10:26	his rod *was* upon the **s**, so shall he lift it	3220
11: 9	of the LORD, as the waters cover the **s**.	3220
11:11	Hamath, and from the islands of the **s**.	3220
11:15	destroy the tongue of the Egyptian **s**;	3220
16: 8	stretched out, they are gone over the **s**.	3220
18: 2	sendeth ambassadors by the **s**, even in	3220
19: 5	the waters shall fail from the **s**, and the	3220
21: 1	The burden of the desert of the **s**.	3220
23: 2	that pass over the **s**, have replenished.	3220
23: 4	the **s** hath spoken, *even* the strength of	3220
23: 4	*even* the strength of the **s**, saying, I travail	3220
23:11	He stretched out his hand over the **s**,	3220
24:14	they shall cry aloud from the **s**.	3220
24:15	LORD God of Israel in the isles of the **s**.	3220
27: 1	he shall slay the dragon that *is* in the **s**.	3220
42:10	ye that go down to the **s**, and all that is	3220
43:16	Which maketh a way in the **s**, and a path	3220
48:18	thy righteousness as the waves of the **s**:	3220
50: 2	at my rebuke I dry up the **s**, I make	3220
51:10	*Art* thou not it which hath dried the **s**,	3220
51:10	hath made the depths of the **s** a way for	3220
51:15	that divided the **s**, whose waves roared:	3220
57:20	wicked *are* like the troubled **s**, when it	3220
60: 5	the abundance of the **s** shall be converted	3220
63:11	of the **s** with the shepherd of his flock?	3220
Jer 5:22	the bound of the **s** *by* a perpetual decree,	3220
6:23	voice roareth like the **s**; and they ride	3220
25:22	kings of the isles which *are* beyond the **s**,	3220
27:19	concerning the **s**, and concerning the	3220
31:35	which divideth the **s** when the waves	3220
33:22	neither the sand of the **s** measured:	3220
46:18	and as Carmel by the **s**, *so* shall he come.	3220
47: 7	against Ashkelon, and against the **s** shore?	3220
48:32	thy plants are gone over the **s**, they reach	3220
48:32	the sea, they reach *even* to the **s** of Jazer:	3220
49:21	the noise thereof was heard in the Red **s**.	3220
49:23	*is* sorrow on the **s**; it cannot be quiet.	3220
50:42	their voice shall roar like the **s**,	3220
51:36	I will dry up her **s**, *so* shall her springs	3220
51:42	The **s** is come up upon Babylon: she is	3220
52:17	the brasen **s** that *was* in the house of	3220
52:20	one **s**, and twelve brasen bulls that *were*	3220
La 2:13	for thy breach *is* great like the **s**: who can	3220
4: 3	Even the **s monsters** draw out the breast,	8577
Eze 25:16	and destroy the remnant of the **s** coast.	3220
26: 3	as the **s** causeth his waves to come up.	3220
26: 5	the spreading of nets in the midst of the **s**:	3220
26:16	all the princes of the **s** shall come down	3220
26:17	which wast strong in the **s**, she and	3220
26:18	isles that *are* in the **s** shall be troubled at	3220
27: 3	thou that art situate at the entry of the **s**,	3220
27: 9	all the ships of the **s** with their mariners	3220
27:29	the mariners, *and* all the pilots of the **s**,	3220
27:32	like the destroyed in the midst of the **s**?	3220
38:20	So that the fishes of the **s**, and the fowls	3220
39:11	of the passengers *on* the east of the **s**:	3220
47: 8	down into the desert, and go into the **s**:	3220
47: 8	*which* being brought forth into the **s**,	3220
47:10	as the fish of the great **s**, exceeding many.	3220
47:15	from the great **s**, the way of Hethlon,	3220
47:17	the border from the **s** shall be Hazar-enan,	3220
47:18	Jordan, from the border unto the east **s**.	3220
47:19	strife *in* Kadesh, *the* river to the great **s**.	3220
47:20	The west side also *shall be* the great **s**	3220
48:28	*and* to the river toward the great **s**.	3220
Da 7: 2	of the heaven strove upon the great **s**.	3221

Ref	Text	Strong
Da 7: 3	four great beasts came up from the **s**,	3221
Hos 1:10	of Israel shall be as the sand of the **s**,	3220
4: 3	fishes of the **s** also shall be taken away.	3220
Joel 2:20	with his face toward the east **s**,	3220
2:20	his hinder part towards the utmost **s**,	3220
Am 5: 8	that calleth for the waters of the **s**,	3220
8:12	they shall wander from **s** to sea,	3220
8:12	they shall wander from sea to **s**,	3220
9: 3	hid from my sight in the bottom of the **s**,	3220
9: 6	he that calleth for the waters of the **s**,	3220
Jnh 1: 4	the LORD sent out a great wind into the **s**,	3220
1: 4	there was a mighty tempest in the **s**,	3220
1: 5	the wares that *were* in the ship into the **s**,	3220
1: 9	which hath made the **s** and the dry *land*.	3220
1:11	thee, that the **s** may be calm unto us?	3220
1:11	for the **s** wrought, and was tempestuous.	3220
1:12	Take me up, and cast me forth into the **s**;	3220
1:12	the sea; so shall the **s** be calm unto you:	3220
1:13	for the **s** wrought, and was tempestuous	3220
1:15	up Jonah, and cast him forth into the **s**:	3220
1:15	the sea: and the **s** ceased from her raging.	3220
Mic 7:12	from **s** to sea, and *from* mountain *to*	3220
7:12	from sea to **s**, and *from* mountain *to*	3220
7:19	cast all their sins into the depths of the **s**.	3220
Na 1: 4	He rebuketh the **s**, and maketh it dry,	3220
3: 8	whose rampart *was* the **s**, *and* her wall	3220
3: 8	the sea, *and* her wall *was* from the **s**?	3220
Hab 1:14	makest men as the fishes of the **s**,	3220
2:14	of the LORD, as the waters cover the **s**.	3220
3: 8	thy wrath against the **s**, that thou didst	3220
3:15	Thou didst walk through the **s** *with* thine	3220
Zep 1: 3	fishes of the **s**, and the stumblingblocks	3220
2: 5	Woe unto the inhabitants of the **s** coast,	3220
2: 6	the coast shall be dwellings *and*	3220
Hag 2: 6	the earth, and the **s**, and the dry *land*;	3220
Zec 9: 4	and he will smite her power in the **s**;	3220
9:10	his dominion *shall be* from **s** *even* to sea,	3220
9:10	his dominion *shall be* from sea *even* to **s**,	3220
10:11	he shall pass through the **s** *with* affliction,	3220
10:11	shall smite the waves in the **s**, and all	3220
14: 8	half of them toward the former **s**,	3220
14: 8	and half of them toward the hinder **s**:	3220
Mt 4:13	Capernaum, which is **upon the s coast**,	3864
4:15	*by* the way of the **s**, beyond Jordan,	2281
4:18	And Jesus, walking by the **s** of Galilee,	2281
4:18	his brother, casting a net into the **s**:	2281
8:24	there arose a great tempest in the **s**,	2281
8:26	arose, and rebuked the winds and the **s**;	2281
8:27	that even the winds and the **s** obey him?	2281
8:32	violently down a steep place into the **s**,	2281
13: 1	out of the house, and sat by the **s** side.	2281
13:47	*that was* cast into the **s**, and gathered of	2281
14:24	the ship was now in the midst of the **s**,	2281
14:25	Jesus went unto them, walking on the **s**.	2281
14:26	the disciples saw him walking on the **s**,	2281
15:29	and came nigh unto the **s** of Galilee;	2281
17:27	go thou to the **s**, and cast a hook,	2281
18: 6	he were drowned in the depth of the **s**.	2281
21:21	removed, and be thou cast into the **s**;	2281
23:15	for ye compass **s** and land to make one	2281
Mk 1:16	Now as he walked by the **s** of Galilee,	2281
1:16	his brother casting a net into the **s**:	2281
2:13	And he went forth again by the **s** side;	2281
3: 7	himself with his disciples to the **s**:	2281
4: 1	And he began again to teach by the **s** side:	2281
4: 1	he entered into a ship, and sat in the **s**;	2281
4: 1	the whole multitude was by the **s** on	2281
4:39	and said unto the **s**, Peace, be still.	2281
4:41	that even the wind and the **s** obey him?	2281
5: 1	came over unto the other side of the **s**,	2281
5:13	violently down a steep place into the **s**,	2281
5:13	two thousand,) and were choked in the **s**.	2281
5:21	unto him: and he was nigh unto the **s**.	2281
6:47	the ship was in the midst of the **s**,	2281
6:48	walking upon the **s**, and would have	2281
6:49	when they saw him walking upon the **s**,	2281
7:31	and Sidon, he came unto the **s** of Galilee,	2281
9:42	his neck, and he were cast into the **s**.	2281
11:23	removed, and be thou cast into the **s**;	2281
Lk 6:17	and *from* the **s coast** of Tyre and Sidon,	3882
17: 2	he cast into the **s**, than that he should	2281
17: 6	by the root, and be thou planted in the **s**;	2281
21:25	the **s** and the waves roaring;	2281
Jn 6: 1	After these *things* Jesus went over the **s**	2281
6: 1	sea of Galilee, *which is* the **s** of Tiberias.	NIG
6:16	his disciples went down unto the **s**,	2281
6:17	and went over the **s** towards Capernaum.	2281
6:18	And the **s** arose by reason of a great wind	2281
6:19	they see Jesus walking on the **s**,	2281
6:22	saw that there was none other boat	
6:25	had found him on the other side of the **s**,	2281
21: 1	again to the disciples at the **s** of Tiberias;	2281
21: 7	naked,) and did cast himself into the **s**.	2281
Ac 4:24	earth, and the **s**, and all that in them is:	2281
7:36	and in the Red **s**, and in the wilderness	2281
10: 6	a tanner, whose house is by the **s** side:	2281
10:32	house of *one* Simon a tanner by the **s** side:	2281
14:15	and the **s**, and all *things* that are therein:	2281
17:14	sent away Paul to go as it were to the **s**:	2281
27: 5	And when we had sailed over the **s** of	3989
27:30	they had let down the boat into the **s**,	2281
27:38	ship, and cast out the wheat into the **s**.	2281
27:40	they committed *themselves* unto the **s**,	2281
27:43	should cast *themselves* first into the **s**,	NIG
28: 4	whom, though he hath escaped the **s**,	2281

Ref	Text	Strong's
Ro	9:27 children of Israel be as the sand of the **s**,	2281
1Co	10: 1 the cloud, and all passed through the **s**,	2281
	10: 2 unto Moses in the cloud and in the **s**;	2281
2Co	11:26 perils in the wilderness, *in* perils in the **s**,	2281
Heb	11:12 as the sand which is by the **s** shore	2281
	11:29 By faith they passed through the Red **s** as	2281
Jas	1: 6 he that wavereth is like a wave of the **s**	2281
	3: 7 and of *things* **in the s**, is tamed,	1724
Jude	1:13 Raging waves of the **s**, foaming out their	2281
Rev	4: 6 before the throne *there was* a **s** of glass	2281
	5:13 such as are in the **s**, and all that are in	2281
	7: 1 the earth, nor on the **s**, nor on any tree.	2281
	7: 2 it was given to hurt the earth and the **s**,	2281
	7: 3 not the earth, neither the **s**, nor the trees,	2281
	8: 8 burning with fire was cast into the **s**:	2281
	8: 8 and the third *part* of the **s** became blood;	2281
	8: 9 *part* of the creatures which were in the **s**,	2281
	10: 2 and he set his right foot upon the **s**,	2281
	10: 5 the angel which I saw stand upon the **s**	2281
	10: 6 the **s**, and the *things* which are therein,	2281
	10: 8 of the angel which standeth upon the **s**.	2281
	12:12 to the inhabiters of the earth and of the **s**!	2281
	13: 1 And I stood upon the sand of the **s**,	2281
	13: 1 and saw a beast rise up out of the **s**,	2281
	14: 7 and the **s**, and the fountains of waters.	2281
	15: 2 And I saw as *it were* a **s** of glass mingled	2281
	15: 2 stand on the **s** of glass, having *the harps*	2281
	16: 3 angel poured out his vial upon the **s**;	2281
	16: 3 and every living soul died in the **s**.	2281
	18:17 and sailors, and as many as trade by **s**,	2281
	18:19 ships in the **s** by reason of her costliness:	2281
	18:21 and cast *it* into the **s**, saying,	2281
	20: 8 number of whom *is* as the sand of the **s**.	2281
	20:13 the **s** gave up the dead which were in	2281
	21: 1 passed away; and there was no more **s**.	2281

SEA COWS See BADGERS'

SEAFARING (1) [FARE, SEA]

| Eze | 26:17 *wast* inhabited of **s** men, the renowned | 3220 |

SEAL (26) [SEALED, SEALEST, SEALETH, SEALING, SEALS]

1Ki	21: 8 sealed *them* with his **s**, and sent the	2368
Ne	9:38 princes, Levites, *and* priests, **s** *unto it.*	2856
Est	8: 8 king's name, and **s** *it* with the king's ring:	2856
Job	38:14 It is turned as clay *to* the **s**; and they	2368
	41:15 pride, shut up *together as with* a close **s**.	2368
SS	8: 6 Set me as a **s** upon thine heart, as a seal	2368
	8: 6 upon thine heart, as a **s** upon thine arm:	2368
Isa	8:16 the law among my disciples.	2856
Jer	32:44 **s** *them*, and take witnesses in the land of	2856
Da	9:24 to **s** **up** the vision and prophecy,	2856
	12: 4 shut up the words, and **s** the book,	2856
Jn	3:33 hath **set to** *his* **s** that God is true.	4972
Ro	4:11 a **s** of the righteousness of the faith which	4973
1Co	9: 2 for the **s** of mine apostleship are ye in	4973
2Ti	2:19 having this **s**, The Lord knoweth them	4973
Rev	5: 3 And when he had opened the second **s**,	4973
	6: 5 And when he had opened the third **s**,	4973
	6: 7 And when he had opened the fourth **s**,	4973
	6: 9 And when he had opened the fifth **s**,	4973
	6:12 I beheld when he had opened the sixth **s**,	4973
	7: 2 the east, having the **s** of the living God:	4973
	8: 1 And when he had opened the seventh **s**,	4973
	9: 4 only *those* men which have not the **s** of	4972
	10: 4 **S** *up* those things which the seven	4972
	20: 3 and shut him up, and **set a s** upon him,	4972
	22:10 **S** not the sayings of the prophecy of this	4972

SEALED (36) [SEAL]

Dt	32:34 with me, *and* **s up** among my treasures?	2856
1Ki	21: 8 **s** *them* with his seal, and sent the letters	2856
Ne	10: 1 Now those that **s** *were*, Nehemiah,	2856
Est	3:12 was it written, and **s** with the king's ring.	2856
	8: 8 with the king's ring, may no man	2856
	8:10 **s** *it* with the king's ring, and sent letters	2856
Job	14:17 My transgression *is* **s up** in a bag,	2856
SS	4:12 *my* spouse; a spring shut up, a fountain **s**.	2856
Isa	29:11 unto you as the words of a book that is **s**,	2856
	29:11 and he saith, I cannot; for it *is* **s**:	2856
Jer	32:10 **s** *it*, and took witnesses, and weighed	2856
	32:11 that which was *according to* the law	2856
	32:14 which is **s**, and this evidence which is	2856
Da	6:17 the king **s** it with his own signet,	2857
	12: 9 closed up and **s** till the time of the end.	2856
Jn	6:27 unto you: for him hath God the Father **s**.	4972
Ro	15:28 and have **s** to them this fruit,	4972
2Co	1:22 Who hath also **s** us, and given the earnest	4972
Eph	1:13 ye were **s** with *that* holy Spirit of promise,	4972
	4:30 whereby ye are **s** unto the day of	4972
Rev	5: 1 and on the backside, **s** with seven seals.	2696
	7: 3 till we have **s** the servants of our God in	4972
	7: 4 heard the number of them which were **s**:	4972
	7: 4 *there were* an hundred *and* forty *and*	4972
	7: 5 Of the tribe of Juda *were* **s** twelve	4972
	7: 5 Of the tribe of Reuben *were* **s** twelve	4972
	7: 6 Of the tribe of Gad *were* **s** twelve	4972
	7: 6 Of the tribe of Aser *were* **s** twelve	4972
	7: 6 Of the tribe of Nephthalim *were* **s** twelve	4972
	7: 6 Of the tribe of Manasses *were* **s** twelve	4972
	7: 7 Of the tribe of Simeon *were* **s** twelve	4972
	7: 7 Of the tribe of Levi *were* **s** twelve	4972
	7: 7 Of the tribe of Isachar *were* **s** twelve	4972
	7: 8 Of the tribe of Zabulon *were* **s** twelve	4972

Rev	7: 8 Of the tribe of Joseph *were* **s** twelve	4972
	7: 8 Of the tribe of Benjamin *were* **s** twelve	4972

SEALEST (1) [SEAL]

| Eze | 28:12 Thou **s** up the sum, full *of* wisdom, | 2856 |

SEALETH (3) [SEAL]

Job	9: 7 and it riseth not; and **s** up the stars.	1157+2856
	33:16 the ears of men, and **s** their instruction.	2856
	37: 7 He **s** up the hand of every man; that all	2856

SEALING (1) [SEAL]

| Mt | 27:66 **s** the stone, and setting a watch. | 4972 |

SEALS (5) [SEAL]

Rev	5: 1 and on the backside, sealed with seven **s**.	4973
	5: 2 open the book, and to loose the **s** thereof?	4973
	5: 5 book, and to loose the seven **s** thereof.	4973
	5: 9 take the book, and to open the **s** thereof:	4973
	6: 1 saw when the Lamb opened one of the **s**,	4973

SEAM (1)

| Jn | 19:23 now the coat was **without s**, woven from | 729 |

SEARCH (48) [SEARCHED, SEARCHEST, SEARCHETH, SEARCHING, SEARCHINGS, UNSEARCHABLE]

Lev	27:33 He shall not **s** whether it be good or bad,	1239
Nu	10:33 to **s** out a resting place for them.	8446
	13: 2 that they may **s** the land of Canaan,	8446
	13:32 through which we have gone to **s** it,	8446
	14: 7 land, which we passed through to **s** it,	8446
	14:36 the men, which Moses sent to **s** the land,	8446
	14:38 which were of the men that went to **s**	8446
Dt	1:22 they shall **s** us **out** the land, and bring us	2658
	1:33 to **s** you **out** a place to pitch your tents *in*,	8446
	13:14 and **make s**, and ask diligently:	2713
Jos	2: 2 children of Israel to **s out** the country.	2658
	2: 3 for they be come to **s out** all the country.	2658
Jdg	18: 2 to spy out the land, and to **s** it;	2713
	18: 2 and they said unto them, Go, **s** the land:	2713
1Sa	23:23 that I will **s** him **out** throughout all	2664
2Sa	10: 3 to **s** the city, and to spy it out,	2713
1Ki	20: 6 they shall **s** thine house, and the houses	2664
2Ki	10:23 **s**, and look that there be here with you	2664
1Ch	19: 3 not his servants come unto thee for to **s**,	2713
Ezr	4:15 That **s** may be **made** in the book of	1240
	4:19 hath been **made**, and it is found that	1240
	5:17 let there be **s made** in the king's treasure	1240
	6: 1 and **s** was **made** in the house of the rolls,	1240
Job	8: 8 prepare *thyself* to the **s** of their fathers:	2714
	13: 9 *Is it* good that he should **s** you **out**?	2713
	38:16 or hast thou walked in the **s** of the depth?	2714
Ps	44:21 Shall not God **s** this **out**? for he knoweth	2713
	64: 6 They **s** out iniquities; they accomplish a	2664
	64: 6 iniquities; they accomplish a diligent **s**:	2665
	77: 6 heart: and my spirit **made diligent s**.	2664
	139:23 **S** me, O God, and know my heart: try me,	2713
Pr	25: 2 the honour of kings *is* to **s** out a matter.	2713
	25:27 *for men* to **s** their own glory *is not* glory.	2714
Ecc	1:13 **s** out by wisdom concerning all *things*	8446
	7:25 to **s**, and to seek out wisdom,	8446
Jer	2:34 I have not found it by **secret s**, but upon	4290
	17:10 I the Lord **s** the heart, *I* try the reins,	2713
	29:13 find *me*, when ye shall **s for** me with all	1875
La	3:40 Let us **s** and try our ways, and turn again	2664
Eze	34: 6 and none did **s** or seek *after* them.	1875
	34: 8 neither did my shepherds **s** for my flock,	1875
	34:11 will both **s** my sheep, and seek them out.	1875
	39:14 after the end of seven months shall they **s**.	2713
Am	9: 3 I will **s** and take them out thence;	2664
Zep	1:12 *that* I will **s** Jerusalem with candles,	2664
Mt	2: 8 Go and **s** diligently for the young child;	1833
Jn	5:39 **S** the Scriptures; for in them ye think ye	2045
	7:52 **S**, and look: for out of Galilee ariseth no	2045

SEARCHED (20) [SEARCH]

Ge	31:34 Laban **s** all the tent, but found *them* not.	4959
	31:35 And he **s**, but found not the images.	2664
	31:37 Whereas thou hast **s** all my stuff, what	4959
	44:12 he **s**, *and* began at the eldest, and left at	2664
Nu	13:21 the land from the wilderness of Zin unto	8446
	13:32 they had **s** unto the children of Israel,	8446
	14: 6 *which were* of them that **s** the land,	8446
	14:34 the number of the days *in* which ye **s**	8446
Dt	1:24 unto the valley of Eshcol, and **s** it **out**.	7270
Job	5:27 we have **s** it, so it *is*; hear it, and know	2713
	28:27 he prepared it, yea, and **s** it **out**.	2713
	29:16 and the cause which I knew not I **s out**.	2713
	32:11 reasons, whilst ye **s out** what to say.	2714
	36:26 can the number of his years be **s out**.	2714
Ps	139: 1 O Lord, thou hast **s** me, and known *me*.	2713
Jer	31:37 foundations of the earth **s out** beneath,	2713
	46:23 saith the Lord, though it cannot be **s**;	2713
Ob	1: 6 How are the *things* of Esau **s out**!	2664
Ac	17:11 and **s** the scriptures daily, whether those	350
1Pe	1:10 prophets have inquired and **s diligently**,	1830

SEARCHEST (2) [SEARCH]

| Job | 10: 6 after mine iniquity, and **s** after my sin? | 1875 |
| Pr | 2: 4 silver, and **s** for her as *for* hid treasures; | 2664 |

SEARCHETH (8) [SEARCH]

1Ch	28: 9 for the Lord **s** all hearts,	1875
Job	28: 3 **s out** all perfection, the stones of darkness	2713
	39: 8 and he **s** after every green thing.	1875

Pr	18:17 but his neighbour cometh and **s** him.	2713
	28:11 poor that hath understanding **s** him **out**.	2713
Ro	8:27 And he that **s** the hearts knoweth what *is*	2045
1Co	2:10 for the Spirit **s** all *things*, yea, the deep	2045
Rev	2:23 shall know that I am he which **s** the reins	2045

SEARCHING (5) [SEARCH]

Nu	13:25 returned from **s** of the land after forty	8446
Job	11: 7 Canst thou *by* **s** find out God? canst thou	2714
Pr	20:27 **s** all the inward parts of the belly.	2664
Isa	40:28 *there is* no **s** of his understanding.	2714
1Pe	1:11 **S** what, or what manner of time the Spirit	2045

SEARCHINGS (1) [SEARCH]

| Jdg | 5:16 of Reuben *there were* great **s** of heart. | 2714 |

SEARED (2)

| 1Ti | 4: 2 their conscience **s with a hot iron**; | 2743 |

SEAS (25) [SEA]

Ge	1:10 together of the waters called he **S**:	3220
	1:22 fill the waters in the **s**, and let fowl	3220
Lev	11: 9 the **s**, and in the rivers, them shall ye eat.	3220
	11:10 all that have not fins nor scales in the **s**,	3220
Dt	33:19 they shall suck *of* the abundance of the **s**,	3220
Ne	9: 6 the **s**, and all that *is* therein,	3220
Ps	8: 8 passeth *through* the paths of the **s**.	3220
	24: 2 for he hath founded it upon the **s**,	3220
	65: 7 Which stilleth the noise of the **s**,	3220
	69:34 the **s**, and every *thing* that moveth	3220
	135: 6 and in earth, in the **s**, and all deep places.	3220
Isa	17:12 make a noise like the noise of the **s**;	3220
Jer	15: 8 increased to me above the sand of the **s**:	3220
Eze	27: 4 Thy borders *are* in the midst of the **s**,	3220
	27:25 made very glorious in the midst of the **s**.	3220
	27:26 hath broken thee in the midst of the **s**.	3220
	27:27 shall fall into the midst of the **s** in the day	3220
	27:33 When thy wares went forth out of the **s**,	3220
	27:34 by the **s** in the depths of the waters,	3220
	28: 2 *in* the seat of God, in the midst of the **s**;	3220
	28: 8 *them that are* slain in the midst of the **s**.	3220
	32: 2 nations, and thou *art* as a whale in the **s**:	3220
Da	11:45 the **s** in the glorious holy mountain;	3220
Jnh	2: 3 me *into* the deep, in the midst of the **s**;	3220
Ac	27:41 falling into a place **where two s** met,	1337

SEASON (56) [SEASONED, SEASONS]

Ge	40: 4 and they continued a **s** in ward.	3117
Ex	13:10 keep this ordinance in his **s** from year to	4150
Lev	2:13 thy meat offering shalt thou **s** with salt;	4414
	26: 4 I will give you rain in **due s**, and the land	6256
Nu	9: 2 keep the passover at his **appointed s**.	4150
	9: 3 even, ye shall keep it in his **appointed s**:	4150
	9: 7 **appointed s** among the children of Israel?	4150
	9:13 offering of the Lord in his **appointed s**,	4150
	28: 2 ye observe to offer unto me in their **due s**.	4150
Dt	11:14 give *you* the rain of your land in his **due s**,	6256
	16: 6 the **s** that thou camest forth out of Egypt.	4150
	28:12 to give the rain unto thy land in his **s**,	6256
Jos	24: 7 and ye dwelt in the wilderness a long **s**.	3117
2Ki	4:16 he said, About this **s**, according to the	4150
	4:17 bare a son at that **s** that Elisha had said	4150
1Ch	21:29 at that **s** in the high place at Gibeon.	6256
2Ch	15: 3 for a long **s** Israel *hath been* without	3117
Job	5:26 like as a shock of corn cometh in in his **s**.	6256
	30:17 bones are pierced in me in the **night s**:	3915
	38:32 thou bring forth Mazzaroth in his **s**?	6256
Ps	1: 3 that bringeth forth his fruit in his **s**;	6256
	22: 2 and in the **night s**, and am not silent.	3915
	104:27 mayest give *them* their meat in **due s**.	6256
	145:15 and thou givest them their meat in **due s**.	6256
Pr	15:23 word *spoken* in **due s**, how good	6256+2050.2
Ecc	3: 1 To every *thing there is* a **s**, and a time to	2165
	10:17 thy princes eat in **due s**, for strength,	6256
Isa	50: 4 **speak** a word in **s** to him *that* is weary:	5790
Jer	5:24 both the former and the latter, in his **s**:	6256
	33:20 should not be day and night in their **s**;	6256
Eze	34:26 cause the shower to come down in his **s**;	6256
Da	7:12 yet their lives were prolonged for a **s** and	2166
Hos	2: 9 my wine in the **s** thereof, and will recover	4150
Mt	24:45 household, to give them meat in **due s**?	2540
Mk	9:50 lost his saltness, wherewith will ye **s** it?	741
	12: 2 And at the **s** he sent to the husbandmen a	2540
Lk	1:20 which shall be fulfilled in their **s**.	2540
	4:13 he departed from him for a **s**.	2540
	12:42 give *them their* portion of meat in **due s**?	2540
	13: 1 There were present at that **s** some that	2540
	20:10 And at the **s** he sent a servant to	2540
	23: 8 he was desirous to see him of a long **s**,	NIG
Jn	5: 4 an angel went down at a *certain* **s** into	2540
	5:35 ye were willing for a **s** to rejoice in his	5610
Ac	13:11 shalt be blind, not seeing the sun for a **s**.	2540
	19:22 but he himself stayed in Asia for a **s**.	5550
	24:25 when I have a **convenient s**, I will call	2540
2Co	7: 8 you sorry, though *it were* but for a **s**.	5610
Gal	6: 9 till we **s** we shall reap, if we faint not.	2540
2Ti	4: 2 be instant **in s**, out of season; reprove,	2122
	4: 2 be instant in season, **out of s**; reprove,	171
Phm	1:15 For perhaps he therefore departed for a **s**,	5610
Heb	11:25 than to enjoy the pleasures of sin for a **s**;	4340
1Pe	1: 6 though now for a **s**, if need be,	3641
Rev	6:11 that they should rest yet for a little **s**,	5550
	20: 3 and after that he must be loosed a little **s**.	5550

S

SEASONED (2) [SEASON]

Lk	14:34	lost his savour, wherewith shall it be s?	741
Col	4: 6	speech *be* alway with grace, **s** with salt,	741

SEASONS (12) [SEASON]

Ge	1:14	signs, and for **s**, and for days, and years:	4150
Ex	18:22	let them judge the people at all **s**:	6256
	18:26	they judged the people at all **s**: the hard	6256
Lev	23: 4	which ye shall proclaim in their **s**.	4150
Ps	16: 7	my reins also instruct me *in* the **night s**.	3915
	104:19	He appointed the moon for **s**: the sun	4150
Da	2:21	he changeth the times and the **s**:	2166
Mt	21:41	shall render him the fruits in their **s**.	2540
Ac	1: 7	is not for you to know the times or the **s**,	2540
	14:17	gave us rain from heaven, and fruitful **s**,	2540
	20:18	manner I have been with you at all **s**,	5550
1Th	5: 1	But of the times and the **s**, brethren,	2540

SEAT (59) [SIT]

Ex	25:17	thou shalt make a **mercy s** *of* pure gold:	3727
	25:18	them, in the two ends of the **mercy s**.	3727
	25:19	*even* of the **mercy s** shall ye make	3727
	25:20	covering the **mercy s** with their wings,	3727
	25:20	toward the **mercy s** shall the faces of	3727
	25:21	thou shalt put the **mercy s** above upon	3727
	25:22	with thee from above the **mercy s**,	3727
	26:34	thou shalt put the **mercy s** upon the ark	3727
	30: 6	before the **mercy s** that *is* over	3727
	31: 7	the **mercy s** that *is* thereupon, and all	3727
	35:12	*with* the **mercy s**, and the vail of	3727
	37: 6	he made the **mercy s** *of* pure gold:	3727
	37: 7	them, on the two ends of the **mercy s**	3727
	37: 8	of the **mercy s** made he the cherubims	3727
	37: 9	with their wings over the **mercy s**,	3727
	39:35	and the staves thereof, and the **mercy s**,	3727
	40:20	and put the **mercy s** above upon the ark:	3727
Lev	16: 2	*place* within the vail before the **mercy s**;	3727
	16: 2	appear in the cloud upon the **mercy s**.	3727
	16:13	that *is* upon the Testimony,	3727
	16:14	*it* with his finger upon the **mercy s**	3727
	16:14	before the **mercy s** shall he sprinkle of	3727
	16:15	sprinkle it upon the **mercy s**, and before	3727
	16:15	the mercy seat, and before the **mercy s**:	3727
Nu	7:89	**mercy s** that *was* upon the ark of	3727
Jdg	3:20	God unto thee. And he arose out of *his* **s**.	3678
1Sa	1: 9	Now Eli the priest sat upon a **s** by a post	3678
	4:13	Eli sat upon a **s** *by* the wayside watching:	3678
	4:18	that he fell from off the **s** backward by	3678
	20:18	be missed, because thy **s** will be empty.	4186
	20:25	the king sat upon his **s**, as at other times,	4186
	20:25	at other times, *even* upon a **s** by the wall:	4186
2Sa	23: 8	The Tachmonite that sat in the **s**,	7675
1Ki	10:19	caused a **s** to be set for the king's mother;	3678
	10:19	stays on either side on the place of the **s**,	7675
1Ch	28:11	and of the place of the **mercy s**,	3727
Est	3: 1	set his **s** above all the princes that *were*	3678
Job	23: 3	find him! *that* I might come *even* to his **s**!	8499
	29: 7	city, when I prepared my **s** in the street;	4186
Ps	1: 1	nor sitteth in the **s** of the scornful.	4186
Pr	9:14	on a **s** in the high places of the city,	3678
Eze	8: 3	where *was* the **s** of the image of jealousy,	4186
	28: 2	said, I *am* a God, I sit *in* the **s** of God,	4186
Am	6: 3	and cause the **s** of violence to come near;	7675
Mt	23: 2	and the Pharisees sit in Moses' **s**:	2515
	27:19	he was set down on the **judgment s**,	968
Jn	19:13	sat down in the **judgment s** in a place	968
Ac	18:12	and brought him to the **judgment s**,	968
	18:16	And he drave them from the **judgment s**.	968
	18:17	and beat *him* before the **judgment s**.	968
	25: 6	the next day sitting in the **judgment s**,	968
	25:10	said Paul, I stand at Cesar's **judgment s**,	968
	25:17	on the morrow I sat on the **judgment s**,	968
Ro	14:10	we shall all stand before the **judgment s**	968
2Co	5:10	appear before the **judgment s** of Christ;	968
Heb	9: 5	of glory shadowing the **mercy s**;	2435
Rev	2:13	*even* where Satan's **s** *is:* and thou holdest	2362
	13: 2	his power, and his **s**, and great authority.	2362
	16:10	out his vial upon the **s** of the beast;	2362

SEATED (1) [SIT]

Dt	33:21	*in* a portion of the lawgiver, *was* he **s**;	5603

SEATS (11) [SIT]

Mt	21:12	and the **s** of them that sold doves,	2515
	23: 6	feasts, and the **chief s** in the synagogues,	4410
Mk	11:15	and the **s** of them that sold doves;	2515
	12:39	And the **chief s** in the synagogues,	4410
Lk	1:52	hath put down the mighty from *their* **s**,	2362
	11:43	for ye love the **uppermost s** in	4410
	20:46	and the **highest s** in the synagogues,	4410
Jas	2: 6	and draw you before the **judgment s**?	2922
Rev	4: 4	about the throne *were* four and twenty **s**:	2362
	4: 4	upon the **s** I saw four and twenty elders	2362
	11:16	which sat before God on their **s**,	2362

SEATWARD (1) [SIT]

Ex	37: 9	*even* toward the **mercy s** were the faces of	3727

SEBA (4)

Ge	10: 7	**S**, and Havilah, and Sabtah, and Raamah,	5434
1Ch	1: 9	**S**, and Havilah, and Sabta, and Raamah,	5434
Ps	72:10	the kings of Sheba and **S** shall offer gifts.	5434
Isa	43: 3	*for* thy ransom, Ethiopia and **S** for thee.	5434

SEBAM See SHEBAM

SEBAT (1)

Zec	1: 7	which *is* the month **S**, in the second year	7627

SECACAH (1)

Jos	15:61	wilderness, Beth-arabah, Middin, and **S**,	5527

SECHU (1)

1Sa	19:22	and came to a great well that *is* in **S**:	7906

SECOND (173) [SECONDARILY, TWO]

Ge	1: 8	and the morning were the **s** day.	8145
	2:13	the name of the **s** river *is* Gihon:	8145
	6:16	**s**, and third *stories* shalt thou make it.	8145
	7:11	in the **s** month, the seventeenth day of	8145
	8:14	in the **s** month, on the seven and	8145
	22:15	unto Abraham out of heaven the **s** time,	8145
	30: 7	conceived again, and bare Jacob a **s** son.	8145
	30:12	Zilpah Leah's maid bare Jacob a **s** son.	8145
	32:19	so commanded he the **s**, and the third,	8145
	41: 5	he slept and dreamed the **s** time:	8145
	41:43	he made him to ride in the **s** chariot	4932
	41:52	the name of the **s** called he Ephraim:	8145
	43:10	surely now we had returned this **s** time.	6471
	47:18	they came unto him the **s** year,	8145
Ex	2:13	when he went out the **s** day, behold,	8145
	16: 1	on the fifteenth day of the **s** month after	8145
	26: 4	*another* curtain, in the coupling of the **s**.	8145
	26: 5	curtain that *is* in the coupling of the **s**;	8145
	26:10	edge of the curtain which coupleth the **s**.	8145
	26:20	for the **s** side of the tabernacle on the	8145
	28:18	the **s** row *shall be* an emerald, a sapphire,	8145
	36:11	*another* curtain, in the coupling of the **s**:	8145
	36:12	which *was* in the coupling of the **s**:	8145
	36:17	edge of the curtain which coupleth the **s**.	8145
	39:11	the **s** row, an emerald, a sapphire,	8145
	40:17	it came to pass in the first month in the **s**	8145
Lev	5:10	he shall offer the **s** *for* a burnt offering,	8145
	13:58	it shall be washed the **s** time, and shall	8145
Nu	1: 1	on the first *day* of the **s** month,	8145
	1: 1	in the **s** year after they were come out of	8145
	1:18	together on the first *day* of the **s** month,	8145
	2:16	And they shall set forth in the **s** rank.	8145
	7:18	On the **s** day Nethaneel the son of Zuar,	8145
	9: 1	in the first month of the **s** year after they	8145
	9:11	The fourteenth day of the **s** month at	8145
	10: 6	When you blow an alarm the **s** time,	8145
	10:11	to pass on the twentieth *day* of the **s**	8145
	10:11	*day* of the **s** month, in the year,	8145
	29:17	on the **s** day ye shall *offer* twelve young	8145
Jos	5: 2	again the children of Israel the **s** time.	8145
	6:14	the **s** day they compassed the city once,	8145
	10:32	which took it on the **s** day, and smote it	8145
	19: 1	the **s** lot came forth to Simeon, *even* for	8145
Jdg	6:25	even the bullock of seven years old,	8145
	6:26	take the **s** bullock, and offer a burnt	8145
	6:28	the **s** bullock was offered upon the altar	8145
	20:24	the children of Benjamin the **s** day.	8145
	20:25	against them out of Gibeah the **s** day,	8145
1Sa	8: 2	was Joel; and the name of his **s**, Abiah:	4932
	20:27	*which* was the **s** *day* of the month,	8145
	20:34	did eat no meat the **s** day of the month:	8145
	26: 8	and I will not *smite* him the **s** time.	8138
2Sa	3: 3	his **s**, Chileab, of Abigail the wife of Nabal	4932
	14:29	when he sent again the **s** time, he would	8145
1Ki	6: 1	in the month Zif, which *is* the **s** month,	8145
	9: 2	LORD appeared to Solomon the **s** time,	8145
	15:25	Israel in the **s** year of Asa king of Judah,	8147
	18:34	he said, Do *it* the **s** time. And they did *it*	8138
	18:34	they **did** *it* **the s time**. And he said, Do *it*	8138
	19: 7	angel of the LORD came again the **s** time,	8145
2Ki	1:17	Jehoram reigned in his stead in the **s** year	8147
	9:19	he sent out a **s** on horseback, which came	8145
	10: 6	he wrote a letter the **s** time to them,	8145
	14: 1	In the **s** year of Joash son of Jehoahaz	8147
	15:32	In the **s** year of Pekah the son of	8145
	19:29	in the **s** year that which springeth of	8145
	23: 4	high priest, and the priests of the **s order**;	4932
	25:17	like unto these had the **s** pillar with	8145
	25:18	Zephaniah the **s** priest, and the three	4932
1Ch	2:13	Abinadab the **s**, and Shimma the third,	8145
	3: 1	the **s** Daniel, of Abigail the Carmelitess:	8145
	3:15	the **s** Jehoiakim, the third Zedekiah,	8145
	7:15	and the name of the **s** *was* Zelophehad:	8145
	8: 1	Ashbel the **s**, and Aharah the third,	8145
	8:39	Jehush the **s**, and Eliphelet the third.	8145
	12: 9	Ezer the first, Obadiah the **s**, Eliab	8145
	15:18	them their brethren of the **s degree**,	4932
	23:11	Jahath the chief, and Zizah the **s**:	8145
	23:19	Jeriah the first, Amariah the **s**, Jahaziel	8145
	23:20	Michah the first, and Jesiah the **s**.	8145
	24: 7	came forth to Jehoiarib, the **s** to Jedaiah,	8145
	24:23	*of* Hebron; Jeriah *the first*, Amariah the **s**,	8145
	25: 9	the **s** *to* Gedaliah, who with his brethren	8145
	26: 2	Jediael the **s**, Zebadiah the third,	8145
	26: 4	Jehozabad the **s**, Joah the third,	8145
	26:11	Hilkiah the **s**, Tebaliah the third,	8145
	27: 4	over the course of the **s** month *was* Dodai	8145
	29:22	the son of David king the **s** time,	8145
2Ch	3: 2	began to build in the **s** *day* of the second	8145
	3: 2	began to build in the second *day* of the	8145
	27: 5	unto him, both the **s** year, and the third.	8145
	30: 2	to keep the passover in the **s** month.	8145
	30:13	feast of unleavened bread in the **s** month,	8145
	30:15	on the fourteenth *day* of the **s** month:	8145
	35:24	and put him in the **s** chariot that he had;	4932

Ezr	1:10	silver basons of a **s** sort four hundred and	4932
	3: 8	Now in the **s** year of their coming unto	8145
	3: 8	in the month, began Zerubbabel the son	8145
	4:24	So it ceased unto the **s** year of the reign	8648
Ne	8:13	on the **s** day were gathered together	8145
	11: 9	Judah the son of Senuah *was* **s** over	4932
	11:17	Bakbukiah the **s** among his brethren,	4932
Est	2:14	the morrow she returned into the **s** house	8145
	2:19	virgins were gathered together the **s time**,	8145
	7: 2	king said again unto Esther on the **s** day	8145
	9:29	to confirm this **s** letter of Purim.	8145
Job	42:14	the name of the **s**, Kezia; and the name of	8145
Ecc	4: 8	There is one *alone*, and *there* is not a **s**;	8145
	4:15	with the **s** child that shall stand *up* in his	8145
Isa	11:11	**s time** to recover the remnant of his	8145
	37:30	the **s** year that which springeth of the	8145
Jer	1:13	of the LORD came unto me the **s time**,	8145
	13: 3	of the LORD came unto me the **s time**,	8145
	33: 1	the LORD came unto Jeremiah the **s time**,	8145
	41: 4	came to pass the **s** day after *he* had slain	8145
	52:22	The **s** pillar also and the pomegranates	8145
	52:24	Zephaniah the **s** priest, and the three	4932
Eze	10:14	the **s** face *was* the face of a man,	8145
	43:22	on the **s** day thou shalt offer a kid of	8145
Da	2: 1	in the **s** year of the reign of	8147
	7: 5	a **s**, like to a bear, and it raised up itself	8578
Jnh	3: 1	of the LORD came unto Jonah the **s time**,	8145
Na	1: 9	affliction shall not rise up the **s time**.	6471
Zep	1:10	howling from the **s**, and a great crashing	4932
Hag	1: 1	In the **s** year of Darius the king, in the	8147
	1:15	in the **s** year of Darius the king.	8147
	2:10	twentieth *day* of the ninth *month*, in the **s**	8147
Zec	1: 1	the eighth month, in the **s** year of Darius,	8147
	1: 7	the month Sebat, in the **s** year of Darius,	8147
	6: 2	and in the **s** chariot black horses;	8145
Mt	21:30	And he came to the **s**,	1208
	22:26	Likewise the **s** also, and the third, unto	1208
	22:39	the **s** *is* like unto it, Thou shalt love thy	1208
	26:42	He went away again the **s time**,	1208+1537
Mk	12:21	the **s** took her, and died, neither left he	1208
	12:31	And the **s** *is* like, *namely* this, Thou shalt	1208
	14:72	And the **s time** the cock crew.	1208+1537
Lk	6: 1	to pass on the **s** sabbath **after the first**,	1207
	12:38	And if he shall come in the **s** watch,	1208
	19:18	And the **s** came, saying, Lord, thy pound	1208
	20:30	And the **s** took her to wife, and he died	1208
Jn	3: 4	can he enter the **s time** into his mother's	1208
	4:54	This *is* again the **s** miracle *that* Jesus did,	1208
	21:16	He saith to him again the **s time**, Simon,	1208
Ac	7:13	at the **s** time Joseph was made known	1208
	10:15	*spake* unto him again the **s time**,	1208+1537
	12:10	they were past the first and the **s** ward,	1208
	13:33	it is also written in the **s** psalm, Thou art	1208
1Co	15:47	the **s** man *is* the Lord from heaven.	1208
2Co	1:15	before, that you might have a **s** benefit;	1208
	1: 2	*you*, as if I were present the **s** *time*;	1208
	13: 2	The **s** *epistle* to the Corinthians was	1208
2Th	3:	The **s** *epistle* to the Thessalonians was	1208
2Ti	4:	The **s** *epistle* unto Timotheus, ordained	1208
	4:	when Paul was brought before Nero the **s**	1208
Tit	3:10	a heretick after the first and **s** admonition,	1208
Heb	8: 7	no place have been sought for the **s**.	1208
	9: 3	after the vail, the tabernacle which *is*	1208
	9: 7	But into the **s** *went* the high priest alone	1208
	9:28	**s time** without sin unto salvation.	1208+1537
2Pe	3: 1	This **s** epistle, beloved, I now write unto	1208
Rev	2:11	that overcometh shall not be hurt of the **s**	1208
	4: 7	and the **s** beast like a calf, and the third	1208
	6: 3	When he had opened the **s** seal, I heard	1208
	6: 3	I heard the **s** beast say, Come and see.	1208
	8: 8	And the **s** angel sounded, and as *it were* a	1208
	11:14	The **s** woe is past; *and* behold, the third	1208
	16: 3	And the **s** angel poured out his vial upon	1208
	20: 6	on such the **s** death hath no power,	1208
	20:14	into the lake of fire. This is the **s** death.	1208
	21: 8	and brimstone: which is the **s** death.	1208
	21:19	the **s**, sapphire; the third, a chalcedony;	1208

SECONDARILY (1) [SECOND]

1Co	12:28	first apostles, **s** prophets, thirdly teachers,	1208

SECRET (68) [SECRETLY, SECRETS]

Ge	49: 6	O my soul, come not thou into their **s**;	5475
Dt	27:15	putteth *it* in a **s** *place*. And all the people	5643
	29:29	The **s** *things belong* unto the LORD our	5641
Jdg	3:19	said, I have a **s** errand unto thee, O king:	5643
	13:18	thou thus after my name, seeing it *is* **s**?	6383
1Sa	5: 9	and they had emerods in their **s parts**.	8368
	19: 2	and abide in a **s place**, and hide thyself:	5643
Job	14:13	that thou wouldest **keep** me **s**, until thy	5641
	15: 8	Hast thou heard the **s** of God? and dost	5475
	15:11	with thee? is there *any* **s** thing with thee?	328
	20:26	All darkness *shall be* hid in his **s places**:	6845
	29: 4	the **s** of God *was* upon my tabernacle;	5475
	40:13	dust together; *and* bind their faces in **s**.	2934
Ps	10: 8	**s places** doth he murder the innocent:	4565
	17:12	it were a young lion lurking in **s places**.	4565
	18:11	made darkness his **s place**; his pavilion	5643
	19:12	*his* errors? cleanse thou me from **s faults**.	5641
	25:14	The **s** of the LORD *is* with them that fear	5475
	27: 5	in the **s** of his tabernacle shall he hide me;	5643
	31:20	Thou shalt hide them in the **s** of thy	5643
	64: 2	me from the **s counsel** of the wicked;	5475
	64: 4	That *they* may shoot in **s** at the perfect:	4565

Ps	81: 7 answered thee in the **s place** of thunder:	5643
	90: 8 our **s** *sins* in the light of thy countenance,	5956
	91: 1 that dwelleth in the **s place** of the most	5643
	139:15 when I was made in **s**,	5643
Pr	3:32 the LORD: but his *is* with the righteous.	5475
	9:17 sweet, and bread *eaten* in **s** is pleasant.	5643
	21:14 A gift in **s** pacifieth anger: and a reward in	5643
	25: 9 and discover not a **s** *to* another:	5475
	27: 5 Open rebuke *is* better than **s** love.	5641
Ecc	12:14 with every *thing*, whether *it be* good,	5956
SS	2:14 in the **s places** of the stairs, let me see	5643
Isa	3:17 the LORD will discover their **s** *parts*.	6596
	45: 3 hidden riches of **s places**, that thou	4565
	45:19 I have not spoken in **s**, in a dark place of	5643
	48:16 I have not spoken in **s** from the beginning;	5643
Jer	2:34 I have not found it by **s search**, but upon	4290
	13:17 my soul shall weep in **s places** for *your*	4565
	23:24 Can any hide himself in **s places** that I	4565
	49:10 I have uncovered his **s places**, and he	4565
La	3:10 lying in wait, *and as* a lion in **s places**.	4565
Eze	7:22 they shall pollute my **s** *place:* for	6845
	28: 3 *is* no **s** *that* they can hide *from* thee:	5640
Da	2:18 of the God of heaven concerning this **s**;	7328
	2:19 *was* the **s** revealed unto Daniel in a night	7328
	2:22 **s** *things:* he knoweth what *is in*	5642
	2:27 The **s** which the king hath demanded	7328
	2:30 **s** *is* not revealed to me for *any* wisdom,	7328
	2:47 seeing thou couldest reveal this **s**.	7328
	4: 9 gods *is* in thee, and no **s** troubleth thee,	7328
Am	3: 7 he revealeth his **s** unto his servants	5475
Mt	6: 4 thine alms may be in **s**: and thy Father	2927
	6: 4 thy Father which seeth in **s** himself shall	2927
	6: 6 thy door, pray to thy Father which is in **s**;	2927
	6: 6 thy Father which seeth in **s** shall reward	2927
	6:18 to fast, but unto thy Father which is in **s**:	2927
	6:18 and thy Father, which seeth in **s**,	2927
	13:35 will utter *things which have been* **kept s**	2928
	24:26 *he is* in the **s chambers**; believe *it*	5009
Mk	4:22 neither was *any* thing **kept s**, but that it	614
Lk	8:17 For nothing is **s**, that shall not be made	2927
	11:33 putteth *it* in a **s place**, neither under a	2927
Jn	7: 4 *is* no *man* doeth *any* thing in **s**,	2927
	7:10 the feast, not openly, but as it were in **s**.	2927
	18:20 resort; and in **s** have I said nothing.	2927
Ro	16:25 which was **kept s** since the world began,	4601
Eph	5:12 those *things* which are done of them in **s**	2931

SECRETLY (20) [SECRET]

Ge	31:27 Wherefore didst thou flee away **s**,	2244
Dt	13: 6 entice thee **s**, saying, Let	5643+871.1+1886.1
	27:24 smiteth his neighbour **s**.	5643+871.1+1886.1
	28:57 of all *things* in the siege	5643+871.1+1886.1
Jos	2: 1 sent out of Shittim two men to spy **s**,	2791
1Sa	18:22 Commune with David **s**,	3909+871.1+1886.1
	23: 9 knew that Saul **s practised** mischief	2790
2Sa	12:12 thou didst *it* **s**: but I will	5643+871.1+1886.1
2Ki	17: 9 the children of Israel did **s** *those* things	2644
Job	4:12 Now a thing was **s brought** to me,	1589
	13:10 if ye do **s** accept persons.	5643+871.1+1886.1
	31:27 my heart hath been **s**	5643+871.1+1886.1
Ps	10: 9 lieth in wait **s** as a lion in	4565+871.1+1886.1
	31:20 thou shalt **keep** them **s** in a pavilion	6845
Jer	37:17 asked him **s** in his house,	5643+871.1+1886.1
	38:16 king sware **s** unto	5643+871.1+1886.1
	40:15 to Gedaliah in Mizpah **s**,	5643+871.1+1886.1
Hab	3:14 as to devour the poor **s**.	4565+871.1+1886.1
Jn	11:28 and called Mary her sister **s**, saying,	2977
	19:38 disciple of Jesus, but **s** for fear of the Jews,	2928

SECRETS (10) [SECRET]

Dt	25:11 forth her hand, and taketh him by the **s**:	4016
Job	11: 6 that he would shew thee the **s** of wisdom,	8587
Ps	44:21 for he knoweth the **s** of the heart.	8587
Pr	11:13 A talebearer revealeth **s**: but he that is of	5475
	20:19 goeth about *as* a talebearer revealeth **s**:	5475
Da	2:28 there is a God in heaven that revealeth **s**,	7328
	2:29 he that revealeth **s maketh** known to thee	7328
	2:47 a Lord of kings, and a revealer of **s**,	7328
Ro	2:16 In the day when God shall judge the **s** of	2927
1Co	14:25 And thus are the **s** of his heart made	2927

SECT (5)

Ac	5:17 him, (which is the **s** of the Sadducees,)	139
	15: 5 But there rose up certain of the **s** of	139
	24: 5 and a ringleader of the **s** of the Nazarenes:	139
	26: 5 after the most straitest **s** of our religion I	139
	28:22 as concerning this **s**, we know that every	139

SECU See SECHU

SECUNDUS (1)

Ac	20: 4 of the Thessalonians, Aristarchus and **S**;	4580

SECURE (7) [SECURELY, SECURITY]

Jdg	8:11 and smote the host: for the host was **s**.	983
	18: 7 the manner of the Zidonians, quiet and **s**;	982
	18:10 ye shall come unto a people **s**, and to a	982
	18:27 unto a people *that were* at quiet and **s**:	982
Job	11:18 thou shalt be **s**, because there is hope; yea,	982
	12: 6 and they that provoke God are **s**;	987
Mt	28:14 we will persuade him, and **s** you.	275+4160

SECURELY (2) [SECURE]

Pr	3:29 seeing he dwelleth **s** by thee.	983+3807.1
Mic	2: 8 that pass by *as men* averse from war.	983

SECURITY (1) [SECURE]

Ac	17: 9 And when they had taken **s** of Jason,	2425

SEDITION (5) [SEDITIONS]

Ezr	4:15 that they have moved **s** within the same	849
	4:19 rebellion and **s** *have* been made therein.	849
Lk	23:19 (Who for a certain **s** made in the city,	4714
	23:25 And he released unto them him that for **s**	4714
Ac	24: 5 a mover of **s** among all the Jews	4714

SEDITIONS (1) [SEDITION]

Gal	5:20 emulations, wrath, strife, **s**, heresies,	1370

SEDUCE (3) [SEDUCED, SEDUCERS, SEDUCETH, SEDUCING]

Mk	13:22 shall shew signs and wonders, to **s**, if *it*	635
1Jn	2:26 unto you concerning them **s** that you.	4105
Rev	2:20 to **s** my servants to commit fornication,	4105

SEDUCED (3) [SEDUCE]

2Ki	21: 9 Manasseh **s** them to do more evil than	8582
Isa	19:13 they have also **s** Egypt, *even they that*	8582
Eze	13:10 even because they have **s** my people,	2937

SEDUCERS (1) [SEDUCE]

2Ti	3:13 men and **s** shall wax worse and worse,	1114

SEDUCETH (1) [SEDUCE]

Pr	12:26 but the way of the wicked **s** them.	8582

SEDUCING (1) [SEDUCE]

1Ti	4: 1 giving heed to **s** spirits, and doctrines of	4108

SEE (597) [EYESIGHT, FORESAW, FORESEEING, FORESEETH, OVERSEE, SAW, SAWEST, SEEING, SEEN, SEER, SEER'S, SEERS, SEEST, SEETH, SIGHT, SIGHTS]

Ge	2:19 brought *them* unto Adam to **s** what he	7200
	8: 8 to **s** if the waters were abated off from	7200
	11: 5 the LORD came down to **s** the city and	7200
	12:12 when the Egyptians shall **s** thee, that	7200
	18:21 whether they have done altogether	7200
	19:21 he said unto him, **S**, I have accepted thee	2009
	21:16 Let me not **s** the death of the child.	7200
	27: 1 his eyes were dim, so that he could not **s**,	7200
	27:27 his raiment, and blessed him, and said, **S**,	7200
	31: 5 unto them, I **s** your father's countenance,	7200
	31:12 he said, Lift up now thine eyes, and **s**,	7200
	31:50 **s**, God *is* witness betwixt me and thee.	7200
	32:20 before me, and afterward I will **s** his face;	7200
	34: 1 went out to **s** the daughters of the land.	7200
	37:14 whether it be well with thy brethren,	7200
	37:20 shall **s** what will become of his dreams.	7200
	39:14 house, and spake unto them, saying, **S**,	7200
	41:41 Pharaoh said unto Joseph, **S**, I have set	7200
	42: 9 to **s** the nakedness of the land you are	7200
	42:12 to **s** the nakedness of the land you are	7200
	43: 3 Ye shall not **s** my face, except your	7200
	43: 5 man said unto us, Ye shall not **s** my face,	7200
	44:23 with you, ye shall **s** my face no more.	7200
	44:26 for we may not **s** the man's face, except	7200
	44:34 lest peradventure I **s** the evil that shall	7200
	45:12 your eyes, **s**, and the eyes of my brother	7200
	45:24 them, **S** that ye fall not out by the way.	NIH
	45:28 alive: I will go and **s** him before I die.	7200
	48:10 were dim for age, *so that* he could not **s**.	7200
	48:11 Joseph, I had not thought to **s** thy face:	7200
Ex	1:16 and **s** *them* upon the stools;	7200
	3: 3 now turn aside, and **s** this great sight,	7200
	3: 4 the LORD saw that he turned aside to **s**,	7200
	4:18 in Egypt, and **s** whether they be yet alive.	7200
	4:21 that thou do all *those* wonders before	7200
	5:19 the officers of the children of Israel did **s**	7200
	6: 1 shalt thou **s** what I will do to Pharaoh:	7200
	7: 1 the LORD said unto Moses, **S**, I have	7200
	10: 5 that *one* cannot be able to **s** the earth:	7200
	10:28 take heed to thyself, **s** my face no more;	7200
	10:29 I will **s** thy face again no more.	7200
	12:13 where you *are:* and when I **s** the blood,	7200
	13:17 the people repent when they **s** war,	7200
	14:13 and **s** the salvation of the LORD,	7200
	14:13 ye shall **s** them again no more for ever.	7200
	16: 7 then ye shall **s** the glory of the LORD;	7200
	16:29 **S**, for that the LORD hath given you	7200
	16:32 that they may **s** the bread wherewith I	7200
	22: 8 *to* **s** whether he have put his hand unto	NIH
	23: 5 If thou **s** the ass of him that hateth thee	7200
	31: 2 **S**, I have called by name Bezaleel the son	7200
	33:12 **S**, thou sayest unto me, Bring up this	7200
	33:20 he said, Thou canst not **s** my face: for	7200
	33:20 for there shall no man **s** me, and live.	7200
	33:23 hand, and thou shalt **s** my back parts:	7200
	34:10 the people among which thou *art* shall **s**	7200
	35:30 Moses said unto the children of Israel, **S**,	7200
Lev	13: 8 *if* the priest **s** that behold, the scab	7200
	13:10 the priest shall **s** *him:* and behold,	7200
	13:17 the priest shall **s** the raw flesh,	7200
	13:17 the priest shall **s** him: and behold,	7200
	13:30 the priest shall **s** the plague: and behold,	7200
	14:36 before the priest go *into it* to **s** the plague,	7200
	14:36 afterward the priest shall go in to **s**	7200
	20:17 her nakedness, and she **s** his	7200
	20:17 her nakedness, and she **s** his nakedness;	7200
Nu	4:20 they shall not go in to **s** when the holy	7200
	11:15 and let me not **s** my wretchedness.	7200

Nu	11:23 thou shalt **s** now whether my word shall	7200
	13:18 the land, what it *is;* and the people that	7200
	14:23 Surely they shall not **s** the land which I	7200
	14:23 shall any of them that provoked me **s** it:	7200
	22:41 that thence he might **s** the utmost part of	7200
	23: 9 For from the top of the rocks I **s** him,	7200
	23:13 from whence thou mayest **s** them:	7200
	23:13 thou shalt **s** but the utmost part of them,	7200
	23:13 part of them, and shalt not **s** them all:	7200
	24:17 I shall **s** him, but not now: I shall behold	7200
	27:12 **s** the land which I have given unto	7200
	32: 8 I sent them from Kadesh-barnea to **s**	7200
	32:11 shall **s** the land which I sware unto	7200
Dt	1:35 of this evil generation **s** that good land,	7200
	1:36 shall **s** it, and to him will I give the land	7200
	3:25 and **s** the good land that *is* beyond Jordan,	7200
	3:28 to inherit the land which thou shalt **s**.	7200
	4:28 and stone, which neither **s**, nor hear,	7200
	18:16 neither let me **s** this great fire any more,	7200
	22: 1 Thou shalt not **s** thy brother's ox or his	7200
	22: 4 Thou shalt not **s** thy brother's ass or his	7200
	23:14 that he **s** no unclean thing in thee,	7200
	28:10 all people of the earth shall **s** that thou art	7200
	28:34 the sight of thine eyes which thou shalt **s**.	7200
	28:67 the sight of thine eyes which thou shalt **s**.	7200
	28:68 unto thee, Thou shalt **s** it no more again:	7200
	29: 4 eyes to **s**, and ears to hear, unto this day.	7200
	29:22 when they **s** the plagues of that land,	7200
	30:15 **S**, I have set before thee *this* day life and	7200
	32:20 I will **s** what their end *shall be:* for they	7200
	32:39 **S** now that I, *even* I, *am* he, and *there is*	7200
	32:52 Yet thou shalt **s** the land before *thee;* but	7200
	34: 4 I have **caused** thee to **s** *it* with thine eyes,	7200
Jos	3: 3 When ye **s** the ark of the covenant of	7200
	6: 2 the LORD said unto Joshua, **S**, I have	7200
	8: 1 **s**, I have given into thy hand the king of	7200
	8: 8 shall ye do. **S**, I have commanded you.	7200
	22:10 an altar by Jordan, a great altar to **s** to.	4758
Jdg	9:37 **S** there come people down by the middle	2009
	14: 8 turned aside to **s** the carcase of the lion:	7200
	16: 5 wherein his great strength *lieth*, and	7200
	21:21 s, and behold, if the daughters of Shiloh	7200
1Sa	2:32 thou shalt **s** an enemy *in my* habitation,	5027
	3: 2 began to **wax** dim, *that* he could not **s**;	7200
	4:15 his eyes were dim, that he could not **s**.	7200
	6: 9 **s**, if it goeth up *by* the way of his own	7200
	6:13 and saw the ark, and rejoiced to **s** *it*.	7200
	10:24 **S** ye him whom the LORD hath chosen,	7200
	12:16 therefore stand and **s** this great thing,	7200
	12:17 and **s** that your wickedness *is* great,	7200
	14:17 Number now, and **s** who is gone from us.	7200
	14:29 **s**, I pray you, how mine eyes have been	7200
	14:38 and **s** wherein this sin hath been *this* day.	7200
	15:35 Samuel came no more to **s** Saul until	7200
	17:28 thou art come down that *thou* mightest **s**	7200
	19: 3 of thee; and what I, that I will tell thee.	7200
	19:15 Saul sent the messengers *again* to **s** David,	7200
	20:29 get away, I pray thee, and **s** my brethren.	7200
	21:14 his servants, Lo, you **s** the man *is* mad:	7200
	23:22 know and **s** his place where his haunt is,	7200
	23:23 **S** therefore, and take knowledge of all	7200
	24:11 Moreover, my father, **s**, yea see the skirt	7200
	24:11 see, yea the skirt of thy robe in my hand:	7200
	24:11 **s** that *there is* neither evil nor	7200
	24:15 **s**, and plead my cause, and deliver me	7200
	25:35 **s**, I have hearkened to thy voice,	7200
	26:16 now **s** where the king's spear *is*, and	7200
2Sa	3:13 of thee, that is, Thou shalt not **s** my face,	7200
	3:13 when thou comest to **s** my face.	7200
	7: 2 **S** now, I dwell in a house of cedar,	7200
	13: 5 thy father cometh to **s** thee, say unto	7200
	13: 5 that I may **s** *it*, and eat *it* at her hand.	7200
	13: 6 the king was come to **s** him, Amnon	7200
	14:24 his own house, and let him not **s** my face.	7200
	14:30 **S**, Joab's field is near mine, and he hath	7200
	14:32 now therefore let me **s** the king's face;	7200
	15: 3 him, **S**, thy matters *are* good and right;	7200
	15:28 **S**, I will tarry in the plain of the	7200
	24: 3 *that* the eyes of my lord the king may **s** *it*:	7200
	24:13 what answer I shall return to him that	7200
1Ki	9:12 Hiram came out from Tyre to **s** the cities	7200
	12:16 now **s** to thine own house, David.	7200
	14: 4 Ahijah could not **s**; for his eyes were set	7200
	17:23 and Elijah said, **S**, thy son liveth.	7200
	20: 7 and **s** how this *man* seeketh mischief:	7200
	20:22 and mark, and **s** what thou doest;	7200
	22:25 Behold, thou shalt **s** in that day,	7200
2Ki	2:10 if thou **s** me *when I am* taken	7200
	3:14 I would not look toward thee, nor **s** thee.	7200
	3:17 Ye shall not **s** wind, neither shall ye see	7200
	3:17 shall not see wind, neither shall ye **s** rain;	7200
	5: 7 **s** how he seeketh a quarrel against me.	7200
	6:17 I pray thee, open his eyes, that he may **s**.	7200
	6:20 the eyes of these *men*, that they may **s**.	7200
	6:32 **S** ye how this son of a murderer hath sent	7200
	7: 2 thou shalt **s** *it* with thine eyes, but shalt	7200
	7:13 that are consumed:) and let us send and **s**.	7200
	7:14 the host of the Syrians, saying, Go and **s**.	7200
	7:19 thou shalt **s** *it* with thine eyes, but shalt	7200
	8:29 to **s** Joram the son of Ahab in Jezreel,	7200
	9:16 king of Judah was come down to **s**	7200
	9:17 Jehu as he came, and said, I **s** a company.	7200
	9:34 **Go, s** now this cursed *woman*, and	6485
	10:16 with me, and **s** my zeal for the LORD.	7200
	19:16 open, LORD, thine eyes, and **s**:	7200

2Ki 22:20 thine eyes shall not **s** all the evil which I — 7200
23:17 he said, What title *is* that that I **s**? — 7200
2Ch 10:16 *and* now, David, **s** to thine own house. — 7200
18:16 I did **s** all Israel scattered upon — 7200
18:24 thou shalt **s** on that day when thou shalt — 7200
20:17 and **s** the salvation of the LORD with you, — 7200
22: 6 to **s** Jehoram the son of Ahab at Jezreel, — 7200
24: 5 to year, and **s** *that* ye haste the matter. — NIH
25:17 Come, let us **s** one another in the face. — 7200
29: 8 and to hissing, as ye **s** with your eyes. — 7200
30: 7 gave them up to desolation, as ye **s**. — 7200
34:28 neither shall thine eyes **s** all the evil that I — 7200
Ezr 4:14 *it was* not meet for us to **s** the king's — 2370
Ne 2:17 I unto them, Ye **s** the distress that we *are* — 7200
4:11 They shall not know, neither **s**, — 7200
9: 9 **s** the affliction of our fathers in Egypt, — 7200
Est 3: 4 to **s** whether Mordecai's matters would — 7200
5:13 long as I **s** Mordecai the Jew sitting at — 7200
8: 6 how can I endure to **s** the evil that shall — 7200
8: 6 how can I endure to **s** the destruction of — 7200
Job 3: 9 neither let it **s** the dawning of the day: — 7200
6:21 ye **s** *my* casting down, and are afraid. — 7200
7: 7 *is* wind: mine eye shall no more **s** good. — 7200
7: 8 eye of him that hath seen me shall **s** me — 7789
9:11 Lo, he goeth by me, and I **s** *him* not: — 7200
9:25 a post: they flee away, they **s** no good. — 7200
10:15 therefore **s** thou mine affliction; — 7200
17:15 my hope? as for my hope, who shall **s** it? — 7789
19:26 this *body*, yet in my flesh shall I **s** God: — 2372
19:27 Whom I shall **s** for myself, and mine eyes — 2372
20: 9 The eye also *which* saw him shall **s** him — NIH
20:17 He shall not **s** the rivers, the floods, — 7200
21:20 His eyes shall **s** his destruction, and he — 7200
22:11 Or darkness, *that* thou canst not **s**; — 7200
22:19 The righteous **s** *it*, and are glad: — 7200
23: 9 *on* the right hand, that I cannot **s** *him*: — 7200
24: 1 do they that know him not **s** his days? — 2372
24:15 the twilight, saying, No eye shall **s** me: — 7789
28:27 did he it, and declare it; he prepared it, — 7200
31: 4 Doth not he **s** my ways, and count all my — 7200
33:26 he shall **s** his face with joy: for he will — 7200
33:28 into the pit, and his life shall **s** the light. — 7200
34:32 *That which* I **s** not teach thou me: if I — 2372
35: 5 Look unto the heavens, and **s**; — 7200
35:14 Although thou sayest thou shalt not **s** him, — 7789
36:25 Every man may **s** it; man may behold *it* — 2372
37:21 *men* **s** not the bright light which *is* in — 7200
Ps 10:11 he hideth his face; he will never **s** *it*. — 7200
14: 2 to **s** if there were *any* that did understand, — 7200
16:10 wilt thou suffer thine Holy One to **s** — 7200
22: 7 All they that **s** me laugh me to scorn: — 7200
27:13 *I had fainted*, unless I had believed to **s** — 7200
31:11 they that did **s** me without fled from me. — 7200
34: 8 O taste and **s** that the LORD *is* good: — 7200
34:12 loveth *many* days, that *he* may **s** good? — 7200
36: 9 of life: in thy light shall we **s** light. — 7200
37:34 the wicked are cut off, thou shalt **s** *it*. — 7200
40: 3 many shall **s** *it*, and fear, and shall trust in — 7200
41: 6 if he come to **s** *me*, he speaketh vanity: — 7200
49: 9 still live for ever, *and* not **s** corruption. — 7200
49:19 of his fathers; they shall never **s** light. — 7200
52: 6 The righteous also shall **s**, and fear, — 7200
53: 2 to **s** if there were *any* that did understand, — 7200
58: 8 of a woman, *that* they may not **s** the sun. — 2372
59:10 God shall let me **s** *my desire* upon mine — 7200
63: 2 To **s** thy power and thy glory, so *as* I have — 7200
64: 5 snares privily; they say, Who shall **s** them? — 7200
64: 8 all that **s** them shall flee away. — 7200
66: 5 and **s** the works of God: *he is* terrible — 7200
69:23 their eyes be darkened, that they **s** not; — 7200
69:32 The humble shall **s** *this, and be* glad: — 7200
74: 9 We **s** not our signs: *there is* no more any — 7200
86:17 that they which hate me may **s** *it*, and — 7200
89:48 *is he that* liveth, and shall not **s** death? — 7200
91: 8 behold and **s** the reward of the wicked. — 7200
92:11 Mine eye also shall **s** *my desire* on mine — 5027
94: 7 Yet they say, The LORD shall not **s**, — 7200
94: 9 he that formed the eye, shall he not **s**? — 5027
97: 6 and all the people **s** his glory. — 7200
106: 5 That *I may* **s** the good of thy chosen, that — 7200
107:24 These **s** the works of the LORD, — 7200
107:42 The righteous shall **s** *it*, and rejoice: — 7200
112: 8 until he **s** *his desire* upon his enemies. — 7200
112:10 The wicked shall **s** *it*, and be grieved; — 7200
115: 5 speak not: eyes have they, but they **s** not: — 7200
118: 7 I **s** *my desire* upon them that hate me. — 7200
119:74 that fear thee will be glad when they **s** — 7200
128: 5 thou shalt **s** the good of Jerusalem all — 7200
128: 6 thou shalt **s** thy children's children, — 7200
135:16 speak not; eyes have they, but they **s** not; — 7200
139:16 Thine eyes did **s** my substance, yet being — 7200
139:24 **s** *if there be any* wicked way in me, — 7200
Pr 24:18 Lest the LORD **s** *it*, and it displease him, — 7200
29:16 but the righteous shall **s** their fall. — 7200
Ecc 1:10 whereof it may be said, **S**, this *is* new? — 7200
2: 3 till I might **s** what *was* that good for — 7200
3:18 that *they* might **s** that they themselves are — 7200
3:22 for who shall bring him to **s** what shall be — 7200
7:11 *by it there is* profit to them that **s** the sun. — 7200
8:16 to **s** the business that is done upon — 7200
SS 2:14 let me **s** thy countenance, let me hear thy — 7200
6:11 I went down into the garden of nuts to **s** — 7200
6:11 and to **s** whether the vine flourished, — 7200
6:13 What will ye **s** in the Shulamite? As it — 2372
7:12 let us **s** if the vine flourish, *whether* — 7200

Isa 5:19 that we may **s** *it*: and let the counsel of — 7200
6: 9 and **s** **indeed**, but perceive not. — 7200+7200
6:10 lest they **s** with their eyes, and hear with — 7200
13: 1 which Isaiah the son of Amoz did **s**. — 2372
14:16 They that **s** thee shall narrowly look upon — 7200
18: 3 world, and dwellers on the earth, **s** ye, — 7200
26:11 thy hand is lifted up, they will not **s**: — 2372
26:11 they shall **s**, and be ashamed for *their* — 2372
29:18 the eyes of the blind shall **s** out of — 7200
30:10 Which say to the seers, **S** not; and to — 7200
30:20 but thine eyes shall **s** thy teachers: — 7200
32: 3 the eyes of them that **s** shall not be dim, — 7200
33:17 Thine eyes shall **s** the king in his beauty: — 2372
33:19 Thou shalt not **s** a fierce people, a people — 7200
33:20 thine eyes shall **s** Jerusalem a quiet — 7200
35: 2 they shall **s** the glory of the LORD, — 7200
37:17 hear; open thine eyes, O LORD, and **s**: — 7200
38:11 I said, I shall not **s** the LORD, *even* — 7200
40: 5 revealed, and all flesh shall **s** *it* together: — 7200
41:20 That they may **s**, and know, and consider, — 7200
42:18 ye deaf; and look, ye blind, that *ye* may **s**. — 7200
44: 9 they **s** not, nor know; that they may be — 7200
44:18 hath shut their eyes, that *they* cannot **s**; — 7200
48: 6 Thou hast heard, **s** all this; and will ye not — 2372
49: 7 a servant of rulers, Kings shall **s** and arise, — 7200
52: 8 for they shall **s** eye to eye, when — 7200
52:10 the ends of the earth shall **s** the salvation — 7200
52:15 had not been told them shall they **s**; — 7200
53: 2 we shall **s** him, *there is* no beauty that — 7200
53:10 he shall **s** *his* seed, he shall prolong *his* — 7200
53:11 He shall **s** of the travail of his soul, — 7200
60: 4 Lift up thine eyes round about, and **s**: — 7200
60: 5 thou shalt **s**, and flow *together*, and — 7200
61: 9 all that **s** them shall acknowledge them, — 7200
62: 2 the Gentiles shall **s** thy righteousness, — 7200
64: 9 , we beseech thee, **s** *we are* all thy — 5027
66:14 when ye **s** *this*, your heart shall rejoice, — 7200
66:18 and they shall **s** my glory. — 7200
Jer 1:10 **S**, I have this day set thee over the nations — 7200
1:11 And I said, I **s** a rod of an almond tree. — 7200
1:13 I said, I **s** a seething pot; and the face — 7200
2:10 For pass over the isles of Chittim, and **s**; — 7200
2:10 and **s** if there be such a *thing*. — 7200
2:19 and **s** that *it is* an evil *thing* and bitter, — 7200
2:23 **s** thy way in the valley, know what thou — 7200
2:31 O generation, **s** ye the word of the LORD. — 7200
3: 2 and **s** where thou hast not been lien with. — 7200
4:21 How long shall I **s** the standard, — 7200
5: 1 **s** now, and know, and seek in the broad — 7200
5:12 neither shall we **s** sword nor famine: — 7200
5:21 which have eyes, and **s** not; which have — 7200
6:16 the ways, and **s**, and ask for the old paths, — 7200
7:12 **s** what I did to it for the wickedness of — 7200
11:20 heart, let me **s** thy vengeance on them: — 7200
12: 4 they said, He shall not **s** our last end. — 7200
14:13 say unto them, Ye shall not **s** the sword, — 7200
17: 6 and shall not **s** when good cometh; — 7200
17: 8 not **s** when heat cometh, but her leaf — 7200
20:12 heart, let me **s** thy vengeance on them: — 7200
20:18 came I forth out of the womb to **s** labour — 7200
22:10 return no more, nor **s** his native country. — 7200
22:12 captive, and shall **s** this land no more. — 7200
23:24 in secret places that I shall not **s** him? — 7200
30: 6 **s** whether a man doth travail with child? — 7200
30: 6 do I **s** every man with his hands — 7200
42:14 land of Egypt, where we shall **s** no war, — 7200
42:18 and ye shall **s** this place no more. — 7200
51:61 shalt **s**, and shalt read all these words; — 7200
La 1:11 **s**, O LORD, and consider; for I am — 7200
1:12 **s** if there be any sorrow like unto my — 7200
Eze 8: 6 *and* thou shalt **s** great*er* abominations. — 7200
8:13 thou shalt **s** great*er* abominations than — 7200
8:15 thou shalt **s** great*er* abominations than — 7200
12: 2 which have eyes to **s**, and see not; — 7200
12: 2 which have eyes to see, and **s** not; — 7200
12: 6 cover thy face, that thou **s** not the ground: — 7200
12:12 that he **s** not the ground with *his* eyes. — 7200
12:13 yet shall he not **s** it, though he shall die — 7200
13: 9 hand shall be upon the prophets that **s** — 2374
13:16 which **s** visions of peace for her, — 2374
13:23 Therefore ye shall **s** no more vanity, — 2372
14:22 and ye shall **s** their way and their doings: — 7200
14:23 when ye **s** their ways and their doings: — 7200
16:37 that they shall **s** all thy nakedness. — 7200
20:48 all flesh shall **s** that I the LORD have — 7200
21:29 Whiles *they* **s** vanity unto thee, whiles — 2372
32:31 Pharaoh shall **s** them, and shall be — 7200
33: 6 if the watchman **s** the sword come, — 7200
39:21 all the heathen shall **s** my judgment that I — 7200
Da 1:10 why should he **s** your faces worse liking — 7200
2: 8 because ye **s** the dream is gone from me. — 2370
3:25 and said, Lo, I **s** four men loose, — 2370
5:23 iron, wood, and stone, which **s** not, — 2370
Joel 2:28 your young men shall **s** visions: — 7200
Am 6: 2 Pass ye unto Calneh, and **s**; — 7200
Jnh 1:10 he might **s** what would become of — 7200
Mic 6: 9 and *the man of* wisdom shall **s** thy name: — 7200
7:10 she that *is* mine enemy shall **s** it, and — 7200
7:16 The nations shall **s** and be confounded at — 7200
Hab 1: 1 which Habakkuk the prophet did **s**. — 2372
1: 2 will watch to **s** what he will say unto me, — 7200
Zep 3:15 of thee: thou shalt not **s** evil any more. — 7200
Hag 2: 3 how do ye **s** it now? *is it* not in your eyes — 7200
Zec 2: 2 to **s** what *is* the breadth thereof, and what — 7200
4:10 shall **s** the plummet in the hand of — 7200

Zec 5: 2 I answered, I **s** a flying roll; the length — 7200
5: 5 and **s** what *is* this that goeth forth. — 7200
9: 5 Ashkelon shall **s** *it*, and fear; Gaza also — 7200
9: 5 Gaza also *shall* **s** *it*, and be very sorrowful, — NIH
10: 7 yea, their children shall **s** *it*, and be glad; — 7200
Mal 2:15 your eyes shall **s**, and ye shall say, — 7200
Mt 5: 8 *are* the pure in heart: for they shall **s** God. — 3700
5:16 that they may **s** your good works, — 1492
7: 5 thou **s clearly** to cast out the mote out — 1227
8: 4 **S** thou tell no *man*; but go thy way, — 3708
9:30 saying, **S** *that* no *man* know *it*. — 3708
11: 4 *those things* which ye do hear and **s**: — 991
11: 7 went ye out into the wilderness to **s**? — 2300
11: 8 But what went ye out for to **s**? A man — 1492
11: 9 But what went ye out for to **s**? A prophet? — 1492
12:38 we would **s** a sign from thee. — 1492
13:13 they seeing **s** not; and hearing they — 991
13:14 seeing ye shall **s**, and shall not perceive: — 991
13:15 lest at any time they should **s** with *their* — 1492
13:16 But blessed *are* your eyes, for they **s**: — 991
13:17 righteous *men* have desired to **s** *those* — 1492
13:17 desired to see those things which ye **s**, — 991
15:31 the lame to walk, and the blind to **s**: — 991
16:28 till they **s** the Son of man coming in his — 1492
22:11 when the king came in to **s** the guests, — 2300
23:39 Ye shall not **s** me henceforth, till ye shall — 1492
24: 2 **S** ye not all these *things*? verily I say unto — 991
24: 6 that ye be not troubled: for all *these* — 3708
24:15 shall **s** the abomination of desolation, — 1492
24:30 they shall **s** the Son of man coming in — 3700
24:33 when ye shall **s** all these *things*, know — 1492
26:58 and sat with the servants, to **s** the end. — 1492
26:64 Hereafter shall ye **s** the Son of man sitting — 3700
27: 4 said, What *is that* to us? thou to that. — 3700
27:24 of the blood of this just *person*: **s** ye to it. — 3700
27:49 let us **s** whether Elias will come to save — 1492
28: 1 and the other Mary to **s** the sepulchre. — 2334
28: 6 Come, **s** the place where the Lord lay. — 1492
28: 7 you into Galilee; there shall ye **s** him: — 3700
28:10 go into Galilee, and there shall they **s** me. — 3700
Mk 1:44 **S** thou say nothing to any *man*: but go thy — 3708
4:12 That seeing they may **s**, and not perceive; — 991
5:14 they went out to **s** what it was that was — 1492
5:15 **s** him that was possessed with the devil, — 2334
5:32 And he looked round about to **s** her that — 1492
6:38 go and **s**. And when they knew, they say, — 1492
8:18 Having eyes, **s** ye not? and having ears, — 991
8:24 and said, I **s** men as trees, walking. — 991
12:15 ye me? bring me a penny, that I may **s** *it*. — 1492
13: 1 **s** what manner of stones and — 2396
13:14 But when ye shall **s** the abomination of — 1492
13:26 shall they **s** the Son of man coming in — 3700
13:29 ye shall **s** these *things* come to pass, — 1492
14:62 ye shall **s** the Son of man sitting on — 3700
15:32 from the cross, that we may **s** and believe. — 1492
15:36 let us **s** whether Elias will come to take — 1492
16: 7 there shall ye **s** him, as he said unto you. — 3700
Lk 2:15 and **s** this thing which is come to pass, — 1492
2:26 that *he* should **s** death, before he had — 1492
3: 6 And all flesh shall **s** the salvation of God. — 3700
6:42 shalt thou **s clearly** to pull out the mote — 1227
7:22 how that the blind **s**, the lame walk, — 308
7:24 went ye out into the wilderness to **s**? — 2300
7:25 But what went ye out for to **s**? A man — 1492
7:26 But what went ye out for to **s**? A prophet? — 1492
8:10 that seeing they might not **s**, — 991
8:16 that they which enter in may **s** the light. — 991
8:20 brethren stand without, desiring to **s** thee. — 1492
8:35 Then they went out to **s** what was done; — 1492
9: 9 such things? And he desired to **s** him. — 1492
9:27 of death, till they **s** the kingdom of God. — 1492
10:23 Blessed *are* the eyes which **s** *the things* — 991
10:23 *are* the eyes which see *the things* that ye **s**: — 991
10:24 kings have desired to **s** *those things* which — 1492
10:24 desired to see *those things* which ye **s**, — 991
11:33 that they which come in may **s** the light. — 991
12:54 When ye a cloud rise out of the west, — 1492
12:55 when *ye* **s** the south wind blow, ye say, — NIG
13:28 when ye shall **s** Abraham, and Isaac, — 3700
13:35 verily I say unto you, Ye shall not **s** me, — 1492
14:18 of ground, and I must needs go and **s** it: — 1492
17:22 when ye shall desire to **s** one of the days — 1492
17:22 of the Son of man, and ye shall not **s** it. — 3700
17:23 And they shall say to you, **S** here; — 2400
17:23 shall say to you, See here; or, **s** there: — 2400
19: 3 he sought to **s** Jesus who he was; — 1492
19: 4 climbed up into a sycomore tree to **s** him: — 1492
20:13 they will reverence *him* when they **s** him. — 1492
21:20 And when ye shall **s** Jerusalem compassed — 1492
21:27 shall they **s** the Son of man coming in a — 3700
21:30 ye **s** and know of your own selves that — 991
21:31 when ye **s** these *things* come to pass, — 1492
23: 8 for he was desirous to **s** him of a long — 1492
24:39 me, and **s**; for a spirit hath not flesh — 1492
24:39 not flesh and bones, as ye **s** me have. — 2334
Jn 1:33 Upon whom thou shalt **s** the Spirit — 1492
1:39 He saith unto them, Come and **s**. — 1492
1:46 Philip saith unto him, Come and **s**. — 1492
1:50 thou shalt **s** greater *things* than these. — 3700
1:51 Hereafter ye shall **s** heaven open, — 3700
3: 3 he cannot **s** the kingdom of God. — 1492
3:36 that believeth not the Son shall not **s** life; — 1492
4:29 Come, **s** a man, which told me all *things* — 1492
4:48 Except ye **s** signs and wonders, ye will not — 1492
6:19 they **s** Jesus walking on the sea, — 2334

S

Jn	6:30 then, that we may **s**, and believe thee?	*1492*
	6:62 if ye shall **s** the Son of man ascend up	*2334*
	7: 3 that thy disciples also may **s** the works	*2334*
	8:51 keep my saying, he shall never **s** death.	*2334*
	8:56 Your father Abraham rejoiced to **s** my day:	*1492*
	9:15 upon mine eyes, and I washed, and do **s**.	*991*
	9:19 was born blind? how then doth he now **s**?	*991*
	9:25 I know, that, whereas I was blind, now I **s**.	*991*
	9:39 world, that they which **s** not might see;	*991*
	9:39 world, that they which see not might **s**;	*991*
	9:39 that they which **s** might be made blind.	*991*
	9:41 but now ye say, We **s**; therefore your sin	*991*
	11:34 They say unto him, Lord, come and **s**.	*1492*
	11:40 thou shouldest **s** the glory of God?	*3700*
	12: 9 but that they might **s** Lazarus also,	*1492*
	12:21 him, saying, Sir, we would **s** Jesus.	*1492*
	12:40 that they should not **s** with *their* eyes,	*1492*
	14:19 world seeth me no more; but ye **s** me:	*2334*
	16:10 I go to my Father, and ye **s** me no more;	*2334*
	16:16 A little while, and ye shall not **s** me:	*2334*
	16:16 and ye shall **s** me, because I go to	*3700*
	16:17 A little while, and ye shall not **s** me:	*2334*
	16:17 again, a little while, and ye shall **s** me:	*3700*
	16:19 said, A little while, and ye shall not **s** me:	*2334*
	16:19 again, a little while, and ye shall **s** me?	*3700*
	16:22 I will **s** you again, and your heart shall	*3700*
	18:26 Did not I **s** thee in the garden with him?	*1492*
	20:25 Except I shall **s** in his hands the print of	*1492*
Ac	2:17 and your young men shall **s** visions,	*3700*
	2:27 wilt thou suffer thine Holy One to **s**	*1492*
	2:31 in hell, neither his flesh did **s** corruption.	*1492*
	2:33 shed forth this, which ye now **s** and hear.	*991*
	3:16 this *man* strong, whom ye **s** and know:	*2334*
	7:56 said, Behold, I **s** the heavens opened,	*2334*
	8:36 and the eunuch said, **S**, *here is* water;	*2400*
	13:35 not suffer thine Holy One to **s** corruption.	*1492*
	15:36 the word of the Lord, and **s** how they do.	NIG
	19:21 I have been there, I must also **s** Rome.	*1492*
	19:26 Moreover ye **s** and hear, that not alone at	*2334*
	20:25 kingdom of God, shall **s** my face no more.	*3700*
	20:38 that they should **s** his face no more.	*2334*
	22:11 when I could not **s** for the glory of that	*1689*
	22:14 and **s** *that* Just One, and shouldest hear	*1492*
	23:22 charged *him*, **S** thou tell no *man* that thou	NIG
	25:24 ye **s** this *man*, about whom all the	*2334*
	28:20 to **s** *you*, and to speak with *you*: because	*1492*
	28:26 and seeing ye shall **s**, and not perceive:	*991*
	28:27 lest they should **s** with *their* eyes,	*1492*
Ro	1:11 For I long to **s** you, that I may impart unto	*1492*
	7:23 But I **s** another law in my members,	*991*
	8:25 But if we hope for that we **s** not, *then* do	*991*
	11: 8 eyes that *they* should not **s**, and ears that	*991*
	11:10 that *they* may not **s**, and bow down their	*991*
	15:21 whom he was not spoken of, they shall **s**:	*3700*
	15:24 for I trust to **s** you in my journey, and to	*2300*
1Co	1:26 ye **s** your calling, brethren, how that not	*991*
	8:10 For if any *man* **s** thee which hast	*1492*
	13:12 For now we **s** through a glass, darkly;	*991*
	16: 7 For I will not **s** you now by the way; but I	*1492*
	16:10 say that he may be with you without fear:	*991*
2Co	8: 7 to us, **s** that ye abound in this grace also.	NIG
Gal	1:18 years I went up to Jerusalem to **s** Peter,	*2477*
	6:11 Ye see how large a letter I have written	*1492*
Eph	3: 9 And to **make** all men **s** what *is*	*5461*
	5:15 then that ye walk circumspectly, not as	*991*
	5:33 wife **s** that she reverence *her* husband.	NIG
Php	1:27 that whether I come and **s** you, or *else* be	*1492*
	2:23 so soon as I shall **s** how it will go with me.	*542*
	2:28 that, when ye **s** him again, ye may rejoice,	*1492*
1Th	2:17 endeavoured the more abundantly to **s**	*1492*
	3: 6 desiring greatly to **s** us, as we also *to see*	*1492*
	3: 6 greatly to see us, as we also *to see* you:	NIG
	3:10 day praying exceedingly that *we* might **s**	*1492*
	5:15 **S** that none render evil for evil unto any	*3708*
1Ti	6:16 whom no man hath seen, nor can **s**:	*1492*
2Ti	1: 4 Greatly desiring to **s** thee, being mindful	*1492*
Heb	2: 8 But now we **s** not yet all *things* put under	*3708*
	2: 9 we **s** Jesus, who was made a little lower	*991*
	3:19 we **s** that they could not enter in because	*991*
	8: 5 for, **S**, saith *he, that* thou make all *things*	*3708*
	10:25 the more, as ye **s** the day approaching.	*991*
	11: 5 was translated that *he* should not **s** death;	*1492*
	12:14 without which no *man* shall **s** the Lord:	*3700*
	12:25 **S** *that* ye refuse not him that speaketh:	*991*
	13:23 whom, *if* he come shortly, I will **s** you.	*3700*
Jas	2:24 Ye **s** then how that by works a man is	*3708*
1Pe	1: 8 in whom, though now ye **s** *him* not,	*3708*
	1:22 ye love one another with a pure	NIG
	3:10 For he that will love life, and **s** good days,	*1492*
2Pe	1: 9 and **cannot s far off**, and hath forgotten	*3467*
1Jn	3: 2 be like him; for we shall **s** him as he is.	*3708*
	5:16 If any *man* **s** his brother sin a sin *which* is	*1492*
3Jn	1:14 But I trust *I* shall shortly **s** thee,	*1492*
Rev	1: 7 and every eye shall **s** him, and they *also*	*3700*
	1:12 And I turned to **s** the voice that spake with	*991*
	3:18 eyes with eyesalve, that thou mayest **s**.	*991*
	6: 1 one of the four beasts saying, Come and **s**.	*991*
	6: 3 I heard the second beast say, Come and **s**.	*991*
	6: 5 I heard the third beast say, Come and **s**.	*991*
	6: 6 and **s** thou hurt not the oil and the wine.	NIG
	6: 7 voice of the fourth beast say, Come and **s**.	*991*
	9:20 which neither can **s**, nor hear, nor walk:	*991*
	11: 9 nations shall **s** their dead bodies three days	*991*
	16:15 lest he walk naked, and they **s** his shame.	*991*
	18: 7 and am no widow, and shall **s** no sorrow.	*1492*

Rev	18: 9 they shall **s** the smoke of her burning,	*991*
	19:10 he said unto me, **S** *thou do it* not: I am	*3708*
	22: 4 And they shall **s** his face; and his name	*3700*
	22: 9 Then saith he unto me, **S** *thou do it* not:	*3708*

SEED (279) [SEED'S, SEEDS, SEEDTIME]

Ge	1:11 the herb yielding **s**, *and* the fruit tree	2233
	1:11 kind, whose **s** *is* in itself, upon the earth:	2233
	1:12 *and* herb yielding **s** after his kind,	2233
	1:12 whose **s** *was* in itself, after his kind:	2233
	1:29 I have given you every herb bearing **s**,	2233
	1:29 the which *is* the fruit of a tree yielding **s**;	2233
	3:15 and between thy **s** and her seed;	2233
	3:15 and between thy seed and her **s**;	2233
	4:25 *said she,* hath appointed me another **s**	2233
	7: 3 to keep **s** alive upon the face of all	2233
	9: 9 with you and with your **s** after you;	2233
	12: 7 and said, Unto thy **s** will I give this land:	2233
	13:15 to thee will I give it, and to thy **s** for ever.	2233
	13:16 I will make thy **s** as the dust of the earth:	2233
	13:16 earth, *then* shall thy **s** also be numbered.	2233
	15: 3 Behold, to me thou hast given no **s**:	2233
	15: 5 and he said unto him, So shall thy **s** be.	2233
	15:13 Know of a surety that thy **s** shall be a	2233
	15:18 saying, Unto thy **s** have I given this land,	2233
	16:10 I will multiply thy **s** exceedingly, that it	2233
	17: 7 thy **s** after thee in their generations for an	2233
	17: 7 a God unto thee, and to thy **s** after thee.	2233
	17: 8 give unto thee, and to thy **s** after thee,	2233
	17: 9 and thy **s** after thee in thy generations.	2233
	17:10 between me and you and thy **s** after thee;	2233
	17:12 of any stranger, which *is* not of thy **s**.	2233
	17:19 *and* with his **s** after him.	2233
	19:32 that we may preserve **s** of our father.	2233
	19:34 that we may preserve **s** of our father.	2233
	21:12 her voice; for in Isaac shall thy **s** be called.	2233
	21:13 will I make a nation, because he *is* thy **s**.	2233
	22:17 in multiplying I will multiply thy **s** as	2233
	22:17 thy **s** shall possess the gate of his enemies;	2233
	22:18 in thy **s** shall all the nations of the earth	2233
	24: 7 saying, Unto thy **s** will I give this land;	2233
	24:60 let thy **s** possess the gate of those which	2233
	26: 3 unto thee, and unto thy **s**, I will give all	2233
	26: 4 I will make thy **s** to multiply as the stars	2233
	26: 4 will give unto thy **s** all these countries;	2233
	26: 4 in thy **s** shall all the nations of the earth	2233
	26:24 multiply thy **s** for my servant Abraham's	2233
	28: 4 Abraham, to thee, and to thy **s** with thee;	2233
	28:13 liest, to thee will I give it, and to thy **s**;	2233
	28:14 thy **s** shall be as the dust of the earth,	2233
	28:14 in thy **s** shall all the families of the earth	2233
	32:12 and make thy **s** as the sand of the sea,	2233
	35:12 to thy **s** after thee will I give the land.	2233
	38: 8 marry her, and raise up **s** to thy brother.	2233
	38: 9 Onan knew that the **s** should not be his;	2233
	38: 9 lest that he should give **s** to his brother.	2233
	46: 6 into Egypt, Jacob, and all his **s** with him:	2233
	46: 7 all his **s** brought he with him into Egypt.	2233
	47:19 give us **s**, that we may live, and not die,	2233
	47:23 lo, *here is* **s** for you, and ye shall sow	2233
	47:24 for **s** of the field, and for your food,	2233
	48: 4 give this land to thy **s** after thee *for* an	2233
	48:11 and lo, God hath shewed me also thy **s**.	2233
	48:19 his **s** shall become a multitude of nations.	2233
Ex	16:31 *was* like coriander **s**, white; and the taste	2233
	28:43 for ever unto him and his **s** after him.	2233
	30:21 and to his **s** throughout their generations.	2233
	32:13 multiply your **s** as the stars of heaven,	2233
	32:13 I have spoken of will I give unto your **s**,	2233
	33: 1 to Jacob, saying, Unto thy **s** will I give it:	2233
Lev	11:37 upon any sowing which is to be sown,	2233
	11:38 if *any* water be put upon the **s**, and *any*	2233
	12: 2 If a woman have **conceived s**, and born	2232
	15:16 if any man's **s** of copulation go out from	2233
	15:17 every skin, whereon is the **s** of copulation,	2233
	15:18 whom man shall lie *with* **s** of copulation,	2233
	15:32 *of him* whose **s** goeth from him, and is	2233
	18:21 shalt not let *any* of thy **s** pass through	2233
	19:19 shalt not **sow** thy field with mingled **s**:	2232
	20: 2 that giveth *any* of his **s** unto Molech;	2233
	20: 3 he hath given of his **s** unto Molech,	2233
	20: 4 when he giveth of his **s** unto Molech,	2233
	21:15 Neither shall he profane his **s** among his	2233
	21:17 Whosoever *he be* of thy **s** in their	2233
	21:21 a blemish, of the **s** of Aaron the priest,	2233
	22: 3 Whosoever *he be* of all your **s** among	2233
	22: 4 What man soever of the **s** of Aaron *is* a	2233
	22: 4 or a man whose **s** goeth from him;	2233+7902
	26:16 ye shall sow your **s** in vain, for your	2233
	27:16 thy estimation shall be according to the **s**	2233
	27:16 homer of barley **s** *shall be valued* at fifty	2233
	27:30 of the **s** of the land, *or* of the fruit	2233
Nu	5:28 shall be free, and shall **conceive s**.	2232+2233
	11: 7 the manna *was* as coriander **s**,	2233
	14:24 he went; and his **s** shall possess it.	2233
	16:40 stranger, which *is* not of the **s** of Aaron,	2233
	18:19 LORD unto thee and to thy **s** with thee.	2233
	20: 5 it *is* no place of **s**, or of figs, or vines,	2233
	24: 7 **s** *shall be* in many waters, and his king	2233
	25:13 he shall have it, and his **s** after him,	2233
Dt	1: 8 give unto them and to their **s** after them.	2233
	4:37 therefore he chose their **s** after them,	2233
	10:15 chose their **s** after them, *even* you above	2233
	11: 9 fathers to give unto them and to their **s**,	2233
	11:10 where thou sowedst thy **s**, and wateredst	2233

Dt	14:22 shalt truly tithe all the increase of thy **s**,	2233
	22: 9 the fruit of *thy* **s** which thou hast sown,	2233
	28:38 shalt carry much **s** out *into* the field,	2233
	28:46 for a wonder, and upon thy **s** for ever.	2233
	28:59 the plagues of thy **s**, *even* great plagues,	2233
	30: 6 the heart of thy **s**, to love the LORD thy	2233
	30:19 that *both* thou and thy **s** may live:	2233
	31:21 be forgotten out of the mouths of their **s**:	2233
	34: 4 Jacob, saying, I will give it unto thy **s**:	2233
Jos	24: 3 and multiplied his **s**, and gave him Isaac.	2233
Ru	4:12 of the **s** which the LORD shall give thee	2233
1Sa	2:20 The LORD give thee **s** of this woman for	2233
	8:15 he will take the tenth of your **s**, and of	2233
	20:42 and between my **s** and thy seed for ever.	2233
	20:42 and between my seed and thy **s** for ever.	2233
	24:21 that thou wilt not cut off my **s** after me,	2233
2Sa	4: 8 the king this day of Saul, and of his **s**.	2233
	7:12 thy fathers, I will set up thy **s** after thee,	2233
	22:51 unto David, and to his **s** for evermore.	2233
1Ki	2:33 Joab, and upon the head of his **s** for ever:	2233
	2:33 upon his **s**, and upon his house,	2233
	11:14 he *was* of the king's **s** in Edom.	2233
	11:39 And I will for this afflict the **s** of David,	2233
	18:32 as would contain two measures of **s**.	2233
2Ki	5:27 cleave unto thee, and unto thy **s** for ever.	2233
	11: 1 she arose and destroyed all the **s** royal.	2233
	17:20 the LORD rejected all the **s** of Israel,	2233
	25:25 of the **s** royal, came, and ten men with	2233
1Ch	16:13 O ye **s** of Israel his servant, ye children of	2233
	17:11 that I will raise up thy **s** after thee,	2233
2Ch	20: 7 gavest it to the **s** of Abraham thy friend	2233
	22:10 destroyed all the **s** royal of the house of	2233
Ezr	2:59 and their **s**, whether they *were* of Israel:	2233
	9: 2 that the holy **s** have mingled themselves	2233
Ne	7:61 nor their **s**, whether they *were* of Israel.	2233
	9: 2 the **s** of Israel separated themselves from	2233
	9: 8 give *it, I say,* to his **s**, and hast performed	2233
Est	6:13 If Mordecai *be* of the **s** of the Jews,	2233
	9:27 upon their **s**, and upon all such as joined	2233
	9:28 the memorial of them perish from their **s**.	2233
	9:31 decreed for themselves and for their **s**,	2233
	10: 3 people, and speaking peace to all his **s**.	2233
Job	5:25 Thou shalt know also that thy **s** *shall be*	2233
	21: 8 Their **s** is established in their sight with	2233
	39:12 that he will bring home thy **s**, and gather	2233
Ps	18:50 to David, and to his **s** for evermore.	2233
	21:10 their **s** from among the children of men.	2233
	22:23 all ye the **s** of Jacob, glorify him;	2233
	22:23 and fear him, all ye the **s** of Israel.	2233
	22:30 A **s** shall serve him; it shall be accounted	2233
	25:13 at ease; and his **s** shall inherit the earth.	2233
	37:25 forsaken, nor his **s** begging bread.	2233
	37:26 and lendeth; and his **s** *is* blessed.	2233
	37:28 but the **s** of the wicked shall be cut off.	2233
	69:36 The **s** also of his servants shall inherit it:	2233
	89: 4 Thy **s** will I stablish for ever, and build	2233
	89:29 His **s** also will I make *to endure* for ever,	2233
	89:36 His **s** shall endure for ever, and his throne	2233
	102:28 their **s** shall be established before thee.	2233
	105: 6 ye **s** of Abraham his servant, ye children	2233
	106:27 To overthrow their **s** also among	2233
	112: 2 His **s** shall be mighty upon earth:	2233
	126: 6 and weepeth, bearing precious **s**,	2233
Pr	11:21 the **s** of the righteous shall be delivered.	2233
Ecc	11: 6 In the morning sow thy **s**, and in	2233
Isa	1: 4 a **s** of evildoers, children that are	2233
	5:10 the **s** of a homer shall yield an ephah.	2233
	6:13 the holy **s** *shall be* the substance thereof.	2233
	14:20 **s** of evildoers shall never be renowned.	2233
	17:11 in the morning shalt thou make thy **s** to	2233
	23: 3 by great waters the **s** of Sihor, the harvest	2233
	30:23 shall he give the rain of thy **s**, that thou	2233
	41: 8 have chosen, the **s** of Abraham my friend.	2233
	43: 5 I will bring thy **s** from the east,	2233
	44: 3 *ground:* I will pour my spirit upon thy **s**,	2233
	45:19 I said not unto the **s** of Jacob, Seek ye me	2233
	45:25 In the LORD shall all the **s** of Israel be	2233
	48:19 Thy **s** also had been as the sand,	2233
	53:10 shall see his **s**, he shall prolong *his* days,	2233
	54: 3 thy **s** shall inherit the Gentiles,	2233
	55:10 that it may give **s** to the sower, and bread	2233
	57: 3 the **s** of the adulterer and the whore.	2233
	57: 4 children of transgression, a **s** of falsehood,	2233
	59:21 thy mouth, nor out of the mouth of thy **s**,	2233
	59:21 nor out of the mouth of thy seed's **s**,	2233
	61: 9 shall be known among the Gentiles,	2233
	61: 9 that they *are* the **s** which the LORD hath	2233
	65: 9 I will bring forth a **s** out of Jacob,	2233
	65:23 for they *are* the **s** of the blessed of	2233
	66:22 so shall your **s** and your name remain.	2233
Jer	2:21 thee a noble vine, wholly a right **s**:	2233
	7:15 *even* the whole **s** of Ephraim.	2233
	22:28 he and his **s**, and are cast into a land	2233
	22:30 for no man of his **s** shall prosper,	2233
	23: 8 which led the **s** of the house of Israel out	2233
	29:32 Shemaiah the Nehelamite, and his **s**:	2233
	30:10 and thy **s** from the land of their captivity;	2233
	31:27 the house of Judah with the **s** of man,	2233
	31:27 the seed of man, and *with* the **s** of beast.	2233
	31:36 the **s** of Israel also shall cease from being	2233
	31:37 I will also cast off all the **s** of Israel for all	2233
	33:22 will I multiply the **s** of David my servant,	2233
	33:26 will I cast away the **s** of Jacob,	2233
	33:26 I will not take *any* of his **s** *to be* rulers	2233
	33:26 seed *to be* rulers over the **s** of Abraham,	2233

Jer	35: 7 nor sow **s**, nor plant vineyard, nor have	2233
	35: 9 neither have we vineyard, nor field, nor **s**:	2233
	36:31 will punish him and his **s** and his servants	2233
	41: 1 of the **s** royal, and the princes of the king,	2233
	46:27 and thy **s** from the land of their captivity;	2233
	49:10 his is spoiled, and his brethren,	2233
Eze	17: 5 He took also of the **s** of the land,	2233
	17:13 hath taken of the king's **s**, and made a	2233
	20: 5 up mine hand unto the **s** of the house	2233
	43:19 the Levites that *be* of the **s** of Zadok,	2233
	44:22 they shall take maidens of the **s** of	2233
Da	1: 3 and of the king's **s**, and of the princes;	2233
	2:43 they shall mingle themselves with the **s** of	2234
	9: 1 son of Ahasuerus, of the **s** of the Medes,	2233
Joel	1:17 The **s** is rotten under their clods, that soweth **s**;	6507
Am	9:13 the treader of grapes him that soweth **s**;	2233
Hag	2:19 *Is* the **s** yet in the barn? yea, as yet the	2233
Zec	8:12 For the **s** *shall be* prosperous; the vine	2233
Mal	2: 3 I *will* corrupt your **s**, and spread dung	2233
	2:15 That he might seek a godly **s**.	2233

Mt	13:19 This is he which **received s** by the way	4687
	13:20 he that **received** the **s** into stony *places*,	4687
	13:22 also that **received s** among the thorns is	4687
	13:23 he that **received s** into the good ground	4687
	13:24 a man which sowed good **s** in his field:	4690
	13:27 Sir, didst not thou sow good **s** in thy field?	4690
	13:31 Heaven is like unto a **grain of** mustard **s**,	2848
	13:37 He that soweth the good **s** is the Son of	4690
	13:38 good **s** are the children of the kingdom;	4690
	17:20 If ye have faith as a **grain of** mustard **s**,	2848
	22:24 his wife, and raise up **s** unto his brother.	4690
Mk	4:26 as if a man should cast **s** into the ground,	4703
	4:27 day, and the **s** should spring and grow up,	4703
	4:31 *It* is like a **grain of** mustard **s**, which,	2848
	12:19 his wife, and raise up **s** unto his brother.	4690
	12:20 the first took a wife, and dying left no **s**.	4690
	12:21 took her, and died, neither left he *any* **s**:	4690
	12:22 And the seven had her, and left no **s**: last	4690
Lk	1:55 to Abraham, and to his **s** for ever.	4690
	8: 5 A sower went out to sow his **s**: and as he	4703
	8:11 parable is this: The **s** is the word of God.	4703
	13:19 is like a **grain of** mustard **s**, which a man	2848
	17: 6 If ye had faith as a **grain of** mustard **s**,	2848
	20:28 *his* wife, and raise up **s** unto his brother.	4690
Jn	7:42 That Christ cometh of the **s** of David,	4690
	8:33 We be Abraham's **s**, and were never in	4690
	8:37 I know that ye are Abraham's **s**; but ye	4690
Ac	3:25 And in thy **s** shall all the kindreds of	4690
	7: 5 and to his **s** after him, when *as yet* he had	4690
	7: 6 his **s** should sojourn in a strange land;	4690
	13:23 Of this *man's* **s** hath God according to *his*	4690
Ro	1: 3 which was made of the **s** of David	4690
	4:13 or to his **s**, through the law, but through	4690
	4:16 the promise might be sure to all the **s**;	4690
	4:18 that which was spoken, So shall thy **s** be.	4690
	9: 7 because they are the **s** of Abraham,	4690
	9: 7 but, In Isaac shall thy **s** be called.	4690
	9: 8 of the promise are counted for the **s**.	4690
	9:29 Except the Lord of sabaoth had left us a **s**,	4690
	11: 1 of the **s** of Abraham, *of* the tribe of	4690
1Co	15:38 pleased him, and to every **s** his own body.	4690
2Co	9:10 he that ministereth **s** to the sower both	4690
	9:10 and multiply your **s sown**, and increase	4703
	11:22 Are they the **s** of Abraham? so am I.	4690
Gal	3:16 and his **s** were the promises made.	4690
	3:16 as of one, And to thy **s**, which is Christ.	4690
	3:19 the **s** should come to whom the promise	4690
	3:29 then are ye Abraham's **s**,	4690
2Ti	2: 8 Remember that Jesus Christ of the **s** of	4690
Heb	2:16 but he took on *him* the **s** of Abraham.	4690
	11:11 herself received strength to conceive **s**,	4690
	11:18 said, That in Isaac shall thy **s** be called:	4690
1Pe	1:23 not of corruptible, but *of* incorruptible,	4701
1Jn	3: 9 commit sin; for his **s** remaineth in him:	4690
Rev	12:17 to make war with the remnant of her **s**,	4690

SEED'S (1) [SEED]

Isa	59:21 nor out of the mouth of thy **s** seed, saith	2233

SEEDS (5) [SEED]

Dt	22: 9 shalt not **sow** thy vineyard with divers **s**:	2232
Mt	13: 4 some **s** fell by the way side, and the fowls	NIG
	13:32 Which indeed is the least of all **s**:	4690
Mk	4:31 is less than all the **s** that be in the earth:	4690
Gal	3:16 He saith not, And to **s**, as of many; but as	4690

SEEDTIME (1) [SEED, TIME]

Ge	8:22 **s** and harvest, and cold and heat,	2233

SEEING (116) [SEE]

Ge	15: 2 **s** I go childless, and the steward of my	2050.1
	18:18 **S** Abraham shall surely become a great	2050.1
	19: 1 Lot *them* rose up to meet them;	7200
	22:12 thou hast not withheld thy son, thine	2050.1
	24:56 **s** the Lord hath prospered my way;	2050.1
	26:27 ye hate me, and have sent me away	2050.1
	28: 8 Esau that the daughters of Canaan	7200
	44:30 **s** that his life *is* bound up in the lad's	2050.1
Ex	4:11 the dumb, or deaf, or the **s**, or the blind?	6493
	21: 8 he hath dealt deceitfully with her:	NIH
	22:10 or be hurt, or driven away, no man **s** *it*:	7200
	23: 9 ye were strangers in the land of Egypt.	3588
Lev	10:17 **s** it *is* most holy, and *God* hath given it	3588
Nu	15:26 **s** all the people were in ignorance,	3588
	16: 3 **s** all the congregation *are* holy, every one	3588

Nu	35:23 **s** him not, and cast *it* upon him, that he	7200
Jos	17:14 portion to inherit, **s** I *am* a great people,	2050.1
	22:18 **s** ye rebel to day against the Lord,	NIH
Jdg	13:18 thou thus after my name, **s** it *is* secret?	2050.1
	17:13 do me good, **s** I have a Levite to *my* priest.	3588
	19:23 **s** that this man is come into mine	310+834
	21: 7 **s** we have sworn by the Lord that *we*	2050.1
	21:16 the women are destroyed out of	3588
Ru	1:21 **s** the Lord hath testified against me,	2050.1
	2:10 knowledge of me, **s** I *am* a stranger?	2050.1
1Sa	16: 1 **s** I have rejected him from reigning over	2050.1
	17:36 he hath defied the armies of the living	3588
	18:23 **s** that I *am* a poor man,	2050.1
	24: 6 **s** he *is* the anointed of the Lord.	3588
	25:26 **s** the Lord hath withholden thee from	834
	28:16 **s** the Lord is departed from thee,	2050.1
2Sa	13:39 concerning Amnon, **s** he was dead.	3588
	15:20 **s** I go whither I may, return thou,	2050.1
	18:22 son, **s** that thou hast no tidings ready?	2050.1
	19:11 **s** the speech of all Israel is come to	2050.1
1Ki	1:48 my throne *this* day, mine eyes even **s** *it*.	7200
	1:18 Solomon **s** the young man that he was	7200
2Ki	10: 2 **s** your master's sons *are* with you,	2050.1
1Ch	12:17 **s** *there* is no wrong in mine hands,	871.1
2Ch	2: 6 **s** the heaven and heaven of heavens	3588
Ezr	9:13 **s** that thou our God hast punished us	3588
Ne	2: 2 countenance sad, **s** thou *art* not sick?	2050.1
Job	14: 5 **s** his days *are* determined, the number of	518
	19:28 the root of the matter is found in me;	2050.1
	21:22 he judgeth those that are high.	2050.1
	21:34 **s** *in* your answers there remaineth	2050.1
	24: 1 times are not hidden from the Almighty,	NIH
	28:21 **S** it is hid from the eyes of all living,	2050.1
Ps	22: 8 let him deliver him, **s** he delighted in him.	3588
	50:17 **S** thou hatest instruction, and castest	2050.1
Pr	3:29 **s** he dwelleth securely by thee.	2050.1
	17:16 to get wisdom, **s** *he hath* no heart to *it*?	2050.1
	20:12 The hearing ear, and the **s** eye, the Lord	7200
Ecc	1: 8 utter *it*: the eye is not satisfied with **s**,	7200
	2:16 **s** that which now *is, in* the days to come	871.1
	6:11 **S** there be many things that increase	3588
Isa	21: 3 hearing *of it*; I was dismayed at the **s** *of it*.	7200
	33:15 of blood, and shutteth his eyes from **s** evil;	7200
	42:20 **S** many *things*, but thou observest not;	7200
	49:21 **s** I have lost my children,	2050.1
Jer	11:15 **s** she hath wrought lewdness *with* many,	NIH
	47: 7 **s** the Lord hath given it a charge	2050.1
Eze	16:30 **s** thou doest all these *things*, the work of	871.1
	17:18 **S** he despised the oath by breaking	2050.1
	21: 4 **S** then that I will cut off from thee	3282
	22:28 them *with* untempered *morter*, **s** vanity,	2374
Da	2:47 secrets, **s** thou couldest reveal this secret.	1768
Hos	4: 6 **s** thou hast forgotten the law of thy God	2050.1
Mt	5: 1 And **s** the multitudes, he went up into a	1492
	9: 2 Jesus **s** their faith said unto the sick of	1492
	13:13 they **s** see not; and hearing they hear	991
	13:14 and **s** ye shall see, and shall not perceive:	991
Mk	4:12 That **s** they may see, and not perceive;	991
	11:13 And **s** a fig tree afar off having leaves,	1492
Lk	1:34 How shall this be, **s** I know not a man?	1492
	5:12 who **s** Jesus fell on *his* face,	1492
	8:10 that **s** they might not see, and hearing they	991
	23:40 **s** thou art in the same condemnation?	3754
Jn	2:18 unto us, **s** that thou doest these *things*?	3754
	9: 7 way therefore, and washed, and came **s**.	991
	21:21 Peter **s** him saith to Jesus, Lord,	1492
Ac	2:15 **s** it is *but* the third hour of the day.	1063
	2:31 **s** this *before*, spake of the resurrection	4275
	3: 3 Who **s** Peter and John about to go into	1492
	7:24 And **s** one *of them* suffer wrong,	1492
	8: 6 hearing and **s** the miracles which he did.	991
	9: 7 hearing a voice, but **s** no *man*.	2334
	13:11 shalt be blind, not **s** the sun for a season.	991
	13:46 but **s** ye put it from *you*, and	1894
	16:27 and **s** the prison doors open, he drew out	1492
	17:24 **s** that he is Lord of heaven and earth,	NIG
	17:25 though he needed any *thing*, **s** he giveth	NIG
	19:36 **S** then that these *things* cannot be spoken	3767
	24: 2 **S** that by thee we enjoy great quietness,	NIG
	28:26 and **s** ye shall see, and not perceive:	991
Ro	3:30 **S** *it* is one God, which shall justify	1897
1Co	14:16 **s** he understandeth not what thou sayest?	1894
2Co	3:12 **S** then that we have such hope, we use	3767
	4: 1 Therefore **s** we have this ministry, as we	2531
	11:18 **S** that many glory after the flesh, I will	1893
	11:19 fools gladly, **s** ye *yourselves* are wise.	NIG
Col	3: 9 that ye have put off the old man with	NIG
2Th	1: 6 **S** *it is* a righteous *thing* with God to	1512
Heb	4: 6 **S** therefore it remaineth that some *must*	1893
	4:14 **S** then that we have a great high priest,	3767
	5:11 to be uttered, **s** ye are dull of hearing.	1893
	6: 6 **s** they crucify to themselves the Son of	NIG
	7:25 **s** he ever liveth to make intercession for	NIG
	8: 4 that there are priests that offer gifts	3708
	11:27 for he endured, as **s** *him who* is invisible.	3708
	12: 1 **Wherefore s** we also are compassed	5105
1Pe	1:22 **S** ye have purified your souls in obeying	NIG
2Pe	2: 8 dwelling among them, in **s** and hearing,	990
	3:11 **S** then that all these *things shall*	NIG
	3:14 **Wherefore**, beloved, **s** that ye look for	1352
	3:17 Ye **therefore**, beloved, **s** ye know *these*	3767

SEEK (244) [SEEKEST, SEEKETH, SEEKING, SOUGHT]

Ge	37:16 he said, I **s** my brethren: tell me, I pray	1245
	43:18 he may **s occasion** against us, and fall	1556

Lev	13:36 the priest shall not **s** for yellow hair;	1239
	19:31 neither **s** after wizards, to be defiled by	1245
Nu	15:39 that ye **s** not after your own heart and	8446
	16:10 with thee: and **s** ye the priesthood also?	1245
	24: 1 to **s** for enchantments; but he set his face	7125
Dt	4:29 If from thence thou shalt **s** the Lord thy	1245
	4:29 thou shalt find *him*, if thou **s** him with all	1875
	12: 5 *even* unto his habitation shall ye **s**,	1875
	22: 2 be with thee until thy brother **s after**	1875
	23: 6 Thou shalt not **s** their peace nor their	1875
Ru	3: 1 My daughter, shall I not **s** rest for thee,	1245
1Sa	9: 3 with thee, and arise, go **s** the asses.	1245
	10: 2 The asses which thou wentest to **s** are	1245
	10:14 he said, To **s** the asses: and when we saw	1245
	16:16 to **s out** a man, *who is* a cunning player	1245
	23:15 David saw that Saul was come out to **s** his	1245
	23:25 his men went to **s** *David*. And they told	1875
	24: 2 to **s** David and his men upon the rocks	1245
	25:26 they that **s** evil to my lord, be as Nabal.	1245
	25:29 is risen to pursue thee, and to **s** thy soul:	1245
	26: 2 to **s** David in the wilderness of Ziph.	1245
	26:20 the king of Israel is come out to **s** a flea,	1245
	27: 1 to **s** me any more in any coast of Israel:	1245
	28: 7 **S** me a woman that hath a familiar spirit,	1875
2Sa	5:17 all the Philistines came up to **s** David;	1245
1Ki	2:40 went to Gath to Achish to **s** his servants:	1245
	18:10 whither my lord hath not sent to **s** thee:	1245
	19:10 left; and they **s** my life, to take it away.	1245
	19:14 left; and they **s** my life, to take it away.	1245
2Ki	2:16 them go, we pray thee, and **s** thy master:	1245
	6:19 I will bring you to the man whom ye **s**.	1245
1Ch	4:39 of the valley, to **s** pasture for their flocks.	1245
	14: 8 all the Philistines went up to **s** David.	1245
	16:10 let the heart of them rejoice that **s**	1245
	16:11 **S** the Lord and his strength, seek his	1875
	16:11 and his strength, his face continually.	1245
	22:19 and your soul to **s** the Lord your God;	1875
	28: 8 **s** for all the commandments of the Lord	1875
	28: 9 if thou **s** him, he will be found of thee;	1875
2Ch	7:14 **s** my face, and turn from their wicked	1245
	11:16 **s** the Lord God of Israel came to	1875
	12:14 he prepared not his heart to **s** the Lord.	1875
	14: 4 commanded Judah to **s** the Lord God of	1875
	15: 2 if ye **s** him, he will be found of you;	1875
	15:12 they entered into a covenant to **s**	1875
	15:13 That whosoever would not **s** the Lord	1875
	19: 3 and hast prepared thine heart to **s** God.	1875
	20: 3 set himself to **s** the Lord,	1875
	20: 4 cities of Judah they came to **s** the Lord.	1245
	30:19 *That* prepareth his heart to **s** God,	1875
	31:21 and in the commandments, to **s** his God,	1875
	34: 3 he began to **s** after the God of David his	1875
Ezr	4: 2 for we **s** your God, as ye *do*; and we do	1875
	6:21 to the Lord God of Israel, did eat,	1875
	7:10 Ezra had prepared his heart to **s** the law	1875
	8:21 to **s** of him a right way for us, and for our	1245
	8:22 God *is* upon all them for good that **s** him;	1245
	9:12 nor **s** their peace or their wealth for ever:	1875
Ne	2:10 to the welfare of the children of Israel.	1245
Job	5: 8 I would **s** unto God, and unto God would	1875
	7:21 thou shalt **s** me **in the morning**, but I	7836
	8: 5 If thou wouldest **s** unto God *betimes*,	7836
	20:10 His children shall **s** *to* please the poor,	NIH
Ps	4: 2 will ye love vanity, *and* **s after** leasing?	1245
	9:10 Lord, hast not forsaken them that **s** thee.	1875
	10: 4 will not **s** *after God*: God *is* not *in* all his	1875
	10:15 evil *man*: **s out** his wickedness *till* thou	1875
	14: 2 were *any* that did understand, *and* **s** God.	1875
	22:26 they shall praise the Lord that **s** him:	1875
	24: 6 This *is* the generation of them that **s** him,	1875
	24: 6 that seek him, that **s** thy face, O Jacob.	1245
	27: 4 I desired of the Lord, that will I **s after**;	1245
	27: 8 *When thou saidst*, **S** ye my face; my heart	1245
	27: 8 said unto thee, Thy face, Lord, will I **s**.	1245
	34:10 they that **s** the Lord shall not want any	1875
	34:14 and do good; **s** peace, and pursue it.	1245
	35: 4 and put to shame that **s after** my soul:	1245
	38:12 They also that **s after** my life lay snares	1245
	38:12 they that **s** my hurt speak mischievous	1875
	40:14 confounded together that **s after** my soul	1245
	40:16 all those that **s** thee rejoice and be glad	1875
	53: 2 *any* that did understand, that did **s** God.	1875
	54: 3 me, and oppressors **s after** my soul:	1245
	63: 1 thou *art* my God; **early** will I **s** thee:	7836
	63: 9 *that* **s** my soul, to destroy *it*, shall go	1245
	69: 6 not those that **s** thee be confounded for	1245
	69:32 and your heart shall live that **s** God.	1875
	70: 2 and confounded that **s after** my soul:	1245
	70: 4 all those that **s** thee rejoice and be glad	1245
	71:13 reproach and dishonour that **s** my hurt.	1245
	71:24 are brought unto shame, that **s** my hurt.	1245
	83:16 that they may **s** thy name, O Lord.	1245
	104:21 *their* prey, and **s** their meat from God.	1245
	105: 3 let the heart of them rejoice that **s**	1245
	105: 4 **S** the Lord, and his strength: seek his	1875
	105: 4 and his strength: **s** his face evermore.	1245
	109:10 let them **s** *their bread* also out of their	1875
	119: 2 and *that* **s** him with the whole heart.	1875
	119:45 I will walk at liberty: for I **s** thy precepts.	1875
	119:155 the wicked: for they **s** not thy statutes.	1875
	119:176 astray like a lost sheep; **s** thy servant;	1245
	122: 9 of the Lord our God I will **s** thy good.	1245
Pr	1:28 they shall **s** me **early**, but they shall not	7836
	7:15 **diligently** to **s** thy face, and I have found	7836
	8:17 and those that **s** me **early** shall find me.	7836

Pr
21: 6 tossed to and fro of them that **s** death. 1245
23:30 at the wine; they that go to **s** mixt wine. 2713
23:35 when shall I awake? I will **s** it yet again. 1245
28: 5 they that **s** the LORD understand all 1245
29:10 hate the upright: but the just **s** his soul. 1245
29:26 Many **s** the ruler's favour; but every 1245

Ecc
1:13 I gave my heart to **s** and search out by 1875
7:25 **s** out wisdom, and the reason of things, 1245
8:17 because though a man labour to **s** it out, 1245

SS
3: 2 I will **s** him whom my soul loveth: 1245
6: 1 aside? that we may **s** him with thee. 1245

Isa
1:17 **s** judgment, relieve the oppressed, judge 1875
8:19 **S** unto them that have familiar spirits, 1875
8:19 should not a people **s** unto their God? 1875
9:13 neither do they **s** the LORD of hosts. 1875
11:10 of the people; to it shall the Gentiles **s**: 1875
19: 3 they shall **s** to the idols, and to 1875
26: 9 my spirit within me will I thee **early**. 7836
29:15 Woe unto them that **s** deep to hide their 6009
31: 1 Holy One of Israel, neither **s** the LORD. 1875
34:16 **S** ye out of the book of the LORD, 1875
41:12 shalt **s** them, and shalt not find them, 1245
41:17 When the poor and needy **s** water, 1245
45:19 unto the seed of Jacob, **S** ye me in vain: 1245
51: 1 after righteousness, ye that **s** the LORD: 1245
55: 6 **S** ye the LORD while he may be found, 1875
58: 2 Yet they **s** me daily, and delight to know 1875

Jer
2:24 all they that **s** her will not weary 1245
2:33 Why trimmest thou thy way to **s** love? 1245
4:30 will despise thee, they will **s** thy life. 1245
5: 1 know, and **s** in the broad places thereof, 1245
11:21 that **s** thy life, saying, Prophesy not in 1245
19: 7 by the hands of them that **s** their lives: 1245
19: 9 they that **s** their lives, shall straiten them. 1245
21: 7 into the hand of those that **s** their life: 1245
22:25 give thee into the hand of them that **s** 1245
29: 7 **s** the peace of the city whither I have 1875
29:13 ye shall **s** me, and find me, when ye shall 1245
30:14 have forgotten thee; they **s** thee not; 1875
34:20 into the hand of them that **s** their life: 1245
34:21 into the hand of them that **s** their life, 1245
38:16 into the hand of these men that **s** thy life. 1245
44:30 and into the hand of them that **s** his life; 1245
45: 5 **s** them not: for behold, I will bring evil 1245
46:26 into the hand of those that **s** their lives, 1245
49:37 and before them that **s** their life: 1245
50: 4 they shall go, and **s** the LORD their God. 1245

La
1:11 All her people sigh, they **s** bread; they 1245

Eze
7:25 shall **s** peace, and there shall be none. 1245
7:26 then shall they **s** a vision of the prophet; 1245
34: 6 and none did search or **s** after them. 1245
34:11 both search my sheep, and **s** them **out**. 1239
34:12 so will I **s** out my sheep, and will deliver 1239
34:16 I will **s** that which was lost, and bring 1245

Da
9: 3 to **s** by prayer and supplications, 1245

Hos
2: 7 she shall **s** them, but shall not find them: 1245
3: 5 the LORD their God, and David their 1245
5: 6 and with their herds to **s** the LORD; 1245
5:15 acknowledge their offence, and **s** my face: 1245
5:15 in their affliction they will **s** me **early**. 7836
7:10 LORD their God, nor **s** him for all this. 1245
10:12 for it is time to **s** the LORD, till he come 1875

Am
5: 4 house of Israel, **S** ye me, and ye shall live: 1875
5: 5 **s** not Beth-el, nor enter into Gilgal, 1875
5: 6 **S** the LORD, and ye shall live; lest he 1875
5: 8 **S** him that maketh the seven stars and NIH
5:14 **S** good, and not evil, that ye may live: 1875
8:12 run to and fro to **s** the word of the LORD, 1245

Na
3: 7 whence shall I **s** comforters for thee? 1245
3:11 thou also shalt **s** strength because of 1245

Zep
2: 3 **S** ye the LORD, all ye meek of the earth, 1245
2: 3 **s** righteousness, seek meekness: 1245
2: 3 seek righteousness, **s** meekness: 1245

Zec
8:21 the LORD, and to **s** the LORD of hosts: 1245
8:22 strong nations shall come to **s** the LORD 1245
11:16 neither shall **s** the young one, nor heal 1245
12: 9 that I will **s** to destroy all the nations that 1245

Mal
2: 7 and they should **s** the law at his mouth: 1245
2:15 That he might **s** a godly seed. 1245
3: 1 the LORD, whom ye **s**, shall suddenly 1245

Mt
2:13 Herod will **s** the young child to destroy 2212
6:32 **after** all these things do the Gentiles **s**): 1934
6:33 But **s** ye first the kingdom of God, 2212
7: 7 **s**, and ye shall find; knock, and it shall be 2212
28: 5 for I know that ye **s** Jesus, which was 2212

Mk
1:37 they said unto him, All men **s** for thee. 2212
3:32 and thy brethren without **s** for thee. 2212
8:12 Why doth this generation **s after** a sign? 1934
16: 6 Ye **s** Jesus of Nazareth, which was 2212

Lk
11: 9 **s**, and ye shall find; knock, and it shall be 2212
11:29 they **s** a sign; and there shall no sign be 1934
12:29 And **s** not ye what ye shall eat, or what ye 2212
12:30 things do the nations of the world **s after**: 1934
12:31 But rather **s** ye the kingdom of God, 2212
13:24 will **s** to enter in, and shall not be able. 2212
15: 8 the house, and **s** diligently till she find it? 2212
17:33 shall **s** to save his life shall lose 2212
19:10 the Son of man is come to **s** and to save 2212
24: 5 Why **s** ye the living among the dead? 2212

Jn
1:38 and saith unto them, What **s** ye? 2212
5:30 is just; because I **s** not mine own will, 2212
5:44 seek not the honour that **cometh** from God 2212
6:26 Ye **s** me, not because ye saw the miracles, 2212
7:25 Is not this he, whom they **s** to kill? 2212
7:34 Ye shall **s** me, and shall not find me: and 2212

Jn
7:36 Ye shall **s** me, and shall not find me: and 2212
8:21 and ye shall **s** me, and shall die in your 2212
8:37 but ye **s** to kill me, because my word hath 2212
8:40 But now ye **s** to kill me, a man that hath 2212
8:50 And I **s** not mine own glory: there is one 2212
13:33 Ye shall **s** me: and as I said unto the Jews, 2212
18: 4 and said unto them, Whom **s** ye? 2212
18: 7 Then asked he them again, Whom **s** ye? 2212
18: 8 told you that I am he: if therefore ye **s** me, 2212

Ac
10:19 said unto him, Behold, three men **s** thee: 2212
10:21 and said, Behold, I am he whom ye **s**: 2212
11:25 departed Barnabas to Tarsus, for to **s** Saul: 327
15:17 That the residue of men might **s after** 1567
17:27 That they should **s** the Lord, if haply they 2212

Ro
2: 7 continuance in well doing **s for** glory 2212
11: 3 and I am left alone, and they **s** my life. 2212

1Co
1:22 a sign, and the Greeks **s after** wisdom: 2212
7:27 **s** not to be loosed. Art thou loosed from a 2212
7:27 Art thou loosed from a wife? **s** not a wife. 2212
10:24 Let no man **s** his own, but every man 2212
14:12 **s** that ye may excel to the edifying of 2212

2Co
12:14 be burdensome to you: for I **s** not yours, 2212
13: 3 ye **s** a proof of Christ speaking in me, 2212

Gal
1:10 do I **s** to please men? for if I yet pleased 2212
2:17 if, while we **s** to be justified by Christ, 2212

Php
2:21 all **s** their own, not the things which are 2212

Col
3: 1 Christ, **s** those things which are above, 2212

Heb
11: 6 a rewarder of them that **diligently** **s** him. 1567
11:14 declare plainly that they **s** a country. 1934
13:14 no continuing city, but we **s** one to come. 1934

1Pe
3:11 do good; let him **s** peace, and ensue it. 2212

Rev
9: 6 And in those days shall men **s** death, 2212

SEEKEST (9) [SEEK]

Ge
37:15 the man asked him, saying, What **s** thou? 1245

Jdg
4:22 I will shew thee the man whom thou **s**. 1245

2Sa
17: 3 the man whom thou **s** is as if all returned: 1245
20:19 thou **s** to destroy a city and a mother in 1245

1Ki
11:22 thou **s** to go to thine own country? 1245

Pr
2: 4 If thou **s** her as silver, and searchest for 1245

Jer
45: 5 seek great things for thyself? seek **them** 1245

Jn
4:27 yet no man said, What **s** thou? 2212
20:15 why weepest thou? whom **s** thou? 2212

SEEKETH (42) [SEEK]

1Sa
19: 2 saying, Saul my father **s** to kill thee: 1245
20: 1 sin before thy father, that he **s** my life? 1245
22:23 for he that **s** my life seeketh thy life: 1245
22:23 for he that seeketh my life **s** thy life: 1245
23:10 servant hath certainly heard that Saul **s** 1245
24: 9 saying, Behold, David **s** thy hurt? 1245

2Sa
4:11 came forth of my bowels, **s** my life: 1245

1Ki
20: 7 you, and see how this man **s** mischief: 1245

2Ki
5: 7 and see how he **s a quarrel** against me: 579

Job
39:29 From thence she **s** the prey, and her eyes 2658
37:32 watcheth the righteous, and **s** to slay him. 1245

Ps

Pr
11:27 that **diligently** **s** good procureth favour: 7836
11:27 that **s** mischief, it shall come unto him. 1875
14: 6 A scorner **s** wisdom, and findeth it not: 1245
15:14 heart of him that hath understanding **s** 1245
17: 9 He that covereth a transgression **s** love; 1245
17:11 An evil man **s** only rebellion: therefore 1245
17:19 he that exalteth his gate **s** destruction. 1245
18: 1 **s** and intermeddleth with all wisdom. 1245
18:15 and the ear of the wise **s** knowledge. 1245
31:13 She **s** wool, and flax, and worketh 1875

Ecc
7:28 Which yet my soul **s**, but I find not: 1245

Isa
40:20 he **s** unto him a cunning workman to 1245

Jer
5: 1 that executeth judgment, that **s** the truth; 2212
30:17 This is Zion, whom no man **s after**. 1875
38: 4 for this man **s** not the welfare of this 1875

La
3:25 that wait for him, to the soul that **s** him. 1875

Eze
14:10 the punishment of him that **s** unto him; 1875
34:12 As a shepherd **s out** his flock in the day 1243

Mt
7: 8 asketh receiveth; and he that **s** findeth: 2212
12:39 and adulterous generation **s after** a sign; 1934
16: 4 and adulterous generation **s after** a sign; 1934
18:12 and **s** that which is gone astray? 2212

Lk
11:10 and he that **s** findeth; and to him that 2212

Jn
4:23 for the Father **s** such to worship him. 2212
7: 4 and he himself **s** to be known openly. 2212
7:18 He that speaketh of himself **s** his own 2212
7:18 but he that **s** his glory that sent him, 2212
8:50 glory: there is one that **s** and judgeth. 2212

Ro
3:11 there is none that **s after** God. NIG

1Co
13: 5 **s** not her own, is not easily provoked, 2212

SEEKING (14) [SEEK]

Est
10: 3 **s** the wealth of his people, 1875

Isa
16: 5 **s** judgment, and hasting righteousness. 1875

Mt
12:43 dry places, **s** rest, and findeth none. 2212
13:45 unto a merchant man, **s** goodly pearls: 2212

Mk
8:11 **s** of him a sign from heaven, tempting 2212

Lk
2:45 turned back again to Jerusalem, **s** him. 2212
11:24 he walketh through dry places, **s** rest; 2212
11:54 to catch something out of his mouth, 2212
13: 7 these three years I come **s** fruit on this fig 2212

Jn
6:24 and came to Capernaum, **s for** Jesus. 2212

Ac
13: 8 **s** to turn away the deputy from the faith. 2212
13:11 he went about **s** to lead him by 2212

1Co
10:33 as I please all men in all things, not **s** 2212

1Pe
5: 8 walketh about, **s** whom he may devour: 2212

SEEM (22) [SEEMED, SEEMETH, SEEMLY, UNSEEMLY]

Ge
27:12 shall **s** to him as a deceiver; 1961+5869+871.1

Dt
15:18 It shall not **s** hard unto thee, 5869+871.1
25: 3 brother should **s** vile **unto** thee. 5869+3807.1

Jos
24:15 if it **s** evil **unto** you to serve 5869+871.1

1Sa
24: 4 to him as it shall **s** good **unto** thee. 5869+871.1

2Sa
19:37 him what shall **s** good **unto** thee. 5869+871.1
19:38 that which shall **s** good **unto** thee: 5869+871.1

1Ki
21: 2 or, if it **s** good to thee, I will give 5869+871.1

1Ch
13: 2 If it **s** good unto you, and that it be of NIH

Ezr
5:17 Now therefore, if it **s** good to the king, NIH
7:18 whatsoever shall **s** good to thee, and to 3191

Ne
9:32 let not all the trouble **s** little before thee, NIH

Est
5: 4 If it **s** good unto the king, let the king and NIH
8: 5 the thing **s** right before the king, and I be 3787

Jer
40: 4 If it **s** good **unto** thee to come 5869+871.1
40: 4 if it **s** ill **unto** thee to come with 5869+871.1

Na
2: 4 shall **s** like torches, they shall run like 4758

1Co
11:16 if any man **s** to be contentious, we have 1380
12:22 which **s** to be more feeble, are necessary: 1380

2Co
10: 9 That I may not **s** as if I would terrify you 1380

Heb
4: 1 any of you should **s** to come short of it. 1380

Jas
1:26 If any man among you **s** to be religious, 1380

SEEMED (16) [SEEM]

Ge
19:14 he **s** as one that mocked 1961+5869+871.1
29:20 they **s** unto him but a few 1961+5869+871.1

2Sa
3:19 in Hebron all that **s** good to Israel, 5869+871.1
3:19 that **s** good to the whole house of 5869+871.1

Ecc
9:13 under the sun, and it **s** great unto me: NIH

Jer
18: 4 as good to the potter to make it. 5869+871.1
27: 5 it unto whom it **s** meet **unto** me. 5869+871.1

Mt
11:26 Father; for so it **s** good in thy sight. 1096

Lk
1: 3 It **s** good to me also, having had perfect 1380
10:21 Father; for so it **s** good in thy sight. 1096
24:11 And their words **s** to them as idle tales, 5316

Ac
15:25 It **s** good unto us, being assembled with 1380
15:28 it **s** good to the Holy Ghost, and to us, 1380

Gal
2: 6 But of these who **s** to be somewhat, 1380
2: 6 for they who **s** to be somewhat in 1380
2: 9 Cephas, and John, who **s** to be pillars, 1380

SEEMETH (28) [SEEM]

Lev
14:35 It **s** to me there is as it were a plague in 7200

Nu
16: 9 **S** it but a small thing unto you, that the NIH

Jos
9:25 It **s** good and right unto thee to do 5869+871.1

Jdg
10:15 us whatsoever **s** good **unto** thee, 5869+871.1
19:24 them what **s** good **unto** you: 5869+871.1

1Sa
1:23 unto her, Do what **s** thee good; 5869+871.1
3:18 let him do what **s** him good. 5869+871.1
11:10 with us all that **s** good **unto** you. 5869+871.1
14:36 Do whatsoever **s** good **unto** you. 5869+871.1
14:40 Do what **s** good **unto** thee. 5869+871.1
18:23 David said, **S** it to you a light thing 5869+871.1

2Sa
10:12 LORD do that which **s** him good. 5869+871.1
15:26 him do to me as **s** good **unto** him. 5869+871.1
18: 4 What ye best I will do. 5869+871.1
24:22 offer up what **s** good **unto** him: 5869+871.1

Est
3:11 do with them as it **s** good to thee. 5869+871.1

Pr
14:12 There is a way which **s** right **unto** 6440+3807.1
16:25 There is a way that **s** right **unto** a 6440+3807.1
18:17 He that is first in his own cause **s** just; NIH

Jer
26:14 me as **s** good and meet **unto** you. 5869+871.1
40: 4 it **s** good and convenient for 5869+871.1
40: 5 wheresoever it **s** convenient **unto** 5869+871.1

Eze
16: 8 **S** it a small thing unto you to have eaten 7200

Lk
8:18 be taken even that which he **s** to have. 1380

Ac
17:18 other some, He **s** to be a setter forth of 1380
25:27 For it **s** to me unreasonable to send a 1380

1Co
3:18 If any man among you **s** to be wise in this 1380

Heb
12:11 Now no chastening for the present **s** to be 1380

SEEMLY (2) [SEEM]

Pr
19:10 Delight is not **s** for a fool; much less for a 5000
26: 1 in harvest, so honour is not **s** for a fool. 5000

SEEN (277) [SEE]

Ge
7: 1 thee have I **s** righteous before me in this 7200
8: 5 were the tops of the mountains **s**. 7200
9:14 that the bow shall be **s** in the cloud: 7200
22:14 In the mount of the LORD it shall be **s**. 7200
31:12 for I have **s** all that Laban doeth unto thee. 7200
31:42 God hath **s** mine affliction and the labour 7200
32:30 I have **s** God face to face, and my life is 7200
33:10 for therefore I have **s** thy face, as though I 7200
33:10 as though I had **s** the face of God, 7200
45:13 glory in Egypt, and of all that you have **s**; 7200
46:30 I have **s** thy face, because thou art yet 7200

Ex
3: 7 I have **surely** **s** the affliction of my 7200+7200
3: 9 I have also **s** the oppression wherewith 7200
3:16 and **s** that which is done to you in Egypt: NIH
10: 6 thy fathers, nor thy fathers' fathers have **s**, 7200
13: 7 there shall no leavened bread be **s** with 7200
13: 7 neither shall there be leaven **s** with thee 7200
14:13 for the Egyptians whom ye have **s** to day, 7200
19: 4 Ye have **s** what I did unto the Egyptians, 7200
20:22 Ye have **s** that I have talked with you 7200
32: 9 I have **s** this people, and behold, it is a 7200
33:23 my back parts: but my face shall not be **s**. 7200
34: 3 neither let any man be **s** throughout all 7200

Lev
13: 1 whether he hath **s** or known of it; if he do 7200
13: 7 after that he hath been **s** of the priest for 7200
13: 7 he shall be **s** of the priest again: 7200

Nu
14:14 that thou LORD art **s** face to face, 7200

Nu	14:22 Because all *those* men which have s my	7200
	23:21 neither hath he s perverseness in Israel;	7200
	27:13 when thou hast s it, thou also shalt be	7200
Dt	1:28 moreover we have s the sons of	7200
	1:31 where thou hast s how that the LORD thy	7200
	3:21 Thine eyes have s all that the LORD your	7200
	4: 3 Your eyes have s what the LORD did	7200
	4: 9 forget the things which thine eyes have s,	7200
	5:24 we have s this day that God doth talk	7200
	9:13 saying, I have s this people, and behold,	7200
	10:21 terrible *things,* which thine eyes have s.	7200
	11: 2 which have not s the chastisement of	7200
	11: 7 your eyes have s all the great acts of	7200
	16: 4 shall be no leavened bread s with thee	7200
	21: 7 this blood, neither have our eyes s it.	7200
	29: 2 Ye have s all that the LORD did before	7200
	29: 3 temptations which thine eyes have s,	7200
	29:17 ye have s their abominations, and their	7200
	33: 9 and to his mother, I have not s him;	7200
Jos	23: 3 ye have s all that the LORD your God	7200
	24: 7 your eyes have s what I have done in	7200
Jdg	2: 7 who had s all the great works of	7200
	5: 8 or spear s among forty thousand in Israel?	7200
	6:22 I have s an angel of the LORD face to	7200
	9:48 What ye have s me do, make haste,	7200
	13:22 shall surely die, because we have s God.	7200
	14: 2 I have s a woman in Timnath of	7200
	18: 9 for we have s the land, and behold, it *is*	7200
	19:30 There was no such *deed* done nor s from	7200
1Sa	6:16 the five lords of the Philistines had s	7200
	16:18 I have s a son of Jesse the Beth-lehemite,	7200
	17:25 Have ye s this man that is come up?	7200
	23:22 his haunt is, *and* who hath s him there:	7200
	24:10 this day thine eyes have s how that	7200
2Sa	17:17 for they might not be s to come into	7200
	18:21 Cushi, Go tell the king what thou hast s.	7200
	22:11 and he was s upon the wings of the wind.	7200
1Ki	6:18 all *was* cedar; there was no stone s.	7200
	8: 8 that the ends of the staves were s out in	7200
	8: 8 the oracle, and they were not s without:	7200
	10: 4 when the queen of Sheba had s all	7200
	10: 7 and mine eyes had s *it:* and behold,	7200
	10:12 almug trees, nor were s unto this day.	7200
	13:12 For his sons had s what way the man of	7200
	20:13 Hast thou s all this great multitude?	7200
2Ki	9:26 Surely I have s yesterday the blood of	7200
	20: 5 have heard thy prayer, I have s thy tears:	7200
	20:15 he said, What have they s in thine house?	7200
	20:15 that *are* in mine house have they s:	7200
	23:29 him at Megiddo, when he had s him.	7200
1Ch	29:17 and now have I s with joy thy people,	7200
2Ch	5: 9 were s from the ark before the oracle;	7200
	5: 9 the oracle; but they were not s without.	7200
	9: 3 the queen of Sheba had s the wisdom	7200
	9: 6 I came, and mine eyes had s *it:* and,	7200
	9:11 there were none such s before in the land	7200
Ezr	3:12 who were ancient men that had s the first	7200
Est	9:26 *of that* which they had s concerning this	7200
Job	4: 8 Even as I have s, they that plow iniquity,	7200
	5: 3 I have s the foolish taking root:	7200
	7: 8 The eye of him that hath s me shall see	7210
	8:18 shall deny him, *saying,* I have not s	7200
	10:18 given up the ghost, and no eye had s me!	7200
	13: 1 mine eye hath s all *this,* mine ear hath	7200
	15:17 and that which I have s I will declare;	2372
	20: 7 they which have s him shall say, Where	7200
	27:12 all ye yourselves have s *it;* why then are	2372
	28: 7 and which the vulture's eye hath not s:	7805
	31:19 If I have s *any* perish for want of clothing,	7200
	33:21 is consumed away, that it cannot be s;	7210
	33:21 and his bones *that* were not s stick out.	7200
	38:17 hast thou s the doors of the shadow of	7200
	38:22 or hast thou s the treasures of the hail,	7200
Ps	10:14 hast s *it;* for thou beholdest mischief	7200
	18:15 the channels of waters were s,	7200
	35:21 *and* said, Aha, aha, our eye hath s *it.*	7200
	35:22 *This* thou hast s, O LORD: keep not	7200
	37:25 yet have I not s the righteous forsaken,	7200
	37:35 I have s the wicked in great power,	7200
	48: 8 have we s in the city of the LORD of	7200
	54: 7 mine eye hath s *his desire* upon mine	7200
	55: 9 for I have s violence and strife in the city.	7200
	63: 2 so *as* I have s thee in the sanctuary,	2372
	68:24 They have s thy goings, O God; *even*	7200
	90:15 *and* the years *wherein* we have s evil.	7200
	98: 3 the ends of the earth have s the salvation	7200
	119:96 I have s an end of all perfection:	7200
Pr	25: 7 of the prince whom thine eyes have s.	7200
Ecc	1:14 I have s all the works that are done under	7200
	3:10 I have s the travail, which God hath given	7200
	3: 4 who hath not s the evil work that is done	7200
	5:13 There is a sore evil *which* I have s under	7200
	5:18 Behold *that* which I have s: *it is* good and	7200
	6: 1 There is an evil which I have s under	7200
	6: 5 Moreover he hath not s the sun, nor	7200
	6: 6 years twice *told,* yet hath he s no good:	7200
	7:15 *things* have I s in the days of my vanity:	7200
	9: 9 All this have I s, and applied my heart	7200
	9:13 This wisdom have I s also under the sun,	7200
	10: 5 There is an evil *which* I have s under	7200
	10: 7 I have s servants upon horses,	7200
Isa	5: 2 for mine eyes have s the King, the LORD	7200
	9: 2 people that walked in darkness have s	7200
	16:12 it is s that Moab is weary on the high	7200
	22: 9 Ye have s also the breaches of the city of	7200

Isa	38: 5 I have heard thy prayer, I have s thy tears:	7200
	39: 4 said he, What have they s in thine house?	7200
	39: 4 All that *is* in mine house have they s:	7200
	44:16 saith, Aha, I am warm, I have s the fire:	7200
	47: 3 be uncovered, yea, thy shame shall be s:	7200
	57:18 I have s his ways, and will heal him:	7200
	60: 2 and his glory shall be s upon thee.	7200
	64: 4 hath the eye s, O God, besides thee,	7200
	66: 8 hath heard such *a thing?* who hath s	7200
	66:19 heard my fame, neither have s my glory;	7200
Jer	1:12 said the LORD unto me, Thou hast well s:	7200
	3: 6 Hast thou s *that* which backsliding Israel	7200
	7:11 Behold, even I have s *it,* saith the LORD.	7200
	12: 3 thou hast s me, and tried mine heart	7200
	13:27 have s thine adulteries, and thy neighings,	7200
	23:13 I have s folly in the prophets of Samaria;	7200
	23:14 I have s also in the prophets of Jerusalem	7200
	44: 2 Ye have s all the evil that I have brought	7200
	46: 5 Wherefore have I s them dismayed *and*	7200
La	1: 8 because they have s her nakedness:	7200
	1:10 she hath s *that* the heathen entered into	7200
	2:14 prophets have s vain and foolish things	2372
	2:14 have s for thee false burdens and causes	2372
	2:16 looked for; we have found, we have s it.	7200
	3: 1 I *am* the man *that* hath s affliction by	7200
	3:59 O LORD, thou hast s my wrong:	7200
	3:60 Thou hast s all their vengeance *and* all	7200
Eze	8:12 thou s what the ancients of the house	7200
	8:15 unto me, Hast thou s *this,* O son of man?	7200
	8:17 unto me, Hast thou s *this,* O son of man?	7200
	11:24 the vision that I had s went up from me.	7200
	13: 3 their own spirit, and have s nothing!	7200
	13: 6 They have s vanity and lying divination,	2372
	13: 7 Have ye not s a vain vision, and have ye	2372
	13: 8 s lies, therefore behold, I *am* against you,	2372
	47: 6 hast thou s *this?* Then he brought me,	7200
Da	2:26 unto me the dream which I have s,	2370
	4: 9 the visions of my dream that I have s,	2370
	4:18 dream I King Nebuchadnezzar have s.	2370
	8: 6 which I had s standing before the river,	7200
	8:15 had s the vision, and sought for	7200
	9:21 I had s in the vision at the beginning,	7200
Hos	6:10 I have s a horrible thing in the house of	7200
Zec	9: 8 for now have I s with mine eyes.	7200
	9:14 the LORD shall be s over them,	7200
	10: 2 diviners have s a lie, and have told false	2372
Mt	2: 2 for we have s his star in the east,	1492
	6: 1 your alms before men, to be s of them:	2300
	6: 5 of the streets, that they may be s of men.	5316
	9:33 saying, It was never so s in Israel.	5316
	13:17 and have not s *them;* and to hear *those*	1492
	21:32 when ye had s *it,* repented not afterward,	1492
	23: 5 But all their works they do for to be s of	2300
Mk	9: 1 till they have s the kingdom of God come	1492
	9: 9 tell no *man* what *things* they had s,	1492
	16:11 and had been s of her, believed not.	2300
	16:14 they believed not them which had s him	2300
Lk	1:22 they perceived that he had s a vision in	3708
	2:17 when they had s, they made known	1492
	2:20 all *the things* that they had heard and s,	1492
	2:26 before he had s the Lord's Christ.	1492
	2:30 For mine eyes have s thy salvation,	1492
	5:26 saying, We have s strange *things* to day.	1492
	7:22 and tell John what *things* ye have s and	1492
	9:36 any of *those things* which they had s.	3708
	10:24 and have not s *them;* and to hear *those*	1492
	19:37 for all the mighty works that they had s;	1492
	23: 8 he hoped to have s some miracle done by	1492
	24:23 that *they* had also s a vision of angels,	3708
	24:37 and supposed that *they* had s a spirit.	2334
Jn	1:18 No *man* hath s God at any time; the only	3708
	3:11 we do know, and testify that we have s;	3708
	3:32 And what he hath s and heard, that he	3708
	4:45 having s all *the things* that he did at	3708
	5:37 his voice at any time, nor s his shape.	3708
	6:14 they had s the miracle that Jesus did,	1492
	6:36 That ye also have s me, and believe not.	3708
	6:46 Not that any *man* hath s the Father, save	3708
	6:46 he which is of God, he hath s the Father.	3708
	8:38 speak *that* which ye have s with my Father:	3708
	8:38 do *that* which ye have s with your father.	3004
	8:57 fifty years old, and hast thou s Abraham?	3708
	9: 8 they which before had s him that he was	2334
	9:37 Thou hast both s him, and it is he that	3708
	11:45 and had s the *things* which Jesus did,	2300
	14: 7 henceforth ye know him, and have s him.	3708
	14: 9 he that hath s me hath seen the Father;	3708
	14: 9 he that hath seen me hath seen the Father;	3708
	15:24 but now have they both s and hated both	3708
	20:18 told the disciples that she had s the Lord,	3708
	20:25 said unto him, We have s the Lord.	3708
	20:29 Thomas, because thou hast s me, thou	3708
	20:29 blessed *are* they that have not s,	1492
Ac	1: 3 being s of them forty days, and speaking	1492
	1:11 come *in* like manner as ye have s him go	2300
	4:20 but speak *the things* which we have s and	1492
	7:34 I have s, I have seen the affliction of my	1492
	7:34 I have s the affliction of my people which	1492
	7:44 it according to the fashion that he had s.	3708
	9:12 And hath s in a vision a man named	1492
	9:27 unto them how he had s the Lord	1492
	10:17 *this* vision which he had s should mean,	1492
	11:13 he shewed us how he had s an angel in	1492
	11:23 and had s the grace of God, was glad,	1492
	13:31 And he was s many days of them which	3700

Ac	16:10 And after he had s the vision,	1492
	16:40 and when they had s the brethren,	1492
	21:29 they had s **before** with him in the city	4308
	22:15 witness unto all men of what thou hast s	3708
	26:16 both of *these things* which thou hast s,	1492
Ro	1:20 the creation of the world are clearly s,	2529
	8:24 hope that is s is not hope: for what a man	991
1Co	2: 9 is written, Eye hath not s, nor ear heard,	1492
	9: 1 have I not s Jesus Christ our Lord? are not	3708
	15: 5 And that he was s of Cephas, then of	3700
	15: 6 he was s of above five hundred brethren	3700
	15: 7 After that, he was s of James; then of all	3700
	15: 8 And last of all he was s of me also, as of	3700
2Co	4:18 we look not at the *things* which are s,	991
	4:18 are seen, but at the *things* which are not s:	991
	4:18 for the *things* which are s *are* temporal;	991
	4:18 but the *things* which are not s *are* eternal.	991
Php	1:30 and received, and heard, and is in me,	1492
Col	2: 1 for as many as have not s my face in	3708
	2:18 into *those things* which he hath not s,	3708
1Ti	3:16 justified in the Spirit, s of angels,	3700
	6:16 whom no man hath s, nor can see:	1492
Heb	11: 1 hoped for, the evidence of things not s.	991
	11: 3 that *things* which are s were not made of	991
	11: 7 warned of God of *things* not s as yet,	991
	11:13 but having s them afar off,	1492
Jas	5:11 of Job, and have s the end of the Lord;	1492
1Pe	1: 8 Whom having not s, ye love; in whom,	1492
1Jn	1: 1 heard, which we have s with our eyes,	3708
	1: 2 and we have s *it,* and bear witness,	3708
	1: 3 *That* which we have s and heard declare	3708
	3: 6 whosoever sinneth hath not s him,	3708
	4:12 No *man* hath s God at any time.	2300
	4:14 And we have s and do testify that	2300
	4:20 loveth not his brother whom he hath s,	3708
	4:20 can he love God whom he hath not s?	3708
3Jn	1:11 but he that doeth evil hath not s God.	3708
Rev	1:19 Write the things which thou hast s,	1492
	1:19 there was s in his temple the ark of his	3700
	22: 8 heard *them.* And when I had heard and s,	991

SEER (21) [SEE]

1Sa	9: 9 he spake, Come, and let us go to the s:	7200
	9: 9 a Prophet was beforetime called a S.)	7200
	9:11 and said unto them, Is the s here?	7200
	9:19 answered Saul, and said, I *am* the s:	7200
2Sa	15:27 unto Zadok the priest, *Art not* thou a s?	7200
	24:11 unto the prophet Gad, David's s, saying,	2374
1Ch	9:22 Samuel the s did ordain in their set office.	7200
	21: 9 LORD spake unto Gad, David's s, saying,	2374
	25: 5 Heman the king's s in the words of God,	2374
	26:28 all that Samuel the s, and Saul the son of	7200
	29:29 *are* written in the book of Samuel the s,	7200
	29:29 prophet, and in the book of Gad the s,	2374
2Ch	9:29 in the visions of Iddo the s against	2374
	12:15 and of Iddo the s concerning genealogies?	2374
	16: 7 that time Hanani the s came to Asa king	7200
	16:10 Asa was wroth with the s, and put him *in*	7200
	19: 2 Jehu the son of Hanani the s went out to	2374
	29:25 of Gad the king's s, and Nathan	2374
	29:30 the words of David, and of Asaph the s.	2374
	35:15 and Heman, and Jeduthun the king's s;	2374
Am	7:12 Amaziah said unto Amos, O thou s,	2374

SEER'S (1) [SEE]

1Sa	9:18 Tell me, I pray thee, where the s house *is.*	7200

SEERS (6) [SEE]

2Ki	17:13 all the prophets, *and by* all the s, saying,	2374
2Ch	33:18 the words of the s that spake to him in	2374
	33:19 *are* written among the sayings of the s.	2374
Isa	29:10 and your rulers, the s hath he covered.	2374
	30:10 Which say to the s, See not; and to	7203
Mic	3: 7 shall the s be ashamed, and the diviners	2374

SEEST (36) [SEE]

Ge	13:15 all the land which thou s, to thee will I	7200
	16:13 that spake unto her, Thou God s me:	7210
	31:43 *are* my cattle, and all that thou s *is* mine:	7200
Ex	10:28 for in *that* day thou s my face thou shalt	7200
Dt	4:19 and when thou s the sun, and the moon,	7200
	12:13 burnt offerings in every place that thou s:	7200
	20: 1 s horses, and chariots, *and* a people more	7200
	21:11 s among the captives a beautiful woman,	7200
Jdg	9:36 Thou s the shadow of the mountains as *if*	7200
1Ki	21:29 s thou how Ahab humbleth himself	7200
Job	10: 4 eyes of flesh? or s thou as man seeth?	7200
Pr	22:29 s thou a man diligent in his business?	2372
	26:12 S thou a man wise in his own conceit?	7200
	29:20 S thou a man that is hasty in his words?	2372
Ecc	5: 8 If thou s the oppression of the poor,	7200
Isa	58: 3 have we fasted, *say they,* and thou s not?	7200
	58: 7 thou s the naked, that thou cover him;	7200
Jer	1:11 unto me, saying, Jeremiah, what s thou?	7200
	1:13 me the second time, saying, What s thou?	7200
	7:17 S thou not what they do in the cities of	7200
	20:12 righteous, *and* s the reins and the heart,	7200
	24: 3 LORD unto me, What s thou, Jeremiah?	7200
	32:24 is come to pass; and behold, thou s *it.*	7200
Eze	8: 6 me, Son of man, s thou what they do?	7200
	40: 4 all that thou s to the house of Israel.	7200
Da	1:13 and as thou s, deal with thy servants.	7200
Am	7: 8 LORD said unto me, Amos, what s thou? And I said,	7200
	8: 2 he said, Amos, what s thou? And I	7200
Zec	4: 2 And said unto me, What s thou? And I	7200

S

Zec 5: 2 he said unto me, What s thou? And I 7200
Mk 5:31 Thou s the multitude thronging thee, 991
 13: 2 unto him, S thou these great buildings? 991
Lk 7:44 said unto Simon, S thou this woman? 991
Ac 21:20 and said unto him, Thou s, brother, 2334
Jas 2:22 S thou how faith wrought with his works, 991
Rev 1:11 and, What thou s, write in a book, 991

SEETH (54) [SEE]

Ge 16:13 Have I also here looked after him that s 7210
 44:31 when he s that the lad is not with us, that 7200
Ex 4:14 he s thee, he will be glad in his heart. 7200
 12:23 when he s the blood upon the lintel, 7200
Lev 13:20 when the priest s it, behold, it be in sight 7200
Dt 32:36 when he s that their power is gone, 7200
1Sa 16: 7 for the LORD s not as man seeth; for man NIH
 16: 7 for the LORD seeth not as man s; for man 7200
2Ki 2:19 of this city is pleasant, as my lord s: 7200
Job 8:17 about the heap, and s the place of stones. 2372
 10: 4 thou eyes of flesh? or seest thou as man s? 7200
 11:11 he s wickedness also; will he not then 7200
 22:14 are a covering to him, that he s not; 7200
 28:10 and his eye s every precious thing. 7200
 28:24 the earth, and s under the whole heaven; 7200
 34:21 the ways of man, and he s all his goings. 7200
 42: 5 of the ear: but now mine eye s thee. 7200
Ps 37:13 at him: for he s that his day is coming. 7200
 49:10 For he s that wise men die, likewise 7200
 58:10 The righteous shall rejoice when he s 2372
Ecc 8:16 also there is that neither day nor night s 7200
Isa 21: 6 a watchman, let him declare what he s. 7200
 28: 4 which when he that looketh upon it s, 7200
 29:15 are in the dark, and they say, Who s us? 7200
 29:23 when he s his children, the work of mine 7200
 47:10 thou hast said, None s me. Thy wisdom 7200
Eze 8:12 for they say, The LORD s us not; 7200
 9: 9 forsaken the earth, and the LORD s not. 7200
 12:27 The vision that he s is for many days to 2372
 18:14 that s all his father's sins which he hath 7200
 33: 3 If when he s the sword come upon the 7200
 39:15 any's a man's bone, then shall he set 7200
Mt 6: 4 thy Father which s in secret himself shall 991
 6: 6 thy Father which s in secret shall reward 991
 6:18 and thy Father, which is in secret, 991
Mk 5:38 and s the tumult, and them that wept and 2334
Lk 16:23 and s Abraham afar off, and Lazarus in his 3708
Jn 1:29 The next day John s Jesus coming unto 991
 5:19 of himself, but what he s the Father do: 991
 6:40 that every one which s the Son, 2334
 9:21 by what means he now s, we know not; 991
 10:12 s the wolf coming, and leaveth the sheep, 2334
 11: 9 because he s the light of this world. 991
 12:45 And he s him that sent me. 2334
 12:45 And he that seeth me s him that sent me. 2334
 14:17 it s him not, neither knoweth him: 2334
 14:19 little while, and the world s me no more; 2334
 20: 1 s the stone taken away from the sepulchre. 2334
 20: 6 the sepulchre, and s the linen clothes lie, 2334
 20:12 s two angels in white sitting, the one at 2334
 21:20 s the disciple whom Jesus loved following; 991
Ro 8:24 what a man s, why doth he yet hope for? 991
2Co 12: 6 of me above that which he s me to be, 991
1Jn 3:17 s his brother hath need, and shutteth up 2334

SEETHE (9) [SEETHING]

Ex 16:23 will bake to day, and s that ye will seethe; 1310
 16:23 will bake to day, and seethe that ye will s; 1310
 23:19 shalt not s a kid in his mother's milk. 1310
 29:31 and s his flesh in the holy place. 1310
 34:26 shalt not s a kid in his mother's milk. 1310
Dt 14:21 shalt not s a kid in his mother's milk. 1310
2Ki 4:38 s pottage for the sons of the prophets. 1310
Eze 24: 5 and let them s the bones of it therein. 1310
Zec 14:21 come and take of them, and s therein: 1310

SEETHING (3) [SEETHE]

1Sa 2:13 servant came, while the flesh was in s, 1310
Job 41:20 goeth smoke, as out of a s pot or caldron. 5301
Jer 1:13 I said, I see a s pot; and the face thereof is 5301

SEGUB (3)

1Ki 16:34 up the gates thereof in his youngest son S, 7687
1Ch 2:21 threescore years old; and she bare him S, 7687
 2:22 S begat Jair, who had three and 7687

SEIR (39)

Ge 14: 6 Horites in their mount S, unto El-paran, 8165
 32: 3 to Esau his brother unto the land of S, 8165
 33:14 endure, until I come unto my lord unto S. 8165
 33:16 Esau returned that day on his way unto S. 8165
 36: 8 dwelt Esau in mount S: Esau is Edom. 8165
 36: 9 the father of the Edomites in mount S: 8165
 36:20 These are the sons of S the Horite, 8165
 36:21 the children of S in the land of Edom. 8165
 36:30 Hori, among their dukes in the land of S. 8165
Nu 24:18 S also shall be a possession for his 8165
Dt 1: 2 the way of mount S unto Kadesh-barnea.) 8165
 1:44 as bees do, and destroyed you in S, 8165
 2: 1 and we compassed mount S many days. 8165
 2: 4 the children of Esau, which dwell in S; 8165
 2: 5 I have given mount S unto Esau for a 8165
 2: 8 which dwelt in S, through the way of 8165
 2:12 The Horims also dwelt in S beforetime; 8165
 2:22 to the children of Esau, which dwelt in S, 8165
 2:29 the children of Esau, which dwell in S, 8165

Dt 33: 2 Sinai, and rose up from S unto them; 8165
Jos 11:17 the mount Halak, that goeth up to S; 8165
 12: 7 the mount Halak, that goeth up to S; 8165
 15:10 from Baalah westward unto mount S, 8165
 24: 4 I gave unto Esau mount S, to possess it; 8165
Jdg 5: 4 LORD, when thou wentest out of S, 8165
1Ch 1:38 the sons of S; Lotan, and Shobal, 8165
 4:42 five hundred men, went to mount S, 8165
2Ch 20:10 of Ammon and Moab and mount S, 8165
 20:22 Moab, and mount S, which were come 8165
 20:23 up against the inhabitants of mount S, 8165
 20:23 had made an end of the inhabitants of S, 8165
 25:11 smote of the children of S ten thousand. 8165
 25:14 he brought the gods of the children of S, 8165
Isa 21:11 He calleth to me out of S, Watchman, 8165
Eze 25: 8 Because that Moab and S do say, Behold, 8165
 35: 2 set thy face against mount S, 8165
 35: 3 Behold, O mount S, I am against thee, 8165
 35: 7 Thus will I make mount S most desolate, 8165
 35:15 O mount S, and all Idumea, even all of it: 8165

SEIRAH See SEIRATH

SEIRATH (1)

Jdg 3:26 beyond the quarries, and escaped unto S. 8167

SEIZE (4) [SEIZED]

Jos 8: 7 up from the ambush, and s upon the city; 3423
Job 3: 6 As for that night, let darkness s upon it; 3947
Ps 55:15 Let death s upon them, and let them go 5377
Mt 21:38 kill him, and let us s on his inheritance. 2722

SEIZED (1) [SEIZE]

Jer 49:24 fear hath s on her: anguish and 2388

SELA (1) [SELA-HAMMAHLEKOTH]

Isa 16: 1 ruler of the land from S to the wilderness, 5554

SELAH (75)

2Ki 14: 7 took S by war, and called the name of it 5554
Ps 3: 2 There is no help for him in God. S. 5542
 3: 4 and he heard me out of his holy hill. S. 5542
 3: 8 thy blessing is upon thy people. S. 5542
 4: 2 ye love vanity, and seek after leasing? S. 5542
 4: 4 own heart upon your bed, and be still. S. 5542
 7: 5 and lay mine honour in the dust. S. 5542
 9:16 the work of his own hands. Higgaion. S. 5542
 9:20 may know themselves to be but men. S. 5542
 20: 3 and accept thy burnt sacrifice. S. 5542
 21: 2 not withholden the request of his lips. S. 5542
 24: 6 seek him, that seek thy face, O Jacob. S. 5542
 24:10 LORD of hosts, he is the King of glory. S. 5542
 32: 4 is turned into the drought of summer. S. 5542
 32: 5 thou forgavest the iniquity of my sin. S. 5542
 32: 7 me about with songs of deliverance. S. 5542
 39: 5 at his best state is altogether vanity. S. 5542
 39:11 like a moth: surely every man is vanity. S. 5542
 44: 8 day long, and praise thy name for ever. S. 5542
 46: 3 shake with the swelling thereof. S. 5542
 46: 7 with us; the God of Jacob is our refuge. S. 5542
 46:11 with us; the God of Jacob is our refuge. S. 5542
 47: 4 excellency of Jacob whom he loved. S. 5542
 48: 8 our God: God will establish it for ever. S. 5542
 49:13 their posterity approve their sayings. S. 5542
 49:15 of the grave: for he shall receive me. S. 5542
 50: 6 for God is judge himself. S. 5542
 52: 3 rather than to speak righteousness. S. 5542
 52: 5 root thee out of the land of the living. S. 5542
 54: 3 they have not set God before them. S. 5542
 55: 7 far off, and remain in the wilderness. S. 5542
 55:19 S. Because they have no changes, 5542
 57: 3 S. God shall send forth his mercy and 5542
 57: 6 whereof they are fallen themselves. S. 5542
 59: 5 merciful to any wicked transgressors. S. 5542
 59:13 in Jacob unto the ends of the earth. S. 5542
 60: 4 may be displayed because of the truth. S. 5542
 61: 4 I will trust in the covert of thy wings. S. 5542
 62: 4 their mouth, but they curse inwardly. S. 5542
 62: 8 before him: God is a refuge for us. S. 5542
 66: 4 unto thee; they shall sing to thy name. S. 5542
 66: 7 let not the rebellious exalt themselves. S. 5542
 66:15 rams; I will offer bullocks with goats. S. 5542
 67: 1 and cause his face to shine upon us; S. 5542
 67: 4 and govern the nations upon earth. S. 5542
 68: 7 didst march through the wilderness; S. 5542
 68:19 benefits, even the God of our salvation. S. 5542
 68:32 the midst of them; O sing praises unto the Lord; S. 5542
 75: 3 are dissolved: I bear up the pillars of it. S. 5542
 76: 3 shield, and the sword, and the battle. S. 5542
 76: 9 to save all the meek of the earth. S. 5542
 77: 3 and my spirit was overwhelmed. S. 5542
 77: 9 in anger shut up his tender mercies? S. 5542
 77:15 people, the sons of Jacob and Joseph. S. 5542
 81: 7 I proved thee at the waters of Meribah. S. 5542
 82: 2 and accept the persons of the wicked? S. 5542
 83: 8 they have holpen the children of Lot. S. 5542
 84: 4 house: they will be still praising thee. S. 5542
 84: 8 my prayer: give ear, O God of Jacob. S. 5542
 85: 2 thou hast covered all their sin. S. 5542
 87: 3 are spoken of thee, O city of God. S. 5542
 87: 6 people, that this man was born there. S. 5542
 88: 7 hast afflicted me with all thy waves. S. 5542
 88:10 shall the dead arise and praise thee? S. 5542
 89: 4 build up thy throne to all generations. S. 5542
 89:37 and as a faithful witness in heaven. S. 5542
 89:45 thou hast covered him with shame. S. 5542

Ps 89:48 his soul from the hand of the grave? S. 5542
 140: 3 adder's poison is under their lips. S. 5542
 140: 5 way side; they have set grins for me. S. 5542
 140: 8 lest they exalt themselves. S. 5542
 143: 6 thirsteth after thee, as a thirsty land. S. 5542
Hab 3: 3 S. His glory covered the heavens, 5542
 3: 9 S. Thou didst cleave the earth with rivers. 5542
 3:13 the foundation unto the neck. S. 5542

SELA-HAMMAHLEKOTH (1) [SELA]

1Sa 23:28 they called that place S. 5555

SELED (2)

1Ch 2:30 the sons of Nadab; S, and Appaim: 5540
 2:30 and Appaim: but S died without children. 5540

SELEUCIA (1)

Ac 13: 4 forth by the Holy Ghost, departed unto S; 4581

SELF (6) [HERSELF, HIMSELF, ITSELF, SELFSAME, SELFWILL, SELFWILLED, SELVES, THEMSELVES, THYSELF, YOURSELVES]

Ex 32:13 to whom thou swarest by thine own s, 3509.2
Jn 5:30 can of mine own s do nothing: as I hear, 1683
 17: 5 glorify thou me with thine own s with 4572
1Co 4: 3 yea, I judge not mine own s. 1683
Phm 1:19 owest unto me even thine own s besides. 4572
1Pe 2:24 Who his own s bare our sins in his own 846

SELF-CONTROL See TEMPERANCE

SELFSAME (15) [SAME, SELF]

Ge 7:13 In the s day entered Noah, and Shem, 6106
 17:23 the flesh of their foreskin in the s day, 6106
 17:26 In the s day was Abraham circumcised, 6106
Ex 12:17 in this s day have I brought your armies 6106
 12:41 years, even the s day it came to pass, 6106
 12:51 it came to pass the s day, that the LORD 6106
Lev 23:14 until the s day that ye have brought an 6106
 23:21 ye shall proclaim on the s day, that it 6106
Dt 32:48 the LORD spake unto Moses that s day, 6106
Jos 5:11 and parched corn in the s day. 6106
Eze 40: 1 in the s day the hand of the LORD was 6106
Mt 8:13 And his servant was healed in the s hour. 1565
1Co 12:11 all these worketh that one and the s Spirit, 846
2Co 5: 5 he that hath wrought us for the s thing, 846
 7:11 For behold this s thing, that ye sorrowed 846

SELFWILL (1) [SELF, WILL]

Ge 49: 6 and in their s they digged down a wall. 7522

SELFWILLED (2) [SELF, WILL]

Tit 1: 7 not s, not soon angry, not given to wine, 829
2Pe 2:10 Presumptuous are they, s, they are not 829

SELL (35) [SALE, SELLER, SELLERS, SELLEST, SELLETH, SOLD]

Ge 25:31 Jacob said, S me this day thy birthright. 4376
 37:27 let us s him to the Ishmeelites, and let not 4376
Ex 21: 7 a man s his daughter to be a maidservant, 4376
 21: 8 to s her unto a strange nation he shall 4376
 21:35 they shall s the live ox, and divide 4376
 22: 1 steal an ox, or a sheep, and kill it, or s it; 4376
Lev 25:14 if thou s ought unto thy neighbour, 4376+4465
 25:15 of years of the fruits he shall s unto thee: 4376
 25:16 the years of the fruits doth he s unto thee. 4376
 25:29 a man s a dwelling house in a walled city, 4376
 25:47 s himself unto the stranger or sojourner 4376
Dt 2:28 Thou shalt s me meat for money, that I 7666
 14:21 eat it; or thou mayest s it unto an alien: 4376
 21:14 shalt not s her at all for money, 4376+4465
Jdg 4: 9 for the LORD shall s Sisera into the hand 4376
1Ki 21:25 did s himself to work wickedness in 4376
2Ki 4: 7 s the oil, and pay thy debt, and live thou 4376
Ne 5: 8 and will you even s your brethren? 4376
 10:31 or any victuals on the sabbath day to s, 4376
Pr 23:23 Buy the truth, and s it not; also wisdom, 4376
Eze 30:12 s the land into the hand of the wicked: 4376
 48:14 they shall not s of it, neither exchange, 4376
Joel 3: 8 I will s your sons and your daughters into 4376
 3: 8 they shall s them to the Sabeans, to a 4376
Am 8: 5 new moon be gone, that we may s corn? 7666
 8: 6 yea, and s the refuse of the wheat? 7666
Zec 11: 5 they that s them say, Blessed be 4376
Mt 19:21 go and s that thou hast, and give to 4453
 25: 9 go ye rather to them that s, and buy for 4453
Mk 10:21 s whatsoever thou hast, and give to 4453
Lk 12:33 S that ye have, and give alms; 4453
 18:22 yet lackest thou one thing: s all that thou 4453
 22:36 let him s his garment, and buy one. 4453
Jas 4:13 there a year, and buy and s, and get gain: 1710
Rev 13:17 And that no man might buy or s, save he 4453

SELLER (4) [SELL]

Isa 24: 2 as with the buyer, so with the s; 4376
Eze 7:12 let not the buyer rejoice, nor the s mourn: 4376
 7:13 For the s shall not return to that which is 4376
Ac 16:14 a s of purple, of the city of Thyatira, 4211

SELLERS (1) [SELL]

Ne 13:20 s of all kind of ware lodged without 4376

SELLEST (1) [SELL]

Ps 44:12 Thou s thy people for nought, and dost 4376

S

SELLETH (7) [SELL]

Ex	21:16 and s him, or if he be found in his hand,	4376
Dt	24: 7 maketh merchandise of him, or s him;	4376
Ru	4: 3 s a parcel of land, which was our brother	4376
Pr	11:26 shall be upon the head of him that s it.	7666
	31:24 s it; and delivereth girdles unto	4376
Na	3: 4 that s nations through her whoredoms,	4376
Mt	13:44 joy thereof goeth and s all that he hath,	4453

SELVEDGE (2)

Ex	26: 4 one curtain from the s in the coupling;	7098
	36:11 of one curtain from the s in the coupling:	7098

SELVES (7) [SELF]

Lk	21:30 know of your own s that summer is now	1438
Ac	20:30 Also of your own s shall men arise,	846
2Co	8: 5 but first gave their own s to the Lord,	1438
	13: 5 ye be in the faith; prove your own s.	1438
	13: 5 Know ye not your own s, how that Jesus	1438
2Ti	3: 2 For men shall be lovers of their own s,	5367
Jas	1:22 not hearers only, deceiving your own s.	1438

SEM (1) [SHEM]

Lk	3:36 was the son of S, which was the son	4590

SEMACHIAH (1)

1Ch 26: 7 brethren were strong men, Elihu, and S.		5565

SEMAKIAH See SEMACHIAH

SEMEI (1)

Lk	3:26 was the son of S, which was the son	4584

SEMEIN See SEMEI

SENAAH (2)

Ezr	2:35 The children of S, three thousand and	5570
Ne	7:38 The children of S, three thousand nine	5570

SENATE (1) [SENATORS]

Ac	5:21 and all the s of the children of Israel,	1087

SENATORS (1) [SENATE]

Ps	105:22 at his pleasure; and teach his s wisdom.	2205

SEND (234) [SENDEST, SENDETH, SENDING, SENT, SENTEST]

Ge	24: 7 he shall s his angel before thee,	7971
	24:12 s me good speed this day,	6440+7136+3807.1
	24:40 will s his angel with thee, and prosper thy	7971
	24:54 and he said, S me away unto my master.	7971
	24:56 s me away that I may go to my master.	5204.1
	27:45 I will s, and fetch thee from thence:	7971
	30:25 that Jacob said unto Laban, S me away,	7971
	37:13 come, and I will s thee unto them.	7971
	38:17 he said, I will s thee a kid from the flock.	7971
	38:17 Wilt thou give me a pledge, till thou s it?	7971
	42:16 S one of you, and let him fetch your	7971
	43: 4 If thou wilt s our brother with us, we will	7971
	43: 5 if thou wilt not s him, we will not go	7971
	43: 8 S the lad with me, and we will arise and	7971
	43:14 that he may s away your other brother,	7971
	45: 5 for God did s me before you to preserve	7971
Ex	3:10 and I will s thee unto Pharaoh,	7971
	4:13 he said, O my Lord, s, I pray thee,	7971
	4:13 by the hand of him whom thou wilt s.	7971
	7: 2 that he s the children of Israel out of his	7971
	8:21 will s swarms of flies upon thee, and	7971
	9:14 I will at this time s all my plagues upon	7971
	9:19 S therefore now, and gather thy cattle,	7971
	12:33 that they might s them out of the land in	7971
	23:20 Behold, I s an Angel before thee, to keep	7971
	23:27 I will s my fear before thee,	7971
	23:28 I will s hornets before thee, which shall	7971
	33: 2 I will s an angel before thee; and I will	7971
	33:12 hast not let me know whom thou wilt s	7971
Lev	16:21 shall s him away by the hand of a fit man	7971
	26:22 I will also s wild beasts among you, which	7971
	26:25 I will s the pestilence among you;	7971
	26:26 when that are left alive of you I will s	935
Nu	13: 2 S thou men, that they may search the land	7971
	13: 2 of every tribe of their fathers shall ye s a	7971
	22:37 earnestly s unto thee to call thee?	7971+7971
	31: 4 the tribes of Israel, shall ye s to the war.	7971
Dt	1:22 We will s men before us, and they shall	7971
	7:20 Moreover the Lord thy God will s	7971
	11:15 I will s grass in thy fields for thy cattle,	5414
	19:12 the elders of his city shall s and fetch him	7971
	24: 1 it in her hand, and s her out of his house.	7971
	28:20 The Lord shall s upon thee cursing,	7971
	28:48 which the Lord shall s against thee,	7971
	32:24 will also s the teeth of beasts upon them,	7971
Jos	18: 4 I will s them, and they shall rise,	7971
Jdg	13: 8 the man of God which thou didst s come	7971
1Sa	5:11 S away the ark of the God of Israel,	7971
	6: 2 tell us wherewith we shall s it to his place.	7971
	6: 3 If ye s away the ark of the God of Israel,	7971
	6: 3 but s it unto him a trespass offering:	7971
	6: 8 thereof; and s it away, that it may go.	7971
	9:16 To morrow about this time I will s thee a	7971
	9:26 saying, Up, that I may s thee away.	7971
	11: 3 that we may s messengers unto all	7971
	12:17 and he shall s thunder and rain;	5414
	16: 1 s thee to Jesse the Beth-lehemite:	7971
	16:11 Samuel said unto Jesse, S and fetch him;	7971
	16:19 said, S me David thy son, which is with	7971

1Sa	20:12 I then s not unto thee, and shew it thee;	7971
	20:13 I will shew it thee, and s thee away,	7971
	20:21 behold, I will s a lad, saying, Go, find out	7971
	20:31 Wherefore now s and fetch him unto me,	7971
	21: 2 thing of the business whereabout I s thee,	7971
	25:25 men of my lord, whom thou didst s.	7971
2Sa	11: 6 to Joab, saying, S me Uriah the Hittite.	7971
	14:32 that I may s thee to the king, to say,	7971
	15:36 by them ye shall s unto me every thing	7971
	17:16 Now therefore s quickly, and tell David,	7971
1Ki	8:44 whithersoever thou shalt s them,	7971
	18: 1 Ahab; and I will s rain upon the earth.	5414
	18:19 therefore s, and gather to me all Israel	7971
	20: 6 Yet I will s my servants unto thee to	7971
	20: 9 All that thou didst s for to thy servant at	7971
	20:34 said Ahab, I will s thee away with this	7971
2Ki	2:16 some valley. And he said, Ye shall not s.	7971
	2:17 urged him till he was ashamed, he said, S.	7971
	4:22 said, S me, I pray thee, one of the young	7971
	5: 5 and I will s a letter unto the king of Israel.	7971
	5: 7 that this man doth s unto me to recover a	7971
	6:13 Go and spy where he is; that I may s and	7971
	7:13 that are consumed:) and let us s and see.	7971
	9:17 s to meet them, and let him say, Is it	7971
	15:37 In those days the Lord began to s	7971
	19: 7 I will s a blast upon him, and he shall hear	5414
1Ch	13: 2 let us s abroad unto our brethren every	7971
2Ch	2: 3 didst s him cedars to build him a house to	7971
	2: 7 S me now therefore a man cunning to	7971
	2: 8 S me also cedar trees, fir trees,	7971
	2:15 spoken of, let him s unto his servants:	7971
	6:27 s rain upon thy land, which thou hast	5414
	6:34 by the way that thou shalt s them,	7971
	7:13 or if I s pestilence among my people;	7971
	28:16 At that time did king Ahaz s unto the	7971
	32: 9 this did Sennacherib king of Assyria s	7971
Ezr	5:17 the king s his pleasure to us concerning	7972
Ne	2: 5 that thou wouldest s me unto Judah,	7971
	2: 6 So it pleased the king to s me; and I set	7971
	8:10 s portions unto them for whom nothing is	7971
	8:12 to s portions, and to make great mirth,	7971
Job	21:11 They s forth their little ones like a flock,	7971
	38:35 Canst thou s lightnings, that they may go,	7971
Ps	20: 2 S thee help from the sanctuary,	7971
	43: 3 O s out thy light and thy truth: let them	7971
	57: 3 He shall s from heaven, and save me from	7971
	57: 3 God shall s forth his mercy and his truth.	7971
	68: 9 Thou, O God, didst s a plentiful rain,	5130
	68:33 lo, he doth s out his voice, and that a	5414
	110: 2 The Lord shall s the rod of thy strength	7971
	118:25 I beseech thee, s now prosperity.	6743
	144: 7 S thine hand from above; rid me,	7971
Pr	10:26 so is the sluggard to them that s him.	7971
	22:21 words of truth to them that s unto thee?	7971
	25:13 a faithful messenger to them that s him:	7971
Ecc	10: 1 cause the ointment of the apothecary	
	to s forth	5042
Isa	6: 8 Whom shall I s, and who will go for us?	7971
	6: 8 go for us? Then I said, Here am I; s me.	7971
	10: 6 I will s him against a hypocritical nation,	7971
	10:16 of hosts, s among his fat ones leanness;	7971
	16: 1 S ye the lamb to the ruler of the land from	7971
	19:20 he shall s them a saviour, and a great one,	7971
	32:20 that s forth thither the feet of the ox and	7971
	37: 7 I will s a blast upon him, and he shall	5414
	57: 9 didst s thy messengers far off,	7971
	66:19 I will s those that escape of them unto	7971
Jer	1: 7 for thou shalt go to all that I shall s thee,	7971
	2:10 s unto Kedar, and consider diligently,	7971
	8:17 For behold, I will s serpents, cockatrices,	7971
	9:16 I will s a sword after them, till I have	7971
	9:17 s for cunning women, that they may	7971
	16:16 Behold, I will s for many fishers, saith	7971
	16:16 after will I s for many hunters,	7971
	24:10 I will s the sword, the famine,	7971
	25: 9 I will s and take all the families of	7971
	25:15 the nations, to whom I s thee, to drink it.	7971
	25:16 of the sword that I will s among them.	7971
	25:27 of the sword which I will s among you.	7971
	27: 3 s them to the king of Edom, and to the	7971
	29:17 Behold, I will s upon them the sword,	7971
	29:31 S to all them of the captivity, saying,	7971
	42: 5 the Lord thy God shall s thee to us.	7971
	42: 6 the Lord our God, to whom we s thee;	7971
	43:10 I will s and take Nebuchadrezzar the king	7971
	48:12 that I will s unto him wanderers,	7971
	49:37 I will s the sword after them, till I have	7971
	51: 2 will s unto Babylon fanners, that shall fan	7971
Eze	2: 3 of man, I s thee to the children of Israel,	7971
	2: 4 I do s thee unto them; and thou shalt say	7971
	5:16 When I shall s upon them the evil arrows	7971
	5:16 and which I will s to destroy you:	7971
	5:17 will I s upon you famine and evil beasts,	7971
	7: 3 I will s mine anger upon thee,	7971
	14:13 will s famine upon it, and will cut off man	7971
	14:19 Or if I s a pestilence into that land,	7971
	14:21 How much more when I s my four sore	7971
	28:23 For I will s into her pestilence,	7971
	39: 6 I will s a fire on Magog, and among them	7971
Hos	8:14 I will s a fire upon his cities, and it shall	7971
Joel	2:19 I will s you corn, and wine, and oil,	7971
Am	1: 4 I will s a fire into the house of Hazael,	7971
	1: 7 I will s a fire on the wall of Gaza,	7971
	1:10 I will s a fire on the wall of Tyrus,	7971
	1:12 will s a fire upon the Teman, which shall	7971

Am	2: 2 I will s a fire upon Moab, and it shall	7971
	2: 5 I will s a fire upon Judah, and it shall	7971
	8:11 that I will s a famine in the land,	7971
Mal	2: 1 will even s a curse upon you,	7971
	3: 1 will s my messenger, and he shall prepare	7971
	4: 5 I will s you Elijah the prophet before	7971
Mt	9:38 that he will s forth labourers into his	1544
	10:16 I s you forth as sheep in the midst of	649
	10:34 Think not that I am come to s peace on	906
	10:34 earth: I came not to s peace, but a sword,	906
	11:10 Behold, I s my messenger before thy face,	649
	12:20 till he s forth judgment unto victory.	1544
	13:41 The Son of man shall s forth his angels,	649
	14:15 s the multitude away, that they may go	630
	15:23 and besought him, saying, S her away;	630
	15:32 I will not s them away fasting, lest they	630
	21: 3 of them; and straightway he will s them.	649
	23:34 s unto you prophets, and wise men, and	649
	24:31 he shall s his angels with a great sound	649
Mk	1: 2 Behold, I s my messenger before thy face,	649
	3:14 and that he might s them forth to preach,	649
	5:10 not s them away out of the country.	649
	5:12 saying, S us into the swine, that we may	3992
	6: 7 began to s them forth by two and two;	649
	6:36 S them away, that they may go into	630
	8: 3 And if I s them away fasting to their own	630
	11: 3 him; and straightway he will s him hither.	649
	12:13 they s unto him certain of the Pharisees	649
	13:27 And then shall he s his angels,	649
Lk	7:27 Behold, I s my messenger before thy face,	649
	9:12 and said unto him, S the multitude away,	630
	10: 2 that he would s forth labourers into his	1544
	10: 3 I s you forth as lambs among wolves.	649
	11:49 I will s them prophets and apostles,	649
	12:49 I am come to s fire on the earth;	906
	16:24 have mercy on me, and s Lazarus,	3992
	16:27 that thou wouldest s him to my father's	3992
	20:13 I will s my beloved son: it may be they	3992
	24:49 I s the promise of my Father upon you:	649
Jn	13:20 that receiveth whomsoever I s receiveth	3992
	14:26 whom the Father will s in my name,	3992
	15:26 whom I will s unto you from the Father,	3992
	16: 7 but if I depart, I will s him unto you.	3992
	17: 8 they have believed that thou didst s me.	649
	20:21 my Father hath sent me, even so s I you.	3992
Ac	3:20 And he shall s Jesus Christ, which before	649
	7:34 And now come, I will s thee into Egypt.	649
	7:35 the same did God s to be a ruler and	649
	10: 5 now s men to Joppa, and call for one	3992
	10:22 a holy angel to s for thee into his house,	3343
	10:32 S therefore to Joppa, and call hither	3992
	11:13 S men to Joppa, and call for Simon,	3992
	11:29 determined to s relief unto the brethren	3992
	15:22 to s chosen men of their own company to	3992
	15:23 brethren s greeting unto the brethren	NIG
	15:25 chosen men unto you with our beloved	3992
	22:21 I will s thee far hence unto the Gentiles.	1821
	25: 3 that he would s for him to Jerusalem,	3343
	25:21 commanded him to be kept till I might s	3992
	25:25 to Augustus, I have determined to s him.	3992
	25:27 For it seemeth to me unreasonable to s a	3992
	26:17 the Gentiles, unto whom now I s thee,	649
1Co	16: 3 them will I s to bring your liberality unto	3992
Php	2:19 I trust in the Lord Jesus to s Timotheus	3992
	2:23 Him therefore I hope to s presently,	3992
	2:25 Yet I supposed it necessary to s to you	3992
2Th	2:11 for this cause God shall s them strong	3992
Tit	3:12 When I shall s Artemas unto thee,	3992
Jas	3:11 Doth a fountain s forth at the same place	1032
Rev	1:11 s it unto the seven churches which are in	3992
	11:10 and shall s gifts one to another;	3992

SENDEST (6) [SEND]

Dt	15:13 when thou s him out free from thee,	7971
	15:18 when thou s him away free from thee;	7971
Jos	1:16 and whithersoever thou s us, we will go.	7971
2Ki	1: 6 thou s to inquire of Baal-zebub the god	7971
Job	14:20 his countenance, and s him away.	7971
Ps	104:30 Thou s forth thy spirit, they are created:	7971

SENDETH (15) [SEND]

Dt	24: 3 it in her hand, and s her out of his house;	7971
1Ki	17:14 until the day that the Lord s rain upon	5414
Job	5:10 the earth, and s waters upon the fields:	7971
	12:15 also he s them out, and they overturn	7971
Ps	104:10 He s the springs into the valleys, which	7971
	147:15 He s forth his commandment upon earth:	7971
	147:18 He s out his word, and melteth them:	7971
Pr	26: 6 He that s a message by the hand of a fool	7971
SS	1:12 my spikenard s forth the smell thereof.	5414
Isa	18: 2 That s ambassadors by the sea, even in	7971
Mt	5:45 and s rain on the just and on the unjust.	1026
Mk	11: 1 of Olives, he s forth two of his disciples,	649
	14:13 And he s forth two of his disciples,	649
Lk	14:32 he s an ambassage, and desireth conditions	649
Ac	23:26 most excellent governor Felix s greeting.	NIG

SENDING (14) [SEND]

2Sa	13:16 this in s me away is greater than	7971
2Ch	36:15 his messengers, rising up betimes, and s;	7971
Est	9:19 day, and of s portions one to another.	4916
	9:22 of s portions one to another, and gifts to	4916
Ps	78:49 and trouble, by s evil angels among them.	4917

Isa	7:25 it shall be for the **s** forth of oxen,	4916
Jer	7:25 daily rising up early and **s** them:	7971
	25: 4 rising early and **s** them; but ye have not	7971
	26: 5 and **s** them, but ye have not hearkened;	7971
	29:19 rising up early and **s** them; but ye would	7971
	35:15 rising up early and **s** them, saying,	7971
	44: 4 rising early and **s** them, saying, Oh, do	7971
Eze	17:15 he rebelled against him in **s** his	7971
Ro	8: 3 God **s** his own Son in the likeness of sinful	3992

SENEH (1)

1Sa	14: 4 was Bozez, and the name of the other **S.**	5573

SENIR (2)

1Ch	5:23 from Bashan unto Baal-hermon and **S,**	8149
Eze	27: 5 made all thy ship boards of fir trees of **S:**	8149

SENNACHERIB (13)

2Ki	18:13 **S** king of Assyria come up against all	5576
	19:16 hear the words of **S,** which hath sent him	5576
	19:20 me against **S** king of Assyria I have heard.	5576
	19:36 So **S** king of Assyria departed, and went	5576
2Ch	32: 1 establishment thereof, **S** king of Assyria	5576
	32: 2 when Hezekiah saw that **S** was come,	5576
	32: 9 After this did **S** king of Assyria send his	5576
	32:10 Thus saith **S** king of Assyria, Whereon do	5576
	32:22 from the hand of **S** the king of Assyria,	5576
Isa	36: 1 that **S** king of Assyria came up against all	5576
	37:17 hear all the words of **S,** which hath sent	5576
	37:21 Whereas thou hast prayed to me against **S**	5576
	37:37 So **S** king of Assyria departed, and went	5576

SENSE (1) [SENSES, SENSUAL]

Ne	8: 8 the **s,** and caused them to understand	7922

SENSELESS See SILLY; SOTTISH

SENSES (1) [SENSE]

Heb	5:14 those who by reason of use have their **s**	145

SENSUAL (2) [SENSE]

Jas	3:15 not from above, but is earthly, **s,** devilish.	5591
Jude	1:19 **s,** having not the Spirit.	5591

SENSUALITY See LASCIVIOUSNESS

SENT (690) [SEND]

Ge	3:23 Therefore the Lord God **s** him forth	7971
	8: 7 he **s** forth a raven, which went forth to	7971
	8: 8 Also he **s** forth a dove from him, to see if	7971
	8:10 again he **s** forth the dove out of the ark;	7971
	8:12 other seven days; and **s** forth the dove;	7971
	12:20 they **s** him away, and his wife, and all	7971
	19:13 and the Lord hath **s** us to destroy it.	7971
	19:29 Lot out of the midst of the overthrow,	7971
	20: 2 Abimelech king of Gerar **s,** and took	7971
	21:14 shoulder, and the child, and **s** her away:	7971
	24:59 they **s** away Rebekah their sister, and her	7971
	25: 6 them away from Isaac his son, while he	7971
	26:27 hate me, and have **s** me away from you?	7971
	26:29 but good, and have **s** thee away in peace:	7971
	26:31 Isaac **s** them away, and they departed	7971
	27:42 she **s** and called Jacob her younger son,	7971
	28: 5 Isaac **s** away Jacob: and he went to	7971
	28: 6 him away to Padan-aram, to take him a	7971
	31: 4 Jacob **s** and called Rachel and Leah to	7971
	31:27 I might have **s** thee away with mirth,	7971
	31:42 surely thou hadst **s** me away now empty.	7971
	32: 3 Jacob **s** messengers before him to Esau his	7971
	32: 5 I have **s** to tell my lord, that I may find	7971
	32:18 it is a present **s** unto my lord Esau:	7971
	32:23 them over the brook, and sent over that	5674
	32:23 over the brook, and **s** over that he had.	5674
	37:14 So he **s** him out of the vale of Hebron,	7971
	37:32 they **s** the coat of many colours,	7971
	38:20 Judah **s** the kid by the hand of his friend	7971
	38:23 I **s** this kid, and thou hast not found her.	7971
	38:25 she **s** to her father in law, saying,	7971
	41: 8 he **s** and called for all the magicians of	7971
	41:14 Pharaoh **s** and called Joseph,	7971
	42: 4 Jacob **s** not with his brethren:	7971
	43:34 and **s** messes unto them from before him:	NIH
	44: 3 men were **s** away, and their asses.	7971
	45: 7 God **s** me before you to preserve you a	7971
	45: 5 So now it was not you that **s** me hither,	7971
	45:23 to his father he **s** after this manner;	7971
	45:24 So he **s** his brethren away,	7971
	45:27 wagons which Joseph had **s** to carry him,	7971
	46: 5 the wagons which Pharaoh had **s** to carry	7971
	46:28 he **s** Judah before him unto Joseph,	7971
	50:16 they **s** a messenger unto Joseph, saying,	6680
Ex	2: 5 the flags, she **s** her maid to fetch it.	7971
	3:12 be a token unto thee, that I have **s** thee:	7971
	3:13 The God of your fathers hath **s** me unto	7971
	3:14 of Israel, I AM hath **s** me unto you.	7971
	3:15 the God of Jacob, hath **s** me unto you:	7971
	4:28 all the words of the Lord who had **s** him,	7971
	5:22 this people? why is it that thou hast **s** me?	7971
	7:16 The Lord God of the Hebrews hath **s** me	7971
	9: 7 Pharaoh sent, and behold, there was not one	7971
	9:23 the Lord **s** thunder and hail, and the fire	5414
	9:27 Pharaoh **s,** and called for Moses and	7971
	18: 2 Moses' wife, after he had **s** her back,	7964
	24: 5 he **s** young men of the children of Israel,	7971
Nu	13: 3 **s** them from the wilderness of Paran:	7971
	13:16 men which Moses **s** to spy out the land.	7971

Nu	13:17 Moses **s** them to spy out the land of	7971
	14:36 men, which Moses **s** to search the land,	7971
	16:12 Moses **s** to call Dathan and Abiram,	7971
	16:28 ye shall know that the Lord hath **s** me.	7971
	16:29 of all men; then the Lord hath not **s** me.	7971
	20:14 Moses **s** messengers from Kadesh unto	7971
	20:16 **s** an angel, and hath brought us forth out	7971
	21: 6 the Lord **s** fiery serpents among	7971
	21:21 Israel **s** messengers unto Sihon king of	7971
	21:32 Moses **s** to spy out Jaazer, and they took	7971
	22: 5 He **s** messengers therefore unto Balaam	7971
	22:10 king of Moab, hath **s** unto me, saying,	7971
	22:15 Balak **s** yet again princes, more,	7971
	22:40 **s** to Balaam, and to the princes that were	7971
	31: 6 Moses **s** them to the war, a thousand of	7971
	32: 8 when I **s** them from Kadesh-barnea to see	7971
Dt	2:26 I **s** messengers out of the wilderness of	7971
	9:23 Likewise when the Lord **s** you from	7971
	24: 4 Her former husband, which **s** her away,	7971
	34:11 which the Lord **s** him to do in the land	7971
Jos	2: 1 Joshua the son of Nun **s** out of Shittim	7971
	2: 3 the king of Jericho **s** unto Rahab, saying,	7971
	2:21 she **s** them away, and they departed:	7971
	6:17 she hid the messengers that we **s.**	7971
	6:25 which Joshua **s** to spy out Jericho.	7971
	7: 2 Joshua **s** men from Jericho to Ai, which is	7971
	7:22 Joshua **s** messengers, and they ran unto	7971
	8: 3 of valour, and **s** them away by night.	7971
	8: 9 Joshua therefore **s** them forth:	7971
	10: 3 Jerusalem **s** unto Hoham king of Hebron,	7971
	10: 6 the men of Gibeon **s** unto Joshua to	7971
	11: 1 things, that he **s** to Jobab king of Madon,	7971
	14: 7 **s** me from Kadesh-barnea to espy out	7971
	14:11 day as I was in the day that Moses **s** me:	7971
	22: 6 Joshua blessed them, and **s** them away:	7971
	22: 7 when Joshua **s** them away also unto their	7971
	22:13 the children of Israel **s** unto the children	7971
	24: 5 I **s** Moses also and Aaron, and I plagued	7971
	24: 9 **s** and called Balaam the son of Beor to	7971
	24:12 I **s** the hornet before you, which drave	7971
Jdg	1:23 the house of Joseph **s** to descry Beth-el.	8446
	3:15 by him the children of Israel **s** a present	7971
	3:18 **s** away the people that bare the present.	7971
	4: 6 **s** and called Barak the son of Abinoam	7971
	5:15 he was **s** on foot into the valley.	7971
	6: 8 That the Lord **s** a prophet unto	7971
	6:14 hand of the Midianites: have not I **s** thee?	7971
	6:35 he **s** messengers throughout all Manasseh;	7971
	6:35 he **s** messengers unto Asher,	7971
	7: 8 he **s** all the rest of Israel every man unto	7971
	7:24 Gideon **s** messengers throughout all	7971
	9:23 God **s** an evil spirit between Abimelech	7971
	9:31 he **s** messengers unto Abimelech privily,	7971
	11:12 Jephthah **s** messengers unto the king of	7971
	11:14 Jephthah **s** messengers again unto the	7971
	11:17 Israel **s** messengers unto the king of	7971
	11:17 like manner they **s** unto the king of Moab	7971
	11:19 Israel **s** messengers unto Sihon king of	7971
	11:28 the words of Jephthah which he **s** him.	7971
	11:38 he **s** her away for two months:	7971
	12: 9 whom he **s** abroad, and took in thirty	7971
	16:18 she **s** and called for the lords of	7971
	18: 2 the children of Dan **s** of their family five	7971
	19:29 and **s** her into all the coasts of Israel.	7971
	20: 6 her throughout all the country of	7971
	20:12 the tribes of Benjamin **s** through all	7971
	21:10 congregation **s** thither twelve thousand	7971
	21:13 the whole congregation **s** some to speak	7971
1Sa	4: 4 So the people **s** to Shiloh, that they might	7971
	5: 8 They **s** therefore and gathered all the lords	7971
	5:10 Therefore they **s** the ark of God to Ekron.	7971
	5:11 they **s** and gathered together all the lords	7971
	6:21 they **s** messengers to the inhabitants of	7971
	10:25 Samuel **s** all the people away, every man	7971
	11: 7 **s** them throughout all the coasts of Israel	7971
	12: 8 then the Lord **s** Moses and Aaron,	7971
	12:11 the Lord **s** Jerubbaal, and Bedan,	7971
	12:18 and the Lord **s** thunder and rain that day:	5414
	13: 2 the rest of the people he **s** every man to	7971
	15: 1 The Lord **s** me to anoint thee to be king	7971
	15:18 the Lord **s** thee on a journey, and said,	7971
	15:20 have gone the way which the Lord **s** me,	7971
	16:12 he **s,** and brought him in. Now he was	7971
	16:19 Wherefore Saul **s** messengers unto Jesse,	7971
	16:20 and **s** them by David his son unto Saul.	7971
	16:22 Saul **s** to Jesse, saying, Let David, I pray	7971
	17:31 them before Saul: and he **s** for him.	3947
	18: 5 David went out whithersoever Saul **s** him,	7971
	19:11 Saul also **s** messengers unto David's	7971
	19:14 when Saul **s** messengers to take David,	7971
	19:15 Saul **s** the messengers again to see David,	7971
	19:17 **s** away mine enemy, that he is escaped?	7971
	19:20 Saul **s** messengers to take David:	7971
	19:21 **s** other messengers, and they prophesied	7971
	19:21 Saul **s** messengers again the third time,	7971
	20:22 thy way: for the Lord hath **s** thee away.	7971
	22:11 the king **s** to call Ahimelech the priest,	7971
	25: 5 David **s** out ten young men, and David	7971
	25:14 David **s** messengers out of the wilderness	7971
	25:32 Israel, which **s** thee this day to meet me:	7971
	25:39 David **s** and communed with Abigail,	7971
	25:40 unto her, saying, David **s** us unto thee,	7971
	26: 2 David therefore **s** out spies,	7971
	30:26 he **s** of the spoil unto the elders of Judah,	7971
	31: 9 **s** into the house of the Philistines round	7971

2Sa	2: 5 David **s** messengers unto the men of	7971
	3:12 Abner **s** messengers to David on his	7971
	3:14 David **s** messengers to Ish-bosheth Saul's	7971
	3:15 Ish-bosheth **s,** and took her from her	7971
	3:21 David **s** Abner away; and he went in	7971
	3:22 he had **s** him away, and he was gone in	7971
	3:23 he hath **s** him away, and he is gone in	7971
	3:24 why is it that thou hast **s** him away,	7971
	3:26 from David, he **s** messengers after Abner,	7971
	5:11 Hiram king of Tyre **s** messengers to David,	7971
	8:10 Toi **s** Joram his son unto king David,	7971
	9: 5 David **s,** and fet him out of the house	7971
	10: 2 David **s** to comfort him by the hand of his	7971
	10: 3 that he hath **s** comforters unto thee?	7971
	10: 3 hath not David rather **s** his servants unto	7971
	10: 4 even to their buttocks, and **s** them away.	7971
	10: 5 he **s** to meet them, because the men were	7971
	10: 6 the children of Ammon **s** and hired	7971
	10: 7 when David heard of it, he **s** Joab, and all	7971
	10:16 Hadarezer **s,** and brought out the Syrians	7971
	11: 1 kings go forth to battle, that David **s** Joab,	7971
	11: 3 David **s** and inquired after the woman.	7971
	11: 4 David **s** messengers, and took her;	7971
	11: 5 **s** and told David, and said, I am with	7971
	11: 6 David **s** to Joab, saying, Send me Uriah	7971
	11: 6 the Hittite. And Joab **s** Uriah to David.	7971
	11:14 to Joab, and **s** it by the hand of Uriah.	7971
	11:18 Joab **s** and told David all the things	7971
	11:22 shewed David all that Joab had **s** him for.	7971
	11:27 David **s** and fet her to his house,	7971
	12: 1 the Lord **s** Nathan unto David. And he	7971
	12:25 he **s** by the hand of Nathan the prophet;	7971
	12:27 Joab **s** messengers to David, and said,	7971
	13: 7 David **s** home to Tamar, saying, Go now	7971
	14: 2 Joab **s** to Tekoah, and fetcht thence a wise	7971
	14:29 Therefore Absalom **s** for Joab, to have sent	7971
	14:29 sent for Joab, to have **s** him to the king;	7971
	14:29 he **s** again the second time, he would	7971
	14:32 I **s** unto thee, saying, Come hither,	7971
	15:10 Absalom **s** spies throughout all the tribes	7971
	15:12 Absalom **s** for Ahithophel the Gilonite,	7971
	18: 2 David **s** forth a third part of the people	7971
	18:29 When Joab **s** the king's servant, and me	7971
	19:11 king David **s** to Zadok and to Abiathar	7971
	19:14 so that they **s** this word unto the king,	7971
	22:15 he **s** out arrows, and scattered them;	7971
	22:17 He **s** from above, he took me; he drew	7971
	24:13 what answer I shall return to him that **s**	7971
	24:15 So the Lord **s** a pestilence upon Israel	5414
1Ki	1:44 hath **s** with him Zadok the priest,	7971
	1:53 king Solomon **s,** and they brought him	7971
	2:25 king Solomon **s** by the hand of Benaiah	7971
	2:29 Solomon **s** Benaiah the son of Jehoiada,	7971
	2:36 the king **s** and called for Shimei,	7971
	2:42 the king **s** and called for Shimei,	7971
	5: 1 Hiram king of Tyre **s** his servants unto	7971
	5: 2 And Solomon **s** to Hiram, saying,	7971
	5: 8 Hiram **s** to Solomon, saying, I have	7971
	5:14 he **s** them to Lebanon, ten thousand a	7971
	7:13 Solomon **s** and fet Hiram out of Tyre.	7971
	8:66 On the eighth day he **s** the people away:	7971
	9:14 Hiram **s** to the king sixscore talents of	7971
	9:27 Hiram **s** in the navy his servants,	7971
	12: 3 they **s** and called him. And Jeroboam	7971
	12:18 king Rehoboam **s** Adoram, who was over	7971
	12:20 that they **s** and called him unto	7971
	14: 6 for I am **s** to thee with heavy tidings.	7971
	15:18 king Asa **s** them to Ben-hadad, the son of	7971
	15:19 I have **s** unto thee a present of silver and	7971
	15:20 **s** the captains of the hosts which he had	7971
	18:10 whither my lord hath not **s** to seek thee:	7971
	18:20 So Ahab **s** unto all the children of Israel,	7971
	19: 2 Jezebel **s** a messenger unto Elijah, saying,	7971
	20: 2 **s** messengers to Ahab king of Israel into	7971
	20: 5 Although I have **s** unto thee, saying,	7971
	20: 7 for he **s** unto me for my wives, and for	7971
	20:10 Ben-hadad **s** unto him, and said, The gods	7971
	20:17 Ben-hadad **s** out, and they told him,	7971
	20:34 a covenant with him, and **s** him away.	7971
	21: 8 **s** the letters unto the elders and to	7971
	21:11 did as Jezebel had **s** unto them, and as it	7971
	21:11 in the letters which she had **s** unto them.	7971
	21:14 **s** to Jezebel, saying, Naboth is stoned,	7971
2Ki	1: 2 he **s** messengers, and said unto them,	7971
	1: 6 turn again unto the king that **s** you,	7971
	1: 9 the king **s** unto him a captain of fifty with	7971
	1:11 also he **s** unto him another captain of	7971
	1:13 he **s** again a captain of the third fifty with	7971
	1:16 Forasmuch as thou hast **s** messengers to	7971
	2: 2 for the Lord hath **s** me to Beth-el.	7971
	2: 4 for the Lord hath **s** me to Jericho.	7971
	2: 6 here; for the Lord hath **s** me to Jordan.	7971
	2:17 They **s** therefore fifty men; and they	7971
	3: 7 and **s** to Jehoshaphat the king of Judah,	7971
	5: 6 I have therewith **s** Naaman my servant to	7971
	5: 8 that he **s** to the king, saying, Wherefore	7971
	5:10 Elisha **s** a messenger unto him, saying,	7971
	5:22 My master hath **s** me, saying, Behold,	7971
	6: 9 the man of God **s** unto the king of Israel,	7971
	6:10 the king of Israel **s** to the place which	7971
	6:14 Therefore he **s** thither horses, and	7971
	6:23 he **s** them away, and they went to their	7971
	6:32 and the king's **s** a man from before him:	7971
	6:32 See ye how this son of a murderer hath **s**	7971
	7:14 the king **s** after the host of the Syrians,	7971

S

2Ki
8: 9 Thy son Ben-hadad king of Syria hath **s** 7971
9:19 he **s** *out* a second on horseback, which 7971
10: 1 Jehu wrote letters, and **s** *to* Samaria, 7971
10: 5 the bringers up *of the children,* **s** to Jehu, 7971
10: 7 in baskets, and **s** *them* to Jezreel. 7971
10:21 Jehu **s** through all Israel: and all 7971
11: 4 the seventh year Jehoiada and fet 7971
12:18 and **s** *it* to Hazael king of Syria: 7971
14: 8 Amaziah **s** messengers to Jehoash, the son 7971
14: 9 Jehoash the king of Israel **s** to Amaziah 7971
14: 9 The thistle that *was* in Lebanon **s** to 7971
14:19 they **s** after him to Lachish, and slew him 7971
16: 7 So Ahaz **s** messengers to Tiglath-pileser 7971
16: 8 **s** *it for* a present to the king of Assyria. 7971
16:10 Ahaz **s** to Urijah the priest the fashion 7971
16:11 all that king Ahaz had **s** from Damascus: 7971
17: 4 for he had **s** messengers to So king of 7971
17:13 which I **s** to you by my servants 7971
17:25 therefore the LORD **s** lions among them, 7971
17:26 therefore he hath **s** lions among them, 7971
18:14 Hezekiah king of Judah **s** to the king of 7971
18:17 the king of Assyria **s** Tartan and Rabsaris 7971
18:27 Hath my master **s** me to thy master, 7971
18:27 *hath* he not **s** *me* to the men which sit on NIH
19: 2 he **s** Eliakim, which *was* over 7971
19: 4 the king of Assyria his master hath **s** 7971
19: 9 he **s** messengers again unto Hezekiah, 7971
19:16 which hath **s** him to reproach the living 7971
19:20 Isaiah the son of Amoz **s** to Hezekiah, 7971
20:12 **s** letters and a present unto Hezekiah: 7971
22: 3 the king **s** Shaphan the son of Azaliah, 7971
22:15 of Israel, Tell the man that **s** you to me, 7971
22:18 the king of Judah which **s** you to inquire 7971
23: 1 king **s**, and they gathered unto him all 7971
23:16 **s**, and took the bones out of the 7971
24: 2 the LORD **s** against him bands of 7971
24: 2 and **s** against Judah to destroy it, 7971

1Ch
8: 8 of Moab, after he had **s** them *away;* 7971
10: 9 **s** into the land of the Philistines round 7971
12:19 Philistines upon advisement **s** him *away,* 7971
14: 1 Now Hiram king of Tyre **s** messengers to 7971
18:10 He **s** Hadoram his son to king David, 7971
19: 2 David **s** messengers to comfort him 7971
19: 3 that he hath **s** comforters unto thee? 7971
19: 4 hard by *their* buttocks, and **s** them *away.* 7971
19: 5 **s** to meet them: for the men were greatly 7971
19: 6 children of Ammon **s** a thousand talents 7971
19: 8 when David heard *of it,* he **s** Joab, and all 7971
19:16 they **s** messengers, and drew forth 7971
21:12 word I shall bring again to him that **s** me. 7971
21:14 So the LORD **s** pestilence upon Israel: 5414
21:15 God **s** an angel unto Jerusalem to destroy 7971

2Ch
2: 3 Solomon **s** to Huram the king of Tyre, 7971
2:11 which he **s** to Solomon, Because 7971
2:13 I have **s** a cunning man, endued with 7971
7:10 he **s** the people *away* into their tents, 7971
8:18 Huram **s** him by the hands of his servants 7971
10: 3 they **s** and called him. So Jeroboam and 7971
10:18 king Rehoboam **s** Hadoram that *was* over 7971
16: 2 and **s** to Ben-hadad king of Syria, 7971
16: 3 behold, I have **s** thee silver and gold; 7971
16: 4 **s** the captains of his armies against 7971
17: 7 in the third year of his reign he **s** to his 7971
17: 8 with them he **s** Levites, *even* Shemaiah, NIH
24:19 Yet he **s** prophets to them, to bring them 7971
24:23 **s** all the spoil of them unto the king of 7971
25:13 of the army which Amaziah **s** *back,* 7725
25:15 he **s** unto him a prophet, which said unto 7971
25:17 **s** to Joash, the son of Jehoahaz, the son of 7971
25:18 Joash king of Israel **s** to Amaziah king of 7971
25:18 **s** to the cedar that *was* in Lebanon, 7971
25:27 they **s** to Lachish after him, and slew him 7971
30: 1 Hezekiah **s** to all Israel and Judah, 7971
32:21 the LORD **s** an angel, which cut off all 7971
32:31 who **s** unto him to inquire of the wonder 7971
34: 8 he **s** Shaphan the son of Azaliah, 7971
34:23 of Israel, Tell ye the man that **s** you to me, 7971
34:26 who **s** you to inquire of the LORD, 7971
34:29 the king **s** and gathered together all 7971
35:21 he **s** ambassadors to him, saying, 7971
36:10 Nebuchadnezzar **s**, and brought him to 7971
36:15 the LORD God of their fathers **s** to them 7971

Ezr
4:11 This *is* the copy of the letter that they **s** 7972
4:14 therefore have we **s** and certified the king; 7972
4:17 *Then* **s** the king an answer unto Rehum 7972
4:18 The letter which ye **s** unto us *hath been* 7972
5: 6 *this* side the river, **s** unto Darius the king: 7972
5: 7 They **s** a letter unto him, wherein *was* 7972
6:13 to that which Darius the king had **s**, 7972
7:14 Forasmuch as *thou art* **s** of the king, 7972
8:16 **s** I for Eliezer, for Ariel, for Shemaiah, 7972
8:17 **s** them **with commandment** unto Iddo 6680

Ne
2: 9 Now the king had **s** captains of the army 7971
6: 2 That Sanballat and Geshem **s** unto me, 7971
6: 3 I **s** messengers unto them, saying, I *am* 7971
6: 4 Yet they **s** unto me four times after this 7971
6: 5 Sanballat his servant unto me in like 7971
6: 8 I **s** unto him, saying, There are no such 7971
6:12 lo, I perceived that God had not **s** him; 7971
6:17 of Judah **s** many letters unto Tobiah, 1980
6:19 And Tobiah **s** letters to put me in fear. 7971

Est
1:22 he **s** letters into all the king's provinces, 7971
3:13 letters were **s** by posts into all the king's 7971
4: 4 she **s** raiment to clothe Mordecai, 7971
5:10 he **s** and called for his friends, and Zeresh 7971

Est
8:10 **s** letters by posts on horseback, 7971
9:20 **s** letters unto all the Jews that *were* in all 7971
9:30 he **s** the letters unto all the Jews, 7971

Job
1: 4 **s** and called for their three sisters to eat 7971
1: 5 Job **s** and sanctified them, and rose up 7971
14: 9 *Yet* through the **s** of water it will bud, 7381
22: 9 Thou hast **s** widows *away* empty, 7971
39: 5 Who hath **s** *out* the wild ass free? 7971

Ps
18:14 he **s** out his arrows, and scattered them; 7971
18:16 He **s** from above, he took me, he drew 7971
59: 7 when Saul **s**, and they watcht the house 7971
77:17 the skies **s** *out* a sound: thine arrows also 5414
78:25 angels' food: he **s** them meat to the full. 7971
78:45 He **s** divers sorts *of* flies among them, 7971
80:11 She **s** *out* her boughs unto the sea, 7971
105:17 He **s** a man before them, *even* Joseph, 7971
105:20 The king **s** and loosed him; *even* the ruler 7971
105:26 He **s** Moses his servant; *and* Aaron whom 7971
105:28 He **s** darkness, and made it dark; 7971
106:15 request; but **s** leanness into their soul. 7971
107:20 He **s** his word, and healed them, 7971
111: 9 He **s** redemption unto his people: he hath 7971
135: 9 *Who* **s** tokens and wonders into the midst 7971

Pr
9: 3 She hath **s** forth her maidens: she crieth 7971
17:11 a cruel messenger shall be **s** against him. 7971

Isa
9: 8 The Lord **s** a word into Jacob, and it hath 7971
20: 1 (when Sargon the king of Assyria **s** him,) 7971
36: 2 the king of Assyria **s** Rabshakeh from 7971
36:12 Hath my master **s** me to thy master and 7971
36:12 *hath* he not **s** *me* to the men that sit upon NIH
37: 2 **s** Eliakim, who *was* over the household, 7971
37: 4 the king of Assyria his master hath **s** 7971
37: 9 when he heard *it,* he **s** messengers to 7971
37:17 which hath **s** to reproach the living God. 7971
37:21 Isaiah the son of Amoz **s** unto Hezekiah, 7971
39: 1 **s** letters and a present to Hezekiah: 7971
42:19 or deaf, as my messenger *that* I **s**? who *is* 7971
43:14 For your sake I have **s** to Babylon, 7971
48:16 the LORD GOD, and his Spirit, hath **s** me. 7971
55:11 it shall prosper *in the thing* whereto I **s** it. 7971
61: 1 hath **s** me to bind up the broken-hearted, 7971

Jer
7:25 I have even **s** unto you all my servants 7971
14: 3 their nobles have **s** their little ones to 7971
14:14 I **s** them not, neither have I commanded 7971
14:15 I **s** them not, yet they say, Sword and 7971
19:14 whither the LORD had **s** him to prophesy; 7971
21: 1 when king Zedekiah **s** unto him Pashur 7971
23:21 I have not **s** *these* prophets, yet they ran: 7971
23:32 yet I **s** them not, nor commanded them: 7971
23:38 have **s** unto you, saying, Ye shall not say, 7971
24: 5 whom I have **s** out of this place *into* 7971
25: 4 the LORD hath **s** unto you all his servants 7971
25:17 to drink, unto whom the LORD had **s** me: 7971
26: 5 whom I **s** unto you, both rising up early, 7971
26:12 The LORD **s** me to prophesy against this 7971
26:15 for of a truth the LORD hath **s** me unto 7971
26:22 Jehoiakim the king **s** men *into* Egypt, 7971
27:15 For I have not **s** them, saith the LORD, 7971
28: 9 that the LORD hath truly **s** him. 7971
28:15 The LORD hath not **s** thee; 7971
29: 1 **s** from Jerusalem unto the residue of 7971
29: 3 whom Zedekiah king of Judah **s** unto 7971
29: 9 I have not **s** them, saith the LORD. 7971
29:19 which I **s** unto them by my servants 7971
29:20 I have **s** from Jerusalem to Babylon: 7971
29:25 Because thou hast **s** letters in thy name 7971
29:28 For therefore he **s** unto us *in* Babylon, 7971
29:31 **s** him not, and he caused you to trust in 7971
35:15 I have **s** also unto you all my servants 7971
36:14 Therefore all the princes **s** Jehudi the son 7971
36:21 So the king **s** Jehudi to fet the roll: 7971
37: 3 Zedekiah the king **s** Jehucal the son of 7971
37: 7 that **s** you unto me to inquire of me; 7971
37:17 Zedekiah the king **s**, and took him *out:* 7971
38:14 Zedekiah the king **s**, and took Jeremiah 7971
39:13 Nebuzar-adan the captain of the guard **s**, 7971
39:14 Even they **s**, and took Jeremiah out of 7971
40:14 **s** Ishmael the son of Nethaniah to slay 7971
42: 9 unto whom ye **s** me to present your 7971
42:20 when ye **s** me unto the LORD your God, 7971
42:21 nor any *thing* for the which he hath **s** me 7971
43: 1 *for* which the LORD their God had **s** him 7971
43: 2 the LORD our God hath not **s** thee to say, 7971
44: 4 Howbeit I **s** unto you all my servants 7971
48:11 in him, and his **s** is not changed. 7381
49:14 an ambassador is **s** unto the heathen, 7971

La
1:13 From above hath he **s** fire into my bones, 7971

Eze
2: 9 I looked, behold, a hand *was* **s** unto me; 7971
3: 5 For thou *art* not **s** to a people of a strange 7971
3: 6 Surely, had I **s** thee to them, they would 7971
13: 6 the LORD hath not **s** them: and they have 7971
23:16 **s** messengers unto them into Chaldea. 7971
23:40 that ye have **s** for men to come from far, 7971
23:40 from far, unto whom a messenger *was* **s**; 7971
31: 4 **s** *out* her little rivers unto all the trees of 7971

Da
3: 2 Nebuchadnezzar the king **s** to gather 7972
3:28 who hath **s** his angel, and delivered his 7972
5:24 *was* the part of the hand **s** from him; 7972
6:22 My God hath **s** his angel, and hath shut 7972
10:11 for unto thee am I now **s**. And when he 7971

Hos
5:13 to the Assyrian, and **s** to king Jareb: 7971
14: 7 the **s** thereof *shall be* as the wine of 2143

Joel
2:25 my great army which I **s** among you. 7971

Am
4:10 I have **s** among you the pestilence after 7971
7:10 Amaziah *the* priest of Beth-el **s** to 7971

Ob
1: 1 an ambassador is **s** among the heathen, 7971

Jnh
1: 4 the LORD **s** *out* a great wind into the sea, 2904

Mic
6: 4 I **s** before thee Moses, Aaron, and Miriam. 7971

Hag
1:12 as the LORD their God had **s** him. 7971

Zec
1:10 These *are they* whom the LORD hath **s** to 7971
2: 8 After the glory hath he **s** me unto 7971
2: 9 know that the LORD of hosts hath **s** me. 7971
2:11 the LORD of hosts hath **s** me unto thee. 7971
4: 9 the LORD of hosts hath **s** me unto you. 7971
6:15 the LORD of hosts hath **s** me unto you. 7971
7: 2 When they had **s** *unto* the house of God 7971
7:12 the words which the LORD of hosts hath **s** 7971
9:11 the blood of thy covenant I have **s** **forth** 7971

Mal
2: 4 ye shall know that I have **s** this 7971

Mt
2: 8 And he **s** them to Bethlehem, and said, 3992
2:16 and **s** forth, and slew all the children that 649
10: 5 These twelve Jesus **s** forth, 649
10:40 that receiveth me receiveth him that **s** me. 649
11: 2 works of Christ, he **s** two of his disciples, 3992
13:36 Then Jesus the multitude **away**, 863
14:10 he **s**, and beheaded John in the prison. 3992
14:22 side, while he **s** the multitudes **away**. 630
14:23 And when he had **s** the multitudes **away**, 630
14:35 they **s** out into all that country round about 649
15:24 I am not **s** but unto the lost sheep of 649
15:39 he **s** away the multitude, and took ship, 630
20: 2 a penny a day, he **s** them into his vineyard. 649
21: 1 mount of Olives, then **s** Jesus two disciples, 649
21:34 he **s** his servants to the husbandmen, 649
21:36 he **s** other servants moe than the first: 649
21:37 But last *of all* he **s** unto them his son, 649
22: 3 And **s** forth his servants to call them that 649
22: 4 Again, he **s** forth other servants, saying, 649
22: 7 and he **s** forth his armies, 3992
22:16 they **s** out unto him their disciples with 649
23:37 and stonest them which are **s** unto thee, 649
27:19 judgment seat, his wife **s** unto him, saying, 649

Mk
1:43 charged him, and forthwith **s** him **away**; 1544
3:31 standing without, **s** unto him, calling him. 649
4:36 And when they had **s** away the multitude, 863
6:17 Herod himself had **s** **forth** and laid hold 649
6:27 immediately the king **s** an executioner, 649
6:45 Bethsaida, while he **s** away the people. 630
6:46 when he had **s** them **away**, he departed 657
8: 9 about four thousand: and he **s** them **away**. 630
8:26 And he **s** him **away** to his house, saying, 649
9:37 receiveth not me, but him that **s** me. 649
12: 2 at the season he **s** to the husbandmen a 649
12: 3 And beat him, and **s** *him* **away** empty. 649
12: 4 And again he **s** unto them another servant; 649
12: 4 and **s** *him* **away** shamefully handled, 649
12: 5 again he **s** another; and him they killed, 649
12: 6 he **s** him also last unto them, saying, 649

Lk
1:19 and am **s** to speak unto thee, and to shew 649
1:26 in the sixth month the angel Gabriel was **s** 649
1:53 and the rich he hath **s** empty **away**. 1821
4:18 he hath **s** me to heal the broken-hearted, 649
4:26 But unto none of them was Elias **s**, 3992
4:43 to other cities also: for therefore am I **s**. 649
7: 3 he **s** unto him *the* elders of the Jews, 649
7: 6 centurion **s** friends to him, saying unto 3992
7:10 And they that were **s**, returning to 3992
7:19 *him* two of his disciples **s** *them* to Jesus, 3992
7:20 John Baptist hath **s** us unto thee, saying, 649
8:38 be with him: but Jesus **s** him away, saying, 630
9: 2 And he **s** them to preach the kingdom of 649
9:48 shall receive me receiveth him that **s** me: 649
9:52 And **s** messengers before his face: 649
10: 1 and **s** them two and two before his face 649
10:16 that despiseth me despiseth him that **s** me. 649
13:34 and stonest them that are **s** unto thee; 649
14:17 And **s** his servant at supper time to say to 649
15:15 and he **s** him into his fields to feed swine. 3992
19:14 and **s** a message after him, saying, 649
19:29 *mount* of Olives, he **s** two of his disciples, 649
19:32 And they that were **s** went their way, 649
20:10 And at the season he **s** a servant to 649
20:10 beat him, and **s** *him* **away** empty. 1821
20:11 And again he **s** another servant: 3992
20:11 *him* shamefully, and **s** *him* **away** empty. 1821
20:12 again he **s** a third: and they wounded 3992
20:20 And they watched *him,* and **s** **forth** spies, 649
22: 8 And he **s** Peter and John, saying, Go and 649
22:35 When I **s** you without purse, and scrip, 649
23: 7 he **s** him to Herod, who himself also was 375
23:11 a gorgeous robe, and **s** him *again* to Pilate. 375
23:15 No, nor yet Herod: for I **s** you to him; 375

Jn
1: 6 There was a man **s** from God, whose name 649
1: 8 but *was* **s** to bear witness of *that* Light. NIG
1:19 when the Jews **s** priests and Levites from 649
1:22 we may give an answer to them that **s** 3992
1:24 And they which were **s** were of 649
1:33 but he that **s** me to baptize with water, 3992
3:17 For God **s** not his Son into the world to 649
3:28 not the Christ, but that I am **s** before him. 649
3:34 he whom God hath **s** speaketh the words 649
4:34 meat is to do the will of him that **s** me, 3992
4:38 I **s** you to reap that whereon ye bestowed 649
5:23 not the Father which hath **s** him. 3992
5:24 and believeth on him that **s** me, 3992
5:30 the will of the Father which hath **s** me. 3992
5:33 Ye **s** unto John, and he bare witness unto 649
5:36 witness of me, that the Father hath **s** me. 649
5:37 And the Father himself, which hath **s** me, 3992
5:38 for whom he hath **s**, him ye believe not. 649

S

Jn	6:29 that ye believe on *him* whom he hath **s**.	649
	6:38 own will, but the will of him that **s** me.	3992
	6:39 And this is the Father's will which hath **s**	3992
	6:40 And this is the will of him that **s** me,	3992
	6:44 except the Father which hath **s** me draw	3992
	6:57 As the living Father hath **s** me, and I live	649
	7:16 doctrine is not mine, but his that **s** me.	3992
	7:18 but he that seeketh his glory that **s** him,	3992
	7:28 he that **s** me is true, whom ye know not.	649
	7:29 for I am from him, and he hath **s** me.	649
	7:32 and the chief priests **s** officers to take him.	649
	7:33 you, and *then* I go unto him that **s** me.	3992
	8:16 not alone, but I and the Father that **s** me.	3992
	8:18 Father that **s** me beareth witness of me.	3992
	8:26 but he that **s** me is true; and I speak to	3992
	8:29 And he that **s** me is with me: the Father	3992
	8:42 neither came I of myself, but he **s** me.	649
	9: 4 I must work the works of him that **s** me,	3992
	9: 7 of Siloam, (which is by interpretation, **S**.)	649
	10:36 and **s** into the world, Thou blasphemest;	649
	11: 3 Therefore *his* sisters **s** unto him, saying,	649
	11:42 that they may believe that thou hast **s** me.	3992
	12:44 not on me, but on him that **s** me.	3992
	12:45 he that seeth me seeth him that **s** me.	3992
	12:49 but the Father which **s** me, he gave me a	3992
	13:16 neither *he that is* **s** greater than he that	652
	13:16 he that is sent greater than he that **s**	3992
	13:20 he that receiveth me receiveth him that **s**	3992
	14:24 is not mine, but the Father's which **s** me.	3992
	15:21 because they know not him that **s** me.	3992
	16: 5 But now I go my way to him that **s** me;	3992
	17: 3 and Jesus Christ, whom thou hast **s**.	649
	17:18 As thou hast **s** me into the world, even *so*	649
	17:18 even *so* have I also **s** them into the world.	649
	17:21 that the world may believe that thou hast **s**	649
	17:23 the world may know that thou hast **s** me,	649
	17:25 these have known that thou hast **s** me.	649
	18:24 Annas had **s** him bound unto Caiaphas	649
	20:21 *my* Father hath **s** me, even *so* send I you.	649
Ac	3:26 raised up his Son Jesus, **s** him to bless you,	649
	5:21 and **s** to the prison to have them brought.	649
	7:12 corn in Egypt, he **s** **out** our fathers first.	1821
	7:14 Then **s** Joseph, and called his father Jacob	649
	8:14 of God, they **s** unto them Peter and John:	649
	9:17 hath **s** me, that thou mightest receive thy	649
	9:30 to Cesarea, and **s** him **forth** to Tarsus.	1821
	9:38 Peter was there, they **s** unto him two men,	649
	10: 8 *things* unto them, he **s** them to Joppa.	649
	10:17 the men which were **s** from Cornelius had	649
	10:20 doubting nothing: for I have **s** them.	649
	10:21 which were **s** unto him from Cornelius;	649
	10:29 without gainsaying, as soon as I was **s** **for**:	3343
	10:29 for what intent ye have **s** **for** me?	3343
	10:33 Immediately therefore I **s** to thee;	3992
	10:36 The word which *God's* unto the children	649
	11:11 where I was, **s** from Cesarea unto me.	649
	11:22 and they **s** **forth** Barnabas, that he should	1821
	11:30 **s** it to the elders by the hands of Barnabas	649
	12:11 that the Lord hath **s** his angel,	1821
	13: 3 *their* hands on them, they **s** *them* **away**.	630
	13: 4 So they, being **s** **forth** by the Holy Ghost,	1599
	13:15 the prophets the rulers of the synagogue **s**	649
	13:26 to you is the word of this salvation **s**.	649
	15:27 We have **s** therefore Judas and Silas,	649
	16:35 the magistrates the serjeants, saying,	649
	16:36 Paul, The magistrates have **s** to let you go:	649
	17:10 the brethren immediately **s** **away** Paul	1599
	17:14 immediately the brethren **s** **away** Paul to	1821
	19:22 So he **s** into Macedonia two of them that	649
	19:31 Asia, which were his friends, **s** unto him,	3992
	20:17 And from Miletus he **s** to Ephesus,	3992
	23:30 I **s** straightway to thee,	3992
	24:24 he **s** **for** Paul, and heard him concerning	3343
	24:26 wherefore he **s** **for** him the oftener,	3343
	28:28 that the salvation of God is **s** unto	649
Ro	10:15 how shall they preach, except they be **s**?	649
	16: 1 **S** **by** Phebe servant of the church at	NIG
1Co	1:17 Christ **s** me not to baptize, but to preach	649
	4:17 this cause have I **s** unto you Timotheus,	3992
2Co	8:18 And we have **s** with them our brother,	4842
	8:22 And we have **s** **with** them our brother,	4842
	9: 3 have I **s** the brethren, lest our boasting	4842
	12:17 you by any of them whom I **s** unto you?	649
	12:18 desired Titus, and with *him* I **s** a brother.	4882
Gal	4: 4 God **s** **forth** his Son, made of a woman,	1821
	4: 6 God hath **s** **forth** the Spirit of his Son into	1821
Eph	6:22 Whom I have **s** unto you for the same	3992
Php	2:28 I **s** him therefore the more carefully, that,	3992
	4:16 For even in Thessalonica ye **s** once and	3992
	4:18 the *things which were* **s** from you,	NIG
Col	4: 8 Whom I have **s** unto you for the same	3992
1Th	3: 2 And **s** Timotheus, our brother,	3992
	3: 5 no longer forbear, I **s** to know your faith,	3992
2Ti	4:12 Tychicus have I **s** to Ephesus.	649
Phm	1:12 Whom I have **s** **again**: thou therefore	375
Heb	1:14 **s** **forth** to minister for them who shall be	649
Jas	2:25 and had **s** *them* **out** another way?	1544
1Pe	1:12 with the Holy Ghost **s** **down** from heaven;	649
	2:14 as unto them that are **s** by him for	3992
1Jn	4: 9 that God **s** his only begotten Son into	649
	4:10 his Son to be the propitiation for our sins.	649
	4:14 do testify that the Father **s** the Son *to be*	649
Rev	1: 1 and signified *it* by his angel unto his	649
	5: 6 which are the seven spirits of God **s** **forth**	649
	22: 6 the Lord God of the holy prophets **s** his	649

Rev	22:16 I Jesus have **s** mine angel to testify unto	3992

SENTENCE (11) [SENTENCES]

Dt	17: 9 they shall shew thee the **s** of judgment:	1697
	17:10 thou shalt do according to the **s**, which	1697
	17:11 According to the **s** of the law which they	NIH
	17:11 thou shalt not decline from the **s** which	1697
Ps	17: 2 Let my **s** come forth from thy presence;	4941
Pr	16:10 A *divine* *is* in the lips of the king:	7081
Ecc	8:11 Because **s** *against* an evil work is not	6599
Jer	4:12 now also will I give **s** against them.	4941
Lk	23:24 Pilate **gave** **s** that it should be as they	1948
Ac	15:19 Wherefore my **s** is, that *we* trouble not	2919
2Co	1: 9 But we had the **s** of death in ourselves,	610

SENTENCES (2) [SENTENCE]

Da	5:12 shewing of **hard** **s**, and dissolving of	280
	8:23 understanding **dark** **s**, shall stand up.	2420

SENTEST (4) [SEND]

Ex	15: 7 thou **s** **forth** thy wrath, *which* consumed	7971
Nu	13:27 came unto the land whither thou **s** us,	7971
	24: 12 to thy messengers which thou **s** unto me,	7971
1Ki	5: 8 have considered *the things* which thou **s**	7971

SENUAH (1)

Ne	11: 9 Judah the son of **S** *was* second over	5574

SEORIM (1)

1Ch	24: 8 The third to Harim, the fourth to **S**,	8188

SEPARATE (32) [SEPARATED, SEPARATETH, SEPARATING, SEPARATION]

Ge	13: 9 **s** thyself, I pray thee, from me: if *thou*	6504
	30:40 Jacob did **s** the lambs, and set the faces of	6504
	49:26 head of him *that was* **s** from his brethren.	5139
Lev	15:31 Thus shall ye **s** the children of Israel from	5144
	22: 2 they **s** themselves from the holy *things*	5144
Nu	6: 2 woman shall **s** *themselves* to vow a vow	6381
	6: 2 to **s** *themselves* unto the LORD:	5144
	6: 3 He shall **s** *himself* from wine and	5144
	8:14 Thus shalt thou **s** the Levites from among	914
	16:21 **S** yourselves from among this congregation,	914
Dt	19: 2 Thou shalt **s** three cities for thee in the	914
	19: 7 Thou shalt **s** three cities for thee.	914
	29:21 the LORD shall **s** him unto evil out of all	914
Jos	16: 9 the cities for the children of Ephraim	3995
1Ki	8:53 For thou didst **s** them from among all	914
Ezr	10: 11 **s** yourselves from the people of the land,	914
Jer	37:12 to **s** himself thence in the midst of	2505
Eze	41:12 **s** place *at* the end toward the west *was*	1508
	41:13 the **s** **place**, and the building, with the	1508
	41:14 the **s** **place** toward the east, an hundred	1508
	41:15 against the **s** **place** which *was* behind it,	1508
	42: 1 that *was* over against the **s** **place**,	1508
	42:10 over against the **s** **place**, and over against	1508
	42:13 which *are* before the **s** **place**,	1508
Mt	25:32 he shall **s** them one from another, as a	873
Lk	6: 22 they shall **s** you *from their company*,	873
Ac	13: 2 **S** me Barnabas and Saul for the work	873
Ro	8:35 Who shall **s** us from the love of Christ?	5563
	8:39 shall be able to **s** us from the love of God,	5563
2Co	6:17 and be ye **s**, saith the Lord, and touch not	873
Heb	7:26 **s** from sinners, and made higher than	5563
Jude	1:19 These be they who **s** themselves, sensual,	592

SEPARATED (33) [SEPARATE]

Ge	13:11 they **s** themselves the one from the other.	6504
	13:14 after that Lot was **s** from him, Lift up now	6504
	25:23 two manner of people shall be **s** from thy	6504
Ex	33:16 so shall we be **s**, I and thy people, from all	6395
Lev	20:24 which have **s** you from *other* people.	914
	20:25 which I have **s** from you as unclean.	914
Nu	16: 9 that the God of Israel hath **s** you from	914
Dt	10: 8 At that time the LORD **s** the tribe of Levi,	914
	32: 8 when he **s** the sons of Adam,	6504
	33:16 head of him *that was* **s** from his brethren.	5139
1Ch	12: 8 the Gadites there **s** themselves unto David	914
	23:13 Aaron was **s**, that he should sanctify	914
	25: 1 the captains of the host **s** to the service of	914
2Ch	25:10 Amaziah **s** them, to wit, the army that was	914
Ezr	6:21 all such as had **s** themselves unto them	914
	8:24 I **s** twelve of the chief of the priests,	914
	9: 1 have not **s** themselves from the people of	914
	10: 8 himself **s** from the congregation of those	914
	10:16 were **s**, and sat down in the first day of	914
Ne	4:19 and large, and we *are* **s** upon the wall,	6504
	9: 2 the seed of Israel **s** themselves from all	914
	10:28 all they that had **s** themselves from	914
	13: 3 that they **s** from Israel all the mixed	914
Pr	18: 1 having **s** himself, seeketh *and*	6504
	19: 4 but the poor is **s** from his neighbour.	6504
Isa	56: 3 The LORD hath **utterly** **s** me from his	914+914
	59: 2 your iniquities have **s** between you and	914
Hos	4:14 for themselves are **s** with whores,	6504
	9:10 and **s** themselves unto *that* shame;	5144
Ac	19: 9 he departed from them, and **s** the disciples,	873
Ro	1: 1 to be an apostle, **s** unto the gospel of God,	873
Gal	1:15 who **s** me from my mother's womb,	873
	2:12 were come, he withdrew and **s** himself,	873

SEPARATETH (5) [SEPARATE]

Nu	6: 5 in the which he **s** *himself* unto the LORD,	5144
	6: 6 All the days that he **s** *himself* unto	5144
Pr	16:28 and a whisperer **s** chief friends.	6504
	17: 9 he that repeateth a matter **s** *very* friends.	6504

Eze	14: 7 which **s** himself from me, and setteth up	5144

SEPARATING (1) [SEPARATE]

Zec	7: 3 **s** myself, as I have done these so	5144

SEPARATION (26) [SEPARATE]

Lev	12: 2 according to the days of the **s** for her	5079
	12: 5 shall be unclean two weeks, as *in* her **s**:	5079
	15:20 *thing* that she lieth upon in her **s** shall	5079
	15:25 blood many days out of the time of her **s**,	5079
	15:25 or if it run beyond the time of her **s**;	5079
	15:25 uncleanness shall be as the uncleanness of her **s**.	5079
	15:26 issue shall be unto her as the bed of her **s**:	5079
	15:26 be unclean, as the uncleanness of her **s**.	5079
Nu	6: 4 All the days of his **s** shall he eat nothing	5145
	6: 5 All the days of the vow of his **s** there shall	5145
	6: 8 All the days of his **s** he *is* holy unto	5145
	6:12 unto the LORD the days of his **s**,	5145
	6:12 shall be lost, because his **s** was defiled.	5145
	6:13 when the days of his **s** are fulfilled:	5145
	6:18 Nazarite shall shave the head of his **s** *at*	5145
	6:18 shall take the hair of the head of his **s**,	5145
	6:19 after *the hair* of his **s** is shaven:	5145
	6:21 *of* his offering unto the LORD for his **s**,	5145
	6:21 so he must do after the law of his **s**.	5145
	19: 9 of the children of Israel for a water of **s**:	5079
	19:13 water of **s** was not sprinkled upon him,	5079
	19:20 water of **s** hath not been sprinkled upon	5079
	19:21 that he that sprinkleth the water of **s** shall	5079
	19:21 the he that toucheth the water of **s** shall be	5079
	31:23 it shall be purified with the water of **s**:	5079
Eze	42:20 to **make** **a** **s** between the sanctuary and	914

SEPHAR (1)

Ge	10:30 as thou goest unto **S**, a mount of the east.	5611

SEPHARAD (1)

Ob	1:20 the captivity of Jerusalem, which *is* in **S**,	5614

SEPHARVAIM (6) [SEPHARVITES]

2Ki	17:24 from **S**, and placed *them* in the cities of	5617
	17:31 and Anammelech, the gods of **S**.	5617
	18:34 where *are* the gods of **S**, Hena, and Ivah?	5617
	19:13 king of the city of **S**, *of* Hena, and Ivah?	5617
Isa	36:19 where *are* the gods of **S**? and have they	5617
	37:13 the king of the city of **S**, Hena, and Ivah?	5617

SEPHARVITES (1) [SEPHARVAIM]

2Ki	17:31 the **S** burnt their children in fire to	5616

SEPULCHRE (54) [SEPULCHRES]

Ge	23: 6 none of us shall withhold from thee his **s**,	6913
Dt	34: 6 no man knoweth of his **s** unto this day.	6900
Jdg	8:32 was buried in the **s** of Joash his father,	6913
1Sa	10: 2 thou shalt find two men by Rachel's **s** in	6900
2Sa	2:32 and buried him in the **s** of his father,	6913
	4:12 and buried *it* in the **s** of Abner in Hebron.	6913
	17:23 died, and was buried in the **s** of his father,	6913
	21:14 in Zelah, in the **s** of Kish his father:	6913
1Ki	13:22 thy carcase shall not come unto the **s** of	6913
	13:31 bury me in the **s** wherein the man of God	6913
2Ki	9:28 buried him in his **s** with his fathers in	6900
	13:21 and they cast the man into the **s** of Elisha:	6913
	21:26 he was buried in his **s** in the garden of	6900
	23:17 *It is* the **s** of the man of God, which came	6913
	23:30 Jerusalem, and buried him in his own **s**.	6900
Ps	5: 9 their throat *is* an open **s**; they flatter with	6913
Isa	22:16 that thou hast hewed thee out a **s** here,	6913
	22:16 *as* he that heweth him out a **s** on high,	6913
Jer	5:16 Their quiver *is* as an open **s**, they *are* all	6913
Mt	27:60 rolled a great stone to the door of the **s**,	3419
	27:61 the other Mary, sitting over against the **s**.	5028
	27:64 the **s** be made sure until the third day,	5028
	27:66 So they went, and made the **s** sure,	5028
	28: 1 and the other Mary to see the **s**.	5028
	28: 8 And they departed quickly from the **s** with	3419
Mk	15:46 laid him in a **s** which was hewn out of a	3419
	15:46 and rolled a stone unto the door of the **s**.	3419
	16: 2 they came unto the **s** at the rising of	3419
	16: 3 us away the stone from the door of the **s**?	3419
	16: 5 And entering into the **s**, they saw a young	3419
	16: 8 went out quickly, and fled from the **s**;	3419
Lk	23:53 and laid it in a *that was* hewn in stone,	3418
	23:55 and beheld the **s**, and how his body was	3419
	24: 1 in the morning, they came unto the **s**,	3418
	24: 2 found the stone rolled away from the **s**.	3419
	24: 9 returned from the **s**, and told all these	3419
	24:12 Then arose Peter, and ran unto the **s**;	3419
	24:22 us astonished, which were early at the **s**;	3419
	24:24 them which were with us went to the **s**,	3419
Jn	19:41 and in the garden a new **s**, wherein was	3419
	19:42 the Jews' preparation *day*; for the **s** was	3419
	20: 1 the **s**, and seeth the stone taken away	3419
	20: 1 seeth the stone taken away from the **s**.	3419
	20: 2 have taken away the Lord out of the **s**,	3419
	20: 3 *that* other disciple, and came to the **s**.	3419
	20: 4 did outrun Peter, and came first to the **s**.	3419
	20: 6 and went into the **s**, and seeth the linen	3419
	20: 8 which came first to the **s**, and he saw,	3419
	20:11 But Mary stood without at the **s** weeping:	3419
	20:11 she stooped down, and looked into the **s**,	3419
Ac	2:29 buried, and his **s** is with us unto this day.	3418
	7:16 laid in the **s** that Abraham bought for a	3418
	13:29 down from the tree, and laid *him* in a **s**.	3419
Ro	3:13 Their throat *is* an open **s**; with their	5028

S

SEPULCHRES (16) [SEPULCHRE]
Ge	23: 6 in the choice of our **s** bury thy dead;	6913
2Ki	23:16 spied the **s** that *were* there in the mount,	6913
	23:16 took the bones out of the **s**, and burnt	6913
2Ch	16:14 they buried him in his own **s**, which he	6913
	21:20 city of David, but not in the **s** of the kings.	6913
	24:25 they buried him not in the **s** of the kings.	6913
	28:27 brought him not into the **s** of the kings	6913
	32:33 they buried him in the chiefest of the **s** of	6913
	35:24 was buried in *one of the* **s** of his fathers.	6913
Ne	2: 3 the place of my fathers' **s**, *lieth* waste,	6913
	2: 5 unto the city of my fathers' **s**, that I may	6913
	3:16 unto *the place* over against the **s** of David,	6913
Mt	23:27 for ye are like unto whited **s**, which	5028
	23:29 and garnish the **s** of the righteous,	3419
Lk	11:47 for ye build the **s** of the prophets,	3419
	11:48 indeed killed them, and ye build their **s**.	3419

SERAH (2)
Ge	46:17 and Ishui, and Beriah, and **S** their sister:	8294
1Ch	7:30 and Ishuai, and Beriah, and **S** their sister.	8294

SERAIAH (20)
2Sa	8:17 *were* the priests; and **S** *was* the scribe;	8304
2Ki	25:18 the captain of the guard took **S** the chief	8304
	25:23 **S** the son of Tanhumeth the Netophathite,	8304
1Ch	4:13 the sons of Kenaz; Othniel, and **S**:	8304
	4:14 **S** begat Joab, the father of the valley of	8304
	4:35 of Josibiah, the son of **S**, the son of Asiel,	8304
	6:14 Azariah begat **S**, and Seraiah begat	8304
	6:14 begat Seraiah, and **S** begat Jehozadak,	8304
Ezr	2: 2 **S**, Reelaiah, Mordecai, Bilshan, Mizpar,	8304
	7: 1 Ezra the son of **S**, the son of Azariah,	8304
Ne	10: 2 **S**, Azariah, Jeremiah,	8304
	11:11 **S** the son of Hilkiah, the son of	8304
	11:11 of Shealtiel, and Jeshua: **S**, Jeremiah, Ezra,	8304
	12:12 of **S**, Meraiah; of Jeremiah, Hananiah;	8304
Jer	36:26 **S** the son of Azriel, and Shelemiah the son	8304
	40: 8 **S** the son of Tanhumeth, and the sons of	8304
	51:59 prophet commanded **S** the son of Neriah,	8304
	51:59 of his reign. And *this* **S** *was* a quiet prince.	8304
	51:61 Jeremiah said to **S**, When thou comest to	8304
	52:24 the captain of the guard took **S** the chief	8304

SERAPHIMS (2)
Isa	6: 2 Above it stood the **s**: each one had six	8314
	6: 6 flew one of the **s** unto me, having a live	8314

SERAPHS See SERAPHIMS

SERED (2)
Ge	46:14 sons of Zebulun; **S**, and Elon, and Jahleel.	5624
Nu	26:26 of **S**, the family of the Sardites: of Elon,	5624

SEREDITE See SARDITES

SERGEANTS (2)
Ac	16:35 the magistrates sent the **s**, saying, Let	4465
	16:38 And the **s** told these words unto	4465

SERGIUS (1)
Ac	13: 7 with the deputy *of the country,* **S** Paulus,	4588

SERIOUSNESS See GRAVITY

SERPENT (38) [SERPENT'S, SERPENTS]
Ge	3: 1 Now the **s** was more subtil than any beast	5175
	3: 2 the woman said unto the **s**, We may eat	5175
	3: 4 the **s** said unto the woman, Ye shall not	5175
	3:13 The **s** beguiled me, and I did eat.	5175
	3:14 the LORD God said unto the **s**,	5175
	49:17 Dan shall be a **s** by the way, an adder in	5175
Ex	4: 3 cast it on the ground, and it became a **s**;	5175
	7: 9 before Pharaoh, *and* it shall become a **s**.	8577
	7:10 before his servants, and it became a **s**.	8577
	7:15 the rod which was turned to a **s** shalt	5175
Nu	21: 8 Make thee a fiery **s**, and set it upon a pole:	NIH
	21: 9 Moses made a **s** of brass, and put it upon	5175
	21: 9 to pass, that if a **s** had bitten *any* man,	5175
	21: 9 when he beheld the **s** of brass, he lived.	5175
2Ki	18: 4 brake in pieces the brasen **s** that Moses	5175
Job	26:13 his hand hath formed the crooked **s**.	5175
Ps	58: 4 Their poison *is* like the poison of a **s**:	5175
	140: 3 have sharpened their tongues like a **s**;	5175
Pr	23:32 At the last it biteth like a **s**,	5175
	30:19 in the air; the way of a **s** upon a rock;	5175
Ecc	10: 8 breaketh a hedge, a **s** shall bite him.	5175
	10:11 the **s** will bite without enchantment;	5175
Isa	14:29 and his fruit *shall be* a **fiery** flying **s**.	8314
	27: 1 shall punish leviathan the piercing **s**,	5175
	27: 1 *even* leviathan *that* crooked **s**;	5175
	30: 6 and old lion, the viper and **fiery** flying **s**,	8314
Jer	46:22 The voice thereof shall go like a **s**; for	5175
Am	5:19 his hand on the wall, and a **s** bit him.	5175
	9: 3 thence will I command the **s**, and he shall	5175
Mic	7:17 They shall lick the dust like a **s**, they shall	5175
Mt	7:10 Or if he ask a fish, will he give him a **s**?	3789
Lk	11:11 ask a fish, will he for a fish give him a **s**?	3789
Jn	3:14 And as Moses lifted up the **s** in	3789
2Co	11: 3 as the beguiled Eve through his subtilty,	3789
Rev	12: 9 the great dragon was cast *out, that* old **s**,	3789
	12:14 and half a time, from the face of the **s**.	3789
	12:15 And the **s** cast out of his mouth water as	3789
	20: 2 *that* old **s**, which is the devil, and Satan,	3789

SERPENT'S (2) [SERPENT]
Isa	14:29 for out of the **s** root shall come forth a	5175
	65:25 dust *shall be* the **s** meat. They shall not	5175

SERPENTS (13) [SERPENT]
Ex	7:12 every man his rod, and they became **s**:	8577
Nu	21: 6 the LORD sent fiery **s** among the people,	5175
	21: 7 that he take away the **s** from us.	5175
Dt	8:15 *wherein were* fiery **s**, and scorpions,	5175
	32:24 them, with the poison of **s** of the dust.	2119
Jer	8:17 For behold, I will send **s**, cockatrices,	5175
Mt	10:16 be ye therefore wise as **s**, and harmless as	3789
	23:33 Ye **s**, ye generation of vipers, how can ye	3789
Mk	16:18 They shall take up **s**; and if they drink any	3789
Lk	10:19 I give unto you power to tread on **s** and	3789
1Co	10: 9 also tempted, and were destroyed of **s**.	3789
Jas	3: 7 of birds, and of **s**, and of *things* in the sea,	2062
Rev	9:19 for their tails *were* like unto **s**,	3789

SERUG (5)
Ge	11:20 lived two and thirty years, and begat **S**:	8286
	11:21 Reu lived after he begat **S** two hundred	8286
	11:22 And **S** lived thirty years, and begat Nahor:	8286
	11:23 **S** lived after he begat Nahor two hundred	8286
1Ch	1:26 **S**, Nahor, Terah,	8286

SERVANT (493) [SERVE]
Ge	9:25 **s** of servants shall he be unto his brethren.	5650
	9:26 God of Shem; and Canaan shall be his **s**.	5650
	9:27 tents of Shem; and Canaan shall be his **s**.	5650
	18: 3 pass not away, I pray thee, from thy **s**:	5650
	18: 5 for therefore are you come to your **s**.	5650
	19:19 thy **s** hath found grace in thy sight,	5650
	24: 2 Abraham said unto his eldest **s** of his	5650
	24: 5 the **s** said unto him, Peradventure	5650
	24: 9 the **s** put his hand under the thigh of	5650
	24:10 the **s** took ten camels of the camels of his	5650
	24:14 *that* thou hast appointed for thy **s** Isaac;	5650
	24:17 the **s** ran to meet her, and said, Let me,	5650
	24:34 And he said, I *am* Abraham's **s**.	5650
	24:52 when Abraham's **s** heard their words,	5650
	24:53 the **s** brought forth jewels of silver,	5650
	24:59 her nurse, and Abraham's **s**, and his men.	5650
	24:61 the **s** took Rebekah, and went his way.	5650
	24:65 For she had said, It *is* my master: therefore	5650
	24:65 she had said, It *is* my master: therefore	5650
	24:66 **s** told Isaac all things that he had done.	5650
	26:24 thy seed for my **s** Abraham's sake.	5650
	32: 4 Thy **s** Jacob saith thus, I have sojourned	5650
	32:10 which thou hast shewed unto thy **s**;	5650
	32:18 thou shalt say, *They be* thy **s** Jacob's; it is	5650
	32:20 Behold, thy **s** Jacob *is* behind us.	5650
	33: 5 which God hath graciously given thy **s**.	5650
	33:14 lord, I pray thee, pass over before his **s**:	5650
	39:17 saying, The Hebrew **s**, which thou hast	5650
	39:19 After this manner did thy **s** to me;	5650
	41:12 a Hebrew, **s** to the captain of the guard;	5650
	43:28 Thy **s** our father *is* in good health, he *is*	5650
	44:10 he with whom it is found shall be my **s**;	5650
	44:17 hand the cup is found, he shall be my **s**;	5650
	44:18 said, O my lord, let thy **s**, I pray thee,	5650
	44:18 and let not thine anger burn against thy **s**:	5650
	44:24 to pass when we came up unto thy **s**	5650
	44:27 thy **s** my father said unto us, Ye know that	5650
	44:30 therefore when I come to thy **s** my father,	5650
	44:31 thy **s** our father with sorrow to the grave.	5650
	44:32 For thy **s** became surety for the lad unto	5650
	44:33 thy **s** abide instead of the lad a bondman	5650
	49:15 to bear, and became a **s** unto tribute.	5647
Ex	4:10 nor since thou hast spoken unto thy **s**:	5650
	12:44 every man's **s** that is bought for money,	5650
	12:45 and a **hired s** shall not eat thereof.	7916
	14:31 and believed the LORD, and his **s** Moses.	5650
	21: 2 If thou buy a Hebrew **s**, six years he shall	5650
	21: 5 if the **s** shall plainly say, I love my master,	5650
	21:20 a man smite his **s**, or his maid, with a rod,	5650
	21:26 if a man smite the eye of his **s**, or the eye	5650
	33:11 **s** Joshua, the son of Nun, a young man,	8334
Lev	22:10 a **hired s**, shall not eat *of* the holy *thing*.	7916
	25: 6 for thy **s**, and for thy maid, and for thy	5650
	25: 6 for thy **hired s**, and for thy stranger that	7916
	25:40 But as a **hired s**, and as a sojourner,	7916
	25:50 according to the time of a **hired s** shall it	7916
	25:53 And as a yearly **hired s** shall he be with	7916
Nu	11:11 Wherefore hast thou afflicted thy **s**?	5650
	11:28 the **s** of Moses, *one* of his young men,	8334
	12: 7 My Moses *is* not so, who *is* faithful in all	5650
	12: 8 were ye not afraid to speak against my **s**	5650
	14:24 my **s** Caleb, because he had another spirit	5650
Dt	3:24 hast begun to shew thy **s** thy greatness,	5650
	5:15 remember that thou wast a **s** in the land	5650
	15:17 the door, and he shall be thy **s** for ever.	5650
	15:18 he hath been worth a double **hired s** *to*	7916
	23:15 shalt not deliver unto his master the **s**	5650
	24:14 Thou shalt not oppress a **hired s** *that is*	7916
	34: 5 So Moses the **s** of the LORD died there in	5650
Jos	1: 1 Now after the death of Moses the **s** of	5650
	1: 2 Moses my **s** is dead; now therefore arise,	5650
	1: 7 which Moses my **s** commanded thee:	5650
	1:13 Remember the word which Moses the **s**	5650
	1:15 which Moses the LORD's **s** gave you on	5650
	5:14 unto him, What saith my lord unto his **s**?	5650
	8:31 As Moses the **s** of the LORD commanded	5650
	8:33 as Moses the **s** of the LORD had	5650
	9:24 his **s** Moses to give you all the land,	5650

Jos	11:12 as Moses the **s** of the LORD commanded.	5650
	11:15 As the LORD commanded Moses his **s**,	5650
	12: 6 Them did Moses the **s** of the LORD and	5650
	12: 6 Moses the **s** of the LORD gave it *for* a	5650
	13: 8 *even* as Moses the **s** of the LORD gave	5650
	14: 7 Forty years old *was* I when Moses the **s**	5650
	18: 7 which Moses the **s** of the LORD gave	5650
	22: 2 Ye have kept all that Moses the **s** of	5650
	22: 4 which Moses the **s** of the LORD gave you	5650
	22: 5 which Moses the **s** of the LORD charged	5650
	24:29 the **s** of the LORD, died, *being* an hundred	5650
Jdg	2: 8 the **s** of the LORD, died, *being* an hundred	5650
	7:10 go thou with Phurah thy **s** down to the	5288
	7:11 went he down with Phurah his **s** unto	5288
	15:18 great deliverance into the hand of thy **s**:	5650
	19: 3 having his **s** with him, and a couple of	5288
	19: 9 and his concubine, and his **s**, his father	5288
	19:11 the **s** said unto his master, Come, I pray	5288
	19:13 he said unto his **s**, Come, and let us draw	5288
Ru	2: 5 said Boaz unto his **s** that was set over	5288
	2: 6 the **s** that was set over the reapers	5288
1Sa	2:13 the priest's **s** came, while the flesh was in	5288
	2:15 the priest's **s** came, and said to the man	5288
	3: 9 that say, Speak, LORD; for thy **s** heareth.	5650
	3:10 answered, Speak; for thy **s** heareth.	5650
	9: 5 said to his **s** that *was* with him, Come,	5288
	9: 7 said Saul to his **s**, But behold, *if* we go,	5288
	9: 8 the **s** answered Saul again, and said,	5288
	9:10 said Saul to his **s**, Well said; come, let us	5288
	9:22 Samuel took Saul and his **s**,	5288
	9:27 Bid the **s** pass on before us, (and	5288
	10:14 Saul's uncle said unto him and to his **s**,	5288
	17:32 thy **s** will go and fight with this Philistine.	5650
	17:34 Thy **s** kept his father's sheep,	5650
	17:36 Thy **s** slew both the lion and the bear:	5650
	17:58 *I am* the son of thy **s** Jesse	5650
	19: 4 him, Let not the king sin against his **s**,	5650
	20: 7 say thus, *It is* well; thy **s** shall have peace:	5650
	20: 8 thou shalt deal kindly with thy **s**;	5650
	20: 8 thou hast brought thy **s** into a covenant	5650
	22: 8 my son hath stirred up my **s** against me,	5650
	22:15 not the king impute *any* thing unto his **s**,	5650
	22:15 for thy **s** knew nothing of all this, less or	5650
	23:10 thy **s** hath certainly heard that Saul seeketh	5650
	23:11 Saul come down, as thy **s** hath heard?	5650
	23:11 God of Israel, I beseech thee, tell thy **s**.	5650
	25:39 of Nabal, and hath kept his **s** from evil:	5650
	25:41 thine handmaid *be* a **s** to wash the feet	8198
	26:18 doth my lord thus pursue after his **s**?	5650
	26:19 my lord the king hear the words of his **s**.	5650
	27: 5 why should thy **s** dwell in the royal city	5650
	27:12 therefore he shall be my **s** for ever.	5650
	28: 2 Surely thou shalt know what thy **s** can do.	5650
	29: 3 this David, the **s** of Saul the king of Israel,	5650
	29: 8 what hast thou found in thy **s** so long as I	5650
	30:13 a young man of Egypt, **s** to an Amalekite;	5650
2Sa	3:18 By the hand of my **s** David I will save my	5650
	7: 5 Go and tell my **s** David, Thus saith	5650
	7: 8 so shalt thou say unto my **s** David,	5650
	7:20 for thou, Lord GOD, knowest thy **s**.	5650
	7:21 great things, to make thy **s** know *them*.	5650
	7:25 that thou hast spoken concerning thy **s**,	5650
	7:26 let the house of thy **s** David be established	5650
	7:27 God of Israel, hast revealed to thy **s**,	5650
	7:27 hath thy **s** found in his heart to pray this	5650
	7:28 hast promised this goodness unto thy **s**:	5650
	7:29 it please thee to bless the house of thy **s**,	5650
	7:29 with thy blessing let the house of thy **s** be	5650
	9: 2 *there was* of the house of Saul a **s** whose	5650
	9: 2 *Art* thou Ziba? And he said, Thy **s** *is* he.	5650
	9: 6 And he answered, Behold thy **s**.	5650
	9: 8 bowed himself, and said, What *is* thy **s**,	5650
	9: 9 called to Ziba, Saul's **s**, and said unto him,	5288
	9:11 my lord the king hath commanded his **s**,	5650
	9:11 commanded his servant, so shall thy **s** do.	5650
	11:21 Thy **s** Uriah the Hittite is dead also.	5650
	11:24 and thy **s** Uriah the Hittite is dead also.	5650
	13:17 he called his **s** that ministered unto him,	5288
	13:18 his **s** brought her out, and bolted the door	8334
	13:24 Behold now, thy **s** hath sheepshearers;	5650
	13:24 and his servants go with thy **s**.	5650
	13:35 king's sons come: as thy **s** said, so it is.	5650
	14:19 for thy **s** Joab, he bade me, and he put all	5650
	14:20 fetch about *this* form of speech hath thy **s**	5650
	14:22 To day thy **s** knoweth that I have found	5650
	14:22 the king had fulfilled the request of his **s**.	5650
	15: 2 Thy **s** *is* of one of the tribes of Israel.	5650
	15: 8 For thy **s** vowed a vow while I abode at	5650
	15:21 or life, even there *also* will thy **s** be.	5650
	15:34 say unto Absalom, I will be thy **s**, O king;	5650
	15:34 as I *have been* thy father's **s** hitherto,	5650
	15:34 hitherto, so *will* I now also *be* thy **s**:	5650
	16: 1 Ziba the **s** of Mephibosheth met him, with	5288
	18:29 When Joab sent the king's **s**, and *me* thy	5650
	18:29 *me* thy **s**, I saw a great tumult, but I knew	5650
	19:17 Ziba the **s** of the house of Saul,	5288
	19:19 do thou remember *that* which thy **s**	5650
	19:20 For thy **s** doth know that I have sinned:	5650
	19:26 My lord, O king, my **s** deceived me:	5650
	19:26 for thy **s** said, I will saddle me an ass, that	5650
	19:26 go to the king; because thy **s** *is* lame.	5650
	19:27 he hath slandered thy **s** unto my lord	5650
	19:28 yet didst thou set thy **s** among them that	5650
	19:35 can thy **s** taste what I eat or what I drink?	5650
	19:35 should thy **s** be yet a burden unto my lord	5650

S

S

| 2Sa | 19:36 | Thy **s** will go a little *way* over Jordan with | 5650 |

2Sa 19:36 Thy **s** will go a little *way* over Jordan with 5650
19:37 Let thy **s**, I pray thee, turn back again, 5650
19:37 behold thy **s** Chimham; let him go over 5650
24:10 O LORD, take away the iniquity of thy **s**; 5650
24:21 is my lord the king come to his **s**? 5650
1Ki 1:19 but Solomon thy **s** hath he not called. 5650
1:26 *even* me thy **s**, and Zadok the priest, 5650
1:26 and thy **s** Solomon, hath he not called. 5650
1:27 and thou hast not shewed *it* to thy **s** do. 5650
1:51 that he will not slay his **s** with the sword. 5650
2:38 lord the king hath said, so will thy **s** do. 5650
3: 6 Thou hast shewed unto thy **s** David my 5650
3: 7 hast made thy **s** king instead of David 5650
3: 8 thy **s** *is* in the midst of thy people which 5650
3: 9 thy **s** an understanding heart to judge thy 5650
8:24 Who hast kept with thy **s** David my father 5650
8:25 keep with thy **s** David my father that thou 5650
8:26 which thou spakest unto thy **s** David my 5650
8:28 have thou respect unto the prayer of thy **s**, 5650
8:28 which thy **s** prayeth before thee to day: 5650
8:29 which thy **s** shall make towards this place. 5650
8:30 hearken thou to the supplication of thy **s**, 5650
8:52 be open unto the supplication of thy **s**, 5650
8:53 thou spakest by the hand of Moses thy **s**, 5650
8:56 he promised by the hand of Moses his **s**. 5650
8:59 that *he* maintain the cause of his **s**, 5650
8:66 that the LORD had done for David his **s**, 5650
11:11 from thee, and will give it to thy **s**. 5650
11:26 an Ephrathite of Zereda, Solomon's **s**, 5650
11:32 (But he shall have one tribe for my **s** 5650
11:36 that David my **s** may have a light alway 5650
11:38 my commandments, as David my **s** did; 5650
12: 7 thou wilt be a **s** unto this people *this* day, 5650
14: 8 *yet* thou hast not been as my **s** David, 5650
14:18 he spake by the hand of his **s** Ahijah 5650
15:29 which he spake by his **s** Ahijah 5650
16: 9 his **s** Zimri, captain of half *his* chariots, 5650
18: 9 that thou wouldest deliver thy **s** into 5650
18:12 but *I* thy **s** fear the LORD from my youth. 5650
18:36 *that* I am thy **s**, and *that* I have done all 5650
18:43 said to his **s**, Go up now, look toward 5288
19: 3 *belongeth* to Judah, and left his **s** there. 5288
20: 9 All that thou didst send for to thy **s** at 5650
20:32 said, Thy **s** Ben-hadad saith, I pray thee, 5650
20:39 **s** went out into the midst of the battle; 5650
20:40 as thy **s** was busy here and there, he was 5650
2Ki 4: 1 saying, Thy **s** my husband is dead; 5650
4: 1 thou knowest that thy **s** did fear 5650
4:12 he said to Gehazi his **s**, Call this 5288
4:24 said to her **s**, Drive, and *go forward;* 5288
4:25 that he said to Gehazi his **s**, Behold, 5288
4:38 he said unto his **s**, Set on the great pot, 5288
5: 6 I have *therewith* sent Naaman my **s** to 5650
5:15 I pray thee, take a blessing of thy **s**. 5650
5:17 be given to thy two mules' burden of 5650
5:17 thy **s** will henceforth offer neither burnt 5650
5:18 In this thing the LORD pardon thy **s**, 5650
5:18 the LORD pardon thy **s** in this thing. 5650
5:20 the **s** of Elisha the man of God, said, 5288
5:25 And he said, Thy **s** went no whither. 5650
6:15 when the **s** of the man of God was risen 8334
6:15 his **s** said unto him, Alas, my master, 5288
8: 4 the king talked with Gehazi the **s** of 5288
8:13 Hazael said, But what, *is* thy **s** a dog, 5650
9:36 he spake by his **s** Elijah the Tishbite, 5650
10:10 done *that* which he spake by his **s** Elijah. 5650
14:25 he spake by the hand of his **s** Jonah, 5650
16: 7 of Assyria, saying, I *am* thy **s** and thy son: 5650
17: 3 Hoshea became his **s**, and gave him 5650
18:12 all that Moses the **s** of the LORD 5650
19:34 own sake, and for my David's sake. 5650
20: 6 own sake, and for my David's sake. 5650
21: 8 according to all the law that my **s** Moses 5650
22:12 and Asahiah a **s** of the king's, saying, 5650
24: 1 and Jehoiakim became his **s** three years: 5650
25: 8 of the king of Babylon, *unto* Jerusalem: 5650
1Ch 2:34 Sheshan had a **s**, an Egyptian, whose 5650
2:35 Sheshan gave his daughter to Jarha his **s** 5650
6:49 according to all that Moses the **s** of God 5650
16:13 O ye seed of Israel his **s**, ye children of 5650
17: 4 Go and tell David my **s**, Thus saith 5650
17: 7 thus shalt thou say unto my **s** David, 5650
17:18 more to thee for the honour of thy **s**? 5650
17:18 of thy servant? for thou knowest thy **s**. 5650
17:23 that thou hast spoken concerning thy **s** 5650
17:24 the house of David thy **s** be established 5650
17:25 hast told thy **s** that *thou* wilt build him a 5650
17:25 thy **s** hath found *in his heart* to pray 5650
17:26 hast promised this goodness unto thy **s**: 5650
17:27 it please thee to bless the house of thy **s**, 5650
21: 8 thee, do away the iniquity of thy **s**; 5650
2Ch 1: 3 which Moses the **s** of the LORD had made 5650
6:15 Thou which hast kept with thy **s** David 5650
6:16 keep with thy **s** David my father *that* 5650
6:17 which thou hast spoken unto thy **s** David. 5650
6:19 therefore to the prayer of thy **s**, 5650
6:19 prayer which thy **s** prayeth before thee: 5650
6:20 to hearken unto the prayer which thy **s** 5650
6:21 therefore unto the supplications of thy **s**, 5650
6:42 remember the mercies of David thy **s**. 5650
13: 6 the **s** of Solomon the son of David, 5650
24: 6 of Moses the **s** of the LORD, 5650
24: 9 **s** of God laid upon Israel in the 5650
32:16 LORD God, and against his **s** Hezekiah. 5650
34:20 and Asaiah a **s** of the king's, saying, 5650

Ne 1: 6 that *thou* mayest hear the prayer of thy **s**, 5650
1: 7 which thou commandedst thy **s** Moses. 5650
1: 8 the word that thou commandedst thy **s** 5650
1:11 ear be attentive to the prayer of thy **s**, 5650
1:11 thy **s** *this* day, and grant him mercy in 5650
2: 5 if thy **s** have found favour in thy sight, 5650
2:10 and Tobiah the **s**, the Ammonite, 5650
2:19 Tobiah the **s**, the Ammonite, 5650
4:22 Let every one with his **s** lodge within 5288
6: 5 sent Sanballat his **s** unto me in like 5288
9:14 and laws, by the hand of Moses thy **s**. 5650
10:29 which was given by Moses the **s** of God, 5650
Job 1: 8 Satan, Hast thou considered my **s** Job, 5650
2: 3 Satan, Hast thou considered my **s** Job, 5650
3:19 there; and the **s** *is* free from his master. 5650
7: 2 As a earnestly desireth the shadow, 5650
19:16 I called my **s**, and he gave *me* no answer; 5650
41: 4 wilt thou take him for a **s** for ever? 5650
42: 7 *the thing that is* right, as my **s** Job *hath.* 5650
42: 8 to my **s** Job, and offer up for yourselves 5650
42: 8 and my **s** Job shall pray for you: 5650
42: 8 *the thing which is* right, like my **s** Job. 5650
Ps 18: T *A Psalm* of David, the **s** of the LORD, 5650
19:11 Moreover by them *is* thy **s** warned: 5650
19:13 Keep back thy **s** also from presumptuous 5650
27: 9 *far* from me; put not thy **s** away in anger: 5650
31:16 Make thy face to shine upon thy **s**: save 5650
35:27 hath pleasure in the prosperity of his **s**. 5650
36: T *A Psalm* of David the **s** of the LORD. 5650
69:17 hide not thy face from thy **s**; for I am in 5650
78:70 He chose David also his **s**, and took him 5650
86: 2 my God, save thy **s** that trusteth in thee. 5650
86: 4 Rejoice the soul of thy **s**: for unto thee, 5650
86:16 give thy strength unto thy **s**, and save 5650
89: 3 chosen, I have sworn unto David my **s**, 5650
89:20 I have found David my **s**; with my holy 5650
89:39 hast made void the covenant of thy **s**: 5650
105: 6 ye seed of Abraham his **s**, ye children of 5650
105:17 *even* Joseph, who was sold for a **s**: 5650
105:26 He sent Moses his **s**; *and* Aaron whom he 5650
105:42 his holy promise, *and* Abraham his **s**. 5650
109:28 let them be ashamed; but let thy **s** rejoice. 5650
116:16 O LORD, truly I *am* thy **s**; I *am* thy 5650
116:16 I *am* thy **s**, *and* the son of thy handmaid: 5650
119:17 Deal bountifully with thy **s**, *that* I may 5650
119:23 *but* thy **s** did meditate in thy statutes. 5650
119:38 Stablish thy word unto thy **s**, who *is* 5650
119:49 Remember the word unto thy **s**, upon 5650
119:65 Thou hast dealt well with thy **s**, O LORD, 5650
119:76 according to thy word unto thy **s**. 5650
119:84 How many are the days of thy **s**? 5650
119:122 Be surety for thy **s** for good: let not 5650
119:124 Deal with thy **s** according unto thy mercy, 5650
119:125 I *am* thy **s**; give me understanding, that I 5650
119:135 Make thy face to shine upon thy **s**; 5650
119:140 *is* very pure: therefore thy **s** loveth it. 5650
119:176 gone astray like a lost sheep; seek thy **s**; 5650
132:10 For thy **s** David's sake turn not away 5650
136:22 *Even* an heritage unto Israel his **s**: for his 5650
143: 2 enter not into judgment with thy **s**: for in 5650
143:12 them that afflict my soul: for I *am* thy **s**. 5650
144:10 delivereth David his **s** from the hurtful 5650
Pr 11:29 the fool *shall be* **s** to the wise of heart. 5650
12: 9 *He that is* despised, and hath a **s**, *is* better 5650
14:35 The king's favour *is* toward a wise **s**: 5650
17: 2 A wise **s** shall have rule over a son that 5650
19:10 less for a **s** to have rule over princes. 5650
22: 7 and the borrower *is* **s** to the lender. 5650
29:19 A **s** will not be corrected by words: 5650
29:21 He that delicately bringeth up his **s** from 5650
30:10 Accuse not a **s** unto his master, lest he 5650
30:22 For a **s** when he reigneth; and a fool 5650
Ecc 7:21 spoken; lest thou hear thy **s** curse thee: 5650
Isa 20: 3 Like as my **s** Isaiah hath walked naked 5650
22:20 that I will call my **s** Eliakim the son of 5650
24: 2 priest; as *with* the **s**, so *with* his master; 5650
37:35 own sake, and for my David's sake. 5650
41: 8 thou, Israel, *art* my **s**, Jacob whom I have 5650
41: 9 and said unto thee, Thou *art* my **s**; 5650
42: 1 Behold my **s**, whom I uphold; mine elect, 5650
42:19 Who *is* blind, but my **s**? or deaf, as my 5650
42:19 is perfect, and blind as the LORD's **s**? 5650
43:10 the LORD, and my **s** whom I have chosen: 5650
44: 1 Yet now hear, O Jacob my **s**; and Israel, 5650
44: 2 Fear not, O Jacob, my **s**; 5650
44:21 O Jacob and Israel; for thou *art* my **s**: 5650
44:21 I have formed thee; thou *art* my **s**: 5650
44:26 That confirmeth the word of his **s**, 5650
48:20 The LORD hath redeemed his **s** Jacob. 5650
49: 3 said unto me, Thou *art* my **s**, O Israel, 5650
49: 5 formed me from the womb *to be* his **s**, 5650
49: 6 a light thing that thou shouldest be my **s** 5650
49: 7 to a of rulers, Kings shall see and arise, 5650
50:10 obeyeth the voice of his **s**, that walketh 5650
52:13 Behold, my **s** shall deal prudently, he 5650
53:11 by his knowledge shall my righteous **s** 5650
Jer 2:14 *Is* Israel a **s**? *is* he a homeborn *slave?* 5650
25: 9 s, and will bring them against this land, 5650
27: 6 the king of Babylon, my **s**; 5650
30:10 thou not, O my **s** Jacob, saith the LORD; 5650
33:21 my covenant be broken with David my **s**, 5650
33:22 so will I multiply the seed of David my **s**, 5650
33:26 David my **s**, *so that* I will make *not any* of 5650
34:16 caused every man his **s**, and every man 5650
43:10 my **s**, and will set his throne upon these 5650

Jer 46:27 O my **s** Jacob, and be not dismayed, 5650
46:28 Fear thou not, O Jacob my **s**, saith 5650
Eze 28:25 their land that I have given to my Jacob. 5650
34:23 and he shall feed them, *even* my **s** David; 5650
34:24 and my **s** David a prince among them; 5650
37:24 David my **s** *shall be* king over them; 5650
37:25 land that I have given unto Jacob my **s**, 5650
37:25 my **s** David *shall be* their prince for ever. 5650
Da 6:20 O Daniel, **s** of the living God, is thy God, 5649
9:11 written in the law of Moses the **s** of God, 5650
9:17 hear the prayer of thy **s**, 5650
10:17 how can the **s** of this my lord talk with 5650
Hag 2:23 will I take thee, O Zerubbabel, my **s**, 5650
Zec 3: 8 I *will* bring forth my **s** the BRANCH. 5650
Mal 1: 6 honoureth *his* father, and a **s** his master: 5650
4: 4 Remember ye the law of Moses my **s**, 5650
Mt 8: 6 Lord, my **s** lieth at home sick of the palsy, 3816
8: 8 the word only, and my **s** shall be healed. 3816
8: 9 and to my **s**, Do this, and he doeth *it.* 1401
8:13 his **s** was healed in the selfsame hour. 3816
10:24 above *his* master, nor the **s** above his lord. 1401
10:25 he be as his master, and the **s** as his lord. 1401
12:18 Behold my **s**, whom I have chosen; 3816
18:26 The **s** therefore fell down, 1401
18:27 Then the lord of that **s** was moved with 1401
18:28 the same **s** went out, and found one of 1401
18:32 said unto him, O *thou* wicked **s**, I forgave 1401
20:27 be chief among you, let him be your **s** 1249
23:11 that is greatest among you shall be your **s**. 1249
24:45 Who then is a faithful and wise **s**, whom 1401
24:46 Blessed *is* that **s**, whom his lord when he 1401
24:48 But *and* if that evil **s** shall say in his heart, 1401
24:50 The lord of that **s** shall come in a day 1401
25:21 Well done, *thou* good and faithful **s**: 1401
25:23 unto him, Well *done,* good and faithful **s**; 1401
25:26 unto him, *Thou* wicked and slothful **s**, 1401
25:30 And cast ye the unprofitable **s** into outer 1401
26:51 and stroke a **s** of the high priest's, 1401
Mk 9:35 *the same* shall be last of all, and **s** of all. 1249
10:44 you will be the chiefest, shall be **s** of all. 1401
12: 2 season he sent to the husbandmen a **s**, 1401
12: 4 And again he sent unto them another **s**; 1401
14:47 smote a **s** of the high priest, and cut off 1401
Lk 1:54 He hath holpen his **s** Israel, 3816
1:69 for us in the house of his **s** David; 3816
2:29 now lettest thou thy **s** depart in peace, 1401
7: 2 a certain centurion's **s**, who was dear 1401
7: 3 him that he would come and heal his **s**. 1401
7: 7 say in a word, and my **s** shall be healed. 3816
7: 8 and to my **s**, Do this, and he doeth *it.* 1401
7:10 found the whole that had been sick. 1401
12:43 Blessed *is* that **s**, whom his lord when he 1401
12:45 But and if that **s** say in his heart, My lord 1401
12:46 The lord of that **s** will come in a day 1401
12:47 And that **s**, which knew his lord's will, 1401
14:17 sent his **s** at supper time to say to them 1401
14:21 So that **s** came, and shewed his lord these 1401
14:21 of the house being angry said to his **s**, 1401
14:22 the **s** said, Lord, it is done as thou hast 1401
14:23 the lord said unto the **s**, Go out into 1401
16:13 No **s** can serve two masters: for either he 3610
17: 7 having a **s** plowing or feeding cattle, 1401
17: 9 Doth he thank that **s** because he did 1401
19:17 And he said unto him, Well, *thou* good **s**: 1401
19:22 mouth will I judge thee, *thou* wicked **s**. 1401
20:10 And at the season he sent a **s** to 1401
20:11 again he sent another **s**: and they beat 1401
22:50 And one of them smote the **s** of the high 1401
Jn 8:34 Whosoever committeth sin is the **s** of sin. 1401
8:35 the **s** abideth not in the house for ever: 1401
12:26 and where I am, there shall also my **s** be: 1249
13:16 you, The **s** is not greater than his lord; 1401
15:15 the **s** knoweth not what his lord doeth: 1401
15:20 you, The **s** is not greater than his lord. 1401
18:10 and smote the high priest's **s**, and cut off 1401
Ac 4:25 by the mouth of thy **s** David hast said, 3816
Ro 1: 1 Paul, a **s** of Jesus Christ, called *to be* an 1401
14: 4 art thou that judgest another *man's* **s**? 3610
16: 1 which is a **s** of the church which is at 1249
16: S by Phebe a **s** of the church at Cenchrea. 1249
1Co 7:21 Art thou called *being* a **s**? care not for it: 1401
7:22 the Lord, *being* a **s**, is the Lord's freeman: 1401
7:22 he that is called, *being* free, is Christ's **s**. 1401
9:19 *men,* yet have I **made** myself a **s** unto all, 1402
Gal 1:10 men, I should not be the **s** of Christ. 1401
4: 1 he is a child, differeth nothing from a **s**, 1401
4: 7 thou art no more a **s**, but a son; 1401
Php 2: 7 and took *upon him* the form of a **s**, 1401
Col 4:12 is *one* of you, a **s** of Christ, saluteth you, 1401
2Ti 2:24 And the **s** of the Lord must not strive; 1401
Tit 1: 1 a **s** of God, and an apostle of Jesus Christ, 1401
Phm 1:16 Not now as a **s**, but above a servant, 1401
1:16 but above a **s**, a brother beloved, 1401
1: S Rome to Philemon, by Onesimus a **s**. 3610
Heb 3: 5 verily was faithful in all his house, as a **s**, 2324
Jas 1: 1 a **s** of God and of the Lord Jesus Christ, 1401
2Pe 1: 1 a **s** and an apostle of Jesus Christ, 1401
Jude 1: 1 the **s** of Jesus Christ, and brother of James, 1401
Rev 1: 1 signified *it* by his angel unto his **s** John: 1401
15: 3 And they sing the song of Moses the **s** of 1401

SERVANT'S (9) [SERVE]

Ge 19: 2 into your **s** house, and tarry all night, 5650
2Sa 7:19 thou hast spoken also of thy **s** house for 5650
1Ki 11:13 one tribe to thy son for David my **s** sake, 5650

1Ki	11:34 all the days of his life for David my **s** sake,	5650
2Ki	8:19 not destroy Judah for David his **s** sake,	5650
1Ch	17:17 thou hast *also* spoken of thy **s** house for	5650
	17:19 for thy **s** sake, and according to thine	5650
Isa	45: 4 For Jacob my **s** sake, and Israel mine elect	5650
Jn	18:10 his right ear. The **s** name was Malchus.	1401

SERVANTS (476) [SERVE]

Ge	9:25 servant of **s** shall he be unto his brethren.	5650
	14:14 he armed his trained **s**, born in his own	NIH
	14:15 he and his **s**, by night, and smote them,	5650
	20: 8 called all his **s**, and told all these things in	5650
	21:25 which Abimelech's **s** had violently taken	5650
	26:14 possession of herds, and great store of **s**:	5657
	26:15 For all the wells which his father's **s** had	5650
	26:19 Isaac's **s** digged in the valley,	5650
	26:25 there: and there Isaac's **s** digged a well.	5650
	26:32 that Isaac's **s** came, and told him	5650
	27:37 all his brethren have I given to him for **s**;	5650
	32:16 he delivered *them* into the hand of his **s**,	5650
	32:16 said unto his **s**, Pass over before me,	5650
	40:20 that he made a feast unto all his **s**:	5650
	40:20 and of the chief baker among his **s**.	5650
	41:10 Pharaoh was wroth with his **s**, and put	5650
	41:37 of Pharaoh, and in the eyes of all his **s**.	5650
	41:38 Pharaoh said unto his **s**, Can we find *such*	5650
	42:10 my lord, but to buy food are thy **s** come.	5650
	42:11 we *are* true men, thy **s** are no spies.	5650
	42:13 they said, Thy **s** *are* twelve brethren,	5650
	44: 7 God forbid that thy **s** should do according	5650
	44: 9 With whom*soever* of thy **s** it be found,	5650
	44:16 God hath found out the iniquity of thy **s**:	5650
	44:16 behold, we *are* my lord's **s**, both we,	5650
	44:19 My lord asked his **s**, saying, Have ye a	5650
	44:21 thou saidst unto thy **s**, Bring him down	5650
	44:23 thou saidst unto thy **s**, Except your	5650
	44:31 that shall bring down the gray hairs of	5650
	45:16 and it pleased Pharaoh well, and his **s**.	5650
	47: 3 Thy **s** *are* shepherds, both we, *and* also	5650
	47: 4 for thy **s** have no pasture for their flocks;	5650
	47: 4 let thy **s** dwell in the land of Goshen.	5650
	47:19 we and our land will be **s** unto Pharaoh:	5650
	47:25 of my lord, and we will be Pharaoh's **s**.	5650
	50: 2 Joseph commanded his **s** the physicians to	5650
	50: 7 with him went up all the **s** of Pharaoh,	5650
	50:17 forgive the trespass of the **s** of the God of	5650
	50:18 face; and they said, Behold, we *be* thy **s**.	5650
Ex	5:15 Wherefore dealest thou thus with thy **s**?	5650
	5:16 *There is* no straw given unto thy **s**,	5650
	5:16 thy **s** *are* beaten; but the fault *is* in	5650
	5:21 in the eyes of his **s**, to put a sword in their	5650
	7:10 and before his **s**, and it became a serpent.	5650
	7:20 sight of Pharaoh, and in the sight of his **s**;	5650
	8: 3 into the house of thy **s**, and upon thy	5650
	8: 4 and upon thy people, and upon all thy **s**.	5650
	8: 9 for thee, and for thy **s**, and for thy people,	5650
	8:11 and from thy **s**, and from thy people;	5650
	8:21 upon thy **s**, and upon thy people,	5650
	8:29 from thy **s**, and from his people;	5650
	8:31 from his **s**, and from his people;	5650
	9:14 and upon thy **s**, and upon thy people;	5650
	9:20 the **s** of Pharaoh made his servants	5650
	9:20 the servants of Pharaoh made his **s**	5650
	9:21 not the word of the LORD left his **s**	5650
	9:30 as for thee and thy **s**, I know that ye will	5650
	9:34 and hardened his heart, he and his **s**.	5650
	10: 1 hardened his heart, and the heart of his **s**,	5650
	10: 6 houses of all thy **s**, and the houses of all	5650
	10: 7 Pharaoh's **s** said unto him, How long	5650
	11: 3 in the sight of Pharaoh's **s**, and in the	5650
	11: 8 all these thy **s** shall come down unto me,	5650
	12:30 he, and all his **s**, and all the Egyptians;	5650
	14: 5 of his **s** was turned against the people,	5650
	32:13 Isaac, and Israel, thy **s**,	5650
Lev	25:42 For they *are* my **s**, which I brought forth	5650
	25:55 For unto me the children of Israel are **s**;	5650
	25:55 they *are* my **s** whom I brought forth out	5650
Nu	22:18 and said unto the **s** of Balak,	5650
	22:22 his ass, and his two **s** *were* with him.	5288
	31:49 Thy **s** have taken the sum of the men of	5650
	32: 4 *is* a land for cattle, and thy **s** have cattle:	5650
	32: 5 let this land be given unto thy **s** for a	5650
	32:25 Thy **s** will do as my lord commandeth.	5650
	32:27 thy **s** will pass over, every man armed for	5650
	32:31 As the LORD hath said unto thy **s**,	5650
Dt	9:27 Remember thy **s**, Abraham, Isaac,	5650
	29: 2 and unto all his **s**, and unto all his land;	5650
	32:36 his people, and repent himself for his **s**,	5650
	32:43 for he will avenge the blood of his **s**,	5650
	34:11 and to all his **s**, and to all his land,	5650
Jos	9: 8 they said unto Joshua, We *are* thy **s**.	5650
	9: 9 From a very far country thy **s** are come	5650
	9:11 and say unto them, We *are* your **s**:	5650
	9:24 said, Because it was certainly told thy **s**,	5650
	10: 6 Slack not thy hand from thy **s**;	5650
Jdg	3:24 When he was gone out, his **s** came;	5650
	6:27 Gideon took ten men of his **s**, and did as	5650
	19:19 for the young man *which is* with thy **s**:	5650
1Sa	4: 9 that ye be not **s** unto the Hebrews,	5647
	8:14 the best *of them*, and give *them* to his **s**.	5650
	8:15 and give to his officers, and to his **s**.	5650
	8:17 tenth of your sheep: and ye shall be his **s**.	5650
	9: 3 Take now one of the **s** with thee, and	5288
	12:19 Pray for thy **s** unto the LORD thy God,	5650
	16:15 Saul's **s** said unto him, Behold now, an	5650

1Sa	16:16 Let our lord now command thy **s** *which*	5650
	16:17 Saul said unto his **s**, Provide me now a	5650
	16:18 answered one of the **s**, and said, Behold,	5288
	17: 8 *am* not I a Philistine, and you **s** to Saul?	5650
	17: 9 and to kill me, then will we be your **s**:	5650
	17: 9 then shall ye be our **s**, and serve us.	5650
	18: 5 people, and also in the sight of Saul's **s**.	5650
	18:22 Saul commanded his **s**, *saying*, Commune	5650
	18:22 delight in thee, and all his **s** love thee:	5650
	18:23 Saul's **s** spake those words in the ears of	5650
	18:24 the **s** of Saul told him, saying, On this	5650
	18:26 when his **s** told David these words,	5650
	18:30 himself more wisely than all the **s** of Saul;	5650
	19: 1 to all his **s**, that they should kill David.	5650
	21: 2 I have appointed *my* **s** to such and such a	5288
	21: 7 Now a *certain* man of the **s** of Saul *was*	5650
	21:11 the **s** of Achish said unto him, *Is* not this	5650
	21:14 said Achish unto his **s**, Lo, you see the	5650
	22: 6 and all his **s** *were* standing about him;)	5650
	22: 7 Saul said unto his **s** that stood about him,	5650
	22: 9 *was* set over the **s** of Saul, and said,	5650
	22:14 *is so* faithful among all thy **s** as David,	5650
	22:17 the **s** of the king would not put forth their	5650
	24: 7 So David stayed his **s** with *these* words,	376
	25: 8 cometh to thine hand unto thy **s**,	5650
	25:10 Nabal answered David's **s**, and said,	5650
	25:10 there be many **s** now a days that break	5650
	25:19 she said unto her **s**, Go on before me;	5288
	25:40 the **s** of David were come to Abigail	5650
	25:41 to wash the feet of the **s** of my lord.	5650
	28: 7 said Saul unto his **s**, Seek me a woman	5650
	28: 7 his **s** said to him, Behold, *there is* a	5650
	28:23 his **s**, together with the woman,	5650
	28:25 brought *it* before Saul, and before his **s**;	5650
	29:10 with thy master's **s** that are come with	5650
2Sa	2:12 and the **s** of Ish-bosheth the son of Saul,	5650
	2:13 the **s** of David, went out, and met	5650
	2:15 son of Saul, and twelve of the **s** of David.	5650
	2:17 the men of Israel, before the **s** of David.	5650
	2:30 there lacked of David's **s** nineteen men	5650
	2:31 the **s** of David had smitten of Benjamin,	5650
	3:22 the **s** of David and Joab came from	5650
	3:38 the king said unto his **s**, Know ye not that	5650
	6:20 in the eyes of the handmaids of his **s**,	5650
	8: 2 so the Moabites became David's **s**,	5650
	8: 6 the Syrians became **s** to David,	5650
	8: 7 of gold that were on the **s** of Hadadezer,	5650
	8:14 and all they of Edom became David's **s**.	5650
	9:10 Thou therefore, and thy sons, and thy **s**,	5650
	9:10 Now Ziba had fifteen sons and twenty **s**.	5650
	9:12 all that dwelt in the house of Ziba *were* **s**	5650
	10: 2 him by the hand of his **s** for his father.	5650
	10: 2 David's **s** came *into* the land of the	5650
	10: 3 not David *rather* sent his **s** unto thee,	5650
	10: 4 Wherefore Hanun took David's **s**,	5650
	10:19 all the kings *that were* **s** to Hadarezer	5650
	11: 1 Joab, and his **s** with him, and all Israel;	5650
	11: 9 the king's house with all the **s** of his lord,	5650
	11:11 my lord Joab, and the **s** of my lord,	5650
	11:13 out to lie on his bed with the **s** of his lord,	5650
	11:17 there fell *some* of the people of the **s** of	5650
	11:24 shooters shot from off the wall upon thy **s**;	5650
	11:24 *some* of the king's **s** be dead,	5650
	12:18 the **s** of David feared to tell him that	5650
	12:19 when David saw that his **s** whispered,	5650
	12:19 therefore David said unto his **s**, Is the	5650
	12:21 said his **s** unto him, What thing *is* this	5650
	13:24 thee, and his **s** go with thy servant.	5650
	13:28 Now Absalom had commanded his **s**,	5288
	13:29 the **s** of Absalom did unto Amnon as	5288
	13:31 all his **s** stood *by* with their clothes rent.	5650
	13:36 the king also and all his **s** wept very sore.	5650
	14:30 Therefore he said unto his **s**, See,	5650
	14:30 And Absalom's **s** set the field on fire.	5650
	14:31 Wherefore have thy **s** set my field on fire?	5650
	15:14 David said unto all his **s** that *were* with	5650
	15:15 the king's **s** said unto the king, Behold,	5650
	15:15 thy **s** *are ready to do* whatsoever my lord	5650
	15:18 all his **s** passed on beside him; and all	5650
	16: 6 at David, and at all the **s** of king David:	5650
	16:11 Abishai, and to all his **s**, Behold, my son,	5650
	17:20 when Absalom's **s** came to the woman to	5650
	18: 7 of Israel were slain before the **s** of David,	5650
	18: 9 Absalom met the **s** of David.	5650
	19: 5 shamed *this* day the faces of all thy **s**,	5650
	19: 6 that thou regardest neither princes nor **s**:	5650
	19: 7 forth, and speak comfortably unto thy **s**:	5650
	19:14 unto the king, Return thou, and all thy **s**.	5650
	19:17 fifteen sons and his twenty **s** with him;	5650
	20: 6 thou thy lord's **s**, and pursue after him,	5650
	21:15 his **s** with him, and fought against	5650
	21:22 hand of David, and by the hand of his **s**.	5650
	24:20 the king and his **s** coming on toward him:	
1Ki	1: 2 Wherefore his **s** said unto him, Let there	5650
	1: 9 and all the men of Judah the king's **s**:	5650
	1:33 Take with you the **s** of your lord,	5650
	1:47 moreover the king's **s** came to bless our	5650
	2:39 that two of the **s** of Shimei ran away unto	5650
	2:39 saying, Behold, thy **s** *be* in Gath.	5650
	2:40 and went to Gath to Achish to seek his **s**:	5650
	2:40 went, and brought his **s** from Gath.	5650
	3:15 and made a feast to all his **s**.	5650
	5: 1 Hiram king of Tyre sent his **s** unto	5650
	5: 6 and my **s** shall be with thy servants:	5650
	5: 6 and my servants shall be with thy **s**:	5650

1Ki	5: 6 unto thee will I give hire for thy **s**	5650
	5: 9 shall bring *them* down from Lebanon	5650
	8:23 mercy with thy **s** that walk before thee	5650
	8:32 do, and judge thy **s**, condemning	5650
	8:36 forgive the sin of thy **s**, and of thy people	5650
	9:22 his **s**, and his princes, and his captains,	5650
	9:27 Hiram sent in the navy his **s**, shipmen that	5650
	9:27 of the sea, with the **s** of Solomon.	5650
	10: 5 the sitting of his **s**, and the attendance of	5650
	10: 8 Happy *are* thy men, happy *are* these thy **s**,	5650
	10:13 went to her own country, she and her **s**.	5650
	11:17 Edomites of his father's **s** with him,	5650
	12: 7 to them, then they will be thy **s** for ever.	5650
	15:18 and delivered them into the hand of his **s**:	5650
	20: 6 Yet I will send my **s** unto thee to morrow	5650
	20: 6 thine house, and the houses of thy **s**;	5650
	20:12 in the pavilions, that he said unto his **s**,	5650
	20:23 the **s** of the king of Syria said unto him,	5650
	20:31 his **s** said unto him, Behold now, we have	5650
	22: 3 the king of Israel said unto his **s**, Know ye	5650
	22:49 Let my **s** go with thy servants in the ships.	5650
	22:49 let my servants go with thy **s** in the ships.	5650
2Ki	1:13 let my life, and the life of these fifty thy **s**,	5650
	2:16 there be with thy **s** fifty strong men;	5650
	3:11 one of the king of Israel's **s** answered and	5650
	5:13 his **s** came near, and spake unto him,	5650
	5:23 and laid *them* upon two of his **s**;	5288
	6: 3 Be content, I pray thee, and go with thy **s**.	5650
	6: 8 took counsel with his **s**, saying, In such	5650
	6:11 called his **s**, and said unto them, Will ye	5650
	6:12 one of his **s** said, None, my lord, O king:	5650
	7:12 arose in the night, and said unto his **s**,	5650
	7:13 one of his **s** answered and said, Let *some*	5650
	9: 7 that I may avenge the blood of my **s**	5650
	9: 7 the blood of all the **s** of the LORD,	5650
	9:11 Jehu came forth to the **s** of his lord:	5650
	9:28 carried him *in a chariot* to Jerusalem,	5650
	10: 5 We *are* thy **s**, and will do all that thou	5650
	10:19 of Baal, all his **s**, and all his priests;	5647
	10:23 here with you none of the **s** of the LORD,	5650
	12:20 his **s** arose, and made a conspiracy,	5650
	12:21 of Shomer, his **s**, smote him, and he died;	5650
	14: 5 he slew his **s** which had slain the king	5650
	17:13 which I sent to you by my **s** the prophets.	5650
	17:23 as he had said by all his **s** the prophets.	5650
	18:24 one captain of the least of my master's **s**,	5650
	18:26 pray thee, to thy **s** in the Syrian language;	5650
	19: 5 So the **s** of king Hezekiah came to Isaiah.	5650
	19: 6 *with* which the **s** of the king of Assyria	5288
	21:10 the LORD spake by his **s** the prophets,	5650
	21:23 the **s** of Amon conspired against him,	5650
	22: 9 Thy **s** have gathered the money that was	5650
	23:30 his **s** carried him *in a chariot* dead from	5650
	24: 2 which he spake by his **s** the prophets.	5650
	24:10 At that time the **s** of Nebuchadnezzar	5650
	24:11 against the city, and his **s** *did* besiege it.	5650
	24:12 his **s**, and his princes, and his officers:	5650
	25:24 Fear not to be the **s** of the Chaldees:	5650
1Ch	18: 2 the Moabites became David's **s**,	5650
	18: 6 the Syrians became David's **s**,	5650
	18: 7 of gold that were on the **s** of Hadarezer,	5650
	18:13 and all the Edomites became David's **s**.	5650
	19: 2 So the **s** of David came into the land of	5650
	19: 3 not his **s** come unto thee for to search,	5650
	19: 4 Wherefore Hanun took David's **s**,	5650
	19:19 when the **s** of Hadarezer saw that they	5650
	19:19 peace with David, and became his **s**.	5647
	20: 8 hand of David, and by the hand of his **s**.	5650
	21: 3 lord the king, *are* they not all my lord's **s**?	5650
2Ch	2: 8 I know that thy **s** can skill to cut timber	5650
	2: 8 behold, my **s** *shall be* with thy servants,	5650
	2: 8 behold, my servants *shall be* with thy **s**,	5650
	2:10 I will give to thy **s**, the hewers that	5650
	2:15 hath spoken of, let him send unto his **s**:	5650
	6:14 and *shewest* mercy unto thy **s**,	5650
	6:23 do, and judge thy **s**, by requiting	5650
	6:27 forgive the sin of thy **s**, and of thy people	5650
	8: 9 did Solomon make no **s** for his work;	5650
	8:18 sent him by the hands of his **s** ships,	5650
	8:18 and **s** that had knowledge of the sea;	5650
	8:18 went with the **s** of Solomon to Ophir,	5650
	9: 4 the sitting of his **s**, and the attendance of	5650
	9: 7 *are* thy men, and happy *are* these thy **s**,	5650
	9:10 the **s** also of Huram, and the servants of	5650
	9:10 the **s** of Solomon, which brought gold	5650
	9:12 away to her own land, she and her **s**.	5650
	9:21 went *to* Tarshish with the **s** of Huram:	5650
	10: 7 words to them, they will be thy **s** for ever.	5650
	12: 8 Nevertheless they shall be his; that they	5650
	24:25 his own **s** conspired against him for	5650
	25: 3 that he slew his **s** that had killed the king	5650
	32: 9 king of Assyria send his **s** to Jerusalem,	5650
	32:16 his **s** spake *yet more* against the LORD	5650
	33:24 his **s** conspired against him, and slew him	5650
	34:16 saying, All that was committed to thy **s**,	5650
	35:23 the king said to his **s**, Have me away; for	5650
	35:24 **s** therefore took him out of *that* chariot,	5650
	36:20 where there were **s** to him and his sons	5650
Ezr	2:55 The children of Solomon's **s**: the children	5650
	2:58 and the children of Solomon's **s**,	5650
	2:65 Beside their **s** and their maids, of whom	5650
	4:11 Thy **s** the men *on this* side the river,	5649
	5:11 We are the **s** of the God of heaven and	5649
	9:11 Which thou hast commanded by thy **s**	5650
Ne	1: 6 for the children of Israel thy **s**,	5650

Ne	1:10	Now these *are* thy **s** and thy people,	5650
	1:11	to the prayer of thy **s**, who desire to fear	5650
	2:20	therefore we his **s** will arise and build:	5650
	4:16	*that* the half of my **s** wrought in the work,	5288
	4:23	So neither I, nor my brethren, nor my **s**,	5288
	5: 5	our sons and our daughters to be **s**,	5650
	5:10	I likewise, *and* my brethren, and my **s**,	5288
	5:15	even their **s** bare rule over the people:	5288
	5:16	all my **s** *were* gathered thither unto	5288
	7:57	The children of Solomon's **s**: the children	5650
	7:60	and the children of Solomon's **s**,	5650
	9:10	on all his **s**, and on all the people of his	5650
	9:36	we *are* this day, and *for* the land that	5650
	9:36	the good thereof, behold, we *are* **s** in it:	5650
	11: 3	and the children of Solomon's **s**.	5650
	13:19	*some* of my **s** set I at the gates, *that* there	5288
Est	1: 3	made a feast unto all his princes and his **s**;	5650
	2: 2	the king's **s** that ministered unto him,	5288
	2:18	a great feast unto all his princes and his **s**,	5650
	3: 2	the king's **s**, that *were* in the king's gate,	5650
	3: 3	king's **s**, which *were* in the king's gate,	5650
	4:11	All the king's **s**, and the people of	5650
	5:11	him above the princes and **s** of the king.	5650
	6: 3	the king's **s** that ministered unto him,	5288
	6: 5	the king's **s** said unto him, Behold,	5288
Job	1:15	they have slain the **s** with the edge of	5288
	1:16	sheep, and the **s**, and consumed them;	5650
	1:17	slain the **s** with the edge of the sword;	5288
	4:18	Behold, he put no trust in his **s**, and in his	5650
Ps	34:22	The LORD redeemeth the soul of his **s**:	5650
	69:36	The seed also of his **s** shall inherit it:	5650
	79: 2	The dead bodies of thy **s** have they given	5650
	79:10	of the blood of thy **s** which is shed.	5650
	89:50	Remember, Lord, the reproach of thy **s**;	5650
	90:13	and let it repent thee concerning thy **s**.	5650
	90:16	Let thy work appear unto thy **s**,	5650
	102:14	For thy **s** take pleasure in her stones,	5650
	102:28	The children of thy **s** shall continue,	5650
	105:25	his people, to deal subtilly with his **s**.	5650
	113: 1	Praise, O ye **s** of the LORD, praise	5650
	119:91	to thine ordinances: for all *are* thy **s**.	5650
	123: 2	as the eyes of **s** *look* unto the hand of	5650
	134: 1	ye the LORD, all ye **s** of the LORD,	5650
	135: 1	praise *him*, O ye **s** of the LORD.	5650
	135: 9	Egypt, upon Pharaoh, and upon all his **s**.	5650
	135:14	he will repent himself concerning his **s**.	5650
Pr	29:12	ruler hearken to lies, all his **s** *are* wicked.	8334
Ecc	2: 7	I got *me* **s** and maidens, and had servants	5650
	2: 7	maidens, and had **s** born in *my* house;	NIH
	10: 7	I have seen **s** upon horses,	5650
	10: 7	and princes walking as **s** upon the earth.	5650
Isa	14: 2	them in the land of the LORD for **s**	5650
	36: 9	one captain of the least of my master's **s**,	5650
	36:11	unto thy **s** in the Syrian language;	5650
	37: 5	So the **s** of king Hezekiah came to Isaiah.	5650
	37: 6	wherewith the **s** of the king of Assyria	5288
	37:24	By thy **s** hast thou reproached the Lord,	5650
	54:17	This *is* the heritage of the **s** of the LORD,	5650
	56: 6	to love the name of the LORD, to be his **s**,	5650
	65: 9	inherit it, and my **s** shall dwell there.	5650
	65:13	my **s** shall eat, but ye shall be hungry:	5650
	65:13	my **s** shall drink, but ye shall be thirsty:	5650
	65:13	my **s** shall rejoice, but ye shall be ashamed:	5650
	65:14	my **s** shall sing for joy of heart, but ye	5650
	65:15	slay thee, and call his **s** by another name:	5650
	66:14	the LORD shall be known towards his **s**,	5650
Jer	7:25	I have even sent unto you all my **s**	5650
	21: 7	his **s**, and the people, and such as are left	5650
	22: 2	thy **s**, and thy people that enter in by	5650
	22: 4	on horses, he, and his **s**, and his people.	5650
	25: 4	the LORD hath sent unto you all his **s**	5650
	25:19	his **s**, and his princes, and all his people;	5650
	26: 5	To hearken to the words of my **s**	5650
	29:19	which I sent unto them by my **s**	5650
	34:11	caused the **s** and the handmaids, whom	5650
	34:11	brought them into subjection for **s** and	5650
	34:16	to be unto you for **s** and for handmaids.	5650
	35:15	I have sent also unto you all my **s**	5650
	36:24	any of his **s** that heard all these words.	5650
	36:31	and his seed and his **s** for their iniquity;	5650
	37: 2	neither he, nor his **s**, nor the people of	5650
	37:18	or against thy **s**, or against this people,	5650
	44: 4	Howbeit I sent unto you all my **s**	5650
	46:26	of Babylon, and into the hand of his **s**:	5650
La	5: 8	**S** have ruled over us: *there is* none that	5650
Eze	38:17	in old time by my **s** the prophets of Israel,	5650
	46:17	a gift of his inheritance to one of his **s**,	5650
Da	1:12	Prove thy, I beseech thee, ten days;	5650
	1:13	and as thou seest, deal with thy **s**.	5650
	2: 4	tell thy **s** the dream, and we will shew	5649
	2: 7	Let the king tell his **s** the dream,	5649
	3:26	ye **s** of the most high God, come forth,	5649
	3:28	delivered his **s** that trusted in him,	5649
	9: 6	Neither have we hearkened unto thy **s**	5650
	9:10	which he set before us by his **s**	5650
Joel	2:29	also upon the **s** and upon the handmaids	5650
Am	3: 7	he revealeth his secret unto his **s**	5650
Mic	6: 4	and redeemed thee out of the house of **s**;	5650
Zec	1: 6	which I commanded my **s** the prophets,	5650
	2: 9	and they shall be a spoil to their **s**:	5647
Mt	13:27	So the **s** of the householder came and	1401
	13:28	The **s** said unto him, Wilt thou then	1401
	14: 2	And said unto his **s**, This is John	3816
	18:23	which would take account of his **s**.	1401
	21:34	he sent his **s** to the husbandmen, that	1401

Mt	21:35	And the husbandmen took his **s**,	1401
	21:36	Again, he sent other **s** moe than the first:	1401
	22: 3	sent forth his **s** to call them that were	1401
	22: 4	Again, he sent forth other **s**, saying,	1401
	22: 6	And the remnant took his **s**,	1401
	22: 8	Then saith he to his **s**, The wedding is	1401
	22:10	So those **s** went out into the *highways*,	1401
	22:13	said the king to the **s**, Bind him hand	1249
	25:14	who called his own **s**, and delivered unto	1401
	25:19	After a long time the lord of those **s**	1401
	26:58	and went in, and sat with the **s**, to see	5257
Mk	1:20	Zebedee in the ship with the **hired s**,	3411
	13:34	and gave authority to his **s**, and to every	1401
	14:54	he sat with the **s**, and warmed himself	5257
	14:65	the **s** did strike him with the palms of	5257
Lk	12:37	Blessed *are* those **s**, whom the lord when	1401
	12:38	and find *them* so, blessed are those **s**.	1401
	15:17	How many hired **s** of my father's have	NIG
	15:19	thy son: make me as one of thy hired **s**.	NIG
	15:22	But the father said to his **s**, Bring forth	1401
	15:26	he called one of the **s**, and asked what	3816
	17:10	say, We are unprofitable **s**:	1401
	19:13	he called his ten **s**, and delivered them	1401
	19:15	he commanded these **s** to be called unto	1401
Jn	2: 5	His mother saith unto the **s**, Whatsoever	1249
	2: 9	(but the **s** which drew the water knew;)	1249
	4:51	his **s** met him, and told *him*, saying,	1401
	15:15	Henceforth I call you not **s**; for the servant	1401
	18:18	the **s** and officers stood *there*, who had	1401
	18:26	One of the **s** of the high priest, being *his*	1401
	18:36	were of this world, then would my **s** fight,	5257
Ac	2:18	And on my **s** and on my handmaidens I	1401
	4:29	grant unto thy **s**, that with all boldness	1401
	10: 7	he called two of his **household s**,	3610
	16:17	men are the **s** of the most high God,	1401
Ro	6:16	to whom ye yield yourselves **s** to obey,	1401
	6:16	to obey, *his* **s** ye are to whom ye obey;	1401
	6:17	that ye were the **s** of sin, but ye have	1401
	6:18	sin, ye became the **s** of righteousness.	1402
	6:19	for as ye have yielded your members **s** to	1401
	6:19	yield your members **s** to righteousness	1401
	6:20	when ye were the **s** of sin, ye were free	1401
	6:22	and become to God, ye have your fruit	1402
1Co	7:23	with a price; be not ye the **s** of men.	1401
2Co	4: 5	and ourselves your **s** for Jesus' sake.	1401
Eph	6: 5	**S**, be obedient to *them that are your*	1401
	6: 6	as the **s** of Christ, doing the will of God	1401
Php	1: 1	Paul and Timotheus, the **s** of Jesus Christ,	1401
Col	3:22	**S**, obey in all *things your* masters	1401
	4: 1	give unto your **s** that which is just and	1401
1Ti	6: 1	Let as many **s** as are under the yoke count	1401
Tit	2: 9	*Exhort* **s** to be obedient unto their own	1401
1Pe	2:16	of maliciousness, but as the **s** of God.	1401
	2:18	**S**, *be* subject to *your* masters with all fear;	3610
2Pe	2:19	they themselves are the **s** of corruption:	1401
Rev	1: 1	to shew unto his **s** *things* which must	1401
	2:20	and to seduce my **s** to commit fornication,	1401
	7: 3	till we have sealed the **s** of our God in	1401
	10: 7	as he hath declared to his **s** the prophets.	1401
	11:18	*thou* shouldest give reward unto thy **s**	1401
	19: 2	avenged the blood of his **s** at her hand.	1401
	19: 5	all ye his **s**, and ye that fear him, both	1401
	22: 3	shall be in it; and his **s** shall serve him:	1401
	22: 6	**s** the *things* which must shortly be done.	1401

SERVANTS' (4) [SERVE]

Ge	46:34	Thy **s** trade hath been about cattle from	5650
Ex	8:24	*into* his **s** houses, and into all the land of	5650
Isa	63:17	Return for thy **s** sake, the tribes of thine	5650
	65: 8	so will I do for my **s** sakes, that *I* may not	5650

SERVE (209) [BONDSERVANT, BONDSERVICE, EYESERVICE, FELLOWSERVANT, FELLOWSERVANTS, MAIDSERVANT, MAIDSERVANT'S, MAIDSERVANTS, MAIDSERVANTS', MANSERVANT, MANSERVANT'S, MANSERVANTS, MENSERVANTS, SERVANT, SERVANT'S, SERVANTS, SERVANTS', SERVED, SERVEDST, SERVEST, SERVETH, SERVICE, SERVILE, SERVING, SERVITOR, SERVITUDE, WOMENSERVANTS]

Ge	15:13	a land *that is* not theirs, and shall **s** them;	5647
	15:14	nation, whom they shall **s**, will I judge:	5647
	25:23	and the elder shall **s** the younger.	5647
	27:29	Let people **s** thee, and nations bow down	5647
	27:40	shalt thou live, and shalt **s** thy brother;	5647
	29:15	shouldest thou therefore **s** me for nought?	5647
	29:18	I will **s** thee seven years for Rachel thy	5647
	29:25	did not I **s** with thee for Rachel?	5647
	29:27	shalt **s** with me yet seven other years.	5647
Ex	1:13	**made** the children of Israel to **s** with	5647
	1:14	their service, wherein they **made** them **s**,	5647
	3:12	ye shall **s** God upon this mountain.	5647
	4:23	thee, Let my son go, that he may **s** me:	5647
	7:16	that they may **s** me in the wilderness:	5647
	8: 1	Let my people go, that they may **s** me.	5647
	8:20	Let my people go, that they may **s** me.	5647
	9: 1	Let my people go, that they may **s** me.	5647
	9:13	Let my people go, that they may **s** me.	5647
	10: 3	Let my people go, that they may **s** me.	5647
	10: 7	that they may **s** the LORD their God:	5647
	10: 8	unto them, Go, **s** the LORD your God:	5647
	10:11	go now ye *that are* men, and **s** the LORD;	5647
	10:24	unto Moses, and said, Go ye, **s** the LORD;	5647
	10:26	for thereof must we take to **s** the LORD	5647

Ex	10:26	we know not with what we must **s**	5647
	12:31	and go, **s** the LORD, as ye have said:	5647
	14:12	us alone, that we may **s** the Egyptians?	5647
	14:12	For *it had been* better for us to **s**	5647
	20: 5	bow down thyself unto them, nor **s** them:	5647
	21: 2	a Hebrew servant, six years he shall **s**:	5647
	21: 6	with an aul; and he shall **s** him for ever.	5647
	23:24	nor **s** them, nor do after their works:	5647
	23:25	ye shall **s** the LORD thy God,	5647
	23:33	for if thou **s** their gods, it will surely be a	5647
Lev	25:39	thou shalt not **compel** him to **s** as	5647+5656
	25:40	*and* shall **s** thee unto the year of jubile:	5647
Nu	4:24	of the Gershonites, to **s**, and for burdens:	5647
	4:26	all that is made for their service: so shall they **s**.	5647
	8:25	the service *thereof*, and shall **s** no more:	5647
	18: 7	altar, and within the vail; and ye shall **s**:	5647
	18:21	for their service which they **s**, *even*	5647
Dt	4:19	be driven to worship them, and **s** them,	5647
	4:28	there ye shall **s** gods, the work of men's	5647
	5: 9	down thyself unto them, nor **s** them:	5647
	6:13	and **s** him, and shalt swear by his name.	5647
	7: 4	following me, that they may **s** other gods:	5647
	7:16	neither shalt thou **s** their gods; for that	5647
	8:19	gods, and **s** them, and worship them,	5647
	10:12	to **s** the LORD thy God with all thy heart	5647
	10:20	him shalt thou **s**, and to him shalt thou	5647
	11:13	to **s** him with all your heart and with all	5647
	11:16	and **s** other gods, and worship them;	5647
	12:30	How did these nations **s** their gods?	5647
	13: 2	thou hast not known, and let us **s** them;	5647
	13: 4	you shall **s** him, and cleave unto him.	5647
	13: 6	saying, Let us go and **s** other gods,	5647
	13:13	saying, Let us go and **s** other gods,	5647
	15:12	be sold unto thee, and **s** thee six years;	5647
	20:11	unto thee, and they shall **s** thee.	5647
	28:14	the left, to go after other gods to **s** them.	5647
	28:36	there shalt thou **s** other gods, wood and	5647
	28:48	Therefore shalt thou **s** thine enemies	5647
	28:64	there thou shalt **s** other gods, which	5647
	29:18	to go *and* **s** the gods of these nations;	5647
	30:17	and worship other gods, and **s** them;	5647
	31:20	**s** them, and provoke me, and break my	5647
Jos	16:10	unto this day, and **s** under tribute.	5647
	22: 5	to **s** him with all your heart and with all	5647
	23: 7	cause to swear *by them*, neither **s** them,	5647
	24:14	and **s** him in sincerity and in truth:	5647
	24:14	and in Egypt; and **s** ye the LORD.	5647
	24:15	if it seem evil unto you to **s** the LORD,	5647
	24:15	choose you *this* day whom ye will **s**;	5647
	24:15	and my house, we will **s** the LORD.	5647
	24:16	should forsake the LORD, to **s** other gods;	5647
	24:18	*therefore* will we also **s** the LORD; for he	5647
	24:19	unto the people, Ye cannot **s** the LORD:	5647
	24:20	**s** strange gods, then he will turn and do	5647
	24:21	Nay; but we will **s** the LORD.	5647
	24:22	ye have chosen you the LORD, to **s** him.	5647
	24:24	The LORD our God will we **s**, and his	5647
Jdg	2:19	in following other gods to **s** them,	5647
	9:28	who *is* Shechem, that we should **s** him?	5647
	9:28	**s** the men of Hamor the father of	5647
	9:28	of Shechem: for why should we **s** him?	5647
	9:38	Who *is* Abimelech, that we should **s** him?	5647
1Sa	7: 3	hearts unto the LORD, and **s** him only:	5647
	10: 7	*that* thou do as **occasion s** thee;	3027+4672
	11: 1	a covenant with us, and we will **s** thee.	5647
	12:10	hand of our enemies, and we will **s** thee.	5647
	12:14	**s** him, and obey his voice, and not rebel	5647
	12:20	but **s** the LORD with all your heart;	5647
	12:24	and **s** him in truth with all your heart:	5647
	17: 9	then shall ye be our servants, and **s** us.	5647
	26:19	of the LORD, saying, Go, **s** other gods.	5647
2Sa	15: 8	*to* Jerusalem, then I will **s** the LORD.	5647
	16:19	whom should I **s**? *should I* not **serve**	5647
	16:19	*should I* not **s** in the presence of his son?	NIH
	22:44	a people *which* I knew not shall **s** me.	5647
1Ki	9: 6	go and **s** other gods, and worship them:	5647
	12: 4	put upon us, lighter, and we will **s** thee.	5647
	12: 7	wilt **s** them, and answer them,	5647
2Ki	10:18	Baal a little; *but* Jehu shall **s** him much.	5647
	17:35	them, nor **s** them, nor sacrifice to them:	5647
	25:24	in the land, and **s** the king of Babylon;	5647
1Ch	28: 9	**s** him with a perfect heart and with a	5647
2Ch	7:19	shall go and **s** other gods,	5647
	10: 4	that he put upon us, and we will **s** thee.	5647
	29:11	to **s** him, and that *you* should minister	8334
	30: 8	**s** the LORD your God, that the fierceness	5647
	33:16	commanded Judah to **s** the LORD God of	5647
	34:33	**made** all that were present in Israel **to s**,	5975
	34:33	to serve, *even* to **s** the LORD their God.	5647
	35: 3	**s** now the LORD your God, and his	5647
Job	21:15	*is* the Almighty, that we should **s** him?	5647
	36:11	**s** *him*, they shall spend their days in	5647
	39: 9	the unicorn be willing to **s** thee,	5647
Ps	2:11	**S** the LORD with fear, and rejoice with	5647
	18:43	a people *whom* I have not known shall **s**	5647
	22:30	A seed shall **s** him; it shall be accounted	5647
	72:11	down before him: all nations shall **s** him.	5647
	97: 7	Confounded be all they that **s** graven	5647
	100: 2	**S** the LORD with gladness: come before	5647
	101: 6	walketh in a perfect way, he shall **s** me.	8334
	102:22	and the kingdoms, to **s** the LORD.	5647
Isa	14: 3	bondage wherein thou wast **made to s**,	5647
	19:23	the Egyptians shall **s** *with* the Assyrians,	5647
	43:23	I have not **caused** thee **to s** with an	5647
	43:24	thou hast **made** me **to s** with thy sins,	5647

Isa 56: 6 to **s** him, and to love the name of 8334
60:12 kingdom that will not **s** thee shall perish; 5647
Jer 5:19 shall ye **s** strangers in a land *that is* not 5647
11:10 and they went after other gods to **s** them: 5647
13:10 gods, to **s** them, and to worship them, 5647
16:13 there shall ye **s** other gods day and night; 5647
17: 4 I will **cause** thee **to s** thine enemies in 5647
25: 6 go not after other gods to **s** them, 5647
25:11 these nations shall **s** the king of Babylon 5647
25:14 great kings shall **s** themselves of them 5647
27: 6 the field have I given him also to **s** him. 5647
27: 7 all nations shall **s** him, and his son, 5647
27: 7 and great kings shall **s** themselves of him. 5647
27: 8 kingdom which will not **s** the same 5647
27: 9 Ye shall not **s** the king of Babylon: 5647
27:11 **s** him, those will I let remain still in their 5647
27:12 and **s** him and his people, and live. 5647
27:13 nation that will not **s** the king of Babylon? 5647
27:14 Ye shall not **s** the king of Babylon: 5647
27:17 them; **s** the king of Babylon, and live: 5647
28:14 that *they* may **s** Nebuchadnezzar king of 5647
28:14 king of Babylon; and they shall **s** him: 5647
30: 8 strangers shall no more **s** themselves of 5647
30: 9 they shall **s** the LORD their God, 5647
34: 9 none should **s** himself of them, *to wit,* 5647
34:10 none should **s** themselves of them any 5647
35:15 go not after other gods to **s** them, 5647
40: 9 saying, Fear not to **s** the Chaldeans: 5647
40: 9 in the land and **s** the king of Babylon, 5647
40:10 I *will* dwell at Mizpah to **s** the Chaldeans, 5975
44: 3 to **s** other gods, whom they knew not, 5647
Eze 20:32 of the countries, to **s** wood and stone. 8334
20:39 **s** ye every one his idols, and hereafter 5647
20:40 of Israel, all of them in the land, **s** me: 5647
29:18 **caused** his army **to s** a great service 5647
48:18 shall be for food unto them that **s** the city. 5647
48:19 they that **s** the city shall serve it out of all 5647
48:19 they that serve the city shall **s** it out of all 5647
Da 3:12 they **s** not thy gods, nor worship the 6399
3:14 and Abed-nego, do not ye **s** my gods, 6399
3:17 our God whom we **s** *is* able to deliver us 6399
3:18 O king, that we will not **s** thy gods, 6399
3:28 they might not **s** nor worship any god, 6399
7:14 and languages, should **s** him: 6399
7:27 and all dominions shall **s** and obey him. 6399
Zep 3: 9 of the LORD, to **s** him *with* one consent. 5647
Mal 3:14 Ye have said, It *is* vain to **s** God: 5647
Mt 4:10 Lord thy God, and him only shalt thou **s**. 3000
6:24 No *man* can **s** two masters: for either he 1398
6:24 Ye cannot **s** God and mammon. 1398
Lk 1:74 of our enemies might **s** him without fear, 3000
4: 8 Lord thy God, and him only shalt thou **s**. 3000
10:40 care that my sister hath left me to **s** alone? 1247
12:37 to meat, and will come forth and **s** them. 1247
15:29 father, Lo, these many years do I **s** thee, 1398
16:13 No servant can **s** two masters: for either 1398
16:13 Ye cannot **s** God and mammon. 1398
17: 8 gird thyself, and **s** me, till I have eaten 1247
22:26 and he that is chief, as he that doth **s**. 1247
Jn 12:26 If any *man* **s** me, let him follow me; 1247
12:26 if any *man* **s** me, him will *my* Father 1247
Ac 6: 2 leave the word of God, and **s** tables. 1247
7: 7 they come forth, and **s** me in this place. 3000
27:23 angel of God, whose I am, and whom I **s**, 3000
Ro 1: 9 whom I **s** with my spirit in the gospel of 3000
6: 6 that henceforth we should not **s** sin. 1398
7: 6 that we should **s** in newness of spirit, 1398
7:25 with the mind I myself **s** the law of God; 1398
9:12 unto her, The elder shall **s** the younger. 1398
16:18 For *they that are* such **s** not our Lord Jesus 1398
Gal 5:13 to the flesh, but by love **s** one another. 1398
Col 3:24 the inheritance: for ye **s** the Lord Christ. 1398
1Th 1: 9 how ye turned to God from idols to **s** 1398
2Ti 1: 3 whom I **s** from *my* forefathers with pure 3000
Heb 8: 5 Who **s** unto the example and shadow of 3000
9:14 from dead works to **s** the living God? 3000
12:28 whereby we may **s** God acceptably with 3000
13:10 whereof they have no right to eat which **s** 3000
Rev 7:15 and **s** him day and night in his temple: 3000
22: 3 shall be in it; and his servants shall **s** him: 3000

SERVED (74) [SERVE]

Ge 14: 4 Twelve years they **s** Chedorlaomer, 5647
29:20 Jacob **s** seven years for Rachel; 5647
29:30 and with him yet seven other years. 5647
30:26 for whom I have **s** thee, and let me go: 5647
30:29 Thou knowest how I have **s** thee, and 5647
31: 6 ye know that with all my power I have **s** 5647
31:41 I **s** thee fourteen years for thy two 5647
39: 4 found grace in his sight, and he **s** him: 8334
40: 4 Joseph with them, and he **s** them: 8334
Dt 12: 2 which ye shall possess **s** their gods, 5647
17: 3 hath gone and **s** other gods, 5647
29:26 For they went and **s** other gods, 5647
Jos 23:16 have gone and **s** other gods, 5647
24: 2 father of Nachor; and they **s** other gods. 5647
24:14 away the gods which your fathers **s** on 5647
24:15 the gods which your fathers **s** that 5647
24:31 Israel **s** the LORD all the days of Joshua, 5647
Jdg 2: 7 the people **s** the LORD all the days of 5647
2:11 in the sight of the LORD, and **s** Baalim: 5647
2:13 the LORD, and **s** Baal and Ashtaroth. 5647
3: 6 daughters to their sons, and **s** their gods. 5647
3: 7 their God, and **s** Baalim and the groves. 5647
3: 8 children of Israel **s** Chushan-rishathaim 5647

Jdg 3:14 the children of Israel **s** Eglon the king of 5647
8: 1 Why hast thou **s** us thus, that *thou* 6213
10: 6 **s** Baalim, and Ashtaroth, and the gods of 5647
10: 6 and forsook the LORD, and **s** not him. 5647
10:10 forsaken our God, and *also* **s** Baalim. 5647
10:13 ye have forsaken me, and **s** other gods: 5647
10:16 gods from among them, and **s** the LORD: 5647
1Sa 7: 4 and Ashtaroth, and **s** the LORD only. 5647
8: 8 **s** other gods, so do they also unto thee. 5647
12:10 and have **s** Baalim and Ashtaroth: 5647
2Sa 16:19 made peace with Israel, and **s** them. 5647
16:19 as I have **s** in thy father's presence, so 5647
1Ki 4:21 and **s** Solomon all the days of his life. 5647
9: 9 and have worshipped them, and **s** them: 5647
16:31 went and **s** Baal, and worshipped him. 5647
22:53 For he **s** Baal, and worshipped him, 5647
2Ki 10:18 and said unto them, Ahab **s** Baal a little; 5647
17:12 For they **s** idols, whereof the LORD had 5647
17:16 all the host of heaven, and **s** Baal. 5647
17:33 feared the LORD, and **s** their own gods, 5647
17:41 their graven images, both their children, 5647
18: 7 against the king of Assyria, and **s** him not. 5647
21: 3 all the host of heaven, and **s** them. 5647
21:21 and **s** the idols that his father **s**, 5647
21:21 and served the idols that his father **s**, 5647
1Ch 19: 5 and told David how the men were **s**. NIH
27: 1 their officers that **s** the king in any matter 8334
2Ch 7:22 and worshipped them, and **s** them: 5647
24:18 of their fathers, and **s** groves and idols: 5647
33: 3 all the host of heaven, and **s** them; 5647
33:22 his father had made, and **s** them; 5647
Ne 9:35 they have not **s** thee in their kingdom, 5647
Est 1:10 the seven chamberlains that **s** in 8334
Ps 106:36 they **s** their idols: which were a snare unto 5647
137: 8 *be,* that rewardeth thee as thou hast **s** us. 1580
Ecc 5: 9 *is* for all: the king *himself* is **s** by the field. 5647
Jer 5:19 strange gods in your land, so shall ye 5647
8: 2 whom they have **s**, and after whom they 5647
16:11 have **s** them, and have worshipped them, 5647
22: 9 and worshipped other gods, and **s** them. 5647
34:14 when he hath **s** thee six years, thou shalt 5647
52:12 **s** the king of Babylon, 5975+6440+3807.1
Eze 29:18 for the service that he had **s** against it: 5647
29:20 *for* his labour wherewith he **s** against it, 5647
34:27 hand of those that **s** themselves of them. 5647
Hos 12:12 Israel **s** for a wife, and for a wife he kept 5647
Lk 2:37 but **s** *God* with fastings and prayers night 3000
Jn 12: 2 they made him a supper; and Martha **s**: 1247
Ac 13:36 after he had **s** his own generation by 5256
Ro 1:25 and **s** the creature more than the Creator, 3000
Php 2:22 father, he hath **s** with me in the gospel. 1398

SERVEDST (1) [SERVE]

Dt 28:47 Because thou **s** not the LORD thy God 5647

SERVEST (2) [SERVE]

Da 6:16 Thy God whom thou **s** continually, 6399
6:20 is thy God, whom thou **s** continually, 6399

SERVETH (9) [SERVE]

Nu 3:36 the vessels thereof, and all that **s** thereto, 5656
Mal 3:17 as a man spareth his own son that **s** him. 5647
3:18 between him that **s** God and *him* that 5647
3:18 that serveth God and *him* that **s** him not. 5647
Lk 22:27 he that sitteth at meat, or he that **s**? 1247
22:27 at meat? but I am among you as he that **s**. 1247
Ro 14:18 For he that in these *things* **s** Christ *is* 1398
1Co 14:22 prophesying **s** not for them that believe not NIG
Gal 3:19 Wherefore then **s** the law? It was added NIG

SERVICE (132) [SERVE]

Ge 29:27 we will give thee this also for the **s** which 5656
30:26 thou knowest my **s** which I have done 5656
Ex 1:14 brick, and in all manner of **s** in the field: 5656
1:14 their **s**, wherein they made them serve, 5656
12:25 hath promised, that ye shall keep this **s**. 5656
12:26 say unto you, What mean you by this **s**? 5656
13: 5 that thou shalt keep this **s** in this month. 5656
27:19 the vessels of the tabernacle in all the **s** 5656
30:16 shalt appoint it for the **s** of the tabernacle 5656
31:10 the clothes of **s**, and the holy garments for 8278
35:19 The clothes of **s**, to do service in the holy 8278
35:19 to do **s** in the holy *place,* the holy 8334
35:21 for all his **s**, and for the holy garments. 5656
35:24 found shittim wood for any work of the **s**, 5656
36: 1 *manner of* work for the **s** of the sanctuary, 5656
36: 3 for the work of the **s** of the sanctuary, 5656
36: 5 more than enough for the **s** of the work, 5656
38:21 *for* the **s** of the Levites, by the hand of 5656
39: 1 and scarlet, they made clothes of **s**, 8278
39: 1 to do **s** in the holy *place,* and made the 8334
39:40 all the vessels of the **s** of the tabernacle, 5656
39:41 The clothes of **s** to do service in the holy 8278
39:41 The clothes of service to do **s** in the holy 8334
Nu 3: 7 to do the **s** of the tabernacle. 5656
3: 8 of Israel, to do the **s** of the tabernacle. 5656
3:26 and the cords of it for all the **s** thereof. 5656
3:31 and the hanging, and all the **s** thereof. 5656
4: 4 This *shall be* the **s** of the sons of Kohath 5656
4:19 appoint them every one to his **s** and to his 5656
4:23 all that enter in to **perform** the **s**, 6633+6635
4:24 This *is* the **s** of the families of the 5656
4:26 all the instruments of their **s**, and all that 5656
4:27 his sons shall be all the **s** of the sons of 5656
4:27 in all their burdens, and in all their **s**: 5656

Nu 4:28 This *is* the **s** of the families of the sons of 5656
4:30 every one that entereth into the **s**, to do 6635
4:31 according to all their **s** in the tabernacle 5656
4:32 all their instruments, and with all their **s**: 5656
4:33 This *is* the **s** of the families of the sons of 5656
4:33 according to all their **s**, in the tabernacle 5656
4:35 old, every one that entereth into the **s**, 6635
4:37 all that *might* **do s** in the tabernacle of 5647
4:39 old, every one that entereth into the **s**, 6635
4:41 of all that *might* **do s** in the tabernacle of 5647
4:43 old, every one that entereth into the **s**, 6635
4:47 every one that came to do the **s** of 5656
4:47 the **s** of the burden in the tabernacle of 5656
4:49 every one according to his **s**, 5656
7: 5 that they may be to do the **s** of 5656
7: 5 to every man according to his **s**. 5656
7: 7 the sons of Gershon, according to their **s**: 5656
7: 8 sons of Merari, according to their **s**, 5656
7: 9 the **s** of the sanctuary belonging unto 5656
8:11 that they may execute the **s** of the LORD. 5656
8:15 that shall the Levites go in to **do the s** 5647
8:19 to do the **s** of the children of Israel in 5656
8:22 that went the Levites in to do their **s** in 5656
8:24 they shall go in to wait upon the **s** 5656
8:25 shall cease waiting upon the **s** *thereof,* 5656
8:26 to keep the charge, and shall do no **s**. 5656
16: 9 to bring you near to himself to do the **s** of 5656
18: 4 for all the **s** of the tabernacle: 5656
18: 6 to do the **s** of the tabernacle of 5656
18: 7 your priest's office *unto you as* a **s** of gift: 5656
18:21 for their **s** which they serve, *even* 5656
18:21 *even* the **s** of the tabernacle of 5656
18:23 the Levites shall do the **s** of the tabernacle 5656
18:31 for it *is* your reward for your **s** in 5656
Jos 22:27 that *we* might do the **s** of the LORD 5656
1Ki 12: 4 make thou the grievous **s** of thy father, 5656
1Ch 6:31 *are they* whom David set over the **s** of 3027
6:48 **s** of the tabernacle of the house of God. 5656
9:13 very able men *for* the work of the **s** of 5656
9:19 Korahites, *were* over the work of the **s**, 5656
23:24 that did the work for the **s** of the house of 5656
23:26 nor any vessels of it for the **s** thereof. 5656
23:28 Aaron for the **s** of the house of the LORD, 5656
23:28 and the work of the **s** of the house of God; 5656
23:32 in the **s** of the house of the LORD. 5656
24: 3 according to their offices in their **s**. 5656
24:19 *were* the orderings of them in their **s** 5656
25: 1 captains of the host separated to the **s** of 5656
25: 1 of the workmen according to their **s** was: 5656
25: 6 and harps, for the **s** of the house of God, 5656
26: 8 able men for strength for the **s**, 5656
26:30 of the LORD, and in the **s** of the king. 5656
28:13 for all the work of the **s** of the house of 5656
28:13 for all the vessels of **s** in the house of 5656
28:14 of **all manner of s**; 5656+5656+2050.1
28:14 of **every kind of s**: 5656+5656+2050.1
28:20 work for the **s** of the house of the LORD. 5656
28:21 *they* shall be with *thee* for all the **s** of 5656
28:21 willing skilful *man,* for any *manner of* **s**: 5656
29: 5 is willing to consecrate his **s** *this* day unto 3027
29: 7 gave for the **s** of the house of God *of* gold 5656
2Ch 8:14 the courses of the priests for their **s**, 5656
12: 8 that they may know my **s**, and the service 5656
12: 8 the **s** of the kingdoms of the countries. 5656
24:12 work of the **s** of the house of the LORD, 5656
29:35 So the **s** of the house of the LORD was set 5656
31: 2 every man according to his **s**, the priests 5656
31:16 daily portion for their **s** in their charges 5656
31:21 in every work that he began in the **s** of 5656
34:13 work in **any manner of s**: 5656+5656+2050.1
35: 2 encouraged them to the **s** of the house of 5656
35:10 the **s** was prepared, and the priests stood 5656
35:15 they might not depart from their **s**; 5656
35:16 So all the **s** of the LORD was prepared 5656
Ezr 6:18 for the **s** of God, which *is* at Jerusalem; 5673
7:19 thee for the **s** of the house of thy God, 6402
8:20 the princes had appointed for the **s** of 5656
Ne 10:32 shekel for the **s** of the house of our God; 5656
Ps 104:14 for the cattle, and herb for the **s** of man: 5656
Jer 22:13 **useth** his neighbour's **s** without wages, 5647
Eze 29:18 his army to serve a great **s** against Tyrus: 5656
29:18 for the **s** that he had served against it: 5656
44:14 for all the **s** thereof, and for all that shall 5656
Jn 16: 2 killeth you will think that he doeth God **s**. 2999
Ro 9: 4 law, and the **s** *of God,* and the promises; 2999
12: 1 unto God, *which is* your reasonable **s**. 2999
15:31 that my **s** which I have for Jerusalem may 1248
2Co 9:12 For the administration of this **s** not only 3009
11: 8 taking wages *of them,* to do you **s**. 1248
Gal 4: 8 ye did **s** unto them which by nature are 1398
Eph 6: 7 With good will **doing s**, as to the Lord, 1398
Php 2:17 upon the sacrifice and **s** of your faith, 3009
2:30 life, to supply your lack of **s** toward me. 3009
1Ti 6: 2 but rather **do them s**, because they are 1398
Heb 9: 1 *covenant* had also ordinances of **divine s**, 2999
9: 6 accomplishing the **s** *of God.* 2999
9: 9 that could not make him that did the **s** 3000
Rev 2:19 I know thy works, and charity, and **s**, 1248

SERVILE (12) [SERVE]

Lev 23: 7 ye shall do no **s** work *therein.* 5656
23: 8 ye shall do no **s** work *therein.* 5656
23:21 ye shall do no **s** work *therein:* it shall be 5656
23:25 Ye shall do no **s** work *therein:* but ye 5656
23:35 ye shall do no **s** work *therein.* 5656

S

Lev 23:36 *and* ye shall do no **s** work *therein.* 5656
Nu 28:18 ye shall do no *manner of* **s** work *therein:* 5656
 28:25 holy convocation; ye shall do no **s** work. 5656
 28:26 holy convocation; ye shall do no **s** work: 5656
 29: 1 holy convocation; ye shall do no **s** work: 5656
 29:12 ye shall do no **s** work, and ye shall keep 5656
 29:35 ye shall do no **s** work *therein:* 5656

SERVING (7) [SERVE]
Ex 14: 5 that we have let Israel go from **s** us? 5647
Dt 15:18 hired servant *to thee*, in **s** thee six years: 5647
Lk 10:40 But Martha was cumbered about much **s**, 1248
Ac 20:19 **S** the Lord with all humility of mind, 1398
 26: 7 instantly **s** *God* day and night, hope to 3000
Ro 12:11 in business; fervent in spirit; **s** the Lord; 1398
Tit 3: 3 deceived, **s** divers lusts and pleasures, 1398

SERVITOR (1) [SERVE]
2Ki 4:43 his **s** said, What, should I set before 8334

SERVITUDE (2) [SERVE]
2Ch 10: 4 ease thou somewhat the grievous **s** of thy 5656
La 1: 3 of affliction, and because of great **s**: 5656

SET (695) [SETTER, SETTEST, SETTETH, SETTING, SETTINGS]
Ge 1:17 God **s** them in the firmament of the 5414
 4:15 the Lord **s** a mark upon Cain, lest any 7760
 6:16 door of the ark shalt thou **s** in the side 7760
 9:13 I do **s** my bow in the cloud, and it shall 5414
 17:21 unto thee at this **s** *time* in the next year. 4150
 18: 8 he had dressed, and **s** *it* before them; 5414
 19:16 him forth, and **s** him without the city. 3240
 21: 2 at the **s** *time* of which God had spoken 4150
 21:28 Abraham **s** seven ewe lambs of the flock 5324
 21:29 lambs which thou hast **s** by themselves? 5324
 24:33 there was **s** *meat* before him to eat: 7760
 28:11 there all night, because the sun was **s**; 935
 28:12 behold a ladder **s** up on the earth, 5324
 28:18 **s** it up *for* a pillar, and poured oil upon 7760
 28:22 this stone, which I have **s** *for* a pillar, 7760
 30:36 he **s** three days' journey betwixt himself 7760
 30:38 he **s** the rods which he had pilled before 3322
 30:40 **s** the faces of the flocks toward 5414
 31:17 and **s** his sons and his wives upon camels; 5375
 31:21 and **s** his face *toward* the mount Gilead. 7760
 31:37 **s** *it* here before my brethren and 7760
 31:45 Jacob took a stone, and **s** it up *for* a pillar. 7311
 35:14 Jacob **s** up a pillar in the place where he 5324
 35:20 Jacob **s** a pillar upon her grave: that *is* 5324
 41:33 wise, and **s** him over the land of Egypt. 7896
 41:41 I have **s** thee over all the land of Egypt. 5414
 43: 9 **s** him before thee, then let me bear 3322
 43:31 refrained himself, and said, **S** on bread. 7760
 43:32 they **s** on for him by himself, and for 7760
 44:21 me, that I may **s** mine eyes upon him. 7760
 47: 7 his father, and **s** him before Pharaoh: 5975
 48:20 and he **s** Ephraim before Manasseh. 7760
Ex 1:11 they did **s** over them taskmasters 7760
 4:20 **s** them upon an ass, and he returned to 7392
 5:14 which Pharaoh's taskmasters had **s** over 7760
 7:23 neither did he **s** his heart to this also. 7896
 9: 5 the Lord appointed a **s** *time*, saying, 4150
 13:12 That thou shalt **s** apart unto the Lord all 5674
 19:12 shalt **s** bounds unto the people round 1379
 19:23 **S** bounds about the mount, and sanctify 1379
 21: 1 judgments which thou shalt **s** before them 7760
 23:31 I will **s** thy bounds from the Red sea even 7896
 25: 7 stones to be **s** in the ephod, and in 4394
 25:30 thou shalt **s** upon the table shewbread 5414
 26:17 board, **s** in order one against another: 7947
 26:35 thou shalt **s** the table without the vail, 7760
 28:11 thou shalt make them to be **s** *in* ouches 5437
 28:17 thou shalt **s** in it settings of stones, 4390
 28:20 they shall be **s** in gold in their inclosings. 7660
 31: 5 to **s** *them*, and in carving of timber, 4390
 32:22 the people, that they *are* **s** on mischief. NIH
 35: 9 stones to be **s** for the ephod, and for 4394
 35:27 stones to be **s**, for the ephod, and for 4394
 35:33 to **s** *them*, and in carving of wood, 4390
 37: 3 of gold, to be **s** by the four corners of it; NIH
 39:10 they **s** in it four rows of stones: *the first* 4390
 39:37 *even with* the lamps to be **s** in order, 4634
 40: 2 **s** up the tabernacle of the tent of 6965
 40: 4 **s** in order the things that are to be set in 6186
 40: 4 things that are to be **s** in order upon it; 6187
 40: 5 shalt **s** the altar of gold for the incense 5414
 40: 6 thou shalt **s** the altar of the burnt offering 5414
 40: 7 thou shalt **s** the laver between the tent of 5414
 40: 8 thou shalt **s** up the court round about, 7760
 40:18 **s** up the boards thereof, and put in the 7760
 40:20 **s** the staves on the ark, and put the mercy 7760
 40:21 **s** up the vail of the covering, 7760
 40:23 he **s** the bread in order upon it 6186+6187
 40:28 he **s** up the hanging at the door of 7760
 40:30 he **s** the laver between the tent of 5414
 40:33 and **s** up the hanging of the court gate. 5414
Lev 17:10 I will even **s** my face against *that* soul that 5414
 20: 3 I will **s** my face against that man, 5414
 20: 5 I will **s** my face against that man, 7760
 20: 6 I will even **s** my face against that soul, 5414
 24: 6 shalt **s** them *in* two rows, six on a row, 7760
 24: 8 Every sabbath he shall **s** it in order 6186
 26: 1 neither shall ye **s** up *any* image of stone 5414
 26:11 I will **s** my tabernacle amongst you: 5414

Lev 26:17 I will **s** my face against you, and ye shall 5414
Nu 1:51 is to be pitched, the Levites shall **s** it **up**: 6965
 2: 9 their armies. *These* shall first **s** forth. 5265
 2:16 And they shall **s** forth in the second rank. 5265
 2:17 **s** forward *with* the camp of the Levites in 5265
 2:17 as they encamp, so shall they **s** forward, 5265
 2:34 so they **s** forward, every one after their 5265
 4:15 sanctuary, as the camp is to **s** forward; 5265
 5:16 her near, and **s** her before the Lord: 5975
 5:18 the priest shall **s** the woman before 5975
 5:30 shall **s** the woman before the Lord, 5975
 7: 1 that Moses had fully **s** up the tabernacle, 6965
 8:13 thou shalt **s** the Levites before Aaron, 5975
 10:17 and the sons of Merari **s** forward, 5265
 10:18 **s** forward according to their armies: 5265
 10:21 the Kohathites **s** forward, bearing 5265
 10:21 *the other* did **s** up the tabernacle against 6965
 10:22 **s** forward according to their armies: 5265
 10:25 camp of the children of Dan **s** forward, 5265
 10:28 to their armies, when they **s** forward. 5265
 10:35 when the ark **s** forward, that Moses said, 5265
 11:24 and **s** them round about the tabernacle. 5975
 21: 8 thee a fiery *serpent*, and **s** it upon a pole: 7760
 21:10 the children of Israel **s** forward, 5265
 22: 1 the children of Israel **s** forward, 5265
 24: 1 but he **s** his face toward the wilderness. 7896
 27:16 all flesh, **s** a man over the congregation, 6485
 27:19 him before Eleazar the priest, and before 5975
 27:22 him before Eleazar the priest, and before 5975
 28:6 shall ordain unto the Lord in your **s** feasts, 4150
Dt 1: 8 Behold, I have **s** the land before you: go 5414
 1:21 the Lord thy God hath **s** the land before 5414
 4: 8 all this law, which I **s** before you *this* day? 5414
 4:44 this *is* the law which Moses **s** before 7760
 7: 7 The Lord did not **s** his *love* upon you, 2836
 11:26 I **s** before you *this* day a blessing and 5414
 11:32 judgments which I **s** before you *this* day. 5414
 14:24 thy God shall choose to **s** his name there, 7760
 16:22 Neither shalt thou **s** thee **up** *any* image; 6965
 17:14 shall say, I will **s** a king over me, 7760
 17:15 Thou shalt **in any wise** *him* king 7760+7760
 17:15 *one* from among thy brethren shalt thou **s** 7760
 17:15 thou mayest not **s** a stranger over thee, 5414
 19:14 which they of old time have **s** in thine 1379
 26: 4 **s** it **down** before the altar of the Lord 3240
 26:10 thou shalt **s** it before the Lord thy God, 3240
 27: 2 that thou shalt **s** up great stones, 6965
 27: 4 *that* ye shall **s** up these stones, which I 6965
 28: 1 that the Lord thy God will **s** thee on high 5414
 28:36 and thy king which thou shalt **s** over thee, 6965
 28:56 which would not adventure to **s** the sole 3322
 30: 1 which I have **s** before thee, and thou shalt 5414
 30:15 I have **s** before thee *this* day life and good, 5414
 30:19 *that* I have **s** before you life and death, 5414
 32: 8 he **s** the bounds of the people according 5324
 32:22 **s** on fire the foundations of the 3857
 32:46 **S** your hearts unto all the words which I 7760
Jos 4: 9 Joshua **s** up twelve stones in the midst of 6965
 6:26 in his youngest *son* shall he **s** up the gates 5324
 8: 8 the city, *that* ye shall **s** the city on fire: 3341
 8:12 **s** them to lie in ambush between Beth-el 7760
 8:13 when they had **s** the people, *even* all 7760
 8:19 took it, and hasted and **s** the city on fire. 3341
 10:18 cave, and **s** men by it for to keep them: 6485
 18: 1 **s** up the tabernacle of the congregation 7931
 24:25 **s** them a statute and an ordinance in 7760
 24:26 stone, and **s** it up there under an oak, 6965
Jdg 1: 8 edge of the sword, and **s** the city on fire. 7971
 6:18 forth my present, and **s** *it* before thee. 3240
 7: 5 dog lappeth, him shalt thou **s** by himself; 3322
 7:19 they had but **newly s** the watch: 6965+6965
 7:22 the Lord **s** every man's sword against 7760
 9:25 men of Shechem **s** liers in wait for him 7760
 9:33 thou shalt rise early, and **s** upon the city: 6584
 9:49 hold, and **s** the hold on fire upon them; 3341
 15: 5 when he had **s** the brands on fire, he let 1197
 16:25 and they **s** him between the pillars. 5975
 18:30 children of Dan **s** up the graven image: 6965
 18:31 they **s** them **up** Micah's graven image, 7760
 20:22 **s** *their* battle again **in array** in the place 6186
 20:29 Israel **s** liers in wait round about Gibeah. 7760
 20:36 in wait which they had **s** beside Gibeah. 7760
 20:48 also they **s** on fire all the cities that they 7971
Ru 2: 5 said Boaz unto his servant that was **s** over 5324
 2: 6 the servant that was **s** over the reapers 5324
1Sa 2: 8 to **s** *them* among princes, and to make 3427
 2: 8 and he hath **s** the world upon them. 7896
 5: 2 the house of Dagon, and **s** it by Dagon. 3322
 5: 3 took Dagon, and **s** him in his place **again**. 7725
 6:18 whereon they **s down** the ark of 3240
 7:12 **s** *it* between Mizpeh and Shen, 7760
 8:12 *will* **s** *them* to ear his ground, and to reap NIH
 9:20 three days ago, **s** not thy mind on them; 7760
 9:23 of which I said unto thee, **S** it by thee. 7760
 9:24 which *was* upon it, and **s** *it* before Saul. 7760
 9:24 which is left; **s** *it* before thee, *and* eat: 7760
 10:19 said unto him, Nay, but **s** a king over us. 7760
 12:13 behold, the Lord hath **s** a king over you. 5414
 13: 8 according to the **s** *time* that Samuel *had* 4150
 15:11 that I have **s** up Saul **to be king**: 4427+4428
 15:12 he **s** him **up** a place, and is gone about, 5324
 17: 2 **s** the battle **in array** against the 6186
 17: 8 are ye come out to **s** *your* battle **in array**? 6186
 18: 5 Saul **s** him over the men of war, and he 7760
 18:30 of Saul; so that his name was much **s** **by**. 3365

1Sa 22: 9 which was **s** over the servants of Saul, 5324
 26:24 thy life was **much s** by this day in mine 1431
 26:24 let my life be **much s** by in the eyes of 1431
 28:22 let me **s** a morsel of bread before thee; 7760
2Sa 3:10 to **s** up the throne of David over Israel 6965
 6: 3 they **s** the ark of God upon a new cart, 7392
 6:17 the ark of the Lord, and **s** it in his place, 3322
 7:12 thy fathers, I will **s** up thy seed after thee, 6965
 10:17 the Syrians **s** **themselves in array** 6186
 11:15 **S** ye Uriah in the forefront of the hottest 3051
 12:20 they **s** bread before him, and he did eat. 7760
 12:30 it was **s** on David's head. And he brought NIH
 14:30 he hath barley there; go and **s** it on fire. 3341
 14:30 And Absalom's servants **s** the field on fire. 3341
 14:31 Wherefore have thy servants **s** my field on 3341
 15:24 they **s down** the ark of God; 3332
 18: 1 **s** captains of thousands and captains of 7760
 18:13 thou thyself wouldest have **s** thyself 3320
 19:28 yet didst thou **s** thy servant among them 7896
 20: 5 he tarried longer than the **s** time which 4150
 23:23 And David **s** him over his guard. 7760
1Ki 2:15 *that* all Israel **s** their faces on me, that *I* 7760
 2:19 **caused** a seat to be **s** for the king's 7760
 2:24 **s** me on the throne of David my father, 3427
 5: 5 I will **s** upon thy throne in thy room, 5414
 6:19 to **s** there the ark of the covenant of 5414
 6:27 **s** the cherubims within the inner house: 5414
 7:16 to **s** upon the tops of the pillars: 5414
 7:21 he **s** up the pillars in the porch of 6965
 7:21 he **s** up the right pillar, and called the 6965
 7:21 he **s** up the left pillar, and called the name 6965
 7:25 the sea *was* **s** above upon them, and all NIH
 7:39 he **s** the sea on the right side of the house 5414
 8:21 I have **s** there a place for the ark, wherein 7760
 9: 6 my statutes which I have **s** before you, 5414
 10: 9 in thee, to **s** thee on the throne of Israel: 5414
 12:29 he **s** the one in Beth-el, and the other put 7760
 14: 4 for his eyes were **s** by reason of his age. 6965
 15: 4 to **s** up his son after him, and to establish 6965
 16:34 **s** up the gates thereof in his youngest *son* 5324
 20:12 **S** *yourselves in array*. And they set 7760
 20:12 Set *yourselves in array*. And they **s** 7760
 21: 9 and **s** Naboth on high among the people: 3427
 21:10 two men, sons of Belial, before him, 3427
 21:12 and **s** Naboth on high among the people. 3427
2Ki 4: 4 and thou shalt **s** aside *that* which *is* full. 5265
 4:10 let us **s** for him there a bed, and a table, 7760
 4:38 **S** on the great pot, and seethe pottage for 8239
 4:43 should I **s** this before an hundred men? 5414
 4:44 So he **s** *it* before them, and they did eat, 5414
 6:22 **s** bread and water before them, that they 7760
 8:12 their strong holds wilt thou **s** on fire, 7971
 10: 3 **s** *him* on his father's throne, and fight for 7760
 12: 4 the money that every man is **s** at, 6187
 12: 9 in the lid of it, and **s** it beside the altar, 5414
 12:17 Hazael **s** his face to go up to Jerusalem. 7760
 17:10 they **s** them **up** images and groves in 5324
 18:23 if thou be able on thy part to **s** riders upon 5414
 20: 1 saith the Lord, **S** thine house in order; 6680
 21: 7 he **s** a graven image of the grove that he 7760
 25:19 of the city he took an officer that was **s** 6496
 25:28 his throne above the throne of the kings 5414
1Ch 6:31 these *are they* whom David **s** over 5975
 9:22 the seer did ordain in their **s** office. 530
 9:26 were in *their* **s** office, and were over 530
 9:31 had the **s** office over the things that were 530
 11:14 they **s** themselves in the midst of *that* 3320
 11:25 three: and David **s** him over his guard. 7760
 16: 1 **s** it in the midst of the tent that David 3322
 19:10 Now when Joab saw that the battle was **s** 6440
 19:11 they **s** *themselves* **in array** against 6186
 19:17 and **s** *the battle* **in array** against them. 6186
 20: 2 in it; and it was **s** upon David's head: NIH
 21:18 **s** up an altar unto the Lord in 6965
 22: 2 he **s** masons to hew wrought stones to 5975
 22:19 Now **s** your heart and your soul to seek 5414
 23: 4 four thousand *were* to **s** forward the 5329
 23:31 moons, and on the **s** feasts, by number, 4150
 29: 2 onyx stones, and *stones* to be **s**, 4394
 29: 3 I have **s** my **affection** to the house of my 7521
2Ch 2:18 he **s** threescore and ten thousand of them 6213
 2:18 overseers to **s** the people **a work**. 5647
 3: 5 and **s** thereon palm trees and chains. 5927
 4: 4 the sea *was* **s** above upon them, and all NIH
 4: 7 **s** *them* in the temple, five on the right 5414
 4:10 he **s** the sea on the right side of the east 5414
 4:19 the tables whereon the shewbread *was* **s**; NIH
 6:10 am **s** on the throne of Israel, as the 3427
 6:13 and had **s** it in the midst of the court: 5414
 7:19 which I have **s** before you, and shall go 5414
 9: 8 which delighted in thee to **s** thee on his 5414
 11:16 their hearts to seek the Lord God of 5414
 13: 3 Abijah **s** the battle **in array** with an army 631
 13: 3 Jeroboam also **s** the battle **in array** against 6186
 13:11 the *shewbread* also **s** *they* in order upon NIH
 14:10 they **s** the battle **in array** in the valley of 6186
 17: 2 **s** garrisons in the land of Judah, and in 5414
 19: 5 he **s** judges in the land throughout all 5975
 19: 8 Moreover in Jerusalem did Jehoshaphat **s** 5975
 20: 3 himself to seek the Lord, 5414
 20:17 Ye shall not need to fight in this *battle:* **s** 3320
 20:22 the Lord **s** ambushments against 5414
 23:10 he **s** all the people, every man having his 5975
 23:14 of hundreds that were **s over** the host, 6485
 23:19 he **s** the porters at the gates of the house 5975

S

2Ch 23:20	s the king upon the throne of the	3427
24: 8	s it without at the gate of the house of	5414
24:13	they s the house of God in his state,	5975
25:14	s them **up** to be his gods, and bowed	5975
29:25	he s the Levites *in* the house of the LORD	5975
29:35	of the house of the LORD was s **in order**.	3559
31: 3	for the new moons, and for the s **feasts**,	4150
31:15	in the cities of the priests, in *their* s **office**,	530
31:18	for in their s **office** they sanctified	530
32: 6	he s captains of war over the people,	5414
33: 7	he s a carved image, the idol which he	7760
33:19	s **up** groves and graven images, before he	5975
34:12	son of the Kohathites, to s *it* forward;	5329
35: 2	he s the priests in their charges,	5975
Ezr 2:68	the house of God to s it **up** in his place:	5975
3: 3	they s the altar upon his bases; for fear	3559
3: 5	of all the s **feasts** of the LORD that were	4150
3: 8	to s **forward** the work of the house of	5329
3: 9	to s **forward** the workmen in the house	5329
3:10	they s the priests in their apparel with	5975
4:10	s in the cities of Samaria, and the rest	3488
4:12	have s **up** the walls *thereof* and joined	3635
4:13	walls s **up** *again, then* will they not pay	3635
4:16	builded *again,* and the walls thereof s **up**,	3635
5:11	a great king of Israel builded and s **up**.	3635
6:11	being s **up**, let him be hanged thereon;	2211
6:18	And they s the priests in their divisions,	6966
7:25	*is* in thine hand, s magistrates and judges,	4483
9: 9	s **up** the house of our God, and to repair	7311
Ne 1: 9	that I have chosen to s my name there.	7931
2: 6	the king to send me; and I s him a time.	5414
3: 1	sanctified it, and s **up** the doors of it;	5975
3: 3	s **up** the doors thereof, the locks thereof,	5975
3: 6	s **up** the doors thereof, and the locks	5975
3:13	they built it, and s **up** the doors thereof,	5975
3:14	he built it, and s **up** the doors thereof,	5975
3:15	covered it, and s **up** the doors thereof,	5975
4: 9	s a watch against them day and night,	5975
4:13	Therefore s I in the lower places behind	5975
4:13	I even s the people after *their* families	5975
5: 7	And I s a great assembly against them.	5414
6: 1	(though at that time I had not s **up**	5975
7: 1	I had s **up** the doors, and the porters and	5975
9:37	unto the kings whom thou hast s over us	5414
10:33	for the s **feasts**, and for the holy *things,*	4150
13:11	them together, and s them in their place.	5975
13:19	*some* of my servants I s at the gates,	5975
Est 2:17	that he s the royal crown upon her head,	7760
3: 1	s his seat above all the princes that *were*	7760
6: 8	the crown royal which is s upon his head:	5414
8: 2	Esther s Mordecai over the house of	7760
Job 5:11	To s **up** on high those that be low;	7760
6: 4	terrors of God do s *themselves* **in array**	6186
7:17	thou shouldest s thine heart upon him?	7896
7:20	hast thou s me as a mark against thee,	7760
9:19	who shall s me a **time** *to* plead?	3259
14:13	that thou wouldest appoint me a **time**,	2706
16:12	me to pieces, and s me **up** for his mark.	6965
19: 8	and he hath s darkness in my paths.	7760
30: 1	to have s with the dogs of my flock.	7896
30:13	my path, they s **forward** my calamity,	3276
33: 5	*if* thy words **in order** before me, stand up.	6186
34:14	If he s his heart upon *man, if* he gather	7760
34:24	number, and s others in their stead.	5975
36:16	*that* which should be s on thy table	5183
38:10	my decreed *place,* and s bars and doors,	7760
38:33	canst thou s the dominion thereof in	7760
Ps 2: 2	The kings of the earth s themselves,	3320
2: 6	Yet have I s my king upon my holy hill of	5258
3: 6	that have s *themselves* against me round	7896
4: 3	know that the LORD hath s **apart** *him*	6395
8: 1	who hast s thy glory above the heavens.	5414
10: 8	his eyes are s **privily** against the poor.	6845
12: 5	will s *him* in safety *from him that* puffeth	7896
16: 8	I have s the LORD always before me:	7737
17:11	they have s their eyes bowing down to	7896
19: 4	In them hath he s a tabernacle for the sun	7760
20: 5	of our God we will s **up** *our* **banners**:	1713
27: 5	he hide me; he shall s me **up** upon a rock.	7311
31: 8	thou hast s my feet in a large room.	5975
40: 2	s my feet upon a rock, *and* established my	6965
50:21	and s *them* **in order** before thine eyes.	6186
54: 3	they have not s God before them. Selah.	7760
57: 4	I lie *even* among them that are s **on fire**,	3857
62:10	s not *your* heart *upon them.*	7896
69:29	thy salvation, O God, s me **up** on high.	7682
73: 9	They s their mouth against the heavens,	8371
73:18	thou didst s them in slippery *places:*	7896
74: 4	s **up** their ensigns *for* signs.	7760
74:17	Thou hast s all the borders of the earth:	5324
78: 7	That they might s their hope in God,	7760
78: 8	a generation *that* s not their heart **aright**,	3559
85:13	and shall s **us** in the way of his steps.	7760
86:14	my soul; and have not s thee before them.	7760
89:25	I will s his hand also in the sea,	7760
89:42	Thou hast s **up** the right hand of his	7311
90: 8	Thou hast s our iniquities before thee,	7896
91:14	Because he hath s his **love** upon me,	2836
91:14	I will s him **on high**, because he hath	7682
101: 3	I will s no wicked thing before mine eyes:	7896
102:13	to favour her, yea, the s **time**, is come.	4150
104: 9	Thou hast s a bound *that* they may not	7760
109: 6	S thou a wicked *man* over him:	6485
113: 8	That *he* may s *him* with princes, *even*	3427
118: 5	answered me, *and* s me in a large place.	NIH

Ps 122: 5	For there are s thrones of judgment,	3427
132:11	Of the fruit of thy body will I s upon thy	7896
140: 5	by the way side; they have s grins for me.	7896
141: 2	Let my prayer be s **forth** before thee as	3559
141: 3	S a watch, O LORD, before my mouth;	7896
Pr 1:25	ye have s at nought all my counsel,	6544
8:23	I was s **up** from everlasting, from	5258
8:27	when he s a compass upon the face of	2710
22:28	landmark, which thy fathers have s.	6213
23: 5	Wilt thou s thine eyes upon that which is	5774
Ecc 3:11	also he hath s the world in their heart,	5414
7:14	God also hath s the one over against	6213
8:11	the heart of the sons of men is **fully** s in	4390
10: 6	Folly is s in great dignity, and the rich sit	5414
12: 9	out, *and* s **in order** many proverbs.	8626
SS 5:12	of waters, washed with milk, *and* fitly s.	3427
5:14	hands *are as* gold rings s with the beryl:	4390
5:15	of marble, s upon sockets of fine gold:	3245
7: 2	thy belly *is like* a heap of wheat s **about**	5473
8: 6	S me as a seal upon thine heart, as a seal	7760
Isa 3:24	instead of **well** s **hair** baldness;	4639+4748
7: 6	s a king in the midst of it, *even*	4427+4428
9:11	Therefore the LORD shall s **up**	7682
11:11	*that* the Lord shall s his hand **again**	3254
11:12	he shall s **up** an ensign for the nations,	5375
14: 1	Israel, and s them in their own land:	3240
17:10	and shalt s it *with* strange slips:	2232
19: 2	will s the Egyptians against the Egyptians:	5526
21: 6	Go, s a watchman, let him declare what	5975
21: 8	and I am s in my ward whole nights:	5324
22: 7	shall s themselves **in array**	7896+7896
22:13	they s **up** the towers thereof, they raised	6965
27: 4	who would s the briers *and* thorns against	5414
27:11	the women come, *and* s them **on fire**:	215
36: 8	if thou be able on thy part to s riders	5414
38: 1	s saith the LORD, S thine house **in order**:	6680
41:19	I will s in the desert the fir tree,	7760
42: 4	till he have s judgment in the earth:	7760
42:25	it hath s him **on fire** round about, yet he	3857
44: 7	shall declare it, and s it **in order** for me,	6186
45:20	have no knowledge that s **up** the wood	5375
46: 7	and s him in his place, and he standeth;	3240
49:22	and s **up** my standard to the people:	7311
50: 7	therefore have I s my face like a flint,	7760
57: 7	and high mountain hast thou s thy bed:	7760
57: 8	posts hast thou s **up** thy remembrance:	7760
62: 6	I have s watchmen upon thy walls,	6485
66:19	I will s a sign among them, and I will	7760
Jer 1:10	I have this day s thee over the nations	6485
1:15	they shall s every one his throne *at*	5414
4: 6	S **up** the standard toward Zion: retire,	5375
5:26	snares; they s a trap, they catch men.	5324
6: 1	and s **up** a sign of fire in Beth-haccerem:	5375
6:17	Also I s watchmen over you,	6965
6:23	s **in array** as men for war against thee,	6186
6:27	have s thee *for* a tower *and* a fortress	5414
7:12	where I s my name at the first, and see	7931
7:30	have s their abominations in the house	7760
9:13	forsaken my law which I s before them,	5414
10:20	tent any more, and to s **up** my curtains.	6965
11:13	have ye s **up** altars to *that* shameful thing,	7760
21: 8	I s before you the way of life, and the way	5414
21:10	For I have s my face against this city for	7760
23: 4	I will s **up** shepherds over them which	6965
24: 1	two baskets of figs *were* s before	3259
24: 6	I will s mine eyes upon them for good,	7760
26: 4	in my law, which I have s before you,	5414
31:21	S thee **up** waymarks, make thee high	5324
31:21	s thine heart toward the highway, *even*	7896
31:29	and the children's teeth are s **on edge**.	6949
31:30	sour grape, his teeth shall be s **on edge**.	6949
32:20	Which hast s signs and wonders in the	7760
32:29	shall come and s fire **on** this city,	3341
32:34	they s their abominations in the house,	7760
34:16	whom ye had s at liberty at their pleasure,	7971
35: 5	s before the sons of the house of	5414
38:22	Thy friends have s thee, **on**,	5496
40:11	that he had s over them Gedaliah the son	6485
42:15	If ye **wholly** s your faces to enter	7760+7760
42:17	So shall it be with all the men that s their	7760
43:10	will s his throne upon these stones that I	7760
44:10	I s before you and before your fathers.	5414
44:11	I will s my face against you for evil,	7760
44:12	that have s their faces to go *into* the land	7760
49:38	I will s my throne in Elam, and will	7760
50: 2	and publish, and s **up** a standard;	5375
50: 9	they shall s *themselves* **in array** against	6186
51:12	S **up** the standard upon the walls of	5375
51:12	s **up** the watchmen, prepare the	6965
51:27	S ye **up** a standard in the land, blow	5375
52:32	s his throne above the throne of the kings	5414
La 2:17	hath s **up** the horn of thine adversaries.	7311
3: 6	hath s me in dark places, as they that be	3427
3:12	bow, and s me as a mark for the arrow.	5324
Eze 2: 2	s me upon my feet, that I heard him that	5975
3:24	s me upon my feet, and spake with me,	5975
4: 2	s the camp also against it, and set	5414
4: 2	s *battering* rams against it round about.	7760
4: 3	s it *for* a wall of iron between thee and	5414
4: 3	s thy face against it, and it shall be	3559
4: 7	Therefore thou shalt s thy face toward	3559
5: 1	I have s it in the midst of the nations and	7760
6: 2	s thy face towards the mountains of Israel,	7760
7:20	beauty of his ornament, he s it in majesty:	7760
7:20	therefore have I s it far from them.	5414

Eze 9: 4	s a mark upon the foreheads of	8420+8427
12: 6	for I have s thee *for* a sign unto the house	5414
13:17	s thy face against the daughters of thy	7760
14: 3	these men have s their idols in their	5927
14: 8	I will s my face against that man,	5414
15: 7	I will s my face against them; they shall	5414
15: 7	when I s my face against them.	7760
16:18	thou hast s mine oil and mine incense	5414
16:19	thou hast even s it before them for a	5414
17: 4	of traffick; he s it in a city of merchants.	7760
17: 5	by great waters, *and* s it *as* a willow tree.	7760
17:22	will s *it;* I will crop off from the top of his	5414
18: 2	and the children's teeth are s **on edge**?	6949
19: 8	the nations s against him on every side	5414
20:46	s thy face toward the south, and drop *thy*	7760
21: 2	s thy face toward Jerusalem, and drop *thy*	7760
21:15	I have s the point of the sword against all	5414
21:16	on the left, whithersoever thy face *is* s.	3259
22: 7	In thee have they s **light** by father and	7043
22:10	her that was s **apart** for pollution.	5079
23:24	which shall s against thee buckler and	7760
23:24	I will s judgment before them,	5414
23:25	I will s my jealousy against thee,	5414
23:41	whereupon thou hast s mine incense and	7760
24: 2	the king of Babylon s himself against	5564
24: 3	S on a pot, set *it* on, and also pour water	8239
24: 3	a pot, s *it* on, and also pour water into it:	8239
24: 7	she s it upon the top of a rock; she poured	7760
24: 8	I have s her blood upon the top of a rock,	5414
24:11	it empty upon the coals thereof, that	5975
24:25	that whereupon they s their minds,	4853
25: 2	s thy face against the Ammonites,	7760
25: 4	they shall s their palaces in thee,	3427
26: 9	shall s engines of war against thy walls,	5414
26:20	shall s thee in the low parts of the earth,	3427
26:20	I shall s glory in the land of the living;	5414
27:10	in thee; they s **forth** thy comeliness.	5414
28: 2	though thou s thine heart as the heart of	5414
28: 6	thou hast s thine heart as the heart	5414
28:14	I have s thee *so:* thou wast upon the holy	5414
28:21	s thy face against Zidon,	7760
29: 2	s thy face against Pharaoh king of Egypt,	7760
30: 8	when I have s a fire in Egypt, and *when*	5414
30:14	will s fire in Zoan, and will execute	5414
30:16	I will s fire in Egypt: Sin shall have great	5414
31: 4	deep s him **up on high** with his rivers	7311
32: 8	s darkness upon thy land, saith the Lord	5414
32:23	Whose graves are s in the sides of the pit,	5414
32:25	They have s her a bed in the midst of	5414
33: 2	coasts, and s him for their watchman:	5414
33: 7	I have s thee a watchman unto the house	5414
34:23	I will s **up** one shepherd over them,	6965
35: 2	s thy face against mount Seir,	7760
37: 1	s me **down** in the midst of the valley	5117
37:26	will s my sanctuary in the midst of them	5414
38: 2	Son of man, s thy face against Gog,	7760
39: 9	shall s **on fire** and burn the weapons,	1197
39:15	bone, then shall he s **up** a sign by it,	1129
39:21	I will s my glory among the heathen,	5414
40: 2	s me upon a very high mountain, by	5117
40: 4	s thine heart upon all that I shall shew	7760
44: 8	ye have s keepers of my charge in my	7760
Da 1:11	the prince of the eunuchs had s over	4487
2:44	shall the God of heaven s **up** a kingdom,	6966
2:49	he s Shadrach, Meshach, and Abed-nego,	4483
3: 1	he s it **up** in the plain of Dura,	6966
3: 2	Nebuchadnezzar the king had s **up**,	6966
3: 3	that Nebuchadnezzar the king had s **up**;	6966
3: 3	image that Nebuchadnezzar had s **up**.	6966
3: 5	that Nebuchadnezzar the king hath s **up**:	6966
3: 7	that Nebuchadnezzar the king had s **up**.	6966
3:12	There are certain Jews whom thou hast s	4483
3:12	the golden image which thou hast s **up**.	6966
3:14	the golden image which I have s **up**?	6966
3:18	the golden image which thou hast s **up**.	6966
5:19	whom he would he s **up**; and whom he	7313
6: 1	It pleased Darius to s over the kingdom	6966
6: 3	the king thought to s him over the whole	6966
6:14	and s *his* heart on Daniel to deliver him:	7761
7:10	the judgment was s, and the books were	3488
8:18	but he touched me, and s me upright.	5975
9: 3	I s my face unto the Lord God, to seek *by*	5414
9:10	which he s before us by his servants	5414
10:10	which s me upon my knees and *upon*	5128
10:12	from the first day that thou didst s thine	5414
10:15	I s my face toward the ground,	5414
11:11	he shall s **forth** a great multitude;	5975
11:13	shall s **forth** a multitude greater than	5975
11:17	He shall also s his face to enter with	7760
12:11	abomination that maketh desolate s **up**,	5414
Hos 2: 3	s her as *in* the day that she was born,	3322
2: 3	s her like a dry land, and slay her with	7896
4: 8	and they s their heart on their iniquity.	5375
6:11	O Judah, he hath s a harvest for thee,	7896
8: 1	*S* the trumpet to thy mouth. *He shall*	NIH
8: 4	They have s **up** kings, but not by me:	4427
11: 8	*how* shall I s thee as Zeboim? mine heart	7760
Joel 2: 5	as a strong people s **in** battle **array**.	6186
Am 7: 8	I *will* s a plumbline in the midst of my	7760
8: 5	the sabbath, that we may s **forth** wheat,	6605
9: 4	I will s mine eyes upon them for evil,	7760
Ob 1: 4	though *thou* s thy nest among the stars,	7760
Na 3: 6	vile, and will s thee as a gazing-stock.	7760
3:13	the gates of thy land shall be s **wide** open	6605
Hab 2: 1	s me upon the tower, and will watch to	3320

S

Hab	2: 9 that he may **s** his nest on high, that *he*	7760
Zec	3: 5 Let them **s** a fair mitre upon his head.	7760
	3: 5 So they **s** a fair mitre upon his head,	7760
	5:11 and **s** there upon her own base.	3240
	6:11 **s** them upon the head of Joshua the son	7760
	8:10 for I **s** all men every one against his	7971
Mal	3:15 yea, they that work wickedness are **s up**;	1129
Mt	5: 1 when he was **s**, his disciples came unto	2523
	5:14 A city that is **s** on a hill cannot be hid.	2749
	10:35 For I am come to **s** a man **at variance**	1369
	18: 2 unto *him*, and **s** him in the midst of them.	2476
	21: 7 their clothes, and they **s** *him* thereon.	1940
	25:33 he shall **s** the sheep on his right hand,	2476
	27:19 he was **s down** on the judgment seat,	2521
	27:37 And **s up** over his head his accusation	2007
Mk	1:32 And at even, when the sun did **s**,	1416
	4:21 a bed? *and* not to be **s** on a candlestick?	2007
	6:41 *them* to his disciples to **s before** them;	3908
	8: 6 gave to his disciples to **s before** *them*;	3908
	8: 6 and they did **s** *them* **before** the people.	3908
	8: 7 commanded to **s** them also **before** them.	3908
	9:12 suffer many *things*, and be **s at nought**;	1847
	9:36 a child, and **s** him in the midst of them:	2476
	12: 1 **s** a hedge **about** *it*, and digged **a place**	4060
Lk	1: 1 **s forth in order** a declaration of those	392
	2:34 this *child* is **s** for the fall and rising again	2749
	4: 9 **s** him on a pinnacle of the temple,	2476
	4:18 to **s at liberty** *them that are bruised*,	649
	7: 8 For I also am a man **s** under authority,	5021
	9:16 gave to the disciples to **s before**	3908
	9:47 heart, took a child, and **s** him by him,	2476
	9:51 he **stedfastly s** his face to go to Jerusalem	4741
	10: 8 eat such things as are **s before** you:	3908
	10:34 and **s** him **on** his own beast,	1913
	11: 6 and I have nothing to **s before** him:	3908
	19:35 the colt, and they **s** Jesus **thereon**.	1913
	22:55 were **s down together**, Peter sat down	4776
	23:11 with his men of war **s** him **at nought**,	1848
Jn	2: 6 And there were **s** there six waterpots of	2749
	2:10 Every man at the beginning doth **s forth**	5087
	3:33 hath **s** to *his* seal that God is true.	4972
	6:11 the disciples to them that were **s down**;	345
	8: 3 and when they had **s** her in the midst,	2476
	13:12 was **s down** again, he said unto them,	377
	19:29 Now there was a vessel full of vinegar:	2749
Ac	4: 7 And when they had **s** them in the midst,	2476
	4:11 This is the stone which was **s at nought**	1848
	5:27 they **s** them before the council:	2476
	6: 6 Whom they **s before** the apostles:	2476
	6:13 And **s up** false witnesses, which said,	2476
	7: 5 in it, no, not so much as to **s** his foot **on**:	968
	7:26 **s** them **at one** *again*, saying,	1515+1519+4900
	12:21 And upon a **s** day Herod, arrayed in royal	5002
	13: 9 with the Holy Ghost, **s** his **eyes** on him,	816
	13:47 *saying*, I have **s** thee to be a light of	5087
	15:16 again the ruins thereof, and I will **s** it **up**:	461
	16:34 **s meat before** *them*, and rejoiced,	3908+5132
	17: 5 and **s** all the city **on an uproar**,	2350
	18:10 and no *man* shall **s** on thee to hurt thee:	2007
	19:27 our craft is in danger to be **s at nought**;	2064
	21: 2 Phenicia, we went aboard, and **s forth**.	321
	22:30 Paul down, and **s** *him* before them.	2476
	23:24 they may **s** Paul on, and bring him safe	1913
	26:32 This man might have been **s at liberty**	630
Ro	3:25 God hath **s forth** *to be* a propitiation	4388
	14:10 why dost thou **s at nought** thy brother?	1848
1Co	4: 9 For I think that God hath **s forth** us	584
	6: 4 **s** them **to judge** who are least esteemed	2523
	10:27 whatsoever is **s before** you, eat, asking	3908
	11:34 the rest will I **s in order** when I come.	1299
	12:18 now hath God **s** the members every one	5087
	12:28 And God hath **s** some in the church,	5087
Gal	3: 1 Jesus Christ hath been **evidently s forth**,	4270
Eph	1:20 **s** him at his own right hand in the	2523
Php	1:17 knowing that I am **s** for the defence of	2749
Col	3: 2 **S** your **affection on** *things* above, not on	5426
Tit	1: 5 that thou shouldest **s in order** the *things*	1930
Heb	2: 7 didst **s** him over the works of thy hands;	2525
	6:18 to lay hold upon the hope **s before** *us*:	4295
	8: 1 who is **s** on the right hand of the throne	2523
	12: 1 with patience the race that is **s before** us,	4295
	12: 2 who for the joy that was **s before** him	4295
	12: 2 is **s down** at the right hand of the throne	2523
	13:23 ye that *our* brother Timothy is **s at liberty**;	630
Jas	3: 6 course of nature; and it is **s on** fire of hell.	5394
Jude	1: 7 strange flesh, are **s forth for** an example,	4295
Rev	3: 8 I have **s** before thee an open door, and no	1325
	3:21 am **s down** with my Father in his throne.	2523
	4: 2 a throne was **s** in heaven, and one sat on	2749
	10: 2 and he **s** his right foot upon the sea,	5087
	20: 3 and shut him up, and **s a seal** upon him,	4972

SETH (8) [SHETH]

Ge	4:25 she bare a son, and called his name **S**:	8352
	4:26 to **S**, to him also there was born a son;	8352
	5: 3 after his image; and called his name **S**.	8352
	5: 4 the days of Adam after he had begotten **S**	8352
	5: 6 **S** lived an hundred and five years,	8352
	5: 7 **S** lived after he begat Enos eight hundred	8352
	5: 8 all the days of **S** were nine hundred	8352
Lk	3:38 *the son* of Enos, which was *the son* of **S**,	4589

SETHUR (1)

Nu	13:13 the tribe of Asher, **S** the son of Michael.	5639

SETTER (1) [SET]

Ac	17:18 other *some*, He seemeth to be a **s forth** of	2604

SETTEST (7) [SET]

Dt	23:20 **s** thine hand to in the land whither thou	4916
	28: 8 and in all that thou **s** thine hand **unto**;	4916
	28:20 all that thou **s** thine hand **unto** for to do,	4916
Job	7:12 or a whale, that thou **s** a watch over me?	7760
	13:27 thou **s** a print upon the heels of my feet.	2707
Ps	21: 3 thou **s** a crown of pure gold on his head.	7896
	41:12 and **s** me before thy face for ever.	5324

SETTETH (22) [SET]

Nu	1:51 the tabernacle **s forward**, the Levites	5265
	4: 5 when the camp **s forward**, Aaron shall	5265
Dt	24:15 for he *is* poor, and **s** his heart upon it:	5375
	27:16 Cursed *be* he that **s light** by his father or	7034
2Sa	22:34 feet: and **s** me upon my high places.	5975
Job	28: 3 He **s** an end to darkness, and searcheth	7760
Ps	18:33 feet, and **s** me upon my high places.	5975
	36: 4 He **s** himself in a way *that is* not good;	3320
	65: 6 by his strength **s fast** the mountains;	3559
	68: 6 God **s** the solitary in families: he bringeth	3427
	75: 7 he putteth down one, and **s up** another.	7311
	83:14 and as the flame **s** the mountains **on fire**;	3857
	107:41 Yet **s** he the poor **on high** from affliction,	7682
Jer	5:26 men: they lay wait, as he that **s** snares;	7918
	43: 3 Baruch the son of Neriah **s** thee **on**	5496
Eze	14: 4 Every man of the house of Israel that **s up**	5927
	14: 7 **s up** his idols in his heart, and putteth	5927
Da	2:21 he removeth kings, and **s up** kings:	6966
	4:17 will, and **s up** over it the basest of men.	6966
Mt	4: 5 and **s** him on a pinnacle of the temple,	2476
Lk	8:16 but **s** *it* on a candlestick, that they	2007
Jas	3: 6 and **s on fire** the course of nature;	5394

SETTING (3) [SET]

Eze	43: 8 In their **s** of their threshold by my	5414
Mt	27:66 sealing the stone, and **s** a watch.	3326
Lk	4:40 Now when the sun was **s**, all they that	1416

SETTINGS (1) [SET]

Ex	28:17 thou shalt set in it **s** of stones, *even* four	4396

SETTLE (10) [SETTLED, SETTLEST]

1Ch	17:14 I will **s** him in mine house and in my	5975
Eze	36:11 I will **s** you after your old estates,	3427
	43:14 *even* to the lower **s** *shall be* two cubits,	5835
	43:14 from the lesser settle *even* to the greater	5835
	43:14 from the lesser settle *even* to the greater **s**	5835
	43:17 the **s** *shall be* fourteen *cubits* long and	5835
	43:20 on the four corners of the **s**, and upon	5835
	45:19 upon the four corners of the **s** of the altar,	5835
Lk	21:14 **S** it therefore in your hearts, not to	5087
1Pe	5:10 you perfect, stablish, strengthen, **s** *you*.	2311

SETTLED (7) [SETTLE]

1Ki	8:13 a **s place** for thee to abide in for ever.	4349
2Ki	8:11 he **s** his countenance stedfastly, until *he*	5975
Ps	119:89 O LORD, thy word *is* **s** in heaven.	5324
Pr	8:25 Before the mountains were **s**, before	2883
Jer	48:11 he hath **s** on his lees, and hath not been	8252
Zep	1:12 punish the men that are **s** on their lees:	7087
Col	1:23 if ye continue in the faith grounded and **s**,	1476

SETTLEMENT See HABITATION

SETTLEST (1) [SETTLE]

Ps	65:10 *thou* **s** the furrows thereof: thou makest it	5181

SEVEN (463) [SEVENFOLD, SEVENS, SEVENTH]

Ge	5: 7 he begat Enos eight hundred and **s** years,	7651
	5:25 lived an hundred eighty and **s** years,	7651
	5:26 Methuselah lived after he begat Lamech **s**	7651
	5:31 all the days of Lamech were **s** hundred	7651
	5:31 were seven hundred seventy and **s** years:	7651
	7: 4 For yet **s** days, *and* I will cause it to rain	7651
	7:10 came to pass after **s** days, that the waters	7651
	8:10 he stayed yet other **s** days; and again he	7651
	8:12 he stayed yet other **s** days; and sent forth	7651
	8:14 on the **s** and twentieth day of the month,	7651
	11:21 he begat Serug two hundred and **s** years,	7651
	21:28 Abraham set **s** ewe lambs of the flock by	7651
	21:29 What *mean* these **s** ewe lambs which	7651
	21:30 For *these* **s** ewe lambs shalt thou take of	7651
	23: 1 an hundred and **s** and twenty years old:	7651
	25:17 an hundred and thirty and **s** years:	7651
	29:18 I will serve thee **s** years for Rachel thy	7651
	29:20 Jacob served **s** years for Rachel;	7651
	29:27 shalt serve with me yet **s** other years.	7651
	29:30 and served with him yet **s** other years.	7651
	31:23 and pursued after him **s** days' journey;	7651
	33: 3 and bowed himself to the ground **s** times,	7651
	41: 2 there came up out of the river **s** well	7651
	41: 3 **s** other kine came up after them out of	7651
	41: 4 leanfleshed kine did eat up the **s** well	7651
	41: 5 **s** ears of corn came up upon one stalk,	7651
	41: 6 **s** thin ears and blasted with the east wind	7651
	41: 7 the **s** thin ears devoured the seven rank	NIH
	41: 7 the seven thin ears devoured the **s** rank	7651
	41:18 there came up out of the river **s** kine,	7651
	41:19 **s** other kine came up after them, poor	7651
	41:20 ill favoured kine did eat up the first **s** fat	7651
	41:22 **s** ears came up in one stalk, full and good:	7651
	41:23 **s** ears, withered, thin, *and* blasted with	7651
	41:24 the thin ears devoured the **s** good ears:	7651

Ge	41:26 The **s** good kine *are* seven years;	7651
	41:26 The seven good kine *are* seven years;	7651
	41:26 and the **s** good ears *are* seven years:	7651
	41:26 and the seven good ears *are* **s** years:	7651
	41:27 **s** thin and ill favoured kine that came up	7651
	41:27 kine that came up after them *are* **s** years,	7651
	41:27 the **s** empty ears blasted with the east	7651
	41:27 the east wind shall be **s** years of famine.	7651
	41:29 there come **s** years of great plenty	7651
	41:30 there shall arise after them **s** years of	7651
	41:34 the land of Egypt in the **s** plenteous years.	7651
	41:36 to the land against the **s** years of famine,	7651
	41:47 in the **s** plenteous years the earth brought	7651
	41:48 he gathered up all the food of the **s** years,	7651
	41:53 the **s** years of plenteousness, that was in	7651
	41:54 the **s** years of dearth began to come,	7651
	46:25 these unto Jacob: all the souls *were* **s**.	7651
	47:28 Jacob was an hundred forty and **s** years.	7651
	50:10 he made a mourning for his father **s** days.	7651
Ex	2:16 the priest of Midian had **s** daughters:	7651
	6:16 Levi *were* an hundred thirty and **s** years.	7651
	6:20 *were* an hundred and thirty and **s** years.	7651
	7:25 **s** days were fulfilled, after *that* the LORD	7651
	12:15 **S** days shall ye eat unleavened bread;	7651
	12:19 **S** days shall there be no leaven found in	7651
	13: 6 **S** days thou shalt eat unleavened bread,	7651
	13: 7 Unleavened bread shall be eaten **s** days;	7651
	22:30 **s** days it shall be with his dam;	7651
	23:15 thou shalt eat unleavened bread **s** days,	7651
	25:37 thou shalt make the **s** lamps thereof:	7651
	29:30 in his stead shall put them on **s** days,	7651
	29:35 **s** days shalt thou consecrate them.	7651
	29:37 **S** days thou shalt make an atonement for	7651
	34:18 **s** days thou shalt eat unleavened bread,	7651
	37:23 he made his **s** lamps, and his snuffers,	7651
	38:24 and **s** hundred and thirty shekels,	7651
	38:25 a thousand **s** hundred and threescore and	7651
	38:28 of the thousand **s** hundred seventy and	7651
Lev	4: 6 sprinkle of the blood **s** times before	7651
	4:17 sprinkle *it* **s** times before the LORD,	7651
	8:11 sprinkled thereof upon the altar **s** times,	7651
	8:33 tabernacle of the congregation *in* **s** days,	7651
	8:33 end: for **s** days shall he consecrate you.	7651
	8:35 of the congregation day and night **s** days,	7651
	12: 2 she shall be unclean **s** days; according to	7651
	13: 4 shut up *him* that hath the plague **s** days:	7651
	13: 5 the priest shall shut him up **s** days more:	7651
	13:21 then the priest shall shut him up **s** days:	7651
	13:26 then the priest shall shut him up **s** days:	7651
	13:31 *that* hath the plague of the scall **s** days:	7651
	13:33 him that hath the scall **s** days more:	7651
	13:50 and shut up *it that* hath the plague **s** days:	7651
	13:54 and he shall shut it up **s** days more:	7651
	14: 7 is to be cleansed from the leprosy **s** times,	7651
	14: 8 shall tarry abroad out of his tent **s** days.	7651
	14:16 shall sprinkle of the oil with his finger **s**	7651
	14:27 in his left hand **s** times before the LORD:	7651
	14:38 the house, and shut up the house **s** days:	7651
	14:51 and sprinkle the house **s** times:	7651
	15:13 he shall number to himself **s** days for his	7651
	15:19 be blood, she shall be put apart **s** days:	7651
	15:24 be upon him, he shall be unclean **s** days,	7651
	15:28 she shall number to herself **s** days,	7651
	16:14 of the blood with his finger **s** times.	7651
	16:19 the blood upon it with his finger **s** times,	7651
	22:27 then it shall be **s** days under the dam;	7651
	23: 6 **s** days ye must eat unleavened bread.	7651
	23: 8 made by fire unto the LORD **s** days:	7651
	23:15 **s** sabbaths shall be complete:	7651
	23:18 ye shall offer with the bread **s** lambs	7651
	23:34 of tabernacles *for* **s** days unto the LORD.	7651
	23:36 **S** days ye shall offer an offering made by	7651
	23:39 ye shall keep a feast unto the LORD **s**	7651
	23:40 rejoice before the LORD your God **s** days.	7651
	23:41 ye shall keep it a feast unto the LORD **s**	7651
	23:42 Ye shall dwell in booths **s** days; all that	7651
	25: 8 thou shalt number **s** sabbaths of years	7651
	25: 8 of years unto thee, **s** times seven years;	7651
	25: 8 of years unto thee, seven times **s** years;	7651
	25: 8 the space of the **s** sabbaths of years shall	7651
	26:18 I will punish you **s** *times* more for your	7651
	26:21 I will bring **s** times moe plagues upon you	7651
	26:24 will punish you *yet* **s** times for your sins.	7651
	26:28 will chastise you **s** *times* for your sins.	7651
Nu	1:31 fifty and **s** thousand and four hundred.	7651
	1:39 and two thousand and **s** hundred.	7651
	2: 8 fifty and **s** thousand and four hundred.	7651
	2:26 and two thousand and **s** hundred.	7651
	2:31 and fifty and **s** thousand and six hundred.	7651
	3:22 were numbered of them *were* **s** thousand	7651
	4:36 families were two thousand **s** hundred	7651
	8: 2 the **s** lamps shall give light over against	7651
	12:14 face, should she not be ashamed **s** days?	7651
	12:14 let her be shut out from the camp **s** days,	7651
	12:15 was shut out from the camp **s** days:	7651
	13:22 were. (Now Hebron was built **s** years	7651
	16:49 were fourteen thousand and **s** hundred,	7651
	19: 4 tabernacle of the congregation **s** times:	7651
	19:11 *body* of any man shall be unclean **s** days.	7651
	19:14 that *is* in the tent, shall be unclean **s** days.	7651
	19:16 a man, or a grave, shall be unclean **s** days.	7651
	23: 1 Build me here **s** altars, and prepare me	7651
	23: 1 I prepare me here **s** oxen and seven rams.	7651
	23: 1 I prepare me here seven oxen and **s** rams.	7651
	23: 4 I have prepared **s** altars, and I have offered	7651

Nu	23:14 built **s** altars, and offered a bullock and	7651
	23:29 Build me here **s** altars, and prepare me	7651
	23:29 me here **s** bullocks and seven rams.	7651
	23:29 me here seven bullocks and **s** rams.	7651
	26: 7 three thousand and **s** hundred and thirty.	7651
	26:34 fifty and two thousand and **s** hundred.	7651
	26:51 and a thousand **s** hundred and thirty.	7651
	28:11 **s** lambs of the first year without spot;	7651
	28:17 **s** days shall unleavened bread be eaten.	7651
	28:19 and one ram, and **s** lambs of the first year:	7651
	28:21 for every lamb, throughout the **s** lambs;	7651
	28:24 ye shall offer daily, *throughout* the **s** days,	7651
	28:27 one ram, **s** lambs of the first year;	7651
	28:29 unto one lamb, throughout the **s** lambs;	7651
	29: 2 **s** lambs of the first year without blemish:	7651
	29: 4 for one lamb, throughout the **s** lambs:	7651
	29: 8 one ram, *and* **s** lambs of the first year;	7651
	29:10 for one lamb, throughout the **s** lambs:	7651
	29:12 ye shall keep a feast unto the LORD **s**	7651
	29:32 on the seventh day **s** bullocks, two rams,	7651
	29:36 lambs of the first year without blemish:	7651
	31:19 do ye abide without the camp **s** days:	7651
	31:36 **s** and thirty thousand and five hundred	7651
	31:43 thirty thousand *and* **s** thousand and	7651
	31:52 was sixteen thousand **s** hundred and	7651
Dt	7: 1 nations greater and mightier than thou;	7651
	15: 1 At the end of *every* **s** years thou shalt	7651
	16: 3 **s** days shalt thou eat unleavened bread	7651
	16: 4 seen with thee in all thy coast **s** days;	7651
	16: 9 **S** weeks shalt thou number unto thee:	7651
	16: 9 begin to number the **s** weeks from *such*	7651
	16:13 observe the feast of tabernacles **s** days,	7651
	16:15 **S** days shalt thou keep a solemn feast	7651
	28: 7 one way, and flee before thee **s** ways.	7651
	28:25 them, and flee **s** ways before them:	7651
	31:10 saying, At the end of *every* **s** years,	7651
Jos	6: 4 **s** priests shall bear before the ark seven	7651
	6: 4 seven priests shall bear before the ark **s**	7651
	6: 4 seventh day ye shall compass the city **s**	7651
	6: 6 let **s** priests bear seven trumpets of rams'	7651
	6: 6 let seven priests bear **s** trumpets of rams'	7651
	6: 8 the **s** priests bearing the seven trumpets	7651
	6: 8 the seven priests bearing the **s** trumpets	7651
	6:13 **s** priests bearing seven trumpets of rams'	7651
	6:13 seven priests bearing **s** trumpets of rams'	7651
	6:15 the city after the same manner **s**	7651
	6:15 on that day they compassed the city **s**	7651
	18: 2 among the children of Israel **s** tribes,	7651
	18: 5 they shall divide it into **s** parts: Judah shall	7651
	18: 6 therefore describe the land *into* **s** parts,	7651
	18: 9 it by cities into **s** parts in a book,	7651
Jdg	6: 1 them into the hand of Midian **s** years.	7651
	6:25 even the second bullock of **s** years old;	7651
	8:26 thousand and **s** hundred *shekels* of gold;	7651
	12: 9 for his sons. And he judged Israel **s** years.	7651
	14:12 it me *within* the **s** days of the feast,	7651
	14:17 wept before him the **s** days, while their	7651
	16: 7 If they bind me with **s** green withs that	7651
	16: 8 green withs which had not been dried,	7651
	16:13 If thou weavest the **s** locks of my head	7651
	16:19 she caused *him* to shave off the **s** locks of	7651
	20:15 *which* were numbered **s** hundred chosen	7651
	20:16 all this people *there were* **s** hundred	7651
Ru	4:15 which *is* better to thee than **s** sons,	7651
1Sa	2: 5 so that the barren hath born **s**; and she	7651
	6: 1 in the country of the Philistines **s** months.	7651
	10: 8 **s** days shalt thou tarry, till I come to thee,	7651
	11: 3 said unto him, Give us **s** days' respite,	7651
	13: 8 he tarried **s** days, according to the set time	7651
	16:10 Jesse made **s** of his sons to pass before	7651
	31:13 under a tree at Jabesh, and fasted **s** days.	7651
2Sa	2:11 over the house of Judah was **s** years	7651
	5: 5 In Hebron he reigned over Judah **s** years	7651
	8: 4 *chariots*, and **s** hundred horsemen,	7651
	10:18 David slew *the men of* **s** hundred chariots	7651
	21: 6 Let **s** men of his sons be delivered unto us	7651
	21: 9 they fell *all* **s** together, and were put to	7651
	23:39 Uriah the Hittite: thirty and **s** *in* all.	7651
	24:13 Shall **s** years of famine come unto thee in	7651
1Ki	2:11 **s** years reigned he in Hebron, and thirty	7651
	6: 6 and the third *was* **s** cubits broad:	7651
	6:38 of it. So was he **s** years in building it.	7651
	7:17 **s** for the one chapiter, and seven for	7651
	7:17 one chapiter, and **s** for the other chapiter.	7651
	8:65 **s** days and seven days, *even* fourteen days	7651
	8:65 seven days and **s** days, *even* fourteen days	7651
	11: 3 he had **s** hundred wives, princesses,	7651
	16:15 of Judah did Zimri reign **s** days in Tirzah.	7651
	18:43 *is* nothing. And he said, Go again **s** times.	7651
	19:18 Yet I have left *me* **s** thousand in Israel,	7651
	20:15 the children of Israel, *being* **s** thousand.	7651
	20:29 they pitched one over against the other **s**	7651
	20:30 and **s** thousand of the men that were left.	7651
2Ki	3: 9 they fetcht a compass of **s** days' journey:	7651
	3:26 he took with him **s** hundred men that	7651
	4:35 the child neesed **s** times, and the child	7651
	5:10 Go and wash in Jordan **s** times,	7651
	5:14 went *himself* **s** times in Jordan,	7651
	8: 1 it shall also come upon the land **s** years.	7651
	8: 2 sojourned in the land of the Philistines **s**	7651
	8: 3 it came to pass at the **s** years' end, that	7651
	11:21 **S** years old *was* Jehoash when he *began*	7651
	24:16 thousand, and craftsmen and smiths	7651
	25:27 it came to pass in the **s** and thirtieth year	7651
	25:27 on the **s** and twentieth *day* of the month,	7651

1Ch	3: 4 there he reigned **s** years and six months:	7651
	3:24 and Johanan, and Dalaiah, and Anani, **s.**	7651
	5:13 Jorai, and Jachan, and Zia, and Heber, **s.**	7651
	5:18 *were* four and forty thousand **s** hundred	7651
	7: 5 genealogies fourscore and **s** thousand.	7651
	9:13 a thousand and **s** hundred and threescore;	7651
	9:25 to come after **s** days from time to time	7651
	10:12 the oak in Jabesh, and fasted **s** days.	7651
	12:25 for the war, **s** thousand and one hundred.	7651
	12:27 him *were* three thousand and **s** hundred;	7651
	12:34 shield and spear thirty and **s** thousand.	7651
	15:26 they offered **s** bullocks and seven rams.	7651
	15:26 they offered seven bullocks and **s** rams.	7651
	18: 4 **s** thousand horsemen, and twenty	7651
	19:18 David slew of the Syrians **s** thousand *men*	7651
	26:30 men of valour, a thousand and **s** hundred,	7651
	26:32 two thousand and **s** hundred chief fathers,	7651
	29: 4 and **s** thousand talents of refined silver,	7651
	29:27 **s** years reigned he in Hebron, and thirty	7651
2Ch	7: 8 same time Solomon kept the feast **s** days,	7651
	7: 9 for they kept the dedication of the altar **s**	7651
	7: 9 the altar seven days, and the feast **s** days.	7651
	13: 9 himself with a young bullock and **s** rams,	7651
	15:11 **s** hundred oxen and seven thousand	7651
	15:11 hundred oxen and **s** thousand sheep.	7651
	17:11 **s** thousand and seven hundred rams,	7651
	17:11 seven thousand and **s** hundred rams,	7651
	17:11 **s** thousand and seven hundred he goats.	7651
	17:11 seven thousand and **s** hundred he goats.	7651
	24: 1 Joash *was* **s** years old when he *began* to	7651
	26:13 and thousand and five hundred,	7651
	29:21 they brought **s** bullocks, and seven rams,	7651
	29:21 **s** rams, and seven lambs, and seven he	7651
	29:21 and **s** lambs, and seven he goats,	7651
	29:21 and seven lambs, and **s** he goats,	7651
	30:21 bread **s** days with great gladness:	7651
	30:22 they did eat throughout the feast **s** days,	7651
	30:23 took counsel to keep other **s** days:	7651
	30:23 and they kept *other* **s** days *with* gladness.	7651
	30:24 thousand bullocks and **s** thousand sheep;	7651
	35:17 the feast of unleavened bread **s** days.	7651
Ezr	2: 5 of Arah, **s** hundred seventy and five.	7651
	2: 9 of Zaccai, **s** hundred and threescore.	7651
	2:25 Beeroth, **s** hundred and forty and three.	7651
	2:33 and Ono, **s** hundred twenty and five.	7651
	2:38 a thousand two hundred forty and **s.**	7651
	2:65 of whom *there were* **s** thousand three	7651
	2:65 thousand three hundred thirty and **s.**	7651
	2:66 horses *were* **s** hundred thirty and six;	7651
	2:67 six thousand **s** hundred and twenty.	7651
	6:22 kept the feast of unleavened bread **s** days	7651
	7:14 of his **s** counsellors, to inquire concerning	7655
	8:35 ninety and six rams, seventy and **s** lambs,	7657
Ne	7:14 of Zaccai, **s** hundred and threescore.	7651
	7:18 Adonikam, six hundred threescore and **s.**	7651
	7:19 of Bigvai, two thousand threescore and **s.**	7651
	7:29 and Beeroth, **s** hundred forty and three.	7651
	7:37 and Ono, **s** hundred twenty and one.	7651
	7:41 a thousand two hundred forty and **s.**	7651
	7:67 of whom *there were* **s** thousand three	7651
	7:67 thousand three hundred thirty and **s.**	7651
	7:68 Their horses, **s** hundred thirty and six:	7651
	7:69 six thousand **s** hundred and twenty asses.	7651
	7:72 and threescore and **s** priests' garments.	7651
	8:18 kept the feast **s** days; and on the eighth	7651
Est	1: 1 *over* an hundred and and	7651
	1: 5 both unto great and small, **s** days,	7651
	1:10 the **s** chamberlains that served in	7651
	1:14 the **s** princes of Persia and Media,	7651
	2: 9 **s** maidens, *which were* meet to be given	7651
	8: 9 an hundred twenty and **s** provinces,	7651
	9:30 **s** provinces of the kingdom of Ahasuerus,	7651
Job	1: 2 there were born unto him **s** sons and	7651
	1: 3 His substance also was **s** thousand sheep,	7651
	2:13 down with him upon the ground **s** days	7651
	2:13 upon the ground seven days and **s** nights,	7651
	5:19 yea, in **s** there shall no evil touch thee.	7651
	42: 8 Therefore take unto you now **s** bullocks	7651
	42: 8 unto you now seven bullocks and **s** rams,	7651
	42:13 He had also **s** sons and three daughters.	7658
Ps	12: 6 in a furnace of earth, purified **s** times.	7659
	119:164 **S** times a day do I praise thee because	7651
Pr	6:16 yea, *are* an abomination unto him:	7651
	9: 1 house, she hath hewn out her **s** pillars:	7651
	24:16 For a just *man* falleth **s** *times*, and riseth	7651
	26:16 than **s** *men* that can render a reason.	7651
	26:25 for *there are* **s** abominations in his heart.	7651
Ecc	11: 2 Give a portion to **s**, and also to eight;	7651
Isa	4: 1 in that day **s** women shall take hold of	7651
	11:15 shall smite it in the **s** streams,	7651
	30:26 shall be sevenfold, as the light of **s** days,	7651
Jer	15: 9 She that hath borne **s** languisheth: she	7651
	34:14 At the end of **s** years let ye go every man	7651
	52:25 **s** men of them that were near the king's	7651
	52:30 away captive *of* the Jews **s** hundred forty	7651
	52:31 it came to pass in the **s** and thirtieth year	7651
Eze	3:15 remained there astonished among them **s**	7651
	3:16 it came to pass at the end of **s** days, that	7651
	29:17 came to pass in the **s** and twentieth year,	7651
	39: 9 they shall burn them with fire **s** years:	7651
	39:12 months shall the house of Israel be	7651
	39:14 the end of **s** months they shall search.	7651
	40:22 they went up unto it by **s** steps;	7651
	40:26 *there were* **s** steps to go up to it,	7651
	41: 3 and the breadth of the door, **s** cubits.	7651

Eze	43:25 **S** days shalt thou prepare every day a goat	7651
	43:26 **S** days shall they purge the altar and	7651
	44:26 they shall reckon unto him **s** days.	7651
	45:21 shall have the passover, a feast of **s** days;	7620
	45:23 **s** days of the feast he shall prepare a burnt	7651
	45:23 **s** bullocks and seven rams without	7651
	45:23 seven rams without blemish daily the seven	7651
	45:23 seven rams without blemish daily the **s**	7651
	45:25 shall he do the like in the feast *of* the **s**	7651
Da	3:19 **s** times more than *it was* wont to be heat.	7655
	4:16 unto him; and let **s** times pass over him.	7655
	4:23 of the field, till **s** times pass over him;	7655
	4:25 heaven, and **s** times shall pass over thee,	7655
	4:32 as oxen, and **s** times shall pass over thee,	7655
	9:25 the Messiah the Prince *shall be* **s** weeks,	7651
Am	5: 8 *Seek him* that maketh the **s** stars	3598
Mic	5: 5 shall we raise against him **s** shepherds,	7651
Zec	3: 9 upon one stone *shall be* **s** eyes:	7651
	4: 2 his **s** lamps thereon, and seven pipes to	7651
	4: 2 and **s** pipes to the seven lamps,	7651
	4: 2 and seven pipes to the **s** lamps,	7651
	4:10 in the hand of Zerubbabel *with* those **s**;	7651
Mt	12:45 taketh with himself **s** other spirits more	2033
	15:34 And they said, **S**, and a few little fishes.	2033
	15:36 And he took the **s** loaves and the fishes,	2033
	15:37 broken *meat* that was left **s** baskets full.	2033
	16:10 Neither the **s** loaves of the four thousand,	2033
	18:21 against me, and I forgive him? till **s** *times*?	2034
	18:22 him, I say not unto thee, Until **s** *times*:	2034
	18:22 seven times: but, Until seventy times **s.**	2033
	22:25 Now there were with us **s** brethren:	2033
	22:28 whose wife shall she be of the **s**?	2033
Mk	8: 5 many loaves have ye? And they said, **S.**	2033
	8: 6 he took the **s** loaves, and gave thanks,	2033
	8: 8 the broken *meat* that was left **s** baskets.	2033
	8:20 And when the **s** among four thousand,	2033
	8:20 fragments took ye up? And they said, **S.**	2033
	12:20 Now there were **s** brethren: and the first	2033
	12:22 And the **s** had her, and left no seed: last	2033
	12:23 she be of them? for the **s** had her to wife.	2033
	16: 9 out of whom he had cast **s** devils.	2033
Lk	2:36 had lived with a husband **s** years from her	2033
	8: 2 out of whom went **s** devils,	2033
	11:26 taketh to *him* **s** other spirits more wicked	2033
	17: 4 And if he trespass against thee **s** times in	2034
	17: 4 and **s** times in a day turn again to thee,	2034
	20:29 There were therefore **s** brethren:	2033
	20:31 took her; and in like manner the **s** also:	2033
	20:33 wife of them is she? for **s** had her to wife.	2033
Ac	6: 3 look ye out among you **s** men of honest	2033
	13:19 And when he had destroyed **s** nations in	2033
	19:14 there were **s** sons of *one* Sceva, a Jew,	2033
	20: 6 in five days; where we abode **s** days.	2033
	21: 4 finding disciples, we tarried there **s** days:	2033
	21: 8 the evangelist, which was *one* of the **s**;	2033
	21:27 And when the **s** days were almost ended,	2033
	28:14 were desired to tarry with them **s** days:	2033
Ro	11: 4 have reserved to myself **s** thousand men,	2035
Heb	11:30 after they were compassed about **s** days.	2033
Rev	1: 4 John to the **s** churches which are in Asia:	2033
	1: 4 from the **s** spirits which are before his	2033
	1:11 send *it* unto the **s** churches which are in	2033
	1:12 being turned, I saw **s** golden candlesticks;	2033
	1:13 And in the midst of the **s** candlesticks one	2033
	1:16 And he had in his right hand **s** stars:	2033
	1:20 The mystery of the **s** stars which thou	2033
	1:20 right hand, and the **s** golden candlesticks.	2033
	1:20 The **s** stars are the angels of the seven	2033
	1:20 The seven stars are the angels of the **s**	2033
	1:20 the **s** candlesticks which thou sawest are	2033
	1:20 which thou sawest are the **s** churches.	2033
	2: 1 These *things* saith he that holdeth the **s**	2033
	2: 1 who walketh in the midst of the **s** golden	2033
	3: 1 *things* saith he that hath the **s** spirits	2033
	3: 1 the seven spirits of God, and the **s** stars;	2033
	4: 5 *there were* **s** lamps of fire burning before	2033
	4: 5 the throne, which are the **s** spirits of God.	2033
	5: 1 and on the backside, sealed with **s** seals.	2033
	5: 5 the book, and to loose the **s** seals thereof.	2033
	5: 6 slain, having **s** horns and seven eyes,	2033
	5: 6 slain, having seven horns and **s** eyes,	2033
	5: 6 which are the **s** spirits of God sent forth	2033
	8: 2 I saw the **s** angels which stood before	2033
	8: 2 and to them were given **s** trumpets.	2033
	8: 6 And the **s** angels which had the seven	2033
	8: 6 And the seven angels which had the **s**	2033
	10: 3 had cried, **s** thunders uttered their voices.	2033
	10: 4 And when the **s** thunders had uttered	2033
	10: 4 Seal *up those things* which the **s** thunders	2033
	11:13 in the earthquake were slain of men **s**	2033
	12: 3 having **s** heads and ten horns,	2033
	12: 3 ten horns, and **s** crowns upon his heads.	2033
	13: 1 having **s** heads and ten horns, and upon	2033
	15: 1 **s** angels having the seven last plagues;	2033
	15: 1 seven angels having the **s** last plagues;	2033
	15: 6 And the **s** angels came out of the temple,	2033
	15: 6 having the **s** plagues, clothed in pure and	2033
	15: 7 one of the four beasts gave unto the **s**	2033
	15: 7 **s** golden vials full of the wrath of God,	2033
	15: 8 till the **s** plagues of the seven angels were	2033
	15: 8 till the seven plagues of the **s** angels were	2033
	16: 1 out of the temple saying to the **s** angels,	2033
	17: 1 And there came one of the **s** angels which	2033
	17: 1 of the seven angels which had the **s** vials,	2033
	17: 3 having **s** heads and ten horns.	2033

Rev 17: 7 which hath the **s** heads and ten horns. — 2033
17: 9 The **s** heads are seven mountains, on — 2033
17: 9 The seven heads are **s** mountains, on — 2033
17:10 And there are **s** kings: five are fallen, — 2033
17:11 and is of the **s**, and goeth into perdition. — 2033
21: 9 there came unto me one of the **s** angels — 2033
21: 9 the **s** vials full of the seven last plagues, — 2033
21: 9 the seven vials full of the **s** last plagues, — 2033

SEVENFOLD (6) [SEVEN]

Ge 4:15 vengeance shall be taken on him **s**. — 7659
4:24 If Cain shall be avenged **s**, truly Lamech — 7659
4:24 truly Lamech seventy and **s**. — 7651
Ps 79:12 render unto our neighbours **s** into their — 7659
Pr 6:31 if he be found, he shall restore **s**; he shall — 7659
Isa 30:26 the light of the sun shall be **s**, as the light — 7659

SEVENS (2) [SEVEN]

Ge 7: 2 thou shalt take to thee **by s**, — 7651+7651
7: 3 Of fowls also of the air **by s**, — 7651+7651

SEVENTEEN (10) [SEVENTEENTH]

Ge 37: 2 Joseph, *being* **s** years old, — 6240+7651
47:28 Jacob lived in the land of Egypt **s** — 6240+7651
Jdg 8:14 **threescore** and **s** men. — 7651+7657+2050.1
1Ki 14:21 he reigned **s** years in Jerusalem, — 6240+7651
2Ki 13: 1 in Samaria, *and reigned* **s** years. — 6240+7651
1Ch 7:11 *were* **s** thousand and two hundred — 6240+7651
2Ch 12:13 he reigned **s** years in Jerusalem, — 6240+7651
Ezr 2:39 of Harim, a thousand and **s**. — 6240+7651
Ne 7:42 of Harim, a thousand *and* **s**. — 6240+7651
Jer 32: 9 *even* **s** shekels of silver. — 6235+7651+2050.1

SEVENTEENTH (6) [SEVENTEEN]

Ge 7:11 the **s** day of the month, — 6240+7651
8: 4 on the **s** day of the month, upon — 6240+7651
1Ki 22:51 **s** year of Jehoshaphat king of Judah, — 6240+7651
2Ki 16: 1 In the **s** year of Pekah the son of — 6240+7651
1Ch 24:15 The **s** to Hezir, the eighteenth to — 6240+7651
25:24 The **s** to Joshbekashah, *he*, his sons, — 6240+7651

SEVENTH (120) [SEVEN]

Ge 2: 2 on the **s** day God ended his work which — 7637
2: 2 he rested on the **s** day from all his work — 7637
2: 3 God blessed the **s** day, and sanctified it: — 7637
8: 4 the ark rested in the **s** month, — 7637
Ex 12:15 bread from the first day until the **s** day, — 7637
12:16 in the **s** day there shall be a holy — 7637
13: 6 in the **s** day *shall be* a feast to the Lord. — 7637
16:26 on the **s** day, *which is* the sabbath, in it — 7637
16:27 of the people on the **s** day for to gather, — 7637
16:29 no man go out of his place on the **s** day. — 7637
16:30 So the people rested on the **s** day. — 7637
20:10 the **s** day *is* the sabbath of the Lord thy — 7637
20:11 all that in them *is*, and rested the **s** day: — 7637
21: 2 in the **s** he shall go out free for nothing. — 7637
23:11 the **s** *year* thou shalt let it rest and lie still; — 7637
23:12 work, and on the **s** day thou shalt rest: — 7637
24:16 the **s** day he called unto Moses out of — 7637
31:15 in the **s** *is* the sabbath of rest, holy to — 7637
31:17 on the **s** day he rested, and was refreshed. — 7637
34:21 work, but on the **s** day thou shalt rest: — 7637
35: 2 on the **s** day there shall be to you a holy — 7637
Lev 13: 5 the priest shall look on him in the **s** day: — 7637
13: 6 priest shall look on him again the **s** day: — 7637
13:27 the priest shall look upon him the **s** day: — 7637
13:32 in the **s** day the priest shall look — 7637
13:34 in the **s** day the priest shall look on — 7637
13:51 he shall look on the plague on the **s** day: — 7637
14: 9 shall be on the **s** day, *that* he shall shave — 7637
14:39 the priest shall come again the **s** day, — 7637
16:29 *that* in the **s** month, on the tenth *day of* — 7637
23: 3 the **s** day *is* the sabbath of rest, a holy — 7637
23: 8 the **s** day *is* a holy convocation: ye shall — 7637
23:16 Even unto the morrow after the **s** sabbath — 7637
23:24 saying, In the **s** month, in the first *day of* — 7637
23:27 on the tenth *day* of this **s** month *there* — 7637
23:34 The fifteenth day of this **s** month *shall be* — 7637
23:39 Also in the fifteenth day of the **s** month, — 7637
23:41 ye shall celebrate it in the **s** month. — 7637
25: 4 in the **s** year shall be a sabbath of rest — 7637
25: 9 to sound on the tenth *day* of the **s** month, — 7637
25:20 ye shall say, What shall we eat the **s** year? — 7637
Nu 6: 9 cleansing, on the **s** day he shall shave it. — 7637
7:48 On the **s** day Elishama the son of — 7637
19:12 and on the **s** day he shall be clean: — 7637
19:12 then the **s** day he shall not be clean. — 7637
19:19 on the third day, and on the **s** day: — 7637
19:19 on the **s** day he shall purify him *self*, and — 7637
28:25 on the **s** day ye shall have a holy — 7637
29: 1 in the **s** month, on the first *day* — 7637
29: 7 ye shall have on the tenth *day* of this **s** — 7637
29:12 on the fifteenth day of the **s** month ye — 7637
29:32 on the **s** day seven bullocks, two rams, — 7637
31:19 on the third day, and on the **s** day. — 7637
31:24 ye shall wash your clothes on the **s** day, — 7637
Dt 5:14 the **s** day *is* the sabbath of the Lord thy — 7637
15: 9 saying, The **s** year, the year of release, is — 7651
15:12 in the **s** year thou shalt let him go free — 7637
16: 8 on the **s** day *shall be* a solemn assembly — 7637
Jos 6: 4 the **s** day ye shall compass the city seven — 7637
6:15 came to pass on the **s** day, that they rose — 7637
6:16 it came to pass at the **s** time, when — 7637
19:40 *And* the **s** lot came out for the tribe of — 7637
Jdg 14:15 came to pass on the **s** day, that they said — 7637

1Sa 14:17 it came to pass on the **s** day, that he told — 7637
14:18 men of the city said unto him on the **s** — 7637
2Sa 12:18 came to pass on the **s** day, that the child — 7637
1Ki 8: 2 month Ethanim, which *is* the **s** month. — 7637
16:10 twenty and **s** year of Asa king of Judah, — 7651
16:15 **s** year of Asa king of Judah did Zimri reign — 7651
18:44 it came to pass at the **s** *time*, that he said, — 7637
20:29 that in the **s** day the battle was joined: — 7637
2Ki 11: 4 the **s** year Jehoiada sent and fet the rulers — 7651
12: 1 In the **s** year of Jehu Jehoash *began* to — 7651
13:10 **s** year of Joash king of Judah *began* — 7651
15: 1 **s** year of Jeroboam king of Israel *began* — 7651
18: 9 *was* the **s** year of Hoshea son of Elah — 7637
25: 8 fifth month, on the **s** *day* of the month, — 7651
25:25 came to pass in the **s** month, *that* Ishmael — 7637
1Ch 2:15 Ozem the sixth, David the **s**: — 7637
12:11 Attai the sixth, Eliel the **s**, — 7637
24:10 The **s** to Hakkoz, the eighth to Abijah, — 7637
25:14 The **s** to Jesharelah, his sons, — 7637
26: 3 Jehohanan the sixth, Elioenai the **s**. — 7637
26: 5 Ammiel the sixth, Issachar the **s**, — 7637
27:10 The **s** *captain* for the seventh month *was* — 7637
27:10 The seventh *captain* for the **s** month *was* — 7637
2Ch 5: 3 in the feast which *was in* the **s** month. — 7637
7:10 twentieth day of the **s** month he sent — 7637
23: 1 in the **s** year Jehoiada strengthened — 7637
31: 7 and finished *them* in the **s** month. — 7637
Ezr 3: 1 when the **s** month was come, — 7637
3: 6 From the first day of the **s** month began — 7637
7: 7 in the **s** year of Artaxerxes the king. — 7651
7: 8 which *was in* the **s** year of the king. — 7637
Ne 7:73 when the **s** month came, the children of — 7637
8: 2 upon the first day of the **s** month. — 7637
8:14 in booths in the feast of the **s** month: — 7637
10:31 *that* we would leave the **s** year, — 7637
Est 1:10 On the **s** day, when the heart of the king — 7637
2:16 month Tebeth, in the **s** year of his reign. — 7651
Jer 28:17 died the same year in the **s** month. — 7637
41: 1 Now it came to pass in the **s** month, — 7637
52:28 in the **s** year three thousand Jews and — 7651
Eze 20: 1 it came to pass in the **s** year, in the fifth — 7637
30:20 in the first *month*, in the **s** *day* of — 7651
45:20 thou shalt do the **s** *day* of the month for — 7651
45:25 In the **s** *month*, in the fifteenth day of — 7637
Hag 2: 1 In the **s** *month*, in the one and twentieth — 7637
Zec 7: 5 in the **s** *month*, even those seventy years, — 7637
8:19 the fast of the **s**, and the fast of the tenth, — 7637
Mt 22:26 the second also, and the third, unto the **s**. — 2033
Jn 4:52 Yesterday at the **s** hour the fever left him. — 1442
Heb 4: 4 he spake in a certain place of the **s** *day* — 1442
4: 4 And God did rest the **s** day from all his — 1442
Jude 1:14 And Enoch also, the **s** from Adam, — 1442
Rev 8: 1 And when he had opened the **s** seal, — 1442
10: 7 But in the days of the voice of the **s** angel, — 1442
11:15 And the **s** angel sounded; and there were — 1442
16:17 And the **s** angel poured out his vial into — 1442
21:20 the sixth, sardius; the **s**, chrysolite; — 1442

SEVENTY (61)

Ge 4:24 truly Lamech **s** and sevenfold. — 7657
5:12 Cainan lived **s** years, and begat — 7657
5:31 days of Lamech were seven hundred **s** — 7657
11:26 Terah lived **s** years, and begat Abram, — 7657
12: 4 Abram *was* **s** and five years old when he — 7657
Ex 1: 5 *out of* the loins of Jacob were **s** souls: — 7657
24: 1 and Abihu, and **s** of the elders of Israel; — 7657
24: 9 and Abihu, and **s** of the elders of Israel: — 7657
38:28 of the thousand seven hundred **s** and — 7657
38:29 the brass of the offering *was* **s** talents, — 7657
Nu 7:13 *shekels*, one silver bowl of **s** shekels, — 7657
7:19 *shekels*, one silver bowl of **s** shekels, — 7657
7:25 *shekels*, one silver bowl of **s** shekels, — 7657
7:31 *shekels*, one silver bowl of **s** shekels, — 7657
7:37 *shekels*, one silver bowl of **s** shekels, — 7657
7:43 thirty *shekels*, a silver bowl of **s** shekels, — 7657
7:49 *shekels*, one silver bowl of **s** shekels, — 7657
7:55 *shekels*, one silver bowl of **s** shekels, — 7657
7:61 *shekels*, one silver bowl of **s** shekels, — 7657
7:67 *shekels*, one silver bowl of **s** shekels, — 7657
7:73 *shekels*, one silver bowl of **s** shekels, — 7657
7:79 *shekels*, one silver bowl of **s** shekels, — 7657
7:85 hundred and thirty *shekels*, each bowl **s**: — 7657
11:16 Gather unto me **s** men of the elders of — 7657
11:24 gathered the **s** men of the elders of — 7657
11:25 upon him, and gave *it* unto the **s** elders: — 7657
31:32 and **s** thousand and five thousand sheep, — 7657
Jdg 9:56 unto his father, in slaying his **s** brethren: — 7657
2Sa 24:15 Dan even to Beer-sheba **s** thousand men. — 7657
2Ki 10: 1 Ahab had **s** sons in Samaria. And Jehu — 7657
10: 6 Now the king's sons, *being* **s** persons, — 7657
10: 7 slew **s** persons, and put their heads in — 7657
1Ch 21:14 and there fell of Israel **s** thousand men. — 7657
Ezr 2: 3 two thousand an hundred **s** and two. — 7657
2: 4 of Shephatiah, three hundred **s** and two. — 7657
2: 5 of Arah, seven hundred **s** and five. — 7657
2:36 of Jeshua, nine hundred **s** and three. — 7657
2:40 the children of Hodaviah, **s** and four. — 7657
8: 7 son of Athaliah, and with him **s** males. — 7657
8:14 and Zabbud, and with them **s** males. — 7657
8:35 ninety and six rams, **s** and seven lambs, — 7651
Ne 7: 8 two thousand an hundred **s** and two. — 7657
7: 9 of Shephatiah, three hundred **s** and two. — 7657
7:39 of Jeshua, nine hundred **s** and three. — 7657
7:43 of the children of Hodevah, **s** and four. — 7657
11:19 the gates, *were* an hundred **s** and two. — 7657

Est 9:16 slew of their foes **s** and five thousand, — 7657
Isa 23:15 that Tyre shall be forgotten **s** years, — 7657
23:15 after the end of **s** years shall Tyre sing as — 7657
23:17 it shall come to pass after the end of **s** — 7657
Jer 25:11 shall serve the king of Babylon **s** years. — 7657
25:12 to pass, when **s** years are accomplished, — 7657
29:10 That after **s** years be accomplished at — 7657
Eze 8:11 there stood before them **s** men of — 7657
41:12 end toward the west *was* **s** cubits broad; — 7657
Da 9: 2 that *he* would accomplish **s** years in — 7657
9:24 **S** weeks are determined upon thy people — 7657
Zec 7: 5 and seventh *month*, even those **s** years, — 7657
Mt 18:22 seven times: but, Until **s** times seven. — 1441
Lk 10: 1 *things* the Lord appointed other **s** also, — 1440
10:17 And the **s** returned *again* with joy, saying, — 1440

SEVER (4) [SEVERED]

Ex 8:22 I will **s** in that day the land of Goshen, — 6395
9: 4 the Lord shall **s** between the cattle of — 6395
Eze 39:14 they shall **s** *out* men of continual — 914
Mt 13:49 and **s** the wicked from among the just, — 873

SEVERAL (12) [SEVERALLY]

Nu 28:13 a **s** tenth deal of flour mingled — 6241+6241
28:21 A **s** tenth deal shalt thou offer for — 6241+6241
28:29 A **s** tenth deal unto one lamb, — 6241+6241
29:10 A **s** tenth deal for one lamb, — 6241+6241
29:15 A **s** tenth deal to each lamb of — 6241+6241
2Ki 15: 5 day of his death, and dwelt in a **s** house. — 2669
2Ch 11:12 every **s** city he put shields — 5892+5892+2050.1
26:21 and dwelt *in* a **s** house, *being* a leper; — 2669
28:25 in every **s** city of Judah he — 5892+5892+2050.1
31:19 in every **s** city, the men — 5892+5892+2050.1
Mt 25:15 to every man according to his **s** ability; — 2398
Rev 21:21 every **s** gate was of one pearl: — 303+1520

SEVERALLY (1) [SEVERAL]

1Co 12:11 dividing to every man **s** as he will. — 2398

SEVERED (3) [SEVER]

Lev 20:26 have **s** you from *other* people, that ye — 914
Dt 4:41 Moses three cities on *this* side Jordan — 914
Jdg 4:11 had **s** himself from the Kenites, — 6504

SEVERITY (2)

Ro 11:22 therefore the goodness and **s** of God: — 663
11:22 on them which fell, **s**; but toward thee, — 663

SEW (2) [SEWED, SEWEST, SEWETH, SOW]

Ecc 3: 7 A time to rent, and a time to **s**; a time to — 8609
Eze 13:18 Woe to *the women* that **s** pillows to all — 8609

SEWED (2) [SEW]

Ge 3: 7 they **s** fig leaves **together**, — 8609
Job 16:15 I have **s** sackcloth upon my skin, — 8609

SEWEST (1) [SEW]

Job 14:17 up in a bag, and thou **s** up mine iniquity. — 2950

SEWETH (1) [SEW]

Mk 2:21 No *man* also **s** a piece of new cloth on an — 1976

SEXUAL IMMORALITY See FORNICATION

SEXUALLY IMMORAL See WHOREMONGER; WHOREMONGERS

SHAALABBIN (1)

Jos 19:42 And **S**, and Aijalon, and Jethlah, — 8169

SHAALBIM (2)

Jdg 1:35 in mount Heres in Aijalon, and in **S**: — 8169
1Ki 4: 9 in **S**, and Beth-shemesh, — 8169

SHAALBONITE (2)

2Sa 23:32 Eliahba the **S**, *of* the sons of Jashen, — 8170
1Ch 11:33 Azmaveth the Baharumite, Eliahba the **S**, — 8170

SHAALIM See SHALIM

SHAAPH (2)

1Ch 2:47 Geshan, and Pelet, and Ephah, and **S**. — 8174
2:49 She bare also **S** the father of Madmannah, — 8174

SHAARAIM (2)

1Sa 17:52 the Philistines fell down by the way to **S**, — 8189
1Ch 4:31 and at Beth-birei, and at **S**. — 8189

SHAASHGAZ (1)

Est 2:14 the custody of **S**, the king's chamberlain, — 8190

SHABBETHAI (3)

Ezr 10:15 Meshullam and **S** the Levite helped them. — 7678
Ne 8: 7 Jamin, Akkub, **S**, Hodijah, Maaseiah, — 7678
11:16 **S** and Jozabad, of the chief of the Levites, — 7678

SHACHIA (1)

1Ch 8:10 Jeuz, and **S**, and Mirma. These *were* his — 7634

SHADE (1) [SHADY]

Ps 121: 5 the Lord *is* thy **s** upon thy right hand. — 6738

SHADOW (73) [OVERSHADOW, SHADOWING, SHADOWS]

Ge 19: 8 came they under the **s** of my roof. — 6738
Jdg 9:15 *then* come *and* put your trust in my **s**: — 6738
9:36 Thou seest the **s** of the mountains as *if* — 6738

S

2Ki	20: 9 shall the **s** go forward ten degrees,	6738
	20:10 It is a light thing for the **s** to go down ten	6738
	20:10 but let the **s** return backward ten degrees.	6738
	20:11 he brought the **s** ten degrees backward,	6738
1Ch	29:15 our days on the earth *are* as a **s**, and *there*	6738
Job	3: 5 Let darkness and the **s of death** stain it;	6757
	7: 2 As a servant earnestly desireth the **s**,)	6738
	8: 9 because our days upon earth *are* as a **s**)	6738
	10:21 the land of darkness and the **s of death**,	6757
	10:22 *and of* the **s of death**, without any order,	6757
	12:22 and bringeth out to light the **s of death**.	6757
	14: 2 he fleeth also as a **s**, and continueth not.	6738
	16:16 and on mine eyelids *is* the **s of death**,	6757
	17: 7 of sorrow, and all my members *are* as a **s**.	6738
	24:17 *is* to them even as the **s of death**:	6757
	24:17 *they are in* the terrors of the **s of death**.	6757
	28: 3 stones of darkness, and the **s of death**.	6757
	34:22 *There is* no darkness, nor **s of death**,	6757
	38:17 thou seen the doors of the **s of death**?	6757
	40:22 The shady trees cover him *with* their **s**;	6752
Ps	17: 8 eye, hide me under the **s** of thy wings,	6738
	23: 4 walk through the valley of the **s of death**,	6757
	36: 7 put their trust under the **s** of thy wings.	6738
	44:19 and covered us with the **s of death**.	6757
	57: 1 the **s** of thy wings will I make my refuge,	6738
	63: 7 in the **s** of thy wings will I rejoice.	6738
	80:10 The hills were covered *with* the **s** of it,	6738
	91: 1 shall abide under the **s** of the Almighty.	6738
	102:11 My days *are* like a **s** that declineth;	6738
	107:10 as sit in darkness and in the **s of death**,	6757
	107:14 them out of darkness and the **s of death**,	6757
	109:23 I am gone like the **s** when it declineth.	6738
	144: 4 his days *are* as a **s** that passeth away.	6738
Ecc	6:12 of his vain life which he spendeth as a **s**?	6738
	8:13 he prolong *his* days, *which are* as a **s**;	6738
SS	2: 3 I sat down under his **s** with great delight,	6738
Isa	4: 6 there shall be a tabernacle for a **s** in	6738
	9: 2 that dwell in the land of the **s of death**,	6757
	16: 3 make thy **s** as the night in the midst of	6738
	25: 4 refuge from the storm, a **s** from the heat,	6738
	25: 5 *even* the heat with the **s** of a cloud:	6738
	30: 2 of Pharaoh, and to trust in the **s** of Egypt.	6738
	30: 3 the trust in the **s** of Egypt *your* confusion.	6738
	32: 2 as the **s** of a great rock in a weary land.	6738
	34:15 lay, and hatch, and gather under her **s**:	6738
	38: 8 I will bring again the **s** of the degrees,	6738
	49: 2 in the **s** of his hand hath he hid me,	6738
	51:16 have covered thee in the **s** of mine hand,	6738
Jer	2: 6 a land of drought, and of the **s of death**,	6757
	13:16 he turn it into the **s of death**, *and* make	6757
	48:45 that fled stood under the **s** of Heshbon	6738
La	4:20 Under his **s** we shall live among	6738
Eze	17:23 in the **s** of the branches thereof shall they	6738
	31: 6 and under his **s** dwelt all great nations.	6738
	31:12 of the earth are gone down from his **s**,	6738
	31:17 *that* dwelt under his **s** in the midst of	6738
Da	4:12 the beasts of the field had **s** under it,	2927
Hos	4:13 and elms, because the **s** thereof *is* good:	6738
	14: 7 They that dwell under his **s** shall return;	6738
Am	5: 8 turneth the **s of death** into the morning,	6757
Jnh	4: 5 him a booth, and sat under it in the **s**,	6738
	4: 6 *it* might be a **s** over his head, to deliver	6738
Mt	4:16 region and **s** of death light is sprung up.	4639
Mk	4:32 of the air may lodge under the **s** of it.	4639
Lk	1:79 that sit in darkness and *in* the **s** of death,	4639
Ac	5:15 that at the least the **s** of Peter passing by	4639
Col	2:17 Which are a **s** of *things* to come;	4639
Heb	8: 5 of heavenly *things*, as Moses was	4639
	10: 1 For the law having a **s** of good *things* to	4639
Jas	1:17 is no variableness, neither **s** of turning.	644

SHADOWING (3) [SHADOW]

Isa	18: 1 Woe to the land **s** with wings, which *is*	6767
Eze	31: 3 with a **s** shrowd, and of a high stature;	6751
Heb	9: 5 And over it the cherubims of glory **s**	2683

SHADOWS (3) [SHADOW]

SS	2:17 the **s** flee away, turn, my beloved, and be	6752
	4: 6 Until the day break, and the **s** flee away,	6752
Jer	6: 4 for the **s** of the evening are stretched out.	6752

SHADRACH (15)

Da	1: 7 to Hananiah, of **S**; and to Mishael,	7714
	2:49 and he set **S**, Meshach, and Abed-nego,	7715
	3:12 of Babylon, **S**, Meshach, and Abed-nego;	7715
	3:13 *his* rage and fury commanded to bring **S**,	7715
	3:14 *Is it* true, O **S**, Meshach, and Abed-nego,	7715
	3:16 **S**, Meshach, and Abed-nego, answered	7715
	3:19 form of his visage was changed against **S**,	7715
	3:20 men that *were* in his army to bind **S**,	7715
	3:22 of the fire slew those men that took up **S**,	7715
	3:23 three men, **S**, Meshach, and Abed-nego,	7715
	3:26 *and* spake, and said, **S**, Meshach,	7715
	3:26 come *hither*. Then **S**, Meshach,	7715
	3:28 said, Blessed *be* the God of **S**, Meshach,	7715
	3:29 any thing amiss against the God of **S**,	7715
	3:30 the king promoted **S**, Meshach,	7715

SHADY (2) [SHADE]

Job	40:21 He lieth under the **s** trees, in the covert	6628
	40:22 The **s** trees cover him *with* their shadow;	6628

SHAFT (4)

Ex	25:31 his **s**, and his branches, his bowls,	3409
	37:17 his **s**, and his branch, his bowls, his knops,	3409

Nu	8: 4 the **s** thereof, unto the flowers thereof,	3409
Isa	49: 2 he hid me, and made me a polished **s**;	2671

SHAGE (1)

1Ch	11:34 Jonathan the son of **S** the Hararite,	7681

SHAGEE See SHAGE

SHAHAR (1)

Ps	22: T To the chief Musician upon Aijeleth **S**,	7837

SHAHARAIM (1)

1Ch	8: 8 **S** begat *children* in the country of Moab,	7842

SHAHAZIMAH (1)

Jos	19:22 to Tabor, and, **S**, and Beth-shemesh;	7831

SHAHAZUMAH See SHAHAZIMAH

SHAKE (39) [SHAKED, SHAKEN, SHAKETH, SHAKING, SHOOK]

Jdg	16:20 out as at other times *before,* and **s** myself.	5287
Ne	5:13 So God **s** out every man from his house,	5287
Job	4:14 which made all my bones to **s**.	6342
	15:33 He shall **s off** his unripe grape as the vine,	2554
	16: 4 against you, and **s** mine head at you.	5128
Ps	22: 7 shoot out the lip, they **s** the head, *saying,*	5128
	46: 3 the mountains **s** with the swelling	7493
	69:23 and make their loins continually **to s**.	4571
	72:16 the fruit thereof shall **s** like Lebanon:	7493
Isa	2:19 when he ariseth to **s terribly** the earth.	6206
	2:21 when he ariseth to **s terribly** the earth.	6206
	10:15 as if the rod should **s** *itself against* them	5130
	10:32 he shall **s** his hand *against* the mount of	5130
	11:15 with his mighty wind shall he **s** his hand	5130
	13: 2 exalt the voice unto them, **s** the hand,	5130
	13:13 I will **s** the heavens, and the earth	7264
	14:16 the earth to tremble, that did **s** kingdoms;	7493
	24:18 and the foundations of the earth do **s**.	7493
	33: 9 and Bashan and Carmel **s off** *their fruits.*	5287
	52: 2 **S** thyself from the dust; arise, *and* sit	5287
Jer	23: 9 because of the prophets; all my bones **s**	7363
Eze	26:10 thy walls shall **s** at the noise of	7493
	26:15 not the isles **s** at the sound of thy fall,	7493
	27:28 suburbs shall **s** at the sound of the cry	7493
	31:16 I made the nations to **s** at the sound of	7493
	38:20 shall **s** at my presence, and the mountains	7493
Da	4:14 **s off** his leaves, and scatter his fruit:	5426
Joel	3:16 and the heavens and the earth shall **s**	7493
Am	9: 1 lintel of the door, that the posts may **s**:	7493
Hag	2: 6 I *will* **s** the heavens, and the earth,	7493
	2: 7 I *will* **s** all nations, and the desire of all	7493
	2:21 I *will* **s** the heavens and the earth;	7493
Zec	2: 9 I *will* **s** mine hand upon them,	5130
Mt	10:14 or city, **s off** the dust of your feet.	1621
	28: 4 And for fear of him the keepers did **s**,	4579
Mk	6:11 **s off** the dust under your feet for a	1621
Lk	6:48 upon that house, and could not **s** it:	4531
	9: 5 **s off** the very dust from your feet for a	660
Heb	12:26 Yet once *more* I **s** not the earth only,	4579

SHAKED (1) [SHAKE]

Ps	109:25 *when* they looked upon me they **s** their	5128

SHAKEN (22) [SHAKE]

Lev	26:36 the sound of a **s** leaf shall chase them;	5086
1Ki	14:15 as a reed is **s** in the water, and he shall	5110
2Ki	19:21 the daughter of Jerusalem hath **s** her head	5128
Ne	5:13 even thus be he **s out**, and emptied.	5287
Job	16:12 set me **to pieces**, and **s** me up for his	6327
	38:13 that the wicked might be **s** out of it?	5287
Ps	18: 7 also of the hills moved and were **s**,	1607
Isa	37:22 the daughter of Jerusalem hath **s** her head	5128
Na	2: 3 and the fir trees shall be **terribly s**.	7477
	3:12 if they be **s**, they shall even fall into	5128
Mt	11: 7 to see? A reed **s** with the wind?	4531
	24:29 and the powers of the heavens shall be **s**:	4531
Mk	13:25 the powers that are in heaven shall be **s**.	4531
Lk	6:38 and **s** *together,* and running over,	4531
	7:24 for to see? A reed **s** with the wind?	4531
	21:26 for the powers of heaven shall be **s**.	4531
Ac	4:31 place was **s** where they were assembled	4531
	16:26 that the foundations of the prison were **s**:	4531
2Th	2: 2 That ye be not soon **s** in mind,	4531
Heb	12:27 the removing of those *things* that are **s**,	4531
	12:27 that those *things* which cannot be **s** may	4531
Rev	6:13 when she is **s** of a mighty wind.	4579

SHAKETH (7) [SHAKE]

Job	9: 6 Which **s** the earth out of her place,	7264
Ps	29: 8 The voice of the LORD **s** the wilderness;	2342
	29: 8 the LORD **s** the wilderness of Kadesh.	2342
	60: 2 heal the breaches thereof; for it **s**.	4131
Isa	10:15 saw magnify itself against him that **s** it?	5130
	19:16 of the LORD of hosts, which he **s** over it.	5130
	33:15 that **s** his hands from holding of bribes,	5287

SHAKING (8) [SHAKE]

Job	41:29 as stubble: he laugheth at the **s** of a spear.	7494
Ps	44:14 a **s** of the head among the people.	4493
Isa	17: 6 the **s** of an olive tree, two or three berries	5363
	19:16 the **s** of the hand of the LORD of hosts,	8573
	24:13 *there shall be* as the **s** of an olive tree,	5363
	30:32 and in battles of **s** shall he fight with it.	8573
Eze	37: 7 behold a **s**, and the bones came together,	7494
	38:19 Surely in that day there shall be a great **s**	7494

SHALEM (1)

Ge	33:18 Jacob came to **S**, a city of Shechem,	8004

SHALIM (1)

1Sa	9: 4 they passed through the land of **S**,	8171

SHALISHA (1) [BAAL-SHALISHA]

1Sa	9: 4 passed through the land of **S**,	8031

SHALL (9838) [SHALT] See Index of Articles, Etc.

SHALLECHETH (1)

1Ch	26:16 with the gate **S**, by the causeway of	7996

SHALLEKETH See SHALLECHETH

SHALLUM (27)

2Ki	15:10 **S** the son of Jabesh conspired against him,	7967
	15:13 **S** the son of Jabesh *began* to reign in	7967
	15:14 smote **S** the son of Jabesh in Samaria,	7967
	15:15 rest of the acts of **S**, and his conspiracy	7967
	22:14 the wife of **S** the son of Tikvah, the son	7967
1Ch	2:40 begat Sisamai, and Sisamai begat **S**,	7967
	2:41 **S** begat Jekamiah, and Jekamiah begat	7967
	3:15 the third Zedekiah, the fourth **S**.	7967
	4:25 **S** his son, Mibsam his son, Mishma his	7967
	6:12 Ahitub begat Zadok, and Zadok begat **S**,	7967
	6:13 **S** begat Hilkiah, and Hilkiah begat Azariah	7967
	7:13 Jahziel, and Guni, and Jezer, and **S**,	7967
	9:17 the porters *were*, **S**, and Akkub,	7967
	9:17 and their brethren: **S** *was* the chief,	7967
	9:19 **S** the son of Kore, the son of Ebiasaph,	7967
	9:31 who *was* the firstborn of **S** the Korahite,	7967
2Ch	28:12 Jehizkiah the son of **S**, and Amasa the son	7967
	34:22 the wife of **S** the son of Tikvath, the son	7967
Ezr	2:42 the children of **S**, the children of Ater,	7967
	7: 2 The son of **S**, the son of Zadok, the son of	7967
	10:24 and of the porters; **S**, and Telem, and Uri.	7967
	10:42 **S**, Amariah, *and* Joseph.	7967
Ne	3:12 next unto him repaired **S** the son of	7967
	7:45 the children of **S**, the children of Ater,	7967
Jer	22:11 For thus saith the LORD touching **S**	7967
	32: 7 Hanameel the son of **S** thine uncle *shall*	7967
	35: 4 the chamber of Maaseiah the son of **S**,	7967

SHALLUN (1)

Ne	3:15 the gate of the fountain repaired **S** the	7968

SHALMAI (2)

Ezr	2:46 the children of **S**, the children of Hanan,	8073
Ne	7:48 the children of Hagaba, the children of **S**,	8014

SHALMAN (1) [SHALMANESER]

Hos	10:14 **S** spoiled Beth-arbel in the day of battle:	8020

SHALMANESER (2) [SHALMAN]

2Ki	17: 3 Against him came up **S** king of Assyria,	8022
	18: 9 *that* **S** king of Assyria came up against	8022

SHALT (1616) [SHALL] See Index of Articles, Etc.

SHAMA (1)

1Ch	11:44 **S** and Jehiel the sons of Hothan	8091

SHAMARIAH (1)

2Ch	11:19 him children; Jeush, and **S**, and Zaham.	8114

SHAMBLES (1)

1Co	10:25 Whatsoever is sold in the **s**, *that* eat,	3111

SHAME (100) [ASHAMED, SHAMED, SHAMEFASTNESS, SHAMEFUL, SHAMEFULLY, SHAMELESSLY, SHAMETH]

Ex	32:25 unto *their* **s** amongst their enemies:)	8103
Jdg	18: 7 that might put *them* **to s** in *any* thing;	3637
1Sa	20:34 because his father had **done** him **s**.	3637
2Sa	13:13 I, whither shall I cause my **s** to go?	2781
2Ch	32:21 So he returned with **s** of face to his own	1322
Job	8:22 that hate thee shall be clothed with **s**;	1322
Ps	4: 2 how long *will ye* turn my glory into **s**?	3639
	35: 4 and **put to s** that seek after my soul:	3637
	35:26 let them be clothed with **s** and	1322
	40:14 and **put to s** that wish me evil.	3637
	40:15 them be desolate for a reward of their **s**	1322
	44: 7 and hast **put** *them* **to s** that hated us.	954
	44: 9 thou hast cast off, and **put us to s**;	3637
	44:15 and the **s** of my face hath covered me,	1322
	53: 5 hast **put** *them* **to s**, because God hath	954
	69: 7 borne reproach; **s** hath covered my face.	3639
	69:19 reproach, and my **s**, and my dishonour:	1322
	70: 3 back for a reward of their **s** that say,	1322
	71:24 for they are **brought unto s**, that seek	2659
	83:16 Fill their faces *with* **s**; that they may seek	7036
	83:17 yea, let them be put to **s**, and perish:	2659
	89:45 thou hast covered him with **s**. Selah.	955
	109:29 Let mine adversaries be clothed with **s**,	3639
	119:31 thy testimonies: O LORD, **put** me not **to s**.	954
	132:18 His enemies will I clothe with **s**:	1322
Pr	3:35 but **s** shall be the promotion of fools.	7036
	9: 7 reproveth a scorner getteth to himself **s**:	7036
	10: 5 sleepeth in harvest *is* a son that **causeth s**.	954
	11: 2 *When* pride cometh, then cometh **s**:	7036
	12:16 but a prudent *man* covereth **s**.	7036
	13: 5 *man* is loathsome, and **cometh to s**.	2659
	13:18 **s** *shall be to* him that refuseth instruction:	7036
	14:35 his wrath is *against* him that **causeth s**.	954

S

Pr	17: 2 shall have rule over a son that **causeth** s,	954
	18:13 he heareth *it*, it *is* folly and s unto him.	3639
	19:26 *is* a son that **causeth** s,	954
	25: 8 when thy neighbour hath **put** thee to s.	3637
	25:10 Lest he heareth *it* **put** thee to s,	2616
	29:15 left *to himself* **bringeth** his mother to s.	954
Isa	20: 4 buttocks uncovered, *to* the s of Egypt.	6172
	22:18 the chariots of thy glory *shall be* the s	7036
	30: 3 shall the strength of Pharaoh be your s,	1322
	30: 5 nor profit, but a s, and also a reproach.	1322
	47: 3 be uncovered, yea, thy s shall be seen:	2781
	50: 6 I hid not my face from s and spitting.	3639
	54: 4 for thou shalt not be **put** to s:	2659
	54: 4 for thou shalt forget the s of thy youth,	1322
	61: 7 For your s *you shall have* double;	1322
Jer	3:24 For s hath devoured the labour of our	1322
	3:25 We lie down in our s, and our confusion	1322
	13:26 upon thy face, that thy s may appear.	7036
	20:18 my days should be consumed with s?	1322
	23:40 perpetual s, which shall not be forgotten.	3640
	46:12 The nations have heard *of* thy s, and thy	7036
	48:39 how hath Moab turned the back with s!	954
	51:51 s hath covered our faces: for strangers are	3639
Eze	7:18 s *shall be* upon all faces, and baldness	955
	16:52 bear thine own s for thy sins that thou	3639
	16:52 be thou confounded also, and bear thy s,	3639
	16:54 That thou mayest bear thine own s,	3639
	16:63 thy mouth any more, because of thy s,	3639
	32:24 yet have they borne their s with them	3639
	32:25 yet have they borne their s with them	3639
	32:30 bear their s with them that go down to	3639
	34:29 bear the s of the heathen any more.	3639
	36: 6 ye have borne the s of the heathen:	3639
	36: 7 that *are* about you, they shall bear their s.	3639
	36:15 in thee the s of the heathen any more,	3639
	39:26 After that they have borne their s, and all	3639
	44:13 holy *place*: but they shall bear their s,	3639
Da	12: 2 and some to s *and* everlasting contempt.	2781
Hos	4: 7 *therefore* will I change their glory into s.	7036
	4:18 her rulers *with* s do love, Give ye.	7036
	9:10 and separated themselves unto *that* s,	1322
	10: 6 Ephraim shall receive s, and Israel shall	1317
Ob	1:10 *thy* violence against thy brother Jacob s	955
Mic	1:11 inhabitant of Saphir, having *thy* s naked:	1322
	2: 6 to them, *that* they shall not take s.	3639
	7:10 and s shall cover her which said unto me,	955
Na	3: 5 thy nakedness, and the kingdoms thy s.	7036
Hab	2:10 Thou hast consulted s to thy house by	1322
	2:16 Thou art filled *with* s for glory: drink thou	7036
Zep	3: 5 faileth not; but the unjust knoweth no s.	1322
	3:19 every land where they have been put to s.	1322
Lk	14: 1 thou begin with s to take the lowest room.	152
Ac	5:41 counted worthy to **suffer** s for his name.	818
1Co	4:14 I write not these *things* to s you, but as	1788
	6: 5 I speak to your s. Is it so, that there is not	1791
	11: 6 but *if* it be a s for a woman to be shorn or	149
	11:14 if a man have long hair, it is a s unto him?	819
	11:22 church of God, and s them that have not?	2617
	14:35 for it is a s for women to speak in	149
	15:34 knowledge of God: I speak *this* to your s.	1791
Eph	5:12 For it is a s even to speak of those *things*	149
Php	3:19 *is their* belly, and *whose* glory *is* in their s,	152
Heb	6: 6 of God afresh, and **put** *him* to an **open** s.	3856
	12: 2 despising the s, and is set down at the	152
Jude	1:13 waves of the sea, foaming out their own s;	152
Rev	3:18 *that* the s of thy nakedness do not appear;	152
	16:15 lest he walk naked, and they see his s.	808

SHAMED (4) [SHAME]

Ge	38:23 Let her take *it* to her, lest we be s:	937
2Sa	19: 5 Thou hast s *this* day the faces of all thy	954
1Ch	8:12 Eber, and Misham, and S, who built Ono,	8106
Ps	14: 6 You have s the counsel of the poor,	954

SHAMEFACEDNESS See SHAMEFASTNESS

SHAMEFASTNESS (1) [SHAME]

1Ti	2: 9 in modest apparel, with s and sobriety;	127

SHAMEFUL (2) [SHAME]

Jer	11:13 have ye set up altars to *that* s thing,	1322
Hab	2:16 s **spuing** *shall be* on thy glory.	7022

SHAMEFULLY (4) [SHAME]

Hos	2: 5 she that conceived them hath **done** s: for	954
Mk	12: 4 the head, and sent *him* away s **handled**.	821
Lk	20:11 and **entreated** *him* s, and sent *him* away	818
1Th	2: 2 and were s **entreated**, as ye know,	5195

SHAMELESSLY (1) [SHAME]

2Sa	6:20 of the vain *fellows* s **uncovereth**	1540+1540

SHAMER (2)

1Ch	6:46 son of Amzi, the son of Bani, the son of S,	8106
	7:34 the sons of S; Ahi, and Rohgah, Jehubbah,	8106

SHAMETH (1) [SHAME]

Pr	28: 7 that *is* a companion of riotous *men* s his	3637

SHAMGAR (2)

Jdg	3:31 after him was S the son of Anath,	8044
	5: 6 In the days of S the son of Anath,	8044

SHAMHUTH (1)

1Ch	27: 8 The fifth captain for the fifth month *was* S	8049

SHAMIR (4)

Jos	15:48 the mountains, S, and Jattir, and Socoh,	8069
Jdg	10: 1 and he dwelt in S in mount Ephraim.	8069
	10: 2 years, and died, and was buried in S.	8069
1Ch	24:24 Michah: of the sons of Michah; S.	8069

SHAMMA (1)

1Ch	7:37 S, and Shilshah, and Ithran, and Beera.	8037

SHAMMAH (8)

Ge	36:13 Nahath, and Zerah, S, and Mizzah:	8048
	36:17 duke Nahath, duke Zerah, duke S,	8048
1Sa	16: 9 Jesse made S to pass by. And he said,	8048
	17:13 next unto him Abinadab, and the third S.	8048
2Sa	23:11 after him was S the son of Agee	8048
	23:25 S the Harodite, Elika the Harodite,	8048
	23:33 S the Hararite, Ahiam the son of Sharar	8048
1Ch	1:37 of Reuel; Nahath, Zerah, S, and Mizzah.	8048

SHAMMAI (6)

1Ch	2:28 the sons of Onam were, S, and Jada.	8060
	2:28 And the sons of S; Nadab, and Abishur.	8060
	2:32 the sons of Jada the brother of S; Jether,	8060
	2:44 father of Jorkoam: and Rekem begat S.	8060
	2:45 the son of S *was* Maon: and Maon *was*	8060
	4:17 and S, and Ishbah the father of Eshtemoa.	8060

SHAMMOTH (1)

1Ch	11:27 S the Harorite, Helez the Pelonite,	8054

SHAMMUA (5)

Nu	13: 4 the tribe of Reuben, S the son of Zaccur.	8051
2Sa	5:14 S, and Shobab, and Nathan, and Solomon,	8051
1Ch	14: 4 S, and Shobab, Nathan, and Solomon,	8051
Ne	11:17 Abda the son of S, the son of Galal,	8051
	12:18 Of Bilgah, S; of Shemaiah, Jehonathan;	8051

SHAMSHERAI (1)

1Ch	8:26 and S, and Shehariah, and Athaliah,	8125

SHAPE (2) [SHAPEN, SHAPES]

Lk	3:22 the Holy Ghost descended in a bodily s	*1491*
Jn	5:37 his voice at any time, nor seen his s.	*1491*

SHAPEN (1) [SHAPE]

Ps	51: 5 Behold, I was s in iniquity; and in sin did	2342

SHAPES (1) [SHAPE]

Rev	9: 7 And the s of the locusts *were* like unto	*3667*

SHAPHAM (1)

1Ch	5:12 S the next, and Jaanai, and Shaphat in	8223

SHAPHAN (30)

2Ki	22: 3 that the king sent S the son of Azaliah,	8227
	22: 8 Hilkiah the high priest said unto S	8227
	22: 8 Hilkiah gave the book to S, and he read	8227
	22: 9 S the scribe came to the king,	8227
	22:10 S the scribe shewed the king, saying,	8227
	22:10 me a book. And S read it before the king.	8227
	22:12 Ahikam the son of S, and Achbor the son	8227
	22:12 S the scribe, and Asahiah a servant of	8227
	22:14 Ahikam, and Achbor, and S, and Asahiah,	8227
	25:22 the son of Ahikam, the son of S, ruler.	8227
2Ch	34: 8 sent S the son of Azaliah, and Maaseiah	8227
	34:15 Hilkiah answered and said to S the scribe,	8227
	34:15 And Hilkiah delivered the book to S.	8227
	34:16 S carried the book to the king,	8227
	34:18 S the scribe told the king, saying,	8227
	34:18 me a book. And S read it before the king.	8227
	34:20 Ahikam the son of S, and Abdon the son	8227
	34:20 S the scribe, and Asaiah a servant of	8227
Jer	26:24 Ahikam the son of S was with Jeremiah,	8227
	29: 3 By the hand of Elasah the son of S,	8227
	36:10 in the chamber of Gemariah the son of S	8227
	36:11 the son of Gemariah, the son of S,	8227
	36:12 Gemariah the son of S, and Zedekiah	8227
	39:14 Gedaliah the son of Ahikam the son of S,	8227
	40: 5 Gedaliah the son of Ahikam the son of S	8227
	40: 9 Gedaliah the son of Ahikam the son of S	8227
	40:11 Gedaliah the son of Ahikam the son of S;	8227
	41: 2 of Ahikam the son of S with the sword,	8227
	43: 6 Gedaliah the son of Ahikam the son of S,	8227
Eze	8:11 of them stood Jaazaniah the son of S,	8227

SHAPHAT (8)

Nu	13: 5 Of the tribe of Simeon, S the son of Hori.	8202
1Ki	19:16 Elisha the son of S of Abel-meholah shalt	8202
	19:19 found Elisha the son of S,	8202
2Ki	3:11 and said, Here *is* Elisha the son of S,	8202
	6:31 if the head of Elisha the son of S shall	8202
1Ch	3:22 Igeal, and Bariah, and Neariah, and S, six.	8202
	5:12 the next, and Jaanai, and S in Bashan.	8202
	27:29 in the valleys *was* S the son of Adlai:	8202

SHAPHER (2)

Nu	33:23 Kehelathah, and pitched in mount S.	8234
	33:24 they removed from mount S,	8234

SHAPHIR See SAPHIR

SHARAI (1)

Ezr	10:40 Machnadebai, Shashai, S,	8298

SHARAIM (1)

Jos	15:36 S, and Adithaim, and Gederah,	8189

SHARAR (1)

2Sa	23:33 Ahiam the son of S the Hararite,	8325

SHARE (1)

1Sa	13:20 sharpen every man his s, and his coulter,	4282

SHAREZER (2)

2Ki	19:37 S his sons smote him with the sword:	8272
Isa	37:38 S his sons smote him with the sword;	8272

SHARON (6) [SHARONITE]

1Ch	5:16 in her towns, and in all the suburbs of S,	8289
	27:29 over the herds that fed in S *was* Shitrai	8289
SS	2: 1 I am the rose of S, *and* the lily of	8289
Isa	33: 9 S is like a wilderness; and Bashan and	8289
	35: 2 the excellency of Carmel and S, they	8289
	65:10 S shall be a fold of flocks, and the valley	8289

SHARONITE (1) [SHARON]

1Ch	27:29 herds that fed in Sharon *was* Shitrai the S:	8290

SHARP (25) [SHARPEN, SHARPENED, SHARPENETH, SHARPER, SHARPLY, SHARPNESS]

Ex	4:25 Zipporah took a s **stone**, and cut off	6864
Jos	5: 2 Make thee s knives, and circumcise	6697
	5: 3 Joshua made him s knives,	6697
1Sa	14: 4 there was a s rock on the one side,	8127
	14: 4 one side, and a s rock on the other side:	8127
Job	41:30 S stones *are* under him: he spreadeth	2303
	41:30 he spreadeth s **pointed** *things* upon	2742
Ps	45: 5 Thine arrows *are* s in the heart of the	8150
	52: 2 like a s razor, working deceitfully.	3913
	57: 4 and arrows, and their tongue a s sword.	2299
	120: 4 S arrows of the mighty, with coals of	8150
Pr	5: 4 as wormwood, s as a twoedged sword.	2299
	25:18 *is* a maul, and a sword, and a s arrow.	8150
Isa	5:28 Whose arrows *are* s, and all their bows	8150
	41:15 I will make thee a new s threshing	2742
	49: 2 he hath made my mouth like a s sword;	2299
Eze	5: 1 thou, son of man, take thee a s knife,	2299
Ac	15:39 And the **contention** was so s *between*	3948
Rev	1:16 of his mouth went a s twoedged sword:	3691
	2:12 These *things* saith he which hath the s	3691
	14:14 golden crown, and in his hand a s sickle.	3691
	14:17 is in heaven, he also having a s sickle.	3691
	14:18 with a loud cry to him that had the s	3691
	14:18 Thrust in thy s sickle, and gather	3691
	19:15 And out of his mouth goeth a s sword,	3691

SHARPEN (2) [SHARP]

1Sa	13:20 to s every man his share, and his coulter,	3913
	13:21 and for the axes, and to s the goads.	5324

SHARPENED (4) [SHARP]

Ps	140: 3 They have s their tongues like a serpent;	8150
Eze	21: 9 A sword, a sword is s, and also furbished;	2300
	21:10 It is s to make a sore slaughter; *it is*	2300
	21:11 this sword is s, and *it is* furbished, to give	2300

SHARPENETH (3) [SHARP]

Job	16: 9 teeth; mine enemy s his eyes upon me.	3913
Pr	27:17 Iron s iron; so a man sharpeneth	2300
	27:17 so a man s the countenance of his friend.	2300

SHARPER (2) [SHARP]

Mic	7: 4 the *most* upright *is* s than a thorn hedge:	NIH
Heb	4:12 and s than any twoedged sword,	*5114*

SHARPLY (2) [SHARP]

Jdg	8: 1 And they did chide with him s.	2394+871.1
Tit	1:13 Wherefore rebuke them s, that they may	*664*

SHARPNESS (1) [SHARP]

2Co	13:10 lest being present I should use s,	*664*

SHARUHEN (1)

Jos	19: 6 Beth-lebaoth, and S; thirteen cities and	8287

SHASHAI (1)

Ezr	10:40 Machnadebai, S, Sharai,	8343

SHASHAK (2)

1Ch	8:14 And Ahio, S, and Jeremoth,	8349
	8:25 And Iphedeiah, and Penuel, the sons of S;	8349

SHATTERED See VEX; VEXATION; VEXED

SHATTERS See SUNDER

SHAUL (7) [SHAULITES]

Ge	46:10 and S the son of a Canaanitish woman.	7586
Ex	6:15 and S the son of a Canaanitish woman.	7586
Nu	26:13 of S, the family of the Shaulites.	7586
1Ch	1:48 S of Rehoboth *by* the river reigned in his	7586
	1:49 when S was dead, Baal-hanan the son of	7586
	4:24 and Jamin, Jarib, Zerah, *and* S:	7586
	6:24 his son, Uzziah his son, and S his son.	7586

SHAULITES (1) [SHAUL]

Nu	26:13 the Zarhites: of Shaul, the family of the S.	7587

SHAVE (14) [SHAVED, SHAVEN]

Lev	13:33 be shaven, but the scall shall he not s;	1548
	14: 8 s off all his hair, and wash *himself* in	1548
	14: 9 *that* he shall s all *off* his head and	1548
	14: 9 even all his hair he shall s off:	1548
	21: 5 neither shall they s off the corner of their	1548

S

Nu 6: 9 he shall **s** his head in the day of his 1548
 6: 9 on the seventh day shall he **s** it. 1548
 6:18 the Nazarite shall **s** the head of his 1548
 8: 7 let them **s** all their flesh, and let 5674+8593
Dt 21:12 she shall **s** her head, and pare her nails; 1548
Jdg 16:19 she **caused** *him* **to s off** the seven locks 1548
Isa 7:20 In the same day shall the Lord **s** with a 1548
Eze 44:20 Neither shall they **s** their heads, nor suffer 1548
Ac 21:24 with them, that they may **s** *their* heads: 3587

SHAVED (4) [SHAVE]

Ge 41:14 he **s** *himself,* and changed his raiment, 1548
2Sa 10: 4 **s** off the *one* half of their beards, 1548
1Ch 19: 4 s them, and cut off their garments in 1548
Job 1:20 **s** his head, and fell down upon the ground 1494

SHAVEH (1) [SHAVEH KIRIATHAIM]

Ge 14:17 at the valley of **S**, which *is* the king's dale. 7740

SHAVEH KIRIATHAIM (1)

Ge 14: 5 in Ham, and the Emims in **S**, 7741

SHAVEN (7) [SHAVE]

Lev 13:33 He shall be **s**, but the scall shall he not 1548
Nu 6:19 after *the hair of* his separation is **s**: 1548
Jdg 16:17 if I be **s**, then my strength will go from 1548
 16:22 head began to grow *again* after he was **s**. 1548
Jer 41: 5 their beards **s**, and their clothes rent, 1548
1Co 11: 5 for *that* is even all one as if she were **s**. 3587
 11: 6 be a shame for a woman to be shorn or **s**, 3587

SHAVSHA (1)

1Ch 18:16 *were* the priests; and **S** *was* scribe; 7798

SHE (981) [HER, HERS, HERSELF] See Index of
Articles, Etc.

SHEAF (9) [SHEAVES]

Ge 37: 7 and lo, my **s** arose, and also stood upright; 485
 37: 7 round about, and made obeisance to my **s**. 485
Lev 23:10 ye shall bring a **s** of the firstfruits of your 6016
 23:11 he shall wave the **s** before the Lord, 6016
 23:12 shall offer that day when ye wave the **s** 6016
 23:15 from the day that ye brought the **s** of 6016
Dt 24:19 forgot a **s** in the field, thou shalt not go 6016
Job 24:10 they take away the **s** *from* the hungry; 6016
Zec 12: 6 the wood, and like a torch of fire in a **s**; 5995

SHEAL (1)

Ezr 10:29 and Adaiah, Jashub, and **S**, and Ramoth. 7594

SHEALTIEL (9)

Ezr 3: 2 Zerubbabel the son of **S**, and his brethren, 7597
 3: 8 began Zerubbabel the son of **S**, 7597
 5: 2 rose up Zerubbabel the son of **S**, 7598
Ne 12: 1 went up with Zerubbabel the son of **S**, 7597
Hag 1: 1 the prophet unto Zerubbabel the son of **S**, 7597
 1:12 Zerubbabel the son of **S**, and Joshua the 7597
 1:14 up the spirit of Zerubbabel the son of **S**, 7597
 2: 2 Speak now to Zerubbabel the son of **S**, 7597
 2:23 O Zerubbabel, my servant, the son of **S**, 7597

SHEAR (4) [SHEARER, SHEARERS, SHEARING,
SHEEPSHEARERS, SHORN]

Ge 31:19 Laban went **s** to his sheep: and Rachel 1494
 38:13 in law goeth up to Timnath to **s** his sheep. 1494
Dt 15:19 bullock, nor **s** the firstling of thy sheep. 1494
1Sa 25: 4 the wilderness that Nabal did **s** his sheep. 1494

SHEARD (1) [SHEARDS]

Isa 30:14 of it a **s** to take fire from the hearth, 2789

SHEARDS (1) [SHEARD]

Eze 23:34 shalt break the **s** thereof, and pluck off 2789

SHEARER (1) [SHEAR]

Ac 8:32 and like a lamb dumb before his **s**, 2751

SHEARERS (3) [SHEAR]

1Sa 31:19 now I have heard that thou hast **s**: now 1494
 25:11 my flesh that I have killed for my **s**, 1494
Isa 53: 7 as a sheep before her **s** is dumb, 1494

SHEARIAH (2)

1Ch 8:38 Ishmael, and **S**, and Obadiah, and Hanan. 8187
 9:44 Ishmael, and **S**, and Obadiah, and Hanan: 8187

SHEARING (3) [SHEAR]

1Sa 25: 2 and he was **s** his sheep in Carmel. 1494
2Ki 10:12 *And* as he was at the **s** house in the way, 1044
 10:14 slew them at the pit of the **s** house, 1044

SHEAR-JASHUB (1)

Isa 7: 3 now to meet Ahaz, thou, and **S** thy son, 7610

SHEATH (8)

1Sa 17:51 it out of the **s** thereof, and slew him, 8593
2Sa 20: 8 fastened upon his loins in the **s** thereof; 8593
1Ch 21:27 put up his sword again into the **s** thereof. 5084
Eze 21: 3 will draw forth my sword out of his **s**, 8593
 21: 4 my sword go forth out of his **s** against 8593
 21: 5 have drawn forth my sword out of his **s**: 8593
 21:30 Shall I cause *it* to return into his **s**? I will 8593
Jn 18:11 unto Peter, Put up thy sword into the **s**: 2336

SHEAVES (9) [SHEAF]

Ge 37: 7 we *were* binding **s** in the field, and lo, 485

 37: 7 your **s** stood round about, 485
Ru 2: 7 gather after the reapers amongst the **s**: 6016
 2:15 Let her glean even among the **s**, 6016
Ne 13:15 and bringing in **s**, and lading asses; 6194
Ps 126: 6 with rejoicing, bringing his **s** *with him.* 485
 129: 7 hand; nor he that **bindeth s** his bosom. 6014
Am 2:13 as a cart is pressed *that* is full *of* **s**. 5995
Mic 4:12 for he shall gather them as the **s** into 5995

SHEBA (32) [BEER-SHEBA]

Ge 10: 7 and the sons of Raamah; **S**, and Dedan. 7614
 10:28 And Obal, and Abimael, and **S**, 7614
 25: 3 Jokshan begat **S**, and Dedan. 7614
Jos 19: 2 inheritance Beer-sheba, or **S**, and 7652
2Sa 20: 1 whose name *was* **S**, the son of Bichri, 7652
 20: 2 *and* followed **S** the son of Bichri: 7652
 20: 6 Now shall **S** the son of Bichri do us more 7652
 20: 7 to pursue after **S** the son of Bichri. 7652
 20:10 Abishai his brother pursued after **S** the 7652
 20:13 to pursue after **S** the son of Bichri. 7652
 20:21 **S** the son of Bichri by name, 7652
 20:22 cut off the head of **S** the son of Bichri, 7652
1Ki 10: 1 when the queen of **S** heard of the fame of 7614
 10: 4 when the queen of **S** had seen all 7614
 10:10 the queen of **S** gave to king Solomon. 7614
 10:13 Solomon gave unto the queen of **S** all 7614
1Ch 1: 9 And the sons of Raamah; **S**, and Dedan. 7614
 1:22 And Ebal, and Abimael, and **S**, 7614
 1:32 And the sons of Jokshan; **S**, and Dedan. 7614
 5:13 and Jorai, and Jachan, and Zia, 7652
2Ch 9: 1 the queen of **S** heard of the fame of 7614
 9: 3 the queen of **S** had seen the wisdom 7614
 9: 9 as the queen of **S** gave king Solomon. 7614
 9:12 Solomon gave to the queen of **S** all her 7614
Job 6:19 the companies of **S** waited for them. 7614
Ps 72:10 the kings of **S** and Seba shall offer gifts. 7614
 72:15 and to him shall be given of the gold of **S**: 7614
Isa 60: 6 and Ephah; all they from **S** shall come: 7614
Jer 6:20 cometh there to me incense from **S**, 7614
Eze 27:22 The merchants of **S** and Raamah, they 7614
 27:23 Eden, the merchants of **S**, Asshur, 7614
 38:13 **S**, and Dedan, and the merchants of 7614

SHEBAH (1) [BEER-SHEBA]

Ge 26:33 called it **S**: therefore the name of the city 7656

SHEBAM (1)

Nu 32: 3 and Elealeh, and **S**, and Nebo, and Beon, 7643

SHEBANIAH (7)

1Ch 15:24 **S**, and Jehoshaphat, and Nethaneel, 7645
Ne 9: 4 Jeshua, and Bani, Kadmiel, **S**, Bunni, 7645
 9: 5 Hodijah, **S**, *and* Pethahiah, said, Stand up 7645
 10: 4 Hattush, **S**, Malluch, 7645
 10:10 **S**, Hodijah, Kelita, Pelaiah, Hanan, 7645
 10:12 Zaccur, Sherebiah, **S**, 7645
 12:14 Of Melicu, Jonathan; of **S**, Joseph; 7645

SHEBARIM (1)

Jos 7: 5 them *from* before the gate *even* unto **S**, 7671

SHEBAT See SEBAT

SHEBER (1)

1Ch 2:48 Caleb's concubine, bare **S**, and Tirhanah. 7669

SHEBNA (9)

2Ki 18:18 **S** the scribe, and Joah the son of Asaph 7644
 18:26 **S**, and Joah, unto Rab-shakeh, Speak, 7644
 18:37 **S** the scribe, and Joah the son of Asaph 7644
 19: 2 **S** the scribe, and the elders of the priests, 7644
Isa 22:15 *even* unto **S**, which *is* over the house, 7644
 36: 3 **S** the scribe, and Joah, Asaph's son, 7644
 36:11 said Eliakim and **S** and Joah unto 7644
 36:22 **S** the scribe, and Joah, the son of Asaph, 7644
 37: 2 **S** the scribe, and the elders of the priests 7644

SHEBUEL (3)

1Ch 23:16 *Of* the sons of Gershom, **S** *was* the chief. 7619
 25: 4 **S**, and Jerimoth, Hananiah, Hanani, 7619
 26:24 **S** the son of Gershom, the son of Moses, 7619

SHECANIAH (2)

1Ch 24:11 The ninth to Jeshua, the tenth to **S**, 7935
2Ch 31:15 Jeshua, and Shemaiah, Amariah, and **S**, 7935

SHECHANIAH (8)

1Ch 3:21 the sons of Obadiah, the sons of **S**. 7935
 3:22 the sons of **S**; Shemaiah: and the sons of 7935
Ezr 8: 3 Of the sons of **S**, of the sons of Pharosh; 7935
 8: 5 Of the sons of **S**; the son of Jahaziel, 7935
 10: 2 of the sons of **S**, *one* of the sons of 7935
Ne 3:29 him repaired also Shemaiah the son of **S**, 7935
 6:18 *was* the son in law of **S** the son of Arah; 7935
 12: 3 **S**, Rehum, Meremoth, 7935

SHECHEM (62) [SHECHEM'S, SHECHEMITES,
SYCHEM]

Ge 33:18 Jacob came to Shalem, a city of **S**, which 7927
 34: 2 when **S** the son of Hamor the Hivite, 7928
 34: 4 **S** spake unto his father Hamor, saying, 7928
 34: 6 Hamor the father of **S** went out unto 7928
 34: 8 The soul of my son **S** longeth for your 7928
 34:11 **S** said unto her father and unto her 7928
 34:13 the sons of Jacob answered **S** and Hamor 7928
 34:18 pleased Hamor, and **S** Hamor's son. 7928

Ge 34:20 **S** his son came unto the gate of their city, 7928
 34:24 unto **S** his son hearkened all that went 7928
 34:26 and **S** his son with the edge of the sword, 7928
 35: 4 hid them under the oak which *was* by **S**. 7927
 37:12 went to feed their father's flock in **S**. 7927
 37:13 Do not thy brethren feed *the flock* in **S**? 7927
 37:14 of the vale of Hebron, and he came to **S**. 7927
Nu 26:31 and *of* **S**, the family of the Shechemites: 7928
Jos 17: 2 for the children of **S**, and for the children 7928
 17: 7 Asher *to* Michmethah, that *lieth* before **S**; 7927
 20: 7 **S** in mount Ephraim, and Kirjath-arba, 7927
 21:21 For they gave them **S** with her suburbs in 7927
 24: 1 gathered all the tribes of Israel to **S**, 7927
 24:25 set them a statute and an ordinance in **S**, 7927
 24:32 brought up out of Egypt, buried they in **S**, 7927
 24:32 father of **S** for an hundred pieces of silver: 7927
Jdg 8:31 his concubine that *was* in **S**, she also bare 7927
 9: 1 Abimelech the son of Jerubbaal went to **S** 7927
 9: 2 I pray you, in the ears of all the men of **S**, 7927
 9: 3 ears of all the men of **S** all these words: 7927
 9: 6 all the men of **S** gathered together, 7927
 9: 6 by the plain of the pillar that *was* in **S**. 7927
 9: 7 them, Hearken unto me, you men of **S**, 7927
 9:18 king over the men of **S**, because he *is* 7927
 9:20 devour the men of **S**, and the house of 7927
 9:20 let fire come out from the men of **S**, 7927
 9:23 between Abimelech and the men of **S**; 7927
 9:23 the men of **S** dealt treacherously with 7927
 9:24 upon the men of **S**, which aided him in 7927
 9:25 the men of **S** set liers in wait for him in 7927
 9:26 with his brethren, and went over to **S**: 7927
 9:26 the men of **S** put their confidence in him. 7927
 9:28 Who *is* Abimelech, and who *is* **S**, that we 7927
 9:28 serve the men of Hamor the father of **S**? 7927
 9:31 of Ebed and his brethren be come to **S**; 7927
 9:34 laid wait against **S** in four companies. 7927
 9:39 Gaal went out before the men of **S**, 7927
 9:41 that *they* should not dwell in **S**. 7927
 9:46 when all the men of the tower of **S** heard 7927
 9:47 that all the men of the tower of **S** were 7927
 9:49 all the men of the tower of **S** died also, 7927
 9:57 the evil of the men of **S** did God render 7927
 21:19 highway that goeth up from Beth-el to **S**, 7927
1Ki 12: 1 Rehoboam went *to* **S**: for all Israel were 7927
 12: 1 for all Israel were come to **S** to make him 7927
 12:25 Jeroboam built **S** in mount Ephraim, 7927
1Ch 6:67 **S** in mount Ephraim with her suburbs; 7927
 7:19 Ahian, and **S**, and Likhi, and Aniam. 7928
 7:28 **S** also and the towns thereof, unto Gaza 7927
2Ch 10: 1 Rehoboam went to **S**: for to Shechem 7927
 10: 1 for to **S** were all Israel come to make him 7927
Ps 60: 6 I will divide **S**, and mete out the valley of 7927
 108: 7 I will divide **S**, and mete out the valley of 7927
Jer 41: 5 That there came certain from **S**, 7927

SHECHEM'S (2) [SHECHEM]

Ge 33:19 **S** father, for an hundred pieces of money. 7928
 34:26 took Dinah out of **S** house, and went out. 7928

SHECHEMITES (1) [SHECHEM]

Nu 26:31 and *of* Shechem, the family of the **S**: 7930

SHED (52) [SHEDDER, SHEDDETH, SHEDDING]

Ge 9: 6 man's blood, by man shall his blood be **s**: 8210
 37:22 **S** no blood, *but* cast him into this pit that 8210
Ex 22: 2 he die, *there shall* no blood *be* **s** for him. NIH
 22: 3 upon him, *there shall* be blood *s* for him; NIH
Lev 17: 4 hath **s** blood; and that man shall be cut 8210
Nu 35:33 be cleansed of the blood that is **s** therein, 8210
 35:33 but by the blood of him that **s** it. 8210
Dt 19:10 That innocent blood be not **s** in thy land, 8210
 21: 7 and say, Our hands have not **s** this blood, 8210
1Sa 25:26 withholden thee from coming to **s** blood, NIH
 25:31 either that thou hast **s** blood causeless, 8210
 25:33 kept me this day from coming to **s** blood, NIH
2Sa 20:10 and **s** out his bowels to the ground, 8210
1Ki 2: 5 **s** the blood of war in peace, and put 7760
 2: 5 Joab **s**, from me, and from the house 8210
2Ki 21:16 Moreover Manasseh **s** innocent blood 8210
 24: 4 also *for* the innocent blood that he **s**: for 8210
1Ch 22: 8 Thou hast **s** blood abundantly, 8210
 22: 8 thou hast **s** much blood upon the earth, 8210
 28: 3 *been* a man of war, and hast **s** blood. 8210
Ps 79: 3 Their blood have they **s** like water round 8210
 79:10 of the blood of thy servants which is **s**. 8210
 106:38 **s** innocent blood, *even* the blood of their 8210
Pr 1:16 run to evil, and make haste to **s** blood. 8210
 6:17 and hands that **s** innocent blood, 8210
Isa 59: 7 and they make haste to **s** innocent blood: 8210
Jer 7: 6 and **s** not innocent blood in this place, 8210
 22: 3 neither **s** innocent blood in this place. 8210
 22:17 to **s** innocent blood, and for oppression, 8210
La 4:13 *have* **s** the blood of the just in the midst 8210
Eze 16:38 break wedlock and **s** blood are judged; 8210
 22: 4 guilty in thy blood that thou hast **s**; 8210
 22: 6 one were in thee to their power to **s** 8210
 22: 9 thee are men that carry tales to **s** blood: 8210
 22:12 In thee have they taken gifts to **s** blood; 8210
 22:27 to **s** blood, *and* to destroy souls, to get 8210
 23:45 after the manner of *women* that **s** blood; 8210
 33:25 your eyes toward your idols, and **s** blood, 8210
 35: 5 hast **s** *the blood of* the children of Israel 5064
 36:18 the blood that they had **s** upon the land, 8210
Joel 3:19 they have **s** innocent blood in their land. 8210
Mt 23:35 all the righteous blood **s** upon the earth, *1632*

Mt	26:28 which is **s** for many for the remission of	1632
Mk	14:24 the new testament, which is **s** for many.	1632
Lk	11:50 which was **s** from the foundation of	1632
	22:20 testament in my blood, which is **s** for you.	1632
Ac	2:33 he hath **s forth** this, which ye now see	1632
	22:20 the blood of thy martyr Stephen was **s**,	1632
Ro	3:15 Their feet *are* swift to **s** blood:	1632
	5: 5 the love of God is **s abroad** in our hearts	1632
Tit	3: 6 he is on us abundantly through Jesus	1632
Rev	16: 6 For they have **s** the blood of saints and	1632

SHEDDER (1) [SHED]

Eze	18:10 a **s** of blood, and *that* doeth the like to	8210

SHEDDETH (2) [SHED]

Ge	9: 6 Whoso **s** man's blood, by man shall his	8210
Eze	22: 3 The city **s** blood in the midst of it, that	8210

SHEDDING (1) [SHED]

Heb	9:22 and without **s of blood** is no remission.	130

SHEDEUR (5)

Nu	1: 5 the tribe of Reuben; Elizur the son of **S**.	7707
	2:10 of Reuben *shall be* Elizur the son of **S**.	7707
	7:30 On the fourth day Elizur the son of **S**,	7707
	7:35 *was* the offering of Elizur the son of **S**.	7707
	10:18 and over his host *was* Elizur the son of **S**.	7707

SHEEP (187) [SHEEP'S, SHEEPCOTE, SHEEPCOTES, SHEEPFOLD, SHEEPFOLDS, SHEEPMASTER, SHEEPSHEARERS, SHEEPSKINS, SHEPHERD, SHEPHERD'S, SHEPHERDS, SHEPHERDS']

Ge	4: 2 Abel was a keeper of **s**, but Cain was a	6629
	12:16 he had **s**, and oxen, and he asses,	6629
	20:14 Abimelech took **s**, and oxen,	6629
	21:27 Abraham took **s** and oxen, and gave *them*	6629
	29: 2 lo, there *were* three flocks of **s** lying by it;	6629
	29: 3 watered the **s**, and put the stone again	6629
	29: 6 Rachel his daughter cometh with the **s**.	6629
	29: 7 water ye the **s**, and go *and* feed *them*.	6629
	29: 8 the well's mouth; then we water the **s**.	6629
	29: 9 them, Rachel came with her father's **s**:	6629
	29:10 the **s** of Laban his mother's brother,	6629
	30:32 all the brown cattle among the **s**,	3775
	30:33 the goats, and brown amongst the **s**,	3775
	30:35 all the brown amongst the **s**, and gave	3775
	31:19 Laban went to shear his **s**: and Rachel	6629
	34:28 They took their **s**, and their oxen, and	6629
	38:13 in law goeth up to Timnah to shear his **s**.	6629
Ex	9: 3 camels, upon the oxen, and upon the **s**:	6629
	12: 5 ye shall take *it* out from the **s**, or from	3532
	20:24 peace offerings, thy **s**, and thine oxen:	6629
	22: 1 steal an ox, or a **s**, and kill it, or sell it;	7716
	22: 1 oxen for an ox, and four **s** for a sheep.	6629
	22: 1 oxen for an ox, and four sheep for a **s**.	7716
	22: 4 hand alive, whether it be ox, or ass, or **s**;	7716
	22: 9 for ass, for **s**, for raiment, *or* for any	7716
	22:10 or an ox, or a **s**, or any beast, to keep;	7716
	22:30 thou do with thine oxen, *and* with thy **s**:	6629
	34:19 thy cattle, *whether* ox or **s**, *that is* male.	7716
Lev	1:10 of the **s**, or of the goats, for a burnt	3775
	7:23 no *manner* fat, of ox, of **s**, or of goat.	3775
	22:19 of the beeves, of the **s**, or of the goats.	3775
	22:21 a freewill offering in beeves or **s**, it shall	6629
	22:27 or a **s**, or a goat, is brought forth, then	3775
	27:26 shall sanctify it; whether *it be* ox, or **s**:	7716
Nu	18:17 or the firstling of a **s**, or the firstling of a	3775
	22:40 Balak offered oxen and **s**, and sent to	6629
	27:17 be not as **s** which have no shepherd.	6629
	31:28 the beeves, and of the asses, and of the **s**:	6629
	31:32 seventy thousand and five thousand **s**,	6629
	31:36 and thirty thousand and five hundred **s**:	6629
	31:37 the LORD's tribute of the **s** was six	6629
	31:43 *and* seven thousand and five hundred **s**,	6629
	32:24 for your little ones, and folds for your **s**;	6792
	32:36 fenced cities: and folds for **s**.	6629
Dt	7:13 of thy kine, and the flocks of thy **s**,	6629
	14: 4 eat: the ox, the **s**, and the goat,	3775+7716
	14:26 or for **s**, or for wine, or for strong drink,	6629
	15:19 bullock, nor shear the firstling of thy **s**.	6629
	17: 1 or **s**, wherein is blemish, *or* any evil	7716
	18: 3 offer a sacrifice, whether *it be* ox or **s**;	7716
	18: 4 thy oil, and the first of the fleece of thy **s**,	6629
	22: 1 not see thy brother's ox or his **s** go astray,	7716
	28: 4 of thy kine, and the flocks of thy **s**.	6629
	28:18 of thy kine, and the flocks of thy **s**.	6629
	28:31 thy **s** *shall be* given unto thine enemies,	6629
	28:51 increase of thy kine, or flocks of thy **s**,	6629
	32:14 Butter of kine, and milk of **s**, with fat of	6629
Jos	6:21 and old, and ox, and **s**, and ass,	7716
	7:24 his **s**, and his tent, and all that he had:	6629
Jdg	6: 4 for Israel, neither **s**, nor ox, nor ass.	7716
1Sa	8:17 He will take the tenth of your **s**:	6629
	14:32 took **s**, and oxen, and calves, and slew	6629
	14:34 every man his **s**, and slay *them* here,	7716
	15: 3 and suckling, ox and **s**, camel and ass.	7716
	15: 9 the best of the **s**, and of the oxen, and of	6629
	15:14 then this bleating of the **s** in mine ears,	6629
	15:15 for the people spared the best of the **s** and	6629
	15:21 the people took of the spoil, **s** and oxen,	6629
	16:11 youngest, and behold, he keepeth the **s**.	6629
	16:19 David thy son, which *is* with the **s**.	6629
	17:15 returned from Saul to feed his father's **s**	6629
	17:20 left the **s** with a keeper, and took, and	6629
	17:28 with whom hast thou left those few **s** in	6629

1Sa	17:34 Thy servant kept his father's **s**,	6629
	22:19 and sucklings, and oxen, and asses, and **s**,	7716
	25: 2 he had three thousand **s**, and a thousand	6629
	25: 2 and he was shearing his **s** in Carmel.	6629
	25: 4 the wilderness that Nabal did shear his **s**.	6629
	25:16 while we were with them keeping the **s**.	6629
	25:18 five **s** ready dressed, and five measures of	6629
	27: 9 took away the **s**, and the oxen,	6629
2Sa	7: 8 from following the **s**, to be ruler over my	6629
	17:29 and **s**, and cheese of kine, for David,	6629
	24:17 these **s**, what have they done? let thine	6629
1Ki	1: 9 Adonijah slew **s** and oxen and fat cattle	6629
	1:19 and fat cattle and **s** in abundance,	6629
	1:25 and fat cattle and **s** in abundance,	6629
	4:23 an hundred **s**, beside harts, and roebucks,	6629
	8: 5 him before the ark, sacrificing **s** and oxen,	6629
	8:63 and an hundred and twenty thousand **s**.	6629
	22:17 the hills, as **s** that have not a shepherd:	6629
2Ki	5:26 **s**, and oxen, and menservants,	6629
1Ch	5:21 of **s** two hundred and fifty thousand,	6629
	12:40 and oil, and oxen, and **s** abundantly:	6629
	17: 7 the sheepcote, *even* from following the **s**,	6629
	21:17 as *for* these **s**, what have they done?	6629
2Ch	5: 6 sacrificed **s** and oxen, which could not be	6629
	7: 5 and an hundred and twenty thousand **s**:	6629
	14:15 carried away **s** and camels in abundance,	6629
	15:11 hundred oxen and seven thousand **s**.	6629
	18: 2 Ahab killed **s** and oxen for him in	6629
	18:16 mountains, as **s** that have no shepherd:	6629
	29:33 six hundred oxen and three thousand **s**.	6629
	30:24 thousand bullocks and seven thousand **s**;	6629
	30:24 a thousand bullocks and ten thousand **s**:	6629
	31: 6 also brought in the tithe of oxen and **s**,	6629
Ne	3: 1 the priests, and they built the **s** gate;	6629
	3:32 unto the **s** gate repaired the goldsmiths	6629
	5:18 *for* me daily *was* one ox *and* six choice **s**;	6629
	12:39 the tower of Meah, even unto the **s** gate:	6629
Job	1: 3 His substance also was seven thousand **s**,	6629
	1:16 hath burnt up the **s**, and the servants,	6629
	31:20 were *not* warmed with the fleece of my **s**;	3532
	42:12 for he had fourteen thousand **s**,	6629
Ps	8: 7 All **s** and oxen, yea, and the beasts of	6792
	44:11 Thou hast given us like **s** appointed for	6629
	44:22 we are counted as **s** for the slaughter.	6629
	49:14 Like **s** they are laid in the grave; death	6629
	74: 1 *why* doth thine anger smoke against the **s**	6629
	78:52 made his own people to go forth like **s**,	6629
	79:13 **s** of thy pasture will give thee thanks for	6629
	95: 7 of his pasture, and the **s** of his hand.	6629
	100: 3 *are* his people, and the **s** of his pasture.	6629
	119:176 I have gone astray like a lost **s**; seek thy	7716
	144:13 *that* our **s** may bring forth thousands and	6629
SS	4: 2 Thy teeth *are* like a flock of **s** that are	NIH
	6: 6 Thy teeth *are* as a flock of **s** which go up	7353
Isa	7:21 shall nourish a young cow, and two **s**;	6629
	13:14 and as as a **s** that no *man* taketh up:	6629
	22:13 killing **s**, eating flesh, and drinking wine:	6629
	53: 6 All we like **s** have gone astray; we have	6629
	53: 7 as a **s** before her shearers is dumb,	7353
Jer	12: 3 pull them out like **s** for the slaughter,	6629
	23: 1 destroy and scatter the **s** of my pasture!	6629
	50: 6 people hath been lost **s**: their shepherds	6629
	50:17 Israel *is* a scattered **s**; the lions have	7716
Eze	34: 6 My **s** wandered through all the	6629
	34:11 both search my **s**, and seek them out.	6629
	34:12 that he is among his **s** *that are* scattered;	6629
	34:12 so will I seek out my **s**, and will deliver	6629
Hos	12:12 for a wife, and for a wife he kept **s**.	NIH
Joel	1:18 yea, the flocks of **s** are made desolate.	6629
Mic	2:12 will put them together as the **s** of Bozrah,	6629
	5: 8 as a young lion among the flocks of **s**:	6629
Zec	13: 7 the shepherd, and the **s** shall be scattered:	6629
Mt	9:36 scattered abroad, as **s** having no shepherd.	4263
	10: 6 But go rather to the lost **s** of the house of	4263
	10:16 send you forth as **s** in the midst of wolves:	4263
	12:11 shall have one **s**, and if it fall into a pit	4263
	12:12 How much then is a man better than a **s**?	4263
	15:24 but unto the lost **s** of the house of Israel.	4263
	18:12 if a man have an hundred **s**, and one of	4263
	18:13 he rejoiceth more of that **s**, than of	NIG
	25:32 a shepherd divideth *his* **s** from the goats:	4263
	25:33 And he shall set the **s** on his right hand,	4263
	26:31 **s** of the flock shall be scattered abroad.	4263
Mk	6:34 they were as **s** not having a shepherd:	4263
	14:27 the shepherd, and the **s** shall be scattered.	4263
Lk	15: 4 What man of you, having an hundred **s**,	4263
	15: 6 for I have found my **s** which was lost.	4263
Jn	2:14 those that sold oxen and **s** and doves,	4263
	2:15 out of the temple, and the **s** and the oxen;	4263
	5: 2 Now there is at Jerusalem by the **s** market	4262
	10: 2 in by the door is the shepherd of the **s**.	4263
	10: 3 porter openeth; and the **s** hear his voice:	4263
	10: 3 and he calleth his own **s** by name,	4263
	10: 4 And when he putteth forth his own **s**,	4263
	10: 4 goeth before them, and the **s** follow him:	4263
	10: 7 I say unto you, I am the door of the **s**.	4263
	10: 8 and robbers: but the **s** did not hear them.	4263
	10:11 the good shepherd giveth his life for the **s**.	4263
	10:12 the shepherd, whose own the **s** are not,	4263
	10:12 coming, and leaveth the **s**, and fleeth:	4263
	10:12 wolf catcheth them, and scattereth the **s**.	4263
	10:13 he is a hireling, and careth not for the **s**.	4263
	10:14 and know my **s**, and am known of mine.	NIG
	10:15 Father: and I lay down my life for the **s**.	4263
	10:16 And other **s** I have, which are not of this	4263

Jn	10:26 because ye are not of my **s**, as I said unto	4263
	10:27 My **s** hear my voice, and I know them,	4263
	21:16 He saith unto him, Feed my **s**.	4263
	21:17 Jesus saith unto him, Feed my **s**.	4263
Ac	8:32 this, He was led as a **s** to the slaughter;	4263
Ro	8:36 we are accounted as **s** for the slaughter.	4263
Heb	13:20 *that* great shepherd of the **s**, through	4263
1Pe	2:25 ye were as **s** going astray; but are now	4263
Rev	18:13 **s**, and horses, and chariots, and slaves,	4263

SHEEP'S (1) [SHEEP]

Mt	7:15 which come to you in **s** clothing,	4263

SHEEPCOTE (2) [SHEEP]

2Sa	7: 8 I took thee from the **s**, from following	5116
1Ch	17: 7 I took thee from the **s**, *even* from	5116

SHEEPCOTES (1) [SHEEP]

1Sa	24: 3 he came to the **s** by the way, where	1448+6629

SHEEPFOLD (1) [FOLD, SHEEP]

Jn	10: 1 not by the door into the **s**,	833+3588+4263

SHEEPFOLDS (3) [FOLD, SHEEP]

Nu	32:16 We will build **s** here for our cattle,	1448+6629
Jdg	5:16 Why abodest thou among the **s**, to hear	4942
Ps	78:70 servant, and took him from the **s**:	4356+6629

SHEEPMASTER (1) [MASTER, SHEEP]

2Ki	3: 4 Mesha king of Moab was a **s**,	5349

SHEEPSHEARERS (3) [SHEAR, SHEEP]

Ge	38:12 went up unto his **s** to Timnath,	1494+6629
2Sa	13:23 that Absalom had **s** in Baal-hazor, which	1494
	13:24 and said, Behold now, thy servant hath **s**;	1494

SHEEPSKINS (1) [SHEEP, SKIN]

Heb	11:37 they wandered about in **s** and goatskins;	3374

SHEERAH See SHERAH

SHEET (2) [SHEETS]

Ac	10:11 as *it had been* a great **s** knit at the four	3607
	11: 5 vessel descend, as *it had been* a great **s**,	3607

SHEETS (2) [SHEET]

Jdg	14:12 I will give you thirty **s** and thirty change	5466
	14:13 shall ye give me thirty **s** and thirty change	5466

SHEHARIAH (1)

1Ch	8:26 And Shamsherai, and **S**, and Athaliah,	7841

SHEKEL (43) [SHEKELS]

Ge	24:22 took a golden earring of **half a s** weight,	1235
Ex	30:13 half a **s** after the shekel of the sanctuary:	8255
	30:13 half a shekel after the **s** of the sanctuary:	8255
	30:13 (a **s** is twenty gerahs:) a half shekel *shall*	8255
	30:13 a half **s** *shall be* the offering of the LORD.	8255
	30:15 the poor shall not give less than half a **s**,	8255
	30:24 cassia five hundred *shekels*, after the **s** of	8255
	38:24 shekels, after the **s** of the sanctuary.	8255
	38:25 shekels, after the **s** of the sanctuary:	8255
	38:26 A bekah for every man, *that is*, half a **s**,	8255
	38:26 half a shekel, after the **s** of the sanctuary,	8255
Lev	5:15 after the **s** of the sanctuary, for a trespass	8255
	27: 3 of silver, after the **s** of the sanctuary.	8255
	27:25 be according to the **s** of the sanctuary:	8255
	27:25 sanctuary: twenty *shekels* shall be the **s**.	8255
Nu	3:47 after the **s** of the sanctuary shalt thou	8255
	3:47 thou take *them*: (the **s** *is* twenty gerahs:)	8255
	3:50 five *shekels*, after the **s** of the sanctuary:	8255
	7:13 after the **s** of the sanctuary;	8255
	7:19 after the **s** of the sanctuary;	8255
	7:25 after the **s** of the sanctuary;	8255
	7:31 after the **s** of the sanctuary;	8255
	7:37 after the **s** of the sanctuary;	8255
	7:43 after the **s** of the sanctuary;	8255
	7:49 after the **s** of the sanctuary;	8255
	7:55 after the **s** of the sanctuary;	8255
	7:61 after the **s** of the sanctuary;	8255
	7:67 after the **s** of the sanctuary;	8255
	7:73 after the **s** of the sanctuary;	8255
	7:79 after the **s** of the sanctuary;	8255
	7:85 four hundred *shekels*, after the **s** of	8255
	7:86 apiece, after the **s** of the sanctuary:	8255
	18:16 after the **s** of the sanctuary, which *is*	8255
1Sa	9: 8 I have here at the fourth part of a **s**	8255
2Ki	7: 1 a measure of fine flour *be sold* for a **s**,	8255
	7: 1 two measures of barley for a **s**, in the gate	8255
	7:16 a measure of fine flour was *sold* for a **s**,	8255
	7:16 two measures of barley for a **s**, according	8255
	7:18 Two measures of barley for a **s**,	8255
	7:18 shekel, and a measure of fine flour for a **s**,	8255
Ne	10:32 **s** for the service of the house of our God;	8255
Eze	45:12 the **s** *shall be* twenty gerahs:	8255
Am	8: 5 the **s** great, and falsifying the balances by	8255

SHEKELS (96) [SHEKEL]

Ge	23:15 the land *is worth* four hundred **s** of silver;	8255
	23:16 four hundred **s** of silver, current *money*	8255
	24:22 bracelets for her hands of ten **s** weight	NIH
Ex	21:32 he shall give unto their master thirty **s** *of*	8255
	30:23 pure myrrh five hundred **s**, and of sweet	NIH
	30:23 two hundred and fifty **s**, and of sweet	NIH
	30:23 of sweet calamus two hundred and fifty **s**,	NIH
	30:24 cassia five hundred **s**, after the shekel of	NIH

Ex 38:24 talents, and seven hundred and thirty **s**, 8255
 38:25 hundred and threescore and fifteen **s**, 8255
 38:28 and five **s** he made hooks for the pillars, NIH
 38:29 and two thousand and four hundred **s**. 8255
Lev 5:15 with thy estimation *by* **s** of silver, after 8255
 27: 3 thy estimation shall be fifty **s** of silver, 8255
 27: 4 then thy estimation shall be thirty **s**. 8255
 27: 5 estimation shall be of the male twenty **s**, 8255
 27: 5 twenty shekels, and for the female ten **s**, 8255
 27: 6 thy estimation *shall be* of the male five **s**, 8255
 27: 6 thy estimation *shall be* three **s** of silver. 8255
 27: 7 thy estimation shall be fifteen **s**, and for 8255
 27: 7 fifteen shekels, and for the female ten **s**, 8255
 27:16 seed *shall be valued* at fifty **s** of silver. 8255
Nu 3:47 Thou shalt even take five **s** apiece for 8255
 3:50 five **s**, after the shekel of the sanctuary: NIH
 7:13 **s**, one silver bowl of seventy shekels, NIH
 7:13 *shekels*, one silver bowl of seventy **s**, 8255
 7:14 One spoon of ten **s** of gold, full *of* incense: NIH
 7:19 **s**, one silver bowl of seventy shekels, NIH
 7:19 *shekels*, one silver bowl of seventy **s**, 8255
 7:20 One spoon of gold of ten **s**, full *of* incense: NIH
 7:25 thirty **s**, one silver bowl of seventy shekels, NIH
 7:25 *shekels*, one silver bowl of seventy **s**, 8255
 7:26 golden spoon of ten **s**, full *of* incense: NIH
 7:31 thirty **s**, one silver bowl of seventy shekels, NIH
 7:31 *shekels*, one silver bowl of seventy **s**, 8255
 7:32 golden spoon *of* ten **s**, full *of* incense: NIH
 7:37 thirty **s**, one silver bowl of seventy shekels, NIH
 7:37 *shekels*, one silver bowl of seventy **s**, 8255
 7:38 golden spoon of ten **s**, full *of* incense: NIH
 7:43 thirty **s**, a silver bowl of seventy shekels, NIH
 7:43 thirty *shekels*, a silver bowl of seventy **s**, 8255
 7:44 golden spoon of ten **s**, full *of* incense: NIH
 7:49 thirty **s**, one silver bowl of seventy shekels, NIH
 7:49 *shekels*, one silver bowl of seventy **s**, 8255
 7:50 golden spoon of ten **s**, full *of* incense: NIH
 7:55 thirty **s**, one silver bowl of seventy shekels, NIH
 7:55 *shekels*, one silver bowl of seventy **s**, 8255
 7:56 One spoon of ten **s**, full *of* incense: NIH
 7:61 thirty **s**, one silver bowl of seventy shekels, NIH
 7:61 *shekels*, one silver bowl of seventy **s**, 8255
 7:62 golden spoon of ten **s**, full *of* incense: NIH
 7:67 thirty **s**, one silver bowl of seventy shekels, NIH
 7:67 *shekels*, one silver bowl of seventy **s**, 8255
 7:68 golden spoon of ten **s**, full *of* incense: NIH
 7:73 thirty **s**, one silver bowl of seventy shekels, NIH
 7:73 *shekels*, one silver bowl of seventy **s**, 8255
 7:74 One golden spoon of ten **s**, full *of* incense: NIH
 7:79 thirty **s**, one silver bowl of seventy shekels, NIH
 7:79 *shekels*, one silver bowl of seventy **s**, 8255
 7:80 One golden spoon of ten **s**, full *of* incense: NIH
 7:85 hundred and thirty **s**, each bowl seventy: NIH
 7:85 four hundred **s**, after the shekel of NIH
 7:86 full *of* incense, *weighing* ten **s** apiece, NIH
 7:86 the spoons *was* an hundred and twenty **s**. NIH
 18:16 thine estimation, *for* the money of five **s**, 8255
 31:52 thousand seven hundred and fifty **s**. 8255
Dt 22:19 they shall amerce him in an hundred **s** of NIH
 22:29 unto the damsel's father fifty **s** of silver, NIH
Jos 7:21 two hundred **s** *of* silver, and a wedge of 8255
 7:21 a wedge of gold of fifty **s** weight, then 8255
Jdg 8:26 a thousand and seven hundred **s** of gold; NIH
 17: 2 The eleven hundred **s** of silver that were NIH
 17: 3 he had restored the eleven hundred **s** NIH
 17: 4 his mother took two hundred **s** of silver, NIH
 17:10 I will give thee ten **s** of silver by the year, NIH
1Sa 17: 5 the weight of the coat *was* five thousand **s** 8255
 17: 7 his spear's head *weighed* six hundred **s** of 8255
2Sa 14:26 *at* two hundred **s** after the king's weight. 8255
 18:11 I would have given thee ten **s** of silver, NIH
 18:12 Though I should receive a thousand **s** of NIH
 21:16 three hundred **s** of brass *in* weight, NIH
 24:24 and the oxen for fifty **s** of silver. 8255
1Ki 10:16 six hundred **s** of gold went to one target. NIH
 10:29 went out of Egypt for six hundred **s** of NIH
2Ki 15:20 of each man fifty **s** *of* silver, to give to 8255
1Ch 21:25 the place six hundred **s** of gold *by* weight. 8255
2Ch 1:17 Egypt a chariot for six hundred **s** of silver, NIH
 3: 9 the weight of the nails *was* fifty **s** of gold. NIH
 9:15 six hundred **s** of beaten gold went to one NIH
 9:16 hundred **s** of gold went to one shield. NIH
Ne 5:15 and wine, beside forty **s** of silver; 8255
Jer 32: 9 the money, *even* seventeen **s** of silver. 8255
Eze 4:10 eat *shall be* by weight, twenty **s** a day: 8255
 45:12 twenty **s**, five and twenty shekels, 8255
 45:12 five and twenty, fifteen shekels, 8255
 45:12 five and twenty shekels, fifteen **s**, 8255

SHELAH (11) [SHELANITES]
Ge 38: 5 and bare a son; and called his name **S**: 7956
 38:11 thy father's house, till **S** my son be grown: 7956
 38:14 for she saw that **S** was grown, and she 7956
 38:26 because that I gave her not to **S** my son. 7956
 46:12 and Onan, and **S**, and Pharez, and Zerah: 7956
Nu 26:20 of **S**, the family of the Shelanites: 7956
1Ch 1:18 Arphaxad begat **S**, and Shelah begat Eber. 7974
 1:18 Arphaxad begat Shelah, and **S** begat Eber. 7974
 1:24 Shem, Arphaxad, **S**, 7974
 2: 3 The sons of Judah; Er, and Onan, and **S**: 7956
 4:21 The sons of **S** the son of Judah *were*, Er 7956

SHELANITES (1) [SHELAH]
Nu 26:20 of Shelah, the family of the **S**: 8024

SHELEMIAH (10)
1Ch 26:14 the lot eastward fell to **S**. Then *for* 8018
Ezr 10:39 And **S**, and Nathan, and Adaiah, 8018
 10:41 Azareel, and **S**, Shemariah, 8018
Ne 3:30 After him repaired Hananiah the son of **S**, 8018
 13:13 **S** the priest, and Zadok the scribe, 8018
Jer 36:14 son of **S**, the son of Cushi, unto Baruch, 8018
 36:26 **S** the son of Abdeel, to take Baruch 8018
 37: 3 the king sent Jehucal the son of **S** 8018
 37:13 the son of **S**, the son of Hananiah; 8018
 38: 1 Jucal the son of **S**, and Pashur the son of 8018

SHELEPH (2)
Ge 10:26 and **S**, and Hazarmaveth, and Jerah, 8026
1Ch 1:20 and **S**, and Hazarmaveth, and Jerah, 8026

SHELESH (1)
1Ch 7:35 Zophah, and Imna, and **S**, and Amal. 8028

SHELOMI (1)
Nu 34:27 children of Asher, Ahihud the son of **S**. 8015

SHELOMITH (9) [SHELOMOTH]
Lev 24:11 his mother's name *was* **S**, the daughter 8019
1Ch 3:19 and Hananiah, and **S** their sister: 8019
 23: 9 Shimei; **S**, and Haziel, and Haran, three. 8019
 23:18 *Of* the sons of Izhar; **S** the chief. 8019
 26:25 his son, and Zichri his son, and **S** his son. 8019
 26:26 Which **S** and his brethren *were* over all 8019
 26:28 anything, it *was* under the hand of **S**, 8019
2Ch 11:20 him Abijah, and Attai, and Ziza, and **S**. 8019
Ezr 8:10 of the sons of **S**; the son of Josiphiah, 8019

SHELOMOTH (2) [SHELOMITH]
1Ch 24:22 Of the Izharites; **S**: of the sons of 8013
 24:22 Shelomoth: of the sons of **S**; Jahath. 8013

SHELTER (2)
Job 24: 8 and embrace the rock for want of a **s**. 4268
Ps 61: 3 thou hast been a **s** for me, *and* a strong 4268

SHELUMIEL (5)
Nu 1: 6 Of Simeon; **S** the son of Zurishaddai. 8017
 2:12 Simeon shall be **S** the son of Zurishaddai. 8017
 7:36 On the fifth day **S** the son of Zurishaddai, 8017
 7:41 this *was* the offering of **S** the son of 8017
 10:19 of Simeon *was* **S** the son of Zurishaddai. 8017

SHEM (17) [SEM]
Ge 5:32 and Noah begat **S**, Ham, and Japheth. 8035
 6:10 begat three sons, **S**, Ham, and Japheth. 8035
 7:13 **S**, and Ham, and Japheth, the sons of 8035
 9:18 of the ark, were **S**, and Ham, and Japheth: 8035
 9:23 **S** and Japheth took a garment, and laid *it* 8035
 9:26 he said, Blessed *be* the LORD God of **S**; 8035
 9:27 and he shall dwell in the tents of **S**; 8035
 10: 1 of the sons of Noah, **S**, Ham, and Japheth: 8035
 10:21 Unto **S** also, the father of all the children 8035
 10:22 The children of **S**; Elam, and Asshur, 8035
 10:31 *are* the sons of **S**, after their families, 8035
 11:10 These *are* the generations of **S**: Shem *was* 8035
 11:10 **S** *was* an hundred years old, 8035
 11:11 **S** lived after he begat Arphaxad five 8035
1Ch 1: 4 Noah, **S**, Ham, and Japheth. 8035
 1:17 The sons of **S**; Elam, and Asshur, 8035
 1:24 **S**, Arphaxad, Shelah, 8035

SHEMA (6)
Jos 15:26 Amam, and **S**, and Moladah, 8090
1Ch 2:43 Korah, and Tappuah, and Rekem, and **S**. 8087
 2:44 **S** begat Raham, the father of Jorkoam: 8087
 5: 8 the son of **S**, the son of Joel, who dwelt 8087
 8:13 Beriah also, and **S**, who *were* heads of 8087
Ne 8: 4 **S**, and Anaiah, and Urijah, and Hilkiah, 8087

SHEMAAH (1)
1Ch 12: 3 then Joash, the sons of **S** the Gibeathite; 8094

SHEMAIAH (41)
1Ki 12:22 the word of God came unto **S** the man of 8098
1Ch 3:22 the sons of Shechaniah; **S**: and the sons 8098
 3:22 the sons of **S**; Hattush, and Igeal, 8098
 4:37 Jedaiah, the son of Shimri, the son of **S**; 8098
 5: 4 **S** his son, Gog his son, Shimei his son, 8098
 9:14 **S** the son of Hasshub, the son of Azrikam 8098
 9:16 Obadiah the son of **S**, the son of Galal, 8098
 15: 8 **S** the chief, and his brethren two hundred 8098
 15:11 and Joel, **S**, and Eliel, and Amminadab, 8098
 24: 6 **S** the son of Nethaneel the scribe, *one* of 8098
 26: 4 the sons of Obed-edom *were*, **S** 8098
 26: 6 Also unto **S** his son were sons born, 8098
 26: 7 The sons of **S**; Othni, and Rephael, 8098
2Ch 11: 2 the word of the LORD came to **S** the man 8098
 12: 5 Then came **S** the prophet to Rehoboam, 8098
 12: 7 the word of the LORD came to **S**, saying, 8098
 12:15 *are* they not written in the book of **S** 8098
 17: 8 *even* **S**, and Nethaniah, and Zebadiah, 8098
 29:14 of the sons of Jeduthun; **S**, and Uzziel. 8098
 31:15 Jeshua, and Amariah, and Shecaniah, 8098
 35: 9 **S** and Nethaneel, his brethren, 8098
Ezr 8:13 and **S**, and with them threescore males. 8098
 8:16 for **S**, and for Elnathan, and for Jarib, 8098
 10:21 and Elijah, and **S**, and Jehiel, and Uzziah. 8098
 10:31 Eliezer, Ishijah, Malchiah, **S**, Shimeon, 8098
Ne 3:29 After him repaired also **S** the son of 8098
 6:10 Afterward I came *unto* the house of **S** 8098

Ne 10: 8 Maaziah, Bilgai, **S**: these *were* the priests. 8098
 11:15 **S** the son of Hashub, the son of Azrikam, 8098
 12: 6 **S**, and Joiarib, Jedaiah, 8098
 12:18 Of Bilgah, Shammua; of **S**, Jehonathan; 8098
 12:34 and Benjamin, and **S**, and Jeremiah, 8098
 12:35 son of **S**, the son of Mattaniah, the son 8098
 12:36 **S**, and Azarael, Milalai, Gilalai, Maai, 8098
 12:42 and Eleazar, and Uzzi, and Jehohanan, 8098
Jer 26:20 Urijah the son of **S** of Kirjath-jearim, 8098
 29:24 *Thus* shalt thou also speak to **S** 8098
 29:31 Thus saith the LORD concerning **S** 8098
 29:31 Because that **S** hath prophesied unto you, 8098
 29:32 I will punish **S** the Nehelamite, and his 8098
 36:12 Delaiah the son of **S**, and Elnathan the 8098

SHEMARIAH (3)
1Ch 12: 5 and **S**, and Shephatiah the Haruphite, 8114
Ezr 10:32 Benjamin, Malluch, *and* **S**. 8114
 10:41 Azareel, and Shelemiah, and **S**, 8114

SHEMEBER (1)
Ge 14: 2 **S** king of Zeboiim, and the king of Bela, 8038

SHEMER (2)
1Ki 16:24 he bought the hill Samaria of **S** for two 8106
 16:24 after the name of **S**, owner of the hill, 8106

SHEMIDA (3) [SHEMIDAITES]
Nu 26:32 of **S**, the family of the Shemidaites: 8061
Jos 17: 2 of Hepher, and for the children of **S**: 8061
1Ch 7:19 the sons of **S** were, Ahian, and Shechem, 8061

SHEMIDAITES (1) [SHEMIDA]
Nu 26:32 of Shemida, the family of the **S**: 8062

SHEMINITH (3)
1Ch 15:21 Azaziah, with harps on the **S** to excel. 8067
Ps 6: T To the chief Musician on Neginoth upon **S**, 8067
 12: T To the chief Musician upon **S**, A Psalm of 8067

SHEMIRAMOTH (4)
1Ch 15:18 **S**, and Jehiel, and Unni, Eliab, 8070
 15:20 **S**, and Jehiel, and Unni, and Eliab, 8070
 16: 5 **S**, and Jehiel, and Mattithiah, and Eliab, 8070
2Ch 17: 8 **S**, and Jehonathan, and Adonijah, 8070

SHEMUEL (3)
Nu 34:20 of Simeon, **S** the son of Ammihud. 8050
1Ch 6:33 a singer, the son of Joel, the son of **S**, 8050
 7: 2 Jeriel, and Jahmai, and Jibsam, and **S**, 8050

SHEN (1)
1Sa 7:12 set *it* between Mizpeh and **S**, and called 8129

SHENAZAR (1)
1Ch 3:18 Pedaiah, and **S**, Jecamiah, Hoshama, 8137

SHENAZZAR See SHENAZAR

SHENIR (2)
Dt 3: 9 call Sirion; and the Amorites call it **S**;) 8149
SS 4: 8 from the top of **S** and Hermon, from 8149

SHEPHAM (2)
Nu 34:10 your east border from Hazar-enan to **S**: 8221
 34:11 the coast shall go down from **S** *to* Riblah, 8221

SHEPHATHIAH (1)
1Ch 9: 8 Meshullam the son of **S**, the son of Reuel, 8203

SHEPHATIAH (12)
2Sa 3: 4 and the fifth, **S** the son of Abital; 8203
1Ch 3: 3 The fifth, **S** of Abital: the sixth, Ithream 8203
 12: 5 and Shemariah, and **S** the Haruphite, 8203
 27:16 of the Simeonites, **S** the son of Maachah: 8203
2Ch 21: 2 and Azariah, and Michael, and **S**: 8203
Ezr 2: 4 The children of **S**, three hundred seventy 8203
 2:57 The children of **S**, the children of Hattil, 8203
 8: 8 of the sons of **S**; Zebadiah the son of 8203
Ne 7: 9 The children of **S**, three hundred seventy 8203
 7:59 The children of **S**, the children of Hattil, 8203
 11: 4 the son of Amariah, the son of **S**, 8203
Jer 38: 1 **S** the son of Mattan, and Gedaliah the son 8203

SHEPHER See SHAPHER

SHEPHERD (43) [HERD, SHEEP]
Ge 46:34 for every **s** *is* an abomination unto 6629+7462
 49:24 (from thence *is* the **s**, the stone of Israel:) 7462
Nu 27:17 LORD be not as sheep which have no **s**. 7462
1Ki 22:17 upon the hills, as sheep that have not a **s**: 7462
2Ch 18:16 the mountains, as sheep that have no **s**: 7462
Ps 23: 1 The LORD *is* my **s**; I shall not want. 7462
 80: 1 Give ear, O **S** of Israel, thou that leadest 7462
Ecc 12:11 assemblies, *which* are given from one **s**. 7462
Isa 40:11 He shall feed his flock like a **s**: he shall 7462
 44:28 He *is* my **s**, and shall perform all my 7462
 63:11 up out of the sea with the **s** of his flock? 7462
Jer 31:10 and keep him as a **s** *doth* his flock. 7462
 43:12 Egypt, as a **s** putteth on his garment; 7462
 49:19 who *is* that **s** that will stand before me? 7462
 50:44 who *is* that **s** that will stand before me? 7462
 51:23 I will also break in pieces with thee the **s** 7462
Eze 34: 5 were scattered, because *there is* no **s**: 7462
 34: 8 because *there was* no **s**, neither did my 7462
 34:12 As a **s** seeketh out his flock in the day 7462
 34:23 I will set up one **s** over them, and he shall 7462

S

Eze	34:23 shall feed them, and he shall be their **s.**	7462
	37:24 over them; and they all shall have one **s:**	7462
Am	3:12 As the **s** taketh out of the mouth of the	7462
Zec	10: 2 were troubled, because *there was* no **s.**	7462
	11:15 thee yet the instruments of a foolish **s.**	7462
	11:16 For lo, I *will* raise up a **s** in the land,	7462
	11:17 Woe to the idol **s** that leaveth the flock!	7473
	13: 7 against my **s,** and against the man *that is*	7462
	13: 7 smite the **s,** and the sheep shall be	7462
Mt	9:36 scattered abroad, as sheep having no **s.**	4166
	25:32 as a **s** divideth *his* sheep from the goats:	4166
	26:31 I will smite the **s,** and the sheep of the	4166
Mk	6:34 they were as sheep not having a **s:**	4166
	14:27 I will smite the **s,** and the sheep shall be	4166
Jn	10: 2 he that entereth in by the door is the **s**	4166
	10:11 I am the good **s:** the good shepherd giveth	4166
	10:11 the good **s** giveth his life for the sheep.	4166
	10:12 But *he that is* a hireling, and not the **s,**	4166
	10:14 I am the good **s,** and know my *sheep,*	4166
	10:16 and there shall be one fold, *and* one **s.**	4166
Heb	13:20 great **s** of the sheep, through the blood	4166
1Pe	2:25 but are now returned unto the **S** and	4166
	5: 4 when the **chief S** shall appear, ye shall	750

SHEPHERD'S (2) [HERD, SHEEP]

1Sa	17:40 put them in a **s** bag which he had, even	7462
Isa	38:12 and is removed from me as a **s** tent:	7473

SHEPHERDS (37) [HERD, SHEEP]

Ge	46:32 the men *are* **s,** for their trade hath	6629+7462
	47: 3 Thy servants *are* **s,** both we,	6629+7462
Ex	2:17 the **s** came and drove them away:	7462
	2:19 delivered us out of the hand of the **s,**	7462
1Sa	25: 7 now thy **s** which were with us, we hurt	7462
Isa	13:20 neither shall the **s** make their fold there.	7462
	31: 4 a multitude of **s** is called forth against	7462
	56:11 and they *are* **s** *that* cannot understand:	7462
Jer	6: 3 The **s** with their flocks shall come unto	7462
	23: 1 I will set up **s** over them which shall feed	7462
	25:34 Howl, ye **s,** and cry; and wallow	7462
	25:35 the **s** shall have no way to flee,	7462
	25:36 A voice of the cry of the **s,** and a howling	7462
	33:12 shall be a habitation of **s** causing *their*	7462
	50: 6 their **s** have caused them to go astray,	7462
Eze	34: 2 prophesy against the **s** of Israel, prophesy,	7462
	34: 2 Thus saith the Lord GOD unto the **s;**	7462
	34: 2 Woe *be* to the **s** of Israel that do feed	7462
	34: 2 should not the **s** feed the flocks?	7462
	34: 7 Therefore, ye **s,** hear the word of	7462
	34: 8 neither did my **s** search for my flock,	7462
	34: 8 **s** fed themselves, and fed not my flock;	7462
	34: 9 Therefore, O ye **s,** hear the word of	7462
	34:10 Behold, I *am* against the **s;** and I will	7462
	34:10 neither shall the **s** feed themselves any	7462
Am	1: 2 the habitations of the **s** mourn,	7462
Mic	5: 5 shall we raise against him seven **s,**	7462
Na	3:18 Thy **s** slumber, O king of Assyria:	7462
Zep	2: 6 shall be dwellings *and* cottages for **s,**	7462
Zec	10: 3 Mine anger was kindled against the **s,**	7462
	11: 3 *There is* a voice of the howling of the **s;**	7462
	11: 5 I am rich: and their own **s** pity them not.	7462
	11: 8 Three **s** also I cut off in one month;	7462
Lk	2: 8 And there were in the same country **s**	4166
	2:15 the **s** said one to another, Let us now go	4166
	2:18 *things* which were told them by the **s.**	4166
	2:20 And the **s** returned, glorifying and	4166

SHEPHERDS' (1) [HERD, SHEEP]

SS	1: 8 and feed thy kids beside the **s** tents.	7462

SHEPHI (1) [SHEPHO]

1Ch	1:40 and Manahath, and Ebal, **S,** and Onam.	8195

SHEPHO (1) [SHEPHI]

Ge	36:23 and Manahath, and Ebal, **S,** and Onam.	8195

SHEPHUPHAN (1)

1Ch	8: 5 And Gera, and **S,** and Huram.	8197

SHERAH (1)

1Ch	7:24 (And his daughter *was* **S,** who built	7609

SHEREBIAH (8)

Ezr	8:18 **S,** with his sons and his brethren,	8274
	8:24 **S,** Hashabiah, and ten of their brethren,	8274
Ne	8: 7 Bani, and **S,** Jamin, Akkub, Shabbethai,	8274
	9: 4 **S,** Bani, *and* Chenani, and cried with a	8274
	9: 5 **S,** Hodijah, Shebaniah, *and* Pethahiah,	8274
	10:12 Zaccur, **S,** Shebaniah,	8274
	12: 8 Binnui, Kadmiel, **S,** Judah, *and* Mattaniah,	8274
	12:24 **S,** and Jeshua the son of Kadmiel,	8274

SHERESH (1)

1Ch	7:16 name of his brother *was* **S;** and his sons	8329

SHEREZER (1)

Zec	7: 2 they had sent *unto* the house of God **S**	8272

SHERIFFS (2)

Da	3: 2 the **s,** and all the rulers of the provinces,	8614
	3: 3 the **s,** and all the rulers of the provinces,	8614

SHESHACH (2)

Jer	25:26 and the king of **S** shall drink after them.	8347
	51:41 How is **S** taken! and *how* is the praise of	8347

SHESHAI (3)

Nu	13:22 Ahiman, **S,** and Talmai, the children	8344
Jos	15:14 **S,** and Ahiman, and Talmai, the children	8344
Jdg	1:10 and they slew **S,** and Ahiman, and Talmai.	8344

SHESHAN (5)

1Ch	2:31 the sons of Ishi; **S.** And the children of	8348
	2:31 Sheshan. And the children of **S;** Ahlai.	8348
	2:34 Now **S** had no sons, but daughters.	8348
	2:34 **S** had a servant, an Egyptian, whose	8348
	2:35 **S** gave his daughter to Jarha his servant to	8348

SHESHBAZZAR (4)

Ezr	1: 8 them unto **S,** the prince of Judah.	8339
	1:11 All *these* did **S** bring up with *them of*	8339
	5:14 delivered unto *one,* whose name *was* **S,**	8340
	5:16 came the same **S,** *and* laid the foundation	8340

SHETH (2) [SETH]

Nu	24:17 of Moab, and destroy all the children of **S.**	8352
1Ch	1: 1 Adam, **S,** Enosh,	8352

SHETHAR (1)

Est	1:14 **S,** Admatha, Tarshish, Meres, Marsena,	8369

SHETHAR-BOZENAI See SHETHAR-BOZNAI

SHETHAR-BOZNAI (4)

Ezr	5: 3 **S,** and their companions, and said thus	8370
	5: 6 **S,** and his companions the Apharsachites,	8370
	6: 6 **S,** and your companions the Apharsachites	8370
	6:13 side the river, **S,** and their companions,	8370

SHEVA (2)

2Sa	20:25 **S** *was* scribe: and Zadok and Abiathar	7724
1Ch	2:49 **S** the father of Machbenah, and the father	7724

SHEW (228) [SHEWBREAD, SHEWED, SHEWEDST, SHEWEST, SHEWETH, SHEWING]

Ge	12: 1 house, unto a land that I will **s** thee:	7200
	20:13 *is* thy kindness which thou shalt **s** unto	6213
	24:12 and **s** kindness unto my master Abraham.	6213
	40:14 kindness, I pray thee, unto me,	6213
	46:31 go up, and **s** Pharaoh, and say unto him,	5046
Ex	7: 9 unto you, saying, **S** a miracle for you:	5414
	9:16 raised thee up, for to **s** *in* thee my power;	7200
	10: 1 that I might **s** these my signs before him:	7896
	13: 8 thou shalt **s** thy son in that day, saying,	5046
	14:13 the LORD, which he will **s** to you to day:	6213
	18:20 shalt **s** them the way *wherein* they must	3045
	25: 9 According to all that I **s** thee, *after*	7200
	33:13 **s** me now thy way, that I may know thee,	3045
	33:18 he said, I beseech thee, **s** me thy glory.	7200
	33:19 **s** mercy on whom I will shew mercy.	7355
	33:19 shew mercy on whom I will **s** mercy.	7355
Nu	16: 5 Even to morrow the LORD will **s** who *are*	3045
Dt	1:33 to **s** you by what way ye should go,	7200
	3:24 thou hast begun to **s** thy servant thy	7200
	5: 5 that time, to **s** you the word of the LORD:	5046
	7: 2 with them, nor **s mercy** unto them:	2603
	13:17 thee mercy, and have compassion upon	5414
	17: 9 shall **s** thee the sentence of judgment:	5046
	17:10 which the LORD shall choose shall **s** thee;	5046
	17:11 the sentence which they shall **s** thee,	5046
	28:50 of the old, nor **s favour** to the young:	2603
	32: 7 ask thy father, and he will **s** thee;	5046
Jos	2:12 that ye will also **s** kindness unto my	6213
	5: 6 sware that *he* would not **s** them the land,	7200
Jdg	1:24 they said unto him, **S** us, we pray thee,	7200
	1:24 the city, and we will **s** thee mercy.	5973+6213
	4:22 I will **s** thee the man whom thou seekest.	7200
	6:17 **s** me a sign that thou talkest with me.	6213
1Sa	3:15 And Samuel feared to **s** Eli the vision.	5046
	8: 9 **s** them the manner of the king that shall	5046
	9: 6 peradventure he can **s** us our way that	5046
	9:27 while, that I may **s** thee the word of God.	8085
	10: 8 to thee, and **s** thee what thou shalt do.	3045
	14:12 Come up to us, and we will **s** you a thing.	3045
	16: 3 and I will **s** thee what thou shalt do:	3045
	20: 2 or small, but that he will **s** it me:	241+1540
	20:12 send unto thee, and **s** it thee;	241+1540
	20:13 I will **s** it thee, and send thee away,	241+1540
	20:14 thou shalt not only while yet I live **s** me	6213
	22:17 he fled, and did not **s** it to me.	241+1540
	25: 8 Ask thy young men, and they will **s** thee.	5046
2Sa	2: 6 now the LORD **s** kindness and truth unto	6213
	3: 8 against Judah do **s** kindness *this* day	6213
	9: 1 that I may **s** him kindness for Jonathan's	6213
	9: 3 I may **s** the kindness of God unto him?	6213
	9: 7 for I will **surely s** thee kindness for	6213+6213
	10: 2 I will **s** kindness unto Hanun the son of	6213
	15:25 and **s** me *both* it, and his habitation:	7200
	22:26 the merciful thou wilt **s** thyself **merciful,**	2616
	22:26 upright man thou wilt **s** thyself **upright.**	8552
	22:27 With the pure thou wilt **s** thyself **pure;**	1305
	22:27 froward thou wilt **s** thyself **unsavoury.**	6617
1Ki	1:52 If he will **s** himself a worthy man,	1961+3807.1
	2: 2 and **s** thyself a man;	1961+3807.1
	2: 7 **s** kindness unto the sons of Barzillai	6213
	18: 1 year, saying, Go, **s** thyself unto Ahab:	7200
	18: 2 Elijah went to **s** himself unto Ahab.	7200
	18:15 I will surely **s** myself unto him to day.	7200
2Ki	6:11 Will ye not **s** me which of us *is* for the	5046
	7:12 I will now **s** you what the Syrians have	5046
1Ch	16:23 **s forth** from day to day his salvation.	1319

1Ch	19: 2 I will **s** kindness unto Hanun the son of	6213
2Ch	16: 9 to **s** himself **strong** in the behalf of *them*	2388
Ezr	2:59 they could not **s** their fathers' house,	5046
Ne	7:61 they could not **s** their fathers' house,	5046
	9:19 **s** them **light,** and the way wherein they	215
Est	1:11 **s** the people and the princes her beauty:	7200
	2:10 had charged her that she should not **s** *it.*	5046
	4: 8 to **s** *it* unto Esther, and to declare *it* unto	5046
Job	10: 2 **s** me wherefore thou contendest with me.	3045
	11: 6 he would **s** thee the secrets of wisdom,	5046
	15:17 I will **s** thee, hear me; and that which I	2331
	32: 6 and durst not **s** you mine opinion.	2331
	32:10 to me; I also will **s** mine opinion.	2331
	32:17 also my part, I also will **s** mine opinion.	2331
	33:23 thousand, to **s** unto man his uprightness:	2331
	36: 2 I will **s** thee that *I have* yet to speak on	2331
Ps	4: 6 many that say, Who will **s** us *any* good?	7200
	9: 1 I will **s forth** all thy marvellous works.	5608
	9:14 That I may **s forth** all thy praise in	5608
	16:11 Thou wilt **s** me the path of life: in thy	3045
	17: 7 **S** thy **marvellous** lovingkindness, O thou	6395
	18:25 the merciful thou wilt **s** thyself **merciful;**	2616
	18:25 upright man thou wilt **s** thyself **upright.**	8552
	18:26 With the pure thou wilt **s** thyself **pure;**	1305
	18:26 the froward thou wilt **s** thyself **froward.**	6617
	25: 4 **S** me thy ways, O LORD; teach me thy	3045
	25:14 fear him; and he will **s** them his covenant.	3045
	39: 6 Surely every man walketh **in a vain s:**	6754
	50:23 *aright* will I **s** the salvation of God.	7200
	51:15 and my mouth shall **s** forth thy praise.	5046
	71:15 My mouth shall **s forth** thy righteousness	5608
	79:13 will **s forth** thy praise to all generations.	5608
	85: 7 **S** us thy mercy, O LORD, and grant us thy	7200
	86:17 **S** me a token for good; that they which	6213
	88:10 Wilt thou **s** wonders to the dead? shall	6213
	91:16 will I satisfy him, and **s** him my salvation.	7200
	92: 2 To **s forth** thy lovingkindness in	5046
	92:15 To **s** that the LORD *is* upright: he *is* my	5046
	94: 1 to whom vengeance belongeth, **s** thyself.	3313
	96: 2 **s forth** his salvation from day to day.	1319
	106: 2 the LORD? *who* can **s forth** all his praise?	8085
	109:16 Because that he remembered not to **s**	6213
Pr	18:24 that hath friends must **s** himself **friendly:**	7462
Isa	3: 9 The **s** of their countenance doth witness	1971
	27:11 that formed them will **s** them no **favour.**	2603
	30:30 shall **s** the lighting down of his arm,	7200
	41:22 them **forth,** and **s** us what shall happen:	5046
	41:22 let them **s** the former **things,** what they	5046
	41:23 **S** the *things* that are to come hereafter,	5046
	41:23 yea, **s** us former *things?* let them bring forth	8085
	43:21 for myself; they shall **s forth** my praise.	5608
	44: 7 and shall come, let them **s** unto them.	5046
	46: 8 Remember this, and **s yourselves men:**	377
	47: 6 thou didst **s** them no mercy; upon	7760
	49: 9 *them* that *are* in darkness, **S** yourselves.	1540
	58: 1 **s** my people their transgression,	5046
	60: 6 they shall **s forth** the praises of	1319
Jer	16:10 when thou shalt **s** this people all these	5046
	16:13 and night; where I will not **s** you favour.	5414
	18:17 I will **s** them the back, and not the face,	7200
	33: 3 **s** thee great and mighty *things,* which	5046
	42: 3 That the LORD thy God may **s** us the way	5046
	42:12 I will **s** mercies unto you, that he may	5414
	50:42 they *are* cruel, and will not **s mercy:**	7355
	51:31 to **s** the king of Babylon that his city is	5046
Eze	22: 2 yea, thou shalt **s** her all her abominations.	3045
	33:31 for with their mouth they **s** much love,	6213
	37:18 Wilt thou not **s** us what thou meanest by	5046
	40: 4 set thine heart upon all that I shall **s** thee;	7200
	40: 4 for to the intent that *I might* **s** *them* unto	7200
	43:10 of man, **s** the house to the house of Israel,	5046
	43:11 **s** them the form of the house,	3045
Da	2: 2 Chaldeans, for to **s** the king his dreams.	5046
	2: 4 dream, and we will **s** the interpretation.	2324
	2: 6 if ye **s** the dream, and the interpretation	2324
	2: 6 therefore **s** me the dream,	2324
	2: 7 and we will **s** the interpretation of it.	2324
	2: 9 I shall know that ye can **s** me	2324
	2:10 is not a man upon the earth that can **s**	2324
	2:11 there is none other that can **s** it before	2324
	2:16 he would **s** the king the interpretation.	2324
	2:24 I will **s** unto the king the interpretation:	2324
	2:27 the soothsayers, **s** unto the king,	2324
	4: 2 I thought it good to **s** the signs and	2324
	5: 7 **s** me the interpretation thereof, shall be	2324
	5:12 called, and he shall **s** the interpretation.	2324
	5:15 they could not **s** the interpretation of	2324
	9:23 I am come to **s** *thee;* for thou *art* greatly	5046
	10:21 I will **s** thee that which is noted in	5046
	11: 2 now will I **s** thee the truth. Behold,	5046
Joel	2:30 I will **s** wonders in the heavens and in	5414
Mic	7:15 Egypt will I **s** unto him marvellous *things.*	7200
Na	3: 5 I will **s** the nations thy nakedness,	7200
Hab	1: 3 Why dost thou **s** me iniquity, and cause	7200
Zec	1: 9 said unto me, I will **s** thee what these *be.*	7200
	7: 9 mercy and compassions every man to	6213
Mt	8: 4 **s** thyself to the priest, and offer the gift	1166
	11: 4 **s** John **again** *those* things which ye do	518
	12:18 and he shall **s** judgment to the Gentiles.	518
	14: 2 works do **s forth** themselves **in** him.	1754
	16: 1 desired him that *he* would **s** them	1925
	16:21 From that time forth began Jesus to **s** unto	1166
	22:19 **S** me the tribute money. And	1925
	24: 1 his disciples came to *him* for to **s** him	1925
	24:24 and shall **s** great signs and wonders;	1325

S

Mk	1:44	**s** thyself to the priest, and offer for thy	1166
	6:14	mighty works do **s** forth themselves in	1754
	13:22	and shall **s** signs and wonders, to seduce,	1325
	14:15	And he will **s** you a large upper room	1166
Lk	1:19	thee, and to **s** thee these **glad tidings**.	2097
	5:14	no *man*: but go, and **s** thyself to the priest,	1166
	6:47	them, I will **s** you to whom he is like:	5263
	8:39	**s** how great *things* God hath done unto	1334
	17:14	them, Go **s** yourselves unto the priests.	1925
	20:24	**S** me a penny. Whose image and	1925
	20:47	and for a **s** make long prayers:	4392
	22:12	And he shall **s** you a large upper room	1166
Jn	5:20	he will **s** him greater works than these,	1166
	7:4	If thou do these *things*, **s** thyself to	5319
	11:57	he should **s** *it*, that they might take him.	3377
	14:8	Lord, **s** us the Father, and it sufficeth us.	1166
	14:9	how sayest thou *then*, **S** us the Father?	1166
	16:13	speak: and he will **s** you *things* to come.	312
	16:14	receive of mine, and shall **s** *it* unto you.	312
	16:15	shall take of mine, and shall **s** *it* unto you.	312
	16:25	but I shall **s** you plainly of the Father.	312
Ac	1:24	which knowest the hearts of all *men*, **s**	322
	2:19	And I will **s** wonders in heaven above,	1325
	7:3	come into the land which I shall **s** thee.	1166
	9:16	For I will **s** him how great *things* he must	5263
	12:17	*Go* **s** these *things* unto James, and to	518
	16:17	which **s** unto us the way of salvation.	2605
	24:27	and Felix, willing to **s** the Jews a pleasure,	2698
	26:23	and should **s** light unto the people,	2605
Ro	2:15	Which **s** the work of the law written in	1731
	9:17	that I might **s** my power in thee,	1731
	9:22	willing to **s** *his* wrath, and to make his	1731
1Co	11:26	ye do **s** the Lord's death till he come.	2605
	12:31	yet **s** I unto you a more excellent way.	1166
	15:51	I **s** you a mystery; We shall not all	3004
2Co	8:24	Wherefore **s** ye to them, and before	1731
Gal	6:12	As many as desire to **make a fair s** in	2146
Eph	2:7	That in the ages to come he might **s**	1731
Col	2:15	and powers, he **made a s** of *them* openly,	1165
	2:23	Which *things* have indeed a **s** of wisdom	3056
1Th	1:9	For they themselves **s** of us what manner	518
1Ti	1:16	that in me first Jesus Christ might **s** **forth**	1731
	5:4	let them learn first to **s** **piety** at home,	2151
	6:15	Which in his times he shall **s**, *who is*	1166
2Ti	2:15	Study to **s** thyself approved unto God,	3936
Heb	6:11	And we desire that every one of you do **s**	1731
	6:17	more abundantly to **s** unto the heirs	1925
Jas	2:18	**s** me thy faith without thy works, and I	1166
	2:18	and I will **s** thee my faith by my works.	1166
	3:13	let him **s** out of a good conversation his	1166
1Pe	2:9	that ye should **s** **forth** the praises of him	1804
1Jn	1:2	witness, and **s** unto you *that* eternal life,	518
Rev	1:1	to **s** unto his servants *things* which must	1166
	4:1	I will **s** thee *things* which must be	1166
	17:1	I will **s** unto thee the judgment of the	1166
	21:9	*Come* hither, I will **s** thee the bride,	1166
	22:6	**s** unto his servants *the things* which must	1166

SHEWBREAD (18) [BREAD, SHEW]

Ex	25:30	shalt set upon the table a **s** before	3899+6440
	35:13	and all his vessels, and the **s**,	3899+6440
	39:36	all the vessels thereof, and the **s**,	3899+6440
Nu	4:7	the table of **s** they shall spread a cloth	6440
1Sa	21:6	no bread there but the **s**,	3899+6440+1886.1
1Ki	7:48	whereupon the **s** *was*,	3899+6440+1886.1
1Ch	9:32	**s**, to prepare *it* every	3899+4635+1886.1
	23:29	Both for the **s**, and for	3899+4635+1886.1
	28:16	weight *he* gave gold for the tables of **s**,	4635
2Ch	2:4	for the continual **s**, and for the burnt	4635
	4:19	whereon the **s** was set;	3899+6440+1886.1
	13:11	the **s**bread also *set they* in order upon	3899
	29:18	the **s** table, with all the vessels thereof.	4635
Ne	10:33	the **s**, and *for* the continual meat	3899+4635
Mt	12:4	did eat the **s**, which was not	740+3588+4286
Mk	2:26	did eat the **s**, which is not	740+3588+4286
Lk	6:4	and did take and eat the **s**,	740+3588+4286
Heb	9:2	and the table, and the **s**;	740+4286

SHEWED (135) [SHEW]

Ge	19:19	which thou hast **s** unto me in saving my	6213
	24:14	thereby shall I know that thou hast **s**	6213
	32:10	which thou hast **s** unto thy servant;	6213
	39:21	**s** him mercy, and gave him favour in	5186
	41:25	God hath **s** Pharaoh what he is about to	5046
	41:39	Forasmuch as God hath **s** thee all this,	3045
	48:11	and lo, God hath **s** me also thy seed.	7200
Ex	15:25	the Lord **s** him a tree, *which* when he	3384
	25:40	which was **s** thee in the mount.	7200
	26:30	thereof which was **s** thee in the mount,	7200
	27:8	as it was **s** thee in the mount, so shall	7200
Lev	13:19	reddish, and it be **s** to the priest;	7200
	13:49	of leprosy, and shall be **s** unto the priest:	7200
	24:12	that the mind of the Lord might be **s**	6567
Nu	8:4	the pattern which the Lord had **s** Moses,	7200
	13:26	and **s** them the fruit of the land.	7200
	14:11	for all the signs which I have **s** among	6213
Dt	4:35	Unto thee it was **s**, that thou mightest	7200
	4:36	upon earth he **s** thee his great fire;	7200
	5:24	the Lord our God hath **s** us his glory and	7200
	6:22	the Lord **s** signs and wonders, great and	5414
	34:1	the Lord **s** him all the land of Gilead,	7200
	34:12	in all the great terror which Moses **s** in	6213
Jos	2:12	the Lord, since I have **s** you kindness,	6213
Jdg	1:25	he **s** them the entrance into the city,	7200
	4:12	they **s** Sisera that Barak the son of	5046

Jdg	8:35	Neither **s** they kindness to the house of	6213
	8:35	the goodness which he had **s** unto Israel.	6213
	13:10	and **s** her husband, and said unto him,	5046
	13:23	would he have **s** us all these *things*,	7200
	16:18	*this* once, for he hath **s** me all his heart.	5046
Ru	2:11	unto me, It hath **fully been s** me,	5046+5046
	2:19	she **s** her mother in law with whom she	5046
	3:10	*for* thou hast **s** **more** kindness in the latter	3190
1Sa	11:9	and **s** *it* to the men of Jabesh;	5046
	15:6	for ye **s** kindness to all the children of	6213
	19:7	and Jonathan **s** him all those *things*.	5046
	22:21	Abiathar **s** David that Saul had slain	5046
	24:18	thou hast **s** *this* day how that thou hast	5046
2Sa	2:5	ye have **s** this kindness unto your lord,	6213
	10:2	Nahash, as his father **s** kindness unto me.	6213
	11:22	and **s** David all that Joab had sent him for.	5046
1Ki	1:27	and thou hast not **s** *it* unto thy servant,	3045
	3:6	Thou hast **s** unto thy servant David my	6213
	16:27	which he did, and his might that he **s**,	6213
	22:45	his might that he **s**, and how he warred,	6213
2Ki	6:6	he **s** him the place. And he cut down a	7200
	8:10	howbeit the Lord hath **s** me that he shall	7200
	8:13	The Lord hath **s** me *that* thou *shalt be*	7200
	11:4	of the Lord, and **s** them the king's son.	7200
	20:13	them all the house of his precious	7200
	20:13	his dominion, that Hezekiah **s** them not.	7200
	20:15	my treasures that I have not **s** them.	7200
	22:10	Shaphan the scribe **s** the king, saying,	5046
1Ch	19:2	because his father **s** kindness to me.	6213
2Ch	1:8	Thou hast **s** great mercy unto David my	6213
	7:10	that the Lord had **s** unto David,	6213
Ezr	9:8	for a little space grace hath been **s** from	NIH
Est	1:4	When he **s** the riches of his glorious	7200
	2:10	Esther had not **s** her people nor her	5046
	2:20	Esther had not yet **s** her kindred nor her	5046
	3:6	they had **s** him the people of Mordecai:	5046
Job	6:14	To him that is afflicted pity *should be* **s**	2617
Ps	31:21	he hath **s** me his **marvellous** kindness	6381
	60:3	Thou hast **s** thy people hard *things*: thou	7200
	71:18	until I have **s** thy strength unto *this*	5046
	71:20	*Thou*, which hast **s** me great and	7200
	78:11	and his wonders that he had **s** them.	7200
	98:2	his righteousness hath he **openly s** in	1540
	105:27	They **s** his signs among them,	7760
	111:6	He hath **s** his people the power of his	5046
	118:27	God *is* the Lord, which hath **s** us **light**:	215
	142:2	before him; I **s** before him my trouble.	5046
Pr	26:26	his wickedness shall be **s** before the *whole*	1540
Ecc	2:19	I have **s** myself **wise** under the sun.	2449
Isa	26:10	Let **favour** be **s** to the wicked, *yet* will	2603
	39:2	**s** them the house of his precious things,	7200
	39:2	his dominion, that Hezekiah **s** them not.	7200
	39:4	my treasures that I have not **s** them.	7200
	40:14	and **s** to him the way of understanding?	3045
	43:12	and have saved, and I have **s**,	8085
	48:3	**s** forth out of my mouth, and I **s** them;	8085
	48:5	to thee; before it came to pass I **s** *it* thee:	8085
	48:6	will not ye declare *it*? I have **s** thee new	8085
Jer	24:1	The Lord **s** me, and, behold, two baskets	7200
	38:21	this *is* the word that the Lord hath **s** me:	7200
Eze	11:25	all the things that the Lord had **s** me.	5046
	20:11	**s** them my judgments, which *if* a man do,	3045
	22:26	neither have they **s** **difference** between	3045
Am	7:1	Thus hath the Lord God **s** unto me;	7200
	7:4	Thus hath the Lord God **s** unto me:	7200
	7:7	Thus he **s** me: and behold, the Lord stood	7200
	8:1	Thus hath the Lord God **s** unto me:	7200
Mic	6:8	He hath **s** thee, O man, what *is* good;	5046
Zec	1:20	And the Lord **s** me four carpenters.	7200
	3:1	he **s** me Joshua the high priest standing	7200
Mt	28:11	**s** unto the chief priests all the *things* that	518
Lk	1:51	He hath **s** strength with his arm; he hath	4160
	1:58	cousins heard how the Lord had **s** **great**	3170
	4:5	**s** unto him all the kingdoms of the world	1166
	7:18	And the disciples of John **s** him of all these	518
	10:37	And he said, He that **s** mercy on him.	4160
	14:21	**s** his lord these *things*. Then the master of	518
	20:37	dead are raised, even Moses **s** at the bush,	3377
	24:40	he **s** them *his* hands and *his* feet.	1925
Jn	10:32	Many good works have I **s** you from my	1166
	20:20	he **s** unto them *his* hands and his side.	1166
	21:1	After these *things* Jesus **s** himself again to	5319
	21:1	of Tiberias; and on this wise **s** he *himself*.	5319
	21:14	This *is* now the third time that Jesus **s**	5319
Ac	1:3	To whom also he **s** himself alive after his	3936
	3:18	those *things*, which God **before** had **s**	4293
	4:22	on whom this miracle of healing was **s**.	1096
	7:26	And the next day he **s** himself unto them	3700
	7:36	after that he had **s** wonders and signs in	4160
	7:52	they have slain them which **s before** of	4293
	10:28	God hath **s** me that *I* should not call any	1166
	10:40	raised him up the third day, and **s** him openly;	1325
	11:13	he **s** us how he had seen an angel in his	518
	19:18	and confessed, and **s** their deeds.	312
	20:20	was profitable *unto you*, but have **s** you,	312
	20:35	I have **s** you all *things*, how that so	5263
	23:22	no *man* that thou hast **s** these *things* to	1718
	26:20	But **s** first unto them of Damascus,	518
	28:2	And the barbarous people **s** us no little	3930
	28:21	neither any of the brethren that came **s** or	518
Ro	1:19	in them; for God hath **s** *it* unto them.	5319
1Co	10:28	eat not for his sake that **s** *it*, and for	3377
Heb	6:10	of love, which ye have **s** toward his name,	1731
	8:5	to the pattern **s** to thee in the mount.	1166
Jas	2:13	without mercy, that hath no mercy;	4160

2Pe	1:14	even as our Lord Jesus Christ hath **s** me.	1213
Rev	21:10	high mountain, and **s** me *that* great city,	1166
	22:1	And he **s** me a pure river of water of life,	1166
	22:8	feet of the angel which **s** me these *things*.	1166

SHEWEDST (2) [SHEW]

Ne	9:10	**s** signs and wonders upon Pharaoh,	5414
Jer	11:18	I know *it*: then thou **s** me their doings.	7200

SHEWEST (5) [SHEW]

2Ch	6:14	and **s** mercy unto thy servants,	NIH
Job	10:16	thou **s** thyself **marvellous** upon me.	6381
Jer	32:18	Thou **s** lovingkindness unto thousands,	6213
Jn	2:18	said unto him, What sign **s** thou unto us,	1166
	6:30	unto him, What sign **s** thou then,	4160

SHEWETH (20) [SHEW]

Ge	41:28	God *is* about to do he **s** unto Pharaoh.	7200
Nu	23:3	whatsoever he **s** me I will tell thee.	7200
1Sa	22:8	*there is* none that **s** that that my son	241+1540
	22:8	**s** unto me that my son hath stirred	241+1540
2Sa	22:51	**s** mercy to his anointed, unto David,	6213
Job	36:9	he **s** them their work,	5046
	36:33	The noise thereof **s** concerning it,	5046
Ps	18:50	**s** mercy to his anointed, to David,	6213
	19:1	and the firmament **s** his handywork.	5046
	19:2	and night unto night **s** knowledge.	2331
	37:21	but the righteous **s** **mercy**, and giveth.	2603
	112:5	A good man **s** **favour**, and lendeth:	2603
	147:19	He **s** his word unto Jacob, his statutes	5046
Pr	12:17	*He that* speaketh truth **s** **forth**	5046
	27:25	the tender grass **s** itself, and herbs of	7200
Isa	41:26	*there is* none that **s**, yea, *there is* none	5046
Mt	4:8	and **s** him all the kingdoms of the world,	1166
Jn	5:20	and **s** him all *things* that himself doeth:	1166
Ro	9:16	that runneth, but of God that **s mercy**.	1653
	9:18	he that **s mercy**, with cheerfulness.	1653

SHEWING (15) [SHEW]

Ex	20:6	**s** mercy unto thousands of them that love	6213
Dt	5:10	**s** mercy unto thousands of them that love	6213
Ps	78:4	**s** to the generation to come the praises of	5608
SS	2:9	windows, **s** himself through the lattice.	6692
Da	4:27	thine iniquities by **s mercy** to the poor;	2604
	5:12	of hard sentences, and dissolving of	263
Lk	1:80	was in the deserts till the day of his **s** unto	323
	8:1	**s the glad tidings** of the kingdom of God:	2097
Ac	9:39	the coats and garments which Dorcas	1925
	18:28	**s** by the scriptures that Jesus was Christ.	1925
2Th	2:4	temple of God, **s** himself that he is God.	584
Tit	2:7	In all *things* **s** thyself a pattern of good	3930
	2:7	in doctrine **s** uncorruptness, gravity,	NIG
	2:10	Not purloining, but **s** all good fidelity;	1731
	3:2	*but* gentle, **s** all meekness unto all men.	1731

SHIBAH See SHEBAH

SHIBBOLETH (1) [SIBBOLETH]

Jdg	12:6	said they unto him, Say now **S**:	7641

SHIBMAH (1)

Nu	32:38	(*their* names being changed,) and **S**:	7643

SHICRON (1)

Jos	15:11	the border was drawn to **S**,	7942

SHIELD (45) [SHIELDS]

Ge	15:1	I *am* thy **s**, *and* thy exceeding great	4043
Dt	33:29	the **s** of thy help, and who *is* the sword	4043
Jdg	5:8	was there a **s** or spear seen among forty	4043
1Sa	17:7	and one bearing a **s** went before him.	6793
	17:41	the man that bare the **s** went before him.	6793
	17:45	a sword, and with a spear, and with a **s**:	3591
2Sa	1:21	for there the **s** of the mighty is vilely cast	4043
	1:21	the **s** of Saul, *as though he had* not *been*	4043
	22:3	*he is* my **s**, and the horn of my salvation,	4043
	22:36	Thou hast also given me the **s** of thy	4043
1Ki	10:17	three pound *of* gold went to one **s**:	4043
2Ki	19:32	an arrow there, nor come before it *with* **s**,	4043
1Ch	12:8	battle, that could handle **s** and buckler,	6793
	12:24	The children of Judah that bare **s** and	6793
	12:34	with them with **s** and spear thirty and	6793
2Ch	9:16	hundred *shekels* of gold went to one **s**.	4043
	17:17	with bow and **s** two hundred thousand.	4043
	25:5	to war, that could handle spear and **s**.	6793
Job	39:23	against him, the glittering spear and the **s**.	3591
Ps	3:3	thou, O Lord, *art* a **s** for me; my glory,	4043
	5:12	favour wilt thou compass him as with a **s**.	6793
	18:35	Thou hast also given me the **s** of thy	4043
	28:7	The Lord *is* my strength and my **s**;	4043
	33:20	for the Lord: he *is* our help and our **s**.	4043
	35:2	Take hold of **s** and buckler, and stand up	4043
	59:11	and bring them down, O Lord our **s**.	4043
	76:3	the **s**, and the sword, and the battle.	4043
	84:9	O God our **s**, and look upon the face of	4043
	84:11	For the Lord God *is* a sun and **s**:	4043
	91:4	his truth *shall be* thy **s** and buckler.	6793
	115:9	in the Lord: he *is* their help and their **s**.	4043
	115:10	in the Lord: he *is* their help and their **s**.	4043
	115:11	in the Lord: he *is* their help and their **s**.	4043
	119:114	Thou *art* my hiding place and my **s**:	4043
	144:2	deliverer; my **s**, and *he in* whom I trust;	4043
Pr	30:5	he *is* a **s** unto them that put their trust in	4043
Isa	21:5	drink: arise, ye princes, *and* anoint the **s**.	4043
	22:6	and horsemen, and Kir uncovered the **s**.	4043
Jer	46:3	Order ye the buckler and **s**, and draw	6793

Jer	46: 9 and the Libyans, that handle the **s**;	4043
Eze	23:24 buckler and **s** and helmet round about:	4043
	27:10 they hanged the **s** and helmet in thee;	4043
	38: 5 with them; all of them *with* **s** and helmet	4043
Na	2: 3 The **s** of his mighty *men is* made red,	4043
Eph	6:16 Above all, taking the **s** of faith,	2375

SHIELD (23) [SHIELD]

2Sa	8: 7 David took the **s** of gold that were on	7982
1Ki	10:17 he made three hundred **s** *of* beaten gold;	4043
	14:26 he took away all the **s** of gold which	4043
	14:27 Rehoboam made in their stead brasen **s**,	4043
2Ki	11:10 the priest give king David's spears and **s**,	7982
1Ch	18: 7 David took the **s** of gold that were on	7982
2Ch	9:16 three hundred **s** *made he of* beaten gold:	4043
	11:12 in every several city *he put* **s** and spears,	6793
	12: 9 he carried away also the **s** of gold which	4043
	12:10 Instead of which king Rehoboam made **s**	4043
	14: 8 that bare **s** and drew bows, two hundred	4043
	23: 9 and **s**, that *had been* king David's,	7982
	26:14 for them throughout all the host **s**,	4043
	32: 5 and made darts and **s** in abundance.	4043
	32:27 **s**, and for all *manner of* pleasant jewels;	4043
Ne	4:16 the **s**, and the bows, and the habergeons;	4043
Ps	47: 9 for the **s** of the earth *belong* unto God:	4043
SS	4: 4 a thousand bucklers, all **s** of mighty *men*.	7982
Isa	37:33 an arrow there, nor come before it *with* **s**,	4043
Jer	51:11 gather the **s**: the LORD hath raised up	7982
Eze	27:11 they hanged their **s** upon thy walls round	7982
	38: 4 a great company *with* bucklers and **s**,	4043
	39: 9 the **s** and the bucklers, the bows and	4043

SHIGGAION (1)

Ps	7: T **S** of David, which he sang unto	7692

SHIGIONOTH (1)

Hab	3: 1 A prayer of Habakkuk the prophet upon **S**.	7692

SHIHOR (1)

1Ch	13: 5 from **S** of Egypt even unto the entering of	7883

SHIHOR-LIBNATH (1)

Jos	19:26 reacheth to Carmel westward, and to **S**;	7884

SHIKKERON See SHICRON

SHILHI (2)

1Ki	22:42 name *was* Azubah the daughter of **S**.	7977
2Ch	20:31 name *was* Azubah the daughter of **S**.	7977

SHILHIM (1)

Jos	15:32 and **S**, and Ain, and Rimmon:	7978

SHILLEM (2) [SHILLEMITES]

Ge	46:24 Jahzeel, and Guni, and Jezer, and **S**.	8006
Nu	26:49 of **S**, the family of the Shillemites.	8006

SHILLEMITES (1) [SHILLEM]

Nu	26:49 of Shillem, the family of the **S**.	8016

SHILOAH (1)

Isa	8: 6 refuseth the waters of **S** that go softly,	7975

SHILOH (33) [SHILONITE, SHILONITES, TAANATH-SHILOH]

Ge	49:10 from between his feet, until **S** come;	7886
Jos	18: 1 of Israel assembled together *at* **S**,	7887
	18: 8 cast lots for you before the LORD in **S**.	7887
	18: 9 came *again* to Joshua to the host *at* **S**.	7887
	18:10 Joshua cast lots for them in **S** before	7887
	19:51 divided for an inheritance by lot in **S**	7887
	21: 2 they spake unto them *at* **S** in the land of	7887
	22: 9 from the children of Israel out of **S**,	7887
	22:12 Israel gathered themselves together *at* **S**,	7887
Jdg	18:31 the time that the house of God was in **S**.	7887
	21:12 they brought them unto the camp *to* **S**,	7887
	21:19 *there is* a feast of the LORD in **S** yearly *in*	7887
	21:21 if the daughters of **S** come out to dance in	7887
	21:21 every man his wife of the daughters of **S**,	7887
1Sa	1: 3 to sacrifice unto the LORD of hosts in **S**.	7887
	1: 9 Hannah rose up after *they* had eaten in **S**,	7887
	1:24 him *unto* the house of the LORD *in* **S**:	7887
	2:14 So they did in **S** unto all the Israelites that	7887
	3:21 the LORD appeared again in **S**:	7887
	3:21 to Samuel in **S** by the word of the LORD.	7887
	4: 3 covenant of the LORD out of **S** unto us,	7887
	4: 4 So the people sent *to* **S**, that they might	7887
	4:12 came *to* **S** the same day with his clothes	7887
	14: 3 the son of Eli, the LORD's priest in **S**,	7887
1Ki	2:27 spake concerning the house of Eli in **S**.	7887
	14: 2 the wife of Jeroboam; and get thee *to* **S**:	7887
	14: 4 *to* **S**, and came *to* the house of Ahijah.	7887
Ps	78:60 So that he forsook the tabernacle of **S**,	7887
Jer	7:12 go ye now unto my place which *was* in **S**,	7887
	7:14 and to your fathers, as I have done to **S**.	7887
	26: 6 will I make this house like **S**, and will	7887
	26: 9 This house shall be like **S**, and this city	7887
	41: 5 from **S**, and from Samaria, *even* fourscore	7887

SHILONI (1)

Ne	11: 5 the son of Zechariah, the son of **S**.	8023

SHILONITE (5) [SHILOH]

1Ki	11:29 that the prophet Ahijah the **S** found him	7888
	12:15 which the LORD spake by the **S**	7888
	15:29 he spake by his servant Ahijah the **S**:	7888

2Ch	9:29 in the prophecy of Ahijah the **S**, and in	7888
	10:15 he spake by the hand of Ahijah the **S**	7888

SHILONITES (1) [SHILOH]

1Ch	9: 5 the **S**; Asaiah the firstborn, and his sons.	7888

SHILSHAH (1)

1Ch	7:37 Shamma, and **S**, and Ithran, and Beera.	8030

SHIMEA (5) [SHIMEAH]

2Sa	21:21 Jonathan the son of **S** the brother of David	8092
1Ch	3: 5 **S**, and Shobab, and Nathan, and Solomon,	8092
	6:30 **S** his son, Haggiah his son, Asaiah his son.	8092
	6:39 Asaph the son of Berachiah, the son of **S**,	8092
	20: 7 Jonathan the son of **S** David's brother	8092

SHIMEAH (3) [SHIMEA]

2Sa	13: 3 Jonadab, the son of **S** David's brother:	8093
	13:32 son of **S** David's brother, answered and	8093
1Ch	8:32 Mikloth begat **S**. And these also dwelt	8039

SHIMEAM (1)

1Ch	9:38 Mikloth begat **S**. And they also dwelt	8043

SHIMEATH (2) [SHIMEATHITES]

2Ki	12:21 For Jozachar the son of **S**,	8100
2Ch	24:26 Zabad the son of **S** an Ammonitess,	8100

SHIMEATHITES (1) [SHIMEATH]

1Ch	2:55 the Tirathites, the **S**, *and* Suchathites.	8101

SHIMEI (42)

Nu	3:18 of Gershon by their families; Libni, and **S**.	8096
2Sa	16: 5 whose name *was* **S**, the son of Gera:	8096
	16: 7 thus said **S** when he cursed, Come out,	8096
	16:13 **S** went along on the hill's side over	8096
	19:16 **S** the son of Gera, a Benjamite, which	8096
	19:18 **S** the son of Gera fell down before the	8096
	19:21 said, Shall not **S** be put to death for this,	8096
	19:23 Therefore the king said unto **S**, Thou	8096
1Ki	1: 8 **S**, and Rei, and the mighty *men* which	8096
	2: 8 *thou hast* with thee **S** the son of Gera,	8096
	2:36 the king sent and called for **S**, and said	8096
	2:38 **S** said unto the king, The saying *is* good:	8096
	2:38 And **S** dwelt in Jerusalem many days.	8096
	2:39 two of the servants of **S** ran away unto	8096
	2:39 they told **S**, saying, Behold, thy servants	8096
	2:40 **S** arose, and saddled his ass, and went to	8096
	2:40 **S** went, and brought his servants from	8096
	2:41 it was told Solomon that **S** had gone from	8096
	2:42 the king sent and called for **S**, and said	8096
	2:44 The king said moreover to **S**, Thou	8096
	4:18 **S** the son of Elah, in Benjamin:	8096
1Ch	3:19 sons of Pedaiah *were*, Zerubbabel, and **S**:	8096
	4:26 his son, Zacchur his son, **S** his son.	8096
	4:27 **S** had sixteen sons and six daughters;	8096
	5: 4 Shemaiah his son, Gog his son, **S** his son,	8096
	6:17 the sons of Gershom; Libni, and **S**.	8096
	6:29 Libni his son, **S** his son, Uzza his son,	8096
	6:42 Ethan, the son of Zimmah, the son of **S**,	8096
	23: 7 Of the Gershonites *were*, Laadan, and **S**.	8096
	23: 9 The sons of **S**; Shelomith, and Haziel,	8096
	23:10 sons of **S** *were*, Jahath, Zina, and Jeush,	8096
	23:10 These four *were* the sons of **S**.	8096
	25:17 The tenth *to* **S**, he, his sons,	8096
	27:27 over the vineyards *was* **S** the Ramathite:	8096
2Ch	29:14 of the sons of Heman; Jehiel, and **S**:	8096
	31:12 ruler, and **S** his brother *was* the next.	8096
	31:13 the hand of Cononiah and **S** his brother,	8096
Ezr	10:23 Jozabad, and **S**, and Kelaiah, (the same *is*	8096
	10:33 Eliphelet, Jeremai, Manasseh, *and* **S**.	8096
	10:38 And Bani, and Binnui, **S**,	8096
Est	2: 5 the son of Jair, the son of **S**, the son of	8096
Zec	12:13 family of **S** apart, and their wives apart;	8097

SHIMEITES See SHIMITES

SHIMEON (1)

Ezr	10:31 Eliezer, Ishijah, Malchiah, Shemaiah, **S**,	8095

SHIMHI (1)

1Ch	8:21 and Beraiah, and Shimrath, the sons of **S**;	8096

SHIMI (1) [SHIMITES]

Ex	6:17 Libni, and **S**, according to their families.	8096

SHIMITES (1) [SHIMI]

Nu	3:21 of the Libnites, and the family of the **S**:	8097

SHIMMA (1)

1Ch	2:13 and Abinadab the second, and **S** the third,	8092

SHIMON (1)

1Ch	4:20 the sons of **S** *were*, Amnon, and Rinnah,	7889

SHIMRATH (1)

1Ch	8:21 Adaiah, and Beraiah, and **S**, the sons of	8119

SHIMRI (3)

1Ch	4:37 of Allon, the son of Jedaiah, the son of **S**,	8113
	11:45 Jediael the son of **S**, and Joha his brother,	8113
2Ch	29:13 of the sons of Elizaphan; **S**, and Jeiel.	8113

SHIMRITH (1)

2Ch	24:26 and Jehozabad the son of **S** a Moabitess.	8116

SHIMRON (5) [SHIMRONITES]

Ge	46:13 Tola, and Phuvah, and Job, and **S**.	8110
Nu	26:24 of **S**, the family of the Shimronites.	8110
Jos	11: 1 to the king of **S**, and to the king of	8110
	19:15 and **S**, and Idalah, and Beth-lehem:	8110
1Ch	7: 1 Tola, and Puah, Jashub, and **S**, four.	8110

SHIMRONITES (1) [SHIMRON]

Nu	26:24 of Shimron, the family of the **S**.	8117

SHIMRON-MERON

Jos	12:20 The king of **S**, one; the king of Achshaph,	8112

SHIMSHAI (4)

Ezr	4: 8 **S** the scribe wrote a letter against	8124
	4: 9 **S** the scribe, and the rest of their	8124
	4:17 *to* **S** the scribe, and *to* the rest of their	8124
	4:23 **S** the scribe, and their companions,	8124

SHINAB (1)

Ge	14: 2 **S** king of Admah, and Shemeber king of	8134

SHINAR (7)

Ge	10:10 and Accad, and Calneh, in the land of	8152
	11: 2 that they found a plain in the land of **S**;	8152
	14: 1 to pass in the days of Amraphel king of **S**,	8152
	14: 9 Amraphel king of **S**, and Arioch king of	8152
Isa	11:11 from **S**, and from Hamath, and from	8152
Da	1: 2 which he carried *into* the land of **S** *to*	8152
Zec	5:11 To build it a house in the land of **S**:	8152

SHINE (32) [SHINED, SHINETH, SHINING, SHONE]

Nu	6:25 The LORD **make** his face **s** upon thee,	215
Job	3: 4 from above, neither let the light **s** upon it.	3313
	10: 3 and **s** upon the counsel of the wicked?	3313
	11:17 thou shalt **s** forth, thou shalt be as	5774
	18: 5 out, and the spark of his fire shall not **s**.	5050
	22:28 and the light shall **s** upon thy ways.	5050
	36:32 commandeth it *not to* **s** *by the cloud* that	NIH
	37:15 and **caused** the light of his cloud to **s**?	3313
	41:18 *By* his neesings a light doth **s**, and his eyes	1984
	41:32 He **maketh** a path to **s** after him; *one*	215
Ps	31:16 **Make** thy face to **s** upon thy servant:	215
	67: 1 *and* **cause** his face to **s** upon us; Selah.	215
	80: 1 dwellest *between* the cherubims, **s** forth.	3313
	80: 3 us again, O God, and **cause** thy face to **s**;	215
	80: 7 O God *of* hosts, and **cause** thy face to **s**;	215
	80:19 O LORD God *of* hosts, **cause** thy face to **s**;	215
	104:15 *and* oil to **make** *his* face to **s**,	6670
	119:135 **Make** thy face to **s** upon thy servant;	215
Ecc	8: 1 a man's wisdom **maketh** his face to **s**,	215
Isa	13:10 the moon shall not **cause** her light to **s**.	5050
	60: 1 Arise, **s**; for thy light is come, and the	215
Jer	5:28 They are waxen fat, they **s**: yea,	6245
Da	9:17 **cause** thy face to **s** upon thy sanctuary	215
	12: 3 they that be wise shall **s** as the brightness	2094
Mt	5:16 Let your light so **s** before men, that they	2989
	13:43 Then shall the righteous **s** forth as the sun	1584
	17: 2 and his face did **s** as the sun,	2989
2Co	4: 4 is the image of God, should **s** unto them.	826
	4: 6 who commanded the light to **s** out of	2989
Php	2:15 among whom ye **s** as lights in the world;	5316
Rev	18:23 the light of a candle shall **s** no more at	5316
	21:23 of the sun, neither of the moon, to **s** in it:	5316

SHINED (9) [SHINE]

Dt	33: 2 he **s** forth from mount Paran, and he	3313
Job	29: 3 When his candle **s** upon my head,	1984
	31:26 If I beheld the sun when it **s**, or the moon	1984
Ps	50: 2 the perfection of beauty, God hath **s**.	3313
Isa	9: 2 of death, upon them hath the light **s**.	5050
Eze	43: 2 waters: and the earth **s** with his glory.	215
Ac	9: 3 suddenly there **s** round about him a light	4015
	12: 7 upon *him*, and a light **s** in the prison:	2989
2Co	4: 6 shine out of darkness, hath **s** in our hearts,	2989

SHINETH (9) [SHINE]

Job	25: 5 Behold *even* to the moon, and it **s** not;	166
Ps	139:12 not from thee; but the night **s** as the day:	215
Pr	4:18 that **s** more and more unto	215+1980
Mt	24:27 out of the east, and **s** *even* unto the west;	5316
Lk	17:24 **s** unto the other *part* under heaven;	2989
Jn	1: 5 And the light **s** in darkness;	5316
2Pe	1:19 as unto a light that **s** in a dark place,	5316
1Jn	2: 8 darkness is past, and the true light now **s**.	5316
Rev	1:16 his countenance *was* as the sun **s** in his	5316

SHINING (11) [SHINE]

2Sa	23: 4 out of the earth by **clear s** after rain.	5051
Pr	4:18 the path of the just *is as* the **s** light,	5051
Isa	4: 5 day, and the **s** of a flaming fire by night:	5051
Joel	2:10 and the stars shall withdraw their **s**:	5051
	3:15 and the stars shall withdraw their **s**.	5051
Hab	3:11 *and* at the **s** of thy glittering spear.	5051
Mk	9: 3 his raiment became **s**, exceeding white	4744
Lk	11:36 as when the **bright s** of a candle doth give	796
	24: 4 two men stood by them in **s** garments:	797
Jn	5:35 was a burning and a **s** light: and ye were	5316
Ac	26:13 **s** round about me and them which	4034

SHION (1)

Jos	19:19 And Hapharaim, and **S**, and Anaharath,	7866

SHIP (71) [FORESHIP, SHIPMASTER, SHIPMEN, SHIPPING, SHIPS, SHIPWRACK]

Pr	30:19 the way of a **s** in the midst of the sea;	591

S

Isa	33:21 neither shall gallant **s** pass thereby.	6716
Eze	27: 5 They have made all thy **s** boards of fir	NIH
Jnh	1: 3 Joppa; and he found a **s** going *to* Tarshish:	591
	1: 4 in the sea, so that the **s** was like to be	591
	1: 5 cast forth the wares that *were* in the **s** into	591
	1: 5 was gone down into the sides of the **s**;	5600
Mt	4:21 brother, in a **s** with Zebedee their father,	4143
	4:22 And they immediately left the **s** and	4143
	8:23 And when he was entered into a **s**,	4143
	8:24 insomuch that the **s** was covered with	4143
	9: 1 And he entered into a **s**, and passed over,	4143
	13: 2 him, so that he went into a **s**, and sat;	4143
	14:13 thence by **s** into a desert place apart:	4143
	14:22 constrained his disciples to get into a **s**,	4143
	14:24 But the **s** was now in the midst of the sea,	4143
	14:29 when Peter was come down out of the **s**,	4143
	14:32 And when they were come into the **s**,	4143
	14:33 Then they that were in the **s** came and	4143
	15:39 and took **s**, and came into the coasts of	4143
Mk	1:19 also *were* in the **s** mending *their* nets.	4143
	1:20 they left their father Zebedee in the **s** with	4143
	3: 9 that a **small s** should wait on him because	4142
	4: 1 so that he entered into a **s**, and sat in	4143
	4:36 they took him *even* as he was in the **s**.	4143
	4:37 the waves beat into the **s**, so that it was	4143
	4:38 And he was in the **hinder part of** the **s**,	4403
	5: 2 And when he was come out of the **s**,	4143
	5:18 when he was come into the **s**, he that	4143
	5:21 when Jesus was passed over again by **s**	4143
	6:32 And they departed into a desert place by **s**	4143
	6:45 constrained his disciples to get into the **s**,	4143
	6:47 the **s** was in the midst of the sea,	4143
	6:51 And he went up unto them into the **s**;	4143
	6:54 And when they were come out of the **s**,	4143
	8:10 And straightway he entered into a **s** with	4143
	8:13 entering into the **s** again departed to	4143
	8:14 neither had they in the **s** with them more	4143
Lk	5: 3 and taught the people out of the **s**.	4143
	5: 7 which were in the other **s**, that *they*	4143
	8:22 that he went into a **s** with his disciples:	4143
	8:37 and he went *up* into the **s**,	4143
Jn	6:17 entered into a **s**, and went over the sea	4143
	6:19 on the sea, and drawing nigh unto the **s**:	4143
	6:21 they willingly received him into the **s**:	4143
	6:21 immediately the **s** was at the land whither	4143
	21: 3 and entered into a **s** immediately;	4143
	21: 6 Cast the net on the right side of the **s**,	4143
	21: 8 And the other disciples came in a **little s**;	4142
Ac	20:13 And we went before to **s**, and sailed unto	4143
	20:38 And they accompanied him unto the **s**.	4143
	21: 2 And finding a **s** sailing over unto Phenicia,	4143
	21: 3 for there the **s** was to unlade *her* burden.	4143
	21: 6 taken our leave one of another, we took **s**;	4143
	27: 2 And entering into a **s** of Adramyttium,	4143
	27: 6 And there the centurion found a **s**	4143
	27:10 not only of the lading and **s**, but also of	4143
	27:11 the master and the **owner of the s**,	3490
	27:15 when the **s** was caught, and could not	4143
	27:17 they used helps, undergirding the **s**;	4143
	27:18 the next *day* they lightened the **s**;	1546+4160
	27:19 with our own hands the tackling of the **s**.	4143
	27:22 of *any man's* life among you, but of the **s**.	4143
	27:30 shipmen were about to flee out of the **s**,	4143
	27:31 the soldiers, Except these abide in the **s**,	4143
	27:37 And we were in all in the **s** two hundred	4143
	27:38 lightened the **s**, and cast out the wheat	4143
	27:39 if it were possible, to thrust in the **s**.	4143
	27:41 two seas met, they ran the **s** aground;	3491
	27:44 and some on broken pieces of the **s**.	4143
	28:11 And after three months we departed in a **s**	4143

SHIPHI (1)

1Ch	4:37 Ziza the son of **S**, the son of Allon, the son	8230

SHIPHMITE (1)

1Ch	27:27 for the wine cellars *was* Zabdi the **S**:	8225

SHIPHRAH (1)

Ex	1:15 of which the name of the one *was* **S**,	8236

SHIPHTAN (1)

Nu	34:24 children of Ephraim, Kemuel the son of **S**.	8204

SHIPMASTER (2) [MASTER, SHIP]

Jnh	1: 6 So the **s** came to him,	2259+7227+1886.1
Rev	18:17 And every **s**, and all the company in ships,	2942

SHIPMEN (3) [MAN, SHIP]

1Ki	9:27 **s** that had knowledge of the sea,	376+591
Ac	27:27 about midnight the **s** deemed that they	3492
	27:30 And as the **s** were about to flee out of	3492

SHIPPING (1) [SHIP]

Jn	6:24 they also **took s**,	1519+1684+3588+4143

SHIPS (39) [SHIP]

Ge	49:13 he *shall be* for a haven of **s**; and his border	591
Nu	24:24 **s** *shall come* from the coast of Chittim,	6716
Dt	28:68 shall bring thee *into* Egypt again with **s**,	591
Jdg	5:17 why did Dan remain *in* **s**? Asher continued	591
1Ki	9:26 king Solomon made a navy of **s** in	NIH
	22:48 Jehoshaphat made **s** of Tharshish to go to	591
	22:48 for the **s** were broken at Ezion-geber.	591
	22:49 my servants go with thy servants in the **s**.	591
2Ch	8:18 sent him by the hands of his servants **s**,	591
	9:21 For the king's went *to* Tarshish with	591

2Ch	9:21 every three years once came the **s** of	591
	20:36 he joined himself with him to make **s** to go	591
	20:36 and they made the **s** in Ezion-geber.	591
	20:37 the **s** were broken, that they were not able	591
Job	9:26 They are passed away as the swift **s**:	591
Ps	48: 7 Thou breakest the **s** of Tarshish with an	591
	104:26 There go the **s**: *there is* that leviathan,	591
	107:23 They that go down to the sea in **s**, that do	591
Pr	31:14 She is like the merchant's **s**; she bringeth	591
Isa	2:16 upon all the **s** of Tarshish, and upon all	591
	23: 1 Howl, ye **s** of Tarshish; for it is laid waste,	591
	23:14 Howl, ye **s** of Tarshish: for your strength is	591
	43:14 and the Chaldeans, whose cry *is* in the **s**.	591
	60: 9 the **s** of Tarshish first, to bring thy sons	591
Eze	27: 9 all the **s** of the sea with their mariners were	591
	27:25 The **s** of Tarshish did sing of thee in thy	591
	27:29 of the sea, shall come down from their **s**,	591
	30: 9 in **s** to make the careless Ethiopians afraid,	6716
Da	11:30 For *the* **s** of Chittim shall come against	6716
	11:40 and with horsemen, and with many **s**;	591
Mk	4:36 there were also with him other **little s**.	4142
Lk	5: 2 And saw two **s** standing by the lake:	4143
	5: 3 he entered into one of the **s**, which was	4143
	5: 7 filled both the **s**, so that they began to	4143
	5:11 when they had brought *their* **s** to land,	4143
Jas	3: 4 Behold also the **s**, which though they be	4143
Rev	8: 9 and the third *part* of the **s** were destroyed.	4143
	18:17 shipmaster, and all the company in **s**,	4143
	18:19 wherein were made rich all that had **s** in	4143

SHIPWRACK (2) [SHIP]

2Co	11:25 thrice I **suffered s**, a night and a day I	3489
1Ti	1:19 put away, concerning faith have **made s**:	3489

SHISHA (1)

1Ki	4: 3 Elihoreph and Ahiah, the sons of **S**,	7894

SHISHAK (7)

1Ki	11:40 unto **S** king of Egypt, and was in Egypt	7895
	14:25 *that* **S** king of Egypt came up against	7895
2Ch	12: 2 *that* in the fifth year of king Rehoboam **S**	7895
	12: 5 together to Jerusalem because of **S**,	7895
	12: 5 have I also left you in the hand of **S**.	7895
	12: 7 out upon Jerusalem by the hand of **S**.	7895
	12: 9 So **S** king of Egypt came up against	7895

SHITRAI (1)

1Ch	27:29 over the herds that fed in Sharon *was* **S**	7861

SHITTAH (1)

Isa	41:19 **s** tree, and the myrtle, and the oil tree;	7848

SHITTIM (32) [ABEL-SHITTIM]

Ex	25: 5 dyed red, and badgers' skins, and **s** wood,	7848
	25:10 they shall make an ark of **s** wood:	7848
	25:13 thou shalt make staves of **s** wood,	7848
	25:23 Thou shalt also make a table *of* **s** wood:	7848
	25:28 thou shalt make the staves *of* **s** wood,	7848
	26:15 for the tabernacle *of* **s** wood standing up.	7848
	26:26 thou shalt make bars *of* **s** wood; five for	7848
	26:32 thou shalt hang it upon four pillars of **s**	7848
	26:37 for the hanging five pillars of **s** *wood*,	7848
	27: 1 thou shalt make an altar *of* **s** wood,	7848
	27: 6 staves of **s** wood, and overlay them with	7848
	30: 1 upon: of **s** wood shalt thou make it.	7848
	30: 5 thou shalt make the staves *of* **s** wood,	7848
	35: 7 dyed red, and badgers' skins, and **s** wood,	7848
	35:24 whom was found **s** wood for any work	7848
	36:20 he made boards for the tabernacle of **s**	7848
	36:31 made bars of **s** wood; five for the boards	7848
	36:36 he made thereunto four pillars of **s** *wood*,	7848
	37: 1 Bezaleel made the ark of **s** wood:	7848
	37: 4 he made staves of **s** wood,	7848
	37:10 he made the table *of* **s** wood: two cubits	7848
	37:15 he made the staves *of* **s** wood,	7848
	37:25 he made the incense altar *of* **s** wood,	7848
	37:28 he made the staves *of* **s** wood,	7848
	38: 1 he made the altar of burnt offering *of* **s**	7848
	38: 6 he made the staves *of* **s** wood,	7848
Nu	25: 1 Israel abode in **S**, and the people begun	7851
Dt	10: 3 I made an ark of **s** wood, and hewed two	7848
Jos	2: 1 Joshua the son of Nun sent out of **S** two	7851
	3: 1 removed from **S**, and came to Jordan,	7851
Joel	3:18 the LORD, and shall water the valley of **S**.	7851
Mic	6: 5 Beor answered him; from **S** unto Gilgal;	7851

SHIVERS (1)

Rev	2:27 of a potter *shall* they be **broken to s**:	4937

SHIZA (1)

1Ch	11:42 Adina the son of **S** the Reubenite,	7877

SHOA (1)

Eze	23:23 all the Chaldeans, Pekod, and **S**, and Koa,	7772

SHOBAB (4)

2Sa	5:14 and **S**, and Nathan, and Solomon,	7727
1Ch	2:18 sons *are* these; Jesher, and **S**, and Ardon.	7727
	3: 5 and **S**, and Nathan, and Solomon, four,	7727
	14: 4 Shammua, and **S**, Nathan, and Solomon,	7727

SHOBACH (2)

2Sa	10:16 **S** the captain of the host of Hadarezer	7731
	10:18 smote **S** the captain of their host, who	7731

SHOBAI (2)

Ezr	2:42 the children of Hatita, the children of **S**,	7630
Ne	7:45 the children of **S**, an hundred thirty and	7630

SHOBAL (9)

Ge	36:20 Lotan, and **S**, and Zibeon, and Anah,	7732
	36:23 the children of **S** were these; Alvan,	7732
	36:29 duke Lotan, duke **S**, duke Zibeon,	7732
1Ch	1:38 **S**, and Zibeon, and Anah, and Dishon,	7732
	1:40 The sons of **S**; Alian, and Manahath,	7732
	2:50 of Ephratah; **S** the father of Kirjath-jearim,	7732
	2:52 **S** the father of Kirjath-jearim had sons;	7732
	4: 1 Hezron, and Carmi, and Hur, and **S**.	7732
	4: 2 Reaiah the son of **S** begat Jahath;	7732

SHOBEK (1)

Ne	10:24 Hallohesh, Pileha, **S**,	7733

SHOBI (1)

2Sa	17:27 that **S** the son of Nahash of Rabbah of	7629

SHOCHO (1)

2Ch	28:18 **S** with the villages thereof, and Timnah	7755

SHOCHOH (2)

1Sa	17: 1 were gathered together *at* **S**,	7755
	17: 1 pitched between **S** and Azekah,	7755

SHOCK (1)

Job	5:26 as a **s of corn** cometh in in his season.	1430

SHOCKS (1)

Jdg	15: 5 burnt up both the **s**, and also the standing	1430

SHOCO (1)

2Ch	11: 7 And Beth-zur, and **S**, and Adullam,	7755

SHOD (4) [UNSHOD]

2Ch	28:15 them, and gave them to eat and to drink	5274
Eze	16:10 thee *with* badgers' *skin*, and I girded	5274
Mk	6: 9 But be **s** with sandals; and not put on two	5265
Eph	6:15 And *your* feet **s** with the preparation of	5265

SHOE (9) [SHOE'S, SHOELATCHET, SHOES]

Dt	25: 9 loose his **s** from off his foot, and spit in	5275
	25:10 The house of him that hath his **s** loosed.	5275
	29: 5 and thy **s** is not waxen old upon thy foot.	5275
Jos	5:15 Joshua, Loose thy **s** from off thy foot;	5275
Ru	4: 7 a man plucked off his **s**, and gave *it* to his	5275
	4: 8 Buy *it* for thee. So he drew off his **s**.	5275
Ps	60: 8 over Edom will I cast out my **s**:	5275
	108: 9 over Edom will I cast out my **s**;	5275
Isa	20: 2 thy loins, and put off thy **s** from thy foot.	5275

SHOE'S (1) [SHOE]

Jn	1:27 **s** latchet I am not worthy to unloose.	5266

SHOELATCHET (1) [LATCHET, SHOE]

Ge	14:23 not *take* from a thread even to a **s**,	5275+8288

SHOES (21) [SHOE]

Ex	3: 5 put off thy **s** from off thy feet, for the place	5275
	12:11 your **s** on your feet, and your staff in your	5275
Dt	33:25 Thy **s** *shall be* iron and brass; and as thy	4515
Jos	9: 5 old **s** and clouted upon their feet,	5275
	9:13 **s** are become old by reason of the very	5275
1Ki	2: 5 loins, and in his **s** that *were* on his feet.	5275
SS	7: 1 How beautiful are thy feet with **s**,	5275
Isa	5:27 nor the latchet of their **s** be broken:	5275
Eze	24:17 put on thy **s** upon thy feet, and cover not	5275
	24:23 your heads, and your **s** upon your feet:	5275
Am	2: 6 for silver, and the poor for a pair of **s**;	5275
	8: 6 for silver, and the needy for a pair of **s**;	5275
Mt	3:11 than I, whose **s** I am not worthy to bear:	5266
	10:10 two coats, neither **s**, nor yet staves:	5266
Mk	1: 7 the latchet of whose **s** I am not worthy to	5266
Lk	3:16 the latchet of whose **s** I am not worthy to	5266
	10: 4 Carry neither purse, nor scrip, nor **s**:	5266
	15:22 put a ring on his hand, and **s** on *his* feet:	5266
	22:35 I sent you without purse, and scrip, and **s**,	5266
Ac	7:33 to him, Put off thy **s** from thy feet:	5266
	13:25 whose **s** of *his* feet I am not worthy to	5266

SHOHAM (1)

1Ch	24:27 Beno, and **S**, and Zaccur, and Ibri.	7719

SHOMER (2)

2Ki	12:21 Jehozabad the son of **S**, his servants,	7763
1Ch	7:32 and **S**, and Hotham, and Shua their sister.	7763

SHONE (7) [SHINE]

Ex	34:29 of his face **s** while he talked with him.	7160
	34:30 saw Moses, behold, the skin of his face **s**;	7160
	34:35 that the skin of Moses' face **s**:	7160
2Ki	3:22 sun **s** upon the water, and the Moabites	2224
Lk	2: 9 glory of the Lord **s** round about them:	4034
Ac	22: 6 suddenly there **s** from heaven a great light	4015
Rev	8:12 and the day **s** not for a third *part* of it,	5316

SHOOK (12) [SHAKE]

2Sa	6: 6 and took hold of it; for the oxen **s** *it*.	8058
	22: 8 the earth **s** and trembled; the foundations	1607
	22: 8 the foundations of heaven moved and **s**,	1607
Ne	5:13 I *my* lap, and said, So God shake out	5287
Ps	18: 7 the earth **s** and trembled; the foundations	1607
	68: 8 The earth **s**, the heavens also dropped at	7493

Ps	77:18 the world: the earth trembled and **s**.	7493
Isa	23:11 his hand over the sea, he **s** the kingdoms:	7264
Ac	13:51 But they **s off** the dust of their feet against	1621
	18: 6 he **s** *his* raiment, and said unto them,	1621
	28: 5 And he **s off** the beast into the fire,	660
Heb	12:26 Whose voice then **s** the earth: but now he	4531

SHOOT (21) [BOWSHOT, SHOOTERS, SHOOTETH, SHOOTING, SHOT]

Ex	36:33 he made the middle bar to **s** through	1272
1Sa	20:20 I will **s** three arrows on the side *thereof*,	3384
	20:36 Run, find out now the arrows which I **s**.	3384
2Sa	11:20 knew ye not that they would **s** from	3384
2Ki	13:17 he opened it. Then Elisha said, **S**. And he	3384
	19:32 nor **s** an arrow there, nor come before it	3384
1Ch	5:18 and to **s** with bow, and skilful in war,	1869
2Ch	26:15 to **s** arrows and great stones withal.	3384
Ps	11: 2 that *they* may privily **s** at the upright in	3384
	22: 7 they **s out** the lip, they shake the head,	6362
	58: 7 *when* he bendeth *his* bow to **s** his arrows,	NIH
	64: 3 *and* bend *their* bows to **s** their arrows,	NIH
	64: 4 That *they* may **s** in secret at the perfect:	3384
	64: 4 suddenly do they **s** at him, and fear not.	3384
	64: 7 God shall **s** at them *with* an arrow;	3384
	144: 6 **s out** thine arrows, and destroy them.	7971
Isa	37:33 nor **s** an arrow there, nor come before it	3384
Jer	50:14 bend the bow, **s** at her, spare no arrows:	3034
Eze	31:14 neither **s up** their top among the thick	5414
	36: 8 ye shall **s forth** your branches,	5414
Lk	21:30 When they now **s forth**, ye see and	4261

SHOOTERS (1) [SHOOT]

2Sa	11:24 the **s** shot from off the wall upon thy	4175

SHOOTETH (3) [SHOOT]

Job	8:16 and his branch **s forth** in his garden,	3318
Isa	27: 8 In measure, when it **s forth**, thou wilt	7971
Mk	4:32 than all herbs, and **s out** great branches;	4160

SHOOTING (2) [SHOOT]

1Ch	12: 2 *hurling* stones and *s* arrows out of a bow,	NIH
Am	7: 1 beginning of the **s up** of the latter growth;	5927

SHOPHACH (2)

1Ch	19:16 **S** the captain of the host of Hadarezer	7780
	19:18 killed **S** the captain of the host.	7780

SHOPHAN See ATROTH SHOPHAN

SHORE (17)

Ge	22:17 and as the sand which *is* upon the sea **s**;	8193
Ex	14:30 saw the Egyptians dead upon the sea **s**.	8193
Jos	11: 4 *even* as the sand that *is* upon the sea **s** in	8193
	15: 2 south border was from the **s** of the salt	7097
Jdg	5:17 Asher continued on the sea **s**, and abode	2348
1Sa	13: 5 people as the sand which *is* on the sea **s**	8193
1Ki	4:29 *even* as the sand that *is* on the sea **s**.	8193
	9:26 on the **s** of the Red sea, in the land of	8193
Jer	47: 7 against Ashkelon, and against the sea **s**?	2348
Mt	13: 2 and the whole multitude stood on the **s**.	123
	13:48 they drew to **s**, and sat down,	123
Mk	6:53 the land of Genesaret, and **drew to** the **s**.	4358
Jn	21: 4 was now come, Jesus stood on the **s**:	123
Ac	21: 5 we kneeled down on the **s**, and prayed.	123
	27:39 they discovered a certain creek with a **s**,	123
	27:40 mainsail to the wind, and made toward **s**.	123
Heb	11:12 as the sand which is by the sea **s**	5491

SHORELANDS See SUBURBS

SHORN (4) [SHEAR]

SS	4: 2 *are* like a flock of *sheep that are* **even s**,	7094
Ac	18:18 having *his* head in Cenchrea: for he had	2751
1Co	11: 6 woman be not covered, let her also be **s**:	2751
	11: 6 but *if* it be a shame for a woman to be **s**	2751

SHORT (13) [SHORTENED, SHORTER, SHORTLY]

Nu	11:23 Is the Lord's hand **waxed s**?	7114
2Ki	10:32 days the Lord began to **cut** Israel **s**:	7096
Job	17:12 day: the light *is* **s**, because of darkness.	7138
	20: 5 the triumphing of the wicked *is* **s**,	4480+7138
Ps	89:47 Remember how **s** my **time** is:	2465
Ro	3:23 and **come s** of the glory of God;	5302
	9:28 the work, and **cut** it **s** in righteousness:	4932
	9:28 **s** work will the Lord make upon the earth.	4932
1Co	7:29 But this I say, brethren, the time *is* **s**:	4958
1Th	2:17 being taken from you for a **s** time in	5610
Heb	4: 1 any of you should seem to **come s** of it.	5302
Rev	12:12 he knoweth that he hath but a **s** time.	3641
	17:10 he cometh, he must continue a **s** *space*.	3641

SHORTENED (9) [SHORT]

Ps	89:45 The days of his youth hast thou **s**: thou	7114
	102:23 my strength in the way; he **s** my days.	7114
Pr	10:27 but the years of the wicked shall be **s**.	7114
Isa	50: 2 Is my hand **s at all**, that *it* cannot	7114+7114
	59: 1 Behold, the Lord's hand is not **s**, that *it*	7114
Mt	24:22 And except those days should be **s**,	2856
	24:22 for the elect's sake those days shall be **s**.	2856
Mk	13:20 except that the Lord had **s** *those* days,	2856
	13:20 he hath chosen, he hath **s** the days.	2856

SHORTER (2) [SHORT]

Isa	28:20 the bed is **s** than that *a man* can stretch	7114
Eze	42: 5 Now the upper chambers *were* **s**:	7114

SHORTLY (15) [SHORT]

Ge	41:32 by God, and God will **s** bring it to pass.	4116
Jer	27:16 now **s** be brought again from Babylon:	4120
Eze	7: 8 Now will I **s** pour out my fury upon	4480+7138
Ac	25: 4 he himself would depart **s** *thither*.	1722+5034
Ro	16:20 shall bruise Satan under your feet **s**.	1722+5034
1Co	4:19 But I will come to you **s**, if the Lord will,	5030
Php	2:19 Lord Jesus to send Timotheus **s** unto you,	5030
	2:24 in the Lord that I also myself shall come **s**.	5030
1Ti	3:14 I unto thee, hoping to come unto thee **s**:	5030
2Ti	4: 9 Do thy diligence to come **s** unto me:	5030
Heb	13:23 with whom, if he come **s**, I will see you.	5030
2Pe	1:14 Knowing that **s** *I* must put off *this* my	5031
3Jn	1:14 But I trust *I* shall **s** see thee, and we shall	2112
Rev	1: 1 *things* which must **s** come to pass;	1722+5034
	22: 6 the *things* which must **s** be done.	1722+5034

SHOSHANNIM (2)

Ps	45: T To the chief Musician upon **S**, for the	7799
	69: T To the chief Musician upon **S**, *A Psalm* of	7799

SHOSHANNIM-EDUTH (1)

Ps	80: T To the chief Musician upon **S**,	5715+7799

SHOT (16) [SHOOT]

Ge	40:10 it budded, *and* her blossoms **s forth**:	5927
	49:23 grieved him, and **s** *at him*, and hated him:	7232
Ex	19:13 surely be stoned, or **s through**;	3384+3384
Nu	21:30 We have **s** at them; Heshbon is perished	3384
1Sa	20:20 the side *thereof*, as *though* I **s** at a mark.	7971
	20:36 as the lad ran, he **s** an arrow beyond him.	3384
	20:37 place of the arrow which Jonathan had **s**,	3384
2Sa	11:24 the shooters **s** from off the wall upon thy	3384
2Ki	13:17 he **s**. And he said, The arrow of	3384
2Ch	35:23 the archers **s** at king Josiah; and the king	3384
Ps	18:14 **s out** lightnings, and discomfited them.	7232
Jer	9: 8 Their tongue *is as* an arrow **s out**;	7819
Eze	17: 6 forth branches, and **s forth** sprigs.	7971
	17: 7 and **s forth** her branches toward him,	7971
	31: 5 the multitude of waters, when he **s forth**.	7971
	31:10 he hath **s up** his top among the thick	5414

SHOULD (783) [SHOULDEST]

Ge	2:18 *It is* not good that the man **s** be alone;	NIH
	4:15 upon Cain, lest any finding him **s** kill him.	NIH
	18:25 that the righteous **s** be as the wicked, that	NIH
	21: 7 that Sarah **s** have given children suck?	NIH
	23: 8 If it be your mind that I **s** bury my dead	NIH
	26: 7 *said he*, the men of the place **s** kill me for	NIH
	27:45 why **s** I be deprived also of you both *in* one	NIH
	29: 7 neither *is it* time that the cattle **s** be	NIH
	29:19 than that I **s** give her to another man:	NIH
	30:38 that they **s** conceive when they came to	NIH
	33:13 if *men* **s** overdrive them one day,	NIH
	34:31 S he deal with our sister as with a harlot?	NIH
	38: 9 Onan knew that the seed **s** not be his;	NIH
	38: 9 lest that he **s** give seed to his brother.	NIH
	40:15 also have I done nothing that they **s** put	NIH
	43:25 for they heard that they **s** eat bread there.	NIH
	44: 7 God forbid that thy servants **s** do	NIH
	44: 8 we steal out of thy lord's house silver or	NIH
	44:17 he said, God forbid that I **s** do so:	NIH
	44:22 for *if* he **s** leave his father, *his father* would	NIH
	47:15 for why **s** we die in thy presence?	NIH
	47:26 that Pharaoh **s** have the fifth *part*; except	NIH
Ex	3:11 that I **s** go unto Pharaoh, and that I should	NIH
	3:11 that I **s** bring forth the children of Israel	NIH
	5: 2 that I **s** obey his voice to let Israel go?	NIH
	14:12 than that we **s** die in the wilderness.	NIH
	22: 3 *for* he **s** make full restitution; if he have	NIH
	32:12 Wherefore **s** the Egyptians speak, and say,	NIH
	35: 1 hath commanded, that *ye* **s** do them.	NIH
	39: 7 *that they* **s** be stones for a memorial to	NIH
	39:23 round about the hole, *that* it **s** not rend.	NIH
Lev	4:13 *concerning things* which **s** not be done,	NIH
	4:22 God *concerning things* which **s** not be	NIH
	9: 6 which the Lord commanded *that* ye **s** do:	NIH
	10:18 indeed have eaten it in the holy *place*,	NIH
	10:19 it have been accepted in the sight of	NIH
	11:43 with them, that *ye* **s** be defiled thereby.	NIH
	20:26 you from *other* people, that *ye* **s** be mine.	NIH
	24:23 that they **s** bring forth him that had cursed	NIH
	26:13 of Egypt, that *ye* **s** not be their bondmen;	NIH
	27:26 which **s** be the Lord's firstling, no man	NIH
Nu	7: 9 *was that* they **s** bear upon *their* shoulders.	NIH
	9: 4 of Israel, that they **s** keep the passover.	NIH
	11:13 Whence **s** I have flesh to give unto all this	NIH
	12:14 her face, **s** she not be ashamed seven days?	NIH
	14: 3 our wives and our children **s** be a prey?	NIH
	14:31 your little ones, which ye said **s** be a prey,	NIH
	15:34 it was not declared what **s** be done to him.	NIH
	20: 4 that we and our cattle **s** die there?	NIH
	23:19 God *is* not a man, that he **s** lie; neither	NIH
	23:19 neither the son of man, that he **s** repent:	NIH
	27: 4 Why **s** the name of our father be done	NIH
	32: 9 that *they* **s** not go into the land which	NIH
	35:28 Because he **s** have remained in the city of	NIH
	35:32 that he **s** come again to dwell in the land,	NIH
Dt	1:18 at that time all the things which ye **s** do.	NIH
	1:33 to shew you by what way ye **s** go, and in	NIH
	1:39 which ye said **s** be a prey,	NIH
	4: 5 that *ye* **s** do in the land whither ye go to	NIH
	4:21 sware that I **s** not go over Jordan, and that	NIH
	4:21 and that *I* **s** not go in unto *that* good land,	NIH
	4:42 which **s** kill his neighbour unawares,	NIH

Dt	5:25 Now therefore why **s** we die? for this great	NIH
	17:16 to the end that he **s** multiply horses:	NIH
	20:18 so **s** ye sin against the Lord your God.	NIH
	25: 3 *if* he **s** exceed, and beat him above these	NIH
	25: 3 then thy brother **s** seem vile unto thee.	NIH
	29:18 Lest there **s** be among you man, or	NIH
	29:18 lest there **s** be among you a root that	NIH
	32:27 lest their adversaries **s** behave themselves	NIH
	32:27 *and* lest they **s** say, Our hand is high,	NIH
	32:30 How **s** one chase a thousand, and two put	NIH
Jos	8:29 Joshua commanded that they **s** take his	NIH
	8:33 that they **s** bless the people of Israel.	NIH
	9:27 this day, in the place which he **s** choose.	NIH
	11:20 that *they* **s** come against Israel *in* battle,	NIH
	22:28 when they **s** *so* say to us or to our	NIH
	22:29 God forbid that we **s** rebel against	NIH
	24:16 God forbid that we **s** forsake the Lord,	NIH
Jdg	8: 6 that we **s** give bread unto thine army?	NIH
	8:15 that we **s** give bread unto thy men *that*	NIH
	9: 9 tree said unto them, **S** I leave my fatness,	NIH
	9:11 **S** I forsake my sweetness, and my good	NIH
	9:13 **S** I leave my wine, which cheereth God	NIH
	9:28 and who *is* Shechem, that we **s** serve him?	NIH
	9:28 of Shechem: for why **s** we serve him?	NIH
	9:38 Who *is* Abimelech, that we **s** serve him?	NIH
	9:41 that *they* **s** not dwell in Shechem.	NIH
	20:38 that they **s** make a great flame with smoke	NIH
	21: 3 that there **s** be to day one tribe lacking in	NIH
	21:22 them at *this* time, *that* you **s** be guilty.	NIH
Ru	1:12 If I say, I have hope, *if* I **s** have a	NIH
	1:12 *if* I **s** have a husband also to night,	NIH
	1:12 also to night, and **s** also bear sons;	NIH
1Sa	2:30 of thy father, **s** walk before me for ever:	NIH
	8: 7 rejected me, that *I* **s** not reign over them.	NIH
	9: 6 he can shew us our way that we **s** go.	NIH
	10:22 if the man yet come thither.	NIH
	12:21 *s ye* go after vain *things*, which cannot	NIH
	12:23 God forbid that I **s** sin against the Lord	NIH
	15:21 the chief of the things which **s** have been	NIH
	15:29 for he *is* not a man, that *he* **s** repent.	NIH
	17:26 he **s** defy the armies of the living God?	NIH
	18:18 in Israel, that I **s** be son in law to the king?	NIH
	18:19 daughter **s** have been given to David,	NIH
	19: 1 to all his servants, that they **s** kill David	NIH
	19:17 said unto me, Let me go; why **s** I kill thee?	NIH
	20: 2 why **s** my father hide this thing from me?	NIH
	20: 5 and I **s** not fail to sit with the king at meat:	NIH
	22:13 that *he* **s** rise against me, to lie in wait,	NIH
	24: 6 The Lord forbid that I **s** do this	NIH
	26:11 The Lord forbid that *I* **s** stretch forth	NIH
	27: 1 *there* is nothing better for me than that I **s**	NIH
	27: 5 why **s** thy servant dwell in the royal city	NIH
	27:11 Lest they **s** tell on us, saying, So did	NIH
	29: 4 for wherewith **s** he reconcile himself unto	NIH
	29: 4 **s** it not *be* with the heads of these men?	NIH
2Sa	2:22 wherefore **s** I smite thee to the ground?	NIH
	2:22 **s** I hold up my face to Joab thy brother?	NIH
	12:23 now he is dead, wherefore **s** I fast? can I	NIH
	13:26 said unto him, Why **s** he go with thee?	NIH
	15:20 **s** I this day make thee go up and down	NIH
	16: 9 Why **s** this dead dog curse my lord	NIH
	16:19 whom **s** I serve? *should I* not *serve* in	NIH
	16:19 *s I* not *serve* in the presence of his son?	NIH
	18:12 Though I **s** receive a thousand *shekels* of	NIH
	18:13 Otherwise I **s** have wrought falsehood	NIH
	19:19 that the king **s** take *it* to his heart.	NIH
	19:22 that ye **s** *this* day be adversaries unto me?	NIH
	19:34 I **s** go up with the king *unto* Jerusalem?	NIH
	19:35 **s** thy servant be yet a burden unto my lord	NIH
	19:36 why **s** the king recompense *it* me *with*	NIH
	19:43 our advice **s** not be first had in bringing	NIH
	20:20 from me, that I **s** swallow up or destroy.	NIH
	21: 5 that devised against us *that* we **s** be	NIH
	23:17 it far from me, O Lord, that I **s** do this:	NIH
1Ki	1:27 who **s** sit on the throne of my lord the	NIH
	2: 1 the days of David drew nigh that *he* **s**	NIH
	2:15 Israel set their faces on me, that *I* **s** reign:	NIH
	6: 6 the beams **s** not be fastened in the walls	NIH
	8:36 them the good way wherein they **s** walk,	NIH
	11:10 thing, that he **s** not go after other gods:	NIH
	14: 2 which told me that I **s** be king over this	NIH
	21: 3 that I **s** give the inheritance of my fathers	NIH
2Ki	3:27 he took his eldest son that **s** have reigned	NIH
	4:43 What, **s** I set this before an hundred men?	NIH
	6:33 what **s** I wait for the Lord any longer?	NIH
	7:19 *if* the Lord **s** make windows in heaven,	NIH
	8:13 a dog, that he **s** do this great thing?	NIH
	11: 9 with them that **s** go out on the sabbath,	NIH
	11:17 that *they* **s** be the Lord's people;	NIH
	17:15 them, that *they* **s** not do like them.	NIH
	17:28 taught them how they **s** fear the Lord.	NIH
	18:35 that the Lord **s** deliver Jerusalem out of	NIH
	22:19 *they* **s** become a desolation and a curse,	NIH
1Ch	9:28 that they **s** bring them in and out by tale.	NIH
	11:19 *I* **s** do this *thing*: shall I drink the blood	NIH
	16:42 cymbals for those that **s** make a sound,	NIH
	21:17 not on thy people, that they **s** be plagued.	NIH
	21:18 that David **s** go up, and set up an altar	NIH
	23:13 that he **s** sanctify the most holy *things*, he	NIH
	23:32 they **s** keep the charge of the tabernacle	NIH
	25: 1 of Jeduthun, who **s** prophesy with harps,	NIH
	29:14 that we **s** be able to offer *so* willingly after	NIH
2Ch	2: 6 who *am* I then, that I **s** build him a house,	NIH
	4:20 that they **s** burn after the manner before	NIH
	6:27 them the good way, wherein they **s** walk;	NIH

Ref	Text	Code
2Ch 15:13	the LORD God of Israel **s** be put to death,	NIH
20:21	that **s** praise the beauty of holiness, as *they*	NIH
23:16	that *they* **s** be the LORD's people.	NIH
23:19	none *which was* unclean in any thing **s**	NIH
25:13	that *they* **s** not go with him to battle, fell	NIH
29:11	that *you* **s** minister unto him,	1961
29:24	the sin offering **s** *be made* for all Israel.	
30: 1	that *they* **s** come to the house of the LORD	NIH
30: 5	that *they* **s** come to keep the passover unto	NIH
32: 4	Why **s** the kings of Assyria come,	NIH
32:14	that your God **s** be able to deliver you out	NIH
Ezr 2:63	that they **s** not eat of the most holy *things*	NIH
4:22	**s** damage grow to the hurt of the kings?	NIH
7:23	for why **s** there be wrath against the realm	NIH
8:17	I told them what they **s** say unto Iddo,	NIH
8:17	that they **s** bring unto us ministers for	NIH
9:14	**S** we again break thy commandments,	NIH
9:14	that *there* **s** be no remnant nor escaping?	NIH
10: 5	to swear that *they* **s** do according to this	NIH
10: 7	*they* **s** gather themselves together *unto*	NIH
10: 8	all his substance be forfeited,	NIH
Ne 2: 3	why **s** not my countenance be sad, when	NIH
5:12	that *they* **s** do according to this promise.	NIH
6: 3	why **s** the work cease, whilst I leave it,	NIH
6:11	I said, **S** such a man as I flee? and who *is*	NIH
6:13	that I **s** be afraid, and do so, and sin,	NIH
7:65	that they **s** not eat of the most holy *things*,	NIH
8:14	the children of Israel **s** dwell in booths	NIH
8:15	they **s** publish and proclaim in all their	NIH
9:12	give them light in the way wherein they **s**	NIH
9:15	them that *they* **s** go in to possess	NIH
9:19	light, and the way wherein they **s** go.	NIH
9:23	fathers, that *they* **s** go in to possess it.	NIH
10:37	*that* we **s** bring the firstfruits of our dough,	NIH
11:23	that a certain portion **s** *be* for the singers,	NIH
13: 1	the Moabite **s** not come into	NIH
13: 2	Balaam against them, that he **s** curse them:	NIH
13:19	I commanded that the gates **s** be shut,	NIH
13:19	charged that they **s** not be opened till after	NIH
13:19	*that* there **s** no burden be brought in on	NIH
13:22	I commanded the Levites that they **s**	1961
13:22	that they **s** come *and* keep the gates,	NIH
Est 1: 8	that *they* **s** do according to every man's	NIH
1:22	every man **s** bear rule in his own house,	NIH
1:22	that it **s** be published according to	NIH
2:10	Mordecai had charged her that she **s** not	NIH
2:11	Esther did, and what **s** become of her.	NIH
3:14	that *they* **s** be ready against that day.	NIH
4: 8	charge her that *she* **s** go in unto the king,	NIH
8:13	the Jews **s** be ready against that day to	NIH
9:21	that they **s** keep the fourteenth day of	1961
9:22	that *they* **s** make them days of feasting and	NIH
9:25	**s** return upon his own head, and that he	NIH
9:25	and his sons be hanged on the gallows.	NIH
9:27	themselves unto them, so as it **s** not fail,	NIH
9:28	*that* these days **s** be remembered and	NIH
9:28	that these days of Purim **s** not fail from	NIH
Job 3:12	or why the breasts that I **s** suck?	NIH
3:13	For now **s** I have lien *still* and been quiet,	NIH
3:13	lien *still* and been quiet, I **s** have slept:	NIH
6:10	**s** I yet have comfort; yea, I would harden	NIH
6:11	What *is* my strength, that I **s** hope?	NIH
6:11	what *is* mine end, that I **s** prolong my life?	NIH
6:14	To him that is afflicted pity **s** *be shewed*	NIH
8: 7	yet thy latter end **s** greatly increase.	NIH
9: 2	a truth: but how **s** man be just with God?	NIH
9:32	I *am, that* I **s** answer him, *and* we should	NIH
9:32	*and* we **s** come together in judgment.	NIH
10:19	I **s** have been as though I had not been;	NIH
10:19	I **s** have been carried from the womb to	NIH
11: 2	**S** not the multitude of words be answered?	NIH
11: 2	and **s** a man full of talk be justified?	NIH
11: 3	**S** thy lies make men hold their peace?	NIH
13: 5	hold your peace, and it **s** be your wisdom.	NIH
13: 9	*Is it* good that he **s** search you out?	NIH
15: 2	**S** a wise *man* utter vain knowledge,	NIH
15: 3	**S** he reason *with* unprofitable talk?	NIH
15:14	What *is* man, that he **s** be clean?	NIH
15:14	born of a woman, that he **s** be righteous?	NIH
16: 5	moving of my lips **s** asswage *your* grief.	NIH
19:28	ye **s** say, Why persecute we him? seeing	NIH
21: 4	*were* so, why **s** not my spirit be troubled?	NIH
21:15	*is* the Almighty, that we **s** serve him?	NIH
21:15	profit **s** we have, if we pray unto him?	NIH
23: 7	so **s** I be delivered for ever from my judge.	NIH
27: 5	God forbid that I **s** justify you: till I die I	NIH
31: 1	eyes; why then **s** I think upon a maid?	NIH
31:28	for I **s** have denied the God *that is* above.	NIH
32: 7	Days **s** speak, and multitude of years	NIH
32: 7	and multitude of years **s** teach wisdom.	NIH
32:13	Lest ye **s** say, We have found out wisdom:	NIH
34: 6	**S** I lie against my right? my wound *is*	NIH
34: 9	It profiteth a man nothing that he **s** delight	NIH
34:10	be it from God, that he **s** *do* wickedness;	NIH
34:10	the Almighty, that he **s** *commit* iniquity.	NIH
34:23	that he **s** enter into judgment with God.	NIH
34:33	**S** it be according to thy mind? he will	NIH
36:16	that which **s** be set on thy table *should be*	NIH
36:16	that which should be set on thy table **s** *be*	NIH
41:11	that I **s** repay *him*? whatsoever *is* under	NIH
Ps 27: 3	Though a host **s** encamp against me,	NIH
27: 3	though war **s** rise against me, in this *will* I	NIH
30: 3	me alive, that I **s** not go down *to* the pit.	NIH
38:16	*Hear me,* lest *otherwise* they **s** rejoice	NIH
49: 5	Wherefore **s** I fear in the days of evil,	NIH
Ps 49: 9	That he **s** still live for ever, *and* not see	NIH
69:22	that which **s** have been for *their* welfare,	NIH
73:15	I **s** offend *against* the generation of thy	NIH
78: 5	that *they* **s** make them known to their	NIH
78: 6	them, *even* the children which **s** be born;	NIH
78: 6	who **s** arise and declare *them* to their	NIH
79:10	Wherefore **s** the heathen say, Where *is*	NIH
81:14	I **s** soon have subdued their enemies,	NIH
81:15	The haters of the LORD **s** have submitted	NIH
81:15	but their time **s** have endured for ever.	NIH
81:16	He **s** have fed them also with the finest of	NIH
81:16	honey out of the rock **s** I have satisfied	NIH
95:11	whom I sware in my wrath that they **s**	NIH
104: 5	earth, that it **s** not be removed for ever.	NIH
106:23	away his wrath, lest he **s** destroy *them*.	NIH
115: 2	Wherefore **s** the heathen say, Where *is*	NIH
119:92	I **s** then have perished in mine affliction.	NIH
139:18	*If* I **s** count them, they are moe in number	NIH
143: 8	me to know the way wherein I **s** walk;	NIH
Pr 8:29	that the waters **s** not pass his	NIH
22: 6	Train up a child in the way he **s** go:	NIH
22:27	why **s** he take away thy bed from under	NIH
Ecc 2: 3	which they **s** do under the heaven all	NIH
2:18	I **s** leave it unto the man that shall be after	NIH
2:24	*than* that he **s** eat and drink, and *that* he	NIH
2:24	that he **s** make his soul enjoy good in his	NIH
3:13	also that every man **s** eat and drink,	NIH
3:22	that a man **s** rejoice in his own works;	NIH
3:14	God doeth *it,* that *men* **s** fear before him.	NIH
5: 6	wherefore **s** God be angry at thy voice,	NIH
7:14	the end that man **s** find nothing after him.	NIH
SS 1: 7	for why **s** I be as one that turneth aside by	NIH
8: 1	when I **s** find thee without, I would kiss	NIH
8: 1	I would kiss thee; yea, I **s** not be despised.	NIH
8: 3	His left hand **s** *be* under my head,	NIH
8: 3	head, and his right hand **s** embrace me.	NIH
Isa 1: 5	Why **s** ye be stricken any more? ye will	NIH
1: 9	we **s** have been as Sodom, *and* we should	NIH
1: 9	*and* we **s** have been like unto Gomorrah.	NIH
5: 2	he looked that *it* **s** bring forth grapes,	NIH
5: 4	when I looked that *it* **s** bring forth grapes,	NIH
8:11	instructed me that I **s** not walk in the way	NIH
8:19	**s** not a people seek unto their God?	NIH
10:15	as if the rod **s** shake *itself against* them	NIH
10:15	as if the staff **s** lift up *itself, as if it were* no	NIH
36:20	that the LORD **s** deliver Jerusalem out of	NIH
41: 7	with nails, *that* it **s** not be moved.	NIH
48:11	I do *it:* for how **s** *my name* be polluted?	NIH
48:19	his name **s** not have been cut off nor	NIH
49:15	that *she* **s** not have compassion on the son	NIH
50: 4	I **s** know how to speak a word in season	NIH
51:14	he **s** not die in the pit, nor that his bread	NIH
51:14	not die in the pit, nor that his bread **s** fail.	NIH
53: 2	*there is* no beauty that we **s** desire him.	NIH
54: 9	of Noah **s** no more go over the earth;	NIH
57: 6	meat offering. **S** I receive comfort in these?	NIH
57:16	for the spirit **s** fail before me, and the souls	NIH
63:13	in the wilderness, *that* they **s** not stumble?	NIH
Jer 5:17	*which* thy sons and thy daughters **s** eat:	NIH
20:18	that my days **s** be consumed with shame?	NIH
23:22	they **s** have turned them from their evil	NIH
25:29	my name, and **s** ye be utterly unpunished?	NIH
26:24	that *they* **s** not give him into the hand of	NIH
27:10	I **s** drive you out, and ye should perish.	NIH
27:10	I should drive you out, and ye **s** perish.	NIH
27:17	live: wherefore **s** this city be laid waste?	NIH
29:26	that ye **s** be officers in the house of	NIH
32:31	that I **s** remove it from before my face,	NIH
32:35	that *they* **s** do this abomination, to cause	NIH
33:20	that there **s** not be day and night in their	NIH
33:21	that he **s** not have a son to reign upon his	NIH
33:24	*they* **s** be no more a nation before them.	NIH
34: 9	That every man **s** let his manservant,	NIH
34: 9	that none **s** serve himself of them, *to wit,*	NIH
34:10	heard that every one **s** let his manservant,	NIH
34:10	that none **s** serve themselves of them any	NIH
37:10	yet **s** they rise up every man in his tent,	NIH
37:21	Zedekiah the king commanded that they **s**	NIH
37:21	that *they* **s** give him daily a piece of bread	NIH
39:14	son of Shaphan, that he **s** carry him home:	NIH
40:15	no man shall know *it:* wherefore **s** he slay	NIH
40:15	are gathered unto thee **s** be scattered,	NIH
44:14	that *they* **s** return *into* the land of Judah,	NIH
46:13	how Nebuchadrezzar king of Babylon **s**	NIH
51:53	Though Babylon **s** mount up to heaven,	NIH
51:53	though she **s** fortify the height of her	NIH
51:60	all the evil that **s** come upon Babylon,	NIH
La 1:10	thou didst command *that* they **s** not	NIH
1:16	the comforter that **s** relieve my soul is far	NIH
1:17	*that* his adversaries **s** be round about him:	NIH
3:26	*It is* good that a man **s** both hope and	NIH
3:44	cloud, that *our* prayer **s** not pass through.	NIH
4:12	the enemy **s** have entered into the gates	NIH
Eze 8: 6	that I **s** go far off from my sanctuary?	NIH
13:19	to slay the souls that **s** not die, and to save	NIH
13:19	and to save the souls alive that **s** not live,	NIH
13:22	that *he* **s** not return from his wicked way,	NIH
14: 3	their face: **s** I be inquired of at all by them?	NIH
14:14	they **s** deliver *but* their own souls by their	NIH
18:23	I any pleasure at all that the wicked **s**	NIH
18:23	*and* not that he **s** return from his ways,	NIH
19: 9	that his voice **s** no more be heard upon	NIH
20: 9	*it* **s** not be polluted before the heathen,	NIH
20:14	*it* **s** not be polluted before the heathen,	NIH
20:22	that *it* **s** not be polluted in the sight of	NIH
Eze 20:25	and judgments whereby they **s** not live;	NIH
21:10	**s** we then make mirth? it contemneth	NIH
22:30	that **s** make up the hedge, and stand in	NIH
22:30	me for the land, that *I* **s** not destroy it:	NIH
24: 8	the top of a rock, that *it* **s** not be covered.	NIH
33:10	pine away in them, how **s** we then live?	NIH
34: 2	**s** not the shepherds feed the flocks?	NIH
Da 1: 3	that *he* **s** bring *certain* of the children of	NIH
1:10	for why **s** he see your faces worse liking	NIH
1:16	their meat, and the wine that they **s** drink;	NIH
1:18	that the king had said *he* **s** bring them in,	NIH
2:13	decree went forth that the wise *men* **s** be	NIH
2:18	his fellows **s** not perish with the rest of	NIH
2:29	thy bed, what **s** come to pass hereafter;	NIH
2:46	commanded that *they* **s** offer an oblation	NIH
3:11	he **s** be cast into the midst of a burning	NIH
3:19	commanded that they **s** heat the furnace	NIH
5:15	that they **s** read this writing,	NIH
5:29	*he* **s** be the third ruler in the kingdom.	NIH
6: 1	which **s** be over the whole kingdom;	NIH
6: 2	them, and the king **s** have no damage.	NIH
6:23	commanded that *they* **s** take Daniel up	NIH
7:14	nations, and languages, **s** serve him:	NIH
Hos 10: 3	the LORD; what then **s** a king do to us?	NIH
10:10	*It is* in my desire that I **s** chastise them;	NIH
13:13	for he **s** not stay long in the *place of*	NIH
Joel 2:17	that the heathen **s** rule over them:	NIH
2:17	wherefore **s** they say among the people,	NIH
Jnh 4:11	**s** not I spare Nineveh, *that* great city,	NIH
Mic 6:16	that I **s** make thee a desolation,	NIH
Zep 3: 7	so their dwelling **s** not be cut off,	NIH
Hag 1: 2	the time that the LORD's house **s** be built.	NIH
Zec 7: 3	**S** I weep in the fifth month,	NIH
7: 7	**S** ye not *hear* the words which the LORD	NIH
7:11	stopped their ears, that they **s** not hear.	NIH
7:12	lest *they* **s** hear the law, and the words	NIH
8: 6	it also be marvellous in my eyes?	NIH
Mal 1:13	**s** I accept this of your hand? saith	NIH
2: 7	For the priest's lips **s** keep knowledge,	NIH
2: 7	and they **s** seek the law at his mouth:	NIH
Mt 2: 4	he demanded of them where Christ **s** be	NIG
2:12	in a dream that *they* **s** not return to Herod,	NIG
5:29	for thee that one of thy members **s** perish,	NIG
5:29	not *that* thy whole body **s** be cast into hell.	NIG
5:30	for thee that one of thy members **s** perish,	NIG
5:30	not *that* thy whole body **s** be cast into hell.	NIG
7:12	whatsoever ye would that men **s** do to you	NIG
11: 3	Art thou he that **s** come, or do we look for	NIG
12:16	charged them that they **s** not make him	NIG
13:15	lest at any time they **s** see with *their* eyes,	NIG
13:15	and **s** understand with *their* heart,	NIG
13:15	**s** be converted, and I should heal them.	NIG
13:15	should be converted, and I **s** heal them.	NIG
15:33	Whence **s** we have so much bread in	NIG
16:11	that ye **s** beware of the leaven of	NIG
16:20	charged he his disciples that they **s** tell	NIG
17:27	Notwithstanding, lest we **s** offend them,	NIG
18:14	that one of these little ones **s** perish.	NIG
18:30	cast him into prison, till he **s** pay the debt.	NIG
18:34	till he **s** pay all that was due unto him.	NIG
19:13	that he **s** put *his* hands on them, and pray:	NIG
20:10	they supposed that they **s** have received	NIG
20:31	because they **s** hold their peace:	NIG
24:22	And except those days **s** be shortened,	302
24:22	be shortened, there **s** no flesh be saved:	302
25:27	at my coming I **s** **have** received mine own	302
26:35	said unto him, Though I **s** die with thee,	1163
27:20	elders persuaded the multitude that they **s**	NIG
Mk 3: 9	that a small ship **s** wait on him because	NIG
3: 9	of the multitude, lest they **s** throng him.	NIG
3:12	he straitly charged them that they **s** not	NIG
3:14	that they **s** be with him, and that he might	NIG
4:12	lest at any time they **s** be converted,	NIG
4:12	and *their* sins **s** be forgiven them.	NIG
4:22	kept secret, but that it **s** come abroad.	NIG
4:26	as if a man **s** cast seed into the ground,	NIG
4:27	And **s** sleep, and rise night and day,	NIG
4:27	day, and the seed **s** spring and grow up,	NIG
5:43	he charged them straitly that no *man* **s**	NIG
5:43	commanded that *something* **s** be given	NIG
6: 8	And commanded them that they **s** take	NIG
6:12	went out, and preached that *men* **s** repent.	NIG
7:36	And he charged them that they **s** tell no	NIG
8:30	he charged them that they **s** tell no *man*	NIG
9: 9	he charged them that they **s** tell no *man*	NIG
9:10	what the rising from the dead **s** mean.	NIG
9:18	I spake to thy disciples that they **s** cast him	NIG
9:30	and he would not that any *man* **s** know *it.*	NIG
9:34	among themselves, who **s** be the greatest.	NIG
10:13	children to him, that he **s** touch them:	NIG
10:32	began to tell them what *things* **s** happen	3195
10:36	What would ye that I **s** do for you?	NIG
10:48	and many charged him that he **s** hold his	NIG
10:51	What wilt thou *that* I **s** do unto thee?	NIG
11:16	And would not suffer that any *man* **s** carry	NIG
12:19	his brother **s** take his wife, and raise up	NIG
13:20	shortened *those* days, no flesh **s** be saved:	302
14:31	If I **s** die with thee, I will not deny thee in	1163
15:11	he **s** rather release Barabbas unto them.	NIG
15:24	lots upon them, what every *man* **s** take.	NIG
Lk 1:29	mind what manner of salutation this **s** be.	NIG
1:43	that the mother of my Lord **s** come to me?	NIG
1:57	Now Elisabeth's full time came that she **s**	NIG
1:71	That we **s** be saved from our enemies,	NIG
2: 1	that all the world **s** be taxed.	NIG

S

Lk
2: 6 the days were accomplished that she **s** be NIG
2:26 *he* **s** not see death, before he had seen NIG
4:42 him, that *he* **s** not depart from them. NIG
5: 7 ship, that *they* **s** come and help them. NIG
6:31 And as ye would that men **s** do to you, NIG
7: 4 he was worthy for whom he **s** do this: NIG
7:19 to Jesus, saying, Art thou he that **s** come? NIG
7:20 thee, saying, Art thou he that **s** come? NIG
8:12 hearts, lest they **s** believe and be saved. NIG
8:56 he charged them that they **s** tell no *man* NIG
9:13 except we **s** go and buy meat for all this NIG
9:31 of his decease which he **s** accomplish 3195
9:46 among them, which of them **s** be greatest. NIG
9:51 when the time was come that he **s** be NIG
15:32 It was meet that *we* **s** make merry, NIG
17: 2 that he **s** offend one of these little ones. NIG
17: 6 thou planted in the sea; and it **s** obey you. 302
17:20 when the kingdom of God **s** come, NIG
18:39 rebuked him, that he **s** hold his peace: NIG
19:11 they thought that the kingdom of God **s** 3195
19:27 which would not that I **s** reign over them, NIG
19:40 I tell you that, if these **s** hold their peace, NIG
20:10 that they **s** give him of the fruit of NIG
20:20 which *s*feign themselves just *men,* that NIG
20:28 his brother **s** take *his* wife, and raise up NIG
22:23 which of them it was that **s** do this *thing.* 3195
22:24 of them **s** be accounted the greatest. NIG
23:24 Pilate gave sentence that it **s** be as they NIG
24:16 But their eyes were holden that they **s** not NIG
24:21 we trusted that it had been he which **s** 3195
24:47 remission of sins **s** be preached in his name NIG

Jn
1:31 but that he **s** be made manifest to Israel, NIG
2:25 And needed not that any **s** testify of man: NIG
3:15 That whosoever believeth in him **s** not NIG
3:16 that whosoever believeth in him **s** not NIG
3:20 to the light, lest his deeds **s** be reproved. NIG
5:23 all *men* **s** honour the Son, even as they NIG
6:14 This is of a truth *that* prophet that **s** come NIG
6:39 that of all which he hath given me I **s** lose NIG
6:39 but **s** raise it up *again* at the last day. NIG
6:64 that believed not, and who **s** betray him. NIG
6:71 for he *it was that* **s** betray him, being one 3195
7:23 that the law of Moses **s** not be broken; NIG
7:39 which they that believe on him **s** receive: 3195
8: 5 law commanded us, that such **s** be stoned: NIG
8:19 me, ye **s** have known my Father also. 302
8:55 and if I **s** say, I know him not, I shall be a NIG
9: 3 that the works of God **s** be made manifest NIG
9:22 he **s** be put out of the synagogue. NIG
9:41 them, If ye were blind, ye **s** have no sin: 302
11:27 Son of God, which **s** come into the world. NIG
11:37 have caused that even this *man* **s** not have NIG
11:50 that one man **s** die for the people, NIG
11:51 he prophesied that Jesus **s** die for *that* 3195
11:52 that also he **s** gather together in one NIG
11:57 he **s** shew *it,* that they might take him. NIG
12: 4 Simon's *son,* which **s** betray him, 3195
12:23 come, that the Son of man **s** be glorified. 3195
12:33 he said, signifying what death he **s** die. 3195
12:40 that they **s** not see with *their* eyes, NIG
12:40 and be converted, and I **s** heal them. NIG
12:42 lest they **s** be put out of the synagogue: NIG
12:46 whosoever believeth on me **s** not abide NIG
12:49 what I **s** say, and what I should speak. NIG
12:49 what I should say, and what I **s** speak. NIG
13: 1 **s** depart out of this world unto the Father, NIG
13:11 For he knew who **s** betray him; therefore NIG
13:15 that ye **s** do as I have done to you. NIG
13:24 *he* **s** ask who it should be of whom he NIG
13:24 *he* should ask who it **s** be of whom he NIG
13:29 or that he **s** give something to the poor. NIG
14: 7 known me, ye **s** have known my Father 302
15:16 that you **s** go and bring forth fruit, NIG
15:16 forth fruit, and *that* your fruit **s** remain: NIG
16: 1 unto you, that ye **s** not be offended. NIG
16:30 and needest not that any *man* **s** ask thee: NIG
17: 2 he **s** give eternal life to as many as thou NIG
18: 4 knowing all *things* that **s** come upon him, NIG
18:14 it was expedient that one man **s** die for NIG
18:28 the judgment hall, lest they **s** be defiled; NIG
18:32 he spake, signifying what death he **s** die. 3195
18:36 that I **s** not be delivered to the Jews: NIG
18:37 that I **s** bear witness unto the truth. NIG
18:39 I **s** release unto you one at the passover: NIG
19:31 the bodies **s** not remain upon the cross NIG
19:36 done, that the scripture **s** be fulfilled, NIG
21:19 signifying by what death he **s** glorify God. NIG
21:23 the brethren, that that disciple **s** not die: NIG
21:25 the which, if they **s** be written every one, NIG
21:25 not contain the books that **s** be written. NIG

Ac
1: 4 commanded them that *they* **s** not depart NIG
2:24 was not possible that he **s** be holden of it. NIG
2:25 on my right hand, that I **s** not be moved: NIG
2:47 to the church daily such as **s** be saved. NIG
3:18 that Christ **s** suffer, he hath so fulfilled. NIG
5:26 the people, lest they **s** have been stoned. NIG
5:28 not we straitly command that *you* **s** NIG
5:40 *them,* they commanded that *they* **s** NIG
6: 2 It is not reason that we **s** leave the word NIG
7: 6 That his seed **s** sojourn in a strange land; NIG
7: 6 and that they **s** bring them into bondage, NIG
7:44 that *he* **s** make it according to the fashion NIG
8:31 How can I, except some *man* **s** guide me? NIG
10:17 *this* vision which he had seen **s** mean, NIG
10:28 God hath shewed me that I **s** not call any NIG

Ac
10:47 forbid water, that these **s** not be baptized, NIG
11:22 that *he* **s** go as far as Antioch. NIG
11:28 signified by the Spirit that there **s** be great 3195
12:19 commanded that *they* **s** be put to death. NIG
13:28 *yet* desired they Pilate that he **s** be slain. NIG
13:46 It was necessary that the word of God **s** NIG
14:15 preach unto you that *ye* **s** turn from these NIG
15: 2 **s** go up to Jerusalem unto the apostles and NIG
15: 7 that the Gentiles by my mouth **s** hear NIG
17:27 That *they* **s** seek the Lord, if haply they NIG
18:14 reason would that I **s** bear with you: NIG
19: 4 that they **s** believe on him which should NIG
19: 4 that they should believe on him which **s** NIG
19:27 of the great goddess Diana **s** be despised, NIG
19:27 and her magnificence **s** be destroyed, 3195
20:38 spake, that they **s** see his face no more. 3195
21: 4 Spirit, that *he* **s** not go up to Jerusalem. NIG
21:16 an old disciple, with whom we **s** lodge. NIG
21:26 until that an offering **s** be offered for every NIG
22:22 the earth: for it is not fit that he **s** live. NIG
22:24 bade that he **s** be examined by scourging; NIG
22:29 from him which **s** have examined him: 3195
23:10 fearing lest Paul **s** have been pulled in NIG
23:27 the Jews, and **s** have been killed of them: 3195
24:23 that *he* **s** forbid none of his acquaintance NIG
24:26 He hoped also that money **s** have been NIG
25: 4 that Paul **s** be kept at Cesarea, and that he NIG
26: 8 Why **s** it be thought *a thing* incredible NIG
26: 8 with you, that God **s** raise the dead? NIG
26:20 that *they* **s** repent and turn to God, NIG
26:22 the prophets and Moses did say **s** come: 3195
26:23 That Christ **s** suffer, *and that* he *should* NIG
26:23 that he **s** *be* the first *that* should rise from NIG
26:23 that he *should be* the first *that* **s** rise from NIG
26:23 and **s** shew light unto the people, and to 3195
27: 1 when it was determined that we **s** sail NIG
27:17 fearing lest they **s** fall into the quicksands, NIG
27:20 lay on *us,* all hope that we **s** be saved was NIG
27:21 *ye* **s** have hearkened unto me, and not 1163
27:29 Then fearing lest we **s** have fallen upon NIG
27:42 lest any *of them* **s** swim out, and escape. NIG
27:43 that they which could swim **s** NIG
28: 6 Howbeit they looked when he **s** have 3195
28:27 lest they **s** see with *their* eyes, and hear NIG
28:27 **s** be converted, and I should heal them. NIG
28:27 should be converted, and I **s** heal them. NIG

Ro
2:21 thou that preachest a *man* **s** not steal, NIG
2:22 Thou that sayest a *man* **s** not commit NIG
4:13 that he **s** be the heir of the world, NIG
6: 4 *even* so we also **s** walk in newness of life. NIG
6: 6 that henceforth we **s** not serve sin. NIG
6:12 that *ye* **s** obey it in the lusts thereof. NIG
7: 4 ye **s** be married to another, *even* to him NIG
7: 4 that we **s** bring forth fruit unto God. NIG
7: 6 that we **s** serve in newness of spirit, NIG
8:26 we know not what we **s** pray for as we NIG
11: 8 that *they* **s** not see, and ears that *they* NIG
11: 8 not see, and ears that *they* **s** not hear;) NIG
11:11 Have they stumbled that they **s** fall? NIG
11:25 that ye **s** be ignorant of this mystery, NIG
11:25 lest ye **s** be wise in your own conceits; NIG
15:16 That I **s** be the minister of Jesus Christ to NIG
15:20 lest I **s** build upon another *man's* NIG

1Co
1:15 Lest any **s** say that I had baptized in mine NIG
1:17 lest the cross of Christ **s** be made of none NIG
1:29 That no flesh **s** glory in his presence. NIG
2: 5 That your faith **s** not stand in the wisdom NIG
4: 3 But with me it is a very small *thing* that I **s** NIG
5: 1 that one **s** have *his* father's wife. NIG
9:10 he that he that ploweth **s** plow in hope; 3784
9:10 he that thresheth in hope **s** be partaker NIG
9:12 all *things,* lest we **s** hinder the gospel NIG
9:14 preach the gospel **s** live of the gospel. NIG
9:15 have I written these *things,* that it **s** be NIG
9:15 that any *man* **s** make my glorying void. NIG
9:27 to others, I myself **s** be a castaway. NIG
10: 1 I would not that ye **s** be ignorant, NIG
10: 6 the intent we **s** not lust after evil *things,* 1510
10:20 I would not that ye **s** have fellowship with NIG
11:31 judge ourselves, we **s** not be judged. 302
11:32 we **s** not be condemned with the world. NIG
12:25 That there **s** be no schism in the body; NIG
12:25 the members **s** have the same care one NIG

2Co
1: 9 we **s** not trust in ourselves, but in God NIG
1:17 that with me there **s** be yea yea, and nay NIG
2: 3 I **s** have sorrow *from them of* whom I NIG
2: 4 not that you **s** be grieved, but that ye NIG
2: 7 comfort *him,* lest perhaps such a one **s** be NIG
2:11 Lest Satan **s** get an advantage of us: for we NIG
4: 4 is the image of God, **s** shine unto them. NIG
5:15 that they which live **s** not henceforth live NIG
8:20 that no *man* **s** blame us in this abundance NIG
9: 3 lest our boasting of you **s** be in vain in this NIG
9: 4 **s** be ashamed in this *same* confident NIG
10: 8 though I **s** boast somewhat more of our NIG
10: 8 for your destruction, I **s** not be ashamed: NIG
11: 3 your minds **s** be corrupted from NIG
12: 6 lest any *man* **s** think of me above *that* NIG
12: 7 And lest I **s** be exalted above measure NIG
12: 7 lest I **s** be exalted above measure. NIG
13: 7 not that we **s** appear approved, but that NIG
13: 7 but that ye **s** do *that which is* honest, NIG
13:10 lest being present I **s** use sharpness, NIG

Gal
1:10 men, I **s** not be the servant of Christ. NIG
2: 2 lest by any means I **s** run, or had run, NIG

Gal
2: 9 that we **s** go unto the heathen, and they NIG
2:10 Only they would that we **s** remember NIG
3: 1 that *you* **s** not obey the truth, NIG
3:17 that *it* **s** make the promise of none effect. NIG
3:19 till the seed **s** come to whom the promise NIG
3:21 righteousness **s** have been by the law. 302
3:23 shut up unto the faith which **s** afterwards NIG
5: 7 who did hinder you that ye **s** not obey NIG
6:12 only lest they **s** suffer persecution for NIG
6:14 But God forbid that I **s** glory, save in NIG

Eph
1: 4 that we **s** be holy and without blame NIG
1:12 That we **s** be to the praise of his glory, NIG
2: 9 Not of works, lest any *man* **s** boast. NIG
2:10 God hath before ordained that we **s** NIG
3: 6 That the Gentiles **s** be fellowheirs, NIG
3: 8 that *I* **s** preach among the Gentiles NIG
5:27 or any such *thing;* but that it **s** be holy NIG

Php
1:12 But I would ye **s** understand, brethren, NIG
2:10 at the name of Jesus every knee **s** bow, NIG
2:11 And *that* every tongue **s** confess that Jesus NIG
2:27 me also, lest I **s** have sorrow upon sorrow. NIG

Col
1:19 For it pleased *the Father* that in him **s** all NIG
2: 4 lest any *man* **s** beguile you with enticing NIG

1Th
3: 3 That no *man* **s** be moved by these NIG
3: 4 we told you before that we **s** suffer 3195
4: 3 that ye **s** abstain from fornication: NIG
4: 4 That every one of you **s** know how to NIG
5: 4 that *that* day **s** overtake you as a thief. NIG
5:10 or sleep, we **s** live together with him. NIG

2Th
2:11 strong delusion, that they **s** believe a lie: NIG
3:10 if any would not work, neither **s** he eat. NIG

1Ti
1:16 for a pattern to them which **s** hereafter NIG

Tit
2:12 and worldly lusts we **s** live soberly, NIG
3: 7 we **s** be made heirs according to the hope NIG

Phm
1:14 that thy benefit **s** not be as *it were of* NIG

Heb
2: 1 lest at any time we **s** let *them* slip. NIG
2: 9 that he by the grace of God **s** taste death NIG
3:18 to whom sware he that *they* **s** not enter NIG
4: 1 any of you **s** seem to come short *of it.* NIG
7:11 priest **s** rise after the order of Melchisedec, NIG
8: 4 if he were on earth, he **s** not be a priest, 302
8: 7 **s** no place **have** been sought for the 302
9:23 in the heavens **s** be purified with these; NIG
9:25 Nor yet that he **s** offer himself often, NIG
10: 2 the worshippers once purged **s** have had NIG
10: 4 of bulls and of goats **s** take away sins. NIG
11: 5 By faith Enoch was translated that *he* **s** not NIG
11: 8 which he **s** after receive for an inheritance, NIG
11:28 lest he that destroyed the firstborn **s** touch NIG
11:40 they without us **s** not be made perfect. NIG
12:19 word **s** not be spoken to them any more: NIG

Jas
1:18 that we **s** be a kind of firstfruits of his NIG

1Pe
1:10 who prophesied of the grace *that* **s** come NIG
1:11 and the glory *that* **s** follow. 3326+3778
2: 9 that ye **s** shew forth the praises of him who NIG
2:21 us an example, that ye **s** follow his steps: NIG
2:24 dead to sins, **s** live unto righteousness: NIG
3: 9 called, that ye **s** inherit a blessing. NIG
4: 2 *he* no longer **s** live the rest of *his* time NIG

2Pe
2: 6 unto those that after **s** live ungodly; NIG
3: 9 not willing that any **s** perish, but that all NIG
3: 9 but that all **s** come to repentance. NIG

1Jn
3: 1 that we **s** be called the sons of God: NIG
3:11 beginning, that we **s** love one another. NIG
3:23 That we **s** believe on the name of his Son NIG
4: 3 whereof you have heard that it **s** come; NIG

2Jn
1: 6 heard from the beginning, ye **s** walk in it. NIG

Jude
1: 3 exhort *you* that ye **s** earnestly contend for NIG
1:18 that they told you there **s** be mockers NIG
1:18 who **s** walk after their own ungodly lusts. NIG

Rev
6: 4 the earth, and that they **s** kill one another: NIG
6:11 that they **s** rest yet for a little season, NIG
6:11 that **s** be killed as they *were,* should be 3195
6:11 that should be killed as they *were,* **s** be NIG
7: 1 the wind **s** not blow on the earth, nor on NIG
8: 3 that he **s** offer *it* with the prayers of all NIG
9: 4 it was commanded them that they **s** not NIG
9: 5 to them it was given that they **s** not kill NIG
9: 5 but that they **s** be tormented five months: NIG
9:20 that they **s** not worship devils, and idols of NIG
10: 6 are therein, that there **s** be time no longer: NIG
10: 7 to sound, the mystery of God **s** be finished, NIG
11:18 that *they* **s** be judged, and that *thou* NIG
12: 6 that they **s** feed her there a thousand two NIG
13:14 that *they* **s** make an image to the beast, NIG
13:15 that the image of the beast **s** both speak, NIG
13:15 worship the image of the beast **s** be killed. NIG
19: 8 to her was granted that she **s** be arrayed NIG
19:15 that with it he **s** smite the nations: NIG
20: 3 that he **s** deceive the nations no more, NIG
20: 3 till the thousand years **s** be fulfilled: NIG

SHOULDER (38) [SHOULDERPIECES, SHOULDERS]

Ge
21:14 putting *it* on her **s**, and the child, 7926
24:15 with her pitcher upon her **s**. 7926
24:45 came forth with her pitcher on her **s**; 7926
24:46 let down her pitcher from her **s**, and said, NIH
49:15 bowed his **s** to bear, and became a servant 7926

Ex
29:22 the fat that *is* upon them, and the right **s**; 7785
29:27 **s** of the heave offering, which is waved, 7785

Lev
7:32 the right **s** shall ye give unto the priest *for* 7785
7:33 the fat, shall have the right **s** for *his* part. 7785
7:34 the heave **s** have I taken of the children 7785
8:25 two kidneys, and their fat, and the right **s**: 7785

Lev	8:26	put *them* on the fat, and upon the right **s**	7785
	9:21	right **s** Aaron waved *for* a wave offering	7785
	10:14	and heave **s** shall ye eat in a clean place;	7785
	10:15	The heave **s** and the wave breast shall	7785
Nu	6:19	priest shall take the sodden **s** of the ram,	2220
	6:20	with the wave breast and heave **s**	7785
	18:18	wave breast and as the right **s** are thine.	7785
Dt	18: 3	and they shall give unto the priest the **s**,	2220
Jos	4: 5	every man of you a stone upon his **s**,	7926
Jdg	9:48	laid *it* on his **s**, and said unto the people	7926
1Sa	9:24	the cook took up the **s**, and *that* which	7785
Ne	9:29	withdrew the **s**, and hardened their neck,	3802
Job	31:22	*Then* let mine arm fall from *my* **s blade**,	7929
	31:36	Surely I would take it upon my **s**,	7926
Ps	81: 6	I removed his **s** from the burden: his	7926
Isa	9: 4	the staff of his **s**, the rod of his oppressor,	7926
	9: 6	and the government shall be upon his **s**:	7926
	10:27	burden shall be taken away from off thy **s**,	7926
	22:22	the house of David will I lay upon his **s**;	7926
	46: 7	They bear him upon the **s**, they carry him,	3802
Eze	12: 7	*and* I bare *it* upon *my* **s** in their sight.	3802
	12:12	them shall bear upon *his* **s** in the twilight,	3802
	24: 4	every good piece, the thigh, and the **s**;	3802
	29: 7	thou didst break, and rent all their **s**:	3802
	29:18	*was* made bald, and every *was* peeled:	3802
	34:21	ye have thrust with side and with **s**,	3802
Zec	7:11	pulled away the **s**, and stopped their ears,	3802

SHOULDERPIECES (4) [PIECE, SHOULDER]

Ex	28: 7	It shall have the two **s** *thereof* joined at	3802
	28:25	put *them* on the **s** of the ephod before it.	3802
	39: 4	They made **s** for it, to couple *it* together;	3802
	39:18	put them on the **s** of the ephod, before it.	3802

SHOULDERS (20) [SHOULDER]

Ge	9:23	laid *it* upon both their **s**,	7926
Ex	12:34	bound up in their clothes upon their **s**.	7926
	28:12	thou shalt put the two stones upon the **s**	3802
	28:12	the Lord upon his two **s** for a memorial.	3802
	39: 7	put them on the **s** of the ephod, *that they*	3802
Nu	7: 9	*was* that they should bear upon *their* **s**.	3802
Dt	33:12	long, and he shall dwell between his **s**.	3802
Jdg	16: 3	bar and all, and put *them* upon his **s**,	3802
1Sa	9: 2	from his **s** and upward *he was* higher than	7926
	10:23	higher than any of the people from his **s**	7926
	17: 6	legs, and a target of brass between his **s**.	3802
1Ch	15:15	God upon their **s** with the staves thereon,	3802
2Ch	35: 3	*it shall not be* a burden upon your **s**:	3802
Isa	11:14	they shall fly upon the **s** of the Philistines	3802
	14:25	and his burden depart from off their **s**.	7926
	30: 6	they will carry their riches upon the **s** of	3802
	49:22	daughters shall be carried upon *their* **s**.	3802
Eze	12: 6	In their sight shalt thou bear *it* upon *thy* **s**,	3802
Mt	23: 4	to be borne, and lay *them* on men's **s**;	5606
Lk	15: 5	he hath found *it*, he layeth *it* on his **s**,	5606

SHOULDEST (73) [SHOULD]

Ge	3:11	I commanded thee that thou **s** not	NIH
	14:23	lest thou say, I have made Abram rich:	NIH
	26:10	thou **s** have brought guiltiness upon us.	NIH
	29:15	thou therefore serve me for nought?	NIH
Nu	11:12	I begotten them, that thou **s** say unto me,	NIH
Dt	4:19	**s** be driven to worship them,	NIH
	26:18	that *thou* **s** keep all his commandments,	NIH
	29:12	That thou **s** enter into covenant with	NIH
	30:12	It *is* not in heaven, that *thou* **s** say,	NIH
	30:13	*is* it beyond the sea, that *thou* **s** say,	NIH
Jdg	11:23	his people Israel, and **s** thou possess it?	NIH
Ru	2:10	that *thou* **s** take knowledge of me, seeing	NIH
1Sa	20: 8	for why **s** thou bring me to thy father?	NIH
2Sa	9: 8	that thou **s** look upon such a dead dog as	NIH
1Ki	1:20	that thou **s** tell them who shall sit on	NIH
2Ki	8:14	He told me *that* thou **s** surely recover.	NIH
	13:19	said, *Thou* **s** have smitten five or six times;	NIH
	14:10	why **s** thou meddle to *thy* hurt, that thou	NIH
	14:10	that thou **s** fall, *even* thou, and Judah with	NIH
	19:25	that thou **s** be to lay waste fenced cities	NIH
1Ch	17: 7	that *thou* **s** be ruler over my people Israel:	NIH
2Ch	19: 2	**S** thou help the ungodly, and love them	NIH
	25:16	forbear; why **s** thou be smitten? Then	NIH
	25:19	why **s** thou meddle to *thine* hurt, that	NIH
	25:19	that thou **s** fall, *even* thou, and Judah with	NIH
Job	7:17	What *is* man, that thou **s** magnify him?	NIH
	7:17	and that thou **s** set thine heart upon him?	NIH
	7:18	*that* thou **s** visit him every morning,	NIH
	10: 3	*Is* it good unto thee that thou **s** oppress,	NIH
	10: 3	thou **s** despise the work of thine hands,	NIH
	38:20	That thou **s** take it to the bound thereof,	NIH
	38:20	that thou **s** know the paths to the house	NIH
Ps	50:16	thou **s** take my covenant in thy mouth?	NIH
	130: 3	If thou, Lord, **s** mark iniquities, O Lord,	NIH
Pr	5: 6	Lest thou **s** ponder the path of life, her	NIH
	25: 7	that thou **s** be put lower in the presence	NIH
	27:22	Though thou **s** bray a fool in a mortar	NIH
Ecc	5: 5	Better *is it* that thou **s** not vow, than that	NIH
	5: 5	vow, than that thou **s** vow and not pay.	NIH
	7:16	over wise: why **s** thou destroy thyself?	NIH
	7:17	why **s** thou die before thy time?	NIH
	7:18	It *is* good that thou **s** take hold of this;	NIH
Isa	37:26	that thou **s** be to lay waste defenced cities	NIH
	48: 5	lest thou say, Mine idol hath done them,	NIH
	48: 7	lest thou say, Behold, I knew them.	NIH
	48:17	which leadeth thee by the way *that* thou **s**	NIH
	49: 6	It is a light thing that thou **s** be my servant	NIH
	51:12	thou **s** be afraid of a man *that* shall die,	NIH

Jer	14: 8	why **s** thou be as a stranger in the land,	NIH
	14: 9	Why **s** thou be as a man astonied, as a	NIH
	29:26	that thou **s** put him in prison, and in	NIH
	49:16	though thou **s** make thy nest as high as	NIH
Ob	1:12	thou **s** not have looked on the day of thy	NIH
	1:12	neither **s** thou have rejoiced over	NIH
	1:12	neither **s** thou have spoken proudly in	NIH
	1:13	Thou **s** not have entered into the gate of	NIH
	1:13	thou **s** not have looked on their affliction	NIH
	1:14	Neither **s** thou have stood in the crossway,	NIH
	1:14	neither **s** thou have delivered up those of	NIH
Mt	8: 8	I am not worthy that thou **s** come under	NIG
	18:33	**S** not thou also **have** had compassion on	*1163*
Mk	10:35	would that thou **s** do for us whatsoever	NIG
Lk	7: 6	I am not worthy that thou **s** enter under	NIG
Jn	11:40	thou **s** see the glory of God?	NIG
	17:15	I pray not that thou **s** take them out of	NIG
	17:15	but that thou **s** keep them from the evil.	NIG
Ac	13:47	be for salvation unto the ends of	NIG
	22:14	that *thou* **s** know his will, and see *that*	NIG
	22:14	and **s** hear the voice of his mouth.	NIG
Tit	1: 5	that thou **s** set in order the *things* that are	NIG
Phm	1:15	a season, that thou **s** receive him for ever;	NIG
Rev	11:18	that thou **s** give reward unto thy servants	NIG
	11:18	**s** destroy them which destroy the earth.	NIG

SHOUT (36) [SHOUTED, SHOUTETH, SHOUTING, SHOUTINGS]

Ex	32:18	*It is* not the voice of *them that* **s** for	6030
Nu	23:21	and the **s** of a king *is* among them.	8643
Jos	6: 5	all the people shall **s** *with* a great shout;	7321
	6: 5	all the people shall shout *with* a great **s**;	8643
	6:10	saying, Ye shall not **s**, nor make any noise	7321
	6:10	of your mouth, until the day I bid you **s**;	7321
	6:10	the day I bid you shout; then shall ye **s**.	7321
	6:16	Joshua said unto the people, **S**;	7321
	6:20	the people shouted *with* a great **s**, that	8643
1Sa	4: 5	all Israel shouted *with* a great **s**, so that	8643
	4: 6	the Philistines heard the noise of the **s**,	8643
	4: 6	What *meaneth* the noise of this great **s** in	8643
2Ch	13:15	men of Judah **gave a s**: and as the men	7321
Ezr	3:11	all the people shouted *with* a great **s**,	8643
	3:13	of joy from the noise of the weeping of	8643
	3:13	for the people shouted *with* a loud **s**,	8643
Ps	5:11	let them ever **s for joy**, because	7442
	32:11	**s for joy**, all *ye that are* upright in heart.	7442
	35:27	Let them **s for joy**, and be glad, that	7442
	47: 1	**s** unto God with the voice of triumph.	7321
	47: 5	God is gone up with a **s**, the Lord with	8643
	65:13	with corn; they **s for joy**, they also sing.	7321
	132: 9	and let thy saints **s for joy**.	7442
	132:16	her saints shall **s aloud for joy**.	7442+7444
Isa	12: 6	Cry out and **s**, thou inhabitant of Zion:	7442
	42:11	let them **s** from the top of the mountains.	6681
	44:23	for the Lord hath done *it*: **s**, ye lower	7321
Jer	25:30	he shall **give a s**, as they that tread	1959+6030
	31: 7	and **s** among the chief of the nations:	6670
	50:15	**S** against her round about: she hath given	7321
	51:14	and they shall lift up a **s** against thee.	1959
La	3: 8	Also when I cry and **s**, he shutteth out	7768
Zep	3:14	**s**, O Israel; be glad and rejoice with all	7321
Zec	9: 9	of Zion; **s**, O daughter of Jerusalem:	7321
Ac	12:22	And the people **gave a s**, *saying, It is*	2019
1Th	4:16	shall descend from heaven with a **s**,	2752

SHOUTED (14) [SHOUT]

Ex	32:17	heard the noise of the people as they **s**,	7452
Lev	9:24	people saw, they, **s**, and fell on their faces.	7442
Jos	6:20	So the people **s** when *the priests* blew	7321
	6:20	the people **s** *with* a great shout, that	7321
Jdg	15:14	unto Lehi, the Philistines **s** against him:	7321
1Sa	4: 5	all Israel **s** *with* a great shout, so that	7321
	10:24	all the people **s**, and said, God save	7321
	17:20	forth to the fight, and **s** for the battle.	7321
	17:52	and **s**, and pursued the Philistines,	7321
2Ch	13:15	as the men of Judah **s**, it came to pass,	7321
Ezr	3:11	all the people **s** *with* a great shout,	7321
	3:12	**s aloud** for joy:	6963+7311+8643+871.1+3807.1
	3:13	for the people **s** *with* a loud shout,	7321
Job	38: 7	and all the sons of God **s for joy**?	7321

SHOUTETH (1) [SHOUT]

Ps	78:65	a mighty *man* that **s** by reason of wine.	7442

SHOUTING (15) [SHOUT]

2Sa	6:15	brought up the ark of the Lord with **s**,	8643
1Ch	15:28	ark of the covenant of the Lord with **s**,	8643
2Ch	15:14	**s**, and with trumpets, and with cornets.	8643
Job	39:25	the thunder of the captains, and the **s**.	8643
Pr	11:10	and when the wicked perish, *there is* **s**.	7440
Isa	16: 9	for the **s** for thy summer fruits and for thy	1959
	16:10	be no singing, neither shall there be **s**:	7321
	16:10	I have made *their* vintage **s** to cease.	1959
Jer	20:16	cry in the morning, and the **s** at noontide;	8643
	48:33	none shall tread *with* **s**; *their* shouting	1959
	48:33	shouting; *their* **s** shall be no shouting.	1959
	48:33	shouting; *their* shouting **s** shall be no **s**.	1959
Eze	21:22	the slaughter, to lift up the voice with **s**,	8643
Am	1:14	thereof, with **s** in the day of battle,	8643
	2: 2	**s**, *and* with the sound of the trumpet:	8643

SHOUTINGS (1) [SHOUT]

Zec	4: 7	bring forth the headstone *thereof* with **s**,	8663

SHOVEL (1) [SHOVELS]

Isa	30:24	which hath been winnowed with the **s**	7371

SHOVELS (9) [SHOVEL]

Ex	27: 3	his **s**, and his basons, and his fleshhooks,	3257
	38: 3	the **s**, and the basons, *and* the fleshhooks,	3257
Nu	4:14	the fleshhooks, and the **s**, and the basons,	3257
1Ki	7:40	the lavers, and the **s**, and the basons.	3257
	7:45	And the pots, and the **s**, and the basons.	3257
2Ki	25:14	the **s**, and the snuffers, and the spoons,	3257
2Ch	4:11	made the pots, and the **s**, and the basons.	3257
	4:16	the **s**, and the fleshhooks, and all their	3257
Jer	52:18	the **s**, and the snuffers, and the bowls,	3257

SHOW See FOREWARN; SHEW

SHOW SYMPATHY See BEMOAN; BEMOANED; BEMOANING

SHOW THE SAME FAVOR See REQUITE; REQUITED; REQUITING

SHOWER (4) [SHOWERS]

Eze	13:11	there shall be an overflowing **s**; and ye,	1653
	13:13	there shall be an overflowing **s** in mine	1653
	34:26	I will cause the **s** to come down in his	1653
Lk	12:54	straightway ye say, There cometh a **s**;	*3655*

SHOWERS (9) [SHOWER]

Dt	32: 2	tender herb, and as the **s** upon the grass:	7241
Job	24: 8	They are wet with the **s** of the mountains,	2230
Ps	65:10	thou makest it soft with **s**: thou blessest	7241
	72: 6	the mown grass: as **s** that water the earth.	7241
Jer	3: 3	Therefore the **s** have been withholden,	7241
	14:22	can the heavens give **s**? *art* not thou he,	7241
Eze	34:26	in his season; there shall be **s** of blessing.	1653
Mic	5: 7	as the **s** upon the grass, that tarrieth not	7241
Zec	10: 1	give them **s** of rain, to every one grass in	4306

SHRANK (2)

Ge	32:32	of Israel eat not *of* the sinew which **s**,	5384
	32:32	of Jacob's thigh in the sinew that **s**.	5384

SHRED (1)

2Ki	4:39	came and **s** *them* into the pot of pottage:	6398

SHREWD See UNSAVOURY

SHRICH (1)

Isa	34:14	the **s** owl also shall rest there, and find	3917

SHRINE PROSTITUTE See SODOMITE; SODOMITES

SHRINES (1)

Ac	19:24	which made silver **s** for Diana,	*3485*

SHROUD (1)

Eze	31: 3	a shadowing **s**, and of a high stature;	2793

SHRUBS (1)

Ge	21:15	and she cast the child under one of the **s**.	7880

SHUA (2) [SHUAH]

1Ch	2: 3	him of the daughter of **S** the Canaanitess.	7770
	7:32	and Hotham, and **S** their sister.	7774

SHUAH (5) [SHUA]

Ge	25: 2	Medan, and Midian, and Ishbak, and **S**.	7744
	38: 2	a certain Canaanite, whose name *was* **S**;	7770
	38:12	process of time the daughter of **S** Judah's	7770
1Ch	1:32	Medan, and Midian, and Ishbak, and **S**.	7744
	4:11	Chelub the brother of **S** begat Mehir,	7746

SHUAL (2) [HAZAR-SHUAL]

1Sa	13:17	that leadeth to Ophrah, unto the land of **S**:	7777
1Ch	7:36	Harnepher, and **S**, and Beri, and Imrah,	7777

SHUBAEL (3)

1Ch	24:20	Levi *were these:* Of the sons of Amram; **S**:	7619
	24:20	Shubael: of the sons of **S**; Jehdeiah.	7619
	25:20	The thirteenth to **S**, *he*, his sons,	7619

SHUHAM (1) [SHUHAMITES]

Nu	26:42	of **S**, the family of the Shuhamites.	7748

SHUHAMITES (2) [SHUHAM]

Nu	26:42	of Shuham, the family of the **S**. These *are*	7749
	26:43	All the families of the **S**, according to	7749

SHUHITE (5)

Job	2:11	Bildad the **S**, and Zophar the Naamathite:	7747
	8: 1	Then answered Bildad the **S**, and said,	7747
	18: 1	Then answered Bildad the **S**, and said,	7747
	25: 1	Then answered Bildad the **S**, and said,	7747
	42: 9	Eliphaz the Temanite and Bildad the **S**	7747

SHULAMITE (2)

SS	6:13	Return, return, O **S**; return, return, that	7759
	6:13	What will ye see in the **S**? As it were	7759

SHULAMMITE See SHULAMITE

SHUMATHITES (1)

1Ch	2:53	the Puhites, and the **S**, and the Mishraites;	8126

SHUN (1) [SHUNNED]

2Ti	2:16	But **s** profane *and* vain babblings: for they	*4026*

SHUNAMMITE (8)

1Ki	1: 3 found Abishag a **S**, and brought her to	7767
	1:15 Abishag the **S** ministered unto the king.	7767
	2:17 that he give me Abishag the **S** to wife.	7767
	2:21 Let Abishag the **S** be given to Adonijah	7767
	2:22 why dost thou ask Abishag the **S** for	7767
2Ki	4:12 he said to Gehazi his servant, Call this **S**.	7767
	4:25 his servant, Behold, *yonder is* that **S**:	7767
	4:36 he called Gehazi, and said, Call this **S**.	7767

SHUNEM (3)

Jos	19:18 toward Jezreel, and Chesulloth, and **S**,	7766
1Sa	28: 4 and came and pitched in **S**:	7766
2Ki	4: 8 it fell on a day, that Elisha passed to **S**,	7766

SHUNI (2) [SHUNITES]

Ge	46:16 **S**, and Ezbon, Eri, and Arodi, and Areli.	7764
Nu	26:15 of **S**, the family of the Shunites:	7764

SHUNITES (1) [SHUNI]

Nu	26:15 the Haggites: of Shuni, the family of the **S**:	7765

SHUNNED (1) [SHUN]

Ac	20:27 For I have not **s** to declare unto you all	*5288*

SHUPHAM (1) [SHUPHAMITES]

Nu	26:39 Of **S**, the family of the Shuphamites:	8197

SHUPHAMITES (1) [SHUPHAM]

Nu	26:39 Of Shupham, the family of the **S**:	7781

SHUPPIM (3)

1Ch	7:12 **S** also, and Huppim, the children of Ir,	8206
	7:15 took to wife *the sister* of Huppim and **S**,	8206
	26:16 To **S** and Hosah *the lot came forth*	8206

SHUR (6)

Ge	16: 7 by the fountain in the way to **S**.	7793
	20: 1 dwelled between Kadesh and **S**,	7793
	25:18 they dwelt from Havilah unto **S**, that *is*	7793
Ex	15:22 they went out into the wilderness of **S**;	7793
1Sa	15: 7 from Havilah *until* thou comest *to* **S**,	7793
	27: 8 inhabitants of the land as thou goest to **S**,	7793

SHUSHAN (21)

Ne	1: 1 twentieth year, as I was in **S** the palace,	7800
Est	1: 2 his kingdom, which *was* in **S** the palace,	7800
	1: 5 people that were present in **S** the palace,	7800
	2: 3 the fair young virgins unto **S** the palace,	7800
	2: 5 *Now* in **S** the palace there was a certain	7800
	2: 8 were gathered together unto **S** the palace,	7800
	3:15 and the decree was given in **S** the palace.	7800
	3:15 to drink; but the city **S** was perplexed.	7800
	4: 8 decree that was given at **S** to destroy them	7800
	4:16 together all the Jews that are present in **S**,	7800
	8:14 and the decree was given at **S** the palace.	7800
	8:15 and the city of **S** rejoiced and was glad.	7800
	9: 6 in **S** the palace the Jews slew and	7800
	9:11 **S** the palace was brought before the king.	7800
	9:12 five hundred men in **S** the palace,	7800
	9:13 it be granted to the Jews which *are* in **S**	7800
	9:14 decree was given at **S**; and they hanged	7800
	9:15 For the Jews that *were* in **S** gathered	7800
	9:15 and slew three hundred men at **S**;	7800
	9:18 Jews that *were* at **S** assembled together	7800
Da	8: 2 when I saw, that I *was* at **S** *in* the palace,	7800

SHUSHAN-EDUTH (1)

Ps	60: T To the chief Musician upon **S**, Michtam	7802

SHUT (105) [SHUTTETH, SHUTTING]

Ge	7:16 commanded him: and the LORD **s** him in.	5462
	19: 6 door unto them, and **s** the door after him,	5462
	19:10 into the house to them, and **s** to the door.	5462
Ex	14: 3 the land, the wilderness hath **s** them in.	5462
Lev	13: 4 the priest shall **s** **up** *him that hath*	5462
	13: 5 priest shall **s** him **up** seven days more:	5462
	13:11 unclean, and shall not **s** him **up**:	5462
	13:21 then the priest shall **s** him **up** seven days:	5462
	13:26 then the priest shall **s** him **up** seven days:	5462
	13:31 the priest shall **s** **up** *him that hath*	5462
	13:33 priest shall **s** *him that hath* the scall	5462
	13:50 **s** **up** *it that hath* the plague seven days:	5462
	13:54 and he shall **s** it **up** seven days more:	5462
	14:38 house, and **s** **up** the house seven days:	5462
	14:46 it is **s** **up** shall be unclean until the even.	5462
Nu	12:14 her be **s** out from the camp seven days,	5462
	12:15 Miriam was **s** out from the camp seven	5462
Dt	11:17 he **s** **up** the heaven, that there be no rain,	6113
	15: 7 nor **s** thine hand from thy poor brother:	7092
	32:30 sold them, and the LORD had **s** them **up**?	5462
	32:36 is gone, and *there is* none **s** **up**, or left.	6113
Jos	2: 7 after them were gone out, they **s** the gate.	5462
	6: 1 Jericho was **straitly s up**	5462+5462+2050.1
Jdg	3:23 the doors of the parlour upon him, and	5462
	9:51 **s** it to them, and gat them up to the top of	5462
1Sa	1: 5 but the LORD had **s up** her womb.	5462
	1: 6 because the LORD had **s up** her womb.	5462
	6:10 to the cart, and **s up** their calves at home:	6113
	23: 7 for he is **s** in, by entering into a town that	5462
2Sa	20: 3 So they were **s up** unto the day of their	6887
1Ki	8:35 heaven is **s up**, and there is no rain,	6113
	14:10 and him that is **s up** and left in Israel,	6113
	21:21 and him that is **s up** and left in Israel,	6113
2Ki	4: 4 thou shalt **s** the door upon thee and	5462
	4: 5 **s** the door upon her and upon her sons,	5462

SHUTHALHITES (1) [SHUTHELAH]

Nu	26:35 of Shuthelah, the family of the **S**:	8364

SHUTHELAH (4) [SHUTHALHITES]

Nu	26:35 of **S**, the family of the Shuthalhites:	7803
	26:36 *are* the sons of **S**: of Eran, the family	7803
1Ch	7:20 **S**, and Bered his son, and Tahath his son,	7803
	7:21 son, and **S** his son, and Ezer, and Elead,	7803

SHUTHELAHITE See SHUTHALHITES

SHUTTETH (8) [SHUT]

Job	12:14 it cannot be built *again*: he **s up** a man,	5462
Pr	16:30 He **s** his eyes to devise froward things:	6095
	17:28 he that **s** his lips *is esteemed* a man of	331
Isa	33:15 of blood, and **s** his eyes from seeing evil;	6105
La	3: 8 when I cry and shout, he **s** out my prayer.	5640
1Jn	3:17 **s up** his bowels *of compassion* from him,	2808
Rev	3: 7 of David, he that openeth, and no *man* **s**;	2808
	3: 7 shutteth; and **s**, and no *man* openeth;	2808

SHUTTING (1) [SHUT]

Jos	2: 5 it came to pass *about the time* of **s** of	5462

SHUTTLE (1)

Job	7: 6 My days are swifter than a **weaver's s**,	708

SIA (1) [SIAHA]

Ne	7:47 the children of **S**, the children of Padon,	5517

SIAHA (1) [SIA]

Ezr	2:44 the children of **S**, the children of Padon,	5517

SIBBECAI (2) [SIBBECHAI]

1Ch	11:29 **S** the Hushathite, Ilai the Ahohite,	5444

2Ki	4:21 and **s** *the* door upon him, and went out.	5462
	4:33 **s** the door upon them twain,	5462
	6:32 **s** the door, and hold him fast at the door:	5462
	9: 8 and *him that is* **s up** and left in Israel:	6113
	14:26 for *there was* not any **s up**, nor any left,	6113
	17: 4 therefore the king of Assyria **s** him **up**,	6113
2Ch	6:26 When the heaven is **s up**, and there is no	6113
	7:13 If I **s up** heaven that there be no rain, or	6113
	28:24 **s up** the doors of the house of the LORD,	5462
	29: 7 they have **s up** the doors of the porch,	5462
Ne	6:10 the son of Mehetabeel, who *was* **s up**;	6113
	6:10 and let us **s** the doors of the temple:	5462
	7: 3 let them **s** the doors, and bar *them*: and	1479
	13:19 I commanded that the gates should be **s**,	5462
Job	3:10 Because it **s** not **up** the doors of my	5462
	11:10 **s up**, or gather together, then who can	5462
	38: 8 Or *who* **s up** the sea with doors, when it	5526
	41:15 pride, **s up** *together as with* a close seal.	5462
Ps	31: 8 hast not **s** me **up** into the hand of	5462
	69:15 and let not the pit **s** her mouth upon me.	332
	77: 9 hath in anger **s up** his tender mercies?	7092
Ecc	12: 4 the doors shall be **s** in the streets, when	5462
SS	4:12 spouse; a spring **s up**, a fountain sealed.	5274
Isa	6:10 make their ears heavy, and **s** their eyes;	8173
	22:22 so he shall open, and none shall **s**;	5462
	22:22 and he shall **s**, and none shall open.	5462
	24:10 every house is **s up**, that no *man may*	5462
	24:22 shall be **s up** in the prison, and after many	5462
	26:20 thy chambers, and **s** thy doors about thee:	5462
	44:18 for he hath **s** their eyes, that *they* cannot	2902
	45: 1 leaved gates; and the gates shall not be **s**;	5462
	52:15 the kings shall **s** their mouths at him:	7092
	60:11 thy gates shall not be **s** day nor night;	5462
	66: 9 forth, and **s** *the* womb? saith thy God.	6113
Jer	13:19 The cities of the south shall be **s up**,	5462
	20: 9 heart as a burning fire **s up** in my bones,	6113
	32: 2 Jeremiah the prophet was **s up** in the	3607
	32: 3 For Zedekiah king of Judah had **s** him **up**,	3607
	33: 1 while he was yet **s up** in the court of	6113
	36: 5 commanded Baruch, saying, I *am* **s up**;	6113
	39:15 he was **s up** in the court of the prison,	6113
Eze	3:24 me, Go, **s** thyself within thine house.	5462
	44: 1 looketh *toward* the east; and it *was* **s**.	5462
	44: 2 This gate shall be **s**, it shall not be opened,	5462
	44: 2 entered in by it, therefore it shall be **s**.	5462
	46: 1 the east shall be **s** the six working days;	5462
	46: 2 the gate shall not be **s** until the evening.	5462
	46:12 after his going forth *one* shall **s** the gate.	5463
Da	6:22 hath the lions' mouths, that they have **s**	5463
	8:26 wherefore **s** thou **up** the vision; for *it shall*	5640
	12: 4 **s up** the words, and seal the book,	5640
Mal	1:10 *is there* even among you that would **s**	5462
Mt	6: 3 thy closet, and when thou hast **s** thy door,	2808
	23:13 for ye **s up** the kingdom of heaven against	2808
	25:10 him to the marriage: and the door was **s**.	2808
Lk	3:20 this above all, that he **s up** John in prison.	2623
	4:25 when the heaven was **s up** three years	2808
	11: 7 the door is now **s**, and my children are	2808
	13:25 hath **s to** the door, and ye begin to stand	608
Jn	20:19 the doors were **s** where the disciples	2808
	20:26 *then* came Jesus, the doors being **s**,	2808
Ac	5:23 prison truly found we **s** with all safety,	2808
	21:30 temple: and forthwith the doors were **s**.	2808
	26:10 many of the saints did I **s up** in prison,	2623
Gal	3:23 **s up** unto the faith which should	4788
Rev	3: 8 thee an open door, and no *man* can **s**:	2808
	11: 6 These have power to **s** heaven, that it rain	2808
	20: 3 into the bottomless *pit*, and **s** him **up**,	2808
	21:25 And the gates of it shall not be **s** at all by	2808

1Ch	27:11 the eighth month *was* **S** the Hushathite,	5444

SIBBECHAI (2) [SIBBECAI]

2Sa	21:18 **S** the Hushathite slew Saph, which *was*	5444
1Ch	20: 4 which time **S** the Hushathite slew Sippai,	5444

SIBBOLETH (1) [SHIBBOLETH]

Jdg	12: 6 he said **S**: for he could not frame to	5451

SIBMAH (4)

Jos	13:19 **S**, and Zareth-shahar in the mount of	7643
Isa	16: 8 of Heshbon languish, *and* the vine of **S**:	7643
	16: 9 with the weeping of Jazer the vine of **S**:	7643
Jer	48:32 O vine of **S**, I will weep for thee with	7643

SIBRAIM (1)

Eze	47:16 Hamath, Berothah, **S**, which *is* between	5453

SICHEM (1)

Ge	12: 6 through the land unto the place of **S**,	7927

SICK (88) [SICKLY, SICKNESS, SICKNESSES]

Ge	48: 1 *one* told Joseph, Behold, thy father *is* **s**:	2470
Lev	15:33 of her that is **s** of her flowers, and of him	1739
1Sa	19:14 to take David, she said, He *is* **s**.	2470
	30:13 left me, because three days agone I **fell s**.	2470
2Sa	11: 6 wife bare unto David, and it was **very s**.	605
	13: 2 vexed, that he **fell s** for his sister Tamar;	2470
	13: 5 down on thy bed, and **make thyself s**:	2470
	13: 6 Amnon lay down, and **made** himself **s**:	2470
1Ki	14: 1 time Abijah the son of Jeroboam **fell s**.	2470
	14: 5 ask a thing of thee for her son; for he *is* **s**:	2470
	17:17 woman, the mistress of the house, **fell s**;	2470
2Ki	1: 2 chamber that *was* in Samaria, and was **s**:	2470
	8: 7 Ben-hadad the king of Syria was **s**;	2470
	8:29 son of Ahab in Jezreel, because he was **s**.	2470
	13:14 Now Elisha was **fallen s** of his sickness	2470
	20: 1 In those days was Hezekiah **s** unto death.	2470
	20:12 he had heard that Hezekiah had been **s**.	2470
2Ch	22: 6 son of Ahab at Jezreel, because he was **s**.	2470
	32:24 those days Hezekiah was **s** to the death,	2470
Ne	2: 2 countenance sad, seeing thou *art* not **s**?	2470
Ps	35:13 *as for* me, when they were **s**, my clothing	2470
Pr	13:12 Hope deferred **maketh** the heart **s**:	2470
	23:35 *shalt* thou *say, and* I was not **s**;	2470
SS	2: 5 me with apples: for I *am* **s** of love.	2470
	5: 8 that ye tell him, that I *am* **s** of love.	2470
Isa	1: 5 the whole head *is* **s**, and the whole heart	2483
	33:24 the inhabitant shall not say, I am **s**:	2470
	38: 1 In those days was Hezekiah **s** unto death.	2470
	38: 9 when he had been **s**, and was recovered	2470
	39: 1 for he had heard that he had been **s**,	2470
Jer	14:18 then behold that are **s** with famine:	8463
Eze	34: 4 neither have ye healed that which was **s**,	2470
	34:16 and will strengthen that which was **s**:	2470
Da	8:27 I Daniel fainted, and was **s** *certain* days;	2470
Hos	7: 5 have **made** *him* **s** with bottles of wine;	2470
Mic	6:13 Therefore also will I **make** *thee* **s** in	2470
Mal	1: 8 if ye offer the lame and **s**, *is it* not evil?	2470
	1:13 *which was* torn, and the lame, and the **s**;	2470
Mt	4:24 they brought unto him all **s** people	2192+2560
	8: 6 my servant lieth at home **s** of the palsy,	3885
	8:14 his wife's mother laid, and **s** of a fever.	4445
	8:16 with his word, and healed all that were **s**:	2560
	9: 2 they brought to him a **man s of the palsy**,	3885
	9: 2 their faith said unto the **s of the palsy**;	3885
	9: 6 (then saith he to the **s of the palsy**,)	3885
	9:12 not a physician, but they that are **s**.	2192+2560
	10: 8 Heal the **s**, cleanse the lepers, raise the	770
	14:14 toward them, and he healed their **s**.	732
	25:36 I was **s**, and ye visited me: I was in prison,	770
	25:39 Or when saw we thee **s**,	772
	25:43 **s**, and in prison, and ye visited me not.	772
	25:44 **s**, or in prison, and did not minister unto	772
Mk	1:30 Simon's wife's mother lay **s of a fever**,	4445
	1:34 And he healed many that were **s** of	2192+2560
	2: 3 bringing **one s of the palsy**, which was	3885
	2: 4 the bed wherein the **s of the palsy** lay.	3885
	2: 5 he said unto the **s of the palsy**,	3885
	2: 9 is it easier to say to the **s of the palsy**,	3885
	2:10 (he saith to the **s of the palsy**,)	3885
	2:17 need of *the* physician, but they that are **s**:	2560
	6: 5 that he laid *his* hands upon a few **s** folk,	732
	6:13 and anointed with oil many that were **s**,	732
	6:55 to carry about in beds those that were **s**,	2560
	6:56 they laid the **s** in the streets,	770
	16:18 they shall lay hands on the **s**, and they	732
Lk	4:40 all they that had *any* **s** with divers diseases	770
	5:24 (he said unto the **s of the palsy**,)	3886
	5:31 not a physician; but they that are **s**.	2192+2560
	7: 2 unto him, was **s**, and ready to die.	2192+2560
	7:10 found the servant whole that had been **s**.	770
	9: 2 the kingdom of God, and to heal the **s**.	770
	10: 9 And heal the **s** that are therein,	772
Jn	4:46 whose son was **s** at Capernaum.	770
	11: 1 Now a certain *man* was **s**, *named* Lazarus,	770
	11: 2 her hair, whose brother Lazarus was **s**.)	770
	11: 3 Lord, behold, he whom thou lovest is **s**.	770
	11: 6 he had heard therefore that he was **s**,	770
Ac	5:15 Insomuch that *they* brought forth the **s** into	772
	5:16 *folks*, and *them* which were vexed	772
	9:33 bed eight years, and was **s of the palsy**.	3886
	9:37 in those days, that she was **s**, and died:	770
	19:12 were brought unto the **s** handkerchiefs	770
	28: 8 that the father of Publius lay **s of** a fever	4912

Php	2:26 that ye had heard that he had been **s**.	770
	2:27 For indeed he was **s** nigh unto death:	770
2Ti	4:20 but Trophimus have I left at Miletum **s**.	770
Jas	5:14 Is any **s** among you? let him call for	770
	5:15 And the prayer of faith shall save the **s**,	2577

SICKLE (12)

Dt	16: 9 as thou beginnest *to* put the **s** to the corn.	2770
	23:25 thou shalt not move a **s** unto thy	2770
Jer	50:16 him that handleth the **s** in the time of	4038
Joel	3:13 Put in the **s**, for the harvest is ripe:	4038
Mk	4:29 immediately he putteth in the **s**, because	1407
Rev	14:14 a golden crown, and in his hand a sharp **s**.	1407
	14:15 was so sore, that thou **s** on the cloud, Thrust in thy **s**, and reap:	1407
	14:16 he that sat on the cloud thrust in his **s**	1407
	14:17 is in heaven, he also having a sharp **s**.	1407
	14:18 a loud cry to him that had the sharp **s**,	1407
	14:18 Thrust in thy sharp **s**, and gather	1407
	14:19 the angel thrust in his **s** into the earth,	1407

SICKLY (1) [SICK]

1Co	11:30 cause many *are* weak and **s** among you,	732

SICKNESS (20) [SICK]

Ex	23:25 I will take **s** away from the midst of thee.	4245
Lev	20:18 man shall lie with a woman **having** her **s**,	1739
Dt	7:15 the LORD will take away from thee all **s**,	2483
	28:61 Also every **s**, and every plague, which *is*	2483
1Ki	8:37 whatsoever plague, whatsoever **s** *there*	4245
	17:17 his **s** was so sore, that there was no breath	2483
2Ki	13:14 Elisha was fallen sick of his **s** whereof	2483
2Ch	6:28 whatsoever sore or whatsoever **s** *there*	4245
	21:15 thou *shalt have* great **s** by disease of thy	2483
	21:15 thy bowels fall out by reason of the **s**	2483
	21:19 his bowels fell out by reason of his **s**:	2483
Ps	41: 3 thou wilt make all his bed in his **s**.	2483
Ecc	5:17 hath much sorrow and wrath with his **s**.	2483
Isa	38: 9 had been sick, and was recovered of his **s**:	2483
	38:12 he will cut me off with *pining* **s**: from day	1803
Hos	5:13 When Ephraim saw his **s**, and Judah *saw*	2483
Mt	4:23 healing all *manner of* **s** and all *manner*	3554
	9:35 and healing every **s** and every disease	3554
	10: 1 to heal all *manner of* **s** and all *manner*	3554
Jn	11: 4 This **s** is not unto death, but for the glory	769

SICKNESSES (4) [SICK]

Dt	28:59 and sore **s**, and of long continuance.	2483
	29:22 the **s** which the LORD hath laid upon it;	8463
Mt	8:17 took our infirmities, and bare our **s**.	3554
Mk	3:15 to have power to heal **s**, and to cast out	3554

SIDDIM (3)

Ge	14: 3 were joined together in the vale of **S**,	7708
	14: 8 joined battle with them in the vale of **S**;	7708
	14:10 the vale of **S** *was* full of slimepits.	7708

SIDE (444) [ASIDE, BACKSIDE, SIDES, WAYSIDE]

Ge	6:16 the door of the ark shalt thou set in the **s**	6654
	38:21 the harlot, that *was* openly by the **way s**?	1870
Ex	2: 5 maidens walked along **by** the river's **s**;	3027
	12: 7 strike *it* on the two **s posts** and on the	4201
	12:22 the two **s posts** with the blood that *is* in	4201
	12:23 on the two **s posts**, the LORD will pass	4201
	17:12 the one on the **one s**, and the other on	2088
	17:12 one side, and the other on the **other s**;	2088
	25:12 two rings *shall be* in the one **s** of it,	6763
	25:12 of it, and two rings in the other **s** of it.	6763
	25:32 of the candlestick out of the one **s**,	6654
	25:32 of the candlestick out of the other **s**:	6654
	26:13 a cubit on the **one s**, and a cubit on	2088
	26:13 a cubit on the **other s** of that which	2088
	26:13 over the sides of the tabernacle on **this s**	2088
	26:13 the tabernacle on this side and on **that s**,	2088
	26:18 twenty boards on the south **s** southward.	6285
	26:20 for the second **s** of the tabernacle on	6763
	26:20 the north **s** *there shall be* twenty boards:	6285
	26:26 five for the boards of the one **s** of	6763
	26:27 five bars for the boards of the other **s** of	6763
	26:27 five bars for the boards of the **s** of	6763
	26:35 the **s** of the tabernacle toward the south:	6763
	26:35 thou shalt put the table on the north **s**.	6763
	27: 9 for the south **s** southward *there shall be*	6285
	27: 9 linen of an hundred cubits long for one **s**:	6285
	27:11 likewise for the north **s** in length *there*	6285
	27:12 *for* the breadth of the court on the west **s**	6285
	27:13 the breadth of the court on the east **s**	6285
	27:14 The hangings of *one* **s** *of the gate shall be*	3802
	27:15 on the other **s** *shall be* hangings,	3802
	28:26 which *is* in the **s** of the ephod inward.	5676
	32:15 on **the one s** and on the other *were* they	2088
	32:26 and said, Who *is* on the **LORD's s**?	3807.1
	32:27 Put every man his sword by his **s**, *and* go	3409
	36:11 likewise he made in the uttermost **s** of	8193
	36:23 twenty boards for the south **s** southward:	6285
	36:25 for the other **s** of the tabernacle, *which is*	6763
	36:31 five for the boards of the one **s** of	6763
	36:32 five bars for the boards of the other **s** of	6763
	37: 3 even two rings upon the one **s** of it,	6763
	37: 3 of it, and two rings upon the other **s** of it.	6763
	37: 8 One cherub on the end on **this s**,	2088
	37: 8 cherub on the *other* end on **that s**:	2088
	37:18 of the candlestick out of the one **s** thereof,	6654
	37:18 the candlestick out of the other **s** thereof:	6654
	38: 9 on the south **s** southward the hangings of	6285
	38:11 for the north **s** *the hangings were* an	6285

Ex	38:12 the west **s** *were* hangings of fifty cubits,	6285
	38:13 And for the east **s** eastward fifty cubits.	6285
	38:14 The hangings of the *one* **s** *of the gate*	3802
	38:15 for the other **s** of the court gate, on this	3802
	39:19 which *was* on the **s** of the ephod inward.	5676
	40:22 upon the **s** of the tabernacle northward,	3409
	40:24 on the **s** of the tabernacle southward.	3409
Lev	1:11 he shall kill it on the **s** of the altar	3409
	1:15 blood thereof shall be wrung out at the **s**	7023
	5: 9 of the sin offering upon the **s** of the altar;	7023
Nu	2: 3 on the **east s** toward the rising of the sun	6924
	2:10 On the **south s** *shall be* the standard of	8486
	2:18 On the **west s** *shall be* the standard of	3220
	2:25 Dan *shall be* on the **north s** by their	6828
	3:29 pitch on the **s** of the tabernacle	3409
	3:35 *these* shall pitch on the **s** of the tabernacle	3409
	10: 6 camps that lie on the **south s** shall take	8486
	11:31 as it were a day's journey on **this s**,	3541
	11:31 as it were a day's journey **on the other s**,	3541
	16:27 Korah, Dathan, and Abiram, on **every s**:	5439
	21:13 and pitched on the *other* **s** of Arnon,	5676
	22: 1 pitched in the plains of Moab on **this s**	5676
	22:24 a wall *being* on **this s**, and a wall on that	2088
	22:24 *being* on this side, and a wall on **that s**.	2088
	24: 6 spread forth, as gardens by the river's **s**,	5104
	32:19 not inherit with them on *yonder* **s** Jordan,	5676
	32:19 our inheritance is fallen to us on **this s**	5676
	32:32 inheritance on **this s** Jordan *may be* ours.	5676
	34:11 Shepham *to* Riblah, on the **east s** of Ain;	6924
	34:11 shall reach unto the **s** of the sea of	3802
	34:15 on **this s** Jordan *near* Jericho eastward,	5676
	35: 5 the city on the east **s** two thousand cubits,	6285
	35: 5 *on* the south **s** two thousand cubits,	6285
	35: 5 *on* the west **s** two thousand cubits,	6285
	35: 5 and *on* the north **s** two thousand cubits;	6285
	35:14 Ye shall give three cities on **this s** Jordan,	5676
Dt	1: 1 Israel on **this s** Jordan in the wilderness,	5676
	1: 5 On **this s** Jordan, in the land of Moab,	5676
	1: 7 vale, and in the south, and by the **sea s**,	2348
	3: 8 the land that *was* on **this s** Jordan,	5676
	4:32 from the one **s** of heaven unto the other,	7097
	4:41 Moses severed three cities on **this s** Jordan	5676
	4:46 On **this s** Jordan, in the valley over against	5676
	4:47 which *were* on **this s** Jordan *toward*	5676
	4:49 all the plain on **this s** Jordan eastward,	5676
	11:30 *Are* they not on the *other* **s** Jordan,	5676
	31:26 put it in the **s** of the ark of the covenant	6654
Jos	1:14 which Moses gave you on **this s** Jordan;	5676
	1:15 you on **this s** Jordan *toward* the sunrising.	5676
	2:10 that *were* on the **other s** Jordan, Sihon	5676
	5: 1 which *were* on the **s** of Jordan westward,	5676
	7: 2 on the **east s** of Beth-el, and spake unto	6924
	7: 7 and dwelt on the **other s** Jordan!	5676
	8: 9 and Ai, on the **west s** of Ai:	3220
	8:11 the city, and pitched on the **north s** of Ai:	6828
	8:12 and Ai, on the **west s** of the city.	3220
	8:22 some **on** this **s**, and some on that **s**:	4480
	8:22 some on this side, and some on that **s**:	4480
	8:33 stood on **this s** the ark and on that side	4480
	8:33 on that **s** before the priests the Levites,	2088
	9: 1 when all the kings which *were* on **this s**	5676
	12: 1 possessed their land on the **other s** Jordan	5676
	12: 7 children of Israel smote on **this s** Jordan	5676
	13:27 Cinnereth on the **other s** Jordan eastward.	5676
	13:32 the **other s** Jordan, *by* Jericho, eastward.	5676
	14: 3 and a half tribe on the **other s** Jordan:	5676
	15: 3 it went out to the **south s** to	5045
	15: 3 ascended up on the **south s** unto	5045
	15: 7 which *is* on the **south s** of the river:	5045
	15: 8 Hinnom unto the south **s** of the Jebusite;	3802
	15:10 passed along unto the **s** of mount Jearim,	3802
	15:10 on the **north s**, and went down	6828+1886.5
	15:11 the border went out unto the **s** of Ekron	3802
	16: 5 on the east **s** was Ataroth-addar,	4217
	16: 6 the sea *to* Michmethah on the **north s**;	6828
	17: 5 which *were* on the **north s** of Jordan;	5676
	17: 9 also *was* on the **north s** of the river,	6828
	18:12 their border on the north **s** was from	6285
	18:12 the border went up to the **s** of Jericho on	3802
	18:12 up to the side of Jericho on the **north s**,	6828
	18:13 to the **s** of Luz, which *is* Beth-el,	3802
	18:13 near the hill that *lieth* on the **south s** of	5045
	18:16 to the **s** of Jebusi on the south,	3802
	18:18 passed along toward the **s** over against	3802
	18:19 the border passed along to the **s** of	3802
	18:20 Jordan was the border of it on the east **s**.	6285
	19:14 border compasseth it on the **north s** *to*	6828
	19:27 toward the **north s** of Beth-emek,	6828
	19:34 and reacheth to Zebulun on the **south s**,	5045
	19:34 reacheth to Asher on the west **s**,	NIH
	20: 8 the **other s** Jordan *by* Jericho eastward,	5676
	22: 4 the LORD gave you on the **other s** Jordan.	5676
	22: 7 their brethren on **this s** Jordan westward.	5676
	24: 2 Your fathers dwelt on the **other s** of	5676
	24: 3 Abraham from the **other s** of the flood,	5676
	24: 8 which dwelt on the **other s** Jordan;	5676
	24:14 fathers served on the **other s** of the flood,	5676
	24:15 that *were* on the **other s** of the flood,	5676
	24:30 on the **north s** of the hill of Gaash.	6828
Jdg	2: 9 on the **north s** of the hill Gaash.	6828
	7: 1 Midianites were on the **north s** of them,	6828
	7:12 as the sand by the **sea s** for multitude.	8193
	7:18 blow ye the trumpets also on **every s**	5439
	7:25 Zeeb to Gideon on the **other s** Jordan.	5676
	8:34 of all their enemies on **every s**:	4480+5439

Jdg	10: 8 *other* **s** Jordan in the land of the Amorites,	5676
	11:18 by the **east s** of the land of Moab,	4217+8121
	11:18 pitched on the **other s** of Arnon,	5676
	19: 1 sojourning on the **s** of mount Ephraim,	3411
	19:18 toward the **s** of mount Ephraim,	3411
	21:19 which *is* on the **north s** of Beth-el,	4480+6828
	21:19 **the east s** of the highway	4217+8121+1886.1
1Sa	4:18 off the seat backward by the **s** of the gate,	3027
	6: 8 in a coffer by the **s** thereof;	6654
	12:11 of the hand of your enemies on **every s**,	5439
	14: 1 Philistines' garrison, that *is on* the other **s**.	5676
	14: 4 *there* was a sharp rock on the one **s**,	5676
	14: 4 one side, and a sharp rock on the other **s**:	5676
	14:40 Be ye on one **s**, and I and Jonathan my	5676
	14:40 Jonathan my son will be on the other **s**.	5676
	14:47 fought against all his enemies on **every s**,	5439
	17: 3 stood on a mountain on the **one s**,	2088
	17: 3 stood on a mountain on the **other s**:	2088
	20:20 I will shoot three arrows on the **s** *thereof*,	6654
	20:21 Behold, the arrows *are* on **this s** of thee,	2008
	20:25 Abner sat by Saul's **s**, and David's place	6654
	23:26 Saul went on this **s** of the mountain,	6654
	23:26 and his men on that **s** of the mountain:	6654
	26:13 David went over *to* the **other s**,	5676
	31: 7 that *were* on the **other s** of the valley,	5676
	31: 7 *they* that *were* on the **other s** Jordan,	5676
2Sa	2:13 the one on the **one s** of the pool,	2088+4480
	2:13 other on the **other s** of the pool.	2088+4480
	2:16 and *thrust* his sword in his fellow's **s**;	6654
	13:34 by the way of the hill **s** behind him.	6654
	16:13 Shimei went along on the hill's **s** over	6763
	18: 4 the king stood by the gate **s**, and all	3027
	24: 5 *on* the **right s** of the city that *lieth* in	3225
1Ki	4:24 over all the **region** on **this s** the river,	5676
	4:24 over all the kings on **this s** the river:	5676
	5: 3 wars which were **about** him on **every s**,	5437
	5: 4 my God hath given me rest on **every s**,	5439
	6: 8 chamber *was* in the right **s** of the house:	3802
	6:31 *and* posts *were* a fifth *part of the wall.	4201
	7: 7 it *was* covered with cedar **from one s** of	4480
	7:30 at the **s** of every addition.	5676
	7:39 put five bases on the right **s** of the house,	3802
	7:39 and five on the left **s** of the house:	3802
	7:39 he set the sea on the right **s** of the house	3802
	7:49 five on the **right s**, and five on the left,	3225
	10:19 on either **s** 2088+2088+4480+4480+2050.1	
	10:20 twelve lions stood there on **the one s**	2088
2Ki	3:22 **on the other s** *as* red as blood:	4480+5048
	9:32 to the window, and said, Who *is* on my **s**?	854
	12: 9 the **right s** as one cometh *into* the house	3225
	16:14 and put it on the **north s** of the altar.	3409
1Ch	4:39 *even* unto the east **s** of the valley, to seek	NIH
	6:78 the **other s** Jordan *by* Jericho, on the east	5676
	6:78 Jordan *by* Jericho, on the east **s** of Jordan,	NIH
	12:18 David, and **on** thy **s**, thou son of Jesse:	5973
	12:37 the **other s** of Jordan, of the Reubenites,	5676
	12:18 he *not* given you not on **every s**?	4480+5439
	26:30 officers among them of Israel on **this s**	5676
2Ch	4: 8 five on the **right s**, and five on the left.	3225
	4:10 set the sea on the right **s** of the east end,	3802
	8:17 to Eloth, at the sea **s** in the land of Edom.	8193
	9:18 **on each s** 2088+2088+4480+4480+2050.1	
	9:19 lions stood there on the **one s**	2088+4480
	11:12 having Judah and Benjamin on his **s**.	3807.1
	14: 7 he hath given us rest on **every s**.	4480+5439
	20: 2 thee from beyond the sea on this **s** Syria;	NIH
	23:10 from the right **s** of the temple to the left	3802
	23:10 of the temple to the left **s** of the temple,	3802
	32:22 and guided them on **every s**.	4480+5439
	32:30 brought it straight down to the west **s** of	NIH
	33:14 on the west **s** of Gihon, in the valley,	NIH
Ezr	4:10 the rest *that are* on **this s** the river,	5675
	4:11 Thy servants the men *on* **this s** the river,	5675
	4:16 shalt have no portion on **this s** the river.	5675
	5: 3 governor on **this s** the river,	5675
	5: 6 governor on **this s** the river,	5675
	6: 6 which *were* on **this s** the river, sent unto	5675
	6:13 Tatnai, governor on **this s** the river,	5675
	8:36 and *to* the governors on **this s** the river:	5676
Ne	3: 7 unto the throne of the governor on **this s**	5676
	4:18 every one had his sword girded by his **s**,	4975
Job	1:10 about all that he hath on **every s**?	4480+5439
	18:11 Terrors shall make him afraid on **every s**,	5439
	18:12 and destruction *shall be* ready at his **s**.	6763
	19:10 He hath destroyed me on **every s**, and I	5439
Ps	12: 8 The wicked walk on **every s**, when	5439
	31:13 fear *was* on **every s**: while they	4480+5439
	65:12 and the little hills rejoice on **every s**.	2296
	71:21 greatness, and comfort me on **every s**.	5437
	91: 7 A thousand shall fall at thy **s**,	6654
	118: 6 The LORD *is* on my **s**; I will not fear:	3807.1
	124: 1 not *been* the LORD who was on our **s**,	3807.1
	124: 2 not *been* the LORD who was on our **s**,	3807.1
	140: 5 have spread a net by the **way s**;	3027+4570
Ecc	4: 1 on the **s** of their oppressors *there was*	3027
Isa	60: 4 thy daughters shall be nursed at thy **s**.	6654
Jer	6:25 the enemy *and* fear *is* on **every s**.	4480+5439
	20:10 defaming of many, fear on **every s**.	4480+5439
	49:29 cry unto them, Fear *is* on **every s**.	4480+5439
	52:23 were ninety and six pomegranates on a **s**;	7307
Eze	1:10 man, and the face of a lion, on the **right s**:	3225
	1:10 four had the face of an ox on the **left s**;	8040
	1:23 which covered on this **s**, and every one	NIH
	1:23 which covered on that **s**, their bodies.	NIH
	4: 4 Lie thou also upon thy left **s**, and lay	6654

S

Eze	4: 6 lie again on thy right **s**, and thou shalt	6654
	4: 8 thou shalt not turn thee from one **s** to	6654
	4: 9 of the days that thou shalt lie upon thy **s**,	6654
	9: 2 linen, with a writer's inkhorn by his **s**:	4975
	9: 3 which *had* the writer's inkhorn by his **s**;	4975
	9:11 which *had* the inkhorn by his **s**, reported	4975
	10: 3 the cherubims stood on the **right s** of	3225
	11:23 which *is* on the **east s** of the city.	6924
	16:33 **on every s** for thy whoredom.	4480+5439
	19: 8 nations set against him **on every s** from	5439
	23:22 them against thee **on every s**;	4480+5439
	25: 9 I *will* open the **s** of Moab from the cities,	3802
	28:23 by the sword upon her **on every s**,	4480+5439
	34:21 Because ye have thrust with **s** and	6654
	36: 3 and swallowed you up **on every s**,	4480+5439
	37:21 will gather them **on every s**,	4480+5439
	39:17 gather yourselves **on every s** to	4480+5439
	40:10 of the gate eastward *were* three on **this s**,	6311
	40:10 three on this side, and three on **that s**,	6311
	40:10 the posts had one measure on **this s** and	6311
	40:10 one measure on this side and on **that s**.	6311
	40:12 little chambers *was* one cubit *on* **this s**,	NIH
	40:12 the space *was* one cubit on **that s**:	6311
	40:12 little chambers *were* six cubits on **this s**,	6311
	40:12 on this side, and six cubits on **that s**.	6311
	40:18 the pavement by the **s** of the gates over	3802
	40:21 chambers thereof *were* three on **this s**	6311
	40:21 three on this side and three on **that s**;	6311
	40:26 one on **this s**, and another on that side,	6311
	40:26 one on this side, and another on **that s**,	6311
	40:34 posts thereof, on **this s**, and on that side:	6311
	40:34 posts thereof, on this side, and on **that s**:	6311
	40:37 posts thereof, on **this s**, and on that side,	6311
	40:37 posts thereof, on this side, and on **that s**:	6311
	40:39 of the gate *were* two tables on **this s**,	6311
	40:39 two tables on **that s**, to slay thereon	6311
	40:40 at the **s** without, as one goeth up to	3802
	40:40 on the other **s**, which *was* at the porch of	3802
	40:41 Four tables *were* on **this s**, and four tables	6311
	40:41 four tables on **that s**, by the side of	6311
	40:41 tables on that side, by the **s** of the gate;	3802
	40:44 which *was* at the **s** of the north gate;	3802
	40:44 one at the **s** of the east gate *having*	3802
	40:48 five cubits on **this s**, and five cubits on	6311
	40:48 on this side, and five cubits on **that s**:	6311
	40:48 of the gate *was* three cubits on **this s**,	6311
	40:48 on this side, and three cubits on **that s**.	6311
	40:49 one on **this s**, and another on that side.	6311
	40:49 one on this side, and another on **that s**.	6311
	41: 1 six cubits broad on the **one s**, and six	6311
	41: 1 and six cubits broad on the **other s**,	6311
	41: 2 of the door *were* five cubits on the **one s**,	6311
	41: 2 one side, and five cubits on the **other s**:	6311
	41: 5 the breadth of *every* **s** chamber,	6763
	41: 5 round about the house **on every s**,	5439
	41: 6 the **s** chambers *were* three, one over	6763
	41: 6 house for the **s** chambers round about,	6763
	41: 7 about still upward to the **s** chambers:	6763
	41: 8 the foundations of the **s** chambers *were*	6763
	41: 9 which *was* for the **s** chamber without,	6763
	41: 9 of the **s** chambers that *were* within.	6763
	41:10 round about the house **on every s**.	5439+5439
	41:11 the doors of the **s** chambers *were* toward	6763
	41:15 the galleries thereof on the **one s** and on	6311
	41:15 on the one side and on the **other s**,	6311
	41:19 *was* toward the palm tree on the **one s**,	6311
	41:19 lion toward the palm tree on the **other s**:	6311
	41:26 palm trees on the **one s** and on the other	6311
	41:26 trees on the one side and on the **other s**,	6311
	41:26 *upon* the **s** chambers of the house,	6763
	42: 9 chambers *was* the entry on the **east s**,	6921
	42:16 He measured the east **s** with the	7307
	42:17 He measured the north **s**, five hundred	7307
	42:18 He measured the south **s**, five hundred	7307
	42:19 He turned about to the west **s**,	7307
	45: 7 for the prince on the **one s**	2088
	45: 7 on the **other s** of the oblation of the holy	2088
	45: 7 from the west westward, and from	6285
	45: 7 and from the east eastward:	6285
	46:19 the entry, which *was* at the **s** of the gate,	3802
	47: 1 from under from the right **s** of the house,	3802
	47: 1 of the house, at the south **s** of the altar.	NIH
	47: 2 there ran out waters on the right **s**.	3802
	47: 7 river *were* very many trees on the **one s**	2088
	47:12 on **this s** and on that side, shall grow all	2088
	47:12 on this side and on **that s**, shall grow all	2088
	47:15 the border of the land toward the north **s**,	6285
	47:17 border of Hamath. And *this is* the north **s**.	6285
	47:18 the east **s** ye shall measure from Hauran,	6285
	47:18 unto the east sea. And *this is* the east **s**.	6285
	47:19 the south **s** southward, from Tamar *even*	6285
	47:19 And *this is* the south **s** southward.	6285
	47:20 The west **s** also *shall be* the great sea from	6285
	47:20 over against Hamath. This *is* the west **s**.	6285
	48: 2 the east side unto the west side, a *portion*	6285
	48: 2 the east side unto the west side, a *portion*	6285
	48: 3 from the east **s** even unto the west side,	6285
	48: 3 from the east side even unto the west **s**,	6285
	48: 4 the east side unto the west side, a *portion*	6285
	48: 4 the east side unto the west side, a *portion*	6285
	48: 5 the east **s** even unto the west side,	6285
	48: 5 the east side even unto the west **s**,	6285
	48: 6 from the east **s** even unto the west side,	6285
	48: 6 from the east side even unto the west **s**,	6285
	48: 7 the east **s** unto the west side, a *portion*	6285

Eze	48: 7 the east side unto the west **s**, a *portion*	6285
	48: 8 Judah, from the east **s** unto the west side,	6285
	48: 8 Judah, from the east side unto the west **s**,	6285
	48: 8 from the east **s** unto the west side:	6285
	48: 8 from the east side unto the west **s**:	6285
	48:16 north **s** four thousand and five hundred,	6285
	48:16 south **s** four thousand and five hundred,	6285
	48:16 on the east **s** four thousand and	6285
	48:16 west **s** four thousand and five hundred.	6285
	48:21 on the **one s** and on the other of the holy	2088
	48:23 from the east side unto the west **s**,	6285
	48:23 from the east **s** unto the west side,	6285
	48:24 from the east side unto the west **s**,	6285
	48:24 from the east **s** unto the west side,	6285
	48:25 from the east side unto the west **s**,	6285
	48:25 from the east **s** unto the west side,	6285
	48:26 from the east side unto the west **s**,	6285
	48:26 from the east **s** unto the west side,	6285
	48:27 from the east side unto the west side, Gad a	6285
	48:27 from the east side unto the west **s**, Gad a	6285
	48:28 border of Gad, at the south **s** southward,	6285
	48:30 on the north **s**, four thousand and	6285
	48:32 at the east **s** four thousand and	6285
	48:33 *at* the south **s** four thousand and	6285
	48:34 At the west **s** four thousand and	6285
Da	7: 5 it raised up itself on one **s**, and *it* had	7859
	10: 4 as I was by the **s** of the great river, which	3027
	11:17 she shall not stand *on his* **s**, neither be for	NIH
	12: 5 the one on **this s** of the bank of the river,	2008
	12: 5 other on **that s** of the bank of the river.	2008
Ob	1:11 the day that thou stoodest on the **other s**,	5048
Jnh	4: 5 sat on the **east s** of the city, and there	6924
Zec	3 one upon the right **s** of the bowl,	NIH
	4: 3 and the other upon the left **s** thereof.	NIH
	4:11 trees upon the right **s** of the candlestick	NIH
	4:11 the candlestick and upon the left **s** thereof?	NIH
	5: 3 shall be cut off *as* on **this s** according to it;	NIH
	5: 3 shall be cut off *as* on that **s** according to it.	NIH
Mt	8:18 to depart unto the **other s**.	4008
	8:28 when he was come to the **other s** into	4008
	13: 1 out of the house, and sat **by** the sea **s**.	3844
	13: 4 *some seeds* fell **by** the way **s**, and the	3844
	13:19 is he which received seed **by** the way **s**.	3844
	14:22 and to go before him unto the **other s**,	4008
	16: 5 his disciples were come to the **other s**,	4008
	20:30 two blind men sitting **by** the way **s**,	3844
Mk	2:13 And he went forth again **by** the sea **s**;	4008
	4: 1 And he began again to teach **by** the sea **s**:	3844
	4: 4 some fell **by** the **way s**, and the fowls of	3598
	4:15 And these are they **by** the **way s**, where	3598
	4:35 Let us pass over unto the **other s**.	4008
	5: 1 And they came over unto the **other s** of	4008
	5:21 over again **by** ship unto the **other s**,	4008
	6:45 go to the **other s** before unto Bethsaida,	4008
	8:13 the ship again departed to the **other s**.	4008
	10: 1 coasts of Judea **by** the **farther s** of Jordan:	4008
	10:46 of Timeus, sat **by** the **high**way **s** begging.	3598
	16: 5 saw a young man sitting on the **right s**,	1188
Lk	1:11 on the **right s** of the altar of incense.	1188
	8: 5 and as he sowed, some fell **by** the **way s**;	3598
	8:12 Those **by** the **way s** are they that hear;	3598
	8:22 us go over unto the **other s** of the lake.	4008
	10:31 saw him, he **passed** by on the **other s**.	492
	10:32 *on him*, and **passed** by on the **other s**.	492
	18:35 a certain blind man sat **by** the **way s**	3598
	19:43 thee round, and keep thee in **on every s**,	3840
Jn	6:22 on the **other s** of the sea saw that there	4008
	6:25 had found him **on the other s** of the sea,	4008
	19:18 with him, **on either s** one,	1782+1782+2532
	19:34 of the soldiers with a spear pierced his **s**,	4125
	20:20 shewed unto them *his* hands and his **s**.	4125
	20:25 and thrust my hand into his **s**, I will not	4125
	20:27 *hither* thy hand, and thrust *it* into my **s**:	4125
Ac	21: 6 Cast the net on the right **s** of the ship,	3313
	10: 6 a tanner, whose house is **by** the sea **s**.	3844
	10:32 house of *one* Simon a tanner **by** the sea **s**:	3844
	12: 7 he smote Peter on the **s**, and raised him	4125
	16:13 we went out of the city **by** a river **s**,	3844
2Co	4: 8 *We are* troubled on every **s**, yet not	NIG
	7: 5 *were* troubled on every **s**; without *were*	NIG
Rev	22: 2 and **of either s** of the river,	1782+1782+2532

SIDES (48) [SIDE]

Ex	25:14 staves into the rings **by** the **s** of the ark,	6763
	25:32 six branches shall come out of the **s** of it;	6654
	26:13 it shall hang over the **s** of the tabernacle	6654
	26:22 for the **s** of the tabernacle westward thou	3411
	26:23 the corners of the tabernacle in the **two s**.	3411
	26:27 of the tabernacle, for the **two s** westward.	3411
	27: 7 the staves shall be upon the **two s** of	6763
	28:27 shalt put them on the **two s** of the ephod	3802
	30: 3 the **s** thereof round about, and the horns	7023
	30: 4 upon the **two s** of it shalt thou make *it;*	6654
	32:15 the tables *were* written on both their **s**;	5676
	36:27 for the **s** of the tabernacle westward he	3411
	36:28 the corners of the tabernacle in the **two s**.	3411
	36:32 of the tabernacle for the **s** westward.	3411
	37: 5 put the staves into the rings **by** the **s** of	6763
	37:18 six branches going out of the **s** thereof;	6654
	37:26 the **s** thereof round about, and the horns	7023
	37:27 two corners of it, upon the **two s** thereof,	6654
	38: 7 he put the staves into the rings on the **s** of	6763
	39:20 put them on the **two s** of the ephod	3802
Nu	33:55 thorns in your **s**, and shall vex you in	6654
Jos	23:13 scourges in your **s**, and thorns in your	6654

Jdg	2: 3 they shall be *as* thorns in your **s**,	6654
	5:30 of divers colours of needlework on both **s**,	NIH
1Sa	24: 3 his men remained in the **s** of the cave.	3411
1Ki	4:24 he had peace on all **s** round about him.	5676
	6:16 built twenty cubits on the **s** of the house,	3411
2Ki	19:23 of the **s** of Lebanon, and will cut down	3411
Ps	48: 2 *is* mount Zion, *on* the **s** of the north,	3411
	128: 3 wife *shall be* as a fruitful vine by the **s**	3411
Isa	14:13 of the congregation, in the **s** of the north:	3411
	14:15 brought down to hell, to the **s** of the pit.	3411
	37:24 of the mountains, *to* the **s** of Lebanon;	3411
	66:12 ye shall be borne upon *her* **s**,	6654
Jer	6:22 a great nation shall be raised from the **s** of	3411
	48:28 her nest in the **s** of the hole's mouth.	5676
	49:32 I will bring their calamity from all **s**	5676
Eze	1: 8 a man under their wings on their four **s**;	7253
	1:17 they went, they went upon their four **s**:	7253
	10:11 they went, they went upon their four **s**:	7253
	32:23 Whose graves are set in the **s** of the pit,	3411
	41: 2 the **s** of the door *were* five cubits on the	3802
	41:26 on the **s** of the porch, and *upon* the side	3802
	42:20 He measured it by the four **s**: it had a wall	7307
	46:19 there *was* a place on the **two s** westward.	3411
	48: 1 these are his **s** east *and* west; a *portion*	6285
Am	6:10 shall say unto *him* that *is* by the **s** of	3411
Jnh	1: 5 But Jonah was gone down into the **s** of	3411

SIDON (14) [SIDONIANS, ZIDON]

Ge	10:15 Canaan begat **S** his firstborn, and Heth,	6721
	10:19 the border of the Canaanites was from **S**,	6721
Mt	11:21 **S** they would have repented long ago in	4605
	11:22 for Tyre and **S** at the day of judgment,	4605
	15:21 departed into the coasts of Tyre and **S**.	4605
Mk	3: 8 and about Tyre and **S**, a great	4605
	7:24 and went into the borders of Tyre and **S**,	4605
	7:31 departing from the coasts of Tyre and **S**,	4605
Lk	4:26 save unto Sarepta, *a city* of **S**, unto a	4605
	6:17 and *from* the sea coast of Tyre and **S**,	4605
	10:13 works had been done in Tyre and **S**,	4605
	10:14 tolerable for Tyre and **S** at the judgment,	4605
Ac	12:20 highly displeased with them of Tyre and **S**:	4606
	27: 3 And the next *day* we touched at **S**.	4605

SIDONIANS (5) [SIDON]

Dt	3: 9 (Which Hermon the **S** call Sirion;	6722
Jos	13: 4 Mearah that *is* beside the **S** unto Aphek,	6722
	13: 6 *and* all the **S**, them will I drive out from	6722
Jdg	3: 3 the **S**, and the Hivites that dwelt in mount	6722
1Ki	5: 6 can skill to hew timber like unto the **S**.	6722

SIEGE (17) [BESIEGE]

Dt	20:19 *is* man's *life*) to employ *them* in the **s**:	4692
	28:53 given thee, in the **s**, and in the straitness,	4692
	28:55 because he hath nothing left him in the **s**,	4692
	28:57 for want of all *things* secretly in the **s**	4692
1Ki	15:27 and all Israel laid **s** to Gibbethon.	6696
2Ch	32: 1 (but he *himself* laid **s** against Lachish,	NIH
	32:10 trust, that ye abide in the **s** in Jerusalem?	4692
Isa	29: 3 will lay **s** against thee *with* a mount,	6696
Jer	19: 9 every one the flesh of his friend in the **s**	4692
Eze	4: 2 lay **s** against it, and build a fort against it,	4692
	4: 3 besieged, and thou shalt lay **s** against it:	6696
	4: 7 set thy face toward the **s** of Jerusalem,	4692
	4: 8 till thou hast ended the days of thy **s**.	4692
	5: 2 when the days of the **s** are fulfilled:	4692
Mic	5: 1 he hath laid **s** against us: they shall smite	4692
Na	3:14 Draw thee waters for the **s**, fortify thy	4692
Zec	12: 2 when they shall be in the **s** both against	4692

SIEGEWORKS See BULWARKS

SIEVE (2)

Isa	30:28 to sift the nations with the **s** of vanity:	5299
Am	9: 9 like as *corn* is sifted in a **s**, yet shall not	3531

SIFT (3) [SIFTED]

Isa	30:28 to **s** the nations with the sieve of vanity:	5130
Am	9: 9 I will **s** the house of Israel among all	5128
Lk	22:31 *to have* you, that *he* may **s** *you* as wheat:	4617

SIFTED (1) [SIFT]

Am	9: 9 like as *corn* is **s** in a sieve, yet shall not	5128

SIGH (7) [SIGHED, SIGHEST, SIGHETH, SIGHING, SIGHS]

Isa	24: 7 vine languisheth, all the merryhearted do **s**.	584
La	1: 4 her virgins *are* afflicted,	584
	1:11 All her people **s**, they seek bread; they have	584
	1:21 They have heard that I **s**; *there is* none to	584
Eze	9: 4 mark upon the foreheads of the men that **s**	584
	21: 6 **S** therefore, thou son of man, with	584
	21: 6 and with bitterness **s** before their eyes.	584

SIGHED (3) [SIGH]

Ex	2:23 the children of Israel **s** by reason of	584
Mk	7:34 he **s**, and saith unto him, EPHPHATHA,	4727
	8:12 And he **s** deeply in his spirit, and saith,	389

SIGHEST (1) [SIGH]

Eze	21: 7 they say unto thee, Wherefore **s** thou?	584

SIGHETH (1) [SIGH]

La	1: 8 yea, she **s**, and turneth backward.	584

SIGHING (7) [SIGH]

Job	3:24 For my **s** cometh before I eat,	585

Ps 12: 5 for the **s** of the needy, now will I arise, 603
31:10 is spent with grief, and my years with **s**: 585
79:11 Let the **s** of the prisoner come before thee, 603
Isa 21: 2 all the **s** thereof have I made to cease. 585
35:10 and sorrow and **s** shall flee away. 585
Jer 45: 3 I fainted in my **s**, and I find no rest. 585

SIGHS (1) [SIGH]
La 1:22 for my **s** *are* many, and my heart *is* faint. 585

SIGHT (333) [SEE]
Ge 2: 9 grow every tree that is pleasant to the **s**, 4758
18: 3 if now I have found favour in thy **s**, 5869
19:19 thy servant hath found grace in thy **s**, 5869
21:11 thing was very grievous in Abraham's **s** 5869
21:12 Let it not be grievous in thy **s** because 5869
23: 4 I may bury my dead out of my **s**. 6440+3807.1
23: 8 should bury my dead out of my **s**; 6440+3807.1
32: 5 tell my lord, that I may find grace in thy **s**. 5869
33: 8 *are* to find grace in the **s** of my lord. 5869
33:10 if now I have found grace in thy **s**, then 5869
33:15 let me find grace in the **s** of my lord. 5869
38: 7 was wicked in the **s** of the LORD, 5869
39: 4 Joseph found grace in his **s**, and he served 5869
39:21 gave him favour in the **s** of the keeper of 5869
47:18 there is not ought left in the **s** of my lord, 6440
47:25 let us find grace in the **s** of my lord, 5869
47:29 If now I have found grace in thy **s**, put, 5869
Ex 3: 3 I will now turn aside, and see this great **s**, 4758
3:21 I will give this people favour in the **s** of 5869
4:30 and did the signs in the **s** of the people. 5869
7:20 in the **s** of Pharaoh, and in the sight of his 5869
7:20 of Pharaoh, and in the **s** of his servants; 5869
9: 8 it towards the heaven in the **s** of Pharaoh. 5869
11: 3 the LORD gave the people favour in the **s** 5869
11: 3 in the **s** of Pharaoh's servants, and in 5869
11: 3 and in the **s** of the people.) 5869
12:36 the LORD gave the people favour in the **s** 5869
15:26 wilt do that which is right in his **s**, 5869
17: 6 Moses did so in the **s** of the elders of 5869
19:11 in the **s** of all the people upon mount 5869
24:17 the **s** of the glory of the LORD *was* like 4758
33:12 and thou hast also found grace in my **s**. 5869
33:13 I pray thee, if I have found grace in thy **s**, 5869
33:13 know thee, that I may find grace in thy **s**? 5869
33:16 and thy people have found grace in thy **s**? 5869
33:17 for thou hast found grace in my **s**, 5869
34: 9 If now I have found grace in thy **s**, 5869
40:38 by night, in the **s** of all the house of Israel, 5869
Lev 10:19 should it have been accepted in the **s** of 5869
13: 3 the plague in **s** be deeper than the skin of 4758
13: 4 in **s** be not deeper than the skin, 5869
13: 5 if the plague in his **s** be at a stay, 5869
13:20 be in **s** lower than the skin, and the hair 4758
13:25 and it be in **s** deeper than the skin; 4758
13:30 behold, if it be in **s** deeper than the skin; 4758
13:31 it be not in **s** deeper than the skin, 4758
13:32 the scall be not in **s** deeper than the skin; 4758
13:34 the skin, nor be in **s** deeper than the skin; 4758
13:37 if the scall be in his **s** at a stay, 5869
14:37 which in **s** *are* lower than the wall; 4758
20:17 shall be cut off in the **s** of their people: 5869
25:53 not rule with rigour over him in thy **s**. 5869
26:45 the land of Egypt in the **s** of the heathen, 5869
Nu 3: 4 office in the **s** of Aaron their father. 6440
11:11 have I not found favour in thy **s**, 5869
11:15 of hand, if I have found favour in thy **s**; 5869
11:33 we were in our own **s** as grasshoppers, 5869
13:33 grasshoppers, and so we were in their **s**. 5869
19: 5 *one* shall burn the heifer in his **s**; her skin, 5869
20:27 went up into mount Hor in the **s** of all 5869
25: 6 a Midianitish *woman* in the **s** of Moses, 5869
25: 6 in the **s** of all the congregation of 5869
27:19 and give him a charge in their **s**. 5869
32: 5 said they, if we have found grace in thy **s**, 5869
32:13 that had done evil in the **s** of the LORD, 5869
33: 3 a high hand in the **s** of all the Egyptians. 5869
Dt 4: 6 your understanding in the **s** of the nations, 5869
4:25 shall do evil in the **s** of the LORD thy 5869
4:37 brought thee out in his **s** with his mighty 6440
6:18 *is* right and good in the **s** of the LORD: 5869
9:18 in doing wickedly in the **s** of the LORD, 5869
12:25 *that which is* right in the **s** of the LORD. 5869
12:28 and right in the **s** of the LORD thy God. 5869
17: 2 that hath wrought wickedness in the **s** of 5869
21: 9 *that which is* right in the **s** of the LORD, 5869
28:34 thou shalt be mad for the **s** of thine 4758
28:67 of thine eyes which thou shalt see. 4758
31: 7 said unto him in the **s** of all Israel, 5869
31:29 ye will do evil in the **s** of the LORD, 5869
34:12 which Moses shewed in the **s** of all Israel. 5869
Jos 3: 7 begin to magnify thee in the **s** of all Israel, 5869
4:14 magnified Joshua in the **s** of all Israel; 5869
10:12 he said in the **s** of Israel, Sun, stand thou 5869
23: 5 drive them from out of your **s**; 6440+3807.1
24:17 which did those great signs in our **s**, 5869
Jdg 2:11 the children of Israel did evil in the **s** of 5869
3: 7 the children of Israel did evil in the **s** 5869
3:12 children of Israel did evil again in the **s** 5869
3:12 they had done evil in the **s** of the LORD. 5869
4: 1 children of Israel again did evil in the **s** 5869
6: 1 the children of Israel did evil in the **s** 5869
6:17 If now I have found grace in thy **s**, then 5869
6:21 angel of the LORD departed out of his **s**. 5869
10: 6 children of Israel did evil again in the **s** 5869

Jdg 13: 1 children of Israel did evil again in the **s** 5869
Ru 2: 2 glean ears of corn after *him* in whose **s** I 5869
2:13 Let me find favour in thy **s**, my lord; 5869
1Sa 1:18 Let thine handmaid find grace in thy **s**. 5869
12:17 which ye have done in the **s** of the LORD, 5869
15:17 When thou *wast* little in thine own **s**, 5869
15:19 and didst evil in the **s** of the LORD? 5869
16:22 for he hath found favour in my **s**. 5869
18: 5 he was accepted in the **s** of all the people, 5869
18: 5 and also in the **s** of Saul's servants. 5869
29: 6 in with me in the host in my **s**: 5869
29: 9 David, I know that thou *art* good in my **s**, 5869
2Sa 6:22 thus, and will be base in mine own **s**: 5869
7: 9 have cut off all thine enemies out of thy **s**, 6440
7:19 this was yet a small thing in thy **s**, O Lord 5869
12: 9 of the LORD, to do evil in his **s**? 5869
12:11 he shall lie with thy wives in the **s** of this 5869
13: 5 give me meat, and dress the meat in my **s**, 5869
13: 6 make *me* a couple of cakes in my **s**, that I 5869
13: 8 kneaded *it*, and made cakes in his **s**, 5869
14:22 knoweth that I have found grace in thy **s**, 5869
16: 4 thee that I may find grace in thy **s**, 5869
16:22 father's concubines in the **s** of all Israel. 5869
22:25 according to my cleanness in his **eye** s. 5869
1Ki 8:25 shall not fail thee a man in my **s** to sit 6440
9: 7 for my name, will I cast out of my **s**; 6440
11: 6 Solomon did evil in the **s** of 5869
11:19 Hadad found great favour in the **s** of 5869
11:38 do that *is* right in my **s**, to keep my 5869
14:22 Judah did evil in the **s** of the LORD, 5869
15:26 he did evil in the **s** of the LORD, 5869
15:34 he did evil in the **s** of the LORD, 5869
16: 7 even for all the evil that he did in the **s** of 5869
16:19 sinned in doing evil in the **s** of the LORD, 5869
16:30 Ahab the son of Omri did evil in the **s** of 5869
21:20 hast sold thyself to work evil in the **s** 5869
21:25 to work wickedness in the **s** of the LORD, 5869
22:52 he did evil in the **s** of the LORD, 5869
2Ki 1:13 fifty thy servants, be precious in thy **s**. 5869
1:14 let my life now be precious in thy **s**. 5869
3: 2 he wrought evil in the **s** of the LORD; 5869
3:18 *but* a light thing in the **s** of the LORD: 5869
8:18 and he did evil in the **s** of the LORD. 5869
8:27 did evil in the **s** of the LORD, as *did* 5869
12: 2 Jehoash did *that* which *was* right in the **s** 5869
13: 2 he did *that* which *was* evil in the **s** of 5869
13:11 he did *that* which *was* evil in the **s** of 5869
14: 3 he did *that* which *was* right in the **s** of 5869
14:24 he did *that* which *was* evil in the **s** of 5869
15: 3 he did *that* which *was* right in the **s** of 5869
15: 9 he did *that* which *was* evil in the **s** of 5869
15:18 he did *that* which *was* evil in the **s** of 5869
15:24 he did *that* which *was* evil in the **s** of 5869
15:28 he did *that* which *was* evil in the **s** of 5869
15:34 he did *that* which *was* right in the **s** of 5869
16: 2 did not *that* which *was* right in the **s** of 5869
17: 2 he did *that* which *was* evil in the **s** of 5869
17:17 sold themselves to do evil in the **s** of 5869
17:18 Israel, and removed them out of his **s**: 6440
17:20 until *he* had cast them out of his **s**. 6440
17:23 the LORD removed Israel out of his **s**, 6440
18: 3 he did *that* which *was* right in the **s** of 5869
20: 3 have done *that* which *is* good in thy **s**. 5869
21: 2 he did *that* which *was* evil in the **s** of 5869
21: 6 he wrought much wickedness in the **s** of 5869
21:15 have done *that* which *was* evil in my **s**, 5869
21:16 in doing *that* which *was* evil in the **s** of 5869
21:20 he did *that* which *was* evil in the **s** of 5869
22: 2 he did *that* which *was* right in the **s** of 5869
23:27 I will remove Judah also out of my **s**, 6440
23:32 he did *that* which *was* evil in the **s** of 5869
23:37 he did *that* which *was* evil in the **s** of 5869
24: 3 to remove *them* out of his **s**, for the sins 6440
24: 9 he did *that* which *was* evil in the **s** of 5869
24:19 he did *that* which *was* evil in the **s** of 5869
1Ch 2: 3 of Judah, was evil in the **s** of the LORD; 5869
19:13 the LORD do *that* which *is* good in his **s**. 5869
22: 8 shed much blood upon the earth in my **s**. 6440
28: 8 in the **s** of all Israel the congregation of 5869
29:25 Solomon exceedingly in the **s** of all Israel, 5869
2Ch 6:16 **s** to sit upon the throne of Israel; 6440+3807.1
7:20 will I cast out of my **s**, and will make it to 6440
20:32 doing *that* which *was* right in the **s** of 5869
22: 4 Wherefore he did evil in the **s** of 5869
24: 2 Joash did *that* which *was* right in the **s** of 5869
25: 2 he did *that* which *was* right in the **s** of 5869
26: 4 he did *that* which *was* right in the **s** of 5869
27: 2 he did *that* which *was* right in the **s** of 5869
28: 1 he did not *that* which *was* right in the **s** 5869
29: 2 he did *that* which *was* right in the **s** of 5869
32:23 he was magnified in the **s** of all nations 5869
33: 2 did *that* which *was* evil in the **s** of 5869
33: 6 he wrought much evil in the **s** of 5869
33:22 he did *that* which *was* evil in the **s** of 5869
34: 2 he did *that* which *was* right in the **s** of 5869
36: 5 he did *that* which *was* evil in the **s** of 5869
36: 9 he did *that* which *was* evil in the **s** of 5869
36:12 he did *that* which *was* evil in the **s** of 5869
Ezr 9: 9 hath extended mercy unto us in the **s** of 5869
Ne 1:11 him mercy in the **s** of this man. 6440+3807.1
2: 5 if thy servant have found favour in thy **s**, 6440
8: 5 Ezra opened the book in the **s** of all 5869
Est 2:15 Esther obtained favour in the **s** of all them 5869
2:17 favour in his **s** more than all the virgins; 6440
5: 2 court, *that* she obtained favour in his **s**: 5869

Est 5: 8 If I have found favour in the **s** of the king, 5869
7: 3 and said, If I have found favour in thy **s**, 5869
8: 5 If I have found favour in his **s**, and the 6440
Job 15:15 yea, the heavens are not clean in his **s**. 5869
18: 3 as beasts, *and* reputed vile in your **s**? 5869
19:15 me for a stranger: I am an alien in their **s**. 5869
21: 8 seed is established in their **s** 6440+3807.1
25: 5 yea, the stars are not pure in his **s**. 5869
34:26 as wicked *men* in the open **s** of others; 7200
41: 9 *not one* be cast down even at the **s** of 4758
Ps 5: 5 The foolish shall not stand in thy **s**: 5869
9:19 let the heathen be judged in thy **s**. 6440
10: 5 thy judgments *are* far above out of his **s**: 5048
19:14 be acceptable in thy **s**, O LORD, 6440
51: 4 have I sinned, and done *this* evil in thy **s**: 5869
72:14 and precious shall their blood be in his **s**. 5869
76: 7 who may stand in thy **s** when once thou 5869
78:12 Marvellous things did he in the **s** of their 5048
79:10 **s** *by* the revenging of the blood of thy 5869
90: 4 For a thousand years in thy **s** *are* but 5869
98: 2 openly shewed in the **s** of the heathen. 5869
101: 7 he that telleth lies shall not tarry in my **s**. 5869
116:15 Precious in the **s** of the LORD *is* the death 5869
143: 2 in thy **s** shall no *man* living be justified. 5869
Pr 1:17 Surely in vain the net *is* spread in the **s** of 5869
3: 4 good understanding in the **s** of God and 5869
4: 3 and only *beloved* in the **s** of my mother. 6440
Ecc 2:26 to a man that *is* good in his **s** wisdom, 6440
6: 9 Better *is* the **s** of the eyes than 4758
8: 3 Be not hasty to go out of his **s**: stand not 6440
11: 9 of thine heart, and in the **s** of thine eyes: 4758
Isa 5:21 own eyes, and prudent in their own **s**! 6440
11: 3 he shall not judge after the **s** of his eyes, 4758
26:17 so have we been in thy **s**, O LORD. 6440
38: 3 have done *that* which *is* good in thy **s**. 5869
43: 4 Since thou wast precious in my **s**, thou 5869
Jer 4: 1 put away thine abominations out of my **s**, 6440
7:15 I will cast you out of my **s**, as I have cast 5869
7:30 children of Judah have done evil in my **s**, 5869
15: 1 cast *them* out of my **s**, and let them go 5869
18:10 If it do evil in my **s**, that *it* obey not my 5869
18:23 blot out their sin from thy **s**, 6440+3807.1
19:10 shalt thou break the bottle in the **s** of 5869
32:12 in the **s** of Hanameel mine uncle's *son,* 5869
34:15 now turned, and had done right in my **s**, 5869
43: 9 Tahpanhes, in the **s** of the men of Judah; 5869
51:24 evil that they have done in Zion in your **s**, 5869
Eze 4:12 dung that cometh out of man, in their **s**. 5869
5: 8 the midst of thee in the **s** of the nations. 5869
5:14 about thee, in the **s** of all that pass by. 5869
10: 2 over the city. And he went in in my **s**. 5869
10:19 and mounted up from the earth in my **s**: 5869
12: 3 removing, and remove by day in their **s**; 5869
12: 3 from thy place to another place in their **s**: 5869
12: 4 thou bring forth thy stuff by day in their **s**, 5869
12: 4 thou shalt go forth at even in their **s**, as 5869
12: 5 Dig thou through the wall in their **s**, 5869
12: 6 In their **s** shalt thou bear *it* upon *thy* 5869
12: 7 *and* I bare *it* upon *my* shoulder in their **s**. 5869
16:41 execute judgments upon thee in the **s** of 5869
20: 9 whom they were, in whose **s** I made 5869
20:14 heathen, in whose **s** I brought them out. 5869
20:22 that *it* should not be polluted in the **s** of 5869
20:22 in whose **s** I brought them forth. 5869
20:43 ye shall lothe yourselves in your own **s** for 6440
21:23 unto them as a false divination in their **s**, 5869
22:16 in thyself in the **s** of the heathen, 5869
28:18 earth in the **s** of all them that behold thee. 5869
28:25 shall be sanctified in them in the **s** of 5869
36:31 shall lothe yourselves in your own **s** for 6440
36:34 whereas it lay desolate in the **s** of all that 5869
39:27 am sanctified in them in the **s** of many 5869
43:11 write *it* in their **s**, that they may keep 5869
Da 4:11 the **s** thereof to the end of all the earth: 2379
4:20 and the **s** thereof to all the earth; 2379
Hos 2: 2 put away her whoredoms out of her **s**, 6440
2:10 will I discover her lewdness in the **s** 5869
6: 2 will raise us up, and we shall live in his **s**. 6440
Am 9: 3 they be hid from my **s** in the bottom 5869
Jnh 2: 4 I am cast out of thy **s**; yet I will look 5869
Mal 2:17 one that doeth evil *is* good in the **s** of 5869
Mt 11: 5 The blind receive their **s**, and the lame 308
11:26 Father: for so it seemed good in thy **s**. 1715
20:34 and immediately their eyes received **s**, 308
Mk 10:51 unto him, Lord, that I might receive my **s**. 308
10:52 And immediately he received his **s**, 308
Lk 1:15 For he shall be great in the **s** of the Lord, 1799
4:18 and recovering of **s** to the blind, 309
7:21 and unto many *that were* blind he gave **s**. 991
10:21 Father: for so it seemed good in thy **s**. 1715
15:21 and in thy **s**, and am no more worthy to 1799
16:15 men is abomination in the **s** of God. 1799
18:41 he said, Lord, that I may receive my **s**. 308
18:42 And Jesus said unto him, **Receive** thy **s**: 308
18:43 And immediately he received his **s**, 308
23:48 the people that came together to that **s**, 2335
24:31 and he **vanished** out of their **s**. 855+1096
Jn 9:11 and I went and washed, and I received **s**. 308
9:15 asked him how he had received his **s**. 308
9:18 he had been blind, and received his **s**, 308
9:18 parents of him that had received his **s**. 308
Ac 1: 9 and a cloud received him out of their **s**. 3788
4:19 Whether it be right in the **s** of God to 1799
7:10 wisdom in the **s** of Pharaoh king of Egypt; 1726
7:31 When Moses saw *it*, he wondered at the **s**: 3705

S

Ac 8:21 for thy heart is not right **in the s** of God. 1799
9: 9 And he was three days without **s**, 991
9:12 hand on him, that he might **receive** his **s**. 308
9:17 that thou mightest **receive** thy **s**, 308
9:18 and he **received s** forthwith, and arose, 308
10:31 alms are had in remembrance **in the s** 1799
22:13 said unto me, Brother Saul, **receive** thy **s**. 308
Ro 3:20 there shall no flesh be justified **in his s**: 1799
12:17 Provide *things* honest **in the s** of all men. 1799
2Co 2:17 **in the s** of God speak we in Christ. 2714
4: 2 every man's conscience **in the s** of God. 1799
5: 7 (For we walk by faith, not by **s**:) 1491
7:12 our care for **you in the s** of God might 1799
8:21 *things*, not only **in the s** of the Lord, 1799
8:21 of the Lord, but also **in the s** of men. 1799
Gal 3:11 is justified by the law **in the s** of God, 3844
Col 1:22 unblameable and unreproveable in his **s**: 2714
1Th 3: 9 **in the s** of God and our Father; 1715
1Ti 2: 3 acceptable **in the s** of God our Saviour; 1799
6:13 I give thee charge **in the s** of God, 1799
Heb 4:13 any creature **s** is not manifest in his **s**: 1799
12:21 And so terrible was the **s**, *that* Moses said, 5324
13:21 in you *that which is* well pleasing in his **s**, 1799
Jas 4:10 Humble yourselves **in the s** of the Lord, 1799
1Pe 3: 4 which is **in the s** of God of great price. 1799
1Jn 3:22 do those *things* that are pleasing in his **s**. 1799
Rev 4: 3 the throne, **in s** like unto an emerald. 3706
13:13 from heaven on the earth **in the s** of men, 1799
13:14 he had power to do **in the s** of the beast. 1799

SIGHTS (1) [SEE]

Lk 21:11 and **fearful s** and great signs shall there be 5400

SIGN (76) [SIGNED, SIGNS]

Ex 4: 8 neither hearken to the voice of the first **s**, 226
4: 8 they will believe the voice of the latter **s**. 226
8:23 and thy people: to morrow shall this **s** be. 226
13: 9 shall be for a **s** unto thee upon thine hand, 226
31:13 it *is* a **s** between me and you throughout 226
31:17 It *is* a **s** between me and the children of 226
Nu 16:38 they shall be a **s** unto the children of Israel. 226
26:10 and fifty men: and they became a **s**. 5251
Dt 6: 8 shalt bind them for a **s** upon thine hand, 226
11:18 and bind them for a **s** upon your hand, 226
13: 1 of dreams, and giveth thee a **s** or a wonder, 226
13: 2 the **s** or the wonder come to pass, whereof 226
28:46 they shall be upon thee for a **s** and for a 226
Jos 4: 6 That this may be a **s** among you, *that* 226
Jdg 6:17 shew me a **s** that thou talkest with me. 226
20:38 Now there was an **appointed s** between 4150
1Sa 2:34 this *shall be* a **s** unto thee, that shall come 226
14:10 our hand: and this *shall be* a **s** unto us. 226
1Ki 13: 3 he gave a **s** the same day, saying, This *is* 4159
13: 3 This *is* the **s** which the LORD hath 4159
13: 5 according to the **s** which the man of God 4159
2Ki 19:29 this *shall be* a **s** unto thee, Ye shall eat *this* 226
20: 8 What *shall be* the **s** that the LORD will heal 226
20: 9 This **s** shalt thou have of the LORD, 226
2Ch 32:24 he spake unto him, and he gave him a **s**. 4159
Isa 7:11 Ask thee a **s** of the LORD thy God; ask it 226
7:14 the Lord himself shall give you a **s**; 226
19:20 it shall be for a **s** and for a witness unto 226
20: 3 barefoot three years *for* a **s** and wonder 226
37:30 this *shall be* a **s** unto thee, Ye shall eat *this* 226
38: 7 this *shall be* a **s** unto thee from the LORD, 226
38:22 What *is* the **s** that I shall go up *to* the 226
55:13 an everlasting **s** *that* shall not be cut off. 226
66:19 I will set a **s** among them, and I will send 226
Jer 6: 1 and set up a **s** of **fire** in Beth-haccerem: 4864
44:29 this *shall be* a **s** unto you, saith the LORD, 226
Eze 4: 3 This *shall be* a **s** to the house of Israel. 226
12: 6 for I have set thee *for* a **s** unto the house 4159
12:11 Say, I *am* your **s**: like as I have done, 4159
14: 8 will make him a **s** and a proverb, and I 226
20:12 sabbaths, to be a **s** between them and them, 226
20:20 they shall be a **s** between me and you, that 226
24:24 Thus Ezekiel is unto you a **s**: according to 4159
24:27 thou shalt be a **s** unto them; and they 4159
39:15 man's bone, then shall he set up a **s** by it, 6725
Da 6: 8 establish the decree, and **s** the writing, 7560
Mt 12:38 Master, we would see a **s** from thee. 4592
12:39 adulterous generation seeketh after a **s**; 4592
12:39 and there shall no **s** be given to it, 4592
12:39 given to it, but the **s** of the prophet Jonas: 4592
16: 1 *he* would shew them a **s** from heaven. 4592
16: 4 adulterous generation seeketh after a **s**; 4592
16: 4 and there shall no **s** be given unto it, 4592
16: 4 unto it, but the **s** of the prophet Jonas. 4592
24: 3 and what *shall be* the **s** of thy coming, 4592
24:30 shall appear the **s** of the Son of man in 4592
26:48 Now he that betrayed him gave them a **s**, 4592
Mk 8:11 seeking of him a **s** from heaven, 4592
8:12 Why doth this generation seek after a **s**? 4592
8:12 There shall no **s** be given unto this 4592
13: 4 what *shall be* the **s** when all these *things* 4592
Lk 2:12 this *shall be* a **s** unto you; Ye shall find 4592
2:34 and for a **s** which shall be spoken against; 4592
11:16 tempting *him*, sought of him a **s** from 4592
11:29 they seek a **s**; and there shall no sign be 4592
11:29 there shall no **s** be given it, but the sign 4592
11:29 given it, but the **s** of Jonas the prophet. 4592
11:30 For as Jonas was a **s** unto the Ninevites, 4592
21: 7 what **s** *will there be* when these *things* 4592
Jn 2:18 unto him, What **s** shewest thou unto us, 4592
6:30 unto him, What **s** shewest thou then, 4592

Ac 28:11 the isle, *whose* **s** was Castor and Pollux. 3902
Ro 4:11 And he received the **s** of circumcision, 4592
1Co 1:22 For the Jews require a **s**, and the Greeks 4592
14:22 Wherefore tongues are for a **s**, not to 4592
Rev 15: 1 And I saw another **s** in heaven, great and 4592

SIGNED (4) [SIGN]

Da 6: 9 Wherefore king Darius **s** the writing and 7560
6:10 Daniel knew that the writing was **s**, 7560
6:12 Hast thou not **s** a decree, that every man 7560
6:13 nor the decree that thou hast **s**, 7560

SIGNET (11) [SIGNETS]

Ge 38:18 Thy **s**, and thy bracelets, and thy staff 2368
38:25 *are* these, the **s**, and bracelets, and staff. 2858
Ex 28:11 in stone, *like* the engravings of a **s**, 2368
28:21 their names, *like* the engravings of a **s**; 2368
28:36 grave upon it, *like* the engravings of a **s**, 2368
39:14 *like* the engravings of a **s**, every one with 2368
39:30 it a writing, *like* to the engravings of a **s**, 2368
Jer 22:24 of Judah were the **s** upon my right hand, 2368
Da 6:17 the king sealed it with his own **s**, 5824
6:17 own signet, and with the **s** of his lords; 5824
Hag 2:23 the LORD, and will make thee as a **s**: 2368

SIGNETS (1) [SIGNET]

Ex 39: 6 graven *as* **s** are graven, with the names of 2368

SIGNIFICATION (1) [SIGNIFY]

1Co 14:10 the world, and none of them *is* **without s**. 880

SIGNIFIED (2) [SIGNIFY]

Ac 11:28 **s** by the Spirit that there should be great 4591
Rev 1: 1 and **s** *it* by his angel unto his servant John: 4591

SIGNIFIETH (1) [SIGNIFY]

Heb 12:27 And this *word*, Yet once *more*, **s** 1213

SIGNIFY (4) [SIGNIFICATION, SIGNIFIED, SIGNIFIETH, SIGNIFYING]

Ac 21:26 to the accomplishment of the days of 1229
23:15 ye with the council **s** to the chief captain 1718
25:27 not withal to **s** the crimes *laid* against him. 4591
1Pe 1:11 Spirit of Christ which was in them did **s**, 1213

SIGNIFYING (4) [SIGNIFY]

Jn 12:33 This he said, **s** what death he should die. 4591
18:32 he spake, **s** what death he should die. 4591
21:19 **s** by what death he should glorify God. 4591
Heb 9: 8 The Holy Ghost this **s**, that the way into 1213

SIGNS (53) [SIGN]

Ge 1:14 let them be for **s**, and for seasons, 226
Ex 4: 9 if they will not believe also these two **s**, 226
4:17 in thine hand, wherewith thou shalt do **s**. 226
4:28 all the **s** which he had commanded him. 226
4:30 and did the **s** in the sight of the people. 226
7: 3 multiply my **s** and my wonders in the land 226
10: 1 that I might shew these my **s** before him: 226
10: 2 my **s** which I have done amongst them; 226
Nu 14:11 for all the **s** which I have shewed among 226
Dt 4:34 by **s**, and by wonders, and by war, and by 226
6:22 the LORD shewed **s** and wonders, great 226
7:19 **s**, and the wonders, and the mighty hand, 226
26: 8 and with **s**, and with wonders: 226
29: 3 have seen, the **s**, and those great miracles: 226
34:11 In all the **s** and the wonders, which 226
Jos 24:17 and which did those great **s** in our sight, 226
1Sa 10: 7 let it be, when these **s** are come unto thee, 226
10: 9 and all those **s** came to pass that day. 226
Ne 9:10 shewedst **s** and wonders upon Pharaoh, 226
Ps 74: 4 they set up their ensigns *for* **s**. 226
74: 9 We see not our **s**: *there is* no more any 226
78:43 How he had wrought his **s** in Egypt, 226
105:27 They shewed his **s** among them, 226
Isa 8:18 whom the LORD hath given me *are* for **s** 226
Jer 10: 2 and be not dismayed at the **s** of heaven; 226
32:20 Which hast set **s** and wonders in the land 226
32:21 Israel out of the land of Egypt with **s**, 226
Da 4: 2 I thought it good to shew the **s** and 852
4: 3 How great *are* his **s**! and how mighty *are* 852
6:27 he worketh **s** and wonders in heaven and 852
Mt 16: 3 but can ye not *discern* the **s** of the times? 4592
24:24 and shall shew great **s** and wonders; 4592
Mk 13:22 and shall shew **s** and wonders, to seduce, 4592
16:17 these **s** shall follow them that believe; 4592
16:20 confirming the word with **s** following. 4592
Lk 1:62 And they **made s** to his father, how he 1770
21:11 and great **s** shall there be from heaven. 4592
21:25 And there shall be **s** in the sun, and in 4592
Jn 4:48 Except ye see **s** and wonders, ye will not 4592
20:30 And many other **s** truly did Jesus in 4592
Ac 2:19 heaven above, and **s** in the earth beneath; 4592
2:22 you by miracles and wonders and **s**, 4592
2:43 and **s** were done by the apostles. 4592
4:30 and that **s** and wonders may be done by 4592
5:12 by the hands of the apostles were many **s** 4592
7:36 wonders and **s** in the land of Egypt, 4592
8:13 the miracles and **s** *which were* done. 4592
14: 3 and granted **s** and wonders to be done by 4592
Ro 15:19 Through mighty **s** and wonders, 4592
2Co 12:12 Truly the **s** of an apostle were wrought 4592
12:12 in **s**, and wonders, and mighty deeds. 4592
2Th 2: 9 with all power and **s** and lying wonders, 4592
Heb 2: 4 both with **s** and wonders, and with divers 4592

SIHON (37)

Nu 21:21 Israel sent messengers unto **S** king of 5511
21:23 would not suffer Israel to pass through 5511
21:23 **S** gathered all his people together, 5511
21:26 For Heshbon *was* the city of **S** the king of 5511
21:27 let the city of **S** be built and prepared: 5511
21:28 of Heshbon, a flame from the city of **S**: 5511
21:29 his daughters into captivity unto **S** king of 5511
21:34 thou shalt do to him as thou didst unto **S** 5511
32:33 the kingdom of **S** king of the Amorites, 5511
Dt 1: 4 After he had slain **S** the king of 5511
2:24 I have given into thy hand **S** the Amorite, 5511
2:26 **S** king of Heshbon *with* words of peace, 5511
2:30 **S** king of Heshbon would not let us pass 5511
2:31 I have begun to give **S** and his land before 5511
2:32 **S** came out against us, he and all his 5511
3: 2 shalt do unto him as thou didst unto **S** 5511
3: 6 as we did unto **S** king of Heshbon, 5511
4:46 in the land of **S** king of the Amorites, 5511
29: 7 **S** the king of Heshbon, and Og the king 5511
31: 4 LORD shall do unto them as he did to **S** 5511
Jos 2:10 **S** and Og, whom ye utterly destroyed. 5511
9:10 to **S** king of Heshbon, and to Og king of 5511
12: 2 **S** king of the Amorites, who dwelt in 5511
12: 5 the border of **S** king of Heshbon. 5511
13:10 all the cities of **S** king of the Amorites, 5511
13:21 all the kingdom of **S** king of the Amorites, 5511
13:21 Hur, and Reba, *which were* dukes of **S**, 5511
13:27 the rest of the kingdom of **S** king of 5511
Jdg 11:19 Israel sent messengers unto **S** king of 5511
11:20 **S** trusted not Israel to pass through his 5511
11:20 **S** gathered all his people together, 5511
11:21 the LORD God of Israel delivered **S** and 5511
1Ki 4:19 in the country of **S** king of the Amorites, 5511
Ne 9:22 so they possessed the land of **S**, 5511
Ps 135:11 **S** king of the Amorites, and Og king of 5511
136:19 **S** king of the Amorites: for his mercy 5511
Jer 48:45 a flame from the midst of **S**, 5511

SIHOR (3)

Jos 13: 3 From **S**, which *is* before Egypt, even unto 7883
Isa 23: 3 by great waters the seed of **S**, the harvest 7883
Jer 2:18 way of Egypt, to drink the waters of **S**? 7883

SILAS (13) [SILVANUS]

Ac 15:22 and **S**, chief *men* among the brethren: 4609
15:27 We have sent therefore Judas and **S**, 4609
15:32 And Judas and **S**, being prophets also 4609
15:34 Notwithstanding it pleased **S** to abide 4609
15:40 And Paul chose **S**, and departed, 4609
16:19 caught Paul and **S**, and drew *them* into 4609
16:25 And at midnight Paul and **S** prayed, 4609
16:29 and fell down before Paul and **S**, 4609
17: 4 and consorted with Paul and **S**; 4609
17:10 sent away Paul and **S** by night unto Berea: 4609
17:14 but **S** and Timotheus abode there still. 4609
17:15 receiving a commandment unto **S** and 4609
18: 5 And when **S** and Timotheus were come 4609

SILENCE (35) [SILENT]

Jdg 3:19 who said, **Keep s**. And all that stood by 2013
Job 4:16 *there was* **s**, and I heard a voice, *saying*, 1827
29:21 and waited, and **kept s** at my counsel. 1826
31:34 I **kept s**, *and* went not out *of* the door? 1826
Ps 31:18 Let the lying lips be **put to s**; which speak 481
32: 3 When I **kept s**, my bones waxed old 2790
35:22 **keep** not **s**: O Lord, be not far from me. 2790
39: 2 I was dumb **with s**, I held my peace, 1747
50: 3 God shall come, and shall not **keep s**: 2790
50:21 *things* hast thou done, and I **kept s**; 2790
83: 1 **Keep** not thou **s**, O God: hold not thy 1824
94:17 my help, my soul had almost dwelt *in* **s**. 1745
115:17 neither any that go down into **s**. 1745
Ecc 3: 7 a time to **keep s**, and a time to speak; 2814
Isa 15: 1 of Moab is laid waste, *and* **brought to s**; 1820
15: 1 of Moab is laid waste, *and* **brought to s**; 1820
41: 1 **Keep s** before me, O islands; and let 2790
62: 6 make mention of the LORD, keep not **s**, 1824
65: 6 I will not keep **s**, but will recompense, 2814
Jer 8:14 for the LORD our God hath **put us to s**, 1826
La 2:10 of Zion sit upon the ground, *and* **keep s**: 1826
3:28 He sitteth alone and **keepeth s**, because 1826
Am 5:13 Therefore the prudent shall **keep s** in that 1826
8: 3 let all the earth **keep s** before him. 2013
Hab 2:20 let all the earth **keep s** before him. 2013
Mt 22:34 heard that he had **put** the Sadducees **to s**, 5392
Ac 15:12 Then all the multitude **kept s**, 4601
21:40 And when there was made a great **s**, 4602
22: 2 tongue to them, they kept the more **s**: 2271
1Co 14:28 interpreter, let him **keep s** in the church; 4601
14:34 Let your women **keep s** in the churches: 4601
1Ti 2:11 Let the woman learn in **s** with all 2271
2:12 authority over the man, but to be in **s**. 2271
1Pe 2:15 that with well doing ye may **put to s** 5392
Rev 8: 1 there was in heaven about the space of 4602

SILENT (9) [SILENCE]

1Sa 2: 9 and the wicked shall be **s** in darkness; 1826
Ps 22: 2 and in the night season, and am not **s**. 1747
28: 1 I cry, O LORD, my rock; be not **s** to me: 2790
28: 1 *if* thou be **s** to me, I become like them 2814
30:12 may sing *praise* to thee, and not be **s**. 1826
31:17 ashamed, *and* let them be **s** in the grave. 1826
Isa 47: 5 Sit thou **s**, and get thee into darkness, 1748
Jer 8:14 the defenced cities, and let us be **s** there: 1826

Zec	2:13 **Be s**, O all flesh, before the LORD: for he	2013

SILK (4)
Pr	31:22 of tapestry; her clothing *is* **s** and purple.	8336
Eze	16:10 fine linen, and I covered thee *with* **s**.	4897
	16:13 *of* fine linen, and, **s**, and broidered work;	4897
Rev	18:12 and **s**, and scarlet, and all thyine wood,	4596

SILLA (1)
2Ki	12:20 house of Millo, which goeth down *to* **S**.	5538

SILLY (3)
Job	5: 2 foolish man, and envy slayeth the **s** one.	6601
Hos	7:11 Ephraim also is like a **s** dove, without	6601
2Ti	3: 6 lead captive **s women** laden with sins,	1133

SILOAH (1) [SILOAM]
Ne	3:15 the wall of the pool of **S** by the king's	7975

SILOAM (3) [SILOAH]
Lk	13: 4 upon whom the tower in **S** fell,	4611
Jn	9: 7 said unto him, Go, wash in the pool of **S**,	4611
	9:11 unto me, Go to the pool of **S**, and wash:	4611

SILVANUS (4) [SILAS]
2Co	1:19 by me and **S** and Timotheus, was not	4610
1Th	1: 1 Paul, and **S**, and Timotheus, unto	4610
2Th	1: 1 Paul, and **S**, and Timotheus, unto	4610
1Pe	5:12 By **S**, a faithful brother unto you, as I	4610

SILVER (320) [SILVERLINGS, SILVERSMITH]
Ge	13: 2 *was* very rich in cattle, in **s**, and in gold.	3701
	20:16 given thy brother a thousand *pieces* of **s**:	3701
	23:15 land *is worth* four hundred shekels of **s**;	3701
	23:16 Abraham weighed to Ephron the **s**,	3701
	23:16 four hundred shekels of **s**, current *money*	3701
	24:35 and gold, and menservants,	3701
	24:53 the servant brought forth jewels of **s**,	3701
	37:28 to the Ishmeelites for twenty *pieces* of **s**:	3701
	44: 2 my cup, the **s** cup, in the sack's mouth	3701
	44: 8 should we steal out of thy lord's house **s**	3701
	45:22 he gave three hundred *pieces* of **s**,	3701
Ex	3:22 jewels of **s**, and jewels of gold.	3701
	11: 2 jewels of **s**, and jewels of gold.	3701
	12:35 borrowed of the Egyptians jewels of **s**,	3701
	20:23 Ye shall not make with me gods of **s**,	3701
	21:32 give unto their master thirty shekels *of* **s**,	3701
	25: 3 shall take of them; gold, and **s**, and brass,	3701
	26:19 thou shalt make forty sockets of **s** under	3701
	26:21 their forty sockets of **s**; two sockets under	3701
	26:25 and their sockets *of* **s**, sixteen sockets;	3701
	26:32 *be* of gold, upon the four sockets of **s**.	3701
	27:10 of the pillars and their fillets *shall be of* **s**.	3701
	27:11 hooks of the pillars and their fillets *of* **s**.	3701
	27:17 about the court *shall be* filleted with **s**;	3701
	27:17 their hooks *shall be of* **s**, and their sockets	3701
	31: 4 to work in gold, and in **s**, and in brass,	3701
	35: 5 of the LORD; gold, and **s**, and brass,	3701
	35:24 Every one that did offer an offering of **s**	3701
	35:32 to work in gold, and in **s**, and in brass,	3701
	36:24 forty sockets of **s** he made under the	3701
	36:26 their forty sockets *of* **s**; two sockets under	3701
	36:30 their sockets *were* sixteen sockets of **s**,	3701
	36:36 and he cast for them four sockets of **s**.	3701
	38:10 of the pillars and their fillets *were of* **s**.	3701
	38:11 hooks of the pillars and their fillets *of* **s**.	3701
	38:12 hooks of the pillars and their fillets *of* **s**;	3701
	38:17 hooks of the pillars and their fillets *of* **s**;	3701
	38:17 the overlaying of their chapiters *of* **s**;	3701
	38:17 pillars of the court *were* filleted with **s**.	3701
	38:19 their hooks *of* **s**, and the overlaying of	3701
	38:19 of their chapiters and their fillets *of* **s**.	3701
	38:25 the **s** of them that were numbered of	3701
	38:27 of the hundred talents of **s** were cast	3701
Lev	5:15 with thy estimation *by* shekels of **s**,	3701
	27: 3 thy estimation shall be fifty shekels of **s**,	3701
	27: 6 shall be of the male five shekels of **s**,	3701
	27: 6 thy estimation *shall be* three shekels of **s**.	3701
	27:16 seed shall be valued at fifty shekels of **s**.	3701
Nu	7:13 his offering *was* one **s** charger, the weight	3701
	7:13 thirty *shekels*, one **s** bowl of seventy	3701
	7:19 He offered *for* his offering one **s** charger,	3701
	7:19 thirty *shekels*, one **s** bowl of seventy	3701
	7:25 His offering *was* one **s** charger, the weight	3701
	7:25 thirty *shekels*, one **s** bowl of seventy	3701
	7:31 His offering *was* one **s** charger of	3701
	7:31 thirty *shekels*, one **s** bowl of seventy	3701
	7:37 His offering *was* one **s** charger, the weight	3701
	7:37 thirty *shekels*, one **s** bowl of seventy	3701
	7:43 His offering *was* one **s** charger of	3701
	7:43 thirty *shekels*, a **s** bowl of seventy	3701
	7:49 His offering *was* one **s** charger, the weight	3701
	7:49 thirty *shekels*, one **s** bowl of seventy	3701
	7:55 His offering *was* one **s** charger of	3701
	7:55 thirty *shekels*, one **s** bowl of seventy	3701
	7:61 His offering *was* one **s** charger, the weight	3701
	7:61 thirty *shekels*, one **s** bowl of seventy	3701
	7:67 His offering *was* one **s** charger, the weight	3701
	7:67 thirty *shekels*, one **s** bowl of seventy	3701
	7:73 His offering *was* one **s** charger, the weight	3701
	7:73 thirty *shekels*, one **s** bowl of seventy	3701
	7:79 His offering *was* one **s** charger, the weight	3701
	7:79 thirty *shekels*, one **s** bowl of seventy	3701
	7:84 twelve chargers of **s**, twelve silver bowls,	3701
	7:84 twelve **s** bowls, twelve spoons of gold:	3701

Nu	7:85 Each charger of **s** weighing an hundred	3701
	7:85 all the **s** vessels *weighed* two thousand	3701
	10: 2 Make thee two trumpets of **s**; of a whole	3701
	22:18 If Balak would give me his house full of **s**	3701
	24:13 If Balak would give me his house full *of* **s**	3701
	31:22 the **s**, the brass, the iron, the tin,	3701
Dt	7:25 thou shalt not desire the **s** or gold *that is*	3701
	8:13 thy **s** and thy gold is multiplied, and all	3701
	17:17 shall he greatly multiply to himself **s**	3701
	22:19 amerce him in an hundred *shekels* of **s**,	3701
	22:29 unto the damsel's father fifty *shekels* of **s**,	3701
	29:17 their idols, wood and stone, **s** and gold,	3701
Jos	6:19 all the **s**, and gold, and vessels of brass	3701
	6:24 only the **s**, and the gold, and the vessels	3701
	7:21 two hundred shekels *of* **s**, and a wedge of	3701
	7:21 the midst of my tent, and the **s** under it.	3701
	7:22 *it was* hid in his tent, and the **s** under it.	3701
	7:24 the **s**, and the garment, and the wedge of	3701
	22: 8 with **s**, and with gold, and with brass,	3701
	24:32 of Shechem for an hundred **pieces** of **s**:	7192
Jdg	9: 4 ten *pieces* of **s** out of the house of	3701
	16: 5 one *of us* eleven hundred *pieces* of **s**.	3701
	17: 2 The eleven hundred *shekels* of **s**,	3701
	17: 2 in mine ears, behold, the **s** *is* with me;	3701
	17: 3 hundred *shekels* of **s** to his mother,	3701
	17: 3 I had wholly dedicated the **s** unto	3701
	17: 4 mother took two hundred *shekels* of **s**,	3701
	17:10 will give thee ten *shekels* of **s** by the year,	3701
1Sa	2:36 crouch to him for a piece of **s** and a	3701
	9: 8 at hand the fourth part of a shekel of **s**:	3701
2Sa	8:10 *Joram* brought with him vessels of **s**,	3701
	8:11 with the **s** and gold that he had dedicated	3701
	18:11 I would have given thee ten *shekels* of **s**,	3701
	18:12 a thousand *shekels* of **s** in mine hand,	3701
	21: 4 We will have no **s** nor gold of Saul, nor of	3701
	24:24 and the oxen for fifty *shekels* of **s**.	3701
1Ki	7:51 *even* the **s**, and the gold, and the vessels,	3701
	10:21 none *were of* **s**: it was nothing accounted	3701
	10:22 and **s**, ivory, and apes, and peacocks.	3701
	10:25 vessels of **s**, and vessels of gold,	3701
	10:27 the king made **s** *to be* in Jerusalem as	3701
	10:29 out of Egypt for six hundred *shekels* of **s**,	3701
	15:15 of the LORD, **s**, and gold, and vessels.	3701
	15:18 Asa took all the **s** and the gold that were	3701
	15:19 I have sent unto thee a present of **s** and	3701
	16:24 Samaria of Shemer for two talents of **s**,	3701
	20: 3 Thy **s** and thy gold *is* mine; thy wives also	3701
	20: 5 Thou shalt deliver me thy **s**, and thy gold,	3701
	20: 7 children, and for my **s**, and for my gold;	3701
	20:39 his life, or else thou shalt pay a talent of **s**.	3701
2Ki	5: 5 took with him ten talents of **s**,	3701
	5:22 talent of **s**, and two changes of garments.	3701
	5:23 and bound two talents of **s** in two bags,	3701
	6:25 head was *sold* for fourscore *pieces* of **s**,	3701
	6:25 a kab of dove's dung for five *pieces* of **s**.	3701
	7: 8 carried thence **s**, and gold, and raiment,	3701
	12:13 *for* the house of the LORD bowls of **s**,	3701
	12:13 any vessels of gold, or vessels of **s**,	3701
	14:14 He took all the gold and **s**, and all	3701
	15:19 gave Pul a thousand talents of **s**, to give to	3701
	15:20 of each man fifty *shekels* of **s**, to give	3701
	16: 8 Ahaz took the **s** and gold that was found	3701
	18:14 king of Judah three hundred talents of **s**	3701
	18:15 Hezekiah gave *him* all the **s** that was	3701
	20:13 the **s**, and the gold, and the spices,	3701
	22: 4 he may sum the **s** which is brought *into*	3701
	23:33 to a tribute of an hundred talents of **s**,	3701
	23:35 Jehoiakim gave the **s** and the gold to	3701
	23:35 exacted the **s** and the gold of the people	3701
	25:15 were *of* gold, *in* gold, and *of* **s**, *in* silver,	3701
	25:15 were *of* gold, *in* gold, and *of* silver, in **s**,	3701
1Ch	18:10 manner *of* vessels of gold and **s** and brass.	3701
	18:11 with the **s** and the gold that he brought	3701
	19: 6 thousand talents of **s** to hire them chariots	3701
	22:14 and a thousand thousand talents *of* **s**;	3701
	22:16 gold, the **s**, and the brass, and the iron,	3701
	28:14 **s** also for all instruments of silver by	NIH
	28:14 silver *also* for all instruments of **s** by	3701
	28:15 for the candlesticks of **s** by weight, *both*	3701
	28:16 and *likewise* **s** for the tables of silver:	3701
	28:16 and *likewise* silver for the tables of **s**.	3701
	28:17 *likewise* **s** by weight for every bason of	NIH
	28:17 *silver* by weight for every bason of **s**:	3701
	29: 2 the **s** for *things of* silver, and the brass for	3701
	29: 2 the silver for *things of* **s**, and the brass for	3701
	29: 3 of mine own proper good, *of* gold and **s**,	3701
	29: 4 and seven thousand talents of refined **s**,	3701
	29: 5 the **s** for *things of* silver, and for all	3701
	29: 5 the silver for *things of* **s**, and for all	3701
	29: 7 *of* **s** ten thousand talents, and *of* brass	3701
2Ch	1:15 the king made **s** and gold at Jerusalem *as*	3701
	1:17 a chariot for six hundred *shekels* of **s**,	3701
	2: 7 **s**, and in brass, and in iron, and in purple,	3701
	2:14 in **s**, in brass, in iron, in stone,	3701
	5: 1 the **s**, and the gold, and all the instruments,	3701
	9:14 country brought gold and **s** to Solomon.	3701
	9:20 none *were of* **s**: it was *not* any thing	3701
	9:21 and **s**, ivory, and apes, and peacocks.	3701
	9:24 vessels of **s**, and vessels of gold,	3701
	9:27 the king made **s** in Jerusalem as stones,	3701
	15:18 had dedicated, **s**, and gold, and vessels.	3701
	16: 2 Asa brought out **s** and gold out of	3701
	16: 3 behold, I have sent thee **s** and gold;	3701
	17:11 Jehoshaphat presents, and tribute **s**;	3701
	21: 3 their father gave them great gifts of **s**,	3701

2Ch	24:14 and spoons, and vessels of gold and **s**.	3701
	25: 6 out of Israel for an hundred talents of **s**.	3701
	25:24 he took all the gold and the **s**, and all	3701
	27: 5 the same year an hundred talents of **s**,	3701
	32:27 he made himself treasuries for **s**,	3701
	36: 3 the land in an hundred talents of **s**	3701
Ezr	1: 4 let the men of his place help him with **s**,	3701
	1: 6 their hands with vessels of **s**,	3701
	1: 9 s thousand chargers of **s**, nine and	3701
	1:10 **s** basons of a second sort four hundred	3701
	1:11 of **s** *were* five thousand and four hundred.	3701
	2:69 five thousand pound *of* **s**, and one	3701
	5:14 also of gold and **s** of the house of God,	3702
	6: 5 and **s** vessels of the house of God,	3702
	7:15 to carry the **s** and gold, which the king	3702
	7:16 all the **s** and gold that thou canst find in	3702
	7:18 to do with the rest of the **s** and gold,	3702
	7:22 Unto an hundred talents of **s**, and to an	3702
	8:25 weighed unto them the **s**, and the gold,	3701
	8:26 hand six hundred and fifty talents *of* **s**,	3701
	8:26 **s** vessels an hundred talents, *and of* gold	3701
	8:28 the **s** and the gold *are* a freewill offering	3701
	8:30 and the Levites the weight of the **s**,	3701
	8:33 Now on the fourth day was the **s** and	3701
Ne	5:15 and wine, beside forty shekels of **s**,	3701
	7:71 thousand and two hundred pound *of* **s**.	3701
	7:72 two thousand pound *of* **s**, and threescore	3701
Est	1: 6 purple to **s** rings and pillars of marble:	3701
	1: 6 the beds *were of* gold and **s**, upon a	3701
	3: 9 I will pay ten thousand talents of **s** to	3701
	3:11 The **s** *is* given to thee, the people also,	3701
Job	3:15 had gold, who filled their houses *with* **s**:	3701
	22:25 and thou shalt have plenty of **s**.	3701
	27:16 Though he heap up **s** as the dust,	3701
	27:17 *it* on, and the innocent shall divide the **s**.	3701
	28: 1 Surely there is a vein for the **s**, and a	3701
	28:15 neither shall **s** be weighed *for* the price	3701
Ps	12: 6 *as* **s** tried in a furnace of earth,	3701
	66:10 proved us: thou hast tried us, as **s** is tried.	3701
	68:13 *be as* the wings of a dove covered with **s**,	3701
	68:30 *every one* submit himself with pieces of **s**:	3701
	105:37 brought them forth also with **s** and gold:	3701
	115: 4 Their idols *are* **s** and gold, the work of	3701
	119:72 unto me than thousands of gold and **s**.	3701
	135:15 The idols of the heathen *are* **s** and gold,	3701
Pr	2: 4 If thou seekest her as **s**, and searchest for	3701
	3:14 of it *is* better than the merchandise of **s**,	3701
	8:10 Receive my instruction, and not **s**;	3701
	8:19 fine gold; and my revenue than choice **s**.	3701
	10:20 The tongue of the just *is as* choice **s**:	3701
	16:16 understanding rather to be chosen than **s**!	3701
	17: 3 The fining pot *is* for **s**, and the furnace for	3701
	22: 1 *and* loving favour rather than **s** and gold.	3701
	25: 4 Take away the dross from the **s**,	3701
	25:11 *is like* apples of gold in pictures of **s**.	3701
	26:23 *are like* a potsherd covered with **s** dross.	3701
	27:21 *As* the fining pot for **s**, and the furnace for	3701
Ecc	2: 8 I gathered me also **s** and gold,	3701
	5:10 He that loveth **s** shall not be satisfied *with*	3701
	5:10 loveth silver shall not be satisfied *with* **s**;	3701
	12: 6 ever the **s** cord be loosed, or the golden	3701
SS	1:11 make thee borders of gold with studs of **s**.	3701
	3:10 made the pillars thereof *of* **s**, the bottom	3701
	8: 9 wall, we will build upon her a palace of **s**:	3701
	8:11 was to bring a thousand *pieces* of **s**.	3701
Isa	1:22 Thy **s** is become dross, thy wine mixt	3701
	2: 7 Their land also is full *of* **s** and gold,	3701
	2:20 In that day a man shall cast his idols of **s**,	3701
	13:17 against them, which shall not regard **s**;	3701
	30:22 the covering of thy graven images of **s**,	3701
	31: 7 every man shall cast away his idols of **s**,	3701
	39: 2 the **s**, and the gold, and the spices,	3701
	40:19 it over with gold, and casteth **s** chains.	3701
	46: 6 weigh **s** in the balance, *and* hire a	3701
	48:10 I have refined thee, but not with **s**;	3701
	60: 9 from far, their **s** and their gold with them,	3701
	60:17 for iron I will bring **s**, and for wood brass,	3701
Jer	6:30 Reprobate **s** shall *men* call them, because	3701
	10: 4 They deck it with **s** and with gold;	3701
	10: 9 **S** spread into plates is brought from	3701
	32: 9 the money, *even* seventeen shekels of **s**.	3701
	52:19 *in* gold, and *that* which *was of* **s**, *in* silver,	3701
	52:19 *in* gold, and *that* which *was of* silver *in* **s**,	3701
Eze	7:19 They shall cast their **s** in the streets,	3701
	7:19 their **s** and their gold shall not be able to	3701
	16:13 Thus wast thou decked *with* gold and **s**;	3701
	16:17 thy fair jewels of my gold and of my **s**,	3701
	22:18 the furnace; they are *even* the dross of **s**.	3701
	22:20 *As they* gather **s**, and brass, and iron,	3701
	22:22 As **s** is melted in the midst of the furnace,	3701
	27:12 with **s**, iron, tin, and lead, they traded in	3701
	28: 4 hast gotten gold and **s** into thy treasures:	3701
	38:13 to carry away **s** and gold, to take *away*	3701
Da	2:32 his breast and his arms of **s**, his belly and	3702
	2:35 the clay, the brass, the **s**, and the gold;	3702
	2:45 the brass, the clay, the **s**, and the gold;	3702
	5: 2 vessels which his father Nebuchadnezzar	3702
	5: 4 of **s**, of brass, of iron, of wood,	3702
	5:23 thou hast praised the gods of **s**, and gold,	3702
	11: 8 *and* with their precious vessels *of* **s** and	3701
	11:38 **s**, and with precious stones, and pleasant	3701
	11:43 power over the treasures of gold and *of* **s**,	3701
Hos	2: 8 and oil, and multiplied her **s** and gold,	3701
	3: 2 I bought her to me for fifteen *pieces* of **s**,	3701
	8: 4 *of* their **s** and their gold have they made	3701

Hos	9: 6 the pleasant *places* for their **s**, nettles	3701	
	13: 2 made them molten images of their **s**,	3701	
Joel	3: 5 Because ye have taken my **s** and my gold,	3701	
Am	2: 6 because they sold the righteous for **s**,	3701	
	8: 6 That *we* may buy the poor for **s**,	3701	
Na	2: 9 Take ye the spoil of **s**, take the spoil of	3701	
Hab	2:19 it *is* laid over *with* gold and **s**, and *there*	3701	
Zep	1:11 cut down; all they that bear **s** are cut off.	3701	
	1:18 Neither their **s** nor their gold shall be able	3701	
Hag	2: 8 The **s** *is* mine, and the gold *is* mine,	3701	
Zec	6:11 take **s** and gold, and make crowns,	3701	
	9: 3 heaped up **s** as the dust, and fine gold as	3701	
	11:12 weighed *for* my price thirty *pieces* of **s**.	3701	
	11:13 I took the thirty *pieces* of **s**, and cast	3701	
	13: 9 will refine them as **s** is refined, and will	3701	
	14:14 gold, and **s**, and apparel, in great	3701	
Mal	3: 3 he shall sit *as* a refiner and purifier of **s**:	3701	
	3: 3 of Levi, and purge them as gold and **s**,	3701	
Mt	10: 9 Provide neither gold, nor **s**, nor brass in	696	
	26:15 covenanted with him for thirty pieces of **s**.	694	
	27: 3 brought again the thirty pieces of **s** to	694	
	27: 5 And he cast down the pieces of **s** in	694	
	27: 6 And the chief priests took the **s** pieces,	694	
	27: 9 And they took the thirty pieces of **s**,	694	
Lk	15: 8 what woman having ten pieces of **s**,	1406	
Ac	3: 6 Then Peter said, **S** and gold have I none;	694	
	17:29 or **s**, or stone, graven by art and	696	
	19:19 and found *it* fifty thousand *pieces* of **s**.	694	
	19:24 which made **s** shrines for Diana,	693	
	20:33 I have coveted no *man's* **s**, or gold,	694	
1Co	3:12 **s**, precious stones, wood, hay, stubble;	696	
2Ti	2:20 there are not only vessels of gold and **of s**,	693	
Jas	5: 3 Your gold and **s** is cankered; and the rust	696	
1Pe	1:18 not redeemed with corruptible *things*, *as* **s**,	694	
Rev	9:20 idols of gold, and **s**, and brass, and stone,	693	
	18:12 and **s**, and precious stones, and of pearls,	696	

SILVERLINGS (1) [SILVER]

Isa	7:23 were a thousand vines at a thousand **s**,	3701	

SILVERSMITH (1) [SILVER, SMITH]

Ac	19:24 For a certain *man* named Demetrius, a **s**,	695	

SIMEON (50) [SIMEONITES]

Ge	29:33 this *son* also: and she called his name **S**.	8095	
	34:25 **S** and Levi, Dinah's brethren, took each	8095	
	34:30 Jacob said to **S** and Levi, Ye have troubled	8095	
	35:23 **S**, and Levi, and Judah, and Issachar,	8095	
	42:24 took from them **S**, and bound him before	8095	
	42:36 **S** is not, and ye will take Benjamin *away*:	8095	
	43:23 And he brought **S** out unto them.	8095	
	46:10 the sons of **S**; Jemuel, and Jamin,	8095	
	48: 5 as Reuben and **S**, they shall be mine.	8095	
	49: 5 **S** and Levi *are* brethren; instruments of	8095	
Ex	1: 2 Reuben, **S**, Levi, and Judah,	8095	
	6:15 the sons of **S**; Jemuel, and Jamin,	8095	
	6:15 these *are* the families of **S**.	8095	
Nu	1: 6 Of **S**; Shelumiel the son of Zurishaddai.	8095	
	1:22 Of the children of **S**, *by* their generations,	8095	
	1:23 *even* of the tribe of **S**, *were* fifty and	8095	
	2:12 pitch by him *shall be* the tribe of **S**:	8095	
	2:12 the captain of the children of **S** *shall be*	8095	
	7:36 prince of the children of **S**, *did offer*:	8095	
	10:19 *was* Shelumiel the son of Zurishaddai.	8095	
	13: 5 Of the tribe of **S**, Shaphat the son of Hori.	8095	
	26:12 The sons of **S** after their families:	8095	
	34:20 of the tribe of the children of **S**,	8095	
Dt	27:12 **S**, and Levi, and Judah, and Issachar,	8095	
Jos	19: 1 the second lot came forth to **S**, *even* for	8095	
	19: 1 *even* for the tribe of the children of **S**	8095	
	19: 8 children of **S** according to their families.	8095	
	19: 9 *was* the inheritance of the children of **S**:	8095	
	19: 9 the children of **S** had their inheritance	8095	
	21: 4 out of the tribe of **S**, and out of the tribe	8099	
	21: 9 out of the tribe of the children of **S**, these	8095	
Jdg	1: 3 Judah said unto **S** his brother, Come up	8095	
	1: 3 thee into thy lot. So **S** went with him.	8095	
	1:17 Judah went with **S** his brother,	8095	
1Ch	2: 1 Reuben, **S**, Levi, and Judah, Issachar,	8095	
	4:24 The sons of **S** *were*, Nemuel, and Jamin,	8095	
	4:42 *even* of the sons of **S**, five hundred men,	8095	
	6:65 and out of the tribe of the children of **S**,	8095	
	12:25 the children of **S**, mighty *men* of valour	8095	
2Ch	15: 9 of Ephraim and Manasseh, and out of **S**:	8095	
	34: 6 and Ephraim, and **S**, even unto Naphtali,	8095	
Eze	48:24 unto the west side, **S** *shall have a portion*.	8095	
	48:25 by the border of **S**, from the east side unto	8095	
	48:33 one gate of **S**, one gate of Issachar, one	8095	
Lk	2:25 a man in Jerusalem, whose name *was* **S**;	4826	
	2:34 And **S** blessed them, and said unto Mary	4826	
	3:30 was *the son* of **S**, which was *the son*	4826	
Ac	13: 1 that was called Niger, and Lucius of	4826	
	15:14 **S** hath declared how God at the first did	4826	
Rev	7: 7 Of the tribe of **S** *were* sealed twelve	4826	

SIMEONITES (3) [SIMEON]

Nu	25:14 a prince of a chief house among the **S**,	8099	
	26:14 These *are* the families of the **S**, twenty	8099	
1Ch	27:16 of the **S**, Shephatiah the son of Maachah:	8099	

SIMILITUDE (11) [SIMILITUDES]

Nu	12: 8 and the **s** of the Lord shall he behold:	8544	
Dt	4:12 the voice of the words, but saw no **s**;	8544	
	4:15 ye saw no *manner of* **s** on the day *that*	8544	
	4:16 the **s** of any figure, the likeness of male	8544	

2Ch	4: 3 under it *was* the **s** of oxen, which did	1823	
Ps	106:20 they changed their glory into the **s** of	8403	
	144:12 polished *after* the **s** of a palace:	8403	
Da	10:16 one like the **s** of the sons of men touched	1823	
Ro	5:14 sinned after the **s** of Adam's transgression,	3667	
Heb	7:15 for that after the **s** of Melchisedec there	3665	
Jas	3: 9 men, which are made after the **s** of God.	3669	

SIMILITUDES (1) [SIMILITUDE]

Hos	12:10 used **s** by the ministry of the prophets.	1819	

SIMON (69) [PETER, SIMON'S]

Mt	4:18 **S** called Peter, and Andrew his brother,	4613	
	10: 2 The first, **S**, who is called Peter,	4613	
	10: 4 **S** the Canaanite, and Judas Iscariot,	4613	
	13:55 James, and Joses, and Judas?	4613	
	16:16 And **S** Peter answered and said, Thou art	4613	
	16:17 unto him, Blessed art thou, **S** Bar-jona:	4613	
	17:25 saying, What thinkest thou, **S**?	4613	
	26: 6 in Bethany, in the house of **S** the leper,	4613	
	27:32 they found a man of Cyrene, **S** by name:	4613	
Mk	1:16 he saw **S** and Andrew his brother casting	4613	
	1:29 they entered into the house of **S** and	4613	
	1:36 And **S** and they that were with him	4613	
	3:16 And he surnamed Peter;	4613	
	3:18 and Thaddeus, and **S** the Canaanite,	4613	
	6: 3 of James, and Joses, and of Juda, and **S**?	4613	
	14:37 and saith unto Peter, **S**, sleepest thou?	4613	
	15:21 And they compel one **S** a Cyrenian,	4613	
Lk	5: 4 he said unto **S**, Launch out into the deep,	4613	
	5: 5 And **S** answering said unto him, Master,	4613	
	5: 8 **S** Peter saw *it*, he fell down at Jesus'	4613	
	5:10 of Zebedee, which were partners with **S**.	4613	
	5:10 And Jesus said unto **S**, Fear not;	4613	
	6:14 **S**, (whom he also named Peter,) and	4613	
	6:15 the *son* of Alpheus, and **S** called Zelotes,	4613	
	7:40 **S**, I have somewhat to say unto thee.	4613	
	7:43 answered and said, I suppose that *he*, to	4613	
	7:44 and said unto **S**, Seest thou this woman?	4613	
	22:31 The Lord said, **S**, Simon, behold, Satan	4613	
	22:31 The Lord said, **S**, Simon, behold, Satan	4613	
	23:26 they laid hold upon one **S**, a Cyrenian,	4613	
	24:34 is risen indeed, and hath appeared to **S**.	4613	
Jn	1:40 was Andrew, **S** Peter's brother.	4613	
	1:41 He first findeth his own brother **S**,	4613	
	1:42 he said, Thou art **S** the son of Jona:	4613	
	6: 8 Andrew, **S** Peter's brother, saith unto	4613	
	6:68 **S** Peter answered him, Lord, to whom	4613	
	6:71 He spake of Judas Iscariot *the son* of **S**:	4613	
	13: 6 cometh he to **S** Peter: and *Peter* saith	4613	
	13: 9 **S** Peter saith unto him, Lord, not my feet	4613	
	13:24 **S** Peter therefore beckoned to him, that	4613	
	13:26 he gave *it* to Judas Iscariot, *the son* of **S**.	4613	
	13:36 **S** Peter said unto him, Lord, whither goest	4613	
	18:10 Then **S** Peter having a sword drew it,	4613	
	18:15 And **S** Peter followed Jesus, and *so*	4613	
	18:25 And **S** Peter stood and warmed himself.	4613	
	20: 2 and cometh to **S** Peter, and to the other	4613	
	20: 6 Then cometh **S** Peter following him,	4613	
	21: 2 There were together **S** Peter,	4613	
	21: 3 **S** Peter saith unto them, I go a fishing.	4613	
	21:11 **S** Peter went up, and drew the net to land	4613	
	21:15 Jesus saith to **S** Peter, Simon, *son* of Jonas,	4613	
	21:15 Jesus saith to Simon Peter, **S**, *son* of Jonas,	4613	
	21:16 **S**, *son* of Jonas, lovest thou me?	4613	
	21:17 time, **S**, *son* of Jonas, lovest thou me?	4613	
Ac	1:13 & Zelotes, and Judas the *brother* of	4613	
	8: 9 But there was a certain man, called **S**,	4613	
	8:13 **S** himself believed also: and when he	4613	
	8:18 when **S** saw that through laying on of	4613	
	8:24 Then answered **S**, and said, Pray ye to	4613	
	9:43 many days in Joppa with one **S** a tanner.	4613	
	10: 5 call for *one* **S**, whose surname is Peter:	4613	
	10: 6 He lodgeth with one **S** a tanner,	4613	
	10:18 And called, and asked whether **S**,	4613	
	10:32 Send therefore to Joppa, and call hither **S**,	4613	
	10:32 is lodged in the house of *one* **S** a tanner	4613	
	11:13 Send men to Joppa, and call for **S**,	4613	
2Pe	1: 1 **S** Peter, a servant and an apostle of Jesus	4826	

SIMON'S (7) [SIMON]

Mk	1:30 But **S** wife's mother lay sick of a fever,	4613	
Lk	4:38 the synagogue, and entered into **S** house.	4613	
	4:38 **S** wife's mother was taken with a great	4613	
	5: 3 was **S**, and prayed him that *he* would	4613	
Jn	12: 4 **S** *son*, which should betray him,	4613	
	13: 2 of Judas Iscariot, **S** *son*, to betray him;	4613	
Ac	10:17 Cornelius had made inquiry for **S** house,	4613	

SIMPLE (20) [SIMPLICITY]

Ps	19: 7 of the Lord *is* sure, making wise the **s**.	6612	
	116: 6 The Lord preserveth the **s**: I was brought	6612	
	119:130 it giveth understanding unto the **s**.	6612	
Pr	1: 4 give subtilty to the **s**, to the young man	6612	
	1:22 How long, ye **s ones**, will ye love	6612	
	1:32 For the turning away of the **s** shall slay	6612	
	7: 7 beheld among the **s ones**, I discerned	6612	
	8: 5 ye **s**, understand wisdom: and, ye fools,	6612	
	9: 4 Whoso *is* **s**, let him turn in hither: *as for*	6612	
	9:13 *she is* **s**, and knoweth nothing.	6615	
	9:16 Whoso *is* **s**, let him turn in hither:	6612	
	14:15 The **s** believeth every word: but the	6612	
	14:18 The **s** inherit folly: but the prudent are	6612	

Pr	19:25 Smite a scorner, and the **s** will beware:	6612	
	21:11 scorner is punished, the **s** is made wise:	6612	
	22: 3 but the **s** pass on, and are punished.	6612	
	27:12 *but* the **s** pass on, *and* are punished.	6612	
Eze	45:20 one that erreth, and for *him that is* **s**:	6612	
Ro	16:18 fair speeches deceive the hearts of the **s**.	172	
	16:19 *that which is* good, and **s** concerning evil.	185	

SIMPLICITY (5) [SIMPLE]

2Sa	15:11 they went in their **s**, and they knew not	8537	
Pr	1:22 How long, ye simple ones, will ye love **s**?	6612	
Ro	12: 8 he that giveth, *let him do it* with **s**; he that	572	
2Co	1:12 in **s** and godly sincerity, not with fleshly	572	
	11: 3 your minds should be corrupted from the **s**	572	

SIMRI (1)

1Ch	26:10 **S** the chief, (for *though* he was not	8113	

SIN (448) [SINFUL, SINNED, SINNER, SINNERS, SINNEST, SINNETH, SINNING, SINS]

Ge	4: 7 if thou doest not well, **s** lieth at the door.	2403	
	18:20 and because their **s** is very grievous;	2403	
	20: 9 on me and on my kingdom a great **s**?	2401	
	31:36 what *is* my **s**, that thou hast so	2403	
	39: 9 this great wickedness, and **s** against God?	2398	
	42:22 saying, Do not **s** against the child;	2398	
	50:17 the trespass of thy brethren, and their **s**;	2403	
Ex	10:17 my **s** only *this* once, and intreat the Lord	2403	
	16: 1 of Israel came unto the wilderness of **S**,	5512	
	17: 1 Israel journeyed from the wilderness of **S**,	5512	
	20:20 may be before your faces, that ye **s** not.	2398	
	23:33 land, lest they **make s** against me:	2398	
	29:14 fire without the camp: it *is* a **s offering**.	2403	
	29:36 a bullock *for* a **s offering** for atonement:	2403	
	30:10 blood of the **s offering** of atonements:	2403	
	32:21 hast brought *so* great a **s** upon them?	2401	
	32:30 the people, Ye have sinned a great **s**:	2401	
	32:30 I shall make an atonement for your **s**.	2403	
	32:31 this people have sinned a great **s**,	2401	
	32:32 Yet now, if thou wilt forgive their **s**;	2403	
	32:34 I visit, I will visit their **s** upon them.	2403	
	34: 7 forgiving iniquity and transgression and **s**,	2403	
	34: 9 pardon our iniquity and our **s**, and take	2403	
Lev	4: 2 If a soul shall **s** through ignorance against	2398	
	4: 3 If the priest that is anointed do **s**	2398	
	4: 3 do sin according to the **s** of the people;	819	
	4: 3 let him bring for his **s**, which he hath	2403	
	4: 3 blemish unto the Lord for a **s offering**.	2403	
	4: 8 the fat of the bullock *for* the **s offering**;	2403	
	4:13 of Israel **s through ignorance**,	7686	
	4:14 When the **s**, which they have sinned	2403	
	4:14 shall offer a young bullock for the **s**,	2403	
	4:20 he did with the bullock for a **s offering**,	2403	
	4:21 it *is* a **s offering** for the congregation.	2403	
	4:23 of his **s**, wherein he hath sinned, come to	2403	
	4:24 before the Lord: it *is* a **s offering**.	2403	
	4:25 blood of the **s offering** with his finger,	2403	
	4:26 an atonement for him as concerning his **s**,	2403	
	4:27 any one of the common people **s** through	2398	
	4:28 Or if his **s**, which he hath sinned, come to	2403	
	4:28 for his **s** which he hath sinned.	2403	
	4:29 his hand upon the head of the **s offering**,	2403	
	4:29 slay the **s offering** in the place of the	2403	
	4:32 if he bring a lamb for a **s offering**, he shall	2403	
	4:33 his hand upon the head of the **s offering**,	2403	
	4:33 slay it for a **s offering** in the place where	2403	
	4:34 blood of the **s offering** with his finger,	2403	
	4:35 priest shall make an atonement for his **s**	2403	
	5: 1 if a soul **s**, and hear the voice of swearing,	2398	
	5: 6 the Lord for his **s** which he hath sinned,	2403	
	5: 6 or a kid of the goats, for a **s offering**;	2403	
	5: 6 an atonement for him concerning his **s**.	2403	
	5: 7 one for a **s offering**, and the other for a	2403	
	5: 8 offer *that* which *is* for the **s offering** first,	2403	
	5: 9 the **s offering** upon the side of the altar;	2403	
	5: 9 the bottom of the altar: it *is* a **s offering**.	2403	
	5:10 for him for his **s** which he hath sinned,	2403	
	5:11 an ephah of fine flour for a **s offering**;	2403	
	5:11 thereon: for it *is* a **s offering**.	2403	
	5:12 by fire unto the Lord: it *is* a **s offering**.	2403	
	5:13 his **s** that he hath sinned in one of these,	2403	
	5:15 a trespass, and **s** through ignorance,	2398	
	5:17 if a soul **s**, and commit any of *these*	2398	
	6: 2 If a soul **s**, and commit a trespass against	2398	
	6:17 as *is* the **s offering**, and as the trespass	2403	
	6:25 This *is* the law of the **s offering**:	2403	
	6:25 the **s offering** be killed before the Lord:	2398	
	6:26 The priest that **offereth** it **for s** shall eat	2398	
	6:30 no **s offering**, whereof *any* of the blood	2403	
	7: 7 As the **s offering** is, so is the trespass	2403	
	7:37 of the **s offering**, and of the trespass	2403	
	8: 2 bullock *for* the **s offering**, and two rams,	2403	
	8:14 he brought the bullock *for* the **s offering**:	2403	
	8:14 the head of the bullock *for* the **s offering**.	2403	
	9: 2 Take thee a young calf for a **s offering**,	2403	
	9: 3 Take ye a kid of the goats for a **s offering**;	2403	
	9: 7 thy **s offering**, and thy burnt offering,	2403	
	9: 8 altar, and slew the calf of the **s offering**	2403	
	9:10 the caul above the liver of the **s offering**,	2403	
	9:15 which *was* the **s offering** for the people,	2403	
	9:15 slew it, and **offered** it **for s**, as the first.	2398	
	9:22 down from offering of the **s offering**,	2403	
	10:16 sought the goat of the **s offering**,	2403	
	10:17 have ye not eaten the **s offering**	2403	
	10:19 day have they offered their **s offering**	2403	

Lev	10:19	if I had eaten the **s offering** to day, 2403
	12: 6	or a turtledove, for a **s offering**, 2403
	12: 8	and the other for a **s offering**; 2403
	14:13	place where they shall kill the **s offering** 2403
	14:13	for as the **s offering** is the priest's, so is 2403
	14:19	the priest shall offer the **s offering**, 2403
	14:22	one shall be a **s offering**, and the other 2403
	14:31	one for a **s offering**, and the other for a 2403
	15:15	one for a **s offering**, and the other for a 2403
	15:30	priest shall offer the one for a **s offering**, 2403
	16: 3	with a young bullock for a **s offering**, and 2403
	16: 5	two kids of the goats for a **s offering**, 2403
	16: 6	shall offer his bullock of the **s offering**, 2403
	16: 9	lot fell, and offer him for a **s offering**. 2403
	16:11	shall bring the bullock of the **s offering** 2403
	16:11	shall kill the bullock of the **s offering** 2403
	16:15	shall he kill the goat of the **s offering**, 2403
	16:25	fat of the **s offering** shall he burn upon 2403
	16:27	bullock for the **s offering**, and the goat 2403
	16:27	offering, and the goat for the **s offering**, 2403
	19:17	thy neighbour, and not suffer **s** upon him. 2399
	19:22	for his **s** which he hath done: 2403
	19:22	**s** which he hath done shall be forgiven 2403
	20:20	they shall bear their **s**; they shall die 2399
	22: 9	lest they bear **s** for it, and die therefore, 2403
	23:19	one kid of the goats for a **s offering**, 2403
	24:15	curseth his God shall bear his **s**. 2399
Nu	5: 6	woman shall commit any **s** that men 2403
	5: 7	they shall confess their **s** which they have 2403
	6:11	priest shall offer the one for a **s offering**, 2403
	6:14	first year without blemish for a **s offering**, 2403
	6:16	shall offer his **s offering**, and his burnt 2403
	7:16	One kid of the goats for a **s offering**: 2403
	7:22	One kid of the goats for a **s offering**: 2403
	7:28	One kid of the goats for a **s offering**: 2403
	7:34	One kid of the goats for a **s offering**: 2403
	7:40	One kid of the goats for a **s offering**: 2403
	7:46	One kid of the goats for a **s offering**: 2403
	7:52	One kid of the goats for a **s offering**: 2403
	7:58	One kid of the goats for a **s offering**: 2403
	7:64	One kid of the goats for a **s offering**: 2403
	7:70	One kid of the goats for a **s offering**: 2403
	7:76	One kid of the goats for a **s offering**: 2403
	7:82	One kid of the goats for a **s offering**: 2403
	7:87	kids of the goats for **s offering** twelve. 2403
	8: 8	bullock shalt thou take for a **s offering**, 2403
	8:12	thou shalt offer the one for a **s offering**, 2403
	9:13	season, that man shall bear his **s**. 2399
	12:11	I beseech thee, lay not the **s** upon us, 2403
	15:24	and one kid of the goats for a **s offering**. 2403
	15:25	their **s offering** before the LORD, 2403
	15:27	if any soul **s** through ignorance, then 2398
	15:27	she goat of the first year for a **s offering**. 2403
	16:22	shall one man **s**, and wilt thou be wroth 2398
	18: 9	every **s offering** of theirs, and every 2403
	18:22	congregation, lest they bear **s**, and die. 2399
	18:32	ye shall bear no **s** by reason of it, when ye 2399
	19: 9	of separation: it is a **purification for s**. 2403
	19:17	of the burnt heifer of **purification for s**, 2403
	27: 3	but died in his own **s**, and had no sons. 2399
	28:15	one kid of the goats for a **s offering** unto 2403
	28:22	one goat for a **s offering**, to make an 2403
	29: 5	one goat for a **s offering**; 2403
	29:11	One kid of the goats for a **s offering**; 2403
	29:11	beside the **s offering** of atonement, 2403
	29:16	one kid of the goats for a **s offering**, 2403
	29:19	one kid of the goats for a **s offering**, 2403
	29:22	one goat for a **s offering**; beside 2403
	29:25	one kid of the goats for a **s offering**; beside 2403
	29:28	one goat for a **s offering**; beside 2403
	29:31	one goat for a **s offering**; beside 2403
	29:34	one goat for a **s offering**; beside 2403
	29:38	one goat for a **s offering**; beside 2403
	32:23	and be sure your **s** will find you out. 2403
	33:11	and encamped in the wilderness of **S**. 5512
	33:12	their journey out of the wilderness of **S**, 5512
Dt	9:21	took your **s**, the calf which ye had made, 2403
	9:27	nor to their wickedness, nor to their **s**: 2403
	15: 9	LORD against thee, and it be **s** unto thee. 2399
	19:15	or for any **s**, in any sin that he sinneth: 2403
	19:15	or for any sin, in any **s** that he sinneth: 2399
	20:18	should ye **s** against the LORD your God. 2398
	21:22	if a man have **committed a s** worthy of 2399
	22:26	is in the damsel no **s** worthy of death: 2399
	23:21	it of thee; and it would be **s** in thee. 2399
	23:22	forbear to vow, it shall be no **s** in thee. 2399
	24: 4	thou shalt not **cause** the land to **s**, 2398
	24:15	thee unto the LORD, and it be **s** unto thee. 2399
	24:16	man shall be put to death for his own **s**. 2399
1Sa	2:17	Wherefore the **s** of the young men was 2403
	2:25	If one man **s** against another, the judge 2398
	2:25	if a man **s** against the LORD, who shall 2398
	12:23	God forbid that I should **s** against 2398
	14:33	Behold, the people **s** against the LORD, 2398
	14:34	**s** not against the LORD in eating with 2398
	14:38	see wherein this **s** hath been this day. 2403
	15:23	For rebellion is as the **s** of witchcraft, 2403
	15:25	pardon my **s**, and turn again with me, 2403
	19: 4	Let not the king **s** against his servant, 2398
	19: 5	then wilt thou **s** against innocent blood, 2398
	20: 1	what is my **s** before thy father, that he 2403
2Sa	12:13	The LORD also hath put away thy **s**; 2403
1Ki	8:34	forgive the **s** of thy people Israel, 2403
	8:35	confess thy name, and turn from their **s**, 2403
	8:36	forgive the **s** of thy servants, and of thy 2403

1Ki	8:46	If they **s** against thee, (for there is no man 2398
	12:30	this thing became a **s**: for the people went 2403
	13:34	this thing became a **s** unto the house of 2403
	14:16	who did **s**, and who **made** Israel to sin. 2398
	14:16	who did sin, and who **made** Israel to **s**. 2398
	15:26	in his **s** wherewith he **made** Israel to sin. 2398
	15:26	in his sin wherewith he **made** Israel to **s**. 2398
	15:30	he sinned, and which he **made** Israel **s**, 2398
	15:34	in his **s** wherewith he **made** Israel to sin. 2403
	15:34	in his sin wherewith he **made** Israel to **s**. 2398
	16: 2	hast **made** my people Israel to **s**, 2398
	16:13	and by which they **made** Israel to **s**, 2398
	16:19	in his **s** which he did, to **make** Israel sin. 2398
	16:19	in his sin which he did, to **make** Israel **s**. 2398
	16:26	in his **s** wherewith he **made** Israel to sin, 2398
	16:26	in his sin wherewith he **made** Israel to **s**, 2398
	17:18	art thou come unto me to call my **s** to 5771
	21:22	me to anger, and **made** Israel to **s**. 2398
	22:52	the son of Nebat, who **made** Israel to **s**: 2398
2Ki	3: 3	the son of Nebat, which **made** Israel to **s**; 2398
	10:29	who **made** Israel to **s**, Jehu departed not 2398
	10:31	sins of Jeroboam, which **made** Israel to **s**. 2403
	12:16	**s** money was not brought into the house 2403
	13: 2	the son of Nebat, which **made** Israel to **s**; 2398
	13: 6	who **made** Israel **s**, but walked therein: 2398
	13:11	the son of Nebat, who **made** Israel to **s**: 2398
	14: 6	man shall be put to death for his own **s**. 2399
	14:24	the son of Nebat, who **made** Israel to **s**. 2398
	15: 9	the son of Nebat, who **made** Israel to **s**. 2398
	15:18	the son of Nebat, who **made** Israel to **s**. 2398
	15:24	the son of Nebat, who **made** Israel to **s**. 2398
	15:28	the son of Nebat, who **made** Israel to **s**. 2398
	17:21	the LORD, and **made** them **s** a great sin. 2398
	17:21	the LORD, and **made** them sin a great **s**. 2401
	21:11	hath **made** Judah also to **s** with his idols: 2398
	21:16	beside his **s** wherewith he **made** Judah to 2403
	21:16	his sin wherewith he **made** Judah to **s**, 2398
	21:17	all that he did, and his **s** that he sinned, 2403
	23:15	who **made** Israel to **s**, had made, both 2398
2Ch	6:22	If a man **s** against his neighbour, 2398
	6:25	forgive the **s** of thy people Israel, 2403
	6:26	confess thy name, and turn from their **s**, 2403
	6:27	forgive the **s** of thy servants, and of thy 2403
	6:36	If they **s** against thee, (for there is no man 2398
	7:14	forgive their **s**, and will heal their land. 2403
	25: 4	but every man shall die for his own **s**. 2399
	29:21	for a **s offering** for the kingdom, 2403
	29:23	he goats for the **s offering** before the 2403
	29:24	**s offering** should be made for all Israel. 2403
	33:19	all his **s**, and his trespass, and the places 2409
Ezr	6:17	for a **s offering** for all Israel, twelve he 2403
	8:35	twelve he goats for a **s offering**: 2403
Ne	4: 5	let not their **s** be blotted out from before 2403
	6:13	**s**, and that they might have matter for an 2398
	10:33	for the **s offerings** to make an atonement 2403
	13:26	Did not Solomon king of Israel **s** by these 2398
	13:26	him did outlandish women **cause** to **s**. 2398
Job	2:10	In all this did not Job **s** with his lips. 2398
	5:24	shalt visit thy habitation, and shalt not **s**. 2398
	10: 6	mine iniquity, and searchest after my **s**? 2403
	10:14	If I **s**, then thou markest me, and thou 2398
	13:23	me to know my transgression and my **s**. 2403
	14:16	my steps: dost thou not watch over my **s**? 2403
	20:11	His bones are full of the **s** of his youth, NIH
	31:30	(Neither have I suffered my mouth to **s** 2398
	34:37	For he addeth rebellion unto his **s**, 2403
	35: 3	shall I have, if I be cleansed from my **s**? 2403
Ps	4: 4	Stand in awe, and **s** not: commune with 2398
	32: 1	is forgiven, whose **s** is covered. 2401
	32: 5	I acknowledged my **s** unto thee, 2403
	32: 5	and thou forgavest the iniquity of my **s**. 2403
	38: 3	any rest in my bones because of my **s**. 2403
	38:18	mine iniquity; I will be sorry for my **s**. 2403
	39: 1	to my ways, that I **s** not with my tongue: 2398
	40: 6	and a **s offering** hast thou not required. 2401
	51: 2	mine iniquity, and cleanse me from my **s**. 2403
	51: 3	and my **s** is ever before me. 2403
	51: 5	and in **s** did my mother conceive me. 2399
	59: 3	my transgression, nor for my **s**, O LORD. 2403
	59:12	For the **s** of their mouth and the words of 2403
	85: 2	thy people, thou hast covered all their **s**. 2403
	109: 7	condemned: and let his prayer become **s**. 2401
	109:14	let not the **s** of his mother be blotted out. 2403
	119:11	heart, that I might not **s** against thee. 2398
Pr	10:16	tendeth to life: the fruit of the wicked to **s**. 2403
	10:19	multitude of words there wanteth not **s**: 6588
	14: 9	Fools make a mock at **s**: but among 817
	14:34	nation: but **s** is a reproach to any people. 2403
	20: 9	my heart clean, I am pure from my **s**? 2403
	21: 4	and the plowing of the wicked, is **s**. 2403
	24: 9	The thought of foolishness is **s**: 2403
Ecc	5: 6	not thy mouth to **cause** thy flesh to **s**; 2398
Isa	3: 9	they declare their **s** as Sodom, they hide 2403
	5:18	vanity, and **s** as it were with a cart rope: 2403
	6: 7	iniquity is taken away, and thy **s** purged. 2403
	27: 9	and this is all the fruit to take away his **s**; 2403
	30: 1	of my Spirit, that they may add **s** to sin: 2403
	30: 1	of my Spirit, that they may add sin to **s**. 2403
	31: 7	own hands have made unto you for a **s**. 2399
	53:10	shalt make his soul an **offering for s**, 817
	53:12	he bare the **s** of many, 2399
Jer	16:10	that we have **committed** against 2398+2403
	16:18	their iniquity and their **s** double; 2403
	17: 1	The **s** of Judah is written with a pen of 2403
	17: 3	thy high places for **s**, throughout all thy 2403

Jer	18:23	neither blot out their **s** from thy sight, 2403
	31:34	and I will remember their **s** no more. 2403
	32:35	do this abomination, to **cause** Judah to **s**. 2398
	36: 3	I may forgive their iniquity and their **s**. 2403
	51: 5	though their land was filled with **s** against 817
La	4: 6	than the **punishment** of the **s** of Sodom, 2403
Eze	3:20	he shall die in his **s**, and his righteousness 2403
	3:21	righteous man, that the righteous **s** not, 2398
	3:21	he doth not **s**, he shall surely live, because 2398
	18:24	in his **s** that he hath sinned, in them shall 2403
	30:15	I will pour my fury upon **S**, the strength 5512
	30:16	**S** shall have great pain, and No shall be 5512
	33:14	if he turn from his **s**, and do that which is 2403
	40:39	the **s offering** and the trespass offering. 2403
	42:13	the **s offering**, and the trespass offering; 2403
	43:19	a young bullock for a **s offering**. 2403
	43:21	take the bullock also of the **s offering**, 2403
	43:22	goats without blemish for a **s offering**; 2403
	43:25	prepare every day a goat for a **s offering**: 2403
	44:27	shall offer his **s offering**, saith the Lord 2403
	44:29	the **s offering**, and the trespass offering; 2403
	45:17	he shall prepare the **s offering**, 2403
	45:19	shall take of the blood of the **s offering**, 2403
	45:22	of the land a bullock for a **s offering**. 2403
	45:23	a kid of the goats daily for a **s offering**. 2403
	45:25	according to the **s offering**, according to 2403
	46:20	the trespass offering and the **s offering**, 2403
Da	9:20	confessing my **s** and the **s** of my people 2403
	9:20	my sin and the **s** of my people Israel, 2403
Hos	4: 8	They eat up the **s** of my people, 2403
	8:11	Ephraim hath made many altars to **s**, 2398
	8:11	altars to sin, altars shall be unto him to **s**. 2398
	10: 8	Aven, the **s** of Israel, shall be destroyed: 2403
	12: 8	find none iniquity in me that were **s**. 2399
	13: 2	now they **s** more and more, and have 2398
	13:12	of Ephraim is bound up; his **s** is hid. 2403
Am	8:14	They that swear by the **s** of Samaria, 819
Mic	1:13	is the beginning of the **s** to the daughter 2403
	3: 8	his transgression, and to Israel his **s**. 2403
	6: 7	the fruit of my body for the **s** of my soul? 2403
Zec	13: 1	to the inhabitants of Jerusalem for **s** and 2403
Mt	12:31	All manner of **s** and blasphemy shall be 266
	18:21	how oft shall my brother **s** against me, 264
Jn	1:29	which taketh away the **s** of the world. 266
	5:14	**s** no more, lest a worse thing come unto 264
	8: 7	them, He that is without **s** among you, 361
	8:11	do I condemn thee: go, and **s** no more. 264
	8:34	Whosoever committeth **s** is the servant of 266
	8:34	committeth sin is the servant of **s**. 266
	8:46	Which of you convinceth me of **s**? And if I 266
	9: 2	saying, Master, who did **s**, this man, or 264
	9:41	If ye were blind, ye should have no **s**: 266
	9:41	ye say, We see; therefore your **s** remaineth. 266
	15:22	and spoken unto them, they had not had **s**: 266
	15:22	but now they have no cloke for their **s**. 266
	15:24	none other man did, they had not had **s**: 266
	16: 8	he will reprove the world of **s**, 266
	16: 9	Of **s**, because they believe not on me; 266
	19:11	delivered me unto thee hath the greater **s**. 266
Ac	7:60	Lord, lay not this **s** to their charge. 266
Ro	3: 9	and Gentiles, that they are all under **s**; 266
	3:20	for by the law is the knowledge of **s**. 266
	4: 8	man to whom the Lord will not impute **s**. 266
	5:12	as by one man **s** entered into the world, 266
	5:12	sin entered into the world, and death by **s**; 266
	5:13	For until the law **s** was in the world: 266
	5:13	but **s** is not imputed when there is no law. 266
	5:20	where **s** abounded, grace did much more 266
	5:21	That as **s** hath reigned unto death, even so 266
	6: 1	Shall we continue in **s**, that grace may 266
	6: 2	How shall we, that are dead to **s**, live any 266
	6: 6	him, that the body of **s** might be destroyed, 266
	6: 6	that henceforth we should not serve **s**. 266
	6: 7	For he that is dead is freed from **s**. 266
	6:10	For in that he died, he died unto **s** once: 266
	6:11	also yourselves to be dead indeed unto **s**, 266
	6:12	Let not **s** therefore reign in your mortal 266
	6:13	as instruments of unrighteousness unto **s**: 266
	6:14	For **s** shall not have dominion over you: 266
	6:15	we **s**, because we are not under the law, 264
	6:16	whether of **s** unto death, or of obedience 266
	6:17	that ye were the servants of **s**, but ye have 266
	6:18	Being then made free from **s**, ye became 266
	6:20	For when ye were the servants of **s**, ye 266
	6:22	But now being made free from **s**, 266
	6:23	For the wages of **s** is death; but the gift of 266
	7: 7	Is the law **s**? God forbid. Nay, I had not 266
	7: 7	I had not known **s**, but by the law: for I 266
	7: 8	**s**, taking occasion by the commandment, 266
	7: 8	For without the law **s** was dead. 266
	7: 9	commandment came, **s** revived, and I died. 266
	7:11	**s**, taking occasion by the commandment, 266
	7:13	**s**, that it might appear sin, working death 266
	7:13	sin, that it might appear **s**, working death 266
	7:13	that **s** by the commandment might become 266
	7:14	is spiritual: but I am carnal, sold under **s**. 266
	7:17	more I that do it, but **s** that dwelleth in me. 266
	7:20	more I that do it, but **s** that dwelleth in me. 266
	7:23	bringing me into captivity to the law of **s** 266
	8: 2	Jesus hath made me free from the law of **s** 266
	8: 3	and for sin, condemned sin in the flesh: 266
	8: 3	and for sin, condemned **s** in the flesh: 266
	8:10	be in you, the body is dead because of **s**; 266
	14:23	of faith: for whatsoever is not of faith is **s**. 266

S

1Co	6:18 Every **s** that a man doeth is without	265
	8:12 But when ye **s** so against the brethren,	264
	8:12 their weak conscience, ye **s** against Christ.	264
	15:34 Awake to righteousness, and **s** not: for	264
	15:56 The sting of death is **s**;	266
	15:56 is sin; and the strength of **s** is the law.	266
2Co	5:21 For he hath made him *to be* **s** for us,	266
	5:21 made him *to be* sin for us, who knew no **s**;	266
Gal	2:17 *is* therefore Christ the minister of **s**?	266
	3:22 the scripture hath concluded all under **s**,	266
Eph	4:26 Be ye angry, and **s** not: let not the sun go	264
2Th	2: 3 and *that* man of **s** be revealed, the son of	264
1Ti	5:20 Them that **s** rebuke before all, that others	264
Heb	3:13 be hardened through the deceitfulness of **s**.	266
	4:15 tempted like as *we are, yet* without **s**.	266
	9:26 to put away **s** by the sacrifice of himself.	266
	9:28 the second time without **s** unto salvation.	266
	10: 6 *sacrifices* for **s** thou hast had no pleasure.	266
	10: 8 and *offering* for **s** thou wouldest not,	266
	10:18 of these *is, there* is no more offering for **s**.	266
	10:26 For if we **s** wilfully after that *we* have	264
	11:25 to enjoy the pleasures of **s** for a season;	266
	12: 1 the **s** which doth so easily beset *us*, and	266
	12: 4 yet resisted unto blood, striving against **s**.	266
	13:11 into the sanctuary by the high priest for **s**,	266
Jas	1:15 lust hath conceived, it bringeth forth **s**:	266
	1:15 and **s**, when it is finished, bringeth forth	266
	2: 9 ye commit **s**, and are convinced of the law	266
	4:17 to do good, and doeth *it* not, to him it is **s**.	266
1Pe	2:22 Who did no **s**, neither was guile found in	266
	4: 1 suffered in the flesh hath ceased from **s**;	266
2Pe	2:14 of adultery and that cannot cease from **s**;	266
1Jn	1: 7 Christ his Son cleanseth us from all **s**.	266
	1: 8 If we say that we have no **s**, we deceive	266
	2: 1 *things* write I unto you, that ye **s** not.	264
	2: 1 if any *man* **s**, we have an advocate with	264
	3: 4 Whosoever committeth **s** transgresseth also	266
	3: 4 law: for **s** is the transgression of the law.	266
	3: 5 to take away our sins; and in him is no **s**.	266
	3: 8 He that committeth **s** is of the devil;	266
	3: 9 is born of God doth not commit **s**;	266
	3: 9 he cannot **s**, because he is born of God.	266
	5:16 If any *man* see his brother **s** a sin *which is*	264
	5:16 If any *man* see his brother sin a **s** *which is*	266
	5:16 he shall give him life for them that **s** not	264
	5:16 There is a **s** unto death: I do not say that	266
	5:17 All unrighteousness is **s**: and there is a sin	266
	5:17 is sin: and there is a **s** not unto death.	266

SINA (2) [SINAI]

Ac	7:30 **S** an angel of the Lord in a flame of fire in	4614
	7:38 angel which spake to him in the mount **S**,	4614

SINAI (37) [HOREB, SINA]

Ex	16: 1 of Sin, which *is* between Elim and **S**,	5514
	19: 1 day came they *into* the wilderness of **S**.	5514
	19: 2 were come to the desert of **S**,	5514
	19:11 the sight of all the people upon mount **S**.	5514
	19:18 mount **S** was altogether on a smoke,	5514
	19:20 the Lord came down upon mount **S**:	5514
	19:23 The people cannot come up to mount **S**:	5514
	24:16 glory of the Lord abode upon mount **S**,	5514
	31:18 of communing with him upon mount **S**,	5514
	34: 2 come up in the morning unto mount **S**,	5514
	34: 4 the morning, and went up unto mount **S**,	5514
	34:29 when Moses came down from mount **S**	5514
	34:32 Lord had spoken with him in mount **S**.	5514
Lev	7:38 the Lord commanded Moses in mount **S**,	5514
	7:38 unto the Lord, in the wilderness of **S**.	5514
	25: 1 the Lord spake unto Moses in mount **S**,	5514
	26:46 the children of Israel in mount **S** by	5514
	27:34 for the children of Israel in mount **S**.	5514
Nu	1: 1 spake unto Moses in the wilderness of **S**,	5514
	1:19 he numbered them in the wilderness of **S**.	5514
	3: 1 the Lord spake with Moses in mount **S**.	5514
	3: 4 in the wilderness of **S**, and they had no	5514
	3:14 spake unto Moses in the wilderness of **S**,	5514
	9: 1 spake unto Moses in the wilderness of **S**,	5514
	9: 5 first month at even in the wilderness of **S**:	5514
	10:12 their journeys out of the wilderness of **S**;	5514
	26:64 children of Israel in the wilderness of **S**.	5514
	28: 6 was ordained in mount **S** for a sweet	5514
	33:15 and pitched in the wilderness of **S**.	5514
	33:16 And they removed from the desert of **S**,	5514
Dt	33: 2 The Lord came from **S**, and rose up	5514
Jdg	5: 5 *even* that **S** from before the Lord God of	5514
Ne	9:13 Thou camest down also upon mount **S**,	5514
Ps	68: 8 **S** itself *was* moved at the presence of	5514
	68:17 *is* among them, *as in* **S**, in the holy *place*.	5514
Gal	4:24 one from the mount **S**, which gendereth	4614
	4:25 For this Agar is mount **S** in Arabia,	4614

SINCE (68) [SITH]

Ge	30:30 Lord hath blessed thee **s** my coming:	3807.1
	44:28 torn in pieces; and I saw him not **s**:	2008+5704
	46:30 I have seen thy face, because thou *art* yet	310
Ex	4:10 **s** thou hast spoken unto thy servant:	227+4480
	5:23 For I came to Pharaoh to speak in	227+4480
	9:18 the foundation	3117+4480+1886.1+3807.1
	9:24 land of Egypt **s** it became a nation.	227+4480
	10: 6 **s** the day that they were upon the earth	4480
Nu	22:30 which thou hast ridden **ever s**?	4480+5750
Dt	4:32 the day that God created man upon	4480
	34:10 there arose not a prophet **s** in Israel like	5750
Jos	2:12 the Lord, **s** I have shewed you kindness,	3588

Jos	14:10 *even* **s** the Lord spake this word	227+4480
Ru	2:11 mother in law **s** the death of thine	310
1Sa	8: 8 **s** the day that I brought them up out of	4480
	9:24 time *hath* it been kept for thee **s** *I* said,	3807.1
	21: 5 I came out, and the vessels of the	871.1
	29: 3 found no *fault* in him **s** he fell	3117+4480
	29: 6 I have not found evil in thee **s** the day of	4480
2Sa	7: 6 **s** the time that I brought up	4480+3801.1
	7:11 *as* **s** the time that I commanded judges	4480
1Ki	8:16 **s** the day that I brought forth my people	4480
2Ki	8: 6 all the fruits of the field **s** the day that she	4480
	21:15 **s** the day their fathers came forth out of	4480
1Ch	17: 5 For I have not dwelt in a house **s** the day	4480
	17:10 **s** the time that I commanded judges *to be*	4480
2Ch	6: 5 **s** the day that I brought forth my people	4480
	30:26 the time of Solomon the son of David	4480
	31:10 **S** *the* people began to bring the offerings	4480
Ezr	4: 2 we do sacrifice unto him **s** the days of	4480
	5:16 **s** that time even until now *hath* it been in	4481
	9: 7 **S** the days of our fathers *have we been* in	4480
Ne	8:17 the days of Jeshua the son of Nun unto	4480
	9:32 **s** the time of the kings of Assyria unto	4480
Job	20: 4 this of old, **s** man was placed upon earth,	4480
	38:12 Hast thou commanded the morning **s** thy	4480
Isa	14: 8 cedars of Lebanon, *saying,* **S** thou	227+4480
	16:13 spoken concerning Moab **s** that time.	4480
	43: 4 **S** thou wast precious in my sight,	834+4480
	44: 7 for me, **s** I appointed the ancient people?	4480
	64: 4 For **s** the beginning of the world	4480+5769
Jer	7:25 **S** the day that your fathers came forth out	4480
	20: 8 For **s** I spake, I cried out, I cried	1767+4480
	31:20 for **s** I spake against him, I do	1767+4480
	44:18 we left off to burn incense to	227+4480
	48:27 for **s** thou spakest of him,	1767+4480
Da	12: 1 such as never was **s** there was a nation	4480
Hag	2:16 **S** those *days* were, when *one* came	1961+4480
Mt	24:21 as was not **s** the beginning of the world	575
Mk	9:21 How long is it ago **s** this came unto him?	5613
Lk	1:70 which have been **s** the world **began**:)	575
	7:45 *woman* **the time** I came in hath	575+3739
	16:16 **s** that time the kingdom of God is	575
	24:21 to day is the third day **s** these *things*	575+3739
Jn	9:32 the world **began** was it not heard that	1537
Ac	3:21 of all his holy prophets **s** the world **began**.	575
	19: 2 Have ye received the Holy Ghost **s** ye	1487
	24:11 twelve days **s** I went up to Jerusalem	575+3739
Ro	16:25 was kept secret **s** the **world began**,	160+5550
1Co	15:21 For **s** by man *came* death, by man *came*	1894
2Co	13: 3 **s** ye seek a proof of Christ speaking in me,	1893
Col	1: 4 **S** we heard of your faith in Christ Jesus,	NIG
	1: 6 **s** the day ye heard of *it*, and knew the	575
	1: 9 **s** the day we heard *it*, do not cease to	575
Heb	7:28 which was **s** the law, *maketh* the Son,	3326
	9:26 he often have suffered **s** the foundation	575
2Pe	3: 4 for the fathers fell asleep, all *things*	575+3739
Rev	16:18 such as was not **s** men were upon	575+3739

SINCERE (2) [SINCERELY, SINCERITY]

Php	1:10 that ye may be **s** and without offence till	1506
1Pe	2: 2 babes, desire the **s** milk of the word,	97

SINCERELY (3) [SINCERE]

Jdg	9:16 if ye have done truly and **s**,	8549+871.1
	9:19 dealt truly and **s** with Jerubbaal	8549+871.1
Php	1:16 one preach Christ of contention, not **s**,	55

SINCERITY (7) [SINCERE]

Jos	24:14 and serve him in **s** and in truth:	8549
1Co	5: 8 but with the unleavened bread of **s** and	1505
2Co	1:12 that in simplicity and godly **s**, not with	1505
	2:17 but as of **s**, but as of God, in the sight of	1505
	8: 8 of others, and to prove the **s** of your love.	1103
Eph	6:24 them that love our Lord Jesus Christ in **s**.	861
Tit	2: 7 doctrine *shewing* uncorruptness, gravity, **s**,	861

SINEW (3) [SINEWS]

Ge	32:32 of Israel eat not *of* the **s** which shrank,	1517
	32:32 of Jacob's thigh in the **s** that shrank.	1517
Isa	48: 4 thy neck *is* an iron **s**, and thy brow brass:	1517

SINEWS (5) [SINEW]

Job	10:11 and hast fenced me with bones and **s**.	1517
	30:17 the night season: and my **s** take no rest.	6207
	40:17 the **s** of his stones are wrapt together.	1517
Eze	37: 6 I will lay **s** upon you, and will bring up	1517
	37: 8 the **s** and the flesh came up upon them,	1517

SINFUL (8) [SIN]

Nu	32:14 your fathers' stead, an increase of **s** men,	2400
Isa	1: 4 Ah **s** nation, a people laden with iniquity,	2398
Am	9: 8 the eyes of the Lord God *are* upon the **s**	2403
Mk	8:38 words in this adulterous and **s** generation;	268
Lk	5: 8 Depart from me; for I am a **s** man, O Lord.	268
	24: 7 must be delivered into the hands of **s** men,	268
Ro	7:13 commandment might become exceeding **s**.	268
	8: 3 sending his own Son in the likeness of **s**	266

SINFUL NATURE See CARNAL; FLESH

SING (119) [SANG, SINGER, SINGERS, SINGETH, SINGING, SONG, SONGS, SUNG]

Ex	15: 1 and spake, saying, I will **s** unto the Lord,	7891
	15:21 answered them, **S** ye to the Lord,	7891
	32:18 *but* the noise of *them that* **s** do I hear.	6031
Nu	21:17 this song, Spring up, O well; **s** ye unto it:	6030
Jdg	5: 3 I, *even* I, will **s** unto the Lord;	7891

Jdg	5: 3 I will **s** *praise* to the Lord God of Israel.	2167
1Sa	21:11 did they not **s** one to another of him in	6030
2Sa	22:50 and I will **s praises** unto thy name.	2167
1Ch	16: 9 **S** unto him, sing psalms unto him, talk	7891
	16: 9 **S** unto him, **s psalms** unto him, talk	2167
	16:23 **S** unto the Lord, all the earth; shew forth	7891
	16:33 shall the trees of the wood **s** out at	7442
2Ch	20:22 when they began to **s** and to praise,	7440
	23:13 of musick, and such as taught to **s** praise.	NIH
	29:30 the princes commanded the Levites to **s**	NIH
Job	29:13 I **caused** the widow's heart **to s for joy**.	7442
Ps	7:17 will I **s** *praise* to the name of the Lord	2167
	9: 2 I will **s** *praise* to thy name, O thou most	2167
	9:11 **S praises** to the Lord, which dwelleth in	2167
	13: 6 I will **s** unto the Lord, because he hath	7891
	18:49 heathen, and **s praises** unto thy name.	2167
	21:13 so will we **s** and praise thy power.	7891
	27: 6 I will **s**, yea, I will sing *praises* unto	7891
	27: 6 yea, I will **s** *praises* unto the Lord,	2167
	30: 4 **S** unto the Lord, O ye saints of his,	2167
	30:12 To the end that *my* glory may **s** *praise* to	2167
	33: 2 **s** unto him with the psaltery *and*	2167
	33: 3 **S** unto him a new song; play skilfully	7891
	47: 6 **S** praises to God, sing *praises*: sing	2167
	47: 6 **s** *praises*: sing *praises* unto our King,	2167
	47: 6 sing *praises*: sing *praises* unto our King,	2167
	47: 6 sing *praises* unto our King, **s** *praises*.	2167
	47: 7 earth: **s** ye *praises* with understanding.	2167
	51:14 my tongue shall **s** *aloud* of thy	7442
	57: 7 my heart is fixed: I will **s** and give praise.	7891
	57: 9 I will **s** unto thee among the nations.	2167
	59:16 I will **s** of thy power; yea, I will sing	7891
	59:16 I will **s** *aloud* of thy mercy in the morning:	7442
	59:17 Unto thee, O my strength, will I **s**:	2167
	61: 8 So will I **s** *praise* unto thy name for ever,	2167
	65:13 with corn; they shout for joy, they also **s**.	7891
	66: 2 **S** forth the honour of his name: make his	2167
	66: 4 shall worship thee, and shall **s** unto thee;	2167
	66: 4 sing unto thee; they shall **s** to thy name.	2167
	67: 4 O let the nations be glad and **s for joy**:	7442
	68: 4 **S** unto God, sing *praises* to his name:	2167
	68: 4 **S** unto God, **s** *praises* to his name:	2167
	68:32 **S** unto God, ye kingdoms of the earth;	7891
	68:32 O **s** *praises* unto the Lord; Selah:	2167
	71:22 unto thee will I **s** with the harp, O thou	2167
	71:23 My lips shall greatly rejoice when I **s** unto	2167
	75: 9 I will **s** *praises* to the God of Jacob.	2167
	81: 1 **S** *aloud* unto God our strength: make a	7442
	89: 1 I will **s** of the mercies of the Lord for	7891
	92: 1 to **s** *praises* unto thy name, O most High:	2167
	95: 1 O come, let us **s** unto the Lord: let us	7442
	96: 1 O **s** unto the Lord a new song: sing unto	7891
	96: 1 new song: **s** unto the Lord, all the earth.	7891
	96: 2 **S** unto the Lord, bless his name;	7891
	98: 1 O **s** unto the Lord a new song; for he	7891
	98: 4 a loud noise, and rejoice, and **s** *praise*.	2167
	98: 5 **S** unto the Lord with the harp; with	2167
	101: 1 I will **s** of mercy and judgment: unto thee,	7891
	101: 1 judgment: unto thee, O Lord, will I **s**.	2167
	104:12 *which* **s** among the branches.	5414+6963
	104:33 I will **s** unto the Lord as long as I live:	7891
	104:33 I will **s** *praise* to my God while I have my	2167
	105: 2 **S** unto him, sing psalms unto him: talk ye	7891
	105: 2 Sing unto him, **s psalms** unto him: talk ye	2167
	108: 1 I will **s** and give praise, even *with* my	7891
	108: 3 I will **s** *praises* unto thee among the.	2167
	135: 3 *praises* unto his name; for *it is* pleasant.	2167
	137: 3 *saying,* **S** us *one* of the songs of Zion.	7891
	137: 4 How shall we **s** the Lord's song in a	7891
	138: 1 before the gods will I **s** *praise* unto thee.	2167
	138: 5 they shall **s** in the ways of the Lord:	7891
	144: 9 I will **s** a new song unto thee, O God:	7891
	144: 9 instrument of ten strings will I **s** *praises*	2167
	145: 7 and shall **s** of thy righteousness.	7442
	146: 2 I will **s** *praises* unto my God while I have	2167
	147: 1 for *it is* good to **s** *praises* unto our God;	2167
	147: 7 **S** unto the Lord with thanksgiving;	6030
	147: 7 **s** *praise* upon the harp unto our God:	2167
	149: 1 **S** unto the Lord a new song,	7891
	149: 3 let them **s** *praises* unto him with the	2167
	149: 5 glory: let them **s** *aloud* upon their beds.	7442
Pr	29: 6 but the righteous doth **s** and rejoice.	7442
Isa	5: 1 Now will I **s** to my wellbeloved a song of	7891
	12: 5 **S** unto the Lord; for he hath done	2167
	23:15 after the end of seventy years shall Tyre **s**	7892
	23:16 make sweet melody, **s** many songs, that	NIH
	24:14 They shall lift up their voice, they shall **s**,	7442
	26:19 Awake and **s**, ye that dwell in dust: for	7442
	27: 2 In that day **s** ye unto her, A vineyard of	6030
	35: 6 as a hart, and the tongue of the dumb **s**	7442
	38:20 **s** my songs *to* **the stringed instruments**	5059
	42:10 **S** unto the Lord a new song,	7891
	42:11 let the inhabitants of the rock **s**, let them	7442
	44:23 **S**, O ye heavens; for the Lord hath done	7442
	49:13 **S**, O heavens; and be joyful, O earth;	7442
	52: 8 *with* the voice together shall they **s**:	7442
	52: 9 Break forth **into joy**, **s** together, ye waste	7442
	54: 1 **S**, O barren, thou *that* didst not bear;	7442
	65:14 my servants shall **s** for joy of heart,	7442
Jer	20:13 **S** unto the Lord, praise ye the Lord:	7891
	31: 7 **S** with gladness for Jacob, and shout	7442
	31:12 shall come and **s** in the height of Zion,	7442
	51:48 and all that *is* therein, shall **s** for Babylon:	7442
Eze	27:25 The ships of Tarshish did **s** of thee *in thy*	7788
Hos	2:15 she shall **s** there, as *in* the days of her	6030

Zep	2:14 *their* voice shall **s** in the windows;	7891
	3:14 **S**, O daughter of Zion; shout, O Israel;	7442
Zec	2:10 **S** and rejoice, O daughter of Zion: for lo,	7442
Ro	15: 9 among the Gentiles, and **s** unto thy name.	5567
1Co	14:15 I will **s** with the spirit, and I will sing with	5567
	14:15 and I will **s** with the understanding also.	5567
Heb	2:12 in the midst of the church will I **s praise**	5214
Jas	5:13 him pray. Is any merry? let him **s psalms.**	5567
Rev	15: 3 they **s** the song of Moses the servant of	103

SINGED (1)
Da	3:27 nor was a hair of their head **s**, neither	2761

SINGER (2) [SING]
1Ch	6:33 Heman a **s**, the son of Joel, the son of	7891
Hab	3:19 the **chief s** on my stringed instruments.	5329

SINGERS (38) [SING]
1Ki	10:12 harps also and psalteries for **s:**	7891
1Ch	9:33 these *are* the **s**, chief of the fathers of	7891
	15:16 *to be* the **s** with instruments of musick,	7891
	15:19 So the **s**, Heman, Asaph, and Ethan,	7891
	15:27 **s**, and Chenaniah the master of the song	7891
	15:27 the master of the song *with* the **s**	7891
2Ch	5:12 Also the Levites *which were* the **s**, all of	7891
	5:13 as the trumpeters and **s** *were* as one,	7891
	9:11 and harps and psalteries for **s:**	7891
	20:21 he appointed **s** unto the LORD,	7891
	23:13 also the **s** with instruments of musick,	7891
	29:28 the **s** sang, and the trumpeters sounded:	7892
	35:15 the **s** the sons of Asaph *were* in their place,	7891
Ezr	2:41 The **s**: the children of Asaph, an hundred	7891
	2:70 the **s**, and the porters, and the Nethinims,	7891
	7: 7 the **s**, and the porters, and the Nethinims,	7891
	7:24 any of the priests and Levites, **s**, porters,	2171
	10:24 Of the **s** also; Eliashib: and of the porters;	7891
Ne	7: 1 the porters and the **s** and the Levites were	7891
	7:44 The **s**: the children of Asaph, an hundred	7891
	7:73 the **s**, and *some* of the people,	7891
	10:28 the priests, the Levites, the porters, the **s**,	7891
	10:39 that minister, and the porters, and the **s:**	7891
	11:22 the **s** *were* over the business of the house	7891
	11:23 that a certain portion *should be* for the **s**,	7891
	12:28 the sons of **s** gathered themselves	7891
	12:29 for the **s** had builded them villages round	7891
	12:42 the **s** sang loud, with Jezrahiah *their*	7891
	12:45 both the **s** and the porters kept the ward	7891
	12:46 and Asaph of old *there were* chief of the **s**,	7891
	12:47 gave the portions of the **s** and the porters,	7891
	13: 5 to the Levites, and the **s**, and the porters;	7891
	13:10 given *them*: for the Levites and the **s**,	7891
Ps	68:25 The **s** went before, the players on	7891
	87: 7 well the **s** as the players on instruments	7891
Ecc	2: 8 I gat me *men* **s** and *women* singers,	7891
	2: 8 I gat me *men* singers and *women* **s**,	7891
Eze	40:44 the chambers of the **s** in the inner court,	7891

SINGETH (1) [SING]
Pr	25:20 so *is* he that **s** songs to a heavy heart.	7891

SINGING (29) [SING]
1Sa	18: 6 **s** and dancing, to meet king Saul,	7891
2Sa	19:35 can I hear any more the voice of **s** *men*	7891
	19:35 singing *men* and **s** *women?* wherefore	7891
1Ch	6:32 the tabernacle of the congregation with **s**,	7892
	13: 8 **s**, and with harps, and with psalteries,	7892
2Ch	23:18 with rejoicing and with **s**, as it was	7892
	30:21 **s** with loud instruments unto the LORD.	NIH
	35:25 all the **s** *men* and the singing *women*	7891
	35:25 the **s** *women* spake of Josiah in their	7891
Ezr	2:65 *were* among them two hundred **s** *men*	7891
	2:65 two hundred singing *men* and **s** *women*.	7891
Ne	7:67 and five **s** *men* and singing *women*.	7891
	7:67 and five singing *men* and **s** *women*.	7891
	12:27 with **s**, with cymbals, psalteries,	7892
Ps	100: 2 come before his presence with **s**.	7445
	126: 2 *with* laughter, and our tongue *with* **s:**	7440
SS	2:12 the time of the **s** *of birds* is come,	2158
Isa	14: 7 rest, *and* is quiet: they break forth **into s**.	7440
	16:10 in the vineyards there shall be no **s**,	7442
	35: 2 and rejoice even *with* joy and **s:**	7444
	44:23 break forth *into* **s**, ye mountains, O forest,	7440
	48:20 with a voice of **s** declare ye, tell this,	7440
	49:13 and break forth *into* **s**, O mountains:	7440
	51:11 shall return, and come with **s** *unto* Zion;	7440
	54: 1 break forth *into* **s**, and cry aloud, thou	7440
	55:12 hills shall break forth before you *into* **s**,	7440
Zep	3:17 in his love, he will joy over thee with **s**.	7440
Eph	5:19 and making melody in your heart to	103
Col	3:16 **s** with grace in your hearts to the Lord.	103

SINGLE (2) [SINGLENESS, SINGULAR]
Mt	6:22 if therefore thine eye be **s**, thy whole body	573
Lk	11:34 therefore when thine eye is **s**, thy whole	573

SINGLENESS (3) [SINGLE]
Ac	2:46 eat *their* meat with gladness and **s** of heart,	858
Eph	6: 5 with fear and trembling, in **s** of your heart,	572
Col	3:22 but in **s** of heart, fearing God:	572

SINGULAR (1) [SINGLE]
Lev	27: 2 When a man shall **make a s vow**,	5088+6381

SINIM (1)
Isa	49:12 the west; and these from the land of **S**.	5515

SINITE (2)
Ge	10:17 And the Hivite, and the Arkite, and the **S**,	5513
1Ch	1:15 And the Hivite, and the Arkite, and the **S**,	5513

SINK (6) [SANK, SUNK]
Ps	69: 2 I **s** in deep mire, where *there is* no	2883
	69:14 me out of the mire, and let me not **s:**	2883
Jer	51:64 Thus shall Babylon **s**, and shall not rise	8257
Mt	14:30 and beginning to **s**, he cried, saying, Lord,	2670
Lk	5: 7 both the ships, so that they began to **s**.	1036
	9:44 Let these sayings **s down** into your ears:	5087

SINNED (119) [SIN]
Ex	9:27 and said unto them, I have **s** *this* time;	2398
	9:34 he yet more, and hardened his heart,	2398
	10:16 I have **s** against the LORD your God,	2398
	32:30 unto the people, Ye have **s** a great sin:	2398
	32:31 this people have **s** a great sin,	2398
	32:33 Whosoever hath **s** against me, him will I	2398
Lev	4: 3 let him bring for his sin, which he hath **s**,	2398
	4:14 which they have **s** against it, is known,	2398
	4:22 When a ruler hath **s**, and done somewhat	2398
	4:23 if his sin, wherein he hath **s**, come to his	2398
	4:28 Or if his sin, which he hath **s**, come to his	2398
	4:28 for his sin which he hath **s**.	2398
	5: 5 shall confess that he hath **s** in that *thing*:	2398
	5: 6 the LORD for his sin which he hath **s**,	2398
	5:10 for him for his sin which he had **s**,	2398
	5:11 he that **s** shall bring for his offering	2398
	5:13 his sin that he hath **s** in one of these,	2398
	6: 4 shall be, because he hath **s**, and is guilty,	2398
Nu	6:11 for that he **s** by the dead, and shall hallow	2398
	12:11 done foolishly, and wherein we have **s**.	2398
	14:40 the LORD hath promised: for we have **s**.	2398
	21: 7 came to Moses, and said, We have **s**,	2398
	22:34 said unto the angel of the LORD, I have **s;**	2398
	32:23 behold, ye have **s** against the LORD:	2398
Dt	1:41 unto me, We have **s** against the LORD,	2398
	9:16 ye had **s** against the LORD your God,	2398
	9:18 because of all your sins which ye **s**,	2398
Jos	7:11 Israel hath **s**, and they have also	2398
	7:20 Indeed I have **s** against the LORD God of	2398
Jdg	10:10 We have **s** against thee, both because	2398
	10:15 of Israel said unto the LORD, We have **s:**	2398
	11:27 Wherefore I have not **s** against thee,	2398
1Sa	7: 6 said there, We have **s** against the LORD.	2398
	12:10 We have **s**, because we have forsaken	2398
	15:24 Saul said unto Samuel, I have **s**: for I have	2398
	15:30 said, I have **s:** *yet* honour me now, I pray	2398
	19: 4 because he hath not **s** against thee,	2398
	24:11 mine hand, and I have not **s** against thee;	2398
	26:21 said Saul, I have **s:** return, my son David:	2398
2Sa	12:13 unto Nathan, I have **s** against the LORD.	2398
	19:20 For thy servant doth know that I have **s**:	2398
	24:10 I have **s** greatly *in* that I have done:	2398
	24:17 Lo, I have **s**, and I have done wickedly:	2398
1Ki	8:33 because they have **s** against thee,	2398
	8:35 no rain, because they have **s** against thee;	2398
	8:47 We have **s**, and have done perversely,	2398
	8:50 forgive thy people that have **s** against	2398
	15:30 of the sins of Jeroboam which he **s**,	2398
	16:13 *by* which they **s**, and *by* which they made	2398
	16:19 For his sins which he **s** in doing evil in	2398
	18: 9 said, What have I **s**, that thou wouldest	2398
2Ki	17: 7 that the children of Israel had **s** against	2398
	21:17 and all that he did, and his sin that he **s**,	2398
1Ch	21: 8 I have **s** greatly, because I have done this	2398
	21:17 I *it is* that have **s** and done evil indeed;	2398
2Ch	6:24 because they have **s** against thee;	2398
	6:26 no rain, because they have **s** against thee;	2398
	6:37 saying, We have **s**, we have done amiss,	2398
	6:39 forgive thy people which have **s** against	2398
Ne	1: 6 of Israel, which we have **s** against thee:	2398
	1: 6 both I and my father's house have **s**.	2398
	9:29 **s** against thy judgments, (which if a man	2398
Job	1: 5 It may be that my sons have **s**,	2398
	1:22 In all this Job **s** not, nor charged God	2398
	7:20 I have **s**; what shall I do unto thee,	2398
	8: 4 If thy children have **s** against him,	2398
	24:19 *so doth* the grave *those which* have **s**.	2398
	33:27 I have **s**, and perverted *that which* was	2398
Ps	41: 4 heal my soul; for I have **s** against thee.	2398
	51: 4 have I **s**, and done *this* evil in thy sight:	2398
	78:17 they yet more against him by provoking	2398
	78:32 For all this they **s** still, and believed not	2398
	106: 6 We have **s** with our fathers, we have	2398
Isa	42:24 the LORD, he against whom we have **s**?	2398
	43:27 Thy first father hath **s**, and thy teachers	2398
	64: 5 behold, thou art wroth; for we have **s**:	2398
Jer	2:35 thee, because thou sayest, I have not **s**.	2398
	3:25 for we have **s** against the LORD our God,	2398
	8:14 because we have **s** against the LORD.	2398
	14: 7 are many; we have **s** against thee.	2398
	14:20 of our fathers: for we have **s** against thee.	2398
	33: 8 whereby they have **s** against me, and I	2398
	33: 8 whereby they have **s**, and whereby they	2398
	40: 3 because ye have **s** against the LORD,	2398
	44:23 because ye have **s** against the LORD,	2398
	50: 7 because they have **s** against the LORD,	2398
	50:14 for she hath **s** against the LORD.	2398
La	1: 8 Jerusalem hath **grievously s;**	2398+2399
	5: 7 Our fathers have **s**, *and are* not;	2398
	5:16 our head: woe unto us, that we have **s!**	2398
Eze	18:24 in his sin that he hath **s**, in them shall	2398
	28:16 of thee *with* violence, and thou hast **s:**	2398

Eze	37:23 they have **s**, and will cleanse them:	2398
Da	9: 5 We have **s**, and have committed iniquity,	2398
	9: 8 fathers, because we have **s** against thee.	2398
	9:11 of God, because we have **s** against him.	2398
	9:15 we have **s**, we have done wickedly,	2398
Hos	4: 7 they were increased, so they **s** against me:	2398
	10: 9 thou hast **s** from the days of Gibeah:	2398
Mic	7: 9 I have **s** against him, until he plead	2398
Hab	2:10 many people, and *hast* **s** *against* thy soul.	2398
Zep	1:17 because they have **s** against the LORD:	2398
Mt	27: 4 have **s** in that I have betrayed the innocent	264
Lk	15:18 I have **s** against heaven, and before thee,	264
	15:21 I have **s** against heaven, and in thy sight,	264
Jn	9: 3 Neither hath this *man* **s**, nor his parents:	264
Ro	2:12 For as many as have **s** without law shall	264
	2:12 many as have **s** in the law shall be judged	264
	3:23 For all have **s**, and come short of the glory	264
	5:12 passed upon all men, for that all have **s:**	264
	5:14 even over them that had not **s** after	264
	5:16 not as *it was* by one that **s**, *so is* the gift:	264
1Co	7:28 But and if thou marry, thou hast not **s;**	264
	7:28 and if a virgin marry, she hath not **s**.	264
2Co	12:21 shall bewail many which have **s already**,	4258
	13: 2 write to them which **heretofore** have **s**,	4258
Heb	3:17 *was it* not with them that had **s**,	264
2Pe	2: 4 For if God spared not the angels that **s**,	264
1Jn	1:10 If we say that we have not **s**, we make him	264

SINNER (21) [SIN]
Pr	11:31 earth: much more the wicked and the **s**.	2398
	13: 6 but wickedness overthroweth the **s**.	2403
	13:22 the wealth of the **s** *is* laid up for the just.	2398
Ecc	2:26 to the **s** he giveth travail, to gather and	2398
	7:26 from her; but the **s** shall be taken by her.	2398
	8:12 Though a **s** do evil an hundred *times*, and	2398
	9: 2 as *is* the good, so *is* the **s;** *and* he that	2398
	9:18 of war: but one **s** destroyeth much good.	2398
Isa	65:20 the **s** *being* an hundred years old shall be	2398
Lk	7:37 a woman in the city, which was a **s**,	268
	7:39 *this is* that toucheth him: for she is a **s**.	268
	15: 7 be in heaven over one **s** that repenteth,	268
	15:10 angels of God over one **s** that repenteth.	268
	18:13 breast, saying, God be merciful to me a **s**.	268
	19: 7 gone to be guest with a man *that is* a **s**.	268
Jn	9:16 can a man *that is* a **s** do such miracles?	268
	9:24 the praise: we know that this man is a **s**.	268
	9:25 said, Whether he be a **s** *or no*, I know not:	268
Ro	3: 7 his glory; why yet am I also judged as a **s**?	268
Jas	5:20 he which converteth the **s** from the error	268
1Pe	4:18 where shall the ungodly and the **s** appear?	268

SINNERS (48) [SIN]
Ge	13:13 and **s** before the LORD exceedingly.	2400
Nu	16:38 The censers of these **s** against their own	2400
1Sa	15:18 and utterly destroy the **s** the Amalekites,	2400
Ps	1: 1 nor standeth in the way of **s**, nor sitteth	2400
	1: 5 nor **s** in the congregation of the righteous.	2400
	25: 8 will he teach **s** in the way.	2400
	26: 9 Gather not my soul with **s**, nor my life	2400
	51:13 and **s** shall be converted unto thee.	2400
	104:35 Let the **s** be consumed out of the earth,	2400
Pr	1:10 My son, if **s** entice thee, consent thou not.	2400
	13:21 Evil pursueth **s**: but to the righteous good	2400
	23:17 Let not thine heart envy **s**: but *be thou* in	2400
Isa	1:28 and of the **s** *shall be* together,	2400
	13: 9 he shall destroy the **s** thereof out of it.	2400
	33:14 The **s** in Zion are afraid; fearfulness hath	2400
Am	9:10 All the **s** of my people shall die by	2400
Mt	9:10 many publicans and **s** came and sat down	268
	9:11 eateth your Master with publicans and **s**?	268
	9:13 to call *the* righteous, but **s** to repentance.	268
	11:19 a winebibber, a friend of publicans and **s**.	268
	26:45 Son of man is betrayed into the hands of **s**.	268
Mk	2:15 and **s** sat also together with Jesus and	268
	2:16 saw him eat with publicans and **s**,	268
	2:16 eateth and drinketh with publicans and **s**?	268
	2:17 to call *the* righteous, but **s** to repentance.	268
	14:41 Son of man is betrayed into the hands of **s**.	268
Lk	5:30 do ye eat and drink with publicans and **s**?	268
	5:32 to call *the* righteous, but **s** to repentance.	268
	6:32 for **s** also love those that love them.	268
	6:33 have ye? for **s** also do *even* the same.	268
	6:34 **s** also to sinners, to receive as much	268
	6:34 sinners also lend to **s**, to receive as much	268
	7:34 a winebibber, a friend of publicans and **s**.	268
	13: 2 Suppose ye that these Galileans were **s**	268
	13: 4 think ye that they were **s** above all men	3781
	15: 1 him all the publicans and **s** for to hear him.	268
	15: 2 *man* receiveth **s**, and eateth with them.	268
Jn	9:31 Now we know that God heareth not **s**:	268
Ro	5: 8 that, while we were yet **s**, Christ died for	268
	5:19 man's disobedience many were made **s**,	268
Gal	2:15 Jews by nature, and not **s** of the Gentiles,	268
	2:17 we ourselves also are found **s**, *is* therefore	268
1Ti	1: 9 for the ungodly and for **s**, for unholy and	268
	1:15 Christ Jesus came into the world to save **s;**	268
Heb	7:26 separate from **s**, and made higher than	268
	12: 3 such contradiction of **s** against himself,	268
Jas	4: 8 Cleanse *your* hands, ye **s;** and purify *your*	268
Jude	1:15 of all *their* hard *speeches* which ungodly **s**	268

SINNEST (1) [SIN]
Job	35: 6 If thou **s**, what doest thou against him?	2398

S

SINNETH (22) [SIN]

Nu	15:28 atonement for the soul that **s ignorantly**,	7683
	15:28 when he **s** by ignorance before the Lord,	2398
	15:29 that **s through ignorance**,	6213+7684+871.1
Dt	19:15 or for any sin, in any sin that he **s**:	2398
1Ki	8:46 (for *there* is no man that **s** not,)	2398
2Ch	6:36 (for *there* is no man which **s** not,)	2398
Pr	8:36 that **s** *against* me wrongeth his own soul:	2398
	14:21 He that despiseth his neighbour **s**:	2398
	19: 2 and he that hasteth with *his* feet, **s**.	2398
	20: 2 provoketh him to anger **s** *against* his	2398
Ecc	7:20 upon earth, that doeth good, and **s** not.	2398
Eze	14:13 The land **s** against me by trespassing	2398
	18: 4 son *is* mine: the soul that **s**, it	2398
	18:20 The soul that **s**, it shall die. The son shall	2398
	33:12 for his *righteousness* in the day that he **s**.	2398
1Co	6:18 that committeth fornication **s** against his	264
	7:36 require, let him do what he will, he **s** not:	264
Tit	3:11 and **s**, being condemned of himself.	264
1Jn	3: 6 Whosoever abideth in him **s** not:	264
	3: 6 whosoever hath not seen him,	264
	3: 8 devil; for the devil **s** from the beginning,	264
	5:18 We know that whosoever is born of God **s**	264

SINNING (2) [SIN]

Ge	20: 6 I also withheld thee from **s** against me:	2398
Lev	6: 3 of all *these* that a man doeth, **s** therein:	2398

SINS (172) [SIN]

Lev	16:16 of their transgressions in all their **s**	2403
	16:21 all their transgressions in all their **s**,	2403
	16:30 ye may be clean from all your **s** before	2403
	16:34 of Israel for all their **s** once a year.	2403
	26:18 punish you seven *times* more for your **s**.	2403
	26:21 plagues upon you according to your **s**.	2403
	26:24 punish you yet seven *times* for your **s**.	2403
	26:28 will chastise you seven *times* for your **s**.	2403
Nu	16:26 theirs, lest ye be consumed in all their **s**.	2403
Dt	9:18 because of all your **s** which ye sinned,	2403
Jos	24:19 forgive your transgressions nor your **s**.	2403
1Sa	12:19 for we have added unto all our **s** *this* evil,	2403
1Ki	14:16 Israel up because of the **s** of Jeroboam,	2403
	14:22 provoked him to jealousy with their **s**	2403
	15: 3 he walked in all the **s** of his father,	2403
	15:30 Because of the **s** of Jeroboam which he	2403
	16: 2 sin, to provoke me to anger with their **s**;	2403
	16:13 all the **s** of Baasha, and the sins of Elah	2403
	16:13 **s** of Elah his son, *by* which they sinned,	2403
	16:19 his **s** which he sinned in doing evil in	2403
	16:31 in the **s** of Jeroboam the son of Nebat,	2403
2Ki	3: 3 Nevertheless he cleaved unto the **s** of	2403
	10:29 Howbeit *from* the **s** of Jeroboam the son	2399
	10:31 he departed not from the **s** of Jeroboam,	2403
	13: 2 followed the **s** of Jeroboam the son of	2403
	13: 6 they departed not from the **s**	2403
	13:11 departed not from all the **s** of Jeroboam	2403
	14:24 departed not from all the **s** of Jeroboam	2403
	15: 9 he departed not from the **s** of Jeroboam	2403
	15:18 he departed not all his days from the **s** of	2403
	15:24 he departed not from the **s** of Jeroboam	2403
	15:28 he departed not from the **s** of Jeroboam	2403
	17:22 the children of Israel walked in all the **s**	2403
	24: 3 for the **s** of Manasseh, according to all	2403
2Ch	28:10 with you, **s** against the Lord your God?	819
	28:13 *already*, ye intend to add *more* to our **s**	2403
Ne	1: 6 confess the **s** of the children of Israel,	2403
	9: 2 stood and confessed their **s**,	2403
	9:37 thou hast set over us because of our **s**:	2403
Job	13:23 How many *are* mine iniquities and **s**?	2403
Ps	19:13 **s**; let them not have dominion over me:	NIH
	25: 7 Remember not the **s** of my youth, nor my	2403
	25:18 and my pain; and forgive all my **s**.	2403
	51: 9 Hide thy face from my **s**, and blot out all	2399
	69: 5 and my **s** are not hid from thee.	819
	79: 9 deliver us, and purge away our **s**, for thy	2403
	90: 8 secret **s** in the light of thy countenance.	NIH
	103:10 He hath not dealt with us after our **s**;	2399
Pr	5:22 shall be holden with the cords of his **s**.	2403
	10:12 stirreth up strifes: but love covereth all **s**.	6588
	28:13 He that covereth his **s** shall not prosper:	6588
Isa	1:18 though your **s** be as scarlet, they shall be	2399
	38:17 thou hast cast all my **s** behind thy back.	2399
	40: 2 of the Lord's hand double for all her **s**.	2403
	43:24 thou hast made me to serve with thy **s**,	2403
	43:25 own sake, and will not remember thy **s**.	2403
	44:22 thy transgressions, and, as a cloud, thy **s**:	2403
	58: 1 and the house of Jacob their **s**.	2403
	59: 2 and your **s** have hid *his* face from you,	2403
	59:12 before thee, and our **s** testify against us:	2403
Jer	5:25 your **s** have withholden good *things* from	2403
	14:10 remember their iniquity, and visit their **s**.	2403
	15:13 *that* for all thy **s**, even in all thy borders.	2403
	30:14 because thy **s** were increased.	2403
	30:15 *because* thy **s** were increased, I have done	2403
	50:20 **s** of Judah, and they shall not be found:	2403
La	3:39 a man for the **punishment** of his **s**?	2399
	4:13 the **s** of her prophets, *and* the iniquities	2403
	4:22 daughter of Edom; he will discover thy **s**.	2403
Eze	16:51 hath Samaria committed half of thy **s**;	2403
	16:52 **s** that thou hast **committed** more	2403
	18:14 that seeth all his father's **s** which he hath	2403
	18:21 if the wicked will turn from all his **s** that	2403
	21:24 that in all your doings your **s** do appear;	2403
	23:49 and ye shall bear the **s** of your idols:	2399
	33:10 our transgressions and our **s** *be* upon us,	2403

Eze	33:16 None of his **s** that he hath committed	2403
Da	4:27 break off thy **s** by righteousness,	2408
	9:16 because for our **s**, and for the iniquities of	2399
	9:24 to make an end of **s**, and to make	2403
Hos	8:13 remember their iniquity, and visit their **s**:	2403
	9: 9 their iniquity, he will visit their **s**.	2403
Am	5:12 transgressions and your mighty **s**:	2403
Mic	1: 5 this, and for the **s** of the house of Israel.	2403
	6:13 in making *thee* desolate because of thy **s**.	2403
	7:19 thou wilt cast all their **s** into the depths	2403
Mt	1:21 for he shall save his people from their **s**.	266
	3: 6 of him in Jordan, confessing their **s**.	266
	9: 2 *be of good cheer; thy* **s** *be forgiven thee.*	266
	9: 5 *is easier, to say, Thy* **s** *be forgiven thee,*	266
	9: 6 *of man hath power on earth to forgive* **s**,	266
	26:28 *is shed for many for the remission of* **s**.	266
Mk	1: 4 of repentance for the remission of **s**.	266
	1: 5 in the river of Jordan, confessing their **s**.	266
	2: 5 of the palsy, *Son, thy* **s** *be forgiven thee.*	266
	2: 7 who can forgive **s** but God only?	266
	2: 9 *sick of the palsy, Thy* **s** *be forgiven thee;*	266
	2:10 *of man hath power on earth to forgive* **s**,	266
	3:28 *All* **s** *shall be forgiven unto the sons of*	265
	4:12 *and their* **s** *should be forgiven them.*	265
Lk	1:77 unto his people by the remission of their **s**,	266
	3: 3 of repentance for the remission of **s**;	266
	5:20 unto him, *Man, thy* **s** *are forgiven thee.*	266
	5:21 *Who can forgive* **s**, *but God alone?*	266
	5:23 *is easier, to say, Thy* **s** *be forgiven thee;*	266
	5:24 *man hath power upon earth to forgive* **s**,	266
	7:47 *Her* **s**, *which are many, are forgiven;*	266
	7:48 *And he said unto her, Thy* **s** *are forgiven.*	266
	7:49 *Who is this that forgiveth* **s** *also?*	266
	11: 4 *And forgive us our* **s**; *for we also forgive*	266
	24:47 *remission of* **s** *should be preached in his*	266
Jn	8:21 ye shall seek me, and shall die in your **s**:	266
	8:24 unto you, that ye shall die in your **s**:	266
	8:24 *not that I am he,* ye shall die in your **s**.	266
	9:34 Thou wast altogether born in **s**, and dost	266
	20:23 *Whose soever* **s** *ye remit, they are remitted*	266
	20:23 *and whose soever* **s** *ye retain, they are*	NIG
Ac	2:38 name of Jesus Christ for the remission of **s**,	266
	3:19 converted, that your **s** may be blotted out,	266
	5:31 repentance to Israel, and forgiveness of **s**.	266
	10:43 in him shall receive remission of **s**.	266
	13:38 is preached unto you the forgiveness of **s**:	266
	22:16 and be baptized, and wash away thy **s**,	266
	26:18 *that they may receive forgiveness of* **s**,	266
Ro	3:25 for the remission of **s** that are past,	265
	4: 7 are forgiven, and whose **s** are covered.	266
	7: 5 the motions of **s**, which were by the law,	266
	11:27 unto them, when I shall take away their **s**.	266
1Co	15: 3 how that Christ died for our **s** according to	266
	15:17 your faith *is* vain; ye are yet in your **s**.	266
Gal	1: 4 Who gave himself for our **s**, that he might	266
Eph	1: 7 the forgiveness of **s**, according to the	3900
	2: 1 who were dead in trespasses and **s**;	266
	2: 5 Even when we were dead in **s**,	3900
Col	1:14 his blood, *even* the forgiveness of **s**:	266
	2:11 putting off the body of the **s** of the flesh,	266
	2:13 being dead in your **s** and	3900
1Th	2:16 might be saved, to fill up their **s** alway:	266
1Ti	5:22 *man*, neither be partaker of other *men's* **s**:	266
	5:24 Some men's **s** are open beforehand,	266
2Ti	3: 6 and lead captive silly women laden with **s**,	266
Heb	1: 3 when he had by himself purged our **s**,	266
	2:17 to make reconciliation for the **s** of	266
	5: 1 he may offer both gifts and sacrifices for **s**:	266
	5: 3 people, so also for himself, to offer for **s**.	266
	7:27 for his own **s**, *and* then for the people's:	266
	8:12 and their **s** and their iniquities will I	266
	9:28 So Christ was once offered to bear the **s** of	266
	10: 2 should have had no more conscience of **s**.	266
	10: 3 a remembrance *again made* of **s** every year.	266
	10: 4 of bulls and of goats should take away **s**.	266
	10:11 which can never take away **s**:	266
	10:12 he had offered one sacrifice for **s** for ever,	266
	10:17 their **s** and iniquities will I remember no	266
	10:26 there remaineth no more sacrifice for **s**,	266
Jas	5:15 and if he have committed **s**, they shall be	266
	5:20 from death, and shall hide a multitude of **s**.	266
1Pe	2:24 his own self bare our **s** in his own body	266
	2:24 that we, being dead to **s**, should live unto	266
	3:18 For Christ also hath once suffered for **s**,	266
	4: 8 for charity shall cover the multitude of **s**.	266
2Pe	1: 9 that *he* was purged from his old **s**.	266
1Jn	1: 9 If we confess our **s**, he is faithful and just	266
	1: 9 he is faithful and just to forgive us *our* **s**,	266
	2: 2 And he is the propitiation for our **s**:	266
	2: 2 but also for the **s** of the whole world.	NIG
	2:12 *your* **s** are forgiven you for his name's sake.	266
	3: 5 that he was manifested to take away our **s**;	266
	4:10 his Son *to be* the propitiation for our **s**.	266
Rev	1: 5 washed us from our **s** in his own blood,	266
	18: 4 that ye be not partakers of her **s**, and that	266
	18: 5 her **s** have reached unto heaven, and God	266

SION (8) [ZION]

Dt	4:48 even unto mount **S**, which *is* Hermon,	7865
Mt	21: 5 Tell ye the daughter of **S**, Behold, thy King	4622
Jn	12:15 Fear not, daughter of **S**: behold, thy King	4622
Ro	9:33 I lay in **S** a stumblingstone and rock of	4622
	11:26 There shall come out of **S** the Deliverer,	4622
Heb	12:22 But ye are come unto mount **S**,	4622
1Pe	2: 6 I lay in **S** a chief corner stone, elect,	4622

Rev	14: 1 and lo, a Lamb stood on the mount **S**,	4622

SIPHMOTH (1)

1Sa	30:28 to *them* which *were* in **S**, and to *them*	8224

SIPPAI (1)

1Ch	20: 4 time Sibbechai the Hushathite slew **S**,	5598

SIR (12) [SIRS]

Ge	43:20 O **s**, we came indeed down at the first	113
Mt	13:27 householder came and said unto him, **S**,	2962
	21:30 And he answered and said, I *go*, **s**:	2962
	27:63 **S**, we remember that that deceiver	2962
Jn	4:11 The woman saith unto him, **S**, thou hast	2962
	4:15 **S**, give me this water, that I thirst not,	2962
	4:19 The woman saith unto him, **S**, I perceive	2962
	4:49 him, **S**, come down ere my child die.	2962
	5: 7 **S**, I have no man, when the water is	2962
	12:21 and desired him, saying, **S**, we would see	2962
	20:15 him to be the gardener, saith unto him, **S**,	2962
Rev	7:14 And I said unto him, **S**, thou knowest.	2962

SIRAH (1)

2Sa	3:26 brought him again from the well of **S**:	5626

SIRION (2)

Dt	3: 9 (*Which* Hermon the Sidonians call **S**;	8303
Ps	29: 6 calf; Lebanon and **S** like a young unicorn.	8303

SIRS (7) [SIR]

Ac	7:26 at one *again*, saying, **S**, ye are brethren;	435
	14:15 And saying, **S**, why do ye these *things*?	435
	16:30 And brought them out, and said, **S**,	2962
	19:25 and said, **S**, ye know that by this craft we	435
	27:10 And said unto them, **S**, I perceive that *this*	435
	27:21 said, **S**, *ye* should have hearkened unto	435
	27:25 **s**, be of good cheer: for I believe	435

SISAMAI (2)

1Ch	2:40 Eleasah begat **S**, and Sisamai begat	5581
	2:40 begat Sisamai, and **S** begat Shallum,	5581

SISERA (21)

Jdg	4: 2 the captain of whose host *was* **S**, which	5516
	4: 7 will draw unto thee to the river Kishon **S**,	5516
	4: 9 for the Lord shall sell **S** into the hand of	5516
	4:12 they shewed **S** that Barak the son of	5516
	4:13 **S** gathered together all his chariots,	5516
	4:14 Lord hath delivered **S** into thine hand:	5516
	4:15 the Lord discomfited **S**, and all *his*	5516
	4:15 so that **S** lighted down off *his* chariot,	5516
	4:16 all the host of **S** fell upon the edge of	5516
	4:17 **S** fled away on his feet to the tent	5516
	4:18 Jael went out to meet **S**, and said unto	5516
	4:22 behold, as Barak pursued **S**, Jael came out	5516
	4:22 **S** lay dead, and the nail *was* in his	5516
	5:20 stars in their courses fought against **S**.	5516
	5:26 with the hammer she smote **S**, she smote	5516
	5:28 The mother of **S** looked out at a window,	5516
	5:30 to **S** a prey of divers colours, a prey of	5516
1Sa	12: 9 he sold them into the hand of **S**, captain	5516
Ezr	2:53 The children of Barkos, the children of **S**,	5516
Ne	7:55 the children of **S**, the children of Tamah,	5516
Ps	83: 9 as *to* **S**, as *to* Jabin, at the brook of Kison:	5516

SISMAI See SISAMAI

SISTER (109) [SISTER'S, SISTERS]

Ge	4:22 iron: and the **s** of Tubal-cain *was* Naamah.	269
	12:13 Say, I pray thee, thou *art* my **s**: that it may	269
	12:19 Why saidst thou, She *is* my **s**? so I might	269
	20: 2 said of Sarah his wife, She *is* my **s**:	269
	20: 5 Said he not unto me, She *is* my **s**? and she,	269
	20:12 indeed *she is* my **s**; she *is* the daughter of	269
	24:30 he heard the words of Rebekah his **s**,	269
	24:59 they sent away Rebekah their **s**, and her	269
	24:60 and said unto her, Thou *art* our **s**,	269
	25:20 of Padan-aram, the **s** to Laban the Syrian.	269
	26: 7 *him* of his wife; and he said, She *is* my **s**:	269
	26: 9 thou saidst thou, She *is* my **s**? And Isaac	269
	28: 9 the **s** of Nebajoth, to be his wife.	269
	30: 1 Jacob no *children*, Rachel envied her **s**,	269
	30: 8 wrestlings have I wrestled with my **s**,	269
	34:13 said, because he had defiled Dinah their **s**:	269
	34:14 to give our **s** to one that is uncircumcised;	269
	34:27 the city, because they had defiled their **s**.	269
	34:31 Should he deal with our **s** as with a harlot?	269
	36: 3 Ishmael's daughter, **s** of Nebajoth.	269
	36:22 and Hemam; and Lotan's **s** *was* Timna.	269
	46:17 and Ishui, and Beriah, and Serah their **s**:	269
Ex	2: 4 his **s** stood afar off, to wit what would be	269
	2: 7 said his **s** to Pharaoh's daughter, Shall I go	269
	6:20 Amram took him Jochebed, his **father's s**	1733
	6:23 of Amminadab, **s** of Naashon, to wife;	269
	15:20 the **s** of Aaron, took a timbrel in her hand;	269
Lev	18: 9 The nakedness of thy **s**, the daughter of	269
	18:11 begotten of thy father, she *is* thy **s**, thou	269
	18:12 uncover the nakedness of thy father's **s**:	269
	18:13 uncover the nakedness of thy mother's **s**:	269
	18:18 Neither shalt thou take a wife to her **s**,	269
	20:17 if a man shall take his **s**, his father's	269
	20:19 uncover the nakedness of thy mother's **s**,	269
	20:19 of thy mother's **s**, nor of thy father's **s**:	269
	21: 3 for his **s** a virgin, that is nigh unto him,	269
Nu	6: 7 for his brother, or for his **s**, when they die:	269
	25:18 the daughter of a prince of Midian, their **s**,	269

Nu 26:59 and Moses, and Miriam their **s**. 269
Dt 27:22 Cursed *be* he that lieth with his **s**, 269
Jdg 15: 2 *is* not her younger **s** fairer than she? 269
Ru 1:15 **s in law** is gone back unto her people, 2994
 1:15 her gods: return thou after thy **s in law**. 2994
2Sa 13: 1 Absalom the son of David had a fair **s**, 269
 13: 2 *so* vexed, that he fell sick for his **s** 269
 13: 4 I love Tamar, my brother Absalom's **s**. 269
 13: 5 let my **s** Tamar come, and give me meat, 269
 13: 6 Tamar my **s** come, and make *me* a couple 269
 13:11 said unto her, Come lie with me, my **s**. 269
 13:20 now thy peace, my **s**: he *is* thy brother; 269
 13:22 because he had forced his **s** Tamar. 269
 13:32 from the day that he forced his **s** Tamar. 269
 17:25 of Nahash, **s** to Zeruiah Joab's mother. 269
1Ki 11:19 that he gave him *to* wife the **s** of his own 269
 11:19 his own wife, the **s** of Tahpenes the queen. 269
 11:20 the **s** of Tahpenes bare him Genubath his 269
2Ki 11: 2 the daughter of king Joram, **s** of Ahaziah, 269
1Ch 1:39 and Homam: and Timna *was* Lotan's **s**. 269
 3: 9 of the concubines, and Tamar their **s**. 269
 3:19 and Hananiah, and Shelomith their **s**: 269
 4: 3 and the name of their **s** *was* Hazelelponi: 269
 4:19 sons of *his* wife Hodiah the **s** of Naham, 269
 7:15 Machir took to wife *the* **s** of Huppim and NIH
 7:18 And his **s** Hammoleketh bare Ishod, and Abiezer, 269
 7:30 and Ishuai, and Beriah, and Serah their **s**. 269
 7:32 Shomer, and Hotham, and Shua their **s**. 269
2Ch 22:11 the priest, (for she was the **s** of Ahaziah,) 269
Job 17:14 the worm, *Thou art* my mother, and my **s**. 269
Pr 7: 4 Say unto wisdom, Thou *art* my **s**; 269
SS 4: 9 hast ravished my heart, my **s**, *my* spouse; 269
 4:10 How fair is thy love, my **s**, *my* spouse! 269
 4:12 A garden inclosed *is* my **s**, *my* spouse: 269
 5: 1 come into my garden, my **s**, *my* spouse: 269
 5: 2 my **s**, my love, my dove, my undefiled: 269
 8: 8 We have a little **s**, and she hath no breasts: 269
 8: 8 what shall we do for our **s** in the day when 269
Jer 3: 7 And her treacherous **s** Judah saw *it*. 269
 3: 8 yet her treacherous **s** Judah feared not, 269
 3:10 yet for all this her treacherous **s** Judah hath 269
 22:18 or, Ah **s**! they shall not lament for him, 269
Eze 16:45 thou *art* the **s** of thy sisters, which lothed 269
 16:46 thine elder **s** *is* Samaria, she and 269
 16:46 thy younger **s**, that dwelleth at thy right 269
 16:48 the Lord GOD, Sodom thy **s** hath not done, 269
 16:49 this was the iniquity of thy **s** Sodom, pride, 269
 16:56 For thy **s** Sodom was not mentioned by thy 269
 22:11 another in thee hath humbled his **s**, 269
 23: 4 Aholah the elder, and Aholibah his **s**: 269
 23:11 her **s** Aholibah saw *this*, she was more 269
 23:11 in her whoredoms more than her **s** in *her* 269
 23:18 like as my mind was alienated from her **s**. 269
 23:31 Thou hast walked in the way of thy **s**; 269
 23:33 desolation, *with* the cup of thy **s** Samaria. 269
 44:25 or for **s** that hath had no husband, 269
Mt 12:50 the same is my brother, and my **s**, and mother. 79
Mk 3:35 same is my brother, and my **s**, and mother. 79
Lk 10:39 she had a **s** called Mary, which also sat at 79
 10:40 dost thou not care that my **s** hath left me to 79
Jn 11: 1 the town of Mary and her **s** Martha. 79
 11: 5 Jesus loved Martha, and her **s**, and Lazarus. 79
 11:28 and called Mary her **s** secretly, saying, 79
 11:39 Martha, the **s** of him that was dead, saith 79
 19:25 and his mother's, Mary the *wife* of 79
Ro 16: 1 I commend unto you Phebe our **s**, which is 79
 16:15 and his **s**, and Olympas, and all the saints 79
1Co 7:15 or a **s** is not under bondage in such *cases*: 79
 9: 5 we not power to lead about a **s**, a wife, 79
Jas 2:15 If a brother or **s** be naked, and destitute of 79
2Jn 1:13 The children of thy elect **s** greet thee. 79

SISTER'S (7) [SISTER]

Ge 24:30 earring and bracelets upon his **s** hands, 269
 29:13 Laban heard the tidings of Jacob his **s** 269
Lev 20:17 he hath uncovered his **s** nakedness; he 269
1Ch 7:15 Shuppim, whose **s** name *was* Maachah;) 269
Eze 23:32 Thou shalt drink *of* thy **s** cup deep and 269
Ac 23:16 when Paul's **s** son heard of *their* lying in 79
Col 4:10 and Marcus, **s son** to Barnabas, 431

SISTERS (19) [SISTER]

Jos 2:13 my **s**, and all that they have, and deliver 269
1Ch 2:16 Whose **s** *were* Zeruiah, and Abigail. 269
Job 1: 4 sent and called for their three **s** to eat and 269
 42:11 all his **s**, and all *they that had been of* his 269
Eze 16:45 *art* the sister of thy **s**, which lothed their 269
 16:51 justified thy **s** in all thine abominations 269
 16:52 Thou also, which hast judged thy **s**, 269
 16:52 shame, in that thou hast justified thy **s**. 269
 16:55 When thy **s**, Sodom and her daughters, 269
 16:61 when thou shalt receive thy **s**, thine elder 269
Hos 2: 1 Ammi; and to your **s**, Ruhamah. 269
Mt 13:56 And his **s**, are they not all with us? Whence 79
 19:29 or **s**, or father, or mother, or wife, or 79
Mk 3: 3 are not his **s** here with us? And they were 79
 10:29 or **s**, or father, or mother, or wife, or 79
 10:30 and mothers, and children, and lands, 79
Lk 14:26 and children, and brethren, and **s**, yea, 79
Jn 11: 3 Therefore *his* **s** sent unto him, saying, Lord, 79
1Ti 5: 2 as mothers; the younger as **s**, with all purity. 79

SIT (113) [DOWNSITTING, SAT, SATEST, SEAT, SEATED, SEATS, SEATWARD, SITTEST, SITTETH, SITTING]

Ge 27:19 I pray thee, **s** and eat of my venison, 3427
Nu 32: 6 brethren go to war, and shall ye **s** here? 3427
Jdg 5:10 that is **s** in judgment, and walk by the way. 3427
Ru 3:18 said she, **S** still, my daughter, until thou 3427
 4: 1 *Ho*, such a one, turn aside, **s down** here. 3427
 4: 2 of the city, and said, **S** ye **down** here. 3427
1Sa 9:22 **made** them **s** in the chiefest place 5414
 16:11 he will not **s down** till he come hither. 5437
 20: 5 I should **not fail to s** with the king 3427+3427
2Sa 19: 8 Behold, the king doth **s** in the gate. 3427
1Ki 1:13 after me, and he shall **s** upon my throne? 3427
 1:17 after me, and he shall **s** upon my throne. 3427
 1:20 *thou* shouldest tell them who shall **s** on 3427
 1:24 after me, and he shall **s** upon my throne. 3427
 1:27 who should **s** on the throne of my lord 3427
 1:30 he shall **s** upon my throne in my stead; 3427
 1:35 that he may come and **s** upon my throne; 3427
 1:48 hath given *one* to **s** on my throne *this* 3427
 3: 6 that thou hast given him a son to **s** on his 3427
 8:20 **s** on the throne of Israel, as the LORD 3427
 8:25 in my sight to **s** on the throne of Israel; 3427
2Ki 7: 3 to another, Why **s** we here until we die? 3427
 7: 4 if we **s** still here, we die also. NIH
 10:30 children of the fourth *generation* shall **s** 3427
 15:12 Thy sons shall **s** on the throne of Israel 3427
 18:27 he not *sent me* to the men which **s** on 3427
1Ch 28: 5 hath chosen Solomon my son to **s** upon 3427
2Ch 6:16 in my sight to **s** upon the throne of Israel; 3427
Ps 26: 5 evildoers; and will not **s** with the wicked. 3427
 69:12 They that **s** in the gate speak against me; 3427
 107:10 Such as **s** in darkness and in the shadow 3427
 110: 1 unto my Lord, **S** thou at my right hand, 3427
 119:23 Princes also did **s** and speak against me: 3427
 127: 2 to **s up** late, to eat the bread of sorrows; 3427
 132:12 their children also shall **s** upon thy throne 3427
Ecc 10: 6 great dignity, and the rich **s** in low place. 3427
Isa 3:26 *being* desolate shall **s** upon the ground. 3427
 14:13 I will **s** also upon the mount of 3427
 16: 5 shall **s** upon it in truth in the tabernacle 3427
 30: 7 this, Their strength *is* to **s still**. 7674
 36:12 he not *sent me* to the men that **s** upon 3427
 42: 7 them that **s** in darkness out of the prison 3427
 47: 1 Come down, and **s** in the dust, O virgin 3427
 47: 1 daughter of Babylon, **s** on the ground: 3427
 47: 5 **S** thou silent, and get thee into darkness, 3427
 47: 8 I shall not **s** *as* a widow, neither shall I 3427
 47:14 a coal to warm at, *nor* fire to **s** before it. 3427
 52: 2 dust; arise, *and* **s down**, O Jerusalem: 3427
Jer 13: 8 Why do we **s still**? assemble yourselves, 3427
 13:13 the kings that **s** upon David's throne, 3427
 13:18 the queen, Humble yourselves, **s down**: 3427
 16: 8 to **s** with them to eat and to drink. 3427
 33:17 David shall never want a man to **s** upon 3427
 36:15 **S down** now, and read it in our ears. 3427
 36:30 He shall have none to **s** upon the throne 3427
 48:18 come down from *thy* glory, and **s** in thirst; 3427
La 1: 1 How doth the city **s** solitary, *that was* full 3427
 2:10 The elders of the daughter of Zion **s** upon 3427
Eze 26:16 they shall **s** upon the ground, 3427
 28: 2 said, I am a God, I **s** in the seat of God, 3427
 33:31 they **s** before thee *as* my people, 3427
 44: 3 he shall **s** in it to eat bread before 3427
Da 7: 9 cast *down*, and the Ancient of days did **s**, 3488
 7:26 the judgment shall **s**, and they shall take 3488
Joel 3:12 for there will I **s** to judge all the heathen 3427
Mic 4: 4 they shall **s** every man under his vine and 3427
 7: 8 when I **s** in darkness, the LORD *shall be* a 3427
Zec 3: 8 thou, and thy fellows that **s** before thee: 3427
 6:13 and shall **s** and rule upon his throne: 3427
Mal 3: 3 shall **s** *as* a refiner and purifier of silver: 3427
Mt 8:11 shall **s down** with Abraham, and Isaac, 347
 14:19 he commanded the multitude to **s down** 347
 15:35 he commanded the multitude to **s down** 377
 19:28 when the Son of man shall **s** in the throne 2523
 19:28 ye also shall **s** upon twelve thrones, 2523
 20:21 Grant that these my two sons may **s**, 2523
 20:23 baptized *with*: but to **s** on my right hand, 2523
 22:44 unto my Lord, **S** thou on my right hand, 2521
 23: 2 and the Pharisees **s** in Moses' seat: 2523
 25:31 shall he **s** upon the throne of his glory: 2523
 26:36 **S**ye here, while I go and pray yonder. 2523
Mk 6:39 **make** all **s down** by companies upon 347
 8: 6 he commanded the people to **s down** 377
 10:37 unto him, Grant unto us that we may **s**, 2523
 10:40 But to **s** on my right hand and on my left 2523
 12:36 said to my Lord, **S** thou on my right hand, 2521
 14:32 his disciples, **S** ye here, while I shall pray. 2523
Lk 1:79 To give light to them that **s** in darkness 2521
 9:14 **Make** them **s down** by fifties in a 2625
 9:15 they did so, and **made** *them* all **s down**. 347
 12:37 and **make** them to **s down to meat**, 347
 13:29 and shall **s down** in the kingdom of God. 347
 14: 8 wedding, **s** not **down** in the highest room; 2625
 14:10 go and **s down** in the lowest room; 377
 14:10 of them that **s at meat with** thee. 4873
 16: 6 and **s down** quickly, and write fifty. 2523
 17: 7 from the field, Go and **s down to meat**? 377
 20:42 said to my Lord, **S** thou on my right hand, 2521
 22:30 **s** on thrones judging the twelve tribes of 2523
 22:69 Hereafter shall the Son of man **s** on 2521
Jn 6:10 And Jesus said, Make the men **s down**. 377

Ac 2:30 would raise up Christ to **s** on his throne; 2523
 2:34 unto my Lord, **S** thou on my right hand, 2521
 8:31 that *he* would come up and **s** with him. 2523
1Co 8:10 knowledge **s at meat** in the idol's temple, 2621
Eph 2: 6 **made** *us* **together** in heavenly *places* 4776
Heb 1:13 **S** on my right hand, until I make thine 2521
Jas 2: 3 say unto him, **S** thou here in a good place; 2521
 2: 3 thou there, or **s** here under my footstool: 2521
Rev 3:21 To him that overcometh will I grant to **s** 2523
 17: 1 I saw a woman upon a scarlet coloured 2521
 18: 7 I **s** a queen, and am no widow, and shall 2521
 19:18 of them that **s** on them, and the flesh of 2521

SITH (3) [SINCE]

Jer 15: 7 **s** they return not from their ways. NIH
 23:38 ye say, The burden of the LORD; 518
Eze 35: 6 **s** thou hast not hated blood, even blood 518

SITHRI See ZITHRI

SITNAH (1)

Ge 26:21 that also: and he called the name of it **S**. 7856

SITTEST (7) [SITH]

Ex 18:14 why **s** thou thyself alone, and all the 3427
Dt 6: 7 shalt talk of them when thou **s** in thine 3427
 11:19 speaking of them when thou **s** in thine 3427
Ps 50:20 Thou **s** *and* speakest against thy brother; 3427
Pr 23: 1 When thou **s** to eat with a ruler, 3427
Jer 22: 2 that **s** upon the throne of David, thou, 3427
Ac 23: 3 for **s** thou to judge me after the law, 2521

SITTETH (42) [SITH]

Ex 11: 5 from the firstborn of Pharaoh that **s** upon 3427
Lev 15: 4 thing, whereon he **s**, shall be unclean. 3427
 15: 6 he that **s** on *any* thing whereon he sat 3427
 15:20 every *thing* also that she **s** upon shall be 3427
 15:23 or on *any* thing whereon she **s**, when he 3427
 15:26 whatsoever she **s** upon shall be unclean, 3427
Dt 17:18 he **s** upon the throne of his kingdom, 3427
1Ki 1:46 also Solomon **s** on the throne of 3427
Est 6:10 Mordecai the Jew, that **s** at the king's 3427
Ps 1: 1 sinners, nor **s** in the seat of the scornful. 3427
 2: 4 He that **s** in the heavens shall laugh: 3427
 10: 8 In the lurking places of the villages: 3427
 29:10 The LORD **s** upon the flood; yea, 3427
 29:10 the flood; yea, the LORD **s** King for ever. 3427
 47: 8 God **s** upon the throne of his holiness. 3427
 99: 1 he **s** *between* the cherubims; let the earth 3427
Pr 9:14 she **s** at the door of her house, on a seat 3427
 20: 8 A king that **s** in the throne of judgment 3427
 31:23 when he **s** among the elders of the land. 3427
SS 1:12 While the king **s** at his table, my NIH
Isa 28: 6 for a spirit of judgment to him that **s** in 3427
 40:22 *It is* he that **s** upon the circle of the earth, 3427
Jer 17:11 *As* the partridge **s** *on* eggs, and 1716
 29:16 the king that **s** upon the throne of David, 3427
La 3:28 He is alone and keepeth silence, because 3427
Zec 1:11 behold, all the earth **s still**, and is at rest. 3427
 5: 7 this *is* a woman that **s** in the midst of 3427
Mt 23:22 of God, and by him that **s** thereon. 2521
Lk 14:28 **s** not **down** first, and counteth the cost, 2523
 14:31 **s** not **down** first, and consulteth whether 2523
 22:27 he that **s at meat**, or he that serveth? 345
 22:27 *is* not he that **s at meat**? but I am among 345
1Co 14:30 If *any* thing be revealed to another that **s** 2521
Col 3: 1 where Christ **s** on the right hand of God, 2521
2Th 2: 4 so that he as God **s** in the temple of God, 2523
Rev 5:13 *be* unto him that **s** upon the throne, 2521
 6:16 hide us from the face of him that **s** 2521
 7:10 Salvation to our God which **s** upon 2521
 7:15 he that **s** on the throne shall dwell among 2521
 17: 1 the great whore that **s** upon many waters: 2521
 17: 9 seven mountains, on which the woman **s**. 2521
 17:15 where the whore **s**, are peoples, 2521

SITTING (43) [SITH]

Dt 22: 6 the dam **s** upon the young, or upon 7257
Jdg 3:20 he was **s** in a summer parlour, which he 4186
1Ki 10: 5 the **s** of his servants, and the attendance 4186
 13:14 of God, and found him **s** under an oak: 3427
 22:19 I saw the LORD **s** on his throne, 3427
2Ki 4:38 sons of the prophets *were* **s** before him: 3427
 9: 5 the captains of the host *were* **s**; 3427
2Ch 9: 4 the **s** of his servants, and the attendance 4186
 9:18 stays on each side of the **s** place, 3427
 18:18 I saw the LORD **s** upon his throne, 3427
Ne 5:13 said unto me, (the queen also **s** by him,) 3427
Est 5:13 long as I see Mordecai the Jew **s** at 3427
Isa 6: 1 I died I saw also the Lord **s** upon a throne, 3427
Jer 17:25 and princes **s** upon the throne of David, 3427
 22: 4 house kings **s** upon the throne of David, 3427
 22:30 **s** upon the throne of David, and ruling 3427
 38: 7 the king then **s** in the gate of Benjamin; 3427
La 3:63 Behold their **s down**, and their rising up; 3427
Mt 9: 9 Matthew, **s** at the receipt of custom; 2521
 11:16 It is like unto children **s** in the markets, 2521
 20:30 two blind men **s** by the way side, 2521
 21: 5 and **s** upon an ass, and a colt the foal of 1910
 26:64 Hereafter shall ye see the Son of man **s** on 2521
 27:36 And **s down** they watched him there; 2521
 27:61 other Mary, **s** over against the sepulchre. 2521
Mk 2: 6 there were certain of the scribes **s** there, 2521
 2:14 he saw Levi the *son* of Alpheus **s** at 2521
 5:15 **s**, and clothed, and in his right mind: 2521
 14:62 ye shall see the Son of man **s** on the right 2521

Mk 16: 5 they saw a young man **s** on the right side, 2521
Lk 2:46 **s** in the midst of the doctors, both 2516
 5:17 doctors of the law *by,* which were come 2521
 5:27 named Levi, **s** at the receipt of custom: 2521
 7:32 They are like unto children **s** in 2521
 8:35 **s** at the feet of Jesus, clothed, and in his 2521
 10:13 ago repented, **s** in sackcloth and ashes. 2521
Jn 2:14 and doves, and the changers of money **s**: 2521
 12:15 thy King cometh, **s** on an ass's colt. 2521
 20:12 seeth two angels in white **s**, the one at 2516
Ac 2: 2 it filled all the house where they were **s**. 2521
 8:28 **s** in his chariot read Esaias the prophet. 2521
 25: 6 and the next day **s** in the judgment seat, 2523
Rev 4: 4 the seats I saw four and twenty elders **s**, 2521

SITUATE (3) [SITUATION]
1Sa 14: 5 The forefront of the one *was* **s** northward 4690
Eze 27: 3 O thou that art **s** at the entry of the sea, 3427
Na 3: 8 No, that was **s** among the rivers, 3427

SITUATION (2) [SITUATE]
2Ki 2:19 I pray thee, the **s** of *this* city *is* pleasant, 4186
Ps 48: 2 Beautiful for **s**, the joy of the whole earth, 5131

SIVAN (1)
Est 8: 9 that *is,* the month **S**, on the three and 5510

SIX (202) [SIXSCORE, SIXTH]
Ge 7: 6 Noah *was* **s** hundred years old when 8337
 7:11 In the **s** hundredth year of Noah's life, 8337
 8:13 it came to pass in the **s** hundredth and 8337
 16:16 Abram *was* fourscore and **s** years old, 8337
 30:20 with me, because I have born him **s** sons: 8337
 31:41 two daughters, and **s** years for thy cattle: 8337
 46:26 all the souls *were* threescore and **s**; 8337
Ex 12:37 about **s** hundred thousand on foot *that* 8337
 14: 7 And he took **s** hundred chosen chariots, 8337
 16:26 **S** days ye shall gather it; but on the 8337
 20: 9 **S** days shalt thou labour, and do all thy 8337
 20:11 For *in* **s** days the LORD made heaven and 8337
 21: 2 a Hebrew servant, **s** years he shall serve: 8337
 23:10 **s** years thou shalt sow thy land, 8337
 23:12 **S** days thou shalt do thy work, and on 8337
 24:16 and the cloud covered it **s** days: 8337
 25:32 **s** branches shall come out of the sides of 8337
 25:33 in the **s** branches that come out of 8337
 25:35 according to the **s** branches that proceed 8337
 26: 9 **s** curtains by themselves, and shalt double 8337
 26:22 westward thou shalt make **s** boards. 8337
 28:10 **S** of their names on one stone, and the 8337
 28:10 *other* **s** names of the rest on the other 8337
 31:15 **S** days may work be done; but in 8337
 31:17 for *in* **s** days the LORD made heaven and 8337
 34:21 **S** days thou shalt work, but on the 8337
 35: 2 **S** days shall work be done, but on 8337
 36:16 and **s** curtains by themselves. 8337
 36:27 tabernacle westward he made **s** boards. 8337
 37:18 **s** branches going out of the sides thereof; 8337
 37:19 throughout the **s** branches going out of 8337
 37:21 according to the **s** branches going out of 8337
 38:26 **s** hundred thousand and three thousand 8337
Lev 12: 5 of her purifying threescore and **s** days. 8337
 23: 3 **S** days work be done: but the 8337
 24: 6 shalt set them *in* two rows, **s** on a row, 8337
 25: 3 **S** years thou shalt sow thy field, 8337
 25: 3 **s** years thou shalt prune thy vineyard, 8337
Nu 1:21 *were* forty and **s** thousand and 8337
 1:25 and five thousand **s** hundred and fifty. 8337
 1:27 and fourteen thousand **s** hundred. 8337
 1:46 all they that were numbered were **s** 8337
 2: 4 and fourteen thousand **s** hundred. 8337
 2: 9 and **s** thousand and four hundred, 8337
 2:11 *were* forty and **s** thousand and 8337
 2:15 five thousand and **s** hundred and fifty. 8337
 2:31 fifty and seven thousand and **s** hundred. 8337
 2:32 their hosts *were* **s** hundred thousand 8337
 3:28 *were* eight thousand and **s** hundred, 8337
 3:34 *were* **s** thousand and two hundred. 8337
 4:40 two thousand and **s** hundred and thirty. 8337
 7: 3 **s** covered wagons, and twelve oxen; 8337
 11:21 amongst whom I *am, are* **s** hundred 8337
 26:41 and five thousand and **s** hundred. 8337
 26:51 **s** hundred thousand and a thousand 8337
 31:32 was **s** hundred thousand and 8337
 31:37 the LORD's tribute of the sheep was **s** 8337
 31:38 the beeves *were* thirty and **s** thousand; 8337
 31:44 And thirty and **s** thousand beeves, 8337
 35: 6 Levites *there* shall *be* **s** cities for refuge, 8337
 35:13 *of these* cities which ye shall give **s** cities 8337
 35:15 These **s** cities shall be a refuge, *both* for 8337
Dt 5:13 **S** days thou shalt labour, and do all thy 8337
 15:12 be sold unto thee, and serve thee **s** years; 8337
 15:18 servant *to thee,* in serving thee **s** years: 8337
 16: 8 **S** days thou shalt eat unleavened bread: 8337
Jos 6: 3 the city once. Thus shalt thou do **s** days. 8337
 6:14 *into* the camp: so they did **s** days. 8337
 7: 5 Ai smote of them about thirty and **s** men: 8337
 15:59 and Eltekon; **s** cities with their villages. 8337
 15:62 and En-gedi; **s** cities with their villages. 8337
Jdg 3:31 which slew *of* the Philistines **s** hundred 8337
 12: 7 Jephthah judged Israel **s** years. Then died 8337
 18:11 **s** hundred men appointed *with* weapons 8337
 18:16 the **s** hundred men appointed *with* their 8337
 18:17 **s** hundred men that were appointed *with* 8337
 20:15 and **s** thousand men that drew sword, 8337

Jdg 20:47 **s** hundred men turned and fled to 8337
Ru 3:15 he measured *measures* of barley, 8337
 3:17 These **s** *measures* of barley gave he me; 8337
1Sa 13: 5 **s** thousand horsemen, and people as 8337
 13:15 present with him, about **s** hundred men. 8337
 14: 2 people that *were* with him *were* about **s** 8337
 17: 4 whose height *was* **s** cubits and a span. 8337
 17: 7 spear's head *weighed* **s** hundred shekels 8337
 23:13 which were about **s** hundred, arose and 8337
 27: 2 he passed over with the **s** hundred men 8337
 30: 9 the **s** hundred men that *were* with him, 8337
2Sa 2:11 of Judah was seven years and **s** months. 8337
 5: 5 over Judah seven years and **s** months: 8337
 6:13 the ark of the LORD had gone **s** paces, 8337
 15:18 **s** hundred men which came after him 8337
 21:20 that had on every hand **s** fingers, 8337
 21:20 on every foot **s** toes, four and twenty in 8337
1Ki 6: 6 middle *was* **s** cubits broad, and the third 8337
 10:14 in one year was **s** hundred threescore 8337
 10:14 hundred threescore and **s** talents of gold, 8337
 10:16 **s** hundred *shekels* of gold went to one 8337
 10:19 The throne had **s** steps, and the top of 8337
 10:20 side and on the other upon the **s** steps: 8337
 9:20 went out of Egypt for **s** hundred *shekels* 8337
 11:16 (For **s** months did Joab remain there with 8337
 16:23 twelve years: **s** years reigned he in Tirzah. 8337
2Ki 5: 5 **s** thousand *pieces* of gold, and ten 8337
 11: 3 her hid *in* the house of the LORD **s** years. 8337
 13:19 shouldest have smitten five or **s** times; 8337
 15: 8 reign over Israel in Samaria **s** months. 8337
1Ch 3: 4 *These* were born unto him in Hebron; 8337
 3: 4 he reigned seven years and **s** months: 8337
 3:22 and Bariah, and Neariah, and Shaphat, **s**. 8337
 4:27 Shimei had sixteen sons and **s** daughters; 8337
 7: 4 and twenty thousand and **s** hundred. 8337
 7: 4 **s** and thirty thousand *men:* for they had 8337
 7:40 to battle *was* twenty and **s** thousand men. 8337
 8:38 Azel had **s** sons, whose names *are* these, 8337
 9: 6 and their brethren, **s** hundred and ninety. 8337
 9: 9 nine hundred and fifty and **s**. 8337
 9:44 Azel had **s** sons, whose names *are* these, 8337
 12:24 spear *were* **s** thousand and eight hundred, 8337
 12:26 of Levi four thousand and **s** hundred. 8337
 12:35 and eight thousand and **s** hundred. 8337
 20: 6 **s** *on each hand,* and six *on each foot:* 8337
 20: 6 six *on each hand,* and **s** *on each foot:* 8337
 21:25 So David gave to Ornan for the place **s** 8337
 23: 4 and **s** thousand *were* officers and judges: 8337
 25: 3 Jeshaiah, Hashabiah, and Mattithiah, **s**, 8337
 26:17 Eastward *were* **s** Levites, northward four 8337
2Ch 1:17 brought forth out of Egypt a chariot for **s** 8337
 2: 2 and **s** hundred to oversee them. 8337
 2:17 and three thousand and **s** hundred. 8337
 2:18 **s** hundred overseers to set the people a 8337
 3: 8 gold, *amounting* to **s** hundred talents. 8337
 9:13 to Solomon in one year was **s** hundred 8337
 9:13 and threescore and **s** talents of gold; 8337
 9:15 **s** hundred *shekels* of beaten gold went to 8337
 9:18 *there were* **s** steps to the throne, with a 8337
 9:19 side and on the other upon the **s** steps. 8337
 16: 1 In the **s** and thirtieth year of the reign of 8337
 22:12 was with them hid in the house of God **s** 8337
 26:12 *were* two thousand and **s** hundred. 8337
 29:33 consecrated *things were* **s** hundred oxen 8337
 35: 8 **s** hundred *small cattle,* and three hundred 8337
Ezr 2:10 children of Bani, **s** hundred forty and two. 8337
 2:11 of Bebai, **s** hundred twenty and three. 8337
 2:13 of Adonikam, **s** hundred sixty and six. 8337
 2:13 of Adonikam, six hundred sixty and **s**. 8337
 2:14 of Bigvai, two thousand fifty and **s**. 8337
 2:22 The men of Netophah, fifty and **s**. 8337
 2:26 and Gaba, **s** hundred twenty and one. 8337
 2:30 of Magbish, an hundred fifty and **s**. 8337
 2:35 three thousand and **s** hundred and thirty. 8337
 2:60 of Nekoda, **s** hundred fifty and two. 8337
 2:66 horses *were* seven hundred thirty and **s**; 8337
 2:67 **s** thousand seven hundred and twenty. 8337
 8:26 even weighed unto their hand **s** hundred 8337
 8:35 ninety and **s** rams, seventy and 8337
Ne 5:18 me daily *was* one ox *and* **s** choice sheep; 8337
 7:10 children of Arah, **s** hundred fifty and two. 8337
 7:15 of Binnui, **s** hundred forty and eight. 8337
 7:16 of Bebai, **s** hundred twenty and eight. 8337
 7:18 **s** hundred threescore and seven. 8337
 7:20 children of Adin, **s** hundred fifty and five. 8337
 7:30 and Geba, **s** hundred twenty and one. 8337
 7:62 of Nekoda, **s** hundred forty and two. 8337
 7:68 Their horses, seven hundred thirty and **s**: 8337
 7:69 **s** thousand seven hundred and twenty 8337
Est 2:12 *to wit,* **s** months with oil of myrrh, 8337
 2:12 **s** months with sweet odours, and with 8337
Job 5:19 He shall deliver thee in **s** troubles: yea, 8337
 42:12 **s** thousand camels, and a thousand yoke 8337
Pr 6:16 These **s** *things* doth the LORD hate: yea, 8337
Isa 6: 2 each one had **s** wings; with twain he 8337
Jer 34:14 he hath served thee **s** years, thou shalt 8337
 52:23 ninety and **s** pomegranates on a side; 8337
 52:30 *were* four thousand and **s** hundred. 8337
Eze 9: 2 **s** men came from the way of the higher 8337
 40: 5 in the man's hand a measuring reed of **s** 8337
 40:12 the little chambers *were* **s** cubits on this 8337
 40:12 on this side, and **s** cubits on that side. 8337
 41: 1 **s** cubits broad on the one side, 8337
 41: 1 and **s** cubits broad on the other side, 8337
 41: 3 the door, **s** cubits; and the breadth of 8337

Eze 41: 5 measured the wall of the house, **s** cubits; 8337
 41: 8 *were* a full reed of **s** great cubits. 8337
 46: 1 the east shall be shut the **s** working days; 8337
 46: 4 day *shall be* **s** lambs without blemish, 8337
 46: 6 without blemish, and **s** lambs, and a ram: 8337
Da 3: 1 *and* the breadth thereof **s** cubits: 8353
Mt 17: 1 And after **s** days Jesus taketh Peter, James, 1803
Mk 9: 2 And after **s** days Jesus taketh with *him* 1803
Lk 4:25 was shut up three years and **s** months, 1803
 13:14 There are **s** days in which men ought to 1803
Jn 2: 6 And there were set there **s** waterpots of 1803
 2:20 and six years was this temple in building, 1803
 12: 1 Jesus **s** days before the passover came 1803
Ac 11:12 Moreover these **s** brethren accompanied 1803
 18:11 he continued *there* a year and **s** months, 1803
Jas 5:17 by the space *of* three years and **s** months. 1803
Rev 4: 8 And the four beasts had each of them **s** 1803
 13:18 *is* **S** hundred threescore *and* six. 5516
 13:18 *is* Six hundred threescore *and* **s**. 5516
 14:20 of a thousand *and* **s** hundred furlongs. 1812

SIXSCORE (2) [SIX]
1Ki 9:14 Hiram sent to the king **s** 3967+6242+2050.1
Jnh 4:11 wherein are more than **s** thousand 6240+8147

SIXTEEN (23) [SIXTEENTH]
Ge 46:18 she bare unto Jacob, *even* **s** souls. 6240+8337
Ex 26:25 sockets *of* silver, **s** sockets; 6240+8337
 36:30 sockets *were* **s** sockets *of* silver, 6240+8337
Nu 26:22 threescore and **s** 7657+8337+2050.1
 31:40 the persons *were* **s** thousand; 6240+8337
 31:46 And **s** thousand persons;) 6240+8337
 31:52 was **s** thousand seven hundred and 6240+8337
Jos 15:41 **s** cities with their villages. 6240+8337
 19:22 Jordan: **s** cities with their villages. 6240+8337
2Ki 13:10 in Samaria, *and reigned* **s** years. 6240+8337
 14:21 *was* **s** years old, and made him 6240+8337
 15: 2 **S** years old was he when he *began* 6240+8337
 15:33 he reigned **s** years in Jerusalem. 6240+8337
 16: 2 reigned **s** years in Jerusalem, 6240+8337
1Ch 4:27 Shimei had **s** sons and six 6240+8337
 24: 4 **s** chief *men* of the house of *their* 6240+8337
2Ch 13:21 two sons, and **s** daughters. 6240+8337
 26: 1 *was* **s** years old, and made him 6240+8337
 26: 3 **S** years old *was* Uzziah when he 6240+8337
 27: 1 he reigned **s** years in Jerusalem. 6240+8337
 27: 8 and reigned **s** years in Jerusalem. 6240+8337
 28: 1 he reigned **s** years in Jerusalem: 6240+8337
Ac 27:37 two hundred threescore and **s** 1440+1803

SIXTEENTH (3) [SIXTEEN]
1Ch 24:14 fifteenth to Bilgah, the **s** to Immer, 6240+8337
 25:23 The **s** to Hananiah, *he,* his sons, 6240+8337
2Ch 29:17 in the **s** day of the first month they 6240+8337

SIXTH (47) [SIX]
Ge 1:31 and the morning were the **s** day. 8345
 30:19 again, and bare Jacob the **s** son. 8345
Ex 16: 5 that on the **s** day they shall prepare *that* 8345
 16:22 *that* on the **s** day they gathered twice as 8345
 16:29 giveth you on the **s** day the bread of two 8345
 26: 9 shalt double the **s** curtain in the forefront 8345
Lev 25:21 my blessing upon you in the **s** year, 8345
Nu 7:42 On the **s** day Eliasaph the son of Deuel, 8345
 29:29 on the **s** day eight bullocks, two rams, 8345
Jos 19:32 The **s** lot came out to the children of 8345
2Sa 3: 5 the **s**, Ithream, by Eglah David's wife. 8345
1Ki 16: 8 year of Asa king of Judah *began* Elah 8337
2Ki 18:10 *even* in the **s** year of Hezekiah, that *is* 8337
1Ch 2:15 Ozem the **s**, David the seventh: 8345
 3: 3 Abital: the **s**, Ithream by Eglah his wife. 8345
 12:11 Attai the **s**, Eliel the seventh, 8345
 24: 9 The fifth to Malchijah, the **s** to Mijamin, 8345
 25:13 The **s** *to* Bukkiah, *he,* his sons, 8345
 26: 3 Elam the fifth, Jehohanan the **s**, 8345
 26: 6 Ammiel the **s**, Issachar the seventh, 8345
 27: 9 The **s** captain for the sixth month *was* Ira 8345
 27: 9 The sixth captain for the **s** month *was* Ira 8345
Ezr 6:15 which *was* in the **s** year of the reign of 8353
Ne 3:30 Hanun the son of Zalaph, another piece. 8165
Eze 4:11 water by measure, the **s** *part* of a hin: 8345
 8: 1 it came to pass in the **s** year, in the sixth 8345
 8: 1 in the **s** *month,* in the fifth *day of* 8345
 39: 2 **leave** but the **s** *part* of thee, and will 8338
 45:13 **s** *part* of an ephah of a homer of wheat, 8345
 45:13 ye shall **give** the **s** *part* of an ephah of a 8341
 46:14 the **s** *part of* an ephah, and the third *part* 8345
Hag 1: 1 in the **s** month, in the first day of 8345
 1:15 four and twentieth day of the **s** month, 8345
Mt 20: 5 Again he went out about the **s** and 1623
 27:45 Now from the **s** hour there was darkness 1623
Mk 15:33 when the **s** hour was come, there was 1623
Lk 1:26 And in the **s** month the angel Gabriel was 1623
 1:36 this is the **s** month with her, who was 1623
 23:44 it was about the **s** hour, and there was 1623
Jn 4: 6 on the well: *and* it was about the **s** hour. 1623
 19:14 of the passover, and about the **s** hour: 1623
Ac 10: 9 upon the house to pray about the **s** hour: 1623
Rev 6:12 And I beheld when he had opened the **s** 1623
 9:13 And the **s** angel sounded, and I heard a 1623
 9:14 Saying to the **s** angel which had 1623
 16:12 And the **s** angel poured out his vial upon 1623
 21:20 The fifth, sardonyx; the **s**, sardius; 1623

SIXTY (15) [SIXTYFOLD, THREESCORE]

Ge	5:15 Mahalaleel lived **s** and five years,	8346
	5:18 Jared lived an hundred **s** and two years,	8346
	5:20 all the days of Jared were nine hundred **s**	8346
	5:21 Enoch lived **s** and five years,	8346
	5:23 the days of Enoch were three hundred **s**	8346
	5:27 days of Methuselah were nine hundred **s**	8346
Lev	27: 3 twenty years old even unto **s** years old,	8346
	27: 7 if *it be* from **s** years old and above; if *it be*	8346
Nu	7:88 twenty and four bullocks, the rams **s**,	8346
	7:88 bullocks, the rams sixty, the he goats **s**,	8346
	7:88 goats sixty, the lambs of the first year **s**.	8346
Ezr	2:13 of Adonikam, six hundred **s** and six.	8346
Mt	13:23 an hundred*fold,* some **s**, some thirty.	1835
Mk	4: 8 and some **s**, and some an hundred.	1835
	4:20 some thirty*fold,* some **s**, and some an	1835

SIXTYFOLD (1) [SIXTY]

Mt	13: 8 some an hundred*fold,* some **s**, some	1835

SIZE (5)

Ex	36: 9 four cubits: the curtains *were* all of one **s**.	4060
	36:15 the eleven curtains *were* of one **s**.	4060
1Ki	6:25 *were* of one measure and one **s**.	7095
	7:37 had one casting, one measure, *and* one **s**.	7095
1Ch	23:29 and for all *manner of* measure and **s**;	4060

SKIES (5) [SKY]

2Sa	22:12 dark waters, *and* thick clouds of the **s**.	7834
Ps	18:11 dark waters *and* thick clouds of the **s**.	7834
	77:17 the **s** sent out a sound: thine arrows also	7834
Isa	45: 8 and let the **s** pour down righteousness:	7834
Jer	51: 9 heaven, and is lifted up *even* to the **s**.	7834

SKILFUL (7) [SKILL]

1Ch	5:18 **s** in war, *were* four and forty thousand	3925
	15:22 about the song, because he *was* **s**.	995
	28:21 willing **s** man, for any *manner of* service:	2451
2Ch	2:14 **s** to work in gold, and in silver, in brass,	3045
Eze	21:31 the hand of brutish *men, and* **s** to destroy.	2796
Da	1: 4 **s** in all wisdom, and cunning in	7919
Am	5:16 such as are **s** of lamentation to wailing.	3045

SKILFULLY (1) [SKILL]

Ps	33: 3 him a new song; play **s** with a loud noise.	3190

SKILFULNESS (1) [SKILL]

Ps	78:72 and guided them by the **s** of his hands.	8394

SKILL (7) [SKILFUL, SKILFULLY, SKILFULNESS, UNSKILFUL]

1Ki	5: 6 **can s** to hew timber like unto	3045
2Ch	2: 7 that can **s** to grave with the cunning *men*	3045
	2: 8 for I know that thy servants can **s** to cut	3045
	34:12 all that could **s** of instruments of musick.	995
Ecc	9:11 nor yet favour to men of **s**;	3045
Da	1:17 and **s** in all learning and wisdom:	7919
	9:22 I am now come forth to **give** thee **s** and	7919

SKIN (77) [FORESKIN, FORESKINS, GOATSKINS, SHEEPSKINS, SKINS]

Ex	22:27 covering only, it *is* his raiment for his **s**:	5785
	29:14 of the bullock, and his **s**, and his dung,	5785
	34:29 that Moses wist not that the **s** of his face	5785
	34:30 Moses, behold, the **s** of his face shone;	5785
	34:35 Moses, that the **s** of Moses' face shone:	5785
Lev	4:11 the **s** of the bullock, and all his flesh,	5785
	7: 8 the priest shall have to himself the **s** of	5785
	11:32 vessel of wood, or raiment, or **s**, or sack,	5785
	13: 2 a man shall have in the **s** of his flesh	5785
	13: 2 it be in the **s** of his flesh like the plague of	5785
	13: 3 the priest shall look on the plague in the **s**	5785
	13: 3 the plague in sight *be* deeper than the **s** of	5785
	13: 4 If the bright spot *be* white in the **s** of his	5785
	13: 4 in sight *be* not deeper than the **s**,	5785
	13: 5 a stay, *and* the plague spread not in the **s**;	5785
	13: 6 and the plague spread not in the **s**,	5785
	13: 7 if the scab spread much abroad in the **s**,	5785
	13: 8 scab spreadeth in the **s**, then the priest	5785
	13:10 *if* the rising *be* white in the **s**, and it have	5785
	13:11 It *is* an old leprosy in the **s** of his flesh,	5785
	13:12 if a leprosy break out abroad in the **s**,	5785
	13:12 the leprosy cover all the **s** of *him that*	5785
	13:18 which, *even* in the **s** thereof, was a boil,	5785
	13:20 *be* in sight lower than the **s**, and the hair	5785
	13:21 *if* it *be* not lower than the **s**, but *be*	5785
	13:22 if it spread much abroad in the **s**, then	5785
	13:24 in the **s** whereof *there is* a hot burning,	5785
	13:25 and it *be* in sight deeper than the **s**;	5785
	13:26 it *be* no lower than the *other* **s**, but *be*	5785
	13:27 *and* if it be spread much abroad in the **s**,	5785
	13:28 spread not in the **s**, but it *be* somewhat	5785
	13:30 behold, *if* it *be* in sight deeper than the **s**;	5785
	13:31 it *be* not in sight deeper than the **s**,	5785
	13:32 the scall *be* not in sight deeper than the **s**;	5785
	13:34 behold, *if* the scall be not spread in the **s**,	5785
	13:34 skin, nor *be* in sight deeper than the **s**;	5785
	13:35 if the scall spread much in the **s** after his	5785
	13:36 behold, *if* the scall be spread in the **s**,	5785
	13:38 woman have in the **s** of their flesh bright	5785
	13:39 *if* the bright spots in the **s** of their flesh *be*	5785
	13:39 it *is* a freckled spot *that* groweth in the **s**:	5785
	13:43 as the leprosy appeareth in the **s** of	5785
	13:48 whether in a **s**, or in any thing made of	5785
	13:48 in a skin, or in any thing made of **s**;	5785

Lev	13:49 or in the **s**, either in the warp, or in	5785
	13:49 or in the woof, or in any thing of **s**;	5785
	13:51 or in a **s**, *or* in any work that is made of	5785
	13:51 a skin, *or* in any work that is made of **s**;	5785
	13:52 in woollen or in linen, or any thing of **s**,	5785
	13:53 in the woof, or in any thing of **s**;	5785
	13:56 out of the **s**, or out of the warp, or out of	5785
	13:57 or in the woof, or in any thing of **s**;	5785
	13:58 whatsoever thing of **s** *it be,* which thou	5785
	15:17 every garment, and every **s**, whereon is	5785
Nu	19: 5 her **s**, and her flesh, and her blood, with	5785
Job	2: 4 the Lord, and said, **S** for skin, yea,	5785
	2: 4 the Lord, and said, Skin for **s**, yea,	5785
	7: 5 my **s** is broken, and become loathsome.	5785
	10:11 Thou hast clothed me with **s** and flesh,	5785
	16:15 I have sewed sackcloth upon my **s**,	1539
	18:13 It shall devour the strength of his **s**:	5785
	19:20 bone cleaveth to my **s** and to my flesh,	5785
	19:20 and I am escaped with the **s** of my teeth.	5785
	19:26 after my **s** *worms* destroy this *body,*	5785
	30:30 My **s** is black upon me, and my bones	5785
	41: 7 Canst thou fill his **s** with barbed irons?	5785
Ps	102: 5 of my groaning my bones cleave to my **s**.	1320
Jer	13:23 Can the Ethiopian change his **s**,	5785
La	3: 4 My flesh and my **s** hath he made old;	5785
	4: 8 their **s** cleaveth to their bones; it is	5785
	5:10 Our **s** was black like an oven because of	5785
Eze	16:10 shod thee *with* badgers' **s**, and I girded	NIH
	37: 6 cover you with **s**, and put breath in you,	5785
	37: 8 them, and the **s** covered them above:	5785
Mic	3: 2 who pluck off their **s** from off them,	5785
	3: 3 my people, and flay their **s** from off them;	5785
Mk	1: 6 and with a girdle of a **s** about his loins;	1193

SKINK See SNAIL

SKINS (24) [SKIN]

Ge	3:21 wife did the Lord God make coats of **s**,	5785
	27:16 she put the **s** of the kids of the goats upon	5785
Ex	25: 5 rams' **s** dyed red, and badgers' skins,	5785
	25: 5 red, and badgers' **s**, and shittim wood,	5785
	26:14 covering for the tent *of* rams' **s** dyed red,	5785
	26:14 and a covering above of badgers' **s**.	5785
	35: 7 rams' **s** dyed red, and badgers' skins,	5785
	35: 7 red, and badgers' **s**, and shittim wood,	5785
	35:23 goats' *hair,* and red **s** of rams,	5785
	35:23 of rams, and badgers' **s**, brought *them.*	5785
	36:19 he made a covering for the tent *of* rams' **s**	5785
	36:19 and a covering of badgers' **s** above *that.*	5785
	39:34 the covering of rams' **s** dyed red,	5785
	39:34 the covering of badgers' **s**, and the vail of	5785
Lev	13:59 *in* the warp, or woof, or any thing of **s**,	5785
	16:27 they shall burn in the fire their **s**, and	5785
Nu	4: 6 put thereon the covering of badgers' **s**,	5785
	4: 8 the same with a covering of badgers' **s**,	5785
	4:10 thereof within a covering of badgers' **s**,	5785
	4:11 cover it with a covering of badgers' **s**,	5785
	4:12 cover them with a covering of badgers' **s**,	5785
	4:14 spread upon it a covering of badgers' **s**,	5785
	4:25 the covering of the **badgers' s** that *is*	8476
	31:20 all that is made of **s**, and all work of goats'	5785

SKIP (1) [SKIPPED, SKIPPEDST, SKIPPING]

Ps	29: 6 He **maketh** them also to **s** like a calf;	7540

SKIPPED (2) [SKIP]

Ps	114: 4 The mountains **s** like rams, *and* the little	7540
	114: 6 Ye mountains, *that* ye **s** like rams;	7540

SKIPPEDST (1) [SKIP]

Jer	48:27 since thou spakest of him, thou **s for joy**.	5110

SKIPPING (1) [SKIP]

SS	2: 8 upon the mountains, **s** upon the hills.	7092

SKIRT (12) [SKIRTS]

Dt	22:30 father's wife, nor discover his father's **s**.	3671
	27:20 because he uncovereth his father's **s**.	3671
Ru	3: 9 therefore thy **s** over thine handmaid;	3671
1Sa	15:27 he laid hold upon the **s** of his mantle,	3671
	24: 4 and cut off the **s** of Saul's robe privily.	3671
	24: 5 him, because he had cut off Saul's **s**.	3671
	24:11 see, yea see the **s** of thy robe in my hand:	3671
	24:11 for in that I cut off the **s** of thy robe,	3671
Eze	16: 8 I spread my **s** over thee, and covered thy	3671
Hag	2:12 If one bear holy flesh in the **s** of his	3671
	2:12 with his **s** do touch bread, or pottage,	3671
Zec	8:23 shall take hold of the **s** of him that is a	3671

SKIRTS (7) [SKIRT]

Ps	133: 2 that went down to the **s** of his garments;	6310
Jer	2:34 in thy **s** is found the blood of the souls	3671
	13:22 the greatness of thine iniquity are thy **s**	7757
	13:26 Therefore will I discover thy **s** upon thy	7757
La	1: 9 filthiness *is* in her **s**; she remembereth	7757
Eze	5: 3 a few in number, and bind them in thy **s**.	3671
Na	3: 5 I will discover thy **s** upon thy face,	7757

SKULL (5)

Jdg	9:53 Abimelech's head, and all to brake his **s**.	1538
2Ki	9:35 they found no more of her than the **s**,	1538
Mt	27:33 that is to say, a place of a **s**,	2898
Mk	15:22 being interpreted, The place of a **s**.	2898
Jn	19:17 forth into a place called *the place* of a **s**,	2898

SKY (7) [SKIES]

Dt	33:26 thy help, and in his excellency *on* the **s**.	7834
Job	37:18 Hast thou with him spread out the **s**,	7834
Mt	16: 2 *It will be* fair weather: for the **s** is red.	3772
	16: 3 for the **s** is red and lowring. O *ye*	3772
	16: 3 ye can discern the face of the **s**;	3772
Lk	12:56 ye can discern the face of the **s** and of	3772
Heb	11:12 *so many* as the stars of the **s** in multitude,	3772

SLACK (8) [SLACKED, SLACKNESS]

Dt	7:10 he will not be **s** to him that hateth him,	309
	23:21 Lord thy God, thou shalt not **s** to pay it:	309
Jos	10: 6 **S** not thy hand from thy servants;	7503
	18: 3 How long *are* you **s** to go to possess	7503
2Ki	4:24 and go *forward;* **s** not *thy* riding for me,	6113
Pr	10: 4 He becometh poor that dealeth *with* a **s**	7423
Zep	3:16 *and to* Zion, Let not thine hands be **s**.	7503
2Pe	3: 9 The Lord is not **s** concerning *his* promise,	1019

SLACKED (1) [SLACK]

Hab	1: 4 Therefore the law is **s**, and judgment doth	6313

SLACKNESS (1) [SLACK]

2Pe	3: 9 *his* promise, as some *men* count **s**;	1022

SLAIN (183) [SLAY]

Ge	4:23 for I have **s** a man to my wounding,	2026
	34:27 The sons of Jacob came upon the **s**,	2491
Lev	14:51 dip them in the blood of the **s** bird,	7819
	26:17 and ye shall be **s** before your enemies:	5062
Nu	11:22 the flocks and the herds be **s** for them,	7819
	14:16 he hath **s** them in the wilderness.	7819
	19:16 whosoever toucheth one *that is* **s** with a	2491
	19:18 a bone, or one **s**, or one dead, or a grave:	2491
	22:33 surely now also I had **s** thee, and saved	2026
	23:24 *of* the prey, and drink the blood of the **s**.	2491
	25:14 Now the name of the Israelite that was **s**,	5221
	25:14 *even* that was **s** with the Midianitish	5221
	25:15 Midianitish woman that was **s** *was* Cozbi,	5221
	25:18 which was **s** in the day of the plague for	5221
	31: 8 beside *the rest of* them that were **s**;	2491
	31:19 whosoever hath touched *any* **s**, purify	2491
Dt	1: 4 After he had **s** Sihon the king of	5221
	21: 1 If *one* be found **s** in the land which	2491
	21: 1 *and* it be not known who hath **s** him:	2491
	21: 2 which *are* round about him that is **s**:	2491
	21: 3 the city *which is* next unto the **s** man,	2491
	21: 6 that *are* next unto the **s** man, shall wash	2491
	28:31 Thine ox *shall be* **s** before thine eyes,	2873
	32:42 *and that* with the blood of the **s** and of	2491
Jos	11: 6 will I deliver them up all **s** before Israel:	2491
	13:22 sword among them that were **s** by them.	2491
Jdg	9:18 his sons, threescore and ten persons,	2026
	15:16 with the jaw of an ass have I **s** a thousand	5221
	20: 4 the husband of the woman that was **s**,	7523
	20: 5 me by night, *and* thought to have **s** me:	2026
1Sa	4:11 sons of Eli, Hophni and Phinehas, were **s**.	4191
	18: 7 Saul hath **s** his thousands, and David his	5221
	19: 6 *As* the Lord liveth, he shall not be **s**.	4191
	19:11 life to night, to morrow thou *shalt* be **s**.	4191
	20:32 said unto him, Wherefore shall he be **s**?	4191
	21:11 Saul hath **s** his thousands, and David his	5221
	22:21 Abiathar shewed David that Saul had **s**	2026
	31: 1 and fell down **s** in mount Gilboa.	2491
	31: 8 when the Philistines came to strip the **s**,	2491
2Sa	1:16 I have **s** the Lord's anointed.	4191
	1:19 The beauty of Israel *is* **s** upon thy high	2491
	1:22 From the blood of the **s**, from the fat of	2491
	1:25 *thou* wast **s** in thine high places.	2491
	3:30 he had **s** their brother Asahel at Gibeon	4191
	4:11 when wicked men have **s** a righteous	2026
	12: 9 hast **s** him with the sword of the children	2026
	13:30 Absalom hath **s** all the king's sons,	5221
	13:32 not my lord suppose *that* they have **s** all	4191
	18: 7 Where the people of Israel were **s** before	5062
	21:12 when the Philistines had **s** Saul in Gilboa:	5221
	21:16 a new *sword,* thought to have **s** David.	2491
1Ki	1:19 he hath **s** oxen and fat cattle and sheep in	2076
	1:25 hath **s** oxen and fat cattle and sheep in	2076
	9:16 the Canaanites that dwelt in the city,	2026
	11:15 of the host was gone up to bury the **s**,	2491
	13:26 which hath torn him, and **s** him,	4191
	16:16 hath conspired, and hath also **s** the king:	5221
	19: 1 withal how he had **s** all the prophets with	2026
	19:10 and **s** thy prophets with the sword;	2026
	19:14 and **s** thy prophets with the sword;	2026
2Ki	3:23 the kings are **surely** **s**, and they	2717+2717
	11: 2 among the king's sons which were **s**;	4191
	11: 2 from Athaliah, so that he was not **s**.	4191
	11: 8 cometh within the ranges, let him be **s**:	4191
	11:15 Let her not be **s** *in* the house of the Lord.	4191
	11:16 the king's house: and there was she **s**.	4191
	14: 5 that he slew his servants which had **s**	5221
1Ch	5:22 For there fell down many **s**, because	2491
	10: 1 and fell down **s** in mount Gilboa.	2491
	10: 8 when the Philistines came to strip the **s**,	2491
	11:11 lift up his spear against three hundred **s**	2491
2Ch	13:17 there fell down **s** of Israel five hundred	2491
	21:13 also hast **s** thy brethren of thy father's	2026
	22: 1 Arabians to the camp had **s** all the eldest.	2026
	22: 9 when they had **s** him, they buried him:	4191
	22:11 from among the king's sons that were **s**,	4191
	23:14 her, let him be **s** with the sword.	4191

S

2Ch 23:21 after that they had **s** Athaliah with | 4191
28: 9 have them in a rage *that* reacheth up | 2026
Est 7: 4 to be destroyed, to be **s**, and to perish. | 2026
9:11 that day the number of those that were **s** | 2026
9:12 The Jews have **s** and destroyed five | 2026
Job 1:15 they have **s** the servants with the edge of | 5221
1:17 **s** the servants with the **e**dge of the sword; | 5221
39:30 blood: and where the **s** *are*, there *is* she. | 2491
Ps 62: 3 ye shall be **s** of all of you: as a bowing wall | 7523
88: 5 the dead, like the **s** that lie in the grave, | 2491
89:10 broken Rahab in pieces, as one that is **s**; | 2491
Pr 7:26 many strong *men have been* **s** by her. | 2026
22:13 a lion without, I shall be **s** in the streets. | 7523
24:11 death, and *those that are* ready to be **s**; | 2027
Isa 10: 4 and they shall fall under the **s**. | 2026
14:19 *and as* the raiment of those that are **s**, | 2026
14:20 destroyed thy land, *and's* thy people: | 2026
22: 2 thy **s** *men are* not slain with the sword, | 2491
22: 2 thy slain *men are* not **s** with the sword, | 2491
26:21 her blood, and shall no more cover her **s**. | 2026
27: 7 is he **s** according to the slaughter of them | 2026
27: 7 the slaughter of them that are **s** by him? | 2026
34: 3 Their **s** also shall be cast out, and their | 2491
66:16 and the **s** of the LORD shall be many. | 2491
Jer 9: 1 night for the **s** of the daughter of my | 2491
14:18 field, then behold the **s** with the sword: | 2491
18:21 *let* their young men be **s** by the sword in | 5221
25:33 the **s** of the LORD shall be at that day | 2491
33: 5 whom I have **s** in mine anger and in my | 5221
41: 4 to pass the second day after *he* had **s** | 4191
41: 9 whom he had **s** because of Gedaliah, | 5221
41: 9 Nethaniah filled it *with them that were* **s**. | 2491
41:16 after *that* he had **s** Gedaliah the son of | 5221
41:18 Ishmael the son of Nethaniah had **s** | 5221
51: 4 Thus the **s** shall fall in the land of | 2491
51:47 and all her **s** shall fall in the midst of her. | 2491
51:49 As Babylon *hath caused* the **s** of Israel to | 2491
51:49 at Babylon shall fall the **s** of all the earth. | 2491
La 2:20 the prophet be **s** in the sanctuary of | 2026
2:21 hast **s** *them* in the day of thine anger; | 2026
3:43 thou hast **s**, thou hast not pitied. | 2026
4: 9 *They that be* **s** with the sword are better | 2491
4: 9 better than *they that be* **s** with hunger: | 2491
Eze 6: 4 I will cast down your **s** *men* before your | 2491
6: 7 the **s** shall fall in the midst of you, | 2491
6:13 their **s** *men* shall be among their idols | 2491
9: 7 the house, and fill the courts with the **s**: | 2491
11: 6 Ye have multiplied your **s** in this city, | 2491
11: 6 have filled the streets thereof *with* the **s**. | 2491
11: 7 Your **s** whom ye have laid in the midst of | 2491
16:21 That thou hast **s** my children, | 7819
21:14 the third time, the sword of the **s**: | 2491
21:14 *is* the sword of the great *men that are* **s**, | 2491
21:29 necks of *them that are* **s**, of the wicked, | 2491
23:39 For when they had **s** their children to | 7819
26: 6 *are* in the field shall be **s** by the sword; | 2026
28: 8 shalt die the deaths of *them that are* **s** | 2491
30: 4 when the **s** shall fall in Egypt, | 2491
30:11 against Egypt, and fill the land *with* the **s**. | 2491
31:17 him unto *them that be* **s** with the sword; | 2491
31:18 with *them that be* **s** with the sword. | 2491
32:20 midst of *them that are* **s** by the sword: | 2491
32:21 they lie uncircumcised, **s** by the sword. | 2491
32:22 all of them, fallen by the sword, | 2491
32:23 all of them, fallen by the sword, | 2491
32:24 all of them, **s** by the sword, | 2491
32:25 the midst of the **s** with all her multitude: | 2491
32:25 of them uncircumcised, **s** by the sword: | 2491
32:25 he is put in the midst of *them that be* **s**. | 2491
32:26 of them uncircumcised, **s** by the sword, | 2490
32:28 shalt lie with *them that are* **s** with | 2491
32:29 laid by *them that were* **s** by the sword: | 2491
32:30 which are gone down with the **s**; | 2491
32:30 lie uncircumcised with *them that be* **s** | 2491
32:31 and all his army by the sword, | 2491
32:32 with *them that are* **s** with the sword, | 2491
35: 8 I will fill his mountains with his **s** *men*: | 2491
35: 8 shall they fall *that are* **s** with the sword. | 2491
37: 9 O breath, and breathe upon these **s**, that | 2026
Da 2:13 went forth that the wise *men* should be **s**; | 6992
2:13 sought Daniel and his fellows to be **s**. | 6992
5:30 Belshazzar the king of the Chaldeans | 6992
7:11 I beheld *even* till the beast *was* **s**, | 6992
11:26 overflow: and many shall fall down **s**. | 2491
Hos 6: 5 I have **s** them by the words of my mouth: | 2026
Am 4:10 your young men have I **s** with the sword, | 2026
Na 3: 3 *there is* a multitude of **s**, and a great | 2491
Zep 2:12 also, ye *shall be* **s** by my sword. | 2491
Lk 9:22 and be **s**, and be raised the third day. | 615
Ac 2:23 and by wicked hands have crucified and **s**: | 337
5:36 was **s**; and all, as many as obeyed him, | 337
7:42 have ye offered to me **s beasts** and | 4968
7:52 they have **s** them which shewed before of | 615
13:28 *yet* desired Pilate that he should be **s**. | 337
23:14 we will eat nothing until we have **s** Paul. | 615
Eph 2:16 by the cross, having **s** the enmity thereby: | 615
Heb 11:37 tempted, were **s** with the sword: | 599+5408
Rev 2:13 who was **s** among you, where Satan | 615
5: 6 a Lamb as *it had been* **s**, having seven | 4969
5: 9 for thou wast **s**, and hast redeemed us to | 4969
5:12 Worthy is the Lamb that was to receive | 4969
6: 9 of them that were **s** for the word of God, | 4969
11:13 in the earthquake were **s** of men seven | 615
13: 8 Lamb **s** from the foundation of the world. | 4969
18:24 and of all that were **s** upon the earth. | 4969

Rev 19:21 the remnant were **s** with the sword of | 615

SLANDER (3) [SLANDERED, SLANDERERS, SLANDEREST, SLANDERETH, SLANDEROUSLY, SLANDERS]

Nu 14:36 by bringing up a **s** upon the land, | 1681
Ps 31:13 I have heard the **s** of many: fear *was* on | 1681
Pr 10:18 lips, and he that uttereth a **s**, *is* a fool. | 1681

SLANDERED (1) [SLANDER]

2Sa 19:27 hath **s** thy servant unto my lord the king; | 7270

SLANDERERS (1) [SLANDER]

1Ti 3:11 grave, not **s**, sober, faithful in all *things*. | 1228

SLANDEREST (1) [SLANDER]

Ps 50:20 thou **s** thine own mother's son. | 1848+5414

SLANDERETH (1) [SLANDER]

Ps 101: 5 Whoso privily **s** his neighbour, him will I | 3960

SLANDEROUSLY (1) [SLANDER]

Ro 3: 8 And not *rather*, (as we be **s reported**, | 987

SLANDERS (2) [SLANDER]

Jer 6:28 *are* all grievous revolters, walking with **s**: | 7400
9: 4 every neighbour will walk with **s**. | 7400

SLANG

1Sa 17:49 **s** *it*, and smote the Philistine in his | 7049

SLAUGHTER (56)

Ge 14:17 his return from the **s** of Chedorlaomer, | 5221
Jos 10:10 and slew them *with* a great **s** at Gibeon, | 4347
10:20 end of slaying them *with* a very great **s**, | 4347
Jdg 11:33 plain of the vineyards, *with* a very great **s**. | 4347
15: 8 smote them hip and thigh *with* a great **s**: | 4347
1Sa 4:10 there was a very great **s**; for there fell of | 4347
4:17 there hath been also a great **s** among | 4046
6:19 smitten *many* of the people *with* a great **s**. | 4347
14:14 **s**, which Jonathan and his |
 armourbearer **made**, | 4347+5221
14:30 had been not been now a much greater **s** | 4347
17:57 as David returned from the **s** of | 5221
18: 6 when David was returned from the **s** of | 5221
19: 8 and slew them *with* a great **s**; | 4347
23: 5 cattle, and smote them *with* a great **s**. | 4347
2Sa 1: 1 when David was returned from the **s** of | 5221
17: 9 There is a **s** among the people that follow | 4046
18: 7 was there a great **s** that day *of* twenty | 4046
1Ki 20:21 and slew the Syrians with a great **s**. | 4347
2Ch 13:17 and his people slew them *with* a great **s**: | 4347
25:14 after that Amaziah was come from the **s** | 5221
28: 5 of Israel, who smote him *with* a great **s**. | 4347
Est 9: 5 and, destruction, and did what they | 2027
Ps 44:22 long; we are counted as sheep for the **s**. | 2878
Pr 7:22 as an ox goeth to the **s**, or as a fool to | 2874
Isa 10:26 to the **s** of Midian at the rock Oreb: | 4347
14:21 Prepare for his children for the iniquity | 4293
27: 7 is he slain according to the **s** of them that | 2027
30:25 of waters in the day of the great **s**, | 2027
34: 2 he hath delivered them to the **s**. | 2874
34: 6 and a great **s** in the land of Idumea. | 2874
53: 7 he is brought as a lamb to the **s**, and as a | 2874
65:12 and ye shall all bow down to the **s**: | 2874
Jer 7:32 of the son of Hinnom, but the valley of **s**: | 2028
11:19 a lamb *or* an ox *that* is brought to the **s**; | 2873
12: 3 pull them out like sheep for the **s**, | 2878
12: 3 and prepare them for the day of **s**. | 2028
19: 6 the son of Hinnom, but The valley of **s**. | 2028
25:34 for the days of your **s** and of your | 2873
48:15 young men are gone down to the **s**, | 2874
50:27 her bullocks; let them go down to the **s**: | 2874
51:40 will bring them down like lambs to the **s**, | 2873
Eze 9: 2 and every man a **s** weapon in his hand; | 4660
21:10 It is sharpened to make a **sore s**; | 2873+2874
21:15 *it is* made bright, *it is* wrapt up for the **s**. | 2874
21:22 to open the mouth in the **s**, | 7524
21:28 for the **s** *it is* furbished, to consume | 2874
26:15 the **s** is **made** in the midst of thee? | 2026+2027
Hos 5: 2 the revolters are profound to make **s**, | 7819
Ob 9 of the mount of Esau may be cut off by **s**. | 6993
Zec 11: 4 LORD my God; Feed the flock of the **s**; | 2028
11: 7 will feed the flock of **s**, *even* you, | 2028
Ac 8:32 was this, He was led as a sheep to the **s**; | 4967
9: 1 and **s** against the disciples of the Lord, | 5408
Ro 8:36 we are accounted as sheep for the **s**. | 4967
Heb 7: 1 met Abraham returning from the **s** of | 2871
Jas 5: 5 nourished your hearts, as in a day of **s**. | 4967

SLAVE (1) [SLAVES]

Jer 2:14 *is* he a homeborn **s**? why is he spoiled? | NIH

SLAVE DRIVERS See TASKMASTERS

SLAVE MASTERS See TASKMASTERS

SLAVE TRADERS See MENSTEALERS

SLAVES (1) [SLAVE]

Rev 18:13 and chariots, and **s**, and souls of men. | 4983

SLAY (117) [MANSLAYER, MANSLAYERS, SLAIN, SLAYER, SLAYETH, SLAYING, SLEW, SLEWEST]

Ge 4:14 every one that findeth me shall **s** me. | 2026
18:25 to **s** the righteous with the wicked: | 4191
20: 4 Lord, wilt thou also **s** a righteous nation? | 2026

Ge 20:11 and they will **s** me for my wife's sake. | 2026
22:10 his hand, and took the knife to **s** his son. | 7819
27:41 at hand; then will I **s** my brother Jacob. | 2026
34:30 together against me, and **s** me; | 5221
37:18 they conspired against him to **s** him. | 4191
37:20 let us **s** him, and cast him into some pit, | 2026
37:26 What profit *is it* if we **s** our brother, | 4191
42:37 saying, **S** my two sons, if I bring him not | 4191
43:16 *these* men home, and **s**, and make ready; | 2873
Ex 2:15 heard this thing, he sought to **s** Moses. | 2026
4:23 I will **s** thy son, *even* thy firstborn. | 2026
5:21 to put a sword in their hand to **s** us. | 2026
21:14 upon his neighbour, to **s** him with guile; | 2026
23: 7 the innocent and righteous **s** thou not: | 2026
29:16 thou shalt **s** the ram, and thou shalt take | 7819
32:12 **s** them in the mountains, and to consume | 2026
32:27 **s** every man his brother, and every man | 2026
Lev 4:29 **s** the sin offering in the place of the burnt | 7819
4:33 **s** it for a sin offering in the place where | 7819
14:13 he shall **s** the lamb in the place where he | 7819
20:15 be put to death: and ye shall **s** the beast. | 7819
Nu 19: 3 and *one* shall **s** her before his face: | 7819
25: 5 **S** ye every one his men that were joined | 2026
35:19 The revenger of blood himself shall **s** | 4191
35:19 when he meeteth him, he shall **s** him. | 4191
35:21 revenger of blood shall **s** the murderer, | 4191
Dt 9:28 he hath brought them out to **s** them in; | 5221+5315
19: 6 because the way is long, and **s** him; | 5221+5315
27:25 *be* he that taketh reward to **s** | 5221+5315
Jos 13:22 the children of Israel **s** with the sword | 2026
Jdg 8:19 had saved them alive, I would not **s** you. | 2026
8:20 unto him his firstborn, Up, *and* **s** them. | 2026
9:54 unto him, Draw thy sword, and **s** me, | 4191
1Sa 2:25 because the LORD would **s** them. | 4191
5:10 of Israel to us, to **s** us and our people. | 4191
5:11 place, that it **s** us not, and our people: | 4191
14:34 his sheep, and **s** *them* here, and eat; | 7819
15: 3 both man and woman, infant and | 4191
19: 5 blood, to **s** David without a cause? | 4191
19:11 watch him, and to **s** him in the morning: | 4191
19:15 up to me in the bed, that I may **s** him. | 4191
20: 8 if there be in me iniquity, **s** me thyself; | 4191
20:33 was determined of his father to **s** David. | 4191
22:17 Turn, and the priests of the LORD; | 4191
2Sa 1: 9 Stand, I pray thee, upon me, and **s** me: | 4191
3:37 not of the king to **s** Abner the son of Ner. | 4191
21: 2 Saul sought to **s** them in his zeal to | 5221
1Ki 1:51 he will not **s** his servant with the sword. | 4191
3:26 living child, and **in** no **wise s** it. | 4191+4191
3:27 living child, and **in** no **wise s** it: | 4191+4191
15:28 of Asa king of Judah did Baasha slay, | 4191
17:18 sin to remembrance, and to **s** my son? | 4191
18: 9 servant into the hand of Ahab, to **s** me? | 4191
18:12 and he cannot find thee, he shall **s** me: | 2026
18:14 Behold, Elijah *is* here: and he shall **s** me. | 2026
19:17 the sword of Hazael shall Jehu **s**: | 4191
19:17 from the sword of Jehu shall Elisha **s**. | 4191
20:36 art departed from me, a lion shall **s** thee. | 5221
2Ki 8:12 young *men* wilt thou **s** with the sword, | 2026
10:25 and to the captains, Go in, *and* **s** them; | 5221
17:26 they **s** them, because they know not | 4191
2Ch 20:23 **utterly to s** and destroy *them*: and | 2763
23:14 **S** her not *in* the house of the LORD. | 4191
Ne 4:11 and **s** them, and cause the work to cease. | 2026
6:10 for they will come to **s** thee; yea, | 2026
6:10 yea, in the night will they come to **s** thee. | 2026
Est 8:11 to destroy, to **s**, and to cause to perish, | 2026
Job 9:23 If the scourge suddenly, he will laugh at | 4191
13:15 Though he **s** me, *yet* will I trust in him: | 6991
20:16 of asps: the viper's tongue shall **s** him. | 2026
Ps 34:21 Evil shall **s** the wicked: and they that hate | 4191
37:14 to such as be of upright conversation. | 2873
37:32 the righteous, and seeketh to **s** him. | 4191
59:11 **S** them not, lest my people forget: | 2026
94: 6 They **s** the widow and the stranger, | 2026
109:16 that *he* might even **s** the broken in heart. | 4191
139:19 Surely thou wilt **s** the wicked, O God: | 6991
Pr 1:32 For the turning away of the simple shall **s** | 2026
Isa 11: 4 with the breath of his lips shall he **s** | 4191
14:30 with famine, and he shall **s** thy remnant, | 2026
27: 1 he shall **s** the dragon that *is* in the sea. | 2026
65:15 for the Lord GOD shall **s** thee, and call his | 4191
Jer 5: 6 Wherefore a lion out of the forest shall **s** | 5221
15: 3 the sword to **s**, and the dogs to tear, | 2026
18:23 me to **s** *me*: forgive not their iniquity, | 4194
20: 4 and shall **s** them with the sword. | 5221
29:21 and he shall **s** them before your eyes; | 5221
40:14 the son of Nethaniah to **s** thee? | 5221+5315
40:15 I will **s** Ishmael the son of Nethaniah, | 5221
40:15 wherefore should he **s** thee, | 5221+5315
41: 8 them that said unto Ishmael, **S** us not: | 4191
50:27 **S** all her bullocks; let them go down to | 2717
Eze 9: 6 **S** utterly old *and* young, both maids, | 2026
13:19 to **s** the souls that should not die, | 4191
23:47 shall **s** their sons and their daughters, | 2026
26: 8 He shall **s** with the sword thy daughters | 2026
26:11 He shall **s** thy people by the sword, | 2026
40:39 to **s** thereon the burnt offering and the sin | 7819
44:11 they shall **s** the burnt offering and | 7819
Da 2:14 which was gone forth to **s** the wise *men* | 6992
Hos 2: 3 her like a dry land, and **s** her with thirst. | 4191
9:16 yet will I **s** *even* the beloved *fruit* of their | 4191
Am 2: 3 will **s** all the princes thereof with him, | 2026
9: 1 I will **s** the last of them with the sword: | 2026
9: 4 command the sword, and it shall **s** them: | 2026

Hab 1:17 not spare continually to **s** the nations? 2026
Zec 11: 5 Whose possessors **s** them, 2026
Lk 11:49 *some of them they shall* **s** *and persecute:* 615
 19:27 bring hither, and **s** *them before me.* 2695
Jn 5:16 and sought to **s** him, because he had done 615
Ac 5:33 *to the heart,* and took counsel to **s** him. 337
 9:29 Grecians: but they went about to **s** him. 337
 11: 7 saying unto me, Arise, Peter; **s** and eat. 2380
Rev 9:15 and a year, for to **s** the third *part* of men. 615

SLAYER (19) [SLAY]

Nu 35:11 that the **s** may flee thither, which killeth 7523
 35:24 congregation shall judge between the **s** 5221
 35:25 the congregation shall deliver the **s** out of 7523
 35:26 if the **s** shall at any time come *without* 7523
 35:27 and the revenger of blood kill the **s** 7523
 35:28 after the death of the high priest the **s** 7523
Dt 4:42 That the **s** might flee thither, which 7523
 19: 3 three parts, that every **s** may flee thither. 7523
 19: 4 this *is* the case of the **s**, which shall flee 7523
 19: 6 the avenger of the blood pursue the **s**, 7523
Jos 20: 3 the **s** that killeth *any* person unawares 7523
 20: 5 shall not deliver the **s** up into his hand; 7523
 20: 6 shall the **s** return, and come unto his own 7523
 21:13 suburbs, *to be* a city of refuge for the **s**; 7523
 21:21 *to be* a city of refuge for the **s**; 7523
 21:27 suburbs, *to be* a city of refuge for the **s** 7523
 21:32 suburbs, *to be* a city of refuge for the **s** 7523
 21:38 suburbs, *to be* a city of refuge for the **s**; 7523
Eze 21:11 to give it into the hand of the **s**. 2026

SLAYETH (5) [SLAY]

Ge 4:15 unto him, Therefore whosoever **s** Cain, 2026
Dt 22:26 and **s** him, even so *is* this matter: 7523
Job 5: 2 the foolish man, and envy **s** the silly one. 4191
Eze 28: 9 Wilt thou yet say before him that **s** thee, 2026
 28: 9 no God, in the hand of him that **s** thee. 2490

SLAYING (7) [SLAY]

Jos 8:24 when Israel had made an end of **s** all 2026
 10:20 children of Israel had made an end of **s** 5221
Jdg 9:56 unto his father, in **s** his seventy brethren: 2026
1Ki 17:20 with whom I sojourn, by **s** her son? 4191
Isa 22:13 and gladness, **s** oxen, and killing sheep, 2026
 57: 5 **s** the children in the valleys under the 7819
Eze 9: 8 while they were **s** them, and I *was* left, 5221

SLEEP (82) [ASLEEP, SLEEPER, SLEEPEST, SLEEPETH, SLEEPING, SLEPT]

Ge 2:21 the Lord God caused a **deep s** to fall 8639
 15:12 going down, a **deep s** fell upon Abram; 8639
 28:11 pillows, and **lay down** in that place to **s**. 7901
 28:16 Jacob awaked out of his **s**, and he said, 8142
 31:40 and my **s** departed from mine eyes. 8142
Ex 22:27 wherein shall he **s**? and it shall come to 7901
Dt 24:12 *be* poor, thou shalt not **s** with his pledge: 7901
 24:13 that he may **s** in his own raiment, 7901
 31:16 Behold, thou shalt **s** with thy fathers; 7901
Jdg 16:14 he awaked out of his **s**, and went away 8142
 16:19 she **made** him **s** upon her knees; 3462
 16:20 he awoke out of his **s**, and said, I will go 8142
1Sa 3: 3 God *was*, and Samuel was laid down to **s**; NIH
 26:12 a **deep s** from the Lord was fallen upon 8639
2Sa 7:12 thou shalt **s** with thy fathers, I will set up 7901
1Ki 1:21 when my lord the king shall **s** with his 7901
Est 6: 1 On that night could not the king **s**, 8142
Job 4:13 the night, when **deep s** falleth on men. 8639
 7:21 for now shall I **s** in the dust; and thou 7901
 14:12 not awake, nor be raised out of their **s**. 8142
 33:15 the night, when **deep s** falleth upon men, 8639
Ps 4: 8 I will both lay me down in peace, and **s**: 3462
 13: 3 mine eyes, lest I **s** the *sleep of* death; 3462
 13: 3 mine eyes, lest I sleep the *s* of death; NIH
 76: 5 are spoiled, they have slept their **s**: 8142
 76: 6 and horse *are* **cast into a dead s**. 7290
 78:65 the Lord awaked as one out of **s**, *and* like 3463
 90: 5 away as with a flood; they are *as* a **s**: 8142
 121: 4 keepeth Israel shall neither slumber nor **s**. 3462
 127: 2 of sorrows: *for so* he giveth his beloved **s**. 8142
 132: 4 I will not give **s** to mine eyes, *or* slumber 8153
Pr 3:24 shalt lie down, and thy **s** shall be sweet. 8142
 4:16 For they **s** not, except they have done 3462
 4:16 their **s** is taken away, unless they cause 8142
 6: 4 Give not **s** to thine eyes, nor slumber to 8142
 6: 9 How long wilt thou **s**, O sluggard? 7901
 6: 9 when wilt thou arise out of thy **s**? 8142
 6:10 a little **s**, a little slumber, a little folding 8142
 6:10 a little folding of the hands to **s**: 7901
 19:15 Slothfulness casteth into a **deep s**: 8639
 20:13 Love not **s**, lest thou come to poverty; 8142
 24:33 a little **s**, a little slumber, a little folding 8142
 24:33 a little folding of the hands to **s**: 7901
Ecc 5:12 The **s** of a labouring *man is* sweet, 8142
 5:12 of the rich will not suffer him to **s**. 3462
 8:16 day nor night seeth **s** with his eyes:) 8142
SS 5: 2 I **s**, but my heart waketh: *it is* the voice 3463
Isa 5:27 none shall slumber nor **s**; neither shall 3462
 29:10 poured out upon you the spirit of **deep s**, 8639
Jer 31:26 beheld; and my **s** was sweet unto me. 8142
 51:39 **s** a perpetual sleep, and not wake, saith 3462
 51:39 sleep a perpetual **s**, and not wake, saith 8142
 51:57 and they shall **s** a perpetual sleep, 3462
 51:57 and they shall sleep a perpetual **s**, 8142
Eze 34:25 in the wilderness, and **s** in the woods. 3462
Da 2: 1 was troubled, and his **s** brake from him. 8142

Da 6:18 before him: and his **s** went from him. 8139
 8:18 I was in a **deep s** on my face toward 7290
 10: 9 I in a **deep s** on my face, and my face 7290
 12: 2 of them that **s** in the dust of the earth 3463
Zec 4: 1 as a man that is wakened out of his **s**, 8142
Mt 1:24 then Joseph being raised from **s** did as 5258
 26:45 unto them, **S** on now, and take your rest: 2518
Mk 4:27 And should **s**, and rise night and day, 2518
 14:41 unto them, **S** on now, and take your rest: 2518
Lk 9:32 that were with him were heavy with **s**: 5258
 22:46 And said unto them, Why **s** ye? rise and 2518
Jn 11:11 but I go, that I may **awake** him **out of s**. 1852
 11:12 disciples, Lord, if he **s**, he shall do well. 2837
 11:13 that he had spoken of taking of rest in **s**. 5258
Ac 13:36 **fell on s**, and was laid unto his fathers, 2837
 16:27 of the prison **awaking out of** his **s**, 1096+1853
 20: 9 Eutychus, being fallen into a deep **s**: 5258
 20: 9 he sunk down with **s**, and fell down from 5258
Ro 13:11 now *it is* high time to awake out of **s**: 5258
1Co 11:30 and sickly among you, and many **s**. 2837
 15:51 We shall not all **s**, but we shall be all 2837
1Th 4:14 them also which **s** in Jesus will God bring 2837
 5: 6 Therefore let us not **s**, as *do* others; 2518
 5: 7 For they that **s** sleep in the night; 2518
 5: 7 For they that sleep in the night; 2518
 5:10 died for us, that, whether we wake or **s**, 2518

SLEEPER (1) [SLEEP]

Jnh 1: 6 said unto him, What meanest thou, O **s**? 7290

SLEEPEST (4) [SLEEP]

Ps 44:23 Awake, why **s** thou, O Lord? arise, cast 3462
Pr 6:22 when thou **s**, it shall keep thee; 7901
Mk 14:37 and saith unto Peter, Simon, **s** thou? 2518
Eph 5:14 Awake thou that **s**, and arise from the 2518

SLEEPETH (7) [SLEEP]

1Ki 18:27 peradventure he **s**, and must be awaked. 3463
Pr 10: 5 he that **s** in harvest *is* a son that causeth 7290
Hos 7: 6 baker **s** all the night; *in* the morning it 3463
Mt 9:24 for the maid is not dead, but **s**. 2518
Mk 5:39 and weep? the damsel is not dead, but **s**. 2518
Lk 8:52 he said, Weep not; she is not dead, but **s**. 2518
Jn 11:11 he saith unto them, Our friend Lazarus **s**; 2837

SLEEPING (6) [SLEEP]

1Sa 26: 7 Saul lay **s** within the trench, and his spear 3463
Isa 56:10 **s**, lying down, loving to slumber. 1957
Mk 13:36 Lest coming suddenly he find you **s**. 2518
 14:37 and findeth them **s**, and saith unto Peter, 2518
Lk 22:45 his disciples, he found them **s** for sorrow, 2837
Ac 12: 6 the same night Peter was **s** between two 2837

SLEIGHT (1)

Eph 4:14 every wind of doctrine, by the **s** of men, 2940

SLEPT (49) [SLEEP]

Ge 2:21 a deep sleep to fall upon Adam, and he **s**: 3462
 41: 5 he **s** and dreamed the second time: 3462
2Sa 11: 9 Uriah **s** *at* the door of the king's house 7901
1Ki 2:10 David **s** with his fathers, and was buried 7901
 3:20 while thine handmaid **s**, and laid it in her 3463
 11:21 when Hadad heard in Egypt that David **s** 7901
 11:43 Solomon **s** with his fathers, and was 7901
 14:20 he **s** with his fathers, and Nadab his son 7901
 14:31 Rehoboam **s** with his fathers, 7901
 15: 8 Abijam **s** with his fathers; and they buried 7901
 15:24 Asa **s** with his fathers, and was buried 7901
 16: 6 So Baasha **s** with his fathers, 7901
 16:28 Omri **s** with his fathers, and was buried 7901
 19: 5 as he lay and **s** under a juniper tree, 3462
 22:40 Ahab **s** with his fathers; and Ahaziah his 7901
 22:50 Jehoshaphat **s** with his fathers, 7901
2Ki 8:24 Joram **s** with his fathers, and was buried 7901
 10:35 Jehu **s** with his fathers: and they buried 7901
 13: 9 Jehoahaz **s** with his fathers; and they 7901
 13:13 Joash **s** with his fathers; and Jeroboam sat 7901
 14:16 Jehoash **s** with his fathers, and was buried 7901
 14:22 after that the king **s** with his fathers. 7901
 14:29 Jeroboam **s** with his fathers, *even* with 7901
 15: 7 So Azariah **s** with his fathers; 7901
 15:22 Menahem **s** with his fathers; 7901
 15:38 Jotham **s** with his fathers, and was buried 7901
 16:20 Ahaz **s** with his fathers, and was buried 7901
 20:21 Hezekiah **s** with his fathers: 7901
 21:18 Manasseh **s** with his fathers: 7901
 24: 6 So Jehoiakim **s** with his fathers: 7901
2Ch 9:31 Solomon **s** with his fathers, and he was 7901
 12:16 Rehoboam **s** with his fathers, 7901
 14: 1 So Abijah **s** with his fathers, 7901
 16:13 Asa **s** with his fathers, and died in the 7901
 21: 1 Now Jehoshaphat **s** with his fathers, 7901
 26: 2 after that the king **s** with his fathers, 7901
 26:23 So Uzziah **s** with his fathers, 7901
 27: 9 Jotham **s** with his fathers, and they buried 7901
 28:27 Ahaz **s** with his fathers, and they buried 7901
 32:33 Hezekiah **s** with his fathers, and they 7901
 33:20 So Manasseh **s** with his fathers, 7901
Job 3:13 lien *still* and been quiet, I should have **s**: 3462
Ps 3: 5 I laid me down and **s**; I awaked; 3462
 76: 5 are spoiled, they have **s** their sleep: 5123
Mt 13:25 But while men **s**, his enemy came and 2518
 25: 5 they all slumbered and **s**. 2518
 27:52 and many bodies of saints which **s** arose, 2837
 28:13 by night, and stole him *away* while we **s**. 2837

1Co 15:20 and become the firstfruits of them that **s**. 2837

SLEW (196) [SLAY]

Ge 4: 8 up against Abel his brother, and **s** him. 2026
 4:25 seed instead of Abel, whom Cain **s**. 2026
 34:25 upon the city boldly, and **s** all the males. 2026
 34:26 they **s** Hamor and Shechem his son with 2026
 38: 7 sight of the Lord; and the Lord **s** him. 4191
 38:10 the Lord: wherefore he **s** him also. 4191
 49: 6 for in their anger they **s** a man, and in 2026
Ex 13:15 that the Lord **s** all the firstborn in 2026
Lev 8:15 he **s** *it;* and Moses took the blood, and 7819
 8:23 he **s** *it;* and Moses took of the blood of it, 7819
 9: 8 the altar, and **s** the calf of the sin offering, 7819
 9:12 he **s** the burnt offering; and Aaron's sons 7819
 9:15 and **s** it, and offered it for sin, as the first. 7819
 9:18 He **s** also the bullock and the ram *for* a 7819
Nu 31: 7 and they **s** all the males. 2026
 31: 8 the kings of Midian, beside the rest 2026
 31: 8 Balaam also the son of Beor they **s** with 2026
Jos 8:21 they turned again, and **s** the men of Ai. 5221
 9:26 children of Israel, that they **s** them not. 2026
 10:10 **s** them *with* a great slaughter at Gibeon, 5221
 10:11 the children of Israel **s** with the sword. 4191
 10:26 **s** them, and hanged them on five trees: 4191
 11:17 he took, and smote them, and **s** them. 4191
Jdg 1: 4 **s** of them in Bezek ten thousand men. 5221
 1: 5 they **s** the Canaanites and the Perizzites. 5221
 1:10 they **s** Sheshai, and Ahiman, and Talmai. 5221
 1:17 they **s** the Canaanites that inhabited 5221
 3:29 they **s** *of* Moab at that time about ten 5221
 3:31 **s** *of* the Philistines six hundred men 5221
 7:25 **s** Oreb upon the rock Oreb, and Zeeb 2026
 7:25 Zeeb they **s** at the winepress of Zeeb, 2026
 8:17 of Penuel, and **s** the men of the city. 2026
 8:18 manner of men *were they* whom ye **s** 2026
 8:21 **s** Zebah and Zalmunna, and took away 2026
 9: 5 **s** his brethren the sons of Jerubbaal, 2026
 9:24 Abimelech their brother, which **s** them; 2026
 9:44 that *were* in the fields, and **s** them. 5221
 9:45 the people that *was* therein, 2026
 9:54 that *men* say not of me, A woman **s** him. 2026
 12: 6 and **s** him at the passages of Jordan: 7819
 14:19 thirty men of them, and took their spoil, 5221
 15:15 took it, and **s** a thousand men therewith. 5221
 16:24 of our country, which **s** many of us. 2491
 16:30 So the dead which he **s** at his death were 4191
 16:30 were moe than *they* which he **s** in his life. 4191
 20:45 and **s** two thousand men of them. 5221
1Sa 1:25 they **s** a bullock, and brought the child to 7819
 4: 2 they **s** of the army in the field about four 5221
 11:11 **s** the Ammonites until the heat of the day: 5221
 14:13 and his armourbearer **s** after him. 4191
 14:32 and calves, and **s** *them* on the ground: 7819
 14:34 ox with him *that* night, and **s** *them* there. 7819
 17:35 by his beard, and smote him, and **s** him. 4191
 17:36 Thy servant **s** both the lion and the bear: 5221
 17:50 and smote the Philistine, and **s** him; 4191
 17:51 and **s** him, and cut off his head therewith. 4191
 18:27 and **s** of the Philistines two hundred men; 5221
 19: 5 **s** the Philistine, and the Lord wrought a 5221
 19: 8 and **s** them *with* a great slaughter; 5221
 22:18 **s** on that day fourscore and five persons 4191
 29: 5 Saul **s** his thousands, and David his ten 5221
 30: 2 they **s** not any, either great or small, 4191
 31: 2 the Philistines **s** Jonathan, and Abinadab, 5221
2Sa 1:10 **s** him, because I was sure that he could 4191
 3:30 So Joab and Abishai his brother **s** Abner, 2026
 4: 7 **s** him, and beheaded him, and took his 4191
 4:10 I took hold of him, and **s** him in Ziklag, 2026
 4:12 they **s** them, and cut off their hands and 2026
 8: 5 David **s** of the Syrians two and 5221
 10:18 David **s** *the men of* seven hundred 2026
 14: 6 but the one smote the other, and **s** him. 4191
 14: 7 for the life of his brother whom he **s**; 5221
 18:15 and smote Absalom, and **s** him. 4191
 21: 1 house, because he **s** the Gibeonites. 4191
 21:18 Sibbechai the Hushathite **s** Saph, 5221
 21:19 *the brother of* Goliath the Gittite, 5221
 21:21 of Shimea the brother of David **s** him. 5221
 23: 8 eight hundred, whom he **s** at one time. 2491
 23:12 and defended it, and **s** the Philistines: 5221
 23:18 **s** them, and had the name among three. 2491
 23:20 acts, he **s** two lionlike men of Moab: 5221
 23:20 **s** a lion in the midst of a pit in time of 5221
 23:21 he **s** an Egyptian, a goodly man: 5221
 23:21 and **s** him with his own spear. 2026
1Ki 1: 9 Adonijah **s** sheep and oxen and fat cattle 2076
 2: 5 whom he **s**, and shed the blood of war in 2026
 2:32 than he, and **s** them with the sword, 2026
 2:34 went up, and fell upon him, and **s** him: 4191
 11:24 when David **s** them *of Zobah:* and 2026
 13:24 a lion met him by the way, and **s** him: 4191
 16:11 *that* he **s** all the house of Baasha: 5221
 18:13 when Jezebel **s** the prophets of the Lord, 2026
 18:40 to the brook Kishon, and **s** them there. 7819
 19:21 **s** them, and boiled their flesh with 2076
 20:20 they **s** every one his man: and the Syrians 5221
 20:21 and **s** the Syrians with a great slaughter. 5221
 20:29 the children of Israel **s** *of* the Syrians an 5221
 20:36 from him, a lion found him, and **s** him. 5221
2Ki 9:31 *Had* Zimri peace, who **s** his master? 2026
 10: 7 **s** seventy persons, and put their heads in 7819
 10: 9 I conspired against my master, and **s** him: 2026

2Ki 10: 9 and slew him: but who **s** all these?	5221
10:11 Jehu **s** all that remained of the house of	5221
10:14 **s** them at the pit of the shearing house,	7819
10:17 he **s** all that remained unto Ahab in	5221
11:18 **s** Mattan the priest of Baal before the	2026
11:20 they **s** Athaliah with the sword *beside*	4191
12:20 **s** Joash *in* the house of Millo,	5221
14: 5 that he **s** his servants which had slain	5221
14: 6 the children of the murderers he **s** not:	4191
14: 7 He **s** of Edom in the valley of salt ten	5221
14:19 sent after him to Lachish, and **s** him there.	4191
15:10 **s** him, and reigned in his stead.	4191
15:14 and **s** him, and reigned in his stead.	4191
15:30 and **s** him, and reigned in his stead,	4191
16: 9 *people* of it captive to Kir, and **s** Rezin.	4191
17:25 among them, which **s** *some* of them.	2026
21:23 and **s** the king in his own house.	4191
21:24 the people of the land **s** all them that had	5221
23:20 he **s** all the priests of the high places that	2076
23:29 he **s** him at Megiddo, when he had seen	4191
25: 7 **s** the sons of Zedekiah before his eyes,	7819
25:21 **s** them at Riblah in the land of Hamath.	5221
1Ch 2: 3 in the sight of the LORD; and he **s** him.	4191
7:21 of Gath that were born in *that* land **s**,	2026
10: 2 the Philistines **s** Jonathan, and Abinadab,	5221
10:14 he **s** him, and turned the kingdom	4191
11:14 and delivered it, and **s** the Philistines;	5221
11:20 **s** *them*, and had a name among the three.	2491
11:22 acts; he **s** two lionlike men of Moab:	5221
11:22 and **s** a lion in a pit in a snowy day.	5221
11:23 he **s** an Egyptian, a man of *great* stature,	5221
11:23 and **s** him with his own spear.	2026
18: 5 David **s** of the Syrians two and	5221
18:12 Moreover Abishai the son of Zeruiah **s** of	5221
19:18 David **s** of the Syrians seven thousand	5221
20: 4 at which time Sibbechai the Hushathite **s**	5221
20: 5 Elhanan the son of Jair **s** Lahmi the	5221
20: 7 the son of Shimea David's brother **s** him.	5221
2Ch 13:17 his people **s** them *with* a great slaughter:	5221
21: 4 **s** all his brethren with the sword,	2026
22: 8 that ministered to Ahaziah, he **s** them.	2026
22:11 him from Athaliah, so that she **s** him not.	4191
23:15 gate *by* the king's house, they **s** her there.	4191
23:17 **s** Mattan the priest of Baal before the	2026
24:22 his father had done to him, but **s** his son.	2026
24:25 and **s** him on his bed, and he died:	2026
25: 3 that he **s** his servants that had killed	2026
25: 4 he **s** not their children, but *did* as it is	4191
25:27 to Lachish after him, and **s** him there.	4191
28: 6 For Pekah the son of Remaliah **s** in Judah	2026
28: 7 Maaseiah the king's son, and Azrikam	2026
32:21 they that came forth of his own bowels **s**	5307
33:24 against him, and **s** him in his own house.	4191
33:25 the people of the land **s** all them that had	4191
36:17 who **s** their young men with the sword in	2026
Ne 9:26 thy prophets which testified against	2026
Est 9: 6 in Shushan the palace the Jews **s** and	2026
9:10 the enemy of the Jews, they;	2026
9:15 and **s** three hundred men at Shushan;	2026
9:16 **s** of their foes seventy and five thousand,	2026
Ps 78:31 the fattest of them, and smote down	2026
78:34 When he **s** them, then they sought him:	2026
105:29 their waters into blood, and **s** their fish.	4191
135:10 smote great nations, and **s** mighty kings;	2026
136:18 **s** famous kings: for his mercy *endureth*	2026
Isa 66: 3 He that killeth an ox *is as if* he **s** a man;	5221
Jer 20:17 Because he **s** me not from the womb;	4191
26:23 who **s** him with the sword, and cast his	5221
39: 6 the king of Babylon **s** the sons of Zedekiah	7819
39: 6 also the king of Babylon **s** all the nobles of	7819
41: 2 **s** him, whom the king of Babylon had	4191
41: 3 Ishmael also **s** all the Jews that were with	5221
41: 7 that Ishmael the son of Nethaniah **s** them,	7819
41: 8 and **s** them not among their brethren.	4191
52:10 the king of Babylon **s** the sons of Zedekiah	7819
52:10 he **s** also all the princes of Judah in Riblah.	7819
La 2: 4 all *that were* pleasant to the eye,	2026
Eze 9: 7 And they went forth, and **s** in the city.	5221
23:10 her daughters, and **s** her with the sword:	2026
40:41 whereupon they **s** *their sacrifices*.	7819
40:42 wherewith they **s** the burnt offering	7819
Da 3:22 the flame of the fire **s** those men that took	6992
5:19 whom he would he **s**; and whom he	6992
Mt 2:16 **s** all the children that were in Bethlehem,	*337*
21:39 cast *him* out of the vineyard, and **s** *him*.	*615*
22: 6 entreated *them* spitefully, and **s** *them*.	*615*
23:35 whom ye **s** between the temple and	*5407*
Lk 13: 4 the tower in Siloam fell, and **s** them,	*615*
Ac 5:30 Jesus, whom ye **s** and hanged on a tree.	*1315*
10:39 whom they **s** and hanged on a tree:	*337*
22:20 and kept the raiment of them that **s** him.	*337*
Ro 7:11 deceived me, and by it **s** *me*.	*615*
1Jn 3:12 was of that wicked one, and **s** his brother.	*4969*
3:12 And wherefore **s** he him? Because his	*4969*

SLEWEST (1) [SLAY]

1Sa 21: 9 whom thou **s** in the valley of Elah,	5221

SLIDDEN (1) [SLIDE]

Jer 8: 5 is this people of Jerusalem **s** back *by* a	7725

SLIDE (3) [BACKSLIDER, BACKSLIDING, BACKSLIDINGS, SLIDDEN, SLIDETH]

Dt 32:35 their foot shall **s** in *due* time:	4131
Ps 26: 1 also in the LORD; *therefore* I shall not **s**.	4571

Ps 37:31 *is* in his heart; none of his steps shall **s**.	4571

SLIDETH (1) [SLIDE]

Hos 4:16 For Israel **s** back as a backsliding heifer:	5637

SLIGHTLY (2)

Jer 6:14 of the daughter of my people **s**,	5921+7043
8:11 of the daughter of my people **s**,	5921+7043

SLIME (2) [SLIMEPITS]

Ge 11: 3 brick for stone, and **s** had they for morter.	2564
Ex 2: 3 daubed it with **s** and with pitch, and put	2564

SLIMEPITS (1) [PIT, SLIME]

Ge 14:10 vale of Siddim *was* **full of s**;	875+875+2564

SLING (8) [SLINGERS, SLINGS, SLINGSTONES]

Jdg 20:16 one could **s** stones at a hair *breadth*,	7049
1Sa 17:40 even in a scrip; and his **s** *was* in his hand:	7050
17:50 prevailed over the Philistine with a **s**	7050
25:29 them shall he **s** out *as out* of the middle	7049
25:29 he sling out *as out* of the middle of a **s**.	7050
Pr 26: 8 As *he that* bindeth a stone in a **s**, so *is* he	4773
Jer 10:18 I will **s** out the inhabitants of the land at	7049
Zec 9:15 shall devour, and subdue *with* **s** stones;	7050

SLINGERS (1) [SLING]

2Ki 3:25 howbeit the **s** went about *it*, and smote it.	7051

SLINGS (1) [SLING]

2Ch 26:14 and bows, and **s** to cast stones.	7050

SLINGSTONES (1) [SLING, STONE]

Job 41:28 **s** are turned with him into stubble.	68+7050

SLIP (5) [SLIPPERY, SLIPPETH, SLIPS, SLIPT]

2Sa 22:37 steps under me; so that my feet did not **s**.	4571
Job 12: 5 He that is ready to **s** with *his* feet *is as* a	4571
Ps 17: 5 in thy paths, *that* my footsteps **s** not.	4131
18:36 steps under me, that my feet did not **s**.	4571
Heb 2: 1 lest at any time we should let *them* **s**.	3901

SLIPPERY (3) [SLIP]

Ps 35: 6 Let their way be dark and **s**: and let	2519
73:18 Surely thou didst set them in **s** *places*:	2513
Jer 23:12 be unto them as **s** *ways* in the darkness:	2519

SLIPPETH (3) [SLIP]

Dt 19: 5 the head **s** from the helve, and lighteth	5394
Ps 38:16 when my foot **s**, they magnify *themselves*	4131
94:18 When I said, My foot **s**; thy mercy,	4131

SLIPS (1) [SLIP]

Isa 17:10 and shalt set it *with* strange **s**:	2156

SLIPT (2) [SLIP]

1Sa 19:10 he **s** away out of Saul's presence,	6362
Ps 73: 2 almost gone; my steps had well nigh **s**.	8210

SLOTHFUL (15) [SLOTHFULNESS]

Jdg 18: 9 be not **s** to go, *and* to enter to possess	6101
Pr 12:24 bear rule: but the **s** shall be under tribute.	7423
12:27 The **s** *man* roasteth not that which he	7423
15:19 The way of the **s** *man* is as a hedge of	2822
18: 9 He also that is **s** in his work *is* brother to	7503
19:24 A **s** *man* hideth his hand in *his* bosom,	6102
21:25 The desire of the **s** killeth him; for his	6102
22:13 The **s** *man* saith, There is a lion without,	6102
24:30 I went by the field of the **s**, and by	376+6102
26:13 **s** *man* saith, There is a lion in the way;	6102
26:14 his hinges, so *doth* the **s** upon his bed.	6102
26:15 The **s** hideth his hand in *his* bosom;	6102
Mt 25:26 unto him, Thou wicked and **s** servant,	*3636*
Ro 12:11 Not **s** in business; fervent in spirit;	*3636*
Heb 6:12 That ye be not **s**, but followers of them	*3576*

SLOTHFULNESS (2) [SLOTHFUL]

Pr 19:15 **S** casteth into a deep sleep; and an idle	6103
Ecc 10:18 By **much s** the building decayeth;	6103

SLOW (15) [SLOWLY]

Ex 4:10 I *am* **s** of speech, of a slow tongue.	3515
4:10 I *am* slow of speech, and of a **s** tongue.	3515
Ne 9:17 **s** to anger, and of great kindness,	750
Ps 103: 8 **s** to anger, and plenteous in mercy.	750
145: 8 **s** to anger, and of great mercy.	750
Pr 14:29 He that is **s** to wrath *is* of great	750
15:18 but *he that is* **s** to anger appeaseth strife.	750
16:32 *He that is* **s** to anger *is* better than	750
Joel 2:13 to anger, and of great kindness,	750
Jnh 4: 2 to anger, and of great kindness,	750
Na 1: 3 The LORD *is* **s** to anger, and great in	750
Lk 24:25 **s** of heart to believe all that the prophets	*1021*
Tit 1:12 *are* alway liars, evil beasts, **s** bellies.	*692*
Jas 1:19 swift to hear, **s** to speak, slow to wrath:	*1021*
1:19 swift to hear, slow to speak, **s** to wrath:	*1021*

SLOWLY (1) [SLOW]

Ac 27: 7 And when we had **sailed s** many days,	*1020*

SLUCES (1)

Isa 19:10 all that make **s** *and* ponds for fish.	7938

SLUG See SNAIL

SLUGGARD (6)

Pr 6: 6 Go to the ant, thou **s**; consider her ways,	6102

Pr 6: 9 How long wilt thou sleep, O **s**? when wilt	6102
10:26 eyes, so *is* the **s** to them that send him.	6102
13: 4 The soul of the **s** desireth, *hath*	6102
20: 4 The **s** will not plow by reason of the cold;	6102
26:16 The **s** *is* wiser in his own conceit than	6102

SLUMBER (10) [SLUMBERED, SLUMBERETH, SLUMBERINGS]

Ps 121: 3 moved: he that keepeth thee will not **s**.	5123
121: 4 he that keepeth Israel shall neither **s** nor	5123
132: 4 sleep to mine eyes, *or* **s** to mine eyelids,	8572
Pr 6: 4 sleep to thine eyes, nor **s** to thine eyelids.	8572
6:10 *Yet* a little sleep, a little **s**, a little folding	8572
24:33 *Yet* a little sleep, a little **s**, a little folding	8572
Isa 5:27 none shall **s** nor sleep; neither shall	5123
56:10 sleeping, lying down, loving to **s**.	5123
Na 3:18 Thy shepherds **s**, O king of Assyria:	5123
Ro 11: 8 God hath given them the spirit of **s**,	*2659*

SLUMBERED (1) [SLUMBER]

Mt 25: 5 bridegroom tarried, they all **s** and slept.	*3573*

SLUMBERETH (1) [SLUMBER]

2Pe 2: 3 lingereth not, and their damnation **s** not.	*3573*

SLUMBERINGS (1) [SLUMBER]

Job 33:15 sleep falleth upon men, in **s** upon the bed;	8572

SLY See BACKBITING; BACKBITINGS

SMALL (97) [SMALLEST]

Ge 19:11 house with blindness, both **s** and great;	6996
30:15 *Is it a* **matter** that thou hast taken my	4592
Ex 9: 9 become **s** dust in all the land of Egypt,	80
16:14 the face of the wilderness *there lay* a **s**	1851
16:14 *as* **s** as the hoar frost on the ground.	1851
18:22 but every **s** matter they shall judge:	6996
18:26 every **s** matter they judged themselves.	6996
30:36 thou shalt beat *some* of it **very s**, and put	1854
Lev 16:12 his hands full of sweet incense **beaten s**,	1851
Nu 16: 9 *Seemeth it but* a **s** thing unto you, that	4592
16:13 *Is it* a **s** thing that thou hast brought us	4592
32:41 and took the **s** towns thereof,	2333
Dt 1:17 you shall hear the **s** as well as the great;	6996
9:21 stamped it, *and* **ground** it *very* **s**,	2912+3190
9:21 very small, *even* until *it was as* **s** as dust:	1854
25:13 in thy bag divers weights, a great and a **s**.	6996
25:14 house divers measures, a great and a **s**.	6996
32: 2 as the **rain** upon the tender herb,	8164
1Sa 5: 9 both **s** and great, and they had emerods	6996
20: 2 father will do nothing *either* great or **s**,	6996
30: 2 either great or **s**, but carried *them* away,	6996
30:19 neither **s** nor great, neither sons nor	6996
2Sa 7:19 this was yet a **s** thing in thy sight, O Lord	6994
17:13 there be not one **s** stone found there.	6872
22:43 I **beat** them *as* **s** as the dust of the earth,	7833
1Ki 2:20 she said, I desire one **s** petition of thee;	6996
19:12 in the fire: and after the fire a still **s** voice.	1851
22:31 saying, Fight neither with **s** nor great,	6996
2Ki 19:26 their inhabitants *were* of **s** power,	7116
23: 2 and all the people, both **s** and great:	6996
23: 6 **stampt** it **s** to powder, and cast the	1854
23:15 *and* **stampt** it **s** to powder, and burnt	1854
25:26 both **s** and great, and the captains of	6996
1Ch 17:17 *yet* this was a **s** thing in thine eyes,	6994
25: 8 ward against **ward**, as well the **s** as	6996
26:13 they cast lots, as well the **s** as the great,	6996
2Ch 15:13 whether **s** or great, whether man or	6996
18:30 saying, Fight ye not with **s** or great,	6996
24:24 For the army of the Syrians came with a **s**	4705
31:15 courses, as well *to* the great as *to* the **s**:	6996
34:30 Levites, and all the people, great and **s**:	6996
35: 8 six hundred **s** cattle, and three hundred	NIH
35: 9 passover *offerings* five thousand **s** cattle,	NIH
Est 1: 5 both unto great and **s**, seven days,	6996
1:20 husbands honour, both to great and **s**.	6996
Job 3:19 The **s** and great *are* there; and the servant	6996
8: 7 Though thy beginning was **s**, yet thy latter	4705
15:11 *Are* the consolations of God **s** with thee?	4592
36:27 For he **maketh** the **s** drops of water:	1639
37: 6 *to* the **s** rain, and *to* the great rain	4306
Ps 18:42 did I **beat** them **s** as the dust before	7833
104:25 both **s** and great beasts.	6996
115:13 that fear the LORD, *both* **s** and great.	6996
119:141 I *am* **s** and despised: *yet* do not I forget	6996
Pr 24:10 in the day of adversity, thy strength *is* **s**.	6862
Ecc 2: 7 **s** cattle above all that were in Jerusalem	6629
Isa 1: 9 left unto us a **very s** remnant,	4592+3509.1
7:13 *Is it* a **s** thing for you to weary men,	4592
16:14 the remnant *shall be* **very s** and feeble,	4213
22:24 and the issue, all vessels of **s** quantity,	6996
29: 5 of thy strangers shall be like **s** dust,	1851
37:27 their inhabitants *were* of **s** power,	7116
40:15 are counted as the **s** dust of the balance:	7834
41:15 **beat** *them* **s**, and shalt make the hills as	1854
43:23 Thou hast not brought me the **s** cattle of	7716
54: 7 For a **s** moment have I forsaken thee;	6996
60:22 a thousand, and a **s** one a strong nation:	6810
Jer 16: 6 the great and the **s** shall die in this land:	6996
30:19 also glorify them, and they shall not be **s**.	6819
44:28 Yet a **s** number that escape the sword	4962
49:15 I will make thee **s** among the heathen,	6996
Eze 16:20 *Is this* of thy whoredoms a **s** **matter**,	4592
34:18 *Seemeth it* a **s** thing unto you to have	4592
Da 11:23 and shall become strong with a **s** people.	4592

Am	7: 2 *by* whom shall Jacob arise? for he *is* **s**.	6996
	7: 5 *by* whom shall Jacob arise? for he *is* **s**.	6996
	8: 5 **making** the ephah **s**, and the shekel great	6994
Ob	1: 2 I have made thee **s** among the heathen:	6996
Zec	4:10 who hath despised the day of **s** *things?*	6996
Mk	3: 9 that a **s ship** should wait on him because	4142
	8: 7 And they had a few **s fishes:**	2485
Jn	2:15 when he had made a scourge of **s cords,**	4979
	6: 9 hath five barley loaves, and two **s fishes?**	3795
Ac	12:18 there was no **s** stir among the soldiers,	3641
	15: 2 and Barnabas had no **s** dissension and	3641
	19:23 And the same time there arose no **s** stir	3641
	19:24 brought no **s** gain unto the craftsmen;	3641
	26:22 this day, witnessing both to **s** and great,	3398
	27:20 no **s** tempest lay on *us*, all hope that we	3641
1Co	4: 3 But with me it is a **very s** *thing* that I	1646
Jas	3: 4 *yet* are they turned about with a **very s**	1646
Rev	11:18 and them that fear thy name, **s** and great;	3398
	13:16 *both* **s** and great, rich and poor, free and	3398
	19: 5 and ye that fear him, both **s** and great.	3398
	19:18 both free and bond, both **s** and great.	3398
	20:12 the dead, **s** and great, stand before God;	3398

SMALL COPPER COINS See MITES

SMALLEST (2) [SMALL]

1Sa	9:21 Benjamite, of the **s** of the tribes of Israel?	6996
1Co	6: 2 are ye unworthy to judge the **s matters?**	1646

SMALLEST LETTER See JOT

SMALLEST STROKE See TITTLE

SMART (1)

Pr	11:15 that is surety for a stranger shall **s**	7321+7451

SMELL (20) [SMELLED, SMELLETH, SMELLING, SWEETSMELLING]

Ge	27:27 he smelled the **s** of his raiment,	7381
	27:27 the **s** of my son *is* as the smell of a field	7381
	27:27 the smell of my son *is* as the smell of a	7381
Ex	30:38 so is thereto, shall even be cut off from his	7306
Lev	26:31 I will not **s** the savour of your sweet	7306
Dt	4:28 neither see, nor hear, nor eat, nor **s**.	7306
Ps	45: 8 All thy garments of myrrh, and aloes,	NIH
	115: 6 hear not: noses have they, but they **s** not:	7306
SS	1:12 my spikenard sendeth forth the **s** thereof.	7381
	2:13 vines *with* the tender grape give a *good* **s**.	7381
	4:10 the **s** of thine ointments than all spices!	7381
	4:11 the **s** of thy garments *is* like the smell of	7381
	4:11 the smell of thy garments *is* like the **s** of	7381
	7: 8 the vine, and the **s** of thy nose like apples;	7381
	7:13 The mandrakes give a **s**, and at our gates	7381
Isa	3:24 instead of **sweet s** there shall be stink;	1314
Da	3:27 nor the **s** of fire had passed on them.	7382
Hos	14: 6 as the olive tree, and his **s** as Lebanon.	7381
Am	5:21 I will not **s** in your solemn assemblies.	7306
Php	4:18 an odour of a **sweet s**, a sacrifice	2175

SMELLED (2) [SMELL]

Ge	8:21 the LORD **s** a sweet savour;	7306
	27:27 he **s** the smell of his raiment,	7306

SMELLETH (1) [SMELL]

Job	39:25 he **s** the battle afar off, the thunder of	7306

SMELLING (3) [SMELL]

SS	5: 5 my fingers *with* **sweet s** myrrh, upon	5674
	5:13 lips *like* lilies, dropping **sweet s** myrrh.	5674
1Co	12:17 whole *were* hearing, where *were* the **s?**	3750

SMITE (125) [SMITERS, SMITEST, SMITETH, SMITING, SMITTEN, SMOTE, SMOTEST]

Ge	8:21 neither will I again **s** any more every	5221
	32: 8 s it, then the *other* company which is left	5221
	32:11 lest he will come and **s** me, *and* the	5221
Ex	3:20 **s** Egypt with all my wonders which I will	5221
	7:17 I will **s** with the rod that *is* in mine hand	5221
	8: 2 behold, I will **s** all thy borders with frogs:	5062
	8:16 thy rod, and **s** the dust of the land,	5221
	9:15 that I may **s** thee and thy people with	5221
	12:12 **s** all the firstborn in the land of Egypt,	5221
	12:13 destroy *you*, when I **s** the land of Egypt.	5221
	12:23 For the LORD will pass through to **s** *you*.	5062
	12:23 to come in unto your houses to **s** *you*.	5062
	17: 6 thou shalt **s** the rock, and there shall	5221
	21:18 another with a stone, or with *his* fist,	5221
	21:20 if a man **s** his servant, or his maid, with a	5221
	21:26 if a man **s** the eye of his servant, or the	5221
	21:27 if he **s** out his manservant's tooth,	5307
Nu	14:12 I will **s** them with the pestilence,	5221
	22: 6 *that* we may **s** them, and *that* I may drive	5221
	24:17 shall **s** the corners of Moab, and destroy	4272
	25:17 Vex the Midianites, and **s** them:	5221
	35:16 if he **s** him with an instrument of iron,	5221
	35:17 if he **s** him with throwing a stone,	5221
	35:18 Or if he **s** him with a hand weapon of	5221
	35:21 Or in enmity **s** him with his hand, that he	5221
Dt	7: 2 shalt them, *and* utterly destroy them;	5221
	13: 5 Thou shalt **surely s** the inhabitants	5221+5221
	19:11 him mortally that he die, and fleeth into	5221
	20:13 thou shalt **s** every male thereof with	5221
	28:22 The LORD shall **s** thee with a	5221
	28:27 The LORD will **s** thee with the botch of	5221
	28:28 The LORD shall **s** thee with madness,	5221
	28:35 The LORD shall **s** thee in the knees,	5221

Dt	33:11 **s** through the loins of them that rise	4272
Jos	7: 3 or three thousand men go up and **s** Ai;	5221
	10: 4 and help me, that we may **s** Gibeon:	5221
	10:19 enemies, and **s** the hindmost of them;	2179
	12: 6 of the LORD and the children of Israel **s**:	5221
	13:12 for these did Moses **s**, and cast them out.	5221
Jdg	6:16 thou shalt **s** the Midianites as one man.	5221
	20:31 they began to **s** of the people, *and* kill,	5221
	20:39 Benjamin began to **s** *and* kill of the men	5221
	21:10 **s** the inhabitants of Jabesh-gilead with	5221
1Sa	15: 3 go and **s** Amalek, and utterly destroy	5221
	17:46 I will **s** thee, and take thine head from	5221
	18:11 I will **s** David even to the wall *with it*.	5221
	19:10 Saul sought to **s** David even to the wall	5221
	20:33 Saul cast a javelin at him to **s** him:	5221
	23: 2 Shall I go and **s** these Philistines?	5221
	23: 2 Go, and **s** the Philistines, and save Keilah.	5221
	26: 8 now therefore let me **s** him, I pray thee,	5221
	26: 8 and I will not **s** him the second time.	NIH
	26:10 the LORD liveth, the LORD shall **s** him;	5062
2Sa	2:22 wherefore should I **s** thee to the ground?	5221
	5:24 thee, to **s** the host of the Philistines.	5221
	13:28 and when I say unto you, **S** Amnon;	5221
	15:14 and **s** the city with the edge of the sword.	5221
	17: 2 him shall flee; and I will **s** the king only:	5221
	18:11 why didst thou not **s** him there to	5221
1Ki	14:15 For the LORD shall **s** Israel, as a reed is	5221
	20:35 the word of the LORD, **S** me, I pray thee.	5221
	20:35 pray thee. And the man refused to **s** him.	5221
	20:37 another man, and said, **S** me, I pray thee.	5221
2Ki	3:19 ye shall **s** every fenced city,	5221
	6:18 said, **S** this people, I pray thee,	5221
	6:21 shall I **s** *them?* shall I smite *them?*	5221
	6:21 shall I smite *them?* shall I **s** *them?*	5221
	6:22 shalt not **s** *them:* wouldest thou smite	5221
	6:22 shalt not smite *them:* wouldest thou **s**	5221
	9: 7 shalt **s** the house of Ahab thy master,	5221
	9:27 and said, **S** him also in the chariot.	5221
	13:17 for thou shalt **s** the Syrians in Aphek,	5221
	13:18 the king of Israel, **S** upon the ground.	5221
	13:19 *it:* whereas now thou shalt **s** Syria	5221
1Ch	14:15 for God is gone forth before thee to **s**	5221
2Ch	21:14 *with* a great plague will the LORD **s** thy	5062
Ps	121: 6 The sun shall not **s** thee by day,	5221
	141: 5 Let the righteous **s** me; *it shall be* a	1986
Pr	19:25 **S** a scorner, and the simple will beware:	5221
Isa	3:17 Therefore the Lord will **s** with a scab	5596
	10:24 he shall **s** thee with a rod, and shall lift	5221
	11: 4 he shall **s** the earth with the rod of his	5221
	11:15 shall **s** it in *the* seven streams,	5221
	19:22 the LORD shall **s** Egypt: *he* shall smite	5062
	19:22 shall **s** and heal *it:* and they shall return	5062
	49:10 neither shall the heat nor sun **s** them:	5221
	58: 4 and to **s** with the fist of wickedness:	5221
Jer	18:18 let us **s** him with the tongue, and let us	5221
	21: 6 I will **s** the inhabitants of this city, both	5221
	21: 7 shall **s** them with the edge of the sword;	5221
	43:11 he shall **s** the land of Egypt,	5221
	46:13 should come and **s** the land of Egypt.	5221
	49:28 Nebuchadrezzar king of Babylon shall **s**,	5221
Eze	5: 2 a third *part, and* **s** about it with a knife:	5221
	6:11 **S** with thine hand, and stamp with thy	5221
	9: 5 Go ye after him through the city, and **s**:	5221
	21:12 my people: **s** therefore upon *thy* thigh.	5606
	21:14 *thine* hands together, and let the sword	5221
	21:17 I will also **s** mine hands together, and I	5221
	32:15 when I shall **s** all them that dwell therein,	5221
	39: 3 I will **s** thy bow out of thy left hand,	5221
Am	3:15 will **s** the winter house with the summer	5221
	6:11 he will **s** the great house with breaches,	5062
	9: 1 he said, **S** the lintel of the door, that	5221
Mic	5: 1 they shall **s** the judge of Israel with a rod	6375
Na	2:10 the knees **together**, and much pain is in	6375
Zec	9: 4 out, and he will **s** her power in the sea;	5221
	10:11 shall **s** the waves in the sea, and all	5221
	11: 6 they shall **s** the land, and out of their	3807
	12: 4 I will **s** every horse with astonishment,	5221
	12: 4 will **s** every horse of the people with	5221
	13: 7 **s** the shepherd, and the sheep shall be	5221
	14:12 **s** all the people that have fought against	5062
	14:18 where *with* the LORD will **s** the heathen	5062
Mal	4: 6 lest I come and **s** the earth *with* a curse.	4474
Mt	5:39 shall **s** thee on thy right cheek,	4474
	24:49 And begin to **s** *his* fellowservants,	5180
	26:31 I will **s** the shepherd, and the sheep of	3960
Mk	14:27 I will **s** the shepherd, and the sheep shall	3960
Lk	22:49 him, Lord, shall we **s** with the sword?	3960
Ac	23: 2 that stood by him to **s** him on the mouth.	5180
	23: 3 God shall **s** thee, *thou* whited wall:	5180
2Co	11:20 exalt himself, if a man **s** you on the face.	1194
Rev	11: 6 to **s** the earth with all plagues, as often	3960
	19:15 that with it he should **s** the nations:	3960

SMITERS (1) [SMITE]

Isa	50: 6 I gave my back to the **s**, and my cheeks to	5221

SMITEST (2) [SMITE]

Ex	2:13 the wrong, Wherefore **s** thou thy fellow?	5221
Jn	18:23 of the evil: but if well, why **s** thou me?	1194

SMITETH (13) [SMITE]

Ex	21:12 He that **s** a man, so that he die, shall be	5221
	21:15 he that **s** his father, or his mother, shall	5221
Dt	25:11 out of the hand of him that **s** him,	5221
	27:24 Cursed *be* he that **s** his neighbour	5221

Jos	15:16 He that **s** Kirjath-sepher, and taketh it,	5221
Jdg	1:12 He that **s** Kirjath-sepher, and taketh it,	5221
2Sa	5: 8 **s** the Jebusites, and the lame and	5221
1Ch	11: 6 Whosoever **s** the Jebusites first shall be	5221
Job	26:12 by his understanding he **s through**	4272
Isa	9:13 the people turneth not unto him that **s**	5221
La	3:30 He giveth *his* cheek to him that **s** him;	5221
Eze	7: 9 ye shall know that I *am* the LORD that **s**.	5221
Lk	6:29 unto him that **s** thee on the *one* cheek	5180

SMITH (3) [COPPERSMITH, GOLDSMITH, GOLDSMITH'S, GOLDSMITHS, SILVERSMITH, SMITHS]

1Sa	13:19 Now there was no **s** found throughout all	2796
Isa	44:12 The **s** with the tongs both worketh	1270+2796
	54:16 have created the **s** that bloweth the coals	2796

SMITHS (4) [SMITH]

2Ki	24:14 and all the craftsmen and **s**:	4525
	24:16 craftsmen and **s** a thousand, all *that were*	4525
Jer	24: 1 with the carpenters and **s**, from Jerusalem	4525
	29: 2 Jerusalem, and the carpenters, and the **s**,	4525

SMITING (5) [SMITE]

Ex	2:11 he spied an Egyptian **s** a Hebrew, *one* of	5221
2Sa	8:13 from **s** of the Syrians in the valley of salt,	5221
1Ki	20:37 smote him, so that in **s** he wounded *him*.	5221
2Ki	3:24 they went forward **s** the Moabites, even	5221
Mic	6:13 Therefore also will I make *thee* sick in **s**	5221

SMITTEN (63) [SMITE]

Ex	7:25 after *that* the LORD had **s** the river.	5221
	9:31 flax and the barley was **s**: for the barley	5221
	9:32 the wheat and the rye were not **s**: for	5221
	22: 2 found breaking up, and be **s** that he die,	5221
Nu	14:42 that ye be not **s** before your enemies.	5062
	22:28 that thou hast **s** me these three times?	5221
	22:32 Wherefore hast thou **s** thine ass these	5221
	33: 4 which the LORD had **s** among them:	5221
Dt	1:42 lest ye be **s** before your enemies.	5062
	28: 7 up against thee or be **s** before thy face:	5062
	28:25 The LORD shall cause thee *to be* **s** before	5062
Jdg	1: 8 **s** it with the edge of the sword, and set	5221
	20:32 They *are* **down** before us, as at the first.	5062
	20:36 of Benjamin saw that they were **s**:	5062
	20:39 Surely they are **down** before us,	5062+5062
1Sa	4: 2 Israel was **s** before the Philistines:	5062
	4: 3 Wherefore hath the LORD **s** us to day	5062
	4:10 Israel was **s**, and they fled every man into	5062
	5:12 the men that died not were **s** with	5221
	6:19 the LORD had **s** *many* of the people *with*	5221
	7:10 and they were **s** before Israel.	5062
	13: 4 all Israel heard say *that* Saul had a **s**	5221
	30: 1 and **s** Ziklag, and burnt it with fire;	5221
2Sa	2:31 the servants of David had **s** of Benjamin,	5221
	8: 9 David had **s** all the host of Hadadezer,	5221
	8:10 fought against Hadadezer, and **s** him:	5221
	10:15 when the Syrians saw that they were **s**	5062
	10:19 saw that they were **s** before Israel,	5062
	11:15 ye from him, that he may be **s**, and die.	5221
1Ki	8:33 When thy people Israel be **s** down before	5062
	11:15 after he had **s** every male in Edom,	5221
2Ki	2:14 he also had **s** the waters, they parted	5221
	3:23 surely slain, and they have **s** one another:	5221
	13:19 *Thou* shouldest have **s** five or six times;	5221
	13:19 thou **s** Syria till *thou* hadst consumed	5221
	14:10 Thou hast **indeed s** Edom,	5221+5221
1Ch	18: 9 **s** all the host of Hadarezer king of Zobah;	5221
	18:10 had fought against Hadarezer, and **s** him;	5221
2Ch	20:22 come against Judah; and they were **s**.	5062
	25:16 forbear; why shouldest thou be **s**? Then	5221
	25:19 sayest, Lo, thou hast **s** the Edomites,	5221
	26:20 to go out, because the LORD had **s** him.	5060
	28:17 the Edomites had come and **s** Judah,	5221
Job	16:10 they have **s** me upon the cheek	5221
Ps	3: 7 for thou hast **s** all mine enemies *upon*	5221
	69:26 they persecute *him* whom thou hast **s**;	5221
	102: 4 My heart is **s**, and withered like grass;	5221
	143: 3 he hath **s** my life **down** to the ground;	1792
Isa	5:25 his hand against them, and hath **s** them:	5221
	24:12 and the gate is **s** *with* destruction.	3807
	27: 7 he **s** him, as he smote those that smote	5221
	53: 4 him stricken, **s** of God, and afflicted.	5221
Jer	2:30 In vain have I **s** your children;	5221
	14:19 hast thou **s** us, and *there is* no healing	5221
	37:10 For though ye had **s** the whole army of	5221
Eze	22:13 I have **s** mine hand at thy dishonest gain	5221
	33:21 came unto me, saying, The city is **s**.	5221
	40: 1 fourteenth year after that the city was **s**,	5221
Hos	6: 1 he hath **s**, and he will bind us up.	5221
	9:16 Ephraim is **s**, their root is dried up,	5221
Am	4: 9 I have **s** you with blasting and mildew:	5221
Ac	23: 3 commandest me to be **s** contrary to	5180
Rev	8:12 and the third *part* of the sun was **s**,	4141

SMOKE (45) [SMOKING]

Ge	19:28 **s** of the country went up as the smoke	7008
	19:28 smoke of the country went up as the **s**	7008
Ex	19:18 mount Sinai was altogether on a **s**,	6225
	19:18 the **s** thereof ascended as the smoke of a	6227
	19:18 the smoke thereof ascended as the **s** of a	6227
Dt	29:20 and his jealousy shall **s** against that man,	6225
Jos	8:20 the **s** of the city ascended up to heaven,	6227
	8:21 that the **s** of the city ascended, then	6227
Jdg	20:38 they should make a great flame with **s**	6227

S

Jdg	20:40 arise up out of the city *with* a pillar of **s**,	6227
2Sa	22: 9 There went up a **s** out of his nostrils,	6227
Job	41:20 Out of his nostrils goeth **s**, as *out of* a	6227
Ps	18: 8 There went up a **s** out of his nostrils,	6227
	37:20 into **s** shall they consume *away*.	6227
	68: 2 As **s** is driven away, *so* drive *them* away:	6227
	74: 1 doth thine anger **s** against the sheep of	6225
	102: 3 For my days are consumed like **s**,	6227
	104:32 he toucheth the hills, and they **s**.	6225
	119:83 For I am become like a bottle in the **s**;	7008
	144: 5 touch the mountains, and they shall **s**.	6225
Pr	10:26 as **s** to the eyes, so *is* the sluggard to	6227
SS	3: 6 out of the wilderness like pillars of **s**,	6227
Isa	4: 5 a cloud and **s** by day, and the shining of a	6227
	6: 4 cried, and the house was filled *with* **s**.	6227
	9:18 shall mount up *like* the lifting up of **s**.	6227
	14:31 for there shall come from the north a **s**,	6227
	34:10 day; the **s** thereof shall go up for ever:	6227
	51: 6 for the heavens shall vanish away like **s**,	6227
	65: 5 These *are* a **s** in my nose, a fire that	6227
Hos	13: 3 floor, and as the **s** out of the chimney.	6227
Joel	2:30 the earth, blood, and fire, and pillars of **s**.	6227
Na	2:13 I will burn her chariots in the **s**,	6227
Ac	2:19 blood, and fire, and vapour of **s**:	2586
Rev	8: 4 the of the incense, *which came* with	2586
	9: 2 and there arose a **s** out of the pit,	2586
	9: 2 out of the pit, as the **s** of a great furnace;	2586
	9: 2 air were darkened by reason of the **s** of	2586
	9: 3 And there came out of the **s** locusts upon	2586
	9:17 mouths issued fire and **s** and brimstone.	2586
	9:18 fire, and by the **s**, and by the brimstone,	2586
	14:11 the **s** of their torment ascendeth up for	2586
	15: 8 And the temple was filled with **s** from	2586
	18: 9 when they shall see the **s** of her burning,	2586
	18:18 And cried when they saw the **s** of her	2586
	19: 3 And her **s** rose up for ever and ever.	2586

SMOKING (5) [SMOKE]

Ge	15:17 behold a **s** furnace, and a burning lamp	6227
Ex	20:18 noise of the trumpet, and the mountain **s**:	6226
Isa	7: 4 for the two tails of these **s** firebrands,	6226
	42: 3 and the **s** flax shall he not quench:	3544
Mt	12:20 not break, and **s** flax shall he not quench,	5188

SMOOTH (6) [SMOOTHER, SMOOTHETH]

Ge	27:11 brother *is* a hairy man, and I *am* a **s** man:	2509
	27:16 his hands, and upon the **s** of his neck:	2513
1Sa	17:40 chose him five **s** stones out of the brook,	2512
Isa	30:10 speak unto us **s** things, prophesy deceits:	2513
	57: 6 Among the **s** *stones* of the stream *is* thy	2511
Lk	3: 5 and the rough ways *shall be* made **s**;	3006

SMOOTHER (2) [SMOOTH]

Ps	55:21 *words of* his mouth were **s** than butter,	2505
Pr	5: 3 honeycomb, and her mouth *is* **s** than oil:	2509

SMOOTHETH (1) [SMOOTH]

Isa	41: 7 that **s** *with* the hammer him that smote	2505

SMOTE (230) [SMITE]

Ge	14: 5 **s** the Rephaims in Ashteroth Karnaim,	5221
	14: 7 **s** all the country of the Amalekites,	5221
	14:15 **s** them, and pursued them unto Hobah,	5221
	19:11 they **s** the men that *were at* the door of	5221
	36:35 who **s** Midian in the field of Moab,	5221
Ex	7:20 and the waters that *were* in the river,	5221
	8:17 **s** the dust of the earth, and it became lice	5221
	9:25 the hail **s** throughout all the land of Egypt	5221
	9:25 the hail **s** every herb of the field, and	5221
	12:27 he **s** the Egyptians, and delivered our	5062
	12:29 that at midnight the LORD **s** all	5221
	21:19 his staff, then shall he that **s** *him* be quit:	5221
Nu	3:13 for on the day that I **s** all the firstborn in	5221
	8:17 on the day that I **s** every firstborn in	5221
	11:33 the LORD **s** the people *with* a very great	5221
	14:45 **s** them, and discomfited them, *even* unto	5221
	20:11 and with his rod he **s** the rock twice:	5221
	21:24 Israel **s** him with the edge of the sword,	5221
	21:35 So they **s** him, and his sons, and all his	5221
	22:23 Balaam **s** the ass, to turn her *into* the	5221
	22:25 foot against the wall: and he **s** her again.	5221
	22:27 kindled, and he **s** the ass with a staff.	5221
	24:10 and he **s** his hands **together**:	5606
	32: 4 *Even* the country which the LORD **s**	5221
	35:21 he that **s** *him* shall surely be put to death;	5221
Dt	2:33 we **s** him, and his sons, and all his people.	5221
	3: 3 we **s** him until none was left to him	5221
	4:46 whom Moses and the children of Israel **s**,	5221
	25:18 by the way, and **s** **the hindmost** of thee,	2179
	29: 7 out against us unto battle, and we **s** them:	5221
Jos	7: 5 the men of Ai **s** of them about thirty and	5221
	7: 5 and **s** them in the going down:	5221
	8:22 they **s** them, so that *they* let none of them	5221
	8:24 Ai, and **s** it with the edge of the sword.	5221
	9:18 the children of Israel **s** them not, because	5221
	10:10 **s** them to Azekah, and unto Makkedah.	5221
	10:26 afterward Joshua **s** them, and slew them,	5221
	10:28 **s** it with the edge of the sword, and the	5221
	10:30 he **s** it with the edge of the sword, and	5221
	10:32 **s** it with the edge of the sword, and all	5221
	10:33 Joshua **s** him and his people, until *he* had	5221
	10:35 **s** it with the edge of the sword, and the	5221
	10:37 **s** it with the edge of the sword, and the	5221
	10:39 they **s** them with the edge of the sword,	5221
	10:40 So Joshua **s** all the country of the hills,	5221

Jos	10:41 Joshua **s** them from Kadesh-barnea even	5221
	11: 8 who **s** them, and chased them unto great	5221
	11: 8 they **s** them, until *they* left them no more	5221
	11:10 and **s** the king thereof with the sword:	5221
	11:11 they **s** all the souls that *were* therein with	5221
	11:12 **s** them with the edge of the sword,	5221
	11:14 every man they **s** with the edge of the	5221
	11:17 he took, and **s** them, and slew them.	5221
	12: 1 which the children of Israel **s**,	5221
	12: 7 children of Israel **s** on *this* side Jordan	5221
	13:21 Moses **s** with the princes of Midian,	5221
	19:47 **s** it with the edge of the sword,	5221
	20: 5 because he **s** his neighbour unwittingly,	5221
Jdg	1:25 **s** the city with the edge of the sword;	5221
	3:13 went and **s** Israel, and possessed the city	5221
	4:21 **s** the nail into his temples, and fastened *it*	8628
	5:26 **s** Sisera, **s** off his head, **s** when she had	1986
	5:26 she **s** **off** his head, when she had pierced	4277
	7:13 and **s** it that it fell, and overturned it,	5221
	8:11 of Nobah and Jogbehah, and **s** the host:	5221
	9:43 and he rose up against them, and **s** them.	5221
	11:21 into the hand of Israel, and they **s** them,	5221
	11:33 he **s** them from Aroer, even till thou	5221
	12: 4 the men of Gilead **s** Ephraim, because	5221
	15: 8 he **s** them hip and thigh *with* a great	5221
	18:27 they **s** them with the edge of the sword,	5221
	20:35 the LORD **s** Benjamin before Israel:	5062
	20:37 **s** all the city with the edge of the sword.	5221
	20:48 **s** them with the edge of the sword, as	5221
1Sa	4: 8 these *are* the Gods that **s** the Egyptians	5221
	5: 6 **s** them with emerods, *even* Ashdod and	5221
	5: 9 he **s** the men of the city, both small and	5221
	6: 9 shall know that *it* is not his hand *that* **s**	5060
	6:19 he **s** the men of Beth-shemesh, because	5221
	6:19 even he **s** of the people fifty thousand	5221
	7:11 pursued the Philistines, and **s** them,	5221
	13: 3 Jonathan **s** the garrison of the Philistines	5221
	14:31 they **s** the Philistines that day from	5221
	14:48 **s** the Amalekites, and delivered Israel out	5221
	15: 7 Saul **s** the Amalekites from Havilah *until*	5221
	17:35 **s** him, and delivered *it* out of his mouth:	5221
	17:35 by his beard, and **s** him, and slew him.	5221
	17:49 and **s** the Philistine in his forehead,	5221
	17:50 stone, and **s** the Philistine, and slew him;	5221
	19:10 and he **s** the javelin into the wall:	5221
	22:19 he with the edge of the sword, both	5221
	23: 5 and **s** them *with* a great slaughter.	5221
	24: 5 that David's heart **s** him, because he had	5221
	25:38 ten days *after*, that the LORD **s** Nabal,	5062
	27: 9 David **s** the land, and left neither man	5221
	30:17 David **s** them from the twilight even unto	5221
2Sa	1:15 **s** him under the fifth *rib*, that he died.	5221
	2:23 **s** him under the fifth *rib*, that the spear	5221
	3:27 **s** him there *under* the fifth *rib*, that he	5221
	4: 6 they **s** him under the fifth *rib*: and Rechab	5221
	4: 7 they **s** him, and slew him,	5221
	5:20 and David **s** them there, and said,	5221
	5:25 the Philistines from Geba until thou	5221
	6: 7 God **s** him there for *his* error; and there	5221
	8: 1 that David **s** the Philistines,	5221
	8: 2 **s** Moab, and measured them with a line,	5221
	8: 3 David **s** also Hadadezer, the son of Rehob	5221
	10:18 Shobach the captain of their host,	5221
	11:21 **s** Abimelech the son of Jerubbesheth?	5221
	14: 6 but the one **s** the other, and slew him.	5221
	14: 7 they said, Deliver him that **s** his brother,	5221
	18:15 armour compassed about and **s** Absalom,	5221
	20:10 so he **s** him therewith in the fifth *rib*, and	5221
	21:17 and **s** the Philistine, and killed him.	5221
	23:10 **s** the Philistines until his hand was weary,	5221
	24:10 David's heart **s** him after that he had	5221
	24:17 when he saw the angel that **s** the people,	5221
1Ki	15:20 **s** Ijon, and Dan, and Abel-beth-maachah,	5221
	15:27 Baasha **s** him at Gibbethon,	5221
	15:29 *that* he **s** all the house of Jeroboam;	5221
	16:10 Zimri went in and **s** him, and killed him,	5221
	20:21 **s** the horses and chariots, and slew	5221
	20:37 the man **s** him, so that in smiting he	5221
	22:24 and **s** Micaiah on the cheek, and said,	5221
	22:34 **s** the king of Israel between the joints of	5221
2Ki	2: 8 **s** the waters, and they were divided hither	5221
	2:14 **s** the waters, and said, Where *is* the LORD	5221
	3:24 the Israelites rose up and **s** the Moabites,	5221
	3:25 the slingers went about *it*, and **s** it.	5221
	6:18 he **s** them with blindness according to	5221
	8:21 the Edomites which compassed him	5221
	9:24 Jehoram between his arms, and the	5221
	10:25 they **s** them with the edge of the sword;	5221
	10:32 Hazael **s** them in all the coasts of Israel;	5221
	12:21 Shomer, his servants, **s** him, and he died;	5221
	13:18 the ground. And he **s** thrice, and stayed.	5221
	15: 5 the LORD **s** the king, so that he was a	5060
	15:10 **s** him before the people, and slew him,	5221
	15:14 Shallum the son of Jabesh in Samaria,	5221
	15:16 Menahem **s** Tiphsah, and all that *were*	5221
	15:16 opened not *to him*, therefore he **s** it; *and*	5221
	15:25 against him, and **s** him in Samaria,	5221
	15:30 **s** him, and slew him, and reigned in his	5221
	18: 8 He **s** the Philistines, *even* unto Gaza,	5221
	19:35 **s** in the camp of the Assyrians an hundred	5221
	19:37 Sharezer *his sons* **s** him with the sword:	5221
	25:21 the king of Babylon **s** them, and slew	5221
	25:25 **s** Gedaliah, that he died, and the Jews	5221
1Ch	1:46 which **s** Midian in the field of Moab,	5221
	4:41 **s** their tents, and the habitations that	5221

1Ch	4:43 they **s** the rest of the Amalekites that	5221
	13:10 he **s** him, because he put his hand to	5221
	14:11 to Baal-perazim; and David **s** them there.	5221
	14:16 they **s** the host of the Philistines from	5221
	18: 1 that David **s** the Philistines,	5221
	18: 2 he **s** Moab; and the Moabites became	5221
	18: 3 David **s** Hadarezer king of Zobah unto	5221
	20: 1 And Joab **s** Rabbah, and destroyed it.	5221
	21: 7 with this thing; therefore he **s** Israel.	5221
2Ch	13:15 that God **s** Jeroboam and all Israel before	5062
	14:12 So the LORD **s** the Ethiopians before Asa,	5062
	14:14 they **s** all the cities round about Gerar;	5221
	14:15 They **s** also the tents of cattle,	5221
	16: 4 they **s** Ijon, and Dan, and Abel-maim,	5221
	18:23 and **s** Micaiah upon the cheek, and said,	5221
	18:33 **s** the king of Israel between the joints of	5221
	21: 9 **s** the Edomites which compassed him in,	5221
	21:18 after all this the LORD **s** him in his	5062
	22: 5 Ramoth-gilead: and the Syrians **s** Joram.	5221
	25:11 **s** *of* the children of Seir ten thousand.	5221
	25:13 **s** three thousand of them, and took much	5221
	28: 5 they **s** him, and carried away a great	5221
	28: 5 Israel, who **s** him *with* a great slaughter.	5221
	28:23 unto the gods of Damascus, which **s** him:	5221
Ne	13:25 **s** certain of them, and pluckt off their hair	5221
Est	9: 5 Thus the Jews **s** all their enemies *with*	5221
Job	1:19 **s** the four corners of the house, and it fell	5060
	2: 7 **s** Job with sore boils from the sole of his	5221
Ps	60: 1 **s** of Edom in the valley of salt twelve	5221
	78:20 Behold, he **s** the rock, that the waters	5221
	78:31 and **s** **down** the chosen *men* of Israel.	3766
	78:51 **s** all the firstborn in Egypt; the chief of	5221
	78:66 he **s** his enemies in the hinder parts:	5221
	105:33 He **s** their vines also and their fig trees;	5221
	105:36 He **s** also all the firstborn in their land,	5221
	135: 8 Who **s** the firstborn of Egypt, both of man	5221
	135:10 Who **s** great nations, and slew mighty	5221
	136:10 To him that **s** Egypt in their firstborn:	5221
	136:17 To him which **s** great kings: for his mercy	5221
SS	5: 7 found me, they **s** me, they wounded me;	5221
Isa	10:20 shall no more again stay upon him that **s**	5221
	14: 6 He who **s** the people in wrath *with* a	5221
	14:29 the rod of him that **s** thee is broken:	5221
	27: 7 him, as he **s** those that smote him?	4347
	27: 7 him, as he smote those that **s** him?	5221
	30:31 be beaten down, *which* **s** with a rod.	5221
	37:36 **s** in the camp of the Assyrians an hundred	5221
	37:38 Sharezer his sons **s** him with the sword;	5221
	41: 7 *with* the hammer him that **s** the anvil,	1986
	57:17 his covetousness was I wroth, and **s** him:	5221
	60:10 for in my wrath I **s** thee, but in my favour	5221
Jer	20: 2 Pashur **s** Jeremiah the prophet, and put	5221
	31:19 that I was instructed, I **s** upon *my* thigh:	5606
	37:15 **s** him, and put *him* in prison *in* the house	5221
	41: 2 **s** Gedaliah the son of Ahikam the son of	5221
	46: 2 which Nebuchadrezzar king of Babylon **s**	5221
	47: 1 Philistines, before that Pharaoh **s** Gaza.	5221
	52:27 the king of Babylon **s** them, and put them	5221
Da	2:34 which **s** the image upon his feet *that*	4223
	2:35 the stone that **s** the image became a great	4223
	5: 6 and his knees **s** one against another.	5368
	8: 7 and **s** the ram, and brake his two horns:	5221
Jnh	4: 7 and it **s** the gourd, that it withered.	5221
Hag	2:17 I **s** you with blasting and with mildew	5221
Mt	26:51 of the high priest's, and **s** off his ear.	851
	26:67 **s** *him* **with the palms** of their **hands**,	4474
	26:68 *thou* Christ, Who is he that **s** thee?	3817
	27:30 took the reed, and **s** him on the head.	5180
Mk	14:47 and **s** a servant of the high priest,	3817
	15:19 And they **s** him on the head with a reed,	5180
Lk	18:13 heaven, but **s** upon his breast, saying,	5180
	22:50 And one of them **s** the servant of the high	3960
	22:63 that held Jesus mocked him, and **s** *him*.	1194
	22:64 saying, Prophesy, who is it that **s** thee?	3817
	23:48 were done, **s** their breasts, and returned.	5180
Jn	18:10 the high priest's servant, and cut off	3817
	19: 3 and they **s** him **with** their **hands**.	1325+4475
Ac	7:24 that was oppressed, and **s** the Egyptian:	3960
	12: 7 he **s** Peter on the side, and raised him	3960
	12:23 and immediately *the* angel of the Lord **s**	3960

SMOTEST (1) [SMITE]

Ex	17: 5 thy rod, wherewith thou **s** the river, take	5221

SMYRNA (2)

Rev	1:11 and unto **S**, and unto Pergamos,	4667
	2: 8 unto the angel of the church in **S** write;	4668

SNAIL (2)

Lev	11:30 and the lizard, and the **s**, and the mole.	2546
Ps	58: 8 As a **s** *which* melteth, let *every one* of	7642

SNARE (47) [ENSNARED, SNARED, SNARES]

Ex	10: 7 How long shall this *man* be a **s** unto us?	4170
	23:33 their gods, it will surely be a **s** unto thee.	4170
	34:12 lest it be for a **s** in the midst of thee:	4170
Dt	7:16 their gods; for that *will be* a **s** to thee.	4170
Jdg	2: 3 and their gods shall be a **s** unto you.	4170
	8:27 which *thing* became a **s** unto Gideon,	4170
1Sa	18:21 that she may be a **s** to him, and that	4170
	28: 9 then **layest** thou a **s** for my life,	5367
Job	18: 8 his own feet, and he walketh upon a **s**.	7639
	18:10 The **s** *is* laid for him in the ground,	2256
Ps	69:22 Let their table become a **s** before them:	6341
	91: 3 Surely he shall deliver thee from the **s** of	6341

Ps	106:36 their idols: which were a **s** unto them.	4170
	119:110 The wicked have laid a **s** for me: yet I	6341
	124: 7 Our soul is escaped as a bird out of the **s**	6341
	124: 7 the **s** is broken, and we are escaped.	6341
	140: 5 The proud have hid a **s** for me, and cords;	6341
	141: 9 Keep me from the **s** *which* they have laid	6341
	142: 3 I walked have they privily laid a **s** for me.	6341
Pr	7:23 as a bird hasteth to the **s**, and knoweth	6341
	18: 7 and his lips *are* the **s** of his soul.	4170
	20:25 *It is* a **s** to the man *who* devoureth *that*	4170
	22:25 learn his ways, and get a **s** to thy soul.	4170
	29: 6 transgression of an evil man *there is* a **s**:	4170
	29: 8 Scornful men **bring** a city **into** a **s**:	6315
	29:25 The fear of man bringeth a **s**:	4170
Ecc	9:12 and as the birds that are caught in the **s**,	6341
Isa	8:14 for a **s** to the inhabitants of Jerusalem.	4170
	24:17 and the pit, and the **s**, *are* upon thee,	6341
	24:18 midst of the pit shall be taken in the **s**:	6341
	29:21 **lay** a **s** for him that reproveth in the gate,	6983
Jer	48:43 Fear, and the pit, and the **s**, *shall be* upon	6341
	48:44 up out of the pit shall be taken in the **s**:	6341
	50:24 I have **laid** a **s** for thee, and thou art also	3369
La	3:47 Fear and a **s** is come upon us, desolation	6354
Eze	12:13 upon him, and he shall be taken in my **s**:	4686
	17:20 he shall be taken in my **s**, and I will bring	4686
Hos	5: 1 because ye have been a **s** on Mizpah,	6341
	9: 8 the prophet *is* a **s** of a fowler in all his	6341
Am	3: 5 Can a bird fall in a **s** upon the earth,	6341
	3: 5 shall *one* take up a **s** from the earth,	6341
Lk	21:35 For as a **s** shall it come on all them that	3803
Ro	11: 9 Let their table be made a **s**, and a trap,	3803
1Co	7:35 not that I may cast a **s** upon you,	1029
1Ti	3: 7 fall into reproach and the **s** of the devil.	3803
	6: 9 will be rich fall into temptation and a **s**,	3803
2Ti	2:26 themselves out of the **s** of the devil.	3803

SNARED (9) [SNARE]

Dt	7:25 take *it* unto thee, lest thou be **s** therein:	3369
	12:30 Take heed to thyself that thou be not **s** by	5367
Ps	9:16 the wicked is **s** in the work of his own	5367
Pr	6: 2 Thou art **s** with the words of thy mouth,	3369
	12:13 The wicked is **s** by the transgression of	4170
Ecc	9:12 so *are* the sons of men **s** in an evil time,	3369
Isa	8:15 be broken, and be **s**, and be taken.	3369
	28:13 and be broken, and **s**, and taken.	3369
	42:22 *they are* all of them **s** in holes, and they	6351

SNARES (14) [SNARE]

Jos	23:13 they shall be **s** and traps unto you,	6341
2Sa	22: 6 me about; the **s** of death prevented me;	4170
Job	22:10 Therefore **s** *are* round about thee,	6341
	40:24 with his eyes: *his* nose pierceth through **s**.	4170
Ps	11: 6 Upon the wicked he shall rain **s**, fire and	6341
	18: 5 me about: the **s** of death prevented me.	4170
	38:12 They also that seek after my life **lay s** *for*	5367
	64: 5 commune of laying **s** privily; they say,	4170
Pr	13:14 of life, to depart from the **s** of death.	4170
	14:27 of life, to depart from the **s** of death.	4170
	22: 5 *and* **s** *are* in the way of the froward:	6341
Ecc	7:26 whose heart *is* **s** and nets, *and* her hands	4685
Jer	5:26 *men:* they lay wait, as he that setteth **s**;	3353
	18:22 a pit to take me, and hid **s** for my feet.	6341

SNATCH (1)

Isa	9:20 shall **s** on the right hand, and be hungry;	1504

SNEERED See DERIDED

SNORTING (1)

Jer	8:16 The **s** of his horses was heard from Dan:	5170

SNOUT (1)

Pr	11:22 *As* a jewel of gold in a swine's **s**, *so is* a fair	639

SNOW (24) [SNOWY]

Ex	4: 6 it out, behold, his hand *was* leprous as **s**.	7950
Nu	12:10 Miriam *became* leprous, *white* as **s**:	7950
2Sa	23:20 a lion in the midst of a pit in time of **s**:	7950
2Ki	5:27 from his presence a leper *as white* as **s**.	7950
Job	6:16 of the ice, *and* wherein the **s** is hid:	7950
	9:30 If I wash myself with **s** water, and make	7950
	24:19 Drought and heat consume the **s** waters:	7950
	37: 6 he saith to the **s**, Be thou *on* the earth;	7950
	38:22 thou entered into the treasures of the **s**?	7950
Ps	51: 7 wash me, and I shall be whiter than **s**.	7949
	68:14 kings in it, it was *white as* **s** in Salmon.	7950
	147:16 He giveth **s** like wool: he scattereth	7950
	148: 8 Fire, and hail; **s**, and vapour; stormy wind	7950
Pr	25:13 As the cold of **s** in the time of harvest,	7950
	26: 1 As **s** in summer, and as rain in harvest,	7950
	31:21 is not afraid of the **s** for her household:	7950
Isa	1:18 be as scarlet, they shall be as white as **s**;	7950
	55:10 the **s** from heaven, and returneth not	7950
Jer	18:14 Will *a man* leave the **s** of Lebanon *which*	7950
La	4: 7 Her Nazarites were purer than **s**, they	7950
Da	7: 9 garment *was* white as **s**, and the hair	8517
Mt	28: 3 like lightning, and his raiment white as **s**:	5510
Mk	9: 3 became shining, exceeding white as **s**;	5510
Rev	1:14 hairs *were* white like wool, *as* white as **s**;	5510

SNOWY (1) [SNOW]

1Ch	11:22 and slew a lion in a pit in a **s** day.	7950

SNUFFDISHES (3) [DISH, SNUFFETH]

Ex	25:38 and the **s** thereof, *shall be of* pure gold.	4289
	37:23 and his snuffers, and his **s**, *of* pure gold.	4289

SNUFFED (2) [SNUFFETH]

Jer	14: 6 they **s** up the wind like dragons;	7602
Mal	1:13 what a weariness *is it!* and ye have **s** at it,	5301

SNUFFERS (6) [SNUFFETH]

Ex	37:23 his **s**, and his snuffdishes, *of* pure gold.	4457
1Ki	7:50 the **s**, and the basons, and the spoons,	4212
2Ki	12:13 **s**, basons, trumpets, any vessels of gold,	4212
	25:14 the **s**, and the basons, and all the vessels	4212
2Ch	4:22 the **s**, and the basons, and the spoons,	4212
Jer	52:18 the **s**, and the bowls, and the spoons,	4212

SNUFFETH (1) [SNUFFDISHES, SNUFFED, SNUFFERS]

Jer	2:24 *that* **s** up the wind at her pleasure;	7602

SO (1689) [FORSOMUCH, HOWSOEVER, INSOMUCH, SOEVER, WHATSOEVER, WHENSOEVER, WHEREINSOEVER, WHERESOEVER, WHITHERSOEVER, WHOMSOEVER, WHOSO, WHOSOEVER]

Ge	1: 7 *were* above the firmament: and it was **s**.	3651
	1: 9 and let the dry *land* appear: and it was **s**.	3651
	1:11 *is* in itself, upon the earth: and it was **s**.	3651
	1:15 to give light upon the earth: and it was **s**.	3651
	1:24 of the earth after his kind: and it was **s**.	3651
	1:27 **S** God created man in his own image,	2050.1
	1:30 every green herb for meat: and it was **s**.	3651
	3:24 **S** he drove out the man; and he placed	2050.1
	6:22 to all that God commanded him, **s** did he.	3651
	8:11 **s** Noah knew that the waters were	2050.1
	11: 8 **S** the Lord scattered them abroad from	2050.1
	12: 4 **S** Abram departed, as the Lord had	2050.1
	12:19 **s** I might have taken her to me to wife:	2050.1
	13: 6 **s** *that* they could not dwell together.	2050.1
	13:16 **s** *that* if a man can number the dust of	834
	15: 5 and he said unto him, **S** shall thy seed be.	3541
	18: 5 And they said, **S** do, as thou hast said.	3651
	19: 7 I pray you, brethren, do not **s** wickedly.	NIH
	19:11 **s** *that* they wearied themselves to find	2050.1
	19:18 Lot said unto them, Oh, not **s**, my Lord:	NIH
	20:17 **S** Abraham prayed unto God:	2050.1
	21: 6 **s** *that* all that hear will laugh with me.	NIH
	22: 8 they went both of them together.	2050.1
	22:19 **S** Abraham returned unto his young	2050.1
	24:46 **s** I drank, and she made the camels	2050.1
	25:22 she said, **If** *it be* **s**, why *am* I thus?	518+3651
	27: 1 eyes were dim, **s** *that* he could **not** see,	4480
	27:20 How is it *that* thou hast found *it* **s** quickly,	NIH
	27:23 brother Esau's hands: **s** he blessed him.	2050.1
	28:21 **S** *that* I come again to my father's	2050.1
	29:26 It must not be **s** done in our country,	3651
	29:28 Jacob did **s**, and fulfilled her week:	3651
	30:33 **S** shall my righteousness answer for me	2050.1
	30:42 the feebler were Laban's,	2050.1
	31:21 **S** he fled with all that he had; and he	2050.1
	31:28 thou hast now done foolishly in **s** doing.	NIH
	31:36 that thou hast **s** hotly pursued after me?	NIH
	32:19 commanded he the second, and the	1571
	32:21 **S** went the present over before him;	2050.1
	33:16 **S** Esau returned that day on his way	2050.1
	34:12 Ask me **never** **s** much dowry and	3966+7235
	35: 6 **S** Jacob came to Luz, which *is* in the	2050.1
	37:14 **S** he sent him out of the vale of Hebron,	2050.1
	40: 7 Wherefore look ye **s** sadly to day?	NIH
	41: 4 and fat kine. **S** Pharaoh awoke.	2050.1
	41:13 to pass, as he interpreted to us, **s** it was;	3651
	41:21 as at the beginning. **S** I awoke.	2050.1
	41:39 *there is* none **s** discreet and wise as thou	NIH
	41:57 that the famine was **s** sore in all lands.	NIH
	42:20 **s** shall your words be verified,	2050.1
	42:20 and ye shall not die. And they did **s**.	3651
	42:34 *that* ye *are* true men: **s** will I deliver you	NIH
	43: 6 Israel said, Wherefore dealt ye **s** ill with	NIH
	43:11 unto them, If *it must be* **s** now, do this;	3651
	43:34 five times **s** much as any of theirs.	4480+7235
	44: 5 he divineth? ye have done evil in **s** doing.	NIH
	44:17 he said, God forbid that I should do **s**:	2063
	45: 8 **S** now *it was* not you *that* sent me	2050.1
	45:21 the children of Israel did **s**: and Joseph	3651
	45:24 **S** he sent his brethren away,	2050.1
	47:13 **s** *that* the land of Egypt and *all* the land	2050.1
	47:20 them: **s** the land became Pharaoh's.	2050.1
	47:28 **s** the whole age of Jacob was an	2050.1
	48:10 were dim for age, **s** *that* he could not see.	NIH
	48:18 said unto his father, Not **s**, my father:	3651
	49:17 **s** *that* his rider shall fall backward.	2050.1
	50: 3 for **s** are fulfilled the days of those which	3651
	50:17 **S** shall ye say unto Joseph, Forgive, I pray	3541
	50:26 **S** Joseph died, *being* an hundred and	2050.1
Ex	1:10 and **s** get them up out of the land.	NIH
	2:18 How *is it that* you are come **s** soon to day?	NIH
	4:26 **S** he let him go: then she said, A bloody	2050.1
	5:12 **S** the people were scattered abroad	2050.1
	5:22 wherefore hast thou **s** evil entreated this	NIH
	6: 9 Moses spake **s** unto the children of Israel:	3651
	7: 6 the Lord commanded them, **s** did they.	3651
	7:10 they did **s** as the Lord had commanded:	3651
	7:20 Moses and Aaron did **s**, as the Lord	3651
	7:22 of Egypt did **s** with their enchantments:	3651
	8: 7 the magicians did **s**	3651
	8:17 they did **s**; for Aaron stretched out his	3651
	8:18 magicians did **s** with their enchantments	3651

Ex	8:18 **s** there were lice upon man,	2050.1
	8:24 the Lord did **s**; and there came a	3651
	8:26 Moses said, It is not meet to **s** to do; for we	3651
	9:24 **S** there was hail, and fire mingled with	2050.1
	10:10 Let the Lord be **s** with you, as I will let	3651
	10:11 Not **s**: go now ye *that are* men,	3651
	10:15 **s** that the land was darkened;	2050.1
	10:20 **s** *that* he would not let the children of	2050.1
	11:10 **s** *that* he would not let the children of	2050.1
	12:28 commanded Moses and Aaron, **s** did they.	3651
	12:36 **s** *that* they lent unto them *such* things	2050.1
	12:50 commanded Moses and Aaron, **s** did they.	3651
	14: 4 know that I *am* the Lord. And they did **s**.	3651
	14:20 **s** *that* the one came not near the other	2050.1
	14:25 the Egyptians said, Let us flee	2050.1
	14:28 remained not **s** much as one of them.	5704
	15:22 **S** Moses brought Israel from the Red sea	2050.1
	16:17 the children of Israel did **s**, and gathered,	3651
	16:30 **S** the people rested on the seventh day.	2050.1
	16:34 **s** Aaron laid it up before the Testimony,	2050.1
	17: 6 Moses did **s** in the sight of the elders of	3651
	17:10 **S** Joshua did as Moses had said to him,	2050.1
	18:22 shall it be easier for thyself,	2050.1
	18:23 God command thee **s**, then thou shalt be	NIH
	18:24 **S** Moses hearkened to the voice of his	2050.1
	19:16 **s** *that* all the people that *was* in the	2050.1
	19:25 **S** Moses went down unto the people,	2050.1
	21:12 He that smiteth a man, **s** that he die,	2050.1
	21:22 **s** *that* her fruit depart *from her,*	2050.1
	22: 6 **s** *that* the stacks of corn, or the standing	2050.1
	25: 9 even **s** shall ye make *it.*	3651
	25:33 **s** in the six branches that come out of	3651
	27: 8 thee in the mount, **s** shall they make *it.*	3651
	28: 7 **s** it shall be joined together.	NIH
	30:21 **S** they shall wash their hands and	2050.1
	30:23 and of sweet cinnamon **half s** much,	4276
	32:21 that thou hast brought **s** great a sin upon	NIH
	32:24 **s** they gave *it* me: then I cast it into	2050.1
	33:16 shall we be separated, I and thy	2050.1
	36: 6 **S** the people were restrained from	2050.1
	36:13 the taches: **s** it became one tabernacle.	2050.1
	37:19 throughout the six branches going out	3651
	39:32 the Lord commanded Moses, **s** did they.	3651
	39:42 **s** the children of Israel made all the work.	3651
	39:43 had commanded, *even* **s** had they done it:	3651
	40:16 that the Lord commanded him, **s** did he.	3651
	40:33 court gate. **S** Moses finished the work.	2050.1
Lev	4:20 for a sin offering, **s** shall he do with this:	3651
	7: 7 As the sin offering *is*, **s** *is* the trespass	3509.1
	8:34 the Lord hath commanded to do,	NIH
	8:35 that ye die not: for **s** I am commanded.	3651
	8:36 **S** Aaron and his sons did all things	2050.1
	10: 5 **S** they went near, and carried them in	2050.1
	10:13 made by fire: for **s** it shall be cleansed.	3651
	11:32 until the even; **s** it shall be cleansed.	2050.1
	14:13 *is* the priest's, **s** *is* the trespass offering:	NIH
	14:21 cannot get **s** much; then he shall take one	NIH
	16: 4 his flesh in water, and **s** put them on.	NIH
	16:16 **s** shall he do for the tabernacle of	3651
	24:19 he hath done, **s** shall it be done to him;	3651
	24:20 in a man, **s** shall it be done to him *again.*	3651
	26:15 **s** *that* ye will not do all my	3807.1
	27:12 valuest it, *who art* the priest, **s** shall it be.	3651
	27:14 the priest shall estimate it, **s** shall it stand.	3651
Nu	1:19 he numbered them in the wilderness	2050.1
	1:45 **S** were all those that were numbered of	2050.1
	1:54 the Lord commanded Moses, **s** did they.	3651
	2:17 as they encamp, **s** shall they set forward,	3651
	2:34 **s** they pitched by their standards, and so	3651
	2:34 they set forward, every one after their	3651
	4:26 that is made for them: **s** shall they serve.	2050.1
	5: 4 the children of Israel did **s**, and put them	3651
	5: 4 unto Moses, **s** did the children of Israel.	3651
	6:21 **s** he must do after the law of his	3651
	8: 3 Aaron did **s**; he lighted the lamps thereof	3651
	8: 4 Moses, **s** he made the candlestick.	3651
	8: 7 clothes, and **s** make themselves clean.	NIH
	8:20 **s** did the children of Israel unto them.	3651
	8:22 the Levites, **s** did they unto them.	3651
	9: 5 **s** did the children of Israel.	3651
	9:14 to the manner thereof, **s** shall he do:	3651
	9:16 **S** it was alway: the cloud covered it *by*	3651
	9:20 **s** it was, when the cloud was a few days	NIH
	9:21 **s** it was, when the cloud abode from even	NIH
	12: 7 My servant Moses *is* not **s**, who *is* faithful	3651
	13:21 **S** they went up, and searched the land	2050.1
	13:33 and **s** we were in their sight.	3651
	14:28 spoken in mine ears, **s** will I do to you:	3651
	15:12 shall ye do to *every* one according to	3602
	15:14 unto the Lord; as ye do, **s** he shall do.	3651
	15:15 as ye *are*, **s** shall the stranger be before	3509.1
	15:20 of the threshingfloor, **s** shall ye heave it.	3651
	16:27 **S** they gat up from the tabernacle of	2050.1
	17:11 Moses did **s**: as the Lord commanded	NIH
	17:11 as the Lord commanded him, **s** did he.	3651
	20: 8 **s** thou shalt give the congregation and	2050.1
	21:35 **S** they smote him, and his sons,	2050.1
	22:30 was I ever wont to do **s** unto thee?	3541
	22:35 **S** Balaam went with the princes of	2050.1
	25: 8 **S** the plague was stayed from the	2050.1
	31: 5 **S** there were delivered out of	2050.1
	32:23 if ye will not do **s**, behold, ye have sinned	3651
	32:28 **S** concerning them Moses commanded	2050.1
	32:31 said unto thy servants, **s** will we do.	3651
	35: 7 **S** all the cities which ye shall give to	NIH

Nu 35:16 of iron, **s that** he die, he *is* a murderer:	2050.1
35:29 S these *things* shall be for a statute of	2050.1
35:33 S ye shall not pollute the land wherein	2050.1
36: 3 **s** shall it be taken from the lot of our	2050.1
36: 4 s shall their inheritance be taken away	2050.1
36: 7 S shall not the inheritance of the	2050.1
36:10 s did the daughters of Zelophehad:	3651
Dt 1:11 **make** you a thousand times **s many moe**	3254
1:15 S I took the chief of your tribes,	2050.1
1:43 S I spake unto you; and you would not	2050.1
1:46 S ye abode in Kadesh many days,	2050.1
2: 5 land, no, not **s much as** a foot breadth;	5704
2:16 S it came to pass, when all the men of	2050.1
3: 3 S the Lord our God delivered into our	2050.1
3:21 s shall the Lord do unto all	3651
3:29 S we abode in the valley over against	2050.1
4: 5 that *ye* should do **s** in the land whither ye	3651
4: 7 For what nation *is there* **s** great, who hath	NIH
4: 7 *so* great, who hath God **s** nigh unto them,	NIH
4: 8 what nation *is there* **s** great, that hath	NIH
4: 8 that hath statutes and judgments **s**	NIH
7: 4 **s** will the anger of the Lord be kindled	2050.1
7:19 s shall the Lord thy God do unto all	3651
8: 5 *s* the Lord thy God chasteneth thee.	NIH
8:20 before your face, **s** shall ye perish;	3651
9: 3 shalt thou drive them out,	2050.1
9: 8 **s that** the Lord was angry with you to	2050.1
9:15 S I turned and came down from	2050.1
12: 4 Ye shall not do **s** unto the Lord your	3651
12:10 round about, **s that** ye dwell in safety;	2050.1
12:22 the hart is eaten, **s** thou shalt eat them:	3651
12:30 their gods? even **s** will I do likewise.	3651
12:31 Thou shalt not do **s** unto the Lord thy	3651
13: 5 S shalt thou put the evil away from	2050.1
14:24 thee, **s that** thou art not able to carry it;	3588
17: 7 S thou shalt put the evil away from	2050.1
18:14 thy God hath not suffered thee **s** *to do.*	3651
19:10 an inheritance, and **s** blood be upon thee.	NIH
19:19 s shalt thou put the evil away your	2050.1
20:18 s should ye sin against the Lord your	2050.1
21: 9 S shalt thou put away the *guilt of*	2050.1
21:21 s shalt thou put evil away from among	2050.1
22: 3 s shalt thou do with his raiment; and	3651
22: 5 for all that do **s** *are* abomination unto	428
22:21 s shalt thou put evil away from among	2050.1
22:22 s shalt thou put away evil from Israel.	2050.1
22:24 s thou shalt put evil away from among	2050.1
22:26 and slayeth him, **even s** *is* this matter:	3651
24: 8 them, *s* ye shall observe to do.	NIH
25: 9 S shall it be done unto *that* man that will	3602
28:34 S that thou shalt be mad for the sight of	2050.1
28:54 S that the man *that is* tender among you,	NIH
28:55 S that *he* will not give to any of them of	NIH
28:63 s the Lord will rejoice over you to	3651
29:22 S that the generation to come of your	2050.1
30:17 s that thou wilt not hear, but shalt be	2050.1
31:17 S that they will say in that day, Are not	2050.1
32:12 S the Lord alone did lead him,	NIH
33:25 and as thy days, *s shall* thy strength *be.*	NIH
34: 5 S Moses the servant of the Lord died	2050.1
34: 8 s the days of weeping and mourning for	2050.1
Jos 1: 5 as I was with Moses, *s* I will be with thee:	NIH
1:17 in all *things,* **s** will we hearken unto thee:	3651
2:21 According unto your words, **s** be it.	3651
2:23 S the two men returned,	2050.1
3: 7 as I was with Moses, **s** I will be with thee.	NIH
4: 8 of Israel did **s** as Joshua commanded,	NIH
5:15 thou standest *is* holy. And Joshua did **s**.	3651
6:11 S the ark of the Lord compassed	2050.1
6:14 *into* the camp: **s** they did six days.	3541
6:20 S the people shouted when *the priests*	2050.1
6:20 **s that** the people went up into the city,	2050.1
6:27 S the Lord was with Joshua;	2050.1
7: 4 S there went up thither of the people	2050.1
7:16 S Joshua rose up early in the morning,	2050.1
7:22 S Joshua sent messengers, and they ran	2050.1
7:26 S the Lord turned from the fierceness	2050.1
8: 3 S Joshua arose, and all the people of	2050.1
8:22 s they were in the midst of Israel,	2050.1
8:22 **s that** *they* let none of them remain or	5704
8:25 *s* it was, *that* all that fell that day, both of	NIH
9:26 s did he unto them, and delivered them	3651
10: 1 king, **s** he had done to Ai and her king;	3651
10: 7 S Joshua ascended from Gilgal, he,	3651
10:13 S the sun stood still in the midst of	2050.1
10:23 they did **s**, and brought forth those five	3651
10:39 s he did to Debir, and to the king thereof;	3651
10:40 S Joshua smote all the country of	2050.1
11: 7 S Joshua came, and all the people of war	2050.1
11:15 s did Moses command Joshua, and so	3651
11:15 command Joshua, and **s** did Joshua;	3651
11:16 S Joshua took all that land, the hills,	2050.1
11:23 S Joshua took the whole land,	2050.1
14: 5 s the children of Israel did,	3651
14:11 even **s** *is* my strength now, for war,	3509.1
14:12 **if s be** the Lord *will be* with me, then	194
15: 7 *s* northward, looking toward Gilgal, that	NIH
16: 4 S the children of Joseph, Manasseh and	2050.1
19:51 S they made an end of dividing	2050.1
21:40 S all the cities for the children of Merari	NIH
22: 6 S Joshua blessed them, and sent them	NIH
22:25 s shall your children make our children	2050.1
22:28 when they should *s* say to us or to our	NIH
23:15 s shall the Lord bring upon you all evil	3651
24:10 s I delivered you out of his hand.	2050.1

Jos 24:25 S Joshua made a covenant with	2050.1
24:28 S Joshua let the people depart, every	2050.1
Jdg 1: 3 into thy lot. S Simeon went with him.	2050.1
1: 7 as I have done, **s** God hath requited me.	3651
1:35 **s that** they became tributaries.	2050.1
2:14 s that they could not any longer stand	2050.1
2:17 of the Lord; *but* they did not **s**.	3651
3:14 S the children of Israel served Eglon	2050.1
3:22 **s that** he could not draw the dagger out	3588
3:30 S Moab was subdued that day under	2050.1
4:14 S Barak went down from mount Tabor,	2050.1
4:15 **s that** Sisera lighted down off *his*	2050.1
4:21 he was fast asleep and weary. S he died.	2050.1
4:23 S God subdued on that day Jabin the	2050.1
5:28 Why is his chariot *s* long in coming?	NIH
5:31 S let all thine enemies perish, O Lord:	3651
6: 3 *s* it was, when Israel had sown, that	NIH
6:20 and pour out the broth. And he did **s**.	3651
6:27 *s* it was, because he feared his father's	NIH
6:38 it was **s**: for he rose up early on	3651
6:40 God did **s** that night: for it was dry upon	3651
7: 1 **s that** the host of the Midianites were	2050.1
7: 5 S he brought down the people unto	2050.1
7: 8 S the people took victuals in their hand,	2050.1
7:15 it was **s**, when Gideon heard the telling of	NIH
7:17 it shall be *that,* as I do, **s** shall ye do.	3651
7:19 S Gideon, and the hundred men that	2050.1
8:18 they answered, As thou *art,* **s** *were* they;	3644
8:21 for as the man **s**, *s* is his strength.	NIH
8:28 **s that** they lifted up their heads no	2050.1
9:49 **s that** all the men of the tower of	2050.1
10: 9 **s that** Israel was sore distressed.	2050.1
11: 5 was, that when the children of Ammon	NIH
11:10 if we do not **s** according to thy words.	3651
11:21 s Israel possessed all the land of	2050.1
11:23 S now the Lord God of Israel hath	2050.1
11:24 s whomsoever the Lord our God shall	2050.1
11:32 S Jephthah passed over unto the	2050.1
12: 5 it was **s**, that when those Ephraimites	NIH
13:19 S Manoah took a kid with a meat	2050.1
14:10 S his father went down unto the	2050.1
14:10 a feast; for **s** used the young men to do.	3651
14:15 called us to take that we have? *is it* not **s**?	NIH
15:11 did unto me, **s** have I done unto them.	3651
16: 9 the fire. S his strength was not known.	2050.1
16:16 *s* that his soul was vexed unto death;	NIH
16:30 S the dead which he slew at his death	2050.1
17:10 and thy victuals. S the Levite went *in.*	2050.1
18:21 S they turned and departed, and put	2050.1
19: 4 s they did eat and drink, and lodged	2050.1
19:21 S he brought him into his house,	2050.1
19:23 nay, I pray you, do not **s** wickedly;	NIH
19:24 but unto this man do not **s** vile a thing.	2063
19:25 s the man took his concubine,	2050.1
19:30 it was **s**, that all that saw it said, There	NIH
20:11 S all the men of Israel were gathered	2050.1
20:36 S the children of Benjamin saw that	2050.1
20:46 S that all which fell that day	2050.1
21:14 and yet **s** they sufficed them not.	3651
21:23 the children of Benjamin did **s**,	3651
Ru 1:17 the Lord do **s** to me, and more also,	3541
1:19 S they two went until they came *to*	2050.1
1:22 S Naomi returned, and Ruth	2050.1
2: 7 she came, and hath continued even	2050.1
2:17 S she gleaned in the field until even,	2050.1
2:23 S she kept fast by the maidens of Boaz	2050.1
4: 8 Buy *it* for thee. S he drew off his shoe.	2050.1
4:13 S Boaz took Ruth, and she was his wife:	2050.1
1Sa 1: 7 *as* he did **s** year by year, when she went	3651
1: 7 house of the Lord, **s** she provoked her;	3651
1: 9 S Hannah rose up after *they* had eaten	2050.1
1:18 S the woman went her way, and did	2050.1
1:23 S the woman abode, and gave her son	2050.1
2: 3 Talk no more **s** exceeding proudly; let *not*	NIH
2: 5 **s that** the barren hath born seven;	5704
2:14 S they did in Shiloh unto all the Israelites	3602
2:21 s that she conceived, and bare three	2050.1
3: 9 S Samuel went and lay down in his	2050.1
3:17 God do **s** to thee, and more also, if thou	3541
4: 4 S the people sent *to* Shiloh, that they	2050.1
4: 5 great shout, **s that** the earth rang again.	2050.1
5: 7 the men of Ashdod saw that *it was* **s**,	3651
5: 9 was **s**, that after they had carried it about,	NIH
5:11 S they sent and gathered together all	2050.1
6:10 the men did **s**; and took two milch kine,	3651
7:13 S the Philistines were subdued,	2050.1
8: 8 other gods, **s** do they also unto thee.	3651
9:10 S they went unto the city where the	2050.1
9:21 s to me? 1697+2088+1886.1+1886.1+3509.1	
9:24 S Saul did eat with Samuel that day.	2050.1
10: 9 it was **s**, that when he had turned his back	NIH
11: 7 s shall it be done unto his oxen.	3541
11:11 it was **s** on the morrow, that Saul put	NIH
11:11 **s that** two of them were not left	2050.1
12:18 S Samuel called unto the Lord;	2050.1
13:22 S it came to pass in the day of battle,	2050.1
14:15 it was a very great trembling.	2050.1
14:23 S the Lord saved Israel that day:	2050.1
14:24 S none of the people tasted *any* food.	2050.1
14:44 Saul answered, God do **s** and more also:	3541
14:45 S the people rescued Jonathan, that he	2050.1
14:47 S Saul took the kingdom over Israel,	2050.1
15: 6 S the Kenites departed from among	2050.1
15:31 S Samuel turned again after Saul;	2050.1
15:33 s shall thy mother be childless among	3651

1Sa 16:13 S Samuel rose up, and went to Ramah.	2050.1
16:23 s Saul was refreshed, and was well,	2050.1
17:27 S shall it be done to the man that killeth	3541
17:50 S David prevailed over the Philistine	2050.1
18:30 Saul; **s that** his name was much set by.	2050.1
19:12 S Michal let David down through a	2050.1
19:17 Why hast thou deceived me **s**,	3602
19:18 S David fled, and escaped, and came to	2050.1
20: 2 father hide this thing from me? it *is* not **s**.	NIH
20:13 The Lord do **s** and much more to	3541
20:16 S Jonathan made *a covenant* with	2050.1
20:24 S David hid himself in the field:	2050.1
20:34 S Jonathan arose from the table in fierce	2050.1
21: 6 S the priest gave him hallowed *bread:*	2050.1
22:14 who *is* **s** faithful among all thy servants as	NIH
23: 5 S David and his men went *to* Keilah.	2050.1
23: 5 S David saved the inhabitants of Keilah.	2050.1
24: 7 S David stayed his servants with *these*	2050.1
25:12 S David's young men turned their way,	2050.1
25:20 it was **s**, *as* she rode on the ass, that she	NIH
25:21 **s that** nothing was missed of all that	2050.1
25:22 S and more also do God unto the enemies	3541
25:25 for as his name *is,* **s** *is* he; Nabal *is* his	3651
25:35 S David received of her hand *that* which	2050.1
26: 7 S David and Abishai came to the people	2050.1
26:12 S David took the spear and the cruse of	2050.1
26:24 s let my life be much set by in the eyes of	3651
26:25 S David went on his way,	2050.1
27: 1 of Israel: **s** shall I escape out of his hand.	2050.1
27:11 S did David, and so *will be* his manner all	3541
27:11 **s** *will be* his manner all the while he	3541
28:23 S he arose from the earth, and sat upon	2050.1
29: 8 **s long as** I have been with thee	3117+4480
29:11 S David and his men rose up early to	2050.1
30: 3 S David and his men came to the city,	2050.1
30: 9 S David went, he and the six hundred	2050.1
30:10 s faint **that** they could **not** go over	4480
30:21 s faint that they could **not** follow David,	4480
30:23 David, Ye shall not do **s**, my brethren,	3651
30:24 s *shall* his part *be* that tarrieth by	2050.1
30:25 it was **s** from that day forward, that he	NIH
31: 6 S Saul died, and his three sons,	2050.1
2Sa 1: 2 s it was, when he came to David, that he	NIH
1:10 S I stood upon him, and slew him,	2050.1
2: 2 S David went up thither, and his two	2050.1
2:16 fellow's side; **s** they fell down together;	2050.1
2:28 S Joab blew a trumpet, and all the	2050.1
2:31 *s that* three hundred and threescore men	NIH
3: 9 S do God to Abner, and more also,	3541
3: 9 hath sworn to David, even **s** I do to him;	3651
3:20 S Abner came to David *to* Hebron,	2050.1
3:30 S Joab and Abishai his brother slew	2050.1
3:34 falleth before wicked men, *s* fellest thou.	NIH
3:35 s do God to me, and more also,	3541
5: 3 S all the elders of Israel came to the	2050.1
5: 9 S David dwelt in the fort, and called it	2050.1
5:25 David did **s**, as the Lord had	3651
6:10 S David would not remove the ark of	2050.1
6:12 S David went and brought up the ark	2050.1
6:13 it was **s**, that when they that bare the ark	NIH
6:15 S David and all the house of Israel	2050.1
6:19 a flagon *of wine.* S the people	2050.1
7: 8 Now therefore **s** shalt thou say unto my	3541
7:17 vision, **s** did Nathan speak unto David.	3651
8: 2 *s* the Moabites became David's servants,	NIH
9:11 his servant, **s** shall thy servant do.	3651
9:13 S Mephibosheth dwelt in Jerusalem:	2050.1
10:14 S Joab returned from the children of	2050.1
10:19 S the Syrians feared to help the children	2050.1
11:12 S Uriah abode in Jerusalem that day,	2050.1
11:20 **if s be that** the king's wrath arise, and he	518
11:20 Wherefore approached ye **s** nigh unto	NIH
11:22 S the messenger went, and came and	2050.1
12:31 S David and all the people returned	2050.1
13: 2 Amnon was **s** vexed, that he fell sick for	NIH
13: 6 S Amnon lay down, and made himself	2050.1
13: 8 S Tamar went *to* her brother Amnon's	2050.1
13:15 **s that** the hatred wherewith he hated her	3588
13:20 S Tamar remained desolate *in* her	2050.1
13:35 sons come: as thy servant said, **s** it is.	3651
13:38 S Absalom fled, and went to Geshur,	2050.1
14: 3 S Joab put the words in her mouth.	2050.1
14: 7 *s* they shall quench my coal which is left,	NIH
14:17 s *is* my lord the king to discern good and	3651
14:23 S Joab arose and went to Geshur,	2050.1
14:24 S Absalom returned to his own house,	2050.1
14:25 **s much** praised as Absalom for his beauty	3966
14:28 S Absalom dwelt two full years in	2050.1
14:33 S Joab came to the king, and told him:	2050.1
15: 2 it was **s**, *that when* any man that had a	NIH
15: 5 it was **s**, that when any man came nigh	NIH
15: 6 s Absalom stole the hearts of the men	2050.1
15: 9 So he arose, and went to Hebron.	2050.1
15:34 s *will* I now also *be* thy servant:	2050.1
15:37 Hushai David's friend came *into*	2050.1
16:10 s let him curse, because the Lord hath	3588
16:10 then say, Wherefore hast thou done **s**?	3651
16:19 s will I be in thy presence.	3651
16:22 S they spread Absalom a tent upon	2050.1
16:23 s *was* all the counsel of Ahithophel both	3651
17: 3 **s** all the people shall be *in* peace.	NIH
17:12 S shall we come upon him in some	2050.1
17:12 there shall not be left **s much as** one.	1571
17:26 S Israel and Absalom pitched *in* the land	2050.1
18: 6 S the people went out *into* the field	2050.1

2Sa 19:13	God do **s** to me, and more also, if thou	3541
19:14	**s that** they sent *this word* unto the	2050.1
19:15	**S** the king returned, and came to	2050.1
20: 2	**S** every man of Israel went up from	2050.1
20: 3	**S** they were shut up unto the day of	2050.1
20: 5	**S** Amasa went to assemble *the men of*	2050.1
20:10	**s** he smote him therewith in the fifth	2050.1
20:10	**S** Joab and Abishai his brother pursued	2050.1
20:18	at Abel: and **s** they ended *the matter.*	3651
20:21	The matter *is* not **s**: but a man of mount	3651
22: 4	**s** shall I be saved from mine enemies.	2050.1
22:35	**s that** a bow of steel is broken *by* mine	2050.1
22:37	under me; **s that** my feet did not slip.	2050.1
23: 5	Although my house *be* not **s** with God;	3651
24: 8	**S when** they had gone through all	2050.1
24:13	**S** Gad came to David, and told him,	2050.1
24:15	**S** the LORD sent a pestilence upon	2050.1
24:24	**S** David bought the threshingfloor and	2050.1
24:25	the LORD was intreated for the land,	2050.1
1Ki 1: 3	**S** they sought for a fair damsel	2050.1
1: 6	time in saying, Why hast thou done **s**?	3602
1:30	**even s** will I certainly do this day.	3588
1:36	LORD God of my lord the king say **s** *too.*	3651
1:37	**even s** be he with Solomon, and make	3651
1:38	**S** Zadok the priest, and Nathan	2050.1
1:40	**s that** the earth rent with the sound of	2050.1
1:45	**s that** the city rang again.	2050.1
1:53	**S** king Solomon sent, and they brought	2050.1
2: 7	**s** they came to me when I fled because	3651
2:10	**S** David slept with his fathers,	2050.1
2:23	God do **s** to me, and more also,	3541
2:27	**S** Solomon thrust out Abiathar from	2050.1
2:34	**S** Benaiah the son of Jehoiada went up,	2050.1
2:38	the king hath said, **s** will thy servant do.	3651
2:46	**S** the king commanded Benaiah the son	2050.1
3: 9	is able to judge this thy **s** great a people?	NIH
3:12	**s that** there was none like thee before	834
3:13	**s that** there shall not be any among the	834
4: 1	**S** king Solomon was king over all Israel.	2050.1
5: 4	**s** *that there is* neither adversary nor evil	NIH
5:10	**S** Hiram gave Solomon cedar trees and	2050.1
5:18	**s** they prepared timber and stones to	2050.1
6: 7	**s that** there was neither hammer nor	2050.1
6: 9	**S** he built the house, and finished it;	2050.1
6:14	**S** Solomon built the house,	2050.1
6:20	**s** covered the altar *which was of* cedar.	NIH
6:21	**S** Solomon overlaid the house within	2050.1
6:26	cubits, and **s** did *it* of the other cherub.	3651
6:27	**s that** the wing of the one touched	2050.1
6:33	**S** also made he for the door of the temple	3651
6:38	**S** was he seven years in building it.	2050.1
7: 9	**s** on the outside toward the great court.	NIH
7:18	and **s** did he for the other chapiter.	3651
7:22	**s** was the work of the pillars finished.	2050.1
7:40	**S** Hiram made an end of doing all	2050.1
7:51	**s** was ended all the work that king	2050.1
8:11	**S that** the priests could not stand to	2050.1
8:25	**s** that thy children take heed to their way,	7535
8:46	**s that** they carry them away captives	2050.1
8:48	**s** return unto thee with all their heart,	NIH
8:54	it was **s**, *that* when Solomon had made an	NIH
8:63	**S** the king and all the children of Israel	2050.1
9:25	the LORD. **S** he finished the house.	2050.1
10:13	**S** she turned and went to her own	2050.1
10:23	**S** king Solomon exceeded all the kings	2050.1
10:29	**s** for all the kings of the Hittites, and for	3651
11:19	**s that** he gave him *to* wife the sister of	3651
12:12	**S** Jeroboam and all the people came to	2050.1
12:16	**S when** all Israel saw that the king	2050.1
12:16	**S** Israel departed unto their tents.	2050.1
12:19	**S** Israel rebelled against the house of	2050.1
12:32	upon the altar. (**s** did he in Beth-el,)	3651
12:33	**S** he offered upon the altar which he	2050.1
13: 4	**s that** he could not pull it in again to	2050.1
13: 9	For **s** was it charged me by the word of	3651
13:10	**S** he went another way, and returned	2050.1
13:13	**S** they saddled him the ass: and he rode	2050.1
13:19	**S** he went back with him, and did eat	2050.1
14: 4	Jeroboam's wife did **s**, and arose,	3651
14: 6	it was **s**, when Ahijah heard the sound of	NIH
14:28	was **s**, when the king went *into* the house	NIH
15:20	**S** Ben-hadad hearkened unto king Asa,	2050.1
16: 6	**S** Baasha slept with his fathers,	2050.1
16:22	**S** Tibni died, and Omri reigned.	2050.1
16:28	**S** Omri slept with his fathers,	2050.1
17: 5	**S** he went and did according unto	2050.1
17:10	**S** he arose and went to Zarephath.	2050.1
17:17	his sickness was **s** sore, that there was no	3966
18: 4	For it was **s**, when Jezebel cut off	NIH
18: 6	**S** they divided the land between them	2050.1
18:12	**s** when I come and tell Ahab, and he	NIH
18:16	**S** Obadiah went to meet Ahab.	2050.1
18:20	**S** Ahab sent unto all the children of	2050.1
18:42	**S** Ahab went up to eat and to drink.	2050.1
19: 2	**S** let the gods do *to me,* and more also,	3541
19:13	it was **s**, when Elijah heard *it,* that he	NIH
19:19	**S** he departed thence, and found Elisha	2050.1
20:10	The gods do **s** unto me, and more also,	3541
20:19	**S** these young men of the princes of	2050.1
20:25	he hearkened unto their voice, and did **s**.	3651
20:29	**s** it was, that in the seventh day the battle	NIH
20:32	**S** they girded sackcloth on their loins,	2050.1
20:34	**S** he made a covenant with him, and	2050.1
20:37	**s that** in smiting he wounded *him.*	2050.1
20:38	**S** the prophet departed, and waited for	2050.1

1Ki 20:40	**S** *shall* thy judgment *be;* thyself hast	3651
21: 5	said unto him, Why is thy spirit **s sad**,	5620
21: 8	**S** she wrote letters in Ahab's name,	2050.1
21: 8	Jehoshaphat said, Let not the king say **s**.	3651
22:12	the prophets prophesied **s**, saying, Go up	3651
22:15	**S** he came to the king. And the king	2050.1
22:22	and prevail also: go forth, and do **s**.	3651
22:29	**S** the king of Israel and Jehoshaphat	2050.1
22:37	**S** the king died, and was brought *to*	2050.1
22:40	**S** Ahab slept with his fathers,	2050.1
2Ki 1:17	**S** he died according to the word of	2050.1
2: 2	**S** they went down *to* Beth-el.	2050.1
2: 4	not leave thee. **S** they came *to* Jericho.	2050.1
2: 8	**s that** they two went over on dry	2050.1
2:10	taken from thee, it shall be **s** unto thee;	3651
2:10	so unto thee; but if not, it shall not be **s**.	NIH
2:22	the waters were healed unto this day,	2050.1
3: 9	**S** the king of Israel went, and the king	2050.1
3:12	**S** the king of Israel and Jehoshaphat and	2050.1
3:24	**s** that they fled before them:	2050.1
4: 5	**S** she went from him, and shut the door	2050.1
4: 8	**s** it was, *that* as oft as he passed by,	NIH
4:25	**S** she went and came unto the man of	2050.1
4:36	**S** he called her. And when she was	2050.1
4:40	**S** they poured out for the men to eat.	2050.1
4:44	**S** he set *it* before them, and they did eat	2050.1
5: 8	it was **s**, when Elisha the man of God had	NIH
5: 9	**S** Naaman came with his horses and	2050.1
5:12	**S** he turned and went away in a rage.	2050.1
5:19	he departed from him a little way.	2050.1
5:21	**S** Gehazi followed after Naaman.	2050.1
6: 4	**S** he went with them. And when they	2050.1
6:23	**S** the bands of Syria came no more into	2050.1
6:29	**S** we boiled my son, and did eat him:	2050.1
6:31	he said, God do **s** and more also to me,	3541
7:10	**S** they came and called unto the porter	2050.1
7:16	**S** a measure of fine flour was *sold* for a	2050.1
7:20	**s** it fell out unto him: for the people trode	3651
8: 6	**S** the king appointed unto her a certain	2050.1
8: 9	**S** Hazael went to meet him, and took a	2050.1
8:14	**S** he departed from Elisha, and came to	2050.1
8:15	spread *it* on his face, **s that** he died:	2050.1
8:21	**S** Joram went over to Zair, and all	2050.1
9: 4	the young man, *even* the young man	2050.1
9:14	**S** Jehu the son of Jehoshaphat the son	2050.1
9:16	**S** Jehu rode *in a chariot,* and went to	2050.1
9:18	**S** there went one on horseback to meet	2050.1
9:22	**s long as** the whoredoms of thy mother	5704
9:22	and her witchcrafts *are* **s** many?	NIH
9:27	*And they did* **s** at the going up to Gur,	NIH
9:33	**S** they threw her down: and *some* of	2050.1
9:37	**s** that they shall not say, This *is* Jezebel.	NIH
10:11	**S** Jehu slew all that remained of the	2050.1
10:16	**S** they made him ride in his chariot.	2050.1
10:21	**s that** there was not a man left but	2050.1
11: 2	from Athaliah, **s that** he was not slain.	2050.1
11: 6	**s** shall ye keep the watch of the house,	2050.1
12: 6	it was **s**, *that* in the three and twentieth	NIH
12:10	it was **s**, when they saw that *there was*	2050.1
13: 5	**s that** they went out from under the	2050.1
13:24	**S** Hazael king of Syria died;	2050.1
15: 5	he was a leper unto the day of his	2050.1
15: 7	**S** Azariah slept with his fathers;	2050.1
15:12	fourth *generation.* And **s** it came to pass.	3651
15:20	**S** the king of Assyria turned back,	2050.1
16: 7	**S** Ahaz sent messengers to	2050.1
16:11	**s** Urijah the priest made *it* against king	3651
17: 4	for he had sent messengers to **S** king of	5471
17: 7	For **s** it was, that the children of Israel	NIH
17:23	**S** was Israel carried away out of their	2050.1
17:25	**s** it was at the beginning of their dwelling	NIH
17:32	**S** they feared the LORD, and made unto	2050.1
17:41	**S** these nations feared the LORD,	2050.1
17:41	did their fathers, **s** do they unto this day.	NIH
18: 5	**s that** after him was none like him	2050.1
18:21	**s** *is* Pharaoh king of Egypt unto all that	3651
19: 5	**S** the servants of king Hezekiah came to	2050.1
19: 8	**S** Rab-shakeh returned, and found	2050.1
19:36	**S** Sennacherib king of Assyria departed,	2050.1
22:14	**S** Hilkiah the priest, and Ahikam,	2050.1
23:18	**S** they let his bones alone, with the	2050.1
24: 6	**S** Jehoiakim slept with his fathers:	2050.1
25: 6	**S** they took the king, and brought him	2050.1
25:21	**S** Judah was carried away out of their	2050.1
1Ch 9:23	**s** all Israel were reckoned by	2050.1
9:23	**S** they and their children had	2050.1
10: 4	**S** Saul took a sword, and fell upon it.	2050.1
10: 6	**S** Saul died, and his three sons, and all	2050.1
10:13	**S** Saul died for his transgression which	2050.1
11: 6	**S** Joab the son of Zeruiah went first up,	2050.1
11: 9	**S** David waxed greater and greater:	2050.1
13: 4	congregation said that *they* would do **s**:	3651
13: 5	**S** David gathered all Israel together,	2050.1
13:13	**S** David brought not the ark *home* to	2050.1
14:11	they came up to Baal-perazim;	2050.1
15:14	**S** the priests and the Levites sanctified	2050.1
15:17	**S** the Levites appointed Heman the son	2050.1
15:19	**S** the singers, Heman, Asaph, and Ethan	2050.1
15:25	**S** David, and the elders of Israel,	2050.1
16: 1	**S** they brought the ark of God, and set	2050.1
16:37	**S** he left there before the ark of	2050.1
17:15	vision, **s** did Nathan speak unto David.	3651
18:14	**S** David reigned over all Israel,	2050.1
19: 2	**S** the servants of David came into	2050.1
19: 7	**S** they hired thirty and two thousand	2050.1

1Ch 19:14	**S** Joab and the people that *were* with	2050.1
19:17	**S when** David had put the battle in	2050.1
20: 3	Even **s** dealt David with all the cities of	3651
21: 3	**make** his people an hundred times **s many moe**	3254
21:11	**S** Gad came to David, and said unto	2050.1
21:14	**S** the LORD sent pestilence upon Israel:	2050.1
21:25	**S** David gave to Ornan for the place six	2050.1
22: 5	**S** David prepared abundantly before his	2050.1
23: 1	**S when** David was old and full *of* days,	2050.1
25: 7	**S** the number of them, with their	2050.1
29:14	that we should be able to offer **s**	NIH
2Ch 1: 3	**S** Solomon, and all the congregation	2050.1
1:10	can judge this thy people, *that is* **s** great?	NIH
1:17	**s** brought they out *horses* for all the kings	3651
2: 3	to dwell therein, *even* **s** deal with me.	3651
5:14	**s that** the priests could not stand to	2050.1
6:16	**s that** thy children take heed to their way	518
6:31	**s long as** they live in	3117+3605+1886.1
7: 5	**s** the king and all the people dedicated	2050.1
7:21	**s that** he shall say, Why hath the LORD	2050.1
8:14	for **s** had David the man of God	3651
8:16	**S** the house of the LORD was perfected.	NIH
9:12	**S** she turned, and went away to her	2050.1
10: 3	**S** Jeroboam and all Israel came and	2050.1
10:12	**S** Jeroboam and all the people came to	2050.1
10:15	**S** the king hearkened not unto the	2050.1
10:16	**S** all Israel went to their tents.	2050.1
11:17	**S** they strengthened the kingdom of	2050.1
12: 9	**S** Shishak king of Egypt came up against	2050.1
12:13	**S** king Rehoboam strengthened himself	2050.1
13: 9	**s** that whosoever cometh to consecrate	NIH
13:13	**s** they were before Judah,	2050.1
13:17	**s** there fell down slain of Israel five	2050.1
14: 1	**S** Abijah slept with his fathers,	2050.1
14: 7	every side. **S** they built and prospered.	2050.1
14:12	**S** the LORD smote the Ethiopians	2050.1
15:10	**S** they gathered themselves together *at*	2050.1
17:10	**s that** they made no war against	2050.1
18: 7	Jehoshaphat said, Let not the king say **s**.	3651
18:11	the prophets prophesied **s**, saying, Go up	3651
18:21	shalt also prevail: go out, and do even **s**.	3651
18:28	**S** the king of Israel and Jehoshaphat	2050.1
18:29	**S** the king of Israel disguised himself;	2050.1
19:10	**s** wrath come upon you, and upon your	NIH
20: 6	**s that** none is able to withstand thee?	2050.1
20:20	your God, **s** shall you be established;	2050.1
20:20	believe his prophets, **s** shall ye prosper.	2050.1
20:25	in gathering of the spoil, it was **s** much.	3588
20:30	**S** the realm of Jehoshaphat was quiet:	2050.1
21:10	**S** the Edomites revolted from under	2050.1
21:17	**s that** there was never a son left him,	2050.1
21:19	he died of sore diseases.	2050.1
22: 1	**S** Ahaziah the son of Jehoram king of	2050.1
22: 9	**S** the house of Ahaziah had no power to	2050.1
22:11	**S** Jehoshabeath, the daughter of king	2050.1
22:11	from Athaliah, **s that** she slew him not.	2050.1
23: 8	**S** the Levites and all Judah did	2050.1
23:15	**S** they laid hands on her; and when she	2050.1
24:13	**S** the workmen wrought, and the work	2050.1
24:24	**S** they executed judgment against Joash.	2050.1
25:21	**S** Joash the king of Israel went up;	2050.1
26:23	**S** Uzziah slept with his fathers,	2050.1
27: 5	**S much** did the children of Ammon pay	2063
27: 6	**S** Jotham became mighty, because	2050.1
28:14	**S** the armed men left the captives and	2050.1
29:17	**s** they sanctified the house of the LORD	2050.1
29:22	**S** they killed the bullocks, and the	2050.1
29:25	for **s** *was* the commandment of the LORD	NIH
29:34	**s that** they could not flay all the burnt	2050.1
29:35	**S** the service of the house of the LORD	2050.1
30: 5	**S** they established a decree to make	2050.1
30: 6	**S** the posts went with the letters from	2050.1
30: 9	**s** that *they shall* come again into this	2050.1
30:10	**S** the posts passed from city to city	2050.1
30:26	**S** there was great joy in Jerusalem:	2050.1
32: 4	**S** there was gathered much people	2050.1
32:17	**s** shall not the God of Hezekiah deliver	3651
32:21	**S** he returned with shame of face to his	2050.1
32:23	**s that** he was magnified in the sight of	2050.1
32:26	**s that** the wrath of the LORD came not	2050.1
33: 8	**s that** they will take heed to do all	518+7535
33: 9	**S** Manasseh made Judah and	2050.1
33:20	**S** Manasseh slept with his fathers,	2050.1
34: 6	**s** *did he* in the cities of Manasseh,	NIH
34:26	of the LORD, **s** shall ye say unto him,	3541
34:28	**S** they brought the king word again.	2050.1
35: 6	**S** kill the passover,	2050.1
35:10	**S** the service was prepared,	2050.1
35:12	And **s** *did they* with the oxen.	3651
35:16	**S** all the service of the LORD was	2050.1
Ezr 2:70	**S** the priests, and the Levites,	2050.1
3:13	**s that** the people could not discern	2050.1
4:13	**s** thou shalt endamage the revenue of	NIH
4:15	shalt thou find in the book of	2050.3
4:24	**S** it ceased unto the second year	1934+2050.3
5:17	whether it be **s**, that a decree *was* made	NIH
6:13	the king had sent, **s** they did speedily.	3660
8:23	**S** we fasted and besought our God for	2050.1
8:30	**S** took the priests and the Levites	2050.1
9: 2	**s that** the holy seed have mingled	2050.1
9:14	**s** that *there should be* no remnant nor	NIH
10:12	voice, As thou hast said, **s** must we do.	3651
10:16	**s** the children of the captivity did **s**.	3651
Ne 2: 4	**S** I prayed to the God of heaven.	2050.1

S

Ne	2: 6 **S** it pleased the king to send me; and I	2050.1
	2:11 **S** I came to Jerusalem, and was there	2050.1
	2:15 by the gate of the valley, and *s* returned.	NIH
	2:18 **S** they strengthened their hands for *this*	2050.1
	4: 6 **S** built we the wall; and all the wall was	2050.1
	4:10 *s* that we are not able to build the wall.	2050.1
	4:18 sword girded by his side, and *s* builded.	NIH
	4:21 **S** we laboured in the work: and half of	2050.1
	4:23 **S** neither I, nor my brethren, nor my	2050.1
	5:12 of them; *s* will we do as thou sayest.	3651
	5:13 **S** God shake out every man from his	3602
	5:15 *s* did not I, because of the fear of God.	3651
	6: 3 great work, **s** that I cannot come down:	2050.1
	6:13 do *s*, and sin, and *that* they might have	3651
	6:15 the wall was finished in the twenty	2050.1
	7:73 **S** the priests, and the Levites,	2050.1
	8: 8 **S** they read in the book in the law of	2050.1
	8:11 the Levites stilled all the people,	2050.1
	8:16 **S** the people went forth,	2050.1
	8:17 day had not the children of Israel done **s**.	3651
	9:10 **S** didst thou get thee a name, as *it is*	2050.1
	9:11 *s* that they went through the midst of	2050.1
	9:21 wilderness, *s that* they lacked nothing;	NIH
	9:22 *s* they possessed the land of Sihon,	2050.1
	9:24 **s** the children went in and possessed	2050.1
	9:25 *s* they did eat, and were filled,	2050.1
	9:28 *s* that they had the dominion over them	2050.1
	12:40 **S** stood the two *companies of them*	2050.1
	12:43 **S** the joy of Jerusalem was heard	2050.1
	13:20 **S** the merchants and sellers of all *kind*	2050.1
	13:21 if ye do *s* again, I will lay hands on you.	NIH
Est	1: 8 for **s** the king had appointed to all	3651
	1:13 (for *s was* the king's manner towards all	3651
	1:17 **s** that *they* shall despise their husbands	3807.1
	2: 4 the thing pleased the king; and he did **s**.	3651
	2: 8 **S** it came to pass, when the king's	2050.1
	2:12 (for *s* were the days of their purifications	3651
	2:16 **S** Esther was taken unto king Ahasuerus	2050.1
	2:17 **s** that he set the royal crown upon her	2050.1
	3: 2 the king had **s** commanded concerning	3651
	4: 4 **S** Esther's maids and her chamberlains	2050.1
	4: 6 **S** Hatach went forth to Mordecai unto	2050.1
	4:16 *s* will I go in unto the king, which *is* not	3651
	4:17 **S** Mordecai went his way,	2050.1
	5: 2 it was **s**, when the king saw Esther	NIH
	5: 2 **S** Esther drew near, and touched the	2050.1
	5: 5 **S** the king and Haman came to	2050.1
	5:13 **s long as** I see Mordecai the Jew	3605+871.1
	6: 6 **S** Haman came in. And the king said	2050.1
	6:10 and do *even* **s** to Mordecai the Jew,	3651
	7: 1 **S** the king and Haman came to banquet	2050.1
	7: 5 that durst presume in his heart to do **s**?	3651
	7:10 **S** they hanged Haman on the gallows	2050.1
	8: 4 **S** Esther arose, and stood before the	2050.1
	8:14 **S** the posts that rode upon mules *and*	NIH
	9:14 the king commanded it **s** to be done:	3651
	9:27 unto them, **s** as it should not fail,	2050.1
Job	1: 3 **s** that this man was the greatest of all	2050.1
	1: 5 it was **s**, when the days of *their* feasting	3588
	1:12 **S** Satan went forth from the presence of	2050.1
	2: 7 **S** went Satan forth from the presence of	2050.1
	2:13 **S** they sat down with him upon	2050.1
	5:12 **s** that their hands cannot perform *their*	2050.1
	5:16 **S** the poor hath hope,	2050.1
	5:27 **s** it *is;* hear it, and know thou *it* for thy	3651
	7: 3 **S** am I made to possess months of vanity,	3651
	7: 9 **s** he that goeth down *to* the grave shall	3651
	7:15 **S** that my soul chooseth strangling,	2050.1
	7:20 **s** that I am a burden to myself?	2050.1
	8: 2 **S** *are* the paths of all that forget God;	3651
	9: 2 I know *it is* **s** of a truth: but how should	3651
	9:30 snow water, and **make** my hands	
	never s clean;	1253+2141+871.1
	9:35 and not fear him; but *it is* not **s** with me.	3651
	13: 9 man mocketh another, do ye **s** mock him?	NIH
	14:12 **S** man lieth down, and riseth not: till	2050.1
	21: 4 if *it were* **s**, why should not my spirit be	NIH
	23: 7 **s** should I be delivered for ever from my	2050.1
	24:19 **s** *doth* the grave *those which* have sinned.	NIH
	24:25 *it be* not **s** now, who will make me a liar,	NIH
	27: 6 shall not reproach *me* **s long as** I live.	4480
	32: 1 **S** these three men ceased to answer Job,	2050.1
	32:22 *in* **s** *doing* my Maker would soon take me	NIH
	33:20 **S** that his life abhorreth bread,	2050.1
	34:25 in the night, **s** that they are destroyed.	2050.1
	34:28 **S** that *they* cause the cry of the poor to	3807.1
	35:15 because *it is* not **s**, he hath visited *in* his	NIH
	36:16 Even **s** would he have removed thee out	637
	41:10 None *is* **s** fierce that dare stir him up:	NIH
	41:16 One is **s** near to another, that no air can	NIH
	42: 7 it was **s**, that after the Lord had spoken	NIH
	42: 9 **S** Eliphaz the Temanite and Bildad	2050.1
	42:12 **S** the Lord blessed the latter end of	2050.1
	42:15 found **s** fair as the daughters of Job:	NIH
	42:17 **S** Job died, *being* old and full of days.	2050.1
Ps	1: 4 The ungodly *are* not **s**: but *are* like the	3651
	7: 7 **S** shall the congregation of the people	2050.1
	18: 3 **s** shall I be saved from mine enemies.	2050.1
	18:34 **s** that a bow of steel is broken *by* mine	2050.1
	21:13 **s** will we sing and praise thy power.	NIH
	22: 1 *why art thou* **s** far from helping me,	NIH
	26: 6 **s** will I compass thine altar, O Lord:	2050.1
	35:25 in their hearts, Ah, **s** would we have it:	NIH
	37: 3 *s* shalt thou dwell in the land,	NIH
	40:12 **s** that I am not able to look *up;* they are	2050.1

Ps	42: 1 **s** panteth my soul after thee, O God.	3651
	45:11 **S** shall the king greatly desire thy	2050.1
	48: 5 They saw *it, and* **s** they marvelled;	3651
	48: 8 **s** have we seen in the city of the Lord of	3651
	48:10 **s** *is* thy praise unto the ends of the earth:	3651
	58: 5 of charmers, charming *never* **s** wisely.	NIH
	58:11 **S** that a man shall say, Verily *there is* a	2050.1
	61: 8 **S** will I sing *praise* unto thy name for	3651
	63: 2 **s** *as* I have seen thee in the sanctuary.	3651
	64: 8 **S** they shall make their own tongue to	2050.1
	65: 9 corn, when thou hast **s** provided for it.	3651
	68: 2 smoke is driven away, **s** *drive them* away.	NIH
	68: 2 *s* let the wicked perish at the presence of	NIH
	72: 7 **s long as** the moon **endureth**.	1097+5704
	73:20 *s*, O Lord, when *thou* awakest, thou shalt	NIH
	73:22 **S** foolish *was* I, and ignorant: I was *as* a	2050.1
	77: 4 I am **s** troubled that I cannot speak.	NIH
	77:13 who *is* **s** great a God as *our* God?	NIH
	78:21 **s** a fire was kindled against Jacob,	2050.1
	78:29 **S** they did eat, and were well filled: for	2050.1
	78:53 them on safely, **s** that they feared not:	2050.1
	78:60 **S** that he forsook the tabernacle of	2050.1
	78:72 **S** he fed them according to the integrity	2050.1
	79:13 **S** we thy people and sheep of thy	NIH
	80:12 **s** that all they which pass by the way do	2050.1
	80:18 **S** will not we go *back* from thee:	2050.1
	81:12 **S** I gave them up unto their own heart's	2050.1
	83:15 **S** persecute them with thy tempest,	3651
	90:11 even according to thy fear, *s* is thy wrath.	NIH
	90:12 **S** teach *us* to number our days, that we	3651
	102: 4 like grass; **s** that I forget to eat my bread.	3588
	102:15 **S** the heathen shall fear the name of	NIH
	103: 5 **s** that thy youth is renewed like the eagle's.	NIH
	103:11 **s** great is his mercy toward them that fear	NIH
	103:12 **s** far hath he removed our transgressions	NIH
	103:13 **s** the Lord pitieth them that fear him.	NIH
	103:15 as a flower of the field, **s** he flourisheth.	3651
	104:25 **S** *is* this great and wide sea, wherein *are*	NIH
	106: 9 **s** he led them through the depths,	2050.1
	106:30 and *s* the plague was stayed.	NIH
	106:32 **s** that it went ill with Moses for their	2050.1
	106:33 **s** that he spake unadvisedly with his	2050.1
	107: 2 Let the redeemed of the Lord say **s**,	NIH
	107:29 calm, **s** that the waves thereof are still.	2050.1
	107:30 **s** he bringeth them unto their desired	2050.1
	107:38 **s** that they are multiplied greatly;	2050.1
	109:17 As he loved cursing, **s** let it come *unto*	2050.1
	109:17 not in blessing, **s** let it be far from him.	2050.1
	109:18 **s** let it come into his bowels like water,	2050.1
	115: 8 **s** *is* every one that trusteth in them.	NIH
	119:27 **S** shall I talk of thy wondrous works.	2050.1
	119:42 **S** shall I have wherewith to answer him	2050.1
	119:44 **S** shall I keep thy law continually for	2050.1
	119:88 **s** shall I keep the testimony of thy	2050.1
	119:134 of man: **s** will I keep thy precepts.	NIH
	123: 2 **s** our eyes *wait* upon the Lord our God,	3651
	125: 2 **s** the Lord *is* round about his people	2050.1
	127: 2 *for* **s** he giveth his beloved sleep.	3651
	127: 4 mighty *man;* **s** *are* children of the youth.	3651
	135:18 **s** *is* every one that trusteth in them.	NIH
	147:20 He hath not dealt **s** with any nation:	3651
Pr	1:19 **S** *are* the ways of every one that is greedy	3651
	2: 2 **S** that *thou* incline thine ear unto	3807.1
	3: 4 **S** shalt thou find favour and	2050.1
	3:10 **S** shall thy barns be filled *with* plenty,	2050.1
	3:22 **S** shall they be life unto thy soul,	2050.1
	6:11 **S** shall thy poverty come as one that	2050.1
	6:29 **S** he that goeth in to his neighbour's wife;	3651
	7:13 **S** she caught him, and kissed him,	2050.1
	10:25 **s** is the wicked *no more:* but the	2050.1
	10:26 **s** *is* the sluggard to them that send him.	3651
	11:19 **s** he that pursueth evil *pursueth it* to	2050.1
	11:22 **s** *is* a fair woman which is without	NIH
	15: 7 but the heart of the foolish *doeth* not **s**.	3651
	19:24 **and** will not **s much as** bring it to his	1571
	20:30 **s** *do* stripes the inward parts of the	2050.1
	23: 7 For as he thinketh in his heart, **s** is he:	3651
	24:14 **S** shall the knowledge of wisdom be unto	3651
	24:29 **s** to him as he hath done to me:	834+3509.1
	24:34 **S** shall thy poverty come *as one* that	2050.1
	25:12 **s** *is* a wise reprover upon an obedient ear.	NIH
	25:13 **s** *is* a faithful messenger to them that send	NIH
	25:16 eat **s much as is sufficient** for thee,	1767
	25:17 lest he be weary of thee, and **s** hate thee.	NIH
	25:20 **s** *is* he that singeth songs to a heavy	2050.1
	25:23 **s** *doth* an angry countenance a	2050.1
	25:25 **s** *is* good news from a far country.	2050.1
	25:27 **s** *for* men to search their own glory	2050.1
	26: 1 **s** honour *is* not seemly for a fool.	3651
	26: 2 **s** the curse causeless shall not come.	3651
	26: 7 **s** *is* a parable in the mouth of fools.	2050.1
	26: 8 sling, **s** *is* he that giveth honour to a fool.	3651
	26: 9 **s** *is* a parable in the mouth of fools.	2050.1
	26:11 his vomit, **s** a fool returneth to his folly.	NIH
	26:14 **s** *doth* the slothful upon his bed.	2050.1
	26:19 **S** *is* the man *that* deceiveth his neighbour,	3651
	26:20 where *there is* no talebearer, the strife	2050.1
	26:21 **s** *is* a contentious man to kindle strife.	2050.1
	27: 8 **s** *is* a man that wandereth from his place.	2050.1
	27: 9 **s** *doth* the sweetness of a man's friend	2050.1
	27:17 **s** a man sharpeneth the countenance of	2050.1
	27:18 **s** he that waiteth on his master shall be	2050.1
	27:19 to face, **s** the heart of man to man.	3651
	27:20 **s** the eyes of man are never satisfied.	2050.1
	27:21 furnace for gold; **s** *is* a man to his praise.	2050.1

Pr	28:15 **s** *is* a wicked ruler over the poor people.	NIH
	30:33 **s** the forcing of wrath bringeth forth	2050.1
	31:11 **s** that he shall have no need of spoil.	2050.1
Ecc	2: 9 **S** I was great, and increased more than	2050.1
	2:15 to the fool, **s** it happeneth even to me;	1571
	3:11 **s** that no man can find out	834+1097+4480
	3:19 as the one dieth, **s** dieth the other; yea,	3651
	3:19 **s** that a man hath no preeminence	2050.1
	4: 1 **S** I returned, and considered all	2050.1
	5:16 in all points as he came, **s** shall he go:	3651
	6: 2 **s** that he wanteth nothing for his soul	2050.1
	6: 3 **s** that the days of his years be many,	2050.1
	7: 6 under a pot, **s** *is* the laughter of the fool:	3651
	8:10 **s** I saw the wicked buried, who had come	3651
	8:10 in the city where they had **s** done:	3651
	9: 2 as *is* the good, **s** *is* the sinner; *and* he	3509.1
	9:12 **s** *are* the sons of men snared in an evil	3509.1
	10: 1 **s** *doth* a little folly *him that is* in	NIH
	11: 5 **even** **s** thou knowest not the works of	3602
SS	2: 2 **s** *is* my love among the daughters.	3651
	2: 3 wood, **s** *is* my beloved among the sons.	3651
	5: 9 beloved, that thou dost **s** charge us?	3602
Isa	5:24 **s** their root shall be as rottenness,	NIH
	6:13 they cast *their leaves:* **s** the holy seed	NIH
	10: 7 Howbeit he meaneth not **s**, neither doth	3651
	10: 7 not so, neither doth his heart think **s**;	3651
	10:11 her idols, **s** do to Jerusalem and her idols?	3651
	10:26 **s** shall he lift it up after the manner of	2050.1
	14:24 as I have thought, **s** shall it come to pass;	3651
	14:24 and as I have purposed, **s** shall it stand:	NIH
	16: 2 **s** the daughters of Moab shall be at	3651
	16: 6 and his wrath: *but* his lies *shall* not *be* **s**.	3651
	18: 4 For **s** the Lord said unto me, I will take	3541
	20: 2 he did **s**, walking naked and barefoot.	3651
	20: 4 **S** shall the king of Assyria lead away	3651
	21: 1 **s** it cometh from the desert, from a terrible	NIH
	22:22 **s** he shall open, and none shall shut;	2050.1
	23: 1 **s** that *there is* no house, no entering in:	NIH
	23: 5 shall they be sorely pained *at* the	3509.1
	24: 2 as *with* the people, **s** *with* the priest;	3509.1
	24: 2 as *with* the servant, **s** *with* his master;	3509.1
	24: 2 as *with* the maid, **s** *with* her mistress;	3509.1
	24: 2 as *with* the buyer, **s** *with* the seller;	3509.1
	24: 2 as *with* the lender, **s** *with* the borrower;	3509.1
	24: 2 usury, **s** *with* the giver of usury to him.	3509.1
	26:17 **s** have we been in thy sight, O Lord.	3651
	28: 8 filthiness, **s** that *there is* no place *clean*.	NIH
	29: 8 **s** shall the multitude of all the nations be,	3651
	30:14 **s** that there shall not be found in	2050.1
	31: 4 **s** shall the Lord of hosts come down to	3651
	31: 5 **s** will the Lord of hosts defend	3651
	36: 6 **s** *is* Pharaoh king of Egypt to all that trust	3651
	37: 5 **S** the servants of king Hezekiah came to	2050.1
	37: 8 **S** Rabshakeh returned, and found the	2050.1
	37:37 **S** Sennacherib king of Assyria departed,	2050.1
	38: 8 **S** the sun returned ten degrees, by	2050.1
	38:13 as a lion, **s** will he break all my bones:	3651
	38:14 Like a crane *or* a swallow, **s** did I chatter:	3651
	38:16 **s** wilt thou recover me, and make me to	2050.1
	40:20 **s** **impoverished** that he hath no oblation	5533
	41: 7 the carpenter encouraged the	2050.1
	47: 7 **s** that thou didst not lay these *things* to	NIH
	47:12 **if** **s** be thou shalt be able to profit, if so	194
	47:12 able to profit, **if** **s** **be** thou mayest prevail.	194
	52:14 his visage *was* **s** marred more than *any*	3651
	52:15 **S** shall he sprinkle many nations;	3651
	53: 7 is dumb, **s** he openeth not his mouth.	2050.1
	54: 9 **s** have I sworn that *I* would not be wroth	3651
	55: 9 **s** are my ways higher than your ways,	3651
	55:11 **S** shall my word be that goeth forth out	3651
	59:19 **S** shall they fear the name of the Lord	2050.1
	60:15 **s** that no man went through thee, I will	2050.1
	61:11 **s** the Lord God will cause righteousness	3651
	62: 5 a virgin, **s** shall thy sons marry thee:	NIH
	62: 5 bride, **s** shall thy God rejoice over thee.	NIH
	63: 8 *that* will not lie: **s** he was their Saviour.	2050.1
	63:14 **s** didst thou lead thy people, to make	3651
	65: 8 **s** will I do for my servants' sakes, that *I*	3651
	66:13 mother comforteth, **s** will I comfort you;	3651
	66:22 **s** shall your seed and your name remain.	3651
Jer	2:26 is found, **s** is the house of Israel ashamed;	3651
	2:36 Why gaddest thou about **s** much to change	NIH
	3:20 **s** have you dealt treacherously with me,	3651
	5:19 **s** shall ye serve strangers in a land *that is*	3651
	5:27 *of* birds, **s** *are* their houses full of deceit:	3651
	5:31 and my people love *to have it* **s**:	3651
	6: 7 **s** she casteth out her wickedness:	3651
	9:10 **s** that none can pass through *them;*	4480
	10:18 will distress them, that they may find *it* **s**.	NIH
	11: 4 **s** shall ye be my people, and I will be	2050.1
	11: 5 answered I, and said, **S** be it, O Lord.	543
	13: 2 **S** I got a girdle, according to the word	2050.1
	13: 5 **S** I went, and hid it by Euphrates,	2050.1
	13:11 have I caused to cleave unto me the	3651
	17:11 **s** he that getteth riches, and not by right,	NIH
	18: 4 **s** he made it again another vessel,	2050.1
	18: 6 *are* in mine hand, O house of Israel.	3651
	19:11 **Even** **s** will I break this people and this	3602
	21: 2 **if** **s** be that the Lord will deal with us	194
	24: 2 could not be eaten, they were **s** bad.	4480
	24: 3 that cannot be eaten, they are **s** evil.	4480
	24: 5 **s** will I acknowledge them that are carried	4480
	24: 8 which cannot be eaten, they are **s** evil;	4480
	24: 8 **S** will I give Zedekiah the king of Judah,	3651
	26: 3 **If** **s** **be** they will hearken, and turn every	194

Jer	26: 7 **S** the priests and the prophets and all	2050.1
	28: 6 the Lord do **s:** the Lord perform thy	3651
	28:11 **Even s** will I break the yoke of	3602
	28:17 **S** Hananiah the prophet died the same	2050.1
	29:17 that cannot be eaten, they are **s** evil.	4480
	30: 7 for that day *is* great, **s that** none *is* like it:	4480
	31:28 s will I watch over them, to build,	3651
	32: 8 **S** Hanameel mine uncle's son came to	2050.1
	32:11 **S** I took the evidence of the purchase,	2050.1
	32:42 s will I bring upon them all the good that	3651
	33:22 s will I multiply the seed of David my	3651
	33:26 **s** that *I* will not take *any* of his seed *to be*	NIH
	34: 5 s shall they burn *odours* for thee;	3651
	35:11 of the Syrians: **s** we dwell at Jerusalem.	2050.1
	36:14 **S** Baruch the son of Neriah took the roll	2050.1
	36:15 our ears. **S** Baruch read *it* in their ears.	2050.1
	36:21 the king sent Jehudi to fet the roll:	2050.1
	37:14 s Irijah took Jeremiah, and brought him	2050.1
	38: 6 but mire: **s** Jeremiah sunk in the mire.	2050.1
	38:11 **S** Ebed-melech took the men with him,	2050.1
	38:12 under the cords. And Jeremiah did **s.**	3651
	38:13 **S** they drew up Jeremiah with cords,	2050.1
	38:16 **S** Zedekiah the king sware secretly unto	2050.1
	38:20 s it shall be well unto thee, and thy soul	2050.1
	38:23 s they *shall* bring out all thy wives and	2050.1
	38:27 **S** they left off speaking with him;	2050.1
	38:28 **S** Jeremiah abode in the court of	2050.1
	39:13 **S** Nebuzar-adan the captain of the guard	2050.1
	39:14 home: **s** he dwelt among the people.	2050.1
	40: 5 **S** the captain of the guard gave him	2050.1
	41: 7 it was **s,** when they came into the midst	NIH
	41: 8 **S** he forbare, and slew them not among	2050.1
	41:14 **S** all the people that Ishmael had carried	2050.1
	42:17 s shall it be with all the men that set	2050.1
	42:18 s shall my fury be poured forth upon you,	3651
	42:20 s declare unto us, and we will do *it.*	3651
	43: 4 **S** Johanan the son of Kareah, and all	2050.1
	43: 7 **S** they came *into* the land of Egypt:	2050.1
	44:14 **s that** none of the remnant of Judah,	2050.1
	44:22 **S** that the Lord could no longer bear,	2050.1
	46:18 as Carmel by the sea, **s** shall he come.	NIH
	48:30 it *shall* not *be* **s;** his lies shall not so	3651
	48:30 *shall* not *be* **s;** his lies shall not **s** effect *it.*	3651
	48:39 s shall Moab be a derision and a	2050.1
	50:40 **s** shall no man abide there, neither shall	NIH
	51: 8 for her pain, **if s be** she may be healed.	194
	51:49 s at Babylon shall fall the slain of all	1571
	51:60 **S** Jeremiah wrote in a book all the evil	2050.1
	52: 5 **S** the city was besieged unto the	2050.1
	52: 6 **s that** there was no bread for the people	2050.1
	52:26 **S** Nebuzar-adan the captain of the guard	2050.1
La	2:22 s that in the day of the Lord's anger	2050.1
	3:29 in the dust; **if s be** there may be hope.	194
	4:14 **s that** *men* could not touch their	871.1
	5:20 us for ever, *and* forsake us **s long** time?	753
Eze	1:18 they were **s** high that they were dreadful;	NIH
	1:28 s *was* the appearance of the brightness	3651
	3: 2 **S** I opened my mouth, and he caused	2050.1
	3:14 **S** the spirit lifted me up, and took me	2050.1
	4: 5 s shalt thou bear the iniquity of the	2050.1
	5:15 **S** it shall be a reproach and a taunt,	2050.1
	5:17 **S** will I send upon you famine and	2050.1
	6:14 **S** will I stretch out mine hand upon	2050.1
	8: 5 **S** I lift up mine eyes this way toward	2050.1
	8:10 **S** I went in and saw; and behold every	2050.1
	11:24 **S** the vision that I had seen went up	2050.1
	12: 7 I did **s** as I was commanded: I brought	3651
	12:11 as I have done, **s** shall it be done unto	3651
	13:14 **S** will I break down the wall that ye	2050.1
	13:14 **s that** the foundation thereof shall be	2050.1
	14:15 spoil it, **s that** it be desolate, that no	2050.1
	14:17 **s that** I cut off man and beast from it:	2050.1
	15: 6 s will I give the inhabitants of Jerusalem.	3651
	16:16 *things* shall not come, neither shall it be **s.**	NIH
	16:42 **S** will I make my fury towards thee to	2050.1
	16:44 As *is* the mother, **s** *is* her daughter.	NIH
	17: 6 s it became a vine, and brought forth	2050.1
	18: 4 s also the soul of the son *is* mine:	3509.1
	18:30 s iniquity shall not be your ruin.	2050.1
	19:14 **s that** she hath no strong rod *to be* a	2050.1
	20:36 s will I plead with you, saith the Lord	3651
	21:24 **s that** in all your doings your sins do	3807.1
	22:20 melt *it;* **s** will I gather *you* in mine anger	3651
	22:22 s ye be melted in the midst thereof;	2050.1
	23:18 **s** she discovered her whoredoms,	2050.1
	23:27 **s** that thou shalt not lift up thine eyes	3651
	23:44 **s** went they in unto Aholah and	3651
	24:18 **S** I spake unto the people in the	2050.1
	24:19 these *things are* to us, that thou doest **s?**	NIH
	28:14 I have set thee **s:** thou wast upon the holy	NIH
	31: 9 **S** that all the trees of Eden, that *were* in	2050.1
	33: 7 **S** thou, O son of man, I have set thee a	2050.1
	34:12 s will I seek out my sheep, and will	3651
	35:15 it was desolate, **s** will I do unto thee:	3651
	36:38 the waste cities be filled *with* flocks	3651
	37: 7 **S** I prophesied as I was commanded:	2050.1
	37:10 **S** I prophesied as he commanded me,	2050.1
	37:23 s shall they be my people, and I will be	2050.1
	38:20 **S that** the fishes of the sea, and the	2050.1
	39: 7 **S** will I make my holy name known in	2050.1
	39:10 **S** that they shall take no wood out of	2050.1
	39:22 **S** the house of Israel shall know that I	2050.1
	39:23 enemies: **s** fell they all by the sword.	2050.1
	40: 5 s he measured the breadth of the	2050.1
	40:47 **S** he measured the court, an hundred	2050.1

Eze	41: 4 **S** he measured the length thereof,	2050.1
	41: 7 s increased *from chamber* to	3651
	41:13 **S** he measured the house, an hundred	2050.1
	41:18 **s that** a palm tree *was* between a	2050.1
	41:19 **S that** the face of a man *was* toward	2050.1
	43: 5 **S** the spirit took me up, and brought me	2050.1
	43:15 **S** the altar *shall be* four cubits;	2050.1
	43:27 *that* upon the eighth day, and **s** forward,	NIH
	45:20 s thou shalt do the seventh *day*	3651
	45:20 simple: **s** shall ye reconcile the house.	2050.1
	47:21 **S** shall ye divide this land unto you	2050.1
Da	1: 5 s nourishing them three years, that at	2050.1
	1:14 **S** he consented to them in this matter,	2050.1
	2: 2 **S** they came and stood before the king.	2050.1
	2:15 Why *is* the decree **s** hasty from the king?	NIH
	2:42 s the kingdom shall be partly strong,	NIH
	3:17 If it be **s,** our God whom we serve *is* able	NIH
	5: 6 **s that** the joints of his loins were loosed	2050.3
	6:23 **S** Daniel was taken up out of the den,	2050.3
	6:28 **S** this Daniel prospered in the reign of	2050.3
	7:16 **S** he told me, and made me know	2050.1
	8: 4 **s that** no beasts might stand before him	2050.1
	8:17 **S** he came near where I stood:	2050.1
	10: 7 **s that** they fled to hide themselves.	2050.1
	11: 9 **S** the king of the south shall come into	2050.1
	11:15 **S** the king of the north shall come,	2050.1
	11:30 s shall he do; he shall even return,	2050.1
Hos	1: 3 **S** he went and took Gomer the daughter	2050.1
	3: 2 **S** I bought her to me for fifteen *pieces*	2050.1
	3: 3 *another* man: **s** *will* I also *be* for thee.	2050.1
	4: 7 increased, **s** they sinned against me:	3651
	6: 9 **s** the company of priests murder in the	NIH
	8: 7 **if s be** it yield, *the* strangers shall swallow	194
	10:15 **S** shall Beth-el do unto you because of	3602
	11: 2 they called them, **s** they went from them:	3651
	13: 6 to their pasture, **s** were they filled;	2050.1
	14: 2 s will we render the calves of our lips.	2050.1
Joel	2: 4 and as horsemen, **s** shall they run.	3651
	3:17 **S** shall ye know that I *am* the Lord	2050.1
Am	3:12 s shall the children of Israel be taken out	3651
	4: 8 **S** two *or* three cities wandered unto one	2050.1
	5: 9 **s that** the spoiled shall come against	2050.1
	5:14 **S** the Lord, the God of hosts, shall be	3651
Ob	1:16 s shall all the heathen drink continually,	NIH
Jnh	1: 3 s he paid the fare thereof, and went	2050.1
	1: 4 **s that** the ship was like to be broken.	2050.1
	1: 6 **S** the shipmaster came to him,	2050.1
	1: 6 **if s be that** God will think upon us,	194
	1: 7 **S** they cast lots, and the lot fell upon	2050.1
	1:12 sea; **s** shall the sea be calm unto you:	2050.1
	1:15 **S** they took up Jonah, and cast him	2050.1
	3: 3 **S** Jonah arose, and went unto Nineveh,	2050.1
	3: 5 **S** the people of Nineveh believed God,	2050.1
	4: 5 **S** Jonah went out of the city, and sat on	2050.1
	4: 6 **S** Jonah was exceeding glad of the	2050.1
Mic	2: 2 s they oppress a man and his house,	2050.1
	5:14 midst of thee: **s** will I destroy thy cities.	2050.1
	7: 3 mischievous desire: **s** they wrap it up.	2050.1
Zep	3: 6 are destroyed, **s** that there is no man,	NIH
	3: 7 s their dwelling should not be cut off,	NIH
Hag	2: 5 s my spirit remaineth among you:	2050.1
	2:14 **S** *is* this people, and so *is* this nation	3651
	2:14 people, and **s** *is* this nation before me,	3651
	2:14 s *is* every work of their hands;	3651
Zec	1: 6 to our doings, **s** hath he dealt with us.	3651
	1:14 **S** the angel that communed with me	2050.1
	1:21 **s that** no man did lift up his head	6310+3509.1
	3: 5 **S** they set a fair mitre upon his head,	2050.1
	4: 4 **S** I answered and spake to the angel	2050.1
	6: 7 **S** they walked to and fro through	2050.1
	7: 3 I have done these **s many** years?	4100+3509.1
	7:13 s they cried, and I would not hear, saith	3651
	8:13 s will I save you, and ye shall be a	3651
	8:15 **S** again have I thought in these days to do	3651
	10: 1 s the Lord *shall* make bright clouds,	NIH
	11:11 s the poor of the flock that waited upon	3651
	11:12 **S** they weighed *for* my price thirty	2050.1
	14:15 s shall be the plague of the horse,	NIH
Mal	3:13 have we spoken **s** much against thee?	NIH
Mt	1:17 **S** all the generations from Abraham to	3767
	3:15 said unto him, Suffer *it to be* **s** now:	NIG
	5:12 for **s** persecuted they the prophets which	3779
	5:16 Let your light **s** shine before men, that	3779
	5:19 and shall teach men **s,**	3779
	5:47 than others? do not even the publicans **s?**	3779
	6:30 if God **s** clothe the grass of the field,	3779
	7:12 should do to you, do ye even **s** to them:	3779
	7:17 s every good tree bringeth forth good	3779
	8:10 I have not found **s great** faith, no not in	5118
	8:13 thou hast believed, **s** be it done unto thee.	3779
	8:28 **s that** no *man* might pass by that way.	5620
	8:31 **S** the devils besought him, saying, If thou	1161
	9:19 and followed him, and **s** did his disciples.	NIG
	9:33 saying, It was never **s** seen in Israel.	3779
	11:26 **Even s,** Father: for **s** it seemed good in	3483
	11:26 Father: for **s** it seemed good in thy sight.	3779
	12:40 s shall the Son of man be three days and	3779
	12:45 *Even* **s** shall it be also unto this wicked	3779
	13: 2 **s that** he went into a ship, and sat;	5620
	13:27 **S** the servants of the householder came	1161
	13:32 **s that** the birds of the air come and lodge	5620
	13:40 s shall it be in the end of this world.	3779
	13:49 **S** shall it be at the end of the world:	3779
	15:33 we have **s much** bread in the wilderness,	5118
	15:33 as to fill **s great** a multitude?	5118

Mt	18:13 And if **s** be that he find it, verily I say unto	NIG
	18:14 *Even* **s** it is not the will of your Father	3779
	18:31 **S** when his fellowservants saw what was	1161
	18:35 **S** likewise shall my heavenly Father do	2532
	19: 8 but from the beginning it was not **s.**	3779
	19:10 If the case of the man be **s** with *his* wife,	3779
	19:12 which were **s** born from *their* mother's	3779
	20: 8 **S** when even was come, the lord of	1161
	20:16 the last shall be first, and the first last:	3779
	20:26 But it shall not be **s** among you:	3779
	20:34 **S** Jesus had compassion *on them,* and	1161
	22:10 **S** those servants went out into	2532
	23:28 ye also outwardly appear righteous	3779
	24:27 s shall also the coming of the Son of man	3779
	24:33 likewise ye, when ye shall see all these	3779
	24:37 But as the days of Noe *were,* **s** shall also	3779
	24:39 s shall also the coming of the Son of man	3779
	24:46 lord when he cometh shall find **s** doing.	3779
	25: 9 *Not* **s;** lest there be not enough for us and	NIG
	25:20 s he that had received five talents came	NIG
	27:64 the last error shall be worse than the	2532
	27:66 **S** they went, and made the sepulchre sure,	1161
	28:15 **S** they took the money, and did as they	1161
Mk	2: 2 *them,* no, **not s much as** about the door:	3366
	2: 8 that they **s** reasoned within themselves,	3779
	3:20 **s that** they could not so much as eat	5620
	3:20 that they could not **s much as** eat bread.	3383
	4: 1 **s** that he entered into a ship, and sat in	5620
	4:17 themselves, and **s** endure but for a time;	NIG
	4:26 he said, **S** is the kingdom of God, as if	3779
	4:32 **s that** the fowls of the air may lodge under	5620
	4:37 beat into the ship, **s that** it was now full.	5620
	4:40 he said unto them, Why are ye **s** fearful?	3779
	6:31 and they had **no** leisure	
	s much as to	2532+3761
	7:18 Are ye **s** without understanding also?	3779
	7:36 s much the more a great deal they	NIG
	8: 8 **S** they did eat, and were filled:	1161
	9: 3 s **as** no fuller on earth can white *them.*	3634
	10: 8 **s then** they are no more twain,	5620
	10:43 But **s** shall it not be among you:	3779
	13:29 **S** ye in like manner, when ye	2532+3779
	13:29 **S** ye in like manner, when ye	2532+3779
	14:59 But neither **s** did their witness agree	3779
	15: 5 answered nothing; **s that** Pilate marvelled.	5620
	15:15 And **s** Pilate, willing to content the people,	NIG
	15:39 saw that he **s** cried out, and gave up	3779
	16:19 **S** then after the Lord had spoken unto	3767
Lk	1:21 that he tarried **s** long in the temple.	NIG
	1:60 said, Not **s;** but he shall be called John.	NIG
	2: 6 And it was **that,** while they were there,	NIG
	2:21 which was **s** named of the angel before he	NIG
	5: 7 both the ships, **s that** they began to sink.	5620
	5:10 And **s** *was* also James, and John, *the* sons	3668
	5:15 But **s** much the more went there a fame	NIG
	6: 3 Have ye not read **s much as** this,	NIG
	6:10 And he did **s:** and his hand was restored	3779
	6:26 s did their fathers to the false	846+2596+3588
	7: 9 I have not found **s great** faith, no, not in	5118
	9:15 they did **s,** and made *them* all sit	3779
	10:21 even **s,** Father; for so it seemed good in	3483
	10:21 Father; for **s** it seemed good in thy sight.	3779
	11: 2 Thy will be done, as in heaven, **s** in earth.	2532
	11:30 s shall also the Son of man be to this	3779
	12:21 **S** is he that layeth up treasure for himself,	3779
	12:28 If then God **s** clothe the grass, which	3779
	12:38 come in the third watch, and find *them* **s,**	3779
	12:43 lord when he cometh shall find **s** doing.	3779
	12:54 say, There cometh a shower; and **s** it is.	2532
	14:21 **S** that servant came, and shewed his lord	2532
	14:33 likewise, whosoever *he be* of you that	3767
	16: 5 **S** he called every one of his lord's debtors	2532
	16:26 **s that** they which would pass from hence	3704
	17:10 **S** likewise ye, when ye shall have done all	3779
	17:24 s shall also the Son of man be in his day.	3779
	17:26 s shall it be also in the days of the Son of	3779
	18:13 would **not** lift up **s much as** *his* eyes unto	3761
	18:39 but he cried **s** much the more, *Thou* Son	NIG
	20:15 **S** they cast him out of the vineyard,	2532
	20:20 that **s** they might deliver him unto	NIG
	21:31 **S** likewise ye, when ye see these *things*	3779
	21:34 and **s** that day come upon you unawares.	NIG
	22:26 ye *shall* not be **s:** but he that is greatest	3779
	24:24 found *it* even **s** as the women had said:	3779
Jn	3: 8 **s** is every one that is born of the Spirit.	3779
	3:14 even **s** must the Son of man be lifted up:	3779
	3:16 For God **s** loved the world, that he gave	3779
	4:40 When the Samaritans were come unto	3767
	4:46 **S** Jesus came again into Cana of Galilee,	3767
	4:53 the father knew that *it was* at the same	3767
	5:21 and quickeneth *them;* even **s** the Son	3779
	5:26 s hath he given to the Son to have life in	3779
	6: 9 but what are they among **s many?**	5118
	6:10 the men sat down, *in* number about	3767
	6:19 **S** when they had rowed about five and	3767
	6:57 s he that eateth me, even he shall live by	2532
	7:43 **S** there was a division among the people	3767
	8: 7 **S** when they continued asking him, he lift	1161
	8:59 the midst of them, and **s** passed by.	3779
	10:15 me, even **s** know I the Father:	2504
	11:28 And when she had **s** said, she went her	3778
	12:37 had done **s many** miracles before them,	5118
	12:50 as the Father said unto me, **s** I speak.	3779
	13:12 **S** after he had washed their feet,	3767
	13:13 and Lord: and ye say well; for **s** I am.	NIG
	13:33 I go, ye cannot come; **s** now I say to you.	2532

S

Jn 14: 2 if *it* were not **s**, I would have told you. NIG
14: 9 Have I been **s** long time with you, 5118
14:31 gave me commandment, *even* **s** I do. 3779
15: 8 much fruit; **s** shall ye be my disciples. 2532
15: 9 Father hath loved me, **s** have I loved you: 2504
17:18 **s** have I also sent them into the world. NIG
18:15 followed Jesus, and **s** did another disciple: NIG
18:22 saying, Answerest thou the high priest **s**? 3779
20: 4 **S** they ran both together: and the other 1161
20:20 And when he had **s** said, he shewed unto 3778
20:21 Father hath sent me, even **s** send I you. NIG
21:11 for **all** there were **s** **many**, *yet* was not 5118
21:15 **S** when they had dined, Jesus saith to 3767
Ac 1:11 shall **s** come *in* like manner as ye have 3779
3:12 why look ye **s** earnestly on us, as though NIG
3:18 Christ should suffer, he hath **s** fulfilled. 3779
4:21 **S** me whether ye sold the land for **s** much? 1161
5: 8 me whether ye sold the land for **s** **much**? 5118
5: 8 so much? And she said, Yea, for **s** **much**. 5118
5:32 and **s** *is* also the Holy Ghost, whom God NIG
7: 1 said the high priest, Are these **things s**? 3779
7: 5 in it, **no**, not **s** much as to set his foot on: 3761
7: 8 and **s** *Abraham* begat Isaac, 3779
7:15 **S** Jacob went down into Egypt, and died, 1161
7:19 **s** that *they* cast out their young children, 3588
7:51 Holy Ghost: as your fathers *did*, **s** do ye. 2532
8:32 his shearer, **s** opened he not his mouth: 3779
10:14 But Peter said, **Not s**, Lord; for I have 3365
11: 8 But I said, **Not s**, Lord: for nothing 3365
12: 8 And **s** he did. And he saith unto him, 3779
12:15 she constantly affirmed that it was *even* **s**. 3779
13: 4 **S** they, being sent forth by the Holy Ghost, 3767
13: 8 But Elymas the sorcerer (for **s** is his name 3779
13:47 For **s** hath the Lord commanded us, 3779
14: 1 and **s** spake, that a great multitude both of 3779
15:30 **S** when they were dismissed, they came to 3767
15:39 And the contention was **s** sharp *between* NIG
15:39 and **s** Barnabas took Mark, and sailed unto NIG
16: 5 **And s** were the churches established in 3767
16:26 **s** that the foundations of the prison were 5620
17:11 whether those *things* were **s**. 3779
17:33 **S** Paul departed from among them. 3779
19: 2 We have **not s** **much as** heard 235+3761
19:10 **s** that all they which dwelt in Asia heard 5620
19:12 **S** that from his body were brought 2532+5620
19:14 Jew, *and* chief of the priests, which did **s**. 3778
19:16 **s** that *they* fled out of that house naked 5620
19:20 **S** mightily grew the word of God and 3779
19:22 **S** he sent into Macedonia two of them 1161
19:27 **S** *that* not only this our craft is in danger 1161
20:11 *even* till break of day, **s** he departed. 3779
20:13 for **s** had he appointed, minding himself 3779
20:24 **s** that *I* might finish my course with joy, 5613
20:35 I have shewed you all *things*, how that **s** 3779
21:11 **S** shall the Jews at Jerusalem bind the man 3779
21:35 when he came upon the stairs, **s** it was, 4819
22:24 know wherefore they cried **s** against him. 3779
23: 7 And when he had **s** said, there arose a 3778
23:11 **s** must thou bear witness also at Rome. 3779
23:18 He took him, and brought *him* to the 3767
23:22 **S** the chief captain then let the young man 3767
24: 9 saying that these *things* were **s**. 3779
24:14 **s** worship I the God of my fathers, 3779
27:17 strake sail, and **s** were driven. 3779
27:44 **s** it came to pass, that *they* escaped all 3779
28: 9 **S** when this was done, others also, 3767
28:14 seven days: and **s** we went toward Rome. 3779
Ro 1:15 **S**, as much as in me is, I am ready to 3779
1:20 **s** that they are without excuse: 1519+3588
4:18 which was spoken, **S** shall thy seed be. 3779
5: 3 not only **s**, but we glory in tribulations NIG
5:11 And not only **s**, but we also joy in God NIG
5:12 **s** death passed upon all men, for that all 3779
5:15 not as the offence, **s** also *is* the free gift. 3779
5:16 as *it was* by one that sinned, **s** *is* the gift: NIG
5:18 **s** by the righteousness of one *the free* 3779
5:19 **s** by the obedience of one shall many be 3779
5:21 **s** even might grace reign through 3779
6: 3 **many** of us **as** were baptized into Jesus 3745
6: 4 *even* **s** we also should walk in newness of 3779
6:19 *even* **s** now yield your members servants 3779
7: 2 the law to *her* husband **s** long as he liveth; NIG
7: 3 **S** then, if, while *her* husband liveth, she be 686
7: 3 **s** that she is no adulteress, though she be 3588
7:25 **S** then with the mind I myself serve the 686
8: 8 **S** then they that are in the flesh cannot 1161
8: 9 if **s** be that the Spirit of God dwell in you. 1512
8:17 if **s** be that we suffer with *him*, that we 1512
9:16 **S** then *it* is not of him that willeth, nor of 686
10:17 **S** then faith *cometh* by hearing, 686
11: 5 **s** then at *this* present time also there is 3779
11:16 if the root *be* holy, **s** *are* the branches. 2532
11:26 And **s** all Israel shall be saved: as it is 3779
11:31 *Even* **s** have these also not now believed, 3779
12: 5 **S** we, *being* many, are one body in Christ, 3779
12:20 for **s** doing thou shalt heap coals of fire 3778
14:12 **S** then every one of us shall give account 686
15:19 **s** that from Jerusalem, and round about 5620
15:20 Yea, **s** I strived to preach the gospel, 5620
1Co 1: 7 **S** that ye come behind in no gift; 5620
2:11 **s** the *things* of God knoweth no *man*, 3779
3: 7 **S** then neither is he that planteth any 5620
3:15 he himself shall be saved; yet **s** as by fire. 3779
4: 1 Let a man **s** account of us, as of 3779
5: 1 fornication as is **not s** **much as** named 3761

1Co 5: 3 him that hath **s** done this *deed*, 3779
6: 5 Is it **s**, that there is not a wise *man* 3779
7:17 hath called every one, **s** let him walk. 3779
7:17 And **s** ordain I in all churches. 3779
7:26 *I say*, that *it* is good for a man **s** to be. 3779
7:36 need require, let him do what he will, 3779
7:37 hath **s** decreed in his heart that *he* will 3778
7:38 **S** then he that giveth *her* in marriage 5620
7:40 But she is happier if she **s** abide, after my 3779
8:12 But when ye sin **s** against the brethren, 3779
9:14 Even **s** hath the Lord ordained that they 3779
9:15 *things*, that it should be **s** done unto me: 3779
9:24 the prize? **S** run, that ye may obtain. 3779
9:26 I therefore **s** run, not as uncertainly; NIG
9:26 **s** fight I, not as one that beateth the air: 3779
11:12 *even* **s** *is* the man also by the woman; 3779
11:28 **s** let him eat of *that* bread, and drink of 3779
12:12 being many, are one body: **s** also *is* Christ. 3779
13: 2 **s** that *I* could remove mountains, 5620
14: 9 **S** likewise you, except ye utter by 3779
14:10 **s** **many** kinds of voices in the world, 5118
14:12 Even **s** ye, forasmuch as ye are zealous of 3779
14:25 and **s** falling down on *his* face he will 3779
15:11 or they, **s** we preach, and so ye believed. 3779
15:11 or they, **s** we preach, and **s** ye believed. 3779
15:15 up, **if s** be that the dead rise not. 686+1512
15:22 even in Christ shall all be made alive. 3779
15:42 **S** also *is* the resurrection of the dead. It is 3779
15:45 And **s** it is written, The first man Adam 1161
15:54 **S** when this corruptible shall have put on 1161
16: 1 to the churches of Galatia, even **s** do ye. 3779
2Co 1: 5 **s** our consolation also aboundeth by 3779
1: 7 **s** *shall ye* be also of the consolation. 3779
1:10 Who delivered us from **s great** a death, 5082
2: 3 **S** that contrariwise *ye ought* rather to 5620
3: 7 **s** that the children of Israel could not 5620
4:12 **S** then death worketh in us, but life in 5620
5: 3 **s** be that being clothed we shall not be 2532
7: 7 toward me; **s** that I rejoiced the more. 5620
7:14 even **s** our boasting, which *I* made before 3779
8: 6 he would also finish in you the same 3779
8:11 **s** *there* may be a performance also out of 3779
9: 7 in *his* heart, **s** let him give; not grudgingly, NIG
10: 7 as he *is* Christ's, even **s** *are* we Christ's. 3779
11: 3 **s** your minds should be corrupted from 3779
11: 9 to you, and **s** will I keep *myself*. NIG
11:22 **s** am I. Are they Israelites? so *am* I. NIG
11:22 **s** am I. Are they the seed of Abraham? NIG
11:22 Are they the seed of Abraham? **s** *am* I. 2504
12:16 But be it **s**, I did not burden you: 1510
Gal 1: 6 I marvel that you are **s** soon removed 3779
1: 9 As we said before, **s** say I now again, If 2532
3: 3 Are ye **s** foolish? having begun in 3779
3: 4 Have ye suffered **s** **many** *things* in vain? 5118
3: 9 **S** then they which be of faith are blessed 5620
4: 3 Even **s** we, when we were children, were 3779
4:29 was *born* after the Spirit, even **s** *it is* now. 3779
4:31 **S** then, brethren, we are not children of 686
5:17 **s** that ye cannot do the *things* that ye 2443
6: 2 and **s** fulfil the law of Christ. 3779
Eph 2:15 of twain one new man, **s** making peace; NIG
4:20 But ye have not **s** learned Christ; NIG
4:21 If **s** be that ye have heard him, 1489
5:24 **s** *let* the wives *be* to their own husbands 3779
5:28 **S** ought men to love their wives as their 3779
5:33 love his wife even as himself; 3779
Php 1:13 **S** that my bonds in Christ are manifest in 3779
1:20 **s** now also Christ shall be magnified in my NIG
2:23 **s** **soon** as I shall see how it will go 302+5613
3:17 mark them which walk **s** as ye have us 3779
4: 1 joy and crown, **s** stand fast in the Lord, 3779
Col 2: 6 Christ Jesus the Lord, **s** walk ye in him: NIG
3:13 even as Christ forgave you, **s** also *do* ye. 3779
1Th 1: 7 **S** that ye were ensamples to all that 5620
1: 8 **S** that we need not to speak any *thing*. 5620
2: 4 in trust with the gospel, *even* **s** we speak; 3779
2: 8 **S** being affectionately desirous of you, 3779
4: 1 **s** ye would abound more and more. NIG
4:14 *even* **s** also which sleep in Jesus will 3779
4:17 and **s** shall we ever be with the Lord. 3779
5: 2 the Lord **s** cometh as a thief in the night. 3779
2Th 1: 4 **S** that we ourselves glory in you in 5620
2: 4 **s** that he as God sitteth in the temple of 5620
3:17 is the token in every epistle: **s** I write. 3779
1Ti 1: 4 than godly edifying which is in faith: **s** do. NIG
3:11 Even **s** *must their* wives *be* grave, 5615
6:20 and oppositions of science falsely called: NIG
2Ti 3: 8 do these also resist the truth: 3779
Heb 1: 4 made **much** better than the angels, 5118
2: 3 we escape, if we neglect **s** great salvation; NIG
3:11 **S** I sware in my wrath, They shall not 5613
3:19 **S** we see that they could not enter in 2532
4: 7 In David, To day, after **s** long a time; 5118
5: 3 **s** also for himself, to offer for sins. 3779
5: 5 **S** also Christ glorified not himself to be 3779
6:15 And **s**, after he had patiently endured, 3779
7: 9 And as *I* may **s** say, Levi also, 2031
7:22 **s** **much** was Jesus made a surety of a 5118
9:28 **S** Christ was once offered to bear the sins 3779
10:25 *one another*: and **s** **much** the more, 5118
10:33 companions of them that were **s** used. 3779
11: 3 **s** that *things* which are seen were 1519+3588
11:12 **s** *many* as the stars of the sky in multitude, NIG
12: 1 about with **s great** a cloud of witnesses, 5118
12: 1 and the sin which doth **s** easily beset *us*, NIG

Heb 12:20 And if **s** much as a beast touch NIG
12:21 terrible was the sight, *that* Moses 3779
13: 6 **S** that we may boldly say, The Lord *is* my 5620
Jas 1:11 **s** also shall the rich *man* fade away in his 3779
2:12 **S** speak ye, and so do, as they that shall be 3779
2:12 So speak ye, and **s** do, as they that shall be 3779
2:17 Even **s** faith, if it hath no works, is dead, 3779
2:26 is dead, **s** faith without works is dead also. 3779
3: 4 which though they be **s great**, 5082
3: 5 Even **s** the tongue is a little member, 3779
3: 6 **s** is the tongue amongst our members, 3779
3:10 brethren, these *things* ought not **s** to be. 3779
3:12 **s** *can* no fountain *both* yield salt water 3779
1Pe 1:15 **s** be ye holy in all *manner of* conversation; 2532
2: 3 **If s** be ye have tasted that the Lord *is* 1512
2:15 For **s** is the will of God, that with well 3779
3:17 For *it* is better, if the will of God be **s s**, 2309
4:10 *even* **s** minister the same one to another, NIG
5:13 saluteth you; and **s** *doth* Marcus my son. NIG
2Pe 1:11 For **s** an entrance shall be ministered unto 3779
1Jn 2: 6 in him ought himself also **s** to walk, 3779
4:11 Beloved, if God **s** loved us, we ought also 3779
4:17 because as he is, **s** are we in this world. 2532
Rev 1: 7 shall wail because of him. **Even s**, Amen. 3483
2:15 **S** hast thou also them that hold the 3779
3:16 **S** *then* because thou art lukewarm, 3779
8:12 **s** as the third *part* of them was darkened 2443
13:13 that he maketh fire come down from 2532
16: 7 **Even s**, Lord God Almighty, true and 3483
16:18 **s** mighty an earthquake, *and* so great. 3779
16:18 so mighty an earthquake, *and* **s** great. 3779
17: 3 **S** he carried me away in the spirit into 2532
18:17 hour **s great** riches is come to nought. 5118
22:20 Amen. **Even s**, come, Lord Jesus. 3483

SOAKED (1)

Isa 34: 7 their land shall be **s** with blood, 7301

SOAP See FULLER; SOPE

SOBER (12) [SOBRIETY]

2Co 5:13 or whether we be **s**, *it is* for your cause. 4993
1Th 5: 6 as do other; but let us watch and be **s**. 3525
5: 8 But let us, who are of the day, be **s**, 3525
1Ti 3: 2 vigilant, **s** of good behaviour, given to 4998
3:11 not slanderers, **s**, faithful in all *things*. 3524
Tit 1: 8 a lover of good *men*, **s**, just, holy, 4998
2: 2 That the aged men be **s**, grave, temperate, 3524
2: 4 may **teach** the young *women* to be **s**, 4994
2: 6 men likewise exhort to be **s** minded. 4993
1Pe 1:13 be **s**, and hope to the end for the grace 3525
4: 7 be ye therefore, and watch unto prayer. 4993
5: 8 Be **s**, be vigilant; because your adversary 3525

SOBERLY (2) [SOBRIETY]

Ro 12: 3 to think **s**, according as God hath dealt 4993
Tit 2:12 and worldly lusts we should live **s**, 4996

SOBERNESS (1) [SOBRIETY]

Ac 26:25 but speak forth *the* words of truth and **s**. 4997

SOBRIETY (2) [SOBER, SOBERLY, SOBERNESS]

1Ti 2: 9 apparel, with shamefastness and **s**; 4997
2:15 in faith and charity and holiness with **s**. 4997

SOCHO (1)

1Ch 4:18 Heber the father of **S**, and Jekuthiel 7755

SOCHOH (1)

1Ki 4:10 to him *pertained* **S**, and all the land of 7755

SOCKET (1) [SOCKETS]

Ex 38:27 of the hundred talents, a talent for a **s**. 134

SOCKETS (54) [SOCKET]

Ex 26:19 thou shalt make forty **s** of silver under 134
26:19 two **s** under one board for his two tenons, 134
26:19 two **s** under another board for his two 134
26:21 their forty **s** *of* silver; two sockets under 134
26:21 two **s** under one board, and two sockets 134
26:21 one board, and two **s** under another board. 134
26:25 and their **s** *of* silver, sixteen sockets; 134
26:25 their sockets *of* silver, sixteen **s**; 134
26:25 two **s** under one board, and two sockets 134
26:25 one board, and two **s** under another board. 134
26:32 shall be *of* gold, upon the four **s** of silver. 134
26:37 and thou shalt cast five **s** of brass for them. 134
27:10 and their twenty **s** *shall be of* brass; 134
27:11 twenty pillars and their twenty **s** *of* brass; 134
27:12 fifty cubits: their pillars ten, and their **s** ten. 134
27:14 their pillars three, and their **s** three. 134
27:15 *cubits*: their pillars three, and their **s** three. 134
27:16 their pillars *shall be* four, and their **s** four. 134
27:17 hooks *shall be of* silver, and their **s** *of* brass. 134
27:18 *of* fine twined linen, and their **s** *of* brass. 134
35:11 his boards, his bars, his pillars, and his **s**, 134
35:17 their **s**, and the hanging for the door of 134
36:24 forty **s** of silver he made under the twenty 134
36:24 two **s** under one board for his two tenons, 134
36:24 two **s** under another board for his two 134
36:26 their forty **s** *of* silver; two sockets under 134
36:26 two **s** under one board, and two sockets 134
36:26 one board, and two **s** under another board. 134
36:30 their **s** *were* sixteen sockets *of* silver, 134
36:30 their sockets *were* sixteen **s** *of* silver, 134

Ex 36:30 sockets *of* silver, under every board two **s**. 134
36:36 gold; and he cast for them four **s** of silver. 134
36:38 with gold: but their five **s** *were of* brass. 134
38:10 *were* twenty, and their **s** of brass twenty; 134
38:11 *were* twenty, and their **s** *of* brass twenty; 134
38:12 fifty cubits, their pillars ten, and their **s** ten; 134
38:14 their pillars three, and their **s** three. 134
38:15 their pillars three, and their **s** three. 134
38:17 the **s** for the pillars *were of* brass; the hooks 134
38:19 pillars *were* four, and their **s** *of* brass four; 134
38:27 of silver were cast the **s** of the sanctuary, 134
38:27 of the sanctuary, and the **s** of the vail; 134
38:27 hundred **s** of the hundred talents, a talent 134
38:30 therewith he made the **s** to the door of 134
38:31 the **s** of the court round about, 134
38:31 the **s** of the court gate, and all the pins of 134
39:33 boards, his bars, and his pillars, and his **s**, 134
39:40 his **s**, and the hanging for the court gate, 134
40:18 his **s**, and set up the boards thereof, 134
Nu 3:36 the **s** thereof, and all the vessels thereof, 134
3:37 and their **s**, and their pins, and their cords. 134
4:31 and the pillars thereof, and **s** thereof, 134
4:32 their **s**, and their pins, and their cords, 134
SS 5:15 *as* pillars of marble, set upon a **s** of fine gold; 134

SOCO See SHOCHO; SHOCO; SOCHO

SOCOH (2)
Jos 15:35 Jarmuth, and Adullam, **S**, and Azekah, 7755
15:48 the mountains, Shamir, and Jattir, and **S**, 7755

SOD (2) [SODDEN]
Ge 25:29 Jacob **s** pottage: and Esau came from 2102
2Ch 35:13 the *other* holy *offerings* **s** they in pots, 1310

SODA See NITRE

SODDEN (6) [SOD]
Ex 12: 9 **s at all** with water, but roast with 1310+1311
Lev 6:28 the earthen vessel wherein it is **s** shall be 1310
6:28 if it be in a brasen pot, it shall be both 1310
Nu 6:19 the priest shall take the **s** shoulder of 1311
1Sa 2:15 he will not have **s** flesh of thee, but raw. 1310
La 4:10 The hands of the pitiful women have **s** 1310

SODERING (1)
Isa 41: 7 the anvil, saying, It *is* ready for the **s**: 1694

SODI (1)
Nu 13:10 the tribe of Zebulun, Gaddiel the son of **S**. 5476

SODOM (48) [SODOMA, SODOMITE, SODOMITES]
Ge 10:19 as thou goest unto **S**, and Gomorrah, 5467
13:10 before the LORD destroyed **S** and 5467
13:12 the plain, and pitched his tent toward **S**. 5467
13:13 the men of **S** were wicked and 5467
14: 2 *That these* made war with Bera king of **S**, 5467
14: 8 there went out the king of **S**, and the king 5467
14:10 the kings of **S** and Gomorrah fled, 5467
14:11 took all the goods of **S** and Gomorrah, 5467
14:12 who dwelt in **S**, and his goods, 5467
14:17 the king of **S** went out to meet him after 5467
14:21 the king of **S** said unto Abram, Give me 5467
14:22 Abram said to the king of **S**, I have lift up 5467
18:16 up from thence, and looked toward **S**: 5467
18:20 Because the cry of **S** and Gomorrah is 5467
18:22 faces from thence, and went toward **S**: 5467
18:26 If I find in **S** fifty righteous within the city, 5467
19: 1 there came two angels to **S** at even; 5467
19: 1 at even; and Lot sat in the gate of **S**: 5467
19: 4 the men of the city, *even* the men of **S**, 5467
19:24 the LORD rained upon **S** and 5467
19:28 he looked toward **S** and Gomorrah, 5467
Dt 29:23 like the overthrow of **S**, and Gomorrah, 5467
32:32 For their vine *is* of the vine of **S**, 5467
Isa 1: 9 we should have been as **S**, *and* we should 5467
1:10 the word of the LORD, ye rulers of **S**; 5467
3: 9 declare their sin as **S**, they hide *it* not. 5467
13:19 shall be as when God overthrew **S** and 5467
Jer 23:14 they are all of them unto me as **S**, 5467
49:18 As *in* the overthrow of **S** and Gomorrah 5467
50:40 As God overthrew **S** and Gomorrah and 5467
La 4: 6 than the punishment of the sin of **S**, 5467
Eze 16:46 at thy right hand, *is* **S** and her daughters. 5467
16:48 the Lord GOD, **S** thy sister hath not done, 5467
16:49 this was the iniquity of thy sister **S**, pride, 5467
16:53 the captivity of **S** and her daughters, 5467
16:55 When thy sisters, **S** and her daughters, 5467
16:56 For thy sister **S** was not mentioned by thy 5467
Am 4:11 as God overthrew **S** and Gomorrah, 5467
Zep 2: 9 Surely Moab shall be as **S**, and the 5467
Mt 10:15 It shall be more tolerable for the land of **S** 4670
11:23 been done in thee, had been done in **S**, 4670
11:24 for the land of **S** in the day of judgment, 4670
Mk 6:11 It shall be more tolerable for **S** 4670
Lk 10:12 it shall be more tolerable in that day for **S**, 4670
17:29 But the *same* day that Lot went out of **S** it 4670
2Pe 2: 6 And turning the cities of **S** and 4670
Jude 1: 7 *Even* as **S** and Gomorrha, and the cities 4670
Rev 11: 8 which spiritually is called **S** and Egypt, 4670

SODOMA (1) [SODOM]
Ro 9:29 we had been as **S**, and been made like 4670

SODOMITE (1) [SODOM]
Dt 23:17 of Israel, nor a **s** of the sons of Israel. 6945

SODOMITES (4) [SODOM]
1Ki 14:24 there were also **s** in the land: *and* they 6945
15:12 he took away the **s** out of the land, 6945
22:46 the remnant of the **s**, which remained in 6945
2Ki 23: 7 he brake down the houses of the **s**, 6945

SOEVER (16) [EVER, SO]
Lev 15: 9 **what** saddle he rideth upon that 834+3605
17: 3 **What man s** *there be* of the house of 376+376
22: 4 **What man s** of the seed of Aaron *is* a 376+376
Dt 12:32 **What** thing s I command you, 834+3605
2Sa 15:35 **what** thing s thou shalt hear out 834+3605
24: 3 how many **s** they be, an hundredfold, 3509.1
1Ki 8:38 and supplication **s** be *made* by any man, 3605
2Ch 6:29 what supplication **s** shall be *made* of any 834
19:10 **what** cause **s** shall come to you of 834+3605
Mk 3:28 blasphemies **wherewith s** they shall 302+3745
6:10 In **what place s** ye enter into a 1437+3699
11:24 What *things* **s** ye desire, when ye pray, 302
Jn 5:19 for what *things* **s** he doeth, these 302+3739
20:23 Whose **s** sins ye remit, they are remitted 302
20:23 whose **s** *sins* ye retain, they are retained. 302
Ro 3:19 we know that **what** *things* **s** the law 3745

SOFT (8) [SOFTER, SOFTLY]
Job 23:16 For God **maketh** my heart **s**, 7401
41: 3 will he speak **s** *words* unto thee? 7390
Ps 65:10 thou **makest** it **s** with showers: 4127
Pr 15: 1 A **s** answer turneth away wrath: 7390
25:15 and a tongue breaketh the bone. 7390
Mt 11: 8 A man clothed in **s** raiment? behold, 3120
11: 8 they that wear **s** *clothing* are in kings' 3120
Lk 7:25 A man clothed in **s** raiment? Behold, 3120

SOFTER (1) [SOFT]
Ps 55:21 his words were **s** than oil, yet *were* they 7401

SOFTLY (7) [SOFT]
Ge 33:14 will lead on **s**, according as 328+3807.1
Jdg 4:21 went **s** unto him, 3814+871.1+1886.1
Ru 3: 7 *of corn:* and she came **s**, 3909+871.1+1886.1
1Ki 21:27 fasted, and lay in sackcloth, and went **s**. 328
Isa 8: 6 the waters of Shiloah that go **s**, 328+3807.1
38:15 himself hath done *it:* I shall **go s** all my 1718
Ac 27:13 And when the south wind **blew s**, 5285

SOIL (1)
Eze 17: 8 It *was* planted in a good **s** by great waters, 7704

SOJOURN (33) [SOJOURNED, SOJOURNER, SOJOURNERS, SOJOURNETH, SOJOURNING]
Ge 12:10 Abram went down into Egypt to **s** there; 1481
19: 9 said *again,* This one *fellow* came in to **s**, 1481
26: 3 **S** in this land, and I will be with thee, 1481
47: 4 For to **s** in the land are we come; 1481
Ex 12:48 when a stranger shall **s** among you, 1481
Lev 17: 8 or of the strangers which **s** among you, 1481
17:10 or of the strangers that **s** among you, 1481
17:13 or of the strangers that **s** among you, 1481
19:33 if a stranger **s** with thee in your land, 1481
20: 2 or of the strangers that **s** in Israel, 1481
25:45 of the strangers that do **s** among you, 1481
Nu 9:14 if a stranger shall **s** among you, 1481
15:14 if a stranger **s** with you, or whosoever *be* 1481
Jdg 17: 8 to **s** where he could find *a place:* 1481
17: 9 I go to **s** where I may find *a place.* 1481
Ru 1: 1 went to **s** in the country of Moab, 1481
1Ki 17:20 evil upon the widow with whom I **s**, 1481
2Ki 8: 1 and wheresoever thou canst sojourn: 1481
8: 1 and sojourn wheresoever thou canst **s**: 1481
Ps 120: 5 Woe is me, that I **s** in Mesech, that I 1481
Isa 23: 7 her own feet shall carry her afar off to **s**. 1481
52: 4 down aforetime *into* Egypt to **s** there; 1481
Jer 42:15 to enter *into* Egypt, and go to **s** there; 1481
42:17 set their faces to go *into* Egypt to **s** there; 1481
42:22 the place whither ye desire to go *and* to **s**. 1481
43: 2 thee to say, Go not *into* Egypt to **s** there: 1481
44:12 to go *into* the land of Egypt to **s** there, 1481
44:14 are gone into the land of Egypt to **s**, 1481
44:28 that are gone into the land of Egypt to **s** 1481
La 4:15 the heathen, They shall no more **s** *there.* 4033
Eze 20:38 forth out of the country where they **s**, 1481
47:22 to the strangers that **s** among you, 1481
Ac 7: 6 his seed should **s** in a strange land; 1510+3941

SOJOURNED (12) [SOJOURN]
Ge 20: 1 between Kadesh and Shur, and **s** in Gerar. 1481
21:23 and to the land wherein thou hast **s**. 1481
21:34 Abraham **s** in the Philistines' land many 1481
32: 4 I have **s** with Laban, and stayed *there* 1481
35:27 *is* Hebron, where Abraham and Isaac **s**. 1481
Dt 18: 6 where he **s**, and come with all the desire 1481
26: 5 **s** there with a few, and became there a 1481
Jdg 17: 7 Judah, who *was* a Levite, and he **s** there. 1481
19:16 of mount Ephraim; and he **s** in Gibeah: 1481
2Ki 8: 2 in the land of the Philistines seven years. 1481
Ps 105:23 Egypt; and Jacob in the land of Ham. 1481
Heb 11: 9 By faith he **s** in the land of promise, as *in* 3939

SOJOURNER (8) [SOJOURN]
Ge 23: 4 I *am* a stranger and a **s** with you: give me 8453
Lev 22:10 eat *of* the holy *thing:* a **s** of the priest's, 8453

Lev 25:35 *though he be* a stranger, or a **s**; that he 8453
25:40 *and* as a **s**, he shall be with thee: 8453
25:47 if a **s** or stranger wax rich by thee, 1616
25:47 sell himself unto the stranger *or* **s** by thee, 8453
Nu 35:15 the stranger, and for the **s** among them: 8453
Ps 39:12 with thee, *and* a **s**, as all my fathers *were.* 8453

SOJOURNERS (3) [SOJOURN]
Lev 25:23 for ye *were* strangers and **s** with me. 8453
2Sa 4: 3 Gittaim, and were **s** there until this day.) 1481
1Ch 29:15 before thee, and **s**, as *were* all our fathers: 8453

SOJOURNETH (15) [SOJOURN]
Ex 3:22 of her that **s** in her house, jewels of silver, 1481
12:49 and unto the stranger that **s** among you. 1481
Lev 16:29 or a stranger that **s** among you: 1481
17:12 neither shall any stranger that **s** among 1481
18:26 nor any stranger that **s** among you: 1481
25: 6 and for thy stranger that **s** with thee, 1481
Nu 15:15 also for the stranger that **s** *with you,* an 1481
15:16 and for the stranger that **s** with you. 1481
15:26 and the stranger that **s** among them; 1481
15:29 and for the stranger that **s** among them. 1481
19:10 unto the stranger that **s** among them, for 1481
Jos 20: 9 and for the stranger that **s** among them, 1481
Ezr 1: 4 remaineth in any place where he **s**, 1481
Eze 14: 7 or of the stranger that **s** in Israel, 1481
47:23 to pass, *that* in what tribe the stranger **s**, 1481

SOJOURNING (3) [SOJOURN]
Ex 12:40 Now the **s** of the children of Israel, 4186
Jdg 19: 1 there was a certain Levite **s** on the side 1481
1Pe 1:17 pass the time of your **s** *here* in fear: 3940

SOLACE (1)
Pr 7:18 the morning: let us **s** ourselves with loves. 5965

SOLD (82) [SELL]
Ge 25:33 to him: and he **s** his birthright unto Jacob. 4376
31:15 for he hath **s** us, and hath quite devoured 4376
37:28 Joseph to the Ishmeelites for twenty 4376
37:36 the Medanites **s** him into Egypt unto 4376
41:56 the storehouses, and **s** unto the Egyptians; 7666
42: 6 *it was* that **s** to all the people of the land: 7666
45: 4 your brother, whom ye **s** into Egypt. 4376
45: 5 angry with yourselves, that ye **s** me hither: 4376
47:20 for the Egyptians **s** every man his field, 4376
47:22 them: wherefore they **s** not their lands. 4376
Ex 22: 3 then he shall be **s** for his theft. 4376
Lev 25:23 The land shall not be **s** for ever: for the 4376
25:25 hath **s** away *some* of his possession, 4376
25:25 shall he redeem **that which** his brother is 4465
25:27 overplus unto the man to whom he **s** it; 4376
25:28 **that which is s** shall remain in the hand 4465
25:29 redeem it within a whole year after it is **s**; 4465
25:33 the house **that was s**, and the city of his 4465
25:34 of the suburbs of their cities may not be **s**; 4376
25:39 thee be waxen poor, and be **s** unto thee; 4376
25:42 they shall not be **s** as bondmen. 4376+4466
25:48 After *that* he is **s** he may be redeemed 4376
25:50 he was **s** to him unto the year of jubile: 4376
27:20 or if he have **s** the field to another man, 4376
27:27 it shall be **s** according to thy estimation. 4376
27:28 of his possession, shall be **s** or redeemed: 4376
Dt 15:12 be **s** unto thee, and serve thee six years; 4376
28:68 there ye shall be **s** unto your enemies for 4376
32:30 except their Rock had **s** them, 4376
Jdg 2:14 he **s** them into the hands of their enemies 4376
3: 8 he **s** them into the hand of 4376
4: 2 the LORD **s** them into the hand of Jabin 4376
10: 7 **s** them into the hands of the Philistines, 4376
1Sa 12: 9 he **s** them into the hand of Sisera, captain 4376
1Ki 21:20 hast **s** thyself to work evil in the sight 4376
2Ki 6:25 until an ass's head was **s** for fourscore NIH
7: 1 a measure of fine flour be **s** for a shekel, NIH
7:16 So a measure of fine flour was **s** for a NIH
17:17 themselves to do evil in the sight of 4376
Ne 5: 8 the Jews, which were **s** unto the heathen; 4376
5: 8 or shall they be **s** unto us? Then held 4376
13:15 them in the day wherein they **s** victuals. 4376
13:16 **s** on the sabbath unto the children of 4376
Est 7: 4 For we are **s**, I and my people, to be 4376
7: 4 if we had been **s** for bondmen and 4376
Ps 105:17 *even* Joseph, *who* was **s** for a servant: 4376
Isa 50: 1 of my creditors *is it* to whom I have **s** 4376
50: 1 for your iniquities have you **s** yourselves, 4376
52: 3 Ye have **s** yourselves for nought; 4376
Jer 34:14 a Hebrew, which hath been **s** unto thee; 4376
La 5: 4 our wood is **s** *unto us.* 4242+871.1+935
Eze 7:13 seller shall not return to that which is **s**, 4465
Joel 3: 3 a girl for wine, that they might drink. 4376
3: 6 the children of Jerusalem have ye **s** unto 4376
3: 7 out of the place whither ye have **s** them, 4376
Am 2: 6 because they **s** the righteous for silver, 4376
Mt 10:29 Are not two sparrows **s** for a farthing? 4453
13:46 went and **s** all that he had, and bought it. 4097
18:25 his lord commanded him to be **s**, 4097
21:12 and cast out all them that **s** and bought in 4453
21:12 and the seats of them that **s** doves, 4453
26: 9 For this ointment might have been **s** for 4097
Mk 11:15 and began to cast out them that **s** and 4453
11:15 and the seats of them that **s** doves; 4453
14: 5 For it might have been **s** for more than 4097
Lk 12: 6 Are not five sparrows **s** for two farthings, 4453
17:28 did eat, they drank, they bought, they **s**, 4453

S

Lk	19:45 and began to cast out them that **s** therein,	4453
Jn	2:14 found in the temple those that **s** oxen	4453
	2:16 And said unto them that **s** doves,	4453
	12: 5 Why was not this ointment **s** for three	4097
Ac	2:45 And **s** their possessions and goods,	4453
	4:34 were possessors of lands or houses **s** them,	4453
	4:34 the prices of the *things* that were **s**,	4453
	4:37 **s** *it*, and brought the money, and laid *it* at	4453
	5: 1 with Sapphira his wife, **s** a possession,	4453
	5: 4 and after it was **s**, was it not in thine own	4097
	5: 8 me whether ye **s** the land for so much?	591
	7: 9 moved with envy, **s** Joseph into Egypt:	591
Ro	7:14 is spiritual: but I am carnal, **s** under sin.	4097
1Co	10:25 Whatsoever is **s** in the shambles, *that* eat,	4453
Heb	12:16 for one morsel of meat **s** his birthright.	591

SOLDIER (5) [FELLOWSOLDIER, SOLDIERS, SOLDIERS']

Jn	19:23 and made four parts, to every **s** a part;	4757
Ac	10: 7 a devout **s** of them that waited on him	4757
	28:16 dwell by himself with a **s** that kept him.	4757
2Ti	2: 3 as a good **s** of Jesus Christ.	4757
	2: 4 him who hath **chosen** *him* to be a **s**.	4758

SOLDIERS (29) [SOLDIER]

1Ch	7: 4 *were* bands of **s** for war, six and	6635
	7:11 two hundred **s**, fit to go out for war	NIH
2Ch	25:13 **s** of the army which Amaziah sent back,	1121
Ezr	8:22 ashamed to require of the king a band *of* **s**	NIH
Isa	15: 4 the **armed s** of Moab shall cry out;	2502
Mt	8: 9 man under authority, having **s** under me:	4757
	27:27 Then the **s** of the governor took Jesus into	4757
	27:27 gathered unto him the whole band *of* **s**.	NIG
	28:12 they gave large money unto the **s**,	4757
Mk	15:16 And the **s** led him away into the hall,	4757
Lk	3:14 And *the* **s** likewise demanded of him,	4754
	7: 8 having under me **s**, and I say unto one,	4757
	23:36 the **s** also mocked him, coming to *him,*	4757
Jn	19: 2 And the **s** platted a crown of thorns,	4757
	19:23 the **s**, when they had crucified Jesus,	4757
	19:24 These *things* therefore the **s** did.	4757
	19:32 Then came the **s**, and brake the legs of	4757
	19:34 But one of the **s** with a spear pierced his	4757
Ac	12: 4 delivered *him* to four quaternions of **s** to	4757
	12: 6 night Peter was sleeping between two **s**,	4757
	12:18 there was no small stir among the **s**,	4757
	21:32 Who immediately took **s** and centurions,	4757
	21:32 they saw the chief captain and the **s**,	4757
	21:35 that he was borne of the **s** for the violence	4757
	23:10 commanded the **s** to go down, and to take	4753
	23:23 Make ready two hundred **s** to go to	4757
	23:31 Then the **s**, as it was commanded them,	4757
	27:31 Paul said to the centurion and to the **s**,	4757
	27:32 the **s** cut off the ropes of the boat,	4757

SOLDIERS' (1) [SOLDIER]

Ac	27:42 the **s** counsel was to kill the prisoners,	4757

SOLE (12) [SOLES]

Ge	8: 9 dove found no rest for the **s** of her foot,	3709
Dt	28:35 from the **s** of thy foot unto the top of thy	3709
	28:56 which would not adventure to set the **s**	3709
	28:65 neither shall the **s** of thy foot have rest:	3709
Jos	1: 3 Every place that the **s** of your foot shall	3709
2Sa	14:25 from the **s** of his foot even to the crown	3709
2Ki	19:24 with the **s** of my feet have I dried up all	3709
Job	2: 7 smote Job with sore boils from the **s** of his	3709
Isa	1: 6 From the **s** of the foot even unto the head	3709
	37:25 with the **s** of my feet have I dried up all	3709
Eze	1: 7 the **s** of their feet *was* like the sole of a	3709
	1: 7 the sole of their feet *was* like the **s** of a	3709

SOLEMN (29) [SOLEMNITIES, SOLEMNITY, SOLEMNLY]

Lev	23:36 it *is* a **s** assembly; *and* ye shall do no	6116
Nu	10:10 in your **s** days, and in the beginnings of	4150
	15: 3 in a freewill offering, or in your **s** feasts,	4150
	29:35 eighth day ye shall have a **s** assembly:	6116
Dt	16: 8 on the seventh day *shall be* a **s** assembly	6116
	16:15 Seven days shalt thou **keep a s** feast unto	2287
2Ki	10:20 Jehu said, Proclaim a **s** assembly for Baal.	6116
2Ch	2: 4 the **s** feasts of the Lord our God.	4150
	7: 9 the eighth day they made a **s** assembly:	6116
	8:13 on the new moons, and on the **s** feasts,	4150
Ne	8:18 on the eighth day *was* a **s** assembly,	6116
Ps	81: 3 in the time appointed, on our **s** feast day.	6116
	92: 3 psaltery; upon the harp with a **s** sound.	1902
Isa	1:13 *it is* iniquity, even the **s** meeting.	6116
La	1: 4 because none come to the **s** feasts:	4150
	2: 6 the Lord hath caused the **s** feasts and	4150
	2: 7 of the Lord, as *in* the day of a **s** feast.	4150
	2:22 Thou hast called as *in* a **s** day my terrors	4150
Eze	36:38 as the flock of Jerusalem in her **s** feasts;	4150
	46: 9 come before the Lord in the **s** feasts,	4150
Hos	2:11 and her sabbaths, and all her **s** feasts.	4150
	9: 5 What will ye do in the **s** day, and in the	4150
	12: 9 tabernacles, *as in* the days of the **s** feast.	4150
Joel	1:14 call a **s** assembly, gather the elders *and*	6116
	2:15 in Zion, sanctify a fast, call a **s** assembly,	6116
Am	5:21 and I will not smell in your **s** assemblies.	6116
Na	1:15 O Judah, keep thy **s** feasts, perform thy	2282
Zep	3:18 *that are* sorrowful for the **s** assembly,	4150
Mal	2: 3 faces, *even* the dung of your **s** feasts;	2282

SOLEMNITIES (3) [SOLEMN]

Isa	33:20 Look upon Zion, the city of our **s**:	4150
Eze	45:17 in the sabbaths in all **s** of the house of	4150
	46:11 the **s** the meat offering shall be an ephah	4150

SOLEMNITY (2) [SOLEMN]

Dt	31:10 in the **s** of the year of release, in the feast	4150
Isa	30:29 as *in* the night when a holy **s** is kept;	2282

SOLEMNLY (2) [SOLEMN]

Ge	43: 3 man did **s protest** unto us, saying,	5749+5749
1Sa	8: 9 howbeit yet **protest s** unto them,	5749+5749

SOLES (7) [SOLE]

Dt	11:24 Every place whereon the **s** of your feet	3709
Jos	3:13 as soon as the **s** of the feet of the priests	3709
	4:18 the **s** of the priests' feet were lift up unto	3709
1Ki	5: 3 until the Lord put them under the **s** of	3709
Isa	60:14 bow themselves down at the **s** of thy feet;	3709
Eze	43: 7 and the place of the **s** of my feet,	3709
Mal	4: 3 for they shall be ashes under the **s** of your	3709

SOLITARILY (1) [SOLITARY]

Mic	7:14 which dwell **s** *in* the wood,	910+3807.1

SOLITARY (7) [SOLITARILY]

Job	3: 7 Lo, let that night be **s**, let no joyful voice	1565
	30: 3 For want and famine *they were* **s**; flying	1565
Ps	68: 6 God setteth the **s** in families: he bringeth	3173
	107: 4 They wandered in the wilderness in a **s**	3452
Isa	35: 1 the **s** place shall be glad *for* them;	6723
La	1: 1 How doth the city sit **s**, *that was* full of	910
Mk	1:35 and departed into a **s** place,	2048

SOLOMON (281) [JEDIDIAH, SOLOMON'S]

2Sa	5:14 and Shobab, and Nathan, and **S**,	8010
	12:24 she bare a son, and he called his name **S**:	8010
1Ki	1:10 and the mighty *men*, and **S** his brother,	8010
	1:11 spake unto Bath-sheba the mother of **S**,	8010
	1:12 thine own life, and the life of thy son **S**.	8010
	1:13 Assuredly **S** thy son shall reign after me,	8010
	1:17 *saying,* Assuredly **S** thy son shall reign	8010
	1:19 but **S** thy servant hath he not called.	8010
	1:21 and my son **S** shall be *counted* offenders.	8010
	1:26 and thy servant **S**, hath he not called.	8010
	1:30 Assuredly **S** thy son shall reign after me,	8010
	1:33 cause **S** my son to ride upon mine own	8010
	1:34 the trumpet, and say, God save king **S**.	8010
	1:37 so be he with **S**, and make his throne	8010
	1:38 caused **S** to ride upon king David's mule,	8010
	1:39 oil out of the tabernacle, and anointed **S**.	8010
	1:39 and all the people said, God save king **S**.	8010
	1:43 Verily our lord king David hath made **S**	8010
	1:46 And **S** sitteth on the throne of the kingdom.	8010
	1:47 God make the name of **S** better than thy	8010
	1:50 Adonijah feared because of **S**, and arose,	8010
	1:51 it was told **S**, saying, Behold,	8010
	1:51 Behold, Adonijah feareth king **S**:	8010
	1:51 Let king **S** swear unto me to day that he	8010
	1:52 **S** said, If he will shew himself a worthy	8010
	1:53 king **S** sent, and they brought him down	8010
	1:53 he came and bowed himself to king **S**:	8010
	1:53 and **S** said unto him, Go to thine house.	8010
	2: 1 and he charged **S** his son, saying,	8010
	2:12 sat **S** upon the throne of David his father;	8010
	2:13 came to Bath-sheba the mother of **S**.	8010
	2:17 said, Speak, I pray thee, unto **S** the king,	8010
	2:19 Bath-sheba therefore went unto king **S**,	8010
	2:22 **S** answered and said unto his mother,	8010
	2:23 king **S** sware by the Lord, saying,	8010
	2:25 **S** sent by the hand of Benaiah the son	8010
	2:27 So **S** thrust out Abiathar from being priest	8010
	2:29 it was told king **S** that Joab was fled unto	8010
	2:29 **S** sent Benaiah the son of Jehoiada,	8010
	2:41 it was told **S** that Shimei had gone from	8010
	2:45 king **S** *shall be* blessed, and the throne of	8010
	2:46 kingdom was established in the hand of **S**.	8010
	3: 1 **S** made affinity with Pharaoh king of	8010
	3: 3 **S** loved the Lord, walking in the statutes	8010
	3: 4 a thousand burnt offerings did **S** offer up	8010
	3: 5 In Gibeon the Lord appeared to **S** in a	8010
	3: 6 **S** said, Thou hast shewed unto thy	8010
	3:10 the Lord, that **S** had asked this thing.	8010
	3:15 **S** awoke; and behold, *it was* a dream.	8010
	4: 1 So king **S** was king over all Israel.	8010
	4: 7 **S** had twelve officers over all Israel, which	8010
	4:11 which had Taphath the daughter of **S** to	8010
	4:15 he also took Basmath the daughter of **S** to	8010
	4:21 **S** reigned over all kingdoms from the river	8010
	4:21 and served **S** all the days of his life.	8010
	4:25 Dan even to Beer-sheba, all the days of **S**.	8010
	4:26 **S** had forty thousand stalls of horses for	8010
	4:27 those officers provided victual for king **S**,	8010
	4:29 God gave **S** wisdom and	8010
	4:34 of all people to hear the wisdom of **S**,	8010
	5: 1 king of Tyre sent his servants unto **S**;	8010
	5: 2 And **S** sent to Hiram, saying,	8010
	5: 7 pass, when Hiram heard the words of **S**,	8010
	5: 8 Hiram sent to **S**, saying, I have considered	8010
	5:10 So Hiram gave **S** cedar trees and fir trees	8010
	5:11 **S** gave Hiram twenty thousand measures	8010
	5:11 oil: thus gave **S** to Hiram year by year.	8010
	5:12 the Lord gave **S** wisdom, as he promised	8010
	5:12 there was peace between Hiram and **S**;	8010
	5:13 king **S** raised a levy out of all Israel:	8010

1Ki	5:15 **S** had threescore and ten thousand that	8010
	6: 2 the house which king **S** built for	8010
	6:11 the word of the Lord came to **S**, saying,	8010
	6:14 So **S** built the house, and finished it.	8010
	6:21 So **S** overlaid the house within with pure	8010
	7: 1 **S** was building his own house thirteen	8010
	7: 8 made also a house for Pharaoh's	8010
	7:13 king **S** sent and fet Hiram out of Tyre.	8010
	7:14 he came to king **S**, and wrought all his	8010
	7:40 made king **S** for the house of the Lord:	8010
	7:45 Hiram made to king **S** for the house	8010
	7:47 **S** left all the vessels *unweighed*, because	8010
	7:48 **S** made all the vessels that *pertained unto*	8010
	7:51 was ended all the work that king **S** made	8010
	7:51 **S** brought in the *things* which David his	8010
	8: 1 **S** assembled the elders of Israel, and all	8010
	8: 1 of Israel, unto king **S** *in* Jerusalem,	8010
	8: 2 king **S** at the feast in the month Ethanim,	8010
	8: 5 king **S**, and all the congregation of Israel,	8010
	8:12 spake **S**, The Lord said that *he* would	8010
	8:22 **S** stood before the altar of the Lord in	8010
	8:54 when **S** had made an end of praying all	8010
	8:63 **S** offered a sacrifice of peace offerings,	8010
	8:65 at that time **S** held a feast, and all Israel	8010
	9: 1 when **S** had finished the building of	8010
	9: 2 That the Lord appeared to **S** the second	8010
	9:10 **S** had built the two houses, the house	8010
	9:11 of Tyre had furnished **S** with cedar trees	8010
	9:11 **S** gave Hiram twenty cities in the land	8010
	9:12 to see the cities which **S** had given him;	8010
	9:15 this *is* the reason of the levy which king **S**	8010
	9:17 **S** built Gezer, and Beth-horon the nether,	8010
	9:19 all the cities of store that **S** had, and cities	8010
	9:19 which **S** desired to build in Jerusalem,	8010
	9:21 upon those did **S** levy a tribute of	8010
	9:22 of the children of Israel did **S** make no	8010
	9:24 unto her house which *S* had built for her:	NIH
	9:25 three times in a year did **S** offer burnt	8010
	9:26 king **S** made a navy *of ships* in	8010
	9:27 of the sea, with the servants of **S**,	8010
	9:28 twenty talents, and brought *it* to king **S**.	8010
	10: 1 of **S** concerning the name of the Lord,	8010
	10: 2 when she was come to **S**, she communed	8010
	10: 3 told her all her questions: there was not	8010
	10:10 which the queen of Sheba gave to king **S**.	8010
	10:13 **S** gave unto the queen of Sheba all her	8010
	10:13 besides *that* which **S** gave her of his royal	8010
	10:14 Now the weight of gold that came to **S** in	8010
	10:16 **S** made two hundred targets *of* beaten	8010
	10:21 nothing accounted of in the days of **S**.	8010
	10:23 So king **S** exceeded all the kings of	8010
	10:24 all the earth sought to **S**, to hear his	8010
	10:26 **S** gathered together chariots and	8010
	10:28 And **S** had horses brought out of Egypt,	8010
	11: 1 king **S** loved many strange women,	8010
	11: 2 their gods: **S** clave unto these in love.	8010
	11: 4 For it came to pass, when **S** was old,	8010
	11: 5 For **S** went after Ashtoreth the goddess	8010
	11: 6 **S** did evil in the sight of the Lord,	8010
	11: 7 did **S** build a high place for Chemosh,	8010
	11: 9 And the Lord was angry with **S**, because	8010
	11:11 Wherefore the Lord said unto **S**,	8010
	11:14 the Lord stirred up an adversary unto **S**,	8010
	11:25 an adversary to Israel all the days of **S**,	8010
	11:27 **S** built Millo, *and* repaired the breaches of	8010
	11:28 seeing the young man that he was	8010
	11:31 rent the kingdom out of the hand of **S**,	8010
	11:40 **S** sought therefore to kill Jeroboam.	8010
	11:40 and was in Egypt until the death of **S**.	8010
	11:41 rest of the acts of **S**, and all that he did,	8010
	11:41 not written in the book of the acts of **S**?	8010
	11:42 the time that **S** reigned in Jerusalem over	8010
	11:43 **S** slept with his fathers, and was buried in	8010
	12: 2 he was fled from the presence of king **S**,	8010
	12: 6 that stood before **S** his father while he *yet*	8010
	12:21 kingdom again to Rehoboam the son of **S**.	8010
	12:23 the son of **S**, king of Judah, and unto all	8010
	14:21 Rehoboam the son of **S** reigned in Judah.	8010
	14:26 all the shields of gold which **S** had made.	8010
2Ki	21: 7 to **S** his son, In this house,	8010
	23:13 which **S** the king of Israel had builded for	8010
	24:13 in pieces all the vessels of gold which **S**	8010
	25:16 the bases which **S** had made for the house	8010
1Ch	3: 5 and Shobab, and Nathan, and **S**, four,	8010
	6:10 in the temple that **S** built in Jerusalem:)	8010
	6:32 until **S** had built the house of the Lord in	8010
	14: 4 Shammua, and Shobab, Nathan, and **S**,	8010
	18: 8 wherewith **S** made the brasen sea,	8010
	22: 5 **S** my son *is* young and tender,	8010
	22: 6 he called for **S** his son, and charged him	8010
	22: 7 David said to **S**, My son, *as for* me, it was	8010
	22: 9 for his name shall be **S**, and I will give	8010
	22:17 all the princes of Israel to help **S** his son,	8010
	23: 1 days, he made **S** his son king over Israel.	8010
	28: 5 hath chosen **S** my son to sit upon	8010
	28: 6 he said unto me, **S** thy son, he shall build	8010
	28: 9 **S** my son, know thou the God of thy	8010
	28:11 David gave to **S** his son the pattern of	8010
	28:20 David said to **S** his son, Be strong and	8010
	29: 1 **S** my son, whom alone God hath chosen,	8010
	29:19 give unto **S** my son a perfect heart,	8010
	29:22 they made **S** the son of David king	8010
	29:23 sat on the throne of the Lord as king	8010
	29:24 submitted themselves unto **S** the king.	8010
	29:25 the Lord magnified **S** exceedingly in	8010

1Ch 29:28	and **S** his son reigned in his stead.	8010
2Ch 1: 1	**S** the son of David was strengthened in	8010
1: 2	**S** spake unto all Israel, to the captains of	8010
1: 3	So **S**, and all the congregation with him,	8010
1: 5	**S** and the congregation sought *unto* it.	8010
1: 6	**S** went up thither to the brasen altar	8010
1: 7	In that night did God appear unto **S**,	8010
1: 8	**S** said unto God, Thou hast shewed great	8010
1:11	God said to **S**, Because this was in thine	8010
1:13	came *from his journey* to the high place	8010
1:14	**S** gathered chariots and horsemen:	8010
1:16	And **S** had horses brought out of Egypt,	8010
2: 1	**S** determined to build a house for the	8010
2: 2	**S** told out threescore and ten thousand	8010
2: 3	**S** sent to Huram the king of Tyre, saying,	8010
2:11	which he sent to **S**, Because the LORD	8010
2:17	**S** numbered all the strangers that *were* in	8010
3: 1	**S** began to build the house of the LORD at	8010
3: 3	Now these *are the things wherein* **S** was	8010
4:11	to make for king **S** for the house of God;	8010
4:16	did Huram his father make to king **S** for	8010
4:18	Thus **S** made all these vessels in great	8010
4:19	**S** made all the vessels that *were for*	8010
5: 1	all the work that **S** made for the house	8010
5: 1	**S** brought in *all the things* that David his	8010
5: 2	**S** assembled the elders of Israel, and all	8010
5: 6	Also king **S**, and all the congregation of	8010
6: 1	said **S**, The LORD hath said that *he* would	8010
6:13	For **S** had made a brasen scaffold, of five	8010
7: 1	Now when **S** had made an end of praying,	8010
7: 5	king **S** offered a sacrifice of twenty and	8010
7: 7	Moreover **S** hallowed the middle of	8010
7: 7	brasen altar which **S** had made was not	8010
7: 8	at the same time **S** kept the feast seven	8010
7:10	and to **S**, and to Israel his people.	8010
7:11	Thus **S** finished the house of the LORD,	8010
7:12	the LORD appeared to **S** by night,	8010
8: 1	wherein **S** had built the house of	8010
8: 2	the cities which Huram had restored to **S**,	8010
8: 2	**S** built them, and caused the children of	8010
8: 3	**S** went *to* Hamath-zobah,	8010
8: 6	all the store cities that **S** had, and all	8010
8: 6	all that **S** desired to build in Jerusalem,	8010
8: 8	them did **S** make to pay tribute until this	8010
8: 9	of the children of Israel did **S** make no	8010
8:11	**S** brought up the daughter of Pharaoh out	8010
8:12	**S** offered burnt offerings unto the LORD	8010
8:16	Now all the work of **S** was prepared unto	8010
8:17	went **S** to Ezion-geber, and to Eloth,	8010
8:18	they went with the servants of **S** to Ophir,	8010
8:18	of gold, and brought *them* to king **S**.	8010
9: 1	queen of Sheba heard of the fame of **S**,	8010
9: 1	she came to prove **S** with hard questions	8010
9: 1	when she was come to **S**, she communed	8010
9: 2	**S** told her all her questions: and there was	8010
9: 2	was nothing hid from **S** which he told	8010
9: 3	queen of Sheba had seen the wisdom of **S**,	8010
9: 9	spice as the queen of Sheba gave king **S**.	8010
9:10	servants of **S**, which brought gold from	8010
9:12	king **S** gave to the queen of Sheba all her	8010
9:13	Now the weight of gold that came to **S** in	8010
9:14	the country brought gold and silver to **S**	8010
9:15	**S** made two hundred targets *of* beaten	8010
9:20	all the drinking vessels of king **S** *were* of	8010
9:20	any thing accounted of in the days of **S**.	8010
9:22	king **S** passed all the kings of the earth in	8010
9:23	of the earth sought the presence of **S**,	8010
9:25	**S** had four thousand stalls for horses and	8010
9:28	they brought unto **S** horses out of Egypt,	8010
9:29	Now the rest of the acts of **S**, first and last,	8010
9:30	**S** reigned in Jerusalem over all Israel forty	8010
9:31	**S** slept with his fathers, and he was buried	8010
10: 2	he had fled from the presence of **S**	8010
10: 6	before **S** his father while he *yet* lived,	8010
11: 3	Speak unto Rehoboam the son of **S**, king	8010
11:17	made Rehoboam the son of **S** strong,	8010
11:17	they walked in the way of David and **S**.	8010
12: 9	the shields of gold which **S** had made.	8010
13: 6	the servant of **S** the son of David, is risen	8010
13: 7	against Rehoboam the son of **S**,	8010
30:26	for since the time of **S** the son of David	8010
33: 7	God had said to David and to **S** his son,	8010
35: 3	Put the holy ark in the house which **S**	8010
35: 4	and according to the writing of **S** his son.	8010
Ne 12:45	commandment of David, *and of* **S** his son.	8010
13:26	not **S** king of Israel sin by these *things*?	8010
Ps 72: T	*A Psalm* for **S**.	8010
127: T	*A Song* of degrees for **S**.	8010
Pr 1: 1	The proverbs of **S** the son of David, king	8010
10: 1	The proverbs of **S**. A wise son maketh a	8010
25: 1	These *are* also proverbs of **S**, which	8010
SS 1: 5	as the tents of Kedar, as the curtains of **S**.	8010
3: 9	**S** made himself a chariot of the wood	8010
3:11	behold king **S** with the crown where*with*	8010
8:11	**S** had a vineyard at Baal-hamon; he let out	8010
8:12	thou, O **S**, *must have* a thousand,	8010
Jer 52:20	which king **S** had made in the house of	8010
Mt 1: 6	David the king begat **S** of *her that had*	4672
1: 7	And **S** begat Roboam; and Roboam begat	4672
6:29	even **S** in all his glory was not arrayed	4672
12:42	of the earth to hear the wisdom of **S**;	4672
12:42	and behold, a greater than **S** *is* here.	4672
Lk 11:31	of the earth to hear the wisdom of **S**;	4672
11:31	and behold, a greater than **S** *is* here.	4672
12:27	*that* **S** in all his glory was not arrayed like	4672

Ac 7:47	But **S** built him a house.	4672

SOLOMON'S (25) [SOLOMON]

1Ki 4:22	**S** provision for one day was thirty	8010
4:27	for all that came unto king **S** table,	8010
4:30	**S** wisdom excelled the wisdom of all	8010
5:16	Besides the chief of **S** officers which *were*	8010
5:18	**S** builders and Hiram's builders did hew	8010
6: 1	in the fourth year of **S** reign over Israel,	8010
9: 1	all **S** desire which he was pleased to do,	8010
9:16	it *for* a present unto his daughter, **S** wife.	8010
9:23	of the officers that *were* over **S** work,	8010
10: 4	when the queen of Sheba had seen all **S**	8010
10:21	all king **S** drinking vessels *were of* gold,	8010
11:26	Ephrathite of Zereda, **S** servant,	8010+3807.1
1Ch 3:10	**S** son *was* Rehoboam, Abia his son, Asa	8010
2Ch 7:11	all that came into **S** heart to make in	8010
8:10	these *were* the chief of king **S**	8010+3807.1
Ezr 2:55	The children of **S** servants: the children of	8010
2:58	and the children of **S** servants,	8010
Ne 7:57	The children of **S** servants: the children	8010
7:60	and the children of **S** servants,	8010
11: 3	and the children of **S** servants.	8010
SS 1: 1	The song of songs, which *is* **S**.	8010+3807.1
3: 7	Behold his bed, which *is* **S**;	8010+3807.1
Jn 10:23	Jesus walked in the temple in **S** porch.	4672
Ac 3:11	unto them in the porch that is called **S**,	4672
5:12	they were all with one accord in **S** porch.	4672

SOME (231) [SOMEBODY, SOMETHING, SOMETIME, SOMETIMES, SOMEWHAT]

Ge 19:19	mountain, lest *s* evil take me, and I die:	NIH
27: 3	go out to the field, and take me *s* venison;	NIH
30:35	*and* every one that had *s* white in it,	NIH
33:15	Let me now leave with thee *s* of the folk	NIH
37:20	and cast him into *s* pit, and we will say,	259
37:20	will say, **S** evil beast hath devoured him:	NIH
47: 2	he took *s* of his brethren, *even* five	4480+7097
Ex 16:17	did so, and gathered, *s*⁵ more, some less.	1886.1
16:17	did so, and gathered, some more, *s*⁵ less.	1886.1
16:20	*s* of them left of it until the morning,	376
16:27	*that* there went out *s* of the people on	NIH
30:36	thou shalt beat *s* of it very small, and put	NIH
Lev 4: 7	the priest shall put *s* of the blood upon	NIH
4:17	the priest shall dip his finger *in s* of	NIH
4:18	he shall put *s* of the blood upon the horns	NIH
14:14	the priest shall take *s* of the blood of	NIH
14:15	the priest shall take *s* of the log of oil,	NIH
14:25	the priest shall take *s* of the blood of	NIH
14:27	priest shall sprinkle with his right finger *s*	NIH
25:25	hath sold away *s* of his possession,	NIH
27:16	if a man shall sanctify unto the LORD *s*	NIH
Nu 5:20	*s* man hath lain with thee beside thine	NIH
21: 1	against Israel, and took *s* of them prisoners.	NIH
27:20	thou shalt put *s* of thine honour upon him,	NIH
31: 3	Arm *s* of yourselves unto the war,	376
Dt 24: 1	he hath found *s* uncleanness in her:	1697
Jos 8:22	*s* on this side, and some on that side:	428
8:22	some on this side, and *s* on that side:	428
Jdg 21:13	the whole congregation sent *s* to speak to	NIH
Ru 2:16	let fall also *s* of the handfuls of purpose for	NIH
1Sa 8:11	and *s* shall run before his chariots.	NIH
13: 7	*s* of the Hebrews went over Jordan *to*	NIH
24:10	*s* bade me kill thee: but *mine eye* spared	NIH
27: 5	let them give me a place in *s* town in	259
2Sa 11:17	there fell *s* of the people of the servants of	NIH
11:24	of the king's servants be dead,	NIH
17: 9	he is hid now in *s* pit, or in some *other*	259
17: 9	is hid now in some pit, or in *s other* place:	259
17: 9	when *s* of them be overthrown at the first,	NIH
17:12	So shall we come upon him in *s* place	259
1Ki 14:13	in him there is found *s* good thing toward	NIH
2Ki 2:16	cast him upon *s* mountain, or into some	259
2:16	him upon some mountain, or into *s* valley.	259
5:13	the prophet had bid thee *do s* great thing,	NIH
7: 9	*s* mischief will come upon us:	NIH
7:13	his servants answered and said, Let *s* take,	NIH
9:33	*s* of her blood was sprinkled on the wall,	NIH
17:25	lions among them, which slew *s* of them.	NIH
1Ch 4:42	*s* of them, *even* of the sons of Simeon,	NIH
9:29	**S** of them also *were* appointed to oversee	NIH
9:30	*s* of the sons of the priests made	NIH
12:19	there fell *s* of Manasseh to David, when he	NIH
2Ch 12: 7	I will grant them *s* deliverance;	4592+3509.1
16:10	of this *thing*. And Asa oppressed *s* of	NIH
17:11	Also *s* of the Philistines brought	NIH
20: 2	there came *s* that told Jehoshaphat, saying,	NIH
Ezr 2:68	*s* of the chief of the fathers, when they	NIH
2:70	*s* of the people, and the singers,	NIH
7: 7	there went up *s* of the children of Israel,	NIH
10:44	*s* of them had wives by *whom* they had	NIH
Ne 2:12	in the night, I and *s* few men with me;	NIH
5: 3	**S** also there were that said, We have	NIH
5: 5	*s* of our daughters are brought unto	NIH
6: 2	us meet together in *s one of* the villages	NIH
7:70	*s* of the chief of the fathers gave	4480+7117
7:71	*s* of the chief of the fathers gave to	NIH
7:73	*s* of the people, and the Nethinims,	NIH
11:25	*s* of the children of Judah dwelt at	NIH
12:44	at that time were *s* appointed over	376
13:15	those days saw I in Judah *s* treading wine	NIH
13:15	of my servants set I at the gates, *that*	NIH
Job 24: 2	**S** remove the landmarks; they violently	NIH
Ps 20: 7	**S** *trust* in chariots, and some in horses:	428
20: 7	Some *trust* in chariots, and *s* in horses:	428

Ps 69:20	I looked *for s* to take pity, but *there was*	NIH
Pr 4:16	is taken away, unless they cause *s* to fall.	NIH
Jer 49: 9	would they not leave *s* gleaning grapes?	NIH
Eze 6: 8	that ye may have *s* that shall escape	NIH
Da 8:10	it cast down *s* of the host and of the stars	NIH
11:35	*s* of them of understanding shall fall, to try	NIH
12: 2	to everlasting life, and some to shame	428
12: 2	and *s* to shame *and* everlasting contempt.	428
Am 4:11	I have overthrown *s* of you, as God	NIH
Ob 1: 5	to thee, would they not leave *s* grapes?	NIH
Mt 13: 4	*s seeds* fell by the way side, and the fowls	3739
13: 5	**S** fell upon stony *places*, where they had	243
13: 7	And *s* fell among thorns; and the thorns	243
13: 8	**S** an hundred*fold*, some sixty*fold*, some	3739
13: 8	some an hundred*fold*, *s* sixty*fold*, some	3739
13: 8	some an hundred*fold*, some sixty*fold*, **s**	3739
13:23	*s* an hundred*fold*, some sixty, some thirty.	3739
13:23	some an hundred*fold*, *s* sixty, some thirty.	3739
13:23	some an hundred*fold*, some sixty, some thirty.	3739
16:14	**S** *say* that thou art John the Baptist:	3588
16:14	*s*, Elias; and others, Jeremias, or one of	243
16:28	I say unto you, There be *s* standing here,	5100
19:12	For there are *s* eunuchs, which were so	NIG
19:12	there are *s* eunuchs, which were made	NIG
23:34	and *s* of them ye shall kill and crucify;	NIG
23:34	of them shall ye scourge in your	NIG
27:47	**S** of them that stood there, when they	5100
28:11	*s* of the watch came into the city,	5100
28:17	they worshipped him: but *s* doubted.	3588
Mk 2: 1	he entered into Capernaum after *s* days;	NIG
4: 4	*s* fell by the way side, and the fowls of	3739
4: 5	And *s* fell on stony ground, where it had	243
4: 7	And *s* fell among thorns, and the thorns grew	243
4: 8	*s* thirty, and some sixty, and some an	1520
4: 8	and *s* sixty, and some an hundred.	1520
4: 8	and some sixty, and *s* an hundred.	1520
4:20	*s* thirty*fold*, some sixty, and some an	1520
4:20	some thirty*fold*, *s* sixty, and some an	1520
4:20	thirty*fold*, some sixty, and *s* an hundred.	1520
7: 2	And when they saw *s* of his disciples eat	5100
8:28	but *s say*, Elias; and others, One of	243
9: 1	That there be *s* of them that stand here,	5100
12: 5	they killed, and many others; beating *s*,	3588
12: 5	many others; beating some, and killing *s*.	3588
14: 4	there were *s* that had indignation	5100
14:65	And *s* began to spit on him, and to cover	5100
15:35	And *s* of them that stood by, when they	5100
Lk 8: 5	and as he sowed, *s* fell by the way side;	3739
8: 6	And *s* fell upon a rock; and as soon as it	2087
8: 7	And *s* fell among thorns; and the thorns	2087
9: 7	because that it was said of *s*,	5100
9: 8	And of *s*, that Elias had appeared;	243
9:19	but *s say*, Elias; and others *say*, that one of	243
9:27	you of a truth, there be *s* standing here,	5100
11:15	But *s* of them said, He casteth out devils	5100
11:49	*s* of them they shall slay and persecute;	NIG
13: 1	There were present at that season *s* that	5100
19:39	And *s* of the Pharisees from among	5100
21: 5	And as *s* spake of the temple, how it was	5100
21:16	*s* of you shall they cause to be put to	NIG
23: 8	he hoped to have seen *s* miracle done by	5100
Jn 3:25	Then there arose a question between *s* of	NIG
6:64	But there are *s* of you that believe not.	5100
7:12	for *s* said, He is a good *man*: others said,	3588
7:25	Then said *s* of them of Jerusalem, Is not	5100
7:41	*s* said, Shall Christ come out of Galilee?	243
7:44	And *s* of them would have taken him;	5100
9: 9	**S** *said*, This is he: others *said*, He is	243
9:16	Therefore said *s* of the Pharisees, This	5100
9:40	*s* of the Pharisees which were with him	NIG
10: 1	climbeth up *s* other way, the same is a	237
11:37	And *s* of them said, Could not this *man*,	5100
11:46	But *s* of them went their ways to	5100
13:29	For *s* *of them* thought, because Judas had	5100
16:17	Then said *s* of his disciples among	5100
Ac 5:15	passing by might overshadow *s* of them.	5100
8: 9	giving out that himself was *s* great one:	5100
8:31	can I, except *s* *man* should guide me?	5100
8:34	of himself, or of *s* other *man*?	5100
11:20	And *s* of them were men of Cyprus and	5100
13:11	he went about seeking *s* to lead him by	NIG
15:36	And *s* days after Paul said unto Barnabas,	5100
17: 4	And *s* of them believed, and consorted	5100
17:18	And said, What will this babbler say?	5100
17:18	other *s*, He seemeth to be a setter forth of	NIG
17:21	but *either* to tell, or to hear *s* new *thing*.)	NIG
17:32	resurrection of the dead, *s* mocked:	3303+3588
18:23	And after he had spent *s* time *there*, he	5100
19:32	**S** therefore cried one *thing*, and	243+3303
19:32	therefore cried one *thing*, and *s* another:	NIG
21:34	And *s* cried one *thing*, some another,	243
21:34	And some cried one *thing*, *s* another,	NIG
27:27	deemed that they drew near to *s* country;	5100
27:34	Wherefore I pray you to take *s* meat: for	NIG
27:36	of good cheer, and they also took *s* meat.	NIG
27:44	*s* on boards, and some on broken pieces	3739
27:44	some on boards, and *s* on broken pieces of the ship.	3739
28:24	And *s* believed the *things* which were	3588
28:24	which were spoken, and *s* believed not.	3588
Ro 1:11	that I may impart unto you *s* spiritual gift,	5100
1:13	that I might have *s* fruit among you also,	5100
3: 3	For what if *s* did not believe? shall their	5100
3: 8	and as *s* affirm that we say,)	5100
5: 7	yet peradventure for a good *man s* would	5100
11:14	*are* my flesh, and might save *s* of them.	5100

Ref	Text	Strong
Ro 11:17	And if **s** of the branches be broken off,	5100
15:15	have written the more boldly unto you in **s**	575
1Co 4:18	**s** are puffed up, as though I would not	5100
6:11	such were **s** of you: but ye are washed,	5100
8: 7	for **s** with conscience of the idol unto this	5100
9:22	all *men*, that I might by all means save **s**.	5100
10: 7	Neither be ye idolaters, as *were* **s** of them;	5100
10: 8	**s** of them committed, and fell in one day	5100
10: 9	as **s** of them also tempted,	5100
10:10	as **s** of them also murmured,	5100
12:28	And God hath set **s** in the church,	3739
15: 6	unto this present, but **s** are fallen asleep.	5100
15:12	how say **s** among you that there is no	5100
15:34	for **s** have not the knowledge of God:	5100
15:35	But **s** *man* will say, How are the dead	5100
15:37	may chance of wheat, or of **s** other *grain*:	5100
2Co 3: 1	as **s** *others*, epistles of commendation to	5100
10: 2	wherewith I think to be bold against **s**,	5100
10:12	compare ourselves with **s** that commend	5100
Gal 1: 7	but there be **s** that trouble you,	5100
Eph 4:11	And he gave **s**, apostles; and some,	3303+3588
4:11	and **s**, prophets; and some, evangelists;	3588
4:11	and **s**, evangelists; and some, pastors and	3588
4:11	evangelists; and **s**, pastors and teachers;	3588
Php 1:15	**S** indeed preach Christ even of envy and	5100
1:15	of envy and strife; and **s** also of good will:	5100
1Th 3: 5	**lest by s means** the tempter have	3381
2Th 3:11	For we hear that *there are* **s** which walk	5100
1Ti 1: 3	thou mightest charge **s** that *they* teach	5100
1: 6	which **s** having swerved have turned	5100
1:19	**s** having put away, concerning faith	5100
4: 1	that in the latter times **s** shall depart from	5100
5:15	For **s** are already turned aside after Satan.	5100
5:24	**S** men's sins are open beforehand,	5100
5:24	to judgment; and **s** *men* they follow after.	5100
5:25	Likewise also the good works of **s** are	NIG
6:10	which while **s** coveted after, they have	5100
6:21	Which **s** professing have erred concerning	5100
2Ti 2:18	past already; and overthrow the faith of **s**.	5100
2:20	and **s** to honour, and some to dishonour.	3739
2:20	and some to honour, and **s** to dishonour.	3739
Heb 3: 4	For every house is builded by **s** *man*; but	5100
3:16	For **s**, when they had heard, did provoke:	5100
4: 6	it remaineth that **s** *must* enter therein,	5100
10:25	as the manner of **s** *is*; but exhorting *one*	5100
11:40	God having provided **s** better *thing* for us,	5100
13: 2	for thereby **s** have entertained angels	5100
1Pe 4:12	as though **s** strange *thing* happened unto	NIG
2Pe 3: 9	*his* promise, as **s** *men* count slackness;	5100
3:16	which are **s** *things* hard to be understood,	NIG
Jude 1:22	of **s** have compassion, making a	3303+3739
Rev 2:10	the devil shall cast **s** of you into prison,	NIG

SOMEBODY (2) [SOME]

| Lk 8:46 | And Jesus said, **S** hath touched me: for I | 5100 |
| Ac 5:36 | rose up Theudas, boasting himself to be **s**; | 5100 |

SOMETHING (8) [SOME, THING]

1Sa 20:26	for he thought, **S** hath **befallen** him, he *is*	4745
Mk 5:43	commanded that **s** should be given her to	NIG
Lk 11:54	and seeking to catch **s** out of his mouth,	5100
Jn 13:29	or that he should give **s** to the poor.	5100
Ac 3: 5	them, expecting to receive **s** of them.	3588
23:15	as though ye would inquire **s** more	3588
23:18	unto thee, who hath **s** to say unto thee.	5100
Gal 6: 3	For if a man think himself to be **s**, when	5100

SOMETIME (3) [SOME, TIME]

Col 1:21	that were **s** alienated and enemies in *your*	4218
3: 7	In the which ye also walked **s**, when ye	4218
1Pe 3:20	Which **s** were disobedient, when once	4218

SOMETIMES (3) [SOME, TIME]

Eph 2:13	But now in Christ Jesus ye who **s** were far	4218
5: 8	For ye were **s** darkness, but now *are ye*	4218
Tit 3: 3	For we ourselves also were **s** foolish,	4218

SOMEWHAT (25) [SOME, WHAT]

Lev 4:13	they have done **s** against any of	259
4:22	done **s** through ignorance against any of	259
4:27	while he doeth **s** against *any of*	259
13: 6	*if* the plague *be* **s** dark, and the plague	3544
13:19	**s** reddish, and it be shewed to the priest;	125
13:21	*be* not lower than the skin, but *be* **s** dark;	3544
13:24	a white bright spot, **s** reddish, or white;	125
13:26	lower than the *other* skin, but *be* **s** dark;	3544
13:28	spread not in the skin, but it *be* **s** dark;	3544
13:56	plague *be* **s** dark after the washing of it;	3544
1Ki 2:14	moreover, I have **s** to **say** unto thee.	1697
2Ki 5:20	I will run after him, and take **s** of him.	3972
2Ch 10: 4	**ease** thou **s** the grievous servitude of thy	7043
10: 9	**Ease** the yoke that thy father did put	7043
10:10	but **make** thou *it* **s** **lighter** for us;	7043
Lk 7:40	him, Simon, I have **s** to say unto thee.	5100
Ac 23:20	as though they would inquire **s** of him	5100
25:26	examination had, I might have **s** to write.	5100
Ro 15:24	first I be **s** filled with your **company**.	575+3313
2Co 5:12	that you may have **s** to *answer* them	NIG
10: 8	For though I should boast **s** more of our	5100
Gal 2: 6	But of these who seemed to be **s**,	NIG
2: 6	they who seemed to be **s** in conference	NIG
Heb 8: 3	that this *man* have **s** also to offer.	5100
Rev 2: 4	Nevertheless I have **s** against thee,	NIG

SON (2374) [SON'S, SONS, SONS']

Ge 4:17	of the city, after the name of his **s**, Enoch.	1121
4:25	She bare a **s**, and called his name Seth:	1121
4:26	to Seth, *to* him also there was born a **s**;	1121
5: 3	and begat *a* **s** in his own likeness,	NIH
5:28	and two years, and begat a **s**:	1121
9:24	knew what his younger **s** had done unto	1121
11:31	Terah took Abram his **s**, and Lot the son	1121
11:31	Lot the **s** of Haran his son's son, and Sarai	1121
11:31	Lot the son of Haran his son's **s**, and Sarai	1121
11:31	his daughter in law, his **s** Abram's wife;	1121
12: 5	Lot his brother's **s**, and all their substance	1121
14:12	they took Lot, Abram's brother's **s**,	1121
16:11	shalt bear a **s**, and shalt call his name	1121
16:15	Hagar bare Abram a **s**: and Abram called	1121
17:16	bless her, and give thee a **s** also of her:	1121
17:19	Sarah thy wife shall bear thee a **s** indeed;	1121
17:23	Abraham took Ishmael his **s**, and all that	1121
17:25	Ishmael his **s** *was* thirteen years old,	1121
17:26	Abraham circumcised, and Ishmael his **s**.	1121
18:10	and lo, Sarah thy wife shall have a **s**.	1121
18:14	the time of life, and Sarah shall have a **s**.	1121
19:12	**s** in law, and thy sons, and thy daughters,	2860
19:37	the firstborn bare a **s**, and called his name	1121
19:38	she also bare a **s**, and called his name	1121
21: 2	and bare Abraham a **s** in his old age,	1121
21: 3	Abraham called the name of his **s** that	1121
21: 4	Abraham circumcised his **s** Isaac being	1121
21: 5	when his **s** Isaac was born unto him.	1121
21: 7	For I have born *him* a **s** in his old age.	1121
21: 9	Sarah saw the **s** of Hagar the Egyptian,	1121
21:10	Cast out this bondwoman and her **s**:	1121
21:10	for the **s** of this bondwoman shall not be	1121
21:10	bondwoman shall not be heir with my **s**,	1121
21:11	in Abraham's sight because of his **s**.	1121
21:13	of the **s** of the bondwoman will I make	1121
21:23	nor with my **s**, nor with my son's son:	5209
21:23	nor with my son, nor with my **son's** son:	5220
22: 2	he said, Take now thy **s**, thine only *son*	1121
22: 2	Take now thy son, thine only **s** Isaac,	NIH
22: 3	Isaac his **s**, and clave the wood for	1121
22: 6	offering, and laid *it* upon Isaac his **s**;	1121
22: 7	he said, Here am I, my **s**. And he said,	1121
22: 8	Abraham said, My **s**, God will provide	1121
22: 9	bound Isaac his **s**, and laid him on the	1121
22:10	his hand, and took the knife to slay his **s**.	1121
22:12	seeing thou hast not withheld thy **s**, thine	1121
22:12	withheld thy **son**, thine only **s** from me.	NIH
22:13	for a burnt offering in the stead of his **s**.	1121
22:16	hast not withheld thy **s**, thine only *son*:	1121
22:16	hast not withheld thy son, thine only **s**	NIH
23: 8	intreat for me to Ephron the **s** of Zohar,	1121
24: 3	thou shalt not take a wife unto my **s** of	1121
24: 4	and take a wife unto my **s** Isaac.	1121
24: 5	I needs bring thy **s** again unto the land	1121
24: 6	Beware thou that thou bring not my **s**	1121
24: 7	thou shalt take a wife unto my **s** from	1121
24: 8	oath: only bring not my **s** thither again.	1121
24:15	**s** of Milcah, the wife of Nahor,	1121
24:24	I *am* the daughter of Bethuel the **s** of	1121
24:36	Sarah my master's wife bare a **s** to my	1121
24:37	Thou shalt not take a wife to my **s** of	1121
24:38	to my kindred, and take a wife unto my **s**.	1121
24:40	thou shalt take a wife for my **s** of my	1121
24:44	hath appointed out for my master's **s**.	1121
24:47	The daughter of Bethuel, Nahor's **s**,	1121
24:48	my master's brother's daughter unto his **s**.	1121
25: 6	sent them away from Isaac his **s**, while he	1121
25: 9	in the field of Ephron the **s** of Zohar	1121
25:11	of Abraham, that God blessed his **s** Isaac;	1121
25:12	Abraham's **s**, whom Hagar the Egyptian,	1121
25:19	*are* the generations of Isaac, Abraham's **s**:	1121
27: 1	he called Esau his eldest **s**, and said unto	1121
27: 1	his eldest son, and said unto him, My **s**.	1121
27: 5	heard when Isaac spake to Esau his **s**.	1121
27: 6	Rebekah spake unto Jacob her **s**, saying,	1121
27: 8	Now therefore, my **s**, obey my voice	1121
27:13	unto him, Upon me *be* thy curse, my **s**:	1121
27:15	took goodly raiment of her eldest **s** Esau,	1121
27:15	and put them upon Jacob her younger **s**:	1121
27:17	prepared, into the hand of her **s** Jacob.	1121
27:18	he said, Here am I; who *art* thou, my **s**?	1121
27:20	Isaac said unto his **s**, How *is it that* thou	1121
27:20	thou hast found *it* so quickly, my **s**?	1121
27:21	I pray thee, that I may feel thee, my **s**,	1121
27:21	whether thou *be* my very **s** Esau or not.	1121
27:24	he said, *Art* thou my very **s** Esau? And he	1121
27:26	Come near now, and kiss me, my **s**.	1121
27:27	the smell of my **s** *is* as the smell of a field	1121
27:32	he said, I *am* thy **s**, thy firstborn Esau.	1121
27:37	and what shall I do now unto thee, my **s**?	1121
27:42	these words of Esau her elder **s** were told	1121
27:42	she sent and called Jacob her younger **s**,	1121
27:43	Now therefore, my **s**, obey my voice;	1121
28: 5	**s** of Bethuel the Syrian, the brother of	1121
28: 9	the daughter of Ishmael Abraham's **s**,	1121
29: 5	them, Know ye Laban the **s** of Nahor?	1121
29:12	and that he *was* Rebekah's **s**:	1121
29:13	heard the tidings of Jacob his sister's **s**,	1121
29:32	bare a **s**, and she called his name Reuben:	1121
29:33	conceived again, and bare a **s**; and said,	1121
29:33	he hath therefore given me this **s** also:	NIH
29:34	conceived again, and bare a **s**; and said,	1121
29:35	She conceived again, and bare a **s**:	1121

Ge 30: 5	And Bilhah conceived, and bare Jacob a **s**.	1121
30: 6	heard my voice, and hath given me a **s**:	1121
30: 7	again, and bare Jacob a second **s**.	1121
30:10	And Zilpah Leah's maid bare Jacob a **s**.	1121
30:12	Zilpah Leah's maid bare Jacob a second **s**.	1121
30:17	she conceived, and bare Jacob the fifth **s**.	1121
30:19	again, and bare Jacob the sixth **s**.	1121
30:23	she conceived, and bare a **s**; and said,	1121
30:24	The LORD shall add to me another **s**.	1121
34: 2	Shechem the **s** of Hamor the Hivite,	1121
34: 8	The soul of my **s** Shechem longeth for	1121
34:18	pleased Hamor, and Shechem Hamor's **s**.	1121
34:20	Shechem his **s** came unto the gate of their	1121
34:24	Shechem his **s** hearkened all that went	1121
34:26	Shechem his **s** with the edge of the sword	1121
35:17	Fear not; thou shalt have this **s** also.	1121
36:10	Eliphaz the **s** of Adah the wife of Esau,	1121
36:10	Reuel the **s** of Bashemath the wife of Esau	1121
36:12	Timna was concubine to Eliphaz Esau's **s**;	1121
36:15	the sons of Eliphaz the firstborn **s** of Esau;	NIH
36:17	these *are* the sons of Reuel Esau's **s**;	1121
36:32	Bela the **s** of Beor reigned in Edom:	1121
36:33	Jobab the **s** of Zerah of Bozrah reigned in	1121
36:35	Husham died, and Hadad the **s** of Bedad,	1121
36:38	Baal-hanan the **s** of Achbor reigned in his	1121
36:39	Baal-hanan the **s** of Achbor died,	1121
37: 3	because he *was* the **s** of his old age:	1121
37:34	loins, and mourned for his **s** many days.	1121
37:35	I will go down into the grave unto my **s**	1121
38: 3	she conceived, and bare a **s**; and he called	1121
38: 4	she conceived again, and bare a **s**;	1121
38: 5	She yet again conceived, and bare a **s**;	1121
38:11	father's house, till Shelah my **s** be grown:	1121
38:26	that I gave her not to Shelah my **s**.	1121
42:38	said, My **s** shall not go down with you;	1121
43:29	Benjamin, his mother's **s**, and said,	1121
43:29	he said, God be gracious unto thee, my **s**.	1121
45: 9	say unto him, Thus saith thy **s** Joseph,	1121
45:28	*It is* enough; Joseph my **s** *is* yet alive:	1121
46:10	and Shaul the **s** of a Canaanitish woman.	1121
47:29	he called his **s** Joseph, and said unto him,	1121
48: 2	Behold, thy **s** Joseph cometh unto thee:	1121
48:19	father refused, and said, I know *it*, my **s**,	1121
49: 9	from the prey, my **s**, thou art gone up:	1121
50:23	**s** of Manasseh were brought up upon	1121
Ex 1:16	stools; if it *be* a **s**, then ye shall kill him	1121
1:22	Every **s** that is born ye shall cast into	1121
2: 2	the woman conceived, and bare a **s**:	1121
2:10	Pharaoh's daughter, and he became her **s**.	1121
2:22	she bare *him* a **s**, and he called his name	1121
4:22	Israel *is* my **s**, *even* my firstborn:	1121
4:23	I say unto thee, Let my **s** go, that he may	1121
4:23	I will slay thy **s**, *even* thy firstborn.	1121
4:25	cut off the foreskin of her **s**, and cast *it* at	1121
6:15	and Shaul the **s** of a Canaanitish woman:	1121
6:25	Eleazar Aaron's **s** took him *one* of	1121
10: 2	that thou mayest tell in the ears of thy **s**,	1121
10: 2	of thy son's **s**, what things I have wrought	1121
13: 8	thou shalt shew thy **s** in that day, saying,	1121
13:14	it shall be when thy **s** asketh thee in time	1121
20:10	thou, nor thy **s**, nor thy daughter,	1121
21: 9	if he have betrothed her unto his **s**, he	1121
21:31	Whether he have gored a **s**, or have gored	1121
23:12	the **s** of thy handmaid, and the stranger,	1121
29:30	*And* that **s** that is priest in his stead shall	1121
31: 2	have called by name Bezaleel the **s** of Uri,	1121
31: 2	of Uri, the **s** of Hur, of the tribe of Judah:	1121
31: 6	the **s** of Ahisamach, of the tribe of Dan:	1121
32:29	even every man upon his **s**, and upon his	1121
33:11	Joshua, the **s** of Nun, a young man,	1121
35:30	hath called by name Bezaleel the **s** of Uri,	1121
35:30	of Uri, the **s** of Hur, of the tribe of Judah;	1121
35:34	*both* he, and Aholiab, the **s** of Ahisamach,	1121
38:21	the hand of Ithamar, **s** to Aaron the priest.	1121
38:22	Bezaleel the **s** of Uri, the son of Hur,	1121
38:22	of Uri, the **s** of Hur, of the tribe of Judah,	1121
38:23	**s** of Ahisamach, of the tribe of Dan,	1121
Lev 12: 6	are fulfilled, for a **s**, or for a daughter,	1121
21: 2	for his **s**, and for his daughter, and for his	1121
24:10	the **s** of an Israelitish woman, whose	1121
24:10	*this* **s** of the Israelitish *woman* and a man	1121
24:11	the Israelitish woman's **s** blasphemed	1121
25:49	Either his uncle, or his uncle's **s**,	1121
Nu 1: 5	tribe *of* Reuben; Elizur the **s** of Shedeur.	1121
1: 6	Simeon; Shelumiel the **s** of Zurishaddai.	1121
1: 7	Of Judah; Nahshon the **s** of Amminadab.	1121
1: 8	Of Issachar; Nethaneel the **s** of Zuar.	1121
1: 9	Of Zebulun; Eliab the **s** of Helon.	1121
1:10	Of Ephraim; Elishama the **s** of Ammihud;	1121
1:10	Of Manasseh; Gamaliel the **s** of Pedahzur.	1121
1:11	Of Benjamin; Abidan the **s** of Gideoni.	1121
1:12	Of Dan; Ahiezer the **s** of Ammishaddai.	1121
1:13	Of Asher; Pagiel the **s** of Ocran.	1121
1:14	Of Gad; Eliasaph the **s** of Deuel.	1121
1:15	Of Naphtali; Ahira the **s** of Enan.	1121
1:20	Israel's **eldest s**, *by* their generations,	1060
2: 3	Nahshon the **s** of Amminadab shall be	1121
2: 5	Nethaneel the **s** of Zuar shall be captain	1121
2: 7	Eliab the **s** of Helon shall be captain of	1121
2:10	Reuben *shall be* Elizur the **s** of Shedeur.	1121
2:12	*shall be* Shelumiel the **s** of Zurishaddai.	1121
2:14	of Gad *shall be* Eliasaph the **s** of Reuel.	1121
2:18	*shall be* Elishama the **s** of Ammihud.	1121
2:20	*shall be* Gamaliel the **s** of Pedahzur.	1121
2:22	shall be Abidan the **s** of Gideoni.	1121

Nu	2:25	*shall be* Ahiezer the **s** of Ammishaddai.	1121
	2:27	of Asher *shall be* Pagiel the **s** of Ocran.	1121
	2:29	of Naphtali *shall be* Ahira the **s** of Enan.	1121
	3:24	*shall be* Eliasaph the **s** of Lael.	1121
	3:30	*shall be* Elizaphan the **s** of Uzziel.	1121
	3:32	Eleazar the **s** of Aaron the priest *shall be*	1121
	3:35	of Merari *was* Zuriel the **s** of Abihail:	1121
	4:16	*to* the office of Eleazar the **s** of Aaron	1121
	4:28	hand of Ithamar the **s** of Aaron the priest.	1121
	4:33	under the hand of Ithamar the **s** of Aaron	1121
	7: 8	under the hand of Ithamar the **s** of Aaron	1121
	7:12	day was Nahshon the **s** of Amminadab,	1121
	7:17	this *was* the offering of Nahshon the **s** of	1121
	7:18	the second day Nethaneel the **s** of Zuar,	1121
	7:23	this *was* the offering of Nethaneel the **s** of	1121
	7:24	On the third day Eliab the **s** of Helon,	1121
	7:29	this *was* the offering of Eliab the **s** of	1121
	7:30	the fourth day Elizur the **s** of Shedeur,	1121
	7:35	this *was* the offering of Elizur the **s** of	1121
	7:36	On the fifth day Shelumiel the **s** of	1121
	7:41	this *was* the offering of Shelumiel the **s** of	1121
	7:42	On the sixth day Eliasaph the **s** of Deuel,	1121
	7:47	this *was* the offering of Eliasaph the **s** of	1121
	7:48	On the seventh day Elishama the **s** of	1121
	7:53	this *was* the offering of Elishama the **s** of	1121
	7:54	the eighth day *offered* Gamaliel the **s** of	1121
	7:59	this *was* the offering of Gamaliel the **s** of	1121
	7:60	On the ninth day Abidan the **s** of Gideoni,	1121
	7:65	this *was* the offering of Abidan the **s** of	1121
	7:66	On the tenth day Ahiezer the **s** of	1121
	7:71	this *was* the offering of Ahiezer the **s** of	1121
	7:72	the eleventh day Pagiel the **s** of Ocran,	1121
	7:77	this *was* the offering of Pagiel the **s** of	1121
	7:78	On the twelfth day Ahira the **s** of Enan,	1121
	7:83	*was* the offering of Ahira the **s** of Enan.	1121
	10:14	over his host *was* Nahshon the **s** of	1121
	10:15	of Issachar *was* Nethaneel the **s** of Zuar.	1121
	10:16	of Zebulun *was* Eliab the **s** of Helon.	1121
	10:18	over his host *was* Elizur the **s** of Shedeur.	1121
	10:19	*was* Shelumiel the **s** of Zurishaddai.	1121
	10:20	of Gad *was* Eliasaph the **s** of Deuel.	1121
	10:22	over his host *was* Elishama the **s** of	1121
	10:23	*was* Gamaliel the **s** of Pedahzur.	1121
	10:24	Benjamin *was* Abidan the **s** of Gideoni.	1121
	10:25	over his host *was* Ahiezer the **s** of	1121
	10:26	of Asher *was* Pagiel the **s** of Ocran.	1121
	10:27	of Naphtali *was* Ahira the **s** of Enan.	1121
	10:29	the **s** of Raguel the Midianite,	1121
	11:28	Joshua the **s** of Nun, the servant of Moses	1121
	13: 4	of Reuben, Shammua the **s** of Zaccur.	1121
	13: 5	tribe of Simeon, Shaphat the **s** of Hori.	1121
	13: 6	tribe of Judah, Caleb the **s** of Jephunneh.	1121
	13: 7	the tribe of Issachar, Igal the **s** of Joseph.	1121
	13: 8	the tribe of Ephraim, Oshea the **s** of Nun.	1121
	13: 9	tribe of Benjamin, Palti the **s** of Raphu.	1121
	13:10	tribe of Zebulun, Gaddiel the **s** of Sodi.	1121
	13:11	tribe of Manasseh, Gaddi the **s** of Susi.	1121
	13:12	tribe of Dan, Ammiel the **s** of Gemalli.	1121
	13:13	tribe of Asher, Sethur the **s** of Michael.	1121
	13:14	tribe of Naphtali, Nahbi the **s** of Vophsi.	1121
	13:15	Of the tribe of Gad, Geuel the **s** of Machi.	1121
	13:16	called Oshea the **s** of Nun, Jehoshua.	1121
	14: 6	Joshua the **s** of Nun, and Caleb the son	1121
	14: 6	of Nun, and Caleb the **s** of Jephunneh,	1121
	14:30	save Caleb the **s** of Jephunneh,	1121
	14:30	of Jephunneh, and Joshua the **s** of Nun.	1121
	14:38	Joshua the **s** of Nun, and Caleb the son	1121
	14:38	of Nun, and Caleb the **s** of Jephunneh,	1121
	16: 1	Now Korah, the **s** of Izhar, the son of	1121
	16: 1	the **s** of Kohath, the son of Levi,	1121
	16: 1	the **s** of Levi, and Dathan and Abiram,	1121
	16: 1	On, the **s** of Peleth, sons of Reuben,	1121
	16:37	Speak unto Eleazar the **s** of Aaron	1121
	20:25	Take Aaron and Eleazar his **s**,	1121
	20:26	and put them upon Eleazar his **s**:	1121
	20:28	and put them upon Eleazar his **s**:	1121
	22: 2	Balak the **s** of Zippor saw all that Israel	1121
	22: 4	Balak the **s** of Zippor *was* king of	1121
	22: 5	unto Balaam the **s** of Beor to Pethor,	1121
	22:10	Balak the **s** of Zippor, king of Moab,	1121
	22:16	to him, Thus saith Balak the **s** of Zippor,	1121
	23:18	hear; hearken unto me, thou **s** of Zippor:	1121
	23:19	the **s** of man, that he should repent:	1121
	24: 3	Balaam the **s** of Beor hath said,	1121
	24:15	Balaam the **s** of Beor hath said,	1121
	25: 7	Phinehas, the **s** of Eleazar, the son of	1121
	25: 7	son of Eleazar, the **s** of Aaron the priest,	1121
	25:11	Phinehas, the **s** of Eleazar, the son of	1121
	25:11	son of Eleazar, the **s** of Aaron the priest	1121
	25:14	Zimri, the **s** of Salu, a prince of a chief	1121
	26: 1	and unto Eleazar the **s** of Aaron the priest,	1121
	26: 5	Reuben, the **eldest** of Israel:	1060
	26:33	Zelophehad the **s** of Hepher had no sons,	1121
	26:65	save Caleb the **s** of Jephunneh,	1121
	26:65	of Jephunneh, and Joshua the **s** of Nun.	1121
	27: 1	the **s** of Hepher, the son of Gilead,	1121
	27: 1	of Gilead, the son of Machir,	1121
	27: 1	the son of Gilead, the **s** of Machir,	1121
	27: 1	the son of Machir, the **s** of Manasseh,	1121
	27: 1	the families of Manasseh the **s** of Joseph:	1121
	27: 4	among his family, because he hath no **s**?	1121
	27: 8	have no **s**, then ye shall cause his	1121
	27:18	Take thee Joshua the **s** of Nun, a man in	1121
	31: 6	and Phinehas the **s** of Eleazar the priest,	1121
	31: 8	Balaam also the **s** of Beor they slew with	1121

Nu	32:12	Save Caleb the **s** of Jephunneh	1121
	32:12	the Kenezite, and Joshua the **s** of Nun:	1121
	32:28	Joshua the **s** of Nun, and the chief fathers	1121
	32:33	unto half the tribe of Manasseh the **s** of	1121
	32:39	the children of Machir the **s** of Manasseh	1121
	32:40	Moses gave Gilead unto Machir the **s** of	1121
	32:41	Jair the **s** of Manasseh went and took	1121
	34:17	the priest, and Joshua the **s** of Nun.	1121
	34:19	tribe of Judah, Caleb the **s** of Jephunneh.	1121
	34:20	of Simeon, Shemuel the **s** of Ammihud.	1121
	34:21	tribe of Benjamin, Elidad the **s** of Chislon.	1121
	34:22	the children of Dan, Bukki the **s** of Jogli.	1121
	34:23	of Manasseh, Hanniel the **s** of Ephod.	1121
	34:24	of Ephraim, Kemuel the **s** of Shiphtan.	1121
	34:25	of Zebulun, Elizaphan the **s** of Parnach.	1121
	34:26	of Issachar, Paltiel the **s** of Azzan.	1121
	34:27	of Asher, Ahihud the **s** of Shelomi.	1121
	34:28	of Naphtali, Pedahel the **s** of Ammihud.	1121
	36: 1	the **s** of Machir, the son of Manasseh,	1121
	36: 1	the son of Machir, the **s** of Manasseh,	1121
	36:12	the sons of Manasseh the **s** of Joseph,	1121
Dt	1:31	as a man doth bear his **s**, in all the way	1121
	1:36	Save Caleb the **s** of Jephunneh, he shall	1121
	1:38	*But* Joshua the **s** of Nun, which standeth	1121
	3:14	Jair the **s** of Manasseh took all the country	1121
	5:14	thou, nor thy **s**, nor thy daughter, nor thy	1121
	6: 2	thou, and thy **s**, and thy son's son,	1121
	6: 2	thou, and thy son, and thy son's **s**,	1121
	6:20	*And* when thy **s** asketh thee in time to	1121
	6:21	thou shalt say unto thy **s**, We were	1121
	7: 3	daughter thou shalt not give unto his **s**,	1121
	7: 3	his daughter shalt thou take unto thy **s**.	1121
	7: 4	For they will turn away thy **s** from	1121
	8: 5	as a man chasteneth his **s**, *so* the LORD	1121
	10: 6	Eleazar his **s** ministered in the priest's	1121
	11: 6	the sons of Eliab, the **s** of Reuben:	1121
	12:18	thy **s**, and thy daughter,	1121
	13: 6	the **s** of thy mother, or thy son,	1121
	13: 6	thy **s**, or thy daughter, or the wife of thy	1121
	16:11	thy **s**, and thy daughter,	1121
	16:14	thy **s**, and thy daughter,	1121
	18:10	among you *any one* that maketh his **s**	1121
	21:15	*if* the firstborn's be hers that was hated:	1121
	21:16	he may not make the **s** of the beloved	1121
	21:16	firstborn before the **s** of the hated,	1121
	21:17	shall acknowledge the **s** of the hated *for*	1121
	21:18	If a man have a stubborn and rebellious **s**,	1121
	21:20	This our **s** *is* stubborn and rebellious,	1121
	23: 4	they hired against thee Balaam the **s** of	1121
	28:56	towards her **s**, and towards her daughter,	1121
	31:23	he gave Joshua the **s** of Nun a charge,	1121
	32:44	the people, he and Hoshea the **s** of Nun.	1121
	34: 9	Joshua the **s** of Nun was full *of* the spirit	1121
Jos	1: 1	that the LORD spake unto Joshua the **s** of	1121
	2: 1	Joshua the **s** of Nun sent out of Shittim	1121
	2:23	came to Joshua the **s** of Nun, and told	1121
	6: 6	Joshua the **s** of Nun called the priests,	1121
	6:26	in his youngest **s** shall he set up the gates	NIH
	7: 1	Achan, the **s** of Carmi, the son of Zabdi,	1121
	7: 1	of Carmi, the **s** of Zabdi, the son of Zerah,	1121
	7: 1	of Carmi, the son of Zabdi, the son of Zerah,	1121
	7:18	Achan, the **s** of Carmi, the son of Zabdi,	1121
	7:18	of Carmi, the **s** of Zabdi, the son of Zerah,	1121
	7:18	of Carmi, the son of Zabdi, the son of Zerah,	1121
	7:19	said unto Achan, My **s**, give, I pray thee,	1121
	7:24	took Achan the **s** of Zerah, and the silver,	1121
	13:22	Balaam also the **s** of Beor, the soothsayer,	1121
	13:31	the children of Machir the **s** of Manasseh,	1121
	14: 1	Joshua the **s** of Nun, and the heads of	1121
	14: 6	Caleb the **s** of Jephunneh the Kenezite	1121
	14:13	unto Caleb the **s** of Jephunneh Hebron	1121
	14:14	became the inheritance of Caleb the **s** of	1121
	15: 6	up *to* the stone of Bohan the **s** of Reuben:	1121
	15: 8	border went up *by* the valley of the **s** of	1121
	15:13	unto Caleb the **s** of Jephunneh he gave a	1121
	15:17	Othniel the **s** of Kenaz, the brother of	1121
	17: 2	Manasseh the **s** of Joseph by their families	1121
	17: 3	Zelophehad, the **s** of Hepher, the son of	1121
	17: 3	the **s** of Gilead, the son of Machir,	1121
	17: 3	the son of Gilead, the **s** of Machir,	1121
	17: 3	the **s** of Manasseh, had no sons,	1121
	17: 4	before Joshua the **s** of Nun, and before	1121
	18:16	before the valley of the **s** of Hinnom,	1121
	18:17	descended *to* the stone of Bohan the **s** of	1121
	19:49	to Joshua the **s** of Nun among them:	1121
	19:51	Joshua the **s** of Nun, and the heads of	1121
	21: 1	unto Joshua the **s** of Nun, and unto	1121
	21:12	gave they to Caleb the **s** of Jephunneh for	1121
	22:13	Phinehas the **s** of Eleazar the priest,	1121
	22:20	Did not Achan the **s** of Zerah commit a	1121
	22:31	Phinehas the **s** of Eleazar the priest said	1121
	22:32	Phinehas the **s** of Eleazar the priest,	1121
	24: 9	Balak the **s** of Zippor, king of Moab, arose	1121
	24: 9	called Balaam the **s** of Beor to curse you:	1121
	24:29	that Joshua the **s** of Nun, the servant of	1121
	24:33	Eleazar the **s** of Aaron died;	1121
	24:33	in a hill that pertained to Phinehas his **s**,	1121
Jdg	1:13	Othniel the **s** of Kenaz, Caleb's younger	1121
	2: 8	Joshua the **s** of Nun, the servant of	1121
	3: 9	*even* Othniel the **s** of Kenaz,	1121
	3:11	And Othniel the **s** of Kenaz died.	1121
	3:15	Ehud the **s** of Gera, a Benjamite, a man	1121
	3:31	after him was Shamgar the **s** of Anath,	1121
	4: 6	called Barak the **s** of Abinoam out of	1121
	4:12	they shewed Sisera that Barak the **s** of	1121

Jdg	5: 1	and Barak the **s** of Abinoam on that day,	1121
	5: 6	In the days of Shamgar the **s** of Anath,	1121
	5:12	thy captivity captive, thou **s** of Abinoam.	1121
	6:11	his **s** Gideon threshed wheat by	1121
	6:29	Gideon the **s** of Joash hath done this	1121
	6:30	Bring out thy **s**, that he may die:	1121
	7:14	save the sword of Gideon the **s** of Joash,	1121
	8:13	Gideon the **s** of Joash returned from battle	1121
	8:22	thou, and thy **s**, and thy son's son also:	1121
	8:22	thou, and thy son, and thy son's **s** also:	1121
	8:23	you, neither shall my **s** rule over you:	1121
	8:29	Jerubbaal the **s** of Joash went and dwelt	1121
	8:31	she also bare him a **s**, whose name he	1121
	8:32	Gideon the **s** of Joash died in a good old	1121
	9: 1	Abimelech the **s** of Jerubbaal went to	1121
	9: 5	yet Jotham the youngest **s**	1121
	9:18	Abimelech, the **s** of his maidservant,	1121
	9:26	Gaal the **s** of Ebed came with his brethren	1121
	9:28	Gaal the **s** of Ebed said, Who *is*	1121
	9:28	*is not he* the **s** of Jerubbaal? and Zebul	1121
	9:30	heard the words of Gaal the **s** of Ebed,	1121
	9:31	Gaal the **s** of Ebed and his brethren be	1121
	9:35	Gaal the **s** of Ebed went out, and stood	1121
	9:57	them came the curse of Jotham the **s**	1121
	10: 1	arose to defend Israel Tola the **s** of Puah,	1121
	10: 1	of Puah, the **s** of Dodo, a man of Issachar;	1121
	11: 1	of valour, and he *was* the **s** of a harlot:	1121
	11: 2	for thou *art* the **s** of a strange woman.	1121
	11:25	thing better than Balak the **s** of Zippor,	1121
	11:34	beside her he had neither **s** nor daughter.	1121
	12:13	after him Abdon the **s** of Hillel,	1121
	12:15	Abdon the **s** of Hillel the Pirathonite died,	1121
	13: 3	but thou shalt conceive, and bear a **s**.	1121
	13: 5	For lo, thou *shalt* conceive, and bear a **s**;	1121
	13: 7	Behold, thou *shalt* conceive, and bear a **s**;	1121
	13:24	the woman bare a **s**, and called his name	1121
	15: 6	the **s in law** of the Timnite, because he	2860
	17: 2	Blessed *be thou* of the LORD, my **s**:	1121
	17: 3	unto the LORD from my hand for my **s**,	1121
	18:30	Jonathan, the **s** of Gershom, the son of	1121
	18:30	the **s** of Manasseh, he and his sons were	1121
	19: 5	the damsel's father said unto his **s in law**,	2860
	20:28	Phinehas, the **s** of Eleazar, the son of	1121
	20:28	the son of Eleazar, the **s** of Aaron,	1121
Ru	4:13	gave her conception, and she bare a **s**.	1121
	4:17	name, saying, There is a **s** born to Naomi;	1121
1Sa	1: 1	the **s** of Jeroham, the son of Elihu, the son	1121
	1: 1	the **s** of Elihu, the son of Tohu, the son of	1121
	1: 1	the **s** of Tohu, the son of Zuph,	1121
	1: 1	son of Tohu, the **s** of Zuph, an Ephrathite:	1121
	1:20	that she bare a **s**, and called his name	1121
	1:23	gave her **s** suck until she weaned him.	1121
	3: 6	he answered, I called not, my **s**; lie down	1121
	3:16	called Samuel, and said, Samuel, my **s**.	1121
	4:16	And he said, What is there done, my **s**?	1121
	4:20	*unto her*, Fear not; for thou hast born a **s**.	1121
	7: 1	sanctified Eleazar his **s** to keep the ark of	1121
	9: 1	the **s** of Abiel, the son of Zeror, the son of	1121
	9: 1	the son of Abiel, the **s** of Zeror, the son of	1121
	9: 1	the son of Zeror, the **s** of Bechorath,	1121
	9: 1	Bechorath, the **s** of Aphiah, a Benjamite,	1121
	9: 2	he had a **s**, whose name *was* Saul,	1121
	9: 3	Kish said to Saul his **s**, Take now one of	1121
	10: 2	for you, saying, What shall I do for my **s**?	1121
	10:11	What *is* this *that* is come unto the **s** of	1121
	10:21	and Saul the **s** of Kish was taken:	1121
	13:16	Jonathan his **s**, and the people that were	1121
	13:22	and with Jonathan his **s** was there found.	1121
	14: 1	that Jonathan the **s** of Saul said unto	1121
	14: 3	Ahiah, the **s** of Ahitub, Ichabod's brother,	1121
	14: 3	of Phinehas, the son of Eli,	1121
	14: 3	of Phinehas, the **s** of Eli,	1121
	14:39	though it be in Jonathan my **s**, he shall	1121
	14:40	Jonathan my **s** will be on the other side.	1121
	14:42	Cast *lots* between me and Jonathan my **s**.	1121
	14:50	*was* Abner, the **s** of Ner, Saul's uncle.	1121
	14:51	the father of Abner *was* the **s** of Abiel.	1121
	16:18	I have seen a **s** of Jesse the Beth-lehemite,	1121
	16:19	said, Send me David thy **s**, which *is* with	1121
	16:20	sent *them* by David his **s** unto Saul.	1121
	17:12	David *was* the **s** of that Ephrathite of	1121
	17:17	Jesse said unto David his **s**, Take now for	1121
	17:55	of the host, Abner, whose **s** *is* this youth?	1121
	17:56	Inquire thou whose **s** the stripling *is*.	1121
	17:58	him, Whose **s** *art* thou, *thou* young man?	1121
	17:58	*I am* the **s** of thy servant Jesse	1121
	18:18	that I should be **s in law** to the king?	2860
	18:21	Thou shalt *this* day be my **s in law** in	2859
	18:22	now therefore be the king's **s in law**.	2859
	18:23	a light *thing* to be a king's **s in law**,	2859
	18:26	David well to be the king's **s in law**:	2859
	18:27	that he might be the king's **s in law**.	2859
	19: 1	Saul spake to Jonathan his **s**, and to all his	1121
	19: 2	Saul's **s** delighted much in David:	1121
	20:27	Saul said unto Jonathan his **s**,	1121
	20:27	Wherefore cometh not the **s** of Jesse to	1121
	20:30	Thou **s** of the perverse rebellious *woman*,	1121
	20:30	the **s** of Jesse to thine own confusion,	1121
	20:31	For as long as the **s** of Jesse liveth upon	1121
	22: 7	will the **s** of Jesse give every one of you	1121
	22: 8	*there is* none that sheweth me that my **s**	1121
	22: 8	hath made *a league* with the **s** of Jesse,	1121
	22: 8	unto me that my **s** hath stirred up	1121
	22: 9	said, I saw the **s** of Jesse coming to Nob,	1121
	22: 9	to Nob, to Ahimelech the **s** of Ahitub:	1121

S

1Sa
22:11 the **s** of Ahitub, and all his father's house, 1121
22:12 Saul said, Hear now, thou **s** of Ahitub. 1121
22:13 thou and the **s** of Jesse, in that thou hast 1121
22:14 which *is* the king's **s in law**, and goeth 2860
22:20 one of the sons of Ahimelech the **s** of 1121
23: 6 when Abiathar the **s** of Ahimelech fled to 1121
23:16 Saul's **s** arose, and went to David 1121
24:16 Saul said, *Is* this thy voice, my **s** David? 1121
25: 8 unto thy servants, and to thy **s** David. 1121
25:10 who *is* the **s** of Jesse? there be many 1121
25:17 for he *is* such a **s** of Belial, that *a man* 1121
25:44 David's wife, to Phalti the **s** of Laish, 1121
26: 5 Abner the **s** of Ner, the captain of his 1121
26: 6 Abishai the **s** of Zeruiah, brother to Joab, 1121
26:14 to Abner the **s** of Ner, saying, Answerest 1121
26:17 and said, *Is* this thy voice, my **s** David? 1121
26:21 return, my **s** David: for I will no more do 1121
26:25 to David, Blessed *be* thou, my **s** David: 1121
27: 2 Achish, the **s** of Maoch, king of Gath. 1121
30: 7 Ahimelech's **s**, I pray thee, bring me 1121

2Sa
1: 4 and Saul and Jonathan his **s** are dead also. 1121
1: 5 that Saul and Jonathan his **s** be dead? 1121
1:12 for Jonathan his **s**, and for the people of 1121
1:13 I *am* the **s** of a stranger, an Amalekite. 1121
1:17 over Saul and over Jonathan his **s**: 1121
2: 8 Abner the **s** of Ner, captain of Saul's host, 1121
2: 8 took Ish-bosheth the **s** of Saul, 1121
2:10 Ish-bosheth Saul's *was* forty years old 1121
2:12 Abner the **s** of Ner, and the servants of 1121
2:12 the servants of Ish-bosheth the **s** of Saul, 1121
2:13 Joab the **s** of Zeruiah, and the servants of 1121
2:15 which *pertained* to Ish-bosheth the **s** of 1121
3: 3 Absalom the **s** of Maachah the daughter of 1121
3: 4 the fourth, Adonijah the **s** of Haggith; 1121
3: 4 and the fifth, Shephatiah the **s** of Abital; 1121
3:14 sent messengers to Ish-bosheth Saul's **s**, 1121
3:15 *even* from Phaltiel the **s** of Laish. 1121
3:23 Abner the **s** of Ner came to the king, 1121
3:25 Thou knowest Abner the **s** of Ner, that 1121
3:28 ever from the blood of Abner the **s** of Ner: 1121
3:37 not of the king to slay Abner the **s** of Ner. 1121
4: 1 Saul's **s** heard that Abner was dead in 1121
4: 2 Saul's **s** had two men *that were* captains 1121
4: 4 Jonathan, Saul's **s**, had a son *that was* 1121
4: 4 had a **s** *that was* lame of *his* feet, 1121
4: 8 Behold the head of Ish-bosheth the **s** of 1121
7:14 I will be his father, and he shall be my **s**. 1121
8: 3 the **s** of Rehob, king of Zobah. 1121
8:10 Toi sent Joram his **s** unto king David, 1121
8:12 of Hadadezer, **s** of Rehob, king of Zobah. 1121
8:16 Joab the **s** of Zeruiah *was* over the host; 1121
8:16 Jehoshaphat the **s** of Ahilud *was* recorder; 1121
8:17 Zadok the **s** of Ahitub, and Ahimelech 1121
8:17 Ahimelech the **s** of Abiathar, *were* 1121
8:18 Benaiah the **s** of Jehoiada *was over* both 1121
9: 3 Jonathan hath yet a **s**, *which is* lame on 1121
9: 4 of Machir, the **s** of Ammiel, in Lo-debar. 1121
9: 5 Machir, the **s** of Ammiel, from Lo-debar. 1121
9: 6 the **s** of Jonathan, the son of Saul, 1121
9: 6 the son of Jonathan, the **s** of Saul, 1121
9: 9 I have given unto thy master's **s** all that 1121
9:10 that thy master's **s** may have food to eat: 1121
9:10 Mephibosheth thy master's **s** shall eat 1121
9:12 Mephibosheth had a young **s**, whose 1121
10: 1 and Hanun his **s** reigned in his stead. 1121
10: 2 I will shew kindness unto Hanun the **s** of 1121
11:21 Who smote Abimelech the **s** of 1121
11:27 she became his wife, and bare him a **s**. 1121
12:24 she bare a **s**, and he called his name 1121
13: 1 that Absalom the **s** of David had a fair 1121
13: 1 and Amnon the **s** of David loved her. 1121
13: 3 the **s** of Shimeah David's brother: 1121
13: 4 Why *art* thou, *being* the king's **s**, lean 1121
13:25 Nay, my **s**, let us not all now go, 1121
13:32 the **s** of Shimeah David's brother, 1121
13:37 the **s** of Ammihud, king of Geshur. 1121
13:37 And *David* mourned for his **s** every day. 1121
14: 1 Now Joab the **s** of Zeruiah perceived that 1121
14:11 destroy any more, lest they destroy my **s**. 1121
14:11 there shall not one hair of thy **s** fall to 1121
14:16 **s** together out of the inheritance of God. 1121
15:27 Ahimaaz thy **s**, and Jonathan the son of 1121
15:27 thy son, and Jonathan the **s** of Abiathar. 1121
15:36 Ahimaaz Zadok's **s**, NIH
15:36 Zadok's *son*, and Jonathan Abiathar's **s**, NIH
16: 3 king said, And where *is* thy master's **s**? 1121
16: 5 whose name *was* Shimei, the **s** of Gera: 1121
16: 8 kingdom into the hand of Absalom thy **s**: 1121
16: 9 Abishai the **s** of Zeruiah unto the king, 1121
16:11 and to all his servants, Behold, my **s**, 1121
16:19 I not *serve* in the presence of his **s**? 1121
17:25 which Amasa *was* a man's **s**, whose name 1121
17:27 that Shobi the **s** of Nahash of Rabbah of 1121
17:27 Machir the **s** of Ammiel of Lo-debar, 1121
18: 2 third part under the hand of Abishai the **s** 1121
18:12 put forth mine hand against the king's **s**: 1121
18:18 I have no **s** to keep my name in 1121
18:19 said Ahimaaz the **s** of Zadok, Let me now 1121
18:20 no tidings, because the king's **s** is dead. 1121
18:22 said Ahimaaz the **s** of Zadok yet again to 1121
18:22 Joab said, Wherefore wilt thou run, my **s**, 1121
18:27 the running of Ahimaaz the **s** of Zadok. 1121
18:33 thus he said, O my **s** Absalom, my **s** 1121
18:33 my son Absalom, my **s**, my son Absalom: 1121
18:33 my son Absalom, my son, my **s** Absalom! 1121

2Sa
18:33 died for thee, O Absalom, my **s**, my son. 1121
18:33 died for thee, O Absalom, my son, my **s**. 1121
19: 2 day how the king was grieved for his **s**. 1121
19: 4 O my **s** Absalom, O Absalom, my son, 1121
19: 4 son Absalom, O Absalom, my son, 1121
19: 4 son Absalom, O Absalom, my son, my **s**. 1121
19:16 Shimei the **s** of Gera, a Benjamite, 1121
19:18 Shimei the **s** of Gera fell down before 1121
19:21 Abishai the **s** of Zeruiah answered and 1121
19:24 Mephibosheth the **s** of Saul came down to 1121
20: 1 *was* Sheba, the **s** of Bichri, a Benjamite: 1121
20: 1 neither have we inheritance in the **s** of 1121
20: 2 *and* followed Sheba the **s** of Bichri: 1121
20: 6 shall Sheba the **s** of Bichri do us more 1121
20: 7 to pursue after Sheba the **s** of Bichri. 1121
20:10 pursued after Sheba the **s** of Bichri. 1121
20:13 to pursue after Sheba the **s** of Bichri. 1121
20:21 Sheba the **s** of Bichri by name, 1121
20:22 they cut off the head of Sheba the **s** of 1121
20:23 Benaiah the **s** of Jehoiada *was* over 1121
20:24 Jehoshaphat the **s** of Ahilud *was* recorder: 1121
21: 7 the **s** of Jonathan the son of Saul, because 1121
21: 7 the son of Jonathan the **s** of Saul, because 1121
21: 7 between David and Jonathan the **s** of Saul. 1121
21: 8 whom she brought up for Adriel the **s** of 1121
21:12 the bones of Jonathan his **s** from the men 1121
21:13 of Saul and the bones of Jonathan his **s**; 1121
21:14 Jonathan his **s** buried they in the country 1121
21:17 Abishai the **s** of Zeruiah succoured him, 1121
21:19 where Elhanan the **s** of Jaare-oregim, 1121
21:21 Jonathan the **s** of Shimea the brother of 1121
23: 1 David the **s** of Jesse said, and the man 1121
23: 9 after him *was* Eleazar the **s** of Dodo 1121
23:11 after him *was* Shammah the **s** of Agee 1121
23:18 the brother of Joab, the **s** of Zeruiah, 1121
23:20 Benaiah the **s** of Jehoiada, the son of a 1121
23:20 the **s** of a valiant man, of Kabzeel, who 1121
23:22 *things* did Benaiah the **s** of Jehoiada, 1121
23:24 Elhanan the **s** of Dodo *of* Beth-lehem, 1121
23:26 the Paltite, Ira the **s** of Ikkesh the Tekoite, 1121
23:29 Heleb the **s** of Baanah, a Netophathite, 1121
23:29 Ittai the **s** of Ribai out of Gibeah of 1121
23:33 Ahiam the **s** of Sharar the Hararite, 1121
23:34 Eliphelet the **s** of Ahasbai, the son of 1121
23:34 son of Ahasbai, the **s** of the Maachathite, 1121
23:34 Eliam the **s** of Ahithophel the Gilonite, 1121
23:36 Igal the **s** of Nathan of Zobah, Bani 1121
23:37 armourbearer to Joab the **s** of Zeruiah, 1121

1Ki
1: 5 Adonijah the **s** of Haggith exalted himself, 1121
1: 7 he conferred with Joab the **s** of Zeruiah, 1121
1: 8 Benaiah the **s** of Jehoiada, and Nathan 1121
1:11 Hast thou not heard that Adonijah the **s** 1121
1:12 own life, and the life of thy **s** Solomon. 1121
1:13 Assuredly Solomon thy **s** shall reign after 1121
1:17 *saying*, Assuredly Solomon thy **s** shall 1121
1:21 my **s** Solomon shall be *counted* offenders. 1121
1:26 Benaiah the **s** of Jehoiada, and thy servant 1121
1:30 Assuredly Solomon thy **s** shall reign after 1121
1:32 the prophet, and Benaiah the **s** of Jehoiada. 1121
1:33 cause Solomon my **s** to ride upon mine 1121
1:36 Benaiah the **s** of Jehoiada answered 1121
1:38 Benaiah the **s** of Jehoiada, 1121
1:42 Jonathan the **s** of Abiathar the priest came: 1121
1:44 Benaiah the **s** of Jehoiada, 1121
2: 1 he charged Solomon his **s**, saying, 1121
2: 5 also what Joab the **s** of Zeruiah did to me, 1121
2: 5 unto Abner the **s** of Ner, and unto Amasa 1121
2: 5 Amasa the **s** of Jether, whom he slew, 1121
2: 8 *thou hast* with thee Shimei the **s** of Gera, 1121
2:13 Adonijah the **s** of Haggith came to 1121
2:22 the priest, and for Joab the **s** of Zeruiah. 1121
2:25 by the hand of Benaiah the **s** of Jehoiada; 1121
2:29 Solomon sent Benaiah the **s** of Jehoiada, 1121
2:32 *thereof, to wit*, Abner the **s** of Ner, 1121
2:32 host of Israel, and Amasa the **s** of Jether, 1121
2:34 So Benaiah the **s** of Jehoiada went up, 1121
2:35 the king put Benaiah the **s** of Jehoiada in 1121
2:39 unto Achish the **s** of Maachah king of Gath. 1121
2:46 So the king commanded Benaiah the **s** 1121
3: 6 that thou hast given him a **s** to sit on his 1121
3:20 midnight, and took my **s** from beside me, 1121
3:21 it was not my **s**, which I did bear. 1121
3:22 the living *is* my **s**, and the dead *is* thy son. 1121
3:22 the living *is* my son, and the dead *is* my **s**. 1121
3:22 the dead *is* thy **s**, and the living *is* my son. 1121
3:22 the dead *is* thy son, and the living *is* my **s**. 1121
3:23 This *is* my **s** that liveth, and thy son *is* 1121
3:23 my son that liveth, and thy **s** *is* the dead: 1121
3:23 thy **s** *is* the dead, and my son *is* the living. 1121
3:23 thy son *is* the dead, and my **s** *is* the living. 1121
3:26 for her bowels yerned upon her **s**, 1121
4: 2 he had; Azariah the **s** of Zadok the priest, 1121
4: 3 Jehoshaphat the **s** of Ahilud, the recorder. 1121
4: 4 Benaiah the **s** of Jehoiada *was* over 1121
4: 5 Azariah the **s** of Nathan *was* over 1121
4: 5 Zabud the **s** of Nathan *was* principal 1121
4: 6 Adoniram the **s** of Abda *was* over 1121
4: 8 The **s** of Hur, in mount Ephraim: 1121
4: 9 The **s** of Dekar, in Makaz, and in 1121
4:10 The **s** of Hesed, in Aruboth; to him 1121
4:11 The **s** of Abinadab, *in* all the region of 1121
4:12 Baana the **s** of Ahilud; *to him* pertained 1121
4:13 The **s** of Geber, in Ramoth-gilead; to him 2860
4:13 to him *pertained* the towns of Jair the **s** 1121
4:14 Ahinadab the **s** of Iddo *had* Mahanaim: 1121

1Ki
4:16 Baanah the **s** of Hushai *was* in Asher and 1121
4:17 Jehoshaphat the **s** of Paruah, in Issachar: 1121
4:18 Shimei the **s** of Elah, in Benjamin: 1121
4:19 Geber the **s** of Uri *was* in the country of 1121
5: 5 unto David my father, saying, Thy **s**, 1121
5: 7 hath given unto David a wise **s** over 1121
7:14 He *was* a widow's **s** of the tribe of 1121
8:19 **s** that shall come forth out of thy loins, 1121
11:12 *but* I will rend it out of the hand of thy **s**. 1121
11:13 will give one tribe to thy **s** for David my 1121
11:20 of Tahpenes bare him Genubath his **s**, 1121
11:23 adversary, Rezon the **s** of Eliadah, 1121
11:26 Jeroboam the **s** of Nebat, an Ephrathite of 1121
11:36 unto his **s** will I give one tribe, that David 1121
11:43 and Rehoboam his **s** reigned in his stead. 1121
12: 2 to pass, when Jeroboam the **s** of Nebat, 1121
12:15 Shilonite unto Jeroboam the **s** of Nebat. 1121
12:16 neither *have we* inheritance in the **s** of 1121
12:21 again to Rehoboam the **s** of Solomon. 1121
12:23 the **s** of Solomon, king of Judah, 1121
13:11 his **s** came and told him all the works that 1121
14: 1 At that time Abijah the **s** of Jeroboam fell 1121
14: 5 cometh to ask a thing of thee for her **s**; 1121
14:20 and Nadab his **s** reigned in his stead. 1121
14:21 Rehoboam the **s** of Solomon reigned in 1121
14:31 And Abijam his **s** reigned in his stead. 1121
15: 1 the **s** of Nebat reigned Abijam over Judah. 1121
15: 4 to set up his **s** after him, and to establish 1121
15: 8 and Asa his **s** reigned in his stead. 1121
15:18 the **s** of Tabrimon, the son of Hezion, 1121
15:18 Tabrimon, the **s** of Hezion, king of Syria, 1121
15:24 and Jehoshaphat his **s** reigned in his stead. 1121
15:25 Nadab the **s** of Jeroboam *began* to reign 1121
15:27 Baasha the **s** of Ahijah, of the house of 1121
15:33 **s** of Ahijah to reign over all Israel in 1121
16: 1 the word of the Lord came to Jehu the **s** 1121
16: 3 like the house of Jeroboam the **s** of Nebat. 1121
16: 6 and Elah his **s** reigned in his stead. 1121
16: 7 also by the hand of the prophet Jehu the **s** 1121
16: 8 of Baasha to reign over Israel in Tirzah, 1121
16:13 sins of Elah his **s**, *by* which they sinned, 1121
16:21 half of the people followed Tibni the **s** of 1121
16:22 people that followed Tibni the **s** of Ginath: 1121
16:26 in all the way of Jeroboam the **s** of Nebat, 1121
16:28 and Ahab his **s** reigned in his stead. 1121
16:29 Ahab the **s** of Omri to reign over Israel: 1121
16:29 Ahab the **s** of Omri reigned over Israel in 1121
16:30 Ahab the **s** of Omri did evil in the sight of 1121
16:31 in the sins of Jeroboam the **s** of Nebat, 1121
16:34 set up the gates thereof in his youngest **s** NIH
16:34 which he spake by Joshua the **s** of Nun. 1121
17:12 I may go in and dress it for me and my **s**, 1121
17:13 and after make for thee and for thy **s**. 1121
17:17 *that* the **s** of the woman, the mistress of 1121
17:18 my sin to remembrance, and to slay my **s**? 1121
17:19 he said unto her, Give me thy **s**. And he 1121
17:20 with whom I sojourn, by slaying her **s**? 1121
17:23 and Elijah said, See, thy **s** liveth. 1121
19:16 Jehu the **s** of Nimshi shalt thou anoint to 1121
19:16 Elisha the **s** of Shaphat of Abel-meholah 1121
19:19 and found Elisha the **s** of Shaphat, 1121
21:22 like the house of Jeroboam the **s** of Nebat, 1121
21:22 like the house of Baasha the **s** of Ahijah, 1121
22: 8 *is* yet one man, Micaiah the **s** of Imlah, 1121
22: 9 Hasten *hither* Micaiah the **s** of Imlah. 1121
22:11 Zedekiah the **s** of Chenaanah made him 1121
22:24 Zedekiah the **s** of Chenaanah went near, 1121
22:26 of the city, and to Joash the king's **s**, 1121
22:40 and Ahaziah his **s** reigned in his stead. 1121
22:41 Jehoshaphat the **s** of Asa *began* to reign 1121
22:50 said Ahaziah the **s** of Ahab unto 1121
22:50 and Jehoram his **s** reigned in his stead. 1121
22:51 Ahaziah the **s** of Ahab *began* to reign 1121
22:52 in the way of Jeroboam the **s** of Nebat, 1121

2Ki
1:17 the **s** of Jehoshaphat king of Judah; 1121
1:17 king of Judah; because he had no **s**. 1121
3: 1 Jehoram the **s** of Ahab began to reign 1121
3: 3 unto the sins of Jeroboam the **s** of Nebat, 1121
3:11 and said, Here is Elisha the **s** of Shaphat, 1121
3:27 he took his eldest **s** that should have 1121
4: 6 that she said unto her **s**, Bring me yet a 1121
4:16 to the time of life, thou shalt embrace a **s**. 1121
4:17 bare a **s** at that season that Elisha had 1121
4:28 she said, Did I desire a **s** of my lord? 1121
4:36 come in unto him, he said, Take up thy **s**. 1121
4:37 and took up her **s**, and went out. 1121
6:28 This woman said unto me, Give thy **s**, 1121
6:28 to day, and we will eat my **s** to morrow. 1121
6:29 So we boiled my **s**, and did eat him: 1121
6:29 day, Give thy **s**, that we may eat him: 1121
6:29 we may eat him: and she hath hid her **s**. 1121
6:31 if the head of Elisha the **s** of Shaphat shall 1121
6:32 See ye how this **s** of a murderer hath sent 1121
8: 1 whose **s** he had restored to life, saying, 1121
8: 5 woman, whose **s** he had restored to life, 1121
8: 5 king, this *is* the woman, and this *is* her **s**, 1121
8: 9 Thy **s** Ben-hadad king of Syria hath sent 1121
8:16 in the fifth year of Joram the **s** of Ahab 1121
8:16 Jehoram the **s** of Jehoshaphat king of 1121
8:24 and Ahaziah his **s** reigned in his stead. 1121
8:25 In the twelfth year of Joram the **s** of Ahab 1121
8:25 **s** of Jehoram king of Judah *begin* to reign. 1121
8:27 for he was the **s in law** of the house of 2860
8:28 he went with Joram the **s** of Ahab to 1121
8:29 Ahaziah the **s** of Jehoram king of Judah 1121

S

2Ki	8:29 to see Joram the **s** of Ahab in Jezreel,	1121
	9: 2 look out there Jehu the **s** of Jehoshaphat	1121
	9: 2 the son of Jehoshaphat the **s** of Nimshi,	1121
	9: 9 the house of Jeroboam the **s** of Nebat,	1121
	9: 9 like the house of Baasha the **s** of Ahijah:	1121
	9:14 So Jehu the **s** of Jehoshaphat the son of	1121
	9:14 So Jehu the **s** of Jehoshaphat the son of	1121
	9:20 driving *is* like the driving of Jehu the **s**	1121
	9:29 the eleventh year of Joram the **s** of Ahab	1121
	10:15 he lighted on Jehonadab the **s** of Rechab	1121
	10:23 went, and Jehonadab the **s** of Rechab,	1121
	10:29 Howbeit *from* the sins of Jeroboam the **s**	1121
	10:35 And Jehoahaz his **s** reigned in his stead.	1121
	11: 1 of Ahaziah saw that her **s** was dead,	1121
	11: 2 took Joash the **s** of Ahaziah, and stale him	1121
	11: 4 the LORD, and shewed them the king's **s**.	1121
	11:12 he brought forth the king's **s**, and put	1121
	12:21 For Jozachar the **s** of Shimeath,	1121
	12:21 Jehozabad the **s** of Shomer, his servants,	1121
	12:21 and Amaziah his **s** reigned in his stead.	1121
	13: 1 twentieth year of Joash the **s** of Ahaziah	1121
	13: 1 of Jehu *began* to reign over Israel in	1121
	13: 2 followed the sins of Jeroboam the **s** of	1121
	13: 3 the hand of Ben-hadad the **s** of Hazael,	1121
	13: 9 and Joash his **s** reigned in his stead.	1121
	13:10 s of Jehoahaz to reign over Israel in	1121
	13:11 all the sins of Jeroboam the **s** of Nebat,	1121
	13:24 and Ben-hadad his **s** reigned in his stead.	1121
	13:25 Jehoash the **s** of Jehoahaz took again out	1121
	13:25 of Ben-hadad the **s** of Hazael the cities,	1121
	14: 1 In the second year of Joash **s** of Jehoahaz	1121
	14: 1 Amaziah the **s** of Joash king of Judah.	1121
	14: 8 the **s** of Jehoahaz son of Jehu, king of	1121
	14: 8 the son of Jehoahaz **s** of Jehu, king of	1121
	14: 9 Give thy daughter to my **s** to wife:	1121
	14:13 the **s** of Jehoash the son of Ahaziah,	1121
	14:13 the son of Jehoash the **s** of Ahaziah,	1121
	14:16 and Jeroboam his **s** reigned in his stead.	1121
	14:17 Amaziah the **s** of Joash king of Judah	1121
	14:17 **s** of Jehoahaz king of Israel fifteen years.	1121
	14:23 In the fifteenth year of Amaziah the **s** of	1121
	14:23 of Joash king of Israel *began* to reign in	1121
	14:24 all the sins of Jeroboam the **s** of Nebat,	1121
	14:25 the **s** of Amittai, the prophet, which *was*	1121
	14:27 by the hand of Jeroboam the **s** of Joash.	1121
	14:29 and Zachariah his **s** reigned in his stead.	1121
	15: 1 of Amaziah king of Judah to reign.	1121
	15: 5 Jotham the king's **s** *was* over the house,	1121
	15: 7 and Jotham his **s** reigned in his stead.	1121
	15: 8 **s** of Jeroboam reign over Israel in Samaria	1121
	15: 9 from the sins of Jeroboam the **s** of Nebat,	1121
	15:10 Shallum the **s** of Jabesh conspired against	1121
	15:13 Shallum the **s** of Jabesh *began* to reign in	1121
	15:14 For Menahem the **s** of Gadi went up from	1121
	15:14 smote Shallum the **s** of Jabesh in Samaria,	1121
	15:17 Menahem the **s** of Gadi to reign over	1121
	15:18 from the sins of Jeroboam the **s** of Nebat,	1121
	15:22 and Pekahiah his **s** reigned in his stead.	1121
	15:23 **s** of Menahem *began* to reign over Israel	1121
	15:24 from the sins of Jeroboam the **s** of Nebat,	1121
	15:25 Pekah the **s** of Remaliah, a captain of his,	1121
	15:27 **s** of Remaliah *began* to reign over Israel in	1121
	15:28 from the sins of Jeroboam the **s** of Nebat,	1121
	15:30 Hoshea the **s** of Elah made a conspiracy	1121
	15:30 against Pekah the **s** of Remaliah,	1121
	15:30 in the twentieth year of Jotham the **s** of	1121
	15:32 In the second year of Pekah the **s** of	1121
	15:32 the **s** of Uzziah king of Judah to reign.	1121
	15:37 of Syria, and Pekah the **s** of Remaliah.	1121
	15:38 and Ahaz his **s** reigned in his stead.	1121
	16: 1 In the seventeenth year of Pekah the **s** of	1121
	16: 1 **s** of Jotham king of Judah *began* to reign.	1121
	16: 3 and made his **s** to pass through the fire,	1121
	16: 5 Pekah **s** of Remaliah king of Israel came	1121
	16: 7 saying, I *am* thy servant and thy **s**:	1121
	16:20 and Hezekiah his **s** reigned in his stead.	1121
	17: 1 of Elah to reign in Samaria over Israel	1121
	17:21 they made Jeroboam the **s** of Nebat king:	1121
	18: 1 year of Hoshea **s** of Elah king of Israel,	1121
	18: 1 *that* Hezekiah the **s** of Ahaz king of Judah	1121
	18: 9 which *was* the seventh year of Hoshea **s**	1121
	18:18 there came out to them Eliakim the **s** of	1121
	18:18 and Joah the **s** of Asaph the recorder.	1121
	18:26 said Eliakim the **s** of Hilkiah, and Shebna,	1121
	18:37 came Eliakim the **s** of Hilkiah, which *was*	1121
	18:37 and Joah the **s** of Asaph the recorder,	1121
	19: 2 to Esai the prophet the **s** of Amoz.	1121
	19:20 Isaiah the **s** of Amoz sent to Hezekiah,	1121
	19:37 And Esarhaddon his **s** reigned in his stead.	1121
	20: 1 the prophet Isaiah the **s** of Amoz came to	1121
	20:12 the **s** of Baladan, king of Babylon,	1121
	20:21 and Manasseh his **s** reigned in his stead.	1121
	21: 6 he made his **s** pass through the fire,	1121
	21: 7 to Solomon his **s**, In this house,	1121
	21:18 and Amon his **s** reigned in his stead.	1121
	21:24 the people of the land made Josiah his **s**	1121
	21:26 and Josiah his **s** reigned in his stead.	1121
	22: 3 the king sent Shaphan the **s** of Azaliah,	1121
	22: 3 of Meshullam, the scribe, *to* the house	1121
	22:12 Ahikam the **s** of Shaphan, and Achbor	1121
	22:12 Achbor the **s** of Michaiah, and Shaphan	1121
	22:14 the wife of Shallum the **s** of Tikvah,	1121
	22:14 the **s** of Harhas, keeper of the wardrobe;	1121
	23:10 that no man might make his **s** or his	1121
	23:15 the high place which Jeroboam the **s** of	1121

2Ki	23:30 people of the land took Jehoahaz the **s**	1121
	23:34 Pharaoh-nechoh made Eliakim the **s** of	1121
	24: 6 and Jehoiachin his **s** reigned in his stead.	1121
	25:22 over them he made Gedaliah the **s** of	1121
	25:22 son of Ahikam, the **s** of Shaphan, ruler.	1121
	25:23 even Ishmael the **s** of Nethaniah,	1121
	25:23 Johanan the **s** of Careah, and Seraiah	1121
	25:23 Seraiah the **s** of Tanhumeth	1121
	25:23 Jaazaniah the **s** of a Maachathite, they	1121
	25:25 Ishmael the **s** of Nethaniah, the son of	1121
	25:25 the **s** of Elishama, of the seed royal, came,	1121
1Ch	1:43 the children of Israel; Bela the **s** of Beor:	1121
	1:44 Jobab the **s** of Zerah of Bozrah reigned in	1121
	1:46 Husham was dead, Hadad the **s** of Bedad,	1121
	1:49 Baal-hanan the **s** of Achbor reigned in his	1121
	2:18 Caleb the **s** of Hezron begat *children* of	1121
	2:45 the **s** of Shammai *was* Maon:	1121
	2:50 were the sons of Caleb the **s** of Hur,	1121
	3: 2 Absalom the **s** of Maachah the daughter	1121
	3: 2 the fourth, Adonijah the **s** of Haggith:	1121
	3:10 Solomon's **s** *was* Rehoboam, Abia his son,	1121
	3:10 Abia his **s**, Asa his son, Jehoshaphat his	1121
	3:10 Abia his son, Asa his **s**, Jehoshaphat his	1121
	3:10 his son, Asa his son, Jehoshaphat his **s**,	1121
	3:11 Joram his **s**, Ahaziah his son, Joash his	1121
	3:11 Joram his son, Ahaziah his **s**, Joash his,	1121
	3:11 his son, Ahaziah his son, Joash his **s**,	1121
	3:12 Amaziah his **s**, Azariah his son, Jotham	1121
	3:12 his son, Azariah his **s**, Jotham his son,	1121
	3:12 his son, Azariah his son, Jotham his **s**,	1121
	3:13 Ahaz his **s**, Hezekiah his son, Manasseh	1121
	3:13 Ahaz his son, Hezekiah his **s**, Manasseh	1121
	3:13 son, Hezekiah his son, Manasseh his **s**,	1121
	3:14 Amon his son, Josiah his son.	1121
	3:14 Amon his son, Josiah his **s**.	1121
	3:16 Jeconiah his **s**, Zedekiah his son.	1121
	3:16 Jeconiah his son, Zedekiah his **s**.	1121
	3:17 the sons of Jeconiah; Assir, Salathiel his **s**,	1121
	3:19 the **s** of Zerubbabel; Meshullam,	1121
	4: 2 Reaiah the **s** of Shobal begat Jahath;	1121
	4: 8 the families of Aharhel the **s** of Harum.	1121
	4:15 the sons of Caleb the **s** of Jephunneh; Iru,	1121
	4:21 The sons of Shelah the **s** of Judah *were*,	1121
	4:25 Shallum his **s**, Mibsam his son, Mishma	1121
	4:25 his son, Mibsam his **s**, Mishma his son,	1121
	4:25 his son, Mibsam his son, Mishma his **s**.	1121
	4:26 Hamuel his **s**, Zacchur his son, Shimei	1121
	4:26 his son, Zacchur his **s**, Shimei his son.	1121
	4:26 his son, Zacchur his son, Shimei his **s**.	1121
	4:34 Jamlech, and Joshah the **s** of Amaziah,	1121
	4:35 Joel, and Jehu the **s** of Josibiah, the son	1121
	4:35 the **s** of Seraiah, the son of Asiel,	1121
	4:35 the son of Seraiah, the **s** of Asiel,	1121
	4:37 Ziza the **s** of Shiphi, the son of Allon,	1121
	4:37 the **s** of Allon, the son of Jedaiah, the son	1121
	4:37 the son of Allon, the **s** of Jedaiah, the son	1121
	4:37 the son of Jedaiah, the **s** of Shimri,	1121
	4:37 the son of Shimri, the **s** of Shemaiah;	1121
	5: 1 unto the sons of Joseph the **s** of Israel:	1121
	5: 4 Shemaiah his **s**, Gog his son, Shimei his	1121
	5: 4 his son, Gog his **s**, Shimei his son,	1121
	5: 4 his son, Gog his son, Shimei his **s**.	1121
	5: 5 Micah his **s**, Reaia his son, Baal his son,	1121
	5: 5 Micah his son, Reaia his **s**, Baal his son,	1121
	5: 5 Micah his son, Reaia his son, Baal his **s**,	1121
	5: 6 Beerah his **s**, whom Tilgath-pilneser king	1121
	5: 8 Bela the **s** of Azaz, the son of Shema,	1121
	5: 8 the **s** of Shema, the son of Joel, who	1121
	5: 8 the son of Shema, the **s** of Joel, who	1121
	5:14 These *are* the children of Abihail the **s** of	1121
	5:14 the **s** of Jaroah, the son of Gilead, the son	1121
	5:14 the son of Jaroah, the **s** of Gilead, the son	1121
	5:14 the son of Gilead, the **s** of Michael,	1121
	5:14 the **s** of Jeshishai, the son of Jahdo, the	1121
	5:14 Jeshishai, the **s** of Jahdo, the son of Buz;	1121
	5:14 Jeshishai, the son of Jahdo, the **s** of Buz;	1121
	5:15 Ahi the **s** of Abdiel, the son of Guni,	1121
	5:15 Ahi the son of Abdiel, the **s** of Guni,	1121
	6:20 Libni his **s**, Jahath his son, Zimmah his	1121
	6:20 Libni his son, Jahath his **s**, Zimmah his	1121
	6:20 his son, Jahath his son, Zimmah his **s**,	1121
	6:21 Joah his **s**, Iddo his son, Zerah his son,	1121
	6:21 Joah his son, Iddo his **s**, Zerah his son,	1121
	6:21 Joah his son, Iddo his son, Zerah his **s**,	1121
	6:21 Iddo his son, Zerah his son, Jeaterai his **s**.	1121
	6:22 Amminadab his **s**, Korah his son, Assir his	1121
	6:22 his son, Korah his **s**, Assir his son,	1121
	6:22 his son, Korah his son, Assir his **s**,	1121
	6:23 Elkanah his **s**, and Ebiasaph his son,	1121
	6:23 and Ebiasaph his **s**, and Assir his son,	1121
	6:23 and Ebiasaph his son, and Assir his **s**,	1121
	6:24 Tahath his **s**, Uriel his son, Uzziah his son,	1121
	6:24 Tahath his son, Uriel his **s**, Uzziah his son,	1121
	6:24 his son, Uzziah his **s**, and Shaul his son.	1121
	6:24 his son, Uzziah his son, and Shaul his **s**.	1121
	6:26 Zophai his **s**, and Nahath his son,	1121
	6:26 Zophai his son, and Nahath his **s**,	1121
	6:27 Eliab his **s**, Jeroham his son, Elkanah his	1121
	6:27 Eliab his son, Jeroham his **s**, Elkanah his	1121
	6:27 his son, Jeroham his son, Elkanah his **s**.	1121
	6:29 Mahli, Libni his **s**, Shimei his son, Uzza	1121
	6:29 Libni his son, Shimei his **s**, Uzza his son,	1121
	6:29 Libni his son, Shimei his son, Uzza his **s**,	1121
	6:30 Shimea his **s**, Haggiah his son, Asaiah his	1121
	6:30 his son, Haggiah his **s**, Asaiah his son.	1121

1Ch	6:30 his son, Haggiah his son, Asaiah his **s**.	1121
	6:33 Heman a singer, the **s** of Joel, the son of	1121
	6:33 singer, the son of Joel, the **s** of Shemuel,	1121
	6:34 The **s** of Elkanah, the son of Jeroham,	1121
	6:34 the **s** of Jeroham, the son of Eliel, the son	1121
	6:34 Jeroham, the son of Eliel, the **s** of Toah,	1121
	6:34 Jeroham, the son of Eliel, the **s** of Toah,	1121
	6:35 The **s** of Zuph, the son of Elkanah, the	1121
	6:35 The son of Zuph, the **s** of Elkanah, the	1121
	6:35 the **s** of Mahath, the son of Amasai,	1121
	6:35 the son of Mahath, the **s** of Amasai,	1121
	6:36 The **s** of Elkanah, the son of Joel, the son	1121
	6:36 the **s** of Joel, the son of Azariah,	1121
	6:36 the son of Joel, the **s** of Azariah,	1121
	6:36 the son of Azariah, the **s** of Zephaniah,	1121
	6:37 The **s** of Tahath, the son of Assir, the son	1121
	6:37 The son of Tahath, the **s** of Assir, the son	1121
	6:37 the son of Assir, the **s** of Ebiasaph, the son	1121
	6:37 the son of Ebiasaph, the **s** of Korah,	1121
	6:38 The **s** of Izhar, the son of Kohath, the son	1121
	6:38 the **s** of Kohath, the son of Levi, the son	1121
	6:38 of Kohath, the son of Levi, the son of Israel.	1121
	6:38 of Kohath, the son of Levi, the **s** of Israel.	1121
	6:39 *even* Asaph the **s** of Berachiah, the son of	1121
	6:39 the son of Berachiah, the **s** of Shimea,	1121
	6:40 The **s** of Michael, the son of Baaseiah,	1121
	6:40 The son of Michael, the **s** of Baaseiah,	1121
	6:40 the son of Baaseiah, the **s** of Malchiah,	1121
	6:41 The **s** of Ethni, the son of Zerah, the son	1121
	6:41 The son of Ethni, the **s** of Zerah, the son	1121
	6:41 of Ethni, the son of Zerah, the **s** of Adaiah,	1121
	6:42 The **s** of Ethan, the son of Zimmah, the	1121
	6:42 The son of Ethan, the **s** of Zimmah, the	1121
	6:42 the son of Zimmah, the **s** of Shimei,	1121
	6:43 The **s** of Jahath, the son of Gershom,	1121
	6:43 the **s** of Gershom, the son of Levi.	1121
	6:43 the son of Gershom, the **s** of Levi.	1121
	6:44 Ethan the **s** of Kishi, the son of Abdi,	1121
	6:44 Kishi, the son of Abdi, the **s** of Malluch,	1121
	6:44 Kishi, the son of Abdi, the **s** of Malluch,	1121
	6:45 The **s** of Hashabiah, the son of Amaziah,	1121
	6:45 the **s** of Amaziah, the son of Hilkiah,	1121
	6:45 the son of Amaziah, the **s** of Hilkiah,	1121
	6:46 The **s** of Amzi, the son of Bani, the son of	1121
	6:46 The son of Amzi, the **s** of Bani, the son of	1121
	6:46 of Amzi, the son of Bani, the **s** of Shamer,	1121
	6:47 The **s** of Mahli, the son of Mushi, the son	1121
	6:47 the **s** of Mushi, the son of Merari, the son	1121
	6:47 of Mushi, the **s** of Merari, the son of Levi.	1121
	6:47 of Mushi, the son of Merari, the **s** of Levi.	1121
	6:50 Eleazar his **s**, Phinehas his son, Abishua	1121
	6:50 Eleazar his son, Phinehas his **s**, Abishua	1121
	6:50 his son, Phinehas his son, Abishua his **s**,	1121
	6:51 Bukki his **s**, Uzzi his son, Zerahiah his	1121
	6:51 Bukki his son, Uzzi his **s**, Zerahiah his	1121
	6:51 his son, Uzzi his son, Zerahiah his **s**,	1121
	6:52 Meraioth his **s**, Amariah his son, Ahitub	1121
	6:52 his son, Amariah his **s**, Ahitub his son,	1121
	6:52 his son, Amariah his son, Ahitub his **s**,	1121
	6:53 Zadok his **s**, Ahimaaz his son.	1121
	6:53 Zadok his son, Ahimaaz his **s**.	1121
	6:56 they gave to Caleb the **s** of Jephunneh.	1121
	7:16 Maachah the wife of Machir bare a **s**,	1121
	7:17 the **s** of Machir, the son of Manasseh.	1121
	7:17 the son of Machir, the **s** of Manasseh.	1121
	7:20 Bered his **s**, and Tahath his son,	1121
	7:20 Tahath his **s**, and Eladah his son,	1121
	7:20 and Eladah his **s**, and Tahath his son,	1121
	7:20 and Eladah his son, and Tahath his **s**,	1121
	7:21 Zabad his **s**, and Shuthelah his son,	1121
	7:21 and Shuthelah his son, and Ezer, and Elead,	1121
	7:23 bare a **s**, and he called his name Beriah,	1121
	7:25 Rephah *was* his **s**, also Resheph,	1121
	7:25 and Telah his **s**, and Tahan his son,	1121
	7:25 and Telah his son, and Tahan his **s**,	1121
	7:26 Laadan his **s**, Ammihud his son,	1121
	7:26 Laadan his son, Ammihud his **s**,	1121
	7:26 son, Ammihud his son, Elishama his **s**,	1121
	7:27 Non his **s**, Jehoshua his son.	1121
	7:27 Non his son, Jehoshua his **s**.	1121
	7:29 these dwelt the children of Joseph the **s**	1121
	7:35 the **s** of his brother Helem; Zophah,	1121
	8:30 his firstborn **s** Abdon, and Zur, and Kish,	1121
	8:34 the **s** of Jonathan *was* Merib-baal;	1121
	8:37 Rapha *was* his **s**, Eleasah his son, Azel his	1121
	8:37 *was* his son, Eleasah his **s**, Azel his son:	1121
	8:37 *was* his son, Eleasah his son, Azel his **s**:	1121
	9: 4 Uthai the **s** of Ammihud, the son of Omri,	1121
	9: 4 the **s** of Omri, the son of Imri, the son of	1121
	9: 4 son of Omri, the **s** of Imri, the son of Bani,	1121
	9: 4 son of Omri, the son of Imri, the **s** of Bani,	1121
	9: 4 of the children of Pharez the **s** of Judah.	1121
	9: 7 Sallu the **s** of Meshullam, the son of	1121
	9: 7 the **s** of Hodaviah, the son of Hasenuah,	1121
	9: 7 the son of Hodaviah, the **s** of Hasenuah,	1121
	9: 8 Ibneiah the **s** of Jeroham, and Elah the	1121
	9: 8 Elah the **s** of Uzzi, the son of Michri,	1121
	9: 8 the **s** of Michri, and Meshullam the son	1121
	9: 8 Meshullam the **s** of Shephathiah, the son	1121
	9: 8 the **s** of Reuel, the son of Ibnijah;	1121
	9: 8 the son of Reuel, the **s** of Ibnijah;	1121
	9:11 Azariah the **s** of Hilkiah, the son of	1121
	9:11 the **s** of Meshullam, the son of Zadok,	1121
	9:11 the **s** of Zadok, the son of Meraioth, the	1121
	9:11 the son of Zadok, the **s** of Meraioth, the	1121

Ref	Text	Strong's
1Ch 9:11	the son of Meraioth, the **s** of Ahitub,	1121
9:12	Adaiah the **s** of Jeroham, the son of	1121
9:12	the **s** of Pashur, the son of Malchijah,	1121
9:12	the **s** of Malchijah, and Maasiai the son of	1121
9:12	Maasiai the **s** of Adiel, the son of Jahzerah,	1121
9:12	of Jahzerah, the son of Meshullam,	1121
9:12	the son of Jahzerah, the **s** of Meshullam,	1121
9:12	the **s** of Meshillemith, the son of Immer;	1121
9:12	the son of Meshillemith, the **s** of Immer;	1121
9:14	Shemaiah the **s** of Hasshub, the son of	1121
9:14	the **s** of Azrikam, the son of Hashabiah,	1121
9:14	the son of Azrikam, the **s** of Hashabiah,	1121
9:15	and Galal, and Mattaniah the **s** of Micah,	1121
9:15	Micah, the **s** of Zichri, the son of Asaph;	1121
9:15	Micah, the son of Zichri, the **s** of Asaph;	1121
9:16	Obadiah the **s** of Shemaiah, the son of	1121
9:16	the **s** of Galal, the son of Jeduthun,	1121
9:16	the **s** of Jeduthun, and Berechiah the son	1121
9:16	Berechiah the **s** of Asa, the son of	1121
9:16	the son of Asa, the **s** of Elkanah,	1121
9:19	Shallum the **s** of Kore, the son of	1121
9:19	the **s** of Ebiasaph, the son of Korah,	1121
9:19	the **s** of Korah, and his brethren,	1121
9:20	Phinehas the **s** of Eleazar the ruler	1121
9:21	And Zechariah the **s** of Meshelemiah *was*	1121
9:36	his firstborn **s** Abdon, then Zur, and Kish,	1121
9:40	the **s** of Jonathan *was* Merib-baal:	1121
9:43	Rephaiah his **s**, Eleasah his son, Azel his	1121
9:43	his son, Eleasah his **s**, Azel his son,	1121
9:43	his son, Eleasah his son, Azel his **s.**	1121
10:14	turned the kingdom unto David the **s** of	1121
11: 6	So Joab the **s** of Zeruiah went first up,	1121
11:12	after him *was* Eleazar the **s** of Dodo,	1121
11:22	Benaiah the **s** of Jehoiada, the son of a	1121
11:22	the **s** of a valiant man of Kabzeel, who	1121
11:24	*things* did Benaiah the **s** of Jehoiada,	1121
11:26	Elhanan the **s** of Dodo of Beth-lehem,	1121
11:28	Ira the **s** of Ikkesh the Tekoite, Abi-ezer	1121
11:30	Heled the **s** of Baanah the Netophathite,	1121
11:31	Ithai the **s** of Ribai of Gibeah,	1121
11:34	Jonathan the **s** of Shage the Hararite,	1121
11:35	Ahiam the **s** of Sacar the Hararite,	1121
11:35	of Sacar the Hararite, Eliphal the **s** of Ur,	1121
11:37	the Carmelite, Naarai the **s** of Ezbai,	1121
11:38	of Nathan, Mibhar the **s** of Haggeri,	1121
11:39	the armourbearer of Joab the **s** of Zeruiah,	1121
11:41	Uriah the Hittite, Zabad the **s** of Ahlai,	1121
11:42	Adina the **s** of Shiza the Reubenite,	1121
11:43	Hanan the **s** of Maachah, and Joshaphat	1121
11:45	Jediael the **s** of Shimri, and Joha his	1121
12: 1	close because of Saul the **s** of Kish:	1121
12:18	David, and on thy side, thou **s** of Jesse:	1121
15:17	So the Levites appointed Heman the **s** of	1121
15:17	of his brethren, Asaph the **s** of Berechiah;	1121
15:17	their brethren, Ethan the **s** of Kushaiah;	1121
16:38	Obed-edom also the **s** of Jeduthun and	1121
17:13	I will be his father, and he shall be my **s:**	1121
18:10	He sent Hadoram his **s** to king David,	1121
18:12	Moreover Abishai the **s** of Zeruiah slew	1121
18:15	Joab the **s** of Zeruiah *was* over the host;	1121
18:15	and Jehoshaphat the **s** of Ahilud, recorder.	1121
18:16	Zadok the **s** of Ahitub, and Abimelech	1121
18:16	Abimelech the **s** of Abiathar, *were*	1121
18:17	Benaiah the **s** of Jehoiada *was* over	1121
19: 1	died, and his **s** reigned in his stead.	1121
19: 2	I will shew kindness unto Hanun the **s** of	1121
20: 5	Elhanan the **s** of Jair slew Lahmi	1121
20: 6	and he also was the **s** of the giant.	3205
20: 7	Jonathan the **s** of Shimea David's brother	1121
22: 5	Solomon my **s** *is* young and tender,	1121
22: 6	he called for Solomon his **s,**	1121
22: 7	David said to Solomon, My **s,** *as for* me,	1121
22: 9	a **s** *shall be* born to thee, who shall	1121
22:10	he shall be my **s**, and I *will be* his father;	1121
22:11	Now, my **s**, the LORD be with thee;	1121
22:17	princes of Israel to help Solomon his **s,**	1121
23: 1	he made Solomon his **s** king over Israel.	1121
24: 6	Shemaiah the **s** of Nethaneel the scribe,	1121
24: 6	Ahimelech the **s** of Abiathar, and *before*	1121
24:29	the **s** of Kish *was* Jerahmeel.	1121
26: 1	the Korhites *was* Meshelemiah the **s** of	1121
26: 6	Also unto Shemaiah his **s** were sons born,	1121
26:14	*for* Zechariah his **s**, a wise counseller,	1121
26:24	Shebuel the **s** of Gershom, the son of	1121
26:24	the **s** of Moses, *was* ruler of the treasures.	1121
26:25	Rehabiah his **s**, and Jeshaiah his son,	1121
26:25	Jeshaiah his **s**, and Joram his son,	1121
26:25	Joram his **s**, and Zichri his son,	1121
26:25	and Zichri his **s**, and Shelomith his son.	1121
26:25	and Zichri his son, and Shelomith his **s.**	1121
26:28	Saul the **s** of Kish, and Abner the son of	1121
26:28	Abner the **s** of Ner, and Joab the son of	1121
26:28	and Joab the **s** of Zeruiah, had dedicated;	1121
27: 2	month *was* Jashobeam the **s** of Zabdiel:	1121
27: 5	month *was* Benaiah the **s** of Jehoiada,	1121
27: 6	and *in* his course *was* Ammizabad his **s.**	1121
27: 7	of Joab, and Zebadiah his **s** after him:	1121
27: 9	*was* Ira the **s** of Ikkesh the Tekoite:	1121
27:16	the Reubenites *was* Eliezer the **s** of Zichri:	1121
27:16	Shephatiah the **s** of Maachah:	1121
27:17	the Levites, Hashabiah the **s** of Kemuel:	1121
27:18	Of Issachar, Omri the **s** of Michael:	1121
27:19	Of Zebulun, Ishmaiah the **s** of Obadiah:	1121
27:19	of Naphtali, Jerimoth the **s** of Azriel:	1121
27:20	of Ephraim, Hoshea the **s** of Azaziah:	1121
1Ch 27:20	tribe of Manasseh, Joel the **s** of Pedaiah:	1121
27:21	in Gilead, Iddo the **s** of Zechariah:	1121
27:21	of Benjamin, Jaasiel the **s** of Abner:	1121
27:22	Of Dan, Azareel the **s** of Jeroham.	1121
27:24	Joab the **s** of Zeruiah began to number,	1121
27:25	treasures *was* Azmaveth the **s** of Adiel:	1121
27:25	castles, *was* Jehonathan the **s** of Uzziah:	1121
27:26	of the ground *was* Ezri the **s** of Chelub:	1121
27:29	in the valleys *was* Shaphat the **s** of Adlai:	1121
27:32	Jehiel the **s** of Hachmoni *was* with	1121
27:34	after Ahithophel *was* Jehoiada the **s** of	1121
28: 5	he hath chosen Solomon my **s** to sit upon	1121
28: 6	he said unto me, Solomon thy **s**, he shall	1121
28: 6	for I have chosen him to be my **s**, and I	1121
28: 9	Solomon my **s**, know thou the God of	1121
28:11	David gave to Solomon his **s** the pattern	1121
28:20	David said to Solomon his **s**, Be strong	1121
29: 1	Solomon my **s**, whom alone God hath	1121
29:19	give unto Solomon my **s** a perfect heart,	1121
29:22	they made Solomon the **s** of David king	1121
29:26	Thus David the **s** of Jesse reigned over all	1121
29:28	and Solomon his **s** reigned in his stead.	1121
2Ch 1: 1	Solomon the **s** of David was strengthened	1121
1: 5	that Bezaleel the **s** of Uri, the son of Hur,	1121
1: 5	the son of Uri, the **s** of Hur, had made,	1121
2:12	hath given to David the king a wise **s,**	1121
2:14	The **s** of a woman of the daughters of	1121
6: 9	thy **s** which shall come forth out of thy	1121
9:29	the seer against Jeroboam the **s** of Nebat?	1121
9:31	and Rehoboam his **s** reigned in his stead.	1121
10: 2	Jeroboam the **s** of Nebat, who *was* in	1121
10:15	the Shilonite to Jeroboam the **s** of Nebat.	1121
10:16	*have* none inheritance in the **s** of Jesse:	1121
11: 3	Speak unto Rehoboam the **s** of Solomon,	1121
11:17	made Rehoboam the **s** of Solomon strong,	1121
11:18	of Jerimoth the **s** of David *to* wife,	1121
11:18	the daughter of Eliab the **s** of Jesse;	1121
11:22	Rehoboam made Abijah the **s** of Maachah	1121
12:16	and Abijah his **s** reigned in his stead.	1121
13: 6	Jeroboam the **s** of Nebat, the servant of	1121
13: 6	the servant of Solomon the **s** of David,	1121
13: 7	against Rehoboam the **s** of Solomon,	1121
14: 1	Asa his **s** reigned in his stead. In his days	1121
15: 1	spirit of God came upon Azariah the **s**	1121
17: 1	Jehoshaphat his **s** reigned in his stead,	1121
17:16	next him *was* Amasiah the **s** of Zichri,	1121
18: 7	the same *is* Micaiah the **s** of Imla.	1121
18: 8	said, Fetch quickly Micaiah the **s** of Imla.	1121
18:10	Zedekiah the **s** of Chenaanah had made	1121
18:23	Zedekiah the **s** of Chenaanah came near,	1121
18:25	of the city, and to Joash the king's **s;**	1121
19: 2	Jehu the **s** of Hanani the seer went out to	1121
19:11	Zebadiah the **s** of Ishmael, the ruler of	1121
20:14	Jahaziel the **s** of Zechariah, the son of	1121
20:14	the **s** of Benaiah, the son of Jeiel, the son	1121
20:14	son of Benaiah, the **s** of Jeiel, the son of	1121
20:14	the son of Jeiel, the **s** of Mattaniah,	1121
20:34	in the book of Jehu the **s** of Hanani,	1121
20:37	Eliezer the **s** of Dodavah of Mareshah	1121
21: 1	And Jehoram his **s** reigned in his stead.	1121
21:17	so that there was never a **s** left him,	1121
22: 1	Ahaziah his youngest **s** king in his stead:	1121
22: 1	Ahaziah the **s** of Jehoram king of Judah	1121
22: 5	went with Jehoram the **s** of Ahab king of	1121
22: 6	Azariah the **s** of Jehoram king of Judah	1121
22: 6	to see Jehoram the **s** of Ahab at Jezreel,	1121
22: 7	Jehoram against Jehu the **s** of Nimshi,	1121
22: 9	said they, he *is the* **s** of Jehoshaphat,	1121
22:10	of Ahaziah saw that her **s** was dead,	1121
22:11	took Joash the **s** of Ahaziah, and stole	1121
23: 1	Azariah the **s** of Jeroham, and Ishmael	1121
23: 1	Ishmael the **s** of Jehohanan, and Azariah	1121
23: 1	Azariah the **s** of Obed, and Maaseiah	1121
23: 1	Maaseiah the **s** of Adaiah, and Elishaphat	1121
23: 1	Elishaphat the **s** of Zichri, into covenant	1121
23: 3	them, Behold, the king's **s** shall reign,	1121
23:11	brought out the king's **s**, and put upon	1121
24:20	spirit of God came upon Zechariah the **s**	1121
24:22	his father had done to him, but slew his **s.**	1121
24:26	Zabad the **s** of Shimeath an Ammonitess,	1121
24:26	Jehozabad the **s** of Shimrith a Moabitess.	1121
24:27	And Amaziah his **s** reigned in his stead.	1121
25:17	sent to Joash, the **s** of Jehoahaz, the son	1121
25:17	the **s** of Jehu, king of Israel, saying, Come,	1121
25:18	Give thy daughter to my **s** to wife:	1121
25:23	the **s** of Joash, the son of Jehoahaz,	1121
25:23	the son of Joash, the **s** of Jehoahaz,	1121
25:25	Amaziah the **s** of Joash king of Judah lived	1121
25:25	**s** of Jehoahaz king of Israel fifteen years.	1121
26:21	Jotham his **s** *was* over the king's house,	1121
26:22	Isaiah the prophet, the **s** of Amoz, write.	1121
26:23	and Jotham his **s** reigned in his stead.	1121
27: 9	and Ahaz his **s** reigned in his stead.	1121
28: 3	incense in the valley of the **s** of Hinnom,	1121
28: 6	For Pekah the **s** of Remaliah slew in Judah	1121
28: 7	slew Maaseiah the king's **s**, and Azrikam	1121
28:12	Azariah the **s** of Johanan, Berechiah	1121
28:12	Berechiah the **s** of Meshillemoth,	1121
28:12	Jehizkiah the **s** of Shallum, and Amasa	1121
28:12	of Shallum, and Amasa the **s** of Hadlai,	1121
28:27	and Hezekiah his **s** reigned in his stead.	1121
29:12	Mahath the **s** of Amasai, and Joel the son	1121
29:12	son of Amasai, and Joel the **s** of Azariah,	1121
29:12	Kish the **s** of Abdi, and Azariah the son of	1121
29:12	of Abdi, and Azariah the **s** of Jehalelel:	1121
2Ch 29:12	Joah the **s** of Zimmah, and Eden the son	1121
29:12	son of Zimmah, and Eden the **s** of Joah:	1121
30:26	for since the time of Solomon the **s** of	1121
31:14	Kore the **s** of Imnah the Levite, the porter	1121
32:20	the prophet Isaiah the **s** of Amoz, prayed	1121
32:32	the **s** of Amoz, *and* in the book of the	1121
32:33	And Manasseh his **s** reigned in his stead.	1121
33: 6	the fire in the valley of the **s** of Hinnom:	1121
33: 7	had said to David and to Solomon his **s,**	1121
33:20	and Amon his **s** reigned in his stead.	1121
33:25	the people of the land made Josiah his **s**	1121
34: 8	he sent Shaphan the **s** of Azaliah,	1121
34: 8	and Joah the **s** of Joahaz the recorder,	1121
34:20	Ahikam the **s** of Shaphan, and Abdon	1121
34:20	Abdon the **s** of Micah, and Shaphan	1121
34:22	the wife of Shallum the **s** of Tikvath,	1121
34:22	of Hasrah, keeper of the wardrobe;	1121
35: 3	the **s** of David king of Israel did build;	1121
35: 4	according to the writing of Solomon his **s.**	1121
36: 1	people of the land took Jehoahaz the **s**	1121
36: 8	and Jehoiachin his **s** reigned in his stead.	1121
Ezr 3: 2	stood up Jeshua the **s** of Jozadak,	1121
3: 2	Zerubbabel the **s** of Shealtiel,	1121
3: 8	began Zerubbabel the **s** of Shealtiel,	1121
3: 8	Jeshua the **s** of Jozadak, and the remnant	1121
5: 1	the prophet, and Zechariah the **s** of Iddo,	1247
5: 2	rose up Zerubbabel the **s** of Shealtiel,	1247
5: 2	Jeshua the **s** of Jozadak, and began to	1247
6:14	the prophet and Zechariah the **s** of Iddo.	1247
7: 1	Ezra the **s** of Seraiah, the son of Azariah,	1121
7: 1	the **s** of Azariah, the son of Hilkiah,	1121
7: 1	the son of Azariah, the **s** of Hilkiah,	1121
7: 2	The **s** of Shallum, the son of Zadok,	1121
7: 2	the **s** of Zadok, the son of Ahitub,	1121
7: 2	the son of Zadok, the **s** of Ahitub,	1121
7: 3	The **s** of Amariah, the son of Azariah,	1121
7: 3	the **s** of Azariah, the son of Meraioth,	1121
7: 3	the son of Azariah, the **s** of Meraioth,	1121
7: 4	The **s** of Zerahiah, the son of Uzzi,	1121
7: 4	the **s** of Uzzi, the son of Bukki,	1121
7: 4	the son of Uzzi, the **s** of Bukki,	1121
7: 5	The **s** of Abishua, the son of Phinehas,	1121
7: 5	the **s** of Phinehas, the son of Eleazar,	1121
7: 5	the son of Phinehas, the **s** of Eleazar,	1121
7: 5	of Eleazar, the **s** of Aaron the chief priest:	1121
8: 4	Elihoenai the **s** of Zerahiah, and with him	1121
8: 5	the **s** of Jahaziel, and with him three	1121
8: 6	Ebed the **s** of Jonathan, and with him fifty	1121
8: 7	Jeshaiah the **s** of Athaliah, and with him	1121
8: 8	Zebadiah the **s** of Michael, and with him	1121
8: 9	Obadiah the **s** of Jehiel, and with him two	1121
8:10	the **s** of Josiphiah, and with him an	1121
8:11	Zechariah the **s** of Bebai, and with him	1121
8:12	Johanan the **s** of Hakkatan, and with him	1121
8:18	of Mahli, the **s** of Levi, the son of Israel;	1121
8:18	the son of Levi, the **s** of Israel;	1121
8:33	of Meremoth the **s** of Uriah the priest;	1121
8:33	with him *was* Eleazar the **s** of Phinehas;	1121
8:33	with him *was* Jozabad the **s** of Jeshua,	1121
8:33	and Noadiah the **s** of Binnui, Levites;	1121
10: 2	Shechaniah the **s** of Jehiel, *one* of the	1121
10: 6	into the chamber of Johanan the **s** of	1121
10:15	Only Jonathan the **s** of Asahel and	1121
10:15	Jahaziah the **s** of Tikvah were employed	1121
10:18	*namely*, of the sons of Jeshua the **s** of	1121
Ne 1: 1	words of Nehemiah the **s** of Hachaliah.	1121
3: 2	to them builded Zaccur the **s** of Imri.	1121
3: 4	unto them repaired Meremoth the **s** of	1121
3: 4	Meremoth the son of Urijah, the **s** of Koz.	1121
3: 4	unto them repaired Meshullam the **s** of	1121
3: 4	son of Berechiah, the **s** of Meshezabeel.	1121
3: 4	next unto them repaired Zadok the **s** of	1121
3: 6	old gate repaired Jehoiada the **s** of Paseah,	1121
3: 6	and Meshullam the **s** of Besodeiah;	1121
3: 8	Next unto him repaired Uzziel the **s** of	1121
3: 9	unto them repaired Rephaiah the **s** of	1121
3:10	next unto them repaired Jedaiah the **s** of	1121
3:10	next unto him repaired Hattush the **s** of	1121
3:11	Malchijah the **s** of Harim, and Hashub	1121
3:11	Hashub the **s** of Pahath-moab, repaired	1121
3:12	next unto him repaired Shallum the **s** of	1121
3:14	the dung gate repaired Malchiah the **s** of	1121
3:15	repaired Shallun the **s** of Col-hozeh,	1121
3:16	After him repaired Nehemiah the **s** of	1121
3:17	repaired the Levites, Rehum the **s** of Bani.	1121
3:18	their brethren, Bavai the **s** of Henadad,	1121
3:19	next to him repaired Ezer the **s** of Jeshua,	1121
3:20	After him Baruch the **s** of Zabbai earnestly	1121
3:21	After him repaired Meremoth the **s** of	1121
3:21	son of Urijah the **s** of Koz another piece,	1121
3:23	After him repaired Azariah the **s** of	1121
3:23	Maaseiah the **s** of Ananiah by his house.	1121
3:24	him repaired Binnui the **s** of Henadad	1121
3:25	Palal the **s** of Uzai, over against the	1121
3:25	After him Pedaiah the **s** of Parosh.	1121
3:29	After them repaired Zadok the **s** of Immer	1121
3:29	After him also repaired Shemaiah the **s** of	1121
3:30	After him repaired Hananiah the **s** of	1121
3:30	Hanun the sixth **s** of Zalaph, another	1121
3:30	After him repaired Meshullam the **s** of	1121
3:31	**s** unto the place of the Nethinims,	1121
6:10	the **s** of Delaiah the son of Mehetabeel,	1121
6:10	the son of Delaiah the **s** of Mehetabeel,	1121
6:18	*was* the **s in law** of Shechaniah the son	2860

Ne	6:18	*was* the son in law of Shechaniah the **s**	1121
	6:18	his **s** Johanan had taken the daughter of	1121
	6:18	of Meshullam the **s** of Berechiah.	1121
	8:17	for since the days of Jeshua the **s** of Nun	1121
	10: 1	the **s** of Hachaliah, and Zidkijah,	1121
	10: 9	both Jeshua the **s** of Azaniah, Binnui of	1121
	10:38	the priest the **s** of Aaron shall be with	1121
	11: 4	Athaiah the **s** of Uzziah, the son of	1121
	11: 4	the **s** of Zechariah, the son of Amariah,	1121
	11: 4	the son of Zechariah, the **s** of Amariah,	1121
	11: 4	the son of Amariah, the **s** of Shephatiah,	1121
	11: 4	son of Shephatiah, the **s** of Mahalaleel,	1121
	11: 5	Maaseiah the **s** of Baruch, the son of	1121
	11: 5	the **s** of Col-hozeh, the son of Hazaiah,	1121
	11: 5	the **s** of Hazaiah, the son of Adaiah, the	1121
	11: 5	the **s** of Adaiah, the son of Joiarib,	1121
	11: 5	the son of Adaiah, the **s** of Joiarib,	1121
	11: 5	the son of Joiarib, the **s** of Zechariah,	1121
	11: 5	the son of Zechariah, the **s** of Shiloni.	1121
	11: 7	Sallu the **s** of Meshullam, the son of Joed,	1121
	11: 7	the **s** of Joed, the son of Pedaiah, the son	1121
	11: 7	the son of Joed, the **s** of Pedaiah, the son	1121
	11: 7	the son of Pedaiah, the **s** of Kolaiah,	1121
	11: 7	the **s** of Maaseiah, the son of Ithiel,	1121
	11: 7	the **s** of Ithiel, the son of Jesaiah.	1121
	11: 7	the son of Ithiel, the **s** of Jesaiah.	1121
	11: 9	Joel the **s** of Zichri *was* their overseer:	1121
	11: 9	Judah the **s** of Senuah *was* second over	1121
	11:10	priests: Jedaiah the **s** of Joiarib, Jachin,	1121
	11:11	Seraiah the **s** of Hilkiah, the son of	1121
	11:11	the **s** of Meshullam, the son of Zadok,	1121
	11:11	the **s** of Zadok, the son of Meraioth,	1121
	11:11	the son of Zadok, the **s** of Meraioth, the	1121
	11:11	the son of Meraioth, the **s** of Ahitub,	1121
	11:12	Adaiah the **s** of Jeroham, the son of	1121
	11:12	the **s** of Pelaliah, the son of Amzi, the son	1121
	11:12	the son of Pelaliah, the **s** of Amzi, the son	1121
	11:12	the son of Amzi, the **s** of Zechariah, the	1121
	11:12	the **s** of Pashur, the son of Malchiah,	1121
	11:12	the son of Pashur, the **s** of Malchiah,	1121
	11:13	Amashai the **s** of Azareel, the son of	1121
	11:13	the **s** of Ahasai, the son of Meshillemoth,	1121
	11:13	the **s** of Meshillemoth, the son of Immer,	1121
	11:13	the son of Meshillemoth, the **s** of Immer,	1121
	11:14	Zabdiel, the **s** of *one of* the great *men.*	1121
	11:15	Shemaiah the **s** of Hashub, the son of	1121
	11:15	the **s** of Azrikam, the son of Hashabiah,	1121
	11:15	the **s** of Hashabiah, the son of Bunni,	1121
	11:15	the son of Hashabiah, the **s** of Bunni;	1121
	11:17	Mattaniah the **s** of Micha, the son of	1121
	11:17	Micha, the **s** of Zabdi, the son of Asaph,	1121
	11:17	Micha, the son of Zabdi, the **s** of Asaph,	1121
	11:17	Abda the **s** of Shammua, the son of Galal,	1121
	11:17	the **s** of Galal, the son of Jeduthun.	1121
	11:17	the son of Galal, the **s** of Jeduthun.	1121
	11:22	at Jerusalem *was* Uzzi the **s** of Bani,	1121
	11:22	the **s** of Hashabiah, the son of Mattaniah,	1121
	11:22	the **s** of Mattaniah, the son of Micha.	1121
	11:22	the son of Mattaniah, the **s** of Micha.	1121
	11:24	Pethahiah the **s** of Meshezabeel,	1121
	11:24	of the children of Zerah the **s** of Judah,	1121
	12: 1	up with Zerubbabel the **s** of Shealtiel,	1121
	12:23	even until the days of Johanan the **s** of	1121
	12:24	Sherebiah, and Jeshua the **s** of Kadmiel,	1121
	12:26	These *were* in the days of Joiakim the **s** of	1121
	12:26	the **s** of Jozadak, and in the days of	1121
	12:35	*namely,* Zechariah the **s** of Jonathan,	1121
	12:35	the **s** of Shemaiah, the son of Mattaniah,	1121
	12:35	the son of Shemaiah, the **s** of Michaiah,	1121
	12:35	the son of Michaiah, the son of Zaccur,	1121
	12:35	the **s** of Zaccur, the son of Asaph:	1121
	12:35	the son of Zaccur, the **s** of Asaph:	1121
	12:45	of David, *and* of Solomon his **s**.	1121
	13:13	next to them *was* Hanan the **s** of Zaccur,	1121
	13:13	the son of Zaccur, the **s** of Mattaniah:	1121
	13:28	of Joiada, the **s** of Eliashib the high priest,	1121
	13:28	*was* **s** in law to Sanballat the Horonite:	2860
Est	2: 5	the **s** of Jair, the son of Shimei, the son of	1121
	2: 5	the son of Jair, the **s** of Shimei, the son of	1121
	2: 5	son of Shimei, the **s** of Kish, a Benjamite;	1121
	3: 1	Haman the **s** of Hammedatha the Agagite,	1121
	3:10	gave it unto Haman the **s** of Hammedatha	1121
	8: 5	Haman the **s** of Hammedatha the Agagite,	1121
	9:10	The ten sons of Haman the **s** of	1121
	9:24	Because Haman the **s** of Hammedatha,	1121
Job	18:19	He shall neither have **s** nor nephew	5209
	25: 6	and the **s** of man, *which is* a worm?	1121
	32: 2	was kindled the wrath of Elihu the **s** of	1121
	32: 6	Elihu the **s** of Barachel the Buzite	1121
	35: 8	thy righteousness *may profit* the **s** of man.	1121
Ps	2: 7	LORD hath said unto me, Thou *art* my **S**;	1121
	2:12	Kiss the **S,** lest he be angry, and ye perish	1248
	3: T	David, when he fled from Absalom his **s**.	1121
	8: 4	and the **s** of man, that thou visitest him?	1121
	50:20	thou slanderest thine own mother's **s**.	1121
	72: 1	and thy righteousness unto the king's **s**.	1121
	72:20	The prayers of David the **s** of Jesse are	1121
	80:17	upon the **s** of man *whom* thou madest	1121
	86:16	and save the **s** of thine handmaid.	1121
	89:22	nor the **s** of wickedness afflict him.	1121
	116:16	thy servant, *and* the **s** of thy handmaid:	1121
	144: 3	the **s** of man, that thou makest account	1121
	146: 3	nor in the **s** of man, in whom *there is* no	1121
Pr	1: 1	The proverbs of Solomon the **s** of David,	1121
	1: 8	My **s,** hear the instruction of thy father,	1121

Pr	1:10	My **s,** if sinners entice thee, consent thou	1121
	1:15	My **s,** walk not thou in the way with	1121
	2: 1	My **s,** if thou wilt receive my words,	1121
	3: 1	My **s,** forget not my law; but let thine	1121
	3:11	My **s,** despise not the chastening of	1121
	3:12	even as a father the **s** *in whom* he	1121
	3:21	My **s,** let not them depart from thine	1121
	4: 3	For I was my father's **s,** tender and	1121
	4:10	Hear, O my **s,** and receive my sayings;	1121
	4:20	My **s,** attend to my words; incline thine	1121
	5: 1	My **s,** attend unto my wisdom,	1121
	5:20	why wilt thou, my **s,** be ravisht with a	1121
	6: 1	My **s,** if thou be surety for thy friend,	1121
	6: 3	Do this now, my **s,** and deliver thyself,	1121
	6:20	My **s,** keep thy father's commandment,	1121
	7: 1	My **s,** keep my words, and lay up my	1121
	10: 1	A wise **s** maketh a glad father: but a	1121
	10: 1	a foolish **s** *is* the heaviness of his mother.	1121
	10: 5	He that gathereth in summer *is* a wise **s:**	1121
	10: 5	he that sleepeth in harvest *is* a that	1121
	13: 1	A wise **s** *heareth his* father's instruction:	1121
	13:24	He that spareth his rod hateth his **s:**	1121
	15:20	A wise **s** maketh a glad father: but a	1121
	17: 2	wise servant shall have rule over a **s** that	1121
	17:25	A foolish **s** *is* a grief to his father,	1121
	19:13	A foolish **s** *is* the calamity of his father:	1121
	19:18	Chasten thy **s** while there is hope,	1121
	19:26	*is* a **s** that causeth shame,	1121
	19:27	Cease, my **s,** to hear the instruction *that*	1121
	23:15	My **s,** if thine heart be wise, my heart	1121
	23:19	my **s,** and be wise, and guide thine heart	1121
	23:26	My **s,** give me thine heart, and let thine	1121
	24:13	My **s,** eat thou honey, because *it is* good;	1121
	24:21	My **s,** fear thou the LORD and the king:	1121
	27:11	My **s,** be wise, and make my heart glad,	1121
	28: 7	Whoso keepeth the law *is* a wise **s:**	1121
	29:17	Correct thy **s,** and he shall give thee rest;	1121
	29:21	shall have him become *his* **s** at the length.	4497
	30: 1	The words of Agur the **s** of Jakeh, *even*	1121
	31: 2	What, my **s?** and what, the son of my	1248
	31: 2	What, my **s?** and what, the son of my	1248
	31: 2	my womb? and what, the **s** of my vows?	1248
Ecc	1: 1	the **s** of David, king in Jerusalem.	1121
	5:14	he begetteth a **s,** and *there is* nothing in	1121
	10:17	when thy king *is* the **s** of nobles,	1121
	12:12	further, by these, my **s,** be admonished:	1121
Isa	1: 1	The vision of Isaiah the **s** of Amoz,	1121
	2: 1	The word that Isaiah the **s** of Amoz saw	1121
	7: 1	came to pass in the days of Ahaz the **s** of	1121
	7: 1	the **s** of Uzziah king of Judah, *that* Rezin	1121
	7: 1	Pekah the **s** of Remaliah, king of Israel,	1121
	7: 3	meet Ahaz, thou, and Shear-jashub thy **s,**	1121
	7: 4	with Syria, and of the **s** of Remaliah.	1121
	7: 5	Ephraim, and the **s** of Remaliah,	1121
	7: 6	in the midst of it, *even* the **s** of Tabeal:	1121
	7: 9	and the head of Samaria *is* Remaliah's **s**.	1121
	7:14	a **S,** and shall call his name Immanuel.	1121
	8: 2	and Zechariah the **s** of Jeberechiah.	1121
	8: 3	and she conceived, and bare a **s**.	1121
	8: 6	and rejoice in Rezin and Remaliah's **s;**	1121
	9: 6	us a child is born, unto us a **S** is given:	1121
	13: 1	which Isaiah the **s** of Amoz did see.	1121
	14:12	from heaven, O Lucifer, **s** of the morning!	1121
	14:22	remnant, and **s,** and nephew, saith	5209
	19:11	I *am* the **s** of the wise, the son of ancient	1121
	19:11	son of the wise, the **s** of ancient kings?	1121
	20: 2	spake the LORD by Isaiah the **s** of Amoz,	1121
	22:20	I will call my servant Eliakim the **s** of	1121
	36: 3	Hilkiah's **s,** which *was* over the house,	1121
	36: 3	and Joah, Asaph's **s,** the recorder.	1121
	36:22	came Eliakim, the **s** of Hilkiah, that *was*	1121
	36:22	and Joah, the **s** of Asaph, the recorder,	1121
	37: 2	unto Isaiah the prophet the **s** of Amoz.	1121
	37:21	Isaiah the **s** of Amoz sent unto Hezekiah,	1121
	37:38	Esar-haddon his **s** reigned in his stead.	1121
	38: 1	Isaiah the prophet the **s** of Amoz came	1121
	39: 1	the **s** of Baladan, king of Babylon,	1121
	49:15	have compassion on the **s** of her womb?	1121
	51:12	of the **s** of man *which* shall be made *as*	1121
	56: 2	and the **s** of man *that* layeth hold on it;	1121
	56: 3	Neither let the **s** of the stranger, that hath	1121
Jer	1: 1	The words of Jeremiah the **s** of Hilkiah,	1121
	1: 2	of Josiah the **s** of Amon king of Judah,	1121
	1: 3	came also in the days of Jehoiakim the **s**	1121
	1: 3	of Zedekiah the **s** of Josiah king of Judah,	1121
	6:26	*as* for an only **s,** most bitter lamentation:	NIH
	7:31	which *is* in the valley of the **s** of Hinnom,	1121
	7:32	nor the valley of the **s** of Hinnom,	1121
	15: 4	of Manasseh the **s** of Hezekiah king of	1121
	19: 2	forth unto the valley of the **s** of Hinnom,	1121
	19: 6	nor The valley of the **s** of Hinnom, but	1121
	20: 1	Now Pashur the **s** of Immer the priest,	1121
	21: 1	sent unto him Pashur the **s** of Melchiah,	1121
	21: 1	Zephaniah the **s** of Maaseiah the priest,	1121
	22:11	Shallum the **s** of Josiah king of Judah,	1121
	22:18	Jehoiakim the **s** of Josiah king of Judah;	1121
	22:24	though Coniah the **s** of Jehoiakim king of	1121
	24: 1	Jeconiah the **s** of Jehoiakim king of Judah,	1121
	25: 1	of Jehoiakim the **s** of Josiah king of Judah,	1121
	25: 3	From the thirteenth year of Josiah the **s** of	1121
	26: 1	**s** of Josiah king of Judah came this word	1121
	26:20	Urijah the **s** of Shemaiah of Kirjath-jearim,	1121
	26:22	*namely,* Elnathan the **s** of Achbor,	1121
	26:24	Nevertheless the hand of Ahikam the **s** of	1121
	27: 1	**s** of Josiah king of Judah came this word	1121

Jer	27: 7	serve him, and his **s,** and his son's son,	1121
	27: 7	serve him, and his son, and his son's **s,**	1121
	27:20	**s** of Jehoiakim king of Judah from	1121
	28: 1	*that* Hananiah the **s** of Azur the prophet,	1121
	28: 4	Jeconiah the **s** of Jehoiakim king of Judah,	1121
	29: 3	By the hand of Elasah the **s** of Shaphan,	1121
	29: 3	Shaphan, and Gemariah the **s** of Hilkiah,	1121
	29:21	Ahab the **s** of Kolaiah, and of Zedekiah,	1121
	29:21	and of Zedekiah, the **s** of Maaseiah,	1121
	29:25	Zephaniah the **s** of Maaseiah the priest,	1121
	31:20	*Is* Ephraim my dear **s?** *is he* a pleasant	1121
	32: 7	Hanameel the **s** of Shallum thine uncle	1121
	32: 8	Hanameel mine uncle's **s** came to me in	1121
	32: 9	the field of Hanameel my uncle's **s,**	1121
	32:12	the purchase unto Baruch the **s** of Neriah,	1121
	32:12	**s** of Maaseiah, in the sight of Hanameel	1121
	32:12	in the sight of Hanameel mine uncle's **s,**	NIH
	32:16	purchase unto Baruch the **s** of Neriah,	1121
	32:35	*are* in the valley of the **s** of Hinnom,	1121
	33:21	that he should not have a **s** to reign upon	1121
	35: 1	of Jehoiakim the **s** of Josiah king of Judah,	1121
	35: 3	I took Jaazaniah the **s** of Jeremiah, the son	1121
	35: 3	the **s** of Habaziniah, and his brethren,	1121
	35: 4	of Hanan, the **s** of Igdaliah, a man of God,	1121
	35: 4	chamber of Maaseiah the **s** of Shallum,	1121
	35: 6	for Jonadab the **s** of Rechab our father	1121
	35: 8	of Rechab our father in all that he hath	1121
	35:14	The words of Jonadab the **s** of Rechab,	1121
	35:16	Because the sons of Jonadab the **s** of	1121
	35:19	Jonadab the **s** of Rechab shall not want a	1121
	36: 1	of Jehoiakim the **s** of Josiah king of Judah,	1121
	36: 4	Jeremiah called Baruch the **s** of Neriah:	1121
	36: 8	Baruch the **s** of Neriah did according to	1121
	36: 9	of Jehoiakim the **s** of Josiah king of Judah,	1121
	36:10	in the chamber of Gemariah the **s** of	1121
	36:11	When Michaiah the **s** of Gemariah, the	1121
	36:11	the son of Gemariah, the **s** of Shaphan,	1121
	36:12	Delaiah the **s** of Shemaiah,	1121
	36:12	Elnathan the **s** of Achbor,	1121
	36:12	Gemariah the **s** of Shaphan,	1121
	36:12	Zedekiah the **s** of Hananiah, and all	1121
	36:14	all the princes sent Jehudi the **s**	1121
	36:14	the **s** of Shelemiah, the son of Cushi,	1121
	36:14	the **s** of Cushi, unto Baruch, saying,	1121
	36:26	So Baruch the **s** of Neriah took the roll in	1121
	36:26	the king commanded Jerahmeel the **s** of	1121
	36:26	Seraiah the **s** of Azriel, and Shelemiah	1121
	36:26	Shelemiah the **s** of Abdeel, to take Baruch	1121
	36:32	it to Baruch the scribe, the **s** of Neriah;	1121
	37: 1	king Zedekiah the **s** of Josiah reigned	1121
	37: 1	instead of Coniah the **s** of Jehoiakim,	1121
	37: 3	Zedekiah the king sent Jehucal the **s** of	1121
	37: 3	Zephaniah the **s** of Maaseiah the priest to	1121
	37:13	the **s** of Shelemiah, the son of Hananiah;	1121
	37:13	the son of Shelemiah, the **s** of Hananiah;	1121
	38: 1	Shephatiah the **s** of Mattan,	1121
	38: 1	Gedaliah the **s** of Pashur, and Jucal the	1121
	38: 1	Jucal the **s** of Shelemiah, and Pashur	1121
	38: 1	the **s** of Malchiah,	1121
	38: 6	him into the dungeon of Malchiah the **s**	1121
	39:14	committed him unto Gedaliah the **s** of	1121
	39:14	the son of Ahikam the **s** of Shaphan,	1121
	40: 5	*he said,* Go back also to Gedaliah the **s** of	1121
	40: 5	the son of Ahikam the **s** of Shaphan,	1121
	40: 6	went Jeremiah unto Gedaliah the **s** of	1121
	40: 7	the **s** of Ahikam governor in the land,	1121
	40: 8	even Ishmael the **s** of Nethaniah,	1121
	40: 8	Seraiah the **s** of Tanhumeth, and the sons	1121
	40: 8	Jezaniah the **s** of a Maachathite, they and	1121
	40: 9	Gedaliah the **s** of Ahikam the son of	1121
	40: 9	Gedaliah the son of Ahikam the **s** of	1121
	40:11	he had set over them Gedaliah the **s** of	1121
	40:11	the son of Ahikam the **s** of Shaphan;	1121
	40:13	Moreover Johanan the **s** of Kareah,	1121
	40:14	Ishmael the **s** of Nethaniah to slay thee?	1121
	40:14	Gedaliah the **s** of Ahikam believed them	1121
	40:15	Johanan the **s** of Kareah spake to Gedaliah	1121
	40:15	I will slay Ishmael the **s** of Nethaniah,	1121
	40:16	Gedaliah the **s** of Ahikam said unto	1121
	40:16	said unto Johanan the **s** of Kareah,	1121
	41: 1	Ishmael the **s** of Nethaniah the son of	1121
	41: 1	the son of Nethaniah the son of	1121
	41: 2	came unto Gedaliah the **s** of Ahikam to	1121
	41: 2	arose Ishmael the **s** of Nethaniah,	1121
	41: 2	smote Gedaliah the **s** of Ahikam the son	1121
	41: 2	Gedaliah the son of Ahikam the **s** of	1121
	41: 6	Ishmael the **s** of Nethaniah went forth	1121
	41: 6	Come to Gedaliah the **s** of Ahikam.	1121
	41: 7	Ishmael the **s** of Nethaniah slew them,	1121
	41: 9	Ishmael the **s** of Nethaniah filled it *with*	1121
	41:10	committed to Gedaliah the **s** of Ahikam:	1121
	41:10	Ishmael the **s** of Nethaniah carried them	1121
	41:11	when Johanan the **s** of Kareah, and all	1121
	41:11	heard of all the evil that Ishmael the **s** of	1121
	41:12	went to fight with Ishmael the **s** of	1121
	41:13	Ishmael saw Johanan the **s** of Kareah,	1121
	41:14	and went unto Johanan the **s** of Kareah.	1121
	41:15	Ishmael the **s** of Nethaniah escaped from	1121
	41:16	took Johanan the **s** of Kareah, and all	1121
	41:16	from Ishmael the **s** of Nethaniah,	1121
	41:16	after *that* he had slain Gedaliah the **s** of	1121
	41:18	Ishmael the **s** of Nethaniah had slain	1121
	41:18	had slain Gedaliah the **s** of Ahikam,	1121
	42: 1	Johanan the **s** of Kareah, and Jezaniah	1121
	42: 1	Jezaniah the **s** of Hoshaiah, and all	1121

Jer	42: 8 called he Johanan the **s** of Kareah,	1121
	43: 2 spake Azariah the **s** of Hoshaiah,	1121
	43: 2 Johanan the **s** of Kareah, and all the	1121
	43: 3 Baruch the **s** of Neriah setteth thee on	1121
	43: 4 So Johanan the **s** of Kareah, and all	1121
	43: 5 Johanan the **s** of Kareah, and all	1121
	43: 6 the **s** of Ahikam the son of Shaphan,	1121
	43: 6 the son of Ahikam the **s** of Shaphan,	1121
	43: 6 the prophet, and Baruch the **s** of Neriah.	1121
	45: 1 spake unto Baruch the **s** of Neriah,	1121
	45: 1 in the fourth year of Jehoiakim the **s** of	1121
	46: 2 Jehoiakim the **s** of Josiah king of Judah.	1121
	49:18 neither shall a **s** of man dwell in it.	1121
	49:33 abide there, nor *any* **s** of man dwell in it.	1121
	50:40 neither shall any **s** of man dwell therein.	1121
	51:43 neither doth *any* **s** of man pass thereby.	1121
	51:59 commanded Seraiah the **s** of Neriah,	1121
	51:59 the son of Neriah, the **s** of Maaseiah,	1121
Eze	1: 3 **s** of Buzi, in the land of the Chaldeans	1121
	2: 1 **S** of man, stand upon thy feet, and I will	1121
	2: 3 he said unto me, **S** of man, I send thee to	1121
	2: 6 thou, **s** of man, be not afraid of them,	1121
	2: 8 hear what I say unto thee;	1121
	3: 1 unto me, **S** of man, eat that thou findest;	1121
	3: 3 said unto me, **S** of man, cause thy belly	1121
	3: 4 said unto me, **S** of man, go, get thee unto	1121
	3:10 Moreover he said unto me, **S** of man,	1121
	3:17 **S** of man, I have made thee a watchman	1121
	3:25 thou, O **s** of man, behold, they shall put	1121
	4: 1 Thou also, **s** of man, take thee a tile,	1121
	4:16 he said unto me, **S** of man, behold,	1121
	5: 1 thou, **s** of man, take thee a sharp knife,	1121
	6: 2 **S** of man, set thy face towards	1121
	7: 2 Also, thou **s** of man, thus saith the Lord	1121
	8: 5 said he unto me, **S** of man, lift up thine	1121
	8: 6 **S** of man, seest thou what they do?	1121
	8: 8 unto me, **S** of man, dig now in the wall:	1121
	8:11 the midst of them stood Jaazaniah the **s**	1121
	8:12 he unto me, **S** of man, hast thou seen	1121
	8:15 me, Hast thou seen *this*, O **s** of man?	1121
	8:17 me, Hast thou seen *this*, O **s** of man?	1121
	11: 1 among whom I saw Jaazaniah the **s** of,	1121
	11: 1 Pelatiah the **s** of Benaiah, princes of	1121
	11: 2 said he unto me, **S** of man, these *are*	1121
	11: 4 against them, prophesy, O **s** of man.	1121
	11:13 that Pelatiah the **s** of Benaiah died.	1121
	11:15 **S** of man, thy brethren, *even* thy brethren	1121
	12: 2 **S** of man, thou dwellest in the midst of a	1121
	12: 3 thou **s** of man, prepare thee stuff	1121
	12: 9 **S** of man, hath not the house of Israel	1121
	12:18 **S** of man, eat thy bread with quaking,	1121
	12:22 **S** of man, what *is* that proverb *that* ye	1121
	12:27 **S** of man, behold, *they* of the house of	1121
	13: 2 **S** of man, prophesy against the prophets	1121
	13:17 Likewise thou **s** of man, set thy face	1121
	14: 3 **S** of man, these men have set up their	1121
	14:13 **S** of man, when the land sinneth against	1121
	14:20 they shall deliver neither **s** nor daughter;	1121
	15: 2 **S** of man, What is the vine tree more than	1121
	16: 2 **S** of man, cause Jerusalem to know her	1121
	17: 2 **S** of man, put forth a riddle, and speak a	1121
	18: 4 father, so also the soul of the **s** *is* mine:	1121
	18:10 If he beget a **s** *that is* a robber, a shedder	1121
	18:14 Now lo, *if* he beget a **s**, that seeth all his	1121
	18:19 doth not the **s** bear the iniquity of	1121
	18:19 the **s** hath done that which is lawful	1121
	18:20 The **s** shall not bear the iniquity of	1121
	18:20 shall the father bear the iniquity of the **s**:	1121
	20: 3 **S** of man, speak unto the elders of Israel,	1121
	20: 4 Wilt thou judge them, **s** of man, wilt thou	1121
	20:27 Therefore, **s** of man, speak unto the house	1121
	20:46 **S** of man, set thy face toward the south,	1121
	21: 2 **S** of man, set thy face toward Jerusalem,	1121
	21: 6 Sigh therefore, thou **s** of man, with	1121
	21: 9 **S** of man, prophesy, and say, Thus saith	1121
	21:10 contemneth the rod of my **s**, *as* every tree.	1121
	21:12 and howl, **s** of man: for it shall be upon	1121
	21:14 **s** of man, prophesy, and smite *thine*	1121
	21:19 thou **s** of man, appoint thee two ways,	1121
	21:28 thou, **s** of man, prophesy and say,	1121
	22: 2 Now, thou **s** of man, wilt thou judge,	1121
	22:18 **S** of man, the house of Israel is to me	1121
	22:24 **S** of man, say unto her, Thou *art* the land	1121
	23: 2 **S** of man, there were two women,	1121
	23:36 **S** of man, wilt thou judge Aholah and	1121
	24: 2 **S** of man, write thee the name of the day,	1121
	24:16 **S** of man, behold, I take away from thee	1121
	24:25 Also, thou **s** of man, *shall it* not *be in*	1121
	25: 2 **S** of man, set thy face against	1121
	26: 2 **S** of man, because that Tyrus hath said	1121
	27: 2 thou **s** of man, take up a lamentation	1121
	28: 2 **S** of man, say unto the prince of Tyrus,	1121
	28:12 **S** of man, take up a lamentation upon	1121
	28:21 **S** of man, set thy face against Zidon,	1121
	29: 2 **S** of man, set thy face against Pharaoh	1121
	29:18 **S** of man, Nebuchadrezzar king of	1121
	30: 2 **S** of man, prophesy and say, Thus saith	1121
	30:21 **S** of man, I have broken the arm of	1121
	31: 2 **S** of man, speak unto Pharaoh king of	1121
	32: 2 **S** of man, take up a lamentation for	1121
	32:18 **S** of man, wail for the multitude of Egypt,	1121
	33: 2 **S** of man, speak to the children of thy	1121
	33: 7 So thou, O **s** of man, I have set thee a	1121
	33:10 Therefore, O thou **s** of man, speak unto	1121
	33:12 Therefore, thou **s** of man, say unto	1121

Eze	33:24 **S** of man, they that inhabit those wastes	1121
	33:30 Also, thou **s** of man, the children of thy	1121
	34: 2 **S** of man, prophesy against the shepherds	1121
	35: 2 **S** of man, set thy face against mount Seir,	1121
	36: 1 Also, thou **s** of man, prophesy unto	1121
	36:17 **S** of man, when the house of Israel dwelt	1121
	37: 3 unto me, **S** of man, can these bones live?	1121
	37: 9 prophesy, **s** of man, and say to the wind,	1121
	37:11 he said unto me, **S** of man, these bones	1121
	37:16 Moreover, thou **s** of man, take thee one	1121
	38: 2 **S** of man, set thy face against Gog, the	1121
	38:14 **s** of man, prophesy and say unto Gog,	1121
	39: 1 Therefore thou **s** of man, prophesy against	1121
	39:17 thou **s** of man, thus saith the Lord GOD;	1121
	40: 4 **S** of man, behold with thine eyes,	1121
	43: 7 he said unto me, **S** of man, the place of	1121
	43:10 of man, shew the house to the house	1121
	43:18 he said unto me, **S** of man, thus saith	1121
	44: 5 **S** of man, mark well, and behold with	1121
	44:25 or for mother, or for **s**, or for daughter,	1121
	47: 6 he said unto me, **S** of man, hast thou	1121
Da	3:25 form of the fourth *is* like the **S** of God.	1247
	5:22 his **s**, O Belshazzar, hast not humbled	1247
	7:13 like the **S** of man came with the clouds	1247
	8:17 he said unto me, Understand, O **s** of man:	1121
	9: 1 In the first year of Darius the **s** of	1121
Hos	1: 1 the **s** of Beeri, in the days of Uzziah,	1121
	1: 1 in the days of Jeroboam the **s** of Joash,	1121
	1: 3 which conceived, and bare him a **s**.	1121
	1: 8 she conceived, and bare a **s**.	1121
	11: 1 I loved him, and called my **s** out of Egypt.	1121
	13:13 he *is* an unwise **s**; for he should not stay	1121
Joel	1: 1 LORD that came to Joel the **s** of Pethuel.	1121
Am	1: 1 the days of Jeroboam the **s** of Joash king	1121
	7:14 no prophet, neither *was* I a prophet's **s**;	1121
	8:10 will make it as the mourning of an only **s**,	NIH
Jnh	1: 1 LORD came unto Jonah the **s** of Amittai,	1121
Mic	6: 5 what Balaam the **s** of Beor answered him;	1121
	7: 6 For the **s** dishonoureth the father,	1121
Zep	1: 1 came unto Zephaniah the **s** of Cushi,	1121
	1: 1 the **s** of Gedaliah, the son of Amariah,	1121
	1: 1 the **s** of Amariah, the son of Hizkiah,	1121
	1: 1 the son of Amariah, the **s** of Hizkiah,	1121
	1: 1 in the days of Josiah the **s** of Amon, king	1121
Hag	1: 1 prophet unto Zerubbabel the **s** of Shealtiel,	1121
	1: 1 to Joshua the **s** of Josedech the high priest,	1121
	1:12 Zerubbabel the **s** of Shealtiel,	1121
	1:12 Joshua the **s** of Josedech the high priest,	1121
	1:14 the spirit of Zerubbabel the **s** of Shealtiel,	1121
	1:14 the spirit of Joshua the **s** of Josedech	1121
	2: 2 now to Zerubbabel the **s** of Shealtiel,	1121
	2: 2 to Joshua the **s** of Josedech the high priest	1121
	2: 4 strong, O Joshua, **s** of Josedech, the high	1121
	2:23 my servant, the **s** of Shealtiel,	1121
Zec	1: 1 the **s** of Berechiah, the son of Iddo	1121
	1: 1 the **s** of Iddo the prophet, saying,	1121
	1: 7 the **s** of Berechiah, the son of Iddo	1121
	1: 7 the **s** of Iddo the prophet, saying,	1121
	6:10 go *into* the house of Josiah the **s** of	1121
	6:11 set *them* upon the head of Joshua the **s** of	1121
	6:14 to Jedaiah, and to Hen the **s** of Zephaniah,	1121
	12:10 as one mourneth for *his* only **s**, and shall	NIH
Mal	1: 6 A **s** honoureth *his* father, and a servant	1121
	3:17 as a man spareth his own **s** that serveth	1121
Mt	1: 1 the **s** of David, the son of Abraham,	5207
	1: 1 the son of David, the **s** of Abraham.	5207
	1:20 saying, Joseph, thou **s** of David, fear not	5207
	1:21 she shall bring forth a **s**, and thou shalt	5207
	1:23 shall bring forth a **s**, and they shall call	5207
	1:25 till she had brought forth her firstborn **s**:	5207
	2:15 saying, Out of Egypt have I called my **s**.	5207
	3:17 saying, This is my beloved **S**, in whom I	5207
	4: 3 to him, he said, If thou be the **S** of God,	5207
	4: 6 If thou be the **S** of God, cast thyself down:	5207
	4:21 James the **s** of Zebedee, and John his	NIH
	7: 9 if his **s** ask bread, will he give him a	5207
	8:20 **S** of man hath not where to lay *his* head.	5207
	8:29 we to do with thee, Jesus, *thou* **S** of God?	5207
	9: 2 **S**, be of good cheer; thy sins be forgiven	5043
	9: 6 But that ye may know that the **S** of man	5207
	9:27 crying, and saying, *Thou* **S** of David,	5207
	10: 2 the **s** of Zebedee, and John his brother;	NIH
	10: 3 James the **s** of Alpheus, and Lebbeus,	NIH
	10:23 cities of Israel, till the **S** of man be come.	5207
	10:37 he that loveth **s** or daughter more than	5207
	11:19 The **S** of man came eating and drinking,	5207
	11:27 no *man* knoweth the **s**, but the Father;	5207
	11:27 save the **S**, and *he* to whomsoever the	5207
	11:27 to whomsoever the **S** will reveal *him*.	5207
	12: 8 For the **S** of man is Lord even of	5207
	12:23 and said, Is this the **s** of David?	5207
	12:32 speaketh a word against the **S** of man,	5207
	12:40 so shall the **S** of man be three days and	5207
	13:37 He that soweth the good seed is the **S** of	5207
	13:41 The **S** of man shall send forth his angels,	5207
	13:55 Is not this the carpenter's **s**? is not his	5207
	14:33 saying, Of a truth thou art the **S** of God.	5207
	15:22 mercy on me, O Lord, *thou* **S** of David;	5207
	16:13 do men say that I the **S** of man am?	5207
	16:16 art the Christ, the **S** of the living God.	5207
	16:27 For the **S** of man shall come in the glory of	5207
	16:28 till they see the **S** of man coming in his	5207
	17: 5 said, This is my beloved **S**, in whom	5207
	17: 9 Tell the vision to no *man*, until the **S** of	5207
	17:12 Likewise shall also the **S** of man suffer of	5207

Mt	17:15 Lord, have mercy on my **s**: for he is	5207
	17:22 The **S** of man shall be betrayed into	5207
	18:11 the **S** of man is come to save that which	5207
	19:28 the **S** of man shall sit in the throne of	5207
	20:18 the **S** of man shall be betrayed unto	5207
	20:28 Even as the **S** of man came not to be	5207
	20:30 mercy on us, O Lord, *thou* **S** of David.	5207
	20:31 mercy on us, O Lord, *thou* **S** of David.	5207
	21: 9 cried, saying, Hosanna to the **s** of David:	5207
	21:15 and saying, Hosanna to the **S** of David;	5207
	21:28 and he came to the first, and said, **S**,	5043
	21:37 But last *of all* he sent unto them his **s**,	5207
	21:37 his son, saying, They will reverence my **s**.	5207
	21:38 But when the husbandmen saw the **s**,	5207
	22: 2 which made a marriage for his **s**,	5207
	22:42 whose is he? They say unto him,	5207
	22:42 They say unto him, *The* **S** of David.	NIG
	22:45 then call him Lord, how is he his **s**?	5207
	23:35 unto the blood of Zacharias the **s** of Barachias,	5207
	24:27 shall also the coming of the **S** of man be.	5207
	24:30 shall appear the sign of the **S** of man in	5207
	24:30 they shall see the **S** of man coming in	5207
	24:37 shall also the coming of the **S** of man be.	5207
	24:39 shall also the coming of the **S** of man be.	5207
	24:44 in such an hour as you think not the **S** of	5207
	25:13 the hour wherein the **S** of man cometh.	5207
	25:31 the **S** of man shall come in his glory,	5207
	26: 2 The **S** of man is betrayed to be crucified.	5207
	26:24 **S** of man goeth as it is written of him:	5207
	26:24 unto that man by whom the **S** of man	5207
	26:45 the **S** of man is betrayed into the hands of	5207
	26:63 whether thou be the Christ, the **S** of God.	5207
	26:64 Hereafter shall ye see the **S** of man sitting	5207
	27:40 If thou be the **S** of God, come down from	5207
	27:43 have him: for he said, I am the **S** of God.	5207
	27:54 saying, Truly this was the **S** of God.	5207
	28:19 and of the **S**, and of the Holy Ghost:	5207
Mk	1: 1 of the gospel of Jesus Christ, the **S** of God;	5207
	1:11 *saying*, Thou art my beloved **S**, in whom I	5207
	1:19 he saw James the **s** of Zebedee, and John	NIG
	2: 5 of the palsy, **S**, thy sins be forgiven thee.	5043
	2:10 But that ye may know that the **S** of man	5207
	2:14 he saw Levi the **s** of Alpheus sitting at	NIG
	2:28 Therefore the **S** of man is Lord also of	5207
	3:11 and cried, saying, Thou art the **S** of God.	5207
	3:17 And James the **s** of Zebedee, and John	NIG
	3:18 James the **s** of Alpheus, and Thaddeus,	NIG
	5: 7 Jesus, *thou* **S** of the most high God?	5207
	6: 3 the **s** of Mary, the brother of James,	5207
	8:31 the **S** of man must suffer many *things*,	5207
	8:38 him also shall the **S** of man be ashamed,	5207
	9: 7 of the cloud, saying, This is my beloved **S**:	5207
	9: 9 till the **S** of man were risen from the dead.	5207
	9:12 and how it is written of the **S** of man,	5207
	9:17 Master, I have brought unto thee my **s**,	5207
	9:31 The **S** of man is delivered into the hands	5207
	10:33 the **S** of man shall be delivered unto	5207
	10:45 For even the **S** of man came not to be	5207
	10:46 blind Bartimeus, the **s** of Timeus,	5207
	10:47 and say, Jesus, *thou* **S** of David,	5207
	10:48 *Thou* **S** of David, have mercy on me.	5207
	12: 6 Having yet therefore one **s**,	5207
	12: 6 saying, They will reverence my **s**.	5207
	12:35 How say the scribes that Christ is the **S** of	5207
	12:37 him Lord; and whence is he *then* his **s**?	5207
	13:12 the brother to death, and the father the **s**;	5043
	13:26 shall they see the **S** of man coming in	5207
	13:32 in heaven, neither the **S**, but the Father.	5207
	13:34 For the **S** of man is as a man taking a far	NIG
	14:21 **S** of man indeed goeth, as it is written	5207
	14:21 to that man by whom the **S** of man is	5207
	14:41 the **S** of man is betrayed into the hands of	5207
	14:61 Art thou the Christ, the **S** of the Blessed?	5207
	14:62 shall see the **S** of man sitting on the right	5207
	15:39 he said, Truly this man was the **S** of God.	5207
Lk	1:13 and thy wife Elisabeth shall bear thee a **s**,	5207
	1:31 bring forth a **s**, and shalt call his name	5207
	1:32 and shall be called the **S** of the Highest:	5207
	1:35 born of thee shall be called the **S** of God.	5207
	1:36 she hath also conceived a **s** in her old age:	5207
	1:57 be delivered; and she brought forth a **s**.	5207
	2: 7 And she brought forth her firstborn **s**,	5207
	2:48 his mother said unto him, **S**, why hast	5043
	3: 2 the word of God came unto John the **s** of	5207
	3:22 which said, Thou art my beloved **S**;	5207
	3:23 the **s** of Joseph, which was *the son of*	5207
	3:23 son of Joseph, which was *the* **s** of Heli,	NIG
	3:24 Which was *the* **s** of Matthat, which was	NIG
	3:24 was *the* **s** of Levi, which was *the* son	NIG
	3:24 son of Levi, which was *the* **s** of Melchi,	NIG
	3:24 which was *the* **s** of Janna, which was	NIG
	3:24 son of Janna, which was *the* **s** of Joseph,	NIG
	3:25 Which was *the* **s** of Mattathias, which was	NIG
	3:25 which was *the* **s** of Amos, which was	NIG
	3:25 which was *the* **s** of Naum, which was	NIG
	3:25 *the son* of Naum, which was *the* **s** of Esli,	NIG
	3:25 *the son* of Esli, which was *the* **s** of Nagge,	NIG
	3:26 Which was *the* **s** of Maath, which was	NIG
	3:26 which was *the* **s** of Mattathias, which was	NIG
	3:26 which was *the* **s** of Semei, which was	NIG
	3:26 which was *the* **s** of Joseph, which was	NIG
	3:26 son of Joseph, which was *the* **s** of Juda,	NIG
	3:27 Which was *the* **s** of Joanna, which was	NIG
	3:27 son of Joanna, which was *the* **s** of Rhesa,	NIG
	3:27 of Rhesa, which was *the* **s** of Zorobabel,	NIG

Lk	3:27	which was *the* **s** of Salathiel, which was	NIG
	3:27	*son* of Salathiel, which was *the* **s** of Neri,	NIG
	3:28	Which was *the* **s** of Melchi, which was	NIG
	3:28	was *the* **s** of Addi, which was *the son*	NIG
	3:28	*son* of Addi, which was *the* **s** of Cosam,	NIG
	3:28	which was *the* **s** of Elmodam, which was	NIG
	3:28	*son* of Elmodam, which was *the* **s** of Er,	NIG
	3:29	was *the* **s** of Jose, which was *the son*	NIG
	3:29	*the son* of Jose, which was *the* **s** of Eliezer,	NIG
	3:29	*son* of Eliezer, which was *the* **s** of Jorim,	NIG
	3:29	which was *the* **s** of Matthat, which was	NIG
	3:29	*son* of Matthat, which was *the* **s** of Levi,	NIG
	3:30	Which was *the* **s** of Simeon, which was	NIG
	3:30	which was *the* **s** of Juda, which was *the*	NIG
	3:30	*son* of Juda, which was *the* **s** of Joseph,	NIG
	3:30	*son* of Joseph, which was *the* **s** of Jonan,	NIG
	3:30	*son* of Jonan, which was *the* **s** of Eliakim,	NIG
	3:31	Which was *the* **s** of Melea, which was	NIG
	3:31	*son* of Melea, which was *the* **s** of Menan,	NIG
	3:31	of Menan, which was *the* **s** of Mattatha,	NIG
	3:31	*son* of Nathan, which was *the* **s** of David,	NIG
	3:32	Which was *the* **s** of Jesse, which was	NIG
	3:32	was *the* **s** of Obed, which was *the son*	NIG
	3:32	*son* of Obed, which was *the* **s** of Booz,	NIG
	3:32	*son* of Booz, which was *the* **s** of Salmon,	NIG
	3:32	of Salmon, which was *the* **s** of Naasson,	NIG
	3:33	which was *the* **s** of Aminadab, which was	NIG
	3:33	which was *the* **s** of Aram, which was	NIG
	3:33	*son* of Aram, which was *the* **s** of Esrom,	NIG
	3:33	which was *the* **s** of Phares, which was	NIG
	3:33	*son* of Phares, which was *the* **s** of Juda,	NIG
	3:34	Which was *the* **s** of Jacob, which was	NIG
	3:34	*son* of Jacob, which was *the* **s** of Isaac,	NIG
	3:34	*son* of Isaac, which was *the* **s** of Abraham,	NIG
	3:34	which was *the* **s** of Thara, which was	NIG
	3:34	*son* of Thara, which was *the* **s** of Nachor,	NIG
	3:35	Which was *the* **s** of Saruch, which was	NIG
	3:35	which was *the* **s** of Ragau, which was	NIG
	3:35	which was *the* **s** of Phalec, which was	NIG
	3:35	which was *the* **s** of Heber, which was	NIG
	3:35	*the son* of Heber, which was *the* **s** of Sala,	NIG
	3:36	Which was *the* **s** of Cainan, which was	NIG
	3:36	which was *the* **s** of Arphaxad, which was	NIG
	3:36	which was *the* **s** of Sem, which was *the*	NIG
	3:36	*the son* of Sem, which was *the* **s** of Noe,	NIG
	3:36	*son* of Noe, which was *the* **s** of Lamech,	NIG
	3:37	Which was *the* **s** of Mathusala, which	NIG
	3:37	which was *the* **s** of Enoch, which	NIG
	3:37	*son* of Enoch, which was *the* **s** of Jared,	NIG
	3:37	*son* of Jared, which was *the* **s** of Maleleel,	NIG
	3:37	of Maleleel, which was *the* **s** of Cainan,	NIG
	3:38	was *the* **s** of Enos, which was *the son*	NIG
	3:38	*the son* of Enos, which was *the* **s** of Seth,	NIG
	3:38	which was *the* **s** of Adam, which was	NIG
	3:38	*son* of Adam, which was *the* **s** of God.	NIG
	4: 3	said unto him, If thou be the **S** of God,	5207
	4: 9	said unto him, If thou be the **S** of God,	5207
	4:22	And they said, Is not this Joseph's **s**?	5207
	4:41	and saying, Thou art Christ the **S** of God.	5207
	5:24	But that ye may know that the **S** of man	5207
	6: 5	That the **S** of man is Lord also of	5207
	6:15	James the **s** of Alpheus, and Simon called	NIG
	6:22	your name as evil, for the **S** of man's sake.	5207
	7:12	the only **s** of his mother, and she was a	5207
	7:34	**S** of man is come eating and drinking;	5207
	8:28	thee, Jesus, *thou* **S** of God most high?	5207
	9:22	The **S** of man must suffer many *things*,	5207
	9:26	of him shall the **S** of man be ashamed,	5207
	9:35	the cloud, saying, This is my beloved **S:**	5207
	9:38	Master, I beseech thee, look upon my **s:**	5207
	9:41	and suffer you? Bring thy **s** hither.	5207
	9:44	for the **S** of man shall be delivered into	5207
	9:56	For the **S** of man is not come to destroy	5207
	9:58	**S** of man hath not where to lay *his* head.	5207
	10: 6	And if the **s** of peace be there, your peace	5207
	10:22	and no *man* knoweth who the **S** is,	5207
	10:22	but the **S**, and *he* to whom the Son will	5207
	10:22	and *he* to whom the **S** will reveal *him.*	5207
	11:11	*If* a **s** shall ask bread of any of you that is	5207
	11:30	shall also the **S** of man be to this	5207
	12: 8	him shall the **S** of man also confess before	5207
	12:10	shall speak a word against the **S** of man,	5207
	12:40	the **S** of man cometh at an hour when ye	5207
	12:53	The father shall be divided against the **s**,	5207
	12:53	the son, and the **s** against the father;	5207
	15:13	And not many days after the younger **s**	5207
	15:19	am no more worthy to be called thy **s:**	5207
	15:21	And the **s** said unto him, Father, I have	5207
	15:21	am no more worthy to be called thy **s.**	5207
	15:24	For this my **s** was dead, and is alive again;	5207
	15:25	his elder **s** was in the field: and as he	5207
	15:30	But as soon as this thy **s** was come,	5207
	15:31	**S**, thou art ever with me, and all that I	5043
	16:25	But Abraham said, **S**, remember that thou	5043
	17:22	to see one of the days of the **S** of man,	5207
	17:24	so shall also the **S** of man be in his day.	5207
	17:26	shall it be also in the days of the **S** of man.	5207
	17:30	thus shall it be in the day when the **S**	5207
	18: 8	Nevertheless when the **S** of man cometh,	5207
	18:31	the **S** of man shall be accomplished.	5207
	18:38	he cried, saying, Jesus, *thou* **S** of David,	5207
	18:39	*so* much the more, *Thou* **S** of David,	5207
	19: 9	forsomuch as he also is a **s** of Abraham.	5207
	19:10	For the **S** of man is come to seek and	5207

Lk	20:13	I will send my beloved **s:** it may be they	5207
	20:41	How say they that Christ is David's **s?**	5207
	20:44	calleth him Lord, how is he then his **s?**	5207
	21:27	shall they see the **S** of man coming in a	5207
	21:36	to pass, and to stand before the **S** of man.	5207
	22:22	And truly the **S** of man goeth, as it was	5207
	22:48	betrayest thou the **S** of man with a kiss?	5207
	22:69	Hereafter shall the **S** of man sit on the	5207
	22:70	said they all, Art thou then the **S** of God?	5207
	24: 7	The **S** of man must be delivered into	5207
Jn	1:18	only begotten **S,** which is in the bosom	5207
	1:34	and bare record that this is the **S** of God.	5207
	1:42	he said, Thou art Simon the **s** of Jona;	5207
	1:45	Jesus of Nazareth, the **s** of Joseph.	5207
	1:49	unto him, Rabbi, thou art the **S** of God;	5207
	1:51	and descending upon the **S** of man.	5207
	3:13	*even* the **S** of man which is in heaven.	5207
	3:14	*even* so must the **S** of man be lifted up:	5207
	3:16	world, that he gave his only begotten **S,**	5207
	3:17	For God sent not his **S** into the world to	5207
	3:18	the name of the only begotten **S** of God.	5207
	3:35	The Father loveth the **S,** and hath given	5207
	3:36	that believeth on the **S** hath everlasting	5207
	3:36	that believeth not the **S** shall not see life;	5207
	4: 5	of ground that Jacob gave to his **s** Joseph.	5207
	4:46	whose **s** was sick at Capernaum.	5207
	4:47	that he would come down, and heal his **s:**	5207
	4:50	saith unto him, Go *thy way*; thy **s** liveth.	5207
	4:51	him, and told *him*, saying, Thy **s** liveth.	3816
	4:53	which Jesus said unto him, Thy **s** liveth:	5207
	5:19	The **S** can do nothing of himself,	5207
	5:19	he doeth, these also doeth the **S** likewise.	5207
	5:20	For the Father loveth the **S,**	5207
	5:21	so the **S** quickeneth whom he will.	5207
	5:22	hath committed all judgment unto the **S:**	5207
	5:23	That all *men* should honour the **S,** even	5207
	5:23	He that honoureth not the **S** honoureth	5207
	5:25	the dead shall hear the voice of the **S**	5207
	5:26	hath he given to the **S** to have life in	5207
	5:27	judgment also, because he is the **S** of man.	5207
	6:27	which the **S** of man shall give unto you:	5207
	6:40	that every one which seeth the **S,**	5207
	6:42	the **s** of Joseph, whose father and mother	5207
	6:53	Except ye eat the flesh of the **S** of man,	5207
	6:62	if ye shall see the **S** of man ascend up	5207
	6:69	art *that* Christ, the **S** of the living God.	5207
	6:71	He spake of Judas Iscariot *the son* of Simon:	NIG
	8:28	When ye have lift up the **S** of man, then	5207
	8:35	the house for ever: *but* the **s** abideth ever.	5207
	8:36	If the **S** therefore shall make you free,	5207
	9:19	they asked them, saying, Is this your **s,**	5207
	9:20	We know that this is our **s,** and that he	5207
	9:35	Dost thou believe on the **S** of God?	5207
	10:36	because I said, I am the **S** of God?	5207
	11: 4	that the **S** of God might be glorified	5207
	11:27	that thou art the Christ, the **S** of God,	5207
	12: 4	Simon's **s,** which should betray him,	NIG
	12:23	that the **S** of man should be glorified.	5207
	12:34	thou, The **S** of man must be lift up?	5207
	12:34	must be lift up? who is this **S** of man?	5207
	13: 2	Judas Iscariot, Simon's **s,** to betray him;	5207
	13:26	gave *it* to Judas Iscariot, *the son* of Simon.	NIG
	13:31	Now is the **S** of man glorified, and God is	5207
	14:13	that the Father may be glorified in the **S.**	5207
	17: 1	glorify thy **S,** that thy Son also may glorify	5207
	17: 1	thy Son, that thy **S** also may glorify thee:	5207
	17:12	of them is lost, but the **s** of perdition;	5207
	19: 7	because he made himself the **S** of God.	5207
	19:26	unto his mother, Woman, behold thy **s.**	5207
	20:31	that Jesus is the Christ, the **S** of God;	5207
	21:15	saith to Simon Peter, Simon, **s** of Jonas,	NIG
	21:16	Simon, **s** of Jonas, lovest thou me?	NIG
	21:17	Simon, **s** of Jonas, lovest thou me?	NIG
Ac	1:13	James the **s** of Alpheus, and Simon	NIG
	3:13	of our fathers, hath glorified his **S** Jesus;	3816
	3:26	first God, having raised up his **S** Jesus,	3816
	4:36	being interpreted, The **s** of consolation,)	5207
	7:21	up, and nourished him for her own **s.**	5207
	7:56	the **S** of man standing on the right hand	5207
	8:37	I believe that Jesus Christ is the **S** of God.	5207
	9:20	in the synagogues, that he is the **S** of God.	5207
	13:21	God gave unto them Saul the **s** of Cis,	5207
	13:22	said, I have found David the **s** of Jesse,	NIG
	13:33	Thou art my **S,** this day have I begotten	5207
	16: 1	the **s** of a certain woman,	5207
	23: 6	I am a Pharisee, the **s** of a Pharisee:	5207
	23:16	And when Paul's sister's **s** heard of *their*	5207
Ro	1: 3	Concerning his **S** Jesus Christ our Lord,	5207
	1: 4	And declared *to be* the **S** of God with	5207
	1: 9	serve with my spirit in the gospel of his **S,**	5207
	5:10	reconciled to God by the death of his **S,**	5207
	8: 3	God sending his own **S** in the likeness of	5207
	8:29	*to be* conformed to the image of his **S,**	5207
	8:32	He that spared not his own **S,**	5207
	9: 9	time I will come, and Sara shall have a **s.**	5207
1Co	1: 9	fellowship of his **S** Jesus Christ our Lord.	5207
	4:17	who is my beloved **s,** and faithful in	5043
	15:28	shall the **S** also himself be subject unto	5207
2Co	1:19	For the **S** of God, Jesus Christ, who was	5207
Gal	1:16	To reveal his **S** in me, that I might preach	5207
	2:20	flesh I live by the faith of the **S** of God,	5207
	4: 4	God sent forth his **S,** made of a woman,	5207
	4: 6	God hath sent forth the Spirit of his **S** into	5207
	4: 7	thou art no more a servant, but a **s;**	5207
	4: 7	and if a **s,** then an heir of God through	5207

Gal	4:30	Cast out the bondwoman and her **s:**	5207
	4:30	for the **s** of the bondwoman shall not be	5207
	4:30	not be heir with the **s** of the freewoman.	5207
Eph	4:13	and of the knowledge of the **S** of God,	5207
Php	2:22	proof of him, that, as a **s** *with the* father,	5043
Col	1:13	*us* into the kingdom of his dear **S:**	5207
	4:10	and Marcus, **sister's s** to Barnabas,	431
1Th	1:10	And to wait for his **S** from heaven,	5207
2Th	2: 3	man of sin be revealed, the **s** of perdition;	5207
1Ti	1: 2	Unto Timothy, *my* own **s** in the faith:	5043
	1:18	charge I commit unto thee, **s** Timothy,	5043
2Ti	1: 2	To Timothy, *my* dearly beloved **s:** Grace,	5043
	2: 1	Thou therefore, my **s,** be strong in the	5043
Tit	1: 4	*mine* own **s** after the common faith:	5043
Phm	1:10	I beseech thee for my **s** Onesimus, whom	5043
Heb	1: 2	in these last days spoken unto us by *his* **S,**	5207
	1: 5	Thou art my **S,** this day have I begotten	5207
	1: 5	him a Father, and he shall be to me a **S?**	5207
	1: 8	unto the **S** *he saith,* Thy throne, O God,	5207
	2: 6	or the **s** of man, that thou visitest him?	5207
	3: 6	But Christ as a **S** over his own house;	5207
	4:14	Jesus the **S** of God, let us hold fast *our*	5207
	5: 5	but he that said unto him, Thou art my **S,**	5207
	5: 8	Though he were a **S,** *yet* learned he	5207
	6: 6	seeing they crucify to themselves the **S** of	5207
	7: 3	of life; but made like unto the **S** of God;	5207
	7:28	which was since the law, *maketh* the **S,**	5207
	10:29	hath trodden under foot the **S** of God,	5207
	11:17	promises offered up *his* only begotten **s,**	NIG
	11:24	refused to be called the **s** of Pharaoh's	5207
	12: 5	My **s,** despise not thou the chastening of	5207
	12: 6	scourgeth every **s** whom he receiveth.	5207
	12: 7	what **s** is *he* whom the father chasteneth	5207
Jas	2:21	when he had offered Isaac his **s** upon	5207
1Pe	5:13	saluteth you; and *so doth* Marcus my **s.**	5207
2Pe	1:17	This is my beloved **S,** in whom I am well	5207
	2:15	the way of Balaam *the* **s** of Bosor,	NIG
1Jn	1: 3	the Father, and with his **S** Jesus Christ.	5207
	1: 7	blood of Jesus Christ his **S** cleanseth us	5207
	2:22	that denieth the Father and the **S.**	5207
	2:23	Whosoever denieth the **S,** the same hath	5207
	2:23	that acknowledgeth the **S** hath the Father	NIG
	2:24	ye also shall continue in the **S,** and in	5207
	3: 8	For this purpose the **S** of God was	5207
	3:23	believe on the name of his **S** Jesus Christ,	5207
	4: 9	that God sent his only begotten **S** into	5207
	4:10	his **S** *to be* the propitiation for our sins.	5207
	4:14	do testify that the Father sent the **S** *to be*	5207
	4:15	Whosoever shall confess that Jesus is the **S**	5207
	5: 5	that believeth that Jesus is the **S** of God?	5207
	5: 9	of God which he hath testified of his **S.**	5207
	5:10	He that believeth on the **S** of God hath	5207
	5:10	not the record that God gave of his **S.**	5207
	5:11	to us eternal life, and this life is in his **S.**	5207
	5:12	He that hath the **S** hath life; *and* he that	5207
	5:12	that hath not the **S** of God hath not life.	5207
	5:13	that believe on the name of the **S** of God;	5207
	5:13	ye may believe on the name of the **S** of	5207
	5:20	And we know that the **S** of God is come,	5207
	5:20	*that is* true, *even* in his **S** Jesus Christ.	5207
2Jn	1: 3	the Father, in truth and love.	5207
	1: 9	Christ, he hath both the Father and the **S.**	5207
Rev	1:13	candlesticks one like unto the **S** of man,	5207
	2:18	These *things* saith the **S** of God, who hath	5207
	14:14	upon the cloud one sat like unto the **S** of	5207
	21: 7	I will be his God, and he shall be my **s.**	5207

SON'S (22) [SON]

Ge	11:31	Lot the son of Haran his **s** son, and Sarai	1121
	16:15	Abram called his **s** name, which Hagar	1121
	21:23	nor with my son, nor with my **s son:**	5220
	24:51	and go, and let her be thy master's **s** wife,	1121
	27:25	near to me, and I will eat of my **s** venison,	1121
	27:31	my father arise, and eat of his **s** venison,	1121
	30:14	Give me, I pray thee, of thy **s** mandrakes.	1121
	30:15	wouldest thou take away my **s** mandrakes	1121
	30:15	lie with thee to night for thy **s** mandrakes.	1121
	30:16	for surely I have hired thee with my **s**	1121
	37:32	know now whether it *be* thy **s** coat or no.	1121
	37:33	he knew it, and said, *It is* my **s** coat;	1121
Ex	10: 2	of thy son, what things I have wrought	1121
Lev	18:10	The nakedness of thy **s** daughter, or of thy	1121
	18:15	she *is* thy **s** wife; thou shalt not uncover	1121
	18:17	neither shalt thou take her **s** daughter,	1121
Dt	6: 2	thou, and thy son, and thy **s** son,	1121
Jdg	8:22	thou, and thy son, and thy **s** son also:	1121
1Ki	11:35	I will take the kingdom out of his **s** hand,	1121
	21:29	in his days will I bring the evil upon his **s**	1121
Pr	30: 4	and what *is* his **s** name, if thou canst tell?	1121
Jer	27: 7	serve him, and his son, and his **s** son,	1121

SONG (78) [SING]

Ex	15: 1	the children of Israel this **s** unto	7892
	15: 2	The LORD *is* my strength and **s,** and he is	2176
Nu	21:17	Israel sang this **s,** Spring up, O well;	7892
Dt	31:19	Now therefore write ye this **s** for you,	7892
	31:19	that this **s** may be a witness for me against	7892
	31:21	that this **s** shall testify against them as a	7892
	31:22	Moses therefore wrote this **s** the same	7892
	31:30	congregation of Israel the words of this **s,**	7892
	32:44	spake all the words of this **s** in the ears of	7892
Jdg	5:12	awake, awake, utter a **s:** arise, Barak,	7892
2Sa	22: 1	**s** in the day *that* the LORD had delivered	7892
1Ch	6:31	the service of **s** *in* the house of the LORD,	7892
	15:22	chief of the Levites, *was* for **s:**	4853

S

1Ch 15:22 he instructed about the **s**, because he *was* 4853
15:27 Chenaniah the master of the **s** *with* 4853
25: 6 father for **s** *in* the house of the LORD, 7892
2Ch 29:27 the **s** of the LORD began *also* with 7892
Job 30: 9 now am I their **s**, yea, I am their byword. 5058
Ps 18: 1 **T s** in the day *that* the LORD delivered him 7892
28: 7 and with my **s** will I praise him. 7892
30: 1 **T S** at the dedication of the house of David. 7892
33: 3 Sing unto him a new **s**; play skilfully with 7892
40: 3 he hath put a new **s** in my mouth, 7892
42: 8 in the night his **s** *shall* be with me, 7892
45: 7 **T** the sons of Korah, Maschil, A **S** of loves. 7892
46: 7 **T** for the sons of Korah, A **S** upon Alamoth. 7892
48: 7 **T A S** *and* Psalm for the sons of Korah. 7892
65: 7 **T** chief Musician, A Psalm *and* **S** of David. 7892
66: 7 **T** To the chief Musician, A **S** *or* Psalm. 7892
67: 7 **T** chief Musician on Neginoth, A Psalm *or* **S**. 7892
68: 7 **T** the chief Musician, A Psalm *or* **S** of David. 7892
69:12 and *I was* the **s** of the drunkards. 5058
69:30 I will praise the name of God with a **s**; 7892
75: 7 **T** Al-taschith, A Psalm *or* **S** of Asaph. 7892
76: 7 **T** on Neginoth, A Psalm *or* **S** of Asaph. 7892
77: 6 I call to remembrance my **s** in the night: 5058
83: 7 **T A S** *or* Psalm of Asaph. 7892
87: 7 **T A** Psalm *or* **S** for the sons of Korah. 7892
88: 7 **T A S** *or* Psalm for the sons of Korah. 7892
92: 7 **T A** Psalm *or* **S** for the sabbath day. 7892
96: 1 O sing unto the LORD a new **s**: sing unto 7892
98: 1 O sing unto the LORD a new **s**; for he 7892
108: 7 **T A** Psalm of David. 7892
118:14 The LORD *is* my strength and **s**, 2176
120: 7 **T A S** of degrees. 7892
121: 7 **T A S** of degrees. 7892
122: 7 **T A S** of degrees of David. 7892
123: 7 **T A S** of degrees. 7892
124: 7 **T A S** of degrees of David. 7892
125: 7 **T A S** of degrees. 7892
126: 7 **T A S** of degrees. 7892
127: 7 **T A S** of degrees for Solomon. 7892
128: 7 **T A S** of degrees. 7892
129: 7 **T A S** of degrees. 7892
130: 7 **T A S** of degrees. 7892
131: 7 **T A S** of degrees of David. 7892
132: 7 **T A S** of degrees. 7892
133: 7 **T A S** of degrees of David. 7892
134: 7 **T A S** of degrees. 7892
137: 3 us away captive required of us a **s**; 1697+7892
137: 4 How shall we sing the LORD'S **s** in a 7892
144: 9 I will sing a new **s** unto thee, O God: 7892
149: 1 Sing unto the LORD a new **s**, 7892
Ecc 7: 5 than for a man to hear the **s** of fools. 7892
SS 1: 1 The **s** of songs, which *is* Solomon's. 7892
Isa 5: 1 Now will I sing to my wellbeloved a **s** of 7892
12: 2 JEHOVAH *is* my strength and *my* **s**; 2176
24: 9 They shall not drink wine with a **s**; 7892
26: 1 In that day shall this **s** be sung in the land 7892
30:29 Ye shall have a **s**, as *in* the night when a 7892
42:10 Sing unto the LORD a new **s**, 7892
La 3:14 to all my people; *and* their **s** all the day. 5058
Eze 33:32 thou *art* unto them as a very lovely **s** of 5058
Rev 5: 9 And they sung a new **s**, saying, Thou art 5603
14: 3 And they sung as *it were* a new **s** before 5603
14: 3 and no *man* could learn *that* **s** but 5603
15: 3 And they sing the **s** of Moses the servant 5603
15: 3 and the **s** of the Lamb, saying, Great and 5603

SONGS (20) [SING]

Ge 31:27 and with **s**, with tabret, and with harp? 7892
1Ki 4:32 and his **s** were a thousand and five. 7892
1Ch 25: 7 *that were* instructed in the **s** of the LORD, 7892
Ne 12:46 of praise and thanksgiving unto God. 7892
Job 35:10 God my Maker, who giveth **s** in the night; 2158
Ps 32: 7 thou shalt compass me about *with* **s** of 7438
119:54 Thy statutes have been my **s** in the house 2158
137: 3 *saying*, Sing us *one* of the **s** of Zion. 7892
Pr 25:20 so *is* he that singeth **s** to a heavy heart. 7892
SS 1: 1 The song of **s**, which *is* Solomon's. 7892
Isa 23:16 make sweet melody, sing many **s**, that 7892
24:16 part of the earth have we heard **s**, 2158
35:10 come *to* Zion with **s** and everlasting joy 7440
38:20 we will sing my **s** *to* the stringed 5058
Eze 26:13 I will cause the noise of thy **s** to cease; 7892
Am 5:23 thou away from me the noise of thy **s**; 7892
8: 3 the **s** of the temple shall be howlings in 7892
8:10 and all your **s** into lamentation; 7892
Eph 5:19 in psalms and hymns and spiritual **s**, 5603
Col 3:16 in psalms and hymns and spiritual **s**, 5603

SONS (1076) [SON]

Ge 5: 4 and he begat **s** and daughters: 1121
5: 7 seven years, and begat **s** and daughters: 1121
5:10 fifteen years, and begat **s** and daughters: 1121
5:13 forty years, and begat **s** and daughters: 1121
5:16 thirty years, and begat **s** and daughters: 1121
5:19 hundred years, and begat **s** and daughters: 1121
5:22 hundred years, and begat **s** and daughters: 1121
5:26 and two years, and begat **s** and daughters: 1121
5:30 and five years, and begat **s** and daughters: 1121
6: 2 the **s** of God saw the daughters of men 1121
6: 4 when the **s** of God came in unto 1121
6:10 Noah begat three **s**, Shem, Ham, 1121
6:18 thy **s**, and thy wife, and thy sons' wives 1121
7: 7 his **s**, and his wife, and his sons' wives 1121
7:13 the **s** of Noah, and Noah's wife, 1121
7:13 the three wives of his **s** with them, into 1121

Ge 8:16 and thy **s**, and thy sons' wives with thee. 1121
8:18 his **s**, and his wife, and his sons' wives 1121
9: 1 God blessed Noah and his **s**, and said unto 1121
9: 8 unto Noah, and to his **s** with him, saying, 1121
9:18 the **s** of Noah, that went forth of the ark, 1121
9:19 These *are* the three **s** of Noah: and of 1121
10: 1 Now these *are* the generations of the **s** of 1121
10: 1 unto them were **s** born after the flood. 1121
10: 2 The **s** of Japheth; Gomer, and Magog, 1121
10: 3 the **s** of Gomer; Ashkenaz, and Riphath, 1121
10: 4 the **s** of Javan; Elishah, and Tarshish, 1121
10: 6 the **s** of Ham; Cush, and Mizraim, 1121
10: 7 the **s** of Cush; Seba, and Havilah, 1121
10: 7 and the **s** of Raamah; Sheba, and Dedan. 1121
10:20 *are* the **s** of Ham, after their families, 1121
10:25 unto Eber were born two **s**: the name of 1121
10:29 and Jobab: all these *were* the **s** of Joktan. 1121
10:31 These *are* the **s** of Shem, after their 1121
10:32 These *are* the families of the **s** of Noah, 1121
11:11 hundred years, and begat **s** and daughters. 1121
11:13 three years, and begat **s** and daughters. 1121
11:15 three years, and begat **s** and daughters. 1121
11:17 thirty years, and begat **s** and daughters. 1121
11:19 nine years, and begat **s** and daughters. 1121
11:21 seven years, and begat **s** and daughters. 1121
11:23 hundred years, and begat **s** and daughters. 1121
11:25 nineteen years, and begat **s** and daughters. 1121
19:12 thy **s**, and thy daughters, 1121
19:14 went out, and spake unto his **s in law**, 2860
19:14 one that mocked unto his **s in law**. 2860
23: 3 and spake unto the **s** of Heth, saying, 1121
23:11 in the presence of the **s** of my people give 1121
23:16 named in the audience of the **s** of Heth, 1121
23:20 of a buryingplace by the **s** of Heth. 1121
25: 3 the **s** of Dedan were Asshurim, 1121
25: 4 the **s** of Midian; Ephah, and Epher, 1121
25: 6 unto the **s** of the concubines, 1121
25: 9 his **s** Isaac and Ishmael buried him in 1121
25:10 Abraham purchased of the **s** of Heth: 1121
25:13 These *are* the names of the **s** of Ishmael, 1121
25:16 These *are* the **s** of Ishmael, and these *are* 1121
27:29 and let thy mother's **s** bow down to thee: 1121
29:34 me, because I have born him three **s**: 1121
30:20 with me, because I have born him six **s**: 1121
30:35 and gave *them* into the hand of his **s**. 1121
31: 1 he heard the words of Laban's **s**, saying, 1121
31:17 and set his **s** and his wives upon camels; 1121
31:28 hast not suffered me to kiss my **s** and my 1121
31:55 kissed his **s** and his daughters, 1121
32:22 his eleven **s**, and passed over the ford 3206
34: 5 his **s** were with his cattle in the field: 1121
34: 7 the **s** of Jacob came out of the field when 1121
34:13 the **s** of Jacob answered Shechem and 1121
34:25 that two of the **s** of Jacob, Simeon and 1121
34:27 The **s** of Jacob came upon the slain, 1121
35: 5 They did not pursue after the **s** of Jacob. 1121
35:22 Israel heard *it*. Now the **s** of Jacob were 1121
35:23 The **s** of Leah; Reuben, Jacob's firstborn, 1121
35:24 The **s** of Rachel; Joseph, and Benjamin: 1121
35:25 the **s** of Bilhah, Rachel's handmaid; Dan, 1121
35:26 the **s** of Zilpah, Leah's handmaid; Gad, 1121
35:26 these *are* the **s** of Jacob, which were born 1121
35:29 and his Esau and Jacob buried him. 1121
36: 5 these *are* the **s** of Esau, which were born 1121
36: 6 his, and his daughters, and the persons 1121
36:10 These *are* the names of Esau's **s**; 1121
36:11 the **s** of Eliphaz were Teman, Omar, 1121
36:12 these *were* the **s** of Adah Esau's wife. 1121
36:13 *are* the **s** of Reuel; Nahath, and Zerah, 1121
36:13 were the **s** of Bashemath Esau's wife. 1121
36:14 these were the **s** of Aholibamah, 1121
36:15 *were* dukes of the **s** of Esau: the sons 1121
36:15 the **s** of Eliphaz the firstborn *son* of Esau; 1121
36:16 land of Edom; these *were* the **s** of Adah. 1121
36:17 these *are* the **s** of Reuel Esau's son; 1121
36:17 these *are* the **s** of Bashemath Esau's wife. 1121
36:18 *are* the **s** of Aholibamah Esau's wife; 1121
36:19 These *are* the **s** of Esau, who *is* Edom, 1121
36:20 These *are* the **s** of Seir the Horite, 1121
37: 2 the lad *was* with the **s** of Bilhah, 1121
37: 2 with the **s** of Zilpah, his father's wives: 1121
37:35 all his **s** and all his daughters rose up to 1121
41:50 unto Joseph were born two **s** before 1121
42: 1 Jacob said unto his **s**, Why do ye look one 1121
42: 5 the **s** of Israel came to buy *corn* among 1121
42:11 We *are* all one man's **s**; we *are* true *men*, 1121
42:13 the **s** of one man in the land of Canaan; 1121
42:32 We *be* twelve brethren, **s** of our father; 1121
42:37 saying, Slay my two **s**, if I bring him not 1121
44:27 Ye know that my wife bare me two **s**. NIH
46: 5 the **s** of Israel carried Jacob their father, 1121
46: 7 His **s**, and his sons' sons with him, 1121
46: 7 His sons, and his sons' **s** with him, 1121
46: 8 which came into Egypt, Jacob and his **s**: 1121
46: 9 the **s** of Reuben; Hanoch, and Phallu, 1121
46:10 the **s** of Simeon; Jemuel, and Jamin, 1121
46:11 the **s** of Levi; Gershon, Kohath, and 1121
46:12 the **s** of Judah; Er, and Onan, and Shelah, 1121
46:12 the **s** of Pharez were Hezron and Hamul. 1121
46:13 the **s** of Issachar; Tola, and Phuvah, 1121
46:14 the **s** of Zebulun; Sered, and Elon, 1121
46:15 *be* the **s** of Leah, which she bare unto 1121
46:15 all the souls of his **s** and his daughters 1121
46:16 the **s** of Gad; Ziphion, and Haggi, Shuni, 1121
46:17 the **s** of Asher; Jimnah, and Ishuah, 1121

Ge 46:17 and the **s** of Beriah; Heber, and Malchiel. 1121
46:18 These *are* the **s** of Zilpah, whom Laban 1121
46:19 The **s** of Rachel Jacob's wife; Joseph, 1121
46:21 the **s** of Benjamin *were* Belah, and Becher, 1121
46:22 *are* the **s** of Rachel, which were born 1121
46:23 And the **s** of Dan; Hushim. 1121
46:24 the **s** of Naphtali; Jahzeel, and Guni, 1121
46:25 These *are* the **s** of Bilhah, which Laban 1121
46:27 the **s** of Joseph, which were born him in 1121
48: 1 he took with him his two **s**, Manasseh 1121
48: 5 now thy two **s**, Ephraim and Manasseh, 1121
48: 8 Israel beheld Joseph's **s**, and said, Who 1121
48: 9 said unto his father, They *are* my **s**, 1121
49: 1 Jacob called unto his **s**, and said, 1121
49: 2 and hear, ye **s** of Jacob; 1121
49:33 had made an end of commanding his **s**, 1121
50:12 his **s** did unto him according as he 1121
50:13 For his **s** carried him into the land of 1121
Ex 3:22 ye shall put *them* upon your **s**, 1121
4:20 Moses took his wife and his **s**, and set 1121
6:14 The **s** of Reuben the firstborn of Israel; 1121
6:15 the **s** of Simeon; Jemuel, and Jamin, 1121
6:16 these *are* the names of the **s** of Levi 1121
6:17 The **s** of Gershon; Libni, and Shimi, 1121
6:18 the **s** of Kohath; Amram, and Izhar, 1121
6:19 the **s** of Merari; Mahali and Mushi: 1121
6:21 the **s** of Izhar; Korah, and Nepheg, 1121
6:22 the **s** of Uzziel; Mishael, and Elzaphan, 1121
6:24 the **s** of Korah; Assir, and Elkanah, 1121
10: 9 old, with our **s** and with our daughters, 1121
12:24 an ordinance to thee and to thy **s** for ever. 1121
18: 3 her two **s**; of which the name of the one 1121
18: 5 came with his **s** and his wife unto Moses 1121
18: 6 and thy wife, and her two **s** with her. 1121
21: 4 and she have born him **s** or daughters; 1121
22:29 the firstborn of thy **s** shalt thou give unto 1121
27:21 his **s** shall order it from evening to 1121
28: 1 his **s** with him, from among the children 1121
28: 1 Abihu, Eleazar and Ithamar, Aaron's **s**. 1121
28: 4 his **s**, that he may minister unto me in 1121
28:40 for Aaron's **s** thou shalt make coats, 1121
28:41 Aaron thy brother, and his **s** with him; 1121
28:43 they shall be upon Aaron, and upon his **s**, 1121
29: 4 his **s** thou shalt bring unto the door of 1121
29: 8 thou shalt bring his **s**, and put coats upon 1121
29: 9 Aaron and his **s**, and put the bonnets on 1121
29: 9 and thou shalt consecrate Aaron and his **s**. 1121
29:10 his **s** shall put their hands upon the head 1121
29:15 his **s** shall put their hands upon the head 1121
29:19 his **s** shall put their hands upon the head 1121
29:20 upon the tip of the right ear of his **s**, 1121
29:21 upon his **s**, and upon the garments of his **s** 1121
29:21 and upon the garments of his **s** with him: 1121
29:21 his **s**, and his sons' garments with him. 1121
29:24 hands of Aaron, and in the hands of his **s**; 1121
29:27 *is* for Aaron, and of *that which is* for his **s**: 1121
29:32 and his **s** shall eat the flesh of the ram, 1121
29:35 shalt thou do unto Aaron, and to his **s**, 1121
29:44 I will sanctify also both Aaron and his **s**, 1121
30:19 and his **s** shall wash their hands and 1121
30:30 thou shalt anoint Aaron and his **s**, 1121
31:10 the garments of his **s**, to minister in 1121
32: 2 of your **s**, and of your daughters, 1121
32:26 all the **s** of Levi gathered themselves 1121
34:16 thou take of their daughters unto thy **s**, 1121
34:16 make thy **s** go a whoring after their gods. 1121
34:20 the firstborn of thy **s** thou shalt redeem: 1121
35:19 the garments of his **s**, to minister in 1121
39:27 *of* woven work for Aaron, and for his **s**, 1121
40:12 his **s** unto the door of the tabernacle of 1121
40:14 thou shalt bring his **s**, and clothe them 1121
40:31 Aaron and his **s** washed their hands and 1121
Lev 1: 5 priests, Aaron's **s**, shall bring the blood, 1121
1: 7 the **s** of Aaron the priest shall put fire 1121
1: 8 the priests, Aaron's **s**, shall lay the parts, 1121
1:11 the priests, Aaron's **s**, shall sprinkle his 1121
2: 2 he shall bring it to Aaron's **s** the priests: 1121
2: 3 Aaron's **s** the priests shall sprinkle 1121
3: 5 Aaron's **s** shall burn it on the altar upon 1121
3: 8 Aaron's **s** shall sprinkle the blood thereof 1121
3:13 the **s** of Aaron shall sprinkle the blood 1121
6: 9 Command Aaron and his **s**, saying, This *is* 1121
6:14 the **s** of Aaron shall offer it before 1121
6:16 thereof shall Aaron and his **s** eat: 1121
6:20 This *is* the offering of Aaron and of his **s**, 1121
6:22 the priest of his **s** that is anointed in his 1121
6:25 Speak unto Aaron and to his **s**, saying, 1121
7:10 and dry, shall all the **s** of Aaron have, 1121
7:33 He among the **s** of Aaron, that offereth 1121
7:34 unto his **s** by a statute for ever from 1121
7:35 of Aaron, and of the anointing of his **s**, 1121
8: 2 Take Aaron and his **s** with him, 1121
8: 6 Moses brought Aaron and his **s**, 1121
8:13 his **s**, and put coats 1121
8:14 his **s** laid their hands upon the head of 1121
8:18 his **s** laid their hands upon the head of 1121
8:22 his **s** laid their hands upon the head of 1121
8:24 he brought Aaron's **s**, and Moses put of 1121
8:30 upon his **s**, and upon his sons' garments 1121
8:30 his **s**, and his sons' garments with him. 1121
8:31 Moses said unto Aaron and to his **s**, 1121
8:31 Aaron and his **s** shall eat it. 1121
8:36 his **s** did all things which the LORD 1121
9: 1 *that* Moses called Aaron and his **s**, 1121
9: 9 the **s** of Aaron brought the blood unto 1121

S

Lev	
9:12	Aaron's s presented unto him the blood, 1121
9:18	Aaron's s presented unto him the blood, 1121
10: 1	Nadab and Abihu, the s of Aaron, 1121
10: 4	the s of Uzziel the uncle of Aaron, 1121
10: 6	unto Eleazar and unto Ithamar his s, 1121
10: 9	strong drink, thou, nor thy s with thee, 1121
10:12	and unto Ithamar his s that were left, 1121
10:14	and thy s, and thy daughters with thee: 1121
10:16	Ithamar the s of Aaron which were left 1121
13: 2	the priest, or unto one of his s the priests 1121
16: 1	after the death of the two s of Aaron, 1121
17: 2	unto his s, and unto all the children of 1121
21: 1	Speak unto the priests the s of Aaron, 1121
21:24	to his s, and unto all the children of Israel. 1121
22: 2	Speak unto Aaron and to his s, that they 1121
22:18	to his s, and unto all the children of Israel, 1121
26:29	shall eat the flesh of your s, and the flesh 1121
Nu	
2:14	captain of the s of Gad after Eliasaph 1121
2:18	the captain of the s of Ephraim *shall be* 1121
2:22	the captain of the s of Benjamin *shall be* 1121
3: 2	these *are* the names of the s of Aaron; 1121
3: 3	These *are* the names of the s of Aaron, 1121
3: 9	give the Levites unto Aaron and to his s: 1121
3:10	And thou shalt appoint Aaron and his s, 1121
3:17	these were the s of Levi by their names; 1121
3:18	these *are* the names of the s of Gershon 1121
3:19	the s of Kohath by their families; Amram, 1121
3:20	the s of Merari by their families; Mahli, 1121
3:25	the charge of the s of Gershon in 1121
3:29	The families of the s of Kohath shall pitch 1121
3:36	charge of the s of Merari *shall be* 1121
3:38	*shall be* Moses, and Aaron and his s, 1121
3:48	*to be* redeemed, unto Aaron and to his s. 1121
3:51	were redeemed unto Aaron and to his s, 1121
4: 2	Take the sum of the s of Kohath from 1121
4: 2	sons of Kohath from among the s of Levi, 1121
4: 4	*shall be* the service of the s of Kohath 1121
4: 5	his s, and they shall take down the 1121
4:15	his s have made an end of covering 1121
4:15	the s of Kohath shall come to bear *it:* but 1121
4:15	These *things are* the burden of the s of 1121
4:19	holy *things:* Aaron and his s shall go in, 1121
4:22	Take also the sum of the s of Gershon, 1121
4:27	his s shall be all the service of the sons of 1121
4:27	his sons shall be all the service of the s of 1121
4:28	*is* the service of the families of the s of 1121
4:29	*As for* the s of Merari, thou shalt number 1121
4:33	*is* the service of the families of the s of 1121
4:34	the s of the Kohathites after their families, 1121
4:38	those that were numbered of the s of 1121
4:41	of the families of the s of Gershon, 1121
4:42	of the families of the s of Merari, 1121
4:45	of the families of the s of Merari, 1121
6:23	Speak unto Aaron and unto his s, saying, 1121
7: 7	four oxen he gave unto the s of Gershon, 1121
7: 8	eight oxen he gave unto the s of Merari, 1121
7: 9	unto the s of Kohath he gave none: 1121
8:13	his s, and offer them *for* an offering 1121
8:19	to his s from among the children of Israel, 1121
8:22	before Aaron, and before his s: 1121
10: 8	the s of Aaron, the priests, shall blow 1121
10:17	the s of Gershon and the sons of Merari 1121
10:17	Gershon and the s of Merari set forward, 1121
13:33	the s of Anak, *which come* of the giants: 1121
16: 1	and Abiram, the s of Eliab, and On, 1121
16: 1	the son of Peleth, s of Reuben, took *men:* 1121
16: 7	*ye take* too much upon you, ye s of Levi. 1121
16: 8	unto Korah, Hear, I pray you, ye s of Levi: 1121
16:10	all thy brethren the s of Levi with thee: 1121
16:12	to call Dathan and Abiram, the s of Eliab: 1121
16:27	and their s, and their little children. 1121
18: 1	Thou and thy s and thy father's house 1121
18: 1	thy s with thee shall bear the iniquity of 1121
18: 2	thy s with thee *shall minister* before 1121
18: 7	thy s with thee shall keep your priest's 1121
18: 8	and to thy s, by an ordinance for ever. 1121
18: 9	*shall be* most holy for thee and for thy s. 1121
18:11	to thy s and to thy daughters with thee, 1121
18:19	and thy s and thy daughters with thee, 1121
21:29	he hath given his s that escaped, 1121
21:35	smote him, and his s, and all his people, 1121
26: 8	And the s of Pallu; Eliab. 1121
26: 9	the s of Eliab; Nemuel, and Dathan, 1121
26:12	The s of Simeon after their families: 1121
26:19	The s of Judah *were* Er and Onan: and Er 1121
26:20	the s of Judah after their families were, 1121
26:21	the s of Pharez were; of Hezron, the 1121
26:23	*Of* the s of Issachar after their families: 1121
26:26	*Of* the s of Zebulun after their families: 1121
26:28	The s of Joseph after their families *were* 1121
26:29	the s of Manasseh: of Machir, the family 1121
26:30	These *are* the s of Gilead: *of* Jeezer, 1121
26:33	Zelophehad the son of Hepher had no s, 1121
26:35	These *are* the s of Ephraim after their 1121
26:36	These *are* the s of Shuthelah: of Eran, 1121
26:37	These *are* the families of the s of Ephraim 1121
26:37	These *are* the s of Joseph after their 1121
26:38	The s of Benjamin after their families: 1121
26:40	the s of Bela were Ard and Naaman: 1121
26:41	These *are* the s of Benjamin after their 1121
26:42	These *are* the s of Dan after their families: 1121
26:45	*Of* the s of Beriah: of Heber, the family of 1121
26:47	These *are* the families of the s of Asher 1121
26:48	*Of* the s of Naphtali after their families: 1121
27: 3	but died in his own sin, and had no s. 1121

Nu	
36: 1	of the families of the s of Joseph, 1121
36: 3	*if* they be married to any of the s of 1121
36: 5	The tribe of the s of Joseph hath said well. 1121
36:11	married unto their father's brothers' s: 1121
36:12	of the s of Manasseh the son of Joseph, 1121
Dt	
1:28	moreover we have seen the s of 1121
2:33	smote him, and his s, and all his people. 1121
4: 9	but teach them thy s, and thy sons' sons; 1121
4: 9	but teach them thy sons, and thy sons' s; 1121
11: 6	unto Dathan and Abiram, the s of Eliab, 1121
12:12	ye, and your s, and of your daughters, 1121
12:31	for even their s and their daughters they 1121
18: 5	of the Lᴏʀᴅ, him and his s for ever. 1121
21: 5	the priests the s of Levi shall come near; 1121
21:16	he maketh his s to inherit *that* which 1121
23:17	of Israel, nor a sodomite of the s of Israel. 1121
28:32	Thy s and thy daughters *shall be* given 1121
28:41	Thou shalt beget s and daughters, 1121
28:53	the flesh of thy s and of thy daughters, 1121
31: 9	delivered it unto the priests the s of Levi, 1121
32: 8	when he separated the s of Adam, 1121
32:19	because of the provoking of his s, 1121
Jos	
7:24	his s, and his daughters, and his oxen, 1121
15:14	Caleb drove thence the three s of Anak, 1121
17: 3	of Manasseh, had no s, but daughters: 1121
17: 6	had an inheritance among his s: 1121
17: 6	the rest of Manasseh's s had the land of 1121
24:32	s of Hamor the father of Shechem for an 1121
Jdg	
1:20	he expelled thence the three s of Anak. 1121
3: 6	gave their daughters to their s, 1121
8:19	my brethren, *even* the s of my mother: 1121
8:30	and ten s of his body begotten: 1121
9: 2	either that all the s of Jerubbaal, *which* 1121
9: 5	slew his brethren the s of Jerubbaal, 1121
9:18	slain his s, threescore and ten persons, 1121
9:24	and ten s of Jerubbaal might come, 1121
10: 4	had thirty s that rode on thirty ass colts, 1121
11: 2	Gilead's wife bare him s; and *his* wife's 1121
11: 2	*his* wife's s grew up, and they thrust out 1121
12: 9	he had thirty s, and thirty daughters, 1121
12: 9	in thirty daughters from abroad for his s. 1121
12:14	he had forty s and thirty nephews, that 1121
17: 5	teraphim, and consecrated one of his s, 1121
17:11	young man was unto him as one of his s. 1121
18:30	his s were priests to the tribe of Dan until 1121
19:22	the men of the city, certain s of Belial, 1121
Ru	
1: 1	of Moab, he, and his wife, and his two s. 1121
1: 2	name of his two s Mahlon and Chilion, 1121
1: 3	and she was left, and her two s. 1121
1: 5	the woman was left of her two s and 3206
1:11	*are there* yet *any* moe s in my womb, 1121
1:12	also to night, and should also bear s; 1121
4:15	which *is* better to thee than seven s, 1121
1Sa	
1: 3	the two s of Eli, Hophni and Phinehas, 1121
1: 4	to all her s and her daughters, portions: 1121
1: 8	*am* not I better to thee than ten s? 1121
2:12	Now the s of Eli *were* sons of Belial; 1121
2:12	Now the sons of Eli *were* s of Belial; 1121
2:21	and bare three s and two daughters. 1121
2:22	and heard all that his s did unto all Israel; 1121
2:24	Nay, my s; for *it is* no good report that I 1121
2:29	honourest thy s above me, to make 1121
2:34	shall come upon thy two s, on Hophni 1121
3:13	because his s made themselves vile, 1121
4: 4	the two s of Eli, Hophni and Phinehas, 1121
4:11	the two s of Eli, Hophni and Phinehas, 1121
4:17	thy two s also, Hophni and Phinehas, 1121
8: 1	that he made his s judges over Israel. 1121
8: 3	his s walked not in his ways, 1121
8: 5	art old, and thy s walk not in thy ways: 1121
8:11	He will take your s, and appoint *them* for 1121
12: 2	and behold, my s *are* with you: 1121
14:49	Now the s of Saul were Jonathan, 1121
16: 1	I have provided me a king among his s. 1121
16: 5	he sanctified Jesse and his s, 1121
16:10	Jesse made seven of his s to pass before 1121
17:12	name *was* Jesse; and he had eight s: 1121
17:13	the three eldest s of Jesse went *and* 1121
17:13	the names of his three s that went to 1121
22:20	one of the s of Ahimelech the son of 1121
28:19	*shalt* thou and thy s *be* with me: 1121
30: 3	wives, and their s, and their daughters, 1121
30: 6	every man for his s and for his daughters: 1121
30:19	neither s nor daughters, neither spoil, 1121
31: 2	followed hard upon Saul and upon his s; 1121
31: 2	and Abinadab, and Malchishua, Saul's s. 1121
31: 6	his three s, and his armourbearer, 1121
31: 7	Saul and his s were dead, they forsook 1121
31: 8	and his three s fallen in mount Gilboa. 1121
31:12	the bodies of his s from the wall of 1121
2Sa	
2:18	there were three s of Zeruiah there, Joab, 1121
3: 2	unto David were s born in Hebron: 1121
3:39	these men the s of Zeruiah *be* too hard for 1121
4: 2	the s of Rimmon a Beerothite, 1121
4: 5	the s of Rimmon the Beerothite, Rechab 1121
4: 9	the s of Rimmon the Beerothite, 1121
5:13	there were yet s and daughters born to 1121
6: 3	Uzzah and Ahio, the s of Abinadab, 1121
8:18	and David's s were chief rulers. 1121
9:10	therefore, and thy s, and thy servants, 1121
9:10	Now Ziba had fifteen s and 1121
9:11	eat at my table, as one of the king's s. 1121
13:23	and Absalom invited all the king's s. 1121
13:27	Amnon and all the king's s go with him. 1121
13:29	all the king's s arose, and every man gat 1121

2Sa	
13:30	Absalom hath slain all the king's s, 1121
13:32	have slain all the young men the king's s; 1121
13:33	to think *that* all the king's s are dead: 1121
13:35	unto the king, Behold, the king's s come: 1121
13:36	the king's s came, and lift up their voice 1121
14: 6	thy handmaid had two s, and they two 1121
14:27	unto Absalom there were born three s, 1121
15:27	your two s with you, Ahimaaz thy son, 1121
15:36	*they have* there with them their two s, 1121
16:10	have I to do with you, ye s of Zeruiah? 1121
19: 5	the lives of thy s and of thy daughters, 1121
19:17	his fifteen s and his twenty servants with 1121
19:22	have I to do with you, ye s of Zeruiah, 1121
21: 6	seven men of his s be delivered unto us, 1121
21: 8	the king took the two s of Rizpah 1121
21: 8	the five s of Michal the daughter of Saul, 1121
21:16	which *was* of the s of the giant, 3211
21:18	Saph, which *was* of the s of the giant. 3211
23: 6	the s *of* Belial *shall be* all of them as NIH
23:32	*of* the s of Jashen, Jonathan, 1121
1Ki	
1: 9	called all his brethren the king's s, and all 1121
1:19	hath called all the s of the king, 1121
1:25	called all the king's s, and the captains 1121
2: 7	shew kindness unto the s of Barzillai 1121
4: 3	Elihoreph and Ahiah, the s of Shisha, 1121
4:31	and Chalcol, and Darda, the s of Mahol: 1121
11:20	household among the s of Pharaoh. 1121
12:31	people, which were not of the s of Levi. 1121
13:12	For his s had seen what way the man of 1121
13:13	he said unto his s, Saddle me the ass. 1121
13:27	spake to his s, saying, Saddle me the ass. 1121
13:31	that he spake to his s, saying, When I am 1121
18:31	the number of the tribes of the s of Jacob, 1121
20:35	a certain man of the s of the prophets said 1121
21:10	set two men, s of Belial, before him, 1121
2Ki	
2: 3	the s of the prophets that *were* at Beth-el 1121
2: 5	the s of the prophets that *were* at Jericho 1121
2: 7	fifty men of the s of the prophets went, 1121
2:15	when the s of the prophets which *were* 1121
4: 1	wives of the s of the prophets unto Elisha, 1121
4: 1	take unto him my two s to be bondmen. 3206
4: 4	shut the door upon thee and upon thy s, 1121
4: 5	shut the door upon her and upon her s, 1121
4:38	the s of the prophets *were* sitting before 1121
4:38	seethe pottage for the s of the prophets. 1121
5:22	two young men of the s of the prophets: 1121
6: 1	the s of the prophets said unto Elisha, 1121
9:26	and the blood of his s, saith the Lᴏʀᴅ; 1121
10: 1	Ahab had seventy s in Samaria. And Jehu 1121
10: 2	seeing your master's s *are* with you, 1121
10: 3	the best and meetest of your master's s, 1121
10: 6	ye the heads of the men your master's s, 1121
10: 6	Now the king's s, *being* seventy persons, 1121
10: 7	that they took the king's s, 1121
10: 8	have brought the heads of the king's s. 1121
11: 2	stale him from among the king's s which 1121
15:12	Thy s shall sit on the throne of Israel unto 1121
17:17	they caused their s and their daughters to 1121
19:37	Sharezer *his s* smote him with the sword: NIH
20:18	of thy s that shall issue from thee, 1121
25: 7	slew the s of Zedekiah before his eyes, 1121
1Ch	
1: 5	The s of Japheth; Gomer, and Magog, 1121
1: 6	the s of Gomer; Ashchenaz, and Riphath, 1121
1: 7	the s of Javan; Elishah, and Tarshish, 1121
1: 8	The s of Ham; Cush, and Mizraim, Put, 1121
1: 9	the s of Cush; Seba, and Havilah, 1121
1: 9	And the s of Raamah; Sheba, and Dedan. 1121
1:17	The s of Shem; Elam, and Asshur, 1121
1:19	unto Eber were born two s: the name of 1121
1:23	and Jobab. All these *were* the s of Joktan. 1121
1:28	The s of Abraham; Isaac, and Ishmael. 1121
1:31	and Kedemah. These *are* the s of Ishmael. 1121
1:32	Now the s of Keturah, 1121
1:32	the s of Jokshan; Sheba, and Dedan. 1121
1:33	the s of Midian; Ephah, and Epher, 1121
1:33	and Eldaah. All these *are* the s of Keturah. 1121
1:34	Isaac. The s of Isaac; Esau and Israel. 1121
1:35	The s of Esau; Eliphaz, Reuel, and Jeush, 1121
1:36	The s of Eliphaz; Teman, and Omar, 1121
1:37	The s of Reuel; Nahath, Zerah, Shammah, 1121
1:38	the s of Seir; Lotan, and Shobal, 1121
1:39	the s of Lotan; Hori, and Homam: 1121
1:40	The s of Shobal; Alian, and Manahath, 1121
1:40	And the s of Zibeon; Aiah, and Anah. 1121
1:41	The s of Anah; Dishon. And the sons of 1121
1:41	the s of Dishon; Amram, and Eshban, 1121
1:42	the s of Ezer; Bilhan, and Zavan, 1121
1:42	Jakan. The s of Dishan; Uz, and Aran. 1121
2: 1	These *are* the s of Israel; Reuben, Simeon, 1121
2: 3	The s of Judah; Er, and Onan, and Shelah: 1121
2: 4	and Zerah. All the s of Judah *were* five. 1121
2: 5	The s of Pharez; Hezron, and Hamul. 1121
2: 6	the s of Zerah; Zimri, and Ethan, 1121
2: 7	the s of Carmi; Achar, the troubler of 1121
2: 8	And the s of Ethan; Azariah. 1121
2: 9	The s also of Hezron, that were born 1121
2:16	the s of Zeruiah; Abishai, and Joab, 1121
2:18	her s *are* these; Jesher, and Shobab, 1121
2:23	All these *belonged to* the s of Machir 1121
2:25	the s of Jerahmeel the firstborn of Hezron 1121
2:27	the s of Ram the firstborn of Jerahmeel 1121
2:28	the s of Onam were, Shammai, and Jada. 1121
2:28	the s of Shammai; Nadab, and Abishur. 1121
2:30	the s of Nadab; Seled, and Appaim: 1121
2:31	the s of Appaim; Ishi. And the sons of Ishi 1121

S

1Ch 2:31 the **s** of Ishi; Sheshan. And the children 1121
2:32 the **s** of Jada the brother of Shammai; 1121
2:33 the **s** of Jonathan; Peleth, and Zaza. 1121
2:33 and Zaza. These were the **s** of Jerahmeel. 1121
2:34 Now Sheshan had no **s**, but daughters. 1121
2:42 Now the **s** of Caleb the brother of 1121
2:42 the **s** of Mareshah the father of Hebron. 1121
2:43 the **s** of Hebron; Korah, and Tappuah, 1121
2:47 the **s** of Jahdai; Regem, and Jotham, 1121
2:50 These were the **s** of Caleb the son of Hur, 1121
2:52 Shobal the father of Kirjath-jearim had **s**; 1121
2:54 The **s** of Salma; Beth-lehem, 1121
3: 1 these were the **s** of David, which were 1121
3: 9 *These were* all the **s** of David, beside 1121
3: 9 beside the **s** of the concubines. 1121
3:15 the **s** of Josiah were, the firstborn Johanan 1121
3:16 the **s** of Jehoiakim: Jeconiah his son, 1121
3:17 the **s** of Jeconiah; Assir, Salathiel his son, 1121
3:19 And the **s** of Pedaiah were, Zerubbabel, 1121
3:21 the **s** of Hananiah; Pelatiah, and Jesaiah: 1121
3:21 the **s** of Rephaiah, the sons of Arnan, 1121
3:21 the **s** of Arnan, the sons of Obadiah, 1121
3:21 the sons of Arnan, the **s** of Obadiah, 1121
3:21 the sons of Obadiah, the **s** of Shechaniah. 1121
3:22 the **s** of Shechaniah; Shemaiah: 1121
3:22 the **s** of Shemaiah; Hattush, and Igeal, 1121
3:23 the **s** of Neariah; Elioenai, and Hezekiah, 1121
3:24 the **s** of Elioenai were, Hodaiah, 1121
4: 1 The **s** of Judah; Pharez, Hezron, and 1121
4: 4 *These are* the **s** of Hur, the firstborn of 1121
4: 6 These were the **s** of Naarah. 1121
4: 7 the **s** of Helah were, Zereth, and Jezoar, 1121
4:13 the **s** of Kenaz; Othniel, and Seraiah: 1121
4:13 Seraiah: and the **s** of Othniel; Hathath. 1121
4:15 the **s** of Caleb the son of Jephunneh; Iru, 1121
4:15 Naam: and the **s** of Elah, even Kenaz. 1121
4:16 the **s** of Jehaleleel; Ziph, and Ziphah, 1121
4:17 the **s** of Ezra were, Jether, and Mered, 1121
4:18 these *are* the **s** of *his* wife Hodiah the daughter of 1121
4:19 the **s** of *his* wife Hodiah the sister of 1121
4:20 the **s** of Shimon were, Amnon, and 1121
4:20 the **s** of Ishi were, Zoheth, and 1121
4:21 The **s** of Shelah the son of Judah were, 1121
4:24 The **s** of Simeon were, Nemuel, and 1121
4:26 the **s** of Mishma; Hamuel his son, 1121
4:27 Shimei had sixteen **s** and six daughters; 1121
4:42 of the **s** of Simeon, five hundred men, 1121
4:42 and Rephaiah, and Uzziel, the **s** of Ishi. 1121
5: 1 the **s** of Reuben the firstborn of Israel, 1121
5: 1 his birthright was given unto the **s** of 1121
5: 3 The **s**, *I say*, of Reuben the firstborn of 1121
5: 4 The **s** of Joel; Shemaiah his son, Gog his 1121
5:18 of Reuben, and the Gadites, 1121
6: 1 The **s** of Levi; Gershon, Kohath, 1121
6: 2 the **s** of Kohath; Amram, Izhar, 1121
6: 3 The **s** also of Aaron; Nadab, and Abihu, 1121
6:16 the **s** of Levi; Gershom, Kohath, 1121
6:17 these *be* the names of the **s** of Gershom; 1121
6:18 the **s** of Kohath were, Amram, and Izhar, 1121
6:19 The **s** of Merari; Mahli, and Mushi. 1121
6:22 The **s** of Kohath; Amminadab his son, 1121
6:25 the **s** of Elkanah; Amasai, and Ahimoth. 1121
6:26 the **s** of Elkanah; Zophai his son, 1121
6:28 the **s** of Samuel; the firstborn Vashni, 1121
6:29 The **s** of Merari; Mahli, Libni his son, 1121
6:33 the of the Kohathites: Heman a singer, 1121
6:44 their brethren the **s** of Merari *stood* on 1121
6:49 his **s** offered upon the altar of the burnt 1121
6:50 these *are* the **s** of Aaron; Eleazar his son, 1121
6:54 of the **s** of Aaron, of the families of 1121
6:57 to the **s** of Aaron they gave the cities of 1121
6:61 unto the **s** of Kohath, which were left of 1121
6:62 to the **s** of Gershom throughout their 1121
6:63 Unto the **s** of Merari were given by lot, 1121
6:66 *the residue* of the families of the **s** of 1121
6:70 for the family of the remnant of the **s** of 1121
6:71 Unto the **s** of Gershom were given out of 1121
7: 1 Now the **s** of Issachar were, Tola, 1121
7: 2 the **s** of Tola; Uzzi, and Rephaiah, 1121
7: 3 the **s** of Uzzi; Izrahiah: and the sons of 1121
7: 3 the **s** of Izrahiah; Michael, and Obadiah, 1121
7: 4 *men:* for they had many wives and **s**. 1121
7: 6 The **s** *of* Benjamin; Bela, and Becher, NIH
7: 7 the **s** of Bela; Ezbon, and Uzzi, and 1121
7: 8 the **s** of Becher; Zemira, and Joash, 1121
7: 8 Alameth. All these *are* the **s** of Becher. 1121
7:10 The **s** also of Jediael; Bilhan: and the sons 1121
7:10 the **s** of Bilhan; Jeush, and Benjamin, 1121
7:11 All these the **s** of Jediael, by the heads of 1121
7:12 children of Ir, *and* Hushim, the **s** of Aher. 1121
7:13 The **s** of Naphtali; Jahziel, and Guni, 1121
7:13 and Jezer, and Shallum, the **s** of Bilhah. 1121
7:14 The **s** of Manasseh; Ashriel, whom she 1121
7:16 and his **s** were Ulam and Rakem. 1121
7:17 The **s** of Ulam; Bedan. These *were* the 1121
7:17 These *were* the **s** of Gilead, the son of 1121
7:19 the **s** of Shemida were, Ahian, 1121
7:20 the **s** of Ephraim; Shuthelah, and Bered 1121
7:30 The **s** of Asher; Imnah, and Isuah, 1121
7:31 the **s** of Beriah; Heber, and Malchiel, 1121
7:33 the **s** of Japhlet; Pasach, and Bimhal, 1121
7:34 the **s** of Shamer; Ahi, and Rohgah, 1121
7:36 The **s** of Zophah; Suah, and Harnepher, 1121
7:38 the **s** of Jether; Jephunneh, and Pispah, 1121
7:39 the **s** of Ulla; Arah, and Haniel, and 1121

1Ch 8: 3 the **s** of Bela were, Addar, and Gera, 1121
8: 6 *are* the **s** of Ehud: these *are* the heads 1121
8:10 These were his **s**, heads of the fathers. 1121
8:12 The **s** of Elpaal; Eber, and Misham, 1121
8:16 and Ispah, and Joha, the **s** of Beriah; 1121
8:18 and Jezliah, and Jobab, the **s** of Elpaal; 1121
8:21 Beraiah, and Shimrath, the **s** of Shimhi; 1121
8:25 and Penuel, the **s** of Shashak; 1121
8:27 and Eliah, and Zichri, the **s** of Jeroham. 1121
8:35 the **s** of Micah were, Pithon, and Melech, 1121
8:38 Azel had six **s**, whose names *are* these, 1121
8:38 and Hanan. All these *were* the **s** of Azel. 1121
8:39 the **s** of Eshek his brother were, Ulam his 1121
8:40 the **s** of Ulam were mighty men of valour, 1121
8:40 archers, and had many **s**, and sons' sons, 1121
8:40 and sons' **s**, an hundred and fifty. 1121
8:40 fifty. All these *are* of the **s** of Benjamin. 1121
9: 5 Asaiah the firstborn, and his **s**. 1121
9: 6 the **s** of Zerah; Jeuel, and their brethren, 1121
9: 7 of the **s** of Benjamin; Sallu the son of 1121
9:14 the son of Hashabiah, of the **s** of Merari; 1121
9:30 *some* of the **s** of the priests made 1121
9:32 of the **s** of the Kohathites, were over 1121
9:41 the **s** of Micah were, Pithon, and Melech, 1121
9:44 Azel had six **s**, whose names *are* these, 1121
9:44 and Hanan: these *were* the **s** of Azel. 1121
10: 2 followed hard after Saul, and after his **s**; 1121
10: 2 and Malchishua, the **s** of Saul. 1121
10: 6 three **s**, and all his house died together. 1121
10: 7 that Saul and his **s** were dead, then 1121
10: 8 and his **s** fallen in mount Gilboa. 1121
10:12 the bodies of his **s**, and brought them to 1121
11:34 The **s** of Hashem the Gizonite, Jonathan 1121
11:44 and Jehiel the **s** of Hothan the Aroerite, 1121
11:46 the **s** of Elnaam, and Ithmah the Moabite, 1121
12: 3 Joash, the **s** of Shemaah the Gibeathite; 1121
12: 3 Jeziel, and Pelet, the **s** of Azmaveth; 1121
12: 7 and Zebadiah, the **s** of Jeroham of Gedor. 1121
12:14 These *were* of the **s** of Gad, captains of 1121
14: 3 and David begat moe **s** and daughters. 1121
15: 5 Of the **s** of Kohath; Uriel the chief, 1121
15: 6 Of the **s** of Merari; Asaiah the chief, 1121
15: 7 Of the **s** of Gershom; Joel the chief, 1121
15: 8 Of the **s** of Elizaphan; Shemaiah the chief, 1121
15: 9 Of the **s** of Hebron; Eliel the chief, 1121
15:10 Of the **s** of Uzziel; Amminadab the chief, 1121
15:17 of the **s** of Merari their brethren, Ethan 1121
16:42 And the **s** of Jeduthun were porters. 1121
17:11 seed after thee, which shall be of thy **s**; 1121
18:17 the **s** of David were chief about the king. 1121
21:20 and his four **s** with him hid themselves. 1121
23: 6 them *into* courses among the **s** of Levi, 1121
23: 8 The **s** of Laadan; the chief *was* Jehiel, 1121
23: 9 The **s** of Shimei; Shelomith, and Haziel, 1121
23:10 And the **s** of Shimei were, Jahath, Zina, 1121
23:10 Beriah. These four *were* the **s** of Shimei. 1121
23:11 Jeush and Beriah had not many **s**; 1121
23:12 The **s** of Kohath; Amram, Izhar, Hebron, 1121
23:13 The **s** of Amram; Aaron and Moses: 1121
23:13 most holy *things*, he and his **s** for ever, 1121
23:14 his **s** were named of the tribe of Levi. 1121
23:15 The **s** of Moses were, Gershom, 1121
23:16 *Of* the **s** of Gershom, Shebuel *was* 1121
23:17 *Of* the **s** of Eliezer were, Rehabiah the chief. 1121
23:17 Eliezer had none other **s**; but the sons of 1121
23:17 but the sons of Rehabiah were very many. 1121
23:18 *Of* the **s** of Izhar; Shelomith the chief. 1121
23:19 *Of* the **s** of Hebron; Jeriah the first, 1121
23:20 *Of* the **s** of Uzziel; Michah the first, 1121
23:21 The **s** of Merari; Mahli, and Mushi. 1121
23:21 Mushi. The **s** of Mahli; Eleazar, and Kish. 1121
23:22 Eleazar died, and had no **s**, but daughters: 1121
23:22 their brethren the **s** of Kish took them. 1121
23:23 The **s** of Mushi; Mahli, and Eder, 1121
23:24 These *were* the **s** of Levi after the house 1121
23:28 Because their office *was* to wait on the **s** 1121
23:32 charge of the **s** of Aaron their brethren, 1121
24: 1 Now *these are* the divisions of the **s** of 1121
24: 1 The **s** of Aaron; Nadab, and Abihu, 1121
24: 3 both Zadok of the **s** of Eleazar, 1121
24: 3 and Ahimelech of the **s** of Ithamar, 1121
24: 4 there were moe chief men found of the **s** 1121
24: 4 sons of Eleazar than of the **s** of Ithamar; 1121
24: 4 Among the **s** of Eleazar *there were* 1121
24: 4 eight among the **s** of Ithamar according to 1121
24: 5 of the **s** of Eleazar, and of the sons of 1121
24: 5 sons of Eleazar, and of the **s** of Ithamar. 1121
24:20 the rest of the **s** of Levi were these: Of 1121
24:20 of Levi were these: Of the **s** of Amram; 1121
24:20 Shubael: of the **s** of Shubael; Jehdeiah. 1121
24:21 of the **s** of Rehabiah, the first *was* Isshiah. 1121
24:22 Shelomoth: of the **s** of Shelomoth; Jahath. 1121
24:23 the **s** *of Hebron;* Jeriah *the first,* Amariah 1121
24:24 *Of* the **s** of Uzziel; Michah: of the sons of 1121
24:24 Michah: of the **s** of Michah; Shamir. 1121
24:25 *was* Isshiah: of the **s** of Isshiah; Zechariah. 1121
24:26 The **s** of Merari were Mahli and Mushi: 1121
24:26 and Mushi: the **s** of Jaaziah; Beno. 1121
24:27 The **s** of Merari by Jaaziah; Beno, 1121
24:28 Of Mahli *came* Eleazar, who had no **s**. 1121
24:30 The **s** also of Mushi; Mahli, and Eder, 1121
24:30 These *were* the **s** of the Levites after 1121
24:31 **s** of Aaron in the presence of David 1121
25: 1 separated to the service of the **s** of Asaph, 1121
25: 2 Of the **s** of Asaph; Zaccur, and Joseph, 1121

1Ch 25: 2 the **s** of Asaph under the hands of Asaph, 1121
25: 3 the **s** of Jeduthun; Gedaliah, and Zeri, 1121
25: 4 the **s** of Heman; Bukkiah, Mattaniah, 1121
25: 5 All these *were* the **s** of Heman the king's 1121
25: 5 God gave to Heman fourteen **s** and 1121
25: 9 with his brethren and **s** *were* twelve: 1121
25:10 he, his **s**, and his brethren, *were* twelve: 1121
25:11 he, his **s**, and his brethren, *were* twelve: 1121
25:12 he, his **s**, and his brethren, *were* twelve: 1121
25:13 he, his **s**, and his brethren, *were* twelve: 1121
25:14 he, his **s**, and his brethren, *were* twelve: 1121
25:15 he, his **s**, and his brethren, *were* twelve: 1121
25:16 he, his **s**, and his brethren, *were* twelve: 1121
25:17 he, his **s**, and his brethren, *were* twelve: 1121
25:18 he, his **s**, and his brethren, *were* twelve: 1121
25:19 he, his **s**, and his brethren, *were* twelve: 1121
25:20 he, his **s**, and his brethren, *were* twelve: 1121
25:21 he, his **s**, and his brethren, *were* twelve: 1121
25:22 he, his **s**, and his brethren, *were* twelve: 1121
25:23 he, his **s**, and his brethren, *were* twelve: 1121
25:24 he, his **s**, and his brethren, *were* twelve: 1121
25:25 he, his **s**, and his brethren, *were* twelve: 1121
25:26 he, his **s**, and his brethren, *were* twelve: 1121
25:27 he, his **s**, and his brethren, *were* twelve: 1121
25:28 he, his **s**, and his brethren, *were* twelve: 1121
25:29 he, his **s**, and his brethren, *were* twelve: 1121
25:30 he, his **s**, and his brethren, *were* twelve: 1121
25:31 he, his **s**, and his brethren, *were* twelve: 1121
26: 1 the son of Kore, of the **s** of Asaph. 1121
26: 2 the **s** of Meshelemiah were, Zechariah 1121
26: 4 Moreover the **s** of Obed-edom were, 1121
26: 6 Also unto Shemaiah his son were **s** born, 1121
26: 7 The **s** of Shemaiah; Othni, and Rephael, 1121
26: 8 All these of the **s** of Obed-edom: they and 1121
26: 8 they and their **s** and their brethren, 1121
26: 9 Meshelemiah had **s** and brethren, 1121
26:10 of the children of Merari, had **s**; 1121
26:11 all the **s** and brethren of Hosah were 1121
26:15 to his **s** the house of Asuppim. 1121
26:19 of the porters among the **s** of Kore, 1121
26:19 sons of Kore, and among the **s** of Merari. 1121
26:21 *As concerning* the **s** of Laadan; the sons 1121
26:21 the **s** of the Gershonite Laadan, 1121
26:22 The **s** of Jehieli; Zetham, and Joel his 1121
26:29 his **s** were for the outward business over 1121
27:32 son of Hachmoni *was* with the king's **s**: 1121
28: 1 of his **s**, with the officers, and 1121
28: 4 among the **s** of my father he liked me to 1121
28: 5 of all my **s**, (for the LORD hath given me 1121
28: 5 (for the LORD hath given me many **s**,) 1121
29:24 and all the **s** likewise of king David, 1121

2Ch 5:12 Jeduthun, with their **s** and their brethren, 1121
11:14 his **s** had cast them off from executing 1121
11:21 begat twenty and eight **s**, 1121
13: 5 to him and to his **s** *by* a covenant of salt? 1121
13: 8 the LORD in the hand of the **s** of David; 1121
13: 9 of Aaron, and the Levites, 1121
13:10 *are* the **s** of Aaron, and the Levites *wait* 1121
13:21 begat twenty and two **s**, 1121
20:14 of Mattaniah, a Levite of the **s** of Asaph, 1121
21: 2 he had brethren the **s** of Jehoshaphat, 1121
21: 2 all these *were* the **s** of Jehoshaphat king 1121
21: 7 to give a light to him and to his **s** for ever. 1121
21:17 house, and his **s** also, and his wives; 1121
21:17 save Jehoahaz, the youngest of his **s**. 1121
22: 8 the **s** of the brethren of Ahaziah, 1121
22:11 stole him from among the king's **s** that 1121
23: 3 as the LORD hath said of the **s** of David. 1121
23:11 Jehoiada and his **s** anointed him, and said, 1121
24: 3 two wives; and he begat **s** and daughters. 1121
24: 7 For the **s** of Athaliah, *that* wicked woman, 1121
24:25 the blood of the **s** of Jehoiada the priest, 1121
24:27 Now *concerning* his **s**, and the greatness 1121
26:18 but to the priests the **s** of Aaron, 1121
28: 8 and daughters, and took also away 1121
29: 9 our **s** and our daughters and our wives 1121
29:11 My **s**, be not now negligent: for the LORD 1121
29:12 son of Azariah, of the **s** of the Kohathites: 1121
29:12 of the **s** of Merari, Kish the son of Abdi, 1121
29:13 of the **s** of Elizaphan; Shimri, and Jeiel: 1121
29:13 of the **s** of Asaph; Zechariah, 1121
29:14 of the **s** of Heman; Jehiel, and Shimei: 1121
29:14 of the **s** of Jeduthun; Shemaiah, and Uzziel. 1121
29:21 he commanded the priests the **s** of Aaron 1121
31:18 wives, and their **s**, and their daughters, 1121
31:19 Also of the **s** of Aaron the priests, 1121
32:33 of the sepulchres of the **s** of David: 1121
34:12 Obadiah, the Levites, of the **s** of Merari; 1121
34:12 Meshullam, of the **s** of the Kohathites, 1121
35:14 the priests the **s** of Aaron were busied in 1121
35:14 and for the priests the **s** of Aaron. 1121
35:15 the singers the **s** of Asaph were in their 1121
36:20 his **s** until the reign of the kingdom of 1121

Ezr 3: 9 stood Jeshua *with* his **s** and his brethren, 1121
3: 9 and his brethren, Kadmiel and his **s**, 1121
3: 9 Kadmiel and his sons, the **s** of Judah, 1121
3: 9 the **s** of Henadad, *with* their sons and 1121
3: 9 their **s** and their brethren the Levites. 1121
3:10 the Levites the **s** of Asaph with cymbals, 1121
6:10 pray for the life of the king, and of his **s**. 1123
7:23 against the realm of the king and his **s**? 1123
8: 2 Of the **s** of Phinehas; Gershom: of the sons 1121
8: 2 Of the **s** of Ithamar; Daniel: of the sons of 1121
8: 2 Daniel: of the **s** of David; Hattush. 1121
8: 3 Of the **s** of Shechaniah, of the sons of 1121

S

Ezr	8: 3 sons of Shechaniah, of the **s** of Pharosh;	1121
	8: 4 the **s** of Pahath-moab; Elihoenai the son of	1121
	8: 5 the **s** of Shechaniah; the son of Jahaziel,	1121
	8: 6 Of the **s** also of Adin; Ebed the son of	1121
	8: 7 of the **s** of Elam; Jeshaiah the son of	1121
	8: 8 the **s** of Shephatiah; Zebadiah the son of	1121
	8: 9 the **s** of Joab; Obadiah the son of Jehiel,	1121
	8:10 the **s** of Shelomith; the son of Josiphiah,	1121
	8:11 of the **s** of Bebai; Zechariah the son of	1121
	8:12 of the **s** of Azgad; Johanan the son of	1121
	8:13 the last **s** of Adonikam, whose names *are*	1121
	8:14 *is* also of Bigvai; Uthai, and Zabbud,	1121
	8:15 and found there none of the **s** of Levi.	1121
	8:18 of the **s** of Mahli, the son of Levi, the son	1121
	8:18 with his **s** and his brethren, eighteen;	1121
	8:19 with him Jeshaiah of the **s** of Merari,	1121
	8:19 Merari, his brethren and their **s**, twenty;	1121
	9: 2 daughters for themselves, and for their **s**:	1121
	9:12 give not your daughters unto their **s**,	1121
	9:12 neither take their daughters unto your **s**,	1121
	10: 2 *one* of the **s** of Elam, answered and	1121
	10:18 among the **s** of the priests there were	1121
	10:18 *namely*, of the **s** of Jeshua the son of	1121
	10:20 of the **s** of Immer; Hanani, and Zebadiah.	1121
	10:21 of the **s** of Harim; Maaseiah, and Elijah,	1121
	10:22 of the **s** of Pashur; Elioenai, Maaseiah,	1121
	10:25 of the **s** of Parosh; Ramiah, and Jeziah,	1121
	10:26 of the **s** of Elam; Mattaniah, Zechariah,	1121
	10:27 of the **s** of Zattu; Elioenai, Eliashib,	1121
	10:28 Of the **s** also of Bebai; Jehohanan,	1121
	10:29 of the **s** of Bani; Meshullam, Malluch,	1121
	10:30 the **s** of Pahath-moab; Adna, and Chelal,	1121
	10:31 *of* the **s** of Harim; Eliezer, Ishijah,	1121
	10:33 Of the **s** of Hashum; Mattenai, Mattathah,	1121
	10:34 the **s** of Bani; Maadai, Amram, and Uel,	1121
	10:43 Of the **s** of Nebo; Jeiel, Mattithiah, Zabad,	1121
Ne	3: 3 the fish gate did the **s** of Hassenaah build,	1121
	4:14 your **s**, and your daughters, your wives,	1121
	5: 2 We, our **s**, and our daughters, *are* many:	1121
	5: 5 we bring into bondage our **s** and our	1121
	10: 9 Binnui of the **s** of Henadad, Kadmiel;	1121
	10:28 their wives, their **s**, and their daughters,	1121
	10:30 land, nor take their daughters for our **s**:	1121
	10:36 Also the firstborn of our **s**, and of our	1121
	11: 6 All the **s** of Perez that dwelt at Jerusalem	1121
	11: 7 these *are* the **s** of Benjamin; Sallu the son	1121
	11:22 Of the **s** of Asaph, the singers *were* over	1121
	12:23 The **s** of Levi, the chief of the fathers,	1121
	12:28 the **s** of the singers gathered themselves	1121
	12:35 *certain* of the priests' **s** with trumpets;	1121
	13:25 shall not give your daughters unto their **s**,	1121
	13:25 nor take their daughters unto your **s**,	1121
	13:28 *one* of the **s** of Joiada, the son of Eliashib	1121
Est	9:10 The ten **s** of Haman the son of	1121
	9:12 the palace, and the ten **s** of Haman;	1121
	9:13 let Haman's ten **s** be hanged upon	1121
	9:14 and they hanged Haman's ten **s**.	1121
	9:25 his **s** should be hanged on the gallows.	1121
Job	1: 2 there were born unto him seven **s** and	1121
	1: 4 his **s** went and feasted *in their* houses,	1121
	1: 5 It may be that my **s** have sinned,	1121
	1: 6 Now there was a day when the **s** of God	1121
	1:13 there was a day when his **s** and	1121
	1:18 Thy **s** and thy daughters *were* eating and	1121
	2: 1 Again there was a day when the **s** of God	1121
	14:21 His **s** come to honour, and he knoweth *it*	1121
	38: 7 and all the **s** of God shouted for joy?	1121
	38:32 or canst thou guide Arcturus with his **s**?	1121
	42:13 He had also seven and three daughters.	1121
	42:16 and saw his **s**, and his sons' sons,	1121
	42:16 and saw his sons, and his sons' **s**,	1121
Ps	4: 2 O ye **s** of men, how long *will ye turn* my	1121
	31:19 that trust in thee before the **s** of men!	1121
	33:13 heaven; he beholdeth all the **s** of men.	1121
	42: T Musician, Maschil, for the **s** of Korah.	1121
	44: T To the chief Musician for the **s** of Korah,	1121
	45: T for the **s** of Korah, Maschil, A Song of	1121
	46: T To the chief Musician for the **s** of Korah.	1121
	47: T Musician, A Psalm for the **s** of Korah.	1121
	48: T A Song *and* Psalm for the **s** of Korah.	1121
	49: T Musician, A Psalm for the **s** of Korah.	1121
	57: 4 *even* the **s** of men, whose teeth *are* spears	1121
	58: 1 do ye judge uprightly, O ye **s** of men?	1121
	77:15 thy people, the **s** of Jacob and Joseph.	1121
	84: T upon Gittith, A Psalm for the **s** of Korah.	1121
	85: T Musician, A Psalm for the **s** of Korah.	1121
	87: T A Psalm *or* Song for the **s** of Korah.	1121
	88: T A Song *or* Psalm for the **s** of Korah.	1121
	89: 6 *who* among the **s** of the mighty can be	1121
	106:37 they sacrificed their **s** and their daughters	1121
	106:38 *even* the blood of their **s** and of their	1121
	144:12 That our **s** *may be* as plants grown up in	1121
	145:12 make known to the **s** of men his mighty	1121
Pr	8: 4 I call; and my voice *is* to the **s** of man.	1121
	8:31 and my delights *were* with the **s** of men.	1121
Ecc	1:13 sore travail hath God given to the **s** of	1121
	2: 3 I might see what *was* that good for the **s** of	1121
	2: 8 and the delights of the **s** of men,	1121
	3:10 God hath given to the **s** of men to be	1121
	3:18 concerning the estate of the **s** of men,	1121
	3:19 For that which befalleth the **s** of men	1121
	8:11 heart of the **s** of men is fully set in them	1121
	9: 3 the heart of the **s** of men is full *of* evil,	1121
	9:12 so *are* the **s** of men snared in an evil time,	1121
SS	2: 3 the wood, so *is* my beloved among the **s**.	1121

Isa	37:38 Sharezer his **s** smote him with the sword;	1121
	39: 7 of thy **s** that shall issue from thee,	1121
	43: 6 bring my **s** from far, and my daughters	1121
	45:11 me of *things* to come concerning my **s**,	1121
	49:22 they shall bring thy **s** in *their* arms,	1121
	51:18 *is* none to guide her among all the **s**	1121
	51:18 hand of all the **s** *that* she hath brought up.	1121
	51:20 Thy **s** have fainted, they lie at the head of	1121
	52:14 and his form more than the **s** of men:	1121
	56: 5 a name better than *of* **s** and *of* daughters:	1121
	56: 6 Also the **s** of the stranger, that join	1121
	57: 3 draw near hither, ye **s** of the sorceress,	1121
	60: 4 thy **s** shall come from far,	1121
	60: 9 to bring thy **s** from far, their silver and	1121
	60:10 the **s** of strangers shall build up thy walls,	1121
	60:14 The **s** also of them that afflicted thee shall	1121
	61: 5 the **s** of the alien *shall be* your plowmen	1121
	62: 5 a virgin, *so* shall thy **s** marry thee:	1121
	62: 8 the **s** of the stranger shall not drink thy	1121
Jer	3:24 their herds, their **s** and their daughters.	1121
	5:17 thy **s** and thy daughters shall eat:	1121
	6:21 and the **s** together shall fall upon them;	1121
	7:31 to burn their **s** and their daughters in	1121
	11:22 their **s** and their daughters shall die by	1121
	13:14 even the fathers and the **s** together, saith	1121
	14:16 them, their wives, nor their **s**, nor their	1121
	16: 2 neither shalt thou have **s** nor daughters in	1121
	16: 3 For thus saith the Lᴏʀᴅ concerning the **s**	1121
	19: 5 burn their **s** with fire *for* burnt offerings	1121
	19: 9 will cause them to eat the flesh of their **s**	1121
	29: 6 Take ye wives, and beget **s** and daughters;	1121
	29: 6 take wives for your **s**, and give your	1121
	29: 6 that they may bear **s** and daughters;	1121
	32:19 open upon all the ways of the **s** of men:	1121
	32:35 cause their **s** and their daughters to pass	1121
	35: 3 all his **s**, and the whole house of	1121
	35: 4 the chamber of the **s** of Hanan, the son	1121
	35: 5 I set before the **s** of the house of	1121
	35: 6 no wine, *neither* ye, nor your **s** for ever:	1121
	35: 8 we, our wives, our **s**, nor our daughters;	1121
	35:14 he commanded his **s** not to drink wine,	1121
	35:16 the **s** of Jonadab the son of Rechab	1121
	39: 6 king of Babylon slew the **s** of Zedekiah	1121
	40: 8 Johanan and Jonathan the **s** of Kareah,	1121
	40: 8 the **s** of Ephai the Netophathite,	1121
	48:46 for thy **s** are taken captives,	1121
	49: 1 thus saith the Lᴏʀᴅ; Hath Israel no **s**?	1121
	52:10 king of Babylon slew the **s** of Zedekiah	1121
La	4: 2 The precious **s** of Zion, comparable to	1121
Eze	5:10 Therefore the fathers shall eat the **s** in	1121
	5:10 of thee, and the **s** shall eat their fathers;	1121
	14:16 they shall deliver neither **s** nor daughters;	1121
	14:18 they shall deliver neither **s** nor daughters,	1121
	14:22 be brought forth, *both* **s** and daughters:	1121
	16:20 Moreover thou hast taken thy **s** and thy	1121
	20:31 when *ye* make your **s** to pass through	1121
	23: 4 mine, and they bare **s** and daughters.	1121
	23:10 took her **s** and her daughters, and slew	1121
	23:25 they shall take thy **s** and thy daughters;	1121
	23:37 have also caused their **s**, whom they bare	1121
	23:47 they shall slay their **s** and their daughters,	1121
	24:21 your **s** and your daughters whom ye have	1121
	24:25 their minds, their **s** and their daughters,	1121
	40:46 *are* the **s** of Zadok among the sons of	1121
	40:46 *are* the sons of Zadok among the **s** of	1121
	44:15 the priests the Levites, the **s** of Zadok,	1121
	46:16 If the prince give a gift unto any of his **s**,	1121
	46:18 he shall give his **s** inheritance out of his	1121
	48:11 that are sanctified of the **s** of Zadok;	1121
Da	5:21 he was driven from the **s** of men;	1123
	10:16 *one* like the similitude of the **s** of men	1121
	11:10 **s** shall be stirred up, and shall assemble	1121
Hos	1:10 unto them, *Ye are* the **s** of the living God.	1121
Joel	1:12 joy is withered away from the **s** of men.	1121
	2:28 your **s** and your daughters shall prophesy,	1121
	3: 8 I will sell your **s** and your daughters into	1121
Am	2:11 I raised up of your **s** for prophets,	1121
	7:17 thy **s** and thy daughters shall fall by	1121
Mic	5: 7 not for man, nor waiteth for the **s** of men.	1121
Zec	9:13 raised up thy **s**, O Zion, against thy sons,	1121
	9:13 O Zion, against thy **s**, O Greece,	1121
Mal	3: 3 he shall purify the **s** of Levi,	1121
	3: 6 therefore ye **s** of Jacob are not consumed.	1121
Mt	20:20 mother of Zebedee's children with her **s**,	5207
	20:21 Grant that these my two **s** may sit,	5207
	21:28 A *certain* man had two **s**; and he came to	5043
	26:37 with *him* Peter and the two **s** of Zebedee,	5207
Mk	3:17 which is, The **s** of thunder:)	5207
	3:28 sins shall be forgiven unto the **s** of men,	5207
	10:35 And James and John, the **s** of Zebedee,	5207
Lk	5:10 also James, and John, the **s** of Zebedee,	5207
	11:19 by whom do your **s** cast *them* out?	5207
	15:11 And he said, A certain man had two **s**:	5207
Jn	1:12 to them gave he power to become the **s** of	5043
	21: 2 and the **s** of Zebedee, and two other of his	NIG
Ac	2:17 and your **s** and your daughters shall	5207
	7:16 the **s** of Emmor the *father* of Sychem.	5207
	7:29 the land of Madian, where he begat two **s**.	5207
	19:14 And there were seven **s** of one Sceva,	5207
Ro	8:14 by the Spirit of God, they are the **s** of God.	5207
	8:19 for the manifestation of the **s** of God.	5207
1Co	4:14 but as my beloved **s** I warn *you*.	5043
2Co	6:18 and ye shall be my **s** and daughters,	5207
Gal	4: 5 that we might receive the **adoption of s**.	5206
	4: 6 And because ye are **s**, God hath sent forth	5207

Gal	4:22 For it is written, that Abraham had two **s**,	5207
Eph	3: 5 was not made known unto the **s** of men,	5207
Php	2:15 harmless, the **s** of God without rebuke,	5043
Heb	2:10 whom *are* all *things*, in bringing many **s**	5207
	7: 5 And verily they that are of the **s** of Levi	5207
	11:21 was a dying, blessed both the **s** of Joseph;	5207
	12: 7 God dealeth with you as with **s**;	5207
	12: 8 then are ye bastards, and not **s**.	5207
1Jn	3: 1 that we should be called the **s** of God:	5043
	3: 2 are we the **s** of God, and it doth not yet	5043

SONS' (26) [SON]

Ge	6:18 and thy wife, and thy **s** wives with thee.	1121
	7: 7 and his wife, and his **s** wives with him,	1121
	8:16 and thy sons, and thy **s** wives with thee,	1121
	8:18 and his wife, and his **s** wives with him:	1121
	46: 7 His sons, and his **s** sons with him,	1121
	46: 7 his **s** daughters, and all his seed brought	1121
	46:26 out of his loins, besides Jacob's **s** wives,	1121
Ex	29:21 his sons, and his **s** garments with him.	1121
	29:28 is **s** by a statute for ever from	1121+3807.1
	29:29 the holy garments of Aaron shall be his **s**	3807.1
	39:41 his **s** garments, to minister in the priest's	3807.1
Lev	2: 3 *shall be* Aaron's and his **s**:	1121+3807.1
	2:10 *shall be* Aaron's and his **s**:	1121+3807.1
	7:31 but the breast shall be Aaron's and his **s**.	1121
	8:27 upon his **s** hands, and waved them *for* a	1121
	8:30 sons, and upon his **s** garments with him;	1121
	8:30 his sons, and his **s** garments with him.	1121
	10:13 because it *is* thy due, and thy **s** due,	1121
	10:14 for *they be* thy due, and thy **s** due,	1121
	10:15 it shall be thine, and thy **s** with thee, by	1121
	24: 9 it shall be Aaron's and his **s**;	1121+3807.1
Dt	4: 9 but teach them thy sons, and thy **s** sons;	1121
1Ch	8:40 and sons, an hundred and fifty.	1121
Job	42:16 and saw his sons, and his **s** sons,	1121
Eze	46:16 inheritance thereof shall be his **s**;	1121+3807.1
	46:17 but his inheritance shall be his **s** for them.	1121

SOON (65) [SOONER]

Ge	18:33 **as s as** he had left communing	834+3509.1
	27:30 **as s as** Isaac had made an end of	834+3509.1
	44: 3 **As s as** the morning was light, the men	2050.1
Ex	2:18 How *is it that* you are come so **s** to day?	4116
	9:29 **As s as** I am gone out of the city,	3509.1
	32:19 **as s as** he came nigh unto the	834+3509.1
Dt	4:26 that ye shall **s** utterly perish from off	4116
Jos	2: 7 **as s as** they which pursued after	834+3509.1
	2:11 **And as s as** we had heard *these things*,	2050.1
	3:13 **as s as** the soles of the feet of the	3509.1
	8:19 they ran **as s as** *he* had stretched out	3509.1
	8:29 **as s as** the sun was down,	3509.1
Jdg	8:33 to pass, **as s as** Gideon was dead,	834+3509.1
	9:33 in the morning, **as s as** the sun is up,	3509.1
1Sa	9:13 **As s as** ye be come *into* the city, ye	3509.1
	13:10 that **as s as** he had made an end of	3509.1
	20:41 *And* **as s as** the lad was gone,	2050.1
	29:10 **and as s as** ye be up early in the	2050.1
2Sa	6:18 **And as s as** David had made an end of	2050.1
	13:36 **as s as** he had made an end of speaking	3509.1
	15:10 **As s as** ye hear the sound of the	3509.1
	22:45 **as s as** they hear, they shall be obedient	3807.1
1Ki	6:11 to reign, **as s as** he sat on his throne,	3509.1
	18:12 to pass, **as s as** I am gone from thee,	NIH
	20:36 behold, **as s as** thou art departed from	2009
	20:36 **as s as** he was departed from me,	2050.1
2Ki	10: 2 Now **as s as** this letter cometh to you,	3509.1
	10:25 **as s as** he had made an end of offering	3509.1
	14: 5 **as s as** the kingdom was	834+3509.1
2Ch	31: 5 **as s as** the commandment came abroad	3509.1
Job	32:22 Maker would **s** take me away.	4592+3509.1
Ps	18:44 **As s as** they hear *of me*, they shall obey	3807.1
	37: 2 they shall **s** be cut down like the grass,	4120
	58: 3 they go astray **as s as** they be **born**,	990+4480
	68:31 Ethiopia shall **s** stretch out her hands unto	NIH
	81:14 I should **s** have subdued their	4592+3509.1
	90:10 for it is **s** cut off, and we fly away.	2440
	106:13 They **s** forgat his works; they waited not	4116
Pr	14:17 He that is **s** angry dealeth foolishly:	7116
Isa	66: 8 **as s as** Zion travailed, she brought forth	1571
Eze	23:16 **as s as** she saw them with her eyes,	3807.1
Mt	21:20 How is the fig tree withered away!	3916
Mk	1:42 And **as s as** he had spoken, immediately	NIG
	5:36 **As s as** Jesus heard the word *that was*	2112
	11: 2 **and as s as** ye be entered into it, ye shall	2112
	14:45 And **as s as** he was come, he goeth	NIG
Lk	1:23 it came to pass that, **as s as** the days of	5613
	1:44 **as s as** the voice of thy salutation sounded	5613
	8: 6 **and as s as** it was sprung up, it withered	NIG
	15:30 But **as s as** this thy son was come,	3753
	22:66 And **as s as** it was day, the elders of	5613
	23: 7 **as s as** he knew that he belonged unto	NIG
Jn	11:20 **as s as** she heard that Jesus was coming,	5613
	11:29 **As s as** she heard that, she arose quickly,	5613
	16:21 but **as s as** she is delivered of the child,	3752
	18: 6 **As s** then **as** he had said unto them, I am	5613
	21: 9 **As s** then **as** they were come to land,	5613
Ac	10:29 without gainsaying, **as s as** I was sent for:	NIG
	12:18 **as s as** it was day, there was no small	NIG
Gal	1: 6 **s** removed from him that called you into	5030
Php	2:23 so **s** as I shall see how it will go	302+5613
2Th	2: 2 That ye be not **s** shaken in mind,	5030
Tit	1: 7 not selfwilled, not **s** angry, not given to	3711
Rev	10:10 and **as s as** I had eaten it, my belly was	3753
	12: 4 to devour her child **as s as** it was born.	3752

S

SOONER (2) [SOON]

Heb	13:19 this, that I may be restored to you the **s**.	5030
Jas	1:11 the sun is no **s** risen with a burning heat,	NIG

SOOTHED See MOLLIFIED

SOOTHSAYER (1) [SOOTHSAYERS, SOOTHSAYING]

Jos	13:22 Balaam also the son of Beor, the **s**,	7080

SOOTHSAYER'S See MEONENIM

SOOTHSAYERS (6) [SOOTHSAYER]

Isa	2: 6 *are* **s** like the Philistines, and they please	6049
Da	2:27 the magicians, the **s**, shew unto the king;	1505
	4: 7 the astrologers, the Chaldeans, and the **s**:	1505
	5: 7 the astrologers, the Chaldeans, and the **s**.	1505
	5:11 astrologers, Chaldeans, *and* **s**;	1505
Mic	5:12 hand; and thou shalt have no *more* **s**:	6049

SOOTHSAYING (1) [SOOTHSAYER]

Ac	16:16 brought her masters much gain by **s**:	3132

SOP (4)

Jn	13:26 He it is, to whom I shall give a **s**,	5596
	13:26 dipped *it*. And when he had dipped the **s**,	5596
	13:27 And after the **s** Satan entered into him.	5596
	13:30 having received the **s** he went immediately	5596

SOPATER (1)

Ac	20: 4 And there accompanied him into Asia **S**	4986

SOPE (2)

Jer	2:22 thee with nitre, and take thee much **s**,	1287
Mal	3: 2 *is* like a refiner's fire, and like fullers' **s**:	1287

SOPHERETH (2)

Ezr	2:55 the children of Sotai, the children of **S**,	5618
Ne	7:57 the children of Sotai, the children of **S**,	5618

SORCERER (2) [SORCERY]

Ac	13: 6 they found a certain **s**, a false prophet,	3097
	13: 8 But Elymas the **s** (for so is his name by	3097

SORCERERS (6) [SORCERY]

Ex	7:11 also called the wise men and the **s**:	3784
Jer	27: 9 nor to your **s**, which speak unto you,	3786
Da	2: 2 and the **s**, and the Chaldeans,	3784
Mal	3: 5 I will be a swift witness against the **s**,	3784
Rev	21: 8 and whoremongers, and **s**, and idolaters,	5332
	22:15 s, and whoremongers, and murderers,	5333

SORCERESS (1) [SORCERY]

Isa	57: 3 draw near hither, ye sons of the **s**,	6049

SORCERIES (5) [SORCERY]

Isa	47: 9 their perfection for the multitude of thy **s**,	3785
	47:12 and with the multitude of thy **s**,	3785
Ac	8:11 long time *he* had bewitched them with **s**.	3095
Rev	9:21 nor of their **s**, nor of their fornication,	5331
	18:23 for by thy **s** were all nations deceived.	5331

SORCERY (1) [SORCERER, SORCERERS, SORCERESS, SORCERIES]

Ac	8: 9 beforetime in the *same* city used **s**,	3096

SORE (98) [SORELY, SORER, SORES]

Ge	19: 9 they pressed **s** upon the man, *even* Lot,	3966
	20: 8 in their ears: and the men were **s** afraid.	3966
	31:30 **s** longedst after thy father's house,	3700+3700
	34:25 when they were **s**, that two of the sons of	3510
	41:56 the famine waxed **s** in the land of Egypt.	2388
	41:57 that the famine was *so* **s** in all lands.	2388
	43: 1 And the famine *was* **s** in the land.	3515
	47: 4 for the famine *is* **s** in the land of Canaan:	3515
	47:13 for the famine *was* very **s**, so that the land	3515
	50:10 with a great and very **s** lamentation.	3515
Ex	14 after them; and they were **s** afraid.	3966
Lev	13:42 or bald forehead, a white reddish **s**;	5061
	13:43 *if* the rising of the **s** *be* white reddish in	5061
Nu	22: 3 Moab was **s** afraid of the people, because	3966
Dt	6:22 shewed signs and wonders, great and **s**,	7451
	28:35 with a botch that cannot be healed,	7451
	28:59 **s** sicknesses, and of long continuance.	7451
Jos	9:24 we were **s** afraid of our lives because of	3966
Jdg	10: 9 Ephraim; so that Israel was **s** distressed.	3966
	14:17 he told her, because she **lay s upon** him:	6693
	15:18 he was **s** athirst, and called on the LORD,	3966
	20:34 men out of all Israel, and the battle was **s**:	3513
	21: 2 up their voices, and **wept s**:	1058+1065+1419
1Sa	1: 6 her adversary also **provoked** her **s**,	3707+3708
	1:10 prayed unto the LORD, and **wept s**.	1058+1058
	5: 7 his hand is **s** upon us, and upon Dagon	7185
	14:52 there was **s** war against the Philistines all	2389
	17:24 man, fled from him, and were **s** afraid.	3966
	21:12 was **s** afraid of Achish the king of Gath.	3966
	28:15 Saul answered, I am **s** distressed;	3966
	28:20 was **s** afraid, because of the words of	3966
	28:21 saw that he was **s** troubled, and said unto	3966
	31: 3 the battle **went s** against Saul,	3513
	31: 3 and he was **s** wounded of the archers.	3966
	31: 4 would not; for he was **s** afraid:	3966
2Sa	2:17 there was a very **s** battle that day;	7186
	13:36 and all his servants **wept** very **s**.	1058+1065
1Ki	17:17 his sickness was so **s**, that there was no	2389
	18: 2 And *there* was a **s** famine in Samaria.	2389

2Ki	3:26 saw that the battle was too **s** for him,	2388
	6:11 of Syria was **s troubled** for this thing;	5590
	20: 3 And Hezekiah **wept s**.	1058+1065+1419
1Ch	10: 3 the battle **went s** against Saul,	3513
	10: 4 would not; for he was **s** afraid.	3966
2Ch	6:28 whatsoever **s** or whatsoever sickness	5061
	6:29 when every one shall know his own **s**	5061
	21:19 so he died of **s** diseases. And his people	7451
	28:19 **transgressed s** against the LORD,	4603+4604
	35:23 Have me away; for I am **s** wounded.	3966
Ezr	10: 1 for the people **wept** very **s**.	1058+1059
Ne	2: 2 of heart. Then I was very **s** afraid,	7235
	13: 8 it grieved me **s**: therefore I cast forth all	3966
Job	2: 7 smote Job with **s** boils from the sole of his	7451
	5:18 For he **maketh s**, and bindeth up:	3510
Ps	6: 3 My soul is also **s** vexed: but thou,	3966
	6:10 mine enemies be ashamed and **s** vexed:	3966
	38: 2 and thy hand **presseth** me **s**.	5181+5921
	38: 8 I am feeble and **s** broken: I have	3966+5704
	38:11 my friends stand aloof from my **s**;	5061
	44:19 thou hast **s broken** us in the place	1794
	55: 4 My heart is **s pained** within me:	2342
	71:20 hast shewed me great and **s** troubles,	7451
	77: 2 my **s** ran in the night, and ceased not:	3027
	118:13 Thou hast **thrust** at me that *I*	1760+1760
	118:18 The LORD hath **chastened** me **s**:	3256+3256
Ecc	1:13 this travail hath God given to the sons	7451
	4: 8 This *is* also vanity, yea, it *is* a **s** travail.	7451
	5:13 There is a **s** evil *which* I have seen under	2470
	5:16 this also *is* a **s** evil, *that* in all points as he	2470
Isa	27: 1 In that day the LORD with his **s** and great	7186
	38: 3 And Hezekiah **wept s**.	1058+1065+1419
	59:11 bears, and **mourn s** like doves:	1897+1897
	64: 9 Be not wroth **very s**, O LORD,	3966+5704
	64:12 thy peace, and afflict us **very s**?	3966+5704
Jer	13:17 eye shall **weep s**, and run down	1830+1830
	22:10 **weep s** for him that goeth away:	1058+1058
	50:12 Your mother shall be **s** confounded;	3966
	52: 6 the famine was **s** in the city, so that there	2388
La	1: 2 She **weepeth s** in the night,	1058+1058
	3:52 Mine enemies **chased** me **s**, like a	6679+6679
Eze	14:21 How much more when I send my four **s**	7451
	21:10 sharpened to make a **s slaughter**;	2873+2874
	27:35 their kings shall be **s afraid**, they	8175+8178
Da	6:14 was **s** displeased with himself, and set *his*	7690
Mic	2:10 it shall **s** displease *you*, even *with* a **s**	4834
Zec	1: 2 The LORD hath been **s displeased**	7107+7110
	1:15 I am very **s displeased**	7107+7110
Mt	17: 6 they fell on their face, and were **s** afraid.	4970
	17:15 he is lunatick, and **s** vexed: for ofttimes	2560
	21:15 the Son of David; they were **s displeased**,	23
Mk	6:51 they were **s** amazed in themselves beyond	3029
	9: 6 wist not to say; for they were **s afraid**.	1630
	9:26 and rent him **s**, and came out of *him*: and	4183
	14:33 and began to be **s amazed**, and to be very	1568
Lk	2: 9 round about them: and they were **s** afraid.	3173
Ac	20:37 And *they* all **wept s**, and fell on Paul's	2425
Rev	16: 2 grievous **s** upon the men which had	1668

SOREK (1)

Jdg	16: 4 that he loved a woman in the valley of **S**,	7796

SORELY (2) [SORE]

Ge	49:23 The archers have **s grieved** him, and shot	4843
Isa	23: 5 they be **s pained** *at* the report of Tyre.	2342

SORER (1) [SORE]

Heb	10:29 Of how much **s** punishment, suppose ye,	5501

SORES (4) [SORE]

Isa	1: 6 *but* wounds, and bruises, and putrifying **s**:	4347
Lk	16:20 which was laid at his gate, **full of s**,	1669
	16:21 moreover the dogs came and licked his **s**.	1668
Rev	16:11 heaven because of their pains and their **s**,	1668

SORROW (70) [SORROWED, SORROWETH, SORROWFUL, SORROWING, SORROWS, SORRY]

Ge	3:16 I will greatly multiply thy **s** and	6093
	3:16 in **s** thou shalt bring forth children;	6089
	3:17 in **s** shalt thou eat *of* it all the days of thy	6093
	42:38 ye bring down my gray hairs with **s** to	3015
	44:29 shall bring down my gray hairs with **s** to	7451
	44:31 thy servant our father with **s** to the grave.	3015
Ex	15:14 **s** shall take hold on the inhabitants of	2427
Lev	26:16 consume the eyes, and **cause s** of heart:	1727
Dt	28:65 and failing of eyes, and **s** of mind:	1671
1Ch	4: 9 saying, Because I bare *him* with **s**.	6090
Ne	2: 2 *this* is nothing *else* but **s** of heart. Then I	7455
Est	9:22 was turned unto them from **s** to joy,	3015
Job	3:10 womb, nor hid **s** from mine eyes.	5999
	6:10 I would harden myself in **s**; let him not	2427
	17: 7 Mine eye also is dim by reason of **s**,	3708
	41:22 and **s** is turned into joy before him.	1670
Ps	13: 2 in my soul, *having* **s** in my heart daily?	3015
	38:17 halt, and my **s** is continually before me.	4341
	39: 2 *even* from good; and my **s** was stirred.	3511
	55:10 mischief also and **s** *are* in the midst of it.	5999
	90:10 yet *is* their strength labour and **s**;	205
	107:39 low through oppression, affliction, and **s**.	3015
	116: 3 gat hold upon me: I found trouble and **s**.	3015
Pr	10:10 He that winketh *with* the eye causeth **s**:	6094
	10:22 maketh rich, and he addeth no **s** with it.	6089
	15:13 but by **s** of the heart the spirit *is* broken.	6094

Pr	17:21 He that begetteth a fool *doeth it* to his **s**:	8424
	23:29 who hath **s**? who hath contentions?	17
Ecc	1:18 that increaseth knowledge increaseth **s**.	4341
	5:17 *hath* much **s** and wrath with his sickness.	3707
	7: 3 **S** *is* better than laughter: for by the	3708
	11:10 Therefore remove **s** from thy heart,	3708
Isa	5:30 behold darkness *and* **s**, and the light is	6862
	14: 3 the LORD shall give thee rest from thy **s**,	6090
	17:11 in the day of grief and of desperate **s**.	3511
	29: 2 and there shall be heaviness and **s**:	592
	35:10 and **s** and sighing shall flee away.	3015
	50:11 have of mine hand; ye shall lie down in **s**.	4620
	51:11 joy; *and* **s** and mourning shall flee away.	3015
	65:14 ye shall cry for **s** of heart, and shall howl	3511
Jer	8:18 *When* I would comfort myself against **s**,	3015
	20:18 out of the womb to see labour and **s**,	3015
	30:15 thy **s** *is* incurable for the multitude of	4341
	31:12 and they shall not **s** any more at all.	1669
	31:13 and make them rejoice from their **s**.	3015
	45: 3 for the LORD hath added grief to my **s**;	4341
	49:23 *there* is **s** on the sea; it cannot be quiet.	1674
	51:29 the land shall tremble and **s**: for every	2342
La	1:12 see if there be any **s** like unto my sorrow,	4341
	1:12 see if there be any sorrow like unto my **s**,	4341
	1:18 I pray you, all people, and behold my **s**:	4341
	3:65 Give them **s** of heart, thy curse unto	4044
Eze	23:33 shalt be filled *with* drunkenness and **s**,	3015
Hos	8:10 they shall **s** a little for the burden of	2490
Lk	22:45 disciples, he found them sleeping for **s**,	3077
Jn	16: 6 *things* ye have, **s** hath filled your heart.	3077
	16:20 but your **s** shall be turned into joy.	3077
	16:21 A woman when she is in travail hath **s**,	3077
	16:22 ye now therefore have **s**: but I will see	3077
Ro	9: 2 heaviness and continual **s** in my heart.	3601
2Co	2: 3 I should have **s** from *them of* whom I	3077
	2: 7 be swallowed up with overmuch **s**.	3077
	7:10 godly **s** worketh repentance to salvation	3077
	7:10 but the **s** of the world worketh death.	3077
Php	2:27 also, lest I should have **s** upon sorrow.	3077
	2:27 also, lest I should have sorrow upon **s**.	3077
1Th	4:13 them which are asleep, that ye **s** not,	3076
Rev	18: 7 so much torment and **s** give her:	3997
	18: 7 and am no widow, and shall see no **s**.	3997
	21: 4 be no more death, neither **s**, nor crying,	3997

SORROWED (2) [SORROW]

2Co	7: 9 made sorry, but that ye **s** to repentance:	3076
	7:11 For behold this selfsame *thing*, that ye **s**	3076

SORROWETH (1) [SORROW]

1Sa	10: 2 **s** for you, saying, What shall I do for my	1672

SORROWFUL (18) [SORROW]

1Sa	1:15 No, my lord, I *am* a woman of a **s** spirit:	7186
Job	6: 7 soul refused to touch *are* as my **s** meat.	1741
Ps	69:29 I *am* poor and **s**: let thy salvation, O God,	3510
Pr	14:13 in laughter the heart is **s**; and the end	3510
Jer	31:25 and I have replenished every **s** soul.	1669
Zep	3:18 I will gather *them that are* **s** for the	3013
Zec	9: 5 Gaza also *shall see it*, and be very **s**,	2342
Mt	19:22 man heard *that* saying, he went away **s**:	3076
	26:22 And they were exceeding **s**,	3076
	26:37 and began to be **s** and very heavy.	3076
	26:38 My soul is **exceeding s**, *even* unto death:	4036
Mk	14:19 they began to be **s**, and to say unto him	3076
	14:34 My soul is **exceeding s** unto death:	4036
Lk	18:23 And when he heard this, he was **very s**:	4036
	18:24 And when Jesus saw that he was **very s**,	4036
Jn	16:20 ye shall be **s**, but your sorrow shall be	3076
2Co	6:10 As **s**, yet alway rejoicing; as poor,	3076
Php	2:28 may rejoice, and *that* I may be the **less s**.	253

SORROWING (2) [SORROW]

Lk	2:48 thy father and I have sought thee **s**.	3600
Ac	20:38 **S** most *of all* for the words which he	3600

SORROWS (22) [SORROW]

Ex	3: 7 of their taskmasters; for I know their **s**;	4341
2Sa	22: 6 The **s** of hell compassed me about;	2256
Job	9:28 I am afraid of all my **s**, I know that thou	6094
	21:17 God distributeth **s** in his anger.	2256
	39: 3 their young ones, they cast out their **s**.	2256
Ps	16: 4 Their **s** shall be multiplied *that* hasten	6094
	18: 4 The **s** of death compassed me,	2256
	18: 5 The **s** of hell compassed me about:	2256
	32:10 Many **s** *shall be* to the wicked: but he	4341
	116: 3 The **s** of death compassed me, and the	2256
	127: 2 early, to sit up late, to eat the bread of **s**:	6089
Ecc	2:23 For all his days *are* **s**, and his travail grief;	4341
Isa	53: 3 a man of **s**, and acquainted with grief:	4341
	53: 4 hath borne our griefs, and carried our **s**:	4341
Jer	13:21 not **s** take thee, as a woman in travail?	2256
	49:24 have taken her as a woman in travail.	2256
Da	10:16 by the vision my **s** are turned upon me,	6735
Hos	13:13 The **s** of a travailing *woman* shall come	2256
Mt	24: 8 All these *are* the beginning of **s**.	5604
Mk	13: 8 troubles: these *are* the beginnings of **s**.	5604
1Ti	6:10 pierced themselves through with many **s**.	3601

SORRY (14) [SORROW]

1Sa	22: 8 *there is* none of you that is **s** for me,	2470
Ne	8:10 neither be ye **s**; for the joy of the LORD *is*	6087
Ps	38:18 mine iniquity; I will be **s** for my sin.	1672
Isa	51:19 come unto thee; who shall be **s** for thee?	5110

S

Mt	14: 9	And the king was **s**: nevertheless for	3076
	17:23	raised *again*. And they were exceeding **s**.	3076
	18:31	they were very **s**, and came and told unto	3076
Mk	6:26	the king was **exceeding s**; *yet* for his	4036
2Co	2: 2	For if I **make** you **s**, who is he then	3076
	2: 2	but *the same* which is **made s** by me?	3076
	7: 8	though I **made** you **s** with a letter, I do	3076
	7: 8	that the same epistle hath **made** you **s**,	3076
	7: 9	not that ye were **made s**, but that ye	3076
	7: 9	for ye were **made s** after a godly manner,	3076

SORT (21) [SORTS]

Ge	6:19	of every **s** shalt thou bring into the ark,	NIH
	6:20	two of every **s** shall come unto thee,	NIH
	7:14	fowl after his kind, every bird of every **s**.	3671
2Ki	24:14	the **poorest s** of the people of the land.	1803
1Ch	24: 5	they divided by lot, one **s** with another;	NIH
	29:14	willingly after this **s**? for all *things come*	NIH
2Ch	30: 5	of a long *time in such* **s** as it was written.	NIH
Ezr	1:10	silver basons of a **second s** four hundred	4932
	4: 8	to Artaxerxes the king **in this s**:	3660
Ne	6: 4	they sent unto me four times after this **s**;	1697
Eze	23:42	the men of the common *were* brought	120
	39: 4	thee unto the ravenous birds of every **s**,	3671
	44:30	of every **s** of your oblations, shall be	NIH
Da	1:10	than the children which *are* of your **s**?	1524
	3:29	other God that can deliver **after** this **s**.	3509.4
Ac	17: 5	*them* certain lewd fellows of the **baser s**,	60
Ro	15:15	the more boldly unto **you in** some **s**,	3313
1Co	3:13	try every man's work of **what s** it is.	3697
2Co	7:11	*thing*, that ye sorrowed **after a** godly **s**,	2596
2Ti	3: 6	For of **this s** are they which creep into	NIG
3Jn	1: 6	forward on their journey **after a** godly **s**,	516

SORTS (7) [SORT]

Dt	22:11	shalt not wear a **garment of divers s**,	8162
Ne	5:18	and once in ten days store of all **s** *of* wine:	NIH
Ps	78:45	He sent **divers s** *of flies* among them,	6157
	105:31	there came **divers s** *of flies, and* lice in	6157
Ecc	2: 8	**musical instruments,** and that of **all s**.	7705+7705
Eze	27:24	*were* thy merchants in **all s of** things,	4360
	38: 4	all of them clothed with **all s** *of armour*,	4358

SOSIPATER (1)

| Ro | 16:21 | Lucius, and Jason, and **S**, my kinsmen, | 4989 |

SOSTHENES (2)

| Ac | 18:17 | all the Greeks took **S**, the *chief* ruler | 4988 |
| 1Co | 1: 1 | the will of God, and **S** *our* brother, | 4988 |

SOTAI (2)

| Ezr | 2:55 | children of **S**, the children of Sophereth, | 5479 |
| Ne | 7:57 | children of **S**, the children of Sophereth, | 5479 |

SOTTISH (1)

| Jer | 4:22 | they *are* **s** children, and they have none | 5530 |

SOUGHT (126) [SEEK]

Ge	43:30	he **s** *where* to weep; and he entered into	1245
Ex	2:15	heard this thing, he **s** to slay Moses.	1245
	4:19	for all the men are dead which **s** thy life.	1245
	4:24	that the Lord met him, and **s** to kill him.	1245
	33: 7	*that* every one which **s** the Lord went	1245
Lev	10:16	Moses **diligently s** the goat of the	1875+1875
Nu	35:23	*was* not his enemy, neither **s** his harm:	1245
Dt	13:10	he hath **s** to thrust thee away from	1245
Jos	2:22	pursuers **s** *them* throughout all the way,	1245
Jdg	14: 4	he **s** an occasion against the Philistines	1245
	18: 1	those days the tribe of the Danites **s** them	1245
1Sa	10:21	when they **s** him, he could not be found.	1245
	13:14	the Lord hath **s** him a man after his own	1245
	14: 4	*by* which Jonathan **s** to go over unto	1245
	19:10	Saul **s** to smite David even to the wall	1245
	23:14	Saul **s** him every day, but God delivered	1245
	27: 4	*to* Gath: and he **s** no more again for him.	1245
2Sa	3:17	Ye **s** **for** David in times past to be king	1245
	4: 8	son of Saul thine enemy, which **s** thy life;	1245
	17:20	they had **s** and could not find *them,*	1245
	21: 2	Saul **s** to slay them in his zeal to	1245
1Ki	1: 2	Let there be **s** for my lord the king a	1245
	1: 3	So they **s for** a fair damsel throughout all	1245
	10:24	all the earth **s** to Solomon, to hear his	1245
	11:40	Solomon **s** therefore to kill Jeroboam.	1245
2Ki	2:17	and they **s** three days, but found him not.	1875
1Ch	15:13	for that we **s** him not after the due order.	1875
	26:31	year of the reign of David they were **s for,**	1875
2Ch	1: 5	Solomon and the congregation **s** *unto* it.	1875
	9:23	all the kings of the earth **s** the presence of	1245
	14: 7	because we have **s** the Lord our God,	1875
	14: 7	we have **s** *him,* and he hath given us rest	1875
	15: 4	Israel, and **s** him, he was found of them.	1245
	15:15	and **s** him with their whole desire;	1245
	16:12	yet in his disease he **s** not *to* the Lord,	1875
	17: 3	his father David, and **s** not unto Baalim;	1875
	17: 4	**s** to the Lord God of his father,	1875
	22: 9	he **s** Ahaziah: and they caught him,	1245
	22: 9	who **s** the Lord with all his heart.	1875
	25:15	Why hast thou **s** after the gods of	1875
	25:20	because they **s after** the gods of Edom.	1875
	26: 5	he **s** God in the days of Zechariah, who	1875
	26: 5	as long as he **s** the Lord, God made him	1875
Ezr	2:62	These **s** their register *among* those that	1245
Ne	7:64	These **s** their register *among* those	1245
	12:27	they **s** the Levites out of all their places,	1245

Est	2: 2	Let there be fair young virgins **s** for	1245
	2:21	and **s** to lay hand on the king Ahasuerus.	1245
	3: 6	Haman **s** to destroy all the Jews	1245
	6: 2	**s** to lay hand on the king Ahasuerus.	1245
	9: 2	to lay hand on such as **s** their hurt:	1245
Ps	34: 4	I **s** the Lord, and he heard me,	1875
	37:36	yea, I **s** him, but he could not be found.	1245
	77: 2	In the day of my trouble I **s** the Lord:	1875
	78:34	When he slew them, then they **s** him:	1875
	86:14	assemblies of violent *men* have **s after**	1245
	111: 2	**s** out of all them that have pleasure	1875
	119:10	With my whole heart have I **s** thee:	1875
	119:94	save me; for I have **s** thy precepts.	1875
Ecc	2: 3	I **s** in mine heart to give myself unto wine	8446
	7:29	but they have **s out** many inventions.	1245
	12: 9	**s out,** *and* set in order many proverbs.	2713
	12:10	The Preacher **s** to find out acceptable	1245
SS	3: 1	By night on my bed I **s** *him* whom my	1245
	3: 1	soul loveth: I **s** him, but I found him not.	1245
	3: 2	soul loveth: I **s** him, but I found him not.	1245
	5: 6	I **s** him, but I could not find him; I called	1245
Isa	62:12	shalt be called, **S** out, A city not forsaken.	1875
	65: 1	I am **s** of *them that* asked not *for me:*	1875
	65: 1	*for me:* I am found of *them that* **s** me not:	1875
	65:10	lie down in, for my people that have **s** me.	1875
Jer	8: 2	whom they have **s**, and whom they have	1875
	10:21	and have not **s** the Lord:	1875
	26:21	his words, the king **s** to put him to death:	1245
	44:30	of Babylon, his enemy, and that **s** his life.	1245
	50:20	the iniquity of Israel shall be **s for,**	1245
La	1:19	while they **s** their meat, to relieve their	1245
Eze	22:30	I **s** for a man among them, that *should*	1245
	26:21	shalt *be no more:* though thou be **s for,**	1245
	34: 4	neither have ye **s** that which was lost;	1245
Da	2:13	they **s** Daniel and his fellows to be slain.	1156
	4:36	my counsellers and my lords **s** unto me;	1156
	6: 4	princes **s** to find occasion against Daniel	1156
	8:15	and **s for** the meaning, then behold,	1245
Ob	1: 6	searched out! *how* are his hid things **s up!**	1158
Zep	1: 6	*those* that have not **s** the Lord,	1245
Zec	6: 7	**s** to go that *they* might walk to and	1245
Mt	2:20	they are dead which **s** the young child's	2212
	21:46	But when they **s** to lay hands on him,	2212
	26:16	And from that time he **s** opportunity to	2212
	26:59	the council, **s** false witness against Jesus,	2212
Mk	11:18	and **s** how they might destroy him:	2212
	12:12	And they **s** to lay hold on him,	2212
	14: 1	the scribes **s** how they might take him by	2212
	14:11	he how he might conveniently betray	2212
	14:55	all the council **s for** witness against Jesus	2212
Lk	2:44	and they **s** him among their kinsfolk and	327
	2:48	thy father and I have **s** thee sorrowing.	2212
	2:49	said unto them, How *is it that* ye **s** me?	2212
	4:42	the people **s** him, and came unto him,	2212
	5:18	they **s** *means* to bring him in, and to lay	2212
	6:19	And the whole multitude **s** to touch him:	2212
	11:16	**s** of him a sign from heaven.	2212
	13: 6	and he came and **s** fruit thereon,	2212
	19: 3	And he **s** to see Jesus who he was;	2212
	19:47	the chief of the people **s** to destroy him,	2212
	20:19	the scribes the same hour **s** to lay hands	2212
	22: 2	and scribes **s** how they might kill him;	2212
	22: 6	opportunity to betray him unto them in	2212
Jn	5:16	and **s** to slay him, because he had done	2212
	5:18	Therefore the Jews **s** the more to kill him,	2212
	7: 1	in Jewry, because the Jews **s** to kill him.	2212
	7:11	Then the Jews **s** him at the feast, and said	2212
	7:30	Then they **s** to take him: but no *man* laid	2212
	10:39	Therefore they **s** again to take him:	2212
	11: 8	Master, the Jews of late **s** to stone thee;	2212
	11:56	Then **s** they **for** Jesus, and spake among	2212
	19:12	And from thenceforth Pilate **s** to release	2212
Ac	12:19	And when Herod had **s for** him,	1934
	17: 5	and **s** to bring them out to the people.	2212
Ro	9:32	Because *they* **s** it not by faith, but as *it*	NIG
	10:20	saith, I was found of them that **s** me not;	2212
1Th	2: 6	Nor of men **s** we glory, neither of you,	2212
2Ti	1:17	was in Rome, he **s** me **out** very diligently,	2212
Heb	8: 7	no place have been **s for** the second.	2212
	12:17	though he **s** it **carefully** with tears.	1567

SOUL (458) [SOUL'S, SOULS]

Ge	2: 7	breath of life; and man became a living **s**.	5315
	12:13	and my **s** shall live because of thee:	5315
	17:14	that **s** shall be cut off from his people;	5315
	19:20	(*is it* not a little one?) and my **s** shall live.	5315
	27: 4	that my **s** may bless thee before I die.	5315
	27:19	of my venison, that thy **s** may bless me.	5315
	27:25	son's venison, that my **s** may bless thee.	5315
	27:31	son's venison, that thy **s** may bless me.	5315
	34: 3	his **s** clave unto Dinah the daughter of	5315
	34: 8	The **s** of my son Shechem longeth for	5315
	35:18	as her **s** was in departing (for she died)	5315
	42:21	in that we saw the anguish of his **s**, when	5315
	49: 6	O my **s**, come not thou into their secret;	5315
Ex	12:15	that **s** shall be cut off from Israel.	5315
	12:19	even that **s** shall be cut off from	5315
	30:12	man a ransom for his **s** unto the Lord,	5315
	31:14	that **s** shall be cut off from amongst his	5315
Lev	4: 2	If a **s** shall sin through ignorance against	5315
	5: 1	If a **s** sin, and hear the voice of swearing,	5315
	5: 2	Or if a **s** touch any unclean thing,	5315
	5: 4	if a **s** swear, pronouncing with *his* lips to	5315
	5:15	If a **s** commit a trespass, and sin through	5315
	5:17	if a **s** sin, and commit any *of these things*	5315

Lev	6: 2	If a **s** sin, and commit a trespass against	5315
	7:18	**s** that eateth of it shall bear his iniquity.	5315
	7:20	**s** that eateth *of* the flesh of the sacrifice	5315
	7:20	that **s** shall be cut off from his people.	5315
	7:21	the **s** that shall touch any unclean	5315
	7:21	that **s** shall be cut off from his people.	5315
	7:25	even the **s** that eateth *it* shall be cut off	5315
	7:27	Whatsoever **s** *it be* that eateth any	5315
	7:27	that **s** shall be cut off from his people.	5315
	17:10	I will even set my face against *that* **s** that	5315
	17:11	*that* maketh an atonement for the **s**.	5315
	17:12	of Israel, No **s** of you shall eat blood,	5315
	17:15	that **s** eateth that which died of itself,	5315
	19: 8	that **s** shall be cut off from among his	5315
	20: 6	the **s** that turneth after such as have	5315
	20: 6	I will even set my face against that **s**,	5315
	22: 3	that **s** shall be cut off from my presence:	5315
	22: 6	The **s** which hath touched *any* such shall	5315
	22:11	if the priest buy *any* **s** with his money,	5315
	23:29	For whatsoever **s** *it be* that shall not be	5315
	23:30	whatsoever **s** *it be* that doeth any work	5315
	23:30	the same **s** will I destroy from among his	5315
	26:11	and my **s** shall not abhor you.	5315
	26:15	or if your **s** abhor my judgments, so that	5315
	26:30	of your idols, and my **s** shall abhor you.	5315
	26:43	and because their **s** abhorred my statutes.	5315
Nu	9:13	even the same **s** shall be cut off from	5315
	11: 6	now our **s** *is* dried away: *there is* nothing	5315
	15:27	if any **s** sin through ignorance, then he	5315
	15:28	priest shall make an atonement for the **s**	5315
	15:30	the **s** that doeth *ought* presumptuously,	5315
	15:30	that **s** shall be cut off from among his	5315
	15:31	that **s** shall utterly be cut off;	5315
	19:13	and that **s** shall be cut off from Israel:	5315
	19:20	that **s** shall be cut off from among	5315
	19:22	the **s** that toucheth *it* shall be unclean	5315
	21: 4	the **s** of the people was much discouraged	5315
	21: 5	and our **s** loatheth this light bread.	5315
	30: 2	swear an oath to bind his **s** with a bond;	5315
	30: 4	bond wherewith she hath bound her **s**,	5315
	30: 4	bond wherewith she hath bound her **s**,	5315
	30: 5	bonds wherewith she hath bound her **s**;	5315
	30: 6	of her lips, wherewith she bound her **s**;	5315
	30: 7	bonds wherewith she bound her **s** shall	5315
	30: 8	wherewith she bound her **s**, of none	5315
	30:10	or bound her **s** by a bond with an oath;	5315
	30:11	bond wherewith she bound her **s** shall	5315
	30:12	or concerning the bond of her **s**, shall not	5315
	30:13	and every binding oath to afflict the **s**,	5315
	31:28	**s** of five hundred, *both of* the persons,	5315
Dt	4: 9	heed to thyself, and keep thy **s** diligently,	5315
	4:29	him with all thy heart and with all thy **s**.	5315
	6: 5	with all thy **s**, and with all thy might.	5315
	10:12	God with all thy heart and with all thy **s**,	5315
	11:13	with all your heart and with all your **s**,	5315
	11:18	my words in your heart and in your **s**,	5315
	12:15	thy gates, whatsoever thy **s** lusteth after,	5315
	12:20	flesh, because thy **s** longeth to eat flesh;	5315
	12:20	eat flesh, whatsoever thy **s** lusteth after.	5315
	12:21	shalt eat in thy gates whatsoever thy **s**	5315
	13: 3	with all your heart and with all your **s**.	5315
	13: 6	or thy friend, which *is* as thine own **s**,	5315
	14:26	money for whatsoever thy **s** lusteth after,	5315
	14:26	or for whatsoever thy **s** desireth:	5315
	26:16	with all thine heart, and with all thy **s**.	5315
	30: 2	with all thine heart, and with all thy **s**,	5315
	30: 6	and with all thy **s**, that thou mayest live	5315
	30:10	with all thine heart, and with all thy **s**.	5315
Jos	22: 5	with all your heart and with all your **s**.	5315
Jdg	5:21	my **s**, thou hast trodden down strength.	5315
	10:16	his **s** was grieved for the misery of Israel.	5315
	16:16	*so* that his **s** was vexed unto death;	5315
1Sa	1:10	she *was* in bitterness of **s**, and prayed	5315
	1:15	have poured out my **s** before the Lord.	5315
	1:26	O my lord, *as* thy **s** liveth, my lord,	5315
	2:16	*then* take as *much* as thy **s** desireth;	5315
	17:55	*As* thy **s** liveth, O king, I cannot tell.	5315
	18: 1	the **s** of Jonathan was knit with the soul	5315
	18: 1	soul of Jonathan was knit with the **s**	5315
	18: 1	and Jonathan loved him as his own **s**.	5315
	18: 3	because he loved him as his own **s**.	5315
	20: 3	thy **s** liveth, *there is* but a step between	5315
	20: 4	Whatsoever thy **s** desireth, I will even do	5315
	20:17	for he loved him as he loved his own **s**.	5315
	23:20	to all the desire of thy **s** to come down;	5315
	24:11	yet thou huntest my **s** to take it.	5315
	25:26	*as* the Lord liveth, and *as* thy **s** liveth,	5315
	25:29	is risen to pursue thee, and to seek thy **s**:	5315
	25:29	the **s** of my lord shall be bound in	5315
	26:21	my **s** was precious in thine eyes this day:	5315
	30: 6	the **s** of all the people was grieved,	5315
2Sa	4: 9	who hath redeemed my **s** out of all	5315
	5: 8	and the blind, *that are* hated of David's **s**,	5315
	11:11	thou livest, and *as* thy **s** liveth, I will not	5315
	13:39	the **s** *of* king David longed to go forth	NIH
	14:19	answered and said, *As* thy **s** liveth,	5315
1Ki	1:29	hath redeemed my **s** out of all distress,	5315
	2: 4	with all their heart and with all their **s**,	5315
	8:48	all their **s**, in the land of their enemies,	5315
	11:37	thou shalt reign according to all that thy **s**	5315
	17:21	let this child's **s** come into him again,	5315
	17:22	the **s** of the child came into him again,	5315
2Ki	2: 2	and *as* thy **s** liveth, I will not leave thee.	5315
	2: 4	and *as* thy **s** liveth, I will not leave thee.	5315
	2: 6	and *as* thy **s** liveth, I will not leave thee.	5315

S

2Ki 4:27 Let her alone; for her **s** *is* vexed within	5315	
4:30 and *as* thy **s** liveth, I will not leave thee.	5315	
23: 3 statutes with all *their* heart and all *their* **s,**	5315	
23:25 with all his **s,** and with all his might,	5315	
1Ch 22:19 and your **s** to seek the LORD your God;	5315	
2Ch 6:38 all their **s** in the land of their captivity,	5315	
15:12 with all their heart and with all their **s;**	5315	
34:31 with all his heart, and with all his **s,**	5315	
Job 3:20 is in misery, and life unto the bitter in **s;**	5315	
6: 7 The things *that* my **s** refused to touch *are*	5315	
7:11 I will complain in the bitterness of my **s.**	5315	
7:15 So that my **s** chooseth strangling,	5315	
9:21 perfect, *yet* would I not know my **s:**	5315	
10: 1 My **s** is weary of my life; I will leave my	5315	
10: 1 I will speak in the bitterness of my **s.**	5315	
12:10 In whose hand *is* the **s** of every living	5315	
14:22 and his **s** within him shall mourn.	5315	
16: 4 I also could speak as ye *do:* if your **s** were	5315	
19: 2 How long will ye vex my **s,** and break me	5315	
21:25 another dieth in the bitterness of his **s,**	5315	
23:13 *what* his **s** desireth, even *that* he doeth.	5315	
24:12 and the **s** of the wounded crieth out:	5315	
27: 2 and the Almighty, *who* hath vexed my **s;**	5315	
27: 8 gained, when God taketh away his **s?**	5315	
30:15 they pursue my **s** as the wind:	5082	
30:16 now my **s** is poured out upon me; the	5315	
30:25 was *not* my **s** grieved for the poor?	5315	
31:30 mouth to sin by wishing a curse to his **s.)**	5315	
33:18 He keepeth back his **s** from the pit,	5315	
33:20 abhorreth bread, and his **s** dainty meat.	5315	
33:22 his **s** draweth near unto the grave,	5315	
33:28 He will deliver his **s** from going into	5315	
33:30 To bring back his **s** from the pit, to be	5315	
Ps 3: 2 Many *there be* which say of my **s,** *There*	5315	
6: 3 My **s** is also sore vexed: but thou,	5315	
6: 4 Return, O LORD, deliver my **s:** O save	5315	
7: 2 Lest he tear my **s** like a lion, rending *it* in	5315	
7: 5 Let the enemy persecute my **s,** and take	5315	
11: 1 how say ye to my **s,** Flee *as* a bird *to* your	5315	
11: 5 and him that loveth violence his **s** hateth.	5315	
13: 2 How long shall I take counsel in my **s,**	5315	
16: 2 *O* my **s,** thou hast said unto the LORD,	NIH	
16:10 For thou wilt not leave my **s** in hell;	5315	
17:13 deliver my **s** from the wicked, *which is*	5315	
19: 7 of the LORD *is* perfect, converting the **s:**	5315	
22:20 Deliver my **s** from the sword; my darling	5315	
22:29 and none can keep alive his own **s.**	5315	
23: 3 He restoreth my **s:** he leadeth me in	5315	
24: 4 who hath not lift up his **s** unto vanity,	5315	
25: 1 Unto thee, O LORD, do I lift up my **s.**	5315	
25:13 His **s** shall dwell at ease; and his seed	5315	
25:20 keep my **s,** and deliver me: let me not be	5315	
26: 9 Gather not my **s** with sinners, nor my life	5315	
30: 3 hast brought up my **s** from the grave;	5315	
31: 7 thou hast known my **s** in adversities;	5315	
31: 9 with grief, *yea,* my **s** and my belly.	5315	
33:19 To deliver their **s** from death, and to keep	5315	
33:20 Our **s** waiteth for the LORD: he *is* our	5315	
34: 2 My **s** shall make her boast in the LORD:	5315	
34:22 The LORD redeemeth the **s** of his	5315	
35: 3 say unto my **s,** I *am* thy salvation.	5315	
35: 4 and put to shame that seek after my **s:**	5315	
35: 7 without cause they have digged for my **s.**	5315	
35: 9 my **s** shall be joyful in the LORD: it shall	5315	
35:12 me evil for good *to* the spoiling of my **s.**	5315	
35:13 I humbled my **s** with fasting; and my	5315	
35:17 rescue my **s** from their destructions,	5315	
40:14 confounded together that seek after my **s**	5315	
41: 4 heal my **s;** for I have sinned against thee.	5315	
42: 1 so panteth my **s** after thee, O God.	5315	
42: 2 My **s** thirsteth for God, for the living God:	5315	
42: 4 these *things,* I pour out my **s** in me:	5315	
42: 5 Why art thou cast down, O my **s?**	5315	
42: 6 O my God, my **s** is cast down within me:	5315	
42:11 Why art thou cast down, O my **s?**	5315	
43: 5 Why art thou cast down, O my **s?**	5315	
44:25 For our **s** is bowed down to the dust:	5315	
49: 8 (For the redemption of their **s** is precious,	5315	
49:15 God will redeem my **s** from the power of	5315	
49:18 Though while he lived he blessed his **s:**	5315	
54: 3 me, and oppressors seek after my **s:**	5315	
54: 4 the Lord *is* with them that uphold my **s.**	5315	
55:18 He hath delivered my **s** in peace from	5315	
56: 6 mark my steps, when they wait for my **s.**	5315	
56:13 For thou hast delivered my **s** from death:	5315	
57: 1 my **s** trusteth in thee: yea, in the shadow	5315	
57: 4 My **s** *is* among lions: *and* I lie *even*	5315	
57: 6 a net for my steps; my **s** is bowed down:	5315	
59: 3 lo, they lie in wait for my **s:** the mighty	5315	
62: 1 Truly my **s** waiteth upon God: from him	5315	
62: 5 My **s,** wait thou only upon God; for my	5315	
63: 1 my **s** thirsteth for thee, my flesh longeth	5315	
63: 5 My **s** shall be satisfied as *with* marrow	5315	
63: 8 My **s** followeth hard after thee: thy right	5315	
63: 9 *that* seek my **s,** to destroy *it,* shall go	5315	
66: 9 Which holdeth our **s** in life,	5315	
66:16 will declare what he hath done for my **s.**	5315	
69: 1 for the waters are come in unto *my* **s.**	5315	
69:10 I wept, *and chastened* my **s** with fasting,	5315	
69:18 Draw nigh unto my **s,** *and* redeem it:	5315	
70: 2 and confounded that seek after my **s:**	5315	
71:10 they that lay wait for my **s** take counsel	5315	
71:13 consumed that are adversaries to my **s;**	5315	
71:23 and my **s,** which thou hast redeemed.	5315	
72:14 he shall redeem their **s** from deceit and	5315	

Ps 74:19 O deliver not the **s** of thy turtledove unto	5315	
77: 2 ceased not: my **s** refused to be comforted.	5315	
78:50 he spared not their **s** from death,	5315	
84: 2 My **s** longeth, yea, even fainteth for	5315	
86: 2 Preserve my **s;** for I *am* holy: O thou my	5315	
86: 4 Rejoice the **s** of thy servant: for unto thee,	5315	
86: 4 for unto thee, O Lord, do I lift up my **s.**	5315	
86:13 thou hast delivered my **s** from the lowest	5315	
86:14 of violent *men* have sought after my **s;**	5315	
88: 3 For my **s** is full of troubles: and my life	5315	
88:14 Lord, why castest thou off my **s?**	5315	
89:48 shall he deliver his **s** from the hand of	5315	
94:17 help, my **s** had almost dwelt in silence.	5315	
94:19 within me thy comforts delight my **s.**	5315	
94:21 together against the **s** of the righteous,	5315	
103: 1 Bless the LORD, O my **s:** and all that is	5315	
103: 2 O my **s,** and forget not all his benefits:	5315	
103:22 of his dominion: bless the LORD, O my **s.**	5315	
104: 1 Bless the LORD, O my **s.** O LORD my	5315	
104:35 Bless thou the LORD, O my **s.** Praise ye	5315	
106:15 request; but sent leanness into their **s.**	5315	
107: 5 and thirsty, their **s** fainted in them.	5315	
107: 9 For he satisfieth the longing **s,**	5315	
107: 9 and filleth the hungry **s** *with* goodness.	5315	
107:18 Their **s** abhorreth all *manner of* meat;	5315	
107:26 their **s** is melted because of trouble.	5315	
109:20 and of them that speak evil against my **s.**	5315	
109:31 save *him* from those that condemn his **s.**	5315	
116: 4 O LORD, I beseech thee, deliver my **s.**	5315	
116: 7 Return unto thy rest, O my **s;**	5315	
116: 8 For thou hast delivered my **s** from death,	5315	
119:20 My **s** breaketh for the longing *that it hath*	5315	
119:25 My **s** cleaveth unto the dust: quicken thou	5315	
119:28 My **s** melteth for heaviness: strengthen	5315	
119:81 My **s** fainteth for thy salvation: *but* I hope	5315	
119:109 My **s** *is* continually in my hand: yet do I	5315	
119:129 therefore doth my **s** keep them.	5315	
119:167 My **s** hath kept thy testimonies; and *I* love	5315	
119:175 Let my **s** live, and it shall praise thee;	5315	
120: 2 Deliver my **s,** O LORD, from lying lips,	5315	
120: 6 My **s** hath long dwelt with him that	5315	
121: 7 thee from all evil: he shall preserve thy **s.**	5315	
123: 4 Our **s** is exceedingly filled *with*	5315	
124: 4 the stream had gone over our **s:**	5315	
124: 5 the proud waters had gone over our **s.**	5315	
124: 7 Our **s** is escaped as a bird out of the snare	5315	
130: 5 **s** doth wait, and in his word do I hope.	5315	
130: 6 My **s** *waiteth* for the Lord more than they	5315	
131: 2 mother: my **s** *is even* as a weaned child.	5315	
138: 3 strengthenedst me *with* strength in my **s.**	5315	
139:14 and *that* my **s** knoweth right well.	5315	
141: 8 thee is my trust; leave not my **s** destitute.	5315	
142: 4 refuge failed me; no man cared for my **s.**	5315	
142: 7 Bring my **s** out of prison, that *I* may praise	5315	
143: 3 For the enemy hath persecuted my **s;**	5315	
143: 6 my **s** *thirsteth* after thee, as a thirsty land.	5315	
143: 8 I trust: walk; for I lift up my **s** unto thee.	5315	
143:11 for thy righteousness' sake bring my **s** out	5315	
143:12 and destroy all them that afflict my **s:**	5315	
146: 1 ye the LORD. Praise the LORD, O my **s.**	5315	
Pr 2:10 and knowledge is pleasant unto thy **s;**	5315	
3:22 So shall they be life unto thy **s,** and grace	5315	
6:30 if he steal to satisfy his **s** when he is	5315	
6:32 he that doeth it destroyeth his own **s.**	5315	
8:36 sinneth *against* me wrongeth his own **s:**	5315	
10: 3 The LORD will not suffer the **s** of	5315	
11:17 merciful man doeth good to his own **s:**	5315	
11:25 liberal **s** shall be made fat: and he that	5315	
13: 2 **s** of the transgressors *shall eat* violence.	5315	
13: 4 The **s** of the sluggard desireth,	5315	
13: 4 but the **s** of the diligent shall be made fat.	5315	
13:19 The desire accomplished is sweet to the **s:**	5315	
13:25 righteous eateth to the satisfying of his **s:**	5315	
15:32 refuseth instruction despiseth his own **s:**	5315	
16:17 he that keepeth his way preserveth his **s.**	5315	
16:24 sweet to the **s,** and health to the bones.	5315	
18: 7 and his lips *are* the snare of his **s.**	5315	
19: 2 *that* the **s** be without knowledge, *it is*	5315	
19: 8 He that getteth wisdom loveth his own **s:**	5315	
19:15 and an idle **s** shall suffer hunger.	5315	
19:16 the commandment keepeth his own **s;**	5315	
19:18 and let not thy **s** spare for his crying.	5315	
20: 2 him to anger sinneth *against* his own **s.**	5315	
21:10 The **s** of the wicked desireth evil:	5315	
21:23 his tongue keepeth his **s** from troubles.	5315	
22: 5 he that doth keep his **s** shall be far from	5315	
22:23 and spoil the **s** of those that spoiled them.	5315	
22:25 learn his ways, and get a snare to thy **s.**	5315	
23:14 the rod, and shalt deliver his **s** from hell.	5315	
24:12 consider *it?* and he that keepeth thy **s,**	5315	
24:14 the knowledge of wisdom be unto thy **s:**	5315	
25:13 for he refresheth the **s** of his masters.	5315	
25:25 *As* cold waters to a thirsty **s,** so *is* good	5315	
27: 7 The full **s** loatheth a honeycomb; but *to*	5315	
27: 7 the hungry **s** every bitter *thing* is sweet.	5315	
29:10 hate the upright: but the just seek his **s.**	5315	
29:17 yea, he shall give delight unto thy **s.**	5315	
29:24 is partner with a thief hateth his own **s:**	5315	
Ecc 2:24 *that* he should make his **s** enjoy good in	5315	
4: 8 do I labour, and bereave my **s** of good?	5315	
6: 2 that he wanteth nothing for his **s** of all	5315	
6: 3 his **s** be not filled with good, and also *that*	5315	
7:28 Which yet my **s** seeketh, but I find not:	5315	
SS 1: 7 Tell me, O thou whom my **s** loveth,	5315	
3: 1 my bed I sought *him* whom my **s** loveth:	5315	

SS 3: 2 I will seek *him* whom my **s** loveth:	5315	
3: 3 *to whom I said,* Saw ye whom my **s**	5315	
3: 4 but I found *him* whom my **s** loveth:	5315	
5: 6 my **s** failed when he spake: I sought him,	5315	
6:12 my **s** made me *like* the chariots of	5315	
Isa 1:14 and your appointed feasts my **s** hateth:	5315	
3: 9 Woe unto their **s!** for they have rewarded	5315	
10:18 and of his fruitful field, both **s** and body;	5315	
26: 8 the desire of *our* **s** *is* to thy name, and to	5315	
26: 9 my **s** have I desired thee in the night;	5315	
29: 8 but he awaketh, and his **s** is empty:	5315	
29: 8 *he is* faint, and his **s** hath appetite:	5315	
32: 6 to make empty the **s** of the hungry,	5315	
38:15 all my years in the bitterness of my **s.**	5315	
38:17 thou hast in love to my **s** *delivered it* from	5315	
42: 1 mine elect, *in whom* my **s** delighteth;	5315	
44:20 that he cannot deliver his **s,** nor say, *Is*	5315	
51:23 which have said to thy **s,** Bow down,	5315	
53:10 when thou shalt make his **s** an offering for	5315	
53:11 He shall see of the travail of his **s,**	5315	
53:12 he hath poured out his **s** unto death:	5315	
55: 2 and let your **s** delight itself in fatness.	5315	
55: 3 and your **s** shall live; and I will make	5315	
58: 3 *wherefore* have we afflicted our **s,**	5315	
58: 5 day for a man to afflict his **s?** *is it* to bow	5315	
58:10 *if* thou draw out thy **s** to the hungry,	5315	
58:10 to the hungry, and satisfy the afflicted **s;**	5315	
58:11 satisfy thy **s** in drought, and make fat thy	5315	
61:10 my **s** shall be joyful in my God;	5315	
66: 3 their **s** delighteth in their abominations.	5315	
Jer 4:10 whereas the sword reacheth unto the **s).**	5315	
4:19 peace, because thou hast heard, O my **s,**	5315	
4:31 for my **s** is wearied because of murderers.	5315	
5: 9 not my **s** be avenged on such a nation	5315	
5:29 not my **s** be avenged on such a nation	5315	
6: 8 O Jerusalem, lest my **s** depart from thee;	5315	
9: 9 not my **s** be avenged on such a nation?	5315	
12: 7 I have given the dearly beloved of my **s**	5315	
13:17 my **s** shall weep in secret places for *your*	5315	
14:19 hath thy **s** lothed Zion? why hast thou	5315	
18:20 for they have digged a pit for my **s.**	5315	
20:13 he hath delivered the **s** of the poor from	5315	
31:12 their **s** shall be as a watered garden;	5315	
31:14 I will satiate the **s** of the priests with	5315	
31:25 I have satiated the weary **s,** and I have	5315	
31:25 and I have replenished every sorrowful **s.**	5315	
32:41 my whole heart and with my whole **s.**	5315	
38:16 *As* the LORD liveth, that made us this **s,**	5315	
38:17 thy **s** shall live, and this city shall not be	5315	
38:20 be well unto thee, and thy **s** shall live.	5315	
50:19 his **s** shall be satisfied upon mount	5315	
51: 6 of Babylon, and deliver every man his **s:**	5315	
51:45 deliver ye every man his **s** from the fierce	5315	
La 1:11 pleasant things for meat to relieve the **s:**	5315	
1:16 comforter that *should* relieve my **s** is far	5315	
2:12 when their **s** was poured out into their	5315	
3:17 hast removed my **s** far off from peace:	5315	
3:20 My **s** hath *them* still in remembrance,	5315	
3:24 The LORD *is* my portion, saith my **s;**	5315	
3:25 wait for him, to the **s** *that* seeketh him.	5315	
3:58 thou hast pleaded the causes of my **s;**	5315	
Eze 3:19 his iniquity; but thou hast delivered thy **s.**	5315	
3:21 is warned; also thou hast delivered thy **s.**	5315	
4:14 behold, my **s** *hath* not *been* polluted:	5315	
18: 4 as the **s** of the father, so also the soul of	5315	
18: 4 the father, so also the **s** of the son *is* mine:	5315	
18: 4 son *is* mine: the **s** that sinneth, it shall die.	5315	
18:20 The **s** that sinneth, it shall die. The son	5315	
18:27 lawful and right, he shall save his **s** alive.	5315	
24:21 your eyes, and that which your **s** pitieth;	5315	
33: 5 he that taketh warning shall deliver his **s.**	5315	
33: 9 his iniquity; but thou hast delivered thy **s.**	5315	
Hos 9: 4 for their bread for their **s** shall not come	5315	
Jnh 2: 5 compassed me about, *even* to the **s:**	5315	
2: 7 When my **s** fainted within me I	5315	
Mic 6: 7 the fruit of my body *for* the sin of my **s?**	5315	
7: 1 to eat: my **s** desired the firstripe fruit.	5315	
Hab 2: 4 his **s** *which* is lifted up is not upright in	5315	
2:10 people, and *hast* sinned *against* thy **s.**	5315	
Zec 11: 8 my **s** lothed them, and their soul also	5315	
11: 8 them, and their **s** also abhorred me.	5315	
Mt 10:28 kill the body, but are not able to kill the **s:**	5590	
10:28 fear him which is able to destroy both **s**	5590	
12:18 beloved, in whom my **s** is well pleased:	5590	
16:26 the whole world, and lose his own **s?**	5590	
16:26 shall a man give in exchange for his **s?**	5590	
22:37 and with all thy **s,** and with all thy mind.	5590	
26:38 My **s** is exceeding sorrowful, *even* unto	5590	
Mk 8:36 the whole world, and lose his own **s?**	5590	
8:37 shall a man give in exchange for his **s?**	5590	
12:30 and with all thy **s,** and with all thy mind,	5590	
12:33 with all the **s,** and with all the strength,	5590	
14:34 My **s** is exceeding sorrowful unto death:	5590	
Lk 1:46 Mary said, My **s** doth magnify the Lord,	5590	
2:35 a sword shall pierce through thy own **s**	5590	
10:27 with all thy **s,** and with all thy strength,	5590	
12:19 And I will say to my **s,** Soul, thou hast	5590	
12:19 And I will say to my soul, **s,** thou hast	5590	
12:20 this night thy **s** shall be required of thee:	5590	
Jn 12:27 Now is my **s** troubled; and what shall I say?	5590	
Ac 2:27 Because thou wilt not leave my **s** in hell,	5590	
2:31 of Christ, that his **s** was not left in hell,	5590	
2:43 And fear came upon every **s:**	5590	
3:23 And it shall come to pass, *that* every **s,**	5590	
4:32 believed were of one heart and of one **s:**	5590	

S

Ro 2: 9 upon every **s** of man that doeth evil, 5590
 13: 1 Let every **s** be subject unto the higher 5590
1Co 15:45 The first man Adam was made a living **s**; 5590
2Co 1:23 I call God for a record upon my **s**, 5590
1Th 5:23 *I pray God* your whole spirit and **s** and 5590
Heb 4:12 piercing even to the dividing asunder of **s** 5590
 6:19 hope we have as an anchor of the **s**, 5590
 10:38 my **s** shall have no pleasure in him. 5590
 10:39 *them* that believe to the saving of the **s**. 5590
Jas 5:20 error of his way shall save a **s** from death, 5590
1Pe 2:11 fleshly lusts, which war against the **s**; 5590
2Pe 2: 8 vexed *his* righteous **s** from day to day 5590
3Jn 1: 2 be in health, even as thy **s** prospereth. 5590
Rev 16: 3 and every living **s** died in the sea. 5590
 18:14 And the fruits that thy **s** lusted after are 5590

SOUL'S (1) [SOUL]
Job 16: 4 as ye *do*: if your soul were in my **s** stead, 5315

SOULS (78) [SOUL]
Ge 12: 5 and the **s** that they had gotten in Haran; 5315
 46:15 all the **s** of his sons and his daughters 5315
 46:18 these she bare unto Jacob, *even* sixteen **s**. 5315
 46:22 born to Jacob: all the **s** *were* fourteen. 5315
 46:25 these unto Jacob: all the **s** *were* seven. 5315
 46:26 All the **s** that came with Jacob into Egypt, 5315
 46:26 all the **s** *were* threescore and six; 5315
 46:27 were born him in Egypt, *were* two **s**: 5315
 46:27 all the **s** of the house of Jacob, which 5315
Ex 1: 5 the **s** that came *out of* the loins of Jacob 5315
 1: 5 *out of* the loins of Jacob were seventy **s**: 5315
 12: 4 take *it* according to the number of the **s**; 5315
 30:15 to make an atonement for your **s**. 5315
 30:16 to make an atonement for your **s**. 5315
Lev 16:29 ye shall afflict your **s**, and do no work at 5315
 16:31 ye shall afflict your **s**, *by* a statute for ever. 5315
 17:11 altar to make an atonement for your **s**: 5315
 18:29 the **s** that commit *them* shall be cut off 5315
 20:25 ye shall not make your **s** abominable by 5315
 23:27 ye shall afflict your **s**, and offer an offering 5315
 23:32 sabbath of rest, and ye shall afflict your **s**: 5315
Nu 16:38 of these sinners against their own **s**, 5315
 29: 7 and ye shall afflict your **s**: 5315
 30: 9 wherewith they have bound their **s**, 5315
 31:50 to make an atonement for our **s** before 5315
Jos 10:28 them, and all the **s** that *were* therein; 5315
 10:30 the sword, and all the **s** that *were* therein; 5315
 10:32 the sword, and all the **s** that *were* therein, 5315
 10:35 all the **s** that *were* therein he utterly 5315
 10:37 and all the **s** that *were* therein. 5315
 10:37 it utterly, and all the **s** that *were* therein. 5315
 10:39 destroyed all the **s** that *were* therein; 5315
 11:11 they smote all the **s** that *were* therein 5315
 23:14 know in all your hearts and in all your **s**, 5315
1Sa 25:29 s of thine enemies, them shall he sling 5315
Ps 72:13 needy, and shall save the **s** of the needy. 5315
 97:10 he preserveth the **s** of his saints; 5315
Pr 11:30 tree of life; and he that winneth **s** *is* wise. 5315
 14:25 true witness delivereth **s**: but a deceitful 5315
Isa 57:16 before me, and the **s** *which* I have made. 5397
Jer 2:34 in thy skirts is found the blood of the **s** 5315
 6:16 and ye shall find rest for your **s**. 5315
 26:19 *might* we procure great evil against our **s**. 5315
 44: 7 commit ye *this* great evil against your **s**, 5315
La 1:19 they sought their meat, to relieve their **s**. 5315
Eze 7:19 they shall not satisfy their **s**, neither fill 5315
 13:18 upon the head of every stature to hunt **s**! 5315
 13:18 Will ye hunt the **s** of my people, and will 5315
 13:18 ye save the **s** alive *that come* unto you? 5315
 13:19 slay the **s** that should not die, and to save 5315
 13:19 to save the **s** alive that should not live, 5315
 13:20 where*with* ye there hunt the **s** to make 5315
 13:20 from your arms, and will let the **s** go, 5315
 13:20 *even* the **s** that ye hunt to make *them* fly. 5315
 14:14 *but* their own **s** by their righteousness. 5315
 14:20 deliver their own **s** by their righteousness. 5315
 18: 4 Behold, all **s** are mine; as the soul of 5315
 22:25 they have devoured **s**; they have taken 5315
 22:27 to shed blood, *and* to destroy **s**, to get 5315
Mt 11:29 heart: and ye shall find rest unto your **s**. 5590
Lk 21:19 In your patience possess ye your **s**. 5590
Ac 2:41 added *unto* them about three thousand **s**. 5590
 7:14 all his kindred, threescore and fifteen **s**. 5590
 14:22 Confirming the **s** of the disciples, 5590
 15:24 subverting your **s**, saying, Ye *must be* 5590
 27:37 two hundred threescore *and* sixteen **s**. 5590
1Th 2: 8 but also our own **s**, because ye were dear 5590
Heb 13:17 for they watch for your **s**, as they that 5590
Jas 1:21 which is able to save your **s**. 5590
1Pe 1: 9 of your faith, *even* the salvation of *your* **s**. 5590
 1:22 Seeing ye have purified your **s** in obeying 5590
 2:25 unto the Shepherd and Bishop of your **s**. 5590
 3:20 that is, eight **s** were saved by water. 5590
 4:19 keeping of their **s** *to him* in well doing, 5590
2Pe 2:14 cease from sin; beguiling unstable **s**: 5590
Rev 6: 9 I saw under the altar the **s** of them that 5590
 18:13 and chariots, and slaves, and **s** of men. 5590
 20: 4 *I saw* the **s** of them that were beheaded 5590

SOUND (89) [SOUNDED, SOUNDETH, SOUNDING, SOUNDNESS, SOUNDS]
Ex 28:35 his **s** shall be heard when he goeth in 6963
Lev 25: 9 thou **cause** the trumpet of the jubile **to s** 5674
 25: 9 **make** the trumpet **s** throughout all your 5674
 26:36 the **s** of a shaken leaf shall chase them; 6963

Nu 10: 7 shall blow, but you shall not **s an alarm**. 7321
Jos 6: 5 *and* when ye hear the **s** of the trumpet, 6963
 6:20 the people heard the **s** of the trumpet, 6963
2Sa 5:24 when thou hearest the **s** of a going in 6963
 6:15 and with the **s** of the trumpet. 6963
 15:10 As soon as ye hear the **s** of the trumpet, 6963
1Ki 1:40 so that the earth rent with the **s** of them. 6963
 1:41 when Joab heard the **s** of the trumpet, 6963
 14: 6 *so*, when Ahijah heard the **s** of her feet, 6963
 18:41 for *there is* a **s** of abundance of rain. 6963
2Ki 6:32 not the **s** of his master's feet behind him? 6963
1Ch 14:15 when thou shalt hear a **s** of going in 6963
 15:19 *appointed* to **s** with cymbals of brass; 8085
 15:28 with **s** of the cornet, and with trumpets, 6963
 16: 5 but Asaph **made a s** with cymbals; 8085
 16:42 cymbals for those that should **make a s**, 8085
2Ch 5:13 to make one **s** to be heard in praising and 6963
Ne 4:20 *therefore* ye hear the **s** of the trumpet, 6963
Job 15:21 A dreadful **s** *is* in his ears: in prosperity 6963
 21:12 harp, and rejoice at the **s** of the organ. 6963
 37: 2 and the **s** *that* goeth out of his mouth. 1899
 39:24 neither believeth he that *it is* the **s** of 6963
Ps 47: 5 shout, the Lᴏʀᴅ with the **s** of a trumpet. 6963
 77:17 the skies sent out a **s**: thine arrows also 6963
 89:15 *is* the people that know the **joyful s**: 8643
 92: 3 psaltery; upon the harp with a **solemn s**. 1902
 98: 6 of cornet make a joyful noise before 6963
 119:80 Let my heart be **s** in thy statutes; that I be 8549
 150: 3 Praise him with the **s** of the trumpet: 8629
Pr 2: 7 He layeth up **s wisdom** for the righteous: 8454
 3:21 eyes: keep **s wisdom** and discretion: 8454
 8:14 Counsel *is* mine, and **s wisdom**: I *am* 8454
 14:30 A **s** heart *is* the life of the flesh: 4832
Ecc 12: 4 when the **s** of the grinding is low, 6963
Isa 16:11 Wherefore my bowels shall **s** like a harp 1993
Jer 4:19 heard, O my soul, the **s** of the trumpet, 6963
 4:21 standard, *and* hear the **s** of the trumpet? 6963
 6:17 *saying*, Hearken to the **s** of the trumpet. 6963
 8:16 the whole land trembled at the **s** of 6963
 25:10 the **s** of the millstones, and the light of 6963
 42:14 nor hear the **s** of the trumpet, nor have 6963
 48:36 Therefore mine heart shall **s** for Moab 1993
 48:36 mine heart shall **s** like pipes for the men 1993
 50:22 A **s** of battle *is* in the land, and of great 6963
 51:54 As of a cry *cometh* from Babylon, 6963
Eze 10: 5 of the cherubims' wings was heard 6963
 26:13 the **s** of thy harps shall be no more heard. 6963
 26:15 not the isles shake at the **s** of thy fall, 6963
 27:28 suburbs shall shake at the **s** of the cry 6963
 31:16 I made the nations to shake at the **s** of his 6963
 33: 4 whosoever heareth the **s** of the trumpet, 6963
 33: 5 He heard the **s** of the trumpet, and took 6963
Da 3: 5 That at what time ye hear the **s** of 7032
 3: 7 when all the people heard the **s** of 7032
 3:10 that every man that shall hear the **s** of 7032
 3:15 at what time ye hear the **s** of the cornet, 7032
Joel 2: 1 and **s an alarm** in my holy mountain: 7321
Am 2: 2 *and* with the **s** of the trumpet: 6963
 6: 5 That chant to the **s** of the viol, *and* invent 6310
Mt 6: 2 alms, do not **s a trumpet** before thee, 4537
 24:31 he shall send his angels with a great **s** 5456
Lk 15:27 because he hath received him *safe and* **s**. 5198
Jn 3: 8 thou hearest the **s** thereof, but canst not 5456
Ac 2: 2 suddenly there came a **s** from heaven 2279
Ro 10:18 their **s** went into all the earth, 5353
1Co 14: 7 *And* even *things* without life giving **s**, 5456
 14: 8 For if the trumpet give an uncertain **s**, 5456
 15:52 the **trumpet** shall **s**, and the dead shall 4537
1Ti 1:10 other *thing* that is contrary to **s** doctrine; 5198
2Ti 1: 7 of power, and of love, and of a **s mind**. 4995
 1:13 Hold fast the form of **s** words, which thou 5198
 4: 3 when they will not endure **s** doctrine; 5198
Tit 1: 9 that he may be able by **s** doctrine both to 5198
 1:13 that they may be in the faith; 5198
 2: 1 speak thou *the things* which become **s** 5198
 2: 2 grave, temperate, **s** in faith, in charity, 5198
 2: 8 **S** speech that cannot be condemned; that 5199
Heb 12:19 And the **s** of a trumpet, and the voice of 2279
Rev 1:15 and his voice as the **s** of many waters. 5456
 8: 6 seven trumpets prepared themselves to **s**. 4537
 8:13 of the three angels, which are yet to **s**. 4537
 9: 9 the **s** of their wings *was* as the sound of 5456
 9: 9 the sound of their wings *was* as the **s** of 5456
 10: 7 when he shall begin to **s**, the mystery of 4537
 18:22 the **s** of a millstone shall be heard no more 5456

SOUNDED (18) [SOUND]
Ex 19:19 when the voice of the trumpet **s long**, 1980
1Sa 20:12 when I have **s** my father about to morrow 2713
2Ch 5:12 and the priests **trumpets** before them, 2690
 13:14 and the priests **s** with the trumpets. 2690
 23:13 of the land rejoiced, and **s** with trumpets, 8628
 29:28 the singers sang, and the trumpeters **s**: 2690
Ne 4:18 And he that **s** the trumpet *was* by me. 8628
Lk 1:44 as soon as the voice of thy salutation **s** in 1096
Ac 27:28 And **s**, and found *it* twenty fathoms: 1001
 27:28 they again, and found *it* fifteen fathoms. 1001
1Th 1: 8 For from you **s out** the word of the Lord 1837
Rev 8: 7 The first angel **s**, and there followed hail 4537
 8: 8 And the second angel **s**, and as *it were* a 4537
 8:10 the third angel **s**, and there fell a great 4537
 8:12 the fourth angel **s**, and the third *part* of 4537
 9: 1 And the fifth angel **s**, and I saw a star fall 4537
 9:13 And the sixth angel **s**, and I heard a voice 4537
 11:15 And the seventh angel **s**; and there were 4537

SOUNDETH (1) [SOUND]
Ex 19:13 when the trumpet **s long**, they shall come 4900

SOUNDING (7) [SOUND]
1Ch 15:16 psalteries and harps and cymbals, **s**, 8085
2Ch 5:12 and twenty priests **s** with trumpets:) 2690
 13:12 his priests with **s** trumpets to cry alarm 8643
Ps 150: 5 praise him upon the **high s** cymbals. 8643
Isa 63:15 the **s** of thy bowels and of thy mercies 1995
Eze 7: 7 and not the **s again** of the mountains. 1906
1Co 13: 1 become *as* **s** brass, or a tinkling 2278

SOUNDNESS (4) [SOUND]
Ps 38: 3 *There is* no **s** in my flesh because of thine 4974
 38: 7 and *there is* no **s** in my flesh. 4974
Isa 1: 6 even unto the head *there is* no **s** in it; 4974
Ac 3:16 this **perfect s** in the presence of you all. 3647

SOUNDS (1) [SOUND]
1Co 14: 7 except they give a distinction in the **s**, 5353

SOUR (5)
Isa 18: 5 and the **s** grape is ripening in the flower, 1155
Jer 31:29 The fathers have eaten a **s grape**, 1155
 31:30 man that eateth the **s grape**, his teeth 1155
Eze 18: 2 The fathers have eaten **s grapes**, 1155
Hos 4:18 Their drink is **s**; they have committed 5493

SOUTH (143) [SOUTHWARD]
Ge 12: 9 going on still toward the **s**. 5045
 13: 1 that he had, and Lot with him, into the **s**. 5045
 13: 3 he went on his journeys from the **s** even 5045
 20: 1 from thence toward the **s** country, 5045
 24:62 for he dwelt in the **s** country. 5045
 28:14 to the east, and to the north, and to the **s**: 5045
Ex 26:18 boards on the **s** side southward. 5045+1886.5
 26:35 the side of the tabernacle toward the **s**: 8486
 27: 9 for the **s** side southward *there shall be* 5045
 36:23 twenty boards for the **s** side southward: 5045
 36: 9 on the **s** side southward the hangings of 5045
Nu 2:10 On the **s** side *shall be* the standard of 8486
 10: 6 the camps that lie on the **s** side shall take 8486
 13:22 they ascended by the **s**, and came unto 5045
 13:29 The Amalekites dwell in the land of the **s**, 5045
 21: 1 Arad the Canaanite, which dwelt *in* the **s**, 5045
 33:40 dwelt in the **s** in the land of Canaan, 5045
 34: 3 s quarter shall be from the wilderness 5045
 34: 3 s border shall be the outmost coast of 5045
 34: 4 your border shall turn from the **s** to 5045
 34: 4 the going forth thereof shall be from the **s** 5045
 35: 5 on the **s** side two thousand cubits, 5045
Dt 1: 7 the vale, and in the **s**, and by the sea side, 5045
 33:23 possess thou the west and the **s**. 1864
 34: 3 s, and the plain of the valley of Jericho, 5045
Jos 10:40 the **s**, and of the vale, and of the springs, 5045
 11: 2 of the plains of Cinneroth, and in 5045
 11:16 all the **s** country, and all the land of 5045
 12: 3 and from the **s**, under Ashdoth-pisgah: 8486
 12: 8 the **s** country; the Hittites, the Amorites, 8486
 13: 4 From the **s**, all the land of the Canaanites, 8486
 15: 1 *was* the uttermost part of the **s** coast. 8486
 15: 2 s border was from the shore of the salt 5045
 15: 3 it went out to the **s** side 5045
 15: 3 ascended up on the **s** side unto 5045
 15: 4 were at the sea: this shall be your **s** coast. 5045
 15: 7 which *is* on the **s** side of the river: 5045
 15: 8 unto the **s** side of the Jebusite; 4480+5045
 15:19 a blessing; for thou hast given me a **s** land; 5045
 18: 5 Judah shall abide in their coast on the **s**, 5045
 18:13 near the hill that *lieth* on the **s** side of 5045
 18:15 the **s** quarter *was* from the end of 5045+1886.5
 18:16 to the side of Jebusi on the **s**, 5045
 18:19 bay of the salt sea at the **s** end of Jordan: 5045
 18:19 south end of Jordan: this *was* the **s** coast. 5045
 19: 8 cities to Baalath-beer, Ramath of the **s**. 5045
 19:34 reacheth to Zebulun on the **s** side, 5045
Jdg 1: 9 and in the **s**, and in the valley. 5045
 1:15 for thou hast given me a **s** land; give me 5045
 1:16 of Judah, which *lieth* in the **s** of Arad; 5045
 21:19 to Shechem, and on the **s** of Lebonah. 5045
1Sa 20:41 David arose out of a *place* toward the **s**, 5045
 23:19 Hachilah, which *is* on the **s** of Jeshimon? 3225
 23:24 Maon, in the plain on the **s** of Jeshimon. 3225
 27:10 Against the **s** of Judah, and against 5045
 27:10 against the **s** of the Jerahmeelites, 5045
 27:10 and against the **s** of the Kenites. 5045
 30: 1 that the Amalekites had invaded the **s**, 5045
 30:14 We made an invasion *upon* the **s** of 5045
 30:14 to Judah, and upon the **s** of Caleb; 5045
 30:27 to *them* which *were* in the **s** of Ramoth, 5045
2Sa 24: 7 they went out to the **s** of Judah, *even* to 5045
1Ki 7:25 three looking toward the **s**, 5045
 7:39 of the house eastward over against the **s**. 5045
1Ch 9:24 toward the east, west, north, and **s**. 5045
2Ch 4: 4 three looking toward the **s**, 5045
 4:10 the east end, over against the **s**. 5045+1886.5
 28:18 of the **s** of Judah, and had taken 5045
Job 9: 9 and Pleiades, and the chambers of the **s**. 8486
 37: 9 Out of the **s** cometh the whirlwind: 2315
 37:17 he quieteth the earth by the **s** *wind*? 1864
 39:26 *and* stretch her wings toward the **s**? 8486
Ps 75: 6 east, nor from the west, nor from the **s**. 4057
 78:26 by his power he brought in the **s wind**. 8486
 89:12 The north and the **s** thou hast created 3225
 107: 3 the west, from the north, and from the **s**. 3220

S

Ps 126: 4 O Lord, as the streams in the **s**.	5045

Ecc 1: 6 The wind goeth toward the **s**, | 1864
1: 6 and turneth about unto the north; |
11: 3 if the tree fall toward the **s**, or toward | 1864

SS 4:16 Awake, O north wind; and come thou **s**; | 8486

Isa 21: 1 As whirlwinds in the **s** pass through; | 5045
30: 6 The burden of the beasts of the **s**: into | 5045
43: 6 Give *up*; and to the **s**, Keep not back: | 8486

Jer 13:19 The cities of the **s** shall be shut up, | 5045
17:26 and from the mountains, and from the **s**, | 5045
32:44 of the valley, and in the cities of the **s**, | 5045
33:13 in the cities of the **s**, and in the land of | 5045

Eze 20:46 set thy face toward the **s**, | 8486+1886.5
20:46 drop *thy* word toward the **s**, | 1864
20:46 prophesy against the forest of the **s** field; | 5045
20:47 say to the forest of the **s**, Hear the word | 5045
20:47 all faces from the **s** to the north shall be | 5045
21: 4 against all flesh from the **s** *to* the north: | 5045
40: 2 which *was* as the frame of a city on the **s**. | 5045
40:24 After that he brought me toward the **s**, | 1864
40:24 the south, and behold a gate toward the **s**: | 1864
40:27 a gate in the inner court toward the **s**: | 1864
40:27 measured from gate to gate toward the **s** | 1864
40:28 he brought me to the inner court by the **s** | 1864
40:28 he measured the **s** gate according to these | 1864
40:44 and their prospect *was* toward the **s**: | 1864
40:45 whose prospect *is* toward the **s**, | 1864
41:11 the north, and another door toward the **s**: | 5045
42:12 the **s** *was* a door in the head of the way, | 1864
42:13 The north chambers *and* the **s** chambers, | 1864
42:18 measured the **s** side, five hundred reeds, | 1864
46: 9 shall go out *by* the way of the **s** gate; | 5045
46: 9 he that entereth *by* the way of the **s** gate | 5045
47: 1 of the house, at the **s** *side* of the altar. | 5045
47:19 is the **s** side southward, from Tamar *even* to | 5045
47:19 *is* the **s** side southward. 8486+1886.5+1886.5

Da 8: 9 toward the **s**, and toward the east, | 5045
48:10 toward the **s** five and twenty thousand *in* | 5045
48:16 the **s** side four thousand and five hundred, | 5045
48:17 toward the **s** two hundred and fifty, | 5045
48:28 border of Gad, at the **s** side southward, | 5045
48:33 the **s** side four thousand and five hundred | 5045

Da 8: 9 toward the **s**, and toward the east, | 5045
11: 5 the king of the **s** shall be strong, *and one* | 5045
11: 6 the king's daughter of the **s** shall come | 5045
11: 9 So the king of the **s** shall come into *his* | 5045
11:11 the king of the **s** shall be moved with | 5045
11:14 many stand up against the king of the **s**: | 5045
11:15 the arms of the **s** shall not withstand, | 5045
11:25 his courage against the king of the **s** with | 5045
11:25 king of the **s** shall be stirred up to battle | 5045
11:29 he shall return, and come toward the **s**; | 5045
11:40 the time of the end shall the king of the **s** | 5045

Ob 1:19 *they* of the **s** shall possess the mount of | 5045
1:20 shall possess the cities of the **s**. | 5045

Zec 6: 6 the grisled go forth toward the **s** country. | 8486
7: 7 when *men* inhabited the **s**, and the plain? | 5045
9:14 and shall go with whirlwinds of the **s**. | 8486
14: 4 the north, and half of it toward the **s**. | 5045
14:10 from Geba to Rimmon **s** of Jerusalem: | 5045

Mt 12:42 *The* queen of the **s** shall rise up in | 3558
Lk 11:31 *The* queen of the **s** shall rise up in | 3558
12:55 when ye see the **s** wind blow, ye say, | 3558
13:29 and *from* the **s**, and shall sit down in | 3558

Ac 8:26 go toward the **s** unto the way that goeth | 3314
27:12 lieth toward the **s** west and north west. | 3047
27:13 And when the **s** wind blew softly, | 3558
28:13 and after one day the **s** wind blew, | 3558

Rev 21:13 the three gates; and on the west three | 3558

SOUTHWARD (24) [SOUTH]

Ge 13:14 **s**, and eastward, and westward: | 5045+1886.5

Ex 26:18 boards on the south side **s**. | 8486+1886.5
27: 9 for the south side *there shall be* | 8486+1886.5
36:23 boards for the south side **s**: | 8486+1886.5
38: 9 on the south side the hangings | 8486+1886.5
40:24 on the side of the tabernacle **s**. | 5045+1886.5

Nu 3:29 on the side of the tabernacle **s**. | 8486+1886.5
13:17 Get you up this *way* **s**, | 5045+871.1+1886.1

Dt 3:27 **s**, and eastward, and behold it | 8486+1886.5

Jos 15: 1 the wilderness of Zin **s** *was* | 5045+1886.5
15: 2 from the bay that looketh **s**: | 5045+1886.5
15:21 coast of Edom **s** were Kabzeel, | 5045+1886.5
17: 9 the river Kanah, **s** of the river: | 5045+1886.5
17:10 **S** it was Ephraim's, | 5045+1886.5
18:13 side of Luz, which *is* Beth-el, **s**; | 5045+1886.5
18:14 the corner of the sea **s**, | 5045+1886.5
18:14 that *lieth* before Beth-horon **s**, | 5045+1886.5

1Sa 14: 5 the other **s** over against Gibeah. | 4480+5045

1Ch 26:15 To Obed-edom; and to his sons | 5045+1886.5
26:17 **s** four a day, and toward Asuppim | 5045+1886.5

Eze 47:19 the south side, from Tamar | 8486+1886.5
47:19 the great sea. And *this is* the south side | 5045
48:28 of Gad, at the south side **s**, | 8486+1886.5

Da 8: 4 and northward, and **s**; | 5045+1886.5

SOW (37) [SEW, SOWED, SOWEDST, SOWER, SOWEST, SOWETH, SOWING, SOWN]

Ge 47:23 *is* seed for you, and ye shall **s** the land. | 2232

Ex 23:10 six years thou shalt **s** thy land, | 2232

Lev 19:19 shalt not **s** thy field **with** mingled **seed**: |
25: 3 Six years thou shalt **s** thy field, | 2232
25: 4 thou shalt neither **s** thy field, nor prune | 2232
25:11 ye shall not **s**, neither reap that which | 2232
25:20 behold, we shall not **s**, nor gather in our | 2232
25:22 ye shall **s** the eighth year, and eat *yet* of | 2232
26:16 ye shall **s** your seed in vain, for your | 2232

Dt 22: 9 not **s** thy vineyard with divers **seeds**:	2232

2Ki 19:29 in the third year **s** ye, and reap, | 2232

Job 4: 8 and wickedness, reap the same. | 2232
31: 8 *Then* let me **s**, and let another eat; yea, | 2232

Ps 107:37 **s** the fields, and plant vineyards, which | 2232
126: 5 They that **s** in tears shall reap in joy. | 2232

Ecc 11: 4 He that observeth the wind shall not **s**; | 2232
11: 6 In the morning **s** thy seed, and in | 2232

Isa 28:24 Doth the plowman plow all day to **s**? | 2232
30:23 that thou shalt **s** the ground withal; | 2232
32:20 Blessed *are* ye that **s** beside all waters, | 2232
37:30 in the third year **s** ye, and reap, | 2232

Jer 4: 3 fallow ground, and **s** not among thorns. | 2232
31:27 that I will **s** the house of Israel and | 2232
35: 7 nor **s** seed, nor plant vineyard, nor have | 2232

Hos 2:23 I will **s** her unto me in the earth; and I | 2232
10:12 **S** to yourselves in righteousness, reap in | 2232

Mic 6:15 Thou shalt **s**, but thou shalt not reap; | 2232

Zec 10: 9 I will **s** them among the people: and they | 2232

Mt 6:26 for they **s** not, neither do they reap, | 4687
13: 3 saying, Behold, a sower went forth to **s**; | 4687
13:27 didst not thou **s** good seed in thy field? | 4687

Mk 4: 3 Behold, there went out a sower to **s**: | 4687

Lk 8: 5 A sower went out to **s** his seed: and as he | 4687
12:24 for they neither **s** nor reap; which neither | 4687
19:21 down, and reapest that thou didst not **s**. | 4687
19:22 not down, and reaping that I did not **s**: | 4687

2Pe 2:22 The **s** that was washed to *her* wallowing | 5300

SOWED (10) [SOW]

Ge 26:12 Isaac **s** in that land, and received in | 2232

Jdg 9:45 beat down the city, and **s** it *with* salt. | 2232

Mt 13: 4 when he **s**, some **seeds** fell by the way | 4687
13:24 a man which **s** good seed in his field: | 4687
13:25 came and **s** tares among the wheat, | 4687
13:31 which a man took, and **s** in his field: | 4687
13:39 The enemy that **s** them is the devil; | 4687
25:26 thou knewest that I reap where I **s** not, | 4687

Mk 4: 4 And it came to pass, as *he* **s**, some fell by | 4687

Lk 8: 5 and as he **s**, some fell by the way side; | 4687

SOWEDST (1) [SOW]

Dt 11:10 where thou **s** thy seed, and wateredst *it* | 2232

SOWER (8) [SOW]

Isa 55:10 that it may give seed to the **s**, and bread | 2232

Jer 50:16 Cut off the **s** from Babylon, and him that | 2232

Mt 13: 3 saying, Behold, a **s** went forth to sow; | 4687
13:18 Hear ye therefore the parable of the **s**. | 4687

Mk 4: 3 Behold, there went out a **s** to sow: | 4687
4:14 The **s** soweth the word. | 4687

Lk 8: 5 A **s** went out to sow his seed: and as he | 4687

2Co 9:10 he that ministereth seed to the **s** both | 4687

SOWEST (3) [SOW]

1Co 15:36 *that* which thou **s** is not quickened, | 4687
15:37 *that* which thou **s**, thou sowest not that | 4687
15:37 thou **s** not that body that shall be, | 4687

SOWETH (5) [SOW]

Pr 6:14 mischief continually; he **s** discord. | 7971
6:19 and he that **s** discord among brethren. | 7971
11:18 him that **s** righteousness *shall be* a sure | 2232
16:28 A froward man **s** strife: and a whisperer | 7971
22: 8 He that **s** iniquity shall reap vanity: | 2232

Am 9:13 and the treader of grapes him that **s** seed; | 4900

Mt 13:37 He that **s** the good seed is the Son of man; | 4687

Mk 4:14 The sower **s** the word. | 4687

Jn 4:36 both he that **s** and he that reapeth may | 4687
4:37 And herein is *that* saying true, One **s**, | 4687

2Co 9: 6 But this *I say*, He which **s** sparingly shall | 4687
9: 6 he which **s** bountifully shall reap also | 4687

Gal 6: 7 for whatsoever a man **s**, that shall he also | 4687
6: 8 For he that **s** to his flesh shall of the flesh | 4687
6: 8 that **s** to the Spirit shall of the Spirit reap | 4687

SOWING (2) [SOW]

Lev 11:37 if *any part* of their carcase fall upon any **s** | 2221
26: 5 the vintage shall reach unto the **s time**: | 2233

SOWN (32) [SOW]

Ex 23:16 labours, which thou hast **s** in the field: | 2232

Lev 11:37 upon any **s**owing seed which is to be **s**, | 2232

Dt 21: 4 which is neither eared nor **s**, and shall | 2232
22: 9 the fruit of *thy* seed which thou hast **s**, | 2232
29:23 salt, *and* burning, *that* it is not **s**, | 2232

Jdg 9: 3 so it was, when Israel had **s**, that | 2232

Ps 97:11 Light is **s** for the righteous, | 2232

Isa 19: 7 every thing **s** by the brooks, shall wither, | 4218
40:24 not be planted; yea, they shall not be **s**: | 2232
61:11 the garden causeth the **things that are s** | 2221

Jer 2: 2 the wilderness, in a land *that was* not **s**. | 2232
12:13 They have **s** wheat, but shall reap thorns: | 2232

Eze 36: 9 unto you, and ye shall be tilled and **s**: | 2232

Hos 8: 7 For they have **s** the wind, and they shall | 2232

Na 1:14 *that* no more of thy name be **s**: | 2232

Hag 1: 6 Ye have **s** much, and bring in little; | 2232

Mt 13:19 away that which was **s** in his heart. | 4687
25:24 reaping where thou hast not **s**, |

Mk 4:15 by the way side, where the word is **s**; | 4687
4:15 taketh away the word that was **s** in their | 4687
4:16 these are they likewise which are **s** on | 4687
4:18 And these are they which are **s** among | 4687
4:20 And these are they which are **s** on good | 4687
4:31 which, when it is **s** in the earth, | 4687

Mk 4:32 But when it is **s**, it groweth up,	4687

1Co 9:11 If we have **s** unto you spiritual *things, is* | 4687
15:42 It is **s** in corruption; it is raised in | 4687
15:43 It is **s** in dishonour; it is raised in glory: it | 4687
15:43 it is **s** in weakness; it is raised in power: | 4687
15:44 It is **s** a natural body; it is raised a spiritual | 4687

2Co 9:10 and multiply your **seed s**, and increase | 4703

Jas 3:18 the fruit of righteousness is **s** in peace | 4687

SPACE (27)

Ge 29:14 And he abode with him the **s** of a month. | 3117
32:16 and put a **s** betwixt drove and drove. | 7305

Lev 25: 8 the **s** of the seven sabbaths of years shall | 3117
25:30 if it be not redeemed within the **s** of a full | 4390

Dt 2:14 the **s** in which we came from | 3117

Jos 3: 4 Yet there shall be a **s** between you and it, | 7350

1Sa 26:13 afar off; a great **s** *being* between them: | 4725

Ezr 9: 8 now for a little **s** grace hath been *shewed* | 7281

Jer 28:11 **within** the **s** of two full years. | 5750+871.1

Eze 40:12 The **s** also before the little chambers *was* | 1366
40:12 and the **s** *was* one cubit on that side: | 1366

Lk 22:59 about the **s** of one hour **after** another | 1339

Ac 5: 7 it was about the **s** of three hours **after**, | 1292
5:34 to put the apostles forth a **little s**; | 1024
7:42 sacrifices *by the* **s** *of* forty years in | NIG
13:20 *them* judges about the **s** *of* four hundred | NIG
13:21 tribe of Benjamin, *by the* **s** *of* forty years. | NIG
15:33 after they had **tarried** *there* a **s**, | 4160+5550
19: 8 spake boldly **for the s** of three months, | 1909
19:10 And this continued **by the s** of two years; | 1909
19:34 with one voice about the **s** of two hours | 1909
20:31 that *by the* **s** *of* three years I ceased not to | NIG

Jas 5:17 it rained not on the earth *by the* **s** *of* three | NIG

Rev 2:21 And I gave her **s** to repent of her | 5550
8: 1 there was silence in heaven about the **s** of | NIG
14:20 by the **s** of a thousand *and* six hundred | 575
17:10 he cometh, he must continue a short **s**. | NIG

SPAIN (2)

Ro 15:24 Whensoever I take my journey into **S**, | 4681
15:28 them this fruit, I will come by you into **S**. | 4681

SPAKE (588) [SPEAK]

Ge 8:15 And God **s** unto Noah, saying, | 1696
9: 8 And God **s** unto Noah, and to his sons with | 559
16:13 she called the name of the Lord that **s** | 1696
18:29 he **s** unto him yet again, and said, | 1696
19:14 Lot went out, and **s** unto his sons in law, | 1696
21:22 Phichol the chief captain of his host **s** unto | 559
22: 7 Isaac **s** unto Abraham his father, and said, | 559
23: 3 and **s** unto the sons of Heth, saying, | 1696
23:13 he **s** unto Ephron in the audience of | 1696
24: 7 **s** unto me, and that sware unto me, | 1696
24:30 sister, saying, Thus **s** the man unto me; | 1696
27: 5 Rebekah heard when Isaac **s** to Esau his | 1696
27: 6 Rebekah **s** unto Jacob her son, saying, | 559
29: 9 he yet **s** with them, Rachel came with | 1696
31:11 the angel of God **s** unto me in a dream, | 559
31:29 God of your father **s** unto me yesternight, | 559
34: 3 the damsel, and **s** kindly unto the damsel. | 1696
34: 4 Shechem **s** unto his father Hamor, saying, | 559
35:15 name of the place where God **s** with him, | 1696
39:10 to pass, as she **s** to Joseph day by day, | 1696
39:14 of her house, and **s** unto them, saying, | 1696
39:17 she **s** unto him according to these words, | 1696
39:19 which she **s** unto him, saying, After this | 1696
41: 9 **s** the chief butler unto Pharaoh, saying, | 1696
42: 7 unto them, and **s** roughly unto them; | 1696
42:14 That *is it* that I **s** unto you, saying, Ye *are* | 559
42:22 **S** I not unto you, saying, Do not sin | 559
42:23 for he **s** **unto** them by an interpreter. | 996
42:30 **s** roughly to us, and took us for spies of | 1696
42:37 Reuben **s** unto his father, saying, Slay my | 559
43: 3 Judah **s** unto him, saying, The man did | 559
43:27 father well, the old man of whom ye **s**? | 559
43:29 younger brother, of whom ye **s** unto me? | 559
44: 6 and he **s** unto them these *same* words. | 1696
46: 2 God **s** unto Israel in the visions of the | 559
47: 5 Pharaoh **s** unto Joseph, saying, Thy father | 559
49:28 this *is it* that their father **s** unto them, | 1696
50: 4 Joseph **s** unto the house of Pharaoh, | 1696
50:17 And Joseph wept when they **s** unto him. | 1696
50:21 comforted them, and **s** kindly unto them. | 1696

Ex 1:15 king of Egypt **s** to the Hebrew midwives, | 559
4:30 Aaron **s** all the words which the Lord | 1696
5:10 and they **s** to the people, saying, | 559
6: 2 God **s** unto Moses, and said unto him, | 1696
6: 9 Moses **s** so unto the children of Israel: | 1696
6:10 And the Lord **s** unto Moses, saying, | 1696
6:12 Moses **s** before the Lord, saying, | 1696
6:13 the Lord **s** unto Moses and unto Aaron, | 1696
6:27 *These are* they which **s** to Pharaoh king | 1696
6:28 Lord **s** unto Moses in the land of Egypt, | 1696
6:29 That the Lord **s** unto Moses, saying, | 1696
7: 7 years old, when they **s** unto Pharaoh. | 1696
7: 8 the Lord **s** unto Moses and unto Aaron, | 559
7:19 the Lord **s** unto Moses, Say unto Aaron, | 559
8: 1 the Lord **s** unto Moses, Go unto Pharaoh, | 559
8: 5 the Lord **s** unto Moses, Say unto Aaron, | 559
12: 1 the Lord **s** unto Moses and Aaron in | 559
13: 1 the Lord **s** unto Moses, saying, | 1696
14: 1 And the Lord **s** unto Moses, saying, | 1696
15: 1 **s**, saying, I will sing unto the Lord, for he | 559
16: 9 Moses **s** unto Aaron, Say unto all | 559
16:10 as Aaron **s** unto the whole congregation | 1696

Ex 16:11 And the LORD **s** unto Moses, saying,	1696
19:19 Moses **s**, and God answered him by a	1696
19:25 down the people, and **s** unto them.	559
20: 1 And God **s** all these words, saying,	1696
25: 1 And the LORD **s** unto Moses, saying,	1696
30:11 And the LORD **s** unto Moses, saying,	1696
30:17 And the LORD **s** unto Moses, saying,	1696
30:22 Moreover the LORD **s** unto Moses,	1696
31: 1 And the LORD **s** unto Moses, saying,	1696
31:12 And the LORD **s** unto Moses, saying,	559
33:11 the LORD **s** unto Moses face to face, as a	1696
34:34 **s** unto the children of Israel *that* which	1696
35: 4 Moses **s** unto all the congregation of	559
36: 5 they **s** unto Moses, saying, The people	559
40: 1 And the LORD **s** unto Moses, saying,	1696
Lev 1: 1 **s** unto him out of the tabernacle of	1696
4: 1 And the LORD **s** unto Moses, saying,	1696
5:14 And the LORD **s** unto Moses, saying,	1696
6: 1 And the LORD **s** unto Moses, saying,	1696
6: 8 And the LORD **s** unto Moses, saying,	1696
6:19 And the LORD **s** unto Moses, saying,	1696
6:24 And the LORD **s** unto Moses, saying,	1696
7:22 And the LORD **s** unto Moses, saying,	1696
7:28 And the LORD **s** unto Moses, saying,	1696
8: 1 And the LORD **s** unto Moses, saying,	1696
10: 3 This *is it* that the LORD **s**, saying,	1696
10: 8 And the LORD **s** unto Aaron, saying,	1696
10:12 Moses **s** unto Aaron, and unto Eleazar	1696
11: 1 the LORD **s** unto Moses and to Aaron,	1696
12: 1 And the LORD **s** unto Moses, saying,	1696
13: 1 the LORD **s** unto Moses and Aaron,	1696
14: 1 And the LORD **s** unto Moses, saying,	1696
14:33 the LORD **s** unto Moses and unto Aaron,	1696
15: 1 the LORD **s** unto Moses and to Aaron,	1696
16: 1 the LORD **s** unto Moses after the death of	1696
17: 1 And the LORD **s** unto Moses, saying,	1696
18: 1 And the LORD **s** unto Moses, saying,	1696
19: 1 And the LORD **s** unto Moses, saying,	1696
20: 1 And the LORD **s** unto Moses, saying,	1696
21:16 And the LORD **s** unto Moses, saying,	1696
22: 1 And the LORD **s** unto Moses, saying,	1696
22:17 And the LORD **s** unto Moses, saying,	1696
22:26 And the LORD **s** unto Moses, saying,	1696
23: 1 And the LORD **s** unto Moses, saying,	1696
23: 9 And the LORD **s** unto Moses, saying,	1696
23:23 And the LORD **s** unto Moses, saying,	1696
23:26 And the LORD **s** unto Moses, saying,	1696
23:33 And the LORD **s** unto Moses, saying,	1696
24: 1 And the LORD **s** unto Moses, saying,	1696
24:13 And the LORD **s** unto Moses, saying,	1696
24:23 Moses **s** to the children of Israel, that	1696
25: 1 The LORD **s** unto Moses in mount Sinai,	1696
27: 1 And the LORD **s** unto Moses, saying,	1696
Nu 1: 1 the LORD **s** unto Moses in the wilderness	1696
2: 1 the LORD **s** unto Moses and unto Aaron,	1696
3: 1 Moses in the day that the LORD **s** with	1696
3: 5 And the LORD **s** unto Moses, saying,	1696
3:11 And the LORD **s** unto Moses, saying,	1696
3:14 the LORD **s** unto Moses in the wilderness	1696
3:44 And the LORD **s** unto Moses, saying,	1696
4: 1 the LORD **s** unto Moses and unto Aaron,	1696
4:17 the LORD **s** unto Moses and unto Aaron,	1696
4:21 And the LORD **s** unto Moses, saying,	1696
5: 1 And the LORD **s** unto Moses, saying,	1696
5: 4 as the LORD **s** unto Moses, so did	1696
5:11 And the LORD **s** unto Moses, saying,	1696
6: 1 And the LORD **s** unto Moses, saying,	1696
6:22 And the LORD **s** unto Moses, saying,	1696
7: 4 And the LORD **s** unto Moses, saying,	559
7:89 the two cherubims: and he **s** unto him.	1696
8: 1 And the LORD **s** unto Moses, saying,	1696
8: 5 And the LORD **s** unto Moses, saying,	1696
8:23 And the LORD **s** unto Moses, saying,	1696
9: 1 the LORD **s** unto Moses in the wilderness	1696
9: 4 Moses **s** unto the children of Israel,	1696
9: 9 And the LORD **s** unto Moses, saying,	1696
10: 1 And the LORD **s** unto Moses, saying,	1696
11:25 unto him, and took of the spirit that	1696
12: 1 and Aaron **s** against Moses because	1696
12: 4 And the LORD **s** suddenly unto Moses,	559
13: 1 And the LORD **s** unto Moses, saying,	1696
14: 7 they **s** unto all the company of the	559
14:26 the LORD **s** unto Moses and unto Aaron,	1696
15: 1 And the LORD **s** unto Moses, saying,	1696
15:17 And the LORD **s** unto Moses, saying,	1696
15:37 And the LORD **s** unto Moses, saying,	559
16: 5 **s** unto Korah and unto all his company,	1696
16:20 the LORD **s** unto Moses and unto Aaron,	1696
16:23 And the LORD **s** unto Moses, saying,	1696
16:26 he **s** unto the congregation, saying,	1696
16:36 And the LORD **s** unto Moses, saying,	1696
16:44 And the LORD **s** unto Moses, saying,	1696
17: 1 And the LORD **s** unto Moses, saying,	1696
17: 6 Moses **s** unto the children of Israel,	1696
17:12 children of Israel **s** unto Moses, saying,	559
18: 8 The LORD **s** unto Aaron, Behold, I also	1696
18:20 the LORD **s** unto Aaron, Thou shalt have	559
18:25 And the LORD **s** unto Moses, saying,	1696
19: 1 the LORD **s** unto Moses and unto Aaron,	1696
20: 3 people chode with Moses, and **s**, saying,	559
20: 7 And the LORD **s** unto Moses, saying,	1696
20:12 the LORD **s** unto Moses and Aaron,	559
20:23 the LORD **s** unto Moses and Aaron in	1696
21: 5 the people **s** against God,	1696

Nu 21:16 that *is* the well whereof the LORD **s** unto	559
22: 7 and **s** unto him the words of Balak.	559
24:12 **S** I not also to thy messengers which thou	1696
25:10 And the LORD **s** unto Moses, saying,	1696
25:16 And the LORD **s** unto Moses, saying,	1696
26: 1 that the LORD **s** unto Moses and	559
26: 3 Eleazar the priest **s** with them in the	1696
26:52 And the LORD **s** unto Moses, saying,	1696
27: 6 And the LORD **s** unto Moses, saying,	1696
27:15 And Moses **s** unto the LORD, saying,	1696
28: 1 And the LORD **s** unto Moses, saying,	1696
30: 1 Moses **s** unto the heads of the tribes	1696
31: 1 And the LORD **s** unto Moses, saying,	1696
31: 3 Moses **s** unto the people, saying, Arm	1696
31:25 And the LORD **s** unto Moses, saying,	559
32: 2 of Reuben came and **s** unto Moses,	559
32:25 the children of Reuben **s** unto Moses,	1696
33:50 the LORD **s** unto Moses in the plains of	1696
34: 1 And the LORD **s** unto Moses, saying,	1696
34:16 And the LORD **s** unto Moses, saying,	1696
35: 1 the LORD **s** unto Moses in the plains of	1696
35: 9 And the LORD **s** unto Moses, saying,	1696
36: 1 before Moses, and before the princes,	1696
Dt 1: 1 These *be* the words which Moses **s** unto	1696
1: 3 *that* Moses **s** unto the children of Israel,	1696
1: 6 The LORD our God **s** unto us in Horeb,	1696
1: 9 I **s** unto you at that time, saying, I am not	559
1:43 So I **s** unto you; and you would not hear,	1696
2: 1 of the Red sea, as the LORD **s** unto me:	1696
2: 2 And the LORD **s** unto me, saying,	559
2:17 That the LORD **s** unto me, saying,	1696
4:12 the LORD **s** unto you out of the midst of	1696
4:15 **s** unto you in Horeb out of the midst of	1696
4:45 Moses **s** unto the children of Israel,	1696
5:22 These words the LORD **s** unto all your	1696
5:28 voice of your words, when ye **s** unto me;	1696
9:10 which the LORD **s** with you in the mount	1696
9:13 Furthermore the LORD **s** unto me, saying,	559
10: 4 which the LORD **s** unto you in the mount	1696
13: 2 to pass, whereof he **s** unto thee, saying,	1696
27: 9 the priests the Levites **s** unto all Israel,	1696
28:68 by the way where*of* I **s** unto thee, Thou	559
31: 1 and **s** these words unto all Israel.	1696
31:30 Moses **s** in the ears of all the congregation	1696
32:44 **s** all the words of this song in the ears of	1696
32:48 the LORD **s** unto Moses that selfsame	1696
Jos 1: 1 that the LORD **s** unto Joshua the son of	559
1:12 the tribe of Manasseh, **s** Joshua, saying,	559
3: 6 Joshua **s** unto the priests, saying, Take up	559
4: 1 that the LORD **s** unto Joshua, saying,	559
4: 8 of Jordan, as the LORD **s** unto Joshua,	1696
4:12 children of Israel, as Moses **s** unto them:	1696
4:15 And the LORD **s** unto Joshua, saying,	559
4:21 he **s** unto the children of Israel, saying,	559
7: 2 **s** unto them, saying, Go up and view	559
9:11 all the inhabitants of our country **s** to us,	559
9:22 for them, and he **s** unto them, saying,	559
10:12 Joshua to the LORD in the day when	1696
14:10 *even* since the LORD **s** this word unto	1696
14:12 whereof the LORD **s** in that day;	1696
17:14 the children of Joseph **s** unto Joshua,	1696
17:17 Joshua **s** unto the house of Joseph, *even* to	559
20: 1 The LORD also **s** unto Joshua, saying,	1696
20: 2 I **s** unto you by the hand of Moses:	1696
21: 2 they **s** unto them at Shiloh in the land of	1696
22: 8 he **s** unto them, saying, Return with much	559
22:15 of Gilead, and they **s** with them, saying,	1696
22:30 of Gad and the children of Manasseh **s**,	1696
23:14 the LORD your God **s** concerning you;	1696
24:27 words of the LORD which he **s** unto us:	1696
Jdg 2: 4 when the angel of the LORD **s** these	1696
8: 8 *to* Penuel, and **s** unto them likewise:	1696
8: 9 he **s** also unto the men of Penuel, saying,	559
9: 3 his mother's brethren **s** of him in the ears	1696
9:37 Gaal **s** again and said, See there come	1696
15:13 they **s** unto him, saying, No; but we will	559
19:22 **s** to the master of the house, the old man,	559
Ru 4: 1 the kinsman of whom Boaz **s** came by;	1696
1Sa 1:13 Now Hannah, she **s** in her heart; only her	1696
7: 3 Samuel **s** unto all the house of Israel,	559
9: 9 thus he **s**, Come, and let us go to the seer:	559
9:17 Behold the man whom I **s** to thee of:	559
10:16 whereof Samuel **s**, he told him not.	559
16: 4 Samuel did *that* which the LORD **s**,	1696
17:23 and **s** according to the same words:	1696
17:26 David **s** to the men that stood by him,	559
17:28 Eliab his eldest brother heard when he **s**	1696
17:30 and **s** after the same manner:	559
17:31 the words were heard which David **s**,	1696
18:23 Saul's servants **s** those words in the ears	1696
18:24 told him, saying, On this manner **s** David.	1696
19: 1 Saul **s** to Jonathan his son, and to all his	1696
19: 4 Jonathan **s** good of David unto Saul his	1696
20:26 Saul **s** not any thing that day:	1696
25: 9 **s** to Nabal according to all those words	1696
25:40 they **s** unto her, saying, David sent us	1696
28:12 the woman **s** to Saul, saying, Why hast	559
28:17 LORD hath done to him, as he **s** by me:	1696
30: 6 for the people **s** of stoning him, because	1696
2Sa 3:19 Abner also **s** in the ears of Benjamin:	1696
5: 1 **s**, saying, Behold, we *are* thy bone and	559
5: 6 which **s** unto David, saying, Except thou	1696
7: 7 **s** I a word with any of the tribes of Israel,	1696
12:18 unto him, and he would not hearken	1696
13:22 Absalom **s** unto his brother Amnon	1696

2Sa 14: 4 when the woman of Tekoah **s** to the king,	559
17: 6 to Absalom, Absalom **s** unto him, saying,	559
20:18 she **s**, saying, They were wont to speak in	559
22: 1 David **s** unto the LORD the words of this	1696
23: 2 The Spirit of the LORD **s** by me,	1696
23: 3 of Israel said, the Rock of Israel **s** to me,	1696
24:17 David **s** unto the LORD when he saw	559
1Ki 1:11 Wherefore Nathan **s** unto Bath-sheba	559
1:42 while he yet **s**, behold, Jonathan the son	1696
2: 4 his word which he **s** concerning me,	1696
2:27 which he **s** concerning the house of Eli in	1696
3:22 *is* my son. Thus they **s** before the king.	1696
3:26 **s** the woman whose the living child *was*	559
4:32 he **s** three thousand proverbs: and his	1696
4:33 he **s** of trees, from the cedar tree that *is*	1696
4:33 he **s** also of beasts, and of fowl,	1696
5: 5 as the LORD **s** unto David my father,	1696
6:12 thee, which I **s** unto David thy father:	1696
8:12 Solomon, The LORD said that *he* would	559
8:15 which **s** with his mouth unto David my	1696
8:20 LORD hath performed his word that he **s**,	1696
12: 3 Israel came, and **s** unto Rehoboam,	1696
12: 7 they **s** unto him, saying, If thou wilt be a	1696
12:10 that were grown up with him **s** unto him,	1696
12:10 thou speak unto this people that **s** unto	1696
12:14 **s** to them after the counsel of the young	1696
12:15 which the LORD **s** by Ahijah the Shilonite	1696
13:18 an angel **s** unto me by the word of	1696
13:26 word of the LORD, which he **s** unto him.	1696
13:27 he **s** to his sons, saying, Saddle me the ass.	1696
13:31 that he **s** to his sons, saying, When I am	559
14:18 which he **s** by the hand of his servant	1696
15:29 which he **s** by his servant Ahijah	1696
16:12 which he **s** against Baasha by Jehu	1696
16:34 which he **s** by Joshua the son of Nun.	1696
17:16 word of the LORD, which he **s** by Elijah.	1696
20:28 **s** unto the king of Israel, and said, Thus	559
21: 2 Ahab **s** unto Naboth, saying, Give me thy	1696
21: 6 Because I **s** unto Naboth the Jezreelite,	1696
21:23 of Jezebel also **s** the LORD, saying,	1696
22:13 that was gone to call Micaiah **s** unto him,	1696
22:38 unto the word of the LORD which he **s**.	1696
2Ki 1: 9 he **s** unto him, Thou man of God, the	1696
2:22 to the saying of Elisha which he **s**.	1696
5:13 and **s** unto him, and said, My father,	1696
7:17 who **s** when the king came down to him.	1696
8: 1 **s** Elisha unto the woman, whose son he	1696
9:12 he said, Thus and thus **s** he to me, saying,	559
9:36 which he **s** by his servant Elijah	1696
10:10 which the LORD **s** concerning the house	1696
10:10 for the LORD hath done *that* which he **s**	1696
10:17 saying of the LORD, which he **s** to Elijah.	1696
14:25 which he **s** by the hand of his servant	1696
15:12 word of the LORD which he **s** unto Jehu,	1696
17:26 Wherefore they **s** to the king of Assyria,	559
18:28 **s**, saying, Hear the word of the great king,	1696
21:10 the LORD **s** by his servants the prophets,	1696
22:19 when thou heardest what I **s** against this	1696
24: 2 which he **s** by his servants the prophets.	1696
25:28 he **s** kindly to him, and set his throne	1696
1Ch 15:16 David **s** to the chief of the Levites to	559
17: 6 **s** I a word to any of the judges of Israel,	1696
21: 9 the LORD **s** unto Gad, David's seer,	1696
21:19 which he **s** in the name of the LORD.	1696
2Ch 2: 1 Solomon **s** unto all Israel, to the captains	559
6: 4 he **s** with his mouth to my father David,	1696
10: 3 and all Israel came and **s** to Rehoboam,	1696
10: 7 they **s** unto him, saying, If thou be kind to	1696
10:10 were brought up with him **s** unto him,	1696
10:10 Thus shalt thou answer the people that **s**	1696
10:15 which he **s** by the hand of Ahijah	1696
18:12 messenger that went to call Micaiah **s** to	1696
18:19 one **s** saying after this manner,	559
30:22 Hezekiah **s** comfortably unto all the	1696
32: 6 city, and **s** comfortably to them, saying,	559
32:16 his servants **s** yet *more* against the LORD	1696
32:19 they **s** against the God of Jerusalem,	1696
32:24 he **s** unto him, and he gave him a sign.	559
33:10 the LORD **s** to Manasseh, and to his	1696
33:18 the words of the seers that **s** to him in	559
34:22 and they **s** to her to *that* effect.	1696
35:25 the singing *women* **s** of Josiah in their	559
Ne 4: 2 he **s** before his brethren and the army of	559
8: 1 they **s** unto Ezra the scribe to bring the	559
13:24 their children **s** half in the speech of	1696
Est 3: 4 when they **s** daily unto him,	559
4:10 Esther **s** unto Hatach, and gave him	559
8: 3 Esther **s** yet again before the king,	1696
Job 2:13 nights, and none **s** a word unto him:	1696
3: 2 And Job **s**, and said,	6030
19:18 I arose, and they **s** against me.	1696
29:22 After my words they **s** not again;	NIH
32:16 (for they **s** not, but stood still,	1696
35: 1 Elihu moreover, and said,	6030
Ps 18: T who **s** unto the LORD the words of this	1696
33: 9 he **s**, and it was *done;* he commanded,	559
39: 3 the fire burned: *then* **s** I with my tongue,	1696
78:19 Yea, they **s** against God; they said,	1696
99: 7 he **s** unto them in the cloudy pillar:	1696
105:31 He **s**, and there came divers sorts *of flies,*	559
105:34 **s**, and the locusts came, and caterpillars,	559
106:33 so that he **s unadvisedly** with his lips.	981
Pr 30: 1 the man **s** unto Ithiel, even unto Ithiel	5002
SS 2:10 My beloved **s**, and said unto me, Rise up	6030
5: 6 my soul failed when he **s**: I sought him,	1696

Isa	7:10	Moreover the Lord **s** again unto Ahaz,	1696
	8: 5	The Lord **s** also unto me again, saying,	1696
	8:11	For the Lord **s** thus to me with a strong	559
	20: 2	At the same time **s** the Lord by Isaiah	1696
	65:12	when I **s**, ye did not hear; but did evil	1696
	66: 4	did answer; when I **s**, they did not hear:	1696
Jer	7:13	I **s** unto you, rising up early and speaking,	1696
	7:22	For I **s** not unto your fathers,	1696
	8: 6	and heard, *but* they **s** not aright:	1696
	14:14	I commanded them, neither **s** unto them:	1696
	19: 5	nor **s** *it*, neither came *it* into my mind:	1696
	20: 8	For since I **s**, I cried out, I cried violence	1696
	22:21	I **s** unto thee in thy prosperity;	1696
	25: 2	which Jeremiah the prophet **s** unto all	1696
	26:11	**s** the priests and the prophets unto	559
	26:12	Jeremiah unto all the princes and to all	559
	26:17	**s** to all the assembly of the people, saying,	559
	26:18	**s** to all the people of Judah, saying,	559
	27:12	I **s** also to Zedekiah king of Judah	1696
	27:16	I **s** to the priests and to all this people,	1696
	28: 1	unto me in the house of the Lord,	559
	28:11	Hananiah **s** in the presence of all the	559
	30: 4	these *are* the words that the Lord **s**	1696
	31:20	for since I **s** against him, I do earnestly	1696
	34: 6	Jeremiah the prophet **s** all these words	1696
	36: 2	all the nations, from the day I **s** unto thee,	1696
	37: 2	which he **s** by the prophet Jeremiah.	1696
	38: 8	king's house, and **s** to the king, saying,	1696
	40:15	Johanan the son of Kareah **s** to Gedaliah	559
	43: 2	**s** Azariah the son of Hoshaiah,	559
	45: 1	The word that Jeremiah the prophet **s**	1696
	46:13	The word that the Lord **s** to Jeremiah	1696
	50: 1	The word that the Lord **s** against	1696
	51:12	that which he **s** against the inhabitants	1696
	52:32	**s** kindly unto him, and set his throne	1696
Eze	1:28	my face, and I heard a voice of one that **s**.	1696
	2: 2	the spirit entered into me when he **s** unto	1696
	2: 2	my feet, that I heard them that **s** unto me.	1696
	3:24	and **s** with me, and said unto me,	1696
	10: 2	he **s** unto the man clothed with linen,	559
	11:25	I **s** unto them of the captivity all the	1696
	24:18	So I **s** unto the people in the morning:	1696
Da	1: 3	king **s** unto Ashpenaz the master of his	559
	2: 4	**s** the Chaldeans to the king in Syriack,	1696
	3: 9	They **s** and said to the king	6032
	3:14	Nebuchadnezzar **s** and said unto them,	6032
	3:19	*therefore* he **s**, and commanded that *they*	6032
	3:24	*and* **s**, and said unto his counsellers,	6032
	3:26	*and* **s**, and said, Shadrach, Meshach,	6032
	3:28	*Then* Nebuchadnezzar **s**, and said,	6032
	4:19	The king **s**, and said, Belteshazzar, let not	6032
	4:30	The king **s**, and said, *Is* not this great	6032
	5: 7	The king **s**, and said to the wise *men* of	6032
	5:10	*and* the queen **s** and said, O king, live for	6032
	5:13	*And* the king **s** and said unto Daniel,	6032
	6:12	**s** before the king concerning the king's	560
	6:16	*Now* the king **s** and said unto Daniel,	6032
	6:20	the king **s** and said to Daniel, O Daniel,	6032
	7: 2	Daniel **s** and said, I saw in my vision by	6032
	7:11	of the great words which the horn **s**:	4449
	7:20	a mouth that **s** very great *things*, whose	4449
	8:13	saint said unto that certain *saint* which **s**,	1696
	9: 6	which **s** in thy name to our kings,	1696
	9:12	which he **s** against us, and against our	1696
	10:16	**s**, and said unto him that stood before me,	1696
Hos	12: 4	him *in* Beth-el, and there he **s** with us;	1696
	13: 1	When Ephraim **s** trembling, he exalted	1696
Jnh	2:10	the Lord **s** unto the fish, and it vomited	559
Hag	1:13	Haggai the Lord's messenger in	559
Zec	1:21	he **s**, saying, These *are* the horns which	559
	3: 4	and **s** unto those that stood before him,	559
	4: 4	and **s** to the angel that talked with me,	559
	4: 6	he answered and **s** unto me, saying, This	559
	6: 8	he upon me, and **s** unto me, saying,	1696
Mal	3:16	they that feared the Lord **s** often one to	1696
Mt	9:18	While he **s** these *things* unto them,	2980
	9:33	when the devil was cast out, the dumb **s**:	2980
	12:22	that the blind and dumb both **s** and saw.	2980
	13: 3	And he **s** many things unto them in	2980
	13:33	Another parable **s** he unto them;	3004
	13:34	All these *things* **s** Jesus unto the	2980
	13:34	without a parable **s** he not unto them:	2980
	14:27	straightway Jesus **s** unto them, saying,	2980
	16:11	is it that ye do not understand that I **s**	3004
	17: 5	While he yet **s**, behold, a bright cloud	2980
	17:13	the disciples understood that he **s** unto	2980
	21:45	they perceived that he **s** of them.	3004
	22: 1	and **s** unto them again by parables,	3004
	23: 1	Then **s** Jesus to the multitude, and to his	2980
	26:47	And while he yet **s**, lo, Judas, one of	2980
	28:18	And Jesus came and **s** unto them, saying,	2980
Mk	3: 9	And he **s** to his disciples, that a small ship	3004
	4:33	with many such parables **s** he the word	2980
	4:34	without a parable **s** he not unto them:	2980
	5:35	While he yet **s**, there came from the ruler	2980
	7:35	of his tongue was loosed, and he **s** plain.	2980
	8:32	And he **s** *that* saying openly. And Peter	2980
	9:18	I **s** to thy disciples that they should cast	2980
	12:26	how in the bush God **s** unto him, saying,	3004
	14:31	he **s** the more vehemently, If I should	3004
	14:39	and prayed, and **s** the same words.	3004
	14:43	while he yet **s**, cometh Judas, one of	2980
Lk	1:42	And she **s** out with a loud voice,	400
	1:55	(As he **s** to our fathers,) to Abraham,	2980
	1:64	and his tongue *loosed*, and he **s**,	2980

Lk	1:70	he **s** by the mouth of his holy prophets,	2980
	2:38	**s** of him to all them that looked for	2980
	2:50	not the saying which he **s** unto them.	2980
	4:36	and **s** among themselves, saying, What a	4814
	5:36	And he **s** also a parable unto them;	3004
	6:39	And he **s** a parable unto them,	3004
	7:39	bidden him saw *it*, he **s** within himself,	3004
	8: 4	him out of every city, he **s** by a parable:	3004
	8:49	While he yet **s**, there cometh one from	2980
	9:11	and **s** unto them of the kingdom of God,	2980
	9:31	**s** of his decease which he should	3004
	9:34	While he thus **s**, there came a cloud,	3004
	11:14	the devil was gone out, the dumb **s**;	2980
	11:27	as he **s** these *things*, a certain woman of	3004
	11:37	And as *he* **s**, a certain Pharisee besought	2980
	12:16	And he **s** a parable unto them, saying,	3004
	13: 6	He **s** also this parable; A certain *man* had	3004
	14: 3	And Jesus answering **s** unto the lawyers	3004
	15: 3	And he **s** this parable unto them, saying,	3004
	18: 1	And he **s** a parable unto them *to this end,*	3004
	18: 9	And he **s** this parable unto certain which	3004
	19:11	these *things*, he added and **s** a parable,	3004
	20: 2	And **s** unto him, saying, Tell us, by what	3004
	21: 5	And as some **s** of the temple, how it was	3004
	21:29	he **s** to them a parable; Behold the fig	3004
	22:47	And while he yet **s**, behold a multitude,	2980
	22:60	while he yet **s**, the cock crew.	2980
	22:65	And many other *things* blasphemously **s**	2980
	23:20	willing to release Jesus, **s** again to *them.*	4377
	24: 6	remember how he **s** unto you when he	2980
	24:36	And as they thus **s**, Jesus himself stood in	2980
	24:44	These *are* the words which I **s** unto you,	2980
Jn	1:15	crying, saying, This was he of whom I **s**,	3004
	2:21	But he **s** of the temple of his body.	3004
	6:71	he **s** of Judas Iscariot *the son of* Simon:	2980
	7:13	Howbeit no *man* **s** openly of him for fear	2980
	7:39	(But this **s** he of the Spirit, which they	3004
	7:46	Never man **s** like this man.	2980
	8:12	Then **s** Jesus again unto them, saying,	2980
	8:20	These words **s** Jesus in the treasury, as he	2980
	8:27	They understood not that he **s** to them of	3004
	8:30	As he **s** these *words,* many believed on	2980
	9:22	These *words* **s** his parents, because	3004
	9:29	We know that God **s** unto Moses: *as for*	2980
	10: 6	This parable **s** Jesus unto them:	3004
	10: 6	*things* they were which he **s** unto them.	2980
	10:41	*things* that John **s** of this *man* were true.	3004
	11:13	Howbeit Jesus **s** of his death:	3004
	11:51	this **s** he not of himself: but being high	3004
	11:56	and **s** among themselves, as they stood in	3004
	12:29	thundered: others said, An angel **s** to him.	2980
	12:36	These *things* **s** Jesus, and departed,	2980
	12:38	which he **s**, Lord, who hath believed our	3004
	12:41	when he saw his glory, and **s** of him.	2980
	13:22	one on another, doubting of whom he **s**.	3004
	13:24	ask who it should be of whom he **s**.	3004
	13:28	knew for what intent he **s** this unto him.	3004
	17: 1	These *words* **s** Jesus, and lift up his eyes	3004
	18: 9	the saying might be fulfilled, which he **s**,	3004
	18:16	and **s** unto her that kept the door,	3004
	18:20	answered him, I **s** openly to the world;	2980
	18:32	he **s**, signifying what death he should	3004
	21:19	This **s** he, signifying by what death he	3004
Ac	1:16	of David **s** before concerning Judas,	4302
	2:31	*this* before, **s** of the resurrection of Christ,	2980
	4: 1	And as they **s** unto the people, the priests,	2980
	4:31	they **s** the word of God with boldness.	2980
	6:10	the wisdom and the spirit by which he **s**.	2980
	7: 6	And God **s** on this wise, That his seed	2980
	7:38	angel which **s** to him in the mount Sina,	2980
	8: 6	heed unto those *things* which Philip **s**,	3004
	8:26	And *the* angel of the Lord **s** unto Philip,	2980
	9:29	And he **s** boldly in the name of the Lord	2980
	10: 7	When the angel which **s** unto Cornelius	2980
	10:15	*the* voice **s** unto him again the second	NIG
	10:44	While Peter yet **s** these words, the Holy	2980
	11:20	unto the Grecians, preaching the Lord	2980
	13:45	**s** against those *things* which were spoken	483
	14: 1	and so **s**, that a great multitude both of	2980
	16:13	**s** unto the women which resorted *thither.*	2980
	16:32	they **s** unto him the word of the Lord,	2980
	18: 9	Then **s** the Lord to Paul in the night by a	3004
	18:25	he **s** and taught diligently the *things* of	2980
	19: 6	and they **s** with tongues, and prophesied.	2980
	19: 8	**s** boldly for the space of three months,	3955
	19: 9	**s** evil of *that* way before the multitude,	2551
	20:38	most *of all* for the words which he **s**,	3004
	21:40	he **s** unto *them* in the Hebrew tongue,	4377
	22: 2	(And when they heard that he **s** in	4377
	22: 9	they heard not the voice of him that **s** to	2980
	26:24	And as he thus **s** for himself, Festus said	626
	28:19	But when the Jews **s** against *it*, I was	483
	28:21	that came shewed or **s** any harm of thee.	2980
	28:25	Well **s** the Holy Ghost by Esaias	2980
1Co	13:11	When I was a child, I **s** as a child,	2980
	14: 5	I would ye all **s** with tongues,	2980
2Co	7:14	but as we **s** all *things* to you in truth,	2980
Gal	4:15	Where is then the blessedness you **s** of?	NIG
Heb	1: 1	in divers manners **s** in time past unto	2980
	4: 7	For he in a certain place of the seventh	3004
	7:14	which tribe Moses **s** nothing concerning	2980
	12:25	who refused not him that **s** on earth,	5537
2Pe	1:21	holy men of God **s** *as they were* moved	2980
Rev	1:12	And I turned to see the voice that **s** with	2980
	10: 8	the voice which I heard from heaven **s**	2980

Rev	13:11	horns like a lamb, and he **s** as a dragon.	2980

SPAKEST (10) [SPEAK]

Jdg	13:11	*Art* thou the man that **s** unto the woman?	1696
	17: 2	**s** of also in mine ears, behold, the silver *is*	559
1Sa	28:21	unto thy words which thou **s** unto me.	1696
1Ki	8:24	thou **s** also with thy mouth,	1696
	8:26	which thou **s** unto thy servant David my	1696
	8:53	thou **s** by the hand of Moses thy servant,	1696
2Ch	6:15	**s** with thy mouth, and hast fulfilled *it*	1696
Ne	9:13	**s** with them from heaven, and gavest	1696
Ps	89:19	thou in vision to thy holy one, and	1696
Jer	48:27	for since thou **s** of him, thou skippedst for	1697

SPAN (8) [SPANNED]

Ex	28:16	a **s** *shall be* the length thereof, and a span	2239
	28:16	and a **s** *shall be* the breadth thereof.	2239
	39: 9	a **s** *was* the length thereof, and a span	2239
	39: 9	**s** the breadth thereof, *being* doubled.	2239
1Sa	17: 4	whose height *was* six cubits and a **s**.	2239
Isa	40:12	meted out heaven with the **s**,	2239
La	2:20	eat their fruit, *and* children of a **s** *long*?	2949
Eze	43:13	the edge thereof round about *shall be* a **s**:	2239

SPANNED (1) [SPAN]

Isa	48:13	and my right hand hath **s** the heavens:	2946

SPARE (40) [SPARED, SPARETH, SPARING, SPARINGLY]

Ge	18:24	not **s** the place for the fifty righteous that	5375
	18:26	then I will **s** all the place for their sakes.	5375
Dt	13: 8	neither shalt thou **s**, neither shalt thou	2550
	29:20	The Lord will not **s** him, but then	5545
1Sa	15: 3	destroy all that they have, and **s** them not;	2550
Ne	13:22	me according to the greatness of	2347+5921
Job	6:10	harden myself in sorrow; let him not **s**:	2550
	16:13	my reins asunder, and doth not **s**;	2550
	20:13	*Though* he **s** it, and forsake it not;	2550
	27:22	For *God* shall cast upon him, and not **s**:	2550
	30:10	far from me, and **s** not to spit in my face.	2820
Ps	39:13	O **s** me, that I may recover strength,	8159
	72:13	He shall **s** the poor and needy,	2347+5921
Pr	6:34	he will not **s** in the day of vengeance.	2550
	19:18	hope, and let not thy soul **s** for his crying.	5375
Isa	9:19	fuel of the fire: no man shall **s** his brother.	2550
	13:18	the womb; their eye shall not **s** children.	2347
	30:14	that is broken in pieces; he shall not **s**:	2550
	54: 2	**s** not, lengthen thy cords,	2820
	58: 1	Cry aloud, **s** not, lift up thy voice like a	2820
Jer	13:14	I will not pity, nor **s**, nor have mercy,	2347
	21: 7	he shall not **s** them, neither have pity,	2347
	50:14	bend the bow, shoot at her, **s** no arrows:	2550
	51: 3	**s** ye not her young men; destroy ye	2550
Eze	5:11	diminish *thee*; neither shall mine eye **s**,	2347
	7: 4	mine eye shall not **s** thee, neither will I	2347
	7: 9	mine eye shall not **s**, neither will I have	2347
	8:18	mine eye shall not **s**, neither will I have	2347
	9: 5	let not your eye **s**, neither have ye pity:	2347
	9:10	*as for* me also, mine eye shall not **s**,	2347
	24:14	neither will I **s**, neither will I repent;	2347
Joel	2:17	**S** thy people, O Lord, and give not thine	2347
Jnh	4:11	should not I **s** Nineveh, *that* great city,	2347
Hab	1:17	and not **s** continually to slay the nations?	2550
Mal	3:17	I will **s** them, as a man spareth his own	2550
Lk	15:17	my father's *have* bread enough and to **s**,	4052
Ro	11:21	take heed lest he also **s** not thee.	5339
1Co	7:28	have trouble in the flesh: but I **s** you.	5339
2Co	1:23	to you I came not as yet unto Corinth.	5339
	13: 2	other, that, if I come again, I will not **s**:	5339

SPARED (12) [SPARE]

1Sa	15: 9	Saul and the people **s** Agag, and the best	2550
	15:15	for the people **s** the best of the sheep and	2550
	24:10	*mine* eye **s** thee; and I said, I will not put	2347
2Sa	12: 4	he to take of his own flock and of his	2550
	21: 7	the king **s** Mephibosheth, the son of	2550
2Ki	5:20	my master hath **s** Naaman this Syrian,	2820
Ps	78:50	he **s** not their soul from death,	2820
Eze	20:17	Nevertheless mine eye **s** them from	2347
Ro	8:32	He that **s** not his own Son,	5339
	11:21	For if God **s** not the natural branches,	5339
2Pe	2: 4	For if God **s** not the angels that sinned,	5339
	2: 5	And **s** not the old world, but saved Noah	5339

SPARETH (4) [SPARE]

Pr	13:24	He that **s** his rod hateth his son: but he	2820
	17:27	He that hath knowledge **s** his words:	2820
	21:26	long: but the righteous giveth and **s** not.	2820
Mal	3:17	as a man **s** his own son that serveth him.	2550

SPARING (1) [SPARE]

Ac	20:29	enter in among you, not **s** the flock.	5339

SPARINGLY (2) [SPARE]

2Co	9: 6	this *I say*, He which soweth **s** shall reap	5340
	9: 6	which soweth sparingly shall reap also **s**;	5340

SPARK (2) [SPARKS]

Job	18: 5	out, and the **s** of his fire shall not shine.	7632
Isa	1:31	the maker of it as a **s**, and they shall both	5213

SPARKLED (1)

Eze	1: 7	they **s** like the colour of burnished brass.	5340

SPARKS (4) [SPARK]

Job	5: 7	unto trouble, as the **s** fly upward.	1121+7565

S

Job	41:19 go burning lamps, *and* **s** of fire leap out.	3590
Isa	50:11 that compass *yourselves* about with **s**:	2131
	50:11 fire, and in the *that* ye have kindled.	2131

SPARROW (2) [SPARROWS]

Ps	84: 3 the **s** hath found a house, and the swallow	6833
	102: 7 and am as a **s** alone upon the housetop.	6833

SPARROWS (4) [SPARROW]

Mt	10:29 Are not two **s** sold for a farthing?	4765
	10:31 ye are of more value than many **s**.	4765
Lk	12: 6 Are not five **s** sold for two farthings,	4765
	12: 7 ye are of more value than many **s**.	4765

SPAT (1) [SPIT]

Jn	9: 6 he **s** on the ground, and made clay of	4429

SPEAK (513) [SPAKE, SPAKEST, SPEAKER, SPEAKEST, SPEAKETH, SPEAKING, SPEAKINGS, SPEECH, SPEECHES, SPEECHLESS, SPOKEN, SPOKESMAN, UNSPEAKABLE]

Ge	18:27 I have taken upon me to **s** unto the Lord,	1696
	18:30 Oh let not the Lord be angry, and I will **s**:	1696
	18:31 I have taken upon me to **s** unto the Lord:	1696
	18:32 be angry, and I will **s** yet but *this* once:	1696
	24:33 have told mine errand. And he said, **S on**.	1696
	24:50 we cannot **s** unto thee bad or good.	1696
	27: 6 I heard thy father **s** unto Esau thy brother,	1696
	31:24 Take heed that thou **s** not to Jacob either	1696
	31:29 Take thou heed that thou **s** not to Jacob	1696
	32: 4 Thus shall ye **s** unto my lord Esau;	559
	32:19 On this manner shall you **s** unto Esau,	1696
	37: 4 and could not **s** peaceably unto him.	1696
	44:16 what shall we **s**? or how shall we clear	1696
	44:18 **s** a word in my lord's ears, and let not	1696
	50: 4 **s**, I pray you, in the ears of Pharaoh,	1696
Ex	4:14 I know that he can **s well**.	1696+1696
	4:15 thou shalt **s** unto him, and put words in	1696
	5:23 For since I came to Pharaoh to **s** in thy	1696
	6:11 Go in, **s** unto Pharaoh king of Egypt,	1696
	6:29 shalt thou unto Pharaoh king of Egypt all that	1696
	7: 2 Thou shalt **s** all that I command thee:	1696
	7: 2 Aaron thy brother shall **s** unto Pharaoh,	1696
	7: 9 When Pharaoh shall **s** unto you, saying,	1696
	11: 2 **S** now in the ears of the people,	1696
	12: 3 **S** ye unto all the congregation of Israel,	1696
	14: 2 **S** unto the children of Israel, that they	1696
	14:15 **s** unto the children of Israel, that they go	1696
	16:12 unto them, saying, At even ye shall eat	1696
	19: 6 These *are* the words which thou shalt **s**	1696
	19: 9 that the people may hear when I **s** with	1696
	20:19 **S** thou with us, and we will hear:	1696
	20:19 but let not God **s** with us, lest we die.	1696
	23: 2 neither shalt thou **s** in a cause to decline	6030
	23:22 indeed obey his voice, and do all that I **s**;	1696
	25: 2 **S** unto the children of Israel, that they	1696
	28: 3 shalt **s** unto all *that are* wise hearted,	1696
	29:42 I will meet you, to **s** there unto thee.	1696
	30:31 thou shalt **s** unto the children of Israel,	1696
	31:13 thou also unto the children of Israel,	1696
	32:12 Wherefore should the Egyptians **s**,	559
	34:34 went in before the Lord to **s** with him,	1696
	34:35 again, until he went in to **s** with him.	1696
Lev	1: 2 **S** unto the children of Israel, and say	1696
	4: 2 **S** unto the children of Israel, saying, If a	1696
	6:25 **S** unto Aaron and to his sons, saying,	1696
	7:23 **S** unto the children of Israel, saying,	1696
	7:29 **S** unto the children of Israel, saying,	1696
	9: 3 unto the children of Israel thou shalt **s**,	1696
	11: 2 **S** unto the children of Israel, saying,	1696
	12: 2 **S** unto the children of Israel, saying, If a	1696
	15: 2 **S** unto the children of Israel, and say unto	1696
	16: 2 unto Moses, **S** unto Aaron thy brother,	1696
	17: 2 **S** unto Aaron, and unto his sons,	1696
	18: 2 **S** unto the children of Israel, and say unto	1696
	19: 2 **S** unto all the congregation of the children	1696
	21: 1 **S** unto the priests the sons of Aaron,	559
	21:17 **S** unto Aaron, saying, Whosoever *he be*	1696
	22: 2 **S** unto Aaron and to his sons, that they	1696
	22:18 **S** unto Aaron, and to his sons, and unto	1696
	23: 2 **S** unto the children of Israel, and say unto	1696
	23:10 **S** unto the children of Israel, and say unto	1696
	23:24 **S** unto the children of Israel, saying,	1696
	23:34 **S** unto the children of Israel, saying,	1696
	24:15 thou shalt **s** unto the children of Israel,	1696
	25: 2 **S** unto the children of Israel, and say unto	1696
	27: 2 **S** unto the children of Israel, and say unto	1696
Nu	5: 6 **S** unto the children of Israel, When a man	1696
	5:12 **S** unto the children of Israel, and say unto	1696
	6: 2 **S** unto the children of Israel, and say unto	1696
	6:23 **S** unto Aaron and unto his sons, saying,	1696
	7:89 of the congregation to **s** with him,	1696
	8: 2 **S** unto Aaron, and say unto him,	1696
	9:10 **S** unto the children of Israel, saying, If any	1696
	12: 6 a vision, *and* will **s** unto him in a dream.	1696
	12: 8 With him will I **s** mouth to mouth,	1696
	12: 8 were ye not afraid to **s** against my servant	1696
	14:15 which have heard the fame of thee will **s**,	559
	15: 2 **S** unto the children of Israel, and say unto	1696
	15:18 **S** unto the children of Israel, and say unto	1696
	15:38 **S** unto the children of Israel, and bid them	1696
	16:24 **S** unto the congregation, saying, Get you	1696
	16:37 **S** unto Eleazar the son of Aaron the priest,	559
	17: 2 **S** unto the children of Israel, and take of	1696
	18:26 **s** unto the Levites, and say unto them,	1696

Nu	19: 2 saying, **S** unto the children of Israel;	1696
	20: 8 and **s** ye unto the rock before their eyes;	1696
	21:27 Wherefore they that **s in proverbs** say,	4911
	22: 8 word again, as the Lord shall **s** unto me:	1696
	22:35 only the word that I shall **s** unto thee,	1696
	22:35 I shall speak unto thee, that thou shalt **s**.	1696
	22:38 God putteth in my mouth, that shall I **s**.	1696
	23: 5 Return unto Balak, and thus thou shalt **s**.	1696
	23:12 Must I not take heed to **s** that which	1696
	24:13 *but* what the Lord saith, that will I **s**?	1696
	27: 7 The daughters of Zelophehad **s** right:	1696
	27: 8 thou shalt **s** unto the children of Israel,	1696
	33:51 **S** unto the children of Israel, and say unto	1696
	35:10 **S** unto the children of Israel, and say unto	1696
Dt	3:26 **s** no more unto me of this matter.	1696
	5: 1 judgments which I **s** in your ears *this* day,	1696
	5:27 **s** thou unto us all that the Lord our God	1696
	5:27 that the Lord our God shall **s** unto thee;	1696
	5:31 I will **s** unto thee all the commandments,	1696
	9: 4 **S** not thou in thine heart, after that	559
	11: 2 for *I* **s** not with your children which have	NIH
	18:18 he shall **s** unto them all that I shall	1696
	18:19 my words which he shall **s** in my name,	1696
	18:20 which shall presume to **s** a word in my	1696
	18:20 which I have not commanded him to **s**,	1696
	18:20 or that shall **s** in the name of other gods,	1696
	20: 2 shall approach and **s** unto the people,	1696
	20: 5 officers shall **s** unto the people, saying,	1696
	20: 8 the officers shall **s** further unto the people,	1696
	25: 8 of his city shall call him, and **s** unto him:	1696
	26: 5 thou shalt **s** and say before the Lord thy	6030
	27:14 Levites shall **s**, and say unto all the men	6030
	31:28 that I may **s** these words in their ears,	1696
	32: 1 Give ear, O ye heavens, and I will **s**;	1696
Jos	4:10 commanded Joshua to **s** unto the people,	1696
	20: 2 **S** to the children of Israel, saying,	1696
	22:24 In time to come your children might **s**	559
Jdg	5:10 **S**, ye that ride on white asses, ye that sit	7878
	6:39 hot against me, and I will **s** but *this* once:	1696
	9: 2 **S**, I pray you, in the ears of all the men of	1696
	19: 3 to **s** friendly unto her, *and* to bring her	1696
	19:30 of it, take advice, and **s** *your minds*.	1696
	21:13 the whole congregation sent some to **s** to	1696
1Sa	3: 9 he call thee, that thou shalt say, **S, Lord**;	1696
	3:10 Samuel answered, **S**; for thy servant	1696
	25:17 son of Belial, that *a man* cannot **s** to him.	1696
	25:24 in thine audience, and hear the words	1696
2Sa	3:19 Abner went also to **s** in the ears of David	1696
	3:27 Joab took him aside in the gate to **s** with	1696
	7:17 this vision, so did Nathan **s** unto David.	1696
	13:13 therefore, I pray thee, **s** unto the king;	1696
	14: 3 the king, and **s** on this manner unto him.	1696
	14:12 **s** *one* word unto my lord the king.	1696
	14:13 the king doth **s** this thing as one which	1696
	14:15 that I am come to **s** of this thing unto my	1696
	14:15 said, I will now **s** unto the king;	1696
	14:18 woman said, Let my lord the king now **s**.	1696
	17: 6 we do *after* his saying? if not; **s** thou.	1696
	19: 7 and **s** comfortably unto thy servants:	1696
	19:10 why **s** ye **not a word** of bringing the king	2790
	19:11 **S** unto the elders of Judah, saying,	1696
	20:16 Come near hither, that I may **s** with thee.	1696
	20:18 were **wont to s** in old time, saying,	1696+1696
1Ki	2:17 he said, **S**, I pray thee, unto Solomon	1696
	2:18 Well; I will **s** for thee unto the king.	1696
	2:19 king Solomon, to **s** unto him for Adonijah.	1696
	12: 7 **s** good words to them, then they will be	1696
	12:10 shalt thou **s** unto this people that spake	559
	12:23 **S** unto Rehoboam, the son of Solomon,	559
	21:19 thou shalt **s** unto him, saying, Thus saith	1696
	21:19 thou shalt **s** unto him, saying, Thus saith	1696
	22:13 of one of them, and **s** *that which is* good.	1696
	22:14 the Lord saith unto me, that will I **s**.	1696
	22:24 of the Lord from me to **s** unto thee?	1696
2Ki	18:19 **S** ye now to Hezekiah, Thus saith the	559
	18:26 and Joah, unto Rab-shakeh, **S**, I pray thee,	1696
	18:27 thy master, and to thee, to **s** these words?	1696
	19:10 Thus shall ye **s** to Hezekiah king of Judah,	559
1Ch	17:15 this vision, so did Nathan **s** unto David.	1696
	17:18 What can David **s** more to thee for	NIH
2Ch	10: 7 please them, and **s** good words to them,	1696
	11: 3 **S** unto Rehoboam the son of Solomon,	559
	18:12 be like one of theirs, and **s** thou good.	1696
	18:13 even what my God saith, that will I **s**.	1696
	18:23 of the Lord from me to **s** unto thee?	1696
	32:17 God of Israel, and to **s** against him, saying,	559
Ne	13:24 could not **s** in the Jews' language,	1696
Est	5:14 to morrow **s** thou unto the king that	559
	6: 4 to **s** unto the king to hang Mordecai on	559
Job	7:11 I will **s** in the anguish of my spirit;	1696
	8: 2 How long wilt thou **s** these *things*? and	4448
	9:19 If *I* **s** of strength, lo, *he is* strong: and if of	NIH
	9:35 would I **s**, and not fear him; but *it is*	1696
	10: 1 I will **s** in the bitterness of my soul.	1696
	11: 5 O that God would **s**, and open his lips	1696
	12: 8 Or **s** to the earth, and it shall teach thee:	7878
	13: 3 Surely I would **s** to the Almighty,	1696
	13: 7 Will you **s** wickedly for God?	1696
	13:13 I may **s**, and let come on what *will*.	1696
	13:22 or let me **s**, and answer thou me.	1696
	16: 4 I also could **s** as ye *do*: if your soul were	1696
	16: 6 Though I **s**, my grief is not assuaged:	1696
	18: 2 words? mark, and afterwards we will **s**.	1696
	21: 3 Suffer me that I may **s**; and after that I	1696
	27: 4 My lips shall not **s** wickedness, nor my	1696

Job	32: 7 Days should **s**, and multitude of years	1696
	32:20 I will **s**, that I may be refreshed: I will	1696
	33:31 unto me: hold thy peace, and I will **s**.	1696
	33:32 answer me: **s**, for I desire to justify thee.	1696
	34:33 not I: therefore **s** what thou knowest.	1696
	36: 2 I will shew thee that *I have* yet to **s** on	4405
	37:20 it be told him that I **s**? if a man speak,	1696
	37:20 if a man **s**, surely he shall be swallowed	559
	41: 3 will he **s** soft words unto thee?	1696
	42: 4 Hear, I beseech thee, and I will **s**: I will	1696
Ps	2: 5 shall he **s** unto them in his wrath,	1696
	5: 6 Thou shalt destroy them that **s** leasing:	1696
	12: 2 They **s** vanity every one with his	1696
	12: 2 *and* with a double heart do they **s**.	1696
	17:10 fat: *with* their mouth they **s** proudly.	1696
	28: 3 which **s** peace to their neighbours,	1696
	29: 9 his temple doth every one **s** of *his* glory.	559
	31:18 which **s** grievous things proudly and	1696
	35:20 For they **s** not peace: but they devise	1696
	35:28 my tongue shall **s** of thy righteousness	1897
	38:12 they that seek my hurt **s** mischievous	1696
	40: 5 **s** *of them*, they are moe than can be	1696
	41: 5 Mine enemies **s** evil of me, When shall he	559
	45: 1 I **s** of the things which I have made	559
	49: 3 My mouth shall **s** of wisdom;	1696
	50: 7 Hear, O my people, and I will **s**; O Israel,	1696
	52: 3 *and* lying rather than to **s** righteousness.	1696
	58: 1 Do ye indeed **s** righteousness,	1696
	59:12 and for cursing and lying *which* they **s**.	5608
	63:11 the mouth of them that **s** lies shall be	1696
	69:12 They that sit in the gate **s** against me;	7878
	71:10 For mine enemies **s** against me; and they	559
	73: 8 and wickedly *concerning* oppression:	1696
	73: 8 *concerning* oppression: they **s** loftily.	1696
	73:15 If I say, I will **s** thus; behold, I should	5608
	75: 5 your horn on high: **s** *not* with a stiff neck.	1696
	77: 4 I am *so* troubled that I cannot **s**.	1696
	85: 8 I will hear what God the Lord will **s**:	1696
	85: 8 for he will **s** peace unto his people,	1696
	94: 4 *long* shall they utter *and* **s** hard *things*?	1696
	109:20 and of them that **s** evil against my soul.	1696
	115: 5 They have mouths, but they **s** not:	1696
	115: 7 neither **s** they through their throat.	1897
	119:23 Princes also did sit *and* **s** against me:	1696
	119:46 will **s** of thy testimonies also before kings,	1696
	119:172 My tongue shall **s** of thy word: for all thy	6030
	120: 7 for peace: but when I **s**, they *are* for war.	1696
	127: 5 they shall **s** with the enemies in the gate.	1696
	135:16 They have mouths, but they **s** not;	1696
	139:20 For they **s** against thee wickedly,	559
	145: 5 I will **s** of the glorious honour of thy	7878
	145: 6 shall **s** of the might of thy terrible acts:	1696
	145:11 They shall **s** of the glory of thy kingdom,	559
	145:21 My mouth shall **s** the praise of the Lord:	1696
Pr	8: 6 Hear, for I will **s** of excellent things;	1696
	8: 7 For my mouth shall **s** truth;	1897
	23: 9 **S** not in the ears of a fool: for he will	1696
	23:16 shall rejoice, when thy lips **s** right things.	1696
Ecc	3: 7 a time to keep silence, and a time to **s**;	1696
SS	7: 9 **causing** the lips of *those that are* asleep to **s**.	1680
Isa	8:10 nought; **s** the word, and it shall not stand:	1696
	8:20 if they **s** not according to this word, *it is*	559
	14:10 All they shall **s** and say unto thee, Art	6030
	19:18 land of Egypt **s** the language of Canaan,	1696
	28:11 another tongue will he **s** to this people.	1696
	29: 4 *and* shalt **s** out of the ground,	1696
	30:10 Prophesy not unto us right *things*, **s** unto	1696
	32: 4 the stammerers shall be ready to **s** plainly.	1696
	32: 6 For the vile person will **s** villany,	1696
	36:11 and Joah unto Rabshakeh, **S**, I pray thee,	1696
	36:11 and **s** not to us in the Jews' language,	1696
	36:12 thy master and to thee to **s** these words?	1696
	37:10 Thus shall ye **s** to Hezekiah king of Judah,	559
	40: 2 **S** ye comfortably to Jerusalem,	1696
	41: 1 let them come near; then let them **s**:	1696
	45:19 I the Lord **s** righteousness, I declare	1696
	50: 4 **s** a word in season to *him that is* weary:	5790
	52: 6 *know* in that day that I *am* he that doth **s**:	1696
	56: 3 hath joined himself to the Lord, **s**, saying,	1696
	59: 4 *they* trust in vanity, and **s** lies;	1696
	63: 1 I *that is* in righteousness, mighty to save.	1696
Jer	1: 6 said I, Ah, Lord God, behold, I cannot **s**:	1696
	1: 7 whatsoever I command thee thou shalt **s**.	1696
	1:17 and **s** unto them all that I command thee:	1696
	5: 5 unto the great men, and will **s** unto them;	1696
	5:14 Because ye **s** this word, behold, I will	1696
	6:10 To whom shall I **s**, and give warning,	1696
	7:27 Therefore thou shalt **s** all these words	1696
	9: 5 his neighbour, and will not **s** the truth:	1696
	9: 5 they have taught their tongue to **s** lies,	1696
	9:22 **S**, Thus saith the Lord, Even	1696
	10: 5 *are* upright as the palm tree, but **s** not:	1696
	11: 2 **s** unto the men of Judah, and to the	1696
	12: 6 though they **s** fair *words* unto thee.	1696
	13:12 Therefore thou shalt **s** unto them this	559
	18: 7 *At what* instant I shall **s** concerning a nation,	1696
	18: 9 *what* instant I shall **s** concerning a nation,	1696
	18:11 to the men of Judah, and to the	559
	18:20 Remember that I stood before thee to **s**	1696
	20: 9 of him, nor **s** any more in his name.	1696
	22: 1 the king of Judah, and **s** there this word,	1696
	23:16 they **s** a vision of their own heart,	1696
	23:28 my word, let him **s** my word faithfully.	1696
	26: 2 and **s** unto all the cities of Judah,	1696

S

Jer	26: 2 the words that I command thee to **s** unto	1696
	26: 8 commanded *him* to **s** unto all the people,	1696
	26:15 unto you to **s** all these words in your ears.	1696
	27: 9 your sorcerers, which **s** unto you, saying,	559
	27:14 the words of the prophets that **s** unto you,	559
	28: 7 thou now this word that I **s** in thine ears,	1696
	29:24 *Thus* shalt thou also **s** to Shemaiah	559
	32: 4 shall **s** with him mouth to mouth,	1696
	34: 2 Go and **s** to Zedekiah king of Judah,	559
	34: 3 he shall **s** with thee mouth to mouth,	1696
	35: 2 **s** unto them, and bring them *into* the	1696
	38:20 voice of the Lord, which I **s** unto thee:	1696
	39:16 Go and **s** to Ebed-melech the Ethiopian,	559
Eze	2: 1 upon thy feet, and I will **s** unto thee.	1696
	2: 7 thou shalt **s** my words unto them,	1696
	3: 1 roll, and go **s** unto the house of Israel.	1696
	3: 4 Israel, and **s** with my words unto them,	1696
	3:10 all my words that I shall **s** unto thee	1696
	3:11 **s** unto them, and tell them, Thus saith	1696
	3:27 I **s** with thee, I will open thy mouth,	1696
	11: 5 Lord fell upon me, and said unto me, **S**;	559
	12:25 I will **s**, and the word that I shall speak	1696
	12:25 the word that I shall **s** shall come to pass;	1696
	14: 4 Therefore **s** unto them, and say unto	1696
	17: 2 **s** a parable unto the house of	4911+4912
	20: 3 **s** unto the elders of Israel, and say unto	1696
	20:27 **s** unto the house of Israel, and say unto	1696
	20:49 they say of me, Doth he not **s** parables?	4911
	24:21 **S** unto the house of Israel, Thus saith	559
	24:27 and thou shalt **s**, and be no more dumb:	1696
	29: 3 **S**, and say, Thus saith the Lord God;	1696
	31: 2 **s** unto Pharaoh king of Egypt, and to his	559
	32:21 The strong among the mighty shall **s** to	1696
	33: 2 **s** to the children of thy people, and say	1696
	33: 8 if thou dost not **s** to warn the wicked	1696
	33:10 son of man, **s** unto the house of Israel;	559
	33:10 Thus ye **s**, saying, If our transgressions	559
	33:24 those wastes of the land of Israel **s**,	559
	33:30 **s** one to another, every one to his brother,	1696
	37:18 the children of thy people shall **s** unto	559
	39:17 **S** unto every feathered fowl, and to every	559
Da	2: 9 and corrupt words to **s** before me,	560
	3:29 which **s** any thing amiss against the God	560
	7:25 he shall **s** great words against the most	4449
	10:11 understand the words that I **s** unto thee,	1696
	10:19 was strengthened, and said, Let my lord **s**;	1696
	11:27 and they shall **s** lies at one table;	1696
	11:36 shall **s** marvellous *things* against the God	1696
Hos	2:14 wilderness, and **s** comfortably unto her.	1696
Hab	2: 3 but at the end it shall **s**, and not lie:	6315
Zep	3:13 of Israel shall not do iniquity, nor **s** lies;	1696
Hag	2: 2 **S** now to Zerubbabel the son of Shealtiel,	559
	2:21 **S** to Zerubbabel, governor of Judah, saying,	559
Zec	2: 4 him, Run, **s** to this young man, saying,	1696
	6:12 **s** unto him, saying, Thus speaketh	559
	7: 3 *And* to **s** unto the priests which *were* in	559
	7: 5 **S** unto all the people of the land, and to	559
	8:16 **S** ye every man the truth to his neighbour;	1696
	9:10 he shall **s** peace unto the heathen:	1696
Mt	8: 8 but **s** the word only, and my servant shall	3004
	10:19 take no thought how or what ye shall **s**:	2980
	10:19 you in that *same* hour what ye shall **s**.	2980
	10:20 For it is not ye that **s**, but the Spirit of	2980
	10:27 I tell you in darkness, *that* **s** ye in light:	3004
	12:34 **s** good *things*? for out of the abundance	2980
	12:36 That every idle word that men shall **s**,	2980
	12:46 stood without, desiring to **s** with him.	2980
	12:47 stand without, desiring to **s** with thee.	2980
	13:13 Therefore **s** I to them in parables: because	2980
	15:31 they saw the dumb to **s**, the maimed	2980
Mk	1:34 and suffered not the devils to **s**, because	2980
	2: 7 Why doth this *man* thus **s** blasphemies?	2980
	7:37 both the deaf to hear, and the dumb to **s**.	2980
	9:39 in my name, that can lightly **s** evil of me.	2551
	12: 1 And he began to **s** unto them by parables.	3004
	13:11 no thought beforehand what ye shall **s**,	2980
	13:11 shall be given you in that hour, that **s** ye:	2980
	13:11 for it is not ye that **s**, but the Holy Ghost.	2980
	14:71 I know not this man of whom ye **s**.	3004
	16:17 out devils; they shall **s** with new tongues;	2980
Lk	1:19 am sent to **s** unto thee, and to shew thee	2980
	1:20 thou shalt be dumb, and not able to **s**,	2980
	1:22 he came out, he could not **s** unto them:	2980
	4:41 he rebuking *them* suffered them not to **s**:	2980
	6:26 you, when all men shall **s** well of you:	3004
	7:15 he that was dead sat up, and began to **s**.	2980
	7:24 he began to **s** unto the people concerning	3004
	11:53 and to **provoke** him to **s** of many *things*:	653
	12:10 And whosoever shall **s** a word against	3004
	12:13 Master, **s** to my brother, that *he* divide	3004
	20: 9 Then began he to **s** to the people this	3004
Jn	1:37 And the two disciples heard him **s**,	2980
	1:40 One of the two which heard John **s**,	NIG
	3:11 We **s** that we do know, and testify *that*	2980
	4:26 saith unto her, I that **s** unto thee am *he*.	2980
	6:63 words that I **s** unto you, *they* are spirit,	2980
	7:17 it be of God, or *whether* I **s** of myself.	2980
	8:26 I **s** to the world those *things* which I	3004
	8:28 Father hath taught me, I **s** these *things*.	2980
	8:38 I **s** *that* which I have seen with my Father:	2980
	9:21 is of age; ask him: he shall **s** for himself.	2980
	12:49 what I should say, and what I should **s**.	2980
	12:50 I **s** therefore, even as the Father	2980
	12:50 even as the Father said unto me, so I **s**.	2980
	13:18 I **s** not of you all: I know whom I have	3004

Jn	14:10 the words that I **s** unto you, I speak not	2980
	14:10 when I speak unto you, I **s** not of myself:	2980
	16:13 for he shall not **s** of himself;	2980
	16:13 whatsoever he shall hear, *that* shall he **s**:	2980
	16:25 when I shall no more **s** unto you in	2980
	17:13 these *things* I **s** in the world, that they	2980
Ac	2: 4 and began to **s** with other tongues,	2980
	2: 6 that every man heard them **s** in his own	2980
	2: 7 that are not all these which **s** Galileans?	2980
	2:11 we do hear them **s** in our tongues	2980
	2:29 let me freely **s** unto you of the patriarch	3004
	4:17 that *they* **s** henceforth to no man in this	2980
	4:18 commanded them not to **s** at all nor teach	5350
	4:20 but **s** *the things* which we have seen and	2980
	4:29 with all boldness *they* may **s** thy word,	2980
	5:20 **s** in the temple to the people all the	2980
	5:40 *they* should not **s** in the name of Jesus,	2980
	6:11 We have heard him **s** blasphemous words	2980
	6:13 This man ceaseth not to **s** blasphemous	2980
	10:32 who, when he cometh, shall **s** unto thee.	2980
	10:46 For they heard them **s** with tongues,	2980
	11:15 And as I began to **s**, the Holy Ghost fell	2980
	14: 9 The same heard Paul **s**: who stedfastly	2980
	18: 9 not afraid, but **s**, and hold not thy peace:	2980
	18:26 he began to **s boldly** in the synagogue:	3955
	21:37 unto the chief captain, May I **s** unto thee?	3004
	21:37 Who said, **Canst** thou **s** Greek?	1097
	21:39 suffer me to **s** unto the people.	2980
	23: 5 Thou shalt not **s** evil of the ruler of thy	3004
	24:10 governor had beckoned unto him to **s**,	3004
	26: 1 Thou art permitted to **s** for thyself.	3004
	26:25 **s forth** the words of truth and soberness.	669
	26:26 these *things*, before whom also I **s** freely:	3955
	28:20 to see *you*, and to **s with** *you*: because	4354
Ro	3: 5 who taketh vengeance? (I **s** as a man)	3004
	6:19 I **s** after the manner of men because of	3004
	7: 1 (for I **s** to them that know the law,)	3004
	11:13 For I **s** to you Gentiles, inasmuch as I am	3004
	15:18 For I will not dare to **s** of any of *those*	3004
1Co	1:10 that ye all **s** the same *thing*, and that	3004
	2: 6 Howbeit we **s** wisdom among *them that*	2980
	2: 7 But we **s** the wisdom of God in a mystery,	2980
	2:13 Which *things* also we **s**, not in the words	2980
	3: 1 could not **s** unto you as unto spiritual,	2980
	6: 5 Is it to your shame. Is it so, that there is not	3004
	7: 6 But I **s** this by permission, *and* not of	2980
	7:12 But to the rest **s** I, not the Lord: If any	3004
	7:35 And this I **s** for your own profit; not that I	3004
	10:15 I **s** as to wise *men*; judge ye what I say.	3004
	12:30 do all **s** with tongues? do all interpret?	2980
	13: 1 Though I **s** with the tongues of men and	2980
	14: 6 except I shall **s** to you either by revelation	2980
	14: 9 what is spoken? for ye shall **s** into the air.	2980
	14:18 I **s** with tongues more than you all:	2980
	14:19 in the church I had rather **s** five words	2980
	14:21 and other lips will I **s** unto this people;	2980
	14:23 and all **s** with tongues, and there come in	2980
	14:27 If any *man* **s** in an *unknown* tongue, *let*	2980
	14:28 and let him **s** to himself, and to God.	2980
	14:29 Let the prophets **s** two or three, and let	2980
	14:34 for it is not permitted unto them to **s**;	2980
	14:35 for it is a shame for women to **s** in	2980
	14:39 and forbid not to **s** with tongues.	2980
	15:34 knowledge of God: I **s** *this* to your shame.	3004
2Co	2:17 of God, in the sight of God **s** we in Christ.	2980
	4:13 spoken; we also believe, and therefore **s**;	2980
	6:13 in the same, (I **s** as unto *my* children,	3004
	7: 3 I **s** not *this* to condemn *you*: for I have	3004
	8: 8 I **s** not by commandment, but by occasion	3004
	11:17 which I **s**, I speak *it* not after the Lord,	2980
	11:17 I **s** *it* not after the Lord, but as *it were*	2980
	11:21 I **s** as concerning reproach, as though we	3004
	11:21 howsoever any is bold, (I **s** foolishly,)	2980
	11:23 (I **s** as a fool) I *am* more; in labours more	2980
	12:19 we **s** before God in Christ: but *we do* all	2980
Gal	3:15 Brethren, I **s** after the manner of men;	2980
Eph	4:25 **s** every man truth with his neighbour;	2980
	5:12 For it is a shame even to **s** of those *things*	3004
	5:32 but I **s** concerning Christ and the church.	3004
	6:20 that therein I may **s boldly**, as I ought to	3955
	6:20 I may speak boldly, as I ought to **s**.	2980
Php	1:14 much more bold to **s** the word without	2980
	4:11 Not that I **s** in respect of want: for I have	3004
Col	4: 3 to **s** the mystery of Christ, for which I am	2980
	4: 4 I may make it manifest, as I ought to **s**.	2980
1Th	1: 8 so that we need not to **s** any *thing*.	2980
	2: 2 we were bold in our God to **s** unto you	2980
	2: 4 put in trust with the gospel, *even* so we **s**;	2980
	2:16 Forbidding us to **s** to the Gentiles that	2980
1Ti	2: 7 (I **s** the truth in Christ, *and* lie not;)	3004
	5:14 to the adversary to **s reproachfully**.	3059
Tit	2: 1 **s** thou *the things* which become sound	2980
	2:15 These *things* **s**, and exhort, and rebuke	2980
	3: 2 To **s** evil of no *man*, to be no brawlers,	987
Heb	5: 5 the world to come, whereof we **s**.	2980
	6: 9 accompany salvation, though we thus **s**.	2980
	9: 5 of which we cannot now **s** particularly.	2980
Jas	1:19 be swift to hear, slow to **s**, slow to wrath:	2980
	2:12 So **s** ye, and so do, as they that shall be	2980
	4:11 **S** not **evil** one of another, brethren.	2635
1Pe	2:12 whereas they **s against** you as evildoers,	2635
	3:10 evil, and his lips that *they* **s** no guile:	2980
	3:16 that, whereas they **s evil** of you, as of	2635
	4:11 If any *man* **s**, *let him speak* as the oracles	2980
	4:11 speak, *let him* **s** as the oracles of God;	NIG

2Pe	2:10 they are not afraid to **s** evil of dignities.	987
	2:12 **s** evil *of the things* that they understand	987
	2:18 For when they **s** great swelling *words* of	5350
1Jn	4: 5 therefore **s** they of the world, and the	2980
2Jn	1:12 **s** face to face, that our joy may be full.	2980
3Jn	1:14 see thee, and we shall **s** face to face.	2980
Jude	1: 8 despise dominion, and **s evil** of dignities.	987
	1:10 But these **s evil** of those *things* which	987
Rev	2:24 not known the depths of Satan, as they **s**;	3004
	13:15 that the image of the beast should both **s**,	2980

SPEAKER (2) [SPEAK]

Ps	140:11 Let not an **evil s** be established in	376+3956
Ac	14:12 Mercurius, because he was the chief **s**.	3056

SPEAKEST (17) [SPEAK]

1Sa	9:21 wherefore then **s** thou so to me?	1696
2Sa	19:29 Why **s** thou any more of thy matters?	1696
2Ki	6:12 the words that thou **s** in thy bedchamber.	1696
Job	2:10 Thou **s** as one of the foolish *women*	1696
Ps	50:20 Thou sittest *and* **s** against thy brother;	1696
	51: 4 thou mightest be justified when thou **s**,	1696
Isa	40:27 Why sayest thou, O Jacob, and **s**, O Israel,	1696
Jer	40:16 do this thing: for thou **s** falsely of Ishmael.	1696
	43: 2 saying unto Jeremiah, Thou **s** falsely:	1696
Eze	3:18 nor **s** to warn the wicked from his wicked	1696
Zec	13: 3 for thou **s** lies in the name of the Lord:	1696
Mt	13:10 Why **s** thou unto them in parables?	1696
Lk	12:41 **s** thou this parable unto us, or even to all?	3004
Jn	16:29 Lo, now **s** thou plainly, and speakest no	2980
	16:29 speakest thou plainly, and **s** no proverb.	3004
	19:10 saith Pilate unto him, **S** thou not unto me?	2980
Ac	17:19 what this new doctrine, whereof thou **s**,	2980

SPEAKETH (74) [SPEAK]

Ge	45:12 that *it is* my mouth that **s** unto you.	1696
Ex	33:11 face to face, as a man **s** unto his friend.	1696
Nu	23:26 saying, All that the Lord **s**, that I must	1696
Dt	18:22 When a prophet **s** in the name	1696
1Ki	20: 5 said, Thus **s** Ben-hadad, saying, Although	559
Job	2:10 speakest as one of the foolish *women* **s**.	1696
	17: 5 He that **s** flattery to *his* friends, even	5046
	33:14 For God **s** once, yea twice, *yet man*	1696
Ps	12: 3 *and* the tongue that **s** proud *things*:	1696
	15: 2 and **s** the truth in his heart.	1897
	37:30 The mouth of the righteous **s** wisdom,	1696
	41: 6 if he come to see *me*, he **s** vanity: his	1696
	144: 8 mouth **s** vanity, and their right hand	1696
	144:11 mouth **s** vanity, and their right hand	1696
Pr	2:12 *man*, from the man that **s** froward *things*;	1696
	6:13 winketh with his eyes, he **s** with his feet,	4448
	6:19 A false witness *that* **s** lies, and he that	6315
	10:32 the mouth of the wicked **s** frowardness.	NIH
	12:17 *that* **s** truth sheweth forth righteousness:	6315
	12:18 is that **s** like the piercings of a sword:	981
	14:25 but a deceitful *witness* **s** lies.	6315
	16:13 of kings; and *they* love him that **s** right.	1696
	19: 5 and he that **s** lies shall not escape.	6315
	19: 9 and *he* that **s** lies shall perish.	6315
	21:28 but the man that heareth, **s** constantly.	1696
	26:25 When he **s** fair, believe him not: for *there*	6963
Isa	9:17 and an evildoer, and every mouth **s** folly.	1696
	32: 7 lying words, even when the needy **s** right.	1696
	33:15 that walketh righteously, and **s** uprightly;	1696
Jer	9: 8 tongue *is as* an arrow shot out; it **s** deceit:	1696
	9: 8 *one* **s** peaceably to his neighbour with his	1696
	10: 1 Hear ye the word which the Lord **s** unto	1696
	28: 2 Thus **s** the Lord of hosts, the God of	559
	29:25 Thus **s** the Lord of hosts, the God of	559
	30: 2 Thus **s** the Lord God of Israel, saying,	559
Eze	10: 5 the voice of the Almighty God when he **s**.	1696
Am	5:10 and they abhor him that **s** uprightly.	1696
Hag	1: 2 Thus **s** the Lord of hosts, saying, This	559
Zec	6:12 Thus **s** the Lord of hosts, saying,	559
	7: 9 Thus **s** the Lord of hosts, saying, Execute	559
Mt	10:20 the Spirit of your Father which **s** in you.	2980
	12:32 whosoever **s** a word against the Son of	3004
	12:32 but whosoever **s** against the Holy Ghost,	3004
	12:34 the abundance of the heart the mouth **s**.	2980
Lk	5:21 saying, Who is this which **s** blasphemies?	2980
	6:45 the abundance of the heart his mouth **s**.	2980
Jn	3:31 of the earth is earthly, and **s** of the earth:	2980
	3:34 he whom God hath sent **s** the words of	2980
	7:18 that **s** of himself seeketh his own glory:	2980
	7:26 **s** boldly, and they say nothing unto him.	2980
	8:44 When he **s** a lie, he speaketh of his own:	2980
	8:44 When he speaketh a lie, he **s** of his own:	2980
	19:12 maketh himself a king **s against**	483
Ac	2:25 For David **s** concerning him, I foresaw	3004
	8:34 I pray thee, of whom **s** the prophet this?	3004
Ro	10: 6 the righteousness which is of faith **s** on	3004
1Co	14: 2 For he that **s** in an *unknown* tongue	2980
	14: 2 in an *unknown* tongue **s** not unto men,	2980
	14: 2 *him*; howbeit in the spirit he **s** mysteries.	2980
	14: 3 But he that prophesieth **s** unto men *to*	2980
	14: 4 He that **s** in an *unknown* tongue edifieth	2980
	14: 5 prophesieth than he that **s** with tongues,	2980
	14:11 I shall be unto him that **s** a barbarian,	2980
	14:11 he that **s** *shall be* a barbarian unto me.	2980
	14:13 Wherefore let him that **s** in an *unknown*	2980
1Ti	4: 1 the Spirit **s** expressly, that in the latter	3004
Heb	11: 4 of his gifts: and by it he being dead yet **s**.	1256
	12: 5 which **s** unto you as unto children,	1256
	12:24 that **s** better *things* than *that of* Abel.	2980
	12:25 See *that* ye refuse not him that **s**: for if	2980

Heb	12:25 turn away from him that **s** from heaven:	NIG
Jas	4:11 He that **s evil** of *his* brother, and judgeth	2635
	4:11 **s evil** of the law, and judgeth the law:	2635
Jude	1:16 mouth **s** great swelling *words,* having	2980

SPEAKING (62) [SPEAK]

Ge	24:15 before I had done **s,** that behold,	1696
	24:45 before I had done **s** in mine heart, behold,	1696
Ex	34:33 *till* Moses had done **s** with them, he put a	1696
Nu	7:89 he heard the voice of one **s** unto him from	1696
	16:31 he had made an end of **s** all these words,	1696
Dt	4:33 *ever* people hear the voice of God **s** out	1696
	5:26 hath heard the voice of the living God **s**	1696
	11:19 **s** of them when thou sittest in thine	1696
	20: 9 when the officers have made an end of **s**	1696
	32:45 Moses made an end of **s** all these words	1696
Jdg	15:17 to pass, when he had made an end of **s,**	1696
Ru	1:18 to go with her, then she left **s** unto her.	1696
1Sa	18: 1 when he made an end of **s** unto Saul,	1696
	24:16 when David had made an end of **s** these	1696
2Sa	13:36 as soon as he had made an end of **s,**	1696
2Ch	36:12 prophet **s** from the mouth of the LORD.	NIH
Est	10: 3 of his people, and **s** peace to all his seed.	1696
Job	1:16 While he *was* yet **s,** there came also	1696
	1:17 While he *was* yet **s,** there came also	1696
	1:18 While he *was* yet **s,** there came also	1696
	4: 2 but who can withhold himself from **s?**	4405
	32:15 they answered no more: they left off **s.**	4405
Ps	34:13 tongue from evil, and thy lips from **s** guile.	1696
	58: 3 go astray as soon as they be born, **s** lies.	1696
Isa	58: 9 putting forth of the finger, and **s** vanity;	1696
	58:13 own pleasure, nor **s** *thine own* words:	1696
	59:13 oppression and revolt, conceiving and	1696
	65:24 and whiles they are yet **s,** I will hear.	1696
Jer	7:13 rising up early and **s,** but ye heard not;	1696
	25: 3 have spoken unto you, rising early and **s;**	1696
	26: 7 the people heard Jeremiah **s** these words	1696
	26: 8 when Jeremiah had made an end of **s** all	1696
	35:14 have spoken unto you, rising early and **s;**	1696
	38: 4 all the people, in **s** such words unto them:	1696
	38:27 So they **left off s** with him; for the matter	2790
	43: 1 *that* when Jeremiah had made an end of **s**	1696
Eze	43: 6 I heard *him* **s** unto me out of the house;	1696
Da	8: 5 eyes of man, and a mouth **s** great *things.*	4449
	8:13 I heard one saint **s,** and another saint said	1696
	8:18 Now as he was **s** with me, I was in a deep	1696
	9:20 whiles I *was* **s,** and praying,	1696
	9:21 whiles I *was* **s** in prayer, even the man	1696
Mt	6: 7 that they shall be heard for their **much s.**	4180
Lk	5: 4 Now when he had left **s,** he said unto	2980
Ac	1: 3 **s** of the *things* pertaining to the kingdom	3004
	7:44 as he had appointed, **s** unto Moses,	2980
	13:43 **s** to them, persuaded them to continue	4354
	14: 3 therefore abode they **s boldly** in the Lord,	3955
	20:30 **s** perverse *things,* to draw away disciples	2980
	26:14 I heard a voice **s** unto me, and saying in	2980
1Co	12: 3 that no man **s** by the Spirit of God calleth	2980
	14: 6 if I come unto you **s** with tongues,	2980
2Co	13: 3 Since ye seek a proof of Christ **s** in me,	2980
Eph	4:15 But **s the truth** in love, may grow *up* into	226
	4:31 and anger, and clamour, and **evil s,**	988
	5:19 **s** to yourselves in psalms and hymns and	2980
1Ti	4: 2 **S lies** in hypocrisy, having their	5573
	5:13 **s** *things* which they ought not.	2980
1Pe	4: 4 to the same excess of riot, **s evil** *of you:*	987
2Pe	2:16 the dumb ass **s** with man's voice forbad	5350
	3:16 **s** in them of these *things;* in which are	2980
Rev	13: 5 And there was given unto him a mouth **s**	2980

SPEAKINGS (1) [SPEAK]

1Pe	2: 1 hypocrisies, and envies, and all **evil s,**	2636

SPEAR (45) [SPEAR'S, SPEARMEN, SPEARS]

Jos	8:18 Stretch out the **s** that *is* in thy hand	3591
	8:18 Joshua stretched out the **s** that *he had* in	3591
	8:26 wherewith he stretched out the **s,**	3591
Jdg	5: 8 or **s** seen among forty thousand in Israel?	7420
1Sa	13:22 there was neither sword nor **s** found in	2595
	17: 7 staff of his **s** *was* like a weaver's beam;	2595
	17:45 a sword, and with a **s,** and with a shield:	2595
	17:47 the LORD saveth not with sword and **s:**	2595
	21: 8 is there not here under thine hand **s** or	2595
	22: 6 his **s** in his hand, and all his servants	2595
	26: 7 his **s** is stuck in the ground *at* his bolster:	2595
	26: 8 with the **s** even to the earth at once,	2595
	26:11 take thou now the **s** that *is at* his bolster,	2595
	26:12 David took the **s** and the cruse of water	2595
	26:16 see where the king's **s** *is,* and the cruse	2595
	26:22 and said, Behold, the king's **s:**	2595
2Sa	1: 6 behold, Saul leaned upon his **s;**	2595
	2:23 **s** smote him under the fifth *rib,* that	2595
	2:23 fifth *rib,* that the **s** came out behind him;	2595
	21:16 the weight of whose **s** *weighed* three	7013
	21:19 the staff of whose **s** *was* like a weaver's	2595
	23: 7 be fenced *with* iron and the staff of a **s;**	2595
	23: 8 *he* lift up his **s** against eight hundred,	NIH
	23:18 he lift up his **s** against three hundred,	2595
	23:21 the Egyptian had a **s** in his hand;	2595
	23:21 plucked the **s** out of the Egyptian's hand,	2595
	23:21 and slew him with his own **s.**	2595
1Ch	11:11 he lift up his **s** against three hundred slain	2595
	11:20 for lifting up his **s** against three hundred,	2595
	11:23 in the Egyptian's *hand was* a **s** like a	2595
	11:23 pluckt the **s** out of the Egyptian's hand,	2595
	11:23 and slew him with his own **s.**	2595

1Ch	12:24 **s** *were* six thousand and eight hundred,	7420
	12:34 shield and **s** thirty and seven thousand.	2595
	20: 5 whose **s** staff *was* like a weaver's beam.	2595
2Ch	25: 5 to war, that could handle **s** and shield.	7420
Job	39:23 him, the glittering **s** and the shield.	2595
	41:26 the **s,** the dart, nor the habergeon.	2595
	41:29 he laugheth at the shaking of a **s.**	3591
Ps	35: 3 Draw out also the **s,** and stop *the way*	2595
	46: 9 the bow, and cutteth the **s** in sunder;	2595
Jer	6:23 They shall lay hold on bow and **s;** they	3591
Na	3: 3 both the bright sword and the glittering **s:**	2595
Hab	3:11 *and* at the shining of thy glittering **s.**	2595
Jn	19:34 But one of the soldiers with a **s** pierced	3057

SPEAR'S (1) [SPEAR]

1Sa	17: 7 his **s** head *weighed* six hundred shekels	2595

SPEARMEN (2) [MAN, SPEAR]

Ps	68:30 Rebuke the company of **s,** the multitude	7070
Ac	23:23 and ten, and **s** two hundred,	1187

SPEARS (16) [SPEAR]

1Sa	13:19 Lest the Hebrews make *them* swords or **s:**	2595
2Ki	11:10 did the priest give king David's **s**	2595
2Ch	11:12 in every several city *he put* shields and **s,**	7420
	14: 8 an army *of men* that bare targets and **s,**	2595
	23: 9 delivered to the captains of hundreds **s,**	2595
	26:14 **s,** and helmets, and habergeons.	7420
Ne	4:13 with their swords, their **s,** and their bows.	7420
	4:16 the *other* half of them held both the **s,**	7420
	4:21 half of them held the **s** from the rising of	7420
Job	41: 7 barbed irons? or his head with fish **s?**	6767
Ps	57: 4 whose teeth *are* **s** and arrows,	2595
Isa	2: 4 and their **s** into pruninghooks:	2595
Jer	46: 4 furbish the **s,** *and* put on the brigandines:	7420
Eze	39: 9 the **s,** and they shall burn them with fire	7420
Joel	3:10 swords, and your pruninghooks into **s:**	7420
Mic	4: 3 their **s** into pruninghooks:	2595

SPECIAL (2) [ESPECIALLY, SPECIALLY]

Dt	7: 6 chosen thee to be a **s** people unto himself,	5459
Ac	19:11 And God wrought **s** miracles	3588+3756+5177

SPECIALLY (6) [SPECIAL]

Dt	4:10 *S* the day that thou stoodest before	NIH
Ac	25:26 and **s** before thee, O king Agrippa, that,	3122
1Ti	4:10 Saviour of all men, **s** of those that believe.	3122
	5: 8 and **s** for those of his own house, he hath	3122
Tit	1:10 and deceivers, **s** they of the circumcision:	3122
Phm	1:16 **s** to me, but how much more unto thee,	3122

SPECK OF SAWDUST See MOTE

SPECKLED (11)

Ge	30:32 removing from thence all the **s** and	5348
	30:32 and the spotted and **s** among the goats:	5348
	30:33 every one that *is* not **s** and spotted	5348
	30:35 all the she goats that were **s** and spotted,	5348
	30:39 forth cattle ringstraked, **s,** and spotted.	5348
	31: 8 If he said thus, The **s** shall be thy wages;	5348
	31: 8 be thy wages; then all the cattle bare **s:**	5348
	31:10 the cattle *were* ringstraked, **s,** and grisled.	5348
	31:12 the cattle *are* ringstraked, **s,** and grisled:	5348
Jer	12: 9 Mine heritage *is* unto me *as* a **s** bird,	6641
Zec	1: 8 him *were there* red horses, **s,** and white.	8320

SPECTACLE (1)

1Co	4: 9 for we are made a **s** unto the world,	2302

SPED (1) [SPEED]

Jdg	5:30 Have they not **s?** have they *not* divided	4672

SPEECH (49) [SPEAK]

Ge	4:23 ye wives of Lamech, hearken unto my **s:**	565
	11: 1 earth was *of* one language, and of one **s.**	1697
	11: 7 they may not understand one another's **s.**	8193
Ex	4:10 but I *am* slow of **s,** and of a slow tongue.	6310
Dt	22:14 give occasions of **s** against her,	1697
	22:17 he hath given occasions of **s** *against her,*	1697
	32: 2 as the rain, my **s** shall distil as the dew,	565
2Sa	14:20 To fetch about *this* form of **s** hath thy	1697
	19:11 the **s** of all Israel is come to the king,	1697
1Ki	3:10 the **s** pleased the Lord, that Solomon had	1697
2Ch	32:18 cried with a loud voice **in the Jews' s**	3066
Ne	13:24 children spake half **in the s of** Ashdod,	797
Job	12:20 He removeth away the **s** of the trusty,	8193
	13:17 Hear diligently my **s,** and my declaration	4405
	21: 2 Hear diligently my **s,** and let this be your	4405
	24:25 me a liar, and make my **s** nothing worth?	4405
	29:22 not again; and my **s** dropped upon them.	4405
	37:19 *for* we cannot order *our* **s** by reason of	NIH
Ps	17: 6 incline thine ear unto me, *and* hear my **s.**	565
	19: 2 Day unto day uttereth **s,** and night unto	562
	19: 3 *There is* no **s** nor language, *where* their	562
Pr	7:21 With her much **fair s** she caused him to	3948
	17: 7 Excellent **s** becometh not a fool: much	8193
SS	4: 3 a thread of scarlet, and thy **s** *is* comely:	4057
Isa	28:23 hear my voice; hearken, and hear my **s.**	565
	29: 4 thy **s** shall be low out of the dust,	565
	29: 4 and thy **s** shall whisper out of the dust.	565
	32: 9 ye careless daughters, give ear unto my **s.**	565
	33:19 a people of a deeper **s** *than* thou canst	8193
Jer	31:23 As yet they shall use this **s** in the land of	1697
Eze	1:24 the voice of **s,** as the noise of a host:	1999
	3: 5 *art* not sent to a people of a strange **s**	8193
	3: 6 Not to many people of a strange **s** and of	8193

Hab	3: 2 I have heard thy **s,** *and* was afraid:	8088
Mt	26:73 art *one* of them; for thy **s** bewrayeth thee.	2981
Mk	7:32 deaf, and had an **impediment in** his **s;**	3424
	14:70 art a Galilean, and thy **s** agreeth *thereto.*	2981
Jn	8:43 Why do ye not understand my **s?** *even*	2981
Ac	14:11 their voices, saying **in the s of** Lycaonia,	3072
	20: 7 and continued *his* **s** until midnight.	3056
1Co	2: 1 came not with excellency of **s** or	3056
	2: 4 And my **s** and my preaching *was* not with	3056
	4:19 not the **s** of them which are puffed up,	3056
2Co	3:12 such hope, we use great **plainness of s:**	3954
	7: 4 Great *is* my **boldness of s** toward you,	3954
	10:10 presence *is* weak, and *his* **s** contemptible.	3056
	11: 6 But though *I be* rude in **s,** yet not in	3056
Col	4: 6 Let your **s** *be* alway with grace,	3056
Tit	2: 8 Sound **s** that cannot be condemned; that	3056

SPEECHES (7) [SPEAK]

Nu	12: 8 even apparently, and not in **dark s;**	2420
Job	6:26 the **s** of one that is desperate, *which are*	561
	15: 3 or *with* **s** wherewith he can do no good?	4405
	32:14 neither will I answer him with your **s.**	561
	33: 1 hear my **s,** and hearken to all my words.	4405
Ro	16:18 and **fair s** deceive the hearts of the simple.	2129
Jude	1:15 of all *their* hard **s** which ungodly sinners	NIG

SPEECHLESS (3) [SPEAK]

Mt	22:12 having a wedding garment? And he was **s.**	5392
Lk	1:22 he beckoned unto them, and remained **s.**	2974
Ac	9: 7 men which journeyed with him stood **s,**	1769

SPEED (11) [SPED, SPEEDILY, SPEEDY]

Ge	24:12 **send me good s** *this* day,	6440+7136+3807.1
1Sa	20:38 after the lad, **Make s,** haste, stay not.	4120
2Sa	15:14 **make s** to depart, lest he overtake us	4116
1Ki	12:18 king Rehoboam **made s** to get	553
2Ch	10:18 king Rehoboam **made s** to get *him* up to	553
Ezr	6:12 have made a decree; let it be done **with s.**	629
Isa	5:19 Let him make **s,** *and* hasten his work,	4116
	5:26 behold, they shall come with swiftly:	4120
Ac	17:15 for to come to him **with all s,**	5030+5613
2Jn	1:10 into *your* house, neither bid him **God s:**	5463
	1:11 For he that biddeth him **God s** is partaker	5463

SPEEDILY (19) [SPEED]

Ge	44:11 they **s** took down every man his sack to	4116
1Sa	27: 1 I **s escape** into the land of	4422+4422
2Sa	17:16 of the wilderness, but **s pass over;**	5674+5674
2Ch	35:13 and **divided** them among all the people.	7323
Ezr	6:13 Darius the king had sent, so they did **s.**	629
	7:17 That thou mayest buy **s** with this money	629
	7:21 heaven, shall require of you, *it* be done **s,**	629
	7:26 let judgment be executed **s** upon him,	629
Est	2: 9 he gave her her things for purification,	926
Ps	31: 2 Bow down thine ear to me; deliver me **s:**	4120
	69:17 servant; for I am in trouble: hear me **s.**	4118
	79: 8 let thy tender mercies **s** prevent us: for	4118
	102: 2 in the day *when* I call answer me **s.**	4118
	143: 7 Hear me **s,** O LORD: my spirit faileth:	4118
Ecc	8:11 *against* an evil work is not executed **s,**	4120
Isa	58: 8 and thine health shall spring forth **s:**	4120
Joel	3: 4 **s** will I return your recompence upon	4120
Zec	8:21 Let us **go s** to pray before	1980+1980
Lk	18: 8 tell you that he will avenge them **s.**	1722+5034

SPEEDY (1) [SPEED]

Zep	1:18 for he shall make even a **s** riddance of all	926

SPELT See RIE

SPEND (7) [SPENDEST, SPENDETH, SPENT]

Dt	32:23 them; I will **s** mine arrows upon them.	3615
Job	21:13 They **s** their days in wealth, and in a	3615
	36:11 serve *him,* they shall **s** their days in	3615
Ps	90: 9 we **s** our years as a tale *that is* told.	3615
Isa	55: 2 Wherefore do ye **s** money for *that which*	8254
Ac	20:16 because he would not **s** the **time** in Asia:	5551
2Co	12:15 And I will very gladly **s** and be spent for	1159

SPENDEST (1) [SPEND]

Lk	10:35 whatsoever thou **s more,** when I come	4325

SPENDETH (3) [SPEND]

Pr	21:20 of the wise; but a foolish man **s** it **up.**	1104
	29: 3 he that keepeth company with harlots **s** *his*	6
Ecc	6:12 all the days of his vain life which he **s** as a	6213

SPENT (19) [SPEND]

Ge	21:15 the water was **s** in the bottle, and she cast	3615
	47:18 *it* from my lord, how that our money is **s;**	8552
Lev	26:20 your strength shall be **s** in vain: for your	8552
Jdg	19:11 they *were* by Jebus, the day was far **s;**	7286
1Sa	9: 7 the bread is **s** in our vessels, and *there is*	235
Job	7: 6 weaver's shuttle, and are **s** without hope.	3615
Ps	31:10 For my life is **s** with grief, and my years	3615
Isa	49: 4 I have **s** my strength for nought,	3615
Jer	37:21 until all the bread in the city were **s.**	8552
Mk	5:26 physicians, and had **s** all that she had,	1159
	6:35 And when the day was now far **s,**	1096
Lk	8:43 had **s** all *her* living upon physicians,	4321
	15:14 when he had **s** all, there arose a mighty	1159
	24:29 and the day is far **s.**	2235+2827
Ac	17:21 strangers which were there **s** their **time**	2119
	18:23 And after he had **s** some time *there,* he	4160
	27: 9 Now when much time was **s,**	1230
Ro	13:12 The night is far **s,** the day is at hand:	4298

2Co 12:15 I will very gladly spend and be **s** for you; *1550*

SPEW See BELCH; SPUE

SPICE (5) [SPICED, SPICERY, SPICES]

Ex	35:28 **s**, and oil for the light, and for the	1314
1Ki	10:15 the traffick of the **s** merchants, and *of* all	NIH
2Ch	9: 9 neither was there any such **s** as the queen	1314
SS	5: 1 I have gathered my myrrh with my **s**;	1313
Eze	24:10 and **s** it well, and let the bones be burnt.	7543

SPICED (1) [SPICE]

SS 8: 2 I would cause thee to drink of **s** wine, 7544

SPICERY (1) [SPICE]

Ge 37:25 from Gilead with their camels bearing **s** 5219

SPICES (31) [SPICE]

Ge	43:11 **s**, and myrrh, nuts, and almonds:	5219
Ex	25: 6 **s** for anointing oil, and for sweet incense,	1314
	30:23 Take thou also unto thee principal **s**,	1314
	30:34 Take unto thee **sweet s**, stacte, and	5561
	30:34 *these* **sweet s** with pure frankincense:	5561
	35: 8 **s** for anointing oil, and for the sweet	1314
	37:29 and the pure incense of **sweet s**,	5561
1Ki	10: 2 *with* camels that bare **s**, and very much	1314
	10:10 of **s** very great store, and precious stones:	1314
	10:10 came no more such abundance of **s** as	1314
	10:25 and armour, and **s**, horses, and mules,	1314
2Ki	20:13 the **s**, and the precious ointment, and all	1314
1Ch	9:29 the oil, and the frankincense, and the **s**.	1314
	9:30 of the priests made the ointment of the **s**.	1314
2Ch	9: 1 *with* camels that bare **s**, and gold in abundance,	1314
	9: 9 of **s** great abundance, and precious stones:	1314
	9:24 harness, and **s**, horses, and mules,	1314
	16:14 divers kinds *of* **s** prepared by	NIH
	32:27 for **s**, and for shields, and for all *manner*	1314
SS	4:10 the smell of thine ointments than all **s**!	1314
	4:14 myrrh and aloes, with all the chief **s**:	1314
	4:16 garden, *that* the **s** thereof may flow out.	1314
	5:13 His cheeks *are* as a bed of **s**, *as* sweet	1314
	6: 2 to the beds of **s**, to feed in the gardens,	1314
	8:14 to a young hart upon the mountains of **s**.	1314
Isa	39: 2 the **s**, and the precious ointment, and all	1314
Eze	27:22 occupied in thy fairs with chief of all **s**,	1314
Mk	16: 1 and Salome, had bought *sweet* **s**, that they	*759*
Lk	23:56 returned, and prepared **s** and ointments;	*759*
	24: 1 bringing the **s** which they had prepared,	*759*
Jn	19:40 and wound it in linen clothes with the **s**,	*759*

SPIDER (1) [SPIDER'S]

Pr 30:28 The **s** taketh hold with her hands, and *is* 8079

SPIDER'S (2) [SPIDER]

Job 8:14 cut off, and whose trust *shall* be a **s** web. 5908
Isa 59: 5 cockatrice' eggs, and weave the **s** web: 5908

SPIED (6) [SPY]

Ex	2:11 he **s** an Egyptian smiting a Hebrew, *one*	7200
Jos	6:22 the two men that had **s** out the country,	7270
2Ki	9:17 he **s** the company of Jehu as he came,	7200
	13:21 they **s** a band *of* men; and they cast the	7200
	23:16 he **s** the sepulchres that *were* there in	7200
	23:24 the abominations that were **s** in the land	7200

SPIES (14) [SPY]

Ge	42: 9 of them, and said unto them, Ye *are* **s**;	7270
	42:11 we *are* true *men*, thy servants are no **s**.	7270
	42:14 that I spake unto you, saying, Ye *are* **s**:	7270
	42:16 else by the life of Pharaoh surely ye *are* **s**.	7270
	42:30 to us, and took us for **s** of the country.	7270
	42:31 unto him, We *are* true *men*; we are no **s**:	7270
	42:34 shall I know that ye *are* no **s**, but *that* ye	7270
Nu	21: 1 *tell* that Israel came *by* the way of the **s**;	871
Jos	6:23 the young men that were **s** went in,	7270
Jdg	1:24 **s** saw a man come forth out of the city,	8104
1Sa	26: 4 David therefore sent out **s**,	7270
2Sa	15:10 Absalom sent **s** throughout all the tribes	7270
Lk	20:20 And they watched *him*, and sent forth **s**,	*1455*
Heb	11:31 when she had received the **s** with peace.	*2685*

SPIKENARD (5)

SS	1:12 my **s** sendeth forth the smell thereof.	5373
	4:13 with pleasant fruits; camphire, with **s**,	5373
	4:14 **S** and saffron; calamus and cinnamon,	5373
Mk	14: 3 box of ointment of **s** very precious;	*3487+4101*
Jn	12: 3 Mary a pound of ointment of **s**,	*3487+4101*

SPILLED (3) [SPILT]

Ge	38: 9 brother's wife, that he **s** *it* on the ground,	7843
Mk	2:22 and the wine is **s**, and the bottles will be	*1632*
Lk	5:37 and be **s**, and the bottles shall perish.	*1632*

SPILT (1) [SPILLED]

2Sa 14:14 die, and *are* as water **s** on the ground, 5064

SPIN (3) [SPUN]

Ex 35:25 the women that were wise hearted did **s** 2901
Mt 6:28 grow; they toil not, neither do they **s**: *3514*
Lk 12:27 they toil not, they **s** not; and yet I say *3514*

SPINDLE (1)

Pr 31:19 She layeth her hands to the **s**, and her 3601

SPIRIT (505) [SPIRITS, SPIRITUAL, SPIRITUALLY]

Ge 1: 2 the **S** of God moved upon the face of 7307

Ge	6: 3 My **s** shall not always strive with man,	7307
	41: 8 it came to pass in the morning that his **s**	7307
	41:38 this *is*, a man in whom the **s** of God *is*?	7307
	45:27 the **s** of Jacob their father revived:	7307
Ex	6: 9 not unto Moses for anguish of **s**,	7307
	28: 3 whom I have filled with the **s** of wisdom,	7307
	31: 3 I have filled him with the **s** of God,	7307
	35:21 every one whom his **s** made willing,	7307
	35:31 he hath filled him *with* the **s** of God,	7307
Lev	20:27 man also or woman that hath a **familiar s**,	178
Nu	5:14 the **s** of jealousy come upon him, and he	7307
	5:14 or if the **s** of jealousy come upon him,	7307
	5:30 Or when the **s** of jealousy cometh upon	7307
	11:17 I will take of the **s** which *is* upon thee,	7307
	11:25 took of the **s** that *was* upon him, and gave	7307
	11:25 pass, that when the **s** rested upon them,	7307
	11:26 the **s** rested upon them; and they *were* of	7307
	11:29 that the LORD would put his **s** upon	7307
	14:24 because he had another **s** with him,	7307
	24: 2 and the **s** of God came upon him.	7307
	27:18 a man in whom *is* the **s**, and lay thine	7307
Dt	2:30 for the LORD thy God hardened his **s**,	7307
	34: 9 Joshua the son of Nun was full *of* the **s** of	7307
Jos	5: 1 neither was there **s** in them any more,	7307
Jdg	3:10 the **s** of the LORD came upon him,	7307
	6:34 the **s** of the LORD came upon Gideon,	7307
	9:23 God sent an evil **s** between Abimelech	7307
	11:29 the **s** of the LORD came upon Jephthah,	7307
	13:25 the **s** of the LORD began to move him at	7307
	14: 6 the **s** of the LORD came mightily upon	7307
	14:19 the **s** of the LORD came upon him,	7307
	15:14 the **s** of the LORD came mightily upon	7307
	15:19 his **s** came again, and he revived:	7307
1Sa	1:15 my lord, I *am* a woman of a sorrowful **s**:	7307
	10: 6 the **s** of the LORD will come upon thee,	7307
	10:10 the **s** of God came upon him,	7307
	11: 6 the **s** of God came upon Saul when he	7307
	16:13 the **s** of the LORD came upon David from	7307
	16:14 the **s** of the LORD departed from Saul,	7307
	16:14 an evil **s** from the LORD troubled him.	7307
	16:15 an evil **s** from God troubleth thee.	7307
	16:16 when the evil **s** from God is upon thee,	7307
	16:23 when the *evil* **s** from God was upon Saul,	7307
	16:23 well, and the evil **s** departed from him.	7307
	18:10 that the evil **s** from God came upon Saul,	7307
	19: 9 the evil **s** from the LORD was upon Saul,	7307
	19:20 the **s** of God was upon the messengers of	7307
	19:23 the **s** of God was upon him also,	7307
	28: 7 Seek me a woman that hath a **familiar s**,	178
	28: 7 *there* is a woman that hath a **familiar s** at	178
	28: 8 divine unto me by the **familiar s**,	178
	30:12 he had eaten, his **s** came again to him:	7307
2Sa	23: 2 The **S** of the LORD spake by me,	7307
1Ki	10: 5 of the LORD; there was no more **s** in her.	7307
	18:12 that the **s** of the LORD shall carry thee	7307
	21: 5 said unto him, Why is thy **s** so sad,	7307
	22:21 there came forth a **s**, and stood before	7307
	22:22 I will be a lying **s** in the mouth of all his	7307
	22:23 the LORD hath put a lying **s** in the mouth	7307
	22:24 Which way went the **s** of the LORD from	7307
2Ki	2: 9 let a double portion of thy **s** be upon me.	7307
	2:15 The **s** of Elijah doth rest on Elisha.	7307
	2:16 lest peradventure the **s** of the LORD hath	7307
1Ch	5:26 the God of Israel stirred up the **s** of Pul	7307
	5:26 the **s** of Tilgath-pilneser king of Assyria,	7307
	10:13 *counsel* of *one that had* a **familiar s**,	178
	12:18 the **s** came upon Amasai, *who was* chief	7307
	28:12 the pattern of all that he had by the **s**,	7307
2Ch	9: 4 of the LORD; there was no more **s** in her.	7307
	15: 1 the **s** of God came upon Azariah the son	7307
	18:20 there came out a **s**, and stood before	7307
	18:21 a lying **s** in the mouth of all his prophets.	7307
	18:22 the LORD hath put a lying **s** in the mouth	7307
	18:23 Which way went the **s** of the LORD from	7307
	20:14 came the **s** of the LORD in the midst of	7307
	21:16 against Jehoram the **s** of the Philistines,	7307
	24:20 the **s** of God came upon Zechariah the	7307
	33: 6 dealt with a **familiar s**, and with wizards:	178
	36:22 the LORD stirred up the **s** of Cyrus king	7307
Ezr	1: 1 the LORD stirred up the **s** of Cyrus king	7307
	1: 5 with all *them* whose **s** God had raised,	7307
Ne	9:20 Thou gavest also thy good **s** to instruct	7307
	9:30 testifiedst against them by thy **s** in thy	7307
Job	4:15 a **s** passed before my face; the hair of my	7307
	6: 4 the poison whereof drinketh up my **s**:	7307
	7:11 I will speak in the anguish of my **s**;	7307
	10:12 and thy visitation hath preserved my **s**.	7307
	15:13 That thou turnest thy **s** against God,	7307
	20: 3 the **s** of my understanding causeth me to	7307
	21: 4 *so*, why should not my **s** be troubled?	7307
	26: 4 and whose **s** came from thee?	5397
	26:13 By his **s** he hath garnished the heavens;	7307
	27: 3 in me, and the **s** of God *is* in my nostrils;	7307
	32: 8 *there* is a **s** in man: and the inspiration of	7307
	32:18 matter, the **s** within me constraineth me.	7307
	33: 4 The **S** of God hath made me, and the	7307
	34:14 upon *man, if* he gather unto himself his **s**	7307
Ps	31: 5 Into thine hand I commit my **s**: thou hast	7307
	32: 2 in whose **s** *there* is no guile.	7307
	34:18 and saveth such as be of a contrite **s**.	7307
	51:10 O God; and renew a right **s** within me.	7307
	51:11 and take not thy holy **S** from me.	7307
	51:12 and uphold me *with thy* free **s**.	7307
	51:17 The sacrifices of God *are* a broken **s**:	7307
	76:12 He shall cut off the **s** of princes: *he is*	7307

Ps	77: 3 complained, and my **s** was overwhelmed.	7307
	77: 6 heart: and my **s** made diligent search.	7307
	78: 8 and whose **s** was not stedfast with God.	7307
	104:30 Thou sendest forth thy **s**, they are created:	7307
	106:33 Because they provoked his **s**, so that he	7307
	139: 7 Whither shall I go from thy **s**?	7307
	142: 3 When my **s** was overwhelmed within me,	7307
	143: 4 Therefore is my **s** overwhelmed within	7307
	143: 7 my **s** faileth: hide not thy face from me,	7307
	143:10 thy **s** *is* good; lead me into the land of	7307
Pr	1:23 I will pour out my **s** unto you, I will	7307
	11:13 he that *is* of a faithful **s** concealeth	7307
	14:29 but *he that is* hasty of **s** exalteth folly.	7307
	15: 4 perverseness therein *is* a breach in the **s**.	7307
	15:13 by sorrow of the heart the **s** *is* broken.	7307
	16:18 and a haughty **s** before a fall.	7307
	16:19 Better *it is to be* of an humble **s** with	7307
	16:32 he that ruleth his **s** than he that taketh a	7307
	17:22 medicine: but a broken **s** drieth the bones.	7307
	17:27 man of understanding is of an excellent **s**.	7307
	18:14 The **s** of a man will sustain his infirmity;	7307
	18:14 but a wounded **s** who can bear?	7307
	20:27 The **s** of man *is* the candle of the LORD,	5397
	25:28 He that *hath* no rule over his own **s** *is* like	7307
	29:23 but honour shall uphold the humble in **s**.	7307
Ecc	1:14 behold, all *is* vanity and vexation of **s**.	7307
	1:17 I perceived that this also *is* vexation of **s**.	7307
	2:11 all *was* vanity and vexation of **s**,	7307
	2:17 for all *is* vanity and vexation of **s**,	7307
	2:26 This also *is* vanity and vexation of **s**.	7307
	3:21 Who knoweth the **s** of man that goeth	7307
	3:21 the **s** of the beast that goeth downward to	7307
	4: 4 This *is* also vanity and vexation of **s**.	7307
	4: 6 hands full *with* travail and vexation of **s**.	7307
	4:16 this also *is* vanity and vexation of **s**.	7307
	6: 9 this *is* also vanity and vexation of **s**.	7307
	7: 8 the patient in **s** *is* better than the proud in	7307
	7: 8 in spirit *is* better than the proud in **s**.	7307
	7: 9 Be not hasty in thy **s** to be angry: for	7307
	8: 8 is no man that hath power over the **s**	7307
	8: 8 hath power over the spirit to retain the **s**;	7307
	10: 4 If the **s** of the ruler rise up against thee,	7307
	11: 5 knowest not what *is* the way of the **s**,	7307
	12: 7 the **s** shall return unto God who gave it.	7307
Isa	4: 4 the midst thereof by the **s** of judgment,	7307
	4: 4 of judgment, and by the **s** of burning.	7307
	11: 2 the **S** of the LORD shall rest upon him,	7307
	11: 2 the **s** of wisdom and understanding,	7307
	11: 2 the **s** of counsel and might,	7307
	11: 2 the **s** of knowledge and of the fear of	7307
	19: 3 the **s** of Egypt shall fail in the midst	7307
	19:14 The LORD hath mingled a perverse **s** in	7307
	26: 9 my **s** within me will I seek thee early:	7307
	28: 6 for a **s** of judgment to him that sitteth in	7307
	29: 4 as of one that hath a **familiar s**, out of	178
	29:10 poured upon you the **s** of deep sleep,	7307
	29:24 They also that erred in **s** shall come to	7307
	30: 1 cover *with* a covering, but not of my **S**,	7307
	31: 3 not God; and their horses flesh, and not **s**.	7307
	32:15 Until the **s** be poured upon us from on	7307
	34:16 and his **s** it hath gathered them.	7307
	38:16 and in all these *things* is the life of my **s**:	7307
	40: 7 the **s** of the LORD bloweth upon it:	7307
	40:13 Who hath directed the **s** of the LORD,	7307
	42: 1 delighteth; I have put my **s** upon him:	7307
	42: 5 upon it, and **s** to them that walk therein:	7307
	44: 3 *ground*: I will pour my **s** upon thy seed,	7307
	48:16 the Lord GOD, and his **S**, hath sent me.	7307
	54: 6 as a woman forsaken and grieved in **s**,	7307
	57:15 also *that is* of a contrite and humble **s**,	7307
	57:15 revive the **s** of the humble, and to revive	7307
	57:16 for the **s** should fail before me,	7307
	59:19 the **s** of the LORD shall lift up a standard	7307
	59:21 My **s** that *is* upon thee, and my words	7307
	61: 1 The **S** of the Lord GOD *is* upon me;	7307
	61: 3 garment of praise for the **s** of heaviness;	7307
	63:10 they rebelled, and vexed his holy **S**:	7307
	63:11 *is* he that put his holy **S** within him?	7307
	63:14 the **S** of the LORD caused him to rest:	7307
	65:14 of heart, and shall howl for vexation of **s**.	7307
	66: 2 to *him that is* poor and of a contrite **s**,	7307
Jer	51:11 the LORD hath raised up the **s** of	7307
Eze	1:12 whither the **s** was to go, they went;	7307
	1:20 Whithersoever the **s** was to go, they went	7307
	1:20 go, they went, thither *was their* **s** to go;	7307
	1:20 for the **s** of the living creature *was* in	7307
	1:21 for the **s** of the living creature *was* in	7307
	2: 2 the **s** entered into me when he spake	7307
	3:12 the **s** took me up, and I heard behind me	7307
	3:14 So the **s** lifted me up, and took me away,	7307
	3:14 I went in bitterness, in the heat of my **s**;	7307
	3:24 the **s** entered into me, and set me upon	7307
	8: 3 the **s** lift me up between the earth and	7307
	10:17 *these* lift up themselves *also*: for the **s** of	7307
	11: 1 Moreover the **s** lift me up, and brought	7307
	11: 5 the **S** of the LORD fell upon me,	7307
	11:19 and I will put a new **s** within you;	7307
	11:24 Afterwards the **s** took me up,	7307
	11:24 brought me in vision by the **S** of God into	7307
	13: 3 that follow their own **s**, and have seen	7307
	18:31 and make you a new heart and a new **s**:	7307
	21: 7 every **s** shall faint, and all knees shall be	7307
	36:26 and a new **s** will I put within you:	7307
	36:27 I will put my **s** within you, and cause you	7307
	37: 1 carried me out in the **s** of the LORD,	7307

Eze	37:14 shall put my **s** in you, and ye shall live,	7307
	39:29 I have poured out my **s** upon the house	7307
	43: 5 So the **s** took me up, and brought me into	7307
Da	2: 1 his **s** was troubled, and his sleep	7307
	2: 3 my **s** was troubled to know the dream.	7307
	4: 8 and in whom *is* the **s** of the holy gods:	7308
	4: 9 that the **s** of the holy gods *is* in thee,	7308
	4:18 for the **s** of the holy gods *is* in thee.	7308
	5:11 in whom *is* the **s** of the holy gods;	7308
	5:12 Forasmuch as an excellent **s**,	7308
	5:14 that the **s** of the gods *is* in thee,	7308
	6: 3 because an excellent **s** *was* in him;	7308
	7:15 I Daniel was grieved in my **s** in the midst	7308
Hos	4:12 for the **s** of whoredoms hath caused *them*	7307
	5: 4 for the **s** of whoredoms *is* in the midst of	7307
Joel	2:28 that I will pour out my **s** upon all flesh;	7307
	2:29 in those days will I pour out my **s**.	7307
Mic	2: 7 of Jacob, is the **s** of the LORD straitened?	7307
	2:11 If a man walking *in* the **s** and falsehood	7307
	3: 8 truly I am full *of* power by the **s** of	7307
Hag	1:14 the LORD stirred up the **s** of Zerubbabel	7307
	1:14 the **s** of Joshua the son of Josedech	7307
	1:14 and the **s** of all the remnant of the people;	7307
	2: 5 of Egypt, so my **s** remaineth among you:	7307
Zec	4: 6 Not by might, nor by power, but by my **s**,	7307
	6: 8 have quieted my **s** in the north country.	7307
	7:12 hath sent in his **s** by the former prophets:	7307
	12: 1 and formeth the **s** of man within him.	7307
	12:10 the **s** of grace and of supplications:	7307
	13: 2 and the unclean **s** to pass out of the land.	7307
Mal	2:15 Yet had he the residue of the **s**.	7307
	2:15 Therefore take heed to your **s**, and let	7307
	2:16 therefore take heed to your **s**, that ye deal	7307
Mt	3:16 he saw the **S** of God descending like a	4151
	4: 1 Then was Jesus led up of the **S** into	4151
	5: 3 Blessed *are* the poor in **s**: for theirs is	4151
	10:20 **S** of your Father which speaketh in you.	4151
	12:18 I will put my **s** upon him, and he shall	4151
	12:28 But if I cast out devils by the **S** of God,	4151
	12:43 When the unclean **s** is gone out of a man,	4151
	14:26 sea, they were troubled, saying, It is a **s**;	5326
	22:43 How then doth David in **s** call him Lord,	4151
	26:41 the **s** indeed *is* willing, but the flesh *is*	4151
Mk	1:10 like a dove descending upon him:	4151
	1:12 And immediately the **S** driveth him into	4151
	1:23 their synagogue a man with an unclean **s**;	4151
	1:26 And when the unclean **s** had torn him,	4151
	2: 8 when Jesus perceived in his **s** that they so	4151
	3:30 Because they said, He hath an unclean **s**.	4151
	5: 2 out of the tombs a man with an unclean **s**,	4151
	5: 8 Come out of the man, *thou* unclean **s**.	4151
	6:49 they supposed *it* had been a **s**,	5326
	7:25 whose young daughter had an unclean **s**,	4151
	8:12 And he sighed deeply in his **s**, and saith,	4151
	9:17 unto thee my son, which hath a dumb **s**;	4151
	9:20 he saw him, straightway the **s** tare him;	4151
	9:25 he rebuked the foul **s**, saying unto him,	4151
	9:25 Thou dumb and deaf **s**, I charge thee,	NIG
	9:26 And the **s** cried, and rent him sore,	4151
	14:38 The **s** truly *is* ready, but the flesh *is* weak.	4151
Lk	1:17 And he shall go before him in the **s** and	4151
	1:47 my **s** hath rejoiced in God my Saviour.	4151
	1:80 And waxed strong in **s**, and was in	4151
	2:27 And he came by the **S** into the temple:	4151
	2:40 waxed strong in **s**, filled with wisdom:	4151
	4: 1 and was led by the **S** into the wilderness,	4151
	4:14 And Jesus returned in the power of the **S**	4151
	4:18 The **S** of the Lord *is* upon me,	4151
	4:33 which had a **s** of an unclean devil,	4151
	8:29 (For he had commanded the unclean **s** to	4151
	8:55 And her **s** came again, and she arose	4151
	9:39 **s** taketh him, and he suddenly crieth out;	4151
	9:42 And Jesus rebuked the unclean **s**,	4151
	9:55 Ye know not what manner of **s** ye are of.	4151
	10:21 In that hour Jesus rejoiced in **s**, and said,	4151
	11:13 give the Holy **S** to them that ask him?	4151
	11:24 When the unclean **s** is gone out of a man,	4151
	13:11 there was a woman which had a **s** of	4151
	23:46 Father, into thy hands I commend my **s**:	4151
	24:37 and supposed that *they* had seen a **s**.	4151
	24:39 for a **s** hath not flesh and bones, as ye see	4151
Jn	1:32 I saw the **S** descending from heaven like a	4151
	1:33 Upon whom thou shalt see the **S**	4151
	3: 5 a man be born of water and *of* the **S**,	4151
	3: 6 and that which is born of the **S** is spirit.	4151
	3: 6 and that which is born of the Spirit is **s**.	4151
	3: 8 so is every one that is born of the **S**.	4151
	3:34 for God giveth not the **S** by measure *unto*	4151
	4:23 worshippers shall worship the Father in **s**	4151
	4:24 God *is* a **S**: and they that worship him	4151
	4:24 that worship him must worship *him* in **s**	4151
	6:63 It is the **s** that quickeneth; the flesh	4151
	6:63 unto you, *they* are **s**, and *they* are life.	4151
	7:39 (But this spake he of the **S**, which they	4151
	11:33 he groaned in the **s**, and was troubled,	4151
	13:21 was troubled in **s**, and testified, and said,	4151
	14:17 the **S** of truth; whom the world cannot	4151
	15:26 the **S** of truth, which proceedeth from	4151
	16:13 Howbeit when he, the **S** of truth, is come,	4151
Ac	2: 4 tongues, as the **S** gave them utterance.	4151
	2:17 I will pour out of my **S** upon all flesh:	4151
	2:18 I will pour out in those days of my **S**;	4151
	5: 9 together to tempt the **S** of the Lord?	4151
	6:10 the wisdom and the **s** by which he spake.	4151
	7:59 and saying, Lord Jesus, receive my **s**.	4151

Ac	8:29 Then the **S** said unto Philip, Go near,	4151
	8:39 the **S** of the Lord caught away Philip,	4151
	10:19 the **S** said unto him, Behold, three men	4151
	11:12 And the **S** bade me go with them,	4151
	11:28 signified by the **S** that there should be	4151
	16: 7 into Bithynia: but the **S** suffered them not.	4151
	16:16 a certain damsel possessed with a **s** of	4151
	16:18 being grieved, turned and said to the **s**,	4151
	17:16 them at Athens, his **s** was stirred in him,	4151
	18: 5 Paul was pressed in **s**, and testified to	4151
	18:25 and being fervent in the **s**, he spake and	4151
	19:15 And the evil **s** answered and said, Jesus I	4151
	19:16 the man in whom the evil **s** was leapt	4151
	19:21 were ended, Paul purposed in the **s**,	4151
	20:22 I go bound in the **s** unto Jerusalem,	4151
	21: 4 who said to Paul through the **S**, that *he*	4151
	23: 8 is no resurrection, neither angel nor **s**:	4151
	23: 9 but if a **s** or an angel hath spoken to him,	4151
Ro	1: 4 according to the **S** of holiness,	4151
	1: 9 whom I serve with my **s** in the gospel of	4151
	2:29 of the heart, in the **s**, *and* not *in* the letter;	4151
	7: 6 that we should serve in newness of **s**,	4151
	8: 1 walk not after the flesh, but after the **S**.	4151
	8: 2 For the law of the **S** of life in Christ Jesus	4151
	8: 4 walk not after the flesh, but after the **S**.	4151
	8: 5 they *that are* after the **S** the *things* of	4151
	8: 5 *are* after the Spirit the *things* of the **S**.	4151
	8: 9 but in the **S**, if so be that the Spirit of God	4151
	8: 9 if so be that the **S** of God dwell in you.	4151
	8: 9 Now if any *man* have not the **S** of Christ,	4151
	8:10 but the **S** *is* life because of righteousness.	4151
	8:11 But if the **S** of him that raised up Jesus	4151
	8:11 bodies by his **S** that dwelleth in you.	4151
	8:13 if ye through the **S** do mortify the deeds	4151
	8:14 For as many as are led by the **S** of God,	4151
	8:15 For ye have not received the **s** of bondage	4151
	8:15 but ye have received the **S** of adoption,	4151
	8:16 The **S** itself beareth witness with our spirit	4151
	8:16 The Spirit itself beareth witness with our **s**	4151
	8:23 which have the firstfruits of the **S**,	4151
	8:26 Likewise the **S** also helpeth our infirmities	4151
	8:26 the **S** itself maketh intercession for us	4151
	8:27 hearts knoweth what *is* the mind of the **S**,	4151
	11: 8 God hath given them the **s** of slumber,	4151
	12:11 in business; fervent in **s**; serving the Lord;	4151
	15:19 wonders, by the power of the **S** of God;	4151
	15:30 Christ's sake, and for the love of the **S**,	4151
1Co	2: 4 in demonstration of the **S** and of power:	4151
	2:10 God hath revealed *them* unto us by his **S**:	4151
	2:10 the **S** searcheth all *things*, yea, the deep	4151
	2:11 a man, save the **s** of man which is in him?	4151
	2:11 God knoweth no *man*, but the **S** of God.	4151
	2:12 not the **s** of the world, but the Spirit	4151
	2:12 of the world, but the **S** which is of God;	4151
	2:14 receiveth not the *things* of the **S** of God:	4151
	3:16 and *that* the **S** of God dwelleth in you?	4151
	4:21 rod, or in love, and *in* the **s** of meekness?	4151
	5: 3 verily, as absent in body, but present in **s**,	4151
	5: 4 when ye are gathered together, and my **s**,	4151
	5: 5 that the **s** may be saved in the day of	4151
	6:11 of the Lord Jesus, and by the **S** of our God.	4151
	6:17 he that is joined unto the Lord is one **s**.	4151
	6:20 body, and in your **s**, which are God's.	4151
	7:34 she may be holy both in body and in **s**:	4151
	7:40 and I think also that *I* have the **S** of God.	4151
	12: 3 that no *man* speaking by the **S** of God	4151
	12: 4 are diversities of gifts, but the same **S**.	4151
	12: 7 But the manifestation of the **S** is given to	4151
	12: 8 For to one is given by the **S** the word of	4151
	12: 8 the word of knowledge by the same **S**;	4151
	12: 9 To another faith by the same **S**; to another	4151
	12: 9 another the gifts of healing by the same **S**;	4151
	12:11 worketh *that* one and the selfsame **S**,	4151
	12:13 For by one **S** are we all baptized into one	4151
	12:13 have been all made to drink into one **S**.	4151
	14: 2 howbeit in the **s** he speaketh mysteries.	4151
	14:14 my **s** prayeth, but my understanding is	4151
	14:15 I will pray with the **s**, and will pray with	4151
	14:15 I will sing with the **s**, and I will sing with	4151
	14:16 Else when thou shalt bless with the **s**,	4151
	15:45 the last Adam *was made* a quickening **s**.	4151
	16:18 For they have refreshed my **s** and yours:	4151
2Co	1:22 given the earnest of the **S** in our hearts.	4151
	2:13 I had no rest in my **s**, because I found not	4151
	3: 3 with ink, but with the **S** of the living God;	4151
	3: 6 not of the letter, but of the **s**:	4151
	3: 6 for the letter killeth, but the **s** giveth life.	4151
	3: 8 How shall not the ministration of the **s** be	4151
	3:17 Now the Lord is *that* **S**: and where	4151
	3:17 where the **S** of the Lord *is*, there *is* liberty.	4151
	3:18 to glory, even as by the **S** of the Lord.	4151
	4:13 having the same **s** of faith, according as	4151
	5: 5 hath given unto us the earnest of the **S**.	4151
	7: 1 from all filthiness of the flesh and **s**,	4151
	7:13 because his **s** was refreshed by you all.	4151
	11: 4 or *if* ye receive another **s**, which ye have	4151
	12:18 walked we not in the same **s**? *walked we*	4151
Gal	3: 2 Received ye the **S** by the works of the law,	4151
	3: 3 having begun in the **S**, are ye now made	4151
	3: 5 He therefore that ministereth to you the **S**,	4151
	3:14 we might receive the promise of the **S**	4151
	4: 6 God hath sent forth the **S** of his Son into	4151
	4:29 persecuted him that was *born* after the **S**,	4151
	5: 5 For we through the **S** wait for the hope of	4151
	5:16 Walk in the **S**, and ye shall not fulfil	4151

Gal	5:17 For the flesh lusteth against the **S**,	4151
	5:17 the Spirit against the flesh:	4151
	5:18 But if ye be led of the **S**, ye are not under	4151
	5:22 But the fruit of the **S** is love, joy, peace,	4151
	5:25 If we live in the **S**, let us also walk in	4151
	5:25 live in the Spirit, let us also walk in the **S**.	4151
	6: 1 restore such a one in the **s** of meekness;	4151
	6: 8 he that soweth to the **S** shall of the Spirit	4151
	6: 8 he that soweth to the Spirit shall of the **S**	4151
	6:18 of our Lord Jesus Christ *be* with your **s**.	4151
Eph	1:13 were sealed with *that* holy **S** of promise,	4151
	1:17 may give unto you the **s** of wisdom and	4151
	2: the **s** that now worketh in the children of	4151
	2:18 have access by one **S** unto the Father.	4151
	2:22 for a habitation of God through the **S**.	4151
	3: 5 his holy apostles and prophets by the **S**;	4151
	3:16 to be strengthened with might by his **S** in	4151
	4: 3 Endeavouring to keep the unity of the **S** in	4151
	4: 4 *There is* one body, and one **S**, even as ye	4151
	4:23 And be renewed in the **s** of your mind;	4151
	4:30 And grieve not the holy **S** of God,	4151
	5: 9 (For the fruit of the **S** *is* in all goodness	4151
	5:18 wherein is excess; but be filled with the **S**;	4151
	6:17 and the sword of the **S**, which is the word	4151
	6:18 with all prayer and supplication in the **S**,	4151
Php	1:19 and the supply of the **S** of Jesus Christ,	4151
	1:27 of your affairs, that ye stand fast in one **s**,	4151
	2: 1 if any fellowship of the **S**, if any bowels	4151
	3: 3 which worship God in the **s**, and rejoice	4151
Col	1: 8 also declared unto you your love in the **S**.	4151
	2: 5 yet am I with you in the **s**, joying and	4151
1Th	4: 8 who hath also given unto us his holy **S**.	4151
	5:19 Quench not the **S**.	4151
	5:23 *I pray God* your whole and soul and	4151
2Th	2: 2 be troubled, neither by **s**, nor by word,	4151
	2: 8 the Lord shall consume with the **s** of	4151
	2:13 to salvation through sanctification of the **S**	4151
1Ti	3:16 justified in the **S**, seen of angels,	4151
	4: 1 Now the **S** speaketh expressly, that in	4151
	4:12 in charity, in **s**, in faith, in purity.	4151
2Ti	1: 7 For God hath not given us the **s** of fear;	4151
	4:22 The Lord Jesus Christ *be* with thy **s**.	4151
Phm	1:25 of our Lord Jesus Christ *be* with your **s**.	4151
Heb	4:12 to the dividing asunder of soul and **s**,	4151
	9:14 who through the eternal **S** offered himself	4151
	10:29 hath done despite unto the **S** of grace?	4151
Jas	2:26 For as the body without the **s** is dead,	4151
	4: 5 the **s** that dwelleth in us lusteth to envy?	4151
1Pe	1: 2 through sanctification of the **S**,	4151
	1:11 what manner of time the **S** of Christ	4151
	1:22 the **S** unto unfeigned love of the brethren,	4151
	3: 4 *even* the ornament of a meek and quiet **s**,	4151
	3:18 death in the flesh, but quickened by the **S**:	4151
	4: 6 flesh, but live according to God in the **s**.	4151
	4:14 *are ye*; for the **s** of glory and of God	4151
1Jn	3:24 in us, by the **S** which he hath given us.	4151
	4: 1 believe not every **s**, but try the spirits	4151
	4: 2 Hereby know ye the **S** of God: Every spirit	4151
	4: 2 Every **s** that confesseth that Jesus Christ is	4151
	4: 3 And every **s** that confesseth not that Jesus	4151
	4: 3 this is *that* **s** of antichrist, whereof you	NIG
	4: 6 Hereby know we the **s** of truth,	4151
	4: 6 we the spirit of truth, and the **s** of error.	4151
	4:13 in us, because he hath given us of his **S**.	4151
	5: 6 it is the **S** that beareth witness, because	4151
	5: 6 beareth witness, because the **S** is truth.	4151
	5: 8 the **S**, and the water, and the blood:	4151
Jude	1:19 sensual, having not the **S**.	4151
Rev	1:10 I was in the **s** on the Lord's day,	4151
	2: 7 let him hear what the **S** saith unto	4151
	2:11 let him hear what the **S** saith unto	4151
	2:17 let him hear what the **S** saith unto	4151
	2:29 let him hear what the **S** saith unto	4151
	3: 6 let him hear what the **S** saith unto	4151
	3:13 let him hear what the **S** saith unto	4151
	3:22 let him hear what the **S** saith unto	4151
	4: 2 And immediately I was in the **s**:	4151
	11:11 a half the **s** of life from God entered into	4151
	14:13 Yea, saith the **S**, that they may rest from	4151
	17: 3 So he carried me away in the **s** into	4151
	18: 2 the hold of every foul **s**, and a cage of	4151
	19:10 for the testimony of Jesus is the **s** of	4151
	21:10 he carried me away in the **s** to a great	4151
	22:17 And the **S** and the bride say, Come.	4151

[HOLY] SPIRIT See [HOLY] GHOST

SPIRITIST See WIZARD

SPIRITS (46) [SPIRIT]

Lev	19:31 Regard not them that have **familiar s**,	178
	20: 6 that turneth after such as have **familiar s**,	178
Nu	16:22 said, O God, the God of the **s** of all flesh,	7307
	27:16 the LORD, the God of the **s** of all flesh,	7307
Dt	18:11 or a consulter with **familiar s**, or a wizard,	178
1Sa	28: 3 had put away those that had **familiar s**,	178
	28: 9 he hath cut off those that have **familiar s**,	178
2Ki	21: 6 and dealt with **familiar s** and wizards:	178
	23:24 Moreover the **workers with familiar s**,	178
Ps	104: 4 Who maketh his angels **s**; his ministers a	7307
Pr	16: 2 own eyes; but the LORD weigheth the **s**.	7307
Isa	8:19 Seek unto them that have **familiar s**,	178
	19: 3 to them that have **familiar s**, and to	178
Zec	6: 5 These *are* the four **s** of the heavens,	7307
Mt	8:16 and he cast out the **s** with *his* word,	4151

Mt	10: 1 he gave them power against unclean **s**,	4151
	12:45 taketh with himself seven other **s** more	4151
Mk	1:27 commandeth he even the unclean **s**,	4151
	3:11 And they saw him,	4151
	5:13 And the unclean **s** went out,	4151
	6: 7 and gave them power over unclean **s**;	4151
Lk	4:36 power he commandeth the unclean **s**;	4151
	6:18 And they that were vexed with unclean **s**:	4151
	7:21 *their* infirmities and plagues, and of evil **s**;	4151
	8: 2 which had been healed of evil **s** and	4151
	10:20 not, that the **s** are subject unto you;	4151
	11:26 taketh to *him* seven other **s** more wicked	4151
Ac	5:16 *them* which were vexed with unclean **s**:	4151
	8: 7 For unclean **s**, crying with loud voice,	4151
	19:12 them, and the evil **s** went out of them;	4151
	19:13 had evil **s** the name of the Lord Jesus,	4151
1Co	12:10 to another discerning of **s**;	4151
	14:32 And the **s** of the prophets are subject to	4151
1Ti	4: 1 giving heed to seducing **s**, and doctrines	4151
Heb	1: 7 maketh his angels **s**, and his ministers	4151
	1:14 Are they not all ministering **s**, sent forth to	4151
	12: 9 be in subjection unto the Father of **s**,	4151
	12:23 and to the **s** of just *men* made perfect,	4151
1Pe	3:19 went and preached unto the **s** in prison;	4151
1Jn	4: 1 but try the **s** whether they are of God:	4151
Rev	1: 4 from the seven **s** which are before his	4151
	3: 1 *things* saith he that hath the seven **s**	4151
	4: 5 the throne, which are the seven **s** of God.	4151
	5: 6 which are the seven **s** of God sent forth	4151
	16:13 And I saw three unclean **s** like frogs *come*	4151
	16:14 For they are the **s** of devils, working	4151

SPIRITUAL (28) [SPIRIT]

Hos	9: 7 the **s** man *is* mad, for the multitude of	7307
Ro	1:11 that I may impart unto you some **s** gift,	4152
	7:14 For we know that the law is **s**: but I am	4152
	15:27 **s** *things*, their duty is also to minister	4152
1Co	2:13 comparing **s** *things* with spiritual.	4152
	2:13 comparing spiritual *things* with **s**.	4152
	2:15 But he that is **s** judgeth all *things*, yet he	4152
	3: 1 could not speak unto you as unto **s**,	4152
	9:11 If we have sown unto you **s** *things, is it* a	4152
	10: 3 And did all eat the same **s** meat;	4152
	10: 4 And did all drink the same **s** drink: for	4152
	10: 4 they drank of *that* **s** Rock that followed	4152
	12: 1 Now concerning **s** *gifts*, brethren, I would	4152
	14: 1 and desire **s** *gifts*, but rather that ye may	4152
	14:12 forasmuch as ye are zealous of **s** *gifts*,	4151
	14:37 *man* think himself to be a prophet, or **s**,	4152
	15:44 sown a natural body; it is raised a **s** body.	4152
	15:44 is a natural body, and there is a **s** body.	4152
	15:46 Howbeit *that was* not first *which is* **s**,	4152
	15:46 is natural; *and* afterward *that which is* **s**.	4152
Gal	6: 1 be overtaken in a fault, ye which are **s**,	4152
Eph	1: 3 who hath blessed us with all **s** blessings	4152
	5:19 in psalms and hymns and **s** songs,	4152
	6:12 against **s** wickedness in high *places*.	4152
Col	1: 9 will in all wisdom and **s** understanding;	4152
	3:16 another in psalms and hymns and **s** songs,	4152
1Pe	2: 5 as lively stones, are built *up* a **s** house,	4152
	2: 5 a holy priesthood, to offer up **s** sacrifices,	4152

SPIRITUALLY (3) [SPIRIT]

Ro	8: 6 but to be **s** minded *is* life and peace.	4151
1Co	2:14 know *them*, because they are **s** discerned.	4153
Rev	11: 8 which **s** is called Sodom and Egypt,	4153

SPIT (11) [SPAT, SPITTED, SPITTING, SPITTLE]

Lev	15: 8 if he that hath the issue **s** upon him that	7556
Nu	12:14 If her father had **but s** in her face,	3417+3417
Dt	25: 9 **s** in his face, and shall answer and say,	3417
Job	30:10 from me, and spare not to **s** in my face.	7536
Mt	26:67 Then did they **s** in his face,	1716
	27:30 And they **s** upon him, and took the reed,	1716
Mk	7:33 ears, and he **s**, and touched his tongue;	4429
	8:23 when he had **s** on his eyes, and put *his*	4429
	10:34 and shall **s** upon him, and shall kill him:	1716
	14:65 some began to **s on** him, and to cover	1716
	15:19 and did **s** upon him, and bowing *their*	1716

SPITE (1) [SPITEFULLY]

Ps	10:14 seen *it*; for thou beholdest mischief and **s**,	3708

SPITEFULLY (2) [SPITE]

Mt	22: 6 and **entreated** *them* **s**, and slew *them*.	5195
Lk	18:32 and **s entreated**, and spitted on:	5195

SPITTED (1) [SPIT]

Lk	18:32 and spitefully entreated, and **s on**:	1716

SPITTING (1) [SPIT]

Isa	50: 6 I hid not my face from shame and **s**.	7536

SPITTLE (3) [SPIT]

1Sa	21:13 and let his **s** fall down upon his beard.	7388
Job	7:19 let me alone till I swallow down my **s**?	7536
Jn	9: 6 and made clay of the **s**, and he anointed	4427

SPLENDID See GOODLIER; GOODLIEST; GOODLY

SPLINT See ROLLER

SPLIT See CLAVE

SPOIL (118) [SPOILED, SPOILER, SPOILERS, SPOILEST, SPOILETH, SPOILING, SPOILS]

Ge	49:27 prey, and at night he shall divide the **s**.	7998
Ex	3:22 and ye shall **s** the Egyptians.	5337
	15: 9 I will overtake, I will divide the **s**;	7998
Nu	31: 9 **took** the **s** of all their cattle, and all their	962
	31:11 they took all the **s**, and all the prey, *both*	7998
	31:12 the prey, and the **s**, unto Moses,	7998
	31:53 the men of war had **taken s**, every man	962
Dt	2:35 and the **s** of the cities which we took.	7998
	3: 7 all the cattle, and the **s** of the cities, we	7998
	13:16 thou shalt gather all the **s** of it into	7998
	13:16 all the **s** thereof every whit, for the Lord	7998
	20:14 that is in the city, *even* all the **s** thereof,	7998
	20:14 thou shalt eat the **s** of thine enemies,	7998
Jos	8: 2 only the **s** thereof, and the cattle thereof,	7998
	8:27 the **s** of that city Israel took for a prey	7998
	11:14 all the **s** of these cities, and the cattle,	7998
	22: 8 divide the **s** of your enemies with your	7998
Jdg	5:30 for the necks of *them* that take the **s**?	7998
	14:19 their **s**, and gave change *of garments*	2488
1Sa	14:30 the **s** of their enemies which they found?	7998
	14:32 people flew upon the **s**, and took sheep,	7998
	14:36 **s** them until the morning light, and let us	962
	15:19 didst fly upon the **s**, and didst evil in	7998
	15:21 the people took of the **s**, sheep and oxen,	7998
	30:16 all the great **s** that they had taken out of	7998
	30:19 neither sons nor daughters, neither **s**,	7998
	30:20 *other* cattle, and said, This *is* David's **s**.	7998
	30:22 we will not give them *ought* of the **s** that	7998
	30:26 he sent of the **s** unto the elders of Judah,	7998
	30:26 Behold a present for you of the **s** of	7998
2Sa	3:22 and brought in a great **s** with them:	7998
	8:12 of Amalek, and of the **s** of Hadadezer,	7998
	12:30 he brought forth the **s** of the city in great	7998
	23:10 the people returned after him only to **s**.	6584
2Ki	3:23 another: now therefore, Moab, to the **s**.	7998
	21:14 a prey and a **s** to all their enemies;	4933
1Ch	20: 2 he brought also exceeding much **s** *out* of	7998
2Ch	14:13 and they carried away very much **s**.	7998
	14:14 for there was *exceeding* much **s** in them.	961
	15:11 of the **s** *which* they had brought,	7998
	20:25 people came to take away the **s** of them,	7998
	20:25 were three days in gathering of the **s**,	7998
	24:23 sent all the **s** of them unto the king of	7998
	25:13 three thousand of them, and took much **s**.	961
	28: 8 took also away much **s** from them,	7998
	28: 8 from them, and brought the **s** to Samaria.	7998
	28:14 the **s** before the princes and all	961
	28:15 with the **s** clothed all *that were* naked	7998
Ezr	9: 7 and to a **s**, and to confusion of face,	961
Est	3:13 and *to take* the **s** of them for a prey.	7998
	8:11 and *to take* the **s** of them for a prey,	7998
	9:10 but on the **s** laid they not their hand.	961
Job	29:17 and pluckt the **s** out of his teeth.	2964
Ps	44:10 and they which hate us **s** for themselves.	8154
	68:12 she that tarried at home divided the **s**.	7998
	89:41 All that pass by the way **s** him: he is a	8155
	109:11 he hath; and let the strangers **s** his labour.	962
	119:162 at thy word, as one that findeth great **s**.	7998
Pr	1:13 we shall fill our houses **with s**:	7998
	16:19 than to divide the **s** with the proud.	7998
	22:23 and **s** the soul of those that spoiled them.	6906
	24:15 of the righteous; **s** not his resting place:	7703
	31:11 in her, so that he shall have no need of **s**.	7998
SS	2:15 the foxes, the little foxes, that **s** the vines:	2254
Isa	3:14 the **s** of the poor *is* in your houses.	1500
	8: 4 the **s** of Samaria shall be taken away	7998
	9: 3 as *men* rejoice when they divide the **s**.	7998
	10: 6 to take the **s**, and to take the prey,	7998
	11:14 they shall **s** them of the east together:	962
	17:14 This *is* the portion of them that **s** us,	8154
	33: 1 when thou shalt cease to **s**, thou shalt be	7703
	33: 4 your **s** shall be gathered *like* the gathering	7998
	33:23 is the prey of a great **s** divided; the lame	7998
	42:22 for a **s**, and none saith, Restore.	4933
	42:24 Who gave Jacob for a **s**, and Israel to	4933
	53:12 and he shall divide the **s** with the strong;	7998
Jer	5: 6 and a wolf of the evenings shall **s** them,	7703
	6: 7 violence and **s** is heard in her; before me	7701
	15:13 thy treasures will I give to the **s** without	957
	17: 3 substance *and* all thy treasures to the **s**,	957
	20: 5 which shall **s** them, and take them,	962
	20: 8 I spake, I cried out, I cried violence and **s**;	7701
	30:16 they that **s** thee shall be a spoil, and all	7601
	30:16 they that spoil thee shall be a **s**, and all	4933
	47: 4 Because of the day that cometh to **s** all	7703
	47: 4 for the Lord *will* **s** the Philistines,	7703
	49:28 go up to Kedar, and **s** the men of the east.	7703
	49:32 and the multitude of their cattle a **s**:	7998
	50:10 Chaldea shall be a **s**: all that spoil her shall	7998
	50:10 all that **s** her shall be satisfied, saith	7997
Eze	7:21 and to the wicked of the earth for a **s**;	7998
	14:15 they **s** it, so that it be desolate, that no	7921
	25: 7 will deliver thee for a **s** to the heathen;	957
	26: 5 and it shall become a **s** to the nations.	957
	26:12 they shall **make** a **s** of thy riches,	7997
	29:19 and **take** her **s**, and take her prey;	7997+7998
	32:12 they shall **s** the pomp of Egypt, and all	7703
	38:12 To **take** a **s**, and to take a prey;	7997+7998
	38:13 thee, Art thou come to **take** a **s**?	7997+7998
	38:13 *away* cattle and goods, to take a great **s**?	7998
	39:10 they shall **s** those that spoiled them,	7997
	45: 9 remove violence and **s**,	7701

Da	11:24 among them the prey, and **s**, and riches:	7998
	11:33 flame, by captivity, and by **s**, *many* days.	961
Hos	10: 2 down their altars, he shall **s** their images.	7703
	13:15 he shall **s** the treasure of all pleasant	8154
Na	2: 9 **Take** ye the **s** of silver, take the spoil of	962
	2: 9 ye the spoil of silver, **take the s** of gold:	962
Hab	2: 8 all the remnant of the people shall **s** thee;	7997
	2:17 the **s** of beasts, *which* made them afraid,	7701
Zep	2: 9 the residue of my people shall **s** them,	962
Zec	2: 9 and they shall be a **s** to their servants:	7998
	14: 1 thy **s** shall be divided in the midst of thee.	7998
Mt	12:29 and **s** his goods, except he first bind	1283
	12:29 **strong** *man*? and then he will **s** his house.	1283
Mk	3:27 and **s** his goods, except he will first bind	1283
	3:27 **strong** *man*; and then he will **s** his house.	1283
Col	2: 8 Beware lest any *man* **s** you through	4812

SPOILED (55) [SPOIL]

Ge	34:27 the city, because they had defiled their	962
	34:29 and **s** even all that *was* in the house.	962
Ex	12:36 *they* required. And they **s** the Egyptians.	5337
Dt	28:29 shalt be only oppressed and **s** evermore,	1497
Jdg	2:14 into the hands of spoilers that **s** them,	8155
	2:16 out of the hand of those that **s** them.	8154
1Sa	14:48 out of the hands of them that **s** them.	8154
	17:53 the Philistines, and they **s** their tents.	8155
2Ki	7:16 went out, and **s** the tents of the Syrians.	962
2Ch	14:14 they **s** all the cities; for there was	962
Job	12:17 He leadeth counsellers away **s**,	7758
	12:19 He leadeth princes away **s**,	7758
Ps	76: 5 The stouthearted are **s**, they have slept	7997
Pr	22:23 and **s** the soul of those that **s** them.	6906
Isa	13:16 their houses shall be **s**, and their wives	8155
	18: 2 down, whose land the rivers have **s**.	958
	18: 7 under foot, whose land the rivers have **s**,	958
	24: 3 be utterly emptied, and **utterly s**:	962+962
	33: 1 to thee that spoilest, and thou *wast* not **s**;	7703
	33: 1 thou shalt cease to spoil, thou shalt be **s**;	7703
	42:22 this *is* a people robbed and **s**; *they are* all	8154
Jer	2:14 *is* he a homeborn *slave*? why is he **s**?	957
	4:13 than eagles. Woe unto us! for we are **s**.	7703
	4:20 is cried; for the whole land is **s**:	7703
	4:20 suddenly are my tents **s**, *and* my curtains	7703
	4:30 when thou art **s**, what wilt thou do?	7703
	9:19 is heard out of Zion, How are we **s**!	7703
	10:20 My tabernacle is **s**, and all my cords are	7703
	21:12 deliver *him* that is **s** out of the hand of	1497
	22: 3 deliver the **s** out of the hand of	1497
	25:36 *shall be heard*: for the Lord *hath* **s** their	7703
	48: 1 for it is **s**: Kiriathaim is confounded *and*	7703
	48:15 Moab is **s**, and gone up *out of* her cities,	7703
	48:20 cry; tell ye *it* in Arnon, that Moab is **s**,	7703
	49: 3 Howl, O Heshbon, for Ai is **s**: cry,	7703
	49:10 his seed is **s**, and his brethren,	7703
	51:55 Because the Lord *hath* **s** Babylon,	7703
Eze	18: 7 hath none by violence, hath given his	1497
	18:12 the poor and needy, hath **s** by violence,	1497
	18:16 neither hath **s** by violence, *but* hath given	1497
	18:18 *his* brother by violence, and did *that*	1497
	23:46 and *will* give them to be removed and **s**.	957
	39:10 they shall spoil those that **s** them,	7997
Hos	10:14 people, and all thy fortresses shall be **s**,	7703
	10:14 as Shalman **s** Beth-arbel in the day of	7701
Am	3:11 from thee, and thy palaces shall be **s**.	962
	5: 9 strengtheneth the **s** against the strong,	7701
	5: 9 that the **s** shall come against the fortress.	7701
Mic	2: 4 and say, We be **utterly s**:	7703+7703
Hab	2: 8 Because thou hast **s** many nations,	7997
Zec	2: 8 he sent me unto the nations which **s** you:	7997
	11: 2 cedar is fallen; because the mighty are **s**:	7703
	11: 3 of the shepherds; for their glory is **s**:	7703
	11: 3 of young lions; for the pride of Jordan is **s**.	7703
Col	2:15 And having **s** principalities and powers,	554

SPOILER (9) [SPOIL]

Isa	16: 4 a covert to them from the face of the **s**:	7703
	16: 4 the extortioner is at an end, the **s** ceaseth,	7701
	21: 2 dealeth treacherously, and the **s** spoileth.	7703
Jer	6:26 for the **s** shall suddenly come upon us.	7703
	15: 8 mother of the young men a **s** at noonday:	7703
	48: 8 the **s** shall come upon every city,	7703
	48:18 for the **s** of Moab shall come upon thee,	7703
	48:32 the **s** is fallen upon thy summer fruits and	7703
	51:56 Because the **s** is come upon her, *even*	7703

SPOILERS (7) [SPOIL]

Jdg	2:14 he delivered them into the hands of **s** that	8154
1Sa	13:17 the **s** came out of the camp of	7843
	14:15 garrison, and the **s**, they also trembled,	7843
2Ki	17:20 and delivered them into the hand of **s**,	8154
Jer	12:12 The **s** are come upon all high places	7703
	51:48 for the **s** shall come unto her from	7703
	51:53 *yet* from me shall **s** come unto her, saith	7703

SPOILEST (1) [SPOIL]

Isa	33: 1 Woe to thee that **s**, and thou *wast* not	7703

SPOILETH (4) [SPOIL]

Ps	35:10 and the needy from him that **s** him?	1497
Isa	21: 2 dealeth treacherously, and the spoiler **s**.	7703
Hos	7: 1 *and* the troop *of robbers* **s** without.	6584
Na	3:16 the cankerworm **s**, and flieth away.	6584

SPOILING (5) [SPOIL]

Ps	35:12 They rewarded me evil for good *to* the **s**	7908

S

Isa 22: 4 of the **s** of the daughter of my people. 7701
Jer 48: 3 from Horonaim, and great destruction. 7701
Hab 1: 3 for **s** and violence *are* before me; 7701
Heb 10:34 and took joyfully the **s** of your goods, *724*

SPOILS (5) [SPOIL]
Jos 7:21 When I saw among the **s** a goodly 7998
1Ch 26:27 Out of the **s won** in battles did they 7998
Isa 25:11 pride together with the **s** of their hands. 698
Lk 11:22 wherein he trusted, and divideth his **s**. 4661
Heb 7: 4 patriarch Abraham gave the tenth of the **s**. 205

SPOKEN (287) [SPEAK]
Ge 12: 4 as the LORD had **s** unto him; 1696
 18:19 Abraham that which he hath **s** of him. 1696
 19:21 *this* city, for the which thou hast **s**. 1696
 21: 1 and the LORD did unto Sarah as he had **s**. 1696
 21: 2 the set time of which God had **s** to him. 1696
 24:51 master's son's wife, as the LORD hath **s**. 1696
 28:15 I have done *that* which I have **s** to thee 1696
 41:28 This *is* the thing which I have **s** unto 1696
 44: 2 according to the word that Joseph had **s**. 1696
Ex 4:10 nor since thou hast **s** unto thy servant: 1696
 4:30 words which the LORD had **s** unto Moses, 1696
 9:12 as the LORD had **s** unto Moses. 1696
 9:35 of Israel go; as the LORD had **s** by Moses. 1696
 10:29 Moses said, Thou hast **s** well, I will see 1696
 19: 8 said, All that the LORD hath **s** we will do. 1696
 32:13 all this land that I have **s** of will I give unto 559
 32:34 *the place* of which I have **s** unto thee: 1696
 33:17 I will do this thing also that thou hast **s**: 1696
 34:32 the LORD had **s** with him in mount Sinai. 1696
Lev 10:11 hath **s** unto them by the hand of Moses. 1696
Nu 1:48 For the LORD had **s** unto Moses, saying, 1696
 10:29 for the LORD hath **s** good concerning 1696
 12: 2 Hath the LORD indeed **s** only by Moses? 1696
 12: 2 hath he not **s** also by us? And the LORD 1696
 14:17 be great, according as thou hast **s**, saying, 1696
 14:28 as ye have **s** in mine ears, so will I do to 1696
 15:22 which the LORD hath **s** unto Moses, 1696
 21: 7 for we have **s** against the LORD, 1696
 23: 2 Balak did as Balaam had **s**; and Balak and 1696
 23:17 said unto him, What hath the LORD **s**? 1696
 23:19 shall he not do *it?* or hath he **s**, and shall 1696
Dt 1:14 The thing which thou hast **s** *is* good *for us* 1696
 5:28 this people, which they have **s** unto thee: 1696
 5:28 they have well *said* all that they have **s**. 1696
 6:19 from before thee, as the LORD hath **s**. 1696
 13: 5 he hath **s** to turn *you* away from 1696
 18:17 They have well *s that* which they have NIH
 18:17 have well *spoken that* which they have **s**. 1696
 18:21 the word which the LORD hath not **s**? 1696
 18:22 *is* the thing which the LORD hath not **s**, 1696
 18:22 the prophet hath **s** it presumptuously: 1696
 26:19 unto the LORD thy God, as he hath **s**. 1696
Jos 6: 8 pass, when Joshua had **s** unto the people, 559
 21:45 the LORD had **s** unto the house of Israel; 1696
Ru 2:13 for that thou hast **s** friendly unto thine 1696
1Sa 1:16 my complaint and grief have I hitherto 1696
 3:12 which I have **s** concerning his house: 1696
 20:23 the matter which thou and I have **s** of, 1696
 25:30 the good that he hath **s** concerning thee, 1696
2Sa 2:27 unless thou hadst **s**, surely then in 1696
 3:18 then do *it:* for the LORD hath **s** of David, 559
 6:22 of the maidservants which thou hast **s** of, 559
 7:19 thou hast **s** also of thy servant's house for 1696
 7:25 the word that thou hast **s** concerning thy 1696
 7:29 hast **s** *it:* and with thy blessing let the 1696
 14:19 from ought that my lord the king hath **s**: 1696
 17: 6 Ahithophel hath **s** after this manner: 1696
1Ki 2:23 Adonijah have not **s** this word against his 1696
 12: 9 this people, who have **s** to me, saying, 1696
 13: 3 This *is* the sign which the LORD hath **s**; 1696
 13:11 the words which he had **s** unto the king, 1696
 14:11 of the air eat: for the LORD hath **s** *it*. 1696
 18:24 the people answered and said, It is well **s**. 1697
 21: 4 which Naboth the Jezreelite had **s** to him: 1696
 22:23 the LORD hath **s** evil concerning thee. 1696
 22:28 all in peace, the LORD hath not **s** by me. 1696
2Ki 1:17 the word of the LORD which Elijah had **s**. 1696
 4:13 wouldest thou be **s** for to the king, or to 1696
 7:18 it came to pass as the man of God had **s** to 1696
 19:21 This *is* the word that the LORD hath **s** 1696
 20: 9 the LORD will do the thing that he hath **s**: 1696
 20:19 the word of the LORD which thou hast **s**. 1696
1Ch 17:17 for thou hast *also* **s** of thy servant's house 1696
 17:23 let the thing that thou hast **s** concerning 1696
2Ch 2:15 and the wine, which my lord hath **s** of, 559
 6:10 hath performed his word that he hath **s**: 1696
 6:17 which thou hast **s** unto thy servant David. 1696
 10: 9 have **s** to me, saying, Ease somewhat 1696
 18:22 and the LORD hath **s** evil against thee. 1696
 18:27 in peace, *then* hath not the LORD **s** by me. 1696
 36:22 that the word of the LORD *s* by the mouth NIH
Ezr 8:22 because we had **s** unto the king, saying, 559
Ne 2:18 as also the king's words that he had **s** unto 559
Est 6:10 let nothing fail of all that thou hast **s**. 1696
 7: 9 who had **s** good for the king, standeth in 1696
Job 21: 3 and after that I have **s**, mock on. 1696
 32: 4 Now Elihu had waited till Job had **s**, 1697
 33: 2 mouth, my tongue hath **s** in my mouth. 1696
 33: 8 Surely thou hast **s** in mine hearing, 559
 34:35 Job hath **s** without knowledge, 1696
 40: 5 Once have I **s**; but I will not answer: yea, 1696
 42: 7 that after the LORD had **s** these words 1696

Job 42: 7 for ye have not **s** of me *the thing that is* 1696
 42: 8 in that ye have not **s** of me *the thing* 1696
Ps 50: 1 hath **s**, and called the earth from the 1696
 60: 6 God hath **s** in his holiness; I will rejoice, 1696
 62:11 God hath **s** once; twice have I heard this; 1696
 66:14 my mouth hath **s**, when I was in trouble. 1696
 87: 3 Glorious *things* are **s** of thee, O city of 1696
 108: 7 God hath **s** in his holiness; I will rejoice, 1696
 109: 2 have **s** against me *with* a lying tongue. 1696
 116:10 believed, therefore have I **s**: I was greatly 1696
Pr 15:23 a word **s** in due season, how good *is it!* NIH
 25:11 A word fitly *is* like apples of gold in 1696
Ecc 7:21 take no heed unto all words that are **s**; 1696
SS 8: 8 sister in the day when she shall be **s** for? 1696
Isa 1: 2 for the LORD hath **s**, I have nourished and 1696
 1:20 for the mouth of the LORD hath **s** *it*. 1696
 16:13 This *is* the word that the LORD hath **s** 1696
 16:14 now the LORD hath **s**, saying, 1696
 21:17 for the LORD God of Israel hath **s** *it*. 1696
 22:25 it shall be cut off: for the LORD hath **s** *it*. 1696
 23: 4 for the sea hath **s**, *even* the strength of 559
 24: 3 for the LORD hath **s** this word. 1696
 25: 8 off all the earth: for the LORD hath **s** *it*. 1696
 31: 4 For thus hath the LORD **s** unto me, Like as 559
 37:22 This *is* the word which the LORD hath **s** 1696
 38: 7 the LORD will do this thing that he hath **s**; 1696
 38:15 he hath both **s** unto me, and himself hath 559
 39: 8 the word of the LORD which thou hast **s**. 1696
 40: 5 for the mouth of the LORD hath **s** *it*. 1696
 45:19 I have not **s** in secret, in a dark place of 1696
 46:11 yea, I have **s** *it*, I will also bring it to pass; 1696
 48:15 I, *even* I, have **s**; yea, I have called him: 1696
 48:16 I have not **s** in secret from the beginning; 1696
 58:14 for the mouth of the LORD hath **s** *it*. 1696
 59: 3 your lips have **s** lies, your tongue hath 1696
Jer 3: 5 thou hast **s** and done evil *things* as thou 1696
 4:28 because I have **s** *it*, I have purposed *it*, 1696
 9:12 to whom the mouth of the LORD hath **s**, 1696
 13:15 be not proud: for the LORD hath **s**. 1696
 23:21 I have not **s** to them, yet they prophesied. 1696
 23:35 and, What hath the LORD **s**? 1696
 23:37 and, What hath the LORD **s**? 1696
 25: 3 I have **s** unto you, rising early and 1696
 26:16 for he hath **s** to us in the name of 1696
 27:13 as the LORD hath **s** against the nation that 1696
 29:23 have **s** lying words in my name, which I 1696
 30: 2 Write thee all the words that I have **s** unto 1696
 32:24 what thou hast **s** is come to pass; 1696
 33:24 thou not what this people have **s**, 1696
 35:14 notwithstanding I have **s** unto you, 1696
 35:17 because I have **s** unto them, but they 1696
 36: 2 write therein all the words that I have **s** 1696
 36: 4 which he had **s** unto him, upon a roll of a 1696
 38: 1 heard the words that Jeremiah had **s** unto 1696
 44:16 *As for* the word that thou hast **s** unto us 1696
 44:25 your wives have both **s** with your mouths, 1696
 48: 8 shall be destroyed, as the LORD hath **s**. 559
 51:62 O LORD, thou hast **s** against this place, 1696
Eze 5:13 they shall know that I the LORD have **s** *it* 1696
 5:15 in furious rebukes. I the LORD have **s** *it*. 1696
 5:17 sword upon thee. I the LORD have **s** *it*. 1696
 12:28 the word which I have **s** shall be done, 1696
 13: 7 have ye not **s** a lying divination, whereas 1696
 13: 7 The LORD saith *it;* albeit I have not **s**? 1696
 13: 8 Because ye have **s** vanity, and seen lies, 1696
 14: 9 if the prophet be deceived when he hath **s** 1696
 17:21 ye shall know that I the LORD have **s** *it*. 1696
 17:24 I the LORD have **s** and have done *it*. 1696
 21:32 for I the LORD have **s** *it*. 1696
 22:14 I the LORD have **s** *it*, and will do *it*. 1696
 22:28 Lord GOD, when the LORD hath not **s**. 1696
 23:34 for I have **s** *it*, saith the Lord GOD. 1696
 24:14 I the LORD have **s** *it:* it shall come to 1696
 26: 5 for I have **s** *it*, saith the Lord GOD: 1696
 26:14 for I the LORD have **s** *it*, saith the Lord 1696
 28:10 for I have **s** *it*, saith the Lord GOD. 1696
 30:12 hand of strangers: I the LORD have **s** *it*. 1696
 34:24 among them; I the LORD have **s** *it*. 1696
 35:12 thou hast **s** against the mountains of Israel, 559
 36: 5 Surely in the fire of my jealousy have I **s** 1696
 36: 6 I have **s** in my jealousy and in my fury, 1696
 36:36 I the LORD have **s** *it*, and I will do *it*. 1696
 37:14 shall ye know that I the LORD have **s** *it*, 1696
 38:17 *Art* thou he of whom I have **s** in old time 1696
 38:19 *and* in the fire of my wrath have I **s**, 1696
 39: 5 for I have **s** *it*, saith the Lord GOD. 1696
 39: 8 this *is* the day whereof I have **s**. 1696
Da 4:31 O king Nebuchadnezzar, to thee it is **s**; 560
 10:11 when he had **s** this word unto me, I stood 1696
 10:15 when he had **s** such words unto me, I set 1696
 10:19 he had **s** unto me, I was strengthened, 1696
Hos 7:13 yet they have **s** lies against me. 1696
 10: 4 They have **s** words, swearing falsely in 1696
 12:10 have also **s** by the prophets, and I have 1696
Joel 3: 8 a people far off: for the LORD hath **s** *it*. 1696
Am 3: 1 Hear this word that the LORD hath **s** 1696
 3: 8 the Lord GOD hath **s**, who can but 1696
 5:14 of hosts, shall be with you, as ye have **s**. 559
Ob 1:12 neither shouldest thou have **s** proudly in 6310
 1:18 house of Esau; for the LORD hath **s** *it*. 1696
Mic 4: 4 the mouth of the LORD of hosts hath **s** *it*. 1696
 6:12 the inhabitants thereof have **s** lies, 1696
Zec 10: 2 the idols have **s** vanity, and the diviners 1696
Mal 3:13 What have we **s** so much against thee? 1696
Mt 1:22 that it might be fulfilled which was **s** of *3004*

Mt 2:15 that it might be fulfilled which was **s** of *3004*
 2:17 Then was fulfilled that which was **s** by *3004*
 2:23 that it might be fulfilled which was **s** by *3004*
 3: 3 For this is he that was **s** of by the prophet *3004*
 4:14 That it might be fulfilled which was **s** by *3004*
 8:17 That it might be fulfilled which was **s** by *3004*
 12:17 That it might be fulfilled which was **s** by *3004*
 13:35 That it might be fulfilled which was **s** by *3004*
 21: 4 that it might be fulfilled which was **s** by *3004*
 22:31 ye not read that which was **s** unto you *3004*
 24:15 **s** of by Daniel the prophet, stand in the *3004*
 26:65 clothes, saying, He hath **s** blasphemy; *987*
 27: 9 Then was fulfilled that which was **s** by *3004*
 27:35 that it might be fulfilled which was **s** by *3004*
Mk 1:42 And as soon as he had **s**, immediately *3004*
 5:36 soon as Jesus heard the word *that was* **s**, *2980*
 12:12 for they knew that he had **s** the parable *3004*
 13:14 **s** of by Daniel the prophet, standing *3004*
 14: 9 also that she hath done shall be **s** of for *2980*
 16:19 So then after the Lord had **s** unto them, *2980*
Lk 2:33 at those *things* which were **s** of him. *2980*
 2:34 and for a sign which shall be **s** *against*; *483*
 12: 3 whatsoever ye have **s** in darkness *3004*
 12: 3 *that* which ye have **s** in the ear in closets *2980*
 18:34 knew they the *things* which were **s**. *3004*
 19:28 And when he had thus **s**, he went before, *2036*
 20:19 they perceived that he had **s** this parable *3004*
 24:25 to believe all that the prophets have **s**: *2980*
 24:40 And when he had thus **s**, he shewed them *2036*
Jn 4:50 the word that Jesus had **s** unto him, *3004*
 9: 6 he had thus **s**, he spat on the ground, *3004*
 11:13 thought that he had **s** of taking of rest *3004*
 11:43 And when he thus had **s**, he cried with a *3004*
 12:48 word that I have **s**, the same shall judge *2980*
 12:49 For I have not **s** of myself; but the Father *2980*
 14:25 These *things* have I **s** unto you, being *yet* *2980*
 15: 3 the word which I have **s** unto you. *2980*
 15:11 *things* have I **s** unto you, that my joy *2980*
 15:22 If I had not come and **s** unto them, they *2980*
 16: 1 These *things* have I **s** unto you, that ye *2980*
 16:25 These *things* have I **s** unto you in proverbs: *2980*
 16:33 These *things* have I **s** unto you, that in *2980*
 18: 1 When Jesus had **s** these *words*, he went *3004*
 18:22 when he had thus **s**, one of the officers *3004*
 18:23 Jesus answered him, If I have **s** evil, *2980*
 20:18 and *that* he had **s** these *things* unto her. *2036*
 21:19 when he had **s** this, he saith unto him, *3004*
Ac 1: 9 when he had **s** these *things*, while they *3004*
 2:16 this is that which was **s** by the prophet *2980*
 3:21 **s** by the mouth of all his holy prophets *2980*
 3:24 those that follow after, as many as have **s**, *2980*
 8:24 that none of *these things* which ye have **s** *2980*
 9:27 and that he had **s** to him, and how he had *2980*
 13:40 upon you, which is **s** of in the prophets; *3004*
 13:45 against those *things* which were **s** by *3004*
 13:46 of God should first have been **s** to you: *2980*
 16:14 unto the *things* which were **s** of Paul. *2980*
 19:36 these *things* **cannot** be **s** against, *368*
 19:41 And when he had thus **s**, he dismissed *3004*
 20:36 when he had thus **s**, he kneeled down, *3004*
 23: 9 but if a spirit or an angel hath **s** to him, *2980*
 26:30 when he had thus **s**, the king rose up, *3004*
 27:11 more than those *things* which were **s** by *3004*
 27:35 And when he had thus **s**, he took bread, *3004*
 28:22 we know that every where it is **s** **against**. *483*
 28:24 some believed the *things* which were **s**, *3004*
 28:25 after that Paul had **s** one word, *3004*
Ro 1: 8 your faith is **s** of throughout the whole *2605*
 4:18 according to that which was **s**, So shall *3004*
 14:16 Let not then your good be **evil s** of: *987*
 15:21 To whom he was not **s** of, they shall see: *312*
1Co 10:30 why am I **evil s** of for *that for* which I *987*
 14: 9 how shall it be known what is **s**? *2980*
2Co 4:13 I believed, *and* therefore have I **s**, *2980*
Heb 2: 2 in these last days **s** unto us by *his* Son, *2980*
 2: 2 For if the word **s** by angels was stedfast, *2980*
 2: 3 at the first began to be **s** by the Lord, *2980*
 3: 5 of those *things* which were to be **s** after; *2980*
 4: 8 would he not afterward have **s** of another *2980*
 7:13 For he of whom these *things* are **s** *3004*
 8: 1 Now of the *things* which we have **s** *this* *3004*
 9:19 For when Moses had **s** every precept to all *2980*
 12:19 the **word** should not be **s** to them any *3056*
 13: 7 who have **s** unto you the word of God: *2980*
Jas 5:10 who have **s** in the name of the Lord, *2980*
1Pe 4:14 on their part he is **evil s** of, but on your *987*
2Pe 2: 2 whom the way of truth shall be **evil s** of. *987*
 3: 2 were **s** *before* by the holy prophets, *4302*
Jude 1:15 which ungodly sinners have **s** against him. *4302*
 1:17 **s** *before* of the apostles of our Lord Jesus *4302*

SPOKES (1)
1Ki 7:33 their naves, and their felloes, and their **s**, 2840

SPOKESMAN (1) [MAN, SPEAK]
Ex 4:16 he shall be thy **s** unto the people: 1696

SPONGE See SPUNGE

SPOON (12) [SPOONS]
Nu 7:14 One **s** of ten *shekels* of gold, full *of* 3709
 7:20 One **s** of gold of ten *shekels*, full *of* 3709
 7:26 golden **s** of ten *shekels*, full *of* incense: 3709
 7:32 golden **s** *of* ten *shekels*, full *of* incense: 3709
 7:38 golden **s** of ten *shekels*, full *of* incense: 3709

Nu	7:44 golden **s** of ten *shekels*, full *of* incense:	3709
	7:50 golden **s** of ten *shekels*, full *of* incense:	3709
	7:56 golden **s** of ten *shekels*, full *of* incense:	3709
	7:62 golden **s** of ten *shekels*, full *of* incense:	3709
	7:68 golden **s** of ten *shekels*, full *of* incense:	3709
	7:74 golden **s** of ten *shekels*, full *of* incense:	3709
	7:80 golden **s** of ten *shekels*, full *of* incense:	3709

SPOONS (12) [SPOON]

Ex	25:29 **s** thereof, and covers thereof,	3709
	37:16 his **s**, and his bowls, and *his* covers to	3709
Nu	4: 7 the **s**, and the bowls, and covers to cover	3709
	7:84 twelve silver bowls, twelve **s** of gold:	3709
	7:86 The golden **s** *were* twelve, full *of* incense,	3709
	7:86 all the gold of the **s** *was* an hundred and	3709
1Ki	7:50 and the **s**, and the censers *of* pure gold;	3709
2Ki	25:14 the **s**, and all the vessels of brass	3709
2Ch	4:22 the basons, and the **s**, and the censers,	3709
	24:14 to offer *withal*, and **s**, and vessels of gold	3709
Jer	52:18 the **s**, and all the vessels of brass	3709
	52:19 the candlesticks, and the **s**, and the cups;	3709

SPORT (6) [SPORTING]

Jdg	16:25 Call for Samson, that he may **make** us **s**.	7832
	16:25 of the prison house; and he **made** them **s**:	6711
	16:27 that beheld while Samson **made s**.	7832
Pr	10:23 *It is* as **s** to a fool to do mischief: but a	7814
	26:19 his neighbour, and saith, Am not I **in s**?	7832
Isa	57: 4 Against whom do ye **s** yourselves?	6026

SPORTING (2) [SPORT]

Ge	26: 8 Isaac *was* **s with** Rebekah his wife.	6711
2Pe	2:13 **s** themselves with their own deceivings	1792

SPOT (25) [SPOTS, SPOTTED, UNSPOTTED]

Lev	13: 2 **bright s**, and it be in the skin of his flesh	934
	13: 4 If the **bright s** *be* white in the skin of his	934
	13:19 a **bright s**, white, *and* somewhat reddish,	934
	13:23 if the **bright s** stay in his place,	934
	13:24 *flesh* that burneth have a white **bright s**,	934
	13:25 *if* the hair in the **bright s** be turned white,	934
	13:26 *there be* no white hair in the **bright s**,	934
	13:28 if the **bright s** stay in his place,	934
	13:39 it *is* a **freckled s** *that* groweth in the skin:	933
	14:56 a rising, and for a scab, and for a **bright s**:	934
Nu	19: 2 they bring thee a red heifer **without s**,	8549
	28: 3 two lambs of the first year **without s** day	8549
	28: 9 two lambs of the first year **without s**,	8549
	28:11 seven lambs of the first year **without s**,	8549
	29:17 fourteen lambs of the first year **without s**:	8549
	29:26 fourteen lambs of the first year **without s**:	8549
Dt	32: 5 their **s** *is not the spot* of his children:	3971
	32: 5 their spot *is not the* **s** of his children:	NIH
Job	11:15 then shalt thou lift up thy face without **s**;	3971
SS	4: 7 *art* all fair, my love; *there is* no **s** in thee.	3971
Eph	5:27 not having **s**, or wrinkle, or any such	4696
1Ti	6:14 thou keep *this* commandment **without s**,	784
Heb	9:14 Spirit offered himself **without s** to God,	299
1Pe	1:19 of a lamb without blemish and **without s**:	784
2Pe	3:14 of him in peace, **without s**, and blameless.	784

SPOTS (6) [SPOT]

Lev	13:38 have in the skin of their flesh **bright s**,	934
	13:38 flesh bright spots, *even* white **bright s**;	934
	13:39 *if* the **bright s** in the skin of their flesh *be*	934
Jer	13:23 change his skin, or the leopard his **s**?	2272
2Pe	2:13 **S** they are and blemishes,	4696
Jude	1:12 These are **s** in your feasts of charity when	4694

SPOTTED (7) [SPOT]

Ge	30:32 from thence all the speckled and **s** cattle,	2921
	30:32 and the **s** and speckled among the goats,	2921
	30:33 *is* not speckled and **s** amongst the goats,	2921
	30:35 the he goats that were ringstraked and **s**,	2921
	30:35 all the she goats that were speckled and **s**,	2921
	30:39 forth cattle ringstraked, speckled, and **s**.	2921
Jude	1:23 hating even the garment **s** by the flesh.	4695

SPOUSE (6) [SPOUSES]

SS	4: 8 *my* **s**, with me from Lebanon.	3618
	4: 9 hast ravished my heart, my sister, *my* **s**;	3618
	4:10 How fair is thy love, my sister, *my* **s**!	3618
	4:11 Thy lips, O *my* **s**, drop *as* the honeycomb:	3618
	4:12 A garden inclosed *is* my sister, *my* **s**;	3618
	5: 1 am come into my garden, my sister, *my* **s**:	3618

SPOUSES (2) [SPOUSE]

Hos	4:13 and your **s** shall commit adultery.	3618
	4:14 nor your **s** when they commit adultery:	3618

SPRANG (8) [SPRING]

Ge	41: 6 with the east wind **s up** after them.	6779
Mk	4: 5 immediately it **s up**, because *it* had no	1816
	4: 8 and did yield fruit that **s up** and increased;	305
Lk	8: 7 the thorns **s up with** *it*, and choked it.	4855
	8: 8 and **s up**, and bare fruit an hundredfold.	5453
Ac	16:29 and **s in**, and came trembling,	1530
Heb	7:14 *it is* evident that our Lord **s** out of Juda;	393
	11:12 Therefore **s** there even of one, and him as	1080

SPREAD (109) [OVERSPREAD, SPREADEST, SPREADETH, SPREADING, SPREADINGS]

Ge	10:18 the families of the Canaanites **s abroad**.	6327
	28:14 thou shalt **s abroad** to the west, and to	6555
	33:19 parcel of a field, where he had **s** his tent,	5186
	35:21 and **s** his tent beyond the tower of Edar.	5186

Ex	9:29 I will **s abroad** my hands unto the Lord;	6566
	9:33 **s abroad** his hands unto the Lord:	6566
	37: 9 the cherubims **s out** *their* wings on high,	6566
	40:19 he **s abroad** the tent over the tabernacle,	6566
Lev	13: 5 at a stay, *and* the plague **s** not in the skin;	6581
	13: 6 and the plague **s** not in the skin,	6581
	13: 7 if the scab **s much abroad** in	6581+6581
	13:22 if it **s much abroad** in the skin,	6581+6581
	13:23 his place, *and* **s** not, it *is* a burning boil;	6581
	13:27 *and* if it be **s much abroad** in	6581+6581
	13:28 and **s** not in the skin, but it *be* somewhat	6581
	13:32 *if* the scall **s** not, and there be in it no	6581
	13:34 behold, *if* the scall be not **s** in the skin,	6581
	13:35 if the scall **s much** in the skin after	6581+6581
	13:36 behold, *if* the scall be **s** in the skin,	6581
	13:51 if the plague be **s** in the garment, either in	6581
	13:53 the plague be not **s** in the garment,	6581
	13:55 his colour, and the plague be not **s**;	6581
	14:39 the plague be **s** in the walls of the house;	6581
	14:44 behold, *if* the plague be **s** in the house,	6581
	14:48 the plague hath not **s** in the house,	6581
Nu	4: 6 shall **s** over *it* a cloth wholly of blue,	6566
	4: 7 upon the table of shewbread they shall **s**	6566
	4: 8 they shall **s** upon them a cloth of scarlet,	6566
	4:11 upon the golden altar they shall **s** a cloth	6566
	4:13 the altar, and **s** a purple cloth thereon:	6566
	4:14 they shall **s** upon it a covering of badgers'	6566
	11:32 they **s** *them* **all abroad** for	7849+7849
	24: 6 As the valleys are they **s forth**, as gardens	5186
Dt	22:17 they shall **s** the cloth before the elders of	6566
Jdg	8:25 We will willingly give *them*. And they **s a**	6566
	15: 9 in Judah, and **s** themselves in Lehi.	5203
Ru	3: 9 therefore thy skirt over thine handmaid;	6566
1Sa	30:16 behold *they were* **s abroad** upon all	5203
2Sa	5:18 **s** themselves in the valley of Rephaim.	5203
	5:22 themselves in the valley of Rephaim.	5203
	16:22 So they **s** Absalom a tent upon the top of	5186
	17:19 and **s** a covering over the well's mouth,	6566
	17:19 well's mouth, and **s** ground corn thereon;	7849
	21:10 and **s** it for her upon the rock,	5186
	22:43 of the street, *and* did **s** them **abroad**.	7554
1Ki	6:32 **s** gold upon the cherubims, and upon	7286
	8: 7 the cherubims **s forth** *their* two wings	6566
	8:22 and **s forth** his hands **toward** heaven:	6566
	8:38 and **s forth** his hands towards this house:	6566
	8:54 kneeling on his knees with his hands **s**	6566
2Ki	8:15 and **s** *it* on his face, so that he died:	6566
	19:14 of the Lord, and **s** it before the Lord.	6566
1Ch	14: 9 themselves in the valley of Rephaim.	6584
	14:13 again **s** themselves **abroad** in the valley.	6584
	28:18 **s** out *their wings*, and covered the ark	6566
2Ch	3:13 **s** themselves **forth** twenty cubits:	6566
	5: 8 For the cherubims **s forth** *their* wings	6566
	6:12 of Israel, and **s forth** his hands:	6566
	6:13 and **s forth** his hands towards heaven,	6566
	6:29 and shall **s forth** his hands in this house:	6566
	26: 8 his name **s abroad** even to the entering	1980
	26:15 his name **s** far abroad; for he was	3318
Ezr	9: 5 **s** out my hands unto the Lord my God,	6566
Job	29:19 My root *was* **s** out by the waters,	6605
	37:18 Hast thou with him **s** out the sky, *which*	7554
Ps	105:39 He **s** a cloud for a covering; and fire to	6566
	140: 5 cords; they have **s** a net by the way side;	6566
Pr	1:17 in vain the net *is* **s** in the sight of any	2219
Isa	1:15 when ye **s forth** your hands, I will hide	6566
	14:11 the worm is **s** under thee, and the worms	3331
	19: 8 they that **s** nets upon the waters shall	6566
	25: 7 and the vail that is **s** over all nations.	5259
	25:11 he shall **s forth** his hands in the midst of	6566
	33:23 their mast, they could not **s** the sail:	6566
	37:14 of the Lord, and **s** it before the Lord.	6566
	42: 5 he that **s forth** the earth, and that *which*	7554
	58: 5 to **s** sackcloth and ashes *under him?* wilt	3331
	65: 2 I have **s** out mine hands all the day unto	6566
Jer	8: 2 they shall **s** them before the sun,	7849
	10: 9 Silver **s into plates** is brought from	7554
	43:10 he shall **s** his royal pavilion over them.	5186
	48:40 an eagle, and shall **s** his wings over Moab.	6566
	49:22 as the eagle, and **s** his wings over Bozrah:	6566
La	1:10 The adversary hath **s** out his hand upon	6566
	1:13 hath **s** a net for my feet, he hath turned	6566
Eze	2:10 he **s** it before me; and it *was* written	6566
	12:13 My net also will I **s** upon him, and he	6566
	16: 8 I **s** my skirt over thee, and covered thy	6566
	17:20 I will **s** my net upon him, and he shall be	6566
	19: 8 the provinces, and **s** their net over him:	6566
	26:14 thou shalt be *a place* to **s** nets **upon**;	4894
	32: 3 **s** out my net over thee with a company	6566
	47:10 they shall be a **place to s forth** nets;	4894
Hos	5: 1 snare on Mizpah, and a net **s** upon Tabor.	6566
	7:12 they shall go, I will **s** my net upon them;	6566
	14: 6 His branches shall **s**, and his beauty shall	1980
Joel	2: 2 as the morning **s** upon the mountains:	6566
Hab	1: 8 their horsemen shall **s** themselves,	6335
Zec	1:17 through prosperity shall yet be **s abroad**;	6327
	2: 6 for I have **s** you **abroad** as the four winds	6566
Mal	2: 3 your seed, and **s** dung upon your faces,	2219
Mt	9:31 **s abroad** his fame in all that country.	1310
	21: 8 a very great multitude **s** their garments	4766
Mk	1:28 And immediately his **fame** **s abroad**	1831
	4:22 *of him;* (for his name was **s abroad**:)	5318
	11: 8 And many **s** their garments in the way:	4766
Lk	19:36 he went, they **s** their clothes in the way.	5291
Ac	4:17 But that it **s** no further among the people,	1268
1Th	1: 8 place your faith to God-ward **s abroad**;	1831

SPREADEST (1) [SPREAD]

Eze	27: 7 that *which* thou **s forth** to be thy sail;	4666

SPREADETH (14) [SPREAD]

Lev	13: 8 the scab **s** in the skin, then the priest	6581
Dt	32:11 **s abroad** her wings, taketh them,	6566
Job	9: 8 Which alone **s** out the heavens,	5186
	26: 9 of *his* throne, *and* **s** his cloud upon it.	6576
	36:30 he **s** his light upon it, and covereth	6566
	41:30 he **s** sharp pointed *things* upon the mire.	7502
Pr	29: 5 man that flattereth his neighbour **s** a net	6566
Isa	25:11 as he that swimmeth **s forth** *his hands* to	6566
	40:19 the goldsmith **s** it **over** with gold,	7554
	40:22 and **s** them **out** as a tent to dwell in:	4969
	44:24 that **s abroad** the earth by myself;	7554
Jer	4:31 *that* bewaileth herself, *that* **s** her hands,	6566
	17: 8 that **s** out her roots by the river,	7971
La	1:17 Zion **s forth** her hands, *and there is* none	6566

SPREADING (4) [SPREAD]

Lev	13:57 it *is* a **s** *plague:* thou shalt burn that	6524
Ps	37:35 and **s** himself like a green bay tree.	6168
Eze	17: 6 grew, and became a **s** vine of low stature,	5628
	26: 5 It shall be *a place for* the **s** of nets in	4894

SPREADINGS (1) [SPREAD]

Job	36:29 Also can *any* understand the **s** of	4666

SPRIGS (2)

Isa	18: 5 he shall both cut off the **s** with pruning	2150
Eze	17: 6 brought forth branches, and shot forth **s**.	6288

SPRING (23) [DAYSPRING, SPRANG, SPRINGETH, SPRINGING, SPRINGS, SPRUNG, WATERSPRINGS, WELLSPRING]

Nu	21:17 Israel sang this song, **S** up, O well; sing ye	5927	
Dt	8: 7 depths that **s** out of the valleys and hills;	3318	
Jdg	19:25 when the day began to **s**, they let her go.	5927	
1Sa	9:26 it came to pass about the **s** of the day,	5927	
2Ki	2:21 he went forth unto the **s** of the waters,	4161	
Job	5: 6 neither doth trouble **s** out of the ground;	6779	
	38:27 **cause** the bud of the tender herb	6779	
		to **s forth**?	
Ps	85:11 Truth shall **s** out of the earth;	6779	
	92: 7 When the wicked **s** as the grass,	6524	
Pr	25:26 *is as* a troubled fountain, and a corrupt **s**.	4726	
SS	4:12 *my* spouse; a **s** shut up, a fountain sealed.	1530	
Isa	42: 9 before they **s forth** I tell you of them.	6779	
	43:19 I will do a new *thing;* now it shall **s forth**;	6779	
	44: 4 they shall **s up** as among the grass,	6779	
	45: 8 and let righteousness **s up** together;	6779	
	45: 8 and thine health shall **s forth** speedily:	6779	
	58:11 like a **s** of water, whose waters fail not.	4161	
	61:11 **causeth** the things that are sown in it	6779	
		to **s forth**;	
	61:11 **cause** righteousness and praise to **s forth**	6779	
Eze	17: 9 it shall wither *in* all the leaves of her **s**,	6780	
Hos	13:15 his **s** shall become dry, and his fountain	4726	
Joel	2:22 for the pastures of the wilderness do **s**,	1876	
Mk	4:27 day, and the seed should **s** and grow up,	985	

SPRINGETH (4) [SPRING]

1Ki	4:33 unto the hyssop that **s** out of the wall:	3318
2Ki	19:29 second year *that which* **s** of the same;	7823
Isa	37:30 second year *that which* **s** of the same:	7823
Hos	10: 4 thus judgment **s up** as hemlock in	6524

SPRINGING (5) [SPRING]

Ge	26:19 and found there a well of **s** water.	2416
2Sa	23: 4 *as* the tender grass **s** out of the earth by	NIH
Ps	65:10 with showers: thou blessest the **s** thereof.	6780
Jn	4:14 a well of water **s up** into everlasting life.	242
Heb	12:15 any root of bitterness **s** up trouble *you*,	5453

SPRINGS (16) [SPRING]

Dt	4:49 the sea of the plain, under the **s** of Pisgah.	794
Jos	10:40 of the vale, and of the **s**, and all their kings:	794
	12: 8 in the **s**, and in the wilderness, and in	794
	15:19 me a south land; give me also **s** of water.	1543
	15:19 he gave her the upper **s**, and the nether	1543
	15:19 her the upper springs, and the nether **s**.	1543
Jdg	1:15 me a south land; give me also **s** of water.	1543
	1:15 Caleb gave her the upper **s** and the nether	1543
	1:15 her the upper springs and the nether **s**.	1543
Job	38:16 Hast thou entered into the **s** of the sea?	5033
Ps	87: 7 shall be there: all my **s** *are* in thee.	4599
	104:10 He sendeth the **s** into the valleys, *which*	4599
Isa	35: 7 a pool, and the thirsty land **s** of water:	4002
	41:18 of water, and the dry land **s** of water.	4161
	49:10 by the **s** of water shall he guide them.	4002
Jer	51:36 I will dry up her sea, and make her **s** dry.	4726

SPRINKLE (31) [SPRINKLED, SPRINKLETH, SPRINKLING]

Ex	9: 8 let Moses **s** it towards the heaven in	2236
	29:16 and **s** it round upon the altar.	2236
	29:20 **s** the blood upon the altar round about.	2236
	29:21 **s** *it* upon Aaron, and upon his garments,	5137
Lev	1: 5 **s** the blood round about upon the altar	2236
	1:11 his blood round about upon the altar.	2236
	3: 2 Aaron's sons the priests shall **s** the blood	2236
	3: 8 Aaron's sons shall **s** the blood thereof	2236
	3:13 the sons of Aaron shall **s** the blood thereof	2236
	4: 6 **s** of the blood seven times before	5137
	4:17 **s** *it* seven times before the Lord,	5137

Lev	5: 9 he shall **s** of the blood of the sin offering 5137
	7: 2 the blood thereof shall **s** round about 2236
	14: 7 he shall **s** upon him that is to be cleansed 5137
	14:16 **s** of the oil with his finger seven times 5137
	14:27 priest shall **s** with his right finger *some* 5137
	14:51 water, and **s** the house seven times: 5137
	16:14 *it* with his finger upon the mercy seat 5137
	16:14 before the mercy seat shall he **s** of 5137
	16:15 **s** it upon the mercy seat, and before 5137
	16:19 he shall **s** of the blood upon it with his 5137
	17: 6 priest shall **s** the blood upon the altar of 2236
Nu	8: 7 **S** water of purifying upon them, 5137
	18:17 thou shalt **s** their blood upon the altar, 2236
	19: 4 **s** of her blood directly before the 5137
	19:18 *it* upon the tent, and upon all the vessels 5137
	19:19 the clean *person* shall **s** upon the unclean 5137
2Ki	9:33 **s** it all the blood of the burnt 2236
Isa	52:15 So shall he **s** many nations; the kings shall 5137
Eze	36:25 will I **s** clean water upon you, and ye shall 2236
	43:18 offerings thereon, and to **s** blood thereon. 2236

SPRINKLED (25) [SPRINKLE]

Ex	9:10 Moses **s** it *up* toward heaven; and it 2236
	24: 6 and half of the blood he **s** on the altar. 2236
	24: 8 blood, and **s** *it* on the people, and said, 2236
Lev	6:27 when there is **s** of the blood thereof upon 5137
	6:27 thou shalt wash that whereon it was **s** in 5137
	8:11 he **s** thereof upon the altar seven times, 2236
	8:19 Moses **s** the blood upon the altar round 2236
	8:24 Moses **s** the blood upon the altar round 2236
	8:30 **s** *it* upon Aaron, *and* upon his garments, 5137
	9:12 which he **s** round about upon the altar. 2236
	9:18 which he **s** upon the altar round about, 2236
Nu	19:13 water of separation was not **s** upon him, 2236
	19:20 the water of separation hath not been **s** 2236
2Ki	9:33 *some* of her blood was **s** on the wall, 5137
	16:13 **s** the blood of his peace offerings, upon 2236
2Ch	29:22 received the blood, and **s** *it* on the altar: 2236
	29:22 the rams, they **s** the blood upon the altar: 2236
	29:22 and they **s** the blood upon the altar. 2236
	30:16 priests **s** the blood, *which they received* 2236
	35:11 the priests **s** *the blood* from their hands, 2236
Job	2:12 **s** dust upon their heads toward heaven. 2236
Isa	63: 3 their blood shall be **s** upon my garments, 5137
Heb	9:19 and **s** both the book, and all the people, 4472
	9:21 Moreover he **s** with blood both 4472
	10:22 having *our* hearts **s** from an evil 4472

SPRINKLETH (2) [SPRINKLE]

Lev	7:14 it shall be the priest's that **s** the blood of 2236
Nu	19:21 that he that **s** the water of separation shall 5137

SPRINKLING (4) [SPRINKLE]

Heb	9:13 and the ashes of a heifer **s** the unclean, 4472
	11:28 he kept the passover, and the **s** of blood, 4378
	12:24 and to the blood of **s**, that speaketh better 4473
1Pe	1: 2 and **s** of the blood of Jesus Christ: 4473

SPROUT (1)

Job	14: 7 that it will **s** again, and that the tender 2498

SPRUNG (7) [SPRING]

Ge	41:23 with the east wind, **s up** after them: 6779
Lev	13:42 it *is* a leprosy **s** in his bald head, or his 6524
Mt	4:16 region and shadow of death light is **s up**. *303*
	13: 5 and forthwith they **s up**, because *they had* *1816*
	13: 7 and the thorns **s up**, and choked them: *305*
	13:26 But when the blade was **s up**, *985*
Lk	8: 6 and as soon as it was **s up**, it withered *5453*

SPUE (4) [SPUED, SPUING]

Lev	18:28 That the land **s** not you **out** also, when ye 6958
	20:22 bring you to dwell therein, **s** you not **out**. 6958
Jer	25:27 a, and fall, and rise no more, because of 7006
Rev	3:16 nor hot, I will **s** thee out of my mouth. *1692*

SPUED (1) [SPUE]

Lev	18:28 it **s** out the nations that *were* before you. 6958

SPUING (1) [SPUE]

Hab	2:16 and **shameful s** *shall be* on thy glory. 7022

SPUN (2) [SPIN]

Ex	35:25 that which they had **s**, *both* of blue, 4299
	35:26 stirred them up in wisdom **s** goats' *hair*. 2901

SPUNGE (3)

Mt	27:48 and took a **s**, and filled *it* with vinegar, *4699*
Mk	15:36 And one ran and filled a **s** *full* of vinegar, *4699*
Jn	19:29 they filled a **s** with vinegar, and put *it* *4699*

SPY (12) [ESPIED, ESPY, SPIED, SPIES]

Nu	13:16 men which Moses sent to **s out** the land. 8446
	13:17 Moses sent him to **s out** the land of 8446
	21:32 Moses sent to **s out** Jaazer, and they took 7270
Jos	2: 1 sent out of Shittim two men to **s** secretly, 7270
	6:25 which Joshua sent to **s out** Jericho. 7270
Jdg	18: 2 to **s out** the land, and to search it; 7270
	18:14 answered the five men that went to **s out** 7270
	18:17 the five men that went to **s out** the land 7270
2Sa	10: 3 and to **s** it **out**, and to overthrow it? 7270
2Ki	6:13 Go and **s** where he *is*, that I may send 7200
1Ch	19: 3 and to overthrow, and to **s out** the land? 7270
Gal	2: 4 who came in privily to **s out** our liberty 2684

SQUADS OF FOUR SOLDIERS See QUATERNIONS

SQUARE (3) [FOURSQUARE, SQUARED, SQUARES, STONESQUARERS]

1Ki	7: 5 all the doors and posts *were* **s**, *with* 7251
Eze	43:16 broad, **s** in the four squares thereof. 7251
	45: 2 five hundred *in breadth*, **s** round about; 7251

SQUARED (1) [SQUARE]

Eze	41:21 The posts of the temple *were* **s**, *and the* 7251

SQUARES (2) [SQUARE]

Eze	43:16 twelve broad, square in the four **s** thereof. 7253
	43:17 and fourteen broad in the four **s** thereof; 7253

STABILITY (1) [STABLE]

Isa	33: 6 and knowledge shall be the **s** of thy times, 530

STABLE (2) [STABILITY, UNSTABLE]

1Ch	16:30 the world also shall be **s**, that it be not 3559
Eze	25: 5 And I will make Rabbah a **s** for camels, 5116

STABLISH (15) [STABLISHED, STABLISHETH]

2Sa	7:13 will **s** the throne of his kingdom for ever. 3559
1Ch	17:11 be of thy sons; and I will **s** his kingdom. 3559
	17:12 a house, and I will **s** his throne for ever. 3559
	18: 3 as he went to **s** his dominion by the river 5324
2Ch	7:18 will I **s** the throne of thy kingdom, 6965
Est	9:21 To **s** *this* among them, that they should 6965
Ps	89: 4 Thy seed will I **s** for ever, and build up 3559
	119:38 **S** thy word unto thy servant, who *is* 6965
Isa	9: 7 to **s** it with judgment and with justice 5582
Ro	16:25 Now to him that is of power to **s** you 4741
1Th	3:13 To the end he may **s** your hearts 4741
2Th	2:17 and **s** you in every good word and work. 4741
	3: 3 who shall **s** you, and keep *you* from evil. 4741
Jas	5: 8 Be ye also patient; **s** your hearts: 4741
1Pe	5:10 you perfect, **s**, strengthen, settle *you*. 4741

STABLISHED (10) [STABLISH]

Lev	25:30 house that *is* in the walled city shall be **s** 6965
Dt	19:15 of three witnesses, shall the matter be **s**. 6965
1Sa	20:31 thou shalt not be **s**, nor thy kingdom. 3559
2Sa	7:16 kingdom shall be **s** for ever before thee: 539
	7:16 before thee: thy throne shall be **s** for ever. 3559
2Ch	17: 5 Therefore the Lord **s** the kingdom in his 3559
Ps	93: 1 world also is, **s**, that it cannot be moved. 3559
	148: 6 He hath also **s** them for ever and ever: 5975
Col	2: 7 and built up in him, and **s** in the faith, 950
2Pe	1:12 know *them*, and be **s** in the present truth. 4741

STABLISHETH (3) [STABLISH]

Pr	29: 4 The king by judgment **s** the land; 5975
Hab	2:12 town with blood, and **s** a city by iniquity! 3559
2Co	1:21 Now he which **s** us with you in Christ, 950

STACHYS (1)

Ro	16: 9 our helper in Christ, and **S** my beloved. 4720

STACKS (1)

Ex	22: 6 that the **s** of corn, or the standing corn, 1430

STACTE (1)

Ex	30:34 spices, **s**, and onycha, and galbanum; 5198

STADIA See FURLONGS

STAFF (43) [HANDSTAVES, STAVES]

Ge	32:10 for with my **s** I passed over this Jordan; 4731
	38:18 bracelets, and thy **s** that *is* in thine hand. 4294
	38:25 *are* these, the signet, and bracelets, and **s**. 4294
Ex	12:11 on your feet, and your **s** in your hand; 4731
	21:19 walk abroad upon his **s**, then shall he that 4938
Lev	26:26 *And* when I have broken the **s** of your 4294
Nu	13:23 and they bare it between two upon a **s**; 4132
	22:27 kindled, and he smote the ass with a **s**. 4731
Jdg	6:21 the end of the **s** that *was* in his hand, 4938
1Sa	17: 7 **s** of his spear *was* like a weaver's beam, 6086
	17:40 he took his **s** in his hand, and chose him 4731
2Sa	3:29 or that leaneth on a **s**, or that falleth on 6418
	21:19 the **s** of whose spear *was* like a weaver's 6086
	23: 7 be fenced with iron and the **s** of a spear; 6086
	23:21 he went down to him with a **s**, 7626
2Ki	4:29 take my **s** in thine hand, and go *thy way*: 4938
	4:29 and lay my **s** upon the face of the child: 4938
	4:31 and laid the **s** upon the face of the child; 4938
	18:21 trustest upon the **s** of this bruised reed, 4938
1Ch	11:23 he went down to him with a **s**, 7626
	20: 5 whose spear *was* like a weaver's beam. 6086
Ps	23: 4 thy rod and thy **s** they comfort me. 4938
	105:16 the land: he brake the whole **s** of bread. 4294
Isa	3: 1 and from Judah the stay and the **s**, 4938
	9: 4 the **s** of his shoulder, the rod of his 4294
	10: 5 the **s** in their hand *is* mine indignation. 4294
	10:15 as if the **s** should lift up *itself, as if it were* 4294
	10:24 shall lift up his **s** against thee, after 4294
	14: 5 The Lord hath broken the **s** of 4294
	28:27 the fitches are beaten out with a **s**, 4294
	30:32 *in every place* where the grounded **s** shall 4294
	36: 6 thou trustest in the **s** of this broken reed, 4938
Jer	48:17 How is the strong **s** broken, 4294
Eze	4:16 I will break the **s** of bread in Jerusalem: 4294
	5:16 upon you, and will break your **s** of bread: 4294
	14:13 will break the **s** of the bread thereof, 4294
	29: 6 have been a **s** of reed to the house of 4938

Hos	4:12 and their **s** declareth unto them: 4731
Zec	8: 4 every man with his **s** in his hand for very 4938
	11:10 I took my **s**, *even* Beauty, and cut it 4731
	11:14 I cut asunder mine other **s**, *even* Bands, 4731
Mk	6: 8 nothing for *their* journey, save a **s** only; *4464*
Heb	11:21 worshipped, *leaning* upon the top of his **s**. *4464*

STAFFS See STAVES

STAG See HART

STAGGER (3) [STAGGERED, STAGGERETH]

Job	12:25 **maketh** them to **s** like a drunken *man*. 8582
Ps	107:27 **s** like a drunken *man*, and are at their 5128
Isa	29: 9 wine; they **s**, but not *with* strong drink. 5128

STAGGERED (1) [STAGGER]

Ro	4:20 He **s** not at the promise of God through *1252*

STAGGERETH (1) [STAGGER]

Isa	19:14 as a drunken *man* **s** in his vomit. 8582

STAIN (3)

Job	3: 5 Let darkness and the shadow of death **s** it; 1350
Isa	23: 9 to **s** the pride of all glory, *and* to bring 2490
	63: 3 my garments, and I will **s** all my raiment. 1351

STAIRS (10)

1Ki	6: 8 they went up with **winding s** into 3883
2Ki	9:13 and put *it* under him on the top of the **s**, 4609
Ne	3:15 unto the **s** that go down from the city of 4609
	9: 4 stood up upon the **s** of the Levites, 4608
	12:37 they went up by the **s** of the city of David, 4609
SS	2:14 in the secret places of the **s**, let me see 4095
Eze	40: 6 went up the **s** thereof, and measured 4609
	43:17 and his **s** *shall* look toward the east. 4609
Ac	21:35 when he came upon the **s**, so it was, 304
	21:40 Paul stood on the **s**, and beckoned with 304

STAKES (2)

Isa	33:20 not one of the **s** thereof shall ever be 3489
	54: 2 lengthen thy cords, and strengthen thy **s**; 3489

STALE (2) [STEAL]

Ge	31:20 Jacob **s away unawares** to Laban 1589+3820
2Ki	11: 2 **s** him from among the king's sons which 1589

STALK (3) [STALKS]

Ge	41: 5 seven ears of corn came up upon one **s**, 7070
	41:22 seven ears came up in one **s**, full and good 7070
Hos	8: 7 it hath no **s**: the bud shall yield no meal: 7054

STALKS (1) [STALK]

Jos	2: 6 hid them with the **s** of flax, which she 6086

STALL (3) [STALLED, STALLS]

Am	6: 4 and the calves out of the midst of the **s**; 4770
Mal	4: 2 go forth, and grow up as calves of the **s**. 4770
Lk	13:15 sabbath loose his ox or *his* ass from the **s**, 5336

STALLED (1) [STALL]

Pr	15:17 love is, than a **s** ox and hatred therewith. 75

STALLS (4) [STALL]

1Ki	4:26 Solomon had forty thousand **s** of horses for 723
2Ch	9:25 Solomon had four thousand **s** for horses 723
	32:28 **s** for all *manner of* beasts, and cotes for 723
Hab	3:17 fold, and *there shall be* no herd in the **s**: 7517

STAMMERERS (1) [STAMMERING]

Isa	32: 4 the tongue of the **s** shall be ready to speak 5926

STAMMERING (2) [STAMMERERS]

Isa	28:11 For with **s** lips and another tongue will he 3934
	33:19 of a **s** tongue, *that thou canst* not 3932

STAMP (2) [STAMPED, STAMPING, STAMPT]

2Sa	22:43 I did **s** them as the mire of the street, 1854
Eze	6:11 thine hand, and **s** with thy foot, and say, 7554

STAMPED (7) [STAMP]

Dt	9:21 fire, and **s** it, *and* ground *it* very small, 3807
2Ch	15:16 and **s** *it*, and burnt *it* at the brook Kidron. 1854
Eze	25: 6 with the feet, and rejoiced in heart with 7554
Da	7: 7 and **s** the residue with the feet of it: 7512
	7:19 in pieces, and **s** the residue with his feet; 7512
	8: 7 down to the ground, and **s** upon him: 7429
	8:10 the stars to the ground, and **s** upon them. 7429

STAMPING (1) [STAMP]

Jer	47: 3 At the noise of the **s** of the hoofs of his 8161

STAMPT (2) [STAMP]

2Ki	23: 6 **s** *it* **small** to powder, and cast the powder 1854
	23:15 *and* **s** *it* **small** to powder, and burnt 1854

STANCHED (1)

Lk	8:44 and immediately her issue of blood **s**. *2476*

STAND (274) [STANDEST, STANDETH, STANDING, STOOD, STOODEST]

Ge	19: 9 they said, **S** back. And they said *again*, 5066
	24:13 I **s** *here* by the well of water; 5324
	24:43 Behold, I **s** by the well of water; and it 5324
Ex	7:15 thou shalt **s** by the river's brink against he 5324
	8:20 in the morning, and **s** before Pharaoh; 3320
	9:11 the magicians could not **s** before Moses 5975

Ex	9:13 and **s** before Pharaoh, and say unto him,	3320
	14:13 **s still**, and see the salvation of the LORD,	3320
	17: 6 I will **s** before thee there upon the rock in	5975
	17: 9 to morrow I will **s** on the top of the hill	5324
	18:14 all the people **s** by thee from morning	5324
	33:10 all the people saw the cloudy pillar **s** *at*	5975
	33:21 by me, and thou shalt **s** upon a rock:	5324
Lev	18:23 neither shall any woman **s** before a beast	5975
	19:16 neither shalt thou **s** against the blood of	5975
	26:37 ye shall have no **power** to **s** before your	8617
	27:14 as the priest shall estimate it, so shall it **s.**	6965
	27:17 according to thy estimation it shall **s.**	6965
Nu	1: 5 *are* the names of the men that shall **s**	5975
	9: 8 **S still**, and I will hear what the LORD	5975
	11:16 that they may **s** there with thee.	3320
	16: 9 to **s** before the congregation to minister	5975
	23: 3 **S** by thy burnt offering, and I will go:	3320
	23:15 unto Balak, **S** here by thy burnt offering,	3320
	27:21 he shall **s** before Eleazar the priest,	5975
	30: 4 all her vows shall **s**, and every bond	6965
	30: 5 she hath bound her soul shall **s**	6965
	30: 5 she hath bound her soul, shall **s:**	6965
	30: 7 that he heard *it:* then her vows shall **s**,	6965
	30: 7 wherewith she bound her soul shall **s.**	6965
	30: 9 bound their souls, shall **s** against her.	6965
	30:11 all her vows shall **s**, and every bond	6965
	30:11 wherewith she bound her soul shall **s**,	6965
	30:12 the bond of her soul, shall not **s:**	6965
	35:12 until he **s** before the congregation in	5975
Dt	5:31 **s** thou here by me, and I will speak unto	5975
	7:24 shall no man *be able to* **s** before thee,	3320
	9: 2 *of whom* thou hast heard *say,* Who can **s**	3320
	10: 8 to **s** before the LORD to minister unto	5975
	11:25 There shall no man *be able to* **s** before	3320
	18: 5 to **s** to minister in the name of the LORD,	5975
	18: 7 as all his brethren the Levites *do,* which **s**	5975
	19:17 between whom the controversy *is,* shall **s**	5975
	24:11 Thou shalt **s** abroad, and the man to	5975
	25: 8 *if* he **s** to *it,* and say, I like not to take her;	5975
	27:12 shall **s** upon mount Gerizzim to bless	5975
	27:13 these shall **s** upon mount Ebal to curse;	5975
	29:10 Ye **s** *this* day all of you before the LORD	5324
Jos	1: 5 shall not any man *be able to* **s** before	3320
	3: 8 water of Jordan, ye shall **s still** in Jordan.	5975
	3:13 from above; and they shall **s** *upon* a heap.	5975
	7:12 the children of Israel could not **s**	6965
	7:13 thou canst not **s** before thine enemies,	6965
	10: 8 shall not a man of them **s** before thee.	5975
	10:12 of Israel, Sun, **s** thou **still** upon Gibeon;	1826
	20: 4 **s** at the entering of the gate of the city,	5975
	20: 6 until he **s** before the congregation for	5975
	23: 9 no man hath *been able to* **s** before you	5975
Jdg	2:14 that they could not any longer **s** before	5975
	4:20 **S** *in* the door of the tent, and it shall be,	5975
1Sa	6:20 Who is able to **s** before this holy LORD	5975
	9:27 **s** thou **still** a while, that I may shew thee	5975
	12: 7 Now therefore **s still**, that I may reason	3320
	12:16 Now therefore **s** and see this great thing,	3320
	14: 9 we will **s still** in our place, and will not	5975
	16:22 Let David, I pray thee, **s** before me;	5975
	19: 3 **s** beside my father in the field where thou	5975
2Sa	1: 9 I pray thee, upon me, and slay me:	5975
	18:30 said *unto him,* Turn aside, *and* **s** here.	3320
1Ki	1: 2 let her **s** before the king, and let her	5975
	8:11 So that the priests could not **s** to minister	5975
	10: 8 which **s** continually before thee,	5975
	17: 1 God of Israel liveth, before whom I **s**,	5975
	18:15 LORD of hosts liveth, before whom I **s**,	5975
	19:11 and **s** upon the mount before the LORD.	5975
2Ki	3:14 of hosts liveth, before whom I **s**, surely,	5975
	5:11 **s**, and call on the name of the LORD his	5975
	5:16 before whom I **s**, I will receive none.	5975
	6:31 the son of Shaphat shall **s** on him *this* day.	5975
	10: 4 not before him: how then shall we **s**?	5975
1Ch	21:16 saw the angel of the LORD **s** between	5975
	23:30 to **s** every morning to thank and praise	5975
2Ch	5:14 So that the priests could not **s** to minister	5975
	7: 6 which **s** continually before them,	5975
	20: 9 before this house, and in thy presence,	5975
	20:17 ye *still,* and see the salvation of	5975
	29:11 for the LORD hath chosen you to **s** before	5975
	34:32 **caused** all that were present in Jerusalem	5975
	and Benjamin to **s**	5975
	35: 5 **s** in the holy *place* according to	5975
Ezr	9:15 *we* cannot **s** before thee because of this.	5975
	10:13 rain, and *we* are not able to **s** without,	5975
	10:14 now our rulers of all the congregation **s**,	5975
Ne	7: 3 while they **s** by, let them shut the doors,	5975
	9: 5 **S** up *and* bless the LORD your God for	6965
Est	3: 4 see whether Mordecai's matters would **s:**	5975
	8:11 to **s** for their life, to destroy, to slay,	5975
Job	8:15 lean upon his house, but it shall not **s:**	5975
	19:25 *that* he shall **s** *at* the latter *day* upon	6965
	30:20 I **s** *up,* and thou regardest me *not.*	5975
	33: 5 set *thy* *words* in order before me, **s up.**	3320
	37:14 **s still**, and consider the wondrous works	5975
	38:14 clay *to* the seal; and they **s** as a garment.	3320
	41:10 him up: who then is able to **s** before me?	3320
Ps	1: 5 Therefore the ungodly shall not **s** in	6965
	4: 4 **S in awe**, and sin not: commune with	7264
	5: 5 The foolish shall not **s** in thy sight:	3320
	20: 8 fallen: but we are risen, and **s upright.**	5749
	24: 3 and who shall **s** in his holy place?	6965
	30: 7 thou hast **made** my mountain to **s** strong:	5975
	33: 8 all the inhabitants of the world **s in awe**	1481

Ps	35: 2 and buckler, and **s up** for mine help.	6965
	38:11 and my friends **s** aloof from my sore;	5975
	38:11 from my sore; and my kinsmen **s** afar off.	5975
	45: 9 hand did **s** the queen in gold of Ophir.	5324
	73: 7 Their eyes **s out** with fatness: they have	3318
	76: 7 may **s** in thy sight when once thou art	5975
	78:13 and he **made** the waters to **s** as a heap.	5324
	89:28 and my covenant *shall* **s** fast with him.	539
	89:43 and hast not **made** *made* to **s** in the battle.	6965
	94:16 who will **s up** for me against the workers	3320
	109: 6 him: and let Satan **s** at his right hand.	5975
	109:31 he shall **s** at the right hand of the poor,	5975
	111: 8 They **s fast** for ever and ever, *and* are	5564
	122: 2 Our feet shall **s** within thy gates,	5975
	130: 3 mark iniquities, O Lord, who shall **s**?	5975
	134: 1 which by night **s** in the house of	5975
	135: 2 Ye that **s** in the house of the LORD,	5975
	147:17 like morsels: who can **s** before his cold?	5975
Pr	12: 7 but the house of the righteous shall **s.**	5975
	19:21 the counsel of the LORD, that shall **s.**	6965
	22:29 he shall **s** before kings; he shall not stand	3320
	22:29 he shall not **s** before mean *men.*	3320
	25: 6 and **s** not in the place of great *men:*	5975
	27: 4 but who is **able to s** before envy?	5975
Ecc	4:15 with the second child that shall **s** *up* in	5975
	8: 3 **s** not in an evil thing; for he doeth	5975
Isa	7: 7 Thus saith the Lord GOD, It shall not **s**,	6965
	8:10 speak the word, and it shall not **s:**	6965
	11:10 which shall **s** for an ensign of the people;	5975
	14:24 and as I have purposed, *so* shall it **s:**	6965
	21: 8 I **s** continually upon the watchtower in	5975
	27: 9 the groves and images shall not **s up.**	6965
	28:18 and your agreement with hell shall not **s**;	6965
	32: 8 and by liberal *things* shall he **s.**	6965
	40: 8 but the word of our God shall **s** for ever.	6965
	44:11 let them **s** *up; yet* they shall fear,	5975
	46:10 My counsel shall **s**, and I will do all my	6965
	47:12 **S** now with thine enchantments,	5975
	47:13 **s** *up,* and save thee from *these things* that	5975
	48:13 *when* I call unto them, they **s** *up* together.	5975
	50: 8 let us **s** together: who *is* mine adversary?	5975
	51:17 Awake, awake, **s up**, O Jerusalem,	6965
	61: 5 strangers shall **s** and feed your flocks,	5975
	65: 5 Which say, **S** by thyself, come not near to	7126
Jer	6:16 **S** ye in the ways, and see, and ask for	5975
	7: 2 **S** in the gate of the LORD's house,	5975
	7:10 come and **s** before me in this house,	5975
	14: 6 the wild asses did **s** in the high places,	5975
	15:19 thee again, *and* thou shalt **s** before me:	5975
	17:19 in the gate of the children of the people,	5975
	26: 2 **S** in the court of the LORD's house,	5975
	35:19 not want a man to **s** before me for ever.	5975
	44:28 shall know whose words shall **s**, mine,	6965
	44:29 shall **surely s** against you for evil: 6965+6965	
	46: 4 and **s forth** with *your* helmets;	3320
	46:14 say ye, **S fast**, and prepare thee;	3320
	46:21 they did not **s**, because the day of their	5975
	48:19 of Aroer, **s** by the way and espy;	5975
	49:19 *is* that shepherd that will **s** before me?	5975
	50:44 *is* that shepherd that will **s** before me?	5975
	51:50 escaped the sword, go *away,* **s** not **still:**	5975
Eze	2: 1 upon thy feet, and I will speak unto	5975
	13: 5 to **s** in the battle in the day of the LORD.	5975
	17:14 that by keeping of his covenant it might **s.**	5975
	22:30 **s** in the gap before me for the land, that *I*	5975
	27:29 their ships, they shall **s** upon the land;	5975
	29: 7 and **madest** all their loins **to be at a s.**	5976
	31:14 neither their trees **s up** in their height,	5975
	33:26 Ye **s** upon your sword, ye work	5975
	44:11 they shall **s** before them to minister unto	5975
	44:15 they shall **s** before me to offer unto me	5975
	44:24 in controversy they shall **s** in judgment;	5975
	46: 2 shall **s** by the post of the gate,	5975
	47:10 the fishers shall **s** upon it from En-gedi	5975
Da	1: 4 such as *had* ability in them to **s**	5975
	1: 5 that at the end thereof they might **s** before	5975
	2:44 all these kingdoms, and it shall **s** for ever.	6966
	7: 4 **made s** upon the feet as a man, and a	6966
	8: 4 so that no beasts might **s** before him,	5975
	8: 7 there was no power in the ram to **s** before	5975
	8:22 kingdoms shall **s up** out of the nation,	5975
	8:23 understanding dark sentences, shall **s up.**	5975
	8:25 he shall also **s up** against the Prince of	5975
	10:11 that I speak unto thee, and **s** upright:	5975
	11: 2 there *shall* **s up** yet three kings in Persia;	5975
	11: 3 a mighty king shall **s up**, that shall rule	5975
	11: 4 when he shall **s up**, his kingdom shall be	5975
	11: 6 of the arm; neither shall he **s**, nor his arm:	5975
	11: 7 of a branch of her roots shall *one* **s up**	5975
	11:14 those times there shall many **s up** against	5975
	11:16 his own will, and none shall **s** before him:	5975
	11:17 shall **s** in the glorious land, which by his	5975
	11:17 she shall not **s** *on his side,* neither be for	5975
	11:20 shall **s up** in his estate a raiser of taxes *in*	5975
	11:21 in his estate shall **s up** a vile person,	5975
	11:25 and mighty army; but he shall not **s:**	5975
	11:31 arms shall **s** on his part, and they shall	5975
	12: 1 at that time shall Michael **s up**, the great	5975
	12:13 and **s** in thy lot at the end of the days.	5975
Am	2:15 Neither shall he **s** that handleth the bow;	5975
Mic	5: 4 he shall **s** and feed in the strength of	5975
Na	1: 6 Who can **s** before his indignation?	5975
	2: 8 **S**, stand, *shall they cry;* but none shall	5975
	2: 8 Stand, **s**, *shall they cry;* but none shall	5975
Hab	2: 1 I will **s** upon my watch, and set me upon	5975

Zec	3: 7 thee places to walk among these that **s** *by.*	5975
	4:14 that **s** by the Lord of the whole earth.	5975
	14: 4 his feet shall **s** in that day upon the mount	5975
	14:12 away while they **s** upon their feet,	5975
Mal	3: 2 who *shall* **s** when he appeareth? for he *is*	5975
Mt	12:25 or house divided against itself shall not **s:**	2476
	12:26 how shall then his kingdom **s**?	2476
	12:47 thy mother and thy brethren **s** without,	2476
	20: 6 unto them, Why **s** ye here all the day idle?	2476
	24:15 **s** in the holy place, (whoso readeth, let	2476
Mk	3: 3 which had the withered hand, **S forth.**	1453
	3:24 against itself, that kingdom cannot **s.**	2476
	3:25 divided against itself, that house cannot **s.**	2476
	3:26 be divided, he cannot **s**, but hath an end.	2476
	9: 1 That there be some of them that **s** here,	2476
	11:25 when ye **s** praying, forgive, if ye have	4739
Lk	1:19 am Gabriel, that **s** in the presence of God;	3936
	6: 8 Rise up, and **s** *forth* in the midst.	2476
	8:20 Thy mother and thy brethren **s** without,	2476
	11:18 against himself, how shall his kingdom **s**?	2476
	13:25 and ye begin to **s** without, and to knock at	2476
	21:36 to pass, and to **s** before the Son of man.	2476
Jn	11:42 the people which **s** by I said *it,* that they	4026
Ac	1:11 Galilee, why ye gazing up into heaven?	2476
	4:10 *even* by him doth this *man* **s** here before	3936
	5:20 **s** and speak in the temple to the people all	2476
	8:38 And he commanded the chariot to **s still:**	2476
	10:26 But Peter took him up, saying, **S up;**	450
	14:10 with a loud voice, **S** upright on thy feet.	450
	25:10 said Paul, I **s** at Cesar's judgment seat,	2476
	26: 6 And now I **s** and am judged for the hope	2476
	26:16 But rise, and **s** upon thy feet: for I have	2476
Ro	5: 2 by faith into this grace wherein we **s**,	2476
	9:11 of God according to election might **s**,	3306
	14: 4 holden up: for God is able to **make** him **s.**	2476
	14:10 for we shall all **s** before the judgment seat	3936
1Co	2: 5 That your faith should not **s** in the wisdom	1510
	15: 1 also you have received, and wherein ye **s;**	2476
	15:30 And why **s** we **in jeopardy** every hour?	2793
	16:13 Watch ye, **s fast** in the faith, quit you like	4739
2Co	1:24 are helpers of your joy: for by faith ye **s.**	2476
Gal	4:20 change my voice; for I **s** in doubt of you.	639
	5: 1 **S fast** therefore in the liberty wherewith	4739
Eph	6:11 that ye may be able to **s** against the wiles	2476
	6:13 in the evil day, and having done all, to **s.**	2476
	6:14 **S** therefore, having your loins girt about	2476
Php	1:27 of your affairs, that ye **s fast** in one spirit,	4739
	4: 1 my joy and crown, so **s fast** in the Lord,	4739
Col	4:12 that ye may **s** perfect and complete in all	2476
1Th	3: 8 For now we live, if ye **s fast** in the Lord.	4739
2Th	2:15 **s fast**, and hold the traditions which ye	2476
Jas	2: 3 **S** thou there, or sit here under my	2476
1Pe	5:12 this is the true grace of God wherein ye **s.**	2476
Rev	3:20 Behold, I **s** at the door, and knock: if any	2476
	6:17 wrath is come; and who shall be able to **s**?	2476
	10: 5 And the angel which I saw **s** upon the sea	2476
	15: 2 **s** on the sea of glass, having *the* harps of	2476
	18:15 shall **s** afar off for the fear of her torment,	2476
	20:12 the dead, small and great, **s** before God;	2476

STANDARD (18) [STANDARD-BEARER, STANDARDS]

Nu	1:52 every man by his own **s**, throughout their	1714
	2: 2 children of Israel shall pitch by his own **s**,	1714
	2: 3 **s** of the camp of Judah pitch throughout	1714
	2:10 the south side *shall be* the **s** of the camp	1714
	2:18 the west side *shall be* the **s** of the camp	1714
	2:25 The **s** of the camp of Dan *shall be* on	1714
	10:14 In the first *place* went the **s** of the camp	1714
	10:18 the **s** of the camp of Reuben set forward	1714
	10:22 the **s** of the camp of the children of	1714
	10:25 the **s** of the camp of the children of Dan	1714
Isa	49:22 Gentiles, and set up my **s** to the people:	5251
	59:19 the spirit of the LORD shall **lift up a s**	5127
	62:10 out the stones; lift up a **s** for the people.	5251
Jer	4: 6 Set up the **s** toward Zion: retire, stay not:	5251
	4:21 How long shall I see the **s**, *and* hear	5251
	50: 2 the nations, and publish, and set up a **s**;	5251
	51:12 Set up the **s** upon the walls of Babylon,	5251
	51:27 Set ye up a **s** in the land, blow the trumpet	5251

STANDARD-BEARER (1) [BEAR, STANDARD]

Isa	10:18 and they shall be as when a **s** fainteth.	5263

STANDARDS (3) [STANDARD]

Nu	2:17 every man in his place by their **s.**	1714
	2:31 They shall go hindmost with their **s.**	1714
	2:34 so they pitched by their **s**, and so they set	1714

STANDEST (6) [STAND]

Ge	24:31 of the LORD; wherefore **s** thou without?	5975
Ex	3: 5 for the place whereon thou **s** is holy	5975
Jos	5:15 for the place whereon thou **s** is holy.	5975
Ps	10: 1 Why **s** thou afar off, O LORD? why hidest	5975
Ac	7:33 for the place where thou **s** is holy ground.	2476
Ro	11:20 they were broken off, and thou **s** by faith.	2476

STANDETH (30) [STAND]

Nu	14:14 *that* thy cloud **s** over them, and *that* thou	5975
Dt	1:38 **s** before thee, he shall go in 5975+3807.1	
	17:12 will not hearken unto the priest that **s** to	5975
	29:15 with *him* that **s** here with us *this* day	5975
Jdg	16:26 feel the pillars whereupon the house **s**,	3559
Est	6: 5 unto him, Behold, Haman **s** in the court.	5975
	7: 9 for the king, **s** in the house of Haman.	5975

Ps	1: 1 nor **s** in the way of sinners, nor sitteth in	5975
	26:12 My foot **s** in an even place:	5975
	33:11 The counsel of the LORD **s** for ever,	5975
	82: 1 God **s** in the congregation of the mighty;	5324
	119:161 cause: but my heart **is in awe** of thy word.	6342
Pr	8: 2 She is in the top of high places by the way,	5324
SS	2: 9 behold, he **s** behind our wall, he looketh	5975
Isa	3:13 The LORD **s** up to plead, and standeth to	5324
	3:13 up to plead, and **s** to judge the people.	5975
	46: 7 and set him in his place, and he **s**;	5975
	59:14 away backward, and justice **s** afar off:	5975
Da	12: 1 the great prince which **s** for the children	5975
Zec	11:16 that is broken, nor feed that that **s still:**	5324
Jn	1:26 there **s** one among you, whom ye know	2476
	3:29 which **s** and heareth him, rejoiceth greatly	2476
Ro	14: 4 to his own master he **s** or falleth. Yea,	4739
1Co	7:37 Nevertheless he that **s** stedfast in his heart	2476
	8:13 I will eat no flesh **while** the world **s,** lest I	1519
	10:12 Wherefore let him that thinketh he **s** take	2476
2Ti	2:19 Nevertheless the foundation of God **s** sure	2476
Heb	10:11 And every priest **s** daily ministering and	2476
Jas	5: 9 the judge **s** before the door.	2476
Rev	10: 8 heard the angel which **s** upon the sea	2476

STANDING (55) [STAND]

Ex	22: 6 stacks of corn, or the **s corn,** or the field,	7054
	26:15 for the tabernacle *of* shittim wood **s up.**	5975
	36:20 for the tabernacle *of* shittim wood, **s up.**	5975
Lev	26: 1 neither rear you up a **s image,**	4676
Nu	22:23 the ass saw the angel of the LORD **s** in	5324
	22:31 he saw the angel of the LORD **s** in	5324
Dt	23:25 When thou comest into the **s corn** of thy	7054
	23:25 a sickle unto thy neighbour's **s corn.**	7054
Jdg	15: 5 he let *them* go into the **s corn** of	7054
	15: 5 also the **s corn,** with the vineyards *and*	7054
1Sa	19:20 Samuel **s** *as* appointed over them, the	5975
	22: 6 and all his servants *were* **s** about him;)	5324
1Ki	13:25 in the way, and the lion **s** by the carcase:	5975
	13:28 and the ass and the lion **s** by the carcase:	5975
	22:19 all the host of heaven **s** by him on his	5975
2Ch	9:18 sitting place, and two lions **s** by the stays:	5975
	18:18 all the host of heaven **s** on his right hand	5975
Est	5: 2 when the king saw Esther the queen **s** in	5975
Ps	69: 2 I sink in deep mire, where *there is* no **s:**	4613
	107:35 He turneth the wilderness into a **s** water,	98
	114: 8 turned the rock *into* a **s** water, the flint	98
Da	8: 6 which I had seen **s** before the river,	5975
Am	9: 1 I saw the Lord **s** upon the altar: and he	5324
Mic	1:11 of Beth-ezel; he shall receive of you his **s.**	5979
	5:13 thy **s images** out of the midst of thee;	4676
Zec	3: 1 he shewed me Joshua the high priest **s**	5975
	3: 1 and Satan **s** at his right hand to resist him.	5975
	6: 5 go forth from **s** before the Lord of all	3320
Mt	6: 5 for they love to pray **s** in the synagogues	2476
	16:28 I say unto you, There be some **s** here,	2476
	20: 3 and saw others **s** idle in the marketplace,	2476
	20: 6 and found others **s** idle, and saith unto	2476
Mk	3:31 brethren and his mother, and, **s** without,	2476
	13:14 Daniel the prophet, **s** where it ought not,	2476
Lk	1:11 **s** on the right side of the altar of incense.	2476
	5: 2 And saw two ships **s** by the lake:	2476
	9:27 I tell you of a truth, there be some **s** here,	2476
	18:13 **s** afar off, would not lift up so much as	2476
Jn	8: 9 left alone, and the woman **s** in the midst.	2476
	19:26 saw *his* mother, and the disciple **s by,**	3936
	20:14 saw Jesus **s,** and knew not that it was	2476
Ac	2:14 But Peter, **s up** with the eleven, lift up	2476
	4:14 beholding the man which was healed **s**	2476
	5:23 the keepers **s** without before the doors:	2476
	5:25 the men whom ye put in prison are **s** in	2476
	7:55 and Jesus on the right hand of God,	2476
	7:56 Son of man **s** on the right hand of God.	2476
	22:20 I also was **s by,** and consenting unto his	2186
	24:21 this one voice, that I cried **s** among them,	2476
Heb	9: 8 while as the first tabernacle was yet **s:**	4714
2Pe	3: 5 and the earth **s** out of the water and in	4921
Rev	7: 1 And after these *things* I saw four angels **s**	2476
	11: 4 the two candlesticks **s** before the God of	2476
	18:10 **S** afar off for the fear of her torment,	2476
	19:17 And I saw an angel **s** in the sun;	2476

STANK (3) [STINK]

Ex	8:14 them together upon heaps: and the land **s.**	887
	16:20 the morning, and it bred worms, and **s:**	887
2Sa	10: 6 the children of Ammon saw that they **s**	887

STAR (15) [STARE, STARS]

Nu	24:17 there shall come a **S** out of Jacob,	3556
Am	5:26 and Chiun your images, the **s** of your god,	3556
Mt	2: 2 for we have seen his **s** in the east,	792
	2: 7 inquired of them diligently what time the **s**	792
	2: 9 and lo, the **s,** which they saw in the east,	792
	2:10 When they saw the **s,** they rejoiced *with*	792
Ac	7:43 of Moloch, and the **s** of your god Remphan,	798
1Co	15:41 *one* **s** differeth from *another* star in glory.	792
	15:41 *one* star differeth from *another* **s** in glory.	5459
2Pe	1:19 and the **day s** arise in your hearts:	5459
Rev	2:28 And I will give him the morning **s.**	792
	8:10 and there fell a great **s** from heaven,	792
	8:11 the name of the **s** is called Wormwood:	792
	9: 1 I saw a **s** fall from heaven unto the earth:	792
	22:16 of David, *and* the bright and morning **s.**	792

STARE (1)

Ps	22:17 all my bones: they look *and* **s** upon me.	7200

STARGAZERS (1) [GAZE, STAR]

Isa	47:13 astrologers, the **s,** 2374+3556+871.1+1886.1	

STARS (51) [STAR]

Ge	1:16 light to rule the night: *he* made the **s** also.	3556
	15: 5 Look now towards heaven, and tell the **s,**	3556
	22:17 multiply thy seed as the **s** of the heaven,	3556
	26: 4 I will make thy seed to multiply as the **s**	3556
	37: 9 and the eleven **s** made obeisance to me.	3556
Ex	32:13 will multiply your seed as the **s** of heaven,	3556
Dt	1:10 you *are this* day as the **s** of heaven for	3556
	4:19 seest the sun, and the moon, and the **s,**	3556
	10:22 thee as the **s** of heaven for multitude.	3556
	28:62 whereas ye were as the **s** of heaven for	3556
Jdg	5:20 **s** in their courses fought against Sisera.	3556
1Ch	27:23 Israel like to the **s** of the heavens.	3556
Ne	4:21 rising of the morning till the **s** appeared.	3556
	9:23 children also multipliedst thou as the **s**	3556
Job	3: 9 Let the **s** of the twilight thereof be dark;	3556
	9: 7 and it riseth not; and sealeth up the **s.**	3556
	22:12 behold the height of the **s,** how high they	3556
	25: 5 yea, the **s** are not pure in his sight.	3556
	38: 7 When the morning **s** sang together,	3556
Ps	8: 3 work of thy fingers, the moon and the **s,**	3556
	136: 9 The moon and **s** to rule by night: for his	3556
	147: 4 He telleth the number of the **s;** he calleth	3556
	148: 3 and moon: praise him, all ye **s** of light.	3556
Ecc	12: 2 sun, or the light, or the moon, or the **s,**	3556
Isa	13:10 For the **s** of heaven and the constellations	3556
	14:13 I will exalt my throne above the **s** of God:	3556
Jer	31:35 the moon and of the **s** for a light by night,	3556
Eze	32: 7 the heaven, and make the **s** thereof dark;	3556
Da	8:10 of the host and of the **s** to the ground,	3556
	12: 3 many to righteousness as the **s** for ever	3556
Joel	2:10 and the **s** shall withdraw their shining:	3556
	3:15 and the **s** shall withdraw their shining.	3556
Am	5: 8 Seek him that maketh the **seven s** and	3598
Ob	1: 4 though *thou* set thy nest among the **s,**	3556
Na	3:16 thy merchants above the **s** of heaven:	3556
Mt	24:29 and the **s** shall fall from heaven,	792
Mk	13:25 the **s** of heaven shall fall,	792
Lk	21:25 in the sun, and in the moon, and in the **s;**	798
Ac	27:20 And when neither sun nor **s** in many days	798
1Co	15:41 of the moon, and another glory of the **s:**	792
Heb	11:12 *so many* as the **s** of the sky in multitude,	798
Jude	1:13 wandering **s,** to whom is reserved	792
Rev	1:16 And he had in his right hand seven **s:**	792
	1:20 The mystery of the seven **s** which thou	792
	1:20 The seven **s** are the angels of the seven	792
	2: 1 *things* saith he that holdeth the seven **s**	792
	3: 1 the seven spirits of God, and the seven **s;**	792
	6:13 And the **s** of heaven fell unto the earth,	792
	8:12 of the moon, and the third *part* of the **s;**	792
	12: 1 and upon her head a crown of twelve **s:**	792
	12: 4 And his tail drew the third *part* of the **s** of	792

STATE (14)

Ge	43: 7 The man asked us straitly of our **s,**	NIH
2Ch	24:13 they set the house of God in his **s,**	4971
Est	1: 7 according to the **s** of the king.	3027
	2:18 gave gifts, according to the **s** of the king.	3027
Ps	39: 5 every man **at his best s** *is* altogether	5324
Pr	27:23 Be thou diligent to know the **s** of thy	6440
	28: 2 the **s** *thereof* shall be prolonged.	3651
Isa	22:19 and from thy **s** shall he pull thee down.	4612
Mt	12:45 last **s** of that man is worse than the first.	NIG
Lk	11:26 last **s** of that man is worse than the first.	NIG
Php	2:19 good comfort, when I know your **s.** 3588+4012	
	2:20 who will naturally care for your **s.** 3588+4012	
	4:11 for I have learned, in whatsoever **s** I am,	NIG
Col	4: 7 All my **s** shall Tychicus declare unto you,	2596

STATELY (1)

Eze	23:41 satest upon a **s** bed, and a table prepared	3520

STATION (1)

Isa	22:19 I will drive thee from thy **s,** and from thy	4673

STATURE (17)

Nu	13:32 that we saw in it *are* men of a **great s.**	4060
1Sa	16: 7 countenance, or on the height of his **s;**	6967
2Sa	21:20 where was a man of great **s,** that had on	4067
1Ch	11:23 a man of great **s,** five cubits *high;* and in	4060
	20: 6 was a man of great **s,** whose fingers	4060
SS	7: 7 This thy **s** is like to a palm tree,	6967
Isa	10:33 the high ones of **s** *shall be* hewn down,	6967
	45:14 of Ethiopia and of the Sabeans, men of **s,**	4060
Eze	13:18 make kerchiefs upon the head of every **s**	6967
	17: 6 and became a spreading vine of low **s,**	6967
	19:11 her **s** was exalted among the thick	6967
	31: 3 a shadowing shrowd, and of a high **s;**	6967
Mt	6:27 thought can add one cubit unto his **s?**	2244
Lk	2:52 and Jesus increased in wisdom and **s,**	2244
	12:25 taking thought can add to his **s** one cubit?	2244
	19: 3 for the press, because he was little of **s.**	2244
Eph	4:13 unto the measure of the **s** of the fulness	2244

STATUTE (35) [STATUTES]

Ex	15:25 there he made for them a **s** and	2706
	27:21 *be* a **s** for ever unto their generations	2708
	28:43 *be* a **s** for ever unto him and his seed	2708
	29: 9 office shall be theirs for a perpetual **s.**	2708
	29:28 sons' by a **s** for ever from the children	2706
	30:21 it shall be a **s** for ever to them, *even* to	2706
Lev	3:17 *It shall be* a perpetual **s** for your	2708

Lev	6:18 *It shall be* a **s** for ever in your generations	2706
	6:22 *it is* a **s** for ever unto the LORD; it shall be	2706
	7:34 unto his sons by a **s** for ever from among	2706
	7:36 a **s** for ever throughout their generations.	2708
	10: 9 *it shall be* a **s** for ever throughout your	2708
	10:15 and thy sons' with thee, by a **s** for ever:	2706
	16:29 *this* shall be a **s** for ever unto you: *that in*	2708
	16:31 ye shall afflict your souls, *by* a **s** for ever.	2708
	16:34 this shall be an everlasting **s** unto you,	2708
	17: 7 This shall be a **s** for ever unto them	2708
	23:14 *It shall be* a **s** for ever throughout your	2708
	23:21 **s** for ever in all your dwellings throughout	2708
	23:31 *It shall be* a **s** for ever throughout your	2708
	23:41 *It shall be* a **s** for ever in your generations:	2708
	24: 3 *it shall be* a **s** for ever in your generations.	2708
	24: 9 the LORD made by fire, *by* a perpetual **s.**	2706
Nu	18:11 to thy daughters with thee, by a **s** for ever:	2706
	18:19 thy daughters with thee, by a **s** for ever:	2706
	18:23 *It shall be* a **s** for ever throughout your	2708
	19:10 sojourneth among them, for a **s** for ever.	2708
	19:21 shall be a perpetual **s** unto them, that he	2708
	27:11 shall be unto the children of Israel a **s** of	2708
	35:29 these *things* shall be for a **s** of judgment	2708
Jos	24:25 set them a **s** and an ordinance in	2706
1Sa	30:25 that he made it a **s** and an ordinance for	2706
Ps	81: 4 For this *was* a **s** for Israel, *and* a law of	2706
Da	6: 7 consulted together to establish a royal **s,**	7010
	6:15 Persians *is,* That no decree nor **s** which	7010

STATUTES (132) [STATUTE]

Ge	26: 5 my commandments, my **s,** and my laws.	2708
Ex	15:26 to his commandments, and keep all his **s,**	2706
	18:16 and I do make *them* know the **s** of God,	2706
Lev	10:11 which the LORD hath spoken unto them	2708
	18: 5 Ye shall therefore keep my **s,** and my	2708
	18:26 Ye shall therefore keep my **s** and my	2708
	19:19 Ye shall keep my **s.** Thou shalt not let	2708
	19:37 Therefore shall ye observe all my **s,** and	2708
	20: 8 ye shall keep my **s,** and do them: I *am*	2708
	20:22 Ye shall therefore keep all my **s,** and all	2708
	25:18 Wherefore ye shall do my **s,** and keep my	2708
	26: 3 If ye walk in my **s,** and keep my	2708
	26:15 if ye shall despise my **s,** or if your soul	2708
	26:43 and because their soul abhorred my **s.**	2708
	26:46 These *are* the **s** and judgments and laws,	2706
Nu	30:16 These *are* the **s,** which the LORD	2706
Dt	4: 1 Israel, unto the **s** and unto the judgments,	2706
	4: 5 I have taught you **s** and judgments,	2706
	4: 6 which shall hear all these **s,** and say,	2706
	4: 8 that hath **s** and judgments *so* righteous as	2706
	4:14 me at that time to teach you **s**	2706
	4:40 Thou shalt keep therefore his **s,** and his	2706
	4:45 and the **s,** and the judgments,	2706
	5: 1 the **s** and judgments which I speak in	2706
	5:31 the **s,** and the judgments, which thou	2706
	6: 1 the **s,** and the judgments,	2706
	6: 2 to keep all his **s** and his commandments,	2708
	6:17 his testimonies, and his **s,** which he hath	2706
	6:20 and the **s,** and the judgments,	2706
	6:24 LORD commanded us to do all these **s,**	2706
	7:11 and the **s,** and the judgments,	2706
	8:11 judgments, and his **s,** which I command	2708
	10:13 commandments of the LORD, and his **s,**	2708
	11: 1 his **s,** and his judgments,	2708
	11:32 ye shall observe to do all the **s** and	2706
	12: 1 These *are* the **s** and judgments, which ye	2706
	16:12 and thou shalt observe and do these **s.**	2706
	17:19 all the words of this law and these **s,**	2706
	26:16 God hath commanded thee to do these **s**	2706
	26:17 to keep his **s,** and his commandments,	2708
	27:10 do his commandments and his **s,** which I	2708
	28:15 and his **s** which I command thee *this* day;	2708
	28:45 and his **s** which he commanded thee:	2708
	30:10 his **s** which are written in this book of	2708
	30:16 and his **s** and his judgments,	2708
2Sa	22:23 *as for* his **s,** I did not depart from them.	2708
1Ki	2: 3 to keep his **s,** *and* his commandments,	2708
	3: 3 walking in the **s** of David his father:	2708
	3:14 to keep my **s** and my commandments,	2708
	6:12 if thou wilt walk in my **s,** and execute	2706
	8:58 and his **s,** and his judgments,	2706
	8:61 to walk in his **s,** and to keep his	2706
	9: 4 and wilt keep my **s** and my judgments:	2708
	9: 6 and my **s** which I have set before you,	2708
	11:11 hast not kept my covenant and my **s,**	2708
	11:33 *to keep* my **s** and my judgments, as *did*	2708
	11:34 he kept my commandments and my **s:**	2708
	11:38 to keep my **s** and my commandments,	2708
2Ki	17: 8 walked in the **s** of the heathen, whom	2708
	17:13 and keep my commandments and my **s,**	2708
	17:15 they rejected his **s,** and his covenant that	2706
	17:19 walked in the **s** of Israel which they made.	2708
	17:34 neither do they after their **s,** or after their	2708
	17:37 the **s,** and the ordinances, and the law,	2706
1Ch	22:13 if thou takest heed to fulfil the **s** and	2706
	29:19 thy **s,** and to do all *these things,* and	2706
2Ch	7:17 shalt observe my **s** and my judgments;	2708
	7:19 forsake my **s** and my commandments,	2708
	19:10 and commandment, **s** and judgments,	2706
	33: 8 according to the whole law and the **s** and	2706
	34:31 testimonies, and his **s,** with all his heart,	2708
Ezr	7:10 to do *it,* and to teach in Israel **s** and	2706
	7:11 of the LORD, and of his **s** to Israel.	2706
Ne	1: 7 nor the **s,** nor the judgments,	2706

S

Ne 9:13 true laws, good **s** and commandments: 2706
 9:14 commandedst them precepts, **s**, and laws, 2706
 10:29 our Lord, and his judgments and his **s**; 2706
Ps 18:22 and I did not put away his **s** from me. 2708
 19: 8 The **s** of the Lord *are* right, rejoicing 6490
 50:16 What hast thou to do to declare my **s**, 2706
 89:31 If they break my **s**, and keep not my 2708
 105:45 That they might observe his **s**, and keep 2706
 119: 5 that my ways were directed to keep thy **s!** 2706
 119: 8 will keep thy **s**: O forsake me not utterly. 2706
 119:12 *art* thou, O Lord: teach me thy **s**. 2706
 119:16 I will delight myself in thy **s**: I will not 2708
 119:23 *but* thy servant did meditate in thy **s**. 2706
 119:26 and thou heardest me: teach me thy **s**. 2706
 119:33 Teach me, O Lord, the way of thy **s**; 2706
 119:48 I have loved; and I will meditate in thy **s**. 2706
 119:54 Thy **s** have been my songs in the house 2706
 119:64 is full *of* thy mercy: teach me thy **s**. 2706
 119:68 *art* good, and doest good; teach me thy **s**. 2706
 119:71 been afflicted; that I might learn thy **s**. 2706
 119:80 Let my heart be sound in thy **s**; that I be 2706
 119:83 in the smoke; *yet* do I not forget thy **s**. 2706
 119:112 have inclined mine heart to perform thy **s** 2706
 119:117 I will have respect unto thy **s** continually. 2706
 119:118 down all them that err from thy **s**: 2706
 119:124 unto thy mercy, and teach me thy **s**. 2706
 119:135 upon thy servant; and teach me thy **s**. 2706
 119:145 hear me, O Lord: I will keep thy **s**. 2706
 119:155 from the wicked: for they seek not thy **s**. 2706
 119:171 when thou hast taught me thy **s**. 2706
 147:19 his **s** and his judgments unto Israel. 2706
Jer 44:10 nor in my **s**, that I set before you and 2708
 44:23 nor walked in his law, nor in his **s**, nor in 2708
Eze 5: 6 my **s** more than the countries that *are* 2708
 5: 6 and my **s**, they have not walked in them. 2708
 5: 7 have not walked in my **s**, neither have 2708
 11:12 for ye have not walked in my **s**, 2706
 11:20 they may walk in my **s**, and keep mine 2708
 18: 9 Hath walked in my **s**, and hath kept my 2708
 18:17 my judgments, hath walked in my **s**; 2708
 18:19 hath kept all my **s**, and hath done them, 2708
 18:21 keep all my **s**, and do that which is lawful 2708
 20:11 I gave them my **s**, and shewed them my 2708
 20:13 walked not in my **s**, and they despised 2708
 20:16 walked not in my **s**, but polluted my 2708
 20:18 Walk ye not in the **s** of your fathers, 2706
 20:19 walk in my **s**, and keep my judgments, 2708
 20:21 they walked not in my **s**, neither kept my 2708
 20:24 had despised my **s**, and had polluted my 2708
 20:25 Wherefore I gave them also **s** *that were* 2706
 33:15 walk in the **s** of life, without committing 2708
 36:27 cause you to walk in my **s**, and ye shall 2706
 37:24 and observe my **s**, and do them. 2708
 44:24 my laws and my **s** in all mine assemblies; 2708
Mic 6:16 For the **s** of Omri are kept, and all 2708
Zec 1: 6 my words and my **s**, which I commanded 2706
Mal 4: 4 for all Israel, *with* the **s** and judgments. 2706

STAVES (49) [STAFF]

Ex 25:13 thou shalt make **s** of shittim wood, 905
 25:14 shalt put the **s** into the rings by the sides 905
 25:15 The **s** shall be in the rings of the ark: 905
 25:27 be for places of the **s** to bear the table. 905
 25:28 thou shalt make the **s** *of* shittim wood, 905
 27: 6 thou shalt make **s** for the altar, staves of 905
 27: 6 of shittim wood, and overlay them with 905
 27: 7 the **s** shall be put into the rings, 905
 27: 7 **s** shall be upon the two sides of the altar, 905
 30: 4 they shall be for places for the **s** to bear it 905
 30: 5 Thou shalt make the **s** *of* shittim wood, 905
 35:12 The ark, and the **s** thereof, *with* the mercy 905
 35:13 **s**, and all his vessels, and the shewbread, 905
 35:15 incense altar and his **s**, and the anointing 905
 35:16 his **s**, and all his vessels, the laver and his 905
 37: 4 he made **s** of shittim wood, 905
 37: 5 he put the **s** into the rings by the sides of 905
 37:14 the places for the **s** to bear the table. 905
 37:15 he made the **s** *of* shittim wood, and 905
 37:27 to be places for the **s** to bear it withal. 905
 37:28 he made the **s** *of* shittim wood, 905
 38: 5 of the grate of brass, *to be* places for the **s**. 905
 38: 6 he made the **s** *of* shittim wood, 905
 38: 7 he put the **s** into the rings on the sides of 905
 39:35 and the **s** thereof, and the mercy seat, 905
 39:39 his **s**, and all his vessels, the laver and his 905
 40:20 set the **s** on the ark, and put the mercy seat 905
Nu 4: 6 of blue, and shall put in the **s** thereof. 905
 4: 8 skins, and shall put in the **s** thereof. 905
 4:11 skins, and shall put to the **s** thereof: 905
 4:14 of badgers' skins, and put to the **s** of it. 905
 21:18 direction of the lawgiver, with their **s**. 4938
1Sa 17:43 I a dog, that thou comest to me with **s**? 4731
1Ki 8: 7 covered the ark and the **s** thereof above. 905
 8: 8 they drew out the **s**, that the ends of 905
 8: 8 that the ends of the **s** were seen out in 905
1Ch 15:15 upon their shoulders with the **s** thereon, 4133
2Ch 5: 8 covered the ark and the **s** thereof above. 905
 5: 9 drew out the **s** *of the ark,* that the ends 905
 5: 9 **s** were seen from the ark before the oracle; 905
Hab 3:14 Thou didst strike through with his **s** 4294
Zec 11:10 I took unto me two **s**; the one I called 4731
Mt 10:10 two coats, neither shoes, nor yet **s**: 4464
 26:47 him a great multitude with swords and **s**, 3586
 26:55 a thief with swords and **s** for to take me? 3586
Mk 14:43 him a great multitude with swords and **s**, 3586

Mk 14:48 thief, with swords and *with* **s** to take me? 3586
Lk 9: 3 neither **s**, nor scrip, neither bread, 4464
 22:52 as against a thief, with swords and **s**? 3586

STAY (33) [STAYED, STAYETH, STAYS]

Ge 19:17 thee, neither **s** thou in all the plain; 5975
Ex 19:28 I will let you go, and ye shall **s** no longer. 5975
Lev 13: 5 *if* the plague in his sight be at a **s**, 5975
 13:23 if the bright spot **s** in his place, 5975
 13:28 if the bright spot **s** in his place, 5975
 13:37 if the scall be in his sight at a **s**, 5975
Jos 10:19 **s** you not, *but* pursue after your enemies, 5975
Ru 1:13 ye **s** for them from having husbands? 5702
1Sa 15:16 **S**, and I will tell thee what the Lord hath 7503
 20:38 after the lad, Make speed, haste, **s** not. 5975
2Sa 22:19 of my calamity: but the Lord was my **s**. 4937
 24:16 **s** now thine hand. And the angel of 7503
1Ch 21:27 it is enough, **s** now thine hand. 7503
Job 37: 4 will not **s** them when his voice is heard. 6117
 38:37 or who can **s** the bottles of heaven, 7901
Ps 18:18 of my calamity: but the Lord was my **s**. 4937
Pr 28:17 shall flee to the pit; let no man **s** him. 8551
SS 2: 5 **S** me with flagons, comfort me with 5564
Isa 3: 1 and from Judah the **s** and the staff, 4937
 3: 1 the whole **s** of bread, and the whole stay 4937
 3: 1 stay of bread, and the whole **s** of water, 4937
 10:20 no more again **s** upon him that smote 8172
 10:20 shall **s** upon the Lord, the Holy One of 8172
 19:13 *even they that are* the **s** of the tribes 6438
 29: 9 **S** yourselves, and wonder; cry ye out, 4102
 30:12 and perverseness, and **s** thereon: 8172
 31: 1 **s** on horses, and trust in chariots, because 8172
 48: 2 and **s** themselves upon the God of Israel; 5564
 50:10 name of the Lord, and **s** upon his God. 8172
Jer 4: 6 retire, **s** not: for I will bring evil from 5975
 20: 9 weary with forbearing, and I could not **s**. NIH
Da 4:35 none can **s** his hand, or say unto him, 4223
Hos 13:13 for he should not **s** long in *the place of* 5975

STAYED (31) [STAY]

Ge 8:10 he **s** yet other seven days; and again he 2342
 8:12 he **s** yet other seven days; and sent forth 3176
 32: 4 with Laban, and **s** *there* until now: 309
Ex 10:24 only let your flocks and your herds be **s**: 3322
 17:12 Aaron and Hur **s up** his hands, the one 8551
Nu 16:48 and the living; and the plague was **s**. 6113
 16:50 the congregation: and the plague was **s**. 6113
 25: 8 So the plague was **s** from the children of 6113
Dt 10:10 I **s** in the mount, according to the first 5975
Jos 10:13 the sun stood still, and the moon **s**, until 5975
1Sa 20:19 *when* thou hast **s three days**, *then* 8027
 24: 7 So David **s** his servants with *these* words, 8156
 30: 9 where those that were left behind **s**. 5975
2Sa 17:17 Jonathan and Ahimaaz **s** by En-rogel; 5975
 24:21 that the plague may be **s** from the people. 6113
 24:25 land, and the plague was **s** from Israel. 6113
1Ki 22:35 the king was **s up** in *his* chariot against 5975
2Ki 4: 6 There *is* not a vessel more. And the oil **s**. 5975
 13:18 the ground. And he smote thrice, and **s**. 5975
 15:20 turned back, and **s** not there in the land. 5975
1Ch 21:22 that the plague may be **s** from the people. 6113
2Ch 18:34 howbeit the king of Israel **s** *himself* up in 5975
Job 38:11 and here shall thy proud waves be **s**? 7896
Ps 106:30 and *so* the plague was **s**. 6113
Isa 26: 3 *whose* mind *is* **s** on thee: because 5564
La 4: 6 as in a moment, and no hands **s** on her. 2342
Eze 31:15 thereof, and the great waters were **s**: 3607
Hag 1:10 Therefore the heaven over you is **s** from 3607
 1:10 dew, and the earth is **s** *from* her fruit. 3607
Lk 4:42 him, and came unto him, and **s** him, 2722
Ac 19:22 but he himself **s** in Asia for a season. 1907

STAYETH (1) [STAY]

Isa 27: 8 he **s** his rough wind in the day of the east 1898

STAYS (4) [STAY]

1Ki 10:19 *there were* **s** on either side on the place 3027
 10:19 the seat, and two lions stood beside the **s**. 3027
2Ch 9:18 **s** on each side of the sitting place, 3027
 9:18 and two lions standing by the **s**: 3027

STEAD (94) [STEADS]

Ge 22:13 up for a burnt offering in the **s** of his son. 8478
 30: 2 he said, *Am* I in God's **s**, who hath 8478
 36:33 son of Zerah of Bozrah reigned in his **s**, 8478
 36:34 of the land of Temani reigned in his **s**. 8478
 36:35 in the field of Moab, reigned in his **s**: 8478
 36:36 and Samlah of Masrekah reigned in his **s**. 8478
 36:37 of Rehoboth *by* the river reigned in his **s**. 8478
 36:38 the son of Achbor reigned in his **s**. 8478
 36:39 Achbor died, and Hadar reigned in his **s**: 8478
Ex 29:30 *And that* son that is priest in his **s** shall 8478
Lev 6:22 priest of his sons that is anointed in his **s** 8478
 16:32 in the priest's office in his father's **s**, 8478
Nu 32:14 ye are risen up in your fathers' **s**, 8478
Dt 2:12 from before them, and dwelt in their **s**; 8478
 2:21 succeeded them, and dwelt in their **s**: 8478
 2:22 and dwelt in their **s** *even* unto this day: 8478
 2:23 destroyed them, and dwelt in their **s**.) 8478
 10: 6 ministered in the priest's office in his **s** 8478
Jos 5: 7 children, *whom* he raised up in their **s**, 8478
2Sa 10: 1 and Hanun his son reigned in his **s**. 8478
 16: 8 of Saul, in whose **s** thou hast reigned; 8478
1Ki 1:30 and he shall sit upon my throne in my **s**; 8478
 1:35 my throne; for he shall be king in my **s**: 8478

1Ki 11:43 and Rehoboam his son reigned **in** his **s**. 8478
 14:20 and Nadab his son reigned **in** his **s**. 8478
 14:27 king Rehoboam made **in** their **s** brasen 8478
 14:31 and Abijam his son reigned **in** his **s**. 8478
 15: 8 David: and Asa his son reigned **in** his **s**. 8478
 15:24 and Jehoshaphat his son reigned **in** his **s**. 8478
 15:28 did Baasha slay him, and reigned **in** his **s**. 8478
 16: 6 Tirzah: and Elah his son reigned **in** his **s**. 8478
 16:10 Asa king of Judah, and reigned **in** his **s**. 8478
 16:28 and Ahab his son reigned **in** his **s**. 8478
 22:40 and Ahaziah his son reigned **in** his **s**. 8478
 22:50 and Jehoram his son reigned **in** his **s**. 8478
2Ki 1:17 Jehoram reigned **in** his **s** in the second 8478
 3:27 son that should have reigned **in** his **s**, 8478
 8:15 that he died: and Hazael reigned **in** his **s**. 8478
 8:24 and Ahaziah his son reigned **in** his **s**. 8478
 10:35 And Jehoahaz his son reigned **in** his **s**. 8478
 12:21 and Amaziah his son reigned **in** his **s**. 8478
 13: 9 and Joash his son reigned **in** his **s**. 8478
 13:24 and Ben-hadad his son reigned **in** his **s**. 8478
 14:16 and Jeroboam his son reigned **in** his **s**. 8478
 14:29 and Zachariah his son reigned **in** his **s**. 8478
 15: 7 and Jotham his son reigned **in** his **s**. 8478
 15:10 and slew him, and reigned **in** his **s**. 8478
 15:14 and slew him, and reigned **in** his **s**. 8478
 15:22 and Pekahiah his son reigned **in** his **s**. 8478
 15:30 and slew him, and reigned **in** his **s**, 8478
 15:38 and Ahaz his son reigned **in** his **s**. 8478
 16:20 and Hezekiah his son reigned **in** his **s**. 8478
 19:37 And Esarhaddon his son reigned **in** his **s**. 8478
 20:21 and Manasseh his son reigned **in** his **s**. 8478
 21:18 Uzza: and Amon his son reigned **in** his **s**. 8478
 21:24 land made Josiah his son king **in** his **s**. 8478
 21:26 Uzza: and Josiah his son reigned **in** his **s**. 8478
 23:30 and made him king **in** his father's **s**. 8478
 24: 6 and Jehoiachin his son reigned **in** his **s**. 8478
 24:17 his father's brother king **in** his **s**, 8478
1Ch 1:44 son of Zerah of Bozrah reigned **in** his **s**. 8478
 1:45 land of the Temanites reigned **in** his **s**. 8478
 1:46 in the field of Moab, reigned **in** his **s**. 8478
 1:47 Samlah of Masrekah reigned **in** his **s**. 8478
 1:48 of Rehoboth *by* the river reigned **in** his **s**. 8478
 1:49 the son of Achbor reigned **in** his **s**. 8478
 1:50 was dead, Hadad reigned **in** his **s**: 8478
 19: 1 Ammon died, and his son reigned **in** his **s**. 8478
 29:28 and Solomon his son reigned **in** his **s**. 8478
2Ch 1: 8 and hast made me to reign **in** his **s**. 8478
 9:31 and Rehoboam his son reigned **in** his **s**. 8478
 12:16 and Abijah his son reigned **in** his **s**. 8478
 14: 1 Asa his son reigned **in** his **s**. In his days 8478
 17: 1 Jehoshaphat his son reigned **in** his **s**, 8478
 21: 1 and Jehoram his son reigned **in** his **s**. 8478
 22: 1 Ahaziah his youngest son king **in** his **s**: 8478
 24:27 And Amaziah his son reigned **in** his **s**. 8478
 26:23 leper: and Jotham his son reigned **in** his **s**. 8478
 27: 9 David: and Ahaz his son reigned **in** his **s**. 8478
 28:27 and Hezekiah his son reigned **in** his **s**. 8478
 32:33 And Manasseh his son reigned **in** his **s**. 8478
 33:20 and Amon his son reigned **in** his **s**. 8478
 33:25 the land made Josiah his son king **in** his **s**. 8478
 36: 1 made him king **in** his father's **s** in 8478
 36: 8 and Jehoiachin his son reigned **in** his **s**. 8478
Job 16: 4 as ye *do*: if your soul were **in** my soul's **s**, 8478
 33: 6 I *am* according to thy wish **in** God's **s**: 3807.1
 34:24 without number, and set others **in** their **s**. 8478
Pr 11: 8 trouble, and the wicked cometh **in** his **s**. 8478
Ecc 4:15 second child that shall stand *up* **in** his **s**. 8478
Isa 37:38 and Esar-haddon his son reigned **in** his **s**. 8478
Jer 29:26 thee priest **in** the **s** of Jehoiada the priest, 8478
2Co 5:20 we pray *you* **in** Christ's **s**, be ye reconciled 5228
Phm 1:13 that in thy **s** he might have ministered 5228

STEADFAST (1) [STEDFAST]

Job 11:15 yea, thou shalt be **s**, and shalt not fear. 3332

STEADS (1) [STEAD]

1Ch 5:22 they dwelt in their **s** until the captivity. 8478

STEADY (1)

Ex 17:12 his hands were **s** until the going down of 530

STEAL (22) [MENSTEALERS, STALE, STEALETH, STEALING, STEALTH, STOLE, STOLEN]

Ge 31:27 flee away secretly, and **s away from** me; 1589
 44: 8 should we **s** out of thy lord's house silver 1589
Ex 20:15 Thou shalt not **s**. 1589
 22: 1 If a man shall **s** an ox, or a sheep, 1589
Lev 19:11 Ye shall not **s**, neither deal falsely, 1589
Dt 5:19 Neither shalt thou **s**. 1589
2Sa 19: 3 as people being ashamed **s away** when 1589
Pr 6:30 he **s** to satisfy his soul when he is hungry; 1589
 30: 9 or, lest I be poor, and **s**, and take the name of my God *in vain*. 1589
Jer 7: 9 Will ye **s**, murder, and commit adultery, 1589
 23:30 that **s** my words every one from his 1589
Mt 6:19 and where thieves break through and **s**: 2813
 6:20 where thieves do not break through nor **s**: 2813
 19:18 not commit adultery, Thou shalt not **s**, 2813
 27:64 and **s** him *away*, and say unto the people, 2813
Mk 10:19 commit adultery, Do not kill, Do not **s**, 2813
Lk 18:20 commit adultery, Do not kill, Do not **s**, 2813
Jn 10:10 but for to **s**, and to kill, and to destroy: 2813
Ro 2:21 thou that preachest *a man* should not **s**, 2813
 2:21 *a man* should not steal, dost thou **s**? 2813
 13: 9 Thou shalt not kill, Thou shalt not **s**, 2813
Eph 4:28 Let him that stole **s** no more: but rather 2813

STEALETH (3) [STEAL]
Ex	21:16 that **s** a man, and selleth him, or if he be	1589
Job	27:20 a tempest **s** him away in the night.	1589
Zec	5: 3 for every one that **s** shall be cut off *as* on	1589

STEALING (2) [STEAL]
Dt	24: 7 If a man be found **s** any of his brethren of	1589
Hos	4: 2 killing, and **s**, and committing adultery,	1589

STEALTH (1) [STEAL]
2Sa	19: 3 the people gat them by **s** that day *into*	1589

STEDFAST (10) [STEADFAST, STEADFASTLY, STEDFASTNESS]
Ps	78: 8 and whose spirit was not **s** with God.	539
	78:37 neither were they **s** in his covenant.	539
Da	6: s for ever, and his kingdom *that* which	7011
1Co	7:37 he that standeth **s** in *his* heart,	1476
	15:58 beloved brethren, be ye **s**, unmoveable,	1476
2Co	1: 7 And our hope of you *is* **s**, knowing, that	949
Heb	2: 2 For if the word spoken by angels was **s**,	949
	3:14 we hold the beginning of *our* confidence **s**	949
	6:19 both sure and **s**, and which entereth into	949
1Pe	5: 9 Whom resist **s** in the faith, knowing that	4731

STEDFASTLY (10) [STEDFAST]
Ru	1:18 she saw that she *was* **s minded** to go	553
2Ki	8:11 he settled his countenance **s**, until *he* was	7760
Lk	9:51 he **s set** his face to go to Jerusalem,	4741
Ac	1:10 while they **looked s** toward heaven as	816
	2:42 And they **continued s** in the apostles'	4342
	6:15 that sat in the council, **looking s** on him,	816
	7:55 **looked** up **s** into heaven, and saw the	816
	9: s **beholding** him, and perceiving that he	816
2Co	3: 7 the children of Israel could not **s behold**	816
	3:13 the children of Israel could not **s look** to	816

STEDFASTNESS (2) [STEDFAST]
Col	2: 5 order, and the **s** of your faith in Christ.	4733
2Pe	3:17 error of the wicked, fall from your own **s**.	4740

STEEL (4)
2Sa	22:35 that a bow of **s** is broken *by* mine arms.	5154
Job	20:24 the bow of **s** shall strike him through.	5154
Ps	18:34 that a bow of **s** is broken *by* mine arms.	5154
Jer	15:12 iron break the northern iron and the **s**?	5178

STEEP (5)
Eze	38:20 **s places** shall fall, and every wall shall	4095
Mic	1: 4 waters *that are* poured down a **s place**.	4174
Mt	8:32 ran violently down a **s place** into the sea,	2911
Mk	5:13 herd ran violently down a **s place** into	2911
Lk	8:33 herd ran violently down a **s place** into	2911

STEM (1)
Isa	11: 1 there shall come forth a rod out of the **s**	1503

STEP (2) [FOOTSTEPS, STEPPED, STEPPETH, STEPS]
1Sa	20: 3 *there is* but a **s** between me and death.	6587
Job	31: 7 If my **s** hath turned out of the way,	838

STEPHANAS (4)
1Co	1:16 And I baptized also the household of **S**:	4734
	16:15 brethren, (ye know the house of **S**,	4734
	16:17 I am glad of the coming of **S** and	4734
	16: **S** was written from Philippi by	4734

STEPHEN (7)
Ac	6: 5 and they chose **S**, a man full of faith and	4736
	6: 8 And **S**, full of faith and power, did great	4736
	6: 9 of Cilicia and of Asia, disputing with **S**.	4736
	7:59 And they stoned **S**, calling upon *God*, and	4736
	8: 2 And devout men carried **S** *to his* burial,	4736
	11:19 arose about **S** travelled as far as Phenice,	4736
	22:20 And when the blood of thy martyr **S** was	4736

STEPPED (1) [STEP]
Jn	5: 4 first after the troubling of the water **s in**,	1684

STEPPETH (1) [STEP]
Jn	5: 7 I am coming, another **s down** before me.	2597

STEPS (38) [STEP]
Ex	20:26 Neither shalt thou go up by **s** unto mine	4609
2Sa	22:37 Thou hast enlarged my **s** under me;	6806
1Ki	10:19 The throne had six **s**, and the top of	4609
	10:20 one side and on the other upon the six **s**:	4609
2Ch	9:18 *there were* six **s** to the throne, with a	4609
	9:19 one side and on the other upon the six **s**:	4609
Job	14:16 For now thou numberest my **s**: dost thou	6806
	18: 7 The **s** of his strength shall be straitened,	838
	23:11 foot hath held my **s**, his way have I kept,	838
	29: 6 When *I* washed my **s** with butter,	1978
	31: 4 not he see my ways, and count all my **s**?	6806
	31:37 declare unto him the number of my **s**;	6806
Ps	17:11 They have now compassed us *in* our **s**:	838
	18:36 Thou hast enlarged my **s** under me, that	6806
	37:23 The **s** of a *good* man are ordered by	4703
	37:31 God *is* in his heart; none of his **s** shall slide.	838
	44:18 neither have our **s** declined from thy way;	838
	56: 6 they hide themselves, they mark my **s**,	6119
	57: 6 They have prepared a net for my **s**;	6471
	73: 2 almost gone; my **s** had well nigh slipt.	838
	85:13 and shall set *us* in the way of his **s**.	6471
	119:133 Order my **s** in thy word: and let not any	6806
Pr	4:12 When thou goest thy **s** shall not be	6806

Pr	5: 5 down *to* death; her **s** take hold on hell.	6806
	16: 9 his way: but the Lord directeth his **s**.	6806
Isa	26: 6 feet of the poor, *and* the **s** of the needy.	6471
Jer	10:23 not in man that walketh to direct his **s**.	6806
La	4:18 They hunt our **s**, that *we* cannot go in	6806
Eze	40:22 they went up unto it by seven **s**;	4609
	40:26 *there were* seven **s** to go up to it,	4609
	40:31 and the going up to it *had* eight **s**.	4609
	40:34 side: and the going up to it *had* eight **s**.	4609
	40:37 side: and the going up to it *had* eight **s**.	4609
	40:49 he brought me by the **s** whereby they	4609
Da	11:43 and the Ethiopians *shall be* at his **s**.	4703
Ro	4:12 who also walk in the **s** of *that* faith of our	2487
2Co	12:18 same spirit? *walked* we not in the same **s**?	2487
1Pe	2:21 an example, that ye should follow his **s**:	2487

STERN (1)
Ac	27:29 they cast four anchors out of the **s**,	4403

STEW See POTTAGE

STEWARD (13) [STEWARDS, STEWARDSHIP]
Ge	15: 2 the **s** of my house *is* this Eliezer of	1121+4943
	43:19 they came near to the **s** of	376+834+5921
	44: 1 he commanded the **s** of his house,	834+5921
	44: 4 Joseph said unto his **s**,	834+1004+5921
1Ki	16: 9 of Arza **s** of *his* house in Tirzah.	834+5921
Mt	20: 8 the lord of the vineyard saith unto his **s**,	2012
Lk	8: 3 And Joanna the wife of Chuza Herod's **s**,	2012
	12:42 Who *then* is *that* faithful and wise **s**,	3623
	16: 1 was a certain rich man, which had a **s**;	3623
	16: 2 for thou mayest be no longer **s**.	3621
	16: 3 Then the **s** said within himself, What shall	3623
	16: 8 And the lord commended the unjust **s**,	3623
Tit	1: 7 bishop must be blameless, as the **s** of God;	3623

STEWARDS (4) [STEWARD]
1Ch	28: 1 the **s** over all the substance and	8269
1Co	4: 1 of Christ, and **s** of the mysteries of God.	3623
	4: 2 Moreover it is required in **s**, that a man be	3623
1Pe	4:10 as good **s** of the manifold grace of God.	3623

STEWARDSHIP (3) [STEWARD]
Lk	16: 2 give an account of thy **s**; for thou mayest	3622
	16: 3 for my lord taketh away from me the **s**:	3622
	16: 4 to do, that, when I am put out of the **s**,	3622

STICK (14) [CANDLESTICK, CANDLESTICKS, STICKETH, STICKS, STUCK]
2Ki	6: 6 he cut down a **s**, and cast *it* in thither;	6086
Job	33:21 and his bones *that* were not seen **s out**.	8192
	41:17 they **s together**, that they cannot be	3920
Ps	38: 2 thine arrows **s fast** in me, and thy hand	5181
La	4: 8 it is withered, it is become like a **s**.	6086
Eze	29: 4 I will **cause** the fish of thy rivers to **s**	1692
	29: 4 all the fish of thy rivers shall unto thy	1692
	37:16 take thee one **s**, and write upon it,	6086
	37:16 take another **s**, and write upon it,	6086
	37:16 the **s** of Ephraim, and *for* all the house of	6086
	37:17 join them one to another into one **s**;	6086
	37:19 I *will* take the **s** of Joseph, which *is*	6086
	37:19 *even* with the **s** of Judah, and make them	6086
	37:19 make them one **s**, and they shall be one	6086

STICKETH (1) [STICK]
Pr	18:24 is a friend *that* **s closer** than a brother.	1695

STICKS (6) [STICK]
Nu	15:32 found a man that gathered **s** upon	6086
	15:33 they that found him gathering **s** brought	6086
1Ki	17:10 widow woman *was* there gathering of **s**:	6086
	17:12 I *am* gathering two **s**, that I may go	6086
Eze	37:20 the **s** whereon thou writest shall be in	6086
Ac	28: 3 when Paul had gathered a bundle of **s**,	5434

STIFF (4) [STIFFENED, STIFFNECKED]
Dt	31:27 For I know thy rebellion, and thy **s** neck:	7186
Ps	75: 5 horn on high: speak *not* with a **s** neck.	6277
Jer	17:23 **made** their neck **s**, that *they* might not	7185
Eze	2: 4 *are* impudent children and **s** hearted.	2389

STIFFENED (1) [STIFF]
2Ch	36:13 he **s** his neck, and hardened his heart	7185

STIFFNECKED (8) [NECK, STIFF]
Ex	32: 9 and behold, it *is* a **s** people:	6203+7186
	33: 3 of thee; for thou *art* a **s** people:	6203+7186
	33: 5 children of Israel, Ye *are* a **s** people:	6203+7186
	34: 9 for it *is* a **s** people; and pardon our	6203+7186
Dt	9: 6 for thou *art* a **s** people.	6203+7186
	9:13 and behold, it *is* a **s** people:	6203+7186
	10:16 of your heart, and be no more **s**.	6203+7185
2Ch	30: 8 Now be ye not **s**, as your fathers	6203+7185
Ac	7:51 Ye **s** and uncircumcised in heart and ears,	4644

STILL (101) [STILLED, STILLEST, STILLETH]
Ge	12: 9 going on *toward* the south.	5265+2050.1
	41:21 *were* **s** ill favoured, as at the beginning.	NIH
Ex	9: 2 to let *them* go, and wilt hold them **s**,	5750
	14:13 **stand s**, and see the salvation of	3320
	15:16 of thine arm they be as **s** as a stone;	1826
	23:11 *year* thou shalt let it rest and **lie s**;	5203
Lev	13:57 if it appear **s** in the garment, either in	5750
Nu	9: 8 **Stand s**, and I will hear what the Lord	5975
	14:38 men that went to search the land, lived **s**.	NIH
Jos	3: 8 of Jordan, ye shall **stand s** in Jordan.	5975

Jos	10:12 of Israel, Sun, **stand** thou **s** upon Gibeon;	1826
	10:13 the sun **stood s**, and the moon stayed,	1826
	10:13 the sun **stood s** in the midst of heaven,	5975
	11:13 *as for* the cities that **stood s** in their	5975
	24:10 therefore he **blessed** you **s**:	1288+1288
Jdg	18: 9 it *is* very good: and *are* ye **s**?	2814
Ru	3:18 said she, Sit **s**, my daughter, until thou	3427
1Sa	9:27 **stand** thou **s** a while, that I may shew	5975
	12: 7 Now therefore **stand s**, that I may reason	3320
	12:25 if ye shall **s do wickedly**, ye shall	7489+7489
	14: 9 we will **stand s** in our place, and will not	5975
	26:25 things, and also shalt **s prevail**.	3201+3201
2Sa	2:23 where Asahel fell down and died **stood s**.	5975
	2:28 all the people **stood s**, and pursued after	5975
	11: 1 But David tarried **s** at Jerusalem.	NIH
	14:32 *been* good for me *to* have been there **s**:	5750
	16: 5 he came forth, and cursed **s** as he came.	NIH
	18:30 And he turned aside, and **stood s**.	5975
	20:12 the man saw that all the people **stood s**,	5975
	20:12 that every one that came by him **stood s**.	5975
1Ki	19:12 the fire: and after the fire a **s** small voice.	1827
	22: 3 we *be* **s**, and take it not out of the hand	2814
2Ki	2:11 **s went on**, and talked, that behold,	1980+1980
	7: 4 if we sit **s** here, we die also.	3427
	12: 3 the people sacrificed and burnt incense	5750
	15: 4 and burnt incense **s** on the high places.	5750
	15:35 and burnt incense **s** in the high places.	5750
2Ch	20:17 stand ye **s**, and see the salvation of	NIH
	22: 9 had no power to **keep s** the kingdom.	6113
	33:17 Nevertheless the people did sacrifice **s** in	5750
Ne	12:39 and they **stood s** in the prison gate.	5975
Job	2: 3 he holdeth fast his integrity,	5750
	2: 9 him, Dost thou **s** retain thine integrity?	5750
	3:13 now should I have lien **s** and been quiet,	NIH
	4:16 It **stood s**, but I could not discern the	5975
	20:13 it not; but **keep** it **s** within his mouth:	4513
	32:16 but **stood s**, *and* answered no more:	5975
	37:14 **stand s**, and consider the wondrous	5975
Ps	4: 4 your own heart upon your bed, and be **s**.	1826
	8: 2 that *thou* mightest **s** the enemy and	7673
	23: 2 he leadeth me beside the **s** waters.	4496
	46:10 Be **s**, and know that *I am* God: I will be	7503
	49: 9 he should **s** live for ever, *and* not see	5750
	68:21 hairy scalp of such a one as **goeth on s**	1980
	76: 8 from heaven; the earth feared, and was **s**,	8252
	78:32 For all this they sinned **s**, and believed not	5750
	83: 1 hold not thy peace, and be not **s**, O God.	8252
	84: 4 they will be **s** praising thee. Selah.	5750
	92:14 They shall **s** bring forth fruit in old age;	5750
	107:29 a calm, so that the waves thereof are **s**.	2814
	139:18 the sand: when I awake, I am **s** with thee.	5750
Ecc	12: 9 he **s** taught the people knowledge;	5750
Isa	5:25 away, but his hand *is* stretched out **s**.	5750
	9:12 away, but his hand *is* stretched out **s**.	5750
	9:17 away, but his hand *is* stretched out **s**.	5750
	9:21 away, but his hand *is* stretched out **s**.	5750
	10: 4 away, but his hand *is* stretched out **s**.	5750
	23: 2 Be **s**, ye inhabitants of the isle; thou	1826
	30: 7 concerning this, Their strength *is* to **sit s**.	7674
	42:14 I have been **s**, and refrained myself:	2790
Jer	8:14 Why do we **sit s**? assemble yourselves,	3427
	23:17 they **say s** unto them that despise	559+559
	27:11 will I let **remain s** in their own land,	3240
	31:20 I do earnestly remember him **s**:	5750
	42:10 If ye will **s** abide in this land, then will I	7725
	47: 6 thyself into thy scabbard, rest, and be **s**.	1826
	51:50 escaped the sword, go *away*, **stand** not **s**:	5975
La	3:20 hath *them* **s** in remembrance,	2142+2142
Eze	33:30 the children of thy people **s** are talking	NIH
	41: 7 winding about **s** upward	4605+1886.5+3807.1
	41: 7 **s** upward round about	4605+1886.5+3807.1
	41: 7 the breadth of the house *was* **s** upward,	NIH
Hab	3:11 *and* moon **stood s** in *their* habitation:	5975
Zec	1:11 all the earth **sitteth s**, and is at rest.	3427
	11:16 is broken, nor feed that that **standeth s**.	5324
Mt	20:32 And Jesus **stood s**, and called them,	2476
Mk	4:39 wind, and said unto the sea, Peace, be **s**.	5392
	10:49 And Jesus **stood s**, and commanded him	2476
Lk	7:14 and they that bare *him* **stood s**. And he	2476
Jn	7: 9 *words* unto them, he abode **s** in Galilee.	NIG
	11: 6 he abode two days **s** in the *same* place	NIG
	11:20 and met him: but Mary sat **s** in the house.	NIG
Ac	8:38 he commanded the chariot to **stand s**:	2476
	15:34 it pleased Silas to abide there **s**.	NIG
	17:14 but Silas and Timotheus **abode** there **s**.	5278
Ro	11:23 they also, if they **bide** not **s** in unbelief,	1961
1Ti	1: 3 As I besought thee to abide **s** at Ephesus,	NIG
Rev	22:11 He that is unjust, let him be unjust **s**:	2089
	22:11 and he which is filthy, let him be filthy **s**:	2089
	22:11 *that is* righteous, let him be righteous **s**:	2089
	22:11 and he that is holy, let him be holy **s**.	2089

STILLBORN See UNTIMELY

STILLED (2) [STILL]
Nu	13:30 Caleb **s** the people before Moses,	2013
Ne	8:11 So the Levites **s** all the people, saying,	2814

STILLEST (1) [STILL]
Ps	89: 9 the waves thereof arise, thou **s** them.	7623

STILLETH (1) [STILL]
Ps	65: 7 Which **s** the noise of the seas, the noise	7623

S

STING (2) [STINGETH, STINGS]
1Co 15:55 death, where *is* thy **s**? O grave, where *is* 2759
15:56 The **s** of death *is* sin; 2759

STINGETH (1) [STING]
Pr 23:32 biteth like a serpent, and **s** like an adder. 6567

STINGS (1) [STING]
Rev 9:10 and there were **s** in their tails: 2759

STINK (8) [STANK, STINKETH, STINKING, STUNK]
Ge 34:30 Ye have troubled me to **make me to s** 887
Ex 7:18 in the river shall die, and the river shall **s**; 887
16:24 it did not **s**, neither was there any worm 887
Ps 38: 5 My wounds *and* are corrupt because of 887
Isa 3:24 instead of sweet smell there shall be **s**; 4716
34: 3 their **s** shall come up *out of* their carcases, 889
Joel 2:20 his **s** shall come up, and his ill savour shall 889
Am 4:10 I have made the **s** of your camps to come 889

STINKETH (2) [STINK]
Isa 50: 2 their fish **s**, because *there is* no water, 887
Jn 11:39 saith unto him, Lord, by this time he **s**: 3605

STINKING (1) [STINK]
Ecc 10: 1 of the apothecary to send forth a **s** savour: 887

STIR (20) [STIRRED, STIRRETH, STIRS]
Nu 24: 9 who shall **s** him up? Blessed *is* he that 6965
Job 17: 8 the innocent shall **s** up himself against 5782
41:10 None *is so* fierce that **dare s** him up: 5782
Ps 35:23 **S** up thyself, and awake to my judgment, 5782
78:38 away, and did not **s** up all his wrath. 5782
80: 2 and Manasseh **s** up thy strength, 5782
Pr 15: 1 wrath: but grievous words **s** up anger. 5927
SS 2: 7 that ye **s** not **up**, nor awake *my* love, 5782
3: 5 that ye **s** not **up**, nor awake *my* love, 5782
8: 4 that ye **s** not **up**, nor awake *my* love, 5782
Isa 10:26 the LORD of hosts shall **s** up a scourge 5782
13:17 I will **s** up the Medes against them, 5782
42:13 he shall **s** up jealousy like a man of war: 5782
Da 11: 2 shall **s** up all against the realm of Grecia. 5782
11:25 he shall **s** up his power and his courage 5782
Ac 12:18 there was no small **s** among the soldiers, 5017
19:23 And the same time there arose no small **s** 5017
2Ti 1: 6 that *thou* **s** up the gift of God, 329
2Pe 1:13 to **s** you up by putting *you* in 1326
3: 1 in both which I **s** up your pure minds by 1326

STIRRED (23) [STIR]
Ex 35:21 every one whose heart **s** him **up**, 5375
35:26 all the women whose heart **s** them **up** in 5375
36: 2 *even* every one whose heart **s** him **up** to 5375
1Sa 22: 8 sheweth unto me that my son hath **s up** 6965
26:19 If the LORD have **s** thee up against me, 5496
1Ki 11:14 the LORD **s** up an adversary unto 6965
11:23 God **s** him up *another* adversary, Rezon 6965
21:25 the LORD, whom Jezebel his wife **s** up. 5496
1Ch 5:26 God of Israel **s** up the spirit of Pul king 5782
2Ch 21:16 Moreover the LORD **s** up against 5782
36:22 the LORD **s** up the spirit of Cyrus king 5782
Ezr 1: 1 the LORD **s** up the spirit of Cyrus king of 5782
Ps 39: 2 *even* from good; and my sorrow was **s**. 5916
Da 11:10 his sons shall be **s** up, and shall assemble 1624
11:10 shall he return, and be **s** up, *even* to his 1624
11:25 king of the south shall be **s** up to battle 1624
Hag 1:14 the LORD **s** up the spirit of Zerubbabel 5782
Ac 6:12 And they **s** up the people, and the elders, 4787
13:50 But the Jews **s** up the devout and 3951
14: 2 the unbelieving Jews **s** up the Gentiles, 1892
17:13 came thither also, and **s** up the people. 4531
17:16 them at Athens, his spirit was **s** in him, 3947
21:27 **s** up all the people, and laid hands on 4797

STIRRETH (8) [STIR]
Dt 32:11 As an eagle **s** up her nest, fluttereth over 5782
Pr 10:12 Hatred **s** up strifes: but love covereth all 5782
15:18 A wrathful man **s** up strife: but *he that is* 1624
28:25 He that is of a proud heart **s** up strife: 1624
29:22 An angry man **s** up strife, and a furious 1624
Isa 14: 9 it **s** up the dead for thee, *even* all the 5782
64: 7 that **s** up himself to take hold of thee: 5782
Lk 23: 5 saying, He **s** up the people, 383

STIRS (1) [STIR]
Isa 22: 2 Thou *that art* full of **s**, a tumultuous city, 8663

STOCK (8) [STOCKS]
Lev 25:47 thee, or to the **s** of the stranger's family: 6133
Job 14: 8 and the **s** thereof die in the ground; 1503
Isa 40:24 their **s** shall not take root in the earth: 1503
44:19 shall I fall down to the **s** of a tree? 944
Jer 2:27 Saying to a **s**, Thou *art* my father; and to 6086
10: 8 and foolish: the **s** *is* a doctrine of vanities. 6086
Ac 13:26 children of the **s** of Abraham, 1085
Php 3: 5 of the **s** of Israel, of the tribe of Benjamin, 1085

STOCKS (9) [STOCK]
Job 13:27 Thou puttest my feet also in the **s**, 5465
33:11 He putteth my feet in the **s**, he marketh 5465
Pr 7:22 or as a fool to the correction of the **s**; 5914
Jer 3: 9 adultery with stones and with **s**. 6086
20: 2 put him in the **s** that *were* in the high 4115
20: 3 brought forth Jeremiah out of the **s**. 4115
29:26 shouldest put him in prison, and in the **s**. 6729
Hos 4:12 My people ask *counsel* at their **s**, 6086

Ac 16:24 and made their feet fast in the **s**. 3586

STOICKS (1)
Ac 17:18 and of the **S**, encountered this. 4770

STOLE (4) [STEAL]
2Sa 15: 6 Absalom **s** the hearts of the men of Israel. 1589
2Ch 22:11 **s** him from among the king's sons that 1589
Mt 28:13 by night, and **s** him *away* while we slept. 2813
Eph 4:28 Let him that **s** steal no more: but rather 2813

STOLEN (15) [STEAL]
Ge 30:33 sheep, that *shall be counted* with me. 1589
31:19 Rachel had **s** the images that *were* her 1589
31:26 thou hast **s away unawares** to 1589+3824
31:30 *yet* wherefore hast thou **s** my gods? 1589
31:32 Jacob knew not that Rachel had **s** them. 1589
31:39 *whether* **s** by day, or stolen by night. 1589
31:39 *whether* stolen by day, or **s** by night. 1589
40:15 For **indeed** I was **s away** out of 1589+1589
Ex 22: 7 keep, and it be **s** out of the man's house; 1589
22:12 if it be **s** from him, he shall make 1589+1589
Jos 7:11 have also **s**, and dissembled also, 1589
2Sa 19:41 brethren the men of Judah **s** thee **away**, 1589
21:12 which had **s** them from the street of 1589
Pr 9:17 **S** waters are sweet, and bread *eaten* in 1589
Ob 1: 5 they not have **s** till they had enough? 1589

STOMACH'S (1) [STOMACHER]
1Ti 5:23 but use a little wine for thy **s** sake and 4751

STOMACHER (1) [STOMACH'S]
Isa 3:24 instead of a **s** a girding of sackcloth; 6614

STONE (192) [BRIMSTONE, CHALKSTONES, HAILSTONES, HAIL-STONES, HEADSTONE, SLINGSTONES, STONE'S, STONED, STONES, STONESQUARERS, STONEST, STONING, STONY, STUMBLINGSTONE]
Ge 2:12 *is* good: there *is* bdellium and the onyx **s**. 68
11: 3 they had brick for **s**, and slime had they for 68
28:18 took the **s** that he had put *for* his pillows, 68
28:22 this **s**, which I have set *for* a pillar, shall be 68
29: 2 and a great *was* upon the well's mouth. 68
29: 3 they rolled the **s** from the well's mouth, 68
29: 3 put the **s** again upon the well's mouth in 68
29: 8 *till* they roll the **s** from the well's mouth; 68
29:10 rolled the **s** from the well's mouth, 68
31:45 Jacob took a **s**, and set it up *for* a pillar. 68
35:14 he talked with him, *even* a pillar of **s**. 68
49:24 thence *is* the shepherd, the **s** of Israel:) 68
Ex 4:25 Zipporah took a **sharp s**, and cut off 6864
7:19 both in *vessels of* wood, and in *vessels of* **s**. 68
8:26 before their eyes, and will they not **s** us? 5619
15: 5 they sank into the bottom as a **s**. 68
15:16 of thine arm they shall be *as* still as a **s**; 68
17: 4 this people? they be almost ready to **s** me. 5619
17:12 they took a **s**, and put *it* under him, and he 68
20:25 if thou wilt make me an altar of **s**, thou 68
20:25 stone, thou shalt not build it of **hewn s**: 1496
21:18 one smite another with a **s**, or with *his* fist, 68
24:10 as it were a paved work of a **sapphire s**, 5601
24:12 and I will give thee tables of **s**, and a law, 68
28:10 Six of their names on one **s**, and the *other* 68
28:10 *other* six names of the rest on the other **s**, 68
28:11 With the work of an engraver in **s**, *like* 68
31:18 two tables of Testimony, tables of **s**, 68
34: 1 Hew thee two tables of **s** like unto the first: 68
34: 4 he hewed two tables of **s** like unto the first: 68
34: 4 and took in his hand the two tables of **s**. 68
Lev 20: 2 the people of the land shall **s** him with 7275
20:27 they shall **s** them with stones: their blood 7275
24:14 head, and let all the congregation **s** him. 7275
24:16 congregation shall **certainly s** him: 7275+7275
24:23 out of the camp, and **s** him with stones. 7275
26: 1 neither shall ye set up *any* image of **s** in 68
Nu 14:10 all the congregation bade **s** them with 7275
15:35 the congregation shall **s** him with stones 7275
35:17 if he smite him with throwing a **s**, 68
35:23 Or with any **s**, wherewith *a man* may die, 68
Dt 4:13 and he wrote them upon two tables of **s**. 68
4:28 wood and **s**, which neither see, nor hear, 68
5:22 he wrote them in two tables of **s**, 68
9: 9 up into the mount to receive the tables of **s**, 68
9:10 the LORD delivered unto me two tables of **s** 68
9:11 *that* the LORD gave me the two tables of **s** 68
10: 1 Hew thee two tables of **s** like unto the first, 68
10: 3 hewed two tables of **s** like unto the first, 68
13:10 thou shalt **s** him with stones, that he die; 5619
17: 5 and shalt **s** them with stones, till they die. 5619
21:21 all the men of his city shall **s** him with 7275
22:21 the men of her city shall **s** her with stones 5619
22:24 ye shall **s** them with stones that they die; 5619
28:36 shalt thou serve other gods, wood and **s**. 68
28:64 thy fathers have known, *even* wood and **s**. 68
29:17 their idols, wood and **s**, silver and gold, 68
Jos 4: 5 take ye up every man of you a **s** upon his 68
15: 6 border went up *to* the **s** of Bohan the son 68
18:17 descended *to* the **s** of Bohan the son of 68
24:26 took a great **s**, and set it up there under an 68
24:27 Behold, this **s** shall be a witness unto us; 68
Jdg 9: 5 threescore and ten persons, upon one **s**: 68
9:18 upon one **s**, and have made Abimelech, 68
1Sa 6:14 stood there, where *there was* a great **s**: 68
6:15 of gold *were*, and put *them* on the great **s**: 68

1Sa 6:18 even unto the great **s** of Abel, NIH
6:18 **s** remaineth unto this day in the field NIH
7:12 Samuel took a **s**, and set *it* between Mizpeh 68
14:33 roll a great **s** unto me this day. 68
17:49 took thence a **s**, and slang *it*, and smote 68
17:49 forehead, that the **s** sunk into his forehead; 68
17:50 over the Philistine with a sling and with a **s**, 68
20:19 was *in* hand, and shalt remain by the **s** Ezel. 68
25:37 died within him, and he became *as* a **s**. 68
2Sa 17:13 there be not one **small s** found there. 6872
20: 8 When they *were* at the great **s** which *is* in 68
1Ki 1: 9 and oxen and fat cattle by the **s** of Zoheleth, 68
6: 7 was built of **s** made ready *before it was* 68
6:18 all *was* cedar; there was no **s** seen. 68
6:36 inner court *with* three rows of **hewed s**, 1496
8: 9 nothing in the ark save the two tables of **s**, 68
21:10 *then* carry him out, and **s** him, that he 5619
2Ki 3:25 good piece of land cast every man his **s**, 68
12:12 hewers of **s**, and to buy timber and 68
12:12 hewed **s** to repair the breaches of the house 68
19:18 but the work of men's hands, wood and **s**: 68
22: 6 buy timber and hewn **s** to repair the house. 68
1Ch 22:14 timber also and **s** have I prepared; 68
22:15 hewers and workers of **s** and timber, 68
2Ch 2:14 silver, in brass, in iron, in **s**, and in timber, 68
34:11 and builders gave they *it*, to buy hewn **s**, 68
Ne 4: 3 up, he shall even break down their **s** wall. 68
9:11 the deeps, as a **s** into the mighty waters. 68
Job 28: 2 the earth, and brass *is* molten *out of* the **s**. 68
38: 6 or who laid the corner **s** thereof; 68
38:30 The waters are hid as *with* a **s**, and the face 68
41:24 His heart is as firm as a **s**; yea, as hard as a 68
Ps 91:12 hands, lest thou dash thy foot against a **s**. 68
118:22 The **s** *which* the builders refused is become 68
118:22 is become the head **s** of the corner. NIH
Pr 17: 8 A gift *is as* a precious **s** in the eyes of him 68
24:31 and the **s** wall thereof was broken down. 68
26: 8 As *he that* bindeth a **s** in a sling, so *is* he 68
26:27 he that rolleth a **s**, it will return upon him. 68
27: 3 A **s** *is* heavy, and the sand *weighty*; 68
Isa 8:14 a **s** of stumbling and for a rock of offence 68
28:16 Behold, I lay in Zion for a foundation a **s**, 68
28:16 in Zion for a foundation a stone, a tried **s**, 68
28:16 a precious corner **s**, a sure foundation: NIH
37:19 but the work of men's hands, wood and **s**: 68
Jer 2:27 and to a **s**, Thou hast brought me forth: 68
51:26 they shall not take of thee a **s** for a corner, 68
51:26 a stone for a corner, nor a **s** for foundations; 68
51:63 *that* thou shalt bind a **s** to it, and cast it into 68
La 3: 9 He hath inclosed my ways with **hewn s**, 1496
3:53 life in the dungeon, and cast a **s** upon me. 68
Eze 1:26 a throne, as the appearance of a sapphire **s**: 68
10: 1 appeared over them as it were a sapphire **s**, 68
10: 9 of the wheels *was* as the colour of a beryl **s**. 68
16:40 they shall **s** thee with stones, and thrust 7275
20:32 of the countries, to serve wood and **s**. 68
23:47 the company shall **s** them with stones, 7275
28:13 every precious **s** *was* thy covering, 68
40:42 the four tables *were* of hewn **s** for the 68
Da 2:34 Thou sawest till that a **s** was cut out 69
2:35 the **s** that smote the image became a great 69
2:45 Forasmuch as thou sawest that the **s** was 69
5: 4 silver, of brass, of iron, of wood, and of **s**. 69
5:23 gold, of brass, iron, wood, and **s**, which see 69
6:17 a **s** was brought, and laid upon the mouth 69
Am 5:11 ye have built houses of **hewn s**, but ye 1496
Hab 2:11 For the **s** shall cry out of the wall, 68
2:19 Awake; to the dumb **s**, Arise, it shall teach! 68
Hag 2:15 from before a **s** was laid upon a stone in 68
2:15 from before a stone was laid upon a **s** in 68
Zec 3: 9 For behold the **s** that I have laid before 68
3: 9 Joshua; upon one **s** *shall be* seven eyes: 68
7:12 they made their hearts *as* an **adamant s**, 8068
12: 3 Jerusalem a burdensome **s** for all people: 68
Mt 4: 6 at any time thou dash thy foot against a **s**. 3037
7: 9 if his son ask bread, will he give him a **s**? 3037
21:42 The **s** which the builders rejected, 3037
21:44 And whosoever shall fall on this **s** shall be 3037
24: 2 There shall not be left here one **s** upon 3037
27:60 he rolled a great **s** to the door of 3037
27:66 sealing the **s**, and setting a watch. 3037
28: 2 came and rolled back the **s** from the door, 3037
Mk 12:10 The **s** which the builders rejected is 3037
13: 2 there shall not be left one **s** upon another, 3037
15:46 rolled a **s** unto the door of the sepulchre. 3037
16: 3 Who shall roll us away the **s** from the 3037
16: 4 they saw that the **s** was rolled away: 3037
Lk 4: 3 command this **s** that it be made bread. 3037
4:11 any time thou dash thy foot against a **s**. 3037
11:11 you that is a father, will he give him a **s**? 3037
19:44 they shall not leave in thee one **s** upon 3037
20: 6 If we say, Of men; all the people will **s** us: 2642
20:17 The **s** which the builders rejected, 3037
20:18 Whosoever shall fall upon that **s** shall be 3037
21: 6 in the which there shall not be left one **s** 3037
23:53 laid it in a sepulchre that was **hewn** in **s**, 2991
24: 2 And they found the **s** rolled away from 3037
Jn 1:42 which is by interpretation, A **s**. 4074
2: 6 there were set there six waterpots of **s**, 3035
8: 7 sin among you, let him first cast a **s** at her. 3035
10:31 Then the Jews took up stones again to **s** 3034
10:32 for which of those works do ye **s** me? 3034
10:33 saying, For a good work we **s** thee not; 3034
11: 8 Master, the Jews of late sought to **s** thee; 3034
11:38 grave. It was a cave, and a **s** lay upon it. 3037

Jn 11:39 Jesus said, Take ye away the **s**. Martha, 3037
11:41 Then they took away the **s** *from the* 3037
20: 1 the **s** taken away from the sepulchre. 3037
Ac 4:11 is the **s** which was set at nought of you 3037
14: 5 to use *them* despitefully, and to **s** them, 3036
17:29 or silver, or **s**, graven by art and 3037
2Co 3: 3 not in tables of **s**, but in fleshy tables of 3035
Eph 2:20 Christ himself being the chief corner **s**; NIG
1Pe 2: 4 To whom coming, *as unto* a living **s**, 3037
2: 6 I lay in Sion a chief corner **s**, elect, 3037
2: 7 the **s** which the builders disallowed, 3037
2: 8 And a **s** of stumbling, and a rock of 3037
Rev 2:17 and will give every man a white **s**, and in 5586
2:17 and in the **s** a new name written, 5586
4: 3 to look upon like a jasper and a sardine **s**: 3037
9:20 idols of gold, and silver, and brass, and **s**, 3035
16:21 *every* **s** about the weight of a talent: NIG
17: 4 with gold and precious **s** and pearls, 3037
18:21 a mighty angel took up a **s** like a great 3037
21:11 her light *was* like unto a **s** most precious, 3037
21:11 *even* like a jasper **s**, clear as crystal; 3037

STONE'S (1) [STONE]

Lk 22:41 he was withdrawn from them about a **s** 3037

STONED (22) [STONE]

Ex 19:13 shall **surely** be **s**, or shot through; 5619+5619
21:28 ox shall be **surely s**, and his flesh 5619+5619
21:29 the ox shall be **s**, and his owner also 5619
21:32 shekels *of* silver, and the ox shall be **s**. 5619
Nu 15:36 and **s** him with stones, and he died; 7275
Jos 7:25 all Israel **s** him *with* stones, 5619
7:25 fire, after they had **s** them with stones. 5619
1Ki 12:18 all Israel **s** him with stones, that he died. 7275
21:13 city, and **s** him with stones, that he died. 5619
21:14 Jezebel, saying, Naboth is **s**, and is dead. 5619
21:15 when Jezebel heard that Naboth was **s**, 5619
2Ch 10:18 the children of Israel **s** him with stones, 7275
24:21 **s** him *with* stones at the commandment 7275
Mt 21:35 one, and killed another, and **s** another. 3036
Jn 8: 5 commanded us, that such should be **s**: 3036
Ac 5:26 the people, lest they should have been **s**. 3034
7:58 and **s** *him:* and the witnesses laid down 3036
7:59 And they **s** Stephen, calling upon *God,* 3036
14:19 and, having **s** Paul, drew *him* out of 3034
2Co 11:25 once was I **s**, thrice I suffered shipwreck, 3034
Heb 11:37 They were **s**, they were sawn asunder, 3034
12:20 it shall be **s**, or thrust through with a dart: 3036

STONES (175) [STONE]

Ge 28:11 he took of the **s** of *that* place, and put *them* 68
31:46 Jacob said unto his brethren, Gather **s**; 68
31:46 and they took **s**, and made a heap: 68
Ex 25: 7 Onyx **s**, and stones to be set in the ephod, 68
25: 7 **s** to be set in the ephod, and in the 68
28: 9 shalt take two onyx **s**, and grave on them 68
28:11 thou engrave the two **s** with the names of 68
28:12 shalt put the two **s** upon the shoulders of 68
28:12 *for* **s** of memorial unto the children of Israel: 68
28:17 thou shalt set in it settings of **s**, *even* four 68
28:17 in it settings of stones, *even* four rows of **s**: 68
28:21 the **s** shall be with the names of the children 68
31: 5 in cutting of **s**, to set *them,* and in carving 68
35: 9 onyx **s**, and stones to be set for the ephod, 68
35: 9 **s** to be set for the ephod, and for 68
35:27 rulers brought onyx **s**, and stones to be set, 68
35:27 **s** to be set, for the ephod, and for 68
35:33 in the cutting of **s**, to set *them,* and in 68
39: 6 they wrought onyx **s** inclosed *in ouches of* 68
39: 7 *that they should be* **s** for a memorial to 68
39:10 they set in it four rows of **s**: the *first* row 68
39:14 the **s** *were* according to the names of 68
Lev 14:40 they take away the **s** in which the plague *is,* 68
14:42 they shall take other **s**, and put *them* in 68
14:42 and put *them* in the place of *those* **s**; 68
14:43 after *that* he hath taken away the **s**, 68
14:45 the **s** of it, and the timber thereof, and all 68
20: 2 people of the land shall stone him with **s**. 68
20:27 they shall stone them with **s**: their blood 68
21:20 scurvy, or scabbed, or hath his **s** broken; 810
24:23 out of the camp, and stone him with **s**. 68
Nu 14:10 the congregation bade stone them with **s**. 68
15:35 all the congregation shall stone him with **s** 68
15:36 camp, and stoned him with **s**, and he died; 68
Dt 8: 9 a land whose *are* iron, and out of whose 68
13:10 thou shalt stone him with **s**, that he die; 68
17: 5 and shalt stone them with **s**, till they die. 68
21:21 the men of his city shall stone him with **s**, 68
22:21 the men of her city shall stone her with **s**: 68
22:24 ye shall stone them with **s** that they die; 68
23: 1 He that is wounded in the **s**, or hath *his* 1795
27: 2 that thou shalt set thee up great **s**, 68
27: 4 ye shall set up these **s**, which I command 68
27: 5 altar unto the LORD thy God, an altar of **s**: 68
27: 6 the altar of the LORD thy God *of* whole **s**: 68
27: 8 thou shalt write upon the **s** all the words of 68
Jos 4: 3 twelve **s**, and ye shall carry them over with 68
4: 6 to come, saying, What mean you by these **s**? 68
4: 7 these **s** shall be for a memorial unto 68
4: 8 took up twelve **s** out of the midst of Jordan, 68
4: 9 set up twelve **s** in the midst of Jordan, 68
4:20 twelve **s**, which they took out of Jordan, 68
4:21 time to come, saying, What *mean* these **s**? 68
7:25 all Israel stoned him *with* **s**, and burned 68
7:25 with fire, after they had stoned them with **s**. 68

Jos 7:26 they raised over him a great heap of **s** unto 68
8:29 thereon a great heap of **s**, *that remaineth* 68
8:31 altar of whole **s**, over which no *man* hath 68
8:32 wrote there upon the **s** a copy of the law of 68
10:11 the LORD cast down great **s** from 68
10:18 Roll great **s** upon the mouth of the cave, 68
10:27 great **s** in the cave's mouth, *which remain* 68
Jdg 20:16 every one could sling **s** at a hair *breadth,* 68
1Sa 17:40 chose him five smooth **s** out of the brook, 68
2Sa 12:30 *was* a talent of gold with the precious **s**: 68
16: 6 he cast **s** at David, and at all the servants of 68
16:13 he went, and threw **s** at him, and cast dust. 68
18:17 and laid a very great heap of **s** upon him: 68
1Ki 5:17 they brought great **s**, costly stones, 68
5:17 great stones, costly **s**, *and* hewed stones, 68
5:17 great stones, costly stones, *and* hewed **s**, 68
5:18 prepared timber and **s** to build the house. 68
7: 9 All these *were* of costly **s**, according to 68
7: 9 according to the measures of **hewed s**, 1496
7:10 the foundation *was* of costly **s**, *even* great 68
7:10 *even* great **s**, stones of ten cubits, 68
7:10 **s** of ten cubits, and stones of eight cubits. 68
7:10 stones of ten cubits, and **s** of eight cubits. 68
7:11 above *were* costly **s**, after the measures of 68
7:11 the measures of **hewed s**, and cedars. 1496
7:12 about *was* with three rows *of* **hewed s**, 1496
10: 2 and very much gold, and precious **s**: 68
10:10 of spices very great store, and precious **s**: 68
10:11 great plenty of almug trees, and precious **s**. 68
10:27 king made silver *to be* in Jerusalem as **s**, 68
12:18 all Israel stoned him with **s**, that he died. 68
15:22 they took away the **s** of Ramah, 68
18:31 Elijah took twelve **s**, according to the 68
18:32 with the **s** he built an altar in the name of 68
18:38 the **s**, and the dust, and licked up the water 68
21:13 city, and stoned him with **s**, that he died. 68
2Ki 3:19 and mar every good piece of land with **s**. 68
3:25 only in Kir-haraseth left *they* the **s** thereof; 68
16:17 under it, and put it upon a pavement of **s**. 68
1Ch 12: 2 the right hand and the left in *hurling* **s** and 68
20: 2 of gold, and *there were* precious **s** in it; 68
22: 2 he set masons to hew wrought **s** to build 68
29: 2 onyx **s**, and *stones* to be set, glistering 68
29: 2 onyx **s**, and **s** to be set, NIH
29: 2 glistering **s**, and of divers colours, 68
29: 2 all *manner of* precious **s**, and marble stones 68
29: 2 precious stones, and marble **s** in abundance. 68
29: 8 they with whom *precious* **s** were found 68
2Ch 1:15 and gold at Jerusalem *as* plenteous as **s**, 68
3: 6 he garnished the house with precious **s** for 68
9: 1 and gold in abundance, and precious **s**: 68
9: 9 of spices great abundance, and precious **s**: 68
9:10 brought algum trees and precious **s**. 68
9:27 the king made silver in Jerusalem as **s**, 68
10:18 the children of Israel stoned him with **s**, 68
16: 6 they carried away the **s** of Ramah, 68
24:21 stoned him *with* **s** at the commandment of 68
26:14 habergeons, and bows, and slings to cast **s**. 68
26:15 to shoot arrows and great **s** withal. 68
32:27 precious **s**, and for spices, and for shields, 68
Ezr 5: 8 which is builded *with* great **s**, and timber *is* 69
6: 4 *With* three rows of great **s**, and a row of 69
Ne 4: 2 will they revive the **s** out of the heaps of 68
Job 5:23 For thou shalt be in league with the **s** of 68
6:12 *Is* my strength the strength of **s**? or *is* my 68
8:17 about the heap, *and* seeth the place of **s**. 68
14:19 The waters wear the **s**: thou washest away 68
22:24 *the gold of* Ophir as the **s** of the brooks. 6697
28: 3 the **s** of darkness, and the shadow of death. 68
28: 6 The **s** of it *are* the place of sapphires: 68
40:17 the sinews of his **s** are wrapt together. 6344
41:30 Sharp **s** *are* under him: he spreadeth 2789
Ps 102:14 For thy servants take pleasure in her **s**, 68
137: 9 and dasheth thy little ones against the **s**. 5553
144:12 *that* our daughters *may be* as **corner s**, 2106
Ecc 3: 5 A time to cast away **s**, and a time to gather 68
3: 5 **s**, and a time to gather **s** together; 68
10: 9 Whoso removeth **s** shall be hurt therewith; 68
Isa 5: 2 **gathered out** the **s** thereof, and planted 5619
9:10 down, but we will build *with* **hewn s**. 1496
14:19 a sword, that go down to the **s** of the pit; 68
27: 9 when he maketh all the **s** of the altar as 68
34:11 line of confusion, and the **s** of emptiness. 68
54:11 I will lay thy **s** with fair colours, and lay thy 68
54:12 and all thy borders of pleasant **s**. 68
57: 6 Among the smooth **s** of the stream *is* thy NIH
60:17 and for wood brass, and for **s** iron: 68
62:10 cast up the highway; gather out the **s**; 68
Jer 3: 9 committed adultery with **s** and with stocks. 68
43: 9 Take great **s** in thine hand, and hide them 68
43:10 will set his throne upon these **s** that I have 68
La 3:16 hath also broken my teeth with **gravel s**, 2687
4: 1 the **s** of the sanctuary are poured out in the 68
Eze 16:40 they shall stone thee with **s**, and thrust thee 68
23:47 And the company shall stone them with **s**, 68
26:12 they shall lay thy **s** and thy timber and 68
27:22 all spices, and with all precious **s**, and gold. 68
28:14 and down in the midst of the **s** of fire. 68
28:16 from the midst of the **s** of fire. 68
Da 11:38 and with precious, and pleasant things. 68
Mic 1: 6 will pour down the **s** thereof into the valley, 68
Zec 5: 4 it with the timber thereof and the **s** thereof. 68
9:15 they shall devour, and subdue *with* sling **s**; 68
9:16 *they shall be* as the **s** of a crown, lifted up 68
Mt 3: 9 that God is able of these **s** to raise up 3037

Mt 4: 3 command that these **s** be made bread. 3037
Mk 5: 5 crying, and cutting himself with **s**. 3037
12: 4 at him they **cast s**, and wounded *him* in 3036
12: 4 what manner of **s** and what buildings 3037
Lk 3: 8 That God is able of these **s** to raise up 3037
19:40 the **s** would immediately cry out. 3037
21: 5 it was adorned with goodly **s** and gifts, 3037
Jn 8:59 Then took they up **s** to cast at him: 3037
10:31 the Jews took up **s** again to stone him. 3037
1Co 3:12 silver, precious **s**, wood, hay, stubble; 3037
2Co 3: 7 written *and* engraven in **s**, was glorious, 3037
1Pe 2: 5 Ye also, as lively **s**, are built up a spiritual 3037
Rev 18:12 and precious **s**, and of pearls, 3037
18:16 with gold, and precious **s**, and pearls: 3037
21:19 garnished with all *manner of* precious **s**. 3037

STONESQUARERS (1) [SQUARE, STONE]

1Ki 5:18 Hiram's builders did hew *them,* and the **s**: 1382

STONEST (2) [STONE]

Mt 23:37 and **s** them which are sent unto thee, 3036
Lk 13:34 and **s** them that are sent unto thee; 3036

STONING (1) [STONE]

1Sa 30: 6 for the people spake of **s** him, because 5619

STONY (7) [STONE]

Ps 141: 6 When their judges are overthrown in **s** 5553
Eze 11:19 will take the **s** heart out of their flesh, 68
36:26 will take away the **s** heart out of your flesh, 68
Mt 13: 5 Some fell upon **s** *places,* where they had 4075
13:20 he that received the seed into **s** *places,* 4075
Mk 4: 5 And some fell on **s ground**, where it had 4075
4:16 likewise which are sown on **s ground**; 4075

STOOD (339) [STAND]

Ge 18: 2 and looked, and lo, three men **s** by him: 5324
18: 8 he **s** by them under the tree, and they did 5975
18:22 but Abraham **s** yet before the LORD. 5975
19:27 to the place where he **s** before the LORD: 5975
23: 3 Abraham **s** up from before his dead, 6965
23: 7 Abraham **s** up, and bowed himself to 6965
24:30 behold, he **s** by the camels at the well. 5975
28:13 the LORD **s** above it, and said, 5324
37: 7 lo, my sheaf arose, and also **s** upright; 5324
37: 7 your sheaves **s** round about, 5437
41: 1 and behold, he **s** by the river. 5975
41: 3 **s** by the *other* kine upon the brink of 5975
41:17 behold, I **s** upon the bank of the river: 5975
41:46 Joseph *was* thirty years old when he **s** 5975
43:15 went down *to* Egypt, and **s** before Joseph. 5975
45: 1 himself before all them that **s** by him; 5324
45: 1 there **s** no man with him, while Joseph 5975
Ex 2: 4 his sister **s** afar off, to wit what would be 3320
2:17 Moses **s** up and helped them, 6965
5:20 met Moses and Aaron, who **s** in the way, 5324
9:10 of the furnace, and **s** before Pharaoh; 5975
14:19 before their face, and **s** behind them: 5975
15: 8 the floods **s** upright as a heap, 5324
18:13 the people **s** by Moses from the morning 5975
19:17 they **s** at the nether part of the mount. 3320
20:18 saw *it,* they removed, and **s** afar off. 5975
20:21 people **s** afar off, and Moses drew near 5975
32:26 Moses **s** in the gate of the camp, and said, 5975
33: 8 every man *at* his tent door, 5324
33: 9 **s** *at* the door of the tabernacle, 5975
34: 5 **s** with him there, and proclaimed the 3320
Lev 9: 5 drew near and **s** before the LORD. 5975
Nu 11:32 the people **s** up all that day, and all *that* 6965
12: 5 **s** *in* the door of the tabernacle, 5975
16:18 **s** *in* the door of the tabernacle of 5975
16:27 **s** *in* the door of their tents, and their 5324
16:48 he **s** between the dead and the living; 5975
22:22 the angel of the LORD **s** in the way for an 3320
22:24 the angel of the LORD **s** in a path of 5975
22:26 went further, and **s** in a narrow place, 5975
23: 6 lo, *he* **s** by his burnt sacrifice, he, 5324
23:17 he **s** by his burnt offering, and the princes 5324
27: 2 they **s** before Moses, and before Eleazar 5975
Dt 4:11 ye came near and **s** under the mountain; 5975
5: 5 (I **s** between the LORD and you at that 5975
31:15 the pillar of the cloud **s** over the door of 5975
Jos 3:16 waters which came down from above **s** 5975
3:17 **s** firm on dry *ground* in the midst of 5975
4: 3 out of the place where the priests' feet **s** 4673
4: 9 which bare the ark of the covenant **s**, 4673
4:10 For the priests which bare the ark **s** in 5975
5:13 there **s** a man over against him with his 5975
8:33 **s** on this side the ark and on that side 5975
10:13 the sun **s still**, and the moon stayed, 1826
10:13 So the sun **s still** in the midst of heaven, 5975
11:13 *for* the cities that **s still** in their strength, 5975
20: 9 blood, until he **s** before the congregation. 5975
21:44 **s** not a man of all their enemies before 5975
24: 1 and **s** by him went out from him. 5975
Jdg 3:19 And all that **s** by him went out from him. 5975
6:31 Joash said unto all that **s** against him, Will 5975
7:21 they **s** every man in his place round about 5975
9: 7 went and **s** in the top of mount Gerizim, 5975
9:35 **s** *in* the entering of the gate of the city: 5975
9:44 **s** *in* the entering of the gate of the city: 5975
16:29 middle pillars upon which the house **s**, 3559
18:16 of Dan, *by* the entering of the gate. 5324
18:17 the priest **s** *in* the entering of the gate 5324
20:28 son of Aaron, **s** before it in those days,) 5975
1Sa 1:26 I *am* the woman that **s** by thee here, 5324

1Sa	3:10	s, and called as at other times, Samuel,	3320

1Sa 3:10 s, and called as at other times, Samuel, 3320
 4:20 the time of her death the *women* that s 5324
 6:14 a Beth-shemite, and s there, where *there* 5975
 10:23 he s among the people, he was higher 3320
 16:21 David came to Saul, and s before him: 5975
 17: 3 the Philistines s on a mountain on the 5975
 17: 3 Israel s on a mountain on the other side: 5975
 17: 8 he s and cried unto the armies of Israel, 5975
 17:26 David spake to the men that s by him, 5975
 17:51 s upon the Philistine, and took his sword, 5975
 22: 7 Saul said unto his servants that s about 5324
 22:17 Saul said to the footmen that s about 5324
 26:13 and s on the top of a hill afar off; 5975
2Sa 1:10 So I s upon him, and slew him, because 5975
 2:23 where Asahel fell down and died s still. 5975
 2:25 one troop, and s on the top of a hill. 5975
 2:28 all the people s still, and pursued after 5975
 13:31 his servants s *by* with their clothes rent. 5324
 15: 2 early, and s beside the way of the gate: 5975
 18: 4 the king s by the gate side, and all 5975
 18:30 And he turned aside, and s still. 5975
 20:11 one of Joab's men s by him, and said, 5975
 20:12 the man saw that all the people s still. 5975
 20:12 that every one that came by him s still. 5975
 20:15 against the city, and it s in the trench: 5975
 23:12 he s in the midst of the ground, 3320
1Ki 1:28 the king's presence, and s before the king. 5975
 3:15 s before the ark of the covenant of 5975
 3:16 unto the king, and s before him. 5975
 7:25 It s upon twelve oxen, three looking 5975
 8:14 (and all the congregation of Israel s;) 5975
 8:22 Solomon s before the altar of the LORD 5975
 8:55 he s, and blessed all the congregation of 5975
 10:19 the seat, and two lions s beside the stays. 5975
 10:20 twelve lions s there on the one side and 5975
 12: 6 that s before Solomon his father while he 5975
 12: 8 up with him, *and* which s before him: 5975
 13: 1 Jeroboam s by the altar to burn incense. 5975
 13:24 was cast in the way, and the ass s by it, 5975
 13:24 stood by it, the lion also s by the carcase. 5975
 19:13 and s *in* the entering in of the cave, 5975
 22:21 s before the LORD, and said, I will 5975
2Ki 2: 7 the prophets went, and s to view afar off: 5975
 2: 7 to view afar off: and they two s by Jordan. 5975
 2:13 went back, and s by the bank of Jordan; 5975
 3:21 armour, and upward, and s in the border. 5975
 4:12 when he had called her, she s before him. 5975
 4:15 when he had called her, she s in the door. 5975
 5: 9 and s *at* the door of the house of Elisha. 5975
 5:15 his company, and came, and s before him: 5975
 5:16 he went in, and s before his master. 5975
 8: 9 and came and s before him, and said, 5975
 9:17 a watchman on the tower in Jezreel, 5975
 10: 4 said, Behold, two kings s not before him: 5975
 10: 9 s, and said to all the people, Ye 5975
 11:11 guard s, every man with his weapons 5975
 11:14 the king s by a pillar, as the manner 5975
 13:21 of Elisha, he revived, and s **up** on his feet. 6965
 18:17 and s by the conduit of the upper pool, 5975
 18:28 Rab-shakeh s and cried with a loud voice 5975
 23: 3 king s by a pillar, and made a covenant 5975
 23: 3 And all the people s to the covenant. 5975
1Ch 6:39 brother Asaph, who s on his right hand, 5975
 6:44 their brethren the sons of Merari *s* on NIH
 21: 1 Satan s **up** against Israel, 5975
 21:15 the angel of the LORD s by 5975
 28: 2 David the king s **up** upon his feet, 6965
2Ch 3:13 they s on their feet, and their faces *were* 5975
 4: 4 It s upon twelve oxen, three looking 5975
 5:12 s *at the east end* of the altar, and with 5975
 6: 3 and all the congregation of Israel s. 5975
 6:12 he s before the altar of the LORD in 5975
 6:13 upon it he s, and kneeled *down* upon his 5975
 7: 6 trumpets before them, and all Israel s. 5975
 9:19 twelve lions s there on the one side and 5975
 10: 6 s before Solomon his father while he *yet* 5975
 10: 8 brought up with him, that s before him. 5975
 13: 4 Abijah s **up** upon mount Zemaraim, 6965
 18:20 s before the LORD, and said, I will entice 5975
 20: 5 Jehoshaphat s in the congregation of 5975
 20:13 all Judah s before the LORD, with their 5975
 20:19 s **up** to praise the LORD God of Israel 6965
 20:20 Jehoshaphat s and said, Hear me, 5975
 20:23 Moab s **up** against the inhabitants of 6965
 23:13 the king s at his pillar at the entering in, 5975
 24:20 which s above the people, and said unto 5975
 28:12 s **up** against them that came from the 6965
 29:26 Levites s with the instruments of David, 5975
 30:16 they s in their place after their manner, 5975
 34:31 the king s in his place, and made a 5975
 35:10 the priests s in their place, and the Levites 5975
Ezr 2:63 holy *things* till there s **up** a priest with 5975
 3: 2 s **up** Jeshua the son of Jozadak, 6965
 3: 9 s Jeshua *with* his sons and his brethren, 5975
 10:10 Ezra the priest s **up**, and said unto them, 6965
Ne 7:65 *things*, till there s **up** a priest with Urim 5975
 8: 4 Ezra the scribe s upon a pulpit of wood, 5975
 8: 4 beside him s Mattithiah, and Shema, 5975
 8: 5 when he opened *it*, all the people s **up:** 5975
 8: 7 the law: and the people s in their place. NIH
 9: 2 s and confessed their sins, and the 5975
 9: 3 they s **up** in their place, and read in 6965
 9: 4 s **up** upon the stairs of the Levites, Jeshua, 6965
 12:39 and they s still in the prison gate. 5975
 12:40 s the two *companies* of them that gave 5975

Est 5: 1 s in the inner court of the king's house, 5975
 5: 9 that he s not **up**, nor moved for him, 6965
 7: 7 Haman s **up** to make request for his life 5975
 8: 4 So Esther arose, and s before the king, 5975
 9:16 s for their lives, and had rest from their 5975
Job 4:15 before my face; the hair of my flesh s **up:** 5568
 4:16 It s still, but I could not discern the form 5975
 29: 8 and the aged arose, *and* s **up.** 6965
 30:28 I s **up**, *and* I cried in the congregation. 6965
 32:16 but s still, *and* answered no more:) 5975
Ps 33: 9 was *done;* he commanded, and it s **fast.** 5975
 104: 6 the waters s above the mountains. 5975
 106:23 had not Moses his chosen s before him in 5975
 106:30 s up Phinehas, and executed judgment; 5975
Isa 6: 2 Above it s the seraphims: each one had 5975
 36: 2 he s by the conduit of the upper pool in 5975
 36:13 Rabshakeh s, and cried with a loud voice 5975
Jer 15: 1 Though Moses and Samuel s before me, 5975
 18:20 Remember that I s before thee to speak 5975
 19:14 he s in the court of the LORD's house; 5975
 23:18 For who hath s in the counsel of 5975
 23:22 if they had s in my counsel, and had 5975
 28: 5 in the presence of all the people that s in 5975
 36:21 the ears of all the princes which s beside 5975
 44:15 the women that s *by*, a great multitude, 5975
 46:15 they s not, because the LORD did drive 5975
 48:45 They that fled s under the shadow of 5975
La 2: 4 he s *with* his right hand as an adversary, 5324
Eze 1:21 when those s, *these* stood; and when 5975
 1:21 when those stood, *these* s; and when 5975
 1:24 when they s, they let down their wings. 5975
 1:25 they s, *and* had let down their wings. 5975
 3:23 behold, the glory of the LORD s there, 5975
 8:11 there s before them seventy men of 5975
 8:11 in the midst of them s Jaazaniah the son 5975
 9: 2 went in, and s beside the brasen altar. 5975
 10: 3 Now the cherubims s on the right side of 5975
 10: 4 *and* s over the threshold of the house; NIH
 10: 6 then he went in, and s beside the wheels. 5975
 10:17 When they s, *these* stood; and when they 5975
 10:17 When they stood, *these* s; and when they 5975
 10:18 of the house, and s over the cherubims. 5975
 10:19 *every one* s *at* the door of the east gate 5975
 11:23 s upon the mountain which *is* on the east 5975
 21:21 For the king of Babylon s at the parting of 5975
 37:10 they lived, and s up upon their feet, 5975
 40: 3 a measuring reed; and he s in the gate. 5975
 43: 6 out of the house; and *the* man s by me. 5975
 47: 1 to the forefront of the house *s toward* NIH
Da 1:19 Azariah: therefore s they before the king. 5975
 2: 2 So they came and s before the king. 5975
 2:31 brightness *was* excellent, s before thee; 6966
 3: 3 they s before the image that 5975
 7:10 ten thousand times ten thousand s before 6966
 7:16 I came near unto one of them that s *by*, 6966
 8: 3 there s before the river a ram which had 5975
 8:15 there s before me as the appearance of a 5975
 8:17 he came near **where I s:** and when he 5977
 8:22 being broken, whereas four s **up** for it, 5975
 10:11 spoken this word unto me, I s trembling. 5975
 10:16 and said unto him that s before me, 5975
 11: 1 I, s to confirm and to strengthen him. 5977
 12: 5 and behold, there s other two, 5975
Hos 10: 9 there they s: the battle in Gibeah against 5975
Am 7: 7 the Lord s upon a wall made by a 5324
Ob 1:14 Neither shouldest thou have s in 5975
Hab 3: 6 He s, and measured the earth: he beheld, 5975
 3:11 sun *and* moon s still in *their* habitation; 5975
Zec 1: 8 he s among the myrtle trees that *were* in 5975
 1:10 the man that s among the myrtle trees 5975
 1:11 the LORD that s among the myrtle trees, 5975
 3: 3 filthy garments, and s before the angel. 5975
 3: 4 and spake unto those that s before him, 5975
 3: 5 And the angel of the LORD s *by*. 5975
Mt 2: 9 and s over where the young child was. 2476
 12:46 *his* mother and his brethren s without, 2476
 13: 2 and the whole multitude s on the shore. 2476
 20:32 Jesus s still, and called them, and said, 2476
 26:73 after a while came unto *him* they that s 2476
 27:11 And Jesus s before the governor: 2476
 27:47 Some of them that s there, when they 2476
Mk 10:49 And Jesus s still, and commanded him to 2476
 11: 5 And certain of them that s there said unto 2476
 14:47 And one of them that s by drew a sword, 3936
 14:60 And the high priest s **up** in the midst, 450
 14:69 began to say to them that s by, This is 3936
 14:70 they that s by said again to Peter, 3936
 15:35 And some of them that s by, when they 3936
 15:39 which s over against him, saw that he so 3936
Lk 4:16 on the sabbath day, and s **up** for to read. 450
 4:39 he s over her, and rebuked the fever; 2186
 5: 1 of God, he s by the lake of Gennesaret, 2476
 6: 8 And he arose and s *forth.* 2476
 6:17 and s in the plain, and the company of 2476
 7:14 and they that bare *him* s still. 2476
 7:38 And s at his feet behind *him* weeping, 2476
 9:32 glory, and the two men that s **with** him. 4921
 10:25 a certain lawyer s **up**, and tempted him, 450
 17:12 men *that were* lepers, which s afar off: 2476
 18:11 The Pharisee s and prayed thus with 2476
 18:40 And Jesus s, and commanded him to be 2476
 19: 8 And Zaccheus s, and said unto the Lord; 2476
 19:24 he said unto them that s by, Take from 3936
 23:10 And the chief priests and scribes s and 2476
 23:35 And the people s beholding. 2476

Lk 23:49 s afar off, beholding these *things.* 2476
 24: 4 two men s by them in shining garments, 2186
 24:36 Jesus himself s in the midst of them, 2476
Jn 1:35 Again the next day *after* John s, and two 2476
 6:22 the people which s on the other side 2476
 7:37 Jesus s and cried, saying, If any *man* thirst 2476
 11:56 as they s in the temple, What think ye, 2476
 12:29 that s *by*, and heard *it*, said that it 2476
 18: 5 which betrayed him, s with them. 2476
 18:16 But Peter s at the door without. 2476
 18:18 officers s there, who had made a fire of 2476
 18:18 Peter s with them, and warmed himself. 2476
 18:22 of the officers which s by stroke Jesus 3936
 18:25 And Simon Peter s and warmed himself. 2476
 19:25 Now there s by the cross of Jesus his 2476
 20:11 But Mary s without at the sepulchre 2476
 20:19 came Jesus and s in the midst, 2476
 20:26 s in the midst, and said, Peace *be* unto 2476
 21: 4 was now come, Jesus s on the shore. 2476
Ac 1:10 two men s by them in white apparel; 3936
 1:15 in those days Peter s **up** in the midst of 450
 3: 8 And he leaping up s, and walked, 2476
 4:26 The kings of the earth s **up**, and the rulers 3936
 5:34 Then s there **up** one in the council, 450
 9: 7 and the men which journeyed with him s 2476
 9:39 and all the widows s by him weeping, 3936
 10:17 and s **before** the gate, 2186
 10:30 a man s before me in bright clothing, 2476
 11:13 which s and said unto him, Send men to 2476
 11:28 there s **up** one of them named Agabus, 450
 12:14 and told how Peter s before the gate. 2476
 13:16 Paul s **up**, and beckoning with *his* hand 450
 14:20 as the disciples s **round about** him, 2944
 16: 9 There s a man of Macedonia, 2476
 17:22 Then Paul s in the midst of Mars' hill, 2476
 21:40 Paul s on the stairs, and beckoned with 2476
 22:13 and s, and said unto me, Brother Saul, 2186
 22:25 Paul said unto the centurion that s *by*, 2476
 23: 2 that s by him to smite him on the mouth. 3936
 23: 4 And they that s by said, Revilest thou 3936
 23:11 the night following the Lord s by him, 2186
 24:20 doing in me, while I s before the council, 2476
 25: 7 down from Jerusalem s **round about**, 4026
 25:18 Against whom when the accusers s **up**, 2476
 27:21 But after long abstinence Paul s *forth* in 2476
 27:23 For there s by me this night the angel of 3936
2Ti 4:16 At my first answer no *man* s **with** me, 4836
 4:17 Notwithstanding the Lord s **with** me, 3936
Heb 9:10 which s only in meats and drinks, NIG
Rev 5: 6 s a Lamb as *it had been* slain, having 2476
 7: 9 s before the throne, and before the Lamb, 2476
 7:11 all the angels s round about the throne, 2476
 8: 2 I saw the seven angels which s before 2476
 8: 3 another angel came and s at the altar, 2476
 11: 1 and the angel s, saying, Rise, 2476
 11:11 into them, and they s upon their feet; 2476
 12: 4 the dragon s before the woman which 2476
 13: 1 And I s upon the sand of the sea, and saw 2476
 14: 1 and lo, a Lamb s on the mount Sion, 2476
 18:17 and as many as trade by sea, s afar off, 2476

STOODEST (3) [STAND]
Nu 22:34 for I knew not that thou s in the way 5324
Dt 4:10 *Specially* the day that thou s before 5975
Ob 1:11 In the day that thou s on the other side, 5975

STOOL (1) [FOOTSTOOL, STOOLS]
2Ki 4:10 and a table, and a s, and a candlestick: 3678

STOOLS (1) [STOOL]
Ex 1:16 Hebrew women, and see *them* upon the s; 70

STOOP (4) [STOOPED, STOOPETH, STOOPING]
Job 9:13 anger, the proud helpers do s under him. 7817
Pr 12:25 in the heart of man **maketh** it s: 7812
Isa 46: 2 They s, they bow down together; 7164
Mk 1: 7 whose shoes I am not worthy to s **down** 2955

STOOPED (7) [STOOP]
Ge 49: 9 he s **down**, he couched as a lion, and as 3766
1Sa 24: 8 David s *with his* face to the earth, 6915
 28:14 he s *with his* face to the ground, 6915
2Ch 36:17 maiden, old man, or him that s **for age:** 3486
Jn 8: 6 Jesus s **down**, and with *his* finger wrote 2955
 8: 8 And again he s **down**, and wrote on 2955
 20:11 s **down, and looked** into the sepulchre, 3879

STOOPETH (1) [STOOP]
Isa 46: 1 Bel boweth down, Nebo s, their idols 7164

STOOPING (2) [STOOP]
Lk 24:12 s **down**, he beheld the linen clothes laid 3879
Jn 20: 5 And he s **down, and looking** in, 3879

STOP (7) [STOPPED, STOPPETH, STOPT, UNSTOPPED]
1Ki 18:44 get thee down, that the rain s thee not. 6113
2Ki 3:19 s all wells of water, and mar every good 5640
2Ch 32: 3 his mighty *men* to s the waters of 5640
Ps 35: 3 s the *way* against them that persecute me: 5462
 107:42 rejoice, and all iniquity shall s her mouth. 7092
Eze 39:11 it *shall* s the noses of the passengers: 2629
2Co 11:10 no *man* shall s me of this boasting in 5420

STOPPED (14) [STOP]
Ge 8: 2 and the windows of heaven were s, 5534

Ge	26:15 the Philistims had **s** them, and filled them	5640
	26:18 the Philistims had **s** them after the death	5640
Lev	15: 3 or his flesh be **s** from his issue, it *is his*	2856
2Ki	3:25 they **s** all the wells of water, and felled all	5640
2Ch	32:30 This same Hezekiah also **s** the upper	5640
Ne	4: 7 *and* that the breaches began to be **s**, then	5640
Ps	63:11 mouth of them that speak lies shall be **s**.	5534
Jer	51:32 *that* the passages are **s**, and the reeds they	8610
Zec	7:11 and **s** their ears, that *they* should not hear.	3513
Ac	7:57 **s** their ears, and ran upon him with	4912
Ro	3:19 that every mouth may be **s**, and all	5420
Tit	1:11 Whose **mouths** must be **s**, who subvert	1993
Heb	11:33 obtained promises, **s** the mouths of lions,	5420

STOPPETH (4) [STOP]

Job	5:16 poor hath hope, and iniquity **s** her mouth.	7092
Ps	58: 4 *they are* like the deaf adder *that* **s** her ear;	331
Pr	21:13 Whoso **s** his ears at the cry of the poor,	331
Isa	33:15 that **s** his ears from hearing of blood,	331

STOPT (1) [STOP]

2Ch	32: 4 who **s** all the fountains, and the brook	5640

STORE (25) [STOREHOUSE, STOREHOUSES]

Ge	26:14 of herds, and **great s** of servants:	7227
	41:36 *that* food shall be for **s** to the land against	6487
Lev	25:22 her fruits come in ye shall eat *of* the old **s**.	NIH
	26:10 ye shall eat **old s**, and bring forth	3462+3465
Dt	28: 5 Blessed *shall be* thy basket and thy **s**.	4863
	28:17 Cursed *shall be* thy basket and thy **s**.	4863
	32:34 *Is* not this **laid up in s** with me,	3647
1Ki	9:19 all the cities of **s** that Solomon had,	4543
	10:10 spices very **great s**, and precious stones:	7235
2Ki	20:17 which thy fathers have **laid up in s** unto	686
1Ch	29:16 all this **s** that we have prepared to build	1995
2Ch	8: 4 all the **s** cities, which he built in Hamath.	4543
	8: 6 all the cities that Solomon had, and all	4543
	11:11 and **s** of victual, and *of* oil and wine.	214
	16: 4 and all the **s** cities of Naphtali.	4543
	17:12 he built in Judah castles, and cities of **s**.	4543
	31:10 and that which is left *is* this **great s**.	1995
Ne	5:18 and once in ten days **s** of all *sorts of* wine:	7235
Ps	144:13 **all manner of s**:	413+2177+2177+4480
Isa	39: 6 which thy fathers have **laid up in s** until	686
Am	3:10 who **s up** violence and robbery in their	686
Na	2: 9 *there is* none end of the **s** *and* glory out	8498
1Co	16: 2 let every one of you lay by him in **s**,	2343
1Ti	6:19 **Laying up in s** for themselves a good	597
2Pe	3: 7 are now, by the same word are **kept in s**,	2343

STOREHOUSE (2) [HOUSE, STORE]

Mal	3:10 Bring ye all the tithes into the **s**,	214+1004
Lk	12:24 which neither have **s** nor barn; and God	5009

STOREHOUSES (6) [HOUSE, STORE]

Ge	41:56 Joseph opened all the **s**,	834+871.1+1992.1
Dt	28: 8 command the blessing upon thee in thy **s**,	618
1Ch	27:25 and over the **s** in the fields, in the cities,	214
2Ch	32:28 **S** also for the increase of corn, and wine,	4543
Ps	33: 7 as a heap: he layeth up the depth in **s**.	214
Jer	50:26 her from the utmost border, open her **s**:	3965

STORIES (5) [STORY]

Ge	6:16 second, and third *s* shalt thou make it.	NIH
Eze	41:16 the galleries round about on their three **s**,	NIH
	42: 3 was gallery against gallery in three **s**.	NIH
	42: 6 they *were* in three **s**, but had not pillars	NIH
Am	9: 6 *It is* he that buildeth his **s** in the heaven,	4609

STORK (5)

Lev	11:19 the **s**, the heron after her kind,	2624
Dt	14:18 the **s**, and the heron after her kind,	2624
Ps	104:17 *as for* the **s**, the fir trees *are* her house.	2624
Jer	8: 7 the **s** in the heaven knoweth her	2624
Zec	5: 9 for they had wings like the wings of a **s**:	2624

STORM (14) [STORMY]

Job	21:18 and as chaff that the **s** carrieth away.	5492
	27:21 and **as a s hurleth** him out of his place.	8175
Ps	55: 8 hasten my escape from the windy **s**.	5584
	83:15 and make them afraid with thy **s**.	5492
	107:29 maketh the **s** a calm, so that the waves	5591
Isa	4: 6 and for a covert from **s** and from rain.	2230
	25: 4 a refuge from the **s**, a shadow from	2230
	25: 4 the blast of the terrible ones *is* as a **s**	2230
	28: 2 as a tempest of hail *and* a destroying **s**,	8178
	29: 6 **with s** and tempest, and the flame of	5492
Eze	38: 9 Thou shalt ascend and come like a **s**,	7722
Na	1: 3 his way in the whirlwind and in the **s**,	8183
Mk	4:37 And there arose a great **s** of wind,	2978
Lk	8:23 there came down a **s** of wind on the lake;	2978

STORMY (4) [STORM]

Ps	107:25 he commandeth, and raiseth the **s** wind,	5591
	148: 8 and vapour; **s** wind fulfilling his word:	5591
Eze	13:11 shall fall; and a **s** wind shall rent *it*.	5591
	13:13 even rent *it with* a **s** wind in my fury;	5591

STORY (2) [STORIES]

2Ch	13:22 *are* written in the **s** of the prophet Iddo.	4097
	24:27 they *are* written in the **s** of the book	4097

STOUT (4) [STOUTHEARTED, STOUTNESS]

Job	4:11 the **lion's** whelps are scattered abroad.	3833
Isa	10:12 I will punish the fruit of the **s** heart of	1433
Da	7:20 whose look *was* more **s** than his fellows.	7260

Mal	3:13 Your words have been **s** against me,	2388

STOUTHEARTED (2) [HEART, STOUT]

Ps	76: 5 The **s** are spoiled, they have slept	47+3820
Isa	46:12 Hearken unto me, ye **s**, that *are* far	47+3820

STOUTNESS (1) [STOUT]

Isa	9: 9 that say in the pride and **s** of heart,	1433

STRAIGHT (28) [STRAIGHTWAY]

Jos	6: 5 shall ascend every man **s** before him.	5048
	6:20 every man **s** before him, and they took	5048
1Sa	6:12 the kine **took** the **s** way to the way of	3474
2Ch	32:30 **brought** it **s** down to the west *side* of	3474
Ps	5: 8 **make** thy way's before my face.	3474
Pr	4:25 and let thine eyelids **look s** before thee.	3474
Ecc	1:15 *which is* crooked cannot be **made s**:	8626
	7:13 for who can **make** that **s**, which he hath	8626
Isa	40: 3 **make s** in the desert a highway for our	3474
	40: 4 the crooked shall be **made s**, and the	4334
	42:16 light before them, and crooked things **s**.	4334
	45: 2 and **make** the crooked places **s**:	3474
Jer	31: 9 to walk by the rivers of waters in a **s** way,	3477
Eze	1: 7 their feet *were* **s** feet; and the sole of their	3477
	1: 9 went every one **s forward**.	413+5676+6440
	1:12 went every one **s forward**;	413+5676+6440
	1:23 under the firmament *were* their wings **s**,	3477
	10:22 went every one **s forward**.	413+5676+6440
Mt	3: 3 ye the way of the Lord, make his paths **s**.	2117
Mk	1: 3 ye the way of the Lord, make his paths **s**.	2117
Lk	3: 4 ye the way of the Lord, make his paths **s**.	2117
	3: 5 and the crooked shall be **made s**,	2117
	13:13 and immediately she was **made s**,	461
Jn	1:23 **Make s** the way of the Lord, as said	2116
Ac	9:11 and go into the street which is called **S**,	2117
	16:11 **came** with a **s course** to Samothracia,	2113
	21: 1 we came with a **s course** unto Cos,	2113
Heb	12:13 And make **s** paths for your feet, lest *that*	3717

STRAIGHTWAY (42) [STRAIGHT]

1Sa	9:13 be come *into* the city, ye shall **s** find him,	3651
	28:20 Saul fell **s** all along on the earth,	4116
Pr	7:22 He goeth after her **s**, as an ox goeth to	6597
Da	10:17 there remained no strength in me,	6258
Mt	3:16 was baptized, went up **s** out of the water:	2112
	4:20 And they left *their* nets,	2112
	14:22 And Jesus constrained his disciples to	2112
	14:27 But **s** Jesus spake unto them, saying,	2112
	21: 2 and ye shall find an ass tied, and a colt	2112
	21: 3 need of them; and **s** he will send them.	2112
	25:15 his several ability; and **s** took his journey.	2112
	27:48 one of them ran, and took a sponge,	2112
Mk	1:10 **s** coming up out of the water, he saw	2112
	1:18 And **s** they forsook their nets,	2112
	1:20 And **s** he called them: and they left their	2112
	1:21 **s** on the sabbath day he entered into	2112
	2: 2 And **s** many were gathered together,	2112
	3: 6 **s** took counsel with the Herodians against	2112
	5:29 the fountain of her blood was dried	2112
	5:42 And the damsel arose, and walked;	2112
	6:25 she came in **s** with haste unto the king,	2112
	6:45 And **s** he constrained his disciples to get	2112
	6:54 come out of the ship, **s** they knew him,	2112
	7:35 And **s** his ears were opened,	2112
	8:10 And **s** he entered into a ship with his	2112
	9:15 And **s** all the people, when they beheld	2112
	9:20 when he saw him, **s** the spirit tare him	2112
	9:24 And **s** the father of the child cried out,	2112
	11: 3 of him; and **s** he will send him hither.	2112
	14:45 he goeth **s** to him, and saith, Master,	2112
	15: 1 **s** in the morning the chief priests held	2112
Lk	5:39 No *man* also having drunk **old wine s**	3916
	8:55 her spirit came again, and she arose: **s**	2112
	12:54 west, **s** ye say, There cometh a shower;	2112
	14: 5 not pull him out on the sabbath day?	2112
Jn	13:32 him in himself, and shall **s** glorify him.	2112
Ac	5:10 Then fell she down **s** at his feet,	3916
	9:20 And **s** he preached Christ in	2112
	16:33 and was baptized, he and all his, **s**.	3916
	22:29 Then **s** they departed from him which	2112
	23:30 I sent **s** to thee, and gave commandment	1824
Jas	1:24 **s** forgetteth what manner of *man* he was.	2112

STRAIN (1)

Mt	23:24 which **s** out a gnat, and swallow a camel.	1368

STRAIT (10) [STRAITEN, STRAITENED, STRAITENETH, STRAITEST, STRAITLY, STRAITNESS, STRAITS]

1Sa	13: 6 men of Israel saw that they were **in a s**,	6887
2Sa	24:14 David said unto Gad, I am in a great **s**:	6887
2Ki	6: 1 place where we dwell with thee is too **s**	6862
1Ch	21:13 David said unto Gad, I am **in a great s**:	6887
Job	36:16 would he have removed thee out of the **s**	6862
Isa	49:20 in thine ears, The place *is* too **s** for me:	6862
Mt	7:13 Enter ye in at the **s** gate: for wide *is*	4728
	7:14 Because **s** *is* the gate, and narrow *is*	4728
Lk	13:24 Strive to enter in at the **s** gate: for many,	4728
Php	1:23 I am **in a s** betwixt two, having a desire	4912

STRAITEN (1) [STRAIT]

Jer	19: 9 that they seek their lives, shall **s** them.	6693

STRAITENED (8) [STRAIT]

Job	18: 7 The steps of his strength shall be **s**,	3334
	37:10 given: and the breadth of the waters is **s**.	4164

Pr	4:12 When thou goest thy steps shall not be **s**;	3334
Eze	42: 6 *the building* was **s** more than the lowest	680
Mic	2: 7 of Jacob, is the spirit of the LORD **s**?	7114
Lk	12:50 and how am I **s** till it be accomplished!	4912
2Co	6:12 Ye are not **s** in us,	4729
	6:12 in us, but ye are **s** in your own bowels.	4729

STRAITENETH (1) [STRAIT]

Job	12:23 enlargeth the nations, and **s** them *again*.	5148

STRAITEST (1) [STRAIT]

Ac	26: 5 that after the **most s** sect of our religion I	196

STRAITLY (11) [STRAIT]

Ge	43: 7 The man **asked** us **s** of our state,	7592+7592
Ex	13:19 for he had **s sworn** the children of	7650+7650
Jos	6: 1 Jericho was **s shut up**	5462+5462+2050.1
1Sa	14:28 **s charged** the people **with an oath**	7650+7650
Mt	9:30 Jesus **s charged** them, saying, See that	1690
Mk	1:43 he **s charged** him, and forthwith sent	1690
	3:12 he **s charged** them that they should not	4183
	5:43 he charged them **s** that no *man* should	4183
Lk	9:21 And he **s charged** them,	2008
Ac	4:17 among the people, let us **s threaten** them,	546
	5:28 Did not we **s command** you that	3852+3853

STRAITNESS (5) [STRAIT]

Dt	28:53 hath given thee, in the siege, and in the **s**,	4689
	28:55 nothing left him in the siege, and in the **s**,	4689
	28:57 of all *things* secretly in the siege and **s**,	4689
Job	36:16 *into* a broad place, where *there is* no **s**;	4164
Jer	19: 9 the flesh of his friend in the siege and **s**,	4689

STRAITS (2) [STRAIT]

Job	20:22 fulness of his sufficiency he shall be **in s**:	3334
La	1: 3 persecutors overtook her between the **s**.	4712

STRAKE (3) [STRIKE]

2Sa	12:15 the LORD **s** the child that Uriah's wife	5062
	20:10 to the ground, and **s** him not again;	NIH
Ac	27:17 the quicksands, **s** sail, and so were driven.	5465

STRAKES (2)

Ge	30:37 pilled white **s** in them, and made the	6479
Lev	14:37 in the walls of the house with **hollow s**,	8258

STRANDS See WIRES

STRANGE (76) [STRANGELY, STRANGER, STRANGER'S, STRANGERS, STRANGERS']

Ge	35: 2 Put away the **s** gods that *are* among you,	5236
	35: 4 they gave unto Jacob all the **s** gods which	5236
	42:7 **made** himself **s** unto them,	5234
Ex	2:22 he said, I have been a stranger in a **s** land.	5237
	18: 3 he said, I have been an alien in a **s** land:	5237
	21: 8 sell her unto a **s** nation he shall have no	5237
	30: 9 Ye shall offer no **s** incense thereon,	2114
Lev	10: 1 offered **s** fire before the LORD,	2114
Nu	3: 4 when they offered **s** fire before the LORD,	2114
	26:61 when they offered **s** fire before the LORD.	2114
Dt	32:12 him, and *there was* no **s** god with him.	5236
	32:16 provoked him to jealousy with **s** *gods*,	2114
Jos	24:20 serve **s** gods, then he will turn and do	5236
	24:23 *said he*, the **s** gods which *are* among you,	5236
Jdg	10:16 put away the **s** gods from among them,	5236
	11: 2 for thou *art* the son of a **s** woman.	312
1Sa	7: 3 *then* put away the **s** gods and Ashtaroth	5236
1Ki	11: 1 king Solomon loved many **s** women,	5237
	11: 8 likewise did he for all his **s** wives,	5237
2Ki	19:24 I have digged and drunk **s** waters,	2114
2Ch	33: 3 For he reared up the altars of the **s** *gods*,	5236
	33:15 he took away the **s** gods, and the idol out	5236
Ezr	10: 2 have taken **s** wives of the people of	5237
	10:10 transgressed, and have taken **s** wives,	5237
	10:11 people of the land, and from the **s** wives.	5237
	10:14 let all *them* which have taken **s** wives in	5237
	10:17 wives by the first day of the first month.	5237
	10:18 there were found that had taken **s** wives:	5237
	10:44 All these had taken **s** wives: and *some* of	5237
Ne	13:27 transgress against our God in marrying **s**	5237
Job	19: 3 *that* you **make** yourselves **s** to me.	1970
	19:17 My breath is **s** to my wife, though I	2114
	31: 3 **punishment** to the workers of iniquity?	5235
Ps	44:20 or stretched out our hands to a **s** god;	2114
	81: 9 There shall no **s** god be in thee;	2114
	81: 9 neither shalt thou worship *any* **s** god.	5236
	114: 1 of Jacob from a people of **s language**;	3937
	137: 4 we sing the LORD's song in a **s** land?	5236
	144: 7 great waters, from the hand of **s** children;	5236
	144:11 deliver me from the hand of **s** children,	5236
Pr	2:16 To deliver thee from the **s** woman,	2114
	5: 3 For the lips of a **s** *woman* drop *as a*	2114
	5:20 be ravisht with a **s** *woman*, and embrace	2114
	6:24 from the flattery of the tongue of a **s**	5237
	7: 5 *they* may keep thee from the **s** *woman*,	5237
	20:16 and take a pledge of him for a **s** *woman*.	5237
	21: 8 The way of man *is* froward and **s**: but *as*	2054
	22:14 The mouth of a **s** *woman is* a deep pit:	2114
	23:27 ditch; and a **s** *woman is* a narrow pit.	5237
	23:33 Thine eyes shall behold **s** *women*, and	5237
	27:13 and take a pledge of him for a **s** *woman*.	5237
Isa	17:10 plants, and shalt set it *with* **s** slips:	2114
	28:21 that *he* may do his work, his work;	2114
	28:21 and bring to pass his act, his **s** act.	5237
	43:12 when *there was* no **s** *god* among you:	2114
Jer	2:21 the degenerate plant of a **s** vine unto me?	5237

S

Jer	5:19	served **s** gods in your land, so shall ye	5236
	8:19	their graven images, *and* with **s** vanities?	5236
Eze	3: 5	For thou *art* not sent to a people of a **s**	6012
	3: 6	Not to many people of a **s** speech and of	6012
Da	11:39	do in the most strong holds with a **s** god,	5236
Hos	5: 7	for they have begotten **s** children: now	2114
	8:12	law, *but* they were counted as as a *thing*.	2114
Zep	1: 8	all such as are clothed with **s** apparel.	5237
Mal	2:11	hath married the daughter of a **s** god.	5236
Lk	5:26	saying, We have seen **s** *things* to day.	3861
Ac	7: 6	That his seed should sojourn in a **s** land;	245
	17:18	He seemeth to be a setter forth of **s** gods:	3581
	17:20	For thou bringest certain **s** *things* to our	3579
	26:11	I persecuted *them* even unto **s** cities.	1854
Heb	11: 9	as *in* a *country*, dwelling in tabernacles	245
	13: 9	carried about with divers and **s** doctrines.	3581
1Pe	4: 4	Wherein they **think it s** that you run not	3579
	4:12	**think it** not **s** concerning the fiery trial	3579
	4:12	as though *some* **s** *thing* happened unto	3581
Jude	1: 7	going after **s** flesh, are set forth for an	2087

STRANGELY (1) [STRANGE]

Dt	32:27	adversaries should **behave** themselves **s**,	5234

STRANGER (129) [STRANGE]

Ge	15:13	Know of a surety that thy seed shall be a **s**	1616
	17: 8	after thee, the land wherein thou art a **s**,	4033
	17:12	or bought with money of any **s**,	1121+5236
	17:27	and bought with money of the **s**,	1121+5236
	23: 4	I *am* a **s** and a sojourner with you: give me	1616
	28: 4	inherit the land wherein thou art a **s**,	4033
	37: 1	in the land wherein his father was a **s**,	4033
Ex	2:22	he said, I have been a **s** in a strange land.	1616
	12:19	whether he be a **s**, or born in the land.	1616
	12:43	There shall no **s** eat thereof:	1121+5236
	12:48	when a **s** shall sojourn with thee,	1616
	12:49	unto the **s** that sojourneth among you.	1616
	20:10	cattle, nor thy **s** that *is* within thy gates:	1616
	22:21	Thou shalt neither vex a **s**, nor oppress	1616
	23: 9	thou shalt not oppress a **s**: for ye know	1616
	23: 9	for ye know the heart of a **s**, seeing ye	1616
	23:12	handmaid, and the **s**, may be refreshed.	1616
	29:33	a **s** shall not eat *thereof*, because they *are*	2114
	30:33	or whosoever putteth *any* of it upon a **s**,	2114
Lev	16:29	or a **s** that sojourneth among you:	1616
	17:12	neither shall any **s** that sojourneth among	1616
	17:15	or a **s**, he shall both wash his clothes,	1616
	18:26	nor any **s** that sojourneth among you:	1616
	19:10	thou shalt leave them for the poor and **s**:	1616
	19:33	if a **s** sojourn with thee in your land,	1616
	19:34	*But* the **s** that dwelleth with you shall be	1616
	22:10	There shall no **s** eat *of* the holy *thing*: a	2114
	22:12	daughter also be *married* unto a **s**,	376+2114
	22:13	but there shall no **s** eat thereof.	2114
	23:22	leave them unto the poor, and to the **s**:	1616
	24:16	well the **s**, as he that is born in the land,	1616
	24:22	as well for the **s**, as for one of your own	1616
	25: 6	and for thy **s** that sojourneth with thee,	8453
	25:35	*yea, though he be* a **s**, or a sojourner;	1616
	25:47	if a sojourner or **s** wax rich by thee,	8453
	25:47	sell himself unto the **s** or sojourner by	1616
Nu	1:51	**s** that cometh nigh shall be put to death.	2114
	3:10	**s** that cometh nigh shall be put to death.	2114
	3:38	**s** that cometh nigh shall be put to death.	2114
	9:14	if a **s** shall sojourn among you,	1616
	9:14	both for the **s**, and for him that was born	1616
	15:14	if a **s** sojourn with you, or whosoever *be*	1616
	15:15	also for the **s** that sojourneth *with you*, an	1616
	15:15	ye *are*, so shall the **s** be before the LORD.	1616
	15:16	and for the **s** that sojourneth with you.	1616
	15:26	and the **s** that sojourneth among them;	1616
	15:29	for the **s** that sojourneth among them.	1616
	15:30	*whether* he *be* born in the land, or a **s**,	1616
	16:40	**s**, which *is* not of the seed of Aaron,	376+2214
	18: 4	and a **s** shall not come nigh unto you.	2114
	18: 7	**s** that cometh nigh shall be put to death.	2114
	19:10	unto the **s** that sojourneth among them,	1616
	35:15	for the **s**, and for the sojourner among	1616
Dt	1:16	his brother, and the **s** that is with him.	1616
	5:14	cattle, nor thy **s** that *is* within thy gates;	1616
	10:18	fatherless and widow, and loveth the **s**,	1616
	10:19	Love ye therefore the **s**: for ye were	1616
	14:21	thou shalt give it unto the **s** that *is* in thy	1616
	14:29	the **s**, and the fatherless, and the widow,	1616
	16:11	the **s**, and the fatherless, and the widow,	1616
	16:14	the **s**, and the fatherless, and the widow,	1616
	17:15	thou mayest not set a **s** over thee,	376+5237
	23: 7	because thou wast a **s** in his land.	1616
	23:20	Unto a **s** thou mayest lend upon usury;	5237
	24:17	shalt not pervert the judgment of the **s**,	1616
	24:19	it shall be for the **s**, for the fatherless,	1616
	24:20	it shall be for the **s**, for the fatherless,	1616
	24:21	it shall be for the **s**, for the fatherless,	1616
	25: 5	shall not marry without unto a **s**,	376+2214
	26:11	the Levite, and the **s** that *is* among you.	1616
	26:12	the **s**, the fatherless, and the widow,	1616
	26:13	unto the **s**, to the fatherless, and to	1616
	27:19	he that perverteth the judgment of the **s**,	1616
	28:43	The **s** that *is* within thee shall get up	1616
	29:11	your wives, and thy **s** that *is* in thy camp,	1616
	29:22	the **s** that shall come from a far land,	5237
	31:12	and thy **s** that *is* within thy gates,	1616
Jos	8:33	as well the **s**, as he that was born among	1616
	20: 9	and for the **s** that sojourneth among them,	1616
Jdg	19:12	not turn aside hither into the city of a **s**,	5237

Ru	2:10	take knowledge of me, seeing I *am* a **s**?	5237
2Sa		king: for thou *art* a **s**, and also an exile.	376+1616
	15:19		
1Ki	3:18	*there* was no **s** with us in the house,	2114
	8:41	Moreover concerning a **s**, that *is* not of	5237
	8:43	according to all that the **s** calleth to thee	5237
2Ch	6:32	Moreover concerning the **s**, which *is* not	5237
	6:33	do according to all that the **s** calleth to	5237
Job	15:19	was given, and no **s** passed among them.	2114
	19:15	and my maidens, count me for a **s**:	2114
	31:32	The **s** did not lodge in the street:	1616
Ps	39:12	for I *am* a **s** with thee, *and* a sojourner,	1616
	69: 8	I am become a **s** unto my brethren,	2114
	94: 6	They slay the widow and the **s**,	1616
	119:19	I *am* a **s** in the earth: hide not thy	1616
Pr	2:16	*even* from the **s** *which* flattereth with her	5237
	5:10	and thy labours *be* in the house of a **s**;	5237
	5:20	and embrace the bosom of a **s**?	5237
	6: 1	if thou hast stricken thy hand with a **s**,	2114
	7: 5	the **s** *which* flattereth with her words.	5237
	11:15	He that is surety for a **s** shall smart *for it*:	2114
	14:10	a **s** doth not intermeddle with his joy.	2114
	20:16	Take his garment that is surety *for* a **s**:	2114
	27: 2	own mouth; a **s**, and not thine own lips.	5237
	27:13	Take his garment that is surety *for* a **s**,	2114
Ecc	6: 2	to eat thereof, but a **s** eateth it:	376+5237
Isa	56: 3	Neither let the son of the **s**, that hath	5236
	56: 6	the sons of the **s**, that join themselves	5236
	62: 8	the sons of the **s** shall not drink thy wine,	5237
Jer	7: 6	If ye oppress not the **s**, the fatherless,	1616
	14: 8	why shouldest thou be as a **s** in the land,	1616
	22: 3	to the **s**, the fatherless, nor the widow,	1616
Eze	14: 7	or of the **s** that sojourneth in Israel,	1616
	22: 7	have they dealt by oppression with the **s**:	1616
	22:29	they have oppressed the **s** wrongfully.	1616
	44: 9	No **s**, uncircumcised in heart,	1121+5236
	44: 9	of any **s** that *is* among the children	1121+5236
	47:23	pass, *that* in what tribe the **s** sojourneth,	1616
Ob	1:12	thy brother in the day that he became a **s**;	5235
Zec	7:10	nor the fatherless, the **s**, nor the poor;	1616
Mal	3: 5	that turn aside the **s** *from his right*, and	1616
Mt	25:35	me drink: I was a **s**, and ye took me in:	3581
	25:38	When saw we thee a **s**, and took *thee* in?	3581
	25:43	I was a **s**, and ye took me not in: naked,	3581
	25:44	or a **s**, or naked, or sick, or in prison,	3581
Lk	17:18	returned to give glory to God, save this **s**.	241
	24:18	Art thou only a **s** in Jerusalem, and hast	3939
Jn	10: 5	And a **s** will they not follow, but will flee	245
Ac	7:29	was a **s** in the land of Madian, where he	3941

STRANGER'S (2) [STRANGE]

Lev	22:25	Neither from a **s** hand shall ye offer	1121+5236
	25:47	by thee, or to the stock of the **s** family:	1616

STRANGERS (79) [STRANGE]

Ge	31:15	Are we not counted of him **s**? for he hath	5237
	36: 7	land wherein they were **s** could not bear	4033
Ex	6: 4	of their pilgrimage, wherein they were **s**.	1481
	22:21	for ye were **s** in the land of Egypt.	1616
	23: 9	seeing ye were **s** in the land of Egypt.	1616
Lev	17: 8	or of the **s** which sojourn among you,	1616
	17:10	or of the **s** that sojourn among you,	1616
	17:13	or of the **s** that sojourn among you,	1616
	19:34	for ye were **s** in the land of Egypt:	1616
	20: 2	of the **s** that sojourn in Israel, that giveth	1616
	22:18	of the house of Israel, or of the **s** in Israel,	1616
	25:23	for ye were **s** and sojourners with me.	1616
	25:45	Moreover of the children of the **s** that do	8453
Dt	10:19	for ye were **s** in the land of Egypt.	1616
	24:14	of thy **s** that *are* in thy land within thy	1616
	31:16	go a whoring after the gods of the **s** of	5236
Jos	8:35	the **s** that were conversant among them.	1616
2Sa	22:45	**S** shall submit themselves unto me:	1121+5236
	22:46	**S** shall fade away, and they shall be	1121+5236
1Ch	16:19	ye were *but* few, even a few, and **s** in it.	1481
	22: 2	commanded to gather together the **s**	1616
	29:15	For we *are* **s** before thee, and sojourners,	1616
2Ch	2:17	Solomon numbered all the **s** that	376+1616
	15: 9	the **s** with them out of Ephraim and	1481
	30:25	the **s** that came out of the land of Israel,	1616
Ne	9: 2	separated themselves from all **s**,	1121+5236
	13:30	Thus cleansed I them from all **s**,	5236
Ps	18:44	**s** shall submit themselves unto me.	1121+5236
	18:45	The **s** shall fade away, and be afraid	1121+5236
	54: 3	For **s** are risen up against me,	2114
	105:12	in number; yea, *very* few, and **s** in it.	1481
	109:11	he hath; and let the **s** spoil his labour.	2114
	146: 9	The LORD preserveth the **s**; he relieveth	1616
Pr	5:10	Lest **s** be filled *with* thy wealth;	2114
Isa	1: 7	**s** devour it in your presence, and *it is*	2114
	1: 7	and *it is* desolate, as overthrown by **s**.	2114
	2: 6	please themselves in the children of **s**.	5237
	5:17	waste places of the fat ones shall **s** eat.	1481
	14: 1	the **s** shall be joined with them,	1616
	25: 2	a palace of **s** to be no city; it shall never	2114
	25: 5	Thou shalt bring down the noise of **s**,	2114
	29: 5	Moreover the multitude of thy **s** shall be	2114
	60:10	the sons of **s** shall build up thy walls,	5236
	61: 5	**s** shall stand and feed your flocks,	2114
Jer	2:25	I have loved **s**, and after them will I go.	2114
	3:13	hast scattered thy ways to the **s** under	2114
	5:19	ye serve **s** in a land *that* is not yours.	2114
	30: 8	**s** no more serve themselves of him:	2114
	35: 7	live many days in the land where ye *be* **s**.	1481
	51:51	for **s** are come into the sanctuaries	2114

La	5: 2	Our inheritance is turned to **s**, our houses	2114
Eze	7:21	I will give it into the hands of the **s** for a	2114
	11: 9	deliver you into the hands of **s**,	2114
	16:32	*which* taketh **s** instead of her husband.	2114
	28: 7	Behold therefore, I *will* bring **s** upon thee,	2114
	28:10	of the uncircumcised by the hand of **s**:	2114
	30:12	and all that is therein, by the hand of **s**:	2114
	31:12	**s**, the terrible of the nations, have cut	2114
	44: 7	have brought *into my sanctuary* **s**,	1121+5236
	47:22	to the **s** that sojourn among you,	1616
Hos	7: 9	**S** have devoured his strength,	2114
	8: 7	if so be it yield, *the* **s** shall swallow it up.	2114
Joel	3:17	shall no **s** pass through her any more.	2214
Ob	1:11	in the day that the **s** carried away captive	2114
Mt	17:25	or tribute? of their own children, or of **s**?	245
	17:26	Peter saith unto him, Of **s**. Jesus saith unto	245
	27: 7	with them the potter's field, to bury **s** in.	3581
Jn	10: 5	him: for they know not the voice of **s**.	245
Ac	2:10	and **s** of Rome, Jews and proselytes,	1927
	13:17	exalted the people when *they* **dwelt as s**	3940
	17:21	which were there spent their time in	3581
Eph	2:12	and **s** from the covenants of promise,	3581
	2:19	Now therefore ye are no more **s** and	3581
1Ti	5:10	brought up children, if she have **lodged s**,	3580
Heb	11:13	and confessed that they were **s** and	3581
	13: 2	Be not forgetful to **entertain s**: for	5381
1Pe	1: 1	to the **s** scattered throughout Pontus,	3927
	2:11	I beseech *you* as **s** and pilgrims,	3941
3Jn	1: 5	thou doest to the brethren, and to **s**;	3581

STRANGERS' (1) [STRANGE]

Pr	5:17	be only thine own, and not **s** with thee.	2114

STRANGLED (4) [STRANGLING]

Na	2:12	**s** for his lionesses, and filled his holes	2614
Ac	15:20	and *from* things **s**, and *from* blood.	4156
	15:29	and from things **s**, and from fornication.	4156
	21:25	and from **s**, and from fornication.	4156

STRANGLING (1) [STRANGLED]

Job	7:15	So that my soul chooseth **s**,	4267

STRAW (16)

Ge	24:25	We have both **s** and provender enough,	8401
	24:32	gave **s** and provender for the camels,	8401
Ex	5: 7	Ye shall no more give the people **s** to	8401
	5: 7	let them go and gather **s** for themselves.	8401
	5:10	Thus saith Pharaoh, I will not give you **s**.	8401
	5:11	get you **s** where you can find *it*: yet not	8401
	5:12	of Egypt to gather stubble instead of **s**.	8401
	5:13	*your* daily tasks, as when there was **s**.	8401
	5:16	There is no **s** given unto thy servants,	8401
	5:18	for there shall no **s** be given you, yet shall	8401
Jdg	19:19	Yet there is both **s** and provender for our	8401
1Ki	4:28	Barley also and **s** for the horses and	8401
Job	41:27	He esteemeth iron as **s**, *and* brass as	8401
Isa	11: 7	and the lion shall eat **s** like the ox.	8401
	25:10	as **s** is trodden down for the dunghill.	4963
	65:25	and the lion shall eat **s** like the bullock.	8401

STRAWED (5) [STROWED]

Ex	32:20	**s** it upon the water, and made the	2219
Mt	21: 8	from the trees, and **s** *them* in the way.	4766
	25:24	and gathering where thou hast not **s**:	1287
	25:26	sowed not, and gather where I have not **s**:	1287
Mk	11: 8	off the trees, and **s** *them* in the way.	4766

STREAKED See RINGSTRAKED

STREAM (12) [STREAMS]

Nu	21:15	*at* the **s** of the brooks that goeth down to	793
Job	6:15	*and* as the **s** of brooks they pass away;	650
Ps	124: 4	the **s** had gone over our soul:	5158
Isa	27:12	channel of the river unto the **s** of Egypt,	5158
	30:28	breath, as an overflowing **s**, shall reach	5158
	30:33	like a **s** of brimstone, doth kindle it.	5158
	57: 6	Among the smooth *stones* of the **s** is thy	5158
	66:12	the glory of the Gentiles like a flowing **s**:	5158
Da	7:10	A fiery **s** issued and came forth from	5103
Am	5:24	waters, and righteousness as a mighty **s**.	5158
Lk	6:48	the **s** beat vehemently upon that house,	4215
	6:49	against which the **s** did beat vehemently,	4215

STREAMS (12) [STREAM]

Ex	7:19	upon their **s**, upon their rivers,	5104
	8: 5	forth thine hand with thy rod over the **s**,	5104
Ps	46: 4	the **s** whereof shall make glad the city of	6388
	78:16	He brought **s** also out of the rock,	5140
	78:20	waters gushed out, and the **s** overflowed;	5158
	126: 4	O LORD, as the **s** in the south.	650
SS	4:15	well of living waters, and **s** from Lebanon.	5140
Isa	11:15	shall smite it in *the* seven **s**, and make	5158
	30:25	of waters in the day of the great	2988
	33:21	*be* unto us a place of broad rivers *and* **s**;	2975
	34: 9	the **s** thereof shall be turned into pitch,	5158
	35: 6	waters break out, and **s** in the desert.	5158

STREET (36) [STREETS]

Ge	19: 2	Nay; but we will abide in the **s** all night.	7339
Dt	13:16	spoil of it into the midst of the **s** thereof,	7339
Jos	2:19	out of the doors of thy house into the **s**,	2351
Jdg	19:15	he sat him down in a **s** of the city:	7339
	19:17	saw a wayfaring man in the **s** of the city:	7339
	19:20	*lie* upon me; only lodge not in the **s**.	7339
2Sa	21:12	which had stolen them from the **s** of	7339
	22:43	I did stamp them as the mire of the **s**,	2351

2Ch 29: 4	gathered them together into the east **s**,	7339
32: 6	gathered them together to him in the **s** of	7339
Ezr 10: 9	all the people sat in the **s** of the house of	7339
Ne 8: 1	into the **s** that *was* before the water gate;	7339
8: 3	he read therein before the **s** that *was*	7339
8:16	in the **s** of the water gate, and in the	7339
8:16	and in the **s** of the gate of Ephraim.	7339
Est 4: 6	forth to Mordecai unto the **s** of the city,	7339
6: 9	bring him on horseback through the **s** of	7339
6:11	brought him on horseback through the **s**	7339
Job 18:17	and he shall have no name in the **s**.	2351
29: 7	city, when I prepared my seat in the **s**;	7339
31:32	The stranger did not lodge in the **s**:	2351
Pr 7: 8	Passing through the **s** near her corner;	7784
Isa 42: 2	nor cause his voice to be heard in the **s**.	2351
51:23	and as the **s**, to them that went over.	2351
59:14	for truth is fallen in the **s**, and equity	7339
Jer 37:21	daily a piece of bread out of the bakers' **s**,	2351
La 2:19	that faint for hunger in the top of every **s**.	2351
4: 1	are poured out in the top of every **s**.	2351
Eze 16:24	hast made thee a high place in every **s**,	7339
16:31	and makest thine high place in every **s**;	7339
Da 9:25	the **s** shall be built again, and the wall,	7339
Ac 9:11	and go into the **s** which is called Straight,	4505
12:10	went out, and passed on through one **s**;	4505
Rev 11: 8	And their dead bodies *shall* lie in the **s** of	4113
21:21	and the **s** of the city were pure gold, as *it*	4113
22: 2	In the midst of the **s** of it, and of either	4113

STREETS (65) [STREET]

2Sa 1:20	Gath, publish *it* not in the **s** of Askelon;	2351
1Ki 20:34	thou shalt make **s** for thee in Damascus,	2351
Ps 18:42	I did cast them out as the dirt in the **s**.	2351
55:11	and guile depart not from her **s**.	7339
144:13	thousands and ten thousands in our **s**:	2351
144:14	That *there be* no complaining in our **s**.	7339
Pr 1:20	she uttereth her voice in the **s**:	7339
5:16	*and* rivers of waters in the **s**.	7339
7:12	now in the **s**, and lieth in wait at every	7339
22:13	*is* a lion without, I shall be slain in the **s**.	7339
26:13	*is* a lion in the way; a lion *is* in the **s**.	7339
Ecc 12: 4	the doors shall be shut in the **s**, when	7784
12: 5	and the mourners go about the **s**:	7784
SS 3: 2	go about the city in the **s** and in the	7784
Isa 5:25	carcases were torn in the midst of the **s**.	2351
10: 6	to tread them down like the mire of the **s**.	2351
15: 3	In their **s** they shall gird themselves with	2351
15: 3	in their **s**, every one shall howl, weeping	7339
24:11	*There is* a crying for wine in the **s**; all joy	2351
51:20	they lie at the head of all the **s**, as a wild	2351
Jer 5: 1	ye to and fro through the **s** of Jerusalem,	2351
7:17	cities of Judah and in the **s** of Jerusalem?	2351
7:34	the **s** of Jerusalem, the voice of mirth,	2351
9:21	*and* the young men from the **s**.	7339
11: 6	in the **s** of Jerusalem, saying, Hear ye	2351
11:13	*according to* the number of the **s** of	2351
14:16	shall be cast out in the **s** of Jerusalem	2351
33:10	in the **s** of Jerusalem, that are desolate,	2351
44: 6	cities of Judah and in the **s** of Jerusalem;	2351
44: 9	land of Judah, and in the **s** of Jerusalem?	2351
44:17	cities of Judah, and in the **s** of Jerusalem:	2351
44:21	the **s** of Jerusalem, ye, and your fathers,	2351
48:38	housetops of Moab, and in the **s** thereof:	7339
49:26	her young men shall fall in her **s**,	7339
50:30	shall her young men fall in the **s**,	7339
51: 4	and *they that are* thrust through in her **s**.	2351
La 2:11	the sucklings swoon in the **s** of the city.	7339
2:12	they swooned as the wounded in the **s**	7339
2:21	and the old lie on the ground in the **s**:	2351
4: 5	did feed delicately are desolate in the **s**:	2351
4: 8	than a coal; they are not known in the **s**:	2351
4:14	have wandered *as* blind *men* in the **s**,	2351
4:18	our steps, that *we* cannot go in our **s**:	7339
Eze 7:19	They shall cast their silver in the **s**,	2351
11: 6	ye have filled the **s** thereof *with* the slain.	2351
26:11	his horses shall he tread down all thy **s**:	2351
28:23	into her pestilence, and blood into her **s**;	2351
Am 5:16	Wailing *shall be* in all **s**; and they shall	7339
Mic 7:10	she be trodden down as the mire of the **s**.	2351
Na 2: 4	The chariots shall rage in the **s**, they shall	2351
3:10	dashed in pieces at the top of all the **s**:	2351
Zep 3: 6	made their **s** waste, that none passeth by:	2351
Zec 8: 4	old women dwell in the **s** of Jerusalem,	7339
8: 5	the **s** of the city shall be full *of* boys and	7339
8: 5	*of* boys and girls playing in the **s** thereof.	7339
9: 3	dust, and fine gold as the mire of the **s**.	2351
10: 5	*enemies* in the mire of the **s** in the battle:	2351
Mt 6: 2	do in the synagogues and in the **s**,	4505
6: 5	synagogues and in the corners of the **s**,	4113
12:19	shall any *man* hear his voice in the **s**.	4113
Mk 6:56	they laid the sick in the **s**, and besought	58
Lk 10:10	go *your* ways out into the **s** of the same,	4113
13:26	presence, and thou hast taught in our **s**.	4113
14:21	Go out quickly into the **s** and lanes of	4113
Ac 5:15	that *they* brought forth the sick into the **s**,	4113

STRENGTH (242) [STRENGTHEN,
STRENGTHENED, STRENGTHENEDST,
STRENGTHENETH, STRENGTHENING, STRONG,
STRONGER, STRONGEST, STRONGLY]

Ge 4:12	shall not henceforth yield unto thee her **s**;	3581
49: 3	my might, and the beginning of my **s**,	202
49:24	his bow abode in **s**, and the arms of his	386
Ex 13: 3	for by **s** of hand the LORD brought you	2392
13:14	By **s** of hand the LORD brought us out	2392

Ex 13:16	for by **s** of hand the LORD brought us	2392
14:27	sea returned to his **s** when the morning	386
15: 2	The LORD *is* my **s** and song, and he is	5797
15:13	thou hast guided *them* in thy **s** unto thy	5797
Lev 26:20	your **s** shall be spent in vain: for your land	3581
Nu 23:22	he hath as it were the **s** of an unicorn.	8443
24: 8	he hath as it were the **s** of an unicorn.	8443
Dt 21:17	for he *is* the beginning of his **s**; the right	202
33:25	brass; and as thy days, *so shall* thy **s** *be*.	1679
Jos 11:13	*as for* the cities that stood still in their **s**,	8510
14:11	as my *was* then, even so *is* my strength	3581
14:11	even so *is* my **s** now, for war, both to go	3581
Jdg 5:21	O my soul, thou hast trodden down **s**.	5797
8:21	for as the man *is, so is* his **s**. And Gideon	1369
16: 5	see wherein his great **s** *lieth*, and by what	3581
16: 6	wherein thy great **s** *lieth*, and	3581
16: 9	the fire. So his **s** was not known.	3581
16:15	not told me wherein thy great **s** *lieth*.	3581
16:17	my **s** will go from me, and I shall become	3581
16:19	to afflict him, and his **s** went from him.	3581
1Sa 2: 4	and they that stumbled are girt with **s**.	2428
2: 9	in darkness; for by **s** shall no man prevail.	3581
2:10	he shall give **s** unto his king, and exalt	5797
15:29	also the **S** of Israel will not lie nor repent:	5331
28:20	there was no **s** in him; for he had eaten	3581
28:22	eat, that thou mayest have **s**, when thou	3581
2Sa 22:33	God *is* my **s** *and* power: and he maketh	4581
22:40	For thou hast girded me with **s** to battle:	2428
1Ki 8:42	went in the **s** of that meat forty days and	3581
2Ki 18:20	*I have* counsel and **s** for the war.	1369
19: 3	the birth, and *there is* not **s** to bring forth.	3581
9:24	drew a bow **with** his **full s**,	3027+4390+871.1
1Ch 16:11	Seek the LORD and his **s**, seek his face	5797
16:27	**s** and gladness *are* in his place.	5797
16:28	give unto the LORD glory and **s**.	5797
26: 8	able men for **s** for the service,	3581
29:12	*it is* to make great, and to **give s** unto all.	2388
2Ch 6:41	resting place, thou, and the ark of thy **s**.	5797
13:20	Neither did Jeroboam recover **s** again in	3581
Ne 4:10	The **s** of the bearers of burdens is decayed	3581
8:10	for the joy of the LORD *is* your **s**.	4581
Job 6:11	What *is* my **s**, that I should hope?	3581
6:12	*Is* my **s** the strength of stones? or *is* my	3581
6:12	*Is* my strength the **s** of stones? or *is* my	3581
9: 4	*He is* wise in heart, and mighty in **s**:	3581
9:19	If *I speak* of **s**, lo, *he is* strong: and if of	3581
12:13	With him *is* wisdom and **s**, he hath	1369
12:16	With him *is* **s** and wisdom: the deceived	5797
12:21	and weakeneth the **s** of the mighty.	4206
18: 7	The steps of his **s** shall be straitened,	202
18:12	His **s** shall be hunger-bitten,	202
18:13	It shall devour the **s** of his skin: *even*	905
18:13	the firstborn of death shall devour his **s**.	905
21:23	dieth in his full **s**, *being* wholly at ease	6106
23: 6	power? No; but he would put **s** in me.	NIH
26: 2	how savest thou the arm *that hath* no **s**?	5797
30: 2	whereto *might* the **s** of their hands profit	3581
36: 5	despiseth not *any: he is* mighty in **s** *and*	3581
36:19	no, not gold, nor all the forces of **s**.	3581
37: 6	small rain, and *to* the great rain of his **s**.	5797
39:11	thou trust him, because his **s** *is* great?	3581
39:19	Hast thou given the horse **s**? hast thou	1369
39:21	in the valley, and rejoiceth in *his* **s**.	3581
40:16	his **s** *is* in his loins, and his force *is* in	3581
41:22	In his neck remaineth **s**, and sorrow is	5797
Ps 8: 2	sucklings hast thou ordained **s** because	5797
18: 1	I will love thee, O LORD, my **s**.	2391
18: 2	my God, my **s**, in whom I will trust;	6697
18:32	*It is* God that girdeth me with **s**,	2428
18:39	For thou hast girded me with **s** unto	2428
19:14	O LORD, my **s**, and my redeemer.	6697
20: 6	with the saving **s** of his right hand.	1369
21: 1	The king shall joy in thy **s**, O LORD;	5797
21:13	Be thou exalted, LORD, in thine own **s**:	5797
22:15	My **s** is dried up like a potsherd;	3581
22:19	O LORD: O my **s**, haste thee to help me.	360
27: 1	the LORD *is* the **s** of my life; of whom	4581
28: 7	The LORD *is* my **s** and my shield;	5797
28: 8	The LORD *is* their **s**, and he *is* the saving	5797
28: 8	and he *is* the saving **s** of his anointed.	4581
29: 1	give unto the LORD glory and **s**.	5797
29:11	The LORD will give **s** unto his people;	5797
31: 4	have laid privily for me: for thou *art* my **s**.	4581
31:10	my **s** faileth because of mine iniquity,	3581
33:16	a mighty *man* is not delivered by much **s**.	3581
33:17	neither shall he deliver *any* by his great **s**.	2428
37:39	*he is* their **s** in the time of trouble.	4581
38:10	My heart panteth, my **s** faileth me: as for	3581
39:13	spare me, that I may **recover s**, before I	1082
43: 2	For thou *art* the God of my **s**: why dost	4581
46: 1	God *is* our refuge and **s**, a very present	5797
52: 7	*this is* the man *that* made not God his **s**;	4581
54: 1	by thy name, and judge me by thy **s**.	1369
59: 9	*Because of* his **s** will I wait upon thee:	5797
59:17	Unto thee, O my **s**, will I sing: for God *is*	5797
67: 7	Ephraim also *is* the **s** of mine head;	4581
60: 7	rock of my **s**, *and* my refuge, *is* in God.	4581
65: 6	Which by his **s** setteth fast the mountains;	5797
68:28	Thy God hath commanded thy **s**:	5797
68:34	Ascribe ye unto God: his excellency *is*	5797
68:34	*is* over Israel, and his **s** *is* in the clouds.	5797
68:35	the God of Israel *is* he that giveth **s** and	5797
71: 9	age; forsake me not when my **s** faileth.	3581
71:16	I will go in the **s** of the Lord GOD: I will	1369
71:18	until I have shewed thy **s** unto *this*	2220

Ps 73: 4	bands in their death: but their **s** *is* firm.	193
73:26	*but* God *is* the **s** of my heart,	6697
74:13	Thou didst divide the sea by thy **s**:	5797
77:14	hast declared thy **s** among the people.	5797
78: 4	his **s**, and his wonderful works that he	5807
78:51	chief of *theirs* in the tabernacles of Ham:	202
78:61	delivered his **s** into captivity, and his glory	5797
80: 2	and Benjamin and Manasseh stir up thy **s**,	1369
81: 1	Sing aloud unto God our **s**: make a joyful	5797
84: 5	Blessed *is* the man whose **s** *is* in thee;	5797
84: 7	They go from **s** to strength, *every one of*	2428
84: 7	They go from strength to **s**, *every one of*	2428
86:16	give thy **s** unto thy servant, and save	5797
88: 4	into the pit: I am as a man *that hath* no **s**:	353
89:17	For thou *art* the glory of their **s**: and in	5797
90:10	if by reason of **s** *they be* fourscore years,	1369
90:10	yet *is* their **s** labour and sorrow;	7296
93: 1	the LORD is clothed with **s**, *wherewith* he	5797
95: 4	of the earth: the **s** of the hills *is* his also.	8443
96: 6	**s** and beauty *are* in his sanctuary.	5797
96: 7	give unto the LORD glory and **s**.	5797
99: 4	The King's **s** also loveth judgment;	5797
102:23	He weakened my **s** in the way;	3581
103:20	the LORD, ye his angels, that excel in **s**,	3581
105: 4	Seek the LORD, and his **s**: seek his face	5797
105:36	in their land, the chief of all their **s**.	202
108: 8	Ephraim also *is* the **s** of mine head;	4581
110: 2	The LORD shall send the rod of thy **s** out	5797
118:14	The LORD *is* my **s** and song,	5797
132: 8	into thy rest; thou, and the ark of thy **s**.	5797
138: 3	and strengthenedst me with **s** in my soul.	5797
140: 7	O GOD the Lord, the **s** of my salvation,	5797
144: 1	Blessed *be* the LORD my **s**,	6697
147:10	He delighteth not in the **s** of the horse:	1369
Pr 8:14	I *am* understanding; I have **s**.	1369
10:29	The way of the LORD *is* **s** to the upright:	4581
14: 4	but much increase *is* by the **s** of the ox.	3581
20:29	The glory of young men *is* their **s**:	3581
21:22	casteth down the **s** of the confidence	5797
24: 5	yea, a man of knowledge increaseth **s**.	3581
24:10	faint in the day of adversity, thy **s** is small.	3581
31: 3	Give not thy **s** unto women, nor thy ways	2428
31:17	She girdeth her loins with **s**,	5797
31:25	**S** and honour *are* her clothing; and she	5797
Ecc 9:16	said I, Wisdom *is* better than **s**:	1369
10:10	the edge, then must he put to more **s**:	2428
10:17	season, for **s**, and not for drunkenness.	1369
Isa 5:22	and men of **s** to mingle strong drink:	2428
10:13	By the **s** of my hand I have done *it*, and	3581
12: 2	for the LORD JEHOVAH *is* my **s** and	5797
17:10	not been mindful of the rock of thy **s**,	4581
23: 4	*even* the **s** of the sea, saying, I travail not,	4581
23:10	daughter of Tarshish: *there is* no more **s**.	4206
23:14	ships of Tarshish: for your **s** is laid waste.	4581
25: 4	For thou hast been a **s** to the poor,	4581
25: 4	a **s** to the needy in his distress, a refuge	4581
26: 4	in the LORD JEHOVAH *is* everlasting **s**:	6697
27: 5	Or let him take hold of my **s**, *that* he may	4581
28: 6	**s** to them that turn the battle to the gate.	1369
30: 2	to strengthen themselves in the **s** of	4581
30: 3	Therefore shall the **s** of Pharaoh be your	4581
30: 7	cried concerning this, Their **s** *is* to sit still.	7293
30:15	and in confidence shall be your **s**:	1369
33: 6	stability of thy times, *and* **s** of salvation:	2633
36: 5	vain words) *I have* counsel and **s** for war:	1369
37: 3	the birth, and *there is* not **s** to bring forth.	3581
40: 9	good tidings, lift up thy voice with **s**,	3581
40:29	*them that have* no might he increaseth **s**.	6109
40:31	wait upon the LORD shall renew *their* **s**;	3581
41: 1	islands; and let the people renew *their* **s**:	3581
42:25	the fury of his anger, and the **s** of battle:	5807
44:12	and worketh it with the **s** of his arms:	3581
44:12	yea, he is hungry, and his **s** faileth:	3581
45:24	in the LORD have I righteousness and **s**:	5797
49: 4	I have spent my **s** for nought, and in vain:	3581
49: 5	of the LORD, and my God shall be my **s**.	5797
51: 9	Awake, awake, put on **s**, O arm of	5797
52: 1	Awake, awake; put on thy **s**, O Zion;	5797
62: 8	by his right hand, and by the arm of his **s**,	5797
63: 1	travelling in the greatness of his **s**?	3581
63: 6	and I will bring down their **s** to the earth.	5332
63:15	where *is* thy zeal and thy **s**, the sounding	1369
Jer 16:19	my **s**, and my fortress, and my refuge in	5797
20: 5	I will deliver all the **s** of this city,	2633
51:53	she should fortify the height of her **s**,	5797
La 1: 6	are gone without **s** before the pursuer.	3581
1:14	he hath made my **s** to fall, the Lord hath	3581
3:18	My **s** and my hope is perished from	5331
Eze 24:21	the excellency of your **s**, the desire of	5797
24:25	in the day when I take from them their **s**,	4581
30:15	pour my fury upon Sin, the **s** of Egypt:	4581
30:18	the pomp of her **s** shall cease in her:	5797
33:28	and the pomp of her **s** shall cease;	5797
Da 2:37	thee a kingdom, power, and **s**, and glory.	8632
2:41	there shall be in it of the **s** of the iron,	5326
10: 8	vision, and there remained no **s** in me:	3581
10: 8	me into corruption, and I retained no **s**.	3581
10:16	upon me, and I have retained no **s**.	3581
10:17	straightway there remained no **s** in me,	3581
11: 2	by his **s** through his riches he shall stir up	2393
11:15	neither *shall there be any* **s** to withstand.	3581
11:17	shall also set his face to enter with the **s**	8633
11:31	they shall pollute the sanctuary of **s**,	4581
Hos 7: 9	Strangers have devoured his **s**,	3581
12: 3	and by his **s** he had power with God:	202

Ro 13:13 and wantonness, not in **s** and envying. 2054
1Co 3: 3 and **s**, and divisions, are ye not carnal, 2054
Gal 5:20 emulations, wrath, **s**, seditions, heresies, 2052
Php 1:15 indeed preach Christ even of envy and **s**; 2054
 2: 3 nothing *be done* through **s** or vainglory; 2052
1Ti 6: 4 cometh envy, **s**, railings, evil surmisings, 2054
Heb 6:16 for confirmation *is* to them an end of all **s**. 485
Jas 3:14 have bitter envying and **s** in your hearts, 2052
 3:16 and **s** *is*, there *is* confusion and every evil 2052

STRIFES (4) [STRIVE]
Pr 10:12 Hatred stirreth up **s**: but love covereth all 4066
2Co 12:20 envyings, wraths, **s**, backbitings, 2052
1Ti 6: 4 doting about questions and **s of words**, 3055
2Ti 2:23 knowing that they do gender **s**. 3163

STRIKE (12) [STRAKE, STRICKEN, STRIKER, STRIKETH, STROKE, STROKES, STROOKE, STRUCK]
Ex 12: 7 **s** *it* on the two side posts and on the 5414
 12:22 **s** the lintel and the two side posts with 5060
Dt 21: 4 shall **s off** the heifer's **neck** there in 6202
2Ki 5:11 **s** his hand over the place, and recover 5130
Job 17: 3 who *is* he *that* will **s** hands with me? 8628
 20:24 *and* the bow of steel shall **s** him **through**. 2498
Ps 110: 5 Lord at thy right hand shall **s** through 4272
Pr 7:23 Till a dart **through** his liver; as a bird 6398
 17:26 *is* not good, *nor* to **s** princes for equity. 5221
 22:26 Be not thou *one* of them that **s** hands, 8628
Hab 3:14 Thou didst **s through** with his staves 5344
Mk 14:65 servants did **s** him **with the palms of** 906+4475
 their **hands**.

STRIKER (2) [STRIKE]
1Ti 3: 3 Not given to wine, no **s**, not greedy of 4131
Tit 1: 7 not soon angry, not given to wine, no **s**, 4131

STRIKETH (3) [STRIKE]
Job 34:26 He **s** them as wicked *men* in the open 5606
Pr 17:18 A man void of understanding **s** hands, 8628
Rev 9: 5 torment of a scorpion, when he **s** a man. 3817

STRING (3) [STRINGED, STRINGS]
Ps 11: 2 they make ready their arrow upon the **s**, 3499
Mk 7:35 and the **s** of his tongue was loosed, 1199

STRINGED (3) [STRING]
Ps 150: 4 praise him with **s instruments** and 4482
Isa 38:20 **sing** my songs *to* the **s instruments** all 5059
Hab 3:19 To the chief singer on my **s instruments**. 5058

STRINGS (4) [STRING]
Ps 21:12 upon thy **s** against the face of them. 4340
 33: 2 the psaltery *and* an **instrument of ten s**. 6218
 92: 3 Upon an **instrument of ten s**, and upon 6218
 144: 9 an **instrument of ten s** will I sing *praises* 6218

STRIP (7) [STRIPPED, STRIPT]
Nu 20:26 **s** Aaron of his garments, and put them 6584
1Sa 31: 8 when the Philistines came to **s** the slain, 6584
1Ch 10: 8 when the Philistines came to **s** the slain, 6584
Isa 32:11 **s** ye, and make ye bare, and gird 6584
Eze 16:39 they shall **s** thee also of thy clothes, 6584
 23:26 They shall also **s** thee **out of** thy clothes, 6584
Hos 2: 3 Lest I **s** her naked, and set her as *in* the 6584

STRIPE (2) [STRIPES]
Ex 21:25 burning, wound for wound, **s** for stripe. 2250
 21:25 burning, wound for wound, stripe for **s**. 2250

STRIPES (17) [STRIPE]
Dt 25: 3 Forty **s** he may **give** him, *and* not exceed: 5221
 25: 3 beat him above these *with* many **s**, then 4347
2Sa 7:14 and with the **s** of the children of men: 5061
Ps 89:32 with the rod, and their iniquity with **s**. 5061
Pr 17:10 a wise *man* than an hundred **s** into a fool. 5221
 19:29 for scorners, and **s** for the back of fools. 4112
 20:30 so *do* **s** the inward parts of the belly. 4347
Isa 53: 5 upon him; and with his **s** we are healed. 2250
Lk 12:47 to his will, shall be beaten with many **s**. NIG
 12:48 and did commit *things* worthy of **s**, 4127
 12:48 shall be beaten with few **s**. For unto NIG
Ac 16:23 when they had laid many **s** upon them, 4127
 16:33 hour of the night, and washed *their* **s**; 4127
2Co 6: 5 In **s**, in imprisonments, in tumults, 4127
 11:23 in **s** above measure, in prisons more 4127
 11:24 Of the Jews five times received I forty **s** NIG
1Pe 2:24 by whose **s** ye were healed. 3468

STRIPLING (1)
1Sa 17:56 king said, Inquire thou whose son the **s** *is*. 5958

STRIPPED (6) [STRIP]
Nu 20:28 Moses **s** Aaron of his garments, 6584
1Sa 31: 9 **s off** his armour, and sent into the land of 6584
1Ch 10: 9 when they had **s** him, they took his head, 6584
Job 22: 6 and the naked of their clothing. 6584
Mt 27:28 And they **s** him, and put on him a scarlet 1562
Lk 10:30 which **s** him **of** his **raiment,** 1562

STRIPT (7) [STRIP]
Ge 37:23 that they **s** Joseph **out of** his coat, 6584
Ex 33: 6 the children of Israel **s** themselves of their 5337
1Sa 18: 4 Jonathan **s** himself of the robe that *was* 6584
 19:24 he **s off** his clothes also, 6584
2Ch 20:25 which they **s off** for themselves, 5337

Job 19: 9 He hath **s** me of my glory, and taken 6584
Mic 1: 8 will wail and howl, I will go **s** and naked: 7758

STRIVE (22) [STRIFE, STRIFES, STRIVED, STRIVEN, STRIVETH, STRIVING, STRIVINGS, STROVE]
Ge 6: 3 My spirit shall not always **s** with man, 1777
 26:20 the herdmen of Gerar did **s** with Isaac's 7378
Ex 21:18 if men **s together**, and one smite another 7378
 21:22 If men **s**, and hurt a woman with child, 5327
Dt 25:11 When men **s** together one with another, 5327
 33: 8 *with* whom thou didst **s** at the waters of 7378
Jdg 11:25 did he **ever s** against Israel, or did 7378+7378
Job 33:13 Why dost thou **s** against him? for he 7378
Ps 35: 1 O LORD, with them that **s** with me: 3401
Pr 3:30 **S** not with a man without cause, if he 7378
 25: 8 Go not forth hastily to **s**, lest *thou know* 7378
Isa 41:11 and they that **s** with thee shall perish. 7379
 45: 9 *Let* the potsherd **s** with the potsherds of NIH
Hos 4: 4 Yet let no man **s**, nor reprove another: 7378
 4: 4 for thy people *are* as they that **s** with 7378
Mt 12:19 He shall not **s**, nor cry; neither shall any 2051
Lk 13:24 **S** to enter in at the strait gate: for many, 75
Ro 15:30 ye **s together with** me in *your* prayers 4865
2Ti 2: 5 if a man also **s for masteries**, *yet* is 118
 2: 5 is he not crowned, except he **s** lawfully. 118
 2:14 that **they**'s not **about words** to no profit, 3054
 2:24 And the servant of the Lord must not **s**; 3164

STRIVED (1) [STRIVE]
Ro 15:20 Yea, so have I **s** to preach the gospel, 5389

STRIVEN (1) [STRIVE]
Jer 50:24 because thou hast **s** against the LORD. 1624

STRIVETH (3) [STRIVE]
Isa 45: 9 Woe unto him that **s** with his maker! 7378
1Co 9:25 And every *man* that **s for the mastery** is 75

STRIVING (3) [STRIVE]
Php 1:27 with one mind **s together** for the faith of 4866
Col 1:29 I also labour, **s** according to his working, 75
Heb 12: 4 not yet resisted unto blood, **s** against sin. 464

STRIVINGS (3) [STRIVE]
2Sa 22:44 Thou also hast delivered me from the **s** of 7379
Ps 18:43 Thou hast delivered me from the **s** of 7379
Tit 3: 9 and contentions, and **s** about the law; 3163

STROKE (14) [STRIKE]
Dt 17: 8 and plea, and between **s** and stroke, 5061
 17: 8 and plea, and between stroke and **s**, 5061
 19: 5 his hand **fetcheth a s** with the axe to cut 5080
 21: 5 every controversy and every **s** be *tried:* 5061
Est 9: 5 all their enemies *with* the **s** of the sword, 4347
Job 23: 2 my **s** is heavier than my groaning. 3027
 36:18 **beware** lest he take thee away with *his* **s**: 5607
Ps 39:10 Remove thy **s** away from me: I am 5061
Isa 14: 6 the people in wrath *with* a continual **s**, 4347
 30:26 and healeth the **s** of their wound. 4273
Eze 24:16 thee the desire of thine eyes with a **s**: 4046
Mt 24:16 thee the desire of thine eyes with a **s**: 4046
Lk 22:64 they **s** him on the face, and asked him, 5180
Jn 18:22 **s** Jesus **with the palm of** his **hand,** 1325+4475

STROKES (1) [STRIKE]
Pr 18: 6 contention, and his mouth calleth for **s**. 4112

STRONG (255) [STRENGTH]
Ge 49:14 Issachar *is* a **s** ass couching down 1634
 49:24 the arms of his hands were **made s** by 6339
Ex 6: 1 for with a **s** hand shall he let them go, 2389
 6: 1 with a **s** hand he drive them out of 2389
 10:19 the LORD turned a mighty **s** west wind, 2389
 13: 9 for with a **s** hand hath the LORD brought 2389
 14:21 LORD caused the sea to go *back* by a **s** 5794
Lev 10: 9 Do not drink wine nor **s drink**, thou, 7941
Nu 6: 3 separate *himself* from wine and **s drink**, 7941
 6: 3 no vinegar of wine, or vinegar of **s drink**, 7941
 13:18 whether they *be* **s** or weak, few or many; 2389
 13:19 dwell in, whether in tents, or in **s holds**; 4013
 13:28 Nevertheless the people *be* **s** that dwell in 5794
 20:20 with much people, and with a **s** hand. 2389
 21:24 border of the children of Ammon *was* **s**. 5794
 24:21 **S** is thy dwelling place, and thou puttest 386
 28: 7 **s wine** to be poured unto the LORD *for* a 7941
Dt 2:36 there was not one city too **s** for us: 7682
 11: 8 that ye may be **s**, and go in and possess 2388
 14:26 or for **s drink**, or for whatsoever thy soul 7941
 29: 6 neither have you drunk wine or **s drink** 7941
 31: 6 Be **s** and of a good courage, fear not, nor 2388
 31: 7 of all Israel, Be **s** and of a good courage: 2388
 31:23 said, Be **s** and of a good courage: 2388
Jos 1: 6 Be **s** and of a good courage: for unto this 2388
 1: 7 Only be thou **s** and very courageous, 2388
 1: 9 Be **s** and of a good courage; be not afraid, 2388
 1:18 to death: only be **s** and of a good courage. 2388
 10:25 be dismayed, be **s** and of a good courage: 2388
 14:11 As yet I *am* as **s** this day as I *was* in the 2389
 17:13 the children of Israel were **waxen s**, 2388
 17:18 have iron chariots, *and* though they *be* **s**. 2389
 19:29 turneth *to* Ramah, and to the **s** city Tyre; 4013
 23: 9 out from before you great nations and **s**: 6099
Jdg 1:28 it came to pass, when Israel was **s**, that 2388
 6: 2 the mountains, and caves, and **s holds**. 4679
 9:51 there was a **s** tower within the city, 5797
 13: 4 drink not wine nor **s drink**, and eat not 7941

Jdg 13: 7 now drink no wine nor **s drink**, neither 7941
 13:14 neither let her drink wine or **s drink**, 7941
 14:14 and out of the **s** came forth sweetness. 5794
 18:26 when Micah saw that they *were* too **s** 2389
1Sa 1:15 I have drunk neither wine nor **s drink**, 7941
 4: 9 Be **s**, and quit yourselves like men, O ye 2388
 14:52 when Saul saw any **s** man, or any valiant 1368
 23:14 David abode in the wilderness in **s holds**, 4679
 23:19 himself with us in **s holds** in the wood, 4679
 23:29 and dwelt in **s holds** at En-gedi. 4679
2Sa 3: 6 Abner **made** himself **s** for the house of 2388
 5: 7 Nevertheless David took the **s hold** of 4686
 10:11 If the Syrians be too **s** for me, then 2388
 10:11 the children of Ammon be too **s** for thee, 2388
 11:25 **make** thy battle *more* **s** against the city, 2388
 15:12 the conspiracy was **s**; for the people 533
 16:21 the hands of all that *are* with thee be **s**. 2388
 22:18 He delivered me from my **s** enemy, 5794
 22:18 that hated me: for they were too **s** for me. 553
 24: 7 came to *the* **s hold** of Tyre, and *to* all 4013
1Ki 2: 2 be thou **s** therefore, and shew thyself a 2388
 8:42 thy **s** hand, and of thy stretched out arm;) 2389
 19:11 a great and a mighty **s** wind rent the mountains, 2389
2Ki 2:16 be with thy servants fifty **s** men; 1121+2428
 8:12 their **s holds** wilt thou set on fire, 4013
 24:16 thousand, all *that were* **s** *and* apt for war, 1368
1Ch 19:12 If the Syrians be too **s** for me, then thou 2388
 19:12 the children of Ammon be too **s** for thee, 2388
 22:13 be **s**, and of good courage; dread not, 2388
 26: 7 whose brethren *were* **s** men, Elihu, 2428
 26: 9 had sons and brethren, **s** men, 2428
 28:10 a house for the sanctuary: be **s**, and do *it*. 2388
 28:20 Be **s** and of good courage, and do *it*: fear 2388
2Ch 11:11 he fortified the **s holds**, and put captains 4694
 11:12 and spears, and **made** them exceeding **s**, 2388
 11:17 **made** Rehoboam the son of Solomon **s**, 553
 15: 7 Be ye therefore, and let not your hands 2388
 16: 9 to **shew** himself **s** in the behalf of *them* 2388
 25: 8 if thou *wilt* go, do *it*, be **s** for the battle: 2388
 26:15 he was marvellously helped, till he was **s**. 2388
 26:16 when he was **s**, his heart was lifted up to 2393
 32: 7 Be **s** and courageous, be not afraid nor 2388
Ezr 9:12 that ye may be **s**, and eat the good of 2388
Ne 1:10 by thy great power, and by thy **s** hand. 2389
 9:25 they took **s** cities, and a fat land, 1219
Job 8: 2 the words of thy mouth *be* like a **s** wind? 3524
 9:19 If *I speak* of strength, lo, *he is* **s**: and if 533
 30:21 with thy **s** hand thou opposest thyself 6108
 33:19 the multitude of his bones with **s pain**: 386
 37:18 which *is*, *and* as a molten looking glass? 2389
 39:28 the crag of the rock, and the **s place**. 4686
 40:18 His bones *are* as **s pieces** of brass; 650
Ps 10:10 that the poor may fall by his **s** ones. 6099
 18:17 He delivered me from my **s** enemy, 5794
 18:17 hated me: for they were too **s** for me. 553
 19: 5 *and* rejoiceth as a *man* to run a race. 1368
 22:12 **bulls** of Bashan have beset me round. 47
 24: 8 the LORD **s** and mighty, the LORD 5808
 30: 7 thou hast made my mountain to stand **s**: 5797
 31: 2 be thou my **s** rock, for a house of defence 4581
 31:21 me his marvellous kindness in a **s** city. 4692
 35:10 the poor from him that is too **s** for him, 2389
 38:19 mine enemies *are* lively, *and* they are **s** 6105
 60: 9 Who will bring me *into* the **s** city? 4692
 61: 3 for me, *and* a **s** tower from the enemy. 5797
 71: 3 Be thou my **s** habitation, whereunto I 6697
 71: 7 unto many; but thou *art* my **s** refuge. 5797
 80:15 the branch *that* thou **madest s** for thyself. 553
 80:17 the son of man *whom* thou **madest s** 553
 89: 8 of hosts, who *is* a **s** LORD like unto thee? 2626
 89:10 hast scattered thine enemies with thy **s** 5797
 89:13 **s** is thy hand, *and* high is thy right hand. 5810
 89:40 thou hast brought his **s holds** to ruin. 4013
 108:10 Who will bring me *into* the **s** city? 4013
 136:12 With a **s** hand, and with a stretched out 2389
 144:14 *That* our oxen *may be* **s** to labour; 5445
Pr 7:26 yea, many **s** *men have been* slain by her. 6099
 10:15 The rich *man's* wealth is his **s** city: 5797
 11:16 honour: and **s** *men* retain riches. 6184
 14:26 In the fear of the LORD *is* **s** confidence: 5797
 18:10 The name of the LORD *is* a **s** tower: 5797
 18:11 The rich *man's* wealth *is* his **s** city, and 5797
 18:19 *is* harder to be won than a **s** city: 5797
 20: 1 Wine *is* a mocker, **s** drink *is* raging: 7941
 21:14 and a reward in the bosom **s** wrath. 5794
 24: 5 A wise man *is* **s**; yea, a man of knowledge 5797
 30:25 The ants *are* a people not **s**, yet they 5794
 31: 4 to drink wine; nor for princes **s drink**: 7941
 31: 6 Give **s drink** unto him that is ready to 7941
Ecc 9:11 nor the battle to the **s**, neither yet bread 1368
 12: 3 the **s** men shall bow themselves, 2428
SS 8: 6 for love *is* **s** as death; jealousy *is* cruel as 5794
Isa 1:31 the **s** shall be as tow, and the maker of it 2634
 5:11 morning, *that* they may follow **s drink**; 7941
 5:22 and men of strength to mingle **s drink**: 7941
 8: 7 **s** and many, *even* the king of Assyria, 6099
 8:11 For the LORD spake thus to me with a **s** 2393
 17: 9 In that day shall his **s** cities be as a 4581
 23:11 *city*, to destroy the **s holds** thereof. 4581
 24: 9 **s drink** shall be bitter to them that drink 7941
 25: 3 Therefore shall the **s** people glorify thee, 5794
 26: 1 We have a **s** city; salvation *is* God 5797
 27: 1 **s** sword shall punish leviathan the 2389
 28: 2 the LORD hath a mighty and **s** one, 533
 28: 7 and through **s drink** are out of the way; 7941

Isa 28: 7 the prophet have erred through **s** drink, · 7941
28: 7 they are out of the way through **s** drink. · 7941
28:22 not mockers, lest your bands be **made s**: · 2388
29: 9 they stagger, but not *with* **s** drink. · 7941
31: 1 in horsemen, because they are very **s**; · 6105
31: 9 he shall pass over *to* his **s** hold for fear, · 5553
35: 4 that are of a fearful heart, Be **s**, fear not: · 2388
40:10 the Lord GOD will come with **s** hand, and · 2389
40:26 of *his* might, for that he *is* **s** in power; · 533
41:21 bring forth your **s** reasons, saith the King · 6110
53:12 and he shall divide the spoil with the **s**; · 6099
56:12 and we will fill ourselves with **s** drink, · 7941
60:22 a thousand, and a small one a **s** nation: · 6099
Jer 8:16 at the sound of the neighing of his **s** ones; · 47
21: 5 an outstretched hand and with a **s** arm, · 2389
32:21 a **s** hand, and with a stretched out arm, · 2389
47: 3 his *horses*, at the rushing of his chariots, · 47
48:14 We *are* mighty and **s** men for the war? · 2428
48:17 How is the **s** staff broken, *and the* · 5797
48:18 thee, *and* he shall destroy thy **s** holds. · 4013
48:41 the **s** holds are surprised, and the mighty · 4679
49:19 of Jordan against the habitation of the **s**: · 386
50:34 Their redeemer *is* **s**; the LORD of hosts *is* · 2389
50:44 of Jordan unto the habitation of the **s**: · 386
51:12 **make** the watch **s**, set up the watchmen, · 2388
La 2: 2 the **s** holds of the daughter of Judah; · 4013
2: 5 he hath destroyed his **s** holds, · 4013
Eze 3: 8 I have made thy face **s** against their faces, · 2389
3: 8 and thy forehead **s** against their foreheads, · 2389
3:14 but the hand of the LORD was **s** upon me. · 2388
7:24 will also make the pomp of the **s** to cease; · 5794
19:11 she had **s** rods for the sceptres of them · 5797
19:12 her **s** rods were broken and withered; · 5797
19:14 that she hath no **s** rod *to be* a sceptre to · 5797
22:14 heart endure, or can thine hands be **s**, · 2388
26:11 **s** garrisons shall go down to the ground. · 5797
26:17 which wast **s** in the sea, the and · 2389
30:21 to bind it, to **make** it **s** to hold the sword. · 2388
30:22 arms, the **s**, and that which was broken; · 2389
32:21 The **s** among the mighty shall speak to · 410
34:16 I will destroy the fat and the **s**; I will feed · 2389
Da 2:40 the fourth kingdom shall be **s** as iron: · 8624
2:42 *so* the kingdom shall be partly **s**, · 8624
4:11 was **s**, and the height thereof reached · 8631
4:20 that thou sawest, which grew, and was **s**, · 8631
4:22 O king, that art grown and become **s**: · 8631
7: 7 dreadful and terrible, and **s** exceedingly; · 8624
8: 8 he was **s**, the great horn was broken; · 6105
10:19 peace *be* unto thee, be **s**, yea, be **s**. · 2388
10:19 peace *be* unto thee, be strong, yea, be **s**. · 2388
11: 5 the king of the south shall be **s**, and *one* · 2388
11: 5 he shall be **s** above him, · 2388
11:23 and shall become **s** with a small people. · 6105
11:24 forecast his devices against the **s** holds, · 4013
11:32 people that do know their God shall be **s**, · 2388
11:39 Thus shall he do in the **most s** holds with · 4581
Joel 1: 6 **s**, and without number, whose teeth *are* · 6099
2: 2 a great people and a **s**; there hath not · 6099
2: 5 stubble, as a **s** people set in battle array. · 6099
2:11 for *he is* **s** that executeth his word: · 6099
3:10 into spears: let the weak say, I *am* **s**. · 1368
Am 2: 9 of the cedars, and he *was* **s** as the oaks; · 2634
2:14 the **s** shall not strengthen his force, · 2389
5: 9 strengtheneth the spoiled against the **s**, · 5794
Mic 2:11 unto thee of wine and of **s** drink; · 7941
4: 3 people, and rebuke **s** nations afar off; · 6099
4: 7 and her that was cast far off a **s** nation: · 6099
4: 8 the **s** hold of the daughter of Zion; · 6077
5:11 thy land, and throw down all thy **s** holds: · 4013
6: 2 and ye **s** foundations of the earth: · 386
Na 1: 7 *is* good, a **s** hold in the day of trouble; · 4581
2: 1 watch the way, **make** *thy* loins **s**, · 2388
3:12 All thy **s** holds *shall be like* fig trees with · 4013
3:14 waters for the siege, fortify thy **s** holds; · 4013
3:14 tread the morter, **make s** the brickkiln. · 2388
Hab 1:10 they shall deride every **s** hold; for they · 4013
Hag 2: 4 Yet now be **s**, O Zerubbabel, saith · 2388
2: 4 be **s**, O Joshua, son of Josedech, the high · 2388
2: 4 be **s**, all ye people of the land, saith · 2388
Zec 8: 9 Let your hands be **s**, ye that hear in these · 2388
8:13 blessing: fear not, *but* let your hands be **s**. · 2388
8:22 **s** nations shall come to seek the LORD of · 6099
9: 3 Tyrus did build herself a **s** hold, · 4692
9:12 Turn ye to the **s** hold, ye prisoners of · 1225
Mt 12:29 Or else how can one enter into a **s** *man's* · 2478
12:29 except he first bind the **s** *man?* and then · 2478
Mk 3:27 No *man* can enter into a **s** *man's* house, · 2478
3:27 except he will first bind the **s** *man;* and · 2478
Lk 1:15 and shall drink neither wine nor **s** drink; · 4608
1:80 and **waxed s** in spirit, and was in · 2901
2:40 and **waxed s** in spirit, filled with wisdom: · 2901
11:21 When a **s** *man* armed keepeth his palace, · 2478
Ac 3:16 faith in his name hath **made s** this man **s**, · 4732
Ro 4:20 but was **s** in faith, giving glory to God; · 1743
15: 1 that are **s** ought to bear the infirmities of · 1415
1Co 4:10 we *are* weak, but ye *are* **s**; ye *are* · 2478
16:13 fast in the faith, quit you like men, be **s**. · 2901
2Co 10: 4 God to the pulling down of **s** holds;) · 3794
12:10 for when I am weak, then am I **s**. · 1415
13: 9 are glad, when we are weak, and ye are **s**: · 1415
Eph 6:10 be **s** in the Lord, and in the power of his · 1743
2Ti 2:11 And for this cause God shall send them **s** · 1753
2Ti 2: 1 be **s** in the grace that is in Christ Jesus. · 1743
Heb 5: 7 and supplications with **s** crying and · 2478
5:12 as have need of milk, and not of **s** meat. · 4731

Heb 5:14 But **s** meat belongeth to *them that are* of · 4731
6:18 too lie, we might have a **s** consolation, · 2478
11:34 out of weakness were **made s**, waxed · 1743
1Jn 2:14 because ye are **s**, and the word of God · 2478
Rev 5: 2 And I saw a **s** angel proclaiming with a · 2478
18: 2 And he cried mightily with a **s** voice, · 3173
18: 8 for **s** *is* the Lord God who judgeth her. · 2478

STRONGER (21) [STRENGTH]

Ge 25:23 *the one* people shall be **s** than *the other* · 553
30:41 whensoever the **s** cattle did conceive, · 7194
30:42 feebler *were* Laban's, and the **s** Jacob's. · 7194
Nu 13:31 against the people; for they *are* **s** than we. · 2389
Jdg 14:18 what *is* **s** than a lion? And he said unto · 5794
2Sa 1:23 than eagles, they were **s** than lions. · 1396
3: 1 David **waxed s** and stronger, and the · 1980
3: 1 David waxed stronger and **s**, and the · 2390
13:14 but, being **s** than she, forced her, · 2388
1Ki 20:23 therefore they were **s** than we; but let us · 2388
20:23 and surely we shall be **s** than they. · 2388
20:25 *and* surely we shall be **s** than they. · 2388
Job 17: 9 clean hands shall be **s** and stronger. · 555+3254
17: 9 clean hands shall be stronger **and s**. · 555+3254
Ps 105:24 **made** them **s** than their enemies. · 6105
142: 6 from my persecutors; for they are **s** than I. · 553
Jer 20: 7 thou art **s** than I, and hast prevailed: I am · 2388
31:11 from the hand of *him that was* **s** than he. · 2389
Lk 11:22 when a **s** than he shall come upon *him,* · 2478
1Co 1:25 and the weakness of God is **s** than men. · 2478
10:22 the Lord to jealousy? are we **s** than he? · 2478

STRONGEST (1) [STRENGTH]

Pr 30:30 A lion *which is* **s** among beasts, · 1368

STRONGLY (1) [STRENGTH]

Ezr 6: 3 and *let* the foundations thereof be **s** laid; · 5446

STROOKE (1) [STRIKE]

1Sa 2:14 he **s** *it* into the pan, or kettle, or caldron, · 5221

STROVE (14) [STRIVE]

Ge 26:20 the well Esek; because they **s** with him. · 6229
26:21 digged another well, and **s** for that also: · 7378
26:22 another well; and for that they **s** not: · 7378
Ex 2:13 two men of the Hebrews **s** together: · 5327
Lev 24:10 a man of Israel **s** together in the camp; · 5327
Nu 20:13 the children of Israel **s** with the LORD, · 7378
26: 9 who **s** against Moses and against Aaron · 5327
26: 9 of Korah, when they **s** against the LORD: · 5327
2Sa 14: 6 they two **s** together in the field, · 5327
Ps 60: T when he **s** with Aram-naharaim and · 5327
Da 7: 2 the four winds of the heaven **s** upon · 1519
Jn 6:52 The Jews therefore **s** amongst themselves, · 3164
Ac 7:26 he shewed himself unto them as they **s**, · 3164
23: 9 and **s**, saying, We find no evil in this man: · 1264

STROWED (1) [STRAWED]

2Ch 34: 4 **s** *it* upon the graves of them that had · 2236

STRUCK (1) [STRIKE]

2Ch 13:20 and the LORD **s** him, and he died. · 5062

STRUGGLED (1)

Ge 25:22 the children **s** together within her; · 7533

STUBBLE (18)

Ex 5:12 Egypt to **gather s** instead of straw. · 7179+7197
15: 7 thy wrath, *which* consumed them as **s**. · 7179
Job 13:25 and fro? and wilt thou pursue the dry **s**? · 7179
21:18 are as **s** before the wind, and as chaff · 8401
41:28 slingstones are turned with him into **s**. · 7179
41:29 Darts are counted as **s**: he laugheth at · 7179
Ps 83:13 like a wheel; as the **s** before the wind. · 7179
Isa 5:24 Therefore as the fire devoureth the **s**, · 7179
33:11 shall conceive chaff, ye shall bring forth **s**: · 7179
40:24 the whirlwind shall take them away as **s**. · 7179
41: 2 to his sword, *and* as driven **s** to his bow. · 7179
47:14 Behold, they shall be as **s**; the fire shall · 7179
Jer 13:24 Therefore will I scatter them as the **s** that · 7179
Joel 2: 5 of a flame of fire that devoureth the **s**, · 7179
Ob 1:18 the house of Esau for **s**, and they shall · 7179
Na 1:10 they shall be devoured as **s** fully dry. · 7179
Mal 4: 1 yea, and all that do wickedly, shall be **s**: · 7179
1Co 3:12 silver, precious stones, wood, hay, **s**; · 2562

STUBBORN (5) [STUBBORNNESS]

Dt 21:18 If a man have a **s** and rebellious son, · 5637
21:20 This our son *is* **s** and rebellious, he will · 5637
Jdg 2:19 their own doings, nor from their **s** way. · 7186
Ps 78: 8 fathers, a **s** and rebellious generation; · 5637
Pr 7:11 (She is loud and **s**; her feet abide not in · 5637

STUBBORNNESS (2) [STUBBORN]

Dt 9:27 look not unto the **s** of this people, nor to · 7190
1Sa 15:23 and **s** *is as* iniquity and idolatry. · 6484

STUCK (2) [STICK]

1Sa 26: 7 his spear **s** in the ground *at* his bolster: · 4600
Ps 119:31 I have **s** unto thy testimonies: O LORD, · 1692
Ac 27:41 and the forepart **s** fast, · 2043

STUDIETH (2) [STUDY]

Pr 15:28 The heart of the righteous **s** to answer: · 1897
24: 2 their heart **s** destruction, and their lips · 1897

STUDS (1)

SS 1:11 We will make thee borders of gold with **s** · 5351

STUDY (3) [STUDIETH]

Ecc 12:12 and much **s** *is* a weariness of the flesh. · 3854
1Th 4:11 And that ye **s** to be quiet, and to do your · 5389
2Ti 2:15 **S** to shew thyself approved unto God, · 4704

STUFF (16)

Ge 31:37 Whereas thou hast searched all my **s**, · 3627
31:37 hast thou found of all thy household **s**? · 3627
45:20 Also regard not your **s**; for the good of all · 3627
Ex 22: 7 unto his neighbour money or **s** to keep, · 3627
36: 7 For the **s** *they had* was sufficient for all · 4399
Jos 7:11 have put *it* even amongst their own **s**. · 3627
1Sa 10:22 Behold, he hath hid himself among the **s**. · 3627
25:13 and two hundred abode by the **s**: · 3627
30:24 so *shall* his part *be* that tarrieth by the **s**: · 3627
Ne 13: 8 I cast forth all the household **s** of Tobiah · 3627
Eze 12: 3 prepare thee **s** for removing, and remove · 3627
12: 4 shalt thou bring forth thy **s** by day in their · 3627
12: 4 by day in their sight, as **s** for removing: · 3627
12: 7 I brought forth my **s** by day, as stuff for · 3627
12: 7 as **s** for captivity, and in the even I digged · 3627
Lk 17:31 the housetop, and his **s** in the house, · 4632

STUMBLE (19) [STUMBLED, STUMBLETH, STUMBLING, STUMBLINGBLOCK, STUMBLINGBLOCKS, STUMBLINGSTONE]

Pr 3:23 *in* thy way safely, and thy foot shall not **s**. · 5062
4:12 and when thou runnest, thou shalt not **s**. · 3782
4:19 darkness: they know not at what they **s**. · 3782
Isa 5:27 None *shall be* weary nor **s** amongst them; · 5062
8:15 many among them shall **s**, and fall, · 3782
28: 7 they err in vision, they **s** *in* judgment. · 6328
59:10 we **s** at noonday as *in* the night; *we are* in · 3782
63:13 in the wilderness, *that* they should not **s**? · 3782
Jer 13:16 your feet **s** upon the dark mountains, · 5062
18:15 they have **caused** them to **s** in their ways · 3782
20:11 therefore my persecutors shall **s**, · 3782
31: 9 a straight way, wherein they shall not **s**: · 3782
46: 6 they shall **s**, and fall toward the north by · 3782
50:32 the most proud shall **s** and fall, · 3782
Da 11:19 but he shall **s** and fall, and not be found. · 3782
Na 2: 5 they shall **s** in their walk; they shall make · 3782
3: 3 *their* corpses; they **s** upon their corpses: · 3782
Mal 2: 8 ye have **caused** many to **s** at the law; · 3782
1Pe 2: 8 *even to them* which **s** at the word, · 4350

STUMBLED (6) [STUMBLE]

1Sa 2: 4 and they that **s** are girt with strength. · 3782
1Ch 13: 9 his hand to hold the ark; for the oxen **s**. · 8058
Ps 27: 2 me to eat up my flesh, they **s** and fell. · 3782
Jer 46:12 for the mighty *man* hath **s** against · 3782
Ro 9:32 For they **s** at *that* stumblingstone; · 4350
11:11 then, Have they **s** that they should fall? · 4417

STUMBLETH (4) [STUMBLE]

Pr 24:17 and let not thine heart be glad when he **s**: · 3782
Jn 11: 9 he **s** not, because he seeth the light of this · 4350
11:10 he **s**, because there is no light in him. · 4350
Ro 14:21 nor *any* thing whereby thy brother **s**, · 4350

STUMBLING (3) [STUMBLE]

Isa 8:14 for a stone of **s** and for a rock of offence to · 5063
1Pe 2: 8 And a stone of **s**, and a rock of offence, · 4348
1Jn 2:10 and there is none **occasion of s** in him. · 4625

STUMBLINGBLOCK (12) [STUMBLE]

Lev 19:14 nor put a **s** before the blind, but shalt fear · 4383
Isa 57:14 take up the **s** out of the way of my people. · 4383
Eze 3:20 and I lay a **s** before him, he shall die: · 4383
7:19 because it is the **s** of their iniquity. · 4383
14: 3 the **s** of their iniquity before their face: · 4383
14: 4 the **s** of his iniquity before his face, · 4383
14: 7 the **s** of his iniquity before his face, · 4383
Ro 11: 9 and a **s**, and a recompence unto them: · 4625
14:13 no *man* put a **s** or an occasion to fall in · 4348
1Co 1:23 unto the Jews a **s**, and unto the Greeks · 4625
8: 9 yours become a **s** to them that are weak. · 4348
Rev 2:14 who taught Balac to cast a **s** before · 4625

STUMBLINGBLOCKS (2) [STUMBLE]

Jer 6:21 I will lay **s** before this people, · 4383
Zep 1: 3 of the sea, and the **s** with the wicked; · 4384

STUMBLINGSTONE (2) [STONE, STUMBLE]

Ro 9:32 For they stumbled at *that* **s**; · 3037+4348
9:33 I lay in Sion a **s** and rock of offence: · 3037+4348

STUMP (3)

1Sa 5: 4 only the **s** of Dagon was left to him. · NIH
Da 4:15 Nevertheless leave the **s** of his roots in · 6136
4:23 yet leave the **s** of the roots thereof in · 6136
4:26 whereas they commanded to leave the **s** · 6136

STUNK (1) [STINK]

Ex 7:21 river **s**, and the Egyptians could not drink · 887

STUPID See UNLEARNED

SUAH (1)

1Ch 7:36 **S**, and Harnepher, and Shual, and Beri, · 5477

SUBDUE (8) [SUBDUED, SUBDUEDST, SUBDUETH]

Ge	1:28 multiply, and replenish the earth, and s it:	3533
1Ch	17:10 Moreover I will s all thine enemies.	3665
Ps	47: 3 He shall s the people under us,	1696
Isa	45: 1 I have holden, to s nations before him;	7286
Da	7:24 from the first, and he shall s three kings.	8214
Mic	7:19 he will s our iniquities; and thou wilt cast	3533
Zec	9:15 they shall devour, and s with sling stones,	3533
Php	3:21 is able even to s all things unto himself.	5293

SUBDUED (19) [SUBDUE]

Nu	32:22 the land be s before the LORD: then	3533
	32:29 and the land shall be s before you;	3533
Dt	20:20 that maketh war with thee, until it be s.	3381
Jos	18: 1 And the land was s before them.	3533
Jdg	3:30 Moab was s that day under the hand of	3665
	4:23 So God s on that day Jabin the king of	3665
	8:28 Thus was Midian s before the children of	3665
	11:33 Thus the children of Ammon were s	3665
1Sa	7:13 the Philistines were s, and they came no	3665
2Sa	8: 1 David smote the Philistines, and s them:	3665
	8:11 had dedicated of all nations which he s;	3533
	22:40 them that rose up against me hast thou s	3766
1Ch	18: 1 s them, and took Gath and her towns out	3665
	20: 4 the children of the giant: and they were s.	3665
	22:18 the land is s before the LORD, and before	3533
Ps	18:39 thou hast s under me those that rose up	3766
	81:14 I should soon have s their enemies,	3665
1Co	15:28 And when all things shall be s unto him,	5293
Heb	11:33 Who through faith s kingdoms,	2610

SUBDUEDST (1) [SUBDUE]

Ne	9:24 thou s before them the inhabitants of	3665

SUBDUETH (3) [SUBDUE]

Ps	18:47 avengeth me, and s the people under me.	1696
	144: 2 I trust; who s my people under me.	7286
Da	2:40 s all things: and as iron that breaketh all	2827

SUBJECT (17) [SUBJECTED, SUBJECTION]

Lk	2:51 came to Nazareth, and was s unto them:	5293
	10:17 even the devils are s unto us through thy	5293
	10:20 rejoice not, that the spirits are s unto you;	5293
Ro	8: 7 for it is not s to the law of God,	5293
	8:20 For the creature was made s to vanity,	5293
	13: 1 every soul be s unto the higher powers.	5293
	13: 5 Wherefore ye must needs be s, not only	5293
1Co	14:32 And the spirits of the prophets are s to	5293
	15:28 shall the Son also himself be s unto him	5293
Eph	5:24 Therefore as the church is s unto Christ,	5293
Col	2:20 in the world, are ye s to ordinances,	1379
Tit	3: 1 Put them in mind to be s to principalities	5293
Heb	2:15 death were all their lifetime s to bondage.	1777
Jas	5:17 Elias was a man s to like passions as we	3663
1Pe	2:18 Servants, be s to your masters with all fear	5293
	3:22 and powers being made s unto him.	5293
	5: 5 all of you be s one to another,	5293

SUBJECTED (1) [SUBJECT]

Ro	8:20 by reason of him who hath s the same,	5293

SUBJECTION (14) [SUBJECT]

Ps	106:42 were brought into s under their hand.	3665
Jer	34:11 brought them into s for servants and	3533
	34:16 to return, and brought them into s, to be	3533
1Co	9:27 keep under my body, and bring it into s:	1396
2Co	9:13 your professed s unto the gospel of Christ,	5292
Gal	2: 5 To whom we gave place by s, no, not for	5292
1Ti	2:11 Let the woman learn in silence with all s.	5292
	3: 4 having his children in s with all gravity;	5292
Heb	2: 5 For unto the angels hath he not put in s	5293
	2: 8 hast put all things in s under his feet.	5293
	2: 8 For in that he put all in s under him,	5293
	12: 9 shall we not much rather be in s unto	5293
1Pe	3: 1 ye wives, be in s to your own husbands;	5293
	3: 5 being in s unto their own husbands.	5293

SUBMISSIVE See SUBJECTION

SUBMIT (12) [SUBMITTED, SUBMITTING]

Ge	16: 9 mistress, and s thyself under her hands.	6031
2Sa	22:45 Strangers shall s themselves unto me.	3584
Ps	18:44 the strangers shall s themselves unto me.	3584
	66: 3 thine enemies s themselves unto thee.	3584
	68:30 till every one s himself with pieces of	7511
1Co	16:16 That ye s yourselves unto such,	5293
Eph	5:22 s yourselves unto your own husbands,	5293
Col	3:18 s yourselves unto your own husbands,	5293
Heb	13:17 have the rule over you, and s yourselves:	5226
Jas	4: 7 S yourselves therefore to God. Resist	5293
1Pe	2:13 S yourselves to every ordinance of man	5293
	5: 5 ye younger, s yourselves unto the elder.	5293

SUBMITTED (3) [SUBMIT]

1Ch	29:24 themselves unto Solomon the king,	5414
Ps	81:15 The haters of the LORD should have s	3584
Ro	10: 3 have not s themselves unto	5293

SUBMITTING (1) [SUBMIT]

Eph	5:21 S yourselves one to another in the fear of	5293

SUBORNED (1)

Ac	6:11 Then they s men, which said, We have	5260

SUBSCRIBE (2) [SUBSCRIBED]

Isa	44: 5 another shall s with his hand unto	3789
Jer	32:44 s evidences, and seal them, and	3789

SUBSCRIBED (2) [SUBSCRIBE]

Jer	32:10 I s the evidence, and sealed it, and	3789
	32:12 in the presence of the witnesses that s	3789

SUBSTANCE (50)

Ge	7: 4 every living s that I have made will I	3351
	7:23 every living s was destroyed which was	3351
	12: 5 all their s that they had gathered,	7399
	13: 6 for their s was great, so that they could	7399
	15:14 shall they come out with great s.	7399
	34:23 Shall not their cattle and their s and	7075
	36: 6 his cattle, and all his beasts, and all his s,	7075
Dt	11: 6 and all the s that was in their possession,	3351
	33:11 his s, and accept the work of his hands:	2428
Jos	14: 4 suburbs for their cattle and for their s.	7075
1Ch	27:31 All these were the rulers of the s which	7399
	28: 1 the stewards over all the s and	7399
2Ch	21:17 carried away all the s that was found in	7399
	31: 3 portion of his s for the burnt offerings,	7399
	32:29 for God had given him s very much.	7399
	35: 7 these were of the king's s.	7399
Ezr	8:21 and for our little ones, and for all our s.	7399
	10: 8 all his s should be forfeited,	7399
Job	1: 3 His s also was seven thousand sheep,	4735
	1:10 hands, and his s is increased in the land.	4735
	5: 5 and the robber swalloweth up their s.	2428
	6:22 or, Give a reward for me of your s?	3581
	15:29 not be rich, neither shall his s continue,	2428
	20:18 according to his s shall the restitution be,	2428
	22:20 Whereas our s is not cut down,	2428
	30:22 me to ride upon it, and dissolvest my s.	8454
Ps	17:14 and leave the rest of their s to their babes.	NIH
	105:21 lord of his house, and ruler of all his s:	7075
	139:15 My s was not hid from thee, when I was	6108
	139:16 eyes did see my s, yet being unperfect;	1564
Pr	1:13 We shall find all precious s, we shall fill	1952
	3: 9 Honour the LORD with thy s,	1952
	6:31 he shall give all the s of his house.	1952
	8:21 may cause those that love me to inherit s;	3426
	10: 3 but he casteth away the s of the wicked.	1942
	12:27 but the s of a diligent man is precious.	1952
	28: 8 by usury and unjust gain increaseth his s,	1952
	29: 3 company with harlots spendeth his s.	1952
SS	8: 7 if a man would give all the s of his house	1952
Isa	6:13 tree, and as an oak, whose s is in them,	4678
	6:13 so the holy seed shall be the s thereof.	4678
Jer	15:13 Thy s and thy treasures will I give to	2428
	17: 3 I will give thy s and all thy treasures to	2428
Hos	12: 8 I am become rich, I have found me out s:	202
Ob	1:13 nor have laid hands on their s in the day	2428
Mic	4:13 their s unto the Lord of the whole earth.	2428
Lk	8: 3 which ministered unto him of their s.	5225
	15:13 and there wasted his s with riotous living.	3776
Heb	10:34 in heaven a better and an enduring s.	5223
	11: 1 Now faith is the s of things hoped for,	5287

SUBTIL (3) [SUBTILTY]

Ge	3: 1 the serpent was more s than any beast	6175
2Sa	13: 3 and Jonadab a very s man.	2450
Pr	7:10 with the attire of a harlot, and s of heart.	5341

SUBTILLY (3) [SUBTILTY]

1Sa	23:22 is told me that he dealeth very s.	6191+6191
Ps	105:25 his people, to deal s with his servants.	5230
Ac	7:19 The same dealt s with our kindred,	2686

SUBTILTY (6) [SUBTIL, SUBTILLY]

Ge	27:35 Thy brother came with s, and hath taken	4820
2Ki	10:19 Jehu did it in s, to the intent that he	6122
Pr	1: 4 To give s to the simple, to the young man	6195
Mt	26: 4 consulted that they might take Jesus by s,	1388
Ac	13:10 And said, O full of all s and all mischief,	1388
2Co	11: 3 as the serpent beguiled Eve through his s,	3834

SUBURBS (115)

Lev	25:34 the field of the s of their cities may not be	4054
Nu	35: 2 ye shall give also unto the Levites s for	4054
	35: 3 the s of them shall be for their cattle,	4054
	35: 4 the s of the cities, which ye shall give	4054
	35: 5 this shall be to them the s of the cities.	4054
	35: 7 cities: them shall ye give with their s.	4054
Jos	14: 4 save cities to dwell in, with their s for	4054
	21: 2 dwell in, with the s thereof for our cattle.	4054
	21: 3 of the LORD, these cities and their s.	4054
	21: 8 unto the Levites these cities with their s,	4054
	21:11 Judah, with the s thereof round about it.	4054
	21:13 of Aaron the priest Hebron with her s,	4054
	21:13 for the slayer; and Libnah with her s,	4054
	21:14 Jattir with her s, and Eshtemoa with her	4054
	21:14 her suburbs, and Eshtemoa with her s,	4054
	21:15 Holon with her s, and Debir with her	4054
	21:15 with her suburbs, Debir with her s,	4054
	21:16 Ain with her s, and Juttah with her	4054
	21:16 Juttah with her s, and Beth-shemesh with	4054
	21:16 suburbs, and Beth-shemesh with her s;	4054
	21:17 Gibeon with her s, Geba with her	4054
	21:17 with her suburbs, Geba with her	4054
	21:18 Anathoth with her s, and Almon with her	4054
	21:18 with her suburbs, and Almon with her s;	4054
	21:19 priests, were thirteen cities with their s.	4054
	21:21 they gave them Shechem with her s in	4054

Jos	21:21 for the slayer; and Gezer with her s,	4054
	21:22 Kibzaim with her s, and Beth-horon with	4054
	21:22 her suburbs, and Beth-horon with her s.	4054
	21:23 of the tribe of Dan, Eltekeh with her s,	4054
	21:23 with her suburbs, Gibbethon with her s,	4054
	21:24 Aijalon with her s, Gath-rimmon with her	4054
	21:24 her suburbs, Gath-rimmon with her s;	4054
	21:25 Tanach with her s, and Gath-rimmon	4054
	21:25 suburbs, and Gath-rimmon with her s:	4054
	21:26 All the cities were ten with their s for	4054
	21:27 they gave Golan in Bashan with her s,	4054
	21:27 and Beeshterah with her s; two cities.	4054
	21:28 Kishon with her s, Dabareh with her	4054
	21:28 with her suburbs, Dabareh with her s,	4054
	21:29 Jarmuth with her s, En-gannim with her	4054
	21:29 with her suburbs, En-gannim with her s;	4054
	21:30 Mishal with her s, Abdon with her	4054
	21:30 with her suburbs, Abdon with her s,	4054
	21:31 Helkath with her s, and Rehob with her	4054
	21:31 with her suburbs, and Rehob with her s;	4054
	21:32 of Naphtali, Kedesh in Galilee with her s,	4054
	21:32 Hammoth-dor with her s, and Kartan	4054
	21:32 with her suburbs, and Kartan with her s:	4054
	21:33 families were thirteen cities with their s.	4054
	21:34 Jokneam with her s, and Kartah with her	4054
	21:34 with her suburbs, and Kartah with her s,	4054
	21:35 Dimnah with her s, Nahalal with her	4054
	21:35 with her suburbs, Nahalal with her s:	4054
	21:36 Bezer with her s, and Jahazah with her	4054
	21:36 with her suburbs, and Jahazah with her s,	4054
	21:37 Kedemoth with her s, and Mephaath with	4054
	21:37 her suburbs, and Mephaath with her s:	4054
	21:38 tribe of Gad, Ramoth in Gilead with her s,	4054
	21:38 for the slayer; and Mahanaim with her s,	4054
	21:39 Heshbon with her s, Jazer with her	4054
	21:39 with her suburbs, Jazer with her s;	4054
	21:41 were forty and eight cities with their s.	4054
	21:42 These cities were every one with their s	4054
2Ki	23:11 which was in the s, and burnt the chariots	6503
1Ch	5:16 in her towns, and in all the s of Sharon,	4054
	6:55 of Judah, and the s thereof round about it.	4054
	6:57 Libnah with her s, and Jattir,	4054
	6:57 and Jattir, and Eshtemoa, with their s,	4054
	6:58 Hilen with her s, Debir with her suburbs,	4054
	6:58 Hilen with her suburbs, Debir with her s,	4054
	6:59 Ashan with her s, and Beth-shemesh with	4054
	6:59 suburbs, and Beth-shemesh with her s:	4054
	6:60 Geba with her s, and Alemeth with her	4054
	6:60 Alemeth with her s, and Anathoth with	4054
	6:60 her suburbs, and Anathoth with her s.	4054
	6:64 to the Levites these cities with their s.	4054
	6:67 Shechem in mount Ephraim with her s;	4054
	6:67 they gave also Gezer with her s,	4054
	6:68 Jokmeam with her s, and Beth-horon	4054
	6:68 her suburbs, and Beth-horon with her s,	4054
	6:69 Aijalon with her s, and Gath-rimmon	4054
	6:69 suburbs, and Gath-rimmon with her s:	4054
	6:70 Aner with her s, and Bileam with her	4054
	6:70 with her suburbs, and Bileam with her s,	4054
	6:71 Golan in Bashan with her s, and	4054
	6:71 her suburbs, and Ashtaroth with her s:	4054
	6:72 Kedesh with her s, Daberath with her	4054
	6:72 with her suburbs, Daberath with her s,	4054
	6:73 Ramoth with her s, and Anem with her	4054
	6:73 with her suburbs, and Anem with her s:	4054
	6:74 Mashal with her s, and Abdon with her	4054
	6:74 with her suburbs, and Abdon with her s,	4054
	6:75 Hukok with her s, and Rehob with her	4054
	6:75 with her suburbs, and Rehob with her s:	4054
	6:76 Kedesh in Galilee with her s, and	4054
	6:76 Hammon with her s, and Kirjathaim with	4054
	6:76 her suburbs, and Kirjathaim with her s:	4054
	6:77 Rimmon with her s, Tabor with her	4054
	6:77 with her suburbs, Tabor with her s:	4054
	6:78 Bezer in the wilderness with her s,	4054
	6:78 with her suburbs, and Jahzah with her s,	4054
	6:79 Kedemoth also with her s, and Mephaath	4054
	6:79 her suburbs, and Mephaath with her s:	4054
	6:80 Ramoth in Gilead with her s,	4054
	6:80 her suburbs, and Mahanaim with her s,	4054
	6:81 Heshbon with her s, and Jazer with her	4054
	6:81 with her suburbs, and Jazer with her s.	4054
	13: 2 Levites which are in their cities and s,	4054
2Ch	11:14 For the Levites left their s and	4054
	31:19 which were in the fields of the s of their	4054
Eze	27:28 The s shall shake at the sound of the cry	4054
	45: 2 fifty cubits round about for the s thereof.	4054
	48:15 place for the city, for dwelling, and for s:	4054
	48:17 the s of the city shall be toward the north	4054

SUBVERT (2) [SUBVERTED, SUBVERTING]

La	3:36 To s a man in his cause, the Lord	5791
Tit	1:11 must be stopped, who s whole houses,	396

SUBVERTED (1) [SUBVERT]

Tit	3:11 Knowing that he that is such is s,	1612

SUBVERTING (2) [SUBVERT]

Ac	15:24 s your souls, saying, Ye must be	384
2Ti	2:14 to no profit, but to the s of the hearers.	2692

SUCATHITES See SUCHATHITES

S

SUCCEED (1) [SUCCEEDED, SUCCEEDEST, SUCCESS]

Dt 25: 6 the firstborn which she beareth shall **s** 6965

SUCCEEDED (3) [SUCCEED]

Dt 2:12 the children of Esau **s** them, when they 3423
 2:21 and they **s** them, and dwelt in their stead: 3423
 2:22 they **s** them, and dwelt in their stead *even* 3423

SUCCEEDEST (2) [SUCCEED]

Dt 12:29 them, and dwellest in their land; 3423
 19: 1 thou **s** them, and dwellest in their cities, 3423

SUCCESS (1) [SUCCEED]

Jos 1: 8 and then thou shalt **have good s.** 7919

SUCCOTH (18)

Ge 33:17 Jacob journeyed to **S**, and built him a 5523
 33:17 the name of the place is called **S.** 5523
Ex 12:37 of Israel journeyed from Rameses to **S**, 5523
 13:20 they took their journey from **S**, 5523
Nu 33: 5 removed from Rameses, and pitched in **S**. 5523
 33: 6 they departed from **S**, and pitched in 5523
Jos 13:27 and Beth-nimrah, and Salom, and Zaphon, 5523
Jdg 8: 5 he said unto the men of **S**, Give, I pray 5523
 8: 6 the princes of **S** said, *Are* the hands of 5523
 8: 8 him as the men of **S** had answered *him*. 5523
 8:14 caught a young man of the men of **S**, 5523
 8:14 he described unto him the princes of **S**, 5523
 8:15 he came unto the men of **S**, and said, 5523
 8:16 and with them he taught the men of **S** 5523
1Ki 7:46 the clay ground between **S** and Zarthan. 5523
2Ch 4:17 in the clay ground between **S** and 5523
Ps 60: 6 and mete out the valley of **S.** 5523
 108: 7 and mete out the valley of **S.** 5523

SUCCOTH-BENOTH (1)

2Ki 17:30 the men of Babylon made **S**, and the men 5524

SUCCOUR (3) [SUCCOURED, SUCCOURER]

2Sa 8: 5 when the Syrians of Damascus came to **s** 5826
 18: 3 now *it is* better that thou **s** us out of 5826
Heb 2:18 he is able to **s** them that are tempted. 997

SUCCOURED (2) [SUCCOUR]

2Sa 21:17 Abishai the son of Zeruiah **s** him, 5826
2Co 6: 2 and in the day of salvation have I **s** thee: 997

SUCCOURER (1) [SUCCOUR]

Ro 16: 2 for she hath been a **s** of many, *4368*

SUCH (249)

Ge 4:20 he was the father of **s** as dwell in tents, NIH
 4:20 as dwell in tents, and of **s** as have cattle. NIH
 4:21 was the father of all **s** as handle the harp NIH
 27: 4 **s** as I love, and bring *it* to me, 834+3509.1
 27: 9 meat for thy father, **s** as he loveth: 834+3509.1
 27:14 savoury meat, **s** as his father loved. 834+3509.1
 27:46 as these *which are* of the daughters of 3509.1
 30:32 the goats: and of **s** shall be my hire. NIH
 41:19 as I never saw in all the land of Egypt 2007
 41:38 Can we find **s** a one as this *is*, a man in NIH
 44:15 wot ye not that **s** a man as I can certainly 834
Ex 9:18 **s** as hath not been in Egypt since 834
 9:24 **s** as there was none like it in all the land 834
 10:14 them there were no **s** locusts as they, 3651
 10:14 as they, neither after them shall be **s**. 3651
 11: 6 **s** as there was none like it, nor shall be 834
 12:36 that they lent unto them **s** things as they NIH
 18:21 **s** as fear God, men of truth, NIH
 18:21 **s** over them, *to be* rulers of thousands, NIH
 34:10 **s** as have not been done in all the earth, NIH
Lev 10:19 and **s** things have befallen me: 3509.1
 11:34 *that* on which **s** water cometh shall be NIH
 11:34 drink that may be drunk in every **s** vessel NIH
 14:22 two young pigeons, **s** as he is able to get; 834
 14:30 or of the young pigeons, **s** as he can get; 4480
 14:31 *Even* **s** as he is able to get, the one *for a* 834
 20: 6 soul that turneth after **s** as have familiar NIH
 22: 6 The soul which hath touched *any* **s** shall 2050.2
 27: 9 all that *any man* giveth of **s** unto NIH
Nu 8:16 instead of **s** as open every womb, NIH
Dt 4:32 whether there hath been *any* **s** thing as NIH
 5:29 O that there were **s** a heart in them, 2088
 13:11 do no more any **s** wickedness as this is 1697
 13:14 **s** abomination is wrought among you; 2063
 16: 9 begin to number the seven weeks from **s** NIH
 17: 4 *that* **s** abomination is wrought in Israel: 2088
 19:20 henceforth commit no more any **s** evil 2088
 25:16 For all that do **s** *things, and* all that do 428
Jdg 3: 2 at the least **s** as before knew nothing 834
 13:23 *at this* time have told us **s** things as these. NIH
 18:23 that thou comest with **s** a company? NIH
 19:30 was no **s** *deed* done 2063+1886.1+3509.1
Ru 4: 1 **s** a one, turn aside, sit down here. 492+6423
1Sa 2:23 he said unto them, Why do ye **s** things? 834
 4: 7 not been **s** *a* thing heretofore. 2088+3509.1
 21: 2 *my* servants to **such and such** 492+6423
 21: 2 *my* servants to **such and s** 492+6423
 25:17 he *is* **s** a son of Belial, that *a man* cannot NIH
2Sa 9: 8 thou shouldest look upon **s** a dead dog NIH
 12: 8 moreover have given unto thee **s** 2007+3509.1
 12: 8 unto thee such and **s things.** 2007+3509.1
 13:12 for no **s** thing ought to be done in Israel: 3651
 13:18 for with **s** robes were the king's daughters 3651

2Sa 14:13 hast thou thought **s** a thing against 3509.1
 16: 2 that **s** as be faint in the wilderness may 1886.1
 19:36 king recompense *it* me with **s** a reward? 2088
1Ki 10:10 came no more **s** abundance of spices 1931
 10:12 there came no **s** almug trees, nor were 3651
2Ki 6: 8 In **s** and such a place *shall be* my camp. 6423
 6: 8 In such and **s** a place *shall be* my camp. 492
 6: 9 Beware that thou pass not **s** a place; 2088
 7:19 windows in heaven, might **s** a thing be? 3509.1
 19:29 year **s** things **as grow of themselves,** 5599
 21:12 I *am* bringing **s** evil upon Jerusalem and NIH
 23:22 there was not holden **s** a passover 3509.1
 25:15 and **s** as *were* of gold, in gold, 834
1Ch 12:33 Of Zebulun, **s** as went forth to battle, NIH
 12:36 **s** as went forth to battle, expert in war, NIH
 29:25 bestowed upon him **s** royal majesty as had NIH
2Ch 1:12 **s** as none of the kings have had that *have* 3651
 4: 6 **s** things as they offered for the burnt NIH
 9: 9 neither was there any **s** spice as the queen 1931
 9:11 were none **s** seen before in the land 3509.1
 11:16 after them out of all the tribes of Israel **s** 1886.1
 23:13 of musick, and **s** as taught to **sing** praise. NIH
 24:12 Jehoiada gave it to **s** as did the work of NIH
 24:12 also **s** as wrought iron and brass to mend NIH
 30: 5 they had not done *it* of a long *time in* **s** NIH
 35:18 neither did all the kings of Israel keep **s** 3509.1
Ezr 4:10 *are* on this side the river, and **at a time.** 3706
 4:11 *on this* side the river, and **at s a time.** 3706
 4:17 beyond the river: Peace, and **at s a time.** 3706
 6:21 all **s** as had separated themselves unto 1886.1
 7:12 of heaven, perfect *peace*, and **at s a time.** 3706
 7:25 river, all **s** as know the laws of thy God; NIH
 7:27 hath put **s** *a* thing as this in the king's NIH
 8:31 and of **s** as lay in wait by the way. NIH
 9:13 and hast given us **s** deliverance as this; NIH
 10: 3 **s** as are born of them, according to 1886.1
Ne 6: 8 There are no **s** things *done* as thou 428+3509.1
 6:11 I said, Should **s** a man **as** I flee? and who 3644
Est 2: 9 with **s things as belonged** to her, and 4490
 4:11 except **s** to whom the king shall hold 834+4480
 4:14 come to the kingdom for **s** a time as this? NIH
 9: 2 to lay hand on **s** as sought their hurt: NIH
 9:27 all **s** as joined themselves unto them, 1886.1
Job 12: 3 yea, who knoweth not **s** things **as** these? 3644
 14: 3 dost thou open thine eyes upon **s** **a one,** 2088
 15:13 and lettest **s** words go out of thy mouth? NIH
 16: 2 I have heard many **s** things: miserable 3509.1
 18:21 Surely **s** *are* the dwellings of the wicked, 428
 23:14 and many **s** things are with him. 2007+3509.1
Ps 25:10 truth unto **s** as keep his covenant and NIH
 27:12 against me, and **s** as breathe out cruelty. NIH
 34:18 and saveth **s** as be of a contrite spirit. NIH
 37:14 to slay **s** as be of upright conversation. NIH
 37:22 For **s** as be blessed of him shall inherit NIH
 40: 4 not the proud, nor **s** as turn aside to lies. NIH
 40:16 let **s** as love thy salvation say continually, NIH
 50:21 thoughtest that I was altogether **s** *a one* NIH
 55:20 He hath put forth his hands against **s** as be NIH
 68:21 the hairy scalp of **s** a one as goeth on still NIH
 70: 4 let **s** as love thy salvation say continually, NIH
 73: 1 to Israel, *even* to **s** as are of a clean heart. NIH
 103:18 To **s** as keep his covenant, and to those NIH
 107:10 **S** as sit in darkness and in the shadow of NIH
 125: 5 As for **s** as turn aside *unto* their crooked 1886.1
 139: 6 **S** knowledge *is* too wonderful for me; it is NIH
 144:15 Happy *is that* people, that is **in s a case:** 3602
Pr 11:20 **s** as are upright in *their* way *are* his NIH
 28: 4 but **s** as keep the law contend with them. NIH
 30:20 **S** *is* the way of an adulterous woman; 3651
 31: 8 of all **s** as *are* appointed to destruction. NIH
Ecc 4: 1 the tears of **s** as were oppressed, 1886.1
Isa 9: 1 the dimness *shall* not *be* **s** as 834
 10:20 **s** as are **escaped** of the house of Jacob, 6413
 20: 6 in that day, Behold, **s** *is* our expectation, 3541
 37:30 shall eat *this* year **s as groweth of itself,** 5599
 58: 5 Is it **s** a fast that I have chosen? 2088+3509.1
 66: 8 Who hath heard **s** a thing? who 2088+3509.1
 66: 8 such *a thing?* who hath **s** things? 428+3509.1
Jer 2:10 and see if there be **s** a thing. 2088+3509.1
 5: 9 soul be avenged on **s** a nation **as** this? 3509.1
 5:29 shall not my soul be avenged on **s** a nation 834
 9: 9 soul be avenged on **s** a nation **as** this? 3509.1
 15: 2 **S as** *are* for death, to death; and such as 834
 15: 2 and **s as** *are* for the sword, to the sword; 834
 15: 2 **s as** *are* for the famine, to the famine; 834
 15: 2 **s as** *are* for the captivity, to the captivity. 834
 18:13 who hath heard **s** things: the virgin 428+3509.1
 21: 7 **s** as are left in this city from 1886.1
 38: 4 in speaking **s** words unto them: 3509.1
 43:11 *and deliver* **s** *as are* for death to death; 834
 43:11 **s** *as are* for captivity to captivity; and such 834
 43:11 and **s** *as are* for the sword to the sword. 834
 44: 7 for none shall return but **s** as shall escape. 518
Eze 17:15 shall he escape that doeth **s** *things?* or 428
 18:14 and considereth, and doeth not **s like,** 3509.1
Da 1: 4 **s** as *had* ability in them to stand in the 834
 2:10 asked **s** things at any magician; 1836+3509.4
 10:15 when he had spoken **s** words unto me, 3509.1
 11:32 **s** as do wickedly against the covenant shall 834
 12: 1 **s** as never was since there was a nation 834
Am 5:16 **s** as are skilful of lamentation to wailing. NIH
Mic 5:15 the heathen, **s** as they have not heard. 834
Zep 1: 8 all **s** as are clothed with strange apparel. 1886.1
Mt 9: 8 which had given **s** power unto men. 5108
 18: 5 whoso shall receive one **s** little child in 5108

Mt 19:14 me: for of **s** is the kingdom of heaven. 5108
 24:21 **s** as was not since the beginning of 3634
 24:44 in **s** an hour as you think not the Son of 3739
 26:18 Go into the city to **s a man**, and say unto 1170
Mk 4:18 sown among thorns; **s** as hear the word, 3588
 4:20 **s** as hear the word, and receive *it*, and 3748
 4:33 And with many **s** parables spake he 5108
 6: 2 that even **s** mighty works are wrought by 5108
 7: 8 cups: and many other **s** like *things* ye do. 5108
 7:13 and many **s** like *things* do ye. 5108
 9:37 Whosoever shall receive one of **s** children 5108
 10:14 them not: for of **s** is the kingdom of God. 5108
 13: 7 for **s** *things* must needs be; but the end NIG
 13:19 **s** as was not from the beginning of 5108
Lk 9: 9 of whom I hear **s** *things?* And he desired 5108
 10: 7 and drinking **s** *things* as they **give:** 3588+3844
 10: 8 eat **s** *things* as are set before you: 3588
 11:41 But rather give alms of **s** *things* as you 3588
 13: 2 because they suffered **s** *things?* 5108
 18:16 them not: for of **s** is the kingdom of God. 5108
Jn 4:23 for the Father seeketh **s** to worship him. 5108
 7:32 murmured **s** *things* concerning him; 3778
 8: 5 commanded us, that **s** should be stoned: 5108
 9:16 How can a man *that is* a sinner do **s** 5108
Ac 2:47 the Lord added to the church daily **s** as 3588
 3: 6 have I none; but **s** as I have give I thee: 3739
 15:24 to whom we gave no **s** commandment: NIG
 16:24 Who, having received **s** a charge, 5108
 18:15 look ye to it; for I will be no judge of **s** 3778
 21:25 concluded that they observe no **s** thing, 5108
 22:22 said, Away with **s** a fellow from the earth: 5108
 25:18 none accusation of **s** things as I supposed: NIG
 25:20 I doubted of **s** *manner* of questions, 3778
 26:29 both almost, and altogether **s** as 3697+5108
 28:10 they laded *us* with **s** things as were 3588
Ro 1:32 they which commit **s** things are worthy 5108
 2: 2 against them which commit **s** *things*. 5108
 2: 3 that judgest them which do **s** things, and 5108
 16:18 *they that are* **s** serve not our Lord Jesus 5108
1Co 5: 1 and **s** fornication as is not so much as 5108
 5: 5 To deliver **s a one** unto Satan for 5108
 5:11 extortioner; with **s a one** no not to eat. 5108
 6:11 And **s** were some of you: but ye are 3778
 7:15 a sister is not under bondage in **s** cases: 5108
 7:28 Nevertheless **s** shall have trouble in 5108
 10:13 taken you but **s** as is common to man: NIG
 11:16 have no **s** custom, neither the churches 5108
 15:48 the earthy, **s** *are they* also *that are* earthy: 5108
 15:48 **s** *are they* also *that are* heavenly. 5108
 16:16 That ye submit yourselves unto **s**, 5108
 16:18 therefore acknowledge ye *them that are* **s**. 5108
2Co 2: 6 Sufficient to **s** a man *is* this punishment, 5108
 2: 7 comfort *him*, lest perhaps **s a one** should 5108
 3: 4 And **s** trust have we through Christ to 5108
 3:12 Seeing then that we have **s** hope, we use 5108
 10:11 Let **s a one** think this, that, such as we 5108
 10:11 as we are in word by letters when we 3634
 10:11 **s** *will we be* also in deed when we are 5108
 11:13 For **s** are false apostles, deceitful workers, 5108
 12: 2 **s** a one caught up to the third heaven. 5108
 12: 3 I knew a man, (whether in the body, 5108
 12: 5 Of **s a one** will I glory: yet of myself I will 5108
 12:20 I shall not find you **s** as I would, and *that* 3634
 12:20 I shall be found unto you **s** as ye would 3634
Gal 5:21 drunkenness, revellings, and **s** like: 3778
 5:21 they which do **s** *things* shall not inherit 5108
 5:23 against **s** there is no law. 5108
 6: 1 restore **s a one** in the spirit of meekness; 5108
Eph 5:27 or any **s** *thing;* but that it should be holy 5108
Php 2:29 all gladness; and hold **s** in reputation: 5108
1Th 4: 6 that the Lord is the avenger of all **s**, 3778
2Th 3:12 Now *them that are* **s** we command and 5108
1Ti 6: 5 is godliness: from **s** withdraw thyself. 5108
2Ti 3: 5 the power thereof: from **s** turn away. 3778
Tit 3:11 Knowing that he *that is* **s** is subverted, 5108
Phm 1: 9 *thee*, being **s a one** as Paul the aged, 5108
Heb 5:12 and are become **s** as have need of milk, NIG
 7:26 a high priest became us, *who is* holy, 5108
 8: 1 We have a high priest, who is set on 5108
 11:14 For they that say **s** things declare plainly 5108
 12: 3 For consider him that endured **s** 5108
 13: 5 and *be* content with **s** *things* as ye have: 3588
 13:16 for with **s** sacrifices God is well pleased. 5108
Jas 4:13 or to morrow we will go into **s** a city, 3592
 4:16 in your boastings: all **s** rejoicing is evil. 5108
2Pe 1:17 when there came **s** a voice to him from 5107
 3:14 that ye look for **s** *things*, be diligent 3778
3Jn 1: 8 We therefore ought to receive **s**, that we 5108
Rev 5:13 and **s** as are in the sea, and all that are in 3739
 16:18 **s** as was not since men were upon the 3634
 20: 6 on **s** the second death hath no power, 3778

SUCHATHITES (1)

1Ch 2:55 the Tirathites, the Shimeathites, *and* **S**. 7756

SUCK (19) [SUCKED, SUCKING, SUCKLING, SUCKLINGS]

Ge 21: 7 that Sarah should have **given** children **s?** 3243
Dt 32:13 he made him to **s** honey out of the rock, 3243
 33:19 for they shall **s** *of* the abundance of 3243
1Sa 1:23 **gave** her son **s** until she weaned him. 3243
1Ki 3:21 I rose in the morning to **give** my child **s**, 3243
Job 3:12 or why the breasts that I should **s?** 3243
 20:16 He shall **s** the poison of asps: the viper's 3243
 39:30 Her young ones also **s up** blood: and 5966

Isa	60:16 Thou shalt also **s** the milk of the Gentiles,	3243
	60:16 Gentiles, and shalt **s** the breast of kings:	3243
	66:11 That ye may **s**, and be satisfied with	3243
	66:12 ye **s**, ye shall be borne upon *her* sides,	3243
La	4: 3 breast, they **give s** to their young ones:	3243
Eze	23:34 Thou shalt even drink it and **s** *it out*,	4680
Joel	2:16 children, and **those that s** the breasts:	3243
Mt	24:19 and to them that **give s** in those days.	2337
Mk	13:17 and to them that **give s** in those days,	2337
Lk	21:23 and to them that **give s**, in those days,	2337
	23:29 and the paps which never **gave s**.	2337

SUCKED (2) [SUCK]

SS	8: 1 brother, that **s** the breasts of my mother!	3243
Lk	11:27 thee, and the paps which thou hast **s**.	2337

SUCKING (5) [SUCK]

Nu	11:12 as a nursing father beareth the **s child**,	3243
1Sa	7: 9 Samuel took a **s** lamb, and offered it *for* a	2461
Isa	11: 8 **s child** shall play on the hole of the asp,	3243
	49:15 Can a woman forget her **s child**, that *she*	5764
La	4: 4 The tongue of the **s child** cleaveth to	3243

SUCKLING (3) [SUCK]

Dt	32:25 the **s** *also* with the man of gray hairs.	3243
1Sa	15: 3 infant and **s**, ox and sheep, camel and ass.	3243
Jer	44: 7 from you man and woman, child and **s**,	3243

SUCKLINGS (4) [SUCK]

1Sa	22:19 children and **s**, and oxen, and asses,	3243
Ps	8: 2 **s** hast thou ordained strength because	3243
La	2:11 and the **s** swoon in the streets of the city.	3243
Mt	21:16 of babes and **s** thou hast perfected praise?	2337

SUDDEN (3) [SUDDENLY]

Job	22:10 about thee, and **s** fear troubleth thee;	6597
Pr	3:25 be not afraid of **s** fear, neither of	6597
1Th	5: 3 then **s** destruction cometh upon them,	160

SUDDENLY (41) [SUDDEN]

Nu	6: 9 if any man die **very s** by 6597+6621+871.1	
	12: 4 the LORD spake **s** unto Moses,	6597
	35:22 if he thrust him **s** without enmity, 6621+871.1	
Dt	7: 4 kindled against you, and destroy thee **s**.	4118
Jos	10: 9 Joshua therefore came unto them **s**,	6597
	11: 7 against them by the waters of Merom **s**,	6597
2Sa	15:14 lest he overtake us **s**, and bring evil upon	4116
2Ch	29:36 people: for the thing was done **s**. 6597+871.1	
Job	5: 3 taking root: but **s** I cursed his habitation.	6597
	9:23 If the scourge slay **s**, he will laugh at	6597
Ps	6:10 let them return and be ashamed **s**.	7281
	64: 4 **s** do they shoot at him, and fear not.	6597
	64: 7 *with* an arrow; **s** shall they be wounded.	6597
Pr	6:15 Therefore shall his calamity come **s**;	6597
	6:15 **s** shall he be broken without remedy.	6621
	24:22 For their calamity shall rise **s**;	6597
	29: 1 shall **s** be destroyed, and that without	6621
Ecc	9:12 an evil time, when it falleth **s** upon them.	6597
Isa	29: 5 away: yea, it shall be at an instant **s**.	6597
	30:13 whose breaking cometh **s** at an instant.	6597
	47:11 desolation shall come upon thee **s**,	6597
	48: 3 I did *them* **s**, and they came to pass.	6597
Jer	4:20 **s** are my tents spoiled, *and* my curtains in	6597
	6:26 for the spoiler shall **s** come upon us.	6597
	15: 8 I have caused *him* to fall upon it **s**,	6597
	18:22 thou shalt bring a troop **s** upon them:	6597
	49:19 I will make him run away from her:	7280
	50:44 I will make them **s** run away from her:	7280
	51: 8 Babylon is **s** fallen and destroyed: howl	6597
Hab	2: 7 Shall they not rise up **s** that *shall* bite	6621
Mal	3: 1 whom ye seek, shall **s** come to his temple,	6597
Mk	9: 8 s, when they had looked round about,	1819
	13:36 Lest coming **s** he find you sleeping.	1810
Lk	2:13 s there was with the angel a multitude	1810
	9:39 a spirit taketh him, and he **s** crieth out;	1810
Ac	2: 2 s there came a sound from heaven as of	869
	9: 3 s there shined round about him a light	1810
	16:26 And **s** there was a great earthquake,	869
	22: 6 s there shone from heaven a great light	1810
	28: 6 have swollen, or fallen down dead **s**:	869
1Ti	5:22 Lay hands **s** on no *man*, neither be	5030

SUE (1)

Mt	5:40 And if any man will **s** thee **at the law**,	2919

SUFFER (96) [LONGSUFFERING, SUFFERED, SUFFEREST, SUFFERETH, SUFFERING, SUFFERINGS]

Ex	12:23 will not **s** the destroyer to come in unto	5414
	22:18 Thou shalt not **s** a witch **to live**.	2421
Lev	2:13 shalt thou **s** the salt of the covenant of thy God **to be lacking**	7673
	19:17 thy neighbour, and not **s** sin upon him.	5375
	22:16 s them **to bear** the iniquity of trespass,	5375
Nu	21:23 Sihon would not **s** Israel to pass through	5414
Jos	10:19 **s** them not to enter into their cities:	5414
Jdg	1:34 they would not **s** them to come down to	5414
	15: 1 But her father would not **s** him to go in.	3240
	16:26 **S** me that I may feel the pillars	3240
2Sa	14:11 that thou wouldest not **s** the revengers	4480
1Ki	15:17 *he* might not **s** *any* to go out or come in	5414
Est	3: 8 it is not for the king's profit to **s** them.	5414
Job	9:18 He will not **s** me to take my breath,	5414
	21: 3 **S** me that I may speak; and after that I	5375
	24:11 *and* tread *their* winepresses, and **s thirst**.	6770
	36: 2 **S** me a little, and I will shew thee that *I*	3803

Ps	9:13 consider my trouble *which I* **s** of them,	NIH
	16:10 neither wilt thou **s** thine Holy One to see	5414
	34:10 The young lions do lack, and **s hunger**:	7456
	55:22 shall never **s** the righteous to be moved.	5414
	88:15 ready to die from *my* youth *up*: while I **s**	5375
	89:33 from him, nor **s** my faithfulness to fail.	8266
	101: 5 high look and a proud heart will not I **s**.	3201
	121: 3 He will not **s** thy foot to be moved: he	5414
Pr	10: 3 not **s** the soul of the righteous to famish:	7456
	19:15 sleep; and an idle soul shall **s hunger**.	7456
	19:19 *A man* of great wrath *shall* **s** punishment:	5375
Ecc	5: 6 **S** not thy mouth to cause thy flesh to sin;	5414
	5:12 the abundance of the rich will not **s** him	3240
Eze	44:20 heads, nor **s** *their* locks **to grow long**;	7971
Mt	3:15 said unto him, **S** it to be so now:	863
	8:21 Lord, **s** me first to go and bury my father.	2010
	8:31 **s** us to go away into the herd of swine.	2010
	16:21 and **s** many *things* of the elders and	3958
	17:12 Likewise shall also the Son of man **s** of	3958
	17:17 how long shall I **s** you? bring him hither to	430
	19:14 **S** little children, and forbid them not,	863
	23:13 **s** ye them that are entering to go in.	863
Mk	7:12 And ye **s** him no more to do ought for his	863
	8:31 that the Son of man must **s** many *things*,	3958
	9:12 that he must **s** many *things*, and be set at	3958
	9:19 how long shall I **s** you? bring him unto me.	430
	10:14 **S** the little children to come unto me,	863
	11:16 would not **s** that any *man* should carry	863
Lk	8:32 they besought him that he would **s** them	2010
	9:22 The Son of man must **s** many *things*, and	3958
	9:41 how long shall I be with you, and **s** you?	430
	9:59 Lord, **s** me first to go and bury my father.	2010
	17:25 But first must he **s** many *things*, and	3958
	18:16 **S** little children to come unto me,	863
	22:15 to eat this passover with you before I **s**:	3958
	22:51 Jesus answered and said, **S** ye thus far.	1439
	24:46 thus it behoved Christ to **s**, and to rise	3958
Ac	2:27 neither wilt thou **s** thine Holy One to see	1325
	3:18 that Christ should **s**, he hath so fulfilled.	3958
	5:41 counted worthy to **s shame** for his name.	818
	7:24 seeing one of *them* **s** wrong, he defended	91
	9:16 *things* he must **s** for my name's sake.	3958
	13:35 not **s** thine Holy One to see corruption.	1325
	21:39 **s** me to speak unto the people.	2010
	26:23 That Christ should **s**, *and* that he *should*	3805
Ro	8:17 be that we **s with** *him*, that we may be	4841
1Co	3:15 work shall be burnt, he shall **s loss**:	2210
	4:12 we bless; being persecuted, we **s** *it*:	430
	6: 7 why do ye not rather **s** *yourselves* to be	NIG
	9:12 all *things*, lest we should hinder	4722
	10:13 who will not **s** you to be tempted above	1439
	12:26 And whether one member **s**,	3958
	12:26 all the members **with** *it*; or one member	4841
2Co	1: 6 of the same sufferings which we also **s**:	3958
	11:19 For ye **s** fools gladly, seeing ye *yourselves*	430
	11:20 For ye **s**, if a man bring you into bondage,	430
Gal	5:11 why do I yet **s persecution**?	1377
	6:12 only lest they should **s persecution** for	1377
Php	1:29 believe on him, but also to **s** for his sake;	3958
	4:12 be hungry, both to abound and to **s need**.	5302
1Th	3: 4 you before that we should **s tribulation**;	2346
2Th	1: 5 the kingdom of God, for which ye also **s**:	3958
1Ti	2:12 I **s** not a woman to teach, nor to usurp	2010
	4:10 therefore we both labour and **s reproach**,	3679
2Ti	1:12 For the which cause I also **s** these *things*:	3958
	2: 9 Wherein I **s trouble**, as an evil doer,	2553
	2:12 If we **s**, we shall also reign with *him*:	5278
	3:12 godly in Christ Jesus shall **s persecution**.	1377
Heb	11:25 Choosing rather to **s affliction** with	4778
	13: 3 with *them*; *and* them which **s adversity**,	2558
	13:22 brethren, **s** the word of exhortation:	430
1Pe	2:20 do well, and **s** *for it*, ye take it patiently,	3958
	3:14 But and if ye **s** for righteousness' sake,	3958
	3:17 ye **s** for well doing, than for evil doing.	3958
	4:15 But let none of you **s** as a murderer, or *as*	NIG
	4:16 Yet if *any man* **s** as a Christian, let him	3958
	4:19 Wherefore let them that **s** according to	3958
Rev	2:10 none *of those things* which thou shalt **s**:	3958
	11: 9 shall not **s** their dead bodies to be put in	863

SUFFERED (50) [SUFFER]

Ge	20: 6 therefore **s** I thee not to touch her.	5414
	31: 7 ten times; but God **s** him not to hurt me.	5414
	31:28 hast not **s** me to kiss my sons and my	5203
Dt	8: 3 **s** thee **to hunger**, and fed thee with	7456
	18:14 the LORD thy God hath not **s** thee so	5414
Jdg	3:28 Moab, and **s** not a man to pass over.	5414
1Sa	24: 7 and **s** them not to rise against Saul.	5414
2Sa	21:10 s neither the birds of the air to rest on	5414
1Ch	16:21 He **s** no man to do them wrong: yea,	3240
Job	31:30 (Neither have I **s** my mouth to sin by	5414
Ps	105:14 He **s** no man to do them wrong:	3240
Jer	15:15 know that for thy sake I have **s** rebuke.	5375
Mt	3:15 to fulfil all righteousness. Then he **s** him.	863
	19: 8 the hardness of your hearts **s** you to put	2010
	24:43 not have **s** his house to be broken up.	1439
	27:19 I have **s** many *things* this day in a dream	3958
Mk	1:34 and **s** not the devils to speak, because	863
	5:19 Jesus him not, but saith unto him,	863
	5:26 had **s** many *things* of many physicians,	3958
	5:37 he **s** no *man* to follow him, save Peter,	863
	10: 4 Moses to write a bill of divorcement,	2010
Lk	4:41 he rebuking *them* **s** them not to speak.	1439
	8:32 them to enter into them. And he **s** them.	2010
	8:51 house, he **s** no *man* to go in, save Peter,	863

Lk	12:39 not have **s** his house to be broken through.	863
	13: 2 the Galileans, because they **s** such *things*?	3958
	24:26 Ought not Christ to have **s** these *things*,	3958
Ac	13:18 he **s** their **manners** in the wilderness.	5159
	14:16 Who in times past **s** all nations to walk in	1439
	16: 7 into Bithynia: but the Spirit **s** them not.	1439
	17: 3 that Christ must needs have **s**,	3958
	19:30 unto the people, the disciples **s** him not.	1439
	28:16 Paul was **s** to dwell by himself with a	2010
2Co	7:12 nor for his cause that **s** wrong, but that	91
	11: 1 thrice I **s shipwrack**, a night and a day I	3489
Gal	3: 4 Have ye **s** so many *things* in vain? if *it be*	3958
Php	3: 8 for whom I have **s** the loss of all *things*,	2210
1Th	2: 2 But even after that we had **s** before,	4310
	2:14 for ye also have **s** like *things* of your own	3958
Heb	2:18 in that he himself hath **s** being tempted,	3958
	5: 8 he obedience by *the things* which he **s**;	3958
	7:23 they were **not s** to continue by reason of	2967
	9:26 must he often have **s** since the foundation	3958
	13:12 with his own blood, **s** without the gate.	3958
1Pe	2:21 because Christ also **s** for us, leaving us an	3958
	2:23 when he **s**, he threatened not;	3958
	3:18 Christ also hath **s** once for sins, the just	3958
	4: 1 then as Christ hath **s** for us in the flesh,	3958
	4: 1 for he that hath **s** in the flesh hath ceased	3958
	5:10 after that ye have **s** a while, make you	3958

SUFFEREST (1) [SUFFER]

Rev	2:20 because thou **s** *that* woman Jezebel,	1439

SUFFERETH (5) [SUFFER]

Ps	66: 9 in life, and **s** not our feet to be moved.	5414
	107:38 and **s** not their cattle **to decrease**.	4591
Mt	11:12 now the kingdom of heaven **s** violence,	971
Ac	28: 4 the sea, yet Vengeance **s** not to live.	1439
1Co	13: 4 Charity **s long**, *and* is kind; charity	3114

SUFFERING (5) [SUFFER]

Ac	27: 7 the wind not **s** us, we sailed under Crete,	4330
Heb	2: 9 for the **s** of death, crowned with glory	3804
Jas	5:10 for an example of **s affliction**,	2552
1Pe	2:19 toward God endure grief, **s** wrongfully.	3958
Jude	1: 7 example, **s** the vengeance of eternal fire.	5254

SUFFERINGS (10) [SUFFER]

Ro	8:18 I reckon that the **s** of *this* present time	3804
2Co	1: 5 For as the **s** of Christ abound in us,	3804
	1: 6 of the same **s** which we also suffer:	3804
	1: 7 that as you are partakers of the **s**,	3804
Php	3:10 resurrection, and the fellowship of his **s**,	3804
Col	1:24 Who now rejoice in my **s** for you,	3804
Heb	2:10 of their salvation perfect through **s**.	3804
1Pe	1:11 it testified beforehand the **s** of Christ,	3804
	4:13 inasmuch as ye are partakers of Christ's **s**;	3804
	5: 1 and a witness of the **s** of Christ, and also	3804

SUFFICE (7) [SUFFICED, SUFFICETH, SUFFICIENCY, SUFFICIENT, SUFFICIENTLY]

Nu	11:22 the herds be slain for them, to **s** them?	4672
	11:22 be gathered together for them, to **s** them?	4672
Dt	3:26 the LORD said unto me, Let it **s** thee;	7227
1Ki	20:10 if the dust of Samaria shall **s** for handfuls	5606
Eze	44: 6 let it **s** you of all your abominations,	7227
	45: 9 Let it **s** you, O princes of Israel:	7227
1Pe	4: 3 the time past of *our* life may **s** us to have	713

SUFFICED (2) [SUFFICE]

Jdg	21:14 and yet so they **s** them not.	4672
Ru	2:14 and she did eat, and was **s**, and left.	7646
	2:18 her that she had reserved after she was **s**.	7648

SUFFICETH (1) [SUFFICE]

Jn	14: 8 Lord, shew us the Father, and it **s** us.	714

SUFFICIENCY (3) [SUFFICE]

Job	20:22 In the fulness of his **s** he shall be in straits:	5607
2Co	3: 5 *thing* as of ourselves; but our **s** *is* of God;	2426
	9: 8 always having all **s** in all *things*, may	841

SUFFICIENT (13) [SUFFICE]

Ex	36: 7 the stuff *they had* was **s** for all the work	1767
Dt	15: 8 shalt surely lend him **s for** his need,	1767
	33: 7 let his hands *be* **s** for him; and be thou a	7227
Pr	25:16 eat **so much as is s** for thee, lest thou be	1767
Isa	40:16 Lebanon *is* not **s** to burn, nor the beasts	1767
	40:16 beasts thereof **s** *for* a burnt offering.	1767
Mt	6:34 of itself. **S** unto the day *is* the evil thereof.	713
Lk	14:28 the cost, whether he have **s** to finish it?	3588
Jn	6: 7 hundred pennyworth of bread is not **s**	714
2Co	2: 6 **S** to such *a man is* this punishment,	2425
	2:16 unto life. And who *is* **s** for these *things*?	2425
	3: 5 Not that we are **s** of ourselves to think	2425
	12: 9 he said unto me, My grace is **s** for thee:	714

SUFFICIENTLY (2) [SUFFICE]

2Ch	30: 3 had not sanctified themselves **s**,	4078+3807.1
Isa	23:18 eat **s**, and for durable clothing.	7654+3807.1

SUIT (3) [SUITS]

Jdg	17:10 and a **s** of apparel, and thy victuals.	6187
2Sa	15: 4 that every man which hath *any* **s** or	7379
Job	11:19 yea, shall **make s** unto thee.	2470

SUITS (1) [SUIT]

Isa	3:22 The **changeable s** of apparel,	4254

SUKKIIMS (1)

2Ch 12: 3 the Lubims, the **S**, and the Ethiopians. 5525

SUKKITES See SUKKIIMS

SULPHUR See BRIMSTONE

SUM (21)

Ex 21:30 If there be laid on him a **s of money**, 3724
 30:12 When thou takest the **s** of the children of 7218
 38:21 This is the **s** of the tabernacle, even of 6485
Nu 1: 2 Take ye the **s** of all the congregation of 7218
 1:49 neither take the **s** of them among 7218
 4: 2 Take the **s** of the sons of Kohath from 7218
 4:22 Take also the **s** of the sons of Gershon, 7218
 26: 2 Take the **s** of all the congregation of 7218
 26: 4 Take **the s of the people**, from twenty NIH
 31:26 Take the **s** of the prey that was taken, 7218
 31:49 Thy servants have taken the **s** of the men 7218
2Sa 24: 9 Joab gave **up** the **s** of the number of 4557
2Ki 4: 7 that he may **s** the silver which is brought 8552
1Ch 21: 5 Joab gave the **s** of the number of the 4557
Est 4: 7 of the **s** of the money that Haman had 6575
Ps 139:17 O God: how great is the **s** of them! 7218
Eze 28:12 Thou sealest up the **s**, full of wisdom, 8508
Da 7: 1 the dream, and told the **s** of the matters. 7217
Ac 7:16 **s** of money of the sons of Emmor the 5092
 22:28 With a great **s** obtained I this freedom. 2774
Heb 8: 1 which we have spoken this is the **s**: 2774

SUMMER (27)

Ge 8:22 **s** and winter, and day and night shall not 7019
Jdg 3:20 he was sitting in a **s** parlour, which he 4747
 3:24 Surely he covereth his feet in his **s** 4747
2Sa 16: 1 hundred of **s fruits**, and a bottle of wine. 7019
 16: 2 and **s fruit** for the young men to eat; 7019
Ps 32: 4 moisture is turned into the drought of **s**. 7019
 74:17 the earth: thou hast made **s** and winter. 7019
Pr 6: 8 Provideth her meat in the **s**, 7019
 10: 5 He that gathereth in **s** is a wise son: 7019
 26: 1 As snow in **s**, and as rain in harvest, 7019
 30:25 yet they prepare their meat in the **s**; 7019
Isa 16: 9 for the shouting for thy **s fruits** and for 7019
 18: 6 the fowls shall **s** upon them, and all 6972
 28: 4 and as the hasty fruit before the **s**, 7019
Jer 8:20 the **s** is ended, and we are not saved. 7019
 40:10 **s fruits**, and oil, and put them in your 7019
 40:12 gathered wine and **s fruits** very much. 7019
 48:32 the spoiler is fallen upon thy **s fruits** and 7019
Da 2:35 became like the chaff of the **s** 7007
Am 3:15 I will smite the winter house with the **s** 7019
 8: 1 unto me: and behold, a basket of **s fruit**. 7019
 8: 2 I said, A basket of **s fruit**. Then said 7019
Mic 7: 1 as when they have gathered the **s fruits**, 7019
Zec 14: 8 hinder sea: in **s** and in winter shall it be. 7019
Mt 24:32 forth leaves, ye know that **s** is nigh: 2330
Mk 13:28 forth leaves, ye know that **s** is near: 2330
Lk 21:30 of your own selves that **s** is now nigh 2330

SUMPTUOUSLY (1)

Lk 16:19 and fine linen, and fared **s** every day: 2988

SUN (160) [SUNRISING]

Ge 15:12 the **s** was going down, a deep sleep 8121
 15:17 when the **s** went down, and it was dark, 8121
 19:23 The **s** was risen upon the earth when Lot 8121
 28:11 there all night, because the **s** was set; 8121
 32:31 as he passed over Penuel the **s** rose upon 8121
 37: 9 the **s** and the moon and the eleven stars 8121
Ex 16:21 and when the **s** waxed hot, it melted. 8121
 17:12 steady until the going down of the **s**. 8121
 22: 3 If the **s** be risen upon him, there shall be 8121
 22:26 shalt deliver it unto him by that the **s** 8121
Lev 22: 7 when the **s** is down, he shall be clean, 8121
Nu 25: 4 the east side toward the **rising of the s** 4217
 25: 4 them up before the LORD against the **s**, 8121
Dt 11:30 by the way where the **s** goeth down, 8121
 16: 6 at the going down of the **s**, at the season, 8121
 17: 3 either the **s**, or moon, or any of the host 8121
 23:11 when the **s** is down, he shall come into 8121
 24:13 the pledge again when the **s** goeth down, 8121
 24:15 hire, neither shall the **s** go down upon it; 8121
 33:14 the precious fruits brought forth by the **s**, 8121
Jos 1: 4 great sea toward the going down of the **s**. 8121
 8:29 as soon as the **s** was down, 8121
 10:12 he said in the sight of Israel, **S**, stand thou 8121
 10:13 the **s** stood still, and the moon stayed, 8121
 10:13 So the **s** stood still in the midst of heaven, 8121
 10:27 at the time of the going down of the **s**, 8121
 12: 1 side Jordan toward the rising of the **s**, 8121
Jdg 5:31 let them that love him be as the **s** when 8121
 8:13 returned from battle before the **s** was up, 2775
 9:33 that in the morning, as soon as the **s** is up, 8121
 14:18 the seventh day before the **s** went down, 2775
 19:14 the **s** went down upon them when they 8121
1Sa 11: 9 To morrow, by that time the **s** be hot, 8121
2Sa 2:24 the **s** went down when they were come 8121
 3: or ought else, till the **s** be down. 8121
 12:11 lie with thy wives in the sight of this **s**. 8121
 12:12 thing before all Israel, and before the **s**. 8121
 23: 4 the **s** riseth, even a morning without 8121
1Ki 22:36 the host about the going down of the **s**, 8121
2Ki 3: the **s** shone upon the water, 8121
 23: 5 to the **s**, and to the moon, and to 8121

2Ki 23:11 that the kings of Judah had given to the **s**, 8121
 23:11 and burnt the chariots of the **s** with fire. 8121
2Ch 18:34 the time of the **s** going down he died. 8121
Ne 7: 3 of Jerusalem be opened until the **s** be hot; 8121
Job 8:16 He is green before the **s**, and his branch 8121
 9: 7 commandeth the **s**, and it riseth not; 8121
 30:28 went mourning without the **s**: I stood up, 2535
 31:26 If I beheld the **s** when it shined, or the 216
Ps 19: 4 In them hath he set a tabernacle for the **s**, 8121
 50: 1 called the earth from the rising of the **s** 8121
 58: 8 of a woman, that they may not see the **s**. 8121
 72: 5 They shall fear thee as long as the **s** and 8121
 72:17 name shall be continued as long as the **s**: 8121
 74:16 thou hast prepared the light and the **s**. 8121
 84:11 For the LORD God is a **s** and shield: 8121
 89:36 and his throne as the **s** before me. 8121
 104:19 seasons: the **s** knoweth his going down. 8121
 104:22 The **s** ariseth, they gather themselves 8121
 113: 3 From the rising of the **s** unto the going 8121
 121: 6 The **s** shall not smite thee by day, 8121
 136: 8 The **s** to rule by day: for his mercy 8121
 148: 3 Praise ye him, **s** and moon: praise him, 8121
Ecc 1: 3 his labour which he taketh under the **s**? 8121
 1: 5 The **s** also ariseth, and the sun goeth 8121
 1: 5 the **s** goeth down, and hasteth to his 8121
 1: 9 and there is no new thing under the **s**. 8121
 1:14 all the works that are done under the **s**; 8121
 2:11 and there was no profit under the **s**. 8121
 2:17 the work that is wrought under the **s** is 8121
 2:18 labour which I had taken under the **s**: 8121
 2:19 have I shewed myself wise under the **s**. 8121
 2:20 all the labour which I took under the **s**. 8121
 2:22 wherein he hath laboured under the **s**? 8121
 3:16 moreover I saw under the **s** the place of 8121
 4: 1 oppressions that are done under the **s**: 8121
 4: 3 the evil work that is done under the **s**. 8121
 4: 7 I returned, and I saw vanity under the **s**. 8121
 4:15 all the living which walk under the **s**, 8121
 5:13 a sore evil which I have seen under the **s**, 8121
 5:18 taketh under the **s** all the days of his life, 8121
 6: 1 is an evil which I have seen under the **s**, 8121
 6: 5 Moreover he hath not seen the **s**, nor 8121
 6:12 man what shall be after him under the **s**? 8121
 7:11 by it there is profit to them that see the **s**. 8121
 8: 9 unto every work that is done under the **s**: 8121
 8:15 a man hath no better thing under the **s**, 8121
 8:15 life, which God giveth him under the **s**. 8121
 8:17 out the work that is done under the **s**: 8121
 9: 3 all things that are done under the **s**, 8121
 9: 6 in any thing that is done under the **s**. 8121
 9: 9 which he hath given thee under the **s**, 8121
 9: 9 thy labour which thou takest under the **s**. 8121
 9:11 I returned, and saw under the **s**, that 8121
 9:13 wisdom have I seen also under the **s**, 8121
 10: 5 is an evil which I have seen under the **s**, 8121
 11: 7 thing it is for the eyes to behold the **s**: 8121
 12: 2 While the **s**, or the light, or the moon, 8121
SS 1: 6 because the **s** hath looked upon me: 8121
 6:10 clear as the **s**, and terrible as an army 2535
Isa 13:10 the **s** shall be darkened in his going forth, 8121
 24:23 shall be confounded, and the **s** ashamed, 2535
 30:26 the moon shall be as the light of the **s**, 2535
 30:26 the light of the **s** shall be sevenfold, 2535
 38: 8 which is gone down in the **s** dial of Ahaz, 8121
 38: 8 So the **s** returned ten degrees, by which 8121
 41:25 from the rising of the **s** shall he call upon 8121
 45: 6 they may know from the rising of the **s**, 8121
 49:10 neither shall the heat nor **s** smite them: 8121
 59:19 and his glory from the rising of the **s**. 8121
 60:19 The **s** shall be no more thy light by day; 8121
 60:20 Thy **s** shall no more go down; neither 8121
Jer 8: 2 they shall spread them before the **s**, 8121
 15: 9 her **s** is gone down while it was yet day: 8121
 31:35 which giveth the **s** for a light by day, 8121
Eze 8:16 they worshipped the **s** towards the east. 8121
 32: 7 I will cover the **s** with a cloud, 8121
Da 6:14 he laboured till the going down of the **s** 8122
Joel 2:10 the **s** and the moon shall be dark, 8121
 2:31 The **s** shall be turned into darkness, 8121
 3:15 The **s** and the moon shall be darkened, 8121
Am 8: 9 I will cause the **s** to go down at noon, 8121
Jnh 4: 8 it came to pass, when the **s** did arise, 8121
 4: 8 the **s** beat upon the head of Jonah, that 8121
Mic 3: 6 the **s** shall go down over the prophets, 8121
Na 3:17 but when the **s** ariseth they flee away, 8121
Hab 3:11 The **s** and moon stood still in their 8121
Mal 1:11 For from the rising of the **s** even unto 8121
 4: 2 unto you that fear my name shall the **S** of 8121
Mt 5:45 for he maketh his **s** to rise on the evil and 2246
 13: 6 And when the **s** was up, they were 2246
 13:43 shall the righteous shine forth as the **s** 2246
 17: 2 and his face did shine as the **s**, 2246
 24:29 of those days shall the **s** be darkened, 2246
Mk 1:32 And at even, when the **s** did set, 2246
 4: 6 But when the **s** was up, it was scorched; 2246
 13:24 the **s** shall be darkened, and the moon 2246
 16: 2 unto the sepulchre at the rising of the **s**. 2246
Lk 4:40 Now when the **s** was setting, all they that 2246
 21:25 And there shall be signs in the **s**, and in 2246
 23:45 And the **s** was darkened, and the vail of 2246
Ac 2:20 The **s** shall be turned into darkness, 2246
 13:11 be blind, not seeing the **s** for a season. 2246
 26:13 the brightness of the **s**, shining round 2246
 27:20 when neither **s** nor stars in many days 2246
1Co 15:41 There is one glory of the **s**, 2246

Eph 4:26 let not the **s** go down upon your wrath: 2246
Jas 1:11 the **s** is no sooner risen with a burning 2246
Rev 1:16 his countenance was as the **s** shineth in 2246
 6:12 the **s** became black as sackcloth of hair, 2246
 7:16 neither shall the **s** light on them, nor any 2246
 8:12 and the third part of the **s** was smitten, 2246
 10: 1 and his face was as it were the **s**, 2246
 12: 1 woman clothed with the **s**, and the moon 2246
 16: 8 angel poured out his vial upon the **s**; 2246
 19:17 And I saw an angel standing in the **s**; 2246
 21:23 the city had no need of the **s**, neither of 2246
 22: 5 need no candle, neither light of the **s**; 2246

SUNDER (7) [SUNDERED]

Ps 46: 9 the bow, and **cutteth** the spear in **s**; 7112
 107:14 of death, and **brake** their bands in **s**. 5423
 107:16 of brass, and **cut** the bars of iron in **s**. 1438
Isa 27: 9 altar as chalkstones that are **beaten** in **s**, 5310
 45: 2 of brass, and **cut** in **s** the bars of iron: 1438
Na 1:13 off thee, and will **burst** thy bonds in **s**. 5423
Lk 12:46 will **cut** him in **s**, and will appoint him 1371

SUNDERED (1) [SUNDER]

Job 41:17 they stick together, that they cannot be **s**. 6504

SUNDRY (1)

Heb 1: 1 God, who at **s** times and in divers 3588

SUNG (6) [SING]

Ezr 3:11 they **s** together by course in praising and 6030
Isa 26: 1 In that day shall this song be **s** in the land 7891
Mt 26:30 when they had **s** a hymn, they went 5214
Mk 14:26 when they had **s** a hymn, they went 5214
Rev 5: 9 And they **s** a new song, saying, Thou art 103
 14: 3 And they **s** as it were a new song before 103

SUNK (7) [SINK]

1Sa 17:49 that the stone **s** into his forehead; 2883
2Ki 9:24 his heart, and he **s down** in his chariot. 3766
Ps 9:15 The heathen are **s down** in the pit that 2883
Jer 38: 6 but mire: so Jeremiah **s** in the mire. 2883
 38:22 thy feet are **s** in the mire, and they are 2883
La 2: 9 Her gates are **s** into the ground; he hath 2883
Ac 20: 9 **s down** with sleep, and fell down 2702

SUNRISING (10) [RISE, SUN]

Nu 21:11 is before Moab, toward the **s**. 4217+8121
 34:15 near Jericho eastward, toward the **s**. 4217
Dt 4:41 on this side Jordan toward the **s**; 4217+8121
 4:47 on this side Jordan toward the **s**; 4217+8121
Jos 1:15 on this side Jordan toward the **s**. 4217+8121
 13: 5 all Lebanon, toward the **s**, 4217+8121+1886.1
 19:12 unto the border of Chisloth-tabor, 4217+8121
 19:27 turneth toward the **s** to 4217+8121+1886.1
 19:34 upon Jordan toward the **s**. 4217+8121+1886.1
Jdg 20:43 over against Gibeah toward the **s**. 4217+8121

SUP (3) [SUPPED, SUPPER]

Hab 1: 9 their faces shall **s up** as the east wind, 4041
Lk 17: 8 Make ready wherewith I may **s**, 1172
Rev 3:20 and will **s** with him, and he with me. 1172

SUPERFLUITY (1) [SUPERFLUOUS]

Jas 1:21 lay apart all filthiness and **s** of naughtiness, 4050

SUPERFLUOUS (3) [SUPERFLUITY]

Lev 21:18 he that hath a flat nose, or any thing **s**, 8311
 22:23 or a lamb that **hath any thing s** or 8311
2Co 9: 1 the saints, it is **s** for me to write to you: 4053

SUPERSCRIPTION (5)

Mt 22:20 unto them, Whose is this image and **s**? 1923
Mk 12:16 unto them, Whose is this image and **s**? 1923
 15:26 And the **s** of his accusation was written 1923
Lk 20:24 Whose image and **s** hath it? 1923
 23:38 also was written over him in letters 1923

SUPERSTITION (1) [SUPERSTITIOUS]

Ac 25:19 questions against him of their own **s**, 1175

SUPERSTITIOUS (1) [SUPERSTITION]

Ac 17:22 I perceive that in all things ye are **too s**. 1174

SUPERVISION See SCHOOLMASTER

SUPPED (1) [SUP]

1Co 11:25 he had **s**, saying, This cup is the new 1172

SUPPER (14) [SUP]

Mk 6:21 Herod on his birthday made a **s** to his 1173
Lk 14:12 thou makest a dinner or a **s**, call not 1173
 14:16 A certain man made a great **s**, 1173
 14:17 And sent his servant at **s** time to say to 1173
 14:24 which were bidden shall taste of my **s**. 1173
 22:20 Likewise also the cup after **s**, saying, 1172
Jn 12: 2 There they made him a **s**; and Martha 1173
 13: 2 And **s** being ended, the devil having now 1173
 13: 4 He riseth from **s**, and laid aside his 1173
 21:20 which also leaned on his breast at **s**, 1173
1Co 11:20 one place, this is not to eat the Lord's **s**. 1173
 11:21 every one taketh before other his own **s**: 1173
Rev 19: 9 called unto the marriage **s** of the Lamb. 1173
 19:17 gather yourselves together unto the **s** of 1173

SUPPLANT (1) [SUPPLANTED]

Jer 9: 4 for every brother will **utterly s**, 6117+6117

SUPPLANTED (1) [SUPPLANT]
Ge 27:36 for he hath **s** me these two times: he took 6117

SUPPLE (1)
Eze 16: 4 wast thou washed in water to **s** *thee*; 4935

SUPPLIANTS (1)
Zep 3:10 From beyond the rivers of Ethiopia my **s**, 6282

SUPPLICATION (39) [SUPPLICATIONS]
1Sa 13:12 and I have not **made s** unto the LORD: 2470
1Ki 8:28 to his **s**, O LORD my God, to hearken 8467
 8:30 hearken thou to the **s** of thy servant, 8467
 8:33 and **make s** unto thee in this house: 2603
 8:38 and **s** soever be *made* by any man, 8467
 8:45 thou *in* heaven their prayer and their **s**, 8467
 8:47 **make s** unto thee in the land of them 2603
 8:49 and their **s** *in* heaven their dwelling place, 8467
 8:52 That thine eyes may be open unto the **s** of 8467
 8:52 unto the **s** of thy people Israel, to hearken 8467
 8:54 all this prayer and **s** unto the LORD, 8467
 8:59 wherewith I have **made s** before 2603
 9: 3 **s**, that thou hast **made** before me: 2603+8467
2Ch 6:19 to his **s**, O LORD my God, to hearken 8467
 6:24 and **make s** before thee in this house; 2603
 6:29 what **s** soever shall be *made* of any man, 8467
 6:35 from the heavens their prayer and their **s**, 8467
 33:13 heard his **s**, and brought him again *to* 8467
Est 4: 8 to **make s** unto him, and to make request 2603
Job 8: 5 and **make** thy **s** to the Almighty; 2603
 9:15 *but* I would **make s** to my judge. 2603
Ps 6: 9 The LORD hath heard my **s**; the LORD 8467
 30: 8 O LORD; and unto the LORD I **made s**. 2603
 55: 1 O God; and hide not thyself from my **s**. 8467
 119:170 Let my **s** come before thee: deliver me 8467
 142: 1 voice unto the LORD did I **make** my **s**. 2603
Isa 45:14 they shall **make s** unto thee, *saying*, 6419
Jer 36: 7 It may be they will present their **s** before 8467
 37:20 let my **s**, I pray thee, be accepted before 8467
 38:26 I presented my **s** before the king, 8467
 42: 2 our **s** be accepted before thee, and pray 8467
 42: 9 unto whom ye sent me to present your **s** 8467
Da 6:11 and **making s** before his God. 2604
 9:20 presenting my **s** before the LORD my God 8467
Hos 12: 4 he wept, and **made s** unto him: he found 2603
Ac 1:14 with one accord in prayer and **s**, 1162
Eph 6:18 always with all prayer and **s** in the Spirit, 1162
 6:18 with all perseverance and **s** for all saints; 1162
Php 4: 6 **s** with thanksgiving let your requests be 1162

SUPPLICATIONS (21) [SUPPLICATION]
2Ch 6:21 Hearken therefore unto the **s** of thy 8469
 6:39 their prayer and their **s**, and maintain 8467
Job 41: 3 Will he make many **s** unto thee? will he 8469
Ps 28: 2 Hear the voice of my **s**, when I cry unto 8469
 28: 6 because he hath heard the voice of my **s**. 8469
 31:22 the voice of my **s** when I cried unto thee. 8469
 86: 6 prayer; and attend to the voice of my **s**. 8469
 116: 1 he hath heard my voice *and* my **s**. 8469
 130: 2 ears be attentive to the voice of my **s**. 8469
 140: 6 my God: hear the voice of my **s**, O LORD. 8469
 143: 1 my prayer, O LORD, give ear to my **s**: 8469
Jer 3:21 weeping *and* **s** of the children of Israel: 8469
 31: 9 weeping, and with **s** will I lead them: 8469
Da 9: 3 to seek *by* prayer and **s**, with fasting, 8469
 9:17 his **s**, and cause thy face to shine upon 8469
 9:18 for we do not present our **s** before thee 8469
 9:23 At the beginning of thy **s** 8469
Zec 12:10 of Jerusalem, the spirit of grace and of **s**: 8469
1Ti 2: 1 therefore that, first of all, **s**, prayers, 1162
 5: 5 and continueth in **s** and prayers night and 1162
Heb 5: 7 up prayers and **s** with strong crying and 2428

SUPPLIED (2) [SUPPLY]
1Co 16:17 was lacking on your part they have **s**. 378
2Co 11: 9 brethren which came from Macedonia **s**: 4322

SUPPLIES See CELLARS; STUFF

SUPPLIETH (2) [SUPPLY]
2Co 9:12 service not only **s** the want of the saints, 4322
Eph 4:16 compacted by that which every joint **s**, 2024

SUPPLY (5) [SUPPLIED, SUPPLIETH]
2Co 8:14 your abundance *may be a s* for their want, NIG
 8:14 that their abundance also may be *a s* for NIG
Php 1:19 and the **s** of the Spirit of Jesus Christ, 2024
 2:30 life, to **s** your lack of service toward me. 378
 4:19 my God shall **s** all your need according 4137

SUPPORT (2)
Ac 20:35 so labouring *ye* ought to **s** the weak, 482
1Th 5:14 comfort the feebleminded, **s** the weak, 472

SUPPORTS See UNDERSETTERS

SUPPOSE (10) [SUPPOSED, SUPPOSING]
2Sa 13:32 Let not my lord **s** *that* they have slain all 559
Lk 7:43 I **s** that *he*, to whom he forgave most. 5274
 12:51 **s** ye that I am come to give peace on 1380
 13: 2 **s** ye that these Galileans were sinners 1380
Jn 21:25 I **s** that even the world itself could not 3633
Ac 2:15 as ye **s**, seeing it is *but* the third hour of 5274
1Co 7:26 I **s** therefore that this is good for the 3543
2Co 11: 5 For I *s* was not a whit behind the very 3049
Heb 10:29 **s** ye, shall he be thought worthy, 1380

1Pe 5:12 as I **s**, I have written briefly, exhorting, 3049

SUPPOSED (8) [SUPPOSE]
Mt 20:10 **s** that they should have received more; 3543
Mk 6:49 they **s** *it* had been a spirit, and cried out: 1380
Lk 3:23 about thirty years of age, being (as was **s**) 3543
 24:37 and **s** that *they* had seen a spirit. 1380
Ac 7:25 For he **s** his brethren would have 3543
 21:29 whom they **s** that Paul had brought into 3543
 25:18 none accusation of *such things* as I **s**: 5282
Php 2:25 Yet I **s** it necessary to send to you 2233

SUPPOSING (7) [SUPPOSE]
Lk 2:44 **s** him to have been in the company, 3543
Jn 20:15 She, him to be the gardener, saith unto 1380
Ac 14:19 *him* out of the city, **s** he had been dead. 3543
 16:27 **s** that the prisoners had been fled. 3543
 27:13 **s** that *they* had obtained *their* purpose, 1380
Php 1:16 **s** to add affliction to my bonds: 3633
1Ti 6: 5 of the truth, **s** that gain is godliness: 3543

SUPREME (1)
1Pe 2:13 sake: whether *it be* to the king, as **s**; 5242

SUPREME COMMANDER See TARTAN

SUR (1)
2Ki 11: 6 a third *part shall be* at the gate of **S**; 5495

SURE (41) [SURELY, SURETIES, SURETISHIP, SURETY]
Ge 23:17 the borders round about, were **made s** 6965
 23:20 were **made s** unto Abraham for 6965
Ex 3:19 I am **s** that the king of Egypt will not let 3045
Nu 32: 23 be **s** your sin will find you out. 3045
Dt 12:23 Only be **s** that thou eat not the blood: 2388
1Sa 2:35 I will build him a **s** house; and he shall 539
 20: 7 be **s** that evil is determined by him. 3045
 25:28 will certainly make my lord a **s** house; 539
2Sa 1:10 I was **s** that he could not live after *that* he 3045
 23: 5 ordered in all *things*, and **s**: 8104
1Ki 11:38 build thee a **s** house, as I built for David, 539
Ne 9:38 because of all this we make a **s** covenant, 548
Job 24:22 he riseth up, and no *man* is **s** of life. 539
Ps 19: 7 The testimony of the LORD *is* **s**, 539
 93: 5 Thy testimonies are very **s**: 539
 111: 7 judgment; all his commandments *are* **s**. 539
Pr 6: 3 humble thyself, and **make s** thy friend. 7292
 11:15 for *it:* and he that hateth suretiship *is* **s**. 982
 11:18 him that soweth righteousness *shall be* a **s** 571
Isa 22:23 I will fasten him as a nail in a **s** place; 539
 22:25 shall the nail that is fastened in the **s** place 539
 28:16 corner *stone*, a **s foundation**: 3245+4143
 32:18 in dwellings, and in quiet resting places; 4009
 33:16 *shall be* given him; his waters *shall be* **s**. 539
 55: 3 with you, *even* the **s** mercies of David. 539
Da 2:45 *is* certain, and the interpretation thereof **s**. 540
 7: thy kingdom *shall be* **s** unto thee, after 7011
Mt 27:64 the sepulchre be **made s** until the third 805
 27:65 go your way, **make** *it* **as s** as you can. 805
 27:66 So they went, and **made** the sepulchre **s**, 805
Lk 10:11 notwithstanding be ye **s** of this, that 1097
Jn 6:69 and are **s** that thou art *that* Christ, 1097
 16:30 are we **s** that thou knowest all *things*, 1492
Ac 13:34 I will give you the **s** mercies of David. 4103
Ro 2: 2 But we are **s** that the judgment of God is 1492
 4:16 to the end the promise might be **s** to all 949
 15:29 And I am **s** that, when I come unto you, 4731
2Ti 2:19 the foundation of God standeth **s**, 949
Heb 6:19 both a and stedfast, and which entereth 804
2Pe 1:10 to make your calling and election **s**: 949
 1:19 We have also a **more s** word of prophecy; 949

SURELY (284) [SURE]
Ge 2:17 eatest thereof thou shalt **s die**: 4191+4191
 3: 4 the woman, Ye shall not **s die**: 4191+4191
 9: 5 **s** your blood of your lives I will require; 389
 18:18 that Abraham shall **s become** 1961+1961
 20: 7 know thou that thou shalt **s die**, 4191+4191
 20:11 **S** the fear of God *is* not in this place; 7535
 26:11 his wife shall **s be put to death**. 4191+4191
 28:16 and he said, **S** the LORD is in this place; 403
 28:22 I will **s give the tenth** unto thee. 6237+6237
 29:14 to him, **S** thou *art* my bone and my flesh. 389
 29:32 **S** the LORD hath looked upon my 3588
 30:16 for **s** I have **hired** thee with my 7936+7936
 31:42 **s** thou hadst sent me away now empty. 3588
 32:12 I will **s do** thee **good**, and make 3190+3190
 42:16 else by the life of Pharaoh **s** ye *are* spies. 3588
 43:10 **s** now we had returned this second time. 3588
 44:28 from me, and I said, **S** he is torn in pieces; 389
 46: 4 I will also **s bring** thee **up** *again:* 5927+5927
 50:24 God will **s visit** you, and bring you 6485+6485
 50:25 God will **s visit** you, and ye shall 6485+6485
Ex 2:14 and said, **S** *this* thing is known. 403
 3: 7 I have **s seen** the affliction of my 7200+7200
 3:16 I have **visited** you, and *seen* that 6485+6485
 4:25 said, **S** a bloody husband *art* thou to me. 3588
 11: 1 **s thrust** you out hence altogether. 1644+1644
 13:19 saying, God will **s visit** you; 6485+6485
 18:18 Thou wilt **s wear away**, both thou, 5034+5034
 19:12 the mount shall be **s put to death**: 4191+4191
 19:13 shall be **stoned**, or shot through; 5619+5619
 21:12 that he die, shall be **s put to death**. 4191+4191
 21:15 mother, shall be **s put to death**. 4191+4191
 21:16 hand, he shall be **s put to death**. 4191+4191

Ex 21:17 mother, shall **s** be **put to death**. 4191+4191
 21:20 his hand; he shall be **s punished**. 5358+5358
 21:22 he shall be **s punished**, according 6064+6064
 21:28 the ox shall be **s stoned**, 5619+5619
 21:36 he shall **s pay** ox for ox; 7999+7999
 22: 6 the fire shall **s make restitution**. 7999+7999
 22:14 with it, he shall **s make** *it* **good**. 7999+7999
 22:16 shall **s endow** her to be his wife. 4117+4117
 22:19 a beast shall **s** be **put to death**. 4191+4191
 22:23 all unto me, I will **s hear** their cry; 8085+8085
 23: 4 shalt **s bring** it **back** to him **again**. 7725+7725
 23: 5 thou shalt **s help** with him. 5800+5800
 23:33 their gods, it will **s** be a snare unto thee. 3588
 31:14 defileth it shall **s** be **put to death**: 4191+4191
 31:15 he shall **s** be **put to death**. 4191+4191
 40:15 anointing shall **s** be an everlasting 1961+1961
Lev 20: 2 he shall **s** be **put to death**: 4191+4191
 20: 9 his mother shall be **s put to death**: 4191+4191
 20:10 adulteress shall be **s put to death**: 4191+4191
 20:11 of them shall be **s put to death**; 4191+4191
 20:12 of them shall be **s put to death**; 4191+4191
 20:13 they shall **s** be **put to death**; their 4191+4191
 20:15 a beast, he shall be **s put to death**: 4191+4191
 20:16 they shall **s** be **put to death**; their 4191+4191
 20:27 a wizard, shall **s** be **put to death**, *and all* 4191+4191
 24:16 he shall **s** be **put to death**, *and all* 4191+4191
 24:17 any man shall **s** be **put to death**. 4191+4191
 27:29 *but* shall **s** be **put to death**. 4191+4191
Nu 13:27 and **s** it floweth with milk and honey; 1571
 14:23 **S** they shall **not** see the land which I sware 518
 14:35 **s** do it unto all this evil congregation, 518+3808
 15:35 The man shall be **s put to death**: 4191+4191
 18:15 of man shalt thou **s redeem**, 6299+6299
 22:33 **s** now also I had slain thee, and saved her 3588
 23:23 **s** *there* is no enchantment against Jacob, 3588
 26:65 They shall **s die** in the wilderness. 4191+4191
 27: 7 thou shalt **s give** them a possession 5414+5414
 32:11 **S none** of the men that came up out of 518
 35:16 murderer shall **s** be **put to death**. 4191+4191
 35:17 murderer shall **s** be **put to death**. 4191+4191
 35:18 murderer shall **s** be **put to death**. 4191+4191
 35:21 smote *him* shall **s** be **put to death**; 4191+4191
 35:31 but he shall be **s put to death**. 4191+4191
Dt 1:35 **S** there shall **not** one of these men of this 518
 4: 6 **S** this great nation *is* a wise and 7535
 8:19 against you *this* day that ye shall **s perish**. 6+6
 13: 9 thou shalt **s kill** him; thine hand 2026+2026
 13:15 Thou shalt **s smite** the inhabitants 5221+5221
 15: 8 shalt **s lend** sufficient for his 5670+5670
 15:10 Thou shalt **s give** him, 5414+5414
 16:15 thine hands, therefore thou shalt **s rejoice**. 389
 22: 4 **s** help him to **lift** *them* **up** again. 6965+6965
 23:21 thy God will **s require** of thee; 1875+1875
 30:18 that ye shall **s perish**, *and that* ye shall 6+6
 31:18 I will **s hide** my face in that day for 5641+5641
Jos 14: 9 **S** the land whereon thy feet have 518+3808
Jdg 3:24 **S** he covereth his feet in *his* summer 389
 4: 9 she said, I will **s go** with thee: 1980+1980
 6:16 **S** I will be with thee, and thou shalt smite 3588
 11:31 shall **s** be the LORD's, and I will offer it NIH
 13:22 **s die**, because we have seen God. 4191+4191
 15:13 **s** we will not **kill** thee. And they 4191+4191
 20:39 said, **S** they are smitten down before us, 389
 21: 5 He shall **s** be **put to death**. 4191+4191
Ru 1:10 **S** we will return with thee unto thy 3588
1Sa 9: 6 all that he saith **cometh s to pass**: 935+935
 14:39 in Jonathan my son, he shall **s die**. 4191+4191
 14:44 for thou shalt **s die**, Jonathan. 4191+4191
 15:32 Agag said, **S** the bitterness of death is past. 403
 16: 6 said, **S** the LORD's anointed *is* before him. 389
 17:25 **s** to defy Israel is he come up: and it shall 3588
 20:26 he *is* not clean; **s** he *is* not clean. 3588
 20:31 him unto me, for he shall **s die**. 1121+4194
 22:16 Thou shalt **s die**, Ahimelech, 4191+4191
 22:22 there, that he would **s tell** Saul: 5046+5046
 24:20 well that thou shalt **s be king**, 4427+4427
 25:21 In vain have I kept all that this *fellow* 389
 25:34 **s** there had not been left unto Nabal by 3588
 28: 2 David said to Achish, **S** thou 3651+3807.1
 29: 6 said unto him, **S**, *as* the LORD liveth, 3588
 30: 8 for thou shalt **s overtake** *them*, 5381+5381
2Sa 2:27 **s** then in the morning the people had 3588
 9: 7 for I will **s shew** thee kindness for 6213+6213
 11:23 **S** the men prevailed against us, 3588
 12: 5 hath done this *thing* shall **s die**: 1121+4194
 12:14 that is born unto thee shall **s die**. 4191+4191
 15:21 **s** in what place my lord the king 518+3588
 18: 2 will **s go forth** with you myself 3318+3318
 20:18 They shall **s ask** *counsel* at Abel: 7592+7592
 24:24 but I will **s buy** *it* of thee at a price: 7069+7069
1Ki 2:37 for certain that thou shalt **s die**: 4191+4191
 2:42 any whither, that thou shalt **s die**? 4191+4191
 8:13 I have **s built** thee a house to dwell 1129+1129
 11: 2 *for* **s** they will turn away your heart after 403
 11:11 I will **s rend** the kingdom from 7167+7167
 13:32 of Samaria, shall **s come to pass**. 1961+1961
 18:15 I will **s shew** myself unto him to day. 3588
 20:23 and **s** we shall be stronger than they. 518+3808
 20:25 *and* **s** we shall be stronger than they. 518+3808
 22:32 that they said, **S** it *is* the king of Israel. 389
2Ki 1: 4 thou art gone up, but shalt **s die**. 4191+4191
 1: 6 thou art gone up, but shalt **s die**. 4191+4191
 1:16 thou art gone up, but shalt **s die**. 4191+4191
 3:14 of hosts liveth, before whom I stand, **s**, 3588
 3:23 the kings are **s slain**, and they have 2717+2717

2Ki	5:11	will **s come out** to me, and, stand,	3318+3318
	8:10	shewed me that he shall **s die**.	4191+4191
	8:14	me *that* thou shouldest **s recover**.	2421+2421
	9:26	S I have seen yesterday the blood of	518+3808
	18:30	The Lord will **s deliver** us,	5337+5337
	23:22	S there was not holden such a passover	3588
	24:	3 S at the commandment of the Lord came	389
Est	6:13	but shalt **s fall** before him.	5307+5307
Job	8:	6 s now he would awake for thee,	3588
	13:	3 S I would speak to the Almighty,	199
	13:10	He will **s reprove** you, if ye do	3198+3198
	14:18	s the mountain falling cometh to nought,	199
	18:21	S such *are* the dwellings of the wicked,	3588
	20:20	S he shall not feel quietness in his belly,	3588
	28:	1 S there is a vein for the silver, and a place	3588
	31:36	S I would take it upon my shoulder,	518+3808
	33:	8 S thou hast spoken in mine hearing,	389
	34:12	s God will not do wickedly, neither will	551
	34:31	S it is *meet to be* said unto God, I have	3588
	35:13	S God will not hear vanity, neither will	389
	37:20	if a man speak, he shall be swallowed	3588
	40:20	S the mountains bring him forth food,	3588
Ps	23:	6 goodness and mercy shall follow me all	389
	32:	6 s in the floods of great waters they shall	7535
	39:	6 S every man walketh in a vain shew:	389
	39:	6 s they are disquieted in vain: he heapeth	389
	39:11	like a moth: **s** every man *is* vanity. Selah.	389
	62:	9 S men of low degree *are* vanity, *and* men	389
	73:18	S thou didst set them in slippery *places*,	389
	76:10	S the wrath of man shall praise thee:	3588
	77:11	s I will remember thy wonders of old.	3588
	85:	9 S his salvation *is* nigh them that fear him;	389
	91:	3 S he shall deliver thee from the snare of	3588
	112:	6 S he shall not be moved for ever:	3588
	131:	2 S I have behaved and quieted myself,	518+3808
	132:	3 S I will **not** come into the tabernacle of my	518
	139:11	If I say, S the darkness shall cover me;	389
	139:19	S thou wilt slay the wicked, O God:	518
	140:13	S the righteous shall give thanks unto thy	389
Pr	1:17	S in vain the net *is* spread in the sight of	3588
	3:34	S he scorneth the scorners: but he giveth	518
	10:	9 He that walketh uprightly walketh **s**:	983
	22:16	giveth to the rich, *shall* **s come** to want.	389
	23:18	**For s** there is an end;	518+3588
	30:	2 S I *am* more brutish than *any* man,	3588
	30:33	S the churning of milk bringeth forth	3588
Ecc	4:16	S this also *is* vanity and vexation of spirit.	3588
	7:	7 S oppression maketh a wise *man* mad;	3588
	8:12	s I know that it shall be well with them	3588
	10:11	s the serpent will bite without	518
Isa	7:	9 not believe, *ye* ye shall not be established.	3588
	14:24	S as I have thought, so shall it come	518+3808
	16:	7 shall ye mourn; **s** *they are* stricken.	389
	19:11	S the princes of Zoan *are* fools, the counsel	389
	22:14	S this iniquity shall **not** be purged from you	518
	22:17	and will **s cover** thee.	5844+5844
	22:18	s **violently turn and toss**	6801+6801+6802
	29:16	S your turning *of things* upside down	518
	36:15	The Lord will **s deliver** us:	5337+5337
	40:	7 bloweth upon it: **s** the people *is* grass.	403
	45:14	unto thee, *saying*, S God *is* in thee;	389
	45:24	S, shall one say, in the Lord have I	389
	49:	4 *yet* **s** my judgment *is* with the Lord,	403
	49:18	thou shalt **s clothe** thee with them all,	NIH
	53:	4 S he hath borne our griefs, and carried	403
	54:15	they shall **s gather together**,	1481+1481
	60:	9 S the isles shall wait for me, and the ships	3588
	62:	8 S I will **no more** give thy corn *to be* meat	518
	63:	8 For he said, S they *are* my people,	389
Jer	2:35	innocent, **s** his anger shall turn from me.	389
	3:20	S *as* a wife treacherously departeth from	403
	4:10	s thou hast greatly deceived this people	403
	5:	2 s they swear falsely,	3651+3807.1
	5:	4 Therefore I said, S these *are* poor; they	389
	8:13	I will **s consume** them, saith	622+5486
	16:19	S our fathers have inherited lies, vanity,	389
	22:	6 *yet* **s** I will make thee a wilderness	518+3808
	22:22	s then shalt thou be ashamed and	3588
	24:	8 s thus saith the Lord, So will I give	3588
	26:	8 took him, saying, Thou shalt **s die**.	4191+4191
	26:15	ye shall **s bring** innocent blood upon	3588
	31:18	have **s heard** Ephraim bemoaning	8085+8085
	31:19	S after that I was turned, I repented;	3588
	31:20	I will **s have mercy** upon him,	7355+7355
	32:	4 shall s **be delivered** into the hand	5414+5414
	34:	3 shalt **s be taken**, and delivered into	8610+8610
	36:16	s **tell** the king of all these words.	5046+5046
	37:	9 Chaldeans shall **s depart** from us:	1980+1980
	38:	3 This city shall **s be given** into	5414+5414
	38:15	wilt thou not s **put** me **to death**?	4191+4191
	39:18	For I will **s deliver** thee,	4422+4422
	44:25	We will **s perform** our vows that we	6213
	44:25	ye will **s accomplish** your vows,	6965+6965
	44:25	and **s perform** your vows.	6213+6213
	44:29	shall **s stand** against you for evil:	6965+6965
	46:18	S as Tabor *is* among the mountains,	3588
	49:12	but thou shalt **s drink** *of it*.	8354+8354
	49:20	S the least of the flock shall draw	518+3808
	49:20	s he shall make their habitations	518+3808
	50:45	S the least of the flock shall draw	518+3808
	50:45	s he shall make *their* habitation	518+3808
	51:14	*saying*, S I will fill thee with men,	3588+3588
	51:56	God of recompences shall **s requite**.	7999+7999
La	3:	3 S against me is he turned; he turneth his	389
Eze	3:	6 S, had I sent thee to them,	518+3808

Eze	3:18	unto the wicked, Thou shalt **s die**;	4191+4191
	3:21	shall **s live**, because he is warned;	2421+2421
	5:11	S, because thou hast defiled my	518+3808
	17:16	s in the place *where* the king	4191+4191
	17:19	s mine oath that he hath despised,	518+3808
	18:	9 he is just, he shall **s live**, saith	2421+2421
	18:13	s **die**; his blood shall be upon him.	4191+4191
	18:17	of his father, he shall **s live**.	2421+2421
	18:19	hath done them, he shall **s live**.	2421+2421
	18:21	is lawful and right, he shall **s live**,	2421+2421
	18:28	he shall **s live**, he shall not die.	2421+2421
	20:33	s with a mighty hand, and with a	518+3808
	31:11	heathen; he shall **s deal** with him:	6213+6213
	33:	8 O wicked *man*, thou shalt **s die**;	4191+4191
	33:13	the righteous, *that* he shall **s live**;	2421+2421
	33:14	unto the wicked, Thou shalt **s die**;	4191+4191
	33:15	he shall **s live**, he shall not die.	2421+2421
	33:16	is lawful and right; he shall **s live**.	2421+2421
	33:27	*they* that *are* in the wastes shall fall	518+3808
	34:	8 s because my flock became a prey,	518+3808
	36:	5 S in the fire of my jealousy have I	518+3808
	36:	7 S the heathen that *are* about you,	518+3808
	38:19	S in that day there shall be a great	518+3808
Hos	5:	9 have I made known that which shall **s** be.	539
	12:11	s they are vanity: they sacrifice bullocks in	389
Am	3:	7 S the Lord God will do nothing, but he	3588
	5:	5 for Gilgal shall **s go into captivity**,	1540+1540
	7:11	Israel shall **s be led away captive**	1540+1540
	7:17	Israel shall **s go into captivity** forth	1540+1540
	8:	7 S I will **never** forget any of	518+5331+3807.1
Mic	2:12	will **s assemble**, O Jacob, all of thee;	622+622
	2:12	will **s gather** the remnant of Israel;	6908+6908
Hab	2:	3 it will **s** come, it will not tarry.	935+935
Zep	2:	9 S Moab shall be as Sodom, and the	3588
	3:	7 S thou wilt fear me, thou wilt receive	389
Mt	26:73	said to Peter, S thou also art *one* of them;	230
Mk	14:70	said again to Peter, S thou art *one* of them:	230
Lk	1:	1 which are **most s believed** among us,	4135
	4:23	Ye will **s** say unto me this proverb,	3843
Jn	17:	8 have known s that I came out from thee,	230
Heb	6:14	S blessing I will bless thee,	2229+3375
Rev	22:20	these *things* saith, S I come quickly.	3483

SURETIES (1) [SURE]

Pr	22:26	hands, *or* of them that are **s** for debts.	6148

SURETISHIP (1) [SURE]

Pr	11:15	smart *for it*: and he that hateth **s** *is* sure.	8628

SURETY (14) [SURE]

Ge	15:13	**Know of a s** that thy seed shall be	3045+3045
	18:13	I **of a s** bear *a child*, which am old?	552+637
	26:	9 and said, Behold, **of a s** she *is* thy wife:	389
	43:	9 I will be **s** for him; of my hand shalt thou	6148
	44:32	For thy servant became **s** for the lad	6148
Job	17:	3 Lay down now, put me **in a s** with thee;	6148
Ps	119:122	Be **s** for thy servant for good: let not	6148
Pr	6:	1 My son, if thou be **s** for thy friend, *if* thou	6148
	11:15	that is **s** for a stranger shall smart *for it*:	6148
	17:18	**becometh s** in the presence of his	6148+6161
	20:16	Take his garment that is **s** for a stranger:	6148
	27:13	Take his garment that is **s** for a stranger,	6148
Ac	12:11	he said, Now I know **of a s**, that the Lord	230
Heb	7:22	much was Jesus made a **s** of a better	1450

SURFEITING (1)

Lk	21:34	time your hearts be overcharged with **s**,	2897

SURMISINGS (1)

1Ti	6:	4 cometh envy, strife, railings, evil **s**,	5283

SURNAME (8) [SURNAMED]

Isa	44:	5 and **s** *himself* by the name of Israel.	3655
Mt	10:	3 and Lebbeus, whose **s** was Thaddeus;	1941
Ac	10:	5 and call for *one* Simon, whose **s** is Peter:	1941
	10:32	and call hither Simon, whose **s** is Peter:	1941
	11:13	and call for Simon, whose **s** is Peter;	1941
	12:12	the mother of John, whose **s** was Mark;	1941
	12:25	took with *them* John, whose **s** was Mark.	1941
	15:37	take with *them* John, whose **s** was Mark.	2564

SURNAMED (8) [SURNAME]

Isa	45:	4 I have **s** thee, though thou hast not	3655
Mk	3:16	And Simon he **s** Peter;	2007
	3:17	(and he **s** them Boanerges, which	2007+3686
Lk	22:	3 Then entered Satan into Judas Iscariot,	1941
Ac	1:23	who was **s** Justus, and Matthias.	1941
	4:36	who by the apostles was **s** Barnabas,	1941
	10:18	which was **s** Peter, were lodged there.	1941
	15:22	namely, Judas Barsabas, and Silas,	1941

SURPRISED (3)

Isa	33:14	afraid; fearfulness hath **s** the hypocrites.	270
Jer	48:41	the strong holds are **s**, and the mighty	8610
	51:41	how is the praise of the whole earth **s**!	8610

SURVIVE See ABIDE; ABIDETH; ABIDING

SURVIVORS See RESIDUE

SUSA See SHUSHAN; SUSANCHITES

SUSANCHITES (1)

Ezr	4:	9 the S, the Dehavites, *and* the Elamites,	7801

SUSANNA (1)

Lk	8:	3 and S, and many others, which ministered	4677

SUSI (1)

Nu	13:11	the tribe of Manasseh, Gaddi the son of S.	5485

SUSPENSE See TARRIED; TARRIEST; TARRIETH; TARRY; TARRYING

SUSPICIONS See SURMISINGS

SUSTAIN (4) [SUSTAINED, SUSTENANCE]

1Ki	17:	9 a widow woman there to **s** thee.	3557
Ne	9:21	forty years didst thou **s** them in	3557
Ps	55:22	upon the Lord, and he shall **s** thee:	3557
Pr	18:14	The spirit of a man will **s** his infirmity;	3557

SUSTAINED (3) [SUSTAIN]

Ge	27:37	and with corn and wine have I **s** him:	5564
Ps	3:	5 and slept; I awaked; for the Lord **s** me.	5564
Isa	59:16	unto him; and his righteousness, it **s** him.	5564

SUSTENANCE (3) [SUSTAIN]

Jdg	6:	4 left no **s** for Israel, neither sheep, nor ox,	4241
2Sa	19:32	he had **provided** the king of **s** while he	3557
Ac	7:11	affliction: and our fathers found no **s**.	5527

SWADDLED (2) [SWADDLING]

La	2:22	those that I have **s** and brought up hath	2946
Eze	16:	4 wast not salted at all, nor **s** at all.	2853+2853

SWADDLING (3) [SWADDLED]

Job	38:	9 and thick darkness a **band** for it,	2854
Lk	2:	7 and **wrapped** him in **s** clothes,	4683
	2:12	find *the* babe **wrapped in s** clothes,	4683

SWALLOW (23) [SWALLOWED, SWALLOWETH]

Nu	16:30	earth open her mouth, and **s** them **up**,	1104
	16:34	for they said, Lest the earth **s** us **up** *also*.	1104
2Sa	20:19	why wilt thou **s** up the inheritance of	1104
	20:20	it from me, that I should **s up** or destroy.	1104
Job	7:19	nor let me alone till I **s down** my spittle?	1104
	20:18	shall he restore, and shall not **s** it **down**:	1104
Ps	21:	9 the Lord shall **s** them **up** in his wrath,	1104
	56:	1 for man would **s** me **up**; he fighting daily	7602
	56:	2 Mine enemies would daily **s** me **up**:	7602
	57:	3 the reproach of him that would **s** me **up**.	7602
	69:15	neither let the deep **s** me **up**, and let not	1104
	84:	3 the **s** a nest for herself, where she may lay	1866
Pr	1:12	Let us **s** them **up** alive as the grave;	1104
	26:	2 as the **s** by flying, so the curse causeless	1866
Ecc	10:12	but the lips of a fool will **s up** himself.	1104
Isa	25:	8 He will **s up** death in victory; and the	1104
	38:14	Like a crane or a **s**, so did I chatter: I did	5693
Jer	8:	7 the **s** observe the time of their coming;	5693
Hos	8:	7 if so be it yield, *the* strangers shall **s** it **up**.	1104
Am	8:	4 Hear this, O ye that **s up** the needy, even	7602
Ob	1:16	they shall **s down**, and they shall be as	3886
Jnh	1:17	that had prepared a great fish to **s up** Jonah.	1104
Mt	23:24	which strain out a gnat, and **s** a camel.	2666

SWALLOWED (26) [SWALLOW]

Ex	7:12	but Aaron's rod **s up** their rods.	1104
	15:12	out thy right hand, the earth **s** them.	1104
Nu	16:32	s them **up**, and their houses, and all	1104
	26:10	s them **up** together with Korah, when	1104
Dt	11:	6 s them **up**, and their households,	1104
2Sa	17:16	lest the king be **s up**, and all the people	1104
Job	6:	3 of the sea: therefore my words are **s up**.	3886
	20:15	He hath **s down** riches, and he shall	1104
	37:20	if a man speak, surely he shall be **s up**.	1104
Ps	35:25	let them not say, We have **s** him **up**.	1104
	106:17	The earth opened and **s up** Dathan,	1104
	124:	3 they had **s** us **up** quick, when their wrath	1104
Isa	28:	7 strong drink, they are **s up** of wine,	1104
	49:19	and they that **s** thee **up** shall be far away.	1104
Jer	51:34	he hath **s** me **up** like a dragon,	1104
	51:44	out of his mouth that which he hath **s up**	1105
La	2:	2 The Lord hath **s up** all the habitations of	1104
	2:	5 he hath **s up** Israel, he hath swallowed up	1104
	2:	5 up Israel, he hath **s up** all her palaces:	1104
	2:16	they say, We have **s** *her* **up**: certainly this	1104
Eze	35:	3 *you* desolate, and **s** you **up** on every side,	7602
Hos	8:	8 Israel is **s up**: now shall they be among	1104
1Co	15:54	that is written, Death is **s up** in victory.	2666
2Co	2:	7 should be **s up** with overmuch sorrow.	2666
	5:	4 that mortality might be **s up** of life.	2666
Rev	12:16	s **up** the flood which the dragon cast out	2666

SWALLOWETH (2) [SWALLOW]

Job	5:	5 and the robber **s up** their substance.	7602
	39:24	He **s** the ground with fierceness and rage:	1572

SWAN (2)

Lev	11:18	the **s**, and the pelican, and the gier eagle,	8580
Dt	14:16	little owl, and the great owl, and the **s**,	8580

SWARE (78) [SWEAR]

Ge	21:31	because there they **s** both of them.	7650
	24:	7 spake unto me, and that **s** unto me,	7650
	24:	9 and **s** to him concerning that matter.	7650
	25:33	Swear to me *this* day; and he **s** to him:	7650
	26:	3 I will perform the oath which I **s** unto	7650
	26:31	in the morning, and **s** one to another:	7650
	31:53	And Jacob **s** by the fear of his father Isaac.	7650
	47:31	he **s** unto him. And Israel bowed himself	7650
	50:24	unto the land which he **s** to Abraham,	7650
Ex	13:	5 which he **s** unto thy fathers to give thee,	7650
	13:11	as he **s** unto thee and to thy fathers,	7650

S

Ex	33: 1	unto the land which I **s** unto Abraham,	7650
Nu	14:16	into the land which he **s** unto them,	7650
	14:23	they shall not see the land which I **s**	7650
	14:30	*concerning* which I **s** to make you	3027+5375
	32:10	kindled the same time, and he **s**, saying,	7650
	32:11	see the land which I **s** unto Abraham,	7650
Dt	1: 8	possess the land which the LORD **s** unto	7650
	1:34	words, and was wroth, and **s**, saying,	7650
	1:35	which I **s** to give unto your fathers,	7650
	2:14	among the host, as the LORD **s** unto them.	7650
	4:21	**s** that I should not go over Jordan,	7650
	4:31	of thy fathers which he **s** unto them,	7650
	6:10	into the land which he **s** unto thy fathers,	7650
	6:18	possess the good land which the LORD **s**	7650
	6:23	to give us the land which he **s** unto our	7650
	7:12	the mercy which he **s** unto thy fathers:	7650
	7:13	in the land which he **s** unto thy fathers to	7650
	8: 1	possess the land which the LORD **s** unto	7650
	8:18	his covenant which he **s** unto thy fathers,	7650
	9: 5	word which the LORD **s** unto thy fathers,	7650
	10:11	which I **s** unto their fathers to give unto	7650
	11: 9	which the LORD **s** unto your fathers to	7650
	11:21	in the land which the LORD **s** unto your	7650
	26: 3	unto our fathers for to give us.	7650
	28:11	in the land which the LORD **s** unto thy	7650
	30:20	land which the LORD **s** unto thy fathers,	7650
	31:20	into the land which I **s** unto their fathers,	7650
	31:21	brought them into the land which I **s**,	7650
	31:23	Israel into the land which I **s** unto them:	7650
	34: 4	This *is* the land which I **s** unto Abraham,	7650
Jos	1: 6	which I **s** unto their fathers to give them.	7650
	5: 6	unto whom the LORD **s** that *he* would not	7650
	5: 6	which the LORD **s** unto their fathers that	7650
	6:22	and all that she hath, as ye **s** unto her.	7650
	9:15	princes of the congregation **s** unto them.	7650
	9:20	of the oath which we **s** unto them.	7650
	14: 9	Moses **s** on that day, saying, Surely	7650
	21:43	land which he **s** to give unto their fathers;	7650
	21:44	to all that he **s** unto their fathers:	7650
Jdg	2: 1	have brought you unto the land which I **s**	7650
1Sa	19: 6	Saul, *As* the LORD liveth, he shall not	7650
	20: 3	David **s** moreover, and said, Thy father	7650
	24:22	David **s** unto Saul. And David went home;	7650
	28:10	Saul **s** to her by the LORD, saying,	7650
2Sa	3:35	David **s**, saying, So do God to me,	7650
	19:23	shalt not die. And the king **s** unto him.	7650
	21:17	the men of David **s** unto him, saying,	7650
1Ki	1:29	the king **s**, and said, *As* the LORD liveth,	7650
	1:30	Even as I **s** unto thee by the LORD God of	7650
	2: 8	and I **s** to him by the LORD, saying,	7650
	2:23	king Solomon **s** by the LORD, saying,	7650
2Ki	25:24	Gedaliah **s** to them, and to their men,	7650
2Ch	15:14	they **s** unto the LORD with a loud voice,	7650
Ezr	10: 5	do according to this word. And they **s**.	7650
Ps	95:11	*Unto* whom I **s** in my wrath that they	7650
	132: 2	How he **s** unto the LORD,	7650
Jer	38:16	So Zedekiah the king **s** secretly unto	7650
	40: 9	Ahikam the son of Shaphan **s** unto them	7650
Eze	16: 8	I **s** unto thee, and entered into a covenant	7650
Da	12: 7	**s** by him that liveth for ever that *it shall*	7650
Mk	6:23	And he **s** unto her, Whatsoever thou shalt	3660
Lk	1:73	oath which he **s** to our father Abraham,	3660
Heb	3:11	So I **s** in my wrath, They shall not enter	3660
	3:18	And to whom **s** he that *they* should not	3660
	6:13	swear by no greater, he **s** by himself,	3660
	7:21	unto him, The Lord **s** and will not repent,	3660
Rev	10: 6	**s** by him that liveth for ever and ever,	3660

SWAREST (5) [SWEAR]

Ex	32:13	to whom thou **s** by thine own self,	7650
Nu	11:12	unto the land which thou **s** unto their	7650
Dt	26:15	as thou **s** unto our fathers, a land that	7650
1Ki	1:17	thou **s** by the LORD thy God unto thine	7650
Ps	89:49	which thou **s** unto David in thy truth?	7650

SWARM (3) [SWARMS]

Ex	8:24	there came a grievous **s** *of flies* into	6157
	8:24	the land was corrupted by reason of the **s**	6157
Jdg	14: 8	*there was* a **s** of bees and honey in	5712

SWARMS (5) [SWARM]

Ex	8:21	I will send a **s** *of flies* upon thee,	6157
	8:21	the Egyptians shall be full of **s** *of flies*,	6157
	8:22	that no **s** *of flies* shall be there;	6157
	8:29	I will intreat the LORD that the **s** *of flies*	6157
	8:31	he removed the **s** *of flies* from Pharaoh,	6157

SWEAR (60) [FORSWEAR, SWARE, SWAREST, SWEARERS, SWEARETH, SWEARING, SWORN]

Ge	21:23	**s** unto me here by God that thou wilt not	7650
	21:24	And Abraham said, I will **s**.	7650
	24: 3	I will **make** thee **s** by the LORD, the God	7650
	24:37	my master **made** me **s**, saying, Thou shalt	7650
	25:33	Jacob said, **S** to me *this* day; and he sware	7650
	47:31	said, **S** unto me. And he sware unto him.	7650
	50: 5	My father **made** me **s**, saying, Lo, I die:	7650
	50: 6	thy father, according as he **made** thee **s**.	7650
Ex	6: 8	the which I did **s** to give	3027+5375
Lev	5: 4	Or if a soul **s**, pronouncing with *his* lips to	7650
	19:12	ye shall not **s** by my name falsely,	7650
Nu	30: 2	or **s** an oath to bind his soul with a bond;	7650
Dt	6:13	and serve him, and shalt **s** by his name.	7650
	10:20	him shalt thou cleave, and **s** by his name.	7650
Jos	2:12	I pray you, **s** unto me by the LORD,	7650
	2:17	thine oath which thou hast **made** us **s**.	7650

Jos	2:20	thine oath which thou hast **made** us to **s**	7650
	23: 7	cause to **s** *by them*, neither serve them.	7650
Jdg	15:12	Samson said unto them, **S** unto me, that	7650
1Sa	20:17	Jonathan caused David to **s** again, because	7650
	24:21	**S** now therefore unto me by the LORD,	7650
	30:15	he said, **S** unto me by God, that thou wilt	7650
2Sa	19: 7	for I **s** by the LORD, if thou go not forth,	7650
1Ki	1:13	O king, **s** unto thine handmaid, saying,	7650
	1:51	Let king Solomon **s** unto me to day that	7650
	2:42	Did I not **make** thee **to s** by the LORD,	7650
	8:31	oath be laid upon him to **cause** him to **s**,	422
2Ch	6:22	an oath be laid upon him to **make** him **s**,	422
	36:13	who had **made** him **s** by God:	7650
Ezr	10: 5	**made** the chief priests, the Levites, and all Israel, **to s**	7650
Ne	13:25	off their hair, and **made** them **s** by God,	7650
Isa	3	In that day shall he **s**, saying, I will not be	5375
	19:18	of Canaan, and **s** to the LORD of hosts:	7650
	45:23	knee shall bow, every tongue shall **s**.	7650
	48: 1	which **s** by the name of the LORD,	7650
	65:16	he that sweareth in the earth shall **s** by	7650
Jer	4: 2	thou shalt **s**, The LORD liveth, in truth,	7650
	5: 2	The LORD liveth; surely they **s** falsely.	7650
	7: 9	**s** falsely, and burn incense unto Baal,	7650
	12:16	to **s** by my name, The LORD liveth;	7650
	12:16	as they taught my people to **s** by Baal;	7650
	22: 5	I **s** by myself, saith the LORD,	7650
	32:22	which thou didst **s** to their fathers to give	7650
Hos	4:15	up *to* Beth-aven, nor **s**, The LORD liveth.	7650
Am	8:14	They that **s** by the sin of Samaria, and say,	7650
Zep	1: 5	that worship *and* that **s** by the LORD,	7650
	1: 5	by the LORD, and that **s** by Malcham;	7650
Mt	5:34	But I say unto you, **S** not at all; neither by	3660
	5:36	Neither shalt thou **s** by thy head, because	3660
	23:16	Whosoever shall **s** by the temple,	3660
	23:16	whosoever shall **s** by the gold of	3660
	23:18	And, Whosoever shall **s** by the altar, it is	3660
	23:20	Whoso therefore shall **s** by the altar,	3660
	23:21	And whoso shall **s** by the temple,	3660
	23:22	he that shall **s** by heaven, sweareth by	3660
	26:74	Then began he to curse and to **s**, *saying*,	3660
Mk	14:71	But he began to curse and to **s**, *saying*, I	3660
Heb	6:13	because he could **s** by no greater, he	3660
	6:16	men verily **s** by the greater: and an oath	3660
Jas	5:12	**s** not, neither by heaven, neither by	3660

SWEARERS (1) [SWEAR]

Mal	3: 5	against false **s**, and against those that	7650

SWEARETH (11) [SWEAR]

Lev	6: 3	and lieth concerning it, and **s** falsely;	7650
Ps	15: 4	*He that s* to his *own* hurt, and changeth	7650
	63:11	God; every one that **s** by him shall glory:	7650
Ecc	9: 2	*and* he that **s**, as he that feareth an oath.	7650
Isa	65:16	that **s** in the earth shall swear by the God	7650
Zec	5: 3	every one that **s** shall be cut off *as* on that	7650
	5: 4	into the house of him that **s** falsely by my	7650
Mt	23:18	whosoever **s** by the gift that is upon it,	3660
	23:20	altar, **s** by it, and by all *things* thereon.	3660
	23:21	**s** by it, and by him that dwelleth therein.	3660
	23:22	**s** by the throne of God, and by him that	3660

SWEARING (4) [SWEAR]

Lev	5: 1	and hear the voice of **s**, and *is* a witness,	423
Jer	23:10	for because of **s** the land mourneth;	423
Hos	4: 2	By **s**, and lying, and killing, and stealing,	422
	10: 4	**s** falsely in making a covenant:	422

SWEAT (3)

Ge	3:19	In the **s** of thy face shalt thou eat bread,	2188
Eze	44:18	*themselves* with any thing that causeth **s**.	3154
Lk	22:44	his **s** was as it were great drops of blood	2402

SWEEP (3) [SWEEPING, SWEPT]

Isa	14:23	I will **s** it with the besom of destruction,	2894
	28:17	the hail shall **s away** the refuge of lies,	3261
Lk	15: 8	**s** the house, and seek diligently till she	4563

SWEEPING (1) [SWEEP]

Pr	28: 3	poor *is like* a **s** rain which leaveth no food.	5502

SWEET (108) [SWEETER, SWEETLY, SWEETNESS, SWEETSMELLING]

Ge	8:21	the LORD smelled a **s** savour;	5207
Ex	15:25	the waters, the waters were **made s**:	4985
	25: 6	spices for anointing oil, and for **s** incense,	5561
	29:18	it *is* a savour, an offering made by fire	5207
	29:25	for a **s** savour before the LORD:	5207
	29:41	the drink offering thereof, for a **s** savour,	5207
	30: 7	Aaron shall burn thereon **s** incense every	5561
	30:23	and of **s** cinnamon half so much,	1314
	30:23	and of **s** calamus two hundred and	1314
	30:34	Take unto thee **s** spices, stacte, and	5561
	30:34	*these* **s** spices with pure frankincense:	5561
	31:11	**s** incense for the holy *place*: according to	5561
	35: 8	for anointing oil, and for the **s** incense,	5561
	35:15	the incense, and the hanging for the	5561
	35:28	the anointing oil, and for the **s** incense.	5561
	37:29	and the pure incense of **s** spices,	5561
	39:38	the incense, and the hanging for	5561
	40:27	he burnt **s** incense thereon; as the LORD	5561
Lev	1: 9	by fire, of a **s** savour unto the LORD.	5207
	1:13	by fire, of a **s** savour unto the LORD.	5207
	1:17	by fire, of a **s** savour unto the LORD.	5207
	2: 2	by fire, of a **s** savour unto the LORD:	5207

Lev	2: 9	by fire, of a **s** savour unto the LORD.	5207
	2:12	they shall not be burnt on the altar for a **s**	5207
	3: 5	by fire, of a **s** savour unto the LORD.	5207
	3:16	of the offering made by fire for a **s** savour:	5561
	4: 7	of the altar of **s** incense before the LORD,	5561
	4:31	priest shall burn *it* upon the altar for a **s**	5207
	6:15	shall burn *it* upon the altar *for a* **s** savour,	5207
	6:21	thou offer *for a* **s** savour unto the LORD.	5207
	8:21	it *was* a burnt sacrifice for a **s** savour,	5207
	8:28	they *were* consecrations for a **s** savour:	5207
	16:12	his hands full of **s** incense beaten small,	5561
	17: 6	burn the fat for a **s** savour unto the LORD,	5207
	23:13	by fire unto the LORD *for a* **s** savour:	5207
	23:18	made by fire, of **s** savour unto the LORD.	5207
	26:31	not smell the savour of your **s** odours.	5207
Nu	4:16	incense, and the daily meat offering,	5561
	15: 3	to make a **s** savour unto the LORD,	5207
	15: 7	*of* wine, for a **s** savour unto the LORD.	5207
	15:10	by fire, of a **s** savour unto the LORD.	5207
	15:13	by fire, of a **s** savour unto the LORD;	5207
	15:14	by fire, of a **s** savour unto the LORD;	5207
	15:24	for a **s** savour unto the LORD, with his	5207
	18:17	by fire, for a **s** savour unto the LORD:	5207
	28: 2	made by fire, *for a* **s** savour unto me,	5207
	28: 6	was ordained in mount Sinai for a **s**	5207
	28: 8	by fire, *of a* **s** savour unto the LORD.	5207
	28:13	*for a* burnt offering *of a* **s** savour,	5207
	28:24	by fire, *of a* **s** savour unto the LORD:	5207
	28:27	ye shall offer the burnt offering for a **s**	5207
	29: 2	shall offer a burnt offering for a **s** savour	5207
	29: 6	unto their manner, for a **s** savour,	5207
	29: 8	offering unto the LORD *for a* **s** savour;	5207
	29:13	by fire, *of a* **s** savour unto the LORD:	5207
	29:36	by fire, *of a* **s** savour unto the LORD.	5207
2Sa	23: 1	of Jacob, and the **s** psalmist of Israel, said,	5273
2Ch	2: 4	*and* to burn before him **s** incense,	5561
	13:11	evening burnt sacrifices and **s** incense:	5561
	16:14	the bed which was filled *with* **s** odours	1314
Ezr	6:10	they may offer sacrifices of **s** savours	5208
Ne	8:10	drink the **s**, and send portions unto *them*	4477
Est	2:12	six months with **s** odours, and with	1314
Job	20:12	Though wickedness be **s** in his mouth,	4985
	21:33	The clods of the valley shall be **s** unto	4985
	38:31	Canst thou bind the **s** influences of	4575
Ps	55:14	We **took** **s** counsel together,	4985
	104:34	My meditation of him shall be **s**: I will be	6149
	119:103	How **s** are thy words unto my taste!	4452
	141: 6	they shall hear my words; for they are **s**.	5276
Pr	3:24	shalt lie down, and thy sleep shall be **s**.	6149
	9:17	Stolen waters are **s**, and bread *eaten* in	4985
	13:19	The desire accomplished is **s** to the soul:	6149
	16:24	**s** to the soul, and health to the bones.	4966
	20:17	Bread of deceit *is* **s** to a man;	6156
	23: 8	thou vomit up, and lose thy **s** words.	5273
	24:13	the honeycomb, *which is* **s** to thy taste:	4966
	27: 7	*to* the hungry soul every bitter *thing is* **s**.	4966
Ecc	5:12	The sleep of a labouring *man is* **s**,	4966
	11: 7	Truly the light *is* **s**, and a pleasant *thing*	4966
SS	2: 3	his fruit *was* **s** to my taste.	4966
	2:14	for **s** *is* thy voice, and thy countenance *is*	6156
	5: 5	my fingers *with* **s smelling** myrrh, upon	5674
	5:13	*are* as a bed of spices, *as* **s** flowers:	4840
	5:13	*like* lilies, dropping **s smelling** myrrh.	5674
	5:16	His mouth *is* most **s**: yea, he *is* altogether	4477
Isa	3:24	instead of **s smell** there shall be stink;	1314
	5:20	that put bitter for **s**, and sweet for bitter!	4966
	5:20	that put bitter for sweet, and **s** for bitter!	4966
	23:16	**make s** melody, sing many songs, that	3190
	43:24	Thou hast bought me no **s** cane with	7070
	49:26	with their own blood, as with **s** wine:	6071
Jer	6:20	**s** cane from a far country?	2896
	6:20	nor your sacrifices **s** unto me.	6149
	31:26	and beheld; and my sleep was **s** unto me.	6149
Eze	6:13	the place where they did offer **s** savour to	5207
	16:19	thou hast even set it before them for a **s**	5207
	20:28	there also they made their **s** savour,	5207
	20:41	I will accept you with your **s** savour,	5207
Da	2:46	offer an oblation and **s** odours unto him.	5208
Am	9:13	the mountains shall drop **s** wine, and all	6071
Mic	6:15	**s** wine, but shalt not drink wine.	8492
Mk	16: 1	Salome, had bought **s** spices, that they	NIG
2Co	2:15	For we are unto God a **s** savour of Christ,	2175
Php	4:18	an odour of a **s smell**, a sacrifice	2175
Jas	3:11	send forth at the same place **s** *water*	1099
Rev	10: 9	but it shall be in thy mouth as honey.	1099
	10:10	it up; and it was in my mouth **s** as honey:	1099

SWEETER (3) [SWEET]

Jdg	14:18	sun went down, What *is* **s** than honey?	4966
Ps	19:10	**s** also than honey and the honeycomb.	4966
	119:103	my taste! *yea*, **s** than honey to my mouth!	NIH

SWEETLY (2) [SWEET]

Job	24:20	him; the worm shall **feed s** on him;	4988
SS	7: 9	my beloved, that goeth *down* **s**,	4339+3807.1

SWEETNESS (5) [SWEET]

Jdg	9:11	Should I forsake my **s**, and my good fruit,	4987
	14:14	and out of the strong came forth **s**.	4966
Pr	16:21	and the **s** of the lips increaseth learning.	4986
	27: 9	*doth* the **s** of a man's friend by hearty	4986
Eze	3: 3	and it was in my mouth as honey for **s**.	4966

SWEETSMELLING (1) [SMELL, SWEET]

Eph	5: 2	and a sacrifice to God for a **s** savour.	2175

S

SWELL (4) [SWELLED, SWELLING, SWELLINGS, SWOLLEN]

Nu	5:21 make thy thigh to rot, and thy belly to **s**;	6639
	5:22 **make** thy belly to **s**, and thy thigh to rot:	6638
	5:27 her belly shall **s**, and her thigh shall rot:	6638
Dt	8: 4 neither did thy foot **s**, these forty years.	1216

SWELLED (1) [SWELL]

Ne	9:21 waxed not old, and their feet **s** not.	1216

SWELLING (7) [SWELL]

Ps	46: 3 *though* the mountains shake with the **s**	1346
Isa	30:13 **s** out in a high wall, whose breaking	1158
Jer	12: 5 then how wilt thou do in the **s** of Jordan?	1347
	49:19 he shall come up like a lion from the **s** of	1347
	50:44 he shall come up like a lion from the **s** of	1347
2Pe	2:18 For when they speak **great** *words* of	5246
Jude	1:16 their mouth speaketh **great s** words,	5246

SWELLINGS (1) [SWELL]

2Co	12:20 backbitings, whisperings, **s**, tumults:	5450

SWEPT (4) [SWEEP]

Jdg	5:21 The river of Kishon **s** them **away**,	1640
Jer	46:15 Why are thy valiant *men* **s away**?	5502
Mt	12:44 he findeth *it* empty, **s**, and garnished.	4563
Lk	11:25 he cometh, he findeth *it* **s** and garnished.	4563

SWERVED (1)

1Ti	1: 6 From which some having **s** have turned	795

SWIFT (20) [SWIFTER, SWIFTLY]

Dt	28:49 end of the earth, *as* **s** as the eagle flieth;	NIH
1Ch	12: 8 *were* as the roes upon the mountains:	4116
Job	9:26 They are passed away as the **s** ships:	16
	24:18 is **s** as the waters; their portion is cursed	7031
Pr	6:18 feet that be **s** in running to mischief,	4116
Ecc	9:11 the sun, that the race *is* not to the **s**,	7031
Isa	18: 2 *saying*, Go, ye **s** messengers, to a nation	7031
	19: 1 the LORD rideth upon a **s** cloud,	7031
	30:16 We will ride upon the **s**; therefore shall	7031
	30:16 therefore shall they that pursue you be **s**.	7043
	66:20 and upon mules, and upon **s beasts**,	3753
Jer	2:23 *art* a **s** dromedary traversing her ways;	7031
	46: 6 Let not the **s** flee away, nor the mighty	7031
	46: 6 the flight shall perish from the **s**,	7031
Am	2:15 *that is* **s** of foot shall not deliver *himself*:	7031
Mic	1:13 Lachish, bind the chariot to the **s beast**:	7409
Mal	3: 5 I will be a **s** witness against the sorcerers,	4116
Ro	3:15 Their feet *are* **s** to shed blood:	3691
Jas	1:19 let every man be **s** to hear, slow to speak,	5036
2Pe	2: 1 and bring upon themselves **s** destruction.	5031

SWIFTER (6) [SWIFT]

2Sa	1:23 were **s** than eagles, they were stronger	7043
Job	7: 6 My days are **s** than a weaver's shuttle,	7043
	9:25 Now my days are **s** than a post: they flee	7043
Jer	4:13 his horses are **s** than eagles. Woe unto us!	7043
La	4:19 Our persecutors are **s** than the eagles of	7031
Hab	1: 8 Their horses also are **s** than the leopards,	7043

SWIFTLY (4) [SWIFT]

Ps	147:15 earth: his word runneth **very s**.	4120+5704
Isa	5:26 behold, they shall come with speed **s**:	7031
Da	9:21 beginning, being caused to fly **s**,	3288+871.1
Joel	3: 4 *and* speedily will I return your	7031

SWIM (6) [SWIMMEST, SWIMMETH]

2Ki	6: 6 and cast *it* in thither; and the iron did **s**.	6687
Ps	6: 6 all the night **make** I my bed to **s**,	7811
Isa	25:11 swimmeth spreadeth forth **his** hands to **s**:	7811
Eze	47: 5 for the waters were risen, waters to **s** in,	7813
Ac	27:42 lest any *of them* should **s** out, and escape.	1579
	27:43 commanded that they which could **s**	2860

SWIMMEST (1) [SWIM]

Eze	32: 6 with thy blood the land wherein thou **s**,	6824

SWIMMETH (1) [SWIM]

Isa	25:11 as he that **s** spreadeth forth *his* hands to	7811

SWINE (16) [SWINE'S]

Lev	11: 7 the **s**, though he divide the hoof,	2386
Dt	14: 8 the **s**, because it divideth the hoof,	2386
Mt	7: 6 neither cast ye your pearls before **s**,	5519
	8:30 off from them a herd of many **s** feeding.	5519
	8:31 suffer us to go away into the herd of **s**.	5519
	8:32 come out, they went into the herd of **s**.	5519
	8:32 the whole herd of **s** ran violently down a	5519
Mk	5:11 the mountains a great herd of **s** feeding.	5519
	5:12 saying, Send us into the **s**, that we may	5519
	5:13 spirits went out, and entered into the **s**:	5519
	5:14 And they that fed the **s** fled, and told *it* in	5519
	5:16 to the devil, and *also* concerning the **s**.	5519
Lk	8:32 And there was there a herd of many **s**	5519
	8:33 out of the man, and entered into the **s**:	5519
	15:15 he sent him into his fields to feed **s**.	5519
	15:16 his belly with the husks that the **s** did eat:	5519

SWINE'S (4) [SWINE]

Pr	11:22 *As* a jewel of gold in a **s** snout, *so is* a fair	2386
Isa	65: 4 eat **s** flesh, and broth of abominable	2386
	66: 3 an oblation, *as if he offered* **s** blood;	2386
	66:17 eating **s** flesh, and the abomination,	2386

SWOLLEN (1) [SWELL]

Ac	28: 6 they looked when he should have **s**,	4092

SWOON (1) [SWOONED]

La	2:11 the sucklings **s** in the streets of the city.	5848

SWOONED (1) [SWOON]

La	2:12 they **s** as the wounded in the streets	5848

SWORD (424) [SWORDS]

Ge	3:24 a flaming **s** which turned every way,	2719
	27:40 by thy **s** shalt thou live, and shalt serve	2719
	31:26 daughters, as captives taken with the **s**?	2719
	34:25 took each man his **s**, and came upon	2719
	34:26 Shechem his son with the edge of the **s**,	2719
	48:22 out of the hand of the Amorite with my **s**	2719
Ex	5: 3 upon us with pestilence, or with the **s**.	2719
	5:21 to put a **s** in their hand to slay us.	2719
	15: 9 I will draw my **s**, my hand shall destroy	2719
	17:13 and his people with the edge of the **s**.	2719
	18: 4 and delivered me from the **s** of Pharaoh:	2719
	22:24 wax hot, and I will kill you with the **s**;	2719
	32:27 Put every man his **s** by his side, *and* go in	2719
Lev	26: 6 neither shall the **s** go through your land.	2719
	26: 7 and they shall fall before you by the **s**.	2719
	26: 8 enemies shall fall before you by the **s**.	2719
	26:25 will bring a **s** upon you, that shall avenge	2719
	26:33 heathen, and will draw out a **s** after you:	2719
	26:36 they shall flee, as fleeing from a **s**;	2719
	26:37 it were before a **s**, when none pursueth:	2719
Nu	14: 3 to fall by the **s**, *that* our wives and	2719
	14:43 before you, and ye shall fall by the **s**.	2719
	19:16 that is slain with a **s** in the open fields,	2719
	20:18 lest I come out against thee with the **s**.	2719
	21:24 Israel smote him with the edge of the **s**,	2719
	22:23 in the way, and his **s** drawn in his hand:	2719
	22:29 I would there were a **s** in mine hand,	2719
	22:31 in the way, and his **s** drawn in his hand:	2719
	31: 8 also the son of Beor they slew with the **s**,	2719
Dt	13:15 of that city with the edge of the **s**,	2719
	13:15 the cattle thereof, with the edge of the **s**:	2719
	20:13 every male thereof with the edge of the **s**:	2719
	28:22 with the **s**, and with blasting,	2719
	32:25 The **s** without, and terror within,	2719
	32:41 If I whet my glittering **s**, and mine hand	2719
	32:42 with blood, and my **s** shall devour flesh;	2719
	33:29 and who *is* the **s** of thy excellency!	2719
Jos	5:13 against him with his **s** drawn in his hand:	2719
	6:21 sheep, and ass, with the edge of the **s**.	2719
	8:24 they were all fallen on the edge of the **s**,	2719
	8:24 Ai, and smote it with the edge of the **s**.	2719
	10:11 the children of Israel slew with the **s**.	2719
	10:28 smote it with the edge of the **s**, and the	2719
	10:30 he smote it with the edge of the **s**, and all	2719
	10:32 smote it with the edge of the **s**, and all	2719
	10:35 smote it with the edge of the **s**, and all	2719
	10:37 smote it with the edge of the **s**, and the	2719
	10:39 they smote them with the edge of the **s**,	2719
	11:10 and smote the king thereof with the **s**:	2719
	11:11 that *were* therein with the edge of the **s**,	2719
	11:12 smote them with the edge of the **s**,	2719
	11:14 man they smote with the edge of the **s**,	2719
	13:22 did the children of Israel slay with the **s**	2719
	19:47 smote it with the edge of the **s**,	2719
	24:12 *but* not with thy **s**, nor with thy bow.	2719
Jdg	1: 8 smitten it with the edge of the **s**, and set	2719
	1:25 smote the city with the edge of the **s**;	2719
	4:15 with the edge of the **s** before Barak;	2719
	4:16 host of Sisera fell upon the edge of the **s**;	2719
	7:14 This *is* nothing else save the **s** of Gideon	2719
	7:18 say, *The* **s** of the LORD, and of Gideon.	NIH
	7:20 The **s** of the LORD, and of Gideon.	2719
	7:22 the LORD set every man's **s** against his	2719
	8:10 and twenty thousand men that drew **s**.	2719
	8:20 the youth drew not his **s**: for he feared,	2719
	9:54 said unto him, Draw thy **s**, and slay me,	2719
	18:27 they smote them with the edge of the **s**,	2719
	20: 2 hundred thousand footmen that drew **s**.	2719
	20:15 and six thousand men that drew **s**,	2719
	20:17 four hundred thousand men that drew **s**:	2719
	20:25 thousand men; all these drew the **s**.	2719
	20:35 an hundred men: all these drew the **s**.	2719
	20:37 smote all the city with the edge of the **s**.	2719
	20:46 and five thousand men that drew the **s**;	2719
	20:48 smote them with the edge of the **s**, as	2719
	21:10 of Jabesh-gilead with the edge of the **s**,	2719
1Sa	13:22 there was neither **s** nor spear found in	2719
	14:20 every man's **s** was against his fellow,	2719
	15: 8 all the people with the edge of the **s**.	2719
	15:33 As thy **s** hath made women childless,	2719
	17:39 David girded his **s** upon his armour,	2719
	17:45 Thou comest to me with a **s**, and with a	2719
	17:47 know that the LORD saveth not with **s**	2719
	17:50 but *there was* no **s** in the hand of David.	2719
	17:51 took his **s**, and drew it out of the sheath	2719
	18: 4 even to his **s**, and to his bow, and to his	2719
	21: 8 not here under thine hand spear or **s**?	2719
	21: 8 for I have neither brought my **s** nor my	2719
	21: 9 priest said, The **s** of Goliath the Philistine,	2719
	22:10 gave him the **s** of Goliath the Philistine.	2719
	22:13 that thou hast given him bread and a **s**,	2719
	22:19 smote he with the edge of the **s**, both	2719
	22:19 asses, and sheep, with the edge of the **s**.	2719
	25:13 his men, Gird you on every man his **s**.	2719
	25:13 they girded on every man his **s**;	2719

1Sa	25:13 **s**; and David also girded on his **s**:	2719
	31: 4 and thrust me through	2719
	31: 4 therefore Saul took a **s**, and fell upon it.	2719
	31: 5 he fell likewise upon his **s**, and died with	2719
2Sa	1:12 Israel; because they were fallen by the **s**.	2719
	1:22 and the **s** of Saul returned not empty.	2719
	2:16 and *thrust* his **s** in his fellow's side;	2719
	2:26 and said, Shall the **s** devour for ever?	2719
	3:29 or that falleth on the **s**, or that lacketh	2719
	11:25 the **s** devoureth one as well as another:	2719
	12: 9 hast killed Uriah the Hittite with the **s**,	2719
	12: 9 hast slain him with the **s** of the children	2719
	12:10 the **s** shall never depart from thine house,	2719
	15:14 and smite the city with the edge of the **s**.	2719
	18: 8 people that day than the **s** devoured.	2719
	20: 8 upon it a girdle with a fastened upon	2719
	20:10 Amasa took no heed to the **s** that *was* in	2719
	21:16 he being girded *with* a new **s**, thought to	NIH
	23:10 weary, and his hand clave unto the **s**:	2719
	24: 9 thousand valiant men that drew the **s**	2719
1Ki	1:51 he will not slay his servant with the **s**.	2719
	2: 8 I will not put thee to death with the **s**.	2719
	2:32 better than he, and slew them with the **s**,	2719
	3:24 the king said, Bring me a **s**. And they	2719
	3:24 And they brought a **s** before the king.	2719
	19: 1 he had slain all the prophets with the **s**.	2719
	19:10 and slain thy prophets with the **s**;	2719
	19:14 and slain thy prophets with the **s**;	2719
	19:17 him that escapeth the **s** of Hazael shall	2719
	19:17 him that escapeth the **s** of Jehu shall slay	2719
2Ki	6:22 whom thou hast taken captive with thy **s**	2719
	8:12 young *men* wilt thou slay with the **s**,	2719
	10:25 they smote them with the edge of the **s**;	2719
	11:15 him that followeth her kill with the **s**.	2719
	11:20 they slew Athaliah with the **s** beside	2719
	19: 7 I will cause him to fall by the **s** in his own	2719
	19:37 Sharezer *his* sons smote him with the **s**,	2719
1Ch	5:18 men *able* to bear buckler and **s**,	2719
	10: 4 Draw thy **s**, and thrust me through	2719
	10: 4 So Saul took a **s**, and fell upon it.	2719
	10: 5 he fell likewise on the **s**, and died.	2719
	21: 5 an hundred thousand men that drew **s**:	2719
	21: 5 and ten thousand men that drew **s**.	2719
	21:12 that *is* of thine enemies overtaketh	2719
	21:12 or else three days the **s** of the LORD,	2719
	21:16 having a drawn **s** in his hand stretched	2719
	21:27 he put up his **s** again into the sheath	2719
	21:30 of the **s** of the angel of the LORD.	2719
2Ch	20: 9 the **s**, judgment, or pestilence, or famine,	2719
	21: 4 slew all his brethren with the **s**,	2719
	23:14 followeth her, let him be slain with the **s**.	2719
	23:21 that they had slain Athaliah with the **s**.	2719
	29: 9 our fathers have fallen by the **s**,	2719
	32:21 own bowels slew him there with the **s**.	2719
	36:17 who slew their young men with the **s** in	2719
	36:20 them that had escaped from the **s** carried	2719
Ezr	9: 7 to the **s**, to captivity, and to a spoil,	2719
Ne	4:18 every one had his **s** girded by his side,	2719
Est	9: 5 all their enemies *with* the stroke of the **s**,	2719
Job	1:15 slain the servants with the edge of the **s**;	2719
	1:17 slain the servants with the edge of the **s**;	2719
	5:15 he saveth the poor from the **s**, from their	2719
	5:20 and in war from the power of the **s**.	2719
	15:22 of darkness, and he *is* waited for of the **s**.	2719
	19:29 Be ye afraid of the **s**: for wrath *bringeth*	2719
	19:29 wrath *bringeth* the punishments of the **s**,	2719
	20:25 the **glistering s** cometh out of his gall:	1300
	27:14 If his children be multiplied, *it is* for the **s**:	2719
	33:18 pit, and his life from perishing by the **s**.	7973
	36:12 shall perish by the **s**, and they shall die	7973
	39:22 neither turneth he back from the **s**.	2719
	40:19 he that made him can make his **s** to	2719
	41:26 The **s** of him that layeth at him cannot	2719
Ps	7:12 If he turn not, he will whet his **s**; he hath	2719
	17:13 my soul from the wicked, *which is* thy **s**:	2719
	22:20 Deliver my soul from the **s**; my darling	2719
	37:14 The wicked have drawn out the **s**,	2719
	37:15 Their **s** shall enter into their own heart,	2719
	42:10 *As* with a **s** in my bones, mine enemies	7524
	44: 3 not the land in possession by their own **s**,	2719
	44: 6 in my bow, neither shall my **s** save me.	2719
	45: 3 Gird thy **s** upon *thy* thigh, O *most* mighty	2719
	57: 4 and arrows, and their tongue a sharp **s**.	2719
	63:10 They shall fall by the **s**: they shall be a	2719
	64: 3 Who whet their tongue like a **s**,	2719
	76: 3 the shield, and the **s**, and the battle.	2719
	78:62 He gave his people over also unto the **s**;	2719
	78:64 Their priests fell by the **s**; and their	2719
	89:43 Thou hast also turned the edge of his **s**,	2719
	144:10 David his servant from the hurtful **s**.	2719
	149: 6 and a twoedged **s** in their hand;	2719
Pr	5: 4 as wormwood, sharp as a twoedged **s**.	2719
	12:18 is that speaketh like the piercings of a **s**:	2719
	25:18 *is* a maul, and a **s**, and a sharp arrow.	2719
SS	3: 8 every man *hath* his **s** upon his thigh	2719
Isa	1:20 rebel, ye shall be devoured *with* the **s**:	2719
	2: 4 nation shall not lift up a **s** against nation,	2719
	3:25 Thy men shall fall by the **s**, and thy	2719
	13:15 is joined *unto* them shall fall by the **s**.	2719
	14:19 thrust through with a **s**, that go down to	2719
	21:15 the drawn **s**, and from the bent bow,	2719
	22: 2 thy slain *men are* not slain with the **s**,	2719
	27: 1 strong **s** shall punish leviathan the	2719
	31: 8 shall the Assyrian fall with the **s**, not of a	2719
	31: 8 **s**, not of a mean man, shall devour him:	2719

Isa 31: 8 shall flee from the **s**, and his young men 2719
34: 5 For my sword shall be bathed in heaven: 2719
34: 6 The **s** of the LORD is filled *with* blood, 2719
37: 7 I will cause him to fall by the **s** in his own 2719
37:38 Sharezer his sons smote him with the **s** 2719
41: 2 he gave *them* as the dust *to* his **s**, 2719
49: 2 he hath made my mouth like a sharp **s**; 2719
51:19 destruction, and the famine, and the **s**: 2719
65:12 Therefore will I number you to the **s**, 2719
66:16 by his **s** will the LORD plead with all 2719

Jer 2:30 your own **s** hath devoured your prophets, 2719
4:10 whereas she **s** reacheth unto the soul). 2719
5:12 neither shall we see **s** nor famine: 2719
5:17 wherein thou trustedst, with the **s**. 2719
6:25 for the **s** of the enemy *and* fear *is* on 2719
9:16 I will send a **s** after them, till I have 2719
11:22 the young men shall die by the **s**; 2719
12:12 for the **s** of the LORD *shall* devour from 2719
14:12 I will consume them by the **s**, and by 2719
14:13 say unto them, Ye shall not see the **s**, 2719
14:15 **S** and famine shall not be in this land; 2719
14:15 By **s** and famine shall those prophets be 2719
14:16 because of the famine and the **s**; 2719
14:18 field, then behold the slain with the **s**! 2719
15: 2 such as *are* for the **s**, to the sword; 2719
15: 2 such as *are* for the sword, to the **s**, 2719
15: 3 the **s** to slay, and the dogs to tear, 2719
15: 9 the residue of them will I deliver to the **s** 2719
16: 4 they shall be consumed by the **s**, 2719
18:21 pour out their *blood* by the force of the **s**; 2719
18:21 *let* their young men *be* slain by the **s** in 2719
19: 7 I will cause them to fall by the **s** before 2719
20: 4 they shall fall by the **s** of their enemies, 2719
20: 4 and shall slay them with the **s**. 2719
21: 7 from the **s**, and from the famine, 2719
21: 7 shall smite them with the edge of the **s**; 2719
21: 9 that abideth in this city shall die by the **s**, 2719
24:10 I will send the **s**, the famine, 2719
25:16 of the **s** that I will send among them. 2719
25:27 of the **s** which I will send among you. 2719
25:29 for I *will* call for a **s** upon all 2719
25:31 will give them *that are* wicked to the **s**, 2719
26:23 slew him with the **s**, and cast his dead 2719
27: 8 with the **s**, and with the famine, 2719
27:13 thou *and* thy people, by the **s**, 2719
29:17 Behold, I will send upon them the **s**, with 2719
29:18 I will persecute them with the **s**, with 2719
31: 2 The people which were left of the **s** found 2719
32:24 because of the **s**, and *of* the famine, 2719
32:36 the hand of the king of Babylon by the **s**, 2719
33: 4 down by the mounts, and by the **s**; 2719
34: 4 of thee, Thou shalt not die by the **s**: 2719
34:17 to the **s**, to the pestilence, and to 2719
38: 2 remaineth in this city shall die by the **s**, 2719
39:18 thou shalt not fall by the **s**, but thy life 2719
41: 2 of Ahikam the son of Shaphan with the **s**, 2719
42:16 come to pass, *that* ye, which ye feared, 2719
42:17 they shall die by the **s**, by the famine, 2719
42:22 know certainly that ye shall die by the **s**, 2719
43:11 and such as *are* for the **s** to the sword. 2719
43:11 and such as *are* for the sword to the **s**. 2719
44:12 they shall *even* be consumed by the **s**, 2719
44:12 the greatest, by the **s** and by the famine: 2719
44:13 by the **s**, by the famine, and by 2719
44:18 have been consumed by the **s** and by 2719
44:27 land of Egypt shall be consumed by the **s** 2719
44:28 Yet a small number that escape the **s** shall 2719
46:10 the **s** shall devour, and it shall be satiate 2719
46:14 for the **s** shall devour round about thee. 2719
46:16 of our nativity, from the oppressing **s**. 2719
47: 6 O thou **s** of the LORD, how long *will it be* 2719
48: 2 O Madmen; the **s** shall pursue thee. 2719
48:10 cursed *be* he that keepeth back his **s** from 2719
49:37 I will send the **s** after them, till I have 2719
50:16 for fear of the oppressing **s** they shall turn 2719
50:35 A **s** *is* upon the Chaldeans, saith 2719
50:36 A **s** *is* upon the liars; and they shall dote: 2719
50:36 a **s** *is* upon her mighty *men*; and they 2719
50:37 A **s** *is* upon their horses, and upon their 2719
50:37 a **s** *is* upon her treasures; and they shall 2719
51:50 Ye that have escaped the **s**, go *away*, 2719

La 1:20 abroad the **s** bereaveth, at home *there is* 2719
2:21 and my young men are fallen by the **s**; 2719
4: 9 *They* that *be* slain with the **s** are better 2719
5: 9 lives because of the **s** of the wilderness. 2719

Eze 5: 2 wind; and I will draw out a **s** after them. 2719
5:12 a third *part* shall fall by the **s** round about 2719
5:12 and I will draw out a **s** after them. 2719
5:17 and I will bring the **s** upon thee. 2719
6: 3 *will* bring a **s** upon you, and I will destroy 2719
6: 8 that shall escape the **s** among the nations, 2719
6:11 for they shall fall by the **s**, by the famine, 2719
6:12 he that *is* near shall fall by the **s**; and he 2719
7:15 The **s** *is* without, and the pestilence and 2719
7:15 he that *is* in the field shall die with the **s**; 2719
11: 8 Ye have feared the **s**; and I will bring a 2719
11: 8 I will bring a **s** upon you, saith the Lord 2719
11:10 Ye shall fall by the **s**; I will judge you in 2719
12:14 and I will draw out the **s** after them. 2719
12:16 will leave a few men of them from the **s**, 2719
14:17 Or *if* I bring a sword upon that land, and say, 2719
14:17 land, and say, **S**, go through the land; 2719
14:21 the **s**, and the famine, and the noisome 2719
17:21 with all his bands shall fall by the **s**, 2719
21: 3 will draw forth my **s** out of his sheath, 2719

Eze 21: 4 shall my **s** go forth out of his sheath 2719
21: 5 have drawn forth my **s** out of his sheath: 2719
21: 9 Say, A **s**, a sword is sharpened, 2719
21: 9 a **s** is sharpened, and also furbished: 2719
21:11 this **s** is sharpened, and *it is* furbished, 2719
21:12 terrors by reason of the **s** shall be upon 2719
21:13 what if *the* **s** contemn even the rod? NIH
21:14 let the **s** be doubled the third time, 2719
21:14 doubled the third time, the **s** of the slain: 2719
21:14 it *is* the **s** of the great *men that are* slain, 2719
21:15 I have set the point of the **s** against all 2719
21:19 the **s** of the king of Babylon may come: 2719
21:20 that the **s** may come to Rabbath of 2719
21:28 even say thou, The **s**, the sword *is* drawn: 2719
21:28 even say thou, The sword, the **s** *is* drawn: 2719
23:10 her daughters, and slew her with the **s**: 2719
23:25 and thy remnant shall fall by the **s**: 2719
24:21 whom ye have left shall fall by the **s**. 2719
25:13 and they of Dedan shall fall by the **s**. 2719
26: 6 *are* in the field shall be slain by the **s**; 2719
26: 8 He shall slay with the **s** thy daughters in 2719
26:11 he shall slay thy people by the **s**, 2719
28:23 of her by the **s** upon her on every side; 2719
29: 8 I *will* bring a **s** upon thee, and cut off 2719
30: 4 the **s** shall come upon Egypt, and great 2719
30: 5 is in league, shall fall with them by the **s**. 2719
30: 6 of Syene shall they fall in it by the **s**, 2719
30:17 and of Phi-beseth shall fall by the **s**: 2719
30:21 to bind it, to make it strong to hold the **s**. 2719
30:22 I will cause the **s** to fall out of his hand. 2719
30:24 of Babylon, and put my **s** in his hand: 2719
30:25 when I shall put my **s** into the hand of 2719
31:17 him unto *them that be* slain with the **s**; 2719
31:18 with *them that be* slain with the **s**. 2719
32:10 when I shall brandish my **s** before them; 2719
32:11 The **s** of the king of Babylon shall come 2719
32:20 the midst of *them that are* slain by the **s**: 2719
32:20 she is delivered to the **s**: draw her and 2719
32:21 they lie uncircumcised, slain by the **s**. 2719
32:22 him: all of them slain, fallen by the **s**: 2719
32:23 all of them slain, fallen by the **s**, 2719
32:24 grave, all of them slain, fallen by the **s**, 2719
32:25 all of them uncircumcised, slain by the **s**: 2719
32:26 all of them uncircumcised, slain by the **s**, 2719
32:28 lie with *them that are* slain with the **s**. 2719
32:29 are laid by *them that were* slain by the **s**: 2719
32:30 with *them that be* slain by the **s**, 2719
32:31 and all his army slain by the **s**, 2719
32:32 with *them that are* slain with the **s**, 2719
33: 2 them, When I bring the **s** upon a land, 2719
33: 3 when he seeth the **s** come upon the land, 2719
33: 4 if the **s** come, and take him away, 2719
33: 6 if the watchman see the **s** come, 2719
33: 6 if the **s** come, and take *any* person from 2719
33:26 Ye stand upon your **s**, ye work 2719
33:27 that *are* in the wastes shall fall by the **s**, 2719
35: 5 of the **s** in the time of their calamity, 2719
35: 8 shall fill *them* that *are* slain with the **s**. 2719
38: 8 the land *that is* brought back from the **s**, 2719
38:21 I will call *for* a **s** against him throughout 2719
38:21 every man's **s** shall be against his brother. 2719
39:23 of their enemies: so fell they all by the **s**. 2719

Da 11:33 yet they shall fall by the **s**, and by flame, 2719
Hos 1: 7 nor by **s**, nor by battle, by horses, nor by 2719
2:18 I will break the bow and the **s** and the 2719
7:16 their princes shall fall by the **s** for the 2719
11: 6 the **s** shall abide on his cities, 2719
13:16 they shall fall by the **s**: their infants shall 2719
Joel 2: 8 when they had fallen upon the **s**, they shall not 7973
Am 1:11 he did pursue his brother with the **s**, 2719
4:10 your young men have I slain with the **s**, 2719
7: 9 against the house of Jeroboam with the **s**. 2719
7:11 Jeroboam shall die by the **s**, and Israel 2719
7:17 and thy daughters shall fall by the **s**, 2719
9: 1 and I will slay the last of them with the **s**: 2719
9: 4 thence will I command the **s**, and it shall 2719
9:10 sinners of my people shall die by the **s**, 2719
Mic 4: 3 nation shall not lift up a **s** against nation, 2719
5: 6 waste the land of Assyria with the **s**, 2719
6:14 thou deliverest will I give up to the **s**. 2719
Na 2:13 and the **s** shall devour thy young lions: 2719
3: 3 The horseman lifteth up both the bright a 2719
3:15 the **s** shall cut thee off, it shall eat thee up 2719
Zep 2:12 Ethiopians also, ye *shall be* slain by my **s**. 2719
Hag 2:22 every one by the **s** of his brother. 2719
Zec 9:13 and made thee as the **s** of a mighty *man*. 2719
11:17 the **s** *shall be* upon his arm, and upon his 2719
13: 7 Awake, O **s**, against my shepherd, 2719
Mt 10:34 earth: I came not to send peace, but a **s**. 3162
26:51 and drew his **s**, and stroke a servant of 3162
26:51 him, Put up again thy **s** into his place: 3162
26:52 for all they that take the **s** shall perish 3162
26:52 take the sword shall perish with the **s**. 3162
Mk 14:47 And one of them that stood by drew a **s**, 3162
Lk 2:35 a **s** shall pierce through thy own soul also 4501
21:24 And they shall fall by the edge of the **s**, 3162
22:36 and he that hath no **s**, let him sell his 3162
22:49 him, Lord, shall we smite with the **s**? 3162
Jn 18:10 Then Simon Peter having a **s** drew it, 3162
18:11 unto Peter, Put up thy **s** into the sheath: 3162
Ac 12: 2 James the brother of John with the **s**. 3162
16:27 he drew out his **s**, and would have killed 3162
Ro 8:35 or famine, or nakedness, or peril, or **s**? 3162
13: 4 be afraid; for he beareth not the **s** in vain: 3162
Eph 6:17 the **s** of the Spirit, which is the word of 3162

Heb 4:12 and sharper than any twoedged **s**, 3162
11:34 violence of fire, escaped the edge of the **s**, 3162
11:37 were tempted, were slain with the **s**: 3162
Rev 1:16 of his mouth went a sharp twoedged **s**: 4501
2:12 *things* saith he which hath the sharp **s** 4501
2:16 will fight against them with the **s** of my 4501
6: 4 and there was given unto him a great **s**. 3162
6: 8 to kill with **s**, and with hunger, 4501
13:10 he that killeth with the **s** must be killed 3162
13:10 with the sword must be killed with the **s**. 3162
13:14 which had the wound by a **s**, and did live. 3162
19:15 And out of his mouth goeth a sharp **s**, 4501
19:21 And the remnant were slain with the **s** of 4501
19:21 which **s** proceeded out of his mouth: NIG

SWORDS (24) [SWORD]

1Sa 13:19 Lest the Hebrews make *them* **s** or spears: 2719
2Ki 3:26 him seven hundred men that drew **s**, 2719
Ne 4:13 the people after *their* families with their **s**, 2719
Ps 55:21 softer than oil, yet *were* they **drawn s** 6609
59: 7 **s** *are* in their lips: for who, *say they*, doth 2719
Pr 30:14 whose teeth *are as* **s**, and their jaw teeth 2719
SS 3: 8 They all hold **s**, *being* expert in war: 2719
Isa 2: 4 they shall beat their **s** into plowshares, 2719
21:15 For they fled from the **s**, from the drawn 2719
Eze 16:40 and thrust thee through with their **s**. 2719
23:47 stones, and dispatch them with their **s**; 2719
28: 7 they shall draw their **s** against the beauty 2719
30:11 they shall draw their **s** against Egypt, 2719
32:12 By the **s** of the mighty will I cause thy 2719
32:27 they have laid their **s** under their heads, 2719
38: 4 and shields, all of them handling **s**: 2719
Joel 3:10 Beat your plowshares into **s**, 2719
Mic 4: 3 they shall beat their **s** into plowshares, 2719
Mt 26:47 with him a great multitude with **s** 3162
26:55 Are ye come out as against a thief with **s** 3162
Mk 14:43 with him a great multitude with **s** and 3162
14:48 thief, with **s** and *with* staves to take me? 3162
Lk 22:38 they said, Lord, behold, here are two **s**. 3162
22:52 as against a thief, with **s** and staves? 3162

SWORN (48) [SWEAR]

Ge 22:16 said, By myself have I **s**, saith the LORD, 7650
Ex 13:19 for he had **straitly s** the children of 7650+7650
17:16 Because the LORD hath **s** 3027+3678+5921
Lev 5: 4 Or all *that* about which he hath **s** falsely; 7650
Dt 7: 8 he would keep the oath which he had **s** 7650
13:17 thee, as he hath **s** unto thy fathers; 7650
19: 8 as he hath **s** unto thy fathers, and give 7650
28: 9 unto himself, as he hath **s** unto thee, 7650
29:13 as he hath **s** unto thy fathers, to Abraham, 7650
31: 7 hath **s** unto their fathers to give them; 7650
Jos 9:18 the princes of the congregation had **s** unto 7650
9:19 We have **s** unto them by the LORD God 7650
2:15 and as the LORD had **s** unto them: 7650
Jdg 21: 1 Now the men of Israel had **s** in Mizpeh, 7650
21: 7 seeing we have **s** by the LORD that we 7650
21:18 for the children of Israel have **s**, saying, 7650
1Sa 3:14 I have **s** unto the house of Eli, 7650
20:42 forasmuch as we have **s** both of us in 7650
2Sa 3: 9 as the LORD hath **s** to David, even so I do 7650
21: 2 the children of Israel had **s** unto them: 7650
2Ch 15:15 for they had **s** with all their heart, 7650
Ne 6:18 *there were* many in Judah **s** unto 1167+7621
9:15 the land which thou hadst **s** to give them. 3027
Ps 24: 4 up his soul unto vanity, nor **s** deceitfully. 7650
89: 3 chosen, I have **s** unto David my servant, 7650
89:35 Once have I **s** by my holiness that I will 7650
102: 8 they that are mad against me are **s** against 7650
110: 4 The LORD hath **s**, and will not repent, 7650
119:106 I have **s**, and I will perform *it*, that *I* will 7650
132:11 The LORD hath **s** *in* truth unto David; 7650
Isa 14:24 The LORD of hosts hath **s**, saying, 7650
45:23 I have **s** by myself, the word is gone out 7650
54: 9 for *as* I have **s** that the waters of Noah 7650
54: 9 have I **s** that *I* would not be wroth with 7650
62: 8 The LORD hath **s** by his right hand, 7650
Jer 5: 7 and **s** by *them that are* no gods: 7650
11: 5 *I* may perform the oath which I have **s** 7650
44:26 Behold, I have **s** by my great name, 7650
49:13 For I have **s** by myself, saith the LORD, 7650
51:14 The LORD of hosts hath **s** by himself, 7650
Eze 21:23 in their sight, to them that have **s** oaths: 7650
Am 4: 2 The Lord GOD hath **s** by his holiness, 7650
6: 8 The Lord GOD hath **s** by himself, saith 7650
8: 7 The LORD hath **s** by the excellency of 7650
Mic 7:20 which thou hast **s** unto our fathers from 7650
Ac 2:30 knowing that God had **s** with an oath to 3660
7:17 which God had **s** to Abraham, the people 3660
Heb 4: 3 *he* said, As I have **s** in my wrath, if they 3660

SYCAMINE (1)

Lk 17: 6 ye might say unto this **s** tree, Be thou 4807

SYCAMORE-FIG See SYCOMORE

SYCHAR (1)

Jn 4: 5 he to a city of Samaria, which is called **S**, 4965

SYCHEM (2) [SHECHEM]

Ac 7:16 And were carried over into **S**, and laid in 4966
7:16 of the sons of Emmor the *father* of **S**. 4966

SYCOMORE (7) [SYCOMORES]

1Ki 10:27 cedars made he *to be* as the **s** trees that 8256
1Ch 27:28 the **s** trees that *were* in the low plains 8256

S

T

2Ch	1:15 cedar trees made he as the **s** trees that	8256
	9:27 cedar trees made he as the **s** trees that	8256
Ps	78:47 with hail, and their **s** trees with frost.	8256
Am	7:14 *was* a herdman, and a gatherer of **s** fruit:	8256
Lk	19: 4 and climbed up into a **s** tree to see him:	4809

SYCOMORES (1) [SYCOMORE]

Isa	9:10 the **s** are cut down, but we will change	8256

SYENE (2)

Eze	29:10 from the tower of **S** even unto the border	5482
	30: 6 from the tower of **S** shall they fall in it by	5482

SYNAGOGUE (43) [SYNAGOGUE'S, SYNAGOGUES]

Mt	12: 9 departed thence, he went into their **s**:	4864
	13:54 he taught them in their **s**, insomuch that	4864
Mk	1:21 on the sabbath day he entered into the **s**,	4864
	1:23 And there was in their **s** a man with an	4864
	1:29 when they were come out of the **s**,	4864
	3: 1 And he entered again into the **s**;	4864
	5:22 there cometh one of the **rulers of the s**,	752
	5:36 he saith unto the **ruler of the s**,	752
	5:38 cometh to the house of the **ruler of the s**,	752
	6: 2 day was come, he began to teach in the **s**:	4864
Lk	4:16 he went into the **s** on the sabbath day,	4864
	4:20 the eyes of all *them that were* in the **s**	4864
	4:28 all *they* in the **s**, when they heard these	4864
	4:33 And in the **s** there was a man, which had	4864
	4:38 he arose out of the **s**, and entered into	4864
	6: 6 that he entered into the **s** and taught:	4864
	7: 5 our nation, and he hath built us a **s**.	4864
	8:41 Jairus, and he was a ruler of the **s**:	4864
	13:14 And the **ruler of the s** answered with	752
Jn	6:59 These *things* said he in the **s**, as he taught	4864
	9:22 *was* Christ, he should be **put out of the s**.	656
	12:42 *him*, lest they should be **put out of the s**:	656
	18:20 I ever taught in the **s**, and in the temple,	4864
Ac	6: 9 Then there arose certain of the **s**, which	4864
	6: 9 which is called the **s** of the Libertines,	NIG
	13:14 and went into the **s** on the sabbath day,	4864
	13:15 the prophets the **rulers of the s** sent unto	752
	13:42 when the Jews were gone out of the **s**,	4864
	14: 1 that they went *both* together into the **s** of	4864
	17: 1 Thessalonica, where was a **s** of the Jews:	4864
	17:10 who coming *thither* went into the **s** of	4864
	17:17 Therefore disputed he in the **s** with	4864
	18: 4 And he reasoned in the **s** every sabbath,	4864
	18: 7 whose house joined hard to the **s**.	4864
	18: 8 And Crispus, the *chief* **ruler of the s**,	752
	18:17 the *chief* **ruler of the s**, and beat *him*	752
	18:19 but he himself entered into the **s**,	4864
	18:26 And he began to speak boldly in the **s**:	4864
	19: 8 And he went into the **s**, and spake boldly	4864
	22:19 in every **s** them that believed on thee:	4864
	26:11 And I punished them oft in every **s**,	4864
Rev	2: 9 Jews are not, but *are* the **s** of Satan.	4864
	3: 9 I *will* make *them* of the **s** of Satan,	4864

SYNAGOGUE'S (2) [SYNAGOGUE]

Mk	5:35 there came from the **ruler of the s** *house*	752
Lk	8:49 there cometh one from the **ruler of the s**	752

SYNAGOGUES (24) [SYNAGOGUE]

Ps	74: 8 they have burnt up all the **s** of God in	4150
Mt	4:23 teaching in their **s**, and preaching the	4864
	6: 2 as the hypocrites do in the **s** and in	4864
	6: 5 for they love to pray standing in the **s**	4864
	9:35 teaching in their **s**, and preaching	4864
	10:17 and they will scourge you in their **s**;	4864
	23: 6 at feasts, and the chief seats in the **s**,	4864
	23:34 *some* of them shall ye scourge in your **s**,	4864
Mk	1:39 And he preached in their **s** throughout all	4864
	12:39 And the chief seats in the **s**;	4864
	13: 9 councils; and in the **s** ye shall be beaten:	4864
Lk	4:15 And he taught in their **s**, being glorified of	4864
	4:44 he preached in the **s** of Galilee.	4864
	11:43 for ye love the uppermost seats in the **s**,	4864
	12:11 And when they bring you unto the **s**,	4864
	13:10 And he was teaching in one of the **s** on	4864
	20:46 the highest seats in the **s**, and the chief	4864
	21:12 persecute *you*, delivering *you* up to *the* **s**,	4864
Jn	16: 2 They shall put you **out of the s**: yea,	656
Ac	9: 2 of him letters to Damascus to the **s**,	4864
	9:20 straightway he preached Christ in the **s**,	4864
	13: 5 they preached the word of God in the **s** of	4864
	15:21 being read in the **s** every sabbath day.	4864
	24:12 people, neither in the **s**, nor in the city:	4864

SYNTYCHE (1)

Php	4: 2 I beseech Euodias, and beseech **S**, that	4941

SYRACUSE (1)

Ac	28:12 And landing at **S**, we tarried *there* three	4946

SYRIA (75) [SYRIA-DAMASCUS, SYRIA-MAACHAH, SYRIACK, SYRIAN, SYRIANS, SYROPHENICIAN]

Jdg	10: 6 the gods of **S**, and the gods of Zidon,	758
2Sa	8: 6 David put garrisons in **S** of Damascus:	758
	8:12 Of **S**, and of Moab, and of the children of	758
	15: 8 vowed a vow while I abode at Geshur in **S**,	758
1Ki	10:29 kings of the Hittites, and for the kings of **S**,	758
	11:25 he abhorred Israel, and reigned over **S**.	758
	15:18 of Tabrimon, the son of Hezion, king of **S**,	758
	19:15 anoint Hazael to be king over **S**:	758
	20: 1 Ben-hadad the king of **S** gathered all his	758

1Ki	20:20 Ben-hadad the king of **S** escaped on a horse	758
	20:22 at the return of the year the king of **S** will	758
	20:23 the servants of the king of **S** said unto him,	758
	22: 1 three years without war between **S**	758
	22: 3 take it not out of the hand of the king of **S**?	758
	22:31 But the king of **S** commanded his thirty	758
2Ki	5: 1 captain of the host of the king of **S**,	758
	5: 1 the Lord had given deliverance unto **S**:	758
	5: 5 king of **S** said, Go to, go, and I will send	758
	6: 8 Then the king of **S** warred against Israel,	758
	6:11 Therefore the heart of the king of **S** was	758
	6:23 So the bands of **S** came no more into	758
	6:24 that Ben-hadad king of **S** gathered all his	758
	7: 5 to the uttermost part of the camp of **S**,	758
	8: 7 Ben-hadad the king of **S** was sick; and it	758
	8: 9 Thy son Ben-hadad king of **S** hath sent me	758
	8:13 shewed me *that* thou *shalt be* king over **S**.	758
	8:28 against Hazael king of **S** in Ramoth-gilead;	758
	8:29 when he fought against Hazael king of **S**.	758
	9:14 and all Israel, because of Hazael king of **S**.	758
	9:15 when he fought with Hazael king of **S**.)	758
	12:17 Hazael king of **S** went up, and fought	758
	12:18 house, and sent *it* to Hazael king of **S**:	758
	13: 3 them into the hand of Hazael king of **S**,	758
	13: 4 because the king of **S** oppressed them.	758
	13: 7 for the king of **S** had destroyed them,	758
	13:17 and the arrow of deliverance from **S**:	758
	13:19 hadst thou smitten **S** till *thou* hadst	758
	13:19 whereas now thou shalt smite **S**	758
	13:22 Hazael king of **S** oppressed Israel all	758
	13:24 Hazael king of **S** died; and Ben-hadad his	758
	15:37 to send against Judah Rezin the king of **S**,	758
	16: 5 Rezin king of **S** and Pekah son of Remaliah	758
	16: 6 that time Rezin king of **S** recovered Elath	758
	16: 6 Rezin king of Syria recovered Elath to **S**,	758
	16: 7 save me out of the hand of the king of **S**,	758
2Ch	1:17 and *for* the kings of **S**, by their means.	758
	16: 2 and sent to Ben-hadad king of **S**,	758
	16: 7 Because thou hast relied on the king of **S**,	758
	16: 7 is the host of the king of **S** escaped out of	758
	18:10 With these thou shalt push **S** until they be	758
	18:30 Now the king of **S** had commanded	758
	20: 2 thee from beyond the sea on this side **S**;	758
	22: 5 against Hazael king of **S** at Ramoth-gilead;	758
	22: 6 when he fought with Hazael king of **S**.	758
	24:23 *that* the host of **S** came up against him:	758
	28: 5 him into the hand of the king of **S**;	758
	28:23 Because the gods of the kings of **S** help	758
Isa	7: 1 *that* Rezin the king of **S**, and Pekah the son	758
	7: 2 **S** is confederate with Ephraim.	758
	7: 4 for the fierce anger of Rezin with **S**,	758
	7: 5 Because **S**, Ephraim, and the son of	758
	7: 8 the head of **S** *is* Damascus, and the head	758
	17: 3 from Damascus, and the remnant of **S**:	758
Eze	16:57 time of *thy* reproach of the daughters of **S**,	758
	27:16 **S** *was* thy merchant by reason of	758
Hos	12:12 Jacob fled *into* the country of **S**,	758
Am	1: 5 the people of **S** shall go into captivity unto	758
Mt	4:24 And his fame went throughout all **S**:	4947
Lk	2: 2 made when Cyrenius was governor of **S**.)	4947
Ac	15:23 the Gentiles in Antioch and **S** and Cilicia;	4947
	18:18 And he went through **S** and Cilicia,	4947
	20: 3 for him, as he was about to sail into **S**,	4947
	21: 3 and sailed thence into **S**, and landed at Tyre:	4947
Gal	1:21 Afterwards I came into the regions of **S**	4947

SYRIACK (1) [SYRIA]

Da	2: 4 spake the Chaldeans to the king **in S**,	762

SYRIA-DAMASCUS (1) [DAMASCUS, SYRIA]

1Ch	18: 6 David put *garrisons* in **S**;	758+1834

SYRIA-MAACHAH (1) [SYRIA]

1Ch	19: 6 and out of **S**, and out of Zobah.	758

SYRIAN (12) [SYRIA]

Ge	25:20 daughter of Bethuel the **S** of Padan-aram,	761
	25:20 of Padan-aram, the sister to Laban the **S**.	761
	28: 5 of Bethuel the **S**, the brother of Rebekah,	761
	31:20 Jacob stole away unawares to Laban the **S**,	761
	31:24 God came to Laban the **S** in a dream by	761
Dt	26: 5 A **S** ready to perish *was* my father,	761
2Ki	5:20 my master hath spared Naaman this **S**,	761
	18:26 thee, to thy servants **in the S** language;	762
Ezr	4: 7 of the letter *was* written **in the S** tongue,	762
	4: 7 and interpreted **in the S** tongue.	762
Isa	36:11 unto thy servants **in the S** language:	762
Lk	4:27 them was cleansed, saving Naaman the **S**.	4948

SYRIAN PHOENICIA See SYROPHENICIAN

SYRIANS (61) [SYRIA]

2Sa	8: 5 when the **S** of Damascus came to succour	758
	8: 5 David slew of the **S** two and	758
	8: 6 the **S** became servants to David,	758
	8:13 from smiting of the **S** in the valley of salt,	758
	10: 6 Ammon saw and hired the **S** of Beth-rehob	758
	10: 6 the **S** of Zoba, twenty thousand footmen,	758
	10: 8 the **S** of Zoba, and of Rehob, and Ish-tob,	758
	10: 9 Israel, and put *them* in array against the **S**:	758
	10:11 If the **S** be too strong for me, then thou	758
	10:13 with him, unto the battle against the **S**:	758
	10:14 the children of Ammon saw that the **S**	758
	10:15 when the **S** saw that they were smitten	758
	10:16 out the **S** that *were* beyond the river:	758

2Sa	10:17 the **S** set *themselves* in array against David,	758
	10:18 the **S** fled before Israel; and David slew	758
	10:18 *the men of* seven hundred chariots of the **S**,	758
	10:19 So the **S** feared to help the children of	758
1Ki	20:20 and the **S** fled; and Israel pursued them:	758
	20:21 and slew the **S** with a great slaughter.	758
	20:26 Ben-hadad numbered the **S**, and went up	758
	20:27 flocks of kids; but the **S** filled the country.	758
	20:28 saith the Lord, Because the **S** have said,	758
	20:29 the children of Israel slew *of* the **S** an	758
	22:11 With these shalt thou push the **S**,	758
	22:35 was stayed up in *his* chariot against the **S**	758
2Ki	5: 2 the **S** had gone out *by* companies,	758
	6: 9 a place; for thither the **S** are come down.	758
	7: 4 come, and let us fall unto the host of the **S**:	758
	7: 5 the twilight, to go unto the camp of the **S**	758
	7: 6 For the Lord had made the host of the **S** to	758
	7:10 We came to the camp of the **S**, and, behold,	758
	7:12 I will now shew you what the **S** have done	758
	7:14 the king sent after the host of the **S**, saying,	758
	7:15 which the **S** had cast away in their haste.	758
	7:16 went out, and spoiled the tents of the **S**.	758
	8:28 Ramoth-gilead; and the **S** wounded Joram.	761
	8:29 which the **S** had given him at Ramah,	761
	9:15 of the wounds which the **S** had given him,	761
	13: 5 went out from under the hand of the **S**:	758
	13:17 for thou shalt smite the **S** in Aphek, till	758
	16: 6 the **S** came *to* Elath, and dwelt there unto	726
	24: 2 bands of the **S**, and bands of the Moabites,	758
1Ch	18: 5 when the **S** of Damascus came to help	758
	18: 5 David slew of the **S** two and	758
	18: 6 the **S** became David's servants,	758
	19:10 Israel, and put *them* in array against the **S**.	758
	19:12 If the **S** be too strong for me, then thou	758
	19:14 him drew nigh before the **S** unto the battle;	758
	19:15 the children of Ammon saw that the **S**	758
	19:16 when the **S** saw that they were put to	758
	19:16 forth the **S** that *were* beyond the river:	758
	19:17 had put the battle in array against the **S**,	758
	19:18 the **S** fled before Israel; and David slew of	758
	19:18 David slew of the **S** seven thousand *men*	758
	19:19 neither would the **S** help the children of	758
2Ch	18:34 in *his* chariot against the **S** until the even:	758
	22: 5 at Ramoth-gilead: and the **S** smote Joram.	7421
	24:24 For the army of the **S** came with a small	758
Isa	9:12 The **S** before, and the Philistines behind;	758
Jer	35:11 and for fear of the army of the **S**:	758
Am	9: 7 from Caphtor, and the **S** from Kir?	758

SYROPHENICIAN (1) [PHENICIA, SYRIA]

Mk	7:26 The woman was a Greek, a **S** by nation;	4949

T

TAANACH (6)

Jos	12:21 The king of **T**, one; the king of Megiddo,	8590
	17:11 the inhabitants of **T** and her towns,	8590
Jdg	1:27 and her towns, nor **T** and her towns,	8590
	5:19 fought the kings of Canaan in **T** by	8590
1Ki	4:12 *to him pertained* **T** and Megiddo,	8590
1Ch	7:29 **T** and her towns, Megiddo and her towns	8590

TAANATH-SHILOH (1) [SHILOH]

Jos	16: 6 the border went about eastward *unto* **T**,	8387

TABALIAH See TEBALIAH

TABBAOTH (2)

Ezr	2:43 children of Hasupha, the children of **T**,	2884
Ne	7:46 children of Hashupha, the children of **T**,	2884

TABBATH (1)

Jdg	7:22 to the border of Abel-meholah, unto **T**.	2888

TABEAL (1)

Isa	7: 6 king in the midst of it, *even* the son of **T**:	2870

TABEEL (1)

Ezr	4: 7 **T**, and the rest of their companions,	2870

TABERAH (2)

Nu	11: 3 he called the name of the place **T**:	8404
Dt	9:22 at **T**, and at Massah,	8404

TABERNACLE (328) [TABERNACLES]

Ex	25: 9 *after* the pattern of the **t**, and the pattern	4908
	26: 1 Moreover thou shalt make the **t** with ten	4908
	26: 6 with the taches: and it shall be one **t**.	4908
	26: 7 *of* goats' hair to be a covering upon the **t**:	4908
	26: 9 the sixth curtain in the forefront of the **t**.	168
	26:12 shall hang over the backside of the **t**.	4908
	26:13 shall hang over the sides of the **t** on this	4908
	26:15 shalt make boards for the **t** *of* shittim	4908
	26:17 thou shalt make for all the boards of the **t**.	4908
	26:18 thou shalt make the boards for the **t**,	4908
	26:20 for the second side of the **t** on the north	4908

Ex	26:22 for the sides of the t westward thou shalt	4908
	26:23 for the corners of the t in the two sides.	4908
	26:26 five for the boards of the one side of the t,	4908
	26:27 for the boards of the other side of the t,	4908
	26:27 five bars for the boards of the side of the t,	4908
	26:30 thou shalt rear up the t according to	4908
	26:35 on the side of the t toward the south:	4908
	27: 9 thou shalt make the court of the t:	4908
	27:19 All the vessels of the t in all the service	4908
	27:21 In the t of the congregation without the	168
	28:43 when they come in unto the t of	168
	29: 4 unto the door of the t of the congregation,	168
	29:10 brought before the t of the congregation:	168
	29:11 *by* the door of the t of the congregation.	168
	29:30 when he cometh into the t of	168
	29:32 *by* the door of the t of the congregation.	168
	29:42 the t of the congregation before the Lord:	168
	29:43 and *the t* shall be sanctified by my glory.	NIH
	29:44 I will sanctify the t of the congregation,	168
	30:16 shalt appoint it for the service of the t of	168
	30:18 thou shalt put it between the t of	168
	30:20 they go into the t of the congregation,	168
	30:26 thou shalt anoint the t of the congregation	168
	30:36 put of it before the Testimony in the t of	168
	31: 7 The t of the congregation, and the ark of	168
	31: 7 *is* thereupon, and all the furniture of the t,	168
	33: 7 Moses took the t, and pitched it without	168
	33: 7 and called the **T** of the Congregation.	168
	33: 7 went out unto the **T** of the Congregation,	168
	33: 8 to pass, when Moses went out unto the t,	168
	33: 8 after Moses, until he was gone into the t.	168
	33: 9 came to pass, as Moses entered into the t,	168
	33: 9 stood *at* the door of the t, and *the Lord*	168
	33:10 saw the cloudy pillar stand *at* the t door:	168
	33:11 a young man, departed not out of the t.	168
	35:11 The t, his tent, and his covering, his	4908
	35:15 for the door at the entering in of the t,	4908
	35:18 The pins of the t, and the pins of the	4908
	35:21 to the work of the t of the congregation,	168
	36: 8 t made ten curtains *of* fine twined linen,	4908
	36:13 with the taches: so it became one t.	4908
	36:14 *of* goats' *hair* for the tent over the t:	4908
	36:20 he made boards for the t *of* shittim wood,	4908
	36:22 did he make for all the boards of the t,	4908
	36:23 he made boards for the t; twenty boards	4908
	36:25 the other side of the t, *which is* toward	4908
	36:27 for the sides of the t westward he made	4908
	36:28 boards made he for the corners of the t	4908
	36:31 five for the boards of the one side of the t,	4908
	36:32 for the boards of the other side of the t,	4908
	36:32 bars for the boards of the t for the sides	4908
	36:37 he made a hanging for the t door *of* blue,	168
	38: 8 which assembled *at* the door of the t of	168
	38:20 the pins of the t, and of the court round	4908
	38:21 This is the sum of the t, *even* of	4908
	38:21 *even* of the t of Testimony, as it was	168
	38:30 to the door of the t of the congregation,	168
	38:31 all the pins of the t, and all the pins of	4908
	39:32 Thus was all the work of the t of the tent	4908
	39:33 they brought the t unto Moses, the tent,	4908
	39:38 and the hanging for the t door,	168
	39:40 and all the vessels of the service of the t,	4908
	40: 2 up the t of the tent of the congregation.	168
	40: 5 and put the hanging of the door to the t.	4908
	40: 6 of the t of the tent of the congregation.	168
	40: 9 anoint the t, and all that *is* therein,	4908
	40:17 his sons unto the door of the t of	168
	40:17 of the month, *that* the t was reared up.	4908
	40:18 Moses reared up the t, and fastened his	4908
	40:19 he spread abroad the tent over the t,	4908
	40:21 he brought the ark into the t, and set up	4908
	40:22 upon the side of the t northward, without	4908
	40:24 the table, on the side of the t southward.	4908
	40:28 he set up the hanging at the door of the t.	4908
	40:29 of the t of the tent of the congregation,	4908
	40:33 he reared up the court round about the t.	4908
	40:34 and the glory of the Lord filled the t.	4908
	40:35 the glory of the Lord filled the t.	4908
	40:36 the cloud was taken up from over the t,	4908
	40:38 For the cloud of the Lord *was* upon the t	4908
Lev	1: 1 spake unto him out of the t of	168
	1: 3 the t of the congregation before the Lord.	168
	1: 5 *is by* the door of the t of the congregation.	168
	3: 2 kill it *at* the door of the t of	168
	3: 8 and kill it before the t of the congregation:	168
	3:13 and kill it before the t of the congregation:	168
	4: 4 the t of the congregation before the Lord;	168
	4: 5 and bring it to the t of the congregation:	168
	4: 7 which *is* in the t of the congregation;	168
	4: 7 which *is* at the door of the t of	168
	4:14 bring him before the t of the congregation:	168
	4:16 bullock's blood to the t of the congregation:	168
	4:18 that *is* in the t of the congregation, and	168
	4:18 which *is* at the door of the t of	168
	6:16 in the court of the t of the congregation	168
	6:26 in the court of the t of the congregation.	168
	6:30 of the congregation to reconcile *withal* in	168
	8: 3 unto the door of the t of the congregation.	168
	8: 4 unto the door of the t of the congregation.	168
	8:10 anointed the t and all that *was* therein,	4908
	8:31 Boil the flesh at the door of the t of	168
	8:33 ye shall not go out of the door of the t of	168
	8:35 Therefore shall ye abide *at* the door of the t	168
	9: 5 before the t of the congregation:	168
	9:23 Aaron went into the t of the congregation,	168

Lev	10: 7 ye shall not go out from the door of the t of	168
	10: 9 when ye go into the t of the congregation,	168
	12: 6 unto the door of the t of the congregation,	168
	14:11 *at* the door of the t of the congregation:	168
	14:23 unto the door of the t of the congregation,	168
	15:14 unto the door of the t of the congregation,	168
	15:29 to the door of the t of the congregation.	168
	15:31 they defile my t that *is* among them.	4908
	16: 7 *at* the door of the t of the congregation.	168
	16:16 so shall he do for the t of the congregation,	168
	16:17 there shall be no man in the t of	168
	16:20 holy *place*, and the t of the congregation,	168
	16:23 Aaron shall come into the t of	168
	16:33 he shall make an atonement for the t of	168
	17: 4 bringeth it not unto the door of the t of	168
	17: 4 the Lord before the t of the Lord;	4908
	17: 5 unto the door of the t of the congregation,	168
	17: 6 *at* the door of the t of the congregation,	168
	17: 9 bringeth it not unto the door of the t of	168
	19:21 unto the door of the t of the congregation,	168
	24: 3 Testimony, in the t of the congregation,	168
	26:11 I will set my t amongst you: and my soul	4908
Nu	1: 1 in the t of the congregation, on the first	168
	1:50 thou shalt appoint the Levites over the t of	4908
	1:50 they shall bear the t, and all the vessels	4908
	1:50 it, and shall encamp round about the t.	4908
	1:51 when the t setteth forward, the Levites	4908
	1:51 when the t is to be pitched, the Levites	4908
	1:53 Levites shall pitch round about the t of	4908
	1:53 Levites shall keep the charge of the t of	4908
	2: 2 far off about the t of the congregation shall	168
	2:17 the t of the congregation shall set forward	168
	3: 7 before the t of the congregation,	168
	3: 7 congregation, to do the service of the t.	4908
	3: 8 they shall keep all the instruments of the t	168
	3: 8 of Israel, to do the service of the t.	4908
	3:23 shall pitch behind the t westward.	4908
	3:25 the charge of the sons of Gershon in the t	168
	3:25 of the congregation *shall* be the t,	4908
	3:25 the hanging for the door of the t of	168
	3:26 which *is* by the t, and by the altar round	4908
	3:29 shall pitch on the side of the t southward.	4908
	3:35 *these* shall pitch on the side of the t	4908
	3:36 sons of Merari *shall be* the boards of the t,	4908
	3:38 those that encamp before the t toward	4908
	3:38 *even* before the t of the congregation	168
	4: 3 to do the work in the t of the congregation.	168
	4: 4 sons of Kohath in the t of the congregation,	168
	4:15 sons of Kohath in the t of the congregation,	168
	4:16 the oversight of all the t, and of all that	4908
	4:23 do the work in the t of the congregation.	168
	4:25 they shall bear the curtains of the t,	4908
	4:25 the t of the congregation, his covering,	168
	4:25 the hanging for the door of the t of	168
	4:26 which *is* by the t and by the altar round	4908
	4:28 of Gershon in the t of the congregation:	168
	4:30 to do the work of the t of the congregation.	168
	4:31 according to all their service in the t of	168
	4:31 the boards of the t, and the bars thereof,	4908
	4:33 their service, in the t of the congregation,	168
	4:35 for the work in the t of the congregation:	168
	4:37 all that *might* do service in the t of	168
	4:39 for the work in the t of the congregation,	168
	4:41 of all that *might* do service in the t of	168
	4:43 for the work in the t of the congregation,	168
	4:47 the service of the burden in the t of	168
	5:17 of the dust that is in the floor of the t	4908
	6:10 to the door of the t of the congregation:	168
	6:13 he shall be brought unto the door of the t	168
	6:18 *at* the door of the t of the congregation,	168
	7: 1 the day that Moses had fully set up the t,	4908
	7: 3 ox: and they brought them before the t.	4908
	7: 5 they may be to do the service of the t of	168
	7:89 when Moses was gone into the t of	168
	8: 9 thou shalt bring the Levites before the t of	168
	8:15 do the service of the t of the congregation:	168
	8:19 of Israel in the t of the congregation,	168
	8:22 in the t of the congregation before Aaron,	168
	8:24 the service of the t of the congregation:	168
	8:26 shall minister with their brethren in the t	168
	9:15 on the day that the t was reared up,	4908
	9:15 the cloud covered the t, *namely*, the tent	4908
	9:15 at even there was upon the t as it were	4908
	9:17 when the cloud was taken up from the t,	168
	9:18 as long as the cloud abode upon the t they	4908
	9:19 when the cloud tarried long upon the t	4908
	9:20 the cloud was a few days upon the t;	4908
	9:22 a year, that the cloud tarried upon the t,	4908
	10: 3 at the door of the t of the congregation.	168
	10:11 *that* the cloud was taken up from off the t	4908
	10:17 the t was taken down; and the sons of	4908
	10:17 sons of Merari set forward, bearing the t.	4908
	10:21 *other* did set up the t against they came.	4908
	11:16 bring them unto the t of the congregation,	168
	11:24 people, and set them round about the t.	168
	11:26 were written, but went not out unto the t:	168
	12: 4 Come out ye three unto the t of	168
	12: 5 stood *in* the door of the t, and called Aaron	168
	12:10 the cloud departed from off the t;	168
	14:10 the glory of the Lord appeared in the t of	168
	16: 9 to do the service of the t of the Lord,	4908
	16:18 *in* the door of the t of the congregation	168
	16:19 unto the door of the t of the congregation:	168
	16:24 Get you up from about the t of Korah,	4908
	16:27 they gat up from the t of Korah, Dathan,	4908

Nu	16:42 that they looked toward the t of	168
	16:43 came before the t of the congregation.	168
	16:50 unto the door of the t of the congregation:	168
	17: 4 thou shalt lay them up in the t of	168
	17: 7 rods before the Lord in the t of Witness.	168
	17: 8 on the morrow Moses went into the t of	168
	17:13 near unto the t of the Lord shall die:	4908
	18: 2 sons with thee *shall minister* before the t	168
	18: 3 thy charge, and the charge of all the t:	168
	18: 4 the charge of the t of the congregation,	168
	18: 4 congregation, for all the service of the t:	168
	18: 6 do the service of the t of the congregation.	168
	18:21 the service of the t of the congregation.	168
	18:22 come nigh the t of the congregation,	168
	18:23 the Levites shall do the service of the t	168
	18:31 it *is* your reward for your service in the t	168
	19: 4 sprinkle of her blood directly before the t	168
	19:13 not himself, defileth the t of the Lord;	4908
	20: 6 unto the door of the t of the congregation,	168
	25: 6 *were* weeping *before* the door of the t	168
	27: 2 *by* the door of the t of the congregation,	168
	31:30 which keep the charge of the t of	4908
	31:47 which kept the charge of the t of	4908
	31:54 brought it into the t of the congregation,	168
Dt	31:14 present yourselves in the t of	168
	31:14 presented themselves in the t of	168
	31:15 the Lord appeared in the t in a pillar of a	168
	31:15 of the cloud stood over the door of the t.	168
Jos	18: 1 and set up the t of the congregation there.	168
	19:51 *at* the door of the t of the congregation.	168
	22:19 wherein the Lord's t dwelleth,	4908
	22:29 of the Lord our God that *is* before his t.	4908
1Sa	2:22 *at* the door of the t of the congregation.	168
2Sa	6:17 the midst of the t that David had pitched	168
	7: 6 but have walked in a tent and in a t.	4908
1Ki	1:39 the priest took a horn of oil out of the t,	168
	2:28 And Joab fled unto the t of the Lord,	168
	2:29 that Joab was fled unto the t of the Lord;	168
	2:30 Benaiah came to the t of the Lord,	168
	8: 4 of the congregation, and all the holy	168
	8: 4 all the holy vessels that *were* in the t,	168
1Ch	6:32 of the t of the congregation with singing,	168
	6:48 *of* service of the t of the house of God.	4908
	9:19 the service, keepers of the gates of the t:	168
	9:21 of the door of the t of the congregation.	168
	9:23 *namely*, the house of the t, by wards.	168
	16:39 before the t of the Lord in the high place	4908
	17: 5 tent to tent, and from *one* to *another*.	4908
	21:29 For the t of the Lord, which Moses	4908
	23:26 *they* shall no *more* carry the t, nor any	4908
	23:32 that they should keep the charge of the t	168
2Ch	1: 3 there was the t of the congregation of	168
	1: 5 he put before the t of the Lord:	4908
	1: 6 which *was* at the t of the congregation,	168
	1:13 from before the t of the congregation,	168
	5: 5 the t of the congregation, and all the holy	168
	5: 5 all the holy vessels that *were* in the t, these	168
	24: 6 congregation of Israel, for the t of Witness?	168
Job	5:24 shalt know that thy t *shall be in* peace;	168
	18: 6 The light shall be dark in his t,	168
	18:14 His confidence shall be rooted out of his t,	168
	18:15 It shall dwell in his t, because *it is* none of	168
	19:12 against me, and encamp round about my t.	168
	20:26 it shall go ill with him that is left in his t.	168
	29: 4 when the secret of God *was* upon my t;	168
	31:31 If the men of my t said not, O that we had	168
	36:29 of the clouds, *or* the noise of his t?	5521
Ps	15: 1 Lord, who shall abide in thy t? who shall	168
	19: 4 In them hath he set a t for the sun,	168
	27: 5 in the secret of his t shall he hide me;	168
	27: 6 will I offer in his t sacrifices of joy;	168
	61: 4 I will abide in thy t for ever: I will trust in	168
	76: 2 In Salem also is his t, and his dwelling	5520
	78:60 that he forsook the t of Shiloh, the tent	4908
	78:67 Moreover he refused the t of Joseph,	168
	132: 3 Surely I will not come into the t of my	168
Pr	14:11 but the t of the upright shall flourish.	168
Isa	4: 6 there shall be a t for a shadow in	5521
	16: 5 shall sit upon it in truth in the t of David,	168
	33:20 a t that shall not be taken down;	168
Jer	10:20 t is spoiled, and all my cords are broken:	168
La	2: 4 to the eye, in the t of the daughter of Zion:	168
	2: 6 he hath violently taken away his t, as *if it*	7900
Eze	37:27 My t also shall be with them: yea, I will be	4908
	41: 1 side, *which was* the breadth of the t.	168
Am	5:26 But ye have borne the t of your Moloch	5522
	9:11 In that day will I raise up the t of David	5521
Ac	7:43 ye took up the t of Moloch, and the star	4633
	7:44 Our fathers had the t of Witness in	4633
	7:46 desired to find a t for the God of Jacob.	4638
	15:16 and will build again the t of David,	4633
2Co	5: 1 our earthly house of *this* t were dissolved,	4636
	5: 4 For we that are in *this* t do groan,	4636
Heb	8: 2 and of the true t, which the Lord pitched,	4633
	8: 5 of God when he was about to make the t:	4633
	9: 2 For there was a t made; the first, wherein	4633
	9: 3 the t which is called the holiest of all;	4633
	9: 6 the priests went always into the first t,	4633
	9: 8 while as the first t was yet standing:	4633
	9:11 by a greater and more perfect t, not made	4633
	9:21 he sprinkled with blood both the t,	4633
	13:10 have no right to eat which serve the t.	4633
2Pe	1:13 that it meet, as long as I am in this t,	4638
	1:14 that shortly *I* must put off *this* my t,	4638
Rev	13: 6 and his t, and them that dwell in heaven.	4633

Rev 15: 5 the temple of the **t** of the testimony in 4633
 21: 3 the **t** of God *is* with men, and he will 4633

TABERNACLES (30) [TABERNACLE]

Lev 23:34 feast of **t** *for*seven days unto the LORD. 5521
Nu 24: 5 are thy tents, O Jacob, *and* thy **t**, O Israel! 4908
Dt 16:13 Thou shalt observe the feast of **t** seven 5521
 16:16 in the feast of weeks, and in the feast of **t**: 5521
 31:10 of the year of release, in the feast of **t**, 5521
2Ch 8:13 in the feast of weeks, and in the feast of **t**, 5521
Ezr 3: 4 kept also the feast of **t**, as it is written, 5521
Job 11:14 and let not wickedness dwell in thy **t**. 168
 12: 6 The **t** of robbers prosper, and they that 168
 15:34 and fire shall consume the **t** of bribery. 168
 22:23 thou shalt put away iniquity far from thy **t**. 168
Ps 43: 3 bring me unto thy holy hill, and to thy **t**. 4908
 46: 4 the holy *place* of the **t** of the most High. 4908
 78:51 the chief of *their* strength in the **t** of Ham: 168
 83: 6 The **t** of Edom, and the Ishmaelites; 168
 84: 1 How amiable *are* thy **t**, O LORD of hosts! 4908
 118:15 and salvation *is* in the **t** of the righteous: 168
 132: 7 We will go into his **t**: we will worship at 4908
Da 11:45 he shall plant the **t** of his palace between 168
Hos 9: 6 possess them: thorns *shall be* in their **t**. 168
 12: 9 of Egypt will yet make thee to dwell in **t**, 168
Zec 14:16 LORD of hosts, and to keep the feast of **t**. 5521
 14:18 that come not up to keep the feast of **t**. 5521
 14:19 that come not up to keep the feast of **t**. 5521
Mal 2:12 out of the **t** of Jacob, and him that offereth 168
Mt 17: 4 if thou wilt, let us make here three **t**: 4633
Mk 9: 5 let us make three **t**; one for thee, 4633
Lk 9:33 and let us make three **t**; one for thee, 4633
Jn 7: 2 Now the Jews' feast of **t** was at hand. 4634
Heb 11: 9 as *in* a strange *country*, dwelling in **t** with 4633

TABITHA (2)

Ac 9:36 was at Joppa a certain disciple named **T**, 5000
 9:40 and turning *him* to the body said, **T**, arise. 5000

TABLE (73) [TABLES]

Ex 25:23 Thou shalt also make a **t** *of*shittim wood: 7979
 25:27 be for places of the staves to bear the **t**. 7979
 25:28 that the **t** may be borne with them. 7979
 25:30 thou shalt set upon the **t** shewbread 7979
 26:35 thou shalt set the **t** without the vail, 7979
 26:35 the candlestick over against the **t** on 7979
 26:35 and thou shalt put the **t** on the north side. 7979
 30:27 **t** and all his vessels, and the candlestick 7979
 31: 8 the **t** and his furniture, and the pure 7979
 35:13 The **t**, and his staves, and all his vessels, 7979
 37:10 made the **t** *of*shittim wood: two cubits 7979
 37:14 the places for the staves to bear the **t**. 7979
 37:15 overlaid them with gold, to bear the **t**. 7979
 37:16 made the vessels which *were* upon the **t**, 7979
 39:36 The **t**, *and* all the vessels thereof, 7979
 40: 4 thou shalt bring in the **t**, and set in order 7979
 40:22 put the **t** in the tent of the congregation, 7979
 40:24 over against the **t**, on the side of 7979
Lev 24: 6 a row, upon the pure **t** before the LORD. 7979
Nu 3:31 the **t**, and the candlestick, and the altars, 7979
 4: 7 upon the **t** of shewbread they shall spread 7979
Jdg 1: 7 cut off, gathered *their* meat under my **t**: 7979
1Sa 20:29 Therefore he cometh not unto the king's **t**. 7979
 20:34 So Jonathan arose from the **t** in fierce 7979
2Sa 9: 7 thou shalt eat bread at my **t** continually. 7979
 9:10 master's son shall eat bread alway at my **t**. 7979
 9:11 *said the king*, he shall eat at my **t**, 7979
 9:13 for he did eat continually at the king's **t**; 7979
 19:28 among them that did eat at thine own **t**. 7979
1Ki 2: 7 and let them be of *those* that eat at thy **t**: 7979
 4:27 for all that came unto king Solomon's **t**, 7979
 7:48 the altar of gold, and the **t** *of* gold, 7979
 10: 5 the meat of his **t**, and the sitting of his 7979
 13:20 it came to pass, as they sat at the **t**, that 7979
 18:19 four hundred, which eat at Jezebel's **t**. 7979
2Ki 4:10 and a **t**, and a stool, and a candlestick: 7979
1Ch 28:16 of shewbread, for **every** **t**; 7979+7979+2050.1
2Ch 4: 8 the meat of his **t**, and the sitting of his 7979
 13:11 also *set they* in order upon the pure **t**; 7979
 29:18 the shewbread **t**, with all the vessels 7979
Ne 5:17 Moreover *there were* at my **t** an hundred 7979
Job 36:16 that which should be set on thy **t** *should* 7979
Ps 23: 5 Thou preparest a **t** before me in 7979
 69:22 Let their **t** become a snare before them: 7979
 78:19 Can God furnish a **t** in the wilderness? 7979
 128: 3 like olive plants round about thy **t**. 7979
Pr 3: 3 write them upon the **t** of thine heart: 3871
 7: 3 write them upon the **t** of thine heart. 3871
 9: 2 her wine; she hath also furnished her **t**. 7979
SS 1:12 While the king *sitteth* at his **t**, my 4524
Isa 21: 5 Prepare the **t**, watch in the watchtower, 7979
 30: 8 write it before them in a **t**, and note it in 3871
 65:11 that prepare a **t** for *that* troop, 7979
Jer 17: 1 *it is* graven upon the **t** of their heart, 3871
Eze 23:41 a stately bed, and a **t** prepared before it, 7979
 39:20 Thus ye shall be filled at my **t** *with* horses 7979
 41:22 This *is* the **t** that *is* before the LORD. 7979
 44:16 they shall come near to my **t**, to minister 7979
Da 11:27 and they shall speak lies at one **t**; 7979
Mal 1: 7 The **t** of the LORD *is* contemptible. 7979
 1:12 ye say, The **t** of the LORD *is* polluted; 7979
Mt 15:27 crumbs which fall from their masters' **t**. 5132
Mk 7:28 yet the dogs under the **t** eat of 5132
Lk 1:63 And he asked for a **writing** **t**, and wrote, 4093
 16:21 crumbs which fell from the rich *man's* **t**: 5132

Lk 22:21 that betrayeth me *is* with me on the **t**. 5132
 22:30 may eat and drink at my **t** in my kingdom, 5132
Jn 12: 2 of them that **sat at the t** with him. 4873
 13:28 no *man* at the **t** knew for what intent he 345
Ro 11: 9 Let their **t** be made a snare, and a trap, 5132
1Co 10:21 ye cannot be partakers of the Lord's **t**, 5132
 10:21 of the Lord's **table**, and of the **t** of devils. 5132
Heb 9: 2 and the **t**, and the shewbread; 5132

TABLES (56) [TABLE, TABLETS]

Ex 24:12 I will give thee **t** of stone, and a law, 3871
 31:18 two **t** of Testimony, tables of stone, 3871
 31:18 two tables of Testimony, **t** of stone, 3871
 32:15 the two **t** of the Testimony *were* in his 3871
 32:15 the **t** *were* written on both their sides; 3871
 32:16 the **t** *were* the work of God, and the 3871
 32:16 the writing of God, graven upon the **t**. 3871
 32:19 he cast the **t** out of his hands, 3871
 34: 1 thee two **t** of stone like unto the first: 3871
 34: 1 I will write upon *these* **t** the words that 3871
 34: 1 tables the words that were in the first **t**, 3871
 34: 4 hewed two **t** of stone like unto the first; 3871
 34: 4 and took in his hand the two **t** of stone. 3871
 34:28 he wrote upon the **t** the words of 3871
 34:29 the two **t** of Testimony in Moses' hand, 3871
Dt 4:13 and he wrote them upon two **t** of stone. 3871
 5:22 he wrote them in two **t** of stone, 3871
 9: 9 into the mount to receive the **t** of stone, 3871
 9: 9 *even* the **t** of the covenant which 3871
 9:10 the LORD delivered unto me two **t** of 3871
 9:11 *that* the LORD gave me the two **t** of stone, 3871
 9:11 of stone, *even* the **t** of the covenant. 3871
 9:15 the two **t** of the covenant *were* in my 3871
 9:17 I took the two **t**, and cast them out of my 3871
 10: 1 thee two **t** of stone like unto the first, 3871
 10: 1 I will write on the **t** the words that were 3871
 10: 2 were in the first **t** which thou brakest, 3871
 10: 3 hewed two **t** of stone like unto the first, 3871
 10: 3 mount, having the two **t** in mine hand. 3871
 10: 4 he wrote on the **t**, according to the first 3871
 10: 5 put the **t** in the ark which I had made; 3871
1Ki 8: 9 was nothing in the ark save the two **t** 3871
1Ch 28:16 *by* weight *he gave* gold for the **t** of 7979
 28:16 and *likewise* silver for the **t** of silver: 7979
2Ch 4: 8 He made also ten **t**, and placed *them* in 7979
 4:19 the **t** whereon the shewbread *was* set; 7979
 5:10 was nothing in the ark save the two **t** 3871
Isa 28: 8 For all **t** are full *of*vomit *and*filthiness, 7979
Eze 40:39 in the porch of the gate *were* two **t** on 7979
 40:39 two **t** on that side, to slay thereon the 7979
 40:40 to the entry of the north gate, *were* two **t**; 7979
 40:40 *was* at the porch of the gate, *were* two **t**. 7979
 40:41 Four **t** *were* on this side, and four tables 7979
 40:41 four **t** on that side, by the side of the gate; 7979
 40:41 eight **t**, whereupon they slew *their* 7979
 40:42 the four **t** *were* of hewn stone for the 7979
 40:43 upon the **t** *was* the flesh of the offering. 7979
Hab 2: 2 the vision, and make *it* plain upon **t**, 3871
Mt 21:12 overthrew the **t** of the moneychangers, 5132
Mk 7: 4 of cups, and pots, brasen vessels, and of **t**. 2825
 11:15 overthrew the **t** of the money-changers, 5132
Jn 2:15 changers' money, and overthrew the **t**; 5132
Ac 6: 2 should leave the word of God, and serve **t**. 5132
2Co 3: 3 not in **t** of stone, but in fleshy tables of 4109
 3: 3 tables of stone, but in fleshy **t** of the heart. 4109
Heb 9: 4 that budded, and the **t** of the covenant; 4109

TABLETS (3) [TABLES]

Ex 35:22 and earrings, and rings, and **t**, 3558
Nu 31:50 and bracelets, rings, earrings, and **t**, 3558
Isa 3:20 and **t**, and the earrings, 1004+5315

TABOR (10) [AZNOTH-TABOR, CHISLOTH-TABOR]

Jos 19:22 the coast reacheth to **T**, and Shahazimah, 8396
Jdg 4: 6 *saying*, Go and draw toward mount **T**, 8396
 4:12 son of Abinoam was gone up to mount **T**. 8396
 4:14 So Barak went down from mount **T**, 8396
 8:18 of men *were they* whom ye slew at **T**? 8396
1Sa 10: 3 thou shalt come to the plain of **T**, 8396
1Ch 6:77 with her suburbs, **T** with her suburbs: 8396
Ps 89:12 **T** and Hermon shall rejoice in thy name. 8396
Jer 46:18 Surely as **T** *is* among the mountains, 8396
Hos 5: 1 on Mizpah, and a net spread upon **T**. 8396

TABRET (4) [TABRETS]

Ge 31:27 and with songs, with **t**, and with harp? 8596
1Sa 10: 5 a **t**, and a pipe, and a harp, before them; 8596
Job 17: 6 of the people; and aforetime I was as a **t**. 8611
Isa 5:12 and the viol, the **t**, and pipe, and wine, 8596

TABRETS (5) [TABRET]

1Sa 18: 6 with **t**, with joy, and with instruments of 8596
Isa 24: 8 The mirth of **t** ceaseth, the noise of them 8596
 30:32 lay upon him, *it* shall be with **t** and harps: 8596
Jer 31: 4 thou shalt again be adorned *with* thy **t**, 8596
Eze 28:13 the workmanship of thy **t** and of thy pipes 8596

TABRIMMON See TABRIMON

TABRIMON (1)

1Ki 15:18 the son of **T**, the son of Hezion, king of 2886

TABRING (1)

Na 2: 7 the voice of doves, **t** upon their breasts. 8608

TACHES (10)

Ex 26: 6 thou shalt make fifty **t** of gold, 7165
 26: 6 couple the curtains together with the **t**: 7165
 26:11 thou shalt make fifty **t** of brass, and put 7165
 26:11 put the **t** into the loops, and couple the 7165
 26:33 thou shalt hang up the vail under the **t**, 7165
 35:11 his **t**, and his boards, his bars, his pillars, 7165
 36:13 he made fifty **t** of gold, and coupled 7165
 36:13 the curtains one unto another with the **t**: 7165
 36:18 he made fifty **t** of brass to couple the tent 7165
 39:33 his **t**, his boards, his bars, and his pillars, 7165

TACHMONITE (1)

2Sa 23: 8 The **T** that sat in the seat, chief among 8461

TACKLING (1) [TACKLINGS]

Ac 27:19 *out* with our own hands the **t** of the ship. 4631

TACKLINGS (1) [TACKLING]

Isa 33:23 Thy **t** are loosed; they could not well 2256

TADMOR (2)

1Ki 9:18 and **T** in the wilderness, in the land, 8412
2Ch 8: 4 he built **T** in the wilderness, and all 8412

TAHAN (2) [TAHANITES]

Nu 26:35 of **T**, the family of the Tahanites. 8465
1Ch 7:25 and Telah his son, and **T** his son, 8465

TAHANITES (1) [TAHAN]

Nu 26:35 of Tahan, the family of the **T**. 8470

TAHAPANES (1) [TAHPANHES]

Jer 2:16 and **T** have broken the crown of thy head. 8471

TAHASH See THAHASH

TAHATH (6)

Nu 33:26 from Makheloth, and encamped at **T**. 8480
 33:27 departed from **T**, and pitched at Tarah. 8480
1Ch 6:24 his son, Uriel his son, Uzziah his son, 8480
 6:37 The son of **T**, the son of Assir, the son of 8480
 7:20 **T** his son, and Eladah his son, 8480
 7:20 son, and Eladah his son, and **T** his son, 8480

TAHKEMONITE See TACHMONITE

TAHPANHES (5) [TAHAPANES, TEHAPHNEHES]

Jer 43: 7 of the LORD: thus came they *even* to **T**. 8471
 43: 8 word of the LORD unto Jeremiah in **T**, 8471
 43: 9 *is* at the entry of Pharaoh's house in **T**, 8471
 44: 1 at **T**, and at Noph, and in the country of 8471
 46:14 in Migdol, and publish in Noph and in **T**: 8471

TAHPENES (3)

1Ki 11:19 of his own wife, the sister of **T** the queen. 8472
 11:20 the sister of **T** bare him Genubath his son, 8472
 11:20 whom **T** weaned in Pharaoh's house: 8472

TAHREA (1)

1Ch 9:41 and Melech, and **T**, *and* Ahaz. 8475

TAHTIM-HODSHI (1)

2Sa 24: 6 they came to Gilead, and to the land of **T**; 8483

TAIL (5)

Ex 4: 4 Put forth thine hand, and take it by the **t**. 2180
Dt 28:13 shall make thee the head, and not the **t**; 2180
 28:44 shall be the head, and thou shalt be the **t**. 2180
Jdg 15: 4 turned **t** to tail, and put a firebrand in 2180
 15: 4 turned tail to **t**, and put a firebrand in 2180
Job 40:17 He moveth his **t** like a cedar: the sinews 2180
Isa 9:14 LORD will cut off from Israel head and **t**, 2180
 9:15 the prophet that teacheth lies, he *is* the **t**. 2180
 19:15 which the head or **t**, branch or rush, 2180
Rev 12: 4 his **t** drew the third *part* of the stars 3769

TAILS (6) [TAIL]

Jdg 15: 4 a firebrand in the midst between two **t**. 2180
Isa 7: 4 neither be fainthearted for the two **t** of 2180
Rev 9:10 And they had **t** like unto scorpions, 3769
 9:10 and there were stings in their **t**: 3769
 9:19 power is in their mouth, and in their **t**: 3769
 9:19 for their **t** *were* like unto serpents, 3769

TAKE (874) [OVERTAKE, TAKEN, TAKER, TAKEST, TAKETH, TAKING, TOOK, TOOKEST, UNTAKEN]

Ge 3:22 **t** also of the tree of life, and eat, 3947
 6:21 **t** thou unto thee of all food that is eaten, 3947
 7: 2 Of every clean beast thou shalt **t** to thee 3947
 12:19 behold thy wife, *her*, and go thy way. 3947
 13: 9 *if thou wilt* **t** the left hand, then I will go NIH
 14:21 me the persons, and **t** the goods to thyself. 3947
 14:23 That I will not **t** from a thread even to a NIH
 14:23 that I will not **t** any thing that *is* thine, 3947
 14:24 and Mamre; let them **t** their portion. 3947
 15: 9 **T** me a heifer of three years old, and a she 3947
 19:15 Arise, **t** thy wife, and thy two daughters, 3947
 19:19 mountain, lest *some* evil **t** me, and I die: 1692
 21:30 For *these* seven ewe lambs shalt thou **t** of 3947
 22: 2 he said, **T** now thy son, thine only *son* 3947
 23:13 **t** *it* of me, and I will bury my dead there. 3947
 24: 3 thou shalt not **t** a wife unto my son of 3947
 24: 4 kindred, and **t** a wife unto my son Isaac. 3947
 24: 7 thou shalt **t** a wife unto my son from 3947
 24:37 Thou shalt not **t** a wife to my son of 3947

Ge
24:38	to my kindred, and t a wife unto my son.	3947
24:40	shalt t a wife for my son of my	3947
24:48	had led me in the right way to t my	3947
24:51	t *her*, and go, and let her be thy master's	5375
27: 3	therefore t, I pray thee, thy weapons,	5375
27: 3	out to the field, and t me *some* venison;	6679
27:46	if Jacob t a wife of the daughters of Heth,	3947
28: 1	Thou shalt not t a wife of the daughters	3947
28: 2	t thee a wife from thence of the daughters	3947
28: 6	Padan-aram, to t him a wife from thence;	3947
28: 6	Thou shalt not t a wife of the daughters	3947
30:15	thou t away my son's mandrakes	3947
31:24	T heed that thou speak not to Jacob	8104
31:29	T heed that thou speak not to Jacob	8104
31:31	Peradventure thou wouldest t by force	1497
31:32	what *is* thine with me, and t *it* to thee.	3947
31:50	if thou shalt t *other* wives beside my	3947
33:11	T, I pray thee, my blessing that is brought	3947
33:12	Let us t our **journey**, and let us go,	5265
34: 9	unto us, and t our daughters unto you.	3947
34:16	we will t your daughters to us, and we	3947
34:17	will we t our daughter, and we will be	3947
34:21	let us t their daughters to us for wives,	3947
38:23	Judah said, Let her t *it* to her, lest we be	3947
41:34	t up the fifth *part* of the land of Egypt in	2567
42:33	t *food* for the famine of your households,	3947
42:36	ye will t Benjamin *away*: all these things	3947
43:11	t of the best fruits in the land in your	3947
43:12	t double money in your hand;	3947
43:13	T also your brother, and arise, go again	3947
43:18	and t us for bondmen, and our asses.	3947
44:29	if ye t this also from me,	3947
45:18	t your father and your households,	3947
45:19	t you wagons out of the land of Egypt for	3947

Ex
2: 9	T this child away, and nurse it for me,	1980
4: 4	Put forth thine hand, and t it by the tail.	270
4: 9	that thou shalt t of the water of the river,	3947
4:17	thou shalt t this rod in thine hand,	3947
6: 7	I will t you to me for a people, and I will	3947
7: 9	T thy rod, and cast *it* before Pharaoh,	3947
7:15	to a serpent shalt thou t in thine hand.	3947
7:19	thy rod, and stretch out thine hand	3947
8: 8	that he may t away the frogs from me,	5493
9: 8	T to you handfuls of ashes of the furnace,	3947
10:17	that he may t away from me this death	5493
10:26	for thereof must we t to serve the LORD	3947
10:28	Get thee from me, t heed to thyself, see	8104
12: 3	the tenth *day* of this month they shall t to	3947
12: 4	his neighbour next unto his house t *it*	3947
12: 5	ye shall t *it* **out** from the sheep, or from	3947
12: 7	they shall t of the blood, and strike *it* on	3947
12:21	t you a lamb according to your families,	3947
12:22	ye shall t a bunch of hyssop, and dip it in	3947
12:32	Also t your flocks and your herds, as ye	3947
15:14	sorrow shall t **hold** on the inhabitants of	270
15:15	Moab, trembling shall t **hold** upon them;	270
16:16	t ye every man for *them* which *are* in his	3947
16:33	T a pot, and put an omer full of manna	3947
17: 5	and t with thee of the elders of Israel;	3947
17: 5	smotest the river, t in thine hand, and go.	3947
19:12	T heed to yourselves, *that ye go not*	8104
20: 7	Thou shalt not t the name of the LORD	5375
21:10	If he t him another *wife*; her food,	3947
21:14	thou shalt t him from mine altar, that he	3947
22:26	**at all** t thy neighbour's raiment	
	to pledge:	2254+2254
23: 8	thou shalt t no gift: for the gift blindeth	3947
23:25	I will t sickness **away** from the midst of	5493
25: 2	with his heart ye shall t my offering.	3947
25: 3	*is* the offering which ye shall t of them;	3947
26: 5	that the loops may t **hold** one of another.	6901
28: 1	thou unto thee Aaron thy brother,	7126
28: 5	they shall t gold, and blue, and purple,	3947
28: 9	thou shalt t two onyx stones, and grave	3947
29: 1	T one young bullock, and two rams	3947
29: 5	thou shalt t the garments, and put upon	3947
29: 7	shalt thou t the anointing oil, and pour *it*	3947
29:12	thou shalt t of the blood of the bullock,	3947
29:13	thou shalt t all the fat that covereth	3947
29:15	Thou shalt also t one ram; and Aaron and	3947
29:16	shalt t his blood, and sprinkle it round	3947
29:19	thou shalt t the other ram; and Aaron and	3947
29:20	t of his blood, and put *it* upon the tip of	3947
29:21	thou shalt t of the blood that *is* upon	3947
29:22	Also thou shalt t of the ram the fat and	3947
29:26	shalt t the breast of the ram of Aaron's	3947
29:31	shalt t the ram of the consecration,	3947
30:16	thou shalt t the atonement money of	3947
30:23	T thou also unto thee principal spices,	3947
30:34	T unto thee sweet spices, stacte,	3947
33:23	I will t away mine hand, and thou shalt	5493
34: 9	our sin, and t us for thine **inheritance**.	5157
34:12	T heed to thyself, lest thou make a	8104
34:16	thou t of their daughters unto thy sons,	3947
35: 5	Ye from amongst you an offering unto	3947
40: 9	thou shalt t the anointing oil, and anoint	3947

Lev
2: 2	shall t thereout his **handful**	4393+7061+7062
2: 9	the priest shall t from the meat offering a	7311
3: 4	with the kidneys, it shall he t **away**.	5493
3: 9	it shall he t **off** hard by the back bone;	5493
3:10	with the kidneys, it shall he t **away**.	5493
3:15	with the kidneys, it shall he t **away**.	5493
4: 5	the priest that is anointed shall t of	3947
4: 8	he shall t **off** from it all the fat of	7311
4: 9	with the kidneys, he shall t **away**,	5493

Lev
4:19	he shall t all his fat from him, and burn *it*	7311
4:25	the priest shall t of the blood of the sin	3947
4:30	the priest shall t of the blood thereof with	3947
4:31	he shall t **away** all the fat thereof, as the	5493
4:34	he shall t of the blood of the sin	3947
4:35	he shall t **away** all the fat thereof, as the	5493
5:12	the priest shall t his **handful**	4393+7061+7062
6:10	t up the ashes which the fire hath	7311
6:15	he shall t of it his handful, of the flour of	7311
7: 4	with the kidneys, it shall he t **away**:	5493
8: 2	T Aaron and his sons with him,	3947
9: 2	T thee a young calf for a sin offering,	3947
9: 3	T ye a kid of the goats for a sin offering,	3947
10:12	the meat offering that remaineth of	3947
14: 4	shall the priest command to t for him that	3947
14: 6	he shall t *it*, and the cedar wood,	3947
14:10	on the eighth day he shall t two he lambs	3947
14:12	priest shall t one he lamb, and offer him	3947
14:14	the priest shall t some of the blood	3947
14:15	the priest shall t some of the log of oil,	3947
14:21	he shall t one lamb *for* a trespass offering	3947
14:24	the priest shall t the lamb of the trespass	3947
14:25	the priest shall t some of the blood of the	3947
14:40	priest shall command that they t **away**	2502
14:42	they shall t other stones, and put *them* in	3947
14:42	they shall t other morter, and plaister	3947
14:49	he shall t to cleanse the house two birds,	3947
14:51	shall t the cedar wood, and the hyssop,	3947
15:14	on the eighth day he shall t to him two	3947
15:29	on the eighth day she shall t unto her two	3947
16: 5	he shall t of the congregation of	3947
16: 7	he shall t the two goats, and present them	3947
16:12	he shall t a censer full of burning coals of	3947
16:14	he shall t of the blood of the bullock,	3947
16:18	shall t of the blood of the bullock,	3947
18:17	neither shalt thou t her son's daughter,	3947
18:18	Neither shalt thou t a wife to her sister,	3947
20:14	if a man t a wife and her mother, it *is*	3947
20:17	if a man shall t his sister, his father's	3947
20:21	if a man shall t his brother's wife, it *is* an	3947
21: 7	They shall not t a wife *that is* a whore,	3947
21: 7	neither shall they t a woman put away	3947
21:13	And he shall t a wife in her virginity.	3947
21:14	he shall t a virgin of his own people to	3947
22: 5	a man of whom he may t **uncleanness**,	2930
23:40	ye shall t you on the first day the boughs	3947
24: 5	thou shalt t fine flour, and bake twelve	3947
25:36	T thou no usury of him, or increase:	3947
25:46	shall t them **as an inheritance** for your	5157

Nu
1: 2	T ye the sum of all the congregation of	5375
1:49	neither t the sum of them among	5375
1:51	forward, the Levites shall t it **down**:	3381
3:40	and t the number of their names.	5375
3:41	thou shalt t the Levites for me (I *am*	3947
3:45	T the Levites instead of all the firstborn	3947
3:47	Thou shalt even t five shekels apiece by	3947
3:47	the shekel of the sanctuary shalt thou t	3947
4: 2	T the sum of the sons of Kohath from	5375
4: 5	they shall t **down** the covering vail,	3381
4: 9	they shall t a cloth of blue, and cover	3947
4:12	shall t all the instruments of ministry,	3947
4:13	shall t **away** the **ashes** from the altar,	1878
4:22	T also the sum of the sons of Gershon,	5375
5:17	the priest shall t holy water in an earthen	3947
5:17	floor of the tabernacle the priest shall t,	3947
5:25	the priest shall t the jealousy offering out	3947
5:26	priest shall t **a handful** of the offering,	7061
6:18	the hair of the head of his separation,	3947
6:19	the priest shall t the sodden shoulder of	3947
7: 5	T *it* of them, that they may be to do	3947
8: 6	T the Levites from among the children of	3947
8: 8	let them t a young bullock with his meat	3947
8: 8	another young bullock shalt thou t for a	3947
10: 6	lie on the south side shall t their **journey**:	5265
11:17	I will t of the spirit which *is* upon thee,	680
16: 3	said unto them, *Ye* t too much upon you,	NIH
16: 6	Ye censers, Korah, and all his	NIH
16: 7	*ye* t too much upon you, ye sons of Levi.	NIH
16:17	every man his censer, and put incense	3947
16:37	he t **up** the censers out of the burning,	7311
16:46	T a censer, and put fire therein from off	3947
17: 2	t of every one of them a rod according to	3947
17:10	thou shalt **quite** t **away** their murmurings	3615
18:26	When ye t of the children of Israel	3947
19: 4	Eleazar the priest shall t of her blood with	3947
19: 6	the priest shall t cedar wood, and hyssop,	3947
19:17	for an unclean *person* they shall t of	3947
19:18	a clean person shall t hyssop, and dip *it* in	3947
20: 8	The rod, and gather thou the assembly	3947
20:25	T Aaron and Eleazar his son,	3947
21: 7	that he t **away** the serpents from us.	5493
23:12	Must I not t **heed** to speak that which	8104
25: 4	T all the heads of the people,	3947
26: 2	T the sum of all the congregation of	5375
26: 4	*T the sum of the people*, from twenty	NIH
27:18	T thee Joshua the son of Nun, a man in	3947
31:26	T the sum of the prey that was taken,	5375
31:29	T of their half, and give *it* unto Eleazar	3947
31:30	thou shalt t one portion of fifty,	3947
34:18	ye shall t one prince of every tribe,	3947
35:31	Moreover ye shall t no satisfaction for	3947
35:32	shall t no satisfaction for him but he is fled	3947

Dt
1: 7	t your **journey**, and go *to* the mount of	5265
1:13	T ye wise men, and understanding,	3051

Dt
1:40	t your **journey** into the wilderness *by*	5265
2: 4	t ye good **heed** unto yourselves therefore:	8104
2:24	t your **journey**, and pass over the river	5265
4: 9	Only t **heed** to thyself, and keep thy soul	8104
4:15	ye therefore good **heed** unto yourselves	8104
4:23	T **heed** unto yourselves, lest ye forget	8104
4:34	t him a nation from the midst of *another*	3947
5:11	Thou shalt not t the name of the LORD	5375
7: 3	nor his daughter shalt thou t unto thy son.	3947
7:15	the LORD will t **away** from thee all	5493
7:25	or gold *that is* on them, nor t *it* unto thee,	3947
10:11	Arise, t thy journey before the people,	1980
11:16	T **heed** to yourselves, that your heart be	8104
12:13	T **heed** to thyself that thou offer not thy	8104
12:19	T **heed** to thyself that thou forsake not	8104
12:26	thou shalt t, and go unto the place which	5375
12:30	T **heed** to thyself that thou be not snared	8104
15:17	thou shalt t an aul, and thrust *it* through	3947
16:19	shalt not respect persons, neither t a gift:	3947
20: 7	die in the battle, and another man t her.	3947
20:14	spoil thereof, shalt thou t unto thyself;	962
20:19	long time, in making war against it to t it,	8610
21: 3	even the elders of that city shall t a heifer,	3947
22: 6	thou shalt not t the dam with the young:	3947
22: 7	let the dam go, and t the young for thee;	3947
22:13	If any man t a wife, and go in unto her,	3947
22:15	t and bring forth the tokens of the	3947
22:18	the elders of that city shall t *that* man and	3947
22:30	A man shall not t his father's wife,	3947
24: 4	may not t her again to be his wife,	3947
24: 6	t the nether or the upper millstone	
	to pledge:	2254
24: 8	T **heed** in the plague of leprosy, that	8104
24:17	nor t a widow's raiment **to pledge:**	2254
25: 5	t her to him to wife, and perform the duty	3947
25: 7	if the man like not to t his brother's wife,	3947
25: 8	he stand *to it*, and say, I like not to t her;	3947
26: 2	That thou shalt t of the first of all the fruit	3947
26: 4	the priest shall t the basket out of thine	3947
27: 9	T **heed**, and hearken, O Israel;	5535
31:26	T this book of the law, and put it in the	3947
32:41	and mine hand t **hold** on judgment;	270

Jos
3: 6	T **up** the ark of the covenant, and pass	5375
3:12	t ye twelve men out of the tribes of Israel,	3947
4: 2	T you twelve men out of the people, out	3947
4: 3	T you hence out of the midst of Jordan,	5375
4: 5	t ye **up** every man of you a stone upon his	7311
6: 6	T **up** the ark of the covenant, and let	5375
6:18	when ye t of the accursed thing,	3947
7:13	until ye t **away** the accursed thing from	5493
7:14	the family which the LORD shall t shall	3920
7:14	the household which the LORD shall t	3920
8: 1	t all the people of war with thee, and	3947
8: 2	shall ye t **for a prey** unto yourselves:	962
8:29	should t his carcase **down** from the tree,	3381
9:11	T victuals with you for the journey,	3947
10:42	and their land did Joshua t *at* one time,	3920
11:12	Joshua t, and smote them with the edge	3920
20: 4	they shall t him into the city unto them,	622
22: 5	t diligent **heed** to do the commandment	8104
22:19	and t **possession** among us:	270
23:11	T good **heed** therefore unto yourselves,	8104

Jdg
4: 6	t with thee ten thousand men of	3947
5:30	for the necks of *them* that t the spoil?	NIH
6:20	T the flesh and the unleavened *cakes*, and	3947
6:25	unto him, T thy father's young bullock,	3947
6:26	t the second bullock, and offer a burnt	3947
7:24	t before them the waters unto Beth-barah	3920
14: 3	that thou goest to t a wife of	3947
14: 8	after a time he returned to t her,	3947
14:15	have ye called us to t that we **have**? *is it*	3423
15: 2	t her, I pray thee, instead of her.	1961+3807.1
19:30	of it, t **advice**, and speak *your* minds.	5779
20:10	we will t ten men of an hundred	3947

Ru
2:10	that *thou* shouldest t **knowledge** of me,	5234
2:19	blessed be he that did t **knowledge**	5234

1Sa
2:16	*then* t as much as thy soul desireth;	3947
2:16	*it* me now: and if not, I will t *it* by force.	3947
6: 7	make a new cart, and t two milch kine,	3947
6: 8	t the ark of the LORD, and lay it upon	3947
8:11	He will t your sons, and appoint *them* for	3947
8:13	he will t your daughters to be	3947
8:14	he will t your fields, and your vineyards,	3947
8:15	he will t **the tenth** of your seed,	6237
8:16	he will t your menservants, and your	3947
8:17	He will t **the tenth** of your sheep:	6237
9: 3	T now one of the servants with thee,	3947
9: 5	*caring* for the asses, and t **thought** for us.	1672
16: 2	LORD said, T a heifer with thee, and say,	3947
17:17	T now for thy brethren an ephah of this	3947
17:18	how thy brethren fare, and t their pledge.	3947
17:46	smite thee, and t thine head from thee;	5493
19: 2	t **heed** to thyself until the morning,	8104
19:14	when Saul sent messengers to t David,	3947
19:20	Saul sent messengers to t David:	3947
20:21	arrows *are* on this side of thee, t them;	3947
21: 9	if thou wilt t that, take *it*: for *there is* no	3947
21: 9	t *it*: for *there is* no other save that here.	3947
23:23	t **knowledge** of all the lurking places	3045
23:26	and his men round about to t them.	8610
24:11	yet thou huntest my soul to t it.	3947
25:11	Shall I then t my bread, and my water,	3947
25:39	with Abigail, to t her to him to wife.	3947
25:40	sent us unto thee, to t thee to him to wife.	3947
26:11	t thou now the spear that *is at* his bolster,	3947

2Sa
2:21 of the young men, and t thee thy armour. 3947
4:11 hand, and t you away from the earth? 1197
5: 6 Except thou t away the blind and the 5493
12: 4 he spared to t of his own flock and of his 3947
12:11 and I will t thy wives before thine eyes, 3947
12:28 and encamp against the city, and t it 3920
12:28 lest I t the city, and it be called after my 3920
13:33 let not my lord the king t the thing to his 7760
15:20 return thou, and t back thy brethren: 7725
16: 9 go over, I pray thee, and t off his head. 5493
19:19 that the king should t it to his heart. 7760
19:30 said unto the king, Yea, let him t all, 3947
20: 6 t thou thy lord's servants, and pursue after 3947
24:10 t away the iniquity of thy servant; 5674
24:22 Let my lord the king t and offer up what 3947

1Ki
1:33 T with you the servants of your lord, 3947
2: 4 If thy children t heed to their way, 8104
2:31 that thou mayest t away the innocent 5493
8:25 so that thy children t heed to their way, 8104
11:31 he said to Jeroboam, T thee ten pieces: 3947
11:34 I will not t the whole kingdom out 3947
11:35 I will t the kingdom out of his son's hand, 3947
11:37 I will t thee, and thou shalt reign 3947
14: 3 t with thee ten loaves, and cracknels, 3947
14:10 will t away the remnant of the house of 1197
16: 3 I will t away the posterity of Baasha, 1197
18:40 said unto them, T the prophets of Baal; 8610
19: 4 is enough; now, O Lord, t away my life; 3947
19:10 left; and they seek my life, to t it away. 3947
19:14 left; and they seek my life, to t it away. 3947
20: 6 shall put it in their hand, and t it away. 3947
20:18 they be come out for peace, t them alive; 8610
20:18 they be come out for war, t them alive. 8610
20:24 this thing, T the kings away, every man 5493
21:15 t possession of the vineyard of Naboth 3423
21:16 Naboth the Jezreelite, to t possession 3423
21:21 will t away thy posterity, and will cut off 1197
22: 3 t it not out of the hand of the king of 3947
22:26 T Micaiah, and carry him back unto 3947

2Ki
2: 1 when the Lord would t up Elijah into 5927
2: 3 Knowest thou that the Lord will t away 3947
2: 5 Knowest thou that the Lord will t away 3947
4: 1 the creditor is come to t unto him my two 3947
4:29 t my staff in thine hand, and go thy way: if 3947
4:36 come in unto him, he said, T up thy son. 5375
5:15 I pray thee, t a blessing of thy servant. 3947
5:16 And he urged him to t it; but he refused. 3947
5:20 run after him, and t somewhat of him. 3947
5:23 Naaman said, Be content, t two talents. 3947
6: 2 thence every man a beam, and let us 3947
6: 7 Therefore said he, T it up to thee. And he 7311
6:32 murderer hath sent to t away mine head? 5493
7:13 servants answered and said, Let some t, 3947
8: 8 T a present in thine hand, and go, meet 3947
9: 1 t this box of oil in thine hand, and go to 3947
9: 3 the box of oil, and pour it on his head, 3947
9:17 T a horseman, and send to meet them, 3947
9:25 T up, and cast him in the portion of 5375
9:26 therefore t and cast him into the plat 5375
10: 6 t ye the heads of the men your master's 3947
10:14 he said, T them alive. And they took them 8610
12: 5 Let the priests t it to them, every man of 3947
13:15 Elisha said unto him, T bow and arrows. 3947
13:18 he said, T the arrows. And he took them. 3947
18:32 t you away to a land like your own land, 3947
19:30 of Judah shall yet again t root downward, 8328
20: 7 Isaiah said, T a lump of figs. And they 3947
20:18 shall they t away; and they shall be 3947

1Ch
7:21 they came down to t away their cattle. 3947
17:13 I will not t my mercy away from him, as 5493
21:23 T it to thee, and let my lord the king do 3947
21:24 for I will not t that which is thine for 5375
28:10 T heed now; for the Lord hath chosen 7200

2Ch
6:16 that thy children t heed to their way to 8104
18:25 T ye Micaiah, and carry him back to 3947
19: 6 said to the judges, T heed what ye do: 7200
19: 7 t heed and do it: for there is no iniquity 8104
20:25 people came to t away the spoil of them, 962
32:18 trouble them; that they might t the city. 3920
33: 8 that they will t heed to do all that I have 8104

Ezr
4:22 T heed now that ye fail not to do this: 2095
5:14 did Cyrus the king t out of the temple 5312
5:15 said unto him, T these vessels, 5376
9:12 neither t their daughters unto your sons, 5375

Ne
5: 2 we t up corn for them, that we may eat, 3947
6: 7 and let us t counsel together. 3289
10:30 land, nor t their daughters for our sons: 3947
10:38 the Levites, when the Levites t tithes, 6237
13:25 nor t their daughters unto your sons, 5375

Est
3:13 and to t the spoil of them for a prey, NIH
4: 4 and to t away his sackcloth from him: 5493
6:10 and t the apparel and the horse, 3947
8:11 and to t the spoil of them for a prey, NIH

Job
7:21 and t away mine iniquity? 5674
9:18 He will not suffer me to t my breath, 7725
9:34 Let him t his rod away from me, and let 5493
10:20 let me alone, that I may t comfort a little, 1082
11:18 and thou shalt t thy rest in safety. 7901
13:14 Wherefore do I t my flesh in my teeth, 5375
18: 9 The grin shall t him by the heel, 270
21:12 They t the timbrel and harp, and rejoice at 5375
23:10 he knoweth the way that I t: when he 5978
24: 2 they violently t away flocks, 1497
24: 3 they t the widow's ox for a pledge. 2254
24: 9 the breast, and t a pledge of the poor. 2254

Job
24:10 they t away the sheaf from the hungry; 5375
27:20 Terrors t hold on him as waters, 5381
30:17 night season: and my sinews t no rest. 7901
31:36 Surely I would t it upon my shoulder, 5375
32:22 doing my Maker would soon t me away. 5375
36:17 judgment and justice t hold on thee. 8551
36:18 lest he t thee away with his stroke: 5496
36:21 T heed, regard not iniquity: for this hast 8104
38:13 it might t hold of the ends of the earth, 270
38:20 That thou shouldest t it to the bound 3947
41: 4 wilt thou t him for a servant for ever? 3947
42: 8 Therefore t unto you now seven bullocks 3947

Ps
2: 2 the rulers t counsel together, against 3245
7: 5 the enemy persecute my soul, and t it; 5381
13: 2 How long shall I t counsel in my soul, 7896
16: 4 not t up their names into my lips. 5375
27:10 forsake me, then the Lord will t me up. 622
31:13 me, they devised to t away my life. 3947
35: 2 T hold of shield and buckler, and stand 2388
39: 1 I said, I will t heed to my ways, that I sin 8104
50: 9 I will t no bullock out of thy house, nor 3947
50:16 that thou shouldest t my covenant in thy 5375
51:11 and t not thy holy Spirit from me. 3947
52: 5 he shall t thee away, and pluck thee out 2846
58: 9 shall t them away as with a whirlwind, 8175
69:20 I looked for some to t pity, but there was 5110
69:24 and let thy wrathful anger t hold of them. 5381
71:10 they that lay wait for my soul t counsel 3289
71:11 persecute and t him; for there is none to 8610
80: 9 didst cause it t deep root, 8327+8328
81: 2 A psalm, and bring hither the timbrel 5375
83:12 t to ourselves the houses of God
 in possession. 3423
89:33 will I not utterly t from him, 6331
102:14 For thy servants t pleasure in her stones, 7521
102:24 t me not away in the midst of my days: 5927
109: 8 days be few; and let another t his office. 3947
116:13 I will t the cup of salvation, and call upon 5375
119:43 t not the word of truth utterly out of my 5337
139: 9 If I t the wings of the morning, and dwell 5375
139:20 and thine enemies t thy name in vain. 5375

Pr
2:19 neither t they hold of the paths of life. 5381
4:13 T fast hold of instruction; let her not go: 2388
5: 5 to death; her steps t hold on hell. 8551
5:22 His own iniquities shall t the wicked 3920
6:25 neither let her t thee with her eyelids. 3947
6:27 Can a man t fire in his bosom, 2846
7:18 let us t our fill of love until the morning: 7301
20:16 T his garment that is surety for a stranger: 3947
20:16 t a pledge of him for a strange woman. 2254
22:27 why should he t away thy bed from 3947
25: 4 T away the dross from the silver, 1898
25: 5 T away the wicked from before the king, 1898
27:13 T his garment that is surety for a stranger, 3947
27:13 t a pledge of him for a strange woman. 2254
30: 9 steal, and t the name of my God in vain. 8610

Ecc
5:15 shall t nothing of his labour, which he 5375
5:19 t his portion, and to rejoice in his labour; 5375
7:18 is good that thou shouldest t hold of this; 270
7:21 Also t no heed unto all words that 3820+5414

SS
2:15 T us the foxes, the little foxes, that spoil 270
7: 8 I will t hold of the boughs thereof: 270

Isa
1:25 away thy dross, and t away all thy tin: 5493
3: 1 doth t away from Jerusalem and 5493
3: 6 When a man shall t hold of his brother of 8610
3:18 that day the Lord will t away the bravery 5493
4: 1 in that day seven women shall t hold of 2388
4: 1 by her name, to t away our reproach. 622
5: 5 I will t away the hedge thereof, and it 5493
5:23 way the righteousness of the righteous 5493
7: 4 say unto him, T heed, and be quiet; 8104
8: 1 T thee a great roll, and write in it with a 3947
8:10 T counsel together, and it shall 5779+6098
10: 2 to t away the right from the poor of my 1497
10: 6 to t the spoil, and to take the prey, 7997
10: 6 to t the prey, and to tread them down like 962
13: 8 sorrows shall t hold of them; they shall be 270
14: 2 the people shall t them, and bring them to 3947
14: 2 shall t them captives, whose captives 7617
14: 4 That thou shalt t up this proverb against 5375
16: 3 T counsel, execute judgment; make thy 935
18: 4 I will t my rest, and I will consider in my 8252
18: 5 and t away and cut down the branches 5493
23:16 T a harp, go about the city, thou harlot 5493
25: 8 the rebuke of his people shall he t away 5493
27: 5 Or let him t hold of my strength, that he 2388
27: 6 cause them that come of Jacob to t root: 8327
27: 9 and this is all the fruit to t away his sin; 5493
28:19 From the time that it goeth forth it shall t 3947
30: 1 the Lord, that t counsel, but not of me; 6213
30:14 of it a sheard to t fire from the hearth, 2846
30:14 or to t water withal out of the pit. 2834
33:23 a great spoil divided; the lame t the prey. 962
36:17 t you away to a land like your own land, 3947
37:31 of Judah shall again t root downward, NIH
38:21 Let them t a lump of figs, and lay it for a 5375
39: 7 which thou shalt beget, shall they t away; 3947
40:24 their stock shall not t root in the earth: 8327
40:24 whirlwind shall t them away as stubble. 5375
44:15 for he will t thereof, and warm himself; 3947
45:21 near; yea, let them t counsel together: 3289
47: 2 T the millstones, and grind meal: 3947
47: 3 I will t vengeance, and I will not meet 3947
56: 4 please me, and t hold of my covenant; 2388
57:13 vanity shall t them: but he that putteth 3947

Isa
57:14 t up the stumblingblock out of the way of 7311
58: 2 they t delight in approaching to God. 2654
58: 9 Here I am. If thou t away from the midst 5493
64: 7 that stirreth up himself to t hold of thee: 2388
66:21 I will also t of them for priests and 3947

Jer
2:22 thee with nitre, and t thee much sope, 7235
3:14 I will t you one of a city, and two of a 3947
4: 4 t away the foreskins of your heart, ye 5493
5:10 t away her battlements; for they are not 5493
7:29 and t up a lamentation on high places; 5375
9: 4 T ye heed every one of his neighbour, 8104
9:10 For the mountains will I t up a weeping 5375
9:18 make haste, and t up a wailing for us, 5375
13: 4 T the girdle that thou hast got, which is 3947
13: 6 Euphrates, and t the girdle from thence, 270
13:21 shall not sorrows t thee, as a woman in 270
15:15 t me not away in thy longsuffering: 3947
15:19 if thou t forth the precious from the vile, 3318
16: 2 Thou shalt not t thee a wife, neither shalt 3947
17:21 T heed to yourselves, and bear no burden 8104
18:22 for they have digged a pit to t me, 3920
19: 1 t of the ancients of the people, and of NIH
20: 5 and t them, and carry them to Babylon. 3947
20:10 and we shall t our revenge on him. 3947
25: 9 send and t all the families of the north, 3947
25:10 I will t from them the voice of mirth, 6
25:15 T the wine cup of this fury at mine hand, 3947
25:28 if they refuse to t the cup at thine hand to 3947
29: 6 T ye wives, and beget sons and daughters 3947
29: 6 t wives for your sons, and give your 3947
32: 3 of the king of Babylon, and he shall t it; 3920
32:14 T these evidences, this evidence of 3947
32:24 they are come unto the city to t it; 3920
32:25 field for money, and t witnesses; 5707+5749
32:28 king of Babylon, and he shall t it: 3920
32:44 t witnesses in the land of 5707+5749
33:26 I will not t any of his seed to be rulers 3947
34:22 against it, and t it, and burn it with fire: 3920
36: 2 T thee a roll of a book, and write therein 3947
36:14 T in thine hand the roll wherein thou hast 3947
36:26 to t Baruch the scribe and Jeremiah 3947
36:28 T thee again another roll, and write in it 3947
37: 8 this city, and t it, and burn it with fire. 3920
38: 3 king of Babylon's army, which shall t it. 3920
38:10 T from hence thirty men with thee, 3947
38:10 t up Jeremiah the prophet out of 5927
39:12 T him, and look well to him, and do him 3947
43: 9 T great stones in thine hand, and hide 3947
43:10 T Nebuchadrezzar the king of Babylon, 3947
44:12 I will t the remnant of Judah, that have 3947
46:11 Go up into Gilead, and t balm, O virgin, 3947
49:29 their flocks shall they t away: they shall 3947
49:29 they shall t to themselves their curtains, 5375
50:15 t vengeance upon her; as she hath done, 5358
51: 8 t balm for her pain, if so be she may be 3947
51:26 shall not t of thee a stone for a corner, 3947
51:36 cause, and t vengeance for thee; 5358+5360

La
2:13 What thing shall I t to witness for thee? 5749

Eze
4: 1 t thee a tile, and lay it before thee, 3947
4: 3 Moreover t thou unto thee an iron pan, 3947
4: 9 T thou also unto thee wheat, and barley, 3947
5: 1 thou, son of man, t thee a sharp knife, 3947
5: 1 t thee a barber's rasor, and cause it to pass 3947
5: 1 t thee balances to weigh, and divide 3947
5: 2 shalt t a third part, and smite about it 3947
5: 3 Thou shalt also t thereof a few in number, 3947
5: 4 t of them again, and cast them into 3947
10: 6 saying, T fire from between the wheels, 3947
11:18 they shall t away all the detestable things 5493
11:19 I will t the stony heart out of their flesh, 5493
14: 5 That I may t the house of Israel in their 8610
15: 3 will men t a pin of it to hang any vessel 3947
16:16 of thy garments thou didst t, 3947
16:39 t thy fair jewels, and leave thee naked 3947
17:22 I will also t of the highest branch of 3947
19: 1 Moreover t thou up a lamentation for 5375
21:26 Remove the diadem, and t off the crown: 7311
22:16 thou shalt t thine inheritance in thyself 2490
23:25 they shall t away thy nose and thine ears; 5493
23:25 they shall t thy sons and thy daughters; 3947
23:26 of thy clothes, and t away thy fair jewels. 3947
23:29 shall t away all thy labour, and shall leave 3947
24: 5 T the choice of the flock, and burn also 3947
24: 8 fury to come up to t vengeance; 5358+5359
24:16 I t away from thee the desire of thine eyes 3947
24:25 shall it not be in the day when I t from 3947
26:17 they shall t up a lamentation for thee, 5375
27: 2 son of man, t up a lamentation for Tyrus; 5375
27:32 in their wailing they shall t up a 5375
28:12 t up a lamentation upon the king of Tyrus 5375
29:19 shall t her multitude, and take her spoil, 5375
29:19 and t her spoil, and take her prey; 7997+7998
29:19 and take her spoil, and t her prey; 957+962
30: 4 they shall t away her multitude, 3947
32: 2 t up a lamentation for Pharaoh king of 5375
33: 2 if the people of the land t a man of their 3947
33: 4 if the sword come, and t him away, 3947
33: 6 and t any person from among them, 3947
36:24 For I will t you from among the heathen, 3947
36:26 I will t away the stony heart out of your 5493
37:16 thee one stick, and write upon it, 3947
37:16 t another stick, and write upon it, 3947
37:19 Behold, I will t the stick of Joseph, 3947
37:21 I will t the children of Israel from among 3947
38:12 To t a spoil, and to take a prey; 7997+7998

T

Eze
38:12 To take a spoil, and to **t** a prey; 957+962
38:13 Art thou come to **t** a spoil? 7997+7998
38:13 gathered thy company to **t** a prey? 957+962
38:13 and gold, to **t** *away* cattle and goods, 3947
38:13 *away* cattle and goods, to **t** a great spoil? 7997
39:10 So that they shall **t** no wood out of 5375
43:20 thou shalt **t** of the blood thereof, and put 3947
43:21 Thou shalt **t** the bullock also of the sin 3947
44:22 Neither shall they **t** for their wives a 3947
44:22 they shall **t** maidens of the seed of 3947
45: 1 ye **t** *away* your exactions from my people, 7311
45:18 thou shalt **t** a young bullock without 3947
45:19 the priest shall **t** of the blood of the sin 3947
46:18 Moreover the prince shall not **t** of 3947

Da
6:23 commanded that *they* should **t** Daniel *up* 5267
7:18 the saints of the most High shall **t** 6902
7:26 shall **t** *away* his dominion, to consume 5709
11:15 up a mount, and **t** the most fenced cities: 3920
11:18 his face unto the isles, and shall **t** many: 3920
11:31 shall **t** *away* the daily *sacrifice,* and 5493

Hos
1: 2 unto thee a wife of whoredoms and 3947
1: 6 but I will **utterly t** them **away.** 5375+5375
2: 9 and **t** *away* my corn in the time thereof, 3947
2:17 For I will **t** *away* the names of Baalim out 5493
4:10 they have left off to **t heed** to the LORD. 8104
4:11 and wine and new wine **t** *away* the heart. 3947
5:14 I will **t** *away,* and none shall rescue him. 5375
7:11 I was to them as they that **t** *off* the yoke 7311
14: 2 **T** with you words, and turn to the LORD: 3947
14: 2 **T** *away* all iniquity, and receive *us* 5375

Am
3: 5 shall *one* **t** *up* a snare from the earth, 5927
4: 2 that he will **t** you *away* with hooks, 5375
5: 1 ye this word which I **t** *up* against you, 5375
5:11 and ye **t** from him burdens of wheat: 3947
5:12 they **t** a bribe, and they turn aside the 5493
5:23 **T** thou *away* from me the noise of thy 5493
6:10 a man's uncle shall **t** him *up,* and he that 5375
9: 2 into hell, thence shall mine hand **t** them; 3947
9: 3 I will search and **t** them out thence; 3947

Jnh
1:12 **T** me *up,* and cast me forth into the sea; 5375
4: 3 O LORD, **t,** I beseech thee, 3947

Mic
2: 2 covet fields, and **t** *them* **by violence;** 1497
2: 2 violence; and houses, and **t** *them* **away:** 5375
2: 4 that day shall *one* **t** *up* a parable against 5375
2: 6 to them, *that* they shall not **t** shame. 5253
6:14 thou shalt **t hold,** but shalt not deliver; 5253

Na
1: 2 The LORD will **t vengeance** on his 5358
2: 9 **T** ye the spoil of silver, take the spoil of 962
2: 9 ye the spoil of silver, **t the spoil** of gold: 962

Hab
1:10 for they shall heap dust, and **t** it. 3920
1:15 They **t** *up* all of them with the angle, 5927
2: 6 Shall not all these **t** *up* a parable against 5375

Zep
3:11 I will **t** *away* out of the midst of thee 5493

Hag
2: 8 I will **t pleasure** in it, and I will be 7521
2:23 will I **t** thee, O Zerubbabel, my servant, 3947

Zec
1: 6 did they not **t hold** of your fathers? 5381
3: 4 **T** *away* the filthy garments from him. 5493
6:10 **T** *of them* of the captivity, *even* of Heldai, 3947
6:11 **t** silver and gold, and make crowns, 3947
8:23 **t hold** out of all languages of the nations, 2388
8:23 shall **t hold** of the skirt of him that is a 2388
9: 7 I will **t** *away* his blood out of his mouth, 5493
11:15 **T** unto thee yet the instruments of a 3947
14:21 that sacrifice shall come and **t** of them, 3947

Mal
2: 3 and *one* shall **t** you *away* with it. 5375
2:15 Therefore **t heed** to your spirit, and let 8104
2:16 therefore **t heed** to your spirit, that ye 8104

Mt
1:20 fear not to **t unto** *thee* Mary thy wife: 3880
2:13 and **t** the young child and his mother, 3880
2:20 and **t** the young child and his mother, 3880
5:40 **t** *away* thy coat, let him have thy *cloke* 2983
6: 1 **T heed** that ye do not your alms before 4337
6:25 **T no thought** for your life, what ye shall 3309
6:28 And why **t** ye **thought** for raiment? 3309
6:31 Therefore **t no thought,** saying, What 3309
6:34 **T** therefore no **thought** for the morrow: 3309
6:34 for the morrow shall **t thought** for 3309
9: 6 **t** *up* thy bed, and go unto thine house. 142
10:19 **t no thought** how or what ye shall speak: 3309
11:12 and the violent **t it by force.** 726
11:29 **T** my yoke upon you, and learn of me; for I 142
15:26 It is not meet to **t** the children's bread, 2983
16: 5 other side, they had forgotten to **t** bread. 2983
16: 6 **T heed** and beware of the leaven of 3708
16:24 and **t** *up* his cross, and follow me. 142
17:25 whom do the kings of the earth **t** custom 2983
17:27 and **t** *up* the fish that first cometh up; 142
17:27 **t,** and give unto them for me and thee. 2983
18:10 **T heed** that ye despise not one of these 3708
18:16 *thee,* then **t** with thee one or two more, 3880
18:23 which would **t** account of his servants. 4868
20:14 **T** *that* thine *is,* and go thy way: I will give 142
22:13 Bind him hand and foot, and **t** him **away,** 142
24: 4 them, **T heed** that no *man* deceive you. 991
24:17 down to **t** any *thing* out of his house: 142
24:18 is in the field return back to **t** his clothes. 142
25:28 **T** therefore the talent from him, and give 142
26: 4 And consulted that they might **t** Jesus by 2902
26:26 gave *it* to the disciples, and said, **T,** eat; 2983
26:45 unto them, Sleep on now, and **t** your **rest:** 373
26:52 for all they that **t** the sword shall perish 2983
26:55 a thief with swords and staves for to **t** me? 4815

Mk
2: 9 to say, Arise, and **t** *up* thy bed, and walk? 142
2:11 **t** *up* thy bed, and go thy way into thine 142
4:24 unto them, **T heed** what you hear: 991
6: 8 And commanded them that they should **t** 142
7:27 for it is not meet to **t** the children's bread, 2983
8:14 the disciples had forgotten to **t** bread, 2983
8:15 And he charged them, saying, **T heed,** 3708
8:34 and **t** *up* his cross, and follow me. 142
10:21 and come, **t** *up* the cross, and follow me. 142
12:19 that his brother should **t** his wife, 2983
13: 5 to say, **T heed** lest any *man* deceive you: 991
13: 9 But **t heed** to yourselves: for they shall 991
13:11 **t** no **thought beforehand** what ye shall 4305
13:15 neither enter *therein,* to **t** any *thing* out of 142
13:16 not turn back again for to **t** *up* his garment. 142
13:23 But **t** ye **heed:** behold, I have foretold you 991
13:33 **T** ye **heed,** watch and pray: for ye know 991
14: 1 the scribes sought how they might **t** him 2902
14:22 and gave to them, and said, **T,** eat: 2983
14:36 unto thee; **t** *away* this cup from me: 3911
14:41 unto them, Sleep on now, and **t** your **rest:** 373
14:44 is he; **t** him, and lead *him* away safely. 2902
14:48 with swords and *with* staves to **t** me? 4815
15:24 lots upon them, what every *man* should **t.** 142
15:36 whether Elias will come to **t** him **down.** 2507
16:18 They shall **t** *up* serpents; and if they drink 142

Lk
1:25 *me,* to **t** *away* my reproach among men. 851
5:24 **t** *up* thy couch, and go into thine house. 142
6: 4 of God, and did **t** and eat the shewbread, 2983
6:29 thy cloke forbid not to **t** *thy* coat also. NIG
8:18 **T heed** therefore how ye hear: 991
9: 3 **T** nothing for *your* journey, neither staves, 142
9:23 him deny himself, and **t** *up* his cross daily, 142
10:35 host, and said unto him, **T care** of him; 1959
11:35 **T heed** therefore that the light which is in 4648
12:11 **t** ye no **thought** how or what *thing* ye 3309
12:15 **T heed,** and beware of covetousness: 3708
12:19 **t** thine *ease,* eat, drink, *and* be merry. 373
12:22 **T no thought** for your life, what ye shall 3309
12:26 is least, why **t** ye **thought** for the rest? 3309
14: 9 thou begin with shame to **t** the lowest 2722
16: 6 **T** thy bill, and sit down quickly, 1209
16: 7 unto him, **T** thy bill, and write fourscore. 1209
17: 3 **T heed** to yourselves: If thy brother 4337
17:31 let him not come down to **t** it **away:** 142
19:24 **T** from him the pound, and give *it* to him 142
20:20 *men,* that they might **t hold** of his words, 1949
20:26 they could not **t hold** of his words 1949
20:28 that his brother should **t** *his* wife, 2983
21: 8 he said, **T heed** that ye be not deceived: 991
21:34 **T heed** to yourselves, lest at any time 4337
22:17 **T** this, and divide *it* among yourselves: 2983
22:36 a purse, let him **t** it, and likewise *his* scrip: 142

Jn
2:16 that sold doves, **T** these *things* hence; 142
5: 8 unto him, Rise, **t** *up* thy bed, and walk, 142
5:11 said unto me, **T** *up* thy bed, and walk. 142
5:12 said unto thee, **T** *up* thy bed, and walk? 142
6: 7 that every one of them may **t** a little. 2983
6:15 that they would come and **t** him **by force,** 726
7:30 they sought to **t** him: but no *man* laid 4084
7:32 and the chief priests sent officers to **t** him. 4084
10:17 I lay down my life, that I might **t** it again. 2983
10:18 it down, and I have power to **t** it again. 4084
10:39 Therefore they sought again to **t** him: 4084
11:39 Jesus said, **T** ye **away** the stone. Martha, 142
11:48 and **t** *away* both our place and nation. 142
11:57 he should shew *it,* that they might **t** him. 4084
16:15 that he shall **t** of mine, and shall shew *it* 2983
17:15 I pray not that thou shouldest **t** them out 142
18:31 **Ye** him, and judge him according to your 2983
19: 6 **Ye** him, and crucify *him:* for I find no 2983
19:38 besought Pilate that he might **t away** 142
20:15 thou hast laid him, and I will **t** him **away.** 142

Ac
1:20 and his bishoprick let another **t.** 2983
1:25 That *he* may **t** part of this ministry and 2983
5:35 heed to yourselves what ye intend to do 4815
12: 3 he proceeded further to **t** Peter also. 4815
15:14 to **t** out of them a people for his name. 2983
15:37 And Barnabas determined to **t with them** 4838
15:38 But Paul thought not good to **t** him with 4838
20:13 unto Assos, there intending to **t** in Paul: 353
20:26 Wherefore I **t** you **to record** this day, 3143
20:28 **T heed** therefore unto yourselves, and to 4337
21:24 Them **t,** and purify thyself with them, 3880
22:26 saying, **T heed** what thou doest: 3708
23:10 and to **t** him **by force** from among them, 726
24: 8 by examining of whom thyself mayest **t** NIG
27:33 Paul besought *them* all to **t** meat, saying, 3335
27:34 Wherefore I pray you to **t** *some* meat: 4355

Ro
11:21 **t** *heed* lest he also spare not thee. NIG
11:27 unto them, when I shall **t away** their sins. 851
15:24 Whensoever I **t** my **journey** into Spain, 4198

1Co
3:10 But let every man **t heed** how he buildeth 991
6: 7 Why do ye not rather **t wrong?** why do 91
6:15 shall I then **t** the members of Christ, 142
8: 9 But **t heed** lest by any means this liberty 991
9: 9 out the corn. Doth God **t care for** oxen? 3199
10:12 thinketh he standeth **t heed** lest he fall. 991
11:24 given thanks, he brake *it,* and said, **T,** eat: 2983

2Co
8: 4 **t** *upon us* the fellowship of the ministering NIG
11:20 if a man devour you, if a man **t** of you, if a 2983
12:10 Therefore I **t pleasure** in infirmities, 2106

Gal
5:15 **t heed** ye be not consumed one of another. 991

Eph
6:13 Wherefore **t unto** *you* the whole armour of 353
6:17 And the helmet of salvation, 1209

Col
4:17 **T heed** to the ministry which thou hast 991

1Ti
3: 5 how shall he **t care of** the church of God? 1959
4:16 **T heed** unto thyself, and unto the 1907

2Ti
4:11 **T** Mark, and bring *him* with thee: for he is 353

Heb
3:12 **T heed,** brethren, lest there be in any of 991
7: 5 **t tithes** of the people according to the law, 586
10: 4 of bulls and of goats should **t away** sins. 851
10:11 which can never **t away** sins: 4014

Jas
5:10 **T,** my brethren, the prophets, who have 2983

1Pe
2:20 for your faults, ye shall **t it patiently?** 5278
2:20 do well, and suffer *for it,* ye **t it patiently,** 5278

2Pe
1:19 whereunto ye do well that ye **t heed,** 4337

1Jn
3: 5 that he was manifested to **t away** our sins; 142

Rev
3:11 thou hast, that no *man* **t** thy crown. 2983
5: 9 art worthy to **t** the book, and to open 2983
6: 4 was given to him that sat thereon to **t** 2983
10: 8 **t** the little book which is open in the hand 2983
10: 9 And he said unto me, **T** *it,* and eat it up; 2983
22:17 let him take the water of life freely. 2983
22:19 if any *man* **t away** from the words 851
22:19 God shall **t away** his part out of the book 851

TAKEN (338) [TAKE]

Ge
2:22 which the LORD God had **t** from man, 3947
2:23 because she was **t** out of Man. 3947
3:19 unto the ground; for out of it wast thou **t:** 3947
3:23 to till the ground from whence he was **t.** 3947
4:15 **vengeance** shall be **t** on him sevenfold. 5358
12:15 the woman was **t** into Pharaoh's house. 3947
12:19 so I might have **t** her to me to wife: 3947
14:14 heard that his brother was **t captive,** 7617
18:27 I have **t upon** me to speak unto the Lord, 2974
18:31 I have **t upon** me to speak unto the Lord: 2974
20: 3 for the woman which thou hast **t;** 3947
21:25 servants had **violently t away.** 1497
27:33 where *is* he that hath **t** venison, 6679
27:35 subtilty, and hath **t away** thy blessing. 3947
27:36 behold, now he hath **t away** my blessing: 3947
27:36 *Is it* a small matter that thou hast **t** my 3947
30:23 and said, God hath **t away** my reproach: 622
31: 1 Jacob hath **t away** all that *was* our 3947
31: 9 Thus God hath **t away** the cattle of your 5337
31:16 For all the riches which God hath **t** from 5337
31:26 daughters, as captives with the sword? NIH
31:34 Rachel had **t** the images, and put them 3947

Ex
14:11 hast thou **t** us **away** to die in 3947
25:15 of the ark: they shall not be **t** from it. 5493
40:36 when the cloud was **t** *up* from over 5927
40:37 if the cloud were not **t** *up,* then 5927
40:37 journeyed not till the day that it was **t** *up.* 5927

Lev
4:10 As it was **t** *off* from the bullock of 7311
4:31 as the fat is **t away** from off the sacrifice 5493
4:35 as the fat of the lamb is **t away** from 5493
6: 2 or in a **thing t away by violence,** 1498
7:34 the heave shoulder have I **t** of the 3947
14:43 after that he hath **t away** the stones, 2502
24: 8 *being* **t** from the children of Israel *by* an NIH

Nu
3:12 I have **t** the Levites from among 3947
5:13 neither she be **t with the manner;** 8610
8:16 children of Israel, have I **t** them unto me. 3947
8:18 I have **t** the Levites for all the firstborn of 3947
9:17 when the cloud was **t** *up* 5927
9:21 the cloud was **t** *up* in the morning, then 5927
9:21 day or by night that the cloud was **t** *up,* 5927
9:22 but when it was **t** *up,* they journeyed. 5927
10:11 *that* the cloud was **t** *up* from off 5927
10:17 the tabernacle was **t** *down;* and the sons 3381
16:15 have I not **t** one ass from them, 5375
18: 6 I have **t** your brethren the Levites from 3947
21:26 **t** all his land out of his hand, *even* unto 3947
31:26 Take the sum of the prey that was **t,** *both* 7628
31:49 Thy servants have **t** the sum of the men of 5375
31:53 the men of war had **t spoil,** every man 962
36: 3 shall their inheritance be **t** from 1639
36: 3 it be **t** from the lot of our inheritance. 1639
36: 4 shall their inheritance be **t away** from 1639

Dt
4:20 the LORD hath **t** you, and brought you 3947
20: 7 hath betrothed a wife, and hath not **t** her? 3947
21:10 and thou hast **t** them **captive,** 7617+7628
24: 1 a man hath **t** a wife, and married her, 3947
24: 5 a man hath **t** a new wife, he shall not 3947
24: 5 shall cheer up his wife which he hath **t.** 3947
26:14 neither have I **t** away *ought* thereof for 1197
28:31 thine ass *shall be* **violently t away** from 1497

Jos
7:11 for they have even **t** of the accursed thing, 3947
7:15 *that* he that is **t** with the accursed thing 3920
7:16 their tribes; and the tribe of Judah was **t:** 3920
7:17 Zarhites man by man; and Zabdi was **t:** 3920
7:18 son of Zerah, of the tribe of Judah, was **t.** 3920
8: 8 it shall be, when ye have **t** the city, *that* 8610
8:21 all Israel saw that the ambush had **t** 3920
10: 1 Jerusalem had heard how Joshua had **t** Ai, 3920

Jdg
1: 8 had **t** it, and smitten it with the edge of 3920
11:36 forasmuch as the LORD hath **t vengeance** 6213
14: 2 told not them that he had **t** the honey out 7287
15: 6 because he had **t** his wife, and given her 3947
17: 2 *shekels* of silver that were **t** from thee, 3947
18:24 Ye have **t away** my gods which I made, 3947

1Sa
4:11 the ark of God was **t;** and the two sons of 3947
4:17 are dead, and the ark of God is **t.** 3947
4:19 the tidings that the ark of God was **t,** 3947
4:21 because the ark of God was **t,** and 3947
4:22 from Israel: for the ark of God is **t.** 3947
7:14 the cities which the Philistines had **t** from 3947
10:20 to come near, the tribe of Benjamin was **t.** 3920
10:21 family of Matri was **t,** and Saul the son 3920
10:21 was taken, and Saul the son of Kish was **t:** 3920
12: 3 whose ox have I **t?** or whose ass have I 3947

T

1Sa 12: 3 or whose ass have I **t**? or whom have I 3947
12: 4 neither hast thou **t** ought of any man's 3947
14:41 perfect *lot*. And Saul and Jonathan were **t**: 3920
14:42 Jonathan my son. And Jonathan was **t**. 3920
21: 6 that was **t** from before the LORD, 5493
21: 6 hot bread in the day when it was **t away**. 5493
30: 2 had **t** the women **captives**, that *were* 7617
30: 3 and their daughters, were **t captives**. 7617
30: 5 David's two wives were **t captives**, 7617
30:16 of all the great spoil that they had **t** out of 3947
30:19 nor any *thing* that they had **t** to them: 3947
2Sa 12: 9 hast **t** his wife to be thy wife, and hast 3947
12:10 hast **t** the wife of Uriah the Hittite to be 3947
12:27 and have **t** the city of waters. 3920
16: 8 and, behold, thou *art* **t** to thy mischief, NIH
18: 9 he was **t up** between the heaven and 5414
18:18 Now Absalom in his lifetime had **t** and 3947
23: 6 because they cannot be **t** with hands: 3947
1Ki 7: 8 he had **t** *to wife*, like unto this porch. 3947
9: 9 have **t hold** upon other gods, 2388
9:16 **t** Gezer, and burnt it with fire, and slain 3920
16:18 pass, when Zimri saw that the city was **t**, 3920
21:19 Hast thou killed, and also **t possession**? 3423
22:43 the high places were not **t away** 5493
2Ki 2: 9 do for thee, before I be **t away** from thee. 3947
2:10 nevertheless, if thou see me *when I am* **t** 3947
2:16 the spirit of the LORD hath **t** him **up**, 5375
4:20 when he had **t** him, and brought him to 5375
6:22 whom thou hast **t captive** with thy sword 7617
12: 3 the high places were not **t away**: the 5493
13:25 he had **t** out of the hand of Jehoahaz 3947
14: 4 Howbeit the high places were not **t away**: 5493
18:10 of Hoshea king of Israel, Samaria was **t**. 3920
18:22 and whose altars Hezekiah hath **t away**, 5493
24: 7 the king of Egypt had **t** from the river 3947
1Ch 24: 6 principal household being **t** for Eleazar, 270
24: 6 taken for Eleazar, and *one* **t** for Ithamar. 270
2Ch 15: 8 of the cities which he had **t** from mount 3920
15:17 the high places were not **t away** out of 5493
17: 2 of Ephraim, which Asa his father had **t**. 3920
19: 3 in that thou hast **t away** the groves out of 1197
20:33 Howbeit the high places were not **t away**, 5493
28:11 which ye have **t captive** of your brethren: 7617
28:18 had **t** Beth-shemesh, and Ajalon, 3920
30: 2 the king had **t counsel**, and his princes, 3289
32:11 Hath not the same Hezekiah **t away** his 5493
Ezr 9: 2 For they have **t** of their daughters for 5375
10: 2 have **t** strange wives of the people of 3427
10:10 and have **t** strange wives, 3427
10:14 let all *them* which have **t** strange wives in 3427
10:17 made an end with all the men that had **t** 3427
10:18 there were found that had **t** strange wives: 3427
10:44 All these had **t** strange wives: and *some* of 5375
Ne 5:15 had **t** of them bread and wine, beside forty 3947
6:18 his son Johanan had **t** the daughter of 3947
Est 2:15 who had **t** *her* for his daughter, was come 3947
2:16 So Esther was **t** unto king Ahasuerus into 3947
8: 2 which he had **t** from Haman, and gave it 5674
Job 1:21 the LORD hath **t** *away*; blessed be 3947
16:12 he hath also **t** *me* by my neck, 270
19: 9 my glory, and the crown *from* my head. 5493
20:19 he hath **violently t away** a house which 1497
22: 6 For thou hast **t a pledge** from thy brother 2254
24:24 they are **t** out of the way as all *other*, and 7092
27: 2 liveth, *who* hath **t away** my judgment; 5493
28: 2 Iron is **t** out of the earth, and brass *is* 3947
30:16 days of affliction have **t hold** upon me. 270
34: 5 and God hath **t away** my judgment. 5493
34:20 the mighty shall be **t away** without hand. 5493
Ps 9:15 the net which they hid is their own foot **t**. 3920
10: 2 let them be **t** in the devices that they have 8610
40:12 mine iniquities have **t hold upon** me, 5381
59:12 words of their lips let them even be **t** in 3920
83: 3 They have **t crafty** counsel against thy 6191
85: 3 Thou hast **t away** all thy wrath: thou hast 622
119:53 Horror hath **t hold upon** me because of 270
119:111 Thy testimonies have I **t as an heritage** 5157
119:143 Trouble and anguish have **t hold** on me: 4672
Pr 3:26 and shall keep thy foot from being **t**. 3921
4:16 their sleep is **t away**, unless they cause 1497
6: 2 thou art **t** with the words of thy mouth, 3920
7:20 He hath **t** a bag of money with him, 3947
11: 6 transgressors shall be **t** in their own 3920
Ecc 2:18 I hated all my labour which I *had* **t** under 6001
3:14 can be put to it, nor any thing **t** from it: 1639
7:26 from her; but the sinner shall be **t** by her. 3920
9:12 as the fishes that are **t** in an evil net, 270
Isa 6: 6 *which* he had **t** with the tongs from off 3947
6: 7 iniquity is **t away**, and thy sin purged. 5493
7: 5 have **t evil counsel** against thee, saying, 3289
8: 4 the spoil of Samaria shall be **t away** before 5375
8:15 and be broken, and be snared, and be **t**. 3920
10:27 his burden shall be **t away** from off thy 5493
10:29 they have **t up** their **lodging** at Geba; 4411
16:10 gladness is **t away**, and joy out of 622
17: 1 Damascus is **t away** *from being* a city, 5493
21: 3 pangs have **t hold upon** me, as the pangs 270
23: 8 Who hath **t** this **counsel** against Tyre, 3289
24:18 the midst of the pit shall be **t** in the snare: 3920
28:13 and be broken, and snared, and **t**. 3920
33:20 a tabernacle *that* shall not be **t down**; 6813
36: 7 and whose altars Hezekiah hath **t away**, 5493
41: 9 *Thou* whom I have **t** from the ends of 2388
49:24 Shall the prey be **t** from the mighty, 3947
49:25 captives of the mighty shall be **t away**, 3947

Isa 51:22 I have **t** out of thine hand the cup of 3947
52: 5 that my people is **t away** for nought? 3947
53: 8 He was **t** from prison and from judgment: 3947
57: 1 merciful men *are* **t away**, none 622
57: 1 considering that the righteous is **t away** 622
64: 6 like the wind, have **t** us **away**. 5375
Jer 6:11 even the husband with the wife shall be **t**, 3920
6:24 anguish hath **t hold** of us, *and* pain, as of 2388
8: 9 are ashamed, they are dismayed and **t**: 3920
8:21 black; astonishment hath **t hold on** me. 2388
12: 2 hast planted them, yea, they have **t root**: 8327
16: 5 I have **t away** my peace from this people, 622
29:22 of them shall be **t up** a curse by all 3947
34: 3 shalt **surely** be **t**, and delivered 8610+8610
38:23 shalt be **t** by the hand of the king of 8610
38:28 prison until the day that Jerusalem was **t**: 3920
38:28 and he was *there* when Jerusalem was **t**. 3920
39: 5 when they had **t** him, they brought him 3947
40: 1 when he had **t** him being bound in chains 8610
40:10 and dwell in your cities that ye have **t**. 3947
48: 1 Kiriathaim is confounded *and* **t**: Misgab 3920
48: 7 and in thy treasures, thou shalt also be **t**: 3920
48:33 and gladness is **t** from the plentiful field, 622
48:41 Kerioth is **t**, and the strong holds are 3920
48:44 that getteth up out of the pit shall be **t** in 3920
48:46 for thy sons are **t** captives, 3947
49:20 of the LORD, that he hath **t** against Edom, 3289
49:24 sorrows have **t** her as a woman in travail. 270
49:30 Babylon hath **t counsel** against you 3289+6098
50: 2 say, Babylon is **t**, Bel is confounded, 3920
50: 9 against her; from thence she shall be **t**: 3920
50:24 thou art also **t**, O Babylon, and thou wast 3920
50:45 the LORD, that he hath **t** against Babylon; 3289
51:31 of Babylon that his city is **t** at *one* end, 3920
51:41 How is Sheshach **t**! and *how* is the praise 3920
51:56 upon Babylon, and her mighty men are **t**, 3920
La 2: 6 he hath **violently t away** his tabernacle, 2554
4:20 was **t** in their pits, *of* whom we said, 3920
Eze 12:13 upon him, and he shall be **t** in my snare: 8610
15: 3 Shall wood be **t** thereof to do *any* work? 3947
16:17 Thou hast also **t** thy fair jewels of my gold 3947
16:20 Moreover thou hast **t** thy sons and thy 3947
16:37 with whom thou hast **t pleasure**, and all 6149
17:12 hath **t** the king thereof, and the princes 3947
17:13 hath **t** of the king's seed, and made a 3947
17:13 with him, and hath **t** an oath of him: 935
17:13 he hath also **t** the mighty of the land: 3947
17:20 he shall be **t** in my snare, and I will bring 8610
18: 8 upon usury, neither hath **t** any increase, 3947
18:13 forth upon usury, and hath **t** increase: 3947
18:17 *That* hath **t off** his hand from the poor, 7725
19: 4 he was **t** in their pit, and they brought 8610
19: 8 their net upon him: he was **t** in their pit. 8610
21:23 the iniquity, that, *they* may be **t**. 8610
21:24 ye shall be **t** with the hand. 8610
22:12 In thee have they **t** gifts to shed blood; 3947
22:12 thou hast **t** usury and increase, 3947
22:25 they have **t** the treasure and 3947
25:15 **t vengeance** with a despiteful 5358+5359
27: 5 they have **t** cedars from Lebanon to make 3947
33: 5 among them, he is **t away** in his iniquity; 3947
36: 3 ye are **t up** in the lips of talkers, and *are* 5927
Da 5: 2 **t** out of the temple which *was* in 5312
5: 3 **t** out of the temple of the house of God 5312
6:23 So Daniel was **t up** out of the den, 5267
7:12 beasts, they had their dominion **t away**: 5709
8:11 by him the daily *sacrifice* was **t away**, 7311
11:12 *And* when he hath **t away** the multitude, 5375
12:11 *that* the daily *sacrifice* shall be **t away**, 5493
Hos 4: 3 the fishes of the sea also shall be **t away**. 622
Joel 3: 5 Because ye have **t** my silver and my gold, 3947
Am 3: 4 cry out of his den, if he have **t** nothing? 3947
3: 5 the earth, and have **t** nothing **at all**? 3920+3920
3:12 shall the children of Israel be **t** out 5337
4:10 the sword, and have **t away** your horses; 7628
6:13 Have we not **t** to us horns by our own 3947
Mic 2: 9 from their children have ye **t** *away* my 3947
4: 9 pangs have **t** thee as a woman in travail. 2388
Zep 3:15 The LORD hath **t away** thy judgments, 5493
Zec 14: 2 the city shall be **t**, and the houses rifled, 3920
Mt 4:24 people that were **t** with divers diseases 4912
9:15 when the bridegroom shall be **t from** 522
13:12 him shall be **t away** even that he hath. 142
16: 7 saying, *It is* because we have **t** no bread. 2983
21:43 The kingdom of God shall be **t** from you, 142
24:40 the one shall be **t**, and the other left. 3880
24:41 *the* one shall be **t**, and *the* other left. 3880
25:29 him that hath not shall be **t away** even 142
27:59 And when Joseph had **t** the body, 2983
28:12 and had **t** counsel, they gave large money 2983
Mk 2:20 when the bridegroom shall be **t away** from 522
4:25 him shall be **t** even *that* which he hath. 142
6:41 And when he had **t** the five loaves and 2983
9:36 when he had **t** him in his **arms**, he said 1723
Lk 1: 1 Forasmuch as many have **t** in **hand** to 2021
4:38 And Simon's wife's mother was **t with a** 4912
5: 5 toiled all the night, and have **t** nothing: 2983
5: 9 the draught of the fishes which they had **t**: 4815
5:18 in a bed a man which was **t with a palsy**: 3886
5:35 the bridegroom shall be **t away** from 522
5:36 piece that was **t** out of the new agreeth NIG
8:18 from him shall be **t** even *that* which he 142
8:37 from them; for they were **t** with great fear: 4912
9:17 there was **t up** of fragments that remained 142
10:42 which shall not be **t away** from her. 851

Lk 11:52 for ye have **t away** the key of knowledge: 142
17:34 the one shall be **t**, and the other shall be 3880
17:35 the one shall be **t**, and the other left. 3880
17:36 the one shall be **t**, and the other left. 3880
19: 8 If any *thing* from any *man*
 by false accusation, 4811
19:26 that he hath shall be **t away** from him. 142
Jn 7:44 And some of them would have **t** him; 4084
8: 3 Pharisees brought unto him a woman **t** in 2638
8: 4 Master, this woman was **t** in adultery, 2638
13:12 and had **t** his garments, and was set down 2983
19:31 be broken, and *that* they might be **t away**. 142
20: 1 seeth the stone **t away** from the sepulchre. 142
20: 2 They have **t away** the Lord out of 142
20:13 Because they have **t away** my Lord, 142
Ac 1: 2 Until the day *in* which he was **t up**, after 353
1: 9 *things*, while they beheld, he was **t up**; 1869
1:11 is **t up** from you into heaven, shall so 353
1:22 *that same* day that he was **t up** from us, 353
2:23 ye have **t**, and by wicked hands have 2983
8: 7 *with them*: and many **t with palsies**, 3886
8:33 his humiliation his judgment was **t away**: 142
8:33 for his life is **t** from the earth. 142
17: 9 And when they had **t** security of Jason, 2983
20: 9 from the third loft, and was **t up** dead. 142
21: 6 And when we had **t** our **leave** one of 782
23:27 This man was **t** of the Jews, 4815
27:17 when they had **t up**, they used helps, 142
27:20 we should be saved was then **t away**. 4014
27:33 and continued fasting, having **t** nothing. 4355
27:40 And when they had **t up** the anchors, 4014
27:40 the word of God hath **t none effect**. 1601
Ro 9: 6 the word of God hath **t none effect**. 1601
1Co 5: 2 deed might be **t away** from among you. 1808
10:13 There hath no temptation **t** you but such 2983
2Co 3:16 turn to the Lord, the vail shall be **t away**. 4014
1Th 2:17 being **t** from you for a short time in 642
2Th 2: 7 *will let*, until he be **t** out of the way. 1096
1Ti 5: 9 Let not a widow be **t into the number** 2639
2Ti 2:26 who are **t captive** by him at his will. 2221
Heb 5: 1 For every high priest **t** from among men 2983
2Pe 2:12 brute beasts, made to be **t** and destroyed, 259
Rev 5: 8 And when he had **t** the book, the four 2983
11:17 thou hast **t** to **thee** thy great power, 2983
19:20 the beast was **t**, and with him the false 4084

TAKER (1) [TAKE]
Isa 24: 2 as *with* the **t** of usury, so *with* the giver 5378

TAKEST (9) [TAKE]
Ex 4: 9 the water which thou **t** out of the river 3947
30:12 When thou **t** the sum of the children of 5375
Jdg 4: 9 notwithstanding the journey that thou **t** 1980
1Ch 22:13 if thou **t heed** to fulfil the statutes and 8104
Ps 104:29 thou **t away** their breath, they die, 622
144: 3 *is* man, that thou **t knowledge** of him? 3045
Ecc 5: 9 in thy labour which thou **t** under the sun. 6001
Isa 58: 3 our soul, and thou **t** no **knowledge**? 3045
Lk 19:21 thou **t up** that thou layedst not down, 142

TAKETH (74) [TAKE]
Ex 20: 7 hold him guiltless that **t** his name in vain. 5375
Dt 5:11 hold *him* guiltless that **t** his name in vain. 5375
10:17 regardeth not persons, nor **t** reward: 3947
24: 6 to pledge: for he **t** a *man's* life **to pledge**. 2254
25:11 forth her hand, and **t** him by the secrets: 2388
27:25 Cursed *be* he that **t** reward to slay an 3947
32:11 **t** them, beareth them on her wings: 3947
Jos 7:14 that the tribe which the LORD **t** shall 3920
15:16 He that smiteth Kirjath-sepher, and **t** it, 3920
Jdg 1:12 He that smiteth Kirjath-sepher, and **t** it, 3920
1Sa 17:26 and **t away** the reproach from Israel? 5493
1Ki 14:10 as *a man* **t away** dung, till it be all gone. 1197
Job 5: 5 **t** it *even* out of the thorns, and the robber 3947
5:13 He **t** the wise in their own craftiness: 3920
9:12 Behold, he **t away**, who can hinder him? 2862
12:20 and **t** *away* the understanding of the aged. 3947
12:24 He **t away** the heart of the chief of 5493
21: 6 afraid, and trembling **t hold on** my flesh. 270
27: 8 hath gained, when God **t away** his soul? 7953
40:24 He **t** it with his eyes: *his* nose pierceth 3947
Ps 15: 3 nor **t up** a reproach against his neighbour. 5375
15: 5 usury, nor **t** reward against the innocent. 3947
118: 7 The LORD **t** my **part** with them that 3807.1
137: 9 Happy *shall* he be that **t** and dasheth thy 270
147:10 he **t** not **pleasure** in the legs of a man. 7521
147:11 The LORD **t pleasure** in them that fear 7521
149: 4 For the LORD **t pleasure** in his people: 7521
Pr 1:19 *which* **t away** the life of the owners 3947
16:32 that ruleth his spirit than he that **t** a city. 3920
17:23 A wicked *man* **t** a gift out of the bosom 3947
25:20 *As* he that **t away** a garment in cold 5710
26:17 to him, *is like* one that **t** a dog by the ears. 2388
30:28 The spider **t hold** with her hands, and *is* 8610
Ecc 1: 3 of all his labour which he **t** under the sun? 5998
2:23 yea, his heart **t** not **rest** in the night. 7901
5:18 enjoy the good of all his labour that he **t** 5998
Isa 13:14 and as a sheep that no *man* **t up**: 6908
40:15 he **t up** the isles as a very little thing. 5190
44:14 cedars, and the cypress and the oak, 3947
51:18 neither *is there any* that **t** her by the hand 2388
56: 6 polluting it, and **t hold** of my covenant; 2388
Eze 16:32 *which* **t** strangers instead of her husband. 3947
33: 4 sound of the trumpet, and **t** not **warning**; 2094
33: 5 he that **t warning** shall deliver his soul. 2094
Am 3:12 As the shepherd **t** out of the mouth of 5337

Mt 4: 5 Then the devil **t** him *up* into the holy city, 3880
 4: 8 the devil **t** him *up* into an exceeding high 3880
 9:16 for that which is put in to fill it up **t** from 142
 10:38 And he that **t** not his cross, 2983
 12:45 with himself seven other spirits more 3880
 17: 1 And after six days Jesus **t** Peter, James, 3880
Mk 2:21 else the new piece that filled it up **t** away 142
 4:15 **t** away the word that was sown in their 142
 5:40 he **t** the father and the mother of 3880
 9: 2 And after six days Jesus **t** with *him* Peter, 3880
 9:18 wheresoever he **t** him, he teareth him: 2638
 14:33 And he **t** with him Peter and James and 3880
Lk 6:29 that **t** away thy cloke forbid not *to take* 142
 6:30 him that **t** away thy *goods* ask *them* not 142
 8:12 and **t** away the word out of their hearts, 142
 9:39 a spirit **t** him, and he suddenly crieth out; 2983
 11:22 he **t** *from him* all his armour wherein he 142
 11:26 **t** *to him* seven other spirits more wicked 3880
 16: 3 my lord **t** away from me the stewardship. 851
Jn 1:29 of God, which **t** away the sin of the world. 142
 10:18 No *man* **t** it from me, but I lay it down of 142
 15: 2 in me that beareth not fruit he **t** away: 142
 16:22 and your joy no *man* **t** from you. 142
 21:13 and **t** bread, and giveth them, 2983
Ro 3: 5 *Is* God unrighteous who **t** vengeance? 2018
1Co 3:19 He is the wise in their own craftiness. 1405
 11:21 For in eating every one **t** *before other* his 4301
Heb 5: 4 And no man **t** this honour unto himself, 2983
 10: 9 He **t** away the first, that he may establish 337

TAKING (20) [TAKE]

2Ch 19: 7 nor respect of persons, nor **t** of gifts. 4727
Job 5: 3 I have seen the foolish **t** root: 8327
Ps 119: 9 by **t** heed *thereto* according to thy word. 8104
Jer 50:46 At the noise of the **t** of Babylon the earth 8610
Eze 25:12 house of Judah by **t** vengeance, 5358+5359
Hos 11: 3 Ephraim also to go, **t** them by their arms; 3947
Mt 6:27 Which of you by **t** thought can add one 3309
Mk 13:34 *Son of man is* as a man **t** a far journey, 590
Lk 4: 5 the devil, **t** him up into a high mountain, 321
 12:25 And which of you with **t** thought can add 3309
 19:22 **t** up that I laid not down, and reaping that 142
Jn 11:13 thought that he had spoken of **t** of rest 2838
Ro 7: 8 But sin, **t** occasion by the commandment, 2983
 7:11 For sin, **t** occasion by the commandment, 2983
2Co 2:13 but **t** my *leave of* them, I went from 657
 11: 8 **t** wages *of them*, to do you service. 2983
Eph 6:16 Above all, **t** the shield of faith, wherewith 353
2Th 1: 8 **t** vengeance on them that know not God, 1325
1Pe 5: 2 the **t** the oversight *thereof*, not by constraint, 1983
3Jn 1: 7 they went forth, **t** nothing of the Gentiles. 2983

TALE (5) [TALEBEARER, TALES]

Ex 5: 8 the **t** of the bricks, which they did make 4971
 5:18 yet shall ye deliver the **t** of bricks. 8506
1Sa 18:27 and they **gave** in full **t** to the king, 4390
1Ch 9:28 they should bring them in and out by **t**. 4557
Ps 90: 9 we spend our years as a **t** *that is told*. 1899

TALEBEARER (6) [BEAR, TALE]

Lev 19:16 go up and down *as a* **t** among thy people: 7400
Pr 11:13 A **t** revealeth secrets: but he that is 1980+7400
 18: 8 The words of a **t** *are* as wounds, 5372
 20:19 that goeth about *as* a **t** revealeth secrets: 7400
 26:20 so where *there is* no **t**, the strife ceaseth. 5372
 26:22 The words of a **t** *are* as wounds, 5372

TALENT (14) [TALENTS]

Ex 25:39 *Of* a **t** of pure gold shall he make it, with 3603
 37:24 *Of* a **t** of pure gold made it, and all 3603
 38:27 of the hundred talents, a **t** for a socket. 3603
2Sa 12:30 the weight whereof *was* a **t** of gold with 3603
1Ki 20:39 his life, or else thou shalt pay a **t** of silver. 3603
2Ki 5:22 a **t** of silver, and two changes of garments. 3603
 23:33 hundred talents of silver, and a **t** of gold. 3603
1Ch 20: 2 found it to weigh a **t** of gold, 3603
2Ch 36: 3 hundred talents of silver and a **t** of gold. 3603
Zec 5: 7 behold, there was lift up a **t** of lead: 3603
Mt 25:24 he which had received the one **t** came 5007
 25:25 and went and hid thy **t** in the earth: 5007
 25:28 Take therefore the **t** from him, and give *it* 5007
Rev 16:21 *every stone* about the **weight of a t**: 5006

TALENTS (51) [TALENT]

Ex 38:24 twenty and nine **t**, and seven hundred 3603
 38:25 of the congregation *was* an hundred **t**, 3603
 38:27 of the hundred **t** of silver were cast 3603
 38:27 an hundred sockets of the hundred **t**, 3603
 38:29 the brass of the offering *was* seventy **t**, 3603
1Ki 9:14 Hiram sent to the king sixscore **t** of gold. 3603
 9:28 four hundred and twenty **t**, and brought 3603
 10:10 the king an hundred and twenty **t** of gold, 3603
 10:14 six hundred threescore and six **t** of gold, 3603
 16:24 hill Samaria of Shemer for **two t** of silver, 3603
2Ki 5: 5 took with him ten **t** of silver, 3603
 5:23 Naaman said, Be content, take **two t**. 3603
 5:23 and bound **two t** of silver in two bags, 3603
 15:19 Menahem gave Pul a thousand **t** of silver 3603
 18:14 king of Judah three hundred **t** of silver 3603
 18:14 talents of silver and thirty **t** of gold. 3603
 23:33 put the land to a tribute of an hundred **t** 3603
1Ch 19: 6 the children of Ammon sent a thousand **t** 3603
 22:14 the Lord an hundred thousand **t** *of* gold, 3603
 22:14 and a thousand thousand **t** *of* silver; 3603
 29: 4 *Even* three thousand **t** of the gold, of the gold 3603

1Ch 29: 4 and seven thousand **t** of refined silver, 3603
 29: 7 the house of God *of* gold five thousand **t** 3603
 29: 7 *of* silver ten thousand **t**, and *of* brass 3603
 29: 7 *of* brass eighteen thousand **t**, 3603
 29: 7 and one hundred thousand **t** *of* iron. 3603
2Ch 3: 8 fine gold, *amounting* to six hundred **t**. 3603
 8:18 thence four hundred and fifty **t** of gold, 3603
 9: 9 the king an hundred and twenty **t** of gold, 3603
 9:13 and threescore and six **t** of gold; 3603
 25: 6 out of Israel for an hundred **t** of silver. 3603
 25: 9 what *shall* we do for the hundred **t** which 3603
 27: 5 him the same year an hundred **t** of silver, 3603
 36: 3 condemned the land in an hundred **t** of 3603
Ezr 7:22 Unto an hundred **t** *of* silver, and to an 3604
 8:26 their hand six hundred and fifty **t** *of* silver, 3603
 8:26 silver vessels an hundred **t** *and of* gold an 3603
 8:26 talents, *and of* gold an hundred **t**; 3603
Est 3: 9 I will pay ten thousand **t** of silver to 3603
Mt 18:24 him, which ought him ten thousand **t**. 5007
 25:15 And unto one he gave five **t**, to another 5007
 25:16 Then he that had received the five **t** went 5007
 25:16 the same, and made *them* other five **t**. 5007
 25:20 *And so* he that had received five **t** came 5007
 25:20 five talents came and brought other five **t**, 5007
 25:20 Lord, thou deliveredst unto me five **t**: 5007
 25:20 I have gained besides them five **t** moe. 5007
 25:22 He also that had received two **t** came and 5007
 25:22 Lord, thou deliveredst unto me two **t**: 5007
 25:22 I have gained two other **t** besides them. 5007
 25:28 and give *it* unto him which hath ten **t**. 5007

TALES (2) [TALE]

Eze 22: 9 are men that **carry t** to shed blood: 7400
Lk 24:11 And their words seemed to them as **idle t**, 3026

TALITHA (1)

Mk 5:41 by the hand, and said unto her, **T** CUMI; 5008

TALK (24) [TALKED, TALKERS, TALKEST, TALKETH, TALKING]

Nu 11:17 I will come down and **t** with thee there: 1696
Dt 5:24 have seen this day that God doth **t** with 1696
 6: 7 shalt **t** of them when thou sittest in thine 1696
1Sa 2: 3 **T** no more *so* exceeding proudly; let *not* 1696
2Ki 18:26 **t** not with us in the Jews' language in 1696
1Ch 16: 9 him, **t** you of all his wondrous works. 7878
Job 11: 2 and should a man **full of t** be justified? 8193
 13: 7 for God? or **t** deceitfully for him? 1696
 15: 3 Should he reason *with* unprofitable **t**? 1697
Ps 69:26 they **t** to the grief of those whom thou 5608
 71:24 My tongue also shall **t** of thy righteousness 1897
 77:12 also of all thy work, and **t** of thy doings. 7878
 105: 2 unto him: **t** ye of all his wondrous works. 7878
 119:27 so shall I **t** of thy wondrous works. 7878
 145:11 glory of thy kingdom, and **t** of thy power; 1696
Pr 6:22 *when* thou awakest, it shall **t** *with* thee. 7878
 14:23 the **t** of the lips *tendeth* only to penury. 1697
 24: 2 and their lips **t** of mischief. 1696
Ecc 10:13 the **t** of his mouth *is* mischievous madness. 6310
Jer 12: 1 yet let me **t** with thee of *thy* judgments. 1696
Eze 3:22 into the plain, and I will there **t** with thee. 1696
Da 10:17 For how can the servant of this my lord **t** 1696
Mt 22:15 how they might entangle him in *his* **t**. 3056
Jn 14:30 Hereafter I will not **t** much with you: 2980

TALKED (42) [TALK]

Ge 4: 8 Cain **t** with Abel his brother: and it came 559
 17: 3 on his face: and God **t** with him, saying, 1696
 35:13 him in the place where he **t** with him. 1696
 35:14 set up a pillar in the place where he **t** 1696
 45:15 and after that his brethren **t** with him. 1696
Ex 20:22 Ye have seen that I have **t** with you from 1696
 33: 9 and the Lord **t** with Moses. 1696
 34:29 of his face shone while he **t** with him. 1696
 34:31 unto him: and Moses **t** with them. 1696
Dt 5: 4 The Lord **t** with you face to face in 1696
Jdg 14: 7 he went down, and **t** with the woman; 1696
1Sa 14:19 came to pass, while Saul **t** unto the priest, 1696
 17:23 as he **t** with them, behold, there came up 1696
1Ki 1:22 lo, while she yet **t** with the king, Nathan 1696
2Ki 2:11 *as* they still went on, and **t**, that behold, 1696
 6:33 while he yet **t** with them, behold, 1696
 8: 4 the king **t** with Gehazi the servant of 1696
2Ch 25:16 it came to pass, as he **t** with him, that 1696
Jer 38:25 if the princes hear that I have **t** with thee, 1696
Da 9:22 he informed *me*, and **t** with me, and said, 1696
Zec 1: 9 the angel that **t** with me said unto me, 1696
 1:13 the Lord answered the angel that **t** with 1696
 1:19 I said unto the angel that **t** with me, 1696
 2: 3 the angel that **t** with me went forth, 1696
 4: 1 the angel that **t** with me came again, 1696
 4: 4 and spake to the angel that **t** with me, 1696
 4: 5 the angel that **t** with me answered and 1696
 4: 5 the angel that **t** with me went forth, 1696
 5:10 I said to the angel that **t** with me, 1696
 6: 4 and said unto the angel that **t** with me, 1696
Mt 12:46 While he yet **t** to the people, behold, 2980
Mk 6:50 And immediately he **t** with them, 2980
Lk 9:30 And behold, there **t** with him two men, 4814
 24:14 And they **t** together of all these *things* 3656
 24:32 while he **t** with us by the way, and while 2980
Jn 4:27 and marvelled that he **t** with *the* woman: 2980
Ac 10:27 And as he **t** with him, he went in, 4926
 20:11 bread, and eaten, and **t** a long while, 3656
 26:31 they **t** between themselves, saying, 2980

Rev 17: 1 and **t** with me, saying unto me, 2980
 21: 9 and **t** with me, saying, *Come* hither, I will 2980
 21:15 he that **t** with me had a golden reed to 2980

TALKERS (2) [TALK]

Eze 36: 3 ye are taken up in the lips of **t**, and *are* an 3956
Tit 1:10 are many unruly and **vain t** and deceivers, 3151

TALKEST (3) [TALK]

Jdg 6:17 then shew me a sign that thou **t** with me. 1696
1Ki 1:14 while thou yet **t** there with the king, 1696
Jn 4:27 seekest thou? or, Why **t** thou with her? 2980

TALKETH (2) [TALK]

Ps 37:30 and his tongue **t** of judgment. 1696
Jn 9:37 seen him, and it is he that **t** with thee. 2980

TALKING (9) [TALK]

Ge 17:22 he left off **t** with him, and God went up 1696
1Ki 18:27 either he is **t**, or he is pursuing, or he is in 7879
Est 6:14 while they *were* yet **t** with him, came 1696
Job 29: 9 princes refrained **t**, and laid *their* hand 4405
Eze 33:30 children of thy people still are **t** against 1696
Mt 17: 3 unto them Moses and Elias **t** with him. 4814
Mk 9: 4 with Moses: and they were **t** with Jesus. 4814
Eph 5: 4 filthiness, nor **foolish t**, nor jesting, 3473
Rev 4: 1 *was* as *it were* of a trumpet **t** with me; 2980

TALL (5) [TALLER]

Dt 2:10 a people great, and many, and **t**, 7311
 2:21 A people great, and many, and **t**, 7311
 9: 2 a people great and **t**, the children of 7311
2Ki 19:23 will cut down the **t** cedar trees thereof, 6967
Isa 37:24 I will cut down the **t** cedars thereof, 6967

TALLER (1)

Dt 1:28 The people *is* greater and **t** than we; 7311

TALMAI (6)

Nu 13:22 where Ahiman, Sheshai, and **T**, 8526
Jos 15:14 Sheshai, and Ahiman, and **T**, the children 8526
Jdg 1:10 they slew Sheshai, and Ahiman, and **T**. 8526
2Sa 3: 3 Maachah the daughter of **T** king of Geshur; 8526
 13:37 Absalom fled, and went to **T**, the son of 8526
1Ch 3: 2 Maachah the daughter of **T** king of 8526

TALMON (5)

1Ch 9:17 and **T**, and Ahiman, and their brethren: 2929
Ezr 2:42 the children of Ater, the children of **T**, 2929
Ne 7:45 the children of Ater, the children of **T**, 2929
 11:19 **T**, and their brethren that kept the gates, 2929
 12:25 Obadiah, Meshullam, **T**, Akkub, 2929

TAMAH (1)

Ne 7:55 the children of Sisera, the children of **T**, 8547

TAMAR (24) [BAAL-TAMAR, HAZAZON-TAMAR, HAZEZON-TAMAR]

Ge 38: 6 for Er his firstborn, whose name *was* **T**. 8559
 38:11 said Judah to **T** his daughter in law, 8559
 38:11 his brethren *did*. And **T** went and 8559
 38:13 it was told **T**, saying, Behold thy father in 8559
 38:24 **T** thy daughter in law hath played 8559
Ru 4:12 of Pharez, whom **T** bare unto Judah, 8559
2Sa 13: 1 had a fair sister, whose name *was* **T**; 8559
 13: 2 *so* vexed, that he fell sick for his sister **T**; 8559
 13: 4 said unto him, I love **T**, my brother 8559
 13: 5 let my sister **T** come, and give me meat, 8559
 13: 6 let **T** my sister come, and make me *a* 8559
 13: 7 David sent home to **T**, saying, Go now *to* 8559
 13: 8 So **T** went *to* her brother Amnon's house; 8559
 13:10 Amnon said unto **T**, Bring the meat *into* 8559
 13:10 **T** took the cakes which she had made, 8559
 13:19 **T** put ashes on her head, and rent her 8559
 13:20 So **T** remained desolate *in* her brother 8559
 13:22 because he had forced his sister **T**. 8559
 13:32 from the day that he forced his sister **T**. 8559
 14:27 and one daughter, whose name *was* **T**: 8559
1Ch 2: 4 **T** his daughter in law bare him Pharez 8559
 3: 9 sons of the concubines, and **T** their sister. 8559
Eze 47:19 from **T** *even* to the waters of strife *in* 8559
 48:28 the border shall be even from **T** *unto* 8559

TAMBOURINE; TAMBOURINES See TABRET; TABRETS; TIMBREL

TAME (2) [TAMED]

Mk 5: 4 in pieces: neither could any *man* **t** him. 1150
Jas 3: 8 the tongue can no man **t**; *it is* an unruly 1150

TAMED (2) [TAME]

Jas 3: 7 is **t**, and hath been tamed of mankind: 1150
 3: 7 is tamed, and hath been **t** of mankind: 1150

TAMMUZ (1)

Eze 8:14 behold, there sat women weeping for **T**. 8542

TANACH (1)

Jos 21:25 **T** with her suburbs, and Gath-rimmon 8590

TANHUMETH (2)

2Ki 25:23 Seraiah the son of **T** the Netophathite, 8576
Jer 40: 8 Seraiah the son of **T**, and the sons of 8576

TANNER (3)

Ac 9:43 many days in Joppa with one Simon a **t**. 1038
 10: 6 He lodgeth with one Simon a **t**, 1038

T

Ac 10:32 he is lodged in the house of *one* Simon a t *1038*

TAPESTRY (2)
Pr 7:16 I have deckt my bed *with* **coverings of** t, 4765
 31:22 She maketh herself **coverings of** t; 4765

TAPHATH (1)
1Ki 4:11 which had **T** the daughter of Solomon to 2955

TAPPUAH (6) [BETH-TAPPUAH]
Jos 12:17 the king of **T**, one; the king of Hepher, 8599
 15:34 Zanoah, and En-gannim, **T**, and Enam, 8599
 16: 8 The border went *out* from **T** westward 8599
 17: 8 *Now* Manasseh had the land of **T**: 8599
 17: 8 **T** on the border of Manasseh *belonged* to 8599
1Ch 2:43 Korah, and **T**, and Rekem, and Shema. 8599

TAR PITS See SLIMEPITS

TARAH (2)
Nu 33:27 departed from Tahath, and pitched at **T**. 8646
 33:28 they removed from **T**, and pitched in 8646

TARALAH (1)
Jos 18:27 And Rekem, and Irpeel, and **T**, 8634

TARE (4) [TEAR]
2Sa 13:31 and **t** his garments, and lay on the earth; 7167
2Ki 2:24 and forty and two children of them. 1234
Mk 9:20 he saw him, straightway the spirit **t** him; *4682*
Lk 9:42 the devil threw him down, **t** *him*. *4952*

TAREA (1)
1Ch 8:35 and Melech, and **T**, and Ahaz. 8390

TARES (8)
Mt 13:25 came and sowed **t** among the wheat, 2215
 13:26 forth fruit, then appeared the **t** also. 2215
 13:27 in thy field? from whence then hath it **t**? 2215
 13:29 while ye gather up the **t**, ye root up also 2215
 13:30 Gather ye together first the **t**, and bind 2215
 13:36 Declare unto us the parable of the **t** 2215
 13:38 the **t** are the children of the wicked one; 2215
 13:40 therefore the **t** are gathered and burnt in 2215

TARGET (3) [TARGETS]
1Sa 17: 6 and a **t** of brass between his shoulders. 3591
1Ki 10:16 hundred *shekels* of gold went to one **t**. 6793
2Ch 9:15 *shekels* of beaten gold went to one **t**. 6793

TARGETS (3) [TARGET]
1Ki 10:16 king Solomon made two hundred **t** *of* 6793
2Ch 9:15 king Solomon made two hundred **t** *of* 6793
 14: 8 Asa had an army *of men* that bare **t** and 6793

TARPELITES (1)
Ezr 4: 9 the **T**, the Apharsites, the Archevites, 2967

TARRIED (32) [TARRY]
Ge 24:54 men that *were* with him, and **t all night**; 3885
 28:11 **t** there **all night**, because the sun was set; 3885
 31:54 eat bread, and **t all night** in the mount. 3885
Nu 9:19 the cloud **t long** upon the tabernacle 748
 9:22 year, that the cloud **t** upon the tabernacle, 748
Jdg 3:25 they **t** till *they* were ashamed: and behold, 2342
 3:26 Ehud escaped while they **t**, and passed 4102
 19: 8 they **t** until afternoon, and they did eat 4102
Ru 2: 7 until now, that she **t** a little in the house. 3427
1Sa 13: 8 he **t** seven days, according to the set time 3176
 14: 2 Saul **t** in the uttermost part of Gibeah 3427
2Sa 11: 1 But David **t** *still* at Jerusalem. 3427
 15:17 after him, and **t** *in* a place that *was* far off. 5975
 15:29 again *to* Jerusalem: and they **t** there. 3427
 20: 5 he **t longer** than the set time which he 309
2Ki 2:18 came again to him, (for he **t** at Jericho,) 3427
1Ch 20: 1 David **t** at Jerusalem. And Joab smote 3427
Ps 68:12 she that **t** at home divided the spoil. 5116
Mt 25: 5 the bridegroom **t**, they all slumbered 5549
Lk 1:21 marvelled that he **t** *so* **long** in the temple. 5549
 2:43 the child Jesus **t behind** in Jerusalem; 5278
Jn 3:22 and there he **t** with them, and baptized. 1304
Ac 9:43 that he **t** many days in Joppa with one 3306
 15:33 And after they had **t** *there* **a space**, 4160+5550
 18:18 Paul *after this* **t** *there* yet a good while, 4357
 20: 5 These going before **t for** us at Troas. 3306
 20:15 we arrived at Samos, and **t** at Trogyllium; 3306
 21: 4 finding disciples, we **t** there seven days: 1961
 21:10 And as we **t** *there* many days, there came 1961
 25: 6 when he had **t** among them more than 1304
 27:33 day is the fourteenth day that ye have **t** 4328
 28:12 landing at Syracuse, we **t** *there* three days. 1961

TARRIEST (1) [TARRY]
Ac 22:16 And now why **t** thou? arise, *3195*

TARRIETH (2) [TARRY]
1Sa 30:24 so *shall* his part *be* that **t** by the stuff: 3427
Mic 5: 7 upon the grass, that **t** not for man, 6960

TARRY (51) [TARRIED, TARRIEST, TARRIETH, TARRYING]
Ge 19: 2 **t all night**, and wash your feet, and ye 3885
 27:44 **t** with him a few days, until thy brother's 3885
 30:27 **t**: *for* I have learned by experience that NIH
 45: 9 of all Egypt: come down unto me, **t** not: 5975
Ex 12:39 were thrust out of Egypt, and could not **t**, 4102

Ex 24:14 he said unto the elders, **T** ye here for us, 3427
Lev 14: 8 shall **t abroad** out of his tent seven days. 3427
Nu 22:19 I pray you, **t** ye also here *this* night, 3427
Jdg 5:28 coming? why *is* the wheels of his chariots? 309
 6:18 he said, I will **t** until thou come again. 3427
 19: 6 **t all night**, and let thine heart be merry. 3885
 19: 9 towards evening, I pray you **t all night**: 3885
 19:10 man would not **t** *that* **night**, but he rose 3885
Ru 1:13 ye **t** for them till they were grown? 7663
 3:13 **T** this night, and it shall be in the 3885
1Sa 1:23 thee good; **t** until thou have weaned him; 3885
 10: 8 seven days shalt thou **t**, till I come to thee 3176
 14: 9 say thus unto us, **T** until we come to you; 1826
2Sa 1: 9 **T** at Jericho until your beards be grown, 3427
 11:12 **T** here to day also, and to morrow I will 3427
 15:28 See, I will **t** in the plain of the wilderness, 4102
 18:14 said Joab, I may not **t** thus with thee. 3176
 19: 7 there will not **t** one with thee *this* night: 3885
2Ki 2: 2 Elijah said unto Elisha, **T** here, I pray thee 3427
 2: 4 said unto him, Elisha, **t** here, I pray thee; 3427
 2: 6 Elijah said unto him, **T**, I pray thee, here; 3427
 7: 9 we **t** till the morning light, *some* mischief 2442
 9: 3 Then open the door, and flee, and **t** not. 2442
 14:10 glory *of this*, and **t** at home: for why 3427
1Ch 19: 5 **T** at Jericho until your beards be grown, 3427
Ps 101: 7 he that telleth lies shall not **t** in my sight. 3559
Pr 23:30 They that **t long** at the wine; they that go 309
Isa 46:13 not be far off, and my salvation shall not **t**: 309
Jer 14: 8 man *that* turneth aside to **t for a night**? 3885
Hab 2: 3 though it **t**, wait for it; because it will 4102
 2: 3 because it will surely come, it will not **t**. 309
Mt 26:38 unto death: **t** ye here, and watch with me. *3306*
Mk 14:34 unto death: **t** ye here, and watch. *3306*
Lk 24:29 far spent. And he went in to **t** with them. *3306*
 24:49 but **t** ye in the city of Jerusalem, until ye *2523*
Jn 4:40 they besought him that *he* would **t** with *3306*
 21:22 If I will that he **t** till I come, what *is that* *3306*
 21:23 but, If I will that he **t** till I come, what *is* *3306*
Ac 10:48 Then prayed they him to **t** certain days. *1961*
 18:20 When they desired *him* to **t** longer time *3306*
 28:14 were desired to **t** with them seven days: *1961*
1Co 11:33 come together to eat, **t** one **for** another. *1551*
 16: 7 I trust to **t** a while with you, if the Lord *1961*
 16: 8 But I will **t** at Ephesus until Pentecost. *1961*
1Ti 3:15 But if I **t long**, that thou mayest know *1019*
Heb 10:37 that shall come will come, and will not **t**. *5549*

TARRYING (2) [TARRY]
Ps 40:17 and my deliverer; **make** no **t**, O my God. 309
 70: 5 and my deliverer; O LORD, **make** no **t**. 309

TARSHISH (24) [THARSHISH]
Ge 10: 4 Elishah, and **T**, Kittim, and Dodanim. 8659
1Ch 1: 7 Elishah, and **T**, Kittim, and Dodanim. 8659
2Ch 9:21 For the king's ships went *to* **T** with 8659
 9:21 three years once came the ships of **T** 8659
 20:36 with him to make ships to go *to* **T**: 8659
 20:37 that they were not able to go to **T**. 8659
Est 1:14 **T**, Meres, Marsena, and Memucan, 8659
Ps 48: 7 Thou breakest the ships of **T** with an east 8659
 72:10 The kings of **T** and of the isles shall bring 8659
Isa 2:16 upon all the ships of **T**, and upon all 8659
 23: 1 Howl, ye ships of **T**; for it is laid waste, 8659
 23: 6 Pass ye over to **T**; howl, ye inhabitants of 8659
 23:10 thy land as a river, O daughter of **T**: 8659
 23:14 Howl, ye ships of **T**: for your strength is 8659
 60: 9 the ships of **T** first, to bring thy sons from 8659
 66:19 *to* **T**, Pul, and Lud, that draw the bow, 8659
Jer 10: 9 spread into plates is brought from **T**, 8659
Eze 27:12 **T** *was* thy merchant by reason of 8659
 27:25 The ships of **T** did sing of thee *in* thy 8659
 38:13 and Dedan, and the merchants of **T**, 8659
Jnh 1: 3 Jonah rose up to flee unto **T** from 8659
 1: 3 *to* Joppa; and he found a ship going *to* **T**: 8659
 1: 3 go with them unto **T** from the presence 8659
 4: 2 Therefore I fled before unto **T**: for I knew 8659

TARSUS (5)
Ac 9:11 house of Judas for *one* called Saul, of **T**: *5018*
 9:30 down to Cesarea, and sent him forth to **T**. *5018*
 11:25 Then departed Barnabas to **T**, for to seek *5018*
 21:39 said, I am a man *which am* a Jew of **T**, *5018*
 22: 3 *am* a Jew, born in **T**, *a city* in Cilicia, *5018*

TARTAK (1)
2Ki 17:31 the Avites made Nibhaz and **T**, 8662

TARTAN (2)
2Ki 18:17 the king of Assyria sent **T** and Rabsaris 8661
Isa 20: 1 In the year that **T** came unto Ashdod, 8661

TASK (2) [TASKMASTERS, TASKS]
Ex 5:14 Wherefore have ye not fulfilled your **t** in 2706
 5:19 *ought* from your bricks of *your* daily **t**. 1697

TASKMASTERS (6) [MASTER, TASK]
Ex 1:11 Therefore they did set over them **t** 4522+8269
 3: 7 have heard their cry by reason of their **t**; 5065
 5: 6 Pharaoh commanded the same day the **t** 5065
 5:10 the **t** of the people went out, 5065
 5:13 the **t** hasted *them*, saying, Fulfil your 5065
 5:14 which Pharaoh's **t** had set over them, 5065

TASKS (1) [TASK]
Ex 5:13 Fulfil your works, *your* daily **t**, as when 1697

TASTE (22) [TASTED, TASTETH]
Ex 16:31 **t** of it *was* like wafers *made* with honey. 2940
Nu 11: 8 and the **t** of it was as the taste of fresh oil. 2940
 11: 8 and the taste of it was as the **t** of fresh oil. 2940
1Sa 14:43 I **did** but **t** a little honey with the 2938+2938
2Sa 3:35 and more also, if I **t** bread, or ought else, 2938
 19:35 thy servant **t** what I eat or what I drink? 2938
Job 6: 6 or is there *any* **t** in the white of an egg? 2940
 6:30 cannot my **t** discern perverse things? 2441
 12:11 ear try words? and the mouth **t** his meat? 2938
Ps 34: 8 O **t** and see that the LORD *is* good: 2938
 119:103 How sweet are thy words unto my **t**! 2441
Pr 24:13 the honeycomb, *which is* sweet to thy **t**: 2441
SS 2: 3 his fruit *was* sweet to my **t**. 2441
Jer 48:11 therefore his **t** remained in him, and 2940
Jnh 3: 7 nor beast, herd nor flock, **t** any thing: 2938
Mt 16:28 standing here, which shall not **t** of death, *1089*
Mk 9: 1 stand here, which shall not **t** of death, *1089*
Lk 9:27 standing here, which shall not **t** of death, *1089*
 14:24 which were bidden shall **t** of my supper. *1089*
Jn 8:52 keep my saying, he shall never **t** of death. *1089*
Col 2:21 (Touch not; **t** not; handle not; *1089*
Heb 2: 9 he by the grace of God should **t** death *1089*

TASTED (8) [TASTE]
1Sa 14:24 So none of the people **t** *any* food. 2938
 14:29 because I **t** a little of this honey. 2938
Da 5: 2 Belshazzar, whiles *he* **t** the wine, 2942
Mt 27:34 he had **t** *thereof*, he would not drink. *1089*
Jn 2: 9 the ruler of the feast had **t** the water *1089*
Heb 6: 4 and have **t** of the heavenly gift, *1089*
 6: 5 And have **t** the good word of God, *1089*
1Pe 2: 3 so be ye have **t** that the Lord *is* gracious. *1089*

TASTELESS See UNSAVOURY

TASTETH (1) [TASTE]
Job 34: 3 the ear trieth words, as the mouth **t** meat. 2938

TASTY See SAVOURY

TATNAI (4)
Ezr 5: 3 At the same time came to them **T**, 8674
 5: 6 The copy of the letter that **T**, governor on 8674
 6: 6 Now *therefore*, **T**, governor beyond 8674
 6:13 **T**, governor on *this* side the river, 8674

TATTENAI See TATNAI

TATTLERS (1)
1Ti 5:13 not only idle, but **t** also and busybodies, *5397*

TAUGHT (81) [TEACH]
Dt 4: 5 I have **t** you statutes and judgments, 3925
 31:22 same day, and **t** it the children of Israel. 3925
Jdg 8:16 and with them he **t** the men of Succoth, 3045
2Ki 17:28 them how they should fear the LORD. 3384
2Ch 6:27 when thou hast **t** them the good way, 3384
 17: 9 **t** in Judah, and *had* the book of the law 3925
 17: 9 all the cities of Judah, and **t** the people, 3925
 23:13 of musick; and such as **t** to *sing* praise. 3045
 30:22 the good **knowledge** of 7919+7922
 35: 3 said unto the Levites that **t** all Israel, 995
Ne 8: 9 the Levites that **t** the people, said unto all 995
Ps 71:17 O God, thou hast **t** me from my youth: 3925
 119:102 from thy judgments: for thou hast **t** me. 3384
 119:171 when thou hast **t** me thy statutes. 3925
Pr 4: 4 He **t** me also, and said unto me, Let thine 3925
 4:11 I have **t** thee in the way of wisdom; I have 3384
 31: 1 the prophecy that his mother **t** him. 3256
Ecc 12: 9 was wise, he still **t** the people knowledge; 3925
Isa 29:13 their fear towards me is **t** *by* the precept 3925
 40:13 or *being* his counsellor hath **t** him? 3045
 40:14 **t** him in the path of judgment, 3925
 40:14 **t** him knowledge, and shewed to him 3925
 54:13 all thy children *shall be* **t** of the LORD; 3928
Jer 2:33 thou also **t** the wicked ones thy ways. 3925
 9: 5 they have **t** their tongue to speak lies, 3925
 9:14 after Baalim, which their fathers **t** them: 3925
 12:16 as they **t** my people to swear by Baal; 3925
 13:21 for thou hast **t** them *to be* captains, 3925
 28:16 thou hast **t** rebellion against the LORD. 1696
 29:32 he hath **t** rebellion against the LORD. 1696
 32:33 though *I* **t** them, rising up early and 3925
Eze 23:48 that all women may be **t** not to do after 3256
Hos 10:11 Ephraim *is as a* heifer *that is* **t**, 3925
 11: 3 I **t** Ephraim also **to go**, taking them by 7270
Zec 13: 5 man **t** me *to keep* cattle from my youth. 7069
Mt 5: 2 he opened his mouth, and **t** them, saying, 1321
 7:29 For he **t** them as *one* having authority, 1321
 13:54 he **t** them in their synagogue, insomuch 1321
 28:15 took the money, and did as they were **t**: 1321
Mk 1:21 day he entered into the synagogue, and **t**. 1321
 1:22 for he **t** them as *one* that had authority, 1321
 2:13 resorted unto him, and he **t** them. 1321
 4: 2 And he **t** them many *things* by parables, 1321
 6:30 what they had done, and what they had **t**. 1321
 9:31 For he **t** his disciples, and said unto them, 1321
 10: 1 and, as he was wont, he **t** them again. 1321
 11:17 And he **t**, saying unto them, Is it not 1321
 12:35 and said, while he **t** in the temple, 1321
Lk 4:15 And he **t** in their synagogues, 1321
 4:31 of Galilee, and **t** them on the sabbath days. 1321
 5: 3 sat down, and **t** the people out of the ship. 1321
 6: 6 that he entered into the synagogue and **t**: 1321
 11: 1 us to pray, as John also **t** his disciples. 1321

Lk	13:26 presence, and thou hast **t** in our streets.	1321
	19:47 And he **t** daily in the temple. But the chief	1321
	20: 1 as he **t** the people in the temple,	1321
Jn	6:45 prophets, And they shall be all **t** of God.	1318
	6:59 in the synagogue, as he **t** in Capernaum.	1321
	7:14 feast Jesus went up into the temple, and **t**.	1321
	7:28 Then cried Jesus in the temple as he **t**,	1321
	8: 2 unto him; and he sat down, and **t** them.	1321
	8:20 Jesus in the treasury, as he **t** in the temple:	1321
	8:28 but as my Father hath **t** me, I speak these	1321
	18:20 in the synagogue, and in the temple,	1321
Ac	4: 2 Being grieved that they **t** the people,	1321
	5:21 the temple early in the morning, and **t**.	1321
	11:26 **t** much people, and the disciples were	1321
	14:21 and had **t** many, they returned *again* to	3100
	15: 1 came down from Judea **t** the brethren,	1321
	18:25 and **t** diligently the *things* of the Lord,	1321
	20:20 and have **t** you publicly, and from house	1321
	22: 3 according to the perfect manner of the	3811
Gal	1:12 neither was I **t** *it*, but by the revelation of	1321
	6: 6 him that is **t** in the word communicate	2727
Eph	4:21 and have been **t** by him, as the truth is in	1321
Col	2: 7 stablished in the faith, as ye have been **t**,	1321
1Th	4: 9 for ye yourselves are **t** of God to love one	2312
2Th	2:15 hold the traditions which ye have been **t**,	1321
Tit	1: 9 fast the faithful word as *he* hath been **t**,	1322
1Jn	2:27 and is no lie, and even as it hath **t** you,	1321
Rev	2:14 who **t** Balac to cast a stumblingblock	1321

TAUNT (2) [TAUNTING]

Jer	24: 9 a reproach and a proverb, a **t** and a curse,	8148
Eze	5:15 So it shall be a reproach and a **t**,	1422

TAUNTING (1) [TAUNT]

Hab	2: 6 and a **t** proverb against him, and say,	4426

TAVERNS (1)

Ac	28:15 us as far as Appii forum, and The three **t**:	4999

TAX BOOTH See RECEIPT OF CUSTOM

TAX COLLECTOR See PUBLICAN

TAXATION (1) [TAXED, TAXES, TAXING]

2Ki	23:35 of every one according to his **t**, to give *it*	6187

TAXED (4) [TAXATION]

2Ki	23:35 he **t** the land to give the money according	6186
Lk	2: 1 that all the world should be **t**.	583
	2: 3 all went to be **t**, every one into his own	583
	2: 5 To be **t** with Mary his espoused wife,	583

TAXES (1) [TAXATION]

Da	11:20 shall stand up in his estate a raiser of **t** *in*	5065

TAXING (2) [TAXATION]

Lk	2: 2 (*And* this **t** was first made when Cyrenius	582
Ac	5:37 rose up Judas of Galilee in the days of the **t**,	582

TEACH (109) [TAUGHT, TEACHER, TEACHERS, TEACHEST, TEACHETH, TEACHING]

Ex	4:12 mouth, and **t** thee what thou shalt say.	3384
	4:15 mouth, and will **t** you what ye shall do.	3384
	18:20 thou shalt **t** them ordinances and laws,	2094
	24:12 I have written; that thou mayest **t** them.	3384
	35:34 he hath put in his heart that *he* may **t**,	3384
Lev	10:11 that *ye* may **t** the children of Israel all	3384
	14:57 To **t** when *it is* unclean, and when *it is*	3384
Dt	4: 1 and unto the judgments, which I **t** you,	3925
	4: 9 but **t** them thy sons, and thy sons' sons;	3045
	4:10 earth, and *that* they may **t** their children.	3925
	4:14 Lord commanded me at that time to **t**	3925
	5:31 the judgments, which thou shalt **t** them,	3925
	6: 1 the Lord your God commanded to **t** you,	3925
	6: 7 thou shalt **t** them **diligently** unto thy	8150
	11:19 ye shall **t** them your children, speaking of	3925
	17:11 sentence of the law which they shall **t**	3384
	20:18 That they **t** you not to do after all their	3925
	24: 8 all that the priests the Levites shall **t** you:	3384
	31:19 for you, and **t** it the children of Israel:	3925
	33:10 They shall **t** Jacob thy judgments,	3384
Jdg	3: 2 to **t** them war, at the least such as before	3925
	3: 8 **t** us what we shall do unto the child that	3384
1Sa	12:23 I will **t** you the good and the right way:	3384
2Sa	1:18 (Also he bade *them* **t** the children of Judah	3925
1Ki	8:36 that thou **t** them the good way wherein	3384
2Ki	17:27 let him **t** them the manner of the God of	3384
2Ch	17: 7 to Michaiah, to **t** in the cities of Judah.	3925
Ezr	7:10 to do *it*, and to **t** in Israel statutes and	3925
	7:25 God; and **t** ye them that know *them* not.	3046
Job	6:24 **T** me, and I will hold my tongue;	3384
	8:10 Shall not they **t** thee, *and* tell thee,	3384
	12: 7 ask now the beasts, and they shall **t** thee;	3384
	12: 8 Or speak to the earth, and it shall **t** thee:	3384
	21:22 Shall *any* **t** God knowledge? seeing he	3925
	27:11 I will **t** you by the hand of God: *that*	3384
	32: 7 and multitude of years should **t** wisdom.	3045
	33:33 hold thy peace, and I shall **t** thee wisdom.	502
	34:32 *That which* I see not **t** thou me: if I have	3384
	37:19 **T** us what we shall say unto him; *for* we	3045
Ps	25: 4 me thy ways, O Lord; **t** me thy paths.	3925
	25: 5 Lead me in thy truth, and **t** me: for thou	3384
	25: 8 will he **t** sinners in the way.	3384
	25: 9 and the meek will he **t** his way.	3925
	25:12 him shall he **t** in the way *that* he shall	3384
	27:11 **T**each me thy way, O Lord, and lead me in a	3384

Ps	32: 8 and **t** thee in the way which thou shalt go:	3384
	34:11 I will you the fear of the Lord.	3925
	45: 4 thy right hand shall **t** thee terrible *things*.	3384
	51:13 Then will I **t** transgressors thy ways;	3925
	60: **T** Michtam of David, to **t**;	3925
	86:11 **T** me thy way, O Lord; I will walk in	3384
	90:12 So **t** *us* to number our days, that we may	3045
	105:22 his pleasure; and **t** his senators **wisdom**.	2449
	119:12 *art* thou, O Lord: **t** me thy statutes.	3925
	119:26 and thou heardest me: **t** me thy statutes.	3925
	119:33 **T** me, O Lord, the way of thy statutes.	3384
	119:64 is full *of* thy mercy: **t** me thy statutes.	3925
	119:66 **T** me good judgment and knowledge: for	3925
	119:68 good, and doest good; **t** me thy statutes.	3925
	119:108 O Lord, and **t** me thy judgments.	3925
	119:124 unto thy mercy, and **t** me thy statutes.	3925
	119:135 upon thy servant; and **t** me thy statutes.	3925
	132:12 and my testimony that I shall **t** them,	3925
	143:10 **T** me to do thy will; for thou *art* my God:	3925
Pr	9: 9 a just *man*, and he will increase in	3045
Isa	2: 3 he will **t** us of his ways, and we will walk	3384
	28: 9 Whom shall he **t** knowledge? and whom	3384
	28:26 instruct him to discretion, *and* doth **t** him.	3384
Jer	9:20 your daughters wailing, and every one	3925
	31:34 they shall **t** no more every man his	3925
Eze	44:23 they shall **t** my people *the difference*	3384
Da	1: 4 whom *they* might **t** the learning and	3925
Mic	3:11 the priests thereof **t** for hire,	3384
	4: 2 he will **t** us of his ways, and we will walk	3384
Hab	2:19 to the dumb stone, Arise, it shall **t**!	3384
Mt	5:19 least commandments, and shall **t** men so,	1321
	5:19 **t** them, the same shall be called great in	1321
	11: 1 he departed thence to **t** and to preach in	1321
	28:19 Go ye therefore, and **t** all nations,	3100
Mk	4: 1 And he began again to **t** by the sea side:	1321
	6: 2 come, he began to **t** in the synagogue:	1321
	6:34 and he began to **t** them many *things*.	1321
	8:31 And he began to **t** them, that the Son of	1321
Lk	11: 1 Lord, **t** us to pray, as John also taught his	1321
	12:12 For the Holy Ghost shall **t** you in the same	1321
Jn	7:35 among the Gentiles, and **t** the Gentiles?	1321
	9:34 altogether born in sins, and dost thou **t** us?	1321
	14:26 he shall **t** you all *things*, and bring all	1321
Ac	1: 1 of all that Jesus began both to do and **t**,	1321
	4:18 commanded them not to speak at all nor **t**	1321
	5:28 you that *you* should not **t** in this name?	1321
	5:42 they ceased not to **t** and preach Jesus	1321
	16:21 **t** customs, which are not lawful for us	2605
1Co	4:17 as I **t** every where in every church.	1321
	11:14 Doth not even nature itself **t** you, that, if	1321
	14:19 that *by my voice* I might **t** others also,	2727
1Ti	1: 3 some that they **t** no **other doctrine**,	2085
	2:12 I suffer not a woman to **t**, nor to usurp	1321
	3: 2 given to hospitality, **apt to t**;	1317
	4:11 These *things* command and **t**.	1321
	6: 2 of the benefit. These *things* **t** and exhort.	1321
	6: 3 If any *man* **t** **otherwise**, and consent not	2085
2Ti	2: 2 who shall be able to **t** others also.	1321
	2:24 be gentle unto all *men*, **apt to t**, patient,	1317
Tit	2: 4 may **t** the young *women* **to be sober**,	4994
Heb	5:12 ye have need that *one* **t** you again which	1321
	8:11 And they shall not **t** every man his	1321
1Jn	2:27 and ye need not that any man **t** you:	1321
Rev	2:20 to **t** and to seduce my servants to commit	1321

TEACHER (6) [TEACH]

1Ch	25: 8 the small as the great, the **t** as the scholar.	995
Hab	2:18 the molten image, and a **t** of lies, that	3384
Jn	3: 2 we know that thou art a **t** come from God:	1320
Ro	2:20 An instructor of the foolish, a **t** of babes,	1320
1Ti	2: 7 a **t** of the Gentiles in faith and verity.	1320
2Ti	1:11 and an apostle, and a **t** of the Gentiles.	1320

TEACHERS (14) [TEACH]

Ps	119:99 I have more understanding than all my **t**:	3925
Pr	5:13 have not obeyed the voice of my **t**,	3384
Isa	30:20 shall not thy **t** be removed into a corner	3384
	30:20 any more, but thine eyes shall see thy **t**:	3384
	43:27 and thy **t** have transgressed against me.	3887
Ac	13: 1 was at Antioch certain prophets and **t**;	1320
1Co	12:28 thirdly **t**, after that miracles, then gifts of	1320
	12:29 are all **t**? are all workers of miracles?	1320
Eph	4:11 evangelists; and some, pastors and **t**;	1320
1Ti	1: 7 Desiring to be **t** **of the law**;	3547
2Ti	4: 3 own lusts shall they heap to themselves **t**,	1320
Tit	2: 3 given to much wine, **t of good things**;	2567
Heb	5:12 For when for the time ye ought to be **t**,	1320
2Pe	2: 1 even as there shall be **false t** among you,	5572

TEACHEST (8) [TEACH]

Ps	94:12 O Lord, and **t** him out of thy law;	3925
Mt	22:16 art true, and **t** the way of God in truth,	1321
Mk	12:14 of men, but **t** the way of God in truth:	1321
Lk	20:21 we know that thou sayest and **t** rightly,	1321
	20:21 person *of any*, but **t** the way of God truly:	1321
Ac	21:21 that thou **t** all the Jews which are among	1321
Ro	2:21 Thou therefore which **t** another,	1321
	2:21 teachest another, **t** thou not thyself?	1321

TEACHETH (16) [TEACH]

2Sa	22:35 He **t** my hands to war; so that a bow of	3925
Job	35:11 **t** us more than the beasts of the earth,	502
	36:22 exalteth by his power: who **t** like him?	3384
Ps	18:34 He **t** my hands to war, so that a bow of	3925
	94:10 he that **t** man knowledge, *shall not* he	3925

Ps	144: 1 which **t** my hands to war, *and* my fingers	3925
	6:13 with his feet, he **t** with his fingers;	3384
Pr	16:23 The heart of the wise **t** his mouth,	7919
Isa	9:15 and the prophet that **t** lies, he *is* the tail.	3384
	48:17 I *am* the Lord thy God which **t** thee to	3925
Ac	21:28 that **t** all *men* every where against	1321
Ro	12: 7 *our* ministering: or he that **t**, on teaching;	1321
1Co	2:13 not in the words which man's wisdom **t**;	1318
	2:13 but which the Holy Ghost **t**;	1318
Gal	6: 6 unto him that **t** in all good *things*.	2727
1Jn	2:27 as the same anointing **t** you of all *things*,	1321

TEACHING (25) [TEACH]

2Ch	15: 3 and without a **t** priest, and without law.	3384
Jer	32:33 **t** them, yet they have not hearkened to	3925
Mt	4:23 in their synagogues, and preaching	1321
	9:35 in their synagogues, and preaching	1321
	15: 9 **t** for doctrines the commandments of men	1321
	21:23 of the people came unto him as he was **t**,	1321
	26:55 I sat daily with you **t** in the temple,	1321
	28:20 **T** them to observe all *things* whatsoever I	1321
Mk	6: 6 And he went round about the villages, **t**.	1321
	7: 7 **t** for doctrines the commandments of men	1321
	14:49 I was daily with you in the temple **t**,	1321
Lk	5:17 as he was **t**, that there were Pharisees and	1321
	13:10 And he was **t** in one of the synagogues on	1321
	13:22 **t**, and journeying towards Jerusalem.	1321
	21:37 in the day time he was **t** in the temple;	1321
	23: 5 up the people, **t** throughout all Jewry,	1321
Ac	5:25 standing in the temple, and **t** the people.	1321
	15:35 and preaching the word of the Lord,	1321
	18:11 months, **t** the word of God among them.	1321
	28:31 **t** those *things* which concern the Lord	1321
Ro	12: 7 *our* ministering; or he that teacheth, on **t**;	1319
Col	1:28 man, and **t** every man in all wisdom;	1321
	3:16 and admonishing one another in psalms	1321
Tit	1:11 **t** *things* which *they* ought not, for filthy	1321
	2:12 **T** us that denying ungodliness and	3811

TEAR (13) [TARE, TEARETH, TEARS, TORN]

Jdg	8: 7 I will **t** your flesh with the thorns of	1758
Ps	7: 2 Lest he **t** my soul like a lion, rending *it* in	2963
	35:15 I knew *it* not; they did **t** *me*, and ceased	7167
	50:22 lest I **t** *you* **in pieces**, and *there be* none	2963
Jer	15: 3 the dogs to **t**, and the fowls of the heaven,	5498
	16: 7 Neither shall *men* **t** *themselves* for them	6536
Eze	13:20 I will **t** them from your arms, and will let	7167
	13:21 Your kerchiefs also will I **t**, and deliver my	7167
Hos	5:14 I, *even* I, will **t** and go away; I will take	2963
	13: 8 like a lion: the wild beast shall **t** them.	1234
Am	1:11 his anger did **t** perpetually, and he kept	2963
Na	2:12 The lion did **t** **in pieces** enough for his	2963
Zec	11:16 of the fat, and **t** their claws **in pieces**.	6561

TEARETH (6) [TEAR]

Dt	33:20 and **t** the arm with the crown of the head.	2963
Job	16: 9 He **t** *me in* his wrath, who hateth me:	2963
	16:14 He **t** himself in his anger: shall the earth	2963
Mic	5: 8 and **t** **in pieces**, and none can deliver.	2963
Mk	9:18 wheresoever he taketh him, he **t** him:	4486
Lk	9:39 and it **t** him that he foameth again,	4682

TEARS (36) [TEAR]

2Ki	20: 5 I have heard thy prayer, I have seen thy **t**:	1832
Est	8: 3 besought him with **t** to put away	1058
Job	16:20 *but* mine eye poureth out **t** unto God.	NIH
Ps	6: 6 to be swim; I water my couch with my **t**.	1832
	39:12 unto my cry; hold not thy peace at my **t**:	1832
	42: 3 My **t** have been my meat day and night,	1832
	56: 8 put thou my **t** into thy bottle: *are they* not	1832
	80: 5 Thou feedest them with the bread of **t**;	1832
	80: 5 givest them to drink in great measure.	1832
	116: 8 eyes from **t**, *and* my feet from falling.	1832
	126: 5 They that sow in **t** shall reap in joy.	1832
Ecc	4: 1 the **t** of such as were oppressed,	1832
Isa	16: 9 I will water thee *with* my **t**, O Heshbon,	1832
	25: 8 the Lord God will wipe away **t** from off	1832
	38: 5 I have heard thy prayer, I have seen thy **t**:	1832
Jer	9: 1 eyes a fountain of **t**, that I might weep	1832
	9:18 that our eyes may run down *with* **t**,	1832
	13:17 run down *with* **t**, because the Lord's	1832
	14:17 Let mine eyes run down *with* **t** night and	1832
	31:16 from weeping, and thine eyes from **t**:	1832
La	1: 2 in the night, and her **t** *are* on her cheeks:	1832
	2:11 Mine eyes do fail with **t**, my bowels are	1832
	2:18 let **t** run down like a river day and night:	1832
Eze	24:16 nor weep, neither shall thy **t** run down.	1832
Mal	2:13 covering the altar of the Lord *with* **t**,	1832
Mk	9:24 cried out, and said with **t**, Lord, I believe;	1144
Lk	7:38 and began to wash his feet with **t**,	1144
	7:44 but she hath washed my feet with **t**,	1144
Ac	20:19 mind, and *with* many **t**, and temptations,	1144
	20:31 to warn every one night and day with **t**.	1144
2Co	2: 4 of heart I wrote unto you with many **t**;	1144
2Ti	1: 4 to see thee, being mindful of thy **t**,	1144
Heb	5: 7 unto him that was able to save him from	1144
	12:17 though he sought it carefully with **t**.	1144
Rev	7:17 God shall wipe away all **t** from their eyes.	1144
	21: 4 And God shall wipe away all **t** from their	1144

TEATS (3)

Isa	32:12 *shall* lament for the **t**, for the pleasant	7699
Eze	23: 3 there they bruised the **t** of their virginity.	1717
	23:21 in bruising thy **t** by the Egyptians for	1717

T

TEBAH (1)
Ge 22:24 bare also **T**, and Gaham, and Thahash, 2875

TEBALIAH (1)
1Ch 26:11 Hilkiah the second, **T** the third, 2882

TEBETH (1)
Est 2:16 which *is* the month **T**, in the seventh year 2887

TEDIOUS (1)
Ac 24: 4 that I be not further **t** unto thee, 1465

TEETH (49) [TOOTH]
Ge 49:12 red with wine, and *his* **t** white with milk. 8127
Nu 11:33 while the flesh *was* yet between their **t**, 8127
Dt 32:24 I will also send the **t** of beasts upon them, 8127
1Sa 2:13 with a fleshhook of three **t** in his hand; 8127
Job 4:10 and the **t** of the young lions, are broken. 8127
13:14 Wherefore do I take my flesh in my **t**, 8127
16: 9 he gnasheth upon me with his **t**; 8127
19:20 and I am escaped with the skin of my **t**. 8127
29:17 wicked, and pluckt the spoil out of his **t**. 8127
41:14 of his face? his **t** *are* terrible round about. 8127
Ps 3: 7 thou hast broken the **t** of the ungodly. 8127
35:16 *they* gnashed upon me *with* their **t**. 8127
37:12 just, and gnasheth upon him *with* his **t**. 8127
57: 4 whose **t** *are* spears and arrows, 8127
58: 6 Break their **t**, O God, in their mouth: 8127
58: 6 break out the **great t** of the young lions, 4459
112:10 he shall gnash *with* his **t**, and melt away: 8127
124: 6 who hath not given us *as* a prey to their **t**. 8127
Pr 10:26 As vinegar to the **t**, and as smoke to 8127
30:14 whose **t** *are as* swords, and their jaw teeth 8127
30:14 *are as* swords, and their **jaw t** *as* knives, 4973
SS 4: 2 Thy **t** *are* like a flock of *sheep that are* 8127
6: 6 Thy **t** *are as* a flock of sheep which go up 8127
Isa 41:15 new sharp threshing instrument having **t**: 6374
Jer 31:29 and the children's **t** are set on edge. 8127
31:30 the sour grape, his **t** shall be set on edge. 8127
La 2:16 they hiss and gnash the **t**: they say, 8127
3:16 He hath also broken my **t** with gravel 8127
Eze 18: 2 and the children's **t** are set on edge? 8127
Da 7: 5 ribs in the mouth of it between the **t** of it: 8128
7: 7 strong exceedingly; and it had great iron **t** 8128
7:19 *it were* of iron, and his nails *of* brass; 8128
Joel 1: 6 the teeth of a lion, and he hath 8127
1: 6 teeth *are* the **t** of a lion, and he hath 8127
Am 4: 6 I also have given you cleanness of **t** in all 8127
Mic 3: 5 that bite with their **t**, and cry, Peace; 8127
Zec 9: 7 and his abominations from between his **t**: 8127
Mt 8:12 there shall be wailing and gnashing of **t**. 3599
13:42 there shall be wailing and gnashing of **t**. 3599
13:50 there shall be wailing and gnashing of **t**. 3599
22:13 there shall be weeping and gnashing of **t**. 3599
24:51 there shall be weeping and gnashing of **t**. 3599
25:30 there shall be weeping and gnashing of **t**. 3599
27:44 crucified with him, **cast** the same **in** his **t**. 3679
Mk 9:18 and gnasheth with his **t**, and pineth away: 3599
Lk 13:28 There shall be weeping and gnashing of **t**, 3599
Ac 7:54 and they gnashed on him *with their* **t**. 3599
Rev 9: 8 their **t** were as *the teeth* of lions. 3599
9: 8 and their teeth were as *the* **t** of lions. NIG

TEHAPHNEHES (1) [TAHPANHES]
Eze 30:18 At **T** also the day shall be darkened, 8471

TEHINNAH (1)
1Ch 4:12 and Paseah, and **T** the father of Irnahash. 8468

TEIL (1)
Isa 6:13 as a **t** *tree*, and as an oak, whose substance 424

TEKEL (2)
Da 5:25 MENE, MENE, **T**, UPHARSIN. 8625
5:27 **T**; Thou art weighed in the balances, 8625

TEKOA (6) [TEKOAH, TEKOITE, TEKOITES]
1Ch 2:24 wife bare him Ashur the father of **T**. 8620
4: 5 Ashur the father of **T** had two wives, 8620
2Ch 11: 6 built even Beth-lehem, and Etam, and **T**, 8620
20:20 and went forth into the wilderness of **T**: 8620
Jer 6: 1 blow the trumpet in **T**, and set up a sign 8620
Am 1: 1 who was among the herdmen of **T**, 8620

TEKOAH (3) [TEKOA]
2Sa 14: 2 Joab sent to **T**, and fetcht thence a wise 8620
14: 4 when the woman of **T** spake to the king, 8621
14: 9 the woman of **T** said unto the king, 8621

TEKOITE (3) [TEKOA]
2Sa 23:26 the Paltite, Ira the son of Ikkesh the **T**, 8621
1Ch 11:28 Ira the son of Ikkesh the **T**, Abi-ezer 8621
27: 9 month *was* Ira the son of Ikkesh the **T**: 8621

TEKOITES (2) [TEKOA]
Ne 3: 5 next unto them the **T** repaired; 8621
3:27 After them the **T** repaired another piece, 8621

TEL-ABIB (1)
Eze 3:15 I came to them of the captivity *at* **T**, 8512

TELAH (1)
1Ch 7:25 and **T** his son, and Tahan his son, 8520

TELAIM (1)
1Sa 15: 4 numbered them in **T**, two hundred 2923

TELASSAR (1) [THELASAR]
Isa 37:12 the children of Eden which *were* in **T**? 8515

TELEM (2)
Jos 15:24 Ziph, and **T**, and Bealoth, 2928
Ezr 10:24 of the porters; Shallum, and **T**, and Uri. 2928

TEL-HARESHA (1) [TEL-HARSA]
Ne 7:61 **T**, Cherub, Addon, and Immer: 8521

TEL-HARSA (1) [TEL-HARESHA]
Ezr 2:59 **T**, Cherub, Addan, *and* Immer: 8521

TELL (217) [FORETELL, FORETOLD, TELLEST, TELLETH, TELLING, TOLD]
Ge 12:18 why didst thou not **t** me that she *was* thy 5046
15: 5 Look now towards heaven, and **t** the stars 5608
21:26 neither didst thou **t** me, neither yet heard 5046
22: 2 of the mountains which I will **t** thee of. 559
24:23 **t** me, I pray thee: is there room *in* thy 5046
24:49 kindly and truly with my master, **t** me: 5046
24:49 if not, **t** me; that I may turn to the right 5046
26: 2 dwell in the land which I shall **t** thee of: 559
29:15 nought? **t** me, what *shall* thy wages *be*? 5046
31:27 not **t** me, that I might have sent thee 5046
32: 5 I have sent to **t** my lord, that I may find 5046
32:29 asked *him*, and said, **T** *me*, I pray thee, 5046
37:16 **t** me, I pray thee, where they feed *their* 5046
40: 8 *belong* to God? **t** me *them*, I pray you. 5608
43: 6 *as* to **t** the man whether ye had yet a 5046
43:22 we cannot **t** who put our money in our 3045
45:13 you shall **t** my father of all my glory in 5046
49: 1 I may **t** you *that* which shall befall you 5046
Ex 9: 1 Moses, Go in unto Pharaoh, and **t** him, 1696
10: 2 that thou mayest **t** in the ears of thy son, 5608
14:12 *Is* not this the word that we did **t** thee in 1696
19: 3 of Jacob, and **t** the children of Israel; 5046
Lev 14:35 the house shall come and **t** the priest, 5046
Nu 14:14 they will **t** *it* to the inhabitants of this land: NIH
21: 1 heard *that* Israel came *by* the way of NIH
23: 3 whatsoever he sheweth me I will **t** thee. 5046
Dt 17:11 to the judgment which they shall **t** 559
32: 7 thee; thy elders, and they will **t** thee. 559
Jos 7:19 **t** me now what thou hast done; hide *it* 5046
Jdg 14:16 nor my mother, and shall I **t** *it* thee? 5046
16: 6 Delilah said to Samson, **T** me, I pray thee, 5046
16:10 now **t** me, I pray thee, wherewith thou 5046
16:13 **t** me wherewith thou mightest be bound. 5046
20: 3 of Israel, **T** *us*, how was this wickedness? 1696
Ru 3: 4 and he will **t** thee what thou shalt do. 5046
4: 4 but if thou wilt not redeem *it, then* **t** me, 5046
1Sa 6: 2 **t** us wherewith we shall send it to his 3045
9: 8 I give to the man of God, to **t** us our way. 5046
9:18 said, **T** me, I pray thee, where the seer's 5046
9:19 and will **t** thee all that *is* in thine heart. 5046
10:15 Saul's uncle said, **T** me, I pray thee, 5046
14:43 to Jonathan, **T** me what thou hast done. 5046
15:16 I will **t** thee what the LORD hath said to 5046
17:55 *As* thy soul liveth, O king, I cannot **t**. 3045
19: 3 of thee; and what I see, that I will **t** thee. 5046
20: 9 upon thee, then would not I **t** it thee? 5046
20:10 said David to Jonathan, Who shall I **t** me? 5046
22:22 that he would **surely** *tell* Saul: 5046+5046
23:11 of Israel, I beseech thee, **t** thy servant. 5046
27:11 saying, Lest they should **t** on us, saying, 5046
2Sa 1: 4 I pray thee, **t** me. And he answered, 5046
1:20 **T** *it* not in Gath, publish *it* not in the 5046
7: 5 Go and **t** my servant David, Thus saith 559
12:18 the servants of David feared to **t** him that 5046
12:18 if we **t** him *that* the child is dead? 559
12:22 Who can **t** *whether* GOD will be gracious 3045
13: 4 wilt thou not **t** me? And Amnon said unto 5046
15:35 thou shalt **t** *it* to Zadok and Abiathar 5046
17:16 therefore send quickly, and **t** David, 5046
18:21 Cushi, Go **t** the king what thou hast seen. 5046
1Ki 1: 20 *thou* shouldest **t** them who shall sit on 5046
14: 3 he shall **t** thee what shall become of 5046
14: 7 Go, **t** Jeroboam, Thus saith the LORD God 559
18: 8 I *am*: go, **t** thy lord, Behold, Elijah *is here.* 559
18:11 Go, **t** thy lord, Behold, Elijah *is here.* 559
18:12 when I come **t** not Ahab, and he cannot 5046
18:14 Go, **t** thy lord, Behold, Elijah *is here:* and 559
20: 9 of Ben-hadad, **T** my lord the king, 559
20:11 **T** *him*, Let not him that girdeth on *his* 1696
22:16 shall I adjure thee, that thou **t** me nothing 1696
22:18 Did I not **t** thee that he would prophesy 559
2Ki 4: 2 **t** me, what hast thou in the house? 5046
7: 9 we may go and **t** the king's household. 5046
8: 4 saying, **T** me, I pray thee, all the great 5608
9:12 said, *It is* false; **t** us now. And he said, 5046
9:15 out of the city to go to **t** *it* in Jezreel. 5046
20: 5 and **t** Hezekiah the captain of my people, 559
22:15 of Israel, **T** the man that sent you to me, 559
1Ch 17: 4 Go and **t** David my servant, Thus saith 559
17:10 Furthermore I **t** thee that the LORD will 559
21:10 Go and **t** David, saying, Thus saith 1696
2Ch 18:17 I not **t** thee *that* he would not prophesy 559
34:23 Israel, **T** ye the man that sent you to me, 559
Job 1:15 and I only am escaped alone to **t** thee. 5046
1:16 and I only am escaped alone to **t** thee. 5046
1:17 and I only am escaped alone to **t** thee. 5046
1:19 and I only am escaped alone to **t** thee. 5046
8:10 **t** thee, and utter words out of their heart? 559
12: 7 the fowls of the air, and they shall **t** thee: 5046
34:34 Let men of understanding **t** me, and let a 559

Ps 22:17 I may **t** all my bones: they look *and* 5608
26: 7 and **t** of all thy wondrous works. 5608
48:12 go round about her: **t** the towers thereof. 5608
48:13 ye may **t** *it* to the generation following. 5608
50:12 If I were hungry, I would not **t** thee: 559
Pr 30: 4 what *is* his son's name, if thou canst **t**? 3045
Ecc 6:12 who can **t** a man what shall be after him 5046
8: 7 for who can **t** him when it shall be? 5046
10:14 a man cannot **t** what shall be; 5046
10:14 what shall be after him, who can **t** him? 5046
10:20 that which hath wings shall **t** the matter. 5046
SS 1: 7 **T** me, O thou whom my soul loveth, 5046
5: 8 that ye **t** him, that I *am* sick of love. 5046
Isa 5: 5 I will **t** you what I *will* do to my vineyard; 3045
6: 9 he said, Go, and **t** this people, Hear ye 559
19:12 thy wise *men*? and let them **t** thee now, 559
42: 9 before they spring forth I **t** you of them. 8085
45:21 **T** ye, and bring *them* near; yea, let them 5046
48:20 with a voice of singing declare ye, **t** this, 8085
Jer 15: 2 thou shalt **t** them, Thus saith the LORD: 559
19: 2 proclaim there the words that I shall **t** 1696
23:27 which they **t** every man to his neighbour, 5608
23:28 that hath a dream, let him **t** a dream; 5608
23:32 do **t** them, and cause my people to err by 5608
28:13 Go and **t** Hananiah, saying, Thus saith 559
34: 2 of Judah, and **t** him, Thus saith the LORD; 559
35:13 Go and **t** the men of Judah and 559
36:16 will **surely t** the king of all these 5046+5046
36:17 they asked Baruch, saying, **T** us now, 5046
48:20 cry; **t** ye *it* in Arnon, that Moab is spoiled, 5046
Eze 3: 1 speak unto them, and **t** them, Thus saith 559
12:23 **T** them therefore, Thus saith the Lord 559
17:12 Know ye not what these *things* mean? **t** 559
24:19 Wilt thou not **t** us what these *things* are 5046
Da 2: 4 **t** thy servants the dream, and we will shew 560
2: 7 Let the king **t** his servants the dream, 560
2: 9 therefore **t** me the dream, and I shall know 560
2:36 we will **t** the interpretation thereof before 560
4: 9 **t** me the visions of my dream that I have 560
Joel 1: 3 **T** your children of it, and *let* your 5608
1: 3 *let* your children **t** their children, NIH
Jnh 1: 8 said they unto him, **T** us, we pray thee, 5046
1:12 Who can **t** *if* God will turn and repent, 3045
Mt 8: 4 See thou **t** no *man;* but go thy way, 3004
10:27 What I **t** you in darkness, *that* speak ye in 3004
16:20 **t** no *man* that he was Jesus the Christ. 3004
17: 9 the vision to no *man,* until the Son of 3004
18:15 go and **t** him his **fault** between thee and 1651
18:17 neglect to hear them, **t** *it* unto the church: 3004
21: 5 **T** ye the daughter of Sion, Behold, 3004
21:24 will ask you one thing, which if ye **t** me, 3004
21:24 I in like wise will **t** you by what authority 3004
21:27 answered Jesus, and said, We cannot **t**. 1492
21:27 Neither **t** I you by what authority I do 3004
22: 4 saying, **T** them which are bidden, Behold, 3004
22:17 **T** us therefore, What thinkest thou? Is it 3004
24: 3 **T** us, when shall these *things* be? 3004
26:63 that thou **t** us whether thou be the Christ, 3004
28: 7 his disciples that he is risen from 3004
28: 9 And as they went to **t** his disciples, behold, 518
28:10 go **t** my brethren that they go into Galilee, 518
Mk 1:30 sick of a fever, and anon they **t** him of her. 3004
5:19 **t** them how great *things* the Lord hath 312
7:36 he charged them that they should **t** no 3004
8:26 into the town, nor **t** *it* to any in the town. 3004
8:30 he charged them that they should **t** no 3004
9: 9 charged them that they should **t** no *man* 1334
10:32 to **t** them what *things* should happen 3004
11:29 I will **t** you by what authority I do these 3004
11:33 and said unto Jesus, We cannot **t**. 1492
11:33 Neither do I **t** you by what authority I do 3004
13: 4 **T** us, when shall these *things* be? 3004
16: 7 **t** his disciples and Peter that he goeth 3004
Lk 4:25 I **t** you of a truth, many widows were in 3004
5:14 And he charged him to **t** no *man:* but go, 3004
7:22 and John what *things* ye have seen and 518
7:42 **T** me therefore, which of them will love 3004
8:56 charged them that they should **t** no *man* 3004
9:21 commanded *them* to **t** no *man* that *thing;* 3004
9:27 But I **t** you of a truth, there be some 3004
10:24 For I **t** you, that many prophets and 3004
12:51 earth? I **t** you, Nay; but rather division: 3004
12:59 I **t** thee, thou shalt not depart thence, 3004
13: 3 I **t** you, Nay: but, except ye repent, ye 3004
13: 5 I **t** you, Nay: but except ye repent, ye shall 3004
13:27 But he shall say, I **t** you, I know you not 3004
13:32 Go ye, and **t** that fox, Behold, I cast out 3004
17:34 I **t** you, in that night there shall be two 3004
18: 8 I **t** you that he will avenge them speedily. 3004
18:14 I **t** you, this man went down to his house 3004
19:40 and said unto them, I **t** you that, 3004
20: 7 that *they* could not **t** whence *it was.* 1492
20: 8 Neither **t** I you by what authority I do 3004
22:34 And he said, I **t** thee, Peter, *the* cock shall 3004
22:67 **t** us. And he said unto them, If I **t** you, 3004
22:67 unto them, If I **t** you, you will not believe: 3004
Jn 3: 8 but canst not **t** whence it cometh, 1492
3:12 ye believe, if I **t** you *of* heavenly *things?* 3004
4:25 when he is come, he will **t** us all *things.* 312
8:14 but ye cannot **t** whence I come, 1492
8:45 And because I **t** *you* the truth, ye believe 3004
10:24 doubt? If thou be the Christ, **t** us plainly. 3004
12:22 and again Andrew and Philip **t** Jesus. 3004
13:19 Now I **t** you before it come, that, when it 3004

Jn 16: 7 Nevertheless I t you the truth; It is 3004
 16:18 A little while? we cannot t what he saith. 1492
 18:34 of thyself, or did others t it thee of me? 3004
 20:15 if thou have borne him hence, t me where 3004
Ac 5: 8 T me whether ye sold the land for so 3004
 10: 6 he shall t thee what thou oughtest to do. 2980
 11:14 Who shall t thee words, whereby thou 2980
 15:27 who shall also t you the same things by 518
 17:21 either to t, or to hear some new thing.) 3004
 22:27 and said unto him, T me, art thou a 3004
 23:17 for he hath a certain thing to t him. 518
 23:19 asked him, What is that thou hast to t me? 518
 23:22 charged him, See thou t no man that thou 1583
2Co 12: 2 ago, (whether in the body, I cannot t; 1492
 12: 2 or whether out of the body, I cannot t: 1492
 12: 3 in the body, or out of the body, I cannot t: 1492
Gal 4:16 your enemy, because I t you the truth? 226
 4:21 T me, ye that desire to be under the law, 3004
 5:21 of the which I t you before, as I have also 4302
Php 3:18 you often, and now I t you even weeping, 3004
Heb 11:32 for the time would fail me to t of Gedeon, 1334
Rev 17: 7 I will t thee the mystery of the woman, 3004

TELLEST (1) [TELL]
Ps 56: 8 Thou t my wanderings: put thou my tears 5608

TELLETH (7) [TELL]
2Sa 7:11 Also the LORD t thee that he will make 5046
2Ki 6:12 the king of Israel the words that thou 5046
Ps 41: 6 to visit; when he goeth abroad, he t it. 1696
 101: 7 he that t lies shall not tarry in my sight. 1696
 147: 4 He t the number of the stars; he calleth 4487
Jer 33:13 hands of him that t them, saith the LORD. 4487
Jn 12:22 Philip cometh and t Andrew: 3004

TELLING (3) [TELL]
Jdg 7:15 when Gideon heard the t of the dream, 4557
2Sa 11:19 When thou hast made an end of t 1696
2Ki 8: 5 as he was t the king how he had restored 5608

TEL-MELAH (2)
Ezr 2:59 these were they which went up from T, 8528
Ne 7:61 were they which went up also from T, 8528

TEMA (5)
Ge 25:15 Hadar, and T, Jetur, Naphish, 8485
1Ch 1:30 and Dumah, Massa, Hadad, and T, 8485
Job 6:19 The troops of T looked, the companies of 8485
Isa 21:14 The inhabitants of the land of T brought 8485
Jer 25:23 T, and Buz, and all that are in the utmost 8485

TEMAH See TAMAH; THAMAH

TEMAN (11) [TEMANI, TEMANITE, TEMANITES]
Ge 36:11 the sons of Eliphaz were T, Omar, Zepho, 8487
 36:15 duke Teman, duke Omar, duke Zepho, 8487
 36:42 Duke Kenaz, duke T, duke Mibzar, 8487
1Ch 1:36 T, and Omar, Zephi, and Gatam, Kenaz, 8487
 1:53 Duke Kenaz, duke T, duke Mibzar, 8487
Jer 49: 7 LORD of hosts; Is wisdom no more in T? 8487
 49:20 purposed against the inhabitants of T: 8487
Eze 25:13 I will make it desolate from T; and they 8487
Am 1:12 I will send a fire upon T, which shall 8487
Ob 1: 9 thy mighty men, O T, shall be dismayed, 8487
Hab 3: 3 God came from T, and the Holy One from 8487

TEMANI (1) [TEMAN]
Ge 36:34 Husham of the land of T reigned in his 8489

TEMANITE (6) [TEMAN]
Job 2:11 Eliphaz the T, and Bildad the Shuhite, 8489
 4: 1 Then Eliphaz the T answered and said, 8489
 15: 1 Then answered Eliphaz the T, and said, 8489
 22: 1 Then Eliphaz the T answered and said, 8489
 42: 7 the LORD said to Eliphaz the T, 8489
 42: 9 So Eliphaz the T and Bildad the Shuhite 8489

TEMANITES (1) [TEMAN]
1Ch 1:45 Husham of the land of the T reigned in 8489

TEMENI (1)
1Ch 4: 6 and Hepher, and T, and Haahashtari. 8488

TEMPER (1) [TEMPERANCE, TEMPERATE, TEMPERED, UNTEMPERED]
Eze 46:14 part of a hin of oil, to t with the fine flour; 7450

TEMPERANCE (4) [TEMPER]
Ac 24:25 t, and judgment to come, Felix trembled, 1466
Gal 5:23 Meekness, t: against such there is no law. 1466
2Pe 1: 6 And to knowledge t; and to temperance 1466
 1: 6 to t patience; and to patience godliness; 1466

TEMPERATE (3) [TEMPER]
1Co 9:25 t in all things. Now they do it to obtain a 1467
Tit 1: 8 a lover of good men, sober, just, holy, t; 1468
 2: 2 grave, t, sound in faith, in charity, 4998

TEMPERED (3) [TEMPER]
Ex 29: 2 cakes unleavened t with oil, 1101
 30:35 apothecary, t together, pure and holy: 4414
1Co 12:24 but God hath t the body together, 4786

TEMPEST (18) [TEMPESTUOUS]
Job 9:17 For he breaketh me with a t, 8183
 27:20 a t stealeth him away in the night. 5492

Ps 11: 6 fire and brimstone, and a horrible t: 7307
 55: 8 my escape from the windy storm and t. 5591
 83:15 So persecute them with thy t, 5591
Isa 28: 2 as a t of hail and a destroying storm, 2230
 29: 6 with storm and t, and the flame of 5591
 30:30 with scattering, and t, and hailstones. 2230
 32: 2 from the wind, and a covert from the t; 2230
 54:11 tossed with t, and not comforted, 5590
Am 1:14 with a t in the day of the whirlwind; 5591
Jnh 1: 4 there was a mighty t in the sea, so that 5591
 1:12 for I know that for my sake this great t is 5591
Mt 8:24 behold, there arose a great t in the sea, 4578
Ac 27:18 we being exceedingly tossed with a t, 5492
 27:20 no small t lay on us, all hope that we 5494
Heb 12:18 nor unto blackness, and darkness, and t, 2366
2Pe 2:17 clouds that are carried with a t; 2978

TEMPESTUOUS (4) [TEMPEST]
Ps 50: 3 and it shall be very t round about him. 8175
Jnh 1:11 unto us? for the sea wrought, and was t. 5590
 1:13 the sea wrought, and was t against them. 5590
Ac 27:14 not long after there arose against it a t 5189

TEMPLE (204) [TEMPLES]
1Sa 1: 9 a seat by a post of the t of the LORD. 1964
 3: 3 ere the lamp of God went out in the t of 1964
2Sa 22: 7 he did hear my voice out of his t, 1964
1Ki 6: 3 The porch before the t of the house, 1964
 6: 5 about, both of the t and of the oracle: 1964
 6:17 house, that is, the t before it, was forty 1964
 6:33 So also made he for the door of the t posts 1964
 7:21 he set up the pillars in the porch of the t: 1964
 7:50 for the doors of the house, to wit, the t 1964
2Ki 11:10 that were in the t of the LORD. 1004
 11:11 from the right corner of the t to the left 1004
 11:11 from the temple to the left corner of the t, 1004
 11:11 of the temple, along by the altar and the t, 1004
 11:13 she came to the people into the t of 1004
 18:16 gold from the doors of the t of the LORD, 1004
 23: 4 to bring forth out of the t of the LORD all 1964
 24:13 of Israel had made in the t of the LORD, 1964
1Ch 6:10 in the t that Solomon built in Jerusalem:) 1004
 10:10 and fastened his head in the t of Dagon. 1004
2Ch 3:17 he reared up the pillars before the t, one 1964
 4: 7 set them in the t, five on the right hand, 1964
 4: 8 placed them in the t, five on the right 1964
 4:22 and the doors of the house of the t, 1964
 23:10 from the right side of the t to the left side 1004
 23:10 side of the temple to the left side of the t, 1004
 23:10 along by the altar and the t, by the king 1004
 26:16 went into the t of the LORD to burn 1964
 27: 2 howbeit he entered not into the t of 1004
 29:16 of the LORD into the court of the house 1004
 35:20 all this, when Josiah had prepared the t, 1004
 36: 7 and put them in his t at Babylon. 1964
Ezr 3: 6 the foundation of the t of the LORD was 1964
 3:10 laid the foundation of the t of the LORD, 1964
 4: 1 the unto the LORD God of Israel; 1964
 5:14 which Nebuchadnezzar took out of the t 1965
 5:14 brought them into the t of Babylon, 1965
 5:14 did Cyrus the king take out of the t of 1965
 5:15 carry them into the t that is in Jerusalem, 1965
 6: 5 forth out of the t at Jerusalem, 1965
 6: 5 brought again unto the t which is at 1965
Ne 6:10 within the t, and let us shut the doors of 1964
 6:10 and let us shut the doors of the t: 1964
 6:11 being as I am, would go into the t to save 1964
Ps 5: 7 thy fear will I worship toward thy holy t. 1964
 11: 4 The LORD is in his holy t, the LORD's 1964
 18: 6 heard my voice out of his t, and my cry 1964
 27: 4 of the LORD, and to inquire in his t. 1964
 29: 9 in his t doth every one speak of his glory. 1964
 48: 9 O God, in the midst of thy t. 1964
 65: 4 goodness of thy house, even of thy holy t. 1964
 68:29 Because of thy t at Jerusalem shall kings 1964
 79: 1 thy holy t have they defiled; they have 1964
 138: 2 I will worship toward thy holy t, 1964
Isa 6: 1 and lifted up, and his train filled the t. 1964
 44:28 and to the t, Thy foundation shall be laid. 1964
 66: 6 of noise from the city, a voice from the t, 1964
Jer 7: 4 saying, The t of the LORD, The temple of 1964
 7: 4 The t of the LORD, The temple of 1964
 7: 4 The t of the LORD, are these. 1964
 24: 1 two baskets of figs were set before the t of 1964
 50:28 LORD our God, the vengeance of his t. 1964
 51:11 of the LORD, the vengeance of his t. 1964
Eze 8:16 behold, at the door of the t of the LORD, 1964
 8:16 with their backs toward the t of 1964
 41: 1 Afterward he brought me to the t, 1964
 41: 4 the breadth, twenty cubits, before the t: 1964
 41:15 with the inner t, and the porches of 1964
 41:20 palm trees made, and on the wall of the t. 1964
 41:21 The posts of the t were squared, 1964
 41:23 the t and the sanctuary had two doors. 1964
 41:25 on the doors of the t, cherubims and 1964
 42: 8 lo, before the t were an hundred cubits. 1964
Da 5: 2 out of the t which was in Jerusalem; 1965
 5: 3 of the house of God which was at 1965
Am 8: 3 the songs of the t shall be howlings in 1964
Jnh 2: 4 yet I will look again toward thy holy t. 1964
 2: 7 came in unto thee, into thine holy t. 1964
Mic 1: 2 against you, the Lord from his holy t. 1964
Hab 2:20 the LORD is in his holy t: let all the earth 1964
Hag 2:15 laid upon a stone in the t of the LORD: 1964
 2:18 the foundation of the LORD's t was laid, 1964

Zec 6:12 and he shall build the t of the LORD: 1964
 6:13 Even he shall build the t of the LORD; 1964
 6:14 for a memorial in the t of the LORD. 1964
 6:15 and build in the t of the LORD, 1964
 8: 9 hosts was laid, that the t might be built. 1964
Mal 3: 1 shall suddenly come to his t, 1964
Mt 4: 5 and setteth him on a pinnacle of the t, 2411
 12: 5 the priests to profane the sabbath, 2411
 12: 6 in this place is one greater than the t. 2411
 21:12 And Jesus went into the t of God, 2411
 21:12 out all them that sold and bought in the t, 2411
 21:14 blind and the lame came to him in the t; 2411
 21:15 the children crying in the t, and saying, 2411
 21:23 when he was come into the t, the chief 2411
 23:16 say, Whosoever shall swear by the t, 3485
 23:16 shall swear by the gold of the t, 3485
 23:17 the gold, or the t that sanctifieth the gold? 3485
 23:21 And whoso shall swear by the t, 3485
 23:35 ye slew between the t and the altar. 3485
 24: 1 Jesus went out, and departed from the t: 2411
 24: 1 for to shew him the buildings of the t. 2411
 26:55 I sat daily with you teaching in the t, 2411
 26:61 I am able to destroy the t of God, 3485
 27: 5 he cast down the pieces of silver in the t, 3485
 27:40 that destroyest the t, and buildest it in 3485
 27:51 the vail of the t was rent in twain from 3485
Mk 11:11 entered into Jerusalem, and into the t: 2411
 11:15 Jesus went into the t, and began to cast 2411
 11:15 out them that sold and bought in the t, 2411
 11:16 should carry any vessel through the t. 2411
 11:27 as he was walking in the t, there come 2411
 12:35 and said, while he taught in the t, 2411
 13: 1 And as he went out of the t, one of his 2411
 13: 3 the mount of Olives over against the t, 2411
 14:49 I was daily with you in the t teaching, 2411
 14:58 destroy this t that is made with hands, 3485
 15:29 that destroyest the t, and buildest it in 3485
 15:38 the vail of the t was rent in twain from 3485
Lk 1: 9 when he went into the t of the Lord. 3485
 1:21 marvelled that he tarried so long in the t. 3485
 1:22 that he had seen a vision in the t: 3485
 2:27 And he came by the Spirit into the t, 2411
 2:37 which departed not from the t, 2411
 2:46 after three days they found him in the t, 2411
 4: 9 and set him on a pinnacle of the t, 2411
 11:51 perished between the altar and the t: 3624
 18:10 Two men went up into the t to pray; 2411
 19:45 And he went into the t, and began to cast 2411
 19:47 And he taught daily in the t. But the chief 2411
 20: 1 as he taught the people in the t, 2411
 21: 5 And as some spake of the t, how it was 2411
 21:37 in the day time he was teaching in the t; 2411
 21:38 came early in the morning to him in the t, 2411
 22:52 and captains of the t, and the elders, 2411
 22:53 When I was daily with you in the t, 2411
 23:45 and the vail of the t was rent in the midst. 3485
 24:53 And were continually in the t, praising 2411
Jn 2:14 found in the t those that sold oxen and 2411
 2:15 drove them all out of the t, and the sheep 2411
 2:19 Destroy this t, and in three days I will 3485
 2:20 Forty and six years was this t in building, 3485
 2:21 But he spake of the t of his body. 3485
 5:14 Afterward Jesus findeth him in the t, 2411
 7:14 of the feast Jesus went up into the t, 2411
 7:28 Then cried Jesus in the t as he taught, 2411
 8: 2 in the morning he came again into the t, 2411
 8:20 These words spake Jesus in the treasury, as he taught in the t: 2411
 8:59 Jesus hid himself, and went out of the t, 2411
 10:23 And Jesus walked in the t in Solomon's 2411
 11:56 as they stood in the t, What think ye, 2411
 18:20 ever taught in the synagogue, and in the t, 2411
Ac 2:46 continuing daily with one accord in the t, 2411
 3: 1 John went up together into the t at the 2411
 3: 2 whom they laid daily at the gate of the t 2411
 3: 2 ask alms of them that entered into the t; 2411
 3: 3 Peter and John about to go into the t, 2411
 3: 8 walked, and entered with them into the t, 2411
 3:10 sat for alms at the Beautiful gate of the t: 2411
 4: 1 the captain of the t, and the Sadducees, 2411
 5:20 speak in the t to the people all the words 2411
 5:21 entered into the t early in the morning, 2411
 5:24 high priest and the captain of the t and 2411
 5:25 ye put in prison are standing in the t, 2411
 5:42 And daily in the t, and in every house, 2411
 19:27 also that the t of the great goddess Diana 2411
 21:26 himself with them entered into the t, 2411
 21:27 when they saw him in the t, stirred up all 2411
 21:28 and further brought Greeks also into the t, 2411
 21:29 supposed that Paul had brought into the t. 2411
 21:30 they took Paul, and drew him out of the t: 2411
 22:17 even while I prayed in the t, I was in a 2411
 24: 6 also hath gone about to profane the t: 2411
 24:12 And they neither found me in the t 2411
 24:18 Jews from Asia found me purified in the t, 2411
 25: 8 neither against the t, nor yet against Cesar, 2411
 26:21 these causes the Jews caught me in the t, 2411
1Co 3:16 Know ye not that ye are the t of God, 3485
 3:17 If any man defile the t of God, him shall 3485
 3:17 for the t of God is holy, which t ye are. 3485
 3:17 the temple of God is holy, which t ye are. NIG
 6:19 know ye not that your body is the t of 3485
 8:10 hast knowledge sit at meat in the idol's t, 1493
 9:13 holy things live of the things of the t? 2411
2Co 6:16 And what agreement hath the t of God 3485
 6:16 for ye are the t of the living God; as God 3485

T

Eph	2:21	groweth unto a holy *t* in the Lord:	3485
2Th	2: 4	so that he as God sitteth in the *t* of God,	3485
Rev	3:12	will I make a pillar in the *t* of my God,	3485
	7:15	and serve him day and night in his *t*:	3485
	11: 1	and measure the *t* of God, and the altar,	3485
	11: 2	But the court which is without the *t* leave	3485
	11:19	And the *t* of God was opened in heaven,	3485
	11:19	there was seen in his the ark of his	3485
	14:15	And another angel came out of the *t*,	3485
	14:17	And another angel came out of the *t*	3485
	15: 5	the *t* of the tabernacle of the testimony in	3485
	15: 6	And the seven angels came out of the *t*,	3485
	15: 8	And the *t* was filled with smoke from	3485
	15: 8	and no *man* was able to enter into the *t*,	3485
	16: 1	And I heard a great voice out of the *t*	3485
	16:17	there came a great voice out of the *t* of	3485
	21:22	And I saw no *t* therein: for the Lord God	3485
	21:22	God Almighty and the Lamb are the *t* of it.	3485

TEMPLE SERVANTS See NETHINIMS

TEMPLES (9) [TEMPLE]

Jdg	4:21	smote the nail into his *t*, and fastened *it*	7541
	4:22	Sisera lay dead, and the nail *was* in his *t*.	7541
	5:26	had pierced and stricken through his *t*.	7541
SS	4: 3	thy *t are* like a piece of a pomegranate	7541
	6: 7	As a piece of a pomegranate *are* thy *t*	7541
Hos	8:14	hath forgotten his Maker, and buildeth *t*;	1964
Joel	3: 5	carried into your *t* my goodly pleasant	1964
Ac	7:48	Howbeit the most High dwelleth not in *t*	3485
	17:24	earth, dwelleth not in *t* made with hands;	3485

TEMPORAL (1)

2Co	4:18	for the *things* which are seen *are t*;	4340

TEMPORARY See TEMPORAL

TEMPORARY RESIDENT See SOJOURN; SOJOURNED; SOJOURNER; SOJOURNERS; SOJOURNETH; SOJOURNING

TEMPT (14) [TEMPTATION, TEMPTATIONS, TEMPTED, TEMPTER, TEMPTETH, TEMPTING]

Ge	22: 1	God did *t* Abraham, and said unto him,	5254
Ex	17: 2	with me? wherefore do ye *t* the LORD?	5254
Dt	6:16	Ye shall not *t* the LORD your God, as ye	5254
Isa	7:12	I will not ask, neither will I *t* the LORD.	5254
Mal	3:15	yea, *they that* *t* God are even delivered.	974
Mt	4: 7	Thou shalt not *t* the Lord thy God.	1598
	22:18	and said, Why *t* ye me, *ye* hypocrites?	3985
Mk	12:15	said unto them, Why *t* ye me?	3985
Lk	4:12	is said, Thou shalt not *t* the Lord thy God.	1598
	20:23	and said unto them, Why *t* ye me?	3985
Ac	5: 9	*is it* that ye have agreed together to *t*	3985
	15:10	therefore why *t* ye God, to put a yoke	3985
1Co	7: 5	Satan *t* you not for your incontinency.	3985
	10: 9	Neither let us *t* Christ, as some of them	1598

TEMPTATION (16) [TEMPT]

Ps	95: 8	*and* as *in* the day of *t* in the wilderness:	4531
Mt	6:13	And lead us not into *t*, but deliver us from	3986
	26:41	Watch and pray, that ye enter not into *t*:	3986
Mk	14:38	Watch ye and pray, lest ye enter into *t*.	3986
Lk	4:13	And when the devil had ended all the *t*,	3986
	8:13	a while believe, and in time of *t* fall away.	3986
	11: 4	And lead us not into *t*; but deliver us from	3986
	22:40	unto them, Pray that *ye* enter not into *t*.	3986
	22:46	sleep ye? rise and pray, lest ye enter into *t*.	3986
1Co	10:13	There hath no *t* taken you but such as is	3986
	10:13	will with the *t* also make a way to escape,	3986
Gal	4:14	And my *t* which was in my flesh ye	3986
1Ti	6: 9	But they that will be rich fall into *t* and	3986
Heb	3: 8	in the day of *t* in the wilderness:	3986
Jas	1:12	Blessed *is* the man that endureth *t*:	3986
Rev	3:10	I also will keep thee from the hour of *t*,	3986

TEMPTATIONS (8) [TEMPT]

Dt	4:34	*t*, by signs, and by wonders, and by war,	4531
	7:19	The great *t* which thine eyes saw,	4531
	29: 3	The great *t* which thine eyes have seen,	4531
Lk	22:28	which have continued with me in my *t*.	3986
Ac	20:19	of mind, and *with* many tears, and *t.*	3986
Jas	1: 2	count *it* all joy when ye fall into divers *t*;	3986
1Pe	1: 6	ye are in heaviness through manifold *t*:	3986
2Pe	2: 9	knoweth *how* to deliver the godly out of *t*,	3986

TEMPTED (25) [TEMPT]

Ex	17: 7	because they *t* the LORD, saying,	5254
Nu	14:22	have *t* me *now* these ten times,	5254
Dt	6:16	LORD your God, as ye *t* *him* in Massah.	5254
Ps	78:18	they *t* God in their heart by asking meat	5254
	78:41	they turned *back* and *t* God, and limited	5254
	78:56	Yet they *t* and provoked the most high	5254
	95: 9	When your fathers *t* me, proved me,	5254
	106:14	in the wilderness, and *t* God in the desert.	5254
Mt	4: 1	into the wilderness to be *t* of the devil.	3985
Mk	1:13	in the wilderness forty days, *t* of Satan;	3985
Lk	4: 2	Being forty days of the devil. And in	3985
	10:25	stood up, and *t* him, saying, Master,	1598
1Co	10: 9	some of them also *t*, and were destroyed	3985
	10:13	who will not suffer you to be *t* above that	3985
Gal	6: 1	considering thyself, lest thou also be *t*.	3985
1Th	3: 5	by some means the tempter have *t* you,	3985
Heb	2:18	in that he himself hath suffered being *t*,	3985
	2:18	he is able to succour them that are *t*.	3985
	3: 9	When your fathers *t* me, proved me,	3985

Heb	4:15	was in all *points* like as *we are, yet*	3985
	11:37	they were sawn asunder, were *t*,	3985
Jas	1:13	Let no *man* say when he is *t*, I am	3985
	1:13	say when he is tempted, I am *t* of God:	3985
	1:13	for God **cannot be** *t* with evil,	551+1510
	1:14	every man is *t*, when he is drawn away	3985

TEMPTER (2) [TEMPT]

Mt	4: 3	And when the *t* came to him, he said,	3985
1Th	3: 5	by some means the *t* have tempted you,	3985

TEMPTETH (1) [TEMPT]

Jas	1:13	tempted with evil, neither *t* he any *man*:	3985

TEMPTING (7) [TEMPT]

Mt	16: 1	*t* desired him that *he* would shew them a	3985
	19: 3	unto him, *t* him, and saying unto him,	3985
	22:35	asked *him a question*, *t* him, and saying,	3985
Mk	8:11	seeking of him a sign from heaven, *t* him.	3985
	10: 2	for a man to put away *his* wife? *t* him.	3985
Lk	11:16	*him*, sought of him a sign from heaven.	3985
Jn	8: 6	This they said, *t* him, that they might have	3985

TEN (248) [TEN'S, TENS, TENTH]

Ge	5:14	of Cainan were nine hundred and *t* years:	6235
	16: 3	after Abram had dwelt *t* years in the land	6235
	18:32	Peradventure *t* shall be found there.	6235
	24:10	the servant took *t* camels of the camels of	6235
	24:22	two bracelets for her hands of *t* *shekels*	6235
	24:55	abide with us *a few* days, at the least *t*;	6218
	31: 7	and changed my wages *t* times;	6235
	31:41	and thou hast changed my wages *t* times.	6235
	32:15	forty kine, and *t* bulls, twenty she asses,	6235
	32:15	ten bulls, twenty she asses, and *t* foals.	6235
	42: 3	Joseph's *t* brethren went down to buy	6235
	45:23	*t* asses laden with the good things of	6235
	45:23	she asses laden with corn and bread and	6235
	46:27	came into Egypt, *were* threescore and *t*.	7657
	50: 3	mourned for him **threescore and** *t*	7657
	50:22	and Joseph lived an hundred and *t* years.	6235
	50:26	*being* an hundred and *t* years old:	6235
Ex	15:27	water, and **threescore and** *t* palm trees:	7657
	26: 1	with *t* curtains of *fine* twined linen,	6235
	26:16	*T* cubits *shall be* the length of a board,	6235
	27:12	their pillars *t*, and their sockets ten.	6235
	27:12	their pillars ten, and their sockets *t*.	6235
	34:28	of the covenant, the *t* commandments.	6235
	36: 8	made *t* curtains of *fine* twined linen,	6235
	36:21	The length of a board *was t* cubits,	6235
	38:12	their pillars *t*, and their sockets ten;	6235
	38:12	their pillars ten, and their sockets *t*;	6235
Lev	26: 8	hundred of you shall put *t* **thousand**	7233
	26:26	*t* women shall bake your bread in one	6235
	27: 5	and for the female *t* shekels.	6235
	27: 7	*t* shekels, and for the female *t* shekels.	6235
Nu	7:14	One spoon of *t* *shekels* of gold, full of	6235
	7:20	One spoon of gold of *t* *shekels*, full of	6235
	7:26	One golden spoon of *t* *shekels*, full of	6235
	7:32	One golden spoon of *t* *shekels*, full of	6235
	7:38	One golden spoon of *t* *shekels*, full of	6235
	7:44	One golden spoon of *t* *shekels*, full of	6235
	7:50	One golden spoon of *t* *shekels*, full of	6235
	7:56	One golden spoon of *t* *shekels*, full of	6235
	7:62	One golden spoon of *t* *shekels*, full of	6235
	7:68	One golden spoon of *t* *shekels*, full of	6235
	7:74	One golden spoon of *t* *shekels*, full of	6235
	7:80	One golden spoon of *t* *shekels*, full of	6235
	7:86	full *of* incense, weighing *t* *shekels* apiece,	6235
	11:19	two days, nor five days, neither *t* days,	6235
	11:32	he that gathered least gathered *t* homers:	6235
	14:22	have tempted me *now* these *t* times,	6235
	29:23	on the fourth day *t* bullocks, two rams,	6235
	33: 9	water, and **threescore and** *t* palm trees;	7657
Dt	4:13	you to perform, *even t* commandments;	6235
	10: 4	to the first writing, the *t* commandments,	6235
	10:22	down into Egypt with **threescore and** *t*	7657
	32:30	two put *t* **thousand** to flight, except their	7233
	33: 2	and he came with *t* **thousands** of saints:	7233
	33:17	they *are* the *t* thousands of Ephraim,	6235
Jos	15:57	and Timnah; *t* cities with their villages.	6235
	17: 5	there fell *t* portions to Manasseh, beside	6235
	21: 5	out of the half tribe of Manasseh, *t* cities.	6235
	21:26	All the cities *were t* with their suburbs for	6235
	22:14	with him *t* princes, of each chief house a	6235
	24:29	died, *being* an hundred and *t* years old.	6235
Jdg	1: 4	slew *of* them in Bezek *t* thousand men.	6235
	1: 7	**Threescore and** *t* kings, having their	7657
	2: 8	died, *being* an hundred and *t* years old.	6235
	3:29	they slew *of* Moab at that time about *t*	6235
	4: 6	take with thee *t* thousand men of	6235
	4:10	went up with *t* thousand men at his feet;	6235
	4:14	and *t* thousand men after him.	6235
	6:27	Gideon took *t* men of his servants,	6235
	7: 3	and there remained *t* thousand.	6235
	8:30	Gideon had **threescore and** *t* sons of his	7657
	9: 2	*which are* **threescore and** *t* persons,	7657
	9: 4	they gave him **threescore and** *t* *pieces*	7657
	9: 5	*being* **threescore and** *t* persons, upon	7657
	9:18	**threescore and** *t* persons, upon one	7657
	9:24	the cruelty *done* to the **threescore and** *t*	7657
	12:11	judged Israel; and he judged Israel *t* years.	6235
	12:14	that rode on **threescore and** *t* ass colts:	7651
	17:10	I will give thee *t* *shekels* of silver by	6235
	20:10	we will take *t* men of an hundred	6235
	20:10	and a thousand out of *t* **thousand**,	7233

Jdg	20:34	there came against Gibeah *t* thousand	6235
Ru	1: 4	and they dwelled there about *t* years.	6235
	4: 2	he took *t* men of the elders of the city,	6235
1Sa	1: 8	*am* not I better to thee than *t* sons?	6235
	6:19	fifty thousand and **threescore and** *t* men:	7657
	15: 4	and *t* thousand men of Judah.	6235
	17:17	of this parched *corn*, and these *t* loaves,	6235
	17:18	carry these *t* cheeses unto the captain of	6235
	18: 7	thousands, and David his *t* thousands,	7233
	18: 8	have ascribed unto David *t* **thousands**,	7233
	21:11	thousands, and David his *t* **thousands**?	7233
	25: 5	David sent out *t* young men,	6235
	25:38	it came to pass about *t* days *after*, that	6235
	29: 5	thousands, and David his *t* **thousands**?	7233
2Sa	15:16	the king left *t* women, *which were*	6235
	18: 3	now *thou art* worth *t* thousand of us:	6235
	18:11	would have given thee *t* *shekels* of silver,	6235
	18:15	*t* young men that bare Joab's armour	6235
	19:43	We have *t* parts in the king, and we have	6235
	20: 3	king took the *t* women *his* concubines,	6235
1Ki	4:23	*t* fat oxen, and twenty oxen out of	6235
	5:14	Lebanon, *t* thousand a month *by* courses:	6235
	5:15	Solomon had **threescore and** *t* thousand	7657
	6: 3	*t* cubits *was* the breadth thereof before	6235
	6:23	cherubims *of* olive tree, each *t* cubits high.	6235
	6:24	uttermost part of the other *were t* cubits.	6235
	6:25	the other cherub *was t* cubits: both	6235
	6:26	The height of the one cherub *was t* cubits,	6235
	7:10	stones of *t* cubits, and stones of eight	6235
	7:23	cubits from the one brim to the other:	6235
	7:24	*t* in a cubit, compassing the sea round	6235
	7:27	he made *t* bases of brass; four cubits *was*	6235
	7:37	After this *manner* he made the *t* bases:	6235
	7:38	made he *t* lavers of brass: one laver	6235
	7:38	upon every one of the *t* bases one laver.	6235
	7:43	the *t* bases, and ten lavers on the bases;	6235
	7:43	the ten bases, and *t* lavers on the bases;	6235
	11:31	he said to Jeroboam, Take thee *t* pieces:	6235
	11:31	of Solomon, and will give *t* tribes to thee:	6235
	11:35	and will give it unto thee, *even t* tribes.	6235
	14: 3	take with thee *t* loaves, and cracknels,	6235
2Ki	5: 5	took with him *t* talents of silver,	6235
	5: 5	*pieces* of gold, and *t* changes of raiment.	6235
	13: 7	and *t* chariots, and ten thousand footmen;	6235
	13: 7	and ten chariots, and *t* thousand footmen;	6235
	14: 7	He slew *of* Edom in the valley of salt *t*	6235
	15:17	Israel, *and reigned t* years in Samaria.	6235
	20: 9	shall the shadow go forward *t* degrees,	6235
	20: 9	forward ten degrees, or go back *t* degrees?	6235
	20:10	for the shadow to go down *t* degrees:	6235
	20:10	let the shadow return backward *t* degrees.	6235
	20:11	brought the shadow *t* degrees backward,	6235
	24:14	*even t* thousand captives, and all	6240
	25:25	and *t* men with him, and smote Gedaliah,	6235
1Ch	6:61	the half *tribe* of Manasseh, by lot, *t* cities.	6235
	21: 5	*was* four hundred **threescore and** *t*	7657
	29: 7	thousand talents and *t* **thousand** drams,	7239
	29: 7	of silver *t* thousand talents, and *of* brass	7657
2Ch	2: 2	Solomon told out **threescore and** *t*	7657
	2:18	he set **threescore and** *t* thousand of	7657
	4: 1	and *t* cubits the height thereof.	6235
	4: 2	he made a molten sea of *t* cubits from	6235
	4: 3	*t* in a cubit, compassing the sea round	6235
	4: 6	He made also *t* lavers, and put five on	6235
	4: 7	made *t* candlesticks of gold according to	6235
	4: 8	He made also *t* tables, and placed *them* in	6235
	14: 1	In his days the land was quiet *t* years.	6235
	25:11	smote *of* the children of Seir *t* thousand.	6235
	25:12	*t* thousand *left* alive did the children	6235
	27: 5	thousand measures of wheat,	6235
	27: 5	of wheat, and *t* thousand of barley.	6235
	29:32	**threescore and** *t* bullocks, an hundred	7657
	30:24	thousand bullocks and *t* thousand sheep:	6235
	36: 9	three months and *t* days in Jerusalem:	6235
	36:21	to fulfil **threescore and** *t* years.	7657
Ezr	1:10	of a second sort four hundred and *t*,	6235
	8:12	and with him an hundred and *t* males.	6235
	8:24	out of their brethren with them,	6235
Ne	4:12	by them came, they said unto us *t* times,	6235
	5:18	once in *t* days store of *all sorts of* wine:	6235
	11: 1	to bring one of *t* to dwell in Jerusalem	6235
Est	3: 9	I will pay *t* thousand talents of silver to	6235
	9:10	The *t* sons of Haman the son of	6235
	9:12	the palace, and the *t* sons of Haman;	6235
	9:13	let Haman's *t* sons be hanged upon	6235
	9:14	and they hanged Haman's *t* sons.	6235
Job	19: 3	These *t* times have ye reproached me:	6235
Ps	3: 6	I will not be afraid of *t* **thousands** of	7233
	33: 2	psaltery *and* an **instrument** of *t* strings.	6218
	90:10	of our years *are* threescore years and *t*;	7657
	91: 7	*t* side, and *t* **thousand** at thy right hand;	7233
	92: 3	Upon an **instrument** of *t* strings,	6218
	144: 9	an **instrument** of *t* strings will I sing	6218
	144:13	and *t* **thousands** in our streets:	7231
Ecc	7:19	strengtheneth the wise more than *t*	6235
SS	5:10	ruddy, the chiefest among *t* **thousand**.	7233
Isa	5:10	*t* acres of vineyard shall yield one bath,	6235
	38: 8	the sun dial of Ahaz, *t* degrees backward.	6235
	38: 8	So the sun returned *t* degrees, by which	6235
Jer	41: 1	princes of the king, even *t* men with him,	6235
	41: 2	the *t* men that were with him,	6235
	41: 8	*t* men were found among them that said	6235
	42: 7	it came to pass after *t* days, that the word	6235
Eze	40:11	breadth of the entry of the gate, *t* cubits;	6235
	41: 2	the breadth of the door *was t* cubits;	6235

Eze	42: 4 the chambers *was* a walk of **t** cubits	6235
	45: 1 and the breadth *shall be* **t** thousand.	6235
	45: 3 and the breadth of **t** thousand:	6235
	45: 5 *the* **t** thousand of breadth, shall also	6235
	45:14 of the cor, *which is* a homer of **t** baths;	6235
	45:14 of ten baths; for **t** baths *are* a homer:	6235
	48: 9 in length, and *of* **t** thousand *in* breadth.	6235
	48:10 toward the west **t** thousand *in* breadth,	6235
	48:10 toward the east **t** thousand *in* breadth:	6235
	48:13 in length, and **t** thousand *in* breadth:	6235
	48:13 and the breadth **t** thousand.	6235
	48:18 *portion shall be* **t** thousand eastward,	6235
	48:18 and **t** thousand westward:	6235
Da	1:12 Prove thy servants, I beseech thee, **t** days;	6235
	1:14 in this matter, and proved them **t** days.	6235
	1:15 at the end of **t** days their countenances	6235
	1:20 he found them **t** times better than all	6235
	7: 7 that *were* before it; and it had **t** horns.	6236
	7:10 **t thousand** times ten thousand stood	7240
	7:10 ten thousand times **t thousand** stood	7240
	7:20 of the **t** horns that *were* in his head,	6236
	7:24 the **t** horns out of this kingdom *are* ten	6236
	7:24 the ten horns out of this kingdom *are* **t**	6236
	11:12 he shall cast down *many* **t thousands:**	7239
Am	5: 3 went forth *by* an hundred shall leave **t**,	6235
	6: 9 if there remain **t** men in one house,	6235
Mic	6: 7 *or* with **t thousands** of rivers of oil?	7233
Hag	2:16 of twenty *measures*, there were but **t**:	6235
Zec	1:12 had indignation these **threescore and t**	7657
	5: 2 and the breadth thereof **t** cubits.	6235
	8:23 In those days *it shall come to pass*, that **t**	6235
Mt	18:24 which ought him **t thousand** talents.	3463
	20:24 when they heard *it*, they were moved	1176
	25: 1 of heaven be likened unto **t** virgins,	1176
	25:28 and give *it* unto him which hath **t** talents.	1176
Mk	10:41 And when the **t** heard *it*, they began to be	1176
Lk	14:31 consulteth whether he be able with **t**	1176
	15: 8 Either what woman having **t** pieces of	1176
	17:12 there met him **t** men *that were* lepers,	1176
	17:17 said, Were there not **t** cleansed?	1176
	19:13 And he called his **t** servants,	1176
	19:13 delivered them **t** pounds, and said unto	1176
	19:16 Lord, thy pound hath gained **t** pounds.	1176
	19:17 little, have thou authority over **t** cities.	1176
	19:24 and give *it* to him that hath **t** pounds.	1176
	19:25 said unto him, Lord, he hath **t** pounds.)	1176
Ac	23:23 and horsemen **threescore** *and* **t**,	1440
	25: 6 had tarried among them more than **t** days,	1176
1Co	4:15 though you have **t thousand** instructors	3463
	14:19 than **t thousand** words in an *unknown*	3463
Jude	1:14 the Lord cometh with **t thousands** of his	3461
Rev	2:10 and ye shall have tribulation **t** days:	1176
	5:11 number of them was **t thousand** times	3461
	5:11 them was ten thousand times **t thousand**,	3461
	12: 3 having seven heads and **t** horns,	1176
	13: 1 having seven heads and **t** horns,	1176
	13: 1 upon his horns **t** crowns, and upon his	1176
	17: 3 having seven heads and **t** horns.	1176
	17: 7 which hath the seven heads and **t** horns.	1176
	17:12 the **t** horns which thou sawest are ten	1176
	17:12 the ten horns which thou sawest are **t**	1176
	17:16 the **t** horns which thou sawest upon	1176

TEN'S (1) [TEN]

Ge	18:32 he said, I will not destroy *it* for **t** sake.	6235

TEND (1) [TENDETH]

Pr	21: 5 The thoughts of the diligent *t* only to	NIH

TENDER (40) [TENDERHEARTED, TENDERNESS]

Ge	18: 7 fetch a calf **t** and good, and gave *it* unto	7390
	29:17 Leah was **t** eyed; but Rachel was beautiful	7390
	33:13 My lord knoweth that the children *are* **t**,	7390
Dt	28:54 *So that* the man *that is* **t** among you,	7390
	28:56 The **t** and delicate *woman* among you,	7390
	32: 2 as the small rain upon the **t herb**, and as	1877
2Sa	3:39 and *as* the **t grass** springing out of the earth	1877
2Ki	22:19 Because thine heart was **t**, and thou hast	7401
1Ch	22: 5 Solomon my son *is* young and **t**,	7390
	29: 1 *is yet* young and **t**, and the work *is* great:	7390
2Ch	13: 7 Rehoboam was young and **t** hearted,	7390
	34:27 Because thine heart was **t**, and thou didst	7401
Job	14: 7 that the **t branch** thereof will not cease.	3127
	38:27 to cause the bud of the **t herb** to spring	1877
Ps	25: 6 thy **t mercies** and thy lovingkindnesses,	7356
	40:11 Withhold not thou thy **t mercies** from	7356
	51: 1 thy **t mercies** blot out my transgressions.	7356
	69:16 to the multitude of thy **t mercies**.	7356
	77: 9 hath he in anger shut up his **t mercies**?	7356
	79: 8 let thy **t mercies** speedily prevent us:	7356
	103: 4 who with lovingkindness and **t mercies**;	7356
	119:77 Let thy **t mercies** come *unto* me, that I	7356
	119:156 Great *are* thy **t mercies**, O LORD:	7356
	145: 9 and his **t mercies** *are* over all his works.	7356
Pr	4: 3 **t** and only *beloved* in the sight of my	7390
	12:10 the **t mercies** of the wicked *are* cruel.	7356
	27:25 the **t grass** sheweth itself, and herbs of	1877
SS	2:13 the vines *with* the **t grape** give a *good*	5563
	2:15 the vines: for our vines *have* **t grapes**.	5563
	7:12 *whether* the **t grape** appear,	5563
Isa	47: 1 for thou shalt no more be called **t** and	7390
	53: 2 he shall grow up before as a **t plant**,	3126
Eze	17:22 from the top of his young twigs a **t** one,	7390
Da	1: 9 **t love** with the prince of the eunuchs.	7356
	4:15 iron and brass, in the **t grass** of the field;	1883

Da	4:23 iron and brass, in the **t grass** of the field;	1883
Mt	24:32 When his branch is yet **t**, and putteth forth	527
Mk	13:28 When her branch is yet **t**, and putteth forth	527
Lk	1:78 Through the **t mercy** of our God;	1656+4698
Jas	5:11 the Lord is very pitiful, and of **t mercy**.	3629

TENDERHEARTED (1) [HEART, TENDER]

Eph	4:32 one to another, **t**, forgiving one another,	2155

TENDERNESS (1) [TENDER]

Dt	28:56 upon the ground for delicateness and **t**,	7391

TENDETH (5) [TEND]

Pr	10:16 The labour of the righteous *t* to life:	NIH
	11:19 As righteousness *t* to life: so he that	NIH
	11:24 more than is meet, but *it t* to poverty.	NIH
	14:23 but the talk of the lips *t* only to penury.	NIH
	19:23 The fear of the LORD *t* to life: and *he* that	NIH

TENONS (6)

Ex	26:17 Two **t** *shall there be* in one board, set in	3027
	26:19 sockets under one board for his two **t**,	3027
	26:19 sockets under another board for his two **t**.	3027
	36:22 One board had two **t**, equally distant one	3027
	36:24 sockets under one board for his two **t**;	3027
	36:24 sockets under another board for his two **t**.	3027

TENOR (2)

Ge	43: 7 we told him according to the **t** of these	6310
Ex	34:27 for after the **t** of these words I have made	6310

TENS (3) [TENS]

Ex	18:21 rulers of fifties, and rulers of **t**:	6235
	18:25 hundreds, rulers of fifties, and rulers of **t**.	6235
Dt	1:15 captains over **t**, and officers among your	6235

TENT (98) [TENTMAKERS, TENTS]

Ge	9:21 and he was uncovered within his **t**.	168
	12: 8 pitched his **t**, *having* Beth-el on the west,	168
	13: 3 unto the place where his **t** had been at	168
	13:12 plain, and **pitched** his **t** toward Sodom.	167
	13:18 Abram **removed** his **t**, and came and	167
	18: 1 he sat *in* the **t** door in the heat of the day;	168
	18: 2 he ran to meet them from the **t** door,	168
	18: 6 Abraham hastened into the **t** unto Sarah,	168
	18: 9 thy wife? And he said, Behold, in the **t**.	168
	18:10 Sarah heard *it* in the **t** door, which *was*	168
	24:67 Isaac brought her into his mother Sarah's **t**,	168
	26:17 **pitched** his **t** in the valley of Gerar,	2583
	26:25 name of the LORD, and pitched his **t** there:	168
	31:25 Now Jacob had pitched his **t** in the mount:	168
	31:33 Laban went into Jacob's **t**, and into Leah's	168
	31:33 Leah's **t**, and into the two maidservants'	168
	31:33 went he out of Leah's **t**, and entered into	168
	31:33 of Leah's **tent**, and entered into Rachel's **t**.	168
	31:34 searched all the **t**, but found *them* not.	168
	33:18 and **pitched** his **t** before the city.	2583
	33:19 parcel of a field, where he had spread his **t**,	168
	35:21 and spread his **t** beyond the tower of Edar.	168
Ex	18: 7 of *their* welfare; and they came into the **t**.	168
	26:11 couple the **t** together, that it may be one.	168
	26:12 that remaineth of the curtains of the **t**,	168
	26:13 in the length of the curtains of the **t**,	168
	26:14 shalt make a covering for the **t** *of* rams'	168
	26:36 shalt make a hanging for the door of the **t**,	168
	33: 8 stood every man *at* his **t** door,	168
	33:10 and worshipped, every man *in* his **t** door.	168
	35:11 his **t**, and his covering, his taches,	168
	36:14 made curtains of goats' **hair** for the **t** over	168
	36:18 made fifty taches of brass to couple the **t**	168
	36:19 he made a covering for the **t** *of* rams' skins	168
	39:32 of the **t** of the congregation finished:	168
	39:33 the **t**, and all his furniture, his taches,	168
	39:40 tabernacle, for the **t** of the congregation,	168
	40: 2 tabernacle of the **t** of the congregation.	168
	40: 6 the tabernacle of the **t** of the congregation.	168
	40: 7 thou shalt set the laver between the **t** of	168
	40:19 he spread abroad the **t** over the tabernacle,	168
	40:19 put the covering of the **t** above *upon* it;	168
	40:22 put the table in the **t** of the congregation,	168
	40:24 he put the candlestick in the **t** of	168
	40:26 he put the golden altar in the **t** of	168
	40:29 the tabernacle of the **t** of the congregation,	168
	40:30 he set the laver between the **t** of	168
	40:32 When they went into the **t** of	168
	40:34 a cloud covered the **t** of the congregation,	168
	40:35 Moses was not able to enter into the **t** of	168
Lev	14: 8 shall tarry abroad out of his **t** seven days.	168
Nu	3:25 the **t**, the covering thereof, and the hanging	168
	9:15 *namely*, the **t** of the Testimony:	168
	11:10 families, every man in the door of his **t**:	168
	19:14 This *is* the law, when a man dieth in a **t**:	168
	19:14 all that come into the **t**, and all that *is* in	168
	19:14 come into the tent, and all that *is* in the **t**,	168
	19:18 sprinkle *it* upon the **t**, and upon all	168
	25: 8 he went after the man of Israel into the **t**,	6898
Jos	7:21 *are* hid in the earth in the midst of my **t**,	168
	7:22 sent messengers, and they ran unto the **t**;	168
	7:22 *it was* hid in his **t**, and the silver under it.	168
	7:23 they took them out of the midst of the **t**,	168
	7:24 his sheep, and his **t**, and all that he had:	168
Jdg	4:11 pitched his **t** unto the plain of Zaanaim,	168
	4:17 Sisera fled away on his feet to the **t**	168
	4:18 when he had turned in unto her into the **t**,	168
	4:20 Stand *in* the door of the **t**, and it shall be,	168

Jdg	4:21 Jael Heber's wife took a nail of the **t**,	168
	4:22 he came into her **t**, behold, Sisera lay	NIH
	5:24 blessed shall she be above women in the **t**.	168
	7: 8 all *the rest of* Israel every man unto his **t**,	168
	7:13 came unto a **t**, and smote it that it fell,	168
	7:13 fell, and overturned it, that the **t** lay along.	168
	20: 8 We will not any *of us* go to his **t**,	168
1Sa	4:10 and they fled every man into his **t**:	168
	13: 2 of the people he sent every man to his **t**.	168
	17:54 Jerusalem; but he put his armour in his **t**.	168
2Sa	7: 6 but have walked in a **t** and in a tabernacle.	168
	16:22 So they spread Absalom a **t** upon the top of	168
	18:17 and all Israel fled every one to his **t**.	168
	19: 8 for Israel had fled every man to his **t**.	168
	20:22 retired from the city, every man to his **t**.	168
2Ki	7: 8 went into one **t**, and did eat and drink,	168
	7: 8 entered into another **t**, and carried thence	168
1Ch	15: 1 for the ark of God, and pitched for it a **t**.	168
	16: 1 set it in the midst of the **t** that David had	168
	17: 5 have gone from **t** to tent, and from *one*	168
	17: 5 have gone from tent to **t**, and from *one*	168
2Ch	1: 4 for he had pitched a **t** for it at Jerusalem.	168
	25:22 and they fled every man to his **t**.	168
Ps	78:60 Shiloh, the **t** *which* he placed among men;	168
Isa	13:20 neither shall the Arabian **pitch t** there;	167
	38:12 and is removed from me as a shepherd's **t**:	168
	40:22 and spreadeth them out as a **t** to dwell in:	168
	54: 2 Enlarge the place of thy **t**, and let them	168
Jer	10:20 *is* none to stretch forth my **t** any more,	168
	37:10 *yet* should they rise up every man in his **t**,	168

TENTH (81) [TENS]

Ge	8: 5 waters decreased continually until the **t**	6224
	8: 5 in the **t** *month*, on the first *day* of	6224
	28:22 I will **surely give** the **t** unto thee.	6237+6237
Ex	12: 3 In the **t** *day* of this month they shall take	6218
	16:36 Now an omer *is* the **t** *part* of an ephah.	6224
	29:40 the one lamb a **t deal** of flour mingled	6241
Lev	5:11 **t** *part* of an ephah of fine flour for a sin	6224
	6:20 the **t** *part* of an ephah of fine flour *for* a	6224
	14:10 **three t deals** of fine flour *for* a	6241+7969
	14:21 **one t deal** of fine flour mingled	259+6241
	16:29 on the **t** *day* of the month, ye shall afflict	6218
	23:13 two **t deals** of fine flour mingled with oil,	6241
	23:17 two wave loaves of two **t deals**:	6241
	23:27 Also on the **t** *day* of this seventh month	6218
	24: 5 two **t deals** shall be *in* one cake.	6241
	25: 9 sound on the **t** *day* of the seventh month,	6218
	27:32 the **t** shall be holy unto the LORD.	6224
Nu	5:15 the **t** *part* of an ephah of barley meal;	6224
	7:66 On the **t** *day* Ahiezer the son of	6224
	15: 4 **t deal** *of* flour mingled with the fourth	6241
	15: 6 **t deals** *of* flour mingled with the third	6241
	15: 9 **t deals** *of* flour mingled with half a hin of	6241
	18:21 I have given the children of Levi all the **t**	4643
	18:26 it for the LORD, *even* a **t** *part* of the tithe.	4643
	28: 5 a **t** *part* of an ephah of flour for a meat	6224
	28: 9 two **t deals** *of* flour *for* a meat offering,	6241
	28:12 three **t deals** *of* flour *for* a meat offering,	6241
	28:12 two **t deals** *of* flour *for* a meat offering,	6241
	28:13 a **several t deal** of flour mingled	6241+6241
	28:20 three **t deals** shall ye offer for a bullock,	6241
	28:20 for a bullock, and two **t deals** for a ram;	6241
	28:21 A **several t deal** shalt thou offer	6241+6241
	28:28 three **t deals** unto one bullock, two tenth	6241
	28:28 one bullock, two **t deals** unto one ram,	6241
	28:29 A **several t deal** unto one lamb,	6241+6241
	29: 3 three **t deals** for a bullock, *and* two tenth	6241
	29: 3 for a bullock, *and* two **t deals** for a ram,	6241
	29: 4 one **t deal** for one lamb, throughout	6241
	29: 7 ye shall have on the **t** *day* of this seventh	6218
	29: 9 three **t deals** to a bullock, *and* two tenth	6241
	29: 9 to a bullock, *and* two **t deals** to one ram,	6241
	29:10 A **several t deal** for one lamb,	6241+6241
	29:14 three **t deals** unto every bullock of	6241
	29:14 two **t deals** to each ram of the two rams,	6241
	29:15 a **several t deal** to each lamb of	6241+6241
Dt	23: 2 even *to* his **t** generation shall he not enter	6224
	23: 3 even *to* their **t** generation shall they not	6224
Jos	4:19 the people came up out of Jordan on the **t**	6218
1Sa	8:15 he will **take** the **t** of your seed, and of	6237
	8:17 He will **take** the **t** of your sheep:	6237
2Ki	25: 1 in the **t** month, in the tenth *day* of	6224
	25: 1 tenth month, in the **t** *day* of	6218
1Ch	12:13 Jeremiah the, Machbanai the eleventh.	6224
	24:11 The ninth to Jeshua, the **t** to Shecaniah,	6224
	25:17 The **t** *to* Shimei, *he*, his sons,	6224
	27:13 The **t** captain for the tenth month *was*	6224
	27:13 the tenth *captain* for the **t** month *was*	6224
Ezr	10:16 sat down in the first day of the **t** month to	6224
Est	2:16 into his house royal in the **t** month,	6224
Isa	6:13 yet in it *shall be* a **t**, and *it* shall return,	6224
Jer	32: 1 in the **t** year of Zedekiah king of Judah,	6224
	39: 1 in the **t** month, came Nebuchadrezzar	6224
	52: 4 in the **t** month, in the tenth *day* of	6224
	52: 4 tenth month, in the **t** *day* of	6218
	52:12 fifth month, in the **t** *day* of the month,	6218
Eze	20: 1 the **t** *month*, the **t** *day* of the month,	6224
	24: 1 Again in the ninth year, in the **t** month,	6224
	24: 1 tenth month, in the **t** *day* of the month,	6218
	29: 1 In the **t** year, in the tenth *month*, in	6224
	29: 1 in the **t** *month*, in the twelfth *day* of	6224
	33:21 in the **t** *month*, in the fifth *day* of	6224
	40: 1 of the year, in the **t** *day* of the month,	6218
	45:11 that the bath may contain the **t part** of a	4643

T

Eze	45:11 and the ephah the **t** *part* of a homer:	6224
	45:14 ye shall *offer* the **t** *part* of a bath out of	4643
Zec	8:19 fast of the seventh, and the fast of the,	6224
Jn	1:39 him that day: for it was about the **t** hour.	1182
Heb	7: 2 whom also Abraham gave a **t** *part* of all;	1181
	7: 4 patriarch Abraham gave the **t** of the spoils.	1181
Rev	11:13 and the **t** *part* of the city fell, and in	1182
	21:20 the ninth, a topaz; the **t**, a chrysoprasus;	1182

TENTMAKERS (1) [MAKE, TENT]

Ac	18: 3 for *by* their occupation they were **t**.	4635

TENTS (66) [TENT]

Ge	4:20 he was the father of such as dwell in **t**,	168
	9:27 and he shall dwell in the **t** of Shem;	168
	13: 5 with Abram, had flocks, and herds, and **t**.	168
	25:27 and Jacob was a plain man, dwelling in **t**.	168
	31:33 and into the two maidservants' **t**;	168
Ex	16:16 ye every man for *them* which *are* in his **t**.	168
Nu	1:52 the children of Israel shall **pitch** their **t**,	2583
	9:17 the children of Israel **pitched** their **t**.	2583
	9:18 upon the tabernacle they **rested** in the **t**.	2583
	9:20 of the Lord they **abode in** their **t**,	2583
	9:22 the children of Israel **abode in** their **t**,	2583
	9:23 of the Lord they **rested in** the **t**,	2583
	13:19 dwell in, whether in **t**, or in strong holds;	4264
	16:26 from the **t** of these wicked men,	168
	16:27 *in* the door of their **t**, and their wives,	168
	24: 2 he saw Israel abiding *in his* **t** according to	NIH
	24: 5 How goodly are thy **t**, O Jacob,	168
Dt	1:27 ye murmured in your **t**, and said,	168
	1:33 search you out a place to **pitch** your **t** *in*,	2583
	5:30 Go say to them, Get you into your **t** again.	168
	11: 6 their **t**, and all the substance that *was* in	168
	16: 7 turn in the morning, and go unto thy **t**.	168
	33:18 in thy going out; and, Issachar, in thy **t**.	168
Jos	3:14 when the people removed from their **t**,	168
	22: 4 get ye unto your **t**, *and* unto the land of	168
	22: 6 them away: and they went unto their **t**.	168
	22: 7 Joshua sent them away also unto their **t**,	168
	22: 8 Return with much riches unto your **t**,	168
	8:11 them that dwelt in **t** on the east of Nobah	168
1Sa	17:53 the Philistines, and they spoiled their **t**.	4264
2Sa	11:11 The ark, and Israel, and Judah, abide in **t**;	5521
	20: 1 son of Jesse: every man to his **t**, O Israel.	168
1Ki	8:66 went unto their **t** joyful and glad of heart	168
	12:16 to your **t**, O Israel: now see to thine own	168
	12:16 David. So Israel departed unto their **t**.	168
2Ki	7: 7 left their **t**, and their horses, and their asses,	168
	7:10 and asses tied, and the **t** as they *were*.	168
	7:16 went out, and spoiled the **t** of the Syrians.	4264
	8:21 chariots: and the people fled into their **t**.	168
	13: 5 the children of Israel dwelt in their **t**,	168
	14:12 and they fled every man to their **t**.	168
1Ch	4:41 smote their **t**, and the habitations that were	168
	5:10 they dwelt in their **t** throughout all the east	168
2Ch	7:10 month he sent the people away into their **t**,	168
	10:16 every man to your **t**, O Israel: *and* now,	168
	10:16 own house. So all Israel went to their **t**.	168
	14:15 They smote also the **t** of cattle,	168
	31: 2 to praise in the gates of the **t** of the Lord.	4264
Ezr	8:15 and there **abode** we in **t** three days:	2583
Ps	69:25 be desolate; *and* let none dwell in their **t**.	168
	78:55 made the tribes of Israel to dwell in their **t**.	168
	84:10 than to dwell in the **t** of wickedness.	168
	106:25 murmured in their **t**, *and* hearkened not	168
	120: 5 *in* Mesech, *that* I dwell in the **t** of Kedar!	168
SS	1: 5 the **t** of Kedar, as the curtains of Solomon.	168
	1: 8 and feed thy kids beside the shepherds' **t**.	4908
Jer	4:20 suddenly are my **t** spoiled, *and* my curtains	168
	6: 3 they shall pitch *their* **t** against her round	168
	30:18 I *will* bring again the captivity of Jacob's **t**,	168
	35: 7 but all your days ye shall dwell in **t**;	168
	35:10 we have dwelt in **t**, and have obeyed,	168
	49:29 Their **t** and their flocks shall they take	168
Hab	3: 7 I saw the **t** of Cushan in affliction:	168
Zec	12: 7 The Lord also shall save the **t** of Judah	168
	14:15 of all the beasts that shall be in these **t**,	4264

TERAH (11) [THARA]

Ge	11:24 lived nine and twenty years, and begat **T**:	8646
	11:25 Nahor lived after he begat **T** an hundred	8646
	11:26 **T** lived seventy years, and begat Abram,	8646
	11:27 Now these *are* the generations of **T**:	8646
	11:27 **T** begat Abram, Nahor, and Haran;	8646
	11:28 Haran died before his father **T** in the land	8646
	11:31 **T** took Abram his son, and Lot the son of	8646
	11:32 the days of **T** were two hundred and	8646
	11:32 five years: and **T** died in Haran.	8646
Jos	24: 2 *even* **T**, the father of Abraham,	8646
1Ch	1:26 Serug, Nahor, **T**,	8646

TERAPHIM (6)

Jdg	17: 5 and **t**, and consecrated one of his sons,	8655
	18:14 **t**, and a graven image, and a molten	8655
	18:17 ephod, and the **t**, and the molten image:	8655
	18:18 ephod, and the **t**, and the molten image:	8655
	18:20 the **t**, and the graven image, and went in	8655
Hos	3: 4 and without an ephod, and *without* **t**:	8655

TEREBINTH See TEIL

TERESH (2)

Est	2:21 Bigthan and **T**, of those which kept	8657
	6: 2 that Mordecai had told of Bigthana and **T**,	8657

TERMED (2)

Isa	62: 4 Thou shalt no more be **t** Forsaken;	559
	62: 4 neither shall thy land any more be **t**	559

TERRACES (1)

2Ch	9:11 the king made *of* the algum trees **t** to	4546

TERRESTRIAL (2)

1Co	15:40 *are* also celestial bodies, and bodies **t**:	1919
	15:40 *is* one, and the *glory* of the **t** *is* another.	1919

TERRIBLE (52) [TERRIFY]

Ex	34:10 for it *is* a **t** thing that I will do with thee.	3372
Dt	1:19 through all that great and **t** wilderness,	3372
	7:21 God *is* among you, a mighty God and **t**.	3372
	8:15 thee through *that* great and **t** wilderness,	3372
	10:17 of lords, a great God, a mighty, and a **t**,	3372
	10:21 and **t** *things*, which thine eyes have seen.	3372
Jdg	13: 6 countenance of an angel of God, very **t**:	3372
2Sa	7:23 to do for you great things and **t**, for thy	3372
Ne	1: 5 great and **t** God, that keepeth covenant	3372
	4:14 which *is* great and **t**, and fight for your	3372
	9:32 the great, the mighty, and the **t** God,	3372
Job	37:22 out of the north: with God *is* **t** majesty.	3372
	39:20 grasshopper? the glory of his nostrils *is* **t**.	367
	41:14 of his face? his teeth *are* **t** round about.	367
Ps	45: 4 thy right hand shall teach thee **t** *things*.	3372
	47: 2 For the Lord most High *is* **t**; *he is* a	3372
	65: 5 By **t** things in righteousness wilt thou	3372
	66: 3 unto God, How **t** *art thou* in thy works!	3372
	66: 5 he *is* **t** in *his* doing toward the children of	3372
	68:35 O God, *thou art* **t** out of thy holy places:	3372
	76:12 of princes: *he is* **t** to the kings of the earth.	3372
	99: 3 Let them praise thy great and **t** name; *for*	3372
	106:22 land of Ham, *and* **t** things by the Red sea.	3372
	145: 6 *men* shall speak of the might of thy **t** *acts*:	3372
SS	6: 4 as Jerusalem, **t** as *an army* with banners.	366
	6:10 as the sun, *and* **t** as *an army* with banners?	366
Isa	13:11 and will lay low the haughtiness of the **t**.	6184
	18: 2 a people **t** from their beginning hitherto;	3372
	18: 7 from a people **t** from their beginning	3372
	21: 1 it cometh from the desert, from a **t** land.	3372
	25: 3 the city of the **t** nations shall fear thee.	6184
	25: 4 when the blast of the **t** ones *is* as a storm	6184
	25: 5 the branch of the **t** ones shall be brought	6184
	29: 5 multitude of the **t** ones *shall be* as chaff	6184
	29:20 For the **t** one is brought to **nought**,	6184
	49:25 and the prey of the **t** shall be delivered:	6184
	64: 3 thou didst **t** *things* which we looked	3372
Jer	15:21 will redeem thee out of the hand of the **t**.	6184
	20:11 the Lord *is* with me as a mighty **t** one:	6184
La	5:10 like an oven because of the **t** famine.	2152
Eze	1:22 creature *was* as the colour of the **t** crystal,	3372
	28: 7 strangers upon thee, the **t** of the nations:	6184
	30:11 his people with him, the **t** of the nations,	6184
	31:12 the **t** of the nations, have cut him	6184
	32:12 to fall, the **t** of the nations, all of them:	6184
Da	2:31 before thee; and the form thereof *was* **t**.	1763
	7: 7 dreadful and **t**, and strong exceedingly;	574
Joel	2:11 the day of the Lord *is* great and very **t**;	3372
	2:31 and *the* **t** day of the Lord come.	3372
Hab	1: 7 They *are* **t** and dreadful: their judgment	366
Zep	2:11 The Lord *will be* **t** unto them: for he will	3372
Heb	12:21 And so **t** was the sight, *that* Moses said,	5398

TERRIBLENESS (3) [TERRIFY]

Dt	26: 8 with great **t**, and with signs,	4172
1Ch	17:21 to make thee a name of greatness and **t**,	3372
Jer	49:16 Thy **t** hath deceived thee, *and* the pride	8606

TERRIBLY (3) [TERRIFY]

Isa	2:19 when he ariseth to **shake t** the earth.	6206
	2:21 when he ariseth to **shake t** the earth.	6206
Na	2: 3 and the fir trees shall be **t shaken**.	7477

TERRIFIED (4) [TERRIFY]

Dt	20: 3 neither be ye **t** because of them;	6206
Lk	21: 9 hear of wars and commotions, be not **t**:	4422
	24:37 But they were **t** and affrighted,	4422
Php	1:28 And in nothing **t** by *your* adversaries:	4426

TERRIFIEST (1) [TERRIFY]

Job	7:14 with dreams, and **t** me through visions:	1204

TERRIFY (4) [TERRIBLE, TERRIBLENESS, TERRIBLY, TERRIFIED, TERRIFIEST, TERROR, TERRORS]

Job	3: 5 upon it; let the blackness of the day **t** it.	1204
	9:34 away from me, and let not his fear **t** me:	1204
	31:34 or did the contempt of families **t** me, that	2865
2Co	10: 9 That I may not seem as if I *would* **t** you *by*	1629

TERROR (29) [TERRIFY]

Ge	35: 5 the **t** of God was upon the cities that *were*	2847
Lev	26:16 even appoint over you **t**, consumption,	928
Dt	32:25 The sword without, and **t** within,	367
	34:12 in all the great **t** which Moses shewed in	4172
Jos	2: 9 that your **t** is fallen upon us, and that all	367
Job	31:23 For destruction *from* God *was* a **t** to me,	6343
	33: 7 Behold, my **t** shall not make thee afraid,	367
Ps	91: 5 Thou shalt not be afraid for the **t** by night;	6343
Isa	10:33 of hosts, shall lop the bough with **t**:	4637
	19:17 the land of Judah shall be a **t** unto Egypt,	2283
	33:18 Thine heart shall meditate **t**. Where *is*	367
	54:14 and from **t**; for it shall not come near thee.	4288
Jer	17:17 Be not a **t** unto me: thou *art* my hope in	4288

TERMED — column 3 continues

Jer	20: 4 I will make thee a **t** to thyself, and to all	4032
	32:21 a stretched out arm, and with great	4172
Eze	26:17 cause their **t** *to be* on all that haunt it.	2851
	26:21 I will make thee a **t**, and thou *shalt be* no	1091
	27:36 thou shalt be a **t**, and never *shalt be* any	1091
	28:19 thou shalt be a **t**, and never *shalt* thou *be*	1091
	32:23 which caused **t** in the land of the living.	2851
	32:24 which caused their **t** in the land of	2851
	32:25 though their **t** was caused in the land of	2851
	32:26 though they caused their **t** in the land of	2851
	32:27 though *they* were the **t** of the mighty in	2851
	32:30 with their **t** *they* are ashamed of their	2851
	32:32 For I have caused my **t** in the land of	2851
Ro	13: 3 For rulers are not a **t** to good works,	5401
2Co	5:11 Knowing therefore the **t** of the Lord,	5401
1Pe	3:14 happy *are ye*: and be not afraid of their **t**,	5401

TERRORS (15) [TERRIFY]

Dt	4:34 by a stretched out arm, and by great **t**,	4172
Job	6: 4 the **t** of God do set *themselves* in array	1161
	18:11 **T** shall make him afraid on every side,	1091
	18:14 and it shall bring him to the king of **t**.	1091
	20:25 cometh out of his gall: **t** *are* upon him.	367
	24:17 if *one* know *them, they are in* the **t** of	1091
	27:20 **T** take hold on him as waters, a tempest	1091
	30:15 **T** are turned upon me: they pursue my	1091
Ps	55: 4 and the **t** of death are fallen upon me.	367
	73:19 they are utterly consumed with **t**.	1091
	88:15 *while* I suffer thy **t** I am distracted.	367
	88:16 goeth over me; thy **t** have cut me off.	1161
Jer	15: 8 fall upon it suddenly, and **t** *upon* the city.	928
La	2:22 Thou hast called as *in* a solemn day my **t**	4032
Eze	21:12 **t** by reason of the sword shall be upon my	4048

TERTIUS (1)

Ro	16:22 I **T**, who wrote *this* epistle, salute you in	5060

TERTULLUS (2)

Ac	24: 1 and *with* a certain orator *named* **T**,	5061
	24: 2 And when he was called *forth*, **T** began	5061

TESTAMENT (14) [TESTIFY]

Mt	26:28 this is my blood of the new **t**, which is	1242
Mk	14:24 unto them, This is my blood of the new **t**,	1242
Lk	22:20 saying, This cup *is* the new **t** in my blood,	1242
1Co	11:25 saying, This cup *is* the new **t** in my blood:	1242
2Co	3: 6 hath made us able ministers of the new **t**;	1242
	3:14 remaineth away in the reading of the old **t**;	1242
Heb	7:22 was Jesus made a surety of a better **t**.	1242
	9:15 this cause he is the mediator of the new **t**,	1242
	9:15 transgressions that were under the first **t**,	1242
	9:16 For where a **t** *is*, there must also of	1242
	9:17 For a **t** *is* of force after *men* are dead:	1242
	9:18 neither the first **t** was dedicated	NIG
	9:20 This *is* the blood of the **t** which God hath	1242
Rev	11:19 was seen in his temple the ark of his **t**:	1242

TESTATOR (2) [TESTIFY]

Heb	9:16 also of necessity be the death of the **t**.	1303
	9:17 is of no strength at all whilst the **t** liveth.	1303

TESTIFIED (24) [TESTIFY]

Ex	21:29 it hath been **t** to his owner, and he hath	5749
Dt	19:18 and hath **t** falsely against his brother;	6030
Ru	1:21 seeing the Lord hath **t** against me,	6030
2Sa	1:16 for thy mouth hath **t** against thee, saying,	6030
2Ki	17:13 Yet the Lord **t** against Israel,	5749
	17:15 his testimonies which he **t** against them;	5749
2Ch	24:19 unto the Lord; and they **t** against them,	5749
Ne	9:26 slew thy prophets which **t** against them to	5749
	13:15 I **t** *against them* in the day wherein they	5749
	13:21 I **t** against them, and said unto them,	5749
Jn	4:39 which **t**, He told me all that ever I did.	3140
	4:44 For Jesus himself **t**, that a prophet hath no	3140
	13:21 and **t**, and said, Verily, verily, I say unto	3140
Ac	8:25 when they had **t** and preached the word	1263
	18: 5 and **t** to the Jews *that* Jesus was Christ.	1263
	23:11 for as thou hast **t** of me in Jerusalem,	1263
	28:23 he expounded and **t** the kingdom of God,	1263
1Co	15:15 we have **t** of God that he raised up Christ:	3140
1Th	4: 6 as we also have forewarned you and **t**.	1263
1Ti	2: 6 a ransom for all, to be **t** in due time.	3142
Heb	2: 6 But one in a certain place **t**, saying, What	1263
1Pe	1:11 when it **beforehand** the sufferings of	4303
1Jn	5: 9 of God which he hath **t** of his Son.	3140
3Jn	1: 3 and **t** of the truth *that is* in thee,	3140

TESTIFIEDST (2) [TESTIFY]

Ne	9:29 **t** against them, that *thou* mightest bring	5749
	9:30 **t** against them by thy spirit in thy prophets	5749

TESTIFIETH (5) [TESTIFY]

Hos	7:10 the pride of Israel **t** to his face: and they	6030
Jn	3:32 what he hath seen and heard, that he **t**;	3140
	21:24 is the disciple which **t** of these *things*,	3140
Heb	7:17 For he **t**, Thou *art* a priest for ever after	3140
Rev	22:20 He which **t** these *things* saith, Surely I	3140

TESTIFY (29) [TESTAMENT, TESTATOR, TESTIFIED, TESTIFIEDST, TESTIFIETH, TESTIFYING, TESTIMONIES, TESTIMONY]

Nu	35:30 one witness shall not **t** against *any* person	6030
Dt	8:19 I **t** against you *this* day that ye shall surely	5749
	19:16 man to **t** against him *that* which *is* wrong;	6030
	31:21 that this song shall **t** against them as a	6030
	32:46 your hearts unto all the words which I **t**	5749

Ne	9:34 where*with* thou didst t against them.	5749
Job	15: 6 not I; yea, thine own lips t against thee.	6030
Ps	50: 7 O Israel, and I will t against thee:	5749
	81: 8 O my people, and I will t unto thee:	5749
Isa	59:12 before thee, and our sins t against us:	6030
Jer	14: 7 though our iniquities t against us,	6030
Hos	5: 5 the pride of Israel doth t to his face:	6030
Am	3:13 Hear ye, and t in the house of Jacob,	5749
Mic	6: 3 have I wearied thee? t against me.	6030
Lk	16:28 that he may t unto them, lest they also	1263
Jn	2:25 and needed not that any should t of man:	3140
	3:11 we do know, and t that we have seen;	3140
	5:39 and they are they which t of me.	3140
	7: 7 but me it hateth, because I t of it, that	3140
	15:26 from the Father, he shall t of me:	3140
Ac	2:40 And with many other words did he t and	1263
	10:42 that it is he which was ordained of God	1263
	20:24 to the gospel of the grace of God.	1263
	26: 5 me from the beginning, if they would t,	3140
Gal	5: 3 For I t again to every man that is	3143
Eph	4:17 This I say therefore, and t in the Lord,	3143
1Jn	4:14 do t that the Father sent the Son *to be*	3140
Rev	22:16 I Jesus have sent mine angel to t unto you	3140
	22:18 For I t unto every *man* that heareth	4828

TESTIFYING (3) [TESTIFY]

Ac	20:21 T both to the Jews, and *also* to the Greeks	1263
Heb	11: 4 that he was righteous, God t of his gifts:	3140
1Pe	5:12 t that this is the true grace of God wherein	1957

TESTIMONIES (36) [TESTIFY]

Dt	4:45 These *are* the t, and the statutes,	5713
	6:17 his t, and his statutes, which he hath	5713
	6:20 What *mean* the t, and the statutes,	5713
1Ki	2: 3 and his judgments, and his t,	5715
2Ki	17:15 and his t which he testified against them;	5715
	23: 3 to keep his commandments and his t and	5715
1Ch	29:19 thy t, and thy statutes, and to do all *these*	5715
2Ch	34:31 his t, and his statutes, with all his heart,	5715
Ne	9:34 unto thy commandments and thy t,	5715
Ps	25:10 unto such as keep his covenant and his t.	5713
	78:56 the most high God, and kept not his t:	5713
	93: 5 Thy t are very sure: holiness becometh	5713
	99: 7 they kept his t, and the ordinance *that* he	5713
	119: 2 Blessed *are* they that keep his t,	5713
	119:14 I have rejoiced in the way of thy t, as	5713
	119:22 and contempt; for I have kept thy t.	5713
	119:24 Thy t also *are* my delight *and*	5713
	119:31 I have stuck unto thy t: O LORD, put me	5715
	119:36 Incline my heart unto thy t, and not to	5715
	119:46 I will speak of thy t also before kings,	5713
	119:59 my ways, and turned my feet unto thy t.	5713
	119:79 me, and those that have known thy t.	5713
	119:95 to destroy me: *but* I will consider thy t.	5713
	119:99 my teachers: for thy t *are* my meditation.	5715
	119:111 Thy t have I taken as an heritage for ever:	5715
	119:119 the earth *like* dross: therefore I love thy t.	5713
	119:125 me understanding, that I may know thy t.	5713
	119:129 Thy t *are* wonderful: therefore doth my	5715
	119:138 Thy t *that* thou hast commanded *are*	5713
	119:144 The righteousness of thy t *is* everlasting:	5715
	119:146 unto thee; save me, and I shall keep thy t.	5713
	119:152 Concerning thy t, I have known of old	5715
	119:157 *yet* do I not decline from thy t.	5715
	119:167 My soul hath kept thy t; and *I* love them	5713
	119:168 I have kept thy precepts and thy t: for all	5715
Jer	44:23 in his law, nor in his statutes, nor in his t;	5715

TESTIMONY (76) [TESTIFY]

Ex	16:34 Aaron laid it up before the T, to be kept.	5715
	25:16 thou shalt put into the ark the T which I	5715
	25:21 in the ark thou shalt put the T that I shall	5715
	25:22 which are upon the ark of the T,	5715
	26:33 in thither within the vail the ark of the T:	5715
	26:34 the ark of the T in the most holy *place*.	5715
	27:21 which *is* before the T, Aaron and his sons	5715
	30: 6 before the vail that *is* by the ark of the T,	5715
	30: 6 before the mercy seat that *is* over the T,	5715
	30:26 and the ark of the T,	5715
	30:36 put of it before the T in the tabernacle of	5715
	31: 7 the ark of the T, and the mercy seat that	5715
	31:18 two tables of T, tables of stone,	5715
	32:15 the two tables of the T *were* in his hand:	5715
	34:29 with the two tables of T in Moses' hand,	5715
	38:21 *even* of the tabernacle of T, as it was	5715
	39:35 The ark of the T, and the staves thereof,	5715
	40: 3 thou shalt put therein the ark of the T,	5715
	40: 5 for the incense before the ark of the T,	5715
	40:20 he took and put the T into the ark,	5715
	40:21 covering, and covered the ark of the T;	5715
Lev	16:13 cover the mercy seat that *is* upon the T,	5715
	24: 3 Without the vail of the T, in the	5715
Nu	1:50 the Levites over the tabernacle of T,	5715
	1:53 pitch round about the tabernacle of T,	5715
	1:53 keep the charge of the tabernacle of T.	5715
	4: 5 and cover the ark of T with it:	5715
	7:89 mercy seat that *was* upon the ark of T,	5715
	9:15 the tabernacle, *namely*, the tent of the T:	5715
	10:11 taken up from off the tabernacle of the T.	5715
	17: 4 of the congregation before the T,	5715
	17:10 Bring Aaron's rod again before the T,	5715
Jos	4:16 the priests that bear the ark of the T,	5715
Ru	4: 7 his neighbour: and this *was* a t in Israel.	8584
2Ki	11:12 the crown upon him, and *gave him* the T;	5715
2Ch	23:11 and *gave him* the T, and made him king.	5715

Ps	19: 7 the t of the LORD *is* sure, making wise	5715
	78: 5 For he established a t in Jacob,	5715
	81: 5 This he ordained in Joseph *for* a t, when	5715
	119:88 so shall I keep the t of thy mouth.	5715
	122: 4 tribes of the LORD, *unto* the t of Israel,	5715
	132:12 and my t that I shall teach them,	5713
Isa	8:16 Bind up the t, seal the law among my	8584
	8:20 the law and to the t: if they speak not	8584
Mt	8: 4 the gift that Moses commanded for a t	3142
	10:18 for a t against them and the Gentiles.	3142
Mk	1:44 Moses commanded, for a t unto them.	3142
	6:11 shake off the dust under your feet for a t	3142
	13: 9 kings for my sake, for a t against them.	3142
Lk	5:14 as Moses commanded, for a t unto them.	3142
	9: 5 dust from your feet for a t against them.	3142
	21:13 And it shall turn to you for a t.	3142
Jn	3:32 he testifieth; and no *man* receiveth his t.	3141
	3:33 He that hath received his t hath set to *his*	3141
	5:34 But I receive not t from man:	3141
	8:17 in your law, that the t of two men is true.	3141
	21:24 *things*: and we know that his t is true.	3141
Ac	13:22 to whom also he *gave* t, and said, I have	3140
	14: 3 which *gave* t unto the word of his grace,	3140
	22:18 for they will not receive thy t concerning	3141
1Co	1: 6 Even as the t of Christ was confirmed in	3142
	2: 1 declaring unto you the t of God.	3142
2Co	1:12 the t of our conscience, that in simplicity	3142
2Th	1:10 (because our t among you was believed)	3142
2Ti	1: 8 therefore ashamed of the t of our Lord,	3142
Heb	3: 5 for a t of those *things* which were to be	3142
	11: 5 for before his translation he had this t,	3140
Rev	1: 2 and of the t of Jesus Christ, and of all	3141
	1: 9 word of God, and for the t of Jesus Christ.	3141
	6: 9 of God, and for the t which they held:	3141
	11: 7 And when they shall have finished their t,	3141
	12:11 of the Lamb, and by the word of their t;	3141
	12:17 of God, and have the t of Jesus Christ.	3141
	15: 5 the temple of the tabernacle of the t in	3142
	19:10 of thy brethren that have the t of Jesus:	3141
	19:10 for the t of Jesus is the spirit of prophecy.	3141

TETRARCH (7)

Mt	14: 1 At that time Herod the t heard of the fame	5076
Lk	3: 1 and Herod being t of Galilee,	5075
	3: 1 and his brother Philip t of Iturea and of	5075
	3: 1 and Lysanias the t of Abilene,	5075
	3:19 Herod the t, being reproved by him for	5076
	9: 7 Herod the t heard of all that was done	5076
Ac	13: 1 had been brought up with Herod the t,	5076

THADDEUS (2)

Mt	10: 3 Lebbeus, whose surname was T;	2280
Mk	3:18 and T, and Simon the Canaanite,	2280

THAHASH (1)

Ge	22:24 and Gaham, and T, and Maachah.	8477

THAMAH (1)

Ezr	2:53 the children of Sisera, the children of T,	8547

THAMAR (1)

Mt	1: 3 And Judas begat Phares and Zara of T;	2283

THAN (483)

Ge	3: 1 Now the serpent was subtil t any	4480
	4:13 My punishment *is* greater t I can bear.	4480
	19: 9 we deal worse with thee, t with them.	4480
	25:23 one people shall be stronger t *the other*	4480
	26:16 from us; for thou art much mightier t we.	4480
	29:19 t that I should give her to another man:	4480
	29:30 he loved also Rachel **more** t Leah,	4480
	34:19 *was* **more** honourable t all the house of	4480
	36: 7 For their riches were more t that they	4480
	37: 3 Now Israel loved Joseph **more** t all his	4480
	37: 4 father loved him **more** t all his brethren,	4480
	38:26 said, She hath been **more** righteous t I;	4480
	39: 9 *There is* none greater in this house t I;	4480
	41:40 only *in* the throne will I be greater t thou.	4480
	48:19 truly his younger brother shall be greater t	4480
Ex	1: 9 of Israel *are* moe and mightier t we:	4480
	14:12 t that we should die in the wilderness.	4480
	18:11 Now I know that the LORD *is* greater t all	4480
	30:15 The poor shall not give less t half a shekel,	4480
	36: 5 The people bring much more t enough for	4480
Lev	13: 3 the plague in sight *be* deeper t the skin of	4480
	13: 4 in sight *be* not deeper t the skin,	4480
	13:20 it *be* in sight lower t the skin, and the hair	4480
	13:21 *if* it *be* not lower t the skin, but *be*	4480
	13:25 and it *be* in sight deeper t the skin;	4480
	13:26 it *be* no lower t the *other* skin, but *be*	4480
	13:30 behold, *if* it *be* in sight deeper t the skin;	4480
	13:31 it *be* not in sight deeper t the skin,	4480
	13:32 the scall *be* not in sight deeper t the skin;	4480
	13:34 the skin, nor *be* in sight deeper t the skin;	4480
	14:37 which in sight *are* lower t the wall;	4480
	27: 8 if he be poorer t thy estimation, then	4480
Nu	3:46 of Israel, which are more t the Levites;	5921
	13:31 the people; for they *are* stronger t we.	4480
	14:12 thee a greater nation and mightier t they.	4480
	22:15 more, and more honourable t they.	4480
	24: 7 his king shall be higher t Agag,	4480
Dt	1:28 The people *is* greater and taller t we;	4480
	4:38 and mightier thou *art*, to bring thee in,	4480
	7: 1 seven nations greater and mightier t thou;	4480
	7: 7 ye were **moe** in number t any people;	4480

Dt	7:17 in thine heart, These nations *are* moe t I;	4480
	9: 1 nations greater and mightier t thyself,	4480
	9:14 thee a nation mightier and greater t they.	4480
	11:23 greater nations and mightier t yourselves.	4480
	20: 1 and chariots, *and* a people more t thou,	4480
Jos	10: 2 because it *was* greater t Ai, and all the	4480
	10:11 *were* moe which died with hailstones t	4480
Jdg	2:19 corrupted *themselves* **more** t their fathers	4480
	8: 2 Ephraim better t the vintage of Abi-ezer?	4480
	11:25 now *art* thou any thing better t Balak	4480
	14:18 went down, What *is* sweeter t honey?	4480
	14:18 what *is* stronger t a lion? And he said	4480
	15: 2 *is* not her younger sister fairer t she?	4480
	15: 3 Now shall I be **more** blameless t	4480
	16:30 were moe t *they* which he slew in his life.	4480
Ru	3:10 in the latter end t at the beginning,	4480
	3:12 howbeit there is a kinsman nearer t I.	4480
	4:15 which *is* better to thee t seven sons,	4480
1Sa	1: 8 am not I better to thee t ten sons?	4480
	9: 2 children of Israel a goodlier person t he:	4480
	9: 2 *he was* higher t any of the people.	4480
	10:23 he was higher t any of the people from	4480
	15:22 obey *is* better t sacrifice, *and* to hearken	4480
	15:22 *and* to hearken t the fat of rams.	4480
	15:28 a neighbour of thine, *that is* better t thou.	4480
	18:30 David behaved himself **more** wisely t	4480
	24:17 to David, Thou *art* **more** righteous t I:	4480
	27: 1 *there is* nothing better for me t that I	3588
2Sa	1:23 they were swifter t eagles, they were	4480
	1:23 than eagles, they were stronger t lions.	4480
	6:22 I will yet be **more** vile t this, and will be	4480
	13:14 but, being stronger t she, forced her,	4480
	13:15 the love wherewith he had loved her.	4480
	13:16 this evil in sending me away *is* greater t	4480
	17:14 is better t the counsel of Ahithophel.	4480
	18: 8 wood devoured more people that day t	4480
	19: 7 that *will be* worse unto thee t all the evil	4480
	19:43 we have also **more** *right* in David t ye:	4480
	19:43 fiercer t the words of the men of Israel.	4480
	20: 5 he tarried longer t the set time which he	4480
	20: 6 Bichri do us **more** harm t *did* Absalom:	4480
	23:23 He was **more** honourable t the thirty,	4480
1Ki	1:37 make his throne greater t the throne of	4480
	1:47 God make the name of Solomon better t	4480
	1:47 and make his throne greater t thy throne.	4480
	2:32 two men **more** righteous and better t	4480
	4:31 For he was wiser t all men; than Ethan	4480
	4:31 t Ethan the Ezrahite, and Heman,	4480
	12:10 My little *finger* shall be thicker t my	4480
	16:25 and did worse t all that *were* before him.	4480
	16:33 t all the kings of Israel that were before	4480
	19: 4 my life; for I *am* not better t my fathers.	4480
	20:23 therefore they were stronger t we; but let	4480
	20:23 and surely we shall be stronger t they,	4480
	20:25 *and* surely we shall be stronger t they.	4480
	21: 2 I will give thee for it a better vineyard t it;	4480
2Ki	5:12 better t all the waters of Israel?	4480
	6:16 for *they* that *be* with us *are* moe t *they*	4480
	9:35 found no more of her t the skull,	518+3588
	21: 9 seduced them to do **more** evil t	4480
1Ch	4: 9 was **more** honourable t his brethren,	4480
	11:21 he was **more** honourable t the two;	871.1
	24: 4 sons of Eleazar t of the sons of Ithamar;	4480
2Ch	10:10 My little *finger* shall be thicker t my	4480
	20:25 **more** t they could carry away:	369+3807.1
	21:13 house, *which were* better t thyself:	4480
	25: 9 is able to give thee much more t this.	4480
	29:34 **more** upright in heart to sanctify themselves t	4480
	30:18 **otherwise** t it was	3808+871.1+3509.1
	32: 7 for *there be* moe with us t with him:	4480
	33: 9 to err, *and* to do worse t the heathen,	4480
Ezr	9:13 punished us less t our iniquities *deserve*,	4480
Est	1:19 estate unto another *that is* better t she.	4480
	2:17 favour in his sight **more** t all the virgins;	4480
	4:13 *in* the king's house, **more** t all the Jews.	4480
	6: 6 delight to do honour **more** t to myself?	3148
Job	3:21 and dig for it **more** t for hid treasures;	4480
	4:17 Shall mortal man be **more** just t God?	4480
	4:17 shall a man be **more** pure t his Maker?	4480
	6: 3 For now it would be heavier t the sand of	4480
	7: 6 My days are swifter t a weaver's shuttle,	4480
	7:15 *and* death **rather** t my life.	4480
	9:25 my days are swifter t a post: they flee	4480
	11: 6 that God exacteth of thee *less* t thine	4480
	11: 8 deeper t hell; what canst thou know?	4480
	11: 9 The measure thereof *is* longer t the earth,	4480
	11: 9 than the earth, and broader t the sea.	4480
	11:17 *thine* age shall be clearer t the noonday;	4480
	15:10 very aged men, much elder t thy father.	4480
	23: 2 my stroke is heavier t my groaning.	5921
	23:12 his mouth **more** t my necessary *food*.	4480
	30: 1 now *they that are* younger t I have me in	4480
	30: 8 of base men: they were viler t the earth.	4480
	32: 2 because he justified himself **rather** t God.	4480
	32: 4 had spoken, because they *were* elder t he.	4480
	33:12 answer thee, that God is greater t man.	4480
	33:25 His flesh shall be fresher t a child's:	4480
	34:19 the rich **more** t the poor?	6440+3807.1
	34:23 he will not lay upon man more t *right;*	NIH
	35: 2 My righteousness *is* **more** t God's?	4480
	35: 5 the clouds *which* are higher t thou.	4480
	35:11 Who teacheth us **more** t the beasts of	4480
	35:11 maketh us wiser t the fowls of heaven?	4480
	36:21 this hast thou chosen **rather** t affliction.	4480

T

Ref	Text	Strong's
Job 42:12	latter end of Job **more t** his beginning:	4480
Ps 4: 7	**more t** in the time that their corn and	4480
8: 5	For thou hast made him a little lower t	4480
19:10	More to be desired are they t gold, yea,	4480
19:10	are they than gold, yea, t much fine gold:	4480
19:10	sweeter also t honey and the honeycomb.	4480
37:16	little that a righteous man hath is better t	4480
40: 5	speak of them, they are moe t can be	4480
40:12	I am not able to look up; they are moe t	4480
45: 2	Thou art fairer t the children of men:	4480
51: 7	wash me, and I shall be whiter t snow.	4480
52: 3	Thou lovest evil **more t** good;	4480
52: 3	and lying **rather t** to speak righteousness.	4480
55:21	The words of his mouth were smoother t	NIH
55:21	his words were softer t oil, yet were they	4480
61: 2	lead me to the rock that is higher t I.	4480
62: 9	they are altogether lighter t vanity.	4480
63: 3	Because thy lovingkindness is better t life,	4480
69: 4	a cause are moe t the hairs of mine head:	4480
69:31	This also shall please the LORD **better t**	4480
73: 7	they **have more t** heart could wish.	5674
76: 4	Thou art **more** glorious and excellent t	4480
84:10	For a day in thy courts is better t a	4480
84:10	t to dwell in the tents of wickedness.	4480
87: 2	of Zion **more** t all the dwellings of Jacob.	4480
89:27	higher t the kings of the earth.	3807.1
93: 4	The LORD on high is mightier t the noise	4480
93: 4	yea, t the mighty waves of the sea.	NIH
105:24	and made them stronger t their enemies.	4480
118: 8	It is better to trust in the LORD t to put	4480
118: 9	It is better to trust in the LORD t to put	4480
119:72	The law of thy mouth is better unto me t	4480
119:98	hast made me wiser t mine enemies.	4480
119:99	I have **more** understanding t all my	4480
119:100	I understand **more** t the ancients,	4480
119:103	yea, sweeter t honey to my mouth!	NIH
130: 6	My soul waiteth for the Lord **more t** they	4480
130: 6	I say, more t they that watch for	NIH
139:18	they are moe in number t the sand:	4480
142: 6	my persecutors; for they are stronger t I.	4480
Pr 3:14	For the merchandise of it is better t	4480
3:14	of silver, and the gain thereof t fine gold.	4480
3:15	She is **more** precious t rubies: and all	4480
5: 3	and her mouth is smoother t oil:	4480
8:10	and knowledge **rather t** choice gold.	4480
8:11	For wisdom is better t rubies; and all	4480
8:19	My fruit is better t gold, yea, than fine	4480
8:19	fruit is better than gold, yea, t fine gold;	4480
8:19	fine gold; and my revenue t choice silver.	4480
11:24	there is that withholdeth **more** t is meet,	4480
12: 9	is better t he that honoureth himself,	4480
12:26	The righteous is **more** excellent t his	4480
15:16	Better is little with the fear of the LORD t	4480
15:17	love is, t a stalled ox and hatred therewith.	4480
16: 8	Better is a little with righteousness t great	4480
16:16	much better is it to get wisdom t gold!	4480
16:16	get understanding **rather** to be chosen t	4480
16:19	t to divide the spoil with the proud.	4480
16:32	He that is slow to anger is better t	4480
16:32	he that ruleth his spirit t he that taketh	4480
17: 1	a house full of sacrifices with strife.	4480
17:10	reproof entereth **more** into a wise man t	4480
17:12	meet a man, rather t a fool in his folly.	408
18:19	A brother offended is harder to be won t	4480
18:24	there is a friend that sticketh closer t a	4480
19: 1	t he that is perverse in his lips, and is a	4480
19:22	and a poor man is better t a liar.	4480
21: 3	**more** acceptable to the LORD t sacrifice.	4480
21: 9	t with a brawling woman in a wide house.	4480
21:19	t with a contentious and an angry woman.	4480
22: 1	good name is **rather** to be chosen t great	4480
22: 1	and loving favour rather t silver and gold.	4480
25: 7	t that thou shouldest be put lower in	4480
25:24	t with a brawling woman and in a wide	4480
26:12	there is **more** hope of a fool t of him.	4480
26:16	The sluggard is wiser in his own conceit t	4480
27: 3	but a fool's wrath is heavier t them both.	4480
27: 5	Open rebuke is better t secret love.	4480
27:10	for better is a neighbour that is near t a	4480
28: 6	t he that is perverse in his ways, though	4480
28:23	afterwards shall find **more** favour t he	4480
29:20	there is **more** hope of a fool t of him.	4480
30: 2	Surely I am **more** brutish t any man,	4480
Ecc 1:16	have gotten more wisdom t all they that	5921
2: 9	increased **more** t all that were before me	4480
2:16	of the wise **more t** of the fool for ever;	5973
2:24	t that he should eat and drink, and that he	NIH
2:25	who else can hasten hereunto, more t I?	4480
3:22	t that a man should rejoice in his own	4480
4: 2	**more** t the living which are yet alive.	4480
4: 3	better is he t both they, which hath not	4480
4: 6	t both the hands full with travail and	4480
4: 9	Two are better t one; because they have a	4480
4:13	and a wise child t an old and foolish king,	4480
5: 1	be **more** ready to hear, t to give	4480
5: 5	t that thou shouldest vow and not pay.	4480
5: 8	for he that is higher t the highest	4480+5921
5: 8	and there be higher t they.	5921
6: 3	I say, that an untimely birth is better t he.	4480
6: 5	known any thing: this hath **more** rest t	4480
6: 7	For what hath the wise more t the fool?	4480
6: 9	Better is the sight of the eyes t	4480
6:10	he contend with him that is mightier t he.	4480
7: 1	good name is better t precious ointment;	4480
7: 1	the day of death t the day of one's birth.	4480
Ecc 7: 2	t to go to the house of feasting:	4480
7: 3	Sorrow is better t laughter: for by	4480
7: 5	t for a man to hear the song of fools.	4480
7: 8	is the end of a thing t the beginning	4480
7: 8	the patient in spirit is better t the proud	4480
7:10	that the former days were better t these?	4480
7:19	Wisdom strengtheneth the wise **more t**	4480
7:26	I find **more** bitter t death the woman,	4480
8:15	t to eat, and to drink, and to be	518+3588
9: 4	for a living dog is better t a dead lion.	4480
9:16	said I, Wisdom is better t strength:	4480
9:17	**more** t the cry of him that ruleth among	4480
9:18	Wisdom is better t weapons of war:	4480
SS 1: 2	t his mouth: for thy love is better t wine.	4480
1: 4	we will remember thy love **more t** wine:	4480
4:10	how much better is thy love t wine! and	4480
4:10	the smell of thine ointments t all spices!	4480
5: 9	What is thy beloved **more t** another	4480
5: 9	What is thy beloved **more t** another	4480
Isa 13:12	I will make a man **more** precious t fine	4480
13:12	even a man t the golden wedge of Ophir.	4480
28:20	For the bed is shorter t that a man can	4480
28:20	covering narrower t that he can wrap	3509.1
33:19	a people of a deeper speech t thou canst	4480
40:17	they are counted to him **less** t nothing,	4480
52:14	visage was so marred **more** t any man,	4480
52:14	and his form **more** t the sons of men:	4480
54: 1	for **more** are the children of the desolate t	4480
55: 9	For as the heavens are higher t the earth,	4480
55: 9	so are my ways higher t your ways,	4480
55: 9	and my thoughts t your thoughts.	4480
56: 5	a name better t of sons and of daughters:	4480
57: 8	discovered thyself to another t me,	854+4480
65: 5	not near to me; for I am holier t thou.	NIH
Jer 3:11	justified herself **more** t treacherous Judah.	4480
4:13	his horses are swifter t eagles. Woe unto	4480
5: 3	have made their faces harder t a rock;	4480
7:26	their neck: they did worse t their fathers.	4480
8: 3	death shall be chosen **rather** t life by all	4480
16:12	ye have done worse t your fathers;	4480
20: 7	thou art **stronger** t I, and hast prevailed:	2388
31:11	the hand of him that was stronger t he.	4480
46:23	because they are **more** t the grasshoppers,	4480
La 4: 6	t the punishment of the sin of Sodom,	4480
4: 7	Her Nazarites were purer t snow, they	4480
4: 7	than snow, they were whiter t milk,	4480
4: 7	they were **more** ruddy in body t rubies,	4480
4: 8	Their visage is blacker t a coal; they are	4480
4: 9	better t they that be slain with hunger:	4480
4:19	Our persecutors are swifter t the eagles of	4480
Eze 3: 9	As an adamant harder t flint have I made	4480
5: 6	into wickedness **more** t the nations,	4480
5: 6	my statutes **more** t the countries that are	4480
5: 7	Because ye multiplied **more** t the nations	4480
6:14	**more** desolate t the wilderness toward	4480
8:15	shalt see greater abominations t these.	4480
15: 2	What is the vine tree **more** t any tree,	4480
15: 2	t a branch which is among the trees of	NIH
16:47	corrupted **more** t they in all thy ways.	4480
16:51	thine abominations **more** t they,	4480
16:52	hast committed **more** abominable t they:	4480
16:52	they are **more** righteous t thou: yea,	4480
23:11	more corrupt in her inordinate love t she,	4480
23:11	in her whoredoms **more** t her sister in	4480
28: 3	thou art wiser t Daniel; there is no	4480
36:11	will do better unto you t at your	4480
42: 5	for the galleries were higher t these,	4480
42: 5	t the lower, and than the middlemost of	4480
42: 5	and t the middlemost of the building.	4480
42: 6	the building was straitened **more** t	4480
Da 1:10	the children which are of your sort?	4480
1:15	fatter in flesh t all the children which did	4480
1:20	he found them ten times better t all	5921
2:30	any wisdom that I have **more** t any living,	4481
3:19	times more t it was wont to be heat.	1768
7:20	whose look was **more** stout t his fellows.	4481
8: 3	was higher t the other, and the higher	4480
11: 8	the fourth shall be far richer t they all:	4480
11: 8	he shall continue more years t the king of	4480
11:13	shall set forth a multitude greater t	4480
Hos 2: 7	then was it better with me t now.	227+4480
6: 6	the knowledge of God **more** t burnt	4480
Am 6: 2	be they better t these kingdoms?	4480
6: 2	or their border greater t your border?	4480
Jnh 4: 3	for it is better for me to die t to live.	4480
4: 8	said, It is better for me to die t to live.	4480
4:11	wherein are more t sixscore thousand	4480
Mic 7: 4	most upright is sharper t a thorn hedge:	4480
Na 3: 8	Art thou better t populous No, that was	4480
Hab 1: 8	horses also are swifter t the leopards,	4480
1: 8	are **more** fierce t the evening wolves:	4480
1:13	Thou art of purer eyes t to behold evil,	4480
1:13	the man that is **more** righteous t he?	4480
Hag 2: 9	house shall be greater t of the former,	4480
Mt 3:11	he that cometh after me is **mightier** t I,	2478
5:37	for whatsoever is **more** t these cometh of	4053
5:47	what do ye more t others? do not even	NIH
6:25	shall put on. Is not the life **more** t meat,	4183
6:25	more than meat, and the body t raiment?	NIG
6:26	Are ye not much better t they?	1308
10:15	in the day of judgment, t for that city.	2228
10:31	ye are of **more value** t many sparrows.	1308
10:37	mother **more** t me is not worthy of me:	5228
10:37	daughter **more** t me is not worthy of me.	5228
11: 9	I say unto you, and **more** t a prophet.	4053
Mt 11:11	not risen a **greater** t John the Baptist:	3187
11:11	in the kingdom of heaven is **greater** t he.	3187
11:22	Sidon at the day of judgment, t for you.	2228
11:24	Sodom in the day of judgment, t for thee.	2228
12: 6	That in this place is one **greater** t	3187
12:12	much then is a man better t a sheep?	1308
12:41	and behold, a **greater** t Jonas is here.	4183
12:42	and behold, a **greater** t Solomon is here.	4183
12:45	other spirits **more wicked** t himself,	4191
12:45	last state of that man is **worse** t the first.	5501
18: 8	rather t having two hands or two feet to	2228
18: 9	rather t having two eyes to be cast into	2228
18:13	he rejoiceth more of that sheep, t of	2228
19:24	t for a rich man to enter into the kingdom	2228
21:36	he sent other servants moe t the first:	4183
23:15	twofold more the child of hell t	1362
26:53	he shall presently give me more t twelve	2228
27:64	so the last error shall be **worse** t the first.	5501
Mk 1: 7	There cometh one **mightier** t I after me,	2478
4:31	is **less** t all the seeds that be in the earth:	3398
4:32	and becometh **greater** t all herbs,	3187
6:11	in the day of judgment, t for that city.	2228
8:14	in the ship with them **more** t one loaf.	1508
9:43	t having two hands to go into hell, into	2228
9:45	t having two feet to be cast into hell,	2228
9:47	t having two eyes to be cast into hell fire:	2228
10:25	t for a rich man to enter into the kingdom	2228
12:31	other commandment **greater** t these.	3187
12:33	is **more** t all whole burnt offerings and	4183
12:43	this poor widow hath cast **more** in, t	4183
14: 5	For it might have been sold for **more** t	1883
Lk 3:13	Exact no more t that which is appointed	3844
3:16	one **mightier** t I cometh, the latchet of	2478
7:26	unto you, and **much more** t a prophet.	4054
7:28	not a **greater** prophet t John the Baptist:	3187
7:28	in the kingdom of God is **greater** t he.	3187
10:12	in that day for Sodom, t for that city.	2228
10:14	and Sidon at the judgment, t for you.	2228
11:22	when a **stronger** t he shall come upon	2478
11:26	other spirits **more wicked** t himself;	4191
11:26	last state of that man is **worse** t the first.	5501
11:31	and behold, a **greater** t Solomon is here.	4183
11:32	and behold, a **greater** t Jonas is here.	4183
12: 7	ye are of **more value** t many sparrows.	1308
12:23	The life is **more** t meat, and the body is	4183
12:23	meat, and the body is **more** t raiment.	NIG
12:24	much more are ye better t the fowls?	1308
14: 8	lest a **more honourable** man t thou be	1784
15: 7	more over ninety and nine just persons	2228
16: 8	generation wiser t the children of light.	2228
16:17	earth to pass, t one tittle of the law to fail.	2228
17: 2	t that he should offend one of these little	2228
18:14	to his house justified rather t the other:	2228
18:25	t for a rich man to enter into the kingdom	2228
21: 3	that this poor widow hath cast in **more** t	4183
Jn 1:50	thou shalt see greater things t these.	3187
3:19	and men loved darkness rather t light,	2228
4: 1	and baptized moe disciples t John,	2228
4:12	Art thou greater t our father Jacob,	3187
5:20	he will shew him greater works t these,	3187
5:36	But I have **greater** witness t that of John:	3187
7:31	will he do moe miracles t these which this	NIG
8:53	Art thou greater t our father Abraham,	3187
10:29	which gave them me, is **greater** t all;	3187
12:43	For they loved the praise of men more t	2260
13:16	The servant is not **greater** t his lord;	3187
13:16	he that is sent **greater** t he that sent	3187
14:12	and **greater** works t these shall he do;	3187
14:28	the Father: for my Father is **greater** t I.	3187
15:13	Greater love hath no man t this, that a	3187
15:20	The servant is not **greater** t his lord.	3187
21:15	of Jonas, lovest thou me **more** t these?	4183
Ac 4:19	to hearken unto you more t unto God,	2228
5:29	said, We ought to obey God rather t men.	3844
15:28	to lay upon you no greater burden t these	4133
17:11	These were **more noble** t those in	2104
20:35	It is more blessed to give t to receive.	2228
23:13	they were more t forty which had made	NIG
23:21	there lie in wait for him of them moe t	NIG
25: 6	had tarried among them more t ten days,	2228
26:22	saying none other things t those which	1622
27:11	more t those things which were spoken	2228
Ro 1:25	served the creature **more** t the Creator,	3844
3: 9	are we better t they? No, in no wise: for	NIG
8:37	**more t conquerors** through him that	5245
12: 3	not to think of himself **more** highly t he	3844
13:11	for now is our salvation nearer t when we	2228
1Co 1:25	Because the foolishness of God is **wiser** t	4680
1:25	the weakness of God is **stronger** t men.	2478
3:11	For other foundation can no man lay t that	3844
7: 9	for it is better to marry t to burn.	2228
9:15	that any man should make my glorying	2228
10:22	Lord to jealousy? are we **stronger** t he?	2478
14: 5	for greater is he that prophesieth t he that	2228
14:18	I speak with tongues **more** t you all:	3123
14:19	ten thousand words in an unknown	2228
15:10	I laboured **more abundantly** t they all:	2228
2Co 1:13	t what you read or acknowledge;	235+2228
Gal 1: 8	preach any other gospel unto you t that	3844
1: 9	any other gospel unto you t that ye have	3844
4:27	she which hath a husband.	2228+3123
Eph 3: 8	who am less the least of all saints,	NIG
Php 2: 3	each esteem other better t themselves,	5242
1Ti 1: 4	rather t godly edifying which is in faith:	2228
5: 8	denied the faith, and is **worse** t an infidel.	5501

T

2Ti	3: 4 lovers of pleasures more **t** lovers of God;	2228
Phm	1:21 knowing that thou wilt also do **more t** I	5228
Heb	1: 4 Being made so much **better t** the angels,	2909
	1: 4 obtained a more excellent name t they.	3844
	2: 7 madest him a little lower **t** the angels;	3844
	2: 9 who was made a little lower **t** the angels,	3844
	3: 3 counted worthy of more glory **t** Moses,	3844
	3: 3 the house hath more honour **t** the house.	NIG
	4:12 and sharper **t** any twoedged sword,	5228
	7:26 and made **higher t** the heavens;	5308
	9:23 themselves with better sacrifices **t** these.	3844
	11: 4 God a more excellent sacrifice **t** Cain,	3844
	11:25 **t** to enjoy the pleasures of sin for a season;	2228
	11:26 **greater** riches **t** the treasures in Egypt:	3187
	12:24 that speaketh better *things* **t** *that of* Abel.	3844
1Pe	1: 7 *being* much more precious **t** of gold that	NIG
	3:17 ye suffer for well doing, **t** for evil doing.	2228
2Pe	2:20 the latter *end* is **worse** with them **t**	5501
	2:21 have known the way of righteousness, **t,**	2228
1Jn	3:20 God is **greater t** our heart, and knoweth	3187
	4: 4 he that is in you, **t** he that is in the world.	2228
3Jn	1: 4 I have no **greater** joy **t** to hear that my	3186
Rev	2:19 and the last *to be* **more t** the first.	4183

THANK (27) [THANKED, THANKFUL,
 THANKFULNESS, THANKING, THANKS,
 THANKSGIVING, THANKSGIVINGS,
 THANKWORTHY, UNTHANKFUL]

1Ch	16: 4 to **t** and praise the LORD God of Israel:	3034
	16: 7 to **t** the LORD into the hand of Asaph	3034
	23:30 to stand every morning to **t** and praise	3034
	29:13 we **t** thee, and praise thy glorious name.	3034
2Ch	29:31 **t** offerings into the house of the LORD.	8426
	29:31 brought in sacrifices and **t offerings;**	8426
	33:16 thereon peace offerings and **t offerings,**	8426
Da	2:23 I **t** thee, and praise thee, O thou God of	3029
Mt	11:25 time Jesus answered and said, **I t thee,**	1843
Lk	6:32 them which love you, what **t** have ye?	5485
	6:33 which do good to you, what **t** have ye?	5485
	6:34 whom ye hope to receive, what **t** have ye?	5485
	10:21 said, **I t thee,** O Father, Lord of heaven	1843
	17: 9 **Doth he t** that servant because he	2192+5485
	18:11 prayed thus with himself, God, **I t thee,**	2168
Jn	11:41 **Father, I t thee** that thou hast heard me.	2168
Ro	1: 8 **I t** my God through Jesus Christ for you	2168
	7:25 **I t** God through Jesus Christ our Lord.	2168
1Co	1: 4 **I t** my God always on your behalf,	2168
	1:14 **I t** God that I baptized none of you,	2168
	14:18 **I t** my God, I speak with tongues more	2168
Php	1: 3 **I t** my God upon every remembrance of	2168
1Th	2:13 For this cause also **I** we **t** God without	2168
2Th	1: 3 We are bound to **t** God always for you,	2168
1Ti	1:12 And **I t** Christ Jesus our Lord,	2192+5485
2Ti	1: 3 **I t** God, whom I serve from *my*	2192+5485
Phm	1: 4 **I t** my God, making mention of thee	2168

THANKED (3) [THANK]

2Sa	14:22 face, and bowed himself, and **t** the king:	1288
Ac	28:15 Paul saw, he **t** God, and took courage.	2168
Ro	6:17 But God be **t,** that ye were the servants of	5485

THANKFUL (3) [THANK]

Ps	100: 4 be **t** unto him, *and* bless his name.	3034
Ro	1:21 glorified *him* not as God, neither were **t;**	2168
Col	3:15 also ye are called in one body; and be ye **t.**	2170

THANKFULNESS (1) [THANK]

Ac	24: 3 in all places, most noble Felix, with all **t.**	2169

THANKING (1) [THANK]

2Ch	5:13 to be heard in praising and **t** the LORD;	3034

THANKS (73) [THANK]

2Sa	22:50 Therefore I will **give t** unto thee,	3034
1Ch	16: 8 **Give t** unto the LORD, call upon his	3034
	16:34 O **give t** unto the LORD; for *he is* good;	3034
	16:35 that *we may* **give t** to thy holy name,	3034
	16:41 to **give t** to the LORD, because his mercy	3034
	25: 3 a harp, to **give t** and to praise the LORD.	3034
2Ch	31: 2 to **give t,** and to praise in the gates of	3034
Ezr	3:11 in praising and **giving t** unto the LORD.	3034
Ne	12:24 over against them, to praise *and* to **give t,**	3034
	12:31 two great *companies of them that gave* **t,**	8426
	12:38 other *company of them that gave* **t** went	8426
	12:40 *of them that gave* **t** in the house of God,	8426
Ps	6: 5 thee: in the grave who shall **give t?**	3034
	18:49 Therefore will I **give t** unto thee,	3034
	30: 4 **give t** at the remembrance of his holiness.	3034
	30:12 my God, I will **give t** unto thee for ever.	3034
	35:18 will **give t** thee in the great congregation:	3034
	75: 1 Unto thee, O God, do we **give t,** *unto*	3034
	75: 1 we give thanks, *unto thee* do we **give t:**	3034
	79:13 sheep of thy pasture will **give t** thee for	3034
	92: 1 *It is* a good *thing* to **give t** unto the LORD,	3034
	97:12 **give t** at the remembrance of his holiness.	3034
	105: 1 O **give t** unto the LORD; call upon his	3034
	106: 1 O **give t** unto the LORD; for *he is* good:	3034
	106:47 to **give t** unto thy holy name,	3034
	107: 1 O **give t** unto the LORD, for *he is* good:	3034
	118: 1 O **give t** unto the LORD; for *he is* good:	3034
	118:29 O **give t** unto the LORD; for *he is* good:	3034
	119:62 At midnight I will rise to **give t** unto thee	3034
	122: 4 to **give t** unto the name of the LORD.	3034
	136: 1 O **give t** unto the LORD; for *he is* good:	3034
	136: 2 O **give t** unto the God of gods: for his	3034

Ps	136: 3 **give t** to the Lord of lords: for his mercy	3034
	136:26 O **give t** unto the God of heaven: for his	3034
	140:13 Surely the righteous shall **give t** unto thy	3034
Da	6:10 prayed, and **gave t** before his God, as he	3029
Mt	15:36 **gave t,** and brake *them,* and gave to his	2168
	26:27 and **gave t,** and gave *it* to them, saying,	2168
Mk	8: 6 and **gave t,** and brake, and gave to his	2168
	14:23 and when he had **given t,** he gave *it* to	2168
Lk	2:38 that instant **gave t** likewise **unto** the Lord,	437
	17:16 down on his face at his feet, **giving** him **t:**	2168
	22:17 and **gave t,** and said, Take this,	2168
	22:19 and **gave t,** and brake *it,* and gave unto	2168
Jn	6:11 when he had **given t,** he distributed to	2168
	6:23 bread, after that the Lord had **given t:**)	2168
Ac	27:35 **gave t** to God in presence of *them* all:	2168
Ro	14: 6 eateth to the Lord, for he **giveth** God **t;**	2168
	14: 6 the Lord he eateth not, and **giveth** God **t.**	2168
	16: 4 unto whom not only I **give t,** but also all	2168
1Co	10:30 evil spoken of for *that for* which I **give t?**	2168
	11:24 And when he had **given t,** he brake *it,*	2168
	14:16 unlearned say Amen at thy **giving of t,**	2169
	14:17 thou verily **givest t** well, but the other	2168
	15:57 But **t** *be* to God, which giveth us	5485
2Co	1:11 **t** may be **given** by many on our behalf.	5485
	2:14 Now **t** *be* unto God, which always causeth	5485
	8:16 **t** *be* to God, which put the same earnest	5485
	9:15 **T** *be* unto God for his unspeakable gift.	5485
Eph	1:16 Cease not to **give t** for you,	2168
	5: 4 are not convenient: but rather **giving** of **t.**	2169
	5:20 **Giving t** always for all *things* unto God	2168
Col	1: 3 We **give t** to God and the Father of our	2168
	1:12 **Giving t** unto the Father, which hath	2168
	3:17 **giving t** to God and the Father by him.	2168
1Th	1: 2 We **give t** to God always for you all,	2168
	3: 9 For what **t** can we render to God again for	2169
	5:18 In every *thing* **give t:** for this *is* the will of	2168
2Th	2:13 But we are bound to **give t** alway to God	2168
1Ti	2: 1 prayers, intercessions, *and* **giving** of **t,**	2169
Heb	13:15 the fruit of *our* lips **giving t** to his name.	3670
Rev	4: 9 and **t** to him that sat on the throne,	2169
	11:17 Saying, We **give t** thee, O Lord God	2168

THANKSGIVING (28) [GIVE, THANK]

Lev	7:12 If he offer it for **t,** then he shall offer	8426
	7:12 he shall offer with the sacrifice of **t**	8426
	7:13 the sacrifice of **t** of his peace offerings.	8426
	7:15 **t** shall be eaten the same day that it is	8426
	22:29 when ye will offer a sacrifice of **t** unto	8426
Ne	11:17 *was* the principal to begin the **t** in prayer:	3034
	12: 8 *was* over the **t,** he and his brethren.	1960
	12:46 and songs of praise and **t** unto God.	3034
Ps	26: 7 That *I* may publish with the voice of **t,**	8426
	50:14 Offer unto God **t;** and pay thy vows unto	8426
	69:30 with a song, and will magnify him with **t.**	8426
	95: 2 Let us come before his presence with **t,**	8426
	100: 4 Enter *into* his gates with **t,** *and* into his	8426
	107:22 let them sacrifice the sacrifices of **t,**	8426
	116:17 I will offer to thee the sacrifice of **t,**	8426
	147: 7 Sing unto the LORD with **t;** sing *praise*	8426
Isa	51: 3 found therein, **t,** and the voice of melody.	8426
Jer	30:19 out of them shall proceed **t** and the voice	8426
Am	4: 5 offer a **sacrifice of t** with leaven,	8426
Jnh	2: 9 will sacrifice unto thee with the voice of **t;**	8426
2Co	4:15 the abundant grace might through the **t**	2169
	9:11 which causeth through us **t** to God.	2169
Php	4: 6 supplication with **t** let your requests be	2169
Col	2: 7 been taught, abounding therein with **t.**	2169
	4: 2 in prayer, and watch in the same with **t;**	2169
1Ti	4: 3 be received with **t** of them which believe	2169
	4: 4 to be refused, if it be received with **t:**	2169
Rev	7:12 and **t,** and honour, and power, and might,	2169

THANKSGIVINGS (2) [GIVE, THANK]

Ne	12:27 both with **t,** and with singing,	8426
2Co	9:12 but is abundant also by many **t** unto God;	2169

THANKWORTHY (1) [THANK, WORTH]

1Pe	2:19 this *is* **t,** if a man for conscience toward	5485

THARA (1) [TERAH]

Lk	3:34 was *the son* of **T,** which was *the son*	2291

THARSHISH (4) [TARSHISH]

1Ki	10:22 For the king had at sea a navy of **T** with	8659
	10:22 once in three years came the navy of **T,**	8659
	22:48 Jehoshaphat made ships of **T** to go to	8659
1Ch	7:10 and Zethan, and **T,** and Ahishahar.	8659

THAT (12914) [THOSE] See Index of Articles, Etc.

THE (64039) See Index of Articles, Etc.

THEATRE (2)

Ac	19:29 they rushed with one accord into the **t.**	2302
	19:31 would not adventure himself into the **t.**	2302

THEBEZ (3)

Jdg	9:50 went Abimelech to **T,**	8405
	9:50 and encamped against **T,** and took it.	8405
2Sa	11:21 him from the wall, that he died in **T?**	8405

THEE (3826) [THOU] See Index of Articles, Etc.

THEE-WARD (1) [THOU]

1Sa	19: 4 his works *have been* to **t** very good:	3509.2

THEFT (2) [THEFTS, THIEF, THIEVES]

Ex	22: 3 nothing, then he shall be sold for his **t.**	1591
	22: 4 the **t** be certainly found in his hand alive,	1591

THEFTS (3) [THEFT]

Mt	15:19 murders, adulteries, fornications, **t,**	2829
Mk	7:22 **T,** covetousness, wickedness, deceit,	2829
Rev	9:21 nor of their fornication, nor of their **t.**	2809

THEIR (3931) [THEY] See Index of Articles, Etc.

THEIRS (21) [THEY]

Ge	15:13 stranger in a land *that is* not **t,**	1992.1+3807.1
	34:23 and every beast of **t** *be* ours?	3963.1
	43:34 was five times so much as any of **t.**	3963.1
Ex	29: 9 the priest's office shall be **t** for	1992.1+3807.1
Lev	18:10 uncover: for **t** *is* thine own nakedness.	2007
Nu	16:26 wicked men, and touch nothing of **t,**	1992.1
	18: 9 every oblation of **t,** every meat offering	3963.1
	18: 9 every meat offering of **t,** and every sin	3963.1
	18: 9 every sin offering of **t,** and every trespass	3963.1
	18: 9 theirs, and every trespass offering of **t,**	3963.1
Jos	21:10 had: for **t** was the first lot.	1992.1+3807.1
1Ch	6:54 Kohathites: for **t** was the lot.	1992.1+3807.1
2Ch	18:12 be like one of **t,** and speak thou good.	1992.1
Jer	44:28 words shall stand, mine, or **t.**	4480+1992.1
Eze	7:11 nor of their multitude, nor of any of **t:**	1992.1
	44:29 thing in Israel shall be **t.**	1992.1+3807.1
Hab	1: 6 the dwelling places *that are* not **t.**	2050.2
Mt	5: 3 in spirit: for **t** is the kingdom of heaven.	846
	5:10 for **t** is the kingdom of heaven.	846
1Co	1: 2 of Jesus Christ our Lord, both **t** and ours:	846
2Ti	3: 9 be manifest unto all *men,* as **t** also was.	1565

THELASAR (1) [TELASSAR]

2Ki	19:12 the children of Eden which *were* in **T?**	8515

THEM (6429) [THEY] See Index of Articles, Etc.

THEMSELVES (409) [SELF, THEY]

Ge	3: 7 fig leaves together, and made **t** aprons.	1992.1
	3: 8 his wife hid **t** from the presence of	NIH
	13:11 they separated **t** the one from the other.	NIH
	19:11 so that they wearied **t** to find the door.	NIH
	21:28 lambs of the flock **by t.**	905+2006.1+3807.1
	21:29 which thou hast set **by t?**	905+3807.1+5089.1
	30:40 he put his own flocks **by t,**	905+3807.1
	32:16 of his servants, every drove **by t;**	905+3807.1
	33: 6 they and their children, and they bowed **t.**	NIH
	33: 7 her children came near, and bowed **t:**	NIH
	33: 7 Joseph near and Rachel, and they bowed **t.**	NIH
	34:30 they shall gather **t** together against me,	NIH
	42: 6 bowed down **t** before him *with* their faces	NIH
	43:26 house, and bowed **t** to him to the earth.	NIH
	43:32 for them **by t,** and for	905+3807.1+3963.1
	43:32 did eat with him, **by t:**	905+3807.1+3963.1
Ex	5: 7 let them go and gather straw for **t.**	1992.1
	11: 8 bow down **t** unto me, saying, Get thee out,	NIH
	12:39 had they prepared for **t** *any* victual.	1992.1
	18:26 but every small matter they judged **t.**	1992
	19:22 which come near to the LORD, sanctify **t,**	NIH
	26: 5 shalt couple five curtains **by t,**	905+3807.1
	26: 9 six curtains **by t,** and shalt double	905+3807.1
	32: 1 people gathered **t** together unto Aaron,	NIH
	32: 7 of the land of Egypt, have corrupted **t**	NIH
	32:26 all the sons of Levi gathered **t** together	NIH
	33: 6 the children of Israel stript **t** of their	NIH
	36:16 he coupled five curtains **by t,**	905+3807.1
	36:16 themselves, and six curtains **by t.**	905+3807.1
Lev	15:18 they shall *both* bathe **t** in water,	NIH
	22: 2 that they separate **t** from the holy *things*	NIH
Nu	6: 2 woman shall separate **t** to vow a vow of a	NIH
	6: 2 a Nazarite, to separate **t** unto the LORD:	NIH
	8: 7 wash their clothes, and *so* make **t** clean.	NIH
	10: 3 all the assembly shall assemble **t** to thee at	NIH
	10: 4 thousands of Israel, shall gather **t** unto	NIH
	11:32 they spread *them* all abroad for **t** round	1992.1
	16: 3 they gathered **t** together against Moses	NIH
	20: 2 they gathered **t** together against Moses	NIH
	27: 3 **t** together against the LORD in	NIH
Dt	7:20 left, and hide **t** from thee, be destroyed.	NIH
	9:12 **t,** they are quickly turned aside out of	NIH
	31:14 presented **t** in the tabernacle of	NIH
	31:20 have eaten and filled **t,** and waxen fat;	NIH
	32: 5 They have corrupted **t,** their spot *is* not	NIH
	32:27 lest their adversaries should behave **t**	NIH
	32:31 Rock, even our enemies **t** *being* judges.	NIH
Jos	8:27 that city Israel took for a prey unto **t,**	1992.1
	9: 2 That they gathered **t** together, to fight	NIH
	10: 5 gathered **t** together, and went up, they	NIH
	10:13 until the people had avenged **t** upon their	NIH
	10:16 fled, and hid **t** in a cave at Makkedah.	NIH
	11:14 children of Israel took for a prey unto **t;**	1992.1
	22:12 of Israel gathered **t** together *at* Shiloh,	NIH
	24: 1 and they presented **t** before God.	NIH
Jdg	2:12 bowed **t** unto them, and provoked	NIH
	2:17 after other gods, and bowed **t** unto them:	NIH
	2:19 and corrupted **t** more than their fathers,	NIH
	5: 2 when the people willingly offered **t.**	NIH
	5: 9 that offered **t** willingly among the people.	NIH
	7: 2 lest Israel vaunt **t** against me, saying,	NIH
	7:23 men of Israel gathered **t** together out of	NIH
	7:24 the men of Ephraim gathered **t** together,	NIH
	10:17 children of Israel assembled **t** together,	NIH
	12: 1 men of Ephraim **gathered t** together,	6817

Jdg 15: 9 pitched in Judah, and spread t in Lehi. NIH
20: 2 presented t in the assembly of the people NIH
20:14 children of Benjamin gathered t together NIH
20:20 the men of Israel put t in array to fight NIH
20:22 people the men of Israel encouraged t, NIH
20:22 where they put t in array the first day. NIH
20:30 put t in array against Gibeah, as at other NIH
20:33 place, and put t in array at Baal-tamar. NIH
20:37 the liers in wait drew t along, and smote NIH
1Sa 2: 5 *They that were* full have hired out t for NIH
3:13 because his sons made t vile, 1992.1
4: 2 the Philistines put t in array against Israel: NIH
8: 4 all the elders of Israel gathered t together, NIH
13: 5 the Philistines gathered t together to fight NIH
13: 6 the people did hide t in caves, NIH
13:11 *that* the Philistines gathered t together *at* NIH
14:11 of them discovered t unto the garrison NIH
14:11 out of the holes where they had hid t. NIH
14:20 people that *were* with him assembled t, NIH
14:22 Israel which had hid t in mount Ephraim, NIH
21: 4 if the young men have kept t at least from NIH
22: 2 *was* discontented, gathered t unto him; NIH
28: 4 Philistines gathered t together, and came NIH
2Sa 2:25 children of Benjamin gathered t together NIH
5:18 and spread t in the valley of Rephaim. NIH
5:22 and spread t in the valley of Rephaim. NIH
10: 8 were **by** t in the field. 905+3807.1+3963.1
10:15 before Israel, they gathered t together. NIH
10:17 the Syrians set t in array against David, NIH
16:14 came weary, and refreshed t there. NIH
22:45 Strangers shall submit t unto me: as soon NIH
1Ki 2: 8 all the men of Israel assembled t unto king NIH
8:47 *Yet* if they shall bethink t in the land 3963.1
18:23 let them choose one bullock for t, 1992.1
18:28 cut t after their manner with knives and NIH
20:12 Set *yourselves* in array. And they set t *in* NIH
2Ki 2:15 and bowed t to the ground before him. NIH
7:12 are they gone out of the camp to hide t NIH
8:20 hand of Judah, and made a king over t. 1992.1
17:17 sold t to do evil in the sight of the LORD, NIH
17:32 unto t of the lowest of them priests 1992.1
19:29 eat *this* year such things as grow of t, 5599
1Ch 11: 1 all Israel gathered t to David unto Hebron, NIH
11:10 who strengthened with him in his NIH
11:14 they set t in the midst of *that* parcel, NIH
12: 8 of the Gadites there separated t unto David NIH
13: 2 suburbs, that they may gather t unto us: NIH
14: 9 and spread t in the valley of Rephaim. NIH
14:13 the Philistines yet again spread t abroad in NIH
15:14 the Levites sanctified t to bring up the ark NIH
19: 6 saw that they had made t odious to David, NIH
19: 7 children of Ammon gathered t together NIH
19: 9 were **by** t in the field. 905+3807.1+3963.1
19:11 they set t in array against the children of NIH
21:20 angel; and his four sons with him hid t. NIH
29:24 submitted t unto Solomon the king. 3027
2Ch 3:13 wings of these cherubims spread t forth NIH
5: 3 all the men of Israel assembled t NIH
6:37 *Yet* if they bethink t in the land whither 3963.1
7: 3 bowed t *with their* faces to the ground NIH
7:14 humble t, and pray, and seek my face, NIH
12: 6 princes of Israel and the king humbled t; NIH
12: 7 when the LORD saw that they humbled t, NIH
12: 7 Shemaiah, saying, They have humbled t, NIH
13: 7 have strengthened t against Rehoboam NIH
14:13 that they could not recover t; 1992.1
15:10 So they gathered t together *at* Jerusalem in NIH
20: 4 Judah gathered t together, to ask *help* of NIH
20:25 which they stript off for t, 1992.1
20:26 on the fourth day they assembled t in NIH
21: 8 dominion of Judah, and made t a king. 1992.1
29:15 their brethren, and sanctified t, and came, NIH
29:29 all that were present with him bowed t, NIH
29:34 until the *other* priests had sanctified t: NIH
29:34 in heart to sanctify t than the priests. NIH
30: 3 the priests had not sanctified t sufficiently, NIH
30: 3 neither had the people gathered t together NIH
30:11 and Manasseh and of Zebulun humbled t, NIH
30:15 sanctified t, and brought in the burnt NIH
30:18 Issachar, and Zebulun, had not cleansed t, NIH
30:24 and a great number of priests sanctified t. NIH
31:18 for in their set office they sanctified t *in* NIH
32: 8 the people rested t upon the words of NIH
35:14 afterward they made ready for t, 1992.1
35:14 therefore the Levites prepared for t, 1992.1
Ezr 3: 1 the people gathered t together as one man NIH
6:20 for their brethren the priests, and for t. 1992.1
6:21 all such as had separated t unto them from NIH
9: 1 have not separated t from the people of NIH
9: 2 they have taken of their daughters for t, 1992.1
9: 2 that the holy seed have mingled t with NIH
10: 7 that *they* should gather t together *unto* NIH
10: 9 Benjamin gathered t together *unto* NIH
Ne 4: 2 will they fortify t? will they sacrifice? 1992.1
8: 1 all the people gathered t together as one NIH
8:16 and brought *them*, and made t booths, 1992.1
9: 2 the seed of Israel separated t from all NIH
9:25 and delighted t in thy great goodness. NIH
10:28 they that had separated t from the people NIH
11: 2 that willingly offered t to dwell at NIH
12:28 the sons of the singers gathered t together, NIH
12:30 the priests and the Levites purified t, NIH
13:22 the Levites that they should cleanse t, NIH
Est 8:11 *were* in every city to gather t together, NIH
8:13 that day to avenge t on their enemies. NIH

Est 9: 2 The Jews gathered t together in their cities NIH
9:15 the Jews that *were* in Shushan gathered t NIH
9:16 in the king's provinces gathered t together, NIH
9:27 upon all such as joined t unto them, so as NIH
9:31 as they had decreed for t and 5315+3963.1
Job 1: 6 God came to present t before the LORD, NIH
2: 1 God came to present t before the LORD, NIH
3:14 which built desolate places for t; 4123.1
6: 4 the terrors of God do set t in array *against* NIH
16:10 they have gathered t together against me. NIH
24: 4 the poor of the earth hide t together. NIH
24:16 *which* they had marked for t in 4123.1
29: 8 The young men saw me, and hid t: NIH
30:14 in the desolation they rolled t *upon* me. NIH
34:22 where the workers of iniquity may hide t. NIH
39: 3 They bow t, they bring forth their young NIH
41:23 are firm in t; they cannot be moved. 2050.2
41:25 by reason of breakings they purify t. NIH
Ps 2: 2 The kings of the earth set t, and the rulers NIH
3: 6 that have set t against me round about. NIH
9:20 the nations may know t *to be but* men. 1992
18:44 the strangers shall submit t unto me. NIH
35:15 they rejoiced, and gathered t together: NIH
35:15 *yea*, the abjects gathered t together against NIH
35:26 and dishonour that magnify t against me. NIH
37:11 shall delight t in the abundance of peace. NIH
38:16 foot slippeth, they magnify t against me. NIH
44:10 and they which hate us spoil for t. 4123.1
49: 6 boast t in the multitude of their riches; NIH
56: 6 They gather t together, they hide NIH
56: 6 they hide t, they mark my steps, when NIH
57: 6 into the midst whereof they are fallen t. NIH
59: 4 They run and prepare t without *my* fault: NIH
64: 5 They encourage t in an evil matter: 4123.1
64: 8 make their own tongue to fall upon t: 4123.1
66: 3 shall thine enemies submit t unto thee. NIH
66: 7 let not the rebellious exalt t. Selah. NIH
80: 6 and our enemies laugh among t. 4123.1
81:15 LORD should have submitted t unto him: NIH
94: 4 *and* all the workers of iniquity boast t? NIH
94:21 They gather t together against the soul of NIH
97: 7 serve graven images, that boast t of idols: NIH
104:22 they gather t together, and lay them down NIH
106:28 They joined t also unto Baal-peor, NIH
109:29 let them cover t *with* their own confusion, NIH
140: 8 not his wicked device; *lest* they exalt t. NIH
Pr 23: 5 riches certainly make t wings; they fly 2050.2
28:28 When the wicked rise, men hide t: NIH
Ecc 3:18 that *they* might see that they t are beasts. 1992
11: 3 full *of* rain, they empty t upon the earth: NIH
12: 3 strong men shall bow t, and the grinders NIH
12: 3 they please t in the children of strangers. NIH
Isa 2: 6 they have rewarded evil unto t. 1992.1
3: 9 for they have rewarded evil unto t. 1992.1
8:21 they shall fret t, and curse their king and NIH
10:31 the inhabitants of Gebim gather t to flee. NIH
15: 3 In their streets they shall gird t with NIH
22: 7 horsemen shall set t in array at the gate. NIH
30: 2 to strengthen t in the strength of Pharaoh, NIH
46: 2 but t are gone into captivity. 5315+3963.1
47:14 they shall not deliver t from 5315+3963.1
48: 2 For they call t of the holy city, NIH
48: 2 city, and stay t upon the God of Israel; NIH
49:18 these gather t together, *and* come to thee. NIH
56: 6 that join t to the LORD, to serve him, NIH
59: 6 neither shall they cover t with their works: NIH
60: 4 they gather t together, they come to thee: NIH
60:14 they that despised thee shall bow t down NIH
66: 3 they t that sanctify t, and purify themselves NIH
66:17 purify t in the gardens behind one *tree* in NIH
Jer 2:24 all they that seek her will not weary t; NIH
4: 2 the nations shall bless t in him, and in him NIH
5: 7 assembled t by troops *in* the harlots' NIH
5:22 though the waves thereof toss t, yet can NIH
7:19 *do they* not *provoke* t to the confusion 3963.1
9: 5 speak lies, *and* weary t to commit iniquity. NIH
11:17 which they have done against t to 1992.1
12:13 have put t to pain, *but* shall not profit: NIH
16: 6 shall *men* lament for them, nor cut t, NIH
16: 6 cut themselves, nor make t bald for them: NIH
16: 7 Neither shall *men* tear t for them in NIH
25:14 and great kings shall serve t of them also: 1992
27: 7 and great kings shall serve t of him. NIH
30: 8 strangers shall no more serve t of him: NIH
30:21 their nobles shall be of t, 5105.2
34:10 none should serve t of them any more, NIH
41: 5 having cut t, with offerings and incense in NIH
49:29 *away:* they shall take to t their curtains, 1992.1
50: 9 they shall set t in array against her; NIH
La 2:10 they have girded t with sackcloth: NIH
4:14 they have polluted t with blood, so that NIH
Eze 6: 9 they shall lothe t for the evils 6440+1992.1
7:18 They shall also gird t with sackcloth, NIH
10:17 these lift up t *also:* for the spirit of 3963.1
10:22 river of Chebar, their appearances and t: 3963.1
14:18 but they only shall be delivered t. 3963.1
26:16 they shall clothe t with trembling; they NIH
27:30 heads, they shall wallow t in the ashes: NIH
27:31 they shall make t utterly bald for thee, NIH
31:14 by the waters exalt t for their height, NIH
34: 2 the shepherds of Israel that do feed t! 3963.1
34: 8 shepherds fed t, and fed not my flock; 3963.1
34:10 shall the shepherds feed t any more; 3963.1
34:27 of the hand of those that served t of them. NIH
37:23 Neither shall they defile t any more with NIH
43:26 and purify it; and they shall consecrate t. 2050.2

Eze 44:18 they shall not gird t with any thing that NIH
44:25 shall come at no dead person to defile t. NIH
44:25 hath had no husband, they may defile t. NIH
45: 5 the ministers of the house, have for t, 1992.1
Da 2:43 they shall mingle t with the seed of men: NIH
10: 7 fell upon them, so that they fled to hide t. NIH
11: 6 the end of years they shall join t together; NIH
11:14 the robbers of thy people shall exalt t to NIH
Hos 1:11 appoint t one head, and they shall come 1992.1
4:14 for t are separated with whores, 1992
7:14 they assemble t for corn and wine, NIH
9: 9 have deeply corrupted t, as *in* the days NIH
9:10 and separated t unto *that* shame; NIH
10:10 *they* shall bind t in their two furrows. 3963.1
Am 2: 8 lay t down upon clothes laid to pledge NIH
6: 4 stretch t upon their couches, and eat NIH
6: 5 *and* invent to t instruments of musick, 1992.1
6: 6 and anoint t *with* the chief ointments: NIH
6: 7 the banquet of them that stretched t shall NIH
9: 3 though they hide t in the top of Carmel, NIH
Mic 3: 4 as they have behaved t ill in their doings. NIH
Hab 1: 7 and their dignity shall proceed of t. 5105.2
1: 8 their horsemen shall spread t, NIH
2:13 the people shall weary t for very vanity? NIH
Zep 2: 8 and magnified t against their border. NIH
2:10 magnified t against the people of NIH
Zec 4:12 pipes empty the golden *oil* out of t? 1992.1
11: 5 possessors slay them, and hold t not guilty: NIH
12: 3 all that burden t with it shall be cut in NIH
12: 7 Jerusalem do not magnify t against Judah. NIH
Mt 9: 3 certain of the scribes said within t, 1438
14: 2 mighty works do shew forth t in him. NIG
14:15 go into the villages, and buy t victuals. 1438
16: 7 And they reasoned among t, saying, *It is* 1438
19:12 which have made t eunuchs for 1438
21:25 And they reasoned with t, saying, If we 1438
21:38 son, they said among t, This is the heir; 1438
23: 4 they t will not move them with *one of* NIG
Mk 1:27 insomuch that *they* questioned among t, 846
2: 8 in his spirit that they so reasoned within t, 1438
4:17 And have no root in t, and so endure but 1438
6:14 mighty works do shew forth t in him. NIG
6:30 And the apostles gathered t together unto NIG
6:36 and *into* the villages, and buy t bread: 1438
6:51 they were sore amazed in t beyond NIH
8:16 And they reasoned among t, saying, *It is* 1438
9: 2 them up into a high mountain apart **by** t: 3441
9: 8 no *man* any more, save Jesus only with t. 1438
9:10 and they kept *that* saying with t, 240
9:34 for by the way they had disputed among t, 240
10:26 saying among t, Who then can be saved? 1438
11:31 And they reasoned with t, saying, If we 1438
12: 7 But those husbandmen said amongst t, 1438
14: 4 were some that had indignation within t, 1438
15:31 mocking said among t with the scribes, 240
16: 3 And they said among t, Who shall roll us 1438
Lk 4:36 spake among t, saying, What a word *is* 240
7:30 rejected the counsel of God against t, 1438
7:49 at meat with *him* began to say within t, 1438
18: 9 trusted in t that they were righteous, 1438
20: 5 And they reasoned with t, saying, If we 1438
20:14 they reasoned among t, saying, This is 1438
20:20 which *should* feign t just *men*, that they 1438
22:23 And they began to inquire among t, which 1438
23:12 for before they were at enmity between t. 1438
24:12 he beheld the linen clothes laid **by** t, 3441
Jn 6:52 The Jews therefore strove amongst t, 240
7:35 Then said the Jews among t, Whither will 1438
11:55 Jerusalem before the passover, to purify t. 1438
11:56 and spake among t, as they stood in 240
12:19 The Pharisees therefore said among t, 1438
16:17 Then said *some* of his disciples among t, 240
17:13 that they might have my joy fulfilled in t. 846
18:18 and they warmed t: and Peter stood with NIG
18:28 they t went not into the judgment hall, 846
19:24 They said therefore among t, Let us not 240
Ac 4:15 out of the council, they conferred among t, 240
5:36 of men, about four hundred, joined t: NIG
11:26 that a whole year they assembled t with NIG
15:32 And Judas and Silas, being prophets also t, 846
16:37 but let them come t and fetch us out. 846
18: 6 when they opposed t, and blasphemed, NIG
21:25 they keep t from things offered to idols, 846
23:12 and bound t under a curse, 1438
23:21 which have bound t with an oath, 1438
24:15 towards God, which they t also allow, 846
26:31 gone aside, they talked between t, saying, 240
27:40 they committed t unto the sea, NIG
27:43 could swim should cast t first into *the sea*, NIG
28: 4 they said among t, No doubt this man is a 240
28:25 And when they agreed not among t, 240
28:29 and had great reasoning among t. 1438
Ro 1:22 Professing t to be wise, they became fools, NIG
1:24 to dishonour their own bodies between t: 1438
1:27 receiving in t that recompence of their 1438
2:14 having not the law, are a law unto t: 1438
10: 3 not submitted t unto the righteousness NIG
13: 2 that resist shall receive to t damnation. 1438
1Co 6: 9 nor abusers of t with mankind, NIG
16:15 they have addicted t to the ministry of 1438
2Co 5:15 live should not henceforth live unto t, 1438
8: 3 beyond *their* power that they *were* willing of t; 830
8: 5 ourselves with some that commend t: 1438
10:12 but they measuring t by themselves, 1438
10:12 but they measuring themselves by t, 1438

2Co 10:12 and comparing t amongst themselves, *1438*
 10:12 and comparing themselves amongst t, *1438*
 11:13 transforming t into the apostles of Christ. NIG
Gal 6:13 For neither they t who are circumcised *3588*
Eph 4:19 Who being past feeling have given t over *1438*
Php 2: 3 mind *let* each esteem other better than t. *1438*
1Th 1: 9 For **they** t shew of us what manner of *846*
1Ti 1:10 for them that defile t with mankind, NIG
 2: 9 that women adorn t in modest apparel, *1438*
 3:13 deacon well purchase to t a good degree, *1438*
 6:10 and pierced t through with many sorrows. *1438*
 6:19 Laying up in store for t a good foundation *1438*
2Ti 2:25 meekness instructing those that **oppose** t; *475*
 2:26 *that* they may recover t out of the snare NIG
 4: 3 after their own lusts shall they heap to t *1438*
Tit 1:12 One of t, *even* a prophet of their own, *846*
Heb 6: 6 seeing they crucify to t the Son of God *1438*
 9:23 the heavenly **things** t with better sacrifices *846*
1Pe 1:12 that not unto t, but unto us they did *1438*
 3: 5 who trusted in God, adorned t, being in *1438*
2Pe 2: 1 and bring upon t swift destruction. *1438*
 2:13 sporting t with their own deceivings while NIG
 2:19 they t are the servants of corruption: *846*
Jude 1: 7 in like manner giving t over to fornication, *3778*
 1:10 beasts, in those **things** they corrupt t. NIG
 1:12 they feast with **you**, feeding t without fear: *1438*
 1:19 These be they who separate t, sensual, *1438*
Rev 6:15 and every free *man*, hid t in the dens and *1438*
 8: 6 the seven trumpets prepared t to sound. *1438*

THEN (2168)

Ge 3: 5 t your eyes shall be opened, and ye shall 2050.1
 4:26 t began *men* to call upon the name of 227
 8: 9 t he put forth his hand, and took her, 2050.1
 12: 6 And the Canaanite *was* t in the land. 227
 13: 7 and the Perizzite dwelled t in the land. 227
 13: 9 the left hand, t I will go to the right; 2050.1
 13: 9 *to* the right hand, t I will go to the left. 2050.1
 13:11 Lot chose him all the plain of Jordan; 2050.1
 13:16 earth, t shall thy seed also be numbered. NIH
 13:18 T Abram removed his tent, and came 2050.1
 17:17 T Abraham fell upon his face, 2050.1
 18:15 T Sarah denied, saying, I laughed not; 2050.1
 18:26 t I will spare all the place for their sakes. 2050.1
 19:15 the angels hastened Lot, saying, Arise, 2050.1
 19:24 The LORD rained upon Sodom and 2050.1
 20: 9 T Abimelech called Abraham, 2050.1
 21:32 t Abimelech rose up, and Phichol 2050.1
 22: 4 T on the third day Abraham lift up his 2050.1
 24: 8 t thou shalt be clear from this my oath: 2050.1
 24:41 T shalt thou be clear from *this* my oath, 227
 24:50 T Laban and Bethuel answered and said, 2050.1
 25: 1 T again Abraham took a wife, 2050.1
 25: 8 T Abraham gave up the ghost, 2050.1
 25:34 T Jacob gave Esau bread and pottage of 2050.1
 26:12 T Isaac sowed in that land, 2050.1
 26:26 T Abimelech went to him from Gerar, 2050.1
 27:41 at hand; t I will slay my brother Jacob. 2050.1
 27:45 t I will send, and fetch thee from thence 2050.1
 28: 9 T went Esau unto Ishmael, and took 2050.1
 28:21 in peace; t shall the LORD be my God: 2050.1
 29: 1 T Jacob went on his journey, 2050.1
 29: 8 the well's mouth; t we water the sheep. 2050.1
 29:25 t hast thou beguiled me? 2050.1
 30:14 T Rachel said to Leah, Give me, I pray 2050.1
 31: 8 thy wages; t all the cattle bare speckled: 2050.1
 31: 8 thy hire; t bare all the cattle ringstraked. 2050.1
 31:16 now t, whatsoever God hath said unto 2050.1
 31:17 T Jacob rose up, and set his sons and his 2050.1
 31:25 T Laban overtook Jacob. Now Jacob had 2050.1
 31:33 T went he out of Leah's tent, 2050.1
 31:54 T Jacob offered sacrifice upon the 2050.1
 32: 7 T Jacob was greatly afraid and distressed 2050.1
 32: 8 t the *other* company which is left shall 2050.1
 32:18 t thou shalt say, *They* be thy servant 2050.1
 33: 6 T the handmaidens came near, they and 2050.1
 33:10 t receive my present at my hand: 2050.1
 34:16 T will we give our daughters unto you, 2050.1
 34:17 t will we take our daughter, and we will 2050.1
 35: 2 T Jacob said unto his household, 2050.1
 37:28 T there passed by Midianites 2050.1
 38:11 t said Judah to Tamar his daughter in 2050.1
 38:21 T he asked the men of that place, 2050.1
 39: 9 how t can I do this great wickedness, 2050.1
 41: 9 T spake the chief butler unto Pharaoh, 2050.1
 41:14 T Pharaoh sent and called Joseph, 2050.1
 42:25 T Joseph commanded to fill their sacks 2050.1
 42:34 t shall I know that ye *are* no spies, 2050.1
 42:38 t shall ye bring down my gray hairs with 2050.1
 43: 9 t let me bear the blame for ever: 2050.1
 44: 8 how t should we steal out of thy lord's 2050.1
 44:11 T they speedily took down every man 2050.1
 44:13 T they rent their clothes, and laded 2050.1
 44:18 T Judah came near unto him, and said, 2050.1
 44:26 brother be with us, t will we go down: 2050.1
 44:32 t I shall bear the blame to my father for 2050.1
 45: 1 T Joseph could not refrain himself 2050.1
 47: 1 T Joseph came and told Pharaoh, 2050.1
 47: 6 t make them rulers over my cattle. 2050.1
 47:23 T Joseph said unto the people, Behold, 2050.1
 49: 4 t defiledst thou *it*: he went up to my 227
Ex 1:16 if *it be* a son, t shall they kill him: 2050.1
 1:16 but if *it be* a daughter, t she shall live. 2050.1
 2: 7 T said his sister to Pharaoh's daughter, 2050.1
 4:25 T Zipporah took a sharp stone, 2050.1

Ex 4:26 t she said, A bloody husband *thou art,* 227
 4:31 t they bowed their heads and 2050.1
 5:15 T the officers of the children of Israel 2050.1
 6: 1 T the LORD said unto Moses, 2050.1
 6:12 how t shall Pharaoh hear me, who *am* 2050.1
 7: 9 t thou shalt say unto Aaron, Take thy 2050.1
 7:11 T Pharaoh also called the wise men and 2050.1
 8: 8 T Pharaoh called for Moses and Aaron, 2050.1
 8:19 T the magicians said unto Pharaoh, 2050.1
 9: 1 T the LORD said unto Moses, Go in 2050.1
 10:16 T Pharaoh called for Moses and Aaron 2050.1
 12:21 T Moses called for all the elders of 2050.1
 12:44 circumcised him, t shall he eat thereof. 227
 12:48 and t let him come near and keep it; 227
 13:13 redeem *it,* t thou shalt break his neck: 2050.1
 15: 1 T sang Moses and the children of Israel 227
 15:15 The dukes of Edom shall be amazed; 227
 16: 4 T said the LORD unto Moses, Behold, 2050.1
 16: 6 t ye shall know that the LORD hath 2050.1
 16: 7 t ye shall see the glory of the LORD; 2050.1
 17: 8 T came Amalek, and fought with Israel 2050.1
 18: 2 T Jethro, Moses' father in law, 2050.1
 18:23 God command thee *so,* t thou shalt be 2050.1
 19: 5 t ye shall be a peculiar treasure unto me 2050.1
 21: 3 his wife shall go out with him. 2050.1
 21: 6 T his master shall bring him unto 2050.1
 21: 8 himself, t shall he let her be redeemed: 2050.1
 21:11 t shall she go out free without money. 2050.1
 21:13 t I will appoint thee a place whither he 2050.1
 21:22 staff, t shall he that smote *him* be quit: 2050.1
 21:23 t thou shalt give life for life, 2050.1
 21:28 the ox shall be surely stoned, 2050.1
 21:30 t he shall give *for* the ransom of his life 2050.1
 21:35 t they shall sell the live ox, and divide 2050.1
 22: 3 t he shall be sold for his theft. 2050.1
 22: 8 t the master of the house shall be 2050.1
 22:11 T shall an oath of the LORD be between NIH
 22:13 t let him bring it *for* witness, *and* he shall NIH
 23:22 t I will be an enemy unto thine enemies 2050.1
 24: 9 T went up Moses, and Aaron, Nadab, 2050.1
 29: 7 T shalt thou take the anointing oil, 2050.1
 29:20 T shalt thou kill the ram, and take of his 2050.1
 29:34 thou shalt burn the remainder with 2050.1
 30:12 t shall they give every man a ransom for 2050.1
 32:24 t I cast it into the fire, and there came 2050.1
 32:26 T Moses stood in the gate of the camp, 2050.1
 34:20 *him* not, t shalt thou break his neck. 2050.1
 36: 1 T wrought Bezaleel and Aholiab, 2050.1
 40:34 T a cloud covered the tent of 2050.1
 40:37 t they journeyed not till the day that it 2050.1
Lev 1:14 t he shall bring his offering of 2050.1
 3: 7 t shall he offer it before the LORD. 2050.1
 3:12 t he shall offer it before the LORD. 2050.1
 4: 3 t let him bring for his sin, which he 2050.1
 4:14 t the congregation shall offer a young 2050.1
 4:28 t he shall bring his offering, a kid of 2050.1
 5: 1 not utter *it,* t he shall bear his iniquity. 2050.1
 5: 3 he knoweth *of it,* t he shall be guilty. 2050.1
 5: 4 when he knoweth *of it,* t he shall be 2050.1
 5: 7 t he shall bring for his trespass, which 2050.1
 5:11 t he that sinned shall bring for his 2050.1
 5:12 T shall he bring it to the priest, 2050.1
 5:15 t he shall bring for his trespass unto 2050.1
 6: 4 T it shall be, because he hath sinned, 2050.1
 7:12 t he shall offer with the sacrifice of 2050.1
 10: 3 T Moses said unto Aaron, This *is it* that 2050.1
 12: 2 t she shall be unclean seven days; 2050.1
 12: 4 she shall *t* continue in the blood of her NIH
 12: 5 t she shall be unclean two weeks, as *in* 2050.1
 12: 8 t she shall bring two turtles, or two 2050.1
 13: 2 t he shall be brought unto Aaron 2050.1
 13: 4 t the priest shall shut up *him that hath* 2050.1
 13: 5 t the priest shall shut him up seven days 2050.1
 13: 8 t the priest shall pronounce him 2050.1
 13: 9 t he shall be brought unto the priest; 2050.1
 13:13 T the priest shall consider: and behold, 2050.1
 13:17 t the priest shall pronounce *him* clean 2050.1
 13:21 t the priest shall shut him up seven 2050.1
 13:22 t the priest shall pronounce him 2050.1
 13:25 T the priest shall look upon it: 2050.1
 13:26 t the priest shall shut him up seven 2050.1
 13:27 t the priest shall pronounce him 2050.1
 13:30 T the priest shall see the plague: 2050.1
 13:30 t the priest shall pronounce him 2050.1
 13:31 t the priest shall shut up *him that hath* 2050.1
 13:34 t the priest shall pronounce him clean: 2050.1
 13:36 T the priest shall look on him: 2050.1
 13:39 T the priest shall look: and behold, 2050.1
 13:43 T the priest shall look upon it: 2050.1
 13:54 T the priest shall command that they 2050.1
 13:56 t the shall rend it out of the garment, 2050.1
 13:58 t it shall be washed the second time, 2050.1
 14: 4 T shall the priest command to take for 2050.1
 14:21 cannot get *so much;* t he shall take one 2050.1
 14:36 T the priest shall command that they 2050.1
 14:38 T the priest shall go out of the house to 2050.1
 14:40 T the priest shall command that they 2050.1
 14:44 T the priest shall come and look, 2050.1
 14:48 t the priest shall pronounce the house 2050.1
 15: 8 t he shall wash his clothes, 2050.1
 15:13 t he shall number to himself seven days 2050.1
 15:16 t he shall wash all his flesh in water, 2050.1
 15:28 t she shall number to herself seven days, 2050.1
 16:15 T he shall kill the goat of the sin 2050.1
 17:15 until the even: t he shall be clean. 2050.1

Lev 17:16 his flesh; t he shall bear his iniquity. 2050.1
 19:23 t ye shall count the fruit thereof as 2050.1
 20: 5 T I will set my face against that man, 2050.1
 22:14 t he shall put the fifth *part* thereof unto 2050.1
 22:27 t it shall be seven days under the dam; 2050.1
 23:10 t ye shall bring a sheaf of the firstfruits 2050.1
 23:19 T ye shall sacrifice one kid of the goats 2050.1
 25: 2 t shall the land keep a sabbath unto 2050.1
 25: 9 T shalt thou cause the trumpet of 2050.1
 25:21 T I will command my blessing upon you 2050.1
 25:25 t shall he redeem that which his brother 2050.1
 25:27 t let him count the years of the sale 2050.1
 25:28 t that which is sold shall remain in 2050.1
 25:29 t he may redeem it within a whole year 2050.1
 25:30 t the house that *is* in the walled city 2050.1
 25:33 t the house that was sold, and the city 2050.1
 25:35 with thee; t thou shalt relieve him: 2050.1
 25:41 t shall he depart from thee, *both* he and NIH
 25:52 t he shall count with him, 2050.1
 25:54 t he shall go out in the year of jubile, 2050.1
 26: 4 T I will give you rain in due season, 2050.1
 26:18 t I will punish you seven *times* more for 2050.1
 26:24 T will I also walk contrary unto you, 2050.1
 26:28 T I will walk contrary unto you **also** in 2050.1
 26:34 T shall the land enjoy her sabbaths, as 227
 26:34 *even* t shall the land rest, and enjoy her 227
 26:41 **if** t their uncircumcised hearts be 176+227
 26:41 they t accept of the punishment of their 227
 26:42 T will I remember my covenant with 2050.1
 27: 4 t thy estimation shall be thirty shekels. 2050.1
 27: 5 t thy estimation shall be of the male 2050.1
 27: 6 t thy estimation shall be of the male five 2050.1
 27: 7 t thy estimation shall be fifteen shekels, 2050.1
 27: 8 t he shall present himself before 2050.1
 27:10 t it and the exchange thereof shall be 2050.1
 27:11 t he shall present the beast before 2050.1
 27:13 t he shall add a fifth *part* thereof unto 2050.1
 27:14 t the priest shall estimate it, whether it 2050.1
 27:15 t he shall add the fifth *part* of the money 2050.1
 27:16 t thy estimation shall be according to 2050.1
 27:18 t the priest shall reckon unto him 2050.1
 27:19 t he shall add the fifth *part* of the money 2050.1
 27:23 T the priest shall reckon unto him 2050.1
 27:27 t he shall redeem *it* according to thine 2050.1
 27:27 t it shall be sold according to thy 2050.1
 27:33 t both it and the change thereof shall be 2050.1
Nu 2: 7 T the tribe of Zebulun: and Eliab the son NIH
 2:14 T the tribe of Gad: and the captain of 2050.1
 2:17 T the tabernacle of the congregation 2050.1
 2:22 T the tribe of Benjamin: and the captain 2050.1
 2:29 T the tribe of Naphtali: and the captain 2050.1
 5: 7 T they shall confess their sin which they 2050.1
 5:15 T shall the man bring his wife unto 2050.1
 5:21 T the priest shall charge the woman 2050.1
 5:25 T the priest shall take the jealousy 2050.1
 5:27 t it shall come to pass, *that,* if she be 2050.1
 5:28 t she shall be free, and shall conceive 2050.1
 5:31 T shall the man be guiltless from 2050.1
 6: 9 t he shall shave his head in the day of 2050.1
 7:89 he heard the voice of one speaking 2050.1
 8: 8 T let them take a young bullock with 2050.1
 9:17 t after that the children of Israel 2050.1
 9:19 t the children of Israel kept the charge 2050.1
 9:21 up in the morning, t they journeyed: 2050.1
 10: 4 *but* with one *trumpet,* t the princes, 2050.1
 10: 5 the camps that lie on the east parts 2050.1
 10: 6 the camps that lie on the south side 2050.1
 10: 9 t ye shall blow an alarm with 2050.1
 11:10 T Moses heard the people weep 2050.1
 12: 8 wherefore t were ye not afraid to speak 2050.1
 14: 5 T Moses and Aaron fell on their faces 2050.1
 14: 8 t he will bring us into this land, 2050.1
 14:13 The Egyptians shall hear *it,* (for thou 2050.1
 14:15 the nations which have heard the fame 2050.1
 14:45 T the Amalekites came down, 2050.1
 15: 4 T shall he that offereth his offering unto 2050.1
 15: 9 T shall he bring with a bullock a meat 2050.1
 15:19 T it shall be, *that* when ye eat of 2050.1
 15:24 T it shall be, if *ought* be committed by 2050.1
 15:27 t he shall bring a she goat of the first 2050.1
 16: 3 wherefore t lift you up yourselves above 2050.1
 16:29 of all men; t the LORD hath not sent me. NIH
 16:30 t ye shall understand that these men 2050.1
 18:26 t ye shall offer up a heave offering of it 2050.1
 18:30 t it shall be counted unto the Levites as 2050.1
 19: 7 T the priest shall wash his clothes, 2050.1
 19:12 the seventh day he shall not be clean. 2050.1
 20: 1 T came the children of Israel, *even* 2050.1
 20:19 drink *of* thy water, t I will pay for it: 2050.1
 21: 1 t he fought against Israel, and took 2050.1
 21: 2 t I will utterly destroy their cities. 2050.1
 21:17 T Israel sang this song, Spring up, O well; 227
 22:31 T the LORD opened the eyes of 2050.1
 27: 1 T came the daughters of Zelophehad, 2050.1
 27: 8 t ye shall cause his inheritance to pass 2050.1
 27: 9 t ye shall give his inheritance unto his 2050.1
 27:10 t ye shall give his inheritance unto his 2050.1
 27:11 t ye shall give his inheritance unto his 2050.1
 30: 4 t all her vows shall stand, and every 2050.1
 30: 7 that he heard *it;* t her vows shall stand, 2050.1
 30: 8 t he shall make her vow which she 2050.1
 30:11 t all her vows shall stand, and every 2050.1
 30:12 t whatsoever proceeded out of her lips NIH
 30:14 t he establisheth all her vows, or all her 2050.1
 30:15 heard *them;* t he shall bear her iniquity. 2050.1

Nu

32:22	t afterward ye shall return,	2050.1
32:29	t ye shall give them the land of Gilead	2050.1
33:52	T ye shall drive out all the inhabitants	2050.1
33:55	T it shall come to pass, that those which	2050.1
34: 3	T your south quarter shall be from	2050.1
35:11	T ye shall appoint you cities to be cities	2050.1
35:24	T the congregation shall judge between	2050.1
36: 3	t shall their inheritance be taken from	2050.1
36: 4	t shall their inheritance be put unto	2050.1

Dt

1:29	T I said unto you, Dread not, neither be	2050.1
1:41	T ye answered and said unto the	2050.1
2: 1	T we turned, and took our journey into	2050.1
2:32	T Sihon came out against us, he and	2050.1
3: 1	T we turned, and went up the way to	2050.1
3:20	t shall ye return every man unto his	NIH
4:41	T Moses severed three cities on this side	227
5:25	our God any more, t we shall die.	2050.1
6:12	T beware lest thou forget the Lord,	NIH
6:21	t thou shalt say unto thy son, We were	2050.1
8:10	t thou shalt bless the Lord thy God for	2050.1
8:14	T thine heart be lifted up, and thou	2050.1
9: 9	t I abode in the mount forty days and	2050.1
9:23	t you rebelled against the	2050.1
11:17	t the Lord's wrath be kindled against	NIH
11:23	T will the Lord drive out all these	2050.1
12:11	T there shall be a place which	2050.1
12:21	t thou shalt kill of thy herd and of thy	2050.1
13:14	T shalt thou inquire, and make search,	2050.1
14:25	T shalt thou turn it into money,	2050.1
15:12	t in the seventh year thou shalt let him	2050.1
15:17	T thou shalt take an aul, and thrust it	2050.1
17: 5	T thou bring forth that man or	2050.1
17: 8	t shalt thou arise, and get thee up into	2050.1
18: 7	T he shall minister in the name of	2050.1
19: 9	t shalt thou add three cities moe for	2050.1
19:12	T the elders of his city shall send and	2050.1
19:17	T both the men, between whom	2050.1
19:19	T shall ye do unto him, as he had	2050.1
20:10	fight against it, t proclaim peace unto it.	2050.1
20:11	peace, and open unto thee, t it shall be,	2050.1
20:12	war against thee, t thou shalt besiege it:	2050.1
21: 2	T thy elders and thy judges shall come	2050.1
21:12	T thou shalt bring her home to thine	2050.1
21:14	t thou shalt let her go whither she will;	2050.1
21:16	T it shall be, when he maketh his sons	2050.1
21:19	T shall his father and his mother lay	2050.1
22: 2	t thou shalt bring it unto thine own	2050.1
22: 8	t thou shalt make a battlement for thy	2050.1
22:15	T shall the father of the damsel,	2050.1
22:21	T they shall bring out the damsel to	2050.1
22:22	t they shall both of them die, both	2050.1
22:24	T ye shall bring them both out unto	2050.1
22:25	T the man only that lay with her shall	2050.1
22:29	T the man that lay with her shall give	2050.1
23: 9	t keep thee from every wicked thing.	2050.1
23:10	t shall he go abroad out of the camp,	2050.1
23:24	t thou mayest eat grapes thy fill at thine	2050.1
23:25	t thou mayest pluck the ears with thine	2050.1
24: 1	t let him write her a bill of divorcement,	2050.1
24: 7	t that thief shall die; and thou shalt put	2050.1
25: 1	t they shall justify the righteous,	2050.1
25: 3	t thy brother should seem vile unto	2050.1
25: 7	t let his brother's wife go up to the gate	2050.1
25: 8	T the elders of his city shall call him,	2050.1
25: 9	T shall his brother's wife come unto	2050.1
25:12	T thou shalt cut off her hand, thine eye	2050.1
26:13	T thou shalt say before the Lord thy	2050.1
28:59	T the Lord will make thy plagues	2050.1
29:20	t the anger of the Lord and his jealousy	227
29:25	T men shall say, Because they have	2050.1
30: 3	That t the Lord thy God will turn thy	2050.1
31:17	T my anger shall be kindled against	2050.1
31:20	t will they turn unto other gods,	2050.1
32:15	thou art covered with fatness; t	2050.1
33:28	Israel t shall dwell in safety alone:	2050.1

Jos

1: 8	t thou shalt make thy way prosperous,	227
1: 8	and t thou shalt have good success.	227
1:10	T Joshua commanded the officers of	2050.1
1:15	t ye shall return unto the land of your	2050.1
2:15	T she let them down by a cord through	2050.1
2:20	t we will be quit of thine oath which	2050.1
3: 3	t ye shall remove from your place,	2050.1
4: 4	T Joshua called the twelve men, whom	2050.1
4: 7	T ye shall answer them, That the waters	2050.1
4:22	T ye shall let your children know,	2050.1
6:10	the day I bid you shout; t shall ye shout.	2050.1
7:21	t I coveted them, and took them;	2050.1
8: 7	T ye shall rise up from the ambush,	2050.1
8:21	t they turned again, and slew the men	2050.1
8:30	T Joshua built an altar unto the Lord God	227
10:12	T spake Joshua to the Lord in the day	227
10:22	T said Joshua, Open the mouth of	2050.1
10:29	T Joshua passed from Makkedah,	2050.1
10:33	T Horam king of Gezer came up to help	227
14: 6	T the children of Judah came unto	2050.1
14:11	as my strength was t, even so is my	227
14:12	t I shall be able to drive them out,	2050.1
15: 1	This t was the lot of the tribe of	2050.1
17:15	t get thee up to the wood country, and	NIH
19:12	t goeth out to Daberath, and goeth up to	NIH
19:29	t the coast turneth to Ramah, and to	NIH
19:34	t the coast turneth westward to	NIH
20: 5	t they shall not deliver the slayer up into	2050.1
20: 6	t shall the slayer return, and come unto	227
21: 1	t came near the heads of the fathers of	2050.1

Jos

22: 1	T Joshua called the Reubenites,	227
22: 7	also unto their tents, t he blessed them,	2050.1
22:19	t pass ye over unto the land of	NIH
22:21	T the children of Reuben and the	2050.1
23:16	t shall the anger of the Lord be	2050.1
24: 9	T Balak the son of Zippor, king of Moab	2050.1
24:20	t he will turn and do you hurt,	2050.1

Jdg

2:18	t the Lord was with the judge,	2050.1
3:23	T Ehud went forth through the porch,	2050.1
4: 8	If thou wilt go with me, t I will go:	2050.1
4: 8	if thou wilt not go with me, t I will not	NIH
4:21	T Jael Heber's wife took a nail of	2050.1
5: 1	T sang Deborah and Barak the son of	2050.1
5: 8	chose new gods; t was war in the gates:	227
5:11	t shall the people of the Lord go down to	227
5:13	T he made him that remaineth have	227
5:19	t fought the kings of Canaan in Taanach	227
5:22	T were the horsehoofs broken by the	227
6:13	be with us, why t is all this befallen us?	2050.1
6:17	t shew me a sign that thou talkest with	2050.1
6:21	T the angel of the Lord put forth	2050.1
6:21	the unleavened cakes. T the angel of	2050.1
6:24	T Gideon built an altar there unto	2050.1
6:27	T Gideon took ten men of his servants,	2050.1
6:30	T the men of the city said unto Joash,	2050.1
6:33	T all the Midianites and the Amalekites	2050.1
6:37	it be dry upon all the earth beside, t	2050.1
7: 1	T Jerubbaal, who is Gideon, and all	2050.1
7:11	T went he down with Phurah his	2050.1
7:18	t blow ye the trumpets also on every	2050.1
7:24	T all the men of Ephraim gathered	2050.1
8: 3	T their anger was abated toward him,	227
8: 7	T I will tear your flesh with the thorns of	2050.1
8:18	T said he unto Zebah and Zalmunna,	2050.1
8:21	T Zebah and Zalmunna said, Rise thou,	2050.1
8:22	T the men of Israel said unto Gideon,	2050.1
9:12	T said the trees unto the vine, Come	2050.1
9:14	T said all the trees unto the bramble,	2050.1
9:15	t come and put your trust in my shadow:	NIH
9:19	If ye t have dealt truly and sincerely	2050.1
9:19	t rejoice ye in Abimelech, and let him also	NIH
9:23	T God sent an evil spirit between	2050.1
9:29	my hand; t would I remove Abimelech.	2050.1
9:33	t mayest thou do to them as thou shalt	2050.1
9:38	T said Zebul unto him, Where is now	2050.1
9:50	T went Abimelech to Thebez,	2050.1
9:54	T he called hastily unto the young man	2050.1
10:17	T the children of Ammon were gathered	2050.1
11: 3	T Jephthah fled from his brethren,	2050.1
11:11	T Jephthah went with the elders of	2050.1
11:17	T Israel sent messengers unto the king	2050.1
11:18	T they went along through	2050.1
11:29	T the spirit of the Lord came upon	2050.1
11:31	T it shall be, that whatsoever cometh	2050.1
12: 3	wherefore t are ye come up unto me	2050.1
12: 4	T Jephthah gathered together all the	2050.1
12: 6	T said they unto him, Say now	2050.1
12: 6	T they took him, and slew him at	2050.1
12: 7	T died Jephthah the Gileadite,	2050.1
12:10	T died Ibzan, and was buried at	2050.1
13: 6	T the woman came and told her	2050.1
13: 8	T Manoah intreated the Lord,	2050.1
13:21	T Manoah knew that he was an angel of	227
14: 3	T his father and his mother said unto	2050.1
14: 5	T went Samson down, and his father	2050.1
14:12	t I will give you thirty sheets and	2050.1
14:13	t shall ye give me thirty sheets and	2050.1
15: 6	T the Philistines said, Who hath done	2050.1
15: 9	T the Philistines went up, and pitched	2050.1
15:11	T three thousand men of Judah went to	2050.1
16: 1	T went Samson to Gaza, and saw there	2050.1
16: 7	T shall I be weak, and be as another	2050.1
16: 8	T the lords of the Philistines brought up	2050.1
16:11	T said he, If they bind me fast with	2050.1
16:17	t my strength will go from me, and I	2050.1
16:18	T the lords of the Philistines came up	2050.1
16:23	T the lords of the Philistines gathered	2050.1
16:31	T his brethren and all the house of his	2050.1
17:13	T said Micah, Now know I that	2050.1
18: 7	T the five men departed, and came to	2050.1
18:14	T answered the five men that went to	2050.1
18:18	T said the priest unto them, What do	2050.1
19:26	T came the woman in the dawning of	2050.1
19:28	T the man took her up upon an ass,	2050.1
20: 1	T all the children of Israel went out,	2050.1
20: 3	T said the children of Israel, Tell us,	2050.1
20:26	T all the children of Israel, and all	2050.1
21:16	T the elders of the congregation said,	2050.1
21:19	T they said, Behold, there is a feast of	2050.1
21:21	t come ye out of the vineyards,	2050.1

Ru

1: 6	T she arose with her daughters in law,	2050.1
1: 9	T she kissed them; and they lift up their	2050.1
1:18	with her, t she left speaking unto her.	2050.1
1:21	Why t call ye me Naomi, seeing the Lord	NIH
2: 5	T said Boaz unto his servant that was	2050.1
2: 8	T said Boaz unto Ruth, Hearest thou	2050.1
2:10	T she fell on her face, and bowed	2050.1
2:13	T she said, Let me find favour in thy	2050.1
3: 1	T Naomi her mother in law said unto	2050.1
3:13	t will I do the part of a kinsman to thee,	2050.1
3:18	T said she, Sit still, my daughter,	2050.1
4: 1	t went Boaz up to the gate, and sat him	2050.1
4: 4	but if thou wilt not redeem it, t tell me,	NIH
4: 5	T said Boaz, What day thou buyest	2050.1

1Sa

1: 8	T said Elkanah her husband to her,	2050.1

1Sa

1:11	t I will give him unto the Lord all	2050.1
1:17	T Eli answered and said, Go in peace:	2050.1
1:22	t I will bring him, that he may appear	NIH
2:16	t take as much as thy soul desireth;	2050.1
2:16	t he would answer him, Nay; but	2050.1
3:10	T Samuel answered, Speak; for thy	2050.1
3:16	T Eli called Samuel, and said, Samuel,	2050.1
6: 3	t ye shall be healed, and it shall be known	227
6: 4	T said they, What shall be the trespass	2050.1
6: 6	Wherefore t do ye harden your hearts,	2050.1
6: 9	t the hath done us this great evil:	NIH
6: 9	t we shall know that it is not his hand	2050.1
7: 3	t put away the strange gods and Ashtaroth	NIH
7: 4	T the children of Israel did put away	2050.1
7:12	T Samuel took a stone, and set it	2050.1
8: 4	T all the elders of Israel gathered	2050.1
9: 4	t they passed through the land of	2050.1
9: 7	T said Saul to his servant, But behold,	2050.1
9:10	T said Saul to his servant, Well said;	2050.1
9:18	T Saul drew near to Samuel in the gate,	2050.1
9:21	t speakest thou so to me?	2050.1
10: 1	T Samuel took a vial of oil, and poured	2050.1
10: 2	t thou shalt find two men by Rachel's	2050.1
10: 3	T shalt thou go on forward from thence,	2050.1
10:11	t the people said one to another,	2050.1
10:25	T Samuel told the people the manner of	2050.1
11: 1	T Nahash the Ammonite came up,	2050.1
11: 3	and t, if there be no man to save us,	2050.1
11: 4	T came the messengers to Gibeah of	2050.1
11:14	T said Samuel to the people, Come,	2050.1
12: 8	t the Lord sent Moses and Aaron,	2050.1
12:14	t shall both ye and also the king that	2050.1
12:15	t shall the hand of the Lord be against	2050.1
12:21	t should ye go after vain things, which	NIH
13: 6	t the people did hide themselves in	2050.1
14: 8	T said Jonathan, Behold, we will pass	2050.1
14: 9	t we will stand still in our place,	2050.1
14:10	Come up unto us; t we will go up:	2050.1
14:17	T said Saul unto the people that were	2050.1
14:28	T answered one of the people, and said,	2050.1
14:29	T said Jonathan, My father hath	2050.1
14:33	T they told Saul, saying, Behold,	2050.1
14:36	T said the priest, Let us draw near	2050.1
14:40	T said he unto all Israel, Be ye on one	2050.1
14:43	T Saul said to Jonathan, Tell me what	2050.1
14:46	T Saul went up from following	2050.1
15:10	T came the word of the Lord unto	2050.1
15:14	meaneth t this bleating of the sheep	2050.1
15:16	T Samuel said unto Saul, Stay, and I will	2050.1
15:19	Wherefore t didst thou not obey the	2050.1
15:30	T he said, I have sinned: yet honour me	2050.1
15:32	T said Samuel, Bring you hither to me	2050.1
15:34	T Samuel went to Ramah; and Saul	2050.1
16: 8	T Jesse called Abinadab, and made him	2050.1
16: 9	T Jesse made Shammah to pass by.	2050.1
16:13	T Samuel took the horn of oil,	2050.1
16:18	T answered one of the servants, and	2050.1
17: 9	to kill me, t will we be your servants:	2050.1
17: 9	t shall ye be our servants, and serve us.	2050.1
17:45	T said David to the Philistine,	2050.1
18: 3	T Jonathan and David made a covenant,	2050.1
18:30	T the princes of the Philistines went	2050.1
19: 5	t wilt thou sin against innocent	2050.1
19:22	T went he also to Ramah, and came to a	2050.1
20: 4	T said Jonathan unto David,	2050.1
20: 6	If thy father at all miss me, t say,	2050.1
20: 7	t be sure that evil is determined by him.	NIH
20: 9	upon thee, t would not I tell it thee?	2050.1
20:10	T said David to Jonathan, Who shall tell	2050.1
20:12	I t send not unto thee, and shew it thee;	227
20:13	t I will shew it thee, and send thee	2050.1
20:18	T Jonathan said to David, To morrow is	2050.1
20:19	t thou shalt go down quickly, and come	NIH
20:21	side of thee, take them; t come thou:	2050.1
20:30	T Saul's anger was kindled against	2050.1
21: 1	T came David to Nob to Ahimelech	2050.1
21:14	T said Achish unto his servants,	2050.1
21:14	t have ye brought him to me?	NIH
22: 5	T David departed, and came into	2050.1
22: 7	T Saul said unto his servants that stood	2050.1
22: 9	T answered Doeg the Edomite, which	2050.1
22:11	T the king sent to call Ahimelech	2050.1
22:14	T Ahimelech answered the king,	2050.1
22:15	Did I t begin to inquire of God	3117+1886.1
23: 1	T they told David, saying, Behold,	2050.1
23: 3	how much more t if we come to Keilah	2050.1
23: 4	T David inquired of the Lord yet	2050.1
23:10	T said David, O Lord God of Israel,	2050.1
23:12	T said David, Will the men of Keilah	2050.1
23:13	T David and his men, which were	2050.1
23:19	T came up the Ziphites to Saul to	2050.1
24: 2	T Saul took three thousand chosen men	2050.1
24: 4	T David arose, and cut off the skirt of	2050.1
25:11	Shall I t take my bread, and my water,	2050.1
25:18	T Abigail made haste, and took two	2050.1
25:31	my lord, t remember thine handmaid.	2050.1
26: 2	T Saul arose, and went down to	2050.1
26: 6	T answered David and said to	2050.1
26: 8	T said Abishai to David, God hath	2050.1
26:13	T David went over to the other side,	2050.1
26:14	T Abner answered and said, Who art	2050.1
26:15	wherefore t hast thou not kept thy lord	2050.1
26:21	T said Saul, I have sinned: return, my	2050.1
26:25	T Saul said to David, Blessed be thou,	2050.1
27: 6	Achish gave him Ziklag that day:	2050.1

T

1Sa	28: 7 **T** said Saul unto his servants, Seek me a	2050.1
	28: 9 wherefore **t** layest thou a snare for my	2050.1
	28:11 **T** said the woman, Whom shall I bring	2050.1
	28:16 **T** said Samuel, Wherefore then dost	2050.1
	28:16 Wherefore I **t** dost thou ask of me,	2050.1
	28:20 **T** Saul fell straightway all along on	2050.1
	28:25 **T** they arose up, and went away that	2050.1
	29: 3 **T** said the princes of the Philistines,	2050.1
	29: 6 **T** Achish called David, and said unto	2050.1
	30: 4 **T** David and the people that *were* with	2050.1
	30:22 **T** answered all the wicked men and	2050.1
	30:23 **T** said David, Ye shall not do so,	2050.1
	31: 4 **T** said Saul unto his armourbearer,	2050.1
2Sa	1:11 **T** David took hold on his clothes,	2050.1
	2:15 **T** there arose and went over by number	2050.1
	2:20 **T** Abner looked behind him, and said,	2050.1
	2:22 how I **t** should I hold up my face to Joab	2050.1
	2:26 **T** Abner called to Joab, and said, Shall	2050.1
	2:26 how long shall it be **t**, ere thou bid	2050.1
	2:27 **t** in the morning the people had gone	227
	3: 8 **T** was Abner very wroth for the words	2050.1
	3:16 **T** said Abner unto him, Go, return.	2050.1
	3:18 Now **t** do *it*: for the Lord hath spoken	2050.1
	3:24 **T** Joab came to the king, and said,	2050.1
	5: 1 **T** came all the tribes of Israel to David	2050.1
	5:24 *that* **t** thou shalt bestir thyself:	227
	5:24 for **t** shall the Lord go out before thee,	227
	6:20 **T** David returned to bless his household	2050.1
	7:18 **T** went king David in, and sat before	2050.1
	8: 6 **T** David put garrisons in Syria of	2050.1
	8:10 **T** Toi sent Joram his son unto king	2050.1
	9: 5 **T** king David sent, and fet him out of	2050.1
	9: 9 **T** the king called to Ziba, Saul's servant,	2050.1
	9:11 **T** said Ziba unto the king, According to	2050.1
	10: 2 **T** said David, I will shew kindness unto	2050.1
	10: 5 until your beards be grown, and **t** return.	NIH
	10:11 too strong for me, **t** thou shalt help me:	2050.1
	10:11 for thee, **t** I will come and help thee.	2050.1
	10:14 **t** fled they *also* before Abishai,	NIH
	11:10 why **t** didst thou not go down unto thine	NIH
	11:11 shall I **t** go into mine house, to eat and	2050.1
	11:18 **T** Joab sent and told David all the things	2050.1
	11:21 **t** say thou, Thy servant Uriah the Hittite	2050.1
	11:25 **T** David said unto the messenger,	2050.1
	12:18 how will he **t** vex himself, if we tell him	2050.1
	12:20 **T** David arose from the earth,	2050.1
	12:20 **t** he came to his own house; and when	2050.1
	12:21 **T** said his servants unto him, What	2050.1
	13: 7 **T** David sent home to Tamar, saying,	2050.1
	13:15 **T** Amnon hated her exceedingly;	2050.1
	13:17 **T** he called his servant that ministered	2050.1
	13:18 **T** his servant brought her out,	2050.1
	13:26 **T** said Absalom, If not, I pray thee,	2050.1
	13:28 Smite Amnon; **t** kill him, fear not:	2050.1
	13:29 **T** all the king's sons arose,	2050.1
	13:31 **T** the king arose, and tare his garments,	2050.1
	14:11 **T** said she, I pray thee, let the king	2050.1
	14:12 **T** the woman said, Let thine handmaid,	2050.1
	14:13 Wherefore **t** hast thou thought such a	2050.1
	14:17 **T** thine handmaid said, The word of my	2050.1
	14:18 **T** the king answered and said unto	2050.1
	14:31 **T** Joab arose, and came to Absalom unto	2050.1
	15: 2 **t** Absalom called unto him, and said,	2050.1
	15: 8 *to* Jerusalem, **t** I will serve the Lord.	2050.1
	15:10 **t** ye shall say, Absalom reigneth in	2050.1
	15:19 **T** said the king to Ittai the Gittite,	2050.1
	15:33 **t** thou shalt be a burden unto me:	2050.1
	15:34 **t** mayest thou for me defeat the counsel	2050.1
	16: 4 **T** said the king to Ziba, Behold, thine	2050.1
	16: 9 **T** said Abishai the son of Zeruiah unto	2050.1
	16:10 Who shall I **t** say, Wherefore hast thou	2050.1
	16:20 **T** said Absalom to Ahithophel,	2050.1
	16:21 **t** shall the hands of all that *are* with thee	2050.1
	17: 5 **T** said Absalom, Call now Hushai	2050.1
	17:13 **t** shall all Israel bring ropes to that city,	2050.1
	17:15 **T** said Hushai unto Zadok and	2050.1
	17:22 **T** David arose, and all the people that	2050.1
	17:24 **T** David came to Mahanaim.	2050.1
	18:14 **T** said Joab, I may not tarry thus with	2050.1
	18:19 **T** said Ahimaaz the son of Zadok, Let	2050.1
	18:21 **T** said Joab to Cushi, Go tell the king	2050.1
	18:22 **T** said Ahimaaz the son of Zadok yet	2050.1
	18:23 **T** Ahimaaz ran *by* the way of the plain,	2050.1
	19: 6 *this* day, **t** it had pleased thee well.	227+3588
	19: 8 **T** the king rose, and sat in the gate.	2050.1
	19:12 wherefore **t** are ye the last to bring back	2050.1
	19:35 and singing *women*? wherefore **t**	2050.1
	19:40 **T** the king went on to Gilgal,	2050.1
	19:42 wherefore **t** be ye angry for this matter?	2050.1
	19:43 why **t** did ye despise us, that our advice	2050.1
	20: 4 **T** said the king to Amasa, Assemble me	2050.1
	20:16 **T** cried a wise woman out of the city,	2050.1
	20:17 I *am* he. **T** she said unto him,	2050.1
	20:18 **T** she spake, saying, They were wont to	2050.1
	20:22 **T** the woman went unto all the people	2050.1
	21: 1 **T** there was a famine in the days of	2050.1
	21:17 **T** the men of David sware unto him,	227
	21:18 **t** Sibbechai the Hushathite slew Saph,	2050.1
	22: 8 **T** the earth shook and trembled;	2050.1
	22:43 **T** did I beat them *as* small as the dust	2050.1
	23:14 David *was* in a hold, and the garrison of	227
	23:14 of the Philistines *was* **t** in Beth-lehem.	227
	24: 6 **T** they came to Gilead, and to the land	2050.1
1Ki	1: 5 **T** Adonijah the son of Haggith exalted	2050.1
	1:13 my throne? why **t** doth Adonijah reign?	2050.1

1Ki	1:28 **T** king David answered and said, Call	2050.1
	1:31 **T** Bath-sheba bowed *with her* face *to*	2050.1
	1:35 **T** ye shall come up after him, that he	2050.1
	2:12 **T** sat Solomon upon the throne of	2050.1
	2:20 **T** she said, I desire one small petition of	2050.1
	2:23 **T** king Solomon sware by the Lord,	2050.1
	2:28 **T** tidings came to Joab: for Joab had	2050.1
	2:29 **T** Solomon sent Benaiah the son of	2050.1
	2:43 Why **t** hast thou not kept the oath of	2050.1
	3:14 did walk, I **t** will lengthen thy days.	2050.1
	3:16 **T** came there two women, *that were*	227
	3:23 **T** said the king, The one saith, This *is*	2050.1
	3:26 **T** spake the woman whose the living	2050.1
	3:27 **T** the king answered and said, Give her	2050.1
	6:10 **t** he built chambers against all the house,	NIH
	6:12 **t** will I perform my word with thee,	2050.1
	7: 7 **T** he made a porch for the throne where	2050.1
	7:38 **T** made he ten lavers of brass: one laver	2050.1
	8: 1 **T** Solomon assembled the elders of Israel,	227
	8:12 **T** spake Solomon, The Lord said that *he*	227
	8:32 **T** hear thou *in* heaven, and do,	2050.1
	8:34 **T** hear thou *in* heaven, and forgive	2050.1
	8:36 **T** hear thou *in* heaven, and forgive the	2050.1
	8:39 **T** hear thou *in* heaven thy dwelling	2050.1
	8:45 **T** hear thou *in* heaven their prayer and	2050.1
	8:49 **T** hear thou their prayer and	2050.1
	9: 5 **T** I will establish the throne of thy	2050.1
	9: 7 **T** will I cut off Israel out of the land	2050.1
	9:11 *that* **t** king Solomon gave Hiram twenty	227
	9:24 had built for her: **t** did he build Millo.	227
	11: 7 **T** did Solomon build a high place for	227
	11:22 **T** Pharaoh said unto him, But what	2050.1
	12: 5 yet *for* three days, **t** come again to me.	2050.1
	12: 7 **t** they will be thy servants for ever.	2050.1
	12:18 **T** king Rehoboam sent Adoram, who	2050.1
	12:25 **T** Jeroboam built Shechem in mount	2050.1
	12:27 **t** shall the heart of this people turn again	2050.1
	13:15 **T** he said unto him, Come home with	2050.1
	13:31 **t** bury me in the sepulchre wherein	2050.1
	15:18 **T** Asa took all the silver and the gold	2050.1
	15:22 **T** king Asa made a proclamation	2050.1
	16: 1 **T** the word of the Lord came to Jehu	2050.1
	16:21 **T** were the people of Israel divided into	227
	18:21 If Baal, **t** follow him. And the people	NIH
	18:22 **T** said Elijah unto the people, I, *even* I	2050.1
	18:38 **T** the fire of the Lord fell,	2050.1
	19: 2 Jezebel sent a messenger unto Elijah,	2050.1
	19: 5 behold **t**, an angel touched him,	2050.1
	19:20 and my mother, and *I* **t** I will follow thee.	NIH
	19:21 **T** he arose, and went after Elijah,	2050.1
	20: 7 **T** the king of Israel called all the elders	2050.1
	20:14 **T** he said, Who shall order the battle?	2050.1
	20:15 **T** he numbered the young men of	2050.1
	20:33 **T** he said, Go ye, bring him.	2050.1
	20:33 Ben-hadad came forth to him;	2050.1
	20:34 **T** *said Ahab,* I will send thee away with	2050.1
	20:36 **T** said he unto him, Because thou hast	2050.1
	20:37 **T** he found another man, and said,	2050.1
	20:39 **t** shall thy life be for his life, or else thou	2050.1
	21:10 **t** carry him out, and stone him, that he	NIH
	21:13 **t** they carried him forth out of the city,	2050.1
	21:14 **t** they sent to Jezebel, saying, Naboth is	2050.1
	22: 6 **T** the king of Israel gathered the	2050.1
	22: 9 **T** the king of Israel called an officer,	2050.1
	22:47 *There was* **t** no king in Edom: a deputy	2050.1
	22:49 **T** said Ahaziah the son of Ahab unto	227
2Ki	1: 1 **T** Moab rebelled against Israel after	2050.1
	1: 9 **T** the king sent unto him a captain of	2050.1
	1:10 **t** let fire come down from heaven,	2050.1
	3:27 **T** he took his eldest son that should	2050.1
	4: 3 **T** he said, Go, borrow thee vessels	2050.1
	4: 7 **T** she came and told the man of God.	2050.1
	4:14 he said, What **t** *is* to be done for her?	2050.1
	4:20 he sat on her knees till noon, and **t** died.	NIH
	4:24 **T** she saddled an ass, and said to her	2050.1
	4:28 **T** she said, Did I desire a son of my	2050.1
	4:29 **T** he said to Gehazi, Gird up thy loins,	2050.1
	4:35 **T** he returned, and walked in the house	2050.1
	4:37 **T** she went in, and fell at his feet,	2050.1
	4:41 said, **T** bring meal. And he cast *it* into	2050.1
	5:13 not have done *it*? how much rather **t**,	2050.1
	5:14 **T** went he down, and dipped *himself*	2050.1
	5:17 Shall there not **t**, I pray thee,	2050.1
	6: 8 **T** the king of Syria warred against Israel,	2050.1
	6:31 **T** he said, God do so and more also to	2050.1
	7: 1 **T** Elisha said, Hear ye the word of	2050.1
	7: 2 **T** a lord on whose hand the king leaned	2050.1
	7: 4 **t** the famine *is* in the city, and we shall	2050.1
	7: 9 **T** they said one to another, We do not	2050.1
	8: 1 **T** spake Elisha unto the woman,	2050.1
	8:16 Jehoshaphat *being* **t** king of Judah,	2050.1
	8:22 **T** Libnah revolted at the same time.	227
	9: 3 **T** take the box of oil, and pour *it* on his	2050.1
	9: 3 **T** open the door, and flee, and tarry not.	2050.1
	9:11 **T** Jehu came forth to the servants of his	2050.1
	9:13 **T** they hasted, and took every man his	2050.1
	9:15 **t** let none go forth *nor* escape out of the	NIH
	9:19 **T** he sent *out* a second on horseback,	2050.1
	9:25 **T** said *Jehu* to Bidkar his captain,	2050.1
	10: 4 not before him: how **t** shall we stand?	2050.1
	10: 1 he wrote a letter the second time to	2050.1
	12: 7 **T** king Jehoash called for Jehoiada	2050.1
	12:17 **T** Hazael king of Syria went up,	227
	13:17 he opened *it*. **T** Elisha said, Shoot.	2050.1
	13:19 **t** hadst thou smitten Syria till *thou* hadst	227

2Ki	14: 8 **T** Amaziah sent messengers to Jehoash,	227
	15:16 **T** Menahem smote Tiphsah, and all that	227
	16: 5 **T** Rezin king of Syria and Pekah son of	227
	17: 5 **T** the king of Assyria came up	2050.1
	17:27 **T** the king of Assyria commanded,	2050.1
	17:28 **T** one of the priests whom they had	2050.1
	18:24 How **t** wilt thou turn away the face of	2050.1
	18:26 **T** said Eliakim the son of Hilkiah,	2050.1
	18:28 **T** Rab-shakeh stood and cried with a	2050.1
	18:31 **t** eat ye every man of his own vine,	NIH
	18:37 **T** came Eliakim the son of Hilkiah,	2050.1
	19:20 **T** Isaiah the son of Amoz sent to	2050.1
	20: 2 **T** he turned his face to the wall,	2050.1
	20:14 **T** came Isaiah the prophet unto king	2050.1
	20:19 **T** said Hezekiah unto Isaiah, Good *is*	2050.1
	23:17 **T** he said, What title *is* that that I see?	2050.1
	24: 1 **t** he turned and rebelled against him.	2050.1
1Ch	1:29 **t** Kedar, and Adbeel, and Mibsam,	2050.1
	2:24 **t** Abiah Hezron's wife bare him Ashur	2050.1
	6:32 **t** they waited on their office according to	NIH
	9:36 **t** Zur, and Kish, and Baal, and Ner,	2050.1
	10: 4 **t** Saul to his armourbearer, Draw	2050.1
	10: 7 **t** they forsook their cities, and fled:	2050.1
	11: 1 **T** all Israel gathered themselves to	2050.1
	11:16 David *was* in the hold, and the	227
	11:16 Philistines' garrison *was* **t** at Beth-lehem.	227
	12: 3 The chief *was* Ahiezer, **t** Joash, the sons	2050.1
	12:18 **T** the spirit came upon Amasai, *who*	2050.1
	12:18 **T** David received them, and made them	2050.1
	14:11 **T** David said, God hath broken in upon	2050.1
	14:15 *that* **t** thou shalt go out to battle:	227
	15: 2 **T** David said, None ought to carry the ark	227
	16: 7 **T** on that day David delivered first *this*	227
	16:33 **t** shall the trees of the wood sing out at	227
	17: 2 **T** Nathan said unto David, Do all that *is*	2050.1
	18: 6 **T** David put *garrisons* in	2050.1
	19: 5 **T** there went *certain,* and told David	2050.1
	19: 5 until your beards be grown, and **t** return.	NIH
	19:12 too strong for me, **t** thou shalt help me:	2050.1
	19:12 be too strong for thee, **t** I will help thee.	2050.1
	19:15 unto the city. **T** Joab came to Jerusalem.	2050.1
	21: 3 why **t** doth my lord require this *thing*?	NIH
	21:16 **T** David and the elders *of Israel, who*	2050.1
	21:18 **T** the angel of the Lord commanded	2050.1
	21:22 **T** David said to Ornan, Grant me	2050.1
	21:28 the Jebusite, **t** he sacrificed there.	2050.1
	22: 1 **T** David said, This *is* the house of	2050.1
	22: 6 **T** he called for Solomon his son,	2050.1
	22:13 **t** shalt thou prosper, if thou takest heed	227
	26:14 *for* Zechariah his son, a wise	2050.1
	28: 2 **T** David the king stood up upon his	2050.1
	28:11 **T** David gave to Solomon his son	2050.1
	29: 5 who **t** is willing to consecrate his service	NIH
	29: 6 **T** the chief of the fathers and princes of	2050.1
	29: 9 **T** the people rejoiced, for that they	2050.1
	29:23 **T** Solomon sat on the throne of	2050.1
2Ch	1: 2 **T** Solomon spake unto all Israel,	2050.1
	1:13 **T** Solomon came *from his journey* to	2050.1
	2: 6 who *am* I **t**, that I should build him a	2050.1
	2:11 **T** Huram the king of Tyre answered in	2050.1
	3: 1 **T** Solomon began to build the house of	2050.1
	5: 2 **T** Solomon assembled the elders of Israel,	227
	5:11 *and* did not **t** wait by course:	NIH
	5:13 that *the* house was filled *with* a cloud,	NIH
	6: 1 **T** said Solomon, The Lord hath said that	227
	6:17 Now **t**, O Lord God of Israel, let thy	2050.1
	6:23 **T** hear thou from heaven, and do,	2050.1
	6:25 **T** hear thou from the heavens,	2050.1
	6:27 **T** hear *thou* from heaven, and forgive	2050.1
	6:29 **T** what prayer *or* what supplication	NIH
	6:30 **T** hear thou from heaven thy dwelling	2050.1
	6:33 **T** hear thou from the heavens, *even*	2050.1
	6:35 **T** hear thou from the heavens their	2050.1
	6:39 **T** hear thou from the heavens, *even*	2050.1
	7: 4 **T** the king and all the people offered	2050.1
	7:14 **t** will I hear from heaven,	2050.1
	7:18 **T** will I stablish the throne of thy	2050.1
	7:20 **T** will I pluck them up by the roots out	2050.1
	8:12 **T** Solomon offered burnt offerings unto	227
	8:17 **T** went Solomon to Ezion-geber,	227
	10:18 **T** king Rehoboam sent Hadoram that	2050.1
	12: 5 **T** came Shemaiah the prophet to	2050.1
	13:15 **T** the men of Judah gave a shout:	2050.1
	14:10 **T** Asa went out against him, and they	2050.1
	16: 2 **T** Asa brought out silver and gold out of	2050.1
	16: 6 **T** Asa the king took all Judah;	2050.1
	16:10 **T** Asa was wroth with the seer,	2050.1
	18:16 **T** he said, I did see all Israel scattered	2050.1
	18:20 **T** there came out a spirit,	2050.1
	18:23 **T** Zedekiah the son of Chenaanah came	2050.1
	18:25 **T** the king of Israel said, Take ye	2050.1
	18:27 **t** hath not the Lord spoken by me.	NIH
	20: 2 **T** there came *some* that told	2050.1
	20: 9 our affliction, **t** thou wilt hear and help.	2050.1
	20:14 **T** upon Jahaziel the son of Zechariah,	2050.1
	20:27 **t** they returned, every man of Judah	2050.1
	20:37 **T** Eliezer the son of Dodavah of	2050.1
	21: 9 **T** Jehoram went forth with his princes,	2050.1
	23:11 **t** they brought out the king's son,	2050.1
	23:13 **T** Athaliah rent her clothes, and said,	2050.1
	23:14 **T** Jehoiada the priest brought out	2050.1
	23:17 **T** all the people went **t** to the house of	2050.1
	24:17 king. **T** the king hearkened unto them.	227
	25:10 **T** Amaziah separated them, to wit,	2050.1
	25:16 **T** the prophet forbare, and said, I know	2050.1

T

Ref	Text	Num
2Ch 25:17	**T** Amaziah king of Judah took advice,	2050.1
26: 1	**T** all the people of Judah took Uzziah,	2050.1
26:19	**T** Uzziah was wroth, and *had* a censer	2050.1
28:12	**T** certain of the heads of the children of	2050.1
28:15	brethren: **t** they returned *to* Samaria.	2050.1
29:12	**T** the Levites arose, Mahath the son of	2050.1
29:18	**T** they went in to Hezekiah the king,	2050.1
29:20	**T** Hezekiah the king rose early,	2050.1
29:31	**T** Hezekiah answered and said, Now ye	2050.1
30:15	**T** they killed the passover on	2050.1
30:27	**T** the priests the Levites arose and	2050.1
36: 1	*all.* **T** all the children of Israel returned,	2050.1
31: 9	**T** Hezekiah questioned with the priests	2050.1
31:11	**T** Hezekiah commanded to prepare	2050.1
32:18	**T** they cried with a loud voice in	2050.1
33:13	**T** Manasseh knew that the Lord he	2050.1
34:18	**T** Shaphan the scribe told the king,	2050.1
34:29	**T** the king sent and gathered together	2050.1
36: 1	**T** the people of the land took Jehoahaz	2050.1
Ezr 1: 5	**T** rose up the chief of the fathers of	2050.1
3: 2	**T** stood up Jeshua the son of Jozadak,	2050.1
3: 9	**T** stood Jeshua *with* his sons and	2050.1
4: 2	**T** they came to Zerubbabel, and to	2050.1
4: 4	**T** the people of the land weakened	2050.1
4: 9	**T** *wrote* Rehum the chancellor,	116
4:13	walls set up *again,* **t** will they not pay toll,	NIH
4:17	**T** sent the king an answer unto Rehum	NIH
4:24	**T** ceased the work of the house of	116+871.2
5: 1	**T** the prophets, Haggai the prophet,	2050.3
5: 2	**T** rose up Zerubbabel the son of	116+871.2
5: 4	**T** said we unto them after this manner,	116
5: 5	**t** they returned answer by letter	116
5: 9	**T** asked we those elders, *and* said unto	116
5:16	**T** came the same Sheshbazzar, *and* laid	116
6: 1	**T** Darius the king made a decree,	116+871.2
6:13	Tatnai, governor on *this* side the river,	116
8:16	**T** sent I for Eliezer, for Ariel,	2050.1
8:21	**T** I proclaimed a fast there, at the river	2050.1
8:24	**T** I separated twelve of the chief of	2050.1
8:31	**T** we departed from the river of Ahava	2050.1
9: 4	**T** were assembled unto me every one	2050.1
10: 5	**T** arose Ezra, and made the chief	2050.1
10: 6	**T** Ezra rose up from before the house	2050.1
10: 9	**T** all the men of Judah and	2050.1
10:12	**T** all the congregation answered and	2050.1
Ne 2: 2	of heart. **T** I was very sore afraid,	2050.1
2: 4	**T** the king said unto me, For what dost	2050.1
2: 9	**T** I came to the governors beyond	2050.1
2:14	**T** I went on to the gate of the fountain,	2050.1
2:15	**T** went I up in the night by the brook,	2050.1
2:17	**T** said I unto them, Ye see the distress	2050.1
2:18	**T** I told them of the hand of my God	2050.1
2:20	**T** answered I them, and said unto them,	2050.1
3: 1	**T** Eliashib the high priest rose up with	2050.1
4: 7	to be stopped, **t** they were very wroth,	2050.1
5: 7	**T** I consulted with myself, and I	2050.1
5: 8	**T** held they their peace,	2050.1
5:12	**T** said they, We will restore *them,* and	2050.1
5:12	**T** I called the priests, and took an oath	2050.1
6: 5	**T** sent Sanballat his servant unto me in	2050.1
6: 8	**T** I sent unto him, saying, There are no	2050.1
8:10	**T** he said unto them, Go *your way,* eat	2050.1
9: 4	**T** stood up upon the stairs of the	2050.1
9: 5	**T** the Levites, Jeshua and Kadmiel,	2050.1
12:31	**T** I brought up the princes of Judah	2050.1
13: 9	**T** I commanded, and they cleansed	2050.1
13:11	**T** contended I with the rulers, and said,	2050.1
13:12	**T** brought all Judah the tithe of the	2050.1
13:17	**T** I contended with the nobles of Judah,	2050.1
13:21	**T** I testified against them, and said unto	2050.1
13:27	Shall we **t** hearken unto you to do all	2050.1
Est 1:13	**T** the king said to the wise *men,* which	2050.1
2: 2	**T** said the king's servants unto	2050.1
2:13	**T** thus came *every* maiden unto the	2050.1
2:18	**T** the king made a great feast unto all	2050.1
2:19	**t** Mordecai sat in the king's gate.	2050.1
3: 3	**T** the king's servants, Which *were* in	2050.1
3: 5	reverence, **t** was Haman full *of* wrath.	NIH
3:12	**T** were the king's scribes called on	2050.1
4: 4	**T** was the queen exceedingly grieved;	2050.1
4: 5	**T** called Esther for Hatach, *one* of	2050.1
4:13	**T** Mordecai commanded to answer	2050.1
4:14	**t** shall there enlargement and	NIH
4:15	**T** Esther bade *them* return Mordecai	2050.1
5: 3	**T** said the king unto her, What wilt	2050.1
5: 5	**T** the king said, Cause Haman to make	2050.1
5: 7	**T** answered Esther, and said, My	2050.1
5: 9	**T** went Haman forth that day joyful and	2050.1
5:14	**T** said Zeresh his wife and all his friends	2050.1
5:14	**t** go thou in merrily with the king unto	2050.1
6: 3	**T** said the king's servants that	2050.1
6:10	**T** the king said to Haman, Make haste,	2050.1
6:11	**T** took Haman the apparel and the	2050.1
6:13	**T** said his wise *men* and Zeresh his wife	2050.1
7: 3	**T** Esther the queen answered and said,	2050.1
7: 5	**T** the king Ahasuerus answered and	2050.1
7: 6	**T** Haman was afraid before the king and	2050.1
7: 8	**T** the king returned out of the palace	2050.1
7: 8	whereon Esther *was.* **T** said the king,	2050.1
7: 9	**T** the king said, Hang him thereon.	2050.1
7:10	**T** was the king's wrath pacified.	2050.1
8: 4	**T** the king held out the golden sceptre	2050.1
8: 7	**T** the king Ahasuerus said unto Esther	2050.1
8: 9	**T** were the king's scribes called at that	2050.1
9:13	**T** said Esther, If it please the king, let it	2050.1
Est 9:29	**T** Esther the queen, the daughter of	2050.1
Job 1: 7	**T** Satan answered the Lord, and said,	2050.1
1: 9	**T** Satan answered the Lord, and said,	2050.1
1:20	**T** Job arose, and rent his mantle,	2050.1
2: 9	**T** said his wife unto him, Dost thou still	2050.1
3:13	I should have slept: **t** had I been at rest,	227
4: 1	**T** Eliphaz the Temanite answered and	2050.1
4:15	**T** a spirit passed before my face;	2050.1
6:10	**T** should I yet have comfort; yea,	2050.1
7:14	**T** thou scarest me with dreams,	2050.1
8: 1	**T** answered Bildad the Shuhite, and	2050.1
8:18	**t** *it* shall deny him, *saying,* I have not	2050.1
9: 1	**T** Job answered and said,	2050.1
9:29	I be wicked, **why t** labour	2088+4100+3807.1
9:35	**T** would I speak, and not fear him; but	NIH
10:14	**t** thou markest me, and thou wilt not	2050.1
10:18	Wherefore **t** hast thou brought me forth	2050.1
10:20	cease **t**, and let me alone, that I may	2050.1
11: 1	**T** answered Zophar the Naamathite,	2050.1
11:10	gather together, **t** who can hinder him?	2050.1
11:11	will he not **t** consider *it?*	2050.1
11:15	**t** shalt thou lift up thy face without spot;	227
13:20	**t** will I not hide myself from thee.	227
13:22	**T** call thou, and I will answer: or let me	2050.1
15: 1	**T** answered Eliphaz the Temanite,	2050.1
16: 1	**T** Job answered and said,	2050.1
16:22	**t** I shall go the way *whence* I shall not	2050.1
18: 1	**T** answered Bildad the Shuhite, and	2050.1
19: 1	**T** Job answered and said,	2050.1
20: 1	**T** answered Zophar the Naamathite,	2050.1
21:34	How **t** comfort ye me in vain, seeing *in*	2050.1
22: 1	**T** Eliphaz the Temanite answered and	2050.1
22:24	**T** shalt thou lay up gold as dust,	2050.1
22:26	For **t** shalt thou have thy delight in	227
22:29	**t** thou shalt say, *There is* lifting up;	2050.1
23: 1	**T** Job answered and said,	2050.1
25: 1	**T** answered Bildad the Shuhite, and	2050.1
25: 4	How **t** can man be justified with God?	2050.1
27:12	why **t** are ye thus altogether vain?	2050.1
28:20	Whence **t** cometh wisdom? and where	2050.1
28:27	**T** did he see it, and declare it; he	227
29:11	When the ear heard *me,* **t** it blessed me;	2050.1
29:18	**T** I said, I shall die in my nest, and I	2050.1
30:26	**t** evil came *unto me:* and when I	2050.1
31: 1	why **t** should I think upon a maid?	2050.1
31: 8	**T** let me sow, and let another eat; yea,	NIH
31:10	**T** let my wife grind unto another,	NIH
31:14	What **t** shall I do when God riseth up?	2050.1
31:22	**T** let mine arm fall from *my* shoulder	NIH
32: 2	**T** was kindled the wrath of Elihu the	2050.1
32: 5	three men, **t** his wrath was kindled.	2050.1
33:16	**T** he openeth the ears of men, and sealeth	227
33:24	**T** he is gracious unto him, and saith,	2050.1
34:29	quietness, who **t** can make trouble?	NIH
34:29	hideth *his* face, who **t** can behold him?	2050.1
36: 9	**T** he sheweth them their work,	2050.1
36:18	**t** a great ransom cannot deliver thee.	2050.1
37: 8	**T** the beasts go into dens, and remain in	2050.1
38: 1	**T** the Lord answered Job out of	2050.1
38:21	thou *it,* because thou wast **t** born?	227
40: 3	**T** Job answered the Lord, and said,	2050.1
40: 6	**T** answered the Lord unto Job out of	2050.1
40:14	**T** will I also confess unto thee that	2050.1
41:10	who **t** is able to stand before me?	2050.1
42: 1	**T** Job answered the Lord, and said,	2050.1
42:11	**T** came there unto him all his brethren,	2050.1
Ps 2: 5	**T** shall he speak unto them in his wrath,	227
18: 7	**T** the earth shook and trembled,	2050.1
18:15	**T** the channels of waters were seen,	2050.1
18:42	**T** did I beat them small as the dust	2050.1
19:13	**t** shall I be upright, and I shall be innocent	227
27:10	**T** the Lord will take me up.	2050.1
39: 3	the fire burned: **t** spake I with my tongue,	NIH
40: 7	**T** said I, Lo, I come: in the volume of	227
43: 4	**T** will I go unto the altar of God,	2050.1
50:18	**t** thou consentedst with him,	2050.1
51:13	**T** will I teach transgressors thy ways;	NIH
51:19	**T** shalt thou be pleased with the sacrifices	227
51:19	burnt offering and whole *burnt offering:* **t**	2050.1
55: 6	for **t** would I fly away, and be at rest.	NIH
55: 7	**t** would I wander far off, *and* remain in	NIH
55:12	**t** I would have borne it: neither *was it*	2050.1
55:12	**t** I would have hid myself from him:	2050.1
56: 9	I cry *unto thee,* **t** shall mine enemies	227
67: 6	**T** shall the earth yield her increase;	NIH
69: 4	**t** I restored *that* which I took not away.	227
73:17	of God; **t** understood I their end.	NIH
78:34	When he slew them, **t** they sought him:	2050.1
78:65	**T** the Lord awaked as one out of sleep,	2050.1
80:12	hast thou **t** broken down her hedges,	NIH
89:19	**T** thou spakest in vision to thy holy one,	227
89:32	**T** will I visit their transgression with	2050.1
96:12	**t** shall all the trees of the wood rejoice	227
106:12	**T** believed they his words; they sang his	2050.1
106:30	**T** stood up Phinehas,	2050.1
107: 6	**T** they cried unto the Lord in their	2050.1
107:13	**T** they cried unto the Lord in their	2050.1
107:19	**T** they cry unto the Lord in their	2050.1
107:28	**T** they cry unto the Lord in their	2050.1
107:30	**T** are they glad because they be quiet;	2050.1
116: 4	**T** called I upon the name of the Lord;	2050.1
119: 6	**T** shall I not be ashamed, when I have	227
119:92	I should **t** have perished in mine affliction.	227
124: 3	**T** they had swallowed us up quick,	233
124: 4	**T** the waters had overwhelmed us,	233
Ps 124: 5	**T** the proud waters had gone over our soul.	233
126: 2	**T** was our mouth filled *with* laughter,	227
126: 2	**t** said they among the heathen, The Lord	227
142: 3	within me, **t** thou knewest my path.	2050.1
Pr 1:28	**T** shall they call upon me, but I will not	227
2: 5	**T** shalt thou understand the fear of	227
2: 9	**T** shalt thou understand righteousness,	227
3:23	**T** shalt thou walk *in* thy way safely,	227
8:30	**T** I was by him, *as* one brought up *with*	2050.1
11: 2	*When* pride cometh, **t** cometh shame:	2050.1
15:11	**how much more t** the hearts of	637+3588
18: 3	**t** cometh also contempt, and with	NIH
20:14	when he is gone his way, **t** he boasteth.	227
20:24	can a man **t** understand his own way?	2050.1
24:14	hast found *it,* **t** there shall be a reward,	2050.1
24:32	**T** I saw, *and* considered *it* well: I looked	2050.1
Ecc 2:11	**T** I looked on all the works that my	2050.1
2:13	**T** I saw that wisdom excelleth folly,	2050.1
2:15	**T** said I in my heart, As it happeneth to	2050.1
2:15	even to me; and why was I **t** more wise?	227
2:15	**T** said I in my heart, that this also *is*	2050.1
4: 7	**T** I returned, and I saw vanity under	2050.1
4:11	Again, if two lie together, **t** they have	2050.1
8:15	**T** I commended mirth, because a man	2050.1
8:17	**T** I beheld all the work of God, that a	2050.1
9:16	said I, Wisdom *is* better than strength	2050.1
10:10	edge, **t** must he put to more strength:	2050.1
12: 7	**T** shall the dust return to the earth as it	2050.1
SS 8:10	**t** was I in his eyes as one that found	227
Isa 5:17	**T** shall the lambs feed after their	2050.1
6: 5	**T** said I, Woe *is* me! for I am undone;	2050.1
6: 6	**T** flew one of the seraphims unto me,	2050.1
6: 8	go for us? **T** I said, Here *am* I; send me.	2050.1
6:11	**T** said I, Lord, how long? And he	2050.1
7: 3	**T** said the Lord unto Isaiah, Go forth	2050.1
8: 3	**T** said the Lord to me, Call his name	2050.1
14:25	**T** shall his yoke depart from off them,	2050.1
14:32	shall *one* **t** answer the messengers	2050.1
24:23	**T** the moon shall be confounded,	2050.1
28:18	**t** ye shall be trodden down by it.	2050.1
30:23	**T** shall he give the rain of thy seed,	2050.1
31: 8	**T** shall the Assyrian fall with the sword,	2050.1
32:16	**T** judgment shall dwell in the	2050.1
33:23	**t** is the prey of a great spoil divided;	227
35: 5	**T** the eyes of the blind shall be opened,	227
35: 6	**T** shall the lame *man* leap as a hart,	227
36: 3	**T** came forth unto him Eliakim,	2050.1
36: 9	How **t** wilt thou turn away the face of	2050.1
36:11	**T** said Eliakim and Shebna and Joah	2050.1
36:13	**T** Rabshakeh stood, and cried with a	2050.1
36:22	**T** came Eliakim, the son of Hilkiah,	2050.1
37:21	**T** Isaiah the son of Amoz sent unto	2050.1
37:36	**T** the angel of the Lord went forth,	2050.1
38: 2	**T** Hezekiah turned his face toward	2050.1
38: 4	**T** came the word of the Lord to Isaiah,	2050.1
39: 3	**T** came Isaiah the prophet unto king	2050.1
39: 3	**T** said he, What have they seen in thine	2050.1
39: 5	**T** said Isaiah to Hezekiah, Hear the	2050.1
39: 8	**T** said Hezekiah to Isaiah, Good *is*	2050.1
40:18	To whom **t** will ye liken God?	2050.1
40:25	To whom **t** will ye liken me, or shall I	2050.1
41: 1	let them come near; **t** let them speak:	227
44:15	**T** shall it be for a man to burn: for he	2050.1
48:18	**t** had thy peace been as a river,	2050.1
49: 4	**T** I said, I have laboured in vain, I have	2050.1
49:21	**t** shalt thou say in thine heart, Who	2050.1
58: 8	**T** shall thy light break forth as the	227
58: 9	**T** shalt thou call, and the Lord shall	227
58:10	**t** shall thy light rise in obscurity,	2050.1
58:14	**T** shalt thou delight thyself in the Lord;	227
60: 5	**T** thou shalt see, and flow *together,* and	227
63:11	**T** he remembered the days of old,	2050.1
66:12	**t** shall ye suck, ye shall be borne upon	2050.1
Jer 1: 4	**T** the word of the Lord came unto me,	2050.1
1: 6	**T** said I, Ah, Lord God, behold,	2050.1
1: 9	**T** the Lord put forth his hand,	2050.1
1:12	**T** said the Lord unto me, Thou hast	2050.1
1:14	**T** the Lord said unto me, Out of	2050.1
2:21	how **t** art thou turned into the	2050.1
4: 1	of my sight, **t** shalt thou not remove.	2050.1
4:10	**T** said I, Ah, Lord God! surely thou	2050.1
5: 7	they **t** committed adultery,	2050.1
5:19	**t** shalt thou answer them, Like as ye	2050.1
7: 7	**T** will I cause you to dwell in this place,	2050.1
7:34	**T** will I cause to cease from the cities of	2050.1
8: 5	Why **t** is this people of Jerusalem slidden	NIH
8:22	why **t** is not the health of the daughter of	3588
11: 5	**T** answered I, and said, So be it,	2050.1
11: 6	**T** the Lord said unto me, Proclaim all	2050.1
11:12	**T** shall the cities of Judah	2050.1
11:15	when thou doest evil, **t** thou rejoicest.	227
11:18	know *it:* **t** thou shewedst me their doings.	227
12: 5	**t** how canst thou contend with horses?	2050.1
12: 5	*they wearied thee,* **t** how wilt thou do	2050.1
12:16	**t** shall they be built in the midst of my	2050.1
13: 7	**t** I went to Euphrates, and digged,	2050.1
13: 8	**T** the word of the Lord came unto me,	2050.1
13:13	**T** shalt thou say unto them, Thus saith	2050.1
13:23	**t** may ye also do good, that are	NIH
14:11	**T** said the Lord unto me, Pray not for	2050.1
14:13	**T** said I, Ah, Lord God! behold,	2050.1
14:14	**T** the Lord said unto me, The prophets	2050.1
14:18	**T** behold the slain with the sword:	2050.1
14:18	**t** behold them that are sick with famine	2050.1
15: 1	**T** said the Lord unto me,	2050.1

Jer	15: 2 t thou shalt tell them, Thus saith	2050.1
	15:19 t will I bring thee again, *and* thou shalt	2050.1
	16:11 T shalt thou say unto them, Because	2050.1
	17:25 T shall there enter into the gates of this	2050.1
	17:27 t will I kindle a fire in the gates thereof,	2050.1
	18: 3 T I went down *to* the potter's house,	2050.1
	18: 5 T the word of the LORD came to me,	2050.1
	18:10 my voice, t I will repent of the good,	2050.1
	18:18 T said they, Come, and let us devise	2050.1
	19:10 T shalt thou break the bottle in the sight	2050.1
	19:14 T came Jeremiah from Tophet,	2050.1
	20: 2 T Pashur smote Jeremiah the prophet,	2050.1
	20: 3 T said Jeremiah unto him, The LORD	2050.1
	20: 9 T I said, I will not make mention of	2050.1
	21: 3 T said Jeremiah unto them, Thus shall	2050.1
	22: 4 t shall there enter in by the gates of this	2050.1
	22: 9 T they shall answer, Because they have	2050.1
	22:15 and justice, *and* t it was well with him?	227
	22:16 t *it was* well *with him: was* not this to	227
	22:22 surely t shalt thou be ashamed and	227
	23:22 t they should have turned them from	2050.1
	23:33 shalt t say unto them, What burden?	2050.1
	24: 3 T said the LORD unto me, What seest	2050.1
	25:17 T took I the cup at the LORD's hand,	2050.1
	25:28 t shalt thou say unto them, Thus saith	2050.1
	26: 6 T will I make this house like Shiloh,	2050.1
	26:10 t they came up from the king's house	2050.1
	26:11 T spake the priests and the prophets	2050.1
	26:12 T spake Jeremiah unto all the princes	2050.1
	26:16 T said the princes and all the people	2050.1
	26:17 T rose up certain of the elders of the	2050.1
	27: 7 *t* many nations and great kings shall serve	NIH
	27:22 t will I bring them up, and restore them	2050.1
	28: 5 T the prophet Jeremiah said unto	2050.1
	28: 9 *t* shall the prophet be known, that	NIH
	28:10 T Hananiah the prophet took the yoke	2050.1
	28:12 T the word of the LORD came unto	2050.1
	28:15 T said the prophet Jeremiah unto	2050.1
	29:12 T shall ye call upon me, and ye shall go	2050.1
	29:30 T came the word of the LORD unto	2050.1
	31:13 T shall the virgin rejoice in the dance,	227
	31:36 *t* the seed of Israel also shall cease from	NIH
	32: 2 For t the king of Babylon's army besieged	227
	32: 8 T I knew that this *was* the word of	2050.1
	32:26 T came the word of the LORD unto	2050.1
	33:21 *T* may also my covenant be broken with	NIH
	33:26 T will I cast away the seed of Jacob,	1571
	34: 6 T Jeremiah the prophet spake all these	2050.1
	34:10 t they obeyed, and let *them* go.	2050.1
	35: 3 T I took Jaazaniah the son of Jeremiah,	2050.1
	35:12 T came the word of the LORD unto	2050.1
	36: 4 T Jeremiah called Baruch the son of	2050.1
	36:10 T read Baruch in the book the words of	2050.1
	36:12 T he went down *into* the king's house,	2050.1
	36:13 T Michaiah declared unto them all	2050.1
	36:18 T Baruch answered them, He	2050.1
	36:19 T said the princes unto Baruch,	2050.1
	36:27 T the word of the LORD came to	2050.1
	36:32 T took Jeremiah another roll, and gave	2050.1
	37: 5 T Pharaoh's army was come forth out of	2050.1
	37: 6 T came the word of the LORD unto	2050.1
	37:12 T Jeremiah went forth out of Jerusalem	2050.1
	37:14 T said Jeremiah, It is false; I fall not	2050.1
	37:17 T Zedekiah the king sent, and took him	2050.1
	37:21 T Zedekiah the king commanded that	2050.1
	38: 1 T Shephatiah the son of Mattan,	2050.1
	38: 5 T Zedekiah the king said, Behold, he *is*	2050.1
	38: 6 T took they Jeremiah, and cast him into	2050.1
	38: 7 king t sitting in the gate of Benjamin;	2050.1
	38:10 T the king commanded Ebed-melech	2050.1
	38:14 T Zedekiah the king sent,	2050.1
	38:15 T Jeremiah said unto Zedekiah, If I	2050.1
	38:17 T said Jeremiah unto Zedekiah,	2050.1
	38:17 t thy soul shall live, and this city shall	2050.1
	38:18 t shall this city be given into the hand of	2050.1
	38:24 T said Zedekiah unto Jeremiah, Let no	2050.1
	38:26 T thou shalt say unto them, I presented	2050.1
	38:27 T came all the princes unto Jeremiah,	2050.1
	39: 4 t they fled, and went forth out of the	2050.1
	39: 6 T the king of Babylon slew the sons of	2050.1
	39: 9 T Nebuzar-adan the captain of the guard	2050.1
	40: 6 T went Jeremiah unto Gedaliah the son	2050.1
	40: 8 T they came to Gedaliah to Mizpah,	2050.1
	40:15 T Johanan the son of Kareah spake to	2050.1
	41: 2 T arose Ishmael the son of Nethaniah,	2050.1
	41:10 T Ishmael carried away captive all	2050.1
	41:12 T they took all the men, and went to	2050.1
	41:13 that *were* with him, t they were glad.	2050.1
	41:16 T took Johanan the son of Kareah,	2050.1
	42: 1 T all the captains of the forces,	2050.1
	42: 4 T Jeremiah the prophet said unto them,	2050.1
	42: 5 T they said to Jeremiah, The LORD be a	2050.1
	42: 8 T called he Johanan the son of Kareah,	2050.1
	42:10 t will I build you, and not pull *you*	2050.1
	42:16 T it shall come to pass, *that* the sword,	2050.1
	43: 2 T spake Azariah the son of Hoshaiah,	2050.1
	43: 8 T came the word of the LORD unto	2050.1
	44:15 T all the men which knew that their	2050.1
	44:17 for *t* had we plenty of victuals,	NIH
	44:20 T Jeremiah said unto all the people,	2050.1
	47: 2 T the men shall cry, and all	2050.1
	49: 1 why *t* doth their king inherit Gad,	NIH
	49: 2 t shall Israel be heir unto them that	2050.1
	51:48 T the heaven and the earth, and all	2050.1
	51:62 T shalt thou say, O LORD, thou hast	2050.1

Jer	52: 7 T the city was broken up, and all the	2050.1
	52: 9 T they took the king, and carried him	2050.1
	52:11 T he put out the eyes of Zedekiah;	2050.1
	52:15 T Nebuzar-adan the captain of the guard	2050.1
La	3:54 over mine head; t I said, I am cut off.	NIH
Eze	3: 3 T did I eat *it;* and it was in my mouth as	2050.1
	3:12 T the spirit took me up, and I heard	2050.1
	3:15 T I came to them of the captivity *at*	2050.1
	3:23 T arose, and went forth into the plain:	2050.1
	3:24 T the spirit entered into me, and set me	2050.1
	4:14 T said I, Ah Lord GOD, behold,	2050.1
	4:15 T he said unto me, Lo, I have given thee	2050.1
	5: 1 t take thee balances to weigh,	2050.1
	5: 4 T take of them again, and cast them into	2050.1
	6:13 T shall ye know that I *am* the LORD,	2050.1
	7:26 t shall they seek a vision of the prophet;	2050.1
	8: 2 T I beheld, and lo, a likeness as	2050.1
	8: 5 T said he unto me, Son of man, lift up	2050.1
	8: 8 T said he unto me, Son of man, dig now	2050.1
	8:12 T said he unto me, Son of man, hast	2050.1
	8:14 T he brought me to the door of the gate	2050.1
	8:15 T he said unto me, Hast thou seen *this,*	2050.1
	8:17 T he said unto me, Hast thou seen *this,*	2050.1
	9: 6 T they began at the ancient men which	2050.1
	9: 9 T said he unto me, The iniquity of	2050.1
	10: 1 T looked, and behold, in the	2050.1
	10: 4 T the glory of the LORD went up from	2050.1
	10: 6 t he went in, and stood beside the	2050.1
	10:18 T the glory of the LORD departed from	2050.1
	11: 2 T said he unto me, Son of man, these	2050.1
	11:13 T fell I down upon my face,	2050.1
	11:22 T did the cherubims lift up their wings,	2050.1
	11:25 T I spake unto them of the captivity all	2050.1
	12: 4 T shalt thou bring forth thy stuff by day	2050.1
	14: 1 T came certain of the elders of Israel	2050.1
	14:13 t will I stretch out mine hand upon it,	2050.1
	16: 9 T washed I thee with water; yea,	2050.1
	16:53 t *will I bring again* the captivity of thy	2050.1
	16:55 t thou and thy daughters shall return to	2050.1
	16:61 T thou shalt remember thy ways,	2050.1
	18:13 shall he t live? he shall not live: he hath	2050.1
	19: 5 t she took another of her whelps,	2050.1
	19: 8 T the nations set against him on every	2050.1
	20: 2 T came the word of the LORD unto me,	2050.1
	20: 7 T said I unto them, Cast ye away every	2050.1
	20: 8 t I said, *I* will pour out my fury upon	2050.1
	20:13 t I said, *I* would pour out my fury upon	2050.1
	20:21 t I said, *I* would pour out my fury upon	2050.1
	20:28 t they saw every high hill, and all	2050.1
	20:29 T I said unto them, What *is* the high	2050.1
	20:49 T said I, Ah Lord GOD, they say of me,	2050.1
	21: 4 *Seeing* t that I will cut off from thee	3282
	21:10 should we t make mirth? it contemneth	176
	22: 3 T say thou, Thus saith the Lord GOD,	2050.1
	23:13 T I saw that she was defiled, *that* they	2050.1
	23:18 t my mind was alienated from her, like	2050.1
	23:39 t they came the same day into my	2050.1
	23:43 T said I unto *her that was* old *in*	2050.1
	24:11 T set it empty upon the coals thereof,	2050.1
	24:20 T I answered them, The word of	2050.1
	26:16 T all the princes of the sea shall come	2050.1
	28:25 t shall they dwell in their land that I	2050.1
	32: 4 T will I leave thee upon the land, I will	2050.1
	32:14 T will I make their waters deep,	227
	32:15 t shall they know that I *am* the LORD.	2050.1
	33: 4 T whosoever heareth the sound of	2050.1
	33:10 away in them, how should we t live?	2050.1
	33:23 T the word of the LORD came unto me,	2050.1
	33:29 T shall they know that I *am* the LORD,	2050.1
	33:33 t shall they know that a prophet hath	2050.1
	36:25 T will I sprinkle clean water upon you,	2050.1
	36:31 T shall ye remember your own evil	2050.1
	36:36 T the heathen that are left round about	2050.1
	37: 9 T said he unto me, Prophesy unto	2050.1
	37:11 T he said unto me, Son of man, these	2050.1
	37:14 t shall ye know that I the LORD have	2050.1
	37:16 t take another stick, and write upon it,	2050.1
	39:15 bone, t shall he set up a sign by it,	2050.1
	39:28 T shall they know that I *am* the LORD	2050.1
	40: 6 T came he unto the gate which looketh	2050.1
	40: 9 T measured he the porch of the gate,	2050.1
	40:13 He measured t the gate from the roof of	2050.1
	40:17 T brought he me into the outward	2050.1
	40:19 T he measured the breadth from	2050.1
	41: 3 T went he inward, and measured the	2050.1
	42: 1 T he brought me forth into the utter	2050.1
	42:13 T said he unto me, The north chambers	2050.1
	42:14 When the priests enter *therein,* t	2050.1
	44: 1 T he brought me back the way of the	2050.1
	44: 2 T said the LORD unto me; This gate	2050.1
	44: 4 T brought he me the way of the north	2050.1
	46: 2 t he shall go forth; but the gate shall not	2050.1
	46:12 shall t open him the gate that looketh	2050.1
	46:12 t he shall go forth; and after his going	2050.1
	46:17 t it shall be his to the year of liberty;	2050.1
	46:20 T said he unto me, This *is* the place	2050.1
	46:21 T he brought me forth into the utter	2050.1
	46:24 T said he unto me, These are the places	2050.1
	47: 2 T brought he me out *of* the way of	2050.1
	47: 6 hast thou seen *this?* T he brought me,	2050.1
	47: 8 T said he unto me, These waters issue	2050.1
Da	1:10 t shall ye make *me* endanger my head to	2050.1
	1:11 T said Daniel to Melzar, whom the	2050.1
	1:13 T let our countenances be looked upon	2050.1
	1:18 t the prince of the eunuchs brought	2050.1

Da	2: 2 T the king commanded to call	2050.1
	2: 4 T spake the Chaldeans to the king in	2050.1
	2:14 T Daniel answered with counsel	116+871.2
	2:15 T Arioch made the thing known to Daniel.	116
	2:16 T Daniel went in, and desired of the	2050.3
	2:17 T Daniel went to his house, and made	116
	2:19 T *was* the secret revealed unto Daniel in a	116
	2:19 T Daniel blessed the God of heaven.	116
	2:25 T Arioch brought in Daniel before the king	116
	2:35 T was the iron, the clay, the brass,	116+871.2
	2:46 T the king Nebuchadnezzar fell	116+871.2
	2:48 T the king made Daniel a great man,	116
	2:49 T Daniel requested of the king, and he	2050.3
	3: 2 T Nebuchadnezzar the king sent to	2050.3
	3: 3 T the princes, the governors and	116+871.2
	3: 4 T a herald cried aloud, To you it is	2050.3
	3:13 T Nebuchadnezzar in *his* rage and	116+871.2
	3:13 T they brought these men	116+871.2
	3:19 T was Nebuchadnezzar full of fury,	116+871.2
	3:21 T these men were bound in their	116+871.2
	3:24 T Nebuchadnezzar the king was astonied,	116
	3:26 T Nebuchadnezzar came near to	116+871.2
	3:26 come *hither.* T Shadrach, Meshach,	116+871.2
	3:28 *T* Nebuchadnezzar spake, and said,	NIH
	3:30 T the king promoted Shadrach,	116+871.2
	4: 7 T came in the magicians,	116
	4:19 T Daniel, whose name *was* Belteshazzar,	116
	5: 3 T they brought the golden vessels	116+871.2
	5: 6 T the king's countenance was changed,	116
	5: 8 T came in all the king's wise *men:* but	116
	5: 9 T *was* king Belshazzar greatly troubled,	116
	5:13 T was Daniel brought in before	116+871.2
	5:17 T Daniel answered and said before	116+871.2
	5:24 T *was* the part of	116+4481+6925+871.2
	5:29 T commanded Belshazzar,	116+871.2
	6: 3 T this Daniel was preferred above	116
	6: 4 T the presidents and princes sought to find	116
	6: 5 T said these men, We shall not find any	116
	6: 6 T these presidents and princes assembled	116
	6:11 T these men assembled, and found Daniel	116
	6:12 T they came near, and spake before	116+871.2
	6:13 T answered they and said before	116+871.2
	6:14 T the king, when he heard *these* words,	116
	6:15 T these men assembled unto the	116+871.2
	6:16 T the king commanded,	116+871.2
	6:18 T the king went to his palace, and passed	116
	6:19 T the king arose very early in	116+871.2
	6:21 T said Daniel unto the king, O king, live	116
	6:23 T was the king exceeding glad for	116+871.2
	6:25 T king Darius wrote unto all people,	116+871.2
	7: 1 visions of his head upon his bed: t	116+871.2
	7:11 I beheld t because of the voice of	116+871.2
	7:19 T I would know the truth of the fourth	116
	8: 3 T I lifted up mine eyes, and saw,	2050.1
	8:13 T I heard one saint speaking,	2050.1
	8:14 t shall the sanctuary be cleansed.	2050.1
	8:15 and sought for the meaning, t behold,	2050.1
	10: 5 T I lift up mine eyes, and looked,	2050.1
	10: 9 t was I in a deep sleep on my face,	2050.1
	10:12 T said he unto me, Fear not, Daniel:	2050.1
	10:16 t I opened my mouth, and spake,	2050.1
	10:18 T there came again and touched me	2050.1
	10:20 T said he, Knowest thou wherefore I	2050.1
	11:10 t shall he return, and be stirred up,	2050.1
	11:19 T he shall turn his face towards the fort	2050.1
	11:20 T shall stand up in his estate a raiser of	2050.1
	11:28 T shall he return *into* his land with	2050.1
	12: 5 T I Daniel looked, and behold,	2050.1
	12: 8 t said I, O my lord, what *shall* be the	2050.1
Hos	1: 9 T said *God,* Call his name Lo-ammi:	2050.1
	1:11 T shall the children of Judah and	2050.1
	2: 7 shall not find *them:* t shall she say,	2050.1
	2: 7 for t *was it* better with me than now.	3588
	3: 1 T said the LORD unto me, Go yet,	2050.1
	5:13 t went Ephraim to the Assyrian,	2050.1
	6: 3 T shall we know, *if* we follow on	2050.1
	7: 1 t the iniquity of Ephraim was	2050.1
	10: 3 the LORD; what t should a king do to us?	NIH
	11: 1 t I loved him, and called my son out of	2050.1
	11:10 t the children shall tremble from the	2050.1
Joel	2:18 T will the LORD be jealous for his land,	2050.1
	2:23 Be glad t, ye children of Zion,	2050.1
	3:17 t shall Jerusalem be holy, and there	2050.1
Am	6: 2 t go down to Gath of the Philistines:	2050.1
	6:10 T shall he say, Hold thy tongue: for *we*	2050.1
	7: 2 t I said, O Lord GOD, forgive, I beseech	2050.1
	7: 5 T said I, O Lord GOD, cease, I beseech	2050.1
	7: 8 T said the Lord, Behold, I *will* set a	2050.1
	7:10 T Amaziah *the* priest of Beth-el sent to	2050.1
	7:14 T answered Amos, and said to Amaziah,	2050.1
	8: 2 T said the LORD, The end is	2050.1
Jnh	1: 5 T the mariners were afraid,	2050.1
	1: 8 T said they unto him, Tell us, we pray	2050.1
	1:10 T were the men exceedingly afraid,	2050.1
	1:11 T said they unto him, What shall we do	2050.1
	1:16 T the men feared the LORD	2050.1
	2: 1 T Jonah prayed unto the LORD his God	2050.1
	2: 4 T I said, I am cast out of thy sight; yet I	2050.1
	4: 4 T said the LORD, Doest thou well to be	2050.1
	4:10 T said the LORD, Thou hast had pity on	2050.1
Mic	3: 4 T shall they cry unto the LORD, but he	227
	3: 7 T shall the seers be ashamed,	2050.1
	5: 3 t the remnant of his brethren shall	2050.1
	5: 5 t shall we raise against him seven	2050.1
	7:10 T she *that is* mine enemy shall see *it,*	2050.1

T

Hab
1:11 T shall *his* mind change, and he shall pass 227

Zep
3: 9 For t will I turn to the people a pure 227
3:11 t I will take away out of the midst of thee 227

Hag
1: 3 T came the word of the LORD by 2050.1
1:12 T Zerubbabel the son of Shealtiel, 2050.1
1:13 T spake Haggai the LORD's messenger 2050.1
2:13 T said Haggai, If *one that is* unclean *by* 2050.1
2:14 T answered Haggai, and said, So *is* this 2050.1

Zec
1: 9 T said I, O my lord, what *are* these? 2050.1
1:12 T the angel of the LORD answered and 2050.1
1:18 T lift I up mine eyes, and saw, 2050.1
1:21 T said I, What come these to do? 2050.1
2: 2 T said I, Whither goest thou? And he 2050.1
3: 7 t thou shalt also judge my house, 2050.1
4: 5 T the angel that talked with me 2050.1
4: 6 T he answered and spake unto me, 2050.1
4:11 T answered I, and said unto him, 2050.1
4:14 T said he, These *are* the two anointed 2050.1
5: 1 T I turned, and lift up mine eyes, 2050.1
5: 3 T said he unto me, This *is* the curse 2050.1
5: 5 T the angel that talked with me went 2050.1
5: 9 T lift I up mine eyes, and looked, 2050.1
5:10 T said I to the angel that talked with 2050.1
6: 4 T I answered and said unto the angel 2050.1
6: 8 T cried he upon me, and spake unto 2050.1
6:11 T take silver and gold, and make 2050.1
7: 4 T came the word of the LORD of hosts 2050.1
11: 9 T said I, I will not feed you: that that 2050.1
11:14 T I cut asunder mine other staff, *even* 2050.1
13: 3 t his father and his mother that begat 2050.1
13: 6 T he shall answer, *Those* with which I 2050.1
14: 3 T shall the LORD go forth, 2050.1

Mal
1: 6 if t I *be* a father, where *is* mine honour? 2050.1
3: 4 T shall the offering of Judah and 2050.1
3:16 T they that feared the LORD spake often 227
3:18 T shall ye return, and discern between 2050.1

Mt
1:19 T Joseph her husband, being a just *man,* 1161
1:24 T Joseph being raised from sleep did as 1161
2: 7 T Herod, when he had privily called 5119
2:16 T Herod, when he saw that he was 5119
2:17 T was fulfilled that which *was* spoken by 5119
3: 5 T went out to him Jerusalem, and all 5119
3:13 T cometh Jesus from Galilee to Jordan 5119
3:15 fulfil all righteousness. T he suffered him. 5119
4: 1 T was Jesus led up of the Spirit into 5119
4: 5 T the devil taketh him *up* into the holy 5119
4:10 T saith Jesus unto him, Get thee hence, 5119
4:11 T the devil leaveth him, and behold, 5119
5:24 thy brother, and t come and offer thy gift. 5119
7: 5 and t shalt thou see clearly to cast out 5119
7:11 T ye t, being evil, know how to give good 3767
7:23 And t will I profess unto them, I never 5119
8:26 T he arose, and rebuked the winds and 5119
9: 6 (t saith he to the sick of the palsy,) 5119
9:14 T came to him the disciples of John, 5119
9:15 be taken from them, and t shall they fast. 5119
9:29 T touched he their eyes, saying, 5119
9:37 T saith he unto his disciples, The harvest 5119
11:20 T began he to upbraid the cities wherein 5119
12:12 How much t is a man better than a sheep? 3767
12:13 T saith he to the man, Stretch forth thine 5119
12:14 T the Pharisees went out, and held a 1161
12:22 T was brought unto him one possessed 5119
12:26 how shall t his kingdom stand? 3767
12:28 t the kingdom of God is come unto you. 686
12:29 strong *man?* and t he will spoil his house. 5119
12:38 T certain of the scribes and of the 5119
12:44 T he saith, I will return into my house 5119
12:45 T goeth he, and taketh with himself seven 5119
12:47 T one said unto him, Behold, thy mother 1161
13:19 t cometh the wicked one, and catcheth NIG
13:26 forth fruit, t appeared the tares also. 5119
13:27 in thy field? from whence t hath it tares? 3767
13:28 thou t *that* we go and gather them up? 3767
13:36 T Jesus sent the multitude away, 5119
13:43 T shall the righteous shine forth as the sun 5119
13:52 T said he unto them, Therefore every 1161
13:56 Whence t hath this *man* all these *things?* 3767
14:33 T they that were in the ship came and 1161
15: 1 T came to Jesus scribes and Pharisees, 5119
15:12 T came his disciples, and said unto him, 5119
15:15 T answered Peter and said unto him, 1161
15:21 T Jesus went thence, and departed into 2532
15:25 T came she and worshipped him, saying, 1161
15:28 T Jesus answered and said unto her, 5119
15:32 T Jesus called his disciples unto *him,* and 1161
16: 6 T Jesus said unto them, Take heed and 1161
16:12 T understood they how that he bade *them* 5119
16:20 T charged he his disciples that they should 5119
16:22 T Peter took him, and began to rebuke 2532
16:24 T said Jesus unto his disciples, If any *man* 5119
16:27 t he shall reward every man according 1161
17: 4 T answered Peter and said unto Jesus, 1161
17:10 Why t say the scribes that Elias must first 3767
17:13 T the disciples understood that he spake 5119
17:17 T Jesus answered and said, O faithless and 1161
17:19 T came the disciples to Jesus apart, 5119
17:26 unto him, T are the children free. 686+1065
18:16 thee, t take with thee one or two more, NIG
18:21 T came Peter to him, and said, Lord, 5119
18:27 T the lord of that servant was moved with 1161
18:32 T his lord, after that he had called him, 5119
19: 7 Why did Moses t command to give a 3767
19:13 T were there brought unto him little 5119
19:23 T said Jesus unto his disciples, Verily I say 1161

Mt
19:25 saying, Who t can be saved? 686
19:27 T answered Peter and said unto him, 5119
20:20 T came to him the mother of Zebedee's 5119
21: 1 T Olives, t sent Jesus two disciples, 5119
21:25 unto us, Why did ye not t believe him? 3767
22: 8 T saith he to his servants, The wedding is 5119
22:13 T said the king to the servants, Bind him 5119
22:15 T went the Pharisees, and took counsel 5119
22:21 T saith he unto them, Render therefore 5119
22:35 T one of them, *which was* a lawyer, 2532
22:43 How t doth David in spirit call him Lord, 3767
22:45 David t call him Lord, how is he his son? 3767
23: 1 T spake Jesus to the multitude, and to his 5119
23:32 Fill ye up t the measure of your fathers. 2532
24: 9 T shall they deliver you up to be afflicted, 5119
24:10 And t shall many be offended, 5119
24:14 unto all nations; and t shall the end come. 5119
24:16 T let them which be in Judea flee into 5119
24:21 For t shall be great tribulation, such as 5119
24:23 T if any *man* shall say unto you, Lo, here 5119
24:30 And t shall appear the sign of the Son of 5119
24:30 t shall all the tribes of the earth mourn, 5119
24:40 T shall two be in the field; the one shall 5119
24:45 Who t is a faithful and wise servant, 686
25: 1 T shall the kingdom of heaven be likened 5119
25: 7 T all those virgins arose, and trimmed 5119
25:16 T he that had received the five talents 1161
25:24 T he which had received the one talent 2532
25:27 t at my coming I should have received NIG
25:31 t shall he sit upon the throne of his glory: 5119
25:34 T shall the King say unto them on his 5119
25:37 T shall the righteous answer him, saying, 5119
25:41 T shall he say also unto them on the left 5119
25:44 T shall they also answer him, saying, Lord, 5119
25:45 T shall he answer them, saying, Verily I 5119
26: 3 T assembled together the chief priests, 5119
26:14 T one of the twelve, called Judas Iscariot, 1161
26:25 T Judas, which betrayed him, answered 1161
26:31 T saith Jesus unto them, All ye shall be 5119
26:36 T cometh Jesus with them unto a place 5119
26:38 T saith he unto them, My soul is 5119
26:45 T cometh he to his disciples, and saith 5119
26:50 T came they, and laid hands on Jesus, 5119
26:52 T said Jesus unto him, Put up again thy 5119
26:54 *But* how t shall the scriptures be fulfilled, 3767
26:56 T all the disciples forsook him, and fled. 5119
26:65 T the high priest rent his clothes, saying, 5119
26:67 T did they spit in his face, 5119
26:74 T began he to curse and to swear, *saying,* 5119
27: 3 T Judas, which had betrayed him, when 5119
27: 9 T was fulfilled that which was spoken by 5119
27:13 T said Pilate unto him, Hearest thou not 5119
27:16 And they had t a notable prisoner, 5119
27:22 What shall I do t with Jesus which is 3767
27:25 T answered all the people, and said, 2532
27:26 T released he Barabbas unto them: 5119
27:27 T the soldiers of the governor took Jesus 5119
27:38 T were there two thieves crucified with 5119
27:58 T Pilate commanded the body to be 5119
28:10 T said Jesus unto them, Be not afraid: 5119
28:16 T the eleven disciples went away into 1161

Mk
2:20 and t shall they fast in those days. 5119
3:27 strong *man;* and t he will spoil his house. 5119
3:31 There came t *his* brethren and his mother, 3767
4:13 and how t will ye know all parables? NIG
4:28 first the blade, t the ear, after that the full 1534
7: 1 T came together unto him the Pharisees, 2532
7: 5 T the Pharisees and scribes asked him, 1899
10: 8 so t they are no more twain, but one flesh 5620
10:21 T Jesus beholding him loved him, 1161
10:26 among themselves, Who t can be saved? 2532
10:28 T Peter began to say unto him, Lo, we 2532
11:31 he will say, Why t did ye not believe him? 3767
12:18 T come unto him the Sadducees, which 2532
12:37 him Lord; and whence is he t his son? NIG
13:14 t let them that be in Judea flee to 5119
13:21 t if any *man* shall say to you, Lo, here 5119
13:26 t shall they see the Son of man coming 5119
13:27 And t shall he send his angels, 5119
14:63 T the high priest rent his clothes, and 1161
15:12 What will ye t that I shall do *unto him* 3767
15:14 T Pilate said unto them, Why, what evil 1161
16:19 So t after the Lord had spoken unto them, 3303

Lk
1:34 T said Mary unto the angel, How shall 1161
2:28 T took he him *up* in his arms, 2532
3: 7 T said he to the multitude that came forth 3767
3:10 asked him, saying, What shall we do t? 3767
3:12 T came also publicans to be baptized, 1161
5:35 and t shall they fast in those days. 5119
5:36 t both the new maketh a rent, and the NIG
6: 9 T said Jesus unto them, I will ask you one 3767
6:42 and t shalt thou see clearly to pull out 5119
7: 6 T Jesus went with them. And when he 1161
7:22 T Jesus answering said unto them, 2532
7:31 Whereunto t shall I liken the men of this 3767
8:12 t cometh the devil, and taketh away 1534
8:19 T came to him *his* mother and his 1161
8:24 Master, master, we perish. T he rose, 1161
8:33 T went the devils out of the man, 1161
8:35 T they went out to see what was done; 1161
8:37 T the whole multitude of the country of 2532
9: 1 T he called his twelve disciples together, 1161
9:12 t came the twelve, and said unto him, 1161
9:16 T he took the five loaves and the two 1161
9:46 T there arose a reasoning among them, 1161

Lk
10:37 T said Jesus unto him, Go, and do thou 3767
11:13 If ye t, being evil, know how to give good 3767
11:26 T goeth he, and taketh to *him* seven 5119
11:45 T answered one of the lawyers, 1161
12:20 t whose shall *those things* be, which thou 1161
12:26 If ye t be not able *to do that thing which* 3767
12:28 If t God so clothe the grass, which is 1161
12:41 T Peter said unto him, Lord, speakest 1161
12:42 Who t is *that* faithful and wise steward, 686
13: 7 T said he unto the dresser of his vineyard, 1161
13: 9 if not, t after that thou shalt cut it down. NIG
13:15 The Lord t answered him, and said, 3767
13:18 T said he, Unto what is the kingdom of 1161
13:23 T said one unto him, Lord, are there few 1161
13:26 T shall ye begin to say, We have eaten 5119
14:10 t shalt thou have worship in the presence 1161
14:12 T said he also to him that bade him, 1161
14:16 T said he unto him, A certain man made 1161
14:21 shewed his lord these *things.* T the master 5119
15: 1 T drew near unto him all the publicans 1161
16: 3 T the steward said within himself, 1161
16: 7 T said he to another, And how much 1899
16:27 T he said, I pray thee therefore, father, 1161
17: 1 T said he unto the disciples, It is 1161
18:26 that heard *it* said, Who t can be saved? 2532
18:28 T Peter said, Lo, we have left all, 1161
18:31 T he took unto *him* the twelve, 1161
19:15 t he commanded these servants to be 2532
19:16 T came the first, saying, Lord, thy pound 1161
19:23 Wherefore t gavest not thou my money 2532
20: 5 he will say, Why t believed ye him not? 3767
20: 9 T began he to speak to the people this 1161
20:13 T said the lord of the vineyard, What shall 1161
20:17 and said, What is this t that is written, 3767
20:27 T came to *him* certain of the Sadducees, 1161
20:39 T certain of the scribes answering said, 1161
20:44 calleth him Lord, how is he t his son? 2532
20:45 T in the audience of all the people he said 1161
21:10 T said he unto them, Nation shall rise 5119
21:20 t know that the desolation thereof is nigh. 5119
21:21 T let them which are in Judea flee to 5119
21:27 t shall they see the Son of man coming 5119
21:28 to pass, t look up, and lift up your heads; NIG
22: 3 T entered Satan into Judas surnamed 1161
22: 7 T came the day of unleavened bread, 1161
22:36 T said he unto them, But now, he that 3767
22:52 T Jesus said unto the chief priests, 1161
22:54 T took they him, and led *him,* and 1161
22:70 T said they all, Art thou then the Son of 1161
22:70 said they all, Art thou t the Son of God? 3767
23: 4 T said Pilate to the chief priests and *to* 1161
23: 9 T he questioned *with* him in many words; 1161
23:30 T shall they begin to say to the mountains, 5119
23:34 T said Jesus, Father, forgive them; for they 1161
24:12 T arose Peter, and ran unto the sepulchre; 1161
24:25 T he said unto them, O fools, and slow of 2532
24:45 T opened he their understanding, that 5119

Jn
1:21 And they asked him, What t? Art thou 3767
1:22 T said they, Who art thou? 3767
1:25 and said unto him, Why baptizest thou t, 3767
1:38 T Jesus turned, and saw them following, 1161
2:10 have well drunk, t that which is worse: 3767
2:18 T answered the Jews and said unto him, 3767
2:20 T said the Jews, Forty and six years was 3767
3:25 T there arose a question between *some* of 3767
4: 5 T cometh he to a city of Samaria, which is 3767
4: 9 T saith the woman of Samaria unto him, 3767
4:11 whence t hast thou that living water? 3767
4:28 The woman t left her waterpot, 3767
4:30 T they went out of the city, and came 3767
4:35 yet four months, and t cometh harvest? NIG
4:45 T when he was come into Galilee, 3767
4:48 T said Jesus unto him, Except ye see signs 3767
4:52 T inquired he of them the hour when he 3767
5: 4 whosoever t first after the troubling of 3767
5:12 T asked they him, What man is that 3767
5:19 T answered Jesus and said unto them, 3767
6: 5 When Jesus t lift up *his* eyes, 3767
6:14 T *those* men, when they had seen 3767
6:21 T they willingly received him into the 3767
6:28 T said they unto him, What shall we do, 3767
6:30 unto him, What sign shewest thou t, 3767
6:32 T Jesus said unto them, Verily, verily, I 3767
6:34 T said they unto him, Lord, evermore 3767
6:41 The Jews t murmured at him, because 3767
6:42 how is it t *that* he saith, I came down 3767
6:53 T Jesus said unto them, Verily, verily, I 3767
6:67 T said Jesus unto the twelve, Will ye also 3767
6:68 T Simon Peter answered him, Lord, 3767
7: 6 T Jesus said unto them, My time is not 3767
7:10 t went he also up unto the feast, not 5119
7:11 T the Jews sought him at the feast, 3767
7:25 T said some of them of Jerusalem, Is not 3767
7:28 T cried Jesus in the temple as he taught, 3767
7:30 T they sought to take him: but no man 3767
7:33 T said Jesus unto them, Yet a little while 3767
7:33 you, and t I go unto him that sent me. NIG
7:35 T said the Jews among themselves, 3767
7:45 T came the officers to the chief priests 3767
7:47 T answered them the Pharisees, Are ye 3767
8:12 T spake Jesus again unto them, saying, 3767
8:19 T said they unto him, Where is thy 3767
8:21 T said Jesus again unto them, I go my 3767
8:22 T said the Jews, Will he kill himself? 3767
8:25 T said they unto him, Who art thou? 3767

Jn	8:28 **T** said Jesus unto them, When ye have lift	3767
	8:28 **t** shall ye know that I am *he*, and *that* I do	5119
	8:31 **T** said Jesus to those Jews which believed	3767
	8:31 in my word, *t* are ye my disciples indeed;	NIG
	8:41 **T** said they to him, We be not born of	3767
	8:48 **T** answered the Jews, and said unto him,	3767
	8:52 **T** said the Jews unto him, Now we know	3767
	8:57 **T** said the Jews unto him, Thou art not	3767
	8:59 **T** took they up stones to cast at him:	3767
	9:12 **T** said they unto him, Where is he?	3767
	9:15 **T** again the Pharisees also asked him how	3767
	9:19 was born blind? how **t** doth he now see?	3767
	9:24 **T** again called they the man that was	3767
	9:26 **T** said they to him again, What did he to	1161
	9:28 **T** they reviled him, and said, Thou art his	3767
	10: 7 **T** said Jesus unto them again, Verily,	3767
	10:24 **T** came the Jews round about him,	3767
	10:31 **T** the Jews took up stones again to stone	3767
	11: 7 **T** after that saith he to *his* disciples,	1899
	11:12 **T** said his disciples, Lord, if he sleep,	3767
	11:14 **T** said Jesus unto them plainly,	3767+5119
	11:16 **T** said Thomas, which is called Didymus,	3767
	11:17 **T** when Jesus came, he found that he had	3767
	11:20 **T** Martha, as soon as she heard that Jesus	3767
	11:21 **T** said Martha unto Jesus, Lord, if thou	3767
	11:31 The Jews **t** which were with her in	3767
	11:32 **T** when Mary was come where Jesus was,	3767
	11:36 **T** said the Jews, Behold, how he loved	3767
	11:41 **t** they took away the stone *from the*	3767
	11:45 **T** many of the Jews which came to Mary,	3767
	11:47 **t** gathered the chief priests and	3767
	11:53 **t** from that day forth they took counsel	3767
	11:56 **T** sought they for Jesus, and spake among	3767
	12: 1 **T** Jesus six days before the passover came	3767
	12: 3 **T** took Mary a pound of ointment of	3767
	12: 4 **T** saith one of his disciples, Judas Iscariot,	3767
	12: 7 **T** said Jesus, Let her alone: against the	3767
	12:16 **t** remembered they that these *things* were	5119
	12:28 **t** came there a voice from heaven,	3767
	12:35 **T** Jesus said unto them, Yet a little while	5119
	13: 6 **t** cometh he to Simon Peter:	3767
	13:14 If I **t**, *your* Lord and Master, have washed	3767
	13:22 the disciples looked one on another,	3767
	13:25 He **t** lying on Jesus' breast saith unto him,	1161
	13:27 **T** said Jesus unto him, That thou doest,	3767
	13:30 He **t** having received the sop went	3767
	14: 9 how sayest thou **t**, Shew us the Father?	NIG
	16:17 **T** said *some* of his disciples among	3767
	18: 3 Judas **t**, having received a band *of men*,	3767
	18: 6 As soon **t** as he had said unto them, I am	3767
	18: 7 **T** asked he them again, Whom seek ye?	3767
	18:10 **T** Simon Peter having a sword drew it,	3767
	18:11 **t** said Jesus unto Peter, Put up thy sword	3767
	18:12 **T** the band and the captain and officers of	3767
	18:16 **t** went out *that* other disciple, which was	3767
	18:17 **T** saith the damsel that kept the door unto	3767
	18:19 The high priest **t** asked Jesus of his	3767
	18:27 Peter **t** denied again: and immediately	3767
	18:28 **T** led they Jesus from Caiaphas unto	3767
	18:29 Pilate **t** went out unto them, and said,	3767
	18:31 **T** said Pilate unto them, Take ye him,	3767
	18:33 **T** Pilate entered into the judgment hall	3767
	18:36 of this world, **t** would my servants fight,	NIG
	18:37 therefore said unto him, Art thou a king **t**?	3766
	18:40 **T** cried they all again, saying, Not this	3767
	19: 1 **T** Pilate therefore took Jesus,	5119
	19: 5 **T** came Jesus forth, wearing the crown of	3767
	19:10 **T** saith Pilate unto him, Speakest thou not	3767
	19:16 **t** delivered he him therefore unto them to	5119
	19:20 This title **t** read many of the Jews:	3767
	19:21 **t** said the chief priests of the Jews to	3767
	19:23 **T** the soldiers, when they had crucified	3767
	19:27 **t** saith he to the disciple, Behold thy	1534
	19:32 **T** came the soldiers, and brake the legs of	3767
	19:40 **T** took they the body of Jesus, and wound	3767
	20: 2 **T** she runneth, and cometh to Simon	3767
	20: 6 **t** cometh Simon Peter following him,	3767
	20: 8 **T** went in also *that* other disciple,	3767+5119
	20:10 **T** the disciples went away again unto their	3767
	20:19 **T** the same day at evening, being the first	3767
	20:20 **t** were the disciples glad, when they saw	3767
	20:21 **T** said Jesus to them again, Peace *be* unto	3767
	20:26 **t** came Jesus, the doors being shut,	NIG
	20:27 **T** saith he to Thomas, Reach hither thy	1534
	21: 5 **T** Jesus saith unto them, Children, have	3767
	21: 9 As soon **t** as they were come to land,	3767
	21:13 Jesus **t** cometh, and taketh bread,	3767
	21:20 **T** Peter, turning about, seeth the disciple	1161
	21:23 **T** went this saying abroad among	3767
Ac	1:12 **T** returned they unto Jerusalem from	5119
	2:38 **T** Peter said unto them, Repent,	1161
	2:41 **T** they that gladly received his word were	3767
	3: 6 **T** Peter said, Silver and gold have I none;	1161
	4: 8 **T** Peter, filled with the Holy Ghost,	5119
	5: 9 **T** Peter said unto her, How *is it* that ye	1161
	5:10 **T** fell she down straightway at his feet,	1161
	5:17 **T** the high priest rose up, and all they that	1161
	5:25 **T** came one and told them, saying,	1161
	5:26 **T** went the captain with the officers,	5119
	5:29 **T** Peter and the *other* apostles answered	1161
	5:34 **T** stood there up one in the council,	1161
	6: 2 **T** the twelve called the multitude of	1161
	6: 9 **T** there arose certain of the synagogue,	1161
	6:11 **T** they suborned men, which said, We	5119
	7: 1 **T** said the high priest, Are these *things* so?	1161

Ac	7: 4 **T** came he out of the land of the	5119
	7:14 **T** sent Joseph, and called his father Jacob	1161
	7:29 **t** fled Moses at this saying, and was a	1161
	7:32 and the God of Jacob. **T** Moses trembled,	1161
	7:33 **T** said the Lord to him, Put off *thy* shoes	1161
	7:42 **T** God turned, and gave them up to	1161
	7:57 **T** they cried out with a loud voice,	1161
	8: 5 **T** Philip went down to the city of Samaria	1161
	8:13 **T** Simon himself believed also:	1161
	8:17 **T** laid they *their* hands on them,	5119
	8:24 **T** answered Simon, and said, Pray ye to	1161
	8:29 **T** the Spirit said unto Philip, Go near,	1161
	8:35 **T** Philip opened his mouth,	1161
	9:13 **T** Ananias answered, Lord, I have heard	1161
	9:19 **t** was Saul certain days with the disciples	1161
	9:25 **T** the disciples took him by night,	1161
	9:31 **T** had the churches rest throughout all	3767
	9:39 **T** Peter arose and went with them. When	1161
	10:21 **T** Peter went down to the men which	1161
	10:23 **T** called he them in, and lodged *them*.	3767
	10:34 **T** Peter opened *his* mouth, and said, Of a	1161
	10:46 and magnify God. **T** answered Peter,	5119
	10:48 **T** prayed they him to tarry certain days.	5119
	11:16 **T** remembered I the word of the Lord,	1161
	11:17 **t** as God gave them the like gift	3767
	11:18 **T** hath God also to the Gentiles granted	686
	11:22 **T** tidings of these *things* came unto the	1161
	11:25 **T** departed Barnabas to Tarsus, for to seek	1161
	11:29 **T** the disciples, every man according to his	1161
	12: 3 (**T** were the days of unleavened bread.)	1161
	12:15 it was *even* so. **T** said they, It is his angel.	1161
	13: 9 **T** Saul, (who also *is called* Paul,)	1161
	13:12 **T** the deputy, when he saw what was	5119
	13:16 **T** Paul stood up, and beckoning with *his*	1161
	13:46 **T** Paul and Barnabas waxed bold, and	1161
	14:13 **T** the priest of Jupiter, which was before	1161
	15:12 **T** all the multitude kept silence,	1161
	15:22 **T** pleased it the apostles and elders,	5119
	16: 1 **T** came he to Derbe and Lystra:	1161
	16:29 **T** he called for a light, and sprang in,	1161
	17:14 And **t** immediately the brethren sent away	5119
	17:18 **T** certain philosophers of the Epicureans,	1161
	17:22 **T** Paul stood in the midst of Mars' hill,	1161
	17:29 **Forasmuch t** as we are the offspring of	3767
	18: 9 **T** spake the Lord to Paul in the night by a	1161
	18:17 **T** all the Greeks took Sosthenes, the *chief*	1161
	18:18 and **t** took his leave of the brethren,	NIG
	19: 3 unto them, Unto what **t** were ye baptized?	3767
	19: 4 **T** said Paul, John verily baptized *with*	1161
	19:13 **T** certain of the vagabond Jews, exorcists,	1161
	19:36 **Seeing t** that these *things* cannot be	3767
	21:13 **T** Paul answered, What mean ye to weep	1161
	21:26 **T** Paul took the men, and the next day	5119
	21:33 **T** the chief captain came near,	5119
	22:22 and **t** lift up their voices, and said,	NIG
	22:27 **T** the chief captain came, and said unto	1161
	22:29 **T** straightway they departed from him	3767
	23: 3 **T** said Paul unto him, God shall smite	5119
	23: 5 **T** said Paul, I wist not, brethren, that he	5037
	23:17 **T** Paul called one of the centurions unto	1161
	23:19 **T** the chief captain took him by the hand,	1161
	23:22 So the chief captain **t** let the young man	NIG
	23:27 **t** came I with an army, and rescued him,	3767
	23:31 **T** the soldiers, as it was commanded	3767
	24:10 **T** Paul, after that the governor had	1161
	25: 2 **T** the high priest and the chief of the Jews	1161
	25:10 **T** said Paul, I stand at Cesar's judgment	1161
	25:12 **T** Festus, when he had conferred with	5119
	25:22 **T** Agrippa said unto Festus, I would also	1161
	26: 1 **T** Agrippa said unto Paul, Thou art	1161
	26: 1 **T** Paul stretched forth the hand,	5119
	26:20 **t** to the Gentiles, that *they* should repent	NIG
	26:28 **T** Agrippa said unto Paul, Almost thou	1161
	26:32 **T** said Agrippa unto Festus, This man	1161
	27:20 we should be saved was **t** taken away.	3062
	27:29 **T** fearing lest we should have fallen upon	5037
	27:32 **T** the soldiers cut off the ropes of the boat,	5119
	27:36 **T** were they all of good cheer,	1161
	28: 1 **t** they knew that the island was called	5119
Ro	3: 1 What advantage **t** hath the Jew?	3767
	3: 6 for **t** how shall God judge the world?	1893
	3: 9 What **t**? are we better *than they*? No, in	3767
	3:27 Where *is* boasting **t**? It is excluded.	3767
	3:31 Do we **t** make void the law through faith?	3767
	4: 1 What shall we say **t** that Abraham our	3767
	4: 9 *Cometh* this blessedness **t** upon	3767
	4:10 How was it **t** reckoned? when he was in	3767
	5: 9 Much more **t**, being now justified by his	3767
	6: 1 What shall we say **t**? Shall we continue in	3767
	6:15 What **t**? shall we sin, because we are not	3767
	6:18 Being **t** made free from sin, ye became	1161
	6:21 What fruit had ye **t** *in* those things	5119
	7: 3 So **t** if, while *her* husband liveth, she be	3767
	7: 7 What shall we say **t**? *Is* the law sin?	3767
	7:13 Was **t** that which is good made death unto	3767
	7:16 If I **t** do that which I would not, I consent	1161
	7:17 Now **t** it is no more I that do it, but sin	1161
	7:21 I find **t** a law, that, when I would do good,	686
	7:25 So **t** with the mind I myself serve the law	1161
	8: 8 So **t** they that are in the flesh cannot	1161
	8:17 And if children; heirs of God,	2532
	8:25 see not, **t** do we with patience wait for *it*.	NIG
	8:31 What shall we say **t** to these *things*?	3767
	9:14 What shall we say **t**? *Is there*	3767
	9:16 So **t** it *is* not of him that willeth, nor of	1161

Ro	9:19 Thou wilt say **t** unto me, Why doth he	3767
	9:30 What shall we say **t**? That the Gentiles,	3767
	10:14 How **t** shall they call on *him* in whom	3767
	10:17 So **t** faith *cometh* by hearing,	686
	11: 1 I say **t**, Hath God cast away his people?	3767
	11: 5 *Even* so **t** at *this* present time also there is	3767
	11: 6 And if by grace, *t is it* no more of works:	NIG
	11: 6 But if *it be* of works, *t* is it no more grace:	NIG
	11: 7 What **t**? Israel hath not obtained that	3767
	11:11 I say **t**, Have they stumbled that they	3767
	11:19 wilt say **t**, The branches were broken	3767
	12: 6 Having **t** gifts differing according to	1161
	13: 3 Wilt thou **t** not be afraid of the power?	1161
	14:12 So **t** every one of us shall give account of	3767
	14:16 Let not **t** your good be evil spoken of:	3767
	15: 1 We **t** that are strong ought to bear	1161
1Co	3: 5 Who **t** is Paul, and who *is* Apollos,	3767
	3: 7 So **t** neither is he that planteth any *thing*,	5620
	4: 5 and **t** shall every man have praise of God.	5119
	5:10 for **t** must ye needs go out of the world.	686
	6: 4 If ye have judgments *of things* pertaining	3767
	6:15 shall I **t** take the members of Christ,	3767
	7:38 So **t** he that giveth *her* in marriage doeth	5620
	9:18 What is my reward **t**? *Verily* that, when I	3767
	10:19 What say I **t**? that the idol is any *thing*, or	3767
	12:28 **t** gifts of healings, helps, governments,	1534
	13:10 **t** that which is in part shall be done away.	5119
	13:12 through a glass, darkly; but **t** face to face:	5119
	13:12 **t** shall I know even as also I am known.	5119
	14:15 What is it **t**? I will pray with the spirit,	3767
	14:26 How is it **t**, brethren? when ye come	3767
	15: 5 he was seen of Cephas, **t** of the twelve:	1534
	15: 7 he was seen of James; **t** of all the apostles.	1534
	15:13 of the dead, **t** is Christ not risen:	3761
	15:14 **t** *is* our preaching vain, and your faith *is*	686
	15:16 if the dead rise not, **t** is **not** Christ raised:	3761
	15:18 They also which are fallen asleep in	686
	15:24 **t** *cometh* the end, when he shall have	1534
	15:28 shall the Son also himself be subject unto	5119
	15:29 why are they **t** baptized for the dead?	2532
	15:54 **t** shall be brought to pass the saying that	5119
2Co	2: 2 who is he **t** that maketh me glad,	2532
	3:12 **Seeing t** that we have such hope, we use	3767
	4:12 So **t** death worketh in us, but life in you.	5620
	5:14 that if one died for all, **t** were all dead:	686
	5:20 Now **t** we are ambassadors for Christ,	3767
	6: 1 We **t**, *as* workers together *with him*,	1161
	12:10 for when I am weak, **t** am I strong.	5119
Gal	1:18 **T** after three years I went up to Jerusalem	1899
	2: 1 **T** fourteen years after I went up again to	1899
	2:21 *come* by the law, **t** Christ is dead in vain.	686
	3: 9 So **t** they which be of faith are blessed	5620
	3:19 Wherefore **t** *serveth* the law? It was added	3767
	3:21 *Is* the law **t** against the promises of God?	3767
	3:29 **t** are ye Abraham's seed, and heirs	686
	4: 7 if a son, **t** an heir of God through Christ.	2532
	4: 8 Howbeit **t**, when ye knew not God,	5119
	4:15 Where is **t** it **t**? the blessedness ye spake of?	3767
	4:29 But as **t** he that was born after the flesh	5119
	4:31 So **t**, brethren, we are not children of	686
	5:11 it is the offence of the cross ceased.	686
	5:16 I say **t**, Walk in the Spirit, and ye shall	1161
	6: 4 and **t** shall he have rejoicing in himself	5119
Eph	5:15 See **t** that ye walk circumspectly, not as	3767
Php	1:18 What **t**? notwithstanding, every way,	1063
Col	3: 1 If ye **t** be risen with Christ, seek those	3767
	3: 4 **t** shall ye also appear with him in glory.	5119
1Th	4: 1 Furthermore **t** we beseech you, brethren,	3767
	4:17 **T** we which are alive *and* remain shall be	1899
	5: 3 **t** sudden destruction cometh upon them,	5119
2Th	2: 8 And **t** shall *that* Wicked be revealed,	5119
1Ti	2:13 For Adam was first formed, **t** Eve.	1534
	3: 2 bishop **t** must be blameless, the husband	3767
	3:10 let them use the office of a deacon,	1534
Heb	2:14 **Forasmuch t** as the children are partakers	3767
	4: 8 **t** would he not afterward have spoken of	NIG
	4:14 **Seeing t** that we have a great high priest,	3767
	7:27 for his own sins, *and* **t** for the people's:	1899
	8: 7 **t** should no place have been sought for	NIG
	9: 1 **T** verily the first *covenant* had also	3767
	9: 9 Which *was* a figure for the time **t** present,	NIG
	9:26 For **t** must he often have suffered since	1893
	10: 2 For **t** would they not have ceased to be	1893
	10: 7 **T** said I, Lo, I come (in the volume of	5119
	10: 9 **T** said he, Lo, I come to do thy will,	5119
	12: 8 partakers, **t** are ye bastards, and not sons.	686
	12:26 Whose voice **t** shook the earth: but now	5119
Jas	1:15 **T** when lust hath conceived, it bringeth	1534
	2: 4 Are ye not **t** partial in yourselves,	2532
	2:24 Ye see **t** how that by works a man is	5106
	3:17 peaceable, gentle, *and* easy to be	1899
	4:14 for a little *time*, and **t** vanisheth away.	1899
1Pe	2: 7 **Forasmuch t** as Christ hath suffered for	3767
2Pe	3: 6 Whereby the world that **t** was,	5119
	3:11 *Seeing* **t** that all these *things* shall be	3767
1Jn	1: 5 This **t** is the message which we have	2532
	3:21 not, **t** have we confidence towards God.	NIG
Rev	3:16 So **t** because thou art lukewarm,	NIG
	22: 9 **t** saith he unto me, See *thou do it* not:	2532

THENCE (145) [THENCEFORTH]

Ge	2:10 from **t** it was parted, and became into	8033
	11: 8 from **t** upon the face of all the earth:	8033
	11: 9 from **t** did the Lᴏʀᴅ scatter them abroad	8033
	12: 8 he removed from **t** unto a mountain on	8033

T

Ge	18:16	men rose up from **t**, and looked toward	8033
	18:22	the men turned their faces from **t**,	8033
	20: 1	Abraham journeyed from **t** toward	8033
	24: 7	shalt take a wife unto my son from **t**.	8033
	26:17	Isaac departed from **t**, and pitched his	4480+8033
	26:22	he removed from **t**, and digged another	8033
	26:23	And he went up from **t** to Beer-sheba.	8033
	27: 9	me from **t** two good kids of the goats;	8033
	27:45	I will send, and fetch thee from **t**:	8033
	28: 2	take thee a wife from **t** of the daughters	8033
	28: 6	to Padan-aram, to take him a wife from **t**;	8033
	30:32	removing from **t** all the speckled and	8033
	42: 2	you down thither, and buy for us from **t**;	8033
	42:26	asses with the corn, and departed **t**.	4480+8033
	49:24	**t** *is* the shepherd, the stone of Israel:)	8033
Nu	13:23	cut down from **t** a branch with one	8033
	13:24	the children of Israel cut down from **t**.	8033
	21:12	From **t** they removed, and pitched in	8033
	21:13	From **t** they removed, and pitched on	8033
	21:16	from **t** *they went* to Beer: that *is* the well	8033
	22:41	that he might see the utmost part	4480+8033
	23:13	see them all: and curse me them from **t**.	8033
	23:27	that thou mayest curse me them from **t**.	8033
Dt	4:29	if from **t** thou shalt seek the Lord thy	8033
	5:15	thee out **t** through a mighty hand	4480+8033
	6:23	he brought us out from **t**, that he might	8033
	10: 7	From **t** they journeyed *unto* Gudgodah;	8033
	19:12	his city shall send and fetch him **t**,	4480+8033
	22: 8	thine house, if any man fall from **t**.	5105.2
	24:18	Lord thy God redeemed thee **t**:	4480+8033
	30: 4	from **t** will the Lord thy God gather	8033
	30: 4	gather thee, and from **t** will he fetch thee:	8033
Jos	6:22	bring out **t** the woman, and all that	4480+8033
	15: 4	*From* **t** it passed toward Azmon,	NIH
	15:14	Caleb drove the three sons of	4480+8033
	15:15	he went up **t** to the inhabitants of	4480+8033
	18:13	the border went over from **t** toward Luz,	8033
	18:14	the border was drawn **t**, and compassed	NIH
	19:13	from **t** passeth on along on the east to	8033
	19:34	goeth out from **t** to Hukkok,	8033
Jdg	1:11	From **t** he went against the inhabitants of	8033
	1:20	expelled **t** the three sons of Anak.	4480+8033
	8: 8	he went up **t** *to* Penuel,	4480+8033
	18:11	there went from **t** of the family of	8033
	18:13	they passed **t** *unto* mount Ephraim,	4480+8033
	19:18	the side of mount Ephraim; from **t** *am* I:	8033
	21:24	children of Israel departed **t** at that time,	8033
	21:24	they went out from **t** every man to his	8033
1Sa	4: 4	that they might bring from **t** the ark of	8033
	10: 3	shalt thou go on forward from **t**,	8033
	10:23	they ran and fetched him **t**:	4480+8033
	17:49	took **t** a stone, and slang *it*, and	4480+8033
	22: 1	David therefore departed **t**, and escaped	8033
	22: 3	David went **t** *to* Mizpeh of Moab:	4480+8033
	23:29	David went up from **t**, and dwelt in	8033
2Sa	6: 2	Judah, to bring up from **t** the ark of God,	8033
	14: 2	fetcht **t** a wise woman, and said	4480+8033
	16: 5	**t** came out a man of the family of	4480+8033
	21:13	he brought up from **t** the bones of Saul	8033
1Ki	1:45	they are come up from **t** rejoicing,	8033
	2:36	and go not forth **t** any whither.	4480+8033
	9:28	fet from **t** gold, four hundred and	8033
	12:25	went out from **t**, and built Penuel.	8033
	19:19	So he departed **t**, and found Elisha	8033
2Ki	2:21	there shall not be from **t** any more death	8033
	2:23	he went up from **t** *unto* Beth-el: and as he	8033
	2:25	he went from **t** to mount Carmel,	8033
	2:25	and from **t** he returned to Samaria.	8033
	6: 2	take **t** every man a beam, and let us	4480+8033
	7: 8	carried **t** silver, and gold,	4480+8033
	7: 8	carried *also*, and went and hid *it*.	4480+8033
	10:15	when he was departed **t**, he lighted on	8033
	17:27	of the priests whom ye brought from **t**;	8033
	17:33	nations whom they carried away from **t**	8033
	23:12	brake *them* down from **t**, and cast the	8033
	24:13	he carried out **t** all the treasures of	4480+8033
1Ch	13: 6	up **t** the ark of God the Lord,	4480+8033
2Ch	8:18	took **t** four hundred and fifty talents	4480+8033
	26:20	and they thrust him out from **t**;	8033
Ezr	6: 6	*are* beyond the river, be ye far from **t**:	8536
Ne	1: 9	will I gather them from **t**, and will bring	8033
Job	39:29	From **t** she seeketh the prey, *and* her eyes	NIH
Isa	52:11	Depart ye, depart ye, go ye out from **t**,	8033
	65:20	There shall be no more **t** an infant	4480+8033
Jer	5: 6	every one that goeth out **t** shall be	2007+4480
	13: 6	to Euphrates, and take the girdle from **t**,	8033
	22:24	hand, yet would I pluck thee **t**;	4480+8033
	36:29	shall cause to cease from **t** man and	5089.1
	37:12	to separate himself **t** in the midst of	4480+8033
	38:11	took **t** old cast clouts and old rotten	4480+8033
	43:12	and he shall go forth from **t** in peace.	8033
	49:16	I will bring thee down from **t**, saith	8033
	49:38	destroy from **t** the king and the princes,	8033
	50: 9	against her; from **t** she shall be taken:	8033
Eze	11:18	and all the abominations thereof from **t**.	5089.1
Hos	2:15	I will give her her vineyards from **t**,	8033
Am	6: 2	and from **t** go ye to Hamath the great:	8033
	9: 2	**t** shall mine hand take them;	4480+8033
	9: 2	heaven, **t** will I bring them down:	4480+8033
	9: 3	will search and take them out **t**;	4480+8033
	9: 3	I will command the serpent,	4480+8033
	9: 4	I will command the sword,	4480+8033
Ob	1: 4	**t** will I bring thee down, saith	4480+8033
Mt	4:21	And going on **from t**, he saw other two	1564
	5:26	Thou shalt by no means come out **t**,	1564

Mt	9: 9	And as Jesus passed forth **from t**, he saw	1564
	9:27	When Jesus departed **t**, two blind men	1564
	10:11	in it is worthy; and there abide till ye **go t**.	1831
	11: 1	he departed **t** to teach and to preach in	1564
	12: 9	when he was departed **t**, he went into	1564
	12:15	knew *it*, he withdrew himself **from t**.	1564
	13:53	had finished these parables, he departed **t**.	1564
	14:13	When Jesus heard *of it*, he departed **t** by	1564
	15:21	Then Jesus went **t**, and departed into	1564
	15:29	And Jesus departed from **t**, and came nigh	1564
	19:15	he laid *his* hands on them, and departed **t**.	1564
Mk	1:19	And when he had gone a little further **t**,	1564
	6: 1	he went out **from t**, and came into his	1564
	6:11	nor hear you, when ye depart **t**,	1564
	7:24	And **from t** he arose, and went into	1564
	9:30	And they departed **t**, and passed through	1564
	10: 1	And he rose **from t**,	2547
Lk	4: 9	ye enter into, there abide, and **t** depart.	1564
	12:59	I tell thee, thou shalt not depart **t**, till thou	1564
	16:26	they pass to us, that *would come* **from t**.	1564
Jn	4:43	Now after two days he departed **t**,	1564
	11:54	went **t** unto a country near to	1564
Ac	7: 4	and **from t**, when his father was dead,	2547
	13: 4	and **from t** they sailed to Cyprus.	1564
	14:26	And **t** sailed to Antioch, from whence	2547
	16:12	And **from t** to Philippi, which is the chief	2547
	18: 7	And he departed **t**, and entered into a	1564
	18:18	and **sailed t** into Syria, and with him	1602
	20:15	And **we sailed t**, and came the next *day*	2547
	21: 1	unto Rhodes, **and from t** unto Patara:	2547
	27: 4	And when we had launched **from t**,	2547
	27:12	the more part advised to depart **t** also,	2547
	27:13	loosing **t**, they sailed close by Crete.	NIG
	28:13	And **from t** we fet a compass,	3606
	28:15	And **from t**, when the brethren heard of	2547
2Co	2:13	of them, I went from **t** into Macedonia.	NIG

THENCEFORTH (4) [THENCE]

Lev	22:27	**t** it shall be accepted for an offering made	1973
2Ch	32:23	in the sight of all nations from **t**.	310+3651
Mt	5:13	it is **t** good for nothing, but to be cast out,	2089
Jn	19:12	*And* **from t** Pilate sought to release	1537+3778

THEOPHILUS (2)

| Lk | 1: 3 | write unto thee in order, most excellent **T**, | 2321 |
| Ac | 1: 1 | The former treatise have I made, O **T**, | 2321 |

THERE (2299)

Ge	1: 3	God said, Let **t** be light: and there was	NIH
	1: 3	God said, Let there be light: and **t** was	NIH
	1: 6	Let **t** be a firmament in the midst of	NIH
	1:14	Let **t** be lights in the firmament of	NIH
	1:30	wherein *t is* life, *I have given* every green	NIH
	2: 5	and **t** was not a man to till the ground.	NIH
	2: 6	**t** went up a mist from the earth,	NIH
	2: 8	**t** he put the man whom he had formed.	8033
	2:11	whole land of Havilah, where **t** *is* gold;	NIH
	2:12	*is* good: **t** *is* bdellium and the onyx stone.	8033
	2:20	for Adam **t** was not found a help meet for	NIH
	4:26	to Seth, *to* him also **t** was born a son;	NIH
	6: 4	**T** were giants in the earth in those days;	NIH
	7: 9	**T** went in two and two unto Noah into	NIH
	9:11	neither shall **t** any more be a flood to	NIH
	11: 2	in the land of Shinar; and they dwelt **t**.	8033
	11: 7	go down, and **t** confound their language,	8033
	11: 9	the Lord did **t** confound the language of	NIH
	11:31	and they came unto Haran, and dwelt **t**.	8033
	12: 7	**t** builded he an altar unto the Lord,	8033
	12: 8	**t** he builded an altar unto the Lord,	8033
	12:10	**t** was a famine in the land: and Abram	NIH
	12:10	Abram went down into Egypt to sojourn **t**;	8033
	13: 4	the altar, which he had made **t** at the first:	8033
	13: 4	**t** Abram called on the name of the Lord.	8033
	13: 7	**t** was a strife between the herdmen of	NIH
	13: 8	Let **t** be no strife, I pray thee, between me	NIH
	13:18	and built **t** an altar unto the Lord.	8033
	14: 8	**t** went out the king of Sodom, and the	NIH
	14:10	of Sodom and Gomorrah fled, and fell **t**;	8033
	14:13	**t** came one that had escaped,	NIH
	18:24	Peradventure **t** **be** fifty righteous within	3426
	18:28	Peradventure **t** shall lack five of the fifty	8033
	18:28	he said, If I find **t** forty and five, I will not	8033
	18:29	Peradventure **t** shall be forty found there.	NIH
	18:29	Peradventure there shall be forty found **t**.	8033
	18:30	Peradventure **t** shall thirty be found there.	NIH
	18:30	Peradventure there shall thirty be found **t**.	8033
	18:30	he said, I will not do *it*, if I find thirty **t**.	8033
	18:31	Peradventure **t** shall be twenty found	NIH
	18:31	there shall be twenty found **t**.	8033
	18:32	Peradventure ten shall be found **t**. And he	8033
	19: 1	**t** came two angels to Sodom at even;	NIH
	19:31	*t is* not a man in the earth to come in unto	NIH
	21:31	because **t** they sware both of them.	8033
	21:33	called **t** on the name of the Lord,	8033
	22: 2	offer him **t** for a burnt offering upon one	8033
	22: 9	Abraham built an altar **t**, and laid the	8033
	23:13	of me, and I will bury my dead **t**.	8033+1886.5
	24:23	**is t** room *in* thy father's house for us to	3426
	24:33	**t** was set *meat* before him to eat:	NIH
	25:10	**t** was Abraham buried,	8033+1886.5
	25:24	behold, *t were* twins in her womb.	NIH
	26: 1	was a famine in the land, besides the first	8033
	26: 8	to pass, when he had been **t** a long time,	8033
	26:17	tent in the valley of Gerar, and dwelt **t**.	8033
	26:19	and found **t** a well of springing water.	8033

Ge	26:25	he builded an altar **t**, and called upon	8033
	26:25	name of the Lord, and pitched his tent **t**,	8033
	26:25	and **t** Isaac's servants digged a well.	NIH
	26:28	we said, Let **t** be now an oath betwixt us,	NIH
	28:11	tarried **t** all night, because the sun was	NIH
	29: 2	lo, **t** were three flocks of sheep lying by it;	NIH
	31:14	*Is t* yet any portion or inheritance for us in	NIH
	31:46	a heap: and they did eat **t** upon the heap.	8033
	32: 4	with Laban, and stayed **t** until now:	NIH
	32:13	he lodged **t** that *same* night; and took of	8033
	32:24	wrestled a man with him until the	8033
	32:29	ask after my name? And he blessed him **t**.	8033
	33:20	he erected **t** an altar, and called it	8033
	35: 1	Arise, go up to Beth-el, and dwell **t**:	8033
	35: 1	make **t** an altar unto God, that appeared	8033
	35: 3	I will make **t** an altar unto God,	8033
	35: 7	he built **t** an altar, and called the place	8033
	35: 7	because **t** God appeared unto him, when	8033
	35:16	**t** was but a little way to come to Ephrath:	NIH
	36:31	before **t** reigned *any* king over the children	NIH
	37:24	the pit *was* empty, **t** *was* no water in it.	NIH
	37:28	**t** passed by Midianites merchantmen;	NIH
	38: 2	Judah saw **t** a daughter of a certain	8033
	38:21	they said, **T** was no harlot in this *place*.	NIH
	38:22	said, *that* **t** was no harlot in this *place*.	NIH
	39: 9	*T is* none greater in this house than I;	NIH
	39:11	**t** was none of the men of the house there	NIH
	39:11	there was none of the men of the house **t**	8033
	39:20	were bound: and he was **t** in the prison.	8033
	39:22	whatsoever they did **t**, he was the doer of	8033
	40: 8	a dream, and *t is* no interpreter of it.	NIH
	40:17	in the uppermost basket **t** *was* of all	NIH
	41: 2	**t** came up out of the river seven well	NIH
	41: 8	**t** *was* none that could interpret them unto	NIH
	41:12	**t** *was* there with us a young man,	NIH
	41:12	*was* **t** with us a young man, a Hebrew,	8033
	41:15	dream, and **t** *is* none that can interpret it:	NIH
	41:18	**t** came up out of the river seven kine,	NIH
	41:24	but **t** *was* none that could declare *it* to me.	NIH
	41:29	**t** come seven years of great plenty	NIH
	41:30	shall arise after them seven years of	NIH
	41:39	*t is* none so discreet and wise as thou *art*:	NIH
	41:54	but in all the land of Egypt **t** was bread.	NIH
	42: 1	Now when Jacob saw that **t** was corn in	3426
	42: 2	I have heard that **t** is corn in Egypt:	3426
	42:22	be proved, whether *t be any* truth in you:	NIH
	43:25	they heard that they should eat bread **t**.	8033
	44:30	into *his* chamber, and wept **t**.	8033+1886.5
	44:14	came to Joseph's house; for he *was* yet **t**:	8033
	45: 1	**t** stood no man with him, while Joseph	NIH
	45: 6	yet **t** *are* five years, *in* the which *there*	NIH
	45: 6	*in* the which **t** *shall* neither *be* earing nor	NIH
	45:11	will I nourish thee; for yet *there are* five	8033
	45:11	for yet *are* five years of famine; lest thou,	NIH
	46: 3	for I will make of thee a great nation.	8033
	47:13	*t was* no bread in all the land; for the	NIH
	47:18	is not ought left in the sight of my lord,	NIH
	48: 7	when yet **t** *was* but a little way to come	NIH
	48: 7	I buried her **t** in the way of Ephrath;	8033
	49:31	**T** they buried Abraham and Sarah	8033+1886.5
	49:31	**t** they buried Isaac and Rebekah	8033+1886.5
	49:31	his wife; and **t** I buried Leah.	8033+1886.5
	50: 5	of Canaan, **t** shalt thou bury me.	8033+1886.5
	50: 9	**t** went up with him both chariots and	NIH
	50:10	they mourned with a great and very sore	8033
Ex	1: 8	Now **t** arose up a new king over Egypt,	NIH
	1:10	to pass, that, when **t** falleth out any war,	NIH
	2: 1	**t** went a man of the house of Levi,	NIH
	2:12	and when he saw that **t** was no man,	NIH
	5: 9	Let **t** more work be laid upon the men,	NIH
	5:13	*your* daily tasks, as when **t** was straw.	NIH
	5:16	**T** is no straw given unto thy servants,	NIH
	5:18	for **t** shall no straw be given you, yet shall	NIH
	7:19	**t** may be blood throughout all the land	NIH
	7:21	**t** was blood throughout all the land of	NIH
	8:10	that thou mayest know that *t is* none like	NIH
	8:15	when Pharaoh saw that **t** was respite,	NIH
	8:18	so **t** were lice upon man, and upon beast.	NIH
	8:22	that no swarms *of flies* shall be **t**;	8033
	8:24	**t** came a grievous swarm *of flies* into	NIH
	8:31	and from his people; **t** remained not one.	NIH
	9: 3	*t shall be* a very grievous murrain.	NIH
	9: 4	**t** shall nothing die of all *that is*	NIH
	9: 7	**t** was not one of the cattle of the Israelites	NIH
	9:14	thou mayest know that *t is* none like me	NIH
	9:22	that **t** may be hail in all the land of Egypt,	NIH
	9:24	**t** was hail, and fire mingled with the hail,	NIH
	9:24	such as **t** was none like it in all the land of	NIH
	9:26	where the children of Israel *were*, *was* **t** no	NIH
	9:28	that **t** be no *more* mighty thunderings and	NIH
	9:29	cease, neither shall **t** be any more hail;	NIH
	10:14	grievous *were* they; before them **t** were	NIH
	10:15	**t** remained not any green thing in the	NIH
	10:19	**t** remained not one locust in all the coasts	NIH
	10:21	that **t** may be darkness over the land of	NIH
	10:22	**t** was a thick darkness in all the land of	NIH
	10:26	with us; **t** shall not a hoof be left behind;	NIH
	11: 6	**t** shall be a great cry throughout all the	NIH
	11: 6	such as **t** was none like it, nor shall be like	NIH
	12:16	in the first day **t** *shall be* a holy	NIH
	12:16	in the seventh day **t** *shall be* a holy	NIH
	12:19	Seven days shall **t** be no leaven found in	NIH
	12:30	and **t** was a great cry in Egypt;	NIH
	12:30	for *t was* not a house where *there was* not	NIH
	12:30	for *there was* not a house where *t was* not	NIH

Ex	12:43 passover: **T** shall no stranger eat thereof:	NIH
	13: 3 *place:* **t** shall no leavened bread be eaten.	NIH
	13: 7 **t** shall no leavened bread be seen with	NIH
	13: 7 neither shall **t** be leaven seen with thee in	NIH
	14:11 Because **t** *were* no graves in Egypt,	NIH
	14:28 **t** remained not so much as one of them.	NIH
	15:25 he made for them a statute and	8033
	15:25 and an ordinance, and **t** he proved them,	8033
	15:27 and they encamped **t** by the waters.	8033
	16:14 upon the face of the wilderness *t lay* a	NIH
	16:24 not stink, neither was **t** any worm therein.	NIH
	16:26 *which is* the sabbath, in it **t** shall be none.	NIH
	16:27 *that* **t** went out *some* of the people on	NIH
	17: 1 *it was* no water for the people to drink.	NIH
	17: 3 the people thirsted **t** for water;	8033
	17: 6 I will stand before thee **t** upon the rock in	8033
	17: 6 the rock, and **t** shall come water out of it,	NIH
	19: 2 and **t** Israel camped before the mount.	8033
	19:13 **T** shall not a hand touch it, but he shall	NIH
	19:16 that **t** were thunders and lightnings,	NIH
	21:30 If **t** be laid on him a sum of money, then	NIH
	22: 2 he die, **t** *shall* no blood *be shed* for him.	NIH
	22: 3 upon him, **t** *shall be* blood *shed* for him;	NIH
	23:26 **T** shall nothing cast their young, nor be	NIH
	24:10 **t** *was* under his feet as it were a paved	NIH
	24:12 Come up to me into the mount, and be **t**:	8033
	25:22 I will meet with thee, and I will	8033
	25:35 **t** *shall be* a knop under two branches of	NIH
	26:17 Two tenons *shall be* in one board, set in	NIH
	26:20 on the north side **t** *shall be* twenty boards:	NIH
	27: 9 for the south side southward **t** *shall be*	NIH
	27:11 likewise for the north side in length **t** *shall*	NIH
	28:32 **t** shall be a hole in the top of it, in the	NIH
	29:42 I will meet you, to speak **t** unto thee.	8033
	29:43 I will meet with the children of	8033+1886.5
	30:12 that **t** be no plague amongst them,	NIH
	30:34 of each shall **t** be a like *weight:*	NIH
	32:17 Moses, **T** *is* a noise of war in the camp.	NIH
	32:24 into the fire, and **t** came out this calf.	NIH
	32:28 **t** fell of the people that day about three	NIH
	33:20 face: for **t** shall no man see me, and live.	NIH
	33:21 **t** *is* a place by me, and thou shalt stand	NIH
	34: 2 present thyself **t** to me in the top of	8033
	34: 5 stood with him **t**, and proclaimed the	8033
	34:28 he was **t** with the LORD forty days and	8033
	35: 2 on the seventh day **t** shall be to you a holy	NIH
	36:30 **t** were eight boards; and their sockets *were*	NIH
	39:23 **t** *was* a hole in the midst of the robe,	NIH
	40:30 and the altar, and put water **t**,	8033+1886.5
Lev	6:27 when **t** is sprinkled of the blood thereof	834
	7: 7 **t** *is* one law for them: the priest that	NIH
	8:31 eat it with the bread that *is* in the basket	8033
	9:24 **t** came a fire out from before the LORD,	NIH
	10: 2 **t** went out fire from the LORD,	NIH
	11:36 or pit, *wherein* **t** *is* plenty of water,	NIH
	13:10 and **t** be quick raw flesh in the rising,	NIH
	13:19 in the place of the boil **t** be a white rising,	NIH
	13:21 **t** *be* no white hairs therein, and *if* it *be* not	NIH
	13:24 Or if **t** *be* any flesh, in the skin whereof	NIH
	13:24 in the skin whereof **t** *is* a hot burning,	NIH
	13:26 **t** *be* no white hair in the bright spot,	NIH
	13:30 **t** *be* in it a yellow thin hair; then the priest	NIH
	13:31 the skin, and *that* **t** *is* no black hair in it;	NIH
	13:32 **t** *be* in it no yellow hair, and the scall *be*	NIH
	13:37 and *that* **t** *is* black hair grown up therein;	NIH
	13:42 if **t** be in the bald head, or bald forehead,	NIH
	14:35 It seemeth to me **t** *is* as it were a plague in	NIH
	16:17 **t** be no man in the tabernacle of	NIH
	16:23 the holy *place,* and shall leave them **t**:	8033
	17: 3 man soever **t** *be* of the house of Israel,	NIH
	17: 8 man **t** *be* of the house of Israel,	NIH
	17:10 man **t** *be* of the house of Israel,	NIH
	17:13 whatsoever man **t** *be* of the children of	NIH
	20:14 that **t** be no wickedness among you.	NIH
	21: 1 **T** shall none be defiled for the dead	NIH
	22:10 **T** shall no stranger eat *of* the holy *thing:* a	NIH
	22:13 but **t** shall no stranger eat thereof.	NIH
	22:21 be accepted; **t** shall be no blemish therein.	NIH
	23:27 month **t** *shall be* a day of atonement:	NIH
	25:51 If **t** *be* yet many years *behind,* according	NIH
	25:52 if **t** remain but few years unto the year of	NIH
Nu	1: 4 with you **t** shall be a man of every tribe;	NIH
	1:53 that **t** be no wrath upon the congregation	NIH
	5:13 be defiled, and **t** *be* no witness against her,	NIH
	6: 5 All the days of the vow of his separation **t**	NIH
	8:19 that **t** be no plague among the children of	NIH
	9: 6 **t** were *certain* men, who were defiled by	NIH
	9:15 at even **t** was upon the tabernacle as it	NIH
	9:17 **t** the children of Israel pitched their tents.	8033
	11: 6 **t** *is* nothing at all, beside *this* manna,	NIH
	11:16 that they may stand **t** with thee.	8033
	11:17 I will come down and talk with thee **t**:	8033
	11:26 remained two *of* the men in the camp,	NIH
	11:27 And **t** ran a young man, and told Moses,	NIH
	11:31 **t** went forth a wind from the LORD,	NIH
	11:34 they buried the people that lusted.	8033
	12: 6 If **t** be a prophet among you, *I* the LORD	NIH
	13:20 lean, whether **t** *be* wood therein, or not.	3426
	13:28 moreover we saw the children of Anak **t**.	8033
	13:33 **t** we saw the giants, the sons of Anak,	NIH
	14:35 shall be consumed, and **t** they shall die.	NIH
	14:43 and the Canaanites *are* **t** before you,	8033
	16:35 And **t** came out a fire from the LORD,	NIH
	16:46 for **t** is wrath gone out from the LORD;	NIH
	18: 5 that **t** be no wrath any more upon	NIH

Nu	19:18 upon the persons that were **t**, and upon	8033
	20: 1 and Miriam died **t**, and was buried there.	8033
	20: 1 and Miriam died there, and was buried **t**.	8033
	20: 2 **t** was no water for the congregation:	NIH
	20: 4 that we and our cattle should die **t**?	8033
	20: 5 neither *is* **t** any water to drink.	NIH
	20:26 gathered *unto his people,* and shall die **t**.	8033
	20:28 and Aaron died **t** in the top of the mount:	8033
	21: 5 **t** *is* no bread, neither *is there any* water;	NIH
	21: 5 *there is* no bread, neither *is* **t** *any* water;	NIH
	21:28 **t** is a fire gone out of Heshbon, a flame	NIH
	21:32 and drove out the Amorites that *were* **t**.	8033
	21:35 his people, until **t** was none left him alive:	NIH
	22: 5 Behold, **t** is a people come out from Egypt:	NIH
	22:11 Behold, **t** *is* a people come out of Egypt,	NIH
	22:29 I would **t** *were* a sword in mine hand,	3426
	23:23 Surely **t** *is* no enchantment against Jacob,	NIH
	23:23 neither *is* **t** any divination against Israel:	NIH
	24:17 **t** shall come a Star out of Jacob,	NIH
	26:62 was no inheritance given them among	NIH
	26:64 among these **t** was not a man of them	NIH
	26:65 was not left a man of them, save Caleb	NIH
	31: 5 So **t** were delivered out of the thousands	NIH
	31:16 **t** was a plague among the congregation of	NIH
	31:49 charge, and **t** lacketh not one man of us.	NIH
	32:26 our cattle, shall be **t** in the cities of Gilead:	8033
	33: 9 and ten palm trees; and they pitched **t**.	8033
	33:38 died **t**, in the fortieth year after the	8033
	35: 6 the Levites **t** *shall be* six cities for refuge,	NIH
Dt	1: 2 (**T** *are* eleven days' *journey* from Horeb *by*	NIH
	1:28 we have seen the sons of the Anakims **t**.	8033
	1:35 Surely **t** shall not one of these men of this	NIH
	1:46 according unto the days that ye abode **t**.	NIH
	2:36 **t** was not one city too strong for us:	NIH
	3: 4 **t** was not a city which we took not from	NIH
	3:24 for what God *is* **t** in heaven or in earth,	NIH
	4: 7 For what nation *is* **t** so great, who hath	NIH
	4: 8 what nation *is* **t** so great, that hath statutes	NIH
	4:28 **t** ye shall serve gods, the work of men's	8033
	4:32 whether **t** hath been *any such thing* as this	NIH
	4:35 he *is* God; **t** *is* none else besides him.	NIH
	4:39 and upon the earth beneath: **t** *is* none else.	NIH
	5:26 For who *is* **t** of all flesh, that hath heard	NIH
	5:29 that **t** were such a heart in them, that they	NIH
	7:14 **t** shall not be male or female barren among	NIH
	7:24 **t** shall no man *be able to* stand before thee,	NIH
	8:15 and drought, where **t** was no water;	NIH
	10: 5 **t** they be, as the LORD commanded me.	8033
	10: 6 Aaron died, and there he was buried;	8033
	10: 6 there Aaron died, and **t** he was buried:	NIH
	11:17 that **t** be no rain, and *that* the land yield	NIH
	11:25 **T** shall no man *be able to* stand before	NIH
	12: 5 out of all your tribes to put his name **t**,	8033
	12: 7 ye shall eat before the LORD your God,	8033
	12:11 **t** shall be a place which the LORD your	NIH
	12:11 shall choose to cause his name to dwell **t**;	8033
	12:14 thou shalt offer thy burnt offerings,	8033
	12:14 thou shalt do all that I command thee,	8033
	12:21 to put his name **t** be too far from thee,	8033
	13: 1 If **t** arise among you a prophet, or a	8033
	13:12 LORD thy God hath given thee to dwell **t**,	8033
	13:17 **t** shall cleave nought of the cursed thing to	NIH
	14:23 which he shall choose to place his name **t**,	8033
	14:24 thy God shall choose to set his name **t**,	8033
	14:26 thou shalt eat **t** before the LORD thy God,	8033
	15: 4 Save when **t** shall be no poor among you;	NIH
	15: 7 If **t** be among you a poor man of one of	NIH
	15: 9 Beware that **t** be not a thought in thy	NIH
	15:21 if **t** be *any* blemish therein, *as if it be* lame,	NIH
	16: 2 LORD shall choose to place his name **t**.	8033
	16: 4 **t** shall be no leavened bread seen for	NIH
	16: 4 neither shall **t** *any thing* of the flesh,	NIH
	16: 6 thou shalt sacrifice the passover at even,	8033
	16:11 thy God hath chosen to place his name **t**.	8033
	17: 2 If **t** be found among you, within any of thy	NIH
	17: 8 If **t** arise a matter too hard for thee in	NIH
	17:12 to minister **t** before the LORD thy God,	8033
	18: 7 *do,* which stand **t** before the LORD.	NIH
	18:10 **T** shall not be found among you *any one*	NIH
	20: 5 What man *is* **t** that hath built a new house,	NIH
	20: 7 what man *is* **t** that hath betrothed a wife,	NIH
	20: 8 What man *is* **t** *that is* fearful and	NIH
	21: 4 shall strike off the heifer's neck **t** in	8033
	22:26 in the damsel no sin *worthy* of death:	NIH
	22:27 damsel cried, and **t** *was* none to save her.	NIH
	23:10 If **t** be among you any man, that is not	NIH
	23:17 **T** shall be no whore of the daughters of	NIH
	25: 1 If **t** be a controversy between men,	NIH
	26: 2 thy God shall choose to place his name **t**.	8033
	26: 5 sojourned **t** with a few, and became there	8033
	26: 5 became **t** a nation, great, mighty,	8033
	27: 5 **t** shalt thou build an altar unto the LORD	NIH
	27: 7 shalt eat **t**, and rejoice before the LORD	NIH
	28:32 and **t** *shall be* no might in thine hand.	NIH
	28:36 shalt thou serve other gods, wood and	8033
	28:64 thou shalt serve other gods, which	8033
	28:65 the LORD shall give thee **t** a trembling	8033
	28:68 ye shall be sold unto your enemies for	8033
	29:18 Lest **t** should be among you man,	3426
	29:18 lest **t** should be among you a root that	3426
	31:26 that it may be **t** for a witness against thee.	8033
	32:12 and **t** *was* no strange god with him.	NIH
	32:28 neither *is* **t** any understanding in them.	NIH
	32:36 is gone, and **t** *is* none shut up, or left.	NIH
	32:39 *even* I, *am* he, and **t** *is* no god with me:	NIH

Dt	32:39 neither *is* **t** any that can deliver out of my	NIH
	33:19 they shall offer sacrifices of	8033
	33:21 because **t**, *in* a portion of the lawgiver,	8033
	33:26 **T** *is* none like unto the God of Jeshurun,	NIH
	34: 5 So Moses the servant of the LORD died **t**	8033
	34:10 **t** arose not a prophet since in Israel like	NIH
Jos	1: 5 **T** shall not any man *be able to* stand	NIH
	2: 1 named Rahab, and lodged **t**.	8033+1886.5
	2: 2 **t** came men in hither to night of the	NIH
	2: 4 **T** came men unto me, but I wist not	NIH
	2:11 neither did **t** remain any more courage in	NIH
	2:16 hide yourselves **t** three days,	8033+1886.5
	2:22 the mountain, and abode **t** three days,	8033
	3: 1 and lodged **t** before they passed over.	8033
	3: 4 Yet **t** shall be a space between you and it,	8033
	4: 8 they lodged, and laid them down **t**.	8033
	4: 9 and they are **t** unto this day.	8033
	5: 1 neither was **t** spirit in them any more,	NIH
	5:13 stood a man over against him with his	NIH
	7: 4 So **t** went up thither of the people about	NIH
	7:13 **T** is an accursed thing in the midst of thee,	NIH
	8:11 now **t** was a valley between them and Ai.	NIH
	8:14 he wist not that **t** *were* liers in ambush	NIH
	8:17 was not a man left in Ai or Beth-el,	NIH
	8:32 he wrote **t** upon the stones a copy of	8033
	8:35 **T** was not a word of all that Moses	NIH
	9:23 **t** shall none of you be freed from being	NIH
	10: 8 **t** shall not a man of them stand before	NIH
	10:14 was no day like that before it or after it,	NIH
	11:11 utterly destroying *them:* **t** was not any left	NIH
	11:19 **T** was not a city that made peace with	NIH
	11:22 **t** was none of the Anakims left in the land	NIH
	11:22 in Gath, and in Ashdod, **t** remained.	NIH
	13: 1 **t** remaineth *yet* very much land to be	NIH
	14:12 in that day how the Anakims *were* **t**,	8033
	17: 1 **T** was also a lot for the tribe of Manasseh;	NIH
	17: 2 **T** was also *a lot* for the rest of the children	NIH
	17: 5 **t** fell ten portions to Manasseh, beside	NIH
	17:15 cut down for thyself **t** in the land of	8033
	18: 1 up the tabernacle of the congregation **t**.	8033
	18: 2 **t** remained among the children of Israel	NIH
	18:10 Joshua divided the land unto the	8033
	21:44 **t** stood not a man of all their enemies	NIH
	21:45 **T** failed not ought of any good thing which	NIH
	22:10 half tribe of Manasseh built **t** an altar by	8033
	22:17 **t** was a plague in the congregation	NIH
	24:26 great stone, and set it up **t** under an oak,	8033
Jdg	1: 7 brought him *to* Jerusalem, and **t** he died.	8033
	2: 5 and they sacrificed **t** unto the LORD.	NIH
	2:10 **t** arose another generation after them,	NIH
	3:29 men of valour; and **t** escaped not a man.	NIH
	4:16 of the sword; *and* **t** was not a man left.	NIH
	4:17 for **t** was peace between Jabin the king of	NIH
	4:20 of thee, and say, **Is** *t* any man here?	3426
	5: 8 was **t** a shield or spear seen among forty	NIH
	5:11 **t** shall they rehearse the righteous acts of	8033
	5:14 Out of Ephraim *was* **t** a root of them,	NIH
	5:15 For the divisions of Reuben **t** *were* great	NIH
	5:16 For the divisions of Reuben **t** *were* great	NIH
	5:27 where he bowed, **t** he fell down dead.	8033
	6:11 **t** came an angel of the LORD,	NIH
	6:21 and **t** rose up fire out of the rock,	NIH
	6:24 Gideon built an altar **t** unto the LORD,	8033
	6:39 and upon all the ground let **t** be dew.	NIH
	6:40 and **t** was dew on all the ground.	NIH
	7: 3 **t** returned of the people twenty and	NIH
	7: 3 thousand; and **t** remained ten thousand.	NIH
	7: 4 the water, and I will try them for thee **t**:	8033
	7:13 **t** was a man that told a dream unto his	NIH
	8:10 for **t** fell an hundred and twenty thousand	NIH
	9:21 and fled, and went to Beer, and dwelt **t**,	8033
	9:36 **t** come people down from the top of	NIH
	9:37 See **t** come people down by the middle of	NIH
	9:51 But **t** was a strong tower within the city,	NIH
	10: 1 after Abimelech **t** arose to defend Israel	NIH
	11: 3 **t** were gathered vain men to Jephthah,	NIH
	12: 5 **t** fell at that time of the Ephraimites forty	NIH
	13: 2 **t** was a certain man of Zorah, of the family	NIH
	14: 3 *Is* **t** never a woman among the daughters	NIH
	14: 8 **t** *was* a swarm of bees and honey in	NIH
	14:10 Samson made **t** a feast; for so used	8033
	15:19 in the jaw, and **t** came water thereout;	NIH
	16: 1 and saw **t** a harlot, and went in unto her.	8033
	16: 9 Now **t** *were* men lying in wait, abiding	NIH
	16:12 **t** *were* liers in wait abiding in the chamber.	NIH
	16:17 **t** hath not come a rasor upon mine head;	NIH
	16:27 lords of the Philistines *were* **t**;	8033+1886.5
	16:27 **t** *were* upon the roof about three thousand	NIH
	17: 1 **t** was a man of mount Ephraim, whose	NIH
	17: 6 In those days **t** *was* no king in Israel,	NIH
	17: 7 **t** was a young man out of	NIH
	17: 7 who *was* a Levite, and he sojourned **t**.	8033
	18: 1 In those days **t** *was* no king in Israel:	NIH
	18: 2 to the house of Micah, they lodged **t**.	8033
	18: 7 **t** *was* no magistrate in the land, that might	NIH
	18:10 place where **t** *is* no want of any thing that	NIH
	18:11 **t** went from thence of the family of	NIH
	18:14 Do ye know that **t** is in these houses an	3426
	18:28 **t** *was* no deliverer, because it *was* far from	NIH
	19: 1 those days, when **t** *was* no king in Israel,	NIH
	19: 1 that **t** was a certain Levite sojourning on	NIH
	19: 2 was **t** four whole months.	8033
	19: 4 so they did eat and drink, and lodged **t**.	8033
	19: 7 urged him: therefore he lodged **t** again.	8033
	19:10 **t** *were* with him two asses saddled,	NIH

T

Ref	Text	Strong's
Jdg 19:15	for *t* was no man that took them into *his*	NIH
19:16	*t* came an old man from his work out of	NIH
19:18	*t* is no man that receiveth me to house.	NIH
19:19	Yet *t* is both straw and provender for our	3426
19:19	*t* is bread and wine also for me, and for	3426
19:19	thy servants: *t* is no want of any thing.	NIH
19:30	T was no such *deed* done nor seen from	NIH
20:16	all this people *t* were seven hundred	NIH
20:26	sat *t* before the Lord, and fasted that day	8033
20:27	the ark of the covenant of God *was* t in	8033
20:34	*t* came against Gibeah ten thousand	NIH
20:38	Now *t* was an appointed sign between	NIH
20:44	*t* fell of Benjamin eighteen thousand men;	NIH
21: 1	T shall not any of us give his daughter	NIH
21: 2	abode *t* till even before God, and lift up	8033
21: 3	that *t* should be to day one tribe lacking in	NIH
21: 4	built *t* an altar, and offered burnt offerings	8033
21: 5	Who *is t* among all the tribes of Israel that	NIH
21: 6	T is one tribe cut off from Israel this day.	NIH
21: 8	What one *is t* of the tribes of Israel that	NIH
21: 8	came none to the camp from	NIH
21: 9	*t* were none of the inhabitants of	NIH
21: 9	none of the inhabitants of Jabesh-gilead *t.*	8033
21:17	T must be an inheritance for them that be	NIH
21:19	*t* is a feast of the Lord in Shiloh yearly *in*	NIH
21:25	In those days *t* was no king in Israel:	NIH
Ru 1: 1	ruled, that *t* was a famine in the land.	NIH
1: 2	the country of Moab, and continued *t.*	8033
1: 4	and they dwelled *t* about ten years.	8033
1:11	*are t* yet *any moe* sons in my womb,	NIH
1:17	diest, will I die, and *t* will I be buried:	8033
3:12	howbeit *t* is a kinsman nearer than I.	3426
4: 1	Boaz up *to* the gate, and sat him down *t:*	8033
4: 4	for *t* is none to redeem *it* besides thee;	NIH
4:17	a name, saying, T is a son born to Naomi;	NIH
1Sa 1: 1	Now *t* was a certain man of	NIH
1: 3	Phinehas, the priests of the Lord, *were t.*	8033
1:11	and *t* shall no rasor come upon his head.	NIH
1:22	before the Lord, and *t* abide for ever.	8033
1:28	And he worshipped the Lord *t.*	8033
2: 2	T is none holy as the Lord: for *there* is	NIH
2: 2	*t* is none beside thee: neither *is there* any	NIH
2: 2	neither *is t* any rock like our God.	NIH
2:27	*t* came a man of God unto Eli, and said	NIH
2:31	*t* shall not be an old man in thine house.	NIH
2:32	*t* shall not be an old man in thine house	NIH
3: 1	in those days; *t* was no open vision.	NIH
4: 4	*t* with the ark of the covenant of God.	8033
4: 7	*t* hath not been such *a thing* heretofore.	NIH
4:10	was a very great slaughter; for *there* fell	NIH
4:10	for *t* fell of Israel thirty thousand footmen.	NIH
4:12	*t* ran a man of Benjamin out of the army,	NIH
4:16	And he said, What is *t* done, my son?	NIH
4:17	*t* hath been also a great slaughter among	NIH
5:11	*t* was a deadly destruction throughout all	NIH
5:11	city; the hand of God was very heavy *t.*	8033
6: 9	on which *t* hath come no yoke, and tie	NIH
6:14	a Beth-shemite, and stood *t,* where *there*	8033
6:14	stood there, where *t was* a great stone:	NIH
7: 6	and fasted on that day, and said *t,*	8033
7:14	was peace between Israel and	NIH
7:17	for *t was* his house; and there he judged	8033
7:17	*t* he judged Israel; and there he built an	8033
7:17	and *t* he built an altar unto the Lord.	8033
9: 1	Now *t* was a man of Benjamin, whose	NIH
9: 2	*t* was not among the children of Israel a	NIH
9: 4	the land of Shalim, and *they* were not:	NIH
9: 6	*t* is in this city a man of God, and *he* is an	NIH
9: 7	*t* is no present to bring to the man of	NIH
9:12	for *t* is a sacrifice of the people to day in	NIH
10: 3	shall meet thee there men going up to	NIH
10:24	*t* is none like him among all the people?	NIH
10:26	*t* went with him a band of men,	NIH
11: 3	then, if *t be* no man to save us, we will	NIH
11:13	T shall not a man be put to death this day:	NIH
11:14	us go *to* Gilgal, and renew the kingdom *t.*	8033
11:15	*t* they made Saul king before the Lord in	8033
11:15	*t* they sacrificed sacrifices *of* peace	8033
11:15	*t* Saul and all the men of Israel rejoiced	8033
13:19	Now *t* was no smith found throughout all	NIH
13:22	*t* was neither sword nor spear found in	NIH
13:22	and with Jonathan his son was *t* found.	NIH
14: 4	*t* was a sharp rock on the one side,	NIH
14: 6	for *t* is no restraint to the Lord to save by	NIH
14:15	was trembling in the host, in the field,	NIH
14:17	and his armourbearer *were* not *t.*	NIH
14:20	and *t was* a very great discomfiture.	NIH
14:25	wood; and *t* was honey upon the ground.	NIH
14:30	for had *t* not been now a much greater	NIH
14:34	ox with him *that* night, and slew *them* *t.*	8033
14:39	*t* was not *a man* among all the people *that*	NIH
14:45	*t* shall not one hair of his head fall to	NIH
14:52	was sore war against the Philistines all	NIH
16:11	T remaineth yet the youngest, and, behold,	NIH
17: 3	side: and *t was* a valley between them.	NIH
17: 4	*t* went out a champion out of the camp of	NIH
17:23	behold, *t* came up the champion,	NIH
17:29	What have I now done? *Is t* not a cause?	NIH
17:34	came a lion and a bear, and took a lamb	NIH
17:46	all the earth may know that *t* is a God	3426
17:50	but *t* was no sword in the hand of David.	NIH
18:10	and *t was* a javelin in Saul's hand.	NIH
19: 8	*t* was war again: and David went out,	NIH
19:16	behold *t was* an image in the bed,	NIH
20: 3	*t is* but a step between me and death.	NIH

Ref	Text	Strong's
1Sa 20: 6	for *t* is a yearly sacrifice there for all	NIH
20: 6	for *there* is a yearly sacrifice for all	8033
20: 8	if *t* be in me iniquity, slay me thyself;	3426
20:12	*if t* be good toward David, and I then	NIH
20:21	for *t* is peace to thee, and no hurt;	NIH
20:29	he hath commanded me *to be t* and now,	NIH
21: 3	bread in mine hand, or what *t* is present.	NIH
21: 4	T is no common bread under mine hand,	NIH
21: 4	mine hand, but *t* is hallowed bread;	3426
21: 6	the priest gave him hallowed *bread:* for *t*	NIH
21: 6	hallowed *bread:* for there was no bread *t*	8033
21: 7	man of the servants of Saul *was t* that day,	8033
21: 8	is *t* not here under thine hand spear or	3426
21: 8	take *it:* for *t is* no other save that here.	NIH
21: 9	David said, T is none like that; give it me.	NIH
22: 2	*t* were with him about four hundred men.	NIH
22: 8	*t* is none that sheweth me that my son	NIH
22: 8	*t* is none of you that is sorry for me,	NIH
22:22	that day, when Doeg the Edomite *was t,*	8033
23:22	his haunt is, *and* who hath seen him *t:*	8033
23:27	came a messenger unto Saul, saying,	NIH
24:11	see that *t* is neither evil nor transgression	NIH
25: 2	*t was* a man in Maon, whose possessions	NIH
25: 7	neither was *t* ought missing unto them,	NIH
25:10	*t* be many servants now a days that break	NIH
25:13	went up after David about four hundred	NIH
25:34	surely *t* had not been left unto Nabal by	NIH
26:15	for *t* came one of the people in to destroy	NIH
27: 1	*t* is nothing better for me than that I	NIH
27: 5	town in the country, that I may dwell *t:*	NIH
28: 7	*t is* a woman that hath a familiar spirit at	NIH
28:10	*t* shall no punishment happen to thee for	NIH
28:20	was no strength in him; for he had eaten	NIH
30:17	*t* escaped not a man of them, save four	NIH
30:19	*t* was nothing lacking to them, neither	NIH
31:12	and came to Jabesh, and burnt them *t.*	8033
2Sa 1:21	Ye mountains of Gilboa, *let t* be no dew,	NIH
1:21	*be* no dew, neither *let t* be rain upon you,	NIH
1:21	for *t* the shield of the mighty is vilely cast	8033
2: 4	*t* they anointed David king over the house	8033
2:15	*t* arose and went over by number twelve	NIH
2:17	*t* was a very sore battle that day;	NIH
2:18	*t* were three sons of Zeruiah there, Joab,	NIH
2:18	there were three sons of Zeruiah *t,* Joab,	8033
2:23	he fell down *t,* and died in the same place:	8033
2:30	*t* lacked of David's servants nineteen men	NIH
3: 1	Now *t* was long war between the house of	NIH
3: 6	*t* was war between the house of Saul	NIH
3:27	smote him *t* under the fifth *rib,* that he	NIH
3:29	let *t* not fail from the house of Joab one	NIH
3:38	Know ye not that *t* is a prince and a great	NIH
4: 3	and were sojourners *t* until this day.)	8033
5:13	*t* were yet sons and daughters born to	NIH
5:20	and David smote them *t,* and said,	8033
5:21	they left their images, and David and	NIH
6: 7	God smote him *t* for *his* error; and there	8033
6: 7	*his* error; and he died by the ark of God.	8033
7:22	for *t* is none like thee, neither *is there* any	NIH
7:22	like thee, neither *is t* any God beside thee,	NIH
9: 1	Is *t* yet *any* that is left of the house of Saul	3426
9: 2	of the house of Saul a servant whose	NIH
9: 3	*Is t* not yet any of the house of Saul,	NIH
10:18	the captain of their host, who died *t.*	8033
11: 8	*t* followed him a mess *of meat* from	NIH
11:17	*t* fell *some* of the people of the servants of	NIH
12: 1	unto him, T were two men in one city;	NIH
12: 4	*t* came a traveller unto the rich man,	NIH
13:16	said unto him, T is no cause: this evil in	NIH
13:30	king's sons, and *t* is not one of them left.	NIH
13:34	*t* came much people by the way of the hill	NIH
13:38	went to Geshur, and was *t* three years.	8033
14: 6	*t was* none to part them, but the one	NIH
14:11	*t* shall not one hair of thy son fall to	NIH
14:25	in all Israel *t* was none to be so	NIH
14:25	of his head *t* was no blemish in him.	NIH
14:27	unto Absalom *t* were born three sons,	NIH
14:30	field is near mine, and he hath barley *t;*	8033
14:32	*had been* good for me *to have been* t still:	8033
14:32	if *t* be *any* iniquity in me, let him kill me.	NIH
15: 3	*t is* no man *deputed* of the king to hear	3426
15:13	*t* came a messenger to David, saying,	NIH
15:21	or life, even *t also* will thy servant be.	NIH
15:28	until *t* come word from you to certify me.	NIH
15:29	again *to* Jerusalem: and they tarried *t.*	8033
15:35	*hast thou* not *t* with thee Zadok and	8033
15:36	*they have t* with them their two sons,	8033
16:14	came *weary,* and refreshed themselves *t.*	8033
17: 9	T is a slaughter among the people that	NIH
17:12	all the men that *are* with him *t* shall not	NIH
17:13	until *t* be not one small stone found there.	NIH
17:13	until there be not one small stone found *t.*	8033
17:22	by the morning light *t* lacked not one *of*	NIH
18: 7	*t* was there a great slaughter that day *of*	NIH
18: 7	there was *t* a great slaughter that day *of*	8033
18: 8	For the battle was *t* scattered over the face	NIH
18:11	why didst thou not smite him *t* to	8033
18:13	for *t* is no matter hid from the king,	NIH
18:25	If he *be* alone, *t* is tidings in his mouth.	NIH
19:17	T will not tarry one with thee *this* night:	NIH
19:17	*t were* a thousand men of Benjamin with	NIH
19:18	*t* went over a ferry boat to carry over	NIH
19:22	shall *t* any man be put to death *this* day in	NIH
20: 1	*t* happened to be there a man of Belial,	8033
20: 1	*t* there happened to be *t* a man of Belial,	NIH
20: 7	*t* went out after him Joab's men,	NIH

Ref	Text	Strong's
2Sa 21: 1	*t* was a famine in the days of David three	NIH
21:18	*t* was again a battle with the Philistines	NIH
21:19	*t* was again a battle in Gob with	NIH
21:20	*t* was yet a battle in Gath, where was a	NIH
22: 9	T went up a smoke out of his nostrils,	NIH
22:42	They looked, but *t* was none to save;	NIH
23: 9	they defied the Philistines *that were* t	8033
24: 9	*t* were in Israel eight hundred thousand	NIH
24:13	that *t* be three days' pestilence in thy land?	NIH
24:15	*t* died of the people from Dan even to	NIH
24:25	And David built *t* an altar unto the Lord,	8033
1Ki 1: 2	Let *t* be sought for my lord the king a	NIH
1:14	while thou yet talkest *t* with the king,	8033
1:34	Nathan the prophet anoint him *t* king	8033
1:52	*t* shall not a hair of him fall to the earth:	NIH
2: 4	their soul, *t* shall not fail thee (said he)	3807.1
2:33	shall *t* be peace for ever from the Lord.	NIH
2:36	dwell *t,* and go not forth thence any	8033
3: 2	was no house built unto the name of	NIH
3: 4	the king went to Gibeon to sacrifice *t;*	8033
3:12	so that *t* was none like thee before thee,	NIH
3:13	*t* shall not be any among the kings like	NIH
3:16	came *t* two women, *that were* harlots,	NIH
3:18	*t* was no stranger with us in the house,	NIH
4:34	*t* came of all people to hear the wisdom of	NIH
5: 4	*t* is neither adversary nor evil occurrent.	NIH
5: 6	thou knowest that *t* is not among us any	NIH
5: 9	will cause them to be discharged *t.*	8033
5:12	*t* was peace between Hiram and Solomon;	NIH
6: 7	that *t* was neither hammer nor axe *nor* any	NIH
6:18	all *was* cedar; *t* was no stone seen.	NIH
6:19	to set *t* the ark of the covenant of	8033
7: 4	*t were* windows in three rows, and light	NIH
7:24	under the brim of it round about *t were*	NIH
7:29	and upon the ledges *t was* a base above:	NIH
7:34	*t were* four undersetters to the four	NIH
7:35	the top of the base was *t* a round compass	NIH
8: 8	seen without: and *t* they are unto this day.	8033
8: 9	T was nothing in the ark save the two	NIH
8: 9	of stone, which Moses put *t* at Horeb,	8033
8:21	I have set *t* a place for the ark, wherein *is*	8033
8:23	*t is* no God like thee, in heaven above,	NIH
8:25	T shall not fail thee a man in my sight to	NIH
8:29	which thou hast said, My name shall be *t:*	8033
8:35	*t* is no rain, because they have sinned	NIH
8:37	If *t* be in the land famine, if there be	NIH
8:37	if *t* be pestilence, blasting, mildew, locust,	NIH
8:37	mildew, locust, *or* if *t* be caterpillar;	NIH
8:37	whatsoever sickness *t* be;	NIH
8:46	(for *t* is no man that sinneth not,)	NIH
8:56	*t* hath not failed one word of all his good	NIH
8:60	the Lord *is* God, *and that t* is none else.	NIH
8:64	for *t* he offered burnt offerings, and meat	8033
9: 3	thou hast built, to put my name *t* for ever;	8033
9: 3	and mine heart shall be *t* perpetually.	8033
9: 5	T shall not fail thee a man upon the	NIH
10: 3	was not *any* thing hid from the king,	NIH
10: 5	of the Lord; *t* was no more spirit in her.	NIH
10:10	came no more such abundance of spices	NIH
10:12	came no such almug trees, nor were seen	NIH
10:19	*t were* stays on either side on the place of	NIH
10:20	twelve lions stood *t* on the one side and	8033
10:20	*t* was not the like made in any kingdom.	NIH
11:16	(For six months did Joab remain *t* with all	8033
11:36	I have chosen me to put my name *t*	NIH
12:20	was none that followed the house of	NIH
13: 1	*t* came a man of God out of Judah by	NIH
13:11	Now *t* dwelt an old prophet in Beth-el;	NIH
13:17	Thou shalt eat no bread nor drink water *t,*	8033
14: 2	*t* is Ahijah the prophet, which told	8033
14:13	in him is found *some* good thing toward	NIH
14:21	all the tribes of Israel, to put his name *t.*	8033
14:24	*t* were also sodomites in the land:	NIH
14:30	*t* was war between Rehoboam and	NIH
15: 6	*t* was war between Rehoboam and	NIH
15: 7	T was war between Abijam and Jeroboam.	NIH
15:16	*t* was war between Asa and Baasha king of	NIH
15:19	T is a league between me and thee,	NIH
15:32	*t* was war between Asa and Baasha king of	NIH
17: 1	*t* shall not be dew nor rain these years,	NIH
17: 4	commanded the ravens to feed thee *t.*	8033
17: 7	because *t* had been no rain in the land.	NIH
17: 9	which *belongeth* to Zidon, and dwell *t:*	8033
17: 9	I have commanded a widow woman *t* to	8033
17:10	the widow woman *was t* gathering of	8033
17:17	so sore, that *t* was no breath left in him.	NIH
18: 2	And *t was* a sore famine in Samaria.	NIH
18:10	thy God liveth, *t* is no nation or kingdom,	3426
18:10	*He is* not *t;* he took an oath of the	NIH
18:26	*t* was no voice, nor any that answered.	NIH
18:29	*t* was neither voice, nor any to answer,	NIH
18:40	to the brook Kishon, and slew them *t.*	8033
18:41	for *t* is a sound of abundance of rain.	NIH
18:43	up, and looked, and said, T is nothing.	NIH
18:44	*t* ariseth a little cloud out of the sea,	NIH
18:45	and wind, and *t* was a great rain.	NIH
19: 3	*belongeth* to Judah, and left his servant *t.*	8033
19: 6	was a cake baken on the coals, and a	NIH
19: 9	he came thither unto a cave, and lodged *t;*	8033
19:13	*t* came a voice unto him, and said,	NIH
20: 1	*t* were thirty and two kings with him,	NIH
20:13	came a prophet unto Ahab king of Israel,	NIH
20:17	T are men come out of Samaria.	NIH
20:28	*t* came a man of God, and spake unto	NIH
20:30	*t* a wall fell upon twenty and	NIH

1Ki 20:40	as thy servant was busy here and t, he	2008
21:13	t came in two men, children of Belial,	NIH
21:25	(But t was none like unto Ahab, which did	NIH
22: 7	*Is t* not here a prophet of the LORD	NIH
22: 8	*T* is yet one man, Micaiah the son of	NIH
22:21	t came forth a spirit, and stood before	NIH
22:36	t went a proclamation throughout the host	NIH
22:47	*T* was then no king in Edom: a deputy	NIH

2Ki 1: 3	*Is it* not because *t is* not a God in Israel,	NIH
1: 6	**T** came a man up to meet us, and said	NIH
1: 6	*Is it* not because *t is* not a God in Israel,	NIH
1:10	t came down fire from heaven,	NIH
1:14	t came fire down from heaven, and burnt	NIH
1:16	*t is* no God in Israel to inquire of his word?	NIH
2:11	t *appeared* a chariot of fire, and horses of	NIH
2:16	t *be* with thy servants fifty strong men;	3426
2:21	cast the salt in t, and said, Thus saith	8033
2:21	t shall not be from thence any more death	NIH
2:23	t came forth little children out of the city,	NIH
2:24	t came forth two she bears out of the	NIH
3: 9	t was no water for the host, and for	NIH
3:11	*Is t* not here a prophet of the LORD,	NIH
3:20	t came water by the way of Edom,	NIH
3:27	t was great indignation against Israel:	NIH
4: 1	Now a certain woman of the wives	NIH
4: 6	he said unto her, *T* is not a vessel more.	NIH
4:10	let us set for him t a bed, and a table,	8033
4:11	into the chamber, and lay t.	8033+1886.5
4:31	but *t was* neither voice, nor hearing.	NIH
4:38	*t was* a dearth in the land; and the sons of	NIH
4:40	O thou man of God, *t is* death in the pot.	NIH
4:41	may eat. And t was no harm in the pot.	NIH
4:42	t came a man from Baal-shalisha,	NIH
5: 8	he shall know that **t is** a prophet in Israel.	3426
5:15	I know that *t is* no God in all the earth,	NIH
5:17	Naaman said, Shall t not then, I pray thee,	NIH
5:18	*into* the house of Rimmon to worship t,	8033
5:22	even now t be come to me from mount	NIH
6: 2	let us make us a place t, where we may	8033
6:10	and warned him of, and saved himself t,	8033
6:25	t was a great famine in Samaria:	NIH
6:26	t cried a woman unto him, saying, Help,	NIH
7: 3	t were four leprous men *at* the entering in	NIH
7: 4	famine is in the city, and we shall die t:	8033
7: 5	of Syria, behold, *t was* no man there.	NIH
7: 5	of Syria, behold, *there* was no man t.	8033
7:10	*t was* no man there, neither voice of	NIH
7:10	*there* was no man t, neither voice	8033
9: 2	look out t Jehu the son of Jehoshaphat	8033
9:10	*t shall* be none to bury *her.*	NIH
9:16	and went to Jezreel; for Joram lay t.	8033
9:17	t stood a watchman on the tower in	NIH
9:18	So t went one on horseback to meet him,	NIH
9:23	said to Ahaziah, *T* is treachery, O Ahaziah.	NIH
9:27	And he fled *to* Megiddo, and died t.	8033
9:32	looked out to him two *or* three eunuchs.	NIH
10: 2	t *are* with you chariots and horses,	NIH
10: 8	t came a messenger, and told him, saying,	NIH
10:10	Know now that t shall fall unto the earth	NIH
10:21	so that t was not a man left that came not.	NIH
10:23	look that t **be** here with you none of	3426
11:16	*into* the king's house: and t was she slain.	8033
12:10	when they saw that *t was* much money in	NIH
12:13	Howbeit t were not made *for* the house of	NIH
13: 6	t remained the grove also in Samaria.)	NIH
14: 9	t passed by a wild beast that was in	NIH
14:19	sent after him to Lachish, and slew him t.	8033
14:26	for *t was* not any shut up, nor any left,	NIH
15:20	turned back, and stayed not t in the land.	8033
16: 6	came *to* Elath, and dwelt t unto this day.	8033
17:11	they burnt incense in all the high places,	8033
17:18	t was none left but the tribe of Judah only.	NIH
17:25	t was at the beginning of their dwelling t,	8033
17:27	let them go and dwell t, and let him teach	8033
18:18	t came out to them Eliakim the son of	NIH
19: 3	birth, and *t is* not strength to bring forth.	NIH
19:32	nor shoot an arrow t, nor come before it	8033
20:13	t was nothing in his house, nor in all his	NIH
20:15	t is nothing among my treasures that	NIH
22: 7	Howbeit t was no reckoning made with	NIH
23:16	he spied the sepulchres that *were* t in	8033
23:20	high places that *were* t upon the altars,	8033
23:22	Surely t was not holden such a passover	NIH
23:25	like unto him was t no king before him,	NIH
23:25	neither after him arose t *any* like him.	NIH
23:27	of which I said, My name shall be t.	8033
23:34	and he came *to* Egypt, and died t.	8033
25: 3	t was no bread for the people of the land.	NIH
25:23	t came to Gedaliah *to* Mizpah, even	NIH

1Ch 3: 4	t he reigned seven years and six months:	8033
4:23	they dwelt with the king for his work.	NIH
4:40	for *they* of Ham had dwelt t of old.	NIH
4:41	the habitations that were found t,	8033+1886.5
4:41	*t was* pasture there for their flocks.	NIH
4:41	*there* was pasture t for their flocks.	8033
4:43	were escaped, and dwelt t unto this day.	8033
5:22	t fell down many slain, because the war	NIH
11:13	the Philistines were gathered together to	NIH
12: 8	of the Gadites t separated themselves unto	NIH
12:16	t came of the children of Benjamin and	NIH
12:17	seeing *t is* no wrong in mine hands,	NIH
12:19	t fell *some* of Manasseh to David, when	NIH
12:20	t fell to him of Manasseh, Adnah,	NIH
12:22	at *that* time day by day t came to David	NIH
12:39	t they were with David three days, eating	8033

1Ch 12:40	sheep abundantly: for *t was* joy in Israel.	NIH
13:10	hand to the ark: and t he died before God.	8033
14:11	to Baal-perazim; and David smote them t.	8033
14:12	they had left their gods t, David gave	NIH
16:37	So he left t before the ark of the covenant	8033
17:20	O LORD, *t is* none like thee, neither *is*	NIH
17:20	thee, neither *is t any* God besides thee,	NIH
19: 5	t went *certain,* and told David how the	NIH
20: 2	of gold, and *t were* precious stones in it;	NIH
20: 4	that t arose war at Gezer with	NIH
20: 5	t was war again with the Philistines;	NIH
20: 6	yet again t was war at Gath, where was a	NIH
21:14	and t fell of Israel seventy thousand men.	NIH
21:26	And David built t an altar unto the LORD,	8033
21:28	Ornan the Jebusite, then he sacrificed t.	NIH
22:15	Moreover *t are* workmen with thee in	NIH
22:16	the brass, and the iron, *t is* no number.	NIH
24: 4	t were moe chief men found of the sons of	NIH
24: 4	Among the sons of Eleazar *t were* sixteen	NIH
26:31	t were found among them mighty *men* of	NIH
27:24	because t fell wrath for it against Israel;	NIH
28:21	*t shall* be with thee for all *manner of*	NIH
29:15	*are* as a shadow, and *t is* none abiding.	NIH

2Ch 1: 3	t was the tabernacle of the congregation	8033
1:12	neither shall t any after thee have the like.	NIH
5: 9	seen without. And t it is unto this day.	8033
5:10	*T* was nothing in the ark save the two	NIH
6: 5	a house *in,* that my name might be t;	8033
6: 6	that my name might be t;	8033
6:14	*t is* no God like thee in the heaven, nor in	NIH
6:16	**T** shall not fail thee a man in my sight to	NIH
6:20	said that *thou* wouldest put thy name t;	8033
6:26	t is no rain, because they have sinned	NIH
6:28	If t be dearth in the land, if there be	NIH
6:28	if t be pestilence, if there be blasting,	NIH
6:28	if t be blasting, or mildew, locusts,	NIH
6:28	or whatsoever sickness t be:	NIH
6:36	(for *t is* no man which sinneth not,)	NIH
7: 7	for he offered burnt offerings, and the fat	8033
7:13	If I shut up heaven that t be no rain, or if I	NIH
7:16	house, that my name may be t for ever:	8033
7:16	and mine heart shall be t perpetually.	NIH
7:18	**T** shall not fail thee a man *to be* ruler in	NIH
8: 2	caused the children of Israel to dwell t.	8033
9: 2	t was nothing hid from Solomon which he	NIH
9: 4	of the LORD; t was no more spirit in her.	NIH
9: 9	neither was t any such spice as the queen	NIH
9:11	t were none such seen before in the land	NIH
9:18	*t were* six steps to the throne, with a	NIH
9:19	twelve lions stood t on the one side and	8033
9:19	t was not the like made in any kingdom.	NIH
12:13	all the tribes of Israel, to put his name t.	8033
12:15	*t were* wars between Rehoboam and	NIH
13: 2	t was war between Abijah and Jeroboam.	NIH
13: 7	t are gathered unto him vain men,	NIH
13: 8	and *t are* with you golden calves,	NIH
13:17	t fell down slain of Israel five hundred	NIH
14: 9	t came out against them Zerah the	NIH
14:14	for t was *exceeding* much spoil in them.	NIH
15: 5	in those times *t was* no peace to him that	NIH
15:19	t was no *more* war unto the five and	NIH
16: 3	*T* is a league between me and thee, as	NIH
16: 3	as *t was* between my father and thy father:	NIH
18: 6	*Is t* not here a prophet of the LORD	NIH
18: 7	*T* is yet one man, by whom we may	NIH
18:20	t came out a spirit, and stood before	NIH
19: 3	Nevertheless t are good things found in	NIH
19: 7	do it: for *t is* no iniquity with the LORD	NIH
20: 2	t came *some* that told Jehoshaphat, saying,	NIH
20: 2	**T** cometh a great multitude against thee	NIH
20: 6	in thine hand *is t* not power and might,	NIH
20:26	of Berachah; for t they blessed the LORD:	8033
21:12	t came a writing to him from Elijah	NIH
21:17	so that t was never a son left him,	NIH
23:15	gate *by* the king's house, they slew her t.	8033
24:11	when they saw that *t was* much money,	NIH
25: 7	t came a man of God to him, saying,	NIH
25:18	t passed by a wild beast that *was* in	NIH
25:27	sent to Lachish after him, and slew him t.	8033
28: 9	a prophet of the LORD was t,	8033
28:10	*are t* not *with* you, *even* with you,	NIH
28:13	great, and *t is* fierce wrath against Israel.	NIH
28:18	and the villages thereof: and they dwelt t.	8033
30:13	t assembled *at* Jerusalem much people to	NIH
30:17	For t were many in the congregation that	NIH
30:26	So t was great joy in Jerusalem: for since	NIH
30:26	of Israel *t was* not the like in Jerusalem.	NIH
32: 4	So t was gathered much people together,	NIH
32: 7	for t be moe with us than with him:	NIH
32:14	Who *was t* among all the gods of those	NIH
32:21	own bowels slew him t with the sword.	8033
32:25	therefore t was wrath upon him,	NIH
34:13	of the Levites *t were* scribes, and officers,	NIH
35:18	t was no passover like to that, kept	NIH
36:16	against his people, till *t was* no remedy.	NIH
36:23	Who *is t* among you of all his people?	NIH

Ezr 1: 3	Who *is t* among you of all his people?	NIH
2:63	*things* till t stood *up* a priest with Urim	NIH
2:65	of whom *t were* seven thousand three	NIH
2:65	*t were* among them two hundred singing	NIH
4:20	**T** have been mighty kings also over	NIH
5:17	let t be search made in the king's treasure	NIH
5:17	which *is t* at Babylon, whether it be *so,*	8536
6: 2	t was found at Achmetha, in the palace	8536
6:12	caused his name to dwell t destroy all	NIH

Ezr 7: 7	t went up *some* of the children of Israel,	NIH
7:23	why should t be wrath against the realm	NIH
8:15	and t abode we in tents three days:	8033
8:15	and found t none of the sons of Levi.	NIH
8:21	I proclaimed a fast t, at the river Ahava,	8033
8:25	his lords, and all Israel *t* present,	NIH
8:32	to Jerusalem, and abode t three days.	8033
9:14	that *t should be* no remnant nor escaping?	NIH
10: 1	t assembled unto him out of Israel a very	NIH
10: 2	yet now t **is** hope in Israel concerning this	3426
10:18	the sons of the priests t were found	8033

Ne 1: 3	remnant that are left of the captivity t	8033
1: 9	though t were of you cast out unto	NIH
1: 9	place that I have chosen to set my name t.	8033
2:10	t was come a man to seek the welfare of	NIH
2:11	came to Jerusalem, and was t three days.	8033
2:12	neither *was t any* beast with me, save	NIH
2:14	*t was* no place for the beast *that was*	NIH
4:10	burdens is decayed, and *t is* much rubbish;	NIH
5: 1	t was a great cry of the people and of their	NIH
5: 2	For t **were** that said, We, our sons,	3426
5: 3	*Some* also t **were** that said, We have	3426
5: 4	**T** were also that said, We have borrowed	3426
5:17	Moreover *t were* at my table an hundred	NIH
6: 1	and *that* t was no breach left therein;	NIH
6: 7	at Jerusalem, saying, *T* is a king in Judah:	NIH
6: 8	**T** are no such things *done* as thou sayest,	NIH
6:11	who *is t,* that, *being* as I *am,* would go	NIH
6:18	*t were* many in Judah sworn unto him,	NIH
7:65	*things,* till t stood *up* a priest with Urim	NIH
7:67	of whom *t were* seven thousand three	NIH
8:17	done so. And t was very great gladness.	NIH
12:46	Asaph of old *t were* chief of the singers,	NIH
13:16	t dwelt men of Tyre also therein, which	NIH
13:19	*that* t should no burden be brought in on	NIH
13:26	many nations was t no king like him,	NIH

Est 1:18	Thus *shall t arise* too much contempt and	NIH
1:19	let t be a royal commandment from him,	NIH
2: 2	Let t be fair young virgins sought for	NIH
2: 5	*Now* in Shushan the palace t was a certain	NIH
3: 8	**T** is a certain people scattered abroad and	3426
3:12	t was written according to all	871.1+2050.2
4: 3	t was great mourning among the Jews,	NIH
4:11	*t is* one law of his to put *him* to death,	NIH
4:14	*then* shall t enlargement and	NIH
6: 3	unto him, *T* is nothing done for him.	NIH
7: 7	for he saw that t was evil determined	NIH

Job 1: 1	*T* was a man in the land of Uz, whose	NIH
1: 2	t were born unto him seven sons and	NIH
1: 6	Now t was a day when the sons of God	NIH
1: 8	*t is* none like him in the earth, a perfect	NIH
1:13	t was a day when his sons and his	NIH
1:14	t came a messenger unto Job, and said,	NIH
1:16	speaking, t came also another, and said,	NIH
1:17	speaking, t came also another, and said,	NIH
1:18	t came also another, and said, Thy sons	NIH
1:19	t came a great wind from the wilderness,	NIH
2: 1	Again t was a day when the sons of God	NIH
2: 3	*t is* none like him in the earth, a perfect	NIH
3: 3	*it was* said, **T** is a man child conceived.	NIH
3:17	**T** the wicked cease *from* troubling;	8033
3:17	troubling; and t the weary be at rest.	8033
3:18	*T* the prisoners rest together; they hear	NIH
3:19	The small and great *are* t; and the servant	8033
4:16	t was silence, and I heard a voice, *saying,*	NIH
5: 1	now, if t **be** *any* that will answer thee;	3426
5: 4	the gate, neither *is t* any to deliver *them.*	NIH
5:19	yea, in seven t shall no evil touch thee.	NIH
6: 6	or *is t* any taste in the white of an egg?	3426
6:30	Is t iniquity in my tongue? cannot my	3426
7: 1	*Is t* not an appointed time to man upon	NIH
9:33	Neither is t *any* daysman betwixt us,	3426
10: 7	*t is* none that can deliver out of thine	NIH
11:18	thou shalt be secure, because t is hope;	3426
12:14	up a man, and t can be no opening.	NIH
12:24	wander in a wilderness *where t is* no way.	3426
14: 7	For t is hope of a tree, if it be cut down,	3426
15:11	with thee? is t *any* secret thing with thee?	NIH
17: 2	*Are* not mockers with me? and *doth not*	NIH
19: 7	heard: I cry aloud, but *t is* no judgment.	NIH
19:29	that ye may know *t is* a judgment.	NIH
20:21	*T shall* none of his meat *be* left; therefore	NIH
21:33	him, as *t are* innumerable before him.	NIH
21:34	seeing in your answers t remaineth	NIH
22:29	then thou shalt say, *T* is lifting up;	NIH
23: 7	**T** the righteous *might* dispute with him;	8033
23: 8	he *is not t,* and backward, but I cannot	NIH
25: 3	*Is t* any number of his armies?	3426
28: 1	Surely t is a vein for the silver, and a	3426
28: 7	*T* is a path which no fowl knoweth,	NIH
30:26	when I waited for light, t came darkness.	NIH
31: 2	For what portion of God *is t* from above?	NIH
32: 5	When Elihu saw that *t was* no answer in	NIH
32: 8	*t is* a spirit in man: and the inspiration of	NIH
32:12	*t was* none of you that convinced Job,	NIH
33: 9	I am innocent; neither is *t* iniquity in me.	NIH
33:23	If t **be** a messenger with him,	3426
34:22	*T* is no darkness, nor shadow of death,	NIH
35:12	**T** they cry, but none giveth answer,	8033
36:16	a broad place, where *t is* no straitness;	NIH
36:18	Because *t is* wrath, *beware* lest he take	NIH
38:26	*on* the wilderness, wherein *t is* no man;	NIH
39:30	blood: and where the slain *are,* t *is* she.	8033
41:33	Upon earth t **is** **not** his like, who is made	369
42:11	came t unto him all his brethren, and all	NIH

T

Ps

3: 2 Many *t* be which say of my soul, There is	NIH
3: 2 of my soul, *T* is no help for him in God.	NIH
4: 6 *T* be many that say, Who will shew us	NIH
5: 9 For *t* is no faithfulness in their mouth;	NIH
6: 5 For in death *t* is no remembrance of thee:	NIH
7: 2 it in pieces, while *t* is none to deliver.	NIH
7: 3 done this; if *t* be iniquity in my hands;	3426
14: 1 fool hath said in his heart, *T* is no God.	NIH
14: 1 *t* is none that doeth good.	NIH
14: 2 to see if *t* were any that did understand,	3426
14: 3 *t* is none that doeth good, no, not one.	NIH
14: 5 *T* were they in great fear: for God is in	8033
16:11 at thy right hand *t* are pleasures for	NIH
18: 8 *T* went up a smoke out of his nostrils,	NIH
18:41 *t* was none to save them: even unto	NIH
19: 3 *T* is no speech nor language, where their	NIH
19: 6 and *t* is nothing hid from the heat thereof.	NIH
19:11 and in keeping of them *t* is great reward.	NIH
22:11 for trouble is near; for *t* is none to help.	NIH
30: 9 What profit is *t* in my blood, when I go	NIH
32: 2 and in whose spirit *t* is no guile.	NIH
33:16 *T* is no king saved by the multitude of a	NIH
34: 9 for *t* is no want to them that fear him.	NIH
36: 1 that *t* is no fear of God before his eyes.	NIH
36:12 *T* are the workers of iniquity fallen:	NIH
38: 3 *T* is no soundness in my flesh because	NIH
38: 3 neither is *t* any rest in my bones because	NIH
38: 7 and *t* is no soundness in my flesh.	NIH
45:12 the daughter of Tyre shall be *t* with a gift;	NIH
46: 4 *T* is a river, the streams whereof shall	NIH
48: 6 Fear took hold upon them *t*, and pain,	8033
50:22 you in pieces, and *t* be none to deliver.	NIH
53: 1 fool hath said in his heart, *T* is no God.	NIH
53: 1 *t* is none that doeth good.	NIH
53: 2 to see if *t* were any that did understand,	3426
53: 3 *t* is none that doeth good, no, not one.	NIH
53: 5 *T* were they in great fear, where no fear	8033
55:18 against me: for *t* were many with me.	NIH
58:11 Verily *t* is a reward for the righteous:	NIH
66: 6 the flood on foot: *t* did we rejoice in him.	8033
68:27 *T* is little Benjamin with their ruler,	8033
69: 2 sink in deep mire, where *t* is no standing:	NIH
69:20 for some to take pity, but *t* was none;	NIH
69:35 that they may dwell *t*, and have it in	8033
71:11 and take him; for *t* is none to deliver him.	NIH
72:16 *T* shall be a handful of corn in the earth	NIH
73: 4 For *t* are no bands in their death:	NIH
73:11 and is *t* knowledge in the most High?	3426
73:25 *t* is none upon earth that I desire beside	NIH
74: 9 *t* is no more any prophet: neither is there	NIH
74: 9 neither is *t* among us any that knoweth	NIH
75: 8 For in the hand of the LORD *t* is a cup,	NIH
76: 3 *T* brake he the arrows of the	8033+1886.5
79: 3 and *t* was none to bury them.	NIH
81: 9 *T* shall no strange god be in thee;	NIH
86: 8 Among the gods *t* is none like unto thee,	NIH
86: 8 are *t* any works like unto thy works.	NIH
87: 4 Tyre, with Ethiopia; this man was born *t*.	8033
87: 6 up the people, that this man was born *t*.	8033
87: 7 shall be *t* all my springs are in thee.	NIH
91:10 *T* shall no evil befall thee, neither shall	NIH
92:15 rock, and *t* is no unrighteousness in him.	NIH
104:26 *T* go the ships: there is that leviathan,	8033
104:26 *t* is that leviathan, whom thou hast made	NIH
105:31 *t* came divers sorts of flies, and lice in all	NIH
105:37 *t* was not one feeble person among their	NIH
106:11 their enemies: *t* was not one of them left.	NIH
107:12 they fell down, and *t* was none to help.	NIH
107:36 *t* he maketh the hungry to dwell, that	8033
107:40 in the wilderness, where *t* is no way.	NIH
109:12 Let *t* be none to extend mercy unto him:	NIH
109:12 neither let *t* be any to favour his fatherless	NIH
112: 4 Unto the upright *t* ariseth light in	NIH
122: 5 For *t* are set thrones of judgment,	8033+1886.5
130: 4 *t* is forgiveness with thee, that thou mayest	NIH
130: 7 for with the LORD *t* is mercy,	NIH
132:17 *T* will I make the horn of David to bud:	8033
133: 3 for *t* the LORD commanded the blessing,	8033
135:17 neither is *t* any breath in their mouths.	3426
137: 1 of Babylon, *t* we sat down, yea, we wept,	8033
137: 3 For they that carried us away captive	8033
139: 4 For *t* is not a word in my tongue, but lo,	NIH
139: 8 If I ascend up into heaven, thou art *t*: if I	8033
139: 8 I make my bed in hell, behold, thou art *t*.	NIH
139:10 Even *t* shall thy hand lead me, and thy	8033
139:16 when as yet *t* was none of them.	NIH
139:24 see if *t* be any wicked way in me,	NIH
142: 4 but *t* was no man that would know me:	NIH
144:14 that *t* be no breaking in, nor going out;	NIH
144:14 that *t* be no complaining in our streets.	NIH
146: 3 in the son of man, in whom *t* is no help.	NIH

Pr

7:10 *t* met him a woman with the attire of a	NIH
8: 8 *t* is nothing froward or perverse in them.	NIH
8:24 *t* were no depths, I was brought forth;	NIH
8:24 when *t* were no fountains abounding with	NIH
8:27 When he prepared the heavens, I was *t*:	8033
9:18 he knoweth not that the dead are *t*;	8033
10:19 the multitude of words *t* wanteth not sin:	NIH
11:10 and when the wicked perish, *t* is shouting.	NIH
11:14 in the multitude of counsellers *t* is safety.	NIH
11:24 *T* is that scattereth, and yet increaseth;	3426
11:24 *t* is that withholdeth more than is meet,	NIH
12:18 *T* is that speaketh like the piercings of a	3426
12:21 *T* shall no evil happen to the just:	NIH
12:28 and in the pathway thereof *t* is no death.	NIH

Pr

13: 7 *T* is that maketh himself rich, yet hath	3426
13: 7 *t* is that maketh himself poor, yet hath	NIH
13:23 *t* is that is destroyed for want of judgment.	3426
14: 9 at sin: but among the righteous *t* is favour.	NIH
14:12 *T* is a way which seemeth right unto a	3426
14:23 In all labour *t* is profit: but the talk of	NIH
16:25 *T* is a way that seemeth right unto a man,	3426
16:27 up evil: and in his lips *t* is as a burning fire.	NIH
17:16 Wherefore is *t* a price in the hand of a fool	NIH
18:24 *t* is a friend that sticketh closer than a	3426
19:18 Chasten thy son while *t* is hope, and let	3426
19:21 *T* are many devices in a man's heart;	NIH
20:15 *T* is gold, and a multitude of rubies:	3426
21:20 *T* is treasure to be desired and oil in	NIH
21:30 *T* is no wisdom nor understanding nor	NIH
22:13 slothful man saith, *T* is a lion without,	NIH
23:18 surely *t* is an end; and thine expectation	3426
24: 6 and in multitude of counsellers *t* is safety.	NIH
24:14 hast found it, then *t* shall be a reward,	3426
24:20 For *t* shall be no reward to the evil man;	NIH
25: 4 *t* shall come forth a vessel for the finer.	NIH
26:12 *t* is more hope of a fool than of him.	NIH
26:13 slothful man saith, *T* is a lion in the way;	NIH
26:20 Where no wood is, *t* the fire goeth out:	NIH
26:20 so where *t* is no talebearer, the strife	NIH
26:25 for *t* are seven abominations in his heart.	NIH
28:12 righteous men do rejoice, *t* is great glory:	NIH
29: 6 In the transgression of an evil man *t* is a	NIH
29: 9 whether he rage or laugh, *t* is no rest.	NIH
29:18 Where *t* is no vision, the people perish:	NIH
29:20 *t* is more hope of a fool than of him.	NIH
30:11 *T* is a generation that curseth their father,	NIH
30:12 *T* is a generation that are pure in their	NIH
30:13 *T* is a generation, O how lofty are their	NIH
30:14 *T* is a generation, whose teeth are as	NIH
30:15 *T* are three things that are never satisfied,	NIH
30:18 *T* be three things which are too wonderful	NIH
30:24 *T* be four things which are little upon	NIH
30:29 *T* be three things which go well, yea,	NIH
30:31 and a king, against whom *t* is no rising up.	NIH

Ecc

1: 9 and *t* is no new thing under the sun.	NIH
1:10 Is *t* any thing whereof it may be said, See,	3426
1:11 *T* is no remembrance of former things;	NIH
1:11 *t* be any remembrance of things that are to	NIH
2:11 spirit, and *t* was no profit under the sun.	NIH
2:16 For *t* is no remembrance of the wise more	NIH
2:21 For *t* is a man whose labour is in wisdom,	3426
2:24 *T* is nothing better for a man, than that he	NIH
3: 1 To every thing *t* is a season, and a time to	NIH
3:12 I know that *t* is no good in them, but for a	NIH
3:16 that wickedness was *t*;	8033+1886.5
3:16 that iniquity was *t*.	8033+1886.5
3:17 for *t* is a time there for every purpose and	NIH
3:17 for there is a time *t* for every purpose and	8033
3:22 Wherefore I perceive that *t* is nothing	NIH
4: 1 the side of their oppressors *t* was power;	NIH
4: 8 *T* is one alone, and there is not a second;	3426
4: 8 There is one alone, and *t* is not a second;	NIH
4: 8 yet is *t* no end of all his labour; neither is	NIH
4:16 *T* is no end of all the people, even of all	NIH
5: 7 and many words *t* are also divers vanities:	NIH
5: 8 regardeth; and *t* be higher than they.	NIH
5:11 what good is *t* to the owners thereof,	NIH
5:13 *T* is a sore evil which I have seen under	3426
5:14 a son, and *t* is nothing in his hand.	NIH
6: 1 *T* is an evil which I have seen under	3426
6:11 Seeing *t* be many things that increase	NIH
7:11 by it *t* is profit to them that see the sun.	NIH
7:15 *t* is a just man that perisheth in his	3426
7:15 *t* is a wicked man that prolongeth his life	3426
7:20 *t* is not a just man upon earth, that doeth	NIH
8: 4 Where the word of a king is, *t* is power:	NIH
8: 6 Because to every purpose *t* is time and	3426
8: 7 For *t* is no man that hath power over the	NIH
8: 8 *t* is no discharge in that war; neither shall	NIH
8: 9 *t* is a time wherein one man ruleth over	NIH
8:14 *T* is a vanity which is done upon the	3426
8:14 *t* be just men, unto whom it happeneth	NIH
8:14 *t* be wicked men, to whom it happeneth	3426
8:16 also *t* is that neither day nor night seeth	NIH
9: 2 *t* is one event to the righteous, and to	NIH
9: 3 under the sun, that *t* is one event unto all:	NIH
9: 4 to him that is joined to all the living *t* is	3426
9:10 *t* is no work, nor device, nor knowledge,	NIH
9:14 *T* was a little city, and few men within it;	NIH
9:14 *t* came a great king against it,	NIH
9:15 Now *t* was found in it a poor wise man,	NIH
10: 5 *T* is an evil which I have seen under	3426
11: 3 place where the tree falleth, *t* it shall be.	8033
12:12 of making many books *t* is no end;	NIH

SS

4: 4 whereon *t* hang a thousand bucklers,	NIH
4: 7 art all fair, my love; *t* is no spot in thee.	NIH
6: 4 and *t* is not one barren among them.	NIH
6: 8 *T* are threescore queens,	NIH
7:12 bud forth: *t* will I give thee my loves.	8033
8: 5 thy mother brought thee forth:	8033+1886.5
8: 5 she brought thee forth that bare	8033+1886.5

Isa

1: 6 even unto the head *t* is no soundness in it;	NIH
2: 7 gold, neither is *t* any end of their treasures;	NIH
2: 7 neither is *t* any end of their chariots:	NIH
3:24 that instead of sweet smell *t* shall be stink;	NIH
4: 6 *t* shall be a tabernacle for a shadow in	NIH
5: 6 but *t* shall come up briers and thorns;	NIH
5: 8 that lay field to field, till *t* be no place,	NIH
6:12 *t* be a great forsaking in the midst of	NIH

Isa

7:23 *t* were a thousand vines at a thousand	NIH
7:25 *t* shall not come thither the fear of briers	NIH
8:20 word, it is because *t* is no light in them.	NIH
9: 7 government and peace *t* shall be no end,	NIH
10:14 *t* was none that moved the wing,	NIH
11: 1 *t* shall come forth a rod out of the stem of	NIH
11:10 in that day *t* shall be a root of Jesse,	NIH
11:16 *t* shall be a highway for the remnant of his	NIH
13:20 neither shall the Arabian pitch tent *t*;	8033
13:20 shall the shepherds make their fold *t*.	8033
13:21 wild beasts of the desert shall lie *t*;	NIH
13:21 owls shall dwell *t*, and satyrs shall dance	8033
13:21 dwell there, and satyrs shall dance *t*.	8033
14:31 for *t* shall come from the north a smoke,	NIH
15: 6 the grass faileth, *t* is no green thing.	NIH
16:10 in the vineyards *t* shall be no singing,	NIH
16:10 be no singing, neither shall *t* be shouting:	NIH
17: 9 children of Israel: and *t* shall be desolation.	NIH
19:15 Neither shall *t* be any work for Egypt,	NIH
19:19 In that day shall *t* be an altar to the LORD	NIH
19:23 In that day shall *t* be a highway out of	NIH
22:18 *t* shalt thou die, and there	8033+1886.5
22:18 the chariots of thy glory shall be	8033+1886.5
23: 1 so that *t* is no house, no entering in:	NIH
23:10 of Tarshish: *t* is no more strength.	NIH
23:12 to Chittim; *t* also shalt thou have no rest.	8033
24:11 *T* is a crying for wine in the streets; all joy	NIH
24:13 *t* shall be as the shaking of an olive tree,	NIH
27:10 *t* shall the calf feed, and there shall he lie	8033
27:10 shall he lie down, and consume	8033
28: 8 and filthiness, so that *t* is no place clean.	NIH
28:10 line upon line; here a little, and *t* a little:	8033
28:13 line upon line; here a little, and *t* a little;	8033
29: 2 and *t* shall be heaviness and sorrow:	NIH
30:14 *t* shall not be found in the bursting of it	NIH
30:25 *t* shall be upon every high mountain,	NIH
30:28 *t* shall be a bridle in the jaws of the	NIH
33:21 *t* the glorious LORD will be unto us a	8033
34:12 none shall be *t*, and all her princes shall	8033
34:14 the shrich owl also shall rest *t*, and find	8033
34:15 *T* shall the great owl make her	8033+1886.5
34:15 *t* shall the vultures also be gathered,	8033
35: 8 a highway shall be *t*, and a way, and it	NIH
35: 9 No lion shall be *t*, nor any ravenous beast	8033
35: 9 go up thereon, it shall be not found *t*:	8033
35: 9 there; but the redeemed shall walk *t*.	NIH
37: 3 birth, and *t* is not strength to bring forth.	NIH
37:33 nor shoot an arrow *t*, nor come before it	8033
39: 2 *t* was nothing in his house, nor in all his	NIH
39: 4 *t* is nothing among my treasures that I	NIH
39: 8 For *t* shall be peace and truth in my days.	NIH
40:28 *t* is no searching of his understanding.	NIH
41:17 *t* is none, and their tongue faileth for thirst	NIH
41:26 yea, *t* is none that sheweth, yea, there is	NIH
41:26 yea, *t* is none that declareth, yea,	NIH
41:26 yea, *t* is none that heareth your words.	NIH
41:28 For I beheld, and *t* was no man;	NIH
41:28 and *t* was no counseller, that,	NIH
43:10 before me *t* was no God formed,	NIH
43:10 no God formed, neither shall *t* be after me.	NIH
43:11 the LORD; and beside me *t* is no saviour.	NIH
43:12 when *t* was no strange god among you:	NIH
43:13 *t* is none that can deliver out of my hand:	NIH
44: 6 I am the last; and besides me *t* is no God.	NIH
44: 8 Is a God besides me? yea, there is no	3426
44: 8 yea, *t* is no God; I know not any.	NIH
44:19 neither *t* knowledge nor understanding	NIH
44:20 nor say, Is *t* not a lie in my right hand?	NIH
45: 5 I am the LORD, and *t* is none else, there is	NIH
45: 5 there is none else, *t* is no God besides me:	NIH
45: 6 from the west, that *t* is none besides me.	NIH
45: 6 I am the LORD, and *t* is none else.	NIH
45:14 thee; and *t* is none else, there is no God.	NIH
45:14 and there is none else, *t* is no God.	NIH
45:18 I am the LORD; and *t* is none else.	NIH
45:21 *t* is no God else beside me; a just God and	NIH
45:21 God and a saviour; *t* is none beside me.	NIH
45:22 the earth: for I am God, and *t* is none else.	NIH
46: 9 I am God, and *t* is none else; I am God,	NIH
46: 9 else; I am God, and *t* is none like me,	NIH
47: 1 *t* is no throne, O daughter of the	NIH
47:14 *t* shall not be a coal to warm at, nor fire to	NIH
48:16 from the time that it was, *t* am I:	8033
48:22 *T* is no peace, saith the LORD, unto	NIH
50: 2 Wherefore, when I came, was *t* no man?	NIH
50: 2 when I called, was *t* none to answer?	NIH
50: 2 because *t* is no water, and dieth for thirst.	NIH
51:18 *T* is none to guide her among all the sons	NIH
51:18 neither is *t* any that taketh her by the	NIH
52: 1 for henceforth *t* shall no more come into	NIH
52: 4 down aforetime into Egypt to sojourn *t*;	8033
53: 2 *t* is no beauty that we should desire him.	NIH
57:10 thy way; yet saidst thou not, *T* is no hope:	NIH
57:21 *T* is no peace, saith my God, to the	NIH
59: 8 and *t* is no judgment in their goings:	NIH
59:11 we look for judgment, but *t* is none:	NIH
59:15 it displeased him that *t* was no judgment.	NIH
59:16 he saw that *t* was no man,	NIH
59:16 and wondered that *t* was no intercessor:	NIH
63: 3 of the people *t* was none with me:	NIH
63: 5 I looked, and *t* was none to help;	NIH
63: 5 I wondered that *t* was none to uphold:	NIH
64: 7 *t* is none that calleth upon thy name,	NIH
65: 9 and my servants shall dwell *t*.	8033+1886.5
65:20 *T* shall be no more thence an infant of	NIH

T

Jer 2:10 and see if t be such a *thing.* NIH
2:25 thou saidst, **T** is no hope: no; for I have NIH
3: 3 and t hath been no latter rain; NIH
3: 6 green tree, and t hath played the harlot. 8033
4:25 lo, *t was* no man, and all the birds of NIH
5: 1 man, if t be *any* that executeth judgment, 3426
6:14 Peace, peace; when *t is* no peace. NIH
6:20 To what purpose cometh t to me incense NIH
7: 2 proclaim t this word, and say, Hear 8033
7:32 shall bury in Tophet, till **t** be no place. 369
8:11 Peace, peace; when *t is* no peace. NIH
8:13 *t shall* be no grapes on the vine, nor figs NIH
8:14 the defenced cities, and let us be silent t: 8033
8:22 *Is t* no balm in Gilead; *is there* no NIH
8:22 balm in Gilead; *is t* no physician there? NIH
8:22 balm in Gilead; *is there* no physician t? 8033
10: 6 Forasmuch as *t is* none like unto thee, NIH
10: 7 their kingdoms, *t is* none like unto thee. NIH
10:13 *t is* a multitude of waters in the heavens, NIH
10:14 *is* falsehood, and *t is* no breath in them. NIH
10:20 *t is* none to stretch forth my tent any NIH
11:23 t shall be no remnant for them: for I will NIH
13: 4 and hide it t in a hole of the rock. 8033
13: 6 which I commanded thee to hide t. 8033
14: 4 t was no rain in the earth, the plowmen NIH
14: 5 and forsook *it,* because t was no grass. NIH
14: 6 their eyes did fail, because *t was* no grass. NIH
14:19 smitten us, and *t is* no healing for us? NIH
14:19 we looked for peace, and *t is* no good; NIH
14:22 **Are** t *any* among the vanities of 3426
16:13 t shall ye serve other gods day and night; 8033
16:19 vanity, and *things* wherein *t is* no profit. NIH
17:25 t enter into the gates of this city kings NIH
18: 2 t I will cause thee to hear my 8033+1886.5
18:12 they said, **T** is no hope: but we will walk NIH
19: 2 proclaim t the words that I shall tell thee, 8033
19:11 *them* in Tophet, till *t be* no place to bury. NIH
20: 6 t thou shalt die, and shalt be buried there, 8033
20: 6 shalt be buried t, thou, and all thy friends, 8033
22: 1 the king of Judah, and speak t this word, 8033
22: 4 shall t enter in by the gates of this house NIH
22:26 ye were not born; and t shall ye die. 8033
26:20 t was also a man that prophesied in NIH
27:22 t shall they be until the day that I 8033+1886.5
29: 6 that ye may be increased t, 8033
30:13 **T** *is* no plead thy cause, that thou NIH
31: 6 For t shall **be** a day, *that* the watchmen 3426
31:17 t **is** hope in thine end, saith the Lord, 3426
31:24 t shall dwell in Judah itself, and *in* all 8033
32: 5 shall he be until I visit him, saith 8033
32:17 arm, *and* t is nothing too hard for thee: NIH
32:27 of all flesh: is t any thing too hard for me? NIH
33:10 Again t shall be heard in this place, which NIH
33:20 that t should not be day and night in their NIH
36:12 lo, all the princes sat t, *even* Elishama 8033
36:22 t was a *fire* on the hearth burning before NIH
36:32 t were added besides unto them many like NIH
37:10 t remained *but* wounded men among NIH
37:13 a captain of the ward *was* t, whose name 8033
37:16 and Jeremiah had remained t many days; 8033
37:17 and said, **Is** t *any* word from the Lord? 3426
37:17 Jeremiah said, **T** is: for, said he, thou NIH
37:20 house of Jonathan the scribe, lest I die t. 8033
38: 6 in the dungeon t was no water, but mire: NIH
38: 9 he is: for *t is* no more bread in the city. NIH
38:26 to return *to* Jonathan's house, to die t. 8033
38:28 and he was t when Jerusalem was taken. NIH
41: 1 t they did eat bread together in Mizpah. 8033
41: 3 the Chaldeans that were found t, 8033
41: 5 **T** that came certain from Shechem, NIH
42:14 hunger of bread; and t will we dwell: 8033
42:15 to enter *into* Egypt, and go to sojourn t; 8033
42:16 shall overtake you t in the land of Egypt, 8033
42:16 shall follow close after you t *in* Egypt; NIH
42:16 after you there *in* Egypt; and t ye shall die. 8033
42:17 their faces to go *into* Egypt to sojourn t; 8033
43: 2 to say, Go not *into* Egypt to sojourn t: 8033
44:12 to go *into* the land of Egypt to sojourn t, 8033
44:14 gone into the land of Egypt to sojourn t, 8033
44:14 they have a desire to return to dwell t: 8033
44:27 by the famine, until t be an end of them. NIH
44:28 gone into the land of Egypt to sojourn t, 8033
46:17 They did cry t, Pharaoh king of Egypt *is* 8033
47: 7 the sea shore? t hath he appointed it. NIH
48: 2 **T** shall be no more praise of Moab: NIH
48:38 **T** *shall be* lamentation generally upon all 8033
49:18 saith the Lord, no man shall abide t, NIH
49:23 *t is* sorrow on the sea; it cannot be quiet. NIH
49:33 t shall no man abide there, nor *any* son of NIH
49:33 there shall no man abide there, nor *any* son of 8033
49:36 shall be no nation whither the outcasts of NIH
50: 3 For out of the north t cometh up a nation NIH
50:20 shall be sought for, and *t shall* be none; NIH
50:39 the wild beasts of the islands shall dwell *t,* NIH
50:40 *so* shall no man abide t, neither shall any 8033
51:16 t is a multitude of waters in the heavens, NIH
51:17 *is* falsehood, and *t is* no breath in them. NIH
52: 6 that t was no bread for the people of NIH
52:23 t were ninety and six pomegranates on a NIH
52:34 t was a continual diet given him of the NIH
La 1:12 if **t** be any sorrow like unto my sorrow, 3426
1:17 her hands, *and t is* none to comfort her: NIH
1:20 sword bereaveth, at home *t is* as death. NIH
1:21 heard that I sigh; *t is* none to comfort me: NIH
3:29 mouth in the dust; if so be t may be hope. NIH

La 4:15 the heathen, They shall no more sojourn *t.* NIH
5: 8 *t is* none that doth deliver *us* out of their NIH
Eze 1: 3 the hand of the Lord was t upon him. 8033
1:25 t was a voice from the firmament *that was* NIH
2: 5 yet shall know that t hath been a prophet NIH
2:10 *t was* written therein lamentations, NIH
3:15 remained t astonished among them seven' 8033
3:22 the hand of the Lord was t upon me; 8033
3:22 into the plain, and I will t talk with thee. 8033
3:23 behold, the glory of the Lord stood t, 8033
4:14 neither came t abominable flesh into my NIH
7:11 theirs: neither *shall t* be wailing for them. NIH
7:25 they shall seek peace, and *t shall* be none. NIH
8: 1 that the hand of the Lord God fell t upon 8033
8: 4 the glory of the God of Israel *was* t, 8033
8:11 t stood before them seventy men of 8033
8:14 t sat women weeping for Tammuz. 8033
10: 1 t appeared over them as it were a sapphire NIH
10: 8 t appeared in the cherubims the form of a NIH
12:13 shall he not see it, though he shall die t. 8033
12:24 For t shall be no more any vain vision nor NIH
12:28 **T** shall none of my words be prolonged NIH
13:10 *t was* no peace; and one built up a wall, NIH
13:11 t shall be an overflowing shower; and ye, NIH
13:13 t shall be an overflowing shower in mine NIH
13:16 and *t is* no peace, saith the Lord God. NIH
13:20 wherewith ye t hunt the souls to make 8033
17: 7 **T** was also another great eagle with great NIH
17:20 will plead with him t *for* his trespass that 8033
20:28 they offered t their sacrifices, 8033
20:28 t they presented the provocation of their 8033
20:28 t also they made their sweet savour, 8033
20:28 and poured out t their drink offerings. 8033
20:35 and t will I plead with you face to face. NIH
20:40 Lord God, t shall all the house of Israel, 8033
20:40 t will I accept them, and there will I 8033
20:40 t will I require your offerings, 8033
20:43 t shall ye remember your ways, and all 8033
22:20 and I will leave *you* t, and melt you. NIH
22:25 **T** *is* a conspiracy of her prophets in NIH
23: 2 Son of man, t were two women, NIH
23: 3 t were their breasts pressed, 8033+1886.5
23: 3 t they bruised the teats of their virginity. 8033
28: 3 *t is* no secret *that* they can hide *from* thee: NIH
28:24 t shall be no more a pricking brier unto NIH
29:14 and they shall be t a base kingdom. NIH
30:13 t shall be no more a prince of the land of NIH
30:18 when I shall break t the yokes of Egypt: 8033
32:22 Asshur *is* t and all her company: his graves 8033
32:24 **T** *is* Elam and all her multitude round 8033
32:26 **T** *is* Meshech, Tubal, and all her 8033
32:29 **T** *is* Edom, her kings, and all her 8033+1886.5
32:30 **T** *be* the princes of the north, all 8033+1886.5
34: 5 were scattered, because *t is* no shepherd: NIH
34: 8 because t was no shepherd, neither did NIH
34:14 t shall they lie in a good fold, and *in* a fat 8033
34:26 his season; t shall be showers of blessing. NIH
35:10 will possess it; whereas the Lord was t: 8033
37: 2 were very many in the open valley; NIH
37: 7 t was a noise, and behold a shaking, NIH
37: 8 them above: but *t was* no breath in them. NIH
38:19 in that day t shall be a great shaking NIH
39:11 I will give unto Gog a place t of graves 8033
39:11 t shall they bury Gog and all his NIH
39:28 and have left none of them any more t. 8033
40: 3 me thither, and behold, *t was* a man, NIH
40:16 t were narrow windows to the little NIH
40:17 t were chambers, and a pavement made NIH
40:25 t were windows in it and in the arches NIH
40:26 t were seven steps to go up to it, NIH
40:27 t was a gate in the inner court toward NIH
40:29 t were windows in it and in the arches NIH
40:33 t were windows therein and in the arches NIH
40:49 t were pillars by the posts, one on this side, NIH
41: 7 t was an enlarging, and a winding about NIH
41:25 t were made on them, on the doors of NIH
41:25 t were thick planks upon the face of NIH
41:26 t were narrow windows and palm trees on NIH
42:13 t shall they lay the most holy *things,* 8033
42:14 t they shall lay their garments wherein 8033
45: 2 Of this t shall be for the sanctuary five NIH
46:19 t was a place on the two sides westward. 8033
46:21 in every corner of the court t was a court. NIH
46:22 In the four corners of the court t were NIH
46:23 t was a row *of building* round about in NIH
47: 2 behold, t ran out waters on the right side. NIH
47: 9 t shall be a very great multitude of fish, 8033
47:23 shall ye give *him* his inheritance, saith NIH
48:35 *that* day *shall* be, The Lord *is* t. 8033+1886.5
Da 2: 9 me the dream, *t is* but one decree for you: NIH
2:10 **T** is not a man upon the earth that can 383
2:10 therefore *t is* no king, lord, nor ruler, NIH
2:11 t is none other that can shew it before NIH
2:28 t is a God in heaven that revealeth secrets, 383
2:41 t shall be in it of the strength of the iron, NIH
3:12 **T** **are** certain Jews whom thou hast set 383
3:29 t is no other God that can deliver after this 383
4:31 t fell a voice from heaven, *saying,* O king NIH
5:11 **T** **is** a man in thy kingdom, in whom *is* 383
6: 4 neither was t any error or fault found in NIH
7: 8 t came up among them another little horn, NIH
7: 8 before whom t were three of the first NIH
7:14 t *was* given him dominion, and glory, NIH
8: 3 t stood before the river a ram which had NIH
8: 4 neither *was t any* that could deliver out of NIH

Da 8: 7 t was no power in the ram to stand before NIH
8: 7 t was none that could deliver the ram out NIH
8:15 t stood before me as the appearance of a NIH
10: 8 and t remained no strength in me: NIH
10:13 and I remained t with the kings of Persia. 8033
10:17 straightway t remained no strength in me, NIH
10:17 in me, neither is t breath left in me. NIH
10:18 t came again and touched me *one* like NIH
10:21 *t is* none that holdeth with me in these NIH
11: 2 t *shall* stand up yet three kings in Persia; NIH
11:14 those times t shall many stand up against NIH
11:15 shall t be *any* strength to withstand. NIH
12: 1 t shall be a time of trouble, such as never NIH
12: 1 as never was since t was a nation *even* NIH
12: 5 and behold, t stood other two, NIH
12:11 *t shall* be a thousand two hundred and NIH
Hos 1:10 not my people, *t* it shall be said unto them, NIH
2:15 she shall sing t, as *in* the days of 8033+1886.5
4: 1 because *t is* no truth, nor mercy, NIH
4: 9 t shall be, like people, like priest: and I NIH
6: 7 t have they dealt treacherously against 8033
6:10 t *is* the whoredom of Ephraim, Israel is 8033
7: 7 t *is* none among them that calleth unto NIH
7: 9 yea, gray hairs are **here and** t upon him, 2236
9:12 *that t shall* not be a man *left:* yea, NIH
9:15 wickedness *is* in Gilgal, for t I hated them: 8033
10: 9 t they stood: the battle in Gibeah against NIH
12: 4 him *in* Beth-el, and t he spake with us; 8033
12:11 *Is* t iniquity *in* Gilead? surely they are NIH
13: 4 but me: for *t is* no saviour beside me. NIH
13: 8 and t will I devour them like a lion: NIH
Joel 2: 2 t hath not been ever the like, neither 1930.2
3: 2 will plead with them t for my people and 8033
3:12 for t will I sit to judge all the heathen 8033
3:17 t shall no strangers pass through her any NIH
Am 3: 6 shall t be evil in a city, and the Lord NIH
3:11 An adversary *t shall be* even round about NIH
4: 7 t *were* yet three months to the harvest: NIH
5: 2 upon her land; *t is* none to raise her up. NIH
5: 6 and *t be* none to quench *it* in Beth-el. NIH
6: 9 t remain ten men in one house, that they NIH
6:10 sides of the house, *Is* t yet *any* with thee? NIH
6:12 will *one* plow t with oxen? for ye have NIH
7:12 and t eat bread, and prophesy there: 8033
7:12 and there eat bread, and prophesy t: 8033
8: 3 *t shall* be many dead bodies in every place; NIH
Ob 1: 7 thee: *t is* none understanding in him. NIH
1:17 be deliverance, and t shall be holiness; NIH
1:18 t shall not be *any* remaining of the house NIH
Jnh 1: 4 was a mighty tempest in the sea, NIH
4: 5 t made him a booth, and sat under it in 8033
Mic 3: 7 cover their lips; for *t is* no answer of God. NIH
4: 9 *is* t no king in thee? is thy counsellor NIH
4:10 to Babylon; t shalt thou be delivered; 8033
4:10 t the Lord shall redeem thee from 8033
6:10 **Are** t yet the treasures of wickedness *in* 786
7: 1 *t is* no cluster to eat: my soul desired NIH
7: 2 *t is* none upright among men: they all lie NIH
Na 1:11 **T** *is* *one* come out of thee, that imagineth NIH
2: 9 for *t is* none end of the store *and* glory out NIH
3: 3 t *is* a multitude of slain, and a great NIH
3: 3 and *t is* none end of *their* corpses; NIH
3:15 **T** shall the fire devour thee; the sword 8033
3:19 **T** *is* no healing of thy bruise; thy wound *is* NIH
Hab 1: 3 t are *that* raise up strife and contention. NIH
2:19 and *t is* no breath at all in the midst of it. NIH
3: 4 hand: and t *was* the hiding of his power. 8033
3:17 fold, and *t shall* be no herd in the stalls: NIH
Zep 1:10 *that t shall* be the noise of a cry from NIH
1:14 the mighty *man* shall cry t bitterly. 8033
2: 5 destroy thee, that t shall be no inhabitant. NIH
2:15 her heart, I *am,* and *t is* none beside me: NIH
3: 6 cities are destroyed, so that t is no man, NIH
3: 6 there is no man, that t is none inhabitant. NIH
Hag 1: 6 *ye* clothe you, but t **is none** warm; and he 369
2:14 *and that* which they offer t *is* unclean. 8033
2:16 came to a heap of twenty *measures,* t were NIH
2:16 *vessels out of* the press, t were *but* twenty. NIH
Zec 1: 8 behind him *were* t red horses, speckled, NIH
5: 7 behold, t *was* lift up a talent of lead: NIH
5: 9 t came out two women, and the wind NIH
5:11 established, and set t upon her own base. 8033
6: 1 t came four chariots out from between NIH
8: 4 **T** shall yet old men and old women dwell NIH
8:10 before these days t was no hire for man, NIH
8:10 neither *was t any* peace to him that went NIH
8:20 *It shall yet come to pass,* that t shall come NIH
10: 2 were troubled, because *t was* no shepherd. NIH
11: 3 **T** *is* a voice of the howling of NIH
12:11 In that day t shall be a great mourning in NIH
13: 1 In that day t shall be a fountain opened to NIH
14: 4 the west, *and t shall be* a very great valley; NIH
14: 9 in that day shall t be one Lord, NIH
14:11 and t shall be no more utter destruction; NIH
14:18 that *have* no *rain;* t shall be the plague, NIH
14:20 In that day shall t be upon the bells of NIH
14:21 that day t shall be no more the Canaanite NIH
Mal 1:10 Who *is* t even among you that would shut NIH
3:10 that t may be meat in mine house, NIH
3:10 that *t shall* not be *room* enough *to receive* NIH
Mt 2: 1 t came wise men from the east to NIG
2:13 and be thou t until I bring thee word: 1563
2:15 And was t until the death of Herod: that it 1563
2:18 In Rama was t a voice heard, lamentation, NIG
4:25 And t followed him great multitudes *of* NIG

T

Mt 5:23 **and** t rememberest that thy brother hath 2546
5:24 Leave t thy gift before the altar, and go 1563
6:21 your treasure is, t will your heart be also. 1563
7: 9 Or what man is t of you, whom if his son NIG
7:13 and many t be which go in thereat: NIG
7:14 leadeth unto life, and few t be that find it. NIG
8: 2 t came a leper and worshipped him, NIG
8: 5 t came unto him a centurion, NIG
8:12 t shall be weeping and gnashing of teeth. 1563
8:24 t arose a great tempest in the sea, NIG
8:26 and the sea; and t was a great calm. NIG
8:28 t met him two possessed with devils, NIG
8:30 t was a good way off from them a herd NIG
9:18 t came a *certain* ruler, and worshipped NIG
10:11 it is worthy; **and** t abide till ye go thence. 2546
10:26 for t is nothing covered, that shall not be NIG
11:11 Among *them that are* born of women t NIG
12:10 t was a man which had *his* hand withered. N.
12:11 them, What man shall t be among you, NIG
12:39 and t shall no sign be given to it, NIG
12:45 himself, and they enter in and dwell t: 1563
13:42 t shall be wailing and gnashing of teeth. 1563
13:50 t shall be wailing and gnashing of teeth. 1563
13:58 And he did not many mighty works t, 1563
14:23 the evening was come, he was t alone. 1563
15:29 went up into a mountain, and sat down t. 1563
16: 4 and t shall no sign be given unto it, NIG
16:28 I say unto you, T be some standing here, NIG
17: 3 t appeared unto them Moses and NIG
17:14 t came to him a *certain* man, kneeling NIG
18:20 in my name, t am I in the midst of them. 1563
19: 2 followed him; and he healed them t. 1563
19:12 For t are *some* eunuchs, which were so NIG
19:12 t are *some* eunuchs, which were made NIG
19:12 and t be eunuchs, which have made NIG
19:13 Then were t brought unto him little NIG
19:17 *it is* none good but one, *that is,* God: NIG
21:17 of the city into Bethany; and he lodged t. 1563
21:33 T was a certain householder, which NIG
22:11 saw t a man which had not on a wedding 1563
22:13 t shall be weeping and gnashing of teeth. 1563
22:23 which say that t is no resurrection, NIG
22:25 Now t were with us seven brethren: NIG
24: 2 T shall not be left here one stone upon NIG
24: 7 and t shall be famines, and pestilences, NIG
24:22 be shortened, t should no flesh be saved: NIG
24:23 shall say unto you, Lo, here *is* Christ, or t; 5602
24:24 For t shall arise false Christs, 5602
24:28 t will the eagles be gathered together. 1563
24:51 t shall be weeping and gnashing of teeth. 1563
25: 6 And at midnight t was a cry made, Behold, NIG
25: 9 lest t be not enough for us and you: NIG
25:25 in the earth: lo, t thou hast *that is* thine. NIG
25:30 t shall be weeping and gnashing of teeth. 1563
26: 5 Not on the feast *day,* lest t be an uproar NIG
26: 7 t came unto him a woman having an NIG
26:13 t shall also *this,* that this *woman* hath NIG
26:71 saw him, and said unto them that were t, 1563
27:36 And sitting down they watched him t; 1563
27:38 were t two thieves crucified with him, NIG
27:45 Now from the sixth hour t was darkness NIG
27:47 of them that stood t, when they heard 1563
27:55 And many women were t beholding afar 1563
27:57 t came a rich man of Arimathea, NIG
27:61 t was Mary Magdalene, and the other NIG
28: 2 And behold, t was a great earthquake: NIG
28: 7 before you into Galilee; t shall ye see him: 1563
28:10 go into Galilee, and t shall they see me. 2546

Mk 1: 5 And t went out unto him all the land of NIG
1: 7 T cometh one mightier than I after me, NIG
1:11 And t came a voice from heaven, NIG
1:13 And he was t in the wilderness forty days, 1563
1:23 And t was in their synagogue a man with NIG
1:35 into a solitary place, **and** t prayed. 2546
1:38 the next towns, that I may preach t **also:** 2546
1:40 t came a leper to him, beseeching him, NIG
2: 2 insomuch that t was no room to receive NIG
2: 6 But t were certain of the scribes sitting NIG
2: 6 there were certain of the scribes sitting t, 1563
2:15 for t were many, and they followed him. NIG
3: 1 t was a man there which had a withered NIG
3: 1 there was a man t which had a withered 1563
3:31 T came then *his* brethren and his mother, NIG
4: 1 was gathered unto him a great multitude, NIG
4: 3 Behold, t went out a sower to sow: NIG
4:22 For t is nothing hid, which shall not be NIG
4:36 And t were also with him other little ships. NIG
4:37 And t arose a great storm of wind, NIG
4:39 the wind ceased, and t was a great calm. NIG
5: 2 immediately t met him out of the tombs a NIG
5:11 Now t was there nigh unto the mountains NIG
5:11 Now there was t nigh unto the mountains 1563
5:22 t cometh one of the rulers of the NIG
5:35 t came from the ruler of the synagogue's NIG
6: 5 And he could t do no mighty work, 1563
6:10 t abide till ye depart from that place. 1563
6:31 for t were many coming and going, and NIG
7: 4 And many other *things* t be, which they NIG
7:15 T is nothing from without a man, NIG
8:12 T shall no sign be given unto this NIG
9: 1 That t be some of them that stand here, NIG
9: 4 And t appeared unto them Elias with NIG
9: 7 t was a cloud that overshadowed them: NIG
9:39 for t is no *man* which shall do a miracle in NIG
10:17 t came one running, and kneeled to him, NIG

Mk 10:18 t *is* none good but one, *that is,* God. NIG
10:29 T is no *man* that hath left house, 1563
11: 5 And certain of them that stood t said unto 1563
11:27 t come to him the chief priests, NIG
12:18 which say t is no resurrection; NIG
12:20 Now t were seven brethren: and the first NIG
12:31 T is none other commandment greater NIG
12:32 for t is one God; and there is none other NIG
12:32 there is one God; and there is none but NIG
12:42 And t came a certain poor widow, NIG
13: 2 t shall not be left one stone upon another, NIG
13: 8 t shall be earthquakes in divers places, NIG
13: 8 and t shall be famines and troubles: NIG
13:21 to you, Lo, here *is* Christ; or lo, *he is* t; 1563
14: 2 Not on the feast *day,* lest t be an uproar of NIG
14: 3 t came a woman having an alabaster box NIG
14: 4 And t were some that had indignation NIG
14:13 t shall meet you a man bearing a pitcher of NIG
14:15 and prepared: t make ready for us. 1563
14:51 And t followed him a certain young man, NIG
14:57 And t arose certain, and bare false witness NIG
14:66 t cometh one of the maids of the high NIG
15: 7 And t was *one* named Barabbas, *which lay* NIG
15:33 t was darkness over the whole land until NIG
15:40 T were also women looking on afar off: NIG
16: 7 t shall ye see him, as he said unto you. 1563

Lk 1: 5 T was in the days of Herod, the king of NIG
1:11 And t appeared unto him an angel of NIG
1:33 and of his kingdom t shall be no end. NIG
1:45 t shall be a performance of those *things* NIG
1:61 T is none of thy kindred that is called by NIG
2: 1 *that* t went out a decree from Cesar NIG
2: 6 And so it was that, while they were t, 1563
2: 7 t was no room for them in the inn. NIG
2: 8 t were in the same country shepherds NIG
2:13 And suddenly t was with the angel a NIG
2:25 And behold, t was a man in Jerusalem, NIG
2:36 And t was *one* Anna, a prophetess, NIG
4:14 t went out a fame of him through all NIG
4:17 And t was delivered unto him the book of NIG
4:33 And in the synagogue t was a man, NIG
5:15 *much* the more went t a fame abroad of NIG
5:17 t were Pharisees and doctors of the law NIG
5:29 t was a great company of publicans and NIG
6: 6 t was a man whose right hand was 1563
6:19 for t went virtue out of him, NIG
7:12 behold, t was a dead man carried out, NIG
7:16 And t came a fear on all: NIG
7:28 Among *those that are* born of women t is NIG
7:41 T was a certain creditor which had two NIG
8:23 t came down a storm of wind on the lake; NIG
8:24 and they ceased, and t was a calm. NIG
8:27 t met him out of the city a certain man, NIG
8:32 And t was there a herd of many swine NIG
8:32 And there was t a herd of many swine 1563
8:41 t came a man named Jairus, and he was a 1563
8:49 t cometh one from the ruler of NIG
9: 4 ye enter into, t abide, and thence depart. 1563
9:17 t was taken up of fragments that remained NIG
9:27 you of a truth, t be some standing here, NIG
9:30 And behold, t talked with him two men, NIG
9:34 t came a cloud, and overshadowed them: NIG
9:35 And t came a voice out of the cloud, NIG
9:46 Then t arose a reasoning among them, NIG
10: 6 And if the son of peace be t, your peace 1563
10:31 by chance t came down a certain priest NIG
11:26 himself; and they enter in, and dwell t: 1563
11:29 and t shall no sign be given it, but the sign NIG
12: 1 when t were gathered together an NIG
12: 2 For t is nothing covered, that shall not be NIG
12:18 and t will I bestow all my fruits and 1563
12:34 your treasure is, t will your heart be also. 1563
12:52 For from henceforth t shall be five in one NIG
12:54 straightway ye say, T cometh a shower; NIG
12:55 south wind blow, ye say, T will be heat; NIG
13: 1 were present at that season some that NIG
13:11 t was a woman which had a spirit of NIG
13:14 T are six days in which *men* ought to NIG
13:23 unto him, Lord, are t few that be saved? NIG
13:28 T shall be weeping and gnashing of teeth, 1563
13:30 t are last which shall be first, and there NIG
13:30 be first, and t are first which shall be last. NIG
13:31 The same day t came certain *of* NIG
14: 2 t was a certain man before him, NIG
14:22 thou hast commanded, and yet t is room. NIG
14:25 And t went great multitudes with him: NIG
15:10 t is joy in the presence of the angels of God NIG
15:13 t wasted his substance with riotous living. 1563
15:14 t arose a mighty famine in that land; NIG
16: 1 T was a certain rich man, which had a NIG
16:19 T was a certain rich man, which was NIG
16:20 t was a certain beggar named Lazarus, NIG
16:26 between us and you t is a great gulf fixed: NIG
17:12 t met him ten men *that were* lepers, NIG
17:17 answering said, Were t not ten cleansed? NIG
17:18 T are not found that returned to give glory NIG
17:21 or, lo t: for behold, the kingdom of God is 1563
17:23 they shall say to you, See here; or, see t: 1563
17:34 that night t shall be two *men* in one bed; NIG
18: 2 Saying, T was in a city a judge, NIG
18: 3 And t was a widow in that city; NIG
18:29 T is no *man* that hath left house, or NIG
19: 2 behold, *t was* a man named Zaccheus, NIG
20:27 which deny that t is any resurrection; NIG
20:29 T were therefore seven brethren: NIG

Lk 21: 6 in the which t shall not be left one stone NIG
21: 7 what sign *will* t be when these *things* NIG
21:11 and great signs shall t be from heaven. NIG
21:18 But t shall not a hair of your head perish. NIG
21:23 for t shall be great distress in the land, NIG
21:25 And t shall be signs in the sun, and in NIG
22:10 t shall a man meet you, bearing a pitcher NIG
22:12 large upper room furnished: t make ready. 1563
22:24 And t was also a strife among them, which NIG
22:43 And t appeared an angel unto him from NIG
23:27 And t followed him a great company of NIG
23:32 And t were also two other, malefactors, NIG
23:33 t they crucified him, and the malefactors, 1563
23:44 t was a darkness over all the earth until NIG
23:50 And behold, *t was* a man named Joseph, NIG
24:18 which are come to pass t in these days? 846

Jn 1: 6 T was a man sent from God, whose name NIG
1:26 but t standeth one among you, whom ye NIG
1:46 t any good *thing* come out of Nazareth? NIG
2: 1 the third day t was a marriage in Cana NIG
2: 1 of Galilee; and the mother of Jesus was t: 1563
2: 6 t were set there six waterpots of stone, NIG
2: 6 there were set t six waterpots of stone, 1563
2:12 and they continued t not many days. 1563
3: 1 T was a man of the Pharisees, NIG
3:22 and t he tarried with them, and baptized. 1563
3:23 Salim, because t was much water there: NIG
3:23 Salim, because there was much water t 1563
3:25 Then t arose a question between *some* of NIG
4: 6 Now Jacob's well was t. Jesus therefore, 1563
4: 7 T cometh a woman of Samaria to draw NIG
4:35 T are yet four months, and *then* cometh NIG
4:40 tarry with them: and he abode t two days. 1563
4:46 And t was a certain nobleman, whose son NIG
5: 1 After this t was a feast of the Jews; NIG
5: 2 t is at Jerusalem by the sheep *market* a NIG
5: 5 And a certain man was t, which had an 1563
5:32 T is another that beareth witness of me; NIG
5:45 t is *one* that accuseth you, *even* Moses, NIG
6: 3 mountain, and t he sat with his disciples. 1563
6: 9 T is a lad here, which hath five barley NIG
6:10 Now t was much grass in the place. NIG
6:22 sea saw that t was none other boat there, NIG
6:22 sea saw that there was none other boat t, 1563
6:23 (Howbeit t came other boats from Tiberias NIG
6:24 therefore saw that Jesus was not t, 1563
6:64 But t are some of you that believe not. NIG
7: 4 For t is no *man that* doeth any *thing* in NIG
7:12 And t was much murmuring among NIG
7:43 So t was a division among the people NIG
8:44 in the truth, because t is no truth in him. NIG
8:50 glory: t is *one* that seeketh and judgeth. NIG
9:16 And t was a division among them. NIG
10:16 and t shall be one fold, *and* one shepherd. NIG
10:19 T was a division therefore again among NIG
10:40 John at first baptized; and t he abode. 1563
10:42 And many believed on him t. 1563
11: 9 Are t not twelve hours in the day? NIG
11:10 he stumbleth, because t is no light in him. NIG
11:15 I am glad for your sakes that I was not t, 1563
11:31 She goeth unto the grave to weep t. 1563
11:54 **and** t continued with his disciples. 2546
12: 2 T they made him a supper; and Martha 1563
12: 9 of the Jews therefore knew that he was t: 1563
12:20 And t were certain Greeks among them NIG
12:26 where I am, t shall also my servant be: 1563
12:28 Then came t a voice from heaven, *saying,* NIG
13:23 Now t was leaning on Jesus' bosom one of NIG
14: 3 that where I am, t ye may be also. NIG
18:18 officers stood *t,* who had made a fire of NIG
19:25 Now t stood by the cross of Jesus his NIG
19:29 Now t was set a vessel full of vinegar: NIG
19:34 and forthwith came t out blood and water. NIG
19:39 And t came also Nicodemus, which at NIG
19:41 Now in the place where he was crucified t NIG
19:42 T laid they Jesus therefore because of 1563
21: 2 T were together Simon Peter, NIG
21: 9 they saw a fire of coals t, and fish laid 2749
21:11 and for all t were so many, *yet* was not NIG
21:25 And t are also many other *things* which NIG

Ac 2: 2 suddenly t came a sound from heaven NIG
2: 3 And t appeared unto them cloven tongues NIG
2: 5 And t were dwelling at Jerusalem Jews, NIG
2:41 same day t were added *unto them* about NIG
4:12 Neither is t salvation in any other: for NIG
4:12 for t is none other name under heaven NIG
4:34 was t any among them that lacked: NIG
5:16 T came also a multitude *out* of the cities NIG
5:34 Then stood t up one in the council, NIG
6: 1 t arose a murmuring of the Grecians NIG
6: 9 Then t arose certain of the synagogue, NIG
7:11 Now t came a dearth over all the land of NIG
7:12 But when Jacob heard that t was corn in NIG
7:30 t appeared to him in the wilderness of NIG
8: 1 At and that time t was a great persecution NIG
8: 8 And t was great joy in that city. NIG
8: 9 But t was a certain man, called Simon, NIG
9: 3 suddenly t shined round about him a light NIG
9:10 And t was a certain disciple at Damascus, NIG
9:18 And immediately t fell from his eyes as it NIG
9:33 And he t found a certain man named 1563
9:36 Now t was at Joppa a certain disciple NIG
9:38 disciples had heard that Peter was t, 846+1722
10: 1 T was a certain man in Cesarea called NIG
10:13 t came a voice to him, Rise, Peter; kill, NIG

Ac	10:18 was surnamed Peter, were lodged **t**.	1759
	11:11 immediately **t** were three men already	NIG
	11:28 stood up one of them named Agabus,	NIG
	11:28 signified by the Spirit that **t** should be great	NIG
	12:18 **t** was no small stir among the soldiers,	NIG
	12:19 down from Judea to Cesarea, and **t** abode.	NIG
	13: 1 Now **t** were in the church that was at	NIG
	13:11 And immediately **t** fell on him a mist and	NIG
	13:25 not *he*. But behold, **t** cometh one after me,	NIG
	14: 5 And when **t** was an assault made both of	NIG
	14: 7 **And t** they preached the gospel.	2546
	14: 8 And **t** sat a certain man at Lystra,	NIG
	14:19 And **t** came thither *certain* Jews from	NIG
	14:28 And **t** abode long time with	1563
	15: 5 But **t** rose up certain of the sect of	NIG
	15: 7 And when **t** had been much disputing,	NIG
	15:33 And after they had tarried **t** a space,	NIG
	15:34 Notwithstanding it pleased Silas to abide **t**.	846
	16: 1 and behold, a certain disciple was **t**,	1563
	16: 9 **T** stood a man of Macedonia,	NIG
	16:15 and abide **t**. And she constrained us.	NIG
	16:26 And suddenly **t** was a great earthquake,	NIG
	17: 7 saying that **t** is another king, *one* Jesus.	NIG
	17:14 but Silas and Timotheus abode **t** still.	1563
	17:21 strangers which **were** t spent their time in	1927
	18:11 And he continued **t** a year and six months,	NIG
	18:18 And Paul *after this* tarried **t** yet a good	NIG
	18:19 And he came to Ephesus, and left them **t**:	846
	18:23 And after he had spent some time **t**,	NIG
	19: 2 much as heard whether **t** be *any* Holy	NIG
	19:14 **t** were seven sons of *one* Sceva, a Jew,	NIG
	19:21 to Jerusalem, saying, After I have been **t**,	1563
	19:23 And the same time **t** arose no small stir	NIG
	19:35 what man is **t** that knoweth not how that	NIG
	19:38 *man*, the law is open, and **t** are deputies:	NIG
	19:40 **t** being no cause whereby we may give an	NIG
	20: 3 And **t** abode three months: and when	NIG
	20: 4 And **t** accompanied him into Asia Sopater	NIG
	20: 8 And **t** were many lights in the upper	NIG
	20: 9 And **t** sat in a window a certain young man	NIG
	20:13 unto Assos, **t** intending to take in Paul:	1564
	20:22 the *things* that shall befall me **t**:	846+1722
	21: 3 for **t** the ship was to unlade *her* burden.	1566
	21: 4 finding disciples, we tarried **t** seven days:	846
	21:10 And as we tarried **t** many days, there came	NIG
	21:10 came down from Judea a certain prophet,	NIG
	21:16 **T** went with us also *certain* of the disciples	NIG
	21:20 how many thousands of Jews **t** are which	NIG
	21:40 And when **t** was made a great silence,	NIG
	22: 5 to Damascus, to bring them which were **t**,	1566
	22: 6 suddenly **t** shone from heaven a great light	NIG
	22:10 **and t** it shall be told thee of all *things*	2546
	22:12 good report of all the Jews which dwelt **t**,	NIG
	23: 7 **t** arose a dissension between the Pharisees	NIG
	23: 8 For the Sadducees say that **t** is no	NIG
	23: 9 And **t** arose a great cry: and the scribes	NIG
	23:10 And when **t** arose a great dissension,	NIG
	23:21 for **t** lie in wait for him of them more *than*	NIG
	24:11 that **t** are *yet* but twelve days since I went	NIG
	24:15 that **t** shall be a resurrection of the dead,	NIG
	25: 5 this man, if **t** be any *wickedness* in him.	NIG
	25: 9 **t** be judged of these *things* before me?	1563
	25:11 for **t** be none of these *things* whereof they	NIG
	25:14 And when they had been **t** many days,	1563
	25:14 **T** is a certain man left in bonds by Felix:	NIG
	25:20 **and t** be judged of these *matters*.	2546
	27: 6 **And t** the centurion found a ship of	2546
	27:12 might attain to Phenice, *and* **t** to winter;	NIG
	27:14 But not long after **t** arose against it a	NIG
	27:22 for **t** shall be no loss of *any man's* life	NIG
	27:23 For **t** stood by me this night *the* angel of	NIG
	27:34 for **t** shall not a hair fall from the head of	NIG
	28: 3 **t** came a viper out of the heat,	NIG
	28:12 at Syracuse, we tarried **t** three days.	NIG
	28:18 because **t** was no cause of death in me.	NIG
	28:23 day, **t** came many to him into *his* lodging;	NIG
Ro	2:11 For **t** is no respect of persons with God.	NIG
	3: 1 Jew? or what profit *is* **t** of circumcision?	NIG
	3:10 written, **T** is none righteous, no, not one:	NIG
	3:11 **T** is none that understandeth, there is	NIG
	3:11 **t** is none that seeketh after God.	NIG
	3:12 **t** is none that doeth good, no, not one.	NIG
	3:18 **T** is no fear of God before their eyes.	NIG
	3:20 Therefore by the deeds of the law **t** shall	NIG
	3:22 them that believe: for **t** is no difference:	NIG
	4:15 for where no law is, *t* is no transgression.	NIG
	5:13 but sin is not imputed when **t** is no law.	NIG
	8: 1 **T** *is* therefore now no condemnation to	NIG
	9:14 *Is* **t** unrighteousness with God? God forbid.	NIG
	9:26 **t** shall they be called the children of	1563
	10:12 For **t** is no difference between the Jew and	NIG
	11: 5 at *this* present time also **t** is a remnant	NIG
	11:26 **T** shall come out of Sion the Deliverer,	NIG
	13: 1 For **t** is no power but of God: the powers	NIG
	13: 9 and if *t* be any other commandment, it is	NIG
	14:14 that **t** is nothing unclean of itself:	NIG
	15:12 **T** shall be a root of Jesse, and he that *shall*	NIG
1Co	1:10 and *that* **t** be no divisions among you;	NIG
	1:11 Chloe, that **t** are contentions among you.	NIG
	3: 3 for whereas **t** is among you envying,	NIG
	5: 1 is reported commonly that **t** is fornication	NIG
	6: 5 so, that **t** is not a wise *man* amongst you?	NIG
	6: 7 therefore **t** is utterly a fault among you,	NIG
	7:34 **T** is difference *also* between a wife and a	NIG
	8: 4 and that *t* is none other God but one.	NIG

1Co	8: 5 For though **t** be that are called gods,	NIG
	8: 5 (as **t** be gods many, and lords many,)	NIG
	8: 6 But to us *t is but* one God, the Father,	NIG
	8: 7 Howbeit *t is* not in every *man that*	NIG
	10:13 **T** hath no temptation taken you but such	NIG
	11:18 I hear that **t** be divisions among you;	NIG
	11:19 For **t** must be also heresies among you,	NIG
	12: 4 Now **t** are diversities of gifts, but the same	NIG
	12: 5 And **t** are differences of administrations,	NIG
	12: 6 And **t** are diversities of operations, but it is	NIG
	12:25 That **t** should be no schism in the body;	NIG
	13: 8 whether **t** *be* prophecies, they shall fail;	NIG
	13: 8 whether **t** *be* tongues, they shall cease;	NIG
	13: 8 whether **t** *be* knowledge, it shall vanish	NIG
	14:10 **T** are, it may be,	NIG
	14:23 and **t** come in *those that are* unlearned,	NIG
	14:24 and **t** come in one that believeth not,	NIG
	14:28 But if **t** be no interpreter, let him keep	NIG
	15:12 how say some among you that **t** is no	NIG
	15:13 But if **t** be no resurrection of the dead,	NIG
	15:39 but *t* is one *kind of* flesh of men,	NIG
	15:40 **T** *are* also celestial bodies,	NIG
	15:41 **T** is one glory of the sun, and another	NIG
	15:44 **T** is a natural body, and there is a spiritual	NIG
	15:44 is a natural body, and **t** is a spiritual body.	NIG
	16: 2 that **t** be no gatherings when I come.	NIG
	16: 9 unto me, and *t* are many adversaries.	NIG
2Co	1:17 that with me **t** should be yea yea, and nay	NIG
	3:17 where the Spirit of the Lord *is*, **t** *is* liberty.	1563
	8:11 perform the doing *of it*; that as **t** *was* a	NIG
	8:11 **t** *may be* a performance also out of that	NIG
	8:12 if **t** be first a willing mind, *it* is accepted	NIG
	8:14 for your want: that **t** may be equality:	NIG
	12: 7 **t** was given to me a thorn in the flesh,	NIG
	12:20 lest **t** *be* debates, envyings, wraths, strifes,	NIG
Gal	1: 7 but **t** be some that trouble you,	NIG
	3:21 for if **t** had been a law given which could	NIG
	3:28 **T** is neither Jew nor Greek, there is	NIG
	3:28 Jew nor Greek, **t** is neither bond nor free,	NIG
	3:28 nor free, **t** is neither male nor female:	NIG
	5:23 against such **t** is no law.	NIG
Eph	4: 4 **T** is one body, and one Spirit, even as ye	NIG
	6: 9 neither is **t** respect of persons with him.	NIG
Php	2: 1 If **t** be therefore any consolation in Christ,	NIG
	4: 8 *t be* any virtue, and if *there be* any praise,	NIG
	4: 8 *there be* any virtue, and if *t be* any praise,	NIG
Col	3:11 Where is neither Greek nor Jew,	NIG
	3:25 hath done: and **t** is no respect of persons.	NIG
2Th	2: 3 for *that* day shall not come, except **t** come	NIG
	3:11 For we hear that **t** *are* some which walk	NIG
1Ti	1:10 if **t** *be* any other *thing that* is contrary to	NIG
	2: 5 **t** is one God, and one mediator between	NIG
2Ti	2:20 But in a great house **t** are not only vessels	NIG
	4: 8 Henceforth **t** is laid up for me a crown of	NIG
Tit	1:10 For **t** are many unruly and vain talkers and	NIG
	3:12 for I have determined **t** to winter.	1563
Phm	1:23 **T** salute thee Epaphras, my fellowprisoner	NIG
Heb	4: 1 lest **t** be in any of you an evil heart of	NIG
	4: 9 **T** remaineth therefore a rest to the people	NIG
	4:13 is **t** any creature that is not manifest	NIG
	7: 8 **t** the *receiveth them*, of whom it is	1563
	7:11 further need *was* **t** that another priest	NIG
	7:12 is made of necessity a change also of	NIG
	7:15 that after the similitude of Melchisedec **t**	NIG
	7:18 For **t** is verily a disannulling of	NIG
	8: 3 seeing that **t** are priests that offer gifts	NIG
	9: 2 For **t** was a tabernacle made; the first,	NIG
	9:16 For where a testament *is*, **t** must also of	NIG
	10: 3 But in those *sacrifices* **t** is a remembrance	NIG
	10:18 Now where remission of these *is*, **t** is no	NIG
	10:26 **t** remaineth no more sacrifice for sins,	NIG
	11:12 Therefore sprang **t** even of one, and him as	NIG
	12:16 Lest **t** *be* any fornicator, or profane *person*,	NIG
Jas	2: 2 For if **t** come unto your assembly a man	NIG
	2: 2 **t** come in also a poor *man* in vile raiment;	NIG
	2: 3 Stand thou **t**, or sit **t** here under my	1563
	2:19 Thou believest that **t** is one God; thou	NIG
	3:16 and strife *is*, **t** *is* confusion and every evil	1563
	4:12 **T** is one lawgiver, who is able to save and	NIG
	4:13 and continue **t** a year, and buy and sell,	1563
2Pe	1:17 when **t** came such a voice to him from	NIG
	2: 1 But **t** were false prophets also among	NIG
	2: 1 as **t** shall be false teachers among you,	NIG
	3: 3 that **t** shall come in the last days scoffers,	NIG
1Jn	2:10 **t** is none occasion of stumbling in him.	NIG
	2:18 even now are **t** many antichrists;	1096
	4:18 **T** is no fear in love; but perfect love	NIG
	5: 7 For **t** are three that bear record in heaven,	NIG
	5: 8 And **t** are three that bear witness in earth,	NIG
	5:16 **T** is a sin unto death: I do not say that he	NIG
	5:17 is sin: and **t** is a sin not unto death.	NIG
2Jn	1:10 If **t** come any unto you, and bring not this	NIG
Jude	1: 4 For **t** are certain men crept in unawares,	NIG
	1:18 How that they told you **t** should be	NIG
Rev	2:14 thou hast **t** them that hold the doctrine of	1563
	4: 3 **t** was a rainbow round about the throne,	NIG
	4: 5 **t** were seven lamps of fire burning before	NIG
	4: 6 And before the throne **t** was a sea of glass	NIG
	6: 4 **t** went out another horse *that was* red:	NIG
	6: 4 and **t** was given unto him a great sword.	NIG
	6:12 seal, and lo, **t** was a great earthquake,	NIG
	7: 4 **t** were sealed an hundred *and* forty *and*	NIG
	8: 1 **t** was silence in heaven about the space of	NIG
	8: 3 and **t** was given unto him much incense,	NIG
	8: 5 and **t** were voices, and thunderings,	NIG

Rev	8: 7 and **t** followed hail and fire mingled with	NIG
	8:10 and **t** fell a great star from heaven,	NIG
	9: 2 and **t** arose a smoke out of the pit,	NIG
	9: 3 And **t** came out of the smoke locusts upon	NIG
	9:10 and **t** were stings in their tails:	NIG
	9:12 behold, **t** come two woes more hereafter.	NIG
	10: 6 therein, that **t** should be time no longer:	NIG
	11: 1 And **t** was given me a reed like unto a rod:	NIG
	11:13 the same hour was **t** a great earthquake,	NIG
	11:15 and **t** were great voices in heaven, saying,	NIG
	11:19 **t** was seen in his temple the ark of his	NIG
	11:19 and **t** were lightnings, and voices,	NIG
	12: 1 And **t** appeared a great wonder in heaven;	NIG
	12: 3 And **t** appeared another wonder in heaven;	NIG
	12: 6 that they should feed her **t** a thousand two	1563
	12: 7 And **t** was war in heaven: Michael and	NIG
	13: 5 And **t** was given unto him a mouth	NIG
	14: 8 And **t** followed another angel, saying,	NIG
	16: 2 **t** fell a noisome and grievous sore upon	NIG
	16:17 **t** came a great voice out of the temple of	NIG
	16:18 And **t** were voices, and thunders,	NIG
	16:18 and **t** was a great earthquake, such as was	NIG
	16:21 And **t** fell upon men a great hail out of	NIG
	17: 1 And **t** came one of the seven angels which	NIG
	17:10 And **t** are seven kings: five are fallen,	NIG
	20:11 and **t** was found no place for them.	NIG
	21: 1 were passed away; and **t** was no more sea.	NIG
	21: 4 and **t** shall be no more death,	NIG
	21: 4 crying, neither shall **t** be any more pain:	NIG
	21: 9 **t** came unto me one of the seven angels	NIG
	21:25 at all by day: for **t** shall be no night there.	NIG
	21:25 at all by day: for **t** shall be no night **t**.	1563
	21:27 **t** shall in no wise enter into it any *thing*	NIG
	22: 2 side of the river, was **t** the tree of life,	NIG
	22: 3 **t** shall be no more curse: but the throne	NIG
	22: 5 **t** shall be no night there; and they need	NIG
	22: 5 there shall be no night **t**; and they need	1563

THEREABOUT (1) [ABOUT]

Lk	24: 4 they were *much* perplexed **t**,	3778+4012

THEREAT (3) [AT]

Ex	30:19 wash their hands and their feet **t**:	4480+5105.2
	40:31 wash their hands and their feet **t**:	4480+5105.2
Mt	7:13 and many there be which go in **t**:	846+1223

THEREBY (21) [BY]

Ge	24:14 that I know that thou hast	871.1+1886.3
Lev	11:43 that ye should be defiled **t**.	871.1+3963.1
Job	22:21 **t** good shall come *unto* thee.	871.1+1992.1
Pr	20: 1 is deceived **t** is not wise.	871.1+2050.2
Ecc	10: 9 wood shall be endangered **t**.	871.1+3963.1
Isa	33:21 oars, neither shall gallant ship pass **t**.	5105.2
Jer	18:16 every one that passeth **t** shall be	5921+1886.3
	19: 8 one that passeth **t** shall be astonished	5921
	51:43 doth *any* son of man pass **t**.	871.1+2006.1
Eze	12: 5 in their sight, and carry out **t**.	871.1+2050.2
	12:12 through the wall to carry out **t**:	871.1+2050.2
	33:12 he shall not fall **t** in the day that	871.1+1886.3
	33:18 he shall even die **t**.	871.1+1992.1
	33:19 is lawful and right, he shall live **t**.	5921+1992.1
Zec	11: 6 Hamath also shall border **t**;	871.1+1886.3
Jn	11: 4 the Son of God might be glorified **t**.	846+1223
Eph	2:16 the cross, having slain the enmity **t**:	846+1722
Heb	12:11 unto them which are exercised **t**.	846+1223
	12:15 up trouble *you*, and **t** many be defiled;	1223
	13: 2 for **t** some have entertained angels	1223
1Pe	2: 2 milk of the word, that ye may grow **t**:	1722

THEREFORE (1237)

Ge	2:24 **T** shall a man leave his father and	3651+5921
	3:23 **T** the Lord God sent him forth from	2050.1
	4:15 the Lord said unto him, **T**	3651+3807.1
	11: 9 **T** is the name of it called Babel;	3651+5921
	12:12 **T** it shall come to pass, when	2050.1
	12:19 now **t** behold thy wife, take *her*, and	2050.1
	17: 9 Thou shalt keep my covenant **t**, thou,	2050.1
	18: 5 for **t** are you come to your servant.	3651+5921
	18:12 **T** Sarah laughed within herself, saying,	2050.1
	19: 8 **t** came they under the shadow of	3651+5921
	19:22 **T** the name of the city was called	3651+5921
	20: 6 thee from sinning against me: **t**	3651+5921
	20: 7 **t** restore the man *his* wife; for he *is*	2050.1
	20: 8 **T** Abimelech rose early in the morning,	2050.1
	21:23 Now **t** swear unto me here by God that	2050.1
	23:15 betwixt me and thee? bury **t** thy dead.	2050.1
	24:65 she took a vail, and covered herself.	2050.1
	25:30 same red *pottage*; for I *am* faint: **t**	3651+5921
	26:33 he called it Shebah: **t** the name of	3651+5921
	27: 3 Now **t** take, I pray thee, thy weapons,	2050.1
	27: 8 **t**, my son, obey my voice according	2050.1
	27:28 **T** God give thee of the dew of heaven,	2050.1
	27:43 **t**, my son, obey my voice; and arise,	2050.1
	29:15 shouldest thou **t** serve me for nought?	2050.1
	29:32 now **t** my husband will love me.	3588
	29:33 he hath **t** given me this *son* also:	2050.1
	29:34 have I born him three sons: **t**	3651+5921
	29:35 Now will I praise the Lord: **t**	3651+5921
	30: 6 a son: **t** called she his name Dan.	3651+5921
	30:15 Rachel said, **T** he shall lie with	3651+3807.1
	31:44 come thou, let us make a covenant,	6258
	31:48 **t** *this* day. **T** was the name of it	3651+5921
	32:32 **T** the children of Israel eat not *of*	3651+5921
	33:10 **t** I have seen thy face, as though I	3651+5921
	33:17 made booths for his cattle: **t**	3651+5921

Ge	34:21 t let them dwell in the land,	2050.1
	37:20 Come now t, and let us slay him,	2050.1
	38:29 t his name was called Pharez.	2050.1
	41:33 Now t let Pharaoh look out a man	2050.1
	42:21 we would not hear; t is this distress	3651+5921
	42:22 t, behold, also his blood is required.	2050.1
	44:30 Now t when I come to thy servant my	3509.1
	44:33 Now t, I pray thee, let thy servant abide	2050.1
	45: 5 Now t be not grieved, nor angry with	2050.1
	47: 4 now t, we pray thee, let thy servants	2050.1
	50: 5 Now t let me go up, I pray thee,	2050.1
	50:21 Now t fear ye not: I will nourish you	2050.1
Ex	1:11 T they did set over them taskmasters to	2050.1
	1:20 T God dealt well with the midwives:	2050.1
	3: 9 Now t, behold, the cry of the children	2050.1
	3:10 Come now t, and I will send thee unto	2050.1
	4:12 Now t go, and I will be with thy mouth,	2050.1
	5: 8 for they be idle; t they cry, saying,	3651+5921
	5:17 ye are idle: t ye say, Let us go and	3651+5921
	5:18 Go t now, and work; for there shall no	2050.1
	9:19 Send t now, and gather thy cattle, and	2050.1
	10:17 Now t forgive, I pray thee, my sin only	2050.1
	12:17 t shall ye observe this day in your	2050.1
	13:10 Thou shalt t keep this ordinance in his	2050.1
	13:15 the firstborn of beast: t I sacrifice to	3651+5921
	15:23 for they were bitter: t the name of	3651+5921
	16:29 hath given you the sabbath, t	3651+5921
	19: 5 Now t, if ye will obey my voice indeed,	2050.1
	31:14 Ye shall keep the sabbath t; for it is holy	2050.1
	32:10 Now t let me alone, that my wrath may	2050.1
	32:34 T now go, lead the people unto the	2050.1
	33: 5 t now put off thy ornaments from thee,	2050.1
	33:13 Now t, I pray thee, if I have found grace	2050.1
Lev	8:35 T shall ye abide at the door of	2050.1
	9: 8 Aaron t went unto the altar, and slew	2050.1
	11:44 ye shall t sanctify yourselves,	2050.1
	11:45 ye shall t be holy, for I am holy.	2050.1
	13:52 He shall t burn that garment,	2050.1
	16: 4 t shall he wash his flesh in water, and	2050.1
	17:12 T I said unto the children of Israel,	3651+5921
	17:14 t I said unto the children of Israel,	2050.1
	18: 5 Ye shall t keep my statutes, and my	2050.1
	18:25 t I do visit the iniquity thereof upon it,	2050.1
	18:26 Ye shall t keep my statutes and my	2050.1
	18:30 T ye shall keep mine ordinance, that ye	2050.1
	19: 8 T every one that eateth it shall bear his	2050.1
	19:37 That shall ye observe all my statutes, and	2050.1
	20: 7 Sanctify yourselves t, and be ye holy:	2050.1
	20:22 Ye shall t keep all my statutes, and all	2050.1
	20:23 all these things, and t I abhorred them.	2050.1
	20:25 Ye shall t put difference between clean	2050.1
	21: 6 they do offer: t they shall be holy.	2050.1
	21: 8 Thou shalt sanctify him; for he offereth	2050.1
	22: 9 They shall t keep mine ordinance,	2050.1
	22: 9 and die t, if they profane it:	871.1+2050.2
	22:31 T shall ye keep my commandments,	2050.1
	25:17 Ye shall not t oppress one another;	2050.1
Nu	3:12 of Israel: t the Levites shall be mine;	2050.1
	11:18 t the LORD will give you flesh,	2050.1
	14:16 t he hath slain them in the wilderness.	2050.1
	14:43 the LORD will not be with you.	2050.1
	16:38 before the LORD, t they are hallowed:	2050.1
	18: 7 T thou and thy sons with thee shall	2050.1
	18:24 given to the Levites to inherit: t	3651+5921
	18:30 T thou shalt say unto them, When ye	2050.1
	20:12 t ye shall not bring this congregation into	3651
	21: 7 The people came to Moses, and said,	2050.1
	22: 5 He sent messengers t unto Balaam	2050.1
	22: 6 Come now t, I pray thee, curse me this	2050.1
	22:17 t, I pray thee, curse me this people.	2050.1
	22:19 t, I pray you, tarry ye also here this	2050.1
	22:34 now t, if it displease thee, I will get me	2050.1
	24:11 T now flee thou to thy place: I thought	2050.1
	24:14 come t, and I will advertise thee what this	NIH
	27: 4 Give unto us t a possession among	NIH
	31:17 Now t kill every male among the little	2050.1
	31:50 We have t brought an oblation for	2050.1
	35:34 Defile not t the land which ye shall	2050.1
Dt	2: 4 take ye good heed unto yourselves t:	2050.1
	4: 1 t hearken, O Israel, unto the statutes	2050.1
	4: 6 Keep t and do them; for this is your	2050.1
	4:15 Take ye t good heed unto yourselves;	2050.1
	4:37 he chose their seed after them,	2050.1
	4:39 Know t this day, and consider it in thine	2050.1
	4:40 Thou shalt keep t his statutes, and his	2050.1
	5:15 by a stretched out arm: t the LORD	3651+5921
	5:25 Now t why should we die? for this great	2050.1
	5:32 Ye shall observe to do t as the LORD	2050.1
	6: 3 Hear t, O Israel, and observe to do it;	2050.1
	7: 9 Know t that the LORD thy God, he is	2050.1
	7:11 Thou shalt t keep the commandments,	2050.1
	8: 6 T thou shalt keep the commandments	2050.1
	9: 3 Understand t this day, that the LORD	2050.1
	9: 6 Understand t, that the LORD thy God	2050.1
	9:26 I prayed t unto the LORD, and said,	2050.1
	10:16 Circumcise t the foreskin of your heart,	2050.1
	10:19 Love ye t the stranger: for ye were	2050.1
	11: 1 T thou shalt love the LORD thy God,	2050.1
	11: 8 T shall ye keep all the commandments	2050.1
	11:18 T shall ye lay up these my words in your	2050.1
	14: 7 not the hoof; t they are unclean unto you.	NIH
	15:11 shall never cease out of the land: t	2050.1
	15:15 LORD thy God redeemed thee: t	3651+5921
	16: 2 Thou shalt t sacrifice the passover unto	2050.1
	16:15 thine hands, t thou shalt surely rejoice.	2050.1

Dt	18: 2 T shall they have no inheritance among	2050.1
	23:14 before thee; t shall thy camp be holy:	2050.1
	24:18 thy God redeemed thee thence: t	3651+5921
	24:22 a bondman in the land of Egypt: t	3651+5921
	25:19 T it shall be, when the LORD thy God	2050.1
	26:16 thou shalt t keep and do them with all	2050.1
	27: 4 T it shall be when ye be gone over	2050.1
	27:10 Thou shalt t obey the voice of	2050.1
	28:48 T shalt thou serve thine enemies which	2050.1
	29: 9 Keep t the words of this covenant,	2050.1
	30:19 t choose life, that both thou and thy	2050.1
	31:19 Now t write ye this song for you,	2050.1
	31:22 Moses t wrote this song the same day,	2050.1
Jos	1: 2 now t arise, go over this Jordan, thou,	2050.1
	2:12 Now t, I pray you, swear unto me by	2050.1
	3:12 Now t take ye twelve men out of	2050.1
	4:17 Joshua t commanded the priests, saying,	2050.1
	7:12 The children of Israel could not stand	2050.1
	7:14 In the morning t ye shall be brought	2050.1
	8: 6 as at the first: t we will flee before them.	2050.1
	8: 9 Joshua t sent them forth: and they went	2050.1
	9: 6 now t make ye a league with us.	6258
	9:11 t now make ye a league with us.	6258
	9:19 of Israel: now t we may not touch them.	6258
	9:23 Now t ye are cursed, and there shall none	6258
	9:24 t we were sore afraid of our lives	2050.1
	10: 5 T the five kings of the Amorites, the	2050.1
	10: 9 Joshua t came unto them suddenly,	2050.1
	13: 7 Now t divide this land for an inheritance	6258
	14: 4 t they gave no part unto the Levites in	2050.1
	14:12 Now t give me this mountain,	2050.1
	14:14 Hebron t became the inheritance of	3651+5921
	17: 1 of war, t he had Gilead and Bashan.	2050.1
	17: 4 t according to the commandment of	2050.1
	18: 6 Ye shall t describe the land into seven	2050.1
	19: 9 t the children of Simeon had their	2050.1
	19:47 the children of Dan went up to fight	2050.1
	22: 4 t now return ye, and get ye unto your	2050.1
	22:26 T we said, Let us now prepare to build	2050.1
	22:28 T said we, that it shall be, when they	2050.1
	23: 6 Be ye t very courageous to keep and	2050.1
	23:11 Take good heed t unto yourselves, that	2050.1
	23:15 T it shall come to pass, that as all good	2050.1
	24:10 unto Balaam: t he blessed you still:	2050.1
	24:14 Now t fear the LORD, and serve him in	2050.1
	24:18 t will we also serve the LORD; for he is	NIH
	24:23 t put away, said he, the strange gods	2050.1
	24:27 it shall be t a witness unto you, lest ye	2050.1
Jdg	2:23 T the LORD left those nations, without	2050.1
	3: 8 T the anger of the LORD was hot	2050.1
	3:25 they took a key, and opened them:	2050.1
	6:32 T on that day he called him Jerubbaal,	2050.1
	7: 3 Now t go to, proclaim in the ears of	2050.1
	8: 7 T when the LORD hath delivered	3651+3807.1
	9:16 Now t, if ye have done truly and	2050.1
	9:32 Now t up by night, thou and the people	2050.1
	11: 8 T we turn again to thee now,	3651+3807.1
	11:13 t restore those lands again peaceably.	2050.1
	11:26 why t did ye not recover them within	2050.1
	13: 4 t beware, I pray thee, and drink not	2050.1
	14: 2 now t get her for me to wife.	2050.1
	15: 2 t I gave her to thy companion:	2050.1
	16:12 Delilah t took new ropes, and bound	2050.1
	17: 3 now t I will restore it unto thee.	2050.1
	18:14 now t consider what ye have to do.	2050.1
	19: 7 urged him: t he lodged there again.	2050.1
	20:13 Now t deliver us the men, the children	2050.1
	20:42 T they turned their backs before the	2050.1
	21:20 T they commanded the children of	2050.1
Ru	3: 3 Wash thyself t, and anoint thee,	2050.1
	3: 9 spread t thy skirt over thine handmaid;	2050.1
	4: 8 T the kinsman said unto Boaz, Buy it for	2050.1
1Sa	1: 7 her; t she wept, and did not eat.	2050.1
	1:13 t Eli thought she had been drunken.	2050.1
	1:28 T also I have lent him to the LORD;	2050.1
	9: 9 T Eli said unto Samuel, Go, lie down:	2050.1
	3:14 t I have sworn unto the house of	3651+3807.1
	5: 5 neither the priests of Dagon,	2050.1
	5: 8 They sent t and gathered all the lords of	2050.1
	5:10 T they sent the ark of God to Ekron.	2050.1
	6: 7 Now t make a new cart, and take two	2050.1
	8: 9 Now t hearken unto their voice:	2050.1
	9:13 Now t get you up; for about this time	2050.1
	10:12 who is their father? T it became a	3651+5921
	10:19 Now t present yourselves before	2050.1
	10:22 T they inquired of the LORD further,	2050.1
	11:10 T the men of Jabesh said, To morrow	2050.1
	12:13 Now t behold the king whom ye have	2050.1
	12:16 Now t stand and see this great thing,	1571
	13:12 T said I, The Philistines will come down	2050.1
	13:12 I forced myself t, and offered a burnt	2050.1
	14:41 T Saul said unto the LORD God of	2050.1
	15: 1 now t hearken thou unto the voice of	2050.1
	15:25 Now t, I pray thee, pardon my sin,	2050.1
	17:51 T David ran, and stood upon	2050.1
	18:13 T Saul removed him from him,	2050.1
	18:22 thee: now t be the king's son in law.	2050.1
	19: 2 now t, I pray thee, take heed to thyself	2050.1
	20: 8 T thou shalt deal kindly with thy	2050.1
	20:29 see my brethren. T he cometh not	3651+5921
	21: 3 t what is under thine hand? give me	2050.1
	22: 1 David t departed thence, and escaped	2050.1
	23: 2 T David inquired of the LORD, saying,	2050.1
	23:20 t, O king, come down according to	2050.1

1Sa	23:23 See t, and take knowledge of all	2050.1
	23:28 went against the Philistines: t	3651+5921
	24:15 The LORD t be judge,	2050.1
	24:15 Swear now t unto me by the LORD,	2050.1
	25:17 t know and consider what thou wilt	2050.1
	25:26 Now t, my lord, as the LORD liveth,	2050.1
	26: 4 David t sent out spies,	2050.1
	26: 8 now t let me smite him, I pray thee,	2050.1
	26:19 Now t, I pray thee, let my lord the king	2050.1
	26:20 Now t, let not my blood fall to the earth	2050.1
	27:12 t he shall be my servant for ever.	2050.1
	28: 2 Achish said to David, T will I	3651+3807.1
	28:15 t I have called thee, that thou mayest	2050.1
	28:18 t hath the LORD done this thing	3651+5921
	28:22 Now t, I pray thee, hearken thou also	2050.1
	31: 4 t Saul took a sword, and fell upon it.	2050.1
2Sa	2: 7 T now let your hands be strengthened,	2050.1
	4:11 shall I not t now require his blood of	2050.1
	5:20 as the breach of waters. T he called	3651+5921
	6:21 t will I play before the LORD.	2050.1
	6:23 T Michal the daughter of Saul had no	2050.1
	7: 8 t so shalt thou say unto my servant	2050.1
	7:27 I will build thee a house: t hath thy	3651+5921
	7:29 T now let it please thee to bless thee	2050.1
	9:10 Thou t, and thy sons, and thy servants,	2050.1
	12:10 Now t the sword shall never depart	2050.1
	12:16 David t besought God for the child;	2050.1
	12:19 t David said unto his servants, Is the	2050.1
	12:28 Now t gather the rest of the people	2050.1
	13:13 Now t, I pray thee, speak unto the king;	2050.1
	13:33 Now t let not my lord the king take	2050.1
	14:15 Now t that I am come to speak of this	2050.1
	14:17 t the LORD thy God will be with thee.	2050.1
	14:21 t, bring the young man Absalom again.	2050.1
	14:26 hair was heavy on him, t he polled it:)	2050.1
	14:29 T Absalom sent for Joab, to have sent	2050.1
	14:30 T he said unto his servants, See,	2050.1
	14:32 now t let me see the king's face;	2050.1
	15:29 Zadok t and Abiathar carried the ark of	2050.1
	15:35 t it shall be, that what thing soever thou	2050.1
	17:11 T I counsel that all Israel be generally	3588
	17:16 Now t send quickly, and tell David,	2050.1
	18: 3 t now it is better that thou succour us	2050.1
	19: 7 Now t arise, go forth,	2050.1
	19:10 Now t why speak ye not a word of	2050.1
	19:20 t, behold, I am come the first this day	2050.1
	19:23 The king said unto Shimei, Thou shalt	2050.1
	19:27 of God: do t what is good in thine eyes.	2050.1
	19:28 What right t have I yet to cry any more	2050.1
	22:25 T the LORD hath recompensed me	2050.1
	22:50 T I will give thanks unto thee,	3651+5921
	23:17 t he would not drink it. These things	2050.1
	23:19 t he was their captain: howbeit he	2050.1
1Ki	1:12 t come, let me, I pray thee, give thee	2050.1
	2: 2 thou strong t, and shew thyself a man;	2050.1
	2: 6 Do t according to thy wisdom, and let	2050.1
	2: 9 Now t hold him not guiltless: for thou	2050.1
	2:19 Bath-sheba t went unto king Solomon,	2050.1
	2:24 Now t, as the LORD liveth, which hath	2050.1
	2:33 Their blood shall t return upon the head	2050.1
	2:44 the LORD shall return thy wickedness	2050.1
	3: 9 Give t thy servant an understanding	2050.1
	5: 6 Now t command thou that they hew	2050.1
	8:25 T now, LORD God of Israel, keep with	2050.1
	8:61 Let your heart t be perfect with	2050.1
	9: 9 served them: t hath the LORD	3651+5921
	10: 9 t made he thee king, to do judgment	2050.1
	11:40 Solomon sought t to kill Jeroboam.	2050.1
	12: 4 t make thou the grievous service of	2050.1
	12:18 T king Rehoboam made speed to get	2050.1
	12:24 They hearkened t to the word of	2050.1
	13:26 t the LORD hath delivered him unto	2050.1
	14:10 T, behold, I will bring evil upon	3651+3807.1
	14:12 Arise thou t, get thee to thine own	2050.1
	18:19 Now t send, and gather to me all Israel	2050.1
	18:23 Let them t give us two bullocks;	2050.1
	20:23 Their gods are gods of the hills; t	3651+5921
	20:28 t will I deliver all this great multitude	2050.1
	20:42 t thy life shall go for his life,	2050.1
	22:19 t the word of the LORD:	3651+3807.1
	22:23 Now t behold, the LORD hath put a	3651+3807.1
2Ki	1: 4 Now t thus saith the LORD,	3651+3807.1
	1: 6 of Baal-zebub the god of Ekron? t	3651+3807.1
	1:14 let my life now be precious in thy	3651+3807.1
	1:16 thou shalt not come down off	3651+3807.1
	2:17 They sent t fifty men; and they sought	2050.1
	3:23 one another: now t, Moab, to the spoil.	2050.1
	4:33 He went in t, and shut the door upon	2050.1
	5:15 now t, I pray thee, take a blessing of thy	2050.1
	5:27 The leprosy t of Naaman shall cleave	2050.1
	6: 7 T said he, Take it up to thee. And he	2050.1
	6:11 T the heart of the king of Syria was sore	2050.1
	6:14 T sent he thither horses, and chariots,	2050.1
	7: 4 t come, and let us fall unto the host	2050.1
	7: 9 now t come, that we may go and tell	2050.1
	7:12 t are they gone out of the camp to hide	2050.1
	7:14 They took t two chariot horses;	2050.1
	9:26 Now t take and cast him into the plat	2050.1
	10:19 Now t call unto me all the prophets of	2050.1
	12: 7 now t receive no more money of your	2050.1
	14:11 T Jehoash king of Israel went up; and	2050.1
	15:16 they opened not to him, t he smote it;	2050.1
	17: 4 the king of Assyria shut him up,	2050.1
	17:18 T the LORD was very angry with Israel,	2050.1
	17:25 t the LORD sent lions among them,	2050.1

T

2Ki		
17:26	t he hath sent lions among them,	2050.1
18:23	Now t, I pray thee, give pledges to my	2050.1
19:18	and stone: t they have destroyed them.	2050.1
19:19	Now t, O LORD our God, I beseech	2050.1
19:26	T their inhabitants *were* of small power,	2050.1
19:28	t I will put my hook in thy nose,	2050.1
19:32	T thus saith the LORD	3651+3807.1
21:12	T thus saith the LORD God of	3651+3807.1
22:17	t my wrath shall be kindled against this	2050.1
22:20	Behold, I will gather thee unto	3651+3807.1

1Ch
10:14	t he slew him, and turned the kingdom	2050.1
11: 3	T came all the elders of Israel to the	2050.1
11: 7	David dwelt in the castle; t	3651+5921
11:19	T he would not drink it. These *things*	2050.1
14:11	like the breaking forth of waters: t	3651+5921
14:14	David inquired again of God;	2050.1
14:16	David t did as God commanded him:	2050.1
17: 7	Now t thus shalt thou say unto my	2050.1
17:23	T now, LORD, let the thing that thou	2050.1
17:25	that *thou* wilt build him a house: t	3651+5921
17:27	let it please thee to bless the house	2050.1
21: 7	with this thing; t he smote Israel.	2050.1
21:12	Now t advise thyself what word I shall	2050.1
22: 5	I will t now make preparation for it.	NIH
22:16	Arise *t*, and be doing, and the LORD be	NIH
22:19	arise t, and build ye the sanctuary of	2050.1
23:11	t they were in one reckoning,	2050.1
24: 2	t Eleazar and Ithamar executed	2050.1
28: 8	Now t in the sight of all Israel	2050.1
29:13	Now t, our God, we thank thee,	2050.1

2Ch
2: 7	Send me now t a man cunning to work	2050.1
2:15	t the wheat, and the barley, the oil,	2050.1
6:10	The LORD t hath performed his word	2050.1
6:16	Now t, O LORD God of Israel,	2050.1
6:19	Have respect t to the prayer of thy	2050.1
6:21	Hearken t unto the supplications of thy	2050.1
6:41	Now t arise, O LORD God, into thy	2050.1
7:22	served them: t hath he brought all	3651+5921
9: 8	t made he thee king over them, to do	2050.1
10: 4	now t ease thou somewhat the grievous	2050.1
12: 5	t have I also left you in the hand of	NIH
12: 7	t I will not destroy them, but I will grant	NIH
14: 7	T he said unto Judah, Let us build these	2050.1
15: 7	Be ye strong t, and let not your hands	2050.1
16: 7	t is the host of the king of Syria	3651+5921
16: 9	t from henceforth thou shalt have wars.	3588
17: 5	T the LORD stablished the kingdom in	2050.1
18: 5	T the king of Israel gathered together of	2050.1
18:12	let thy word t, I pray thee, be like one	2050.1
18:16	let them return t every man to his house	3651+3807.1
18:18	Again he said, t hear the word of	3651+3807.1
18:22	Now t behold, the LORD hath put a	2050.1
18:31	They compassed about him to fight:	2050.1
18:33	t he said to *his* chariot man, Turn thine	2050.1
19: 2	*is* wrath upon thee from	2063+871.1+2050.1
20:26	for there they blessed the LORD: t	3651+5921
28:11	hear me t, and deliver the captives	2050.1
28:23	*t* will I sacrifice to them, that they may	NIH
30: 7	*who* t gave them up to desolation, as ye	2050.1
30:17	t the Levites had the charge of the	2050.1
32:15	Now t let not Hezekiah deceive you,	2050.1
32:25	t there was wrath upon him,	2050.1
34:25	t my wrath shall be poured out upon	2050.1
35:14	t the Levites prepared for themselves,	2050.1
35:24	His servants t took him out of *that*	2050.1
36:17	T he brought upon them the king of	2050.1

Ezr
2:62	t were they, as polluted, put from	2050.1
4:14	t have we sent and certified the	1836+5922
5:17	Now t, if *it seem* good to the king,	2050.3
6: 6	Now *t*, Tatnai, governor beyond the river,	NIH
9:12	Now t give not your daughters unto your	6258
10: 3	Now t let us make a covenant with our	2050.1
10:11	Now t make confession unto the LORD	2050.1

Ne
2:20	t we his servants will arise and build:	2050.1
4:13	T set I in the lower places behind	2050.1
4:20	In what place *t* ye hear the sound of	NIH
5: 2	t we take up corn *for them*, that we	2050.1
6: 7	Come now t, and let us take counsel	2050.1
6: 9	Now t, O God, strengthen my hands.	2050.1
6:13	T *was* he hired, that I should be	4616+3807.1
7:64	t were they, as polluted, put from	2050.1
9:27	t thou deliveredst them into the hand	2050.1
9:28	t leftest thou them in the hand of their	2050.1
9:30	t gavest thou them into the hand of	2050.1
9:32	Now t, our God, the great, the mighty,	2050.1
13: 8	t I cast forth all the household stuff of	2050.1
13:28	the Horonite: t I chased him from me.	2050.1

Est
1:12	t was the king very wroth, and his	2050.1
2:23	t they were both hanged on a tree:	2050.1
3: 8	t it *is* not for the king's profit to suffer	2050.1
9:19	T the Jews of the villages, that	3651+5921
9:26	T for all the words of this letter,	3651+5921

Job
5:17	t despise not thou the chastening of	2050.1
6: 3	t my words are swallowed up.	3651+5921
6:28	Now t be content, look upon me; for	2050.1
7:11	T I will not refrain my mouth; I will speak	1571
9:22	This is one *thing*, t I said *it*, He	2050.1
10:15	of confusion; t see thou mine affliction;	2050.1
11: 6	Know t that God exacteth of thee *less*	3588
17: 4	their heart from understanding: t	3651+5921
20: 2	T do my thoughts cause me to	3651+3807.1
20:21	t shall no *man* look for his goods.	2050.1
21:14	T they say unto God, Depart from us;	2050.1
22:10	T snares *are* round about thee,	2050.1
23:15	T am I troubled at his presence;	3651+5921

Job
32:10	T I said, Hearken to me; I also	3651+3807.1
34:10	T hearken unto me, ye men of	3651+3807.1
34:25	T he knoweth their works,	3651+3807.1
34:33	and not I: t speak what thou knowest.	2050.1
35:14	*is* before him; t trust thou in him.	2050.1
35:16	T doth Job open his mouth in vain;	2050.1
37:24	Men do t fear him: he respecteth	3651+3807.1
42: 3	counsel without knowledge? t	2050.1
42: 8	T take unto you now seven bullocks	2050.1

Ps
1: 5	T the ungodly shall not stand in	3651+5921
2:10	Be wise now t, O ye kings: be	2050.1
7: 7	for their sakes t return thou on high.	2050.1
16: 9	T my heart is glad, and my glory	3651+3807.1
18:24	T hath the LORD recompensed me	3651+5921
18:49	T will I give thanks unto thee,	3651+5921
21:12	T shalt thou make them turn their back,	3588
25: 8	Good and upright *is* the LORD: t	3651+5921
26: 1	in the LORD; *t* I shall not slide.	NIH
27: 6	t will I offer in his tabernacle sacrifices	2050.1
28: 7	t my heart greatly rejoiceth; and with	2050.1
31: 3	t for thy name's sake lead me,	2050.1
36: 7	t the children of men put their trust	2050.1
40:12	of mine head: t my heart faileth me.	2050.1
42: 6	t will I remember thee from the	3651+5921
45: 2	grace is poured into thy lips: t	3651+5921
45: 7	hatest wickedness: t God, thy God,	3651+5921
45:17	remembered in all generations: t	3651+5921
46: 2	T will not we fear, though the earth	3651+5921
55:19	have no changes, t they fear not God.	2050.1
59: 5	Thou t, O LORD God of hosts, the God	2050.1
63: 7	t in the shadow of thy wings will I	2050.1
73: 6	T pride compasseth them about	3651+3807.1
73:10	T his people return hither:	3651+3807.1
78:21	T the LORD heard *this*, and	3651+3807.1
78:33	T their days did he consume in vanity,	3651+5921
91:14	his love upon me, t will I deliver him:	2050.1
106:23	T he said that *he* would destroy them,	2050.1
106:26	T he lifted up his hand against them,	2050.1
106:40	T was the wrath of the LORD kindled	2050.1
107:12	T he brought down their heart with	2050.1
110: 7	drink of the brook in the way: t	3651+5921
116: 2	t will I call upon *him* as long as I live.	2050.1
116:10	I believed, t have I spoken: I was greatly	3588
118: 7	t shall I see *my desire* upon them that	2050.1
119:104	thy precepts I get understanding: t	3651+5921
119:119	wicked of the earth *like* dross: t	3651+3807.1
119:127	I love thy commandments above	3651+5921
119:128	T I esteem all *thy* precepts	3651+5921
119:129	t doth my soul keep them.	3651+5921
119:140	*is* very pure: t thy servant loveth it.	2050.1
139:19	God: depart from me t, ye bloody men.	2050.1
143: 4	T is my spirit overwhelmed within me;	2050.1

Pr
1:31	T shall they eat of the fruit of their own	2050.1
4: 7	*is* the principal thing; *t* get wisdom:	NIH
5: 7	Hear me now t, O ye children,	2050.1
6:15	T shall his calamity come suddenly;	3651+5921
6:34	t he will not spare in the day of	2050.1
7:15	t came I forth to meet thee,	3651+5921
7:24	Hearken unto me now t, O ye children,	2050.1
8:32	Now t hearken unto me, O ye children:	2050.1
17:11	t a cruel messenger shall be sent against	2050.1
17:14	t leave off contention, before *it be*	2050.1
20: 4	t shall he beg in harvest,	2050.1
20:19	t meddle not with him that flattereth	2050.1

Ecc
2: 1	prove thee with mirth, t enjoy pleasure:	2050.1
2:17	T I hated life; because the work that is	2050.1
2:20	T I went about to cause my heart to	2050.1
5: 2	upon earth: t let thy words be few.	3651+5921
8: 6	t the misery of man *is* great upon him.	3588
8:11	t the heart of the sons of men is	3651+5921
11:10	T remove sorrow from thy heart,	2050.1

SS
1: 3	t do the virgins love thee.	3651+5921

Isa
1:24	T saith the Lord, the LORD	3651+3807.1
2: 6	T thou hast forsaken thy people the house	3588
2: 9	humbleth himself; t forgive them not.	2050.1
3:17	T the Lord will smite with a scab	2050.1
5:13	T my people are gone into	3651+3807.1
5:14	T hell hath enlarged herself,	3651+3807.1
5:24	T as the fire devoureth the	3651+3807.1
5:25	T is the anger of the LORD kindled	3651+5921
7:14	T the Lord himself shall give you	3651+3807.1
8: 7	t behold, the Lord bringeth up	3651+3807.1
9:11	T the LORD shall set up the adversaries	2050.1
9:14	T the LORD will cut off from Israel	2050.1
9:17	T the Lord shall have no joy in their	3651+5921
10:16	T shall the Lord, the Lord of	3651+3807.1
10:24	T thus saith the Lord GOD of	3651+3807.1
12: 3	T with joy shall ye draw water out of	2050.1
13: 7	T shall all hands be faint,	3651+5921
13:13	T I will shake the heavens,	3651+5921
15: 4	t the armed soldiers of Moab shall	2050.1
15: 7	T the abundance they have gotten,	3651+5921
16: 7	T shall Moab howl for Moab,	3651+5921
16: 9	T I will bewail with the weeping of	3651+5921
17:10	t shalt thou plant pleasant plants,	2050.1
21: 3	T are my loins filled *with* pain:	3651+5921
22: 4	I said, Look away from me; I will	3651+5921
24: 6	T hath the curse devoured the	3651+5921
24: 6	t the inhabitants of the earth are	3651+5921
25: 3	T shall the strong people glorify	3651+5921
26:14	t hast thou visited and	2050.1
27: 9	By this t shall the iniquity of Jacob	3651+3807.1
27:11	*is* a people of no understanding: t	2050.1
28:16	T thus saith the Lord GOD,	3651+3807.1
28:22	t be ye not mockers, lest your bands	2050.1

Isa
29:14	T, behold, I will proceed to do a	3651+3807.1
29:22	T thus saith the LORD,	2050.1
30: 3	T shall the strength of Pharaoh be your	2050.1
30: 7	t have I cried concerning this,	3651+3807.1
30:13	T this iniquity shall be to you as a	3651+3807.1
30:16	will flee upon horses; t shall ye flee:	3651+5921
30:16	t shall they that pursue you be	3651+5921
30:18	t will the LORD wait, that *he* may	3651+3807.1
30:18	you, and t will he be exalted,	3651+3807.1
36: 8	Now t give pledges, I pray thee, to my	2050.1
37:19	and stone: t they have destroyed them.	2050.1
37:20	Now t, O LORD our God, save us from	2050.1
37:27	T their inhabitants *were* of small power,	2050.1
37:29	t will I put my hook in thy nose,	2050.1
37:33	T thus saith the LORD	2050.1
38:20	t we will sing my songs *to* the stringed	2050.1
42:25	T he hath poured upon him the fury of	2050.1
43: 4	t will I give men for thee, and people for	2050.1
43:12	T ye *are* my witnesses, saith the LORD,	2050.1
43:28	T I have profaned the princes of	2050.1
47: 8	T hear now this, *thou that art* given to	2050.1
47:11	T shall evil come upon thee; thou shalt	2050.1
50: 7	For the Lord GOD will help me; t	3651+3807.1
50: 7	shall I not be confounded: t	3651+3807.1
51:11	T the redeemed of the LORD shall	2050.1
51:21	T hear now this, thou afflicted,	3651+3807.1
52: 5	Now t, what have I here, saith	2050.1
52: 6	T my people shall know my	3651+3807.1
52: 6	my people shall know now t: my name:	3651+3807.1
53:12	T will I divide him a *portion* with	3651+3807.1
57:10	hast found the life of thine hand; t	3651+5921
59: 9	Is judgment far from us,	3651+5921
59:16	t this arm brought salvation unto him;	2050.1
60:11	T thy gates shall be open continually;	2050.1
61: 7	shall rejoice in their portion: t	3651+3807.1
63: 5	t mine own arm brought salvation unto	2050.1
63:10	t he was turned to be their enemy,	2050.1
65: 7	t will I measure their former work into	2050.1
65:12	T will I number you to the sword,	2050.1
65:13	T thus saith the Lord GOD,	3651+3807.1

Jer
1:17	Thou t gird up thy loins, and arise,	2050.1
2:19	know t and see that *it is* an evil *thing*	2050.1
2:33	thou thy way to seek love? t	3651+5921
3: 3	T the showers have been withholden,	2050.1
5: 4	T said, Surely these *are* poor; they are	2050.1
5:27	so *are* their houses full *of* deceit: t	3651+5921
6:11	T I am full *of* the fury of the LORD;	2050.1
6:15	neither could they blush: t	3651+3807.1
6:18	T hear, ye nations, and know,	3651+3807.1
6:21	T thus saith the LORD, Behold,	3651+3807.1
7:14	T will I do unto *this* house, which is	2050.1
7:16	T pray not thou for this people, neither	2050.1
7:20	T thus saith the Lord GOD;	3651+3807.1
7:27	T thou shalt speak all these words unto	2050.1
7:32	T, behold, the days come, saith	3651+3807.1
8:10	T will I give their wives unto	3651+3807.1
8:12	neither could they blush: t	3651+3807.1
9: 7	T thus saith the LORD of hosts,	3651+3807.1
9:15	T thus saith the LORD of hosts,	3651+3807.1
10:21	have not sought the LORD: t	3651+5921
11: 8	t I will bring upon them all the words of	2050.1
11:11	T thus saith the LORD, Behold,	3651+3807.1
11:14	T pray not thou for this people, neither	2050.1
11:21	T thus saith the LORD of the men	3651+3807.1
11:22	T thus saith the LORD of hosts,	3651+3807.1
12: 8	out against me: t have I hated it.	2050.1
13:12	T thou shalt speak unto them this word;	2050.1
13:24	T will I scatter them as the stubble that	2050.1
13:26	T will I discover thy skirts upon	1571+2050.1
14:10	t the LORD doth not accept them;	2050.1
14:15	T thus saith the LORD	2050.1
14:17	T thou shalt say this word unto them;	2050.1
14:22	t we will wait upon thee: for thou hast	2050.1
15: 6	t I will stretch out my hand against thee	2050.1
15:19	T thus saith the LORD, If thou	3651+5921
16:13	T will I cast you out of this land into a	2050.1
16:14	T behold, the days come, saith	3651+3807.1
16:21	T behold, I *will* this once cause	3651+3807.1
18:11	Now t go to, speak to the men of Judah,	2050.1
18:13	T thus saith the LORD; Ask ye	3651+3807.1
18:21	T deliver up their children to	3651+3807.1
19: 6	T behold, the days come, saith	3651+3807.1
20:11	with me as a mighty terrible one: t	3651+5921
22:18	T thus saith the LORD	3651+3807.1
23: 2	T thus saith the LORD God of	3651+3807.1
23: 7	T, behold, the days come, saith	3651+3807.1
23:15	T thus saith the LORD of hosts	3651+3807.1
23:30	T, behold, I *am* against	3651+3807.1
23:32	t they shall not profit this people at all,	2050.1
23:38	t thus saith the LORD;	3651+3807.1
23:39	T behold, I, even I, will utterly	3651+3807.1
25: 8	T thus saith the LORD of hosts;	3651+3807.1
25:27	T thou shalt say unto them, Thus saith	2050.1
25:30	T prophesy thou against them all these	2050.1
26:13	T now amend your ways and	2050.1
27: 9	T hearken not ye to your prophets, nor	2050.1
27:14	T hearken not unto the words of	2050.1
28:16	T thus saith the LORD; Behold,	3651+3807.1
29:20	Hear ye t the word of the LORD, all *ye*	2050.1
29:27	Now t why hast thou not reproved	6258
29:28	For the sent unto us in Babylon,	3651+5921
29:32	T thus saith the LORD; Behold,	3651+3807.1
30:10	T fear thou not, O my servant Jacob,	2050.1
30:16	T all they that devour thee shall	3651+3807.1
31: 3	t *with* lovingkindness have I drawn	3651+5921

Jer 31:12	**T** they shall come and sing in the height 2050.1
31:20	I do earnestly remember him still: **t** 3651+5921
32:23	**t** thou hast caused all this evil to come 2050.1
32:28	**T** thus saith the LORD; Behold, 3651+3807.1
32:36	now **t** thus saith the LORD, 3651+3807.1
34:12	**T** the word of the LORD came to 2050.1
34:17	**T** thus saith the LORD; Ye have 3651+3807.1
35:17	**T** thus saith the LORD God of 3651+3807.1
35:19	**T** thus saith the LORD of hosts, 3651+3807.1
36: 6	**T** go thou, and read in the roll, 2050.1
36:14	**T** all the princes sent Jehudi the son of 2050.1
36:30	**T** thus saith the LORD of 3651+3807.1
37:20	**T** hear now, I pray thee, O my lord 2050.1
38: 4	**T** the princes said unto the king, 2050.1
40: 3	his voice, **t** this thing is come upon you. 2050.1
42:15	now **t** hear the word of 2050.1
42:22	Now **t** know certainly that ye shall die 2050.1
44: 7	**T** now thus saith the LORD, the God of 2050.1
44:11	**T** thus saith the LORD of hosts, 3651+3807.1
44:22	**t** is your land a desolation, and an 2050.1
44:23	**t** this evil is happened unto you, 3651+5921
44:26	**T** hear ye the word of the LORD, 3651+3807.1
48:11	**t** his taste remained in him, 3651+5921
48:12	**T** behold, the days come, saith 3651+3807.1
48:31	**T** will I howl for Moab, and I will 3651+5921
48:36	**T** mine heart shall sound for Moab 3651+5921
49: 2	**T** behold, the days come, saith 3651+5921
49:20	**T** hear the counsel of the LORD, 3651+3807.1
49:26	**T** her young men shall fall in her 3651+5921
50:18	**T** thus saith the LORD of hosts, 3651+3807.1
50:30	**T** shall her young men fall in 3651+5921
50:39	**T** the wild beasts of the desert 3651+5921
50:45	**T** hear ye the counsel of 3651+3807.1
51: 7	of her wine; **t** the nations are mad. 3651+5921
51:36	**T** thus saith the LORD; Behold, 3651+3807.1
51:47	**T** behold, the days come, that I 3651+3807.1
La 1: 8	grievously sinned; **t** she is removed: 3651+5921
1: 9	last end; **t** she came down wonderfully: 2050.1
2: 8	**t** he made the rampart and the wall to 2050.1
3:21	This I recall to my mind, I have **t** 3651+5921
3:24	saith my soul; **t** will I hope in him. 3651+5921
Eze 3:17	**t** hear the word at my mouth, 2050.1
4: 7	**t** thou shalt set thy face toward the 2050.1
5: 7	**T** thus saith the Lord GOD; 3651+3807.1
5: 8	**T** thus saith the Lord GOD; 3651+3807.1
5:10	**T** the fathers shall eat the sons in 3651+3807.1
5:11	**t** will I also diminish *thee*; neither shall 2050.1
7:20	of their detestable things therein: **t** 3651+5921
8:18	**T** will I also deal in fury: mine eye shall 1571
11: 4	**T** prophesy against them, 3651+3807.1
11: 7	**T** thus saith the Lord GOD; 3651+3807.1
11:16	**T** say, Thus saith the Lord GOD; 3651+3807.1
11:17	**T** say, Thus saith the Lord GOD; 3651+3807.1
12: 3	**T** thou son of man, prepare thee stuff 2050.1
12:23	Tell them **t**, Thus saith the Lord 3651+3807.1
12:28	**T** say unto them, Thus saith 3651+3807.1
13: 8	**T** thus saith the Lord GOD; 3651+3807.1
13: 8	seen lies, **t** behold, I *am* against 3651+5921
13:13	**T** thus saith the Lord GOD; I will 3651+3807.1
13:23	**T** ye shall see no more vanity, 3651+3807.1
14: 4	**T** speak unto them, and say unto 3651+3807.1
14: 6	**T** say unto the house of Israel, 3651+3807.1
15: 6	**T** thus saith the Lord GOD; 3651+3807.1
16:27	Behold **t**, I have stretched out my hand 2050.1
16:34	is given unto thee, **t** thou art contrary. 2050.1
16:37	Behold **t**, I will gather all thy 3651+3807.1
16:43	fretted me in all these *things;* behold **t**, 2050.1
16:50	**t** I took them away as I saw *good.* 2050.1
17:19	**T** thus saith the Lord GOD; *As* I 3651+3807.1
18:30	**T** I will judge you, O house of 3651+3807.1
20:27	**T**, son of man, speak unto 3651+3807.1
21: 4	**t** shall my sword go forth out of 3651+3807.1
21: 6	Sigh **t**, thou son of man, with 2050.1
21:12	people: smite **t** upon *thy* thigh. 3651+3807.1
21:14	Thou **t**, son of man, prophesy, 2050.1
21:24	**T** thus saith the Lord GOD; 3651+3807.1
22: 4	art come *even* unto thy years: **t** 3651+5921
22:13	Behold **t**, I have smitten mine hand at 2050.1
22:19	**T** thus saith the Lord GOD; 3651+3807.1
22:19	ye are all become dross, behold **t**, 3651+3807.1
22:31	**T** have I poured out mine indignation 2050.1
23:22	**T**, O Aholibah, thus saith the 3651+3807.1
23:31	**t** will I give her cup into thine hand. 3651+5921
23:35	**T** thus saith the Lord GOD; 3651+3807.1
23:35	**t** bear thou also thy lewdness and thy 2050.1
24: 9	**T** thus saith the Lord GOD; 3651+3807.1
25: 4	Behold **t**, I *will* deliver thee to 3651+3807.1
25: 7	Behold **t**, I will stretch out mine 3651+3807.1
25: 9	**T** behold, I *will* open the side of 3651+3807.1
25:13	Thus saith the Lord GOD; I will 3651+3807.1
25:16	Thus saith the Lord GOD; 3651+3807.1
26: 3	**T** thus saith the Lord GOD; 3651+3807.1
28: 6	**T** thus saith the Lord GOD; 3651+3807.1
28: 7	Behold **t**, I *will* bring strangers 3651+3807.1
28:16	**t** I will cast thee as profane out of 2050.1
28:18	**t** will I bring forth a fire from the midst 2050.1
29: 8	**T** thus saith the Lord GOD; 3651+3807.1
29:10	Behold **t**, I *am* against thee, 3651+3807.1
29:19	**T** thus saith the Lord GOD; 3651+3807.1
30:22	**T** thus saith the Lord GOD; 3651+3807.1
31: 5	**T** his height was exalted above all 3651+5921
31:10	**T** thus saith the Lord GOD; 3651+3807.1
31:11	have I delivered him into the hand of 2050.1
32: 3	I will **t** spread out my net over thee 2050.1
33: 7	**t** thou shalt hear the word at my mouth, 2050.1

Eze 33:10	**T**, O thou son of man, speak unto 2050.1
33:12	**T**, thou son of man, say unto the 2050.1
34: 7	**T**, ye shepherds, hear the word of 3651+3807.1
34: 9	**T**, O ye shepherds, hear the word 3651+3807.1
34:20	**T** thus saith the Lord GOD unto 3651+3807.1
34:22	**T** will I save my flock, and they shall no 2050.1
35: 6	**T**, *as* I live, saith the Lord GOD, 3651+3807.1
35:11	**T**, *as* I live, saith the Lord GOD, 3651+3807.1
36: 3	**T** prophesy and say, Thus saith 3651+3807.1
36: 4	**T**, ye mountains of Israel, hear 3651+3807.1
36: 5	**T** thus saith the Lord GOD; 3651+3807.1
36: 6	Prophesy **t** concerning the land 2050.1
36: 7	**T** thus saith the Lord GOD; 3651+3807.1
36:14	**T** thou shalt devour men no 3651+3807.1
36:22	**t** say unto the house of Israel, 3651+3807.1
37:12	**T** prophesy and say unto them, 3651+3807.1
38:14	**t**, son of man, prophesy and 3651+3807.1
39: 1	**T** thou son of man, prophesy against 2050.1
39:23	**t** hid I my face from them, and gave 2050.1
39:25	**T** thus saith the Lord GOD; 3651+3807.1
41: 7	the breadth of the house *was still* 3651+5921
42: 6	pillars as the pillars of the courts: **t** 3651+5921
44: 2	hath entered in by it, **t** it shall be shut. 2050.1
44:12	house of Israel to fall into iniquity; **t** 3651+5921
Da 1: 8	**t** the requested of the prince of 2050.1
1:19	Azariah: **t** stood they before the king. 2050.1
2: 6	**t** shew me the dream, and the 3861
2: 9	**t** tell me the dream, and I shall know that 3861
2:10	*there is* no king, lord, 1768+3606+6903
2:24	**T** Daniel went in unto 1836+3606+6903
3: 7	**T** at that time, when all 1836+3606+6903
3:19	**t** he spake, and commanded that *they* NIH
3:22	**T** because the king's 1836+3606+6903
3:29	**T** I make a decree, That every people, 2050.3
4: 6	**T** made I a decree to bring in all 4481+2050.3
8: 8	**T** the he goat waxed very great: 2050.1
9:11	the curse is poured upon us, 2050.1
9:14	**T** hath the LORD watched upon 2050.1
9:17	Now **t**, O our God, hear the prayer of 2050.1
9:23	**t** understand the matter, and consider 2050.1
9:25	Know **t** and understand, *that* from 2050.1
10: 8	**T** I was left alone, and saw this great 2050.1
11:30	**t** he shall be grieved, and return, 2050.1
11:44	**t** he shall go forth with great fury to 2050.1
Hos 2: 2	let her **t** put away her whoredoms out 2050.1
2: 6	**T** behold, I will hedge up thy way 3651+3807.1
2: 9	**T** will I return, and take *away* my 3651+3807.1
2:14	**T**, behold, I, *will* allure her, 3651+3807.1
4: 3	**T** shall the land mourn, 2050.1
4: 5	**t** shalt thou fall *in* the day, 2050.1
4: 7	**t** will I change their glory into shame. NIH
4:13	the shadow thereof *is* good: **t** 3651+5921
4:14	**t** the people *that* doth not understand 2050.1
5: 5	**t** shall Israel and Ephraim fall in their 2050.1
5:10	**t** I will pour out my wrath upon them like NIH
5:12	**T** will I *be* unto Ephraim as a moth, 2050.1
6: 5	**T** have I hewed *them* by 3651+5921
8: 6	the workman made it; **t** it *is* not God: 2050.1
9: 9	**t** he will remember their iniquity, he will NIH
10:14	**T** shall a tumult arise among thy people, 2050.1
12: 6	**T** turn thou to thy God: keep mercy and 2050.1
12:14	**t** shall he leave his blood upon him, 2050.1
13: 3	**T** they shall be as the morning 3651+3807.1
13: 6	their heart was exalted; **t** have they 3651+5921
13: 7	**T** I will be unto them as a lion: as a 2050.1
Joel 2:12	**T** also now, saith the LORD, turn ye 2050.1
Am 2:14	**T** the flight shall perish from the swift, 2050.1
3: 2	of all the families of the earth: **t** 3651+5921
3:11	**T** thus saith the Lord GOD; 3651+3807.1
4:12	**T** thus will I do unto thee, 3651+3807.1
5:11	Forasmuch **t** as your treading *is* upon 3282
5:13	**T** the prudent shall keep silence 3651+3807.1
5:16	**T** the LORD, the God of hosts, 3651+3807.1
5:27	**T** will I cause you to go into captivity 2050.1
6: 7	**T** now shall they go captive with 3651+3807.1
6: 8	**t** will I deliver up the city with all that is 2050.1
7:16	Now **t** hear thou the word of the LORD: 2050.1
7:17	**T** thus saith the LORD; Thy wife 3651+3807.1
Jnh 4: 2	**T** I fled before unto Tarshish: 3651+5921
4: 3	**T** now, O LORD, take, I beseech thee, 2050.1
Mic 1: 6	**T** I will make Samaria as a heap of 2050.1
1: 8	**T** I will wail and howl, I will go 2088+5921
1:14	**t** shalt thou give presents to 3651+5921
2: 3	**T** thus saith the LORD; Behold, 3651+3807.1
2: 5	**T** thou shalt have none that shall 3651+3807.1
3: 6	**T** night *shall be* unto you, that *ye* 3651+3807.1
3:12	**T** shall Zion for your sake be 3651+3807.1
5: 3	**T** will he give them up, until 3651+3807.1
6:13	**T** also will I make *thee* sick in smiting 2050.1
6:16	**t** ye shall bear the reproach of my 2050.1
7: 7	**T** I will look unto the LORD; I will wait 2050.1
Hab 1: 4	**T** the law is slacked, 3651+5921
1: 4	**t** wrong judgment proceedeth. 3651+5921
1:15	**t** they rejoice and are glad. 3651+5921
1:16	**T** they sacrifice unto their net, 3651+5921
1:17	Shall they **t** empty their net, 3651+5921
Zep 1:13	**T** their goods shall become a booty, 2050.1
2: 9	**T** *as* I live, saith the LORD of 3651+3807.1
3: 8	**T** wait ye upon me, saith 3651+3807.1
Hag 1: 5	Now **t** thus saith the LORD of hosts; 2050.1
1:10	**T** the heaven over you is stayed 3651+5921
Zec 1: 3	**T** say thou unto them, Thus saith 2050.1
1:16	**T** thus saith the LORD; I am 3651+3807.1
7:12	**t** came a great wrath from the LORD of 2050.1
7:13	**T** it is come to pass, *that* as he cried, 2050.1

Zec 8:19	feasts; **t** love the truth and peace. 2050.1
10: 2	they comfort in vain: **t** they went 3651+5921
Mal 2: 9	**T** have I also made you contemptible 2050.1
2:15	**T** take heed to your spirit, and let none 2050.1
2:16	**T** take heed to your spirit, that ye deal 2050.1
3: 6	**t** ye sons of Jacob are not consumed. 2050.1
Mt 3: 8	Bring forth **t** fruits meet for repentance: 3767
3:10	**t** every tree which bringeth not forth good 3767
5:19	Whosoever **t** shall break one of these least 3767
5:23	**T** if thou bring thy gift to the altar, 3767
5:48	Be ye **t** perfect, even as your Father which 3767
6: 2	**T** when thou doest *thine* alms, do not 3767
6: 8	Be not ye **t** like unto them: for your Father 3767
6: 9	After this manner **t** pray ye: Our Father 3767
6:22	if **t** thine eye be single, thy whole body 3767
6:23	If **t** the light that is in thee be darkness, 3767
6:25	**T** I say unto you, Take no thought 1223+3778
6:31	**T** take no thought, saying, What shall we 3767
6:34	Take **t** no thought for the morrow: 3767
7:12	**T** all *things* whatsoever ye would that 3767
7:24	**T** whosoever heareth these sayings of 3767
9:38	Pray ye **t** the Lord of the harvest, that he 3767
10:16	be ye **t** wise as serpents, and harmless as 3767
10:26	Fear them not **t**: for there is nothing 3767
10:31	Fear ye not **t**, ye are of more value than 3767
10:32	Whosoever **t** shall confess me before men, 3767
12:27	**t** they shall be your judges. 1223+3778
13:13	**T** speak I to them in parables: 1223+3778
13:18	Hear ye **t** the parable of the sower. 3767
13:40	As **t** the tares are gathered and burnt in 1223+3778
13:52	**T** every scribe *which is* instructed 3767
14: 2	and **t** mighty works do shew forth 1223+3778
18:4	Whosoever **t** shall humble himself as this 3767
18:23	**T** is the kingdom of heaven likened 1223+3778
18:26	The servant **t** fell down, 3767
19: 6	What **t** God hath joined together, let not 3767
19:27	and followed thee; what shall we have **t**? 686
21:40	When the lord **t** of the vineyard cometh, 3767
21:43	**T** say I unto you, The kingdom of 1223+3778
22: 9	Go ye **t** into the highways, 3767
22:17	Tell us **t**, What thinkest thou? Is it lawful 3767
22:21	Render **t** unto Cesar the *things* which are 3767
22:28	**T** in the resurrection whose wife shall she 3767
23: 3	All **t** whatsoever they bid you observe, 3767
23:14	**t** ye shall receive the greater damnation. 1223
23:20	Whoso **t** shall swear by the altar, 3767
24:15	When ye **t** shall see the abomination of 1223+3778
24:42	Watch **t**: for ye know not what hour your 3767
24:44	**T** be ye also ready: for in such an 1223+3778
25:13	Watch **t**, for ye know neither the day nor 3767
25:27	Thou oughtest **t** to have put my money to 3767
25:28	Take **t** the talent from him, and give *it* 3767
27:17	**T** when they were gathered together, 3767
27:64	Command **t** that the sepulchre be made 3767
28:19	Go ye **t**, and teach all nations, 3767
Mk 1:38	preach there also: for **t** came I forth. 1519+3778
2:28	**T** the Son of man is Lord also of 5620
6:14	and **t** mighty works do shew forth 1223+3778
6:19	**T** Herodias had a quarrel against him, 1161
8:38	Whosoever **t** shall be ashamed of me and 1063
10: 9	What **t** God hath joined together, let not 3767
11:24	**T** I say unto you, What *things* 1223+3778
12: 6	Having yet **t** one son, his wellbeloved, 3767
12: 9	What shall **t** the lord of the vineyard do? 3767
12:23	In the resurrection **t**, when they shall rise, 3767
12:24	Do ye not **t** err, because ye know 1223+3778
12:27	**t** the God of the living: ye **t** do greatly err. 3767
12:37	David **t** himself calleth him Lord; 3767
13:35	Watch ye **t**: for ye know not when 3767
Lk 1:35	**t** also that holy thing which shall be born 1352
3: 8	Bring forth **t** fruits worthy of repentance, 3767
3: 9	every tree **t** which bringeth not forth good 3767
4: 7	If thou **t** wilt worship me, all shall be 3767
4:43	to other cities also: for **t** am I sent. 1519+3778
6:36	Be ye **t** merciful, as your Father also is 3767
7:42	Tell me **t**, which of them will love him 3767
8:18	Take heed **t** how ye hear: for whosoever 3767
10: 2	**t** said he unto them, The harvest truly *is* 3767
10: 2	pray ye **t** the Lord of the harvest, that he 3767
10:40	serve alone? bid her **t** that she help me. 3767
11:19	**t** shall they be your judges. 1223+3778
11:34	**t** when thine eye is single, thy whole body 3767
11:35	Take heed **t** that the light which is in thee 3767
11:36	If thy whole body **t** be full of light, 3767
11:49	**T** also said the wisdom of God, 1223+3778
12: 3	**T** whatsoever ye have spoken in 473+3739
12: 7	Fear not **t**: ye are of more value than 3767
12:22	**T** I say unto you, Take no thought 1223+3778
12:40	Be ye **t** ready also: for the Son of man 3767
13:14	in them **t** come and be healed, and not on 3767
14:20	a wife, and **t** I cannot come. 1223+3778
15:28	came his father out and intreated him. 3767
16:11	If **t** ye have not been faithful in 3767
16:27	he said, I pray thee **t**, father, that thou 3767
19:12	He said **t**, A certain nobleman went into a 3767
20:15	and killed *him*. What shall **t** the lord of 3767
20:25	Render **t** unto Cesar the *things* which be 5106
20:29	There were **t** seven brethren: and the first 3767
20:33	**T** in the resurrection whose wife of them 3767
20:44	David **t** calleth him Lord, how is he then 3767
21: 8	time draweth near: go ye not **t** after them. 3767
21:14	Settle *it* **t** in your hearts, not to meditate 3767
21:36	Watch ye **t**, and pray always, that ye may 3767
23:16	I will **t** chastise him, and release *him*. 3767
23:20	Pilate **t**, willing to release Jesus, spake 3767

Lk	23:22 I will t chastise him, and let *him* go.	3767
Jn	1:31 t am I come baptizing with water.	1223+3767
	2:22 When t he was risen from the dead,	3767
	3:29 this my joy t is fulfilled.	3767
	4: 1 When t the Lord knew how the Pharisees	3767
	4: 6 Jesus t, being wearied with *his* journey,	3767
	4:33 T said the disciples one to another,	3767
	5:10 The Jews t said unto him that was cured,	3767
	5:16 And t did the Jews persecute Jesus,	1223+3767
	5:18 The Jews sought the more to kill	1223+3767
	6:13 T they gathered *them* together,	3767
	6:15 When Jesus t perceived that they would	3767
	6:24 When the people t saw that Jesus was not	3767
	6:30 They said t unto him, What sign shewest	3767
	6:43 Jesus t answered and said unto them,	3767
	6:45 Every *man* t that hath heard,	3767
	6:52 The Jews t strove amongst themselves,	3767
	6:60 Many t of his disciples, when they had	3767
	6:65 And he said, T said I unto you,	1223+3767
	7: 3 His brethren t said unto him, Depart	3767
	7:22 Moses t gave unto you circumcision	1223+3767
	7:40 Many of the people t, when they heard	3767
	8:13 The Pharisees t said unto him, Thou	3767
	8:24 I said t unto you, that ye shall die in your	3767
	8:36 If the Son t shall make you free, ye shall	3767
	8:47 ye t hear *them* not, because ye are	1223+3767
	9: 7 He went his way t, and washed,	3767
	9: 8 The neighbours t, and they which before	3767
	9:10 T said they unto him, How were thine	3767
	9:16 T said some of the Pharisees, This man is	3767
	9:23 T said his parents, He is of age;	3767
	9:41 now ye say, We see; t your sin remaineth.	3767
	10:17 T doth *my* Father love me, because	1223+3767
	10:19 There was a division t again among	3767
	10:39 T they sought again to take him:	3767
	11: 3 His sisters sent unto him, saying, Lord,	3767
	11: 6 When he had heard t that he was sick,	3767
	11:33 When Jesus t saw her weeping,	3767
	11:38 Jesus t again groaning in himself cometh	3767
	11:54 Jesus t walked no more openly among	3767
	12: 9 of the Jews t knew that he was there:	3767
	12:17 The people t that was with him when he	3767
	12:19 The Pharisees t said among themselves,	3767
	12:21 The same came t to Philip, which was of	3767
	12:29 The people t, that stood *by*, and heard *it*,	3767
	12:39 T they could not believe, because	1223+3767
	12:50 whatsoever I speak t, even as the Father	3767
	13:11 t said he, Ye are not all clean.	1223+3767
	13:24 Simon Peter t beckoned to him, that *he*	3767
	13:31 T, when he was gone out, Jesus said,	3767
	15:19 the world, t the world hateth you.	1223+3767
	16:15 t said I, that he shall take of mine,	1223+3767
	16:18 They said t, What is this that he saith,	3767
	16:22 And ye now t have sorrow: but I will see	3767
	18: 4 Jesus t, knowing all *things* that should	3767
	18: 8 told you that I am *he*: if t ye seek me,	3767
	18:25 They said t unto him, Art not thou also	3767
	18:31 The Jews t said unto him, It is not lawful	3767
	18:37 Pilate t said unto him, Art thou a king	3767
	18:39 will ye t *that* I release unto you the King	3767
	19: 1 Then Pilate t took Jesus,	3767
	19: 4 Pilate t went forth again, and saith unto	3767
	19: 6 the chief priests t and officers saw him,	3767
	19: 8 When Pilate t heard that saying, he was	3767
	19:11 t he that delivered me unto thee	1223+3767
	19:13 Pilate t heard that saying, he brought	3767
	19:16 Then delivered he him t unto them to be	3767
	19:24 They said t among themselves, Let us not	3767
	19:24 cast lots. These *things* t the soldiers did.	3767
	19:26 When Jesus t saw *his* mother,	3767
	19:30 When Jesus t had received the vinegar,	3767
	19:31 The Jews t, because it was the preparation	3767
	19:38 He came t, and took the body of Jesus.	3767
	19:42 There laid they Jesus t because of the	3767
	20: 3 Peter t went forth, and *that* other disciple,	3767
	20:25 The other disciples t said unto him,	3767
	21: 6 They cast t, and now they were not able	3767
	21: 7 That disciple whom Jesus loved saith	3767
Ac	1: 6 When they t were come together,	3767
	2:26 T did my heart rejoice,	1223+3767
	2:30 T being a prophet, and knowing that God	3767
	2:33 T being by the right hand of God exalted,	3767
	2:36 T let all the house of Israel know	3767
	3:19 Repent ye t, and be converted, that your	3767
	8: 4 They that were scattered abroad went	235
	8:22 Repent t of this thy wickedness,	3767
	10:20 Arise t, and get *thee* down, and go with	235
	10:29 T came I *unto you* without	1352+2532
	10:29 I ask t for what intent ye have sent for me?	3767
	10:32 Send t to Joppa, and call hither Simon,	3767
	10:33 Immediately t I sent to thee; and thou hast	3767
	10:33 Now t are we all here present before God,	3767
	12: 5 Peter t was kept in prison: but prayer was	3767
	13:38 Be it known unto you t, men *and*	3767
	13:40 Beware t, lest that come upon you, which	3767
	14: 3 Long time t abode they speaking boldly in	3767
	15: 2 When t Paul and Barnabas had no small	3767
	15:10 Now t why tempt ye God, to put a yoke	3767
	15:27 We have sent t Judas and Silas, who shall	3767
	16:11 T loosing from Troas, we came with a	3767
	16:36 let you go: now t depart, and go in peace.	3767
	17:12 T many of them believed; also of	3767
	17:17 T disputed he in the synagogue with	3767
	17:20 would know t what these *things* mean.	3767
	17:23 Whom t ye ignorantly worship, him	3767

Ac	19:32 t cried one *thing*, and some another:	3767
	20:11 When he t was come up *again*, and	1161
	20:28 Take heed t unto yourselves, and to all	3767
	20:31 T watch, and remember, that *by the*	1352
	21:22 What is it t? the multitude must needs	3767
	21:23 Do t this that we say to thee: We have	3767
	23:15 Now t ye with the council signify to	3767
	25: 5 Let them t, said he, which among you are	3767
	25:17 T, when they were come hither,	3767
	26:22 Having t obtained help of God, I continue	3767
	28:20 For this cause t have I called for you, to	3767
	28:28 Be it known t unto you, that the salvation	3767
Ro	2: 1 T thou art inexcusable, O man,	1352
	2:21 Thou t which teachest another,	3767
	2:26 T if the uncircumcision keep	3767
	3:20 T by the deeds of the law there shall no	1360
	3:28 T we conclude that a man is justified by	3767
	4:16 T it is of faith, that *it might be* by	1223+3767
	4:22 And t it was imputed to him for	1352
	5: 1 T being justified by faith, we have peace	3767
	5:18 T as by the offence of one *judgment*	686+3767
	6: 4 T we are buried with him by baptism into	3767
	6:12 Let not sin t reign in your mortal body,	3767
	8: 1 T *is* now no condemnation to them	686
	8:12 T, brethren, we are debtors, not to	686+3767
	9:18 T hath he mercy on whom he will	686+3767
	11:22 the goodness and severity of God:	3767
	12: 1 I beseech you t, brethren, by the mercies	3767
	12:20 T if thine enemy hunger, feed him; if he	3767
	13: 2 Whosoever t resisteth the power,	3767
	13: 7 Render t to all *their* dues: tribute to whom	3767
	13:10 t love *is* the fulfilling of the law.	3767
	13:12 let us t cast off the works of darkness,	3767
	14: 8 we live t, or die, we are the Lord's.	3767
	14:13 Let us not t judge one another any more:	3767
	14:19 Let us t follow *after* the *things*	686+3767
	15:17 I have t whereof *I* may glory through Jesus	3767
	15:28 When t I have performed this,	3767
	16:19 unto all *men*. I am glad t on your behalf:	3767
1Co	3:21 T let no *man* glory in men. For all *things*	5620
	4: 5 T judge nothing before the time, until	5620
	5: 7 Purge out t the old leaven, that ye may be	3767
	5: 8 T let us keep the feast, not with old	5620
	5:13 T put away from among yourselves *that*	2532
	6: 7 Now t there is utterly a fault among you,	3767
	6:20 T glorify God in your body, and in your	1211
	7: 8 I say t to the unmarried and widows, It is	1161
	7:26 I suppose t that this is good for the present	3767
	8: 4 As concerning t the eating of those *things*	3767
	9:26 I t so run, not as uncertainly; so fight I,	5106
	10:31 Whether t ye eat, or drink,	3767
	11:20 When ye come together t into one place,	3767
	12:15 of the body; is it t not of the body?	3778+3844
	12:16 of the body; is it t not of the body?	3778+3844
	14:11 T if I know not the meaning of the voice,	3767
	14:23 If t the whole church be come together	3767
	15:11 T whether *it were* I or they, so we preach,	3767
	15:58 T, my beloved brethren, be ye stedfast,	5620
	16:11 Let no *man* t despise him: but conduct	3767
	16:18 t acknowledge ye them that are such.	3767
2Co	4: 1 T seeing we have this ministry,	1223+3767
	4:13 is written, I believed, *and* t have I spoken;	1352
	4:13 I spoken: we also believe, and t speak;	1352
	5: 6 T *we are* always confident, knowing that,	3767
	5:11 Knowing t the terror of the Lord,	3767
	5:17 T if any *man* be in Christ, *he is* a new	5620
	7: 1 Having t these promises, dearly beloved,	3767
	7:13 T we were comforted in your	1223+3767
	7:16 I rejoice t that I have confidence in you in	3767
	8: 7 T, as ye abound in every *thing, in* faith,	235
	8:11 Now t perform the doing *of it;* that as	2532
	9: 5 T I thought it necessary to exhort	3767
	11:15 T *it is* no great *thing* if his ministers also	3767
	12: 9 Most gladly t will I rather glory in my	3767
	12:10 T I take pleasure in infirmities,	1352
	13:10 T I write these *things* being absent,	1223+3767
Gal	2:17 sinners, *is* t Christ the minister of sin?	687
	3: 5 He t that ministereth to you the Spirit,	3767
	3: 7 Know ye t that they which are of faith,	686
	4:16 Am I t become your enemy, because I tell	5620
	5: 1 Stand fast t in the liberty wherewith	3767
	6:10 As we have t opportunity, let us do	686+3767
Eph	2:19 Now t ye are no more strangers and	3767
	4: 1 I t, the prisoner of the Lord, beseech you	3767
	4:17 This I say t, and testify in the Lord, that	3767
	5: 1 Be ye t followers of God, as dear children;	3767
	5: 7 Be not ye t partakers with them.	3767
	5:24 T as the church is subject unto Christ,	235
	6:14 Stand t, having your loins girt about with	3767
Php	2: 1 If *there be* t any consolation in Christ,	3767
	2:23 Him t I hope to send presently, so soon as	3767
	2:28 I sent him t the more carefully, that,	3767
	2:29 Receive him t in the Lord with all	3767
	3:15 Let us t, as many as *be* perfect, be thus	3767
	4: 1 T, my brethren dearly beloved and	5620
Col	2: 6 As ye have t received Christ Jesus	3767
	2:16 Let no *man* t judge you in meat,	3767
	3: 5 Mortify t your members which are upon	3767
	3:12 Put on t, as the elect of God, holy and	3767
1Th	3: 7 T, brethren, we were comforted	1223+3767
	4: 8 He t that despiseth, despiseth not man,	5105
	5: 6 T let us not sleep, as *do* others;	686+3767
2Th	2:15 T, brethren, stand fast, and hold	686+3767
1Ti	2: 1 I exhort t, first of all, supplications,	3767

1Ti	2: 8 I will t that men pray every where,	3767
	4:10 For t we both labour and	1519+3767
	5:14 I will t that the younger *women* marry,	3767
2Ti	1: 8 Be not thou t ashamed of the testimony	3767
	2: 1 Thou t, my son, be strong in the grace	3767
	2: 3 Thou t endure hardness, as a good soldier	3767
	2:10 T I endure all *things* for the elects'	1223+3767
	2:21 If a man t purge himself from these,	3767
	4: 1 I charge t before God, and the Lord	3767
Phm	1:12 thou t receive him, that is, mine own	1161
	1:15 For perhaps he t departed for a	1223+3767
	1:17 If thou count me t a partner, receive him	3767
Heb	1: 9 t God, *even* thy God, hath anointed	1223+3767
	2: 1 T we ought to give the more	3767
	4: 1 Let us t fear, lest, a promise being left *us*	3767
	4: 6 Seeing t it remaineth that some *must*	3767
	4: 9 There remaineth t a rest to the people of	686
	4:11 Let us labour t to enter into that rest,	3767
	4:16 Let us t come boldly unto the throne of	3767
	6: 1 T leaving the principles of the doctrine of	1352
	7:11 If t perfection were by the Levitical	3767
	9:23 *It was* t necessary that the patterns of	3767
	10:19 Having t, brethren, boldness to enter into	3767
	10:35 Cast not away t your confidence,	3767
	11:12 T sprang there even of one, and him as	1352
	13:13 Let us go forth t unto him without	5106
	13:15 By him t let us offer the sacrifice of praise	3767
Jas	4: 4 whosoever t will be a friend of the world	3767
	4: 7 Submit yourselves t to God. Resist	3767
	4:17 T to him that knoweth to do good,	3767
1Pe	2: 7 Unto you t which believe *he is* precious:	3767
	4: 7 be ye t sober, and watch unto prayer.	3767
	5: 6 Humble yourselves t under the mighty	3767
2Pe	3:17 Ye t, beloved, **seeing** ye know *these*	3767
1Jn	2:24 Let *that* t abide in you, which ye have	3767
	3: 1 t the world knoweth us not,	1223+3767
	4: 5 t speak they of the world,	1223+3767
3Jn	1: 8 We t ought to receive such, that we might	NIG
Jude	1: 5 I will t put you in remembrance, though	NIG
Rev	2: 5 Remember t from whence thou art fallen,	3767
	3: 3 Remember t how thou hast received and	3767
	3: 3 If t thou shalt not watch, I will come on	3767
	3:19 and chasten: be zealous t, and repent.	3767
	7:15 are they before the throne of God	1223+3767
	12:12 T rejoice, ye heavens, and ye that	1223+3767
	18: 8 T shall her plagues come in one	1223+3767

THEREFROM (3) [FROM]

Jos	23: 6 ye turn not aside t *to* the right	4480+5105.2
2Ki	3: 3 Israel to sin; he departed not t.	4480+5089.1
	3: 3 Israel to sin; he departed not t.	4480+5089.1

THEREIN (230) [IN]

Ge	9: 7 in the earth, and multiply t.	871.1+1886.3
	18:24 for the fifty righteous that *are* t?	7130+871.1
	23:11 the cave that *is* t, I give it thee;	871.1+2050.2
	23:17 the cave which *was* t, and all	871.1+2050.2
	23:20 the field, and the cave that *is* t,	871.1+2050.2
	34:10 dwell and trade you t, and get you	1886.3
	34:10 and get you possessions t.	871.1+1886.3
	34:21 let them dwell in the land, and trade t;	1886.3
	47:27 they had possession t, and grew,	871.1+1886.3
	49:32 of the cave that *is* t *was* from	871.1+2050.2
Ex	2: 3 with pitch, and put the child t;	871.1+1886.3
	5: 9 the men, that they may labour t;	871.1+2050.2
	16:24 neither was there any worm t:	871.1+2050.2
	16:33 put an omer full of manna t,	8033+1886.5
	21:33 it, and an ox or an ass fall t;	8033+1886.5
	29:20 to be anointed t, and to	871.1+1992.1
	30:18 altar, and thou shalt put water t.	8033+1886.5
	31:14 for whosoever doeth *any* work t,	871.1+1886.3
	35: 2 whosoever doeth work t shall be	871.1+2050.2
	40: 3 thou shalt put t the ark of the Testimony,	8033
	40: 7 and the altar, and shalt put water t.	8033
	40: 9 all that *is* t, and shalt hallow it,	871.1+2050.2
Lev	6: 3 a man doeth, sinning t:	2007+871.1+1886.1
	6: 7 he hath done in trespassing t.	871.1+1886.3
	8:10 the tabernacle and all that *was* t,	871.1+2050.2
	10: 1 put fire t, and put incense	871.1+2006.1
	13:21 *there be* no white hairs t, and *if*	871.1+1886.3
	13:37 there is black hair grown up t;	871.1+2050.2
	18: 4 keep mine ordinances, to walk t:	871.1+1992.1
	18:30 that ye defile not yourselves t:	871.1+1992.1
	20:22 whither I bring you to dwell t,	871.1+1886.3
	22:21 there shall be no blemish t.	871.1+2050.2
	23: 3 ye shall do no work *t* it *is* the sabbath of	NIH
	23: 7 ye shall do no servile work *t*.	NIH
	23: 8 ye shall do no servile work *t*.	NIH
	23:21 ye shall do no servile work *t* it shall be a	NIH
	23:25 Ye shall do no servile work *t* but ye shall	NIH
	23:35 ye shall do no servile work *t*.	NIH
	23:36 *and* ye shall do no servile work *t*.	NIH
	25:19 eat *your* fill, and dwell t in safety.	5921+1886.3
	26:32 your enemies which dwell t shall	871.1+1886.3
Nu	4:16 of all that *is*, in the sanctuary,	871.1+2050.2
	13:18 and the people that dwelleth t,	5921+1886.3
	13:20 whether there be wood t, or not.	871.1+1886.3
	14:30 I sware to make you dwell t,	871.1+1886.3
	16: 7 put fire t, and put incense in	871.1+2006.1
	16:46 put fire t from off the altar,	5921+1886.3
	28:18 ye shall do no *manner of* servile work *t*.	NIH
	29: 7 your souls: ye shall not do any work *t*.	NIH
	29:35 ye shall do no servile work *t*.	NIH
	32:40 son of Manasseh; and he dwelt t.	871.1+1886.3

T

Nu	33:53 *of* the land, and dwell **t**:	871.1+1886.3
	35:33 of the blood that is shed **t**,	871.1+1886.3
Dt	2:10 The Emims dwelt **t** in times past,	871.1+1886.3
	2:20 giants dwelt **t** in old time;	871.1+1886.3
	7:25 unto thee, lest thou be snared **t**:	871.1+2050.2
	8:12 and hast built goodly houses, dwelt **t**,	NIH
	10:14 the earth *also*, with all that *is*.	871.1+1886.3
	11:31 ye shall possess it, and dwell **t**.	871.1+1886.3
	13:15 all that *is* **t**, and the cattle	871.1+1886.3
	15:21 if there be *any* blemish **t**, *as if it*	871.1+2050.2
	16: 8 LORD thy God: thou shalt do no work **t**	NIH
	17:14 and shalt dwell **t**, and shalt say,	871.1+1886.3
	17:19 read **t** all the days of his life:	871.1+2050.2
	20:11 all the people that is found **t**	871.1+1886.3
	26: 1 and possessest it, and dwellest **t**;	871.1+1886.3
	28:30 and thou shalt not dwell **t**.	871.1+2050.2
	29:23 nor any grass groweth **t**,	871.1+1886.3
Jos	1: 8 thou shalt meditate **t** day and	871.1+2050.2
	1: 8 according to all that is written **t**:	871.1+2050.2
	6:17 all that *are* **t**, to the LORD:	834+871.1+1886.3
	6:24 city with fire, and all that *was* **t**:	871.1+1886.3
	10:28 and all the souls that *were* **t**;	871.1+1886.3
	10:30 and all the souls that *were* **t**;	871.1+1886.3
	10:32 and all the souls that *were* **t**;	871.1+1886.3
	10:35 the souls that *were* **t** he utterly	871.1+1886.3
	10:37 all the souls that *were* **t**.	871.1+1886.3
	10:37 all the souls that *were* **t**.	871.1+1886.3
	10:39 all the souls that *were* **t**;	871.1+1886.3
	11:11 smote all the souls that *were* **t**	871.1+1886.3
	19:47 dwelt **t**, and called Leshem, Dan,	871.1+1886.3
	19:50 he built the city, and dwelt **t**.	871.1+1886.3
	21:43 they possessed it, and dwelt **t**.	871.1+1886.3
Jdg	2:22 the way of the LORD to walk **t**,	871.1+3963.1
	8:25 cast **t** every man the earrings of	8033+1886.5
	9:45 slew the people that *was* **t**,	871.1+1886.3
	16:30 upon all the people that *were* **t**.	871.1+2050.2
	18: 7 the people that *were* **t**,	7130+871.1+1886.3
	18:28 they built a city, and dwelt **t**.	871.1+1886.3
1Sa	30: 2 women captives, that *were* **t**.	871.1+1886.3
2Sa	12:31 forth the people that *were* **t**,	871.1+1886.3
1Ki	8:16 build a house, that my name might be **t**;	8033
	11:24 **t**, and reigned in Damascus.	871.1+1886.3
	12:25 in mount Ephraim, and dwelt **t**;	871.1+1886.3
2Ki	2:20 Bring me a new cruse, and put salt **t**.	8033
	12: 9 priests that kept the door put **t**	8033+1886.5
	13: 6 made Israel sin, *but* walked **t**.	871.1+1886.3
	13:11 made Israel sin: *but* he walked **t**.	871.1+1886.3
	15:16 all that *were* **t**, and the coasts	871.1+1886.3
	15:16 all the women **t** that were with child he	1886.3
1Ch	16:32 fields rejoice, and all that *is* **t**.	871.1+2050.2
	21:22 build an altar **t** unto the LORD:	871.1+2050.2
2Ch	2: 5 to build him a house to dwell **t**,	871.1+2050.2
	5:10 two tables which Moses put **t** at Horeb,	NIH
	20: 8 dwelt **t**, and have built thee a	871.1+1886.3
	20: 8 thee a sanctuary **t** for thy name,	871.1+1886.3
Ezr	4:19 and sedition have *been* made **t**.	871.2+1886.9
	6: 2 **t** *was* a record thus	1459+871.2+1886.9
Ne	6: 1 *that* there was no breach left **t**;	871.1+1886.3
	7: 4 the people *were* few **t**,	8432+871.1+1886.3
	7: 5 at the first, and found written **t**,	871.1+2050.2
	8: 3 read **t** before the street that *was*	871.1+2050.2
	9: 6 all *things* that *are* **t**, the seas,	5921+1886.3
	9: 6 all that *is* **t**, and thou preservest	871.1+1992.1
	13: 1 **t** was found written, that	871.1+2050.2
	13:16 There dwelt men of Tyre also **t**,	871.1+1886.3
Job	3: 7 let no joyful voice come **t**.	871.1+2050.2
	20:18 restitution *be*, and he shall not rejoice **t**.	NIH
Ps	24: 1 the world, and they that dwell **t**.	871.1+1886.3
	37:29 the land, and dwell **t** for ever.	5921+1886.3
	68:10 Thy congregation hath dwelt **t**:	871.1+1886.3
	69:34 and every *thing* that moveth **t**.	871.1+3963.1
	69:36 that love his name shall dwell **t**.	871.1+1886.3
	96:12 field be joyful, and all that *is* **t**:	871.1+2050.2
	98: 7 the world, and they that dwell **t**.	871.1+1886.3
	104:26 *whom* thou hast made to play **t**.	871.1+1886.3
	107:34 wickedness of them that dwell **t**.	871.1+1886.3
	111: 2 out of all them that have pleasure **t**.	1992.1
	119:35 for **t** do I delight.	871.1+2050.2
	146: 6 earth, the sea, and all that *is*:	871.1+3963.1
Pr	15: 4 **t** *is* a breach in the spirit.	871.1+1886.3
	22:14 is abhorred of the LORD shall fall **t**.	8033
	26:27 Whoso diggeth a pit shall fall **t**:	871.1+2050.2
Ecc	2:21 **t** shall he leave it *for* his portion.	871.1+2050.2
Isa	5: 2 and also made a winepress **t**:	871.1+2050.2
	7: 6 let us make a breach **t** for us, and set a	5089.1
	24: 6 they that dwell **t** are desolate:	871.1+1886.3
	33:24 the people that dwell **t** *shall be*	871.1+1886.3
	34: 1 let the earth hear, and **all that is** **t**:	4393
	34:17 to generation shall they dwell **t**.	871.1+1886.3
	35: 8 though fools, shall not err **t**.	NIH
	42:10 that go down to the sea, and **all that is** **t**;	4393
	44:23 O forest, and every tree **t**:	871.1+2050.2
	51: 3 joy and gladness shall be found **t**,	871.1+1886.3
	51: 6 that dwell **t** shall die in like manner:	1886.3
	59: 8 goeth **t** shall not know peace.	871.1+1886.3
Jer	4:29 and not a man dwell **t**.	871.1+2006.1
	6:16 walk **t**, and ye shall find rest for	871.1+1886.3
	6:16 But they said, We will not walk **t**.	NIH
	8:16 the city, and those that dwell **t**.	871.1+1886.3
	9:13 my voice, neither walked **t**;	871.1+1886.3
	12: 4 wickedness of them that dwell **t**?	871.1+1886.3
	17:24 sabbath day, to do no work **t**;	871.1+2050.2
	23:12 shall be driven on, and fall **t**:	871.1+1886.3
	27:11 they shall till they land, and dwell **t**.	871.1+1886.3

Jer	36: 2 write **t** all the words that I have	413+1886.3
	36:29 Why hast thou written **t**, saying,	5921+1886.3
	36:32 who wrote **t** from the mouth of	5921+1886.3
	44: 2 and no man dwelleth **t**,	871.1+1992.1
	47: 2 shall overflow the land, and **all that is** **t**;	4393
	47: 2 the city, and them that dwell **t**:	871.1+1886.3
	48: 9 without any to dwell **t**.	871.1+2006.1
	50: 3 and none shall dwell **t**:	871.1+1886.3
	50:39 and the owls shall dwell **t**:	871.1+1886.3
	50:40 shall any son of man dwell **t**.	871.1+1886.3
	51:48 and the earth, and all that *is* **t**,	871.1+1992.1
Eze	2: 9 and lo, a roll of a book *was* **t**;	871.1+1886.3
	2:10 *there was* written **t** lamentations,	413+1886.3
	7:20 *and* of their detestable things **t**:	871.1+2050.2
	12:19 land may be desolate from **all that is** **t**,	4393
	12:19 violence of all them that dwell **t**.	871.1+1886.3
	14:22 **t** shall be left a remnant that shall	871.1+1886.3
	20:47 to the north shall be burnt **t**.	871.1+1886.3
	24: 5 seethe the bones of it **t**.	8432+871.1+1886.3
	24: 6 to the pot whose scum *is* **t**,	871.1+1886.3
	28:26 they shall dwell safely **t**,	5921+1886.3
	30:12 **all that is** **t**, by the hand of strangers:	4393
	32:15 shall smite all them that dwell **t**,	871.1+1886.3
	37:25 they shall dwell **t**, *even* they,	5921+1886.3
	40:33 *there were* windows **t** and in	2050.2+3807.1
	42:14 When the priests enter **t**, then shall they	NIH
	44:14 and for all that shall be done **t**.	871.1+1886.3
Da	5: 2 his concubines, might drink **t**.	871.2+1952.1
Hos	4: 3 that dwelleth **t** shall languish,	871.1+1886.3
	14: 9 but the transgressors shall fall **t**.	871.1+3963.1
Am	6: 8 I deliver up the city with **all that is** **t**.	4393
	8: 8 every one mourn that dwelleth **t**?	871.1+1886.3
	9: 5 and all that dwell **t** shall mourn:	871.1+1886.3
Mic	1: 2 hearken, O earth, and **all that is** **t**:	4393
	7:13 desolate because of them that dwell **t**,	1886.3
Na	1: 5 the world, and all that dwell **t**.	871.1+1886.3
Hab	2: 8 the city, and *of* all that dwell **t**.	871.1+1886.3
	2:17 the city, and *of* all that dwell **t**.	871.1+1886.3
	2:18 the maker of his work trusteth **t**,	5921+2050.2
Zec	2: 4 of men and cattle **t**:	8432+871.1+1886.3
	6: 6 The black horses which *are* **t** go	871.1+1886.3
	13: 8 parts **t** shall be cut off *and* die;	871.1+1886.3
	13: 8 die; but the third shall be left **t**.	871.1+1886.3
	14:21 and take of them, and seethe **t**.	871.1+1992.1
Mt	23:21 sweareth by it, and by him that dwelleth **t**.	846
Mk	10:15 as a little child, he shall not enter **t**.	846+1519
	13:15 neither enter **t**, to take any *thing* out of his	NIG
Lk	1:20 And heal the sick that are **t**,	846+1722
	18:17 a little child shall in no wise enter **t**.	846+1519
	19:45 began to cast out them that sold **t**,	846+1722
Jn	12: 6 had the bag, and bare what was put **t**.	NIG
Ac	1:20 be desolate, and let no man dwell **t**:	846+1722
	14:15 and the sea, and all *things* that are **t**:	846+1722
	17:24 that made the world and all *things* **t**,	846+1722
	27: 6 sailing into Italy; and he put us **t**.	846+1519
Ro	1:17 For **t** is the righteousness of God	846+1722
	6: 2 are dead to sin, live any longer **t**?	846+1722
1Co	7:24 he is called, **t** abide with God.	1722+3778
Eph	6:20 that I **t** may speak boldly, as I ought	846+1722
Php	1:18 I do rejoice, yea, and will rejoice.	1722+3778
Col	2: 7 abounding **t** with thanksgiving.	846+1722
Heb	4: 6 it remaineth that some *must* enter **t**,	846+1519
	10: 8 neither hadst pleasure **t**: which are offered	NIG
	13: 9 profited them that have been **occupied** **t**.	4043
Jas	1:25 continueth **t**, he being not a forgetful	NIG
2Pe	2:20 they are again entangled **t**, and overcome,	3778
	3:10 and the works that are **t** shall be burnt up.	1722
Rev	1: 3 those *things* which are written **t**:	846+1722
	10: 6 the *things* that are **t**, and the earth,	846+1722
	10: 6 the *things* that are **t**, and the sea,	846+1722
	10: 6 the sea, and the *things* which are **t**,	846+1722
	11: 1 the altar, and them that worship **t**.	846+1722
	13:12 them which dwell **t** to worship	846+1722
	21:22 And I saw no temple **t**: for the Lord	846+1722

THEREINTO (1) [INTO]

Lk	21:21 that are in the countries enter **t**.	846+1519

THEREOF (908) [OF]

Ge	2:17 in the day that thou eatest **t** thou shalt	4480
	2:19 living creature, that *was* the name **t**.	2050.2
	2:21 ribs, and closed up the flesh instead **t**;	5089.1
	3: 5 know that in the day ye eat **t**,	4480+5105.2
	3: 6 she took of the fruit **t**, and did eat,	2050.2
	4: 4 the firstlings of his flock and of the fat **t**.	2006.1
	6:16 of the ark shalt thou set in the side **t**;	1886.3
	9: 4 flesh with the life **t**, *which is* the blood	2050.2
	9: 4 *which* is the blood **t**, shall you not eat.	2050.2
	40:10 the clusters **t** brought forth ripe grapes:	1886.3
	40:18 and said, This *is* the interpretation **t**:	2050.2
	41: 8 of Egypt, and all the wise men **t**:	1886.3
	45:16 the fame **t** was heard *in* Pharaoh's house,	NIH
	47:21 of Egypt even to the *other* end **t**.	1930.2
Ex	3:20 wonders which I will do in the midst **t**:	2050.2
	5: 8 you shall not diminish *ought* **t**:	4480+5105.2
	9:18 since the foundation **t** even until now.	1886.3
	10:26 for **t** must we take to serve	4480+5105.2
	12: 9 his legs, and with the purtenance **t**.	2050.2
	12:43 There shall no stranger eat **t**:	871.1+2050.2
	12:44 then shall he eat **t**.	871.1+2050.2
	12:45 a hired servant shall not eat **t**.	871.1+2050.2
	12:46 neither shall ye break a bone **t**.	871.1+1886.3
	12:48 uncircumcised person shall eat **t**.	871.1+2050.2
	16:31 the house of Israel called the name **t**	2050.2
	19:18 the smoke **t** ascended as the smoke of a	2050.2

Ex	22:11 owner of it shall accept **t**, and he shall	NIH
	22:12 make restitution unto the owner **t**.	2050.2
	22:14 or die, the owner **t** *being* not with it,	2050.2
	22:15 if the owner **t** *be* with it, he shall not	2050.2
	23:10 thy land, and shalt gather in the fruits **t**:	1886.3
	25: 9 the pattern of all the instruments, even	2050.2
	25:10 cubits and a half *shall be* the length **t**,	2050.2
	25:10 a cubit and a half the breadth **t**,	2050.2
	25:10 a cubit and a half the height **t**.	2050.2
	25:12 it, and put *them* in the four corners **t**;	2050.2
	25:17 cubits and a half *shall be* the length **t**,	1886.3
	25:17 a cubit and a half the breadth **t**.	1886.3
	25:19 make the cherubims on the two ends **t**.	2050.2
	25:23 two cubits *shall be* the length **t**,	2050.2
	25:23 a cubit the breadth **t**, and a cubit and	2050.2
	25:23 a cubit and a half the height **t**.	2050.2
	25:25 golden crown to the border **t** round	2050.2
	25:26 four corners that *are* on the four feet **t**.	2050.2
	25:29 thou shalt make the dishes **t**,	2050.2
	25:29 spoons **t**, and covers thereof,	2050.2
	25:29 and covers **t**, and bowls thereof,	2050.2
	25:29 and covers thereof, and bowls **t**,	2050.2
	25:37 thou shalt make the seven lamps **t**:	1886.3
	25:37 shall light the lamps **t**, that they may	1886.3
	25:38 the tongs **t**, and the snuffdishes thereof,	1886.3
	25:38 the snuffdishes **t**, *shall be* of pure gold.	1886.3
	26:30 **t** which was shewed thee in the mount.	2050.2
	27: 1 and the height **t** *shall be* three cubits.	2050.2
	27: 2 of it upon the four corners **t**:	4480+5105.2
	27: 3 all the vessels **t** thou shalt make *of* brass.	2050.2
	27: 4 four brasen rings in the four corners **t**.	2050.2
	27:10 the twenty pillars **t** and their twenty	2050.2
	27:19 of the tabernacle in all the service **t**,	2050.2
	27:19 the pins **t**, and all the pins of the court,	2050.2
	28: 7 shall have the two shoulderpieces **t** joined	2050.2
	28: 7 *thereof* joined to the two edges **t**;	2050.2
	28: 8 be of the same, according to the work **t**;	1930.2
	28:16 a span *shall be* the length **t**, and a span	2050.2
	28:16 and a span *shall be* the breadth **t**.	2050.2
	28:26 ends of the breastplate in the border **t**,	2050.2
	28:27 towards the forepart **t**, over against	2050.2
	28:27 over against the *other* coupling **t**,	2050.2
	28:28 **t** unto the rings of the ephod with a lace	2050.2
	28:32 be a hole in the top of it, in the midst **t**:	2050.2
	28:33 and of scarlet, round about the hem **t**;	2050.2
	29:33 a stranger shall not eat **t**, because they *are*	NIH
	29:41 according to the drink offering **t**	1886.3+3807.1
	30: 2 A cubit *shall be* the length **t**, and a cubit	2050.2
	30: 2 thereof, and a cubit the breadth **t**;	2050.2
	30: 2 two cubits *shall be* the height **t**: the	2050.2
	30: 2 the horns **t** *shall be* of the same.	2050.2
	30: 3 the top **t**, and the sides thereof round	2050.2
	30: 3 the sides **t** round about, and the horns	2050.2
	30: 3 thereof round about, and the horns **t**;	2050.2
	30: 4 the two corners **t**, upon the two sides	2050.2
	30:37 according to the composition **t**:	1886.3
	36: 2 ark, and the staves **t**, *with* the mercy	2050.2
	36:29 coupled together at the head **t**, to one	2050.2
	37: 6 two cubits and a half *was* the length **t**,	1886.3
	37: 6 and one cubit and a half the breadth **t**.	1886.3
	37: 8 he the cherubims on the two ends **t**;	2050.2
	37:10 two cubits *was* the length **t**, and a cubit	2050.2
	37:10 a cubit the breadth **t**, and a cubit and	2050.2
	37:10 and a cubit and a half the height **t**.	2050.2
	37:12 made a crown of gold for the border **t**.	2050.2
	37:13 four corners that *were* in the four feet **t**.	2050.2
	37:18 six branches going out of the sides **t**;	1886.3
	37:18 of the candlestick out of the one side **t**,	1886.3
	37:18 of the candlestick out of the other side **t**:	1886.3
	37:24 gold made he it, and all the vessels **t**.	1886.3
	37:25 of it; the horns **t** were of the same.	2050.2
	37:26 sides **t** round about, and the horns of	2050.2
	37:27 rings of gold for it under the crown **t**,	2050.2
	37:27 two corners of it, upon the two sides **t**,	2050.2
	38: 1 five cubits *was* the length **t**,	2050.2
	38: 1 and five cubits the breadth **t**;	2050.2
	38: 1 and three cubits the height **t**.	2050.2
	38: 2 made the horns **t** on the four corners of	2050.2
	38: 2 of it; the horns **t** were of the same:	2050.2
	38: 3 all the vessels **t** made he *of* brass.	2050.2
	38: 4 compass **t** beneath unto the midst of it.	2050.2
	39: 5 of the same, according to the work **t**;	1930.2
	39: 9 a span *was* the length **t**, and a span	2050.2
	39: 9 a span the breadth **t**, *being* doubled.	2050.2
	39:20 of it, over against the *other* coupling **t**,	2050.2
	39:35 and the staves **t**, and the mercy seat,	2050.2
	39:36 all the vessels **t**, and the shewbread,	2050.2
	39:37 The pure candlestick, *with* the lamps **t**,	1886.3
	39:37 all the vessels **t**, and the oil for light,	1886.3
	40: 4 in the candlestick, and light the lamps **t**.	1886.3
	40: 9 shalt hallow it, and all the vessels **t**:	2050.2
	40:18 set up the boards **t**, and put in the bars	2050.2
	40:18 put in the bars **t**, and reared up his	2050.2
Lev	1:15 blood **t** shall be wrung out at the side	2050.2
	1:17 he shall cleave it with the wings **t**,	2050.2
	2: 2 take thereout his handful of the flour **t**,	1886.3
	2: 2 of the oil **t**, with all the frankincense	1886.3
	2: 2 all thereof, with all the frankincense **t**;	1886.3
	2: 9 from the meat offering a memorial **t**,	1886.3
	2:16 *part* of the beaten corn **t**, and *part* of	1886.3
	2:16 corn thereof, and *part* of the oil **t**,	1886.3
	2:16 oil thereof, with all the frankincense **t**:	1886.3
	3: 8 Aaron's sons shall sprinkle the blood **t**	2050.2
	3: 9 the fat **t**, and the whole rump, it shall	2050.2
	3:13 the blood **t** upon the altar round about.	2050.2

Lev 3:14 he shall offer t his offering, 4480+5105.2
4:30 the priest shall take of the blood t with 1886.3
4:30 shall pour out all the blood t at 1886.3
4:31 shall take away all the fat t, as the fat 1886.3
4:34 shall pour out all the blood t at 1886.3
4:35 shall take away all the fat t, as the fat 1886.3
5:12 a memorial t, and burn *it* on the altar, 1886.3
6:15 of the oil t, and all the frankincense 1886.3
6:16 the remainder t shall Aaron and 4480+5089.1
6:20 of it in the morning, and half t at night. 1886.3
6:27 Whatsoever shall touch the flesh t shall 1886.3
6:27 when there is sprinkled of the blood t 1886.3
6:29 the males among the priests shall eat t: 1886.3
7: 2 blood t shall he sprinkle round about 2050.2
7: 3 he shall offer of it all the fat t; the rump, 2050.2
7: 6 Every male among the priests shall eat t: 5105.2
7:19 for the flesh, all that be clean shall eat t. 1320
8:11 sprinkled t upon the altar seven 4480+5089.1
9:13 him, with the pieces t, and the head: 1886.3
9:17 took a handful t, and burnt *it* 4480+5089.1
11:39 he that toucheth the carcase t shall 1886.3
13: 4 and the hair t be not turned white; 1886.3
13:18 in which, *even* in the skin t, was a boil, 3588
13:20 the skin, and the hair t be turned white; 1886.3
14:45 the timber t, and all the morter of 2050.2
17:13 he shall even pour out the blood t, 2050.2
17:14 all flesh; the blood of it *is* for the life t: 2050.2
17:14 for the life of all flesh *is* the blood t: 2050.2
18:25 I do visit the iniquity t upon it, 1886.3
19:23 shall count the fruit t as uncircumcised: 2050.2
19:24 in the fourth year all the fruit t shall be 2050.2
19:25 the fifth year shall ye eat of the fruit t, 2050.2
19:25 *it* may yield unto you the increase t: 2050.2
22:13 but there shall no stranger eat t. 871.1+2050.2
22:14 he shall put the fifth *part* t unto it, 2050.2
22:24 neither shall you make *any* offering t in NIH
23:10 shall reap the harvest t, then ye shall 1886.3
23:13 the meat offering t *shall be* two tenth 2050.2
23:13 the drink offering t *shall be* of wine, 1886.4
24: 5 take fine flour, and bake twelve cakes t: 1886.3
25: 3 thy vineyard, and gather in the fruit t; 1886.3
25: 7 thy land, shall all the increase t be meat. 1886.3
25:10 *all* the land unto all the inhabitants t. 1886.3
25:12 shall eat the increase t out of the field. 1886.3
25:16 of years thou shalt increase the price t, 2050.2
25:27 let him count the years of the sale t, 2050.2
27:10 then it and the exchange t shall be holy. 2050.2
27:13 he shall add a fifth *part* t unto thy 2050.2
27:16 shall be according to the seed t: 2050.2
27:21 the possession t shall be the priest's. 2050.2
27:31 he shall add thereto the fifth *part* t. 2050.2
27:33 both it and the change t shall be holy; 2050.2
Nu 1:50 over all the vessels t, and over all 2050.2
1:50 the tabernacle, and all the vessels t; 2050.2
2: 6 those that were numbered t, *were* fifty 2050.2
2: 8 those that were numbered t, *were* fifty 2050.2
2:11 those that were numbered t, *were* forty 2050.2
3:25 the covering t, and the hanging for 1930.2
3:26 and the cords of it for all the service t. 2050.2
3:31 and the hanging, and all the service t. 2050.2
3:36 the bars t, and the pillars thereof, 2050.2
3:36 the pillars t, and the sockets thereof, 2050.2
3:36 sockets t, and all the vessels thereof, 2050.2
3:36 all the vessels t, and all that serveth 2050.2
4: 6 of blue, and shall put in the staves t. 2050.2
4: 8 and shall put in the staves t. 2050.2
4: 9 his snuffdishes, and all the oil vessels t, 1886.3
4:10 all the vessels t within a covering of 1886.3
4:11 and shall put to the staves t: 2050.2
4:14 they shall put upon it all the vessels t, 2050.2
4:16 is, in the sanctuary, and in the vessels t. 2050.2
4:31 the bars t, and the pillars thereof, 2050.2
4:31 and the pillars t, and sockets thereof, 2050.2
4:31 the pillars thereof, and sockets t, 2050.2
5: 7 his trespass with the principal t, 2050.2
5: 7 add unto it the fifth *part* t, and give *it* 2050.2
5:26 *even* the memorial t, and burn *it* upon 1886.3
7: 1 sanctified it, and all the instruments t, 2050.2
7: 1 both the altar and all the vessels t, 2050.2
7:13 the weight t *was* an hundred and 1886.3
8: 3 he lighted the lamps t over against 1886.3
8: 4 the shaft t, unto the flowers thereof, 1886.3
8: 4 unto the flowers t, *was* beaten work: 1886.3
8:25 shall cease waiting upon the service t, NIH
9: 3 according to all the ceremonies t, shall 2050.2
9:14 according to the manner t, so shall he 2050.2
11: 7 the colour t as the colour of bdellium. 2050.2
13:32 a land that eateth up the inhabitants t; 1886.3
18:28 ye shall give the LORD's heave 4480+5105.2
18:29 of all the best t, *even* the hallowed *part* 2050.2
18:29 *even* the hallowed *part* t out of it. 2050.2
18:30 When ye have heaved the best t from it, 2050.2
21:25 in Heshbon, and in all the villages t. 1886.3
21:32 they took the villages t, and drove out 1886.3
26:56 to the lot shall the possession t 1886.3
28: 7 the drink offering t *shall be* the fourth 2050.2
28: 8 morning, and as the drink offering t, 2050.2
28: 9 with oil, and the drink offering t: 2050.2
29:19 the meat offering t, and their drink 1886.3
32:33 the land, with the cities t in the coasts, 1886.3
32:41 and took the small towns t, 1992.1
32:42 and the villages t, and called it Nobah, 1886.3
34: 2 the land of Canaan with the coasts t:) 1886.3
34: 3 the going forth t shall be from the south 2050.2
34:12 this shall be your land with the coasts t 1886.3

Dt 3:11 nine cubits *was* the length t, 1886.3
3:12 half mount Gilead, and the cities t, gave 2050.2
3:17 the coast t, from Chinnereth even unto NIH
9:21 I cast the dust t into the brook that 2050.2
12:15 the unclean and the clean may eat t, as 5105.2
13:15 and all that *is* therein, and the cattle t, 1886.3
13:16 spoil of it into the midst of the street t, 1886.3
13:16 all the spoil t every whit, for the LORD 1886.3
15:23 Only thou shalt not eat the blood t: 2050.2
20:13 thou shalt smite every male t with 1886.3
20:14 all that is in the city, *even* all the spoil t, 1886.3
20:19 thou shalt not destroy the trees t by 1886.3
26:14 not eaten t in my mourning, 4480+5105.2
26:14 have I taken away *ought* t 4480+5105.2
26:14 nor given *ought* t for the dead: 4480+5105.1
28:30 and shalt not gather the grapes t. 5105.2
28:31 eyes, and thou shalt not eat t: 4480+5105.2
29:23 *And that* the whole land t *is* brimstone, 1886.3
33:16 things of the earth and fulness t, 1886.3
Jos 6: 2 king t, *and* the mighty *men* of valour. 1886.3
6:26 he shall lay the foundation t in his 5089.1
7:14 shall come according to the families t, NIH
8: 2 only the spoil t, and the cattle thereof, 1886.3
8: 2 only the spoil thereof, and the cattle t, 1886.3
9: 1 the Hivite, and the Jebusite, heard t, NIH
10: 2 than Ai, and all the men t *were* mighty. 1886.3
10:28 the king t he utterly destroyed, them, 1886.3
10:30 the king t, into the hand of Israel; 1886.3
10:30 unto the king t as he did unto the king 1886.3
10:37 the king t, and all the cities thereof, 1886.3
10:37 the cities t, and all the souls that *were* 1886.3
10:39 and the king t, and all the cities thereof; 1886.3
10:39 and the king thereof, and all the cities t; 1886.3
10:39 so he did to Debir, and to the king t; 1886.3
11:10 and smote the king t with the sword: 1886.3
13:23 the border t. This *was* the inheritance of NIH
13:23 their families, the cities and villages t. 2006.1
15: 7 and the goings out t were at En-rogel: 2050.2
15:12 the coast t. This is the coast of the children NIH
15:47 and the great sea, and the border t. NIH
16: 3 and the goings out t are at the sea. 2050.2
16: 8 and the goings out t are at the sea. 2050.2
18:12 the goings out t were at the wilderness of NIH
18:14 the goings out t were at Kirjath-baal, 2050.2
18:20 by the coasts t round about, according to 1886.3
19:14 the outgoings t are *in* the valley of 2050.2
19:29 the outgoings t are at the sea from 2050.2
19:33 and the outgoings t were at Jordan: 2050.2
21: 2 with the suburbs t for our cattle. 2006.1
21:11 with the suburbs t round about it. 1886.3
21:12 the fields of the city, and the villages t, 1886.3
22: 7 unto the *other* half t gave Joshua among 2050.2
23:14 and not one thing hath failed t. 4480+5105.2
Jdg 1:18 Also Judah took Gaza with the coast t, 1886.3
1:18 Askelon with the coast t, and Ekron 1886.3
1:18 thereof, and Ekron with the coast t. 1886.3
1:26 built a city, and called the name t Luz: 1886.3
1:26 which *is* the name t unto this day. 1886.3
3: 2 the least such as before knew nothing t: 3963.1
5:23 curse ye bitterly the inhabitants t, 1886.3
7:15 the interpretation t, that he worshipped, 2050.2
8:14 the elders t, *even* threescore 1886.3
8:27 Gideon made an ephod t, and put it in 2050.2
14: 9 took t in his hands, and went on eating, NIH
15:19 wherefore he called the name t 1886.3
17: 4 made t a graven image and a molten 1930.2
1Sa 5: 6 *even* Ashdod and the coasts t. 1886.3
6: 1 offering, in a coffer by the side t; 2050.2
7:14 the coasts t did Israel deliver out of 4993.1
17:51 drew it out of the sheath t, and slew 1886.3
20:20 I will shoot three arrows on the side t, NIH
28:24 and did bake unleavened bread t: 1930.2
2Sa 20: 8 fastened upon his loins in the sheath t; 1886.3
23:16 nevertheless he would not drink t, 3963.1
1Ki 2:32 my father David not knowing t, *to wit*, NIH
3:27 in no wise slay it: she *is* the mother t. 2050.2
6: 2 the length t *was* threescore cubits, 2050.2
6: 2 breadth t twenty *cubits*, and the height 2050.2
6: 2 and the height t thirty cubits. 2050.2
6: 3 twenty cubits *was* the length t, 2050.2
6: 3 ten cubits *was* the breadth t before 2050.2
6:20 and twenty cubits in the height t: 2050.2
6:38 finished throughout all the parts t, 2050.2
7: 2 the length t *was* an hundred cubits, 2050.2
7: 2 breadth t fifty cubits, and the height 2050.2
7: 2 cubits, and the height t thirty cubits, 2050.2
7: 6 the length t *was* fifty cubits, 2050.2
7: 6 and the breadth t thirty cubits: 2050.2
7:21 pillar, and called the name t Jachin: 2050.2
7:21 left pillar, and called the name t Boaz. 2050.2
7:26 brim t was wrought like the brim of a 1886.3
7:27 four cubits the breadth t, and three 1886.3
7:30 the four corners t had undersetters: 2050.2
7:31 the mouth t *was* round *after* the work 1886.3
7:35 on the top of the base the ledges t and 1886.3
7:35 and the borders t *were* of the same. 1886.3
7:36 For on the plates of the ledges t, 1886.3
7:36 on the borders t, he graved cherubims, 1886.3
8: 7 covered the ark and the staves t above. 2050.2
13:26 him back from the way heard t, he said, NIH
15:21 when Baasha heard t, that he left off NIH
15:22 the timber t, wherewith Baasha had NIH
16:34 he laid the foundation t in Abiram his 1886.3
16:34 set up the gates t in his youngest *son* 1886.3
17:13 make me t a little cake first, 4480+8033

2Ki 2:12 chariot of Israel, and the horsemen t. 2050.2
3:25 in Kir-haraseth left *they* the stones t; 1886.3
4:39 gathered t wild gourds his lap full 4480+5105.2
4:40 death in the pot. And they could not eat t. NIH
4:42 and full ears of corn in the husk t. 2050.2
4:43 They shall eat, and shall leave t. NIH
4:44 left t, according to the word of the LORD. NIH
7: 2 with thine eyes, but shalt not eat t. 4480+8033
7:19 with thine eyes, but shalt not eat t. 4480+8033
13:14 chariot of Israel, and the horsemen t. 2050.2
15:16 and the coasts t from Tirzah: 1886.3
16:10 according to all the workmanship t. 1930.2
17:24 and dwelt in the cities t. 1886.3
18: 8 *even* unto Gaza, and the borders t, 1886.3
19:23 will cut down the tall cedar trees t, 2050.2
19:23 trees thereof, *and* the choice fir trees t: 2050.2
19:29 and plant vineyards, and eat the fruits t. 3963.1
22:16 this place, and upon the inhabitants t, 2050.2
22:19 against the inhabitants t, that *they* 2050.2
23: 6 cast the powder t upon the graves of 1886.3
1Ch 2:23 them, with Kenath, and the towns t. 1886.3
6:55 and the suburbs t round about it. 1886.3
6:56 the fields of the city, and the villages t, 1886.3
7:28 were, Beth-el and the towns t, 1886.3
7:28 and westward Gezer, with the towns t; 1886.3
7:28 Shechem also and the towns t, unto 1886.3
7:28 thereof, unto Gaza and the towns t: 1886.3
8:12 built Ono, and Lod, with the towns t: 1886.3
9:27 the opening *every* morning pertained to NIH
16:32 Let the sea roar, and the fulness t: 2050.2
21:27 put up his sword again into the sheath t. 1886.3
23:26 nor any vessels of it for the service t. 2050.2
28:11 of the houses t, and of the treasuries 2050.2
28:11 of the treasuries t, and of the upper 2050.2
28:11 the upper chambers t, and of the inner 2050.2
28:11 the inner parlours t, and of the place of 2050.2
28:15 every candlestick, and *for* the lamps t: 1886.3
28:15 candlestick, and *also for* the lamps t, 1886.3
2Ch 3: 7 and the walls t, and the doors thereof, 2050.2
3: 7 thereof, and the doors t, with gold; 2050.2
3: 8 and the breadth t twenty cubits: 2050.2
4: 1 twenty cubits the length t, 2050.2
4: 1 twenty cubits the breadth t, and ten 2050.2
4: 1 and ten cubits the height t. 2050.2
4: 2 in compass, and five cubits the height t; 2050.2
4:22 inner doors t for the most holy *place*, 2050.2
5: 8 covered the ark and the staves t above. 2050.2
13:11 the candlestick of gold with the lamps t, 1886.3
13:19 Beth-el with the towns t, and Jeshanah 1886.3
13:19 Jeshanah with the towns t, and Ephrain 1886.3
13:19 and Ephrain with the towns t. 1886.3
16: 6 the timber t, wherewith Baasha was a 1886.3
28:18 Shocho with the villages t, and Timnah 1886.3
28:18 Timnah with the villages t, Gimzo also 1886.3
28:18 Gimzo also with the villages t: 1886.3
29:18 all the vessels t, and the shewbread 2050.2
29:18 shewbread table, with all the vessels t. 2050.2
32: 1 the establishment t, Sennacherib king of NIH
34:24 this place, and upon the inhabitants t, 2050.2
34:27 against the inhabitants t, 2050.2
36:19 burnt all the palaces t with fire, 1886.3
36:19 and destroyed all the goodly vessels t. 1886.3
Ezr 4:12 have set up the walls t, and joined NIH
4:16 be builded *again*, and the walls t set up, 1886.7
6: 3 *let* the foundations *be* strongly laid; 1958.2
6: 3 the height t threescore cubits, 1886.8
6: 3 *and* the breadth t threescore cubits; 1886.8
9: 9 repair the desolations t, and to give us 2050.2
10:14 elders of every city, and the judges t, 1886.3
Ne 1: 3 and the gates t are burnt with fire. 1886.3
2: 3 and the gates t are consumed with fire? 1886.7
2:13 the gates t were consumed with fire. 1886.3
2:17 and the gates t are burnt with fire: 1886.3
3: 3 who *also* laid the beams t, and set up 1930.2
3: 3 set up the doors t, the locks thereof, 2050.2
3: 3 the locks t, and the bars thereof. 2050.2
3: 3 the locks thereof, and the bars t. 2050.2
3: 6 laid the beams t, and set up the doors 1930.2
3: 6 up the doors t, and the locks thereof, 2050.2
3: 6 and the locks t, and the bars thereof. 2050.2
3: 6 and the locks thereof, and the bars t. 2050.2
3:13 they built it, and set up the doors t, 2050.2
3:13 the locks t, and the bars thereof, 2050.2
3:13 the bars t, and a thousand cubits on 2050.2
3:14 he built it, and set up the doors t, 2050.2
3:14 the locks t, and the bars thereof. 2050.2
3:14 the locks thereof, and the bars t. 2050.2
3:15 and covered it, and set up the doors t, 2050.2
3:15 the locks t, and the bars thereof, 2050.2
3:15 the bars t, and the wall of the pool of 2050.2
4: 6 wall was joined together unto the half t: 1886.3
6:16 that when all our enemies heard t, NIH
9:36 gavest unto our fathers to eat the fruit t 1886.3
9:36 to eat the fruit thereof and the good t, 1886.3
11:25 *in* the villages t, and at Dibon, and *in* 1886.3
11:25 *in* the villages t, and at Jekabzeel, 1886.3
11:25 and at Jekabzeel, and *in* the villages t, 1886.3
11:27 and at Beer-sheba, and *in* the villages t, 1886.3
11:28 and at Mekonah, and in the villages t, 1886.3
11:30 fields t, *at* Azekah, and in the villages 1886.3
11:30 at Azekah, and *in* the villages t. 1886.3
13:14 house of my God, and for the offices t. 2050.2
Est 1:22 province according to the writing t, 1886.3
2:22 Esther certified the king *t* in Mordecai's NIH
3:12 province according to the writing t, 1886.3

Est
8: 9 the three and twentieth *day* t; 871.1+2050.2
8: 9 province according to the writing t, 1886.3
9:18 together on the thirteenth *day* t, 871.1+2050.2
9:18 and on the fourteenth t; 871.1+2050.2

Job
3: 9 Let the stars of the twilight t be dark; 2050.2
4:12 and mine ear received a little t. 4480+1930.2
4:16 but I could not discern the form t: 1930.2
9: 6 of her place, and the pillars t tremble. 1886.3
9:24 he covereth the faces of the judges t; 1886.3
11: 9 The measure t *is* longer than the earth, 1886.3
14: 7 that the tender branch t will not cease. 2050.2
14: 8 Though the root t wax old in the earth, 2050.2
14: 8 and the stock t die in the ground; 2050.2
15:29 neither shall he prolong the perfection t 3963.1
24: 2 violently take away flocks, and feed *t*. NIH
24:13 they know not the ways t, nor abide in 2050.2
24:13 ways thereof, nor abide in the paths t 2050.2
26: 5 under the waters, and the inhabitants t. 1992.1
28:13 Man knoweth not the price t; neither is 1886.3
28:15 shall silver be weighed *for* the price t. 1886.3
28:22 have heard the fame t with our ears. 1886.3
28:23 God understandeth the way t, 1886.3
28:23 thereof, and he knoweth the place t. 1886.3
31:17 the fatherless hath not eaten t; 4480+5089.1
31:38 or that the furrows likewise t complain; 1886.3
31:39 I have eaten the fruits t without money, 1886.3
31:39 caused the owners t to lose their life: 1886.3
36:27 down rain according to the vapour t. 2050.2
36:33 The noise t sheweth concerning it, 2050.2
38: 5 Who hath laid the measures t, if thou 1886.3
38: 6 Whereupon are the foundations t 1886.3
38: 6 or who laid the corner stone t; 1886.3
38: 9 When I made the cloud the garment t, 2050.2
38:19 *as for* darkness, where *is* the place t, 2050.2
38:20 thou shouldest take it to the bound t, 2050.2
38:20 know the paths to the house t? 2050.2
38:33 thou set the dominion t in the earth? 2050.2

Ps
19: 6 and there is nothing hid from the heat t. 2050.2
24: 1 earth *is* the LORD's, and the fulness t; 1886.3
34: 2 The humble shall hear *t*, and be glad. NIH
46: 3 the waters t roar *and* be troubled, 2050.2
46: 3 mountains shake with the swelling t. 2050.2
48:12 go round about her: tell the towers t. 1886.3
50: 1 rising of the sun unto the going down t. 2050.2
50:12 for the world *is* mine, and the fulness t. 1886.3
55:10 night they go about it upon the walls t: 1886.3
55:11 Wickedness *is* in the midst t: deceit and 1886.3
60: 2 heal the breaches t; for it shaketh. 1886.3
65:10 *Thou* waterest the ridges t abundantly: 1886.3
65:10 settlest the furrows t: thou makest it 1886.3
65:10 thou blessest the springing t. 1886.3
71:15 all the day; for I know not the numbers *t*. NIH
72:16 the fruit t shall shake like Lebanon: 2050.2
74: 6 they break down the carved work t 1886.3
75: 3 and all the inhabitants t *are* dissolved: 1886.3
75: 8 the dregs t, all the wicked of the earth 1886.3
80:10 boughs t *were like* the goodly cedars. 1886.3
89: 9 the waves t arise, thou stillest them. 2050.2
89:11 *as for* the world and the fulness t, 1886.3
96:11 glad; let the sea roar, and the fulness t. 2050.2
97: 1 let the multitude of isles be glad *t*. NIH
98: 7 Let the sea roar, and the fulness t; 2050.2
102:14 in her stones, and favour the dust t. 1886.3
103:16 and the place t shall know it no more. 2050.2
107:25 which lifteth up the waves t. 2050.2
107:29 a calm, so that the waves t are still. 1992.1
137: 2 harps upon the willows in the midst t. 1886.3
137: 7 rase *it*, *even* to the foundation t. 871.1+1886.3

Pr
1:19 taketh away the life of the owners t. 2050.2
3:14 of silver, and the gain t than fine gold. 1886.3
12:28 and *in* the pathway t *there is* no death. NIH
14:12 but the end t *are* the ways of death. 1886.3
16:25 but the end t *are* the ways of death. 1886.3
16:33 the whole disposing t *is* of the LORD. 2050.2
18:21 and they that love it shall eat the fruit t. 1886.3
20:21 but the end t shall not be blessed. 1886.3
21:22 down the strength of the confidence t. 1886.3
24:31 *and* nettles had covered the face t, 2050.2
24:31 and the stone wall t was broken down. 2050.2
25: 8 *thou know not* what to do in the end t, 1886.3
27:18 keepeth the fig tree shall eat the fruit t: 1886.3
28: 2 of a land many *are* the princes t: 1886.3
28: 2 knowledge the state *t* shall be prolonged. NIH

Ecc
5:11 what good *is there* to the owners t, 1886.3
5:13 *namely,* riches kept for the owners t to 2050.2
5:19 hath given him power to eat t, 4480+5105.2
6: 2 giveth him not power to eat t, 4480+5105.2
7: 8 the end of a thing than the beginning t: 2050.2

SS
1:12 my spikenard sendeth forth the smell t. 2050.2
3:10 made the pillars t *of* silver, the bottom 2050.2
3:10 the bottom t *of* gold, the covering of it 2050.2
3:10 the midst t being paved *with* love, 2050.2
4:16 garden, *that* the spices t may flow out. 2050.2
7: 8 I will take hold of the boughs t: 2050.2
8: 6 the coals t *are* coals of fire, *which hath a* 1886.3
8:11 every one for the fruit t was to bring a 2050.2
8:12 those that keep the fruit t two hundred. 2050.2

Isa
3:14 ancients of his people, and the princes t: 2050.2
4: 4 the midst t by the spirit of judgment, 1886.3
5: 2 gathered out the stones t, and planted it 1930.2
5: 5 I *will* take away the hedge t, and it shall 2050.2
5: 5 break down the wall t, and it shall be 2050.2
5:30 the light is darkened in the heavens t. 1886.3
6:13 the holy seed *shall be* the substance t. 1886.3
13: 9 he shall destroy the sinners t out of it. 1886.3

13:10 the constellations t shall not give their 1992.1
14:17 a wilderness, and destroyed the cities t; 2050.2
15: 8 the howling t unto Eglaim, 1886.3
15: 8 and the howling *unto* Beer-elim. 1886.3
16: 8 have broken down the principal plants t, 1886.3
17: 6 *or* five in the outmost fruitful branches t, 1886.3
19: 3 spirit of Egypt shall fail in the midst t: 2050.2
19: 3 and I will destroy the counsel t: 2050.2
19:10 they shall be broken *in* the purposes t, 1886.3
19:13 *they that are* the stay of the tribes t. 1886.3
19:14 mingled a perverse spirit in the midst t: 1886.3
19:14 caused Egypt to err in every work t, 1930.2
19:17 every one that maketh mention t shall 1886.3
19:19 and a pillar at the border t to the LORD. 1886.3
21: 2 all the sighing t have I made to cease. 1886.3
22:11 ye have not looked unto the Maker t, 1886.3
23:11 *city,* to destroy the strong holds t. 1886.3
23:13 they set up the towers t, they raised up 2050.2
23:13 they raised up the palaces t; 1886.3
24: 1 and scattereth abroad the inhabitants t. 1886.3
24: 5 also is defiled under the inhabitants t; 1886.3
24:20 transgression t shall be heavy upon it; 1886.3
27:10 lie down, and consume the branches t. 1886.3
27:11 When the boughs t are withered, 1886.3
28:25 When he hath made plain the face t, 1886.3
30:27 his anger, and the burden *t is* heavy: NIH
30:33 the pile t *is* fire and much wood; 1886.3
31: 4 fight for mount Zion, and for the hill t. 1886.3
33:20 not one of the stakes t shall ever be 2050.2
33:20 shall any of the cords t be broken. 2050.2
34: 9 the streams t shall be turned into pitch, 1886.3
34: 9 the dust t into brimstone, and the land 1886.3
34: 9 the land t shall become burning pitch. 1886.3
34:10 day; the smoke t shall go up for ever: 1886.3
34:12 They shall call the nobles t *to* 1886.3
34:13 nettles and brambles in the fortresses t: 1886.3
37:24 I will cut down the tall cedars t, 2050.2
37:24 cedars thereof, *and* the choice fir trees t: 2050.2
37:30 and plant vineyards, and eat the fruit t. 3963.1
40: 6 all the goodliness t *is* as the flower of 2050.2
40:16 nor the beasts t sufficient *for* a burnt 2050.2
40:22 the inhabitants t *are* as grasshoppers; 1886.3
41: 9 called thee from the chief men t, 1886.3
42:10 therein; the isles, and the inhabitants t. 1992.1
42:11 cities t lift up *their voice,* the villages 2050.2
44:15 for he will take t, 4480+1992.1
44:16 He burneth part t in the fire; with part 1992.1
44:16 with part t he eateth flesh; he roasteth 2050.2
44:17 the residue t he maketh a god, *even* his 2050.2
44:19 I have baked bread upon the coals t; 2050.2
44:19 have made the residue t an abomination? 2050.2
44:26 and I will raise up the decayed places t: 1886.3
48:19 offspring of thy bowels like the gravel t; 2050.2
62: 1 until the righteousness t go forth as 1886.3
62: 1 the salvation t as a lamp *that* burneth. 1886.3

Jer
1:13 and the face t *is* towards the north. 2050.2
1:15 against all the walls t round about, 1886.3
1:18 against the princes t, against the priests 1886.3
1:18 against the priests t, and against 1886.3
2: 7 eat the fruit t and the goodness thereof; 1886.3
2: 7 the fruit thereof and the goodness t; 1886.3
4:26 all the cities t were broken down at 2050.2
5: 1 know, and seek in the broad places t, 1886.3
5:22 though the waves t toss themselves, 2050.2
5:31 *it* so: and what will ye do in the end t? 1886.3
6:24 We have heard the fame t: our hands 2050.2
11:19 Let us destroy the tree with the fruit t, 2050.2
14: 2 mourneth, and the gates t languish; 1886.3
14: 8 Israel, the saviour t in time of trouble, 2050.2
17:27 will I kindle a fire in the gates t, 1886.3
19: 8 and hiss because of all the plagues t. 1886.3
19:12 to the inhabitants t, and *even* make this 2050.2
20: 5 all the labours t, and all the precious 1886.3
20: 5 all the precious things t, and all 1886.3
21:14 I will kindle a fire in the forest t, 1886.3
23:14 and the inhabitants t as Gomorrah. 1886.3
25: 9 against the inhabitants t, and against all 1886.3
25:18 and the kings t, *and* the princes thereof, 1886.3
25:18 and the kings thereof, *and* the princes t, 1886.3
26:15 this city, and upon the inhabitants t: 1886.3
29: 7 for in the peace t shall ye have peace. 1886.3
30:18 palace shall remain after the manner t. 2050.2
31:23 in the land of Judah and in the cities t, 2050.2
31:24 *in* all the cities t together, husbandmen, 2050.2
31:35 divideth the sea when the waves t 2050.2
33: 2 Thus saith the LORD the maker t, 2050.2
33:12 without beast, and in all the cities t, 2050.2
34: 1 and against all the cities t, saying, 1886.3
34:18 twain, and passed between the parts t, 1886.3
46: 8 the city and the inhabitants t. 871.1+1886.3
46:22 The voice t shall go like a serpent; 1886.3
48: 9 for the cities t shall be desolate, without 1886.3
48:38 housetops of Moab, and in the streets t: 1886.3
49:13 all the cities t shall be perpetual wastes. 1886.3
49:17 and shall hiss at all the plagues t. 1886.3
49:18 Gomorrah and the neighbour *cities* t, 1886.3
49:21 the noise t was heard in the Red sea. 1886.3
49:32 will bring their calamity from all sides t, 1886.3
50:29 round about; let none t escape: 1886.3+3807.1
50:40 Gomorrah and the neighbour *cities* t, 1886.3
51:28 the captains t, and all the rulers thereof, 1886.3
51:28 all the rulers t, and all the land of his 1886.3
51:42 with the multitude of the waves t. 2050.2
52:21 and the thickness t *was* four fingers: 2050.2

La
2: 2 polluted the kingdom and the princes t. 1886.3

4:11 and it hath devoured the foundations t. 1886.3

Eze
1: 4 of the midst t as the colour of amber, 1886.3
1: 5 out of the midst t *came* the likeness 1886.3
4: 9 in one vessel, and make thee bread t, 3963.1
4: 9 and ninety days shalt thou eat t. 5105.2
5: 3 Thou shalt also take t a few in 4480+8033
5: 4 shall a fire come forth into all 4480+5105.2
7:12 for wrath *is* upon all the multitude t. 1886.3
7:13 *is* touching the whole multitude t, 1886.3
7:14 for my wrath *is* upon all the multitude t. 1886.3
9: 4 that be done in the midst t. 1886.3
10: 7 took *t*, and put *it* into the hands of *him* NIH
11: 6 ye have filled the streets t *with* the slain. 1886.3
11: 9 I will bring you out of the midst t, 1886.3
11:11 shall ye be the flesh in the midst t; 1886.3
11:18 take away all the detestable things t 1886.3
11:18 and all the abominations t from thence. 1886.3
13:14 so that the foundation t shall be 2050.2
13:14 ye shall be consumed in the midst t: 1886.3
14:13 break the staff of the bread t, 1886.3+3807.1
15: 3 Shall wood be taken t to do *any* 4480+5105.2
17: 6 and the roots t were under him: 1886.3
17: 9 he not pull up the roots t, and cut off 1886.3
17: 9 and cut off the fruit t, that it wither? 1886.3
17: 9 people to pluck it up by the roots t. 1886.3
17:12 hath taken the king t, and the princes 1886.3
17:12 the princes t, and led them with him to 1886.3
17:23 in the shadow of the branches t shall 1886.3
19: 7 the land was desolate, and the fulness t, 1886.3
20:29 name is called Bamah unto this day. 1886.3
22:21 and ye shall be melted in the midst t, 1886.3
22:22 so shall ye be melted in the midst t; 1886.3
22:25 of her prophets in the midst t, 1886.3
22:25 made her many widows in the midst t. 1886.3
22:27 princes in the midst t *are* like wolves 1886.3
23:34 thou shalt break the sheards t, 1886.3
24: 4 Gather the pieces t into it, *even* every 1886.3
24:11 set it empty upon the coals t, that 1886.3
27: 9 the wise men t were in thee thy calkers: 1886.3
31:15 I restrained the floods t, and the great 1886.3
32: 7 the heaven, and make the stars t dark; 1992.1
32:12 all the multitude t shall be destroyed. 1886.3
32:13 I will destroy also all the beasts t from 1886.3
38:13 with all the young lions t, shall say unto 1886.3
40: 6 went up the stairs t, and measured 2050.2
40: 9 posts t, two cubits; and the porch of 2050.2
40:20 measured the length t, and the breadth 2050.2
40:20 the length thereof, and the breadth t. 2050.2
40:21 the little chambers t *were* three on this 2050.2
40:21 the posts t and the arches thereof were 2050.2
40:21 the arches t *were* after the measure of 2050.2
40:21 the length t *was* fifty cubits, 2050.2
40:22 and the arches t *were* before them. 2050.2
40:24 he measured the posts t and the arches 2050.2
40:24 arches t according to these measures. 2050.2
40:25 in it and in the arches t round about, 2050.2
40:26 to it, and the arches t *were* before them: 2050.2
40:26 another on that side, upon the posts t. 2050.2
40:29 the little chambers t, and the posts 2050.2
40:29 the posts t, and the arches thereof, 2050.2
40:29 the posts thereof, and the arches t, 2050.2
40:29 in it and in the arches t round about: 2050.2
40:31 arches t *were* toward the utter court; 2050.2
40:31 and palm trees *were* upon the posts t: 2050.2
40:33 the little chambers t, and the posts 2050.2
40:33 and the posts t, and the arches thereof, 2050.2
40:33 and the posts thereof, and the arches t, 2050.2
40:33 and in the arches t round about: 2050.2
40:34 the arches t *were* toward the outward 2050.2
40:34 palm trees *were* upon the posts t, on 2050.2
40:36 The little chambers t, the posts thereof, 2050.2
40:36 the posts t, and the arches thereof, 2050.2
40:36 the arches t, and the windows to it 2050.2
40:37 the posts t *were* toward the utter court; 2050.2
40:37 palm trees *were* upon the posts t, on 2050.2
40:38 entries t *were* by the posts of the gates, 1886.3
41: 2 he measured the length t, forty cubits: 2050.2
41: 4 So he measured the length t, 2050.2
41:12 and the length t ninety cubits. 2050.2
41:13 and the building, with the walls t, 1886.3
41:15 the galleries t on the one side and on 1886.3
41:22 cubits high, and the length t two cubits; 2050.2
41:22 the corners t, and the length thereof, 2050.2
41:22 the length t, and the walls thereof, 2050.2
41:22 and the walls t, *were of* wood: 2050.2
42: 7 the length t *was* fifty cubits. 2050.2
43:11 fashion t, and the goings out thereof, 2050.2
43:11 the goings out t, and the comings in 2050.2
43:11 the comings in t, and all the forms 2050.2
43:11 all the forms t, and all the ordinances 2050.2
43:11 all the ordinances t, and all the forms 2050.2
43:11 all the forms t, and all the laws thereof: 2050.2
43:11 all the forms thereof, and all the laws t: 2050.2
43:11 that they may keep the whole form t, 2050.2
43:11 and all the ordinances t, and do them. 2050.2
43:12 limit t round about *shall be* most holy. 2050.2
43:13 the border t by the edge thereof round 1886.3
43:13 the border thereof by the edge t round 1886.3
43:16 broad, square in the four squares t. 2050.2
43:17 fourteen broad in the four squares t; 1886.3
43:17 the bottom t *shall be* a cubit about; 1886.3
43:20 thou shalt take of the blood t, and put *it* 2050.2
44: 5 house of the LORD, and all the laws t; 2050.2
44:14 for all the service t, and for all that shall 2050.2
45: 1 This *shall be* holy in all the borders t 1886.3

T

Eze 45: 2 cubits round about *for* the suburbs **t**. 2050.2
45:11 the measure **t** shall be after the homer. 2050.2
46: 8 and he shall go forth by the way **t**. 2050.2
46:12 the inheritance **t** shall be his sons'; 2050.2
47:11 miry places **t** and the marishes thereof 2050.2
47:11 and the marishes **t** shall not be healed; 2050.2
47:12 the river upon the bank **t**, on this side 2050.2
47:12 neither shall the fruit **t** be consumed: 2050.2
47:12 the fruit **t** shall be for meat, and the leaf 2050.2
47:12 be for meat, and the leaf **t** for medicine. 1930.2
48:10 of the LORD shall be in the midst **t**. 2050.2
48:15 and the city shall be in the midst **t**. 2050.2
48:16 these *shall be* the measures **t**; the north 1886.3
48:18 increase **t** shall be for food unto them 2050.2
48:21 of the house *shall be* in the midst **t**. 2050.2
Da 1: 5 that at the end **t** they might stand before 3963.1
2: 5 with the interpretation **t**, ye shall be cut 1886.8
2: 6 the dream, and the interpretation **t**, 1886.8
2: 6 me the dream, and the interpretation **t**. 1886.8
2: 9 ye can shew me the interpretation **t**. 1886.8
2:26 I have seen, and the interpretation **t**? 1886.8
2:31 before thee; and the form **t** *was* terrible. 1886.8
2:36 we will tell the interpretation **t** before 1886.8
2:45 *is* certain, and the interpretation **t** sure. 1886.8
3: 1 *and* the breadth **t** six cubits: 1886.8
4: 7 known unto me the interpretation **t**. 1886.8
4: 9 I have seen, and the interpretation **t** 1886.8
4:10 of the earth, and the height **t** *was* great. 1886.8
4:11 the height **t** reached unto heaven, 1886.8
4:11 the sight **t** to the end of all the earth: 1886.8
4:12 The leaves **t** *were* fair, and the fruit **t** 1886.8
4:12 the fruit **t** much, and in it *was* meat for 1886.8
4:12 of the heaven dwelt in the boughs **t**, 1958.2
4:18 Belteshazzar, declare the interpretation **t**, NIH
4:19 or the interpretation **t**, trouble thee. NIH
4:19 the interpretation **t** to thine enemies. 1886.8
4:20 heaven, and the sight **t** to all the earth; 1886.8
4:21 the fruit **t** much, and in it *was* meat for 1886.8
4:23 yet leave the stump of the roots **t** in 1958.2
5: 7 shew me the interpretation **t**, shall be 1886.8
5: 8 known to the king the interpretation **t**. 1886.8
5:15 known unto me the interpretation **t**, 1886.8
5:16 make known to me the interpretation **t**, 1886.8
7: 4 I beheld till the wings **t** were pluckt, 1886.9
9:26 the end **t** *shall be* with a flood, 2050.2
Hos 2: 9 take *away* my corn in the time **t**, 2050.2
2: 9 wine in the season **t**, and will recover 2050.2
4:13 and elms, because the shadow **t** *is* good: 1886.3
8:14 and it shall devour the palaces **t**: 1886.3
9: 4 all that eat **t** shall be polluted: 2050.2
10: 5 for the people **t** shall mourn over it, 2050.2
10: 5 the priests *that* rejoiced on it, 5921+2050.2
10: 5 for the glory **t**, because it is departed from NIH
14: 7 sent **t** *shall be* as the wine of Lebanon. 2050.2
Joel 1: 7 *it* away; the branches **t** are made white. 1886.3
Am 1: 3 I will not turn away *the punishment* **t**; 5105.2
1: 6 I will not turn away *the punishment* **t**; 5105.2
1: 7 Gaza, which shall devour the palaces **t**: 1886.3
1: 9 I will not turn away *the punishment* **t**; 5105.2
1:10 which shall devour the palaces **t**. 1886.3
1:11 I will not turn away *the punishment* **t**; 5105.2
1:13 I will not turn away *the punishment* **t**; 5105.2
1:14 it shall devour the palaces **t**, 1886.3
2: 1 I will not turn away *the punishment* **t**; 5105.2
2: 3 I will cut off the judge from the midst **t**, 1886.3
2: 3 will slay all the princes **t** with him, 1886.3
2: 4 I will not turn away *the punishment* **t**; 5105.2
2: 6 I will not turn away *the punishment* **t**; 5105.2
3: 9 behold the great tumults in the midst **t**, 1886.3
3: 9 and the oppressed in the midst **t**. 1886.3
8:10 an only *son*, and the end **t** as a bitter day. NIH
9:11 is fallen, and close up the breaches **t**; 2006.1
9:14 plant vineyards, and drink the wine **t**; 3963.1
Jnh 1: 3 he paid the fare **t**, and went down into 1886.3
Mic 1: 6 I will pour down the stones **t** into 1886.3
1: 6 and I will discover the foundations **t**. 1886.3
1: 7 the graven images **t** shall be beaten to 1886.3
1: 7 the hires **t** shall be burnt with the fire, 1886.3
1: 7 and all the idols **t** will I lay desolate: 1886.3
3:11 The heads **t** judge for reward, 1886.3
3:11 the priests **t** teach for hire, 1886.3
3:11 and the prophets **t** divine for money: 1886.3
5: 6 the land of Nimrod in the entrances **t**: 1886.3
6:12 For the rich *men* **t** are full *of* violence, 1886.3
6:12 the inhabitants **t** have spoken lies, 1886.3
6:16 and the inhabitants **t** a hissing: 1886.3
Na 1: 8 he will make an utter end of the place **t**, 1886.3
2: 5 they shall make haste *to* the wall **t**, 1886.3
Hab 2:18 image that the maker **t** hath graven it; 2050.2
Zep 1:13 vineyards, but not drink the wine **t**. 3963.1
3: 5 The just LORD *is* in the midst **t**; he will 1886.3
Zec 2: 2 to see what *is* the breadth **t**, and what *is* 1886.3
2: 2 thereof, and what *is* the length **t**. 1886.3
3: 9 behold, I *will* engrave the graving **t**, 1886.3
4: 2 lamps, which *were* upon the top **t**: 1886.3
4: 3 and the other upon the left *side* **t**. 1886.3
4: 7 he shall bring forth the headstone **t** *with* NIH
4:11 the candlestick and upon the left *side* **t**? 1886.3
5: 2 the length **t** *is* twenty cubits, 1886.3
5: 2 and the breadth **t** ten cubits. 1886.3
5: 4 shall consume it with the timber **t** and 2050.2
5: 4 with the timber thereof and the stones **t**. 2050.2
5: 8 the weight of lead upon the mouth **t**. 1886.3
7: 7 and the cities **t** round about her, 1886.3
8: 5 *of* boys and girls playing in the streets **t**. 1886.3

Zec 9: 1 and Damascus *shall be* the rest **t**: 2050.2
14: 4 cleave in the midst **t** toward the east 2050.2
Mal 1:12 fruit **t**, *even* his meat, *is* contemptible. 2050.2
Mt 2:16 and in all the coasts **t**, from two years old 846
6:34 Sufficient unto the day *is* the evil **t**. 846
12:36 they shall give account **t** in the day of 4012
13:32 the air come and lodge in the branches **t**. 846
13:44 and for joy **t** goeth and selleth all that he 846
14:13 the people had heard **t**, they followed NIG
21:43 to a nation bringing forth the fruits **t**. 846
22: 7 But when the king heard **t**, he was wroth: NIG
27:34 when he had tasted **t**, he would not drink. NIG
Mk 6:16 when Herod heard **t**, he said, It is John, NIG
Lk 19:33 the owners **t** said unto them, Why loose ye 846
21:20 then know that the desolation **t** is nigh. 846
22:16 unto you, I will not any more eat **t**, 846+1537
Jn 3: 8 thou hearest the sound **t**, but canst not 846
4:12 drank **t** himself, and his children, 846+1537
6:50 *from* heaven, that a man may eat **t**, 846+1537
7: 7 I testify of it, that the works **t** are evil. 846
Ac 15:16 and I will build again the ruins **t**, and I will 846
Ro 6:12 that *ye* should obey it in the lusts **t**. 846
13:14 provision for the flesh, to *fulfil* the lusts **t**. NIG
1Co 9: 7 a vineyard, and eateth not of the fruit **t**? 846
9:23 that I might be partaker **t** with *you*. 846
10:26 the earth *is* the Lord's, and the fulness **t**. 846
10:28 the earth *is* the Lord's, and the fulness **t**: 846
2Ti 3: 5 form of godliness, but denying the power **t**: 846
Heb 7:18 for the weakness and unprofitableness **t**. 846
Jas 1:11 and the flower **t** falleth, and the grace of 846
1Pe 1:24 and the flower **t** falleth away: 846
5: 2 taking the oversight **t**, not by constraint, NIG
1Jn 2:17 And the world passeth away, and the lust **t**: 846
Rev 5: 2 to open the book, and to loose the seals **t**? 846
5: 5 the book, and to loose the seven seals **t**. 846
5: 9 to take the book, and to open the seals **t**: 846
16:12 the water **t** was dried up, that the way of 846
16:21 for the plague **t** was exceeding great. 846
21:15 city, and the gates **t**, and the wall thereof. 846
21:15 city, and the gates thereof, and the wall **t**. 846
21:17 And he measured the wall **t**, an hundred 846
21:23 did lighten it, and the Lamb *is* the light **t**. 846

THEREON (66) [ON]

Ge 35:14 he poured a drink offering **t**, 5921+1886.3
35:14 and he poured oil **t**. 5921+1886.3
Ex 17:12 put *it* under him, and he sat **t**; 5921+1886.3
20:24 sacrifice **t** thy burnt offerings, 5921+2050.2
20:26 nakedness be not discovered **t**. 5921+2050.2
30: 7 Aaron shall burn **t** sweet incense 5921+2050.2
30: 9 shall offer no strange incense **t**, 5921+2050.2
30: 9 shall ye pour drink offering **t**. 5921+2050.2
40:27 he burnt sweet incense **t**; 5921+2050.2
40:35 because the cloud abode **t**, 5921+2050.2
Lev 2: 1 upon it, and put frankincense **t**: 5921+1886.3
2: 6 part it in pieces, and pour oil **t**: 5921+1886.3
2:15 upon it, and lay frankincense **t**: 5921+1886.3
5:11 shall he put *any* frankincense **t**: 5921+1886.3
6:12 shall burn **t** the fat of the peace 5921+1886.3
10: 1 put incense **t**, and offered strange 5921+1886.3
11:38 *any part* of their carcase fall **t**, it *shall be* 5921
Nu 4: 6 put **t** the covering of badgers' 5921+2050.2
4: 7 put **t** the dishes, and the spoons, 5921+2050.2
4: 7 the continual bread shall be **t**: 5921+2050.2
4:13 and spread a purple cloth **t**: 5921+2050.2
5:15 upon it, nor put frankincense **t**; 5921+2050.2
9:22 remaining **t**, the children of Israel 5921+1992.1
16:18 laid incense **t**, and stood *in* 5921+1992.1
Dt 27: 6 thou shalt offer burnt offerings **t** 5921+2050.2
Jos 8:29 raise **t** a great heap of stones, 5921
8:31 they offered **t** burnt offerings unto 5921+2050.2
22:23 or if to offer **t** burnt offering or 5921+2050.2
22:23 or if to offer peace offerings **t**, 5921+2050.2
2Sa 17:19 and spread ground corn **t**; 5921+2050.2
19:26 I may ride **t**, and go to the king; 5921+1886.3
1Ki 6:35 he carved **t** cherubims and palm trees and NIH
13:13 the ass: and he rode **t**, 5921+2050.2
2Ki 16:12 to the altar, and offered **t**. 5921+2050.2
1Ch 12:17 the God of our fathers look **t**, and rebuke NIH
15:15 their shoulders with the staves **t**, 5921+1992.1
2Ch 3: 5 and set **t** palm trees and chains. 5921+2050.2
3:14 and wrought cherubims **t**. 5921+2050.2
33:16 sacrificed **t** peace offerings and 5921+2050.2
Ezr 2: 3 Israel, to offer burnt offerings **t**, 5921+2050.2
3: 3 they offered burnt offerings **t** 5921+2050.2
6:11 being set up, let him be hanged **t**; 5922+1958.2
Est 5:14 that Mordecai may be hanged **t**: 5921+2050.2
7: 9 Then the king said, Hang him **t**. 5921+2050.2
Isa 30:12 and perverseness, and stay **t**: 5921+2050.2
35: 9 nor *any* ravenous beast shall go up **t**, 5089.1
Eze 15: 3 a pin of it to hang any vessel **t**? 5921+2050.2
40:39 to slay **t** the burnt offering and 413+1992.1
43:18 to offer burnt offerings **t**, 5921+2050.2
43:18 and to sprinkle blood **t**. 5921+2050.2
Zec 4: 2 his seven lamps **t**, and seven pipes to 1886.3
Mt 21: 7 on them their clothes, and they set *him* **t**. 1883
21:19 he came to it, and found nothing **t**, 846+1722
23:20 sweareth by it, and by all *things* **t**. 1883
23:22 of God, and by him that sitteth **t**. 846+1883
Mk 11:13 if haply he might find any *thing* **t**: 846+1722
11:13 when he came to it, he found nothing **t**, 1911
Lk 13: 6 and he came and sought fruit **t**, 846+1722
19:35 upon the colt, and they set Jesus **t**. 1913
Jn 12:14 he had found a young ass, sat **t**; 846+1909
21: 9 of coals there, and fish laid **t**, and bread. 1945

1Co 3:10 the foundation, and another **buildeth t**. 2026
Rev 5: 3 able to open the book, neither to look **t**. 846
5: 4 and to read the book, neither to look **t**. 846
6: 4 *power* was given to him that sat **t** to take 1909
21:12 twelve angels, and names **written t** on, 1924

THEREOUT (2) [OUT]

Lev 2: 2 he shall take **t** his handful of 4480+8033
Jdg 15:19 the jaw, and there came water **t**; 4480+5105.2

THERETO (20) [TO]

Ex 25:24 make **t** a crown *of* gold round about. 2050.2
29:41 shalt do **t** according to the meat offering of NIH
30:38 to smell **t**, shall even be cut off 871.1+1886.3
Lev 5:16 and shall add the fifth *part* **t**, 5921+2050.2
6: 5 shall add the fifth *part* more **t**, *and* give 2050.2
18:23 stand before a beast to lie down **t**: 1886.3
20:16 lie down **t**, thou shalt kill the woman 1886.3
27:27 and shall add a fifth *part* of it **t**: 5921
27:31 shall add **t** the fifth *part* thereof. 5921+2050.2
Nu 3:36 vessels thereof, and all that serveth **t**, 2050.2
19:17 water shall be put **t** in a vessel: 5921+2050.2
Dt 12:32 not add **t**, nor diminish from it. 5921+2050.2
Jdg 11:17 the king of Edom would not hearken **t**. NIH
1Ch 22:14 I prepared; and thou mayest add **t**. 5921+1992.1
2Ch 10:14 your yoke heavy, but I will add **t**: 5921+2050.2
21:11 commit fornication, and compelled Judah **t**. NIH
Ps 119: 9 by taking heed **t** according to thy word. NIG
Isa 44:15 image, and falleth down **t**. 3807.1+4123.1
Mk 14:70 art a Galilean, and thy speech agreeth **t**. NIG
Gal 3:15 no *man* disannulleth, or added **t**. NIG

THEREUNTO (9) [UNTO]

Ex 32: 8 have sacrificed **t**, and said, 2050.2+3807.1
36:36 he made **t** four pillars of shittim 1886.3+3807.1
37:11 **t** a crown *of* gold round about. 2050.2+3807.1
37:12 Also he made **t** a border of a 2050.2+3807.1
Dt 1: 7 unto all *the places* nigh **t**, in the plain, 2050.2
Eph 6:18 and watching **t** with all 846+1519+3778
1Th 3: 3 know that we are appointed **t**. 1519+3778
Heb 10: 1 continually make the comers **t** perfect. NIG
1Pe 3: 9 knowing that ye are **t** called, that ye 1519+3778

THEREUPON (5) [UPON]

Ex 31: 7 the mercy seat that *is* **t**, and all 5921+2050.2
Eze 16:16 and playedst the harlot **t**: 5921+1992.1
Zep 2: 7 house of Judah; they shall feed **t**: 5921+1992.1
1Co 3:10 every man take heed how he **buildeth t**. 2026
3:14 *man's* work abide which he hath **built t**, 2026

THEREWITH (36) [WITH]

Ex 22: 6 be consumed **t**; he that kindled the fire NIH
30:26 tabernacle of the congregation **t**, 871.1+2050.2
38:30 **t** he made the sockets to the 871.1+1886.3
Lev 7: 7 priest that maketh atonement **t** 871.1+2050.2
8: 7 and bound *it* unto him **t**. 871.1+2050.2
15:32 goeth from him, and is defiled **t**; 871.1+1886.3
18:23 with any beast to defile *thyself* **t**: 871.1+1886.3
22: 8 shall not eat to defile *himself* **t**: 871.1+2050.2
Dt 16: 3 thou eat unleavened bread **t**, 5921+2050.2
23:13 thou shalt dig **t**, and shalt turn 871.1+1886.3
Jdg 15:15 and slew a thousand men **t**. 871.1+1886.3
16:12 bound him **t**, and said unto him, 871.1+1992.1
1Sa 12: 3 *any* bribe to blind mine eyes **t**? 871.1+2050.2
17:51 slew him, and cut off his head **t**. 871.1+1886.3
31: 4 and thrust me through **t**; 871.1+1886.3
2Sa 20:10 he smote him **t** in the fifth *rib*, 871.1+1886.3
2Ki 5: 6 I have **t** sent Naaman my servant to thee, NIH
5:12 house of the LORD. 871.1+2050.2
1Ch 10: 4 and thrust me through **t**; 871.1+1886.3
23: 5 which I made, *said David*, to praise **t**. NIH
2Ch 16: 6 and he built **t** Geba and Mizpah. 871.1+1992.1
Pr 15:16 than great treasure and trouble **t**. 871.1+2050.2
15:17 than a stalled ox and hatred **t**. 871.1+2050.2
17: 1 *is* a dry morsel, and quietness **t**, 871.1+1886.3
25:16 lest thou be filled **t**, and vomit it. 5105.2
Ecc 1:13 to the sons of man to be exercised **t**. 871.1
2: 6 to water **t** the wood that bringeth forth 4480
10: 9 removeth stones shall be hurt **t**; 871.1+1992.1
Isa 10:15 itself against him that heweth **t**? 871.1+1992.1
Eze 4:15 and thou shalt prepare thy bread **t**. 5921+1992.1
Joel 2:19 and oil, and ye shall be satisfied **t**: 854+2050.2
Php 4:11 in whatsoever *state* I am, **t** to be content. NIG
1Ti 6: 8 food and raiment let us be **t** content. 3778
Jas 3: 9 **T** bless we God, even the Father; 846+1722
3: 9 and **t** curse we men, which are made 846+1722
3Jn 1:10 and not content **t**, neither doth he 1909+3778

THESE (1225) [THIS]

Ge 2: 4 **T** *are* the generations of the heavens and 428
6: 9 **T** *are* the generations of Noah: Noah was a 428
9:19 **T** *are* the three sons of Noah: and of them 428
10: 1 Now **t** *are* the generations of the sons of 428
10: 5 By **t** were the isles of the Gentiles divided 428
10:20 **T** *are* the sons of Ham, after their families, 428
10:29 and Jobab: all **t** *were* the sons of Joktan. 428
10:31 **T** *are* the sons of Shem, after their families, 428
10:32 **T** *are* the families of the sons of Noah, 428
10:32 by **t** were the nations divided in the earth 428
11:10 **T** *are* the generations of Shem: Shem *was* 428
11:27 Now **t** *are* the generations of Terah: 428
14: 2 *That* **t** made war with Bera king of Sodom, NIH
14: 3 All **t** were joined together in the vale of 428
14:13 and **t** *were* confederate with Abram. 1992
15: 1 After **t** things the word of the LORD came 428

T

Ge	15:10 he took unto him all **t**, and divided them in	428
	19: 8 only unto **t** men do nothing; for therefore	411
	20: 8 and told all **t** things in their ears:	428
	21:29 What *mean* **t** seven ewe lambs which thou	428
	21:30 For **t** seven ewe lambs shalt thou take of	428
	22: 1 it came to pass after **t** things, that God did	428
	22:20 it came to pass after **t** things, that it was	428
	22:23 **t** eight Milcah did bear to Nahor,	428
	23: 1 **t** *were* the years of the life of Sarah.	NIH
	24:28 told *them of* her mother's house **t** things.	428
	25: 4 All **t** *were* the children of Keturah.	428
	25: 7 **t** *are* the days of the years of Abraham's life	428
	25:12 Now **t** *are* the generations of Ishmael,	428
	25:13 **t** *are* the names of the sons of Ishmael,	428
	25:16 **T** *are* the sons of Ishmael, and these *are*	428
	25:16 **t** *are* their names, by their towns,	428
	25:17 **t** *are* the years of the life of Ishmael,	428
	25:19 **t** *are* the generations of Isaac,	428
	26: 3 I will give all **t** countries, and I will perform	411
	26: 4 and will give unto thy seed all **t** countries;	411
	27:36 for he hath supplanted me **t** two times:	2088
	27:42 **t** words of Esau her elder son were told to	NIH
	27:46 such as **t** *which are* of the daughters of	428
	29:13 to his house. And he told Laban all **t** things.	428
	31:43 **T** daughters *are* my daughters, and *these*	NIH
	31:43 **t** children *are* my children, and *these* cattle	NIH
	31:43 **t** cattle *are* my cattle, and all that thou	NIH
	31:43 can I do *this* day unto **t** my daughters,	428
	32:17 goest thou? and whose *are* **t** before thee?	428
	33: 8 **T** *are* to find grace in the sight of my lord.	NIH
	34:21 **T** men *are* peaceable with us; therefore	428
	35:26 **t** *are* the sons of Jacob, which were born	428
	36: 1 Now **t** *are* the generations of Esau, who *is*	428
	36: 5 **t** *are* the sons of Esau, which were born	428
	36: 9 **t** *are* the generations of Esau the father of	428
	36:10 **T** *are* the names of Esau's sons; Eliphaz	428
	36:12 **t** *were* the sons of Adah Esau's wife.	428
	36:13 **t** *are* the sons of Reuel; Nahath, and Zerah,	428
	36:13 **t** were the sons of Bashemath Esau's wife.	428
	36:14 **t** were the sons of Aholibamah,	428
	36:15 **t** *were* dukes of the sons of Esau: the sons	428
	36:16 **t** *are* the dukes *that came* of Eliphaz in	428
	36:16 the land of Edom; **t** *were* the sons of Adah.	428
	36:17 **t** *are* the dukes *that came* of Reuel Esau's son;	428
	36:17 **t** *are* the dukes *that came* of Reuel in	428
	36:17 **t** *are* the sons of Bashemath Esau's wife.	428
	36:18 **t** *are* the sons of Aholibamah Esau's wife;	428
	36:18 **t** *were* the dukes *that came* of Aholibamah	428
	36:19 **T** *are* the sons of Esau, who *is* Edom,	428
	36:19 Esau, who *is* Edom, and **t** *are* their dukes.	428
	36:20 **T** *are* the sons of Seir the Horite,	428
	36:21 **t** *are* the dukes of the Horites, the children	428
	36:23 the children of Shobal *were* **t**; Alvan,	428
	36:24 the children of Zibeon; both Aiah,	428
	36:25 the children of Anah *were* **t**; Dishon,	428
	36:26 the children of Dishon; Hemdan,	428
	36:27 The children of Ezer *are* **t**; Bilhan,	428
	36:28 The children of Dishan *are* **t**; Uz, and Aran.	428
	36:29 **T** *are* the dukes *that came* of the Horites;	428
	36:30 **t** *are* the dukes *that came* of Hori,	428
	36:31 **t** *are* the kings that reigned in the land of	428
	36:40 **t** *are* the names of the dukes *that came* of	428
	36:43 **t** *be* the dukes of Edom, according to their	428
	37: 2 **T** *are* the generations of Jacob. Joseph,	428
	38:25 By the man, whose **t** *are*, am I with child:	428
	38:25 whose *are* **t**, the signet, and bracelets,	428
	39: 7 it came to pass after **t** things, that his	428
	39:17 she spake unto him according to **t** words,	428
	40: 1 came to pass after **t** things, *that* the butler	428
	42:36 ye will take Benjamin *away*: all **t things**	5089.1
	43: 7 we told him according to the tenor of **t**	428
	43:16 Bring **t** men home, and slay,	NIH
	43:16 for **t** men shall dine with me at noon.	NIH
	44: 6 and he spake unto them **t** *same* words.	428
	44: 7 him, Wherefore saith my lord **t** words?	428
	45: 6 For **t** two years *hath* the famine *been* in	2088
	46: 8 **t** *are* the names of the children of Israel,	428
	46:15 **T** *be* the sons of Leah, which she bare unto	428
	46:18 **T** *are* the sons of Zilpah, whom Laban gave	428
	46:18 she bare unto Jacob, *even* sixteen souls.	428
	46:22 **T** *are* the sons of Rachel, which were born	428
	46:25 **T** *are* the sons of Bilhah, which Laban gave	428
	46:25 his daughter, and she bare **t** unto Jacob:	428
	48: 1 it came to pass after **t** things, that *one* told	428
	48: 8 beheld Joseph's sons, and said, Who *are* **t**?	428
	49:28 All **t** *are* the twelve tribes of Israel:	428
Ex	1: 1 Now **t** *are* the children of	428
	4: 9 if they will not believe also **t** two signs,	428
	6:14 **T** *be* the heads of their fathers' houses:	428
	6:14 and Carmi: **t** *be* the families of Reuben.	428
	6:15 **t** *are* the families of Simeon.	428
	6:16 **t** *are* the names of the sons of Levi	428
	6:19 **t** *are* the families of Levi according to their	428
	6:24 Abiasaph: **t** *are* the families of the Korhites.	428
	6:25 **t** *are* the heads of the fathers of the Levites	428
	6:26 **T** *are* that Aaron and Moses, to whom	NIH
	6:27 **T** *are* they which spake to Pharaoh king of	NIH
	6:27 from Egypt: **t** *are* that Moses and Aaron.	NIH
	10: 1 that I might shew **t** my signs before him:	428
	11: 8 all **t** thy servants shall come down unto	428
	11:10 Aaron did all **t** wonders before Pharaoh:	428
	14:20 to them, but it gave light by night *to* **t**.	NIH
	15:26 I will put none of **t** diseases upon thee,	NIH
	19: 6 **t** *are* the words which thou shalt speak	428
	19: 7 laid before their faces all **t** words which	428

Ex	20: 1 And God spake all **t** words, saying,	428
	21: 1 Now **t** *are* the judgments which thou shalt	428
	21:11 if he do not **t** three unto her, then shall she	428
	24: 8 made with you concerning all **t** words.	428
	25:39 gold shall he make it, with all **t** vessels.	428
	28: 4 **t** *are* the garments which they shall make;	428
	30:34 **t** sweet spices with pure frankincense:	NIH
	32: 4 they said, **T** *be* thy gods, O Israel,	428
	32: 8 and said, **T** *be* thy gods, O Israel,	428
	33: 4 when the people heard **t** evil tidings, they	2088
	34: 1 I will write upon **t** tables the words that	NIH
	34:27 said unto Moses, Write thou **t** words:	428
	34:27 for after the tenor of **t** words I have made	428
	35: 1 **t** *are* the words which the LORD hath	428
Lev	2: 8 that is made of **t** *things* unto the LORD:	428
	5: 4 of it, then he shall be guilty in one of **t**.	428
	5: 5 when he shall be guilty in one of **t** *things*,	428
	5:13 his sin that he hath sinned in one of **t**,	428
	5:17 any *of* **t** *things* which are forbidden	NIH
	6: 3 in any of all **t** *that* a man doeth, sinning	NIH
	11: 2 **T** *are* the beasts which ye shall eat among	2063
	11: 4 Nevertheless **t** shall ye not eat of them	2088
	11: 9 **T** shall ye eat of all that *are* in the waters:	2088
	11:13 **t** *are* they which ye shall have in	428
	11:21 Yet **t** may ye eat of every flying creeping	2088
	11:22 *Even* **t** of them ye may eat; the locust after	428
	11:24 for **t** ye shall be unclean:	428
	11:29 **T** also *are* unclean unto you among	2088
	11:31 **T** *are* unclean to you among all that creep:	428
	16: 4 **t** *are* holy garments; therefore shall he	1992
	18:24 Defile not you yourselves in any of **t** *things*:	428
	18:24 **t** the nations are defiled which I cast out	428
	18:26 shall not commit any of **t** abominations;	428
	18:27 (For all **t** abominations have the men of	411
	18:29 For whosoever shall commit any of **t**	428
	18:30 ye commit not *any one* of **t** abominable	NIH
	20:23 for they committed all **t** *things*, and	428
	21:14 or profane, *or* a harlot, **t** shall he not take:	428
	22:22 ye shall not offer **t** unto the LORD,	428
	22:25 ye offer the bread of your God of any of **t**;	428
	23: 2 *be* holy convocations, *even* **t** *are* my feasts.	428
	23: 4 **T** *are* the feasts of the LORD, *even* holy	428
	23:37 **T** *are* the feasts of the LORD, which ye	428
	25:54 if he be not redeemed in **t** *years*, then	428
	26:14 and will not do all **t** commandments;	428
	26:23 ye will not be reformed by me by **t** *things*,	428
	26:46 **T** *are* the statutes and judgments and laws,	428
	27:34 **T** *are* the commandments, which the LORD	428
Nu	1: 5 **t** *are* the names of the men that shall stand	428
	1:16 **T** *were* the renowned of the congregation,	428
	1:17 Aaron took **t** men which are expressed by	428
	1:44 **T** *are* those that were numbered,	428
	2: 9 their armies. **T** shall first set forth.	NIH
	2:32 **T** *are* those which were numbered of	428
	3: 1 **T** also *are* the generations of Aaron and	428
	3: 2 **t** *are* the names of the sons of Aaron;	428
	3: 3 **T** *are* the names of the sons of Aaron,	428
	3:17 **t** were the sons of Levi by their names;	428
	3:18 **t** *are* the names of the sons of Gershon by	428
	3:20 **T** *are* the families of the Levites according	428
	3:21 **t** *are* the families of the Gershonites.	428
	3:27 **t** *are* the families of the Kohathites.	428
	3:33 the Mushites: **t** *are* the families of Merari.	428
	3:35 **t** shall pitch on the side of the tabernacle	NIH
	4:15 **T** *things are* the burden of the sons of	428
	4:37 **T** *were* they that were numbered of	428
	4:41 **t** are they that were numbered of	428
	4:45 **T** *be* those that were numbered of	428
	5:23 the priest shall write **t** curses in a book,	428
	13: 4 **t** were their names: of the tribe of Reuben,	428
	13:16 **T** *are* the names of the men which Moses	428
	14:22 have tempted me *now* **t** ten times,	2088
	14:39 Moses told **t** sayings unto all the children	428
	15:13 All that are born of the country shall do **t**	428
	15:22 and not observed all **t** commandments,	428
	16:14 wilt thou put out the eyes of **t** men?	1992
	16:26 from the tents of **t** wicked men,	428
	16:28 the LORD hath sent me to do all **t** works;	428
	16:29 If **t** *men* die the common death of all men,	428
	16:30 ye shall understand that **t** men have	428
	16:31 as he had made an end of speaking all **t**	428
	16:38 The censers of **t** sinners against their own	428
	21:25 Israel took all **t** cities: and Israel dwelt in	428
	22: 9 and said, What men *are* **t** with thee?	428
	22:28 that thou hast smitten me **t** three times?	2088
	22:32 Wherefore hast thou smitten thine ass **t**	2088
	22:33 me, and turned from me **t** three times:	2088
	24:10 thou hast altogether blessed *them* **t** three	2088
	26: 7 **T** *are* the families of the Reubenites.	428
	26:14 **T** *are* the families of the Simeonites.	428
	26:18 **T** *are* the families of the children of Gad	428
	26:22 **T** *are* the families of Judah according to	428
	26:25 **T** *are* the families of Issachar according to	428
	26:27 **T** *are* the families of the Zebulunites	428
	26:30 **T** *are* the sons of Gilead: *of* Jeezer,	428
	26:34 **T** *are* the families of Manasseh,	428
	26:35 **T** *are* the sons of Ephraim after their	428
	26:36 **t** *are* the sons of Shuthelah: of Eran,	428
	26:37 **T** *are* the families of the sons of Ephraim	428
	26:37 **T** *are* the sons of Joseph after their families.	428
	26:41 **T** *are* the sons of Benjamin after their	428
	26:42 **T** *are* the families of Dan after their families:	428
	26:42 **T** *are* the families of Dan after their	428
	26:47 **T** *are* the families of the sons of Asher	428
	26:50 **T** *are* the families of Naphtali according to	428

Nu	26:51 **T** *were* the numbered of the children of	428
	26:53 Unto **t** the land shall be divided for an	428
	26:57 **t** *are* they that were numbered of the	428
	26:58 **T** *are* the families of the Levites: the family	428
	26:63 **T** *are* they that were numbered by Moses	428
	26:64 among **t** there was not a man of them	428
	27: 1 **t** *are* the names of his daughters; Mahlah,	428
	28:23 Ye shall offer **t** beside the burnt offering in	428
	29:39 **T** *things* ye shall do unto the LORD in your	428
	30:16 **T** *are* the statutes, which the LORD	428
	31:16 Behold, **t** caused the children of Israel,	2007
	33: 1 **T** *are* the journeys of the children of Israel,	428
	33: 2 **t** *are* their journeys according to their	428
	34:17 **T** *are* the names of the men which shall	428
	34:19 the names of the men *are* **t**: Of the tribe of	428
	34:29 **T** *are* they whom the LORD commanded to	428
	35:13 *of* **t** cities which ye shall give six cities	NIH
	35:15 **T** six cities shall be a refuge, *both* for	428
	35:24 the revenger of blood according to **t**	428
	35:29 So **t** *things* shall be for a statute of	428
	36:13 **T** *are* the commandments and the	428
Dt	1: 1 **T** *be* the words which Moses spake unto	428
	1:35 Surely there shall not one of **t** men of this	428
	2: 7 **t** forty years the LORD thy God *hath been*	2088
	3: 5 All **t** cities *were* fenced *with* high walls,	428
	3:21 your God hath done unto **t** two kings:	428
	4: 6 which shall hear all **t** statutes, and say,	428
	4:30 all **t** things are come upon thee, *even* in	428
	4:42 fleeing unto one of **t** cities he might live:	411
	4:45 **T** *are* the testimonies, and the statutes,	428
	5:22 **T** words the LORD spake unto all your	428
	6: 1 **t** *are* the commandments, the statutes,	2088
	6: 6 **t** words, which I command thee *this* day,	428
	6:24 the LORD commanded us to do all **t**	2088
	6:25 if we observe to do all **t** commandments	2088
	7:12 if ye hearken to **t** judgments, and keep,	428
	7:17 in thine heart, **T** nations *are* moe than I;	428
	8: 2 led thee **t** forty years in the wilderness,	2088
	8: 4 neither did thy foot swell, **t** forty years.	2088
	9: 4 for the wickedness of **t** nations the LORD	428
	9: 5 for the wickedness of **t** nations the LORD	428
	10:21 that hath done for thee **t** great and terrible	428
	11:18 Therefore shall ye lay up **t** my words in	428
	11:22 For if ye shall diligently keep all **t**	2088
	11:23 will the LORD drive out all **t** nations from	428
	12: 1 **T** *are* the statutes and judgments, which ye	428
	12:28 hear all **t** words which I command thee,	428
	12:30 How did **t** nations serve their gods?	428
	14: 4 **T** *are* the beasts which ye shall eat:	2088
	14: 7 Nevertheless **t** ye shall not eat of them	428
	14: 9 **T** ye shall eat of all that *are* in the waters:	2088
	14:12 **t** *are they* of which ye shall not eat:	2088
	15: 5 to observe to do all **t** commandments	2088
	16:12 and thou shalt observe and do **t** statutes.	428
	17:19 all the words of this law and **t** statutes,	428
	18:12 For all that do **t** *things* are an abomination	428
	18:12 of **t** abominations the LORD thy God doth	428
	18:14 For **t** nations, which thou shalt possess,	428
	19: 9 If thou shalt keep all **t** commandments to	2088
	19: 9 three cities moe for thee, beside **t** three:	428
	19:11 that he die, and fleeth into one of **t** cities:	411
	20:15 which are not of the cities of **t** nations.	428
	20:16 of the cities of **t** people, which the LORD	428
	22:17 *yet* **t** *are* the tokens of my daughter's	428
	23:18 for even both **t** *are* abomination unto	1992.1
	25: 3 and beat him above **t** *with* many stripes,	428
	26:16 God hath commanded thee to do **t** statutes	428
	27: 4 *that* ye shall set up **t** stones, which I	428
	27:12 **T** shall stand upon mount Gerizzim to	428
	27:13 **t** shall stand upon mount Ebal to curse;	428
	28: 2 all **t** blessings shall come on thee,	428
	28:15 that all **t** curses shall come upon thee,	428
	28:45 all **t** curses shall come upon thee,	428
	28:65 among **t** nations shalt thou find no ease,	1992
	29: 1 **T** *are* the words of the covenant, which	428
	29:18 to go *and* serve the gods of **t** nations;	1992
	30: 1 when all **t** things are come upon thee,	428
	30: 7 the LORD thy God will put all **t** curses	428
	31: 1 and spake **t** words unto all Israel.	428
	31: 3 he will destroy **t** nations from before thee,	428
	31:17 Are not **t** evils come upon us, because our	428
	31:28 that I may speak **t** words in their ears,	428
	32:45 Moses made an end of speaking all **t** words	428
Jos	2:11 as soon as we had heard **t** *things*, our	NIH
	4: 6 saying, What mean you by **t** stones?	428
	4: 7 **t** stones shall be for a memorial unto	428
	4:21 time to come, saying, What *mean* **t** stones?	428
	9:13 **t** bottles of wine, which we filled, *were*	428
	9:13 **t** our garments and our shoes are become	428
	10:16 **t** five kings fled, and hid themselves in a	428
	10:24 put your feet upon the necks of **t** kings.	428
	10:42 all **t** kings and their land did Joshua take *at*	428
	11: 5 when all **t** kings were met together,	428
	11:14 all the spoil of **t** cities, and the cattle,	428
	12: 1 Now **t** *are* the kings of the land, which	428
	12: 7 **t** *are* the kings of the country which Joshua	428
	13:12 did Moses smite, and cast them out.	3963.1
	13:32 **T** *are* the countries which Moses did	428
	14: 1 **t** *are* the countries which the children of	428
	14:10 me alive, as he said, **t** forty and five years,	2088
	17: 2 **t** were the male children of Manasseh	428
	17: 3 **t** *are* the names of his daughters, Mahlah,	428
	17: 9 **t** cities of Ephraim *are* among the cities of	428
	19: 8 the villages that *were* round about **t** cities	428
	19:16 to their families, **t** cities with their villages.	428

T

Jos	19:31 to their families, t cities with their villages.	428
	19:48 to their families, t cities with their villages.	428
	19:51 T *are* the inheritances, which Eleazar	428
	20: 9 T were the cities appointed for all	428
	21: 3 of the LORD, t cities and their suburbs.	428
	21: 8 unto the Levites t cities with their suburbs,	428
	21: 9 t cities which are *here* mentioned by	428
	21:42 T cities were every one with their suburbs	428
	21:42 round about them: thus *were* all t cities.	428
	23: 3 have not left your brethren t many days	2088
	23: 3 your God hath done unto all t nations	428
	23: 4 I have divided unto you *by lot* t nations that	428
	23: 7 That *ye* come not among t nations, these	428
	23: 7 these nations, t that remain amongst you;	428
	23:12 cleave unto the remnant of t nations,	428
	23:12 *even* t that remain among you,	428
	23:13 drive out *any of* t nations from before you;	428
	24:26 Joshua wrote t words in the book of the	428
	24:29 it came to pass after t things, that Joshua	428
Jdg	2: 4 when the angel of the LORD spake t words	428
	3: 1 Now t *are* the nations which the LORD left,	428
	9: 3 ears of all the men of Shechem all t words:	428
	13:23 would he have shewed us all t *things,*	428
	13:23 *at this* time have told us *such things* as t.	2063
	16:15 thou hast mocked me t three times,	2088
	18:14 Do ye know that there is in t houses an	428
	18:18 t went *into* Micah's house, and fetched	428
	19:13 let us draw near to one of t places to lodge	NIH
	20:17 that drew sword: all t *were* men of war.	2088
	20:25 thousand men; all t drew the sword.	428
	20:35 an hundred men; all t drew the sword.	428
	20:44 thousand men; all t *were* men of valour.	428
	20:46 drew the sword; all t *were* men of valour.	428
Ru	3:17 T six *measures* of barley gave he me;	428
	4:18 Now t *are* the generations of Pharez:	428
1Sa	4: 8 who shall deliver us out of the hand of t	428
	4: 8 are the Gods that smote the Egyptians	428
	6:17 t *are* the golden emerods which	428
	10: 7 let it be, when t signs are come unto thee,	428
	14: 6 let us go over unto the garrison of t	428
	14: 8 we will pass over unto t men, and we will	428
	14:49 the names of his two daughters *were* t,	NIH
	16:10 unto Jesse, The LORD hath not chosen t.	428
	17:17 of this parched *corn,* and t ten loaves,	2088
	17:18 carry t ten cheeses unto the captain of	428
	17:39 David said unto Saul, I cannot go with t;	428
	18:26 when his servants told David t words,	428
	21: 5 kept from us about t **three days,**	8032+8543
	21:12 David laid up t words in his heart,	428
	23: 2 Shall I go and smite t Philistines?	428
	24: 7 So David stayed his servants with *t* words,	NIH
	24:16 David had made an end of speaking t	428
	25:37 wife had told him t things, that his heart	428
	29: 3 What *do* t Hebrews *here*? And Achish said	428
	29: 3 which hath been with me t days,	2088
	29: 3 t years, and I have found no *fault* in him	2088
	29: 4 *should it* not be with the heads of t men?	1992
	31: 4 lest t uncircumcised come and thrust me	428
2Sa	3: 5 T were born to David in Hebron.	428
	3:39 t men the sons of Zeruiah *be* too hard for	428
	5:14 t *be* the names of those that were born	428
	7:17 According to all t words, and according to	428
	7:21 heart, hast thou done all t great things,	2088
	13:21 when king David heard of all t things,	428
	14:19 he put all t words in the mouth of thine	428
	16: 2 said unto Ziba, What meanest thou by t?	428
	21:22 T four were born to the giant in Gath,	428
	23: 1 Now t *be* the last words of David. David	428
	23: 8 T *be* the names of the mighty *men* whom	428
	23:17 T *things* did *these* three mighty *men.*	428
	23:17 These *things* did *t* three mighty *men.*	NIH
	23:22 T *things* did Benaiah the son of Jehoiada,	428
	24:17 t sheep, what have they done?	428
	24:23 All *t things* did Araunah, *as* a king,	NIH
1Ki	4: 2 t *were* the princes which he had; Azariah	428
	4: 8 t *are* their names: The son of Hur, in	428
	7: 9 All t *were of* costly stones, according to	428
	7:45 all t vessels, which Hiram made to king	428
	8:59 let t my words, wherewith I have made	428
	9:13 What cities *are* t which thou hast given	428
	9:23 T were of the officers that *were*	428
	10: 8 *are* thy men, happy *are* t thy servants,	428
	10:10 t which the queen of Sheba gave to king	428
	11: 2 gods: Solomon clave unto t in love.	1992.1
	17: 1 there shall not be dew nor rain t years,	428
	17:17 it came to pass after t things, *that* the son	428
	18:36 *that* I have done all t things at thy word.	428
	20:19 So t young men of the princes of	428
	21: 1 it came to pass after t things, *that* Naboth	428
	22:11 With t shalt thou push the Syrians,	428
	22:17 the LORD said, T have no master: let them	428
	22:23 spirit in the mouth of all t thy prophets,	428
2Ki	1: 7 up to meet you, and told you t words?	428
	1:13 my life, and the life of t fifty thy servants,	428
	2:21 saith the LORD, I have healed t waters;	428
	3:10 that the LORD hath called t three kings	428
	3:13 for the LORD hath called t three kings	428
	6:20 open the eyes of t *men,* that they may see.	428
	7: 8 when t lepers came to the uttermost part	428
	10: 9 and slew him: but who slew all t?	428
	17:41 So t nations feared the LORD, and served	428
	18:27 thy master, and to thee, to speak t words?	428
	20:14 and said unto him, What said t men?	428
	21:11 Manasseh king of Judah hath done t	428
	23:16 proclaimed, who proclaimed t words.	428

2Ki	23:17 proclaimed t things that thou hast done	428
	25:16 brass of all t vessels was without weight.	428
	25:17 like unto t had the second pillar with	428
	25:20 captain of the guard took t,	3963.1
1Ch	1:23 and Jobab. All t *were* the sons of Joktan.	428
	1:29 T *are* their generations: The firstborn of	428
	1:31 and Kedemah. T *are* the sons of Ishmael.	428
	1:33 and Eldaah. All t *are* the sons of Keturah.	428
	1:43 t *are* the kings that reigned in the land	428
	1:54 duke Iram. T *are* the dukes of Edom.	428
	2: 1 T *are* the sons of Israel: Reuben, Simeon,	428
	2:18 her sons *are* t; Jesher, and Shobab,	428
	2:23 All t *belonged to* the sons of Machir	428
	2:33 and Zaza. T were the sons of Jerahmeel.	428
	2:50 T were the sons of Caleb the son of Hur,	428
	2:55 T *are* the Kenites that came of Hemath,	1992
	3: 1 t were the sons of David, which were	428
	3: 4 T six *were* born unto him in Hebron;	NIH
	3: 5 t were born unto him in Jerusalem:	428
	3: 9 T *were* all the sons of David, beside	NIH
	4: 2 T are the families of the Zorathites.	428
	4: 3 t *were of* the father of Etam; Jezreel,	428
	4: 4 T *are* the sons of Hur, the firstborn of	428
	4: 6 Haahashtari. T were the sons of Naarah.	428
	4:12 of Irnahash. T *are* the men of Rechah.	428
	4:18 t *are* the sons of Bithiah the daughter of	428
	4:22 Jashubi-lehem. And t *are* ancient things.	NIH
	4:23 T were the potters, and those that dwelt	1992
	4:31 T *were* their cities unto the reign of David.	428
	4:33 T *were* their habitations,	2088
	4:38 T mentioned by *their* names *were* princes	428
	4:41 t written by name came in the days of	428
	5:14 T *are* the children of Abihail the son of	428
	5:17 All t were reckoned by genealogies in	3963.1
	5:24 t were the heads of the house of their	428
	6:17 t *be* the names of the sons of Gershom;	428
	6:19 t *are* the families of the Levites according	428
	6:31 t *are they* whom David set over the service	428
	6:33 t *are they* that waited with their children.	428
	6:50 t *are* the sons of Aaron; Eleazar his son,	428
	6:54 t *are* their dwelling places throughout	428
	6:64 the children of Israel gave to the Levites t	NIH
	6:65 t cities, which are called by *their* names.	428
	7: 8 and Alameth. All t *are* the sons of Becher.	428
	7:11 t the sons of Jediael, by the heads of	428
	7:17 T *were* the sons of Gilead, the son of	428
	7:29 In t dwelt the children of Joseph the son of	428
	7:33 and Ashvath. T *are* the children of Japhlet.	428
	7:40 All t *were* the children of Asher, heads of	428
	8: 6 t *are* the sons of Ehud: these *are* the heads	428
	8: 6 t *are* the heads of the fathers of	428
	8:10 T *were* his sons, heads of the fathers.	428
	8:28 T *were* heads of the fathers, by their	428
	8:28 chief *men.* T dwelt in Jerusalem.	428
	8:32 t also dwelt with their brethren in	1992
	8:38 whose names *are* t, Azrikam, Bocheru,	428
	8:38 and Hanan. All t *were* the sons of Azel.	428
	8:40 and fifty. All t *are* of the sons of Benjamin.	428
	9: 9 All t men *were* chief of the fathers in	428
	9:22 All t which were set to be porters in	3963.1
	9:22 T were reckoned by their genealogy in	1992
	9:26 For t Levites, the four chief porters, *were*	1992
	9:33 t *are* the singers, chief of the fathers of	428
	9:34 T chief fathers of the Levites were chief	428
	9:34 their generations; t dwelt at Jerusalem.	428
	9:44 whose names *are* t, Azrikam, Bocheru,	428
	9:44 and Hanan: t *were* the sons of Azel.	428
	10: 4 lest t uncircumcised come and abuse me.	428
	11:10 T also *are* the chief of the mighty *men*	428
	11:19 t men that have put their lives in jeopardy?	428
	11:19 drink it. T *things* did *these* three mightiest.	428
	11:19 drink it. These *things* did *t* three mightiest.	NIH
	11:24 T *things* did Benaiah the son of Jehoiada,	428
	12: 1 Now t *are* they that came to David to	428
	12:14 T *were* of the sons of Gad, captains of	428
	12:15 T *are* they that went over Jordan in the	428
	12:23 t *are* the numbers of the bands that were	428
	12:38 All t men of war, that could keep rank,	428
	14: 4 Now t *are* the names of *his* children which	428
	17:15 According to all t words, and according to	428
	17:19 in making known all *t* great things.	NIH
	18:11 the gold that he brought from all *t* nations;	NIH
	20: 8 T were born unto the giant in Gath;	411
	21:17 *as for* t sheep, what have they done?	428
	23: 9 T *were* the chief of the fathers of Laadan.	428
	23:10 and Beriah. T four *were* the sons of Shimei.	428
	23:24 T *were* the sons of Levi after the house of	428
	24: 1 Now t *are* the divisions of the sons of	NIH
	24:19 T *were* the orderings of them in their	428
	24:20 the rest of the sons of Levi *were* t:	NIH
	24:30 T *were* the sons of the Levites after	428
	24:31 t likewise cast lots over against their	1992
	25: 5 All t *were* the sons of Heman the king's	428
	25: 6 All t *were* under the hands of their father	428
	26: 8 All t of the sons of Obed-edom: they and	428
	26:12 Among t *were* the divisions of the porters,	428
	26:19 T *are* the divisions of the porters among	428
	27:22 T *were* the princes of the tribes of Israel.	428
	27:31 All t *were* the rulers of the substance	428
	29:17 heart I have willingly offered all t *things:*	428
	29:19 to do all *t things,* and to build the palace,	NIH
2Ch	3: 3 Now t *are* the things wherein Solomon	428
	3:13 The wings of t cherubims spread	428
	4:18 Thus Solomon made all t vessels in great	428
	5: 5 t did the priests *and* the Levites bring	3963.1

2Ch	8:10 t *were* the chief of king Solomon's officers,	428
	9: 7 *are* thy men, and happy *are* t thy servants,	428
	14: 7 Let us build t cities, and make about *them*	428
	14: 8 all t were mighty *men* of valour.	428
	15: 8 when Asa heard t words, and the prophecy	428
	17:14 t *are* the numbers of them according to	428
	17:19 T waited on the king, besides *those* whom	428
	18:10 With t thou shalt push Syria until they be	428
	18:16 the LORD said, T have no master; let them	428
	18:22 lying spirit in the mouth of t thy prophets,	428
	21: 2 all t *were* the sons of Jehoshaphat king of	428
	24:26 t *are* they that conspired against him;	428
	29:32 all t *were* for a burnt offering to the LORD.	428
	32: 1 After t things, and the establishment	428
	35: 7 t *were* of the king's substance.	428
	36:18 of his princes; all *t* he brought *to* Babylon.	NIH
Ezr	1:11 All *t* did Sheshbazzar bring up with *them*	NIH
	2: 1 t *are* the children of the province that	428
	2:59 t *were* they which went up from Tel-melah	428
	2:62 T sought their register *among* those that	428
	4:21 Give ye now commandment to cause t	479
	5: 9 build this house, and to make up t walls?	1836
	5:11 build the house that was builded t many	1836
	5:15 said unto him, Take t vessels, go, carry	412
	6: 8 t Jews for the building of this house of God	479
	6: 8 forthwith expences be given unto t men,	479
	7: 1 after t things, in the reign of Artaxerxes	428
	8: 1 T *are* now the chief of their fathers,	428
	8:13 whose names *are* t, Eliphelet, Jeiel,	428
	9: 1 when t *things* were done, the princes	428
	9:14 join in affinity with the people of t	428
	10:44 All t had taken strange wives: and *some* of	428
Ne	1: 4 when I heard t words, *that* I sat down and	428
	1:10 Now t *are* thy servants and thy people,	1992
	4: 2 and said, What do t feeble Jews?	NIH
	5: 6 angry when I heard their cry and t words.	428
	6: 6 mayest be their king, according to t words.	428
	6: 7 reported to the king according to t words.	428
	6:14 and Sanballat according to t their works,	428
	6:16 all the heathen that *were* about us saw *t*	NIH
	7: 6 T *are* the children of the province, that	428
	7:61 t *were* they which went up *also* from	428
	7:64 T sought their register *among* those that	428
	10: 8 Bilgai, Shemaiah: t *were* the priests.	428
	11: 3 Now t *are* the chief of the province that	428
	11: 7 t *are* the sons of Benjamin; Sallu the son of	428
	12: 1 Now t *are* the priests and the Levites that	428
	12: 7 T *were* the chief of the priests and of their	428
	12:26 T *were* in the days of Joiakim the son of	428
	13:26 Did not Solomon king of Israel sin by t	428
Est	1: 5 when t days were expired, the king made a	428
	2: 1 After t things, when the wrath of king	428
	3: 1 After t things did king Ahasuerus promote	428
	4:11 to come in unto the king t thirty days.	2088
	9:20 Mordecai wrote t things, and sent letters	428
	9:26 Wherefore they called t days Purim after	428
	9:27 they would keep t two days according to	428
	9:28 *that* t days *should* be remembered and	428
	9:28 *that* t days of Purim should not fail from	428
	9:31 To confirm t days of Purim in their times	428
	9:32 the decree of Esther confirmed t matters	428
Job	8: 2 How long wilt thou speak t *things?* and	428
	10:13 t *things* hast thou hid in thine heart:	428
	12: 3 yea, who knoweth not such *things* as t?	428
	12: 9 Who knoweth not in all t that the hand of	428
	19: 3 T ten times have ye reproached me: you	2088
	26:14 Lo, t *are* parts of his ways: but how little a	428
	32: 1 So t three men ceased to answer Job,	428
	32: 5 no answer in the mouth of *t* three men,	NIH
	33:29 all t *things* worketh God oftentimes with	428
	42: 7 that after the LORD had spoken t words	428
Ps	15: 5 that doeth t *things* shall never be moved.	428
	42: 4 When I remember t *things,* I pour out my	428
	50:21 T *things* hast thou done, and I kept	428
	57: 1 my refuge, until t calamities be overpast.	NIH
	73:12 Behold, t *are* the ungodly, who prosper in	428
	104:27 T wait all upon thee; that *thou* mayest	3963.1
	107:24 T see the works of the LORD,	1992
	107:43 will observe t *things,* even they shall	428
Pr	6:16 T six *things* doth the LORD hate: yea,	2007
	24:23 T *things* also belong to the wise. *It is* not	428
	25: 1 T *are* also proverbs of Solomon, which	428
Ecc	7:10 that the former days were better than t?	428
	11: 9 for all t *things* God will bring thee into	428
	12:12 further, by t, my son, be admonished:	1992
Isa	7: 4 be fainthearted for the two tails of t	428
	34:16 no one of t shall fail, none shall want her	2007
	36:12 thy master and to thee to speak t words?	428
	36:20 Who *are they* amongst all the gods of t	428
	38: 6 by t things men live, and in all these	1992.1
	38:16 and in all t *things is* the life of my spirit:	2006.1
	39: 3 and said unto him, What said t men?	428
	40:26 behold who hath created t *things,* that	428
	42:16 T things will I do unto them, and not	428
	44:21 Remember t, O Jacob and Israel; for thou	428
	45: 7 and create evil: I the LORD do all t things.	428
	47: 7 that thou didst not lay t *things* to thy heart,	428
	47: 9 two *things* shall come to thee *in* a	428
	47:13 save thee from t things that shall come	NIH
	48:14 which among them hath declared t *things?*	428
	49:12 Behold, t shall come from far: and lo,	428
	49:12 lo, t from the north and from the west;	428
	49:12 the west; and t from the land of Sinim.	428
	49:18 all t gather themselves together,	3963.1
	49:21 Who hath begotten me t, seeing I have lost	428

T

Isa
49:21 who hath brought up t? Behold, I was left 428
49:21 I was left alone; t, where *had* they *been?* 428
51:19 Two *things* are come unto thee; who 2007
57: 6 meat offering. Should I receive comfort in t? 428
60: 8 Who *are* t *that* fly as a cloud, and as 428
64:12 Wilt thou refrain thyself for t *things,* O 428
65: 5 T *are* a smoke in my nose, a fire that 428

Jer
2:34 found it by secret search, but upon all t. 428
3: 7 I said after she had done all t *things,* Turn 428
3:12 Go and proclaim t words toward the north, 428
4:18 doings have procured t *things* unto thee; 428
5: 4 Therefore I said, Surely t *are* poor; they 1992
5: 5 t have altogether broken the yoke, 1992
5: 9 Shall I not visit for t *things?* saith 428
5:19 Wherefore doth the Lord our God all t 428
5:25 Your iniquities have turned away t *things,* 428
5:29 Shall I not visit for t *things?* saith 428
7: 2 that enter in at t gates to worship 428
7: 4 The temple of the Lord, *are* t. 1992
7:10 We are delivered to do all t abominations! 428
7:13 now, because ye have done all t works, 428
7:27 Therefore thou shalt speak all t words unto 428
9: 9 Shall I not visit them for t *things?* saith 428
9:24 for in t *things* I delight, saith the Lord. 428
9:26 for all t *nations are* uncircumcised. NIH
10:11 from the earth, and from under t heavens. 429
11: 6 Proclaim all t words in the cities of Judah, 428
13:22 Wherefore come t *things* upon me? 428
14:22 upon thee: for thou hast made all t *things.* 428
16:10 thou shalt shew this people all t words, 428
17:20 of Jerusalem, that enter in by t gates: 428
20: 1 heard *that* Jeremiah prophesied t things. 428
22: 2 and thy people that enter in by t gates: 428
22: 5 if ye will not hear t words, I swear by 428
23:21 I have not sent t *prophets,* yet they ran: NIH
24: 5 Like t good figs, so will I acknowledge 428
25: 9 against all t nations round about, 428
25:11 t nations shall serve the king of Babylon 428
25:30 Therefore prophesy thou against them all t 428
26: 7 all the people heard Jeremiah speaking t 428
26:10 When the princes of Judah heard t things, 428
26:15 unto you to speak all t words in your ears. 428
27: 6 now have I given all t lands into the hand 428
27:12 king of Judah according to all t words, 428
28:14 yoke of iron upon the neck of all t nations, 428
29: 1 Now t *are* the words of the letter that 428
30: 4 t *are* the words that the Lord spake 428
30:15 I have done t **things** unto thee. 428
31:21 O virgin of Israel, turn again to t thy cities, 428
32:14 Take t evidences, this evidence of 428
36: 6 Jeremiah the prophet spake all t words 428
36: 7 for t defenced cities remained of the cities 2007
36:16 We will surely tell the king of all t words. 428
36:17 How didst thou write all t words at his 428
36:18 He pronounced all t words unto me with 428
36:24 any of his servants that heard all t words. 428
38: 9 t men have done evil in all that they have 428
38:12 Put now t *old* cast clouts and rotten rags NIH
38:16 neither will I give thee into the hand of t 428
38:24 Let no man know of t words, and thou 428
38:27 he told them according to all t words that 428
43: 1 had sent him to them, *even* all t words; 428
43:10 will set his throne upon t stones that I have 428
45: 1 when he had written t words in a book at 428
51:60 *even* all t words that are written against 428
51:61 and shalt see, and shalt read all t words; 428
52:20 brass of all t vessels was without weight. 428
52:22 and the pomegranates *were* like unto t. 428

La
1:16 For t *things* I weep; mine eye, mine eye 428
4: 9 for t pine away, stricken through for *want* 1992
5:17 heart is faint; for t *things* our eyes are dim. 428

Eze
1:21 When those went, t went; and when NIH
1:21 when those stood, t stood; and when NIH
8:15 shalt see greater abominations than t. 428
10:17 When they stood, t stood; and when they NIH
10:17 lift up themselves *also:* for the spirit of NIH
11: 2 t *are* the men that devise mischief, and 428
14: 3 t men have set up their idols in their heart, 428
14:14 three men, Noah, Daniel, and Job, 428
14:16 *Though* t three men *were* in it, *as* I live, 428
14:18 Though t three men *were* in it, *as* I live, 428
16: 5 eye pitied thee, to do any of t unto thee, 428
16:20 t hast thou sacrificed unto them to be 3963.1
16:30 seeing thou doest all t *things,* the work of 428
16:43 hast fretted me in all t *things;* behold 428
17:12 Know ye not what t *things mean?* tell 428
17:18 hath done all t *things,* he shall not escape. 428
18:10 *that* doeth the like to *any* one of t *things,* 428
18:13 he hath done all t abominations; he shall 428
23:10 T discovered her nakedness: they took her 1992
23:30 *I will* so do t *things* unto thee, because 428
24:19 Wilt thou not tell us what t *things are* to 428
27:21 goats: in t *were they* thy merchants. 3963.1
27:24 T *were* thy merchants in all sorts of 1992
30:17 and t *cities* shall go into captivity. 2007
35:10 Two nations and these two countries 1886.1
35:10 and t two countries shall be mine, NIH
36:20 T *are* the people of the Lord, 428
37: 3 unto me, Son of man, can t bones live? 428
37: 4 Prophesy upon t bones, and say unto 428
37: 5 Thus saith the Lord God unto t bones; 428
37: 9 breath, and breathe upon t slain, that they 428
37:11 t bones *are* the whole house of Israel. 428
37:18 thou not shew us what thou meanest by t? 428
40:24 the arches thereof according to t measures. 428

Eze
40:28 he measured the south gate according to t 428
40:29 arches thereof, according to t measures: 428
40:32 he measured the gate according to t 428
40:33 *were* according to t measures: 428
40:35 and measured *it* according to t measures; 428
40:46 t *are* the sons of Zadok among the sons of 1992
42: 5 for the galleries were higher than t, than 2007
42: 9 from under t chambers *was* the entry on 428
43:13 t *are* the measures of the altar after 428
43:18 T *are* the ordinances of the altar in the day 428
43:27 when t days are expired, it shall be, NIH
46:22 t four corners *were* of one measure. 3963.1
46:24 me, T *are* the places of them that boil, 428
47: 8 T waters issue out toward the east country 428
47: 9 of fish, because t waters shall come thither: 428
48: 1 Now t *are* the names of the tribes. From 428
48: 1 for t are his sides east *and* west; a *portion* NIH
48:16 t *shall* be the measures thereof; the north 428
48:29 t are their portions, saith the Lord God. 428
48:30 t *are* the goings out of the city: on the 428

Da
1: 6 Now among t were of the children of 1992.1
1:17 As for t four children, God gave them 428
2:28 visions of thy head upon thy bed, *are* t; 1836
2:40 all *things:* and as iron that breaketh all t, 459
2:44 in the days of t kings shall the God of 581
2:44 in pieces and consume all t kingdoms, 459
3:12 t men, O king, have not regarded thee: 479
3:13 Then they brought t men before the king. 479
3:21 t men were bound in their coats, their 479
3:23 three men, Shadrach, Meshach, 479
3:27 being gathered together, saw t men, 479
6: 2 over t three presidents; of whom Daniel 1952.1
6: 5 said t men, We shall not find any occasion 479
6: 6 t presidents and princes assembled 459
6:11 t men assembled, and found Daniel praying 479
6:14 the king, when he heard t words, was sore NIH
6:15 t men assembled unto the king, and said 479
7:17 T great beasts, which *are* four, *are* four 459
10:21 *there is* none that holdeth with me in t 428
11: 6 and he that strengthened her in t times. NIH
11:27 both t kings' hearts *shall be* to do 1992.1
11:41 shall escape out of his hand, *even* Edom, 428
12: 6 How long *shall it be* to the end of t NIH
12: 7 holy people, all t *things* shall be finished. 428
12: 8 my lord, what *shall be* the end of t *things?* 428

Hos
2:12 T *are* my rewards that my lovers have NIH
14: 9 he shall understand t *things?* prudent, 428

Am
3: 2 be *they* better than t kingdoms? 428

Mic
2: 7 *are* t his doings? do not my words do good 428

Hab
2: 6 Shall not all t take up a parable against 3963.1

Hag
2:13 is unclean *by* a dead body touch any of t, 428

Zec
1: 9 said I, O my lord, what *are* t? And the 428
1: 9 said unto me, I will shew thee what t be. 428
1:10 T *are they* whom the Lord hath sent to 428
1:12 *against* which thou hast had indignation t 2088
1:19 the angel that talked with me, What *be* t? 428
1:19 T *are* the horns which have scattered 428
1:21 said I, What come t to do? And he spake, 428
1:21 T *are* the horns which have scattered 428
1:21 t are come to fray them, to cast out the 428
3: 7 I will give thee places to walk among t that 428
4: 4 with me, saying, What *are* t, my lord? 428
4: 5 Knowest thou not what t *be?* And I said, 428
4:11 What *are* t two olive trees upon the right 428
4:12 What *be* t two olive branches which NIH
4:13 Knowest thou not what t *be?* And I said, 428
4:14 said he, T *are* the two anointed ones, 428
5:10 with me, Whither do t bear the ephah? 1992
6: 4 that talked with me, What *are* t, my lord? 428
6: 5 T *are* the four spirits of the heavens, 428
6: 8 t that go toward the north country have NIH
7: 3 as I have done t so many years? 2088
8: 6 of the remnant of this people in t days, 1992
8: 9 ye that hear in t days these words by 428
8: 9 ye that hear in these days t words by 428
8:10 For before t days there was no hire for 1992
8:12 of this people to possess all t *things.* 428
8:15 again have I thought in t days to do well 428
8:16 T *are* the things that ye shall do; Speak ye 428
8:17 for all t *are things* that I hate, saith 428
13: 6 him, What *are* t wounds in thine hands? 428
14:15 of all the beasts that shall be in t tents, 1992

Mt
1:20 But while he thought on t *things,* behold, 3778
2: 3 When Herod the king had heard t *things,* NIG
3: 9 that God is able of t stones to raise up 3778
4: 3 command that t stones be made bread. 3778
4: 9 unto him, All t *things* will I give thee, 3778
5:19 shall break one of t least commandments, 3778
5:37 for whatsoever is more than t cometh of 3778
6:29 all his glory was not arrayed like one of t. 3778
6:32 after all t *things* do the Gentiles seek): 3778
6:32 knoweth that ye have need of all t *things.* 3778
6:33 and all t *things* shall be added unto you. 3778
7:24 Therefore whosoever heareth t sayings of 3778
7:26 And every one that heareth t sayings of 3778
7:28 to pass, when Jesus had ended t sayings, 3778
9:18 While he spake t *things* unto them, 3778
10: 2 the names of the twelve apostles are t; 3778
10: 5 T twelve Jesus sent forth, 3778
10:42 t little ones a cup of cold *water* only in 3778
11:25 thou hast hid t *things* from the wise and 3778
13:34 All t *things* spake Jesus unto the 3778
13:51 Have ye understood all t *things?* 3778
13:53 *that* when Jesus had finished t parables, 3778
13:54 *man* this wisdom, and t mighty works? NIG

Mt
13:56 Whence then hath this *man* all t *things?* 3778
15:20 T are *the things* which defile a man: 3778
18: 6 But whoso shall offend one of t little ones 3778
18:10 heed that ye despise not one of t little 3778
18:14 that one of t little ones should perish. 3778
19: 1 *that* when Jesus had finished t sayings, 3778
19:20 All t *things* have I kept from my youth up: 3778
20:12 T last have wrought *but* one hour, 3778
20:21 him, Grant that t my two sons may sit, 3778
21:16 said unto him, Hearest thou what t say? 3778
21:23 By what authority doest thou t *things?* 3778
21:24 tell you by what authority I do t *things.* 3778
21:27 Neither tell I you by what authority I do t 3778
22:22 When they had heard t words, they NIG
22:40 On t two commandments hang all the law 3778
23:23 t ought *ye* to have done, and not to leave 3778
23:36 All t *things* shall come upon this 3778
24: 2 See ye not all t *things?* verily I say unto 3778
24: 3 Tell us, when shall t *things* be? 3778
24: 6 for all t *things* must come to pass, NIG
24: 8 All t *are* the beginning of sorrows. 3778
24:33 when ye shall see all t *things,* know that 3778
24:34 shall not pass, till all t *things* be fulfilled. 3778
25:40 *it* unto one of the least of t my brethren, 3778
25:45 as ye did *it* not to one of the least of t, 3778
25:46 And t shall go away into everlasting 3778
26: 1 when Jesus had finished all t sayings, 3778
26:62 what *is it which* t witness against thee? 3778

Mk
2: 8 Why reason ye t *things* in your hearts? 3778
4:11 all t *things* are done in parables: NIG
4:15 And t are they by the way side, where 3778
4:16 And t are they likewise which are sown 3778
4:18 And t are they which are sown among 3778
4:20 And t are they which are sown on good 3778
6: 2 From whence hath this *man* t *things?* 3778
7:23 All t evil *things* come from within, 3778
8: 4 From whence can a man satisfy t men 3778
9:42 And whosoever shall offend one of t little NIG
10:20 all t have I observed from my youth. 3778
11:28 By what authority doest thou t *things?* 3778
11:28 gave thee this authority to do t *things?* 3778
11:29 I will tell you by what authority I do t 3778
11:33 I tell you by what authority I do t *things.* 3778
12:31 none other commandment greater than t. 3778
12:40 t shall receive greater damnation. 3778
13: 2 unto him, Seest thou t great buildings? 3778
13: 4 Tell us, when shall t *things* be? 3778
13: 4 what *shall* be the sign when all t *things* 3778
13: 8 troubles: t *are* the beginnings of sorrows. 3778
13:29 when ye shall see t *things* come to pass, 3778
13:30 shall not pass, till all t *things* be done. 3778
14:60 what *is it which* t witness against thee? 3778
16:17 t signs shall follow them that believe; 3778

Lk
1:19 unto thee, and to shew thee t glad tidings. 3778
1:20 until the day that t *things* shall be 3778
1:65 all t sayings were noised abroad 3778
2:19 But Mary kept all t *things,* 3778
2:51 his mother kept all t sayings in her heart. 3778
3: 8 That God is able of t stones to raise up 3778
4:28 when they heard t *things,* were filled with 3778
5:27 And after t *things* he went forth, and saw 3778
7: 9 When Jesus heard t *things,* he marvelled 3778
7:18 of John shewed him of all t *things.* 3778
8: 8 when he said t *things,* he cried, He that 3778
8:13 and t have no root, which for a while 3778
8:21 my brethren are t which hear the word of 3778
9:28 to pass about an eight days after t sayings, 3778
9:44 Let t sayings sink down into your ears: 3778
10: 1 After t *things* the Lord appointed other 3778
10:21 that thou hast hid t *things* from the wise 3778
10:36 Which now of t three, thinkest thou, 3778
11:27 as he spake t *things,* a certain woman of 3778
11:42 t ought *ye* to have done, and not to leave 3778
11:53 And as he said t *things* unto them, 3778
12:27 all his glory was not arrayed like one of t. 3778
12:30 all t *things* do the nations of the world 3778
12:30 Father knoweth that ye have need of t 3778
12:31 and all t *things* shall be added unto you. 3778
13: 2 Suppose ye that t Galileans were sinners 3778
13: 7 t three years I come seeking fruit on this NIG
13:16 Satan hath bound, lo t eighteen years, NIG
13:17 And when he had said t *things,* all his 3778
14: 6 they could not answer him again to t 3778
14:15 *him* heard t *things,* he said unto him, 3778
14:21 shewed his lord t *things.* Then the master 3778
15:26 and asked what t *things* meant. 3778
15:29 father, Lo, t **many** years do I serve thee, 5118
16:14 heard all t *things:* and they derided him. 3778
17: 2 than that he should offend one of t little 3778
18:21 All t have I kept from my youth up. 3778
18:22 Now when Jesus heard t *things,* he said 3778
18:34 And they understood none of t *things:* 3778
19:11 And as they heard t *things,* he added and 3778
19:15 commanded t servants to be called unto 3778
19:40 I tell you that, if t should hold their peace, 3778
20: 2 by what authority doest thou t *things?* or 3778
20: 8 Neither tell I you by what authority I do t 3778
20:16 He shall come and destroy t husbandmen, 3778
21: 4 For all t have of their abundance cast in 3778
21: 6 *As for* t *things* which ye behold, the days 3778
21: 7 Master, but when shall t *things* be? 3778
21: 7 what sign *will there be* when t *things* 3778
21: 9 for t *things* must first come to pass; 3778
21:12 But before all t, they shall lay their hands 3778
21:22 For t be *the* days of vengeance, that all 3778

Lk	21:28 And when t *things* begin to come to pass,	3778
	21:31 when ye see t *things* come to pass,	3778
	21:36 escape all t *things* that shall come to pass,	3778
	23:31 For if they do t *things* in a green tree,	3778
	23:49 stood afar off, beholding t *things*.	3778
	24: 9 and told all t *things* unto the eleven,	3778
	24:10 which told t *things* unto the apostles.	3778
	24:14 And they talked together of all t *things*	3778
	24:17 What *manner of* communications *are* t	3778
	24:18 which are come to pass there in t days?	3778
	24:21 to day is the third day since t *things* were	3778
	24:26 Ought not Christ to have suffered t *things*,	3778
	24:44 T *are* the words which I spake unto you,	3778
	24:48 And ye are witnesses of t *things*.	3778
Jn	1:28 T *things* were done in Bethabara beyond	3778
	1:50 thou shalt see greater *things* than t.	3778
	2:16 that sold doves, Take t *things* hence;	3778
	2:18 unto us, seeing that thou doest t *things*?	3778
	3: 2 for no *man* can do t miracles that thou	3778
	3: 9 and said unto him, How can t *things* be?	3778
	3:10 of Israel, and knowest not t *things*?	3778
	3:22 After t *things* came Jesus and his disciples	3778
	5: 3 In t lay a great multitude of impotent *folk*,	3778
	5:16 he had done t *things* on the sabbath day.	3778
	5:19 he doeth, t also doeth the Son likewise.	3778
	5:20 he will shew him greater works than t,	3778
	5:34 but t *things* I say, that ye might be saved.	3778
	6: 1 After t *things* Jesus went over the sea of	3778
	6: 5 shall we buy bread, that t may eat?	3778
	6:59 T *things* said he in the synagogue, as he	3778
	7: 1 After t *things* Jesus walked in Galilee:	3778
	7: 4 If thou do t *things*, shew thyself to	3778
	7: 9 When he had said t *words* unto them,	3778
	7:31 will he do moe miracles than t which this	3778
	8:20 T *words* spake Jesus in the treasury, as he	3778
	8:28 Father hath taught me, I speak t *things*.	3778
	8:30 As he spake t *words*, many believed on	3778
	9:22 T *words* spake his parents, because	3778
	9:40 which were with him heard t *words*,	3778
	10:19 again among the Jews for t sayings.	3778
	10:21 T are not the words of him that hath a	3778
	11:11 T *things* said he: and after that he saith	3778
	12:16 T *things* understood not his disciples at	3778
	12:16 they that t *things* were written	3778
	12:16 and *that* they had done t *things* unto him.	3778
	12:36 T *things* spake Jesus, and departed.	3778
	12:41 T *things* said Esaias, when he saw his	3778
	13:17 If ye know t *things*, happy are ye if ye do	3778
	14:12 and greater *works* than t shall he do;	3778
	14:25 T *things* have I spoken unto you, being	3778
	15:11 T *things* have I spoken unto you, that my	3778
	15:17 T *things* I command you, that ye love one	3778
	15:21 But all t *things* will they do unto you for	3778
	16: 1 T *things* have I spoken unto you, that ye	3778
	16: 3 And t *things* will they do unto you,	3778
	16: 4 But t *things* have I told you, that when	3778
	16: 4 And t *things* I said not unto you at	3778
	16: 6 But because I have said t *things* unto you,	3778
	16:25 T *things* have I spoken unto you in	3778
	16:33 T *things* I have spoken unto you, that in	3778
	17: 1 T *words* spake Jesus, and lift up his eyes	3778
	17:11 but t are in the world, and I come to thee.	3778
	17:13 t *things* I speak in the world, that they	3778
	17:20 Neither pray I for t alone, but for them	3778
	17:25 and t have known that thou hast sent me.	3778
	18: 1 When Jesus had spoken t *words*, he went	3778
	18: 8 therefore ye seek me, let t go their way:	3778
	19:24 T *things* therefore the soldiers did.	3778
	19:36 For t *things* were done, that the scripture	3778
	20:18 and *that* he had spoken t *things* unto her.	3778
	20:31 But t are written, that ye might believe	3778
	21: 1 After t *things* Jesus shewed himself again	3778
	21:15 *son of* Jonas, lovest thou me more than t?	3778
	21:24 This is the disciple which testifieth of t	3778
	21:24 and wrote t *things*: and we know that his	3778
Ac	1: 9 And when he had spoken t *things*, while	3778
	1:14 T all continued with one accord in prayer	3778
	1:21 Wherefore of t men which have	NIG
	1:24 shew whether of t two thou hast chosen,	3778
	2: 7 are not all t which speak Galileans?	3778
	2:13 mocking said, *T* men are full of new wine.	NIG
	2:15 For t are not drunken, as ye suppose,	3778
	2:22 Ye men of Israel, hear t words; Jesus of	3778
	3:24 have likewise foretold of t days.	3778
	4:16 Saying, What shall we do to t men?	3778
	5: 5 And Ananias hearing t words fell down,	3778
	5: 5 great fear came on all them that heard t	3778
	5:11 and upon as many as heard t *things*.	3778
	5:24 and the chief priests heard t things,	3778
	5:32 we are his witnesses of t things; and *so*	3778
	5:35 what ye intend to do as touching t men.	3778
	5:36 For before t days rose up Theudas,	3778
	5:38 Refrain from t men, and let them alone:	3778
	7: 1 Then said the high priest, Are t things so?	3778
	7:50 Hath not my hand made all t *things*?	3778
	7:54 When they heard t *things*, they were cut	3778
	8:24 none of t *things* which ye have spoken	NIG
	10: 8 when he had declared all t *things* unto	NIG
	10:44 While Peter yet spake t words, the Holy	3778
	10:47 water, that t should not be baptized,	3778
	11:12 Moreover t six brethren accompanied me,	3778
	11:18 When they heard t *things*, they held their	3778
	11:22 Then tidings of t *things* came unto the	846
	11:27 And in t days came prophets from	3778
	12:17 *Go* shew t *things* unto James, and to	3778

Ac	13:42 the Gentiles besought that t words might	3778
	14:15 why do ye t *things*? We also are men of	3778
	14:15 unto you that *ye* should turn from t	3778
	14:18 And with t sayings scarce restrained they	3778
	15:17 saith the Lord, who doeth all t *things*.	3778
	15:28 to lay upon you no greater burden than t	3778
	16:17 T men are the servants of the most high	3778
	16:20 saying, T men, being Jews, do exceedingly	3778
	16:38 And the sergeants told t words unto	3778
	17: 6 T that have turned the world upside down	3778
	17: 7 t all do contrary to the decrees of Cesar,	3778
	17: 8 of the city, when they heard t *things*.	3778
	17:11 T were more noble than those in	3778
	17:20 know therefore what t *things* mean.	3778
	18: 1 After t *things* Paul departed from Athens,	3778
	19:21 After t *things* were ended, Paul purposed	3778
	19:28 And when they heard t *sayings*, they were	NIG
	19:36 that t *things* cannot be spoken against,	3778
	19:37 For ye have brought *hither* t men,	3778
	20: 5 going before tarried for us at Troas.	3778
	20:24 none of t *things* move me, neither count	NIG
	20:34 that t hands have ministered unto my	3778
	21:12 And when we heard t *things*, both we,	3778
	21:38 which before t days madest an uproar,	3778
	23:22 that thou hast shewed t *things* to me.	3778
	24: 8 of all t *things*, whereof we accuse him.	3778
	24: 9 assented, saying that t *things* were so.	3778
	24:20 Or else let t same *here* say, if they have	3778
	24:22 And when Felix heard t *things*, having	3778
	25: 9 there be judged of t *things* before me?	3778
	25:11 if there be none *of* t *things* whereof these	NIG
	25:11 if there be none of *these things* whereof t	3778
	25:20 and there be judged of t *matters*.	3778
	26:16 a witness both of t *things* which thou hast	NIG
	26:21 For t causes the Jews caught me in	3778
	26:26 For the king knoweth of t *things*, before	3778
	26:26 for I am persuaded that none of t *things*	3778
	26:29 altogether such as I am, except t bonds.	3778
	27:31 to the soldiers, Except t abide in the ship,	3778
	28:29 And when he had said t *words*, the Jews	3778
Ro	2:14 t, having not the law, are a law unto	3778
	8:31 then say to t *things*? If God *be* for us,	3778
	8:37 all t *things* we are more than conquerors	3778
	9: 8 of the flesh, these *are* not the children of God:	3778
	11:24 how much more shall t, which be	3778
	11:31 *Even* so have t also now not believed,	3778
	14:18 For he that in t *things* serveth Christ *is*	3778
	15:23 But now having no more place in t parts,	3778
	15:23 having a great desire t many years to come	NIG
1Co	4: 6 And t *things*, brethren, I have in a figure	3778
	4:14 I write not t *things* to shame you,	3778
	9: 8 Say I t *things* as a man? or saith not the	3778
	9:15 But I have used none of t *things*: neither	3778
	9:15 have I written t *things*, that it should be	3778
	10: 6 Now t *things* were our examples,	3778
	10:11 Now all t *things* happened unto them for	3778
	12: 2 carried away unto t *dumb* idols, *even* as	NIG
	12:11 all t worketh *that* one and the selfsame	3778
	12:23 upon t we bestow more abundant honour;	3778
	13:13 now abideth faith, hope, charity, t three;	3778
	13:13 these three; but the greatest of t *is* charity.	3778
2Co	2:16 And who *is* sufficient for t *things*?	3778
	7: 1 Having therefore t promises,	3778
	13:10 Therefore I write t *things* being absent,	3778
Gal	2: 6 But of t who seemed to be somewhat,	3588
	4:24 for t are the two covenants; the one from	3778
	5:17 and t are contrary the one to the other:	3778
	5:19 which are t, Adultery, fornication,	NIG
Eph	5: 6 of t *things* cometh the wrath of God upon	3778
Php	4: 8 if *there be* any praise, think on t *things*.	3778
Col	3: 8 now you also put off all t, anger, wrath,	NIG
	3:14 And above all t *things* put on charity,	3778
	4:11 T only *are my* fellowworkers unto	3778
1Th	3: 3 That no *man* should be moved by t	3778
	4:18 Wherefore comfort one another with t	3778
2Th	2: 5 I was yet with you, I told you t *things*?	3778
1Ti	3:10 let t also first be proved; then let them	3778
	3:14 T *things* write I unto thee, hoping to	3778
	4: 6 t *things*, thou shalt be a good minister of	3778
	4:11 T *things* command and teach.	3778
	4:15 Meditate upon t *things*; give thyself	3778
	5: 7 And t *things* give in charge, that they may	3778
	5:21 that thou observe t *things* without	3778
	6: 2 of the benefit. T *things* teach and exhort.	3778
	6:11 flee t *things*; and follow *after*	3778
2Ti	1:12 For the which cause I also suffer t *things*:	3778
	2:14 Of t *things* put *them* in remembrance,	3778
	2:21 If a man therefore purge himself from t,	3778
	3: 8 so do t also resist the truth:	3778
Tit	2:15 T *things* speak, and exhort, and rebuke	3778
	3: 8 t *things* I will that thou affirm constantly,	3778
	3: 8 T *things* are good and profitable unto	3778
Heb	1: 2 Hath in t last days spoken unto us by *his*	3778
	7:13 For he of whom t *things* are spoken	3778
	9: 6 Now when t *things* were thus ordained,	3778
	9:23 in the heavens should be purified with t;	3778
	9:23 themselves with better sacrifices than t.	3778
	10:18 Now where remission of t *is, there is* no	3778
	11:13 T all died in faith, not having received	3778
	11:39 And t all, having obtained a good report	3778
Jas	3:10 My brethren, t *things* ought not so to be.	3778
1Pe	1:20 but was manifest in t last times for you,	NIG
2Pe	1: 4 that by t you might be partakers of	3778
	1: 8 For if t *things* be in you, and abound,	3778
	1: 9 But he that lacketh t *things* is blind,	3778

2Pe	1:10 for if ye do t *things*, ye shall never fall:	3778
	1:12 of t *things*, though ye know *them*,	3778
	1:15 to have t *things* always in remembrance.	3778
	2:12 But t, as natural brute beasts, made to be	3778
	2:17 T are wells without water, clouds that are	3778
	3:11 then that all t *things shall* be dissolved,	3778
	3:16 speaking in them t *things*; in which are	3778
	3:17 beloved, seeing ye know *t things* before,	NIG
1Jn	1: 4 And t *things* write we unto you, that your	3778
	2: 1 T *things* write I unto you, that ye sin not.	3778
	2:26 T *things* have I written unto you	3778
	5: 7 and the Holy Ghost: and t three are one.	3778
	5: 8 and the blood: and t three agree in one.	NIG
	5:13 T *things* have I written unto you that	3778
Jude	1: 8 Likewise also t *filthy* dreamers defile	3778
	1:10 But t speak evil of those *things* which they	3778
	1:12 T are spots in your feasts of charity when	3778
	1:14 prophesied of t, saying, Behold,	3778
	1:16 T are murmurers, complainers,	3778
	1:19 T be they who separate themselves,	3778
Rev	2: 1 T *things* saith he that holdeth the seven	3592
	2: 8 T *things* saith the first and the last,	3592
	2:12 T *things* saith he which hath the sharp	3592
	2:18 T *things* saith the Son of God, who hath	3592
	3: 1 T *things* saith he that hath the seven	3592
	3: 7 T *things* saith he *that is* holy, he *that is*	3592
	3:14 T *things* saith the Amen, the faithful and	3592
	7: 1 And after t *things* I saw four angels	3778
	7:13 What are t which are arrayed in white	3778
	7:14 T are they which came out of great	3778
	9:18 By t three was the third *part* of men killed	3778
	9:20 t plagues *yet* repented not of the works of	3778
	11: 4 T are the two olive trees, and the two	3778
	11: 6 T have power to shut heaven, that it rain	3778
	11:10 t two prophets tormented them that dwelt	3778
	14: 4 T are they which were not defiled with	3778
	14: 4 T are they which follow the Lamb	3778
	14: 4 T were redeemed from among men,	3778
	16: 9 of God, which hath power over t plagues:	3778
	17:13 T have one mind, and shall give their	3778
	17:14 T shall make war with the Lamb,	3778
	17:16 t shall hate the whore, and shall make her	3778
	18: 1 after t *things* I saw another angel come	3778
	18:15 The merchants of t *things*, which were	3778
	19: 1 And after t *things* I heard a great voice of	3778
	19: 9 unto me, T are the true sayings of God.	3778
	19:20 T both were cast alive into a lake of fire	NIG
	21: 5 Write: for t words are true and faithful.	3778
	22: 6 unto me, T sayings *are* faithful and true:	3778
	22: 8 And I John saw t *things*, and heard *them*.	3778
	22: 8 of the angel which shewed me t *things*.	3778
	22:16 testify unto you t *things* in the churches.	3778
	22:18 If any *man* shall add unto t *things*, God	3778
	22:20 He which testifieth t *things* saith, Surely I	3778

THESSALONIANS (5) [THESSALONICA]

Ac	20: 4 and of the T, Aristarchus and Secundus;	2331
1Th	1: 1 unto the church of the T which is in God	2331
	5: S The first *epistle* unto the T was written	2331
2Th	1: 1 the church of the T in God our Father	2331
	3: S The second *epistle* to the T was written	2331

THESSALONICA (6) [THESSALONIANS]

Ac	17: 1 and Apollonia, they came to T,	2332
	17:11 These were more noble than those in T,	2332
	17:13 But when the Jews of T had knowledge	2332
	27: 2 a Macedonian of T, being with us.	2331
Php	4:16 For even in T ye sent once and again	2332
2Ti	4:10 present world, and is departed unto T;	2332

THEUDAS (1)

Ac	5:36 For before these days rose up T,	2333

THEY (7376) [THEIR, THEIRS, THEM, THEMSELVES]
See Index of Articles, Etc.

THICK (39) [THICKER, THICKNESS]

Ex	10:22 there was a t darkness in all the land of	653
	19: 9 Lo, I come unto thee in a t cloud,	5645
	19:16 a t cloud upon the mount, and the voice	3515
	20:21 Moses drew near unto the t darkness	6205
Lev	23:40 the boughs of t trees, and willows of	5687
Dt	4:11 *with* darkness, clouds, and t darkness.	6205
	5:22 of the cloud, and of the t darkness, *with*	6205
	32:15 thou art waxed fat, thou art grown t,	5666
2Sa	18: 9 the mule went under the t boughs of a	7730
	22:12 dark waters, *and* t clouds of the skies.	5645
1Ki	7: 6 the t beam *were* before them.	5646
	7:26 it *was* a handbreadth t, and the brim	5672
	8:12 that *he* would dwell in the t **darkness**.	6205
2Ki	8:15 he took a t **cloth**, and dipt *it* in water,	4346
2Ch	6: 1 that *he* would dwell in the t **darkness**.	6205
Ne	8:15 palm branches, and branches of t trees,	5687
Job	15:26 neck, upon the t bosses of his bucklers;	5672
	22:14 T **clouds** *are* a covering to him, that he	5645
	26: 8 bindeth up the waters in his t **clouds**;	5645
	37:11 by watering he wearieth the t **cloud**:	5645
	38: 9 and t **darkness** a swaddling band for it,	6205
Ps	18:11 dark waters *and* t **clouds** of the skies.	5645
	18:12 *that was* before him his t **clouds** passed,	5645
	74: 5 as he had lifted up axes upon the t **trees**.	5442
Isa	44:22 I have blotted out, as a t **cloud**,	5645
Eze	6:13 every green tree, and under every t oak,	5687
	8:11 hand; and a t **cloud** of incense went up.	6282
	19:11 was exalted among the t **branches**,	5688

T

Eze	20:28 all the t trees, and they offered there their	5687
	31: 3 and his top was among the t **boughs.**	5688
	31:10 hath shot up his top among the t **boughs,**	5688
	31:14 shoot up their top among the t **boughs,**	5688
	41:12 the wall of the building *was* five cubits t	7341
	41:25 *there were* t planks upon the face of	5646
	41:26 side chambers of the house, and t **planks.**	5646
Joel	2: 2 a day of clouds and of t **darkness,**	6205
Hab	2: 6 to him that ladeth himself with t **clay!**	5671
Zep	1:15 a day of clouds and t **darkness,**	6205
Lk	11:29 the people were **gathered** t **together,**	*1865*

THICKER (2) [THICK]

1Ki	12:10 My little *finger* shall be t than my father's	5666
2Ch	10:10 My little *finger* shall be t than my father's	5666

THICKET (2) [THICKETS]

Ge	22:13 behold behind *him* a ram caught in a t by	5442
Jer	4: 7 The lion is come up from his t,	5441

THICKETS (4) [THICKET]

1Sa	13: 6 in t, and in rocks, and in high places,	2337
Isa	9:18 shall kindle in the t of the forest,	5442
	10:34 he shall cut down the t of the forest with	5442
Jer	4:29 they shall go into t, and climb up upon	5645

THICKNESS (4) [THICK]

2Ch	4: 5 the t of it *was* a handbreadth, and the	5672
Jer	52:21 and the t thereof *was* four fingers:	5672
Eze	41: 9 The t of the wall, which *was* for the side	7341
	42:10 The chambers *were* in the t of the wall of	7341

THIEF (28) [THEFT]

Ex	22: 2 If a t be found breaking up, and be	1590
	22: 7 if the t be found, let him pay double.	1590
	22: 8 If the t be not found, then the master of	1590
Dt	24: 7 that t shall die; and thou shalt put evil	1590
Job	24:14 and needy, and in the night is as a t;	1590
	30: 5 (they cried after them as *after* a t;)	1590
Ps	50:18 When thou sawest a t, then	1590
Pr	6:30 do not despise a t, if he steal to satisfy	1590
	29:24 Whoso is partner with a t hateth his own	1590
Jer	2:26 As the t is ashamed when he is found,	1590
Hos	7: 1 the t cometh in, *and* the troop *of robbers*	1590
Joel	2: 9 shall enter in at the windows like a t.	1590
Zec	5: 4 and it shall enter into the house of the t,	1590
Mt	24:43 known in what watch the t would come,	2812
	26:55 ye come out as against a t with swords	3027
Mk	14:48 against a t, with swords and *with* staves	3027
Lk	12:33 where no t approacheth, neither moth	2812
	12:39 had known what hour the t would come,	2812
	22:52 as against a t, with swords and staves?	3027
Jn	10: 1 other way, the same is a t and a robber.	2812
	10:10 The t cometh not, but for to steal,	2812
	12: 6 but because he was a t, and had the bag,	2812
1Th	5: 2 of the Lord so cometh as a t in the night.	2812
	5: 4 that *that* day should overtake you as a t.	2812
1Pe	4:15 as a t, or *as* an evildoer, or as a busybody	2812
2Pe	3:10 But the day of the Lord will come as a t in	2812
Rev	3: 3 I will come on thee as a t, and thou shalt	2812
	16:15 Behold, I come as a t. Blessed *is* he that	2812

THIEVES (16) [THEFT]

Isa	1:23 *are* rebellious, and companions of t:	1590
Jer	48:27 was he found among t? for since thou	1590
	49: 9 if t by night, they will destroy till they	1590
Ob	1: 5 If t came to thee, if robbers by night,	1590
Mt	6:19 and where t break through and steal:	2812
	6:20 where t do not break through nor steal:	2812
	21:13 of prayer; but ye have made it a den of t.	3027
	27:38 Then were there two t crucified with him,	3027
	27:44 The t also, which were crucified with him,	3027
Mk	11:17 of prayer? but ye have made it a den of t.	3027
	15:27 And with him they crucify two t; the one	3027
Lk	10:30 and fell among t, which stripped him of	3027
	10:36 neighbour unto him that fell among the t?	3027
	19:46 of prayer: but ye have made it a den of t.	3027
Jn	10: 8 All that ever came before me are t and	2812
1Co	6:10 Nor t, nor covetous, nor drunkards,	2812

THIGH (21) [THIGHS]

Ge	24: 2 Put, I pray thee, thy hand under my t:	3409
	24: 9 the servant put his hand under the t of	3409
	32:25 him, he touched the hollow of his t;	3409
	32:25 the hollow of Jacob's t was out of joint,	3409
	32:31 rose upon him, and he halted upon his t.	3409
	32:32 which *is* upon the hollow of the t, unto	3409
	32:32 he touched the hollow of Jacob's t in	3409
	47:29 thy hand under my t, and deal kindly and	3409
Nu	5:21 when the Lord doth make thy t to rot,	3409
	5:22 make *thy* belly to swell, and *thy* t to rot:	3409
	5:27 her belly shall swell, and her t shall rot:	3409
Jdg	3:16 gird it under his raiment upon his right t.	3409
	3:21 took the dagger from his right t,	3409
	15: 8 them hip and t *with* a great slaughter:	3409
Ps	45: 3 Gird thy sword upon *thy* t, O *most*	3409
SS	3: 8 every man *hath* his sword upon his t	3409
Isa	47: 2 locks, make bare the leg, uncover the t,	7785
Jer	31:19 that I was instructed, I smote upon *my* t:	3409
Eze	21:12 my people: smite therefore upon *thy* t.	3409
	24: 4 every good piece, the t, and the shoulder;	3409
Rev	19:16 *his* vesture and on his t a name written,	3382

THIGHS (3) [THIGH]

Ex	28:42 from the loins even unto the t they shall	3409
SS	7: 1 joints of thy t *are* like jewels, the work	3409

Da	2:32 arms of silver, his belly and his t of brass,	3410

THIMNATHAH (1)

Jos	19:43 And Elon, and T, and Ekron,	8553

THIN (9)

Ge	41: 6 seven t ears and blasted with the east	1851
	41: 7 the seven t ears devoured the seven rank	1851
	41:23 t, *and* blasted with the east wind,	1851
	41:24 the t ears devoured the seven good ears:	1851
	41:27 seven t and ill favoured kine that came	7534
Ex	39: 3 they did beat the gold into t **plates,**	6341
Lev	13:30 *be* in it a yellow t hair; then the priest	1851
1Ki	7:29 oxen *were* certain additions **made** of	4174
Isa	17: 4 that the glory of Jacob shall be **made** t,	1809

THINE (933) [THOU]

Ge	13:14 Lift up now t eyes, and look from	3509.2
	14:20 which hath delivered t enemies into thy	3509.2
	14:23 will not take any thing that *is* t,	3509.2+3807.1
	15: 4 him, saying, This shall not be t heir;	3509.2
	15: 4 he that shall come forth out of t **own**	3509.2
	15: 4 out of thine own bowels shall be t heir.	3509.2
	20: 7 die, thou, and all that *are* t.	3509.2+3807.1
	21:18 lift up the lad, and hold him in t hand;	3509.3
	22: 2 Take now thy son, t only *son* Isaac,	3509.2
	22:12 he said, Lay not t hand upon the lad,	3509.2
	22:12 withheld thy son, t only *son* from me.	3509.2
	22:16 hast not withheld thy son, t only *son:*	3509.2
	30:27 If I have found favour in t eyes,	3509.2
	31:12 he said, Lift up now t eyes, and see,	3509.2
	31:32 discern thou what *is* t with me,	3509.2+3807.1
	38:18 and thy staff that *is* in t hand.	3509.2
	40:13 three days shall Pharaoh lift up t head,	3509.2
	44:18 let not t anger burn against thy servant:	3509.2
	46: 4 Joseph shall put his hand upon t eyes.	3509.2
	47:19 Wherefore shall we die before t eyes,	3509.2
	48: 6 shall be t, *and* shall be called	3509.2+3807.1
	49: 8 thy hand *shall be* in the neck of t	3509.2
Ex	4: 2 said unto him, What *is* that in t hand?	3509.2
	4: 4 Put forth t hand, and take it by the tail.	3509.2
	4: 6 him, Put now t hand into thy bosom.	3509.2
	4: 7 said, Put t hand into thy bosom again.	3509.2
	4:17 thou shalt take this rod in t hand,	3509.2
	4:21 which I have put in t hand:	3509.2
	5:16 but the fault *is* in t **own** people.	3509.2
	7: 5 to a serpent shalt take in t hand.	3509.2
	7:19 stretch out t hand upon the waters of	3509.2
	8: 3 shall go up and come into t house,	3509.2
	8: 3 into t ovens, and into thy	3509.2
	8: 5 Stretch forth t hand with thy rod over	3509.2
	9:14 time send all my plagues upon t heart,	3509.2
	9:22 Stretch forth t hand toward heaven,	3509.2
	10:12 Stretch out t hand over the land of	3509.2
	10:21 Stretch out t hand toward heaven,	3509.2
	13: 9 it shall be for a sign unto thee upon t	3509.2
	13: 9 for a memorial between t eyes, that	3509.2
	13:16 it shall be for a token upon t hand,	3509.2
	13:16 and for frontlets between t eyes:	3509.2
	14:16 stretch out t hand over the sea,	3509.2
	14:26 Stretch out t hand over the sea,	3509.2
	15: 7 in the greatness of t excellency thou	3509.2
	15:16 by the greatness of t arm they shall be	3509.2
	15:17 them in the mountain of t inheritance,	3509.2
	17: 5 the river, take in t hand, and go.	3509.2
	20:24 peace offerings, thy sheep, and t oxen:	3509.2
	22:30 Likewise shalt thou do with t oxen,	3509.2
	23: 1 put not t hand with the wicked to be an	3509.2
	23: 4 If thou meet t enemy's ox or his ass	3509.2
	23:12 that t ox and thine ass may rest,	3509.2
	23:12 that thine ox and t ass may rest,	3509.2
	23:22 I will be an enemy unto t enemies,	3509.2
	23:22 and an adversary unto t adversaries.	3509.2
	23:27 I will make all t enemies turn their	3509.2
	32:13 to whom thou swarest by t **own self,**	3509.2
	34: 9 our sin, and take us for t inheritance.	NIH
Lev	2:13 with all t offerings thou shalt offer salt.	3509.2
	10:15 it shall be t, and thy sons' with	3509.2+3807.1
	18:10 for theirs *is* t **own** nakedness.	3509.2
	18:14 not approach to his wife: she *is* t aunt.	3509.2
	19:17 shalt not hate thy brother in t heart:	3509.2
	27:23 he shall give t estimation in that day,	3509.2
	27:27 he shall redeem *it* according to t	3509.2
Nu	5:20 some man hath lain with thee beside t	3509.3
	10:35 Lord, and let t enemies be scattered;	3509.2
	18: 9 This shall be t of the most holy	3509.2+3807.1
	18:11 this *is* t; the heave offering of	3509.2+3807.1
	18:13 unto the Lord, shall be t;	3509.2+3807.1
	18:13 one *that is* clean in t house shall eat	3509.2
	18:14 devoted in Israel shall be t.	3509.2+3807.1
	18:15 *be* of men or beasts, shall be t:	3509.2+3807.1
	18:16 according to t estimation, *for* the money	3509.2
	18:18 the flesh of them shall be t,	3509.2+3807.1
	18:18 and as the right shoulder are t.	3509.2+3807.1
	18:20 t inheritance among the children of	3509.2
	22:30 the ass said unto Balaam, *Am* not I t ass,	3509.2
	22:30 ridden ever since *I was* t unto this day?	3509.2
	22:32 Wherefore hast thou smitten t ass these	3509.2
	27:18 *is* the spirit, and lay t hand upon him;	3509.2
	27:20 thou shalt put *some* of t honour upon	3509.2
Dt	3:21 T eyes have seen all that the Lord	3509.2
	3:27 lift up t eyes westward, and northward,	3509.2
	3:27 eastward, and behold *it* with t eyes:	3509.2
	4: 9 lest thou forget the things which t eyes	3509.2
	4:19 lest thou lift up t eyes unto heaven,	3509.2

Dt	4:39 *this* day, and consider *it* in t heart,	3509.2
	5:14 thy maidservant, nor t ox, nor thine ass,	3509.2
	5:14 thy maidservant, nor thine ox, nor t ass,	3509.2
	6: 5 love the Lord thy God with all t heart,	3509.2
	6: 6 thee *this* day, shall be in t heart:	3509.2
	6: 7 shalt talk of them when thou sittest in t	3509.2
	6: 8 thou shalt bind them for a sign upon t	3509.2
	6: 8 they shall be as frontlets between t eyes.	3509.2
	6:19 To cast out all t enemies from before	3509.2
	7:13 land, thy corn, and thy wine, and t oil,	3509.2
	7:16 t eye shall have no pity upon them:	3509.2
	7:17 thou shalt say in t heart, These nations	3509.2
	7:19 The great temptations which t eyes saw,	3509.2
	7:24 he shall deliver their kings into t hand,	3509.2
	7:26 thou bring an abomination into t house,	3509.2
	8: 2 thee, to know what *was* in t heart,	3509.2
	8: 5 Thou shalt also consider in t heart, that,	3509.2
	8:14 t heart be lifted up, and thou forget	3509.2
	8:17 thou say in t heart, My power and	3509.2
	9: 4 Speak not thou in t heart, after that	3509.2
	9: 5 or for the uprightness of t heart,	3509.2
	9:26 destroy not thy people and t inheritance,	3509.2
	9:29 they *are* thy people and t inheritance,	3509.2
	10:21 terrible *things,* which t eyes have seen.	3509.2
	11:14 in thy corn, and thy wine, and t oil.	3509.2
	11:19 speaking of them when thou sittest in t	3509.2
	11:20 them upon the door posts of t house,	3509.2
	12:17 or heave offering of t hand:	3509.2
	12:18 in all that thou puttest t hands unto.	3509.2
	13: 6 or thy friend, which *is* as t **own** soul,	3509.2
	13: 8 neither shall t eye pity him, neither shalt	3509.2
	13: 9 t hand shall be first upon him to put him	3509.2
	13:17 nought of the cursed thing to t hand:	3509.2
	14:23 of t oil, and the firstlings of thy herds	3509.2
	14:25 bind up the money in t hand, and shalt	3509.2
	14:26 thou shalt rejoice, thou and t household,	3509.2
	14:28 all the tithe of t increase the same year,	3509.2
	14:29 all the work of t hand which thou doest.	3509.2
	15: 3 which is t with thy brother thine hand	3509.2
	15: 3 which is thine with thy brother t hand	3509.2
	15: 7 nor shut t hand from thy poor brother:	3509.2
	15: 8 thou shalt open t hand wide unto him,	3509.2
	15: 9 t eye be evil against thy poor brother,	3509.2
	15:10 t heart shall not be grieved when thou	3509.2
	15:10 and in all that thou puttest t hand unto.	3509.2
	15:11 Thou shalt open t hand wide unto thy	3509.2
	15:16 because he loveth thee and t house,	3509.2
	16:10 a tribute of a freewill offering of t hand,	3509.2
	16:15 in all the works of t hands, therefore	3509.2
	18:21 if thou say in t heart, How shall we	3509.2
	19:13 T eye shall not pity him, but thou shalt	3509.2
	19:14 which they of old time have set in t	3509.2
	19:21 t eye shall not pity; *but* life shall go for	3509.2
	20: 1 When thou goest out to battle against t	3509.2
	20:13 thy God hath delivered it into t hands,	3509.2
	20:14 thou shalt eat the spoil of t enemies,	3509.2
	21:10 When thou goest forth to war against t	3509.2
	21:10 God hath delivered them into t hands,	3509.2
	21:12 thou shalt bring her home to t house;	3509.2
	21:13 shall remain in t house, and bewail her	3509.2
	22: 2 thou shalt bring it unto t **own** house,	3509.2
	23: 9 When the host goeth forth against t	3509.2
	23:14 and to give up t enemies before thee;	3509.2
	23:20 t hand to in the land whither thou goest	3509.2
	23:24 thou mayest eat grapes thy fill at t **own**	3509.2
	23:25 thou mayest pluck the ears with t hand;	3509.2
	24:19 When thou cuttest down t harvest in	3509.2
	24:19 may bless thee in all the work of t hands.	3509.2
	24:20 When thou beatest t olive tree, thou	3509.2
	25:12 cut off her hand, t eye shall not pity *her.*	3509.2
	25:14 Thou shalt not have in t house divers	3509.2
	25:19 rest from all t enemies round about,	3509.2
	26: 4 the priest shall take the basket out of t	3509.2
	26:11 unto t house, thou, and the Levite,	3509.2
	26:12 all the tithes of t increase the third year,	3509.2
	26:16 keep and do them with all t heart,	3509.2
	28: 7 The Lord shall cause t enemies that	3509.2
	28: 8 and in all that thou settest t hand unto;	3509.2
	28:12 and to bless all the work of t hand:	3509.2
	28:20 that thou settest t hand unto for to do,	3509.2
	28:25 thee to be smitten before t enemies:	3509.2
	28:31 T ox *shall be* slain before thine eyes,	3509.2
	28:31 Thine ox *shall be* slain before t eyes,	3509.2
	28:31 t ass *shall be* violently taken away from	3509.2
	28:31 thy sheep *shall be* given unto t enemies,	3509.2
	28:32 t eyes shall look, and fail *with* longing	3509.2
	28:32 and *there shall be* no might in t hand.	3509.2
	28:34 the sight of t eyes which thou shalt see.	3509.2
	28:40 the oil; for t olive shall cast *his* fruit.	3509.2
	28:48 Therefore shalt thou serve t enemies	3509.2
	28:53 thou shalt eat the fruit of t **own** body,	3509.2
	28:53 wherewith t enemies shall distress thee:	3509.2
	28:55 wherewith t enemies shall distress thee	3509.2
	28:57 wherewith t enemy shall distress thee	3509.2
	28:67 for the fear of t heart wherewith thou	3509.2
	28:67 the sight of t eyes which thou shalt see.	3509.2
	29: 3 The great temptations which t eyes have	3509.2
	30: 2 with all t heart, and with all thy soul;	3509.2
	30: 4 If *any* of t be driven out unto the	3509.2
	30: 6 the Lord thy God will circumcise t	3509.2
	30: 6 to love the Lord thy God with all t	3509.2
	30: 7 will put all these curses upon t enemies,	3509.2
	30: 9 thee plenteous in every work of t hand,	3509.2
	30:10 unto the Lord thy God with all t heart,	3509.2

Dt 30:17 if t heart turn away, so that thou wilt	3509.2
33:10 and whole *burnt sacrifice* upon t altar.	3509.2
33:29 t enemies shall be found liars unto thee;	3509.2
34: 4 I have caused thee to see *it* with t eyes,	3509.2
Jos 2: 3 to thee, which are entered into t house:	3509.3
2:17 We *will be* blameless of this t oath	3509.3
2:20 we will be quit of t oath which thou	3509.3
6: 2 I have given into t hand Jericho,	3509.2
7:13 thou canst not stand before t enemies,	3509.2
8:18 toward Ai; for I will give it into t hand.	3509.2
9:25 now, behold, we *are* in t hand: as it	3509.2
10: 8 for I have delivered them into t hand;	3509.2
14: 9 trodden shall be t inheritance,	3509.2+3807.1
17:18 the mountain shall be t; for it *is* a wood,	3509.2
17:18 the outgoings of it shall be t:	3509.2+3807.1
Jdg 4: 7 and I will deliver him into t hand.	3509.2
4: 9 thou takest shall not be for t honour;	3509.2
4:14 LORD hath delivered Sisera into t hand:	3509.2
5:31 So let all t enemies perish, O LORD:	3509.2
6:39 Let not t anger be hot against me,	3509.2
7: 7 and deliver the Midianites into t hand:	3509.2
7: 9 for I have delivered it into t hand.	3509.2
7:11 afterward shall t hands be strengthened	3509.2
8: 6 of Zebah and Zalmunna now in t hand,	3509.2
8: 6 that we should give bread unto t army?	3509.2
8:15 of Zebah and Zalmunna now in t hand,	3509.2
9:29 Increase t army, and come out.	3509.2
11:36 taken vengeance for thee of t enemies,	3509.2
12: 1 will burn t house upon thee with fire.	3509.2
16:15 love thee, when t heart *is not* with me?	3509.2
18:19 lay t hand upon thy mouth, and go with	3509.2
19: 5 Comfort t heart *with* a morsel of bread,	3509.2
19: 6 tarry all night, and let t heart be merry.	3509.2
19: 8 father said, Comfort t heart, I pray thee.	3509.2
19: 9 lodge here, that t heart may be merry;	3509.2
19:22 forth the man that came into t house,	3509.2
20:28 for to morrow I will deliver them into t	3509.2
Ru 2: 9 *Let* t eyes *be* on the field that they do	3509.3
2:10 Why have I found grace in t eyes,	3509.2
2:11 in law since the death of t husband:	3509.3
2:13 for that thou hast spoken friendly unto t	3509.2
3: 9 she answered, I *am* Ruth t handmaid:	3509.2
3: 9 spread therefore thy skirt over t	3509.2
4:11 that is come into t house like Rachel	3509.2
4:15 of *thy* life, and a nourisher of t old age:	3509.3
1Sa 1:11 look on the affliction of t handmaid,	3509.2
1:11 not forget t handmaid, but wilt give	3509.2
1:11 wilt give unto t handmaid a man child,	3509.2
1:16 Count not t handmaid for a daughter of	3509.2
1:18 Let t handmaid find grace in thy sight.	3509.2
2:31 that I will cut off t arm, and the arm of	3509.2
2:31 that there shall not be an old man in t	3509.2
2:32 there shall not be an old man in t house	3509.2
2:33 the man of t, *whom* I shall not cut off	3509.2
2:33 *be* to consume t eyes, and to grieve	3509.2
2:33 thine eyes, and to grieve t heart:	3509.2
2:33 all the increase of t house shall die in	3509.2
2:36 every one that is left in t house shall	3509.2
9:19 and will tell thee all that *is* in t heart.	3509.2
9:20 as for t asses that were lost three days	3509.2
14: 7 said unto him, Do all that *is* in t heart:	3509.2
14:19 said unto the priest, Withdraw t hand.	3509.2
15:17 When thou *wast* little in t own sight,	3509.2
15:28 hath given it to a neighbour of t, *that is*	3509.2
16: 1 fill t horn *with* oil, and go, I will send	3509.2
17:28 pride, and the naughtiness of t heart;	3509.2
17:46 smite thee, and take t head from thee;	3509.2
20: 3 that I have found grace in t eyes;	3509.2
20:29 now, if I have found favour in t eyes,	3509.2
20:30 the son of Jesse to t own confusion,	3509.2
21: 3 Now therefore what is under t hand?	3509.2
21: 8 is there not here under t hand spear or	3509.2
22:14 bidding, and *is* honourable in t house?	3509.2
23: 4 I will deliver the Philistines into t hand.	3509.2
24: 4 I will deliver t enemy into thine hand,	3509.2
24: 4 I will deliver thine enemy into t hand,	3509.2
24:10 this day t eyes have seen how that	3509.2
24:15 my cause, and deliver me out of t hand.	3509.2
24:18 the LORD had delivered me into t hand,	3509.2
24:20 of Israel shall be established in t hand.	3509.2
25: 6 peace *be to* t house, and peace *be unto*	3509.2
25: 8 let the young men find favour in t eyes:	3509.2
25: 8 whatsoever cometh to t hand unto thy	3509.2
25:24 *let this* iniquity *be:* and let t handmaid,	3509.2
25:24 speak in t audience, and hear the words	3509.2
25:24 and hear the words of t handmaid.	3509.2
25:25 I t handmaid saw not the young men of	3509.2
25:26 *from* avenging thyself with t own hand,	3509.2
25:26 let t enemies, and they that seek evil	3509.2
25:27 this blessing which t handmaid hath	3509.2
25:28 forgive the trespass of t handmaid:	3509.2
25:29 souls of t enemies, them shall he sling	3509.2
25:31 my lord, then remember t handmaid.	3509.2
25:35 unto her, Go up in peace to t house:	3509.3
25:41 *let* t handmaid *be* a servant to wash	3509.2
26: 8 God hath delivered t enemy into thine	3509.2
26: 8 God hath delivered thine enemy into t	3509.2
26:21 my soul was precious in t eyes this day:	3509.2
27: 5 If I have now found grace in t eyes,	3509.2
28:16 from thee, and is become t enemy?	3509.2
28:17 hath rent the kingdom out of t hand,	3509.2
28:21 t handmaid hath obeyed thy voice,	3509.2
28:22 hearken thou also unto the voice of t	3509.2
2Sa 1:14 wast thou not afraid to stretch forth t	3509.2
1:25 *thou wast* slain in t high places.	3509.2

2Sa 3:21 thou mayest reign over all that t heart	3509.2
4: 8 of Ish-bosheth the son of Saul t enemy,	3509.2
5:19 deliver the Philistines into t hand.	3509.2
7: 3 to the king, Go, do all that *is* in t heart;	3509.2
7: 9 cut off all t enemies out of thy sight,	3509.2
7:11 caused thee to rest from all t enemies.	3509.2
7:16 t house and thy kingdom shall be	3509.2
7:21 and according to t own heart,	3509.2
11:10 didst thou not go down unto t house?	3509.2
12:10 sword shall never depart from t house,	3509.2
12:11 up evil against thee out of t own house,	3509.2
12:11 I will take thy wives before t eyes,	3509.2
13:10 the chamber, that I may eat of t hand.	3509.3
14: 7 the whole family is risen against t	3509.2
14: 8 Go to t house, and I will give charge	3509.3
14:17 said, Let t handmaid, I pray thee,	3509.2
14:17 t handmaid said, The word of my lord	3509.2
14:19 he put all these words in the mouth of t	3509.2
16: 4 Behold, t *are* all that *pertained*	3509.2+3807.1
17:11 *that* thou go to battle in t own person.	3509.2
19: 6 In that thou lovest t enemies, and hatest	3509.2
19:27 do therefore what *is* good in t eyes.	3509.2
19:28 among them that did eat at t own table.	3509.2
20:17 him, Hear the words of t handmaid.	3509.2
22:28 t eyes *are* upon the haughty, *that* thou	3509.2
24:13 wilt thou flee three months before t	3509.2
24:16 stay now t hand. And the angel of	3509.2
24:17 let t hand, I pray thee, be against me,	3509.2
1Ki 1:12 that thou mayest save t own life,	3509.3
1:13 O king, swear unto t handmaid, saying,	3509.2
1:17 by the LORD thy God unto t handmaid,	3509.2
1:53 Solomon said unto him, Go to t house.	3509.3
2:26 Get thee *to* Anathoth, unto t own fields;	3509.2
2:37 thy blood shall be upon t own head.	3509.2
2:44 knowest all the wickedness which t	3509.2
2:44 thy wickedness upon t own head;	3509.2
3:11 nor hast asked the life of t enemies;	3509.2
3:20 while t handmaid slept, and laid it in her	3509.2
3:26 neither mine nor t, *but* divide	3509.3+3807.1
8:18 it was in t heart to build a house	3509.2
8:18 thou didst well that it was in t heart.	3509.2
8:24 hast fulfilled *it* with t hand, as *it is* this	3509.2
8:29 That t eyes may be open toward this	3509.2
8:31 oath come before t altar in this house:	3509.2
8:51 they *be* thy people, and t inheritance,	3509.2
8:52 That t eyes may be open unto	3509.2
8:53 to be t inheritance, as thou	3509.2+3807.1
11:22 thou seekest to go to t own country?	3509.2
12:16 now see to t own house, David.	3509.2
13: 8 If thou wilt give me half t house, I will	3509.2
13:18 Bring him back with thee into t house,	3509.2
14:12 thou therefore, get thee to t own house:	3509.3
17:11 I pray thee, a morsel of bread in t hand.	3509.3
19:10 thrown down t altars, and slain thy	3509.2
19:14 thrown down t altars, and slain thy	3509.2
20: 4 I *am* t, and all that I have.	3509.2+3807.1
20: 6 shall search t house, and the houses	3509.2
20: 6 *that* whatsoever *is* pleasant in t eyes,	3509.2
20:13 behold, I will deliver it into t hand this	3509.2
20:28 I deliver all this great multitude into t	3509.2
21: 7 *and* eat bread, and let t heart be merry:	3509.2
21:19 Naboth shall dogs lick thy blood, even t.	859
21:22 will make t house like the house of	3509.2
22:34 Turn t hand, and carry me out of the	3509.2
2Ki 4: 2 t handmaid hath not any thing in	3509.2
4:16 of God, do not lie unto t handmaid.	3509.2
4:29 take my staff in t hand, and go *thy way:*	3509.2
7: 2 shalt see *it* with t eyes, but shalt not	3509.2
7:19 shalt see *it* with t eyes, but shalt not	3509.2
8: 1 go thou and t household,	3509.3
8: 8 Take a present in t hand, and go, meet	3509.2
9: 1 take this box of oil in t hand, and go *to*	3509.2
10: 5 do thou *that* which *is* good in t eyes.	3509.2
10:15 and said to him, Is t heart right,	3509.2
10:15 If it be, give *me* t hand. And he gave	3509.2
13:16 king of Israel, Put t hand upon the bow.	3509.2
14:10 and t heart hath lifted thee up:	3509.2
19:16 bow down t ear, and hear: open,	3509.2
19:16 open, LORD, t eyes, and see:	3509.2
19:22 thy voice, and lift up t eyes on high?	3509.2
20: 1 saith the LORD, Set t house in order;	3509.2
20:15 said, What have they seen in t house?	3509.2
20:17 all that *is* in t house, and that which	3509.2
22:19 Because t heart was tender, and thou	3509.2
22:20 t eyes shall not see all the evil which I	3509.2
1Ch 4:10 that t hand might be with me,	3509.2
12:18 of the captains, and he said, T	3509.2+3807.1
12:18 *be* unto thee, and peace *be to* t helpers;	3509.2
14:10 up; for I will deliver them into t hand.	3509.2
17: 2 said unto David, Do all that *is* in t heart;	3509.2
17: 8 cut off all t enemies from before thee,	3509.2
17:10 Moreover I will subdue all t enemies.	3509.2
17:17 *yet* this was a small thing in t eyes,	3509.2
17:19 and according to t own heart,	3509.2
17:22 make t own people for ever;	3509.2+3807.1
21:12 while that the sword of t enemies	3509.2
21:15 *It* is enough, stay now t hand.	3509.2
21:17 let t hand, I pray thee, O LORD my	3509.2
21:24 I will not take that which *is* t	3509.2+3807.1
29:11 T, O LORD, *is* the greatness,	3509.2+3807.1
29:11 in the earth *is* t; thine *is* the kingdom,	NIH
29:11 earth *is thine;* t *is* the kingdom,	3509.2+3807.1
29:12 in t hand *is* power and might; and in	3509.2
29:12 in t hand *it is* to make great, and to give	3509.2
29:14 thee, and of t own have we given thee.	3509.2

1Ch 29:16 for t holy name *cometh* of thine hand,	3509.2
29:16 for thine holy name *cometh* of t hand,	3509.2
29:16 *cometh* of thine hand, and *is* all t own.	3509.2
2Ch 1:11 Because this was in t heart, and thou	3509.2
1:11 or honour, nor the life of t enemies;	3509.2
6: 8 Forasmuch as it was in t heart to build a	3509.2
6: 8 thou didst well *in* that it was in t heart:	3509.2
6:15 hast fulfilled *it* with t hand, as *it is* this	3509.2
6:20 t eyes may be open upon this house	3509.2
6:22 oath come before t altar in this house;	3509.2
6:40 let t eyes be open, and *let* thine ears be	3509.2
6:40 *let* t ears be attent unto the prayer *that*	3509.2
6:42 turn not away the face of t anointed:	3509.2
9: 5 I heard in mine own land of t acts,	3509.2
10:16 *and* now, David, see to t own house.	3509.2
16: 7 the king of Syria escaped out of t hand.	3509.2
16: 8 he delivered them into t hand.	3509.2
18:33 he said to *his* chariot man, Turn t hand,	3509.2
19: 3 and hast prepared t heart to seek God.	3509.2
20: 6 in t hand *is there not* power and might,	3509.2
25:15 deliver their own people out of t hand?	3509.2
25:19 and t heart lifteth thee up to boast:	3509.2
25:19 why shouldest thou meddle to t hurt,	NIH
26:18 neither *shall it be* for t honour from	3509.2
34:27 Because t heart was tender,	3509.2
34:28 neither shall t eyes see all the evil that I	3509.2
Ezr 7:14 the law of thy God which *is* in t hand;	3509.5
7:25 *is* in t hand, set magistrates and judges,	3509.5
Ne 1: 6 Let t ear now be attentive, and thine	3509.2
1: 6 ear now be attentive, and t eyes open,	3509.2
1:11 let now t ear be attentive to the prayer	3509.2
6: 8 thou feignest them out of t own heart.	3509.2
Job 1:11 put forth t hand now, and touch all that	3509.2
1:12 only upon himself put not forth t hand.	3509.2
2: 5 put forth t hand now, and touch his	3509.2
2: 6 said unto Satan, Behold, he *is* in t hand;	3509.2
2: 9 Dost thou still retain t integrity?	3509.2
5:25 and t offspring as the grass of the earth.	3509.2
7: 8 see me no *more:* t eyes *are* upon me,	3509.2
7:17 thou shouldest set t heart upon him?	3509.2
10: 3 thou shouldest despise the work of t	3509.2
10: 7 *is* none that can deliver out of t hand.	3509.2
10: 8 T hands have made me and fashioned	3509.2
10:13 these *things* hast thou hid in t heart:	3509.2
10:17 and increasest t indignation upon me;	3509.2
11: 4 *is* pure, and I am clean in t eyes.	3509.2
11: 6 that God exacteth of thee *less* than t	3509.2
11:13 If thou prepare t heart, and stretch out	3509.2
11:13 and stretch out t hands toward him;	3509.2
11:14 If iniquity *be* in t hand, put it far away,	3509.2
11:17 t *age* shall be clearer than the noonday;	NIH
13:21 Withdraw t hand far from me: and let	3509.2
13:24 thy face, and holdest me for t enemy?	3509.2
14: 3 dost thou open t eyes upon such a one,	3509.2
14:15 thou wilt have a desire to the work of t	3509.2
15: 5 For thy mouth uttereth t iniquity,	3509.2
15: 6 T own mouth condemneth thee,	3509.2
15: 6 yea, t own lips testify against thee.	3509.2
15:12 Why doth t heart carry thee away?	3509.2
15:12 thee away? and what do t eyes wink at,	3509.2
22: 5 and t iniquities infinite?	3509.2
22:22 and lay up his words in t heart.	3509.2
22:30 is delivered by the pureness of t hands.	3509.2
35: 7 or what receiveth he of t hand?	3509.2
40:14 will I also confess unto thee that t own	3509.2
41: 3 t hand upon him, remember	3509.2
Ps 2: 8 I shall give *thee* the heathen *for* t	3509.2
6: 1 O LORD, rebuke me not in t anger,	3509.2
7: 6 Arise, O LORD, in t anger, lift up	3509.2
8: 2 ordained strength because of t enemies,	3509.2
10:12 Arise, O LORD; O God, lift up t hand:	3509.2
10:17 their heart, thou wilt cause t ear to hear:	3509.2
16:10 neither wilt thou suffer t Holy One to	3509.2
17: 2 t eyes behold the things that are equal.	3509.2
17: 6 t ear unto me, *and* hear my speech.	3509.2
20: 4 Grant thee according to t own heart,	3509.2
21: 8 T hand shall find out all thine enemies:	3509.2
21: 8 Thine hand shall find out all t enemies:	3509.2
21: 9 as a fiery oven in the time of t anger:	3509.2
21:12 thou shalt make ready t arrows upon	NIH
21:13 thou exalted, LORD, in t own strength:	3509.2
26: 6 so will I compass t altar, O LORD:	3509.2
26: 8 and the place where t honour dwelleth.	3509.2
27:14 and he shall strengthen t heart:	3509.2
28: 5 Save thy people, and bless t inheritance.	3509.2
31: 2 Bow down t ear to me; deliver me	3509.2
31: 5 Into t hand I commit my spirit: thou	3509.2
31:22 haste, I am cut off from before t eyes:	3509.2
37: 4 he shall give thee the desires of t heart.	3509.2
38: 2 For t arrows stick fast in me,	3509.2
38: 3 in my flesh because of t anger;	3509.2
39:10 I am consumed by the blow of t hand.	3509.2
44: 3 t arm, and the light of thy countenance,	3509.2
45: 5 T arrows *are* sharp in the heart of	3509.2
45:10 and consider, and incline t ear;	3509.3
45:10 forget also t own people, and thy	3509.2
50:20 thou slanderest t own mother's son.	3509.2
50:21 and set *them* in order before t eyes.	3509.2
51:19 shall they offer bullocks upon t altar.	3509.2
56: 7 in t anger cast down the people, O God.	NIH
66: 3 the greatness of thy power shall t	3509.2
68: 9 thou didst confirm t inheritance,	3509.2
68:23 may be dipped in the blood of t enemies,	NIH
69: 9 the zeal of t house hath eaten me up;	3509.2
69:24 Pour out t indignation upon them,	3509.2

T

Ps
71: 2 incline t ear unto me, and save me. 3509.2
71:16 of thy righteousness, *even* of t only. 3509.2
74: 1 doth t anger smoke against the sheep 3509.2
74: 2 the rod of t inheritance, *which* thou 3509.2
74: 4 T enemies roar in the midst of thy 3509.2
74:16 The day *is* t, the night also *is* 3509.2+3807.1
74:16 day *is* thine, the night also *is* t: 3509.2+3807.1
74:22 Arise, O God, plead t own cause. 3509.2
74:23 Forget not the voice of t enemies: 3509.2
77:15 hast with t arm redeemed thy people. NIH
77:17 out a sound: t arrows also went abroad. 3509.2
79: 1 the heathen are come into t inheritance; 3509.2
83: 2 For lo, t enemies make a tumult: 3509.2
84: 3 *even* t altars, O LORD of hosts, 3509.2
84: 9 and look upon the face of t anointed. 3509.2
85: 3 *thyself* from the fierceness of t anger. 3509.2
85: 4 and cause t anger towards us to cease. 3509.2
85: 5 wilt thou draw out t anger to all 3509.2
86: 1 Bow down t ear, O LORD, hear me: 3509.2
86:16 and save the son of t handmaid. 3509.2
88: 2 before thee: incline t ear unto my cry; 3509.2
89:10 thou hast scattered t enemies with thy 3509.2
89:11 The heavens *are* t, the earth 3509.2+3807.1
89:11 *are* thine, the earth also is t: 3509.2+3807.1
89:38 thou hast been wroth with t anointed. 3509.2
89:51 Wherewith t enemies have reproached, 3509.2
89:51 reproached the footsteps of t anointed. 3509.2
90: 7 For we are consumed by t anger, 3509.2
90:11 Who knoweth the power of t anger? 3509.2
91: 8 Only with t eyes shalt thou behold and 3509.2
92: 9 For lo, t enemies, O LORD, for lo, 3509.2
92: 9 O LORD, for lo, t enemies shall perish; 3509.2
93: 5 holiness becometh t house, O LORD, 3509.2
94: 5 O LORD, and afflict t heritage. 3509.2
102: 2 I am in trouble; incline t ear unto me: 3509.2
102:10 Because of t indignation and thy wrath: 3509.2
103: 3 Who forgiveth all t iniquities; 3509.3
104:28 thou openest t hand, they are filled *with* 3509.2
106: 5 that *I* may glory with t inheritance. 3509.2
110: 1 until I make t enemies thy footstool. 3509.2
110: 2 rule thou in the midst of t enemies. 3509.2
119:91 They continue *this* day according to t 3509.2
119:94 I am t, save me; for I have 3509.2+3807.1
119:173 Let t hand help me; for I have chosen 3509.2
128: 2 For thou shalt eat the labour of t hands: 3509.2
128: 3 as a fruitful vine by the sides of t house: 3509.2
130: 2 let t ears be attentive to the voice of my 3509.2
132:10 turn not away the face of t anointed. 3509.2
138: 7 thou shalt stretch forth t hand against 3509.2
138: 8 forsake not the works of t own hands. 3509.2
139: 5 and before, and laid t hand upon me. 3509.2
139:16 T eyes did see my substance, yet being 3509.2
139:20 *and* t enemies take *thy* name in vain. 3509.2
144: 6 shoot out t arrows, and destroy them. 3509.2
144: 7 Send t hand from above; rid me, 3509.2
145:16 Thou openest t hand, and satisfiest 3509.2

Pr
2: 2 So that *thou* incline t ear unto wisdom, 3509.2
2: 2 *and* apply t heart to understanding; 3509.2
2:10 When wisdom entereth into t heart, 3509.2
3: 1 let t heart keep my commandments; 3509.2
3: 3 write them upon the table of t heart: 3509.2
3: 5 Trust in the LORD with all t heart; 3509.2
3: 5 lean not unto t own understanding. 3509.2
3: 7 Be not wise in t own eyes: fear 3509.2
3: 9 and with the firstfruits of all t increase: 3509.2
3:21 son, let not them depart from t eyes: 3509.2
3:27 it is in the power of t hand to do *it.* 3509.2
4: 4 unto me, Let t heart retain my words: 3509.2
4: 9 She shall give to t head an ornament of 3509.2
4:20 words; incline t ear unto my sayings. 3509.2
4:21 Let them not depart from t eyes; 3509.2
4:21 keep them in the midst of t heart. 3509.2
4:25 Let t eyes look right on, and let thine 3509.2
4:25 let t eyelids look straight before thee. 3509.2
5: 1 *and* bow t ear to my understanding: 3509.2
5: 9 Lest thou give t honour unto others, 3509.2
5:15 Drink waters out of t own cistern, 3509.2
5:15 and running waters out of t own well. 3509.2
5:17 Let them be only t own, 3509.2+3807.1
6: 4 Give not sleep to t eyes, nor slumber to 3509.2
6: 4 to thine eyes, nor slumber to t eyelids. 3509.2
6:21 Bind them continually upon t heart, 3509.2
6:25 Lust not after her beauty in t heart; 3509.2
7: 2 live; and my law as the apple of t eye. 3509.2
7: 3 write them upon the table of t heart. 3509.2
7:25 Let not t heart decline to her ways, go 3509.2
20:13 open t eyes, *and* thou shalt be satisfied 3509.2
22:17 Bow down t ear, and hear the words of 3509.2
22:17 and apply t heart unto my knowledge. 3509.2
23: 4 to be rich: cease from t own wisdom. 3509.2
23: 5 Wilt thou set t eyes upon that which is 3509.2
23:12 Apply t heart unto instruction, 3509.2
23:12 and t ears to the words of knowledge. 3509.2
23:15 My son, if t heart be wise, my heart 3509.2
23:17 Let not t heart envy sinners: but be 3509.2
23:18 and t expectation shall not be cut off. 3509.2
23:19 be wise, and guide t heart in the way. 3509.2
23:26 give me t heart, and let thine eyes 3509.2
23:26 and let t eyes observe my ways. 3509.2
23:33 T eyes shall behold strange *women,* 3509.2
23:33 and t heart shall utter perverse things. 3509.2
24:17 Rejoice not when t enemy falleth, 3509.2
24:17 not t heart be glad when he stumbleth: 3509.2
24:27 the field; and afterwards build t house. 3509.2
25: 7 of the prince whom t eyes have seen. 3509.2

Pr
25:10 to shame, and t infamy turn not away. 3509.2
25:21 If t enemy be hungry, give him bread to 3509.2
27: 2 *man* praise thee, and not t own mouth; 3509.2
27: 2 a stranger, and not t own lips. 3509.2
27:10 T own friend, and thy father's friend, 3509.2
30:32 thought evil, *lay* t hand upon thy mouth. NIH

Ecc
5: 2 not t heart be hasty to utter *any* thing 3509.2
5: 6 and destroy the work of t hands? 3509.2
7:18 also from this withdraw not t hand: 3509.2
7:22 oftentimes also t own heart knoweth 3509.2
11: 6 in the evening withhold not t hand: 3509.2
11: 9 walk in the ways of t heart, and in 3509.2
11: 9 of thine heart, and in the sight of t eyes: 3509.2

SS
4: 9 hast ravished my heart with one of t 3509.2
4:10 the smell of t ointments than all spices! 3509.3
6: 5 Turn away t eyes from me, for they 3509.3
7: 4 t eyes like the fishpools in Heshbon, 3509.3
7: 5 T head upon thee *is* like Carmel, 3509.3
7: 5 and the hair of t head like purple; 3509.3
8: 2 Set me as a seal upon t heart, as a seal 3509.2
8: 6 upon thine heart, as a seal upon t arm: 3509.2

Isa
6: 7 t iniquity is taken away, and thy sin 3509.2
12: 1 t anger is turned away, 3509.2
14:13 thou hast said in t heart, I will ascend 3509.2
26:11 the fire of t enemies shall devour them. 3509.2
30:20 but t eyes shall see thy teachers: 3509.2
30:21 t ears shall hear a word behind thee, 3509.2
33:17 T eyes shall see the king in his beauty: 3509.2
33:18 T heart shall meditate terror. Where *is* 3509.2
33:20 t eyes shall see Jerusalem a quiet 3509.2
37:17 Incline t ear, O LORD, and hear; 3509.2
37:17 hear; open t eyes, O LORD, and see: 3509.2
37:23 thy voice, and lifted up t eyes on high? 3509.2
38: 1 saith the LORD, Set t house in order: 3509.2
39: 4 he, What have they seen in t house? 3509.2
39: 6 all that *is in* t house, and *that* which 3509.2
42: 6 will hold t hand, and will keep thee, 3509.2
43:24 thou hast wearied me with t iniquities. 3509.2
44: 3 and my blessing upon t offspring: 3509.2
45:14 unto thee, and they shall be t: 3509.3+3807.1
47: 6 and given them into t hand: 3509.2
47: 8 sayest in t heart, I *am,* and none else 1886.3
47: 9 the great abundance of t enchantments. 3509.2
47:10 thou hast said in t heart, I *am,* and 3509.2
47:12 Stand now with t enchantments, 3509.2
48: 8 that time *that* t ear was not opened: 3509.2
49:18 Lift up t eyes round about, and behold: 3509.3
49:20 lost the other, shall say again in t ears, 3509.2
49:21 shalt thou say in t heart, Who hath 3509.3
51:22 I have taken out of t hand the cup of 3509.2
54: 2 let them stretch forth the curtains of t 3509.3
54: 5 For thy Maker *is* t husband; the LORD 3509.2
57:10 thou hast found the life of t hand; 3509.2
58: 7 thou hide not thyself from t own flesh? 3509.2
58: 8 and t health shall spring forth speedily: 3509.2
58:13 honour him, not doing t own ways, 3509.2
58:13 own ways, nor finding t own pleasure, 3509.2
58:13 pleasure, nor speaking t own words: NIH
60: 4 Lift up t eyes round about, and see: 3509.3
60: 5 flow *together,* and t heart shall fear, 3509.3
60:17 and t exactors righteousness. 3509.3
60:20 for the LORD shall be t 3509.3+3807.1
62: 8 give thy corn *to be* meat for t enemies; 3509.3
63: 2 Wherefore *art thou* red in t apparel, 3509.2
63:17 sake, the tribes of t inheritance. 3509.2
63:19 We are t: thou never barest rule over NIH
64: 2 make thy name known to t adversaries, 3509.2
64: 8 and we all *are* the work of t hand. 3509.2

Jer
2: 2 of thy youth, the love of t espousals, 3509.3
2:19 T own wickedness shall correct thee, 3509.3
2:22 *yet* t iniquity *is* marked before me, 3509.3
2:37 from him, and t hands upon thine head: 3509.3
2:37 from him, and thine hands upon t head: 3509.3
3: 2 Lift up t eyes unto the high places, 3509.3
3:13 Only acknowledge t iniquity, that thou 3509.3
4: 1 if thou wilt put away t abominations 3509.2
4:14 wash t heart from wickedness, 3509.2
4:18 bitter, because it reacheth unto t heart. 3509.3
5: 3 O LORD, *are* not t eyes upon the truth? 3509.2
5:17 shall eat up t harvest, and thy bread, 3509.2
5:17 they shall eat up thy flocks and t herds: 3509.2
6: 9 turn back t hand as a grapegatherer into 3509.2
7:29 Cut off t hair, *O Jerusalem,* and cast *it* 3509.2
9: 6 T habitation *is* in the midst of deceit; 3509.2
10:24 not in t anger, lest thou bring me to 3509.2
13:22 if thou say in t heart, Wherefore come 3509.3
13:22 For the greatness of t iniquity are thy 3509.3
13:27 I have seen t adulteries, 3509.3
13:27 t abominations on the hills in the fields. 3509.3
15:14 I will make *thee* to pass with t enemies 3509.2
17: 4 shalt discontinue from t heritage that I 3509.2
17: 4 I will cause thee to serve t enemies in 3509.2
18:23 *thus* with them in the time of t anger. 3509.2
20: 4 t eyes *shall* behold *it;* and I will give all 3509.2
20: 6 all that dwell in t house shall go into 3509.2
22:17 t eyes and thine heart *are* not but for 3509.2
22:17 thine eyes and t heart *are* not but for 3509.2
25:28 if they refuse to take the cup at t hand 3509.2
28: 7 now this word that I speak in t ears, 3509.2
30:14 one, for the multitude of t iniquity; 3509.3
30:15 Why criest thou for t affliction? 3509.3
30:15 incurable for the multitude of t iniquity: 3509.3
30:16 all adversaries, every one of them, 3509.2
31:16 from weeping, and t eyes from tears: 3509.3
31:17 there is hope in t end, saith the LORD, 3509.3

Jer
31:21 set t heart toward the highway, *even* 3509.3
32: 7 Hanameel the son of Shallum t uncle 3509.3
32: 7 of redemption *is* to buy *it.* 3509.2+3807.1
32: 8 for the right of inheritance *is* t, 3509.2+3807.1
32: 8 thine, and the redemption *is* t; 3509.2+3807.1
32:19 for t eyes *are* open upon all the ways of 3509.2
34: 3 t eyes shall behold the eyes of the king 3509.2
36:14 Take in t hand the roll wherein thou 3509.2
38:12 rotten rags under t armholes under 3509.2
38:17 fire; and thou shalt live, and t house: 3509.2
40: 4 the chains which *were* upon t hand. 3509.2
42: 2 a few of many, as t eyes do behold us:) 3509.2
43: 9 Take great stones in t hand, 3509.2
49:16 deceived thee, *and* the pride of t heart, 3509.3
51:13 t end is come, *and* the measure of thy 3509.3

La
2:14 they have not discovered t iniquity, 3509.3
2:16 All t enemies have opened their mouth 3509.3
2:17 hath caused t enemy to rejoice over thee, NIH
2:17 he hath set up the horn of t adversaries. 3509.3
2:18 no rest; let not the apple of t eye cease. 3509.3
2:19 pour out t heart like water before the 3509.3
2:21 hast slain *them* in the day of t anger; 3509.2
3:56 hide not t ear at my breathing, at my 3509.3
4:22 The punishment of t iniquity is 3509.3
4:22 he will visit t iniquity, O daughter of 3509.3

Eze
3:10 shall speak unto thee receive in t heart, 3509.2
3:10 in thine heart, and hear with t ears. 3509.2
3:18 but his blood will I require at t hand. 3509.2
3:20 but his blood will I require at t hand. 3509.2
3:24 me, Go, shut thyself within t house. 3509.2
4: 7 t arm *shall be* uncovered, and thou shalt 3509.2
5: 1 cause *it* to pass upon t head and upon 3509.2
5: 9 the like, because of all t abominations. 3509.2
5:11 with all t abominations, therefore will I 3509.2
6:11 Smite with t hand, and stamp with thy 3509.2
7: 3 will recompense upon thee all t 3509.3
7: 4 t abominations shall be in the midst of 3509.3
7: 8 will recompense thee for all t 3509.3
7: 9 t abominations *that* are in the midst of 3509.3
8: 5 lift up t eyes now the way towards 3509.2
10: 2 fill t hand *with* coals of fire from 3509.2
16: 6 and saw thee polluted in t own blood, 3509.3
16: 7 t hair is grown, whereas thou *wast* 3509.3
16:11 I put bracelets upon t hands, and a 3509.3
16:12 earrings in t ears, and a beautiful crown 3509.3
16:12 and a beautiful crown upon t head. 3509.3
16:15 thou didst trust in t own beauty, 3509.3
16:22 all t abominations and thy whoredoms 3509.3
16:27 have diminished t ordinary *food,* and 3509.3
16:30 How weak is t heart, saith the Lord 3509.3
16:31 In that thou buildest t eminent place in 3509.3
16:31 and makest t high place in every street; 3509.3
16:39 they shall throw down t eminent place, 3509.3
16:41 they shall burn t houses with fire, 3509.3
16:43 will recompense thy way upon t head, NIH
16:43 this lewdness above all t abominations. 3509.3
16:46 t elder sister *is* Samaria, she and 3509.3
16:51 thou hast multiplied t abominations 3509.3
16:51 hast justified thy sisters in all t 3509.3
16:52 bear t own shame for thy sins that thou 3509.3
16:54 That thou mayest bear t own shame, 3509.3
16:58 borne thy lewdness and t abominations, 3509.3
16:61 thy sisters, t elder and thy younger: 3509.3
21:14 smite t hands together, and let the NIH
22: 4 hast defiled *thyself* in t idols which thou 3509.3
22:14 Can t heart endure, or can thine hands 3509.3
22:14 heart endure, or can t hands be strong, 3509.3
22:16 thou shalt take t inheritance in thyself in NIH
23:25 they shall take away thy nose and t ears; 3509.3
23:27 thou shalt not lift up t eyes unto them, 3509.3
23:31 therefore will I give her cup into t hand. 3509.3
23:34 and pluck off t own breasts: 3509.3
24:16 take away from thee the desire of t eyes 3509.2
24:17 bind the tire of t head upon thee, 3509.2
24:26 to cause *thee* to hear *it* with t ears? NIH
25: 6 Because thou hast clapped t hands, NIH
27: 6 *Of* the oaks of Bashan have they made t 3509.3
27:10 and of Lud and of Phut were in t army, 3509.3
27:11 The men of Arvad with t army were upon NIH
27:15 isles *were* the merchandise of t hand: 3509.3
28: 2 Because t heart is lifted up, and thou 3509.2
28: 2 thou set t heart as the heart of God: 3509.2
28: 4 with understanding thou hast gotten 3509.2
28: 5 t heart is lifted up because of thy riches: 3509.2
28: 6 Because thou hast set t heart as the 3509.2
28:17 T heart was lifted up because of thy 3509.2
28:18 by the multitude of t iniquities, 3509.2
33: 8 but his blood will I require at t hand. 3509.2
35:11 I will even do according to t anger, 3509.2
35:11 according to t envy which thou hast 3509.2
37:17 and they shall become one in t hand. 3509.2
37:20 shall be in t hand before their eyes. 3509.2
38: 4 and all t army, horses and horsemen, 3509.2
38:12 to turn t hand upon the desolate places 3509.2
39: 3 cause t arrows to fall out of thy right 3509.2
40: 4 behold with t eyes, and hear with thine 3509.2
40: 4 hear with t ears, and set thine heart 3509.2
40: 4 set t heart upon all that I shall shew 3509.2
44: 5 behold with t eyes, and hear with thine 3509.2
44: 5 hear with t ears all that I say unto thee 3509.2
44:30 he may cause the blessing to rest in t 3509.2

Da
2:38 of the heaven hath he given into t hand, 3509.5
3:17 he will deliver *us* out of t hand, O king. 3509.5
4:19 the interpretation thereof to t enemies. 3509.5
4:27 t iniquities by shewing mercy to the 3509.5

T

Da	5:22	O Belshazzar, hast not humbled t heart,	3509.5
	9:16	let t anger and thy fury be turned away	3509.2
	9:18	O my God, incline t ear, and hear;	3509.2
	9:18	open t eyes, and behold our desolations,	3509.2
	9:19	defer not, for t own sake, O my God:	3509.2
	10:12	from the first day that thou didst set t	3509.2
Hos	9: 7	for the multitude of t iniquity,	3509.2
	13: 9	destroyed thyself; but in me *is* t help.	3509.2
	14: 1	God; for thou hast fallen by t iniquity.	3509.2
Joel	2:17	and give not t heritage to reproach,	3509.2
Ob	1: 3	The pride of t heart hath deceived thee,	3509.2
	1:15	reward shall return upon t own head.	3509.2
Jnh	1: 8	evil *is* upon us; What *is* t occupation?	3509.2
	2: 7	came in unto thee, into t holy temple.	3509.2
Mic	4:10	thee from the hand of t enemies.	3509.2
	4:13	for I will make t horn iron, and I will	3509.3
	5: 9	T hand shall be lift up upon thine	3509.2
	5: 9	Thine hand shall be lift up upon t	3509.2
	5: 9	and all t enemies shall be cut off.	3509.2
	5:12	I will cut off witchcrafts out of t hand;	3509.2
	5:13	shalt no more worship the work of t	3509.2
	7:14	with thy rod, the flock of t heritage,	3509.2
Na	3:13	shall be set wide open unto t enemies:	3509.3
Hab	3: 8	*was* t anger against the rivers? *was* thy	3509.2
	3: 8	that thou didst ride upon t horses *and*	3509.2
	3:11	at the light of t arrows they went,	3509.2
	3:13	*even* for salvation with t anointed;	3509.2
	3:15	Thou didst walk through the sea *with* t	3509.2
Zep	3:15	judgments, he hath cast out t enemy:	3509.3
	3:16	and to Zion, Let not t hands be slack.	3509.3
Zec	3: 4	I have caused t iniquity to pass from	3509.2
	5: 5	Lift up now t eyes, and see what *is* this	3509.2
	13: 6	What *are* these wounds in t hands?	3509.2
Mt	5:25	Agree with t adversary quickly, whiles	4771
	5:33	but shalt perform unto the Lord t oaths:	4771
	5:43	love thy neighbour, and hate t enemy.	4771
	6: 2	Therefore when thou doest *t* alms, do not	NIG
	6: 4	That t alms may be in secret:	4771
	6:13	For t is the kingdom, and the power,	4771
	6:17	anoint t head, and wash thy face;	4771
	6:22	if therefore t eye be single, thy whole body	4771
	6:23	if t eye be evil, thy whole body shall be	4771
	7: 3	considerest not the beam that is in t own	4774
	7: 4	Let me pull out the mote out of t eye;	4771
	7: 4	and behold, a beam *is* in t own eye?	4771
	7: 5	first cast out the beam out of t own eye;	4771
	9: 6	take up thy bed, and go unto t house.	4771
	12:13	saith he to the man, Stretch forth t hand.	4771
	18: 9	And if t eye offend thee, pluck it out,	4771
	20:14	Take *that* t *is*, and go thy way: I will give	4674
	20:15	what I will with mine own? Is t eye evil,	4771
	22:44	till I make t enemies thy footstool?	4771
	25:25	in the earth: lo, *there* thou hast *that* t.	4674
Mk	2:11	up thy bed, and go thy way into t house.	4771
	3: 5	saith unto the man, Stretch forth t hand.	4771
	9:47	And if t eye offend thee, pluck it out: it is	4771
	12:36	till I make t enemies thy footstool.	4771
Lk	4:27	therefore wilt worship me, all shall be t.	4771
	5:24	take up thy couch, and go into t house.	4674
	5:33	of the Pharisees; but t eat and drink?	4674
	6:41	perceivest not the beam that is in t own	2398
	6:42	let me pull out the mote that is in t eye,	4771
	6:42	not the beam that is in t own eye?	4771
	6:42	cast out first the beam out of t own eye,	4771
	7:44	I entered into t house, thou gavest me no	4771
	8:39	Return to t own house, and shew how	4771
	11:34	therefore when t eye is single, thy whole	4771
	11:34	but when *t eye* is evil, thy body also *is* full	NIG
	12:19	take t ease, eat, drink, *and* be merry.	NIG
	12:58	When thou goest with t adversary to	4771
	15:31	art ever with me, and all that I have is t.	4674
	19:22	Out of t own mouth will I judge thee,	4771
	19:42	but now they are hid from t eyes.	4771
	19:43	that t enemies shall cast a trench about	4771
	20:43	Till I make t enemies thy footstool.	4771
	22:42	nevertheless not my will, but t, be done.	4674
Jn	2:17	The zeal of t house hath eaten me up.	4771
	8:10	Woman, where are those t accusers?	4771
	9:10	they unto him, How were t eyes opened?	4771
	9:17	thou of him, that he hath opened t eyes?	4771
	9:26	did he to thee? how opened he t eyes?	4771
	17: 5	glorify thou me with t own self with	4572
	17: 6	t they were, and thou gavest them me;	4674
	17: 9	which thou hast given me; for they are t.	4674
	17:10	And all mine are t, and thine are mine;	4674
	17:10	And all mine are thine, and t are mine;	4674
	17:11	keep through t own name those whom	4771
	18:35	**T** own nation and the chief priests have	4674
Ac	2:27	neither wilt thou suffer t Holy One to see	4771
	4:30	By stretching forth t hand to heal;	4771
	5: 3	why hath Satan filled t heart to lie to	4771
	5: 4	Whiles it remained, was it not t own?	4771
	5: 4	it was sold, was it not in t own power?	4674
	5: 4	why hast thou conceived this thing in t	4771
	8:22	if perhaps the thought of t heart may be	4771
	8:37	If thou believest with all t heart,	NIG
	10: 4	t alms are come up for a memorial before	4771
	10:31	t alms are had in remembrance in the	4771
	13:35	not suffer t Holy One to see corruption.	4771
	23:35	said he, when t accusers are also come.	4771
Ro	10: 6	Say not in t heart, Who shall ascend into	4771
	10: 9	believe in t heart that God hath raised	4771
	11: 3	thy prophets, and digged down t altars;	4771
	12:20	Therefore if t enemy hunger, feed him;	4771
1Co	10:29	I say, not t **own**, but of the other's:	1438

1Ti	5:23	thy stomach's sake and t often infirmities.	4771
Phm	1:19	owest unto me even t **own self** besides.	4572
Heb	1:10	and the heavens are the works of t hands:	4771
	1:13	until I make t enemies thy footstool?	4771
Rev	3:18	and anoint t eyes *with eyesalve, that thou*	4771

THING (548) [ANYTHING, NOTHING, SOMETHING, THINGS, THINGS']

Ge	1:24	**creeping** t, and beast of the earth after	7431
	1:25	every t **that creepeth** upon the earth	7431
	1:26	over every **creeping** t that creepeth upon	7431
	1:28	over every **living** t that moveth upon	2416
	1:30	to every *t* that creepeth upon the earth,	NIH
	1:31	God saw **every** t that he had made,	3605
	6: 7	the **creeping** t, and the fowls of the air;	7431
	6:17	*and* every *t* that is in the earth shall die.	NIH
	6:19	of every **living** *t* of all flesh, two of every	NIH
	6:20	of every **creeping** t of the earth after his	7431
	7: 8	of every *t* that creepeth upon the earth,	NIH
	7:14	every **creeping** t that creepeth upon	7431
	7:21	of every **creeping** t that creepeth upon	8318
	8: 1	every **living** t, and all the cattle that *was*	2416
	8:17	Bring forth with thee every **living** t that	2416
	8:17	of every **creeping** t that creepeth upon	7431
	8:19	every **creeping** t, and every fowl,	7431
	8:21	neither will I again smite any more every *t*	NIH
	9: 3	Every **moving** t that liveth shall be meat	7431
	14:23	that I will not take **any** t that *is* thine,	3605
	18:14	Is **any** t too hard for the LORD?	1697
	18:17	Shall I hide from Abraham that *t* which I	NIH
	19:21	I have accepted thee concerning this t,	1697
	19:22	for I cannot do **any** t till thou be come	1697
	20:10	sawest thou, that thou hast done this t?	1697
	21:11	was very grievous in Abraham's sight	1697
	21:26	I wot not who hath done this t:	1697
	22:12	the lad, neither do thou **any** t unto him:	3972
	22:16	for because thou hast done this t,	1697
	24:50	said, The t proceedeth from the LORD:	1697
	30:31	Jacob said, Thou shalt not give me **any** t:	3972
	30:31	if thou wilt do this t for me, I will again	1697
	34: 7	**which** t ought not to be done.	3651
	34:14	they said unto them, We cannot do this t,	1697
	34:19	the young man deferred not to do the t,	1697
	38:10	the *t* which he did displeased the LORD:	NIH
	39: 9	neither hath he kept back **any** t from me	3972
	39:23	to **any** t *that was* under his hand;	3605+3972
	41:28	This *is* the t which I have spoken unto	1697
	41:32	*it is* because the t is established by God,	1697
	41:37	the t was good in the eyes of Pharaoh,	1697
	44: 7	thy servants should do according to this t:	1697
Ex	1:18	Why have ye done this t, and have saved	1697
	2:14	and said, Surely *this* t is known.	1697
	2:15	when Pharaoh heard this t, he sought	1697
	9: 5	To morrow the LORD shall do this t in	1697
	9: 6	the LORD did that t on the morrow,	1697
	10:15	remained not any **green** t in the trees,	3418
	12:24	ye shall observe this t for an ordinance to	1697
	16:14	the wilderness *there lay* a small **round** t,	2636
	16:16	This *is* the t which the LORD hath	1697
	16:32	This *is* the t which the LORD	1697
	18:11	for in the t wherein they dealt proudly *he*	1697
	18:14	is this t that thou doest to the people?	1697
	18:17	him, The t that thou doest *is* not good.	1697
	18:18	*this* t *is* too heavy for thee; thou art not	1697
	18:23	If thou shalt do this t, and God command	1697
	20: 4	any likeness of *any* t that *is* in heaven	NIH
	20:17	his ass, nor **any** t that *is* thy neighbour's.	3605
	22: 9	for any manner of lost t, which *another*	NIH
	22:15	if it *be* a hired *t*, it came for his hire.	NIH
	29: 1	this *is* the t that thou shalt do unto them	1697
	33:17	I will do this t also that thou hast spoken:	1697
	34:10	for it *is* a terrible t that I will do with thee.	NIH
	35: 4	This *is* the t which the LORD	1697
Lev	2: 3	*it is* a t most holy of the offerings of	NIH
	2:10	*it is* a **most holy** of the offerings	6944+6944
	4:13	the t be hid from the eyes of the assembly,	1697
	5: 2	Or if a soul touch any unclean t, whether	1697
	5: 5	shall confess that he hath sinned in that *t*.	NIH
	5:16	the harm that he hath done in the holy *t*,	NIH
	6: 2	or in a t **taken away by violence**,	1498
	6: 4	**the** t which he hath deceitfully gotten,	1886.1
	6: 4	him to keep, or the lost *t* which he found,	NIH
	6: 7	it shall be forgiven him for any *t* of all that	NIH
	7:19	the flesh that toucheth any unclean *t* shall	NIH
	7:21	any unclean *t*, as the uncleanness of man,	NIH
	7:21	or any abominable unclean *t*, and eat of	NIH
	8: 5	This *is* the t which the LORD commanded	1697
	9: 6	This *is* the t which the LORD commanded	1697
	11:10	and of any living t which *is* in the waters,	5315
	11:21	flying **creeping** t that goeth upon all four,	8318
	11:35	every *t* whereupon *any part* of their	NIH
	11:41	every **creeping** t that creepeth upon	8318
	11:43	with any **creeping** t that creepeth,	8318
	11:44	**creeping** t that creepeth upon the earth.	8318
	12: 4	she shall touch no hallowed *t*, nor come	NIH
	13:48	in a skin, or in **any** t made of skin;	3605
	13:49	warp, or in the woof, or in any t of skin;	3627
	13:52	in woollen or in linen, or any t of skin,	3627
	13:53	warp, or in the woof, or in any t of skin;	3627
	13:54	priest shall command that they wash the *t*	NIH
	13:57	warp, or in the woof, or in any t of skin;	3627
	13:58	whatsoever t of skin *it be*, which thou	3627
	13:59	*in* the warp, or woof, or any t of skins,	3627
	15: 4	every t, whereon he sitteth, shall be	3627
	15: 6	that sitteth on *any* t whereon he sat that	3627

Lev	15:10	whosoever toucheth any *t* that was under	NIH
	15:20	every t that she lieth upon in her	NIH
	15:20	every *t* also that she sitteth upon shall be	NIH
	15:22	whosoever toucheth any *t* that she sat	3627
	15:23	or on *any* t whereon she sitteth, when he	3627
	17: 2	This *is* the t which the LORD hath	1697
	19: 8	he hath profaned the hallowed *t* of	NIH
	19:26	Ye shall not eat *any* t with the blood:	NIH
	20:17	is a **wicked** t; and they shall be cut off in	2617
	20:21	take his brother's wife, it *is* an **unclean** t:	5079
	20:25	by any *manner of living* t that creepeth on	NIH
	21:18	that hath a flat nose, or any t superfluous,	NIH
	22: 4	whoso toucheth any *t that is* unclean by	NIH
	22: 5	Or whosoever toucheth any **creeping** t,	8318
	22:10	There shall no stranger eat *of* the holy *t*.	NIH
	22:10	a hired servant, shall not eat *of* the holy *t*.	NIH
	22:14	if a man eat *of* the holy *t* unwittingly,	NIH
	22:14	give *it* unto the priest with the holy *t*.	NIH
	22:23	or a lamb that **hath any** t **superfluous** or	8311
	23:37	and drink offerings, **every** t upon his day:	1697
	27:23	in that day, *as* a holy *t* unto the LORD.	1697
	27:28	Notwithstanding no **devoted** t, that a	2764
	27:28	every **devoted** t *is* most holy unto	2764
Nu	4:15	shall not touch *any* holy *t*, lest they die.	NIH
	16: 9	*Seemeth it but* a **small** t unto you, that	4592
	16:13	*Is it* a **small** t that thou hast brought us	4592
	16:30	if the LORD make a **new** t, and the earth	1278
	17:13	Whosoever cometh **any** t near unto	3605
	18: 7	your priest's office for every t of the altar,	1697
	18:14	**Every** t devoted in Israel shall be thine.	3605
	18:15	**Every** t that openeth the matrix in all	3605
	20:19	without *doing any* t *else*, go through on	1697
	22:38	have I now any power at all to say **any** t?	3972
	30: 1	This *is* the t which the LORD doth	1697
	31:23	Every t that may abide the fire, ye shall	1697
	32:20	Moses said unto them, If ye will do this t,	1697
	35:22	have cast upon him any t without laying	3627
	36: 6	This *is* the t which the LORD doth	1697
Dt	1:14	t which thou hast spoken *is* good *for us*	1697
	1:32	Yet in this t ye did not believe the LORD	1697
	4:18	The likeness of any *t* that creepeth on	NIH
	4:23	the likeness of any *t*, which the LORD thy	NIH
	4:25	the likeness of any *t*, and shall do evil in	NIH
	4:32	whether there hath been *any such t* as	NIH
	4:32	been *any such thing* as this great t *is*,	1697
	5: 8	any likeness of *any* t that *is* in heaven	NIH
	5:21	or his ass, or any t that *is* thy neighbour's.	NIH
	7:26	house, lest thou be a **cursed** t like it;	2764
	7:26	shalt utterly abhor it; for it *is* a **cursed** t.	2764
	8: 9	thou shalt not lack *any t* in it;	NIH
	12:32	What t soever I command you, observe to	1697
	13:14	behold, *if it be* truth, *and* the t certain,	1697
	13:17	there shall cleave nought of the **cursed** t	2764
	14: 3	Thou shalt not eat any abominable *t*.	NIH
	14:19	every **creeping** t is unclean	8318
	14:21	shall not eat of **any** t that dieth of itself:	3605
	15:10	that for this t the LORD thy God shall	1697
	15:15	I command thee this t to day.	1697
	16: 4	neither shall there *any* t of the flesh,	NIH
	17: 4	and behold, *it is* true, *and* the t certain,	1697
	17: 5	which have committed that wicked t,	1697
	18:22	if the t follow not, nor come to pass, that	1697
	18:22	that *is* the t which the LORD hath not	NIH
	22: 3	with all lost t of thy brother's, which he	NIH
	22:20	if this be true, *and the tokens of* virginity	1697
	23: 9	then keep thee from every wicked t.	1697
	23:14	that he see no unclean t in thee,	1697
	23:19	usury of any t that is lent upon usury:	1697
	24:10	When thou dost lend thy brother **any** t,	3972
	24:18	I command thee to do this t.	1697
	24:22	I command thee to do this t.	1697
	26:11	thou shalt rejoice in every good *t* which	NIH
	31:13	which have not known *any* t, may hear,	NIH
	32:47	For it *is* not a vain t for you; because it *is*	1697
	32:47	through this t ye shall prolong *your* days	1697
Jos	4:10	until every t was finished that the LORD	1697
	6:18	keep *yourselves* from the **accursed** t,	2764
	6:18	when ye take of the **accursed** t,	2764
	7: 1	committed a trespass in the **accursed** t:	2764
	7: 1	tribe of Judah, took of the **accursed** t:	2764
	7:11	they have even taken of the **accursed** t,	2764
	7:13	is an **accursed** t in the midst of thee,	2764
	7:13	until ye take away the **accursed** t from	2764
	7:15	*that* he that is taken with the **accursed** t	2764
	9:24	because of you, and have done this t.	1697
	14: 6	Thou knowest the t that the LORD said	1697
	21:45	There failed not ought of any good t	1697
	22:20	commit a trespass in the **accursed** t,	2764
	22:24	have not *rather* done it for fear of *this* t,	1697
	22:33	And the t pleased the children of Israel;	1697
	23:14	that not one t hath failed of all the good	1697
	23:14	you, *and* not one t hath failed thereof.	1697
Jdg	6:29	said one to another, Who hath done this t?	1697
	6:29	Gideon the son of Joash hath done this t.	1697
	8:27	which *t* became a snare unto Gideon,	NIH
	11:25	*art* thou **any** t **better** than Balak	2896+2896
	11:37	unto her father, Let this t be done for me:	1697
	13: 4	strong drink, and eat not any unclean *t*.	NIH
	13: 7	neither eat any unclean *t*: for the child	NIH
	13:14	She may not eat of any *t* that cometh of	NIH
	13:14	eat any unclean *t*: all that I commanded	NIH
	18: 7	that might put *them* to shame in *any* t;	1697
	18:10	place where *there is* no want of any t that	1697
	19:19	thy servants: *there is* no want of any t.	1697
	19:24	but unto this man do not so vile a t.	1697

Jdg 20: 9 now this *shall be* the t which we will do 1697
 21:11 this *is* the t that ye shall do, Ye shall 1697
Ru 3:18 rest, until I have finished the t *this* day. 1697
1Sa 3:11 to Samuel, Behold, I will do a t in Israel, 1697
 3:17 What *is* the t that the LORD hath said 1697
 3:17 if thou hide *any* t from me of all the 1697
 4: 7 there hath not been such *a* t heretofore. NIH
 8: 6 the t displeased Samuel, when they said, 1697
 12:16 Now therefore stand and see this great t, 1697
 14:12 Come up to us, and we will shew you a t. 1697
 15: 9 every t *that was* vile and refuse, that they 4399
 18:20 and they told Saul, and the t pleased him. 1697
 18:23 Seemeth it to you a light *t* to be a king's NIH
 20: 2 should my father hide this t from me? 1697
 20:26 Nevertheless Saul spake not **any** t that 3972
 20:39 the lad knew not **any** t: only Jonathan 3972
 21: 2 Let no man know **any** t of the business 3972
 22:15 let not the king impute *any* t unto his 1697
 24: 6 The LORD forbid that I should do this t 1697
 25:15 were not hurt, neither missed we **any** t, 3972
 26:16 This t *is* not good that thou hast done. 1697
 28:10 no punishment happen to thee for this t. 1697
 28:18 hath the LORD done this t unto thee this 1697
 30:19 nor any t that they had taken to them: NIH
2Sa 2: 6 this kindness, because ye have done this t. 1697
 3:13 one t I require of thee, that is, Thou shalt 1697
 7:19 this was yet a **small** t in thy sight, O Lord 6994
 11:11 and *as* thy soul liveth, I will not do this t. 1697
 11:25 say unto Joab, Let not this t displease thee, 1697
 11:27 the t that David had done displeased 1697
 12: 5 the man that hath done this *t* shall surely NIH
 12: 6 because he did this t, and because he had 1697
 12:12 I will do this t before all Israel, 1697
 12:21 What *is* this that thou hast done? 1697
 13: 2 thought it hard for him to do **any** t 3972
 13:12 for no such t ought to be done in Israel: NIH
 13:20 he *is* thy brother; regard not this t. 1697
 13:33 let not my lord the king take the t to his 2088
 14:13 hast thou thought such a t against 1697
 14:13 for the king doth speak this t as one 1697
 14:15 that I am come to speak of this t unto my 1697
 14:18 I pray thee, the t that I shall ask thee. 1697
 14:20 speech hath thy servant Joab done this t: 1697
 14:21 unto Joab, Behold now, I have done this t: 1697
 15:11 their simplicity, and they knew not any t. 1697
 15:35 *that* what t soever thou shalt hear out of 1697
 15:36 by them ye shall send unto me every t 1697
 17:19 corn thereon; and the t was not known. 1697
 24: 3 doth my lord the king delight in this t? 1697
1Ki 1:27 Is this t done by my lord the king, 1697
 3:10 the Lord, that Solomon had asked this t. 1697
 3:11 Because thou hast asked this t, and hast 1697
 10: 3 there was not *any* t hid from the king, 1697
 11:10 had commanded him concerning this t, 1697
 12:24 man to his house; for this t is from me. 1697
 12:30 this t became a sin: for the people went 1697
 13:33 After this t Jeroboam returned not from 1697
 13:34 this t became sin unto the house of 1697
 14: 5 the wife of Jeroboam cometh to ask a t of 1697
 14:13 in him there is found *some* good t toward 1697
 15: 5 turned not aside from any t that he NIH
 16:31 as if it had been a **light** t for him to walk 7043
 20: 9 this t I may not do. And the messengers 1697
 20:24 do this t, Take the kings away, every man 1697
 20:33 whether *any* t would come from him, NIH
2Ki 2:10 he said, Thou hast asked a **hard** t: 7185
 3:18 *but* a **light** t in the sight of the LORD: 7043
 4: 2 Thine handmaid hath not **any** t in 3605
 5:13 the prophet had bid thee *do some* great t, 1697
 5:18 In this t the LORD pardon thy servant, 1697
 5:18 the LORD pardon thy servant in this t. 1697
 6:11 king of Syria was sore troubled for this t; 1697
 7: 2 make windows in heaven, might this t be? 1697
 7:19 in heaven, might such a t be? 1697+1886.1
 8: 9 even *of* every **good** t of Damascus, 2898
 8:13 a dog, that he should do this great t? 1697
 11: 5 saying, This *is* the t that ye shall do; 1697
 17:12 had said unto them, Ye shall not do this t. 1697
 20: 9 that the LORD will do the t that he hath 1697
 20:10 It is a **light** t for the shadow to go down 7043
1Ch 2: 7 who transgressed in the t **accursed.** 2764
 11:19 that *I* should do this *t* shall I drink NIH
 13: 4 for the t was right in the eyes of all 1697
 17:17 this was a **small** t in thine eyes, O God; 6994
 17:23 let the t that thou hast spoken concerning 1697
 21: 3 doth my lord require this *t*? why will he NIH
 21: 7 God was displeased with this t; therefore 1697
 21: 8 sinned greatly, because I have done this t: 1697
2Ch 9:20 it was *not* **any** t accounted of in the days 3972
 11: 4 man to his house, for this t is done of me. 1697
 16:10 of this t. And Asa oppressed *some* of NIH
 23: 4 This *is* the t that ye shall do; A third *part* 1697
 23:19 that none *which was* unclean in any t 1697
 29:36 the people: for the t was *done* suddenly. NIH
 30: 4 the t pleased the king and all 1697
Ezr 7:27 hath put *such a t* as this in the king's NIH
 9: 3 when I heard this t, I rent my garment 1697
 10: 2 there is hope in Israel concerning this *t.* 1697
 10:13 are many that have transgressed in this t. 1697
Ne 2:19 and said, What *is* this t that ye do? 1697
 13:17 What evil t *is* this that ye do, 1697
Est 2: 4 And the t pleased the king; and he did so. 1697
 2:22 the t was known to Mordecai, who told 1697
 5:14 the t pleased Haman; and he caused 1697
 6:13 his friends every *t* that had befallen him. NIH

Est 8: 5 the t seem right before the king, and I *be* 1697
Job 3:25 For the t which I greatly feared is come NIH
 4:12 Now a t was secretly brought to me, 1697
 6: 8 God would grant *me* the t that I **long for!** 8615
 9:22 This *is* one t, therefore I said *it,* He NIH
 12:10 whose hand *is* the soul of every living *t,* NIH
 13:28 as a **rotten** t, consumeth, as a garment 7538
 14: 4 can bring a clean *t* out of an unclean? NIH
 15:11 with thee? is there *any* secret t with thee? 1697
 22:28 Thou shalt also decree a t, and it shall be 562
 23:14 he performeth the **t that is appointed** 2706
 26: 3 thou plentifully declared the **t** as it is? 8454
 28:10 and his eye seeth every **precious** t. 3366
 28:11 t **that is hid** bringeth he forth *to* light. 8587
 33:32 If *thou* hast **any** t **to say**, answer me: 4405
 39: 8 and he searcheth after every **green** t. 3387
 42: 2 I know that thou canst do every *t,* NIH
 42: 7 for ye have not spoken of me *the t that is* NIH
 42: 8 in that ye have not spoken of me *the t* NIH
Ps 2: 1 and the people imagine a vain *t*? NIH
 27: 4 One t have I desired of the LORD, that NIH
 33:17 A horse *is a* **vain** t for safety: neither shall 8267
 34:10 seek the LORD shall not want any good *t.* NIH
 38:20 because I follow *the t that* good *is.* NIH
 69:34 the seas, and every *t* that moveth therein. NIH
 84:11 no good *t* will he withhold from them that NIH
 89:34 nor alter the **t that is gone out** of my lips. 4161
 92: 1 *It is a* good *t* to give thanks unto NIH
 101: 3 I will set no wicked t before mine eyes: 1697
 141: 4 Incline not my heart to *any* evil t, 1697
 145:16 and satisfiest the desire of every **living** t. 2416
 150: 6 Let every *t that hath* breath praise NIH
Pr 4: 7 Wisdom *is* the **principal** t; therefore 7225
 18:22 *Whoso* findeth a wife findeth a good *t,* NIH
 22:18 For *it is* a pleasant *t* if thou keep them NIH
 25: 2 *It is* the glory of God to conceal a t: 1697
 27: 7 *to* the hungry soul every bitter *t is* sweet. NIH
Ecc 1: 9 The t that hath been, *it is* that which shall 4100
 1: 9 there *is* no new *t* under the sun. NIH
 1:10 Is there *any* t whereof it may be said, See, 1697
 3: 1 To every *t there* is a season, and a time to NIH
 3:11 He hath made every *t* beautiful in his time: NIH
 3:14 put to it, **nor** any *t* taken from it: 369+2050.1
 3:19 beasts; even **one** t befalleth them: 259
 5: 2 let not thine heart be hasty to utter *any* t 1697
 6: 5 nor known *any t* this hath more rest than NIH
 7: 8 Better *is* the end of a t than the beginning 1697
 8: 1 who knoweth the interpretation of a t? 1697
 8: 3 stand not in an evil t; for he doeth 1697
 8: 5 the commandment shall feel no evil t: 1697
 8:15 a man hath no better t under the sun, NIH
 9: 5 the dead know not **any** t, neither have 3972
 9: 6 ever in any t that is done under the sun. NIH
 11: 7 a pleasant *t it is* for the eyes to behold NIH
 12:14 with every secret *t*, whether *it be* good, NIH
Isa 7:13 *Is it a* **small** t for you to weary men, 4592
 15: 6 the grass faileth, there is no **green** t. 3418
 17:13 and like a **rolling** t before the whirlwind. 1534
 19: 7 **every** t sown by the brooks, shall wither, 3605
 29:16 shall the t **framed** say of him that framed 3336
 29:21 and turn aside the just for a t **of nought.** 8414
 38: 7 that the LORD will do this t that he hath 1697
 40:15 he taketh up the isles as a **very little** t. 1851
 41:12 shall be as nothing, and as a t **of nought.** 657
 43:19 I will do a new t, now it shall spring forth; NIH
 49: 6 It is a light t that thou shouldest be my NIH
 52:11 touch no unclean *t*, go ye out of the midst NIH
 55:11 it shall prosper *in* the t whereto I sent it. NIH
 64: 6 we are all as an unclean *t*, and all our NIH
 66: 8 Who hath heard such *a t*? who hath seen NIH
Jer 2:10 and see if there be such a t. NIH
 2:19 and see that *it is* an evil *t* and bitter, NIH
 5:30 and **horrible** t is committed in the land; 8186
 7:23 this t commanded I them, saying, Obey 1697
 11:13 have ye set up altars to *that* **shameful** t, 1322
 14:14 t **of nought**, and the deceit of their heart. 457
 18:13 of Israel hath done a very **horrible** t. 8186
 22: 4 For if ye do this t indeed, then shall there 1697
 23:14 in the prophets of Jerusalem a **horrible** t: 8186
 31:22 for the LORD hath created a new t in 1697
 32:27 of all flesh: is there any t too hard for me? 1697
 33:14 I will perform *that* good t which I have 1697
 38: 5 for the king *is not he that* can do *any* t 1697
 38:14 said unto Jeremiah, I *will* ask thee a t; 1697
 40: 3 voice, therefore this t is come upon you. 1697
 40:16 son of Kareah, Thou shalt not do this t: 1697
 42: 3 we may walk, and the t that we may do. 1697
 42: 4 *that* whatsoever t the LORD shall answer 1697
 42:21 nor any t for the which he hath sent me NIH
 44: 4 Oh, do not this abominable t that I hate. 1697
 44:17 we will certainly do whatsoever t goeth 1697
La 2:13 What *t* shall I take to witness for thee? NIH
 2:13 what *t* shall I liken to thee, O daughter of NIH
Eze 8:17 Is it a **light** t to the house of Judah that 7043
 14: 9 be deceived when he hath spoken a t, 1697
 16:47 as *if that were* a very little t, thou wast NIH
 34:18 *Seemeth it* a **small** t unto you to have 4592
 44:18 they shall not gird *themselves* with any t NIH
 44:29 every **dedicate** t in Israel shall be theirs. 2764
 44:31 The priests shall not eat *of* **any** t that is 3605
 47: 9 *that* every t liveth, which moveth, 5315
 47: 9 every t shall live whither the river cometh. NIH
 48:12 *a t* most holy by the border of the Levites. NIH
Da 2: 5 to the Chaldeans, The t is gone from me: 4406
 2: 8 because ye see the t is gone from me. 4406

Da 2:11 And *it is* a rare t that the king requireth, 4406
 2:15 then Arioch made the t known to Daniel. 4406
 2:17 made the t known to Hananiah, Mishael, 4406
 3:29 which speak **any** t amiss against the God 7960
 4:33 The same hour was the t fulfilled upon 4406
 5:15 could not shew the interpretation of the t: 4406
 5:26 This *is* the interpretation of the t: MENE; 4406
 6:12 The king answered and said, The t *is* true, 4406
 10: 1 the third year of Cyrus king of Persia a t 1697
 10: 1 the t *was* true, but the time appointed 1697
 10: 1 understood the t, and had understanding 1697
Hos 6:10 I have seen a **horrible** t in the house of 8186
 8: 3 Israel hath cast off *the t that is* good: NIH
 8:12 *but* they were counted as a strange *t.* NIH
Am 6:13 Ye which rejoice in a t of nought, 1697
Jnh 3: 7 nor beast, herd nor flock, taste **any** t: 3972
Mal 1:14 sacrificeth unto the Lord a corrupt *t* for I NIH
Mt 8:33 and told every *t,* and what was befallen to NIG
 18:19 earth as touching any t that they shall ask, 4229
 19:16 Good Master, what good *t* shall I do, NIG
 20:20 and desiring a certain t of him. NIG
 21:24 said unto them, I also will ask you one t, 3056
 24:17 come down to take any *t* out of his house: NIG
Mk 1:27 among themselves, saying, What *t* is this? NIG
 4:22 neither was *any t* kept secret, but that it NIG
 5:32 about to see her that had done this t. NIG
 7:18 whatsoever *t* from without entereth into NIG
 9:22 if thou canst do any *t,* have compassion on NIG
 10:21 and said unto him, One *t* thou lackest: NIG
 11:13 if haply he might find any *t* thereon: NIG
 13:15 neither enter *therein,* to take any *t* out of NIG
 16: 8 neither said they any *t* to any *man;* for NIG
 16:18 if they drink any deadly *t,* it shall not hurt NIG
Lk 1:35 *that* **holy** t which shall be born of thee 40
 2:15 and see this t which is come to pass, 4487
 6: 9 I will ask you one *t*, Is it lawful on NIG
 8:17 neither *any t* hid, that shall not be known NIG
 9:21 commanded *them* to tell no man that *t,* NIG
 10:42 one *t* is needful: and Mary hath chosen NIG
 12:11 no thought how or what *t* ye shall answer, NIG
 12:26 be not able *to do that t which is* least, NIG
 18:22 Yet lackest thou one *t:* sell all that thou NIG
 19: 8 if I have taken any *t* from any *man* by false NIG
 20: 3 said unto them, I will also ask you one t; 3056
 22:23 of them it was that should do this t. NIG
 22:35 and shoes, lacked ye any *t*? And they said, NIG
Jn 1: 3 without him was not any *t* made that was NIG
 1:46 there any good *t* come out of Nazareth? NIG
 5:14 no more, lest a worse *t* come unto thee. NIG
 7: 4 For there is no *man* that doeth any *t* in NIG
 9:25 one *t* I know, that, whereas I was blind, NIG
 9:30 Why herein is a marvellous *t,* that ye NIG
 14:14 If ye shall ask any *t* in my name, I will do NIG
 18:34 answered him, Sayest thou this *t* of thyself, NIG
Ac 5: 4 why hast thou conceived this t in thine 4229
 10:14 I have never eaten any *t that is* common NIG
 10:28 Ye know how that it is an unlawful *t* for a NIG
 12:12 when he had considered *the t,* he came NIG
 17:21 but *either* to tell, or to hear some new *t*) NIG
 17:25 as though he needed any *t,* seeing he NIG
 19:32 Some therefore cried one *t,* NIG
 19:39 But if ye inquire any *t* concerning other NIG
 21:25 concluded that they observe no such *t,* NIG
 21:34 And some cried one *t,* some another, NIG
 23:17 for he hath a certain *t* to tell him. NIG
 25: 8 against Cesar, have I offended any *t at all.* NIG
 25:11 or have committed any *t* worthy of death, NIG
 25:26 Of whom I have no certain *t* to write unto NIG
 26: 8 Why should it be thought *a t* incredible NIG
 26:10 Which *t* I also did in Jerusalem: NIG
 26:26 for this *t* was not done in a corner. NIG
Ro 7:18 dwelleth no good *t* for to will is present NIG
 8:33 Who shall lay any t to the charge of God's NIG
 9:20 Shall **the** t formed say to him that formed 3588
 13: 6 attending continually upon this very *t.* NIG
 13: 8 Owe no *man* any *t,* but to love one NIG
 14:14 to him that esteemeth any *t* to be unclean, NIG
 14:21 nor *any t* whereby thy brother stumbleth, NIG
 14:22 not himself in *that t* which he alloweth. NIG
1Co 1: 5 That in every *t* ye are enriched by him, NIG
 1:10 that ye all speak the same *t,* and *that* there NIG
 2: 2 I determined not to know any *t* among NIG
 3: 7 neither is he that planteth any *t,* neither NIG
 4: 3 with me it is a very small *t* that I should NIG
 8: 2 if any *man* think that *he* knoweth any *t,* NIG
 8: 7 hour, eat *it* as a t **offered unto an idol;** 1494
 9:11 great *t* if we shall reap your carnal *things?* NIG
 9:17 For if I do this *t* willingly, I have a reward: NIG
 10:19 that the idol is any *t,* or that which is NIG
 10:19 is offered in sacrifice to idols is any *t*? NIG
 14:30 If *any t* be revealed to another that sitteth NIG
 14:35 And if they will learn any *t,* let them ask NIG
2Co 2:10 To whom ye forgive any *t,* I *forgive* also: NIG
 2:10 for if I forgave any *t,* to whom I forgave *it,* NIG
 3: 5 of ourselves to think any *t* as of ourselves; NIG
 5: 5 hath wrought us for the selfsame *t* is God, NIG
 6: 3 Giving no offence in any *t,* that the NIG
 6:17 and touch not the unclean *t,* and I will NIG
 7:11 For behold this selfsame *t,* that ye NIG
 7:14 For if I have boasted any *t* to him of you, NIG
 8: 7 as ye abound in every *t, in* faith, NIG
 9:11 Being enriched in every *t* to all NIG
 10: 5 **every** high t that exalteth itself against 3956
 11:15 Therefore *it is* no great *t* if his ministers NIG
 12: 8 For this *t* I besought the Lord thrice, that it NIG

T

Gal	4:18 to be zealously affected always in a good *t*,	NIG
	5: 6 availeth any *t*, nor uncircumcision;	NIG
	6:15 availeth any *t*, nor uncircumcision:	NIG
Eph	4:28 with *his* hands the *t which is* good,	NIG
	5:24 *be* to their own husbands in every *t*.	NIG
	5:27 any such *t*; but that it should be holy and	NIG
	6: 8 Knowing that whatsoever good *t* any man	NIG
Php	1: 6 Being confident of this very *t*, that he	NIG
	3:13 *this* one *t I do*, forgetting those *things*	NIG
	3:15 and if in any *t* ye be otherwise minded,	NIG
	3:16 by the same rule, *let us* mind the same *t*.	NIG
	4: 6 but in every *t* by prayer and supplication	NIG
1Th	1: 8 so that we need not to speak any *t*.	NIG
	5:18 In every *t* give thanks: for this *is* the will	NIG
2Th	1: 6 Seeing *it is* a righteous *t* with God to	NIG
1Ti	1:10 if there be any other *t* that is contrary to	NIG
2Ti	1:14 *That* good *t* which was committed unto	2570
Tit	2: 8 ashamed, having no evil *t* to say of you.	NIG
Phm	1: 6 every good *t* which is in you in Christ	NIG
Heb	10:29 an unholy *t*, and hath done despite unto	NIG
	10:31 *It is* a fearful *t* to fall into the hands of	NIG
	11:40 God having provided some better *t* for us,	NIG
	13: 9 For it *is* a good *t* that the heart be	NIG
Jas	1: 7 that he shall receive any *t* of the Lord.	NIG
1Pe	4:12 as though *some* strange *t* happened unto	NIG
2Pe	3: 8 be not ignorant of this one *t*, that one day	NIG
1Jn	2: 8 you, which *t* is true in him and in you:	NIG
	5:14 that, if we ask any *t* according to his will,	NIG
Rev	2:15 doctrine of the Nicolaitans, which *t* I hate.	NIG
	9: 4 neither any green *t*, neither any tree;	NIG
	21:27 there shall in no wise enter into it any *t*	NIG

THINGS (1161) [THING]

Ge	7:23 **creeping** *t*, and the fowl of the heaven;	7431
	9: 3 as the green herb have I given you all *t*.	NIH
	15: 1 After these *t* the word of the Lord came	1697
	20: 8 and told all these *t* in their ears:	1697
	22: 1 it came to pass after these *t*, that God did	1697
	22:20 it came to pass after these *t*, that it was	1697
	24: 1 the Lord had blessed Abraham in **all** *t*.	3605
	24:28 told *them* of her mother's house these *t*.	1697
	24:53 her brother and to her mother **precious** *t*.	4030
	24:66 servant told Isaac all *t* that he had done.	1697
	29:13 his house. And he told Laban all these *t*.	1697
	39: 7 it came to pass after these *t*, that his	1697
	40: 1 it came to pass after these *t*, that the butler	1697
	42:36 ye will take Benjamin *away*: all **these** *t*	5089.1
	45:23 ten asses laden with the **good** *t* of Egypt,	2898
	48: 1 it came to pass after these *t*, that *one* told	1697
Ex	10: 2 **what** *t* I have wrought in Egypt, and my	834
	12:36 that they lent unto them *such t as* they	NIH
	23:13 in all *t* that I have said unto you be	NIH
	25:22 of all *t* which I will give thee in	NIH
	28:38 *t*, which the children of Israel shall hallow	NIH
	29:33 they shall eat those *t* wherewith	NIH
	29:35 to all *t* which I have commanded	NIH
	40: 4 set in order the *t* that are to be set in order	NIH
Lev	2: 8 that is made of these *t* unto the Lord:	NIH
	4: 2 (*concerning t* which ought not to be done)	NIH
	4:13 *concerning t* which should not be done,	NIH
	4:22 *concerning t* which should not be done,	NIH
	4:27 *concerning t* which ought not to be done,	NIH
	5: 2 or the carcase of unclean **creeping** *t*,	8318
	5: 5 when he shall be guilty in one of these *t*,	NIH
	5:15 in the holy *t* of the Lord,	NIH
	5:17 commit any of *these t* which are forbidden	NIH
	8:36 his sons did all *t* which the Lord	1697
	10:19 the Lord; and such *t* have befallen me:	428
	11:23 all *other* flying **creeping** *t*, which have	8318
	11:29 the **creeping** *t* that creep upon the earth;	8318
	11:42 all **creeping** *t* that creep upon the earth,	8318
	14:11 those *t*, before the Lord, *at* the door of	NIH
	15:10 that beareth *any* of those *t* shall wash his	NIH
	15:27 whosoever toucheth those *t* shall be	NIH
	18:24 Defile not you yourselves in any of these *t*:	NIH
	20:23 they committed all these *t*, and therefore	NIH
	22: 2 from the holy *t* of the children of Israel,	NIH
	22: 2 *in* those *t* which they hallow unto me:	NIH
	22: 3 that goeth unto the holy *t* which the	NIH
	22: 4 he shall not eat of the holy *t*, until he be	NIH
	22: 6 shall not eat of the holy *t*, unless he wash	NIH
	22: 7 shall afterward eat of the holy *t*, because	NIH
	22:12 may not eat of an offering of the holy *t*.	NIH
	22:15 they shall not profane the holy *t* of	NIH
	22:16 when they eat their holy *t*: for I the Lord	NIH
	26:23 ye will not be reformed by me by these *t*,	NIH
Nu	1:50 and over all *t* that *belong* to it:	NIH
	4: 4 the congregation, *about* the most holy *t*.	NIH
	4:15 These *t are* the burden of the sons of	NIH
	4:19 they approach unto the most holy *t*:	NIH
	4:20 shall not go in to see when the holy *t*	NIH
	5: 9 every offering of all the holy *t* of	NIH
	5:10 every man's hallowed *t* shall be his:	NIH
	15:13 country shall do these *t* after this manner,	NIH
	18: 8 all the hallowed *t* of the children of Israel,	NIH
	18: 9 This shall be thine of the most holy *t*,	NIH
	18:19 All the heave offerings of the holy *t*, which	NIH
	18:32 neither shall ye pollute the holy *t* of	NIH
	29:39 These *t* ye shall do unto the Lord in your	NIH
	31:20 of goats' *hair*, and all **made** of wood.	3627
	35:29 These *t* shall be for a statute of judgment	NIH
Dt	1:18 I commanded you at that time all the *t*	1697
	4: 7 as the Lord our God *is* in all *t* that we	NIH
	4: 9 lest thou forget the *t* which thine eyes	1697
	4:30 all these *t* are come upon thee, *even* in	1697

Dt	6:11 houses full *of* all good *t*, which thou	NIH
	10:21 and terrible *t*, which thine eyes have seen.	NIH
	12: 8 Ye shall not do after all *the t* that we do	NIH
	12:26 Only thy holy *t* which thou hast,	NIH
	18:12 For all that do these *t are* an abomination	NIH
	25:16 For all that do such *t*, *and* all that do	NIH
	26:13 I have brought away the hallowed *t* out of	NIH
	28:47 of heart, for the abundance of all *t*;	NIH
	28:48 in want of all *t*, and he shall put a yoke of	NIH
	28:57 for she shall eat them for want of all *t*	NIH
	29:29 The secret *t belong* unto the Lord our	NIH
	29:29 *those t* which are revealed *belong* unto us	NIH
	30: 1 when all these *t* are come upon thee,	1697
	32:35 the *t* that shall come upon them make	6264
	33:13 the **precious** *t* of heaven, for the dew,	4022
	33:14 for the **precious** *t* put forth by the moon,	4022
	33:15 for the **chief** *t* of the ancient mountains,	7218
	33:15 and for the **precious** *t* of the lasting hills,	4022
	33:16 for the **precious** *t* of the earth and	4022
Jos	1:17 as we hearkened unto Moses in all *t*,	NIH
	2:11 soon as we had heard *these t*, our hearts	NIH
	2:23 of Nun, and told him all *t* that befell them:	NIH
	11: 1 Jabin king of Hazor had heard *those t*,	NIH
	23:14 *t* which the Lord your God spake	1697
	23:15 *that* as all good *t* are come upon you,	1697
	23:15 shall the Lord bring upon you all evil *t*,	1697
	24:29 it came to pass after these *t*, that Joshua	1697
Jdg	13:23 would he have shewed us all these *t*,	NIH
	13:23 as *at this* time have told us *such t* as these.	NIH
	18:27 they took *the t* which Micah had made,	NIH
Ru	4: 7 concerning changing, for to confirm all *t*;	1697
1Sa	2:23 he said unto them, Why do ye such *t*?	NIH
	3:12 In that day I will perform against Eli all *t*	NIH
	3:17 if thou hide *any* thing from me of all the *t*	1697
	12:21 *should* ye go after vain *t*, which cannot	NIH
	12:24 for consider how **great** *t* he hath **done** for	1431
	15:21 *t* which should have been	
	utterly destroyed,	2764
	19: 7 and Jonathan shewed him all those *t*.	1697
	25:37 wife had told him these *t*, that his heart	1697
	26:25 thou shalt both **do great** *t*,	6213+6213
2Sa	7:21 heart, hast thou done all these **great** *t*,	1420
	7:23 to do for you **great** *t* and terrible, for thy	1420
	11:18 told David at the *t* **concerning** the war;	1697
	12: 8 given unto thee such and **such** *t*.	2007+3509.1
	13:21 when king David heard of all these *t*,	1697
	14:20 of God, to know all *t* that *are* in the earth.	NIH
	23: 5 ordered in all *t*, and sure:	NIH
	23:17 These *t* did *these* three mighty *men*.	NIH
	23:22 These *t* did Benaiah the son of Jehoiada,	NIH
	24:12 offer thee three *t*: choose thee one of them,	NIH
	24:23 All *these t* did Araunah, *as* a king, give	NIH
1Ki	4:33 and of fowl, and of **creeping** *t*.	7431
	5: 8 I have considered *the t* which thou sentest	NIH
	7:51 Solomon brought in the *t* which David his	NIH
	15:15 he brought in the *t* which his father had	NIH
	15:15 the *t* which himself had dedicated, *into*	NIH
	17:17 came to pass after these *t*, *that* the son of	1697
	18:36 *that* I have done all these *t* at thy word.	1697
	21: 1 it came to pass after these *t*, *that* Naboth	1697
	21:26 according to all *t* as did the Amorites,	1697
2Ki	8: 4 all the great *t* that Elisha hath done.	NIH
	11: 9 all *t* that Jehoiada the priest commanded:	NIH
	12: 4 All the money of the dedicated *t* that is	NIH
	12:18 took all the hallowed *t* that Jehoshaphat,	NIH
	12:18 his own hallowed *t*, and all the gold that	NIH
	14: 3 he did according to all *t* as Joash his father	NIH
	17: 9 the children of Israel did secretly *those* t	NIH
	17:11 wrought wicked *t* to provoke the Lord	1697
	19:29 *this* year **such** *t* as grow of themselves,	5599
	20:13 them all the house of his **precious** *t*,	5238
	20:15 All *the t* that *are* in mine house have they	NIH
	23:17 proclaimed these *t* that thou hast done	1697
	25:15 such *t as were* of gold, *in* gold, and of	NIH
1Ch	4:22 Jashubi-lehem. And *these are* ancient *t*.	1697
	9:31 over the *t* **that were made** in the pans.	4639
	11:19 These *t* did *these* three mightiest.	NIH
	11:24 These *t* did Benaiah the son of Jehoiada,	1420
	17:19 in making known all *these* **great** *t*.	NIH
	21:10 offer thee three *t*: choose thee one of them,	NIH
	21:13 that he should sanctify the most holy *t*,	NIH
	23:28 in the purifying of all holy *t*, and the work	NIH
	26:20 and over the treasures of the dedicate *t*.	NIH
	26:26 of the dedicate *t*, which David the king,	NIH
	28:12 and of the treasuries of the dedicate *t*:	NIH
	28:14 *He* gave of gold by weight for *t* of gold,	NIH
	29: 2 my God the gold for *t* to be made of gold,	NIH
	29: 2 the silver for *t* of silver, and the brass for	NIH
	29: 2 brass for *t* of brass, the iron for *things* of	NIH
	29: 2 iron for *t* of iron, and wood for *things* of	NIH
	29: 2 for *things* of iron, and wood for *t* of wood;	NIH
	29: 5 The gold for *t* of gold, and the silver for	NIH
	29: 5 the silver for *t* of silver, and for all *manner*	NIH
	29:14 willingly after this *sort*? for all *t* **come** of	NIH
	29:17 heart I have willingly offered all these *t*:	NIH
	29:19 to do all *these t*, and to build the palace,	NIH
2Ch	3: 3 Now these are *the t* **wherein** Solomon	NIH
	4: 6 such *t* as they **offered** for the burnt	4639
	5: 1 Solomon brought in *all the t* that David	NIH
	12:12 and also in Judah *t* went well.	1697
	15:18 brought *into* the house of God *the t* that	NIH
	19: 3 there are good *t* found in thee,	1697
	21: 3 of gold, and of **precious** *t*, with fenced	4030
	23: 8 Judah did according to all *t* that Jehoiada	NIH
	24: 7 also all the dedicate *t* of the house of	NIH

2Ch	29:33 the consecrated *t were* six hundred oxen	NIH
	31: 5 tithe of all *t* brought they in abundantly.	NIH
	31: 6 tithe of holy *t* which were consecrated	NIH
	31:12 and the tithes and the dedicate *t* faithfully:	NIH
	31:14 of the Lord, and the most holy *t*	NIH
	32: 1 After these *t*, and the establishment	1697
Ezr	1: 6 and with beasts, and with **precious** *t*,	4030
	2:63 they should not eat of the most holy *t*	NIH
	7: 1 Now after these *t*, in the reign of	1697
	9: 1 Now when these *t* were done, the princes	1697
Ne	6: 8 There are no such *t* done as thou sayest,	1697
	6:16 they were much cast down in their own	NIH
	7:65 they should eat of the most holy *t*,	NIH
	9: 6 all *t* that *are* therein, the seas, and all that	NIH
	10:33 for the holy *t*, and for the sin offerings to	NIH
	12:47 they sanctified *holy t* unto the Levites;	NIH
	13:26 *t*: yet among many nations was there no	NIH
Est	2: 1 After these *t*, when the wrath of king	1697
	2: 3 their *t* for purification be given *them*:	8562
	2: 9 speedily gave her her *t* for **purification**,	8562
	2: 9 with **such** *t* as belonged to her, and	4490
	2:12 with *other t* for the **purifying** of	8562
	3: 1 After these *t* did king Ahasuerus promote	1697
	5:11 all *the t* wherein the king had promoted	NIH
	9:20 Mordecai wrote these *t*, and sent letters	1697
Job	5: 9 Which doeth great *t* and unsearchable;	NIH
	5: 9 marvellous *t* without number:	NIH
	6: 7 **The t** *that* my soul refused to touch *are* as	1992
	6:30 cannot my taste discern **perverse** *t*?	1942
	8: 2 How long wilt thou speak these *t*?	NIH
	9:10 Which doeth great *t* past finding out; yea,	NIH
	10:13 these *t* hast thou hid in thine heart:	NIH
	12: 3 yea, who knoweth not such *t* as these?	NIH
	12:22 He discovereth deep *t* out of darkness,	NIH
	13:20 Only do not two *t* unto me: then will I not	NIH
	13:26 For thou writest bitter *t* against me,	NIH
	14:19 thou washest away the *t* **which grow** out	5599
	16: 2 I have heard many such *t*: miserable	NIH
	22:18 Yet he filled their houses with good *t*:	NIH
	23:14 for me: and many such *t are* with him.	NIH
	26: 5 Dead *t* are formed from under the waters,	NIH
	33:29 all these *t* worketh God oftentimes with	NIH
	37: 5 great *t* doeth he, which we cannot	NIH
	41:30 spreadeth sharp pointed *t* upon the mire.	NIH
	41:34 He beholdeth all high *t*: he *is* a king over	NIH
	42: 3 too wonderful for me, which I knew not.	NIH
Ps	8: 6 hands; thou hast put all *t* under his feet:	NIH
	12: 3 *and* the tongue that speaketh proud *t*:	NIH
	15: 5 that doeth these *t* shall never be moved.	NIH
	17: 2 thine eyes behold the *t* **that are equal**.	4339
	31:18 which speak **grievous** *t* proudly and	6277
	35:11 they laid to my charge *t* that I knew not.	NIH
	38:12 that seek my hurt speak **mischievous** *t*,	1942
	42: 4 When I remember these *t*, I pour out my	NIH
	45: 1 I speak of the *t* which I have **made**	4639
	45: 4 thy right hand shall teach thee terrible *t*.	NIH
	50:21 These *t* hast thou done, and I kept silence;	NIH
	57: 2 unto God that performeth *all t* for me.	NIH
	60: 3 Thou hast shewed thy people hard *t*: thou	NIH
	65: 5 *By* terrible *t* in righteousness wilt thou	NIH
	71:19 very high, who hast done great *t*: O God,	NIH
	72:18 God of Israel, who only doeth wondrous *t*.	NIH
	78:12 **Marvellous** *t* did he in the sight of their	6382
	86:10 and doest wondrous *t*: thou *art* God alone.	NIH
	87: 3 Glorious *t* are spoken of thee, O city of	NIH
	94: 4 *long* shall they utter *and* speak hard *t*?	NIH
	98: 1 for he hath done marvellous *t*: his right	NIH
	103: 5 Who satisfieth thy mouth with good *t*;	NIH
	104:25 wherein *are* t **creeping** innumerable,	7431
	106:21 which had done great *t* in Egypt;	NIH
	106:22 land of Ham, *and* terrible *t* by the Red sea.	NIH
	107:43 will observe these *t*, even they shall	NIH
	113: 6 humbleth *himself* to behold the *t* that	NIH
	119:18 that I may behold wondrous *t* out of thy	NIH
	119:128 *thy* precepts concerning all *t* to be right;	NIH
	126: 2 The Lord hath done great *t* for them.	NIH
	126: 3 The Lord hath done great *t* for us;	NIH
	131: 1 in great *matters*, or in *t* too high for me.	NIH
	148:10 all cattle; **creeping** *t*, and flying fowl:	7431
Pr	2:12 from the man that speaketh **froward** *t*;	8419
	3:15 all the *t* thou canst desire are not to be	NIH
	6:16 These six *t* doth the Lord hate: yea,	NIH
	8: 6 Hear, for I will speak of **excellent** *t*;	5057
	8: 6 the opening of my lips *shall be* **right** *t*.	4339
	8:11 all the *t* that may be desired are not to be	NIH
	16: 4 The Lord hath made all *t* for himself:	NIH
	16:30 He shutteth his eyes to devise **froward** *t*:	8419
	22:20 Have not I written to thee **excellent** *t* in	7991
	23:16 shall rejoice, when thy lips speak **right** *t*.	4339
	23:33 and thine heart shall utter **perverse** *t*.	8419
	24:23 These *t* also *belong* to the wise. *It is* not	NIH
	26:10 The great *God* that formed all *t* both	NIH
	28: 5 they that seek the Lord understand all *t*.	NIH
	28:10 upright shall have good *t* in possession.	NIH
	30: 7 Two *t* have I required of thee; deny me	NIH
	30:15 There are three *t* that are never satisfied,	NIH
	30:15 *yea*, four *t* say not, *It is* enough:	NIH
	30:18 There be three *t* which are too wonderful	NIH
	30:21 For three *t* the earth is disquieted,	NIH
	30:24 There be four *t* which are little upon	NIH
	30:29 There be three *t* which go well, yea, four	NIH
Ecc	1: 8 All *t are* full of labour; man cannot utter	1697
	1:11 *There is* no remembrance of former *t*;	NIH
	1:11 *t* that are to come with *those* that shall	NIH

Ecc	1:13 search out by wisdom concerning all *t* that	NIH
	6:11 Seeing there be many *t* that increase	1697
	7:15 All *t* have I seen in the days of my vanity:	NIH
	7:25 reason *of t,* and to know the wickedness	NIH
	9: 2 All *t come* alike to all: *there* is one event	NIH
	9: 3 This *is* an evil among all *t* that are done	NIH
	10:19 maketh merry: but money answereth all *t.*	NIH
	11: 9 that for all these *t* God will bring thee into	NIH
Isa	12: 5 the Lord; for he hath done **excellent t:**	1348
	25: 1 name; for thou hast done **wonderful t;**	6382
	25: 6 hosts make unto all people a feast of **fat t,**	8081
	25: 6 wines on the lees, of **fat t** full of marrow,	8081
	29:16 Surely your turning *of t* upside down shall	NIH
	30:10 Prophesy not unto us right *t,* speak unto us	NIH
	30:10 speak unto us smooth *t,* prophesy deceits:	NIH
	32: 8 the liberal deviseth liberal *t;* and by liberal	NIH
	32: 8 *things,* and by liberal *t* shall he stand.	NIH
	34: 1 the world, and **all** *t* that come forth of it.	3605
	38:16 by these *t* men live, and in all these *things*	NIH
	38:16 and in all these *t* is the life of my spirit:	NIH
	39: 2 shewed them the house of his **precious t,**	5238
	40:26 behold who hath created these *t,* that	NIH
	41:22 let them shew us the former *t,* what they *be,*	NIH
	41:22 end of them; or declare us *t* for to come.	NIH
	41:23 Shew the *t* that are to come hereafter,	NIH
	42: 9 the former *t* are come to pass,	NIH
	42: 9 are come to pass, and new *t* do I declare:	NIH
	42:16 light before them, and **crooked t** straight.	4625
	42:16 These *t* will I do unto them, and not	1697
	42:20 Seeing many *t,* but thou observest not;	NIH
	43: 9 shew us former *t?* let them bring forth	NIH
	43:18 Remember ye not the former *t,* neither	NIH
	43:18 *things,* neither consider the *t* of old.	NIH
	44: 7 the *t* that are coming, and shall come,	NIH
	44: 9 their delectable *t* shall not profit;	NIH
	44:24 I *am* the Lord that maketh all *t,*	NIH
	45: 7 and create evil: I the Lord do all these *t.*	NIH
	45: 9 Ask me of *t* to come concerning my sons,	NIH
	45:19 I declare it **that are right.**	4339
	46: 9 Remember the former *t* of old: for I *am*	NIH
	46:10 from ancient times *the t* that are not yet	NIH
	47: 7 that thou didst not lay these *t* to thy heart,	NIH
	47: 9 two *t* shall come to thee *in* a moment	NIH
	47:13 save thee from *these t* that shall come	NIH
	48: 3 I have declared the former *t* from	NIH
	48: 6 I have shewed thee new *t* from this time,	NIH
	48: 6 even hidden *t,* and thou didst not know	NIH
	48:14 which among them hath declared these *t?*	NIH
	51:19 These two *t* are come unto thee; who	NIH
	56: 4 choose the *t* that please me, and take hold	NIH
	61:11 the garden causeth the **t that are sown**	2221
	64: 3 When thou didst **terrible t** *which* we	3372
	64:11 and all our **pleasant t** are laid waste.	4261
	64:12 Wilt thou refrain thyself for these *t,*	NIH
	65: 4 broth of abominable *t is in* their vessels;	NIH
	66: 2 For all those *t* hath mine hand made,	NIH
	66: 2 and all those *t* have been, saith the Lord:	NIH
	66: 8 *t?* Shall the earth be made to bring forth in	NIH
Jer	2: 8 and walked after *t* that do not profit.	NIH
	3: 5 and done evil *t* as thou couldest.	NIH
	3: 7 I said after she had done all these *t,* Turn	NIH
	4:18 doings have procured these *t* unto thee;	NIH
	5: 9 Shall I not visit for these *t?* saith	NIH
	5:19 the Lord our God all these *t* unto us?	NIH
	5:25 Your iniquities have turned away these *t,*	NIH
	5:25 sins have withholden good *t* from you.	NIH
	5:29 Shall I not visit for these *t?* saith	NIH
	8:13 the *t that* I have given them shall pass	NIH
	9: 9 Shall I not visit for these *t?* saith	NIH
	9:24 for in these *t* I delight, saith the Lord.	NIH
	10:16 for he *is* the former of all *t;* and Israel *is*	NIH
	13:22 Wherefore come these *t* upon me?	NIH
	14:22 upon thee: for thou hast made all these *t.*	NIH
	16:18 of their detestable and **abominable t.**	8441
	16:19 vanity, and *t* wherein *there* is no profit.	NIH
	17: 9 The heart *is* deceitful above all *t,*	NIH
	18:13 who hath heard such a *t* the virgin of Israel	NIH
	20: 1 heard *that* Jeremiah prophesied these *t.*	1697
	20: 5 all the **precious t** thereof, and all	3366
	21:14 and it shall devour **all** *t* round about it.	3605
	26:10 When the princes of Judah heard these *t,*	1697
	30:15 I have done **these** *t* unto thee.	428
	31: 5 and shall **eat** *them* **as common t.**	2490
	33: 3 and mighty *t,* which thou knowest not.	NIH
	42: 5 if we do not even according to all *t* *for*	1697
	44:18 we have wanted all *t,* and have been	NIH
	45: 5 seekest thou great *t* for thyself? seek *them*	NIH
	51:19 for he *is* the former of all *t,* and *Israel is*	NIH
La	1: 7 of her miseries all her **pleasant t** that she	4262
	1:10 out his hand upon all her **pleasant t:**	4261
	1:11 they have given their **pleasant t** for meat	4261
	1:16 For these *t* I weep; mine eye, mine eye	NIH
	2:14 have seen vain and **foolish t** for thee:	8602
	5:17 heart is faint; for these *t* our eyes are dim.	NIH
Eze	5:11 my sanctuary with all thy **detestable t,**	8251
	7:20 *and* of their **detestable t** therein:	8251
	8:10 behold every form of **creeping t,**	7431
	11: 5 I know the **t that come into** your mind,	4609
	11:18 they shall take away all the **detestable t**	8251
	11:21 after the heart of their **detestable t**	8251
	11:25 spake unto them of the captivity all the **t**	1697
	16:16 the *like t* shall not come, neither shall it be	NIH
	16:30 seeing thou doest all these *t,* the work of	NIH
	16:43 hast fretted me in all these *t,* behold	NIH
	17:12 Know ye not what these *t mean?* tell	NIH

Eze	17:15 shall he escape that doeth such *t?* or shall	NIH
	17:18 hath done all these *t,* he shall not escape.	NIH
	18:10 *that* doeth the like to *any* one of these *t,*	NIH
	20:40 of your oblations, with all your holy *t.*	NIH
	22: 8 Thou hast despised mine holy *t,* and hast	NIH
	22:25 have taken the treasure and **precious t;**	3366
	22:26 have profaned mine holy *t:* they have put	NIH
	23:30 I will go do these *t* unto thee, because thou	NIH
	24:19 Wilt thou not tell us what these *t are* to us,	NIH
	27:24 *were* thy merchants in **all sorts of t,**	4360
	37:23 nor with their **detestable t,** nor with any	8251
	38:10 *that* at the same time shall *t* come into thy	1697
	38:20 all **creeping t** that creep upon the earth,	7431
	42:13 *t* there shall they lay the most holy *things,*	NIH
	42:13 there shall they lay the most holy *t,*	NIH
	42:14 shall approach to *those t* which *are* for	NIH
	44: 8 have not kept the charge of mine holy *t:*	NIH
	44:13 nor to come near to any of my holy *t,*	NIH
	44:30 And the first of all the firstfruits of all *t,*	NIH
Da	2:10 *that* asked such *t* at any magician,	4406
	2:22 secret *t:* he knoweth what *is* in the	NIH
	2:40 subdueth all *t* and as iron that breaketh	NIH
	7: 8 of man, and a mouth speaking great *t.*	NIH
	7:16 me know the interpretation of the *t.*	4406
	7:20 mouth that spake very great *t,* whose look	NIH
	10:21 *is* none that holdeth with me in these *t,*	NIH
	11:36 shall speak marvellous *t* against the God of	NIH
	11:38 and with precious stones, and **pleasant t.**	2532
	11:43 and over all the precious *t* of Egypt:	NIH
	12: 7 holy people, all these *t* shall be finished.	NIH
	12: 8 my lord, what *shall be* the end of these *t?*	NIH
Hos	2:18 and *with* the **creeping t** of the ground:	7431
	8:12 written to him the **great t** of my law,	7230
	9: 3 and they shall eat unclean *t* in Assyria.	NIH
	14: 9 he shall understand these *t?* prudent,	NIH
Joel	2:20 come up, because he hath done **great t.**	1431
	2:21 and rejoice: for the Lord will do **great t.**	1431
	3: 5 into your temples my goodly **pleasant t.**	4261
Ob	1: 6 How are the *t* of Esau searched out! how	NIH
	1: 6 how *are* his **hid t** sought up!	4710
Mic	7:15 Egypt will I shew unto him marvellous *t.*	NIH
Hab	1:14 as the **creeping t,** *that have* no ruler over	7431
Zep	1: 2 I will utterly consume all *t* from off	NIH
Zec	4:10 For who hath despised the day of small *t?*	NIH
	8:12 of this people to possess all these *t.*	NIH
	8:16 These *are* the *t* that ye shall do; Speak ye	1697
	8:17 for all these *are t* that I hate, saith	NIH
Mt	1:20 But while he thought on these *t,* behold,	NIG
	2: 3 When Herod the king had heard *these t,*	NIG
	4: 9 saith unto him, All these *t* will I give thee,	NIG
	6: 8 for your Father knoweth what *t* ye have	NIG
	6:32 (For after all these *t* do the Gentiles seek):	NIG
	6:32 knoweth that ye have need of all these *t.*	NIG
	6:33 and all these *t* shall be added unto you.	NIG
	6:34 the morrow shall take thought for the *t*	NIG
	7:11 heaven give good *t* to them that ask him?	NIG
	7:12 Therefore all *t* whatsoever ye would that	NIG
	9:18 While he spake these *t* unto them, behold,	NIG
	11: 4 shew John again *those t* which ye do hear	NIG
	11:25 thou hast hid these *t* from the wise and	NIG
	11:27 All *t* are delivered unto me of my Father:	NIG
	12:34 speak good *t?* for out of the abundance of	NIG
	12:35 treasure of the heart bringeth forth good *t.*	NIG
	12:35 of the evil treasure bringeth forth evil *t.*	NIG
	13: 3 he spake many *t* unto them in parables,	NIG
	13:17 righteous *men* have desired to see *those t*	NIG
	13:17 and to hear *those t* which ye hear,	NIG
	13:34 All these *t* spake Jesus unto the multitude	NIG
	13:35 I will utter *t which have been* kept secret	NIG
	13:41 out of his kingdom all **t that offend,**	4625
	13:51 Have ye understood all these *t?* They say	NIG
	13:52 which bringeth forth out of his treasure *t*	NIG
	13:56 Whence then hath this *man* all these *t?*	NIG
	15:18 those *t* which proceed out of the mouth	NIG
	15:20 These are the *t* which defile a man:	NIG
	16:21 and suffer many *t* of the elders and	NIG
	16:23 thou savourest not the *t* that be of God,	NIG
	17:11 truly shall first come, and restore all *t.*	NIG
	19:20 All these *t* have I kept from my youth up:	NIG
	19:26 but with God all *t* are possible.	NIG
	21:15 scribes saw the wonderful *t* that he did,	NIG
	21:22 all *t,* whatsoever ye shall ask in prayer,	NIG
	21:23 By what authority doest thou these *t?*	NIG
	21:24 tell you by what authority I do these *t.*	NIG
	21:27 tell I you by what authority I do these *t*	NIG
	22: 4 *my* fatlings *are* killed, and all *t are* ready:	NIG
	22:21 unto Cesar the *t* which are Cesar's;	NIG
	22:21 and unto God the *t* that are God's.	NIG
	23:20 sweareth by it, and by all *t* thereon.	NIG
	23:36 these *t* shall come upon this generation.	NIG
	24: 2 See ye not all *these t?* verily I say unto you	NIG
	24: 3 Tell us, when shall these *t* be?	NIG
	24: 6 for all *these t* must come to pass,	NIG
	24:33 ye shall see all these *t,* know that it is	NIG
	24:34 shall not pass, till all these *t* be fulfilled.	NIG
	25:21 thou hast been faithful over a few *t,* I will	NIG
	25:21 many *t:* enter thou into the joy of thy lord.	NIG
	25:23 thou hast been faithful over a few *t,* I will	NIG
	25:23 many *t:* enter thou into the joy of thy lord.	NIG
	27:13 Hearest thou not how many *t* they witness	NIG
	27:19 I have suffered many *t* this day in a dream	NIG
	27:54 and *those t* that were done, they feared	NIG
	28:11 shewed unto the chief priests all the *t*	NIG
	28:20 Teaching them to observe all *t* whatsoever	NIG
Mk	1:44 for thy cleansing *those t* which Moses	NIG

Mk	2: 8 Why reason ye these *t* in your hearts?	NIG
	3: 8 when they had heard what great *t* he did,	NIG
	4: 2 And he taught them many *t* by parables,	NIG
	4:11 without, all *these t* are done in parables:	NIG
	4:19 and the lusts of other *t* entering in,	NIG
	4:34 he expounded all *t* to his disciples.	NIG
	5:19 tell them how great *t* the Lord hath done	NIG
	5:20 began to publish in Decapolis how great *t*	NIG
	5:26 And had suffered many *t* of many	NIG
	6: 2 From whence hath this *man* these *t?*	NIG
	6:20 he did many *t,* and heard him gladly.	NIG
	6:30 told him all *t,* both what they had done,	NIG
	6:34 and he began to teach them many *t.*	NIG
	7: 4 many other *t* there be, which they have	NIG
	7: 8 cups: and many other such like *t* ye do.	NIG
	7:13 delivered: and many such like *t* do ye.	NIG
	7:15 but the *t* which come out of him, those	NIG
	7:23 All these evil *t* come from within,	NIG
	7:37 saying, He hath done all *t* well:	NIG
	8:31 that the Son of man must suffer many *t,*	NIG
	8:33 for thou savourest not the *t* that be of God,	NIG
	8:33 that be of God, but the *t* that be of men.	NIG
	9: 9 should tell no *man* what *t* they had seen,	NIG
	9:12 and restoreth all *t;* and how it is written of	NIG
	9:12 that he must suffer many *t,* and be set at	NIG
	9:23 all *t* are possible to him that believeth.	NIG
	10:27 with God: for with God all *t* are possible.	NIG
	10:32 began to tell them what *t* should happen	NIG
	11:11 he had looked round about upon all *t,*	NIG
	11:23 shall believe that *those t* which he saith	NIG
	11:24 What *soever* ye desire, when ye pray,	NIG
	11:28 By what authority doest thou these *t?*	NIG
	11:28 who gave thee this authority to do these *t?*	NIG
	11:29 will tell you by what authority I do these *t.*	NIG
	11:33 do I tell you by what authority I do these *t.*	NIG
	12:17 Render to Cesar the *t* that are Cesar's,	NIG
	12:17 Cesar's, and to God the *t* that are God's.	NIG
	13: 4 Tell us, when shall these *t* be?	NIG
	13: 4 *shall be* the sign when all these *t* shall	NIG
	13: 7 *such t* must needs be; but the end *shall*	NIG
	13:23 ye heed: behold, I have foretold you all *t.*	NIG
	13:29 when ye shall see these *t* come to pass,	NIG
	13:30 shall not pass, till all these *t* be done.	NIG
	14:36 Abba, Father, all *t* are possible unto thee;	NIG
	15: 3 the chief priests accused him of many *t:*	NIG
	15: 4 behold how many *t* they witness against	NIG
Lk	1: 1 *t* which are most surely believed among	4229
	1: 3 having had perfect understanding of all *t*	NIG
	1: 4 mightest know the certainty of *those* t,	3056
	1:20 the day that these *t* shall be performed,	NIG
	1:45 for there shall be a performance of those *t*	NIG
	1:49 he *that is* mighty hath done to me **great t;**	3167
	1:53 he hath filled the hungry with good *t;*	NIG
	2:18 *t* which were told them by the shepherds.	NIG
	2:19 But Mary kept all these *t,*	4487
	2:20 praising God for all *the t* that they had	NIG
	2:33 his mother marvelled at those *t* which	NIG
	2:39 And when they had performed all *t*	NIG
	3:18 And many other *t* in his exhortation	NIG
	4:28 when they heard these *t,* were filled with	NIG
	5:26 saying, We have seen strange *t* to day.	NIG
	5:27 And after these *t* he went forth, and saw a	NIG
	6:46 Lord, Lord, and do not *the t* which I say?	NIG
	7: 9 When Jesus heard these *t,* he marvelled at	NIG
	7:18 disciples of John shewed him of all these *t.*	NIG
	7:22 tell John what *t* ye have seen and heard;	NIG
	8: 8 And when he had said these *t,* he cried,	NIG
	8:39 how great *t* God hath done unto thee.	NIG
	8:39 city how great *t* Jesus had done unto him.	NIG
	9: 9 of whom I hear such *t?* And he desired to	NIG
	9:22 The Son of man must suffer many *t,*	NIG
	9:36 told no *man* in those days any of *those t*	NIG
	9:43 while they wondered every one at all *t*	NIG
	10: 1 After these *t* the Lord appointed other	NIG
	10: 7 eating and drinking such *t* as they give:	NIG
	10: 8 you, eat such *t* as are set before you:	NIG
	10:21 that thou hast hid these *t* from the wise	NIG
	10:22 All *t* are delivered to me of my Father:	NIG
	10:23 Blessed *are* the eyes which see the *t* that	NIG
	10:24 kings have desired to see *those t* which ye	NIG
	10:24 and to hear *those t* which ye hear,	NIG
	10:41 art careful and troubled about many *t:*	NIG
	11:27 as he spake these *t,* a certain woman of	NIG
	11:41 But rather give alms *of such t as you* have;	NIG
	11:41 and behold, all *t* are clean unto you.	NIG
	11:53 as he said these *t* unto them, the scribes	NIG
	11:53 and to provoke him to speak of many *t*	NIG
	12:15 abundance of the *t* which he possesseth.	NIG
	12:20 then whose *shall those t* be, which thou	NIG
	12:30 For all these *t* do the nations of the world	NIG
	12:30 knoweth that ye have need of these *t.*	NIG
	12:31 and all these *t* shall be added unto you.	NIG
	12:48 and did commit *t* worthy of stripes,	NIG
	13: 2 Galileans, because they suffered such *t?*	NIG
	13:17 And when he had said these *t,* all his	NIG
	13:17 the people rejoiced for all the glorious *t*	NIG
	14: 6 could not answer him again to these *t.*	NIG
	14:15 with *him* heard these *t,* he said unto him,	NIG
	14:17 bidden, Come; for all *t* are now ready.	NIG
	14:21 shewed his lord these *t.* Then the master	NIG
	15:26 servants, and asked what these *t* meant.	NIG
	16:14 heard all these *t:* and they derided him.	NIG
	16:25 thou in thy lifetime receivedst thy good *t,*	NIG
	16:25 and likewise Lazarus evil *t:* but now he is	NIG
	17: 9 he did the *t* that were commanded him?	NIG

Lk 17:10 when ye shall have done all those *t* which NIG
17:25 But first must he suffer many *t,* NIG
18:22 Now when Jesus heard these *t,* he said NIG
18:27 The *t which are* unpossible with men are NIG
18:31 all *t* that are written by the prophets NIG
18:34 And they understood none of these *t.* NIG
18:34 knew they the *t* which were spoken. NIG
19:11 And as they heard these *t,* he added and NIG
19:42 day, the *t* which belong unto thy peace! NIG
20: 2 by what authority doest thou these *t?* NIG
20: 8 tell I you by what authority I do these *t.* NIG
20:25 unto Cesar the *t* which be Cesar's, NIG
20:25 and unto God the *t* which be God's. NIG
21: 6 *As for* these *t* which ye behold, the days NIG
21: 7 saying, Master, but when shall these *t* be? NIG
21: 7 what sign *will there be* when these *t* shall NIG
21: 9 for these *t* must first come to pass; NIG
21:22 all *t* which are written may be fulfilled. NIG
21:26 *for* looking after those *t* which are coming NIG
21:28 And when these *t* begin to come to pass, NIG
21:31 when ye see these *t* come to pass, NIG
21:36 escape all these *t* that shall come to pass, NIG
22:37 for the *t* concerning me have an end. NIG
22:65 And many other *t* blasphemously spake NIG
23: 8 because *he* had heard many *t* of him; NIG
23:14 *touching* those *t* whereof ye accuse him: NIG
23:31 For if they do these *t* in a green tree, NIG
23:48 beholding the *t* which were done, NIG
23:49 stood afar off, beholding these *t.* NIG
24: 9 and told all these *t* unto the eleven, NIG
24:10 which told these *t* unto the apostles. NIG
24:14 And they talked together of all these *t* NIG
24:18 not known the *t* which are come to pass NIG
24:19 unto them, What *t?* And they said unto NIG
24:21 to day is the third day since these *t* were NIG
24:26 Ought not Christ to have suffered these *t,* NIG
24:27 all the scriptures the *t* concerning himself. NIG
24:35 they told what *t were* done in the way, NIG
24:44 yet with you, that all *t* must be fulfilled, NIG
24:48 And ye are witnesses of these *t.* NIG
Jn 1: 3 All *t* were made by him; and without him NIG
1:28 These *t* were done in Bethabara beyond NIG
1:50 thou shalt see greater *t* than these. NIG
2:16 them that sold doves, Take these *t* hence; NIG
2:18 unto us, seeing that thou doest these *t?* NIG
3: 9 and said unto him, How can these *t* be? NIG
3:10 master of Israel, and knowest not these *t?* NIG
3:12 If I have told you earthly *t,* and ye believe NIG
3:12 shall ye believe, if I tell you *of* heavenly *t?* NIG
3:22 After these *t* came Jesus and his disciples NIG
3:35 the Son, and hath given all *t* into his hand. NIG
4:25 when he is come, he will tell us all *t.* NIG
4:29 a man, which told me all *t* that ever I did: NIG
4:45 seen all *the t* that he did at Jerusalem NIG
5:16 he had done these *t* on the sabbath day. NIG
5:19 what *t* soever he doeth, these also doeth NIG
5:20 and sheweth him all *t* that himself doeth: NIG
5:34 but these *t* I say, that ye might be saved. NIG
6: 1 After these *t* Jesus went over the sea of NIG
6:59 These *t* said he in the synagogue, as he NIG
7: 1 After these *t* Jesus walked in Galilee: for NIG
7: 4 If thou do these *t,* shew thyself to the NIG
7:32 people murmured such *t* concerning him; NIG
8:26 I have many *t* to say and to judge of you: NIG
8:26 I speak to the world those *t* which I have NIG
8:28 my Father hath taught me, I speak these *t.* NIG
8:29 for I do always those *t* that please him. NIG
10: 6 they understood not what *t* they were NIG
10:41 all *t* that John spake of this *man* were true. NIG
11:11 These *t* said he: and after that he saith unto NIG
11:45 and had seen the *t* which Jesus did, NIG
11:46 and told them what *t* Jesus had done. NIG
12:16 These *t* understood not his disciples at NIG
12:16 remembered they that these *t* were written NIG
12:16 and *that* they had done these *t* unto him. NIG
12:36 These *t* spake Jesus, and departed, NIG
12:41 These *t* said Esaias, when he saw his glory, NIG
13: 3 knowing that the Father had given all *t* NIG
13:17 If ye know these *t,* happy are ye if ye do NIG
13:29 Buy *those t* that we have need of against NIG
14:25 These *t* have I spoken unto you, being *yet* NIG
14:26 shall teach you all *t,* and bring all *things* NIG
14:26 and bring all *t* to your remembrance, NIG
15:11 These *t* have I spoken unto you, that my NIG
15:15 for all *t* that I have heard of my Father I NIG
15:17 These *t* I command you, that ye love one NIG
15:21 But all these *t* will they do unto you for NIG
16: 1 These *t* have I spoken unto you, that ye NIG
16: 3 And these *t* will they do unto you, because NIG
16: 4 But these *t* have I told you, that when NIG
16: 4 And these *t* I said not unto you at NIG
16: 6 But because I have said these *t* unto you, NIG
16:12 I have yet many *t* to say unto you, NIG
16:13 he speak: and he will shew you *t* to come. NIG
16:15 All *t* that the Father hath are mine: NIG
16:25 These *t* have I spoken unto you in NIG
16:30 Now are we sure that thou knowest all *t,* NIG
16:33 These *t* I have spoken unto you, that in NIG
17: 7 they have known that all *t* whatsoever NIG
17:13 and these *t* I speak in the world, that they NIG
18: 4 knowing all *t* that should come upon him, NIG
19:24 These *t* therefore the soldiers did. NIG
19:28 Jesus knowing that all *t* were now NIG
19:36 For these *t* were done, that the scripture NIG
20:18 and *that* he had spoken these *t* unto her. NIG

Jn 21: 1 After these *t* Jesus shewed himself again to NIG
21:17 thou knowest all *t,* thou knowest that I NIG
21:24 is the disciple which testifieth of these *t,* NIG
21:24 and wrote these *t:* and we know that his NIG
21:25 there are also many other *t* which Jesus NIG
Ac 1: 3 speaking of the *t* pertaining to the kingdom NIG
1: 9 when he had spoken these *t,* while they NIG
2:44 were together, and had all *t* common; NIG
3:18 *those t,* which God before had shewed NIG
3:21 *t,* which God hath spoken by the mouth NIG
3:22 him shall ye hear in all *t* whatsoever he NIG
4:20 but speak *the t* which we have seen and NIG
4:25 and the people imagine vain *t?* NIG
4:32 said any *of them* that ought of the *t* NIG
4:32 was his own; but they had all *t* common. NIG
4:34 brought the prices of the *t* that were sold, NIG
5: 5 fear came on all them that heard these *t.* NIG
5:11 and upon as many as heard these *t.* NIG
5:24 and the chief priests heard these *t,* 3056
5:32 we are his witnesses of these *t;* and so 4487
7: 1 Then said the high priest, Are these *t* so? NIG
7:50 Hath not my hand made all these *t?* NIG
7:54 When they heard these *t,* they were cut to NIG
8: 6 heed unto those *t* which Philip spake, NIG
8:12 the *t* concerning the kingdom of God, NIG
8:24 that none of *these t* which ye have spoken NIG
9:16 For I will shew him how great *t* he must NIG
10: 8 when he had declared all *these t* unto NIG
10:12 and **creeping** *t,* and fowls of the air. 2062
10:33 to hear all *t* that are commanded thee of NIG
10:39 we are witnesses of all *t* which he did NIG
11: 6 and **creeping** *t,* and fowls of the air. 2062
11:18 When they heard these *t,* they held their NIG
11:22 Then tidings of these *t* came unto the ears NIG
12:17 *Go* shew these *t* unto James, and to NIG
13:39 *t, from* which ye could not be justified by NIG
13:45 spake against those *t* which were spoken NIG
14:15 why do ye these *t?* We also are men of like NIG
14:15 and the sea, and all *t* that are therein: NIG
15: 4 they declared all *t* that God had done with NIG
15:17 saith the Lord, who doeth all these *t.* NIG
15:20 and *from* t strangled, and *from* blood. 3588
15:27 shall also tell *you* the same *t* by mouth. NIG
15:28 no greater burden than these necessary *t,* NIG
15:29 from *t* **strangled,** and from fornication: 4156
16:14 that *she* attended unto the *t* which were NIG
17: 8 of the city, when they heard these *t.* NIG
17:11 scriptures daily, whether those *t* were so. NIG
17:20 For thou bringest certain strange *t* to our NIG
17:20 would know therefore what these *t* mean. NIG
17:22 I perceive that in all *t* ye are too NIG
17:24 God that made the world and all *t* therein, NIG
17:25 he giveth to all life, and breath, and all *t;* NIG
18: 1 After these *t* Paul departed from Athens, NIG
18:17 And Gallio cared for none of those *t.* NIG
18:25 and taught diligently the *t* of the Lord, NIG
19: 8 persuading the *t* concerning the kingdom NIG
19:21 After these *t* were ended, Paul purposed in NIG
19:36 then that these *t* cannot be spoken against, NIG
20:22 knowing the *t* that shall befall me there: NIG
20:24 none of these *t* move me, neither count NIG
20:30 speaking perverse *t,* to draw away disciples NIG
20:35 I have shewed you all *t,* how that so NIG
21:12 And when we heard these *t,* both we, NIG
21:19 he declared particularly what *t* God had NIG
21:24 all may know that those *t,* whereof they NIG
21:25 keep themselves from *t* **offered to idols,** 1494
22:10 there it shall be told thee of all *t* which are NIG
23:22 no *man* that thou hast shewed these *t* to NIG
24: 8 of all these *t,* whereof we accuse him. NIG
24: 9 also assented, saying that these *t* were so. NIG
24:13 Neither can they prove the *t* whereof they NIG
24:14 believing all *t* which are written in the law NIG
24:22 when Felix heard these *t,* having more NIG
25: 9 and there be judged of these *t* before me? NIG
25:11 if there be none *of these t* whereof these NIG
25:18 none accusation of *such t* as I supposed: NIG
26: 2 all the *t* whereof I am accused of the Jews: NIG
26: 9 that *I* ought to do many *t* contrary to NIG
26:16 a witness both of *these t* which thou hast NIG
26:16 *of those t* in the which I will appear unto NIG
26:22 saying none other *t* than those which NIG
26:26 For the king knoweth of these *t,* before NIG
26:26 for I am persuaded that none of these *t* are NIG
27:11 more than those *t* which were spoken by NIG
28:10 laded *us* with such *t* as were necessary. NIG
28:24 And some believed the *t* which were NIG
28:31 teaching those *t* which concern the Lord NIG
Ro 1:20 For the invisible *t* of him from the creation NIG
1:20 being understood by the *t* **that are made,** 4161
1:23 and fourfooted beasts, and **creeping** *t.* 2062
1:28 to do those *t* which are not convenient; NIG
1:30 inventors of evil *t,* disobedient to parents, NIG
1:32 they which commit such *t* are worthy of NIG
2: 1 for thou that judgest doest the same *t.* NIG
2: 2 truth against them which commit such *t.* NIG
2: 3 that judgest them which do such *t,* NIG
2:14 do by nature the *t* contained in the law, NIG
2:18 approvest the *t* that are more excellent, NIG
3:19 Now we know that what *t* soever the law NIG
4:17 calleth those *t* which be not as though NIG
6:21 *in those t* whereof ye are now ashamed? NIG
6:21 for the end of those *t* is death. NIG
8: 5 after the flesh do mind the *t* of the flesh; NIG
8: 5 they *that are* after the Spirit the *t* of NIG

Ro 8:28 And we know that all *t* work together for NIG
8:31 then say to these *t?* If God *be* for us, NIG
8:32 he not with him also freely give us all *t?* NIG
8:37 in all these *t* we are more than conquerors NIG
8:38 principalities, nor powers, nor *t* present, NIG
8:38 nor *things* present, nor *t* to come, NIG
10: 5 the man which doeth those *t* shall live NIG
10:15 of peace, and bring glad tidings of good *t!* NIG
11:36 him, *are* all *t:* to whom *be* glory for ever. NIG
12:16 Mind not high *t,* but condescend to *men* NIG
12:17 Provide *t* honest in the sight of all men. NIG
14: 2 For one believeth that *he* may eat all *t:* NIG
14:18 For he that in these *t* serveth Christ *is* NIG
14:19 follow *after* the *t* which make for peace, NIG
14:19 and *t* wherewith one may edify another. NIG
14:20 All *t* indeed *are* pure; but *it is* evil for that NIG
15: 4 For whatsoever *t* were written aforetime NIG
15:17 Christ *in those t* which pertain to God. NIG
15:18 I will not dare to speak of any of *those t* NIG
15:27 *their* duty is also to minister unto them NIG
15:27 is also to minister unto them in carnal *t.* NIG
1Co 1:27 But God hath chosen the foolish *t* of NIG
1:27 God hath chosen the weak *t* of the world NIG
1:27 world to confound the *t which are* mighty; NIG
1:28 And base *t* of the world, and *things* which NIG
1:28 *t* which are despised, hath God chosen, NIG
1:28 God chosen, *yea,* and *t* which are not, NIG
1:28 are not, to bring to nought *t* that are: NIG
2: 9 the *t* which God hath prepared for them NIG
2:10 for the Spirit searcheth all *t,* yea, the deep NIG
2:10 all *things,* yea, the **deep** *t* of God. 899
2:11 For what man knoweth the *t* of a man, NIG
2:11 even so the *t* of God knoweth no *man,* NIG
2:12 that we might know the *t* that are freely NIG
2:13 Which *t* also we speak, not in the words NIG
2:13 comparing spiritual *t* with spiritual. NIG
2:14 But the natural man receiveth not the *t* of NIG
2:15 But he that is spiritual judgeth all *t,* yet he NIG
3:21 no *man* glory in men. For all *t* are yours; NIG
3:22 or death, or *t* present, or *things* to come; NIG
3:22 or death, or *things* present, or *t* to come; NIG
4: 5 who both will bring to light the hidden *t* NIG
4: 6 And these *t,* brethren, I have in a figure NIG
4:13 *are* the offscouring of all *t* unto this day. NIG
4:14 I write not these *t* to shame you, but as NIG
6: 3 how much more *t* that pertain to *this* life? NIG
6: 4 ye have judgments *of t* pertaining to *this* NIG
6:12 All *t* are lawful unto me, but all *things* are NIG
6:12 lawful unto me, but all *t* are not expedient: NIG
6:12 all *t* are lawful for me, but I will not be NIG
7: 1 Now concerning *the t* whereof ye wrote NIG
7:32 He *that is* unmarried careth for the *t* that NIG
7:33 But he that is married careth for the *t* that NIG
7:34 The unmarried *woman* careth for the *t* of NIG
7:34 she that is married careth for the *t* of NIG
8: 1 Now as touching *t* **offered unto idols,** 1494
8: 4 *t* that are **offered in sacrifice unto idols,** 1494
8: 6 of whom *are* all *t,* and we in him; NIG
8: 6 by whom *are* all *t,* and we by him. NIG
8:10 to eat those *t* which are **offered to idols;** 1494
9: 8 Say I these *t* as a man? or saith not the law NIG
9:11 If we have sown unto you spiritual *t, is it* a NIG
9:11 a great *thing* if we shall reap your carnal *t?* NIG
9:12 suffer all *t,* lest we should hinder the NIG
9:13 holy *t* live of the *things* of the temple? NIG
9:13 holy *things* live of the *t* of the temple? NIG
9:15 But I have used none of these *t:* neither NIG
9:15 have I written these *t,* that it should be NIG
9:22 I am made all *t* to all *men,* that I might by NIG
9:25 *t.* Now they do *it* to obtain a corruptible NIG
10: 6 Now these *t* were our examples, NIG
10: 6 the intent we should not lust after evil *t,* NIG
10:11 Now all these *t* happened unto them for NIG
10:20 But *I* say, that the *t* which the Gentiles NIG
10:23 All *t* are lawful for me, but all *things* are NIG
10:23 lawful for me, but all *t* are not expedient: NIG
10:23 all *t* are lawful for me, but all *things* edify NIG
10:23 are lawful for me, but all *t* edify not. NIG
10:33 as I please all *men* in all *t,* not seeking NIG
11: 2 that you remember me in all *t,* and keep NIG
11:12 man also by the woman; but all *t* of God. NIG
13: 7 Beareth all *t,* believeth all *things,* hopeth NIG
13: 7 Beareth all *things,* believeth all *t,* hopeth NIG
13: 7 *things,* hopeth all *t,* endureth all *things.* NIG
13: 7 *things,* hopeth all *things,* endureth all *t.* NIG
13:11 I became a man, I put away childish *t.* NIG
14: 7 *And* even *without* life giving sound, NIG
14:26 Let all *t* be done unto edifying. NIG
14:37 let him acknowledge that *the t* that I NIG
14:40 Let all *t* be done decently and in order. NIG
15:27 For he hath put all *t* under his feet. NIG
15:27 all *t* are put under *him, it is* manifest that NIG
15:27 is excepted, which did put all *t* under him. NIG
15:28 And when all *t* shall be subdued unto him, NIG
15:28 subject unto him that put all *t* under him, NIG
16:14 Let all *your t* be done with charity. NIG
2Co 1:13 For we write none other *t* unto you, NIG
1:17 or *the t* that I purpose, do I purpose NIG
2: 9 of you, whether ye be obedient in all *t.* NIG
2:16 unto life. And who *is* sufficient for these *t?* NIG
4: 2 But have renounced the hidden *t* of NIG
4:15 For all *t are* for your sakes, that NIG
4:18 While we look not at the *t* which are seen, NIG
4:18 are seen, but at the *t* which are not seen: NIG
4:18 for the *t* which are seen *are* temporal; NIG

2Co	4:18	but the *t* which are not seen *are* eternal. NIG
	5:10	every one may receive the *t* done in *his* NIG
	5:17	old *t* are past away; behold, all *things* are NIG
	5:17	past away; behold, all *t* are become new. NIG
	5:18	And all *t* are of God, who hath reconciled NIG
	6: 4	But in all *t* approving ourselves as NIG
	6:10	as having nothing, and *yet* possessing all *t*. NIG
	7:11	In all *t* ye have approved yourselves to be NIG
	7:14	but as we spake all *t* to you in truth, even NIG
	7:16	that I have confidence in you in all *t*. NIG
	8:21	Providing for honest *t*, not only in the sight NIG
	8:22	have oftentimes proved diligent in many *t*, NIG
	9: 8	always having all sufficiency in all *t*, NIG
	10: 7	Do ye look on *t* after the outward NIG
	10:13	But we will not boast of *t* without our NIG
	10:15	Not boasting of *t* without our measure, NIG
	10:16	not to boast in another *man's* line of *t* NIG
	11: 6	made manifest among you in all *t*. NIG
	11: 9	in all *t* I have kept myself from being NIG
	11:28	Besides those *t* that are without, NIG
	11:30	I will glory of the *t* which concern mine NIG
	12:19	but *we do* all *t*, dearly beloved, for your NIG
	13:10	Therefore I write these *t* being absent, NIG
Gal	1:20	Now the *t* which I write unto you, behold, NIG
	2:18	For if I build again the *t* which I destroyed, NIG
	3: 4	Have ye suffered so many *t* in vain? if *it be* NIG
	3:10	*t* which are written in the book of the law NIG
	4:24	Which *t* are an allegory: for these are NIG
	5:17	so that ye cannot do the *t* that ye would. NIG
	5:21	that they which do such *t* shall not inherit NIG
	6: 6	unto him that teacheth in all good *t*. NIG
Eph	1:10	might gather together in one all *t* in Christ, NIG
	1:11	all *t* after the counsel of his own will: NIG
	1:22	And hath put all *t* under his feet, NIG
	1:22	gave him *to be* the head over all *t* to NIG
	3: 9	in God, who created all *t* by Jesus Christ: NIG
	4:10	above all heavens, that he might fill all *t*) NIG
	4:15	may grow *up* into him *in* all *t*, which is NIG
	5: 6	of these *t* cometh the wrath of God upon NIG
	5:12	For it is a shame even to speak of those *t* NIG
	5:13	But all *t* that are reproved are made NIG
	5:20	Giving thanks always for all *t* unto God NIG
	6: 9	And, ye masters, do the same *t* unto them, NIG
	6:21	in the Lord, shall make known to you all *t* NIG
Php	1:10	That ye may approve *t* that are excellent; NIG
	1:12	that the *t* which happened unto me have NIG
	2: 4	Look not every man on his own *t*, NIG
	2: 4	but every man also on the *t* of others. NIG
	2:10	of *t* in heaven, and *things* in earth, NIG
	2:10	and *t* in earth, and *things* under the earth; NIG
	2:10	and *things* in earth, and *t* under the earth; NIG
	2:14	Do all *t* without murmurings and NIG
	2:21	not the *t* which are Jesus Christ's. NIG
	3: 1	To write the same *t* to you, to me indeed NIG
	3: 7	what *t* were gain to me, those I counted NIG
	3: 8	I count all *t but* loss for the excellency NIG
	3: 8	for whom I have suffered the loss of all *t*, NIG
	3:13	one *thing* I do, forgetting those *t* which NIG
	3:13	reaching forth unto those *t* which are NIG
	3:19	*is* in their shame, who mind earthly *t*.) NIG
	3:21	is able even to subdue all *t* unto himself. NIG
	4: 8	Finally, brethren, whatsoever *t* are true, NIG
	4: 8	whatsoever *t* are honest, whatsoever NIG
	4: 8	whatsoever *t* are just, whatsoever *things* NIG
	4: 8	*things* are just, whatsoever *t* are pure, NIG
	4: 8	*things* are pure, whatsoever *t* are lovely, NIG
	4: 8	lovely, whatsoever *t* are of good report; NIG
	4: 8	if *there be* any praise, think on these *t*. NIG
	4: 9	Those *t*, which ye have both learned, NIG
	4:12	in all *t* I am instructed both to be full and NIG
	4:13	I can do all *t* through Christ which NIG
	4:18	received of Epaphroditus the *t* which NIG
Col	1:16	For by him were all *t* created, that are in NIG
	1:16	all *t* were created by him, and for him: NIG
	1:17	he is before all *t*, and by him all *things* NIG
	1:17	before all *things*, and by him all *t* consist. NIG
	1:18	in all *t* the might have the preeminence. NIG
	1:20	by him to reconcile all *t* unto himself; NIG
	1:20	*I say*, whether *they be* in earth, or *things* NIG
	1:20	*they be* things in earth, or *t* in heaven. NIG
	2:17	Which are a shadow of *t* to come; NIG
	2:18	intruding into *those t* which he hath not NIG
	2:23	Which *t* have indeed a shew of wisdom in NIG
	3: 1	with Christ, seek those *t* which are above, NIG
	3: 2	Set your affection on *t* above, not on NIG
	3: 2	on *things* above, not on *t* on the earth. NIG
	3:14	And above all these *t* put on charity, NIG
	3:20	obey *your* parents in all *t* for this is well NIG
	3:22	obey in all *t your* masters according to NIG
	4: 9	They shall make known to you all *t* NIG
1Th	2:14	for ye also have suffered like *t* of your own NIG
	5:21	Prove all *t*, hold fast *that which is* good. NIG
2Th	2: 5	I was yet with you, I told you these *t*? NIG
	3: 4	will do the *t* which we command you. NIG
1Ti	3:11	not slanderers, sober, faithful in all *t*. NIG
	3:14	These *t* write I unto thee, hoping to come NIG
	4: 6	thou shalt be a good minister of Jesus NIG
	4: 8	godliness is profitable unto all *t*, having NIG
	4:11	These *t* command and teach. NIG
	4:15	Meditate upon these *t*; give thyself wholly NIG
	5: 7	And these *t* give in charge, that they may NIG
	5:13	speaking *t* which they ought not. NIG
	5:21	thou observe these *t* without preferring NIG
	6: 2	of the benefit. These *t* teach and exhort. NIG
	6:11	flee these *t*; and follow after righteousness; NIG

1Ti	6:13	who quickeneth all *t*, and before Christ NIG
	6:17	who giveth us richly all *t* to enjoy; NIG
2Ti	1:12	For the which cause I also suffer these *t*. NIG
	1:18	in how many *t* he ministered *unto me* at NIG
	2: 2	the *t* that thou hast heard of me among NIG
	2: 7	The Lord give thee understanding in all *t*. NIG
	2:10	I endure all *t* for the elects' sakes, NIG
	2:14	Of these *t* put *them* in remembrance, NIG
	3:14	continue thou in the *t* which thou hast NIG
Tit	1: 5	thou shouldest set in order the *t* that are NIG
	1:11	teaching *t* which *they* ought not, for filthy NIG
	1:15	Unto the pure all *t* are pure: but unto NIG
	2: 1	But speak thou *the t* which become sound NIG
	2: 3	given to much wine, teachers of good *t*; 2567
	2: 7	In all *t* shewing thyself a pattern of good NIG
	2: 9	to please *them* well in all *t*, not answering NIG
	2:10	the doctrine of God our Saviour in all *t*. NIG
	2:15	These *t* speak, and exhort, and rebuke NIG
	3: 8	these I *t* will that thou affirm constantly, NIG
	3: 8	These *t* are good and profitable unto men. NIG
Heb	1: 2	whom he hath appointed heir of all *t*, NIG
	1: 3	upholding all *t* by the word of his power, NIG
	2: 1	heed to the *t* which we have heard, NIG
	2: 8	Thou hast put all *t* in subjection under his NIG
	2: 8	now we see not yet all *t* put under him. NIG
	2:10	for whom *are* all *t*, and by whom *are* all NIG
	2:10	by whom *are* all *t*, in bringing many sons NIG
	2:17	Wherefore in all *t* it behoved him to be NIG
	2:17	faithful high priest *in t* pertaining to God, NIG
	3: 4	by some *man*; but he that built all *t* is God. NIG
	3: 5	for a testimony of those *t* which were to NIG
	4:13	all *t* are naked and opened unto the eyes NIG
	5: 1	is ordained for men in *t* pertaining to God, NIG
	5: 8	learned he obedience by the *t* which he NIG
	5:11	Of whom we have **many t** to say, 4183
	6: 9	we are persuaded better *t* of you, NIG
	6: 9	*t* that accompany salvation, though we NIG
	6:18	That by two immutable *t*, in which *it was* 4229
	7:13	For he of whom these *t* are spoken NIG
	8: 1	Now of the *t* which we have spoken *this* NIG
	8: 5	shadow of heavenly *t*, as Moses was NIG
	8: 5	saith *he*, that thou make all *t* according to NIG
	9: 6	Now when these *t* were thus ordained, NIG
	9:11	being come a high priest of good *t* to come, NIG
	9:22	And almost all *t* are by the law purged NIG
	9:23	necessary that the patterns of *t* in NIG
	9:23	the heavenly *t* themselves with better NIG
	10: 1	For the law having a shadow of good *t* to NIG
	10: 1	to come, *and* not the very image of the *t*, 4229
	11: 1	Now faith is the substance of *t* hoped for, NIG
	11: 1	hoped for, the evidence of *t* not seen. 4229
	11: 3	that *t* which are seen were not made of NIG
	11: 3	seen were not made of *t* which do appear. NIG
	11: 7	being warned of God of *t* not seen as yet, NIG
	11:14	For they that say such *t* declare plainly NIG
	11:20	and Esau concerning *t* to come. NIG
	12:24	that speaketh better *t* than *that of* Abel. NIG
	12:27	The removing of those *t* that are shaken, NIG
	12:27	as of *t* that are made, that those *things* NIG
	12:27	that those *t* which cannot be shaken may NIG
	13: 5	*and* be content with such *t* as ye have: NIG
	13:18	in all *t* willing to live honestly. NIG
Jas	2:16	notwithstanding ye give them not those *t* NIG
	3: 2	For in many *t* we offend all. If any *man* NIG
	3: 5	is a little member, and boasteth **great t**. 3173
	3: 7	of *t* in the sea, is tamed, and hath been NIG
	3:10	My brethren, these *t* ought not so to be. NIG
	5:12	But above all *t*, my brethren, swear not, NIG
1Pe	1:12	but unto us they did minister the *t*, 846
	1:12	which *the* angels desire to look into. NIG
	1:18	not redeemed with corruptible *t*, as silver NIG
	4: 7	But the end of all *t* is at hand: be ye NIG
	4: 8	above all *t* have fervent charity among NIG
	4:11	that God in all *t* may be glorified through NIG
2Pe	1: 3	given unto us all *t* that *pertain* unto life NIG
	1: 8	For if these *t* be in you, and abound, NIG
	1: 9	But he that lacketh these *t* is blind, NIG
	1:10	for if ye do these *t*, ye shall never fall: NIG
	1:12	of these *t*, though ye know *them*, NIG
	1:15	to have these *t* always in remembrance. NIG
	2:12	evil of the *t* that they understand not; NIG
	3: 4	all *t* continue as *they were* from NIG
	3:11	then that all these *t shall* be dissolved, NIG
	3:14	seeing that ye look for such *t*, be diligent NIG
	3:16	speaking in them of these *t*; in which are NIG
	3:16	in which are some *t* hard to be understood, NIG
	3:17	beloved, seeing ye know these *t* before, NIG
1Jn	1: 4	These *t* write we unto you, that your joy NIG
	2: 1	These *t* write I unto you, that ye sin not. NIG
	2:15	world, neither the *t* that are in the world. NIG
	2:20	from the Holy One, and ye know all *t*. NIG
	2:26	These *t* have I written unto you concerning NIG
	2:27	as the same anointing teacheth you of all *t*, NIG
	3:20	greater than our heart, and knoweth all *t*. NIG
	3:22	do those *t* that are pleasing in his sight. NIG
	5:13	These *t* have I written unto you that NIG
2Jn	1: 8	that we lose not *those t* which we have NIG
	1:12	Having many *t* to write unto you, I would NIG
3Jn	1: 2	I wish above all *t* that thou mayest prosper NIG
	1:13	I had many *t* to write, NIG
Jude	1:10	But these speak evil of those *t* which they NIG
	1:10	in those *t* they corrupt themselves. NIG
Rev	1: 1	to shew unto his servants *t* which must NIG
	1: 2	of Jesus Christ, and of all *t* that he saw. NIG

Rev	1: 3	keep those *t* which are written therein: NIG
	1:19	Write the *t* which thou hast seen, NIG
	1:19	and *the t* which are, and *the things* which NIG
	1:19	and *the t* which shall be hereafter; NIG
	2: 1	These *t* saith he that holdeth the seven NIG
	2: 8	These *t* saith the first and the last, NIG
	2:10	Fear none *of those t* which thou shalt NIG
	2:12	These *t* saith he which hath the sharp NIG
	2:14	But I have a few *t* against thee, because NIG
	2:14	to eat *t* sacrificed unto idols, 1494
	2:18	These *t* saith the Son of God, who hath NIG
	2:20	Notwithstanding I have a few *t* against NIG
	2:20	and to eat *t* sacrificed unto idols. 1494
	3: 1	These *t* saith he that hath the seven spirits NIG
	3: 2	and strengthen the *t* which remain, NIG
	3: 7	These *t* saith he *that is* holy, he *that is* true NIG
	3:14	These *t* saith the Amen, the faithful and NIG
	4: 1	I will shew thee *t* which must be hereafter. NIG
	4:11	for thou hast created all *t*, and for thy NIG
	7: 1	after these *t* I saw four angels standing NIG
	10: 4	Seal *up those t* which the seven thunders NIG
	10: 6	and the *t* that therein are, and the earth, NIG
	10: 6	and the *t* that therein are, and the sea, NIG
	10: 6	and the sea, and the *t* which are therein, NIG
	13: 5	given unto him a mouth speaking great *t* NIG
	18: 1	after these *t* I saw another angel come NIG
	18:14	all *t* which *were* dainty and goodly are NIG
	18:15	The merchants of these *t*, which were NIG
	19: 1	And after these *t* I heard a great voice of NIG
	20:12	the dead were judged out of those *t* which NIG
	21: 4	pain: for the former *t* are passed away. NIG
	21: 5	the throne said, Behold, I make all *t* new. NIG
	21: 7	He that overcometh shall inherit all *t*, NIG
	22: 6	servants the *t* which must shortly be done. NIG
	22: 8	And I John saw these *t*, and heard *them*. NIG
	22: 8	of the angel which shewed me these *t*. NIG
	22:16	to testify unto you these *t* in the churches. NIG
	22:18	If any *man* shall add unto these *t*, God NIG
	22:19	*from* the *t* which are written in this book. NIG
	22:20	He which testifieth these *t* saith, Surely I NIG

THINGS' (1) [THING]

Col	3: 6	For which *t* sake the wrath of God cometh NIG

THINK (65) [BETHINK, THINKEST, THINKETH, THINKING, THOUGHT, THOUGHTEST, THOUGHTS]

Ge	40:14	*t* on me when it shall be well with thee, 2142
Nu	36: 6	marry to whom they **t best**; 2896+5869+871.1
2Sa	13:33	to *t* that all the king's sons are dead: 559
2Ch	13: 8	now ye *t* to withstand the kingdom of 559
Ne	5:19	**T** upon me, my God, for good, *according* 2142
	6: 6	saith *it, that* thou and the Jews to rebel: 2803
	6:14	thou upon Tobiah and Sanballat 2142
Est	4:13	**T** not with thyself that *thou* shalt escape 1819
Job	31: 1	eyes; why then should I *t* upon a maid? 995
	41:32	him; *one* would *t* the deep to be hoary. 2803
Ecc	8:17	though a wise *man t* to know *it*, yet shall 559
Isa	10: 7	not so, neither doth his heart *t* so; 2803
Jer	23:27	Which *t* to cause my people to forget my 2803
	29:11	For I know the thoughts that I *t* towards 2803
Eze	38:10	mind, and thou shalt *t* an evil thought: 2803
Da	7:25	High, and *t* to change times and laws: 5452
Jnh	1: 6	if so be that God will *t* upon us, that we 6245
Zec	11:12	If ye *t* good, give *me* my price; 5869+871.1
Mt	3: 9	And *t* not to say within yourselves, 1380
	5:17	**T** not that I am come to destroy the law, 3543
	6:	as the heathen *do:* for they *t* that they 1380
	9: 4	Wherefore *t* ye evil in your hearts? 1760
	10:34	**T** not that I am come to send peace on 3543
	18:12	How *t* ye? if a man have an hundred 1380
	21:28	But what *t* you? A *certain* man had two 1380
	22:42	Saying, What *t* ye of Christ? whose son is 1380
	24:44	for in such an hour as you *t* not the Son of 1380
	26:66	What *t* ye? They answered and said, He 1380
Mk	14:64	what *t* ye? And they all condemned him 5316
Lk	12:40	of man cometh at an hour when ye *t* not. 1380
	13: 4	*t* ye that they were sinners above all men 1380
Jn	5:39	for in them ye *t* ye have eternal life: 1380
	5:45	Do not *t* that I will accuse you to 1380
	11:56	as they stood in the temple, What *t* ye, 1380
	16: 2	that whosoever killeth you will *t* that he 1380
Ac	13:25	*his* course, he said, Whom *t* ye that I am? 5282
	17:29	we ought not to *t* that the Godhead is like 3543
	26: 2	I *t* myself happy, king Agrippa, because 2233
Ro	12: 3	not to *t* of *himself* more **highly** than he 5252
	12: 3	of *himself* more highly than he ought to *t*; 5426
	12: 3	but to *t* soberly, according as God hath 5426
1Co	4: 9	For I *t* that God hath set forth us 1380
	7:36	But if any *man t* that *he* behaveth himself 3543
	7:40	and I *t* also that I have the Spirit of God. 1380
	8: 2	And if any *man t* that *he* knoweth any 1380
	12:23	body, which we *t* to be less honourable, 1380
	14:37	If any *man t* himself to be a prophet, 1380
2Co	3: 5	Not that we are sufficient of ourselves to *t* 3049
	10: 2	wherewith I *t* to be bold against some, 3049
	10: 2	which I of us as if we walked according to 3049
	10: 7	let him of himself *t* this again, that, as he 3049
	10:11	Let such a one *t* this, that such as we are 3049
	11:16	I say again, Let no *man t* me a fool; 1380
	12: 6	lest any *man* should *t* of me above *that* 3049
	12:19	*t* you that we excuse ourselves unto you? 1380
Gal	6: 3	For if a man *t* himself to be something, 1380
Eph	3:20	abundantly above all that we ask or *t*, 3539

T

Php 1: 7 as it is meet for me to **t** this of you all, 5426
 4: 8 if *there* be any praise, **t** on these *things*. 3049
Jas 1: 7 For let not that man **t** that he shall receive 3633
 4: 5 Do ye **t** that the scripture saith in vain, 1380
1Pe 4: 4 Wherein they **t it** strange that you run 3579
 4:12 **t** it not **strange** concerning the fiery trial 3579
2Pe 1:13 Yea, I **t** it meet, as long as I am in this 2233

THINKEST (9) [THINK]

2Sa 10: 3 said unto Hanun their lord, **T** 5869+871.1
1Ch 19: 3 **T** thou that David doth honour thy 5869+871.1
Job 35: 2 **T** thou this to be right, *that* thou saidst, 2803
Mt 17:25 saying, What **t** thou, Simon? 1380
 22:17 Tell us therefore, What **t** thou? Is it lawful 1380
 26:53 **T** thou that I cannot now pray to my 1380
Lk 10:36 Which now of these three, **t** thou, 1380
Ac 28:22 But we desire to hear of thee what thou **t**: 5426
Ro 2: 3 And **t** thou this, O man, that judgest them 3049

THINKETH (6) [THINK]

2Sa 18:27 Me **t** the running of the foremost *is* like 7200
Ps 40:17 and needy; *yet* the Lord **t** upon me: 2803
Pr 23: 7 For as he **t** in his heart, so *is* he: Eat and 8176
1Co 10:12 Wherefore let him that **t** he standeth take 1380
 13: 5 her own, is not easily provoked, **t** no evil; 3049
Php 3: 4 If any other *man* **t** that *he* hath whereof 1380

THINKING (2) [THINK]

2Sa 4:10 to have brought good tidings, 5869+871.1
 5: 6 in hither: **t**, David cannot come in hither. 559

THIRD (182) [THREE]

Ge 1:13 and the morning were the **t** day. 7992
 2:14 the name of the **t** river *is* Hiddekel: that 7992
 6:16 second, and **t** *stories* shalt thou make it. 7992
 22: 4 on the **t** day Abraham lift up his eyes, 7992
 31:22 it was told Laban on the **t** day that Jacob 7992
 32:19 the **t**, and all that followed the droves, 7992
 34:25 it came to pass on the **t** day, when they 7992
 40:20 it came to pass the **t** day, *which was* 7992
 42:18 Joseph said unto them the **t** day, This do, 7992
 50:23 Joseph saw Ephraim's children of the **t** 8029
Ex 19: 1 In the **t** month, when the children of 7992
 19:11 ready against the **t** day: for the third day 7992
 19:11 for the **t** day the LORD will come down in 7992
 19:15 the people, Be ready against the **t** day: 7969
 19:16 came to pass on the **t** day in the morning, 7992
 20: 5 the fathers upon the children unto the **t** 8029
 28:19 the **t** row a ligure, an agate, 7992
 34: 7 unto the **t** and to the fourth *generation*. 8029
 39:12 the **t** row, a ligure, an agate, 7992
Lev 7:17 on the **t** day shall be burnt with fire. 7992
 7:18 offerings be eaten at all on the **t** day, 7992
 19: 6 if ought remain until the **t** day, it shall be 7992
 19: 7 if it be eaten at all on the **t** day, it *is* 7992
Nu 2:24 And they shall go forward in the **t** **rank**. 7992
 7:24 On the **t** day Eliab the son of Helon, 7992
 14:18 the fathers upon the children unto the **t** 8029
 15: 6 mingled with the **t** *part* of a hin of oil. 7992
 15: 7 for a drink offering thou shalt offer the **t** 7992
 19:12 shall purify himself with it on the **t** day, 7992
 19:12 if he purify not himself the **t** day, then 7992
 19:19 sprinkle upon the unclean on the **t** day, 7992
 28:14 the **t** *part* of a hin unto a ram, and a 7992
 29:20 on the **t** day eleven bullocks, two rams, 7992
 31:19 and your captives on the **t** day, 7992
Dt 5: 9 the fathers upon the children unto the **t** 8029
 23: 8 of the LORD *in* their **t** generation. 7992
 26:12 all the tithes of thine increase the **t** year, 7992
Jos 9:17 and came unto their cities on the **t** day, 7992
 19:10 the **t** lot came up for the children of 7992
Jdg 20:30 the children of Benjamin on the **t** day, 7992
1Sa 3: 8 the LORD called Samuel again the **t** **time**. 7992
 17:13 unto him Abinadab, and the **t** Shammah. 7992
 19:21 Saul sent messengers again the **t** **time**, 7992
 20: 5 myself in the fields unto the **t** *day* at even. 7992
 20:12 or the **t** *day*, and, behold, *if there be* good 7992
 30: 1 his men were come *to* Ziklag on the **t** day, 7992
2Sa 1: 2 it came even to pass on the **t** day, that 7992
 3: 3 the **t**, Absalom the son of Maacah 7992
 18: 2 Joab sent forth a **t** **part** of the people 7992
 18: 2 a **t** **part** under the hand of Abishai the son 7992
 18: 2 a **t** **part** under the hand of Ittai the Gittite. 7992
1Ki 3:18 it came to pass the **t** day after that I was 7992
 6: 6 and the **t** *was* seven cubits broad: 7992
 6: 8 and out of the middle into the **t** 7992
 12:12 the people came to Rehoboam the **t** day, 7992
 12:12 saying, Come to me again the **t** day. 7992
 15:28 in the **t** year of Asa king of Judah did 7969
 15:33 In the **t** year of Asa king of Judah began 7969
 18: 1 of the LORD came to Elijah in the **t** year, 7992
 18:34 he said, **Do** *it* **the t time**. And they did *it* 8027
 18:34 third time. And they **did** *it* **the t time**. 8027
 22: 2 it came to pass on the **t** year, that 7992
2Ki 1:13 he sent again a captain of the **t** fifty with 7992
 1:13 the **t** captain of fifty went up, and came 7992
 11: 5 a **t** *part* of you that enter in on the sabbath 7992
 11: 6 a **t** *part shall be* at the gate of Sur; 7992
 11: 6 a **t** *part* at the gate behind the guard: 7992
 18: 1 it came to pass in the **t** year of Hoshea 7969
 19:29 in the **t** year sow ye, and reap, 7992
 20: 5 on the **t** day thou shalt go up *unto* 7992
 20: 8 up *into* the house of the LORD the **t** day? 7992
1Ch 2:13 Abinadab the second, and Shimma the **t**, 7992
 3: 2 The **t**, Absalom the son of Maacah 7992

1Ch 3:15 the **t** Zedekiah, the fourth Shallum. 7992
 8: 1 Ashbel the second, and Aharah the **t**, 7992
 8:39 Jehush the second, and Eliphelet the **t**. 7992
 12: 9 the first, Obadiah the second, Eliab the **t**, 7992
 23:19 Jahaziel the **t**, and Jekameam the fourth. 7992
 24: 8 The **t** to Harim, the fourth to Seorim, 7992
 24:23 Jahaziel the **t**, Jekameam the fourth. 7992
 25:10 The **t** *to* Zaccur, *he*, his sons, 7992
 26: 2 Jediael the second, Zebadiah the **t**, 7992
 26: 4 Joah the **t**, and Sacar the fourth, 7992
 26:11 Hilkiah the second, Tebaliah the **t**, 7992
 27: 5 The **t** captain of the host for the third 7992
 27: 5 third captain of the host for the **t** month 7992
2Ch 10:12 the people came to Rehoboam on the **t** 7992
 10:12 saying, Come again to me on the **t** day. 7992
 15:10 together *at* Jerusalem in the **t** month, 7969
 17: 7 in the **t** year of his reign he sent to his 7969
 23: 4 A **t** *part* of you entering on the sabbath, 7992
 23: 5 a **t** *part shall be* at the king's house; 7992
 23: 5 and a **t** *part* at the gate of the foundation: 7992
 27: 5 him, both the second year, and the **t**. 7992
 31: 7 In the **t** month they began to lay 7992
Ezr 6:15 this house was finished on the **t** day of 8532
Ne 10:32 charge ourselves yearly with the **t** *part* of 7992
Est 1: 3 In the **t** year of his reign, he made a feast 7969
 5: 1 Now it came to pass on the **t** day, 7992
 8: 9 scribes called at that time in the **t** month, 7992
Job 42:14 and the name of the **t**, Keren-happuch. 7992
Isa 19:24 In that day shall Israel be the **t** with Egypt 7992
 37:30 in the **t** year sow ye, and reap, 7992
Jer 38:14 entry that *is* in the house of the LORD: 7992
Eze 5: 2 Thou shalt burn with fire a **t** *part* in 7992
 5: 2 thou shalt burn a **t** *part*, and smite about it 7992
 5: 2 a **t** *part* thou shalt scatter in the wind; 7992
 5:12 A **t** *part* thou shalt die with 7992
 5:12 a **t** *part* shall fall by the sword round about 7992
 5:12 I will scatter a **t** *part* into all the winds, 7992
 10:14 the face of a lion, and the fourth 7992
 21:14 let the sword be doubled the **t time**, 7992
 31: 1 the **t** *month*, in the first *day* of the month, 7992
 46:14 of an ephah, and the **t** *part* of a hin of oil, 7992
Da 1: 1 In the **t** year of the reign of Jehoiakim 7969
 2:39 another **t** kingdom of brass, which shall 8523
 5: 7 and shall be the **t** ruler in the kingdom. 8523
 5:16 and shalt be the **t** ruler in the kingdom. 8531
 5:29 *he* should be the **t** ruler in the kingdom. 8531
 8: 1 the **t** year of the reign of king Belshazzar 7969
 10: 1 In the **t** year of Cyrus king of Persia a 7969
Hos 6: 2 in the **t** day he will raise us up, and we 7992
Zec 6: 3 in the **t** chariot white horses; and in 7992
 13: 8 and die; but the **t** shall be left therein. 7992
 13: 9 I will bring the **t** *part* through the fire, 7992
Mt 16:21 be killed, and be raised *again* the **t** day. 5154
 17:23 the **t** day he shall be raised *again*. 5154
 20: 3 And he went out about the **t** hour, 5154
 20:19 and the **t** day he shall rise again. 5154
 22:26 second also, and the **t**, unto the seventh. 5154
 26:44 away again, and prayed the **t time**, 1537+5154
 27:64 the sepulchre be made sure until the **t** 5154
Mk 9:31 that he is killed, he shall rise the **t** day. 5154
 10:34 kill him: and the **t** day he shall rise again. 5154
 12:21 left he *any* seed: and the **t** likewise. 5154
 14:41 And he cometh the **t time**, and saith unto 5154
 15:25 And it was the **t** hour, and they crucified 5154
Lk 9:22 and be slain, and be raised the **t** day. 5154
 12:38 or come in the **t** watch, and find *them* so, 5154
 13:32 and the **t** *day* I shall be perfected. 5154
 18:33 to death: and the **t** day he shall rise again. 5154
 20:12 And again he sent a **t**: and they wounded 5154
 20:31 And the **t** took her; and in like manner 5154
 23:22 And he said unto them the **t** time, Why, 5154
 24: 7 and be crucified, and the **t** day rise again. 5154
 24:21 to day is the **t** day since these *things* were 5154
 24:46 and to rise from the dead the **t** day: 5154
Jn 2: 1 the **t** day there was a marriage in Cana 5154
 21:14 This *is* now the **t time** *that* Jesus shewed 5154
 21:17 He saith unto him the **t time**, Simon, 5154
 21:17 because he said unto him the **t time**, 5154
Ac 2:15 seeing it is *but* the **t** hour of the day. 5154
 10:40 Him God raised up the **t** day, 5154
 20: 9 and fell down from the **t** loft, 5152
 23:23 two hundred, at the **t** hour of the night; 5154
 27:19 And the **t** *day* we cast *out* with our own 5154
1Co 15: 4 that he rose *again* the **t** day according to 5154
2Co 12: 2 such a one caught up to the **t** heaven. 5154
 12:14 the **t** *time* I am ready to come to you; 5154
 13: 1 This *is* the **t** *time* I am coming to you. 5154
Rev 4: 7 and the **t** beast had a face as a man, 5154
 6: 5 when he had opened the **t** seal, I heard 5154
 6: 5 I heard the **t** beast say, Come and see. 5154
 8: 7 the **t** *part* of trees was burnt up, and all 5154
 8: 8 and the **t** *part* of the sea became blood; 5154
 8: 9 the **t** *part* of the creatures which were 5154
 8: 9 and the **t** *part* of the ships were destroyed. 5154
 8:10 And the **t** angel sounded, and there fell a 5154
 8:10 and it fell upon the **t** *part* of the rivers, 5154
 8:11 **t** *part* of the waters became wormwood; 5154
 8:12 and the **t** *part* of the sun was smitten, 5154
 8:12 and the **t** *part* of the moon, and the third 5154
 8:12 of the moon, and the **t** *part* of the stars; 5154
 8:12 so as the **t** *part* of them was darkened 5154
 8:12 and the day shone not for a **t** *part* of it, 5154
 9:15 and a year, for to slay the **t** *part* of men. 5154
 9:18 these three was the **t** *part* of men killed, 5154
 11:14 *and* behold, the **t** woe cometh quickly. 5154

Rev 12: 4 And his tail drew the **t** *part* of the stars of 5154
 14: 9 *the* **t** angel followed them, saying with 5154
 16: 4 And the **t** angel poured out his vial upon 5154
 21:19 the second, sapphire; the **t**, a chalcedony; 5154

THIRDLY (1) [THREE]

1Co 12:28 **t** teachers, after that miracles, then gifts of 5154

THIRST (31) [ATHIRST, BLOODTHIRSTY, THIRSTED, THIRSTETH, THIRSTY]

Ex 17: 3 and our children and our cattle with **t**? 6772
Dt 28:48 in **t**, and in nakedness, and in want of all 6772
 29:19 of mine heart, to add drunkenness *to* **t**: 6771
Jdg 15:18 shall I die for **t**, and fall into the hand 6772
2Ch 32:11 over yourselves to die by famine and by **t**, 6772
Ne 9:15 water for them out of the rock for their **t**, 6772
 9:20 and gavest them water for their **t**. 6772
Job 24:11 *and* tread *their* winepresses, and **suffer** **t**. 6770
Ps 69:21 and in my **t** they gave me vinegar to drink. 6772
 104:11 of the field: the wild asses quench their **t**. 6772
Isa 5:13 and their multitude dried up with **t**. 6772
 41:17 is none, *and* their tongue faileth for **t**, 6770
 49:10 They shall not hunger nor **t**; neither shall 6770
 50: 2 because *there* is no water, and dieth for **t**. 6772
Jer 2:25 from being unshod, and thy throat from **t**: 6773
 48:18 come down from *thy* glory, and sit in **t**; 6772
La 4: 4 cleaveth to the roof of his mouth for **t**: 6772
Hos 2: 3 her like a dry land, and slay her with **t**. 6772
Am 8:11 nor a **t** for water, but of hearing the words 6772
 8:13 the fair virgins and young men faint for **t**. 6772
Mt 5: 6 do hunger and **t** after righteousness: 1372
Jn 4:13 Whosoever drinketh of this water shall **t** 1372
 4:14 water that I shall give him shall never **t**; 1372
 4:15 Sir, give me this water, that I **t** not, 1372
 6:35 and he that believeth on me shall never **t**. 1372
 7:37 Jesus stood and cried, saying, If any *man* **t**, 1372
 19:28 the scripture might be fulfilled, saith, I **t**. 1372
Ro 12:20 feed him; if he **t**, give him drink: 1372
1Co 4:11 and **t**, and are naked, and are buffeted, 1372
2Co 11:27 in hunger and **t**, in fastings often, in cold 1373
Rev 7:16 shall hunger no more, neither **t** any more; 1372

THIRSTED (2) [THIRST]

Ex 17: 3 there **t** there for water: and the 6770
Isa 48:21 they **t** not *when* he led them through 6770

THIRSTETH (4) [THIRST]

Ps 42: 2 My soul **t** for God, for the living God: 6770
 63: 1 my soul **t** for thee, my flesh longeth for 6770
 143: 6 my soul **t** after thee, as a thirsty land. NIH
Isa 55: 1 every one that **t**, come ye to the waters, 6771

THIRSTY (17) [THIRST]

Jdg 4:19 thee, a little water to drink; for I am **t**. 6770
2Sa 17:29 and weary, and **t**, in the wilderness. 6771
Ps 63: 1 in a dry and **t** land, where no water is; 5889
 107: 5 Hungry and **t**, their soul fainted in them. 6771
 143: 6 my soul *thirsteth* after thee, as a **t** land. 5889
Pr 25:21 and if he be **t**, give him water to drink: 6770
 25:25 *As* cold waters to a **t** soul, so *is* good news 5889
Isa 21:14 of Tema brought water to him that was **t**, 6771
 29: 8 as when a *man* dreameth, and, behold, 6771
 32: 6 and he will cause the drink of the **t** to fail. 6771
 35: 7 a pool, and the **t** land springs of water: 6774
 44: 3 For I will pour water upon *him* that is **t**, 6771
 65:13 my servants shall drink, but ye shall be **t**: 6770
Eze 19:13 in the wilderness, in a dry and **t** ground. 6772
Mt 25:35 I was **t**, and ye gave me drink: I was a 1372
 25:37 and fed *thee*? or **t**, and gave *thee* drink? 1372
 25:42 meat: I was **t**, and ye gave me no drink: 1372

THIRTEEN (15) [THIRTEENTH]

Ge 17:25 Ishmael his son *was* **t** years old, 6240+7969
Nu 3:43 and **threescore** and **t**. 7657+7969+2050.1
 3:46 **threescore** and **t** 7657+7969+1886.1+2050.1
 29:13 **t** young bullocks, two rams, 6240+7969
 29:14 every bullock of the **t** bullocks, 6240+7969
Jos 19: 6 Sharuhen; **t** cities and their villages: 6240+7969
 21: 4 of the tribe of Benjamin, **t** cities. 6240+7969
 21: 6 of Manasseh in Bashan, **t** cities. 6240+7969
 21:19 *were* **t** cities with their suburbs. 6240+7969
 21:33 *were* **t** cities with their suburbs. 6240+7969
1Ki 7: 1 building his own house **t** years, 6240+7969
1Ch 6:60 their families *were* **t** cities. 6240+7969
 6:62 of Manasseh in Bashan, **t** cities. 6240+7969
 26:11 and brethren of Hosah *were* **t**. 6240+7969
Eze 40:11 and the length of the gate, **t** cubits. 6240+7969

THIRTEENTH (11) [THIRTEEN]

Ge 14: 4 and *in* the **t** year they rebelled. 6240+7969
1Ch 24:13 to Huppah, the fourteenth to 6240+7969
 25:20 The **t** *to* Shubael, *he*, his sons, 6240+7969
Est 3:12 on the **t** day of the first month, 6240+7969
 3:13 the **t** *day* of the twelfth month, 6240+7969
 8:12 upon the **t** *day* of the twelfth 6240+7969
 9: 1 on the **t** day of the same, 6240+7969
 9:17 On the **t** day of the month Adar; 6240+7969
 9:18 together on the **t** *day* thereof, 6240+7969
Jer 1: 2 of Judah, in the **t** year of his reign. 6240+7969
 25: 3 From the **t** year of Josiah the son of 6240+7969

THIRTIETH (9) [THIRTY]

2Ki 15:13 nine and **t** year of Uzziah king of Judah; 7970
 15:17 **t** year of Azariah king of Judah began 7970
 25:27 **t** year of the captivity of Jehoiachin king 7970
2Ch 15:19 the five and **t** year of the reign of Asa. 7970

T

2Ch 16: 1 t year of the reign of Asa Baasha king of	7970	
Ne 5:14 the two and t year of Artaxerxes the	7970	
13: 6 t year of Artaxerxes king of Babylon came	7970	
Jer 52:31 t year of the captivity of Jehoiachin king	7970	
Eze 1: 1 Now it came to pass in the t year,	7970	

THIRTY (174) [THIRTIETH, THIRTYFOLD]

Ge 5: 3 Adam lived an hundred and t years,	7970	
5: 5 lived were nine hundred and t years:	7970	
5:16 he begat Jared eight hundred and t years,	7970	
6:15 it fifty cubits, and the height of it t cubits.	7970	
11:12 Arphaxad five and t years,	7970	
11:14 And Salah lived t years, and begat Eber:	7970	
11:16 Eber lived four and t years,	7970	
11:17 he begat Peleg four hundred and t years,	7970	
11:18 And Peleg lived t years, and begat Reu:	7970	
11:20 Reu lived two and t years, and begat	7970	
11:22 And Serug lived t years, and begat Nahor:	7970	
18:30 Peradventure there shall be found there.	7970	
18:30 he said, I will not do it, if I find t there.	7970	
25:17 an hundred and t and seven years:	7970	
32:15 T milch camels with their colts, forty	7970	
41:46 Joseph was t years old when he stood	7970	
46:15 sons and his daughters were t and three.	7970	
47: 9 my pilgrimage are an hundred and t years:	7970	
Ex 6:16 years of the life of Levi were an hundred t	7970	
6:18 of the life of Kohath were an hundred t	7970	
6:20 were an hundred and t and seven years.	7970	
12:40 in Egypt, was four hundred and t years.	7970	
12:41 at the end of the four hundred and t years,	7970	
21:32 he shall give unto their master t shekels	7970	
26: 8 length of one curtain shall be t cubits,	7970	
36:15 The length of one curtain was t cubits,	7970	
38:24 and seven hundred and t shekels.	7970	
Lev 12: 4 blood of her purifying three and t days;	7970	
27: 4 then thy estimation shall be t shekels.	7970	
Nu 1:35 t and two thousand and two hundred.	7970	
1:37 t and five thousand and four hundred.	7970	
2:21 t and two thousand and two hundred.	7970	
2:23 t and five thousand and four hundred.	7970	
4: 3 From t years old and upward even until	7970	
4:23 From t years old and upward until fifty	7970	
4:30 From t years old and upward even unto	7970	
4:35 From t years old and upward even unto	7970	
4:39 From t years old and upward even unto	7970	
4:40 two thousand and six hundred and t.	7970	
4:43 From t years old and upward even unto	7970	
4:47 From t years old and upward even unto	7970	
7:13 t shekels, one silver bowl of seventy	7970	
7:19 t shekels, one silver bowl of seventy	7970	
7:25 t shekels, one silver bowl of seventy	7970	
7:31 t shekels, one silver bowl of seventy	7970	
7:37 t shekels, one silver bowl of seventy	7970	
7:43 t shekels, a silver bowl of seventy shekels,	7970	
7:49 t shekels, one silver bowl of seventy	7970	
7:55 t shekels, one silver bowl of seventy	7970	
7:61 t shekels, one silver bowl of seventy	7970	
7:67 t shekels, one silver bowl of seventy	7970	
7:73 t shekels, one silver bowl of seventy	7970	
7:79 t shekels, one silver bowl of seventy	7970	
7:85 and t shekels, each bowl seventy:	7970	
20:29 they mourned for Aaron t days, even all	7970	
26: 7 three thousand and seven hundred and t.	7970	
26:37 t and two thousand and five hundred.	7970	
26:51 and a thousand seven hundred and t.	7970	
31:35 t and two thousand persons in all,	7970	
31:36 seven and t thousand and five hundred	7970	
31:38 the beeves were t and six thousand;	7970	
31:39 asses were t thousand and five hundred;	7970	
31:40 of which the LORD's tribute was t and	7970	
31:43 t thousand and seven thousand and	7970	
31:44 And t and six thousand beeves,	7970	
31:45 And t thousand asses and five hundred,	7970	
Dt 2:14 the brook Zered, was t and eight years,	7970	
34: 8 for Moses in the plains of Moab t days:	7970	
Jos 7: 5 the men of Ai smote of them about t and	7970	
8: 3 Joshua chose out t thousand mighty men	7970	
12:24 of Tirzah, one: all the kings t and one.	7970	
Jdg 10: 4 he had t sons that rode on thirty ass colts,	7970	
10: 4 he had thirty sons that rode on t ass colts,	7970	
10: 4 they had t cities, which are called	7970	
12: 9 he had t sons, and thirty daughters,	7970	
12: 9 t daughters, whom he sent abroad,	7970	
12: 9 took in t daughters from abroad for his	7970	
12:14 had forty sons and t nephews, that rode	7970	
14:11 they brought t companions to be with	7970	
14:12 I will give you t sheets and thirty change	7970	
14:12 thirty sheets and t change of garments.	7970	
14:13 ye give me t sheets and thirty change	7970	
14:13 thirty sheets and t change of garments.	7970	
14:19 slew t men of them, and took their spoil,	7970	
20:31 Gibeah in the field, about t men of Israel.	7970	
20:39 kill of the men of Israel about t persons:	7970	
1Sa 4:10 for there fell of Israel t thousand footmen.	7970	
9:22 bidden, which were about t persons.	7970	
11: 8 and the men of Judah t thousand.	7970	
13: 5 t thousand chariots, and six thousand	7970	
2Sa 5: 4 David was t years old when he began to	7970	
5: 5 in Jerusalem he reigned t and three years	7970	
6: 1 all the chosen men of Israel, t thousand.	7970	
23:13 three of the t chief went down, and came	7970	
23:23 He was more honourable than the t,	7970	
23:24 the brother of Joab was one of the t;	7970	
23:39 Uriah the Hittite: t and seven in all.	7970	
1Ki 2:11 t and three years reigned he in Jerusalem.	7970	

1Ki 4:22 Solomon's provision for one day was t	7970	
5:13 Israel; and the levy was t thousand men.	7970	
6: 2 and the height thereof t cubits.	7970	
7: 2 cubits, and the height thereof t cubits,	7970	
7: 6 and the breadth thereof t cubits:	7970	
7:23 a line of t cubits did compass it round	7970	
16:23 In the t and first year of Asa king of Judah	7970	
16:29 in the t and eighth year of Asa king of	7970	
20: 1 there were t and two kings with him,	7970	
20:15 and they were two hundred and t two:	7970	
20:16 the t and two kings that helped him.	7970	
22:31 the king of Syria commanded his t and	7970	
22:42 Jehoshaphat was t and five years old	7970	
2Ki 8:17 T and two years old was he when he	7970	
13:10 In the t and seventh year of Joash king of	7970	
15: 8 In the t and eighth year of Azariah king of	7970	
18:14 talents of silver and t talents of gold.	7970	
22: 1 he reigned t and one years in Jerusalem.	7970	
1Ch 3: 4 in Jerusalem he reigned t and three years.	7970	
7: 4 t thousand men: for they had many wives	7970	
7: 4 and two thousand and t and four.	7970	
11:15 Now three of the t captains went down to	7970	
11:25 he was honourable among the t,	7970	
11:42 captain of the Reubenites, and t with him,	7970	
12: 4 a mighty man among the t, and over	7970	
12: 4 man among the thirty, and over the t;	7970	
12:34 shield and spear t and seven thousand.	7970	
15: 7 and his brethren an hundred and t:	7970	
19: 7 they hired t and two thousand chariots,	7970	
23: 3 were numbered from the age of t years	7970	
23: 3 man by man, was t and eight thousand.	7970	
27: 6 who was mighty among the t,	7970	
27: 6 mighty among the thirty, and above the t:	7970	
29:27 t and three years reigned he in Jerusalem.	7970	
2Ch 3:15 he made before the house two pillars of t	7970	
4: 2 a line of t cubits did compass it round	7970	
16:12 Asa in the t and ninth year of his reign	7970	
20:31 he was t and five years old when he	7970	
21: 5 Jehoram was t and two years old when he	7970	
21:20 T and two years old was he when he	7970	
24:15 and t years old was he when he died.	7970	
34: 1 he reigned in Jerusalem one and t years.	7970	
35: 7 to the number of t thousand,	7970	
Ezr 1: 9 t chargers of gold, a thousand chargers of	7970	
1:10 T basons of gold, silver basons of a second	7970	
2:35 three thousand and six hundred and t.	7970	
2:42 of Shobai, in all an hundred t and nine.	7970	
2:65 were seven thousand three hundred t	7970	
2:66 horses were seven hundred t and six;	7970	
2:67 Their camels, four hundred t and five;	7970	
Ne 7:38 three thousand nine hundred and t.	7970	
7:45 of Shobai, an hundred t and eight.	7970	
7:67 were seven thousand three hundred t	7970	
7:68 Their horses, seven hundred t and six:	7970	
7:69 Their camels, four hundred t and five:	7970	
7:70 five hundred and t priests' garments.	7970	
Est 4:11 to come in unto the king these t days.	7970	
Jer 38:10 Take from hence t men with thee,	7970	
52:29 captive from Jerusalem eight hundred t	7970	
Eze 40:17 t chambers were upon the pavement.	7970	
41: 6 one over another, and t in order;	7970	
46:22 joined of forty cubits long and t broad:	7970	
Da 6: 7 a petition of any God or man for t days,	8533	
6:12 petition of any God or man within t days,	8533	
12:12 three hundred and five and t days.	7970	
Zec 11:12 So they weighed for my price t pieces of	7970	
11:13 I took the t pieces of silver, and cast them	7970	
Mt 13:23 some an hundredfold, some sixty, some t.	5144	
26:15 they covenanted with him for t pieces	5144	
27: 3 brought again the t pieces of silver to	5144	
27: 9 And they took the t pieces of silver,	5144	
Mk 4: 8 some t, and some sixty, and some an	5144	
Lk 3:23 And Jesus himself began to be about t	5144	
Jn 5: 5 which had an infirmity t and eight years.	5144	
6:19 rowed about five and twenty or t furlongs,	5144	
Gal 3:17 which was four hundred and t years after,	5144	

THIRTYFOLD (2) [THIRTY]

Mt 13: 8 hundredfold, some sixtyfold, some t.	5144	
Mk 4:20 some t, some sixty, and some an	5144	

THIS (2786) [THESE]

Ge 2:23 T is now bone of my bones, and flesh of	2063	
3:13 woman, What is t that thou hast done?	2088	
3:14 Because thou hast done t, thou art cursed	2088	
4:14 hast driven me out t day from the face	NIH	
5: 1 Is the book of the generations of Adam.	2088	
5:29 T same shall comfort us concerning our	2088	
6:15 t is the fashion which thou shalt make it	2088	
7: 1 seen righteous before me in t generation.	2088	
9:12 T is the token of the covenant which I	2088	
9:17 Noah, T is the token of the covenant,	2088	
11: 6 all one language; and t they begin to do:	2088	
12: 7 and said, Unto thy seed will I give t land:	2063	
12:12 see thee, that they shall say, T is his wife:	2088	
12:18 What is t that thou hast done unto me?	2088	
15: 2 the steward of my house is t Eliezer of	1931	
15: 4 him, saying, T shall not be thine heir;	2088	
15: 7 to give thee t land to inherit it.	2088	
15:18 saying, Unto thy seed have I given t land,	2088	
17:10 T is my covenant, which ye shall keep,	2088	
17:21 which Sarah shall bear unto thee at t set	2088	
18:25 be far from thee to do after t manner,	2088	
18:32 be angry, and I will speak yet but t once:	NIH	
19: 5 the men which came in to thee t night?	1886.1	

Ge 19: 9 they said again, T one fellow came in to	NIH	
19:12 hast in the city, bring them out of t place:	NIH	
19:13 For we will destroy t place, because the	2088	
19:14 and said, Up, get ye out of t place;	2088	
19:14 for the LORD will destroy t city.	1886.1	
19:20 t city is near to flee unto, and it is a little	2088	
19:21 I have accepted thee concerning t thing,	2088	
19:21 that I will not overthrow t city,	NIH	
19:34 let us make him drink wine t night also;	1886.1	
19:37 same is the father of the Moabites unto t	NIH	
19:38 of the children of Ammon unto t day.	NIH	
20: 5 and innocency of my hands have I done t.	NIH	
20: 6 I know that thou didst t in the integrity of	2088	
20:10 sawest thou, that thou hast done t thing?	2088	
20:11 Surely the fear of God is not in t place;	2088	
20:13 T is thy kindness which thou shalt shew	2088	
21:10 Cast out t bondwoman and her son:	2088	
21:10 for the son of t bondwoman shall not be	2088	
21:26 I not wot who hath done t thing:	2088	
21:30 unto me, that I have digged t well.	2088	
22:14 as it is said to t day, In the mount of	NIH	
22:16 for because thou hast done t thing,	2088	
23:19 after t, Abraham buried Sarah his wife in	3651	
24: 5 not be willing to follow me unto t land:	2088	
24: 7 saying, Unto thy seed will I give t land;	2088	
24: 8 then thou shalt be clear from t my oath:	2088	
24:12 send me good speed t day,	NIH	
24:41 shalt thou be clear from t my oath,	2088	
24:42 I came t day unto the well, and said,	1886.1	
24:58 said unto her, Wilt thou go with t man?	2088	
24:65 What man is t that walketh in the field to	1976	
25:31 Jacob said, Sell me t day thy birthright.	NIH	
25:32 and what profit shall t birthright do to me?	2088	
25:33 said, Swear to me t day; and he sware	NIH	
26: 3 Sojourn in t land, and I will be with thee,	2088	
26:10 What is t thou hast done unto us?	2088	
26:11 He that toucheth t man or his wife shall	2088	
26:33 the name of the city is Beer-sheba unto t	2088	
28:15 and will bring thee again into t land;	2088	
28:16 he said, Surely the LORD is in t place;	2088	
28:17 and said, How dreadful is t place!	2088	
28:17 is none other but the house of God,	2088	
28:17 house of God, and t is the gate of heaven.	2088	
28:20 will keep me in t way that I go,	2088	
28:22 t stone, which I have set for a pillar,	2088	
29:25 What is t thou hast done unto me?	2088	
29:27 we will give thee t also for the service	2063	
29:33 he hath therefore given me t son also:	2088	
29:34 Now t time will my husband be joined	NIH	
30:31 if thou wilt do t thing for me, I will again	2088	
31: 1 of our father's hath he gotten all t glory.	2088	
31:13 get thee out from t land, and return unto	2088	
31:38 T twenty years have I been with thee;	2088	
31:43 what can I do t day unto these my	NIH	
31:48 T heap is a witness between me and thee	2088	
31:48 is a witness between me and thee t day.	NIH	
31:51 Behold t heap, and behold this pillar,	2088	
31:51 Behold this heap, and behold t pillar,	NIH	
31:52 T heap be witness, and this pillar be	2088	
31:52 heap be witness, and t pillar be witness,	NIH	
31:52 that I will not pass over t heap to thee,	2088	
31:52 that thou shalt not pass over t heap and	2088	
31:52 pass over this heap and t pillar unto me,	2088	
32: 2 Jacob saw them, he said, T is God's host:	2088	
32:10 for with my staff I passed over t Jordan;	2088	
32:19 On t manner shall you speak unto Esau,	2088	
32:32 upon the hollow of the thigh, unto t day:	2088	
33: 8 What meanest thou by all t drove which	2088	
34: 4 saying, Get me t damsel to wife.	2088	
34:14 said unto them, We cannot do t thing,	2088	
34:15 in t will we consent unto you: If ye will	2063	
35:17 Fear not; thou shalt have t son also.	2088	
35:20 that is the pillar of Rachel's grave unto t	2088	
36:24 t was that Anah that found the mules in	1931	
37: 6 pray you, t dream which I have dreamed:	2088	
37:10 What is t dream that thou hast dreamed?	2088	
37:19 to another, Behold, t dreamer cometh.	1976	
37:22 him into t pit that is in the wilderness,	2088	
37:32 their father; and said, T have we found:	2088	
38:21 they said, There was no harlot in t place.	NIH	
38:22 that there was no harlot in t place.	2088	
38:23 I sent t kid, and thou hast not found her.	2088	
38:28 a scarlet thread, saying, T came out first.	2088	
38:29 t breach be upon thee: therefore his name	NIH	
39: 9 There is none greater in t house than I;	2088	
39: 9 how then can I do t great wickedness,	2088	
39:11 it came to pass about t time, that Joseph	NIH	
39:19 After t manner did thy servant to me;	428	
40:12 unto him, T is the interpretation of it:	2088	
40:14 Pharaoh, and bring me out of t house:	2088	
40:18 and said, T is the interpretation thereof:	2088	
41: 9 I do remember my faults t day:	NIH	
41:24 I told t unto the magicians; but there was	NIH	
41:28 T is the thing which I have spoken unto	1931	
41:34 Let Pharaoh do t, and let him appoint	NIH	
41:38 Can we find such a one as t is, a man in	2088	
41:39 Forasmuch as God hath shewed thee all t,	2088	
42:13 the youngest is t day with our father,	2088	
42:18 unto them the third day, T do, and live;	2088	
42:21 therefore is t distress come upon us.	2088	
42:28 What is t that God hath done unto us?	2088	
42:32 the youngest is t day with our father in	NIH	
43:10 now we had returned t second time.	2088	
43:11 unto them, If it must be so now, do t;	2088	
43:29 and said, Is t your younger brother,	2088	

Ge 44: 5 *Is not t it* in which my lord drinketh, — 2088
44: 7 servants should do according to t thing: — 2088
44:15 What deed *is t* that ye have done? — 2088
44:29 if ye take t also from me, — 2088
45:17 Say unto thy brethren, **T** do ye; — 2088
45:19 Now thou art commanded, t do ye; — 2088
45:23 to his father he sent after t manner; — 2063
47:23 I have bought you t day and your land for — NIH
47:26 it a law over the land of Egypt unto t day, — 2088
48: 4 will give t land to thy seed after thee *for* — 2088
48: 9 whom God hath given me in t place. — 2088
48:15 which fed me all my life long unto t day, — 2088
48:18 for t *is* the firstborn; put thy right hand — 2088
49:28 t *is it* that their father spake unto them, — 2088
50:11 **T** *is* a grievous mourning to the Egyptians: — 2088
50:20 unto good, to bring to pass, as *it is* t day, — 2088
50:24 bring you out of t land unto the land — 2088

Ex 1:18 Why have ye done t thing, and have saved — 2088
2: 6 said, **T** *is one* of the Hebrews' children. — 2088
2: 9 Take t child away, and nurse it for me, — 2088
2:12 he looked t **way** and that way, and when — 3541
2:14 and said, Surely t thing is known. — NIH
2:15 Now when Pharaoh heard t thing, — 2088
3: 3 will now turn aside, and see t great sight, — 2088
3:12 t *shall be* a token unto thee, that I have — 2088
3:12 ye shall serve God upon t mountain. — 2088
3:15 t *is* my name for ever, and this *is* my — 2088
3:15 and t *is* my memorial unto all generations. — 2088
3:21 I will give t people favour in the sight of — 2088
4:17 thou shalt take t rod in thine hand, — 2088
5:22 hast thou *so* evil entreated t people? — 2088
5:23 thy name, he hath done evil to t people; — 2088
7:17 In t thou shalt know that I *am* the LORD: — 2088
7:23 neither did he set his heart to t also. — 2063
8:19 said unto Pharaoh, **T** *is* the finger of God: — 1931
8:23 and thy people: to morrow shall t sign be. — 2088
8:32 Pharaoh hardened his heart at t time also, — 2088
9: 5 To morrow the LORD shall do t thing in — 2088
9:14 For I will at t time send all my plagues — 2088
9:16 in very deed for t cause have I raised thee — 2088
9:18 to morrow about t time I will cause it to — NIH
9:27 and said unto them, I have sinned t time: — NIH
10: 6 that they were upon the earth unto t day. — NIH
10: 7 How long shall t *man* be a snare unto us? — 2088
10:17 my sin only t once, and intreat the LORD — NIH
10:17 that he may take away from me t death — 2088
12: 2 **T** month *shall be* unto you the beginning — 2088
12: 3 In the tenth *day* of t month they shall take — 2088
12:12 I will pass through the land of Egypt t — 2088
12:14 t day shall be unto you for a memorial; — 2088
12:17 for in t selfsame day have I brought your — 2088
12:17 shall ye observe t day in your generations — 2088
12:24 ye shall observe t thing for an ordinance — 2088
12:25 promised, that ye shall keep t service. — 2088
12:26 unto you, What mean you by t service? — 2088
12:42 t *is* that night of the LORD to be observed — 2088
12:43 Aaron, **T** *is* the ordinance of the passover: — 2088
13: 3 said unto the people, Remember t day, — 2088
13: 3 t *place*: there shall no leavened bread be — 2088
13: 4 t day came ye out in the month Abib. — NIH
13: 5 thou shalt keep t service in this month. — 2088
13: 5 thou shalt keep this service in t month. — 2088
13: 8 **T** *is done* because of that *which* the LORD — NIH
13:10 keep t ordinance in his season from year — 2088
13:14 thee in time to come, saying, What *is* t? — 2088
14: 5 They said, Why have we done t thing, — 2088
14:12 *Is* not the word that we did tell thee in — 2088
15: 1 the children of Israel t song unto — 2088
16: 3 for ye have brought us forth into t — 2088
16: 3 to kill t whole assembly with hunger. — 2088
16: 8 **T** *shall be*, when the LORD shall give you — NIH
16:15 **T** *is* the bread which the LORD hath — 1931
16:16 **T** *is* the thing which the LORD hath — 2088
16:23 **T** *is that* which the LORD hath said, — 1931
16:32 **T** *is* the thing which the LORD — 2088
17: 3 Wherefore *is t that* thou hast brought us — 2088
17: 4 What shall I do unto t people? — 2088
17:14 Write t *for* a memorial in a book, — 2088
18:14 What *is t* thing that thou doest to — 2088
18:18 both thou, and t people that *is* with thee: — 2088
18:18 for t thing *is* too heavy for thee; thou art — NIH
18:23 If thou shalt do t thing, and God — 2088
18:23 all t people shall also go to their place in — 2088
21:31 according to t judgment shall it be done — 2088
25: 3 t *is* the offering which ye shall take of — 2088
26:13 over the sides of the tabernacle on t **side** — 2088
28:17 and a carbuncle: t *shall be* the first row. — NIH
29: 1 t *is* the thing that thou shalt do unto them — 2088
29:38 Now t *is that* which thou shalt offer upon — 2088
29:42 **T** *shall be* a continual burnt offering — NIH
30:13 **T** they shall give, every one that passeth — 2088
30:31 **T** shall be a holy anointing oil unto me — 2088
32: 1 for *as for* t Moses, the man that brought — 2088
32: 9 I have seen t people, and behold, it *is a* — 2088
32:12 shall repent of t evil against thy people. — NIH
32:13 all t land that I have spoken of will I give — 2088
32:21 What did t people unto thee, that thou — 2088
32:23 for *as for* t Moses, the man that brought — 2088
32:24 it into the fire, and there came out t calf. — NIH
32:29 that he may bestow upon you a blessing t — 2088
32:31 t people have sinned a great sin, — 2088
33:12 thou sayest unto me, Bring up t people: — 2088
33:13 and consider that t nation *is* thy people. — 2088
33:17 will do t thing also that thou hast spoken: — 2088
34:11 thou that which I command thee t — NIH

Ex 35: 4 **T** *is* the thing which the LORD — 2088
37: 8 One cherub on the end on t **side**, — 2088
38:15 on t **hand** and that hand, *were* hangings — 2088
38:21 **T** *is* the sum of the tabernacle, *even* of — 428
39:10 topaz, and a carbuncle: t *was* the first row. — NIH

Lev 4:20 for a sin offering, so shall he do with t: — 2050.2
6: 9 **T** *is* the law of the burnt offering: — 2088
6:14 t *is* the law of the meat offering: the sons — 2088
6:20 **T** *is* the offering of Aaron and his sons, — 2088
6:25 **T** *is* the law of the sin offering: — 2088
7: 1 Likewise t *is* the law of the trespass — 2088
7:11 t *is* the law of the sacrifice of peace — 2088
7:35 **T** *is the portion* of the anointing of Aaron, — 2088
7:37 **T** *is* the law of the burnt offering, — 2088
8: 5 **T** *is* the thing which the LORD — 2088
8:34 As he hath done t day, *so* the LORD hath — 2088
9: 6 **T** *is* the thing which the LORD — 2088
10: 3 **T** *is it* that the LORD spake, saying, — 1931
10:19 t day have they offered their sin offering — NIH
11:46 **T** *is* the law of the beasts, and of the fowl, — 2088
12: 7 **T** *is* the law for her that hath born a male — 2088
13:59 **T** *is* the law of the plague of leprosy in a — 2088
14: 2 **T** shall be the law of the leper in the day — 2088
14:32 **T** *is* the law *of him* in whom *is* the plague — 2088
14:54 **T** *is* the law for all *manner of* plague of — 2088
14:57 when *it is* clean: t *is* the law of leprosy. — 2088
15: 3 t shall be his uncleanness in his issue: — 2088
15:32 **T** *is* the law of him that hath an issue, — 2088
16:29 t shall be a statute for ever unto you: *that* — NIH
16:34 t shall be an everlasting statute unto you, — 2088
17: 2 **T** *is* the thing which the LORD hath — 2088
17: 7 **T** shall be a statute for ever unto them — 2088
23:27 Also on the tenth *day* of t seventh month — 2088
23:34 The fifteenth day of t seventh month *shall* — 2088
24:10 t *son* of the Israelitish woman and a man — NIH
25:13 In the year of t jubile ye shall return every — 2088
26:16 I also will do t unto you; I will even — 2088
26:18 if ye will not yet for *all* t hearken unto me, — 428
26:27 if ye will not for *all* t hearken unto me, — 2088

Nu 4: 4 **T** *shall be* the service of the sons of — 2088
4:24 **T** *is* the service of the families of — 2088
4:28 **T** *is* the service of the families of the sons — 2088
4:31 t *is* the charge of their burden, according — 2088
4:33 **T** *is* the service of the families of the sons — 2088
5:19 thou free from t bitter water that causeth — 428
5:22 t water that causeth the curse shall go into — 428
5:29 **T** *is* the law of jealousies, when a wife — 2088
5:30 the priest shall execute upon her all t law. — 2088
5:31 and t woman shall bear her iniquity. — 1931
6:13 t *is* the law of the Nazarite, when the — 2088
6:20 t *is* holy for the priest, with the wave — 1931
6:21 **T** *is* the law of the Nazarite who hath — 2088
6:23 **On** t **wise** ye shall bless the children of — 3541
7:17 t *was* the offering of Nahshon the son of — 2088
7:23 t *was* the offering of Nethaneel the son of — 2088
7:29 t *was* the offering of Eliab the son of — 2088
7:35 t *was* the offering of Elizur the son of — 2088
7:41 t *was* the offering of Shelumiel the son of — 2088
7:47 t *was* the offering of Eliasaph the son of — 2088
7:53 t *was* the offering of Elishama the son of — 2088
7:59 t *was* the offering of Gamaliel the son of — 2088
7:65 t *was* the offering of Abidan the son of — 2088
7:71 t *was* the offering of Ahiezer the son of — 2088
7:77 t *was* the offering of Pagiel the son of — 2088
7:83 t *was* the offering of Ahira the son of — 2088
7:84 **T** *was* the dedication of the altar, in the — 2088
7:88 **T** *was* the dedication of the altar, after — 2088
8: 4 work of the candlestick *was of* beaten — 2088
8:24 **T** *is it* that *belongeth* unto the Levites: — 2088
9: 3 In the fourteenth day of t month, at even, — 2088
11: 6 at all, beside t manna, *before* our eyes. — NIH
11:11 that *thou* layest the burden of all t people — 2088
11:12 Have I conceived all t people? — 2088
11:13 I have flesh to give unto all t people? — 2088
11:14 I am not able to bear all t people alone, — 2088
11:31 as it were a day's journey **on** t **side**, — 3541
13:17 Get you up t *way* southward, and go up — 2088
13:27 milk and honey; and t *is* the fruit of it. — 2088
14: 2 would God we had died in t wilderness! — 2088
14: 3 t *hath* the LORD brought us unto t land, — 2088
14: 8 he will bring us into t land, and give it us; — 2088
14:11 How long will t people provoke me? — 2088
14:13 t people in thy might from among them;) — 2088
14:14 they will tell *it* to the inhabitants of t land: — 2088
14:14 heard that thou *hast* t *art* among t people, — 2088
14:15 Now *if* thou shalt kill *all* t people as one — 2088
14:16 Because the LORD was not able to bring t — 2088
14:19 the iniquity of t people according unto — 2088
14:19 as thou hast forgiven t people, from Egypt — 2088
14:27 How long *shall I bear* with t evil — 2088
14:29 Your carcases shall fall in t wilderness; — 2088
14:32 they shall fall in t wilderness. — 2088
14:35 I will surely do it unto all t evil — 2088
14:35 in t wilderness they shall be consumed, — 2088
15:13 shall do these *things* **after t manner**, — 3602
16: 6 **T** do; Take you censers, Korah, and all his — 2088
16:21 Separate yourselves from among t — 2088
16:45 Get you up from among t congregation, — 2088
18: 9 **T** shall be thine of the most holy *things*, — 2088
18:11 t *is* thine; the heave offering of their gift, — 2088
18:27 t your heave offering shall be reckoned — NIH
19: 2 **T** *is* the ordinance of the law which — 2088
19:14 **T** *is* the law, when a man dieth in a tent: — 2088
20: 4 of the LORD into t wilderness, — 2088
20: 5 of Egypt, to bring us in unto t evil place? — 2088

Nu 20:10 must we fetch you water out of t rock? — 2088
20:12 shall not bring t congregation into — 2088
20:13 **T** *is* the water of Meribah; because — 1992
21: 2 If thou wilt indeed deliver t people into — 2088
21: 5 and our soul loatheth t light bread. — NIH
21:17 Israel sang t song, Spring up, O well; — 2088
22: 1 pitched in the plains of Moab on t side — NIH
22: 4 Now shall t company lick up all *that are* — NIH
22: 6 for I pray thee, curse me t people; — 2088
22: 8 Lodge here t night, and I will bring you — NIH
22:17 I pray thee, curse me t people. — 2088
22:19 I pray you, tarry ye also here t night, — NIH
22:24 a wall *being* on t side, and a wall on that — 2088
22:30 ridden ever since *I was* thine unto t day? — 2088
23:23 according to t time it shall be said of Jacob — NIH
24:14 I will advertise thee what t people shall do — 2088
24:23 Alas, who shall live when God doeth t! — 2050.2
26: 9 **T** *is* that Dathan and Abiram, *which were* — 1931
27:12 Get thee up into t mount Abarim, — 2088
28: 3 **T** *is* the offering made by fire which ye — 2088
28:10 **T** *is* the burnt offering of every sabbath, — NIH
28:14 t *is* the burnt offering of every month — 2088
28:17 In the fifteenth day of t month *is* the feast: — 2088
28:24 After t manner ye shall offer daily, — 428
29: 7 ye shall have on the tenth *day* of t seventh — 2088
30: 1 **T** *is* the thing which the LORD hath — 2088
31:21 **T** *is* the ordinance of the law which — 2088
32: 5 let t land be given unto thy servants for a — 2088
32:15 and ye shall destroy all t people. — 2088
32:19 our inheritance is fallen to us on t side — NIH
32:20 said unto them, If ye will do t thing, — 2088
32:22 t land shall be your possession before — 2088
32:32 the possession of our inheritance on t — NIH
34: 2 (t *is* the land that shall fall unto you for — 2088
34: 6 for a border: t shall be your west border. — 2088
34: 7 t shall be your north border: from the — 2088
34: 9 Hazar-enan: t shall be your north border. — 2088
34:12 t shall be your land with the coasts — 2088
34:13 **T** *is* the land which ye shall inherit by lot, — 2088
34:15 on t side Jordan *near* Jericho eastward, — NIH
35: 5 t shall be to them the suburbs of the — 2088
35:14 Ye shall give three cities on t side Jordan, — NIH
36: 6 **T** *is* the thing which the LORD doth — 2088

Dt 1: 1 Israel on t side Jordan in the wilderness, — NIH
1: 5 On t side Jordan, in the land of Moab, — NIH
1: 5 began Moses to declare t law, saying, — 2088
1: 6 Ye have dwelt long enough in t mount: — 2088
1:10 Ye *are* t day as the stars of heaven for — NIH
1:31 that ye went, until ye came into t place. — 2088
1:32 Yet in t thing ye did not believe — 2088
1:35 there shall not one of these men of t — 2088
2: 3 Ye have compassed t mountain long — 2088
2: 7 he knoweth thy walking *through* t great — 2088
2:18 over *through* Ar, the coast of Moab, t day: — NIH
2:22 and dwelt in their stead *even* unto t day: — 2088
2:25 **T** day will I begin to put the dread of thee — 2088
2:30 him into thy hand, as *appeareth* t day. — 2088
3: 8 the land that *was* on t side Jordan, — NIH
3:12 t land, *which* we possessed at that time, — 2088
3:14 name, Bashan-havoth-jair, unto t day. — 2088
3:18 The LORD your God hath given you t — 2088
3:26 speak no more unto me of t matter. — 2088
3:27 for thou shalt not go over t Jordan. — 2088
3:28 for he shall go over before t people, — 2088
4: 4 your God *are* alive every one of you t day. — NIH
4: 6 and do *them*; for t *is* your wisdom and — 1931
4: 6 Surely t great nation *is* a wise and — 2088
4: 8 and judgments *so* righteous as all t law, — 2088
4: 8 all this law, which I set before you t day? — NIH
4:20 a people of inheritance, as *ye are* t day. — NIH
4:22 I *must* die in t land, I *must* not go over — 2088
4:26 and earth to witness against you t day, — NIH
4:32 there hath been *any such thing* as t — 2088
4:38 their land *for* an inheritance, as *it is* t day. — 2088
4:39 Know therefore t day, and consider *it* in — NIH
4:40 which I command thee t day, — NIH
4:41 Moses severed three cities on t side Jordan — NIH
4:44 t *is* the law which Moses set before — 2088
4:46 On t side Jordan, in the valley over against — NIH
4:47 which *were* on t side Jordan toward — NIH
4:49 all the plain on t side Jordan eastward, — NIH
5: 1 which I speak in your ears t day, — NIH
5: 3 The LORD made not t covenant with our — 2088
5: 3 *even* us, who *are* all of us here alive t day. — NIH
5:24 we have seen t day that God doth talk — 2088
5:25 t great fire will consume us: if we hear — 2088
5:28 I have heard the voice of the words of t — 2088
6: 6 words, which I command thee t day, — NIH
6:24 might preserve us alive, as *it is* at t day. — 2088
7:11 which I command thee t day, to do them. — NIH
8: 1 command thee t day shall ye observe to — NIH
8:11 his statutes, which I command thee t day: — NIH
8:17 the might of mine hand hath gotten me t — 2088
8:18 he sware unto thy fathers, as *it is* t day. — NIH
8:19 I testify against you t day that ye shall — NIH
9: 1 Thou art to pass over Jordan t day, to go — NIH
9: 3 Understand therefore t day, that the LORD — NIH
9: 4 hath brought me in to possess t land: — 2088
9: 6 the LORD thy God giveth thee not t — 2088
9: 7 until ye came unto t place, ye have been — 2088
9:13 saying, I have seen t people, and behold, — 2088
9:27 not unto the stubbornness of t people, — 2088
10: 8 and to bless in his name, unto t day. — 2088
10:13 I command thee t day for thy good? — NIH
10:15 *even* you above all people, as *it is* t day. — 2088

T

Dt
11: 2 know you *t* day: for *I speak* not with your NIH
11: 4 LORD hath destroyed them unto *t* day; 2088
11: 5 the wilderness, until ye came into *t* place; 2088
11: 8 which I command you *t* day, NIH
11:13 which I command you *t* day, NIH
11:26 before you *t* day a blessing and a curse; NIH
11:27 your God, which I command you *t* day: NIH
11:28 of the way which I command you *t* day, NIH
11:32 judgments which I set before you *t* day. NIH
12: 8 after all *the things* that we do here *t* day, NIH
13:11 do no more any such wickedness as *t* 2088
13:18 which I command thee *t* day, NIH
15: 2 *t* is the manner of the release: 2088
15: 5 which I command thee *t* day, NIH
15:10 that for *t* thing the LORD thy God shall 2088
15:15 I command thee *t* thing to day. 2088
17:18 that he shall write him a copy of *t* law in 2088
17:19 to keep all the words of *t* law and 2088
18: 3 *t* shall be the priest's due from the people, 2088
18:16 neither let me see *t* great fire any more, 2088
19: 4 *t* is the case of the slayer, which shall flee 2088
19: 9 which I command thee *t* day, to love NIH
20: 3 you approach *t* day unto battle against NIH
21: 7 and say, Our hands have not shed *t* blood, 2088
21:20 T our son *is* stubborn and rebellious, 2088
22:14 I took *t* woman, and when I came to her, 2088
22:16 I gave my daughter unto *t* man to wife, 2088
22:20 if *t* thing be true, *and the tokens of* 2088
22:26 and slayeth him, even so *is t* matter: 2088
24:18 I command thee to do *t* thing. 2088
24:22 I command thee to do *t* thing. 2088
26: 3 I profess *t* day unto the LORD thy God, NIH
26: 9 he hath brought us into *t* place, 2088
26: 9 hath given us *t* land, *even* a land that 2088
26:16 T day the LORD thy God hath 2088
26:17 Thou hast avouched the LORD *t* day to be NIH
26:18 the LORD hath avouched thee *t* day to be NIH
27: 1 which I command you *t* day. NIH
27: 4 I command you *t* day, in mount Ebal, NIH
27: 8 stones all the words of *t* law very plainly. 2088
27: 9 *t* day thou art become the people of 2088
27:10 his statutes, which I command thee *t* day. NIH
27:26 not *all* the words of *t* law to do them. 2088
28: 1 which I command thee *t* day, NIH
28:13 which I command thee *t* day, to observe NIH
28:14 of the words which I command thee *t* day, NIH
28:15 his statutes which I command thee *t* day; NIH
28:58 words of *t* law that are written in this 2088
28:58 of this law that are written in *t* book, 2088
28:58 *thou* mayest fear *t* glorious and fearful 2088
28:61 which *is* not written in the book of *t* law, 2088
29: 4 yet to see, and ears to hear, unto *t* day. 2088
29: 7 ye came unto *t* place, Sihon the king 2088
29: 9 Keep therefore the words of *t* covenant, 2088
29:10 Ye stand *t* day all of you before the LORD NIH
29:12 LORD thy God maketh with thee *t* day: NIH
29:14 with you only do I make *t* covenant 2088
29:14 only do I make this covenant and *t* oath; 2088
29:15 with *him* that standeth here with us *t* day NIH
29:15 with *him* that *is* not here with us *t* day; NIH
29:18 whose heart turneth away *t* day from NIH
29:19 when he heareth the words of *t* curse, 2088
29:20 all the curses that are written in *t* book 2088
29:21 that are written in *t* book of the law: 2088
29:24 hath the LORD done thus unto *t* land? 2088
29:24 what *meaneth* the heat of *t* great anger? 2088
29:27 of the LORD was kindled against *t* land, 1931
29:27 it all the curses that are written in *t* book: 2088
29:28 cast them into another land, as *it is t* day. 2088
29:29 that we may do all the words of *t* law. 2088
30: 2 to all that I command thee *t* day, NIH
30: 8 which I command thee *t* day. NIH
30:10 his statutes which are written in *t* book of 2088
30:11 *t* commandment which I command thee NIH
30:11 which I command thee *t* day, NIH
30:15 I have set before thee *t* day life and good, NIH
30:16 In that I command thee *t* day to love NIH
30:18 I denounce unto you *t* day, that ye shall NIH
30:19 and earth to record *t* day against you, NIH
31: 2 An hundred and twenty years old *t* day; NIH
31: 2 unto me, Thou shalt not go over *t* Jordan. 2088
31: 7 for thou must go with *t* people unto 2088
31: 9 Moses wrote *t* law, and delivered it unto 2088
31:11 thou shalt read *t* law before all Israel in 2088
31:12 and observe to do all the words of *t* law: 2088
31:16 *t* people will rise up, and go a whoring 2088
31:19 Now therefore write ye *t* song for you, 2088
31:19 that *t* song may be a witness for me 2088
31:21 that *t* song shall testify against them as a 2088
31:22 Moses therefore wrote *t* song the same 2088
31:24 of writing the words of *t* law in a book, 2088
31:26 Take *t* book of the law, and put it in 2088
31:27 while I am yet alive with you *t* day, NIH
31:30 congregation of Israel the words of *t* song, 2088
32:27 is high, and the LORD hath not done all *t*. 2088
32:29 they were wise, *that* they understood *t*, 2088
32:34 *Is* not *t* laid up in store with me, 1931
32:44 spake all the words of *t* song in the ears 2088
32:46 words which I testify among you *t* day, NIH
32:46 to observe to do, all the words of *t* law. 2088
32:47 through *t* thing ye shall prolong *your* days 2088
32:49 Get thee up into *t* mountain Abarim, 2088
33: 1 *t is* the blessing, wherewith Moses the 2088
33: 7 *t is the blessing* of Judah: and he said, 2088

Dt
34: 4 T *is* the land which I sware unto 2088
34: 6 no man knoweth of his sepulchre unto *t* 2088
Jos
1: 2 go over *t* Jordan, thou, and all this people, 2088
1: 2 go over this Jordan, thou, and all *t* people, 2088
1: 4 and *t* Lebanon even unto the great river, 2088
1: 6 for unto *t* people shalt thou divide for an 2088
1: 8 T book of the law shall not depart out of 2088
1:11 for within three days ye shall pass over *t* 2088
1:13 given you rest, and hath given you *t* land. 2088
1:14 which Moses gave you on *t* side Jordan; NIH
1:15 you on *t* side Jordan *toward* the sunrising. NIH
2:14 for yours, if ye utter not *t* our business. 2088
2:17 We *will be* blameless of *t* thine oath 2088
2:18 thou shalt bind *t* line of scarlet thread in 2088
2:20 if thou utter *t* our business, then we will 2088
3: 4 for ye have not passed *t* way heretofore. 2088
3: 7 T day will I begin to magnify thee in 2088
4: 3 where you shall lodge *t* night. NIH
4: 6 That *t* may be a sign among you, *that* 2088
4: 9 and they are there unto *t* day. 2088
4:22 Israel came over *t* Jordan on dry *land.* 2088
5: 4 *t is* the cause why Joshua did circumcise: 2088
5: 9 T day have I rolled away the reproach of NIH
5: 9 of the place is called Gilgal unto *t* day. 2088
6:25 she dwelleth in Israel *even* unto *t* day; 2088
6:26 that riseth up and buildeth *t* city Jericho: 2088
7: 7 hast thou at all brought *t* people 2088
7:25 the LORD shall trouble thee *t* day. And all 2088
7:26 him a great heap of stones unto *t* day. 2088
7:26 called, The valley of Achor, unto *t* day. 2088
8:20 they had no power to flee *t* **way** or 2008
8:22 some on *t* side, and some on that side: 2088
8:28 for ever, *even* a desolation unto *t* day. 2088
8:29 heap of stones, *that remaineth* unto *t* day. 2088
8:33 stood on *t* side the ark and on that side 2088
9: 1 when all the kings which *were* on *t* side NIH
9:12 T our bread we took hot for our provision 2088
9:20 T we will do to them; we will even let 2088
9:24 because of you, and have done *t* thing. 2088
9:27 the altar of the LORD, *even* unto *t* day, 2088
10:13 *Is* not *t* written in the book of Jasher? 1931
10:27 *which remain* until *t* very day. 2088
11: 6 for to morrow about *t* time will I deliver 2088
12: 7 children of Israel smote on *t* side Jordan NIH
13: 2 T is the land that *yet* remaineth: 2088
13: 7 divide *t* land for an inheritance unto 2088
13:13 dwell among the Israelites until *t* day.) NIH
13:23 border *thereof.* T *was* the inheritance of 2088
13:28 T *is* the inheritance of the children of Gad 2088
13:29 *t* was *the possession* of the half tribe of NIH
14:10 *even* since the LORD spake *t* word unto 2088
14:10 I *am t* day fourscore and five years old. NIH
14:11 As yet I am *as* strong *t* day as *I was* in NIH
14:12 Now therefore give me *t* mountain, 2088
14:14 of Jephunneh the Kenezite unto *t* day, 2088
15: 1 T *then* was the lot of the tribe of NIH
15: 4 at the sea: *t* shall be your south coast. 2088
15:12 the coast *thereof.* T *is* the coast of 2088
15:20 T *is* the inheritance of the tribe of 2088
15:63 children of Judah at Jerusalem unto *t* day. 2088
16: 8 T *is* the inheritance of the tribe of 2088
16:10 dwell among the Ephraimites unto *t* day, 2088
18:14 children of Judah: *t was* the west quarter. 2088
18:19 end of Jordan: *t was* the south coast. 2088
18:20 T *was* the inheritance of the children of 2088
18:28 T *is* the inheritance of the children of 2088
19: 8 T *is* the inheritance of the tribe of 2088
19:16 T *is* the inheritance of the children of 2088
19:23 T *is* the inheritance of the tribe of 2088
19:31 T *is* the inheritance of the tribe of 2088
19:39 T *is* the inheritance of the tribe of 2088
19:48 T *is* the inheritance of the tribe of 2088
22: 3 brethren these many days unto *t* day, 2088
22: 7 their brethren on *t* side Jordan westward. NIH
22:16 What trespass *is t* that ye have committed 2088
22:16 to turn away *t* day from following NIH
22:16 that ye might rebel *t* day against NIH
22:17 which we are not cleansed until *t* day, 2088
22:18 ye must turn away *t* day from following 2088
22:22 against the LORD, (save us not *t* day,) 2088
22:24 if we have not *rather* done it for fear of *t* 2088
22:29 turn *t* day from following the LORD, NIH
22:31 T day we perceive that the LORD *is* NIH
22:31 ye have not committed *t* trespass against 2088
23: 8 your God, as ye have done unto *t* day. 2088
23: 9 *been able* to stand before you unto *t* day. 2088
23:13 until ye perish from off *t* good land which 2088
23:14 *t* day I am going the way of all the earth: NIH
23:15 he have destroyed you from off *t* good 2088
24:15 choose you *t* day whom you will serve; NIH
24:27 *t* stone shall be a witness unto us; NIH
Jdg
1:21 of Benjamin in Jerusalem unto *t* day. 2088
1:26 which *is* the name thereof unto *t* day. 2088
2: 2 no league with the inhabitants of *t* land; 2088
2: 2 obeyed my voice: why have ye done *t*? 2088
2:20 Because that *t* people hath transgressed 2088
4:14 for *t is* the day in which the LORD hath 2088
6:13 be with us, why then is all *t* befallen us? 2088
6:14 Go in *t* thy might, and thou shalt save 2088
6:20 and lay *them* upon *t* rock, 1975
6:24 unto *t* day it *is* yet in Ophrah of 2088
6:26 the LORD thy God upon the top of *t* rock, 2088
6:29 one to another, Who hath done *t* thing? 2088
6:29 Gideon the son of Joash hath done *t* thing. 2088
6:39 against me, and I will speak but *t* once: NIH

Jdg
6:39 I pray thee, but *t* once with the fleece; NIH
7: 4 T shall go with thee, the same shall go 2088
7: 4 T shall not go with thee, the same shall 2088
7:14 T *is* nothing else save the sword of 2088
8: 9 again in peace, I will break down *t* tower. 2088
9:18 are risen up against my father's house *t* NIH
9:19 with Jerubbaal and with his house *t* day, 2088
9:29 would to God *t* people were under my 2088
9:38 not to the people that thou hast despised? 2088
10: 4 which are called Havoth-jair unto *t* day, 2088
10:15 deliver us only, we pray thee, *t* day. NIH
11:27 the LORD the Judge be judge *t* day 2088
11:37 her father, Let *t* thing be done for me: 2088
12: 3 are ye come up unto me *t* day, 2088
13:23 at *t* time have told us *such things* as these. NIH
15: 6 the Philistines said, Who hath done *t*? 2088
15: 7 Though ye have done *t*, yet will I be 2063
15:11 what *is t* that thou hast done unto us? 2088
15:18 Thou hast given *t* great deliverance into 2088
15:19 which *is* in Lehi unto *t* day. 2088
16:18 Come up *t* once, for he hath shewed NIH
16:28 I pray thee, only *t* once, O God, 2088
18: 3 what makest thou in *t* place? and what 2088
18:12 called that place Mahaneh-dan unto *t* day: 2088
18:24 what *is t* that ye say unto me, What aileth 2088
19:11 let us turn in into *t* city of the Jebusites, 2088
19:23 that *t* man is come into mine house, 2088
19:23 is come into mine house, do not *t* folly. 2088
19:24 but unto *t* man do not so vile a thing. 2088
19:30 up out of the land of Egypt unto *t* day: 2088
20: 3 of Israel, Tell *us*, how was *t* wickedness? 2088
20: 9 now *t shall be* the thing which we will do 2088
20:12 What wickedness *is t* that is done among 2088
20:16 Among all *t* people *there were* seven 2088
21: 3 of Israel, why is *t* come to pass in Israel, 2088
21: 6 There is one tribe cut off from Israel *t* day. NIH
21:11 it is the thing that ye shall do, Ye shall 2088
21:22 for ye did not give unto them at *t* time, NIH
Ru
1:19 about them, and they said, *Is t* Naomi? 2088
2: 5 set over the reapers, Whose damsel *is t*? 2088
3:13 Tarry *t* night, and it shall be in the NIH
3:18 until he have finished the thing *t* day. 2088
4: 7 Now *t was the manner* in former time in 2088
4: 7 and *t was* a testimony in Israel. 2088
4: 9 all the people, Ye *are* witnesses *t* day, NIH
4:10 gate of his place: ye *are* witnesses *t* day. NIH
4:12 LORD shall give thee of *t* young woman. 2088
4:14 which hath not left thee *t* day without a NIH
1Sa
1: 3 *t* man went up out of his city yearly to 1931
1:27 For *t* child I prayed; and the LORD hath 2088
2:20 The LORD give thee seed of *t* woman for 2088
2:23 for I hear of your evil dealings by all *t* 428
2:34 *t shall be* a sign unto thee, that shall 2088
4: 6 What *meaneth* the noise of *t* great shout 2088
4:14 What *meaneth* the noise of *t* tumult? 2088
5: 5 threshold of Dagon in Ashdod unto *t* day. 2088
6: 9 *then* he hath done us *t* great evil: 2088
6:18 *which stone* remaineth unto *t* day in 2088
6:20 Who is able to stand before *t* holy LORD 2088
8: 8 them up out of Egypt even unto *t* day, 2088
8:11 T will be the manner of the king that shall 2088
9: 6 *there is* in *t* city a man of God, and *he is* 2088
9:13 you up; for about *t* time ye shall find him. NIH
9:16 To morrow about *t* time I will send thee a NIH
9:17 thee of: *t same* shall reign over my people. 2088
9:24 for unto *t* time *hath it* been kept for thee NIH
10:11 What *is t that* is come unto the son of 2088
10:19 ye have *t* day rejected your God, NIH
10:27 of Belial said, How shall *t man* save us? 2088
11: 2 On *t* condition will I make *a covenant* 2063
11:13 shall not a man be put to death *t* day: 2088
12: 2 you from my childhood unto *t* day. 2088
12: 5 and his anointed *is* witness *t* day, 2088
12: 6 of Egypt, and made them dwell in *t* place. 2088
12:16 therefore stand and see *t* great thing, 2088
12:19 for we have added unto all our sins *t* evil, NIH
12:20 have done all *t* wickedness: yet turn not 2088
14:10 our hand: and *t shall be* a sign unto us. 2088
14:28 Cursed *be* the man that eateth *any* food *t* NIH
14:29 because I tasted a little of *t* honey. 2088
14:33 roll a great stone unto me *t* day. NIH
14:38 and see wherein *t* sin hath been *this* day. 2088
14:38 and see wherein this sin hath been *t* day. NIH
14:45 who hath wrought *t* great salvation in 2088
14:45 for he hath wrought with God *t* day. 2088
15:14 then *t* bleating of the sheep in mine ears, 2088
15:16 what the LORD hath said to me *t* night. NIH
15:28 rent the kingdom of Israel from thee *t* day, NIH
16: 8 he said, Neither hath the LORD chosen *t*. 2088
16: 9 he said, Neither hath the LORD chosen *t*. 2088
16:12 LORD said, Arise, anoint him: for *t is* he. 2088
17:10 I defy the armies of Israel *t* day; 2088
17:17 Take now for thy brethren an ephah of *t* 2088
17:25 Have ye seen *t* man that is come up? 2088
17:26 shall be done to the man that killeth *t* 1975
17:26 for who *is t* uncircumcised Philistine, 2088
17:27 the people answered him after *t* manner, 2088
17:32 servant will go and fight with *t* Philistine. 2088
17:33 Thou art not able to go against *t* Philistine 2088
17:36 *t* uncircumcised Philistine shall be as one 2088
17:37 he will deliver me out of the hand of *t* 2088
17:46 T day will the LORD deliver thee into 2088
17:46 Philistines *t* day unto the fowls of the air, 2088
17:47 all *t* assembly shall know that the LORD 2088
17:55 of the host, Abner, whose son *is t* youth? 2088

1Sa	18:21 Thou shalt *t* day be my son in law in *the*	NIH
	18:24 him, saying, On t manner spake David.	428
	20: 2 why should my father hide t thing from	2088
	20: 3 he saith, Let not Jonathan know t, lest he	2088
	20:21 Behold, the arrows *are* **on t side** of thee,	2008
	21: 5 it were sanctified t day in the vessel.	NIH
	21:11 *Is* not t David the king of the land?	2088
	21:15 that ye have brought t *fellow* to play	2088
	21:15 shall t *fellow* come into my house?	2088
	22: 8 against me, to lie in wait, as at t day?	2088
	22:13 rise against me, to lie in wait, as at t day?	2088
	22:15 for thy servant knew nothing of all t, less	2088
	23:26 Saul went on t side of the mountain,	2088
	24: 6 The Lord forbid that I should do t thing	2088
	24:10 t day thine eyes have seen how that	NIH
	24:16 that Saul said, *Is* t thy voice, my son	2088
	24:18 thou hast shewed t day how that thou	NIH
	24:19 for that thou hast done unto me t day.	2088
	25:21 Surely in vain have I kept all that t *fellow*	2088
	25:24 *upon* me t iniquity *be*: and let thine	NIH
	25:25 I pray thee, regard t man of Belial,	2088
	25:27 now t blessing which thine handmaid	2088
	25:31 That t shall be no grief unto thee,	2088
	25:32 Israel, which sent thee t day to meet me:	2088
	25:33 which hast kept me t day from coming to	2088
	26: 8 thine enemy into thine hand t day:	NIH
	26:16 T thing *is* not good that thou hast done.	2088
	26:17 and said, *Is* t thy voice, my son David?	2088
	26:19 for they have driven me out t day from	NIH
	26:21 my soul was precious in thine eyes t day:	2088
	26:24 as thy life was much set by t day in mine	2088
	27: 6 unto the kings of Judah unto t day.	NIH
	28:10 punishment happen to thee for t thing.	2088
	28:18 hath the Lord done t thing unto thee this	2088
	28:18 hath the Lord done this thing unto thee t	2088
	29: 3 *Is* not t David, the servant of Saul the	2088
	29: 3 in him since he fell *unto* me unto t day?	2088
	29: 4 Make t fellow return, that he may go	NIH
	29: 5 *Is* not t David, of whom they sang one to	2088
	29: 6 day of thy coming unto me unto t day:	2088
	29: 8 long as I have been with thee unto t day,	2088
	30: 8 Shall I pursue after t troop?	NIH
	30:15 Canst thou bring me down to t company?	2088
	30:15 and I will bring thee down to t company.	2088
	30:20 *other* cattle, and said, T *is* David's spoil.	2088
	30:24 who will hearken unto you in t matter?	2088
	30:25 and an ordinance for Israel unto t day.	2088
2Sa	1:17 David lamented with t lamentation over	2088
	2: 1 came to pass after t, that David inquired	3651
	2: 5 that ye have shewed t kindness unto your	2088
	2: 6 I also will requite you t kindness, because	2088
	2: 6 kindness, because ye have done t thing.	2088
	3: 8 against Judah do shew kindness t day	NIH
	3: 8 to day with a fault concerning t woman?	NIH
	3:38 and a great *man* fallen t day in Israel?	2088
	3:39 I *am* t day weak, though anointed king;	NIH
	4: 3 and were sojourners there until t day.)	
	4: 4 Lord hath avenged my lord the king t	2088
	6: 8 *name* of the place Perez-uzzah to t day.	
	7: 6 even to t day, but have walked in a tent	2088
	7:17 according to all t vision, so did Nathan	2088
	7:19 t was yet a small thing in thy sight,	2088
	7:19 *is* t the manner of man, O Lord God?	2088
	7:27 thy servant found in his heart to pray t	2088
	7:28 thou hast promised t goodness unto thy	2088
	8: 1 after t it came to pass, that David smote	3651
	10: 1 it came to pass after t, that the king of	3651
	11: 3 said, *Is* not t Bath-sheba, the daughter	2088
	11:11 *as* thy soul liveth, I will not do t thing.	2088
	11:25 unto Joab, Let not t thing displease thee,	2088
	12: 5 man that hath done t *thing* shall surely	2088
	12: 6 because he did t thing, and because he	2088
	12:11 shall lie with thy wives in the sight of t	2088
	12:12 I will do t thing before all Israel,	2088
	12:14 by t deed thou hast given great occasion	2088
	12:21 What thing *is* t that thou hast done?	2088
	13: 1 came to pass after t, that Absalom the son	3651
	13:12 to be done in Israel: do not thou t folly.	2088
	13:16 t evil in sending me away *is* greater than	1886.1
	13:17 Put now t *woman* out from me, and bolt	2088
	13:20 he *is* thy brother; regard not t thing.	2088
	13:32 for by the appointment of Absalom t hath	NIH
	14: 3 king, and speak on t manner unto him.	2088
	14:13 for the king doth speak t thing as one	2088
	14:15 I am come to speak of t thing unto my	2088
	14:19 *Is* not the hand of Joab with thee in all t?	2088
	14:20 To fetch about t form of speech hath thy	NIH
	14:20 speech hath thy servant Joab done t thing:	2088
	14:21 Joab, Behold now, I have done t thing:	2088
	15: 1 it came to pass after t, that Absalom	3651
	15: 6 on t manner did Absalom to all Israel that	2088
	15:20 should I t day make thee go up and	NIH
	16: 9 Why should t dead dog curse my lord	NIH
	16:11 how much more now *may* t Benjamite *do*	NIH
	16:12 will requite me good for his cursing t day.	2088
	16:17 to Hushai, *Is* t thy kindness to thy friend?	2088
	16:18 t people, and all the men of Israel,	
	17: 1 I will arise and pursue after David t night:	NIH
	17: 2 Ahithophel hath spoken after t manner:	2088
	17: 7 hath given t is not good at t time.	2088
	17:16 Lodge not t night in the plains of	NIH
	18:18 it is called unto t day, Absalom's place.	2088
	18:20 Thou *shalt* not bear tidings t day,	2088
	18:20 but t day thou shalt bear no tidings,	2088
	18:31 for the Lord hath avenged t day of	NIH

2Sa	19: 5 Thou hast shamed t day the faces of all	NIH
	19: 5 which t day have saved thy life,	NIH
	19: 6 for thou hast declared t day, that thou	NIH
	19: 6 if I perceive, that if Absalom had	NIH
	19: 6 all we had died t day, then it had pleased	NIH
	19: 7 there will not tarry one with thee t night:	NIH
	19:14 so that they sent t word unto the king,	NIH
	19:20 I am come the first t day of all the house	2088
	19:21 Shall not Shimei be put to death for t,	2088
	19:22 ye should t day be adversaries unto me?	NIH
	19:22 shall there any man be put to death t day	NIH
	19:22 for do not I know that I *am* t day king over	NIH
	19:35 I *am* t day fourscore years old: *and* can I	NIH
	19:42 wherefore then be ye angry for t matter?	2088
	21:18 it came to pass after t, that there was again	3651
	22: 1 spake unto the Lord the words of t	2088
	23: 5 for t is all my salvation, and all *my* desire,	NIH
	23:17 far from me, O Lord, that I should do t:	2088
	23:17 *is not* t the blood of the men that went in	NIH
	24: 3 why doth my lord the king delight in t	2088
1Ki	1:25 For he is gone down t day, and hath slain	NIH
	1:27 Is t thing done by my lord the king,	2088
	1:30 my stead; even so will I certainly do t day.	2088
	1:41 Wherefore *is* t noise of the city being in an	NIH
	1:45 T is the noise that ye have heard.	1931
	1:48 hath given *one* to sit on my throne t	NIH
	2:23 if Adonijah have not spoken t word	NIH
	2:24 Adonijah shall be put to death t day.	NIH
	2:26 I will not at t time put thee to death,	2088
	3: 6 thou hast kept for him t great kindness,	2088
	3: 6 a son to sit on his throne, as *it is* t day.	2088
	3: 9 for who is able to judge t thy *so* great a	2088
	3:10 the Lord, that Solomon had asked t thing.	2088
	3:11 Because thou hast asked t thing,	2088
	3:17 lord, I and t woman dwell in one house;	2088
	3:18 that t woman was delivered also:	2088
	3:19 t woman's child died in the night;	2088
	3:22 t said, No; but the dead *is* thy son,	2088
	3:23 T *is* my son that liveth, and thy son *is*	2088
	4:24 he had dominion over all *the region* on t	NIH
	4:24 over all the kings on t side the river:	NIH
	5: 7 and said, Blessed *be* the Lord t day,	NIH
	5: 7 unto David a wise son over t great people.	2088
	6:12 *Concerning* t house which thou art in	2088
	7: 8 whom he had taken *to wife*, like unto t	2088
	7:28 the work of the bases *was* on t *manner:*	NIH
	7:37 After t *manner* he made the ten bases:	2088
	8: 8 without: and there they are unto t day.	2088
	8:24 fulfilled *it* with thine hand, as *it is* t day.	2088
	8:27 much less t house that I have builded?	2088
	8:29 That thine eyes may be open toward t	2088
	8:29 thy servant shall make towards t place.	2088
	8:30 when they shall pray towards t place:	2088
	8:31 oath come before thine altar in t house:	2088
	8:33 make supplication unto thee in t house:	2088
	8:35 if they pray towards t place,	2088
	8:38 spread forth his hands towards t house:	2088
	8:42 he shall come and pray towards t house;	2088
	8:43 that *they* may know that t house, which I	2088
	8:54 had made an end of praying all t prayer	2088
	8:61 to keep his commandments, as at t day.	2088
	9: 3 I have hallowed t house, which thou hast	2088
	9: 7 t house, which I have hallowed for my	NIH
	9: 8 at t house, *which* is high, every one that	NIH
	9: 8 Why hath the Lord done thus unto t	2088
	9: 8 done thus unto this land, and to t house?	2088
	9: 9 hath the Lord brought upon them all t	2088
	9:13 called them the land of Cabul unto t day.	NIH
	9:15 t *is* the reason of the levy which king	2088
	9:21 levy a tribute of bondservice unto t day.	NIH
	10:12 almug trees, nor were seen unto t day.	2088
	11:10 had commanded him concerning t thing,	2088
	11:11 Forasmuch as t is done of thee,	2088
	11:27 t *was* the cause that he lift up *his* hand	2088
	11:39 I will for t afflict the seed of David,	2088
	12: 6 How do you advise that *I* may answer t	2088
	12: 7 thou wilt be a servant unto t people this	2088
	12: 7 thou wilt be a servant unto this people	NIH
	12: 9 counsel give ye that we may answer t	2088
	12:10 Thus shalt thou speak unto t people that	2088
	12:19 against the house of David unto t day.	2088
	12:24 man to his house; for t thing is from me.	2088
	12:27 If t people go up to do sacrifice in	2088
	12:27 shall the heart of t people turn again unto	2088
	12:30 t thing became a sin: for the people went	2088
	13: 3 T *is* the sign which the Lord hath	2088
	13: 8 will I eat bread nor drink water in t	2088
	13:16 nor drink water with thee in t place:	2088
	13:33 After t thing Jeroboam returned not from	NIH
	13:34 t thing became sin unto the house of	2088
	14: 2 which told me that I should be king over t	NIH
	14:15 he shall root up Israel out of t good land,	2088
	17:21 let t child's soul come into him again.	2088
	17:24 Now *by* t I know that thou *art* a man of	NIH
	18:36 let it be known t day that thou *art* God in	NIH
	18:37 that t people may know that thou *art*	NIH
	19: 2 of one of them *by* to morrow about t time,	NIH
	20: 5 servants unto thee to morrow about t time,	NIH
	20: 7 and see how t *man* seeketh mischief:	2088
	20: 9 t thing I may not do. And the messengers	NIH
	20:12 when *Ben-hadad* heard t message, as he	2088
	20:13 Hast thou seen all t great multitude?	NIH
	20:13 I will deliver it into thine hand t day;	NIH
	20:24 do t thing, Take the kings away, every	2088
	20:28 I deliver all t great multitude into thine	

1Ki	20:34 said Ahab, I will send thee away with t	NIH
	20:39 a man unto me, and said, Keep t man:	2088
	22:20 one said on t **manner**, and another said	3541
	22:27 Put t *fellow* in the prison, and feed him	2088
2Ki	1: 2 Ekron whether I shall recover of t disease.	2088
	2:19 thee, the situation of t *city is* pleasant,	NIH
	2:22 So the waters were healed unto t day,	2088
	3:16 the Lord, Make t valley full of ditches.	2088
	3:18 t is *but* a light thing in the sight of	2088
	3:23 they said, T *is* blood: the kings are surely	NIH
	4: 9 I perceive that t *is* a holy man of God,	1931
	4:12 to Gehazi his servant, Call t Shunammite.	2088
	4:13 hast been careful for us with all t care;	2088
	4:16 he said, About t season, according to	2088
	4:36 Gehazi, and said, Call t Shunammite.	2088
	4:43 should I set t before an hundred men?	2088
	5: 6 Now when t letter is come unto thee,	2088
	5: 7 that t *man* doth send unto me to recover	2088
	5:18 In t thing the Lord pardon thy servant,	2088
	5:18 the Lord pardon thy servant in t thing.	2088
	5:20 my master hath spared Naaman t Syrian,	2088
	6:11 king of Syria was sore troubled for t thing;	2088
	6:18 said, Smite t people, I pray thee,	2088
	6:19 T *is* not the way, neither *is* this the city:	2088
	6:19 This *is* not the way, neither *is* t the city:	2090
	6:24 came to pass after t, that Ben-hadad king	3651
	6:28 T woman said unto me, Give thy son,	2088
	6:31 son of Shaphat shall stand on him t day.	NIH
	6:32 See ye how t son of a murderer hath sent	2088
	6:33 he said, Behold, t evil *is* of the Lord;	2088
	7: 1 To morrow about t time *shall* a measure	NIH
	7: 2 windows in heaven, might t thing be?	2088
	7: 9 t day *is* a day of good tidings, and we	2088
	7:18 be to morrow about t time in the gate	NIH
	8: 5 king, t *is* the woman, and this *is* her son,	2088
	8: 5 king, this *is* the woman, and t *is* her son,	2088
	8: 8 him, saying, Shall I recover of t disease?	2088
	8: 9 thee, saying, Shall I recover of t disease?	2088
	8:13 a dog, that he should do t great thing?	2088
	8:22 from under the hand of Judah unto t day.	2088
	9: 1 take t box of oil in thine hand, and go *to*	2088
	9:11 wherefore came t mad *fellow* to thee?	2088
	9:25 the Lord laid t burden upon him;	2088
	9:26 I will requite thee in t plat, saith	2088
	9:27 when Ahaziah the king of Judah saw t,	NIH
	9:34 see now t cursed *woman,* and bury her:	2088
	9:36 he said, T *is* the word of the Lord,	1931
	9:37 *so* that they shall not say, T *is* Jezebel.	2088
	10: 2 Now as soon as t letter cometh to you,	2088
	10: 6 to me to Jezreel by to morrow t time.	NIH
	10:27 and made it a draught house unto t day.	NIH
	11: 5 saying, T *is* the thing that ye shall do;	2088
	14: 7 called the name of it Joktheel unto t day.	NIH
	14:10 glory *of* t, and tarry at home: for why	NIH
	15:12 T *was* the word of the Lord which he	1931
	16: 6 to Elath, and dwelt there unto t day.	2088
	17:12 said unto them, Ye shall not do t thing.	2088
	17:23 of their own land to Assyria unto t day.	2088
	17:34 Unto t day they do after the former	2088
	17:41 did their fathers, *so* do they unto t day.	2088
	18:19 confidence *is* t where*in* thou trustest?	2088
	18:21 thou trustest upon the staff of t bruised	2088
	18:22 Ye shall worship before t altar in	2088
	18:25 the Lord against t place to destroy it?	2088
	18:25 me, Go up against t land, and destroy it.	2088
	18:30 t city shall not be delivered into the hand	2088
	19: 3 T day *is* a day of trouble, and of rebuke,	2088
	19:21 T *is* the word that the Lord hath spoken	2088
	19:29 t *shall be* a sign unto thee, Ye shall eat	2088
	19:29 Ye shall eat t year such things as grow of	NIH
	19:31 the zeal of the Lord *of* hosts shall do t.	2088
	19:32 He shall not come into t city, nor shoot	2088
	19:33 shall not come into t city, saith the Lord.	2088
	19:34 I will defend t city, to save it, for mine	2088
	20: 6 t city out of the hand of the king of	2088
	20: 6 I will defend t city for mine own sake,	2088
	20: 9 T sign shalt thou have of the Lord,	2088
	20:17 fathers have laid up in store unto t day,	2088
	21: 7 his son, In t house, and in Jerusalem,	2088
	21:15 came forth out of Egypt, even unto t day.	2088
	22:13 concerning the words of t book that is	2088
	22:13 not hearkened unto the words of t book,	2088
	22:16 I will bring evil upon t place, and upon	2088
	22:17 my wrath shall be kindled against t place,	2088
	22:19 thou heardest what I spake against t	2088
	22:20 the evil which I will bring upon t place.	2088
	23: 3 to perform the words of t covenant that	2088
	23: 3 this covenant that were written in t book.	2088
	23:21 as it is written in the book of t covenant.	2088
	23:23 where*in* t passover was holden to	2088
	23:27 will cast off t city Jerusalem which I have	2088
	24: 3 of the Lord came t upon Judah,	NIH
1Ch	4:41 destroyed them utterly unto t day,	2088
	4:43 escaped, and dwelt there unto t day.	2088
	5:26 Hara, and to the river Gozan, unto t day.	2088
	11:11 t *is* the number of the mighty *men* whom	428
	11:19 that *I* should do t *thing:* shall I drink	2063
	13:11 that place is called Perez-uzza to t day.	2088
	16: 7 on that day David delivered first t *psalm*	NIH
	17: 5 day that I brought up Israel unto t day;	2088
	17:15 according to all t vision, so did Nathan	2088
	17:17 *yet* was a small thing in thine eyes,	2088
	17:19 own heart, hast thou done all t greatness,	2088
	17:26 promised t goodness unto thy servant:	2088
	18: 1 Now after t it came to pass, that David	3651

T

1Ch 19: 1 Now it came to pass after *t*, that Nahash 3651
20: 4 came to pass after *t*, that there arose war 3651
21: 3 doth my lord require *t* thing? why will 2088
21: 7 God was displeased with *t* thing; 2088
21: 8 greatly, because I have done *t* thing: 2088
21:22 Grant me the place of *t* threshingfloor, NIH
22: 1 *T* is the house of the Lord God, 2088
22: 1 *t* is the altar of the burnt offering for 2088
26:30 officers among them of Israel on *t* side NIH
27: 6 *T* is that Benaiah, who was mighty 1931
28: 7 and my judgments, as at *t* day. 2088
28: 8 that ye may possess *t* good land, NIH
28:19 All *t*, said David, the Lord made me NIH
28:19 upon me, even all the works of *t* pattern. NIH
29: 5 is willing to consecrate his service *t* day NIH
29:14 willingly after *t* sort? for all things come 2088
29:16 all *t* store that we have prepared to build 2088
29:18 keep *t* for ever in the imagination of 2088
2Ch 1:10 I may go out and come in before *t* people: 2088
1:10 for who can judge *t* thy people, that is so 2088
1:11 Because *t* was in thine heart, and thou 2088
2: 4 *T* is an ordinance for ever to Israel. 2088
5: 9 seen without. And there it is unto *t* day. 2088
6:15 fulfilled *it* with thine hand, as it is *t* day. 2088
6:18 much less *t* house which I have built? 2088
6:20 thine eyes may be open upon *t* house 2088
6:20 thy servant prayeth towards *t* place. 2088
6:21 which they shall make towards *t* place: 2088
6:22 oath come before thine altar in *t* house; 2088
6:24 make supplication before thee in *t* house; 2088
6:26 yet if they pray towards *t* place, 2088
6:29 shall spread forth his hands in *t* house: 2088
6:32 out arm; if they come and pray in *t* house; 2088
6:33 know that *t* house which I have built is 2088
6:34 they pray unto thee toward *t* city which 2088
6:40 unto the prayer that is made in *t* place. 2088
7:12 have chosen *t* place to myself for a house 2088
7:15 unto the prayer that is made in *t* place. 2088
7:16 now have I chosen and sanctified *t* house, 2088
7:20 *t* house, which I have sanctified for my 2088
7:21 *t* house, which is high, shall be an 2088
7:21 Why hath the Lord done thus unto *t* 2088
7:21 thus unto this land, and unto *t* house? 2088
7:22 hath he brought all *t* evil upon them. 2088
8: 8 did Solomon make to pay tribute until *t* 2088
10: 6 give ye *me* to return answer to *t* people? 2088
10: 7 If thou be kind to *t* people, 2088
10: 9 ye that we may return answer to *t* people, 2088
10:19 against the house of David unto *t* day. 2088
11: 4 to his house, for *t* thing is done of me. 2088
14:11 in thy name we go against *t* multitude. 2088
16:10 of *t* thing. And Asa oppressed some of 2088
18:19 one spake saying after *t* manner, 3602
18:26 Put *t* fellow in the prison, and feed him 2088
19:10 to do, and ye shall not trespass. 3541
20: 1 came to pass after *t* also, that the children 3651
20: 2 thee from beyond the sea on *t* side Syria; NIH
20: 7 didst drive out the inhabitants of *t* land 2088
20: 9 we stand before *t* house, and in thy 2088
20: 9 thy presence, (for thy name is in *t* house,) 2088
20:12 for we have no might against *t* great 2088
20:15 Be not afraid nor dismayed by reason of *t* 2088
20:17 Ye shall not need to fight in *t* battle: set 2063
20:26 The valley of Berachah, unto *t* day. NIH
20:35 after *t* did Jehoshaphat king of Judah join 3651
21:10 from under the hand of Judah unto *t* day. 2088
21:18 after all *t* the Lord smote him in his 2088
23: 4 *T* is the thing that ye shall do; A third 2088
24: 4 it came to pass after *t*, that Joash was 3651
24:18 and Jerusalem for *t* their trespass. 2088
25: 9 is able to give thee much more than *t*. 2088
25:16 because thou hast done *t*, and hast not 2088
28:22 against the Lord: *t* is that king Ahaz. 1931
29: 9 and our wives are in captivity for *t*. 2088
29:28 all *t* continued until the burnt offering NIH
30: 9 so that they shall come again into *t* land: 2088
31: 1 Now when all *t* was finished, all Israel 2088
31:10 and that which is left is *t* great store. 2088
32: 9 After *t* did Sennacherib king of Assyria 2088
32:15 nor persuade you on *t* manner, neither 2088
32:20 for *t* cause Hezekiah the king, NIH
32:30 *T* same Hezekiah also stopped the upper 1931
33: 7 his son, in *t* house, and in Jerusalem, 2088
33:14 after *t* he built a wall without the city 3651
34:21 to do after all that is written in *t* book. 2088
34:24 I will bring evil upon *t* place, and upon 2088
34:25 wrath shall be poured out upon *t* place, 2088
34:27 when thou heardest his words against *t* 2088
34:28 all the evil that I will bring upon *t* place, 2088
34:31 the covenant which are written in *t* book. 2088
35:19 of the reign of Josiah was *t* passover kept. 2088
35:20 After all *t*, when Josiah had prepared 2088
35:21 I come not against thee *t* day, NIH
35:25 of Josiah in their lamentations to *t* day, NIH
Ezr 1: 9 is the number of them: thirty chargers of 428
3:12 when the foundation of *t* house was laid 2088
4: 8 Jerusalem to Artaxerxes the king in *t* sort: 3660
4:10 the rest that are on *t* side the river, NIH
4:11 *T* is the copy of the letter that they sent 1836
4:11 Thy servants the men on *t* side the river, NIH
4:13 if *t* city be builded, and the walls set up 1791
4:15 and know that *t* city is a rebellious city, 1791
4:15 for which cause was *t* city destroyed. 1791
4:16 if *t* city be builded again, and the walls 1791
4:16 by *t* means thou shalt have no portion on 1836

4:16 shalt have no portion on *t* side the river. NIH
4:19 it is found that *t* city of old time hath 1791
4:21 that *t* city be not builded, until another 1791
4:22 Take heed now that ye fail not to do *t*: 1836
5: 3 governor on *t* side the river, NIH
5: 3 hath commanded you to build *t* house, 1836
5: 3 build this house, and to make up *t* wall? 1836
5: 4 said we unto them after *t* manner, 3660
5: 4 are the names of the men that make *t* 1836
5: 5 returned answer by letter concerning *t* 1836
5: 6 governor on *t* side the river, NIH
5: 6 which were on *t* side the river, sent unto NIH
5: 8 *t* work goeth fast on, and prospereth in 1791
5: 9 Who commanded you to build *t* house, 1836
5:12 who destroyed *t* house, and carried 1836
5:13 made a decree to build *t* house of God. 1836
5:17 king to build *t* house of God at Jerusalem, 1791
5:17 his pleasure to us concerning *t* matter. 1836
6: 7 Let the work of *t* house of God alone; 1791
6: 7 elders of the Jews build *t* house of God 1791
6: 8 Jews for the building of *t* house of God: 1791
6:11 decree, that whosoever shall alter *t* word, 1836
6:11 let his house be made a dunghill for *t*. 1836
6:12 to destroy *t* house of God which is at 1791
6:13 Tatnai, governor on *t* side the river, NIH
6:15 *t* house was finished on the third day of 1836
6:16 kept the dedication of *t* house of God with 1836
6:17 offered at the dedication of *t* house of God 1836
7: 6 *T* Ezra went up from Babylon; and he was 1931
7:11 it is the copy of the letter that the king 2088
7:17 That thou mayest buy speedily with *t* 1836
7:24 or ministers of *t* house of God, 1836
7:27 which hath put such a thing as in *t* 2088
8: 1 *t* is the genealogy of them that went up NIH
8:23 So we fasted and besought our God for *t*: 2088
8:35 all *t* was a burnt offering unto the Lord. NIH
8:36 and to the governors on *t* side the river: NIH
9: 2 and rulers hath been chief in *t* trespass. 2088
9: 3 when I heard *t* thing, I rent my garment 2088
9: 7 we been in a great trespass unto *t* day; 2088
9: 7 and to confusion of face, as it is *t* day. 2088
9:10 O our God, what shall we say after *t*? 2088
9:13 and hast given us such deliverance as *t*; 2088
9:15 for we remain yet escaped, as it is *t* day: 2088
9:15 we cannot stand before thee because of *t*. 2088
10: 2 now there is hope in Israel concerning *t* 2088
10: 4 Arise; for *t* matter belongeth unto thee: NIH
10: 5 swear that they should do according to *t* 2088
10: 9 trembling because of *t* matter, and for 2088
10:13 neither is *t* a work of one day or two: NIH
10:13 we are many that have transgressed in *t* 2088
10:14 until the fierce wrath of our God for *t* 2088
10:15 of Tikvah were employed about *t* matter: 2088
Ne 1:11 thy servant *t* day, and grant him mercy in NIH
1:11 and grant him mercy in the sight of *t* man. 2088
2: 2 *t* is nothing else but sorrow of heart. 2088
2:18 they strengthened their hands for *t* good 2088
2:19 and said, What is *t* thing that ye do? 2088
3: 7 unto the throne of the governor on *t* side NIH
5:10 corn: I pray you, let us leave off *t* usury. 2088
5:11 Restore, I pray you, to them, even *t* day, NIH
5:12 they should do according to *t* promise. 2088
5:13 his labour, that performeth not *t* promise, 2088
5:13 the people did according to *t* promise. 2088
5:16 Yea also I continued in the work of *t* wall, 2088
5:18 yet for all *t* required not I the bread of 2088
5:18 the bondage was heavy upon *t* people. 2088
5:19 according to all that I have done for *t* 2088
6: 4 what they sent unto me four times after *t* 2088
6:12 he pronounced *t* prophecy against me: NIH
6:16 they perceived that *t* work was wrought 2088
7: 7 of the men of the people of Israel was *t* NIH
8: 9 *T* day is holy unto the Lord your God; NIH
8:10 for *t* day is holy unto our Lord: neither be NIH
9: 1 day of *t* month the children of Israel 2088
9:10 didst thou get thee a name, as it is *t* day. 2088
9:18 *T* is thy God that brought thee up out of 2088
9:32 the time of the kings of Assyria unto *t* 2088
9:36 we are servants *t* day, and for the land NIH
9:38 because of all *t* we make a sure covenant, 2088
13: 4 before I, Eliashib the priest, having 2088
13: 6 in all *t* time was not I at Jerusalem: for in 2088
13:14 concerning *t*, and wipe not out my good 2088
13:17 What evil thing is *t* that ye do, 2088
13:18 did not our God bring all *t* evil upon us, 2088
13:18 all this evil upon us, and upon *t* city? 2088
13:22 concerning *t* also, and spare me 2088
13:27 hearken unto you to do all *t* great evil, 2088
Est 1: 1 *t* is Ahasuerus which reigned, from India 1931
1:17 For *t* deed of the queen shall come abroad NIH
1:18 Media say *t* day unto all the king's NIH
4:14 if thou altogether holdest thy peace at *t* NIH
4:14 come to the kingdom for such a time as *t*? NIH
4:15 Esther bade them return Mordecai *t* NIH
5: 4 Haman come *t* day unto the banquet that NIH
5:13 Yet all *t* availeth me nothing, so long as I NIH
6: 3 dignity hath been done to Mordecai for *t*? NIH
6: 9 let *t* apparel and horse be delivered to NIH
7: 6 and enemy is *t* wicked Haman. 2088
9: 4 for *t* man Mordecai waxed greater and NIH
9:13 morrow also according unto *t* day's decree, NIH
9:21 To stablish *t* among them, that they should NIH
9:26 Therefore for all the words of *t* letter, 2088
9:26 of that which they had seen concerning *t* 3602
9:29 to confirm *t* second letter of Purim. 2088

Job 1: 3 that *t* man was the greatest of all the men 1931
1:22 In all *t* Job sinned not, nor charged God 2088
2:10 In all *t* did not Job sin with his lips. 2088
2:11 when Job's three friends heard of all *t* 2088
3: 1 After *t* opened Job his mouth, 3651
4: 6 Is not *t* thy fear, thy confidence, thy hope; NIH
5:27 Lo *t*, we have searched it, so it is; hear it, 2088
8:19 *t* is the joy of his way, and out of the earth 1931
9:22 *T* is one thing, therefore I said it, He 1931
10:13 in thine heart: I know that *t* is with thee. 2088
12: 9 that hand of the Lord hath wrought *t*? 2088
13: 1 mine eye hath seen all *t*, mine ear hath NIH
17: 8 Upright men shall be astonied at *t*, 2088
18:21 is the place of him that knoweth not 2088
19:26 after my skin worms destroy *t* body, 2088
20: 2 me to answer, and for *t* I make haste. NIH
20: 4 Knowest thou not *t* of old, since man was 2088
20:29 *T* is the portion of a wicked man from 2088
21: 2 my speech, and let *t* be your consolations. 2088
27:13 *T* is the portion of a wicked man with 2088
31:11 For *t* is a heinous crime; yea, it is an 1931
31:28 *T* also were an iniquity to be punished by 1931
33:12 in *t* thou art not just: I will answer 2088
34:16 If now thou hast understanding, hear *t*: 2088
35: 2 Thinkest thou *t* to be right, that thou 2088
36:21 *t* hast thou chosen rather than affliction. NIH
37: 1 At *t* also my heart trembleth, and is 2063
37:14 Hearken unto *t*, O Job: stand still, 2088
38: 2 Who is *t* that darkeneth counsel by words 2088
42:16 After *t* lived Job an hundred and 2088
Ps 2: 7 art my Son; *t* day have I begotten thee. NIH
7: 3 O Lord my God, if I have done *t*; 2088
11: 6 *t* shall be the portion of their cup. 2098
12: 7 shalt preserve them from *t* generation 2098
17:14 which have their portion in *t* life, 2088
18: T who spake unto the Lord the words of *t* 2088
22:31 that shall be born, that he hath done *t*. NIH
24: 6 *T* is the generation of them that seek him, 2088
24: 8 Who is *t* King of glory? The Lord strong 2088
24:10 Who is *t* King of glory? The Lord of 2088
27: 3 rise against me, in *t* will I be confident. 2088
32: 6 For *t* shall every one that is godly pray 2088
34: 6 *T* poor man cried, and the Lord heard 2088
35:22 *T* thou hast seen, O Lord: keep not NIH
41:11 By *t* I know that thou favourest me, 2088
44:17 All *t* is come upon us; yet have we not 2088
44:21 Shall not God search *t* out? for he 2088
48:14 For *t* God is our God for ever and ever: 2088
49: 1 Hear *t*, all ye people; give ear, all ye 2088
49:13 *T* their way is their folly: yet their 2088
50:22 Now consider *t*, ye that forget God, lest I 2088
51: 4 have I sinned, and done *t* evil in thy sight: NIH
52: 7 *t* is the man that made not God his NIH
56: 9 turn back: *t* I know; for God is for me. 2088
62:11 hath spoken once; twice have I heard *t*; 2098
68:16 *t* is the hill which God desireth to dwell in; NIH
69:31 *T* also shall please the Lord better than NIH
69:32 The humble shall see *t*, and be glad: NIH
71:18 until I have shewed thy strength unto *t* NIH
73:16 When I thought to know *t*, it was too 2088
74: 2 *t* mount Zion, wherein thou hast dwelt. 2088
74:18 Remember *t*, that the enemy hath 2088
77:10 I said, *T* is my infirmity: but I will 1931
78:21 Therefore the Lord heard *t*, NIH
78:32 For all *t* they sinned still, and believed not 2088
78:54 even to *t* mountain, which his right hand 2088
78:59 When God heard *t*, he was wroth, NIH
80:14 from heaven, and behold, and visit *t* vine; 2088
81: 4 For *t* was a statute for Israel, and a law of 1931
81: 5 The ordained in Joseph for a testimony, NIH
87: 4 with Ethiopia; *t* man was born there. 2088
87: 5 be said, *T*'s and that man was born in her: 376
87: 6 up the people, that *t* man was born there. 2088
92: 6 neither doth a fool understand *t*. 2088
95:10 Forty years long was I grieved with *t* NIH
102:18 *T* shall be written for the generation to 2088
104:25 So is *t* great and wide sea, wherein are 2088
109:20 Let *t* be the reward of mine adversaries 2088
109:27 That they may know that *t* is thy hand; 2088
113: 2 the name of the Lord from *t* time forth 6258
115:18 we will bless the Lord from *t* time forth 6258
118:20 *T* gate of the Lord, into which 2088
118:23 *T* is the Lord's doing; it is marvellous 2088
118:24 *T* is the day which the Lord hath made; 2088
119:50 *T* is my comfort in my affliction: for thy 2088
119:56 *T* I had, because I kept thy precepts. 2088
119:91 They continue *t* day according to thine NIH
121: 8 and thy coming in from *t* time forth, 6258
132:14 *T* is my rest for ever: here will I dwell; 2088
149: 9 *t* honour have all his saints. Praise ye 1931
Pr 6: 3 Do *t* now, my son, and deliver thyself, 2088
7:14 with me; *t* day have I payed my vows. NIH
22:19 I have made known to thee *t* day, even to NIH
Ecc 1:10 whereof it may be said, See, *t* is new? 2088
1:13 *t* sore travail hath God given to the sons 1931
1:17 I perceived that *t* also is vexation of spirit. 2088
2: 1 pleasure: and behold, *t* also is vanity. 1931
2:10 and *t* was my portion of all my labour. 2088
2:15 I said in my heart, that *t* also is vanity. 2088
2:19 wise under the sun. *T* is also vanity. 2088
2:21 *T* also is vanity and a great evil. 2088
2:23 not rest in the night. *T* is also vanity. 2088
2:24 *T* also I saw, that it was from the hand of 2090
2:26 *T* also is vanity and vexation of spirit. 2088
4: 4 for *t* a man is envied of his neighbour. 1931

Ecc	4: 4 **T** *is* also vanity and vexation of spirit.	2088
	4: 8 **T** *is* also vanity, yea, it *is* a sore travail.	2088
	4:16 Surely **t** also *is* vanity and vexation of	2088
	5:10 abundance *with* increase: **t** *is* also vanity.	2088
	5:16 **t** also *is* a sore evil, *that* in all points as he	2090
	5:19 rejoice in his labour; **t** *is* the gift of God.	2090
	6: 2 **t** *is* vanity, and it *is* an evil disease.	2088
	6: 5 nor known *any thing*: **t** hath more rest	2088
	6: 9 **t** *is* also vanity and vexation of spirit.	2088
	6:12 who knoweth what *is* good for man in **t**	NIH
	7: 6 *is* the laughter of the fool: **t** also *is* vanity.	2088
	7:10 thou dost not inquire wisely concerning **t.**	2088
	7:18 *is* good that thou shouldest take hold of **t;**	2088
	7:18 yea, also from **t** withdraw not thine hand:	2088
	7:23 All **t** have I proved by wisdom: I said,	2090
	7:27 Behold, **t** have I found, saith the Preacher,	2088
	7:29 Lo, **t** only have I found, that God hath	2088
	8: 9 All **t** have I seen, and applied my heart	2088
	8:10 where they had so done: **t** *is* also vanity.	2088
	8:14 the righteous: I said that **t** also *is* vanity.	2088
	9: 1 For all **t** I considered in my heart even to	2088
	9: 1 in my heart even to declare all **t,**	2088
	9: 3 **T** *is* an evil among all *things* that are	2088
	9: 9 for that *is* thy portion in **t** life, and in thy	NIH
	9:13 **T** wisdom have I seen also under the sun,	2090
	11: 6 either **t** or that, or whether they both	2088
	12:13 for **t** *is* the whole *duty of* man.	2088
SS	3: 6 Who *is* **t** that cometh out of the	2088
	5:16 **T** *is* my beloved, and this *is* my friend,	2088
	5:16 This *is* my beloved, and **t** *is* my friend,	2088
	7: 7 **T** thy stature is like to a palm tree,	2088
	8: 5 Who *is* **t** that cometh up from	2088
Isa	1:12 hath required **t** at your hand, to tread	2088
	3: 6 ruler, and *let* **t** ruin *be* under thy hand:	2088
	5:25 For all **t** his anger is not turned away,	2088
	6: 7 and said, Lo, **t** hath touched thy lips;	2088
	6: 9 he said, Go, and tell **t** people, Hear ye	2088
	6:10 Make the heart of **t** people fat,	2088
	8: 6 Forsomuch as **t** people refuseth the waters	2088
	8:11 *I* should not walk in the way of **t** people,	2088
	8:12 to all *them* to whom **t** people shall say,	2088
	8:20 if they speak not according to **t** word, *it is*	2088
	9: 5 but **t** shall be with burning *and* fuel of fire.	NIH
	9: 7 zeal of the LORD of hosts will perform **t.**	2088
	9:12 For all **t** his anger is not turned away,	2088
	9:16 For the leaders of **t** people cause *them* to	2088
	9:17 For all **t** his anger is not turned away,	2088
	9:21 For all **t** his anger is not turned away,	2088
	10: 4 For all **t** his anger is not turned away,	2088
	12: 5 things: **t** *is* known in all the earth.	2088
	14: 4 That thou shalt take up **t** proverb against	2088
	14:16 *Is* **t** the man that made the earth to	2088
	14:26 **T** *is* the purpose that is purposed upon	2088
	14:26 **t** *is* the hand that is stretched out upon	2088
	14:28 In the year that king Ahaz died was **t**	2088
	16:13 **T** *is* the word that the LORD hath spoken	2088
	17:14 **T** *is* the portion of them that spoil us,	2088
	20: 6 inhabitant of **t** isle shall say in that day,	2088
	22:14 Surely **t** iniquity shall not be purged from	2088
	22:15 Go, get thee unto **t** treasurer, *even* unto	2088
	23: 7 *Is* **t** your joyous *city,* whose antiquity *is* of	2088
	23: 8 Who hath taken **t** counsel against Tyre,	2088
	23:13 **t** people was not, *till* the Assyrian	2088
	24: 3 for the LORD hath spoken **t** word.	2088
	25: 6 in **t** mountain shall the LORD of hosts	2088
	25: 7 he will destroy in **t** mountain the face of	2088
	25: 9 shall be said in that day, Lo, **t** *is* our God;	2088
	25: 9 **t** *is* the LORD; we have waited for him,	2088
	25:10 For in **t** mountain shall the hand of	2088
	26: 1 In that day shall **t** song be sung in the	2088
	27: 9 By **t** therefore shall the iniquity of Jacob	2063
	27: 9 and **t** *is* all the fruit to take away his sin;	2088
	28:11 another tongue will he speak to **t** people.	2088
	28:12 **T** *is* the rest *wherewith* ye may cause	2088
	28:12 the weary to rest; and **t** *is* the refreshing:	2088
	28:14 that rule **t** people which *is* in Jerusalem.	2088
	28:29 **T** also cometh forth from the LORD of	2088
	29:11 that is learned, saying, Read **t,** I pray thee:	2088
	29:12 is not learned, saying, Read **t,** I pray thee:	2088
	29:13 Forasmuch as **t** people draw near *me* with	2088
	29:14 do a marvellous work amongst **t** people,	2088
	30: 7 therefore have I cried concerning **t,**	2063
	30: 9 **t** *is* a rebellious people, lying children,	1931
	30:12 Because ye despise **t** word, and trust in	2088
	30:13 Therefore **t** iniquity shall be to you as a	2088
	30:21 **T** *is* the way, walk ye in it, when ye	2088
	36: 4 confidence *is* **t** where*in* thou trustest?	2088
	36: 6 thou trustest in the staff of **t** broken reed,	2088
	36: 7 Ye shall worship before **t** altar?	2088
	36:10 The LORD against **t** land to destroy it?	2088
	36:10 Go up against **t** land, and destroy it.	2088
	36:15 **t** city shall not be delivered into the hand	2088
	37: 3 **T** day *is* a day of trouble, and of rebuke,	2088
	37:22 **T** *is* the word which the LORD hath	2088
	37:30 **t** *shall be* a sign unto thee, Ye shall eat	2088
	37:30 Ye shall eat **t** year such as groweth of itself;	NIH
	37:32 the zeal of the LORD of hosts shall do **t.**	2088
	37:33 He shall not come into **t** city, nor shoot an	2088
	37:34 shall not come into **t** city, saith the LORD.	2088
	37:35 For I will defend **t** city to save it for mine	2088
	38: 6 **t** city out of the hand of the king of	2088
	38: 6 king of Assyria: and I will defend **t** city.	2088
	38: 7 **t** *shall be* a sign unto thee from	2088
	38: 7 that the LORD will do **t** thing that he hath	2088
	38:19 living, he shall praise thee, as I *do* **t** day:	NIH

Isa	39: 6 fathers have laid up in store until **t** day,	2088
	41:20 that the hand of the LORD hath done **t,**	2088
	42:22 **t** *is* a people robbed and spoiled; *they are*	1931
	42:23 Who among you will give ear to **t?**	2088
	43: 9 who among them can declare **t,**	2088
	43:21 **T** people have I formed for myself;	2098
	45:21 who hath declared **t** from ancient time?	2088
	46: 8 Remember **t,** and shew yourselves men:	2088
	47: 8 Therefore hear now **t,** *thou that art* given	2088
	48: 1 Hear ye **t,** O house of Jacob, which are	2088
	48: 6 Thou hast heard, see all **t;** and will not	1886.3
	48: 6 shewed thee new *things* from **t** time,	6258
	48:16 Come ye near unto me, hear ye **t;** I have	2088
	48:20 with a voice of singing declare ye, tell **t,**	2088
	50:11 **T** shall ye have of mine hand; ye shall lie	2088
	51:21 Therefore hear now **t,** thou afflicted,	2088
	54: 9 For **t** *is* as the waters of Noah unto me:	2088
	54:17 **T** *is* the heritage of the servants of	2088
	56: 2 Blessed *is* the man *that* doeth **t,** and the	2088
	56:12 to morrow shall be as **t** day,	2088
	58: 4 ye shall not fast as *ye do* **t** day, to make	NIH
	58: 5 ashes *under him?* wilt thou call **t** a fast,	2088
	58: 6 *Is* not **t** the fast that I have chosen?	2088
	59:21 As for me, **t** *is* my covenant with them,	2088
	63: 1 Who *is* **t** *that* cometh from Edom,	2088
	63: 1 **t** *that is* glorious in his apparel, travelling	2088
	66: 2 to **t** *man* will I look, *even* to *him that is*	2088
	66:14 when ye see **t,** your heart shall rejoice,	NIH
Jer	1:10 I have **t** day set thee over the nations and	2088
	1:18 have made thee **t** day a defenced city,	NIH
	2:12 O ye heavens, at **t,** and be horribly afraid,	2088
	2:17 Hast thou not procured **t** unto thyself,	6258
	3: 4 Wilt thou not from **t** time cry unto me,	6258
	3:10 yet for all **t** her treacherous sister Judah	2088
	3:25 from our youth even unto **t** day,	2088
	4: 8 For **t** gird you with sackcloth, lament and	2088
	4:10 surely thou hast greatly deceived **t** people	2088
	4:11 At that time shall it be said to **t** people	2088
	4:18 **t** *is* thy wickedness, because *it is* bitter,	2088
	4:28 For **t** shall the earth mourn, and the	2088
	5: 7 How shall I pardon thee for **t?**	2063
	5: 9 soul be avenged on such a nation as **t?**	2088
	5:14 Because ye speak **t** word, behold, I will	2088
	5:14 **t** people wood, and it shall devour them.	2088
	5:20 Declare **t** in the house of Jacob,	2088
	5:21 Hear now **t,** O foolish people,	2088
	5:23 **t** people hath a revolting and a rebellious	2088
	5:29 my soul be avenged on such a nation as **t?**	2088
	6: 6 **t** *is* the city to be visited; she *is* wholly	1931
	6:19 behold, I will bring evil upon **t** people,	2088
	6:21 I will lay stumblingblocks before **t** people,	2088
	7: 2 proclaim there **t** word, and say, Hear	2088
	7: 3 and I will cause you to dwell in **t** place.	2088
	7: 6 and shed not innocent blood in **t** place,	2088
	7: 7 will I cause you to dwell in **t** place,	2088
	7:10 come and stand before me in **t** house,	2088
	7:11 Is **t** house, which is called by my name,	2088
	7:14 Therefore will I do unto **t** house, which is	NIH
	7:16 Therefore pray not thou for **t** people,	2088
	7:20 my fury *shall be* poured out upon **t** place,	2088
	7:23 **t** thing commanded I them, saying,	2088
	7:25 forth out of the land of Egypt unto **t** day,	2088
	7:28 **T** *is* a nation that obeyeth not the voice	2088
	7:33 the carcases of **t** people shall be meat for	2088
	8: 3 of them that remain of **t** evil family,	2088
	8: 5 is **t** people of Jerusalem slidden back *by* a	2088
	9: 9 my soul be avenged on such a nation as **t?**	2088
	9:12 *is* the wise man, that may understand **t?**	2088
	9:15 Behold, I *will* feed them, *even* **t** people,	2088
	9:24 let him that glorieth glory in **t,** that *he*	2088
	10:18 sling out the inhabitants of the land at **t**	2088
	10:19 said, Truly **t** *is* a grief, and I must bear it.	2088
	11: 2 Hear ye the words of **t** covenant,	2088
	11: 3 that obeyeth not the words of **t** covenant,	2088
	11: 5 with milk and honey, as *it is* **t** day.	2088
	11: 6 Hear ye the words of **t** covenant,	2088
	11: 7 unto **t** day, rising early and protesting,	2088
	11: 8 I will bring upon them all the words of **t**	2088
	11:14 Therefore pray not thou for **t** people,	2088
	13: 9 After **t** manner will I mar the pride of	3602
	13:10 **T** evil people, which refuse to hear my	2088
	13:10 to worship them, shall even be as **t** girdle,	2088
	13:12 Therefore thou shalt speak unto them **t**	2088
	13:13 I *will* fill all the inhabitants of **t** land,	2088
	13:25 **T** *is* thy lot, the portion of thy measures	2088
	14:10 Thus saith the LORD unto **t** people, Thus	2088
	14:11 Pray not for **t** people for *their* good.	2088
	14:13 I will give you assured peace in **t** place.	2088
	14:15 Sword and famine shall not be in **t** land;	2088
	14:17 thou shalt say **t** word unto them;	2088
	15: 1 my mind *could* not *be* toward **t** people:	2088
	15:20 I will make thee unto **t** people a fenced	2088
	16: 2 thou have sons nor daughters in **t** place.	2088
	16: 3 the daughters that are born in **t**	2088
	16: 3 their fathers that begat them in **t**	2088
	16: 5 for I have taken away my peace from **t**	2088
	16: 6 the great and the small shall die in **t** land:	2088
	16: 9 I will cause to cease out of **t** place in your	2088
	16:10 when thou shalt shew **t** people all these	2088
	16:10 hath the LORD pronounced all **t**	2088
	16:13 Therefore will I cast you out of **t** land into	2088
	16:21 I *will* once cause them to know,	2088
	17:24 bring in no burden through the gates of **t**	2088
	17:25 shall there enter into the gates of **t** city	2088
	17:25 and **t** city shall remain for ever.	2088

Jer	18: 6 of Israel, cannot I do with you as **t** potter?	2088
	19: 3 Behold, I *will* bring evil upon **t** place,	2088
	19: 4 have estranged **t** place, and have burnt	2088
	19: 4 have filled **t** place *with* the blood of	2088
	19: 6 **t** place shall no more be called Tophet,	2088
	19: 7 counsel of Judah and Jerusalem in **t** place;	2088
	19: 8 I will make **t** city desolate, and a hissing;	2088
	19:11 Even so will I break **t** people and this city,	2088
	19:11 Even so will I break this people and **t** city,	2088
	19:12 Thus will I do unto **t** place, saith	2088
	19:12 and *even* make **t** city as Tophet:	2088
	19:15 I will bring upon **t** city and upon all her	2088
	20: 5 I will deliver all the strength of **t**	2088
	21: 4 I will assemble them into the midst of **t**	2088
	21: 6 I will smite the inhabitants of **t** city, both	2088
	21: 7 as are left in **t** city from the pestilence,	2088
	21: 8 unto **t** people thou shalt say, Thus saith	2088
	21: 9 He that abideth in **t** city shall die by	2088
	21:10 For I have set my face against **t** city for	2088
	22: 1 the king of Judah, and speak there **t** word,	2088
	22: 3 neither shed innocent blood in **t** place.	2088
	22: 4 if ye do **t** thing indeed, then shall there	2088
	22: 4 shall there enter in by the gates of **t** house	2088
	22: 5 that **t** house shall become a desolation,	2088
	22: 8 many nations shall pass by **t** city,	2088
	22: 8 the LORD done thus unto **t** great city?	2088
	22:11 his father, which went forth out of **t** place;	2088
	22:12 him captive, and shall see **t** land no more.	2088
	22:16 *it was* well *with* him: *was* not **t** to know	1931
	22:21 **T** *hath been* thy manner from thy youth,	2088
	22:28 *Is* **t** man Coniah a despised broken idol?	2088
	22:30 saith the LORD, Write ye **t** man childless,	2088
	23: 6 **t** *is* his name whereby he shall be called,	2088
	23:26 How long shall **t** be in the heart of	NIH
	23:32 they shall not profit **t** people at all,	2088
	23:33 when **t** people, or the prophet, or a priest,	2088
	23:38 Because you say **t** word, The burden of	2088
	24: 5 whom I have sent out of **t** place *into*	2088
	24: 6 and I will bring them again to **t** land:	2088
	24: 8 that remain in **t** land, and them that dwell	2088
	25: 3 even unto **t** day, that *is* the three and	2088
	25: 9 will bring them against **t** land,	2088
	25:11 **t** whole land shall be a desolation,	2088
	25:13 *even* all that is written in **t** book, which	2088
	25:15 Take the wine cup of **t** fury at mine hand,	2088
	25:18 a hissing, and a curse; as *it is* **t** day;	2088
	26: 1 of Judah came **t** word from the LORD,	2088
	26: 6 will I make **t** house like Shiloh, and will	2088
	26: 6 will make **t** city a curse to all the nations	2088
	26: 9 **T** house shall be like Shiloh, and this city	2088
	26: 9 **t** city shall be desolate without an	2088
	26:11 people, saying, **T** man *is* worthy to die;	2088
	26:11 for he hath prophesied against **t** city, as ye	2088
	26:12 The LORD sent me to prophesy against **t**	2088
	26:12 against **t** city all the words that ye have	2088
	26:15 upon **t** city, and upon the inhabitants	2088
	26:16 the prophets; **T** man *is* not worthy to die:	2088
	26:20 who prophesied against **t** city and	2088
	26:20 against **t** land according to all the words	2088
	27: 1 **t** word unto Jeremiah from the LORD,	2088
	27:16 I spake to the priests and to all **t** people,	2088
	27:17 wherefore should **t** city be laid waste?	2088
	27:19 residue of the vessels that remain in **t** city,	2088
	27:22 them up, and restore them to **t** place.	2088
	28: 3 two full years *will* I bring again into **t**	2088
	28: 3 king of Babylon took away from **t** place,	2088
	28: 4 I *will* bring again to **t** place Jeconiah	2088
	28: 6 away captive, from Babylon into **t** place.	2088
	28: 7 Nevertheless hear thou now **t** word that I	2088
	28:15 but thou makest **t** people to trust in a lie.	2088
	28:16 **t** year thou *shalt* die, because thou hast	NIH
	29:10 in causing you to return to **t** place.	2088
	29:16 of all the people that dwelleth in **t** city,	2088
	29:28 us *in* Babylon, saying, **T** *captivity* is long:	1931
	29:29 Zephaniah the priest read **t** letter in the	2088
	29:32 he shall not have a man to dwell among **t**	2088
	30:17 called thee an Outcast, *saying,* **T** *is* Zion,	1931
	30:21 for who *is* **t** that engaged his heart to	1931
	31:23 As yet they shall use **t** speech in the land	2088
	31:26 Upon **t** I awaked, and beheld; and my	2088
	31:33 **t** *shall be* the covenant that I will make	2088
	32: 3 I *will* give **t** city into the hand of the king	2088
	32: 8 I knew that **t** *was* the word of the LORD.	1931
	32:14 evidence of the purchase, both which is	2088
	32:14 is sealed, and **t** evidence which is open;	2088
	32:15 vineyards shall be possessed again in **t**	2088
	32:20 *even* unto **t** day, and in Israel,	2088
	32:20 and hast made thee a name, as *at* **t** day;	2088
	32:22 hast given them **t** land, which thou didst	2088
	32:23 thou hast caused all **t** evil to come upon	2088
	32:28 I *will* give **t** city into the hand of	2088
	32:29 that fight against **t** city, shall come and	2088
	32:29 come and set fire on **t** city, and burn it	2088
	32:31 **t** city hath been to me *as* a provocation	2088
	32:31 the day that they built it even unto **t** day;	2088
	32:35 *they* should do **t** abomination, to cause	2088
	32:36 Israel, concerning **t** city, whereof ye say,	2088
	32:37 I will bring them again unto **t** place,	2088
	32:41 I will plant them in **t** land assuredly with	2088
	32:42 Like as I have brought all **t** great evil	2088
	32:42 brought all this great evil upon **t** people,	2088
	32:43 fields shall be bought in **t** land, whereof	2088
	33: 4 concerning the houses of **t** city,	2088
	33: 5 I have hid my face from **t** city.	2088
	33:10 Again there shall be heard in **t** place,	2088

T

T

Jer	33:12 Again in t place, *which is* desolate	2088
	33:16 t *is the name* wherewith she shall be	2088
	33:24 Considerest thou not what t people have	2088
	34: 2 I *will* give t city into the hand of the king	2088
	34: 8 *T is* the word that came unto Jeremiah	NIH
	34:22 and cause them to return to t city;	2088
	35:14 for unto t day they drink none,	2088
	35:16 but t people hath not hearkened unto me:	2088
	36: 1 that t word came unto Jeremiah from	2088
	36: 2 from the days of Josiah, even unto t day.	2088
	36: 7 LORD hath pronounced against t people.	2088
	36:29 Thou hast burnt t roll, saying, Why hast	2088
	36:29 shall certainly come and destroy t land,	2088
	37: 8 fight against t city, and take it, and burn it	2088
	37:10 man in his tent, and burn t city with fire.	2088
	37:18 against thy servants, or against t people,	2088
	37:19 not come against you, nor against t land?	2088
	38: 2 He that remaineth in t city shall die by	2088
	38: 3 T city shall surely be given into the hand	2088
	38: 4 beseech thee, let t man be put to death:	2088
	38: 4 of the men of war that remain in t city,	2088
	38: 4 for t man seeketh not the welfare of this	2088
	38: 4 for this man seeketh not the welfare of t	2088
	38:16 As the LORD liveth, that made us t soul,	2088
	38:17 and t city shall not be burnt with fire;	2088
	38:18 shall t city be given into the hand of	2088
	38:21 t *is* the word that the LORD hath shewed	2088
	38:23 shalt cause t city to be burnt with fire.	2088
	39:16 I *will* bring my words upon t city for evil,	2088
	40: 2 The LORD thy God hath pronounced t	2088
	40: 2 hath pronounced this evil upon t place.	2088
	40: 3 therefore t thing is come upon you.	2088
	40: 4 I loose thee t day from the chains which	NIH
	40:16 son of Kareah, Thou shalt not do t thing:	2088
	42: 2 LORD thy God, *even* for all t remnant;	2088
	42:10 If ye will still abide in t land, then will I	2088
	42:13 if ye say, We will not dwell in t land,	2088
	42:18 and ye shall see t place no more.	2088
	42:19 certainly that I have admonished you t	NIH
	42:21 And *now* I have t day declared *it* to you;	NIH
	44: 2 t day they *are* a desolation, and no man	2088
	44: 4 Oh, do not t abominable thing that I hate.	2088
	44: 6 they are wasted *and* desolate, as *at* t day.	2088
	44: 7 Wherefore commit ye t great evil against	NIH
	44:10 They are not humbled *even* unto t day,	2088
	44:22 curse, without an inhabitant, as *at* t day.	2088
	44:23 therefore t evil is happened unto you,	2088
	44:23 evil is happened unto you, as *at* t day.	2088
	44:29 t *shall be* a sign unto you, saith	2088
	44:29 that I will punish you in t place,	2088
	45: 4 I *will* pluck up, even t whole land.	1931
	46: 7 Who *is* t *that* cometh up as a flood,	2088
	46:10 For t *is* the day of the Lord GOD of hosts,	1931
	50:17 last t Nebuchadrezzar king of Babylon	2088
	50:25 for t *is* the work of the Lord GOD of hosts	1931
	51: 6 for t *is* the time of the LORD's	1931
	51:59 And t Seraiah *was* a quiet prince.	NIH
	51:62 thou hast spoken against t place,	2088
	51:63 when thou hast made an end of reading t	2088
	52:28 T *is* the people whom Nebuchadrezzar	2088
La	2:15 saying, *Is* t the city that *men* call The	2088
	2:16 certainly t *is* the day that we looked for;	2088
	2:20 and consider to whom thou hast done t.	3541
	3:21 T I recall to my mind, therefore have I	2088
	5:17 For t our heart is faint; for these *things*	2088
Eze	1: 5 t *was* their appearance; they had	2088
	1:23 which covered on t side, and every one	2007
	1:28 T *was* the appearance of the likeness of	1931
	2: 3 against me, *even* unto t very day.	2088
	3: 1 eat t roll, and go speak unto the house of	2088
	3: 3 fill thy bowels with t roll that I give thee.	2088
	4: 3 T *shall be* a sign to the house of Israel.	1931
	5: 5 Thus saith the Lord GOD; T *is* Jerusalem:	2088
	6:10 I have not said in vain that I *would* do t	2088
	8: 5 at the gate of the altar t image of	2088
	8:15 unto me, Hast thou seen t, O son of man?	NIH
	8:17 unto me, Hast thou seen t, O son of man?	NIH
	10:15 T *is* the living creature that I saw by	1931
	10:20 T *is* the living creature that I saw under	1931
	11: 2 give wicked counsel in t city:	2088
	11: 3 t *city* is the caldron, and we *be* the flesh.	1931
	11: 6 Ye have multiplied your slain in t city,	2088
	11: 7 *are* the flesh, and t *city* is the caldron:	1931
	11:11 T *city* shall not be your caldron,	1931
	11:15 unto us is t land given in possession.	1931
	12:10 T burden *concerneth* the prince in	2088
	12:23 I will make t proverb to cease,	2088
	16:20 *Is* t of thy whoredoms a small matter,	NIH
	16:43 shalt not commit t lewdness above all	NIH
	16:44 every one that useth proverbs shall use t	NIH
	16:49 t was the iniquity of thy sister Sodom,	2088
	17: 7 t vine did bend her roots toward him,	2088
	18: 2 ye use t proverb concerning the land of	2088
	18: 2 Hath t have *occasion* any more to use t	2088
	19:14 T *is* a lamentation, and shall be for a	1931
	20:27 in t your fathers have blasphemed me,	2088
	20:29 the name thereof is called Bamah unto t	NIH
	20:31 with all your idols, *even* unto t day:	NIH
	21:11 t sword is sharpened, and it *is* furbished,	1931
	21:26 t *shall* not be the same: exalt *him that is*	2063
	23:11 when her sister Aholibah saw t, she was	NIH
	23:38 Moreover t they have done unto me:	2088
	24: 2 the name of the day, *even* of t same day:	2088
	24: 2 set himself against Jerusalem t same day.	2088
	24:24 when t cometh, ye shall know that I *am*	1886.3

Eze	31:18 T *is* Pharaoh and all his multitude, saith	1931
	32:16 T *is* the lamentation wherewith they shall	1931
	33:33 when t cometh to pass, (lo, it will come)	1886.3
	36:22 I do not t for your sakes, O house of Israel,	NIH
	36:32 Not for your sakes do I t, saith the Lord	NIH
	36:35 T land that was desolate is become like	1977
	36:37 I will yet for t be inquired of by the house	2088
	39: 8 t *is* the day whereof I have spoken.	1931
	40:10 of the gate eastward *were* three on t side,	6311
	40:10 the posts had one measure on t side and	6311
	40:12 little chambers *was* one cubit on t side,	NIH
	40:12 little chambers *were* six cubits on t side,	6311
	40:21 chambers thereof *were* three on t side	6311
	40:26 one on t side, and another on that side,	6311
	40:34 posts thereof, on t side, and on that side:	6311
	40:37 posts thereof, on t side, and on that side:	6311
	40:39 of the gate *were* two tables on t side,	6311
	40:41 Four tables *were* on t side, and four	6311
	40:45 he said unto me, T chamber,	2090
	40:48 five cubits on t side, and five cubits on	6311
	40:48 of the gate *was* three cubits on t side,	6311
	40:49 one on t side, and another on that side.	6311
	41: 4 he said unto me, T *is* the most holy *place.*	2088
	41:22 T *is* the table that *is* before the LORD.	2088
	43:12 T *is* the law of the house; Upon the top of	2088
	43:12 Behold, t *is* the law of the house.	2088
	43:13 and t *shall* be the higher place of the altar.	2088
	44: 2 T gate shall be shut, it shall not be	2088
	45: 1 T *shall* be holy in all the borders thereof	1931
	45: 2 Of there shall be for the sanctuary five	2088
	45: 3 t measure shalt thou measure the length	2088
	45:13 T *is* the oblation that ye shall offer;	2088
	45:16 All the people of the land shall give t	2088
	46: 3 of t gate before the LORD in the sabbaths	1931
	46:20 T *is* the place where the priests shall boil	2088
	47: 6 hast thou seen t? Then he brought me,	NIH
	47:12 on t side and on that side, shall grow all	2088
	47:13 T *shall* be the border, whereby ye shall	1454
	47:14 t land shall fall unto you for inheritance.	2088
	47:15 t *shall* be the border of the land toward	2088
	47:17 border of Hamath. And t *is* the north side.	NIH
	47:18 unto the east sea. And t *is* the east side.	NIH
	47:19 And t *is* the south side southward.	NIH
	47:20 over against Hamath. T *is* the west side.	NIH
	47:21 So shall ye divide t land unto you	2088
	48:10 for the priests, shall *be* t holy oblation;	NIH
	48:12 t oblation of the land that is offered shall	NIH
	48:29 T *is* the land which ye shall divide *by lot*	2088
Da	1:14 So he consented to them in t matter,	2088
	2:12 For t cause the king was 1836+3600+6903	
	2:18 of the God of heaven concerning t secret;	1836
	2:30 t secret *is* not revealed to me for *any*	1836
	2:31 T great image, whose brightness *was*	1797
	2:32 T image's head *was* of fine gold, his breast	0.2
	2:36 T *is* the dream; and we will tell	1836
	2:38 over them all. Thou *art* t head of gold.	1932
	2:47 seeing thou couldest reveal t secret.	1836
	3:16 we *are* not careful to answer thee in t	1836
	3:29 is no other God that can deliver after t	1836
	4:17 T matter *is* by the decree of the watchers,	NIH
	4:18 T dream I king Nebuchadnezzar have	1836
	4:24 T *is* the interpretation, O king, and this *is*	1836
	4:24 and t *is* the decree of the most High,	1932
	4:28 All t came upon the king Nebuchadnezzar.	0.2
	4:30 spake, and said, *Is* not t great Babylon,	1668
	5: 7 Whosoever shall read t writing,	1836
	5:15 that they should read t writing,	1836
	5:22 thine heart, though thou knewest all t;	1836
	5:24 sent from him; and t writing *was* written.	1836
	5:25 t *is* the writing that *was* written, MENE,	1836
	5:26 T *is* the interpretation of the thing:	1836
	6: 3 t Daniel was preferred above the	1836
	6: 5 We shall not find any occasion against t	1836
	6:28 So t Daniel prospered in the reign of	1836
	7: 6 After t I beheld, and lo another, like a	1836
	7: 7 After t I saw in the night visions,	1836
	7: 8 in t horn *were* eyes like the eyes of man,	1668
	7:16 stood *by*, and asked him the truth of all t.	1836
	7:24 the ten horns out of t kingdom *are* ten	1886.7
	8:16 make t man to understand the vision.	1975
	9: 7 but unto us confusion of faces, as *at* t day;	2088
	9:13 law of Moses, all t evil is come upon us:	2088
	9:15 and hast gotten thee renown, as *at* t day;	2088
	10: 8 saw t great vision, and there remained no	2088
	10:11 when he had spoken t word unto me,	2088
	10:17 For how can the servant of t my lord talk	2088
	10:17 servant of this my lord talk with t my lord?	2088
	11:18 After t shall he turn his face unto	2050.1
	12: 5 the one on t side of the bank of the river,	2008
Hos	5: 1 Hear ye t, O priests; and hearken,	2088
	7:10 LORD their God, nor seek him for all t.	2088
	7:16 t *shall* be their derision in the land of	2097
Joel	1: 2 Hear t, ye old men, and give ear, all ye	2088
	1: 2 Hath t been in your days, or even in	2088
	3: 9 Proclaim ye t among the Gentiles;	2088
Am	3: 1 Hear t word that the LORD hath spoken	2088
	4: 1 Hear t word, ye kine of Bashan, that *are*	2088
	4: 5 for t liketh you, O ye children of Israel,	3651
	4:12 because I will do t unto thee, prepare to	2088
	5: 1 Hear ye t word which I take up against	2088
	7: 3 The LORD repented for t: It shall not be,	2088
	7: 6 The LORD repented for t: This also shall	2088
	7: 6 T also shall not be, saith the Lord GOD.	1931
	8: 4 Hear t, O ye that swallow up the needy,	2088
	8: 8 Shall not the land tremble for t,	2088

Am	9:12 by my name, saith the LORD that doeth t.	2088
Ob	1:20 the captivity of t host of the children of	2088
Jnh	1: 7 we may know for whose cause t evil *is*	2088
	1: 8 thee, for whose cause t evil *is* upon us;	2088
	1:10 said unto him, Why hast thou done t?	2088
	1:12 I know that for my sake t great tempest	2088
	1:14 let us not perish for t man's life, and lay	2088
	4: 2 pray thee, O LORD, *was* not t my saying,	2088
Mic	1: 5 For the transgression of Jacob *is* all t,	2088
	2: 3 against t family do I devise an evil,	2088
	2: 3 shall ye go haughtily: for t time *is* evil.	1931
	2:10 Arise ye, and depart; for t *is* not your rest:	2088
	2:11 he shall even be the prophet of t people.	2088
	5: 5 T *man* shall be the peace, when the	2088
	5: 5 t hath power into his god.	2098
Hab	1:11 *imputing* this his power into his god.	2098
Zep	1: 4 I will cut off the remnant of Baal from t	2088
	2:10 T shall they have for their pride, because	2088
	2:15 T *is* the rejoicing city that dwelt carelessly,	2088
Hag	1: 2 T people say, The time is not come,	2088
	1: 4 your cieled houses, and t house *lie* waste?	2088
	2: 3 Who *is* left among you that saw t house	2088
	2: 7 I will fill t house *with* glory, saith	2088
	2: 9 The glory of t latter house shall be greater	2088
	2: 9 in t place will I give peace, saith	2088
	2:14 So *is* t people, and so *is* this nation before	2088
	2:14 this people, and so *is* t nation before me,	2088
	2:15 you, consider from t day and upward,	2088
	2:18 Consider now from t day and upward,	2088
	2:19 brought forth: from t day will I bless *you.*	2088
Zec	2: 4 Run, speak to t young man, saying,	1975
	3: 2 *is* not t a brand pluckt out of the fire?	2088
	4: 6 T *is* the word of the LORD unto	2088
	4: 9 have laid the foundation of t house;	2088
	5: 3 T *is* the curse that goeth forth over the	2088
	5: 3 be cut off as on t side according to it;	2088
	5: 3 and see what *is* t that goeth forth.	2088
	5: 6 he said, T *is* an ephah that goeth forth.	2088
	5: 7 t *is* their resemblance through all the	2088
	5: 7 t *is* a woman that sitteth in the midst of	2088
	5: 8 said, T *is* wickedness. And he cast it into	2088
	6:15 t shall come to pass, if ye will diligently	NIH
	8: 6 of the remnant of t people in these days,	2088
	8:11 now I *will* not *be* unto the residue of t	2088
	8:12 I will cause the remnant of t people to	2088
	14:12 t shall be the plague wherewith the LORD	2088
	14:15 that shall be in these tents, as t plague.	2088
	14:19 T shall be the punishment of Egypt,	2088
Mal	1: 9 t hath been by your means: will he regard	2088
	1:13 should I accept t of your hand? saith	1886.3
	2: 1 O ye priests, t commandment *is* for you.	2088
	2: 4 ye shall know that I have sent t	2088
	2:12 LORD will cut off the man that doth t,	5089.1
	2:13 t have ye done again, covering the altar	2088
	3: 7 *have* robbed me, *even* t whole nation.	1886.1
	4: 3 that I *shall* do t, saith the LORD of hosts.	NIH
Mt	1:18 the birth of Jesus Christ was on t wise:	3779
	1:22 Now all t was done, that it might be	3778
	3: 3 For t is he that was spoken of by	3778
	3:17 T is my beloved Son, in whom I am	3778
	6: 9 **After t manner** therefore pray ye:	3779
	6:11 Give us t day our daily bread.	4594
	7:12 to them: for t is the law and the prophets.	3778
	8: 9 and I say to t man, Go, and he goeth;	3778
	8: 9 and to my servant, Do t, and he doeth *it.*	3778
	8:27 What manner of man is t, that even	3778
	9: 3 within themselves, T man blasphemeth.	3778
	9:28 Believe ye that I am able to do t?	3778
	10:23 But when they persecute you in t city,	3778
	11:10 For t is *he,* of whom it is written, Behold,	3778
	11:14 And if ye will receive *it,* t is Elias,	846
	11:16 But whereunto shall I liken t generation?	3778
	11:23 it would have remained until t day.	4594
	12: 6 That in t place is *one* greater than	5602
	12: 7 if ye had known what t meaneth, I will	NIG
	12:23 and said, Is t the son of David?	3778
	12:24 T fellow doth not cast out devils, but by	3778
	12:32 not be forgiven him, neither in t world,	3778
	12:41 shall rise in judgment with t generation,	3778
	12:42 rise up in the judgment with t generation,	3778
	12:45 shall it be also unto t wicked generation.	3778
	13:15 For t people's heart is waxed gross,	3778
	13:19 t is he which received seed by the way	3778
	13:22 and the care of t world,	3778
	13:28 said unto them, An enemy hath done t.	3778
	13:40 fire; so shall it be in the end of t world.	3778
	13:54 Whence hath t man this wisdom,	3778
	13:54 Whence hath this man t wisdom,	3778
	13:55 Is not t the carpenter's son? is not his	3778
	13:56 Whence then hath t man all these *things?*	3778
	14: 2 unto his servants, T is John the Baptist;	3778
	14:15 T is a desert place, and the time is now	NIG
	15: 8 T people draweth nigh unto me with their	3778
	15:11 out of the mouth, t defileth a man.	3778
	15:12 were offended, after they heard t saying?	NIG
	15:15 said unto him, Declare unto us t parable.	3778
	16:18 and upon t rock I will build my church;	3778
	16:22 from thee, Lord: t shall not be unto thee.	3778
	17: 5 said, T is my beloved Son, in whom	3778
	17:20 ye shall say unto t mountain,	3778
	17:21 Howbeit t kind goeth not out but by	3778
	18: 4 shall humble himself as t little child,	3778
	19: 5 For t cause shall a man leave	1752+3778
	19:11 them, All *men* cannot receive t saying,	3778
	19:26 said unto them, With men t is unpossible;	3778

Mt	20:14	I will give unto t last, even as unto thee.	3778

Mt
20:14 I will give unto t last, even as unto thee. 3778
21: 4 All t was done, that it might be fulfilled 3778
21:10 all the city was moved, saying, Who is t? 3778
21:11 T is Jesus the prophet of Nazareth of 3778
21:21 ye shall not only do t which is done to 3588
21:21 but also if ye shall say unto t mountain, 3778
21:23 and gave thee t authority? 3778
21:38 they said among themselves, T is the heir; 3778
21:42 t is the Lord's doing, and it is marvellous 3778
21:44 whosoever shall fall on t stone shall be 3778
22:20 Whose is t image and superscription? 3778
22:33 when the multitude heard t, they were NIG
22:38 T is the first and great commandment. 3778
23:36 All these things shall come upon t 3778
24:14 And t gospel of the kingdom shall be 3778
24:21 beginning of the world to t time, 3568+3588
24:34 say unto you, T generation shall not pass, 3778
24:43 But know t, that if the goodman of 1565
26: 8 saying, To what purpose is t waste? 3778
26: 9 For t ointment might have been sold for 3778
26:12 For in that she hath poured t ointment on 3778
26:13 Wheresoever t gospel shall be preached in 3778
26:13 there shall also t, that this woman hath NIG
26:13 there shall also this, that t woman hath 3778
26:26 and said, Take, eat; t is my body. 3778
26:28 For t is my blood of the new testament, 3778
26:29 I will not drink henceforth of t fruit of 3778
26:31 shall be offended because of me t night: 3778
26:34 That t night, before the cock crow, 3778
26:39 if it be possible, let t cup pass from me: 3778
26:42 if t cup may not pass away from me, 3778
26:56 But all t was done, that the scriptures of 3778
26:61 And said, T fellow said, I am able to 3778
26:71 T fellow was also with Jesus of Nazareth. 3778
27: 8 called, The field of blood, unto t day. 4594
27:19 suffered many things t day in a dream 4594
27:24 am innocent of the blood of t just person: 3778
27:37 T IS JESUS THE KING OF THE JEWS. 3778
27:47 heard that, said, T man calleth for Elias. 3778
27:54 saying, Truly t was the Son of God. 3778
28:14 And if t come to the governor's ears, 3778
28:15 t saying is commonly reported among 3778
28:15 reported among the Jews until t day. 4594

Mk
1:27 themselves, saying, What thing is t? 3778
1:27 what new doctrine is t? for with authority 3778
2: 7 Why doth t man thus speak blasphemies? 3778
2:12 saying, We never saw it on t fashion. 3779
4:13 said unto them, Know ye not t parable? 3778
4:19 And the cares of t world, 3778
4:41 What manner of man is t, that even 3778
5:32 about to see her that had done t thing. 3778
5:39 them, Why make ye t ado, and weep? NIG
6: 2 From whence hath t man these things? 3778
6: 2 wisdom is t which is given unto him, NIG
6: 3 Is not t the carpenter, the son of Mary, 3778
6:35 T is a desert place, and now the time is far NIG
7: 6 T people honoureth me with their lips, 3778
7:29 he said unto her, For t saying go thy way; 3778
8:12 Why doth t generation seek after a sign? 3778
8:12 There shall no sign be given unto t 3778
8:38 and of my words in t adulterous and 3778
9: 7 of the cloud, saying, T is my beloved Son: 3778
9:21 How long is it ago since t came unto him? 3778
9:29 T kind can come forth by nothing, but by 3778
10: 5 of your heart he wrote you t precept. 3778
10: 7 For t cause shall a man leave his 1752+3778
10:30 he shall receive an hundredfold now in t 3778
11: 3 if any man say unto you, Why do ye t? 3778
11:23 whosoever shall say unto t mountain, 3778
11:28 who gave thee t authority to do these 3778
12: 7 said amongst themselves, T is the heir; 3778
12:10 have ye not read t scripture; The stone 3778
12:11 T was the Lord's doing, and it is 3778
12:16 Whose is t image and superscription? 3778
12:30 thy strength: t is the first commandment. 3778
12:31 And the second is like, namely t, 3778
12:43 That t poor widow hath cast more in, 3778
13:19 which God created unto t time, 3568+3588
13:30 unto you, that t generation shall not pass, 3778
14: 4 Why was t waste of the ointment made? 3778
14: 9 Wheresoever t gospel shall be preached 3778
14: 9 t also that she hath done shall be spoken NIG
14:22 to them, and said, Take, eat: t is my body. 3778
14:24 T is my blood of the new testament, 3778
14:27 shall be offended because of me t night: 3778
14:30 unto thee, That t day, even in this night, 4594
14:30 unto thee, That this day, even in t night, 3778
14:36 unto thee; take away t cup from me: 3778
14:58 I will destroy t temple that is made with 3778
14:69 to them that stood by, T is one of them. 3778
14:71 saying, I know not t man of whom ye 3778
15:39 he said, Truly t man was the Son of God. 3778

Lk
1:18 unto the angel, Whereby shall I know t? 3778
1:29 what manner of salutation t should be. 3778
1:34 How shall t be, seeing I know not a man? 3778
1:36 and t is the sixth month with her, who 3778
1:43 And whence is t to me, that the mother 3778
1:61 of thy kindred that is called by t name. 3778
1:66 saying, What manner of child shall t be! 3778
2: 2 (And t taxing was first made when 3778
2:11 For unto you is born t day in the city of 4594
2:12 And t shall be a sign unto you; Ye shall 3778
2:15 and see t thing which is come to pass, 3778
2:17 which was told them concerning t child. 3778
2:34 t child is set for the fall and rising again of 3778

Lk
3:20 Added yet t above all, that he shut up 3778
4: 3 command t stone that it be made bread. 3778
4: 6 All t power will I give thee, and the glory 3778
4:21 T day is this scripture fulfilled in your 4594
4:21 This day is t scripture fulfilled in your 3778
4:22 And they said, Is not t Joseph's son? 3778
4:23 Ye will surely say unto me t proverb, 3778
4:36 saying, What a word is t! 3778
5: 6 And when they had t done, they inclosed 3778
5:21 Who is t which speaketh blasphemies? 3778
6: 3 Have ye not read so much as t, what 3778
7: 4 he was worthy for whom he should do t: 3778
7: 8 and to my servant, Do t, and he doeth it. 3778
7:17 t rumour of him went forth throughout 3778
7:27 T is he, of whom it is written, Behold, 3778
7:31 then shall I liken the men of t generation? 3778
7:39 saying, T man, if he were a prophet, 3778
7:39 what manner of woman t is that toucheth NIG
7:44 said unto Simon, Seest thou t woman? 3778
7:45 t woman since the time I came in hath 3778
7:46 t woman hath anointed my feet with 3778
7:49 Who is t that forgiveth sins also? 3778
8: 9 saying, What might t parable be? 3778
8:11 the parable is t: The seed is the word 3778
8:14 cares and riches and pleasures of t life, NIG
8:25 one to another, What manner of man is t? 3778
9: 9 but who is t, of whom I hear such things? 3778
9:13 should go and buy meat for all t people. 3778
9:35 of the cloud, saying, T is my beloved Son: 3778
9:45 But they understood not t saying, 3778
9:48 Whosoever shall receive t child in my 3778
9:54 disciples James and John saw t, they said, NIG
10: 5 ye enter, first say, Peace be to t house. 3778
10:11 notwithstanding be ye sure of t, that 3778
10:20 Notwithstanding in t rejoice not, that 3778
10:28 answered right: t do, and thou shalt live. 3778
11:29 he began to say, T is an evil generation: 3778
11:30 shall also the Son of man be to t 3778
11:31 judgment with the men of t generation, 3778
11:32 rise up in the judgment with t generation, 3778
11:50 world, may be required of t generation; 3778
11:51 It shall be required of t generation. 3778
12:18 And said, T will I do: I will pull down 3778
12:20 t night thy soul shall be required of thee: 3778
12:39 And t know, that if the goodman of 3778
12:41 speakest thou t parable unto us, or even 3778
12:56 how is it that ye do not discern t time? 3778
13: 6 He spake also t parable; A certain man 3778
13: 7 these three years I come seeking fruit on t 3778
13: 8 Lord, let it alone t year also, till I shall dig 3778
13:16 And ought not t woman, being a daughter 3778
13:16 loosed from t bond on the sabbath day? 3778
14: 9 and say to thee, Give t man place; 3778
14:30 T man began to build, and was not able to 3778
15: 2 T man receiveth sinners, and eateth with 3778
15: 3 And he spake t parable unto them, saying, 3778
15:24 For t my son was dead, and is alive again; 3778
15:30 But as soon as t thy son was come, 3778
15:32 for t thy brother was dead, and is alive 3778
16: 2 unto him, How is it that I hear t of thee? 3778
16: 8 for the children of t world are in their 3778
16:24 my tongue; for I am tormented in t flame. 3778
16:26 besides all t, between us and you there 3778
16:28 they also come into t place of torment. 3778
17: 6 might say unto t sycamine tree, Be thou 3778
17:18 to give glory to God, save t stranger. 3778
17:25 and be rejected of t generation. 3778
18: 1 he spake a parable unto them to t end, NIG
18: 5 Yet because t widow troubleth me, I will 3778
18: 9 And he spake t parable unto certain which 3778
18:11 unjust, adulterers, or even as t publican. 3778
18:14 t man went down to his house justified 3778
18:23 And when he heard t, he was very 3778
18:30 Who shall not receive manifold more in t 3778
18:34 and t saying was hid from them, 3778
19: 9 T day is salvation come to this house, 4594
19: 9 This day is salvation come to t house, 3778
19:14 We will not have t man to reign over us. 3778
19:42 even thou, at least in t thy day, 3778
20: 2 or who is t that gave thee t authority? 3778
20: 9 Then began he to speak to the people t 3778
20:14 among themselves, saying, T is the heir: 3778
20:17 and said, What is t then that is written, 3778
20:19 for they perceived that he had spoken t 3778
20:34 The children of t world marry, 3778
21: 3 that t poor widow hath cast in more than 3778
21:23 in the land, and wrath upon t people. 3778
21:32 T generation shall not pass away, till all 3778
21:34 and cares of t life, and so that day come NIG
22:15 desire I have desired to eat t passover 3778
22:17 Take t, and divide it among yourselves: 3778
22:19 T is my body which is given for you: 3778
22:19 for you: t do in remembrance of me. 3778
22:20 T cup is the new testament in my blood, 3778
22:23 which of them it was that should do t 3778
22:34 Peter, the cock shall not crow t day, 4594
22:37 that t that is written must yet be 3778
22:42 if thou be willing, remove t cup from me: 3778
22:53 but t is your hour, and the power of 3778
22:56 and said, T man was also with him. 3778
22:59 Of a truth t fellow also was with him: 3778
23: 2 We found t fellow perverting the nation, 3778
23: 4 to the people, I find no fault in t man. 3778
23: 5 beginning from Galilee to t place. 5602
23:14 them, Ye have brought t man unto me, 3778

Lk
23:14 found no fault in t man touching those 3778
23:18 Away with t man, and release unto us 3778
23:38 Hebrew, T IS THE KING OF THE JEWS. 3778
23:41 but t man hath done nothing amiss. 3778
23:47 saying, Certainly t was a righteous man. 3778
23:52 T man went unto Pilate, and begged 3778
24:21 beside all t, to day is the third day since 3778
Jn
1:15 cried, saying, T was he of whom I spake, 3778
1:19 is the record of John, when the Jews 3778
1:30 T is he of whom I said, After me cometh 3778
1:34 and bare record that t is the Son of God. 3778
2:11 T beginning of miracles did Jesus in Cana 3778
2:12 After t he went down to Capernaum, 3778
2:19 Destroy t temple, and in three days I will 3778
2:20 and six years was t temple in building, 3778
2:22 disciples remembered that he had said t 3778
3:19 And t is the condemnation, that light is 3778
3:29 t my joy therefore is fulfilled. 3778
4:13 Whosoever drinketh of t water shall thirst 3778
4:15 Sir, give me t water, that I thirst not, 3778
4:20 Our fathers worshipped in t mountain; 3778
4:21 when ye shall neither in t mountain, 3778
4:27 And upon t came his disciples, 3778
4:29 things that ever I did: is not t the Christ? 3778
4:42 and know that t is indeed the Christ, 3778
4:54 T is again the second miracle that Jesus 3778
5: 1 After t there was a feast of the Jews; 3778
5:28 Marvel not at t: for the hour is coming, 3778
6: 6 And t he said to prove him: for he himself 3778
6:14 T is of a truth that prophet that should 3778
6:29 and said unto them, T is the work of God, 3778
6:34 unto him, Lord, evermore give us t bread. 3778
6:39 And t is the Father's will which hath sent 3778
6:40 And t is the will of him that sent me, 3778
6:42 And they said, Is not t Jesus, the son of 3778
6:50 T is the bread which cometh down from 3778
6:51 if any man eat of t bread, he shall live for 3778
6:52 How can t man give us his flesh to eat? 3778
6:58 T is that bread which came down from 3778
6:58 he that eateth of t bread shall live for ever. 3778
6:60 of his disciples, when they had heard t, NIG
6:60 had heard this, said, T is a hard saying; 3778
6:61 it, he said unto them, Doth t offend you? 3778
7: 8 Go ye up unto t feast: I go not up yet unto 3778
7: 8 I go not up yet unto t feast; for my time is 3778
7:15 saying, How knoweth t man letters, 3778
7:25 Is not t he, whom they seek to kill? 3778
7:26 Do the rulers know indeed that t is 3778
7:27 Howbeit we know t man whence he is: 3778
7:31 he do moe miracles than these which t 3778
7:36 What manner of saying is t that he said, 3778
7:39 (But t spake he of the Spirit, which they 3778
7:40 when they heard t saying, said, Of a truth NIG
7:40 saying, said, Of a truth t is the Prophet. 3778
7:41 Others said, T is the Christ. But some 3778
7:46 Never man spake like t man. 3778
7:49 But t people who knoweth not the law 3778
8: 4 Master, t woman was taken in adultery, 3778
8: 6 T they said, tempting him, that they might 3778
8:23 ye are of t world; I am not of this world. 3778
8:23 ye are of this world; I am not of t world. 3778
8:40 I have heard of God: t did not Abraham. 3778
9: 2 who did sin, t man, or his parents, 3778
9: 3 Neither hath t man sinned, nor his 3778
9: 8 said, Is not t he that sat and begged? 3778
9: 9 Some said, T is he: others said, He is like 3778
9:16 T man is not of God, because he keepeth 3778
9:19 they asked them, saying, Is t your son, 3778
9:20 We know that t is our son, and that he 3778
9:24 praise: we know that t man is a sinner. 3778
9:29 as for t fellow, we know not from 3778
9:33 If t man were not of God, he could do 3778
9:39 For judgment I am come into t world, 3778
10: 6 T parable spake Jesus unto them: 3778
10:16 sheep I have, which are not of t fold: 3778
10:18 t commandment have I received of my 3778
10:41 all things that John spake of t man were 3778
11: 4 T sickness is not unto death, but for 3778
11: 9 because he seeth the light of t world. 3778
11:26 in me shall never die. Believest thou t? 3778
11:37 Could not t man, which opened the eyes 3778
11:37 have caused that even t man should not 3778
11:39 unto him, Lord, by t time he stinketh: 2235
11:47 do we? for t man doeth many miracles. 3778
11:51 And t spake he not of himself: 3778
12: 5 Why was not t ointment sold for three 3778
12: 6 T he said, not that he cared for the poor; 3778
12: 7 the day of my burying hath she kept t. 846
12:18 For t cause the people also met 1223+3778
12:18 for that they heard that he had done t 3778
12:25 that hateth his life in t world shall keep 3778
12:27 Father, save me from t hour: but for this 3778
12:27 For t cause came I unto this hour. 1223+3778
12:27 but for this cause came I unto t hour. 3778
12:30 T voice came not because of me, 3778
12:31 is the judgment of t world: now shall 3778
12:31 shall the prince of t world be cast out. 3778
12:33 T he said, signifying what death he should 3778
12:34 man must be lift up? who is t Son of man? 3778
13: 1 I depart out of t world unto the Father, 3778
13:28 knew for what intent he spake t unto him. 3778
13:35 By t shall all men know that ye are my 3778
14:30 for the prince of t world cometh; 3778
15:12 T is my commandment, That ye love one 3778
15:13 Greater love hath no man than t, that a 3778

Jn
15:25	t *cometh to pass*, that the word might be	NIG
16:11	because the prince of t world is judged.	3778
16:17	What is t he saith unto us, A little	3778
16:18	What is t that he saith, A little while?	3778
16:30	by t we believe that thou camest forth	3778
17: 3	And t is life eternal, that they might know	3778
18:17	Art not thou also *one* of t man's disciples?	3778
18:29	What accusation bring you against t man?	3778
18:34	Sayest thou t *thing* of thyself,	3778
18:36	My kingdom is not of t world:	3778
18:36	world: if my kingdom were of t world,	3778
18:37	To t end was I born, and for this cause	3778
18:37	for t cause came I into the world,	1519+3778
18:38	when he had said t, he went out again	3778
18:40	all again, saying, Not t man, but Barabbas.	3778
19:12	cried out, saying, If thou let t *man* go,	3778
19:20	T title then read many of the Jews:	3778
19:28	After t, Jesus knowing that all *things* were	3778
19:38	And after t Joseph of Arimathea, being a	3778
20:22	And when he had said t, he breathed on	3778
20:30	which are not written in t book:	3778
21: 1	and **on t wise** shewed he *himself*.	3779
21:14	T *is* now the third time *that* Jesus shewed	3778
21:19	T spake he, signifying by what death he	3778
21:19	And when he had spoken t, he saith unto	3778
21:21	to Jesus, Lord, and what *shall* t man do?	3778
21:23	Then went t saying abroad among	3778
21:24	T is the disciple which testifieth of these	3778

Ac
1: 6	wilt thou at t time restore again	3778
1:11	t *same* Jesus, which is taken up from you	3778
1:16	t scripture must needs have been fulfilled,	3778
1:17	us, and had obtained part of t ministry.	3778
1:18	Now t *man* purchased a field with	3778
1:25	That *he* may take part of t ministry and	3778
2: 6	Now when t was noised abroad,	3778
2:12	saying one to another, What meaneth t?	3778
2:14	be t known unto you, and hearken to my	3778
2:16	But t is that which was spoken by	3778
2:29	and his sepulchre is with us unto t day.	3778
2:31	He seeing t before, spake of the	NIG
2:32	T Jesus hath God raised up, whereof we	3778
2:33	he hath shed forth t, which ye now see	3778
2:37	when they heard t, they were pricked	NIG
2:40	Save yourselves from t untoward	3778
3:12	Y men of Israel, why marvel ye at t?	3778
3:12	or holiness we had made t *man* to walk?	846
3:16	faith in his name hath made t man strong,	3778
3:16	faith which is by him hath given him t	3778
4: 7	or by what *name*, have ye done t?	3778
4: 9	If we t **day** be examined of the good deed	4594
4:10	*even* by him doth t *man* stand here before	3778
4:11	T is the stone which was set at nought of	3778
4:17	that *they* speak henceforth to no man in t	3778
4:22	whom t miracle of healing was shewed.	3778
5: 4	why hast thou conceived t thing in thine	3778
5:20	temple to the people all the words of t life.	3778
5:24	they doubted of them whereunto t would	3778
5:28	you that *you* should not teach in t name?	3778
5:28	intend to bring t man's blood upon us.	3778
5:37	After t *man* rose up Judas of Galilee in	3778
5:38	for if t counsel or this work be of men,	3778
5:38	for if this counsel or t work be of men,	3778
6: 3	whom we may appoint over t business.	3778
6:13	T man ceaseth not to speak blasphemous	3778
6:13	blasphemous words against t holy place,	3778
6:14	that t Jesus of Nazareth shall destroy this	3778
6:14	that this Jesus of Nazareth shall destroy t	3778
7: 4	he removed him into t land, wherein ye	3778
7: 6	And God spake **on t wise**, That his seed	3779
7: 7	they come forth, and serve me in t place.	3778
7:29	Then fled Moses at t saying, and was a	3778
7:35	T Moses whom they refused, saying,	3778
7:37	T is *that* Moses, which said unto	3778
7:38	T is he, that was in the church in	3778
7:40	for *as for* t Moses, which brought us out	3778
7:60	Lord, lay not t sin to their charge.	3778
7:60	And when he had said t, he fell asleep.	3778
8:10	saying, T *man* is the great power of God.	3778
8:19	Saying, Give me also t power, that on	3778
8:21	Thou hast neither part nor lot in t matter:	3778
8:22	Repent therefore of t thy wickedness,	3778
8:29	Go near, and join thyself to t chariot.	3778
8:32	of the scripture which he read was t,	3778
8:34	thee, of whom speaketh the prophet t?	3778
9: 2	that if he found any of t way, whether	NIG
9:13	Lord, I have heard by many of t man,	3778
9:21	Is not t he that destroyed them which	3778
9:21	which called on t name in Jerusalem,	3778
9:22	at Damascus, proving that t is *very* Christ.	3778
9:36	t *woman* was full of good works and	3778
10:16	T was done thrice: and the vessel was	3778
10:17	while Peter doubted in himself what *t*	NIG
10:30	Four days ago I was fasting until t hour;	3778
11:10	And t was done three times: and all were	3778
13:17	The God of t people of Israel chose our	3778
13:23	Of t *man's* seed hath God according to	3778
13:26	to you is the word of t salvation sent.	3778
13:33	art my Son, t **day** have I begotten thee.	4594
13:34	to return to corruption, he said **on t wise**,	3779
13:38	that through t man is preached unto you	3778
13:48	And when the Gentiles heard t, they were	NIG
15: 2	the apostles and elders about t question.	3778
15: 6	elders came together for to consider of t	3778
15:15	And to t agree the words of the prophets;	3778
15:16	After t I will return, and will build again	3778

Ac
15:23	wrote *letters* by them **after t manner**;	3592
16:18	And t did she many days. But Paul,	3778
16:36	And the keeper of the prison told t saying	3778
17: 3	and that t Jesus, whom I preach unto you,	3778
17:18	And some said, What will t babbler say?	3778
17:19	May we know what t new doctrine,	3739
17:23	I found an altar with t inscription,	3739
17:30	And the times of t ignorance God winked	NIG
17:32	We will hear thee again of t matter.	3778
18:10	thee: for I have much people in t city.	3778
18:13	T *fellow* persuadeth men to worship God	3778
18:18	And Paul *after t* tarried *there* yet a good	NIG
18:21	I must by all means keep t feast that	NIG
18:25	T *man* was instructed in the way of	3778
19: 5	When they heard t, they were baptized in	NIG
19:10	t continued by the space of two years;	3778
19:17	And t was known to all the Jews and	3778
19:25	know that by t craft we have our wealth.	3778
19:26	t Paul hath persuaded and turned away	3778
19:27	So *that* not only t our craft is in danger to	3778
19:40	to be called in question for t **day's** uproar,	4594
19:40	we may give an account of t concourse.	3778
20:26	I take you to record t **day**,	2250+4594
20:29	I know t, that after my departing shall	3778
21:11	bind the man that oweth t girdle,	3778
21:23	Do therefore t that we say to thee: We	3778
21:28	T is the man, that teacheth all *men* every	3778
21:28	the people, and the law, and t place:	3778
21:28	temple, and hath polluted t holy place.	3778
22: 3	yet brought up in t city at the feet of	3778
22: 3	zealous towards God, as ye all are t **day**.	4594
22: 4	And I persecuted t way unto the death,	3778
22:22	And they gave him audience unto t word,	3778
22:26	what thou doest: for t man is a Roman.	3778
22:28	With a great sum obtained I t freedom.	3778
23: 1	good conscience before God until t day.	3778
23: 9	strove, saying, We find no evil in t man:	3778
23:13	*than* forty which had made t conspiracy.	3778
23:17	Bring t young man unto the chief captain:	3778
23:18	me to bring t young man unto thee,	3778
23:25	And he wrote a letter after t manner:	3778
23:27	T man was taken of the Jews,	3778
24: 2	that very worthy deeds are done unto t	3778
24: 5	we have found t man a pestilent *fellow*,	3778
24:10	been of many years a judge unto t nation,	3778
24:14	t I confess unto thee, that after the way	3778
24:21	Except *it be* for t one voice, that I cried	3778
24:21	I am called in question by you t **day**.	4594
24:25	and answered, Go *thy way* for t time;	NIG
25: 5	go down with *me*, and accuse t man,	3778
25:24	see t *man*, about whom all the multitude	3778
26: 2	I shall answer for myself t **day** before thee	4594
26:16	I have appeared unto thee for t *purpose*,	3778
26:22	help of God, I continue unto t day,	3778
26:26	for t *thing* was not done in a corner.	3778
26:29	but also all that hear me t **day**, were both	4594
26:31	T man doeth nothing worthy of death or	3778
26:32	T man might have been set at liberty,	3778
27:10	I perceive that t voyage will be with hurt	NIG
27:21	and to have gained t harm and loss.	3778
27:23	For there stood by me t night the angel of	3778
27:33	T **day** is the fourteenth day that ye have	4594
27:34	for t is for your health: for there shall not	3778
28: 4	No doubt t man is a murderer, whom,	3778
28: 9	when t was done, others also, which had	3778
28:20	For t cause therefore have I called for you,	3778
28:20	for the hope of Israel I am bound with t	3778
28:22	for as concerning t sect, we know that	3778
28:26	Saying, Go unto t people, and say,	3778
28:27	For the heart of t people is waxed gross,	3778

Ro
1:26	For t cause God gave them up	1223+3778
2: 3	And thinkest thou t, O man, that judgest	3778
3:26	*I say*, at t time his righteousness:	3568+3588
4: 9	Cometh t blessedness then upon	3778
5: 2	whom also we have access by faith into t	3778
6: 6	Knowing t, that our old man is crucified	3778
7:24	who shall deliver me from the body of t	3778
8:18	For I reckon that the sufferings of t *present*	NIG
9: 9	For t *is* the word of promise, At this time	3778
9: 9	At t time will I come, and Sara shall have	3778
9:10	And not only *t*, but when Rebecca also	NIG
9:17	Even for t same *purpose* have I raised	3778
10: 6	which is of faith speaketh **on t wise**,	3779
11: 5	at t present time also there is a remnant	3778
11: 8	*they* should not hear;) unto t **day**.	2250+4594
11:25	that ye should be ignorant of t mystery,	3778
11:27	For t *is* my covenant unto them, when I	3778
12: 2	And be not conformed to t world: but be	3778
13: 6	for **for t cause** pay you tribute also:	1223+3778
13: 6	attending continually upon t very *thing*.	3778
13: 9	For t, Thou shalt not commit adultery,	NIG
13: 9	it is briefly comprehended in t saying,	3778
14: 9	For **to t end** Christ both died,	1519+3778
14:13	but judge t rather, that no *man* put a	3778
15: 9	For **for t cause** I will confess to thee	1223+3778
15:28	When therefore I have performed t,	3778
15:28	and have sealed to them t fruit,	3778
16:22	I Tertius, who wrote t epistle, salute you	NIG

1Co
1:12	Now I say, that every one of you saith,	3778
1:20	where is the disputer of t world? hath not	3778
1:20	not God made foolish the wisdom of t	3778
2: 6	yet not the wisdom of t world, nor of	3778
2: 6	nor of the princes of t world, that come	3778
2: 8	none of the princes of t world knew:	3778
3:12	Now if any *man* build upon t foundation	3778

1Co
3:18	among you seemeth to be wise in t world,	3778
3:19	For the wisdom of t world is foolishness	3778
4:11	Even unto t present hour we both hunger,	3588
4:13	*are* the offscouring of all *things* unto t day.	737
4:17	For t cause have I sent unto you	1223+3778
5: 2	he that hath done t deed might be taken	3778
5: 3	*concerning* him that hath so done t *deed*,	3778
5:10	Yet not altogether with the fornicators of t	3778
6: 3	much more *things* that pertain to t life?	NIG
6: 4	have judgments *of things* pertaining to t	NIG
7: 6	But I speak t by permission, *and* not of	3778
7: 7	proper gift of God, one **after t manner**,	3779
7:26	that t is good for the present distress,	3778
7:29	But t I say, brethren, the time *is* short:	3778
7:31	they that use t world, as not abusing *it*:	3778
7:31	not abusing *it*: for the fashion of t world	3778
7:35	And t I speak for your own profit; not that	3778
8: 7	with conscience of the idol unto t *hour*,	737
8: 9	But take heed lest by any means t liberty	3778
9: 3	answer to them that do examine me is t:	3778
9:10	For our sakes, no doubt, t is written: that	NIG
9:12	If others be partakers of t power over you,	NIG
9:12	Nevertheless we have not used t power;	3778
9:17	For if I do t *thing* willingly, I have a	3778
9:23	And t I do for the gospel's sake, that I	3778
10:28	T is offered in sacrifice unto idols,	3778
11:10	**For t cause** ought the woman to	1223+3778
11:17	Now in t that I declare unto you I praise	3778
11:20	one place, t is not to eat the Lord's supper.	NIG
11:22	shall I praise you in t? I praise you not.	3778
11:24	t is my body, which is broken for you:	3778
11:24	for you: t do in remembrance of me.	3778
11:25	T cup is the new testament in my blood:	3778
11:25	t do ye, as oft as ye drink *it*, in	3778
11:26	For as often as ye eat t bread, and drink	3778
11:26	often as ye eat this bread, and drink t cup,	3778
11:27	Wherefore whosoever shall eat t bread,	3778
11:27	and drink t cup of the Lord unworthily,	NIG
11:30	**For t cause** many *are* weak and	1223+3778
14:21	and other lips will I speak unto t people;	3778
15: 6	the greater part remain unto t **present**,	737
15:19	If in t life only we have hope in Christ,	3778
15:34	of God: I speak t to your shame.	NIG
15:50	Now t I say, brethren, that flesh and	3778
15:53	corruptible must put on incorruption,	3778
15:53	and t mortal *must* put on immortality.	3778
15:54	So when t corruptible shall have put on	3778
15:54	t mortal shall have put on immortality,	3778
16:12	*his* will was not at all to come at t time;	3568

2Co
1:12	For our rejoicing is t, the testimony of our	3778
1:15	in t confidence I was minded to come	3778
2: 1	But I determined t with myself, that *I*	3778
2: 3	And I wrote t same unto you, lest, when I	3778
2: 6	Sufficient to such *a man* is t punishment,	3778
2: 9	For **to t end** also did I write, that I	1519+3778
3:10	made glorious had no glory in t respect,	3778
3:14	for until t **day** remaineth the same	2250+4594
3:15	But *even* unto t **day**, when Moses is read,	4594
4: 1	Therefore seeing we have t ministry, as	3778
4: 4	In whom the god of t world hath blinded	3778
4: 7	But we have t treasure in earthen vessels,	3778
5: 1	For we know that if our earthly house of t	NIG
5: 2	For in t we groan, earnestly desiring to be	3778
5: 4	For we that are in t tabernacle do groan,	NIG
7: 3	I speak not t to condemn *you:* for I have	NIG
7:11	For behold t selfsame *thing*, that ye	3778
7:11	yourselves to be clear in t matter.	NIG
8: 5	And t *they* did, not as we hoped,	NIG
8: 7	to us, *see* that ye abound in t grace also.	3778
8:10	t is expedient for you, who have begun	3778
8:14	now at t time your abundance *may be* a	NIG
8:19	churches to travel with us with t grace,	3778
8:20	Avoiding t, that no *man* should blame us	3778
8:20	that no *man* should blame us in t	3778
9: 3	of you should be in vain in t behalf;	3778
9: 4	should be ashamed in t *same* confident	3778
9: 6	But I *say*, He which soweth sparingly	3778
9:12	For the administration of t service not	3778
9:13	by the experiment of t ministration	3778
10: 7	let him of himself think t again, that, as	3778
10:11	Let such a one think t, that, such as we	3778
11:10	no *man* shall stop me of t boasting in	3778
11:17	*were* foolishly, in t confidence of boasting.	3778
12: 8	For t *thing* I besought the Lord thrice,	3778
12:13	burdensome to you? forgive me t wrong.	3778
13: 1	T *is* the third *time* I am coming to you.	3778
13: 9	and t also we wish, *even* your perfection.	3778

Gal
1: 4	he might deliver us from t present evil	NIG
3: 2	T only would I learn of you, Received ye	3778
3:17	And t I say, *that* the covenant, that was	3778
4:25	For t Agar is mount Sinai in Arabia,	NIG
5: 8	T persuasion *cometh* not of him that	NIG
5:14	*even* in t, Thou shalt love thy neighbour	NIG
5:16	T I say then, Walk in the Spirit, and ye	NIG
5:21	and such like: of the which I tell you	NIG

Eph
1:21	not only in t world, but also in that which	3778
2: 2	walked according to the course of t world,	3778
3: 1	For t cause I Paul, the prisoner of Jesus	3778
3: 8	than the least of all saints, is t grace given,	3778
3:14	For t cause I bow my knees unto the	3778
4:17	T I say therefore, and testify in the Lord,	3778
5: 5	For t ye know, that no whoremonger,	3778
5:31	For t cause shall a man leave his father	3778
5:32	T is a great mystery: but I speak	3778
6: 1	your parents in the Lord: for t is right.	3778

T

Eph	6:12 against the rulers of the darkness of t	3778
Php	1: 6 Being confident of t very *thing*, that he	3778
	1: 7 Even as it is meet for me to think t of you	3778
	1: 9 And t I pray, that your love may abound	3778
	1:19 I know that t shall turn to my salvation	3778
	1:22 live in the flesh, t *is* the fruit of my labour:	3778
	1:25 And having t confidence, I know that I	3778
	2: 5 Let t mind be in you, which *was* also in	3778
	3:13 t one *thing* I do, forgetting those *things*	NIG
	3:15 God shall reveal even t unto you.	3778
Col	1: 9 For t cause we also, since the day	1223+3778
	1:27 the glory of t mystery among the Gentiles;	3778
	2: 4 And t I say, lest any *man* should beguile	3778
	3:20 obey *your* parents in all *things*: for t is well	3778
	4:16 And when t epistle is read amongst you,	NIG
1Th	2:13 For t cause also thank we God	1223+3778
	3: 5 For t cause, when I could no	1223+3778
	4: 3 For t is the will of God, *even* your	3778
	4:15 For t we say unto you, by the word of	3778
	5:18 for t is the will of God in Christ Jesus	3778
	5:27 I charge you by the Lord that t epistle be	NIG
2Th	1:11 our God would count you worthy of t	NIG
	2:11 For t cause God shall send them	1223+3778
	3:10 t we commanded you, that if any would	3778
	3:14 And if any *man* obey not our word by t	NIG
1Ti	1: 9 Knowing t, that the law is not made for a	3778
	1:15 *T* is a faithful saying, and worthy of all	NIG
	1:16 Howbeit for t cause I obtained	1223+3778
	1:18 T charge I commit unto thee, son Timothy	NIG
	2: 3 For t is good and acceptable in the sight of	3778
	3: 1 *T* is a true saying, If a man desire the office	NIG
	4: 9 *T* is a faithful saying and worthy of all	NIG
	4:16 for in doing t thou shalt both save thyself,	NIG
	6: 7 For we brought nothing into t world,	NIG
	6:14 That thou keep t commandment without	NIG
	6:17 Charge *them that are* rich in t world,	3568
2Ti	1:15 T thou knowest, that all they which are in	3778
	2: 4 entangleth himself with the affairs of t life;	NIG
	2:19 having t seal, The Lord knoweth them	3778
	3: 1 T know also, that in the last days perilous	3778
	3: 6 For of t sort are they which creep into	3778
	4:10 having loved t present world,	NIG
Tit	1: 5 For t cause left I thee in Crete, that thou	3778
	1:13 T witness is true. Wherefore rebuke them	3778
	2:12 and godly, in t present world;	NIG
	3: 8 *T* is a faithful saying, and these *things* I	NIG
Heb	1: 5 art my Son, t **day** have I begotten thee?	4594
	3: 3 For t *man* was counted worthy of more	3778
	4: 4 place of the seventh *day* on t wise,	3779
	4: 5 in t *place* again, If they shall enter into	3778
	5: 4 no *man* taketh t honour unto himself,	NIG
	6: 3 And t will we do, if God permit.	3778
	7: 1 For Melchisedec, king of Salem, priest of	3778
	7: 4 Now consider how great t *man was*, unto	3778
	7:21 t with an oath by him that said unto him,	3588
	7:24 But t *man*, because he continueth ever,	846
	7:27 for t he did once, when he offered up	3778
	8: 1 of the *things* which we have spoken t	NIG
	8: 3 wherefore *it is* of necessity that t *man*	3778
	8:10 For t *is* the covenant that I will make with	3778
	9: 8 The Holy Ghost t signifying, that the way	NIG
	9:11 hands, that is to say, not of t building,	3778
	9:15 For t cause he is the mediator of	1223+3778
	9:20 T *is* the blood of the testament which God	3778
	9:27 men once to die, but after t the judgment:	3778
	10:12 t *man*, after he had offered one sacrifice	846
	10:16 T *is* the covenant that I will make with	3778
	11: 5 before his translation he had t testimony,	NIG
	12:27 And t *word*, Yet once *more*, signifieth	3588
	13:19 But I beseech *you* the rather to do t, that	3778
Jas	1: 3 Knowing t, that the trying of your faith	NIG
	1:25 t *man* shall be blessed in his deed.	3778
	1:26 his own heart, t *man's* religion *is* vain.	3778
	1:27 undefiled before God and the Father is t	3778
	2: 5 Hath not God chosen the poor of t world	3778
	3:15 T wisdom descendeth not from above,	3778
	4:15 Lord will, we shall live, and do t, or that.	3778
1Pe	1:25 And t is the word which by the gospel is	3778
	2:19 For t *is* thankworthy, if a man for	3778
	2:20 take it patiently, t *is* acceptable with God.	3778
	3: 5 For **after t manner** in the old time the	3779
	4: 6 For **for t cause** was the gospel	1519+3778
	4:16 but let him glorify God on t behalf.	3778
	5:12 testifying that t is the true grace of God	3778
2Pe	1: 5 And beside t, giving all diligence, add to	3778
	1:13 it meet, as long as I am in t tabernacle,	3778
	1:14 Knowing that shortly *I* must put off t my	NIG
	1:17 T is my beloved Son, in whom I am well	3778
	1:18 And t voice which came from heaven we	3778
	1:20 Knowing t first, that no prophecy of	3778
	3: 1 T second epistle, beloved, I now write	3778
	3: 3 Knowing t first, that there shall come in	NIG
	3: 5 For t they willingly are ignorant of, that by	3778
	3: 8 not ignorant of t one *thing*, that one day	NIG
1Jn	1: 5 T then is the message which we have	3778
	2:25 is the promise that he hath promised	3778
	3: 3 And every *man* that hath t hope in him	3778
	3: 8 For t purpose the Son of God was	3778
	3:10 In t the children of God are manifest,	3778
	3:11 For t is the message that ye heard from	3778
	3:17 But whoso hath t world's good,	NIG
	3:23 And t is his commandment, That we	3778
	4: 3 t is *that spirit* of antichrist, whereof ye	3778
	4: 9 In t was manifested the love of God	3778
	4:17 because as he is, so are we in t world.	3778

1Jn	4:21 And t commandment have we from him,	3778
	5: 2 By t we know that we love the children	3778
	5: 3 For t is the love of God, that we keep his	3778
	5: 4 t is the victory that overcometh the world,	3778
	5: 6 T is he that came by water and blood,	3778
	5: 9 for t is the witness of God which he hath	3778
	5:11 And t is the record, that God hath given to	3778
	5:11 to us eternal life, and t life is in his Son.	3778
	5:14 And t is the confidence that we have in	3778
	5:20 T is the true God, and eternal life.	3778
2Jn	1: 6 And t is love, that we walk after his	3778
	1: 6 T is the commandment, That, as ye have	3778
	1: 7 the flesh. T is a deceiver and an antichrist.	3778
	1:10 any unto you, and bring not t doctrine,	3778
Jude	1: 4 who were before of old ordained to t	3778
	1: 5 ye once knew t, how that the Lord,	3778
Rev	1: 3 they that hear the words of t prophecy,	NIG
	2: 6 t thou hast, that thou hatest the deeds	3778
	2:24 as many as have not t doctrine,	3778
	4: 1 After t I looked, and behold, a door *was*	3778
	7: 9 After t I beheld, and lo, a great multitude,	3778
	11: 5 them, he must **in t manner** be killed.	3779
	11:15 The kingdoms of t world are become	3778
	18:18 saying, What *city* is like unto t great city?	NIG
	20: 5 were finished. T is the first resurrection.	3778
	20:14 the lake of fire. T is the second death.	3778
	22: 7 the sayings of the prophecy of t book.	3778
	22: 9 of them which keep the sayings of t book:	3778
	22:10 Seal not the sayings of the prophecy of t	3778
	22:18 the words of the prophecy of t book,	3778
	22:18 him the plagues that are written in t book:	3778
	22:19 from the words of the book of t prophecy,	3778
	22:19 the *things* which are written in t book.	3778

THISTLE (5) [THISTLES]

2Ki	14: 9 The t that *was* in Lebanon sent to the	2336
	14: 9 *was* in Lebanon, and trode down the t.	2336
2Ch	25:18 The t that *was* in Lebanon sent to the	2336
	25:18 *was* in Lebanon, and trode down the t.	2336
Hos	10: 8 and the t shall come up on their altars;	1863

THISTLES (3) [THISTLE]

Ge	3:18 and t shall it bring forth to thee;	1863
Job	31:40 Let t grow instead of wheat,	2336
Mt	7:16 men gather grapes of thorns, or figs of t?	5146

THITHER (95) [THITHERWARD]

Ge	19:20 Oh, let me escape t, (is it not a	8033+1886.5
	19:22 Haste thee, escape t; for I cannot	8033+1886.5
	19:22 do any thing till thou be come t.	8033+1886.5
	24: 6 thou bring not my son t again.	8033+1886.5
	24: 8 only bring not my son t again.	8033+1886.5
	29: 3 t were all the flocks gathered:	8033+1886.5
	39: 1 which had brought him down t.	8033+1886.5
	42: 2 get you down t, and buy for us	8033+1886.5
Ex	10:26 serve the Lord, until we come t.	8033+1886.5
	26:33 thou mayest bring in t within	8033+1886.5
Nu	35: 6 manslayer, that he may flee t:	8033+1886.5
	35:11 the slayer may flee t, which	8033+1886.5
	35:15 *any* person unawares may flee t.	8033+1886.5
Dt	1:37 saying, Thou also shalt not go in t.	8033
	1:38 before thee, he shall go in t:	8033
	1:39 they shall go in t, and unto them	8033+1886.5
	4:42 That the slayer might flee t,	8033+1886.5
	12: 5 ye seek, and t thou shalt come:	8033+1886.5
	12: 6 t ye shall bring your burnt	8033+1886.5
	12:11 t shall ye bring all that I	8033+1886.5
	19: 3 that every slayer may flee t.	8033+1886.5
	19: 4 shall flee t, that he may live:	8033+1886.5
	32:52 thou shalt not go t unto the land	8033+1886.5
	34: 4 but thou shalt not go over t.	8033+1886.5
Jos	7: 3 not all the people to labour t;	8033+1886.5
	7: 5 So there went up t of the people	8033+1886.5
	20: 3 *and* unwittingly may flee t:	8033+1886.5
	20: 9 person at unawares might flee t,	8033+1886.5
Jdg	8:27 all Israel went a t whoring after it:	8033
	9:51 t fled all the men and women,	8033+1886.5
	18: 3 they turned in t, and said unto him,	8033
	18:17 came in t, *and* took the graven	8033+1886.5
	19:15 they turned aside t, to go in *and* to lodge	8033
	21:10 the congregation sent t twelve thousand	8033
1Sa	2:14 Shiloh unto all the Israelites that came t.	8033
	5: 8 the ark of the God of Israel about t.	NIH
	9: 6 now let us go t; peradventure he can	8033
	10: 5 to pass, when thou art come t *to* the city,	8033
	10:10 when they came t to the hill, behold,	8033
	10:22 if the man should yet come t.	1988
	19:23 he went t to Naioth in Ramah: and the	8033
	22: 1 they went down t to him.	8033+1886.5
	30: 7 Abiathar **brought** t the ephod to David.	5066
2Sa	2: 2 David went up t, and his two wives also,	8033
	4: 6 they came t into the midst of the house,	2007
1Ki	5: 7 stone made ready *before* it was brought t.	NIH
	19: 9 he came t unto a cave, and lodged there;	8033
2Ki	2: 8 they were divided hither and t, so that	2008
	2:14 the waters, they parted hither and t:	2008
	4: 8 he turned in t to eat bread.	8033+1886.5
	4:10 to us, *that* he shall turn in t.	8033+1886.5
	4:11 he came t, and he turned into	8033+1886.5
	6: 4 cut down a stick, and cast *it* in t;	8033+1886.5
	6: 9 a place; for t the Syrians are come down.	8033
	6:14 Therefore sent he t horses,	8033+1886.5
	9: 2 thou comest t, look out there	8033+1886.5
	17:27 Carry t one of the priests whom	8033+1886.5
2Ch	1: 6 Solomon went up t to the brasen altar	8033

Ezr	10: 6 when he came t, he did eat no bread,	8033
Ne	4:20 the trumpet, resort ye t unto us:	8033+1886.5
	5:16 all my servants *were* gathered t unto	8033
	13: 9 t brought I again the vessels of the house	8033
Job	1:21 and naked shall I return t:	8033+1886.5
	6:20 they came t, and were ashamed.	5704+1886.5
Ecc	1: 7 the rivers come, t they return again.	8033
Isa	7:24 and with bows shall *men* come t;	8033+1886.5
	7:25 there shall not come t the fear of	8033+1886.5
	32:20 that send forth t the feet of the ox and	NIH
	55:10 returneth not t, but watereth	8033+1886.5
	57: 7 even t wentest thou up to offer sacrifice.	8033
Jer	22:11 this place; He shall not return t any more:	8033
	22:27 to return, t shall they not return.	8033+1886.5
	31: 8 a great company shall return t.	2008
	40: 4 convenient for thee to go, t go.	8033+1886.5
Eze	1:20 they went, t *was their* spirit to go;	8033+1886.5
	11:18 they shall come t, and they shall	8033+1886.5
	40: 1 was upon me, and brought me t.	8033+1886.5
	40: 3 he brought me t, and behold,	8033+1886.5
	47: 9 these waters shall come t:	8033+1886.5
Joel	3:11 t cause thy mighty ones to come	8033+1886.5
Mt	2:22 his father Herod, he was afraid to go t:	1563
Mk	6:33 and ran afoot t out of all cities,	1563
Lk	17:37 Wheresoever the body *is*, t will the eagles	1563
	21: 2 certain poor widow casting in t two mites.	1563
Jn	7:34 where I am, t ye cannot come.	NIG
	7:36 *me:* and where I am, t ye cannot come?	NIG
	11: 8 to stone thee; and goest thou t again?	1563
	18: 2 for Jesus ofttimes resorted t with his	1563
	18: 3 cometh t with lanterns and torches and	1563
Ac	17: 6 Philip ran t to *him*, and heard him read	NIG
	14:19 And there **came** t *certain* Jews from	1904
	16:13 spake unto the women which resorted t.	NIG
	17:10 who coming t went into the synagogue of	NIG
	17:13 came t also, and stirred up the people.	2546
	25: 4 that he himself would depart shortly t.	NIG

THITHERWARD (3) [THITHER]

Jdg	18:15 they turned t, and came to	8033+1886.5
Jer	50: 5 ask the way to Zion with their faces t,	2008
Ro	15:24 be brought on my way t by you,	1563

THOMAS (12)

Mt	10: 3 T, and Matthew the publican;	2381
Mk	3:18 and T, and James the *son* of Alpheus,	2381
Lk	6:15 Matthew and T, James the *son* of	2381
Jn	11:16 Then said T, which is called Didymus,	2381
	14: 5 T saith unto him, Lord, we know not	2381
	20:24 But T, one of the twelve, called Didymus,	2381
	20:26 disciples were within, and T with them:	2381
	20:27 saith he to T, Reach hither thy finger,	2381
	20:28 And T answered and said unto him,	2381
	20:29 T, because thou hast seen me, thou hast	2381
	21: 2 and T called Didymus, and Nathanael of	2381
Ac	1:13 and John, and Andrew, Philip, and T,	2381

THONG; THONGS See LATCHET; SHOELATCHET; WITHS

THONGS (1)

Ac	22:25 And as they bound him with t, Paul said	2438

THORN (7) [THORNS]

Job	41: 2 nose? or bore his jaw through with a t?	2336
Pr	26: 9 t goeth up into the hand of a drunkard,	2336
Isa	55:13 Instead of the t shall come up the fir tree,	5285
Eze	28:24 nor *any* grieving t of all *that* are round	6975
Hos	10: 8 and the thistle shall come up on	6975
Mic	7: 4 *most* upright *is sharper* than a t hedge:	4534
2Co	12: 7 there was given to me a t in the flesh,	4647

THORNBUSH See BRAMBLE

THORNS (50) [THORN]

Ge	3:18 T also and thistles shall it bring forth to	6975
Ex	22: 6 catch in t, so that the stacks of corn,	6975
Nu	33:55 t in your sides, and shall vex you in	6796
Jos	23:13 scourges in your sides, and t in your eyes,	6796
Jdg	2: 3 they shall be *as* t in your sides,	NIH
	8: 7 I will tear your flesh with the t of	6975
	8:16 t of the wilderness and briers,	6975
2Sa	23: 6 the sons of Belial *shall be* all of them as t	6975
2Ch	33:11 which took Manasseh among the t,	2336
Job	5: 5 taketh it *even* out of the t, and the robber	6791
Ps	58: 9 Before your pots can feel the t, he shall	329
	118:12 bees; they are quenched as the fire of t:	6975
Pr	15:19 way of the slothful *man is* as a hedge of t:	2312
	22: 5 T *and* snares *are* in the way of the	6791
	24:31 it was all grown over *with* t, *and* nettles	7063
Ecc	7: 6 For as the crackling of t under a pot,	5518
SS	2: 2 As the lily among t, so *is* my love among	2336
Isa	5: 6 but there shall come up briers and t:	7898
	7:19 and upon all, t, and upon all bushes.	5285
	7:23 it shall *even* be for briers and t.	7898
	7:24 all the land shall become briers and t.	7898
	7:25 not come thither the fear of briers and t:	7898
	9:18 it shall devour the briers and t,	7898
	10:17 shall burn and devour his t and his briers	7898
	27: 4 set the briers *and* t against me in battle?	7898
	32:13 the land of my people shall come up t	6975
	33:12 *as* t cut up shall they be burnt in the fire.	6975
	34:13 t shall come up *in* her palaces, nettles and	5518
Jer	4: 3 your fallow ground, and sow not among t.	6975
	12:13 They have sown wheat, but shall reap t:	6975
Eze	2: 6 though briers and t *be* with thee,	5544

Hos	2: 6 I will hedge up thy way with **t**, and make	5518
	9: 6 them: **t** *shall be* in their tabernacles.	2336
Na	1:10 For while *they be* folden together *as* **t**,	5518
Mt	7:16 Do *men* gather grapes of **t**, or figs of	173
	13: 7 And some fell among **t**; and the thorns	173
	13: 7 and the **t** sprung up, and choked them:	173
	13:22 He also that received seed among the **t** is	173
	27:29 And when they had platted a crown of **t**,	173
Mk	4: 7 some fell among **t**, and the thorns grew	173
	4: 7 and the **t** grew up, and choked it,	173
	4:18 these are they which are sown among **t**;	173
	15:17 platted a crown of **t**, and put *it* about his	174
Lk	6:44 For of **t** *men* do not gather figs, nor of a	173
	7: 7 And some fell among **t**; and the thorns	173
	8: 7 and the **t** sprang up with *it*, and choked it.	173
	8:14 And that which fell among **t** are they,	173
Jn	19: 2 And the soldiers platted a crown of **t**,	173
	19: 5 wearing the crown of **t**, and the purple	174
Heb	6: 8 But that which beareth **t** and briers *is*	173

THOROUGHLY (2) [THROUGHLY]

Ge	11: 3 and **burn** *them* **t**.	8313+8316+3807.1
Ex	21:19 shall **cause** *him* **to be t** healed.	7495+7495

THOSE (465) [THAT]

Ge	6: 4 There were giants in the earth in **t** days;	1992
	15:17 burning lamp that passed between **t** pieces.	428
	19:25 he overthrew **t** cities, and all the plain,	411
	24:60 thy seed possess the gate of **t** which hate	NIH
	33: 5 children; and said, Who *are* **t** with thee?	428
	41:35 let them gather all the food of **t** good years	428
	42: 5 sons of Israel came to buy *corn* among **t**	NIH
	50: 3 are fulfilled the days of **t** which are	NIH
Ex	2:11 it came to pass in **t** days, when Moses	1992
	4:21 see that thou do all **t** wonders before	NIH
	29:33 they shall eat **t** *things* wherewith	NIH
	35:35 of **t that devise cunning work.**	2803+4284
Lev	11:27 that go on *all* four, **t** are unclean unto you:	1992
	14:11 **t** *things*, before the LORD, *at* the door	3963.1
	14:42 and put *them* in the place of **t** stones;	NIH
	15:10 that beareth *any of* **t** *things* shall wash	3963.1
	15:27 whosoever toucheth **t** *things* shall be	3963.1
	22: 2 that they profane not my holy name in **t**	NIH
Nu	1:21 **T** that were numbered of them, *even* of	NIH
	1:22 fathers, **t** that were numbered of them,	NIH
	1:23 **T** that were numbered of them, *even* of	NIH
	1:25 **T** that were numbered of them, *even* of	NIH
	1:27 **T** that were numbered of them,	NIH
	1:29 **T** that were numbered of them,	NIH
	1:31 **T** that were numbered of them,	NIH
	1:33 **T** that were numbered of them,	NIH
	1:35 **T** that were numbered of them, *even* of	NIH
	1:37 **T** that were numbered of them,	NIH
	1:39 **T** that were numbered of them, *even* of	NIH
	1:41 **T** that were numbered of them,	NIH
	1:43 **T** that were numbered of them, *even* of	NIH
	1:44 These *are* **t** that were numbered,	NIH
	1:45 So were all **t** that were numbered of	NIH
	2: 4 host, and **t** that were numbered of them,	NIH
	2: 5 **t** that do pitch next unto him *shall be*	NIH
	2: 6 **t** that were numbered thereof, *were* fifty	NIH
	2: 8 **t** that were numbered thereof, *were* fifty	NIH
	2:11 **t** that were numbered thereof, *were* forty	NIH
	2:12 **t** which pitch by him *shall be* the tribe	1886.1
	2:13 **t** that were numbered of them, *were* fifty	NIH
	2:15 **t** that were numbered of them, *were* forty	NIH
	2:19 host, and **t** that were numbered of them,	NIH
	2:21 **t** that were numbered of them, *were* thirty	NIH
	2:23 **t** that were numbered of them, *were* thirty	NIH
	2:26 host, and **t** that were numbered of them,	NIH
	2:27 **t** that encamp by him *shall be* the tribe of	NIH
	2:28 **t** that were numbered of them, *were* forty	NIH
	2:30 **t** that were numbered of them, *were* fifty	NIH
	2:32 These *are* **t** which were numbered of	NIH
	2:32 all **t** that were numbered of the camps	NIH
	3:22 **T** that were numbered of them, according	NIH
	3:22 *even* **t** that were numbered of them *were*	NIH
	3:34 **t** that were numbered of them, according	NIH
	3:38 **t** that encamp before the tabernacle toward	NIH
	3:43 upward, of **t** that were numbered of them,	NIH
	3:46 for **t that are** *to be* **redeemed** of the two	6302
	4:36 **t** that were numbered of them by their	NIH
	4:38 **t** that were numbered of the sons of	NIH
	4:40 Even **t** that were numbered of them,	NIH
	4:42 **t** that were numbered of the families of	NIH
	4:44 Even **t** that were numbered of them after	NIH
	4:45 These *be* **t** that were numbered of	NIH
	4:46 All **t** that were numbered of the Levites,	NIH
	4:48 Even **t** that were numbered of them,	NIH
	9: 7 **t** men said unto him, We *are* defiled by	1992
	13: 3 all **t** men *were* heads of the children of	3963.1
	14:22 Because all **t** men which have seen my	NIH
	14:37 **t** men that did bring up the evil report	NIH
	18:16 **t** that are *to be* redeemed from a month	2050.2
	25: 9 **t** that died in the plague were twenty and	NIH
	26:18 according to **t** that were numbered of	NIH
	26:22 according to **t** that were numbered of	NIH
	26:25 according to **t** that were numbered of	NIH
	26:27 according to **t** that were numbered of	NIH
	26:34 **t** that were numbered of them, fifty and	NIH
	26:37 according to **t** that were numbered of	NIH
	26:43 according to **t** that were numbered of	NIH
	26:47 according to **t** that were numbered of	NIH
	26:54 according to **t** that were numbered of him.	NIH
	26:62 **t** that were numbered of them were	NIH

Nu	33:55 that **t** which ye let remain of them *shall be*	NIH
Dt	7:22 the LORD thy God will put out **t** nations	411
	17: 9 unto the judge that shall be in **t** days,	1992
	18: 9 to do after the abominations of **t** nations.	1992
	19: 5 he shall flee unto one of **t** cities, and live:	428
	19:17 and the judges, which shall be in **t** days;	1992
	19:20 **t** which remain shall hear, and fear,	1886.1
	26: 3 shalt go unto the priest that shall be in **t**	1992
	29: 3 have seen, the signs, and **t** great miracles:	1992
	29:29 **t** *things* which are revealed *belong* unto	NIH
	32:21 I will move them to jealousy with **t** *which*	NIH
Jos	3:16 **t** that came down toward the sea of	1886.1
	4:20 **t** twelve stones, which they took out of	1886.1
	10:22 bring out **t** five kings unto me out of	428
	10:23 brought forth **t** five kings unto him out of	428
	10:24 they brought out **t** kings unto Joshua,	428
	11: 1 when Jabin king of Hazor had heard **t**	NIH
	11:10 for Hazor beforetime was the head of all **t**	428
	11:12 all the cities of **t** kings, and all the kings of	428
	11:18 Joshua made war a long time with all **t**	428
	17:12 not drive out *the inhabitants of* **t** cities;	428
	20: 4 when he that doth flee unto one of **t** cities	428
	20: 6 of the high priest that shall be in **t** days:	1992
	21:16 her suburbs; nine cities out of **t** two tribes.	428
	24:17 and which did **t** great signs in our sight,	428
Jdg	2:16 which delivered them out of the hand of **t**	NIH
	2:23 Therefore the LORD left **t** nations, without	428
	7: 8 tent, and retained **t** three hundred men:	NIH
	11:13 restore *t* *lands* again peaceably.	2006.1
	12: 5 that when **t** Ephraimites which were	NIH
	17: 6 In **t** days *there was* no king in Israel,	1992
	18: 1 In **t** days *there was* no king in Israel,	1992
	18: 1 in **t** days the tribe of the Danites sought	1992
	19: 1 it came to pass in **t** days, when *there was*	1992
	20:27 the covenant of God *was* there in **t** days,	1992
	20:28 son of Aaron, stood before it in **t** days,)	1992
	21:25 In **t** days *there was* no king in Israel:	1992
1Sa	3: 1 the word of the LORD was precious in **t**	1992
	7:16 Mizpeh, and judged Israel in all **t** places.	428
	10: 9 and all **t** signs came to pass that day.	428
	11: 6 came upon Saul when he heard **t** tidings,	428
	17:11 all Israel heard **t** words of the Philistine,	428
	17:28 with whom hast thou left **t** few sheep in	2007
	18:23 Saul's servants spake **t** words in the ears of	428
	19: 7 and Jonathan shewed him all **t** things.	428
	25: 9 spake to Nabal according to all **t** words	428
	25:12 and came and told him all **t** sayings.	428
	27: 8 for **t** *nations were* of old the inhabitants	2007
	28: 1 came to pass in **t** days, that the Philistines	1992
	28: 3 Saul had put away **t** that had familiar	NIH
	28: 9 how he hath cut off **t** that have familiar	1886.1
	30: 9 where **t** that were left behind stayed.	NIH
	30:20 *which* they drave before **t** *other* cattle,	1931
	30:22 of **t**^s that went with David, and said,	376
2Sa	5:14 these *be* the names of **t** that were born	NIH
	16:23 which he counselled in **t** days,	1992
1Ki	2: 7 and let them be of **t** that eat at thy table:	NIH
	3: 2 unto the name of the LORD, until **t** days.	1992
	4:27 officers provided victual for king Solomon,	428
	8: 4 even **t** did the priests and the Levites	3963.1
	9:21 upon **t** did Solomon levy a tribute of	3963.1
	21:27 it came to pass, when Ahab heard **t** words,	428
2Ki	4: 4 shalt pour out into all **t** vessels,	428
	6:22 **t** whom thou hast taken captive with thy	NIH
	10:32 In **t** days the LORD began to cut Israel	1992
	15:37 In **t** days the LORD began to send against	1992
	17: 9 the children of Israel did secretly **t** *things*	NIH
	18: 4 for unto **t** days the children of Israel did	1992
	20: 1 In **t** days was Hezekiah sick unto death.	1992
	24:15 **t** carried he *into* captivity from Jerusalem	NIH
1Ch	4:23 **t** that dwelt amongst plants and hedges:	NIH
	16:42 cymbals for **t** that should make a sound,	NIH
2Ch	6: 4 had rest, and he had no war in **t** years;	428
	15: 5 in **t** times *there was* no peace to him that	1992
	17:19 besides **t** whom the king put in the fenced	NIH
	20:29 fear of God was on all the kingdoms of **t**	NIH
	32:13 were the gods of the nations of **t** lands any	428
	32:14 Who *was* there among all the gods of **t**	428
	32:24 In **t** days Hezekiah was sick to the death,	1992
Ezr	1: 8 Even **t** did Cyrus king of Persia bring forth	NIH
	2: 1 *of* **t** which had been **carried away,**	1473
	2:62 These sought their register *among* **t** that	1886.1
	3: 3 because of the people of **t** countries:	NIH
	5: 9 asked we **t** elders, *and* said unto them	479
	5:14 did Cyrus the king take out of the temple	1994
	7:19 **t** deliver thou before the God of Jerusalem.	NIH
	8:35 the children of **t** that had been carried	NIH
	9: 2 themselves with the people of **t** lands:	NIH
	9: 4 of the transgression of **t** that had been	NIH
	10: 3 of **t** that tremble at the commandment of	NIH
	10: 8 of **t** that had been **carried away.**	1473
Ne	4:17 they that bare burdens, *with* **t** that laded,	871.1
	5:17 besides **t**^s that came unto us from among	376
	6:17 Moreover in **t** days the nobles of Judah	1992
	7: 6 *of* **t** that had been **carried away,**	1473
	7:64 These sought their register *among* **t** that	NIH
	8: 3 the women, and **t** that could understand;	NIH
	10: 1 Now **t** that sealed *were*, Nehemiah,	NIH
	13:15 In **t** days saw I in Judah *some* treading	1992
	13:23 In **t** days saw I Jews that had married	1992
Est	1: 2 *That* in **t** days, when the king Ahasuerus	1992
	2:21 In **t** days, while Mordecai sat in the king's	1992
	2:21 and Teresh, of **t** which kept the door,	1992
	3: 9 of **t** that have the charge of the business,	NIH
	9: 5 what they would unto **t** that hated them.	NIH

Est	9:11 On that day the number of **t** that were	1886.1
Job	5:11 To set up on high **t** that be low; that those	NIH
	5:11 that **t** which mourn may be exalted *to*	NIH
	21:22 seeing he judgeth **t** that are high.	NIH
	24:13 They are of **t** that rebel against the light;	1992
	24:19 *so doth* the grave **t** *which* have sinned.	NIH
	27:15 **T** that remain of him shall be buried in	NIH
Ps	5:11 let all **t** that put their trust in thee rejoice:	NIH
	13: 4 **t** that trouble me rejoice when I am	NIH
	17: 7 *in* thee from **t** that rise up *against* them.	NIH
	18:30 he *is* a buckler to all **t** that trust in him.	NIH
	18:39 thou hast subdued under me **t** that rose up	NIH
	18:48 thou liftest me up above **t** that rise up	NIH
	21: 8 right hand shall find out **t** that hate thee.	NIH
	37: 9 **t** that wait upon the LORD, they shall	NIH
	40:16 Let all **t** that seek thee rejoice and be glad	NIH
	50: 5 **t** that have made a covenant with me by	NIH
	61: 5 hast given *me* the heritage of **t** that fear	NIH
	63: 9 **t** *that* seek my soul, to destroy *it*, shall go	1992
	68: 6 he bringeth out **t** which are bound with	NIH
	68:11 great *was* the company of **t** that	1886.1
	69: 6 let not **t** that seek thee be confounded for	NIH
	69:26 they talk to the grief of **t** whom thou hast	NIH
	70: 4 Let all **t** that seek thee rejoice and be glad	NIH
	74:23 the tumult of **t** that rise up against thee	NIH
	79:11 preserve thou **t** that are appointed to die;	NIH
	92:13 **T** that be planted in the house of	NIH
	102:20 to loose **t** that are appointed to death;	NIH
	103:18 to **t** that remember his commandments to	NIH
	106:46 He made them also to be pitied of all **t** that	NIH
	109:31 to save *him* from **t** that condemn his soul.	NIH
	119:79 Let **t** that fear thee turn unto me,	NIH
	119:79 and **t** that have known thy testimonies.	NIH
	119:132 as thou usest to do unto **t** that love thy	NIH
	123: 4 *with* the scorning of **t** that are at ease,	NIH
	125: 4 unto **t** that *be* good, and to *them that are*	NIH
	139:21 not I grieved with **t** that rise up against	NIH
	140: 9 *for* the head of **t** that compass me about,	NIH
	143: 3 in darkness, as **t** that have been long dead.	NIH
	145:14 and raiseth up all **t** that be bowed down.	1886.1
	147:11 that fear him, in **t** that hope in his mercy.	NIH
Pr	1:12 and whole, as **t** that go down into the pit:	NIH
	4:22 For they *are* life unto **t** that find them,	NIH
	8:17 and **t** that seek me early shall find me.	NIH
	8:21 That *I* may cause **t** that love me to inherit	NIH
	22:23 and spoil the soul of **t** that spoiled them.	NIH
	24:11 death, and **t** *that are* ready to be slain;	NIH
	26:28 A lying tongue hateth **t** *that are* afflicted	NIH
	31: 6 and wine unto **t** that be of heavy hearts.	NIH
Ecc	1:11 are to come with **t** that shall come after.	NIH
	5:14 **t** riches perish by evil travail:	1931
	7:28 a woman among all **t** have I not found.	NIH
	8: 8 wickedness deliver **t that are given to** it.	1167
	12: 3 **t** that look out of the windows be	NIH
SS	7: 9 the lips of **t** *that are* asleep to speak.	NIH
	8:12 **t** that keep the fruit thereof two hundred.	NIH
Isa	3:14 *and as* the raiment of **t** that are slain,	NIH
	27: 7 him, as he smote **t** that smote him?	NIH
	35: 8 not pass over it; but it *shall be* for **t**:	4123.1
	38: 1 In **t** days was Hezekiah sick unto death.	1992
	40:11 *and* shall gently lead **t** that are with young.	NIH
	56: 8 him, besides **t** that are gathered unto him.	NIH
	60:12 yea, **t** nations shall be utterly wasted.	NIH
	64: 5 **t** *that* remember thee in thy ways:	NIH
	64: 5 in **t** is continuance, and we shall be	1992.1
	66: 2 For all **t** *things* hath mine hand made,	428
	66: 2 and all **t** *things* have been, saith the LORD:	428
	66:19 I will send **t** that escape of them unto	NIH
Jer	3:16 in the land, in **t** days, saith the LORD,	1992
	3:18 In **t** days the house of Judah shall walk	1992
	4:12 *Even* a full wind from **t** *places* shall come	428
	5:18 Nevertheless in **t** days, saith the LORD,	1992
	8:16 is in it; the city, and **t** that dwell therein.	NIH
	14:15 and famine shall **t** prophets be consumed.	1992
	21: 7 and into the hand of **t** that seek their life:	NIH
	27:11 **t** will I let remain still in their own land,	2050.2
	31:29 In **t** days they shall say no more,	1992
	31:33 After **t** days, saith the LORD, I will put	1992
	31:36 If **t** ordinances depart from before me,	428
	33:15 In **t** days, and at that time, will I cause	1992
	33:16 In **t** days shall Judah be saved,	1992
	38:22 **t** *women shall* say, Thy friends have set	2007
	39: 9 **t** that fell away, that fell to him, with	NIH
	46:26 I will deliver them into the hand of **t** that	NIH
	49: 5 of hosts, from all **t** that be about thee;	NIH
	49:36 and will scatter them towards all **t** winds;	428
	50: 4 In **t** days, and in that time, saith	1992
	50:20 In **t** days, and in that time, saith	1992
	52:15 that fell away, that fell to the king of	1992
La	2:22 **t** that I have swaddled and brought up hath	834
	3:62 The lips of **t** that rose up against me,	NIH
Eze	1:21 When **t** went, *these* went; and when	3963.1
	1:21 when **t** stood, *these* stood;	3963.1
	1:21 when **t** were lifted up from the earth,	3963.1
	18:11 that doeth not any of **t** *duties*, but even	428
	22: 5 **T** that be near, and *those that be* far from	NIH
	22: 5 *it that be* far from thee, shall mock thee,	NIH
	28:26 I have executed judgments upon all **t**	NIH
	33:24 that inhabit **t** wastes of the land of Israel	428
	34:27 delivered them out of the hand of **t** that	NIH
	38:17 which prophesied in **t** days *many* years,	1992
	39:10 they shall spoil **t** that spoiled them,	NIH
	39:10 and rob **t** that robbed them, saith the Lord	NIH
	39:14 **t** that remain upon the face of the earth,	NIH
	40:25 thereof round about, like **t** windows:	428

T

Eze 42:14 shall approach to *t things* which *are* for — NIH
Da 3:22 flame of the fire slew *t* men that took up — 479
4:37 *t* that walk in pride he *is* able to abase. — 1768
6:24 they brought *t* men which had accused — 479
10: 2 In *t* days I Daniel was mourning three full — 1992
11: 4 be pluckt up, even for others besides *t*. — 428
11:14 in *t* times there shall many stand up — 1992
Joel 2:16 the children, and *t that suck* the breasts: — 3243
2:29 upon the handmaids in *t* days will I pour — 1992
3: 1 For behold, in *t* days, and in that time, — 1992
Ob 1:14 to cut off *t* of his that did escape; — NIH
1:14 neither shouldest thou have delivered up *t* — NIH
Zep 1: 6 *t* that have not sought the LORD, — NIH
1: 9 In the same day also will I punish all *t* that — NIH
Hag 2:16 Since *t* days were, when *one* came to a — 3963.1
2:22 the chariots, and *t* that ride in them; — NIH
Zec 3: 4 and spake unto *t* that stood before him, — 1886.1
4:10 in the hand of Zerubbabel *with* *t* seven; — 428
7: 5 and seventh *month*, even *t* seventy years, — 2088
8:23 In *t* days *it shall come* to pass, that ten — 1992
11:16 *which* shall not visit *t* that be cut off, — NIH
13: 6 *T* with which I was wounded *in* the — NIH
14: 3 go forth, and fight against *t* nations, — 1992
Mal 3: 5 against *t* that oppress the hireling in *his* — NIH
Mt 3: 1 In *t* days came John the Baptist, — 1565
4:24 and *t* which were possessed with devils, — NIG
4:24 and *t* which were lunatick, and those that — NIG
4:24 were lunatick, and *t* that had the palsy; — NIG
11: 4 shew John again *t things* which ye do hear — NIG
13:17 righteous *men* have desired to see *t things* — NIG
13:17 and to hear *t things* which ye hear, — NIG
15:18 But *t things* which proceed out of — 3588
15:30 having with them *t that were* lame, blind, — NIG
16:23 that be of God, but *t* that be of men. — 1565
21:40 what will he do unto *t* husbandmen? — 1565
21:41 He will miserably destroy *t* wicked *men*, — 846
22: 7 and destroyed *t* murderers, and burnt up — 1565
22:10 So *t* servants went out into the *highways*, — 1565
24:19 and to them that give suck in *t* days. — 1565
24:22 And except *t* days should be shortened, — 1565
24:22 for the elect's sake *t* days shall be — 1565
24:29 Immediately after the tribulation of *t* days — 1565
25: 7 Then all *t* virgins arose, and trimmed their — 1565
25:19 After a long time the lord of *t* servants — 1565
27:54 and *t things* that were done, they feared — 1565
Mk 1: 9 And it came to pass in *t* days, *that* Jesus — 1565
1:44 for thy cleansing *t things* which Moses — NIG
2:20 and then shall they fast in *t* days. — 1565
6:55 began to carry about in beds *t* that were — 3588
7:15 out of him, *t* are they that defile the man. — 3588
8: 1 In *t* days the multitude being very great, — 1565
10:13 *his* disciples rebuked *t* that brought *them*. — 3588
11:23 shall believe that *t things* which he saith — 3588
12: 7 But *t* husbandmen said amongst — 1565
13:17 and to them that give suck in *t* days. — 1565
13:19 in *t* days shall be affliction, such as was — 1565
13:20 except that the Lord had shortened *t* — 1565
13:24 in *t* days, after that tribulation, the sun — 1565
Lk 1: 1 *t* things which are most surely believed — 3588
1: 4 thou mightest know the certainty of *t* — NIG
1:24 And after *t* days his wife Elisabeth — 3778
1:39 And Mary arose in *t* days, and went into — 3778
1:45 there shall be a performance of *t* things — 3588
2: 1 And it came to pass in *t* days, *that* there — 1565
2:18 And all they that heard *it* wondered at *t* — 3588
2:33 his mother marvelled at *t things* which — 3588
4: 2 in *t* days he did eat nothing: — 1565
5:35 and then shall they fast in *t* days. — 1565
6:12 it came to pass in *t* days, *that* he went — 3778
6:32 for sinners also love *t* that love them. — 1565
7:28 Among *t that are* born of women there is — NIG
8:12 *T* by the way side are they that hear; then — 3588
9:36 told no man in *t* days any of *those things* — 1565
9:36 told no *man* in those days any of *t things* — NIG
10:24 kings have desired to see *t things* which — NIG
10:24 and to hear *t things* which ye hear, — NIG
12:20 then whose shall *t things* be, which thou — NIG
12:37 Blessed *are t* servants, whom the lord — 1565
12:38 and find *them* so, blessed are *t* servants. — 1565
13: 4 Or *t* eighteen, upon whom the tower in — 3588
14: 7 he put forth a parable to *t* which were — 3588
14:24 That none of *t* men which were bidden — 3588
17:10 ye shall have done all *t things* which — 3588
19:27 *t* mine enemies, which would not that I — 1565
20: 1 And it came to pass, *that* on one of *t* days, — 1565
21:23 and to them that give suck, in *t* days, — 1565
21:26 looking after *t things* which are coming — 3588
23:14 found no fault in this man *touching t* — NIG
Jn 2:14 And found in the temple *t* that sold oxen — NIG
6:14 *t* men, when they had seen the miracle — NIG
8:10 Woman, where are *t* thine accusers? — NIG
8:26 I speak to the world *t things* which I have — 3778
8:29 for I do always *t things* that please him. — 3588
8:31 Then said Jesus to *t* Jews which believed — 3588
10:32 for which of *t* works do ye stone me? — 846
13:29 Buy *t things* that we have need of against — 846
17:11 keep through thine own name *t* whom — 846
17:12 *t* that thou gavest me I have kept, — NIG
Ac 1:15 In *t* days Peter stood up in the midst of — 3778
2:18 on my handmaidens I will pour out in *t* — NIG
3:18 *t things*, which God before had shewed — NIG
3:24 from Samuel and *t* that follow after, — 3588
6: 1 in *t* days, when the number of — 3778
7:41 And they made a calf in *t* days, — 1565
8: 6 heed unto *t things* which Philip spake, — 3588

Ac 9:37 it came to pass in *t* days, that she was — 1565
13:45 spake against *t* things which were spoken — 3588
16: 3 of the Jews which were in *t* quarters: — 1565
16:35 sent the sergeants, saying, Let *t* men go. — 1565
17:11 These were more noble than *t* in — 3588
17:11 scriptures daily, whether *t* things were so. — 3778
18:17 And Gallio cared for none of *t* things. — 3778
20: 2 And when he had gone over *t* parts, — 1565
21: 5 And when we had accomplished *t* days, — NIG
21:15 And after *t* days we took up our carriages, — 3778
21:24 all may know that *t things*, whereof they — NIG
26:16 *of t things* in the which I will appear unto — NIG
26:22 saying none other *things* than *t* which — 3588
27:11 more than *t things* which were spoken by — 3588
28:31 teaching *t things* which concern the Lord — 3588
Ro 1:28 to do *t things* which are not convenient; — 3588
4:17 calleth *t things* which be not as though — 3588
6:13 as *t that are* alive from the dead, — NIG
6:21 in *t things* whereof ye are now ashamed? — NIG
6:21 for the end of *t things* is death. — 1565
10: 5 the man which doeth *t things* shall live — 846
15:17 *I* may glory through Jesus Christ in *t* — NIG
15:18 For I will not dare to speak of any of *t* — NIG
1Co 8: 4 the eating of *t things* that are offered in — 3588
8:10 to eat *t* things which are offered to idols; — 3588
12:22 Nay, much more *t* members of the body, — NIG
12:23 And *t members* of the body, which we — 3739
14:23 and there come in *t that are* unlearned, — NIG
2Co 7: 6 that comforteth *t that are* cast down, — 3588
11:28 Besides *t things* that are without, — 3588
Eph 5:12 For it is a shame even to speak of *t things* — 3588
Php 3: 7 gain to me, *t* I counted loss for Christ. — 3778
3:13 *this* one *thing I do*, forgetting *t things* — 3588
3:13 reaching forth unto *t things which are* — 3588
4: 3 help *t women* which laboured with me in — 846
4: 9 *T things*, which ye have both learned, — 3778
Col 2:18 intruding into *t things* which he hath not — NIG
3: 1 Christ, seek *t things* which are above, — 3588
1Ti 4:10 of all men, specially of *t* that believe. — 3588
5: 8 specially for *t* of his own house, he hath — NIG
2Ti 2:25 In meekness instructing *t* that oppose — 3588
3: 3 fierce, despisers of *t that are* good, — NIG
Heb 3: 5 for a testimony of *t things* which were to — 3588
5:14 *even* to who by reason of use have their — NIG
6: 4 For *it* is impossible for *t* who were once — 3588
7:21 (For *t* priests were made without an oath; — 3588
7:27 as *t* high priests, to offer up sacrifice, — NIG
8:10 make with the house of Israel after *t* days, — 1565
10: 1 can never with *t* sacrifices which they — 846
10: 3 But in *t sacrifices there is* a remembrance — 846
10:16 that I will make with them after *t* days, — 1565
12:27 the removing of *t things* that are shaken, — 3588
12:27 that *t things* which cannot be shaken may — 3588
13:11 For the bodies of *t* beasts, whose blood is — 3778
Jas 2:16 notwithstanding ye give them not *t things* — 3588
2Pe 2: 6 unto *t that* after should *live ungodly*; — 764
2:18 *t* that were clean escaped from them who — 3588
1Jn 3:22 do *t things* that are pleasing in his sight. — 3588
2Jn 1: 8 that we lose not *t things* which we have — NIG
Jude 1:10 But these speak evil of *t things* which they — NIG
1:10 in *t things* they corrupt themselves. — 3778
Rev 1: 3 keep *t things* which are written therein: — 3588
2:10 *Fear none of t things* which thou shalt — NIG
2:13 even in *t* days wherein Antipas *was* my — NIG
4: 9 And when *t* beasts give glory and honour — NIG
9: 4 *t* men which have not the seal of God — NIG
9: 6 And in *t* days shall men seek death, — 1565
10: 7 when *t things* which the seven thunders — NIG
13:14 *t* miracles which he had power to do in — 3588
20:12 the dead were judged out of *t things* — 3588

THOU (5474) [THEE, THEE-WARD, THINE, THY, THYSELF, YOU] See Index of Articles, Etc.

THOUGH (233) [ALTHOUGH]

Ge 31:30 *t* thou wouldest needs be gone, because — NIH
33:10 as *t* I had seen the face of God, — 3509.1
40:10 it *was* as *t* it budded, *and* her blossoms — 3509.1
Lev 5:17 *t* he wist *it* not, yet is he guilty, — 2050.1
11: 7 he divide the hoof, and *be* clovenfooted, — 3588
35:25 yea, *t* he *be* a stranger, or a sojourner; — NIH
Nu 18:27 as *t* it were the corn of the — 3509.1
Dt 29:19 I walk in the imagination of mine heart, — 3588
Jos 17:18 they have iron chariots, *and though* they — 3588
17:18 have iron chariots, *and* *t* they be strong. — 3588
Jdg 13:16 *T* thou detain me, I will not eat of thy — 518
15: 3 *t* I do them a displeasure. — 3588+5973
15: 7 *T* ye have done this, yet will I be avenged — 518
Ru 1: 8 *t* I be not like unto one of thy — 2050.1
1Sa 14:39 *t* it be in Jonathan my son, he shall — 518+3588
20:20 on the side *thereof*, as *t* I shot at a mark. — NIH
21: 5 it were sanctified *this* day in — 637+3588
2Sa 1:21 as *t* he *had* not *been* anointed with oil. — 2050.1
3:39 I *am this* day weak, *t* anointed king; — 2050.1
4: 6 as *t* they would have fetched wheat; — NIH
18:12 *T* I should receive a thousand — 3863+2050.1
1Ki 2:28 *t* he turned not after Absalom. — 2050.1
1Ch 26:10 the chief, (for *t* he was not the firstborn, — 2050.1
2Ch 30:19 *t* he *be* not *cleansed* according to — 2050.1
Ne 1: 9 *t* there were of you cast out unto — 518
6: 1 (at that time I had not set up the doors — 1571
Est 9: 1 (*t* it was turned *to the contrary*, that — 2050.1
Job 8: 7 *T* thy beginning was small, yet thy latter — 2050.1
9:15 Whom, *t* I were righteous, *yet* would I not — 518
9:21 *T* I *were* perfect, *yet* would I not know — NIH

Job 10:19 I should have been *as t* I had not — 834+3509.1
11:12 man be born *like* a wild ass's colt. — 2050.1
13:15 The slay me, *yet* will I trust in him: — 2005
14: 8 *T* the root thereof wax old in the earth, — 518
16: 6 *T* I speak, my grief is not assuaged: — 518
16: 6 and *t* I forbear, what am I eased? — NIH
19:17 *t* I intreated for the children's *sake* of — 2050.1
19:26 *t* after my skin *worms* destroy this *body*, — NIH
19:27 *t* my reins be consumed within me. — NIH
20: 6 *T* his excellency mount up to the heavens, — 518
20:12 *T* wickedness be sweet in his mouth, — 518
20:12 his mouth, *t* he hide it under his tongue; — NIH
20:13 *T* he spare it, and forsake it not; but keep — NIH
24:23 *T* it be given him *to be* in safety, — NIH
27: 8 *t* he hath gained, when God taketh away — 3588
27:16 *T* he heap up silver as the dust, — 518
30:24 to the grave, *t* they cry in his destruction. — 518
39:16 her young ones, as *t* they were not hers: — 3807.1
Ps 23: 4 *t* I walk through the valley of the shadow — 3588
27: 3 *T* a host should encamp against me, — 518
27: 3 *t* war should rise against me, in this *will* I — 518
35:14 behaved myself *as t* he had been my — 3509.1
37:24 *T* he fall, he shall not be utterly cast — 3588
44:19 *t* thou hast sore broken us in the place of — 3588
46: 2 the earth be removed, and though — 871.1
46: 2 *t* the mountains be carried into the midst — 871.1
46: 3 *T* the waters thereof roar *and* be troubled, — NIH
46: 3 *t* the mountains shake with the swelling — NIH
49:18 *T* whiles he lived he blessed his soul: — 3588
68:13 *T* ye have lien among the pots, *yet shall* — 518
78:23 *T* he had commanded the clouds from — 2050.1
99: 8 *t* thou tookest vengeance of their — 2050.1
138: 6 The LORD *be* high, yet hath he respect — 3588
138: 7 *T* I walk in the midst of trouble, thou wilt — 3588
Pr 6:35 he rest content, *t* thou givest many gifts. — 3588
11:21 *T* hand *join* in hand, the wicked shall not — NIH
16: 5 *t* hand *join* in hand, he shall not be — NIH
27:22 *T* thou shouldest bray a fool in a mortar — NIH
28: 6 *that is* perverse in *his* ways, *t* he *be* rich. — 2050.1
29:19 for *t* he understand he will not answer. — 2050.1
Ecc 6: 6 he live a thousand years twice *told*, — 432
8:12 *T* a sinner do evil an hundred *times*, and — 834
8:17 because *t* a man labour to seek *it* — 834+3807.1
8:17 *t* a wise *man* think to know *it*, yet shall he — 518
Isa 1:18 your sins be as scarlet, they shall be as — 518
1:18 *t* they be red like crimson, they shall be as — 518
10:22 *For t* thy people Israel be as the sand — 518+3588
12: 1 *t* thou wast angry with me, thine anger is — 3588
30:20 *t* the Lord give you the bread of adversity, — NIH
35: 8 the wayfaring men, *t* fools, shall not err — 2050.1
45: 4 thee, *t* thou hast not known me. — 2050.1
45: 5 girded thee *t* thou hast not known me: — 2050.1
49: 5 again to him, *T* Israel be not gathered, — 2050.1
63:16 *t* Abraham be ignorant of us, — 3588
Jer 2:22 For *t* thou wash thee with nitre, — 518
4:30 *T* thou clothest thyself with crimson, — 3588
4:30 *t* thou deckest thee with ornaments of, — 3588
4:30 *t* thou rentest thy face with painting, in — 3588
5: 2 *t* they say, The LORD liveth; surely they — 518
5:22 and *t* the waves thereof toss themselves, — 2050.1
5:22 *t* they roar, yet can they not pass over it? — 2050.1
11:11 and *t* they shall cry unto me, I will not — 2050.1
12: 6 not, *t* they speak fair *words* unto thee. — 3588
14: 7 O LORD, *t* our iniquities testify against us, — 518
15: 1 *T* Moses and Samuel stood before me, — 518
22:24 Coniah the son of Jehoiakim king — 518+3588
30:11 I make a full end of all nations whither I — 3588
32: 5 ye fight with the Chaldeans, ye shall not — 3588
32:33 *t* I taught them, rising up early and — 2050.1
37:10 For *t* ye had smitten the whole army of — 518
46:23 saith the LORD, *t* it cannot be searched; — 3588
49:16 thou shouldest make thy nest as high as — 3588
51: 5 their land was filled *with* sin against — 3588
51:53 *T* Babylon should mount up *to* heaven, — 3588
51:53 *t* she should fortify the height of her — 3588
La 3:32 the cause grief, yet will he have — 518
Eze 2: 6 briers and thorns *be* with thee, — 3588
2: 6 at their looks, *t* they *be* a rebellious house. — 3588
3: 9 at their looks, *t* they *be* a rebellious house. — 3588
8:18 and *t* they cry in mine ears *with* a loud — 2050.1
12: 3 will consider, *t* they *be* a rebellious house. — 3588
12:13 shall he not see it, *t* he shall die there. — 2050.1
14:14 *T* these three men, Noah, Daniel, — 2050.1
14:16 *T* these three men *were* in it, *as* I live, — NIH
14:18 *T* these three men *were* in it, *as* I live, — 2050.1
14:20 *T* Noah, Daniel, and Job, *were* in it, — 2050.1
26:21 *shalt* be no *more*: *t* thou be sought for, — 2050.1
28: 2 *t* thou set thine heart as the heart of — 2050.1
32:25 their terror was caused in the land of — 3588
32:26 *t* they caused their terror in the land of — 3588
32:27 *t* they were the terror of the mighty in — 3588
Da 5:22 *t* thou knewest all this; — 1768+3606+6903
9: 9 we have rebelled against him; — 3588
Hos 4:15 *T* thou, Israel, play the harlot, *yet* let not — 518
5: 2 *t* I *have been* a rebuker of them all. — 2050.1
7:13 *t* I have redeemed them, yet they have — 2050.1
7:15 *T* I have bound *and* strengthened their — 2050.1
8:10 *t* they have hired among the nations, — 2050.1
9:12 *T* they bring up their children, yet — 518+3588
9:16 yea, *t* they bring forth, yet will I slay *even* — 2050.1
11: 7 *t* they called them to the most High, — 2050.1
13:15 *T* he be fruitful among *his* brethren, and — 3588
Am 5:22 *T* ye offer me burnt offerings and — 518+3588
9: 2 *T* they dig into hell, thence shall mine — 518
9: 2 *t* they climb up *to* heaven, — 518+2050.1

T

Am
9: 3 t they hide themselves in the top of 518
9: 3 t hide him from my sight in the bottom 518
9: 4 t they go into captivity before their 518
Ob
1: 4 T thou exalt *thyself* as the eagle, 518
1: 4 t *thou* set thy nest among the stars, 518
1:16 they shall be as t they had not been. 3509.1
Mic
5: 2 t be little among the thousands of NIH
Na
1:12 T *they* be quiet, and likewise many, yet 518
1:12 T I have afflicted thee, I will afflict thee 2050.1
Hab
1: 5 *which* ye will not believe, t it be told *you.* 3588
2: 3 t it tarry, wait for it; because it will surely 518
Zec
2: 9 and Zidon, t it be very wise. 3588
10: 6 be as t I had not cast them off: 834+3509.1
12: 3 t all the people of the earth be gathered 2050.1
Mt
26:33 T all *men* shall be offended because 1499
26:35 said unto him, T I should die with thee, 2579
26:60 t many false witnesses came, *yet* found 2532
Lk
9:53 face was *as t he* would go to Jerusalem. NIG
11: 8 T he will not rise and give him, because 1499
16:31 be persuaded, t one rose from the dead. 1437
18: 4 T I fear not God, nor regard man; 1499
18: 7 night unto him, t he bear long with them? 2532
24:28 made as t he would have gone further. 4364
Jn
4: 2 (T Jesus himself baptized not, 2544
8: 6 on the ground, as *t he heard them not.* NIG
8:14 said unto them, T I bear record of myself, 2579
10:38 But if I do, t ye believe not me, believe 2579
11:25 in me, t he were dead, *yet* shall he live: 2579
12:37 But t he had done so many miracles 1161
Ac
3:12 as t by our own power or holiness we 5613
13:28 t they found no cause of death *in him,* NIG
13:41 wise believe, t a man declare it unto you. 1437
17:25 as t he needed any *thing,* seeing he giveth NIG
17:27 find *him,* t he be not far from every one of 2544
23:15 as t ye would inquire something more 5613
23:20 as t they would inquire somewhat of him 5613
27:30 under colour *as t* they would have cast 5613
28: 4 whom, t he hath escaped the sea, NIG
28:17 t I have committed nothing against NIG
Ro
4:11 that believe, t they be not circumcised; 1223
4:17 calleth those *things* which be not as t 5613
7: 3 t she be married to another man. NIG
9: 6 Not as t the word of God hath taken none 3754
9:27 T the number of the children of Israel be 1437
1Co
4:15 For t you have ten thousand instructors in 1437
4:18 puffed up, *as t* I would not come to you. 5613
5: 3 have judged already, *as t* I were present, 5613
7:29 both they that have wives be *as t* they 5613
7:30 And they that weep, *as t* they wept not; 5613
7:30 they that rejoice, *as t* they rejoiced not; 5613
7:30 they that buy, *as t* they possessed not; 5613
8: 5 For t there be that are called gods, 1512+2532
9:16 For t I preach the gospel, I have nothing to 1437
9:19 For t I be free from all *men,* yet have I NIG
13: 1 T I speak with the tongues of men and 1437
13: 2 And t I have *the gift of* prophecy, 1437
13: 2 t I have all faith, so that *I* could remove 1437
13: 3 And t I bestow all my goods to feed 2579
13: 3 and t I give my body to be burned, 1437
2Co
4:16 but t our outward man perish, 1499
5:16 t we have known Christ after the flesh, 1499
5:20 Christ, **as t** God did beseech *you* by us: 5613
7: 8 For t I made you sorry with a letter, I do 1499
7: 8 a letter, I do not repent, t I did repent: 1499
7: 8 you sorry, t *it were* **but** for a season. 1499
7:12 Wherefore, t I wrote unto you, *I did it* 1499
8: 9 that, t he was rich, *yet* for your sakes he NIG
10: 3 For t we walk in the flesh, we do not war NIG
10: 8 For t I should boast somewhat more of 1437
10:14 *measure,* **as t** we reached not unto you: 5613
11: 6 But t *I be* rude in speech, 1161+1487+2532
11:21 as t we had been weak. 3754
12: 6 For t I would desire to glory, I shall not be 1437
12:11 the very chiefest apostles, t I be nothing. 1499
12:15 t the more abundantly I love you, the less 1499
13: 4 For t he was crucified through weakness, 2532
13: 7 *which* is honest, t we be as reprobates. 1161
Gal
1: 8 But t we, or an angel from heaven, 1437+2532
3:15 T *it be but* a man's covenant, *yet if it be* 3676
4: 1 nothing from a servant, t he be lord of all; NIG
Php
3: 4 T I *might* also have confidence in the 2539
3:12 Not as t I had already attained, either 3754
Col
2: 5 For t I be absent in the flesh, yet 1487+2532
2:20 as t living in the world, are ye subject 5613
Phm
1: 8 t I might be much bold in Christ to enjoin NIG
Heb
5: 8 T he were a Son, *yet* learned he obedience 2539
6: 9 accompany salvation, t we thus speak. 1499
7: 5 t they come out of the loins of Abraham: 2539
12:17 he sought it carefully with tears. 2539
Jas
2:14 t a man say *he* hath faith, and have not 1437
3: 4 which t they be so great, and are driven of NIG
1Pe
1: 6 t now for a season, if need be, NIG
1: 7 t it be tried with fire, might be found unto 1161
1: 8 in whom, t now ye see *him* not, NIG
4:12 as t *some* strange *thing* happened unto 5613
2Pe
1:12 of these things, t ye know *them,* 2539
2Jn
1: 5 not as t I wrote a new commandment, 5613
Jude
1: 5 t ye once knew this, how that the Lord, NIG

THOUGHT (81) [THINK]
Ge
20:11 Abraham said, Because I t, Surely the fear 559
38:15 Judah saw her, he t her to be a harlot; 2803
48:11 unto Joseph, I had not t to see thy face: 6419
50:20 as for you, ye t evil against me; 2803
Ex
32:14 the LORD repented of the evil which he t 1696

Nu
24:11 I t to promote thee unto great honour; 559
33:56 I shall do unto you, as I t to do unto them. 1819
Dt
15: 9 Beware that there be not a t in thy wicked 1697
19:19 as he had t to have done unto his brother: 2161
Jdg
15: 2 **verily** I t that thou hadst utterly hated 559+559
20: 5 upon me by night, *and* t to have slain me: 1819
Ru
4: 4 I t to advertise thee, saying, Buy it before 559
1Sa
1:13 therefore Eli t she had been drunken. 2803
9: 5 caring for the asses, and **take** t for us. 1672
18:25 Saul t to make David fall by the hand of 2803
20:26 for he t, Something hath befallen him, 559
2Sa
4:10 t that I would have given him a reward NIH
13: 2 Amnon t it hard for him to do any 5869+871.1
14:13 hast thou t such a thing against the people 2803
19:18 and to do what the t good. 5869+871.1
21:16 being girded *with* a new *sword,* t to have 559
2Ki
5:11 and went away, and said, Behold, I t, 559
2Ch
11:22 his brethren: for *he t* to make him king. NIH
32: 1 cities, and t to win them for himself. 2803
Ne
6: 2 of Ono. But they t to do me mischief. 2803
Est
6: 6 t scorn to lay hands on Mordecai 5869+871.1
6: 6 Now Haman t in his heart, To whom 559
Job
12: 5 despised in the t of him that is at ease. 6248
42: 2 that no t can be withholden from thee. 4209
Ps
48: 9 We have t of thy lovingkindness, O God, 1819
49:11 Their inward t *is, that* their houses *shall* NIH
64: 6 both the inward *t* of every one *of them,* NIH
73:16 When I t to know this, it *was* too painful 2803
119:59 I t on my ways, and turned my feet unto 2803
139: 2 thou understandest my t afar off. 7454
Pr
24: 9 The t of foolishness *is* sin: and the scorner 2154
30:32 or if thou hast **t** evil, *lay thine* hand upon 2161
Ecc
10:20 Curse not the king, no not in thy t; 4093
Isa
14:24 Surely as I have t, so shall it come to pass; 1819
Jer
18: 8 I will repent of the evil that I t to do unto 2803
Eze
38:10 thy mind, and thou shalt think an evil t: 4284
Da
4: 2 I t it good to shew the signs and 6925
6: 3 king t to set him over the whole realm. 6246
Am
4:13 and declareth unto man what *is his t,* 7808
Zec
1: 6 As I was the LORD of hosts t to do unto us, 2161
8:14 As I t to punish you, when your fathers 2161
8:15 So again have I t in these days to do well 2161
Mal
3:16 the LORD, and that t upon his name. 2803
Mt
1:20 But while he t on these *things,* behold, 1760
6:25 Take no t for your life, what ye shall eat, 3309
6:27 Which of you by **taking** t can add one 3309
6:28 And why **take** ye t for raiment? 3309
6:31 Therefore **take** no t, saying, What shall 3309
6:34 **Take** therefore no t for the morrow: 3309
6:34 for the morrow shall **take** t for the *things* 3309
10:19 **take** no t how or what ye shall speak: 3309
Mk
13:11 **take** no t beforehand what ye shall 4305
14:72 And when he t thereon, he wept. 1911
Lk
7: 7 Wherefore neither t I myself **worthy** 515
9:47 And Jesus, perceiving the t of their heart, 1261
12:11 **take** ye no t how or what *thing* ye shall 3309
12:17 he t within himself, saying, What shall 1260
12:22 **Take** no t for your life, what ye shall eat; 3309
12:25 And which of you with **taking** t can add 3309
12:26 *which is* least, why **take** ye t for the rest? 3309
19:11 they t that the kingdom of God should 1380
Jn
11:13 they t that he had spoken of taking of rest 1380
13:29 For some *of them* t, because Judas had 1380
Ac
8:20 thou hast t that the gift of God may be 3543
8:22 if perhaps the t of thine heart may be 1963
10:19 While Peter t on the vision, the Spirit said 1760
12: 9 done by the angel; but t he saw a vision. 1380
15:38 Paul t not **good** to take him with *them,* 515
26: 8 Why should it be t a *thing* incredible with 2919
26: 9 I verily t with myself, that *I* ought to do 1380
1Co
13:11 I understood as a child, I t as a child: 3049
2Co
1:17 Therefore I t it necessary to exhort 2233
10: 5 bringing into captivity every t to 3540
Php
2: 6 it not robbery to be equal with God: 2233
1Th
3: 1 we t it **good** to be left at Athens alone; 2106
Heb
10:29 suppose ye, shall he be t **worthy,** 515

THOUGHTEST (1) [THINK]
Ps
50:21 thou t that I was altogether *such a one* as 1819

THOUGHTS (57) [THINK]
Ge
6: 5 *that* every imagination of the t of his heart 4284
Jdg
5:15 of Reuben *there were* great t of heart. 2711
1Ch
28: 9 all the imaginations of the t: 4284
29:18 of the t of the heart of thy people, 4284
Job
4:13 In t from the visions of the night, 5587
17:11 are broken off, *even* the t of my heart. 4180
20: 2 Therefore do my t cause me to answer, 5587
21:27 I know your t, and the devices *which ye* 4284
Ps
10: 4 not seek *after God:* God *is* not *in* all his t. 4209
33:11 the t of his heart to all generations. 4284
40: 5 done, and thy t *which are* to us-ward: 4284
56: 5 all their t *are* against me for evil. 4284
92: 5 are thy works! *and* thy t are very deep. 4284
94:11 The LORD knoweth the t of man, 4284
94:19 In the multitude of my t within me thy 8312
119:113 I hate vain t: but thy law do I love. 5588
139:17 How precious also are thy t unto me, 7454
139:23 know my heart: try me, and know my t: 8312
146: 4 to his earth; in that *very* day his t perish. 6250
Pr
12: 5 The t of the righteous *are* right: 4284
15:26 The t of the wicked *are* an abomination to 4284
16: 3 the LORD, and thy t shall be established. 4284
21: 5 The t of the diligent *tend* only to 4284
Isa
55: 7 his way, and the unrighteous man his t: 4284

Isa
55: 8 For my t *are* not your thoughts, neither 4284
55: 8 For my thoughts *are* not your t, neither 4284
55: 9 your ways, and my t than your thoughts. 4284
55: 9 your ways, and my thoughts than your t. 4284
59: 7 their t *are* thoughts of iniquity; wasting 4284
59: 7 their thoughts *are* t of iniquity; wasting 4284
65: 2 way *that was* not good, after their own t; 4284
66:18 For I *know* their works and their t: it shall 4284
Jer
4:14 How long shall thy vain t lodge within 4284
6:19 the fruit of their t, because they have 4284
23:20 till he have performed the t of his heart: 4209
29:11 For I know the t that I think towards you, 4284
29:11 the LORD, t of peace, and not of evil, 4284
Da
2:29 thy t came *into thy mind* upon thy bed, 7476
2:30 thou mightest know the t of thy heart. 7476
4: 5 the t upon my bed and the visions of my 2031
4:19 for one hour, and his t troubled him. 7476
5: 6 his t troubled him, so that the joints of his 7476
5:10 let not thy t trouble thee, nor let thy 7476
Mic
4:12 they know not the t of the LORD, 4284
Mt
9: 4 And Jesus knowing their t, said, 1761
12:25 Jesus knew their t, and said unto them, 1761
15:19 out of the heart proceed evil t, murders, 1261
Mk
7:21 proceed evil t, adulteries, fornications, 1261
Lk
2:35 that the t of many hearts may be revealed. 1261
5:22 But when Jesus perceived their t, 1261
6: 8 But he knew their t, and said to the man 1261
11:17 But he, knowing their t, said unto them, 1270
24:38 and why do t arise in your hearts? 1261
Ro
2:15 and *their* t the mean while accusing or 3053
1Co
3:20 The Lord knoweth the t of the wise, 1261
Heb
4:12 and *is* a discerner of the t and intents of 1761
Jas
2: 4 and are become judges of evil t? 1261

THOUSAND (521) [THOUSANDS]
Ge
20:16 I have given thy brother a t *pieces of* silver: 505
Ex
12:37 about six hundred t on foot *that were* men, 505
32:28 fell of the people that day about three t 505
38:25 a t seven hundred and threescore and 505
38:26 for six hundred t and three thousand and 505
38:26 three t and five hundred and fifty *men.* 505
38:28 of the t seven hundred seventy and 505
38:29 and **two** t and four hundred shekels. 505
Lev
26: 8 an hundred of you shall put **ten** t to flight: 7233
Nu
1:21 were forty and six t and five hundred. 505
1:23 were fifty and nine t and three hundred. 505
1:25 were forty and five t six hundred and fifty. 505
1:27 and fourteen t and six hundred. 505
1:29 were fifty and four t and four hundred. 505
1:31 were fifty and seven t and four hundred. 505
1:33 of Ephraim, *were* forty t and five hundred. 505
1:35 were thirty and two t and two hundred. 505
1:37 were thirty and five t and four hundred. 505
1:39 and two t and seven hundred. 505
1:41 were forty and one t and five hundred. 505
1:43 were fifty and three t and four hundred. 505
1:46 that were numbered were six hundred t 505
1:46 and three t and five hundred and fifty. 505
2: 4 and fourteen t and six hundred. 505
2: 6 were fifty and four t and two hundred. 505
2: 8 were fifty and seven t and four hundred. 505
2: 9 in the camp of Judah *were* an hundred t 505
2: 9 fourscore and six thousand and 505
2: 9 and six t and four hundred, 505
2:11 were forty and six t and five hundred. 505
2:13 were fifty and nine t and three hundred. 505
2:15 were forty and five t and six hundred and 505
2:16 in the camp of Reuben *were* an hundred t 505
2:16 fifty and one t and four hundred and fifty, 505
2:19 of them, *were* forty t and five hundred. 505
2:21 were thirty and two t and two hundred. 505
2:23 were thirty and five t and four hundred. 505
2:24 of the camp of Ephraim *were* an hundred t 505
2:24 and eight t and an hundred, 505
2:26 and two t and seven hundred. 505
2:28 were forty and one t and five hundred. 505
2:30 were fifty and three t and four hundred. 505
2:31 in the camp of Dan *were* an hundred t 505
2:31 and fifty and seven t and six hundred. 505
2:32 throughout their hosts *were* six hundred t 505
2:32 and three t and five hundred and fifty. 505
3:22 that were numbered of them were seven t 505
3:28 and upward, *were* eight t and six hundred, 505
3:34 and upward, *were* six t and two hundred. 505
3:39 and upward, *were* twenty and two t. 505
3:43 two t two hundred and threescore and 505
3:50 a t three hundred and threescore and 505
4:36 by their families were **two** t seven hundred 505
4:40 were **two** t and six hundred and thirty. 505
4:44 families, were three t and two hundred. 505
4:48 eight t and five hundred and fourscore. 505
7:85 all the silver vessels *weighed* **two** t and 505
11:21 amongst whom I *am, are* six hundred t 505
16:49 they that died in the plague were fourteen t 505
25: 9 died in the plague were twenty and four t. 505
26: 7 and three t and seven hundred and thirty. 505
26:14 twenty and two t and two hundred. 505
26:18 of them, forty t and five hundred. 505
26:22 threescore and sixteen t and five hundred. 505
26:25 threescore and four t and three hundred. 505
26:27 of them, threescore t and five hundred. 505
26:34 them, fifty and two t and seven hundred. 505
26:37 of them, thirty and two t and five hundred. 505
26:41 *were* forty and five t and six hundred. 505
26:43 threescore and four t and four hundred. 505

T

Nu 26:47 *were* fifty and three t and four hundred.	505
26:50 *were* forty and five t and four hundred.	505
26:51 six hundred t and a thousand seven	505
26:51 and a t seven hundred and thirty.	505
26:62 of them were twenty and three t,	505
31: 4 Of every tribe a t, throughout all the tribes	505
31: 5 a t of *every* tribe, twelve thousand armed	505
31: 5 of *every* tribe, twelve t armed for war.	505
31: 6 a t of *every* tribe, them and Phinehas the	505
31:32 was six hundred and seventy thousand	505
31:32 and seventy t and five thousand sheep,	505
31:32 and seventy thousand and five t sheep,	505
31:33 And threescore and twelve t beeves,	505
31:34 And threescore and one t asses,	505
31:35 thirty two t persons in all, of women	505
31:36 was *in* number three hundred t and seven	505
31:36 seven and thirty t and five hundred sheep:	505
31:38 The beeves *were* thirty and six t; of which	505
31:39 The asses *were* thirty t and five hundred;	505
31:40 the persons *were* sixteen t; of which	505
31:43 unto the congregation was three hundred t	505
31:43 thirty t *and* seven thousand and five	505
31:43 thirty thousand *and* seven t and five	505
31:44 And thirty and six t beeves,	505
31:45 And thirty t asses and five hundred,	505
31:46 And sixteen t persons;)	505
31:52 was sixteen t seven hundred and	505
35: 4 city and outward a t cubits round about.	505
35: 5 the city *on the* east side **two** t cubits,	505
35: 5 *on the* south side **two** t cubits, and *on*	505
35: 5 *on the* west side **two** t cubits, and *on*	505
35: 5 and *on the* north side **two** t cubits;	505
Dt 1:11 God of your fathers make you a t times	505
7: 9 keep his commandments to a t generations;	505
32:30 How should one chase a t, and two put	505
32:30 two put **ten** t to flight, except their Rock	7233
Jos 3: 4 and it, about **two** t cubits by measure:	505
4:13 About forty t prepared for war passed over	505
7: 3 *but* let about **two** or three t men go up	505
7: 4 up thither of the people about three t men:	505
8: 3 Joshua chose out thirty t mighty *men of*	505
8:12 took about five t men, and set them to lie	505
8:25 both of men and women, *were* twelve t,	505
23:10 One man of you shall chase a t:	505
Jdg 1: 4 and they slew *of* them in Bezek ten t men.	505
3:29 they slew *of* Moab at that time about ten t	505
4: 6 take with thee ten t men of the children of	505
4:10 and he went up with ten t men at his feet:	505
4:14 mount Tabor, and ten t men after him.	505
5: 8 or spear seen among forty t in Israel?	505
7: 3 returned of the people twenty and two t;	505
7: 3 two thousand; and there remained ten t.	505
8:10 about fifteen t *men*, all that were left of all	505
8:10 and twenty t men that drew sword.	505
8:26 golden earrings that he requested was a t	505
9:49 died also, about a t men and women.	505
12: 6 time of the Ephraimites forty and two t.	505
15:11 three t men of Judah went to the top of	505
15:15 and took it, and slew a t men therewith.	505
15:16 with the jaw of an ass have I slain a t men.	505
16:27 *were* upon the roof about three t men	505
20: 2 four hundred t that drew sword.	505
20:10 an hundred of a t, and a thousand out of	505
20:10 of a thousand, and a t out of ten thousand,	505
20:10 a thousand, and a thousand out of **ten t**,	7233
20:15 twenty and six t men that drew sword,	505
20:17 were numbered four hundred t men that	505
20:21 Israelites that day twenty and two t men.	505
20:25 the children of Israel again eighteen t men;	505
20:34 came against Gibeah ten t chosen men	505
20:35 twenty and five t and an hundred men:	505
20:44 there fell of Benjamin eighteen t men;	505
20:45 gleaned of them in the highways five t	505
20:45 unto Gidom, and slew two t of them.	505
20:46 and five t men that drew the sword;	505
21:10 the congregation sent thither twelve t men	505
1Sa 4: 2 of the army in the field about four t men.	505
4:10 for there fell of Israel thirty t footmen.	505
6:19 even he smote of the people fifty t	505
11: 8 the children of Israel were three hundred t,	505
11: 8 and the men of Judah thirty t.	505
13: 2 Saul chose him three *men* of Israel;	505
13: 2 **two** t were with Saul in Michmash	505
13: 2 a t were with Jonathan in Gibeah of	505
13: 5 thirty t chariots, and six thousand	505
13: 5 six t horsemen, and people as the sand	505
15: 4 two hundred t footmen, and ten thousand	505
15: 4 thousand footmen, and ten t men of Judah.	505
17: 5 the weight of the coat *was* five t shekels *of*	505
17:18 ten cheeses unto the captain of *their* t,	505
18:13 him, and made him captain over a t;	505
24: 2 Saul took three t chosen men out of all	505
25: 2 he had three t sheep, and a thousand goats:	505
25: 2 he had three thousand sheep, and a t goats:	505
26: 2 having three t chosen men of Israel with	505
2Sa 6: 1 all the chosen *men* of Israel, thirty t.	505
6: 4 David took from him a t *chariots*, and	505
8: 4 hundred horsemen, and twenty t footmen:	505
8: 5 slew of the Syrians two and twenty t men.	505
8:13 in the valley of salt, *being* eighteen t men.	505
10: 6 twenty t footmen, and of king Maacah a	505
10: 6 of king Maacah a t men, and of Ish-tob	505
10: 6 men, and of Ish-tob twelve t men.	505
10:18 forty t horsemen, and smote Shobach	505
17: 1 Let me now choose out twelve t men,	505

2Sa 18: 3 but now *thou art* worth ten t of us:	505
18: 7 a great slaughter that day of twenty t *men.*	505
18:12 I should receive a t shekels of silver	505
19:17 *there were* a t men of Benjamin with him,	505
24: 9 were in Israel eight hundred t valiant	505
24: 9 the men of Judah *were* five hundred t men.	505
24:15 Dan even to Beer-sheba seventy t men.	505
1Ki 3: 4 a burnt offerings did Solomon offer up on	505
4:26 Solomon had forty t stalls of horses for his	505
4:26 for his chariots, and twelve t horsemen.	505
4:32 he spake three t proverbs: and his songs	505
4:32 and his songs were a t and five.	505
5:11 Solomon gave Hiram twenty t measures of	505
5:13 of all Israel; and the levy was thirty t men.	505
5:14 to Lebanon, ten a month *by* courses:	505
5:15 had threescore and ten t that bare burdens,	505
5:15 and fourscore t hewers in the mountains;	505
5:16 three t and three hundred, which ruled	505
7:26 flowers of lilies: it contained **two** t baths.	505
8:63 two and twenty t oxen, and an hundred	505
8:63 and an hundred and twenty t sheep.	505
10:26 he had a t and four hundred chariots,	505
10:26 hundred chariots, and twelve t horsemen,	505
12:21 fourscore t chosen *men,* which were	505
19:18 Yet I have left *me* seven t in Israel,	505
20:15 all the children of Israel, *being* seven t.	505
20:29 Syrians an hundred t footmen in one day.	505
20:30 and seven t of the men that were left.	505
2Ki 3: 4 unto the king of Israel an hundred t	505
3: 4 and an hundred t rams, *with* the wool.	505
5: 5 six t *pieces* of gold, and ten changes of	505
13: 7 and ten chariots, and ten t footmen;	505
14: 7 He slew of Edom in the valley of salt ten t,	505
15:19 Menahem gave Pul a t talents of silver,	505
18:23 and I will deliver thee **two** t horses,	505
19:35 Assyrians an hundred fourscore and five t:	505
24:14 *even* ten t captives, and all the craftsmen	505
24:16 *even* seven t, and craftsmen and smiths a	505
24:16 craftsmen and smiths a t, all *that* were	505
1Ch 5:18 *were* four and forty t seven hundred and	505
5:21 *of* their camels fifty t, and *of* sheep two	505
5:21 *of* sheep two hundred and fifty t,	505
5:21 *of* asses **two** t, and *of* men an hundred	505
5:21 two thousand, and *of* men an hundred t.	505
7: 2 David two and twenty t and six hundred.	505
7: 4 thirty t *men:* for they had many wives and	505
7: 5 by their genealogies fourscore and seven t.	505
7: 7 and two t and thirty and four.	505
7: 9 of valour, *was* twenty t and two hundred.	505
7:11 seventeen t and two hundred *soldiers,*	505
7:40 *and* to battle *was* twenty and six t men.	505
9:13 a t and seven hundred and threescore;	505
12:14 over an hundred, and the greatest over a t.	505
12:24 and spear *were* six t and eight hundred,	505
12:25 for the war, seven t and one hundred.	505
12:26 Of the children of Levi four t and	505
12:27 with him *were* three t and seven hundred;	505
12:29 of Benjamin, the kindred of Saul, three t:	505
12:30 of the children of Ephraim twenty t and	505
12:31 of the half tribe of Manasseh eighteen t,	505
12:33 of war, fifty t, which could keep rank:	505
12:34 of Naphtali a t captains, and with them	505
12:34 with shield and spear thirty and seven t.	505
12:35 in war twenty and eight t and six hundred,	505
12:36 went forth to battle, expert in war, forty t.	505
12:37 for the battle, an hundred and twenty t.	505
16:15 the word *which* he commanded to a t	505
18: 4 David took from him a t chariots,	505
18: 4 seven t horsemen, and twenty thousand	505
18: 4 thousand horsemen, and twenty t footmen:	505
18: 5 slew of the Syrians two and twenty t men.	505
18:12 the Edomites in the valley of salt eighteen t.	505
19: 6 the children of Ammon sent a t talents of	505
19: 7 So they hired thirty and two t chariots,	505
19:18 David slew of the Syrians seven t *men*	505
19:18 forty t footmen, and killed Shophach	505
21: 5 all *they of* Israel were a t thousand and	505
21: 5 all *they of* Israel were a thousand t and	505
21: 5 and an hundred t men that drew sword:	505
21: 5 and ten t men that drew sword.	505
21:14 and there fell of Israel seventy t men.	505
22:14 of the LORD an hundred t talents *of* gold,	505
22:14 *of* gold, and a thousand talents *of* silver;	505
22:14 *of* gold, and a thousand talents *of* silver;	505
23: 3 man by man, was thirty and eight t.	505
23: 4 four t *were* to set forward the work of	505
23: 4 and six t *were* officers and judges:	505
23: 5 Moreover four t *were* porters;	505
23: 5 four t praised the LORD with	505
26:30 men of valour, a t and seven hundred,	505
26:32 men of valour, and seven hundred chief fathers,	505
27: 1 *of* every course *were* twenty and four t.	505
27: 2 and in his course *were* twenty and four t.	505
27: 3 his course likewise *were* twenty and four t.	505
27: 5 and in his course *were* twenty and four t.	505
27: 7 and in his course *were* twenty and four t.	505
27: 8 and in his course *were* twenty and four t.	505
27: 9 and in his course *were* twenty and four t.	505
27:10 and in his course *were* twenty and four t.	505
27:11 and in his course *were* twenty and four t.	505
27:12 and in his course *were* twenty and four t.	505
27:13 and in his course *were* twenty and four t.	505
27:14 and in his course *were* twenty and four t.	505
27:15 and in his course *were* twenty and four t.	505
29: 4 *Even* three t talents of gold, of the gold of	505

1Ch 29: 4 and seven t talents of refined silver,	505
29: 7 of the house of God *of* gold five t talents	505
29: 7 five thousand talents and **ten** t drams,	7239
29: 7 of silver ten t talents, and *of* brass eighteen	505
29: 7 *of* brass **eighteen** t	505+7239+8083+2050.1
29: 7 and one hundred t talents *of* iron.	505
29:21 *even* a t bullocks, a thousand rams,	505
29:21 a t rams, *and* a thousand lambs, with their	505
29:21 thousand rams, *and* a t lambs, with their	505
2Ch 1: 6 and offered a t burnt offerings upon it.	505
1:14 he had a t and four hundred chariots,	505
1:14 hundred chariots, and twelve t horsemen,	505
2: 2 threescore and ten t men to bear burdens,	505
2: 2 fourscore t to hew in the mountain,	505
2: 2 three t and six hundred to oversee them.	505
2:10 twenty t measures of beaten wheat,	505
2:10 twenty t measures of barley,	505
2:10 twenty t baths of wine, and twenty	505
2:10 baths of wine, and twenty t baths of oil.	505
2:17 fifty t and three thousand and six hundred.	505
2:17 fifty thousand and three t and six hundred.	505
2:18 and ten t of them *to be* bearers of burdens,	505
2:18 fourscore t *to be* hewers in the mountain,	505
2:18 three t and six hundred overseers to set	505
4: 5 *and* it received and held three t baths.	505
7: 5 a sacrifice of twenty and two t oxen,	505
7: 5 and an hundred and twenty t sheep:	505
9:25 And Solomon had four t stalls for horses	505
9:25 and chariots, and twelve t horsemen;	505
11: 1 fourscore chosen *men,* which were	505
12: 3 chariots, and threescore t horsemen:	505
13: 3 of war, *even* four hundred t chosen men:	505
13: 3 him with eight hundred t chosen men,	505
13:17 fell down slain of Israel five hundred t	505
14: 8 and spears, out of Judah three hundred t;	505
14: 8 drew bows, two hundred and fourscore t:	505
14: 9 the Ethiopian with a host of a t thousand,	505
14: 9 the Ethiopian with a host of a thousand t,	505
15:11 seven hundred oxen and seven t sheep.	505
17:11 seven t and seven hundred rams,	505
17:11 and seven t and seven hundred he goats.	505
17:14 mighty *men* of valour three hundred t.	505
17:15 with him two hundred and fourscore t.	505
17:16 with him two hundred t mighty *men* of	505
17:17 *men* with bow and shield two hundred t.	505
17:18 and fourscore t ready prepared for the war.	505
25: 5 found them three hundred t choice men,	505
25: 6 He hired also an hundred t mighty *men* of	505
25:11 and smote *of* the children of Seir ten t.	505
25:12 ten t *left* alive did the children of Judah	505
25:13 three t of them, and took much spoil.	505
26:12 of the mighty *men* of valour were **two** t	505
26:13 three hundred and seven thousand and	505
26:13 and seven t and five hundred,	505
27: 5 ten t measures of wheat, and ten thousand	505
27: 5 measures of wheat, and ten t of barley.	505
28: 6 in Judah an hundred and twenty t in one	505
28: 8 captive of their brethren two hundred t,	505
29:33 *were* six hundred oxen and three t sheep.	505
30:24 did give to the congregation a t bullocks	505
30:24 a thousand bullocks and seven t sheep;	505
30:24 the princes gave to the congregation a t	505
30:24 a thousand bullocks and ten t sheep:	505
35: 7 the number of thirty t, and three thousand	505
35: 7 of thirty thousand, and three t bullocks:	505
35: 8 the priests for the passover *offerings* **two** t	505
35: 9 for passover *offerings* five t *small cattle,*	505
Ezr 1: 9 a t chargers of silver, nine and	505
1:10 hundred and ten, *and* other vessels a t.	505
1:11 and of silver *were* five t and four hundred.	505
2: 3 **two** t an hundred seventy and two.	505
2: 6 *and* Joab, **two** t eight hundred and twelve.	505
2: 7 of Elam, a t two hundred fifty and four.	505
2:12 of Azgad, a t two hundred twenty and two.	505
2:14 The children of Bigvai, **two** t fifty and six.	505
2:31 other Elam, a t two hundred fifty and four.	505
2:35 Senaah, three t and six hundred and thirty.	505
2:37 The children of Immer, a t fifty and two.	505
2:38 of Pashur, a t two hundred forty and seven.	505
2:39 The children of Harim, a t and seventeen.	505
2:64 together *was* **forty** *and* **two** t	505+702+7239
2:65 of whom *there were* seven t three hundred	505
2:67 *their* asses, six t seven hundred and twenty.	505
2:69 threescore and one t drams *of* gold,	
	505+7239+8337+2050.1
2:69 five t pound *of* silver, and one hundred	505
8:27 Also twenty basons of gold, of a t drams;	505
Ne 3:13 a t cubits on the wall unto the dung gate.	505
7: 8 **two** t an hundred seventy and two.	505
7:11 **two** t and eight hundred *and* eighteen.	505
7:12 of Elam, a t two hundred fifty and four.	505
7:17 **two** t three hundred twenty and two.	505
7:19 of Bigvai, **two** t threescore and seven.	505
7:34 other Elam, a t two hundred fifty and four.	505
7:38 of Senaah, three t nine hundred and thirty.	505
7:40 The children of Immer, a t fifty and two.	505
7:41 of Pashur, a t two hundred forty and seven.	505
7:42 The children of Harim, a t *and* seventeen.	505
7:66 together *was* **forty** *and* **two** t	505+702+7239
7:67 of whom *there were* seven t three hundred	505
7:69 five: six t seven hundred and twenty asses.	505
7:70 Tirshatha gave to the treasure a t drams	505
7:71 of the work twenty t drams *of* gold,	7239
7:71 **two** t and two hundred pound *of* silver.	505
7:72 people gave *was* twenty t drams *of* gold,	7239

T

Ne	7:72	**two** t pound *of* silver, and threescore and	505
Est	3: 9	will pay ten t talents of silver to the hands	505
	9:16	and slew of their foes seventy and five t,	505
Job	1: 3	His substance also was seven t sheep,	505
	1: 3	three t camels, and five hundred yoke of	505
	9: 3	him, he cannot answer him one of a t.	505
	33:23	with him, an interpreter, one among a t,	505
	42:12	he had fourteen t sheep, and six thousand	505
	42:12	six t camels, and a thousand yoke of oxen,	505
	42:12	a yoke of oxen, and a thousand she asses.	505
	42:12	a thousand yoke of oxen, and a t she asses.	505
Ps	50:10	forest *is* mine, *and* the cattle upon a t hills.	505
	60: T	of Edom in the valley of salt twelve t.	505
	68:17	The chariots of God *are* **twenty t**,	7239
	84:10	For a day in thy courts *is* better than a t.	505
	90: 4	a t years in thy sight *are but* as yesterday	505
	91: 7	A t shall fall at thy side, and ten thousand	505
	91: 7	at thy side, and **ten** t at thy right hand;	7233
	105: 8	the word *which* he commanded to a t	505
Ecc	6: 6	though he live a t years twice *told,* yet	505
	7:28	one man among a t have I found;	505
SS	4: 4	there hang a t bucklers, all shields	505
	5:10	and ruddy, the chiefest among **ten t**.	7233
	8:11	thereof was to bring a t *pieces* of silver.	505
	8:12	have a t, and those that keep the fruit	505
Isa	7:23	where there were a t vines at a thousand	505
	7:23	where there were a thousand vines at a t	505
	30:17	One t *shall flee* at the rebuke of one;	505
	36: 8	Assyria, and I will give thee **two** t horses,	505
	37:36	an hundred and fourscore and five t:	505
	60:22	A little one shall become a t, and a small	505
Jer	52:28	in the seventh year three t Jews and three	505
	52:30	the persons *were* four t and six hundred.	505
Eze	45: 1	twenty t *reeds,* and the breadth *shall be*	505
	45: 1	and the breadth *shall be* ten t.	505
	45: 3	measure the length of five and twenty t,	505
	45: 3	twenty thousand, and the breadth of ten t	505
	45: 5	*the* five and twenty t of length, and *the* ten	505
	45: 5	*the* ten t of breadth, shall also the Levites,	505
	45: 6	the possession of the city five t broad,	505
	45: 6	broad, and five and twenty t long,	505
	47: 3	forth east*ward,* he measured a t cubits,	505
	47: 4	Again he measured a t, and brought me	505
	47: 4	Again he measured a t, and brought me	505
	47: 5	he measured a t; *and it was* a river	505
	48: 8	offer *of* five and twenty t *reeds* in breadth,	505
	48: 9	*shall be of* five and twenty t in length,	505
	48: 9	thousand in length, and *of* ten t in breadth.	505
	48:10	the north five and twenty t *in length,* and	505
	48:10	and toward the west ten t *in breadth,*	505
	48:10	toward the east ten t *in breadth,*	505
	48:10	the south five and twenty t *in length:*	505
	48:13	*shall have* five and twenty t *in length,*	505
	48:13	thousand *in length,* and ten t *in breadth:*	505
	48:13	all the length *shall be* five and twenty t,	505
	48:13	twenty thousand, and the breadth ten t.	505
	48:15	the five t, that are left in the breadth over	505
	48:15	breadth over against the five and twenty t,	505
	48:16	the north side four t and five hundred,	505
	48:16	the south side four t and five hundred,	702
	48:16	on the east side four t and five hundred,	505
	48:16	and the west side four t and five hundred.	505
	48:18	of the holy *portion shall be* ten t eastward,	505
	48:18	thousand eastward, and ten t westward:	505
	48:20	and twenty t by five and twenty thousand:	505
	48:20	and twenty thousand by five and twenty t:	505
	48:21	twenty t of the oblation toward the east	505
	48:21	five and twenty t toward the west border,	505
	48:30	side, four t and five hundred measures.	505
	48:32	at the east side four t and five hundred:	505
	48:33	*at* the south side four t and five hundred	505
	48:34	*At* the west side four t and five hundred,	505
	48:35	*It was* round about eighteen t *measures:*	505
Da	5: 1	the king made a great feast to a t	506
	5: 1	of his lords, and drank wine before the **t**.	506
	7:10	t thousands ministered unto him,	506
	7:10	**ten** t times ten thousand stood before	7240
	7:10	ten thousand times **ten** t stood before	7240
	8:14	me, Unto **two** t and three hundred days;	505
	12:11	*there shall be* a t two hundred and	505
	12:12	cometh to the t three hundred *and* five and	505
Am	5: 3	The city that went out *by* a t shall leave an	505
Jnh	4:11	wherein are more than sixscore t persons	7239
Mt	14:21	they that had eaten were about **five t**	4000
	15:38	And they that did eat were four t men,	5070
	16: 9	remember the five loaves of the **five t,**	4000
	16:10	Neither the seven loaves of the **four t,**	5070
	18:24	unto him, which ought him ten t talents.	3463
Mk	5:13	into the sea, (they were about **two t,)**	1367
	6:44	eat *of* the loaves were about **five t** men.	4000
	8: 9	they that had eaten were about **four t**	5070
	8:19	I brake the five loaves among **five t,**	4000
	8:20	And when the seven among **four t,**	5070
Lk	9:14	For they were about **five t** men. And he	4000
	14:31	consulteth whether he be able with ten t	5505
	14:31	that cometh against him with twenty t?	5505
Jn	6:10	men sat down, *in* number about **five t**	4000
Ac	2:41	added *unto* them about **three t** souls.	5153
	4: 4	the number of the men was about five t.	5505
	19:19	and found *it* **fifty t** *pieces* of silver.	3461+4002
	21:38	leddest out into the wilderness four t men	5070
Ro	11: 4	I have reserved to myself **seven t** men,	2035
1Co	4:15	For though ye have **ten t** instructors in	3463
	10: 8	and fell in one day three and twenty t,	5505
	14:19	than **ten t** words in an *unknown* tongue.	3463

2Pe	3: 8	that one day *is* with the Lord as a t years,	5507
	3: 8	a thousand years, and a t years as one day.	5507
Rev	5:11	the number of them was **ten** t times ten	3461
	5:11	of them was ten thousand times **ten t,**	3461
	7: 4	four t of all the tribes of the children of	5505
	7: 5	Of the tribe of Juda *were* sealed twelve t.	5505
	7: 5	the tribe of Reuben *were* sealed twelve t.	5505
	7: 5	Of the tribe of Gad *were* sealed twelve t.	5505
	7: 6	Of the tribe of Aser *were* sealed twelve t.	5505
	7: 6	tribe of Nephthalim *were* sealed twelve t.	5505
	7: 6	tribe of Manasses *were* sealed twelve t.	5505
	7: 7	the tribe of Simeon *were* sealed twelve t.	5505
	7: 7	Of the tribe of Levi *were* sealed twelve t.	5505
	7: 7	the tribe of Isachar *were* sealed twelve t.	5505
	7: 8	the tribe of Zabulon *were* sealed twelve t.	5505
	7: 8	tribe of Joseph *were* sealed twelve t.	5505
	7: 8	tribe of Benjamin *were* sealed twelve t.	5505
	9:16	were **two hundred t thousand:**	1417+3461
	9:16	were **two hundred thousand t:**	1417+3461
	11: 3	they shall prophesy a t two hundred *and*	5507
	11:13	the earthquake were slain of men seven t:	5507
	12: 6	that they should feed her there a t two	5507
	14: 1	and with him an hundred forty *and* four t,	5505
	14: 3	but the hundred *and* forty *and* four t,	5505
	14:20	by the space of a t and six hundred	5507
	20: 2	and Satan, and bound him a t years,	5507
	20: 3	no more, till the t years should be fulfilled:	5507
	20: 4	lived and reigned with Christ a t years.	5507
	20: 5	not again until the t years were finished.	5507
	20: 6	and shall reign with him a t years.	5507
	20: 7	And when the t years are expired, Satan	5507
	21:16	the city with the reed, twelve t furlongs.	5505

THOUSANDS (62) [THOUSAND]

Ge	24:60	be thou *the mother of* t millions,	505
Ex	18:21	*to be* rulers of t, *and* rulers of hundreds,	505
	18:25	rulers of t, rulers of hundreds, rulers of	505
	20: 6	mercy unto t of them that love me,	505
	34: 7	Keeping mercy for t, forgiving iniquity and	505
Nu	1:16	tribes of their fathers, heads of t in Israel.	505
	10: 4	*which are* heads of the t of Israel,	505
	10:36	Return, O Lord, *unto* the many t of Israel.	505
	31: 5	there were delivered out of the t of Israel,	505
	31:14	*with* the captains over t, and captains over	505
	31:48	the officers which *were* over t of the host,	505
	31:48	the captains of t, and captains of hundreds,	505
	31:52	of the captains of t, and of the captains of	505
	31:54	the priest took the gold of the captains of t	505
Dt	1:15	captains over t, and captains over	505
	5:10	mercy unto t of them that love me	505
	33: 2	and he came with **ten** t of saints:	7233
	33:17	they *are* the **ten** t of Ephraim, and they	7233
	33:17	Ephraim, and they *are* the t of Manasseh.	505
Jos	22:14	house of their fathers among the t of Israel.	505
	22:21	and said unto the heads of the t of Israel,	505
	22:30	heads of the t of Israel which *were* with	505
1Sa	8:12	And he will appoint him captains over t,	505
	10:19	the Lord by your tribes, and by your t.	505
	18: 7	Saul hath slain his t, and David his ten	505
	18: 7	slain his thousands, and David his **ten t**,	7233
	18: 8	They have ascribed unto David **ten t,**	7233
	18: 8	and to me they have ascribed *but* t:	505
	21:11	Saul hath slain his t, and David his ten	505
	21:11	slain his thousands, and David his **ten t**?	7233
	22: 7	*and* make you all captains of t,	505
	23:23	I will search him out throughout all the t	505
	29: 2	passed on by hundreds, and by t:	505
	29: 5	Saul slew his t, and David his ten	505
	29: 5	slew his thousands, and David his **ten t**?	7233
2Sa	18: 1	set captains of t and captains of hundreds	505
	18: 4	the people came out by hundreds and by t.	505
1Ch	12:20	captains of the t that *were* of Manasseh.	505
	13: 1	David consulted with the captains of t and	505
	15:25	the elders of Israel, and the captains over t,	505
	26:26	the captains over t and hundreds,	505
	27: 1	fathers and captains of t and hundreds,	505
	28: 1	the captains over the t, and captains over	505
	29: 6	and the captains of t and of hundreds,	505
2Ch	1: 2	to the captains of t and of hundreds,	505
	17:14	Of Judah, the captains of t; Adnah the chief,	505
	25: 5	made them captains over t, and captains	505
Ps	3: 6	I will not be afraid of **ten** t of people,	7233
	68:17	God *are* twenty thousand, *even* t of angels:	505
	119:72	thy mouth *is* better unto me than t of gold	505
	144:13	*that* our sheep may **bring forth** t and	503
	144:13	forth thousands and **ten** t in our streets:	7231
Jer	32:18	Thou shewest lovingkindness unto t,	505
Da	7:10	thousand t ministered unto him,	506
	11:12	and he shall cast down *many* **ten** t:	7239
Mic	5: 2	*though thou* be little among the t of Judah,	505
	6: 7	Will the Lord be pleased with t of rams,	505
	6: 7	of rams, *or* with **ten** t of rivers of oil?	7233
Ac	21:20	how many t of Jews there are which	3461
Jude	1:14	the Lord cometh with **ten** t of his saints,	3461
Rev	5:11	times ten thousand, and t of thousands;	5505
	5:11	times ten thousand, and thousands of t;	5505

THREAD (7)

Ge	14:23	That I will not *take* from a t even to a	2339
	38:28	bound upon his hand a **scarlet t,**	8144
	38:30	that had the **scarlet** t upon his hand:	8144
Jos	2:18	thou shalt bind this line of scarlet t in	2339
Jdg	16: 9	as a t of tow is broken when it toucheth	6616
	16:12	he brake them from off his arms like a t.	2339
SS	4: 3	Thy lips *are* like a t of scarlet,	2339

THREATEN (1) [THREATENED, THREATENING, THREATENINGS]

Ac	4:17	among the people, let us **straitly** t them,	546

THREATENED (2) [THREATEN]

Ac	4:21	So when they had **further** t them, they let	4324
1Pe	2:23	when he suffered, he t not;	546

THREATENING (1) [THREATEN]

Eph	6: 9	do the same *things* unto them, forbearing t:	547

THREATENINGS (2) [THREATEN]

Ac	4:29	And now, Lord, behold their t:	547
	9: 1	yet breathing out t and slaughter against	547

THREE (485) [THIRD, THIRDLY, THREEFOLD, THRICE]

Ge	5:22	he begat Methuselah t hundred years,	7969
	5:23	the days of Enoch were t hundred sixty	7969
	6:10	Noah begat t sons, Shem, Ham,	7969
	6:15	of the ark *shall be* t hundred cubits,	7969
	7:13	the t wives of his sons with them, into	7969
	9:19	These *are* the t sons of Noah: and of them	7969
	9:28	Noah lived after the flood t hundred and	7969
	11:13	he begat Salah four hundred and t years,	7969
	11:15	he begat Eber four hundred and t years,	7969
	14:14	t hundred and eighteen, and pursued	7969
	15: 9	Take me a heifer of t **years old,** and a she	8027
	15: 9	a she goat of t **years old,** and a ram of	8027
	15: 9	a ram of t **years old,** and a turtle-dove,	8027
	18: 2	and looked, and lo, t men stood by him:	7969
	18: 6	Make ready quickly t measures of fine	7969
	29: 2	there *were* t flocks of sheep lying by it;	7969
	29:34	unto me, because I have born him t sons:	7969
	30:36	he set t days' journey betwixt himself and	7969
	38:24	it came to pass about t months after, that	7969
	40:10	in the vine *were* t branches: and it *was* as	7969
	40:12	of it: The t branches *are* three days:	7969
	40:12	of it: The three branches *are* t days:	7969
	40:13	Yet within t days shall Pharaoh lift up	7969
	40:16	behold, *I had* t white baskets on my head:	7969
	40:18	The t baskets *are* three days:	7969
	40:18	The three baskets *are* t days:	7969
	40:19	Yet within t days shall Pharaoh lift up thy	7969
	42:17	he put them all together into ward t days.	7969
	45:22	to Benjamin he gave t hundred *pieces* of	7969
	46:15	sons and his daughters *were* thirty and t.	7969
Ex	2: 2	*a goodly child,* she hid him t months.	7969
	3:18	t days' journey into the wilderness,	7969
	5: 3	t days' journey into the desert,	7969
	6:18	*were* an hundred thirty and t years.	7969
	7: 7	Aaron fourscore and t years old, when	7969
	8:27	We will go t days' journey into	7969
	10:22	darkness in all the land of Egypt t days:	7969
	10:23	neither rose any from his place for t days:	7969
	15:22	they went t days in the wilderness,	7969
	21:11	if he do not these t unto her, then shall	7969
	23:14	T times thou shalt keep a feast unto me in	7969
	23:17	T times in the year all thy males shall	7969
	25:32	t branches of the candlestick out of the	7969
	25:32	t branches of the candlestick out of	7969
	25:33	T bowls made like unto almonds, *with* a	7969
	25:33	t bowls made like almonds in the other	7969
	27: 1	and the height thereof *shall be* t cubits.	7969
	27:14	their pillars t, and their sockets three.	7969
	27:14	their pillars three, and their sockets t.	7969
	27:15	fifteen *cubits:* their pillars t,	7969
	27:15	their pillars three, and their sockets t.	7969
	32:28	there fell of the people that day about t	7969
	37:18	t branches of the candlestick out of the	7969
	37:18	t branches of the candlestick out of	7969
	37:19	T bowls made after the fashion of	7969
	37:19	t bowls made like almonds in another	7969
	38: 1	and t cubits the height thereof.	7969
	38:14	their pillars t, and their sockets three.	7969
	38:14	their pillars three, and their sockets t.	7969
	38:15	their pillars t, and their sockets three.	7969
	38:15	their pillars three, and their sockets t.	7969
	38:26	t thousand and five hundred and fifty	7969
Lev	12: 4	continue in the blood of her purifying t	7969
	14:10	t **tenth deals** of fine flour *for a*	6241+7969
	19:23	t years shall it be as uncircumcised unto	7969
	25:21	it shall bring forth fruit for t years.	7969
	27: 6	for the female thy estimation *shall be* t	7969
Nu	1:23	fifty and nine thousand and t hundred.	7969
	1:43	fifty and t thousand and four hundred.	7969
	1:46	and t thousand and five hundred and fifty.	7969
	2:13	fifty and nine thousand and t hundred.	7969
	2:30	fifty and t thousand and four hundred.	7969
	2:32	and t thousand and five hundred and fifty.	7969
	3:50	a thousand t hundred and threescore and	7969
	4:44	were t thousand and two hundred.	7969
	10:33	the mount of the Lord t days' journey:	7969
	10:33	went before them *in* the t days' journey,	7969
	12: 4	Come out ye t unto the tabernacle of	7969
	12: 4	of the congregation. And they t came out.	7969
	15: 9	t **tenth deals** *of* flour mingled with half a	7969
	22:28	that thou hast smitten me these t times?	7969
	22:32	hast thou smitten thine ass these t times?	7969
	22:33	me, and turned from me these t times:	7969
	24:10	thou hast altogether blessed *them* these t	7969
	26: 7	t thousand and seven hundred and thirty.	7969
	26:25	and four thousand and t hundred.	7969
	26:47	fifty and t thousand and four hundred.	7969
	26:62	of them were twenty and t thousand,	7969

Ref	Text	Strong
Nu	28:12 **t** tenth deals *of* flour *for* a meat offering,	7969
	28:20 **t** tenth deals shall ye offer for a bullock,	7969
	28:28 **t** tenth deals unto one bullock, two tenth	7969
	29: 3 **t** tenth deals for a bullock, *and* two tenth	7969
	29: 9 **t** tenth deals to a bullock, *and* two tenth	7969
	29:14 **t** tenth deals unto every bullock of	7969
	31:36 was *in* number **t** hundred thousand and	7969
	31:43 the congregation was **t** hundred thousand	7969
	33: 8 went **t** days' journey in the wilderness of	7969
	33:39 **t** years old when he died in mount Hor.	7969
	35:14 Ye shall give **t** cities on *this* side Jordan,	7969
	35:14 **t** cities shall ye give in the land of Canaan,	7969
Dt	4:41 Moses severed **t** cities on *this* side Jordan	7969
	14:28 At the end of **t** years thou shalt bring forth	7969
	16:16 **T** times in a year shall all thy males appear	7969
	17: 6 mouth of two witnesses, or **t** witnesses,	7969
	19: 2 Thou shalt separate **t** cities for thee in	7969
	19: 3 **divide** the coasts . . . **into t parts**,	8027
	19: 7 Thou shalt separate **t** cities for thee.	7969
	19: 9 shalt thou add **t** cities moe for thee,	7969
	19: 9 three cities moe for thee, beside these **t**:	7969
	19:15 or at the mouth of **t** witnesses, shall	7969
Jos	1:11 for within **t** days ye shall pass over this	7969
	2:16 hide yourselves there **t** days, until	7969
	2:22 the mountain, and abode there **t** days,	7969
	3: 2 it came to pass after **t** days, that the	7969
	7: 3 or **t** thousand men go up and smite Ai;	7969
	7: 4 of the people about **t** thousand men:	7969
	9:16 it came to pass at the end of **t** days after	7969
	15:14 Caleb drove thence the **t** sons of Anak,	7969
	17:11 and her towns, *even* **t** countries.	7969
	18: 4 Give out from among you **t** men for *each*	7969
	21:32 and Kartan with her suburbs; **t** cities.	7969
Jdg	1:20 he expelled thence the **t** sons of Anak.	7969
	7: 6 to their mouth, were **t** hundred men:	7969
	7: 7 By the **t** hundred men that lapped will I	7969
	7: 8 tent, and retained *those* **t** hundred men:	7969
	7:16 he divided the **t** hundred men *into* three	7969
	7:16 he divided the three hundred men *into* **t**	7969
	7:20 the **t** companies blew the trumpets,	7969
	7:22 the **t** hundred blew the trumpets,	7969
	8: 4 the **t** hundred men that *were* with him,	7969
	9:22 When Abimelech had reigned **t** years	7969
	9:43 divided them into **t** companies,	7969
	10: 2 he judged Israel twenty and **t** years,	7969
	11:26 by the coasts of Arnon, **t** hundred years?	7969
	14:14 could not *in* **t** days expound the riddle.	7969
	15: 4 Samson went and caught **t** hundred foxes	7969
	15:11 thousand men of Judah went to the top	7969
	16:15 thou hast mocked me these **t** times,	7969
	16:27 *were* upon the roof about **t** thousand	7969
	19: 4 and he abode with him **t** days:	7969
1Sa	1:24 with **t** bullocks, and one ephah of flour,	7969
	2:13 with a fleshhook of **t** teeth in his hand;	7969
	2:21 and bare **t** sons and two daughters.	7969
	9:20 for thine asses that were lost **t** days ago,	7969
	10: 3 shall meet thee **t** men going up to God	7969
	10: 3 one carrying **t** kids, and another carrying	7969
	10: 3 another carrying **t** loaves of bread,	7969
	11: 8 the children of Israel were **t** hundred	7969
	11:11 that Saul put the people *in* **t** companies;	7969
	13: 2 Saul chose him **t** thousand *men* of Israel;	7969
	13:17 camp of the Philistines in **t** companies:	7969
	17:13 the **t** eldest sons of Jesse went *and*	7969
	17:13 the names of his **t** sons that went to	7969
	17:14 and the **t** eldest followed Saul.	7969
	20:19 *when* thou hast **stayed t** days, *then*	8027
	20:20 I will shoot **t** arrows on the side *thereof*,	7969
	20:41 the ground, and bowed himself **t** times:	7969
	21: 5 kept from us about **these t days**,	8032+8543
	24: 2 Saul took **t** thousand chosen men out of	7969
	25: 2 he had **t** thousand sheep, and a thousand	7969
	26: 2 having **t** thousand chosen men of Israel	7969
	30:12 drunk *any* water, **t** days and three nights.	7969
	30:12 drunk *any* water, three days and **t** nights.	7969
	30:13 left me, because **t** days agone I fell sick.	7969
	31: 6 his **t** sons, and his armourbearer, and all	7969
	31: 8 and his **t** sons fallen in mount Gilboa.	7969
2Sa	2:18 there were **t** sons of Zeruiah there, Joab,	7969
	2:31 that **t** hundred and threescore men died.	7969
	5: 5 and **t** years over all Israel and Judah.	7969
	6:11 house of Obed-edom the Gittite **t** months:	7969
	13:38 went to Geshur, and was there **t** years.	7969
	14:27 unto Absalom there were born **t** sons,	7969
	18:14 took **t** darts in his hand, and thrust them	7969
	20: 4 Assemble me the men of Judah *within* **t**	7969
	21: 1 there was a famine in the days of David **t**	7969
	21:16 the weight of whose spear *weighed* **t**	7969
	23: 9 *one* of the mighty *men* with David,	7969
	23:13 **t** of the thirty chief went down, and came	7969
	23:16 the mighty *men* brake through the host	7969
	23:17 These *things* did *these* **t** mighty *men*.	7969
	23:18 the son of Zeruiah, *was* chief among **t**.	7969
	23:18 he lift up his spear against **t** hundred,	7969
	23:18 slew them, and had the name among **t**.	7969
	23:19 Was he not most honourable of **t**?	7969
	23:19 howbeit he attained not unto the *first* **t**.	7969
	23:22 and had the name among **t** mighty *men*.	7969
	23:23 thirty, but he attained not to the *first* **t**.	7969
	24:12 I offer thee **t** *things;* choose thee one of	7969
	24:13 wilt thou flee **t** months before thine	7969
	24:13 there be **t** days' pestilence in thy land?	7969
1Ki	2:11 thirty and **t** years reigned he in Jerusalem.	7969
	2:39 it came to pass at the end of **t** years,	7969
	4:32 he spake **t** thousand proverbs: and his	7969

Ref	Text	Strong
1Ki	5:16 **t** thousand and three hundred, which	7969
	5:16 three thousand and **t** hundred, which	7969
	6:36 he built the inner court *with* **t** rows of	7969
	7: 4 *there were* windows *in* **t** rows,	7969
	7: 4 and light *was* against light *in* **t** ranks.	7969
	7: 5 and light *was* against light *in* **t** ranks.	7969
	7:12 great court round about *was* with **t** rows	7969
	7:25 **t** looking toward the north,	7969
	7:25 **t** looking toward the west,	7969
	7:25 **t** looking toward the south,	7969
	7:25 the south, and **t** looking toward the east:	7969
	7:27 and **t** cubits the height of it.	7969
	9:25 **t** times in a year did Solomon offer burnt	7969
	10:17 *made* **t** hundred shields of beaten gold;	7969
	10:17 **t** pound *of* gold went to one shield:	7969
	10:22 in **t** years came the navy of Tharshish,	7969
	11: 3 princesses, and **t** hundred concubines:	7969
	12: 5 Depart yet *for* **t** days, then come again to	7969
	15: 2 **T** years reigned he in Jerusalem. And his	7969
	17:21 stretched himself upon the child **t** times,	7969
	22: 1 continued **t** years without war between	7969
2Ki	2:17 they sought **t** days, but found him not.	7969
	3:10 that the LORD hath called these **t** kings	7969
	3:13 for the LORD hath called these **t** kings	7969
	9:32 looked out to him two *or* **t** eunuchs.	7969
	12: 6 was so, *that* in the **t** and twentieth year of	7969
	13: 1 In the **t** and twentieth year of Joash the	7969
	13:25 **T** times did Joash beat him,	7969
	17: 5 up *to* Samaria, and besieged it **t** years.	7969
	18:10 at the end of **t** years they took it: *even* in	7969
	18:14 king of Judah **t** hundred talents of silver	7969
	23:31 and **t** years old when he *began* to reign;	7969
	23:31 and he reigned **t** months in Jerusalem.	7969
	24: 1 and Jehoiakim became his servant **t** years:	7969
	24: 8 and he reigned **t** months in Jerusalem.	7969
	25:17 the height of the chapiter **t** cubits;	7969
	25:18 priest, and the **t** keepers of the door:	7969
1Ch	2: 3 *which* **t** were born unto him of the	7969
	2:16 Abishai, and Joab, and Asahel, **t**.	7969
	2:22 who had **t** and twenty cities in the land of	7969
	3: 4 in Jerusalem he reigned thirty and **t** years.	7969
	3:23 Elioenai, and Hezekiah, and Azrikam, **t**.	7969
	7: 6 Bela, and Becher, and Jediael, **t**.	7969
	10: 6 his **t** sons, and all his house died together.	7969
	11:11 he lift up his spear against **t** hundred slain	7969
	11:12 Ahohite, who *was* one of the **t** mighties.	7969
	11:15 Now **t** of the thirty captains went down to	7969
	11:18 the **t** brake through the host of	7969
	11:19 These *things* did *these* **t** mightiest.	7969
	11:20 the brother of Joab, he was chief of the **t**:	7969
	11:20 for lifting up his spear against **t** hundred,	7969
	11:20 slew *them*, and had a name among the **t**.	7969
	11:21 Of the **t**, he was more honourable than	7969
	11:21 howbeit he attained not to the *first* **t**.	7969
	11:24 and had the name among the **t** mighties.	7969
	11:25 the thirty, but attained not to the *first* **t**:	7969
	12:27 with him *were* **t** thousand and	7969
	12:29 the kindred of Saul, **t** thousand:	7969
	12:39 there they were with David **t** days, eating	7969
	13:14 of Obed-edom in his house **t** months.	7969
	21:10 I offer thee **t** *things:* choose thee one of	7969
	21:12 Either **t** years' famine; or three months to	7969
	21:12 **t** months to be destroyed before thy foes,	7969
	21:12 or else **t** days the sword of the LORD,	7969
	23: 8 chief *was* Jehiel, and Zetham, and Joel, **t**.	7969
	23: 9 Shelomith, and Haziel, and Haran, **t**.	7969
	23:23 Mushi; Mahli, and Eder, and Jeremoth, **t**.	7969
	24:18 The **t** and twentieth to Delaiah, the four	7969
	25: 5 to Heman fourteen sons and **t** daughters.	7969
	25:30 The **t** and twentieth to Mahazioth, he, his	7969
	29: 4 **t** thousand talents of gold, of the gold	7969
	29:27 thirty and **t** *years* reigned he in Jerusalem.	7969
2Ch	2: 2 **t** thousand and six hundred to oversee	7969
	2:17 and **t** thousand and six hundred.	7969
	2:18 **t** thousand and six hundred overseers to	7969
	4: 4 **t** looking toward the north,	7969
	4: 4 **t** looking toward the west,	7969
	4: 4 **t** looking toward the south,	7969
	4: 4 the south, and **t** looking toward the east:	7969
	4: 5 *and* it received and held **t** thousand baths.	7969
	6:13 **t** cubits high, and had set it in the midst	7969
	7:10 on the **t** and twentieth day of the seventh	7969
	8:13 on the solemn feasts, **t** times in the year,	7969
	9:16 **t** hundred shields *made he of* beaten gold:	7969
	9:16 **t** hundred *shekels* of gold went to one	7969
	9:21 every **t** years once came the ships of	7969
	10: 5 Come again unto me after **t** days.	7969
	11:17 the son of Solomon strong, **t** years:	7969
	11:17 **t** years they walked in the way of David	7969
	13: 2 He reigned **t** years in Jerusalem.	7969
	14: 8 spears, out of Judah **t** hundred thousand;	7969
	14: 9 thousand, and **t** hundred chariots;	7969
	17:14 him mighty *men* of valour **t** hundred	7969
	20:25 they were **t** days in gathering of the spoil,	7969
	25: 5 found them **t** hundred thousand choice	7969
	25:13 smote **t** thousand of them, and took much	7969
	26:13 **t** hundred thousand and seven thousand	7969
	29:33 six hundred oxen and **t** thousand sheep.	7969
	31:16 of males, from **t** years old and upward,	7969
	35: 7 thirty thousand, and **t** thousand bullocks:	7969
	35: 8 hundred *small cattle*, and **t** hundred oxen.	7969
	36: 2 and **t** years old when he *began* to reign,	7969
	36: 2 and he reigned **t** months in Jerusalem.	7969
	36: 9 he reigned **t** months and ten days in	7969
Ezr	2: 4 of Shephatiah, **t** hundred seventy and two.	7969

Ref	Text	Strong
Ezr	2:11 of Bebai, six hundred twenty and **t**.	7969
	2:17 of Bezai, **t** hundred twenty and three.	7969
	2:17 of Bezai, three hundred twenty and **t**.	7969
	2:19 of Hashum, **t** hundred twenty and **t**.	7969
	2:21 of Beth-lehem, an hundred twenty and **t**.	7969
	2:25 Beeroth, seven hundred and forty and **t**.	7969
	2:28 and Ai, two hundred twenty and **t**.	7969
	2:32 children of Harim, **t** hundred and twenty.	7969
	2:34 of Jericho, **t** hundred forty and five.	7969
	2:35 **t** thousand and six hundred and thirty.	7969
	2:36 of Jeshua, nine hundred seventy and **t**.	7969
	2:58 *were* **t** hundred ninety and two.	7969
	2:64 two thousand **t** hundred *and* threescore,	7969
	2:65 of whom *there were* seven thousand **t**	7969
	6: 4 *With* **t** rows of great stones, and a row of	8532
	8: 5 Jahaziel, and with him **t** hundred males.	7969
	8:15 and there abode we in tents **t** days:	7969
	8:32 *to* Jerusalem, and abode there **t** days.	7969
	10: 8 *that* whosoever would not come within **t**	7969
	10: 9 together *unto* Jerusalem within **t** days.	7969
Ne	2:11 I came to Jerusalem, and was there **t** days.	7969
	7: 9 of Shephatiah, **t** hundred seventy and two.	7969
	7:17 two thousand **t** hundred twenty and two.	7969
	7:22 of Hashum, **t** hundred twenty and eight.	7969
	7:23 of Bezai, **t** hundred twenty and four.	7969
	7:29 and Beeroth, seven hundred forty and **t**.	7969
	7:32 Beth-el and Ai, an hundred twenty and **t**.	7969
	7:35 children of Harim, **t** hundred and twenty.	7969
	7:36 of Jericho, **t** hundred forty and five.	7969
	7:38 **t** thousand nine hundred and thirty.	7969
	7:39 of Jeshua, nine hundred seventy and **t**.	7969
	7:60 *were* **t** hundred ninety and two.	7969
	7:66 two thousand **t** hundred and threescore,	7969
	7:67 of whom *there were* seven thousand **t**	7969
Est	4:16 neither eat nor drink **t** days, night or day;	7969
	8: 9 on the **t** and twentieth *day* thereof;	7969
	9:15 and slew **t** hundred men at Shushan;	7969
Job	1: 2 born unto him seven sons and **t** daughters.	7969
	1: 3 **t** thousand camels, and five hundred yoke	7969
	1: 4 sent and called for their **t** sisters to eat and	7969
	1:17 The Chaldeans made out **t** bands,	7969
	2:11 Now when Job's **t** friends heard of all this	7969
	32: 1 So these **t** men ceased to answer Job,	7969
	32: 3 Also against his **t** friends was his wrath	7969
	32: 5 no answer in the mouth of *these* **t** men,	7969
	42:13 He had also seven sons and **t** daughters.	7969
Pr	30:15 There are **t** *things that* are never satisfied,	7969
	30:18 There be **t** *things which* are too wonderful	7969
	30:21 For **t** *things* the earth is disquieted,	7969
	30:29 There be **t** *things* which go well, yea,	7969
Isa	15: 5 *flee* unto Zoar, a heifer of **t years old**:	7992
	16:14 saying, Within **t** years, as the years of a	7969
	17: 6 **t** berries in the top of the uppermost	7969
	20: 3 barefoot **t** years *for* a sign and wonder	7969
Jer	25: 3 this day, that *is* the **t** and twentieth year,	7969
	36:23 when Jehudi had read **t** or four leaves,	7969
	48:34 unto Horonaim, *as* a heifer of **t years old**:	7992
	52:24 priest, and the **t** keepers of the door:	7969
	52:28 in the seventh year **t** thousand Jews and	7969
	52:28 three thousand Jews and **t** and twenty:	7969
	52:30 In the **t** and twentieth year of	7969
Eze	4: 5 of the days, **t** hundred and ninety days:	7969
	4: 9 **t** hundred and ninety days shalt thou eat	7969
	14:14 Though these **t** men, Noah, Daniel,	7969
	14:16 *Though* these **t** men *were* in it, *as* I live,	7969
	14:18 Though these **t** men *were* in it, *as* I live,	7969
	40:10 of the gate eastward *were* **t** on this side,	7969
	40:10 three on this side, and **t** on that side;	7969
	40:10 on that side; they **t** *were* of one measure:	7969
	40:21 the little chambers thereof *were* **t** on this	7969
	40:21 *were* three on this side and **t** on that side;	7969
	40:48 breadth of the gate *was* **t** cubits on this	7969
	40:48 on this side, and **t** cubits on that side.	7969
	41: 6 side chambers *were* **t**, one over another,	7969
	41: 6 galleries round about on their **t** *stories*,	7969
	41:22 The altar *of* wood *was* **t** cubits high,	7969
	42: 3 *was* gallery against gallery in **t** *stories*.	7992
	42: 6 For they *were* in **t** *stories*, but had not	8027
	48:31 **t** gates northward; one gate of Reuben,	7969
	48:32 **t** gates; and one gate of Joseph, one gate	7969
	48:33 **t** gates; one gate of Simeon, one gate of	7969
	48:34 and **t** hundred, *with* their **t** gates;	7969
Da	1: 5 nourishing them **t** years, that at the end	7969
	3:23 these **t** men, Shadrach, Meshach,	8532
	3:24 Did not we cast **t** men bound into the	8532
	6: 2 over these **t** presidents; of whom Daniel	8532
	6:10 he kneeled upon his knees **t** times a day,	8532
	6:13 but maketh his petition **t** times a day.	8532
	7: 5 *it had* **t** ribs in the mouth of it between	8532
	7: 8 whom there were **t** of the first horns	8532
	7:20 which came up, and before whom **t** fell;	8532
	7:24 from the first, and he shall subdue **t** kings.	8532
	8:14 Unto two thousand and **t** hundred days;	7969
	10: 2 In those days I Daniel was mourning **t** full	7969
	10: 3 at all, till **t** whole weeks were fulfilled.	7969
	11: 2 there *shall* stand up yet **t** kings in Persia;	7969
	12:12 to the thousand **t** hundred *and* five	7969
Am	1: 3 For **t** transgressions of Damascus,	7969
	1: 6 For **t** transgressions of Gaza, and for four,	7969
	1: 9 For **t** transgressions of Tyrus, and for four,	7969
	1:11 For **t** transgressions of Edom, and for four,	7969
	1:13 For **t** transgressions of the children of	7969
	2: 1 For **t** transgressions of Moab, and for four,	7969
	2: 4 For **t** transgressions of Judah, and for four,	7969
	2: 6 For **t** transgressions of Israel, and for four,	7969

T

Am	4: 4 *and* your tithes after *t* years:	7969
	4: 7 when *there were* yet *t* months to	7969
Jnh	1:17 Jonah was in the belly of the fish three days	7969
	1:17 belly of the fish three days and *t* nights.	7969
	3: 3 an exceeding great city of *t* days' journey.	7969
Zec	13: 8 shepherds also I cut off in one month;	7969
Mt	12:40 as Jonas was *t* days and three nights in	5140
	12:40 three days and *t* nights in the whale's	5140
	12:40 so shall the Son of man be *t* days and	5140
	12:40 and *t* nights in the heart of the earth.	5140
	13:33 took, and hid in *t* measures of meal,	5140
	15:32 they continue with me now *t* days,	5140
	17: 4 thou wilt, let us make here *t* tabernacles:	5140
	18:16 *t* witnesses every word may be established	5140
	18:20 or *t* are gathered together in my name,	5140
	26:61 temple of God, and to build it in *t* days.	5140
	27:40 and buildest *it* in *t* days, save thyself.	5140
	27:63 yet alive, After *t* days I will rise *again*.	5140
Mk	8: 2 they have now been with me *t* days,	5140
	8:31 and be killed, and after *t* days rise again.	5140
	9: 5 let us make *t* tabernacles; one for thee,	5140
	14: 5 sold for more than *t* **hundred** pence,	5145
	14:58 within *t* days I will build another made	5140
	15:29 the temple, and buildest *it* in *t* days,	5140
Lk	1:56 Mary abode with her about *t* months,	5140
	2:46 *that* after *t* days they found him in	5140
	4:25 when the heaven was shut up *t* years and	5140
	9:33 let us make *t* tabernacles; one for thee,	5140
	10:36 Which now of these *t*, thinkest thou,	5140
	11: 5 say unto him, Friend, lend me *t* loaves;	5140
	12:52 *t* against two, and two against three.	5140
	12:52 three against two, and two against *t*.	5140
	13: 7 *t* years I come seeking fruit on this fig	5140
	13:21 took and hid in *t* measures of meal,	5140
Jn	2: 6 Jews, containing two or *t* firkins apiece.	5140
	2:19 temple, and in *t* days I will raise it up.	5140
	2:20 and wilt thou rear it up in *t* days?	5140
	12: 5 this ointment sold for *t* **hundred** pence,	5145
Ac	2:41 added *unto* them about *t* **thousand** souls.	5153
	5: 7 it was about the space of *t* hours after,	5140
	7:20 up in his father's house *t* months:	5140
	9: 9 And he was *t* days without sight,	5140
	10:19 said unto him, Behold, *t* men seek thee:	5140
	11:10 And this was done *t* **times**: 1909+5151	
	11:11 immediately there were *t* men already	5140
	17: 2 *t* sabbath days reasoned with them out of	5140
	19: 8 spake boldly for the space of *t* months,	5140
	20: 3 And *there* abode *t* months: and when	5140
	20:31 that *by* the space of *t* **years** I ceased not	5148
	25: 1 after *t* days he ascended from Cesarea to	5140
	28: 7 and lodged *us t* days courteously.	5140
	28:11 after *t* months we departed in a ship of	5140
	28:12 at Syracuse, we tarried *there t* days.	5140
	28:15 as far as Appii forum, and The *t* taverns,	5140
	28:17 that after *t* days Paul called the chief of	5140
1Co	10: 8 and fell in one day *t* and twenty thousand.	5140
	13:13 now abideth faith, hope, charity, these *t*;	5140
	14:27 or at the most *by t*, and *that* by course;	5140
	14:29 Let the prophets speak two or *t*, and let	5140
2Co	13: 1 *t* witnesses shall every word be	5140
Gal	1:18 Then after *t* years I went up to Jerusalem	5140
1Ti	5:19 but before two or *t* witnesses.	5140
Heb	10:28 without mercy under two or *t* witnesses:	5140
	11:23 was hid *t* **months** of his parents, because	5150
Jas	5:17 rained not on the earth *by* the space of *t*	5140
1Jn	5: 7 For there are *t* that bear record in heaven,	5140
	5: 7 and the Holy Ghost: and these *t* are one.	5140
	5: 8 And there are *t* that bear witness in earth,	5140
	5: 8 and the blood: and *these t* agree in one.	5140
Rev	6: 6 and *t* measures of barley for a penny;	5140
	8:13 other voices of the trumpet of the *t* angels,	5140
	9:18 By these *t* was the third *part* of men killed,	5140
	11: 9 nations shall see their dead bodies *t* days	5140
	11:11 And after *t* days and a half the spirit of life	5140
	16:13 And I saw *t* unclean spirits like frogs *come*	5140
	16:19 And the great city was *divided* into *t* parts,	5140
	21:13 the east *t* gates; on the north three gates;	5140
	21:13 the east three gates; on the north *t* gates;	5140
	21:13 the south three gates; and on the west three	5140
	21:13 south three gates; and on the west *t* gates.	5140

THREEFOLD (1) [THREE]

Ecc	4:12 and a *t* cord is not quickly broken.	8027

THREESCORE (93) [SIXTY]

Ge	25: 7 hundred *t* **and fifteen** 2568+7657+2050.1	
	25:26 Isaac *was t* years old when she bare them.	8346
	46:26 sons' wives, all the souls *were t* and six;	8346
	46:27 which came into Egypt, *were t* and ten.	7657
	50: 3 The Egyptians mourned for him *t* **and ten**	7657
Ex	15:27 wells of water, and *t* **and ten** palm trees;	7657
	38:25 and *t* **and fifteen** 2568+7657+2050.1+2050.1	
Lev	12: 5 continue in the blood of her purifying *t*	8346
Nu	1:27 *t* **and fourteen** thousand 702+7657+2050.1	
	1:39 *were t* and two thousand and	8346
	2: 4 *t* **and fourteen** thousand 702+7657+2050.1	
	2:26 *were t* and two thousand and	8346
	3:43 and *t* **and thirteen** 7657+7969+2050.1	
	3:46 *t* **and thirteen** of 7657+7969+1886.1+2050.1	
	3:50 a thousand three hundred and *t* and	8346
	26:22 and *t* **and sixteen** thousand 7657+8337+2050.1	
	26:25 *t* and four thousand and three hundred.	8346
	26:27 of them, *t* thousand and five hundred.	8346

Nu	26:43 *t* and four thousand and four hundred.	8346
	31:33 *t* **and twelve** thousand 7657+8147+2050.1	
	31:34 And *t* and one thousand asses,	8346
	31:37 *and t* **and fifteen**. 2568+7657+2050.1	
	31:38 tribute *was t* **and twelve**. 7657+8147+2050.1	
	31:39 tribute *was t* **and one**. 259+8346+2050.1	
Dt	33: 9 of water, and *t* **and ten** palm trees;	7657
	3: 4 *t* cities, all the region of Argob,	8346
	10:22 went down into Egypt with *t* **and ten**	7657
Jos	13:30 of Jair, which *are* in Bashan, *t* cities:	8346
Jdg	1: 7 **T and ten** kings, having their thumbs	7657
	8:14 *t* **and seventeen** men. 7651+7657+2050.1	
	8:30 Gideon had *t* **and ten** sons of his body	7657
	9: 2 which *are t* **and ten** persons, reign over	7657
	9: 4 gave him *t* **and ten** *pieces* of silver out	7657
	9: 5 *being t* **and ten** persons, upon one stone:	7657
	9:18 *t* **and ten** persons, upon one stone,	7657
	9:24 the cruelty *done* to the *t* **and ten** sons	7657
	12:14 that rode on *t* **and ten** ass colts;	7651
1Sa	6:19 people fifty thousand and *t* **and ten** men:	7657
2Sa	2:31 *so that* three hundred and *t* men died.	8346
1Ki	4:13 *t* great cities *with* walls and brasen bars:	8346
	4:22 of fine flour, and *t* measures of meal,	8346
	5:15 Solomon had *t* **and ten** thousand that	7657
	6: 2 the length thereof *was t* cubits,	8346
	10:14 to Solomon in one year was six hundred *t*	8346
2Ki	25:19 *t* men of the people of the land that were	8346
1Ch	2:21 he married when he *was t* years old;	8346
	2:23 and the towns thereof, *even t* cities.	8346
	5:18 and forty thousand seven hundred and *t*,	8346
	9:13 a thousand and seven hundred and *t*;	8346
	16:38 with their brethren, *t* and eight;	8346
	21: 5 *was* four hundred *t* **and ten** thousand	7657
	26: 8 service, *were t* and two of Obed-edom.	8346
2Ch	2: 2 Solomon told out *t* **and ten** thousand	7657
	2:18 he set *t* **and ten** thousand of them *to be*	7657
	3: 3 cubits after the first measure *was t* cubits,	8346
	9:13 six hundred and *t* and six talents of gold;	8346
	11:21 he took eighteen wives, and *t* concubines;	8346
	11:21 and eight sons, and *t* daughters.)	8346
	12: 3 chariots, and *t* thousand horsemen:	8346
	29:32 was *t* **and ten** bullocks, an hundred rams,	7657
	36:21 she kept sabbath, to fulfil *t* **and ten** years.	7657
Ezr	2: 9 children of Zaccai, seven hundred and *t*.	8346
	2:64 *and* two thousand three hundred and *t*,	8346
	2:69 *t* **and one thousand** 505+7239+8337+2050.1	
	6: 3 height thereof *t* cubits, *and* the breadth	8361
	6: 3 *and* the breadth thereof *t* cubits;	8361
	8:10 and with him an hundred and *t* males.	8346
	8:13 and Shemaiah, and with them *t* males.	8346
Ne	7:14 children of Zaccai, seven hundred and *t*.	8346
	7:18 of Adonikam, six hundred *t* and seven.	8346
	7:19 of Bigvai, two thousand *t* and seven.	8346
	7:66 *and* two thousand three hundred and *t*,	8346
	7:72 silver, and *t* and seven priests' garments.	8346
	11: 6 dwelt at Jerusalem *were* four hundred *t*	8346
Ps	90:10 The days of our years *are t* years and **ten**;	7657
SS	3: 7 *t* valiant *men are* about it, of the valiant	8346
	6: 8 There *are t* queens,	8346
Isa	7: 8 within *t* and five years shall Ephraim be	8346
Jer	52:25 *t* men of the people of the land, that were	8346
Eze	40:14 He made also posts *of t* cubits, even unto	8346
Da	3: 1 height *was t* cubits, *and* the breadth	8361
	5:31 *being* about *t* and two year old.	8361
	9:25 *be* seven weeks, and *t* and two weeks:	8346
	9:26 after *t* and two weeks shall Messiah be	8346
Zec	1:12 thou hast had indignation these *t* **and ten**	7657
Lk	24:13 was from Jerusalem *about t* furlongs.	
Ac	7:14 all his kindred, *t* **and fifteen** souls. 1440+4002	
	23:23 horsemen *t* **and ten**, and spearmen two	1440
	27:37 the ship two hundred *t* **and sixteen** 1440+1803	
1Ti	5: 9 taken into the number under *t* years old,	1835
Rev	11: 3 a thousand two hundred *and t* days,	1835
	12: 6 there a thousand two hundred *and t* days.	1835
	13:18 his number *is* **Six hundred** *t* *and* **six**.	5516

THRESH (4) [THRESHED, THRESHETH, THRESHING, THRESHINGFLOOR, THRESHINGFLOORS, THRESHINGPLACE]

Isa	41:15 thou shalt *t* the mountains, and beat	1758
Jer	51:33 *is* like a threshingfloor, *it is* time to *t* her;	1869
Mic	4:13 Arise and *t*, O daughter of Zion: for I will	1758
Hab	3:12 thou didst *t* the heathen in anger.	1758

THRESHED (3) [THRESH]

Jdg	6:11 his son Gideon *t* wheat by the winepress,	2251
Isa	28:27 For the fitches are not *t* with a threshing	1758
Am	1: 3 they have *t* Gilead with threshing	1758

THRESHETH (1) [THRESH]

1Co	9:10 that he that *t* in hope should be partaker of	248

THRESHING (10) [THRESH]

Lev	26: 5 And your *t* shall reach unto the vintage,	1786
2Sa	24:22 *t* **instruments** and *other* instruments of	4173
2Ki	13: 7 and had made them like the dust by *t*.	1758
1Ch	21:20 hid themselves. Now Ornan was *t* wheat.	1758
	21:23 the *t* **instruments** for wood, and the	4173
Isa	21:10 O my *t*, and the corn of my floor:	4098
	28:27 For the fitches are not threshed with a *t*	2742
	28:28 because he will not ever be *t* it, 156+156	
	41:15 will make thee a new sharp *t* **instrument**	4173
Am	1: 3 they have threshed Gilead with *t*	2742

THRESHINGFLOOR (17) [FLOOR, THRESH]

Ge	50:10 came to the *t* of Atad, which *is* beyond	1637
Nu	15:20 as *ye do* the heave offering of the *t*,	1637
	18:27 as though it were the corn of the *t*,	1637
	18:30 unto the Levites as the increase of the *t*,	1637
Ru	3: 2 he winnoweth barley to night in the *t*,	1637
2Sa	6: 6 when they came to Nachon's *t*, Uzzah	1637
	24:18 rear an altar unto the LORD in the *t* of	1637
	24:21 David said, To buy the *t* of thee, to build	1637
	24:24 David bought the *t* and the oxen for fifty	1637
1Ch	13: 9 when they came unto the *t* of Chidon,	1637
	21:15 the angel of the LORD stood by the *t* of	1637
	21:18 set up an altar unto the LORD in the *t* of	1637
	21:21 went out of the *t*, and bowed himself to	1637
	21:22 to Ornan, Grant me the place of *this t*,	1637
	21:28 him in the *t* of Ornan the Jebusite,	1637
2Ch	3: 1 place that David had prepared in the *t*	1637
Jer	51:33 The daughter of Babylon *is* like a *t*, *it is*	1637

THRESHINGFLOORS (2) [FLOOR, THRESH]

1Sa	23: 1 fight against Keilah, and they rob the *t*.	1637
Da	2:35 became like the chaff of the summer *t*;	147

THRESHINGPLACE (1) [PLACE, THRESH]

2Sa	24:16 the angel of the LORD was by the *t* of	1637

THRESHOLD (14) [THRESHOLDS]

Jdg	19:27 house, and her hands *were* upon the *t*.	5592
1Sa	5: 4 of his hands *were* cut off upon the *t*;	4670
	5: 5 tread on the *t* of Dagon in Ashdod unto	4670
1Ki	14:17 *and* when she came to the *t* of the door,	5592
Eze	9: 3 whereupon he was, to the *t* of the house.	4670
	10: 4 *and* stood over the *t* of the house;	4670
	10:18 departed from off the *t* of the house,	5592
	40: 6 and measured the *t* of the gate,	5592
	40: 6 other *t* of *the gate, which was* one reed	5592
	40: 7 the *t* of the gate by the porch of the gate	5592
	43: 8 In their setting of their *t* by my thresholds,	5592
	46: 2 and he shall worship at the *t* of the gate:	4670
	47: 1 waters issued out from under the *t* of	4670
Zep	1: 9 will I punish all those that leap on the *t*,	4670

THRESHOLDS (3) [THRESHOLD]

Ne	12:25 *were* porters keeping the ward at the *t* of	624
Eze	43: 8 In their setting of their threshold by my *t*,	5592
Zep	2:14 the windows; desolation *shall be* in the *t*:	5592

THREW (6) [THROW]

2Sa	16:13 went, and *t* stones at him, and cast dust.	5619
2Ki	9:33 they *t* her **down**: and *some* of her blood	8058
2Ch	31: 1 *down* the high places and the altars out	5422
Mk	12:42 and she *t* in two mites, which make a	906
Lk	9:42 the devil *t* him **down**, and tare *him*.	4486
Ac	22:23 *off their* clothes, and *t* dust into the air,	906

THREWEST (1) [THROW]

Ne	9:11 and their persecutors thou *t* into the deeps, 7993	

THRICE (15) [THREE]

Ex	34:23 **T** in the year shall all your men 6471+7969	
	34:24 the LORD thy God *t* in the year. 6471+7969	
2Ki	13:18 And he smote *t*, and stayed. 6471+7969	
	13:19 now thou shalt smite Syria *but t*. 6471+7969	
Mt	26:34 the cock crow, thou shalt deny me *t*.	5151
	26:75 the cock crow, thou shalt deny me *t*.	5151
Mk	14:30 cock crow twice, thou shalt deny me *t*.	5151
	14:72 cock crow twice, thou shalt deny me *t*.	5151
Lk	22:34 before that thou shalt *t* deny that *thou*	5151
	22:61 the cock crow, thou shalt deny me *t*.	5151
Jn	13:38 shall not crow, till thou hast denied me *t*.	5151
Ac	10:16 This was done *t*: and the vessel was 1909+5151	
2Co	11:25 **T** was I beaten with rods, once was I	5151
	11:25 *t* I suffered shipwrack, a night and a day I	5151
	12: 8 For this *thing* I besought the Lord *t*, that it	5151

THROAT (7)

Ps	5: 9 their *t is* an open sepulchre; they flatter	1627
	69: 3 my *t* is dried: mine eyes fail while *I* wait	1627
	115: 7 neither speak they through their *t*.	1627
Pr	23: 2 put a knife to thy *t*, if thou *be* a man	3930
Jer	2:25 from being unshod, and thy *t* from thirst:	1627
Mt	18:28 on him, and took *him* by the *t*, saying,	4155
Ro	3:13 Their *t is* an open sepulchre; with their	2995

THRONE (176) [THRONES]

Ge	41:40 only in the *t* will I be greater than thou.	3678
Ex	11: 5 of Pharaoh that sitteth upon his *t*,	3678
	12:29 *t* unto the firstborn of the captive that	3678
Dt	17:18 he sitteth upon the *t* of his kingdom,	3678
1Sa	2: 8 and to make them inherit the *t* of glory:	3678
2Sa	3:10 to set up the *t* of David over Israel and	3678
	7:13 will stablish the *t* of his kingdom for ever.	3678
	7:16 thy *t* shall be stablished for ever.	3678
	14: 9 and the king and his *t be* guiltless.	3678
1Ki	1:13 reign after me, and he shall sit upon my *t*?	3678
	1:17 reign after me, and he shall sit upon my *t*.	3678
	1:20 sit on the *t* of my lord the king after him.	3678
	1:24 reign after me, and he shall sit upon my *t*?	3678
	1:27 should sit on the *t* of my lord the king	3678
	1:30 and he shall sit upon my *t* in my stead;	3678
	1:35 that he may come and sit upon my *t*;	3678
	1:37 make his *t* greater than the throne of my	3678
	1:37 make his throne greater than the *t* of my	3678
	1:46 also Solomon sitteth on the *t* of	3678
	1:47 and make his *t* greater than thy throne.	3678

1Ki	1:47 and make his throne greater than thy t.	3678
	1:48 which hath given *one* to sit on my t *this*	3678
	2: 4 fail thee (said he) a man on the t of Israel.	3678
	2:12 Solomon upon the t of David his father;	3678
	2:19 sat down on his t, and caused a seat to be	3678
	2:24 set me on the t of David my father,	3678
	2:33 and upon his house, and upon his t,	3678
	2:45 the t of David shall be established before	3678
	3: 6 thou hast given him a son to sit on his t,	3678
	5: 5 whom I will set upon thy t in thy room,	3678
	7: 7 he made a porch for the t where he might	3678
	8:20 sit on the t of Israel, as the LORD	3678
	8:25 a man in my sight to sit on the t of Israel;	3678
	9: 5 I will establish the t of thy kingdom upon	3678
	9: 5 shall not fail thee a man upon the t of	3678
	10: 9 in thee, to set thee on the t of Israel:	3678
	10:18 the king made a great t of ivory,	3678
	10:19 The t had six steps, and the top of	3678
	10:19 and the top of the t *was* round behind:	3678
	16:11 *began* to reign, as soon as he sat on his t,	3678
	22:10 the king of Judah sat each on his t,	3678
	22:19 I saw the LORD sitting on his t,	3678
2Ki	10: 3 set *him* on his father's t, and fight for	3678
	10:30 *generation* shall sit on the t of Israel.	3678
	11:19 And he sat on the t of the kings.	3678
	13:13 his fathers; and Jeroboam sat upon his t.	3678
	15:12 Thy sons shall sit on the t of Israel unto	3678
	25:28 set his t above the throne of the kings that	3678
	25:28 set his throne above the t of the kings that	3678
1Ch	17:12 a house, and I will stablish his t for ever.	3678
	17:14 his t shall be established for evermore.	3678
	22:10 I will establish the t of his kingdom over	3678
	28: 5 t of the kingdom of the LORD over Israel.	3678
	29:23 Solomon sat on the t of the LORD as king	3678
2Ch	6:10 am set on the t of Israel, as the LORD	3678
	6:16 man in my sight to sit upon the t of Israel;	3678
	7:18 will I stablish the t of thy kingdom,	3678
	9: 8 delighted in thee to set thee on his t,	3678
	9:17 the king made a great t of ivory,	3678
	9:18 there were six steps to the t, with a	3678
	9:18 *which were* fastened to the t, and stays	3678
	18: 9 king of Judah sat either of them on his t,	3678
	18:18 I saw the LORD sitting upon his t,	3678
	23:20 set the king upon the t of the kingdom.	3678
Ne	3: 7 unto the t of the governor on *this* side	3678
Est	1: 2 the king Ahasuerus sat on the t of his	3678
	5: 1 the king sat upon his royal t in the royal	3678
Job	26: 9 He holdeth back the face of *his* t,	3678
	36: 7 with kings *are* they on the t; yea, he doth	3678
Ps	9: 4 cause; thou satest in the t judging right.	3678
	9: 7 he hath prepared his t for judgment.	3678
	11: 4 holy temple, the LORD'S t *is* in heaven.	3678
	45: 6 Thy t, O God, *is* for ever and ever:	3678
	47: 8 God sitteth upon the t of his holiness.	3678
	89: 4 and build up thy t to all generations.	3678
	89:14 and judgment *are* the habitation of thy t:	3678
	89:29 for ever, and his t as the days of heaven.	3678
	89:36 for ever, and his t as the sun before me.	3678
	89:44 cease, and cast his t down to the ground.	3678
	93: 2 Thy t is established of old: thou *art* from	3678
	94:20 Shall the t of iniquity have fellowship	3678
	97: 2 and judgment *are* the habitation of his t.	3678
	103:19 The LORD hath prepared his t in	3678
	132:11 the fruit of thy body will I set upon thy t.	3678
	132:12 their children also shall sit upon thy t for	3678
Pr	16:12 for the t is established by righteousness.	3678
	20: 8 A king that sitteth in the t of judgment	3678
	20:28 the king: and his t is upholden by mercy.	3678
	25: 5 his t shall be established in righteousness.	3678
	29:14 poor, his t shall be established for ever.	3678
Isa	6: 1 died I saw also the Lord sitting upon a t,	3678
	9: 7 the t of David, and upon his kingdom,	3678
	14:13 I will exalt my t above the stars of God:	3678
	16: 5 And in mercy shall the t be established:	3678
	22:23 he shall be for a glorious t to his father's	3678
	47: 1 *is* no t, O daughter of the Chaldeans;	3678
	66: 1 The heaven *is* my t, and the earth *is* my	3678
Jer	1:15 shall set every one his t *at* the entering	3678
	3:17 that time they shall call Jerusalem the t	3678
	13:13 even the kings that sit upon David's t,	3678
	14:21 do not disgrace the t of thy glory:	3678
	17:12 A glorious high t from the beginning *is*	3678
	17:25 and princes sitting upon the t of David,	3678
	22: 2 that sittest upon the t of David, thou,	3678
	22: 4 house kings sitting upon the t of David,	3678
	22:30 sitting upon the t of David, and ruling	3678
	29:16 the king that sitteth upon the t of David,	3678
	33:17 to sit upon the t of the house of Israel;	3678
	33:21 not have a son to reign upon his t;	3678
	36:30 He shall have none to sit upon the t of	3678
	43:10 will set his t upon these stones that I have	3678
	49:38 I will set my t in Elam, and will destroy	3678
	52:32 set his t above the throne of the kings that	3678
	52:32 set his throne above the t of the kings that	3678
La	5:19 thy t from generation to generation.	3678
Eze	1:26 over their heads *was* the likeness of a t,	3678
	1:26 upon the likeness of the t *was* the	3678
	10: 1 as the appearance of the likeness of a t.	3678
	43: 7 place of my t, and the place of the soles	3678
Da	5:20 he was deposed from his kingly t,	3764
	7: 9 his t *was like* the fiery flame,	3764
Jnh	3: 6 he arose from his t, and he laid his robe	3678
Hag	2:22 I will overthrow the t of kingdoms,	3678
Zec	6:13 glory, and shall sit and rule upon his t:	3678
	6:13 he shall be a priest upon his t:	3678

Mt	5:34 at all; neither by heaven; for it is God's t:	2362
	19:28 when the Son of man shall sit in the t of	2362
	23:22 sweareth by the t of God, and by him that	2362
	25:31 then shall he sit upon the t of his glory:	2362
Lk	1:32 the Lord God shall give unto him the t of	2362
Ac	2:30 he would raise up Christ to sit on his t;	2362
	7:49 Heaven *is* my t, and earth *is* my footstool:	2362
	12:21 sat upon his t, and made an oration unto	968
Heb	1: 8 But unto the Son *he saith*, Thy t, O God,	2362
	4:16 therefore come boldly unto the t of grace,	2362
	8: 1 who is set on the right hand of the t of	2362
	12: 2 is set down at the right hand of the t of	2362
Rev	1: 4 the seven spirits which are before his t;	2362
	3:21 will I grant to sit with me in my t,	2362
	3:21 and am set down with my Father in his t.	2362
	4: 2 a t was set in heaven, and one sat on	2362
	4: 2 was set in heaven, and one sat on the t.	2362
	4: 3 *there was* a rainbow round about the t,	2362
	4: 4 And round about the t *were* four and	2362
	4: 5 And out of the t proceeded lightnings and	2362
	4: 5 seven lamps of fire burning before the t,	2362
	4: 6 And before the t *there was* a sea of glass	2362
	4: 6 and in the midst of the t, and round about	2362
	4: 6 of the throne, and round about the t,	2362
	4: 9 and thanks to him that sat on the t,	2362
	4:10 fall down before him that sat on the t,	2362
	4:10 ever, and cast their crowns before the t,	2362
	5: 1 him that sat on the t a book written	2362
	5: 6 the midst of the t and of the four beasts,	2362
	5: 7 the right hand of him that sat upon the t.	2362
	5:11 voice of many angels round about the t	2362
	5:13 *be* unto him that sitteth upon the t,	2362
	6:16 from the face of him that sitteth on the t,	2362
	7: 9 stood before the t, and before the Lamb,	2362
	7:10 to our God which sitteth upon the t,	2362
	7:11 all the angels stood round about the t,	2362
	7:11 and fell before the t on their faces,	2362
	7:15 Therefore are they before the t of God,	2362
	7:15 he that sitteth on the t shall dwell among	2362
	7:17 the Lamb which is in the midst of the t	2362
	8: 3 the golden altar which was before the t.	2362
	12: 5 was caught up unto God, and to his t.	2362
	14: 3 sung as *it were* a new song before the t,	2362
	14: 5 for they are without fault before the t of	2362
	16:17 of heaven, from the t, saying, It is done.	2362
	19: 4 and worshipped God that sat on the t,	2362
	19: 5 And a voice came out of the t, saying,	2362
	20:11 I saw a great white t, and him that sat	2362
	21: 5 And he that sat upon the t said, Behold,	2362
	22: 1 proceeding out of the t of God and of	2362
	22: 3 the t of God and of the Lamb shall be in	2362

THRONES (9) [THRONE]

Ps	122: 5 there are set t of judgment, the thrones	3678
	122: 5 of judgment, the t of the house of David.	3678
Isa	14: 9 it hath raised up from their t all the kings	3678
Eze	26:16 the sea shall come down from their t,	3764
Da	7: 9 I beheld till the t were cast *down*, and	2362
Mt	19:28 ye also shall sit upon twelve t, judging	2362
Lk	22:30 sit on t judging the twelve tribes of Israel.	2362
Col	1:16 whether *they be* t, or dominions,	2362
Rev	20: 4 And I saw t, and they sat upon them,	2362

THRONG (2) [THRONGED, THRONGING]

Mk	3: 9 of the multitude, lest they should t him.	2346
Lk	8:45 the multitude t thee and press *thee*, and	4912

THRONGED (2) [THRONG]

Mk	5:24 much people followed him, and t him.	4918
Lk	8:42 a dying. (But as he went the people t him.	4846

THRONGING (1) [THRONG]

Mk	5:31 Thou seest the multitude t thee,	4918

THROUGH (463) [THROUGHOUT]

Ge	6:13 the earth is filled *with* violence t	4480+6440
	12: 6 Abram passed t the land unto the place	871.1
	13:17 walk t the land in the length of it and in	871.1
	30:32 I will pass t all thy flock to day,	871.1
	41:36 that the land perish not t the famine.	871.1
Ex	10:15 herbs of the field, t all the land of Egypt.	871.1
	12:12 For I will pass t the land of Egypt this	871.1
	12:23 For the LORD will **pass** t to smite	5674
	13:17 God led them not t the way of the land	NIH
	13:18 t the way of the wilderness of the Red sea:	NIH
	14:16 go on dry *ground* t the midst of the sea.	871.1
	14:24 host of the Egyptians t the pillar of fire	871.1
	19:13 he shall surely be stoned, or **shot** t;	3384+3384
	19:21 lest they **break** t unto the LORD to gaze,	2040
	19:24 the people **break** t to come up unto	2040
	21: 6 master shall **bore** his ear t with an aul;	7527
	36:33 he made the middle bar to shoot t	8432+871.1
Lev	4: 2 If a soul sin t ignorance against any	871.1
	4:13 congregation of Israel **sin** t **ignorance**,	7686
	4:22 done somewhat t ignorance against any	871.1
	4:27 if any one of the common people sin t	871.1
	5:15 commit a trespass, and sin t ignorance,	871.1
	18:21 thou shalt not let *any* of thy seed **pass** t	5674
	26: 6 neither shall the sword go t your land.	871.1
Nu	13:32 which we have gone to search it,	871.1
	14: 7 The land, which we passed t to search it,	871.1
	15:27 if any soul sin t ignorance, then he shall	871.1
	15:29 that **sinneth** t **ignorance**	6213+7684+871.1
	20:17 Let us pass, I pray thee, t thy country:	871.1
	20:17 we will not pass t the fields, or through	871.1

Nu	20:17 through the fields, or t the vineyards,	871.1
	20:19 without *doing any* thing *else*, **go** t on my	5674
	20:20 he said, Thou shalt not **go** t. And Edom	5674
	20:21 Edom refused to give Israel passage t	871.1
	21:22 Let me **pass** t thy land: we will not turn	871.1
	21:23 Sihon would not suffer Israel to pass t his	871.1
	24: 8 and **pierce** *them* t with his arrows.	4272
	25: 8 **thrust** both of them t, the man of Israel,	1856
	25: 8 man of Israel, and the woman t her belly.	413
	31:16 of Israel, t the counsel of Balaam,	871.1
	31:23 ye shall **make** *it* **go** t the fire, and it shall	5674
	31:23 not the fire ye shall **make** **go** t the water.	5674
	33: 8 **passed** t the midst of the sea into	5674
Dt	1:19 we went t all that great and terrible	NIH
	2: 4 Ye are to pass t the coast of your brethren	871.1
	2: 7 he knoweth thy walking t this great	NIH
	2: 8 t the way of the plain from Elath,	4480
	2:18 Thou art to pass over t Ar, the coast of	NIH
	2:27 Let me pass t thy land: I will go along by	871.1
	2:28 I may drink: only I will **pass** t on my feet;	5674
	5:15 brought thee out thence t a mighty hand	871.1
	8:15 Who led thee t *that* great and terrible	871.1
	9:26 thou hast redeemed t thy greatness,	871.1
	15:17 thrust *it* t his son or his daughter **to pass** t	5674
	18:10 **maketh** t his son or his daughter **to pass** t	5674
	29:16 how we came t the nations which	7130+871.1
	31:29 to provoke him to anger t the work of	871.1
	32:47 t this thing ye shall prolong *your* days in	871.1
	33:11 smite t the loins of them that rise against	NIH
Jos	1:11 Pass t the host, and command	7130+871.1
	2:15 let them down by a cord t the window:	1157
	3: 2 that the officers went t the host;	7130+871.1
	18: 4 go t the land, and describe it according to	871.1
	18: 8 Go and walk t the land, and describe it,	871.1
	18: 9 the men went and **passed** t the land,	5674
	18:12 and went up t the mountains westward;	871.1
	24:17 all the people t whom we passed:	7130+871.1
Jdg	2:22 That t them I may prove Israel,	871.1
	3:23 Ehud went forth t the porch, and shut	1886.5
	5: 6 and the travellers walked t byways.	NIH
	5:26 had pierced and **stricken** t his temples.	2498
	5:28 cried t the lattice, Why is his chariot *so*	1157
	9:54 his young man **thrust** him t, and he died.	1856
	11:16 t the wilderness unto the Red sea,	871.1
	11:17 Let me, I pray thee, pass t thy land:	871.1
	11:18 they went along t the wilderness,	871.1
	11:19 we pray thee, t thy land into my place.	871.1
	11:20 trusted not Israel to pass t his coast:	871.1
	20:12 tribes of Israel sent men t all the tribe	871.1
1Sa	9: 4 he passed t mount Ephraim,	871.1
	9: 4 passed t the land of Shalisha,	871.1
	9: 4 they passed t the land of Shalim,	871.1
	9: 4 he passed t the land of the Benjamites,	871.1
	19:12 So Michal let David down t a window:	1157
	31: 4 thy sword, and **thrust** me t therewith;	1856
	31: 4 uncircumcised come and **thrust** me t,	1856
2Sa	2:29 his men walked all that night t the plain,	871.1
	2:29 went t all Bithron, and they came to	NIH
	4: 7 and gat them away t the plain all night.	1870
	6:16 Saul's daughter looked t a window,	1157
	12:31 and made them pass t the brickkiln:	871.1
	18:14 and thrust them t the heart of Absalom,	871.1
	20:14 went t all the tribes of Israel unto Abel,	5674
	22:13 T the brightness before him were coals of	4480
	22:30 by thee I have run t a troop: by my God	NIH
	23:16 the three mighty *men* brake t the host of	871.1
	24: 2 him, Go now t all the tribes of Israel,	871.1
	24: 8 So when they had gone t all the land,	871.1
2Ki	1: 2 Ahaziah fell down t a lattice in his upper	1157
	3: 8 The way t the wilderness of Edom.	NIH
	3:26 to **break** t *even* unto the king of Edom:	1234
	10:21 Jehu sent t all Israel: and all	871.1
	16: 3 yea, and made his son to pass t the fire,	871.1
	17:17 and their daughters to pass t the fire,	871.1
	21: 6 he made his son pass t the fire,	871.1
	23:10 his daughter to pass t the fire to Molech.	871.1
	24:20 For t the anger of the LORD it came to	5921
1Ch	10: 4 thy sword, and **thrust** me t therewith;	1856
	11:18 three brake t the host of the Philistines,	871.1
2Ch	9: 4 he went out again t the people from	871.1
	23:20 they came t the high gate *into*	8432+871.1
	24: 9 they made a proclamation t Judah and	871.1
	30:10 So the posts passed from city to city t	871.1
	31:18 their daughters, t all the congregation:	3807.1
	32: 4 the brook that ran t the midst of the land,	871.1
	33: 6 he caused his children to pass t the fire in	871.1
Ezr	6:14 they prospered t the prophesying of	871.2
Ne	9:11 that they **went** t the midst of the sea on	5674
Est	6: 9 bring him on horseback t the street of	871.1
	6:11 brought him on horseback t the street of	871.1
Job	7:14 with dreams, and terrifiest me t visions:	4480
	14: 9 *Yet* t the scent of water it will bud,	4480
	20:24 *and* the bow of steel shall **strike** him t.	2498
	22:13 can he judge t the dark *cloud?*	1157
	24:16 In the dark *they* dig t houses, *which* they	NIH
	26:12 by his understanding he **smiteth** t	4272
	29: 3 *when* by his light I walked t darkness;	NIH
	29: 7 When I went out *to* the gate t the city,	5921
	40:24 with his eyes: *his* nose pierceth t snares.	871.1
	41: 2 his nose? or **bore** his jaw t with a thorn?	5344
Ps	8: 8 *whatsoever* passeth t the paths of the seas.	734
	10: 4 The wicked, t the pride of his	3509.1
	18:29 For by thee I have run t a troop; and by	NIH
	19: 4 Their line is gone out t all the earth,	871.1
	21: 7 t the mercy of the most High he shall not	871.1

T

Ps
23: 4 though I walk t the valley of the shadow — 871.1
32: 3 my bones waxed old t my roaring all — 871.1
44: 5 T thee will we push down our enemies: — 871.1
44: 5 t thy name will we tread them under that — 871.1
60:12 T God we shall do valiantly: for he it is — 871.1
66: 3 t the greatness of thy power shall thine — 871.1
66: 6 dry land: they went t the flood on foot: — 871.1
66:12 we went t fire and through water: — 871.1
66:12 we went through fire and t water: — 871.1
68: 7 when thou didst march t the wilderness; — 871.1
73: 9 and their tongue walketh t the earth. — 871.1
78:13 the sea, and caused them to pass t; — 5674
81: 5 when he went out t the land of Egypt: — 5921
84: 6 Who passing t the valley of Baca make it — 871.1
92: 4 Lord, hast made me glad t thy work: — 871.1
106: 9 so he led them t the depths, as through — 871.1
106: 9 through the depths, as t the wilderness. — NIH
107:39 minished and brought low t oppression, — 4480
108:13 T God we shall do valiantly: — 871.1
109:24 My knees are weak t fasting; and my flesh — 4480
110: 5 The Lord at thy right hand shall strike t — 4272
115: 7 not: neither speak they t their throat. — 871.1
119:98 Thou t thy commandments hast made me — NIH
119:104 Thy precepts I get understanding: — 4480
136:14 made Israel to pass t the midst of it: — 5674
136:16 To him which led his people t — 871.1

Pr
7: 6 at the window of my house I looked t — 1157
7: 8 Passing t the street near her corner; — 871.1
7:23 Till a dart strike t his liver; as a bird — 6398
11: 9 t knowledge shall the just be delivered. — 871.1
18: 1 T desire a man, having separated — 3807.1
24: 3 T wisdom is a house builded; — 871.1

Ecc
5: 3 For a dream cometh t the multitude of — 871.1
10:18 t idleness of the hands the house — 871.1
10:18 of the hands the house droppeth t. — 1811

SS
4: 2 windows, shewing himself t the lattice. — 4480

Isa
8: 8 he shall pass t Judah; he shall overflow — 871.1
8:21 they shall pass t it, hardly bestead and — 871.1
9:19 the wrath of the Lord of hosts is — 871.1
13:15 Every one that is found shall be thrust t; — 1856
14:19 thrust t with a sword, that go down to — 2944
16: 8 Jazer, they wandered t the wilderness: — NIH
21: 1 As whirlwinds in the south pass t; — 2498
23:10 Pass t thy land as a river, O daughter of — 5674
27: 4 I would go t them, I would burn them — 871.1
28: 7 they also have erred t wine, — 871.1
28: 7 and t strong drink are out of the way; — 871.1
28: 7 the prophet have erred t strong drink, — 871.1
28: 7 they are out of the way t strong drink; — 4480
28:15 the overflowing scourge shall pass t, — 5674
28:18 the overflowing scourge shall pass t, — 5674
30:31 For t the voice of the Lord shall — 4480
34:10 none shall pass t it for ever and ever. — 871.1
43: 2 When thou passest t the waters, I will be — 871.1
43: 2 the rivers, they shall not overflow thee: — 871.1
43: 2 thou walkest t the fire, thou shalt not — 1119
48:21 they thirsted not when he led them t — 871.1
60:15 no man went t thee, I will make thee — 5674
62:10 Go t, go through the gates; prepare you — 871.1
62:10 Go through, go t the gates; prepare you — 871.1
63:13 That led them t the deep, as a horse in — 871.1

Jer
2: 6 led us t the wilderness, through a land — 871.1
2: 6 t a land of deserts and of pits, through a — 871.1
2: 6 t a land of drought, and of the shadow of — 871.1
2: 6 t a land that no man passed through, — 871.1
2: 6 through a land that no man passed t, — 4480
3: 9 it came to pass t the lightness of her — 871.1
5: 1 Run ye to and fro t the streets of — 871.1
9: 6 t deceit they refuse to know me, saith — 871.1
9:10 that none can pass t them; neither can — 5674
9:12 like a wilderness, that none passeth t? — 5674
12:12 upon all high places t the wilderness: — 871.1
17:24 bring in no burden t the gates of this city — 871.1
32:35 cause their sons and their daughters
 to pass t — 5674
51: 4 and they that are thrust t in her streets. — 1856
51:52 t all her land the wounded shall groan. — 871.1
52: 3 For t the anger of the Lord it came to — 5921

La
3:44 cloud, that our prayer should not pass t. — 871.1
4: 9 stricken t for want of the fruits of the — 1856
4:21 of Uz; the cup also shall pass t unto thee: — 5674

Eze
5:17 pestilence and blood shall pass t thee; — 871.1
6: 8 ye shall be scattered t the countries. — 871.1
9: 4 Go t the midst of the city through the — 5674
9: 4 Go through the midst of the city t the — 871.1
9: 5 Go ye after him t the city, and smite: — 871.1
12: 5 Dig thou t the wall in their sight, — 871.1
12: 7 in the even I digged t the wall with mine — 871.1
12:12 they shall dig t the wall to carry out — 871.1
14: 5 are all estranged from me t their idols. — 871.1
14:15 I cause noisome beasts to pass t the land, — 871.1
14:15 that no man may pass t because of — 5674
14:17 that land, and say, Sword, go t the land; — 871.1
16:14 for it was perfect t my comeliness, which — 871.1
16:21 delivered them to cause them to pass t — 5674
16:36 nakedness discovered t thy whoredoms — 871.1
16:40 and thrust thee t with their swords. — 1333
20:23 and disperse them t the countries; — 871.1
20:26 in that they caused to pass t the fire all — 5674
20:31 ye make your sons to pass t the fire, — 5674
23:37 caused their sons, whom they bare
 unto me, to pass for them t — 5674
29:11 No foot of man shall pass t it, nor foot of — 5674
29:11 through it, nor foot of beast shall pass t it, — 871.1
29:12 and will disperse them t the countries. — 871.1

Eze
30:23 and will disperse them t the countries. — 871.1
33:28 shall be desolate, that none shall pass t. — 5674
34: 6 My sheep wandered t all the mountains, — 871.1
36:19 and they were dispersed t the countries: — 871.1
39:14 passing t the land to bury with — 5674
39:15 the passengers that pass t the land, — 5674
41:19 it was made t all the house round about. — 413
46:19 After, he brought me t the entry, — 871.1
47: 3 and he brought me t the waters; — 871.1
47: 4 thousand, and brought me t the waters; — 871.1
47: 4 measured a thousand, and brought me t; — 871.1

Da
8:25 t his policy also he shall cause craft to — 5921
9: 7 t all the countries whither thou hast — 871.1
11: 2 his strength t his riches he shall stir up — 871.1
11:10 certainly come, and overflow, and pass t: — 5674

Joel
3:17 there shall no strangers pass t her any — 871.1

Am
2:10 led you forty years t the wilderness, — 871.1
5:17 I will pass t thee, saith the Lord. — 7130+871.1

Jnh
3: 7 published t Nineveh by the decree of — 871.1

Mic
2:13 passed t the gate, and are gone out by — 5674
5: 8 who, if he go t, both treadeth down, — 5674
7:12 he shall be cut down, when he shall pass t. — 5674

Na
1:12 they be cut down, yet thus shall he pass t, — 871.1
1:15 for the wicked shall no more pass t thee; — 871.1
3: 4 that selleth nations t her whoredoms, — 871.1
3: 4 and families t her witchcrafts. — 871.1

Hab
1: 6 shall march t the breadth of the land, — 3807.1
3:12 didst march t the land in indignation, — 6805
3:14 didst strike t with his staves the head — 5344
3:15 Thou didst walk t the sea with thine — 871.1
3:15 thine horses, t the heap of great waters. — NIH

Zec
1:10 hath sent to walk to and fro t the earth. — 871.1
1:11 We have walked to and fro t the earth, — 871.1
1:17 My cities t prosperity shall yet be spread — 4480
4:10 which run to and fro t the whole earth. — 871.1
4:12 the two golden pipes empty — 3027+871.1
5: 6 This is their resemblance t all the earth. — 871.1
6: 7 they might walk to and fro t the earth: — 871.1
6: 7 Get ye hence, walk to and fro t the earth. — 871.1
6: 7 So they walked to and fro t the earth. — 871.1
7:14 that no man passed t nor returned: — 5674
9: 8 no oppressor shall pass t them any more: — 5921
9:15 shall drink, and make a noise as t wine; — NIH
10: 7 and their heart shall rejoice as t wine: — NIH
10:11 he shall pass t the sea with affliction, — 871.1
13: 3 shall thrust him t when he prophesieth. — 1856
13: 9 I will bring the third part t the fire, — 871.1

Mt
6:19 and where thieves break t and steal: — 1358
6:20 where thieves do not break t nor steal: — 1358
9:34 He casteth out the devils t the prince of — 1722
12: 1 Jesus went on the sabbath day t the corn; — 1223
12:43 he walketh t dry places, seeking rest, — 1330
19:24 It is easier for a camel to go t the eye — 1330

Mk
2:23 he went t the corn fields on the sabbath — 1223
6:55 And ran t that whole region round about, — 4063
7:13 Making the word of God of none effect t — NIG
7:31 the midst of the coasts of Decapolis. — 303
9:30 departed thence, and passed t Galilee; — 1223
10:25 It is easier for a camel to go t the eye of a — 1330
11:16 man should carry any vessel t the temple. — 1223

Lk
1:78 T the tender mercy of our God; — 1223
2:35 a sword shall pierce t thy own soul also,) — 1330
4:14 there went out a fame of him t all — 2596
4:30 But he passing t the midst of them — 1330
5:19 let him down t the tiling with his couch — 1223
6: 1 that he went t the corn fields; — 1279
9: 6 they departed, and went t the towns, — 1330
10:17 even the devils are subject unto us t thy — 1722
11:15 He casteth out devils t Beelzebub the chief — 1722
11:18 ye say that I cast out devils t Beelzebub. — 1722
11:24 walketh t dry places, seeking rest; — 1330
12:39 have suffered his house to be broken t. — 1358
13:22 And he went t the cities and villages, — 2596
17: 1 but woe unto him, t whom they come. — 1223
17:11 that he passed t the midst of Samaria — 1330
18:25 it is easier for a camel to go t a needle's — 1223
19: 1 And Jesus entered and passed t Jericho. — 1330

Jn
1: 7 Light, that all men t him might believe. — 1223
3:17 but that the world t him might be saved. — 1223
4: 4 And he must needs go t Samaria. — 1223
8:59 going t the midst of them, and so — 1223
15: 3 ye are clean t the word which I have — 1223
17:11 keep t thine own name those whom thou — 1722
17:17 Sanctify them t thy truth: thy word is — 1722
17:19 that they also might be sanctified t — 1722
17:20 for them also which shall believe on me t — 1223

Ac
1: 2 after that he t the Holy Ghost had given — 1722
3:16 his name t faith in his name hath made — 1909
3:17 I wot that t ignorance ye did it, as did also — 2596
4: 2 preached t Jesus the resurrection from — 1722
8:18 And when Simon saw that t laying on of — 1223
8:40 passing t he preached in all the cities, — 1330
10:43 that t his name whosoever believeth in — 1223
12:10 they went out, and passed on t one street; — NIG
13: 6 And when they had gone t the isle unto — 1330
13:38 that t this man is preached unto you — 1223
14:22 that we must t much tribulation enter into — 1223
15: 3 they passed t Phenice and Samaria, — 1330
15:11 But we believe that t the grace of the Lord — 1223
15:41 And he went t Syria and Cilicia, — 1330
16: 4 And as they went t the cities, — 1279
17: 1 Now when they had passed t Amphipolis — 1353
18:27 helped them much which had believed t — 1223
19: 1 Paul having passed t the upper coasts — 1330
19:21 when he had passed t Macedonia and — 1330

Ac
20: 3 he purposed to return t Macedonia. — 1223
21: 4 said to Paul t the Spirit, that he should — 1223

Ro
1: 8 I thank my God t Jesus Christ for you all, — 1223
1:24 uncleanness t the lusts of their own hearts — 1722
2:23 t breaking the law dishonourest thou God? — 1223
2:24 is blasphemed among the Gentiles t you, — 1223
3: 7 more abounded t my lie unto his glory; — 1722
3:24 Being justified freely by his grace t — 1223
3:25 to be a propitiation t faith in his blood, — 1722
3:25 that are past, t the forbearance of God; — 1722
3:30 by faith, and uncircumcision t faith. — 1223
3:31 Do we then make void the law t faith? — 1223
4:13 to him, but through the righteousness — 1223
4:13 the law, but t the righteousness of faith. — 1223
4:20 He staggered not at the promise of God t — NIG
5: 1 we have peace with God t our Lord Jesus — 1223
5: 9 we shall be saved from wrath t him. — 1223
5:11 we also joy in God t our Lord Jesus Christ, — 1223
5:15 For if t the offence of one many be dead, — 1223
5:21 might grace reign t righteousness unto — 1223
6:11 but alive unto God t Jesus Christ our Lord. — 1722
6:23 the gift of God is eternal life t Jesus Christ — 1722
7:25 I thank God t Jesus Christ our Lord. — 1223
8: 3 not do, in that it was weak t the flesh, — 1223
8:13 if ye t the Spirit do mortify the deeds of — NIG
8:37 more than conquerors t him that loved us. — 1223
11:11 rather t their fall salvation is come unto — NIG
11:30 yet have now obtained mercy t their — NIG
11:31 that t your mercy they also may obtain — NIG
11:36 For of him, and t him, and to him, are all — 1223
12: 3 For I say, t the grace given unto me, — 1223
15: 4 that we t patience and comfort of — 1223
15:13 in hope, t the power of the Holy Ghost. — 1722
15:17 whereof I may glory t Jesus Christ in — 1722
15:19 T mighty signs and wonders, by the power — 1223
16:27 only wise, be glory t Jesus Christ for ever. — 1223

1Co
1: 1 called to be an apostle of Jesus Christ t — 1223
4:15 for in Christ Jesus I have begotten you t — 1223
8:11 t thy knowledge shall the weak brother — 1909
10: 1 under the cloud, and all passed t the sea; — 1223
13:12 For now we see t a glass, darkly; — 1223
15:57 which giveth us the victory t our Lord — 1223
16: 5 unto you, when I shall pass t Macedonia: — 1330
16: 5 for I do pass t Macedonia. — 1330

2Co
3: 4 And such trust have we t Christ to — 1223
4:15 that the abundant grace might t — 1223
8: 9 that ye t his poverty might be rich. — NIG
9:11 which causeth t us thanksgiving to God. — 1223
10: 4 mighty t God to the pulling down of — NIG
11: 3 as the serpent beguiled Eve t his subtilty, — 1722
11:33 t a window in a basket was I let down — 1223
12: 7 the abundance of the revelations, — NIG
13: 4 For though he was crucified t weakness, — 1537

Gal
2:19 For I t the law am dead to the law, that I — 1223
3: 8 that God would justify the heathen t faith, — 1537
3:14 might come on the Gentiles t Jesus Christ; — 1722
3:14 receive the promise of the Spirit t faith. — 1223
4: 7 and if a son, then an heir of God t Christ. — 1223
4:13 Ye know how t infirmity of the flesh I — NIG
5: 5 For we t the Spirit wait for the hope of — NIG
5:10 I have confidence in you t the Lord, — 1722

Eph
1: 7 In whom we have redemption t his blood, — 1223
2: 7 in his kindness towards us t Christ Jesus. — 1223
2: 8 For by grace are ye saved t faith; — 1223
2:18 t him we both have access by one Spirit — 1223
2:22 for a habitation of God t the Spirit. — 1722
4: 6 who is above all, and t all, and in you all. — 1223
4:18 being alienated from the life of God t — 1223

Php
1:19 shall turn to my salvation t your prayer, — 1223
2: 3 Let nothing be done t strife or vainglory; — 2596
3: 9 but that which is t the faith of Christ, — 1223
4: 7 keep your hearts and minds t Christ Jesus. — 1722
4:13 I can do all things t Christ which — 1722

Col
1:14 In whom we have redemption t his blood, — 1223
1:20 made peace t the blood of his cross, — 1223
1:22 In the body of his flesh t death, to present — 1223
2: 8 lest any man spoil you t philosophy — 1223
2:12 wherein also ye are risen with him t — 1223

2Th
2:13 to salvation t sanctification of the Spirit — 1722
2:16 and good hope t grace, — 1223

1Ti
6:10 pierced themselves t with many sorrows. — 4044

2Ti
1:10 and immortality to light t the gospel: — 1223
3:15 salvation t faith which is in Christ Jesus. — 1223

Tit
1: 3 hath in due times manifested his word t — 1722
3: 6 Which he shed on us abundantly t Jesus — 1223

Phm
1:22 for I trust that t your prayers I shall be — 1223

Heb
2:10 of their salvation perfect t sufferings. — 1223
2:14 that t death he might destroy him that had — 1223
2:15 And deliver them who t fear of death were — 1223
3:13 lest any of you be hardened t — NIG
6:12 but followers of them who t faith and — 1223
9:14 who t the eternal Spirit offered himself — 1223
10:10 By the which will we are sanctified t — 1223
10:20 for us, t the vail, that is to say, his flesh; — 1223
11: 3 T faith we understand that the worlds — NIG
11:11 T faith also Sara herself received strength — NIG
11:28 T faith he kept the passover, — NIG
11:29 By faith they passed t the Red sea as by — 1224
11:33 Who t faith subdued kingdoms, — 1223
11:39 having obtained a good report t faith, — 1223
12:20 it shall be stoned, or thrust t with a dart: — 2700
13:20 the blood of the everlasting covenant, — 1722
13:21 is well pleasing in his sight, t Jesus Christ; — 1223

1Pe
1: 2 t sanctification of the Spirit, unto — 1722
1: 5 Who are kept by the power of God t faith — 1223

T

1Pe	1: 6 are in heaviness **t** manifold temptations:	1722
	1:22 t the Spirit unto unfeigned love of	1223
	4:11 that God in all *things* may be glorified **t**	1223
2Pe	1: 1 faith with us **t** the righteousness of God	1722
	1: 2 peace be multiplied unto you **t**	1223
	1: 3 **t** the knowledge of him that hath called	1223
	1: 4 the corruption that is in the world **t** lust:	1722
	2: 3 **t** covetousness shall they with feigned	1722
	2:18 they allure **t** the lusts of the flesh,	1722
	2:18 the lusts of the flesh, **t** much wantonness,	1722
	2:20 of the world **t** the knowledge of the Lord	1722
1Jn	4: 9 into the world, that we might live **t** him.	1223
Rev	8:13 heard an angel flying **t** the midst of heaven,	1722
	18: 3 merchants of the earth are waxed rich **t**	1537
	22:14 and may enter in **t** the gates into the city.	1525

THROUGHLY (12) [THOROUGHLY]

2Ki	11:18 and his images brake they in pieces **t**,	3190
Job	6: 2 Oh that my grief were **t** weighed,	8254+8254
Ps	51: 2 Wash me **t** from mine iniquity,	7235
Jer	6: 9 They shall **t** glean the remnant of	5953+5953
	7: 5 For if you **t** amend your ways and	3190+3190
	7: 5 if you **t** execute judgment between	6213+6213
	50:34 he shall **t** plead their cause, that he	7378+7378
Eze	16: 9 I **t** washed away thy blood from thee,	7857
Mt	3:12 he will **t** purge his floor, and gather his	1245
Lk	3:17 and he will **t** purge his floor,	1245
2Co	1: 6 we *have been* **t** made manifest	1722+3956
2Ti	3:17 **t** furnished unto all good works.	1822

THROUGHOUT (162) [THROUGH]

Ge	41:29 come seven years of great plenty **t** all	871.1
	41:46 and **went t** all the land of Egypt.	5674+871.1
	45: 8 and a ruler **t** all the land of Egypt.	871.1
Ex	5:12 So the people were scattered abroad **t** all	871.1
	7:19 *that* there may be blood **t** all the land of	871.1
	7:21 there was blood **t** all the land of Egypt.	871.1
	8:16 that it may become lice **t** all the land of	871.1
	8:17 all the dust of the land became lice **t** all	871.1
	9: 9 and upon beast, **t** all the land of Egypt.	871.1
	9:16 that my name may be declared **t** all	871.1
	9:22 herb of the field, **t** the land of Egypt.	871.1
	9:25 the hail smote **t** all the land of Egypt all	871.1
	11: 6 there shall be a great cry **t** all the land of	871.1
	12:14 you shall keep it a feast to the LORD **t**	3807.1
	29:42 *shall be* a continual burnt offering **t**	3807.1
	30: 8 a perpetual incense before the LORD **t**	3807.1
	30:10 atonement upon it **t** your generations:	3807.1
	30:21 him and to his seed **t** their generations.	3807.1
	30:31 oil unto me **t** your generations;	3807.1
	31:13 me and you **t** your generations;	3807.1
	31:16 observe the sabbath **t** their generations,	3807.1
	32:27 in and out from gate to gate **t** the camp,	871.1
	34: 3 let any man be seen **t** all the mount;	871.1
	35: 3 Ye shall kindle no fire **t** your	3605+871.1
	36: 6 caused it to be proclaimed **t** the camp,	871.1
	37:19 the six branches going out of	3807.1
	40:15 priesthood **t** their generations.	3807.1
	40:38 the house of Israel, **t** all their journeys.	871.1
Lev	3:17 generations **t** all your dwellings,	3605+871.1
	3:17 *by* a statute for **ever t** their generations.	5769
	10: 9 *it shall be* a statute for **ever t** your	5769
	17: 7 for ever unto them **t** their generations.	3807.1
	23:14 *it shall be* a statute for ever **t** your	3807.1
	23:21 in all your dwellings **t** your generations.	3807.1
	23:31 *it shall be* a statute for ever **t** your	3807.1
	25: 9 make the trumpet sound **t** all your land.	871.1
	25:10 proclaim liberty **t** *all* the land unto all	871.1
	25:30 to him that bought it **t** his generations:	3807.1
Nu	1:42 **t** their generations, after their families,	NIH
	1:52 man by his own standard, **t** their hosts.	3807.1
	2: 3 the camp of Judah pitch **t** their armies:	3807.1
	2: 9 and four hundred, **t** their armies.	3807.1
	2:16 four hundred and fifty, **t** their armies.	3807.1
	2:24 and an hundred, **t** their armies.	3807.1
	2:32 **t** their hosts *were* six hundred thousand	3807.1
	3:39 **t** their families, all the males from a	3807.1
	4:22 **t** the houses of their fathers, by their	3807.1
	4:38 **t** their families, and by the house of their	3807.1
	4:40 **t** their families, by the house of their	3807.1
	4:42 **t** their families, by the house of their	3807.1
	10: 8 an ordinance for ever **t** your generations.	3807.1
	10:25 *was* the rereward of all the camps **t**	3807.1
	11:10 Moses heard the people weep **t** their	3807.1
	15:38 of their garments **t** their generations,	3807.1
	18:23 *it shall be* a statute for ever **t** your	3807.1
	26: 2 and upward, **t** their fathers' house,	3807.1
	28:14 *is* the burnt offering of every month **t**	3807.1
	28:21 offer for every lamb, **t** the seven lambs;	3807.1
	28:24 ye shall offer daily, **t** the seven days,	NIH
	28:29 deal unto one lamb, **t** the seven lambs	3807.1
	29: 4 deal unto one lamb, **t** the seven lambs	3807.1
	29:10 deal unto one lamb, **t** the seven lambs	3807.1
	31: 4 tribes of Israel, shall ye send to	3807.1
	35:29 **t** your generations in all your dwellings.	3807.1
Dt	16:18 LORD thy God giveth thee, **t** thy tribes:	3807.1
	28:40 shalt have olive trees **t** all thy coasts,	871.1
	28:52 wherein thou trustedst, **t** all thy land:	871.1
	28:52 he shall besiege thee in all thy gates **t** all	871.1
Jos	2:22 the pursuers sought *them* **t** all the way,	871.1
	6:27 his fame was *noised* **t** all the country.	871.1
	16: 1 goeth out from Jericho **t** mount Beth-el,	871.1
	22:14 of each chief house a prince **t** all	3807.1
	24: 3 led him **t** all the land of Canaan,	871.1
Jdg	6:35 he sent messengers **t** all Manasseh;	871.1

Jdg	7:22 against his fellow, even **t** all the host:	871.1
	7:24 Gideon sent messengers **t** all mount	871.1
	20: 6 sent her **t** all the country of the	871.1
	20:10 will take ten men of an hundred **t** all	3807.1
1Sa	5:11 for there was a deadly destruction **t** all	871.1
	11: 7 sent *them* **t** all the coasts of Israel by	871.1
	13: 3 And Saul blew the trumpet **t** all the land,	871.1
	13:19 Now there was no smith found **t** all	871.1
	23:23 that I will search him out **t** all	871.1
2Sa	8:14 **t** all Edom put he garrisons, and all they	871.1
	15:10 Absalom sent spies **t** all the tribes of	871.1
	19: 9 the people were at strife **t** all the tribes	871.1
1Ki	1: 3 So they sought for a fair damsel **t** all	871.1
	6:38 was the house finished **t** all the parts	3807.1
	15:22 Asa made a proclamation **t** all Judah;	3605
	18: 6 the land between them to pass **t** it:	871.1
	22:36 went a proclamation **t** the host about	871.1
2Ki	17: 5 the king of Assyria came up **t** all the land,	871.1
1Ch	5:10 dwelt in their tents **t** all the east	5921+6440
	6:54 Now these *are* their dwelling places **t**	3807.1
	6:60 All their cities **t** their families *were*	871.1
	6:62 to the sons of Gershom **t** their families	3807.1
	6:63 **t** their families, out of the tribe of	871.1
	7:40 number **t** the **genealogy** of them *that*	3187
	9:34 Levites *were* chief **t** their generations;	3807.1
	12:30 famous **t** the house of their fathers.	3807.1
	21: 4 went **t** all Israel, and came to Jerusalem.	871.1
	21:12 the angel of the LORD destroying **t** all	871.1
	22: 5 of fame and of glory **t** all countries:	3807.1
	26: 6 that ruled **t** the house of their father:	3807.1
	27: 1 out month by month **t** all the months	3807.1
2Ch	2: 6 and **t** all the land of his dominion.	871.1
	11:23 dispersed of all his children **t** all	3807.1
	16: 9 LORD run to and fro **t** the whole earth,	871.1
	17: 9 went about **t** all the cities of Judah,	871.1
	17:19 king put in the fenced cities **t** all Judah.	871.1
	19: 5 he set judges in the land **t** all the fenced	871.1
	20: 3 and proclaimed a fast **t** all Judah.	5921
	25: 5 *their* fathers, **t** all Judah and Benjamin.	3807.1
	26:14 Uzziah prepared for them **t** all the host	3807.1
	30: 5 decree to make proclamation **t** all Israel,	871.1
	30: 6 and his princes **t** all Israel and Judah,	871.1
	30:22 they did eat **t** the feast seven days,	NIH
	31:20 thus did Hezekiah **t** all Judah,	3807.1
	34: 7 cut down all the idols **t** all the land of	871.1
	36:22 that he made a proclamation **t** all his	871.1
Ezr	1: 1 that he made a proclamation **t** all his	871.1
	10: 7 they made proclamation **t** Judah and	871.1
Est	1:20 make shall be published **t** all his empire,	871.1
	3: 6 **t** the whole kingdom of Ahasuerus,	871.1
	9: 2 **t** all the provinces of the king Ahasuerus,	871.1
	9: 4 his fame went out **t** all the provinces:	871.1
	9:28 and kept **t** every generation,	871.1
Ps	72: 5 moon endure, **t all generations.**	1755+1755
	102:24 my days: thy years *are* **t** all generations.	871.1
	135:13 O LORD, **t** all generations.	3807.1
	145:13 thy dominion *endureth* **t** all generations.	871.1
	145:13 thy high places for sin, **t** all thy borders.	871.1
Jer	17: 3 thy high places for sin, **t** all thy borders.	871.1
Eze	38:21 I will call *for* a sword against him **t** all	3807.1
Mt	4:24 And his fame went **t** all Syria:	1519
Mk	1:28 **t** all the region round about Galilee.	1519+3837
	1:39 And he preached in their synagogues **t** all	1519
	14: 9 shall be preached **t** the whole world,	1519
Lk	1:65 all these sayings were noised abroad **t** all	1722
	4:25 when great famine was **t** all the land;	1909
	7:17 And this rumour of him went forth **t** all	1722
	7:17 all Judea, and **t** all the region round about.	1722
	8: 1 that he **went t** every city and village,	1353
	8:39 published **t** the whole city how great	2596
	23: 5 stirreth up the people, teaching **t** all Jewry,	2596
Jn	19:23 seam, woven from the top **t**.	1223+3650
Ac	8: 1 they were all scattered abroad **t** the	2596
	9:31 Then had the churches rest **t** all Judea and	2596
	9:32 as Peter passed **t** all *quarters*, he came	1223
	9:42 And it was known **t** all Joppa;	2596
	10:37 which was published **t** all Judea,	2596
	11:28 should be great dearth **t** all the world:	1909
	13:49 And the word of the Lord was published **t**	1223
	14:24 And after they had **passed t** Pisidia,	1330
	16: 6 Now when they had **gone t** Phrygia and	1330
	19:26 but almost **t** all Asia, this Paul hath	NIG
	24: 5 a mover of sedition among all the Jews **t**	2596
	26:20 and **t** all the coasts of Judea, and *then* to	1519
Ro	1: 8 that your faith is spoken of **t** the whole	1722
	9:17 that my name might be declared **t** all	1722
2Co	8:18 whose praise *is* in the gospel **t** all	1223
Eph	3:21 in the church by Christ Jesus **t** all ages,	1519
1Pe	1: 1 to the strangers **scattered t** Pontus,	1290

THROW (9) [OVERTHROW, THREWEST, THROWING, THROWN]

Jdg	2: 2 in this land; you shall **t down** their altars:	5422
	6:25 **t down** the altar of Baal that thy father	2040
2Sa	20:15 with Joab battered the wall, to **t** *it* **down**.	5307
2Ki	9:33 he said, **T** her **down**. So they threw her	8058
Jer	1:10 and to **t down**, to build, and to plant.	2040
	31:28 to **t down**, and to destroy, and to afflict;	2040
Eze	16:39 they shall **t down** thine eminent place,	2040
Mic	5:11 thy land, and **t** all thy strong holds:	2040
Mal	1: 4 They shall build, but I will **t down**;	2040

THROWING (1) [THROW]

Nu	35:17 if he smite him with **t** a stone,	3027

THROWN (19) [THROW]

Ex	15: 1 and his rider hath he **t** into the sea.	7411
	15:21 and his rider hath he **t** into the sea.	7411
Jdg	6:32 because he hath **t down** his altar.	5422
2Sa	20:21 his head *shall be* **t** to thee over the wall.	7993
1Ki	19:10 **t down** thine altars, and slain thy	2040
	19:14 **t down** thine altars, and slain thy	2040
Jer	31:40 up, nor **t down** any more for ever.	2040
	33: 4 which are **t down** by the mounts,	5422
	50:15 are fallen, her walls are **t down**:	2040
La	2: 2 he hath **t down** in his wrath the strong	2040
	2:17 he hath **t down**, and hath not pitied:	2040
Eze	29: 5 I will leave thee **t** into the wilderness,	NIH
	38:20 the mountains shall be **t down**,	2040
Na	1: 6 fire, and the rocks are **t down** by him.	5422
Mt	24: 2 upon another, that shall not be **t down**.	2647
Mk	13: 2 upon another, that shall not be **t down**.	2647
Lk	4:35 when the devil had **t** him in the midst,	4496
	21: 6 upon another, that shall not be **t down**.	2647
Rev	18:21 shall *that* great city Babylon be **t down**,	906

THRUST (50) [THRUSTETH]

Ex	11: 1 **surely t** you out hence altogether.	1644+1644
	12:39 because they were **t out** of Egypt,	1644
Nu	22:25 she herself unto the wall,	3905
	25: 8 **t** both of them **through**, the man of Israel,	1856
	35:20 if he **t** him of hatred, or hurl at him by	1920
	35:22 if he **t** him suddenly without enmity,	1920
Dt	13: 5 to **t** thee out of the way which the LORD	5080
	13:10 he hath sought to **t** thee **away** from	5080
	15:17 **t** *it* through his ear unto the door,	5414
	33:27 shall **t out** the enemy from before thee;	1644
Jdg	3:21 from his right thigh, and **t** it into his belly:	8628
	6:38 the fleece **together**, and wringed the	2115
	9:41 Zebul **t out** Gaal and his brethren, that	1644
	9:54 young man **t** him **through**, and he died.	1856
	12: 2 they **t out** Jephthah, and said unto him,	1644
1Sa	11: 2 that I may **t out** all your right eyes,	5365
	31: 4 thy sword, and **t** me **through** therewith;	1856
	31: 4 uncircumcised come and **t** me **through**,	1856
2Sa	2:16 and **t** his sword in his fellow's side;	NIH
	18:14 and **t** them through the heart of Absalom,	8628
	23: 6 *shall be* all of them as thorns **t away**,	5074
1Ki	2: 7 So Solomon **t out** Abiathar from being	1644
2Ki	4:27 Gehazi came near to **t** her **away**.	1920
1Ch	10: 4 thy sword, and **t** me **through** therewith;	1856
2Ch	26:20 and they **t** him **out** from thence;	926
Ps	118:13 Thou hast **t** sore at me that *I* might	1760+1760
Isa	13:15 one that is found shall be **t through**;	1856
	14:19 **t through** with a sword, that go down to	2944
Jer	51: 4 *they that are* **t through** in her streets.	1856
Eze	16:40 and **t** thee **through** with their swords.	1333
	34:21 Because ye have **t** with side and	1920
	46:18 by oppression to **t** them out of their	NIH
Joel	2: 8 Neither shall one **t** another; they shall	1766
Zec	13: 3 shall **t** him **through** when he prophesieth.	1856
Lk	4:29 **t** him **out** of the city, and led him unto	1544
	5: 3 prayed him that *he* would **t out** a little	1877
	10:15 to heaven, shalt be **t down** to hell.	2601
	13:28 of God, and you yourselves **t out**.	1544
Jn	20:25 and **t** my hand into his side, I will not	906
	20:27 *hither* thy hand, and **t** *it* into my side:	906
Ac	7:27 that did his neighbour wrong **t** him **away**,	683
	7:39 but **t** *him* **from** *them*, and in their hearts	683
	16:24 them into the inner prison, and made	906
	16:37 and now do they **t** us **out** privily?	1544
	27:39 if it were possible, to **t** in the ship.	1856
Heb	12:20 shall be stoned, or **t through** with a dart:	2700
Rev	14:15 on the cloud, **T** in thy sickle, and reap:	3992
	14:16 And he that sat on the cloud **t** in his sickle	906
	14:18 **T** in thy sharp sickle, and gather	3992
	14:19 thy sickle into the earth,	906

THRUSTETH (1) [THRUST]

Job	32:13 out wisdom: God **t** him **down**, not man.	5086

THUMB (6) [THUMBS]

Ex	29:20 upon the **t** of their right hand, and upon	931
Lev	8:23 upon the **t** of his right hand, and upon	931
	14:14 upon the **t** of his right hand, and upon	931
	14:17 upon the **t** of his right hand, and upon	931
	14:25 upon the **t** of his right hand, and upon	931
	14:28 upon the **t** of his right hand, and upon	931

THUMBS (3) [THUMB]

Lev	8:24 upon the **t** of their right hands, and upon	931
Jdg	1: 6 and cut off his **t** and his great toes.	931+3027
	1: 7 their **t** and their great toes cut off,	931+3027

THUMMIM (5)

Ex	28:30 of judgment the Urim and the **T**;	8550
Lev	8: 8 put in the breastplate the Urim and the **T**.	8550
Dt	33: 8 *Let* thy **T** and thy Urim *be* with thy holy	8550
Ezr	2:63 stood *up* a priest with Urim and with **T**.	8550
Ne	7:65 there stood *up* a priest with Urim and **T**.	8550

THUNDER (19) [THUNDERBOLTS, THUNDERED, THUNDERETH, THUNDERINGS, THUNDERS]

Ex	9:23 the LORD sent **t** and hail, and the fire ran	6963
	9:29 the **t** shall cease, neither shall there be	6963
1Sa	2:10 out of heaven shall he **t** upon them:	7481
	7:10 the LORD thundered with a great **t** on that	6963
	12:17 the LORD, and he shall send **t** and rain;	6963
	12:18 and the LORD sent **t** and rain that day:	6963
Job	26:14 the **t** of his power who can understand?	7482

Job 28:26 and a way for the lightning of the **t**: 6963
38:25 of waters, or a way for the lightning of **t**; 6963
39:19 hast thou clothed his neck with **t**? 7483
39:25 the **t** of the captains, and the shouting. 7482
40: 9 or, canst thou **t** with a voice like him? 7481
Ps 77:18 The voice of thy **t** *was* in the heaven: 7482
81: 7 I answered thee in the secret place of **t**: 7482
104: 7 at the voice of thy **t** they hasted away. 7482
Isa 29: 6 be visited of the Lᴏʀᴅ of hosts with **t**, 7482
Mk 3:17 Boanerges, which is, The sons of **t**:) 1027
Rev 6: 1 and I heard, as *it were* the noise of **t**, one 1027
14: 2 many waters, and as the voice of a great **t**: 1027

THUNDERBOLTS (1) [THUNDER]
Ps 78:48 also to the hail, and their flocks to **hot t**. 7565

THUNDERED (4) [THUNDER]
1Sa 7:10 the Lᴏʀᴅ **t** with a great thunder on that 7481
2Sa 22:14 The Lᴏʀᴅ **t** from heaven, and the most 7481
Ps 18:13 The Lᴏʀᴅ also **t** in the heavens, 7481
Jn 12:29 stood *by*, and heard *it*, said that it **t**: 1027+1096

THUNDERETH (3) [THUNDER]
Job 37: 4 he **t** with the voice of his excellency; 7481
37: 5 God **t** marvellously with his voice; 7481
Ps 29: 3 the God of glory **t**: the Lᴏʀᴅ *is* upon 7481

THUNDERINGS (6) [THUNDER]
Ex 9:28 that there be no *more* mighty **t** and hail; 6963
20:18 the people saw the **t**, and the lightnings, 6963
Rev 4: 5 proceeded lightnings and **t** and voices: 1027
8: 5 and **t**, and lightnings, and an earthquake. 1027
11:19 and **t**, and an earthquake, and great hail. 1027
19: 6 and as the voice of mighty **t**, saying, 1027

THUNDERS (7) [THUNDER]
Ex 9:33 the **t** and hail ceased, and the rain was not 6963
9:34 rain and the hail and the **t** were ceased, 6963
19:16 there were **t** and lightnings, and a thick 6963
Rev 10: 3 he had cried, seven **t** uttered their voices. 1027
10: 4 And when the seven **t** had uttered their 1027
10: 4 Seal *up those things* which the seven **t** 1027
16:18 there were voices, and **t**, and lightnings; 1027

THUS (737)
Ge 2: 1 **T** the heavens and the earth were 2050.1
6:22 **T** did Noah; according to all that God 2050.1
19:36 **T** were both the daughters of Lot with 2050.1
20:16 and with all *other*: **t** she was reproved. 2050.1
21:32 **T** they made a covenant at Beer-sheba: 2050.1
24:30 sister, saying, **T** spake the man unto me; 3541
25:22 and she said, If *it be* so, why *am* I **t**? 2088
25:34 his way: **t** Esau despised *his* birthright. 2050.1
31: 8 If he said **t**, The speckled shall be thy 3541
31: 8 If he said **t**, The ringstraked shall be thy 3541
31: 9 **T** God hath taken away the cattle of 2050.1
31:40 **T** I was in the day, the drought consumed NIH
31:41 **T** have I been twenty years in thy house; 2088
32: 4 **T** shall ye speak unto my lord Esau; 3541
32: 4 Thy servant Jacob saith **t**, I have 3541
36: 8 **T** dwelt Esau in mount Seir: Esau *is* 2050.1
37:35 mourning. **T** his father wept for him. 2050.1
42:25 for the way: and **t** did he unto them. 3651
45: 9 and say unto him, **T** saith thy son Joseph, 3541
Ex 3:14 **T** shalt thou say unto the children of 3541
3:15 **T** shalt thou say unto the children of 3541
4:22 **T** saith the Lᴏʀᴅ, Israel *is* my son, 3541
5: 1 **T** saith the Lᴏʀᴅ God of Israel, 3541
5:10 to the people, saying, **T** saith Pharaoh, 3541
5:15 dealest thou **t** with thy servants? 3541
7:17 **T** saith the Lᴏʀᴅ, In this thou shalt know 3541
8: 1 and say unto him, **T** saith the Lᴏʀᴅ, 3541
8:20 say unto him, **T** saith the Lᴏʀᴅ, Let my 3541
9: 1 **T** saith the Lᴏʀᴅ God of the Hebrews, 3541
9:13 **T** saith the Lᴏʀᴅ God of the Hebrews, 3541
10: 3 **T** saith the Lᴏʀᴅ God of the Hebrews, 3541
11: 4 Moses said, **T** saith the Lᴏʀᴅ, 3541
12:11 **t** shall ye eat it; *with* your loins girded, 3602
12:50 **T** did all the children of Israel; 2050.1
14:11 hast thou dealt **t** with us, to carry 2063
14:30 **T** the Lᴏʀᴅ saved Israel that day out of 2050.1
19: 3 **T** shalt thou say to the house of Jacob, 3541
20:22 **T** thou shalt say unto the children of 3541
26:17 **t** shalt thou make for all the boards of 3651
26:24 **t** shall it be for them both; they shall be 3651
29:35 **t** shalt thou do unto Aaron, and to his NIH
32:27 **T** saith the Lᴏʀᴅ God of Israel, 3541
36:22 **t** did he make for all the boards of 3651
36:29 **t** he did to both of them in both the 3651
39:32 **T** was all the work of the tabernacle of 2050.1
40:16 **T** did Moses: according to all that 2050.1
Lev 15:31 **T** shall ye separate the children of Israel 2050.1
16: 3 **T** shall Aaron come into the holy 2063+871.1
Nu 4:19 **t** do unto them, that they may live, 2088
4:49 **t** *were they* numbered of him, 2050.1
8: 7 **t** shalt thou do unto them, to cleanse 3541
8:14 **T** shalt thou separate the Levites from 2050.1
8:26 **t** shalt thou do unto the Levites touching 3602
10:28 **T** *were* the journeyings of the children of 428
11:15 if thou deal **t** with me, kill me, I pray 3602
15:11 **T** shall it be done for one bullock, 3602
18:26 **t** speak unto the Levites, and say unto 2050.1
18:28 **T** you also shall offer a heave offering 3651
20:14 **T** saith thy brother Israel, Thou knowest 3541
20:21 **T** Edom refused to give Israel passage 2050.1

Nu 21:31 **T** Israel dwelt in the land of 2050.1
22:16 to him, **T** saith Balak the son of Zippor, 3541
23: 5 Return unto Balak, and **t** thou shalt speak. 3541
23:16 and said, Go again unto Balak, and say **t**. 3541
32: 8 **T** did your fathers, when I sent them from 3541
Dt 7: 5 **t** shall ye deal with them; ye shall destroy 3541
9:25 I fell down before the Lᴏʀᴅ forty 2050.1
20:15 **T** shalt thou do unto all the cities *which* 3651
29:24 Wherefore hath the Lᴏʀᴅ done **t** unto 3602
32: 6 Do ye **t** requite the Lᴏʀᴅ, O foolish 2088
Jos 2: 4 hid them, and said **t**, There came men 3651
6: 3 the city once. **T** shalt thou do six days. 3541
7:10 wherefore liest thou **t** upon thy face? 2088
7:13 for **t** saith the Lᴏʀᴅ God of Israel, 3541
7:20 and **t** and **t** have I done: 2088+3509.1
7:20 and **t** and **t** have I done: 2088+3509.1
10:25 for **t** shall the Lᴏʀᴅ do to all your 3602
16: 5 **t** even the border of their inheritance on NIH
21:13 They gave to the children of Aaron 2050.1
21:42 round about them: **t** *were* all these cities. 3651
22:16 **T** saith the whole congregation of 3541
24: 2 **T** saith the Lᴏʀᴅ God of Israel, 3541
Jdg 6: 8 **T** saith the Lᴏʀᴅ God of Israel, 3541
8: 1 thou served us **t**, 1697+2088+1886.1+1886.1
8:28 **T** was Midian subdued before 2050.1
9:56 **T** God rendered the wickedness of 2050.1
11:15 unto him, **T** saith Jephthah, Israel took 3541
11:33 **T** the children of Ammon were subdued 2050.1
13:18 Why askest thou **t** after my name, seeing 2088
18: 4 **T** and **t** dealeth Micah with 2090+3509.1
18: 4 **T** and **t** dealeth Micah with 2088+3509.1
20:43 **T** *they* inclosed the Benjamites round NIH
1Sa 2:27 and said unto him, **T** saith the Lᴏʀᴅ, 3541
9: 9 **t** he spake, Come, and let us go to the 3541
10:18 **t** saith the Lᴏʀᴅ God of Israel, I brought 3541
11: 9 **T** shall ye say unto the men of 3541
14: 9 If they say **t** unto us, Tarry until we come 3541
14:10 If they say **t**, Come up unto us; then we 3541
15: 2 **T** saith the Lᴏʀᴅ of hosts, I remember 3541
18:25 Saul said, **T** shall ye say to David, The 3541
20: 7 If he say **t**, *It is* well; thy servant shall 3541
20:22 if I say **t** unto the young man, Behold, 3541
25: 6 **t** shall ye say to him that liveth *in* 3541
26:18 Wherefore doth my lord **t** pursue after his 2088
2Sa 6:22 I will yet be more vile than **t**, and will be 2063
7: 5 tell my servant David, **T** saith the Lᴏʀᴅ, 3541
7: 8 **T** saith the Lᴏʀᴅ of hosts, I took thee 3541
11:25 **t** shalt thou say unto Joab, Let not this 3541
12: 7 **T** saith the Lᴏʀᴅ God of Israel, 3541
12:11 **T** saith the Lᴏʀᴅ, Behold, I will raise up 3541
12:31 **t** did he unto all the cities of the children 3651
15:26 if he **t** say, I have no delight in thee; 3541
16: 7 **t** said Shimei when he cursed, Come out, 3541
17:15 **T** and thus did Ahithophel 2088+3509.1
17:15 **t** did Ahithophel counsel Absalom 2088+3509.1
17:15 and **t** and thus have I counselled. 2088+3509.1
17:15 and thus and **t** have I counselled. 2088+3509.1
17:21 for **t** hath Ahithophel counselled against 3602
18:14 said Joab, I may not tarry **t** with thee. 3651
18:33 as he went, **t** he said, O my son Absalom, 3541
24:12 and say unto David, **T** saith the Lᴏʀᴅ, 3541
1Ki 1:48 also **t** said the king, Blessed *be* the Lᴏʀᴅ 3602
2:30 unto him, **T** saith the king, Come forth. 3541
2:30 **T** said Joab, and thus he answered me. 3541
2:30 Thus said Joab, and **t** he answered me. 3541
3:22 *is* my son. **T** they spake before the king. 2050.1
5:11 **t** gave Solomon to Hiram year by year. 3541
9: 8 Why hath the Lᴏʀᴅ done **t** unto this land, 3602
11:31 for **t** saith the Lᴏʀᴅ, the God of Israel, 3541
12:10 **T** shalt thou speak unto this people that 3541
12:10 **t** shalt thou say unto them, My little 3541
12:24 **T** saith the Lᴏʀᴅ, Ye shall not go up, 3541
13: 2 and said, O altar, altar, **t** saith the Lᴏʀᴅ; 3541
13:21 from Judah, saying, **T** saith the Lᴏʀᴅ, 3541
14: 5 he *is* sick: **t** and thus shalt thou 2090+3509.1
14: 5 thus and **t** shalt thou say unto 2090+3509.1
14: 7 **T** saith the Lᴏʀᴅ God of Israel, 3541
16:12 **T** did Zimri destroy all the house of 2050.1
17:14 For **t** saith the Lᴏʀᴅ God of Israel, 3541
20: 2 and said unto him, **T** saith Ben-hadad, 3541
20: 5 said, **T** speaketh Ben-hadad, saying, 3541
20:13 saying, **T** saith the Lᴏʀᴅ, Hast thou seen 3541
20:14 he said, **T** saith the Lᴏʀᴅ, *Even* by 3541
20:28 of Israel, and said, **T** saith the Lᴏʀᴅ, 3541
20:42 he said unto him, **T** saith the Lᴏʀᴅ, 3541
21:19 saying, **T** saith the Lᴏʀᴅ, Hast thou 3541
21:19 unto him, saying, **T** saith the Lᴏʀᴅ, 3541
22:11 he said, **T** saith the Lᴏʀᴅ, With these 3541
22:27 say, **T** saith the king, Put this *fellow in* 3541
2Ki 1: 4 Now therefore **t** saith the Lᴏʀᴅ, 3541
1: 6 **T** saith the Lᴏʀᴅ, *Is it* not because 3541
1:11 O man of God, **t** hath the king said, 3541
1:16 he said unto him, **T** saith the Lᴏʀᴅ, 3541
2:21 salt in there, and said, **T** saith the Lᴏʀᴅ, 3541
3:16 he said, **T** saith the Lᴏʀᴅ, Make this 3541
3:17 For **t** saith the Lᴏʀᴅ, Ye shall not see 3541
4:43 for **t** saith the Lᴏʀᴅ, They shall eat, 3541
5: 4 and **t** said the maid that *is* 2088+3509.1
5: 4 said the maid that *is* of the land 2088+3509.1
7: 1 **T** saith the Lᴏʀᴅ, To morrow about *this* 3541
9: 3 **t** it on his head, and say, **T** saith the Lᴏʀᴅ, 3541
9: 6 **T** saith the Lᴏʀᴅ God of Israel, 3541
9:12 **T** and thus spake he to me, 2088+3509.1
9:12 Thus and **t** spake he to me, 2088+3509.1
9:12 spake he to me, saying, **T** saith the Lᴏʀᴅ, 3541

2Ki 9:18 and said, **T** saith the king, *Is it* peace? 3541
9:19 and said, **T** saith the king, *Is it* peace? 3541
10:28 **T** Jehu destroyed Baal out of Israel. 2050.1
16:16 **T** did Urijah the priest, according to all 2050.1
18:19 **T** saith the great king, the king of Assyria, 3541
18:29 **T** saith the king, Let not Hezekiah deceive 3541
18:31 for **t** saith the king of Assyria, Make *an* 3541
19: 3 they said unto him, **T** saith Hezekiah, 3541
19: 6 **T** shall ye say to your master, Thus saith 3541
19: 6 ye say to your master, **T** saith the Lᴏʀᴅ, 3541
19:10 **T** shall ye speak to Hezekiah king of 3541
19:20 **T** saith the Lᴏʀᴅ God of Israel, 3541
19:32 Therefore **t** saith the Lᴏʀᴅ concerning 3541
20: 1 said unto him, **T** saith the Lᴏʀᴅ, 3541
20: 5 **T** saith the Lᴏʀᴅ, the God of David thy 3541
21:12 Therefore **t** saith the Lᴏʀᴅ God of Israel, 3541
22:15 **T** saith the Lᴏʀᴅ God of Israel, 3541
22:16 **T** saith the Lᴏʀᴅ, Behold, I will bring 3541
22:18 **t** shall ye say to him, Thus saith 3541
22:18 to him, **T** saith the Lᴏʀᴅ God of Israel, 3541
1Ch 15:28 **T** all Israel brought up the ark of 2050.1
17: 4 tell David my servant, **T** saith the Lᴏʀᴅ, 3541
17: 7 **t** shalt thou say unto my servant David, 3541
17: 7 **T** saith the Lᴏʀᴅ of hosts, I took thee 3541
18: 6 **T** the Lᴏʀᴅ preserved David 2050.1
18:13 **T** the Lᴏʀᴅ preserved David 2050.1
21:10 and tell David, saying, **T** saith the Lᴏʀᴅ, 3541
21:11 unto him, **T** saith the Lᴏʀᴅ, Choose thee 3541
24: 4 sons of Ithamar; and **t** *were* they divided. NIH
24: 5 **T** were they divided by lot, one *sort* 2050.1
29:26 The son of Jesse reigned over all 2050.1
2Ch 4:18 **T** Solomon made all these vessels in 2050.1
5: 1 **T** all the work that Solomon made for 2050.1
7:11 **T** Solomon finished the house of 2050.1
7:21 Why hath the Lᴏʀᴅ done **t** unto this land, 3602
10:10 **T** shalt thou answer the people that spake 3541
10:10 **t** shalt thou say unto them, My little 3541
11: 4 **T** saith the Lᴏʀᴅ, Ye shall not go up, 3541
12: 5 and said unto them, **T** saith the Lᴏʀᴅ, 3541
13:18 **T** the children of Israel were brought 2050.1
18:10 said, **T** saith the Lᴏʀᴅ, With these thou 3541
18:26 say, **T** saith the king, Put this *fellow in* 3541
19: 9 **T** shall ye do in the fear of the Lᴏʀᴅ, 3541
20:15 **T** saith the Lᴏʀᴅ unto you, 3541
21:12 **T** saith the Lᴏʀᴅ God of David thy 3541
24:11 **T** they did day by day, and gathered 3541
24:20 and said unto them, **T** saith God, 3541
24:22 **T** Joash the king remembered not 2050.1
31:20 **t** did Hezekiah throughout all 2088+3509.1
32:10 **T** saith Sennacherib king of Assyria, 3541
32:22 **T** the Lᴏʀᴅ saved Hezekiah and 2050.1
34:23 **T** saith the Lᴏʀᴅ God of Israel, 3541
34:24 **T** saith the Lᴏʀᴅ, Behold, I will bring 3541
34:26 **T** saith the Lᴏʀᴅ God of Israel 3541
36:23 **T** saith Cyrus king of Persia, 2050.1
Ezr 1: 2 **T** saith Cyrus king of Persia, The Lᴏʀᴅ 3541
5: 3 their companions, and said **t** unto them, 3652
5: 7 unto him, wherein *was* written **t**: 1836+3509.4
5: 9 we those elders, *and* said unto them **t**, 3660
5:11 they returned us answer, saying, We are 3660
6: 2 a roll, and therein *was* a record **t** written: 3652
Ne 5:13 even **t** be he shaken out, and emptied. 3602
13:18 Did not your fathers **t**, and *did not* our God 2050.1
13:30 **T** cleansed I them from all strangers, 2050.1
Est 1:18 **T** *For this day* arise too much contempt 2050.1
2:13 **t** came *every* maiden unto the king 2088+871.1
6: 9 **T** shall it be done to the man whom 3602
6:11 **T** shall it be done unto the man whom 3602
9: 5 The Jews smote all their enemies *with* 2050.1
Job 1: 5 in their hearts. **T** did Job continually. 3602
27:12 why then are ye **t** altogether vain? 2088
Ps 38:14 **T** I was as a man that heareth not, 2050.1
63: 4 **T** will I bless thee while I live: I will lift 3651
73:15 If I say, I will speak **t**; behold, I should 3644
73:21 **T** my heart was grieved, and I was 3588
106:20 **T** they changed their glory into 2050.1
106:29 **T** they provoked *him* to anger with 2050.1
106:39 **T** were they defiled with their own 2050.1
128: 4 **t** shall the man be blessed that feareth 3651
Isa 7: 7 **T** saith the Lord Gᴏᴅ, It shall not stand, 3541
8:11 For the Lᴏʀᴅ spake **t** to me with a strong 3541
10:24 Therefore **t** saith the Lord Gᴏᴅ of hosts, 3541
21: 6 For **t** hath the Lord said unto me, Go, set 3541
21:16 For **t** hath the Lord said unto me, Within 3541
22:15 **T** saith the Lord Gᴏᴅ of hosts, 3541
24:13 When **t** it shall be in the midst of the land 3541
28:16 Therefore **t** saith the Lord Gᴏᴅ, Behold, 3541
29:22 Therefore **t** saith the Lᴏʀᴅ, 3541
30:12 Wherefore **t** saith the Holy One of Israel, 3541
30:15 For **t** saith the Lord Gᴏᴅ, the Holy One 3541
31: 4 For **t** hath the Lᴏʀᴅ spoken unto me, 3541
36: 4 **T** saith the great king, the king of Assyria, 3541
36:14 **T** saith the king, Let not Hezekiah deceive 3541
36:16 for **t** saith the king of Assyria, Make *an* 3541
37: 3 they said unto him, **T** saith Hezekiah, 3541
37: 6 **T** shall ye say unto your master, Thus 3541
37: 6 say unto your master, **T** saith the Lᴏʀᴅ, 3541
37:10 **T** shall ye speak to Hezekiah king of 3541
37:21 **T** saith the Lᴏʀᴅ God of Israel, 3541
37:33 Therefore **t** saith the Lᴏʀᴅ concerning 3541
38: 1 said unto him, and say, **T** saith the Lᴏʀᴅ, 3541
38: 5 and say to Hezekiah, **T** saith the Lᴏʀᴅ, 3541
42: 5 **T** saith God the Lᴏʀᴅ, he that created 3541
43: 1 now **t** saith the Lᴏʀᴅ that created thee, 3541
43:14 **T** saith the Lᴏʀᴅ, your redeemer, 3541

T

Isa		
43:16	T saith the LORD, which maketh a way in	3541
44: 2	T saith the LORD that made thee,	3541
44: 6	T saith the LORD the King of Israel,	3541
44:24	T saith the LORD, thy redeemer,	3541
45: 1	T saith the LORD to his anointed,	3541
45:11	T saith the LORD, the Holy One of Israel,	3541
45:14	T saith the LORD, The labour of Egypt,	3541
45:18	For t saith the LORD that created	3541
47:15	T shall they be unto thee *with* whom	3651
48:17	T saith the LORD, thy redeemer, the Holy	3541
49: 7	T saith the LORD, the redeemer of Israel,	3541
49: 8	T saith the LORD, In an acceptable time	3541
49:22	T saith the Lord GOD, Behold, I will lift	3541
49:25	t saith the LORD, Even the captives of	3541
50: 1	T saith the LORD, Where *is* the bill of	3541
51:22	T saith thy Lord the LORD, and thy God	3541
52: 3	For t saith the LORD, Ye have sold	3541
52: 4	For t saith the Lord GOD, My people	3541
56: 1	T saith the LORD, Keep ye judgment,	3541
56: 4	For t saith the LORD unto the eunuchs	3541
57:15	For t saith the high and lofty One that	3541
65: 8	T saith the LORD, As the new wine is	3541
65:13	Therefore t saith the Lord GOD, Behold,	3541
66: 1	T saith the LORD, The heaven *is* my	3541
66:12	For t saith the LORD, Behold, I will	3541

Jer		
2: 2	of Jerusalem, saying, T saith the LORD;	3541
2: 5	T saith the LORD, What iniquity have	3541
4: 3	For t saith the LORD to the men of Judah	3541
4:27	For t hath the LORD said, The whole land	3541
5:13	not in them: t shall it be done unto them.	3541
5:14	Wherefore t saith the LORD God of hosts,	3541
6: 6	For t hath the LORD of hosts said,	3541
6: 9	T saith the LORD of hosts, They shall	3541
6:16	T saith the LORD, Stand ye in the ways,	3541
6:21	Therefore t saith the LORD, Behold,	3541
6:22	T saith the LORD, Behold, a people	3541
7: 3	T saith the LORD of hosts, the God of	3541
7:20	Therefore t saith the Lord GOD; Behold,	3541
7:21	T saith the LORD of hosts, the God of	3541
8: 4	shalt say unto them, T saith the LORD;	3541
9: 7	T saith the LORD of hosts,	3541
9:15	Therefore t saith the LORD of hosts,	3541
9:17	T saith the LORD of hosts, Consider ye,	3541
9:22	Speak, T saith the LORD, Even	3541
9:23	T saith the LORD, Let not the wise *man*	3541
10: 2	T saith the LORD, Learn not the way of	3541
10:11	T ye say unto them, The	1836+3509.4
10:18	For t saith the LORD, Behold, I will sling	3541
11: 3	T saith the LORD God of Israel;	3541
11:11	Therefore t saith the LORD, Behold,	3541
11:21	Therefore t saith the LORD of the men of	3541
11:22	Therefore t saith the LORD of hosts,	3541
12:14	T saith the LORD against all mine evil	3541
13: 1	T saith the LORD unto me, Go and	3541
13: 9	T saith the LORD, After this manner will	3541
13:12	T saith the LORD God of Israel,	3541
13:13	say unto them, T saith the LORD, Behold,	3541
14:10	T saith the LORD unto this people, Thus	3651
14:10	T have they loved to wander, they have	3651
14:15	Therefore t saith the LORD concerning	3541
15: 2	thou shalt tell them, T saith the LORD;	3541
15:19	Therefore t saith the LORD, If thou	3541
16: 3	For t saith the LORD concerning the sons	3541
16: 5	For t saith the LORD, Enter not *into*	3541
16: 9	For t saith the LORD of hosts, the God of	3541
17: 5	T saith the LORD; Cursed *be* the man that	3541
17:19	T said the LORD unto me; Go and	3541
17:21	T saith the LORD; Take heed to	3541
18:11	of Jerusalem, saying, T saith the LORD;	3541
18:13	Therefore t saith the LORD; Ask ye now	3541
18:23	deal *t* with them in the time of thine	NIH
19: 1	T saith the LORD, Go and get a potter's	3541
19: 3	T saith the LORD of hosts, the God of	3541
19:11	say unto them, T saith the LORD of hosts;	3541
19:12	T will I do unto this place, saith	3651
19:15	T saith the LORD of hosts, the God of	3541
20: 4	For t saith the LORD, Behold, I will make	3541
21: 3	unto them, T shall ye say to Zedekiah:	3541
21: 4	T saith the LORD God of Israel; Behold,	3541
21: 8	people thou shalt say, T saith the LORD;	3541
21:12	O house of David, t saith the LORD;	3541
22: 1	T saith the LORD; Go down *to* the house	3541
22: 3	T saith the LORD; Execute ye judgment	3541
22: 6	For t saith the LORD unto the king's	3541
22: 8	Wherefore hath the LORD done t unto	3602
22:11	For t saith the LORD touching Shallum	3541
22:18	Therefore t saith the LORD concerning	3541
22:30	T saith the LORD, Write ye this man	3541
23: 2	Therefore t saith the LORD God of Israel	3541
23:15	Therefore t saith the LORD of hosts	3541
23:16	T saith the LORD of hosts, Hearken not	3541
23:35	T shall ye say every one to his neighbour,	3541
23:37	T shalt thou say to the prophet, What	3541
23:38	the LORD; therefore t saith the LORD;	3541
24: 5	T saith the LORD, the God of Israel;	3541
24: 8	surely t saith the LORD, So will I give	3541
25: 8	Therefore t saith the LORD of hosts;	3541
25:15	For t saith the LORD God of Israel unto	3541
25:27	T saith the LORD of hosts, the God of	3541
25:28	say unto them, T saith the LORD of hosts;	3541
25:32	T saith the LORD of hosts, Behold,	3541
26: 2	T saith the LORD; Stand in the court of	3541
26: 4	shalt say unto them, T saith the LORD;	3541
26:18	saying, T saith the LORD of hosts;	3541
26:19	T *might* we procure great evil against	2050.1

Jer		
27: 2	T saith the LORD to me; Make thee	3541
27: 4	T saith the LORD of hosts, the God of	3541
27: 4	of Israel; T shall ye say unto your masters;	3541
27:16	all this people, saying, T saith the LORD;	3541
27:19	For t saith the LORD of hosts concerning	3541
27:21	Yea, t saith the LORD of hosts, the God	3541
28: 2	T speaketh the LORD of hosts, the God of	3541
28:11	all the people, saying, T saith the LORD;	3541
28:13	tell Hananiah, saying, T saith the LORD;	3541
28:14	For t saith the LORD of hosts, the God of	3541
28:16	Therefore t saith the LORD; Behold,	3541
29: 4	T saith the LORD of hosts, the God of	3541
29: 8	For t saith the LORD of hosts, the God of	3541
29:10	For t saith the LORD, That after seventy	3541
29:16	*Know* that t saith the LORD of the king	3541
29:17	T saith the LORD of hosts; Behold, I will	3541
29:21	T saith the LORD of hosts, the God of	3541
29:24	*T* shalt thou also speak to Shemaiah	NIH
29:25	T speaketh the LORD of hosts, the God of	3541
29:31	T saith the LORD concerning Shemaiah	3541
29:32	Therefore t saith the LORD, Behold,	3541
30: 2	T speaketh the LORD God of Israel,	3541
30: 5	For t saith the LORD; We have heard a	3541
30:12	For t saith the LORD, Thy bruise *is*	3541
30:18	T saith the LORD: Behold, I *will* bring	3541
31: 2	T saith the LORD, The people which	3541
31: 7	For t saith the LORD; Sing with gladness	3541
31:15	T saith the LORD; A voice was heard in	3541
31:16	T saith the LORD, Refrain thy voice from	3541
31:18	himself *t*, Thou hast chastised me,	NIH
31:23	T saith the LORD of hosts, the God of	3541
31:35	T saith the LORD, which giveth the sun	3541
31:37	T saith the LORD; If heaven above can be	3541
32: 3	and say, T saith the LORD, Behold,	3541
32:14	T saith the LORD of hosts, the God of	3541
32:15	For t saith the LORD of hosts, the God of	3541
32:28	Therefore t saith the LORD; Behold,	3541
32:36	now therefore t saith the LORD, the God	3541
32:42	For t saith the LORD; Like as I have	3541
33: 2	T saith the LORD the maker thereof,	3541
33: 4	For t saith the LORD, the God of Israel,	3541
33:10	T saith the LORD; Again there shall be	3541
33:12	T saith the LORD of hosts; Again in this	3541
33:17	For t saith the LORD; David shall never	3541
33:20	T saith the LORD; If you can break my	3541
33:24	t they have despised my people, that	2050.1
33:25	T saith the LORD; If my covenant *be* not	3541
34: 2	T saith the LORD, the God of Israel;	3541
34: 2	of Judah, and tell him, T saith the LORD;	3541
34: 4	T saith the LORD of thee, Thou shalt not	3541
34:13	T saith the LORD, the God of Israel;	3541
34:17	Therefore t saith the LORD; Ye have not	3541
35: 8	T have we obeyed the voice of Jonadab	2050.1
35:13	T saith the LORD of hosts, the God of	3541
35:17	Therefore t saith the LORD God of hosts,	3541
35:18	T saith the LORD of hosts, the God of	3541
35:19	Therefore t saith the LORD of hosts,	3541
36:29	king of Judah, T saith the LORD;	3541
36:30	Therefore t saith the LORD of Jehoiakim	3541
37: 7	T saith the LORD, the God of Israel;	3541
37: 7	T shall ye say to the king of Judah,	3541
37: 9	T saith the LORD; Deceive not	3541
37:21	Jeremiah remained in the court of	2050.1
38: 2	T saith the LORD, He that remaineth in	3541
38: 3	T saith the LORD, This city shall surely	3541
38: 4	for t he weakeneth the hands of the men	3651
38:17	T saith the LORD, the God of hosts,	3541
39:16	saying, T saith the LORD of hosts,	3541
42: 9	T saith the LORD, the God of Israel,	3541
42:15	T saith the LORD of hosts, the God of	3541
42:18	For t saith the LORD of hosts, the God of	3541
43: 7	t came they *even* to Tahpanhes.	2050.1
43:10	T saith the LORD of hosts, the God of	3541
44: 2	T saith the LORD of hosts, the God of	3541
44: 7	Therefore now t saith the LORD, the God	3541
44:11	Therefore t saith the LORD of hosts,	3541
44:25	T saith the LORD of hosts, the God of	3541
44:30	T saith the LORD; Behold, I *will* give	3541
45: 2	T saith the LORD, the God of Israel,	3541
45: 4	T shalt thou say unto him, The LORD	3541
45: 4	thou say unto him, The LORD saith t;	3541
47: 2	T saith the LORD; Behold, waters rise up	3541
48: 1	Against Moab t saith the LORD of hosts,	3541
48:40	For t saith the LORD; Behold, he shall fly	3541
48:47	T *far* is the judgment of Moab.	2008+5704
49: 1	the Ammonites, t saith the LORD;	3541
49: 7	t saith the LORD of hosts;	3541
49:12	For t saith the LORD; Behold, they whose	3541
49:28	of Babylon shall smite, t saith the LORD;	3541
49:35	the LORD of hosts; Behold, I *will*	3541
50:18	Therefore t saith the LORD of hosts,	3541
50:33	T saith the LORD of hosts; The children	3541
51: 1	T saith the LORD; Behold, I *will* raise up	3541
51: 4	T the slain shall fall in the land of	2050.1
51:33	For t saith the LORD of hosts, the God of	3541
51:36	Therefore t saith the LORD; Behold,	3541
51:58	T saith the LORD of hosts; The broad	3541
51:64	T shall Babylon sink, and shall not rise	3602
51:64	T *far* are the words of Jeremiah.	2008+5704
52:27	T Judah was carried away captive out	2050.1

Eze		
1:11	T *were* their faces: and their wings	2050.1
2: 4	say unto them, T saith the Lord GOD.	3541
3:11	and tell them, T saith the Lord GOD;	3541
3:27	say unto them, T saith the Lord GOD;	3541
4:13	*Even* t shall the children of Israel eat	3602

Eze		
5: 5	T saith the Lord GOD; This *is* Jerusalem:	3541
5: 7	Therefore t saith the Lord GOD;	3541
5: 8	Therefore t saith the Lord GOD; Behold,	3541
5:13	T shall mine anger be accomplished,	2050.1
6: 3	T saith the Lord GOD to the mountains,	3541
6:11	T saith the Lord GOD; Smite with thine	3541
6:12	t will I accomplish my fury upon them.	2050.1
7: 2	t saith the Lord GOD unto the land of	3541
7: 5	T saith the Lord GOD; An evil, an only	3541
11: 5	said unto me, Speak; T saith the LORD;	3541
11: 5	T have ye said, O house of Israel:	3651
11: 7	Therefore t saith the Lord GOD;	3541
11:16	Therefore say, T saith the Lord GOD;	3541
11:17	Therefore say, T saith the Lord GOD;	3541
12:10	thou unto them, T saith the Lord GOD;	3541
12:19	T saith the Lord GOD, of the inhabitants	3541
12:23	them therefore, T saith the Lord GOD;	3541
12:28	say unto them, T saith the Lord GOD;	3541
13: 3	T saith the Lord GOD; Woe unto	3541
13: 8	Therefore t saith the Lord GOD;	3541
13:13	Therefore t saith the Lord GOD; I will	3541
13:15	T will I accomplish my wrath upon	2050.1
13:18	say, T saith the Lord GOD; Woe to	3541
13:20	Wherefore t saith the Lord GOD; Behold,	3541
14: 4	and say unto them, T saith the Lord GOD;	3541
14: 6	the house of Israel, T saith the Lord GOD;	3541
14:21	For t saith the Lord GOD; How much	3541
15: 6	Therefore t saith the Lord GOD;	3541
16: 3	T saith the Lord GOD unto Jerusalem;	3541
16:13	T wast thou decked *with* gold and silver	2050.1
16:19	and *t* it was, saith the Lord GOD.	NIH
16:36	T saith the Lord GOD; Because thou	3541
16:59	For t saith the Lord GOD; I will even deal	3541
17: 3	say, T saith the Lord GOD; A great eagle	3541
17: 9	Say thou, T saith the Lord GOD; Shall it	3541
17:19	Therefore t saith the Lord GOD; *As* I live,	3541
17:22	T saith the Lord GOD; I will also take of	3541
20: 3	and say unto them, T saith the Lord GOD;	3541
20: 5	say unto them, T saith the Lord GOD;	3541
20:27	and say unto them, T saith the Lord GOD;	3541
20:30	the house of Israel, T saith the Lord GOD;	3541
20:39	O house of Israel, t saith the Lord GOD;	3541
20:47	T saith the Lord GOD; Behold, I *will*	3541
21: 3	to the land of Israel, T saith the LORD;	3541
21: 9	prophesy, and say, T saith the LORD;	3541
21:24	Therefore t saith the Lord GOD;	3541
21:26	T saith the Lord GOD; Remove	3541
21:28	T saith the Lord GOD concerning	3541
22: 3	say thou, T saith the Lord GOD, The city	3541
22:19	Therefore t saith the Lord GOD;	3541
22:28	unto them, saying, T saith the Lord GOD,	3541
23: 4	*were* their names; Samaria *is* Aholah,	2050.1
23: 7	T she committed her whoredoms with	2050.1
23:21	t thou calledst to remembrance	2050.1
23:22	O Aholibah, t saith the Lord GOD;	3541
23:27	T will I make thy lewdness to cease	2050.1
23:28	For t saith the Lord GOD; Behold, I *will*	3541
23:32	T saith the Lord GOD; Thou shalt drink	3541
23:35	Therefore t saith the Lord GOD;	3541
23:39	t have they done in the midst of mine	3651
23:46	For t saith the Lord GOD; *I will* bring up	3541
23:48	T will I cause lewdness to cease out of	2050.1
24: 3	and say unto them, T saith the Lord GOD;	3541
24: 6	Wherefore t saith the Lord GOD; Woe to	3541
24: 9	Therefore t saith the Lord GOD; Woe to	3541
24:21	the house of Israel, T saith the Lord GOD;	3541
24:24	T Ezekiel is unto you a sign: according	2050.1
25: 3	T saith the Lord GOD; Because thou	3541
25: 6	For t saith the Lord GOD; Because thou	3541
25: 8	T saith the Lord GOD; Because that Moab	3541
25:12	T saith the Lord GOD; Because that	3541
25:13	Therefore t saith the Lord GOD; I will	3541
25:15	T saith the Lord GOD; Because	3541
25:16	Therefore t saith the Lord GOD; Behold,	3541
26: 3	Therefore t saith the Lord GOD; Behold,	3541
26: 7	For t saith the Lord GOD; Behold, I *will*	3541
26:15	T saith the Lord GOD to Tyrus; Shall not	3541
26:19	For t saith the Lord GOD; When I shall	3541
27: 3	for many isles, T saith the Lord GOD;	3541
28: 2	prince of Tyrus, T saith the Lord GOD;	3541
28: 6	Therefore t saith the Lord GOD;	3541
28:12	and say unto him, T saith the Lord GOD;	3541
28:22	say, T saith the Lord GOD; Behold, I *am*	3541
28:25	T saith the Lord GOD; When I shall have	3541
29: 3	Speak, and say, T saith the Lord GOD;	3541
29: 8	Therefore t saith the Lord GOD; Behold,	3541
29:13	Yet t saith the Lord GOD; At the end of	3541
29:19	Therefore t saith the Lord GOD; Behold,	3541
30: 2	prophesy, and say, T saith the Lord GOD;	3541
30: 6	T saith the LORD; They also that uphold	3541
30:10	T saith the Lord GOD; I will also make	3541
30:13	T saith the Lord GOD; I will also destroy	3541
30:19	T will I execute judgments in Egypt:	2050.1
30:22	Therefore t saith the Lord GOD; Behold,	3541
31: 7	T was he fair in his greatness,	2050.1
31:10	Therefore t saith the Lord GOD;	3541
31:15	T saith the Lord GOD; In the day when	3541
31:18	To whom art thou t like in glory and	3602
32: 3	T saith the Lord GOD; I will therefore	3541
32:11	For t saith the Lord GOD; The sword of	3541
33:10	T ye speak, saying, If our transgressions	3651
33:25	say unto them, T saith the Lord GOD;	3541
33:27	Say thou unto them, Thus saith the Lord	3541
33:27	thus unto them, T saith the Lord GOD;	3541
34: 2	T saith the Lord GOD unto the shepherds;	3541

T

Eze 34:10 **T** saith the Lord God; Behold, I *am* 3541
34:11 For t saith the Lord God; Behold, 3541
34:17 O my flock, t saith the Lord God; 3541
34:20 Therefore **t** saith the Lord God unto 2050.1
34:30 **T** shall they know that I the Lord their 2050.1
35: 3 say unto it, **T** saith the Lord God; 3541
35: 7 **T** will I make mount Seir most desolate, 2050.1
35:13 **T** with your mouth ye have boasted 2050.1
35:14 **T** saith the Lord God; When the whole 3541
36: 2 **T** saith the Lord God; Because 3541
36: 3 and say, **T** saith the Lord God; 3541
36: 4 **T** saith the Lord God to the mountains, 3541
36: 5 Therefore **t** saith the Lord God; Surely in 3541
36: 6 and to the valleys, **t** saith the Lord God; 3541
36: 7 Therefore **t** saith the Lord God; I have 3541
36:13 **T** saith the Lord God; Because they say 3541
36:22 the house of Israel, **T** saith the Lord God; 3541
36:33 **T** saith the Lord God; In the day that I 3541
36:37 **T** saith the Lord God; I will yet *for* this 3541
37: 5 **T** saith the Lord God unto these bones; 3541
37: 9 say to the wind, **T** saith the Lord God; 3541
37:12 and say unto them, **T** saith the Lord God; 3541
37:19 Say unto them, **T** saith the Lord God; 3541
37:21 say unto them, **T** saith the Lord God; 3541
38: 3 say, **T** saith the Lord God; Behold, I *am* 3541
38:10 **T** saith the Lord God; It shall also come 3541
38:14 and say unto Gog, **T** saith the Lord God; 3541
38:17 **T** saith the Lord God; *Art* thou he of 3541
38:23 **T** will I magnify myself, 2050.1
39: 1 and say, **T** saith the Lord God; 3541
39:16 **T** shall they cleanse the land. 2050.1
39:17 thou son of man, t saith the Lord God; 3541
39:20 **T** ye shall be filled at my table *with* 2050.1
39:25 Therefore **t** saith the Lord God; Now will 3541
43:18 Son of man, t saith the Lord God; 3541
43:20 t shalt thou cleanse and purge it. 2050.1
44: 6 the house of Israel, t saith the Lord God; 3541
44: 9 **T** saith the Lord God; No stranger, 3541
45: 9 **T** saith the Lord God; Let it suffice you, 3541
45:18 **T** saith the Lord God; In the first *month*, 3541
46: 1 **T** saith the Lord God; The gate of 3541
46:15 **T** shall they prepare the lamb, 2050.1
46:16 **T** saith the Lord God; If the prince give a 3541
47:13 **T** saith the Lord God; This *shall be* 3541
Da 1:16 **T** Melzar took away the portion of their 2050.1
2:24 he went and said t unto him; Destroy not 3652
2:25 said t unto him, I have found a man of 3652
4:10 **T** *were* the visions of mine head in my 2050.3
4:14 He cried aloud, and said t, Hew down 3652
6: 6 said t unto him, King Darius, live for ever. 3652
7: 5 they said t unto it, Arise, devour much 3652
7:23 **T** he said, The fourth beast shall be 3652
11:17 upright with him; t shall he do: 2050.1
11:39 **T** shall he do in the most strong holds 2050.1
Hos 10: 4 t judgment springeth up as hemlock in 2050.1
Am 1: 3 **T** saith the Lord; For three 3541
1: 6 **T** saith the Lord; For three 3541
1: 9 **T** saith the Lord; For three 3541
1:11 **T** saith the Lord; For three 3541
1:13 **T** saith the Lord; For three 3541
2: 1 **T** saith the Lord; For three 3541
2: 4 **T** saith the Lord; For three 3541
2: 6 **T** saith the Lord; For three 3541
2:11 *Is it* not even t, O ye children of Israel? 2088
3:11 Therefore **t** saith the Lord God; 3541
3:12 **T** saith the Lord; As the shepherd taketh 3541
4:12 Therefore t will I do unto thee, O Israel; 3541
5: 3 For t saith the Lord God; The city that 3541
5: 4 For t saith the Lord unto the house of 3541
5:16 the God of hosts, the Lord, saith t; 3541
7: 1 **T** hath the Lord God shewed unto me; 3541
7: 4 **T** hath the Lord God shewed unto me: 3541
7: 7 **T** he shewed me: and behold, the Lord 3541
7:11 For **T** Amos saith, Jeroboam shall die by 3541
7:17 Therefore t saith the Lord; Thy wife 3541
8: 1 **T** hath the Lord God shewed unto me: 3541
Ob 1: 1 **T** saith the Lord God concerning Edom; 3541
Mic 2: 3 Therefore **t** saith the Lord; Behold, 3541
3: 5 **T** saith the Lord concerning 3541
5: 6 t shall he deliver *us* from the Assyrian, 2050.1
Na 1:12 **T** saith the Lord; Though *they be* quiet, 3541
1:12 yet t shall they be cut down, 3651
Hag 1: 2 **T** speaketh the Lord of hosts, saying, 3541
1: 5 Now therefore t saith the Lord of hosts; 3541
1: 7 **T** saith the Lord of hosts; Consider your 3541
2: 6 For t saith the Lord of hosts; Yet once, 3541
2:11 **T** saith the Lord of hosts; Ask now 3541
Zec 1: 3 unto them, **T** saith the Lord of hosts; 3541
1: 4 saying, **T** saith the Lord of hosts; 3541
1:14 saying, **T** saith the Lord of hosts; 3541
1:16 Therefore t saith the Lord; I am returned 3541
1:17 saying, **T** saith the Lord of hosts; After 3541
2: 8 For t saith the Lord of hosts; After 3541
3: 7 **T** saith the Lord of hosts; If thou wilt 3541
6:12 **T** speaketh the Lord of hosts, saying, 3541
7: 9 **T** speaketh the Lord of hosts, saying, 3541
7:14 t the land was desolate after them, that 2050.1
8: 2 **T** saith the Lord of hosts; I was jealous 3541
8: 3 **T** saith the Lord; I am returned unto 3541
8: 4 **T** saith the Lord of hosts; There shall 3541
8: 6 **T** saith the Lord of hosts; If it be 3541
8: 7 **T** saith the Lord of hosts; Behold, I *will* 3541
8: 9 **T** saith the Lord of hosts; Let your 3541
8:14 For t saith the Lord of hosts; As I 3541
8:19 **T** saith the Lord of hosts; The fast of 3541

Zec 8:20 **T** saith the Lord of hosts; *It shall* yet 3541
8:23 **T** saith the Lord of hosts; In those days 3541
11: 4 **T** saith the Lord my God; Feed the flock 3541
Mal 1: 4 t saith the Lord of hosts; They shall 3541
1:13 and the sick; t ye brought an offering: 2050.1
Mt 2: 5 of Judea: for **t** it is written by the prophet, 3779
3:15 for t it becometh us to fulfil all 3779
15: 6 he shall be free. **T** have ye made 2532
26:54 scriptures be fulfilled, that t it must be? 3779
Mk 2: 7 Why doth this *man* t speak blasphemies? 3779
Lk 1:25 **T** hath the Lord dealt with me in the days 3779
2:48 Son, why hast thou t dealt with us? 3779
9:34 While he t spake, there came a cloud, 3778
11:45 Master, t saying thou reproachest us also. 3778
17:30 Even t shall it be in the day when 2590+5024
18:11 Pharisee stood and prayed t with himself, 3778
19:28 when he had t spoken, he went before, 3778
19:31 Why do ye loose *him?* t shall ye say unto 3779
22:51 and said, Suffer ye t far. 2193+3778
23:46 and having said t, he gave up the ghost. 3778
24:36 And as they t spake, Jesus himself stood 3778
24:40 And when he had t spoken, he shewed 3778
24:46 **T** it is written, and thus it behoved Christ 3779
24:46 t it behoved Christ to suffer, and to rise 3779
Jn 4: 6 with *his* journey, sat t on the well: 3779
9: 6 When he had t spoken, he spat on 3778
11:43 when he t had spoken, he cried with a 3778
11:48 If we let him t alone, all *men* will believe 3779
13:21 When Jesus had t said, he was troubled in 3778
18:22 And when he had t spoken, one of 3778
20:14 when she had t said, she turned herself 3778
Ac 19:41 And when he had t spoken, he dismissed 3778
20:36 And when he had t spoken, he kneeled 3778
21:11 And feet, and said, **T** saith the Holy Ghost, 3592
26:24 And as he t spake for himself, Festus said 3778
26:30 And when he had t spoken, the king rose 3778
27:35 when he had t spoken, he took bread, 3778
Ro 9:20 that formed *it*, Why hast thou made me t? 3779
1Co 14:25 And t are the secrets of his heart made 3779
2Co 1:17 When I therefore was t minded, did I use 3778
5:14 because we t judge, that if one died for all, 3778
Php 3:15 as many as *be* perfect, be t minded: 3778
Heb 6: 9 accompany salvation, though we t speak. 3779
9: 6 Now when these *things* were t ordained, 3779
Rev 9:17 And t I saw the horses in the vision, 3779
16: 5 and shalt be, because thou hast judged t. 3778
18:21 **T** with violence shall *that* great city 3779

THWART See DISANNUL; DISANNULLED

THWARTED See NOUGHT

THY (4607) [THOU] See Index of Articles, Etc.

THYATIRA (4)
Ac 16:14 a seller of purple, of the city of **T**, 2363
Rev 1:11 and unto **T**, and unto Sardis, 2363
2:18 And unto the angel of the church in **T** 2363
2:24 But unto you I say, and unto the rest in **T**, 2363

THYINE (1)
Rev 18:12 and all t wood, and all *manner* vessels of 2367

THYSELF (215) [SELF, THOU]
Ge 13: 9 separate t, I pray thee, from me: if *thou* NIH
14:21 me the persons, and take the goods to t. 3509.2
16: 9 mistress, and submit t under her hands. NIH
33: 9 my brother; keep that thou hast unto t. 3509.2
Ex 9:17 As yet exaltest thou t against my people, NIH
10: 3 How long wilt thou refuse to humble t NIH
10:28 Get thee from me, take heed to t, see 3509.2
18:14 why sittest thou t alone, and all the people 859
18:18 thou art not able to perform it t alone. 3509.2
18:22 so shall it be easier for t, and they shall 3509.2
20: 5 Thou shalt not bow down t to them, NIH
34: 2 present t there to me in the top of NIH
34:12 Take heed to t, lest thou make a 3509.2
Lev 9: 7 make an atonement for t, and for 3509.2
18:20 thy neighbour's wife, to defile *t* with her. NIH
18:23 lie with any beast to defile *t* therewith: NIH
19:18 but thou shalt love thy neighbour as t: 3509.2
19:34 and thou shalt love him as t; 3509.2
Nu 11:17 with thee, that thou bear *it* not t alone. 3509.2
16:13 except thou make t altogether a prince NIH
Dt 4: 9 Only take heed to t, and keep thy soul 3509.2
5: 9 Thou shalt not bow down t unto them, NIH
7: 1 nations greater and mightier than t, 3509.2
12:13 Take heed to t that thou offer not thy 3509.2
12:19 Take heed to t that thou forsake not 3509.2
12:30 Take heed to t that thou be not snared 3509.2
20:14 the spoil thereof, shalt thou take unto t; 3509.2
22: 1 his sheep go astray, and hide t from them: NIH
22: 3 thou do likewise: thou mayest not hide t. NIH
22: 4 down by the way, and hide t from them: NIH
22:12 of thy vesture, wherewith thou coverest *t*. NIH
23:13 it shall be, when thou wilt ease t abroad, 3509.2
28:40 but thou shalt not anoint *t* with the oil; NIH
Jos 17:15 cut down for t there in the land of 3509.2
Ru 3: 3 Wash *t* therefore, and anoint thee, NIH
3: 3 *but* make not t known unto the man, until NIH
4: 6 redeem thou my right to t; for I cannot 3509.2
1Sa 19: 2 take heed to t until the morning, NIH
19: 2 and abide in a secret place, and hide t: NIH
20: 8 if there be in me iniquity, slay me t; 859
20:19 come to the place where thou didst hide t NIH
25:26 *from* avenging t with thine 3509.2+3807.1

2Sa 5:24 trees, *that* then thou shalt bestir t: NIH
7:24 For thou hast confirmed to t thy people 3509.2
13: 5 *thee* down on thy bed, and make t sick: NIH
14: 2 feign to be a mourner, and put on now NIH
14: 2 anoint not *t* with oil, but be as a woman NIH
18:13 thou t wouldest have set thyself against 859
18:13 thou thyself wouldest have set t against NIH
22:26 the merciful thou wilt shew t merciful, NIH
22:26 with the upright man thou wilt shew t NIH
22:27 With the pure thou wilt shew t pure; NIH
22:27 with the froward thou wilt shew t NIH
1Ki 2: 2 thou strong therefore, and shew t a man; NIH
2: 3 and whithersoever thou turnest t: NIH
3:11 hast not asked for t long life; NIH
3:11 neither hast asked riches for t, nor hast 3509.2
3:11 hast asked for t understanding to discern 3509.2
13: 7 refresh t, and I will give thee a reward. NIH
14: 2 his wife, Arise, I pray thee, and disguise t, NIH
14: 6 why feignest thou t to be another? NIH
17: 3 and hide t by the brook Cherith, NIH
18: 1 third year, saying, Go, shew t unto Ahab, NIH
20:22 strengthen t, and mark, and see what thou NIH
20:40 So *shall* thy judgment *be;* t hast decided *it.* 859
21:20 thou hast sold t to work evil in the sight 3509.2
22:25 shalt go into an inner chamber to hide t. NIH
2Ki 22:19 and thou hast humbled t before the Lord, NIH
1Ch 21:12 advise t what word I shall bring again to NIH
2Ch 1:11 hast asked wisdom and knowledge for t, 3509.2
18:24 shalt go into an inner chamber to hide t. NIH
20:37 Because thou hast joined t with Ahaziah, 3509.2
21:13 house, *which were* better than t: 3509.2
34:27 and thou didst humble t before God, NIH
34:27 humbledst t before me, and didst rend thy NIH
Est 4:13 Think not with t that *thou* shalt 5315+3509.3
Job 8: 8 and prepare *t* to the search of their fathers: NIH
10:16 again thou shewest t marvellous upon me. NIH
15: 8 and dost thou restrain wisdom to t? 3509.2
22:21 Acquaint now t with him, and be at peace: NIH
30:21 thy strong hand thou opposest t against NIH
40:10 Deck t now with majesty and excellency; NIH
40:10 and array t with glory and beauty. NIH
Ps 7: 6 lift up t because of the rage of mine NIH
10: 1 *why* hidest thou *t* in times of trouble? NIH
18:25 the merciful thou wilt shew t merciful; NIH
18:25 with an upright man thou wilt shew t NIH
18:26 With the pure thou wilt shew t pure; NIH
18:26 the froward thou wilt shew t froward. NIH
35:23 Stir up t, and awake to my judgment, NIH
37: 1 Fret not t because of evildoers, neither be NIH
37: 4 Delight t also in the Lord; and he shall NIH
37: 7 fret not t because of him who prospereth NIH
37: 8 fret not t in any wise to do evil. NIH
49:18 praise thee, when thou doest well to t. 3509.2
50:21 that I was altogether *such a one* as t: 3509.2
52: 1 Why boastest thou t in mischief, O mighty NIH
55: 1 hide not t from my supplication. NIH
60: 1 hast been displeased; O turn t to us again. NIH
80:15 the branch *that* thou madest strong for t. 3509.2
80:17 of man *whom* thou madest strong for t. 3509.2
85: 3 thou hast turned *t* from the fierceness of NIH
89:46 wilt thou hide t, for ever? shall thy wrath NIH
94: 1 to whom vengeance belongeth, shew t. NIH
94: 2 Lift up t, thou judge of the earth: render a NIH
104: 2 Who coverest *t* with light as with a NIH
Pr 6: 3 Do this now, my son, and deliver t, NIH
6: 3 go, humble t, and make sure thy friend. NIH
6: 5 Deliver t as a roe from the hand of NIH
9:12 If thou be wise, thou shalt be wise for t: 3509.2
24:19 Fret not t because of evil *men*, neither be NIH
24:27 and make it fit for t in the field; 3509.2
25: 6 Put not forth t in the presence of the king, NIH
27: 1 Boast not t of to morrow; for thou knowest NIH
30:32 If thou hast done foolishly in lifting up t, NIH
Ecc 7:16 over much; neither make t over wise: NIH
7:16 over wise: why shouldest thou destroy t? 859
7:22 that thou likewise hast cursed others. NIH
Isa 26:20 hide t as it were for a little moment, NIH
33: 3 at the lifting up of t the nations were 3509.2
45:15 Verily thou *art* a God that hidest t, O God NIH
52: 2 Shake t from the dust; arise, *and* sit down, NIH
52: 2 loose t from the bands of thy neck, NIH
57: 8 for thou hast discovered *t* to another than NIH
57: 9 far off, and didst debase *t even* unto hell. NIH
58: 7 that thou hide not t from thine own flesh? NIH
58:14 Then shalt thou delight t in the Lord; NIH
63:14 thy people, to make t a glorious name. 3509.2
64:12 Wilt thou refrain t for these *things*, O NIH
65: 5 Which say, Stand by t, come not near to 3509.2
Jer 2:17 Hast thou not procured this unto t, in 3509.3
4:30 Though thou clothest t with crimson, NIH
4:30 painting, in vain shalt thou make t fair; NIH
6:26 with sackcloth, and wallow t in ashes: NIH
17: 4 even t, shalt discontinue from thine 3509.2
20: 4 I will make thee a terror to t, and to all 3509.2
22:15 reign, because thou closest t in cedar? NIH
32: 8 and the redemption *is* thine; buy *it* for t. 3509.2
45: 5 seekest thou great *things* for t? seek 3509.2
46:19 In Egypt, furnish t to go into captivity: 3509.3
47: 5 of their valley: how long wilt thou cut t? NIH
47: 6 put up t into thy scabbard, rest, and be NIH
La 2:18 give t no rest; let not the apple of thine 3509.2
3:44 hast covered t with a cloud, *that our* 3509.2
4:21 shalt be drunken, and shalt make t naked. NIH
Eze 3:24 unto me, Go, shut t within thine house. NIH
16:17 madest to t images of men, 3509.2

T

Eze	22: 4	defiled *t* in thine idols which thou hast	NIH
	22:16	thou shalt take thine inheritance in *t* in	3509.3
	23:40	for whom thou didst wash *t*, paintedst thy	NIH
	23:40	thy eyes, and deckedst *t* with ornaments,	NIH
	31:10	because thou hast lifted up *t* in height,	NIH
	38: 7	prepare for *t*, thou, and all thy company	3509.2
Da	5:17	thy gifts be to *t*, and give thy rewards	3509.5
	5:23	lifted up *t* against the Lord of heaven;	NIH
	10:12	to chasten *t* before thy God, thy words	NIH
Hos	13: 9	Israel, *thou* hast destroyed *t*; but in me	3509.2
Ob	1: 4	Though thou exalt *t* as the eagle,	NIH
Mic	1:10	in the house of Aphrah roll *t* in the dust.	NIH
	5: 1	Now gather *t* in troops, O daughter of	NIH
Na	3:15	make *t* many as the cankerworm,	NIH
	3:15	make *t* many as the locusts.	NIH
Zec	2: 7	Deliver *t*, O Zion, that dwellest *with*	NIH
Mt	4: 6	If thou be the Son of God, cast *t* down:	4572
	5:33	shalt not forswear *t*, but shalt perform	NIG
	8: 4	shew *t* to the priest, and offer the gift that	4572
	19:19	and, Thou shalt love thy neighbour as *t*.	4572
	22:39	it, Thou shalt love thy neighbour as *t*.	4572
	27:40	and buildest *it* in three days, save *t*.	4572
Mk	1:44	shew *t* to the priest, and offer for thy	4572
	12:31	Thou shalt love thy neighbour as *t*.	4572
	15:30	Save *t*, and come down from the cross.	4572
Lk	4: 9	the Son of God, cast *t* down from hence:	4572
	4:23	unto me this proverb, Physician, heal *t*:	4572
	5:14	no *man*: but go, and shew *t* to the priest,	4572
	6:42	when thou *t* beholdest not the beam that	846
	7: 6	him, saying unto him, Lord, trouble not *t*:	NIG
	10:27	with all thy mind; and thy neighbour as *t*.	4572
	17: 8	and gird *t*, and serve me, till I have eaten	NIG
	23:37	If thou be the King of the Jews, save *t*.	4572
	23:39	saying, If thou be Christ, save *t* and us.	4572
Jn	1:22	them that sent us. What sayest thou of *t*?	4572
	7: 4	thou do these *things*, shew *t* to the world.	4572
	8:13	said unto him, Thou bearest record of *t*;	4572
	8:53	prophets are dead: whom makest thou *t*?	4572
	10:33	that thou, being a man, makest *t* God.	4572
	14:22	how is it that thou wilt manifest *t* unto us,	4572
	18:34	answered him, Sayest thou this *thing* of *t*,	1438
	21:18	thou girdedst *t*, and walkedst whither	4572
Ac	8:29	Go near, and join *t* to this chariot.	NIG
	12: 8	unto him, Gird *t*, and bind on thy sandals.	NIG
	16:28	with a loud voice, saying, Do *t* no harm:	4572
	21:24	and purify *t* with them, and be at charges	NIG
	21:24	but *that* thou *t* also walkest orderly,	846
	24: 8	by examining of whom *t* mayest take	846
	26: 1	Thou art permitted to speak for *t*.	4572
	26:24	a loud voice, Paul, thou art **beside** *t*;	3105
Ro	2: 1	thou judgest another, thou condemnest *t*;	4572
	2: 5	impenitent heart treasurest up unto *t*	4572
	2:19	art confident that thou *t* art a guide of	4572
	2:21	teachest another, teachest thou not *t*?	4572
	13: 9	Thou shalt love thy neighbour as *t*.	4572
	14:22	have *it* to *t* before God. Happy *is* he that	4572
Gal	5:14	*this*; Thou shalt love thy neighbour as **t**.	4572
	6: 1	considering *t*, lest thou also be tempted.	4572
1Ti	3:15	oughtest to behave *t* in the house of God,	NIG
	4: 7	and exercise *t* *rather* unto godliness.	4572
	4:15	Meditate upon these *things*; give *t* wholly	NIG
	4:16	Take heed unto *t*, and unto the doctrine;	4572
	4:16	for in doing this thou shalt both save *t*,	4572
	5:22	partaker of other *men's* sins: keep *t* pure.	4572
	6: 5	gain is godliness: from such withdraw *t*.	NIG
2Ti	2:15	Study to shew *t* approved unto God,	4572
Tit	2: 7	In all *things* shewing *t* a pattern of good	4572
Jas	2: 8	Thou shalt love thy neighbour as *t*, ye do	4572

TIBERIAS (3)

Jn	6: 1	the sea of Galilee, *which is the sea* of T.	5085
	6:23	(Howbeit there came other boats from T	5085
	21: 1	again to the disciples at the sea of T;	5085

TIBERIUS (1)

Lk	3: 1	Now in the fifteenth year of the reign of T	5086

TIBHATH (1)

1Ch	18: 8	Likewise from T, and from Chun, cities of	2880

TIBNI (3)

1Ki	16:21	half of the people followed T the son of	8402
	16:22	people that followed T the son of Ginath:	8402
	16:22	of Ginath: so T died, and Omri reigned.	8402

TIDAL (2)

Ge	14: 1	king of Elam, and T king of nations;	8413
	14: 9	T king of nations, and Amraphel king	8413

TIDINGS (46)

Ge	29:13	Laban heard the *t* of Jacob his sister's	8088
Ex	33: 4	when the people heard these evil *t*, they	1697
1Sa	4:19	when she heard the *t* that the ark of God	8052
	11: 4	and told the *t* in the ears of the people:	1697
	11: 5	they told him the *t* of the men of Jabesh.	1697
	11: 6	came upon Saul when he heard those *t*,	1697
	27:11	bring *t* to Gath, saying, Lest they should	NIH
2Sa	4: 4	five years old when the *t* came of Saul	8052
	4:10	is dead, thinking to have **brought good** *t*,	1319
	4:10	would have given him a **reward for** *his t*:	1309
	13:30	in the way, that *t* came to David, saying,	8052
	18:19	Let me now run, and **bear** the king *t*,	1319
	18:20	Thou *shalt* not bear *t* this day,	1309
	18:20	day, but thou shalt **bear** *t* another day:	1319
	18:20	this day thou shalt **bear** no *t*, because	1319

2Sa	18:22	my son, seeing that thou hast no *t* ready?	1309
	18:25	If he *be* alone, *there is t* in his mouth.	1309
	18:26	And the king said, He also **bringeth** *t*.	1319
	18:27	*is* a good man, and cometh with good *t*.	1309
	18:31	and Cushi said, T, my lord the king:	1319
1Ki	1:42	*art* a valiant man, and **bringest** good *t*.	1319
	2:28	came to Joab: for Joab had turned after	8052
	14: 6	for I *am* sent to thee *with* heavy *t*.	NIH
2Ki	7: 9	this day *is* a day of **good** *t*, and we hold	1309
1Ch	10: 9	to **carry** *t* unto their idols, and to	1319
Ps	112: 7	He shall not be afraid of evil *t*: his heart is	8052
Isa	40: 9	O Zion, that **bringest good** *t*, get thee up	1319
	40: 9	O Jerusalem, that **bringest good** *t*, lift up	1319
	41:27	to Jerusalem one that **bringeth good** *t*.	1319
	52: 7	are the feet of him that **bringeth good** *t*,	1319
	52: 7	that **bringeth good** *t* of good;	1319
	61: 1	me to **preach good** *t* unto the meek;	1319
Jer	20:15	Cursed *be* the man who **brought** *t* to my	1319
	37: 5	that besieged Jerusalem heard *t* of them,	8088
	49:23	for they have heard evil *t*: they are	8052
Eze	21: 7	that thou shalt answer, For the *t*; because	8052
Da	11:44	*t* out of the east and out of the north shall	8052
Na	1:15	the feet of him that **bringeth good** *t*,	1319
Lk	1:19	unto thee, and to **shew** thee these **glad** *t*.	2097
	2:10	behold, I **bring** you good *t* of great joy,	2097
	8: 1	**shewing the glad** *t* of the kingdom of	2097
Ac	11:22	Then *t* of these *things* came unto the ears	3056
	13:32	we **declare** unto you **glad** *t*, how that	2097
	21:31	*t* came unto the chief captain of the band,	5334
Ro	10:15	peace, and **bring glad** *t* of good *things*!	2097
1Th	3: 6	and **brought** us **good** *t* of your faith and	2097

TIE (2) [TIED]

1Sa	6: 7	the kine to the cart, and bring their	631
Pr	6:21	thine heart, *and* *t* them about thy neck.	6029

TIED (8) [TIE]

Ex	39:31	they *t* unto it a lace of blue, to fasten *it on*	5414
1Sa	6:10	*t* them to the cart, and shut up their calves	631
2Ki	7:10	horses *t*, and asses tied, and the tents as	631
	7:10	and asses *t*, and the tents as they were,	631
Mt	21: 2	and straightway ye shall find an ass *t*,	1210
Mk	11: 2	ye shall find a colt *t*, whereon never man	1210
	11: 4	found the colt *t* by the door without in a	1210
Lk	19:30	at your entering ye shall find a colt *t*,	1210

TIGLATH-PILESER (3) [PUL, TILGATH-PILNESER]

2Ki	15:29	the days of Pekah king of Israel came T	8407
	16: 7	So Ahaz sent messengers to T king of	8407
	16:10	king Ahaz went *to* Damascus to meet T	8407

TIGRIS See HIDDEKEL

TIKVAH (2) [TIKVATH]

2Ki	22:14	the wife of Shallum the son of T, the son	8616
Ezr	10:15	Jahaziah the son of T were employed	8616

TIKVATH (1) [TIKVAH]

2Ch	34:22	the wife of Shallum the son of T, the son	8616

TILE (1) [TILING]

Eze	4: 1	take thee a *t*, and lay it before thee,	3843

TILGATH-PILNESER (3) [TIGLATH-PILESER]

1Ch	5: 6	whom T king of Assyria carried away	8407
	5:26	the spirit of T king of Assyria,	8407
2Ch	28:20	T king of Assyria came unto him,	8407

TILING (1) [TILE]

Lk	5:19	let him down through the *t* with *his* couch	2766

TILL (169) [TILLAGE, TILLED, TILLER, TILLEST, TILLETH]

Ge	2: 5	and *there was* not a man to *t* the ground.	5647
	3:19	eat bread, *t* thou return unto the ground;	5704
	3:23	the ground from whence he was taken.	5647
	19:22	for I cannot do any thing *t* thou be come	5704
	29: 8	*t* they roll the stone from the well's	NIH
	38:11	father's house, *t* Shelah my son be grown:	5704
	38:17	thou give me *a* pledge, *t* thou send *it?*	5704
Ex	15:16	*t* thy people pass over, O Lord, till	5704
	15:16	O Lord, *t* the people pass over,	5704
	16:19	Let no man leave of it *t* the morning.	5704
	16:24	they laid it up *t* the morning, as Moses	5704
	34:33	*t* Moses had done speaking with them,	NIH
	40:37	they journeyed not *t* the day that it was	5704
Nu	12:15	the people journeyed not *t* Miriam was	5704
Dt	17: 5	shalt stone them with stones, *t* they die.	NIH
	28:45	and overtake thee, *t* thou be destroyed;	5704
Jos	5: 1	*t* all the people *that were* men of war,	5704
	5: 8	places in the camp, *t* they were whole.	5704
	8: 6	we have drawn them from the city;	5704
	10:20	they were consumed, that the rest	5704
Jdg	3:25	they tarried *t* *they* were ashamed:	5704
	6: 4	*t* thou come *unto* Gaza, and left no	5704
	11:33	thou come *t* Minnith, *even* twenty	5704
	16: 3	Samson lay *t* midnight, and arose at	5704
	19:26	house where her lord *was*, *t* it was light.	5704
	21: 2	abode there *t* even before God, and lift up	5704
Ru	1:13	Would ye tarry for them *t* they were	834+5704
1Sa	1:22	*t* I come to thee, and shew thee what	5704
	16:11	for we will not sit down *t* he come hither.	5704
	22: 3	*t* I know what God will do for me.	834+5704
2Sa	3:35	or ought else, *t* the sun be down.	6440+3807.1
	9:10	shall *t* the land for him, and thou shalt	5647
1Ki	14:10	*a* man taketh away dung, *t* it be all gone.	5704

1Ki	18:28	*t* the blood gushed out upon them.	5704
2Ki	2:17	when they urged him *t* *he* was ashamed,	5704
	4:20	sat on her knees *t* noon, and *then* died.	5704
	7: 9	if we tarry *t* the morning light,	5704
	10:17	*t* *he* had destroyed him, according to	5704
	13:17	in Aphek, *t* *thou* hast consumed *them*.	5704
	13:19	hadst thou smitten Syria *t* *thou* hadst	5704
	21:16	*t* he had filled Jerusalem from one	834+5704
2Ch	26:15	*t* I die I will be was strong.	3588+5704
	29:34	the work was ended, and until the *other*	5704
	36:16	against his people, *t* there was no remedy.	5704
Ezr	2:63	*things t* there stood *up* a priest with Urim	5704
	5: 5	to cease, *t* the matter came to Darius:	5705
	9:14	wouldest thou not be angry with us *t*	5704
Ne	2: 7	that they may convey me over *t* I	834+5704
	4:11	we come in the midst among them,	834+5704
	4:21	rising of the morning *t* the stars appeared.	5704
	7:65	there stood *up* a priest with Urim	5704
	13:19	charged that they should not be opened *t*	5704
Job	7:19	nor let me alone *t* I swallow down my	5704
	8:21	T he fill thy mouth *with* laughing,	5704
	14: 6	*t* he shall accomplish, as a hireling, his	5704
	14:12	the heavens be no more, they shall not	5704
	14:14	time will I wait, *t* my change come.	5704
	27: 5	*t* I die I will not remove my integrity from	5704
	32: 4	Now Elihu had waited *t* Job had spoken,	871.1
Ps	10:15	evil *man*: seek out his wickedness *t* thou	NIH
	18:37	neither did I turn again *t* they were	5704
	68:30	*t* *every one* submit himself with pieces of	NIH
Pr	7:23	T a dart strike through his liver; as a bird	NIH
	29:11	but a wise *man* keepeth it in *t* afterwards.	NIH
Ecc	2: 3	*t* I might see what *was* that good for	834+5704
SS	2: 7	nor awake *my* love, *t* he please.	5704+7945
	3: 5	nor awake *my* love, *t* he please.	5704+7945
Isa	5: 8	*that* lay field to field, *t* there be no place,	NIH
	5:11	continue until night, *t* wine inflame them!	NIH
	22:14	shall not be purged from you *t* ye die,	5704
	23:13	*t* the Assyrian founded it for them that	NIH
	30:17	*t* ye be left as a beacon upon the top	518+5704
	38:13	I reckoned *t* morning, *that*, as a lion,	5704
	42: 4	*t* he have set judgment in the earth:	5704
	62: 1	*t* the establish, and till he make Jerusalem	5704
	62: 7	*t* he make Jerusalem a praise in the earth.	5704
Jer	7:32	shall bury in Tophet, *t* there be no place.	4480
	9:16	after them, *t* I have consumed them.	5704
	19:11	in Tophet, *t* there *be* no place to bury.	4480
	23:20	*t* he have performed the thoughts of his	5704
	24:10	*t* they be consumed from off the land that	5704
	27:11	and they shall *t* it, and dwell therein.	5647
	49: 9	they will destroy *t* they have enough.	NIH
	49:37	after them, *t* I have consumed them:	5704
	52: 3	*t* he had cast them out from his presence,	5704
	52:11	put him in prison *t* the day of his death.	5704
La	3:50	The Lord look down, and behold from	5704
Eze	4: 8	*t* thou hast ended the days of thy siege.	5704
	4:14	for from my youth *up* even *t* now have I	5704
	24:13	I have caused my fury to rest upon thee.	5704
	28:15	wast created, *t* iniquity was found in thee.	5704
	34:21	*t* ye have scattered them abroad;	834+5704
	39:15	the buriers have buried in the valley of	5704
	39:19	ye shall eat fat *t* *ye* be full,	3807.1
	39:19	be full, and drink blood *t* *ye* be drunken,	3807.1
	47:20	*t* a *man* come over against Hamath.	5704
Da	2: 9	before me, *t* the time be changed:	1768+5705
	2:34	Thou sawest *t* that a stone was cut out	5705
	4:23	*t* seven times pass over him;	1768+5705
	4:25	*t* thou know that the most High	1768+5705
	4:33	*t* his hairs were grown like eagles'	1768+5705
	5:21	*t* he knew that the most high God	5705
	6:14	he laboured *t* the going down of the sun	5705
	7: 4	I beheld *t* the wings thereof were	1768+5705
	7: 9	I beheld *t* the thrones were cast	1768+5705
	7:11	I beheld *even* the beast *was* slain,	1768+5705
	10: 3	at all, *t* three whole weeks were fulfilled.	5704
	11:36	shall *t* prosper *t* the indignation be	5704
	12: 9	closed up and sealed *t* the time of the end.	5704
	12:13	go thou thy way *t* the end *be*: for thou	3807.1
Hos	5:15	*t* they acknowledge their offence,	834+5704
	10:12	*t* he come and rain righteousness upon	5704
Ob	1: 5	would they not have stolen *t* they had	NIH
Jnh	4: 5	*t* he might see what would become	834+5704
Zep	3: 3	they gnaw not the bones *t* the morrow.	3807.1
Mt	1:25	And knew her not *t* she had brought	2193+5704
	2: 9	*t* it came and stood over where the young	2193
	5:18	T heaven and earth pass, one jot or	302+2193
	5:18	pass from the law, *t* all be fulfilled.	302+2193
	5:26	*t* thou hast paid the uttermost	302+2193
	10:11	and there abide *t* ye go thence.	302+2193
	10:23	of Israel, *t* the Son of man be come.	302+2193
	12:20	*t* he send forth judgment unto	302+2193
	13:33	of meal, *t* the whole was leavened.	2193+3739
	16:28	*t* they see the Son of man coming in	302+2193
	18:21	and I forgive him? *t* seven times?	2193
	18:30	into prison, *t* he should pay the debt.	2193
	18:34	*t* he should pay all that was due	2193+3739
	22:44	*t* I make thine enemies thy footstool?	302+2193
	23:39	not see me henceforth, *t* ye shall say,	302+2193
	24:34	pass, *t* all these *things* be fulfilled.	302+2193
Mk	6:10	abide *t* ye depart from that place.	302+2193
	9: 1	*t* they have seen the kingdom of God	302+2193
	9: 9	*t* the Son of man were risen from	1508+3752
	12:36	*t* I make thine enemies thy footstool.	302+2193
	13:30	not pass, *t* all these *things* be done.	3360+3739
Lk	1:80	in the deserts *t* the day of his shewing	2193
	9:27	*t* they see the kingdom of God.	302+2193

Lk	12:50 I straitened t it be accomplished!	2193+3748
	12:59 t thou hast paid the very last mite.	2193
	13: 8 t I shall dig about it, and dung it:	2193+3748
	13:21 of meal, t the whole was leavened.	2193+3739
	15: 8 and seek diligently t she find it?	2193+3739
	17: 8 serve me, t I have eaten and drunken;	2193
	19:13 and seek unto them, Occupy t I come.	2193
	20:43 T I make thine enemies thy footstool	302+2193
	21:32 shall not pass away, t all be fulfilled.	302+2193
Jn	13:38 t thou hast denied me thrice.	2193+3739
	21:22 If I will that he tarry t I come, what is	2193
	21:23 If I will that he tarry t I come, what is	2193
Ac	7:18 T another king arose, which knew	891+3739
	8:40 in all the cities, t he came to Cesarea.	2193
	20:11 even t break of day, so he departed.	891
	21: 5 and children, t we were out of the city:	2193
	23:12 eat nor drink t they had killed Paul.	2193+3739
	23:21 they will neither eat nor drink t	2193+3739
	25:21 I commanded him to be kept t I	2193+3739
	28:23 of the prophets, from morning t evening.	2193
1Co	11:26 do shew the Lord's death t he come.	891+3739
	15:25 t he hath put all enemies under his	891+3739
Gal	3:19 t the seed should come to whom	891+3739
Eph	4:13 T we all come in the unity of the faith,	3360
Php	1:10 and without offence t the day of Christ;	1519
1Ti	4:13 T I come, give attendance to reading,	2193
Heb	10:13 From henceforth expecting t his enemies	2193
Rev	2:25 have already hold fast t I come.	302+891+3739
	7: 3 t we have sealed the servants of our God	891
	15: 8 the seven plagues of the seven angels	891
	20: 3 t the thousand years should be fulfilled:	891

TILLAGE (3) [TILL]

1Ch	27:26 t of the ground was Ezri the son of	5656
Ne	10:37 have the tithes in all the cities of our t.	5656
Pr	13:23 Much food is in the t of the poor:	5215

TILLED (1) [TILL]

Eze	36: 9 turn unto you, and ye shall be t and sown:	5647
	36:34 the desolate land shall be t, whereas it lay	5647

TILLER (1) [TILL]

Ge	4: 2 of sheep, but Cain was a t of the ground.	5647

TILLEST (1) [TILL]

Ge	4:12 When thou tillest the ground, it shall not	5647

TILLETH (2) [TILL]

Pr	12:11 He that t his land shall be satisfied with	5647
	28:19 He that t his land shall have plenty of	5647

TILON (1)

1Ch	4:20 and Rinnah, Ben-hanan, and T.	8436

TIMBER (26)

Ex	31: 5 of stones, to set them, and in carving of t,	6086
Lev	14:45 the t thereof, and the morter of	6086
1Ki	5: 6 can skill to hew t like unto the Sidonians.	6086
	5: 8 I will do all thy desire concerning t of	6086
	5: 8 timber of cedar, and concerning t of fir.	6086
	5:18 so they prepared t and stones to build	6086
	6:10 they rested on the house with t of cedar.	6086
	15:22 the t thereof, wherewith Baasha had	6086
2Ki	12:12 to buy t and hewed stone to repair	6086
	22: 6 to buy t and hewn stone to repair the	6086
1Ch	22: 14 t of cedars, with masons and carpenters,	6086
	22:14 t also and stone have I prepared;	6086
	22:15 hewers and workers of stone and t,	6086
2Ch	2: 8 thy servants can skill to cut t in Lebanon;	6086
	2: 9 Even to prepare me t in abundance:	6086
	2:10 give to thy servants, the hewers that cut t,	6086
	2:14 silver, in brass, in iron, in stone, and in t,	6086
	16: 6 the t thereof, wherewith Baasha was a	6086
	34:11 t for couplings, and to floor the houses	6086
Ezr	5: 8 t is laid in the walls, and this work goeth	636
	6: 4 rows of great stones, and a row of new t:	636
	6:11 let it be pulled down from his house,	636
Ne	2: 8 that he may give me t to make beams for	6086
Eze	26:12 they shall lay thy stones and thy t and	6086
Hab	2:11 and the beam out of the t shall answer it.	6086
Zec	5: 4 shall consume it with the t thereof and	6086

TIMBREL (5) [TIMBRELS]

Ex	15:20 the sister of Aaron, took a t in her hand;	8596
Job	21:12 They take the t and harp, and rejoice at	8596
Ps	81: 2 Take a psalm, and bring hither the t,	8596
	149: 3 let them sing praises unto him with the t	8596
	150: 4 Praise him with the t and dance: praise	8596

TIMBRELS (5) [TIMBREL]

Ex	15:20 all the women went out after her with t	8596
Jdg	11:34 his daughter came out to meet him with t	8596
2Sa	6: 5 and on t, and on cornets, and on cymbals.	8596
1Ch	13: 8 with t, and with cymbals,	8596
Ps	68:25 them were the damsels playing with t.	8608

TIME (619) [BEFORETIME, BETIMES, DAYTIME, LIFETIME, MEALTIME, OFTENTIMES, OFTTIMES, SEEDTIME, SOMETIME, SOMETIMES, TIMES, UNTIMELY]

Ge	4: 3 in process of t it came to pass, that Cain	3117
	17:21 unto thee at this set t in the next year.	4150
	18:10 return unto thee according to the t of life;	6256
	18:14 At the t appointed I will return unto	4150
	18:14 according to the t of life, and Sarah shall	6256
	21: 2 at the set t of which God had spoken to	4150
Ge	21:22 it came to pass at that t, that Abimelech	6256
	22:15 Abraham out of heaven the second t,	8145
	24:11 by a well of water at the t of the evening,	6256
	24:11 even the t that women go out to draw	6256
	26: 8 to pass, when he had been there a long t,	3117
	29: 7 neither is it t that the cattle should be	6256
	29:34 Now this t will my husband be joined	6471
	30:33 righteousness answer for me in t to come,	3117
	31:10 it came to pass at the t that the cattle	6256
	38: 1 it came to pass at that t, that Judah went	6256
	38:12 in process of the	3117+7235+1886.1
	38:27 it came to pass in the t of her travail, that,	6256
	39: 5 came to pass from the t that he had made	227
	39:11 it came to pass about this t, that Joseph	3117
	41: 5 he slept and dreamed the second t:	8145
	43:10 now we had returned this second t.	6471
	43:18 our sacks at the first t are we brought in;	8462
	43:20 came indeed down at the first t to buy	8462
	47:29 the t drew nigh that Israel must die:	3117
Ex	2:23 in process of t,	3117+7227+1886.1+1886.1
	8:32 Pharaoh hardened his heart at this t also,	6471
	9: 5 the Lord appointed a set t, saying,	4150
	9:14 For I will at this t send all my plagues	6471
	9:18 about this t I will cause it to rain	6256
	9:27 and said unto them, I have sinned this t:	6471
	13:14 when thy son asketh thee in t to come,	4279
	21:19 only he shall pay for the loss of his t,	7674
	21:29 push with his horn in t past,	4480+8032+8543
	21:36 hath used to push in t past,	4480+8032+8543
	23:15 in the t appointed of the month Abib;	4150
	34:18 in the t of the month Abib:	4150
	34:21 in earing t and in harvest thou shalt rest.	2758
Lev	13:58 it shall be washed the second t,	8145
	15:25 many days out of the t of her separation,	6256
	15:25 or if it run beyond the t of her separation;	NIH
	18:18 besides the other in her life t.	NIH
	25:32 may the Levites redeem at any t.	5769
	25:50 according to the t of a hired servant shall	3117
	26: 5 the vintage shall reach unto the sowing t;	2233
Nu	10: 6 When you blow an alarm the second t,	8145
	13:20 Now the t was the t of the first ripe	3117
	13:20 Now the time was the t of the first ripe	3117
	14:14 by day t in a pillar of a cloud, and in a	3119
	20:15 and we have dwelt in Egypt a long t;	3117
	22: 4 Zippor was king of the Moabites at that t.	6256
	23:23 according to this t shall be said of Jacob	6256
	26:10 what t the fire devoured two hundred	871.1
	32:10 Lord's anger was kindled the same t,	6256
	35:26 if the slayer shall at any t come	3318+3318
Dt	1: 9 I spake unto you at that t, saying, I am not	6256
	1:16 I charged your judges at that t, saying,	6256
	1:18 I commanded you at that t all the things	6256
	2:20 giants dwelt therein in old t,	6440+3807.1
	2:34 we took all his cities at that t,	6256
	3: 4 we took all his cities at that t, there was	6256
	3: 8 we took at that t out of the hand of the	6256
	3:12 which we possessed at that t, from Aroer,	6256
	3:18 I commanded you at that t, saying,	6256
	3:21 I commanded Joshua at that t, saying,	6256
	3:23 I besought the Lord at that t, saying,	6256
	4:14 the Lord commanded me at that t to	6256
	5: 5 between the Lord and you at that t,	6256
	6:20 when thy son asketh thee in t to come,	4279
	9:19 the Lord hearkened unto me at that t	6471
	9:20 and I prayed for Aaron also the same t.	6256
	10: 1 At that t the Lord said unto me,	6256
	10: 8 At that t the Lord separated the tribe of	6256
	10:10 according to the first t, forty days and	3117
	10:10 the Lord hearkened unto me at that t	6471
	16: 9 t as thou beginnest to put the sickle to	NIH
	19: 4 he hated not in t past,	4480+8032+8543
	19: 6 he hated him not in t past,	4480+8032+8543
	19:14 which they of old t have set in thine	7223
	20:19 When thou shalt besiege a city a long t,	3117
	22:35 recompence; their foot shall slide in due t:	6256
Jos	2: 5 it came to pass about the t of shutting of	NIH
	2: 5 all his banks all the t of harvest,)	3117
	4: 6 children ask their fathers in t to come,	4279
	4:21 shall ask their fathers in t to come,	4279
	5: 2 At that t the Lord said unto Joshua,	6256
	5: 2 again the children of Israel the second t.	8145
	6:16 it came to pass at the seventh t, when	6471
	6:26 Joshua adjured them at that t, saying,	6256
	8:14 he and all his people, at a t appointed,	4150
	10:27 came to pass at the t of the going down of	6256
	10:42 and their land did Joshua take at one t,	6471
	11: 6 for to morrow about this t will I deliver	6256
	11:10 Joshua at that t turned back,	6256
	11:18 Joshua made war a long t with all those	3117
	11:21 at that t came Joshua, and cut off	6256
	22:24 In t to come your children might speak	4279
	22:27 may not say to our children in t to come,	4279
	22:28 to us or to our generations in t to come,	4279
	23: 1 it came to pass a long t after that	3117
	24: 2 on the other side of the flood in old t,	5769
Jdg	3:29 they slew of Moab at that t about ten	6256
	4: 4 of Lapidoth, she judged Israel at that t.	6256
	9: 8 trees went forth on a t to anoint	1980+1980
	10:14 let them deliver you in the t of your	6256
	11: 4 it came to pass in process of t,	3117+4480
	11:26 did ye not recover them within that t?	6256
	12: 6 there fell at that t of the Ephraimites forty	6256
	13:23 as at this t have told us such things as	6256
	14: 4 for at that t the Philistines had dominion	6256
	14: 8 after a t he returned to take her,	3117
Jdg	15: 1 in the t of wheat harvest, that Samson	3117
	18:31 all the t that the house of God was in	3117
	20:15 numbered at that t out of the cities twenty	3117
	21:14 Benjamin came again at that t;	6256
	21:22 for ye did not give unto them at this t,	6256
	21:24 of Israel departed thence at that t,	6256
Ru	4: 7 in former t in Israel concerning	6440+3807.1
1Sa	1: 4 when the t was that Elkanah offered,	3117
	1:20 when the t was come about after Hannah	3117
	3: 2 it came to pass at that t, when Eli was laid	3117
	3: 8 Lord called Samuel again the third t.	7992
	4:20 about the t of her death the women that	6256
	7: 2 in Kirjath-jearim, that the t was long:	3117
	9:13 you up; for about this t ye shall find him.	3117
	9:16 To morrow about this t I will send thee a	6256
	9:24 for unto this t hath it been kept for thee	4150
	11: 9 To morrow, by that t the sun be hot, ye	NIH
	13: 8 according to the set t that Samuel had	4150
	14:18 For the ark of God was at that t with	3117
	14:21 Philistines before that t,	865+8032+3509.1
	18:19 it came to pass at the t when Merab Saul's	6256
	19:21 Saul sent messengers again the third t,	7992
	20:12 sounded my father about to morrow any t,	6256
	20:35 the field at the t appointed with David,	4150
	26: 8 and I will not smite him the second t.	8138
	27: 7 t that David dwelt in the country	3117+4557
2Sa	2:11 t that David was king in Hebron	3117+4557
	5: 2 Also in t past, when Saul	865+1571+8032
	7: 6 t that I brought up the children of Israel	3117
	7:11 as since the t that I commanded judges to	3117
	11: 1 at the t when kings go forth to battle, that	6256
	14: 2 be as a woman that had a long t mourned	3117
	14:29 when he sent again the second t, he	8145
	17: 7 hath given is not good at this t.	6471
	20: 5 he tarried longer than the set t which he	4150
	20:18 They were wont to speak in old t, saying,	7223
	23: 8 eight hundred, whom he slew at one t.	6471
	23:13 came to David in the harvest t unto	7105
	23:20 slew a lion in the midst of a pit in t of	3117
	24:15 from the morning even to the t appointed:	6256
1Ki	1: 6 father had not displeased him at any t in	3117
	2:26 I will not at this t put thee to death,	3117
	8:65 at that t Solomon held a feast, and all	6256
	9: 2 Lord appeared to Solomon the second t,	8145
	11:29 it came to pass at that t when Jeroboam	6256
	11:42 the t that Solomon reigned in Jerusalem	3117
	14: 1 At that t Abijah the son of Jeroboam fell	6256
	15:23 Nevertheless in the t of his old age he was	6256
	18:29 they prophesied until the t of the offering	NIH
	18:34 he said, Do it the second t. And they did	8138
	18:34 they did it the second t. And they did, Do	8138
	18:34 he said, Do it the third t. And they did it	8027
	18:34 third time. And they did it the third t.	8027
	18:36 it came to pass at the t of the offering of	NIH
	18:44 came to pass at the seventh t, that he said,	NIH
	19: 2 of one of them by to morrow about this t.	6256
	19: 7 of the Lord came again the second t,	8145
	20: 5 servants unto thee to morrow about this t,	6256
2Ki	3: 6 Jehoram went out of Samaria the same t,	3117
	4:16 this season, according to the t of life,	6256
	4:17 said unto her, according to the t of life.	6256
	5:26 Is it a t to receive money, and to receive	6256
	7: 1 To morrow about this t shall a measure of	6256
	7:18 shall be to morrow about this t in the gate	6256
	8:22 Then Libnah revolted at the same t.	6256
	10: 6 he wrote a letter the second t to them,	8145
	10: 6 to me to Jezreel by to morrow this t.	6256
	10:36 the t that Jehu reigned over Israel in	3117
	16: 6 At that t Rezin king of Syria recovered	6256
	18:16 At that t did Hezekiah cut off the gold	6256
	20:12 At that t Berodach-baladan, the son of	6256
	24:10 At that t the servants of Nebuchadnezzar	6256
1Ch	9:20 the ruler over them in t past,	6440+3807.1
	9:25 were to come after seven days from t to	6256
	9:25 after seven days from time to t with them.	6256
	11: 2 moreover in t past, even when	8032+8543
	11:11 three hundred slain by him at one t.	6471
	12:22 For at that t day by day there came to	6256
	17:10 since the t that I commanded judges to be	3117
	20: 1 at the t that kings go out to battle, Joab led	6256
	20: 4 at which t Sibbechai the Hushathite slew	227
	21:28 At that t when David saw that the Lord	6256
	29:22 the son of David king the second t,	8145
	29:27 the t that he reigned over Israel was forty	3117
2Ch	7: 8 Also at the same t Solomon kept the feast	6256
	13:18 of Israel were brought under at that t,	6256
	15:11 they offered unto the Lord the same t,	3117
	16: 7 at that t Hanani the seer came to Asa king	6256
	16:10 oppressed some of the people the same t.	6256
	18:34 of the sun going down he died.	6256
	21:10 The same t also did Libnah revolt from	6256
	21:19 in process of t,	3117+3117+4480+3807.1
	24:11 that at what t the chest was brought unto	6256
	25:27 Now after the t that Amaziah did turn	6256
	28:16 At that t did king Ahaz send unto the	6256
	28:22 in the t of his distress did he trespass yet	6256
	30: 3 For they could not keep it at that t,	6256
	30: 5 they had not done it of a long t in such	NIH
	30:26 since the t of Solomon the son of David	3117
	35:17 were present kept the passover at that t,	6256
Ezr	4:10 are on this side the river, and at such a t.	3706
	4:11 on this side the river, and at such a t.	3706
	4:15 moved sedition within the same of old t:	3118
	4:17 beyond the river: Peace, and at such a t.	3706
	4:19 it is found that this city of old t hath made	3118

T

Ezr
5: 3 At the same **t** came to them Tatnai, 2166
5:16 since **that t** even until now *hath it been* in 116
7:12 of heaven, perfect *peace,* and **at such a t.** 3706
8:34 and all the weight was written at that **t.** 6256
10:13 *it is a* **t** of much rain, and *we are* not able 6256

Ne
2: 6 the king to send me; and I set him a **t.** 2165
4:16 it came to pass from that **t** forth, *that* 3117
4:22 Likewise at the same **t** said I unto 6256
5:14 Moreover from the **t** that I was appointed 3117
6: 1 (though at that **t** I had not set up the doors 6256
6: 5 the fifth **t** with an open letter in his hand; 6471
9:27 in the **t** of their trouble, when they cried 6256
9:32 since the **t** of the kings of Assyria unto this 3117
12:44 at that **t** were some appointed over 3117
13: 6 in all this **t** was not I at Jerusalem: for in NIH
13:21 From that **t** forth came they no *more* on 6256

Est
2:19 were gathered together the **second t,** 8145
4:14 thou altogether holdest thy peace at this **t,** 6256
4:14 come to the kingdom for *such* a **t** as this? 6256
8: 9 were the king's scribes called at that **t** in 6256
9:27 according to their **appointed t** every year; 2165

Job
6:17 What **t** they wax warm, they vanish: 6256
7: 1 *Is there* not an **appointed t** to man upon 6635
9:19 judgment, who shall **set** me a **t** *to plead?* 3259
14:13 that thou wouldest appoint me a **set t,** 2706
14:14 all the days of my **appointed t** will I wait, 6635
15:32 It shall be accomplished before his **t,** 3117
22:16 Which were cut down out of **t,** 6256
30: 3 flying *into* the wilderness **in former t** 570
38:23 Which I have reserved against the **t** of 6256
39: 1 Knowest thou the **t** when the wild goats 6256
39: 2 knowest thou the **t** when they bring forth? 6256
39:18 What **t** she lifteth up herself on high, 6256

Ps
4: 7 more than *in* the **t** *that* their corn and 6256
21: 9 as a fiery oven in the **t** of thine anger: 6256
27: 5 For in the **t** of trouble shall hide me in 3117
32: 6 thee in a **t** when thou mayest be found: 6256
37:19 They shall not be ashamed in the evil **t:** 6256
37:39 *he is* their strength in the **t** of trouble. 6256
41: 1 The LORD will deliver him in **t** of trouble. 3117
56: 3 *What* **t** I am afraid, I will trust in thee. 3117
69:13 *is* unto thee, O LORD, *in an* acceptable **t:** 6256
71: 9 Cast me not off in the **t** of old age; 6256
78:38 **many a t** turned he his anger away, 7235
81: 3 in the **t appointed,** on our solemn feast 3677
81:15 but their **t** should have endured for ever. 6256
89:47 Remember how **short** my **t** is: 2465
102:13 for the **t** to favour her, yea, the set time, 6256
102:13 time to favour her, yea, the **set t,** is come. 4150
105:19 Until the **t** that his word came: the word 6256
113: 2 the name of the LORD **from this t forth** 6258
115:18 we will bless the LORD from **this t forth** 6258
119:126 *It is* **t** for *thee,* LORD, to work: *for* they 6256
121: 8 and thy coming in from **this t forth,** 6258
129: 1 **Many a t** have they afflicted me from my 7227
129: 2 **Many a t** have they afflicted me from my 7227

Pr
25:13 As the cold of snow in the **t** of harvest, 3117
25:19 Confidence in an unfaithful *man* in **t** of 3117
31:25 and she shall rejoice in **t** to come. 3117

Ecc
1:10 it hath been already **of old t,** 5769+3807.1
3: 1 to every purpose under the heaven: 6256
3: 2 A **t** to be born, and a time to die; a time to 6256
3: 2 A time to be born, and a **t** to die; a time to 6256
3: 2 a **t** to plant, and a time to pluck up *that* 6256
3: 2 and a **t** to pluck up *that which* is planted; 6256
3: 3 A **t** to kill, and a time to heal; a time to 6256
3: 3 A time to kill, and a **t** to heal; a time to 6256
3: 3 to break down, and a time to build *up;* 6256
3: 3 a time to break down, and a **t** to build *up;* 6256
3: 4 A **t** to weep, and a time to laugh; a time to 6256
3: 4 A time to weep, and a **t** to laugh; a time to 6256
3: 4 laugh; a **t** to mourn, and a time to dance; 6256
3: 4 laugh; a time to mourn, and a **t** to dance; 6256
3: 5 A **t** to cast away stones, and a time to 6256
3: 5 and a **t** to gather stones together; 6256
3: 5 a **t** to embrace, and a time to refrain from 6256
3: 5 and a **t** to refrain from embracing; 6256
3: 6 A **t** to get, and a time to lose; a time to 6256
3: 6 A time to get, and a **t** to lose; a time to 6256
3: 6 lose; a **t** to keep, and a time to cast away; 6256
3: 6 lose; a time to keep, and a **t** to cast away; 6256
3: 7 A **t** to rent, and a time to sew; a time to 6256
3: 7 A time to rent, and a **t** to sew; a time to 6256
3: 7 a **t** to keep silence, and a time to speak; 6256
3: 7 a time to keep silence, and a **t** to speak; 6256
3: 8 A **t** to love, and a time to hate; a time of 6256
3: 8 A time to love, and a **t** to hate; a time of 6256
3: 8 to hate; a **t** of war, and a time of peace. 6256
3: 8 to hate; a time of war, and a **t** of peace. 6256
3:11 hath made every *thing* beautiful in his **t:** 6256
3:17 for *there is* a **t** there for every purpose and 6256
7:17 why shouldest thou die before thy **t?** 6256
8: 5 a wise *man's* heart discerneth *both* **t** and 6256
8: 6 Because to every purpose there is a **t** and 6256
8: 9 *there is* a **t** wherein one man ruleth over 6256
9:11 but **t** and chance happeneth to them all. 6256
9:12 For man also knoweth not his **t:** 6256
9:12 so *are* the sons of men snared in an evil **t,** 6256

SS
2:12 the **t** of the singing *of birds* is come, 6256

Isa
11:11 **second t** to recover the remnant of his 8145
13:22 her **t** *is* near to come, and her days shall 6256
16:13 spoken concerning Moab since that **t.** 227
18: 7 In that **t** shall the present be brought unto 6256
20: 2 At the same **t** spake the LORD by Isaiah 6256
26:17 *that* **draweth near the t** of her delivery, 7126

Isa
28:19 From the **t** that it goeth forth it shall take 1767
30: 8 that it may be for the **t** to come for ever 3117
33: 2 our salvation also in the **t** of trouble. 6256
39: 1 At that **t** Merodach-baladan, the son of 6256
42:14 I have **long** holden my peace; I have 5769
42:23 will hearken and hear for the **t to come?** 268
44: 8 have not I told thee from **that t,** 227
45:21 who hath declared this from **ancient t?** 6924
45:21 *who* hath told it from **that t?** *have* not I 227
48: 6 have shewed thee new *things* from **this t,** 6258
48: 8 from **that t** *that* thine ear was not opened: 227
48:16 from the **t** that it was, there *am* I: 6256
49: 8 In an acceptable **t** have I heard thee, 6256
60:22 I the LORD will hasten it in his **t.** 6256

Jer
1:13 of the LORD came unto me the **second t,** 8145
2:20 For **of old t** I have broken thy yoke, 4480+5769
2:27 of their trouble they will say, Arise, 6256
2:28 they can save thee in the **t** of thy trouble: 6256
3: 4 Wilt thou not from **this t** cry unto me, 6258
3:17 At that **t** they shall call Jerusalem 6256
4:11 At that **t** shall it be said to this people and 6256
6:15 at the **t** *that* I visit them they shall be cast 6256
8: 1 At that **t,** saith the LORD, they shall bring 6256
8: 7 swallow observe the **t** of their coming; 6256
8:12 the **t** of their visitation they shall be cast 6256
8:15 but no good *came; and* for a **t** of health, 6256
10:15 the **t** of their visitation they shall perish. 6256
11:12 they shall not save them at all in the **t** of 6256
11:14 for I will not hear *them* in the **t** that they 6256
13: 3 of the LORD came unto me the **second t,** 8145
14: 3 Israel, the saviour thereof in **t** of trouble, 6256
14:19 for the **t** of healing, and behold trouble. 6256
15:11 enemy to entreat thee *well* in the **t** of evil, 6256
15:11 the time of evil, and in the **t** of affliction. 6256
18:23 thus with them in the **t** of thine anger. 6256
27: 7 son, until the very **t** of his land come: 6256
30: 7 it is even the **t** of Jacob's trouble; 6256
31: 1 At the same **t,** saith the LORD, will I be 6256
33: 1 LORD came unto Jeremiah the **second t,** 8145
33:15 In those days, and at that **t,** will I cause 6256
39:10 them vineyards and fields at the same **t.** 3117
46:17 a noise; he hath passed the **t appointed.** 4150
46:21 upon them, *and* the **t** of their visitation. 6256
49: 8 Esau upon him, the **t** *that* I will visit him. 6256
49:19 who will **appoint** me the **t?** and who *is* 3259
50: 4 In those days, and in that **t,** saith 6256
50:16 him that handleth the sickle in the **t** of 6256
50:20 In those days, and in that **t,** saith 6256
50:27 their day is come, the **t** of their visitation. 6256
50:31 thy day is come, the **t** *that* I will visit thee. 6256
50:44 who will **appoint** me the **t?** and who *is* 3259
51: 6 for this *is* the **t** of the LORD's vengeance; 6256
51:18 the **t** of their visitation they shall perish: 6256
51:33 like a threshingfloor, *it is* **t** to thresh her: 6256
51:33 and the **t** of her harvest shall come. 6256

La
5:20 us for ever, *and* forsake us so long **t?** 3117

Eze
4:10 a day: from **t** to time shalt thou eat it. 6256
4:10 a day: from time to **t** shalt thou eat it. 6256
4:11 of a hin: from **t** to time shalt thou drink. 6256
4:11 of a hin: from time to **t** shalt thou drink. 6256
7: 7 the **t** is come, the day of trouble *is* near, 6256
7:12 The **t** is come, the day draweth near: let 6256
16: 8 behold, thy **t** was the time of love; 6256
16: 8 behold, thy time *was* the **t** of love; 6256
16:57 as *at the* **t** of thy reproach of the daughters 6256
21:14 let the sword be doubled the **third t,** 7992
22: 3 that her **t** may come, and maketh idols 6256
26:20 with the people of **old t,** and shall set thee 5769
27:34 *In the* **t** when *thou shalt be* broken by 6256
30: 3 day; it shall be the **t** of the heathen. 6256
35: 5 of the sword in the **t** of their calamity, 6256
35: 5 in the **t** *that* their iniquity *had* an end: 6256
38:10 *that* at the same **t** shall things come into 3117
38:17 thou he of whom I have spoken in old **t** 3117
38:18 it shall come to pass at the same **t** when 3117

Da
2: 8 of certainty that ye would gain the **t,** 5732
2: 9 to speak before me, till the **t** be changed: 5732
2:16 of the king that he would give him **t,** 2166
3: 5 *That at what* **t** ye hear 0.2+1768+5732+871.2
3: 8 Therefore at that **t,** when all the people 2166
3: 8 Wherefore at that **t** certain Chaldeans 2166
3:15 Now if ye be ready that at what **t** ye hear 5732
4:36 At the same **t** my reason returned unto 2166
7:12 lives were prolonged for a season and **t.** 5732
7:22 the **t** came that the saints possessed 2166
7:25 they shall be given into his hand until a **t** 5732
7:25 a time and times and the dividing of **t.** 5732
8:17 for at the **t** of the end *shall be* the vision. 6256
8:19 for at the **t appointed** the end *shall be.* 4150
8:23 in the **latter t** of their kingdom, when 319
9:21 touched me about the **t** of the evening 6256
10: 1 *was* true, but the **t appointed** *was* long: 6635
11:24 against the strong holds, even for a **t.** 6256
11:27 yet the end *shall be* at the **t appointed.** 4150
11:29 At the **t appointed** he shall return, 6256
11:35 *them* white, *even* to the **t** of the end: 6256
11:35 end: because *it is* yet for a **t appointed.** 4150
11:40 at the **t** of the end shall the king of 6256
12: 1 at that **t** shall Michael stand up, the great 6256
12: 1 there shall be a **t** of trouble, such as never 6256
12: 1 there was a nation *even* to that same **t:** 6256
12: 1 at that **t** thy people shall be delivered, 6256
12: 4 seal the book, *even* to the **t** of the end: 6256
12: 7 that liveth for ever that *it shall be* for a **t,** 4150
12: 9 closed up and sealed till the **t** of the end. 6256

Da
12:11 from the **t** *that* the daily *sacrifice* shall be 6256

Hos
2: 9 take *away* my corn in the **t** thereof, 6256
9:10 as the firstripe in the fig tree at her **first t:** 7225

Joel
3: 1 For behold, in those days, and in that **t,** 6256

Am
5:13 the prudent shall keep silence in that **t;** 6256
5:13 keep silence in that time; for it *is* an evil **t.** 6256

Jnh
3: 1 the LORD came unto Jonah the **second t,** 8145

Mic
2: 3 shall ye go haughtily: for this **t** is evil. 6256
3: 4 will even hide his face from them at that **t,** 6256
5: 3 until the **t** that she which travaileth hath 6256

Na
1: 9 affliction shall not rise up the **second t.** 6471

Hab
2: 3 For the vision *is* yet for an **appointed t,** 4150

Zep
1:12 it shall come to pass at that **t,** *that* I will 6256
3:19 at that **t** I *will* undo all that afflict thee: 6256
3:20 At that **t** will I bring you **again,** even in 6256
3:20 you **again,** even in the **t** that I gather you: 6256

Hag
2: 1 This people say, The **t** is not come, 6256
1: 2 the **t** that the LORD's house should be 6256
1: 4 *Is it* **t** for you, O ye, to dwell in your 6256

Zec
10: 1 Ask ye of the LORD rain in the **t** of 6256
14: 7 to pass, *that* at evening **t** it shall be light. 6256

Mal
3:11 vine **cast her fruit before the t** in the 7921

Mt
1:11 **about the t** they were carried away to 1909
2: 7 inquired of them diligently what the **t** the star 5550
2:16 according to the **t** which he had diligently 5550
4: 6 **lest at any t** thou dash thy foot against a 3379
4:17 From **that t** Jesus began to preach, 5119
5:21 heard that it was said by them of **old t,** 744
5:25 **lest at any t** the adversary deliver thee to 3379
5:27 heard that it was said by them of **old t,** 744
5:33 that it hath been said by them of **old t,** 744
8:29 come hither to torment us before the **t?** 2540
11:25 At that **t** Jesus answered and said, I thank 2540
12: 1 At that **t** Jesus went on the sabbath day 2540
13:15 **lest at any t** they should see with *their* 3379
13:30 in the **t** of harvest I will say to the reapers, 2540
14: 1 At that **t** Herod the tetrarch heard of 2540
14:15 is a desert place, and the **t** is now past; 5610
16:21 From **that t** forth began Jesus to shew 5119
18: 1 At the same **t** came the disciples unto 5610
21:34 And when the **t** of the fruit drew near, 2540
24:21 the beginning of the world to **this t,** 3568+3588
25:19 After a long **t** the lord of those servants 5550
26:16 And from that **t** he sought opportunity to 5119
26:18 The Master saith, My **t** is at hand; 2540
26:42 He went away again the **second t,** 1208+1537
26:44 away again, and prayed the **third t,** 1537+5154

Mk
1:15 and saying, The **t** is fulfilled, 2540
4:12 **lest at any t** they should be converted, 3379
4:17 in themselves, and so endure but for a **t;** 4340
6:35 a desert place, and now the **t** is far passed: 5610
10:30 shall receive an hundredfold now in **this t,** 2540
11:13 but leaves; for the **t** of figs was not *yet.* 2540
13:19 which God created unto **this t,** 3568+3588
13:33 and pray: for ye know not when the **t** is. 2540
14:41 And he cometh the **third t,** and saith unto 5154
14:72 And the **second t** *the* cock crew. 1208+1537

Lk
1:10 were praying without at the **t** of incense. 5610
1:57 Elisabeth's full **t** came that she should 5550
4: 5 kingdoms of the world in a moment of **t.** 5550
4:11 **lest at any t** thou dash thy foot against a 3379
4:27 And many lepers were in Israel **in the t of** 1909
7:45 this *woman* **since the** **t** I came in 575+3739
8:13 and in **t** of temptation fall away. 5550
8:27 which had devils long **t,** and ware no 5550
9:51 when the **t** was come that he should be 2250
12: 1 **In the mean t,** when there were 1722+3739
12:56 but how *is it that* ye do not discern **this t?** 2540
13:35 me, until the **t** come when ye shall say, NIG
14:17 And sent his servant at supper **t** to say to 5610
15:29 **neither** transgressed I **at any t** 2532+3763
16:16 since **that t** the kingdom of God is 5119
18:30 receive manifold more in this **present t,** 2540
19:44 thou knewest not the **t** of thy visitation. 5550
20: 9 and went into a far country for a long **t.** 5550
21: 8 I am *Christ;* and the **t** draweth near: 2540
21:34 **lest at any t** your hearts be overcharged 3379
21:37 And in the **day t** he was teaching in 2250
23: 7 himself also was at Jerusalem at that **t.** 2250
23:22 And he said unto them the **third t,** Why, 5154

Jn
1:18 No *man* hath seen God at any **t;** the only 4455
3: 4 he enter the **second t** into his mother's 1208
5: 6 knew that he had been now a long **t** in 5550
5:37 Ye have neither heard his voice **at any t,** 4455
6:66 that *t* many of his disciples went back, NIG
7: 6 said unto them, My **t** is not yet come: 2540
7: 6 is not yet come: but your **t** is alway ready. 2540
7: 8 this feast; for my **t** is not yet full come. 2540
11:39 unto him, Lord, **by this** **t** he stinketh: 2235
14: 9 Have I been so long **t** with you, 5550
16: 2 yea, the **t** cometh, that whosoever killeth 5610
16: 4 I told you, that when the **t** shall come, 5610
16:25 but the **t** cometh, when I shall no more 5610
21:14 This is now the **third t** *that* Jesus shewed 5154
21:16 He saith to him again the **second t,** 1208
21:17 He saith unto him the **third t,** Simon, 5154
21:17 because he said unto him the **third t,** 5154

Ac
1: 6 thou at this **t** restore again the kingdom 5550
1:21 with us all the **t** that the Lord Jesus went 5550
7:13 And at the second **t** Joseph was made NIG
7:17 But when the **t** of the promise drew nigh, 5550
7:20 In which **t** Moses was born, 2540
8: 1 at that **t** there was a great persecution 2250
8:11 that of long **t** *he* had bewitched them with 5550

T

Ac	10:15 spake unto him again the **second t**,	1208+1537
	11: 8 **nothing** common or unclean hath	
	at any t	3763+3956
	12: 1 about that t Herod the king stretched	2540
	13:18 And about the t of forty years suffered he	5550
	14: 3 Long t therefore abode they speaking	5550
	14:28 And there they abode long t with	5550
	15:21 For Moses of old t hath in every city them	1074
	17:21 strangers which were there **spent** their **t**	2119
	18:20 When they desired *him* to tarry longer **t**	5550
	18:23 And after he had spent some t *there,* he	5550
	19:23 And the same t there arose no small stir	2540
	20:16 he would not **spend** the t in Asia:	5551
	24:25 and answered, Go *thy way* for *this* t;	3568
	27: 9 Now when much t was spent,	5550
Ro	3:26 declare, *I say,* at this t his righteousness:	2540
	5: 6 in due t Christ died for the ungodly.	2540
	8:18 t *are* not worthy to be compared with	2540
	9: 9 At this t will I come, and Sara shall have a	2540
	11: 5 at *this* present t also there is a remnant	2540
	13:11 that, knowing the t, that *now it is* high	2540
	13:11 now *it is* **high t** to awake out of	2235+5610
1Co	4: 5 Therefore judge nothing before the t,	2540
	7: 5 other, except *it be* with consent for a t,	2540
	7:29 But this I say, brethren, the t *is* short:	2540
	9: 7 Who goeth a warfare **any t** at his own	4218
	15: 8 of me also, as of one **born out of due t**.	1626
	16:12 *his* will was not at all to come **at this t**;	3568
	16:12 come when he shall **have convenient t.**	2119
2Co	6: 2 I have heard thee in a t accepted, and in	2540
	6: 2 behold, now *is* the accepted t; behold,	2540
	8:14 *that* now at *this* t your abundance *may*	2540
	12:14 the third t I am ready to come to you;	NIV
	13: 1 This *is* the third t I am coming to you.	NIV
	13: 2 *you,* as if I were present the second **t,**	NIV
Gal	1:13 conversation **in t past** in the Jews'	4218
	4: 2 governors until the **t appointed** of	4287
	4: 4 But when the fulness of the t was come,	5550
	5:21 as I have also **told** *you* **in t past,**	4302
Eph	2: 2 Wherein **in t past** we walked according to	4218
	2:11 that ye *being* **in t past** Gentiles in	4218
	2:12 That at that t ye were without Christ,	2540
	5:16 Redeeming the **t**, because the days are	2540
Col	4: 5 them that are without, redeeming the **t.**	2540
1Th	2: 5 For neither **at any t** used we flattering	4218
	2:17 being taken from you for a short t in	2540
2Th	2: 6 that he might be revealed in his t.	2540
1Ti	2: 6 a ransom for all, to be testified in due t.	2540
	6:19 a good foundation against the **t to come,**	3195
2Ti	4: 3 For the t will come when they will not	2540
	4: 6 and the t of my departure is at hand.	2540
	4: S was brought before Nero the second t.	NIV
Phm	1:11 Which **in t past** was to thee unprofitable,	4218
Heb	1: 1 **in t** past unto the fathers by the prophets,	3588
	1: 5 unto which of the angels said he **at any t,**	4218
	1:13 to which of the angels said he **at any t,**	4218
	2: 1 **lest at any t** we should let *them* slip.	3379
	4: 7 saying in David, To day, after so long a t;	5550
	4:16 and find grace to help in **t of need.**	2121
	5:12 when for the t ye ought to be teachers,	5550
	9: 9 Which *was* a figure for the **t** *then* present,	2540
	9:10 *on them* until the t of reformation.	2540
	9:28 **second t** without sin unto salvation	1208+1537
	11:32 for the t would fail me to tell of Gedeon,	5550
Jas	4:14 that appeareth for a little *t,* and then	NIV
1Pe	1: 5 salvation ready to be revealed in the last t.	2540
	1:11 what manner of t the Spirit of Christ	2540
	1:17 pass the t of your sojourning *here* in fear:	5550
	2:10 Which **in t past** *were* not a people,	4218
	3: 5 For after this manner **in the old t** the holy	4218
	4: 2 *his* t in the flesh to the lusts of men,	2540
	4: 3 For the t past of *our* life may suffice us to	5550
	4:17 the t *is come* that judgment must begin	2540
	5: 6 of God, that he may exalt you in **due t:**	2540
2Pe	1:21 For the prophecy came not in old t by	4218
	2: 3 whose judgment now **of a long t** lingereth	1597
	2:13 that count it pleasure to riot in the day t.	NIV
1Jn	2:18 Little children, it is the last t: and as ye	5610
	2:18 whereby we know that it is the last t.	5610
	4:12 No *man* hath seen God **at any t.**	4455
Jude	1:18 you there should be mockers in the last t,	5550
Rev	1: 3 are written herein: for the t *is* at hand.	2540
	10: 6 therein, that there should be t no longer:	5550
	11:18 thy wrath is come, and the t of the dead,	2540
	12:12 he knoweth that he hath *but* a short t.	2540
	12:14 where she is nourished for a t, and times,	2540
	12:14 and times, and half a t, from the face of	2540
	14:15 for the t is come for thee to reap;	5610
	22:10 prophecy of this book: for the t is at hand.	2540

TIMES (146) [TIME]

Ge	27:36 for he hath supplanted me these **two t.**	6471
	31: 7 me, and changed my wages ten t;	4489
	31:41 and thou hast changed my wages ten t.	4489
	33: 3 and bowed himself to the ground seven t,	6471
	43:34 Benjamin's mess was five t so much as	3027
Ex	23:14 Three t thou shalt keep a feast unto me in	7272
	23:17 Three t in the year all thy males shall	6471
Lev	4: 6 sprinkle of the blood seven t before	6471
	4:17 sprinkle *it* seven t before the LORD,	6471
	8:11 sprinkled thereof upon the altar seven t,	6471
	14: 7 is to be cleansed from the leprosy seven t,	6471
	14:16 with his finger seven t before the LORD:	6471
	14:27 in his left hand seven t before the LORD:	6471
	14:51 and sprinkle the house seven t:	6471

Lev	16: 2 he come not at all t into the holy *place*	6256
	16:14 of the blood with his finger seven t,	6471
	16:19 the blood upon it with his finger seven t,	6471
	19:26 shall ye use enchantment, nor **observe t.**	6049
	25: 8 of years unto thee, seven t seven years;	6471
	26:18 will punish you seven *t* more for your sins.	NIV
	26:21 I will bring seven *t* moe plagues upon you	NIV
	26:24 will punish you yet seven *t* for your sins.	NIV
	26:28 will chastise you seven *t* for your sins.	NIV
Nu	14:22 have tempted me *now* these ten t,	6471
	19: 4 tabernacle of the congregation seven t:	6471
	22:28 that thou hast smitten me these three t?	7272
	22:32 hast thou smitten thine ass these three t?	7272
	22:33 me, and turned from me these three t?	7272
	24: 1 he went not, as **at other t,**	6471+6471+871.1
	24:10 altogether blessed *them* these three t.	6471
Dt	1:11 of your fathers make you a thousand t	6471
	2:10 Emims dwelt therein **in t past,**	6440+3807.1
	4:42 hated him not **in t past;**	4480+8032+8543
	16:16 Three t in a year shall all thy males appear	6471
	18:10 *or* an **observer of t,** or an enchanter,	6049
	18:14 hearkened unto **observers of t.**	6049
Jos	6: 4 day ye shall compass the city seven t,	6471
	6:15 the city after the same manner seven t:	6471
	6:15 that day they compassed the city seven t.	6471
Jdg	13:25 to **move** him **at t** in the camp of Dan,	6470
	16:15 thou hast mocked me these three t,	6471
	16:20 I will go out as **at other t**	6471+6471+871.1
	20:30 Gibeah, as **at other t.**	6471+6471+871.1
	20:31 as **at other t,** in the	6471+6471+871.1
1Sa	18:10 and called as **at other t:**	6471+6471+871.1
	18:10 his hand, as **at other t:**	3117+3117+871.1
	19: 7 he was in his presence, as **in t past.**	865+8032
	20:25 **at other t,** *even* upon a seat	6471+6471+871.1
	20:41 to the ground, and bowed himself three t:	6471
2Sa	3:17 **in t past** to be king	1571+1571+8032+8543
1Ki	8:59 of his people Israel **at all t,**	3117+3117+871.1
	9:25 three t in a year did Solomon offer burnt	6471
	17:21 stretched himself upon the child three t,	6471
	18:43 *is* nothing. And he said, Go again seven t.	6471
	22:16 How many t shall I adjure thee that thou	6471
2Ki	4:35 the child neesed seven t, and the child	6471
	5:10 Go and wash in Jordan seven t,	6471
	5:14 and dipped *himself* seven t in Jordan,	6471
	13:19 *Thou* shouldest have smitten five or six t;	6471
	13:25 Three t did Joash beat him,	6471
	19:25 *and* of ancient t that I have formed it?	3117
	21: 6 **observed t,** and used enchantments,	6049
1Ch	12:32 *men* that had understanding of the t,	6256
	21: 3 The LORD make his people an hundred t	6471
	29:30 the t that went over him, and over Israel,	6256
2Ch	8:13 on the solemn feasts, three t in the year,	6471
	15: 5 in those t *there was* no peace to him that	6256
	18:15 How many t shall I adjure thee that thou	6471
	33: 6 he **observed t,** and used enchantments,	6049
Ezr	10:14 wives in our cities come at appointed t,	6256
Ne	4:12 by them came, they said unto us ten t,	6471
	6: 4 they sent unto me four t after this sort;	6471
	9:28 many t didst thou deliver them according	6256
	10:34 of our fathers, at t appointed year by year,	6256
	13:31 at t appointed, and for the firstfruits.	6256
Est	1:13 said to the wise *men,* which knew the t,	6256
	9:31 To confirm these days of Purim in their t	2165
Job	19: 3 These ten t have ye reproached me: you	6471
	24: 1 seeing t are not hidden from the Almighty,	6256
Ps	9: 9 for the oppressed, a refuge in t of trouble.	6256
	10: 1 *why* hidest thou *thyself* in t of trouble?	6256
	12: 6 in a furnace of earth, purified seven t.	7659
	31:15 My t *are* in thy hand: deliver me from	6256
	34: 1 I will bless the LORD at all t: his praise	6256
	44: 1 thou didst in their days, in the t of old.	3117
	62: 8 Trust in him at all t; ye people, pour out	6256
	77: 5 the days of old, the years of **ancient t.**	5769
	106: 3 *and* he that doeth righteousness at all t.	6256
	106:43 Many t did he deliver them;	6471
	119:20 *that it hath* unto thy judgments at all t.	6256
	119:164 Seven *t* a day do I praise thee because	NIV
Pr	5:19 let her breasts satisfy thee at all t;	6256
	17:17 A friend loveth at all t, and a brother is	6256
	24:16 For a just *man* falleth seven *t,* and riseth	NIV
Ecc	8:12 Though a sinner do evil an hundred *t,*	NIV
Isa	14:31 none *shall* be alone in his **appointed t.**	4151
	33: 6 knowledge shall be the stability of thy t,	6256
	37:26 *and* of ancient t, that I have formed it?	3117
	46:10 from **ancient t** the *things* that are not yet	6924
Jer	8: 7 in the heaven knoweth her **appointed t,**	4150
Eze	12:27 he prophesieth of the t *that are* far off.	6256
Da	1:20 he found them ten t better than all	3027
	2:21 he changeth the t and the seasons:	5732
	3:19 seven *t* more than *it* was wont to be heat.	NIV
	4:16 unto him; and let seven t pass over him.	5732
	4:23 of the field, till seven t pass over him;	5732
	4:25 heaven, and seven t shall pass over thee,	5732
	4:32 as oxen, and seven t shall pass over thee,	5732
	6:10 he kneeled upon his knees three t a day,	2166
	6:13 but maketh his petition three t a day.	2166
	7:10 ten thousand t ten thousand stood before	NIV
	7:25 High, and think to change t and laws:	2166
	7:25 a time and t and the dividing of time.	5732
	9:25 and the wall, even in troublous t.	6256
	11: 6 and he that strengthened her in *these* t.	6256
	11:14 in those t there shall many stand up	6256
	12: 7 that *it shall* be for a time, t, and a half;	4150
Mt	16: 3 but can ye not *discern* the signs of the t?	2540
	18:21 me, and I forgive him? till **seven t?**	2034

Mt	18:22 him, I say not unto thee, Until **seven t:**	2034
	18:22 seven times: but, Until **seventy t** seven.	1441
Lk	17: 4 if he trespass against thee **seven t** in a	2034
	17: 4 and **seven t** in a day turn again to thee,	2034
	21:24 until the t of the Gentiles be fulfilled.	2540
Ac	1: 7 It is not for you to know the *t* or	5550
	3:19 when the *t* of refreshing shall come from	2540
	3:21 the heaven must receive until the t	5550
	11:10 And this was done three *t*:	1909+4513
	14:16 Who in t past suffered all nations to walk	1074
	17:26 hath determined the t before appointed,	2540
	17:30 the t of *this* ignorance God winked at;	5550
Ro	11:30 For as ye **in t past** have not believed God,	4218
2Co	11:24 Of the Jews **five** t received I forty *stripes*	3999
Gal	1:23 he which persecuted us **in t past** now	4218
	4:10 days, and months, and t, and years.	2540
Eph	1:10 That in the dispensation of the fulness of t	2540
	2: 3 **in t past** in the lusts of our flesh,	4218
1Th	5: 1 But of the t and the seasons, brethren,	5550
1Ti	4: 1 that in the latter t some shall depart from	2540
	6:15 Which in his t he shall shew, *who is*	2540
2Ti	3: 1 that in the last days perilous t shall come.	2540
Tit	1: 3 But hath in due t manifested his word	2540
Heb	1: 1 who at sundry t and in divers manners	4181
1Pe	1:20 but was manifest in *these* last t for you,	5550
Rev	5:11 number of them was ten thousand t ten	NIV
	12:14 and t, and half a time, from the face of	2540

TIMEUS (1)

Mk	10:46 of people, blind Bartimeus, the son of T,	5090

TIMNA (4)

Ge	36:12 **T** was concubine to Eliphaz Esau's son;	8555
	36:22 and Hemam; and Lotan's sister *was* **T.**	8555
1Ch	1:36 and Gatam, Kenaz, and **T**, and Amalek.	8555
	1:39 and Homam: and **T** *was* Lotan's sister.	8555

TIMNAH (5)

Ge	36:40 duke **T**, duke Alvah, duke Jetheth,	8555
Jos	15:10 to Beth-shemesh, and passed on *to* **T.**	8553
	15:57 Cain, Gibeah, and **T**; ten cities with their	8553
1Ch	1:51 duke **T**, duke Aliah, duke Jetheth,	8555
2Ch	28:18 **T** with the villages thereof, Gimzo also	8553

TIMNATH (8)

Ge	38:12 and went up unto his sheepshearers to **T**,	8553
	38:13 Behold thy father in law goeth up to **T** to	8553
	38:14 an open place, which *is* by the way to **T**;	8553
Jdg	14: 1 Samson went down *to* **T**, and saw a	8553
	14: 1 saw a woman in **T** of the daughters	8553
	14: 2 have seen a woman in **T** of the daughters	8553
	14: 5 *to* **T**, and came to the vineyards of	8553
	14: 5 and came to the vineyards of **T**:	8553

TIMNATH-HERES (1) [TIMNATH-SERAH]

Jdg	2: 9 him in the border of his inheritance in **T**,	8556

TIMNATH-SERAH (2) [TIMNATH-HERES]

Jos	19:50 he asked, *even* **T** in mount Ephraim:	8556
	24:30 him in the border of his inheritance in **T**,	8556

TIMNITE (1)

Jdg	15: 6 the son in law of the **T**, because he had	8554

TIMON (1)

Ac	6: 5 and **T**, and Parmenas, and Nicolas a	5096

TIMOTHEUS (19) [TIMOTHY]

Ac	16: 1 named **T**, the son of a certain woman,	5095
	17:14 the sea: but Silas and **T** abode there still.	5095
	17:15 and **T** for to come to him with all speed,	5095
	18: 5 and **T** were come from Macedonia,	5095
	19:22 that ministered unto him, **T** and Erastus;	5095
	20: 4 and Gaius of Derbe, and **T**; and of Asia,	5095
Ro	16:21 **T** my workfellow, and Lucius, and Jason,	5095
1Co	4:17 For this cause have I sent unto you **T**,	5095
	16:10 Now if **T** come, see that he may be with	5095
	16: S and Fortunatus, and Achaicus, and **T**.	5095
2Co	1:19 *even* by me and Silvanus and **T**, was not	5095
Php	1: 1 Paul and **T**, the servants of Jesus Christ,	5095
	2:19 But I trust in the Lord Jesus to send **T**	5095
Col	1: 1 by the will of God, and **T** *our* brother,	5095
1Th	1: 1 Paul, and Silvanus, and **T**, unto the church	5095
	3: 2 And sent **T**, our brother, and minister of	5095
	3: 6 But now when **T** came from you unto us,	5095
2Th	1: 1 Paul, and Silvanus, and **T**, unto the church	5095
2Ti	4: S The second *epistle* unto **T**, ordained	5095

TIMOTHY (9) [TIMOTHEUS]

2Co	1: 1 **T** *our* brother, unto the church of God	5095
1Ti	1: 2 Unto **T**, *my* own son in the faith: Grace,	5095
	1:18 This charge I commit unto thee, son **T**,	5095
	6:20 O **T**, keep that which is committed to *thy*	5095
	6: S The first to **T** was written from Laodicea,	5095
2Ti	1: 2 To **T**, *my* dearly beloved son: Grace,	5095
Phm	1: 1 prisoner of Jesus Christ, and **T** *our* brother,	5095
Heb	13:23 ye that *our* brother **T** is set at liberty;	5095
	13: S Written to the Hebrews from Italy by **T**.	5095

TIN (5)

Nu	31:22 the brass, the iron, the **t**, and the lead,	913
Isa	1:25 away thy dross, and take away all thy **t**	913
Eze	22:18 all they *are* brass, and **t**, and iron, and lead,	913
	22:20 and brass, and iron, and lead, and **t**,	913
	27:12 with silver, iron, **t**, and lead, they traded in	913

TINDER See TOW

TINGLE (3)
1Sa 3:11 ears of every one that heareth it shall **t**. 6750
2Ki 21:12 heareth of it, both his ears shall **t**. 6750
Jer 19: 3 which whosoever heareth, his ears shall **t**. 6750

TINKLING (3)
Isa 3:16 they go, and **making a t** with their feet; 5913
 3:18 of *their* **ornaments** *about their feet*, 5914
1Co 13: 1 become *as* sounding brass, or a **t** cymbal. 214

TIP (9)
Ex 29:20 put *it* upon the **t** of the *right* ear of Aaron, 8571
 29:20 upon the **t** of the right ear of his sons, 8571
Lev 8:23 put *it* upon the **t** of Aaron's right ear, 8571
 8:24 Moses put of the blood upon the **t** of their 8571
 14:14 priest shall put *it* upon the **t** of the right 8571
 14:17 **t** of the right ear of him that is to be 8571
 14:25 put *it* upon the **t** of the right ear of him 8571
 14:28 **t** of the right ear of him that is to be 8571
Lk 16:24 that he may dip the **t** of his finger in water, 206

TIPHSAH (2)
1Ki 4:24 from **T** even to Azzah, over all the kings 8607
2Ki 15:16 Menahem smote **T**, and all that *were* 8607

TIRAS (2)
Ge 10: 2 Javan, and Tubal, and Meshech, and **T**. 8494
1Ch 1: 5 Javan, and Tubal, and Meshech, and **T**. 8494

TIRATHITES (1)
1Ch 2:55 the **T**, the Shimeathites, *and* Suchathites. 8654

TIRE (1) [TIRED, TIRES]
Eze 24:17 bind the **t** of thine **head** upon thee, 6287

TIRED (1) [TIRE]
2Ki 9:30 **t** her head, and looked out at a window. 3190

TIRES (2) [TIRE]
Isa 3:18 and *their* **round t** like the moon, 7720
Eze 24:23 your **t** *shall be* upon your heads, 6287

TIRHAKAH (2)
2Ki 19: 9 when he heard say of **T** king of Ethiopia, 8640
Isa 37: 9 he heard say concerning **T** king of 8640

TIRHANAH (1)
1Ch 2:48 Caleb's concubine, bare Sheber, and **T**. 8647

TIRIA (1)
1Ch 4:16 Ziph, and Ziphah, **T**, and Asareel. 8493

TIRSHATHA (5)
Ezr 2:63 **T** said unto them, that they should not 8660
Ne 7:65 **T** said unto them, that they should not 8660
 7:70 The **T** gave to the treasure a thousand 8660
 8: 9 which *is* the **T**, and Ezra the priest 8660
 10: 1 the **T**, the son of Hachaliah, and Zidkijah, 8660

TIRZAH (18)
Nu 26:33 and Noah, Hoglah, Milcah, and **T**. 8656
 27: 1 Noah, and Hoglah, and Milcah, and **T**. 8656
 36:11 **T**, and Hoglah, and Milcah, and Noah, 8656
Jos 12:24 The king of **T**, one: all the kings thirty 8656
 17: 3 Noah, Hoglah, Milcah, and **T**. 8656
1Ki 14:17 wife arose, and departed, and came to **T**: 8656
 15:21 off building of Ramah, and dwelt in **T**. 8656
 15:33 son of Ahijah to reign over all Israel in **T**, 8656
 16: 6 with his fathers, and was buried in **T**: 8656
 16: 8 son of Baasha to reign over Israel in **T**, 8656
 16: 9 conspired against him, as he *was* in **T**, 8656
 16: 9 house of Arza steward of *his* house in **T**. 8656
 16:15 of Judah did Zimri reign seven days in **T**. 8656
 16:17 all Israel with him, and they besieged **T**. 8656
 16:23 twelve years: six years reigned he in **T**. 8656
2Ki 15:14 the son of Gadi went up from **T**, 8656
 15:16 therein, and the coasts thereof from **T**: 8656
SS 6: 4 Thou *art* beautiful, O my love, as **T**, 8656

TISHBITE (6)
1Ki 17: 1 Elijah the **T**, *who was* of the inhabitants 8664
 21:17 word of the Lord came to Elijah the **T**, 8664
 21:28 word of the Lord came to Elijah the **T**, 8664
2Ki 1: 3 angel of the Lord said to Elijah the **T**, 8664
 1: 8 his loins. And he said, It *is* Elijah the **T**. 8664
 9:36 he spake by his servant Elijah the **T**, 8664

TITHE (14) [TITHES, TITHING]
Lev 27:30 all the **t** of the land, *whether* of the seed 4643
 27:32 the **t** of the herd, or of the flock, 4643
Nu 18:26 it for the Lord, *even* a tenth *part* of the **t**. 4643
Dt 12:17 mayest not eat within thy gates the **t** 4643
 14:22 Thou shalt **truly t** all the increase 6237+6237
 14:23 thy corn, of thy wine, and of thine 4643
 14:28 all the **t** of thine increase the same year, 4643
2Ch 31: 5 the **t** of all *things* brought they in 4643
 31: 6 they also brought in the **t** of oxen and 4643
 31: 6 of holy *things* which were 4643
Ne 10:38 Levites shall bring up the **t** of the tithes 4643
 13:12 Then brought all Judah the **t** of the corn 4643
Mt 23:23 ye **pay t of** mint and anise and cummin, 586
Lk 11:42 for ye **t** mint and rue and all *manner of* 586

TITHES (24) [TITHE]
Ge 14:20 into thy hand. And he gave him **t** of all. 4643
Lev 27:31 if a man will at all redeem *ought* of his **t**, 4643
Nu 18:24 the **t** of the children of Israel, which they 4643
 18:26 ye take of the children of Israel the **t** 4643
 18:28 offering unto the Lord of all your **t**, 4643
Dt 12: 6 your **t**, and heave offerings of your hand, 4643
 12:11 **t**, and the heave offering of your hand, 4643
 26:12 all the **t** of thine increase the third year, 4643
2Ch 31:12 brought in the offerings and the **t** and 4643
Ne 10:37 the **t** of our ground unto the Levites, 4643
 10:37 the same Levites *might* have the **t** in all 6237
 10:38 with the Levites, when the Levites **take t** 6237
 10:38 the Levites shall bring up the tithe of the **t** 4643
 12:44 for the firstfruits, and for the **t**, 4643
 13: 5 the vessels, and the **t** of the corn, the new 4643
Am 4: 4 morning, *and* your **t** after three years: 4643
Mal 3: 8 have we robbed thee? In **t** and offerings. 4643
 3:10 Bring ye all the **t** into the storehouse, that 4643
Lk 18:12 in the week, I **give t** of all that I possess. 586
Heb 7: 5 **take t** of the people according to the law, 1183
 7: 6 from them **received t** of Abraham, 1183
 7: 8 And here men that die receive **t**; 1181
 7: 9 *I* may so say, Levi also, who receiveth **t**, 1181
 7: 9 receiveth tithes, **payed t** in Abraham. 1183

TITHING (2) [TITHE]
Dt 26:12 When thou hast made an end of **t** all 6237
 26:12 *which is* the year of **t**, and hast given *it* 4643

TITLE (3) [TITLES]
2Ki 23:17 he said, What *is* that that I see? 6725
Jn 19:19 And Pilate wrote a **t**, and put *it* on 5102
 19:20 This **t** then read many of the Jews: 5102

TITLES (2) [TITLE]
Job 32:21 neither let me **give flattering t** unto man. 3655
 32:22 For I know not to **give flattering t**; *in so* 3655

TITTLE (2)
Mt 5:18 one **t** shall in no wise pass from the law, 2762
Lk 16:17 earth to pass, than one **t** of the law to fail. 2762

TITUS (15)
2Co 2:13 because I found not **T** my brother: 5103
 7: 6 comforted us by the coming of **T**; 5103
 7:13 the more joyed we for the joy of **T**, 5103
 7:14 so our boasting, which *I made* before **T**, 5103
 8: 6 Insomuch that we desired **T**, that as he 5103
 8:16 earnest care into the heart of **T** for you. 5103
 8:23 Whether *any do* inquire of **T**, *he is* my 5103
 12:18 I desired **T**, and with *him* I sent a brother. 5103
 12:18 Did **T** make a gain of you? walked we not 5103
 13: S *a city* of Macedonia, by **T** and Lucas. 5103
Gal 2: 1 with Barnabas, and took **T** with *me* also. 5103
 2: 3 But neither **T**, who was with me, being a 5103
2Ti 4:10 Crescens to Galatia, **T** unto Dalmatia. 5103
Tit 1: 4 To **T**, *mine* own son after the common 5103
 3: S It was written to **T**, ordained the first 5103

TIZITE (1)
1Ch 11:45 son of Shimri, and Joha his brother, the **T**, 8491

TO (13641) [HERETOFORE, HITHERTO, INTO, THERETO, WHERETO] See Index of Articles, Etc.

TOAH (1)
1Ch 6:34 of Jeroham, the son of Eliel, the son of **T**, 8430

TOB (2)
Jdg 11: 3 his brethren, and dwelt in the land of **T**: 2897
 11: 5 to fetch Jephthah out of the land of **T**: 2897

TOB-ADONIJAH (1)
2Ch 17: 8 and Adonijah, and Tobijah, and **T**, Levites; 2899

TOBIAH (15)
Ezr 2:60 the children of **T**, the children of Nekoda, 2900
Ne 2:10 and **T** the servant, the Ammonite, 2900
 2:19 **T** the servant, the Ammonite, 2900
 4: 3 Now **T** the Ammonite *was* by him, 2900
 4: 7 **T**, and the Arabians, and the Ammonites, 2900
 6: 1 **T**, and Geshem the Arabian, and the rest 2900
 6:12 for **T** and Sanballat had hired him. 2900
 6:14 think thou upon **T** and Sanballat 2900
 6:17 nobles of Judah sent many letters unto **T**, 2900
 6:17 and *the letters* of **T** came unto them. 2900
 6:19 *And* **T** sent letters to put me in fear. 2900
 7:62 the children of **T**, the children of Nekoda, 2900
 13: 4 the house of our God, *was* allied unto **T**: 2900
 13: 7 of the evil that Eliashib did for **T**, 2900
 13: 8 I cast forth all the household stuff of **T** 2900

TOBIJAH (3)
2Ch 17: 8 and **T**, and Tob-adonijah, Levites; 2900
Zec 6:10 *even* of Heldai, of **T**, and of Jedaiah, 2900
 6:14 to **T**, and to Jedaiah, and to Hen the son 2900

TOCHEN (1)
1Ch 4:32 Ain, Rimmon, and **T**, and Ashan, 8507

TODAY See TO DAY

TOE (6) [TOES]
Ex 29:20 upon the **great t** of their right foot, 931
Lev 8:23 and upon the **great t** of his right foot. 931

Lev 14:14 and upon the **great t** of his right foot: 931
 14:17 and upon the **great t** of his right foot: 931
 14:25 and upon the **great t** of his right foot: 931
 14:28 and upon the **great t** of his right foot, 931

TOES (7) [TOE]
Lev 8:24 upon the **great t** of their right feet: 931
Jdg 1: 6 and cut off his thumbs and his **great t**. 7272
 1: 7 their thumbs and their **great t** cut off, 7272
2Sa 21:20 on every foot six **t**, four and twenty *in* 676
1Ch 20: 6 **fingers and t** *were* four and twenty, 676
Da 2:41 whereas thou sawest the feet and **t**, part 677
 2:42 And *as* the **t** of the feet *were* part of iron, 677

TOGARMAH (4)
Ge 10: 3 of Gomer; Ashkenaz, and Riphath, and **T**. 8425
1Ch 1: 6 Gomer; Ashchenaz, and Riphath, and **T**. 8425
Eze 27:14 They of the house of **T** traded in thy fairs 8425
 38: 6 house of **T** *of* the north quarters, and all 8425

TOGETHER (484) [ALTOGETHER]
Ge 1: 9 the heaven be **gathered t** unto one place, 6960
 1:10 the **gathering t** of the waters called he 4723
 3: 7 they **sewed** fig leaves t, 8609
 13: 6 to bear them, that they might dwell **t**: 3162
 13: 6 was great, so that they could not dwell **t**. 3162
 14: 3 All these were **joined t** in the vale of 2266
 22: 6 a knife; and they went both of them **t**. 3162
 22: 8 offering: so they went both of them **t**. 3162
 22:19 they rose up and went **t** to Beer-sheba; 3162
 25:22 the children **struggled t** within her; 7533
 29: 7 time that the cattle should be **gathered t**: 622
 29: 8 until all the flocks be **gathered t**, 622
 29:22 Laban **gathered t** all the men of the place, 622
 34:30 they shall **gather** themselves **t** against me, 622
 36: 7 were more than that they might dwell **t**; 3162
 42:17 he **put** them **all t** into ward three days. 622
 49: 1 his sons, and said, **Gather** yourselves **t**, 622
 49: 2 **Gather** yourselves **t**, and hear, ye sons of 6908
Ex 2:13 two men of the Hebrews **strove t**: 5327
 3:16 **gather** the elders of Israel **t**, and say unto 622
 4:29 **gathered t** all the elders of the children of 622
 8:14 they **gathered** them **t** upon heaps: 6651
 15: 8 thy nostrils the waters were **gathered t**, 6192
 19: 8 all the people answered it, and said, All 3162
 21:18 if men **strive t**, and one smite another 7378
 26: 3 The five curtains shall be **coupled t** 2266
 26: 6 the curtains **t** with the taches: 269+413+802
 26:11 and **couple** the tent **t**, that it may be one. 2266
 26:24 they shall be **coupled t** beneath, 8382
 26:24 they shall be **coupled t** above 3162+8535
 28: 7 edges thereof; and *so* it shall be **joined t**. 2266
 30:35 apothecary, **tempered t**, pure *and* holy: 4414
 32: 1 the people **gathered** themselves **t** unto 6950
 32:26 all the sons of Levi **gathered** themselves **t** 622
 35: 1 **gathered** all the congregation of 6950
 the children of Israel **t**, 6950
 36:18 fifty taches of brass to **couple** the tent **t**, 2266
 39: 4 coupled **t** at the head thereof, to one ring: 3162
 39: 4 made shoulderpieces for it, to **couple** it **t**: 2266
 39: 4 by the two edges was it **coupled t**. 2266
Lev 8: 3 **gather** thou all the congregation **t** unto 6950
 8: 4 assembly was **gathered t** unto the door 6950
 24:10 and a man of Israel **strove t** in the camp 5327
 26:25 when ye are **gathered t** within your cities, 6950
Nu 1:18 they **assembled** all the congregation **t** on 6950
 8: 9 **gather** the whole assembly of 6950
 the children of Israel **t**: 6950
 10: 7 the congregation is to be **gathered t**, 6950
 11:22 all the fish of the sea be **gathered t** for 622
 14:35 that are **gathered t** against me: 3259
 16: 3 **gathered** themselves **t** against Moses 6950
 16:11 all thy company *are* **gathered t** against 3259
 20: 2 **gathered** themselves **t** against Moses 6950
 20: 8 **gather** thou the assembly **t**, thou, 6950
 20:10 Aaron **gathered** the congregation **t** before 6950
 21:16 **Gather** the people **t**, and I will give them 622
 21:23 Sihon **gathered** all his people **t**, 622
 24:10 against Balaam, and he **smote** his hands **t** 5606
 26:10 swallowed them up **t** with Korah, 2050.1
 27: 3 **gathered** themselves **t** against the Lord 3259
Dt 4:10 **Gather** me the people **t**, and I will make 6950
 22:10 shalt not plow with an ox and an ass **t**. 3162
 22:11 of divers sorts, *as* of woollen and linen **t**. 3162
 25: 5 If brethren dwell **t**, and one of them die, 3162
 25:11 When men **strive t** one with another, 3162
 31:12 **Gather** the people **t**, men, and women, 6950
 33: 5 *and* the tribes of Israel were **gathered t**, 3162
 33:17 with them he shall push the people **t** *to* 3162
Jos 8:16 the people that *were* in Ai were called **t** NIH
 9: 2 That they **gathered** themselves **t**, to fight 3162
 10: 5 **gathered** themselves **t**, and went up, they 622
 10: 6 the mountains are **gathered t** against us, 6908
 11: 5 all these kings were **met t**, they came 3259
 11: 5 and pitched **t** at the waters of Merom, 3162
 17:10 they **met t** in Asher on the north, 6293
 18: 1 children of Israel **assembled t** *at* Shiloh, 6950
 22:12 Israel **gathered** themselves **t** *at* Shiloh, 6950
Jdg 4:13 Sisera **gathered t** all his chariots, *even* 2199
 6:33 the children of the east were **gathered t**, 3162
 6:38 **thrust** the fleece **t**, and wringed the dew 2115
 7:23 men of Israel **gathered** themselves **t** out 6817
 7:24 men of Ephraim **gathered** themselves **t**, 6817
 9: 6 And all the men of Shechem **gathered t**, 622
 9:47 the tower of Shechem were **gathered t**. 6908

T

Jdg 10:17 the children of Ammon were **gathered t**, 6817
10:17 children of Israel **assembled** themselves t, 622
11:20 Sihon **gathered** all his people t, 622
12: 1 men of Ephraim **gathered themselves t**, 6817
12: 4 Jephthah **gathered t** all the men of Gilead 6908
16:23 lords of the Philistines **gathered** them t 622
18:22 near to Micah's house were **gathered t**, 2199
19: 6 and did eat and drink both of them **t**; 3162
19:29 divided her, *t* with her bones, into twelve NIH
20: 1 the congregation was **gathered t** as one 6950
20:11 against the city, **knit t** as one man. 2270
20:14 **gathered** themselves t out of the cities 622

1Sa 5:11 **gathered t** all the lords of the Philistines, 622
7: 6 **gathered t** to Mizpeh, and drew water, 6908
7: 7 of Israel were **gathered t** to Mizpeh, 6908
8: 4 elders of Israel **gathered** themselves t, 6908
10:17 Samuel **called** the people t unto 6817
11:11 so that two of them were not left t. 3162
13: 4 the people were **called** t after Saul *to* 6817
13: 5 the Philistines **gathered** themselves t to 622
13:11 the Philistines **gathered** themselves t *at* 622
15: 4 Saul **gathered** the people t, 8085
17: 1 the Philistines **gathered** their armies 622
17: 1 were **gathered t** at Shochoh, 622
17: 2 and the men of Israel were **gathered t**, 622
17:10 give me a man, that we may fight **t**. 3162
23: 8 Saul **called** all the people t to war, to go 8085
25: 1 all the Israelites were **gathered t**, 6908
28: 1 the Philistines **gathered** their armies t 6908
28: 4 the Philistines **gathered** themselves t 6908
28: 4 Saul **gathered** all Israel t, and they 6908
28:23 **t** with the woman, compelled 1571+2050.1
29: 1 Now the Philistines **gathered t** all their 6908
31: 6 all his men, that *same* day t. 3162

2Sa 2:13 out, and met by the pool of Gibeon: 3162
2:16 in his fellow's side; so they fell down t: 3162
2:25 **gathered** themselves t after Abner, 6908
2:30 when he had **gathered** all the people t, 6908
6: 1 David **gathered t** all the chosen *men* of 622
10:15 before Israel, they gathered themselves t 3162
10:17 he **gathered** all Israel t, and passed over 622
12: 3 it grew up t with him, and with his 3162
12:28 therefore **gather** the rest of the people t, 622
12:29 David **gathered** all the people t, and went 622
14: 6 they two **strove** t in the field, and *there* 5327
14:16 my son t out of the inheritance of God. 3162
20:14 they were **gathered** t, and went also after 6950
21: 9 they fell all seven t, and were put to death 3162
23: 9 *that* were there **gathered t** to battle, 622
23:11 Philistines were **gathered t** into a troop, 622

1Ki 3:18 we *were* t; *there* was no stranger with us 3162
5:12 and they two made a league t. NIH
10:26 Solomon **gathered t** chariots and 622
11: 1 *t* with the daughter of Pharaoh, 2050.1
18:20 **gathered** the prophets t unto mount 6908
20: 1 the king of Syria **gathered** all his host t: 6908
22: 6 king of Israel **gathered** the prophets t, 6908

2Ki 2: 8 **wrapt** *it* t, and smote the waters, 1563
3:10 *t*, to deliver them into the hand of Moab. NIH
3:13 *t*, to deliver them into the hand of Moab. NIH
9:25 and thou rode t after Ahab his father, 6776
10:18 Jehu **gathered** all the people t, 6908

1Ch 10: 6 his three sons, and all his house died t. 3162
11:13 there the Philistines were **gathered t** to 622
13: 5 David **gathered** all Israel t, from Shihor 6950
15: 3 David **gathered** all Israel t to Jerusalem, 6950
16:35 **gather** us t, and deliver us from 6908
19: 7 **gathered** themselves t from their cities, 622
22: 2 David commanded to **gather t** the 3664
23: 2 he **gathered t** all the princes of Israel, 622

2Ch 12: 5 that were **gathered t** to Jerusalem because 622
15:10 they **gathered** themselves t *at* Jerusalem 622
18: 5 Therefore the king of Israel **gathered t** of 6908
20: 4 Judah **gathered** themselves t, to ask *help* 6908
24: 5 he **gathered t** the priests and the Levites, 6908
25: 5 Moreover Amaziah **gathered** Judah t, 6908
28:24 Ahaz **gathered t** the vessels of the house 622
29: 4 and **gathered** them t into the east street, 622
30: 3 **gathered** themselves t to Jerusalem. 6908
32: 4 So there was **gathered** much people t, 6908
32: 6 **gathered** them t to him in the street of 6908
34:17 they have **gathered t** the money that was 5413
34:29 **gathered t** all the elders of Judah and 622

Ezr 2:64 whole congregation *t was* forty 259+3509.1
3: 1 the people **gathered** themselves t as one 622
3: 9 and his sons, the sons of Judah, t, 259+3509.1
3:11 they sung t by course in praising and NIH
4: 3 we ourselves t will build unto the LORD 259+3509.1
6:20 and the Levites were purified, t, 259+3509.1
7:28 I **gathered t** out of Israel chief *men* to go 6908
8:15 I **gathered** them t to the river that 6908
10: 7 that *they* should **gather** themselves t 6908
10: 9 Benjamin **gathered** themselves t *unto* 6908

Ne 4: 6 all the wall was **joined** t unto the half 7194
4: 8 conspired all of them t to come *and* to 3162
6: 2 let us meet t in *some one of* the villages 3162
6: 7 now therefore, and let us take counsel t. 3162
6:10 said, Let us **meet** t in the house of God, 3259
7: 5 my God put into mine heart to **gather t** 6908
7:66 whole congregation *t was* forty 259+3509.1
8: 1 the people **gathered** themselves t as one 622
8:13 the second day were **gathered t** the chief 622
12:28 sons of the singers **gathered** themselves t, 622
13:11 I **gathered** them t, and set them in their 6908

Est 2: 3 that they may **gather t** all the fair young 6908

Est 2: 8 many maidens were **gathered t** unto 6908
2:19 when the virgins were **gathered t** 6908
4:16 **gather t** all the Jews that are present in 3664
8:11 in every city to **gather** themselves t 6950
9: 2 The Jews **gathered** themselves t in their 6950
9:15 **gathered** themselves t on the fourteenth 6950
9:16 king's provinces **gathered** themselves t, 6950
9:18 Jews that *were* at Shushan **assembled t** 6950

Job 2:11 for they had made an appointment t to 3162
3:18 *There* the prisoners rest t; they hear not 3162
6: 2 my calamity laid in the balances t! 3162
9:32 *and* we should come t in judgment. 3162
10: 8 me and fashioned me t round about; 3162
11:10 or **gather t**, then who can hinder him? 6950
16:10 they have gathered themselves t against 3162
17:16 of the pit, when *our* rest t *is* in the dust. 3162
19:12 His troops come t, and raise up their way 3162
24: 4 the poor of the earth hide themselves t. 3162
30: 7 under the nettles they were **gathered t**. 5596
34:15 All flesh shall perish t, and man shall turn 3162
38: 7 When the morning stars sang t, and all 3162
38:38 into hardness, and the clods **cleave fast** t? 1692
40:13 Hide them in the dust t; *and* bind their 3162
40:17 the sinews of his stones are **wrapt** t. 8276
41:15 *his* pride, shut up *t* as with a close seal. NIH
41:17 they **stick** t, that they cannot be sundered 3920
41:23 The flakes of his flesh are **joined** t: they 1692

Ps 2: 2 the rulers take counsel t, against 3162
14: 3 all gone aside, they are all t become filthy: 3162
31:13 while they took counsel t against me, 3162
33: 7 He **gathereth** the waters of the sea as a 3664
34: 3 with me, and let us exalt his name t. 3162
35:15 they rejoiced, and **gathered** themselves t: 622
35:15 *yea*, the abjects **gathered** themselves t 622
35:26 brought to confusion t that rejoice at mine 3162
37:38 the transgressors shall be destroyed t: 3162
40:14 confounded t that seek after my soul to 3162
41: 7 All that hate me whisper t against me: 3162
47: 9 The princes of the people are **gathered t**, 622
48: 4 kings were assembled, they passed by t. 3162
49: 2 Both low and high, rich and poor, t. 3162
50: 5 Gather my saints t unto me; those that NIH
55:14 We took sweet counsel t, *and* walked 3162
56: 6 They **gather** themselves t, they hide 1481
71:10 that lay wait for my soul take counsel t, 3162
74: 8 said in their hearts, Let us destroy them t: 3162
83: 5 they have consulted t *with one* consent: 3162
85:10 Mercy and truth are **met** t; righteousness 6298
88:17 like water; they compassed me about t. 3162
94:21 They **gather** themselves t against the soul 1413
98: 8 clap *their* hands: let the hills be joyful t 3162
102:22 When the people are gathered t, 3162
104:22 they **gather** themselves t, and lay them 622
122: 3 *is* builded as a city that is compact t: 3162
133: 1 *it is* for brethren to dwell t **in unity**. 3162
140: 2 continually are they **gathered t** *for* war. 1481
147: 2 he **gathereth** t the outcasts of Israel. 3664

Pr 22: 2 The rich and poor **meet** t: the LORD is 6298
29:13 The poor and the deceitful man **meet** t: 6298

Ecc 3: 5 stones, and a time to **gather** stones t; 3664
4: 5 The fool **foldeth** his hands t, and eateth 2263
4:11 again, if two lie t, then they have heat: 7901

Isa 1:18 Come now, and let us **reason** t, saith 3198
1:28 and of the sinners shall be t, 3162
1:31 they shall both burn t, and none shall 3162
8:10 **Take counsel** t, and it shall come 5779+6098
9:11 Rezin against him, and **join** his enemies t; 5526
9:21 *and* they *t shall* be against Judah. For all 3162
11: 6 calf and the young lion and the fatling t; 3162
11: 7 their young ones shall lie down t: 3162
11:12 **gather** t the dispersed of Judah from 6908
11:14 west; they shall spoil them of the east t: 3162
13: 4 of the kingdoms of nations **gathered t**: 622
18: 6 They shall be left t unto the fowls of 3162
22: 3 All thy rulers are fled t, they are bound by 3162
22: 3 all that are found in thee are bound t, 3162
22: 9 **gathered** t the waters of the lower pool. 6908
24:22 they shall be **gathered** t, *as* prisoners 622+626
26:19 *t* with my dead body shall they arise. NIH
27: 4 go through them, I would burn them t. 3162
31: 3 shall fall down, and they all shall fail t. 3162
34: 4 the heavens shall be **rolled** t as a scrole: 1556
40: 5 be revealed, and all flesh shall see *it* t. 3162
41: 1 speak: let us come near t to judgment. 3162
41:19 fir tree, *and* the pine, and the box tree t: 3162
41:20 know, and consider, and understand t, 3162
41:23 we may be dismayed, and behold *it* t. 3162
43: 9 Let all the nations be gathered t, and let 3162
43:17 they shall lie down t, they shall not rise: 3162
43:26 let us plead t: declare thou, that thou 3162
44:11 let them all be **gathered** t, let them stand 6908
44:11 shall fear, *and* they shall be ashamed t. 3162
45: 8 and let righteousness spring up t; 3162
45:16 shall go to confusion t *that are* makers 3162
45:20 draw near t, ye that *are* escaped of 3162
45:21 *them* near; yea, let them take counsel t: 3162
46: 2 They stoop, they bow down t; they could 3162
48:13 *when* I call unto them, they stand *up* t. 3162
49:18 all these **gather** themselves t, *and* come 6908
50: 8 let us stand t: who *is* mine adversary? 3162
52: 8 the voice; with the voice they shall sing: 3162
52: 9 Break forth into joy, sing t, ye waste 3162
54:15 shall **surely gather** t, *but* not by 1481+1481
54:15 whosoever shall **gather** t against thee 1481

Isa 60: 4 all they **gather** themselves t, they come 6908
60: 5 flow *t*, and thine heart shall fear, NIH
60: 7 the flocks of Kedar shall be **gathered t** 6908
60:13 the fir tree, the pine tree, and the box t, 3162
62: 9 they that have **brought** it t shall drink t 6908
65: 7 and the iniquities of your fathers t, 3162
65:25 The wolf and the lamb shall feed t, 259+3509.1
66:17 and the mouse, shall be consumed t, 3162

Jer 3:18 they shall come t out of the land of 3162
4: 5 cry, **gather** t, and say, 4390
6:11 and upon the assembly of young men t: 3162
6:12 unto others, *with their* fields and wives t: 3162
6:21 and the sons t shall fall upon them; 3162
13:14 even the fathers and the sons t, saith 3162
31: 8 and her that travaileth with child t: 3162
31:12 shall flow *t* to the goodness of the LORD, NIH
31:13 in the dance, both young men and old t: 3162
31:24 *in* all the cities thereof t, husbandmen, 3162
41: 1 and there they did eat bread t in Mizpah. 3162
46:12 the mighty, *and* they are fallen both t. 3162
46:21 also are turned back, *and* are fled away t; 3162
48: 7 captivity *with* his priests and his princes t. 3162
49: 3 *and* his priests and his princes t. 3162
49:14 **Gather** ye t, and come against her, 6908
50: 4 they and the children of Judah t, going 3162
50:29 **Call** t the archers against Babylon: all ye 8085
50:33 the children of Judah *were* oppressed t: 3162
51:27 **call** t against her the kingdoms of Ararat, 8085
51:38 They shall roar t like lions: they shall yell 3162
51:44 the nations shall not flow *t* any more unto NIH

La 2: 8 and the wall to lament; they languished t. 3162

Eze 21:14 smite *thine* **hands** t, and let 413+3709+3709
21:17 will also smite mine **hands** t, 413+3709+3709
29: 5 thou shalt not be **brought** t, nor gathered: 622
37: 7 and the bones **came** t, bone to his bone. 7126

Da 2:35 broken to pieces t, and became 2298+3509.4
3: 2 Nebuchadnezzar the king sent to **gather** t 3673
3: 3 were **gathered** t unto the dedication of 3673
3:27 being **gathered** t, saw these men, 3673
6: 6 princes assembled *t* to the king, NIH
6: 7 have **consulted** t to establish a royal 3272
11: 6 end of years they shall **join** themselves t, 2266

Hos 1:11 and the children of Israel be gathered t, 3162
11: 8 within me, my repentings are kindled t. 3162

Joel 3:11 and **gather** yourselves t round about: 6908

Am 1:15 he and his princes t, saith the LORD. 3162
3: 3 Can two walk t, except they be agreed? 3162

Mic 2:12 I will put them t as the sheep of Bozrah: 3162

Na 1:10 For while *they be* **folden** t *as* thorns, 5440
2:10 the knees **smite** t, and much pain *is* in all 6375

Zep 2: 1 **Gather** yourselves t, yea, gather together, 7197
2: 1 yea, **gather** t, O nation not desired; 7197

Zec 10: 4 battle bow, out of him every oppressor t. 3162
12: 2 people of the earth be **gathered** t against 622
14:14 heathen round about shall be **gathered** t, 622

Mt 1:18 before they **came** t, she was found with 4905
2: 4 **gathered** all the chief priests and 4863
scribes of the people t,
13: 2 great multitudes were **gathered** t unto 4863
13:30 Let both **grow** t until the harvest: and in 4885
13:30 **Gather** ye t first the tares, and bind 4863
18:20 or three are **gathered** t in my name, 4863
19: 6 What therefore God hath **joined** t, let not 4801
22:10 and **gathered** t all as many as they found, 4863
22:34 silence, they were **gathered** t. 846+1909+3588
22:41 the Pharisees were **gathered** t, Jesus 4863
23:37 would I have **gathered** thy children t, 1996
24:28 there will the eagles be **gathered** t. 4863
24:31 they shall **gather** t his elect from the four 1996
26: 3 Then **assembled** t the chief priests, 4863
27:17 Therefore when they were **gathered** t, 4863
27:62 and Pharisees **came** t unto Pilate, 4863

Mk 1:33 all the city was **gathered** t at the door. 1996
2: 2 And straightway many were **gathered** t, 4863
2:15 and sinners **sat also t with** Jesus and 4873
3:20 And the multitude **cometh** t again, 4905
6:30 And the apostles **gathered** themselves t 4863
6:33 and outwent them, and **came** t unto him. 4905
7: 1 Then **came** t unto him the Pharisees, 4863
9:25 saw that the people **came running** t, 1998
10: 9 What therefore God hath **joined** t, let not 4801
12:28 and having heard them **reasoning** t, 4802
13:27 **gather** t his elect from the four winds, 1996
14:56 but *their* witness **agreed** not t. 1510+2470
14:59 so did their witness **agree** t. 1510+2470
15:16 and they **call** t the whole band. 4779

Lk 5:15 and great multitudes **came** t to hear, 4905
6:38 and shaken t, and running over, NIG
8: 4 And when much people were **gathered** t, 4896
9: 1 Then he **called** his twelve disciples t, 4779
11:29 when the people were **gathered** thick t, 1865
12: 1 when there were **gathered** t an 1996
13:11 was **bowed** t, and could in no wise lift 4794
13:34 would I have **gathered** thy children t, 1996
15: 6 he **calleth** t *his* friends and neighbours, 4779
15: 9 **calleth** *her* friends and *her* neighbours t, 4779
15:13 days after the younger son **gathered** all t, 4863
17:35 women shall be grinding t; 846+1909+3588
17:37 *is*, thither will the eagles be **gathered** t. 4863
22:55 were **set down** t, Peter sat down among 4776
22:66 the chief priests and the scribes **came** t, 4863
23:12 and Herod were made friends t: 240+3326
23:13 when he had **called** t the chief priests 4779
23:48 all the people that **came** t to that sight, 4836
24:14 And they talked t of all these *things* 240+4314

Lk	24:15 while they communed *t* and reasoned,	NIG
	24:33 and found the eleven **gathered** t,	4867
Jn	4:36 he that reapeth may rejoice t,	3674
	6:13 Therefore they **gathered** them t,	4863
	11:52 that also he should **gather** t in one	4863
	11:53 **took counsel** t for to put him to death.	4823
	20: 4 So they ran both t: and the other disciple	3674
	20: 7 but **wrapped** t in a place by itself.	1794
	21: 2 There were t Simon Peter,	3674
Ac	1: 4 And, being **assembled** t with them,	4871
	1: 6 When they therefore were **come** t,	4905
	1:15 (the number of names t were	846+1909+3588
	2: 6 the multitude **came** t,	4905
	2:44 And all that believed were t,	846+1909+3588
	3: 1 went up t into the temple	846+1909+3588
	3:11 the people **ran** t unto them in the porch	4936
	4: 6 priest, were **gathered** t at Jerusalem.	4863
	4:26 **gathered** t against the Lord,	846+1909+3588
	4:27 and the people of Israel, were **gathered** t,	4863
	4:31 shaken where they were **assembled** t;	4863
	5: 9 How *is it* that ye have **agreed** t to tempt	4856
	5:21 **called** the council t, and all the senate	4779
	10:24 and had **called** t his kinsmen and near	4779
	10:27 and found many that were **come** t.	4905
	12:12 where many were **gathered** t praying.	4867
	13:44 came almost the whole city t to hear	4905
	14: 1 that they went *both* t into	846+2596+3588
	14:27 come, and had **gathered** the church t,	4863
	15: 6 **came** t for to consider of this matter.	4863
	15:30 when they had **gathered** the multitude t,	4863
	16:22 the multitude **rose up** t against them:	4911
	19:19 used curious arts **brought** their books t,	4851
	19:25 Whom he **called** t with the workmen of	4867
	19:32 knew not wherefore they were **come** t.	4905
	20: 7 the disciples **came** t to break bread,	4863
	20: 8 where they were **gathered** t.	4863
	21:22 the multitude must needs **come** t: for	4905
	21:30 was moved, and the people **ran** t:	1096+4890
	23:12 certain of the Jews **banded** t,	4160+4963
	28:17 days Paul **called** the chief of the Jews t:	4779
	28:17 when they were **come** t, he said unto	4905
Ro	1:12 that *I* may be **comforted** t with you by	4837
	3:12 the way, they are t become unprofitable;	260
	6: 5 For if we have been **planted** t in	4854
	8:17 *him*, that we may be also **glorified** t.	4888
	8:22 and **travaileth in pain** t until now.	4944
	8:28 And we know that all *things* **work** t for	4903
	15:30 that ye **strive** t with me in your prayers	4865
1Co	1:10 *that* ye be **perfectly joined** t in the same	2675
	3: 9 For we are **labourers** t with God: ye are	4904
	5: 4 when ye are **gathered** t, and my spirit,	4863
	7: 5 and prayer, and come t again,	846+1909+3588
	11:17 that you **come** t not for the better,	4905
	11:18 first of all, when ye **come** t in the church,	4905
	11:20 When ye **come** t therefore into one place,	4905
	11:33 my brethren, when ye **come** t to eat,	4905
	11:34 that ye **come** not t unto condemnation.	4905
	12:24 but God hath **tempered** the body t,	4786
	14:23 whole church be **come** t into one place,	4905
	14:26 **come** t, every one of you hath a	4905
2Co	1:11 You also **helping** t by prayer for us,	4943
	6: 1 as **workers** t with him, beseech *you* also	4903
	6:14 Be ye not **unequally yoked** t with	2086
Eph	1:10 might **gather** t in one all *things* in Christ,	346
	2: 5 hath **quickened** *us* t with Christ,	4806
	2: 6 And hath **raised** *us* up t, and made *us* sit	4891
	2: 6 **made** *us* sit t in heavenly *places* in Christ	4776
	2:21 In whom all the building **fitly framed** t,	4883
	2:22 In whom you also are **builded** t for a	4925
	4:16 whom the whole body **fitly joined** t,	4883
Php	1:27 with one mind **striving** t for the faith of	4866
	3:17 be **followers** t of me, and mark them	4831
Col	2: 2 being **knit** t in love, and unto all riches of	4822
	2:13 flesh, hath **quickened** t with him,	4806
	2:19 and **knit** t, increaseth *with* the increase of	4822
1Th	4:17 remain shall be caught up t with them in	260
	5:10 wake or sleep, we should live t with him.	260
	5:11 Wherefore comfort **yourselves** t,	240
2Th	2: 1 and *by* our **gathering** t unto him,	1997
Heb	10:25 forsaking the **assembling** of ourselves t,	1997
Jas	5: 3 ye have **heaped treasure** t for the last	2343
1Pe	3: 7 and as *being* **heirs** t of the grace of life;	4789
	5:13 **elected** t with you, saluteth you;	4899
Rev	6:14 departed as a scrole when it is **rolled** t;	1507
	16:16 he **gathered** them t into a place called	4863
	19:17 **gather** **yourselves** t unto the supper of	4863
	19:19 **gathered** t to make war against him that	4863
	20: 8 and Magog, to **gather** them t to battle:	4863

TOHU (1)

1Sa	1: 1 is the son of **T**, the son of Zuph,	8459

TOI (3) [TOU]

2Sa	8: 9 **T** king of Hamath heard that David	8583
	8:10 **T** sent Joram his son unto king David,	8583
	8:10 for Hadadezer had wars with **T**.	8583

TOIL (4) [TOILED, TOILING]

Ge	5:29 concerning our work and t of our hands,	6093
	41:51 *said he*, hath made me forget all my t,	5999
Mt	6:28 grow; they t not, neither do they spin:	2872
Lk	12:27 they t not, they spin not; and yet I say	2872

TOILED (1) [TOIL]

Lk	5: 5 we have t all the night, and have taken	2872

TOILING (1) [TOIL]

Mk	6:48 And he saw them t in rowing; for the wind	928

TOKEN (14) [TOKENS]

Ge	9:12 This *is* the t of the covenant which I make	226
	9:13 It shall be for a t of a covenant between me	226
	9:17 unto Noah, This *is* the t of the covenant,	226
	17:11 it shall be a t of the covenant betwixt me	226
Ex	3:12 this *shall be* a t unto thee, that I have sent	226
	12:13 the blood shall be to you for a t upon	226
	13:16 it shall be for a t upon thine hand,	226
Nu	17:10 to be kept for a t against the rebels;	226
Jos	2:12 my father's house, and give me a true t:	226
Ps	86:17 Shew me a t for good; that they which	226
Mk	14:44 he that betrayed him had given them a t,	4953
Php	1:28 is to them an **evident** t of perdition,	1732
2Th	1: 5 *Which is* a **manifest** t of the righteous	1730
	3:17 own hand, which is the t in every epistle:	4592

TOKENS (7) [TOKEN]

Dt	22:15 bring forth the t of the damsel's virginity	NIH
	22:17 *yet* these *are* the t of my daughter's	NIH
	22:20 the t of virginity be not found for	NIH
Job	21:29 by the way? and do ye not know their t,	226
Ps	65: 8 in the uttermost parts are afraid at thy t:	226
	135: 9 *Who* sent t and wonders into the midst of	226
Isa	44:25 That frustrateth the t of the liars,	226

TOKHATH See TIKVATH

TOLA (6) [TOLAITES]

Ge	46:13 **T**, and Phuvah, and Job, and Shimron.	8439
Nu	26:23 *of* **T**, the family of the Tolaites: of Pua,	8439
Jdg	10: 1 arose to defend Israel **T** the son of Puah,	8439
1Ch	7: 1 Now the sons of Issachar *were*, **T**,	8439
	7: 2 And the sons of **T**; Uzzi, and Rephaiah,	8439
	7: 2 heads of their fathers' house, *to wit*, of **T**:	8439

TOLAD (1)

1Ch	4:29 And at Bilhah, and at Ezem, and at **T**,	8434

TOLAITES (1) [TOLA]

Nu	26:23 *of* Tola, the family of the **T**: of Pua,	8440

TOLD (283) [TELL]

Ge	3:11 he said, Who t thee that thou *wast* naked?	5046
	9:22 father, and t his two brethren without.	5046
	14:13 had escaped, and t Abram the Hebrew;	5046
	20: 8 and t all these things in their ears:	1696
	22: 3 unto the place which God had t him.	559
	22: 9 came to the place which God had t him	559
	22:20 that it was t Abraham, saying, Behold,	5046
	24:28 t *them of* her mother's house these	5046
	24:33 I will not eat, until I have t mine errand.	1696
	24:66 the servant t Isaac all things that he had	5608
	26:32 t him concerning the well which they had	5046
	27:42 words of Esau her elder son were t to	5046
	29:12 Jacob t Rachel that he *was* her father's	5046
	29:12 son: and she ran and t her father.	5046
	29:13 And he t Laban all these things.	5608
	31:20 Syrian, in that he t him not that he fled.	5046
	31:22 it was t Laban on the third day that Jacob	5046
	37: 5 dreamed a dream, and he t *it* his brethren:	5046
	37: 9 t it his brethren, and said, Behold, I have	5608
	37:10 he t *it* to his father, and to his brethren:	5608
	38:13 it was t Tamar, saying, Behold thy father	5046
	38:24 months after, that it was t Judah, saying,	5046
	40: 9 the chief butler t his dream to Joseph,	5608
	41: 8 Pharaoh t them his dream; but *there was*	5608
	41:12 we t him, and he interpreted to us our	5608
	41:24 I t *this* unto the magicians; but *there was*	559
	42:29 and t him all that befell unto them;	5046
	43: 7 we t him according to the tenor of these	5046
	44:24 my father, we t him the words of my lord.	5046
	45:26 t him, saying, Joseph *is* yet alive, and he	1696
	45:27 they t him all the words of Joseph,	1696
	47: 1 Joseph came and t Pharaoh, and said,	5046
	48: 1 *one* t Joseph, Behold, thy father *is* sick:	559
	48: 2 *one* t Jacob, and said, Behold, thy son	5046
Ex	4:28 Moses t Aaron all the words of the LORD	5046
	5: 1 and Aaron went in, and t Pharaoh,	559
	14: 5 it was t the king of Egypt that the people	5046
	16:22 of the congregation came and t Moses.	5046
	18: 8 Moses t his father in law all that	5608
	18: 9 Moses t the words of the people unto	5046
	24: 3 the people all the words of the LORD,	5608
Lev	21:24 Moses t *it* unto Aaron, and to his sons,	1696
Nu	11:24 t the people the words of the LORD,	1696
	11:27 t Moses, and said, Eldad and Medad do	5046
	13:27 they t him, and said, We came unto	5608
	14:39 Moses t these sayings unto all the	1696
	23:26 and said unto Balak, **T** not I thee, saying,	1696
	29:40 Moses t the children of Israel according to	559
Dt	17: 4 it be t thee, and thou hast heard *of it*, and	5046
Jos	2: 2 it was t the king of Jericho, saying, Behold,	559
	2:23 and t him all *things* that befell them:	5608
	9:24 it was **certainly** t thy servants,	5046+5046
	10:17 it was t Joshua, saying, The five kings are	5046
Jdg	6:13 *be* all his miracles which our fathers' t	5608
	7:13 *there was* a man that t a dream unto his	5608
	9: 7 when they t *it* to Jotham, he went and	5046
	9:25 way by them: and it was t Abimelech.	5046
	9:42 out *into* the field; and they t Abimelech.	5046
	9:47 it was t Abimelech, that all the men of	5046
	13: 6 the woman came and t her husband,	559

Jdg	13: 6 him not whence he *was*, neither the	5046
	13:23 *this* time have t us *such things* as these.	8085
	14: 2 and t his father and his mother, and said,	5046
	14: 6 he t not his father or his mother what he	5046
	14: 9 he t not them that he had taken the	5046
	14:16 of my people, and hast not t *it* me.	5046
	14:16 it my father nor my mother,	5046
	14:17 that he t her, because she lay sore upon	5046
	14:17 she t the riddle to the children of her	5046
	16: 2 *it was* t the Gazites, saying, Samson is	NIH
	16:10 thou hast mocked me, and t me lies:	1696
	16:13 thou hast mocked me, and t me lies:	1696
	16:15 hast not t me wherein thy great strength	5046
	16:17 That he t her all his heart, and said unto	5046
	16:18 Delilah saw that he had t her all his	5046
Ru	3:16 t her all that the man had done to her.	5046
1Sa	3:13 I have t him that I will judge his house	5046
	3:18 Samuel t him every whit, and hid nothing	5046
	4:13 into the city, and t *it*, all the city cried out.	5046
	4:14 And the man came in hastily, and t Eli.	5046
	8:10 Samuel t all the words of the LORD unto	559
	9:15 Now the LORD had t Samuel **in** his ear a	1540
	10:16 t us **plainly** that the asses were	5046+5046
	10:16 whereof Samuel spake, he t him not.	5046
	10:25 Samuel t the people the manner of	1696
	11: 4 and t the tidings in the ears of the people:	1696
	11: 5 t him the tidings of the men of Jabesh.	5608
	14: 1 on the other side. But he t not his father.	5046
	14:33 they t Saul, saying, Behold, the people sin	5046
	14:43 Jonathan t him, and said, I did but taste a	5046
	15:12 it was t Samuel, saying, Saul came to	5046
	18:20 they t Saul, and the thing pleased him.	5046
	18:24 servants of Saul t him, saying, On this	5046
	18:26 when his servants t David these words,	5046
	19: 2 Jonathan t David, saying, Saul my father	5046
	19:11 Michal David's wife t him, saying, If thou	5046
	19:18 and t him all that Saul had done to him.	5046
	19:19 it was t Saul, saying, Behold, David *is* at	5046
	19:21 when it was t Saul, he sent other	5046
	23: 1 they t David, saying, Behold,	5046
	23: 7 it was t Saul that David was come to	5046
	23:13 it was t Saul that David was escaped from	5046
	23:22 for it is t me *that* he dealeth very subtilly.	559
	23:25 his men went to seek *him*. And they t	5046
	24: 1 that it was t him, saying, Behold, David *is*	5046
	25:12 and came and t him all those sayings.	5046
	25:14 one of the young men t her about Abigail.	5046
	25:19 But she t not her husband Nabal.	5046
	25:36 she t him nothing, less or more,	5046
	25:37 his wife had t him these things, that his	5046
	27: 4 it was t Saul that David was fled *to* Gath:	5046
2Sa	1: 5 said unto the young man that t him,	5046
	1: 6 the young man that t him said, As I	5046
	1:13 said unto the young man that t him,	5046
	2: 4 they t David, saying, *That* the men of	5046
	3:23 they t Joab, saying, Abner the son of Ner	5046
	4:10 When one t me, saying, Behold, Saul is	5046
	6:12 it was t king David, saying, The LORD	5046
	10: 5 When they t *it* unto David, he sent to	5046
	10:17 it was t David, he gathered all Israel	5046
	11: 5 and t David, and said, I *am* with child.	5046
	11:10 when they had t David, saying, Uriah	5046
	11:18 t David all the things concerning the war;	5046
	14:33 So Joab came to the king, and t him:	5046
	15:31 *one* t David, saying, Ahithophel *is* among	5046
	17:17 a wench went and t them; and they went	5046
	17:17 them; and they went and t king David.	5046
	17:18 a lad saw them, and t Absalom:	5046
	17:21 went and t king David, and said unto	5046
	18:10 a certain man saw *it*, and t Joab, and said,	5046
	18:11 Joab said unto the man that t him,	5046
	18:25 the watchman cried, and t the king.	5046
	19: 1 it was t Joab, Behold, the king weepeth	5046
	19: 8 they t unto all the people, saying, Behold,	5046
	21:11 it was t David what Rizpah the daughter	5046
	24:13 to David, and t him, and said unto him,	5046
1Ki	1:23 they t the king, saying, Behold Nathan	5046
	1:51 it was t Solomon, saying, Behold,	5046
	2:29 it was t king Solomon that Joab was fled	5046
	2:39 they t Shimei, saying, Behold, thy servants	5046
	2:41 it was t Solomon that Shimei had gone	5046
	8: 5 that could not be t nor numbered for	5608
	10: 3 Solomon t her all her questions: there was	5046
	10: 3 hid from the king, which he t her not.	5046
	10: 7 and behold, the half was not t me:	5046
	13:11 t him all the works that the man of God	5608
	13:11 the king, them they t also to their father.	5608
	13:25 t *it* in the city where the old prophet	1696
	14: 2 which t me that I should be king over	1696
	18:13 Was it not t my lord what I did when	5046
	18:16 Obadiah went to meet Ahab, and t him:	5046
	19: 1 Ahab t Jezebel all that Elijah had done,	5046
	20:17 Ben-hadad sent out, and they t him,	5046
2Ki	1: 7 up to meet you, and t you these words?	1696
	4: 7 she came and t the man of God. And he	5046
	4:27 hath hid *it* from me, and hath not t me.	5046
	4:31 him, saying, The child is not awaked.	5046
	5: 4 t his lord, saying, Thus and thus said	5046
	6:10 to the place which the man of God t him	559
	6:13 it was t him, saying, Behold, *he is* in	5046
	7:10 t them, saying, We came to the camp	5046
	7:11 and t *it* to the king's house within.	5046
	7:15 the messengers returned, and t the king.	5046
	8: 6 the king asked the woman, she t him.	5608
	8: 7 it was t him, saying, The man of God is	5046

Ref	Text	Strong
2Ki	8:14 t me *that* thou shouldest surely recover.	559
	9:18 the watchman t, saying, The messenger	5046
	9:20 the watchman t, saying, He came even	5046
	9:36 Wherefore they came again, and t him.	5046
	10: 8 there came a messenger, and t him,	5046
	12:10 t the money that was found *in* the house	4487
	12:11 they gave the money, being t, into	8505
	18:37 and t him the words of Rab-shakeh.	5046
	23:17 men of the city t him, *It is* the sepulchre	559
1Ch	17:25 t thy servant that *thou* wilt build	241+1540
	19: 5 and t David how the men were served.	5046
	19:17 it was t David; and he gathered all Israel,	5046
2Ch	2: 2 Solomon **t out** threescore and ten	5608
	5: 6 which could not be t nor numbered for	5608
	9: 2 Solomon t her all her questions:	5046
	9: 2 hid from Solomon which he t her not.	5046
	9: 6 greatness of thy wisdom was not t me:	5046
	20: 2 there came *some* that t Jehoshaphat,	5046
	34:18 Shaphan the scribe t the king, saying,	5046
Ezr	8:17 t them what they should say	6310+7760+871.1
Ne	2:12 neither t I *any* man what my God had put	5046
	2:16 neither had I as yet t *it* to the Jews, nor to	5046
	2:18 I t them of the hand of my God which	5046
Est	2:22 who t *it* unto Esther the queen;	5046
	3: 4 not unto them, that they t Haman,	5046
	3: 4 for he had t them that he *was* a Jew.	5046
	4: 4 and her chamberlains came and t *it* her.	5046
	4: 7 Mordecai t him of all that had happened	5046
	4: 9 and t Esther the words of Mordecai.	5046
	4:12 And they t to Mordecai Esther's words.	5046
	5:11 Haman t them of the glory of his riches,	5608
	6: 2 that Mordecai had t of Bigthana and	5046
	6:13 Haman t Zeresh his wife and all his	5046
	8: 1 for Esther had t what he *was* unto her.	5046
Job	15:18 Which wise men have t from their fathers,	5046
	37:20 Shall it be t him that I speak? if a man	5608
Ps	44: 1 our ears, O God, our fathers have t us,	5608
	52: T when Doeg the Edomite came and t Saul,	5046
	78: 3 and known, and our fathers have t us.	5608
	90: 9 we spend our years as a tale *that is* t.	NIH
Ecc	6: 6 though he live a thousand years twice *t,*	NIH
Isa	7: 2 it was t the house of David, saying, Syria	5046
	36:22 and t him the words of Rabshakeh.	5046
	40:21 hath it not been t you from the beginning?	5046
	44: 8 have not I t thee from that time,	8085
	45:21 *who* hath t it from that time? *have* not I	5046
	52:15 for *that* which had not been t them shall	5608
Jer	36:20 and t all the words in the ears of the king.	5046
	38:27 he t them according to all these words	5046
Da	4: 7 I t the dream before them; but they *did*	560
	4: 8 and before him I t the dream, *saying,*	560
	7: 1 the dream, *and* t the sum of the matters.	560
	7:16 So he t me, and made me know	560
	8:26 and the morning which was t *is* true:	559
Jnh	1:10 of the LORD, because he had t them.	5046
Hab	1: 5 ye will not believe, though it be t *you.*	5608
Zec	10: 2 have seen a lie, and have t false dreams;	1696
Mt	8:33 and t every *thing,* and what was befallen	518
	12:48 answered and said unto him that t him,	3004
	14:12 and buried it, and went and t Jesus.	518
	18:31 and t unto their lord all that was done.	1285
	24:25 Behold, I have t you **before.**	4302
	26:13 hath done, be t for a memorial of her.	2980
	28: 7 there shall ye see him: lo, I have t you.	3004
Mk	5:14 and t *it* in the city, and in the country.	312
	5:16 they that saw *it* t them how it befell to	1334
	5:33 down before him, and t him all the truth.	3004
	6:30 t him all *things,* both what they had done,	518
	9:12 And he answered and t them, Elias verily	3004
	16:10 went and t them that had been with him,	518
	16:13 And they went and t *it* unto the residue:	518
Lk	1:45 *things* which were t her from the Lord.	2980
	2:17 which was t them concerning this child.	2980
	2:18 which were t them by the shepherds.	2980
	2:20 heard and seen, as it was t unto them.	2980
	8:20 And it was t him *by certain* which said,	518
	8:34 and went and t *it* in the city and in	518
	8:36 They also which saw *it* t them by what	518
	9:10 returned, t him all that they had done.	1334
	9:36 t no *man* in those days any of *those things*	518
	13: 1 were present at that season some that t	518
	18:37 And they t him, that Jesus of Nazareth	518
	24: 9 and t all these *things* unto the eleven,	518
	24:10 which t these *things* unto the apostles.	3004
	24:35 And they t what *things* were done in	1834
Jn	3:12 If I have t you earthly *things,* and	3004
	4:29 man, which t me all *things* that ever I did:	3004
	4:39 which testified, He t me all that ever I did.	3004
	4:51 met him, and t *him,* saying, Thy son liveth.	518
	5:15 and t the Jews that it was Jesus,	312
	8:40 a man that hath t you the truth, which I	2980
	9:27 I have t you already, and ye did not hear:	3004
	10:25 them, I t you, and ye believe not:	3004
	11:46 and t them what *things* Jesus had done.	3004
	14: 2 if *it were* not so, I would have t you.	3004
	14:29 And now I have t you before it come to	3004
	16: 4 But these *things* have I t you, that when	2980
	16: 4 we may remember that I t you of them.	3004
	18: 8 I have t you that I am *he:* if therefore	3004
Ac	20:18 the disciples that he had seen the Lord,	518
	5:22 not in the prison, they returned, and t,	518
	5:25 Then came one and t them, saying,	518
	9: 6 it shall be t thee what thou must do.	2980
	12:14 and t **how** Peter stood before the gate.	518
	16:36 And the keeper of the prison t this saying to	518

Ref	Text	Strong
Ac	16:38 And the sergeants t these words unto	312
	22:10 there it shall be t thee of all *things* which	2980
	22:26 heard *that,* he went and t the chief captain,	518
	23:16 and entered into the castle, and t Paul.	518
	23:30 And when it was t me how that the Jews	3377
	27:25 that it shall be even as it was t me.	2980
2Co	7: 7 when he t us your earnest desire, your	312
	13: 2 I t *you* before, and foretell *you,* as if I	4302
Gal	5:21 as I have also t *you* in time past,	4302
Php	3:18 of whom I have t you often, and now tell	3004
1Th	3: 4 we t you **before** that we should suffer	4302
2Th	2: 5 I was yet with you, I t you these *things?*	3004
Jude	1:18 How that they t you there should be	3004

TOLERABLE (6)

Ref	Text	Strong
Mt	10:15 It shall be **more t** for the land of Sodom	414
	11:22 It shall be **more t** for Tyre and Sidon at	414
	11:24 It shall be **more t** for the land of Sodom	414
Mk	6:11 It shall be **more t** for Sodom and	414
Lk	10:12 It shall be **more t** in that day for Sodom,	414
	10:14 it shall be **more t** for Tyre and Sidon at	414

TOLL (3)

Ref	Text	Strong
Ezr	4:13 set up *again, then* will they not pay t,	4061
	4:20 t, tribute, and custom, *was* paid unto	4061
	7:24 it *shall* not be lawful to impose t, tribute,	4061

TOMB (3) [TOMBS]

Ref	Text	Strong
Job	21:32 to the grave, and shall remain in the t.	1430
Mt	27:60 And laid it in his own new t, which he	3419
Mk	6:29 and took up his corpse, and laid in a t.	3419

TOMBS (6) [TOMB]

Ref	Text	Strong
Mt	8:28 coming out of the t, exceeding fierce,	3419
	23:29 because ye build the t of the prophets,	5028
Mk	5: 2 immediately there met him out of the t a	3419
	5: 3 Who had *his* dwelling among the t;	3419
	5: 5 and in the t, crying, and cutting himself	3418
Lk	8:27 neither abode in *any* house, but in the t.	3418

TOMORROW See TO MORROW

TONGS (5)

Ref	Text	Strong
Ex	25:38 the t thereof, and the snuffdishes thereof,	4457
Nu	4: 9 his t, and his snuffdishes, and all the oil	4457
1Ki	7:49 and the lamps, and the t *of* gold,	4457
2Ch	4:21 the flowers, and the lamps, and the t,	4457
Isa	6: 6 which he had taken with the t from off	4457
	44:12 The smith *with* the t both worketh in	4621

TONGUE (129) [DOUBLETONGUED, TONGUES]

Ref	Text	Strong
Ge	10: 5 every one after his t, after their families,	3956
Ex	4:10 but I *am* slow of speech, and of a slow t.	3956
	11: 7 of Israel shall not a dog move his t,	3956
Dt	28:49 nation whose t thou shalt not understand;	3956
Jos	10:21 none moved his t against any of	3956
Jdg	7: 5 one that lappeth of the water with his t,	3956
2Sa	23: 2 spake by me, and his word *was* in my t.	3956
Ezr	4: 7 of the letter *was* written **in the Syrian** t,	762
	4: 7 and interpreted **in the** Syrian t.	762
Est	7: 4 and bondwomen, I had **held** my t.	2790
Job	5:21 shalt be hid from the scourge of the t:	3956
	6:24 Teach me, and I will **hold** my t:	2790
	6:30 Is there iniquity in my t? cannot my taste	2790
	13:19 for now, if I **hold** my t, I shall give up	2790
	15: 5 and thou choosest the t of the crafty.	3956
	20:12 his mouth, *though* he hide it under his t;	3956
	20:16 poison of asps: the viper's t shall slay him.	3956
	27: 4 speak wickedness, nor my t utter deceit.	3956
	29:10 their t cleaved to the roof of their mouth.	3956
	33: 2 mouth, my t hath spoken in my mouth.	3956
	41: 1 his t with a cord *which* thou lettest down?	3956
Ps	5: 9 open sepulchre; they flatter with their t.	3956
	10: 7 fraud: under his t *is* mischief and vanity.	3956
	12: 3 *and* the t that speaketh proud *things:*	3956
	12: 4 have said, With our t will we prevail;	3956
	15: 3 *that* backbiteth not with his t, nor doeth	3956
	22:15 my t cleaveth to my jaws; and thou hast	3956
	34:13 Keep thy t from evil, and thy lips from	3956
	35:28 my t shall speak of thy righteousness and	3956
	37:30 and his t talketh of judgment.	3956
	39: 1 to my ways, that *I* sin not with my t:	3956
	39: 3 the fire burned: *then* spake I with my t,	3956
	45: 1 king: my t *is* the pen of a ready writer.	3956
	50:19 mouth to evil, and thy t frameth deceit.	3956
	51:14 my t shall sing aloud of thy righteousness.	3956
	52: 2 Thy t deviseth mischiefs; like a sharp	3956
	52: 4 all devouring words, O thou deceitful t.	3956
	57: 4 and arrows, and their t a sharp sword.	3956
	64: 3 Who whet their t like a sword,	3956
	64: 8 they shall make their own t to fall upon	3956
	66:17 mouth, and he was extolled with my t.	3956
	68:23 *and* the t of thy dogs in the same.	3956
	71:24 My t also shall talk of thy righteousness	3956
	73: 9 and their t walketh through the earth.	3956
	109: 2 have spoken against me *with* a lying t.	3956
	119:172 My t shall speak of thy word: for all thy	3956
	120: 2 from lying lips, *and* from a deceitful t.	3956
	120: 3 shall be done unto thee, thou false t?	3956
	126: 2 *with* laughter, and our t *with* singing:	3956
	137: 6 let my t cleave to the roof of my mouth;	3956
	139: 4 For *there* is not a word in my t, *but* lo,	3956
Pr	6:17 a lying t, and hands that shed innocent	3956
	6:24 from the flattery of the t of a strange	3956
	10:20 The t of the just *is as* choice silver:	3956
	10:31 but the froward t shall be cut out.	3956

Ref	Text	Strong
Pr	12:18 of a sword: but the t of the wise *is* health.	3956
	12:19 for ever: but a lying t *is* but for a moment.	3956
	15: 2 The t of the wise useth knowledge aright:	3956
	15: 4 A wholesome t *is* a tree of life:	3956
	16: 1 the answer of the t, *is* from the LORD.	3956
	17: 4 *and* a liar giveth ear to a naughty t.	3956
	17:20 he that hath a perverse t falleth into	3956
	18:21 Death and life *are* in the power of the t:	3956
	21: 6 The getting of treasures by a lying t *is* a	3956
	21:23 and his t keepeth his soul from troubles.	3956
	25:15 and a soft t breaketh the bone.	3956
	25:23 an angry countenance a backbiting t.	3956
	26:28 A lying t hateth *those that are* afflicted by	3956
	28:23 favour than he that flattereth with the t.	3956
	31:26 and in her t *is* the law of kindness.	3956
SS	4:11 honey and milk *are* under thy t;	3956
Isa	3: 8 their t and their doings *are* against	3956
	11:15 the LORD shall utterly destroy the t of	3956
	28:11 another t will he speak to this people.	3956
	30:27 indignation, and his t *as* a devouring fire:	3956
	32: 4 the t of the stammerers shall be ready to	3956
	33:19 of a stammering t, *that* thou canst not	3956
	35: 6 leap as a hart, and the t of the dumb sing:	3956
	41:17 *there is* none, *and* their t faileth for thirst,	3956
	45:23 every knee shall bow, every t shall swear.	3956
	50: 4 The Lord GOD hath given me the t of	3956
	54:17 every t *that* shall rise against thee in	3956
	57: 4 ye a wide mouth, *and* draw out the t?	3956
	59: 3 your t hath muttered perverseness.	3956
Jer	9: 5 they have taught their t to speak lies,	3956
	9: 8 Their t *is* as an arrow shot out; it speaketh	3956
	18:18 let us smite him with the t, and let us not	3956
La	4: 4 The t of the sucking child cleaveth to	3956
Eze	3:26 I will make thy t cleave to the roof of thy	3956
Da	1: 4 the learning and the t of the Chaldeans.	3956
Hos	7:16 fall by the sword for the rage of their t:	3956
Am	6:10 shall he say, **Hold** thy t: for *we may* not	2013
Mic	6:12 and their t *is* deceitful in their mouth.	3956
Hab	1:13 **holdest** thy t when the wicked devoureth	2790
Zep	3:13 neither shall a deceitful t be found in their	3956
Zec	14:12 their t shall consume away in their mouth.	3956
Mk	7:33 his ears, and he spit, and touched his t;	1100
	7:35 and the string of his t was loosed,	1100
Lk	1:64 and his t *loosed,* and he spake,	1100
	16:24 tip of his finger in water, and cool my t;	1100
Jn	5: 2 is called **in the Hebrew** t Bethesda,	1447
Ac	1:19 as that field is called in their proper t,	1258
	2: 8 how hear we every man in our own t,	1258
	2:26 did my heart rejoice, and my t was glad;	1100
	21:40 he spake unto *them* in the Hebrew t,	1258
	22: 2 that he spake in the Hebrew t to them,	1258
	26:14 and saying in the Hebrew t, Saul, Saul,	1258
Ro	14:11 to me, and every t shall confess to God.	1100
1Co	14: 2 For he that speaketh in an *unknown* t	1100
	14: 4 He that speaketh in an *unknown* t edifieth	1100
	14: 9 except ye utter by the t words easy to be	1100
	14:13 in an *unknown* t pray that he may interpret.	1100
	14:14 For if I pray in an *unknown* t, my spirit	1100
	14:19 ten thousand words in an *unknown* t.	1100
	14:26 a doctrine, hath a t, hath a revelation,	1100
	14:27 If any *man* speaketh in an *unknown* t, *let it*	1100
Php	2:11 And that every t should confess that Jesus	1100
Jas	1:26 bridleth not his t, but deceiveth his own	1100
	3: 5 Even so the t is a little member,	1100
	3: 6 And the t *is* a fire, a world of iniquity:	1100
	3: 6 so is the t amongst our members, that it	1100
	3: 8 the t can no man tame; *it* is an unruly	1100
1Pe	3:10 let him refrain his t from evil, and his lips	1100
1Jn	3:18 let us not love in word, neither in t;	1100
Rev	5: 9 and t, and people, and nation;	1100
	9:11 name **in the Hebrew** t *is* Abaddon,	1447
	9:11 in the Greek t hath *his* name Apollyon.	NIG
	14: 6 and kindred, and t, and people,	1100
	16:16 called **in the Hebrew** t Armageddon.	1447

TONGUES (36) [TONGUE]

Ref	Text	Strong
Ge	10:20 after their t, in their countries, *and* in	3956
	10:31 after their t, in their lands, after their	3956
Ps	31:20 secretly in a pavilion from the strife of t.	3956
	55: 9 Destroy, O Lord, *and* divide their t: for I	3956
	78:36 and they lied unto him with their t.	3956
	140: 3 have sharpened their t like a serpent;	3956
Isa	66:18 that *I* will gather all nations and t;	3956
Jer	9: 3 they bend their t *like* their bow *for* lies:	3956
	23:31 that use their t, and say, He saith.	3956
Mk	16:17 out devils; they shall speak with new t;	1100
Ac	2: 3 there appeared unto them cloven t like	1100
	2: 4 and began to speak with other t,	1100
	2:11 we do hear them speak in our t	1100
	10:46 For they heard them speak with t,	1100
	19: 6 and they spake with t, and prophesied.	1100
Ro	3:13 with their t they have used deceit;	1100
1Co	12:10 of spirits; to another *divers* kinds of t;	1100
	12:10 to another the interpretation of t:	1100
	12:28 helps, governments, diversities of t.	1100
	12:30 do all speak with t? do all interpret?	1100
	13: 1 Though I speak with the t of men and	1100
	13: 8 whether *there be* t, they shall cease;	1100
	14: 5 I would that ye all spake with t, but rather	1100
	14: 5 prophesieth than he that speaketh with t,	1100
	14: 6 if I come unto you speaking with t,	1100
	14:18 my God, I speak with t more than you all:	1100
	14:21 With men *of* other t and other lips will I	2084
	14:22 Wherefore t are for a sign, not to them	1100
	14:23 and all speak with t, and there come in	1100

1Co	14:39 prophesy, and forbid not to speak with t.	1100
Rev	7: 9 nations, and kindreds, and people, and t,	1100
	10:11 and nations, and t, and kings.	1100
	11: 9 *the* of the people and kindreds and t and	1100
	13: 7 him over all kindreds, and t, and nations.	1100
	16:10 and they gnawed their t for pain,	1100
	17:15 and multitudes, and nations, and t.	1100

TOO (51)

Ge	18:14 Is any thing t hard for the LORD?	4480
Ex	12: 4 if the household be t little for the lamb,	4480
	18:18 for *this* thing *is* t heavy for thee; thou art	4480
	36: 7 for all the work to make it, and t **much**.	3498
Nu	11:14 people alone, because *it is* t heavy for me.	4480
	16: 3 unto them, Ye take t **much** upon you,	7227
	16: 7 take t **much** upon you, ye sons of Levi.	7227
	22: 6 this people; for they *are* t mighty for me:	4480
Dt	1:17 the cause that is t hard for you, bring *it*	4480
	2:36 there was not one city t strong for us:	4480
	12:21 to put his name there be t far from thee,	4480
	14:24 if the way be t long for thee, so that thou	4480
	14:24 or if the place be t far from thee, which	NIH
	17: 8 If there arise a matter t hard for thee in	4480
Jos	17:15 if mount Ephraim be t narrow for thee.	3588
	19: 9 children of Judah was t **much** for them:	7227
	19:47 coast of the children of Dan went out t	NIH
	22:17 *Is* the iniquity of Peor t little for us,	NIH
Jdg	7: 2 The people that *are* with thee *are* t **many**	7227
	7: 4 unto Gideon, The people *are* yet t many;	NIH
	18:26 when Micah saw that they *were* t strong	4480
Ru	1:12 go *your way*; for I am t old to have a	4480
2Sa	3:39 these men the sons of Zeruiah *be* t hard	4480
	10:11 If the Syrians be t strong for me, then	4480
	10:11 if the children of Ammon be t strong for	4480
	12: 8 if *that had been* t little, I would moreover	NIH
	22:18 hated me: for they were t strong for me.	4480
1Ki	1:36 LORD God of my lord the king say so t.	NIH
	8:64 *was* t little to receive the burnt offerings,	4480
	12:28 *It is* t **much** for you to go up *to* Jerusalem:	4480
	19: 7 because the journey *is* t great for thee.	4480
2Ki	3:26 saw that the battle was t sore for him,	4480
	6: 1 the place where we dwell with thee is t	4480
1Ch	19:12 If the Syrians be t strong for me, then	4480
	19:12 if the children of Ammon be t strong for	4480
2Ch	29:34 priests were t few, so that they could not	NIH
Est	1:18 Thus *shall there arise* t **much** contempt	3509.1
Job	42: 3 *things* wonderful for me, which I knew	4480
Ps	18:17 hated me: for they were t strong for me.	4480
	35:10 deliverest the poor from him that is t	4480
	38: 4 a heavy burden they *are* t heavy for me.	4480
	73:16 to know this, it *was* t painful for me;	NIH
	131: 1 great *matters*, or in *things* t high for me.	4480
	139: 6 *Such* knowledge *is* t wonderful for me;	4480
Pr	24: 7 Wisdom *is* t high for a fool: he openeth not	NIH
	30:18 be three *things* which *are* t wonderful	4480
Isa	49:19 shall even now be t narrow by reason of	NIH
	49:20 in thine ears, The place *is* t strait for me:	NIH
Jer	32:17 *and* there is nothing t hard for thee:	4480
	32:27 all flesh: is there any thing t hard for me?	4480
Ac	17:22 that in all *things* ye are t **superstitious**.	1174

TOOK (752) [TAKE]

Ge	2:15 the LORD God t the man, and put him	3947
	2:21 he t one of his ribs, and closed up the	3947
	3: 6 she t of the fruit thereof, and did eat,	3947
	4:19 Lamech t unto him two wives: the name	3947
	5:24 with God: and he *was* not; for God t him.	3947
	6: 2 they t them wives of all which they chose.	3947
	8: 9 t her, and pulled her in unto him into	3947
	8:20 t of every clean beast, and of every clean	3947
	9:23 Shem and Japheth t a garment, and laid *it*	3947
	11:29 Abram and Nahor t them wives: the name	3947
	11:31 Terah t Abram his son, and Lot the son of	3947
	12: 5 Abram t Sarai his wife, and Lot his	3947
	14:11 they t all the goods of Sodom and	3947
	14:12 they t Lot, Abram's brother's son,	3947
	15:10 he t unto him all these, and divided them	3947
	16: 3 Sarai Abram's wife t Hagar her maid	3947
	17:23 Abraham t Ishmael his son, and all that	3947
	18: 8 he t butter, and milk, and the calf which	3947
	20: 2 Abimelech king of Gerar sent, and t Sarah.	3947
	20:14 Abimelech t sheep, and oxen,	3947
	21:14 t bread, and a bottle of water, and gave *it*	3947
	21:21 his mother t him a wife out of the land of	3947
	21:27 Abraham t sheep and oxen, and gave	3947
	22: 3 t two of his young men with him, and	3947
	22: 6 Abraham t the wood of the burnt offering,	3947
	22: 6 he t the fire in his hand, and a knife;	3947
	22:10 his hand, and t the knife to slay his son.	3947
	22:13 Abraham went and t the ram,	3947
	24: 7 which t me from my father's house,	3947
	24:10 the servant t ten camels of the camels of	3947
	24:22 that the man t a golden earring of half a	3947
	24:61 the servant t Rebekah, and went his way.	3947
	24:65 therefore she t a vail, and covered herself.	3947
	24:67 and t Rebekah, and she became his wife;	3947
	25: 1 Abraham t a wife, and her name *was*	3947
	25:20 Isaac was forty years old when he t	3947
	25:26 and his hand t **hold** on Esau's heel;	270
	26:34 Esau was forty years old when he t to wife	3947
	27:15 Rebekah t goodly raiment of her eldest son	3947
	27:36 he t **away** my birthright; and behold,	3947
	28: 9 t unto the wives which he had Mahalath	3947
	28:11 he t of the stones of *that* place,	3947
	28:18 t the stone that he had put *for* his pillows,	3947

Ge	29:23 he t Leah his daughter, and brought her	3947
	30: 9 she t Zilpah her maid, and gave her Jacob	3947
	30:37 Jacob t him rods of green poplar, and of	3947
	31:23 he t his brethren with him,	3947
	31:45 Jacob t a stone, and set it up *for* a pillar.	3947
	31:46 and they t stones, and made a heap:	3947
	32:13 t of that which came to his hand a present	3947
	32:22 t his two wives, and his two	3947
	32:23 he t them, and sent them over the brook,	3947
	33:11 And he urged him, and he t *it*.	3947
	34: 2 he t her, and lay with her, and defiled her.	3947
	34:25 t each man his sword, and came upon	3947
	34:26 t Dinah out of Shechem's house,	3947
	34:28 They t their sheep, and their oxen, and	3947
	34:29 their wives t they **captive**, and spoiled	7617
	36: 2 Esau t his wives of the daughters of	3947
	36: 6 Esau t his wives, and his sons, and his	3947
	37:24 they t him, and cast him into a pit:	3947
	37:31 they t Joseph's coat, and killed a kid of	3947
	38: 2 and he t her, and went in unto her.	3947
	38: 6 Judah t a wife for Er his firstborn,	3947
	38:28 the midwife t and bound upon his hand a	3947
	39:20 Joseph's master t him, and put him into	3947
	40:11 I t the grapes, and pressed them into	3947
	41:42 Pharaoh t **off** his ring from his hand,	5493
	42:24 t from them Simeon, and bound him	3947
	42:30 to us, and t us for spies of the country.	5414
	43:15 the men t that present, and they took	3947
	43:15 they t double money in their hand,	3947
	43:34 he t *and sent* messes unto them from	5375
	44:11 they speedily t **down** every man his sack	3381
	46: 1 Israel t his **journey** with all that he had,	5265
	46: 6 they t their cattle, and their goods,	3947
	47: 2 he t some of his brethren, *even* five men,	3947
	48: 1 he t with him his two sons, Manasseh and	3947
	48:13 Joseph t them both, Ephraim in his right	3947
	48:22 which I t out of the hand of the Amorite	3947
	50:25 Joseph t **an oath** of the children of Israel,	7650
Ex	2: 1 of Levi, and t *to wife* a daughter of Levi.	3947
	2: 3 she t for him an ark of bulrushes,	3947
	2: 9 And the woman t the child, and nursed it.	3947
	4: 6 when he t it **out**, behold, his hand *was*	3318
	4:20 Moses t his wife and his sons, and set	3947
	4:20 and Moses t the rod of God in his hand.	3947
	4:25 Zipporah t a sharp stone, and cut off	3947
	6:20 Amram t him Jochebed his father's sister	3947
	6:23 Aaron t him Elisheba, daughter of	3947
	6:25 Eleazar Aaron's son t him *one* of	3947
	9:10 they t ashes of the furnace,	3947
	10:19 which t **away** the locusts, and cast them	5375
	12:34 the people t their dough before it was	3947
	13:19 Moses t the bones of Joseph with him:	3947
	13:20 And they t their **journey** from Succoth,	5265
	13:22 He t not **away** the pillar of the cloud by	4185
	14: 6 his chariot, and t his people with him:	3947
	14: 7 he t six hundred chosen chariots, and all	3947
	14:25 t off their chariot wheels, that they drave	5493
	15:20 sister of Aaron, t a timbrel in her hand;	3947
	16: 1 they t their **journey** from Elim, and	5265
	17:12 they t a stone, and put *it* under him,	3947
	18: 2 father in law, t Zipporah, Moses' wife,	3947
	18:12 t a burnt offering and sacrifices for God:	3947
	24: 6 Moses t half of the blood, and put *it* in	3947
	24: 7 he t the book of the covenant, and read in	3947
	24: 8 Moses t the blood, and sprinkled *it* on	3947
	32:20 he t the calf which they had made,	3947
	33: 7 Moses t the tabernacle, and pitched it	3947
	34: 4 and t in his hand the two tables of stone.	3947
	34:34 the vail **off**, until he came out.	5493
	40:20 he t and put the Testimony into the ark,	3947
Lev	6: 4 that which he t **violently away**,	1497+1500
	8:10 Moses t the anointing oil, and anointed	3947
	8:15 slew *it*; and Moses t the blood, and put *it*	3947
	8:16 he t all the fat that *was* upon the inwards,	3947
	8:23 he slew *it*; and Moses t of the blood of it,	3947
	8:25 he t the fat, and the rump, and all the fat	3947
	8:26 he t one unleavened cake, and a cake of	3947
	8:28 Moses t them from off their hands,	3947
	8:29 Moses t the breast, and waved it *for* a	3947
	8:30 Moses t of the anointing oil, and of	3947
	9:15 the people's offering, and t the goat,	3947
	9:17 t a **handful** thereof, and burnt *it*	3709+4390
	10: 1 either of them his censer, and put fire	3947
Nu	1:17 Aaron t these men which are expressed by	3947
	3:49 Moses t the redemption money of them	3947
	3:50 Of the firstborn of the children of Israel t	3947
	7: 6 Moses t the wagons and the oxen,	3947
	10:12 the children of Israel t their journeys out	5265
	10:13 they first t their **journey** according to	5265
	11:25 of the spirit that *was* upon him, and gave	680
	16: 1 the son of Peleth, sons of Reuben, t *men:*	3947
	16:18 they t every man his censer, and put fire	3947
	16:39 Eleazar the priest t the brasen censers,	3947
	16:47 Aaron t as Moses commanded, and ran	3947
	17: 9 and they looked, and t every man his rod.	3947
	20: 9 Moses t the rod from before the LORD,	3947
	21: 1 and t *some* of them **prisoners**.	7617+7628
	21:25 Israel t all these cities: and Israel dwelt in	3947
	21:32 they t the villages thereof, and drove out	3920
	22:41 that Balak t Balaam, and brought him up	3947
	23: 7 he t up his parable, and said, Balak	5375
	23:11 I t thee to curse mine enemies,	3947
	23:18 he t up his parable, and said, Rise up,	5375
	24: 3 he t up his parable, and said, Balaam	5375
	24:15 he t up his parable, and said, Balaam	5375

Nu	24:20 on Amalek, he t **up** his parable, and said,	5375
	24:21 t **up** his parable, and said, Strong *is* thy	5375
	24:23 he t **up** his parable, and said, Alas,	5375
	25: 7 and t a javelin in his hand;	3947
	27:22 he t Joshua, and set him before Eleazar	3947
	31: 9 Israel t *all* the women of Midian **captives**,	7617
	31: 9 the **spoil** of all their cattle, and all their	962
	31:11 they t all the spoil, and the prey, both	3947
	31:27 between them that t the war upon them,	8610
	31:47 Moses t one portion of fifty, *both* of man	3947
	31:51 and Eleazar the priest t the gold of them,	3947
	32:39 t it, and dispossessed the Amorite which	3920
	32:41 and t the small towns thereof,	3920
	32:42 Nobah went and t Kenath, and the	3920
	33:12 they t their **journey** out of the wilderness	5265
Dt	1:15 So I t the chief of your tribes, wise men,	3947
	1:23 I t twelve men of you, one of a tribe:	3947
	1:25 they t of the fruit of the land in their	3947
	2: 1 t our **journey** into the wilderness *by*	5265
	2:34 we t all his cities at that time,	3920
	2:35 Only the cattle we t **for a prey**	962
	2:35 and the spoil of the cities which we t.	3920
	3: 4 we t all his cities at that time, there was	3920
	3: 4 there was not a city which we t not from	3947
	3: 7 of the cities, we t **for a prey** to ourselves.	962
	3: 8 we t at that time out of the hand of the	3947
	3:14 Jair the son of Manasseh t all the country	3947
	9:17 I t the two tables, and cast them out of	8610
	9:21 I t your sin, the calf which ye had made,	3947
	10: 6 the children of Israel t their **journey**	5265
	22:14 I t this woman, and when I came to her,	3947
	24: 1 husband die, which I t her *to be* his wife;	3947
	29: 8 we t their land, and gave it for an	3947
Jos	2: 4 the woman t the two men, and hid them,	3947
	3: 6 they t up the ark of the covenant,	5375
	4: 8 t **up** twelve stones out of the midst of	5375
	4:20 twelve stones, which they t out of Jordan,	3947
	6:12 and the priests t **up** the ark of the LORD.	5375
	6:20 straight before him, and they t the city.	3920
	7: 1 the tribe of Judah, t of the accursed thing:	3947
	7:17 and he t the family of the Zarhites:	3920
	7:21 then I coveted them, and t them;	3947
	7:23 they t them out of the midst of the tent,	3947
	7:24 t Achan the son of Zerah, and the silver,	3947
	8:12 he t about five thousand men, and set	3947
	8:19 t it, and hasted and set the city on fire.	3920
	8:23 the king of Ai they t alive, and brought	8610
	8:27 spoil of that city Israel t **for a prey** unto	962
	9: 4 t old sacks upon their asses,	3947
	9:12 This our bread we t hot for our **provision**	6679
	9:14 the men t of their victuals, and asked not	3947
	10:27 they t them **down** off the trees,	3381
	10:28 that day Joshua t Makkedah, and smote it	3920
	10:32 which t it on the second day, and smote it	3920
	10:35 they t it on that day, and smote it with	3920
	10:37 they t it, and smote it with the edge of	3920
	10:39 he t it, and the king thereof, and all	3920
	11:10 t Hazor, and smote the king thereof with	3920
	11:14 the children of Israel t **for a prey** unto	962
	11:16 So Joshua t all that land, the hills, and all	3947
	11:17 all their kings he t, and smote them,	3920
	11:19 of Gibeon: all *other* they t in battle.	3947
	11:23 Joshua t the whole land, according to all	3947
	15:17 son of Kenaz, the brother of Caleb, t it:	3920
	16: 4 and Ephraim, t their **inheritance**.	5157
	19:47 t it, and smote it with the edge of	3920
	24: 3 I your father Abraham from the *other*	3947
	24:26 t a great stone, and set it up there under	3947
Jdg	1:13 of Kenaz, Caleb's younger brother, t it:	3920
	1:18 Also Judah t Gaza with the coast thereof,	3920
	3: 6 they t their daughters to be their wives,	3947
	3:21 t the dagger from his right thigh,	3947
	3:25 therefore they t a key, and opened *them:*	3947
	3:28 t the fords of Jordan toward Moab,	3920
	4:21 Jael Heber's wife t a nail of the tent,	3947
	4:21 t a hammer in her hand, and went softly	7760
	5:19 of Megiddo; they t no gain of money.	3947
	6:27 Gideon t ten men of his servants, and did	3947
	7: 8 So the people t victuals in their hand,	3947
	7:24 t the waters unto Beth-barah and Jordan.	3920
	7:25 they t two princes of the Midianites, Oreb	3920
	8:12 t the two kings of Midian, Zebah and	3920
	8:16 he t the elders of the city, and thorns of	3947
	8:21 t **away** the ornaments that *were* on their	3947
	9:43 he t the people, and divided them into	3947
	9:45 he t the city, and slew the people that	3920
	9:48 Abimelech t an axe in his hand,	3947
	9:48 t it, and laid *it* on his shoulder,	5375
	9:50 and encamped against Thebez, and t it.	3920
	11:13 Because Israel t **away** my land, when	3947
	11:15 Israel t not **away** the land of Moab,	3947
	12: 5 the Gileadites t the passages of Jordan	3920
	12: 6 t him, and slew him at the passages	270
	12: 9 t in thirty daughters from abroad for his	935
	13:19 So Manoah t a kid with a meat offering,	3947
	14: 9 he t thereof in his hands, and went on	7287
	14:19 their spoil, and gave change of *garments*	3947
	15: 4 t firebrands, and turned tail to tail,	3947
	15:15 t it, and slew a thousand men therewith.	3947
	16: 3 the doors of the gate of the city,	270
	16:12 Delilah therefore t new ropes,	3947
	16:21 the Philistines t him, and put out his eyes,	270
	16:29 Samson t **hold** of the two middle pillars	3943
	16:31 t him, and brought *him* up, and buried	5375

T

Jdg 17: 2	behold, the silver *is* with me; I **t** it.	3947
17: 4	mother **t** two hundred *shekels* of silver,	3947
18:17	*and* **t** the graven image, the ephod,	3947
18:20	he **t** the ephod, and the teraphim,	3947
18:27	they **t** *the things* which Micah had made,	3947
19: 1	who **t** to him a concubine out of	3947
19:15	for *there was* no man that **t** them into *his*	622
19:25	the man **t** his concubine, and brought *her*	2388
19:28	man **t** her *up* upon an ass, and the man	3947
19:29	he **t** a knife, and laid hold on his	3947
20: 6	I **t** my concubine, and cut her in pieces,	270
21:23	**t** *them* wives, according to their number,	5375
Ru 1: 4	**t** them wives of the women of Moab;	5375
2:18	she **t** *it* up, and went *into* the city:	3947
4: 2	he **t** ten men of the elders of the city,	3947
4:13	So Boaz **t** Ruth, and she was his wife:	3947
4:16	Naomi **t** the child, and laid it in her	3947
1Sa 1:24	him **up** with her, with three bullocks,	5927
2:14	that the fleshhook brought up the priest **t**	3947
5: 1	the Philistines **t** the ark of God,	3947
5: 2	When the Philistines **t** the ark of God,	3947
5: 3	they **t** Dagon, and set him in his place	3947
6:10	two milch kine, and tied them to the	3947
6:12	the kine **t** the **straight** way to the way of	3474
6:15	the Levites **t** **down** the ark of the LORD,	3381
7: 9	Samuel **t** a sucking lamb, and offered it	3947
7:12	Samuel **t** a stone, and set *it* between	3947
8: 3	and **t** bribes, and perverted judgment.	3947
9:22	Samuel **t** Saul and his servant,	3947
9:24	the cook **t** **up** the shoulder, and *that*	7311
10: 1	Samuel **t** a vial of oil, and poured *it* upon	3947
11: 7	he **t** a yoke of oxen, and hewed them in	3947
14:32	**t** sheep, and oxen, and calves,	3947
14:47	So Saul **t** the kingdom over Israel,	3920
14:52	or any valiant man, he **t** him unto him.	622
15: 8	he **t** Agag the king of the Amalekites alive,	8610
15:21	the people **t** of the spoil, sheep and oxen,	3947
16:13	Samuel **t** the horn of oil, and anointed	3947
16:20	Jesse **t** an ass *laden* with bread, and	3947
16:23	that David **t** a harp, and played with his	3947
17:20	the sheep with a keeper, and **t**, and went,	5375
17:34	and a bear, and **t** a lamb out of the flock:	5375
17:40	he **t** his staff in his hand, and chose him	3947
17:49	**t** thence a stone, and slang *it*, and smote	3947
17:51	**t** his sword, and drew it out of the sheath	3947
17:54	David **t** the head of the Philistine,	3947
17:57	Abner **t** him, and brought him before Saul	3947
18: 2	Saul **t** him that day, and would let him go	3947
19:13	Michal **t** an image, and laid *it* in the bed,	3947
24: 2	Saul **t** three thousand chosen men out of	3947
25:18	**t** two hundred loaves, and two bottles of	3947
25:43	David also **t** Ahinoam of Jezreel;	3947
26:12	David **t** the spear and the cruse of water	3947
27: 9	**t** **away** the sheep, and the oxen,	3947
28:24	flour, and kneaded *it*, and did bake	3947
30:20	David **t** all the flocks and the herds,	3947
31: 4	therefore Saul **t** a sword, and fell upon it.	3947
31:12	the body of Saul and the bodies of his	3947
31:13	they **t** their bones, and buried *them* under	3947
2Sa 1:10	I **t** the crown that *was* upon his head,	3947
1:11	David **t** **hold** on his clothes, and rent	2388
2: 8	**t** Ish-bosheth the son of Saul,	3947
2:32	they **t** **up** Asahel, and buried him in	5375
3:15	and **t** her from *her* husband,	3947
3:27	Joab **t** him **aside** in the gate to speak with	5186
3:36	all the people **t** **notice** *of it*, and it pleased	5234
4: 4	Jezreel, and his nurse **t** him *up*, and fled:	5375
4: 7	**t** his head, and gat them away through	3947
4:10	I **t** **hold** of him, and slew him in Ziklag,	270
4:12	they **t** the head of Ish-bosheth, and buried	3947
5: 7	Nevertheless David **t** the strong hold of	3920
5:13	David **t** *him* mo concubines and wives out	3947
6: 6	*hand* to the ark of God, and **t** **hold** of it;	270
7: 8	I **t** thee from the sheepcote, from	3947
7:15	as I **t** *it* from Saul, whom I put away	5493
8: 1	David **t** Metheg-ammah out of the hand	3947
8: 4	David **t** from him a thousand *chariots,*	3920
8: 7	David **t** the shields of gold that were on	3947
8: 8	king David **t** exceeding much brass.	3947
10: 4	Wherefore Hanun **t** David's servants,	3947
11: 4	David sent messengers, and **t** her;	3947
12: 4	**t** the poor man's lamb, and dressed it for	3947
12:26	children of Ammon, and **t** the royal city.	3920
12:29	to Rabbah, and fought against it, and **t** it.	3920
12:30	he **t** their king's crown from off his head,	3947
13: 8	she **t** flour, and kneaded *it*, and made	3947
13: 9	she **t** a pan, and poured *them* out before	3947
13:10	Tamar **t** the cakes which she had made,	3947
13:11	he **t** **hold** of her, and said unto her,	2388
15: 5	his hand, and **t** him, and kissed him.	2388
17:19	the woman **t** and spread a covering over	3947
18:14	he **t** three darts in his hand, and thrust	3947
18:17	they **t** Absalom, and cast him into a great	3947
20: 3	the king **t** the ten women *his* concubines,	3947
20: 9	Joab **t** Amasa by the beard with the right	270
20:10	Amasa **t** no **heed** to the sword that *was*	8104
21: 8	the king **t** the two sons of Rizpah	3947
21:10	Rizpah the daughter of Aiah **t** sackcloth,	3947
21:12	David went and **t** the bones of Saul and	3947
22:17	He sent from above, he **t** me; he drew me	3947
23:16	the gate, and **t** *it*, and brought *it* to David:	5375
1Ki 1:39	Zadok the priest **t** a horn of oil out of	3947
3: 1	Pharaoh's daughter, and brought her	3947
3:20	midnight, and **t** my son from beside me,	3947
4:15	also **t** Basmath the daughter of Solomon	3947

1Ki 8: 3	Israel came, and the priests **t** **up** the ark.	5375
11:18	they **t** men with them out of Paran,	3947
12:28	Whereupon the king **t** **counsel,**	3289
12:29	the prophet **t** **up** the carcase of the man	5375
14:26	he **t** **away** the treasures of the house of	3947
14:26	of the king's house; he even **t** **away** all:	3947
14:26	he **t** **away** all the shields of gold which	3947
15:12	he **t** **away** the sodomites out of the land,	5674
15:18	Asa **t** all the silver and the gold that were	3947
15:22	they **t** **away** the stones of Ramah,	5375
16:31	that he **t** **to** wife Jezebel the daughter of	3947
17:19	he **t** him out of her bosom, and carried	3947
17:23	Elijah **t** the child, and brought him down	3947
18: 4	that Obadiah **t** an hundred prophets,	3947
18:10	*He is* not *there;* he **t** **an oath** of	7650
18:26	they **t** the bullock which was given them,	3947
18:31	Elijah **t** twelve stones, according to	3947
18:40	they **t** them: and Elijah brought them	8610
19:21	**t** a yoke of oxen, and slew them, and	3947
20:34	which my father **t** from thy father,	3947
20:41	and **t** the ashes **away** from his face;	5493
22:46	of his father Asa, he **t** **out** of the land.	1197
2Ki 2: 8	Elijah **t** his mantle, and wrapt *it* together,	3947
2:12	he **t** **hold** of his own clothes, and rent	2388
2:13	He **t** **up** also the mantle of Elijah that fell	7311
2:14	he **t** the mantle of Elijah that fell from	3947
3:26	he **t** with him seven hundred men that	3947
3:27	he **t** his eldest son that should have	3947
4:37	ground, and **t** **up** her son, and went out.	5375
5: 5	**t** with him ten talents of silver,	3947
5:24	he **t** *them* from their hand,	3947
6: 7	to thee. And he put out his hand, and **t** it.	3947
6: 8	**t** **counsel** with his servants, saying, In	3289
7:14	They **t** therefore two chariot horses;	3947
8: 9	to meet him, and **t** a present with him,	3947
8:15	he **t** a thick cloth, and dipt *it* in water,	3947
9:13	every man his garment, and put *it* under	3947
10: 7	that they **t** the king's sons,	3947
10:14	they **t** them alive, and slew them at the	8610
10:15	and he **t** him **up** to him into the chariot.	5927
10:31	Jehu **t** no **heed** to walk in the law of	8104
11: 2	**t** Joash the son of Ahaziah, and stale him	3947
11: 4	**t** **an oath** of them in the house of	7650
11: 9	they **t** every man his men that were to	3947
11:19	he **t** the rulers over hundreds,	3947
12: 9	Jehoiada the priest **t** a chest, and bored a	3947
12:17	and fought against Gath, and **t** it:	3920
12:18	Jehoash king of Judah **t** all the hallowed	3947
13:15	And he **t** unto him bow and arrows.	3947
13:18	he **t** *them*. And he said unto the king of	3947
13:25	Jehoash the son of Jehoahaz **t** again out of	3947
14: 7	**t** Selah by war, and called the name of it	8610
14:13	Jehoash king of Israel **t** Amaziah king of	8610
14:14	he **t** all the gold and silver, and all	3947
14:21	all the people of Judah **t** Azariah, which	3947
15:29	**t** Ijon, and Abel-beth-maachah, and	3947
16: 8	Ahaz **t** the silver and gold that was found	3947
16: 9	**t** it, and carried the *people of* it captive to	8610
16:17	**t** **down** the sea from off the brasen oxen	3381
17: 6	the king of Assyria **t** Samaria,	3920
18:10	at the end of three years they **t** it: *even* in	3920
18:13	all the fenced cities of Judah, and **t** them.	8610
20: 7	they **t** and laid *it* on the boil,	3947
23:11	he **t** **away** the horses that the kings of	7673
23:16	the bones out of the sepulchres,	3947
23:19	Josiah **t** **away,** and did to them according	5493
23:30	the people of the land **t** Jehoahaz the son	3947
23:34	**t** Jehoahaz *away:* and he came *to* Egypt,	3947
24:12	king of Babylon **t** him in the eighth year	3947
25: 6	So they **t** the king, and brought him up to	8610
25:14	wherewith they ministered, **t** they **away.**	3947
25:15	in silver, the captain of the guard **t** **away.**	3947
25:18	captain of the guard **t** Seraiah the chief	3947
25:19	out of the city he **t** an officer that was set	3947
25:20	Nebuzar-adan captain of the guard **t** these	3947
1Ch 2:19	Caleb **t** unto him Ephrath, which bare	3947
2:23	he **t** Geshur, and Aram, with the towns	3947
4:18	the daughter of Pharaoh, whom Mered **t.**	3947
5:21	they **t** **away** their cattle; *of* their camels	7617
7:15	Machir **t** to wife *the sister* of Huppim and	3947
10: 4	So Saul **t** a sword, and fell upon it.	3947
10: 9	they **t** his head, and his armour,	5375
10:12	they **t** the body of Saul, and the bodies	5375
11: 5	Nevertheless David **t** the castle of Zion,	3920
11:18	the gate, and **t** *it*, and brought *it* to David:	5375
14: 3	David **t** moe wives at Jerusalem:	3947
17: 7	I **t** thee from the sheepcote, *even* from	3947
17:13	as I **t** *it* from *him* that was before thee:	5493
18: 1	**t** Gath and her towns out of the hand of	3947
18: 4	David **t** from him a thousand chariots,	3920
18: 7	David **t** the shields of gold that were on	3947
19: 4	Wherefore Hanun **t** David's servants,	3947
20: 2	David **t** the crown of their king from off	3947
23:22	their brethren the sons of Kish **t** them.	5375
27:23	David **t** not the number of them from	5375
2Ch 5: 4	Israel came; and the Levites **t** **up** the ark.	5375
8:18	thence four hundred and fifty talents of	3947
10: 6	Rehoboam **t** **counsel** **with** the old men	3289
10: 8	**t** **counsel** **with** the young men that were	3289
11:18	Rehoboam **t** him Mahalath the daughter	3947
11:20	after her he **t** Maachah the daughter of	3947
11:21	(for he **t** eighteen wives,	5375
12: 4	he **t** the fenced cities which *pertained* to	3920
12: 9	**t** **away** the treasures of the house of	3947
12: 9	the treasures of the king's house; he **t** all:	3947

2Ch 13:19	**t** cities from him, Beth-el with the towns	3920
14: 3	For he **t** **away** the altars of the strange	5493
14: 5	he **t** **away** out of all the cities of Judah	5493
15: 8	**t** **courage,** and put away the abominable	2388
16: 6	Asa the king **t** all Judah; and they carried	3947
17: 6	moreover he **t** **away** the high places and	5493
22:11	Joash the son of Ahaziah, and stole him	3947
23: 1	**t** the captains of hundreds, Azariah the	3947
23: 8	every man his men that were to come in	3947
23:20	he **t** the captains of hundreds,	3947
24: 3	Jehoiada **t** for him two wives; and he	5375
24:11	and **t** it, and carried it to his place again.	5375
25:13	three thousand of them, and **t** much spoil.	962
25:17	Amaziah king of Judah **t** **advice,**	3289
25:23	Joash the king of Israel **t** Amaziah king of	8610
25:24	he **t** all the gold and the silver, and all	NIH
26: 1	all the people of Judah **t** Uzziah, who *was*	3947
28: 8	also **away** much spoil from them,	962
28:15	the captives, and with the spoil clothed	2388
28:21	For Ahaz **t** **away** a portion *out of*	2505
29:16	the Levites **t** *it*, to carry *it* out abroad into	6901
30:14	**t** **away** the altars that *were* in Jerusalem,	5493
30:14	all the altars for incense **t** they **away,**	5493
30:23	the whole assembly **t** **counsel** to keep	3289
32: 3	he **t** **counsel** with his princes and	3289
33:11	which **t** Manasseh among the thorns,	3920
33:15	he **t** **away** the strange gods, and the idol	5493
34:33	Josiah **t** **away** all the abominations out of	5493
35:24	therefore **t** him out of *that* chariot,	5674
36: 1	the people of the land **t** Jehoahaz the son	3947
36: 4	Necho **t** Jehoahaz his brother,	3947
Ezr 2:61	which **t** a wife of the daughters of Barzillai	3947
5:14	Nebuchadnezzar **t** out of the temple	5312
6: 5	which Nebuchadnezzar **t** **forth** out of	5312
8:30	the priests and the Levites **t** the weight	6901
Ne 2: 1	I **t** **up** the wine, and gave *it* unto the king.	5375
4: 1	**t** great **indignation,** and mocked the Jews	3707
5:12	I called the priests, and **t** **an oath** of them,	7650
7:63	which **t** *one* of the daughters of Barzillai	3947
9:25	they **t** strong cities, and a fat land,	3920
Est 2: 7	were dead, **t** for his own daughter.	3947
3:10	the king **t** his ring from his hand,	5493
6:11	Haman the apparel and the horse,	3947
8: 2	king **t** **off** his ring, which he had taken	5493
9:27	**t** upon them, and upon their seed,	6901
Job 1:15	fell *upon them,* and **t** them **away;**	3947
2: 8	he **t** him a potsherd to scrape himself	3947
Ps 18:16	He sent from above, he **t** me, he drew me	3947
22: 9	thou *art* he that **t** me **out** of the womb:	1518
31:13	while they **t** **counsel** together against me,	3245
48: 6	Fear **t** **hold** **upon** them there, *and* pain,	270
55:14	We **t** **sweet** counsel together,	4985
56: 1	David, when the Philistines **t** him in Gath.	270
69: 4	then I restored *that* which I **t** not away.	NIH
71: 6	thou art he that **t** me out of my mother's	1491
78:70	servant, and **t** him from the sheepfolds:	3947
Pr 12:27	roasteth not that which he **t** in **hunting:**	6718
Ecc 2:20	of all the labour which I **t** under the sun.	5998
SS 5: 7	the keepers of the walls **t** **away** my vail	5375
Isa 8: 2	I **t** unto me faithful witnesses **to record,**	5749
20: 1	and fought against Ashdod, and **t** it;	3920
36: 1	the defenced cities of Judah, and **t** them.	8610
40:14	With whom he **t** **counsel,**	3289
Jer 13: 7	the girdle from the place where I had	3947
25:17	**t** I the cup at the LORD's hand,	3947
26: 8	and the prophets and all the people **t** him,	8610
27:20	Which Nebuchadnezzar king of Babylon **t**	3947
28: 3	king of Babylon **t** **away** from this place,	3947
28:10	Hananiah the prophet **t** the yoke from off	3947
31:32	in the day *that* I **t** them by the hand,	2388
32:10	sealed *it*, and **t** **witnesses,**	5707+5375
32:11	So I **t** the evidence of the purchase, *both*	3947
35: 3	I **t** Jaazaniah the son of Jeremiah, the son	3947
36:14	Baruch the son of Neriah **t** the roll in his	3947
36:21	he **t** it out of Elishama the scribe's	3947
36:32	Jeremiah another roll, and gave it to	3947
37:13	he **t** Jeremiah the prophet, saying,	8610
37:14	so Irijah **t** Jeremiah, and brought him to	8610
37:17	**t** him *out:* and the king asked him	3947
38: 6	they **t** Jeremiah, and cast him into	3947
38:11	So Ebed-melech **t** the men with him,	3947
38:11	thence old cast clouts and old rotten rags	3947
38:13	and **t** him **up** out of the dungeon:	5927
38:14	**t** Jeremiah the prophet unto him into	3947
39:14	**t** Jeremiah out of the court of the prison,	3947
40: 2	the captain of the guard **t** Jeremiah,	3947
41:12	they **t** all the men, and went to fight with	3947
41:16	**t** Johanan the son of Kareah, and all	3947
43: 5	of the forces, **t** all the remnant of Judah,	3947
50:33	all that **t** them **captives** held them fast;	7617
50:43	anguish **t** **hold** of him, *and* pangs as of a	2388
52: 9	they **t** the king, and carried him up unto	8610
52:18	wherewith they ministered, **t** they **away.**	3947
52:19	in silver, **t** the captain of the guard **away.**	3947
52:24	the captain of the guard **t** Seraiah	3947
52:25	He **t** also out of the city a man eunuch,	3947
52:26	Nebuzar-adan the captain of the guard **t**	3947
La 5:13	They **t** the young men to grind,	5375
Eze 3:12	the spirit **t** me **up,** and I heard behind me	5375
3:14	**t** me **away,** and I went in bitterness,	5375
8: 3	a hand, and **t** me by a lock of mine head;	3947
10: 7	*thereof*, and put *it* into the hands of *him*	5375
10: 7	with linen: who **t** *it*, and went out.	3947
11:24	Afterwards the spirit **t** me **up,**	5375
16:50	therefore I **t** them **away** as I saw *good.*	5493

Eze	17: 3 and t the highest branch of the cedar:	3947
	17: 5 he t also of the seed of the land,	3947
	19: 5 she t another of her whelps, *and* made	3947
	23:10 they t her sons and her daughters, and	3947
	23:13 was defiled, *that* they t both one way,	3807.1
	29: 7 When they t **hold** of thee by thy hand,	8610
	33: 5 sound of the trumpet, and t not **warning**;	2094
	43: 5 So the spirit t me **up**, and brought me into	5375
Da	1:16 Thus Melzar t **away** the portion of their	5375
	3:22 fire slew those men that t **up** Shadrach,	5267
	5:20 and they t his glory from him:	5709
	5:31 Darius the Median t the kingdom,	6902
Hos	1: 3 and t Gomer the daughter of Diblaim;	3947
	12: 3 t his brother **by the heel** in the womb,	6117
	13:11 mine anger, and t *him away* in my wrath.	3947
Am	7:15 the LORD t me as I followed the flock,	3947
Jnh	1:15 they t **up** Jonah, and cast him forth into	5375
Zec	11: 7 I t unto me two staves; the one I called	3947
	11:10 I t my staff, *even* Beauty, and cut it	3947
	11:13 I t the thirty *pieces* of silver, and cast	3947
Mt	1:24 had bidden him, and t **unto** him his wife:	3880
	2:14 he t the young child and his mother by	3880
	2:21 and t the young child and his mother,	3880
	8:17 saying Himself t our infirmities,	2983
	9:25 and t her by the hand, and the maid arose.	2902
	13:31 which a man t, and sowed in his field:	2983
	13:33 which a woman t, and hid in three	2983
	14:12 And his disciples came, and t **up** the body,	142
	14:19 and the five loaves, and the two fishes,	2983
	14:20 they t up of the fragments that remained	142
	15:36 And he t the seven loaves and the fishes,	2983
	15:37 they t **up** of the broken *meat* that was left	142
	15:39 and t ship, and came into the coasts of	1684
	16: 9 and how many baskets ye t **up**?	2983
	16:10 and how many baskets ye t **up**?	2983
	16:22 Peter t him, and began to rebuke him,	4355
	18:28 on him, and t *him* **by the throat,** saying,	4355
	20:17 And Jesus going up to Jerusalem t	3880
	21:35 And the husbandmen t his servants,	2983
	21:46 because they t him for a prophet.	2192
	22: 6 And the remnant t his servants,	2902
	22:15 t counsel how they might entangle him in	2983
	24:39 until the flood came, and t *them* all **away**;	142
	25: 1 t their lamps, and went forth to meet	2983
	25: 3 They that *were* foolish t their lamps,	2983
	25: 3 took their lamps, and t no oil with them:	2983
	25: 4 the wise t oil in their vessels with their	2983
	25:15 and straightway t his **journey.**	589
	25:35 drink: I was a stranger, and ye t me in:	4863
	25:38 saw we thee a stranger, and t *thee* in?	4863
	25:43 was a stranger, and ye t me not in: naked,	4863
	26:26 Jesus t bread, and blessed *it,* and brake *it,*	2983
	26:27 And he t the cup, and gave thanks,	2983
	26:37 And he t **with** *him* Peter and the two sons	3880
	26:50 and laid hands on Jesus, and t him.	2902
	27: 1 elders of the people t counsel against Jesus	2983
	27: 6 And the chief priests t the silver pieces,	2983
	27: 7 And they t counsel, and bought with them	2983
	27: 9 And they t the thirty pieces of silver,	2983
	27:24 he t water, and washed his hands before	2983
	27:27 Then the soldiers of the governor t Jesus	3880
	27:30 t the reed, and smote him on the head.	2983
	27:31 they t the robe **off** from him, and put his	1562
	27:48 and t a spunge, and filled *it* with vinegar,	2983
	28:15 So they t the money, and did as they were	2983
Mk	1:31 And he came and t her by the hand,	2902
	2:12 t **up** the bed, and went forth before *them*	142
	3: 6 straightway t counsel with the Herodians	4160
	4:36 they t him *even* as he was in the ship.	3880
	5:41 And he t the damsel by the hand,	2902
	6:29 heard *of it,* they came and t **up** his corpse,	142
	6:43 And they t **up** twelve baskets full of	142
	7:33 And he t him aside from the multitude,	618
	8: 6 he t the seven loaves, and gave thanks,	2983
	8: 8 they t **up** of the broken *meat* that was left	142
	8:19 many baskets full of fragments t ye **up**?	142
	8:20 many baskets full of fragments t ye **up**?	142
	8:23 he t the blind man by the hand, and led	1949
	8:32 Peter t him, and began to rebuke him.	4355
	9:27 Jesus t him by the hand, and lifted him	2902
	9:36 And he t a child, and set him in the midst	2983
	10:16 And he t them **up in** his **arms,** put *his*	1723
	10:32 he t again the twelve, and began to tell	3880
	12: 8 And they t him, and killed *him,* and	2983
	12:20 and the first a t a wife, and dying left no	2983
	12:21 the second t her, and died, neither left	2983
	14:22 Jesus t bread, and blessed, and brake *it,*	2983
	14:23 And he t the cup, and when he had given	2983
	14:46 they laid their hands on him, and t him.	2902
	14:49 in the temple teaching, and ye t me not:	2902
	15:20 they t **off** the purple **from** him, and put	1562
	15:46 and t him **down**, and wrapped *him* in	2507
Lk	2:28 Then t he him *up* in his arms,	1209
	5:25 and t **up** *that* whereon he lay,	142
	8:54 and t her by the hand, and called, saying,	2902
	9:10 And he t them, and went aside privately	3880
	9:16 Then he t the five loaves and the two	2983
	9:28 he t Peter and John and James, and went	3880
	9:47 their heart, t a child, and set him by him,	1949
	10:34 brought him to an inn, and t care of him.	1959
	10:35 he t out two pence, and gave *them* to	1544
	13:19 which a man t, and cast into his garden;	2983
	13:21 a woman t and hid in three measures	2983
	14: 4 he t him, and healed him, and let *him*	1949
	15:13 and t his **journey** into a far country,	589

Lk	18:31 Then he t **unto** him the twelve,	3880
	20:29 and the first a t a wife, and died without	2983
	20:30 And the second t her to wife, and he died	2983
	20:31 And the third t her; and in like manner	2983
	22:17 And he t the cup, and gave thanks,	1209
	22:19 And he t bread, and gave thanks,	2983
	22:54 Then t they him, and led *him,* and	4815
	23:53 he t it **down**, and wrapped it in linen,	2507
	24:30 he t bread, and blessed *it,* and brake,	2983
	24:43 And he t *it,* and did eat before them.	2983
Jn	5: 9 whole, and t **up** his bed, and walked:	142
	6:11 And Jesus t the loaves; and when he had	2983
	6:24 they also t **shipping,** *1519+1684+3588+4143*	
	8:59 Then t they **up** stones to cast at him:	142
	10:31 Then the Jews t **up** stones again to stone	941
	11:41 Then they t **away** the stone *from the place*	142
	11:53 t counsel **together** for to put him to	4823
	12: 3 Then t Mary a pound of ointment of	2983
	12:13 T branches of palm trees, and went forth	2983
	13: 4 and t a towel, and girded himself.	2983
	18:12 captain and officers of the Jews t Jesus,	4815
	19: 1 Then Pilate therefore t Jesus,	2983
	19:16 And they t Jesus, and led him away.	3880
	19:23 t his garments, and made four parts,	2983
	19:27 from that hour that disciple t her unto	2983
	19:38 He came therefore, and t the body of Jesus.	142
	19:40 t they the body of Jesus, and wound it	2983
Ac	1:16 which was guide to them that t Jesus.	4815
	3: 7 he t him by the right hand, and lift *him*	4084
	4:13 and they t **knowledge** of them, that they	1921
	5:33 to the heart, and t **counsel** to slay them.	1011
	7:21 Pharaoh's daughter t him **up,**	337
	7:43 ye t **up** the tabernacle of Moloch,	353
	9:23 the Jews t **counsel** to kill him:	4823
	9:25 Then the disciples t him by night,	2983
	9:27 But Barnabas t him, and brought *him* to	1949
	10:26 But Peter t him **up,** saying, Stand up;	1453
	12:25 and t **with** *them* John, whose surname	4838
	13:29 they t him **down** from the tree,	2507
	15:39 and *so* Barnabas t Mark, and sailed unto	3880
	16: 3 and t and circumcised him because of	2983
	16:33 And he t them the same hour of the night,	3880
	17: 5 t **unto** *them* certain lewd fellows of	4355
	17:19 And they t him, and brought him unto	1949
	18:17 Then all the Greeks t Sosthenes, the *chief*	1949
	18:18 and then t his **leave** of the brethren,	657
	18:26 they t him unto *them,* and expounded	4355
	19:13 t **upon** *them* to call over them which had	2021
	20:14 Assos, we t him in, and came to Mitylene.	353
	21: 6 taken our leave one of another, we t ship;	1910
	21:11 he t Paul's girdle, and bound his *own* hands	142
	21:15 after those days we t **up** our **carriages,**	643
	21:26 Then Paul t the men, and the next day	3880
	21:30 and they t Paul, and drew him out of	1949
	21:32 immediately t soldiers and centurions,	3880
	21:33 and t him, and commanded *him* to be	1949
	23:18 So he t him, and brought him to the chief	3880
	23:19 Then the chief captain t him by the hand,	1949
	23:31 t Paul, and brought *him* by night to	353
	24: 6 whom we t, and would have judged	2902
	24: 7 with great violence t *him* **away** out of our	520
	27:35 he t bread, and gave thanks to God in	2983
	27:36 of good cheer, and they also t *some* meat.	4355
	28:15 Paul saw, he thanked God, and t courage.	2983
1Co	11:23 night in which he was betrayed t bread:	2983
	11:25 After the same manner also *he t* the cup,	NIG
Gal	2: 1 with Barnabas, and t Titus **with** *me* also.	4838
Php	2: 7 and t **upon** *him* the form of a servant,	2983
Col	2:14 t it out of the way, nailing it to *his* cross;	142
Heb	2:14 also himself likewise t **part** of the same;	3348
	2:16 For verily he t not **on** *him the nature of*	1949
	2:16 but he t **on** *him* the seed of Abraham.	1949
	8: 9 t them by the hand to lead them out of	1949
	9:19 he t the blood of calves and of goats,	2983
	10:34 and t joyfully the spoiling of your goods,	4327
Rev	5: 7 t the book out of the right hand of him	2983
	8: 5 And the angel t the censer, and filled it	2983
	10:10 And I t the little book out of the angel's	2983
	18:21 a mighty angel t **up** a stone like a great	142

TOOKEST (2) [TAKE]

Ps	99: 8 though thou t **vengeance** of their	5358
Eze	16:18 t thy broidered garments,	3947

TOOL (4)

Ex	20:25 for if thou lift up thy t upon it, thou hast	2719
	32: 4 fashioned it with a **graving** t, after he had	2747
Dt	27: 5 shalt not lift up *any iron t* upon them.	NIH
1Ki	6: 7 axe *nor* any t of iron heard in the house,	3627

TOOTH (11) [CHEEK-TEETH, TEETH, TOOTH'S]

Ex	21:24 Eye for eye, t for tooth, hand for hand,	8127
	21:24 Eye for eye, tooth for t, hand for hand,	8127
	21:27 if he smite out his manservant's t,	8127
	21:27 tooth, or his maidservant's t;	8127
Lev	24:20 Breach for breach, eye for eye, t for tooth:	8127
	24:20 Breach for breach, eye for eye, tooth for t:	8127
Dt	19:21 eye for eye, t for tooth, hand for hand,	8127
	19:21 eye for eye, tooth for t, hand for hand,	8127
Pr	25:19 man in time of trouble *is like* a broken t,	8127
Mt	5:38 An eye for an eye, and a t for a tooth:	3599
	5:38 An eye for an eye, and a tooth for a t:	3599

TOOTH'S (1) [TOOTH]

Ex	21:27 he shall let him go free for his t sake.	8127

TOP (90) [HOUSETOP, HOUSETOPS, TOPS]

Ge	11: 4 a tower, whose t *may reach* unto heaven;	7218
	28:12 earth, and the t of it reached to heaven:	7218
	28:18 a pillar, and poured oil upon the t of it.	7218
Ex	17: 9 to morrow I will stand on the t of the hill	7218
	17:10 and Hur went up *to* the t of the hill.	7218
	19:20 upon mount Sinai, on the t of the mount:	7218
	19:20 the LORD called Moses *up* to the t of	7218
	24:17 t of the mount in the eyes of the children	7218
	28:32 there shall be a hole in the t of it,	7218
	30: 3 the t thereof, and the sides thereof round	1406
	34: 2 present thyself there to me in the t of	7218
	37:26 of it, and the sides thereof round	1406
Nu	14:40 gat them up into the t of the mountain,	7218
	14:44 they presumed to go up unto the hill t:	7218
	20:28 Aaron died there in the t of the mount:	7218
	21:20 in the country of Moab, *to* the t of Pisgah,	7218
	23: 9 For from the t of the rocks I see him,	7218
	23:14 to the t of Pisgah, and built seven altars,	7218
	23:28 Balak brought Balaam *unto* the t of Peor,	7218
Dt	3:27 Get thee up *into* the t of Pisgah, and lift	7218
	28:35 sole of thy foot unto the t of thy **head.**	6936
	33:16 upon the t **of the head** of him *that was*	6936
	34: 1 to the t of Pisgah, that *is* over against	7218
Jos	15: 8 border went up to the t of the mountain	7218
	15: 8 border was drawn from the t of the hill	7218
Jdg	6:26 the LORD thy God upon the t of this rock,	7218
	9: 7 and stood in the t of mount Gerizim,	7218
	9:25 in wait for him in the t of the mountains,	7218
	9:36 there come people down from the t of	7218
	9:51 and gat them up to the t of the tower.	1406
	15: 8 and dwelt in the t of the rock Etam.	5585
	15:11 thousand men of Judah went to the t	5585
	16: 3 carried them up to the t of a hill that *is*	7218
1Sa	9:25 with Saul upon the t **of the house.**	1406
	9:26 Samuel called Saul to the t **of the house,**	1406
	26:13 and stood on the t of a hill afar off;	7218
2Sa	2:25 one troop, and stood on the t of a hill.	7218
	15:32 that *when* David was come to the t *of*	7218
	16: 1 when David was a little past the t *of*	7218
	16:22 Absalom a tent upon the t **of the house;**	1406
1Ki	7:17 the chapiters which *were* upon the t	7218
	7:18 cover the chapiters that *were* upon the t,	7218
	7:19 the chapiters that *were* upon the t of	7218
	7:22 upon the t of the pillars *was* lily work:	7218
	7:35 in the t of the base *was* there a round	7218
	7:35 on the t of the base the ledges thereof and	7218
	7:41 that *were* on the t of the *two* pillars;	7218
	7:41 which *were* upon the t of the pillars;	7218
	10:19 and the t of the throne *was* round behind:	7218
	18:42 Elijah went up to the t of Carmel;	7218
2Ki	1: 9 behold, he sat on the t of a hill. And he	7218
	9:13 put *it* under him on the t of the stairs,	1634
	23:12 the altars that *were* on the t of the upper	1406
2Ch	3:15 the chapiter that *was* on the t *of each* of	7218
	4:12 the chapiters *which were* on the t of the	7218
	4:12 which *were* on the t of the pillars;	7218
	25:12 brought them unto the t of the rock,	7218
	25:12 cast them down from the t of the rock,	7218
Est	5: 2 near, and touched the t of the sceptre.	7218
Ps	72:16 in the earth upon the t of the mountains;	7218
Pr	8: 2 She standeth in the t of high places by	7218
	23:34 or as he that lieth upon the t of a mast.	7218
SS	4: 8 look from the t of Amana, from the top of	7218
	4: 8 from the t of Shenir and Hermon, from	7218
Isa	2: 2 be established in the t of the mountains,	7218
	17: 6 three berries in the t of the uppermost	7218
	30:17 till ye be left as a beacon upon the t of a	7218
	42:11 them shout from the t of the mountains.	7218
La	2:19 faint for hunger in the t of every street.	7218
	4: 1 are poured out in the t of every street.	7218
Eze	17: 4 He cropt the t of his young twigs,	7218
	17:22 will set *it;* I will crop off from the t of his	7218
	24: 7 she set it upon the t of a rock; she poured	6706
	24: 8 I have set her blood upon the t of a rock,	6706
	26: 4 her, and make her like the t of a rock.	6706
	26:14 I will make thee like the t of a rock:	6706
	31: 3 and his t was among the thick boughs.	6788
	31:10 he hath shot up his t among the thick	6788
	31:14 neither shoot up their t among the thick	6788
	43:12 Upon the t of the mountain the whole	7218
Am	1: 2 and the t of Carmel shall wither.	7218
	9: 3 though they hide themselves in the t of	7218
Mic	4: 1 be established in the t of the mountains,	7218
Na	3:10 dashed in pieces at the t of all the streets:	7218
Zec	4: 2 with a bowl upon the t of it, and his seven	7218
	4: 2 which *were* upon the t thereof:	7218
Mt	27:51 rent in twain from the t to the bottom;	509
Mk	15:38 rent in twain from the t to the bottom.	509
Jn	19:23 seam, woven from the t throughout.	509
Heb	11:21 worshipped, *leaning* upon the t of his staff.	206

TOPAZ (5)

Ex	28:17 *shall be* a sardius, a t, and a carbuncle:	6357
	39:10 row *was* a sardius, a t, and a carbuncle:	6357
Job	28:19 The t of Ethiopia shall not equal it,	6357
Eze	28:13 t, and the diamond, the beryl, the onyx,	6357
Rev	21:20 the eighth, beryl; the ninth, a t; the tenth,	5116

TOPHEL (1)

Dt	1: 1 T, and Laban, and Hazeroth, and Dizahab.	8603

TOPHET (9) [TOPHETH]

Isa	30:33 For T *is* ordained of old; yea, for the king	8613
Jer	7:31 they have built the high places of T,	8612

T

Jer　　7:32 that it shall no more be called **T**,　　8612
　　　　7:32 for they shall bury in **T**, till there be no　　8612
　　　19: 6 that this place shall no more be called **T**,　　8612
　　　19:11 they shall bury *them* in **T**, till *there* be no　　8612
　　　19:12 and *even* make this city as **T**:　　8612
　　　19:13 shall be defiled as the place of **T**, because　　8612
　　　19:14 came Jeremiah from **T**, whither the LORD　　8612

TOPHETH (1) [TOPHET]
2Ki 23:10 he defiled **T**, which *is* in the valley of　　8612

TOPMOST See OUTMOST; UPPERMOST

TOPS (10) [TOP]
Ge　　8: 5 were the **t** of the mountains seen.　　7218
2Sa　 5:24 of a going in the **t** of the mulberry trees,　　7218
1Ki　 7:16 to set upon the **t** of the pillars,　　7218
1Ch 14:15 of going in the **t** of the mulberry trees,　　7218
Job 24:24 and cut off as the **t** of the ears of corn.　　7218
Isa　 2:21 into the **t** of the ragged rocks, for fear of　　5585
　　　15: 3 on the **t** of their **houses**, and in their　　1406
Eze　 6:13 in all the **t** of the mountains,　　7218
Hos　 4:13 sacrifice upon the **t** of the mountains,　　7218
Joel　 2: 5 Like the noise of chariots on the **t** of　　7218

TORCH (1) [TORCHES]
Zec 12: 6 the wood, and like a **t** of fire in a sheaf;　　3940

TORCHES (3) [TORCH]
Na　　2: 3 the chariots *shall be* with flaming **t** in　　6393
　　　　2: 4 they shall seem like **t**, they shall run like　　3940
Jn　　18: 3 thither with lanterns and **t** and weapons.　　2985

TORMENT (11) [TORMENTED, TORMENTORS, TORMENTS]
Mt　　8:29 thou come hither to **t** us before the time?　　928
Mk　　5: 7 I adjure thee by God, that thou **t** me not.　　928
Lk　　8:28 God most high? I beseech thee, **t** me not.　　928
　　　16:28 lest they also come into this place of **t**.　　931
1Jn　 4:18 because fear hath **t**. He that feareth is not　　2851
Rev　 9: 5 their **t** *was* as the torment of a scorpion,　　929
　　　　9: 5 their torment *was* as the **t** of a scorpion,　　929
　　　14:11 And the smoke of their **t** ascendeth up for　　929
　　　18: 7 so much **t** and sorrow give her:　　929
　　　18:10 Standing afar off for the fear of her **t**,　　929
　　　18:15 shall stand afar off for the fear of her **t**,　　929

TORMENTED (8) [TORMENT]
Mt　　8: 6 at home sick of the palsy, grievously **t**.　　928
Lk　 16:24 cool my tongue; for I am **t** in this flame.　　3600
　　　16:25 but now he is comforted, and thou art **t**.　　3600
Heb 11:37 and goatskins; being destitute, afflicted, **t**;　　2558
Rev　 9: 5 but that they should be **t** five months:　　928
　　　11:10 these two prophets **t** them that dwelt on　　928
　　　14:10 and he shall be **t** with fire and brimstone in　　928
　　　20:10 and shall be **t** day and night for ever and　　928

TORMENTORS (1) [TORMENT]
Mt 18:34 lord was wroth, and delivered him to the **t**,　　930

TORMENTS (2) [TORMENT]
Mt　　4:24 that were taken with divers diseases and **t**,　　931
Lk　 16:23 being in **t**, and seeth Abraham afar off,　　931

TORN (17) [TEAR]
Ge　 31:39 **That which was t** *of beasts* I brought　　2966
　　　44:28 and I said, Surely he is **t in pieces**;　　2963+2963
Ex　 22: 13 If it be **t in pieces**, *then* let him　　2963+2963
　　　22:13 he shall not make good that which was **t**,　　2966
　　　22:31 neither shall ye eat *any* flesh *that is* **t** of　　2966
Lev　 7:24 the fat of **that which is t** with *beasts*,　　2966
　　　17:15 that which was **t** with *beasts*, whether　　2966
　　　22: 8 is **t** *with beasts*, he shall not eat to defile　　2966
1Ki 13:26 which hath **t** him, and slain him,　　7665
　　　13:28 had not eaten the carcase, nor **t** the ass.　　7665
Isa　 5:25 their carcases were **t** in the midst of　　5478
Jer　 5: 6 goeth out thence shall be **t in pieces**:　　2963
Eze　 4:14 which dieth of itself, or is **t in pieces**;　　2966
　　　44:31 of itself, or **t**, whether it be fowl or beast.　　2966
Hos　 6: 1 for he hath **t**, and he will heal us; he hath　　2963
Mal　 1:13 brought *that which was* **t**, and the lame,　　1497
Mk　 1:26 And when the unclean spirit had **t** him,　　4682

TORTOISE (1)
Lev 11:29 and the mouse, and the **t** after his kind,　　6632

TORTURED (1)
Heb 11:35 and others were **t**, not accepting　　5178

TOSS (2) [TOSSED, TOSSINGS]
Isa 22:18 **surely violently turn and t**　　6801+6801+6802
Jer　 5:22 though the waves thereof **t** themselves,　　1607

TOSSED (7) [TOSS]
Ps 109:23 I am **t up and down** as the locust.　　5287
Pr　 21: 6 by a lying tongue *is* a vanity **t to and fro**　　5086
Isa　 54:11 **t with tempest**, *and* not comforted,　　5590
Mt　 14:24 now in the midst of the sea, **t** with waves:　　928
Ac　 27:18 we being exceedingly **t with a tempest**,　　5492
Eph　 4:14 **t to and fro**, and carried about with every　　2831
Jas　　1: 6 of the sea driven with the wind and **t**.　　4494

TOSSINGS (1) [TOSS]
Job　 7: 4 I am full of **t to and fro** unto the dawning　　5076

TOTTERING (1)
Ps　 62: 3 bowing wall *shall ye be, and as* a **t** fence.　　1760

TOU (2) [TOI]
1Ch 18: 9 Now when **T** king of Hamath heard how　　8583
　　　18:10 (for Hadarezer had war with **T**;) and　　8583

TOUCH (48) [TOUCHED, TOUCHETH, TOUCHING]
Ge　　3: 3 eat of it, neither shall ye **t** it, lest ye die.　　5060
　　　20: 6 therefore suffered I thee not to **t** her.　　5060
Ex　 19:12 up into the mount, or **t** the border of it:　　5060
　　　19:13 There shall not a hand **t** it, but he shall　　5060
Lev　 5: 2 Or if a soul **t** any unclean thing, whether　　5060
　　　　5: 3 Or if he **t** the uncleanness of man,　　5060
　　　　6:27 Whatsoever shall **t** the flesh thereof shall　　5060
　　　　7:21 Moreover the soul that shall **t** any unclean　　5060
　　　11: 8 not eat, and their carcase shall ye not **t**;　　5060
　　　11:31 doth **t** them, when they be dead,　　5060
　　　12: 4 shall **t** no hallowed *thing*, nor come into　　5060
　　　12:4 shall not **t** any *holy thing*, lest they die.　　5060
Nu　 16:26 wicked men, and **t** nothing of theirs,　　5060
Dt　 14: 8 eat of their flesh, nor **t** their dead carcase.　　5060
Jos　 9:19 Israel: now therefore we may not **t** them.　　5060
Ru　　2: 9 the young men that *they* shall not **t** thee?　　5060
2Sa 14:10 to me, and he shall **t** thee any more.　　5060
　　　18:12 Beware *that* none **t** the young man　　NIH
　　　23: 7 the man *that* shall **t** them must be fenced　　5060
1Ch 16:22 *Saying*, **T** not mine anointed, and do my　　5060
Job　 1:11 **t** all that he hath, and he will curse thee to　　5060
　　　　2: 5 his bone and his flesh, and he will curse　　5060
　　　　5:19 yea, in seven there shall no evil **t** thee.　　5060
　　　　6: 7 The things *that* my soul refused to **t** *are* as　　5060
Ps 105:15 *Saying*, **T** not mine anointed, and do my　　5060
　　　144: 5 the mountains, and they shall smoke.　　5060
Isa 52:11 **t** no unclean *thing*; go ye out of the midst　　5060
Jer 12:14 that **t** the inheritance which I have caused　　5060
La　　4:14 so that *men* could not **t** their garments.　　5060
　　　　4:15 depart, depart, **t** not, when they fled away　　5060
Hag　 2:12 with his skirt do **t** bread, or pottage,　　5060
　　　　2:13 If *one that* is unclean *by* a dead body **t** any　　5060
Mt　　9:21 If I may but **t** his garment, I shall be whole.　　681
　　　14:36 And besought him that they might only **t**　　681
Mk　　3:10 that *they* pressed upon him for to **t**　　681
　　　　5:28 For she said, If I may but **t** his clothes,　　681
　　　　6:56 besought him that they might **t** if it were　　681
　　　　8:22 man unto him, and besought him to **t** him.　　681
　　　10:13 children to him, that he should **t** them:　　681
Lk　　6:19 And the whole multitude sought to **t** him:　　681
　　　11:46 ye yourselves **t** not the burdens with one　　4379
　　　18:15 him also infants, that he would **t** them:　　681
Jn　 20:17 Jesus saith unto her, **T** me not; for I am　　681
1Co　 7: 1 *It is* good for a man not to **t** a woman.　　681
2Co　 6:17 and **t** not the unclean *thing*; and I will　　681
Col　 2:21 (**T** not; taste not; handle not;　　681
Heb 11:28 the fat that destroyed the firstborn should **t**　　2345
　　　12:20 And if *so much as* a beast **t** the mountain,　　2345

TOUCHED (49) [TOUCH]
Ge　 26:29 as we have not **t** thee, and as we have　　5060
　　　32:25 against him, he **t** the hollow of his thigh;　　5060
　　　32:32 the hollow of Jacob's thigh in　　5060
Lev 22: 6 The soul which hath **t** *any* such shall be　　5060
Nu　 19:18 upon him that **t** a bone, or one slain, or　　5060
　　　31:19 whosoever hath **t** *any* slain, purify *both*　　5060
Jdg　 6:21 the flesh and the unleavened *cakes;* and　　5060
1Sa 10:26 a band of men, whose hearts God had **t**.　　5060
1Ki　 6:27 so that the wing of the one **t** the *one* wall,　　5060
　　　　6:27 the wing of the other cherub **t** the other　　5060
　　　　6:27 their wings **t** one another in the midst of　　5060
　　　19: 5 an angel **t** him, and said unto him, Arise　　5060
　　　19: 7 and **t** him, and said, Arise *and* eat;　　5060
2Ki 13:21 the bones of Elisha, he revived,　　5060
Est　 5: 2 drew near, and **t** the top of the sceptre.　　5060
Job 19:21 my friends; for the hand of God hath **t** me.　　5060
Isa　 6: 7 mouth, and said, Lo, this hath **t** thy lips;　　5060
Jer　 1: 9 put forth his hand, and **t** my mouth.　　5060
Eze　 3:13 of the living creatures that **t** one another,　　5401
Da　　8: 5 of the whole earth, and **t** not the ground:　　5060
　　　　8:18 ground: but he **t** me, and set me upright.　　5060
　　　　9:21 **t** me about the time of the evening　　5060
　　　10:10 a hand **t** me, which set me upon my　　5060
　　　10:16 like the similitude of the sons of men **t**　　5060
　　　10:18 **t** me *one* like the appearance of a man,　　5060
Mt　　8: 3 forth *his* hand, and **t** him, saying, I will;　　681
　　　　8:15 And he **t** her hand, and the fever left her:　　681
　　　　9:20 behind *him*, and **t** the hem of his garment:　　681
　　　　9:29 Then **t** he their eyes, saying, According to　　681
　　　14:36 as many as **t** were made perfectly whole.　　681
　　　17: 7 Jesus came and **t** them, and said, Arise,　　681
　　　20:34 had compassion *on them*, and **t** their eyes:　　681
Mk　　1:41 and saith unto him, I will;　　681
　　　　5:27 in the press behind, and **t** his garment.　　681
　　　　5:30 in the press, and said, Who **t** my clothes?　　681
　　　　5:31 thee, and sayest thou, Who **t** me?　　681
　　　　6:56 and as many as **t** him were made whole.　　681
　　　　7:33 into his ears, and he spit, and **t** his tongue;　　681
Lk　　5:13 forth *his* hand, and **t** him, saying, I will:　　681
　　　　7:14 And he came and **t** the bier: and they that　　681
　　　　8:44 him, and **t** the border of his garment:　　681
　　　　8:45 Jesus said, Who **t** me? When all denied,　　681
　　　　8:45 press *thee*, and sayest thou, Who **t** me?　　681
　　　　8:46 And Jesus said, Somebody hath **t** me: for I　　681
　　　　8:47 the people for what cause she had **t** him,　　681
　　　22:51 And he **t** his ear, and healed him.　　681

Ac　 27: 3 And the next *day* we **t** at Sidon.　　2609
Heb　 4:15 be **t with the feeling** of our infirmities;　　4834
　　　12:18 come unto the mount that might be **t**,　　5584

TOUCHETH (40) [TOUCH]
Ge　 26:11 He that **t** this man or his wife shall surely　　5060
Ex　 19:12 whosoever **t** the mount shall be surely put　　5060
　　　29:37 whatsoever **t** the altar shall be holy.　　5060
　　　30:29 holy: whatsoever **t** them shall be holy.　　5060
Lev　 6:18 fire: every one that **t** them shall be holy.　　5060
　　　　7:19 the flesh that **t** any unclean *thing* shall not　　5060
　　　11:24 whosoever **t** the carcase of them shall be　　5060
　　　11:26 every one that **t** them shall be unclean.　　5060
　　　11:27 whoso **t** their carcase shall be unclean.　　5060
　　　11:36 which **t** their carcase shall be unclean.　　5060
　　　11:39 he that **t** the carcase thereof shall be　　5060
　　　15: 5 **t** his bed shall wash his clothes,　　5060
　　　15: 7 that **t** the flesh of him that hath the issue　　5060
　　　15:10 whosoever **t** any *thing* that was under　　5060
　　　15:11 whomsoever he that hath the issue **t**,　　5060
　　　15:12 that he **t** which hath the issue, shall be　　5060
　　　15:19 whosoever **t** her shall be unclean until　　5060
　　　15:21 her bed shall wash his clothes,　　5060
　　　15:22 whosoever **t** any thing that she sat upon　　5060
　　　15:23 thing whereon she sitteth, when he **t** it,　　5060
　　　15:27 whoso **t** *those things* shall be unclean,　　5060
　　　22: 4 whoso **t** any *thing that is* unclean by　　5060
　　　22: 5 Or whosoever **t** any creeping thing,　　5060
Nu　 19:11 He that **t** the dead *body* of any man shall　　5060
　　　19:13 Whosoever **t** the dead *body* of *any* man　　5060
　　　19:16 whosoever **t** one that is slain with a sword　　5060
　　　19:21 he that **t** the water of separation shall be　　5060
　　　19:22 whatsoever the unclean *person* **t** shall be　　5060
　　　19:22 soul that **t** *it* shall be unclean until even.　　5060
Jdg 16: 9 as a thread of tow is broken when it **t**　　7306
Job　 4: 5 it **t** thee, and thou art troubled.　　5060
Ps 104:32 trembleth: he **t** the hills, and they smoke.　　5060
Pr　 6:29 whosoever **t** her shall not be innocent.　　5060
Eze 17:10 utterly wither, when the east wind **t** it?　　5060
Hos　 2: 2 they break out, and blood **t** blood.　　5060
Am　　9: 5 the Lord GOD of hosts *is* he that **t**　　5060
Zec　 2: 8 for he that **t** you **toucheth** the apple of his　　5060
　　　　2: 8 for he that **toucheth** you **t** the apple of his　　5060
Lk　　7:39 what manner of woman *this is* that **t** him:　　681
1Jn　 5:18 and *that* wicked one **t** him not.　　681

TOUCHING (30) [TOUCH]
Ge　 27:42 Behold, thy brother Esau, **as t** thee,　　3807.1
Lev　 5:13 as **t** his sin that he hath committed in one of　　5921
Nu　　8:26 shalt thou do unto the Levites **t** their　　871.1
1Sa 20:23 as **t** the matter which thou and I have　　NIH
2Ki 22:18 **As t** the words which thou hast heard;　　NIH
Ezr　 7:24 **t** any of the priests and Levites, singers,　　NIH
Job 37:23 **T** the Almighty, we cannot find him out:　　NIH
Ps　 45: 1 I speak of the things which I have made **t**　　3807.1
Isa　 5: 1 a song of my beloved **t** his vineyard.　　3807.1
Jer　 1:16 will utter my judgments against them **t** all　　5921
　　　21:11 **t** the house of the king of Judah,　　3807.1
　　　22:11 For thus saith the LORD **t** Shallum the son　　413
Eze　 7:13 for the vision *is* **t** the whole multitude　　413
Mt　 18:19 if two of you shall agree on earth **as t**　　4012
　　　22:31 But **as t** the resurrection of the dead,　　4012
Mk　 12:26 And **as t** the dead, that they rise: have ye　　4012
Lk　 23:14 have found no fault in this man **t** *those*　　NIG
Ac　　5:35 what ye intend to do **as t** these men.　　1909
　　　21:25 the Gentiles which believe, we have　　4012
　　　24:21 **T** the resurrection of the dead I am called　　4012
　　　26: 2 **t** all *the things* whereof I am accused of　　4012
Ro　 11:28 but **as t** the election, *they are* beloved for　　2596
1Co　 8: 1 Now **as t** things offered unto idols,　　4012
　　　16:12 **As t** *our* brother Apollos, I greatly desired　　4012
2Co　 9: 1 For **as t** the ministering to the saints, it is　　4012
Php　 3: 5 of the Hebrews; **as t** the law, a Pharisee;　　2596
　　　　3: 6 **t** the righteousness which is in the law,　　2596
Col　 4:10 (**t** whom ye received commandments;)　　4012
1Th　 4: 9 But **as t** brotherly love ye need not that I　　4012
2Th　 3: 4 we have confidence in the Lord **t** you,　　1909

TOW (3)
Jdg 16: 9 a thread of **t** is broken when it toucheth　　5296
Isa　 1:31 strong shall be as **t**, and the maker of it　　5296
　　　43:17 they are extinct, they are quenched as **t**.　　6594

TOWARD (265) [TOWARDS]
Ge　　2:14 *is it* which goeth to the **east** of Assyria.　　6926
　　　12: 9 going on still **t** the south.　　1886.5
　　　13:12 the plain, and pitched his tent **t** Sodom.　　5704
　　　18: 2 and bowed himself **t** the ground,　　1886.5
　　　18:16 from thence, and looked **t** Sodom:　　5921+6440
　　　18:22 faces from thence, and went **t** Sodom:　　1886.5
　　　19: 1 he bowed himself with his face **t**　　1886.5
　　　19:28 he looked **t** Sodom and Gomorrah,　　5921+6440
　　　19:28 **t** all the land of the plain, and　　5921+6440
　　　20: 1 Abraham journeyed from thence **t**　　1886.5
　　　28:10 out from Beer-sheba, and went **t** Haran.　　1886.5
　　　30:40 set the faces of the flocks **t** the ringstraked,　　413
　　　31: 2 and behold, it *was* not **t** him as before.　　5973
　　　31: 5 that it *is* not **t** me as before;　　413
　　　31:21 and set his face **t** the mount Gilead.　　NIH
　　　48:13 Ephraim in his right hand **t** Israel's left　　4480
Ex　　9:10 Moses sprinkled it *up* **t** heaven;　　1886.5
　　　　9:22 Stretch forth thine hand **t** heaven,　　5921
　　　　9:23 Moses stretched forth his rod **t** heaven;　　5921
　　　10:21 Stretch out thine hand **t** heaven,　　5921
　　　10:22 Moses stretched forth his hand **t** heaven;　　5921

Ex	16:10 that they looked *t* the wilderness,	413
	25:20 t the mercy seat shall the faces of	413
	26:35 on the side of the tabernacle *t* the south:	1886.5
	34: 8 bowed his head *t* the earth,	1886.5
	36:25 which is *t* the north corner, he made	3807.1
	39:20 t the forepart of it, over against the *other*	4480
Lev	13:41 off from the part of *his head t* his face,	NIH
Nu	2: 3 on the east side *t* the rising of the sun	1886.5
	3:38 that encamp before the tabernacle *t*	1886.5
	16:42 that they looked *t* the tabernacle of	413
	21:11 which *is* before Moab, *t* the sunrising.	4480
	21:20 Pisgah, which looketh *t* Jeshimon.	5921+6440
	23:28 of Peor, that looketh *t* Jeshimon.	5921+6440
	24: 1 but he set his face *t* the wilderness.	413
	32:14 yet the fierce anger of the Lord *t* Israel.	413
	34:15 *near* Jericho eastward, *t* the sunrising.	1886.5
Dt	4:41 cities on *this* side Jordan *t* the sunrising;	1886.5
	4:47 which *were* on *this* side Jordan *t*	NIH
	28:54 his eye shall be evil *t* his brother,	871.1
	28:54 t the wife of his bosom, and towards	871.1
Jos	1: 4 unto the great sea *t* the going down of	NIH
	1:15 you on *this* side Jordan *t* the sunrising.	NIH
	3:16 that came down *t* the sea of the plain,	5921
	8:18 out the spear that *is* in thy hand *t* Ai;	413
	8:18 spear that *he had* in his hand *t* the city.	413
	12: 1 *other* side Jordan *t* the rising of the sun,	1886.5
	13: 5 and all Lebanon, *t* the sunrising,	NIH
	15: 4 *From thence* it passed *t* Azmon,	1886.5
	15: 7 the border went up *t* Debir from	1886.5
	15: 7 northward, looking *t* Gilgal, that *is* before	413
	15:21 *t* the coast of Edom southward were	413
	16: 6 the border went out *t* the sea *to*	1886.5
	18:13 the border went over from thence *t* Luz,	1886.5
	18:17 *t* En-shemesh, and went forth *t* Geliloth,	413
	18:18 passed along *t* the side over against Arabah	413
	19:11 their border went up *t* the sea,	1886.5
	19:12 turned from Sarid eastward *t* the sunrising	NIH
	19:18 their border was *t* Jezreel,	1886.5
	19:27 turneth *t* the sunrising *to* Beth-dagon,	NIH
	19:27 to the valley of Jiphthah-el *t* the north	1886.5
	19:34 and to Judah upon Jordan *t* the sunrising.	NIH
Jdg	3:28 took the fords of Jordan *t* Moab,	3807.1
	4: 6 *saying,* Go and draw *t* mount Tabor,	871.1
	5: 9 My heart *is t* the governors of Israel,	3807.1
	8: 3 their anger was abated *t* him,	4480+5921
	13:20 when the flame went up *t* heaven from	1886.5
	19:18 We are passing from Beth-lehem-judah *t*	5704
	20:43 ease over against Gibeah *t* the sunrising.	4480
	20:45 fled *t* the wilderness unto the rock of	1886.5
1Sa	13:18 to the valley of Zeboim *t* the wilderness.	1886.5
	17:48 and ran *t* the army to meet the Philistine.	NIH
	20:12 *if there be* good *t* David, and I then send	413
	20:41 David arose out of a *place t* the south,	681
2Sa	14: 1 that the king's heart *was t* Absalom.	5921
	15:23 t the way of the wilderness.	5921+6440
	24: 5 the midst of the river of Gad, and *t* Jazer:	413
	24:20 king and his servants coming on *t* him:	5921
1Ki	7: 9 and *so* on the outside *t* the great court.	5704
	7:25 three looking *t* the north,	1886.5
	7:25 three looking *t* the west,	1886.5
	7:25 three looking *t* the south,	1886.5
	7:25 the south, and three looking *t* the east:	1886.5
	8:22 and stretched forth his hands *t* heaven:	NIH
	8:29 That thine eyes may be open *t* this house	413
	8:29 even *t* the place of which thou hast said,	413
	8:44 shall pray unto the Lord *t* the city which	1870
	8:44 *t* the house that I have built for thy name:	NIH
	8:48 and pray unto thee *t* their land,	1870
	14:13 in him there is found *some* good thing *t*	413
	18:43 to his servant, Go up now, look *t* the sea.	1870
2Ki	3:14 I would not look *t* thee, nor see thee.	413
	4:39 and the *king* went the way *t* the plain.	NIH
1Ch	9:24 the east, west, north, and south.	1886.5
	12:15 *both t* the east, and toward the west.	3807.1
	12:15 *both* toward the east, and *t* the west.	3807.1
	26:17 four a day, and *t* Asuppim two *and* two.	3807.1
2Ch	4: 4 three looking *t* the north,	1886.5
	4: 4 three looking *t* the west,	1886.5
	4: 4 three looking *t* the south,	1886.5
	4: 4 the south, and three looking *t* the east:	1886.5
	6:34 they pray unto thee *t* this city which thou	1870
	6:38 pray *t* their land, which thou gavest unto	1870
	6:38 *t* the city which thou hast chosen,	NIH
	6:38 to the house which I have built for thy	3807.1
	20:24 when Judah came *t* the watch tower in	5921
Ne	3:14 Imnah the Levite, the porter *t* the east,	1886.5
	3:26 over against the water gate *t* the east,	3807.1
	12:31 hand upon the wall *t* the dung gate:	3807.1
Est	8: 4 the king held out the golden sceptre *t*	413
Job	2:12 dust upon their heads *t* heaven.	1886.5
	11:13 and stretch out thine hands *t* him;	413
	39:26 *and* stretch her wings *t* the south?	3807.1
Ps	5: 7 in thy fear will I worship *t* thy holy temple.	413
	28: 2 when I lift up my hands *t* thy holy oracle.	413
	66: 5 *he is* terrible *in his* doing *t* the children of	5921
	86:13 For great *is* thy mercy *t* me: and thou hast	5921
	98: 3 and his truth *t* the house of Israel:	3807.1
	103:11 *so* great is his mercy *t* them that fear him.	5921
	117: 2 For his merciful kindness is great *t* us:	5921
	138: 2 I will worship *t* thy holy temple,	413
Pr	14:35 The king's favour *is t* a wise servant:	3807.1
	23: 5 they fly away as an eagle *t* heaven.	NIH
Ecc	1: 6 The wind goeth *t* the south,	413
	11: 3 if the tree fall *t* the south, or toward	871.1
	11: 3 tree fall toward the south, or *t* the north,	871.1

SS	7: 4 of Lebanon which looketh *t* Damascus.	6440
Isa	11:14 shoulders of the Philistines *t* the west;	1886.5
	38: 2 Hezekiah turned his face *t* the wall,	413
	49:23 down to thee *with their* face *t* the earth,	NIH
Jer	3:12 and proclaim these words *t* the north,	1886.5
	4: 6 Set up the standard *t* Zion: retire,	1886.5
	4:11 wilderness *t* the daughter of my people,	1870
	15: 1 *yet* my mind *could* not *be t* this people:	413
	31:21 set thine heart *t* the highway, *even*	3807.1
	46: 6 fall *t* the north by the river Euphrates.	1886.5
La	2:19 lift up thy hands *t* him for the life of thy	413
Eze	1:23 their wings straight, the one *t* the other:	413
	4: 7 Therefore thou shalt set thy face *t* the siege	413
	6:14 more desolate than the wilderness *t*	1886.5
	8: 3 the door of the inner gate that looketh *t*	1886.5
	8: 5 I lift up mine eyes the way *t* the north,	1886.5
	8:16 *with* their backs *t* the temple of the Lord,	413
	9: 2 which lieth *t* the north, and every man a	1886.5
	12:14 I will scatter *t* every wind all that *are*	3807.1
	16:63 when I am pacified *t* thee for all that	3807.1
	17: 6 branches turned *t* him, and the roots	413
	17: 7 this vine did bend her roots *t* him,	5921
	17: 7 and shot forth her branches *t* him,	3807.1
	20:46 set thy face *t* the south, and drop *thy word*	1870
	20:46 drop *thy word t* the south,	413
	21: 2 set thy face *t* Jerusalem, and drop *thy word*	413
	21: 2 drop *thy word t* the holy places,	413
	33:25 lift up your eyes *t* your idols,	413
	40: 6 came he unto the gate which looketh *t*	1870
	40:20 gate of the outward court that looked *t*	1870
	40:23 *was* over against the gate *t* the north,	3807.1
	40:23 gate toward the north, and *t* the east;	3807.1
	40:24 After that he brought me *t* the south,	1870
	40:24 the south, and behold a gate *t* the south:	1870
	40:27 *there was* a gate in the inner court *t*	1870
	40:27 he measured from gate to gate *t* the south	1870
	40:31 the arches thereof *were t* the utter court;	413
	40:32 he brought me into the inner court *t*	1870
	40:34 the arches thereof *were t* the outward	3807.1
	40:37 the posts thereof *were t* the utter court;	3807.1
	40:44 and their prospect *was t* the south:	1870
	40:44 east gate *having* the prospect *t* the north.	1870
	40:45 whose prospect *is t* the south,	1870
	40:46 the chamber whose prospect *is t* the north	1870
	41:11 the doors of the side chambers *were t*	3807.1
	41:11 one door *t* the north, and another door	1870
	41:11 the north, and another door *t* the south:	3807.1
	41:12 end *t* the west *was* seventy cubits broad;	1870
	41:14 of the separate place *t* the east,	413
	41:19 that the face of a man *was t* the palm tree	413
	41:19 the face of a young lion *t* the palm tree on	413
	42: 1 into the utter court, the way *t* the north:	1870
	42: 1 which *was* before the building *t* the north.	3807.1
	42: 4 of one cubit; and their doors *t* the north,	3807.1
	42:10 of the wall of the court *t* the east,	1870
	42:11 of the chambers which *were t* the north,	1870
	42:12 *t* the south *was* a door in the head of	1870
	42:12 *even* the way directly before the wall *t*	1870
	42:15 he brought me forth *t* the gate whose	1870
	42:15 the gate whose prospect *is t* the east,	1870
	43: 1 *even* the gate that looketh *t* the east:	1870
	43: 4 of the gate whose prospect *is t* the east.	1870
	43:17 and his stairs **look** *t* the east.	6437
	44: 1 sanctuary which looketh *t* the east;	NIH
	46: 1 The gate of the inner court that looketh *t*	NIH
	46:12 open him the gate that looketh *t* the east,	NIH
	46:19 of the priests, which **looked** *t* the north:	6437
	47: 1 for the forefront of the house *stood t*	NIH
	47: 8 These waters issue out *t* the east country,	413
	47:15 this *shall be* the border of the land *t*	3807.1
	48:10 *t* the north five and twenty thousand *in*	1886.5
	48:10 and *t* the west ten thousand *in* breadth,	1886.5
	48:10 the east ten thousand *in* breadth,	1886.5
	48:10 the south five and twenty thousand *in*	1886.5
	48:17 suburbs of the city shall be *t* the north	1886.5
	48:17 *t* the south two hundred and fifty,	1886.5
	48:17 the east two hundred and fifty,	1886.5
	48:17 and *t* the west two hundred and fifty.	1886.5
	48:21 twenty thousand of the oblation *t* the east	5704
	48:21 and twenty thousand *t* the west border,	5921
	48:28 in Kadesh, *and to* the river *t* the great sea.	5921
Da	4: 2 wonders that the high God hath wrought *t*	5974
	6:10 his windows being open in his chamber *t*	5049
	8: 8 it came up four notable ones *t* the four	3807.1
	8: 9 *t* the south, and toward the east,	413
	8: 9 the east, and toward the pleasant *land.*	413
	8: 9 toward the east, and *t* the pleasant *land.*	413
	8:18 I was in a deep sleep on my face *t*	1886.5
	10: 9 on my face, and my face *t* the ground.	1886.5
	10:15 I set my face *t* the ground, and I became	1886.5
	11: 4 be divided *t* the four winds of heaven;	3807.1
	11:29 he shall return, and come *t* the south;	871.1
Hos	3: 1 according to the love of the Lord *t*	NIH
	5: 1 for judgment *is t* you, because ye have	3807.1
Joel	2:20 with his face *t* the east sea, and his hinder	413
Jnh	2: 4 yet I will look again *t* thy holy temple.	413
Zec	6: 6 the grisled go forth *t* the south country.	413
	6: 8 these that go *t* the north country have	413
	9: 1 the tribes of Israel, *shall be t* the Lord.	3807.1
	14: 4 cleave in the midst thereof *t* the east	1886.5
	14: 4 thereof toward the east and *t* the west,	1886.5
	14: 4 half of the mountain shall remove *t*	1886.5
	14: 4 the north, and half of it *t* the south.	1886.5
	14: 8 half of them *t* the former sea, and half of	413
	14: 8 sea, and half of them *t* the hinder sea:	413

Mt	12:49 And he stretched forth his hand *t* his	1909
	14:14 and was moved with compassion *t* them,	1909
Mk	6:34 and was moved with compassion *t* them,	1909
Ac	1:10 And while they looked stedfastly *t* heaven	1519
	8:26 go *t* the south unto the way that goeth	2596
	20:21 repentance *t* God, and faith toward our	1519
	20:21 and faith *t* our Lord Jesus Christ.	1519
	24:16 always a conscience void of offence *t* God,	4314
	24:16 void of offence toward God, and *t* men.	NIG
	27:12 and faith *t* the south west and north west.	2596
	27:40 mainsail to the wind, and made *t* shore.	NIH
	28:14 them seven days: and so we went *t* Rome.	NIH
Ro	5: 8 God commendeth his love *t* us, in that,	1519
	11:22 but *t* thee, goodness, if thou continue in	1909
1Co	7:36 *he* behaveth himself uncomely *t* his virgin,	1909
2Co	1:16 of you to be brought on *my* way *t* Judea.	1519
	1:18 true, our word *t* you was not yea and nay.	4314
	7: 4 Great *is* my boldness of speech *t* you,	4314
	7: 7 your mourning, your fervent mind *t* me;	5228
	7:15 inward affection is more abundant *t* you,	1519
	10: 1 but being absent am bold *t* you:	1519
	13: 4 live with him by the power of God *t* you.	1519
Eph	1: 8 Wherein he hath abounded *t* us in all	1519
Php	2:30 life, to supply your lack of service *t* me.	4314
	3:14 I press *t* the mark for the prize of the high	2596
Col	4: 5 Walk in wisdom *t* them that are without,	4314
1Th	4:12 That ye may walk honestly *t* them that are	4314
	5:14 support the weak, be patient *t* all *men.*	4314
Tit	3: 4 *love* of God our Saviour *t* man appeared,	5363
Phm	1: 5 which thou hast *t* the Lord Jesus,	4314
	1: 5 toward the Lord Jesus, and *t* all saints;	1519
Heb	6:10 of love, which ye have shewed *t* his name,	1519
1Pe	2:19 if a man for conscience *t* God endure grief,	NIG
	3:21 the answer of a good conscience *t* God,)	1519

TOWARDS (81) [TOWARD]

Ge	15: 5 Look now *t* heaven, and tell the stars,	1886.5
	25:18 *is* before Egypt, as thou goest *t* Assyria:	1886.5
	48:13 Manasseh in his left hand *t* Israel's right	4480
Ex	8: let Moses sprinkle it *t* the heaven in	1886.5
	28:27 the forepart thereof, over against	4136+4480
Lev	9:22 And Aaron lift up his hand *t* the people,	413
Dt	28:54 the remnant of his children which he	871.1
	28:56 her eye shall be evil *t* the husband of her	871.1
	28:56 and *t* her son, and towards her daughter,	871.1
	28:56 and towards her son, and *t* her daughter,	871.1
	28:57 *t* her young one that cometh out from	871.1
	28:57 and her children which she shall bear:	871.1
Jos	15: 7 the border passed *t* the waters of	413
Jdg	5:11 *even* the righteous acts *t* the inhabitants of	NIH
	19: 9 Behold now, the day draweth *t* evening,	3807.1
1Sa	17:30 he turned from him *t* another,	413+4136
1Ki	8:29 which thy servant shall make *t* this place.	413
	8:30 when they shall pray *t* this place:	413
	8:35 if they pray *t* this place, and confess thy	413
	8:38 and spread forth his hands *t* this house:	413
	8:42 when he shall come and pray *t* this house;	413
2Ch	6:13 and spread forth his hands *t* heaven,	1886.5
	6:20 which thy servant prayeth *t* this place.	413
	6:21 which their make *t* this place:	413
	6:26 *yet* if they pray *t* this place, and confess thy	413
	16: 9 behalf of *them* whose heart *is* perfect *t* him.	413
	16: 9 toward God, and *towards* his house.	5973
	24:16 Israel, both towards God, and *t* his house.	NIH
Ezr	3:11 for his mercy *endureth* for ever *t* Israel.	5921
Est	1:13 king's manner *t* all that knew law	6440+3807.1
Ps	25:15 Mine eyes *are* ever *t* the Lord; for he	413
	85: 4 and cause thine anger *t* us to cease.	5973
	116:12 unto the Lord *for* all his benefits *t* me?	5921
SS	7:10 I *am* my beloved's, and his desire *is t* me.	5921
Isa	7: 1 I went up *t* Jerusalem to war against it,	NIH
	29:13 their fear *t* me is taught *by* the precept of	NIH
	63: 7 The great goodness *t* the house of Israel,	3807.1
	63:15 of thy bowels and of thy mercies *t* me?	413
	66:14 the hand of the Lord shall be known *t* his	NIH
	66:14 and *his* indignation *t* his enemies.	NIH
Jer	1:13 and the face thereof *is t* the north.	4480+6440
	12: 3 hast seen me, and tried mine heart *t* thee:	854
	29:10 perform my good word *t* you, in causing	5921
	29:11 For I know the thoughts that I think *t* you,	5921
	31:40 unto the corner of the horse gate *t*	1886.5
	49:36 and will scatter them *t* all those winds;	3807.1
Eze	6: 2 set thy face *t* the mountains of Israel,	413
	8: 5 up thine eyes now the way *t* the north.	1886.5
	8:14 Lord's house which *was t* the north;	1886.5
	8:16 of the Lord, and their faces *t* the east;	1886.5
	8:16 and they worshipped the sun *t* the east.	1886.5
	16:42 So will I make my fury *t* thee to rest,	871.1
	17:21 they that remain shall be scattered *t* all	3807.1
	24:23 your iniquities, and mourn one *t* another.	413
	40:22 of the gate that looketh *t* the east;	1870
	42: 7 the utter court on the forepart of	1870
Da	11:19 he shall turn his face *t* the fort of	3807.1
Joel	2:20 his hinder part *t* the utmost sea, and his	413
Mt	28: 1 as it began to dawn *t* the first *day of*	1519
Lk	2:14 and on earth peace, good will *t* men.	1722
	12:21 treasure for himself, and is not rich *t* God.	
	13:22 teaching, and journeying *t* Jerusalem.	1519
	24:29 for it is *t* evening, and the day is far spent.	4314
Jn	6:17 ship, and went over the sea *t* Capernaum.	1519
Ac	22: 3 and was zealous *t* God, as ye all are this	NIG
	24:15 And have hope *t* God, which they	1519
Ro	1:27 burned in their lust one *t* another;	1519
	12:16 *Be* of the same mind one *t* another.	1519
	15: 5 one *t* another according to Christ Jesus:	1722

2Co	2: 8 that *you* would confirm *your* love t him.	1519
	9: 8 God *is* able to make all grace abound t	1519
Gal	2: 8 *same* was mighty in me t the Gentiles:)	1519
Eph	2: 7 in *his* kindness t us through Christ Jesus.	1909
1Th	3:12 and abound in love one t another,	1519
	3:12 and t all *men*, even as we *do* towards you:	1519
	3:12 and towards all *men*, even as we *do* t you:	1519
	4:10 indeed ye do it t all the brethren which	1519
2Th	1: 3 the charity of every one of you all t each	1519
Heb	6: 1 from dead works, and of faith t God,	1909
1Jn	3:21 us not, *then* have we confidence t God.	4314
	4: 9 this was manifested the love of God t us,	1722

TOWEL (2)

Jn	13: 4 and took a t, and girded himself.	3012
	13: 5 to wipe *them* with the t wherewith he	3012

TOWER (48) [TOWERS, WATCHTOWER]

Ge	11: 4 Go to, let us build us a city and a t,	4026
	11: 5 came down to see the city and the t,	4026
	35:21 and spread his tent beyond the t of Edar.	4026
Jdg	8: 9 again in peace, I will break down this t.	4026
	8:17 he beat down the t of Penuel, and slew	4026
	9:46 all the men of the t of Shechem heard	4026
	9:47 that all the men of the t of Shechem were	4026
	9:49 that all the men of the t of Shechem died	4026
	9:51 But there was a strong t within the city,	4026
	9:51 them, and gat them up to the top of the t.	4026
	9:52 Abimelech came unto the t,	4026
	9:52 hard unto the door of the t to burn it	4026
2Sa	22: 3 my **high** t, and my refuge, my saviour;	4869
	22:51 *He is* the t of salvation for his king:	4024
2Ki	5:24 when he came to the t, he took *them*	6076
	9:17 stood a watchman on the t in Jezreel,	4026
	17: 9 from the t of the watchmen to the fenced	4026
	18: 8 from the t of the watchmen to the fenced	4026
2Ch	20:24 when Judah came toward the **watch** t in	4707
Ne	3: 1 even unto the t of Meah they sanctified it,	4026
	3: 1 they sanctified it, unto the t of Hananeel.	4026
	3:11 the other piece, and the t of the furnaces.	4026
	3:25 the t which lieth out from the king's high	4026
	3:26 toward the east, and the t that lieth out.	4026
	3:27 over against the great t that lieth out,	4026
	12:38 from beyond the t of the furnaces even	4026
	12:39 the t of Hananeel, and the tower of Meah,	4026
	12:39 the tower of Hananeel, and the t of Meah,	4026
Ps	18: 2 the horn of my salvation, *and* my **high** t.	4869
	61: 3 for me, *and* a strong t from the enemy.	4026
	144: 2 my **high** t, and my deliverer; my shield,	4869
Pr	18:10 The name of the LORD *is* a strong t:	4026
SS	4: 4 Thy neck *is* like the t of David builded for	4026
	7: 4 Thy neck *is* as a t of ivory; thine eyes *like*	4026
	7: 4 thy nose *is* as the t of Lebanon which	4026
Isa	2:15 upon every high t, and upon every fenced	4026
	5: 2 built a t in the midst of it, and also made	4026
Jer	6:27 I have set thee *for* a t *and* a fortress	969
	31:38 t of Hananeel unto the gate of the corner.	4026
Eze	29:10 from the t of Syene even unto the border	4024
	30: 6 from the t of Syene shall they fall in it by	4024
Mic	4: 8 thou, O t of the flock, the strong hold of	4026
Hab	2: 1 set me upon the t, and will watch to see	4692
Zec	14:10 *from* the t of Hananeel unto the king's	4026
Mt	21:33 built a t, and let it out to husbandmen,	4444
Mk	12: 1 built a t, and let it out to husbandmen,	4444
Lk	13: 4 upon whom the t in Siloam fell,	4444
	14:28 For which of you, intending to build a t,	4444

TOWERS (17) [TOWER]

2Ch	14: 7 about *them* walls, and t, gates, and bars,	4026
	26: 9 Moreover Uzziah built t in Jerusalem at	4026
	26:10 Also he built t in the desert,	4026
	26:15 invented by cunning *men*, to be on the t	4026
	27: 4 and in the forests he built castles and t.	4026
	32: 5 raised *it* up to the t, and another wall	4026
Ps	48:12 and go round about her: tell the t thereof.	4026
SS	8:10 I *am* a wall, and my breasts like t: then	4026
Isa	23:13 they set up the t thereof, they raised up	971
	30:25 day of the great slaughter, when the t fall.	4026
	32:14 the forts and t shall be for dens for ever,	975
	33:18 where *is* he that counted the t?	4026
Eze	26: 4 the walls of Tyrus, and break down her t:	4026
	26: 9 with his axes he shall break down thy t.	4026
	27:11 and the Gammadims were in thy t:	4026
Zep	1:16 the fenced cities, and against the high t.	6438
	3: 6 their t are desolate; I made their streets	6438

TOWN (13) [TOWNCLERK, TOWNS]

Jos	2:15 for her house *was* upon the t wall,	7023
1Sa	16: 4 the elders of the t trembled at his coming,	5892
	23: 7 entering into a t that hath gates and bars.	5892
	27: 5 let them give me a place in some t in	5892
Hab	2:12 Woe to him that buildeth a t with blood,	5892
Mt	10:11 into whatsoever city or t ye shall enter,	2968
Mk	8:23 by the hand, and led him out of the t;	2968
	8:26 saying, Neither go into the t, nor tell *it* to	2968
	8:26 into the town, nor tell *it* to any in the t.	2968
Lk	5:17 were come out of every t of Galilee,	2968
Jn	7:42 out of the t of Bethlehem, where David	2968
	11: 1 the t of Mary and her sister Martha.	2968
	11:30 Now Jesus was not yet come into the t,	2968

TOWNCLERK (1) [TOWN]

Ac	19:35 And when the t had appeased the people,	1122

TOWNS (45) [TOWN]

Ge	25:16 names, by their t, and by their castles;	2691
Nu	32:41 and took the **small** t thereof,	2333
Dt	3: 5 and bars; beside unwalled t a great many.	5892
Jos	13:30 all the t of Jair, which *are* in Bashan,	2333
	15:45 Ekron, with her t and her villages:	1323
	15:47 Ashdod *with* her t and her villages,	1323
	15:47 Gaza with her t and her villages,	1323
	17:11 and in Asher Beth-shean and her t,	1323
	17:11 Ibleam and her t, and the inhabitants of	1323
	17:11 the inhabitants of Endor and her t,	1323
	17:11 the inhabitants of Taanach and her t,	1323
	17:11 and the inhabitants of Megiddo and her t,	1323
	17:16 *they* who *are* of Beth-shean and her t,	1323
Jdg	1:27 *the inhabitants of* Beth-shean and her t,	1323
	1:27 and her towns, nor Taanach and her t,	1323
	1:27 nor the inhabitants of Dor and her t,	1323
	1:27 nor the inhabitants of Ibleam and her t,	1323
	1:27 nor the inhabitants of Megiddo and her t:	1323
1Ki	11:26 While Israel dwelt in Heshbon and her t,	1323
	11:26 in Aroer and her t, and in all the cities	1323
	4:13 to him *pertained* the t of Jair the son of	2333
1Ch	2:23 Aram, with the t of Jair, from them,	2333
	2:23 them, with Kenath, and the t thereof,	1323
	5:16 in her t, and in all the suburbs of Sharon,	1323
	7:28 *were*, Beth-el and the t thereof,	1323
	7:28 and westward Gezer, with the t thereof;	1323
	7:28 Shechem also and the t thereof, unto	1323
	7:28 thereof, unto Gaza and the t thereof:	1323
	7:29 Beth-shean and her t, Taanach and	1323
	7:29 Taanach and her t, Megiddo and her	1323
	7:29 Megiddo and her t, Dor and her towns.	1323
	7:29 Megiddo and her towns, Dor and her t.	1323
	8:12 Ono, and Lod, with the t thereof:	1323
	18: 1 her t out of the hand of the Philistines.	1323
2Ch	13:19 Beth-el with the t thereof, and Jeshanah	1323
	13:19 Jeshanah with the t thereof, and Ephrain	1323
	13:19 and Ephrain with the t thereof.	1323
Est	9:19 the villages, that dwelt in the unwalled t,	5892
Jer	19:15 upon all her t all the evil that I have	5892
Zec	2: 4 *as* t **without walls** for the multitude of	6519
Mk	1:38 said unto them, Let us go into the next t,	2969
	8:27 his disciples, into the t of Cesarea Philippi:	2968
Lk	9: 6 they departed, and went through the t,	2968
	9:12 that they may go into the t and	2968

TRACHONITIS (1)

Lk	3: 1 tetrarch of Iturea and of the region of T,	5139

TRACONITIS See TRACHONITIS

TRADE (5) [TRADED, TRADING]

Ge	34:10 dwell and t you therein, and get you	5503
	34:21 let them dwell in the land, and t therein;	5503
	46:32 for their t hath been to feed cattle;	376+4735
	46:34 servants' t hath been **about cattle**	376+4735
Rev	18:17 and sailers, and as many as t by sea,	2038

TRADED (5) [TRADE]

Eze	27:12 iron, tin, and lead, they t in thy fairs.	5414
	27:13 they t the persons of men and vessels of	5414
	27:14 They of the house of Togarmah t in thy	5414
	27:17 they t in thy market wheat of Minnith,	5414
Mt	25:16 the five talents went and t with the same,	2038

TRADERS See TRAFFICK; TRAFFICKERS

TRADING (1) [TRADE]

Lk	19:15 how much every *man* had **gained by t**.	1281

TRADITION (11) [TRADITIONS]

Mt	15: 2 Why do thy disciples transgress the t of	3862
	15: 3 the commandment of God by your t?	3862
	15: 6 of God of none effect by your t.	3862
Mk	7: 3 eat not, holding the t of the elders.	3862
	7: 5 disciples according to the t of the elders,	3862
	7: 8 hold the t of men, *as* the washing of pots	3862
	7: 9 of God, that ye may keep your own t.	3862
	7:13 of God of none effect through your t,	3862
Col	2: 8 and vain deceit, after the t of men,	3862
2Th	3: 6 not after the t which he received of us.	3862
1Pe	1:18 **received by t** from your **fathers**;	3970

TRADITIONS (2) [TRADITION]

Gal	1:14 being more exceedingly zealous of the t of	3862
2Th	2:15 and hold the t which ye have been taught,	3862

TRAFFICK (5) [TRAFFICKERS]

Ge	42:34 your brother, and ye shall t in the land.	5503
1Ki	10:15 *of* the t of the *spice* merchants, and *of* all	4536
Eze	17: 4 twigs, and carried it into a land of t;	3667
	28: 5 by thy t hast thou increased thy riches,	7404
	28:18 of thine iniquities, by the iniquity of thy t;	7404

TRAFFICKERS (1) [TRAFFICK]

Isa	23: 8 whose t *are* the honourable of the earth?	3667

TRAIN (3) [TRAINED]

1Ki	10: 2 she came to Jerusalem with a very great t,	2428
Pr	22: 6 T up a child in the way he should go:	2596
Isa	6: 1 and lifted up, and his t filled the temple.	7757

TRAINED (1) [TRAIN]

Ge	14:14 he armed his t *servants*, born in his own	2593

TRAITOR (1) [TRAITORS, TREASON]

Lk	6:16 and Judas Iscariot, which also was the t.	4273

TRAITORS (1) [TRAITOR]

2Ti	3: 4 T, heady, highminded, lovers of pleasures	4273

TRAMPLE (3)

Ps	91:13 and the dragon shalt thou t **under feet**.	7429
Isa	63: 3 in mine anger, and t them in my fury;	7429
Mt	7: 6 lest they t them under their feet,	2662

TRANCE (5)

Nu	24: 4 falling *into a* t, but having his eyes open:	NIH
	24:16 falling *into a* t, but having his eyes open:	NIH
Ac	10:10 while they made ready, he fell into a t,	1611
	11: 5 and in a t I saw a vision, A certain vessel	1611
	22:17 while I prayed in the temple, I was in a t;	1611

TRANQUILLITY (1)

Da	4:27 poor; if it may be a lengthening of thy t.	7963

TRANSFER See TRANSLATE

TRANSFERRED (1)

1Co	4: 6 I have **in a figure** t to myself and	3345

TRANSFIGURED (2)

Mt	17: 2 And was t before them: and his face did	3339
Mk	9: 2 by themselves: and he was t before them.	3339

TRANSFORMED (3) [TRANSFORMING]

Ro	12: 2 but be ye t by the renewing of your mind,	3339
2Co	11:14 for Satan himself is t into an angel of light.	3345
	11:15 also be t as the ministers of righteousness;	3345

TRANSFORMING (1) [TRANSFORMED]

2Co	11:13 t themselves into the apostles of Christ.	3345

TRANSGRESS (14) [TRANSGRESSED, TRANSGRESSEST, TRANSGRESSETH, TRANSGRESSING, TRANSGRESSION, TRANSGRESSIONS, TRANSGRESSOR, TRANSGRESSORS]

Nu	14:41 now do ye t the commandment	5674
1Sa	2:24 I hear: ye **make** the LORD'S people to t.	5674
2Ch	24:20 Why t ye the commandments of	5674
Ne	1: 8 saying, *If* ye t, I will scatter you abroad	4603
	13:27 to t against our God in marrying strange	4603
Ps	17: 3 I am purposed *that* my mouth shall not t.	5674
	25: 3 them be ashamed which t without cause.	898
Pr	28:21 for for a piece of bread *that* man will t.	6586
Jer	2:20 thy bands; and thou saidst, I will not t;	6586
Eze	20:38 the rebels, and them that t against me:	6586
Am	4: 4 Come to Beth-el, and t; *at* Gilgal multiply	6586
Mt	15: 2 Why do thy disciples t the tradition of	3845
	15: 3 Why do you also t the commandment of	3845
Ro	2:27 the letter and circumcision dost t the law?	3848

TRANSGRESSED (34) [TRANSGRESS]

Dt	26:13 I have not t thy commandments,	5674
Jos	7:11 they have also t my covenant which I	5674
	7:15 he hath t the covenant of the LORD,	5674
	23:16 When ye have t the covenant of the	5674
Jdg	2:20 Because that this people hath t my	5674
1Sa	14:33 said, Ye have t: roll a great stone unto me	898
	15:24 for I have t the commandment of	5674
1Ki	8:50 their transgressions wherein they have t	6586
2Ki	18:12 t his covenant, *and* all that Moses	5674
1Ch	2: 7 of Israel, who t in the thing accursed.	4603
	5:25 they t against the God of their fathers,	4603
2Ch	12: 2 because they had t against the LORD,	4603
	26:16 for he t against the LORD his God,	4603
	28:19 and t sore against the LORD.	4603+4604
	36:14 t very **much** after all	4603+4604
Ezr	10:10 Ye have t, and have taken strange wives,	4603
	10:13 for we are many that have t in this thing.	6586
Isa	24: 5 because they have t the laws, changed	5674
	43:27 and thy teachers have t against me.	6586
	66:24 carcases of the men that have t against me	6586
Jer	2: 8 the pastors also t against me,	6586
	2:29 ye all have t against me, saith the LORD.	6586
	3:13 that thou hast t against the LORD thy	6586
	33: 8 whereby they have t against me.	6586
	34:18 I will give the men that have t my	5674
La	3:42 We have t and have rebelled: thou hast	6586
Eze	2: 3 they and their fathers have t against me,	6586
	18:31 your transgressions, whereby ye have t;	6586
Da	9:11 Yea, all Israel have t thy law, even by	5674
Hos	6: 7 they like men have t the covenant:	5674
	7:13 because they have t against me: though I	6586
	8: 1 because they have t my covenant,	6586
Zep	3:11 doings, wherein thou hast t against me:	6586
Lk	15:29 neither t I at any time thy commandment:	3928

TRANSGRESSEST (1) [TRANSGRESS]

Est	3: 3 Why t thou the king's commandment?	5674

TRANSGRESSETH (4) [TRANSGRESS]

Pr	16:10 of the king: his mouth t not in judgment.	4603
Hab	2: 5 also, because he t *by* wine, *he is* a proud	898
1Jn	3: 4 committeth sin t also the **law**:	458+4160
2Jn	1: 9 Whosoever t,	3845

TRANSGRESSING (2) [TRANSGRESS]

Dt	17: 2 of the LORD thy God, in t his covenant,	5674
Isa	59:13 In t and lying against the LORD,	6586

TRANSGRESSION (51) [TRANSGRESS]

Ex	34: 7 forgiving iniquity and t and sin,	6588
Nu	14:18 forgiving iniquity and t, and by no means	6588
Jos	22:22 in rebellion, or if in t against the LORD,	4604
1Sa	24:11 see that *there is* neither evil nor t in mine	6588
1Ch	9: 1 were carried away to Babylon for their t.	4604
	10:13 t which he **committed** against	4603+4604
2Ch	29:19 Ahaz in his reign did cast away in his t,	4604
Ezr	9: 4 of those that had been carried away;	4604
	10: 6 the t of them that had been carried away.	4604
Job	7:21 why dost thou not pardon my t,	6588
	8: 4 and he have cast them away for their t;	6588
	13:23 sins? make me to know my t and my sin.	6588
	14:17 My t *is* sealed up in a bag, and thou	6588
	33: 9 I am clean without t, I *am* innocent;	6588
	34: 6 right? my wound *is* incurable without t.	6588
Ps	19:13 and I shall be innocent from the great t.	6588
	32: 1 Blessed *is* he whose t *is* forgiven,	6588
	36: 1 The t of the wicked saith within my heart,	6588
	59: 3 not *for* my t, nor *for* my sin, O LORD.	6588
	89:32 will I visit their t with the rod,	6588
	107:17 Fools because of their t, and	1870+6588
Pr	12:13 The wicked is snared by the t of *his* lips:	6588
	17: 9 He that covereth a t seeketh love;	6588
	17:19 He loveth t that loveth strife: *and* he that	6588
	19:11 and *it is* his glory to pass over a t.	6588
	28: 2 For the t of a land many *are* the princes	6588
	28:24 father or his mother, and saith, *It is* no t;	6588
	29: 6 In the t of an evil man *there is* a snare:	6588
	29:16 the wicked are multiplied, t increaseth:	6588
	29:22 strife, and a furious man aboundeth in t.	6588
Isa	24:20 and the t thereof shall be heavy upon it;	6588
	53: 8 for the t of my people was he stricken.	6588
	57: 4 ye not children of t, a seed of falsehood,	6588
	58: 1 shew my people their t, and the house of	6588
	59:20 unto them that turn from t in Jacob,	6588
Eze	33:12 shall not deliver him in the day of his t:	6588
Da	8:12 against the daily *sacrifice* by reason of t,	6588
	8:13 the daily *sacrifice*, and the t of desolation,	6588
	9:24 to finish the t, and to make an end of sins,	6588
Am	4: 4 *at* Gilgal multiply t; and bring your	6586
Mic	1: 5 the t of Jacob *is* all this, and for the sins	6588
	1: 5 What *is* the t of Jacob? *is it* not Samaria?	6588
	3: 8 to declare unto Jacob his t, and to Israel	6588
	6: 7 shall I give my firstborn *for* my t, the fruit	6588
	7:18 passeth by the t of the remnant of his	6588
Ac	1:25 apostleship, from which Judas **by t** fell,	3845
Ro	4:15 for where no law is, *there is* no t.	3847
	5:14 sinned after the similitude of Adam's t,	3847
1Ti	2:14 the woman being deceived was in the t.	3847
Heb	2: 2 and every t and disobedience received a	3847
1Jn	3: 4 also the law: for sin is t of the **law**.	458

TRANSGRESSIONS (48) [TRANSGRESS]

Ex	23:21 him not; for he will not pardon your t:	6588
Lev	16:16 and because of their t in all their sins:	6588
	16:21 all their t in all their sins, putting them	6588
Jos	24:19 he will not forgive your t nor your sins.	6588
1Ki	8:50 all their t wherein they have transgressed	6588
Job	31:33 If I covered my t as Adam, by hiding mine	6588
	35: 6 or *if* thy t be multiplied, what doest thou	6588
	36: 9 and their t that they have exceeded.	6588
Ps	5:10 cast them out in the multitude of their t;	6588
	25: 7 not the sins of my youth, nor my t:	6588
	32: 1 I said, I will confess my t unto the LORD;	6588
	39: 8 Deliver me from all my t: make me not	6588
	51: 1 of thy tender mercies blot out my t.	6588
	51: 3 I acknowledge my t: and my sin *is* ever	6588
	65: 3 *as for* our t, thou shalt purge them away.	6588
	103:12 *so* far hath he removed our t from us.	6588
Isa	43:25 he that blotteth out thy t for mine own	6588
	44:22 cloud, thy t, and, as a cloud, thy sins:	6588
	50: 1 and for your t *is* your mother put away.	6588
	53: 5 *was* wounded for our t, he *was* bruised	6588
	59:12 For our t are multiplied before thee,	6588
	59:12 for our t *are* with us; and *as for* our	6588
Jer	5: 6 because their t are many,	6588
La	1: 5 afflicted her for the multitude of her t:	6588
	1:14 The yoke of my t is bound by his hand:	6588
	1:22 as thou hast done unto me for all my t:	6588
Eze	14:11 be polluted any more with all their t;	6588
	18:22 All his t that he hath committed, they	6588
	18:28 turneth away from all his t that he hath	6588
	18:30 and turn *yourselves* from all your t;	6588
	18:31 Cast away from you all your t, whereby	6588
	21:24 in that your t are discovered, so that in all	6588
	33:10 If our t and our sins *be* upon us,	6588
	37:23 detestable things, nor with any of their t:	6588
	39:24 according to their t have I done unto	6588
Am	1: 3 For three t of Damascus, and for four, I	6588
	1: 6 For three t of Gaza, and for four, I	6588
	1: 9 For three t of Tyrus, and for four, I will	6588
	1:11 For three t of Edom, and for four, I will	6588
	1:13 For three t of the children of Ammon,	6588
	2: 1 For three t of Moab, and for four, I will	6588
	2: 4 For three t of Judah, and for four, I will	6588
	2: 6 For three t of Israel, and for four, I will	6588
	3:14 That in the day that I shall visit the t of	6588
	5:12 For I know your manifold t and	6588
Mic	1:13 for the t of Israel were found in thee.	6588
Gal	3:19 It was added because of t, till the seed	3847
Heb	9:15 the redemption of the t that were under	3847

TRANSGRESSOR (5) [TRANSGRESS]

Pr	21:18 for the righteous, and the t for the upright.	898
	22:12 and he overthroweth the words of the t.	898
Isa	48: 8 wast called a t from the womb.	6586
Gal	2:18 which I destroyed, I make myself a t.	3848
Jas	2:11 *if* thou kill, thou art become a t of the law.	3848

TRANSGRESSORS (20) [TRANSGRESS]

Ps	37:38 shall be destroyed together: the end	6586
	51:13 Then will I teach t thy ways;	6586
	59: 5 be not merciful to any wicked t. Selah.	898
	119:158 I beheld the t, and was grieved; because	898
Pr	2:22 earth, and the t shall be rooted out of it.	898
	11: 3 the perverseness of t shall destroy them.	898
	11: 6 t shall be taken in their own naughtiness.	898
	13: 2 but the soul of the t *shall eat* violence.	898
	13:15 giveth favour: but the way of t is hard.	898
	23:28 a prey, and increaseth the t among men.	898
	26:10 both rewardeth the fool, and rewardeth t.	5674
Isa	1:28 the destruction of the t and of the sinners	6586
	46: 8 bring *it* again to mind, O ye t.	6586
	53:12 he was numbered with the t; and he bare	6586
	53:12 of many, and made intercession for the t.	6586
Da	8:23 when the t are come to the full, a king of	6586
Hos	14: 9 walk in them: but the t shall fall therein.	6586
Mk	15:28 And he was numbered with the t.	459
Lk	22:37 in me, And he was reckoned among the t:	459
Jas	2: 9 and are convinced of the law as t.	3848

TRANSLATE (1) [TRANSLATED, TRANSLATION]

2Sa	3:10 To t the kingdom from the house of Saul,	5674

TRANSLATED (3) [TRANSLATE]

Col	1:13 hath t us into the kingdom of his dear Son:	3179
Heb	11: 5 By faith Enoch was t that he should	3346
	11: 5 was not found, because God had t him:	3346

TRANSLATION (1) [TRANSLATE]

Heb	11: 5 for before his t he had this testimony,	3331

TRANSPARENT (1)

Rev	21:21 the city *was* pure gold, as *it were* t glass.	1307

TRAP (4) [TRAPS]

Job	18:10 in the ground, and a t for him in the way.	4434
Ps	69:22 been for *their* welfare, *let it become* a t.	4170
Jer	5:26 snares; they set a t, they catch men.	4889
Ro	11: 9 and a t, and a stumblingblock, and a	2339

TRAPS (1) [TRAP]

Jos	23:13 they shall be snares and t unto you,	4170

TRAVAIL (31) [TRAVAILED, TRAVAILEST, TRAVAILETH, TRAVAILING]

Ge	38:27 it came to pass in the time of her t, that,	3205
Ex	18: 8 all the t that had come upon them by	8513
Nu	20:14 Thou knowest all the t that hath befallen	8513
Ps	48: 6 them there, *and* pain, as of a woman in t.	3205
Ecc	1:13 this sore t hath God given to the sons of	6045
	2:23 all his days *are* sorrows, and his t grief;	6045
	2:26 to the sinner he giveth t, to gather and	6045
	3:10 I have seen the t, which God hath given	6045
	4: 4 I considered all t, and every right work,	5999
	4: 6 than both the hands full *with* t and	5999
	4: 8 This *is* also vanity, yea, it *is* a sore t.	6045
	5:14 those riches perish by evil t:	6045
Isa	23: 4 saying, I t not, nor bring forth children,	2342
	53:11 He shall see of the t of his soul,	5999
	54: 1 aloud, thou *that* didst not t **with child**:	2342
Jer	4:31 I have heard a voice as of a woman in t,	2470
	6:24 hold of us, *and* pain, as of a woman in t.	3205
	13:21 not sorrows take thee, as a woman in t?	3205
	22:23 upon thee, the pain as of a woman in t!	3205
	30: 6 see whether a man doth t **with child**?	3205
	30: 6 as a woman in t, and all faces are turned	3205
	49:24 sorrows have taken her as a woman in t.	3205
	50:43 of him, *and* pangs as of a woman in t.	8513
La	3: 5 and compassed *me* with gall and t.	3205
Mic	4: 9 pangs have taken thee as a woman in t:	3205
	4:10 O daughter of Zion, like a woman in t:	3205
Jn	16:21 A woman when she is in t hath sorrow,	5088
Gal	4:19 of whom I t in birth again until Christ be	5605
1Th	2: 9 ye remember, brethren, our labour and t:	3449
	5: 3 them, as t upon a *woman* with child;	5604
2Th	3: 8 wrought with labour and t night and day,	3449

TRAVAILED (5) [TRAVAIL]

Ge	35:16 and Rachel t, and she had hard labour.	3205
	38:28 it came to pass, when she t, that *the one*	3205
1Sa	4:19 were dead, she bowed herself and t.	3205
Isa	66: 7 Before she t, she brought forth; before her	2342
	66: 8 as soon as Zion t, she brought forth her	2342

TRAVAILEST (1) [TRAVAIL]

Gal	4:27 break forth and cry, thou that t not:	5605

TRAVAILETH (7) [TRAVAIL]

Job	15:20 The wicked *man* t **with pain** all his days,	2342
Ps	7:14 he t with iniquity, and hath conceived	2254
Isa	13: 8 they shall be in pain as a woman that t:	3205
	21: 3 upon me, as the pangs of a woman that t:	3205
Jer	31: 8 and her that t **with child** together:	3205
Mic	5: 3 the time that she which t hath brought	3205
Ro	8:22 and t **in pain together** until now.	4944

TRAVAILING (3) [TRAVAIL]

Isa	42:14 *now* will I cry like a t **woman**; I will	3205
Hos	13:13 The sorrows of a t *woman* shall come	3205

Rev	12: 2 t **in birth**, and pained to be delivered.	5605

TRAVEL (2) [TRAVELLED, TRAVELLER, TRAVELLERS, TRAVELLEST, TRAVELLETH, TRAVELLING]

Ac	19:29 of Macedonia, Paul's **companions in** t,	4898
2Co	8:19 the churches to t **with** us with this grace,	4898

TRAVELLED (1) [TRAVEL]

Ac	11:19 arose about Stephen t as far as Phenice,	1330

TRAVELLER (2) [TRAVEL]

2Sa	12: 4 there came a t unto the rich man,	1982
Job	31:32 the street: *but* I opened my doors to the t.	734

TRAVELLERS (1) [TRAVEL]

Jdg	5: 6 and the t walked *through* byways.	1980+5410

TRAVELLETH (2) [TRAVEL]

Pr	6:11 So shall thy poverty come as one that t,	1980
	24:34 So shall thy poverty come *as* one that t;	1980

TRAVELLING (3) [TRAVEL]

Isa	21:13 ye lodge, O ye t **companies** of Dedanim.	736
	63: 1 t in the greatness of his strength?	6808
Mt	25:14 *of heaven is as a man* t **into a far country,**	589

TRAVERSING (1)

Jer	2:23 thou art a swift dromedary t her ways;	8308

TRAYS See SNUFFDISHES

TREACHEROUS (9) [TREACHERY]

Isa	21: 2 the t dealer dealeth treacherously,	898
	24:16 the t **dealers** have dealt treacherously;	898
	24:16 **dealers** have dealt very treacherously.	898
Jer	3: 7 And her t sister Judah saw *it*.	901
	3: 8 yet her t sister Judah feared not, but went	898
	3:10 yet for all this her t sister Judah hath not	901
	3:11 hath justified herself more than t Judah.	898
	9: 2 be all adulterers, an assembly of t **men**.	898
Zep	3: 4 Her prophets *are* light *and* t persons:	900

TREACHEROUSLY (23) [TREACHERY]

Jdg	9:23 men of Shechem **dealt** t with Abimelech:	898
Isa	21: 2 the treacherous dealer **dealeth** t,	898
	24:16 the treacherous dealers have **dealt** t; yea,	898
	24:16 treacherous dealers have **dealt very** t.	898+899
	33: 1 **dealest** t, and they dealt not treacherously	898
	33: 1 and they **dealt** not t with thee!	898
	33: 1 when thou shalt make an end to **deal** t,	898
	33: 1 they shall **deal** t with thee.	898
	48: 8 knew *that* thou wouldest **deal very** t,	898+898
Jer	3:20 Surely *as* a wife t departeth from her	898
	3:20 so have you **dealt** t with me, O house of	898
	5:11 the house of Judah have **dealt very** t	898+899
	12: 1 are all they happy that **deal very** t?	898+899
	12: 6 father, even they have **dealt** t with thee;	898
La	1: 2 all her friends have **dealt** t with her,	898
Hos	5: 7 They have **dealt** t against the LORD:	898
	6: 7 there have they **dealt** t against me.	898
Hab	1:13 lookest thou upon them that **deal** t,	898
Mal	2:10 why do we **deal** t every man against his	898
	2:11 Judah hath **dealt** t, and an abomination is	898
	2:14 youth, against whom thou hast **dealt** t:	898
	2:15 none **deal** t against the wife of his youth.	898
	2:16 take heed to your spirit, that ye **deal** not t.	898

TREACHERY (1) [TREACHEROUS, TREACHEROUSLY]

2Ki	9:23 said to Ahaziah, There is t, O Ahaziah.	4820

TREAD (33) [TREADER, TREADERS, TREADETH, TREADING, TRODDEN, TRODE]

Dt	11:24 soles of your feet shall t shall be yours:	1869
	11:25 you upon all the land that ye shall t upon,	1869
	33:29 and thou shalt t upon their high places.	1869
Jos	1: 3 that the sole of your foot shall t **upon,**	1869
1Sa	5: 5 t on the threshold of Dagon in Ashdod	1869
Job	24:11 *and their* winepresses, and suffer thirst.	
	40:12 and t **down** the wicked in their place.	1915
Ps	7: 5 let him t **down** my life upon the earth,	7429
	44: 5 through thy name will we t them **under**	947
	60:12 for he *it is that* shall t **down** our enemies.	947
	91:13 Thou shalt t upon the lion and adder;	1869
	108:13 for he *it is that* shall t **down** our enemies.	947
Isa	1:12 required this at your hand, to t my courts?	7429
	10: 6 t them **down** like the mire of	4823+7760
	14:25 upon my mountains t him **under foot**:	947
	16:10 the treaders shall t out no wine in *their*	1869
	26: 6 The foot shall t it **down,** *even* the feet of	7429
	63: 3 for I will t them in mine anger,	1869
	63: 6 I will t **down** the people in mine anger,	947
Jer	25:30 as they that t *the grapes,* against all	1869
	48:33 none shall t *with* shouting; *their* shouting	1869
Eze	26:11 the hoofs of his horses shall he t **down**	7429
	34:18 must t **down** with your feet the residue	7429
Da	7:23 shall t it **down,** and break it in pieces.	1759
Hos	10:11 *and* loveth to t **out** *the corn;* but I passed	1758
Mic	1: 3 and t upon the high places of the earth.	1869
	5: 5 when he shall t in our palaces, then	1869
	6:15 thou shalt t the olives, but thou shalt not	1869
Na	3:14 into clay, and t the morter, make strong	7429
Zec	10: 5 shall be as mighty *men,* which t **down**	947
Mal	4: 3 ye shall t **down** the wicked; for they shall	6072
Lk	10:19 I give unto you power to t **on** serpents and	3961
Rev	11: 2 the holy city shall they t **under foot** forty	3961

TREADER (1) [TREAD]
Am 9:13 and the **t** of grapes him that soweth seed; 1869

TREADERS (1) [TREAD]
Isa 16:10 the **t** shall tread out no wine in *their* 1869

TREADETH (10) [TREAD]
Dt 25: 4 muzzle the ox when he **t** out *the corn.* 1758
Job 9: 8 and **t** upon the waves of the sea. 1869
Isa 41:25 as *upon* morter, and as the potter **t** clay. 7429
 63: 2 garments like him that **t** in the winefat? 1869
Am 4:13 **t** upon the high places of the earth, 1869
Mic 5: 6 land, and when he **t** within our borders. 1869
 5: 8 both **t down,** and teareth in pieces, 7429
1Co 9: 9 the mouth of the ox that **t out the corn.** *248*
1Ti 5:18 not muzzle the ox that **t out the corn.** *248*
Rev 19:15 he **t** the winepress of the fierceness and *3961*

TREADING (4) [TREAD]
Ne 13:15 In those days saw I in Judah *some* **t** wine 1869
Isa 7:25 forth of oxen, and for the **t** of lesser cattle. 4823
 22: 5 of **t down,** and of perplexity by the Lord 4001
Am 5:11 as your **t** *is* upon the poor, 1318

TREASON (5) [TRAITOR]
1Ki 16:20 acts of Zimri, and his **t** that he wrought, 7195
2Ki 11:14 rent her clothes, and cried, **T,** Treason. 7195
 11:14 rent her clothes, and cried, Treason, **T.** 7195
2Ch 23:13 rent her clothes, and said, **T,** Treason. 7195
 23:13 rent her clothes, and said, Treason, **T.** 7195

TREASURE (37) [TREASURED, TREASURER, TREASURERS, TREASURES, TREASUREST, TREASURIES, TREASURY]
Ge 43:23 father, hath given you **t** in your sacks: 4301
Ex 1:11 they built for Pharaoh **t** cities, Pithom and 4543
 19: 5 ye shall be a **peculiar t** unto me above all 5459
Dt 28:12 The Lord shall open unto thee his good **t,** 214
1Ch 29: 8 *them* to the **t** of the house of the Lord, 214
Ezr 2:69 They gave after their ability unto the **t** of 214
 5:17 let there be search made in the king's **t** 1596
 7:20 bestow *it* out of the king's **t** house. 1596
Ne 7:70 Tirshatha gave to the **t** a thousand drams 214
 7:71 of the chief of the fathers gave to the **t** house. 214
 10:38 our God, to the chambers, unto the **t.** 214
Ps 17:14 whose belly thou fillest *with* thy hid **t** they NIH
 135: 4 unto himself, *and* Israel for his **peculiar t.** 5459
Pr 15: 6 *In* the house of the righteous *is* much **t:** 2633
 15:16 little with the fear of the Lord than great **t** 214
 21:20 *There is* **t** to be desired and oil in 214
Ecc 2: 8 the **peculiar t** of kings and of 5459
Isa 33: 6 of salvation: the fear of the Lord *is* his **t.** 214
Eze 22:25 they have taken the **t** and precious things; 2633
Da 1: 2 he brought the vessels *into* the **t** house of 214
Hos 13:15 he shall spoil the **t** of all pleasant vessels. 214
Mt 6:21 where your **t** is, there will your heart be 2344
 12:35 A good man out of the good **t** of the heart 2344
 12:35 an evil man out of the evil **t** bringeth forth 2344
 13:44 kingdom of heaven is like unto **t** hid in 2344
 13:52 which bringeth forth out of his **t** *things* 2344
 19:21 the poor, and thou shalt have **t** in heaven: 2344
Mk 10:21 the poor, and thou shalt have **t** in heaven: 2344
Lk 6:45 A good man out of the good **t** of his heart 2344
 6:45 an evil man out of the evil **t** of his heart 2344
 12:21 So *is* he that **layeth up t** for himself, 2343
 12:33 a **t** in the heavens that faileth not, where 2344
 12:34 where your **t** is, there will your heart be 2344
 18:22 the poor, and thou shalt have **t** in heaven: 2344
Ac 8:27 who had the charge of all her **t,** and had 1047
2Co 4: 7 But we have this **t** in earthen vessels, 2344
Jas 5: 3 ye have **heaped t together** for the last 2343

TREASURED (1) [TREASURE]
Isa 23:18 it shall not be **t** nor laid up; for her 686

TREASURER (2) [TREASURE]
Ezr 1: 8 forth by the hand of Mithredath the **t,** 1489
Isa 22:15 get thee unto this **t,** *even* unto Shebna, 5532

TREASURERS (4) [TREASURE]
Ezr 7:21 do make a decree to all the **t** which *are* 1490
Ne 13:13 I **made t** over the treasuries, Shelemiah 686
Da 3: 2 and the captains, the judges, the **t,** 1411
 3: 3 and captains, the judges, the **t,** 1411

TREASURES (62) [TREASURE]
Dt 32:34 store with me, *and* sealed up among my **t?** 214
 33:19 of the seas, and *of* **t** hid in the sand. 8226
1Ki 7:51 did he put among the **t** of the house of 214
 14:26 he took away the **t** of the house of 214
 14:26 of the Lord, and the **t** of the king's house; 214
 15:18 the gold that were left in the **t** of the house 214
 15:18 **t** of the king's house, and delivered them 214
2Ki 12:18 all the gold that was found in the **t** of 214
 14:14 in the **t** of the king's house, and hostages, 214
 16: 8 in the **t** of the king's house, and sent *it for* 214
 18:15 the Lord, and in the **t** of the king's house. 214
 20:13 his armour, and all that was found in his **t:** 214
 20:15 there is nothing among my **t** that I have not 214
 24:13 he carried out thence all the **t** of the house 214
 24:13 the **t** of the king's house, and cut in pieces 214
1Ch 26:20 Ahijah *was* over the **t** of the house of God, 214
 26:20 and over the **t** of the dedicate *things.* 214
 26:22 *which were* over the **t** of the house of 214
 26:24 the son of Moses, *was* ruler of the **t.** 214

1Ch 26:26 his brethren *were* over all the **t** of 214
 27:25 over the king's **t** *was* Azmaveth the son of 214
2Ch 5: 1 put he among the **t** of the house of God. 214
 8:15 concerning any matter, or concerning the **t.** 214
 12: 9 took away the **t** of the house of the Lord, 214
 12: 9 of the Lord, and the **t** of the king's house; 214
 16: 2 gold out of the **t** of the house of the Lord 214
 25:24 the **t** of the king's house, the hostages also, 214
 36:18 the **t** of the house of the Lord, 214
 36:18 and the **t** of the king, and of his princes; 214
Ezr 6: 1 where the **t** were laid up in Babylon. 1596
Ne 12:44 appointed over the chambers for the **t,** 214
Job 3:21 and dig for it more than for **hid t;** 4301
 38:22 Hast thou entered into the **t** of the snow? 214
 38:22 snow? or hast thou seen the **t** of the hail, 214
Pr 2: 4 silver, and searchest for her as *for* **hid t;** 4301
 8:21 to inherit substance; and I will fill their **t.** 214
 10: 2 **T** of wickedness profit nothing: 214
 21: 6 getting of **t** by a lying tongue *is* a vanity 214
Isa 2: 7 gold, neither *is there any* end of their **t;** 214
 10:13 have robbed their **t,** and I have put down 6259
 30: 6 their **t** upon the bunches of camels, to a 214
 39: 2 his armour, and all that was found in his **t:** 214
 39: 4 there is nothing among my **t** that I have not 214
 45: 3 I will give thee the **t** of darkness, 214
Jer 10:13 and bringeth forth the wind out of his **t.** 214
 15:13 thy **t** will I give to the spoil without price, 214
 17: 3 give thy substance *and* all thy **t** to the spoil, 214
 20: 5 all the **t** of the kings of Judah will I give into 214
 41: 8 for we have **t** in the field, *of* wheat, 4301
 48: 7 thou hast trusted in thy works and in thy **t,** 214
 49: 4 that trusted in her **t,** *saying,* Who shall 214
 50:37 a sword *is* upon her **t;** and they shall be 214
 51:13 abundant in **t,** thine end is come, 214
 51:16 and bringeth forth the wind out of his **t.** 214
Eze 28: 4 and hast gotten gold and silver into thy **t:** 214
Da 11:43 he shall have power over the **t** of gold and 4362
Mic 6:10 Are there yet the **t** of wickedness *in* 214
Mt 2:11 and when they had opened their **t,** 2344
 6:19 Lay not up for yourselves **t** upon earth, 2344
 6:20 But lay up for yourselves **t** in heaven, 2344
Col 2: 3 In whom are hid all the **t** of wisdom and 2344
Heb 11:26 Christ greater riches than the **t** in Egypt: 2344

TREASUREST (1) [TREASURE]
Ro 2: 5 impenitent heart **t** up unto thyself wrath 2343

TREASURIES (10) [TREASURE]
1Ch 9:26 the chambers and **t** of the house of God. 214
 28:11 thereof, and of the upper chambers 1597
 28:12 of the **t** of the house of God, and of 214
 28:12 of God, and of the **t** of the dedicate *things:* 214
2Ch 32:27 he made himself **t** for silver, and for gold, 214
Ne 13:12 and the new wine and the oil unto the **t.** 214
 13:13 I made treasurers over the **t,** Shelemiah 214
Est 3: 9 the business, to bring *it* into the king's **t** 1595
 4: 7 to pay to the king's **t** for the Jews, 1595
Ps 135: 7 the rain; he bringeth the wind out of his **t.** 214

TREASURY (9) [TREASURE]
Jos 6:19 they shall come *into* the **t** of the Lord. 214
 6:24 they put *into* the **t** of the house of 214
Jer 38:11 *into* the house of the king under the **t,** 214
Mt 27: 6 It is not lawful for to put them into the **t,** 2878
Mk 12:41 And Jesus sat over against the **t,** 1049
 12:41 how the people cast money into the **t:** 1049
 12:43 than all they which have cast into the **t:** 1049
Lk 21: 1 the rich *men* casting their gifts into the **t.** 1049
Jn 8:20 These words spake Jesus in the **t,** as he 1049

TREATISE (1)
Ac 1: 1 The former **t** have I made, O Theophilus, 3056

TREATY See LEAGUE

TREE (201) [TREES]
Ge 1:11 *and* the fruit **t** yielding fruit after his kind, 6086
 1:12 the **t** yielding fruit, whose seed *was* in 6086
 1:29 upon the face of all the earth, and every **t,** 6086
 1:29 the which *is* the fruit of a **t** yielding seed; 6086
 2: 9 grow every **t** that is pleasant to the sight, 6086
 2: 9 **t** of life also in the midst of the garden, 6086
 2: 9 and the **t** of knowledge of good and evil. 6086
 2:16 every **t** of the garden thou mayest freely 6086
 2:17 the **t** of the knowledge of good and evil, 6086
 3: 1 Ye shall not eat of every **t** of the garden? 6086
 3: 3 the fruit of the **t** which *is* in the midst of 6086
 3: 6 when the woman saw that the **t** *was* good 6086
 3: 6 a **t** to be desired to make *one* wise, she 6086
 3:11 Hast thou eaten of the **t,** whereof I 6086
 3:12 me, she gave me of the **t,** and I did eat. 6086
 3:17 eaten of the **t,** of which I commanded 6086
 3:22 take also of the **t** of life, and eat, 6086
 3:24 way, to keep the way of the **t** of life. 6086
 18: 4 your feet, and rest yourselves under the **t:** 6086
 18: 8 he stood by them under the **t,** and they 6086
 30:37 and of the hazel and **chesnut t;** 6196
 40:19 from off thee, and shall hang thee on a **t;** 6086
Ex 9:25 of the field, and brake every **t** of the field. 6086
 10: 5 shall eat every **t** which groweth for you 6086
 15:25 the Lord shewed him a **t,** *which* when he 6086
Lev 27:30 *or* of the fruit of the **t,** *is* the Lord's: 6086
Nu 6: 4 he eat nothing that is made of the vine **t,** 1612
Dt 12: 2 upon the hills, and under every green **t:** 6086
 19: 5 a stroke with the axe to cut down the **t,** 6086
 20:19 thou shalt not cut them down (for the **t** of 6086

Dt 21:22 put to death, and thou hang him on a **t:** 6086
 21:23 body shall not remain all night upon the **t,** 6086
 22: 6 to be before thee in the way in any **t,** 6086
 24:20 When thou beatest thine **olive t,** thou 2132
Jos 8:29 the king of Ai he hanged on a **t** until 6086
 8:29 should take him carcase down from the **t,** 6086
Jdg 4: 5 she dwelt under the **palm t** of Deborah 8560
 9: 8 they said unto the **olive t,** Reign thou 2132
 9: 9 the **olive t** said unto them, Should I leave 2132
 9:10 the trees said to the **fig t,** Come thou, 8384
 9:11 the **fig t** said unto them, Should I forsake 8384
1Sa 14: 2 a **pomegranate t** which *is* in Migron: 7416
 22: 6 (now Saul abode in Gibeah under a **t** in 815
 31:13 buried *them* under a **t** at Jabesh, 815
1Ki 4:25 man under his vine and under his **fig t,** 8384
 4:33 from the **cedar t** that *is* in Lebanon even 730
 6:23 oracle he made two cherubims *of* olive **t,** 6086
 6:31 of the oracle he made doors of olive **t:** 6086
 6:32 The two doors also *were* of olive **t;** 6086
 6:33 for the door of the temple posts of olive **t,** 6086
 6:34 the two doors *were* of fir **t:** the two leaves 6086
 14:23 every high hill, and under every green **t.** 6086
 19: 4 came and sat down under a **juniper t.** 7574
 19: 5 as he lay and slept under a **juniper t,** 7574
2Ki 3:19 shall fell every good **t,** and stop all wells 6086
 16: 4 and on the hills, and under every green **t.** 6086
 17:10 every high hill, and under every green **t:** 6086
 18:31 every one of his **fig t,** and drink ye every 8384
2Ch 3: 5 the greater house he cieled with fir **t,** 6086
 28: 4 and on the hills, and under every green **t.** 6086
Est 2:23 therefore they were both hanged on a **t:** 6086
Job 14: 7 For there is hope of a **t,** if it be cut down, 6086
 19:10 and mine hope hath he removed like a **t.** 6086
 24:20 and wickedness shall be broken as a **t.** 6086
Ps 1: 3 he shall be like a **t** planted by the rivers of 6086
 37:35 and spreading himself like a green **bay t.** 249
 52: 8 I *am* like a green **olive t** in the house of 2132
 92:12 righteous shall flourish like the **palm t:** 8558
Pr 3:18 She *is* a **t** of life to them that lay hold 6086
 11:30 The fruit of the righteous *is* a **t** of life; 6086
 13:12 *when* the desire cometh, *it is* a **t** of life. 6086
 15: 4 A wholesome tongue *is* a **t** of life: 6086
 27:18 Whoso keepeth the **fig t** shall eat the fruit 8384
Ecc 11: 3 if the **t** fall toward the south, or toward 6086
 11: 3 *in* the place where the **t** falleth, there it 6086
 12: 5 the **almond t** shall flourish, 8247
SS 2: 3 As the **apple t** among the trees of 8598
 2:13 The **fig t** putteth forth her green figs, 8384
 7: 7 This thy stature is like to a **palm t,** 8558
 7: 8 I will go up to the **palm t,** I will take 8558
 8: 5 I raised thee up under the **apple t:** there 8598
Isa 6:13 as a **teil t,** and as an oak, whose substance 424
 17: 6 as the shaking of an **olive t,** two *or* 2132
 24:13 *shall be* as the shaking of an **olive t,** 2132
 34: 4 vine, and as a falling *fig* from the **fig t.** 8384
 36:16 every one *of* his **fig t,** and drink ye every 8384
 40:20 no oblation chooseth a **t** *that* will not rot; 6086
 41:19 the **shittah t,** and the myrtle, and the oil 7848
 41:19 shittah tree, and the myrtle, and the oil **t;** 6086
 41:19 I will set in the desert the **fir t,** 1265
 41:19 *and* the pine, and the **box t** together: 8391
 44:19 shall I fall down to the stock of a **t?** 6086
 44:23 mountains, O forest, and every **t** therein: 6086
 55:13 of the thorn shall come up the **fir t,** 1265
 55:13 of the brier shall come up the **myrtle t:** 1918
 56: 3 let the eunuch say, Behold, I *am* a dry **t.** 6086
 57: 5 yourselves with idols under every green **t,** 6086
 60:13 **fir t,** the pine tree, and the box together, 1265
 60:13 fir tree, the **pine t,** and the box together, 8410
 65:22 for as the days of a **t** *are* the days of my 6086
 66:17 in the gardens behind one **t** in the midst, NIH
Jer 1:11 And I said, I see a rod of an **almond t.** 8247
 2:20 and under every green **t** thou wanderest, 6086
 3: 6 high mountain and under every green **t,** 6086
 3:13 to the strangers under every green **t,** 6086
 8:13 figs on the **fig t,** and the leaf shall fade; 8384
 10: 3 for *one* cutteth a **t** out of the forest, 6086
 10: 5 They *are* upright as the **palm t,** 8560
 11:16 A green **olive t,** fair, *and* of goodly fruit: 2132
 11:19 *saying,* Let us destroy the **t** with the fruit 6086
 17: 8 he shall be as a **t** planted by the waters, 6086
Eze 6:13 under every green **t,** and under every 6086
 15: 2 What is the vine **t** more than any tree, 6086
 15: 2 What is the vine tree more than any **t,** 6086
 15: 6 As the vine **t** among the trees of the forest, 6086
 17: 5 by great waters, *and* set it *as* a **willow t.** 6851
 17:24 The Lord have brought down the high **t,** 6086
 17:24 have exalted the low **t,** have dried up 6086
 17:24 have dried up the green **t,** and have made 6086
 17:24 and have made the dry **t** to flourish: 6086
 20:47 it shall devour every green **t** in thee, 6086
 20:47 every green tree in thee, and every dry **t:** 6086
 21:10 contemneth the rod of my son, *as every* **t.** 6086
 31: 8 nor any **t** in the garden of God was like 6086
 34:27 the **t** of the field shall yield her fruit, 6086
 36:30 I will multiply the fruit of the **t,** 6086
 41:18 so that a **palm t** *was* between a cherub 8561
 41:19 *was* toward the **palm t** on the one side, 8561
 41:19 face of a young lion toward the **palm t** 8561
Da 4:10 a **t** in the midst of the earth, and the height 363
 4:11 The **t** grew, and was strong, and the height 363
 4:14 Hew down the **t,** and cut off his branches, 363
 4:20 The **t** that thou sawest, which grew, 363
 4:23 saying, Hew the **t** down, and destroy it; 363
 4:26 to leave the stump of the **t** roots, 363

Hos	9:10 the firstripe in the **fig t** at her first time:	8384
	14: 6 his beauty shall be as the **olive t**, and his	2132
	14: 8 I *am* like a green **fir t**. From me is thy	1265
Joel	1: 7 laid my vine waste, and barked my **fig t**:	8384
	1:12 vine is dried up, and the **fig t** languisheth;	8384
	1:12 the **pomegranate t**, the palm tree also,	7416
	1:12 the **palm t** also, and the apple tree,	8558
	1:12 the palm tree also, and the **apple t**,	8598
	2:22 for the t beareth her fruit, the fig tree and	6086
	2:22 the **fig t** and the vine do yield their	8384
Mic	4: 4 man under his vine and under his **fig t**;	8384
Hab	3:17 Although the **fig t** shall not blossom,	8384
Hag	2:19 the **fig t**, and the pomegranate,	8384
	2:19 and the pomegranate, and the olive, the	6086
Zec	3:10 under the vine and under the **fig t**.	8384
	11: 2 Howl, **fir t**; for the cedar is fallen; because	1265
Mt	3:10 every t which bringeth not forth good fruit	*1186*
	7:17 so every good **t** bringeth forth good fruit;	*1186*
	7:17 but a corrupt **t** bringeth forth evil fruit.	*1186*
	7:18 A good **t** cannot bring forth evil fruit,	*1186*
	7:18 neither *can* a corrupt **t** bring forth good	*1186*
	7:19 Every **t** that bringeth not forth good fruit	*1186*
	12:33 Either make the **t** good, and his fruit good;	*1186*
	12:33 or else make the **t** corrupt, and his fruit	*1186*
	12:33 corrupt: for the **t** is known by *his* fruit.	*1186*
	13:32 becometh a **t**, so that the birds of the air	*1186*
	21:19 And when he saw a **fig t** in the way,	*4808*
	21:19 And presently the **fig t** withered away.	*4808*
	21:20 How soon is the **fig t** withered away!	*4808*
	21:21 only do this which is done to the **fig t**,	*4808*
	24:32 Now learn a parable of the **fig t**; When	*4808*
Mk	11:13 And seeing a **fig t** afar off having leaves,	*4808*
	11:20 they saw the **fig t** dried up from the roots.	*4808*
	11:21 the **fig t** which thou cursedst is withered	*4808*
	13:28 Now learn a parable of the **fig t**; When	*4808*
Lk	3: 9 every t therefore which bringeth not forth	*1186*
	6:43 For a good **t** bringeth not forth corrupt	*1186*
	6:43 neither doth a corrupt **t** bring forth good	*1186*
	6:44 For every **t** is known by his own fruit.	*1186*
	13: 6 A certain *man* had a **fig t** planted in his	*4808*
	13: 7 years I come seeking fruit on this **fig t**,	*4808*
	13:19 and it grew, and waxed a great t;	*1186*
	17: 6 might say unto this **sycamine t**, Be thou	*4807*
	19: 4 climbed up into a **sycomore t** to see him:	*4809*
	21:29 parable; Behold the **fig t**, and all the trees;	*4808*
	23:31 For if they do these *things* in a green **t**,	*3586*
Jn	1:48 thou wast under the **fig t**, I saw thee.	*4808*
	1:50 I saw thee under the **fig t**, believest thou?	*4808*
Ac	5:30 Jesus, whom ye slew and hanged on a **t**.	*3586*
	10:39 whom they slew and hanged on a **t**:	*3586*
	13:29 they took *him* down from the **t**,	*3586*
Ro	11:17 thou, being a **wild olive t**, wert graffed in	65
	11:17 of the root and fatness of the **olive t**;	*1636*
	11:24 out of the **olive t which is wild** by nature,	65
	11:24 contrary to nature into a **good olive t**,	*2565*
	11:24 be graffed into their own **olive t**?	*1636*
Gal	3:13 Cursed *is* every one that hangeth on a **t**:	*3586*
Jas	3:12 Can the **fig t**, my brethren, bear olive	*4808*
1Pe	2:24 bare our sins in his own body on the **t**,	*3586*
Rev	2: 7 will I give to eat of the **t** of life,	*3586*
	6:13 *even* as a **fig t** casteth her untimely figs,	*4808*
	7: 1 on the earth, nor on the sea, nor on any **t**.	*1186*
	9: 4 neither any green *thing*, neither any **t**;	*1186*
	22: 2 side of the river, *was there* the **t** of life,	*3586*
	22: 2 the leaves of the **t** *were* for the healing of	*3586*
	22:14 that they may have right to the **t** of life,	*3586*

TREES (157) [TREE]

Ge	2: 9 We may eat of the fruit of the **t** of	6086
	3: 8 LORD God amongst the **t** of the garden.	6086
	23:17 and all the **t** that *were* in the field,	6086
Ex	10:15 the fruit of the **t** which the hail had left:	6086
	10:15 remained not any green thing in the **t**,	6086
	15:27 of water, and threescore and ten **palm t**:	8558
Lev	19:23 have planted all *manner of* **t** for food,	6086
	23:40 on the first day the boughs of goodly **t**,	6086
	23:40 branches of **palm t**, and the boughs of	8558
	23:40 the boughs of thick **t**, and willows of	6086
	26: 4 and the **t** of the field shall yield their fruit.	6086
	26:20 neither shall the **t** of the land yield their	6086
Nu	24: 6 as the **t of lign aloes** *which* the LORD hath	174
	24: 6 *and* as **cedar t** beside the waters.	730
	33: 9 of water, and threescore and ten **palm t**;	8558
Dt	6:11 thou diggedst not, vineyards and **olive t**,	2132
	8: 8 and vines, and **fig t**, and pomegranates;	8384
	16:21 Thou shalt not plant thee a grove *of* any **t**	6086
	20:19 thou shalt not destroy the **t** thereof by	6086
	20:20 Only the **t** which thou knowest that they	6086
	20:20 thou knowest that they *be* not **t** for meat,	6086
	28:40 Thou shalt have **olive t** throughout all	2132
	28:42 All thy **t** and fruit of thy land shall	6086
	34: 3 of Jericho, the city of **palm t**, unto Zoar.	8558
Jos	10:26 slew them, and hanged them on five **t**:	6086
	10:26 they were hanging upon the **t** until	6086
	10:27 they took them down off the **t**,	6086
Jdg	1:16 went up out of the city of **palm t** with	8558
	3:13 and possessed the city of **palm t**.	8558
	9: 8 The **t** went forth on a time to anoint a	6086
	9: 9 man, and go to be promoted over the **t**?	6086
	9:10 the **t** said to the fig tree, Come thou,	6086
	9:11 and go to be promoted over the **t**?	6086
	9:12 said the **t** unto the vine, Come thou,	6086
	9:13 man, and go to be promoted over the **t**?	6086
	9:14 said all the **t** unto the bramble, Come	6086
	9:15 the bramble said unto the **t**, If in truth ye	6086

Jdg	9:48 cut down a bough from the **t**, and took it,	6086
2Sa	5:11 and cedar **t**, and carpenters, and masons:	6086
	5:23 upon them over against the **mulberry t**.	1057
	5:24 of a going in the tops of the **mulberry t**,	1057
1Ki	4:33 he spake of **t**, from the cedar tree that *is*	6086
	5: 6 command thou that they hew me **cedar t**	730
	5:10 So Hiram gave Solomon cedar **t** and	6086
	5:10 and fir **t** *according to* all his desire.	6086
	6:29 cherubims and **palm t** and open flowers,	8561
	6:32 cherubims and **palm t** and open flowers,	8561
	6:32 the cherubims, and upon the **palm t**.	8561
	6:35 and **palm t** and open flowers:	8561
	7:36 he graved cherubims, lions, and **palm t**,	8561
	9:11 Tyre had furnished Solomon with cedar **t**	6086
	9:11 Solomon with cedar trees and fir **t**,	6086
	10:11 in from Ophir great plenty of almug **t**,	6086
	10:12 the king made *of* the almug **t** pillars for	6086
	10:12 there came no such almug **t**, nor were	6086
	10:27 cedars made he *to be* as the **sycomore t**	8256
2Ki	3:25 wells of water, and felled all the good **t**:	6086
	19:23 will cut down the tall **cedar t** thereof,	730
	19:23 trees thereof, *and* the choice **fir t** thereof:	1265
1Ch	14:14 upon them over against the **mulberry t**,	1057
	14:15 of going in the tops of the **mulberry t**,	1057
	16:33 shall the **t** of the wood sing out at	6086
	22: 4 Also cedar **t** in abundance:	6086
	27:28 over the **olive t** and the sycomore trees	2132
	27:28 **sycomore t** that *were* in the low plains	8256
2Ch	1:15 **cedar t** made he as the sycomore trees	730
	1:15 cedar trees made he as the **sycomore t**	8256
	2: 8 Send me also cedar **t**, fir trees,	6086
	2: 8 **fir t**, and algum trees, out of Lebanon:	1265
	2: 8 fir trees, and **algum t**, out of Lebanon.	418
	3: 5 and set thereon **palm t** and chains.	8561
	9:10 brought algum **t** and precious stones.	6086
	9:11 the king made *of* the algum **t** terraces to	6086
	9:27 **cedar t** made he as the sycomore trees	730
	9:27 cedar trees made he as the **sycomore t**	8256
	28:15 the city of **palm t**, to their brethren:	8558
Ezr	3: 7 to bring cedar **t** from Lebanon to the sea	6086
Ne	8:15 palm branches, and branches of thick **t**,	6086
	9:25 and oliveyards, and fruit **t** in abundance:	6086
	10:35 the firstfruits of all fruit of all **t**, year by	6086
	10:37 the fruit of all *manner of* **t**, of wine and	6086
Job	40:21 He lieth under the **shady t**, in the covert	6628
	40:22 The **shady t** cover him *with* their shadow	6628
Ps	74: 5 as he had lifted up axes upon the thick **t**.	6086
	78:47 hail, and their **sycomore t** with frost.	8256
	96:12 shall all the **t** of the wood rejoice	6086
	104:16 The **t** of the LORD are full *of sap*;	6086
	104:17 *as for* the stork, the **fir t** *are* her house.	1265
	105:33 He smote their vines also and their **fig t**;	8384
	105:33 fig trees; and brake the **t** of their coasts.	6086
	148: 9 all hills; fruitful **t**, and all cedars:	6086
Ecc	2: 5 I planted **t** in them of all *kind of* fruits:	6086
	2: 6 therewith the wood that bringeth forth **t**:	6086
SS	2: 3 the apple tree among the **t** of the wood,	6086
	4:14 and cinnamon, with all **t** of frankincense;	6086
Isa	7: 2 as the **t** of the wood are moved with	6086
	10:19 the rest of the **t** of his forest shall be few,	6086
	14: 8 the **fir t** rejoice at thee, *and* the cedars of	1265
	37:24 thereof, *and* the choice **fir t** thereof:	1265
	44:14 for himself among the **t** of the forest:	6086
	55:12 all the **t** of the field shall clap *their* hands.	6086
	61: 3 they might be called **t** of righteousness,	352
Jer	5:17 they shall eat up thy vines and thy **fig t**:	8384
	6: 6 Hew ye down **t**, and cast a mount against	6097
	7:20 upon the **t** of the field, and upon the fruit	6086
	17: 2 their groves by the green **t** upon the high	6086
Eze	15: 2 than a branch which is among the **t** of	6086
	15: 6 As the vine tree among the **t** of the forest,	6086
	17:24 all the **t** of the field shall know that I	6086
	20:28 all the thick **t**, and they offered there their	6086
	27: 5 have made all thy *ship* boards of **fir t**	1265
	31: 4 sent out her little rivers unto all the **t** of	6086
	31: 5 was exalted above all the **t** of the field,	6086
	31: 8 the **fir t** were not like his boughs,	1265
	31: 8 the **chesnut t** were not like his branches:	6196
	31: 9 so that all the **t** of Eden, that *were* in	6086
	31:14 To the end that none of all the **t** by	6086
	31:14 neither their **t** stand up in their height,	352
	31:15 and all the **t** of the field fainted for him.	6086
	31:16 all the **t** of Eden, the choice and best of	6086
	31:18 and in greatness among the **t** of Eden?	6086
	31:18 shalt thou be brought down with the **t** of	6086
	40:16 and upon *each* post were **palm t**.	8561
	40:22 and their arches, and their **palm t**,	8561
	40:26 it had **palm t**, one on this side,	8561
	40:31 and **palm t** *were* upon the posts thereof:	8561
	40:34 **palm t** *were* upon the posts thereof, on	8561
	40:37 **palm t** *were* upon the posts thereof, on	8561
	41:18 it *was* made *with* cherubims and **palm t**,	8561
	41:20 door *were* cherubims and **palm t** made,	8561
	41:25 of the temple, cherubims and **palm t**,	8561
	41:26 **palm t** on the one side and on the other	8561
	47: 7 at the bank of the river *were* very many **t**	6086
	47:12 and on that side, shall grow all **t** for meat,	6086
Hos	2:12 I will destroy her vines and her **fig t**,	8384
Joel	1:12 *even* all the **t** of the field, are withered:	6086
	1:19 the flame hath burnt all the **t** of the field.	
Am	4: 9 and your vineyards and your **fig t** and	8384
	4: 9 your fig trees and your **olive t** increased,	2132
Na	2: 3 and the **fir t** shall be terribly shaken.	
	3:12 All thy strong holds *shall be like* **fig t** with	8384
Zec	1: 8 he stood among the **myrtle t** that *were* in	1918

Zec	1:10 the man that stood among the **myrtle t**	1918
	1:11 the LORD that stood among the **myrtle t**,	1918
	4: 3 two **olive t** by it, one upon the right *side*	2132
	4:11 What *are* these two **olive t** upon the right	2132
Mt	3:10 also the axe is laid unto the root of the **t**:	*1186*
	21: 8 others cut down branches from the **t**,	*1186*
Mk	8:24 and said, I see men as **t**, walking.	*1186*
	11: 8 and others cut down branches off the **t**,	*1186*
Lk	3: 9 also the axe is laid unto the root of the **t**:	*1186*
	21:29 parable; Behold the fig tree, and all the **t**;	*1186*
Jn	12:13 Took branches of **palm t**, and went forth	*5404*
Jude	1:12 whose fruit withereth, without fruit,	*1186*
Rev	7: 3 not the earth, neither the sea, nor the **t**,	*1186*
	8: 7 the third *part* of **t** was burnt up, and all	*1186*
	11: 4 These are the two **olive t**, and the two	*1636*

TREMBLE (29) [TREMBLED, TREMBLETH, TREMBLING]

Dt	2:25 shall **t**, and be in anguish because of thee.	7264
	20: 3 not, and do not **t**, neither be ye terrified	2648
Ezr	9: 3 of those that **t** at the commandment of	2730
Job	9: 6 out of her place, and the pillars thereof **t**.	6426
	26:11 The pillars of heaven **t** and are astonished	7322
Ps	60: 2 Thou hast **made** the earth to **t**; thou hast	7493
	99: 1 The LORD reigneth; let the people **t**:	7264
	114: 7 **T**, thou earth, at the presence of the Lord,	2342
Ecc	12: 3 when the keepers of the house shall **t**,	2111
Isa	5:25 hills did **t**, and their carcases were torn	7264
	14:16 *Is* this the man that **made** the earth to **t**,	7264
	32:11 **T**, ye *women* that are at ease; be troubled	2729
	64: 2 *that* the nations may **t** at thy presence!	7264
	66: 5 word of the LORD, ye that **t** at his word;	2730
Jer	5:22 will ye not **t** at my presence, which have	2342
	10:10 at his wrath the earth shall **t**,	7493
	33: 9 shall fear and **t** for all the goodness and	7264
	51:29 the land shall **t** and sorrow: for every	7493
Eze	26:16 **t** at every moment, and be astonished	2729
	26:18 Now shall the isles **t** *in* the day of thy fall;	7493
	32:10 they shall **t** at every moment, every man	2729
Da	6:26 in every dominion of my kingdom *men* **t**	2112
Hos	11:10 then the children shall **t** from the west.	2729
	11:11 They shall **t** as a bird out of Egypt, and as	2729
Joel	2: 1 let all the inhabitants of the land **t**:	7264
	2:10 quake before them; the heavens shall **t**:	7493
Am	8: 8 Shall not the land **t** for this, and every one	7264
Hab	3: 7 the curtains of the land of Midian did **t**.	7264
Jas	2:19 doest well: the devils also believe, and **t**.	*5425*

TREMBLED (21) [TREMBLE]

Ge	27:33 Isaac **t** very exceedingly, and said,	2729+2731
Ex	19:16 that all the people that *was* in the camp **t**.	2729
Jdg	5: 4 the earth **t**, and the heavens dropped,	7493
1Sa	4:13 for his heart **t** for the ark of God.	1961+2730
	14:15 they also **t**, and the earth quaked:	2729
	16: 4 the elders of the town **t** at his coming,	2729
	28: 5 he was afraid, and his heart greatly **t**.	2729
2Sa	22: 8 the earth shook and **t**; the foundations of	7493
Ezr	9: 4 were assembled unto me every one that **t**	2730
Ps	18: 7 the earth shook and **t**; the foundations	7493
	77:18 the world: the earth **t** and shook.	7264
	97: 4 the world: the earth saw, and **t**.	2342
Jer	4:24 lo, they **t**, and all the hills moved lightly.	7493
	8:16 the whole land **t** at the sound of	7493
Da	5:19 languages, **t** and feared before him:	2112
Hab	3:10 The mountains saw thee, *and* they **t**:	2342
	3:16 I heard, my belly **t**; my lips quivered	7264
	3:16 entered into my bones, and I **t** in myself,	7264
Mk	16: 8 for they **t** and were amazed:	2192+5156
Ac	7:32 the God of Jacob. Then Moses **t**,	1096+1790
	24:25 and judgment to come, Felix **t**,	1096+1719

TREMBLETH (4) [TREMBLE]

Job	37: 1 At this also my heart **t**, and is moved out	2729
Ps	104:32 He looketh on the earth, and it **t**:	7460
	119:120 My flesh **t** for fear of thee; and I am afraid	5568
Isa	66: 2 and of a contrite spirit, and **t** at my word.	2730

TREMBLING (26) [TREMBLE]

Ex	15:15 of Moab, **t** shall take hold upon them;	7461
Dt	28:65 the LORD shall give thee there a **t** heart,	7268
1Sa	13: 7 Gilgal, and all the people followed him **t**.	2729
	14:15 And there was **t** in the host, in the field,	2731
	14:15 the earth quaked: so it was a very great **t**.	2731
Ezr	10: 9 **t** because of *this* matter, and for the great	7460
Job	4:14 Fear came upon me, and **t**, which made	7461
	21: 6 I am afraid, and **t** taketh hold on my flesh.	6427
Ps	2:11 the LORD with fear, and rejoice with **t**.	7461
	55: 5 Fearfulness and **t** are come upon me,	7461
Isa	51:17 hast drunken the dregs of the cup of **t**,	8653
	51:22 have taken out of thine hand the cup of **t**,	8653
Jer	30: 5 We have heard a voice of **t**, of fear,	2731
Eze	12:18 drink thy water with **t** and with	7269
	26:16 they shall clothe themselves with **t**;	2731
Da	10:11 had spoken this word unto me, I stood **t**.	7460
Hos	13: 1 When Ephraim spake **t**, he exalted	7578
Zec	12: 2 I *will* make Jerusalem a cup of **t** unto all	7478
Mk	5:33 But the woman fearing and **t**,	*5141*
Lk	8:47 she came **t**, and falling down before him,	*5141*
Ac	9: 6 And he **t** and astonished said, Lord,	*5141*
	16:29 and came **t**, and fell down before Paul and	*1790*
1Co	2: 3 in weakness, and in fear, and in much **t**.	*5156*
2Co	7:15 how with fear and **t** you received him.	*5156*
Eph	6: 5 with fear and **t**, in singleness of your heart,	*5156*
Php	2:12 out your own salvation with fear and **t**.	*5156*

T

TRENCH (8)
1Sa	17:20 he came to the **t**, as the host was going	4570
	26: 5 Saul lay in the **t**, and the people pitched	4570
	26: 7 Saul lay sleeping within the **t**, and his	4570
2Sa	20:15 bank against the city, and it stood in the **t**:	2426
1Ki	18:32 he made a **t** about the altar, as great as	8585
	18:35 altar; and he filled the **t** also *with* water.	8585
	18:38 and licked up the water that *was* in the **t**.	8585
Lk	19:43 thine enemies shall cast a **t** about thee,	5482

TRESPASS (82) [TRESPASSED, TRESPASSES, TRESPASSING]
Ge	31:36 and said to Laban, What *is* my **t**?	6588
	50:17 the **t** of thy brethren, and their sin;	6588
	50:17 forgive the **t** of the servants of the God of	6588
Ex	22: 9 For all manner of **t**, *whether it be* for ox,	6588
Lev	5: 6 he shall bring his **t offering** unto the LORD	817
	5: 7 he shall bring for his **t**, which he hath	817
	5:15 If a soul **commit a t**, and sin	4603+4604
	5:15 he shall bring for his **t** unto the LORD a	817
	5:15 shekel of the sanctuary, for a **t offering**:	817
	5:16 for him with the ram of the **t offering**,	817
	5:18 for a **t offering**, unto the priest:	817
	5:19 *is* a **t offering**: he hath certainly trespassed	817
	6: 2 **commit a t** against the LORD,	4603+4604
	6: 5 it appertaineth, in the day of his **t offering**.	819
	6: 6 he shall bring his **t offering** unto	817
	6: 6 for a **t offering**, unto the priest:	817
	6:17 as *is* the sin offering, and as the **t offering**:	817
	7: 1 Likewise this *is* the law of the **t offering**:	817
	7: 2 burnt offering shall they kill the **t offering**,	817
	7: 5 by fire unto the LORD: it *is* a **t offering**.	817
	7: 7 As the sin offering *is*, so *is* the **t offering**:	817
	7:37 of the **t offering**, and of the consecrations,	817
	14:12 offer him for a **t offering**, and the log of oil,	817
	14:13 offering *is* the priest's, *so is* the **t offering**:	817
	14:14 take *some* of the blood of the **t offering**,	817
	14:17 right foot, upon the blood of the **t offering**:	817
	14:21 he shall take one lamb *for* a **t offering** to	817
	14:24 priest shall take the lamb of the **t offering**,	817
	14:25 he shall kill the lamb of the **t offering**,	817
	14:25 take *some* of the blood of the **t offering**,	817
	14:28 the place of the blood of the **t offering**:	817
	19:21 he shall bring his **t offering** unto	817
	19:21 *even* a ram for a **t offering**.	817
	19:22 **t offering** before the LORD for his sin	817
	26:40 with their **t** which they trespassed against	4604
Nu	5: 6 to **do a t** against the LORD,	4603+4604
	5: 7 shall recompense his **t** with the principal	817
	5: 8 have no kinsman to recompense the **t** unto,	817
	5: 8 *let* the **t** be recompensed unto the LORD,	817
	5:12 and **commit a t** against him,	4603+4604
	5:27 have **done t** against her husband,	4603+4604
	6:12 a lamb of the first year for a **t offering**:	817
	18: 9 of theirs, and every **t offering** of theirs,	817
	31:16 to commit **t** against the LORD in	4604
Jos	7: 1 children of Israel **committed a t**	4603+4604
	22:16 What *is* this that ye have committed	4604
	22:20 **commit a t** in the accursed thing,	4604
	22:31 have not **committed** this **t** against	4603+4604
1Sa	6: 3 but in any wise return him a **t offering**:	817
	6: 4 What *shall* be the **t offering** which we	817
	6: 8 gold, which ye return him *for* a **t offering**,	817
	6:17 returned *for* a **t offering** unto the LORD;	817
	25:28 pray thee, forgive the **t** of thine handmaid:	6588
1Ki	8:31 If any man **t** against his neighbour,	2398
2Ki	12:16 The **t** money and sin money was not	817
1Ch	21: 3 why will he be a **cause of t** to Israel?	819
2Ch	19:10 ye shall even warn them that they **t** not	816
	19:10 your brethren; this do, and ye shall not **t**.	816
	24:18 upon Judah and Jerusalem for this their **t**.	819
	28:13 to add *more* to our sins and to our **t**:	819
	28:13 for our **t** is great, and *there is* fierce wrath	819
	28:22 the time of his distress did he **t** yet more	4603
	33:19 his **t**, and the places wherein he built high	4604
Ezr	9: 2 and rulers hath been chief in this **t**.	4604
	9: 6 and our **t** is grown up unto the heavens.	819
	9: 7 *have* we *been* in a great **t** unto this day;	819
	9:13 us for our evil deeds, and for our great **t**,	819
	10:10 strange wives, to increase the **t** of Israel.	819
	10:19 *they offered* a ram of the flock for their **t**.	819
Eze	15: 8 because they have **committed a t**,	4603+4604
	17:20 will plead with him there *for* his **t** that he	4604
	18:24 in his **t** that he hath trespassed, and in his	4604
	20:27 in that they have **committed a t**	4603+4604
	40:39 and the sin offering and the **t offering**.	817
	42:13 and the sin offering, and the **t offering**;	817
	44:29 and the sin offering, and the **t offering**;	817
	46:20 where the priests shall boil the **t offering**	817
Da	9: 7 their **t** that they have trespassed against	4604
Mt	18:15 Moreover if thy brother shall **t against** thee,	264
Lk	17: 3 If thy brother **t** against thee, rebuke him;	264
	17: 4 if he **t** against thee seven times in a day,	264

TRESPASSED (15) [TRESPASS]
Lev	5:19 he hath **certainly t** against the LORD.	816+816
	26:40 their trespass which they **t** against me,	4603
Nu	5: 7 give *it* unto *him* against whom he **hath t**.	816
Dt	32:51 Because ye **t** against me among	4603
2Ch	26:18 go out of the sanctuary; for thou hast **t**;	4603
	29: 6 For our fathers have **t**, and done *that*	4603
	30: 7 which **t** against the LORD God of their	4603
	33:23 but Amon **t** more and more.	819
Ezr	10: 2 We have **t** against our God, and have	4603

TRESPASSES (12) [TRESPASS]
Ezr	9:15 behold, we *are* before thee in our **t**: for we	819
Ps	68:21 of such a one as goeth on still in his **t**.	817
Eze	39:26 all their **t** whereby they have trespassed	4604
Mt	6:14 if ye forgive men their **t**, your heavenly	3900
	6:15 But if ye forgive not men their **t**,	3900
	6:15 neither will your Father forgive your **t**.	3900
	18:35 forgive not every one his brother their **t**.	3900
Mk	11:25 is in heaven may forgive you your **t**.	3900
	11:26 Father which is in heaven forgive your **t**.	3900
2Co	5:19 not imputing their **t** unto them;	3900
Eph	2: 1 *hath* he quickened, who were dead in **t**	3900
Col	2:13 with him, having forgiven you all **t**;	3900

TRESPASSING (2) [TRESPASS]
Lev	6: 7 thing of all that he hath done in **t** therein.	819
Eze	14:13 sinneth against me by **t grievously**,	4603+4604

TRIAL (6) [TRY]
Job	9:23 he will laugh at the **t** of the innocent.	4531
Eze	21:13 Because *it is* a **t**, and what if *the sword*	974
2Co	8: 2 How that in a great **t** of affliction	1382
Heb	11:36 And others had **t** of *cruel* mockings and	3984
1Pe	1: 7 That the **t** of your faith, *being* much more	1383
	4:12 think it not strange concerning the **fiery t**	4451

TRIBE (242) [TRIBES]
Ex	31: 2 of Uri, the son of Hur, of the **t** of Judah:	4294
	31: 6 the son of Ahisamach, of the **t** of Dan;	4294
	35:30 of Uri, the son of Hur, of the **t** of Judah;	4294
	35:34 the son of Ahisamach, of the **t** of Dan.	4294
	38:22 of Uri, the son of Hur, of the **t** of Judah,	4294
	38:23 the **t** of Dan, an engraver, and a cunning	4294
Lev	24:11 the daughter of Dibri, of the **t** of Dan:)	4294
Nu	1: 4 with you there shall be a man of every **t**;	4294
	1: 5 of *the* **t** of Reuben; Elizur the son of	NIH
	1:21 *even* of the **t** of Reuben, were forty and	4294
	1:23 *even* of the **t** of Simeon, were fifty and	4294
	1:25 *even* of the **t** of Gad, were forty and	4294
	1:27 *even* of the **t** of Judah, were threescore	4294
	1:29 *even* of the **t** of Issachar, were fifty and	4294
	1:31 *even* of the **t** of Zebulun, were fifty and	4294
	1:33 *even* of the **t** of Ephraim, were forty	4294
	1:35 *even* of the **t** of Manasseh, were thirty	4294
	1:37 *even* of the **t** of Benjamin, were thirty and	4294
	1:39 *even* of the **t** of Dan, were threescore and	4294
	1:41 *even* of the **t** of Asher, were forty and	4294
	1:43 *even* of the **t** of Naphtali, were fifty and	4294
	1:47 the Levites after the **t** of their fathers were	4294
	1:49 Only thou shalt not number the **t** of Levi,	4294
	2: 5 next unto him *shall* be the **t** of Issachar:	4294
	2: 7 the **t** of Zebulun: and Eliab the son of	4294
	2:12 those which pitch by him *shall* be the **t** of	4294
	2:14 the **t** of Gad: and the captain of the sons	4294
	2:20 by him *shall* be the **t** of Manasseh:	4294
	2:22 the **t** of Benjamin: and the captain of	4294
	2:27 those that encamp by him *shall* be the **t** of	4294
	2:29 the **t** of Naphtali: and the captain of	4294
	3: 6 Bring the **t** of Levi near, and present them	4294
	4:18 Cut ye not off the **t** of the families of	7626
	7:12 the son of Amminadab, of the **t** of Judah:	4294
	10:15 over the host of the **t** of the children of	4294
	10:16 over the host of the **t** of the children of	4294
	10:19 over the host of the **t** of the children of	4294
	10:20 over the host of the **t** of the children of	4294
	10:23 over the host of the **t** of the children of	4294
	10:24 over the host of the **t** of the children of	4294
	10:26 over the host of the **t** of the children of	4294
	10:27 over the host of the **t** of the children of	4294
	13: 2 of every **t** of their fathers shall ye send a	4294
	13: 4 of the **t** of Reuben, Shammua the son of	4294
	13: 5 Of the **t** of Simeon, Shaphat the son of	4294
	13: 6 Of the **t** of Judah, Caleb the son of	4294
	13: 7 the **t** of Issachar, Igal the son of Joseph.	4294
	13: 8 Of the **t** of Ephraim, Oshea the son of Nun.	4294
	13: 9 Of the **t** of Benjamin, Palti the son of	4294
	13:10 Of the **t** of Zebulun, Gaddiel the son of	4294
	13:11 Of the **t** of Joseph, *namely*, of the tribe of	4294
	13:11 *namely*, of the **t** of Manasseh, Gaddi	4294
	13:12 Of the **t** of Dan, Ammiel the son of	4294
	13:13 Of the **t** of Asher, Sethur the son of	4294
	13:14 Of the **t** of Naphtali, Nahbi the son of	4294
	13:15 Of the **t** of Gad, Geuel the son of Machi.	4294
	18: 2 brethren also *of* the **t** of Levi, the tribe	4294
	18: 2 of thy father, bring thou with thee,	7626
	31: 4 Of every **t** a thousand, throughout all	4294
	31: 5 a thousand of *every* **t**, twelve thousand	4294
	31: 6 a thousand of *every* **t**, them and Phinehas	4294
	32:33 unto half the **t** of Manasseh the son of	7626
	34:13 unto the nine tribes, and *to* the half **t**:	4294
	34:14 For the **t** of the children of Reuben	4294
	34:14 the **t** of the children of Gad according to	4294
	34:14 half the **t** of Manasseh have received their	4294
	34:15 half **t** have received their inheritance on	4294
	34:18 ye shall take one prince of every **t**,	4294
	34:19 Of the **t** of Judah, Caleb the son of	4294
	34:20 Of the **t** of the children of Simeon,	4294
	34:21 Of the **t** of Benjamin, Elidad the son of	4294
	34:22 the prince of the **t** of the children of Dan,	4294
	34:23 for the **t** of the children of Manasseh,	4294
	34:24 the prince of the **t** of the children of	4294
	34:25 the prince of the **t** of the children of	4294
	34:26 the prince of the **t** of the children of	4294
	34:27 prince of the **t** of the children of Asher,	4294
	34:28 the prince of the **t** of the children of	4294
	36: 3 shall be put to the inheritance of the **t**	4294
	36: 4 of the **t** whereunto they are received:	4294
	36: 4 the inheritance of the **t** of our fathers.	4294
	36: 5 The **t** of the sons of Joseph hath said well.	4294
	36: 6 only to the family of the **t** of their father	4294
	36: 7 children of Israel remove from **t** to tribe:	4294
	36: 7 children of Israel remove from tribe to **t**:	4294
	36: 7 to the inheritance of the **t** of his fathers.	4294
	36: 8 that possesseth an inheritance in any **t** of	4294
	36: 8 be wife unto one of the family of the **t**	4294
	36: 9 remove from *one* **t** to another tribe;	4294
	36: 9 remove from *one* tribe to another **t**;	4294
	36:12 their inheritance remained in the **t** of	4294
Dt	1:23 I took twelve men of you, one of a **t**:	7626
	3:13 of Og, gave I unto the half **t** of Manasseh;	7626
	10: 8 At that time the LORD separated the **t** of	7626
	18: 1 priests the Levites, *and* all the **t** of Levi,	7626
	29: 8 Gadites, and to the half **t** of Manasseh.	7626
	29:18 you man, or woman, or family, or **t**,	7626
Jos	1:12 to half the **t** of Manasseh, spake Joshua,	7626
	3:12 the tribes of Israel, out of every **t** a man.	7626
	4: 2 out of the people, out of every **t** a man,	7626
	4: 4 children of Israel, out of every **t** a man:	7626
	4:12 of Gad, and half the **t** of Manasseh,	7626
	7: 1 the son of Zerah, of the **t** of Judah:	4294
	7:14 *that* the **t** which the LORD taketh shall	7626
	7:16 their tribes; and the **t** of Judah was taken:	4294
	7:18 son of Zerah, of the **t** of Judah, was taken.	4294
	12: 6 the Gadites, and the half **t** of Manasseh.	7626
	13: 7 nine tribes, and the half **t** of Manasseh,	7626
	13:14 Only unto the **t** of Levi he gave none	7626
	13:15 Moses gave unto the **t** of the children of	4294
	13:24 Moses gave *inheritance* unto the **t** of Gad	4294
	13:29 Moses gave *inheritance* unto the half **t** of	7626
	13:29 *this* was the possession of the half **t** of	7626
	13:33 unto the **t** of Levi Moses gave not *any*	7626
	14: 2 for the nine tribes, and *for* the half,	4294
	14: 3 and a half **t** on the *other* side Jordan:	4294
	15: 1 the lot of the **t** of the children of Judah	4294
	15:20 This *is* the inheritance of the **t** of	4294
	15:21 uttermost cities of the **t** of the children	4294
	16: 8 This *is* the inheritance of the **t** of	4294
	17: 1 was also a lot for the **t** of Manasseh;	4294
	18: 4 from among you three men for *each* **t**:	7626
	18: 7 and Reuben, and half the **t** of Manasseh,	7626
	18:11 the lot of the **t** of the children of Benjamin	4294
	18:21 Now the cities of the **t** of the children of	4294
	19: 1 *even* for the **t** of the children of Simeon	4294
	19: 8 This *is* the inheritance of the **t** of	4294
	19:23 This *is* the inheritance of the **t** of	4294
	19:24 the fifth lot came out for the **t** of	4294
	19:31 This *is* the inheritance of the **t** of	4294
	19:39 This *is* the inheritance of the **t** of	4294
	19:40 *And* the seventh lot came out for the **t** of	4294
	19:48 This *is* the inheritance of the **t** of	4294
	20: 8 upon the plain out of the **t** of Reuben,	4294
	20: 8 Ramoth in Gilead out of the **t** of Gad,	4294
	20: 8 Golan in Bashan out of the **t** of Manasseh.	4294
	21: 4 by lot out of the **t** of Judah, and out of	4294
	21: 4 out of the **t** of Simeon, and out of the	4294
	21: 4 out of the **t** of Benjamin, thirteen cities.	4294
	21: 5 lot out of the families of the **t** of Ephraim,	4294
	21: 5 out of the **t** of Dan, and out of the half	4294
	21: 5 out of the half **t** of Manasseh, ten cities.	4294
	21: 6 lot out of the families of the **t** of Issachar,	4294
	21: 6 out of the **t** of Asher, and out of the tribe	4294
	21: 6 out of the **t** of Naphtali, and out of the	4294
	21: 6 out of the half **t** of Manasseh in Bashan,	4294
	21: 7 their families *had* out of the **t** of Reuben,	4294
	21: 7 out of the **t** of Gad, and out of the tribe of	4294
	21: 7 and out of the **t** of Zebulun, twelve cities.	4294
	21: 9 they gave out of the **t** of the children of	4294
	21: 9 out of the **t** of the children of Simeon,	4294
	21:17 out of the **t** of Benjamin, Gibeon with her	4294
	21:20 cities of their lot out of the **t** of Ephraim.	4294
	21:23 out of the **t** of Dan, Eltekeh with her	4294
	21:25 out of the half **t** of Manasseh, Tanach	4294
	21:27 out of the *other* half **t** of Manasseh they	4294
	21:28 out of the **t** of Issachar, Kishon with her	4294
	21:30 out of the **t** of Asher, Mishal with her	4294
	21:32 out of the **t** of Naphtali, Kedesh in Galilee	4294
	21:34 rest of the Levites, out of the **t** of Zebulun,	4294
	21:36 out of the **t** of Reuben, Bezer with her	4294
	21:38 out of the **t** of Gad, Ramoth in Gilead	4294
	22: 1 the Gadites, and the half **t** of Manasseh,	4294
	22: 7 Now to the *one* half of the **t** of Manasseh	7626
	22: 9 Gad and the half **t** of Manasseh returned,	7626
	22:10 the half **t** of Manasseh built there an altar	7626
	22:11 the half **t** of Manasseh have built an altar	7626
	22:13 of Gad, and to the half **t** of Manasseh,	7626
	22:15 of Gad, and to the half **t** of Manasseh,	7626
	22:21 and the half **t** of Manasseh answered,	7626
Jdg	18: 1 in those days the **t** of the Danites sought	7626
	18:19 that thou be a priest unto a **t** and a family	7626
	18:30 his sons were priests to the **t** of Dan until	7626
	20:12 sent men through all the **t** of Benjamin,	7626
	21: 3 that there should be to day one **t** lacking	7626
	21: 6 There is one **t** cut off from Israel *this* day.	7626

Jdg	21:17	that a **t** be not destroyed out of Israel.	7626
	21:24	every man to his **t** and to his family,	7626
1Sa	9:21	of all the families of the **t** of Benjamin?	7626
	10:20	come near, the **t** of Benjamin was taken.	7626
	10:21	When he had caused the **t** of Benjamin to	7626
1Ki	7:14	*was* a widow's son of the **t** of Naphtali,	4294
	11:13	will give one **t** to thy son for David my	7626
	11:32	(But he shall have one **t** for my servant	7626
	11:36	unto his son will I give one **t**, that David	7626
	12:20	house of David, but the **t** of Judah only.	7626
	12:21	with the **t** of Benjamin, an hundred and	7626
2Ki	17:18	was none left but the **t** of Judah only.	7626
1Ch	5:18	the Gadites, and half the **t** of Manasseh,	7626
	5:23	children of the half **t** of Manasseh dwelt	7626
	5:26	the half **t** of Manasseh, and brought them	7626
	6:60	out of the **t** of Benjamin; Geba with her	4294
	6:61	which were left of the family of *that* **t**,	4294
	6:61	*were cities given* out of the half **t**,	4294
	6:61	namely, *out of* the half of Manasseh,	NIH
	6:62	their families of the **t** of Issachar,	4294
	6:62	out of the **t** of Asher, and out of the tribe	4294
	6:62	out of the **t** of Naphtali, and out of the	4294
	6:62	out of the **t** of Manasseh in Bashan,	4294
	6:63	out of the **t** of Reuben, and out of the	4294
	6:63	out of the **t** of Gad, and out of the tribe of	4294
	6:63	and out of the **t** of Zebulun, twelve cities.	4294
	6:65	they gave by lot out of the **t** of the	4294
	6:65	out of the **t** of the children of Simeon,	4294
	6:65	out of the **t** of the children of Benjamin,	4294
	6:66	of their coasts out of the **t** of Ephraim.	4294
	6:70	out of the half **t** of Manasseh; Aner with	4294
	6:71	of the family of the half **t** of Manasseh,	4294
	6:72	out of the **t** of Issachar; Kedesh with her	4294
	6:74	out of the **t** of Asher; Mashal with her	4294
	6:76	out of the **t** of Naphtali; Kedesh in Galilee	4294
	6:77	Merari *were given* out of the **t** of Zebulun,	4294
	6:78	*were given them* out of the **t** of Reuben,	4294
	6:80	out of the **t** of Gad; Ramoth in Gilead	4294
	12:31	of the half **t** of Manasseh eighteen	4294
	12:37	Gadites, and of the half **t** of Manasseh,	7626
	23:14	his sons were named of the **t** of Levi.	7626
	26:32	the Gadites, and the half **t** of Manasseh,	7626
	27:20	Of the half **t** of Manasseh, Joel the son of	7626
	27:21	Of the half **t** of Manasseh in Gilead,	NIH
Ps	78:67	of Joseph, and chose not the **t** of Ephraim:	7626
	78:68	chose the **t** of Judah, the mount Zion	7626
Eze	47:23	*that* in what **t** the stranger sojourneth,	7626
Lk	2:36	the daughter of Phanuel, of the **t** of Aser:	5443
Ac	13:21	a man of the **t** of Benjamin, *by the space*	5443
Ro	11:1	the seed of Abraham, *of* the **t** of Benjamin.	5443
Php	3:5	of the stock of Israel, of the **t** of Benjamin,	5443
Heb	7:13	things are spoken pertaineth to another **t**,	5443
	7:14	of which **t** Moses spake nothing	5443
Rev	5:5	behold, the Lion of the **t** of Juda, the root	5443
	7:5	Of the **t** of Juda *were* sealed twelve	5443
	7:5	Of the **t** of Reuben *were* sealed twelve	5443
	7:5	Of the **t** of Gad *were* sealed twelve	5443
	7:6	Of the **t** of Aser *were* sealed twelve	5443
	7:6	Of the **t** of Nephthalim *were* sealed twelve	5443
	7:6	Of the **t** of Manasses *were* sealed twelve	5443
	7:7	Of the **t** of Simeon *were* sealed twelve	5443
	7:7	Of the **t** of Levi *were* sealed twelve	5443
	7:7	Of the **t** of Isachar *were* sealed twelve	5443
	7:8	Of the **t** of Zabulon *were* sealed twelve	5443
	7:8	Of the **t** of Joseph *were* sealed twelve	5443
	7:8	Of the **t** of Benjamin *were* sealed twelve	5443

TRIBES (112) [TRIBE]

Ge	49:16	judge his people, as one of the **t** of Israel.	7626
	49:28	All these *are* the twelve **t** of Israel:	7626
Ex	24:4	according to the twelve **t** of Israel.	7626
	28:21	shall they be according to the twelve **t**.	7626
	39:14	with his name, according to the twelve **t**.	7626
Nu	1:16	princes of the **t** of their fathers, heads of	4294
	7:2	who *were* the princes of the **t**, and were	4294
	24:2	abiding *in his tents* according to their **t**;	7626
	26:55	according to the names of the **t** of their	4294
Dt	1:13	known among your **t**, and I will make	7626
	1:15	So I took the chief of your **t**, wise men,	7626
	1:15	over tens, and officers among your **t**.	7626
	5:23	*even* all the heads of your **t**,	7626
	12:5	out of all your **t** to put his name there,	7626
	12:14	the LORD shall choose in one of thy **t**,	7626
	16:18	thy God giveth thee, throughout thy **t**:	7626
	18:5	thy God hath chosen him out of all thy **t**,	7626
	29:10	your captains of your **t**, your elders,	7626
	29:21	him unto evil out of all the **t** of Israel,	7626
	31:28	Gather unto me all the elders of your **t**,	7626
	33:5	*and* the **t** of Israel were gathered together.	7626
Jos	3:12	take ye twelve men out of the **t** of Israel,	7626
	4:5	according unto the number of the **t** of	7626
	4:8	according to the number of the **t** of	7626
	7:14	ye shall be brought according to your **t**:	7626
	7:16	the morning, and brought Israel by their **t**;	7626
	11:23	according to their divisions by their **t**.	7626
	12:7	which Joshua gave the **t** of Israel *for*	7626
	13:7	land for an inheritance unto the nine **t**,	7626

Jos	14:1	the heads of the fathers of the **t** of	4294
	14:2	for the nine **t**, and *for* the half tribe.	4294
	14:3	Moses had given the inheritance of two **t**	4294
	14:4	For the children of Joseph were two **t**,	4294
	18:2	among the children of Israel seven **t**,	7626
	19:51	the heads of the fathers of the **t** of	4294
	21:1	unto the heads of the fathers of the **t** of	4294
	21:16	her suburbs; nine cities out of those two **t**.	4294
	22:14	a prince throughout all the **t** of Israel:	7626
	23:4	be an inheritance for your **t**, from Jordan,	7626
	24:1	Joshua gathered all the **t** of Israel to	7626
Jdg	18:1	not fallen unto them among the **t** of Israel.	7626
	20:2	of all the people, *even* of all the **t** of Israel,	7626
	20:10	an hundred throughout all the **t** of Israel,	7626
	20:12	the **t** of Israel sent men through all the	7626
	21:5	Who *is there* among all the **t** of Israel that	7626
	21:8	What one *is there* of the **t** of Israel that	7626
	21:15	that the LORD had made a breach in the **t**	7626
1Sa	2:28	did I choose him out of all the **t** of Israel	7626
	9:21	of the smallest of the **t** of Israel?	7626
	10:19	yourselves before the LORD by your **t**,	7626
	10:20	when Samuel had caused all the **t** of Israel	7626
	15:17	*wast* thou not *made* the head of the **t** of	7626
2Sa	5:1	came all the **t** of Israel to David unto	7626
	7:7	spake I a word with any of the **t** of Israel,	7626
	15:2	Thy servant *is* of one of the **t** of Israel.	7626
	15:10	Absalom sent spies throughout all the **t** of	7626
	19:9	were at strife throughout all the **t** of Israel,	7626
	20:14	he went through all the **t** of Israel unto	7626
	24:2	Go now through all the **t** of Israel,	7626
1Ki	8:1	elders of Israel, and all the heads of the **t**,	4294
	8:16	I chose no city out of all the **t** of Israel to	7626
	11:31	of Solomon, and will give ten **t** to thee:	7626
	11:32	city which I have chosen out of all the **t**	7626
	11:35	and will give it unto thee, *even* ten **t**.	7626
	14:21	LORD did choose out of all the **t** of Israel,	7626
	18:31	according to the number of the **t** of the	7626
2Ki	21:7	which I have chosen out of all the **t** of Israel,	7626
1Ch	27:16	Furthermore over the **t** of Israel: the ruler	7626
	27:22	These *were* the princes of the **t** of Israel.	7626
	28:1	the princes of the **t**, and the captains of	7626
	29:6	of the fathers and princes of the **t** of Israel,	7626
2Ch	5:2	elders of Israel, and all the heads of the **t**,	4294
	6:5	of Israel to build a house *in*, that my	7626
	11:16	after them out of all the **t** of Israel such as	7626
	12:13	had chosen out of all the **t** of Israel,	7626
	33:7	which I have chosen before all the **t** of	7626
Ezr	6:17	according to the number of the **t** of Israel.	7625
Ps	78:55	made the **t** of Israel to dwell in their tents.	7626
	105:37	was not *one* feeble *person* among their **t**.	7626
	122:4	Whither the **t** go up, the tribes of	7626
	122:4	the tribes go up, the **t** of the LORD,	7626
Isa	19:13	*they that are* the stay of the **t** thereof.	7626
	49:6	be my servant to raise up the **t** of Jacob,	7626
	63:17	servants' sake, the **t** of thine inheritance.	7626
Eze	37:19	his fellows, and will put	7626
	45:8	to the house of Israel according to their **t**.	7626
	47:13	land according to the twelve **t** of Israel:	7626
	47:21	land unto you according to the **t** of Israel:	7626
	47:22	inheritance with you among the **t** of Israel.	7626
	48:1	Now these *are* the names of the **t**. From	7626
	48:19	city shall serve it out of all the **t** of Israel.	7626
	48:23	As for the rest of the **t**, from the east side	7626
	48:29	*by lot* unto the **t** of Israel for inheritance,	7626
	48:31	*shall* be after the names of the **t** of Israel:	7626
Hos	5:9	among the **t** of Israel have I made known	7626
Hab	3:9	*according to* the oaths of the **t**, *even* thy	4294
Zec	9:1	the eyes of man, as of all the **t** of Israel,	7626
Mt	19:28	judging the twelve **t** of Israel.	5443
	24:30	then shall all the **t** of the earth mourn,	5443
Lk	22:30	on thrones judging the twelve **t** of Israel.	5443
Ac	26:7	Unto which *promise* our **twelve t**,	1429
Jas	1:1	to the twelve **t** which are scattered abroad,	5443
Rev	7:4	four thousand of all the **t** of the children of	5443
	21:12	which are *the names* of the twelve **t** of	5443

TRIBULATION (22) [TRIBULATIONS]

Dt	4:30	When thou art in **t**, and all these things	6862
Jdg	10:14	let them deliver you in the time of your **t**.	6869
1Sa	26:24	and let him deliver me out of all **t**.	6869
Mt	13:21	for when **t** or persecution ariseth because	2347
	24:21	For then shall be great **t**, such as was not	2347
	24:29	Immediately after the **t** of those days shall	2347
Mk	13:24	in those days, after that **t**, the sun shall	2347
Jn	16:33	In the world ye shall have **t**: but be of	2347
Ac	14:22	that we must through much **t** enter into	2347
Ro	2:9	**T** and anguish, upon every soul of man	2347
	5:3	knowing that **t** worketh patience;	2347
	8:35	*shall* **t**, or distress, or persecution,	2347
	12:12	Rejoicing in hope; patient in **t**;	2347
2Co	1:4	Who comforteth us in all our **t**, that we	2347
	7:4	I am exceeding joyful in all our **t**.	2347
1Th	3:4	told you before that we should **suffer t**;	2346
2Th	1:6	to recompense **t** to them that trouble you;	2347
Rev	1:9	and companion in **t**, and in the kingdom	2347
	2:9	and **t**, and poverty, (but thou art rich)	2347
	2:10	may be tried; and ye shall have **t** ten days:	2347
	2:22	that commit adultery with her into great **t**,	2347
	7:14	These are they which came out of great **t**,	2347

TRIBULATIONS (4) [TRIBULATION]

1Sa	10:19	you out of all your adversities and your **t**;	6869
Ro	5:3	And not only *so*, but we glory in **t** also;	2347
Eph	3:13	I desire that *ye* faint not at my **t**	2347
2Th	1:4	all your persecutions and **t** that ye endure;	2347

TRIBUTARIES (4) [TRIBUTE]

Dt	20:11	that is found therein shall be **t** unto thee,	4522
Jdg	1:30	dwelt among them, and became **t**.	4522
	1:33	and of Beth-anath became **t** unto them.	4522
	1:35	Joseph prevailed, so that they became **t**.	4522

TRIBUTARY (1) [TRIBUTE]

La	1:1	the provinces, *how* is she become **t**!	4522

TRIBUTE (37) [TRIBUTARIES, TRIBUTARY]

Ge	49:15	to bear, and became a servant unto **t**.	4522
Nu	31:28	levy a **t** unto the LORD of the men of war	4371
	31:37	the LORD's **t** of the sheep was six	4371
	31:38	of which the LORD's **t** was threescore	4371
	31:39	of which the LORD's **t** was threescore	4371
	31:40	of which the LORD's **t** was thirty and	4371
	31:41	Moses gave the **t**, *which was* the LORD's	4371
Dt	16:10	a of a freewill offering of thine hand,	4530
Jos	16:10	unto this day, and serve under **t**.	4522
	17:13	that they put the Canaanites to **t**,	4522
Jdg	1:28	that they put the Canaanites to **t**,	4522
2Sa	20:24	Adoram *was* over the **t**:	4522
1Ki	4:6	Adoniram the son of Abda *was* over the **t**.	4522
	9:21	upon those did Solomon levy a **t** of	4522
	12:18	sent Adoram, who *was* over the **t**;	4522
2Ki	23:33	put the land to a **t** of an hundred talents	6066
2Ch	8:8	them did Solomon make to pay **t** until this	4522
	10:18	sent Hadoram that *was* over the **t**;	4522
	17:11	Jehoshaphat presents, and silver;	4853
Ezr	4:13	**t**, and custom, and *so* thou shalt	1093
	4:20	toll, **t**, and custom, *was* paid unto them.	1093
	6:8	*even* of **t** beyond the river,	4061
	7:24	to impose toll, **t**, or custom, upon them.	1093
Ne	5:4	have borrowed money for the king's **t**,	4060
Est	10:1	the king Ahasuerus laid a **t** upon the land,	4522
Pr	12:24	rule: but the slothful shall be under **t**.	4522
Mt	17:24	that received **t money** came to Peter,	1323
	17:24	and said, Doth not your master pay **t**?	1323
	17:25	the kings of the earth take custom or **t**?	2778
	22:17	Is it lawful to give **t** unto Cesar, or not?	2778
	22:19	Shew me the **t** money. And they brought	2778
Mk	12:14	Is it lawful to give **t** to Cesar, or not?	2778
Lk	20:22	Is it lawful for us to give **t** unto Cesar,	5411
	23:2	and forbidding to give **t** to Cesar, saying	5411
Ro	13:6	For for this cause pay you **t** also: for they	5411
	13:7	**t** to whom tribute *is due*; custom to	5411
	13:7	tribute to whom **t** *is due*; custom to	5411

TRICKERY See GUILE

TRICKLETH (1)

La	3:49	Mine eye **t** down, and ceaseth not,	5064

TRIED (20) [TRY]

Dt	21:5	every controversy and every stroke be **t**	NIH
2Sa	22:31	way *is* perfect; the word of the LORD *is* **t**:	6884
Job	23:10	*when* he hath **t** me, I shall come forth as	974
	34:36	My desire *is that* Job may be **t** unto the	974
Ps	12:6	*as* silver **t** in a furnace of earth,	6884
	17:3	thou hast **t** me, *and* shalt find nothing;	6884
	18:30	the word of the LORD is **t**: he *is* a buckler	6884
	66:10	proved us: thou hast **t** us, as silver is tried.	6884
	66:10	proved us: thou hast **t** us, as silver is **t**.	6884
	105:19	word came: the word of the LORD **t** him.	6884
Isa	28:16	in Zion for a foundation stone, a **t** stone,	976
Jer	12:3	seen me, and **t** mine heart towards thee:	974
Da	12:10	shall be purified, and made white, and **t**;	6884
Zec	13:9	is refined, and will try them as gold is **t**:	974
Heb	11:17	when he was **t**, offered up Isaac:	3985
Jas	1:12	when he is **t**, he shall receive the crown	1384
1Pe	1:7	though it be **t** with fire, might be found	1381
Rev	2:2	thou hast **t** them which say *they are*	3985
	2:10	*some* of you into prison, that ye may be **t**;	3985
	3:18	I counsel thee to buy of me gold **t** in	4448

TRIEST (3) [TRY]

1Ch	29:17	that thou **t** the heart, and hast pleasure in	974
Jer	11:20	that **t** the reins and the heart,	974
	20:12	that **t** the righteous, *and* seest the reins	974

TRIETH (5) [TRY]

Job	34:3	For the ear **t** words, as the mouth tasteth	974
Ps	7:9	the righteous God **t** the hearts and reins.	974
	11:5	The LORD **t** the righteous: but the wicked	974
Pr	17:3	for gold: but the LORD **t** the hearts.	974
1Th	2:4	men, but God, which **t** our hearts.	1381

TRIMMED (2) [TRIMMEST]

2Sa	19:24	nor **t** his beard, nor washed his clothes,	6213
Mt	25:7	all those virgins arose, and **t** their lamps.	2885

TRIMMEST (1) [TRIMMED]

Jer	2:33	Why **t** thou thy way to seek love?	3190

TRIPOLIS See TARPELITES

TRIUMPH (10) [TRIUMPHED, TRIUMPHING]

2Sa	1:20	lest the daughters of the uncircumcised **t**.	5937
Ps	25:2	let not mine enemies **t** over me.	5970
	41:11	because mine enemy doth not **t** over me.	7321
	47:1	shout unto God with the voice of **t**.	7440
	60:8	my shoe: Philistia, **t** thou because of me.	7321
	92:4	work: I will **t** in the works of thy hands.	7442
	94:3	the wicked, how long shall the wicked **t**?	5937
	106:47	unto thy holy name, *and* to **t** in thy praise.	7623
	108:9	I cast out my shoe; over Philistia will I **t**.	7321

2Co 2:14 which always **causeth** us **to** t in Christ, 2358

TRIUMPHED (2) [TRIUMPH]
Ex 15: 1 the LORD, for he hath **t gloriously**; 1342+1342
15:21 the LORD, for he hath **t gloriously**; 1342+1342

TRIUMPHING (2) [TRIUMPH]
Job 20: 5 That the **t** of the wicked *is* short, 7445
Col 2:15 a shew of *them* openly, **t over** them in it. 2358

TROAS (6)
Ac 16: 8 they passing by Mysia came down to **T**. 5174
16:11 Therefore loosing from **T**, we came with a 5174
20: 5 These going before tarried for us at **T**. 5174
20: 6 and came unto them to **T** in five days; 5174
2Co 2:12 I came to **T** to *preach* Christ's gospel, 5174
2Ti 4:13 The cloke that I left at **T** with Carpus, 5174

TRODDEN (27) [TREAD]
Dt 1:36 to him will I give the land that he hath **t** 1869
Jos 14: 9 Surely the land whereon thy feet have **t** 1869
Jdg 5:21 O my soul, thou hast **t down** strength. 1869
Job 22:15 the old way which wicked men have **t**? 1869
28: 8 The lion's whelps have not **t** it, 1869
Ps 119:118 Thou hast **t down** all them that err from 5541
Isa 5: 5 the wall thereof, and it shall be **t down**: 4823
14:19 stones of the pit; as a carcase **t under feet**. 947
18: 2 a nation meted out and **t down**, whose 4001
18: 7 a nation meted out and **t under foot**, 4001
25:10 Moab shall be **t down** under him, *even* as 1758
25:10 *even* as straw is **t down** for the dunghill. 1758
28: 3 of Ephraim, shall be **t** under feet: 7429
28:18 through, then ye shall be **t down** by it. 4823
63: 3 I have **t** the winepress alone; and of 1869
63: 3 adversaries have **t down** thy sanctuary. 947
Jer 12:10 they have **t** my portion **under foot**, 947
La 1:15 The Lord hath **t under foot** all my mighty 5541
1:15 the Lord hath **t** the virgin, the daughter of 1869
Eze 34:19 they eat **that which** ye have **t** with your 4823
Da 8:13 and the host to be **t under foot**? 4823
Mic 7:10 now shall she be **t down** as the mire of 4823
Mt 5:13 cast out, and to be **t under foot** of men. 2662
Lk 8: 5 it was **t down**, and the fowls of the air 2662
21:24 Jerusalem shall be **t down** of the Gentiles, 3961
Heb 10:29 who hath **t under foot** the Son of God, 2662
Rev 14:20 And the winepress was **t** without the city, 3961

TRODE (8) [TREAD]
Jdg 9:27 **t** *the grapes*, and made merry, 1869
20:43 **t** them **down** with ease over against 1869
2Ki 7:17 the people **t upon** him in the gate, 7429
7:20 for the people **t upon** him in the gate, 7429
9:33 on the horses: and he **t** her **under foot**. 7429
14: 9 *was* in Lebanon, and **t down** the thistle, 7429
2Ch 25:18 *was* in Lebanon, and **t down** the thistle, 7429
Lk 12: 1 insomuch that *they* **t** one **upon** another, 2662

TROGYLLIUM (1)
Ac 20:15 *day* we arrived at Samos, and tarried at **T**; 5175

TROOP (13) [TROOPS]
Ge 30:11 Leah said, A **t** cometh: and she called his 1409
49:19 Gad, a **t** shall overcome him: but he shall 1416
1Sa 30: 8 saying, Shall I pursue after this **t**? 1416
2Sa 2:25 one **t**, and stood on the top of a hill. 92
3:22 of David and Joab came from *pursuing* a **t**, 1416
22:30 For by thee I have run **through** a **t**; 1416
23:11 Philistines were gathered together into a **t**, 2416
23:13 **t** of the Philistines pitched in the valley 2416
Ps 18:29 For by thee I have run **through** a **t**; 1416
Isa 65:11 that prepare a table for that **t**, 1409
Jer 18:22 when thou shalt bring a **t** suddenly upon 1416
Hos 7: 1 *and* the **t** of *robbers* spoileth without. 1416
Am 9: 6 and hath founded his **t** in the earth; 92

TROOPS (7) [TROOP]
Job 6:19 The **t** of Tema looked, the companies of 734
19:12 His **t** come together, and raise up their 1416
Jer 5: 7 **assembled** themselves **by t** *in* the harlots' 1413
Hos 6: 9 as **t** of *robbers* wait for a man, 1416
Mic 5: 1 Now **gather** thyself in **t**, O daughter of 1413
5: 1 gather thyself in troops, O daughter of **t**: 1416
Hab 3:16 people, he will **invade** them **with** his **t**. 1464

TROPHIMUS (3)
Ac 20: 4 Timotheus; and of Asia, Tychicus and **T**. 5161
21:29 before with him in the city **T** an Ephesian, 5161
2Ti 4:20 but **T** have I left at Miletum sick. 5161

TROUBLE (110) [TROUBLED, TROUBLEDST, TROUBLER, TROUBLES, TROUBLEST, TROUBLETH, TROUBLING, TROUBLOUS]
Jos 6:18 make the camp of Israel a curse, and **t** it. 5916
7:25 the LORD shall **t** thee this day. And all 5916
Jdg 11:35 and thou art one of them that **t** me: 5916
2Ki 19: 3 This day *is* a day of **t**, and of rebuke, 6869
1Ch 22:14 in my **t** I have prepared for the house of 6040
2Ch 15: 4 when they in their **t** did turn unto 6862
29: 8 and he hath delivered them to **t**, 2189
32:18 the wall, to affright them, and to **t** them; 926
Ne 9:27 in the time of their **t**, when they cried 6869
9:32 let not all the **t** seem little before thee, 8513
Job 3:26 had I rest, neither was I quiet; yet **t** came. 7267
5: 6 neither doth **t** spring out of the ground; 5999
5: 7 Yet man is born unto **t**, as the sparks fly 5999
14: 1 of a woman *is* of few days, and full of **t**. 7267

Job 15:24 **T** and anguish shall make him afraid; 6862
27: 9 Will God hear his cry when **t** cometh 6869
30:25 not I weep for him that was **in t**? 3117+7186
34:29 giveth quietness, who then can **make t**? 7561
38:23 I have reserved against the time of **t**, 6862
Ps 3: 1 LORD, how are they increased that **t** me! 6862
9: 9 for the oppressed, a refuge in times of **t**. 6869
9:13 consider my **t** *which I suffer* of them that 6040
10: 1 *why* hidest thou *thyself* in times of **t**? 6869
13: 4 those that **t** me rejoice when I am moved. 6862
20: 1 The LORD hear thee in the day of **t**; 6869
22:11 Be not far from me; for **t** *is* near; for *there* 6869
27: 5 For in the time of **t** he shall hide me in his 7451
31: 7 for thou hast considered my **t**; thou hast 6040
31: 9 mercy upon me, O LORD, for I am in **t**: 6887
32: 7 place; thou shalt preserve me from **t**; 6862
37:39 *he is* their strength in the time of **t**. 6869
41: 1 the LORD will deliver him in time of **t**. 7451
46: 1 and strength, a very present help in **t**. 6869
50:15 call upon me in the day of **t**: I will deliver 6869
54: 7 For he hath delivered me out of all **t**: 6869
59:16 my defence and refuge in the day of my **t**. 6862
60:11 Give us help from **t**: for vain *is* the help of 6862
66:14 my mouth hath spoken, when I was in **t**. 6862
69:17 thy face from thy servant; for I am in **t**: 6887
73: 5 They *are not* in **t** as other men; neither 5999
77: 2 In the day of my **t** I sought the Lord: 6869
78:33 he consume in vanity, and their years in **t**. 928
78:49 wrath, and indignation, and **t**, *by* sending 6869
81: 7 Thou calledst in **t**, and I delivered thee; 6869
86: 7 In the day of my **t** I will call upon thee: 6869
91:15 I *will be* with him in **t**; I will deliver him, 6869
102: 2 face from me in the day *when* I am in **t**; 6862
107: 6 they cried unto the LORD in their **t**, 6862
107:13 they cried unto the LORD in their **t**, 6862
107:19 they cry unto the LORD in their **t**, 6862
107:26 depths: their soul is melted because of **t**. 7451
107:28 they cry unto the LORD in their **t**, 6862
108:12 Give us help from **t**: for vain *is* the help of 6862
116: 3 gat hold upon me: I found **t** and sorrow. 6869
119:143 **T** and anguish have taken hold on me: 6862
138: 7 Though I walk in the midst of **t**, thou wilt 6869
142: 2 before him; I shewed before him my **t**. 6869
143:11 righteousness' sake bring my soul out of **t**. 6869
Pr 11: 8 The righteous is delivered out of **t**, 6869
12:13 of *his* lips: but the just shall come out of **t**. 6869
15: 6 but in the revenues of the wicked *is* **t**. 5916
15:16 LORD than great treasure and **t** therewith. 4103
25:19 *man* in time of **t** *is like* a broken tooth, 6869
Isa 1:14 they are a **t** unto me; I am weary to bear 2960
8:22 and darkness, dimness of anguish; 6869
17:14 behold at eveningtide **t**; *and before* 1091
22: 5 For *it is* a day of **t**, and of treading down, 4103
26:16 LORD, in **t** have they visited thee, 6862
30: 6 into the land of **t** and anguish, from 6869
33: 2 our salvation also in the time of **t**. 6869
37: 3 This day *is* a day of **t**, and of rebuke, 6869
46: 7 he not answer, nor save him out of his **t**. 6869
65:23 not labour in vain, nor bring forth for **t**; 928
Jer 2:27 in the time of their **t** they will say, Arise, 7451
2:28 if they can save thee in the time of thy **t**: 7451
8:15 *and* for a time of health, and behold **t**! 1205
11:12 not save them at all in the time of their **t**. 7451
11:14 the time that they cry unto me for their **t**. 7451
14: 8 of Israel, the saviour thereof in time of **t**, 6869
14:19 and for the time of healing, and behold **t**! 1205
30: 7 it *is* even the time of Jacob's **t**; but he 6869
51: 2 for in the day of **t** they shall be against her 7451
La 1:21 all mine enemies have heard of my **t**: 7451
Eze 7: 7 The day of **t** *is* near, and not the sounding 4103
32:13 neither shall the foot of man **t** them any 1804
32:13 any more, nor the hoofs of beasts **t** them. 1804
Da 4:19 or the interpretation thereof, **t** thee. 927
5:10 let not thy thoughts **t** thee, nor let thy 927
11:44 of the east and out of the north shall **t** him: 926
12: 1 there shall be a time of **t**, such as never 6869
Na 1: 7 *is* good, a strong hold in the day of **t**; 6869
Hab 3:16 in myself, that I might rest in the day of **t**: 6869
Zep 1:15 a day of **t** and distress, a day of wasteness 7451
Mt 26:10 unto them, Why **t** ye the woman? 2873+3930
Mk 14: 6 Let her alone; why **t** you her? 2873+3930
Lk 7: 6 him, saying unto him, Lord, **t** not thyself: 4660
8:49 Thy daughter is dead; **t** not the Master. 4660
11: 7 **shall answer and say, T** me not: 2873+3930
Ac 15:19 my sentence is, that *we* **t** not them, 3926
16:20 being Jews, do **exceedingly t** our city, 1613
20:10 and embracing *him* said, **T** not yourselves; 2350
1Co 7:28 Nevertheless such shall have **t** in the flesh: 2347
2Co 1: 4 able to comfort them which are in any **t**, 2347
1: 8 have you ignorant of our **t** which came to 2347
Gal 1: 7 but there be some that **t** you, 5015
5:12 would they were even cut off which **t** you. 387
6:17 From henceforth let no *man* **t** me: 2873+3930
2Th 1: 7 recompense tribulation to them that **t** you; 2346
2Ti 2: 9 Wherein I **suffer t**, as an evil doer, 2553
Heb 12:15 lest any root of bitterness springing up **t** 1776

TROUBLED (68) [TROUBLE]
Ge 34:30 Ye have **t** me to make me to stink among 5916
41: 8 pass in the morning that his spirit was **t**; 6470
45: 3 him; for they were **t** at his presence. 926
Ex 14:24 cloud, and the host of the Egyptians, 2000
Jos 7:25 Joshua said, Why hast thou **t** us? 5916
1Sa 14:29 said Jonathan, My father hath **t** the land: 5916
16:14 and an evil spirit from the LORD **t** him. 1204

1Sa 28:21 saw that he was sore **t**, and said unto him, 926
4: 1 were feeble, and all the Israelites were **t**. 926
1Ki 18:18 he answered, I have not **t** Israel; but thou, 5916
2Ki 6:11 the king of Syria was sore **t** for this thing; 5590
Ezr 4: 4 people of Judah, and **t** them in building, 926
Job 4: 5 faintest; it toucheth thee, and thou art **t**. 926
21: 4 *it so*, why should not my spirit be **t**? 7114
23:15 Therefore am I **t** at his presence: when I 926
34:20 the people shall be **t** at midnight, 1607
Ps 30: 7 thou didst hide thy face, *and* I was **t**. 926
38: 6 I am **t**; I am bowed down greatly; I go 5753
46: 3 *Though* the waters thereof roar *and* be **t**, 2560
48: 5 they were **t**, *and* hasted away. 926
77: 3 I remembered God, and was **t**: 1993
77: 4 waking: I am *so* **t** that I cannot speak. 6470
77:16 they were afraid: the depths also were **t**. 7264
83:17 Let them be confounded and **t** for ever; 926
90: 7 by thine anger, and by thy wrath are we **t**. 926
104:29 Thou hidest thy face, they are **t**: thou 926
Pr 25:26 down before the wicked *is as* a **t** fountain, 7515
Isa 32:10 Many days and years shall ye be **t**, 7264
32:11 that are at ease; be **t**, ye careless ones: 7264
57:20 the wicked *are* like the sea, when it 1644
Jer 31:20 therefore my bowels are **t** for him; I will 1993
La 1:20 my bowels are **t**; mine heart is turned 2560
2:11 eyes do fail with tears, my bowels are **t**, 2560
Eze 7:27 hands of the people of the land shall be **t**: 926
26:18 the isles that *are* in the sea shall be **t** at thy 926
27:35 they shall be **t** in *their* countenance. 7481
Da 2: 1 wherewith his spirit was **t**, and his sleep 6470
2: 3 and my spirit was to know the dream; 6470
4: 5 my bed and the visions of my head **t** me. 927
4:19 for one hour, and his thoughts **t** him. 927
5: 6 his thoughts **t** him, so that the joints of his 927
5: 9 *was* king Belshazzar greatly **t**, 927
7:15 *my* body, and the visions of my head **t** me. 927
7:28 my cogitations much **t** me, 927
Zec 10: 2 were **t**, because *there was* no shepherd. 6031
Mt 2: 3 the king had heard *these things*, he was **t**, 5015
14:26 the sea, they were **t**, saying, It is a spirit; 5015
24: 6 see that ye be not **t**: for all *these things* 2360
Mk 6:50 For they all saw him, and were **t**. 5015
13: 7 of wars and rumours of wars, be ye not **t**: 2360
Lk 1:12 And when Zacharias saw *him*, he was **t**, 5015
1:29 And when she saw *him*, she was **t** at his 1298
10:41 thou art careful and **t** about many *things*: 5182
24:38 he said unto them, Why are ye **t**? 5015
Jn 5: 4 season into the pool, and **t** the water: 5015
5: 7 Sir, I have no man, when the water is **t**, 5015
11:33 he groaned in the spirit, and was **t**, 5015
12:27 Now is my soul **t**; and what shall I say? 5015
13:21 he was **t** in spirit, and testified, and said, 5015
14: 1 Let not your heart be **t**: ye believe in God, 5015
14:27 Let not your heart be **t**, neither let it be 5015
Ac 15:24 certain which went out from us have **t** 5015
17: 8 And they **t** the people and the rulers of 5015
2Co 4: 8 *We are* **t** on every *side*, yet not distressed; 2346
4: 8 we are **t** on every *side*; without were 2346
2Th 1: 7 And to you who are **t** rest with us, when 2346
2: 2 or be **t**, neither by spirit, nor by word, 2360
1Pe 3:14 be not afraid of their terror, neither be **t**; 5015

TROUBLEDST (1) [TROUBLE]
Eze 32: 2 **t** the waters with thy feet, and fouledst 1804

TROUBLEMAKER See PESTILENT

TROUBLER (1) [TROUBLE]
1Ch 2: 7 Achar, the **t** of Israel, who transgressed in 5916

TROUBLES (12) [TROUBLE]
Dt 31:17 and many evils and **t** shall befall them; 6869
31:21 when many evils and **t** are befallen them, 6869
Job 5:19 He shall deliver thee in six **t**: yea, 6869
Ps 25:17 The **t** of my heart are enlarged: O bring 6869
25:22 Redeem Israel, O God, out of all his **t**. 6869
34: 6 heard *him*, and saved him out of all his **t**. 6869
34:17 and delivereth them out of all their **t**. 6869
71:20 which hast shewed me great and sore **t**, 6869
88: 3 For my soul is full of **t**: and my life 7451
Pr 21:23 and his tongue keepeth his soul from **t**. 6869
Isa 65:16 because the former **t** are forgotten, 6869
Mk 13: 8 and there shall be famines and **t**: 5016

TROUBLEST (1) [TROUBLE]
Mk 5:35 dead: why **t** thou the Master any further? 4660

TROUBLETH (10) [TROUBLE]
1Sa 16:15 now, an evil spirit from God **t** thee. 1204
1Ki 18:17 said unto him, *Art* thou he that **t** Israel? 5916
Job 22:10 round about thee, and sudden fear **t** thee; 926
23:16 my heart soft, and the Almighty **t** me: 926
Pr 11:17 but *he that is* cruel **t** his own flesh. 5916
11:29 He that **t** his own house shall inherit 5916
15:27 He that is greedy of gain **t** his own house; 5916
Da 4: 9 holy gods *is* in thee, and no secret **t** thee, 598
Lk 18: 5 Yet because this widow **t** me, I will 2873+3930
Gal 5:10 but he that **t** you shall bear *his* judgment, 5015

TROUBLING (2) [TROUBLE]
Job 3:17 there the wicked cease *from* **t**; 7267
Jn 5: 4 first after the **t** of the water stepped in, 5016

TROUBLOUS (1) [TROUBLE]
Da 9:25 built again, and the wall, even in **t** times. 6695

T

TROUGH (1) [KNEADINGTROUGHS, TROUGHS]
Ge 24:20 emptied her pitcher into the **t**, and ran　8268

TROUGHS (2) [TROUGH]
Ge 30:38 watering it when the flocks came to drink,　8268
Ex 2:16 filled the **t** to water their father's flock.　7298

TROUSERS See HOSEN

TROW (1)
Lk 17: 9 *things that were commanded him? I t not.*　1380

TRUCEBREAKERS (1) [BREAK]
2Ti 3: 3 **t**, false accusers, incontinent, fierce,　786

TRUE (81) [TRUTH]
Ge 42:11 we *are* **t** men, thy servants are no spies.　3651
42:19 If ye *be* **t** men, let one of your brethren be　3651
42:31 unto him, We *are* **t** men; we are no spies.　3651
42:33 Hereby shall I know that ye *are* **t** men;　3651
42:34 *that* ye *are* **t** men: so will I deliver you　3651
Dt 17: 4 and behold, *it* is **t**, *and* the thing certain,　571
22:20 this thing be **t**, *and the tokens* of virginity　571
Jos 2:12 my father's house, and give me a **t** token:　571
Ru 3:12 now it is **t** that I *am thy* near kinsman:　551
2Sa 7:28 thy words be **t**, and thou hast promised　571
1Ki 10: 6 It was a **t** report that I heard in mine own　571
22:16 *that which* is **t** in the name of the LORD?　571
2Ch 9: 5 *It was* a **t** report which I heard in mine　571
15: 3 season Israel *hath been* without the **t** God,　571
Ne 9:13 **t** laws, good statutes and commandments;　571
Ps 19: 9 the judgments of the LORD *are* **t** and　571
119:160 Thy word *is* **t** *from* the beginning:　571
Pr 14:25 A **t** witness delivereth souls: but a deceitful　571
Jer 10:10 the LORD *is* the **t** God, he *is* the living　571
42: 5 The LORD be a **t** and faithful witness　571
Eze 18: 8 hath executed **t** judgment between man　571
Da 3:14 *Is it* **t**, O Shadrach, Meshach,　6656
3:24 and said unto the king, **T**, O king.　3330
6:12 king answered and said, The thing *is* **t**,　3330
8:26 and the morning which was told *is* **t**:　571
10: 1 the thing *was* **t**, but the time appointed　571
Zec 7: 9 Execute **t** judgment, and shew mercy and　571
Mt 22:16 we know that thou art **t**, and teachest　227
Mk 12:14 we know that thou art **t**, and carest for no　227
Lk 16:11 who will commit to your trust the **t** *riches*?　228
Jn 1: 9 *That* was the **t** Light, which lighteth every　228
3:33 testimony hath set to *his* seal that God is **t**.　227
4:23 when the **t** worshippers shall worship　228
4:37 And herein is *that* saying **t**, One soweth,　228
5:31 bear witness of myself, my witness is not **t**.　227
5:32 the witness which he witnesseth of me is **t**.　227
6:32 my Father giveth you the **t** bread from　228
7:18 the same is **t**, and no unrighteousness is in　227
7:28 he that sent me is **t**, whom ye know not.　228
8:13 record of thyself; thy record is not **t**.　227
8:14 I bear record of myself, *yet* my record is **t**;　227
8:16 And yet if I judge, my judgment is **t**: for I　227
8:17 law, that the testimony of two men is **t**.　227
8:26 but he that sent me is **t**; and I speak to　227
10:41 *things* that John spake of this *man* were **t**.　227
15: 1 I am the **t** vine, and my Father is　228
17: 3 that they might know thee the only **t** God,　228
19:35 that saw *it* bare record, and his record is **t**:　228
19:35 he knoweth that he saith, that ye might　227
21:24 and we know that his testimony is **t**.　227
Ac 12: 9 wist not that it was **t** which was done by　227
Ro 3: 4 yea, let God be **t**, but every man a liar; as it　227
2Co 1:18 But *as* God *is* **t**, our word toward you was　4103
6: 8 and good report: as deceivers, and *yet* **t**;　227
Eph 4:24 is created in righteousness and **t** holiness.　225
Php 4: 3 And I intreat thee also, **t** yokefellow,　1103
4: 8 Finally, brethren, whatsoever *things* are **t**,　227
1Th 1: 9 from idols to serve the living and **t** God,　228
1Ti 3: 1 *This* is a **t** saying, If a man desire the office　4103
Tit 1:13 This witness is **t**. Wherefore rebuke them　227
Heb 8: 2 and of the **t** tabernacle, which the Lord　228
9:24 with hands, *which are* the figures of the **t**;　228
10:22 Let us draw near with a **t** heart in full　228
1Pe 5:12 testifying that this is the **t** grace of God　227
2Pe 2:22 unto them according to the **t** proverb,　227
1Jn 2: 8 you, which *thing* is **t** in him and in you:　227
2: 8 is past, and the **t** light now shineth.　228
5:20 that we may know him *that is* **t**, and we　228
5:20 and we are in him *that is* **t**, *even* in his Son　228
5:20 This is the **t** God, and eternal life.　228
3Jn 1:12 record; and ye know that our record is **t**.　228
Rev 3: 7 he *that is* **t**, he that hath the key of David,　228
3:14 saith the Amen, the faithful and **t** witness,　228
6:10 saying, How long, O Lord, holy and **t**,　228
15: 3 just and **t** *are* thy ways, thou King of saints.　228
16: 7 **t** and righteous *are* thy judgments.　228
19: 2 For **t** and righteous *are* his judgments: for　228
19: 9 unto me, These are the **t** sayings of God.　228
19:11 sat upon him *was* called Faithful and **T**,　228
21: 5 Write: for these words are **t** and faithful.　228
22: 6 unto me, These sayings *are* faithful and **t**:　228

TRULY (42) [TRUTH]
Ge 4:24 **t** Lamech seventy and sevenfold.　2050.1
24:49 if ye will deal kindly and **t** with my master,　571
47:29 my thigh, and deal kindly and **t** with me;　571
48:19 his younger brother shall be greater than　199
Nu 14:21 *as* **t** *as* I live, all the earth shall be filled　199
14:28 Say unto them, *As* **t** *as* I live, saith　NIH

Dt 14:22 Thou shalt **t** tithe all the increase　6237+6237
Jos 2:14 that we will deal kindly and **t** with thee.　571
2:24 **T** The LORD hath delivered into our hands　3588
Jdg 9:16 if ye have done **t** and sincerely,　571+871.1
9:19 If ye then have dealt **t** and sincerely　571+871.1
1Sa 20: 3 **t** *as* the LORD liveth, and *as* thy soul　199
Job 36: 4 For **t** my words *shall* not be false: *he that*　551
Ps 62: 1 **T** my soul waiteth upon God: from him　389
73: 1 **T** God *is* good to Israel, *even* to such as　389
116:16 Oh LORD, **t** I *am* thy servant; I *am* thy　3588
Pr 12:22 but they that deal **t** *are* his delight.　530
Ecc 11: 7 **T** the light *is* sweet, and a pleasant　2050.1
Jer 3: 23 **T** in vain *is* salvation hoped *for* from　403
3:23 **t** in the LORD our God *is* the salvation of　403
10:19 I said, **T** this *is* a grief, and I must bear it.　389
28: 9 that the LORD hath **t** sent him.　571+871.1
Eze 18: 9 and hath kept my judgments, to deal **t**;　571
Mic 3: 8 **t** I am full *of* power by the spirit of　199
Mt 9:37 harvest **t** is plenteous, but the labourers　3303
17:11 Elias **t** shall first come, and restore all　3303
27:54 saying, **T** this was the Son of God.　230
Mk 14:38 The spirit **t** is ready, but the flesh is weak.　3303
15:39 he said, **T** this man was the Son of God.　230
Lk 10: 2 The harvest **t** is great, but the labourers　3303
11:48 Ye bear witness that ye allow the deeds　686
20:21 *any*, but teachest the way of God **t**:　225+1909
22:22 And **t** the Son of man goeth, as it was　3303
Jn 4:18 is not thy husband: *in* that saidst thou **t**.　227
20:30 And many other signs **t** did Jesus in　3303
Ac 1: 5 John **t** baptized with water; but ye shall　3303
3:22 For Moses **t** said unto the fathers,　3303
5:23 The prison **t** found we shut with all safety,　3303
2Co 12:12 **T** the signs of an apostle were wrought　3303
Heb 7:23 And they **t** were many priests, because　3303
11:15 And **t**, if they had been mindful of that　3303
1Jn 1: 3 and **t** our fellowship *is* with the Father,　NIG

TRUMP (2) [TRUMPET]
1Co 15:52 in the twinkling of an eye, at the last **t**:　4536
1Th 4:16 of the archangel, and with the **t** of God:　4536

TRUMPET (61) [TRUMP, TRUMPETERS, TRUMPETS]
Ex 19:13 the **t** soundeth long, they shall come　3104
19:16 and the voice of the **t** exceeding loud;　7782
19:19 when the voice of the **t** sounded long,　7782
20:18 the noise of the **t**, and the mountain　7782
Lev 25: 9 thou cause the **t** of the jubile to sound　7782
25: 9 the day of atonement shall ye make the **t**　7782
Nu 10: 4 blow *but* with one **t**, then the princes,　NIH
Jos 6: 5 *and* when ye hear the sound of the **t**,　7782
6:20 the people heard the sound of the **t**,　7782
Jdg 3:27 that he blew a **t** in the mountain of　7782
6:34 came upon Gideon, and he blew a **t**;　7782
7:16 put a **t** in every man's hand, with empty　7782
7:18 When I blow with a **t**, I and all that *are*　7782
1Sa 13: 3 Saul blew the **t** throughout all the land,　7782
2Sa 2:28 So Joab blew a **t**, and all the people stood　7782
6:15 shouting, and with the sound of the **t**.　7782
15:10 As soon as ye hear the sound of the **t**,　7782
18:16 Joab blew the **t**, and the people returned　7782
20: 1 he blew a **t**, and said, We have no part in　7782
20:22 blew a **t**, and they retired from the city,　7782
1Ki 1:34 ye with the **t**, and say, God save king　7782
1:39 they blew the **t**; and all the people said,　7782
1:41 Joab heard the sound of the **t**, he said,　7782
Ne 4:18 And he that sounded the **t** *was* by me.　7782
4:20 *therefore* ye hear the sound of the **t**,　7782
Job 39:24 believeth he that *it is* the sound of the **t**.　7782
Ps 47: 5 a shout, the LORD with the sound of a **t**.　7782
81: 3 Blow up the **t** in the new moon, in the　7782
150: 3 Praise him with the sound of the **t**:　7782
Isa 18: 3 and when *he* bloweth a **t**, hear ye.　7782
27:13 *that* the great **t** shall be blown,　7782
58: 1 lift up thy voice like a **t**, and shew my　7782
Jer 4: 5 and say, Blow ye the **t** in the land:　7782
4:19 hast heard, O my soul, the sound of the **t**,　7782
4:21 the standard, *and* hear the sound of the **t**?　7782
6: 1 blow the **t** in Tekoa, and set up a sign of　7782
6:17 *saying*, Hearken to the sound of the **t**.　7782
42:14 hear the sound of the **t**, nor have hunger　7782
51:27 blow the **t** among the nations, prepare　7782
Eze 7:14 They have blown the **t**, even to make all　8619
33: 3 he blow the **t**, and warn the people;　7782
33: 4 whosoever heareth the sound of the **t**,　7782
33: 5 He heard the sound of the **t**, and took not　7782
33: 6 blow not the **t**, and the people be not　7782
Hos 5: 8 the cornet in Gibeah, *and* the **t** in Ramah:　2689
8: 1 *Set* the **t** to thy mouth. He shall come as　7782
Joel 2: 1 Blow ye the **t** in Zion, and sound an alarm　7782
2:15 Blow the **t** in Zion, sanctify a fast, call a　7782
Am 2: 2 shouting, *and* with the sound of the **t**:　7782
3: 6 Shall a **t** be blown in the city,　7782
Zep 1:16 A day of the **t** and alarm against the　7782
Zec 9:14 the Lord GOD shall blow the **t**,　7782
Mt 6: 2 *thine* alms, do not sound a **t** before thee,　4537
24:31 send his angels with a great sound of a **t**,　4536
1Co 14: 8 For if the **t** give an uncertain sound,　4537
15:52 for the **t** shall sound, and the dead shall　4537
Heb 12:19 And the sound of a **t**, and the voice of　4536
Rev 1:10 heard behind me a great voice, as of a **t**,　4536
4: 1 was as *it were* of a **t** talking with me;　4536
8:13 other voices of the **t** of the three angels,　4536
9:14 Saying to the sixth angel which had the **t**,　4536

TRUMPETERS (4) [TRUMPET]
2Ki 11:14 and the princes and the **t** by the king,　2689
2Ch 5:13 to pass, as the **t** and singers *were* as one,　2690
29:28 and the singers sang, and the **t** sounded:　2689
Rev 18:22 and musicians, and of pipers, and **t**,　4538

TRUMPETS (51) [TRUMPET]
Lev 23:24 a memorial of **blowing of t**, a holy　8643
Nu 10: 2 Make thee two **t** of silver; of a whole　2689
10: 8 Aaron, the priests, shall blow with the **t**;　2689
10: 9 then ye shall blow an alarm with the **t**;　2689
10:10 ye shall blow with the **t** over your burnt　2689
29: 1 it is a day of **blowing t** unto you.　8643
31: 6 and the **t** to blow in his hand.　2689
Jos 6: 4 before the ark seven **t** of rams' horns　7782
6: 4 and the priests shall blow with the **t**.　7782
6: 6 seven priests bear seven **t** of rams' horns　7782
6: 8 that the seven priests bearing the seven **t**　7782
6: 8 on before the LORD, and blew with the **t**:　7782
6: 9 before the priests that blew *with* the **t**,　7782
6: 9 *priests* going on, and blowing with the **t**,　7782
6:13 priests bearing seven **t** of rams' horns　7782
6:13 on continually, and blew with the **t**:　7782
6:13 *priests* going on, and blowing with the **t**:　7782
6:16 when the priests blew with the **t**, Joshua　7782
6:20 when the *priests* blew with the **t**:　7782
Jdg 7: 8 took victuals in their hand, and their **t**:　7782
7:18 blow ye the **t** also on every side of all　7782
7:19 they blew the **t**, and brake the pitchers　7782
7:20 the three companies blew the **t**,　7782
7:20 the **t** in their right hands to blow *withal*:　7782
7:22 the three hundred blew the **t**,　7782
2Ki 9:13 and blew with **t**, saying, Jehu is king.　7782
11:14 of the land rejoiced, and blew with **t**:　2689
12:13 snuffers, basons, **t**, any vessels of gold,　2689
1Ch 13: 8 and with cymbals, and with **t**.　2689
15:24 did blow with the **t** before the ark of God:　2689
15:28 the cornet, and with **t**, and with cymbals,　2689
16: 6 Jahaziel the priests with **t** continually　2689
16:42 with them Heman and Jeduthun *with* **t**　2689
2Ch 5:12 and twenty priests sounding with **t**:)　2689
5:13 when *they* lift up *their* voice with the **t**　2689
7: 6 the priests **sounded t** before them,　2690
13:12 his priests with sounding **t** to cry alarm　2689
13:14 and the priests sounded with the **t**.　2689
15:14 shouting, and with **t**, and with cornets.　2689
20:28 and **t** unto the house of the LORD.　2689
23:13 and the princes and the **t** by the king:　2689
23:13 of the land rejoiced, and sounded with **t**,　2689
29:26 of David, and the priests with the **t**.　2689
29:27 song of the LORD began *also* with the **t**,　2689
Ezr 3:10 they set the priests in their apparel with **t**,　2689
Ne 12:35 *certain* of the priests' sons with **t**;　2689
12:41 Zechariah, *and* Hananiah, with **t**;　2689
Job 39:25 He saith among the **t**, Ha, ha;　7782
Ps 98: 6 With **t** and sound of cornet make a joyful　2689
Rev 8: 2 and to them were given seven **t**.　4536
8: 6 the seven angels which had the seven **t**　4536

TRUST (134) [TRUSTED, TRUSTEDST, TRUSTEST, TRUSTETH, TRUSTING, TRUSTY]
Jdg 9:15 *then* come *and* put your **t** in my shadow:　2620
Ru 2:12 under whose wings thou art come to **t**.　2620
2Sa 22: 3 The God of my rock; in him will I **t**: *he is*　2620
22:31 he *is* a buckler to all them that **t** in him.　2620
2Ki 18:20 Now on whom dost thou **t**, that thou　982
18:21 *is* Pharaoh king of Egypt unto all that **t** on　982
18:22 say unto me, We **t** in the LORD our God:　982
18:24 **put** thy **t** on Egypt for chariots and　982
18:30 Neither let Hezekiah **make** you **t** in　982
1Ch 5:20 of them; because they **put** their **t** in him.　982
2Ch 32:10 Whereon do ye **t**, that ye abide in the siege　982
Job 4:18 Behold, he **put** no **t** in his servants;　539
8:14 off, and, whose **t** *shall be* a spider's web.　4009
13:15 Though he slay me, *yet* will I **t** in him:　3176
15:15 Behold, he **putteth** no **t** in his saints; yea,　539
15:31 Let not him that is deceived **t** in vanity:　539
35:14 *is* before him; therefore **t** thou in him.　2342
39:11 Wilt thou **t** him, because his strength *is*　982
Ps 2:12 blessed *are* all they that **put** their **t** in him.　2620
4: 5 and **put** your **t** in the LORD.　982
5:11 all those that **put** their **t** in thee rejoice:　2620
7: 1 O LORD my God, in thee do I **put** my **t**:　2620
9:10 they that know thy name will **put** their **t**　982
11: 1 In the LORD **put** I my **t**: how say ye to　2620
16: 1 O God: for in thee do I **put** my **t**.　2620
17: 7 **put** their **t** *in them* from those that rise up　2620
18: 2 my God, my strength, in whom I will **t**;　2620
18:30 he *is* a buckler to all those that **t** in him.　2620
20: 7 Some *t* in chariots, and some in horses:　NIH
25: 2 O my God, I **t** in thee: let me not be　982
25:20 not be ashamed; for I **put** my **t** in thee.　2620
31: 1 In thee, O LORD, do I **put** my **t**; let me　2620
31: 6 regard lying vanities: but I **t** in the LORD.　982
31:19 thou hast wrought for them that **t** in　2620
34:22 of them that **t** in him shall be desolate.　2620
36: 7 the children of men **put** their **t** under　2620
37: 3 **T** in the LORD, and do good; *so* shalt thou　982
37: 5 **t** also in him; and he shall bring *it* to pass.　982
37:40 and save them, because they **t** in him.　2620
40: 3 see *it*, and fear, and shall **t** in the LORD.　982
40: 4 *is that* man that maketh the LORD his **t**,　4009
44: 6 For I will not **t** in my bow, neither shall　982
49: 6 They that **t** in their wealth,　982
52: 8 I **t** in the mercy of God for ever and ever.　982

Ps	55:23 live out half their days; but I will **t** in thee.	982
	56: 3 *What* time I am afraid, I will **t** in thee.	982
	56: 4 praise his word, in God I have **put** my **t**;	982
	56:11 In God I have **put** my **t**: I will not be afraid	982
	61: 4 I will **t** in the covert of thy wings. Selah.	2620
	62: 8 **T** in him at all times; ye people, pour out	982
	62:10 **T** not in oppression, and become not vain	982
	64:10 be glad in the Lord, and shall **t** in him;	2620
	71: 1 In thee, O Lord, do I **put** my **t**: let me	2620
	71: 5 Lord God: *thou art* my **t** from my youth.	4009
	73:28 I have put my **t** in the Lord God, that *I*	4268
	91: 2 and my fortress: my God; in him will I **t**.	982
	91: 4 and under his wings shalt thou **t**:	2620
	115: 9 O Israel, **t** thou in the Lord: he *is* their	982
	115:10 O house of Aaron, **t** in the Lord: he *is*	982
	115:11 Ye that fear the Lord, **t** in the Lord:	982
	118: 8 *It is* better to **t** in the Lord than to put	2620
	118: 9 *It is* better to **t** in the Lord than to put	2620
	119:42 that reproacheth me: for I **t** in thy word.	982
	125: 1 They that **t** in the Lord *shall be* as mount	982
	141: 8 in thee is my **t**; leave not my soul	2620
	143: 8 in the morning; for in thee do I **t**:	982
	144: 2 my shield, and *he* in whom I **t**;	2620
	146: 3 **Put** not your **t** in princes, *nor* in the son of	982
Pr	3: 5 **T** in the Lord with all thine heart;	982
	22:19 That thy **t** may be in the Lord, I have	4009
	28:25 he that **putteth** his **t** in the Lord shall be	982
	29:25 whoso **putteth** his **t** in the Lord shall be	982
	30: 5 he *is* a shield unto them that **put** their **t**	2620
	31:11 heart of her husband doth *safely* **t** in her,	982
Isa	12: 2 *is* my salvation; I will **t**, and not be afraid:	982
	14:32 and the poor of his people shall **t** in it.	2620
	26: 4 **T** ye in the Lord for ever: for in	982
	30: 2 and to **t** in the shadow of Egypt.	2620
	30: 3 the **t** in the shadow of Egypt *your*	2622
	30:12 **t** in oppression and perverseness,	982
	31: 1 and **t** in chariots, because *they are* many;	982
	36: 5 on whom dost thou **t**, that thou rebellest	982
	36: 6 Pharaoh king of Egypt to all that **t** in him.	982
	36: 7 say to me, We **t** in the Lord our God:	982
	36: 9 **put** thy **t** on Egypt for chariots and	982
	36:15 Neither let Hezekiah **make** you **t** in	982
	42:17 that **t** in graven images, that say to	982
	50:10 let him **t** in the name of the Lord,	982
	51: 5 upon me, and on mine arm shall they **t**.	3176
	57:13 he that **putteth** his **t** in me shall possess	2620
	59: 4 *they* **t** in vanity, and speak lies;	982
Jer	7: 4 **T** ye not in lying words, saying, The temple	982
	7: 8 Behold, ye **t** in lying words, *that* cannot	982
	7:14 wherein ye **t**, and unto the place which I	982
	9: 4 his neighbour, and **t** ye not in any brother:	982
	28:15 but thou **makest** this people to **t** in a lie.	982
	29:31 him not, and he **caused** you to **t** in a lie:	982
	39:18 because thou hast **put** thy **t** in me, saith	982
	46:25 even Pharaoh, and *all* them that **t** in him:	982
	49:11 *them* alive; and let thy widows **t** in me.	982
Eze	16:15 thou didst **t** in thine own beauty,	982
	33:13 if he **t** to his own righteousness,	982
Hos	10:13 because thou didst **t** in thy way,	982
Am	6: 1 in Zion, and **t** in the mountain of Samaria,	982
Mic	7: 5 **T** ye not in a friend, put ye not confidence	539
Na	1: 7 and he knoweth them that **t** in him.	2620
Zep	3:12 and they shall **t** in the name of the Lord.	2620
Mt	12:21 And in his name shall the Gentiles **t**.	1679
Mk	10:24 how hard is it for them that **t** in riches to	3982
Lk	16:11 will **commit** to your **t** the true *riches*?	4100
Jn	5:45 accuseth you, *even* Moses, in whom ye **t**.	1679
Ro	15:12 the Gentiles; in him shall the Gentiles **t**.	1679
	15:24 for I **t** to see you in my journey, and to be	1679
1Co	16: 7 I **t** to tarry a while with you, if the Lord	1679
2Co	1: 9 that we should not **t** in ourselves,	3982
	1:10 in whom we **t** that he will yet deliver *us*;	1679
	1:13 I **t** you shall acknowledge even to the end;	1679
	3: 4 And such **t** have we through Christ to	4006
	5:11 **t** it also are made manifest in your	1679
	10: 7 If any *man* **t** to himself that *he* is Christ's,	3982
	13: 6 But I **t** that ye shall know that we are not	1679
Php	2:19 I **t** in the Lord Jesus to send Timotheus	1679
	2:24 But I **t** in the Lord that I also myself shall	3982
	3: 4 *he* hath *whereof* he might **t** in the flesh,	3982
1Th	2: 4 of God to be **put in t** with the gospel,	4100
1Ti	1:11 which was **committed** to my **t**.	4100
	4:10 because we **t** in the living God,	1679
	6:17 nor **t** in uncertain riches, but in the living	1679
	6:20 keep that which is **committed** to *thy* **t**,	3872
Phm	1:22 for I **t** that through your prayers I shall be	1679
Heb	2:13 And again, I will **put** my **t** in him.	3982
	13:18 for we **t** we have a good conscience, in all	3982
2Jn	1:12 I **t** to come unto you, and speak face to	1679
3Jn	1:14 I **t** *I* shall shortly see thee, and we shall	1679

TRUSTED (29) [TRUST]

Dt	32:37 *are* their gods, *their* rock in whom they **t**,	2620
Jdg	11:20 Sihon **t** not Israel to pass through his coast:	539
	20:36 they **t** unto the liers in wait which they had	982
2Ki	18: 5 He **t** in the Lord God of Israel;	982
Ps	13: 5 I have **t** in thy mercy; my heart shall rejoice	982
	22: 4 Our fathers **t** in thee: they trusted,	982
	22: 4 thee: they **t**, and thou didst deliver them.	982
	22: 5 they **t** in thee, and were not confounded.	982
	22: 8 He **t** on the Lord *that* he would deliver	1556
	26: 1 I have **t** also in the Lord; *therefore* I shall	982
	28: 7 my heart **t** in him, and I am helped:	982
	31:14 I **t** in thee, O Lord: I said, Thou *art* my	982
	33:21 him, because we have **t** in his holy name.	982

Ps	41: 9 mine own familiar friend, in whom I **t**,	982
	52: 7 in the abundance of his riches,	982
	78:22 not in God, and **t** not in his salvation:	982
Isa	47:10 For thou hast **t** in thy wickedness: thou	982
Jer	13:25 thou hast forgotten me, and **t** in falsehood.	982
	48: 7 For because thou hast **t** in thy works and	982
	49: 4 that **t** in her treasures, *saying*, Who shall	982
Da	3:28 delivered his servants that **t** in him,	7365
Zep	3: 2 not correction; she **t** not in the Lord;	982
Mt	27:43 He is God; let him deliver him now, if	3982
Lk	11:22 *from him* all his armour wherein he **t**,	3982
	18: 9 **t** in themselves that they were righteous,	3982
	24:21 But we **t** that it had been he which should	1679
Eph	1:12 praise of his glory, who **first t** in Christ:	4276
	1:13 In whom ye also **t**, after that ye heard	NIG
1Pe	3: 5 who **t** in God, adorned themselves, being	1679

TRUSTEDST (3) [TRUST]

Dt	28:52 wherein thou **t**, throughout all thy land:	982
Jer	5:17 cities, wherein thou **t**, with the sword.	982
	12: 5 *wherein* thou **t**, *they* wearied thee, then	982

TRUSTEST (6) [TRUST]

2Ki	18:19 What confidence *is* this where*in* thou **t**?	982
	18:21 thou **t** upon the staff of this bruised reed,	982
	19:10 Let not thy God in whom thou **t** deceive	982
Isa	36: 4 What confidence *is* this where*in* thou **t**?	982
	36: 6 Lo, thou **t** in the staff of this broken reed,	982
	37:10 in whom thou **t**, deceive thee, saying,	982

TRUSTETH (17) [TRUST]

Job	40:23 he **t** that he can draw up Jordan into his	982
Ps	21: 7 For the king **t** in the Lord,	982
	32:10 he that **t** in the Lord, mercy shall compass	982
	34: 8 *is* good: blessed *is* the man that **t** in him.	2620
	57: 1 for my soul **t** in thee: yea, in the shadow	2620
	84:12 of hosts, blessed *is* the man that **t** in thee.	982
	86: 2 my God, save thy servant that **t** in thee.	982
	115: 8 unto them; *so is* every one that **t** in them.	982
	135:18 unto them; *so is* every one that **t** in them.	982
Pr	11:28 He that **t** in his riches shall fall:	982
	16:20 and whoso **t** in the Lord, happy *is* he.	982
	28:26 He that **t** in his own heart *is* a fool:	982
Isa	26: 3 *is* stayed *on thee*: because he **t** in thee.	982
Jer	17: 5 Cursed *be* the man that **t** in man,	982
	17: 7 Blessed *is* the man that **t** in the Lord,	982
Hab	2:18 lies, that the maker of his work **t** therein,	982
1Ti	5: 5 **t** in God, and continueth in supplications	1679

TRUSTING (1) [TRUST]

Ps	112: 7 his heart is fixed, **t** in the Lord.	982

TRUSTY (1) [TRUST]

Job	12:20 He removeth away the speech of the **t**,	539

TRUTH (235) [TRUE, TRULY, TRUTH'S]

Ge	24:27 destitute my master of his mercy and his **t**:	571
	32:10 of all the **t**, which thou hast shewed unto	571
	42:16 be proved, whether *there be any* **t** in you:	571
Ex	18:21 such as fear God, men of **t**,	571
	34: 6 abundant in goodness and **t**,	571
Dt	13:14 behold, *if it be* **t**, *and* the thing certain,	571
	32: 4 a God of **t** and without iniquity, just and	530
Jos	24:14 and serve him in sincerity and in **t**:	571
Jdg	9:15 If in **t** ye anoint me king over you, *then*	571
1Sa	21: 5 and serve him in **t** with all your heart:	571
	21: 5 *Of a* **t** women *have been* kept from	518+3588
2Sa	2: 6 The Lord shew kindness and **t** unto you:	571
	15:20 thy brethren: mercy and **t** be with thee.	571
1Ki	2: 4 to walk before me in **t** with all their heart	571
	3: 6 according as he walked before thee in **t**,	571
	17:24 the word of the Lord in thy mouth *is* **t**.	571
2Ki	19:17 *Of a* **t**, Lord, the kings of Assyria have	551
	20: 3 now how I have walked before thee in **t**	571
	20:19 *not good*, *If* peace and **t** be in my days?	571
2Ch	18:15 but the **t** to me in the name of the Lord?	571
	31:20 and right and **t** before the Lord his God.	571
Est	9:30 of Ahasuerus, *with* words of peace and **t**,	571
Job	9: 2 I know *it is* so of a **t**: but how should man	551
Ps	15: 2 and speaketh the **t** in his heart.	571
	25: 5 Lead me in thy **t**, and teach me: for thou	571
	25:10 unto such as keep his covenant and	571
	26: 3 mine eyes: and I have walked in thy **t**.	571
	30: 9 the dust praise thee? shall it declare thy **t**?	571
	31: 5 thou hast redeemed me, O Lord God of **t**.	571
	33: 4 *is* right; and all his works *are* done in **t**.	530
	40:10 and thy **t** from the great congregation.	571
	40:11 and thy **t** continually preserve me.	571
	43: 3 send out thy light and thy **t**: let them lead	571
	45: 4 because of **t** and meekness *and*	571
	51: 6 Behold, thou desirest **t** in the inward parts:	571
	54: 5 unto mine enemies: cut them off in thy **t**.	571
	57: 3 God shall send forth his mercy and his **t**.	571
	57:10 the heavens, and thy **t** unto the clouds.	571
	60: 4 that *it may* be displayed because of the **t**.	7189
	61: 7 prepare mercy and **t**, *which* may preserve	571
	69:13 mercy hear me, in the **t** of thy salvation.	571
	71:22 with the psaltery, *even* thy **t**, O my God:	571
	85:10 Mercy and **t** are met together;	571
	85:11 **T** shall spring out of the earth;	571
	86:11 me thy way, O Lord; I will walk in thy **t**:	571
	86:15 and plenteous in mercy and **t**.	571
	89:14 mercy and **t** shall go before thy face.	571
	89:49 *which* thou swarest unto David in thy **t**?	530
	91: 4 his **t** *shall be thy* shield and buckler.	571

Ps	96:13 righteousness, and the people with his **t**.	530
	98: 3 his **t** toward the house of Israel:	530
	100: 5 his **t** *endureth* to all generations.	530
	108: 4 and thy **t** *reacheth* unto the clouds.	571
	111: 8 ever, *and are* done in **t** and uprightness.	571
	117: 2 the **t** of the Lord *endureth* for ever.	571
	119:30 I have chosen the way of **t**: thy judgments	530
	119:43 take not the word of **t** utterly out of my	571
	119:142 and thy law *is* the **t**.	571
	119:151 O Lord; and all thy commandments *are* **t**.	571
	132:11 The Lord hath sworn in **t** unto David;	571
	138: 2 name for thy lovingkindness and for thy **t**:	571
	145:18 upon him, to all that call upon him in **t**.	571
	146: 6 that therein is: which keepeth **t** for ever:	571
Pr	3: 3 Let not mercy and **t** forsake thee: bind	571
	8: 7 For my mouth shall speak **t**;	571
	12:17 *He that* speaketh **t** sheweth forth	530
	12:19 The lip of **t** shall be established for ever:	571
	14:22 and **t** *shall be* to them that devise good.	571
	16: 6 By mercy and **t** iniquity is purged:	571
	20:28 Mercy and **t** preserve the king:	571
	22:21 thee know the certainty of the words of **t**;	571
	22:21 that *thou* mightest answer the words of **t**	571
	23:23 Buy the **t**, and sell *it* not; *also* wisdom,	571
Ecc	12:10 *was* written *was* upright, *even* words of **t**.	571
Isa	5: 9 **Of a t** many houses shall be desolate,	518+3808
	10:20 the Lord, the Holy One of Israel, in **t**.	571
	16: 5 he shall sit upon it in **t** in the tabernacle of	571
	25: 1 *thy* counsels of old *are* faithfulness *and* **t**.	544
	26: 2 the righteous nation which keepeth the **t**	529
	37:18 *Of a* **t**, Lord, the kings of Assyria have	551
	38: 3 how I have walked before thee in **t** and	571
	38:18 go down into the pit cannot hope for thy **t**.	571
	38:19 to the children shall make known thy **t**.	571
	39: 8 For there shall be peace and **t** in my days.	571
	42: 3 he shall bring forth judgment unto **t**.	571
	43: 9 justified: or let them hear, and say, *It is* **t**.	571
	48: 1 of Israel, *but* not in **t**, nor in righteousness.	571
	59: 4 calleth for justice, nor any pleadeth for **t**:	530
	59:14 for **t** is fallen in the street, and equity	571
	59:15 **t** faileth; and *he that* departeth from evil	571
	61: 8 I will direct their work in **t**, and I will	571
	65:16 earth shall bless himself in the God of **t**;	543
	65:16 in the earth shall swear by the God of **t**;	543
Jer	4: 2 in **t**, in judgment, and in righteousness;	571
	5: 1 executeth judgment, that seeketh the **t**;	530
	5: 3 O Lord, *are* not thine eyes upon the **t**?	530
	7:28 **t** is perished, and is cut off from their	530
	9: 3 are not valiant for the **t** upon the earth;	571
	9: 5 his neighbour, and will not speak the **t**:	571
	26:15 for of a **t** the Lord hath sent me unto you	571
	33: 6 unto them the abundance of peace and **t**.	571
Da	2:47 *Of a* **t** *it is*, that your God *is* a God	4481+7187
	4:37 all whose works *are* **t**, and his ways	7187
	7:16 stood *by*, and asked him the **t** of all this.	3330
	7:19 I would *know* the **t** of the fourth beast,	3321
	8:12 and it cast down the **t** to the ground;	571
	9:13 from our iniquities, and understand thy **t**.	571
	10:21 that which is noted in the scripture of **t**:	571
	11: 2 now will I shew thee the **t**. Behold,	571
Hos	4: 1 because *there is* no **t**, nor mercy,	571
Mic	7:20 Thou wilt perform the **t** to Jacob,	571
Zec	8: 3 and Jerusalem shall be called a city of **t**;	571
	8: 8 be their God, in **t** and in righteousness.	571
	8:16 Speak ye every man the **t** to his neighbour;	571
	8:16 execute the judgment of **t** and peace in	571
	8:19 therefore love the **t** and peace.	571
Mal	2: 6 The law of **t** was in his mouth,	571
Mt	14:33 saying, **Of a t** thou art the Son of God.	230
	15:27 And she said, **T**, Lord: yet the dogs eat of	3483
	22:16 art true, and teachest the way of God in **t**,	571
Mk	5:33 down before him, and told him all the **t**.	225
	12:14 of men, but teachest the way of God in **t**:	225
	12:32 him, Well, Master, thou hast said the **t**:	225
Lk	4:25 But I tell you of a **t**, many widows were in	225
	9:27 I tell you of a **t**, there be some standing	230
	12:44 **Of a t** I say unto you, that he will make	230
	21: 3 he said, **Of a t** I say unto you, that this	230
	22:59 **Of a t** this *fellow* also was with him:	225+1909
Jn	1:14 begotten of the Father,) full of grace and **t**.	225
	1:17 *but* grace and **t** came by Jesus Christ.	225
	3:21 But he that doeth **t** cometh to the light,	225
	4:23 shall worship the Father in spirit and *in* **t**:	225
	4:24 him must worship *him* in spirit and *in* **t**.	225
	5:33 unto John, and he bare witness unto the **t**.	225
	6:14 This is *of a* **t** *that* prophet that should come	230
	7:40 *this* saying, said, **Of a t** this is the Prophet.	230
	8:32 ye shall know the **t**, and the truth shall	225
	8:32 the truth, and the **t** shall make you free.	225
	8:40 a man that hath told you the **t**, which I	225
	8:44 and abode not in the **t**, because there is no	225
	8:44 in the **t**, because there is no **t** in him.	225
	8:45 And because I tell *you* the **t**, ye believe me	225
	8:46 if I say the **t**, why do ye not believe me?	225
	14: 6 unto him, I am the way, and the **t**, and the life:	225
	14:17 the Spirit of **t**; whom the world cannot	225
	15:26 the Spirit of **t**, which proceedeth from	225
	16: 7 Nevertheless I tell you the **t**; It is expedient	225
	16:13 Howbeit when he, the Spirit of **t**, is come,	225
	16:13 **t**, is come, he will guide you into all **t**:	225
	17:17 Sanctify them through thy **t**: thy word is **t**.	225
	17:17 them through thy truth: thy word is **t**.	225
	17:19 also might be sanctified through the **t**.	225
	18:37 that I should bear witness unto the **t**.	225
	18:37 Every one that is of the **t** heareth my voice.	225

T

Jn	18:38 Pilate saith unto him, What is **t**? And when	225
Ac	4:27 **of a t** against thy holy child Jesus,	225+1909
	10:34 **Of a t** I perceive that God is no	225+1909
	26:25 but speak forth the *words* of **t** and	225
Ro	1:18 men, who hold the **t** in unrighteousness;	225
	1:25 Who changed the **t** of God into a lie,	225
	2: 2 against them which commit such *things*.	225
	2: 8 and do not obey the **t**,	225
	2:20 form of knowledge and of the **t** in the law.	225
	3: 7 For if the **t** of God hath *more* abounded	225
	9: 1 I say the **t** in Christ, I lie not, my	225
	15: 8 of the circumcision for the **t** of God,	225
1Co	5: 8 the unleavened bread of sincerity and **t**.	225
	13: 6 not in iniquity, but rejoiceth in the **t**;	225
	14:25 and report that God is in you **of a t**.	3689
2Co	4: 2 by manifestation of the **t** commending	225
	6: 7 By the word of **t**, by the power of God,	225
	7:14 but as we spake all *things* to you in **t**, even	225
	7:14 which *I* made before Titus, is found a **t**.	225
	11:10 the **t** of Christ is in me, no *man* shall stop	225
	12: 6 I will *not* be a fool; for I will say the **t**:	225
	13: 8 For we can do nothing against the **t**,	225
	13: 8 do nothing against the truth, but for the **t**.	225
Gal	2: 5 that the **t** of the gospel might continue	225
	2:14 uprightly according to the **t** of the gospel,	225
	3: 1 that *you* should not obey the **t**,	225
	4:16 your enemy, because I **tell you the t**?	226
	5: 7 hinder you that *ye* should not obey the **t**?	225
Eph	1:13 *trusted*, after that ye heard the word of **t**,	225
	4:15 But **speaking the t** in love, may grow *up*	226
	4:21 been taught by him, as the **t** is in Jesus:	225
	4:25 speak every man **t** with his neighbour:	225
	5: 9 *is* in all goodness and righteousness and **t**;)	225
	6:14 having your loins girt about with **t**,	225
Php	1:18 in pretence, or in **t**, Christ is preached;	225
Col	1: 5 ye heard before in the word of the **t**	225
	1: 6 of *it*, and knew the grace of God in **t**:	225
1Th	2:13 of men, but as it is in **t**, the word of God,	230
2Th	2:10 because they received not the love of the **t**,	225
	2:12 might be damned who believed not the **t**,	225
	2:13 of the Spirit and belief of the **t**:	225
1Ti	2: 4 and to come unto the knowledge of the **t**.	225
	2: 7 (I speak the **t** in Christ, *and* lie not;)	225
	3:15 living God, the pillar and ground of the **t**.	225
	4: 3 of them which believe and know the **t**.	225
	6: 5 destitute of the **t**, supposing that gain is	225
2Ti	2:15 be ashamed, rightly dividing the word of **t**.	225
	2:18 Who concerning the **t** have erred, saying	225
	2:25 repentance to the acknowledging of the **t**;	225
	3: 7 able to come to the knowledge of the **t**.	225
	3: 8 so do these also resist the **t**:	225
	4: 4 they shall turn away *their* ears from the **t**,	225
Tit	1: 1 the acknowledging of the **t** which is after	225
	1:14 of men, that turn from the **t**.	225
Heb	10:26 *we* have received the knowledge of the **t**,	225
Jas	1:18 own will begat he us with the word of **t**,	225
	3:14 glory not, and lie *not* against the **t**.	225
	5:19 if any of you do err from the **t**,	225
1Pe	1:22 **t** through the Spirit unto unfeigned love of	225
2Pe	1:12 and be stablished in the present **t**.	225
	2: 2 reason of whom the way of **t** shall be evil	225
1Jn	1: 6 walk in darkness, we lie, and do not the **t**:	225
	1: 8 deceive ourselves, and the **t** is not in us.	225
	2: 4 is a liar, and the **t** is not in him.	225
	2:21 unto you because ye know not the **t**,	225
	2:21 ye know it, and that no lie is of the **t**.	225
	2:27 teacheth you of all *things*, and is **t**,	227
	3:18 neither in tongue; but in deed and in **t**.	225
	3:19 And hereby we know that we are of the **t**,	225
	4: 6 Hereby know we the spirit of **t**, and the	225
	5: 6 beareth witness, because the Spirit is **t**.	225
2Jn	1: 1 and her children, whom I love in the **t**;	225
	1: 1 but also all they that have known the **t**;	225
	1: 3 the Son of the Father, in **t** and love.	225
	1: 4 that I found of thy children walking in **t**,	225
3Jn	1: 1 wellbeloved Gaius, whom I love in the **t**.	225
	1: 3 and testified of the **t** *that is* in thee,	225
	1: 3 *is* in thee, even as thou walkest in the **t**.	225
	1: 4 joy than to hear that my children walk in **t**.	225
	1: 8 that we might be fellowhelpers to the **t**.	225
	1:12 good report of all *men*, and of the **t** itself:	225

TRUTH'S (2) [TRUTH]

Ps	115: 1 glory, for thy mercy, *and* for thy **t** sake.	571
2Jn	1: 2 For the **t** sake, which dwelleth in us,	225

TRY (17) [TRIAL, TRIED, TRIEST, TRIETH, TRYING]

Jdg	7: 4 water, and I will **t** them for thee there:	6884
2Ch	32:31 God left him, to **t** him, that *he* might	5254
Job	7:18 every morning, *and* **t** him every moment?	974
	12:11 Doth not the ear **t** words? and the mouth	974
Ps	11: 4 his eyes behold, his eyelids **t**, the children	974
	26: 2 and prove me; **t** my reins and my heart.	6884
	139:23 my heart: **t** me, and know my thoughts:	974
Jer	6:27 that thou mayest know and **t** their way.	974
	9: 7 Behold, I will melt them, and **t** them;	974
	17:10 I the LORD search the heart, *I* **t** the reins,	974
La	3:40 Let us search and **t** our ways,	2713
Da	11:35 to **t** them, and to purge, and to make	6884
Zec	13: 9 is refined, and will **t** them as gold is tried:	974
1Co	3:13 the fire shall **t** every man's work of what	1381
1Pe	4:12 concerning the fiery trial which is to **t** you,	3986
1Jn	4: 1 but **t** the spirits whether they are of God:	1381
Rev	3:10 to **t** them that dwell upon the earth.	3985

TRYING (1) [TRY]		
Jas	1: 3 Knowing *this*, that the **t** of your faith	1383
TRYPHENA (1)		
Ro	16:12 Salute **T** and Tryphosa, who labour in	5170
TRYPHOSA (1)		
Ro	16:12 Salute Tryphena and **T**, who labour in	5173

TUBAL (8)

Ge	10: 2 Javan, and **T**, and Meshech, and Tiras.	8422
1Ch	1: 5 Javan, and **T**, and Meshech, and Tiras.	8422
Isa	66:19 Lud, that draw the bow, to **T**, and Javan,	8422
Eze	27:13 Javan, **T**, and Meshech, they *were* thy	8422
	32:26 *is* Meshech, **T**, and all her multitude:	8422
	38: 2 the chief prince of Meshech and **T**:	8422
	38: 3 Gog, the chief prince of Meshech and **T**:	8422
	39: 1 Gog, the chief prince of Meshech and **T**:	8422

TUBAL-CAIN (2)

Ge	4:22 Zillah, she also bare **T**, an instructor of	8423
	4:22 iron: and the sister of **T** *was* Naamah.	8423

TUCKED INTO BELT See GIRDED

TUMBLED (1)

Jdg	7:13 a cake of barley bread **t** into the host of	2015

TUMORS See EMERODS

TUMULT (16) [TUMULTS, TUMULTUOUS]

1Sa	4:14 said, What *meaneth* the noise of this **t**?	1995
2Sa	18:29 saw a great **t**, but I knew not what *it was*.	1995
2Ki	19:28 and thy **t** is come up into mine ears,	7600
Ps	65: 7 of their waves, and the **t** of the people.	1995
	74:23 the **t** of those that rise up against thee	7588
	83: 2 For lo, thine enemies **make a t**:	1995
Isa	33: 3 At the noise of the **t** the people fled;	1995
	37:29 thy **t**, is come up into mine ears, therefore	7600
Jer	11:16 with the noise of a great **t** he hath kindled	1999
Hos	10:14 Therefore shall a **t** arise among thy people,	7588
Am	2: 2 Moab shall die with **t**, with shouting,	7588
Zec	14:13 *that* a great **t** from the LORD shall be	4103
Mt	27:24 *that* rather a **t** was made, he took water,	2351
Mk	5:38 and seeth *the* **t**, and them that wept and	2351
Ac	21:34 he could not know the certainty for the **t**,	2351
	24:18 neither with multitude, nor with **t**.	2351

TUMULTS (3) [TUMULT]

Am	3: 9 behold the great **t** in the midst thereof,	4103
2Co	6: 5 in **t**, in labours, in watchings, in fastings;	181
	12:20 backbitings, whisperings, swellings, **t**:	181

TUMULTUOUS (3) [TUMULT]

Isa	13: 4 a **t** noise of the kingdoms of nations	7588
	22: 2 *that art* full *of* stirs, a **t** city, a joyous city:	1993
Jer	48:45 and the crown of the head of the **t** ones.	7588

TUNNEL See CONDUIT

TURBAN See MITRE

TURBANS See BONNETS; TIRES

TURN (283) [OVERTURN, TURNED, TURNEST, TURNETH, TURNING]

Ge	19: 2 Behold now, my lords, **t** in, I pray you,	5493
	24:49 I may **t** to the right hand, or to the left.	6437
	27:44 few days, until thy brother's fury **t** away;	7725
	27:45 thy brother's anger **t** away from thee,	7725
Ex	3: 3 I will now **t** aside, and see this great	5493
	14: 2 that they **t** and encamp before Pi-hahiroth,	7725
	23:27 will make all thine enemies **t** their **backs**	6203
	32:12 **T** from thy fierce wrath, and repent of	7725
Lev	13:16 if the raw flesh **t** again, and be changed	7725
	19: 4 **T** ye not unto idols, nor make to	6437
Nu	14:25 To morrow **t** you, and get you *into*	6437
	20:17 we will not **t** to the right hand nor *to*	5186
	21:22 we will not **t** into the fields, or into	5186
	22:23 smote the ass, to **t** her *into* the way.	5186
	22:26 where *was* no way to **t** *either* to the right	5186
	32:15 For if ye **t** away from after him, he will	7725
	34: 4 your border shall **t** from the south to	5437
Dt	1: 7 **T** you, and take your journey, and go *to*	6437
	1:40 **t** ye, and take your journey into	5265
	2: 3 mountain long enough: **t** you northward.	6437
	2:27 I will neither **t** *unto* the right hand nor *to*	5493
	4:30 if thou **t** to the LORD thy God,	7725
	5:32 ye shall not **t** aside *to* the right hand or	5493
	7: 4 For they will **t** away thy son from	5493
	11:16 ye **t** aside, and serve other gods,	5493
	11:28 **t** aside out of the way which I command	5493
	13: 5 he hath spoken to **t** *you* away from	5627
	13:17 that the LORD may **t** from the fierceness	7725
	14:25 shalt thou **t** *it* into money, and bind up	5414
	16: 7 thou shalt **t** in the morning, and go unto	6437
	17:17 to himself, that his heart **t** not away:	5493
	17:20 *he* **t** not aside from the commandment,	5493
	23:13 shalt **t** back and cover that which cometh	7725
	23:14 thing in thee, and **t** away from thee.	7725
	30: 3 the LORD thy God will **t** thy captivity,	7725
	30:10 if thou **t** unto the LORD thy God with all	7725
	30:17 if thine heart **t** away, so that thou wilt	6437
	31:20 they **t** unto other gods, and serve them,	6437
	31:29 **t** aside from the way which I have	5493
Jos	1: 7 **t** not from it *to* the right hand or *to* the	5493
	22:16 **t** away *this* day from following	7725

Jos	22:18 that ye must **t** away *this* day from	7725	
	22:23 That we have built us an altar to **t** from	7725	
	22:29 **t** *this* day from following the LORD,	7725	
	23: 6 that *ye* **t** not aside therefrom *to* the right	5493	
	24:20 he will **t** and do you hurt,	7725	
Jdg	4:18 unto him, **T** in, my lord, turn in to me;	5493	
	4:18 unto him, Turn in, my lord, **t** in to me;	5493	
	11: 8 Therefore we **t** again to thee now, that	7725	
	19:11 let us **t** in into this city of the Jebusites,	5493	
	19:12 We will not **t** aside hither into the city of	5493	
	20: 8 We will not any of *us* **t** into his house.	5493	
Ru	1:11 Naomi said, **T** again, my daughters:	7725	
	1:12 **T** again, my daughters, go *your way*; for I	7725	
	4: 1 *Ho*, such a one, **t** aside, sit down here.	5493	
1Sa	12:20 yet **t** not aside from following the LORD,	5493	
	12:21 **t** ye not aside: for *then* should ye go after	5493	
	14: 7 **t** thee; behold, I *am* with thee according	5186	
	15:25 pardon my sin, and **t** again with me,	7725	
	15:30 and before Israel, and **t** again with me,	7725	
	22:17 **T**, and slay the priests of the LORD;	5437	
	22:18 to Doeg, **T** thou, and fall upon the priests.	5437	
2Sa	2:21 **T** thee aside to thy right hand or to thy	5186	
	2:21 Asahel would not **t** aside from following	5493	
	2:22 Asahel, **T** thee aside from following me:	5493	
	2:23 Howbeit he refused to **t** aside:	5493	
	14:19 none can **t** to the right hand or to the	3231	
	14:24 Let him **t** to his own house, and let him	5437	
	15:31 **t** the counsel of Ahithophel	5528	
		into foolishness.	5528
	18:30 the king said *unto* him, **T** aside,	5437	
	19:37 Let thy servant, I pray thee, **t** back again,	7725	
1Ki	8:33 **t** again to thee, and confess thy name,	7725	
	8:35 confess thy name, and **t** from their sin,	7725	
	9: 6 shall **at all t** from following me,	7725+7725	
	11: 2 surely they will **t** away your heart after	5186	
	12:27 shall the heart of this people **t** again unto	7725	
	13: 9 nor **t** again by the *same* way that thou	7725	
	13:17 nor **t** again to go by the way that thou	7725	
	17: 3 **t** thee eastward, and hide thyself by	6437	
	22:34 **T** thine hand, and carry me out of the	2015	
2Ki	1: 6 **t** again unto the king that sent you,	7725	
	4:10 he cometh to us, *that* he shall **t** in thither.	5493	
	9:18 **t** thee behind me. And the watchman	5437	
	9:19 thou to do with peace? **t** thee behind me.	5437	
	17:13 **T** ye from your evil ways, and keep my	7725	
	18:24 wilt thou **t** away the face of one captain	7725	
	19:28 I will **t** thee **back** by the way by which	7725	
	20: 5 **T** again, and tell Hezekiah the captain of	5437	
1Ch	12:23 Hebron, to **t** the kingdom of Saul to him,	5437	
	14:14 **t** away from them, and come upon them	5437	
2Ch	6:26 confess thy name, *and* **t** from their sin,	7725	
	6:37 **t** and pray unto thee in the land of their	7725	
	6:42 **t** not away the face of thine anointed:	7725	
	7:14 my face, and **t** from their wicked ways;	7725	
	7:19 if ye **t** away, and forsake my statutes and	7725	
	15: 4 when they in their trouble did **t** unto	7725	
	18:33 he said to *his* chariot man, **T** thine hand,	2015	
	25:27 after the time that Amaziah did **t** away	5493	
	29:10 that his fierce wrath may **t** away from us.	7725	
	30: 6 **t** again unto the LORD God of Abraham,	7725	
	30: 8 the fierceness of his wrath may **t** away	7725	
	30: 9 For if ye **t** again unto the LORD,	7725	
	30: 9 and will not **t** away *his* face from you,	5493	
	35:22 Nevertheless Josiah would not **t** his face	5437	
Ne	1: 9 *if* ye **t** unto me, and keep my	7725	
	4: 4 their reproach upon their own head,	7725	
	9:26 testified against them to **t** them to thee,	7725	
Est	2:12 Now when every maid's **t** was come to	8447	
	2:15 Now when the **t** of Esther, the daughter	8447	
Job	5: 1 and to which of the saints wilt thou **t**?	6437	
	14: 6 **T** from him, that he may rest, till he shall	8159	
	23:13 he *is* in one *mind*, and who can **t** him?	7725	
	24: 4 They **t** the needy out of the way: the poor	5186	
	34:15 and man shall **t** again unto dust.	7725	
Ps	4: 2 how long *will ye* **t** my glory into shame?	NIH	
	7:12 If he **t** not, he will whet his sword; he	7725	
	18:37 neither did I **t** again till they were	7725	
	21:12 Therefore shalt thou **make** them their	7896	
	22:27 shall remember and **t** unto the LORD:	7725	
	25:16 **T** thee unto me, and have mercy upon	6437	
	40: 4 not the proud, nor such as **t** aside to lies.	7750	
	44:10 makest us to **t** back from the enemy:	7725	
	56: 9 *thee*, then shall mine enemies **t** back:	7725	
	60: 1 been displeased; O **t** thyself to us **again**.	7725	
	69:16 **t** unto me according to the multitude of	6437	
	80: 3 **T** us **again**, O God, and cause thy face to	7725	
	80: 7 **T** us **again**, O God *of* hosts, and cause	7725	
	80:19 **T** us **again**, O LORD God *of* hosts,	7725	
	85: 4 **T** us, O God of our salvation,	7725	
	85: 8 saints: but let them not **t** *again* to folly.	7725	
	86:16 O **t** unto me, and have mercy upon me;	6437	
	101: 3 I hate the work of them that **t** aside;	7750	
	104: 9 *that* they **t** not again to cover the earth.	7725	
	106:23 **t** away his wrath, lest he should destroy	7725	
	119:37 **T** away mine eyes from beholding vanity;	5674	
	119:39 **T** away my reproach which I fear: for thy	5674	
	119:79 Let those that fear thee **t** unto me,	7725	
	125: 5 As for such as **t** aside *unto* their crooked	5186	
	126: 4 **T** again our captivity, O LORD,	7725	
	132:10 For thy servant David's sake **t** not **away**	7725	
	132:11 *in* truth unto David; he will not **t** from it;	7725	
Pr	1:23 **T** you at my reproof: behold, I will pour	7725	
	4:15 pass not by it, **t** from it, and pass away.	7847	
	4:27 **T** not to the right hand nor *to* the left:	5186	
	9: 4 Whoso *is* simple, let him **t** in hither:	5493	

Pr
9:16 Whoso *is* simple, let him **t in** hither: 5493
24:18 and he **t away** his wrath from him. 7725
25:10 to shame, and thine infamy **t** not **away.** 7725
29: 8 into a snare: but wise *men* **t away** wrath. 7725
Ecc 3:20 all are of the dust, and all **t** to dust **again.** 7725
SS 2:17 **t**, my beloved, and be thou like a roe or a 5437
6: 5 **T away** thine eyes from me, for they have 5437
Isa 1:25 I will **t** my hand upon thee, and purely 7725
10: 2 To **t aside** the needy from judgment, 5186
13:14 they shall every man **t** to his own people, 6437
14:27 *is* stretched out, and who shall **t it back?** 7725
19: 6 they shall **t** the rivers **far away;** 2186
22:18 **surely violently t** and toss 6801+6801+6802
23:17 she shall **t** to her hire, and shall commit 7725
28: 6 for strength to them that **t** the battle to 7725
29:21 and **t aside** the just for a thing of nought. 5186
30:11 ye out of the way, **t aside** out of the path, 5186
30:21 when ye **t** to **the right hand,** and when 541
30:21 the right hand, and when ye **t to the left.** 8041
31: 6 **T** ye unto *him from* whom the children 7725
36: 9 wilt thou **t away** the face of one captain 7725
37:29 I will **t** thee **back** by the way by which 7725
58:13 If thou **t away** thy foot from the sabbath, 7725
59:20 unto them that **t from** transgression in 7725
Jer 2:24 *in* her occasion who can **t** her **away?** 7725
2:35 surely his anger shall **t** from me. 7725
3: 7 after she had done all these *things,* **T** 7725
3:14 **T**, O backsliding children, saith 7725
3:19 father; and shalt not **t away** from me. 7725
4:28 not repent, neither will I **t back** from it. 7725
6: 9 **t** back thine hand as a grapegatherer into 7725
8: 4 arise? shall he **t away,** and not return? 7725
13:16 he **t it** into the shadow of death, *and* make 7760
18: 8 I have pronounced, **t** from their evil, 7725
18:20 *and* to **t away** thy wrath from them. 7725
21: 4 I *will* **t back** the weapons of war *that are* 5437
25: 5 **T** ye **again** now every one from his evil 7725
26: 3 and **t** every man from his evil way, 7725
29:14 I will **t away** your captivity, and I will 7725
31:13 for I will **t** their mourning into joy, 2015
31:18 as a bullock unaccustomed *to the yoke;* **t** 7725
31:21 **t again,** O virgin of Israel, turn again to 7725
31:21 virgin of Israel, **t again** to these thy cities, 7725
32:40 that I will not **t away** from them, to do 7725
44: 5 nor inclined their ear to **t** from their 7725
49: 8 Flee ye, **t back,** dwell deep, O inhabitants 6437
50:16 fear of the oppressing sword they shall **t** 6437
La 2:14 thine iniquity, to **t away** thy captivity; 7725
3:35 To **t aside** the right of a man before 5186
3:40 try our ways, and **t again** to the LORD. 7725
5:21 **T** thou us unto thee, O LORD, 7725
Eze 3:19 he **t** not from his wickedness, nor from 7725
3:20 When a righteous *man* doth **t** from his 7725
4: 8 thou shalt not **t** thee from one side to 2015
7:22 My face will I **t** also from them, 5437
8: 6 **t** thee yet **again,** *and* thou shalt see 7725
8:13 **T** thee yet **again,** *and* thou shalt see 7725
8:15 **t** thee yet **again,** *and* thou shalt see 7725
14: 6 Repent, and **t** *yourselves* from your idols; 7725
14: 6 **t away** your faces from all your 7725
18:21 if the wicked will **t** from all his sins *that* 7725
18:30 **t** *yourselves* from all your transgressions; 7725
18:32 wherefore **t** *yourselves,* and live ye. 7725
33: 9 if thou warn the wicked of his way to **t** 7725
33: 9 if he do not **t** from his way, he shall die in 7725
33:11 that the wicked **t** from his way and live: 7725
33:11 **t** ye, turn ye from your evil ways; for why 7725
33:11 turn ye, **t** ye from your evil ways; for why 7725
33:14 if he **t** from his sin, and do that which is 7725
33:19 if the wicked **t** from his wickedness, 7725
36: 9 I will **t** unto you, and ye shall be tilled 6437
38: 4 I will **t** thee **back,** and put hooks into thy 7725
38:12 to **t** thine hand upon the desolate places 7725
39: 2 I will **t** thee **back,** and leave but the sixth 7725
Da 9:13 that *we* might **t** from our iniquities, 7725
11:18 After this shall he **t** his face unto the isles, 7725
11:18 reproach he shall **cause** *it* to **t** upon him. 7725
11:19 he shall **t** his face towards the fort of his 7725
12: 3 they that **t** many to **righteousness** as 6663
Hos 5: 4 They will not frame their doings to **t** unto 7725
12: 6 Therefore **t** thou to thy God: keep mercy 7725
14: 2 Take with you words, and **t** to the LORD: 7725
Joel 2:12 **t** ye *even* to me with all your heart, 7725
2:13 and **t** unto the LORD your God: 7725
Am 1: 3 I will not **t away** *the punishment* thereof; 7725
1: 6 I will not **t away** *the punishment* thereof; 7725
1: 8 and I will **t** mine hand against Ekron; 7725
1: 9 I will not **t away** *the punishment* thereof; 7725
1:11 I will not **t away** *the punishment* thereof; 7725
1:13 I will not **t away** *the punishment* thereof; 7725
2: 1 I will not **t away** *the punishment* thereof; 7725
2: 4 I will not **t away** *the punishment* thereof; 7725
2: 6 I will not **t away** *the punishment* thereof; 7725
2: 7 poor, and **t aside** the way of the meek: 5186
5: 7 *Ye* who **t** judgment to wormwood, 2015
5:12 they **t aside** the poor in the gate *from* 5186
8:10 I will **t** your feasts into mourning, 2015
Jnh 3: 8 let them **t** every one from his evil way, 7725
3: 9 Who can tell *if* God will **t** and repent, 7725
3: 9 repent, and **t away** from his fierce anger, 7725
Mic 7:19 He will **t again,** he will have compassion 7725
Zep 2: 7 visit them, and **t away** their captivity. 7725
3: 9 will I **t** to the people a pure language, 2015
3:20 when I **t back** your captivity before your 7725
Zec 1: 3 **T** ye unto me, saith the LORD of hosts,

Zec
1: 3 I will **t** unto you, saith the LORD of hosts. 7725
1: 4 **T** ye now from your evil ways, 7725
9:12 **T** ye to the strong hold, ye prisoners of 7725
10: 9 shall live with their children, and **t again.** 7725
13: 7 I will **t** mine hand upon the little ones. 7725
Mal 2: 6 and did **t** many **away** from iniquity. 7725
3: 5 that **t aside** the stranger *from his right,* 5186
4: 6 he shall **t** the heart of the fathers to 7725
Mt 5:39 on thy right cheek, **t** to him the other also. 4762
5:42 would borrow of thee **t** not thou **away.** 654
6: 8 under their feet, and **t** *again* and rent you. 4762
Mk 13:16 And let him that is in the field not **t back** 1994
Lk 1:16 shall he **t** to the Lord their God. 1994
1:17 to **t** the hearts of the fathers **to** 1994
10: 9 rest upon it: if not, it shall **t** to you **again.** 344
17: 4 and seven times in a day **t again** to thee, 1994
21:13 And it shall **t** to you for a testimony. 576
Ac 13: 8 to **t away** the deputy from the faith. 1294
13:46 of everlasting life, lo, we **t** to the Gentiles. 4762
14:15 from these vanities **unto** the living 1994
26:18 *and* to **t** *them* from darkness to light, 1994
26:20 that *they* should repent and **t** to God, 1994
Ro 11:26 and shall **t away** ungodliness from Jacob: 654
2Co 3:16 Nevertheless when *it* shall **t** to the Lord, 1994
Gal 4: 9 how **t** ye again to the weak and 1994
Php 1:19 For I know that this shall **t** to my salvation 576
2Ti 3: 5 the power thereof: **from** such **t away.** 665
4: 4 And they shall **t away** *their* ears from 654
Tit 1:14 of men, that **t from** the truth. 654
Heb 12:25 **t away** from him that *speaketh* from 654
Jas 3: 4 and we **t** about their whole body. 3329
2Pe 2:21 they have known *it,* to **t** from the holy 1994
Rev 11: 6 power over waters to **t** them to blood, 4762

TURNED (287) [TURN]

Ge
3:24 a flaming sword which **t every way,** 2015
18:22 the men **t** their **faces** from thence, 6437
19: 3 they **t in** unto him, and entered into his 5493
38: 1 **t in** to a certain Adullamite, whose name 5186
38:16 he **t** unto her by the way, and said, Go to, 5186
42:24 he **t** himself **about** from them, and wept; 5437
Ex 3: 4 when the LORD saw that he **t aside** 5493
4: 7 behold, it was **t again** as his *other* flesh. 7725
7:15 the rod which was **t** to a serpent shall 2015
7:17 in the river, and they shall be **t** to blood. 2015
7:20 the waters *that were* in the river were **t** 2015
7:23 Pharaoh **t** and went into his house, 6437
10: 6 he **t** himself, and went out from Pharaoh. 6437
10:19 the LORD **t** a mighty strong west wind, 2015
14: 5 of his servants was **t** against the people, 2015
32: 8 They have **t aside** quickly out of the way 5493
32:15 Moses **t,** and went down from the mount, 6437
33:11 he **t again** into the camp: but his servant 7725
Lev 13: 3 *when* the hair in the plague is **t** white, 2015
13: 4 skin, and the hair thereof be not **t** white; 2015
13:10 have **t** the hair white, and *there be* quick 2015
13:13 the plague: it is all **t** white: he *is* clean. 2015
13:17 behold, *if* the plague be **t** into white; then 2015
13:20 the skin, and the hair thereof be **t** white; 2015
13:25 *if* the hair in the bright spot be **t** white, 2015
Nu 14:43 because ye are **t away** from the LORD, 7725
20:21 wherefore Israel **t away** from him. 5186
21:33 they **t** and went up *by* the way of Bashan: 6437
22:23 the ass **t aside** out of the way, 5186
22:33 saw me, and **t** from me these three times: 5186
22:33 unless she had **t** from me, surely now also 5186
25: 4 of the LORD may be **t away** from Israel. 7725
25:11 hath **t** my wrath **away** from the children 7725
33: 7 **t again** unto Pi-hahiroth, which *is* before 7725
Dt 1:24 they **t** and went up into the mountain, 6437
2: 1 we **t,** and took our journey into 6437
2: 8 we **t** and passed *by* the way of 6437
3: 1 we **t,** and went up the way to Bashan: 6437
9:12 **t aside** out of the way which I 5493
9:15 So I **t** and came down from the mount, 6437
9:16 ye had **t aside** quickly out of the way 5493
10: 5 I **t** myself and came down from the mount, 6437
23: 5 the LORD thy God **t** the curse into a 2015
31:18 in that they are **t** unto other gods. 6437
Jos 7:12 *but* **t** their backs before their enemies, 6437
7:26 So the LORD **t** from the fierceness of his 7725
8:20 the wilderness **t back** upon the pursuers. 2015
8:21 they **t again,** and slew the men of Ai. 7725
11:10 Joshua at that time **t back,** and took 7725
19:12 **t** from Sarid eastward *toward* the 7725
Jdg 2:17 they **t** quickly out of the way which their 5493
15 he himself **t again** from the quarries that 7725
4:18 when he had **t in** unto her into the tent, 5493
8:33 that the children of Israel **t again,** 7725
14: 8 he **t aside** to see the carcase of the lion: 5493
15: 4 tail to tail, and put a firebrand in 6437
18: 3 they **t in** thither, and said unto him, 5493
18:15 they **t** thitherward, and came to the house 5493
18:21 So they **t** and departed, and put the little 6437
18:23 they **t** their faces, and said unto Micah, 5437
18:26 him, he **t** and went back unto his house. 6437
19:15 they **t aside** thither, to go in *and* to lodge 5493
20:41 when the men of Israel **t again,** the men 2015
20:42 Therefore they **t** *their backs* before the 6437
20:45 they **t** and fled toward the wilderness 6437
20:47 six hundred men **t** and fled to 6437
20:48 the men of Israel **t** again upon the 7725
Ru 3: 8 that the man was afraid, and **t** himself: 3943
4: 1 here. And he **t aside,** and sat down. 5493
1Sa 6:12 **t** not **aside** *to* the right hand or *to* the left; 5493

1Sa
8: 3 **t aside** after lucre, and took bribes, 5186
10: 6 them, and shalt be **t** into another man. 2015
10: 9 that when he had **t** his back to go from 6437
13:17 one company **t** unto the way that leadeth 6437
13:18 another company **t** the way to Beth-horon: 6437
13:18 another company **t** *to* the way of the 6437
14:21 they also **t** to be with the Israelites that NIH
14:47 whithersoever he **t** himself, he vexed 6437
15:11 for he is **t back** from following me, 7725
15:27 Samuel **t about** to go away, he laid hold 5437
15:31 So Samuel **t again** after Saul; 7725
17:30 he **t** from him towards another, 5437
22:18 Doeg the Edomite **t,** and he fell upon 5437
25:12 So David's young men **t** their way, 2015
2Sa 1:22 the bow of Jonathan **t** not back, 7734
2:19 in going he **t** not to the right hand nor to 5186
18:30 And he **t aside,** and stood still. 5437
19: 2 the victory that day was **t** into mourning NIH
22:38 I **t** not **again** until I had consumed them. 7725
1Ki 2:15 howbeit the kingdom is **t about,** 5437
2:28 for Joab had **t** after Adonijah, though he 5186
2:28 though he **t** not after Absalom. 5186
8:14 the king **t** his face **about,** and blessed all 5437
10:13 So she **t** and went to her own country, 6437
11: 3 and his wives **t away** his heart. 5186
11: 4 *that* his wives **t away** his heart after other 5186
11: 9 his heart was **t** from the LORD God of 5186
15: 5 **t** not **aside** from any *thing* that he 5493
18:37 *that* thou hast **t** their heart **back** again. 5437
20:39 man **t aside,** and brought a man unto me, 5493
21: 4 **t away** his face, and would eat no bread. 7725
22:32 they **t aside** to fight against him: 5493
22:33 that they **t back** from pursuing him. 7725
22:43 he **t** not **aside** from it, doing *that* which 5493
2Ki 1: 5 when the messengers **t back** unto him, 7725
1: 5 said unto them, Why are ye now **t back?** 7725
2:24 he **t** back, and looked on them, 6437
4: 8 he passed by, he **t in** thither to eat bread. 5493
4:11 he **t** into the chamber, and lay there. 5493
5:12 clean? So he **t** and went away in a rage. 6437
5:26 **t** *again* from his chariot to meet thee? 2015
9:23 Joram **t** his hands, and fled, and said to 2015
15:20 So the king of Assyria **t back,** 7725
16:18 he **t** the *from* the house of the LORD for 5437
20: 2 he **t** his face to the wall, and prayed unto 5437
22: 2 **t** not **aside** *to* the right hand or *to* the 5493
23:16 Josiah **t** himself, he spied the sepulchres 6437
23:25 that **t** to the LORD with all his heart, 7725
23:26 Notwithstanding the LORD **t** not from 7725
23:34 **t** his name *to* Jehoiakim, and took 5437
24: 1 then he **t** and rebelled against him. 7725
1Ch 10:14 the kingdom unto David the son of 5437
21:20 Ornan **t back,** and saw the angel; 7725
2Ch 6: 3 the king **t** his face, and blessed the whole 5437
9:12 So she **t,** and went away to her own land, 2015
12:12 the wrath of the LORD **t** from him, 7725
18:32 they **t back** *again* from pursuing him. 7725
20:10 they **t** from them, and destroyed them 5493
29: 6 have **t away** their faces from the 5437
29: 6 habitation of the LORD, and **t** *their* backs. 5414
36: 4 Jerusalem, and **t** his name *to* Jehoiakim. 5437
Ezr 6:22 the heart of the king of Assyria unto 5437
10:14 of our God for this matter be **t** from us. 7725
Ne 2:15 **t back,** and entered by the gate of 7725
9:35 neither **t** they from their wicked works. 7725
13: 2 our God the curse into a blessing. 2015
Est 9: 1 (though it was **t** *to the contrary,* that 2015
9:22 the month which was **t** unto them from 2015
Job 6:18 The paths of their way are **t aside;** they 3943
6:11 me **over** into the hands of the wicked. 3399
19:19 and they whom I loved are **t** against me. 2015
20:14 his meat in his bowels is **t,** *it is* the gall 2015
28: 5 and under it is **t up** as it were fire. 2015
30:15 Terrors are **t** upon me: they pursue my 2015
30:31 My harp also is **t** to mourning, NIH
31: 7 If my step hath **t** out of the way, 5186
34:27 Because they **t back** from him, 7725
37:12 it is **t** round about by his counsels: that 2015
38:14 It is **t** as clay *to the* seal; and they stand as 2015
41:22 and sorrow is **t** into joy before him. 1750
42:10 the LORD **t** the captivity of Job, when he 7725
Ps 9: 3 When mine enemies are **t back,** they shall 7725
9:17 The wicked shall be **t** into hell, *and* all 7725
30:11 Thou hast **t** for me my mourning into 2015
32: 4 my moisture is **t** into the drought of 2015
35: 4 them be **t back** and brought to confusion 5472
44:18 Our heart is not **t back,** neither have our 5472
66: 6 He **t** the sea into dry *land:* they went 2015
66:20 God, which hath not **t away** my prayer, 5493
70: 2 let them be **t backward,** and put to 5472
70: 3 Let them be **t back** for a reward of their 7725
78: 9 carrying bows, **t** *back* in the day of battle. 2015
78:38 many a time he **t** his anger **away,** 7725
78:41 they **t back,** and tempted God, 7725
78:44 had **t** their rivers into blood; 2015
78:57 **t** back, and dealt unfaithfully like their 5472
78:57 they were **t aside** like a deceitful bow. 2015
81:14 and **t** my hand against their adversaries. 7725
85: 3 thou hast **t** *thyself* from the fierceness of 7725
89:43 Thou hast also **t** the edge of his sword, 7725
105:25 He **t** their heart to hate his people, to deal 2015
105:29 He **t** their waters into blood, and slew 2015
114: 8 Which **t** the rock *into* a standing water, 2015
119:59 and **t** my feet unto thy testimonies. 7725

T

Ps	126: 1 When the LORD **t again** the captivity of	7725
	129: 5 be confounded and **t** back that hate Zion.	5472
Ecc	2:12 **t** myself to behold wisdom, and madness,	6437
SS	6: 1 whither is thy beloved **t aside**? that we	6437
Isa	5:25 For all this his anger is not **t away**,	7725
	9:12 For all this his anger is not **t away**,	7725
	9:17 For all this his anger is not **t away**,	7725
	9:21 For all this his anger is not **t away**,	7725
	10: 4 For all this his anger is not **t away**,	7725
	12: 1 anger is **t away**, and thou comfortedst	7725
	21: 4 night of my pleasure hath he **t** into fear	7760
	28:27 is a cart wheel **t about** upon the cummin;	5437
	29:17 Lebanon shall be **t** into a fruitful field,	7725
	34: 9 the streams thereof shall be **t** into pitch,	2015
	38: 2 Hezekiah **t** his face toward the wall,	6437
	42:17 They shall be **t** back, they shall be greatly	5472
	44:20 a deceived heart hath **t** him **aside**, that	5186
	50: 5 I was not rebellious, neither **t away** back.	5472
	53: 6 we have **t** every one to his own way;	6437
	59:14 judgment is **t away** backward,	5253
	63:10 therefore he was **t** to be their enemy,	2015
Jer	2:21 art thou **t** *into* the degenerate plant of a	2015
	2:27 for they have **t** *their* back unto me,	6437
	3:10 hath not **t** unto me with her whole heart,	7725
	4: 8 anger of the LORD is not **t back** from us.	7725
	5:25 Your iniquities have **t away** these *things*,	5186
	6:12 their houses shall be **t** unto others,	5437
	8: 6 every one **t** to his course, as the horse	7725
	11:10 They are **t back** to the iniquities of their	7725
	23:22 they should have **t** them from their evil	7725
	30: 6 in travail, and all faces are **t** into paleness?	7725
	31:18 *the yoke*; turn thou me, and I shall be **t**;	7725
	31:19 Surely after that I was **t**, I repented;	7725
	32:33 they have **t** unto me the back, and not	6437
	34:11 afterwards they **t**, and caused the servants	7725
	34:15 ye were now **t**, and had done right in my	7725
	34:16 ye **t** and polluted my name,	7725
	38:22 in the mire, and they are **t away** back.	5472
	46: 5 I seen them dismayed *and* **t away** back?	5472
	46:21 for they also are **t back**, *and* are fled	6437
	48:39 how hath Moab **t** the back with shame!	6437
	50: 6 have **t** them *away* **on** the mountains:	7725
La	1:13 a net for my feet, he hath **t** me back;	7725
	1:20 are troubled; mine heart is **t** within me;	2015
	3: 3 Surely against me is he **t**; he turneth his	7725
	3:11 He hath **t aside** my ways, and pulled me	5493
	5: 2 Our inheritance is **t** to strangers, our	2015
	5:15 is ceased; our dance is **t** into mourning.	2015
	5:21 us unto thee, O LORD, and we shall be **t**;	2015
Eze	1: 9 they **t** not when they went; they went	5437
	1:12 went; *and* they **t** not when they went.	5437
	1:17 sides: *and* they **t** not when they went.	5437
	10:11 they **t** not as they went, but *to* the place	5437
	10:11 they followed it; they **t** not as they went.	5437
	10:16 the same wheels also **t** not from beside	5437
	17: 6 whose branches **t** toward him, and the	6437
	26: 2 she is **t** unto me: I shall be replenished,	5437
	42:19 He **t about** to the west side,	5437
Da	9:16 fury be **t away** from thy city Jerusalem,	7725
	10: 8 for my comeliness was **t** in me into	2015
	10:16 by the vision my sorrows are **t** upon me,	2015
Hos	7: 8 the people; Ephraim is a cake not **t**.	2015
	11: 8 mine heart is **t** within me, my repentings	2015
	14: 4 for mine anger is **t away** from him.	7725
Joel	2:31 The sun shall be **t** into darkness,	2015
Am	6:12 for ye have **t** judgment into gall,	2015
Jnh	3:10 works, that they **t** from their evil way;	7725
Na	2: 2 For the LORD hath **t** *away* the excellency	7725
Hab	2:16 LORD's right hand shall be **t** unto thee,	5472
Zep	1: 6 And them that are **t back** from the LORD;	5472
Hag	2:17 yet ye **t** *not* to me, saith the LORD.	NIH
Zec	5: 1 I **t**, and lift up mine eyes, and looked,	7725
	6: 1 I **t**, and lift up mine eyes, and looked,	7725
	14:10 All the land shall be **t** as a plain from Geba	5437
Mt	2:22 dream, he **t aside** into the parts of Galilee:	402
	9:22 But Jesus **t** him **about**, and when he saw	1994
	16:23 But he **t**, and said unto Peter, Get thee	4762
Mk	5:30 **t** him **about** in the press, and said,	1994
	8:33 But when he had **t about** and looked on	1994
Lk	2:45 they **t back again** to Jerusalem,	5290
	7: 9 and **t** him *about*, and said unto the people	4762
	7:44 And he **t** to the woman, and said unto	4762
	9:55 But he **t**, and rebuked them, and said,	4762
	10:23 And he **t** him unto *his* disciples,	4762
	14:25 with him: and he **t**, and said unto them,	4762
	17:15 **t back**, and with a loud voice glorified	5290
	22:61 And the Lord **t**, and looked upon Peter.	4762
Jn	1:38 Then Jesus **t**, and saw them following,	4762
	16:20 but your sorrow shall be **t** into joy.	1096
	20:14 she had thus said, she **t** herself back,	4762
	20:16 She **t** herself, and saith unto him, Rabboni;	4762
Ac	2:20 The sun shall be **t** into darkness,	3344
	7:39 and in their hearts **t back again** into Egypt,	4762
	7:42 Then God **t**, and gave them up to worship	4762
	9:35 Saron saw him, and **t** to the Lord.	1994
	11:21 and **t** unto the Lord.	1994
	15:19 among the Gentiles are **t** to God:	1994
	16:18 being grieved, **t** and said to the spirit,	1994
	17: 6 that have **t** the world **upside down** are	387
	19:26 hath persuaded and **t away** much people,	3179
1Th	1: 9 how ye **t** to God from idols to serve	1994
1Ti	1: 6 swerved have **t aside** unto vain jangling;	1624
	5:15 For some are already **t aside** after Satan.	1624
2Ti	1:15 which are in Asia be **t away from** me;	654
	4: 4 from the truth, and shall be **t** unto fables.	1624

Heb	11:34 fight, **t to flight** the armies of the aliens.	2827
	12:13 *that which is* lame be **t out of the way**;	1624
Jas	3: 4 *yet* are they **t about** with a very small	3329
	4: 9 let your laughter be **t** to mourning,	3344
2Pe	2:22 The dog *is* **t** to his own vomit **again**;	1994
Rev	1:12 I **t** to see the voice that spake with me.	1994
	1:12 And being **t**, I saw seven golden	1994

TURNEST (3) [TURN]

1Ki	2: 3 and whithersoever thou **t** thyself:	6437
Job	15:13 That thou **t** thy spirit against God,	7725
Ps	90: 3 Thou **t** man to destruction; and sayest,	7725

TURNETH (33) [TURN]

Lev	20: 6 the soul that **t** after such as have familiar	6437
Dt	29:18 whose heart **t away** *this* day from	6437
Jos	7: 8 when Israel **t** *their* backs before their	2015
	19:27 **t** *toward* the sunrising to Beth-dagon,	7725
	19:29 the coast **t** *to* Ramah, and to the strong	7725
	19:29 the coast **t** *to* Hosah; and the outgoings	7725
	19:34 the coast westward **to** Aznoth-tabor,	7725
Job	39:22 neither **t** he **back** from the sword.	7725
Ps	107:33 He **t** rivers into a wilderness,	7760
	107:35 He **t** the wilderness into a standing water,	7760
	146: 9 the way of the wicked he **t upside down**.	5791
Pr	15: 1 A soft answer **t away** wrath:	7725
	17: 8 hath it: whithersoever it **t**, it prospereth.	6437
	21: 1 of water: he **t** it whithersoever he will.	5186
	26:14 *As* the door **t** upon his hinges, so *doth*	5437
	28: 9 He that **t away** his ear from hearing	5493
	30:30 among beasts, and **t** not away for any;	7725
Ecc	1: 6 the south, and **t about** unto the north;	5437
SS	1: 7 why should I be as one that **t aside**	5844
Isa	9:13 the people **t** not unto him that smiteth	7725
	24: 1 it upside down, and scattereth abroad	5753
	44:25 that **t** wise *men* backward, and maketh	7725
Jer	14: 8 as a wayfaring man *that* **t aside** to tarry	5186
	49:24 and **t** herself to flee, and fear hath seized	6437
La	1: 8 yea, she sigheth, and **t** backward.	7725
	3: 3 he **t** his hand *against me* all the day.	2015
Eze	18:24 when the righteous **t away** from his	7725
	18:26 When a righteous *man* **t away** from his	7725
	18:27 when the wicked *man* **t away** from his	7725
	18:28 **t away** from all his transgressions that he	7725
	33:12 shall not fall thereby in the day that he **t**	7725
	33:18 When the righteous **t** from his	7725
Am	5: 8 the shadow of death into the morning,	2015

TURNING (18) [TURN]

2Ki	21:13 a dish, wiping *it*, and **t** *it* upside down.	2015
2Ch	9: 8 at the **t** *of the wall*, and fortified them.	4740
	36:13 hardened his heart from **t** unto the LORD	7725
Ne	3:19 up to the armoury at the **t** *of the wall*.	4740
	3:20 from the **t** *of the wall* unto the door of	4740
	3:24 from the house of Azariah unto the **t** of	4740
	3:25 against the **t** *of the wall*, and the tower	4740
Pr	1:32 For the **t away** of the simple shall slay	4878
Isa	29:16 Surely your **t** *of things* **upside down** shall	2017
Eze	41:24 the doors had two leaves *apiece*, two **t**	5437
Mic	2: 4 **t away** he hath divided our fields.	7725
Lk	23:28 But Jesus **t** unto them, said, Daughters of	4762
Jn	21:20 Then Peter, **t about**, seeth the disciple	1994
Ac	3:26 in **t away** every one of you from *his*	654
	9:40 and **t** *him* to the body said, Tabitha, arise.	1994
Jas	1:17 is no variableness, neither shadow of **t**.	5157
2Pe	2: 6 **t** the cities of Sodom and Gomorrha into ashes	5077
Jude	1: 4 ungodly *men*, **t** the grace of our God into	3346

TURTLE (2) [TURTLEDOVE, TURTLE-DOVE, TURTLEDOVES, TURTLES]

SS	2:12 the voice of the **t** is heard in our land;	8449
Jer	8: 7 **t** and the crane and the swallow observe	8449

TURTLEDOVE, TURTLE-DOVE (3) [TURTLE]

Ge	15: 9 years old, and a **t**, and a young pigeon.	8449
Lev	12: 6 a young pigeon, or a **t**, for a sin offering,	8449
Ps	74:19 O deliver not the soul of thy **t** unto	8449

TURTLEDOVES (7) [TURTLE]

Lev	1:14 he shall bring his offering of **t**, or of young	8449
	5: 7 two **t**, or two young pigeons, unto	8449
	5:11 if he be not able to bring two **t**, or two	8449
	14:22 two **t**, or two young pigeons, such as he	8449
	14:30 he shall offer the one of the **t**, or a	8449
	15:14 the eighth day he shall take to him two **t**,	8449
Lk	2:24 Lord, A pair of **t**, or two young pigeons.	5167

TURTLES (3) [TURTLE]

Lev	12: 8 she shall bring two **t**, or two young	8449
	15:29 eighth day she shall take unto her two **t**,	8449
Nu	6:10 on the eighth day he shall bring two **t**,	8449

TUTORS (1)

Gal	4: 2 is under **t** and governors until the time	2012

TWAIN (17) [TWO]

1Sa	18:21 day be my son in law in *the* one of *the* **t**.	8147
2Ki	4:33 shut the door upon them **t**, and prayed	8147
Isa	6: 2 with **t** he covered his face, and with twain	8147
	6: 2 with **t** he covered his feet, and with twain	8147
	6: 2 he covered his feet, and with **t** he did fly.	8147
Jer	34:18 when they cut the calf in **t**,	8147
Eze	21:19 **both t** shall come forth out of one land:	8147
Mt	5:41 compel thee to go a mile, go with him **t**.	1417
	19: 5 to his wife: and they **t** shall be one flesh?	1417

Mt	19: 6 Wherefore they are no more **t**,	1417
	21:31 Whether of them **t** did the will of *his*	1417
	27:21 Whether of the **t** will ye *that* I release unto	1417
	27:51 the vail of the temple was rent in **t** from	1417
Mk	10: 8 And they **t** shall be one flesh: so then	1417
	10: 8 so then they are no more **t**, but one flesh.	1417
	15:38 And the vail of the temple was rent in **t**	1417
Eph	2:15 for to make in himself of **t** one new man,	1417

TWELFTH (23) [TWELVE]

Nu	7:78 On the **t** day Ahira the son of Enan,	6240+8147
1Ki	19:19 before him, and he with the **t**.	6240+8147
2Ki	8:25 In the **t** year of Joram the son of	6240+8147
	17: 1 In the **t** year of Ahaz king of Judah	6240+8147
	25:27 In the **t** month, on the seven and	6240+8147
1Ch	24:12 eleventh to Eliashib, the **t** to Jakim,	6240+8147
	25:19 The **t** to Hashabiah, *he*, his sons,	6240+8147
	27:15 The **t** *captain* for the twelfth	6240+8147
	27:15 twelfth *captain* for the **t** month	6240+8147
2Ch	34: 3 **t** year he began to purge Judah and	6240+8147
Ezr	8:31 on the **t** day of the first month,	6240+8147
Est	3: 7 in the **t** year of king Ahasuerus,	6240+8147
	3: 7 the **t** *month, that is,* the month	6240+8147
	3:13 upon the thirteenth *day* of the **t**	6240+8147
	8:12 the thirteenth *day* of the **t** month,	6240+8147
	9: 1 Now in the **t** month, that *is*,	6240+8147
Jer	52:31 in the **t** month, in the five and	6240+8147
Eze	29: 1 in the tenth *month*, in the **t** *day* of	6240+8147
	32: 1 it came to pass in the **t** year,	6240+8147
	32: 1 in the **t** month, in the first *day* of	6240+8147
	32:17 It came to pass also in the **t** year,	6240+8147
	33:21 It came to pass in the **t** year of our	6240+8147
Rev	21:20 the eleventh, a jacinth; the **t**, an amethyst.	1428

TWELVE (189) [TWELFTH]

Ge	5: 8 were nine hundred and **t** years:	6240+8147
	14: 4 **T** years they served Chedorlaomer,	6240+8147
	17:20 **t** princes shall he beget, and I will	6240+8147
	25:16 **t** princes according to their nations.	6240+8147
	35:22 *it*. Now the sons of Jacob were **t**:	6240+8147
	42:13 they said, Thy servants *are* **t**	6240+8147
	42:32 *be* **t** brethren, sons of our father;	6240+8147
	49:28 All these *are* the **t** tribes of Israel:	6240+8147
Ex	15:27 where *were* **t** wells of water,	6240+8147
	24: 4 an altar under the hill, and **t** pillars,	6240+8147
	24: 4 according to the **t** tribes of Israel.	6240+8147
	28:21 **t**, according to their names, *like*	6240+8147
	28:21 they be according to the **t** tribes.	6240+8147
	39:14 **t**, according to their names, *like*	6240+8147
	39:14 his name, according to the **t** tribes.	6240+8147
Lev	24: 5 fine flour, and bake **t** cakes thereof:	6240+8147
Nu	1:44 the princes of Israel, *being* **t** men:	6240+8147
	7: 3 six covered wagons, and **t** oxen:	6240+8147
	7:84 **t** chargers of silver, twelve silver	6240+8147
	7:84 silver bowls, twelve spoons of	6240+8147
	7:84 silver bowls, **t** spoons of gold:	6240+8147
	7:86 The golden spoons *were* **t**, full of	6240+8147
	7:87 the burnt offering *were* **t** bullocks,	6240+8147
	7:87 rams **t**, the lambs of the first year	6240+8147
	7:87 the lambs of the first year **t**,	6240+8147
	7:87 kids of the goats for sin offering **t**.	6240+8147
	17: 2 to the house of their fathers **t** rods:	6240+8147
	17: 6 their fathers' houses, *even* **t** rods:	6240+8147
	29:17 day ye shall offer **t** young bullocks,	6240+8147
	31: 5 **t** thousand armed for war.	8147
	31:33 threescore and **t**	7657+8147+2050.1
	31:38 *was* threescore and **t**.	7657+8147+2050.1
	33: 9 in Elim *were* **t** fountains of water,	6240+8147
Dt	1:23 I took **t** men of you, one of a tribe:	6240+8147
Jos	3:12 ye **t** men out of the tribes of Israel,	6240+8147
	4: 2 Take you **t** men out of the people,	6240+8147
	4: 3 **t** stones, ye shall carry them	6240+8147
	4: 4 Joshua called the **t** men, whom he	6240+8147
	4: 8 **t** stones out of the midst of Jordan,	6240+8147
	4: 9 Joshua set up **t** stones in the midst	6240+8147
	4:20 those **t** stones, which they took out	6240+8147
	8:25 both of men and women, *were* **t**	6240+8147
	18:24 Gaba; **t** cities with their villages.	6240+8147
	19:15 **t** cities with their villages.	6240+8147
	21: 7 out of the tribe of Zebulun, **t** cities.	6240+8147
	21:40 Levites, were *by* their lot **t** cities.	6240+8147
Jdg	19:29 into **t** pieces, and sent her into all	6240+8147
	21:10 the congregation sent thither **t**	6240+8147
2Sa	2:15 over by number **t** of Benjamin,	6240+8147
	2:15 and **t** of the servants of David.	6240+8147
	10: 6 and of Ish-tob **t** thousand men.	6240+8147
	17: 1 Let me now choose out **t** thousand	6240+8147
1Ki	4: 7 Solomon had **t** officers over all	6240+8147
	4:26 and **t** thousand horsemen.	6240+8147
	7:15 a line of **t** cubits did compass either	6240+8147
	7:25 It stood upon **t** oxen, three looking	6240+8147
	7:44 one sea, and **t** oxen under the sea;	6240+8147
	10:20 **t** lions stood there on the one side	6240+8147
	10:26 and **t** thousand horsemen,	6240+8147
	11:30 *was* on him, and rent it in **t** pieces:	6240+8147
	16:23 Omri to reign over Israel, **t** years:	6240+8147
	18:31 Elijah took **t** stones, according to	6240+8147
	19:19 who *was* plowing *with* **t** yoke of	6240+8147
2Ki	3: 1 king of Judah, and reigned **t** years.	6240+8147
	21: 1 Manasseh *was* **t** years old when he	6240+8147
1Ch	6:63 out of the tribe of Zebulun, **t** cities.	6240+8147
	9:22 the gates *were* two hundred and **t**	6240+8147
	15:10 and his brethren an hundred and **t**.	6240+8147
	25: 9 with his brethren and sons *were* **t**:	6240+8147
	25:10 his sons, and his brethren, *were* **t**:	6240+8147

T

1Ch 25:11 his sons, and his brethren, *were* t: 6240+8147
25:12 his sons, and his brethren, *were* t: 6240+8147
25:13 his sons, and his brethren, *were* t: 6240+8147
25:14 his sons, and his brethren, *were* t: 6240+8147
25:15 his sons, and his brethren, *were* t: 6240+8147
25:16 his sons, and his brethren, *were* t: 6240+8147
25:17 his sons, and his brethren, *were* t: 6240+8147
25:18 his sons, and his brethren, *were* t: 6240+8147
25:19 his sons, and his brethren, *were* t: 6240+8147
25:20 his sons, and his brethren, *were* t: 6240+8147
25:21 his sons, and his brethren, *were* t: 6240+8147
25:22 his sons, and his brethren, *were* t: 6240+8147
25:23 his sons, and his brethren, *were* t: 6240+8147
25:24 his sons, and his brethren, *were* t: 6240+8147
25:25 his sons, and his brethren, *were* t: 6240+8147
25:26 his sons, and his brethren, *were* t: 6240+8147
25:27 his sons, and his brethren, *were* t: 6240+8147
25:28 his sons, and his brethren, *were* t: 6240+8147
25:29 his sons, and his brethren, *were* t: 6240+8147
25:30 his sons, and his brethren, *were* t: 6240+8147
25:31 his sons, and his brethren, *were* t: 6240+8147
2Ch 1:14 and t thousand horsemen, 6240+8147
4: 4 It stood upon t oxen, three looking 6240+8147
4:15 One sea, and t oxen under it. 6240+8147
9:19 t lions stood there on the one side 6240+8147
9:25 chariots, and t thousand horsemen; 6240+8147
12: 3 With t hundred chariots, 505+3967+2050.1
33: 1 Manasseh *was* t years old when he 6240+8147
Ezr 2: 6 two thousand eight hundred and t. 6240+8147
2:18 children of Jorah, an hundred and t. 6240+8147
6:17 sin offering for all Israel, t he goats, 6236+8648
8:24 I separated t of the chief of 6240+8147
8:35 t bullocks for all Israel, ninety and 6240+8147
8:35 t he goats *for* a sin offering; 6240+8147
Ne 5:14 *that is,* t years, I and my brethren 6240+8147
7:24 of Hariph, an hundred and t. 6240+8147
Est 2:12 after that she had been t months, 6240+8147
Ps 60: T of Edom in the valley of salt t 6240+8147
Jer 52:20 t brasen bulls that *were* under 6240+8147
52:21 a fillet of t cubits did compass it; 6240+8147
Eze 43:16 the altar *shall be* t cubits long, 6240+8147
43:16 t broad, square in the four squares 6240+8147
47:13 according to the t tribes of Israel: 6240+8147
Da 4:29 At the end of t months he walked 6236+8648
Mt 9:20 was diseased with an issue of blood t 1427
10: 1 And when he had called unto *him* his t 1427
10: 2 Now the names of the t apostles are these; 1427
10: 5 These t Jesus sent forth, 1427
11: 1 an end of commanding his t disciples, 1427
14:20 the fragments that remained t baskets full. 1427
19:28 ye also shall sit upon t thrones, judging 1427
19:28 judging the t tribes of Israel. 1427
20:17 Jesus going up to Jerusalem took the t 1427
26:14 Then one of the t, called Judas Iscariot, 1427
26:20 even was come, he sat down with the t. 1427
26:47 one of the t, came, and with him a great 1427
26:53 he shall presently give me more than t 1427
Mk 3:14 he ordained t, that they should be with 1427
4:10 they that were about him with the t asked 1427
5:25 which had an issue of blood t years, 1427
5:42 walked; for she was *of the age of* t years. 1427
6: 7 he calleth unto *him* the t, and began to 1427
6:43 And they took up t baskets full of 1427
8:19 took ye up? They say unto him, **T.** 1427
9:35 and called the t, and saith unto them, 1427
10:32 And he took again the t, and began to tell 1427
11:11 he went out unto Bethany with the t. 1427
14:10 And Judas Iscariot, one of the t, went unto 1427
14:17 And in the evening he cometh with the t. 1427
14:20 and said unto them, *It is* one of the t, 1427
14:43 one of the t, and with him a great 1427
Lk 2:42 when he was t years old, they went up 1427
6:13 of them he chose t, whom also he 1427
8: 1 of God: and the t *were* with him, 1427
8:42 about t years of age, and she lay a dying. 1427
8:43 And a woman having an issue of blood t 1427
9: 1 Then he called his t disciples together, 1427
9:12 then came the t, and said unto him, 1427
9:17 fragments that remained to them t baskets. 1427
18:31 Then he took unto *him* the t, and said 1427
22: 3 being of the number of the t. 1427
22:14 he sat down, and the t apostles with him. 1427
22:30 sit on thrones judging the t tribes of Israel. 1427
22:47 one of the t, went before them, 1427
Jn 6:13 filled t baskets with the fragments of 1427
6:67 Then said Jesus unto the t, Will ye also go 1427
6:70 Have not I chosen you t, and one of you is 1427
6:71 *that* should betray him, being one of the t. 1427
11: 9 Are there not t hours in the day? 1427
20:24 But Thomas, one of the t, called Didymus, 1427
Ac 6: 2 Then the t called the multitude of 1427
7: 8 and Jacob *begat* the t patriarchs. 1427
19: 7 And all the men were about t. 1427
24:11 t days since I went up to Jerusalem for to 1177
26: 7 Unto which *promise* our t tribes, 1429
1Co 15: 5 that he was seen of Cephas, then of the t: 1427
Jas 1: 1 to the t tribes which are scattered abroad, 1427
Rev 7: 5 the tribe of Juda *were* sealed t thousand. 1427
7: 5 tribe of Reuben *were* sealed t thousand. 1427
7: 5 the tribe of Gad *were* sealed t thousand. 1427
7: 6 the tribe of Aser *were* sealed t thousand. 1427
7: 6 of Nephthalim *were* sealed t thousand. 1427
7: 6 tribe of Manasses *were* sealed t thousand. 1427
7: 7 tribe of Simeon *were* sealed t thousand. 1427
7: 7 the tribe of Levi *were* sealed t thousand. 1427

Rev 7: 7 the tribe of Isachar *were* sealed t thousand. 1427
7: 8 tribe of Zabulon *were* sealed t thousand. 1427
7: 8 the tribe of Joseph *were* sealed t thousand. 1427
7: 8 tribe of Benjamin *were* sealed t thousand. 1427
12: 1 and upon her head a crown of t stars; 1427
21:12 and had t gates, and at the gates twelve 1427
21:12 at the gates t angels, and names written 1427
21:12 which are *the names* of the t tribes of 1427
21:14 And the wall of the city had t foundations, 1427
21:14 in them the names of the t apostles of 1427
21:16 the city with the reed, t thousand furlongs. 1427
21:21 And the t gates *were* twelve pearls; 1427
21:21 the t gates *were* twelve pearls; 1427
22: 2 which bare t *manner of* fruits, 1427

TWENTIETH (36) [TWENTY]

Ge 8:14 on the seven and t day of the month, 6242
Ex 12:18 the one and t day of the month at even. 6242
Nu 10:11 it came to pass on the t *day* of the second 6242
1Ki 15: 9 in the t year of Jeroboam king of Israel 6242
2Ki 12: 6 t year of king Jehoash the priests had not 6242
13: 1 t year of Joash the son of Ahaziah king of 6242
15:30 in the t year of Jotham the son of Uzziah. 6242
25:27 on the seven and t *day* of the month, 6242
1Ch 24:16 to Pethahiah, the t to Jehezekel, 6242
24:17 The one and t to Jachin, the two and 6242
24:17 to Jachin, the two and t to Gamul, 6242
24:18 The three and t to Delaiah, the four and 6242
24:18 to Delaiah, the four and t to Maaziah. 6242
25:27 The t to Eliathah, *he,* his sons, 6242
25:28 The one and t to Hothir, *he,* his sons, 6242
25:29 The two and t to Giddalti, *he,* his sons, 6242
25:30 three and t to Mahazioth, *he,* his sons, 6242
25:31 The four and t to Romamti-ezer, *he,* his 6242
2Ch 7:10 t day of the seventh month he sent 6242
Ezr 10: 9 ninth month, on the t *day* of the month; 6242
Ne 1: 1 in the t year, as I was in Shushan 6242
2: 1 in the t year of Artaxerxes the king, 6242
5:14 from the t year even unto the two 6242
Est 8: 9 on the three and t *day* thereof; 6242
Jer 25: 3 unto this day, that *is* the three and t year, 6242
52:30 t year of Nebuchadrezzar Nebuzar-adan 6242
52:31 in the five and t *day* of the month, 6242
Eze 29:17 it came to pass in the seven and t year, 6242
40: 1 In the five and t year of our captivity, 6242
Da 10: 4 in the four and t day of the first month, 6242
Hag 1:15 In the four and t day of the sixth month, 6242
2: 1 *month,* in the one and t *day* of the month, 6242
2:10 t day of the ninth *month,* in the second 6242
2:18 t day of the ninth *month, even* from the 6242
2:20 Haggai in the four and t *day* of the month, 6242
Zec 1: 7 the four and t day of the eleventh month, 6242

TWENTY (293) [TWENTIETH, TWENTY'S]

Ge 6: 3 his days shall be an hundred and t years. 6242
11:24 Nahor lived nine and t years, 6242
18:31 Peradventure there shall be t found there. 6242
23: 1 an hundred and seven and t years old: 6242
31:38 This t years have I *been* with thee; thy 6242
31:41 Thus have I *been* t years in thy house; 6242
32:14 the goats, two hundred ewes, 6242
32:14 he goats, two hundred ewes, and t rams, 6242
32:15 and ten bulls, t she asses, and ten foals. 6242
37:28 sold Joseph to the Ishmeelites for t *pieces* 6242
Ex 26: 2 of one curtain *shall be* eight and t cubits, 6242
26:18 t boards on the south side southward. 6242
26:19 forty sockets of silver under the t boards; 6242
26:20 on the north side *there shall be* t boards: 6242
27:10 t pillars thereof and their twenty sockets 6242
27:10 and their t sockets *shall be of* brass; 6242
27:11 his t pillars and their t sockets *of* brass; 6242
27:11 twenty pillars and their t sockets *of* brass; 6242
27:16 of the court *shall be* a hanging of t cubits, 6242
30:13 (a shekel *is* t gerahs:) a half shekel *shall* 6242
30:14 from t years old and above, shall give an 6242
36: 9 The length of one curtain *was* t and 6242
36:23 t boards for the south side southward: 6242
36:24 forty sockets of silver he made under the t 6242
36:25 the north corner, he made t boards, 6242
38:10 Their pillars *were* t, and their brasen 6242
38:10 *were* twenty, and their brasen sockets t; 6242
38:11 their pillars *were* t, and their sockets *of* 6242
38:11 *were* twenty, and their sockets *of* brass t; 6242
38:18 t cubits *was* the length, and the height in 6242
38:24 was t and nine talents, and seven hundred 6242
38:26 from t years old and upward, for six 6242
Lev 27: 3 the male from t years old even unto sixty 6242
27: 5 if *it be* from five years old even unto t 6242
27: 5 thy estimation shall be of the male t 6242
27:25 the sanctuary: t gerahs shall be the shekel. 6242
Nu 1: 3 From t years old and upward, all that *are* 6242
1:18 t years old and upward, by their polls. 6242
1:20 every male from t years old and upward, 6242
1:22 every male from t years old and upward, 6242
1:24 from t years old and upward, all that 6242
1:26 from t years old and upward, all that 6242
1:28 from t years old and upward, all that 6242
1:30 from t years old and upward, all that 6242
1:32 from t years old and upward, all that 6242
1:34 from t years old and upward, all that 6242
1:36 from t years old and upward, all that 6242
1:38 from t years old and upward, all that 6242
1:40 from t years old and upward, all that 6242
1:42 from t years old and upward, all that 6242
1:45 fathers, from t years old and upward, 6242

Nu 3:39 and upward, *were* t and two thousand. 6242
3:43 and t and two thousand two hundred 6242
3:47 thou take *them:* (the shekel *is* t gerahs:) 6242
7:86 the spoons *was* an hundred and t shekels. 6242
7:88 the sacrifice of the peace offerings *were* t 6242
8:24 from t and five years old and upward they 6242
11:19 nor five days, neither ten days, nor t days; 6242
14:29 from t years old and upward, 6242
18:16 shekel of the sanctuary, which *is* t gerahs. 6242
25: 9 those that died in the plague were t and 6242
26: 2 from t years old and upward, throughout 6242
26: 4 *Take* the sum of the people, from t years 6242
26:14 t and two thousand and two hundred. 6242
26:62 that were numbered of them were t 6242
32:11 from t years old and upward, shall see 6242
33:39 Aaron *was* an hundred and t 6242
Dt 31: 2 I *am* an hundred and t years old *this* day; 6242
34: 7 an hundred and t years old when he died: 6242
Jos 15:32 all the cities *are* t and nine, with their 6242
19:30 Rehob: t and nine cities with their villages. 6242
Jdg 4: 3 t years he mightily oppressed the children 6242
7: 3 there returned of the people t and 6242
8:10 and t thousand men that drew sword. 6242
10: 2 judged Israel t and three years, and died, 6242
10: 3 t and judged Israel t and two years. 6242
11:33 *even* t cities, and unto the plain of 6242
15:20 Israel in the days of the Philistines t years. 6242
16:31 his father. And he judged Israel t years. 6242
20:15 numbered at that time out of the cities t 6242
20:21 to the ground of the Israelites that day t 6242
20:35 destroyed of the Benjamites that day t 6242
20:46 all which fell that day of Benjamin were t 6242
1Sa 7: 2 it was t years: and all the house of Israel 6242
14:14 armourbearer made, was about t men, 6242
2Sa 3:20 to David *to* Hebron, and t men with him. 6242
8: 4 and t thousand footmen: 6242
8: 5 of the Syrians two and t thousand men. 6242
9:10 Now Ziba had fifteen sons and t servants. 6242
10: 6 t thousand footmen, and of king Maachah 6242
18: 7 slaughter that day *of* t thousand *men.* 6242
19:17 fifteen sons and his t servants with him; 6242
21:20 every foot six toes, four and t *in* number; 6242
24: 8 at the end of nine months and t days. 6242
1Ki 4:23 t oxen out of the pastures, and an 6242
5:11 Solomon gave Hiram t thousand 6242
5:11 household, and t measures of pure oil: 6242
6: 2 breadth thereof t cubits, and the height 6242
6: 3 t cubits *was* the length thereof, according 6242
6:16 he built t cubits on the sides of the house, 6242
6:20 the oracle in the forepart *was* t cubits in 6242
6:20 t cubits in breadth, and twenty cubits in 6242
6:20 and t cubits in the height thereof: 6242
8:63 two and t thousand oxen, and an 6242
8:63 an hundred and t thousand sheep. 6242
9:10 it came to pass at the end of t years, 6242
9:11 king Solomon gave Hiram t cities in 6242
9:28 four hundred and t talents, and brought 6242
10:10 the king an hundred and t talents of gold, 6242
14:20 Jeroboam reigned *were* two and t years, 6242
15:33 over all Israel in Tirzah, and t and four years. 6242
16: 8 In the t and sixth year of Asa king of 6242
16:10 in the t and seventh year of Asa king of 6242
16:15 In the t and seventh year of Asa king of 6242
16:29 of Omri reigned over Israel in Samaria t 6242
20:30 a wall fell upon t and seven thousand 6242
22:42 he reigned t and five years in Jerusalem. 6242
2Ki 4:42 t loaves of barley, and full ears of corn in 6242
8:26 t years old *was* Ahaziah when he *began* 6242
10:36 Jehu reigned over Israel in Samaria *was* t 6242
14: 2 He was t and five years old when he 6242
14: 2 and reigned t and nine years in Jerusalem. 6242
15: 1 In the t and seventh year of Jeroboam 6242
15:27 Israel in Samaria, *and reigned* t years. 6242
15:33 t years old was he when he *began* to 6242
16: 2 T years old *was* Ahaz when he *began* to 6242
18: 2 T and five years old was he when he 6242
18: 2 he reigned t and nine years in Jerusalem. 6242
21:19 Amon *was* t and two years old when he 6242
23:31 Jehoahaz *was* t and three years old when 6242
23:36 Jehoiakim *was* t and five year old when 6242
24:18 Zedekiah *was* t and one years old when 6242
1Ch 2:22 three and t cities in the land of Gilead. 6242
7: 2 two and t thousand and six hundred. 6242
7: 7 were reckoned by their genealogies t and 6242
7: 9 valour, *was* t thousand and two hundred. 6242
7:40 *and* to battle *was* t and six thousand men. 6242
12:28 of his father's house t and two captains. 6242
12:30 of the children of Ephraim t thousand and 6242
12:35 of the Danites expert in war t and 6242
12:37 for the battle, an hundred and t thousand. 6242
15: 5 his brethren an hundred and t: 6242
15: 6 and his brethren two hundred and t: 6242
18: 4 and t thousand footmen: 6242
18: 5 of the Syrians two and t thousand men. 6242
20: 6 whose fingers and toes were four and t, 6242
23: 4 t and four thousand *were* to set forward 6242
23:24 from the age of t years and upward. 6242
23:27 Levites *were* numbered from t years old 6242
27: 1 *of* every course *were* t and four thousand. 6242
27: 2 in his course *were* t and four thousand: 6242
27: 4 in his course likewise *were* t and 6242
27: 5 in his course *were* t and four thousand. 6242
27: 7 in his course *were* t and four thousand. 6242
27: 7 in his course *were* t and four thousand. 6242
27: 8 in his course *were* t and four thousand. 6242
27: 9 in his course *were* t and four thousand. 6242

T

1Ch 27:10	in his course *were* t and four thousand.	6242
27:11	in his course *were* t and four thousand.	6242
27:12	in his course *were* t and four thousand.	6242
27:13	in his course *were* t and four thousand.	6242
27:14	in his course *were* t and four thousand.	6242
27:15	in his course *were* t and four thousand.	6242
27:23	took not the number of them from t	6242
2Ch 2:10	t thousand measures of beaten wheat,	6242
2:10	t thousand measures of barley,	6242
2:10	t thousand baths of wine,	6242
2:10	baths of wine, and t thousand baths of oil.	6242
3: 3	threescore cubits, and the breadth t cubits.	6242
3: 4	t cubits, and the height *was* an hundred	6242
3: 4	and the height *was* an hundred and t:	6242
3: 8	t cubits, and the breadth thereof twenty	6242
3: 8	and the breadth thereof t cubits.	6242
3:11	the wings of the cherubims *were* t cubits	6242
3:13	spread themselves forth t cubits:	6242
4: 1	t cubits the length thereof,	6242
4: 1	t cubits the breadth thereof, and ten	6242
5:12	and t priests sounding with trumpets:)	6242
7: 5	king Solomon offered a sacrifice of t and	6242
7: 5	and an hundred and t thousand sheep.	6242
8: 1	it came to pass at the end of t years,	6242
9: 9	the king an hundred and t talents of gold,	6242
11:21	begat t and eight sons,	6242
13:21	begat t and two sons,	6242
20:31	he reigned t and five years in Jerusalem.	6242
25: 1	Amaziah *was* t and five years old *when* he	6242
25: 1	he reigned t and nine years in Jerusalem.	6242
25: 5	he numbered them from t years old and	6242
27: 1	Jotham *was* t and five years old when he	6242
27: 8	and t years old when he *began* to reign,	6242
28: 1	Ahaz *was* t years old when he *began* to	6242
28: 6	an hundred and t thousand in one day,	6242
29: 1	to reign *when he was* five and t years old,	6242
29: 1	he reigned nine and t years in Jerusalem.	6242
31:17	the Levites from t years old and upward,	6242
33:21	and t years old when he *began* to reign,	6242
36: 2	Jehoahaz *was* t and three years old when	6242
36: 5	Jehoiakim *was* t and five years old when	6242
36:11	and t years old when he *began* to reign,	6242
Ezr 1: 9	chargers of silver, nine and t knives,	6242
2:11	of Bebai, six hundred t and three.	6242
2:12	a thousand two hundred t and two.	6242
2:17	of Bezai, three hundred t and three.	6242
2:19	of Hashum, two hundred t and three.	6242
2:21	of Beth-lehem, an hundred t and three.	6242
2:23	of Anathoth, an hundred t and eight.	6242
2:26	Ramah and Gaba, six hundred t and one.	6242
2:27	men of Michmas, an hundred t and two.	6242
2:28	Beth-el and Ai, two hundred t and three.	6242
2:32	children of Harim, three hundred and t.	6242
2:33	and Ono, seven hundred t and five.	6242
2:41	of Asaph, an hundred t and eight.	6242
2:67	six thousand seven hundred t and t.	6242
3: 8	appointed the Levites from t years old and	6242
8:11	of Bebai, and with him t and eight males.	6242
8:19	of Merari, his brethren and their sons, t;	6242
8:20	Levites, two hundred and t Nethinims:	6242
8:27	t basons of gold, of a thousand drams;	6242
Ne 6:15	So the wall was finished in the t and	6242
7:16	children of Bebai, six hundred t and eight.	6242
7:17	two thousand three hundred t and two.	6242
7:22	of Hashum, three hundred t and eight.	6242
7:23	of Bezai, three hundred t and four.	6242
7:27	men of Anathoth, an hundred t and eight.	6242
7:30	Ramah and Geba, six hundred t and one.	6242
7:31	of Michmas, an hundred t and two.	6242
7:32	of Beth-el and Ai, an hundred t and three.	6242
7:35	children of Harim, three hundred and t.	6242
7:37	and Ono, seven hundred and t asses.	6242
7:69	six thousand seven hundred and t asses.	6242
7:71	of the work t thousand drams of gold,	8147
7:72	which the rest of the people gave *was* t	8147
9: 1	Now in the t and fourth day of this month	6242
11: 8	Sallai, nine hundred t and eight.	6242
11:12	work of the house *were* eight hundred t	6242
11:14	*men* of valour, an hundred t and eight:	6242
Est 1: 1	an hundred and seven and t provinces:)	6242
8: 9	an hundred and seven provinces,	6242
9:30	to the hundred t and seven provinces of	6242
Ps 68:17	The chariots of God *are* t **thousand,**	7239
Jer 52: 1	and t year old when he *began* to reign,	6242
52:28	year three thousand Jews and three and t:	6242
Eze 4:10	eat *shall be* by weight, t shekels a day:	6242
8:16	and the altar, *were* about five and t men,	6242
11: 1	at the door of the gate five and t men;	6242
40:13	the breadth *was* five and t cubits,	6242
40:21	and the breadth thereof t cubits.	6242
40:25	and the breadth five and t cubits.	6242
40:29	cubits long, and five and t cubits broad.	6242
40:30	round about *were* five and t cubits long,	6242
40:33	cubits long, and five and t cubits broad.	6242
40:36	and the breadth five and t cubits.	6242
40:49	The length of the porch *was* t cubits,	6242
41: 2	forty cubits: and the breadth, t cubits.	6242
41: 4	he measured the length thereof, t cubits;	6242
41: 4	the breadth, t cubits, before the temple:	6242
41:10	the chambers *was* the wideness of t	6242
42: 3	Over against the t cubits which *were* for	6242
45: 1	t thousand *reeds,* and the breadth *shall*	6242
45: 3	measure the length of five and t thousand,	6242
45: 5	*the* five and t thousand of length,	6242
45: 5	for a possession for t chambers.	6242

Eze 45: 6	and five and t thousand long,	6242
45:12	shekel *shall be* t gerahs: twenty shekels,	6242
45:12	t shekels, five and twenty shekels,	6242
45:12	five and t shekels, fifteen shekels,	6242
48: 8	*of* five and t thousand reeds in breadth,	6242
48: 9	*shall be of* five and t thousand in length,	6242
48:10	the north five and t thousand *in length,*	6242
48:10	the south five and t thousand *in length:*	6242
48:13	all have five and t thousand *in length,*	6242
48:13	all the length *shall be* five and t thousand,	6242
48:15	over against the five and t thousand,	6242
48:20	t thousand by five and twenty thousand:	6242
48:20	twenty thousand by five and t thousand:	6242
48:21	t thousand of the oblation toward the east	6242
48:21	t thousand toward the west border,	6242
Da 6: 1	the kingdom an hundred and t princes,	6243
10:13	of Persia withstood me one and t days:	6242
Hag 2:16	when one came to a heap of t *measures,*	6242
2:16	*vessels* out *of* the press, there were *but* t.	6242
Zec 5: 2	the length thereof *is* t cubits,	6242
Lk 14:31	that cometh against him with t thousand?	1501
Jn 6:19	rowed about five and t or thirty furlongs,	1501
Ac 1:15	together were about an hundred and t,)	1501
27:28	And sounded, and found *it* t fathoms:	1501
1Co 10: 8	and fell in one day three and t thousand.	1501
Rev 4: 4	about the throne *were* four and t seats:	1501
4: 4	the seats I saw four and t elders sitting,	1501
4:10	t elders fall down before him that sat on	1501
5: 8	*and* t elders fell down before the Lamb,	1501
5:14	And the four *and* t elders fell down and	1501
11:16	And the four and t elders, which sat before	1501
19: 4	And the four and t elders and the four	1501

TWENTY'S (1) [TWENTY]

Ge 18:31	he said, I will not destroy *it* for t sake.	6242

TWICE (17) [TWO]

Ge 41:32	the dream was doubled unto Pharaoh t;	6471
Ex 16: 5	it shall be t as much as they gather daily.	4932
16:22	sixth day they gathered t **as much** bread,	4932
Nu 20:11	and with his rod he smote the rock t:	6471
1Sa 18:11	And David avoided out of his presence t.	6471
1Ki 11: 9	of Israel, which had appeared unto him t,	6471
2Ki 6:10	and saved himself there, not once nor t.	8147
Ne 13:20	ware lodged without Jerusalem once or t.	8147
Job 33:14	For God speaketh once, yea t,	8147+871.1
40: 5	yea, t; but I will proceed no further.	8147
42:10	also the Lord gave Job t as much as he	4932
Ps 62:11	God hath spoken once; t have I heard	8147
Ecc 6: 6	though he live a thousand years t *told,* yet	6471
Mk 14:30	even in this night, before the cock crow t,	1364
14:72	Before the cock crow t, thou shalt deny	1364
Lk 18:12	I fast t in the week, I give tithes of all that	1364
Jude 1:12	without fruit, t dead, plucked up by	1364

TWIGS (2)

Eze 17: 4	He cropt off the top of his **young** t,	3242
17:22	from the top of his **young** t a tender one,	3127

TWILIGHT (9)

1Sa 30:17	David smote them from the t even unto	5399
2Ki 7: 5	they rose up in the t, to go unto the camp	5399
7: 7	Wherefore they arose and fled in the t,	5399
Job 3: 9	Let the stars of the t thereof be dark; let it	5399
24:15	eye also of the adulterer waiteth for the t,	5399
Pr 7: 9	In the t, in the evening, in the black and	5399
Eze 12: 6	*thy* shoulders, *and* carry *it* forth in the t:	5939
12: 7	I brought *it* forth in the t, *and* I bare *it*	5939
12:12	them shall bear upon *his* shoulder in the t,	5939

TWINED (21)

Ex 26: 1	tabernacle *with* ten curtains *of* fine linen,	7806
26:31	scarlet, and fine t linen *of* cunning work:	7806
26:36	and purple, and scarlet, and fine t linen,	7806
27: 9	t linen of an hundred cubits long for one	7806
27:16	and purple, and scarlet, and fine t linen,	7806
27:18	the height five cubits *of* fine t linen,	7806
28: 6	and *of* purple, *of* scarlet, and fine t linen,	7806
28: 8	and purple, and scarlet, and fine t linen.	7806
28:15	purple, and *of* scarlet, and *of* fine t linen,	7806
36: 8	made ten curtains *of* fine t linen,	7806
36:35	and purple, and scarlet, and fine t linen,	7806
36:37	purple, and scarlet, and fine t linen,	7806
38: 9	hangings of the court *were of* fine t linen,	7806
38:16	court round about *were of* fine t linen.	7806
38:18	and purple, and scarlet, and fine t linen:	7806
39: 2	and purple, and scarlet, and fine t linen.	7806
39: 5	and purple, and scarlet, and fine t linen;	7806
39: 8	and purple, and scarlet, and fine t linen;	7806
39:24	and purple, and scarlet, and t linen.	7806
39:28	and linen breeches *of* fine t linen,	7806
39:29	a girdle *of* fine t linen, and blue,	7806

TWINKLING (1)

1Co 15:52	In a moment, in the t of an eye, at the last	4493

TWINS (6)

Ge 25:24	behold, *there* were t in her womb.	8380
38:27	that, behold, t *were* in her womb.	8380
SS 4: 2	whereof every one **beareth** t, and none	8382
4: 5	breasts *are* like two young roes *that are* t,	8380
6: 6	whereof every one **beareth** t, and *there*	8382
7: 3	breasts *are* like two young roes *that are* t.	8380

TWIST See WREST

TWISTED See PLATTED; TWINED

TWO (835) [SECOND, TWAIN, TWICE, TWOEDGED, TWOFOLD]

Ge 1:16	God made t great lights; the greater light	8147
4:19	Lamech took unto him t wives: the name	8147
5:18	Jared lived an hundred sixty and t years,	8147
5:20	Jared were nine hundred sixty and t years:	8147
5:26	Lamech seven hundred eighty and t years,	8147
5:28	lived an hundred eighty and t years,	8147
6:19	t of every *sort* shalt thou bring into the	8147
6:20	t of every *sort* shall come unto thee,	8147
7: 2	of beasts that *are* not clean by t, the male	8147
7: 9	There went in t and two unto Noah into	8147
7: 9	went in two and t unto Noah into the ark,	8147
7:15	and two of all flesh, wherein *is* the	8147
7:15	two and t of all flesh, wherein *is* the	8147
9:22	father, and told his t brethren without.	8147
10:25	unto Eber were born t sons: the name of	8147
11:10	begat Arphaxad t years after the flood:	8141
11:19	Peleg lived after he begat Reu t **hundred**	3967
11:20	Reu lived t and thirty years,	8147
11:21	Reu lived after he begat Serug t **hundred**	3967
11:23	lived after he begat Nahor t **hundred**	3967
11:32	the days of Terah were t **hundred** and	3967
19: 1	there came t angels to Sodom at even;	8147
19: 8	I have t daughters which have not known	8147
19:15	Arise, take thy wife, and thy t daughters,	8147
19:16	and upon the hand of his t daughters;	8147
19:30	mountain, and his t daughters with him;	8147
19:30	dwelt in a cave, he and his t daughters.	8147
22: 3	took t of his young men with him,	8147
24:22	t bracelets for her hands of ten *shekels*	8147
25:23	**T** nations *are* in thy womb, and two	8147
25:23	t manner of people shall be separated	8147
27: 9	fetch me from thence t good kids of	8147
27:36	for he hath supplanted me these t *times*:	6471
29:16	Laban had t daughters: the name of	8147
31:33	and into the t maidservants' tents;	8147
31:41	I served thee fourteen years for thy t	8147
32: 7	and herds, and the camels, into t bands;	8147
32:10	Jordan; and now I am become t bands.	8147
32:14	**T hundred** she goats, and twenty he	3967
32:14	t hundred ewes, and twenty rams,	3967
32:22	took his t wives, and his two	8147
32:22	his t womenservants, and his eleven sons,	8147
33: 1	unto Rachel, and unto the t handmaids.	8147
34:25	that t of the sons of Jacob, Simeon and	8147
40: 2	Pharaoh was wroth against t *of* his officers	8147
41: 1	to pass at the end of t **full years,**	3117+8141
41:50	unto Joseph were born t sons before	8147
42:37	saying, Slay my t sons, if I bring him not	8147
44:27	Ye know that my wife bare me t *sons:*	8147
45: 6	For these t **years** *hath* the famine been	8141
46:27	were born him in Egypt, *were* t souls:	8147
48: 1	he took with him his t sons, Manasseh	8147
48: 5	now thy t sons, Ephraim and Manasseh,	8147
49:14	ass couching down between t **burdens:**	4942
Ex 2:13	t men of the Hebrews strove together:	8147
4: 9	if they will not believe also these t signs,	8147
12: 7	strike *it* on the t side posts and on the	8147
12:22	the t side posts with the blood that *is* in	8147
12:23	on the t side posts, the Lord will pass	8147
16:22	t omers for one *man*: and all the rulers of	8147
16:29	you on the sixth day the bread of t **days;**	3117
18: 3	her t sons; of which the name of the one	8147
18: 6	and thy wife, and her t sons with her.	8147
21:21	Notwithstanding, if he continue a day or t,	3117
25:10	t **cubits** and a half *shall be* the length	520
25:12	t rings *shall be* in the one side of it,	8147
25:12	of it, and t rings in the other side of it.	8147
25:17	t **cubits** and a half *shall be* the length	520
25:18	thou shalt make t cherubims *of* gold,	8147
25:18	them, in the t ends of the mercy seat.	8147
25:19	make the cherubims on the t ends thereof.	8147
25:22	from between the t cherubims which *are*	8147
25:23	t **cubits** *shall be* the length thereof,	520
25:35	there shall be a knop under t branches of	8147
25:35	a knop under t branches of the same,	8147
25:35	and a knop under t branches of the same,	8147
26:17	**T** tenons *shall there* be in one board, set	8147
26:19	t sockets under one board for his two	8147
26:19	two sockets under one board for his t	8147
26:19	t sockets under another board for his two	8147
26:19	two sockets under another board for his t	8147
26:21	t sockets under one board, and two	8147
26:21	and t sockets under another board.	8147
26:23	t boards shalt thou make for the corners	8147
26:23	corners of the tabernacle in the t **sides.**	3411
26:24	them both; they shall be for the t corners.	8147
26:25	t sockets under one board, and two	8147
26:25	and t sockets under another board.	8147
26:27	the tabernacle, for the t **sides** westward.	3411
27: 7	the staves shall be upon the t *sides* of	8147
28: 7	It shall have the t shoulderpieces *thereof*	8147
28: 7	*thereof* joined at the t edges thereof;	8147
28: 9	thou shalt take t onyx stones, and grave	8147
28:11	shalt thou engrave the t stones with	8147
28:12	thou shalt put the t stones upon	8147
28:12	upon his t shoulders for a memorial.	8147
28:14	t chains *of* pure gold at the ends;	8147
28:23	shalt make upon the breastplate t rings	8147
28:23	shalt put the t rings on the two ends of	8147
28:23	shalt put the two rings on the t ends of	8147

Ref	Text	Strong's
Ex 28:24	shalt put the t wreathen *chains of* gold	8147
28:24	t rings *which are* on the ends of	8147
28:25	*other* t ends of the two wreathen *chains*	8147
28:25	*other* two ends of the t wreathen *chains*	8147
28:25	*chains* thou shalt fasten in the t ouches,	8147
28:26	thou shalt make t rings of gold,	8147
28:26	thou shalt put them upon the t ends of	8147
28:27	t *other* rings of gold thou shalt make,	8147
28:27	shalt put them on the t sides of the ephod	8147
29: 1	bullock, and t rams without blemish,	8147
29: 3	basket, with the bullock and the t rams.	8147
29:13	t kidneys, and the fat that *is* upon them,	8147
29:22	t kidneys, and the fat that *is* upon them,	8147
29:38	t lambs of the first year day by day	8147
30: 2	t cubits *shall be* the height thereof:	520
30: 4	t golden rings shalt thou make to it under	8147
30: 4	by the t corners thereof, upon the two	8147
30: 4	upon the t sides of it shalt thou make *it;*	8147
30:23	*even* t hundred and fifty *shekels,* and	3967
30:23	and of sweet calamus t hundred and	3967
31:18	t tables of Testimony, tables of stone,	8147
32:15	the t tables of the Testimony *were* in his	8147
34: 1	Hew thee t tables of stone like unto	8147
34: 4	he hewed t tables of stone like unto	8147
34: 4	and took in his hand the t tables of stone.	8147
34:29	the t tables of Testimony in Moses' hand,	8147
36:22	One board had t tenons, equally distant	8147
36:24	t sockets under one board for his two	8147
36:24	two sockets under one board for his t	8147
36:24	two sockets under another board for his two	8147
36:24	two sockets under another board for his t	8147
36:26	t sockets under one board, and two	8147
36:26	and t sockets under another board.	8147
36:28	t boards made he for the corners of	8147
36:28	corners of the tabernacle in the t sides.	3411
36:30	*of* silver, under every board t sockets.	8147
37: 1	t cubits and a half *was* the length of it,	520
37: 3	even t rings upon the one side of it,	8147
37: 3	of it, and t rings upon the other side of it.	8147
37: 6	t cubits and a half *was* the length thereof,	520
37: 7	he made t cherubims *of* gold, beaten out	8147
37: 7	he them, on the t ends of the mercy seat;	8147
37: 8	he the cherubims on the t ends thereof.	8147
37:10	t cubits *was* the length thereof, and a	520
37:21	a knop under t branches of the same,	8147
37:21	a knop under t branches of the same,	8147
37:21	and a knop under t branches of the same,	8147
37:25	and t cubits *was* the height of it;	520
37:27	he made t rings of gold for it under	8147
37:27	by the t corners of it, upon the two sides	8147
37:27	two corners of it, upon the t sides thereof,	8147
38:29	t thousand and four hundred shekels.	505
39: 4	by the t edges was it coupled together.	8147
39:16	they made t ouches *of* gold, and two gold	8147
39:16	two ouches *of* gold, and t gold rings;	8147
39:16	put the t rings in the two ends of	8147
39:16	put the two rings in the t ends of	8147
39:17	they put the t wreathen *chains of* gold in	8147
39:17	the t rings on the ends of the breastplate.	8147
39:18	the t ends of the two wreathen *chains*	8147
39:18	the two ends of the t wreathen *chains*	8147
39:18	*chains* they fastened in the t ouches,	8147
39:19	they made t rings of gold, and put *them*	8147
39:19	put *them* on the t ends of the breastplate,	8147
39:20	they made t *other* golden rings,	8147
39:20	put them on the t sides of the ephod	8147
Lev 3: 4	the t kidneys, and the fat that *is* on them,	8147
3:10	t kidneys, and the fat that *is* upon them,	8147
3:15	t kidneys, and the fat that *is* upon them,	8147
4: 9	t kidneys, and the fat that *is* upon them,	8147
5: 7	t turtledoves, or two young pigeons,	8147
5: 7	two turtledoves, or t young pigeons,	8147
5:11	if he be not able to bring t turtledoves,	8147
5:11	or t young pigeons, then he that sinned	8147
7: 4	the t kidneys, and the fat that *is* on them,	8147
8: 2	t rams, and a basket of unleavened bread;	8147
8:16	the t kidneys, and their fat,	8147
8:25	the t kidneys, and their fat, and the right	8147
12: 5	she shall be unclean t weeks, as *in* her	7620
12: 8	she shall bring t turtles, or two young	8147
12: 8	shall bring two turtles, or t young pigeons;	8147
14: 4	for him that is to be cleansed t birds alive	8147
14:10	on the eighth day he shall take t he lambs	8147
14:22	t turtledoves, or two young pigeons,	8147
14:22	two turtledoves, or t young pigeons,	8147
14:49	he shall take to cleanse the house t birds,	8147
15:14	on the eighth day he shall take to him t	8147
15:14	t young pigeons, and come before	8147
15:29	the eighth day she shall take unto her t	8147
15:29	or t young pigeons, and bring them unto	8147
16: 1	after the death of the t sons of Aaron,	8147
16: 5	Israel t kids of the goats for a sin offering,	8147
16: 7	shall take the t goats, and present them	8147
16: 8	Aaron shall cast lots upon the t goats;	8147
23:13	the meat offering thereof *shall be* t tenth	8147
23:17	Ye shall bring out of your habitations t	8147
23:17	two wave loaves of t tenth deals:	8147
23:18	and one young bullock, and t rams:	8147
23:19	t lambs of the first year for a sacrifice of	8147
23:20	before the LORD, with the t lambs:	8147
24: 5	t tenth deals shall be *in* one cake.	8147
24: 6	shalt set them *in* t rows, six on a row,	8147
Nu 1:35	*were* thirty and t thousand and	8147
1:35	and two thousand and t hundred.	3967
1:39	and t thousand and seven hundred.	8147

Ref	Text	Strong's
Nu 2:21	*were* thirty and t thousand and	8147
2:21	and two thousand and t hundred.	3967
2:26	and t thousand and seven hundred.	8147
3:34	*were* six thousand and t hundred.	3967
3:39	and upward, *were* twenty and t thousand.	8147
3:43	thousand two hundred and threescore	8147
3:43	two thousand t hundred and threescore	3967
3:46	that are *to be* redeemed of the t hundred	3967
4:36	families were t thousand seven hundred	505
4:40	t thousand and six hundred and thirty.	505
4:44	were three thousand and t hundred.	3967
6:10	on the eighth day he shall bring t turtles,	8147
6:10	or t young pigeons, to the priest,	8147
7: 3	a wagon for t of the princes, and for *each*	8147
7: 7	T wagons and four oxen he gave unto	8147
7:17	t oxen, five rams, five he goats, five lambs	8147
7:23	t oxen, five rams, five he goats, five lambs	8147
7:29	t oxen, five rams, five he goats, five lambs	8147
7:35	t oxen, five rams, five he goats, five lambs	8147
7:41	t oxen, five rams, five he goats, five lambs	8147
7:47	t oxen, five rams, five he goats, five lambs	8147
7:53	t oxen, five rams, five he goats, five lambs	8147
7:59	t oxen, five rams, five he goats, five lambs	8147
7:65	t oxen, five rams, five he goats, five lambs	8147
7:71	t oxen, five rams, five he goats, five lambs	8147
7:77	t oxen, five rams, five he goats, five lambs	8147
7:83	t oxen, five rams, five he goats, five lambs	8147
7:85	all the silver vessels *weighed* t thousand	505
7:89	from between the t cherubims:	8147
9:22	Or *whether it were* t days, or a month,	3117
10: 2	Make thee t trumpets of silver; of a whole	8147
11:19	nor t days, nor five days, neither ten days,	3117
11:26	there remained t *of* the men in the camp,	8147
11:31	as it were t cubits *high* upon the face of	520
13:23	and they bare it between t upon a staff;	8147
15: 6	thou shalt prepare *for* a meat offering t	8147
16: 2	t hundred and fifty princes of	3967
16:17	his censer, t hundred and fifty censers;	3967
16:35	consumed the t hundred and fifty men	3967
22:22	his ass, and his t servants *were* with him.	8147
26:10	what time the fire devoured t hundred	3967
26:14	twenty and t thousand and two hundred.	8147
26:14	twenty and two thousand and t hundred.	3967
26:34	fifty and t thousand and seven hundred.	8147
26:37	thirty and t thousand and five hundred.	8147
28: 3	t lambs of the first year without spot day	8147
28: 9	on the sabbath day t lambs of the first year	8147
28: 9	t tenth deals *of* flour *for* a meat offering,	8147
28:11	t young bullocks, and one ram, seven	8147
28:12	t tenth deals *of* flour *for* a meat offering,	8147
28:19	t young bullocks, and one ram,	8147
28:20	for a bullock, and t tenth deals for a ram;	8147
28:27	t young bullocks, one ram, seven lambs of	8147
28:28	one bullock, t tenth deals unto one ram,	8147
29: 3	for a bullock, *and* t tenth deals for a ram,	8147
29: 9	to a bullock, *and* t tenth deals to one ram,	8147
29:13	t rams, *and* fourteen lambs of the first	8147
29:14	t tenth deals to each ram of the two rams,	8147
29:14	two tenth deals to each ram of the t rams,	8147
29:17	t rams, fourteen lambs of the first year	8147
29:20	on the third day eleven bullocks, t rams,	8147
29:23	t rams, *and* fourteen lambs of the first	8147
29:26	t rams, *and* fourteen lambs of the first	8147
29:29	t rams, *and* fourteen lambs of the first	8147
29:32	t rams, *and* fourteen lambs of the first	8147
31:27	divide the prey into t parts; between	2673
31:35	thirty and t thousand persons in all,	8147
31:40	LORD's tribute *was* thirty and t persons.	8147
34:15	t tribes and the half tribe have received	8147
35: 5	the city *on* the east side t thousand cubits,	505
35: 5	and *on* the south side t thousand cubits,	505
35: 5	*on* the west side t thousand cubits,	505
35: 5	and *on* the north side t thousand cubits;	505
35: 6	to them ye shall add forty and t cities.	8147
Dt 3: 8	took at that time out of the hand of the t	8147
3:21	your God hath done unto these t kings:	8147
4:13	and he wrote them upon t tables of stone.	8147
4:47	king of Bashan, t kings of the Amorites,	8147
5:22	he wrote them in t tables of stone,	8147
9:10	the LORD delivered unto me t tables of	8147
9:11	*that* the LORD gave me the t tables of	8147
9:15	the t tables of the covenant *were* in my	8147
9:15	two tables of the covenant *were* in my t	8147
9:17	I took the t tables, and cast them out of	8147
9:17	cast them out of my t hands,	8147
10: 1	Hew thee t tables of stone like unto	8147
10: 3	hewed t tables of stone like unto the first,	8147
10: 3	having the t tables in mine hand.	8147
14: 6	cleaveth the cleft *into* t claws,	8147
17: 6	At the mouth of t witnesses,	8147
18: 3	and the t cheeks, and the maw.	3895
19:15	at the mouth of t witnesses, or at the	8147
21:15	If a man have t wives, one beloved,	8147
32:30	t put ten thousand to flight, except their	8147
Jos 2: 1	the son of Nun sent out of Shittim t	8147
2: 4	the woman took the t men, and hid them,	8147
2:10	what you did unto the t kings of	8147
2:23	the t men returned, and descended from	8147
3: 4	it, about t thousand cubits by measure:	505
6:22	Joshua had said unto the t men that had	8147
7: 3	let about t or three thousand men go up	505
7:21	t hundred shekels *of* silver, and a wedge	3967
9:10	all that he did to the t kings of	8147
14: 3	For Moses had given the inheritance of t	8147
14: 4	For the children of Joseph were t tribes,	8147

Ref	Text	Strong's
Jos 15:60	and Rabbah; t cities with their villages.	8147
19:30	twenty and t cities with their villages.	8147
21:16	suburbs; nine cities out of those t tribes.	8147
21:25	Gath-rimmon with her suburbs; t cities.	8147
21:27	and Beeshterah with her suburbs; t cities.	8147
24:12	*even* the t kings of the Amorites;	8147
Jdg 3:16	Ehud made him a dagger which had t	8147
5:30	the prey; to every man a damsel or t's;	7361
7: 3	of the people twenty and t thousand	8147
7:25	they took t princes of the Midianites, Oreb	8147
8:12	took the t kings of Midian, Zebah and	8147
9:44	the t *other* companies ran upon all	8147
10: 3	and judged Israel twenty and t years.	8147
11:37	let me alone t months, that I may go up	8147
11:38	he sent her away *for* t months:	8147
11:39	it came to pass at the end of t months,	8147
12: 6	of the Ephraimites forty and t thousand.	8147
15: 4	a firebrand in the midst between t tails.	8147
15:13	they bound him with t new cords,	8147
16: 3	the t posts, and went away with them,	8147
16:28	avenged of the Philistines for my t eyes.	8147
16:29	Samson took hold of the t middle pillars	8147
17: 4	his mother took t hundred *shekels* of	3967
19:10	*there were* with him t asses saddled,	6776
20:21	that day twenty and t thousand men.	8147
20:45	and slew t thousand men of them.	505
Ru 1: 1	of Moab, he, and his wife, and his t sons.	8147
1: 2	name of his t sons Mahlon and Chilion,	8147
1: 3	and she was left, and her t sons.	8147
1: 5	the woman was left of her t sons and	8147
1: 7	and her t daughters in law with her;	8147
1: 8	Naomi said unto her t daughters in law,	8147
1:19	So they t went until they came to	8147
4:11	which t did build the house of Israel:	8147
1Sa 1: 2	he had t wives; the name of the one *was*	8147
1: 3	the t sons of Eli, Hophni and Phinehas,	8147
2:21	and bare three sons and t daughters.	8147
2:34	shall come upon thy t sons, on Hophni	8147
4: 4	the t sons of Eli, Hophni and Phinehas,	8147
4:11	the t sons of Eli, Hophni and Phinehas,	8147
4:17	thy t sons also, Hophni and Phinehas,	8147
6: 7	make a new cart, and take t milch kine,	8147
6:10	t milch kine, and tied them to the cart,	8147
10: 2	shalt find t men by Rachel's sepulchre	8147
10: 4	thee, and give thee t *loaves* of bread;	8147
11:11	so that t of them were not left together.	8147
13: 1	when he had reigned t years over Israel,	8147
13: 2	*whereof* t thousand were with Saul in	505
14:49	the names of his t daughters were these;	8147
15: 4	t hundred thousand footmen,	3967
18:27	slew of the Philistines t hundred men;	3967
23:18	they t made a covenant before the LORD:	8147
25:13	and t hundred abode by the stuff.	3967
25:18	took t hundred loaves, and two bottles	3967
25:18	t bottles of wine, and five sheep ready	8147
25:18	t hundred cakes *of figs,* and laid *them*	3967
27: 3	*even* David with his t wives, Ahinoam	8147
28: 8	t men with him, and they came to	8147
30: 5	David's t wives were taken captives,	8147
30:10	t hundred abode *behind,* which were so	3967
30:12	of a cake *of figs,* and t clusters of raisins:	8147
30:18	and David rescued his t wives.	8147
30:21	David came to the t hundred men,	3967
2Sa 1: 1	and David had abode t days in Ziklag;	8147
2: 2	his t wives also, Ahinoam the Jezreelitess,	8147
2:10	to reign over Israel, and reigned t years.	8147
4: 2	Saul's son had t men *that were* captains	8147
8: 2	*even* with t lines measured he to put to	8147
8: 5	David slew of the Syrians t and	8147
12: 1	unto him, There were t men in one city;	8147
13:23	it came to pass after t full years,	3117+8141
14: 6	thy handmaid had t sons, and they two	8147
14: 6	they t strove together in the field,	8147
14:26	t hundred shekels after the king's weight.	3967
14:28	So Absalom dwelt t full years in	3117+8141
15:11	with Absalom went t hundred men out of	3967
15:27	your t sons with you, Ahimaaz thy son,	8147
15:36	*they have* there with them their t sons,	8147
16: 1	upon them t hundred *loaves of* bread,	3967
18:24	David sat between the t gates:	8147
21: 8	the king took the t sons of Rizpah	8147
23:20	he slew t lionlike men of Moab:	8147
1Ki 2: 5	what he did to the t captains of the hosts	8147
2:32	who fell upon t men more righteous and	8147
2:39	that t of the servants of Shimei ran away	8147
3:16	came there t women, *that were* harlots,	8147
3:18	us in the house, save we t in the house.	8147
3:25	Divide the living child in t, and give half	8147
5:12	and they t made a league *together.*	8147
5:14	were in Lebanon, *and* t months at home:	8147
6:23	within the oracle he made t cherubims *of*	8147
6:32	The t doors also *were* of olive tree;	8147
6:34	the t doors *were* of fir tree: the two leaves	8147
6:34	the t leaves of the one door were folding,	8147
6:34	the t leaves of the other door *were* folding	8147
7:15	For he cast t pillars, of eighteen	8147
7:16	made t chapiters *of* molten brass, to set	8147
7:18	t rows round about upon the one	8147
7:20	the chapiters upon the t pillars *had*	8147
7:20	pomegranates *were* t hundred *in* rows	3967
7:24	knops *were* cast *in* t rows, when it was	8147
7:26	of lilies: it contained t thousand baths.	505
7:41	The t pillars, and the two bowls of	8147
7:41	the t bowls of the chapiters that *were* on	8147
7:41	that *were* on the top of the t pillars;	NIH

1Ki
7:41 the t networks, to cover the two bowls of 8147
7:41 to cover the t bowls of the chapiters 8147
7:42 four hundred pomegranates for the t 8147
7:42 even t rows *of* pomegranates for one 8147
7:42 to cover the t bowls of the chapiters that 8147
8: 7 *their* t **wings** over the place of the ark, 3671
8: 9 *There was* nothing in the ark save the t 8147
8:63 t and twenty thousand oxen, 8147
9:10 when Solomon had built the t houses, 8147
10:16 king Solomon made t **hundred** targets *of* 3967
10:19 seat, and t lions stood beside the stays. 8147
11:29 and they t *were* alone in the field: 8147
12:28 t calves of gold, and said unto them, 8147
14:20 the days which Jeroboam reigned *were* t 8147
15:25 of Judah, and reigned over Israel t **years**. 8141
16: 8 to reign over Israel in Tirzah, t **years**. 8141
16:21 the people of Israel divided into t **parts**. 2677
16:24 Samaria of Shemer for t **talents** of silver, 3603
16:29 over Israel in Samaria twenty and t years. 8147
17:12 behold, I *am* gathering t sticks, that I may 8147
18:21 How long halt ye between t opinions? 8147
18:23 Let them therefore give us t bullocks; 8147
18:32 as great as would contain t **measures** of 5429
20: 1 *there were* thirty and t kings with him, 8147
20:15 and they were t **hundred** and thirty two: 3967
20:15 and they were two hundred and thirty t: 8147
20:16 the thirty and t kings that helped him. 8147
20:27 before them like t little flocks of kids; 8147
21:10 set t men, sons of Belial, before him, 8147
21:13 there came in t men, children of Belial, 8147
22:31 t captains that had rule over *his* chariots, 8147
22:51 of Judah, and reigned t **years** over Israel. 8141

2Ki
1:14 burnt up the t captains of the former 8147
2: 6 I will not leave thee. And they t went on. 8147
2: 7 view afar off: and they t stood by Jordan. 8147
2: 8 so that they t went over on dry *ground*. 8147
2:12 own clothes, and rent them in t pieces. 8147
2:24 there came forth t she bears out of 8147
2:24 and tare forty and t children of them. 8147
4: 1 creditor is come to take unto him my t 8147
5:17 be given to thy servant t mules' burden? 6776
5:22 t young men of the sons of the prophets: 8147
5:22 talent of silver, and t changes of garments. 8147
5:23 Naaman said, Be content, take t **talents**. 3603
5:23 and bound t **talents** of silver in two bags, 3603
5:23 and bound two talents of silver in t bags, 8147
5:23 with t changes of garments, and laid 8147
5:23 and laid *them* upon t of his servants; 8147
7: 1 t **measures** of barley for a shekel, 5429
7:14 They took therefore t chariot horses; 8147
7:16 t **measures** of barley for a shekel, 5429
7:18 T **measures** of barley for a shekel, 5429
8:17 t years old was he when he *began* to 8147
8:26 T and twenty years old *was* Ahaziah 8141
9:32 looked out to him t *or* three eunuchs. 8147
10: 4 Behold, t kings stood not before him: 8147
10: 8 Lay ye them *in* t heaps *at* the entering in 8147
10:14 the shearing house, *even* t and forty men; 8147
11: 7 t parts of all you that go forth on 8147
15: 2 he reigned t and fifty years in Jerusalem. 8147
15:23 Israel in Samaria, *and* reigned t **years**, 8141
15:27 In the t and fiftieth year of Azariah king 8147
17:16 *even* t calves, and made a grove, 8147
18:23 and I will deliver thee t **thousand** horses, 505
21: 5 in the t courts of the house of the Lord. 8147
21:19 and t years old when he *began* to reign, 8147
21:19 and he reigned t years in Jerusalem. 8147
23:12 in the t courts of the house of the Lord, 8147
25: 4 *by* the way of the gate between t **walls**, 2346
25:16 The T pillars, one sea, and the bases 8147

1Ch
1:19 unto Eber were born t sons: the name of 8147
4: 5 Ashur the father of Tekoa had t wives, 8147
5:21 *of* sheep t **hundred** and fifty thousand, 3967
5:21 asses t **thousand**, and *of* men an hundred 505
7: 2 whose number *was* in the days of David t 8147
7: 7 and t thousand and thirty and four. 8147
7: 9 was twenty thousand and t **hundred**. 3967
7:11 t **hundred** *soldiers*, fit to go out *for* war 3967
9:22 be porters in the gates *were* t **hundred** 3967
11:21 he was more honourable than the t; 8147
11:22 acts; he slew t lionlike men of Moab. 8147
12:28 his father's house twenty and t captains. 8147
12:32 the heads of them *were* t **hundred**; 3967
15: 6 and his brethren t **hundred** and twenty. 3967
15: 8 the chief, and his brethren t **hundred**: 3967
18: 5 David slew of the Syrians t and 8147
19: 7 they hired thirty and t thousand chariots, 8147
24:17 to Jachin, the t and twentieth to Gamul, 8147
25: 7 was t **hundred** fourscore and eight. 3967
25:29 The t and twentieth to Giddalti, *he*, his 8147
26: 8 *were* threescore and t of Obed-edom. 8147
26:17 a day, and toward Asuppim t *and* two. 8147
26:17 a day, and toward Asuppim two *and* t. 8147
26:18 four at the causeway, *and* t at Parbar. 8147
26:32 *were* t **thousand** and seven hundred chief 505

2Ch
3:10 in the most holy house he made t 8147
3:15 Also he made before the house t pillars of 8147
4: 3 T rows *of* oxen *were* cast, when it was 8147
4:12 *To wit*, the t pillars, and the pommels, 8147
4:12 chapiters which *were* on the top of the t 8147
4:12 the t wreaths to cover the two pommels 8147
4:12 the two wreaths to cover the t pommels 8147
4:13 four hundred pomegranates on the t 8147
4:13 t rows *of* pomegranates on each wreath, 8147
4:13 to cover the t pommels of the chapiters 8147

2Ch
5:10 *There was* nothing in the ark save the t 8147
7: 5 a sacrifice of twenty and t thousand oxen, 8147
8:10 *even* t hundred and fifty, that bare rule 3967
9:15 king Solomon made t **hundred** targets *of* 3967
9:18 and t lions standing by the stays: 8147
13:21 begat twenty and t sons, 8147
14: 8 t **hundred** and fourscore thousand: 3967
17:15 with him t **hundred** and 3967
17:16 with him t **hundred** thousand mighty 3967
17:17 bow and shield t **hundred** thousand. 3967
21: 5 and t years old when he *began* to reign, 8147
21:19 in process of time, after the end of t years, 8147
21:20 t *years* old *was* he when he *began* to 8147
22: 2 t years old *was* Ahaziah when he *began* 8147
24: 3 Jehoiada took for him t wives; and he 8147
26: 3 he reigned fifty and t years in Jerusalem. 8147
26:12 mighty *men* of valour *were* t **thousand** 505
28: 8 of their brethren t **hundred** thousand, 3967
29:32 an hundred rams, *and* t **hundred** lambs: 3967
33: 5 in the t courts of the house of the Lord. 8147
33:21 Amon *was* t and twenty years old when 8147
33:21 to reign, and reigned t years in Jerusalem. 8147
35: 8 for the passover *offerings* t **thousand** 505

Ezr
2: 3 t **thousand** an hundred seventy and two. 505
2: 3 two thousand an hundred seventy and t. 8147
2: 4 Shephatiah, three hundred seventy and t. 8147
2: 6 t **thousand** eight hundred and twelve. 505
2: 7 a thousand t **hundred** fifty and four. 3967
2:10 children of Bani, six hundred forty and t. 8147
2:12 a thousand t **hundred** twenty and two. 3967
2:12 a thousand two hundred twenty and t. 8147
2:14 of Bigvai, t **thousand** fifty and six. 505
2:19 of Hashum, t **hundred** twenty and three. 3967
2:24 The children of Azmaveth, forty and t. 8147
2:27 of Michmas, an hundred twenty and t. 8147
2:28 and Ai, t **hundred** twenty and three. 3967
2:29 The children of Nebo, fifty and t. 8147
2:31 a thousand t **hundred** fifty and four. 3967
2:37 children of Immer, a thousand fifty and t. 8147
2:38 a thousand t **hundred** forty and seven. 3967
2:58 *were* three hundred ninety and t. 8147
2:60 of Nekoda, six hundred fifty and t. 8147
2:64 was **forty** *and* t **thousand** 505+702+7239
2:65 *were* among them t **hundred** singing 3967
2:66 six; their mules, t **hundred** forty and five; 3967
6:17 t hundred rams, four hundred lambs; 3969
8: 4 and with him t **hundred** males. 3967
8: 9 with him t **hundred** and eighteen males. 3967
8:20 hundred and twenty Nethinims: 3967
8:27 t vessels of fine copper, precious as gold. 8147
10:13 neither *is this* a work of one day or t: 8147

Ne
5:14 from the twentieth year even unto the t 8147
6:15 *day* of the month Elul, in fifty and t days. 8147
7: 8 t **thousand** an hundred seventy and two. 505
7: 8 two thousand an hundred seventy and t. 8147
7: 9 Shephatiah, three hundred seventy and t. 8147
7:10 children of Arah, six hundred fifty and t. 8147
7:11 t **thousand** and eight hundred and 505
7:12 a thousand t **hundred** fifty and four. 3967
7:17 thousand three hundred twenty and 505
7:17 two thousand three hundred twenty and t. 8147
7:19 Bigvai, t **thousand** threescore and seven. 505
7:28 The men of Beth-azmaveth, forty and t. 8147
7:31 Michmas, an hundred and twenty and t. 8147
7:33 The men of the other Nebo, fifty and t. 8147
7:34 a thousand t **hundred** fifty and four. 3967
7:40 children of Immer, a thousand fifty and t. 8147
7:41 a thousand t **hundred** forty and seven. 3967
7:60 *were* three hundred ninety and t. 8147
7:62 of Nekoda, six hundred forty and t. 8147
7:66 was **forty** *and* t **thousand** 505+702+7239
7:67 they had t **hundred** forty and five singing 3967
7:68 six: their mules, t **hundred** forty and five: 3967
7:71 t **thousand** and two hundred pound of 505
7:71 and t **hundred** pound *of* silver. 3967
7:72 t **thousand** pound *of* silver, and threescore 505
11:12 house *were* eight hundred twenty and t: 8147
11:13 of the fathers, t **hundred** forty and two: 3967
11:13 of the fathers, two hundred forty and t: 8147
11:18 in the holy city *were* t **hundred** fourscore 3967
11:19 the gates, *were* an hundred seventy and t. 8147
12:31 appointed t great *companies of them* that 8147
12:40 stood the t *companies of them* that gave 8147
13: 6 in the t and thirtieth year of Artaxerxes 8147

Est
2:21 t of the king's chamberlains, Bigthan and 8147
6: 2 and Teresh, t of the king's chamberlains, 8147
9:27 they would keep these t days according 8147

Job
13:20 Only do not t *things* unto me: then will I 8147
42: 7 against thee, and against thy t friends: 8147

Pr
30: 7 T *things* have I required of thee; deny me 8147
30:15 The horseleach hath t daughters, 8147

Ecc
4: 9 T are better than one; because they have 8147
4:11 if t lie together, then they have heat: 8147
4:12 against him, t shall withstand him; 8147

SS
4: 5 Thy t breasts *are* like two young roes *that* 8147
4: 5 Thy two breasts *are* like t young roes *that* 8147
6:13 As it were the company of t **armies**. 4264
7: 3 Thy t breasts *are* like two young roes 8147
7: 3 Thy two breasts *are* like t young roes *that* 8147
8:12 that keep the fruit thereof t **hundred**. 3967

Isa
7: 4 neither be fainthearted for the t tails of 8147
7:21 shall nourish a young cow, and t sheep; 8147
17: 6 t *or* three berries in the top of 8147
22:11 Ye made also a ditch between the t **walls** 2346
36: 8 and I will give thee t **thousand** horses, 505

Isa
45: 1 to open before him the t **leaved gates**; 1817
47: 9 these t *things* shall come to thee *in* a 8147
51:19 These t *things* are come unto thee; 8147

Jer
2:13 For my people have committed t evils; 8147
3:14 t of a family, and I will bring you *to* Zion: 8147
24: 1 t baskets of figs *were* set before the 8147
28: 3 Within t **full years** *will* I bring again 3117+8141
28:11 within the space of t **full years**. 3117+8141
33:24 The t families which the Lord hath 8147
39: 4 by the gate betwixt the t **walls**: 2346
52: 7 the way of the gate between the t **walls**, 2346
52:20 The t pillars, one sea, and twelve brasen 8147
52:29 eight hundred thirty and t persons: 8147

Eze
1:11 t wings of every one *were* joined one to 8147
1:11 to another, and t covered their bodies. 8147
1:23 every one had t, which covered on this 8147
1:23 on this *side*, and every one had t, 8147
21:19 thou son of man, appoint thee t ways, 8147
21:21 the head of the t ways, to use divination: 8147
23: 2 Son of man, there were t women, 8147
35:10 These t nations and these two countries 8147
35:10 and these t countries shall be mine, 8147
37:22 they shall be no more t nations, 8147
37:22 neither shall they be divided into t 8147
40: 9 the posts thereof, t cubits; and the porch 8147
40:39 in the porch of the gate *were* t tables on 8147
40:39 t tables on that side, to slay thereon 8147
40:40 the entry of the north gate, *were* t tables; 8147
40:40 at the porch of the gate, *were* t tables. 8147
41: 3 measured the post of the door, t cubits; 8147
41:18 a cherub; and *every* cherub had t faces; 8147
41:22 high, and the length thereof t cubits; 8147
41:23 the temple and the sanctuary had t doors. 8147
41:24 doors had t leaves *apiece*, two turning 8147
41:24 doors had two leaves *apiece*, t turning 8147
41:24 t leaves for the one door, and two leaves 8147
41:24 one door, and t leaves for the other *door*. 8147
43:14 *even* to the lower settle *shall be* t cubits, 8147
45:15 lamb out of the flock, out of t **hundred**, 3967
46:19 was a place on the t **sides** westward. 3411
47:13 of Israel: Joseph *shall have* t portions. NIH
48:17 city shall be toward the north t **hundred** 3967
48:17 toward the south t **hundred** and fifty, 3967
48:17 toward the east t **hundred** and fifty, 3967
48:17 and toward the west t **hundred** and fifty. 3967

Da
5:31 being about threescore and t year old. 8648
8: 3 before the river a ram which had t **horns**: 7161
8: 3 t **horns** *were* high; but one *was* higher 7161
8: 6 he came to the ram that had t **horns**, 7161
8: 7 and smote the ram, and brake his t **horns**: 8147
8:14 Unto t **thousand** and three hundred days; 505
8:20 ram which thou sawest having t **horns** 7161
9:25 seven weeks, and threescore and t weeks: 8147
9:26 and t weeks shall Messiah be cut off, 8147
12: 5 and behold, there stood other t, 8147
12:11 *there shall be* a thousand t **hundred** and 3967

Hos
6: 2 After t days will he revive us: in the third 3117
10:10 when *they* shall bind themselves in their t 8147

Am
1: 1 of Israel, t **year** before the earthquake. 8141
3: 3 t walk together, except they be agreed? 8147
3:12 taketh out of the mouth of the lion t legs, 8147
4: 8 t *or* three cities wandered unto one city, 8147

Zec
4: 3 t olive trees by it, one upon the right *side* 8147
4:11 What *are* these t olive trees upon the 8147
4:12 What *be these* t olive branches which 8147
4:12 t golden pipes empty the golden *oil* out of 8147
4:14 said he, These *are* the t anointed ones, 8147
5: 9 came out t women, and the wind *was* 8147
6: 1 came four chariots out from between t 8147
11: 7 I took unto me t staves; the one I called 8147
13: 8 t parts therein shall be cut off *and* die; 8147

Mt
2:16 thereof, from t **years old** and under, 1332
4:18 saw t brethren, Simon called Peter, 1417
4:21 he saw other t brethren, James the *son of* 1417
6:24 No *man* can serve t masters: for either he 1417
8:28 there met him t possessed with devils, 1417
9:27 t blind men followed him, crying, 1417
10:10 neither t coats, neither shoes, nor yet 1417
10:29 Are not t sparrows sold for a farthing? 1417
11: 2 works of Christ, he sent t of his disciples, 1417
14:17 We have here but five loaves, and t fishes. 1417
14:19 and the t fishes, and looking up to heaven, 1417
18: 8 rather than having t hands or two feet to 1417
18: 8 t feet to be cast into everlasting fire. 1417
18: 9 than having t eyes to be cast into hell 1417
18:16 *then* take with thee one or t more, 1417
18:16 that in the mouth of t or three witnesses 1417
18:19 That if t of you shall agree on earth as 1417
18:20 For where t or three are gathered together 1417
20:21 Grant that these my t sons may sit, 1417
20:24 with indignation against the t brethren. 1417
20:30 t blind men sitting by the way side, 1417
21: 1 of Olives, then sent Jesus t disciples, 1417
21:28 A *certain* man had t sons; and he came to 1417
22:40 On these t commandments hang all the 1417
24:40 shall t be in the field; the one shall be 1417
24:41 T *women shall be* grinding at the mill; 1417
25:15 to another t, and to another one; 1417
25:17 likewise he that *had received* t, he also 1417
25:17 had received two, he also gained other t. 1417
25:22 He also that had received t talents came 1417
25:22 Lord, thou deliveredst unto me t talents: 1417
25:22 have gained t other talents besides them. 1417
26: 2 Ye know that after t days is *the feast of* 1417
26:37 with *him* Peter and the t sons of Zebedee, 1417

T

U

Mt 26:60 At the last came t false witnesses, 1417
27:38 Then were there t thieves crucified with 1417
Mk 5:13 the sea, (they were about **t thousand**,) 1367
6: 7 began to send them forth by two and two; 1417
6: 7 began to send them forth by two and t; 1417
6: 9 shod with sandals; and not put on t coats. 1417
6:37 and buy **t hundred** pennyworth of bread, 1250
6:38 they knew, they say, Five, and t fishes. 1417
6:41 had taken the five loaves and the t fishes 1417
6:41 the t fishes divided he among *them* all. 1417
9:43 than having t hands to go into hell, into 1417
9:45 than having t feet to be cast into hell, 1417
9:47 than having t eyes to be cast into hell fire: 1417
11: 1 he sendeth forth t of his disciples, 1417
11: 4 door without in a place where t ways met; NIG
12:42 and she threw in t mites, which make a 1417
14: 1 After t days the *feast of the passover,* 1417
14:13 And he sendeth forth t of his disciples, 1417
15:27 And with him they crucify t thieves; 1417
16:12 appeared in another form unto t of them, 1417
Lk 2:24 A pair of turtledoves, or t young pigeons. 1417
3:11 and saith unto them, He that hath t coats, 1417
5: 2 And saw t ships standing by the lake: 1417
7:19 John calling unto *him* t of his disciples 1417
7:41 There was a certain creditor which had t 1417
9: 3 money; neither have t coats apiece. 1417
9:13 have no more but five loaves and t fishes; 1417
9:16 he took the five loaves and the t fishes, 1417
9:30 And behold, there talked with him t men, 1417
9:32 and the t men that stood with him. 1417
10: 1 sent them t and two before his face into 1417
10: 1 and t before his face into every city and 1417
10:35 he took out t pence, and gave *them* to 1417
12: 6 Are not five sparrows sold for t farthings, 1417
12:52 three against t, and two against three. 1417
12:52 three against two, and t against three. 1417
15:11 And he said, A certain man had t sons: 1417
16:13 No servant can serve t masters: for either 1417
17:34 in that night there shall be t men in one 1417
17:35 T women shall be grinding together; 1417
17:36 T men shall be in the field; the one shall 1417
18:10 T men went up into the temple to pray; 1417
19:29 *mount* of Olives, he sent t of his disciples, 1417
21: 2 poor widow casting in thither t mites. 1417
22:38 they said, Lord, behold, here *are* t swords. 1417
23:32 And there were also t other, malefactors, 1417
24: 4 t men stood by them in shining garments: 1417
24:13 t of them went *that* same day to a village 1417
Jn 1:35 day *after* John stood, and t of his disciples; 1417
1:37 And the t disciples heard him speak, 1417
1:40 One of the t which heard John speak, 1417
2: 6 containing t or three firkins apiece. 1417
4:40 with them: and he abode there t days. 1417
4:43 Now after t days he departed thence, 1417
6: 7 T hundred pennyworth of bread is not 1250
6: 9 hath five barley loaves, and t small fishes: 1417
8:17 that the testimony of t men is true. 1417
11: 6 he abode t days still in the *same place* 1417
19:18 and t other with him, on either side one, 1417
20:12 seeth t angels in white sitting, the one 1417
21: 2 of Zebedee, and t other of his disciples. 1417
21: 8 land, but as it were t hundred cubits,) 1250
Ac 1:10 t men stood by them in white apparel; 1417
1:23 And they appointed t, Joseph called 1417
1:24 shew whether of these t thou hast chosen, 1417
7:29 land of Madian, where he begat t sons. 1417
9:38 Peter was there, they sent unto him t men, 1417
10: 7 he called t of his household servants, 1417
12: 6 Peter was sleeping between t soldiers, 1417
12: 6 two soldiers, bound with t chains: 1417
19:10 this continued by the space of t years; 1417
19:22 So he sent into Macedonia t of them that 1417
19:34 all with one voice about the space of t 1417
21:33 *him* to be bound with t chains; 1417
23:23 And he called unto *him* t centurions, 1417
23:23 Make ready **t hundred** soldiers to go to 1250
23:23 and ten, and spearmen **t hundred,** 1250
24:27 But after **t years** Porcius Festus came into 1333
27:37 And we were in all in the ship **t hundred** 1250
27:41 falling into a place **where t seas met,** 1337
28:30 And Paul dwelt t whole **years** in his own 1333
1Co 6:16 body? for t, saith *he,* shall be one flesh. 1417
14:27 *let it be* by t, or at the most *by* three, 1417
14:29 Let the prophets speak t or three, 1417
2Co 13: 1 In the mouth of t or three witnesses shall 1417
Gal 4:22 For it is written, that Abraham had t sons, 1417
4:24 for these are the t covenants; the one from 1417
Eph 5:31 unto his wife, and they t shall be one flesh. 1417
Php 1:23 For I am in a strait betwixt t, having a 1417
1Ti 5:19 but before t or three witnesses. 1417
Heb 6:18 That by t immutable things, in which *it* 1417
10:28 Moses' law died without mercy under t 1417
Rev 2:12 hath the sharp sword with t edges; 1366
9:12 behold, there come t woes more hereafter. 1417
9:16 **t hundred thousand:** 1417+3461
11: 2 they tread under foot forty *and* t months. 1417
11: 3 I will give *power* unto my t witnesses, 1417
11: 3 they shall prophesy a thousand **t hundred** 1250
11: 4 These are the t olive trees, and the two 1417
11: 4 t candlesticks standing before the God 1417
11:10 these t prophets tormented them that 1417
12: 6 feed her there a thousand **t hundred** 1250
12:14 And to the woman were given t wings of 1417
13: 5 unto him to continue forty *and* t months. 1417
13:11 and he had t horns like a lamb, 1417

TWOEDGED (4) [EDGE, TWO]

Ps 149: 6 their mouth, and a t sword in their hand; 6374
Pr 5: 4 is bitter as wormwood, sharp as a t sword. 6310
Heb 4:12 powerful, and sharper than any t sword, 1366
Rev 1:16 out of his mouth went a sharp t sword: 1366

TWOFOLD (1) [TWO]

Mt 23:15 make him t more *the* child of hell **than** 1362

TYCHICUS (7)

Ac 20: 4 Timotheus; and of Asia, T and Trophimus. 5190
Eph 6:21 ye also, T, a beloved brother and 5190
6: S from Rome unto the Ephesians by T. 5190
Col 4: 7 All my state shall T declare unto you, 5190
4: S Written from Rome to the Colossians by T 5190
2Ti 4:12 And T have I sent to Ephesus, 5190
Tit 3:12 I shall send Artemas unto thee, or T, 5190

TYRANNUS (1)

Ac 19: 9 disputing daily in the school of one T. 5181

TYRE (37) [TYRUS]

Jos 19:29 *to* Ramah, and to the strong city T; 6865
2Sa 5:11 Hiram king of T sent messengers to David 6865
24: 7 came *to* the strong hold of T, and *to* all 6865
1Ki 5: 1 Hiram king of T sent his servants unto 6865
7:13 Solomon sent and fet Hiram out of T. 6865
7:14 his father *was* a man **of** T, a worker in 6876
9:11 (*Now* Hiram the king of T had furnished 6865
9:12 Hiram came out from T to see the cities 6865
1Ch 14: 1 Now Hiram king of T sent messengers to 6865
22: 4 they of T brought much cedar wood to 6876
2Ch 2: 3 Solomon sent to Huram the king of T, 6865
2:11 Huram the king of T answered in writing, 6865
2:14 his father *was* a man of T, skilful to work 6876
Ezr 3: 7 unto them of Zidon, and to them of T, 6865
Ne 13:16 There dwelt **men of** T also therein, 6876
Ps 45:12 daughter of T *shall be there* with a gift; 6865
83: 7 the Philistines with the inhabitants of T; 6865
87: 4 behold Philistia, and T, with Ethiopia; 6865
Isa 23: 1 The burden of T. Howl, ye ships of 6865
23: 5 they be sorely pained *at* the report of T, 6865
23: 8 Who hath taken this counsel against T, 6865
23:15 that T shall be forgotten seventy years, 6865
23:15 after the end of seventy years shall T sing 6865
23:17 *that* the LORD will visit T, and she shall 6865
Joel 3: 4 O T, and Zidon, and all the coasts of 6865
Mt 11:21 had been done in T and Sidon they would 5184
11:22 It shall be more tolerable for T and Sidon 5184
15:21 and departed into the coasts of T and 5184
Mk 3: 8 and they about T and Sidon, a great 5184
7:24 and went into the borders of T and Sidon, 5184
7:31 departing from the coasts of T and Sidon, 5184
Lk 6:17 and *from* the sea coast of T and Sidon, 5184
10:13 if the mighty works had been done in T 5184
10:14 But it shall be more tolerable for T and 5184
Ac 12:20 was highly displeased with them **of** T 5183
21: 3 and sailed into Syria, and landed at T: 5184
21: 7 when we had finished *our* course from T, 5184

TYRUS (22) [TYRE]

Jer 25:22 all the kings of T, and all the kings of 6865
27: 3 to the king of T, and to the king of Zidon, 6865
47: 4 *and* to cut off from T and Zidon every 6865
Eze 26: 2 that T hath said against Jerusalem, 6865
26: 3 T, and will cause many nations to come 6865
26: 4 they shall destroy the walls of T, 6865
26: 7 I *will* bring upon T Nebuchadrezzar king 6865
26:15 Thus saith the Lord GOD to T; Shall not 6865
27: 2 son of man, take up a lamentation for T; 6865
27: 3 say unto T, O thou that art situate at 6865
27: 3 T, thou hast said, I *am* of perfect beauty. 6865
27: 8 thy wise *men*, O T, *that* were in thee, 6865
27:32 over thee, *saying*, What *city is* like T, 6865
28: 2 Son of man, say unto the prince of T, 6865
28:12 take up a lamentation upon the king of T, 6865
29:18 army to serve a great service against T: 6865
29:18 yet had he no wages, nor his army, for T, 6865
Hos 9:13 Ephraim, as I saw T, *is* planted in a 6865
Am 1: 9 For three transgressions of T, and for four, 6865
1:10 I will send a fire on the wall of T, 6865
Zec 9: 2 T, and Zidon, though it be very wise. 6865
9: 3 T did build herself a strong hold, 6865

U

UCAL (1)

Pr 30: 1 spake unto Ithiel, even unto Ithiel and U. 401

UEL (1)

Ezr 10:34 the sons of Bani; Maadai, Amram, and U, 177

UGLY See NOISOME

ULAI (2)

Da 8: 2 in a vision, and I was by the river of U. 195

Da 8:16 a man's voice between *the banks of* U, 195

ULAM (4)

1Ch 7:16 and his sons *were* U and Rakem. 198
7:17 the sons of U; Bedan. These *were* the sons 198
8:39 the sons of Eshek his brother *were,* U his 198
8:40 the sons of U were mighty men of valour, 198

ULLA (1)

1Ch 7:39 sons of U; Arah, and Haniel, and Rezia. 5925

UMMAH (1)

Jos 19:30 U also, and Aphek, and Rehob: twenty 5981

UNACCUSTOMED (1) [ACCUSTOMED]

Jer 31:18 as a bullock u *to the yoke;* turn 3808+3925

UNADVISEDLY (1) [ADVISE]

Ps 106:33 his spirit, so that he **spake** u with his lips. 981

UNAWARES (12) [AWARE]

Ge 31:20 Jacob **stale away** u to Laban 1589+3820
31:26 thou hast **stolen away** u to me, 1589+3824
Nu 35:11 thither, which killeth *any* person u 6310
35:15 *any* person u may flee thither. 7684+871.1
Dt 4:42 should kill his neighbour u, 1097+1847+871.1
Jos 20: 3 the slayer that killeth *any* person u 7684+871.1
20: 9 that whosoever killeth *any* person at u 7684
Ps 35: 8 destruction come upon him at u; 3045+3808
Lk 21:34 life, and *so* that day come upon you u. 160
Gal 2: 4 because of false brethren u **brought in,** 3920
Heb 13: 2 thereby some have entertained angels u. 2990
Jude 1: 4 For there are certain men **crept in** u, 3921

UNBELIEF (16) [BELIEVE, UNBELIEVERS, UNBELIEVING]

Mt 13:58 mighty works there, because of their u. 570
17:20 Jesus said unto them, Because of your u: 570
Mk 6: 6 And he marvelled because of their u. 570
9:24 tears, Lord, I believe; help thou mine u. 570
16:14 and upbraided them with their u and 570
Ro 3: 3 shall their u make the faith of God without 570
4:20 not at the promise of God through u; 570
11:20 because of u they were broken off, 570
11:23 And they also, if they bide not still in u, 570
11:30 have now obtained mercy through their u: 543
11:32 For God hath concluded *them* all in u, 570
1Ti 1:13 because I did *it* ignorantly in u. 570
Heb 3:12 there be in any of you an evil heart of u, 570
3:19 that they could not enter in because of u. 570
4: 6 first preached entered not in because of u, 543
4:11 any *man* fall after the same example of u. 543

UNBELIEVER See INFIDEL

UNBELIEVERS (4) [UNBELIEF]

Lk 12:46 will appoint *him* his portion with the u. 571
1Co 6: 6 to law with brother, and that before the u. 571
14:23 or u, will they not say that ye are mad? 571
2Co 6:14 ye not unequally yoked together with u: 571

UNBELIEVING (6) [UNBELIEF]

Ac 14: 2 But the u Jews stirred up the Gentiles, 544
1Co 7:14 the u husband is sanctified by the wife, 571
7:14 the u wife is sanctified by the husband; 571
7:15 But if the u depart, let him depart. 571
Tit 1:15 that are defiled and u *is* nothing pure; 571
Rev 21: 8 and u, and the abominable, and murderers, 571

UNBLAMEABLE (2) [BLAME, UNBLAMEABLY]

Col 1:22 to present you holy and u and 299
1Th 3:13 To the end *he* may stablish your hearts u 273

UNBLAMEABLY (1) [UNBLAMEABLE]

1Th 2:10 u we behaved ourselves among you that 274

UNCERTAIN (2) [CERTAIN, UNCERTAINLY]

1Co 14: 8 For if the trumpet give an u sound, who 82
1Ti 6:17 nor trust in u riches, but in the living God, 83

UNCERTAINLY (1) [UNCERTAIN]

1Co 9:26 I therefore so run, not as u; so fight I, not 84

UNCHANGEABLE (1) [CHANGE]

Heb 7:24 he continueth ever, hath an u priesthood. 531

UNCIRCUMCISED (43) [CIRCUMCISE, UNCIRCUMCISION]

Ge 17:14 the u man *child* whose flesh of his 6189
34:14 thing, to give our sister to one that is u; 6190
Ex 6:12 shall Pharaoh hear me, who *am* of u lips? 6189
6:30 I *am* of u lips, and how shall Pharaoh 6189
12:48 land: for no u *person* shall eat thereof. 6189
Lev 19:23 shall **count** the fruit thereof **as** u: 6188+6190
19:23 three years shall it be as u unto you: 6189
26:41 if *then* their u hearts be humbled, and 6189
Jos 5: 7 for they *were* u, because they had not 6189
Jdg 14: 3 that thou goest to take a wife of the u 6189
15:18 for thirst, and fall into the hand of the u? 6189
1Sa 14: 6 let us go over unto the garrison of these u: 6189
17:26 for who *is* this u Philistine, that he should 6189
17:36 this u Philistine shall be as one of them, 6189
31: 4 lest these u come and thrust me through, 6189
2Sa 1:20 lest the daughters of the u triumph. 6189
1Ch 10: 4 lest these u come and abuse me. 6189
Isa 52: 1 there shall no more come into thee the u 6189

Jer	6:10 their ear *is* **u**, and they cannot hearken:	6189
	9:25 *them which are* circumcised with the **u**	6190
	9:26 all *these* nations *are* **u**, and all the house	6189
	9:26 all the house of Israel *are* **u** in the heart.	6189
Eze	28:10 Thou shalt die the deaths of the **u** by	6189
	31:18 thou shalt lie in the midst of the **u** with	6189
	32:19 go down, and be thou laid with the **u**	6189
	32:21 gone down, they lie **u**, slain by the sword.	6189
	32:24 which are gone down **u** into the nether	6189
	32:25 all of them **u**, slain by the sword.	6189
	32:26 all of them **u**, slain by the sword,	6189
	32:27 with the mighty *that are* fallen of the **u**,	6189
	32:28 thou shalt be broken in the midst of the **u**,	6189
	32:29 they shall lie with the **u**, and with them	6189
	32:30 they lie **u** with *them that be* slain by	6189
	32:32 he shall be laid in the midst of the **u** with	6189
	44: 7 **u** in heart, and uncircumcised in flesh,	6189
	44: 7 **u** in flesh, to be in my sanctuary,	6189
	44: 9 stranger, **u** in heart, nor uncircumcised	6189
	44: 9 uncircumcised in heart, nor **u** in flesh,	6189
Ac	7:51 Ye stiffnecked and **u** in heart and ears,	564
	11: 3 Saying, Thou wentest in to men **u**,	203+2192
Ro	4:11 of the faith which he had *yet* being **u**:	203
	4:12 which he had being *yet* **u**.	203+1722
1Co	7:18 let him not **become u**. Is any called in	1986

UNCIRCUMCISION (16) [UNCIRCUMCISED]

Ro	2:25 of the law, thy circumcision is made **u**.	203
	2:26 Therefore if the **u** keep the righteousness	203
	2:26 not his **u** be counted for circumcision?	203
	2:27 shall not **u** which is by nature, if it fulfil	203
	3:30 circumcision by faith, and **u** through faith.	203
	4: 9 the circumcision *only*, or upon the **u** also?	203
	4:10 when he was in circumcision, or in **u**?	203
	4:10 Not in circumcision, but in **u**.	203
1Co	7:18 Is any called in **u**? let him not be	203
	7:19 and **u** is nothing, but the keeping of	203
Gal	2: 7 when they saw that the gospel of the **u**	203
	5: 6 circumcision availeth any *thing*, nor **u**;	203
	6:15 circumcision availeth any *thing*, nor **u**,	203
Eph	2:11 who are called **U** by that which is called	203
Col	2:13 dead in *your* sins and **u** of your flesh,	203
	3:11 circumcision nor **u**, barbarian, Scythian,	203

UNCLE (10) [UNCLE'S]

Lev	10: 4 the sons of Uzziel the **u** of Aaron,	1730
	25:49 Either his **u**, or his uncle's son,	1730
1Sa	10:14 Saul's **u** said unto him and to his servant,	1730
	10:15 Saul's **u** said, Tell me, I pray thee,	1730
	10:16 Saul said unto his **u**, He told us plainly	1730
	14:50 host *was* Abner, the son of Ner, Saul's **u**.	1730
1Ch	27:32 Also Jonathan David's **u** *was* a counsellor,	1730
Est	2:15 the daughter of Abihail the **u** of Mordecai,	1730
Jer	32: 7 Hanameel the son of Shallum thine **u** *shall*	1730
Am	6:10 a man's **u** shall take him up, and he that	1730

UNCLE'S (7) [UNCLE]

Lev	20:20 if a man shall lie with his **u wife**, he hath	1733
	20:20 he hath uncovered his **u** nakedness:	1730
	25:49 Either his uncle, or his **u** son, may redeem	1730
Est	2: 7 Hadassah, that *is*, Esther, his **u** daughter:	1730
Jer	32: 8 So Hanameel mine **u** son came to me in	1730
	32: 9 I bought the field of Hanameel my **u** son,	1730
	32:12 in the sight of Hanameel mine **u** *son*, and	1730

UNCLEAN (194) [CLEAN, UNCLEANNESS, UNCLEANNESSES]

Lev	5: 2 Or if a soul touch any **u** thing, whether	2931
	5: 2 whether *it be* a carcase of an **u** beast, or a	2931
	5: 2 or a carcase of an **u** cattle, or the carcase of	2931
	5: 2 or the carcase of **u** creeping things, and	2931
	5: 2 from him; he also shall be **u**, and guilty.	2931
	7:19 the flesh that toucheth any **u** *thing* shall	2931
	7:21 Moreover the soul that shall touch any **u**	2931
	7:21 *any* **u** beast, or any abominable unclean	2931
	7:21 or any abominable **u** *thing*, and eat of	2931
	10:10 and unholy, and between **u** and clean;	2931
	11: 4 divideth not the hoof; he *is* **u** unto you.	2931
	11: 5 divideth not the hoof; he *is* **u** unto you.	2931
	11: 6 divideth not the hoof; he *is* **u** unto you.	2931
	11: 7 he cheweth not the cud; he *is* **u** to you.	2931
	11: 8 shall ye not touch; they *are* **u** to you.	2931
	11:24 these ye shall be **u**: whosoever toucheth	2930
	11:24 carcase of them shall be **u** until the even.	2930
	11:25 wash his clothes, and be **u** until the even.	2930
	11:26 nor cheweth the cud, *are* **u** unto you:	2931
	11:26 every one that toucheth them shall be **u**.	2930
	11:27 that go on *all* four, those *are* **u** unto you:	2931
	11:27 whoso toucheth their carcase shall be **u**	2930
	11:28 wash his clothes, and be **u** until the even:	2930
	11:28 until the even: they *are* **u** unto you.	2931
	11:29 These also *shall be* **u** unto you among	2931
	11:31 These *are* **u** to you among all that creep:	2931
	11:31 they be dead, shall be **u** until the even.	2930
	11:32 they are dead, doth fall, it shall be **u**;	2930
	11:32 water, and it shall be **u** until the even;	2930
	11:33 falleth, whatsoever *is* in it shall be **u**;	2930
	11:34 *which there is* water cometh shall be **u**:	2930
	11:34 be drunk in every *such* vessel shall be **u**.	2930
	11:35 *any part* of their carcase falleth shall be **u**;	2931
	11:35 *for* they *are* **u**, and shall be unclean unto	2931
	11:35 they *are* unclean, and shall be **u** unto you.	2931
	11:36 which toucheth their carcase shall be **u**.	2930
	11:38 fall thereon, it *shall be* **u** unto you.	2931
	11:39 carcase thereof shall be **u** until the even.	2930
Lev	11:40 wash his clothes, and be **u** until the even:	2930
	11:40 wash his clothes, and be **u** until the even.	2930
	11:43 neither shall ye **make** yourselves **u** with	2933
	11:47 To make a difference between the **u** and	2931
	12: 2 she shall be **u** seven days; according to	2930
	12: 2 separation for her infirmity shall she be **u**.	2930
	12: 5 she shall be **u** two weeks, as *in* her	2930
	13: 3 shall look on him, and **pronounce** him **u**:	2930
	13: 8 then the priest shall **pronounce** him **u**:	2930
	13:11 the priest shall **pronounce** him **u**,	2930
	13:11 *and* shall not shut him up: for he *is* **u**.	2930
	13:14 raw flesh appeareth in him, he shall be **u**.	2930
	13:15 raw flesh, and **pronounce** him to be **u**:	2930
	13:15 *for* the raw flesh *is* **u**: it *is* a leprosy.	2931
	13:20 the priest shall **pronounce** him **u**:	2930
	13:22 then the priest shall **pronounce** him **u**:	2930
	13:25 then the priest shall **pronounce** him **u**:	2930
	13:27 then the priest shall **pronounce** him **u**:	2930
	13:30 then the priest shall **pronounce** him **u**:	2930
	13:36 shall not seek for yellow hair: he *is* **u**.	2930
	13:44 He *is* a leprous man, he *is* **u**: the priest	2931
	13:44 shall **pronounce** him **utterly, u**,	2930+2930
	13:45 *his* upper lip, and shall cry, **U**, unclean.	2931
	13:45 *his* upper lip, and shall cry, Unclean, **u**.	2931
	13:46 be in him he shall be defiled; he *is* **u**:	2931
	13:51 the plague *is* a fretting leprosy; it *is* **u**.	2931
	13:55 and the plague be not spread; it *is* **u**;	2931
	13:59 pronounce it clean, or to **pronounce** it **u**.	2930
	14:36 all that *is* in the house be not *made* **u**:	2930
	14:40 shall cast them into an **u** place without	2931
	14:41 scrape off without the city into an **u** place:	2931
	14:44 it *is* a fretting leprosy in the house: it *is* **u**.	2931
	14:45 *them* forth out of the city into an **u** place.	2931
	14:46 that it is shut up shall be **u** until the even.	2930
	14:57 teach when *it is* **u**, and when *it is* clean:	2931
	15: 2 of his flesh, *because of* his issue he *is* **u**.	2931
	15: 4 whereon he lieth that hath the issue, is **u**:	2930
	15: 4 thing, whereon he sitteth, shall be **u**.	2930
	15: 5 *himself* in water, and be **u** until the even.	2930
	15: 6 *himself* in water, and be **u** until the even.	2930
	15: 7 *himself* in water, and be **u** until the even.	2930
	15: 8 *himself* in water, and be **u** until the even.	2930
	15: 9 rideth upon that hath the issue shall be **u**.	2930
	15:10 was under him shall be **u** until the even:	2930
	15:10 *himself* in water, and be **u** until the even.	2930
	15:11 *himself* in water, and be **u** until the even.	2930
	15:16 his flesh in water, and be **u** until the even.	2930
	15:17 with water, and be **u** until the even.	2930
	15:18 in water, and be **u** until the even.	2930
	15:19 whosoever toucheth her shall be **u** until	2930
	15:20 lieth upon in her separation shall be **u**:	2930
	15:20 *thing* also that she sitteth upon shall be **u**.	2930
	15:21 *himself* in water, and be **u** until the even.	2930
	15:22 *himself* in water, and be **u** until the even.	2930
	15:23 toucheth it, he shall be **u** until the even.	2930
	15:24 be upon him, he shall be **u** seven days;	2930
	15:24 all the bed whereon he lieth shall be **u**.	2930
	15:25 the days of her separation: she *shall be* **u**.	2931
	15:26 whatsoever she sitteth upon shall be **u**,	2931
	15:27 toucheth those *things* shall be **u**,	2930
	15:27 *himself* in water, and be **u** until the even.	2930
	15:33 and of him that lieth with her which is **u**.	2931
	17:15 *himself* in water, and be **u** until the even:	2930
	20:21 take his brother's wife, it *is* an **u thing**:	5079
	20:25 difference between clean beasts and **u**,	2931
	20:25 and between **u** fowls and clean:	2931
	20:25 which I have separated from you as **u**.	2930
	22: 4 whoso toucheth any *thing that is* **u** by	2931
	22: 5 whereby he may be **made u**, or a man of	2930
	22: 6 touched *any* such shall be **u** until even,	2930
	27:11 if *it be* any **u** beast, of which they do not	2931
	27:27 of an **u** beast, then he shall redeem *it*	2931
Nu	6: 7 shall not **make** himself **u** for his father,	2930
	9:10 of your posterity be **u** by reason of a	2931
	18:15 the firstling of **u** beasts shalt thou redeem.	2931
	19: 7 and the priest shall be **u** until the even.	2930
	19: 8 in water, and shall be **u** until the even.	2930
	19:10 wash his clothes, and be **u** until the even:	2930
	19:11 *body* of any man shall be **u** seven days.	2930
	19:13 not sprinkled upon him, he shall be **u**;	2930
	19:14 that is in the tent, shall be **u** seven days.	2930
	19:15 hath no covering bound upon it, *is* **u**.	2931
	19:16 a man, or a grave, shall be **u** seven days.	2930
	19:17 an **u** *person* they shall take of the ashes	2931
	19:19 clean *person* shall sprinkle upon the **u**	2931
	19:20 man that shall be **u**, and shall not purify	2930
	19:20 not been sprinkled upon him; he *is* **u**.	2931
	19:21 water of separation shall be **u** until even.	2930
	19:22 whatsoever the **u** *person* toucheth shall	2931
	19:22 the unclean *person* toucheth shall be **u**;	2930
	19:22 the soul that toucheth *it* shall be **u** until	2930
Dt	12:15 the **u** and the clean may eat thereof, as of	2931
	12:22 the **u** and the clean shall eat of them	2931
	14: 7 the hoof; *therefore* they *are* **u** unto you.	2931
	14: 8 yet *cheweth* not the cud, it *is* **u** unto you:	2931
	14:10 scales ye may not eat; it *is* **u** unto you.	2931
	14:19 every creeping thing that flieth *is* **u** unto	2931
	15:22 the **u** and the clean *person* shall eat it	2931
	23:14 that he see no **u** thing in thee,	6172
	26:14 **u** *use*, nor given *ought* thereof for the	2931
Jos	22:19 if the land of your possession *be* **u**, then	2931
Jdg	13: 4 nor strong drink, and eat not any **u** thing:	2931
	13: 7 neither eat any **u** *thing*: for the child shall	2932
	13:14 nor eat any **u** *thing*: all that I commanded	2932
2Ch	23:19 none *which was* **u** in any thing should	2931
Ezr	9:11 an **u** land with the filthiness of the people	5079
Job	14: 4 Who can bring a clean *thing* out of an **u**?	2931
	36:14 in youth, and their life *is* among the **u**.	6945
Ecc	9: 2 the good and to the clean, and to the **u**;	2931
Isa	6: 5 because I *am* a man of **u** lips, and I dwell	2931
	6: 5 I dwell in the midst of a people of **u** lips:	2931
	35: 8 the **u** shall not pass over it; but it *shall be*	2931
	52: 1 into thee the uncircumcised and the **u**.	2931
	52:11 touch no **u** *thing*; go ye out of the midst	2931
	64: 6 we are all as an **u** *thing*, and all our	2931
La	4:15 *it is* **u**; depart, depart, touch not, when	2931
Eze	22:26 they shewed *difference* between the **u**	2931
	44:23 cause them to discern between the **u** and	2931
Hos	9: 3 and they shall eat **u** *things* in Assyria.	2931
Hag	2:13 If *one that is* **u** *by* a dead body touch any	2931
	2:13 body touch any of these, shall it be **u**?	2930
	2:13 priests answered and said, It shall be **u**.	2930
	2:14 and *that which* they offer there *is* **u**.	2931
Zec	13: 2 and the **u** spirit to pass out of the land.	2932
Mt	10: 1 gave them power against **u** spirits, to cast	169
	12:43 When the **u** spirit is gone out of a man,	169
Mk	1:23 in their synagogue a man with an **u** spirit;	169
	1:26 And when the **u** spirit had torn him,	169
	1:27 with authority commandeth he even the **u**	169
	3:11 **u** spirits, when they saw him, fell down	169
	3:30 Because they said, He hath an **u** spirit.	169
	5: 2 out of the tombs a man with an **u** spirit,	169
	5: 8 Come out of the man, *thou* **u** spirit.	169
	5:13 the **u** spirits went out, and entered into	169
	6: 7 two; and gave them power over **u** spirits;	169
	7:25 whose young daughter had an **u** spirit,	169
Lk	4:33 which had a spirit of an **u** devil,	169
	4:36 and power he commandeth the **u** spirits,	169
	6:18 And they that were vexed with **u** spirits:	169
	8:29 he had commanded the **u** spirit to come	169
	9:42 tare *him*. And Jesus rebuked the **u** spirit,	169
	11:24 When the **u** spirit is gone out of a man,	169
Ac	5:16 *them* which were vexed with **u** spirits:	169
	8: 7 For **u** spirits, crying with loud voice,	169
	10:14 eaten any *thing that is* common or **u**.	169
	10:28 *I* should not call any man common or **u**.	169
	11: 8 **u** hath at any time entered into my mouth.	169
Ro	14:14 Jesus, *that there is* nothing **u** of itself:	2839
	14:14 to him that esteemeth any *thing* to be **u**,	2839
	14:14 any *thing* to be unclean, to him it *is* **u**.	2839
1Co	7:14 else were your children **u**; but now are	169
2Co	6:17 touch not the **u** *thing*; and I will receive	169
Eph	5: 5 nor **u** *person*, nor covetous man who is	169
Heb	9:13 and the ashes of a heifer sprinkling the **u**,	2840
Rev	16:13 I saw three **u** spirits like frogs *come* out	169
	18: 2 and a cage of every **u** and hateful bird.	169

UNCLEANNESS (40) [UNCLEAN]

Lev	5: 3 Or if he touch the **u** of man,	2932
	5: 3 whatsoever **u** *it be* that a man shall be	2932
	7:20 unto the LORD, having his **u** upon him,	2932
	7:21 any unclean *thing*, *as* the **u** of man,	2932
	14:19 for him that is to be cleansed from his **u**;	2932
	15: 3 this shall be his **u** in his issue: *whether*	2932
	15: 3 flesh be stopped from his issue, it *is* his **u**.	2932
	15:25 all the days of the issue of her **u** shall be	2932
	15:26 be unclean, as the **u** of her separation.	2932
	15:30 before the LORD for the issue of her **u**.	2932
	15:31 the children of Israel from their **u**;	2932
	15:31 they die not in their **u**, when they defile	2932
	16:16 because of the **u** of the children of Israel,	2932
	16:16 among them in the midst of their **u**.	2932
	16:19 hallow it from the **u** of the children of	2932
	18:19 as long as she is put apart for her **u**.	2932
	22: 3 having his **u** upon him, that soul shall be	2932
	22: 5 or a man of whom he may **take u**,	2930
	22: 5 take uncleanness, whatsoever **u** he hath;	2932
Nu	5:19 if thou hast not gone aside to **u** with	2932
	19:13 shall be unclean; his **u** is yet upon him.	2932
Dt	23:10 that is not clean by reason of **u** that	NIH
	24: 1 because he hath found some **u** in her:	6172
2Sa	11: 4 with her; for she was purified from her **u**	2932
2Ch	29:16 brought out all the **u** that they found in	2932
Ezr	9:11 it from one end to another with their **u**,	2932
Eze	36:17 their way was before me as the **u** of a	2932
	39:24 According to their **u** and according to	2932
Zec	13: 1 inhabitants of Jerusalem for sin and for **u**.	5079
Mt	23:27 full of dead *men's* bones, and of all **u**.	167
Ro	1:24 Wherefore God also gave them up to **u**	167
	6:19 have yielded your members servants to **u**	167
2Co	12:21 and have not repented of the **u** and	167
Gal	5:19 fornication, **u**, lasciviousness,	167
Eph	4:19 to work all **u** with greediness.	167
	5: 3 But fornication, and all **u**, or covetousness,	167
Col	3: 5 fornication, **u**, inordinate affection,	167
1Th	2: 3 *was* not of deceit, nor of **u**, nor in guile:	167
	4: 7 For God hath not called us unto **u**,	167
2Pe	2:10 that walk after the flesh in the lust of **u**,	3394

UNCLEANNESSES (1) [UNCLEAN]

Eze	36:29 I will also save you from all your **u**:	2932

UNCLOTHED (1) [CLOTHE]

2Co	5: 4 not for that we would be **u**,	1562

UNCOMELY (2) [COMELINESS]

1Co	7:36 *he* **behaveth** himself **u** toward his virgin,	807
	12:23 **u** *parts* have more abundant comeliness.	809

U

UNCONDEMNED (2) [CONDEMN]

Ac	16:37 They have beaten us openly **u**,	*178*
	22:25 to scourge a man *that is* a Roman, and **u**?	*178*

UNCORRUPTIBLE (1) [CORRUPT, UNCORRUPTNESS]

Ro	1:23 And changed the glory of the **u** God into	*862*

UNCORRUPTNESS (1) [UNCORRUPTIBLE]

Tit	2: 7 in doctrine *shewing* **u**, gravity, sincerity,	*90*

UNCOVER (26) [COVER, UNCOVERED, UNCOVERETH]

Lev	10: 6 unto Ithamar his sons, **U** not your heads,	6544
	18: 6 near of kin to him, to **u** *their* nakedness.	1540
	18: 7 of thy mother, shalt thou not **u**:	1540
	18: 7 mother; thou shalt not **u** her nakedness.	1540
	18: 8 of thy father's wife shalt thou not **u**:	1540
	18: 9 *even* their nakedness thou shalt not **u**.	1540
	18:10 *even* their nakedness thou shalt not **u**:	1540
	18:11 thy sister, thou shalt not **u** her nakedness.	1540
	18:12 Thou shalt not **u** the nakedness of thy	1540
	18:13 Thou shalt not **u** the nakedness of thy	1540
	18:14 Thou shalt not **u** the nakedness of thy	1540
	18:15 Thou shalt not **u** the nakedness of thy	1540
	18:15 wife; thou shalt not **u** her nakedness.	1540
	18:16 Thou shalt not **u** the nakedness of thy	1540
	18:17 shalt not **u** the nakedness of a woman	1540
	18:17 daughter's daughter, to **u** her nakedness;	1540
	18:18 to vex *her*, to **u** her nakedness, besides	1540
	18:19 unto a woman to **u** her nakedness;	1540
	20:18 her sickness, and shall **u** her nakedness;	1540
	20:19 thou shalt not **u** the nakedness of thy	1540
	21:10 shall not **u** his head, nor rend his clothes;	6544
Nu	5:18 **u** the woman's head, and put the offering	6544
Ru	4: 4 go in, and **u** his feet, and lay them down;	1540
Isa	47: 2 thy locks, make bare the leg, uncover	1540
	47: 2 thy locks, make bare the leg, the thigh,	1540
Zep	2:14 for he shall **u** the cedar work.	6168

UNCOVERED (17) [UNCOVER]

Ge	9:21 drunken; and he was **u** within his tent.	1540
Lev	20:11 wife hath **u** his father's nakedness.	1540
	20:17 he hath **u** his sister's nakedness; he shall	1540
	20:18 and she hath **u** the fountain of her blood;	1540
	20:20 he hath **u** his uncle's nakedness:	1540
	20:21 he hath **u** his brother's nakedness:	1540
Ru	3: 7 and **u** his feet, and laid her down.	1540
2Sa	6:20 who **u** himself to day in the eyes of	1540
Isa	20: 4 and barefoot, even with *their* buttocks **u**,	2834
	22: 6 men and horsemen, and Kir **u** the shield.	6168
	47: 3 Thy nakedness shall be **u**, yea, thy shame	1540
Jer	49:10 I have **u** his secret places, and he shall not	1540
Eze	4: 7 thine arm *shall be* **u**, and thou shalt	2834
Hab	2:16 thou also, and let thy **foreskin** be **u**:	6188
Mk	2: 4 the press, they **u** the roof where he was:	648
1Co	11: 5 prophesieth with *her* head **u** dishonoureth	177
	11:13 it comely that a woman pray unto God **u**?	177

UNCOVERETH (3) [UNCOVER]

Lev	20:19 for he **u** his near kin: they shall bear their	6168
Dt	27:20 because he **u** his father's skirt.	1540
2Sa	6:20 of the vain *fellows* **shamelessly u**	1540+1540

UNCTION (1)

1Jn	2:20 But ye have an **u** from the Holy One,	*5545*

UNDEFILED (7) [DEFILE]

Ps	119: 1 Blessed are the **u** in the way, who walk in	8549
SS	5: 2 to me, my sister, my love, my dove, my **u**:	8535
	6: 9 My dove, my **u** *is but* one; she *is* the *only*	8535
Heb	7:26 *who is* holy, harmless, **u**, separate from	283
	13: 4 *is* honourable in all, and the bed **u**:	283
Jas	1:27 Pure religion and **u** before God and	283
1Pe	1: 4 and **u**, and that fadeth not away, reserved	283

UNDER (392)

Ge	1: 7 divided the waters which *were* **u**	4480+8478
	1: 9 Let the waters **u** the heaven be	4480+8478
	6:17 *is* the breath of life, from **u** heaven;	8478
	7:19 that *were* **u** the whole heaven,	8478
	16: 9 and submit thyself **u** her hands.	8478
	18: 4 your feet, and rest yourselves **u** the tree:	8478
	18: 8 he stood by them **u** the tree, and they did	8478
	19: 8 came they **u** the shadow of my roof.	871.1
	21:15 she cast the child **u** one of the shrubs.	8478
	24: 2 Put, I pray thee, thy hand **u** my thigh:	8478
	24: 9 the servant put his hand **u** the thigh of	8478
	35: 4 Jacob hid them **u** the oak which *was* by	8478
	35: 8 she was buried beneath Beth-el **u** an oak:	8478
	39:23 not to any thing *that was* **u** his hand;	871.1
	41:35 lay up corn **u** the hand of Pharaoh,	8478
	47:29 thy hand **u** my thigh, and deal kindly and	8478
	49:25 blessings of the deep that lieth **u**,	8478
Ex	6: 6 I will bring you out from **u** the burdens	8478
	6: 7 bringeth you out from **u** the burdens	8478
	17:12 and put *it* **u** him, and he sat thereon;	8478
	17:14 remembrance of Amalek from **u** heaven.	8478
	18:10 who hath delivered the people from **u**	8478
	20: 4 or that *is* in the water **u** the earth:	4480+8478
	21:20 maid, with a rod, and he die **u** his hand;	8478
	23: 5 him that hateth thee lying **u** his burden,	8478
	24: 4 builded an altar **u** the hill,	8478
	24:10 *was* **u** his feet as it were a paved work	8478
	25:35 *there* shall be a knop **u** two branches of	8478

Ex	25:35 and a knop **u** two branches of the same,	8478
	25:35 and a knop **u** two branches of the same,	8478
	26:19 thou shalt make forty sockets of silver **u**	8478
	26:19 sockets **u** one board for his two tenons,	8478
	26:19 two sockets **u** another board for his two	8478
	26:21 two sockets **u** one board, and two sockets	8478
	26:21 and two sockets **u** another board.	8478
	26:25 two sockets **u** one board, and two sockets	8478
	26:25 and two sockets **u** another board.	8478
	26:33 thou shalt hang up the vail **u** the taches,	8478
	27: 5 thou shalt put it **u** the compass of the altar	8478
	30: 4 thou make to it **u** the crown of it,	4480+8478
	36:24 sockets of silver he made **u** the twenty	8478
	36:24 two sockets **u** one board for his two	8478
	36:24 two sockets **u** another board for his two	8478
	36:26 two sockets **u** one board, and two sockets	8478
	36:26 and two sockets **u** another board.	8478
	36:30 *of* silver, **u** every board two sockets.	8478
	37:21 a knop **u** two branches of the same,	8478
	37:21 and a knop **u** two branches of the same,	8478
	37:21 and a knop **u** two branches of the same,	8478
	37:27 he made two rings of gold for it **u**	4480+8478
	38: 4 the compass thereof beneath unto	8478
Lev	15:10 whosoever toucheth any *thing* that was **u**	8478
	22:27 then it shall be seven days **u** the dam;	8478
	27:32 *even of* whatsoever passeth **u** the rod,	8478
Nu	3:36 **u** the custody and charge of the sons of	NIH
	4:28 charge *shall be* **u** the hand of Ithamar	871.1
	4:33 the hand of Ithamar the son of Aaron	871.1
	6:18 put *it* in the fire which *is* **u** the sacrifice	8478
	7: 8 the hand of Ithamar the son of Aaron	871.1
	16:31 that the ground clave asunder that *was* **u**	8478
	22:27 of the LORD, she fell down **u** Balaam:	8478
	31:49 the men of war which *are* **u** our charge,	871.1
	33: 1 with their armies **u** the hand of Moses	871.1
Dt	2:25 fear of thee upon the nations that *are* **u**	8478
	3:17 the salt sea, **u** Ashdoth-pisgah eastward.	8478
	4:11 ye came near and stood **u** the mountain;	8478
	4:19 unto all nations **u** the whole heaven.	8478
	4:49 sea of the plain, **u** the springs of Pisgah.	8478
	7:24 thou shalt destroy their name from **u**	8478
	9:14 and blot out their name from **u** heaven:	8478
	12: 2 upon the hills, and **u** every green tree:	8478
	25:19 remembrance of Amalek from **u** heaven;	8478
	28:23 and the earth that *is* **u** thee *shall be* iron.	8478
	29:20 the LORD shall blot out his name from **u**	8478
Jos	7:21 the midst of my tent, and the silver **u** it.	8478
	7:22 *it was* hid in his tent, and the silver **u** it.	8478
	11: 3 *to* the Hivite **u** Hermon in the land of	8478
	11:17 the valley of Lebanon **u** mount Hermon:	8478
	12: 3 and from the south, **u** Ashdoth-pisgah:	8478
	13: 5 from Baal-gad **u** mount Hermon unto	8478
	16:10 unto this day, and serve **u** tribute.	3807.1
	24:26 a great stone, and set it up there **u** an oak,	8478
Jdg	1: 7 cut off, gathered *their meat* **u** my table:	8478
	3:16 he did gird it **u** his raiment upon	4480+8478
	3:30 Moab was subdued that day **u** the hand	8478
	4: 5 she dwelt **u** the palm tree of Deborah	8478
	6:11 sat **u** an oak which *was* in Ophrah,	8478
	6:19 brought *it* out unto him **u** the oak,	413+8478
	9:29 to God this people were **u** my hand;	871.1
Ru	2:12 whose wings thou art come to trust.	8478
1Sa	7:11 until *they came* **u** Beth-car.	4480+8478
	14: 2 a pomegranate tree which *is* in Migron:	8478
	21: 3 Now therefore what is **u** thine hand?	8478
	21: 4 *There is* no common bread **u** mine	413+8478
	21: 8 is there not here **u** thine hand spear or	8478
	22: 6 (now Saul abode in Gibeah **u** a tree in	8478
	31:13 buried *them* **u** a tree at Jabesh,	8478
2Sa	2:23 the fifth *rib*, that the spear came out	413
	3:27 smote him there **u** the fifth *rib*, that he	NIH
	4: 6 smote him **u** the fifth *rib*: and Rechab	413
	12:31 put *them* **u** saws, and under harrows of	871.1
	12:31 **u** harrows of iron, and under axes of	871.1
	12:31 **u** axes of iron, and made them pass	871.1
	18: 2 part of the people **u** the hand of Joab,	871.1
	18: 2 third part **u** the hand of Abishai the son	871.1
	18: 2 third part **u** the hand of Ittai the Gittite.	871.1
	18: 9 the mule went **u** the thick boughs of a	8478
	18: 9 and the mule that *was* **u** him went away.	8478
	22:10 came down; and darkness *was* **u** his feet.	8478
	22:37 Thou hast enlarged my steps **u** me;	8478
	22:39 not arise: yea, they are fallen **u** my feet.	8478
	22:40 up against me hast thou subdued **u** me.	8478
	22:48 and that bringeth down the people **u** me,	8478
1Ki	4:25 man **u** his vine and under his fig tree,	8478
	4:25 man under his vine and **u** his fig tree,	8478
	5: 3 until the LORD **u** the soles of his	8478
	7:24 **u** the brim of it round about *there*	4480+8478
	7:30 corners thereof had undersetters: **u**	4480+8478
	7:32 the borders *were* **u** four wheels;	4480+8478
	7:44 And one sea, and twelve oxen **u** the sea;	8478
	8: 6 to the most holy *place*, even **u**	413+8478
	13:14 of God, and found him sitting **u** an oak:	8478
	14:23 on every high hill, and **u** every green tree.	8478
	18:23 put no fire **u**, and I will dress the other	NIH
	18:23 and lay *it* on wood, and put no fire **u**.	NIH
	18:25 the name of your gods, but put no fire **u**.	NIH
	19: 4 and came and sat down **u** a juniper tree:	8478
	19: 5 as he lay and slept **u** a juniper tree,	8478
2Ki	8:20 his days Edom revolted from **u** the hand	8478
	8:22 Yet Edom revolted from **u** the hand of	8478
	9:13 and put *it* **u** him on the top of the stairs,	8478
	9:33 on the horses: and he **trode** her **u** foot.	7429
	13: 5 that they went out from **u** the hand of	8478

2Ki	14:27 out the name of Israel from **u** heaven:	8478
	16: 4 and on the hills, and **u** every green tree.	8478
	16:17 from off the brasen oxen that *were* **u** it,	8478
	17: 7 **u** the hand of Pharaoh king of Egypt,	8478
	17:10 in every high hill, and **u** every green tree:	8478
1Ch	10:12 buried their bones **u** the oak in Jabesh,	8478
	17: 1 of the LORD *remaineth* **u** curtains.	8478
	24:19 their manner, **u** Aaron their father,	3027+871.1
	25: 2 the sons of Asaph **u** the hands of Asaph,	5921
	25: 3 six, **u** the hands of their father Jeduthun,	5921
	25: 6 All these *were* **u** the hands of their father	5921
	26:28 had dedicated *anything, it was* **u**	5921
	27:23 of them from twenty years old and **u**:	4295
2Ch	4: 3 **u** it was the similitude of oxen, which did	8478
	4:15 One sea, and twelve oxen **u** it.	8478
	5: 7 the most holy *place*, even **u** the wings	8478
	13:18 the children of Israel were **brought u**	3665
	21: 8 In his days the Edomites revolted from **u**	8478
	21:10 So the Edomites revolted from **u** the hand	8478
	21:10 also did Libnah revolt from **u** his hand;	8478
	26:11 the ruler, **u** the hand of Hananiah,	5921
	26:13 **u** their hand *was* an army, three hundred	5921
	28: 4 and on the hills, and **u** every green tree.	8478
	28:10 now ye purpose to **keep u** the children	3533
	31:13 *were* overseers **u** the hand of Cononiah	4480
Ne	2:14 *was* no place for the beast *that was* **u**	8478
	8:17 made booths, and sat **u** the booths:	871.1
Job	9:13 the proud helpers do stoop **u** him.	8478
	20:12 mouth, *though* he hide it **u** his tongue;	8478
	26: 5 *things* are formed from **u** the waters,	8478
	26: 8 and the cloud is not rent **u** them.	8478
	28: 5 and it is turned up as it were fire.	8478
	28:24 the earth, *and* seeth **u** the whole heaven;	8478
	30: 7 **u** the nettles they were gathered together.	8478
	37: 3 He directeth it **u** the whole heaven,	8478
	40:21 He lieth **u** the shady trees, in the covert	8478
	41:11 that I should repay *him*? *whatsoever is* **u**	8478
	41:30 Sharp stones *are* **u** him: he spreadeth	8478
Ps	8: 6 thou hast put all *things* **u** his feet:	8478
	10: 7 **u** his tongue *is* mischief and vanity.	8478
	17: 8 hide me **u** the shadow of thy wings,	871.1
	18: 9 came down: and darkness *was* **u** his feet.	8478
	18:36 Thou hast enlarged my steps **u** me, that	8478
	18:38 not able to rise: they are fallen **u** my feet.	8478
	18:39 hast subdued **u** me those that rose up	8478
	18:47 and subdueth the people **u** me.	8478
	36: 7 the children of men put their trust **u**	871.1
	44: 5 through thy name will we **tread** them **u**	947
	45: 5 *whereby* the people fall **u** thee.	8478
	47: 3 He shall subdue the people **u** us,	8478
	47: 3 and the nations **u** our feet.	8478
	91: 1 shall abide **u** the shadow of the Almighty.	871.1
	91: 4 and **u** his wings shalt thou trust:	8478
	91:13 the dragon shalt thou **trample u** feet.	7429
	106:42 they were brought into subjection **u** their	8478
	140: 3 a serpent; adder's poison *is* **u** their lips.	8478
	144: 2 I trust; who subdueth my people **u** me.	8478
Pr	12:24 but the slothful shall be **u** tribute.	3807.1
	22:27 why should he take away thy bed from **u**	8478
Ecc	1: 3 all his labour which he taketh **u** the sun?	8478
	1: 9 and *there is* no new *thing* **u** the sun.	8478
	1:13 all *things* that are done **u** heaven:	8478
	1:14 I have seen all the works that are done **u**	8478
	2: 3 which they should do **u** the heaven all	8478
	2:11 spirit, and *there was* no profit **u** the sun.	8478
	2:17 the work that is wrought **u** the sun *is*	8478
	2:18 hated all my labour which I *had* taken **u**	8478
	2:19 where*in* I have shewed myself wise **u**	8478
	2:20 of all the labour which I took **u** the sun.	8478
	2:22 wherein he *hath* laboured **u** the sun?	8478
	3: 1 a time to every purpose **u** the heaven:	8478
	3:16 moreover I saw **u** the sun the place of	8478
	4: 1 the oppressions that *are* done **u** the sun:	8478
	4: 3 seen the evil work that is done **u** the sun.	8478
	4: 7 I returned, and I saw vanity **u** the sun.	8478
	4:15 I considered all the living which walk **u**	8478
	5:13 There is a sore evil *which* I have seen **u**	8478
	5:18 he taken **u** the sun all the days of his life,	8478
	6: 1 There is an evil which I have seen **u**	8478
	6:12 a man what shall be after him **u** the sun?	8478
	7: 6 For as the crackling of thorns **u** a pot,	8478
	8: 9 unto every work that is done **u** the sun:	8478
	8:15 a man hath no better *thing* **u** the sun,	8478
	8:15 his life, which God giveth him **u** the sun.	8478
	8:17 find out the work that is done **u** the sun:	8478
	9: 3 among all *things* that are done **u** the sun,	8478
	9: 6 ever in any *thing* that is done **u** the sun,	8478
	9: 9 which he hath given thee **u** the sun,	8478
	9: 9 thy labour which thou takest **u** the sun.	8478
	9:11 and saw **u** the sun, that the race	8478
	9:13 This wisdom have I seen also **u** the sun,	8478
	10: 5 There is an evil *which* I have seen **u**	8478
SS	2: 3 I sat down **u** his shadow with great	871.1
	2: 6 His left hand *is* **u** my head, and his right	8478
	4:11 honey and milk *are* **u** thy tongue;	8478
	8: 3 His left hand *should be* **u** my head,	8478
	8: 5 I raised thee up **u** the apple tree: there	8478
Isa	3: 6 our ruler, and *let* this ruin *be* **u** thy hand:	8478
	10: 4 Without me they shall bow down **u**	8478
	10: 4 prisoners, and they shall fall **u** the slain.	8478
	10:16 **u** his glory he shall kindle a burning like	8478
	14:11 worm is spread **u** thee, and the worms	8478
	14:19 of the pit; as a carcase **trodden u** feet.	947
	14:25 upon my mountains **tread** him **u** foot:	947
	18: 7 a nation meted out and **trodden u** foot,	4001

Ref	Text	Num
Isa 24: 5	The earth also is defiled **u** the inhabitants	8478
25:10	Moab shall be trodden down **u** him,	8478
28: 3	of Ephraim, shall be trodden **u** feet:	871.1
28:15	and **u** falsehood have we hid ourselves:	871.1
34:15	and hatch, and gather **u** her shadow:	871.1
57: 5	Inflaming yourselves with idols **u** every	8478
57: 5	slaying the children in the valleys **u**	8478
58: 5	and ashes **u** him? wilt thou call this a fast,	NIH
Jer 2:20	and **u** every green tree thou wanderest,	8478
3: 6	high mountain and **u** every green tree,	8478
3:13	hast scattered thy ways to the strangers **u**	8478
10:11	from the earth, and from **u** these heavens.	8460
12:10	they have **trodden** my portion **u** foot,	947
27: 8	that will not put their neck **u** the yoke of	871.1
27:11	nations that bring their neck **u** the yoke	871.1
27:12	Bring your necks **u** the yoke of the king	871.1
33:13	shall the flocks pass again **u** the hands of	5921
38:11	went into the house of the king **u**	413+8478
38:12	rotten rags **u** thine armholes under	8478
38:12	rotten rags under thine armholes **u**	4480+8478
48:45	They that fled stood **u** the shadow of	871.1
52:20	twelve brasen bulls that were **u** the bases,	8478
La 1:15	The Lord hath **trodden u** foot all my	5541
3:34	To crush **u** his feet all the prisoners of	8478
3:66	destroy them in anger from **u** the heavens	8478
4:20	**U** his shadow we shall live among	871.1
5: 5	Our necks are **u** persecution: we labour,	5921
5:13	grind, and the children fell **u** the wood.	871.1
Eze 1: 8	they had the hands of a man **u**	4480+8478
1:23	the firmament were their wings straight,	8478
6:13	**u** every green tree, and under every thick	8478
6:13	every green tree, and **u** every thick oak,	8478
10: 2	even **u** the cherub, and fill thine hand	8478
10: 8	the form of a man's hand **u** their wings.	8478
10:20	This is the living creature that I saw **u**	8478
10:21	the likeness of the hands of a man was **u**	8478
17: 6	and the roots thereof were **u** him:	8478
17:23	**u** it shall dwell all fowl of every wing;	8478
20:37	I will cause you to pass **u** the rod, and I	8478
24: 5	burn also the bones **u** it, and make it boil	8478
31: 6	In his branches did all the beasts of the	8478
31: 6	and **u** his shadow dwelt all great nations.	871.1
31:17	that dwelt **u** his shadow in the midst of	871.1
32:27	they have laid their swords **u** their heads,	8478
42: 9	from **u** these chambers was the entry on	8478
46:23	it was made with boiling places **u**	4480+8478
47: 1	waters issued out from **u** the threshold of	8478
47: 1	the waters came down from **u** from	4480
Da 4:12	the beasts of the field had shadow **u** it,	8460
4:14	let the beasts get away from **u** it,	8479
4:21	**u** which the beasts of the field dwelt,	8460
7:27	the greatness of the kingdom **u** the whole	8460
8:13	and the host to be **trodden u** foot?	4823
Hos 9:12	**u** the whole heaven hath not been done	8478
4:12	they have gone a whoring from **u** their	8478
4:13	**u** oaks and poplars and elms, because	8478
14: 7	that dwell **u** his shadow shall return;	871.1
Joel 1:17	The seed is rotten **u** their clods, the	8478
Am 2:13	Behold, I am pressed **u** you, as a cart is	8478
Ob 1: 7	that eat thy bread have laid a wound **u**	8478
Jnh 4: 5	him a booth, and sat **u** it in the shadow,	8478
Mic 1: 4	the mountains shall be molten **u** him,	8478
4: 4	they shall sit every man **u** his vine and	8478
4: 4	man under his vine and **u** his fig tree;	8478
Zec 3:10	**u** the vine and under the fig tree.	8478
3:10	under the vine and **u** the fig tree.	8478
Mal 4: 3	for they shall be ashes **u** the soles of your	8478
Mt 2:16	coasts thereof, from two years old and **u**,	2736
5:13	out, and to be **trodden u foot** of men.	2662
5:15	put it **u** a bushel, but on a candlestick;	5259
7: 6	lest they trample them **u** their feet,	1722
8: 8	not worthy that thou shouldest come **u**	5259
8: 9	I am a man **u** authority, having soldiers	5259
8: 9	under authority, having soldiers **u** me:	5259
23:37	as a hen gathereth her chickens **u** her	5259
Mk 4:21	Is a candle brought to be put **u** a bushel,	5259
4:21	to be put under a bushel, or **u** a bed?	5259
4:32	that the fowls of the air may lodge **u**	5259
6:11	shake off the dust **u** your feet for a	5270
7:28	the dogs **u** the table eat of the children's	5259
Lk 7: 6	that thou shouldest enter **u** my roof:	5259
7: 8	For I also am a man set **u** authority,	5259
7: 8	having **u** me soldiers, and I say unto one,	5259
8:16	it with a vessel, or putteth it **u** a bed;	5270
11:33	neither **u** a bushel, but on a candlestick,	5259
13:34	a hen doth gather her brood **u** her wings,	5259
17:24	lighteneth out of the one part **u** heaven,	5259
17:24	shineth unto the other part **u** heaven;	5259
Jn 1:48	when thou wast **u** the fig tree, I saw thee.	5259
1:50	I saw thee **u** the fig tree, believest thou?	5270
Ac 2: 5	devout men, out of every nation **u** heaven.	5259
4:12	for there is none other name **u** heaven	5259
8:27	an eunuch of great authority **u** Candace	NIG
332		332
23:12	and **bound** themselves **u** a curse,	332
23:14	**bound** ourselves **u** a great curse,	331+332
27: 4	we **sailed u** Cyprus, because the winds	5284
27: 7	we **sailed u** Crete, over against Salmone;	5284
27:16	And **running u** a certain island which is	5295
27:30	**u** colour as though they would have cast	4392
Ro 3: 9	and Gentiles, that they are all **u** sin;	5259
3:13	the poison of asps is **u** their lips:	5259
3:19	it saith to them who are **u** the law:	1722
6:14	for ye are not **u** the law, but under grace.	5259
6:14	for ye are not under the law, but **u** grace.	5259
6:15	because we are not **u** the law,	5259

Ref	Text	Num
Ro 6:15	we are not under the law, but **u** grace?	5259
7:14	law is spiritual: but I am carnal, sold **u** sin.	5259
16:20	And the God of peace shall bruise Satan **u**	5259
1Co 6:12	I will not be **brought u the power** of any.	1850
7:15	or a sister is not **u bondage** in such cases:	1402
9:20	them that are **u** the law, as under the law,	5259
9:20	them that are under the law, as **u** the law,	5259
9:20	that I might gain them that are **u** the law;	5259
9:21	law to God, but **u** the **law** to Christ,)	1772
9:27	But I **keep u** my body, and bring it into	5299
10: 1	how that all our fathers were **u** the cloud,	5259
14:34	they are commanded to be **u obedience**,	5293
15:25	till he hath put all enemies **u** his feet.	5259
15:27	For he hath put all things **u** his feet.	5259
15:27	all things are put **u** him, it is manifest that	5293
15:27	excepted, which did **put** all things **u** him.	5293
15:28	subject unto him that **put** all things **u** him,	5293
2Co 11:32	Damascus the governor **u** Aretas the king	NIG
Gal 3:10	of the works of the law are **u** the curse:	5259
3:22	But the scripture hath concluded all **u** sin,	5259
3:23	faith came, we were kept **u** the law,	5259
3:25	come, we are no longer **u** a schoolmaster.	5259
4: 2	is **u** tutors and governors until the time	5259
4: 3	were in bondage **u** the elements of	5259
4: 4	Son, made of a woman, made **u** the law,	5259
4: 5	To redeem them that were **u** the law,	5259
4:21	Tell me, ye that desire to be **u** the law,	5259
5:18	be led of the Spirit, ye are not **u** the law.	5259
Eph 1:22	And hath put all things **u** his feet,	5259
Php 2:10	things in earth, and things **u the earth**;	2709
Col 1:23	every creature which is **u** heaven;	5259
1Ti 5: 9	not a widow be taken into the number **u**	1640
6: 1	Let as many servants as are **u** the yoke	5259
Heb 2: 8	Thou hast put all things **in subjection u** his	5270
2: 8	For in that he **put** all **in subjection u** him,	5293
2: 8	he left nothing that is **not put u** him.	506
2: 8	But now we see not yet all things **put u**	5293
7:11	(for **u** it the people received the law,)	1909
9:15	that were **u** the first testament,	1909
10:28	Moses' law died without mercy **u** two	1909
10:29	who hath **trodden u foot** the Son of God,	2662
Jas 2: 3	thou there, or sit here **u** my footstool:	5259
1Pe 5: 6	therefore **u** the mighty hand of God,	5259
Jude 1: 6	he hath reserved in everlasting chains **u**	5259
Rev 5: 3	heaven, nor in earth, neither **u** the earth,	5270
5:13	the earth, and such as are in the sea,	5270
6: 9	I saw **u** the altar the souls of them that	5270
11: 2	the holy city shall they **tread u foot** forty	3961
12: 1	the moon **u** her feet, and upon her head	5270

UNDERGARMENT See BREECHES

UNDERGIRDING (1) [GIRD]
| Ac 27:17 | had taken up, they used helps, **u** the ship; | 5269 |

UNDERNEATH (3)
Ex 28:27	two sides of the ephod **u**,	4295+4480+3807.1
39:20	two sides of the ephod **u**,	4295+4480+3807.1
Dt 33:27	and **u** are the everlasting arms:	4480+8478

UNDERSETTERS (4)
1Ki 7:30	the four corners thereof had **u**: under	3802
7:30	to the laver **u** molten, at the side	3802
7:34	were four **u** to the four corners of one	3802
7:34	and the **u** were of the very base itself.	3802

UNDERSTAND (91) [UNDERSTANDEST, UNDERSTANDETH, UNDERSTANDING, UNDERSTOOD]
Ge 11: 7	they may not **u** one another's speech.	8085
41:15	that thou canst **u** a dream to interpret it.	8085
Nu 9:20	they shall **u** that these men have provoked	3045
Dt 9: 3	**U** therefore this day, that the Lord thy	3045
9: 6	**U** therefore, that the Lord thy God	3045
28:49	a nation whose tongue thou shalt not **u**;	8085
2Ki 18:26	for we **u** it: and talk not with us in	8085
1Ch 28:19	**made** me **u** in writing by his hand upon	7919
Ne 8: 3	and the women, and those that could **u**;	995
8: 7	Levites, **caused** the people to **u** the law:	995
8: 8	sense, and **caused** them to **u** the reading.	995
8:13	scribe, even to **u** the words of the law.	7919
Job 6:24	and **cause** me to **u** wherein I have erred.	995
23: 5	and **u** what he would say unto me.	995
26:14	but the thunder of his power who can **u**?	995
32: 9	neither do the aged **u** judgment.	995
36:29	can any **u** the spreadings of the clouds,	995
Ps 14: 2	to see if there were any that did **u**,	7919
19:12	Who can **u** his errors? cleanse thou me	995
53: 2	to see if there were any that did **u**, that	7919
82: 5	They know not, neither will they **u**;	995
92: 6	knoweth not; neither doth a fool **u** this.	995
94: 8	**U**, ye brutish among the people:	995
107:43	will observe these things, even they shall **u**	995
119:27	**Make** me to **u** the way of thy precepts:	995
119:100	I **u** more than the ancients, because I keep	995
Pr 1: 6	To **u** a proverb, and the interpretation;	995
2: 5	shalt thou **u** the fear of the Lord,	995
2: 9	shalt thou **u** righteousness, and judgment,	995
8: 5	ye simple, **u** wisdom: and, ye fools, be ye	995
14: 8	The wisdom of the prudent is to **u** his way:	995
19:25	and he will **u** knowledge.	995
20:24	how can a man then **u** his own way?	995
28: 5	Evil men **u** not judgment: but they that	995
28: 5	but they that seek the Lord **u** all things.	995
29:19	for though he **u** he will not answer.	995

Ref	Text	Num
Isa 6: 9	tell this people, Hear ye indeed, but **u** not;	995
6:10	**u** with their heart, and convert,	995
28: 9	whom shall he **make** to **u** doctrine?	995
28:19	it shall be a vexation only to **u** the report.	995
32: 4	heart also of the rash shall **u** knowledge,	995
33:19	stammering tongue, that thou canst not **u**.	998
36:11	we **u** it: and speak not to us in the Jews'	8085
41:20	and know, and consider, and **u** together,	7919
43:10	and believe me, and that I am he:	995
44:18	and their hearts, that they cannot **u**.	995
56:11	they are shepherds that cannot **u**:	995+3045
Jer 9:12	Who is the wise man, that may **u** this?	995
Eze 3: 6	whose words thou canst not **u**.	8085
Da 8:16	Gabriel, **make** this man to **u** the vision.	995
8:17	he said unto me, **U**, O son of man: for at	995
9:13	turn from our iniquities, and **u** thy truth.	7919
9:23	therefore **u** the matter, and consider	995
9:25	Know therefore and **u**, that from the going	7919
10:11	**u** the words that I speak unto thee,	995
10:12	day that thou didst set thine heart to **u**,	995
10:14	I am come to **make** thee **u** what shall	995
11:33	that **u** among the people shall instruct	7919
12:10	none of the wicked shall **u**; but the wise	995
12:10	shall understand; but the wise shall **u**.	995
Hos 4:14	the people that doth not **u** shall fall.	995
14: 9	he shall **u** these things? prudent, and he	995
Mic 4:12	of the Lord, neither **u** they his counsel:	995
Mt 13:13	hearing they hear not, neither do they **u**.	4920
13:14	By hearing ye shall hear, and shall not **u**;	4920
13:15	and should **u** with their heart,	4920
15:10	and said unto them, Hear, and **u**:	4920
15:17	Do not ye yet **u**, that whatsoever entereth	3539
16: 9	Do ye not yet **u**, neither remember the	3539
16:11	How is it that ye do not **u** that I spake it	3539
24:15	holy place, (whoso readeth, let him **u**:)	3539
Mk 4:12	and hearing they may hear, and not **u**;	4920
7:14	unto me every one of you, and **u**:	4920
8:17	perceive ye not yet, neither **u**? have ye	4920
8:21	unto them, How is it that ye do not **u**?	4920
13:14	it ought not, (let him that readeth **u**,)	3539
14:68	I know not, neither **u** I what thou sayest.	1987
Lk 8:10	not see, and hearing they might not **u**.	4920
24:45	that they might **u** the scriptures,	4920
Jn 8:43	Why do ye not **u** my speech? even	1097
12:40	nor **u** with their heart, and be converted,	3539
Ac 24:11	Because that thou mayest **u**, that there	1097
28:26	Hearing ye shall hear, and shall not **u**;	4920
28:27	and **u** with their heart, and should be	4920
Ro 15:21	and they that have not heard shall **u**.	4920
1Co 12: 3	Wherefore I **give** you to **u**, that no man	1107
13: 2	and **u** all mysteries, and all knowledge;	1492
Eph 3: 4	ye may **u** my knowledge in the mystery of	3539
Php 1:12	But I would ye should **u**, brethren,	1097
Heb 11: 3	Through faith we **u** that the worlds were	3539
2Pe 2:12	speak evil of the things that they **u** not;	50

UNDERSTANDEST (4) [UNDERSTAND]
Job 15: 9	not? what **u** thou, which is not in us?	995
Ps 139: 2	mine uprising, thou **u** my thought afar off.	995
Jer 5:15	knowest not, neither **u** what they say.	8085
Ac 8:30	and said, **U** thou what thou readest?	1097

UNDERSTANDETH (11) [UNDERSTAND]
1Ch 28: 9	and **u** all the imaginations of the thoughts:	995
Job 28:23	God **u** the way thereof, and he knoweth	995
Ps 49:20	Man that is in honour, and **u** not, is like	995
Pr 8: 9	They are all plain to him that **u**, and right	995
14: 6	but knowledge is easy unto him that **u**.	995
Jer 9:24	glory in this, that he **u** and knoweth me,	7919
Mt 13:19	**u** it not, then cometh the wicked one,	4920
13:23	and **u** it; which also beareth fruit,	4920
Ro 3:11	There is none that **u**, there is none that	4920
1Co 14: 2	for no man **u** him; howbeit in the spirit	191
14:16	seeing he **u** not what thou sayest?	1492

UNDERSTANDING (160) [UNDERSTAND]
Ex 31: 3	in **u**, and in knowledge, and in all	8394
35:31	in **u**, and in knowledge, and in all	8394
36: 1	**u** to know how to work all manner of	8394
Dt 1:13	**u**, and known among your tribes, and I	995
4: 6	and your **u** in the sight of the nations,	998
4: 6	this great nation is a wise and **u** people.	995
32:28	counsel, neither is there any **u** in them.	8394
1Sa 25: 3	she was a woman of good **u**, and of a	7922
1Ki 3: 9	thy servant an **u** heart to judge thy people,	8085
3:11	asked for thyself **u** to discern judgment;	995
3:12	I have given thee a wise and an **u** heart;	8394
4:29	Solomon wisdom and **u** exceeding much,	8394
7:14	**u**, and cunning to work all works in	8394
1Ch 12:32	were men that had **u** of the times,	998+3045
22:12	Only the Lord give thee wisdom and **u**,	998
2Ch 2:12	endued with prudence and **u**, that might	998
2:13	endued with **u**, of Huram my father's,	998
26: 5	who had **u** in the visions of God:	995
Ezr 8:16	for Joiarib, and for Elnathan, men of **u**.	995
8:18	God upon us they brought us a man of **u**,	7922
Ne 8: 2	women, and all that could hear with **u**,	995
10:28	one having knowledge, and having **u**;	995
Job 12: 3	I have **u** as well as you; I am not inferior	3824
12:12	is wisdom; and in length of days **u**.	8394
12:13	and strength, he hath counsel and **u**.	8394
12:20	and taketh away the **u** of the aged.	2940
17: 4	For thou hast hid their heart from **u**:	7922
20: 3	the spirit of my **u** causeth me to answer.	998
26:12	by his **u** he smiteth through the proud.	8394

Ref	Text	Strong's
Job 28:12	be found? and where *is* the place of **u**?	998
28:20	and where *is* the place of **u**?	998
28:28	*is* wisdom; and to depart from evil *is* **u**.	995
32: 8	inspiration of the Almighty **giveth** them **u**.	995
34:10	Therefore hearken unto me, ye men of **u**.	3824
34:16	If now *thou hast* **u**, hear this: hearken to	998
34:34	Let men of **u** tell me, and let a wise man	3824
38: 4	of the earth? declare, if thou hast **u**.	998
38:36	or who hath given **u** to the heart?	998
39:17	neither hath he imparted to her **u**.	995
Ps 32: 9	horse, *or* as the mule, *which have* no **u**:	995
47: 7	of all the earth: sing ye *praises* with **u**.	7919
49: 3	the meditation of my heart *shall be* of **u**.	8394
111:10	a good **u** have all they that do *his*	7922
119:34	**Give** me **u**, and I shall keep thy law; yea,	995
119:73	give me **u**, that I may learn thy	995
119:99	I **have** more **u** than all my teachers: for	7919
119:104	Through thy precepts I get **u**: therefore I	995
119:125	give me **u**, that I may know thy	995
119:130	giveth light; it **giveth u** unto the simple.	995
119:144	*is* everlasting: **give** me **u**, and I shall live.	995
119:169	O Lord: **give** me **u** according to thy word.	995
147: 5	and of great power: his **u** *is* infinite.	8394
Pr 1: 2	instruction; to perceive the words of **u**;	998
1: 5	a man of **u** shall attain unto wise counsels:	995
2: 2	unto wisdom, *and* apply thine heart to **u**;	8394
2: 3	*and* liftest up thy voice for **u**;	8394
2: 6	of his mouth *cometh* knowledge and **u**.	8394
2:11	shall preserve thee, **u** shall keep thee:	8394
3: 4	and good in the sight of God and man.	7922
3: 5	heart; and lean not unto thine own **u**.	998
3:13	wisdom, and the man *that* getteth **u**.	8394
3:19	by **u** hath he established the heavens.	8394
4: 1	of a father, and attend to know **u**.	998
4: 5	Get wisdom, get **u**: forget *it* not;	998
4: 7	get wisdom: and with all thy getting get **u**.	998
5: 1	my wisdom, *and* bow thine ear to my **u**:	8394
6:32	adultery with a woman lacketh **u**:	3820
7: 4	*art* my sister; and call **u** *thy* kinswoman:	998
7: 7	the youths, a young man void of **u**,	3820
8: 1	wisdom cry? and **u** put forth her voice?	8394
8: 5	and, ye fools, be ye of an **u** heart.	995
8:14	sound wisdom: I *am* **u**; I have strength.	998
9: 4	*for* him that wanteth **u**, she saith to him,	3820
9: 6	foolish, and live; and go in the way of **u**.	998
9:10	and the knowledge of the holy *is* **u**.	998
9:16	*for* him that wanteth **u**, she saith to him,	3820
10:13	In the lips of him that **hath u** wisdom is	995
10:13	is for the back of him that is void of **u**.	3820
10:23	do mischief: but a man of **u** hath wisdom.	8394
11:12	but a man of **u** holdeth his peace.	8394
12:11	that followeth vain *persons is* void of **u**.	3820
13:15	Good **u** giveth favour: but the way of	7922
14:29	*He that is* slow to wrath *is* of great **u**:	8394
14:33	resteth in the heart of him that **hath u**:	995
15:14	The heart of him that **hath u** seeketh	995
15:21	but a man of **u** walketh uprightly.	8394
15:32	but he that heareth reproof getteth **u**.	3820
16:16	to get **u** rather to be chosen than silver!	998
16:22	**U** *is* a wellspring of life unto him that	7922
17:18	A man void of **u** striketh hands,	3820
17:24	Wisdom *is* before him that **hath u**;	995
17:27	*and* a man of **u** is of an excellent spirit.	8394
17:28	shutteth his lips *is esteemed a man* of **u**.	8394
18: 2	A fool hath no delight in **u**, but that his	8394
19: 8	soul: he that keepeth **u** shall find good.	8394
19:25	reprove one that **hath u**, *and* he will	998
20: 5	water; but a man of **u** will draw it out.	8394
21:16	man that wandereth out of the way of **u**	7919
21:30	*There is* no wisdom nor **u** nor counsel	8394
23:23	not; *also* wisdom, and instruction, and **u**.	998
24: 3	a house builded; and by **u** it is established:	8394
24:30	by the vineyard of the man void of **u**;	3820
28: 2	by a man of **u** *and* knowledge the state	995
28:11	the poor that hath **u** searcheth him out.	995
28:16	The prince that wanteth **u** *is* also a great	8394
30: 2	*any* man, and have not the **u** of a man.	998
Ecc 9:11	to the wise, nor yet riches to men of **u**,	995
Isa 11: 2	the spirit of wisdom and **u**, the spirit of	998
11: 3	shall **make** him **of quick u** in the fear of	7306
27:11	for it *is a* people of no **u**: therefore he that	998
29:14	the **u** of their prudent *men* shall be hid.	995
29:16	say of him that framed it, He had no **u**?	995
29:24	that erred in spirit shall **come** to **u**,	998+3045
40:14	and shewed to him the way of **u**?	8394
40:28	is weary? *there is* no searching of his **u**.	8394
44:19	neither *is there* knowledge nor **u** to say,	8394
Jer 3:15	shall feed you with knowledge and **u**.	7919
4:22	sottish children, and they **have** none **u**:	995
5:21	this, O foolish people, and without **u**;	3820
51:15	hath stretched out the heaven by his **u**.	8394
Eze 28: 4	with thine **u** thou hast gotten thee riches,	8394
Da 1: 4	**u** science, and such as *had* ability in them	995
1:17	and Daniel had **u** in all visions and dreams.	995
1:20	all matters of wisdom *and* **u**, that the king	998
2:21	and knowledge to them that know **u**:	999
4:34	mine **u** returned unto me, and I blessed	4486
5:11	days of thy father light and **u** and wisdom,	7924
5:12	knowledge, and **u**, interpreting of dreams,	7924
5:14	*that* light and **u** and excellent wisdom is	7924
8:23	and **u** dark sentences, shall stand up.	995
9:22	now come forth to give thee skill and **u**.	998
10: 1	the thing, and had **u** of the vision.	998
11:35	*some* of them of **u** shall fall, to try them,	7919
Hos 13: 2	idols according to their own **u**, all of it	8394

Ref	Text	Strong's
Ob 1: 7	under thee: *there is* none **u** in him.	8394
1: 8	of Edom, and **u** out of the mount of Esau?	8394
Mt 15:16	And Jesus said, Are ye also yet **without u**?	801
Mk 7:18	saith unto them, Are ye so **without u** also?	801
12:33	and with all the **u**, and with all the soul,	4907
Lk 1: 3	having had perfect **u** of all *things* from	3877
2:47	that heard him were astonished at his **u**	4907
24:45	Then opened he their **u**, that *they* might	3563
Ro 1:31	**Without u**, covenant-breakers,	801
1Co 1:19	bring to nothing the **u** of the prudent.	4907
14:14	my spirit prayeth, but my **u** is unfruitful.	3563
14:15	the spirit, and I will pray with the **u** also:	3563
14:15	the spirit, and I will sing with the **u** also.	3563
14:19	I had rather speak five words with my **u**,	3563
14:20	Brethren, be not children in **u**: howbeit in	5424
14:20	in malice be ye children, but in **u** be men.	5424
Eph 1:18	The eyes of your **u** being enlightened;	1271
4:18	Having the **u** darkened, being alienated	1271
5:17	but **u** what the will of the Lord *is*.	4920
Php 4: 7	which passeth all **u**, shall keep your hearts	3563
Col 1: 9	of his will in all wisdom and spiritual **u**;	4907
2: 2	unto all riches of the full assurance of **u**,	4907
1Ti 1: 7	**u** neither what they say, nor whereof they	3539
2Ti 2: 7	and the Lord give thee **u** in all *things*.	4907
1Jn 5:20	hath given us an **u**, that we may know	1271
Rev 13:18	Let him that hath **u** count the number of	3563

UNDERSTOOD (37) [UNDERSTAND]

Ref	Text	Strong's
Ge 42:23	they knew not that Joseph **u** *them*; for he	8085
Dt 32:29	O that they were wise, *that* they **u** this,	7919
1Sa 4: 6	they **u** that the ark of the Lord was come	3045
26: 4	and **u** that Saul was come in very deed.	3045
2Sa 3:37	all Israel **u** that day that it was not of	3045
Ne 8:12	they had **u** the words that were declared	995
13: 7	**u** of the evil that Eliashib did for Tobiah,	995
Job 13: 1	seen all *this*, mine ear hath heard and **u** it.	995
42: 3	therefore have I uttered that I **u** not;	995
Ps 73:17	the sanctuary of God; *then* **u** I their end.	995
81: 5	*where* I heard a language *that* I **u** not.	3045
106: 7	Our fathers **u** not thy wonders in Egypt;	7919
Isa 40:21	have ye not **u** from the foundations of	995
44:18	They have not known nor **u**: for he hath	995
Da 8:27	astonished at the vision, but none **u** *it*.	995
9: 2	In the first year of his reign I Daniel **u** by	995
10: 1	he **u** the thing, and had understanding of	995
12: 8	heard, but I **u** not: then said I, O my lord,	995
Mt 13:51	Have ye **u** all these *things?* They say unto	4920
16:12	Then **u** they how that he bade *them* not	4920
17:13	Then the disciples **u** that he spake unto	4920
26:10	When Jesus **u** *it*, he said unto them,	1097
Mk 9:32	they **u** not *that* saying, and were afraid to	50
Lk 2:50	And they **u** not the saying which he spake	4920
9:45	But they **u** not this saying, and it was hid	50
18:34	And they **u** none of these *things*: and	4920
Jn 8:27	They **u** not that he spake to them of	1097
10: 6	they **u** not what *things* they were which	1097
12:16	These *things* **u** not his disciples at the first:	1097
Ac 7:25	he supposed his brethren would have **u**	4920
7:25	hand would deliver them: but they **u** not.	4920
23:27	having **u** that he was a Roman.	3129
23:34	and when he **u** that he was of Cilicia;	4441
Ro 1:20	being **u** by the things that are made,	3539
1Co 13:11	I spake as a child, I **u** as a child, I thought	5426
14: 9	utter by the tongue words **easy to be u**,	2154
2Pe 3:16	in which are some *things* **hard to be u**,	1425

UNDERTAKE (1) [UNDERTOOK]

Ref	Text	Strong's
Isa 38:14	O Lord, I am oppressed; **u** for me.	6148

UNDERTOOK (1) [UNDERTAKE]

Ref	Text	Strong's
Est 9:23	the Jews **u** to do as they had begun,	6901

UNDO (2) [DO, UNDONE]

Ref	Text	Strong's
Isa 58: 6	to **u** the heavy burdens, and to let	5425
Zep 3:19	that time I *will* **u** all that afflict thee:	854+6213

UNDONE (5) [UNDO]

Ref	Text	Strong's
Nu 21:29	thou art **u**, O people of Chemosh: he hath	6
Jos 11:15	he **left** nothing **u** of all that the Lord	5493
Isa 6: 5	for I am **u**; because I *am* a man of unclean	1820
Mt 23:23	to have done, and not to **leave** the other **u**.	863
Lk 11:42	to have done, and not to **leave** the other **u**.	863

UNDRESSED (2) [DRESS]

Ref	Text	Strong's
Lev 25: 5	neither gather the grapes of thy **vine u**:	5139
25:11	nor gather *the grapes* in it of thy **vine u**.	5139

UNEQUAL (2) [EQUAL, UNEQUALLY]

Ref	Text	Strong's
Eze 18:25	way equal? are not your ways **u**?	3808+8505
18:29	ways equal? are not your ways **u**?	3808+8505

UNEQUALLY (1) [UNEQUAL]

Ref	Text	Strong's
2Co 6:14	Be ye not **u yoked together** with	2086

UNFAILING LOVE See LOVINGKINDNESS

UNFAITHFUL (1) [FAITH, UNFAITHFULLY]

Ref	Text	Strong's
Pr 25:19	Confidence in an **u** *man* in time of trouble	898

UNFAITHFULLY (1) [UNFAITHFUL]

Ref	Text	Strong's
Ps 78:57	turned *back*, and **dealt u** like their fathers:	898

UNFAITHFULNESS See WHOREDOM

UNFEIGNED (4) [FEIGN]

Ref	Text	Strong's
2Co 6: 6	by kindness, by the Holy Ghost, by love **u**,	505

Ref	Text	Strong's
1Ti 1: 5	and *of* a good conscience, and *of* faith **u**:	505
2Ti 1: 5	When I call to remembrance thy faith **u**	505
1Pe 1:22	the Spirit unto **u** love of the brethren,	505

UNFIT See REPROBATE; REPROBATES

UNFORGIVING See TRUCEBREAKERS

UNFORMED See UNPERFECT

UNFRUITFUL (6) [FRUIT]

Ref	Text	Strong's
Mt 13:22	choke the word, and he becometh **u**.	175
Mk 4:19	choke the word, and it becometh **u**.	175
1Co 14:14	spirit prayeth, but my understanding is **u**.	175
Eph 5:11	have no fellowship with the **u** works of	175
Tit 3:14	for necessary uses, that they be not **u**.	175
2Pe 1: 8	**u** in the knowledge of our Lord Jesus	175

UNGIRDED (1) [GIRD]

Ref	Text	Strong's
Ge 24:32	he **u** *his* camels, and gave straw and	6605

UNGODLINESS (4) [GOD, UNGODLY]

Ref	Text	Strong's
Ro 1:18	God is revealed from heaven against all **u**	763
11:26	and shall turn away **u** from Jacob:	763
2Ti 2:16	for they will increase unto more **u**.	763
Tit 2:12	Teaching us that denying **u** and worldly	763

UNGODLY (27) [UNGODLINESS]

Ref	Text	Strong's
2Sa 22: 5	the floods of **u** men made me afraid;	1100
2Ch 19: 2	Shouldest thou help the **u**, and love them	7563
Job 16:11	God hath delivered me to the **u**,	5760
34:18	*art* wicked? *and* to princes, *Ye are* **u**?	7563
Ps 1: 1	that walketh not in the counsel of the **u**,	7563
1: 4	The **u** *are* not so: but *are* like the chaff	7563
1: 5	Therefore the **u** shall not stand in	7563
1: 6	but the way of the **u** shall perish.	7563
3: 7	thou hast broken the teeth of the **u**.	7563
18: 4	and the floods of **u** men made me afraid.	1100
43: 1	I plead my cause against an **u** nation:	2623+3808
73:12	Behold, these *are* the **u**, who prosper in	7563
Pr 16:27	An **u** man diggeth up evil: and in his lips	1100
19:28	An **u** witness scorneth judgment:	1100
Ro 4: 5	but believeth on him that justifieth the **u**,	765
5: 6	in due time Christ died for the **u**.	765
1Ti 1: 9	for the **u** and for sinners, for unholy and	765
1Pe 4:18	where shall the **u** and the sinner appear?	765
2Pe 2: 5	in the flood upon the world of the **u**;	765
2: 6	unto **those that** after should **live u**;	764
3: 7	day of judgment and perdition of **u** men.	765
Jude 1: 4	**u** men, turning the grace of our God into	765
1:15	convince all *that are* **u** among them of all	765
1:15	**u** deeds which they have ungodly	763
1:15	deeds which they have **u committed**,	764
1:15	of all *their* hard *speeches* which **u** sinners	765
1:18	who should walk after their own **u** lusts.	763

UNGRATEFUL See UNTHANKFUL

UNHOLY (4) [HOLY]

Ref	Text	Strong's
Lev 10:10	may put difference between holy and **u**,	2455
1Ti 1: 9	and for sinners, for **u** and profane,	462
2Ti 3: 2	disobedient to parents, unthankful, **u**,	462
Heb 10:29	an **u** *thing*, and hath done despite unto	2839

UNICORN (6) [UNICORNS]

Ref	Text	Strong's
Nu 23:22	he hath as it were the strength of an **u**.	7214
24: 8	he hath as it were the strength of an **u**:	7214
Job 39: 9	Will the **u** be willing to serve thee,	7214
39:10	Canst thou bind the **u** with his band in	7214
Ps 29: 6	a calf; Lebanon and Sirion like a young **u**.	7214
92:10	shalt thou exalt like *the horn of* an **u**:	7214

UNICORNS (3) [UNICORN]

Ref	Text	Strong's
Dt 33:17	and his horns *are like* the horns of **u**:	7214
Ps 22:21	hast heard me from the horns of the **u**.	7214
Isa 34: 7	the **u** shall come down with them,	7214

UNINTENTIONALLY See UNAWARES

UNITE (1) [UNITED, UNITY]

Ref	Text	Strong's
Ps 86:11	in thy truth: **u** my heart to fear thy name.	3161

UNITED (1) [UNITE]

Ref	Text	Strong's
Ge 49: 6	assembly, mine honour, be not thou **u**:	3161

UNITY (3) [UNITE]

Ref	Text	Strong's
Ps 133: 1	*it is* for brethren to dwell **together in u**.	3162
Eph 4: 3	Endeavouring to keep the **u** of the Spirit	1775
4:13	Till we all come in the **u** of the faith,	1775

UNJUST (17) [JUST, UNJUSTLY]

Ref	Text	Strong's
Ps 43: 1	deliver me from the deceitful and **u** man.	5766
Pr 11: 7	and the hope of **u** *men* perisheth.	205
28: 8	and **u** gain increaseth his substance,	8636
29:27	An **u** man is an abomination to the just:	5766
Zep 3: 5	faileth not; but the **u** knoweth no shame.	5767
Mt 5:45	and sendeth rain on the just and *on* the **u**.	94
Lk 16: 8	And the lord commended the **u** steward,	93
16:10	that is **u** in the least is unjust also in much.	94
16:10	that is unjust in the least is **u** also in much.	94
18: 6	the Lord said, Hear what the **u** judge saith.	93
18:11	**u**, adulterers, or even as this publican.	94
Ac 24:15	of the dead, both of the just and **u**.	94
1Co 6: 1	go to law before the **u**, and not before	94
1Pe 3:18	the just for the **u**, that he might bring us to	94
2Pe 2: 9	to reserve the **u** unto the day of judgment	94
Rev 22:11	He that is **u**, let him be unjust still:	91

Rev 22:11 He that is unjust, let him be **u** still: 91

UNJUSTLY (2) [UNJUST]
Ps 82: 2 How long will ye judge **u**, and accept 5766
Isa 26:10 in the land of uprightness will he **deal u**, 5765

UNKNOWN (9) [KNOW]
Ac 17:23 altar with this inscription, TO *THE* **U** GOD. 57
1Co 14: 2 For he that speaketh in an **u** tongue NIG
 14: 4 He that speaketh in an **u** tongue edifieth NIG
 14:13 Wherefore let him that speaketh in an **u** NIG
 14:14 For if I pray in an **u** tongue, my spirit NIG
 14:19 than ten thousand words in an **u** tongue. NIG
 14:27 If any *man* speak in an **u** tongue, *let it be* NIG
2Co 6: 9 As **u**, and *yet* well known; as dying, 50
Gal 1:22 was **u** by face unto the churches of Judea 50

UNLADE (1) [LADE]
Ac 21: 3 for there the ship was to **u** *her* burden. 670

UNLAWFUL (2) [LAW]
Ac 10:28 Ye know how that it is an **u** thing for a 111
2Pe 2: 8 soul from day to day with *their* **u** deeds;) 459

UNLEARNED (6) [LEARN]
Ac 4:13 and perceived that they were **u** and 62
1Co 14:16 of the **u** say Amen at thy giving of thanks, 2399
 14:23 and there come in *those that are* **u**, 2399
 14:24 or *one* **u**, he is convinced of all, he is 2399
2Ti 2:23 But foolish and **u** questions avoid, 521
2Pe 3:16 which *they that are* **u** and unstable wrest, 261

UNLEAVENED (61) [LEAVEN]
Ge 19: 3 and did bake **u** bread, and they did eat. 4682
Ex 12: 8 that night, roast with fire, and **u** bread; 4682
 12:15 Seven days shall ye eat **u** bread; even 4682
 12:17 ye shall observe the *feast of* **u** bread; for 4682
 12:18 ye shall eat **u** bread, until the one and 4682
 12:20 all your habitations shall ye eat **u** bread. 4682
 12:39 they baked **u** cakes of the dough which 4682
 13: 6 Seven days thou shalt eat **u** bread, 4682
 13: 7 **U** bread shall be eaten seven days; 4682
 23:15 Thou shalt keep the feast of **u** bread: 4682
 23:15 thou shalt eat **u** bread seven days, as I 4682
 29: 2 **u** bread, and cakes unleavened tempered 4682
 29: 2 cakes **u** tempered with oil, 4682
 29: 2 with oil, and wafers **u** anointed with oil: 4682
 29:23 wafer out of the basket of the **u** bread 4682
 34:18 The feast of **u** bread shalt thou keep: 4682
 34:18 seven days thou shalt eat **u** bread, as I 4682
Lev 2: 4 *it shall be* **u** cakes of fine flour mingled 4682
 2: 4 with oil, or **u** wafers anointed with oil. 4682
 2: 5 shall be *of* fine flour **u**, mingled with oil. 4682
 6:16 *with* **u** bread shall it be eaten in the holy 4682
 7:12 of thanksgiving **u** cakes mingled with oil, 4682
 7:12 **u** wafers anointed with oil, 4682
 8: 2 and two rams, and a basket of **u** bread; 4682
 8:26 out of the basket of **u** bread, that *was* 4682
 8:26 he took one **u** cake, and a cake of oiled 4682
 23: 6 *is* the feast of **u** bread unto the LORD: 4682
 23: 6 seven days ye must eat **u** bread. 4682
Nu 6:15 a basket of **u** bread, cakes *of* fine flour 4682
 6:15 wafers of **u** bread anointed with oil, 4682
 6:17 the LORD, with the basket of **u** bread: 4682
 6:19 one **u** cake out of the basket, 4682
 6:19 one **u** wafer, and shall put *them* upon 4682
 9:11 *and* eat it with **u** bread and bitter *herbs*. 4682
 28:17 seven days shall **u** bread be eaten. 4682
Dt 16: 3 seven days shalt thou eat **u** bread 4682
 16: 8 Six days thou shalt eat **u** bread: and on 4682
 16:16 in the feast of **u** bread, and in the feast of 4682
Jos 5:11 **u** cakes, and parched *corn* in the selfsame 4682
Jdg 6:19 a kid, and **u** cakes *of* an ephah of flour: 4682
 6:20 Take the flesh and the **u** cakes, and 4682
 6:21 touched the flesh and the **u** cakes; and 4682
 6:21 the **u** cakes. Then the angel of the LORD 4682
1Sa 28:24 kneaded *it*, and did bake **u** bread thereof: 4682
2Ki 23: 9 they did eat of the **u** bread among their 4682
1Ch 23:29 for the **u** cakes, and for *that which is* 4682
2Ch 8:13 *even* in the feast of **u** bread, and in 4682
 30:13 the feast of **u** bread in the second month, 4682
 30:21 **u** bread seven days with great gladness: 4682
 35:17 and the feast of **u** bread seven days. 4682
Ezr 6:22 kept the feast of **u** bread seven days with 4682
Eze 45:21 of seven days; **u** bread shall be eaten. 4682
Mt 26:17 Now the first *day* of the *feast of* **u** bread 106
Mk 14: 1 the *feast of* the passover, and *of* **u** bread: 106
 14:12 And the first day of **u** bread, when they 106
Lk 22: 1 Now the feast of **u** bread drew nigh, 106
 22: 7 Then came the day of **u** bread, when 106
Ac 12: 3 These were the days of **u** bread.] 106
 20: 6 from Philippi after the days of **u** bread, 106
1Co 5: 7 that ye may be a new lump, as ye are **u**. 106
 5: 8 with the **u** bread of sincerity and truth. 106

UNLESS (8)
Lev 22: 6 shall not eat of the holy *things*, **u** he 518+3588
Nu 22:33 **u** she had turned from me, surely now I 194
2Sa 2:27 thou hadst spoken, surely then 3588+3884
Ps 27:13 *I had fainted*, **u** I had believed to see 3884
 94:17 **U** the LORD *had been* my help, my soul 3884
 119:92 **U** thy law *had been* my delights, I should 3884
Pr 4:16 away, **u** they cause *some* to fall. 518+3808
1Co 15: 2 **u** ye have believed in vain. 1487+1622+3361

UNLOAD See UNLADE

UNLOADED See UNGIRDED

UNLOOSE (3) [LOOSE]
Mk 1: 7 I am not worthy to stoop down and **u**. 3089
Lk 3:16 of whose shoes I am not worthy to **u**: 3089
Jn 1:27 shoe's latchet I am not worthy to **u**. 3089

UNMARRIED (4) [MARRY]
1Co 7: 8 I say therefore to the **u** and widows, It is 22
 7:11 let her remain **u**, or be reconciled to *her* 22
 7:32 He *that is* **u** careth for the *things* that 22
 7:34 The **u** *woman* careth for the *things* of 22

UNMERCIFUL (1) [MERCY]
Ro 1:31 without natural affection, implacable, **u**: 415

UNMINDFUL (1) [MIND]
Dt 32:18 Of the Rock *that* begat thee thou art **u**, 7876

UNMOVEABLE (2) [MOVE]
Ac 27:41 and remained **u**, but the hinder part was 761
1Co 15:58 my beloved brethren, be ye stedfast, **u**, 277

UNNI (3)
1Ch 15:18 **U**, Eliab, and Benaiah, and Maaseiah, 6042
 15:20 **U**, and Eliab, and Maaseiah, and Benaiah, 6042
Ne 12: 9 Bakbukiah and **U**, their brethren, *were* 6042

UNOCCUPIED (1) [OCCUPY]
Jdg 5: 6 the highways were **u**, and the travellers 2308

UNPERFECT (1) [PERFECT]
Ps 139:16 eyes did see my **substance, yet being u**; 1564

UNPLOWED See FALLOW

UNPOSSIBLE (4) [IMPOSSIBLE, POSSIBLE]
Mt 17:20 and nothing shall be **u** unto you. 101
 19:26 and said unto them, With men this is **u**; 102
Lk 1:37 For with God nothing shall be **u**. 101
 18:27 The *things which are* **u** with men are 102

UNPREPARED (1) [PREPARE]
2Co 9: 4 and find you **u**, we (that we say not, you) 532

UNPRESENTABLE See UNCOMELY

UNPROFITABLE (7) [PROFIT, UNPROFITABLENESS]
Job 15: 3 Should he reason *with* **u** talk? 3808+5532
Mt 25:30 And cast ye the **u** servant into outer 888
Lk 17:10 commanded you, say, We are **u** servants: 888
Ro 3:12 of the way, they are together become **u**; 889
Tit 3: 9 about the law; for they are **u** and vain. 512
Phm 1:11 Which in time past was to thee **u**, 890
Heb 13:17 and not with grief: for that *is* **u** for you. 255

UNPROFITABLENESS (1) [UNPROFITABLE]
Heb 7:18 before for the weakness and **u** thereof. 512

UNPUNISHED (11) [PUNISH]
Pr 11:21 *join* in hand, the wicked shall not be **u**: 5352
 16: 5 hand *join* in hand, he shall not be **u**. 5352
 17: 5 that is glad at calamities shall not be **u**. 5352
 19: 5 A false witness shall not be **u**, and *he that* 5352
 19: 9 A false witness shall not be **u**, and *he that* 5352
Jer 25:29 and should ye be **utterly u**? 5352+5352
 25:29 shall not be **u**: for I *will* call for a sword 5352
 30:11 will not **leave** thee **altogether u**. 5352+5352
 46:28 will I not **leave** thee **wholly u**. 5352+5352
 49:12 he *that* shall **altogether go u**? 5352+5352
 49:12 thou shalt not **go u**, but thou shalt surely 5352

UNQUENCHABLE (2) [QUENCH]
Mt 3:12 but will burn up the chaff with **u** fire. 762
Lk 3:17 but the chaff he will burn with fire **u**. 762

UNREASONABLE (2) [REASON]
Ac 25:27 For it seemeth to me **u** to send a prisoner, 249
2Th 3: 2 And that we may be delivered from **u** and 824

UNREBUKEABLE (1) [REBUKE]
1Ti 6:14 **u**, until the appearing of our Lord Jesus 423

UNREPENTANT See IMPENITENT

UNREPROVEABLE (1) [REPROVE]
Col 1:22 holy and unblameable and **u** in his sight: 410

UNRIGHTEOUS (9) [RIGHT, UNRIGHTEOUSLY, UNRIGHTEOUSNESS]
Ex 23: 1 hand with the wicked to be an **u** witness. 2555
Job 27: 7 and he that riseth up against me as the **u**. 5767
Ps 71: 4 out of the hand of the **u** and cruel *man*. 5765
Isa 10: 1 Woe unto them that decree **u** decrees, 205
 55: 7 his way, and the **u** man his thoughts: 205
Lk 16:11 ye have not been faithful in the **u** mammon, 94
Ro 3: 5 *Is* God **u** who taketh vengeance? (I speak as 94
1Co 6: 9 Know ye not that the **u** shall not inherit 94
Heb 6:10 For God *is* not **u** to forget your work and 94

UNRIGHTEOUSLY (1) [UNRIGHTEOUS]
Dt 25:16 all that do such *things, and* all that do **u**, 5766

UNRIGHTEOUSNESS (21) [UNRIGHTEOUS]
Lev 19:15 Ye shall do no **u** in judgment: thou shalt 5766
 19:35 shall do no **u** in judgment, in meteyard, 5766

Ps 92:15 *he is* my rock, and *there is* no **u** in him. 5766
Jer 22:13 him that buildeth his house by **u**, 3808+6664
Lk 16: 9 to yourselves friends of the mammon of **u**; 93
Jn 7:18 him, the same is true, and no **u** is in him. 93
Ro 1:18 heaven against all ungodliness and **u** of men, 93
 1:18 of men, who hold the truth in **u**; 93
 1:29 Being filled with all **u**, fornication, 93
 2: 8 truth, but obey **u**, indignation and wrath, 93
 3: 5 But if our **u** commend the righteousness of 93
 6:13 your members *as* instruments of **u** unto sin: 93
 9:14 say then? *Is there* **u** with God? God forbid. 93
2Co 6:14 what fellowship hath righteousness with **u**? 458
2Th 2:10 And with all deceivableness of **u** in them 93
 2:12 not the truth, but had pleasure in **u**. 93
Heb 8:12 I will be merciful to their **u**, and their sins 93
2Pe 2:13 shall receive the reward of **u**, *as* they that 93
 2:15 *the son* of Bosor, who loved the wages of **u**; 93
1Jn 1: 9 us *our* sins, and to cleanse us from all **u**. 93
 5:17 All **u** is sin: and there is a sin not unto death. 93

UNRIPE (1) [RIPE]
Job 15:33 He shall shake off his **u** grape as the vine, 1154

UNRULY (4)
1Th 5:14 you, brethren, warn *them that are* **u**, 813
Tit 1: 6 faithful children not accused of riot or **u**. 506
 1:10 For there are many **u** and vain talkers and 506
Jas 3: 8 *it is* an **u** evil, full of deadly poison. 183

UNSANDALED See SHOE; SHOE'S; SHOES

UNSATIABLE (1) [SATIATE]
Eze 16:28 the Assyrians, because thou wast **u**; 1115+7654

UNSAVOURY (2) [SAVOUR]
2Sa 22:27 the froward thou wilt **shew** thyself **u**. 6617
Job 6: 6 that which is **u** be eaten without salt? 8602

UNSCHOOLED See UNLEARNED

UNSEARCHABLE (5) [SEARCH]
Job 5: 9 Which doeth great *things* and **u**; 369+2714
Ps 145: 3 to be praised; and his greatness *is* **u**. 369+2714
Pr 25: 3 for depth, and the heart of kings *is* **u**. 369+2714
Ro 11:33 how **u** *are* his judgments, and his ways 419
Eph 3: 8 *I* should preach among the Gentiles the **u** 421

UNSEEMLY (2) [SEEM]
Ro 1:27 men with men working that which is **u**, 808
1Co 13: 5 Doth not **behave** itself **u**, seeketh not her 807

UNSHOD (1) [SHOD]
Jer 2:25 Withhold thy foot from being **u**, 3182

UNSKILFUL (1) [SKILL]
Heb 5:13 For every one that useth milk *is* **u** in 552

UNSPEAKABLE (3) [SPEAK]
2Co 9:15 Thanks *be* unto God for his **u** gift. 411
 12: 4 and heard **u** words, which *it is* not lawful 731
1Pe 1: 8 ye rejoice with joy **u** and full of glory: 412

UNSPIRITUAL See CARNAL

UNSPOTTED (1) [SPOT]
Jas 1:27 *and* to keep himself **u** from the world. 784

UNSTABLE (4) [STABLE]
Ge 49: 4 **U** as water, thou shalt not excel; because 6349
Jas 1: 8 A double minded man *is* **u** in all his ways. 182
2Pe 2:14 cannot cease from sin; beguiling **u** souls: 793
 3:16 which *they that are* unlearned and **u** wrest, 793

UNSTOPPED (1) [STOP]
Isa 35: 5 and the ears of the deaf shall be **u**. 6605

UNTAKEN (1) [TAKE]
2Co 3:14 **u** away in the reading of the old 343+3361

UNTEMPERED (5) [TEMPER]
Eze 13:10 and lo, others daubed it *with* **u** morter: 8602
 13:11 unto them which daub *it with* **u** morter, 8602
 13:14 wall that ye have daubed *with* **u** morter, 8602
 13:15 upon them that have daubed it *with* **u** 8602
 22:28 her prophets have daubed them *with* **u** 8602

UNTENDED See UNDRESSED

UNTHANKFUL (2) [THANK]
Lk 6:35 for he is kind unto the **u** and *to* the evil. 884
2Ti 3: 2 disobedient to parents, **u**, unholy, 884

UNTIL (366)
Ge 8: 5 waters decreased continually **u** 5704+2050.1
 8: 7 **u** the waters were dried up from off 5704
 24:19 **u** they have done drinking. 518+5704
 24:33 not eat, **u** I have told mine errand. 518+5704
 26:13 grew **u** he became very great: 3588+5704
 27:44 **u** thy brother's fury turn away; 834+5704
 27:45 **U** thy brother's anger turn away from 5704
 28:15 **u** I have done *that* which I 518+834+5704
 29: 8 **u** all the flocks be gathered together, 834+5704
 32: 4 with Laban, and stayed *there* **u** now: 5704
 32:24 there wrestled a man with him **u** 5704
 33: 3 times, **u** he came near to his brother. 5704
 33:14 **u** I come unto my lord unto Seir. 834+5704
 34: 5 Jacob held his peace **u** they were come. 5704

U

Ge 39:16 garment by her, **u** his lord came home. 5704
41:49 very much, **u** he left numbering; 3588+5704
46:34 about cattle from our youth even **u** now, 5704
49:10 between his feet, **u** Shiloh come; 3588+5704

Ex 9:18 since the foundation thereof even **u** now. 5704
10:26 must serve the Lord, **u** we come thither. 5704
12: 6 ye shall keep it *up* **u** the fourteenth day of 5704
12:10 ye shall let nothing of it remain **u** 5704
12:10 that which remaineth of it **u** the morning 5704
12:15 bread from the first day **u** the seventh day, 5704
12:18 the one and twentieth day of the month 5704
12:22 at the door of his house **u** the morning. 5704
16:20 some of them left of it **u** the morning, 5704
16:23 lay up for you to be kept **u** the morning. 5704
16:35 **u** they came to a land inhabited; 5704
16:35 **u** they came unto the borders of the land 5704
17:12 his hands were steady **u** the going down 5704
23:18 fat of my sacrifice remain **u** the morning. 5704
23:30 **u** thou be increased, and inherit 834+5704
24:14 for us, **u** we come again unto you: 834+5704
33: 8 **u** he was gone into the tabernacle. 5704
34:34 he took the vail off, **u** he came out. 5704
34:35 again, **u** he went in to speak with him. 5704

Lev 7:15 he shall not leave *any* of it **u** the morning. 5704
8:33 **u** the days of your consecration be at an 5704
11:24 of them shall be unclean **u** the even. 5704
11:25 his clothes, and be unclean **u** the morning. 5704
11:27 their carcase shall be unclean **u** the even: 5704
11:28 his clothes, and be unclean **u** the morning. 5704
11:31 they be dead, shall be unclean **u** the even. 5704
11:32 and it shall be unclean **u** the even; 5704
11:39 thereof shall be unclean **u** the even. 5704
11:40 his clothes, and be unclean **u** the even: 5704
11:40 his clothes, and be unclean **u** the even. 5704
12: 4 **u** the days of her purifying be fulfilled. 5704
14:46 it is shut up shall be unclean **u** the even. 5704
15: 5 in water, and be unclean **u** the even. 5704
15: 6 in water, and be unclean **u** the even. 5704
15: 7 in water, and be unclean **u** the even. 5704
15: 8 in water, and be unclean **u** the even. 5704
15:10 under him shall be unclean **u** the even: 5704
15:10 in water, and be unclean **u** the even. 5704
15:11 in water, and be unclean **u** the even. 5704
15:16 in water, and be unclean **u** the even. 5704
15:17 with water, and be unclean **u** the even. 5704
15:18 in water, and be unclean **u** the even. 5704
15:19 toucheth her shall be unclean **u** 5704
15:21 in water, and be unclean **u** the even. 5704
15:22 in water, and be unclean **u** the even. 5704
15:23 it, he shall be unclean **u** the even. 5704
15:27 in water, and be unclean **u** the even. 5704
16:17 in the holy *place,* **u** he come out, 5704
17:15 in water, and be unclean **u** the morning. 5704
19: 6 if ought remain **u** the third day, it shall be 5704
19:13 abide with thee all night **u** the morning. 5704
22: 4 he shall not eat of the holy *things,* **u** 834+5704
22: 6 touched *any* such shall be unclean **u** even, 5704
22:30 ye shall leave none of it **u** the morrow: 5704
23:14 the selfsame day that ye have brought 5704
25:22 and eat *yet* of old fruit **u** the ninth year; 5704
25:22 **u** her fruits come in ye shall eat *of* the old 5704
25:28 that hath bought it **u** the year of jubile: 5704

Nu 4: 3 and upward even **u** fifty years old, 5704
4:23 u fifty years old shalt thou number 5704
6: 5 **u** the days be fulfilled, *in* the which he 5704
9:15 the appearance of fire, **u** the morning. 5704
11:20 **u** it come out at your nostrils, and it 834+5704
14:19 this people, from Egypt even **u** now. 5704
14:33 **u** your carcases be wasted in 5704
19: 7 the priest shall be unclean **u** the even. 5704
19: 8 in water, and shall be unclean **u** the even. 5704
19:10 his clothes, and be unclean **u** the even: 5704
19:21 of separation shall be unclean **u** even. 5704
19:22 soul that toucheth *it* shall be unclean **u** 5704
20:17 left, **u** we have passed thy borders. 834+5704
21:22 *high* way, **u** we be past thy borders. 834+5704
21:35 people, **u** there was none left him alive: 5704
23:24 shall not lie down **u** he eat *of* the prey, 5704
24:22 **u** Asshur shall carry thee away 4100+5704
32:13 **u** all the generation, that had done evil in 5704
32:17 **u** we have brought them unto 518+834+5704
32:18 **u** the children of Israel have inherited 5704
32:21 **u** he hath driven out his enemies from 5704
35:12 **u** he stand before the congregation in 5704
35:28 his refuge **u** the death of the high priest: 5704
35:32 in the land, **u** the death of the priest. 5704

Dt 1:31 that ye went, **u** ye came into this place. 5704
2:14 **u** we were come over the brook 834+5704
2:14 **u** all the generation of the men of war 5704
2:15 among the host, **u** they were consumed. 5704
2:29 **u** I shall pass over Jordan into the 834+5704
3: 3 we smote him **u** none was left to him 5704
3:20 **U** the Lord have given rest unto 834+5704
3:20 **u** they also possess the land which NIH
7:20 **u** they that are left, and hide themselves 5704
7:23 mighty destruction, **u** they be destroyed. 5704
7:24 before **u** thou have destroyed them. 5704
9: 7 ye came unto this place, ye have been 5704
9:21 *even* **u** *it was as* small as dust: 834+5704
11: 5 the wilderness, **u** ye came into this place; 5704
16: 4 at even, remain all night **u** the morning. 3807.1
20:20 maketh war with thee, **u** it be subdued. 5704
22: 2 it shall be with thee **u** thy brother seek 5704
28:20 **u** thou be destroyed, and until thou perish 5704
28:20 be destroyed, and **u** thou perish quickly; 5704

Dt 28:21 **u** he have consumed thee from off the 5704
28:22 and they shall pursue thee **u** thou perish. 5704
28:24 down upon thee, **u** thou be destroyed. 5704
28:48 upon thy neck, **u** he have destroyed thee. 5704
28:51 the fruit of thy land, **u** thou be destroyed: 5704
28:51 of thy sheep, **u** he have destroyed thee. 5704
28:52 thy high and fenced walls come down, 5704
28:61 bring upon thee, **u** thou be destroyed. 5704
31:24 this law in a book, **u** they were finished, 5704
31:30 words of this song, **u** they were ended. 5704

Jos 1:15 **U** the Lord have given your 834+5704
2:16 three days, **u** the pursuers be returned: 5704
2:22 three days, **u** the pursuers were returned: 5704
3:17 **u** all the people were passed clean 834+5704
4:10 **u** every thing was finished that the Lord 5704
4:23 **u** ye were passed over, as the Lord your 5704
4:23 up from before us, **u** we were gone over: 5704
5: 1 **u** we were passed over, that their heart 5704
6:10 of your mouth, **u** the day I bid you shout; 5704
7: 6 the ark of the Lord **u** the eventide, 5704
7:13 ye take away the accursed thing from 5704
8:24 **u** they were consumed, that all 5704
8:26 **u** he had utterly destroyed all 834+5704
8:29 the king of Ai he hanged on a tree **u** 5704
10:13 the people had avenged themselves 5704
10:26 they were hanging upon the trees **u** 5704
10:27 *which* remain **u** this very day. 5704
10:33 **u** he had left him none remaining. 5704
11: 8 *they* left them none remaining. 5704
11:14 they had destroyed them, neither left 5704
13:13 dwell among the Israelites **u** this day.) 5704
20: 6 he stand before the congregation **u** 5704
20: 6 the death of the high priest that shall be 5704
20: 9 he stood before the congregation. 5704
22:17 which we are not cleansed **u** this day, 5704
23:13 u ye perish from off this good land which 5704
23:15 **u** he have destroyed you from off this good 5704

Jdg 4:24 **u** they had destroyed Jabin king of 834+5704
5: 7 ceased in Israel, **u** that I Deborah arose, 5704
6:18 **u** I come unto thee, and bring forth my 5704
6:18 he said, I will tarry **u** thou come again. 5704
13:15 **u** we shall have made ready a kid for 2050.1
18:30 his sons were priests to the tribe of Dan **u** 5704
19: 8 they tarried **u** afternoon, and they did eat 5704
19:25 abused her all the night **u** the morning: 5704
20:23 and wept before the Lord **u** even, 5704
20:26 fasted that day **u** even, and offered burnt 5704

Ru 1:19 So they two went **u** they came *to* 5704
2: 7 even from the morning **u** now, 5704+2050.1
2:17 So she gleaned in the field **u** even, 5704
2:21 **u** they have ended all my harvest. 518+5704
3: 3 **u** he shall have done eating and drinking. 5704
3:13 the Lord liveth: lie down **u** the morning. 5704
3:14 she lay *at* his feet **u** the morning: 5704
3:18 **u** thou know how the matter will 834+5704
3:18 **u** he have finished the thing *this* day. 518+3588

1Sa 1:22 *I will not go up* **u** the child be weaned, 5704
1:23 good; tarry **u** thou have weaned him; 5704
1:23 gave her son suck **u** she weaned him. 5704
3:15 Samuel lay **u** the morning, and opened 5704
7:11 smote them, **u** *they came* under Beth-car. 5704
9:13 for the people will not eat **u** he come, 5704
11:11 the Ammonites **u** the heat of the day: 5704
14: 9 thus unto us, Tarry **u** we come to you; 5704
14:24 Cursed *be* the man that eateth *any* food **u** 5704
14:36 spoil them **u** the morning light, and let us 5704
15: 7 Saul smote the Amalekites from Havilah **u** NIH
15:18 fight against them **u** they be consumed. 5704
15:35 came no more to see Saul **u** the day 5704
17:52 **u** thou come *to* the valley, and to the 5704
19: 2 take heed to thyself **u** the morning, 871.1
19:23 **u** he came to Naioth in Ramah. 5704
20:41 one with another, **u** David exceeded. 5704
25:36 less or more, **u** the morning light. 5704
30: 4 **u** they had no more power to weep. 834+5704

2Sa 1:12 wept, and fasted **u** even, for Saul, 5704
4: 3 and were sojourners there **u** this day.) 5704
5:25 smote the Philistines from Geba **u** thou 5704
10: 5 Tarry at Jericho **u** your beards be grown, 5704
15:24 **u** all the people had done passing out of 5704
15:28 **u** there come word from you to certify 5704
17:13 there be not one small stone found 834+5704
19: 7 that befell thee from thy youth **u** now. 5704
19:24 from the day the king departed **u** the day 5704
21:10 from the beginning of harvest **u** water 5704
22:38 turned not again **u** I had consumed them. 5704
23:10 Philistines **u** his hand was weary, 3588+5704

1Ki 3: 1 **u** he had made an end of building his own 5704
3: 2 unto the name of the Lord, **u** those days. 5704
5: 3 **u** the Lord put them under the soles of 5704
6:22 with gold, **u** he had finished all the house: 5704
10: 7 **u** I came, and mine eyes had seen *it:* 834+5704
11:16 **u** he had cut off every male in Edom:) 5704
11:40 and was in Egypt **u** the death of Solomon. 5704
15:29 **u** *he* had destroyed him, according unto 5704
17:14 the day *that* the Lord sendeth rain 5704
18:26 name of Baal from morning even **u** noon, 5704
18:29 they prophesied **u** *the time* of the offering 5704
22:11 the Syrians, **u** thou have consumed them. 5704
22:27 with water of affliction, **u** I come in peace. 5704

2Ki 6:25 **u** an ass's head was *sold* for fourscore 5704
7: 3 one to another, Why sit we here **u** we die? 5704
8: 6 the day that she left the land, even **u** now. 5704
8:11 stedfastly, **u** *he* was ashamed. 5704
10: 8 the entering in of the gate **u** the morning. 5704

2Ki 10:11 his priests, **u** *he* left him none remaining. 5704
17:20 *he* had cast them out of his sight. 834+5704
17:23 **U** the Lord removed Israel out of 834+5704
18:32 **U** I come and take you away to a land like 5704
24:20 **u** he had cast them out from his presence, 5704

1Ch 5:22 they dwelt in their steads in the captivity. 5704
6:32 **u** Solomon had built the house of 5704
12:22 **u** it was a great host, like the host of God. 5704
19: 5 Tarry at Jericho **u** your beards be 834+5704
28:20 **u** *thou* hast finished all the work for 5704

2Ch 8: 8 them did Solomon make to pay tribute **u** 5704
8:16 house of the Lord, and **u** it was finished. 5704
9: 6 **u** I came, and mine eyes had seen *it:* 834+5704
16:12 **u** his disease *was* exceeding *great:* yet in 5704
18:10 With these thou shalt push Syria **u** they 5704
18:26 water of affliction, **u** I return in peace. 5704
18:34 *his* chariot against the Syrians **u** the even: 5704
21:15 thy bowels fall out by reason of 5704
24:10 into the chest, **u** *they* had made an end. 5704
29:28 all *this continued* **u** the burnt offering 5704
29:34 the *other* priests had sanctified 5704
31: 1 **u** *they* had utterly destroyed *them all.* 5704
35:14 of burnt offerings and the fat **u** night: 5704
36:16 the wrath of the Lord arose against his 5704
36:20 his sons **u** the reign of the kingdom of 5704
36:21 the land had enjoyed her sabbaths: 5704

Ezr 4: 5 even **u** the reign of Darius king of Persia. 5704
4:21 *another* commandment shall be given 5705
5:16 since that time even **u** now *hath it been* 5705
8:29 keep *them,* **u** ye weigh *them* before 5704
9: 4 and I sat astonied **u** the evening sacrifice. 5704
10:14 the fierce wrath of our God for this 5704

Ne 7: 3 not the gates of Jerusalem be opened **u** 5704
8: 3 water gate from the morning **u** midday, 5704
12:23 even **u** the days of Johanan the son of 5704

Job 14:13 keep me secret, **u** thy wrath be past, 5704
26:10 the day and night come to an end. 5704

Ps 36: 2 **u** his iniquity be found to be hateful. NIH
57: 1 my refuge, **u** *these* calamities be overpast. 5704
71:18 **u** I have shewed thy strength unto *this* 5704
73:17 **U** I went into the sanctuary of God; *then* 5704
94:13 the pit be digged for the wicked. 5704
104:23 his work and to his labour **u** the evening. 5704
105:19 **U** the time that his word came: the word 5704
110: 1 **u** I make thine enemies thy footstool. 5704
112: 8 **u** he see *his desire* upon his enemies 834+5704
123: 2 our God, **u** that he have mercy upon us. 5704
132: 5 **U** I find out a place for the Lord, 5704

Pr 7:18 let us take our fill of love **u** the morning: 5704

SS 2:17 **U** the day break, and the shadows 5704+7945
3: 4 **u** I had brought him into my 5704+7945
4: 6 **U** the day break, and the shadows 5704+7945
8: 4 nor awake *my* love, **u** he please. 5704+7945

Isa 5:11 that continue **u** night, *till* wine inflame 871.1
6:11 **U** the cities be wasted without 518+834+5704
26:20 the indignation be overpast. 5704
32:15 **U** the spirit be poured upon us from on 5704
36:17 **U** I come and take you away to a land 5704
39: 6 fathers have laid up in store **u** this day, 5704
62: 1 **u** the righteousness thereof go forth as 5704

Jer 23:20 **u** he have executed, and till he have 5704
27: 7 son, **u** the very time of his land come: 5704
27: 8 **u** I have consumed them by his hand. 5704
27:22 there shall they be **u** the day that I visit 5704
30:24 **u** he have done *it,* and until he have 5704
30:24 he have performed the intents of his 5704
32: 5 there shall he be **u** I visit him, saith 5704
36:23 **u** all the roll was consumed in the fire 5704
37:21 all the bread in the city were spent. 5704
38:28 prison **u** the day that Jerusalem was taken: 5704
44:27 by the famine, **u** there be an end of them. 5704
52:34 every day a portion **u** the day of his death, 5704

Eze 21:27 shall be no *more,* **u** he come whose right 5704
33:22 **u** *he* came to me in the morning; 5704
46: 2 the gate shall not be shut **u** the evening. 5704

Da 4:32 **u** thou know that the most High 1768+5705
7:22 **U** the Ancient of days came, 1768+5705
7:25 they shall be given into his hand **u** a time 5705
9:27 even **u** the consummation, 5704

Hos 7: 4 hath kneaded the dough, **u** it be leavened. 5704

Mic 5: 3 the time *that* she which travaileth hath 5704
7: 9 he plead my cause, 834+5704

Zep 3: 8 **u** the day that I rise up to the prey: 3807.1

Mt 1:17 from David **u** the carrying away into 2193
2:13 be thou there **u** I bring thee word: 302+2193
2:15 And was there **u** the death of Herod: that 2193
11:12 And from the days of John the Baptist **u** 2193
11:13 and the law prophesied **u** John. 2193
11:23 it would have remained **u** this day. 3360
13:30 Let both grow together **u** the harvest: 3360
17: 9 the vision to no *man,* **u** the Son 2193+3739
18:22 I say not unto thee, **U** seven times: 2193
18:22 seven times: but, **U** seventy times seven. 2193
24:38 the day that Noe entered into the ark, 891
24:39 And knew not **u** the flood came, 2193
26:29 **u** that day when I drink it new with you 2193
27:64 the sepulchre be made sure **u** the third 2193
28:15 reported among the Jews **u** this day. 3360

Mk 14:25 the day *that* I drink it new in 2193
15:33 there was darkness over the whole land **u** 2193

Lk 1:20 **u** the day that these *things* shall be 891
13:35 me, **u** *the time* come when ye shall say, 2193
15: 4 go after that which is lost, **u** he find it? 2193
16:16 The law and the prophets *were* **u** John: 2193
17:27 **u** the day that Noe entered into 891+3739

Lk 21:24 u the times of the Gentiles be 891+3739
 22:16 u it be fulfilled in the kingdom of 2193+3748
 22:18 u the kingdom of God shall come. 2193+3739
 23:44 there was a darkness over all the earth u 2193
 24:49 ye be endued with power from 2193+3739
Jn 2:10 but thou hast kept the good wine u now. 2193
 9:18 they called the parents of him 2193+3748
Ac 1: 2 U the day in which he was taken up, 891
 2:35 U I make thy foes thy footstool. 302+2193
 3:21 Whom the heaven must receive u the 891
 10:30 Four days ago I was fasting u this hour; 3360
 13:20 and fifty years, u Samuel the prophet. 2193
 20: 7 and continued his speech u midnight. 3360
 21:26 u that an offering should be offered for 2193
 23: 1 all good conscience before God u this day. 891
 23:14 that we will eat nothing u we have 2193+3739
Ro 5:13 For u the law sin was in the world: but sin 891
 8:22 and travaileth in pain together u now. 891
 11:25 u the fulness of the Gentiles be come 891+3739
1Co 4: 5 before the time, u the Lord come, 302+2193
 16: 8 But I will tarry at Ephesus u Pentecost. 2193
2Co 3:14 for u this day remaineth the same vail 891
Gal 4: 2 u the time appointed of the father. 891
 4:19 of whom I travail in birth again u 891+3739
Eph 1:14 u the redemption of the purchased 1519
Php 1: 5 in the gospel from the first day u now; 891
 1: 6 will perform it u the day of Jesus Christ; 891
2Th 2: 7 only he who now letteth will let, u he be 2193
1Ti 6:14 u the appearing of our Lord Jesus Christ: 3360
Heb 1:13 u I make thine enemies thy footstool? 302+2193
 9:10 on them u the time of reformation. 3360
Jas 5: 7 u he receive the early and latter rain. 302+2193
2Pe 1:19 u the day dawn, and the day star 2193+3739
1Jn 2: 9 his brother, is in darkness even u now. 2193
Rev 6:11 u their fellowservants also and their 2193
 17:17 u the words of God shall be fulfilled. 891
 20: 5 But the rest of the dead lived not again u 2193

UNTIMELY (4) [TIME]

Job 3:16 Or as a hidden u birth I had not been; 5309
Ps 58: 8 like the u birth of a woman, that they 5309
Ecc 6: 3 I say, that an u birth is better than he. 5309
Rev 6:13 even as a fig tree casteth her u figs, when 3653

UNTO (9005) [HEREUNTO, THEREUNTO, WHEREUNTO] See Index of Articles, Etc.

UNTOWARD (1)

Ac 2:40 Save yourselves from this u generation. 4646

UNWALLED (3) [WALL]

Dt 3: 5 and bars; beside u towns a great many. 6521
Est 9:19 of the villages, that dwelt in the u towns, 6519
Eze 38:11 I will go up to the land of u villages; 6519

UNWASHEN (3) [WASH]

Mt 15:20 but to eat with u hands defileth not a man. 449
Mk 7: 2 is to say, with u, hands, they found fault. 449
 7: 5 of the elders, but eat bread with u hands? 449

UNWEIGHED (1) [WEIGH]

1Ki 7:47 Solomon left all the vessels u, because NIH

UNWISE (4) [WISDOM]

Dt 32: 6 the LORD, O foolish people and u? 2450+3808
Hos 13:13 is an u son; for he should not stay 2450+3808
Ro 1:14 barbarians; both to the wise, and to the u. 453
Eph 5:17 Wherefore be ye not u, 878

UNWITTINGLY (3) [WIT]

Lev 22:14 if a man eat of the holy thing u, 7684+871.1
Jos 20: 3 and u may flee thither: 1097+1847+871.1
 20: 5 he smote his neighbour u, 1097+1847+871.1

UNWORTHILY (2) [UNWORTHY]

1Co 11:27 and drink this cup of the Lord u, shall be 371
 11:29 For he that eateth and drinketh u, eateth 371

UNWORTHY (2) [UNWORTHILY, WORTH]

Ac 13:46 judge yourselves of everlasting life, 514+3756
1Co 6: 2 are ye u to judge the smallest matters? 370

UP (2381) [UPON, UPPER, UPPERMOST, UPSIDE, UPWARD] See Index of Articles, Etc.

UPBRAID (2) [UPBRAIDED, UPBRAIDETH]

Jdg 8:15 with whom ye did u me, saying, 2778
Mt 11:20 began he to u the cities wherein most 3679

UPBRAIDED (1) [UPBRAID]

Mk 16:14 and u them with their unbelief and 3679

UPBRAIDETH (1) [UPBRAID]

Jas 1: 5 that giveth to all men liberally, and u not; 3679

UPHARSIN (1)

Da 5:25 MENE, MENE, TEKEL, U. 6537+2050.3

UPHAZ (2)

Jer 10: 9 gold from U, the work of the workman, 210
Da 10: 5 loins were girded with fine gold of U: 210

UPHELD (1) [UPHOLD]

Isa 63: 5 salvation unto me; and my fury, it u me. 5564

UPHOLD (8) [UPHELD, UPHOLDEN, UPHOLDEST, UPHOLDETH, UPHOLDING]

Ps 51:12 salvation; and u me with thy free spirit. 5564
 54: 4 the Lord is with them that u my soul. 5564
 119:116 U me according unto thy word, that I 5564
Pr 29:23 but honour shall u the humble in spirit. 8551
Isa 41:10 I will u thee with the right hand of my 8551
 42: 1 Behold my servant, whom I u; mine elect, 8551
 63: 5 and I wondered that there was none to u: 5564
Eze 30: 6 They also that u Egypt shall fall; 5564

UPHOLDEN (2) [UPHOLD]

Job 4: 4 Thy words have u him that was falling, 6965
Pr 20:28 the king: and his throne is u by mercy. 5582

UPHOLDEST (1) [UPHOLD]

Ps 41:12 thou u me in mine integrity, and settest 8551

UPHOLDETH (4) [UPHOLD]

Ps 37:17 be broken: but the LORD u the righteous. 5564
 37:24 for the LORD u him with his hand. 5564
 63: 8 hard after thee: thy right hand u me. 8551
 145:14 The LORD u all that fall, and raiseth up 5564

UPHOLDING (1) [UPHOLD]

Heb 1: 3 and u all things by the word of his power, 5342

UPON (2763) [THEREUPON, UP, WHEREUPON] See Index of Articles, Etc.

UPPER (25) [UP]

Ex 12: 7 and on the u door post of the houses, 4947
Lev 13:45 he shall put a covering upon his u lip, 8222
Dt 24: 6 the nether or the u millstone to pledge: 7393
Jos 15:19 he gave her the u springs, and the nether 5942
 16: 5 Ataroth-addar, unto Beth-horon the u; 5945
Jdg 1:15 Caleb gave her the u springs and the 5942
2Ki 1: 2 in his u chamber that was in Samaria, 5944
 18:17 and stood by the conduit of the u pool, 5945
 23:12 on the top of the u chamber of Ahaz, 5944
1Ch 7:24 the nether, and the u, and Uzzen-sherah.) 5945
 28:11 the u chambers thereof, and of the inner 5944
2Ch 3: 9 he overlaid the u chambers with gold. 5944
 8: 5 Also he built Beth-horon the u, 5945
 32:30 This same Hezekiah also stopped the u 5945
Isa 7: 3 at the end of the conduit of the u pool in 5945
 36: 2 he stood by the conduit of the u pool in 5945
Eze 42: 5 Now the u chambers were shorter: 5945
Zep 2:14 bittern shall lodge in the u lintels of it; 3730
Mk 14:15 And he will shew you a large u room 508
Lk 22:12 And he shall shew you a large u room 508
Ac 1:13 went up into an u room, where abode 5253
 9:37 washed, they laid her in an u chamber. 5253
 9:39 they brought him into the u chamber: 5253
 19: 1 Paul having passed through the u coasts 510
 20: 8 there were many lights in the u chamber, 5253

UPPERMOST (6) [UP]

Ge 40:17 in the u basket there was of all manner 5945
Isa 17: 6 or three berries in the top of the u bough, 534
 17: 9 an u branch, which they left because of NIH
Mt 23: 6 And love the u rooms at feasts, 4411
Mk 12:39 synagogues, and the u rooms at feasts: 4411
Lk 11:43 ye love the u seats in the synagogues, 4410

UPRIGHT (68) [UPRIGHTNESS]

Ge 37: 7 and lo, my sheaf arose, and also stood u; 5324
Ex 15: 8 the floods stood u as a heap, and the 5324
Lev 26:13 bands of your yoke, and made you go u. 6968
1Sa 29: 6 thou hast been u, and thy going out and 3477
2Sa 22:24 I was also u before him, and have kept 8549
 22:26 with the u man thou wilt shew thyself 8549
 22:26 upright man thou wilt shew thyself u. 8552
2Ch 29:34 for the Levites were more u in heart to 3477
Job 1: 1 that man was perfect and u, and one that 3477
 1: 8 a perfect and an u man, one that feareth 3477
 2: 3 a perfect and an u man, one that feareth 3477
 8: 6 If thou wert pure and u; surely now he 3477
 12: 4 the just u man is laughed to scorn. 8549
 17: 8 U men shall be astonied at this, 3477
Ps 7:10 is of God, which saveth the u in heart. 3477
 11: 2 they may privily shoot at the u in heart. 3477
 11: 7 his countenance doth behold the u. 3477
 18:23 I was also u before him, and I kept myself 8549
 18:25 with an u man thou wilt shew thyself 8549
 18:25 an upright man thou wilt shew thyself u; 8552
 19:13 shall I be u, and I shall be innocent from 8552
 20: 8 and fallen: but we are risen, and stand u. 5749
 25: 8 Good and u is the LORD: therefore 3477
 32:11 shout for joy, all ye that are u in heart. 3477
 33: 1 righteous: for praise is comely for the u. 3477
 36:10 and thy righteousness to the u in heart. 3477
 37:14 and to slay such as be of u conversation. 3477
 37:18 The LORD knoweth the days of the u: 8549
 37:37 Mark the perfect man, and behold the u: 3477
 49:14 the u shall have dominion over them in 3477
 64:10 in him; and all the u in heart shall glory. 3477
 92:15 To shew that the LORD is u: he is my 3477
 94:15 and all the u in heart shall follow it. 3477
 97:11 and gladness for the u in heart. 3477
 111: 1 in the assembly of the u, and in 3477
 112: 2 the generation of the u shall be blessed. 3477
 112: 4 Unto the u there ariseth light in 3477
 119:137 O LORD, and u are thy judgments. 3477
 125: 4 and to them that are u in their hearts. 3477

Ps 140:13 name: the u shall dwell in thy presence. 3477
Pr 2:21 For the u shall dwell in the land, 3477
 10:29 The way of the LORD is strength to the u: 8537
 11: 3 The integrity of the u shall guide them: 3477
 11: 6 The righteousness of the u shall deliver 3477
 11:11 By the blessing of the u the city is exalted: 3477
 11:20 such as are u in their way are his delight. 8549
 12: 6 but the mouth of the u shall deliver them. 3477
 13: 6 Righteousness keepeth him that is u in 8537
 14:11 but the tabernacle of the u shall flourish. 3477
 15: 8 but the prayer of the u is his delight. 3477
 16:17 highway of the u is to depart from evil: 3477
 21:18 and the transgressor for the u. 3477
 21:29 but as for the u, he directeth his way. 3477
 28:10 u shall have good things in possession. 8549
 29:10 The bloodthirsty hate the u: but the just 8535
 29:27 he that is u in the way is abomination to 3477
Ecc 7:29 have I found, that God hath made man u; 3477
 12:10 which was written was u, even words 3476
SS 1: 4 love more than wine: the u love thee. 4339
Isa 26: 7 thou, most u, dost weigh the path of 3477
Jer 10: 5 are u as the palm tree, but speak not: 4749
Da 8:18 but he touched me, and set me u. 5921+5977
 10:11 that I speak unto thee, and stand u: 5921+5977
 11:17 whole kingdom, and u ones with him; 3477
Mic 7: 2 there is none u among men: they all lie 3477
 7: 4 the most u is sharper than a thorn hedge: 3477
Hab 2: 4 his soul which is lifted up is not u in him: 3474
Ac 14:10 with a loud voice, Stand u on thy feet. 3717

UPRIGHTLY (12) [UPRIGHTNESS]

Ps 15: 2 He that walketh u, 8549
 58: 1 do ye judge u, O ye sons of men? 4339
 75: 2 receive the congregation I will judge u. 4339
 84:11 withhold from them that walk u. 8549+871.1
Pr 2: 7 he is a buckler to them that walk u. 8537
 10: 9 He that walketh u walketh surely: 8537+871.1
 15:21 but a man of understanding walketh u. 3474
 28:18 Whoso walketh u shall be saved: 8549
Isa 33:15 that walketh righteously, and speaketh u; 4339
Am 5:10 and they abhor him that speaketh u. 8549
Mic 2: 7 my words do good to him that walketh u? 3477
Gal 2:14 But when I saw that they walked not u 3716

UPRIGHTNESS (19) [UPRIGHT, UPRIGHTLY]

Dt 9: 5 or for the u of thine heart, 3476
1Ki 3: 6 in u of heart with thee, 3483
 9: 4 in integrity of heart, and in u, 3476
1Ch 29:17 triest the heart, and hast pleasure in u. 4339
 29:17 in the u of mine heart I have willingly 3476
Job 4: 6 thy hope; and the u of thy ways? 8537
 33: 3 My words shall be of the u of my heart: 3476
 33:23 a thousand, to shew unto man his u: 3476
Ps 9: 8 minister judgment to the people in u. 4339
 25:21 Let integrity and u preserve me; for I wait 3476
 111: 8 and ever, and are done in truth and u. 3477
 119: 7 I will praise thee with u of heart, when I 3476
 143:10 spirit is good; lead me into the land of u. 4334
Pr 2:13 Who leave the paths of u, to walk in 3476
 14: 2 He that walketh in his u feareth 3476
 28: 6 Better is the poor that walketh in his u, 8537
Isa 26: 7 way of the just is u: thou, most upright, 4339
 26:10 in the land of u will he deal unjustly, 5229
 57: 2 in their beds, each one walking in his u. 5228

UPRISING (1)

Ps 139: 2 knowest my downsitting and mine u, 6965

UPROAR (8)

1Ki 1:41 is this noise of the city being in an u? 1993
Mt 26: 5 Not on the feast day, lest there be an u 2351
Mk 14: 2 Not on the feast day, lest there be an u of 2351
Ac 17: 5 set all the city on an u, and assaulted 2350
 19:40 be called in question for this day's u, 4714
 20: 1 And after the u was ceased, Paul called 2351
 21:31 the band, that all Jerusalem was in an u. 4797
 21:38 which before these days madest an u, 387

UPSIDE (5) [UP]

2Ki 21:13 wiping it, and turning it u down. 5921+6440
Ps 146: 9 way of the wicked he turneth u down. 5791
Isa 24: 1 turneth it u down, and scattereth abroad 6440
 29:16 Surely your turning of things u down 2017
Ac 17: 6 These that have turned the world u down 387

UPWARD (61) [UP]

Ge 7:20 Fifteen cubits u 4480+4605+1886.5+3807.1
Ex 38:26 from twenty years old and u, 4605+1886.5
Nu 1: 3 From twenty years old and u, 4605+1886.5
 1:18 years old and u, by their polls. 4605+1886.5
 1:20 from twenty years old and u, 4605+1886.5
 1:22 from twenty years old and u, 4605+1886.5
 1:24 from twenty years old and u, 4605+1886.5
 1:26 from twenty years old and u, 4605+1886.5
 1:28 from twenty years old and u, 4605+1886.5
 1:30 from twenty years old and u, 4605+1886.5
 1:32 from twenty years old and u, 4605+1886.5
 1:34 from twenty years old and u, 4605+1886.5
 1:36 from twenty years old and u, 4605+1886.5
 1:38 from twenty years old and u, 4605+1886.5
 1:40 from twenty years old and u, 4605+1886.5
 1:42 from twenty years old and u, 4605+1886.5
 1:45 from twenty years old and u, 4605+1886.5
 3:15 and u shalt thou number them. 4605+1886.5
 3:22 males, from a month old and u, 4605+1886.5

Nu	3:28 from a month old and **u**, were	4605+1886.5
	3:34 from a month old and **u**, were six	4605+1886.5
	3:39 males from a month old and **u**,	4605+1886.5
	3:40 Israel from a month old and **u**,	4605+1886.5
	3:43 from a month old and **u**, of those	4605+1886.5
	4: 3 and **u** even until fifty years old,	4605+1886.5
	4:23 **u** until fifty years old shalt thou	4605+1886.5
	4:30 **u** even unto fifty years old shalt	4605+1886.5
	4:35 and **u** even unto fifty years old,	4605+1886.5
	4:39 and **u** even unto fifty years old,	4605+1886.5
	4:43 and **u** even unto fifty years old,	4605+1886.5
	4:47 and **u** even unto fifty years old,	4605+1886.5
	8:24 **u** they shall go in to wait upon	4605+1886.5
	14:29 from twenty years old and **u**,	4605+1886.5
	26: 2 from twenty years old and **u**,	4605+1886.5
	26:62 males from a month old and **u**:	4605+1886.5
	32:11 from twenty years old and **u**,	4605+1886.5
Jdg	1:36 Akrabbim, from the rock, and **u**.	4605+1886.5
1Sa	9: 2 **u** he was higher than any of	4605+1886.5
	10:23 people from his shoulders and **u**.	4605+1886.5
2Ki	3:21 **u**, and stood in the border.	4605+1886.5
	19:30 and bear fruit **u**.	4605+1886.5+3807.1
1Ch	23: 3 the age of thirty years and **u**:	4605+1886.5
	23:24 the age of twenty years and **u**.	4605+1886.5
2Ch	31:16 three years old and **u**,	4605+1886.5+3807.1
	31:17 twenty years old and **u**,	4605+1886.5+3807.1
Ezr	3: 8 from twenty years old and **u**,	4605+1886.5
Job	5: 7 born unto trouble, as the sparks fly **u**.	1361
Ecc	3:21 of man that goeth **u**,	4605+1886.5+3807.1
Isa	8:21 their God, and look **u**.	4605+1886.5+3807.1
	37:31 and bear fruit **u**.	4605+1886.5+3807.1
	38:14 mine eyes fail with looking **u**: O Lᴏʀᴅ,	4791
Eze	1:11 were stretched **u**;	4480+4605+3807.1
	1:27 of his loins even **u**,	4605+1886.5+3807.1
	8: 2 from his loins even **u**,	4605+1886.5+3807.1
	41: 7 a winding about still **u**	4605+1886.5+3807.1
	41: 7 **u** round about the house	4605+1886.5+3807.1
	41: 7 of the house was still **u**,	4605+1886.5+3807.1
	43:15 **u** shall be four horns.	4605+1886.5+3807.1
Hag	2:15 consider from this day and **u**,	4605+1886.5
	2:18 now from this day and **u**,	4605+1886.5

UR (5)

Ge	11:28 land of his nativity, in **U** of the Chaldees.	218
	11:31 they went forth with them from **U** of	218
	15: 7 I am the Lᴏʀᴅ that brought thee out of **U**	218
1Ch	11:35 of Sacar the Hararite, Eliphal the son of **U**,	218
Ne	9: 7 broughtest him forth out of **U** of	218

URBAN (1)

Ro	16: 9 Salute **U** our helper in Christ,	3773

URBANUS See URBAN

URGE (1) [URGED]

Lk	11:53 the Pharisees began to **u** him vehemently,	1758

URGED (6) [URGE]

Ge	33:11 And he **u** him, and he took it.	6484
Jdg	16:16 **u** him, so that his soul was vexed unto	509
	19: 7 rose up to depart, his father in law **u** him:	6484
2Ki	2:17 when they **u** him till he was ashamed,	6484
	5:16 And he **u** him to take it; but he refused.	6484
	5:23 he **u** him, and bound two talents of silver	6555

URGENT (2)

Ex	12:33 the Egyptians were **u** upon the people,	2388
Da	3:22 the king's commandment was **u**,	2685

URI (8)

Ex	31: 2 have called by name Bezaleel the son of **U**,	221
	35:30 hath called by name Bezaleel the son of **U**,	221
	38:22 Bezaleel the son of **U**, the son of Hur,	221
1Ki	4:19 Geber the son of **U** was in the country of	221
1Ch	2:20 And Hur begat **U**, and Uri begat Bezaleel.	221
	2:20 And Hur begat Uri, and **U** begat Bezaleel.	221
2Ch	1: 5 that Bezaleel the son of **U**, the son of Hur,	221
Ezr	10:24 of the porters; Shallum, and Telem, and **U**.	221

URIAH (26) [URIAH'S, URIAS, URIJAH]

2Sa	11: 3 of Eliam, the wife of **U** the Hittite?	223
	11: 6 sent to Joab, saying, Send me **U** the Hittite.	223
	11: 6 the Hittite. And Joab sent **U** to David.	223
	11: 7 when **U** was come unto him, David	223
	11: 8 David said to **U**, Go down to thy house,	223
	11: 8 And **U** departed out of the king's house,	223
	11: 9 **U** slept at the door of the king's house with	223
	11:10 saying, **U** went not down unto his house,	223
	11:10 David said unto **U**, Camest thou not from	223
	11:11 **U** said unto David, The ark, and Israel,	223
	11:12 David said to **U**, Tarry here to day also,	223
	11:12 So **U** abode in Jerusalem that day,	223
	11:14 letter to Joab, and sent it by the hand of **U**.	223
	11:15 Set ye **U** in the forefront of the hottest	223
	11:16 that he assigned **U** unto a place where he	223
	11:17 of David; and **U** the Hittite died also.	223
	11:21 Thy servant **U** the Hittite is dead also.	223
	11:24 and thy servant **U** the Hittite is dead also.	223
	11:26 when the wife of **U** heard that Uriah her	223
	11:26 when the wife of Uriah heard that **U** her	223
	12: 9 hast killed **U** the Hittite with the sword,	223
	12:10 hast taken the wife of **U** the Hittite to be	223
	23:39 **U** the Hittite: thirty and seven in all.	223
1Ch	11:41 **U** the Hittite, Zabad the son of Ahlai,	223
Ezr	8:33 hand of Meremoth the son of **U** the priest;	223

Isa	8: 2 **U** the priest, and Zechariah the son of	223

URIAH'S (1) [URIAH]

2Sa	12:15 the Lᴏʀᴅ strake the child that **U** wife bare	223

URIAS (1) [URIAH]

Mt	1: 6 of her that had been the wife of **U**;	3774

URIEL (4)

1Ch	6:24 Tahath his son, **U** his son, Uzziah his son,	222
	15: 5 Of the chief, and his brethren an hundred	222
	15:11 **U**, Asaiah, and Joel, Shemaiah, and Eliel,	222
2Ch	13: 2 was Michaiah the daughter of **U** of Gibeah.	222

URIJAH (12) [URIAH]

1Ki	15: 5 save only in the matter of **U** the Hittite.	223
2Ki	16:10 Ahaz sent to **U** the priest the fashion of	223
	16:11 **U** the priest built an altar according to all	223
	16:11 **U** the priest made it against king Ahaz	223
	16:15 king Ahaz commanded **U** the priest,	223
	16:16 Thus did **U** the priest, according to all that	223
Ne	3: 4 them repaired Meremoth the son of **U**,	223
	3:21 After him repaired Meremoth the son of **U**	223
	8: 4 Anaiah, and **U**, and Hilkiah, and Maaseiah,	223
Jer	26:20 **U** the son of Shemaiah of Kirjath-jearim,	223
	26:21 when **U** heard it, he was afraid, and fled,	223
	26:23 they fet forth **U** out of Egypt,	223

URIM (7)

Ex	28:30 put in the breastplate of judgment the **U**	224
Lev	8: 8 also he put in the breastplate the **U** and	224
Nu	27:21 after the judgment of **U** before the Lᴏʀᴅ:	224
Dt	33: 8 and thy **U** be with thy holy one,	224
1Sa	28: 6 by dreams, nor by **U**, nor by prophets.	224
Ezr	2:63 things till there stood up a priest with **U**	224
Ne	7:65 things, till there stood up a priest with **U**	224

URINE See PISS

US (1449) [WE] See Index of Articles, Etc.

USE (35) [USED, USES, USEST, USETH, USING]

Lev	7:24 with beasts, may be used in any other **u**:	4399
	19:26 neither shall ye **u** enchantment,	5172
Nu	10: 2 that thou mayest **u** them for	1961+3807.1
	15:39 eyes, after which ye **u** to go a whoring:	NIH
Dt	26:14 **u**, nor given ought thereof for the dead:	NIH
2Sa	1:18 the children of Judah the **u** of the bow:	NIH
1Ch	12: 2 could **u** both the right hand and the left	3231
	28:15 according to the **u** of every candlestick.	5656
Jer	23:31 that **u** their tongues, and say, He saith.	3947
	31:23 As yet they shall use this speech in the land	559
	46:11 in vain shalt thou **u** many medicines;	7235
Eze	12:23 they shall no more **u** it as a proverb in	4911
	16:44 proverbs shall **u** this proverb against thee,	4911
	18: 2 that ye **u** this proverb concerning	4911+4912
	18: 3 more to **u** this proverb in Israel.	4911+4912
	21:21 of the two ways, to **u** divination:	7080+7081
Mt	5:44 pray for them which despitefully **u** you,	1908
	6: 7 when ye pray, **u** not vain repetitions,	945
Lk	6:28 pray for them which despitefully **u** you.	1908
Ac	14: 5 **u** them despitefully, and to stone them,	5195
Ro	1:26 natural **u** into that which is against nature:	5540
	1:27 leaving the natural **u** of the woman,	5540
1Co	7:21 if thou mayest be made free, **u** it rather.	5530
	7:31 And they that **u** this world, as not abusing	5530
2Co	1:17 was thus minded, did I **u** lightness?	5530
	3:12 hope, we **u** great plainness of speech:	5530
	13:10 lest being present I should **u** sharpness,	5530
Gal	5:13 only **u** not liberty for an occasion to	NIG
Eph	4:29 that which is good to the **u** of edifying,	5532
1Ti	1: 8 the law is good, if a man **u** it lawfully;	5530
	3:10 then let them **u** the office of a deacon,	1247
	5:23 but **u** a little wine for thy stomach's sake	5530
2Ti	2:21 and meet for the master's **u**,	2173
Heb	5:14 even those who by reason of **u** have their	1838
1Pe	4: 9 **U** hospitality one to another without	NIG

USED (22) [USE]

Ex	21:36 if it be known that the ox hath **u** to push	5056
Lev	7:24 with beasts, may be **u** in any other use:	6213
Jdg	14:10 a feast; for so **u** the young men to do.	6213
	14:20 whom he had **u** as his friend.	3807.1
2Ki	17:17 **u** divination and enchantments,	7080+7081
	21: 6 **u** enchantments, and dealt with familiar	5172
2Ch	33: 6 **u** enchantments, and used witchcraft,	5172
	33: 6 **u** witchcraft, and dealt with a familiar	3784
Jer	2:24 A wild ass **u** to the wilderness,	3928
Eze	22:29 of the land have **u** oppression,	6231+6233
	35:11 according to thine envy which thou hast **u**	6213
Hos	12:10 **u** similitudes by the ministry of	1819
Mk	2:18 of John and of the Pharisees **u** to fast:	1510
Ac	8: 9 beforetime in the same city **u** sorcery,	3096
	19:19 Many also of them which **u** curious arts	4238
	27:17 they **u** helps, undergirding the ship;	5530
Ro	3:13 with their tongues they have **u** deceit;	1387
1Co	9:12 Nevertheless we have not **u** this power;	5530
	9:15 But I have **u** none of these things: neither	5530
1Th	2: 5 For neither at any time **u** we flattering	1096
1Ti	3:13 they that have **u** the office of a deacon	1247
Heb	10:33 companions of them that were so **u**.	390

USELESS See NOUGHT

USES (1) [USE]

Tit	3:14 to maintain good works for necessary **u**,	5532

USEST (1) [USE]

Ps	119:132 as thou **u** to do unto those that love thy	4941

USETH (7) [USE]

Dt	18:10 that **u** divination, or an observer	7080+7081
Est	6: 8 be brought which the king **u** to wear,	NIH
Pr	15: 2 tongue of the wise **u** knowledge aright:	3190
	18:23 The poor **u** intreaties; but the rich	1696+8469
Jer	22:13 that **u** his neighbour's service without	5647
Eze	16:44 every one that **u** proverbs shall use this	4911
Heb	5:13 For every one that **u** milk is unskilful in	3348

USING (2) [USE]

Col	2:22 Which all are to perish with the **u**;) after	671
1Pe	2:16 not **u** your liberty for a cloke of	2192

USUAL See WONT

USURER (1) [USURY]

Ex	22:25 thou shalt not be to him as an **u**,	5383

USURP (1)

1Ti	2:12 nor to **u** authority over the man, but to be	831

USURY (24) [USURER]

Ex	22:25 neither shalt thou lay upon him **u**.	5392
Lev	25:36 Take thou no **u** of him, or increase:	5392
	25:37 shalt not give him thy money upon **u**,	5392
Dt	23:19 shalt not lend upon **u** to thy brother;	5391
	23:19 **u** of money, usury of victuals, usury of	5392
	23:19 of money, **u** of victuals, usury of	5392
	23:19 **u** of any thing that is lent upon usury:	5392
	23:20 a stranger thou mayest lend upon **u**;	5391
	23:20 thy brother thou shalt not lend upon **u**:	5391
Ne	5: 7 rulers, and said unto them, You exact **u**,	4855
	5:10 corn: I pray you, let us leave off this **u**.	4855
Ps	15: 5 He that putteth not out his money to **u**,	5392
Pr	28: 8 He that by **u** and unjust gain increaseth	5392
Isa	24: 2 as with the **taker of u**, so with the giver	5378
	24: 2 of usury, so with the **giver of u** to him.	5383
Jer	15:10 I have neither **lent on u**, nor men have	5383
	15:10 on usury, nor men have **lent** to me **on u**.	5383
Eze	18: 8 He that hath not given forth upon **u**,	5392
	18:13 Hath given forth upon **u**, and hath taken	5392
	18:17 that hath not received **u** nor increase,	5392
	22:12 thou hast taken **u** and increase,	5392
Mt	25:27 I should have received mine own with **u**.	5110
Lk	19:23 I might have required mine own with **u**?	5110

US-WARD (3) [WE]

Ps	40: 5 and thy thoughts which are to **u**:	413+5105.1
Eph	1:19 greatness of his power to **u** who believe,	1473
2Pe	3: 9 but is longsuffering to **u**, not willing that	1473

UTENSILS See FURNITURE

UTHAI (2)

1Ch	9: 4 **U** the son of Ammihud, the son of Omri,	5793
Ezr	8:14 **U**, and Zabbud, and with them seventy	5793

UTMOST (11) [UTTER]

Ge	49:26 unto the **u** bound of the everlasting hills:	8379
Nu	22:36 border of Arnon, which is in the **u** coast.	7097
	22:41 that thence he might see the **u** part of	7097
	23:13 thou shalt see but the **u** part of them,	7097
Dt	34: 2 and all the land of Judah, unto the **u** sea,	314
Jer	9:26 Moab, and all that are in the **u** corners,	7112
	25:23 Buz, and all that are in the **u** corners,	7112
	49:32 all winds them that are in the **u** corners;	7112
	50:26 Come against her from the **u** border,	7093
Joel	2:20 his hinder part towards the **u** sea,	314
Lk	11:31 she came from the **u** parts of the earth	4009

UTTER (46) [UTMOST, UTTERANCE, UTTERED, UTTERETH, UTTERING, UTTERLY, UTTERMOST]

Lev	5: 1 or known of it; if he do not **u** it, then	5046
Jos	2:14 life for yours, if ye **u** not this our business.	5046
	2:20 if thou **u** this our business, then we will be	5046
Jdg	5:12 awake, awake, **u** a song: arise, Barak,	1696
1Ki	20:42 whom I **appointed** to **u** destruction,	2764
Job	8:10 tell thee, and **u** words out of their heart?	3318
	15: 2 Should a wise man **u** vain knowledge,	6030
	27: 4 wickedness, nor my tongue **u** deceit.	1897
	33: 3 and my lips shall **u** knowledge clearly.	4448
Ps	78: 2 in a parable: I will **u** dark sayings of old:	5042
	94: 4 How long shall they **u** and speak hard	5042
	106: 2 Who can **u** the mighty acts of the Lᴏʀᴅ?	4448
	119:171 My lips shall **u** praise, when thou hast	5042
	145: 7 They shall **abundantly u** the memory of	5042
Pr	14: 5 will not lie: but a false witness will **u** lies.	6315
	23:33 and thine heart shall **u** perverse things.	1696
Ecc	1: 8 man cannot **u** it: the eye is not satisfied	1696
	5: 2 let not thine heart be hasty to **u** any thing	3318
Isa	32: 6 and to **u** error against the Lᴏʀᴅ,	1696
	48:20 tell this, **u** it even to the end of the earth;	3318
Jer	1:16 will **u** my judgments against them	1696
	25:30 and **u** his voice from his holy habitation;	5414
Eze	10: 5 wings was heard even to the **u** court,	2435
	24: 3 a parable unto the rebellious house,	4911
	40:31 arches thereof were toward the **u** court;	2435
	40:37 posts thereof were toward the **u** court,	2435
	42: 1 he brought me forth into the **u** court,	2435
	42: 3 the pavement which was for the **u** court,	2435
	42: 7 towards the **u** court on the forepart of	2435
	42: 8 that were in the **u** court was fifty cubits:	2435

U

Eze 42: 9 as one goeth into them from the **u** court,	2435	
42:14 go out of the holy *place* into the **u** court,	2435	
44:19 when they go forth into the **u** court,	2435	
44:19 *even* into the **u** court to the people,	2435	
46:20 *they* bear not out into the **u** court,	2435	
46:21 he brought me forth into the **u** court,	2435	
47: 2 led me about the way without unto the **u**	2351	
Joel 2:11 the LORD shall **u** his voice before his	5414	
3:16 of Zion, and **u** his voice from Jerusalem;	5414	
Am 1: 2 Zion, and **u** his voice from Jerusalem;	5414	
Na 1: 8 will make an **u** end of the place thereof,	3617	
1: 9 he *will* make an **u** end: affliction shall not	3617	
Zec 14:11 there shall be no more **u** destruction;	2764	
Mt 13:35 I will **u** things which have been kept	2044	
1Co 14: 9 except ye **u** by the tongue words easy to	1325	
2Co 12: 4 which *it is* not lawful for a man to **u**.	2980	

UTTERANCE (5) [UTTER]

Ac 2: 4 other tongues, as the Spirit gave them **u**.	669	
1Co 1: 5 by him, in all **u**, and *in* all knowledge;	3056	
2Co 8: 7 **u**, and knowledge, and *in* all diligence,	3056	
Eph 6:19 that **u** may be given unto me,	3056	
Col 4: 3 that God would open unto us a door of **u**,	3056	

UTTERED (17) [UTTER]

Nu 30: 6 she vowed, or **u ought out** of her lips,	4008	
30: 8 **that which** she **u** with her lips,	4008	
Jdg 11:11 Jephthah **u** all his words before the LORD	1696	
2Sa 22:14 and the most High **u** his voice.	5414	
Ne 6:19 deeds before me, and **u** my words to him.	3318	
Job 26: 4 To whom hast thou **u** words?	5046	
42: 3 therefore have I **u** that I understood not;	5046	
Ps 46: 6 he **u** his voice, the earth melted.	5414	
66:14 Which my lips have **u**, and my mouth	6475	
Jer 48:34 *even* unto Jahaz, have they **u** their voice,	5414	
51:55 great waters, a noise of their voice is **u**:	5414	
Hab 3:10 the deep **u** his voice, *and* lift up his hands	5414	
Ro 8:26 for us with groanings which **cannot be u**.	3004	
Heb 5:11 and hard to be **u**, seeing ye are dull of	3004	
Rev 10: 3 had cried, seven thunders **u** their voices.	2980	
10: 4 And when the seven thunders had **u** their	2980	
10: 4 *those things* which the seven thunders **u**,	2980	

UTTERETH (9) [UTTER]

Job 15: 5 For thy mouth **u** thine iniquity,	502	
Ps 19: 2 Day unto day **u** speech, and night unto	5042	
Pr 1:20 she **u** her voice in the streets:	5414	
1:21 in the city she **u** her words, *saying,*	559	
10:18 lips, and he that **u** a slander, *is* a fool.	3318	
29:11 A fool **u** all his mind: but a wise *man*	3318	
Jer 10:13 When he **u** his voice, *there is* a multitude	5414	
51:16 When he **u** *his* voice, *there is* a multitude	5414	
Mic 7: 3 great *man,* he **u** his mischievous desire;	1696	

UTTERING (1) [UTTER]

Isa 59:13 and **u** from the heart words of falsehood.	1897	

UTTERLY (101) [UTTER]

Ex 17:14 I will **u put out** the remembrance	4229+4229	
22:17 If her father **u refuse** to give her	3985+3985	
22:20 the LORD only, he shall be **u destroyed**.	2763	
23:24 thou shalt **u overthrow** them,	2040+2040	
Lev 13:44 shall **pronounce** him **u unclean**,	2930+2930	
26:44 to **destroy** them **u**, and to break my	3615	
Nu 15:31 that soul shall be **u** cut off;	3772+3772	
21: 2 hand, then I will **u destroy** their cities.	2763	
21: 3 they **u destroyed** them and their cities:	2763	
30:12 **u** made them **void** on the day he	6565+6565	
Dt 2:34 **u destroyed** the men, and the women,	2763	
3: 6 we **u destroyed** them, as we did unto	2763	
3: 6 **u destroying** the men, women,	2763	
4:26 ye shall soon **u perish** from off the land	6+6	
4:26 *your* days upon it, but shall be **u** destroyed.	NIH	
7: 2 shalt smite them, *and* **u destroy**	2763+2763	
7:26 *but* thou shalt **u detest** it,	8262+8262	
7:26 detest it, and thou shalt **u abhor** it;	8581+8581	
12: 2 Ye shall **u destroy** all the places,	6+6	
13:15 **destroying** it **u**, and all that *is* therein,	2763	
20:17 thou shalt **u destroy** them;	2763+2763	
31:29 death ye will **u corrupt** *yourselves,*	7843+7843	
Jos 2:10 and Og, whom ye **u destroyed**.	2763	
6:21 they **u destroyed** all that *was* in the city,	2763	
8:26 *he* had **u destroyed** all the inhabitants	2763	
10: 1 had taken Ai, and had **u destroyed** it;	2763	
10:28 the king thereof he **u destroyed**, them,	2763	
10:35 *were* therein he **u destroyed** that day,	2763	
10:37 **destroyed** it **u**, and all the souls that	2763	
10:39 **u destroyed** all the souls that *were*	2763	
10:40 but **u destroyed** all that breathed,	2763	
11:11 **u destroying** *them:* there was not any	2763	
11:12 of the sword, *and* he **u destroyed** them,	2763	
11:20 that *he* might **destroy** them **u**, *and* that	2763	
11:21 **destroyed** them **u** with their cities.	2763	
17:13 but did not **u drive** them **out**.	3423+3423	
Jdg 1:17 inhabited Zephath, and **u destroyed** it:	2763	
1:28 and did not **u drive** them **out**.	3423+3423	
15: 2 that thou hadst **u hated** her;	8130+8130	
21:11 Ye shall **u destroy** every male,	2763	
1Sa 15: 3 **u destroy** all that they have,	2763	
15: 8 **u destroyed** all the people with the edge	2763	
15: 9 good, and would not **u destroy** them:	2763	
15: 9 vile and refuse, that **destroyed** they **u**.	2763	
15:15 God; and the rest we have **u destroyed**.	2763	
15:18 and **u destroy** the sinners the Amalekites,	2763	
15:20 and have **u destroyed** the Amalekites.	2763	

1Sa 15:21 **things** which should have		
been **u destroyed**,	2764	
27:12 **made** his people Israel **u** to abhor	887+887	
2Sa 17:10 as the heart of a lion, shall **u melt**:	4549+4549	
23: 7 they shall be **u burnt** with fire in	8313+8313	
1Ki 9:21 of Israel also were not able **u** to **destroy**,	2763	
2Ki 19:11 done to all lands, by **destroying** them **u**:	2763	
1Ch 4:41 **destroyed** them **u** unto this day,	2763	
2Ch 20:23 **u** to **slay** and destroy *them:* and when	2763	
31: 1 until *they* had **u destroyed** *them all.*	3615	
32:14 nations that my fathers **u destroyed**,	2763	
Ne 9:31 sake thou didst not **u consume** them,	3617	
Ps 37:24 he fall, he shall not be **u cast down**:	2904	
73:19 they are **u consumed** with terrors.	8552	
89:33 lovingkindness will I not **u take** from him,	6331	
119: 8 thy statutes: O forsake me not **u**.	3966+5704	
119:43 take not the word of truth **u** out of	3966+5704	
SS 8: 7 for love, it would **u** be **contemned**.	936+936	
Isa 2:18 And the idols he shall **u** abolish.	3632	
6:11 without man, and the land be **u** desolate,	8077	
11:15 the LORD shall **u destroy** the tongue of	2763	
24: 3 The land shall be **u emptied**,	1238+1238	
24: 3 be utterly emptied, and **u spoiled**:	962+962	
24:19 The earth is **u broken down**,	7489+7489	
34: 2 he hath **u destroyed** them, he hath	2763	
37:11 done to all lands by **destroying** them **u**;	2763	
40:30 and the young men shall **u fall**:	3782+3782	
56: 3 The LORD hath **u separated** me from	914+914	
60:12 *those* nations shall be **u wasted**.	2717+2717	
Jer 9: 4 for every brother will **u supplant**,	6117+6117	
12:17 I will **u pluck up** and destroy that	5428+5428	
14:19 Hast thou **u rejected** Judah?	3988+3988	
23:39 will **u forget** you, and I will forsake	5377+5382	
25: 9 will **u destroy** them, and make them an	2763	
25:29 and should ye be **u unpunished**?	5352+5352	
50:21 waste and **u destroy** after them, saith	2763	
50:26 cast her up as heaps, and **destroy** her **u**:	2763	
51: 3 her young men; **destroy** ye **u** all her host.	2763	
51:58 walls of Babylon shall be **u broken**,	6209+6209	
La 5:22 thou hast **u rejected** us; thou art	3988+3988	
Eze 9: 6 Slay **u** old *and* young, both	4889+3807.1	
17:10 it not **u wither**, when the east	3001+3001	
27:31 they shall **make** themselves **u bald**	7139+7139	
29:10 make the land of Egypt **u waste**	2721+2723	
11:44 to destroy, and **u** to **make away** many.	2763	
Hos 1: 6 but I will **u take** them **away**.	5375+5375	
10:15 shall the king of Israel **u** be **cut off**.	1820+1820	
Am 9: 8 saving that I will not **u destroy**	8045+8045	
Mic 2: 4 *and* say, We be **u spoiled**:	7703+7703	
Na 1:15 more pass through thee; he is **u** cut off.	3605	
Zep 2: 1 I will **u consume** all *things* from off the	622	
Zec 11:17 his right eye shall be **u darkened**.	3543+3543	
1Co 6: 7 therefore there is **u** a fault among you,	3654	
2Pe 2:12 shall **u perish** in their own corruption;	2704	
Rev 18: 8 and she shall be **u burnt** with fire:	2618	

UTTERMOST (28) [UTTER]

Ex 26: 4 likewise shalt thou make in the **u** edge of	7020	
36:11 likewise he made in the **u** side of *another*	7020	
36:17 he made fifty loops upon the **u** edge of	7020	
Nu 11: 1 consumed *them that were* in the **u parts**	7097	
20:16 in Kadesh, a city in the **u** of thy border:	7097	
Dt 11:24 even unto the **u** sea shall your coast be.	314	
Jos 15: 1 *was* the **u part** of the south *coast.*	4480+7097	
15: 5 the bay of the sea at the **u part** of Jordan:	7097	
15:21 the **u** cities of the tribe of	4480+7097	
1Sa 14: 2 Saul tarried in the **u part** of Gibeah under	7097	
1Ki 6:24 from the **u part** of the one wing unto	7098	
6:24 unto the **u part** of the other *were* ten	7098	
2Ki 7: 5 when they were come to the **u part** of	7097	
7: 8 when these lepers came to the **u part** of	7097	
Ne 1: 9 cast out unto the **u part** of the heaven,	7097	
Ps 2: 8 the **u parts** of the earth *for* thy possession.	657	
65: 8 They also that dwell in the **u parts** are	7099	
139: 9 *and* dwell in the **u parts** of the sea;	319	
Isa 7:18 that *is* in the **u part** of the rivers of Egypt,		
24:16 From the **u part** of the earth have we	3671	
Mt 5:26 thence, till thou hast paid the **u** farthing.	2078	
12:42 for she came from the **u parts** of the earth	4009	
Mk 13:27 the **u part** of the earth to the uttermost	206	
13:27 part of the earth to the **u part** of heaven.	206	
Ac 1: 8 and unto the **u part** of the earth.	2078	
24:22 I will **know** the **u** of your matter.	1231	
1Th 2:16 the wrath is come upon them to the **u**.	5056	
Heb 7:25 to the **u** that come unto God by him,	3838	

UZ (7)

Ge 10:23 **U**, and Hul, and Gether, and Mash.	5780	
36:28 children of Dishan *are* these; **U**, and Aran.	5780	
1Ch 1:17 **U**, and Hul, and Gether, and Meshech.	5780	
1:42 Jakan. The sons of Dishan; **U**, and Aran.	5780	
Job 1: 1 There was a man in the land of **U**,	5780	
Jer 25:20 all the kings of the land of **U**, and all	5780	
La 4:21 of Edom, that dwellest in the land of **U**;	5780	

UZAI (1)

Ne 3:25 Palal the son of **U**, over against the turning	186	

UZAL (2)

Ge 10:27 And Hadoram, and **U**, and Diklah,	187	
1Ch 1:21 Hadoram also, and **U**, and Diklah,	187	

UZZA (10) [UZZAH]

2Ki 21:18 of his own house, in the garden of **U**:	5798	
21:26 buried in his sepulchre in the garden of **U**:	5798	

1Ch 6:29 Libni his son, Shimei his son, **U** his son,	5798	
8: 7 removed them, and begat **U**, and Ahihud.	5798	
13: 7 and **U** and Ahio drave the cart.	5798	
13: 9 **U** put forth his hand to hold the ark;	5798	
13:10 of the LORD was kindled against **U**,	5798	
13:11 the LORD had made a breach upon **U**.	5798	
Ezr 2:49 The children of **U**, the children of Paseah,	5798	
Ne 7:51 the children of **U**, the children of Phaseah,	5798	

UZZAH (4) [PEREZ-UZZA, PEREZ-UZZAH, UZZA]

2Sa 6: 3 **U** and Ahio, the sons of Abinadab,	5798	
6: 6 **U** put forth *his* hand to the ark of God,	5798	
6: 7 of the LORD was kindled against **U**;	5798	
6: 8 the LORD had made a breach upon **U**.	5798	

UZZEN SHEERAH See UZZEN-SHERAH

UZZEN-SHERAH (1)

1Ch 7:24 the nether, and the upper, and **U**.)	242	

UZZI (11)

1Ch 6: 5 Abishua begat Bukki, and Bukki begat **U**,	5813	
6: 6 **U** begat Zerahiah, and Zerahiah begat	5813	
6:51 his son, **U** his son, Zerahiah his son,	5813	
7: 2 **U**, and Rephaiah, and Jeriel, and Jahmai,	5813	
7: 3 the sons of **U**; Izrahiah: and the sons of	5813	
7: 7 **U**, and Uzziel, and Jerimoth, and Iri, five;	5813	
9: 8 Elah the son of **U**, the son of Michri,	5813	
Ezr 7: 4 Zerahiah, the son of **U**, the son of Bukki,	5813	
Ne 11:22 at Jerusalem *was* **U** the son of Bani,	5813	
12:19 And of Joiarib, Mattenai; of Jedaiah, **U**;	5813	
12:42 **U**, and Jehohanan, and Malchijah,	5813	

UZZIA (1)

1Ch 11:44 **U** the Ashterathite, Shama and Jehiel	5814	

UZZIAH (27) [AZARIAH]

2Ki 15:13 and thirtieth year of **U** king of Judah;	5818	
15:30 twentieth year of Jotham the son of **U**.	5818	
15:32 Jotham the son of **U** king of Judah to	5818	
15:34 did according to all that his father **U** had	5818	
1Ch 6:24 his son, **U** his son, and Shaul his son.	5818	
27:25 the castles, *was* Jehonathan the son of **U**:	5818	
2Ch 26: 1 all the people of Judah took **U**, who *was*	5818	
26: 3 Sixteen years old *was* **U** when he *began*	5818	
26: 8 the Ammonites gave gifts to **U**:	5818	
26: 9 Moreover **U** built towers in Jerusalem at	5818	
26:11 Moreover **U** had a host of fighting *men,*	5818	
26:14 **U** prepared for them throughout all the	5818	
26:18 they withstood **U** the king, and said unto	5818	
26:18 unto him, *It pertaineth* not unto thee, **U**,	5818	
26:19 **U** was wroth, and *had* a censer in his	5818	
26:21 **U** the king was a leper unto the day of	5818	
26:22 the rest of the acts of **U**, first and last,	5818	
26:23 **U** slept with his fathers, and they buried	5818	
27: 2 according to all that his father **U** did:	5818	
Ezr 10:21 Elijah, and Shemaiah, and Jehiel, and **U**.	5818	
Ne 11: 4 Athaiah the son of **U**, the son of	5818	
Isa 1: 1 and Jerusalem in the days of **U**,	5818	
6: 1 In the year that king **U** died I saw also	5818	
7: 1 the son of **U** king of Judah, that Rezin	5818	
Hos 1: 1 in the days of **U**, Jotham, Ahaz,	5818	
Am 1: 1 Israel in the days of **U** king of Judah,	5818	
Zec 14: 1 earthquake in the days of **U** king of Judah:	5818	

UZZIEL (16) [UZZIELITES]

Ex 6:18 Amram, and Izhar, and Hebron, and **U**:	5816	
6:22 the sons of **U**; Mishael, and Elzaphan.	5816	
Lev 10: 4 the sons of **U** the uncle of Aaron,	5816	
Nu 3:19 Amram, and Izehar, Hebron, and **U**.	5816	
3:30 *shall be* Elizaphan the son of **U**.	5816	
1Ch 4:42 Neariah, and Rephaiah, and **U**, the sons	5816	
6: 2 Amram, Izhar, and Hebron, and **U**.	5816	
6:18 and Izhar, and Hebron, and **U**.	5816	
7: 7 Uzzi, and **U**, and Jerimoth, and Iri, five;	5816	
15:10 Of the sons of **U**; Amminadab the chief,	5816	
23:12 Amram, Izhar, Hebron, and **U**, four.	5816	
23:20 *Of* the sons of **U**; Michah the first,	5816	
24:24 *Of* the sons of **U**; Michah: of the sons of	5816	
25: 4 **U**, Shebuel, and Jerimoth, Hananiah,	5816	
2Ch 29:14 the sons of Jeduthun; Shemaiah, and **U**.	5816	
Ne 3: 8 Next unto him repaired **U** the son of	5816	

UZZIELITES (2) [UZZIEL]

Nu 3:27 the Hebronites, and the family of the **U**:	5817	
1Ch 26:23 the Izharites, the Hebronites, *and* the **U**:	5817	

V

VAGABOND (3) [VAGABONDS]

Ge 4:12 fugitive and a **v** shalt thou be in the earth.	5110	
4:14 I shall be a fugitive and a **v** in the earth;	5110	
Ac 19:13 Then certain of the **v** Jews, exorcists,	4022	

VAGABONDS (1) [VAGABOND]

Ps 109:10 Let his children be **continually v**,	5128+5128	

VAIL (45) [VAILS]

Ge 24:65 she took a **v**, and covered herself. 6809
38:14 covered her with a **v**, and wrapped 6809
38:19 laid by her **v** from her, and put on 6809
Ex 26:31 thou shalt make a **v** of blue, and purple, 6532
26:33 thou shalt hang up the **v** under the taches, 6532
26:33 within the **v** the ark of the Testimony, 6532
26:33 the **v** shall divide unto you between 6532
26:35 thou shalt set the table without the **v**, 6532
27:21 of the congregation without the **v**, 6532
30: 6 thou shalt put it before the **v** that *is* by 6532
34:33 with them, he put a **v** on his face. 4533
34:34 he took the **v** off, until he came out. 4533
34:35 Moses *put* the **v** upon his face again, 4533
35:12 the mercy seat, and the **v** of the covering, 6532
36:35 he made a **v** of blue, and purple, 6532
38:27 of the sanctuary, and the sockets of the **v**; 6532
39:34 badgers' skins, and the **v** of the covering, 6532
40: 3 and cover the ark with the **v**. 6532
40:21 set up the **v** of the covering, 6532
40:22 the tabernacle northward, without the **v**. 6532
40:26 the tent of the congregation before the **v**: 6532
Lev 4: 6 the LORD, before the **v** of the sanctuary. 6532
4:17 times before the LORD, *even* before the **v**. 6532
16: 2 *place* within the **v** before the mercy seat, 6532
16:12 beaten small, and bring *it* within the **v** 6532
16:15 bring his blood within the **v**, and do with 6532
21:23 Only he shall not go in unto the **v**, 6532
24: 3 Without the **v** of the Testimony, 6532
Nu 4: 5 they shall take down the covering **v**, 6532
18: 7 every thing of the altar, and within the **v**; 6532
Ru 3:15 Bring the **v** that *thou* hadst upon thee, 4304
2Ch 3:14 he made the **v** of blue, and purple, 6532
SS 5: 7 the keepers of the walls took away my **v** 7289
Isa 25: 7 and the **v** that is spread over all nations. 4541
Mt 27:51 the **v** of the temple was rent in twain from 2665
Mk 15:38 And the **v** of the temple was rent in twain 2665
Lk 23:45 the **v** of the temple was rent in the midst. 2665
2Co 3:13 not as Moses, *which* put a **v** over his face, 2571
3:14 for until this day remaineth the same **v** 2571
3:14 which **v** is done away in Christ. NIG
3:15 Moses is read, the **v** is upon their heart. 2571
3:16 to the Lord, the **v** shall be taken away. 2571
Heb 6:19 which entereth into that within the **v**; 2665
9: 3 And after the second **v**, the tabernacle 2665
10:20 through the **v**, that is to say, his flesh; 2665

VAILS (1) [VAIL]

Isa 3:23 the fine linen, and the hoods, and the **v**. 7289

VAIN (112) [VAINGLORY, VAINLY, VANITIES, VANITY]

Ex 5: 9 and let them not regard **v** words. 8267
20: 7 take the name of the LORD thy God in **v**; 7723
20: 7 him guiltless that taketh his name in **v**. 7723
Lev 26:16 ye shall sow your seed in **v**, for your 7385
26:20 your strength shall be spent in **v**: for your 7385
Dt 5:11 take the name of the LORD thy God in **v**: 7723
5:11 *him* guiltless that taketh his name in **v**. 7723
32:47 For it *is* not a **v** thing for you; because it *is* 7386
Jdg 9: 4 wherewith Abimelech hired **v** and 7386
11: 3 there were gathered **v** men to Jephthah, 7386
1Sa 12:21 *should* ye go after **v** *things*, which cannot 8414
12:21 cannot profit nor deliver; for they *are* **v**. 8414
25:21 Surely in **v** have I kept 8267+1886.1+3807.1
2Sa 6:20 as one of the **v** *fellows* shamelessly 7386
2Ki 17:15 became **v**, and *went* after the heathen that 1891
18:20 Thou sayest, (but *they are but* **v** words,) 8193
2Ch 13: 7 there are gathered unto him **v** men, 7386
Job 9:29 *If* I be wicked, why then labour I in **v**? 1892
11:11 For he knoweth **v** men: he seeth 7723
11:12 For **v** man would be wise, though man be 5014
15: 2 Should a wise *man* utter **v** knowledge, 7307
16: 3 Shall **v** words have an end? 7307
21:34 How then comfort ye me in **v**, seeing *in* 1892
27:12 why then are ye thus **altogether v**? 1891+1892
35:16 Therefore doth Job open his mouth in **v**; 1892
39:16 not hers: her labour *is* in **v** without fear; 7385
41: 9 Behold, the hope of him is in **v**: shall *not* 3576
Ps 2: 1 and the people imagine a **v** *thing*? 7385
26: 4 I have not sat with **v** persons, neither will 7723
33:17 A horse *is* a **v** *thing* for safety: neither 8267
39: 6 Surely every man walketh **in a v shew**: 6754
39: 6 surely they are disquieted **in v**: he heapeth 1892
60:11 from trouble: for **v** *is* the help of man. 7723
62:10 and become not **v** in robbery: 1891
73:13 Verily I have cleansed my heart *in* **v**, 7385
89:47 wherefore hast thou made all men in **v**? 7723
108:12 from trouble: for **v** *is* the help of man. 7723
119:113 I hate **v** thoughts: but thy law do I love. NIH
127: 1 the house, they labour in **v** that build it: 7723
127: 1 the city, the watchman waketh *but* **in v**. 7723
127: 2 *It is* **v** for you to rise up early, to sit up 7723
139:20 *and* thine enemies take *thy* name in **v**. 7723
Pr 1:17 Surely in **v** the net *is* spread in the sight 2600
12:11 he that followeth **v** *persons is* void of 7386
28:19 he that followeth after **v** *persons* shall 7386
30: 9 steal, and take the name of my God *in* **v**. NIH
31:30 Favour *is* deceitful, and beauty *is* **v**: 1892
Ecc 6:12 all the days of his **v** life which he 1892
Isa 1:13 Bring no more **v** oblations; incense *is* an 7723
30: 7 For the Egyptians shall help in **v**, and to 1892
36: 5 *sayest thou*, (but *these are but* **v** words) 8193
45:18 hath established it, he created it not **in v**, 8414
45:19 unto the seed of Jacob, Seek ye **in v**: 8414

Isa 49: 4 I said, I have laboured in **v**, I have spent 7385
49: 4 spent my strength for nought, and **in v**: 1892
65:23 They shall not labour **in v**, nor bring forth 7385
Jer 2: 5 walked after vanity, and are **become v**? 1891
2:30 **In v** have I smitten your 7723+1886.1+3807.1
3:23 Truly in **v** *is salvation hoped for* from 8267
4:14 How long shall thy **v** thoughts lodge 205
4:30 in **v** shalt thou make thyself fair; 7723
6:29 founder melteth **in v**: 7723+1886.1+3807.1
8: 8 certainly **in v** made he *it*; the pen of 8267
8: 8 made he *it*; the pen of the scribes *is* **in v**. 8267
10: 3 For the customs of the people *are* **v**: for 1892
23:16 they **make** you **v**: they speak a vision of 1891
46:11 in **v** shalt thou use many medicines; 7723
50: 9 expert *man*; none shall return **in v**. 7387
51:58 the people shall labour in **v**, and the folk 7385
La 2:14 Thy prophets have seen **v** and 7723
4:17 our eyes as yet failed for our **v** help: 1892
Eze 6:10 I have not said in **v** that *I* would do this 2600
12:24 For there shall be no more any **v** vision 7723
13: 7 Have ye not seen a **v** vision, and have ye 7723
Zec 10: 2 have told falsely; they comfort in **v**: 1892
Mal 3:14 Ye have said, It *is* **v** to serve God: 7723
Mt 6: 7 But when ye pray, **use not v repetitions**, 945
15: 9 But **in v** they do worship me, teaching for 3155
Mk 7: 7 Howbeit **in v** do they worship me, 3155
Ac 4:25 and the people imagine **v** *things*? 2756
Ro 1:21 but became **v** in their imaginations, 3154
13: 4 afraid; for he beareth not the sword **in v**: 1500
1Co 3:20 the thoughts of the wise, that they are **v**. 3152
15: 2 unto you, unless ye have believed **in v**. 1500
15:10 was *bestowed* upon me was not **in v**; 2756
15:14 then *is* our preaching **v**, and your faith *is* 2756
15:14 preaching **v**, and your faith *is* also **v**. 2756
15:17 And if Christ be not raised, your faith *is* **v**; 3152
15:58 that your labour is not **in v** in the Lord. 2756
2Co 6: 1 that ye receive not the grace of God in **v**. 2756
9: 3 lest our boasting of you should be **in v** 2758
Gal 2: 2 any means I should run, or had run, **in v**. 2756
2:21 *come by* the law, then Christ is dead **in v**. 1432
3: 4 Have ye suffered so many *things* **in v**? 1500
3: 4 so many *things* in vain? if *it be* yet **in v**. 1500
4:11 I have bestowed upon you labour **in v**. 1500
5:26 Let us not be desirous of **v glory**, 2755
Eph 5: 6 Let no *man* deceive you with **v** words: 2756
Php 2:16 that I have not run **in v**, neither laboured 2756
2:16 not run in vain, neither laboured **in v**. 2756
Col 2: 8 you through philosophy and **v** deceit, 2756
1Th 2: 1 entrance in unto you, that it was not **in v**: 2756
2: 3 avoiding tempted you, and our labour be **in v**. 2756
1Ti 1: 6 have turned aside unto **v jangling**: 3150
6:20 avoiding profane *and* **v babblings**, 2757
2Ti 2:16 But shun profane *and* **v babblings**: for 2757
Tit 1:10 many unruly and **v talkers** and deceivers, 3151
3: 9 the law; for they are unprofitable and **v**. 3152
Jas 1:26 his own heart, this *man's* religion *is* **v**. 3152
2:20 But wilt thou know, O **v** *man*, that faith 2756
4: 5 Do ye think that the scripture saith **in v**, 2761
1Pe 1:18 from your **v** conversation received by 3152

VAINGLORY (1) [GLORY, VAIN]

Php 2: 3 *Let* nothing *be done* through strife or **v**; 2754

VAINLY (1) [VAIN]

Col 2:18 not **v** puft up by his fleshly mind, 1500

VAIZATHA See VAJEZATHA

VAJEZATHA (1)

Est 9: 9 and Arisai, and Aridai, and **V**, 2055

VALE (9) [VALLEY]

Ge 14: 3 All these were joined together in the **v** of 6010
14: 8 they joined battle with them in the **v** of 6010
14:10 the **v** of Siddim *was* full of slimepits; 6010
37:14 So he sent him out of the **v** of Hebron, 6010
Dt 1: 7 in the, and in the south, and by the sea 8219
Jos 10:40 of the **v**, and of the springs, and all their 8219
1Ki 10:27 *be* as the sycomore trees that *are* in the **v**, 8219
2Ch 1:15 trees that *are* in the **v**, for abundance. 8219
Jer 33:13 in the cities of the **v**, and in the cities of 8219

VALIANT (31) [VALOUR]

1Sa 14:52 or any **v** man, he took him unto him. 2428
16:18 a mighty **v** *man*, and a man of war, 2428
18:17 only be thou **v** for me, and fight 1121+2428
26:15 David said to Abner, *Art* not thou a **v** man? NIH
31:12 All the **v** men arose, and went all night, 2428
2Sa 2: 7 hands be strengthened, and be ye **v**: 1121+2428
11:16 a place where he knew that **v** men *were*. 2428
13:28 be courageous, and be **v**. 1121+2428
17:10 he also *that is* **v**, whose heart *is* as 1121+2428
17:10 and *they* which *be* with him *are* **v** men. 2428
23:20 the son of a **v** man, of Kabzeel, who had 2428
24: 9 *thousand* **v** men that drew the sword; 2428
1Ki 1:42 for thou *art* a **v** man, and bringest good 2428
1Ch 5:18 of **v** men, men able to bear buckler and 2428
7: 2 *they were* **v** men of might in their 1368
10:12 all the **v** men, and took away the body of 2428
11:22 the son of a **v** man of Kabzeel, who had 2428
11:26 the **v** men of the armies *were*, Asahel 1368
28: 1 the mighty *men*, and with all the **v** men, 2428
2Ch 13: 3 in array with an army of **v** men of war, 1368
26:17 priests of the LORD, *that were* **v** men: 2428
28: 6 in one day, *which were* all **v** men; 2428
Ne 11: 6 four hundred threescore and eight **v** men. 2428

VALIANTEST (1) [VALOUR]

Jdg 21:10 twelve thousand men of the **v**, 1121+2428

VALIANTLY (6) [VALOUR]

Nu 24:18 for his enemies; and Israel shall do **v**. 2428
1Ch 19:13 let us **behave** ourselves **v** for our people, 2388
Ps 60:12 Through God we shall do **v**: for he *it is* 2428
108:13 Through God we shall do **v**: for he *it is* 2428
118:15 the right hand of the LORD doeth **v**. 2428
118:16 the right hand of the LORD doeth **v**. 2428

VALLEY (140) [VALE, VALLEYS]

Ge 14:17 the **v** of Shaveh, which *is* the king's dale. 6010
26:17 pitched his tent in the **v** of Gerar. 5158
26:19 Isaac's servants digged in the **v**, 5158
Nu 14:25 and the Canaanites dwelt in the **v**.) 6010
21:12 and pitched in the **v**, that *is* in the country 5158
21:20 Bamoth *in the* **v**, that *is in* the country 1516
32: 9 For when they went up unto the **v** of 5158
Dt 1:24 came unto the **v** of Eshcol, and searched 5158
3:16 half the **v**, and the border, even unto 5158
3:29 So we abode in the **v** over against 1516
4:46 in the **v** over against Beth-peor, 1516
21: 4 bring down the heifer unto a rough **v**, 5158
21: 4 strike off the heifer's neck there in the **v**: 5158
21: 6 over the heifer that is beheaded in the **v**: 5158
34: 3 south, and the plain of the **v** of Jericho, 1237
34: 6 he buried him in a **v** in the land of Moab, 1516
Jos 7:24 they brought them *unto* the **v** of Achor. 6010
7:26 was called, The **v** of Achor, unto this day. 6010
8:11 now *there was* a **v** between them and Ai. 1516
8:13 went that night into the midst of the **v**. 6010
10:12 and thou, Moon, in the **v** of Ajalon. 6010
11: 2 in the **v**, and in the borders of Dor on 8219
11: 8 and unto the **v** of Mizpeh eastward; 1237
11:16 the **v**, and the plain, and the mountain of 8219
11:16 mountain of Israel, and the **v** of the same; 8219
11:17 even unto Baal-gad in the **v** of Lebanon 1237
12: 7 from Baal-gad in the **v** of Lebanon even 1237
13:19 and Zareth-shahar in the mount of the **v**, 6010
13:27 in the **v**, Beth-aram, and Beth-nimrah, 1516
15: 7 border went up toward Debir from the **v** 6010
15: 8 the border went up *by* the **v** of the son of 1516
15: 8 lieth before the **v** of Hinnom westward, 1516
15: 8 which *is* at the end of the **v** of the giants 6010
15:33 And in the **v**, Eshtaol, and Zoreah, 8219
17:16 in the land of the **v** have chariots of iron, 6010
17:16 and *they* who *are* of the **v** of Jezreel. 6010
18:16 lieth before the **v** of the son of Hinnom, 1516
18:16 is in the **v** of the giants on the north, 6010
18:21 and Beth-hoglah, and the **v** of Keziz, 6010
19:14 the outgoings thereof are *in* the **v** 1516
19:27 to the **v** of Jiphthah-el toward the north 1516
Jdg 1: 9 mountain, and in the south, and in the **v**, 8219
1:19 not drive out the inhabitants of the **v**, 6010
1:34 not suffer them to come down to the **v**: 6010
5:15 he was sent on foot into the **v**. 6010
6:33 went over, and pitched in the **v** of Jezreel. 6010
7: 1 of them, by the hill of Moreh, in the **v**. 6010
7: 8 host of Midian was beneath him in the **v**. 6010
7:12 the children of the east lay along in the **v** 6010
16: 4 that he loved a woman in the **v** of Sorek, 5158
18:28 it was in the **v** that *lieth* by Beth-rehob. 6010
1Sa 6:13 *were* reaping *their* wheat harvest in the **v**: 6010
13:18 to the **v** of Zeboim toward the wilderness. 1516
15: 5 to a city of Amalek, and laid wait in the **v**. 5158
17: 2 pitched by the **v** of Elah, and set the battle 1516
17: 3 side: and *there was* a **v** between them. 1516
17:19 the men of Israel, *were* in the **v** of Elah, 6010
17:52 until thou come to the **v**, and to the gates 1516
21: 9 whom thou slewest in the **v** of Elah, 6010
31: 7 Israel that *were* on the *other* side of the **v**, 6010
2Sa 5:18 spread themselves in the **v** of Rephaim. 6010
5:22 spread themselves in the **v** of Rephaim. 6010
8:13 from smiting of the Syrians in the **v** of salt, 1516
23:13 troop of the Philistines pitched in the **v** 6010
2Ki 3:16 upon some mountain, or into some **v**. 1516
3:16 the LORD, Make this **v** full of ditches. 5158
3:17 yet that **v** shall be filled *with* water, that 5158
14: 7 He slew *of* Edom in the **v** of salt ten 1516
23:10 is in the **v** of the children of Hinnom, 1516
1Ch 4:14 the father of the **v** of Charashim, 1516
4:39 *even* unto the east *side* of the **v**, to seek 1516
10: 7 that *were* in the **v** saw that they fled, 6010
11:15 Philistines encamped in the **v** of Rephaim. 6010
14: 9 spread themselves in the **v** of Rephaim. 6010
14:13 again spread themselves abroad in the **v**. 6010
18:12 Edomites in the **v** of salt eighteen 1516
2Ch 14:10 they set the battle in array in the **v** of 1516
20:26 themselves in the **v** of Berachah; 6010
20:26 The **v** of Berachah, unto *this* day. 6010
25:11 went to the **v** of salt, and smote *of* the 1516
26: 9 at the **v** gate, and at the turning *of* the 1516
28: 3 Moreover he burnt incense in the **v** of 1516
33: 6 the fire in the **v** of the son of Hinnom: 1516

2Ch 33:14 on the west *side* of Gihon, in the **v**, even | 5158
35:22 and came to fight in the **v** of Megiddo, | 1237
Ne 2:13 I went out by night by the gate of the **v**, | 1516
2:15 entered by the gate of the **v**, and *so* | 1516
3:13 The **v** gate repaired Hanun, | 1516
11:30 they dwelt from Beer-sheba unto the **v** of | 1516
11:35 Lod, and Ono, the **v** of craftsmen. | 1516
Job 21:33 The clods of the **v** shall be sweet unto | 5158
39:21 He paweth in the **v**, and rejoiceth in *his* | 6010
Ps 23: 4 I walk through the **v** of the shadow | 6010
60: T smote of Edom in the **v** of salt twelve | 1516
60: 6 and mete out the **v** of Succoth. | 6010
84: 6 *Who* passing through the **v** of Baca make | 6010
108: 7 and mete out the **v** of Succoth. | 6010
Pr 30:17 the ravens of the **v** shall pick it out, | 5158
SS 6:11 garden of nuts to see the fruits of the **v**, | 5158
Isa 17: 5 shall be as he that gathereth ears in the **v** | 6010
22: 1 The burden of the **v** of vision. What aileth | 1516
22: 5 the Lord God of hosts in the **v** of vision, | 1516
28: 4 which *is* on the head of the fat **v**, shall be | 1516
28:21 he shall be wroth as *in* the **v** of Gibeon, | 6010
40: 4 Every **v** shall be exalted, | 1516
63:14 As a beast goeth down into the **v**, the | 1237
65:10 the **v** of Achor a place for the herds to lie | 6010
Jer 2:23 see thy way in the **v**, know what thou | 1516
7:31 which *is* in the **v** of the son of Hinnom, | 1516
7:32 nor the **v** of the son of Hinnom, | 1516
7:32 the son of Hinnom, but the **v** of slaughter: | 1516
19: 2 go forth unto the **v** of the son of Hinnom, | 1516
19: 6 nor The **v** of the son of Hinnom, but The | 1516
19: 6 son of Hinnom, but The **v** of slaughter. | 1516
21:13 inhabitant of the **v**, *and* rock of the plain, | 6010
31:40 the whole **v** of the dead bodies, and of | 6010
32:35 which *are* in the **v** of the son of Hinnom, | 1516
32:44 in the cities of the **v**, and in the cities of | 8219
47: 5 is cut off *with* the remnant of their **v**: | 6010
48: 8 the **v** also shall perish, and the plain shall | 6010
49: 4 thy flowing **v**, Õ backsliding daughter? | 6010
Eze 37: 1 set me down in the midst of the **v** which | 1237
37: 2 *there were* very many in the open **v**; | 1237
39:11 the **v** of the passengers *on* the east of | 1516
39:11 and they shall call *it* The **v** of Hamon-gog. | 1516
39:15 till the buriers have buried it in the **v** of | 1516
Hos 1: 5 that I will break the bow of Israel in the **v** | 6010
2:15 and the **v** of Achor for a door of hope: | 6010
Joel 3: 2 will bring them down into the **v** of | 6010
3:12 and come up to the **v** of Jehoshaphat: | 6010
3:14 multitudes in the **v** of decision: | 6010
3:14 for the day of the Lord *is* near in the **v** of | 6010
3:18 and shall water the **v** of Shittim. | 5158
Mic 1: 6 pour down the stones thereof into the **v**, | 1516
Zec 12:11 the mourning of Hadadrimmon in the **v** | 1237
14: 4 west, *and there shall be* a very great **v**; | 1516
14: 5 ye shall flee *to* the **v** of the mountains; | 1516
14: 5 for the **v** of the mountains shall reach | 1516
Lk 3: 5 Every **v** shall be filled, and every | 5327

VALLEYS (28) [VALLEY]
Nu 24: 6 As the **v** are they spread forth, as gardens | 5158
Dt 8: 7 depths that spring out of the **v** and hills; | 1237
11:11 a land of hills and **v**, *and* drinketh water | 1237
Jos 9: 1 in the **v**, and in all the coasts of the great | 8219
12: 8 in the **v**, and in the plains, and in | 8219
1Ki 20:28 he *is* not God of the **v**, therefore will I | 6010
1Ch 12:15 they put to flight all *them* of the **v**, | 6010
27:29 over the herds *that were* in the **v** *was* | 6010
Job 30: 6 To dwell in the clifts of the **v**, *in* caves of | 5158
39:10 or will he harrow the **v** after thee? | 6010
Ps 65:13 the **v** also are covered with corn; | 6010
104: 8 they go down *by* the **v** unto the place | 1237
104:10 He sendeth the springs into the **v**, | 5158
SS 2: 1 the rose of Sharon, *and* the lily of the **v**. | 6010
Isa 7:19 shall rest all of them in the desolate **v**, | 5158
22: 7 thy choicest **v** shall be full *of* chariots, | 6010
28: 1 *are* on the head of the fat **v** of them | 1516
41:18 and fountains in the midst of the **v**: | 1237
57: 5 slaying the children in the **v** under the | 5158
Jer 49: 4 Wherefore gloriest thou in the **v**, | 6010
Eze 6: 3 to the hills, to the rivers, and to the **v**; | 1516
7:16 be on the mountains like doves of the **v**, | 1516
31:12 and in all the **v** his branches are fallen, | 1516
32: 5 and fill the **v** *with* thy height. | 1516
35: 8 in thy **v**, and in all thy rivers, shall they | 1516
36: 4 to the hills, to the rivers, and to the **v**, | 1516
36: 6 to the hills, to the rivers, and to the **v**, | 1516
Mic 1: 4 the **v** shall be cleft, as wax before the fire, | 6010

VALOUR (37) [VALIANT, VALIANTEST, VALIANTLY]
Jos 1:14 all the mighty *men* of **v**, and help them; | 2428
6: 2 king thereof, *and* the mighty *men* of **v**. | 2428
8: 3 out thirty thousand mighty *men* of **v**. | 2428
10: 7 with him, and all the mighty *men* of **v**. | 2428
Jdg 3:29 thousand men, all lusty, and all men of **v**: | 2428
6:12 Lord *is* with thee, thou mighty *man* of **v**. | 2428
11: 1 the Gileadite was a mighty *man* of **v**, | 2428
18: 2 men of **v**, from Zorah and from Eshtaol, | 2428
20:44 thousand men; all these *were* men of **v**. | 2428
20:46 drew the sword; all these *were* men of **v**. | 2428
1Ki 11:28 man Jeroboam *was* a mighty *man* of **v**: | 2428
2Ki 5: 1 he was also a mighty *man* in **v**, but he | 2428
24:14 the princes, and all the mighty *men* of **v**. | 2428
1Ch 5:24 Hodaviah, and Jahdiel, mighty *men* of **v**, | 2428
7: 5 house of *their* fathers, mighty *men* of **v**; | 2428
7: 9 mighty *men* of **v**, *was* twenty thousand | 2428

1Ch 7:11 mighty *men* of **v**, *were* seventeen | 2428
7:40 choice *and* mighty *men* of **v**, chief of | 2428
8:40 the sons of Ulam were mighty *men* of **v**, | 2428
12:21 for they *were* all mighty *men* of **v**, | 2428
12:25 mighty *men* of **v** for the war, | 2428
12:28 a young man mighty of **v**, and *of* his | 2428
12:30 and eight hundred, mighty *men* of **v**, | 2428
26: 6 father: for they *were* mighty *men* of **v**. | 2428
26:30 men of **v**, a thousand and seven hundred, | 2428
26:31 them mighty *men* of **v** at Jazer of Gilead. | 2428
26:32 brethren, men of **v**, were two thousand | 2428
2Ch 13: 3 chosen men, *being* mighty *men* of **v**. | 2428
14: 8 all these *were* mighty *men* of **v**. | 2428
17:13 the men of war, mighty *men* of **v**, *were* | 2428
17:14 with him mighty *men* of **v** three hundred | 2428
17:16 two hundred thousand mighty *men* of **v** | 2428
17:17 Eliada a mighty *man* of **v**, and with him | 2428
25: 6 **v** out of Israel for an hundred talents of | 2428
26:12 the mighty *men* of **v** *were* two thousand | 2428
32:21 which cut off all the mighty *men* of **v**, | 2428
Ne 11:14 mighty *men* of **v**, an hundred twenty and | 2428

VALUE (7) [VALUED, VALUEST]
Lev 27: 8 the priest, and the priest shall **v** him; | 6186
27: 8 ability that vowed shall the priest **v** him. | 6186
27:12 the priest shall **v** it, whether it be good or | 6186
Job 13: 4 of lies, ye *are* all physicians **of no v**. | 457
Mt 10:31 ye are of **more v than** many sparrows. | 1308
27: 9 whom they of the children of Israel did **v**; | 5091
Lk 12: 7 ye are of **more v than** many sparrows. | 1308

VALUED (4) [VALUE]
Lev 27:16 a homer of barley seed *shall be v* at fifty | NIH
Job 28:16 It cannot be **v** with the gold of Ophir, | 5541
28:19 neither shall it be **v** with pure gold. | 5541
Mt 27: 9 of silver, the price of him that was **v**, | 5091

VALUEST (1) [VALUE]
Lev 27:12 as thou **v** it, *who art* the priest, so shall it | 6187

VANIAH (1)
Ezr 10:36 **V**, Meremoth, Eliashib, | 2057

VANISH (3) [VANISHED, VANISHETH]
Job 6:17 What time they wax warm, they **v**: when | 6789
Isa 51: 6 for the heavens shall **v away** like smoke, | 4414
1Co 13: 8 *there be* knowledge, it shall **v away**. | 2673
Heb 8:13 and waxeth old *is* ready to **v away**. | 854

VANISHED (2) [VANISH]
Jer 49: 7 from the prudent? is their wisdom **v**? | 5628
Lk 24:31 him; and he **v out** of their **sight**. | 855+1096

VANISHETH (2) [VANISH]
Job 7: 9 *As* the cloud is consumed and **v away**: | 1980
Jas 4:14 for a little *time*, and then **v away**. | 853

VANITIES (13) [VAIN]
Dt 32:21 have provoked me to anger with their **v**: | 1892
1Ki 16:13 Lord God of Israel to anger with their **v**. | 1892
16:26 Lord God of Israel to anger with their **v**. | 1892
Ps 31: 6 I have hated them that regard lying **v**: | 1892
Ecc 1: 2 Vanity of **v**, saith the Preacher, vanity of | 1892
1: 2 vanities, saith the Preacher, vanity of **v**; | 1892
5: 7 and many words *there are* also *divers* **v**: | 1892
12: 8 Vanity of **v**, saith the Preacher; all *is* | 1892
Jer 8:19 their graven images, *and* with strange **v**? | 1892
10: 8 and foolish: the stock *is* a doctrine of **v**. | 1892
14:22 Are there *any* among the **v** of the Gentiles | 1892
Jnh 2: 8 They that observe lying **v** forsake their | 1892
Ac 14:15 turn from these **v** unto the living God, | 3152

VANITY (86) [VAIN]
2Ki 17:15 they followed **v**, and became vain, | 1892
Job 7: 3 So am I made to possess months of **v**, | 7723
7:16 alway: let me alone; for my days *are* **v**. | 1892
15:31 Let not him that is deceived trust in **v**: | 7723
15:31 in vanity: for **v** shall be his recompence. | 7723
15:35 bring forth **v**, and their belly prepareth | 205
31: 5 If I have walked with **v**, or *if* my foot hath | 7723
35:13 Surely God will not hear **v**, neither will | 7723
Ps 4: 2 *how* long will ye love **v**, and seek after | 7385
10: 7 fraud: under his tongue *is* mischief and **v**. | 205
12: 2 They speak **v** every one with his | 7723
24: 4 who hath not lift up his soul unto **v**, | 7723
39: 5 every man at his best state *is* altogether **v**. | 1892
39:11 like a moth: surely every man *is* **v**. Selah. | 1892
41: 6 if he come to see *me*, he speaketh **v**: | 7723
62: 9 Surely men of low degree *are* **v**, *and* men | 1892
62: 9 *are* altogether *lighter* than **v**. | 1892
78:33 Therefore their days did he consume in **v**, | 1892
94:11 the thoughts of man, that they *are* **v**. | 1892
119:37 Turn away mine eyes from beholding **v**; | 7723
144: 4 Man is like to **v**: his days *are* as a shadow | 1892
144: 8 Whose mouth speaketh **v**, and their right | 7723
144:11 whose mouth speaketh **v**, and their right | 7723
Pr 13:11 Wealth *gotten* by **v** shall be diminished: | 1892
21: 6 treasures by a lying tongue *is* a **v** tossed to | 1892
22: 8 He that soweth iniquity shall reap **v**: | 205
30: 8 Remove far from me **v** and lies: give me | 7723
Ecc 1: 2 **V** of vanities, saith the Preacher, vanity of | 1892
1: 2 vanities, saith the Preacher, **v** of vanities; | 1892
1: 2 the Preacher, vanity of vanities; all *is* **v**. | 1892
1:14 and behold, all *is* **v** and vexation of spirit. | 1892
2: 1 enjoy pleasure: and behold, this also *is* **v**. | 1892
2:11 all *was* **v** and vexation of spirit, | 1892

Ecc 2:15 Then I said in my heart, that this also *is* **v**. | 1892
2:17 unto me: for all *is* **v** and vexation of spirit. | 1892
2:19 myself wise under the sun. This *is* also **v**. | 1892
2:21 his portion. This also *is* **v** and a great evil. | 1892
2:23 taketh not rest in the night. This *is* also **v**. | 1892
2:26 This also *is* **v** and vexation of spirit. | 1892
3:19 no preeminence above a beast: for all *is* **v**. | 1892
4: 4 This *is* also **v** and vexation of spirit. | 1892
4: 7 I returned, and I saw **v** under the sun. | 1892
4: 8 This *is* also **v**, yea, it *is* a sore travail. | 1892
4:16 Surely this also *is* **v** and vexation of spirit. | 1892
5:10 abundance *with* increase: this *is* also **v**. | 1892
6: 2 eateth it: this *is* **v**, and it *is* an evil disease. | 1892
6: 4 For he cometh in with **v**, and departeth in | 1892
6: 9 this *is* also **v** and vexation of spirit. | 1892
6:11 there be many things that increase **v**, | 1892
7: 6 so *is* the laughter of the fool: this also *is* **v**. | 1892
7:15 All *things* have I seen in the days of my **v**: | 1892
8:10 city where they had so done: this *is* also **v**. | 1892
8:14 There is a **v** which is done upon the earth; | 1892
8:14 of the righteous: I said that this also *is* **v**. | 1892
9: 9 thou lovest all the days of the life of thy **v**, | 1892
9: 9 thee under the sun, all the days of thy **v**: | 1892
11: 8 they shall be many. All that cometh *is* **v**. | 1892
11:10 thy flesh: for childhood and youth *are* **v**. | 1892
12: 8 **V** of vanities, saith the Preacher; all *is* | 1892
12: 8 of vanities, saith the Preacher; all *is* **v**. | 1892
Isa 5:18 them that draw iniquity with cords of **v**, | 7723
30:28 to sift the nations with the sieve of **v**: | 7723
40:17 counted to him less than nothing, and **v**. | 8414
40:23 he maketh the judges of the earth as **v**. | 205
41:29 Behold, they *are* all **v**; their works *are* | 205
44: 9 make a graven image *are* all of them **v**; | 8414
57:13 **v** shall take *them*: but he that putteth his | 1892
58: 9 forth of the finger, and speaking **v**; | 205
59: 4 *they* trust in **v**, and speak lies; | 8414
Jer 2: 5 walked after **v**, and are become vain? | 1892
10:15 They *are* **v**, and the work of errors: | 1892
16:19 **v**, and *things* wherein *there is* no profit. | 1892
18:15 They have burnt incense to **v**, and they | 7723
51:18 They *are* **v**, the work of errors: in the time | 1892
Eze 13: 6 They have seen **v** and lying divination, | 7723
13: 8 Because ye have spoken **v**, and seen lies, | 7723
13: 9 shall be upon the prophets that see **v**, | 7723
13:23 Therefore ye shall see no more **v**, | 7723
21:29 Whiles *they* see **v** unto thee, whiles *they* | 7723
22:28 them *with* untempered *morter*, seeing **v**, | 7723
Hos 12:11 surely they are **v**: they sacrifice bullocks in | 7723
Hab 2:13 people shall weary themselves for very **v**? | 7385
Zec 10: 2 the idols have spoken **v**, and the diviners | 205
Ro 8:20 For the creature was made subject to **v**, | 3153
Eph 4:17 Gentiles walk, in the **v** of their mind, | 3153
2Pe 2:18 they speak great swelling *words* of **v**, | 3153

VAPOUR (5) [VAPOURS]
Job 36:27 they pour down rain according to the **v** | 108
36:33 the cattle also concerning the **v**. | 5927
Ps 148: 8 Fire, and hail; snow, and **v**; stormy wind | 7008
Ac 2:19 blood, and fire, and **v** of smoke: | 822
Jas 4:14 It is even a **v**, that appeareth for a little | 822

VAPOURS (3) [VAPOUR]
Ps 135: 7 He causeth the **v** to ascend from the ends | 5387
Jer 10:13 he causeth the **v** to ascend from the ends | 5387
51:16 he causeth the **v** to ascend from the ends | 5387

VARIABLENESS (1) [VARIANCE]
Jas 1:17 with whom is no **v**, neither shadow of | 3883

VARIANCE (2) [VARIABLENESS]
Mt 10:35 For I am come to **set** a man **at v** against | 1369
Gal 5:20 Idolatry, witchcraft, hatred, **v**, emulations, | 2054

VARIED See DIVERS; DIVERSE

VASHNI (1)
1Ch 6:28 of Samuel; the firstborn **V**, and Abiah. | 2059

VASHTI (7)
Est 1: 9 Also **V** the queen made a feast for | 2060
1:11 To bring **V** the queen before the king | 2060
1:12 queen **V** refused to come at the king's | 2060
1:15 What shall we do unto the queen **V** | 2060
1:16 **V** the queen hath not done wrong to | 2060
1:17 The king Ahasuerus commanded **V** | 2060
1:19 That **V** come no *more* before king | 2060
2: 1 remembered **V**, and what she had done, | 2060
2: 4 pleaseth the king be queen instead of **V**. | 2060
2:17 head, and made her queen instead of **V**. | 2060

VAT; VATS See CELLARS; FATS; LIQUORS; PRESSES

VAUNT (1) [VAUNTETH]
Jdg 7: 2 lest Israel **v** themselves against me, saying, | 6286

VAUNTETH (1) [VAUNT]
1Co 13: 4 charity **v** not itself, is not puffed up, | 4068

VEGETABLES See PULSE

VEHEMENT (3) [VEHEMENTLY]
SS 8: 6 coals of fire, *which hath* a **most v flame**. | 7957
Jnh 4: 8 arise, that God prepared a **v** east wind; | 2759
2Co 7:11 yea, *what* fear, yea, *what* **v desire**, yea, | 1972

VEHEMENTLY (5) [VEHEMENT]
Mk 14:31 he spake the more **v**, If I should | 1537+4053

Lk 6:48 the stream **beat v upon** that house, 4366
 6:49 against which the stream did **beat v**, 4366
 11:53 and the Pharisees began to urge *him* v, 1171
 23:10 and scribes stood and **v** accused him. 2159

VEIL, VEILS See KERCHIEFS; LOCKS; MUFFLERS; VAIL; VAILS

VEIN (1)
Job 28: 1 Surely there is a **v** for the silver, 4161

VENGEANCE (45) [AVENGE, AVENGED, AVENGER, AVENGETH, AVENGING, REVENGE, REVENGED, REVENGER, REVENGERS, REVENGES, REVENGETH, REVENGING]
Ge 4:15 **v** shall be **taken** on him sevenfold. 5358
Dt 32:35 To me *belongeth* **v**, and recompence; 5359
 32:41 I will render **v** to mine enemies, 5359
 32:43 will render **v** to his adversaries, and will 5359
Jdg 11:36 forasmuch as the Lord hath taken **v** for 5360
Ps 58:10 shall rejoice when he seeth the **v**: 5359
 94: 1 O Lord God, to whom **v** belongeth; 5360
 94: 1 God, to whom **v** belongeth, shew thyself. 5360
 99: 8 thou **tookest v** of their inventions. 5358
 149: 7 To execute **v** upon the heathen, 5360
Pr 6:34 therefore he will not spare in the day of **v**. 5359
Isa 34: 8 For *it is* the day of the Lord's **v**, 5359
 35: 4 behold, your God will come *with* **v**, 5359
 47: 3 I will take **v**, and I will not meet *thee as* a 5359
 59:17 he put on the garments of **v** *for* clothing, 5359
 61: 2 the Lord, and the day of **v** of our God; 5359
 63: 4 For the day of **v** *is* in mine heart, 5359
Jer 11:20 and the heart, let me see thy **v** on them: 5360
 20:12 and the heart, let me see thy **v** on them: 5360
 46:10 a day of **v**, that *he* may avenge him of his 5360
 50:15 for it *is* the **v** of the Lord: 5360
 50:15 **take v** upon her; as she hath done, do 5358
 50:28 to declare in Zion the **v** of the Lord our 5360
 50:28 of the Lord our God, the **v** of his temple. 5360
 51: 6 for this *is* the time of the Lord's **v**; 5360
 51:11 because it *is* the **v** of the Lord, 5360
 51:11 of the Lord, the **v** of his temple. 5360
 51:36 thy cause, and **take v** for thee; 5358+5360
La 3:60 Thou hast seen all their **v** *and* all their 5360
Eze 24: 8 cause fury to come up to **take v**; 5358+5359
 25:12 the house of Judah by taking **v**, 5358+5359
 25:14 I will lay my **v** upon Edom by the hand of 5360
 25:14 they shall know my **v**, saith the Lord 5360
 25:15 **taken v** with a despiteful heart, 5358+5359
 25:17 I will execute great **v** upon them with 5360
 25:17 when I shall lay my **v** upon them. 5360
Mic 5:15 I will execute **v** in anger and fury upon 5359
Na 1: 2 the Lord will **take v** on his adversaries, 5358
Lk 21:22 For these be *the* days of **v**, that all *things* 1557
Ac 28: 4 the sea, yet **V** suffereth not to live. 1349
Ro 3: 5 *Is* God unrighteous who taketh **v**? (I speak 3709
 12:19 for it is written, **V** *is* mine; I will repay, 1557
2Th 1: 8 taking **v** on them that know not God, 1557
Heb 10:30 **V** *belongeth* unto me, I will recompense, 1557
Jude 1: 7 an example, suffering the **v** of eternal fire. 1349

VENISON (8)
Ge 25:28 loved Esau, because he did eat of *his* **v**: 6718
 27: 3 go out to the field, and take *me* some **v**; 6718
 27: 5 Esau went to the field to hunt for **v**, 6718
 27: 7 Bring me **v**, and make me savoury meat, 6718
 27:19 arise, I pray thee, sit and eat of my **v**, that 6718
 27:25 *it* near to me, and I will eat of my son's **v**, 6718
 27:31 Let my father arise, and eat of his son's **v**, 6718
 27:33 *is* he that hath taken **v**, and brought *it* 6718

VENOM (1) [VENOMOUS]
Dt 32:33 poison of dragons, and the cruel **v** of asps. 7219

VENOMOUS (1) [VENOM]
Ac 28: 4 And when the barbarians saw the **v** beast NIG

VENT (1)
Job 32:19 my belly *is* as wine *which* hath no **v**; 6605

VENTURE (2)
1Ki 22:34 a *certain* man drew a bow at a **v**, 8537
2Ch 18:33 a *certain* man drew a bow at a **v**, 8537

VERIFIED (3) [VERITY]
Ge 42:20 so shall your words be **v**, and ye shall not 539
1Ki 8:26 of Israel, let thy word, I pray thee, be **v**, 539
2Ch 6:17 O Lord God of Israel, let thy word be **v**, 539

VERILY (140) [VERITY]
Ge 42:21 We *are* **v** guilty concerning our brother, 61
Ex 31:13 saying, **V** my sabbaths ye shall keep: 389
Jdg 15: 2 I **v thought** that thou hadst utterly 559+559
1Ki 1:43 **V** our lord king David hath made Solomon 61
2Ki 4:14 **V** she hath no child, and her husband is old. 61
1Ch 21:24 but I will **v buy** *it* for the full price: 7069+7069
Job 19:13 acquaintance are **v** estranged from me. 389
Ps 37: 3 dwell in the land, and **v** thou shalt be fed. 530
 39: 5 every man at his best state *is* altogether 389
 58:11 **V** *there* is a reward for the righteous: 389
 58:11 **v** he is a God that judgeth in the earth. 389
 66:19 *But* **v** God hath heard *me*; he hath attended 403
 73:13 **V** I have cleansed my heart *in* vain, 389
Isa 45:15 **V** thou *art* a God that hidest thyself, O God 403
Jer 15:11 **V** it shall be well with thy remnant; 518+3808
 15:11 **v** I will cause the enemy to entreat 518+3808

Mt 5:18 For **v** I say unto you, Till heaven and earth 281
 5:26 **V** I say unto thee, Thou shalt by no means 281
 6: 2 **V** I say unto you, They have their reward. 281
 6: 5 **V** I say unto you, They have their reward. 281
 6:16 **V** I say unto you, They have their reward. 281
 8:10 **V** I say unto you, I have not found so 281
 10:15 **V** I say unto you, It shall be more tolerable 281
 10:23 for **v** I say unto you, Ye shall not have gone 281
 10:42 **v** I say unto you, he shall in no wise lose 281
 11:11 **V** I say unto you, Among *them that are* 281
 13:17 For **v** I say unto you, That many prophets 281
 17:20 for **v** I say unto you, If ye have faith as a 281
 18: 3 And said, **V** I say unto you, Except ye be 281
 18:13 if so be that he find it, **v** I say unto you, 281
 18:18 **V** I say unto you, Whatsoever ye shall bind 281
 19:23 Jesus unto his disciples, **V** I say unto you, 281
 19:28 Jesus said unto them, **V** I say unto you, 281
 21:21 and said unto them, **V** I say unto you, 281
 21:31 **V** I say unto you, That the publicans and 281
 23:36 **V** I say unto you, All these *things* shall 281
 24: 2 ye not all these *things?* **v** I say unto you, 281
 24:34 **V** I say unto you, This generation shall not 281
 24:47 **V** I say unto you, That he shall make him 281
 25:12 he answered and said, **V** I say unto you, 281
 25:40 and say unto them, **V** I say unto you, 281
 25:45 he answer them, saying, **V** I say unto you, 281
 26:13 **V** I say unto you, Wheresoever this gospel 281
 26:21 as they did eat, he said, **V** I say unto you, 281
 26:34 him, **V** I say unto thee, That this night, 281
Mk 3:28 **V** I say unto you, All sins shall be forgiven 281
 6:11 **V** I say unto you, It shall be more tolerable 281
 8:12 **v** I say unto you, There shall no sign be 281
 9: 1 he said unto them, **V** I say unto you, That 281
 9:12 Elias **v** cometh first, and restoreth all 3303
 9:41 ye belong to Christ, **v** I say unto you, 281
 10:15 **V** I say unto you, Whosoever shall not 281
 10:29 Jesus answered and said, **V** I say unto you, 281
 11:23 For **v** I say unto you, That whosoever shall 281
 12:43 and saith unto them, **V** I say unto you, 281
 13:30 **V** I say unto you, that this generation shall 281
 14: 9 **V** I say unto you, Wheresoever this gospel 281
 14:18 and did eat, Jesus said, **V** I say unto you, 281
 14:25 **V** I say unto you, I will drink no more of 281
 14:30 **V** I say unto thee, That this day, *even* 281
Lk 4:24 he said, **V** I say unto you, No prophet is 281
 11:51 **v** I say unto you, It shall be required of 3483
 12:37 **v** I say unto you, that he shall gird himself, 281
 13:35 and **v** I say unto you, Ye shall not see me, 281
 18:17 **V** I say unto you, Whosoever shall not 281
 18:29 And he said unto them, **V** I say unto you, 281
 21:32 **V** I say unto you, This generation shall not 281
 23:43 And Jesus said unto him, **V** I say unto thee, 281
Jn 1:51 saith unto him, **V**, verily, I say unto you, 281
 1:51 saith unto him, Verily, **v**, I say unto you, 281
 3: 3 answered and said unto him, **V**, verily, 281
 3: 3 answered and said unto him, Verily, **v**, 281
 3: 5 Jesus answered, **V**, verily, I say unto thee, 281
 3: 5 Jesus answered, Verily, **v**, I say unto thee, 281
 3:11 **V**, verily, I say unto thee, We speak that 281
 3:11 Verily, **v**, I say unto thee, We speak that 281
 5:19 said unto them, **V**, verily, I say unto you, 281
 5:19 said unto them, Verily, **v**, I say unto you, 281
 5:24 **V**, verily, I say unto you, He that heareth 281
 5:24 Verily, **v**, I say unto you, He that heareth 281
 5:25 **V**, verily, I say unto you, The hour is 281
 5:25 Verily, **v**, I say unto you, The hour is 281
 6:26 Jesus answered them and said, **V**, verily, 281
 6:26 Jesus answered them and said, Verily, **v**, 281
 6:32 said unto them, **V**, verily, I say unto you, 281
 6:32 said unto them, Verily, **v**, I say unto you, 281
 6:47 **V**, verily, I say unto you, He that believeth 281
 6:47 Verily, **v**, I say unto you, He that believeth 281
 6:53 said unto them, **V**, verily, I say unto you, 281
 6:53 said unto them, Verily, **v**, I say unto you, 281
 8:34 answered them, **V**, verily, I say unto you, 281
 8:34 answered them, Verily, **v**, I say unto you, 281
 8:51 **V**, verily, I say unto you, If a man keep my 281
 8:51 Verily, **v**, I say unto you, If a man keep my 281
 8:58 said unto them, **V**, verily, I say unto you, 281
 8:58 said unto them, Verily, **v**, I say unto you, 281
 10: 1 **V**, verily, I say unto you, He that entereth 281
 10: 1 Verily, **v**, I say unto you, He that entereth 281
 10: 7 **V**, verily, I say unto you, I am the door of 281
 10: 7 Verily, **v**, I say unto you, I am the door of 281
 12:24 **V**, verily, I say unto you, Except a corn of 281
 12:24 Verily, **v**, I say unto you, Except a corn of 281
 13:16 **V**, verily, I say unto you, The servant is not 281
 13:16 Verily, **v**, I say unto you, The servant is not 281
 13:20 **V**, verily, I say unto you, He that receiveth 281
 13:20 Verily, **v**, I say unto you, He that receiveth 281
 13:21 and testified, and said, **V**, verily, I say unto 281
 13:21 and testified, and said, Verily, **v**, I say unto 281
 13:38 **V**, verily, I say unto thee, The cock shall 281
 13:38 Verily, **v**, I say unto thee, The cock shall 281
 14:12 **V**, verily, I say unto you, He that believeth 281
 14:12 Verily, **v**, I say unto you, He that believeth 281
 16:20 **V**, verily, I say unto you, That ye shall 281
 16:20 Verily, **v**, I say unto you, That ye shall 281
 16:23 **V**, verily, I say unto you, Whatsoever ye 281
 16:23 Verily, **v**, I say unto you, Whatsoever ye 281
 21:18 **V**, verily, I say unto thee, When thou wast 281
 21:18 Verily, **v**, I say unto thee, When thou wast 281
Ac 16:37 nay **v**; but let them come themselves and 1063
 19: 4 John **v** baptized *with* the baptism of 3303

Ac 22: 3 I am **v** a man *which am* a Jew, born in 3303
 26: 9 I **v** myself, that *I* ought to do 3303
Ro 2:25 For circumcision **v** profiteth, if thou keep 3303
 10:18 **Yes v**, their sound went into all the earth, 3304
 15:27 It hath pleased them **v**; and their debtors 1063
1Co 5: 3 For I **v**, as absent in body, but present in 3303
 9:18 **V** that, when I preach the gospel, I may NIG
 14:17 thou **v** givest thanks well, but the other 3303
Gal 3:21 **v** righteousness should have been by 3689
1Th 3: 4 For, when we were with you, we told 2532
Heb 2:16 For **v** he took not on *him* the nature of 1222
 3: 5 And Moses *was* faithful in all his house, 3303
 6:16 men **v** swear by the greater: and an oath 3303
 7: 5 And **v** they that are of the sons of Levi 3303
 7:18 For there is a **v** disannulling of 3303
 9: 1 Then **v** the first *covenant* had also 3303
 12:10 they **v** for a few days chastened *us* after 3303
1Pe 1:20 Who **v** was foreordained before 3303
1Jn 2: 5 in him **v** is the love of God perfected: 230

VERITY (2) [VERIFIED, VERILY]
Ps 111: 7 works of his hands *are* **v** and judgment; 571
1Ti 2: 7 a teacher of the Gentiles in faith and **v**. 225

VERMILION (2)
Jer 22:14 *is* cieled with cedar, and painted with **v**. 8350
Eze 23:14 of the Chaldeans pourtrayed with **v**, 8350

VERY (257)
Ge 1:31 he had made, and behold, *it was* **v** good. 3966
 4: 5 Cain was **v** wroth, and his countenance 3966
 12:14 beheld the woman that she *was* **v** fair. 3966
 13: 2 Abram *was* **v** rich in cattle, in silver, 3966
 18:20 great, and because their sin is **v** grievous; 3966
 21:11 the thing was **v** grievous in Abraham's 3966
 24:16 the damsel *was* **v** fair to look upon, 3966
 26:13 and grew until he became **v** great: 3966
 27:21 whether thou *be* my **v** son Esau or not. 2088
 27:24 he said, *Art* thou my **v** son Esau? And he 2088
 27:33 Isaac trembled **v** exceedingly, 3966+5704
 34: 7 they were **v** wroth, because he had 3966
 41:19 poor and **v** ill favoured and leanfleshed, 3966
 41:31 following; for it *shall be* **v** grievous. 3966
 41:49 the sea, **v** much, until he left numbering; 3966
 47:13 the famine *was* **v** sore, so that the land 3966
 50: 9 horsemen: and it was a **v** great company. 3966
 50:10 with a great and **v** sore lamentation: 3966
Ex 1:20 people multiplied, and waxed **v** mighty. 3966
 8:28 only ye shall not go **v far away**; 7368+7368
 9: 3 *there shall be* a **v** grievous murrain. 3966
 9:16 in **v deed** for this cause have I raised thee 199
 9:18 I will cause it to rain a **v** grievous hail, 3966
 9:24 fire mingled with the hail, **v** grievous, 3966
 10:14 **v** grievous *were* they; before them there 3966
 11: 3 Moreover the man Moses *was* **v** great in 3966
 12:38 and flocks, and herds, *even* **v** much cattle. 3966
 30:36 thou shalt beat *some* of it **v** small, 1854
Nu 6: 9 if any man die **v suddenly** 6597+6621+871.1
 11:33 the Lord smote the people *with* a **v** great 3966
 12: 3 (Now the man Moses *was* **v** meek, 3966
 13:28 and the cities *are* walled, *and* **v** great: 3966
 16:15 Moses was **v** wroth, and said unto 3966
 22:17 For I will promote thee unto **v great** 3966
 32: 1 children of Gad had a **v** great multitude 3966
Dt 9:20 the Lord was angry with Aaron to 3966
 9:21 stamped it, *and* **ground** it **v** small, 2912+3190
 20:15 all the cities *which* are **v** far off from thee, 3966
 27: 8 stones all the words of this law **v** plainly. 3190
 28:43 above thee **v high** 4605+4605+1886.5+1886.5
 28:43 thou shalt come down **v low**. 4295+4295
 28:54 **v** delicate, his eye shall be evil toward his 3966
 30:14 word *is* **v** nigh unto thee, in thy mouth, 3966
 32:20 *be:* for they *are* a **v** froward generation, 8419
Jos 1: 7 Only be thou strong and **v** courageous, 3966
 3:16 stood *and* rose up *upon* a heap **v** far, 3966
 8: 4 go not **v** far from the city, but be ye all 3966
 9: 9 From a **v** far country thy servants are 3966
 9:13 shoes are become old by reason of the **v** 3966
 10:20 of slaying them *with* a **v** great slaughter, 3966
 10:27 *which* remain until this **v** day. 6106
 11: 4 with horses and chariots **v** many. 3966
 13: 1 there remaineth *yet* **v** much land to be 3966
 22: 8 with **v** much cattle, with silver, 3966
 22: 8 and with iron, and with **v** much raiment: 3966
 23: 6 Be ye therefore **v** courageous to keep and 3966
Jdg 3:17 king of Moab: and Eglon *was* a **v** fat man. 3966
 11:33 of the vineyards, *with* a **v** great slaughter. 3966
 11:35 thou hast **brought** me **v** low, 3766+3766
 13: 6 of an angel of God, **v** terrible: 3966
 18: 9 seen the land, and, behold, it *is* **v** good: 3966
Ru 1:20 for the Almighty hath dealt **v** bitterly with 3966
1Sa 2:17 the sin of the young men was **v** great 3966
 2:22 Now Eli was **v** old, and heard all that his 3966
 4:10 there was a **v** great slaughter; for there fell 3966
 5: 9 against the city *with* a **v** great destruction: 3966
 5:11 the hand of God was **v** heavy there. 3966
 14:15 quaked: so it was a **v great** trembling. 430
 14:20 *and there was* a **v** great discomfiture. 3966
 14:31 to Aijalon: and the people were **v** faint. 3966
 18: 8 Saul was **v** wroth, and the saying 3966
 18:15 saw that he behaved himself **v** wisely, 3966
 19: 4 his works *have* been to thee-ward **v** good: 3966
 20: 7 if he be **v wroth**, *then* be sure that 2734+2734
 23:22 told me *that* he **dealeth v** subtilly. 6191+6191

1Sa	25: 2 the man *was* **v** great, and he had three	3966
	25:15 the men *were* **v** good unto us, and we	3966
	25:34 For in **v deed**, *as the* LORD God of Israel	199
	25:36 within him, for he *was* **v** drunken:	3966+5704
	26: 4 understood that Saul was come in **v deed**.	3559
2Sa	1:26 **v** pleasant hast thou been unto me:	3966
	2:17 there was a **v** sore battle that day;	3966+5704
	3: 8 was Abner **v** wroth for the words of	3966
	11: 2 the woman *was* **v** beautiful to look upon.	3966
	12:15 the babe unto David, and it was **v sick**.	605
	13: 3 and Jonadab *was* a **v** subtil man.	3966
	13:21 heard of all these things, he was **v** wroth.	3966
	13:36 and all his servants wept **v** sore.	1419+3966
	18:17 laid a **v** great heap of stones upon him:	3966
	19:32 Now Barzillai was a **v** aged man,	3966
	19:32 at Mahanaim; for he *was* a **v** great man.	3966
	24:10 of thy servant; for I have done **v** foolishly.	3966
1Ki	1: 4 the damsel *was* **v** fair,	3966+5704
	1: 6 he also *was* a **v** goodly *man; and his*	3966
	1:15 the king was **v** old; and Abishag	3966
	7:34 the undersetters *were* of the **v** base itself.	NIH
	10: 2 came to Jerusalem with a **v** great train,	3966
	10: 2 and **v** much gold, and precious stones:	3966
	10:10 spices **v** great store, and precious stones:	3966
	19:10 I have been **v jealous** for the LORD	7065+7065
	19:14 I have been **v jealous** for the LORD	7065+7065
	21:26 he did **v** abominably in following idols,	3966
2Ki	14:26 the affliction of Israel, *that it was* **v** bitter:	3966
	17:18 Therefore the LORD was **v** angry with	3966
	21:16 Manasseh shed innocent blood **v** much,	3966
1Ch	9:13 **v able** men *for* the work of the service of	2428
	18: 8 Hadarezer, brought David **v** much brass,	3966
	21: 8 of thy servant; for I have done **v** foolishly.	3966
	21:13 of the LORD; for **v** great *are* his mercies:	3966
	23:17 Rehabiah were **v** many.	4605+1886.5+3807.1
2Ch	6:18 will God in **v deed** dwell with men on	552
	7: 8 all Israel with him, a **v** great congregation,	3966
	9: 1 with a **v** great company, and camels that	3966
	14:13 and they carried away **v** much spoil.	3966
	16: 8 with **v** many chariots and horsemen?	3966
	16:14 a **v** great burning for him.	3966+5704+3807.1
	20:35 king of Israel, who did **v wickedly**:	7561
	24:24 the LORD delivered a **v** great host into	3966
	30:13 the second month, a **v** great congregation.	3966
	32:29 for God had given him substance **v** much.	3966
	33:14 raised it up a **v** great height,	3966
	36:14 transgressed **v** much after all	7235
Ezr	10: 1 there assembled unto him out of Israel a **v**	3966
	10: 1 and children: for the people wept **v** sore.	7235
Ne	1: 7 We have **dealt v corruptly** against	2254+2254
	2: 2 sorrow of heart. Then I was **v** sore afraid,	3966
	4: 7 to be stopped, then they were **v** wroth,	3966
	5: 6 I was **v** angry when I heard their cry and	3966
	8:17 done so. And there was **v** great gladness.	3966
Est	1:12 therefore was the king **v** wroth,	3966
Job	1: 3 she asses, and a **v** great household;	3966
	2:13 for they saw that *his* grief was **v** great.	3966
	15:10 *are* both the grayheaded and **v aged men,**	3453
	32: 6 and said, I *am* young, and ye *are* **v** old;	3453
Ps	5: 9 their inward *part is* **v** wickedness;	NIH
	35: 8 into that **v** destruction let him fall.	NIH
	46: 1 and strength, a **v** present help in trouble.	3966
	50: 3 shall be **v** tempestuous round about him.	3966
	71:19 also, O God, *is* **v** high,	4791+5704
	79: 8 prevent us: for we are brought **v** low.	3966
	89: 2 faithfulness shalt thou establish in the **v**	NIH
	92: 5 thy works! *and* thy thoughts are **v** deep.	3966
	93: 5 Thy testimonies are **v** sure:	3966
	104: 1 O LORD my God, thou art **v** great;	3966
	105:12 in number; yea, **v** few, and strangers in it.	NIH
	119:107 I am afflicted **v much**: quicken me,	3966+5704
	119:138 commanded *are* righteous and **v** faithful.	3966
	119:140 Thy word *is* **v** pure: therefore thy servant	3966
	142: 6 unto my cry; for I am brought **v** low:	3966
	146: 4 his earth; in that **v** day his thoughts perish.	NIH
	147:15 his word runneth **v** swiftly.	4120+5704
Pr	17: 9 repeateth a matter separateth **v friends.**	441
	27:15 A continual dropping in a **v rainy** day and	5464
Isa	1: 9 left unto us a **v small** remnant,	4592+3509.1
	5: 1 hath a vineyard in a **v fruitful** hill:	1121+8081
	10:25 For yet a **v little while**,	4213+4592
	16: 6 heard of the pride of Moab; *he is* **v** proud:	3966
	16:14 the remnant *shall be* **v** small *and* feeble.	4592
	24:16 dealers have **dealt v treacherously.**	898+899
	29:17 *Is it* not yet a **v little while**,	4213+4592
	30:19 he will be **v** gracious unto thee at	2603+2603
	31: 1 in horsemen, because they are **v** strong;	3966
	33:17 shall behold the land that is **v far off.**	4801
	40:15 he taketh up the isles as a **v little thing.**	1851
	47: 6 upon the ancient hast thou **v** heavily laid	3966
	48: 8 wouldest **deal v treacherously**,	898+898
	52:13 be exalted and extolled, and be **v** high.	3966
	64: 9 Be not wroth **v sore**, O LORD,	3966+5704
	64:12 thy peace, and afflict us **v sore?**	3966+5704
Jer	2:12 be ye **v** desolate, saith the LORD.	3966
	4:19 am pained *at* my **v heart**; my heart	3820+7023
	5:11 have **dealt v treacherously** against	898+898
	12: 1 happy that **deal v treacherously?**	898+899
	14:17 a great breach, *with* a **v** grievous blow.	3966
	18:13 of Israel hath done a **v** horrible thing.	3966
	20:15 unto thee; **making** him **v** glad.	8055+8055
	24: 2 One basket *had* **v** good figs, *even* like	3966
	24: 2 the other basket *had* **v** naughty figs,	3966
	24: 3 the good figs, **v** good; and the evil,	3966
	24: 3 the evil, **v** evil, that cannot be eaten,	3966

Jer	27: 7 son, until the **v** time of his land come:	1931
	40:12 gathered wine and summer fruits **v** much.	3966
	46:20 Egypt *is like* a **v fair** heifer,	3304
La	5:22 thou art **v** wroth against us.	3966+5704
Eze	2: 3 against me, *even* unto this **v** day.	6106
	16:47 as *if that were* a **v little** thing, thou	4592+6985
	27:25 made **v** glorious in the midst of the seas.	3966
	33:32 thou *art* unto them as a **v lovely** song of	5690
	37: 2 there were **v** many in the open valley;	3966
	37: 2 the open valley; and lo, *they* were **v** dry.	3966
	40: 2 set me upon a **v** high mountain, by which	3966
	47: 7 at the bank of the river *were* **v** many trees	3966
	47: 9 there shall be a **v** great multitude of fish,	3966
Da	2:12 cause the king was angry and **v** furious,	7690
	6:19 the king arose **v** early in the morning,	8238
	7:20 a mouth that spake **v** great *things*, whose	7229
	8: 8 the he goat waxed **v** great:	3966+5704
	11:25 stirred up to battle with a **v** great	3966+5704
Joel	2:11 for his camp *is* **v** great: for *he is* strong	3966
	2:11 day of the LORD *is* great and **v** terrible;	3966
Am	5:20 even **v** dark, and no brightness in it?	651
Jnh	4: 1 Jonah exceedingly, and he was **v angry.**	2734
Hab	2:13 that the people shall labour in the **v** fire,	1767
	2:13 the people shall weary themselves for **v**	1767
Zec	1:15 I am **v** sore displeased with the heathen	1419
	8: 4 every man with his staff in his hand for **v**	7230
	9: 2 and Zidon, though it be **v** wise.	3966
	9: 5 Gaza also *shall see it*, and be **v** sorrowful,	3966
	14: 4 west, *and there shall be* a **v** great valley;	3966
Mt	10:30 But the **v** hairs of your head are all	2532
	15:28 was made whole from that **v** hour.	NIG
	17:18 and the child was cured from that **v** hour.	NIG
	18:31 they were **v** sorry, and came and told unto	4970
	21: 8 And a **v great** multitude spread their	4183
	24:24 *they shall* deceive the **v** elect.	2532
	26: 7 an alabaster box of **v precious** ointment,	927
	26:37 and began to be sorrowful and **v heavy.**	85
Mk	8: 1 In those days the multitude being **v** great,	3827
	14: 3 box of ointment of spikenard **v precious**;	4185
	14:33 to be sore amazed, and to be **v heavy**;	85
	16: 2 And **v** early in the morning the first *day* of	3029
	16: 4 stone was rolled away: for it was **v** great.	4970
Lk	1: 3 of all *things* from the **v** first,	509
	9: 5 **shake off** the **v** dust from your feet for a	2532
	10:11 the **v** dust of your city, which cleaveth	NIG
	12: 7 But even the **v** hairs of your head are all	NIG
	12:59 till thou hast paid the **v** last mite.	NIG
	18:23 when he heard this, he was **v sorrowful**:	4036
	18:23 he was **v** sorrowful: for he was **v** rich.	4970
	18:24 when Jesus saw that he was **v sorrowful**,	4036
	19:17 thou hast been faithful in a **v little**,	1646
	19:48 for all the people were **v attentive** to hear	1582
	24: 1 **v early in the morning**, they came	901+3722
Jn	7:26 the rulers know indeed that this is the **v**	230
	8: 4 was taken in adultery, **in the v** act.	1888
	12: 3 **v costly**, and anointed the feet of Jesus,	4186
	14:11 or else believe me for the **v** works' sake.	846
Ac	9:22 at Damascus, proving that this is **v** Christ.	NIG
	10:10 And he became **v** hungry, and would have	NIG
	24: 2 that **v worthy deeds** are done unto this	2735
	25:10 I done no wrong, as thou **v well** knowest.	2573
Ro	10:20 Esaias is **v bold**, and saith, I was found	662
	15: 8 attendance continually upon this **v** thing.	846
1Co	4: 3 But with me it is a **v small** thing that I	1646
2Co	9: 2 and your zeal hath provoked **v many.**	4183
	11: 5 I suppose *I* was not a whit behind the **v**	5228
	12:11 for *in* nothing am I behind the **v** chiefest	5228
	12:15 And I will **gladly** spend and be spent for	2236
Php	1: 6 Being confident of this **v** thing, that he	846
1Th	5:13 And to esteem them **v** highly in love for	5228
	5:23 And the **v** God of peace sanctify you	846
2Ti	1:17 in Rome, he sought me out **v diligently**,	4706
	1:18 *unto* me at Ephesus, thou knowest **v well**.	957
Heb	10: 1 to come, *and* not the **v** image of the things,	846
Jas	3: 4 yet are they turned about with a **v small**	1646
	5:11 that the Lord is **v pitiful**, and of tender	4184

VESSEL (46) [VESSELS]

Lev	6:28 the earthen **v** wherein it is sodden shall	3627
	11:32 whether *it be* any **v** of wood, or raiment,	3627
	11:32 whatsoever **v** *it be*, wherein *any* work is	3627
	11:33 every earthen **v**, whereinto *any* of them	3627
	11:34 drink that may be drunk in every *such* **v**	3627
	14: 5 killed in an earthen **v** over running water:	3627
	14:50 birds in an earthen **v** over running water:	3627
	15:12 the **v** of earth, that he toucheth which	3627
	15:12 every **v** of wood shall be rinsed in water.	3627
Nu	5:17 shall take holy water in an earthen **v**;	3627
	19:15 every open **v**, which hath no covering	3627
	19:17 running water shall be put thereto in a **v**:	3627
Dt	23:24 but thou shalt not put *any* in thy **v**.	3627
1Sa	21: 5 though it were sanctified *this* day in the **v**.	3627
1Ki	17:10 Fetch me, I pray thee, a little water in a **v**,	3627
2Ki	4: 6 she said unto her son, Bring me yet a **v**.	3627
	4: 6 he said unto her, There is not a **v** more.	3627
Ps	2: 9 shalt dash them in pieces like a potter's **v**.	3627
	31:12 man out of mind: I am like a broken **v**.	3627
Pr	25: 4 there shall come forth a **v** for the finer.	3627
Isa	30:14 of the potters' **v** that is broken in pieces;	5035
	66:20 in a clean **v** *into* the house of the LORD.	3627
Jer	18: 4 the **v** that he made of clay was marred in	3627
	18: 4 so he made it again another **v**, as seemed	3627
	19:11 this city, as *one* breaketh a potter's **v**,	3627
	22:28 *is he* a **v** wherein *is* no pleasure?	3627
	25:34 And ye shall fall like a pleasant **v**.	3627

Jer	32:14 put them in an earthen **v**, that they may	3627
	48:11 hath not been emptied from **v** to vessel,	3627
	48:11 hath not been emptied from vessel to **v**,	3627
	48:38 for I have broken Moab like a **v** wherein	3627
	51:34 me, he hath made me an empty **v**,	3627
Eze	4: 9 both in **v** of one, and make thee bread	3627
	15: 3 will *men* take a pin of it to hang any **v**	3627
Hos	8: 8 shall they be among the Gentiles as a **v**	3627
Mk	11:16 should carry *any* **v** through the temple.	4632
Lk	8:16 covereth it with a **v**, or putteth *it* under a	4632
Jn	19:29 Now there was set a **v** full of vinegar:	4632
Ac	9:15 Go *thy way*: for he is a chosen **v** unto me,	4632
	10:11 and a certain **v** descending unto him,	4632
	10:16 the **v** was received up again into heaven.	4632
	11: 5 trance I saw a vision, A certain **v** descend,	4632
Ro	9:21 of the same lump to make one **v** unto	4632
1Th	4: 4 how to possess his **v** in sanctification	4632
2Ti	2:21 he shall be a **v** unto honour, sanctified,	4632
1Pe	3: 7 as unto the weaker **v**, and as *being* heirs	4632

VESSELS (154) [VESSEL]

Ge	43:11 of the best fruits in the land in your **v**,	3627
Ex	7:19 both in **v** of wood, and in *vessels* of stone,	NIH
	7:19 both in *vessels of* wood, and in **v** of stone,	NIH
	25:39 gold shall he make it, with all these **v**.	3627
	27: 3 all the **v** thereof thou shalt make *of* brass.	3627
	27:19 All the **v** of the tabernacle in all the	3627
	30:27 the table and all his **v**, and the candlestick	3627
	30:27 the candlestick and his **v**, and the altar of	3627
	30:28 the altar of burnt offering with all his **v**,	3627
	35:13 staves, and all his **v**, and the shewbread,	3627
	35:16 and all his **v**, the laver and his foot,	3627
	37:16 made the **v** which *were* upon the table,	3627
	37:24 gold made he it, and all the **v** thereof.	3627
	38: 3 he made all the **v** of the altar, the pots,	3627
	38: 3 all the **v** thereof made he *of* brass.	3627
	38:30 grate for it, and all the **v** of the altar,	3627
	39:36 all the **v** thereof, and the shewbread,	3627
	39:37 and all the **v** thereof, and the oil for light,	3627
	39:39 and all his **v**, the laver and his foot,	3627
	39:40 all the **v** of the service of the tabernacle,	3627
	40: 9 shalt hallow it, and all the **v** thereof:	3627
	40:10 and all his **v**, and sanctify the altar:	3627
Lev	8:11 anointed the altar and all his **v**, both	3627
Nu	1:50 over all the **v** thereof, and over all *things*	3627
	1:50 bear the tabernacle, and all the **v** thereof;	3627
	3:31 the **v** of the sanctuary wherewith they	3627
	3:36 all the **v** thereof, and all that serveth	3627
	4: 9 his snuffdishes, and all the oil **v** thereof,	3627
	4:10 all the **v** thereof within a covering of	3627
	4:14 they shall put upon it all the **v** thereof,	3627
	4:14 and the basons, all the **v** of the altar;	3627
	4:15 all the **v** of the sanctuary, as the camp is	3627
	4:16 *is*, in the sanctuary, and in the **v** thereof.	3627
	7: 1 both the altar and all the **v** thereof,	3627
	7:85 all the silver **v** weighed two thousand	3627
	18: 3 only they shall not come nigh the **v** of	3627
	19:18 upon all the **v**, and upon the persons that	3627
Jos	6:19 silver, and gold, and **v** of brass and iron,	3627
	6:24 the gold, and the **v** of brass and of iron,	3627
Ru	2: 9 go unto the **v**, and drink of *that* which	3627
1Sa	9: 7 for the bread is spent in our **v**, and *there*	3627
	21: 5 the **v** of the young men are holy,	3627
2Sa	8:10 *Joram* brought with him **v** of silver,	3627
	8:10 and **v** of gold, and vessels of brass:	3627
	8:10 and vessels of gold, and **v** of brass:	3627
	17:28 earthen **v**, and wheat, and barley,	3627
1Ki	7:45 all these **v**, which Hiram made to king	3627
	7:47 Solomon left all the **v** *unweighed*, because	3627
	7:48 Solomon made all the **v** that *pertained*	3627
	7:51 *even* the silver, and the gold, and the **v**,	3627
	8: 4 all the holy **v** that *were* in the tabernacle,	3627
	10:21 king Solomon's drinking **v** *were* of gold,	3627
	10:21 all the **v** of the house of the forest of	3627
	10:25 **v** of silver, and vessels of gold,	3627
	10:25 **v** of gold, and garments, and armour,	3627
	15:15 of the LORD, silver, and gold, and **v**.	3627
2Ki	4: 3 thee **v** abroad of all thy neighbours,	3627
	4: 3 of all thy neighbours, *even* empty **v**;	3627
	4: 4 shalt pour out into all those **v**,	3627
	4: 5 upon her sons, who brought *the* **v** to her;	NIH
	4: 6 it came to pass, when the **v** were full,	3627
	7:15 lo, all the way *was* full *of* garments and **v**,	3627
	12:13 any **v** of gold, or vessels of silver,	3627
	12:13 any vessels of gold, or **v** of silver,	3627
	14:14 all the **v** that were found *in* the house of	3627
	23: 4 LORD all the **v** that were made for Baal,	3627
	24:13 cut in pieces all the **v** of gold which	3627
	25:14 all the **v** of brass wherewith they	3627
	25:16 brass of all these **v** was without weight.	3627
1Ch	9:28 them had the charge of the ministering **v**,	3627
	9:29 also *were* appointed to oversee the **v**,	3627
	18: 8 and the pillars, and the **v** of brass.	3627
	18:10 *him* all *manner of* **v** of gold and silver	3627
	22:19 of the LORD, and the holy **v** of God,	3627
	23:26 nor any **v** of it for the service thereof.	3627
	28:13 for all the **v** of service in the house of	3627
2Ch	4:18 Thus Solomon made all these **v** in great	3627
	4:19 Solomon made all the **v** that *were for*	3627
	5: 5 all the holy **v** that *were* in the tabernacle,	3627
	9:20 all the drinking **v** of king Solomon *were*	3627
	9:20 all the **v** of the house of the forest of	3627
	9:24 **v** of silver, and vessels of gold,	3627
	9:24 **v** of gold, and raiment, harness, and	3627
	15:18 had dedicated, silver, and gold, and **v**.	3627

V

2Ch	24:14 whereof were made **v** for the house of	3627
	24:14 to minister, and to offer *withal,*	3627
	24:14 and spoons, and **v** of gold and silver.	3627
	25:24 all the **v** that were found in the house of	3627
	28:24 Ahaz gathered together the **v** of the	3627
	28:24 cut in pieces the **v** of the house of God,	3627
	29:18 with all the **v** thereof, and the shewbread	3627
	29:18 shewbread table, with all the **v** thereof.	3627
	29:19 Moreover all the **v**, which king Ahaz in	3627
	36: 7 Nebuchadnezzar also carried of the **v** of	3627
	36:10 with the goodly **v** of the house of	3627
	36:18 all the **v** of the house of God, great and	3627
	36:19 and destroyed all the goodly **v** thereof.	3627
Ezr	1: 6 strengthened their hands with **v** of silver,	3627
	1: 7 Also Cyrus the king brought forth the **v** of	3627
	1:10 and ten, *and* other **v** a thousand.	3627
	1:11 All the **v** of gold and of silver *were* five	3627
	5:14 the **v** also of gold and of silver the house	3984
	5:15 unto him, Take these **v**, go, carry them	3984
	6: 5 golden and silver **v** of the house of God,	3984
	7:19 The **v** also that *are* given thee for	3984
	8:25 them the silver, and the gold, and the **v**,	3627
	8:26 silver **v** an hundred talents, *and of* gold	3627
	8:27 two **v** of fine copper, precious as gold.	3627
	8:28 the **v** *are* holy also; and the silver and	3627
	8:30 of the silver, and the gold, and the **v**,	3627
	8:33 the **v** weighed in the house of our God by	3627
Ne	10:39 where *are* the **v** of the sanctuary,	3627
	13: 5 the **v**, and the tithes of the corn, the new	3627
	13: 9 thither brought I again the **v** of the house	3627
Est	1: 7 *they* gave *them* drink in **v** of gold,	3627
	1: 7 (the **v** being diverse one from another,)	3627
Isa	18: 2 even in **v** of bulrushes upon the waters,	3627
	22:24 and the issue, all **v** of small quantity,	3627
	22:24 of small quantity, from the **v** of cups,	3627
	22:24 of cups, even to all the **v** of flagons.	3627
	52:11 be ye clean, that bear the **v** of the L<small>ORD</small>.	3627
	65: 4 broth of abominable *things is in* their **v**;	3627
Jer	14: 3 water; they returned *with* their **v** empty;	3627
	27:16 the **v** of the L<small>ORD</small>'s house *shall* now	3627
	27:18 that the **v** which are left in the house of	3627
	27:19 concerning the residue of the **v** that	3627
	27:21 concerning the **v** that remain in the house	3627
	28: 3 this place all the **v** of the L<small>ORD</small>'s house,	3627
	28: 6 to bring again the **v** of the L<small>ORD</small>'s house,	3627
	40:10 oil, and put *them* in your **v**, and dwell in	3627
	48:12 shall empty his **v**, and break their bottles.	3627
	49:29 and all their **v**, and their camels;	3627
	52:18 all the **v** of brass wherewith they	3627
	52:20 brass of all these **v** was without weight.	3627
Eze	27:13 of men and **v** of brass in thy market.	3627
Da	1: 2 with part of the **v** of the house of God:	3627
	1: 2 he brought the **v** *into* the treasure house	3627
	5: 2 silver **v** which his father Nebuchadnezzar	3984
	5: 3 they brought the golden **v** that were taken	3984
	5:23 they have brought the **v** of his house	3984
	11: 8 *and* with their precious **v** of silver and	3627
Hos	13:15 he shall spoil the treasure of all pleasant **v**.	3627
Hag	2:16 for to draw out fifty **v** *out of* the press,	NIH
Mt	13:48 gathered the good into **v**, but cast the bad	30
	25: 4 But the wise took oil in their **v** with their	30
Mk	7: 4 of cups, and pots, **brasen v**, and of tables.	5473
Ro	9:22 endured with much longsuffering the **v** of	4632
	9:23 the riches of his glory on the **v** of mercy,	4632
2Co	4: 7 But we have this treasure in earthen **v**,	4632
2Ti	2:20 in a great house there are not only **v** of	4632
Heb	9:21 tabernacle, and all the **v** of the ministry.	4632
Rev	2:27 as the **v** of a potter *shall* they be broken to	4632
	18:12 all *manner* of ivory, and all *manner*	4632
	18:12 and *manner* of most precious wood,	4632

VESTMENTS (2) [VESTURE]

2Ki	10:22 Bring forth **v** for all the worshippers of	3830
	10:22 of Baal. And he brought them forth **v**.	4403

VESTRY (1) [VESTURE]

2Ki	10:22 he said unto *him* that *was* over the **v**,	4458

VESTURE (8) [VESTMENTS, VESTRY, VESTURES]

Dt	22:12 fringes upon the four quarters of thy **v**,	3682
Ps	22:18 among them, and cast lots upon my **v**.	3830
	102:26 as a **v** shalt thou change them,	3830
Mt	27:35 and upon my **v** did they cast lots.	2441
Jn	19:24 and for my **v** they did cast lots.	2441
Heb	1:12 And as a **v** shalt thou fold them up,	4018
Rev	19:13 he *was* clothed with a **v** dipt in blood:	2440
	19:16 he hath on *his* **v** and on his thigh a	2440

VESTURES (1) [VESTURE]

Ge	41:42 arrayed him in **v** of fine linen, and put a	899

VEX (15) [VEXATION, VEXATIONS, VEXED]

Ex	22:21 shalt neither **v** a stranger, nor oppress	3238
Lev	18:18 to **v** *her*, to uncover her nakedness,	6887
	19:33 thee in your land, ye shall not **v** him.	3238
Nu	25:17 **V** the Midianites, and smite them:	6887
	25:18 For they **v** you with their wiles,	6887
	33:55 shall **v** you in the land wherein ye dwell.	6887
2Sa	12:18 how will he then **v** himself, if we	6213+7451
2Ch	15: 6 for God did **v** them with all adversity.	2000
Job	19: 2 How long will ye **v** my soul, and break me	3013
Ps	2: 5 wrath, and **v** them in his sore displeasure.	926
Isa	7: 6 **v** it, and let us make a breach therein for	6973
	11:13 Judah, and Judah shall not **v** Ephraim.	6887
Eze	32: 9 I will also **v** the hearts of many people,	3707

Hab	2: 7 awake that *shall* **v** thee, and thou shalt be	2111
Ac	12: 1 forth *his* hands to **v** certain of the church.	2559

VEXATION (14) [VEX]

Dt	28:20 send upon thee cursing, **v**, and rebuke,	4103
Ecc	1:14 and behold, all *is* vanity and **v** of spirit.	7469
	1:17 I perceived that this also *is* **v** of spirit.	7475
	2:11 all *was* vanity and **v** of spirit, and *there*	7469
	2:17 unto me: for all *is* vanity and **v** of spirit.	7469
	2:22 of all his labour, and of the **v** of his heart,	7475
	2:26 This also *is* vanity and **v** of spirit.	7469
	4: 4 This *is* also vanity and **v** of spirit.	7469
	4: 6 the hands full *with* travail and **v** of spirit.	7469
	4:16 Surely this also *is* vanity and **v** of spirit.	7475
	6: 9 desire: this *is* also vanity and **v** of spirit.	7469
Isa	9: 1 dimness *shall* not *be* such as *was* in her **v**,	4164
	28:19 shall be a **v** only *to* understand the report.	2113
	65:14 of heart, and shall howl for **v** of spirit.	7667

VEXATIONS (1) [VEX]

2Ch	15: 5 great **v** *were* upon all the inhabitants of	4103

VEXED (22) [VEX]

Nu	20:15 and the Egyptians **v** us, and our fathers:	7489
Jdg	2:18 of them that oppressed them and **v** them.	1766
	10: 8 year they **v** and oppressed the children	7492
	16:16 *so* that his soul was **v** unto death;	7114
1Sa	14:47 he turned himself, he **v** *them*.	7561
2Sa	13: 2 Amnon was so **v**, that he fell sick for his	3334
2Ki	4:27 Let her alone; for her soul *is* **v** within her:	4843
Ne	9:27 the hand of their enemies, who **v** them:	6887
Job	27: 2 and the Almighty, *who* hath **v** my soul;	4843
Ps	6: 2 O L<small>ORD</small>, heal me; for my bones are **v**.	926
	6: 3 My soul is also sore **v**: but thou, O L<small>ORD</small>,	926
	6:10 all mine enemies be ashamed and sore **v**:	926
Isa	63:10 they rebelled, and **v** his holy Spirit:	6087
Eze	22: 5 thee, *which art* infamous *and* much **v**.	4103
	22: 7 in thee have they **v** the fatherless and	3238
	22:29 and have **v** the poor and needy:	3238
Mt	15:22 my daughter is grievously **v** **with a devil**.	1139
	17:15 for he is lunatick, and sore **v**: for ofttimes	3958
Lk	6:18 And they that were **v** with unclean spirits:	3791
Ac	5:16 them which were **v** with unclean spirits:	3791
2Pe	2: 7 **v** with the filthy conversation of	2669
	2: 8 **v** *his* righteous soul from day to day with	928

VIAL (8) [VIALS]

1Sa	10: 1 Samuel took a **v** of oil, and poured *it* upon	6378
Rev	16: 2 and poured out his **v** upon the earth;	5357
	16: 3 And the second angel poured out his **v**	5357
	16: 4 And the third angel poured out his **v** upon	5357
	16: 8 And the fourth angel poured out his **v** upon	5357
	16:10 And the fifth angel poured out his **v** upon	5357
	16:12 And the sixth angel poured out his **v** upon	5357
	16:17 the seventh angel poured out his **v** into	5357

VIALS (5) [VIAL]

Rev	5: 8 and golden **v** full of odours, which are	5357
	15: 7 seven golden **v** full of the wrath of God,	5357
	16: 1 pour out the **v** of the wrath of God upon	5357
	17: 1 the seven angels which had the seven **v**,	5357
	21: 9 the seven **v** full of the seven last plagues,	5357

VICTORY (12)

2Sa	19: 2 the **v** that day was *turned* into mourning	8668
	23:10 the L<small>ORD</small> wrought a great **v** that day;	8668
	23:12 and the L<small>ORD</small> wrought a great **v**.	8668
1Ch	29:11 and the glory, and the **v**, and the majesty:	5331
Ps	98: 1 and his holy arm, hath **gotten** him the **v**.	3467
Isa	25: 8 He will swallow up death in **v**;	5331
Mt	12:20 till he send forth judgment unto **v**.	3534
1Co	15:54 is written, Death is swallowed up in **v**.	3534
	15:55 *is* thy sting? O grave, where *is* thy **v**?	3534
	15:57 which giveth us the **v** through our Lord	3534
1Jn	5: 4 this is the **v** that overcometh the world,	3529
Rev	15: 2 that had **gotten** the **v** over the beast,	3528

VICTUAL (5) [VICTUALS]

Ex	12:39 had they prepared for themselves any **v**.	6720
Jdg	20:10 fetch **v** for the people, that *they* may do,	6720
1Ki	4:27 those officers **provided v** for king	3557
2Ch	11:11 them, and store of **v**, and *of* oil and wine.	3978
	11:23 he gave them **v** in abundance. And he	4202

VICTUALS (17) [VICTUAL]

Ge	14:11 and all their **v**, and went their way.	400
Lev	25:37 usury, nor lend him thy **v** for increase.	400
Dt	23:19 usury of money, usury of **v**, usury of any	400
Jos	1:11 the people, saying, Prepare you **v**;	6720
	9:11 Take **v** with you for the journey, and go	6720
	9:14 the men took of their **v**, and asked not	6718
Jdg	7: 8 So the people took **v** in their hand, and	6720
	17:10 the year, and a suit of apparel, and thy **v**.	4241
1Sa	22:10 gave him **v**, and gave him the sword of	6720
1Ki	4: 7 which **provided v** for the king and his	3557
	11:18 and appointed him **v**, and gave him land.	3899
Ne	10:31 or any **v** on the sabbath day to sell,	7668
	13:15 *them* in the day wherein they sold **v**.	6718
Jer	40: 5 So the captain of the guard gave him **v**	737
	44:17 *then* had we plenty of **v**, and were well,	3899
Mt	14:15 go into the villages, and buy themselves **v**.	1033
Lk	9:12 round about, and lodge, and get **v**:	1979

VIEW (4) [VIEWED]

Jos	2: 1 Go **v** the land, even Jericho.	7200
	7: 2 them, saying, Go up and **v** the country.	7270

2Ki	2: 7 and stood to **v** afar off:	4480+5048
	2:15 were to **v** at Jericho saw him,	4480+5048

VIEWED (4) [VIEW]

Jos	7: 2 And the men went up and **v** Ai.	7270
Ezr	8:15 I **v** the people, and the priests,	995
Ne	2:13 dung port, and **v** the walls of Jerusalem,	7663
	2:15 **v** the wall, and turned back, and entered	7663

VIGILANT (2)

1Ti	3: 2 **v**, sober, of good behaviour, given to	3524
1Pe	5: 8 Be sober, be **v**; because your adversary	1127

VIGOROUS See LIVELY

VIGOROUSLY See THROUGHLY

VILE (19) [VILELY, VILER, VILEST]

Dt	25: 3 thy brother should seem **v** unto thee.	7034
Jdg	19:24 but unto this man do not so **v** a thing.	5039
1Sa	3:13 because his sons **made** themselves **v**,	7043
	15: 9 every thing *that was* **v** and refuse, that	5240
2Sa	6:22 I will yet be more **v** than thus, and will	7043
Job	18: 3 as beasts, *and* **reputed v** in your sight?	2933
	40: 4 Behold, I am **v**; what shall I answer thee?	7043
Ps	15: 4 In whose eyes a **v** person is contemned;	3988
Isa	32: 5 The **v person** shall be no more called	5036
	32: 6 For the **v person** will speak villany,	5036
Jer	15:19 if thou take forth the precious from the **v**,	2151
	29:17 and will make them like **v** figs,	8182
La	1:11 and consider; for I am become **v**.	2151
Da	11:21 in his estate shall stand up a **v person**,	959
Na	1:14 I will make thy grave; for thou art **v**.	7043
	3: 6 **make** thee **v**, and will set thee as a	5034
Ro	1:26 For this cause God gave them up unto **v**	819
Php	3:21 Who shall change our **v** body, that it may	5014
Jas	2: 2 come in also a poor *man* in **v** raiment;	4508

VILELY (1) [VILE]

2Sa	1:21 the shield of the mighty is **v** cast away,	1602

VILER (1) [VILE]

Job	30: 8 of base men: they were **v** than the earth.	5217

VILEST (1) [VILE]

Ps	12: 8 every side, when the **v** men are exalted.	2149

VILLAGE (10) [VILLAGES]

Mt	21: 2 Go into the **v** over against you,	2968
Mk	11: 2 Go your way into the **v** over against you:	2968
Lk	8: 1 he went throughout every city and **v**,	2968
	9:52 and entered into a **v** of the Samaritans,	2968
	9:56 to save *them*. And they went to another **v**.	2968
	10:38 went, that he entered into a certain **v**:	2968
	17:12 And as he entered into a certain **v**,	2968
	19:30 Go ye into the **v** over against *you*; in	2968
	24:13 two of them went *that* same day to a **v**	2968
	24:28 And they drew nigh unto the **v**,	2968

VILLAGES (75) [VILLAGE]

Ex	8:13 out of the **v**, and out of the fields.	2691
Lev	25:31 the houses of the **v** which have no wall	2691
Nu	21:25 in Heshbon, and in all the **v** thereof.	1323
	21:32 they took the **v** thereof, and drove out	1323
	32:42 and the **v** thereof, and called it Nobah,	1323
Jos	13:23 their families, the cities and **v** thereof.	2691
	13:28 after their families, the cities, and their **v**.	2691
	15:32 cities *are* twenty and nine, with their **v**.	2691
	15:36 Gederothaim; fourteen cities with their **v**.	2691
	15:41 Makkedah; sixteen cities with their **v**.	2691
	15:44 and Mareshah; nine cities with their **v**.	2691
	15:45 Ekron, with her towns and her **v**:	2691
	15:46 all that *lay* near Ashdod, with their **v**:	2691
	15:47 Ashdod *with* her towns and her **v**,	2691
	15:47 Gaza *with* her towns and her **v**,	2691
	15:51 and Giloh; eleven cities with their **v**.	2691
	15:54 Hebron, and Zior; nine cities with their **v**.	2691
	15:57 and Timnah; ten cities with their **v**.	2691
	15:59 and Elteton; six cities with their **v**.	2691
	15:60 and Rabbah; two cities with their **v**.	2691
	15:62 salt, and En-gedi; six cities with their **v**.	2691
	16: 9 of Manasseh, all the cities with their **v**.	2691
	18:24 and Gaba; twelve cities with their **v**.	2691
	18:28 *and* Kirjath; fourteen cities with their **v**.	2691
	19: 6 and Sharuhen; thirteen cities and their **v**:	2691
	19: 7 Ether, and Ashan; four cities and their **v**:	2691
	19: 8 all the **v** that *were* round about these	2691
	19:15 Beth-lehem: twelve cities with their **v**.	2691
	19:16 to their families, these cities and their **v**.	2691
	19:22 at Jordan: sixteen cities with their **v**.	2691
	19:23 to their families, the cities and their **v**.	2691
	19:30 twenty and two cities with their **v**.	2691
	19:31 to their families, these cities and their **v**.	2691
	19:38 nineteen cities with their **v**.	2691
	19:39 to their families, these cities and their **v**.	2691
	19:48 to their families, these cities with their **v**.	2691
	21:12 the fields of the city, and the **v** thereof,	2691
Jdg	5: 7 *The* inhabitants of the **v** ceased, they	6520
	5:11 towards the inhabitants of his **v** in Israel:	6520
1Sa	6:18 *both* of fenced cities, and of country **v**,	3724
1Ch	4:32 their **v** *were*, Etam, and Ain, Rimmon,	2691
	4:33 all their **v** that *were* round about the	2691
	6:56 the fields of the city, and the **v** thereof,	2691
	9:16 that dwelt in the **v** of the Netophathites,	2691
	9:22 reckoned by their genealogy in their **v**,	2691
	9:25 their brethren, *which were* in their **v**,	2691

1Ch 27:25	the cities, and in the **v**, and in the castles,	3723
2Ch 28:18	Shocho with the **v** thereof, and Timnah	1323
28:18	Timnah with the **v** thereof, Gimzo also	1323
28:18	Gimzo also and the **v** thereof:	1323
Ne 6: 2	us meet together in *some one of* the **v** in the	3715
11:25	for the **v**, with their fields, *some* of	2691
11:25	*in* the **v** thereof, and at Dibon, and *in*	1323
11:25	*in* the **v** thereof, and at Jekabzeel, and *in*	1323
11:25	and at Jekabzeel, and *in* the **v** thereof,	2691
11:27	and at Beer-sheba, and *in* the **v** thereof,	1323
11:28	and at Mekonah, and *in* the **v** thereof,	1323
11:30	Zanoah, Adullam, and *in* their **v**,	2691
11:30	*at* Azekah, and *in* the **v** thereof:	1323
11:31	and Aija, and Beth-el, and *in* their **v**,	1323
12:28	and from the **v** of Netophathi;	2691
12:29	for the singers had builded them **v** round	2691
Est 9:19	Therefore the Jews of the **v**, that dwelt in	6521
Ps 10: 8	He sitteth in the lurking places of the **v**:	2691
SS 7:11	forth *into* the field; let us lodge in the **v**.	3723
Isa 42:11	the cities thereof lift up *their voice*, the **v**	2691
Eze 38:11	I will go up to the land of **unwalled v**;	6519
Hab 3:14	through with his staves the head of his **v**:	6518
Mt 9:35	And Jesus went about all the cities and **v**,	2968
14:15	that they may go into the **v**,	2968
Mk 6: 6	And he went round about the **v**, teaching.	2968
6:36	and *into* the **v**, and buy themselves bread:	2968
6:56	he entered, into **v**, or cities, or country,	2968
Lk 13:22	And he went through the cities and **v**,	2968
Ac 8:25	preached the gospel in many **v** of	2968

VILLANY (2)

Isa 32: 6	For the vile person will speak **v**,	5039
Jer 29:23	Because they have committed **v** in Israel,	5039

VINE (61) [VINEDRESSERS, VINES, VINEYARD, VINEYARDS, VINTAGE]

Ge 40: 9	In my dream, behold, a **v** *was* before me;	1612
40:10	In the **v** *were* three branches: and it *was*	1612
49:11	Binding his foal unto the **v**, and his ass's	1612
49:11	and his ass's colt unto the **choice v**;	8322
Lev 25: 5	gather the grapes of thy **v undressed**:	5139
25:11	the grapes in it of thy **v undressed**.	5139
Nu 6: 4	he eat nothing that is made of the **v** tree,	3196
Dt 32:32	For their **v** *is* of the vine of Sodom,	1612
32:32	For their vine *is* of the **v** of Sodom,	1612
Jdg 9:12	said the trees unto the **v**, Come thou,	1612
9:13	the **v** said unto them, Should I leave my	1612
13:14	of any *thing* that cometh of the **v**,	1612+3196
1Ki 4:25	every man under his **v** and under his fig	1612
2Ki 4:39	found a wild **v**, and gathered thereof wild	1612
18:31	*then* eat ye every man of his own **v**,	1612
Job 15:33	shall shake off his unripe grape as the **v**,	1612
Ps 80: 8	Thou hast brought a **v** out of Egypt:	1612
80:14	from heaven, and behold, and visit this **v**;	1612
128: 3	Thy wife *shall be* as a fruitful **v** by the	1612
SS 6:11	*and* to see whether the **v** flourished,	1612
7: 8	thy breasts shall be as clusters of the **v**,	1612
7:12	let us see if the **v** flourish, *whether*	1612
Isa 5: 2	planted it *with* the **choicest v**, and built a	8321
16: 8	Heshbon languish, *and* the **v** of Sibmah:	1612
16: 9	the weeping of Jazer the **v** of Sibmah:	1612
24: 7	new wine mourneth, the **v** languisheth,	1612
32:12	for the pleasant fields, for the fruitful **v**.	1612
34: 4	as the leaf falleth off from the **v**, and as a	1612
36:16	eat ye every one *of* his **v**, and every one	1612
Jer 2:21	Yet I had planted thee a **noble v**, wholly	8321
2:21	degenerate **plant of** a strange **v** unto me?	1612
6: 9	glean the remnant of Israel as a **v**:	1612
8:13	*there shall be* no grapes on the **v**, nor figs	1612
48:32	O **v** of Sibmah, I will weep for thee with	1612
Eze 15: 2	What is the **v** tree more than any tree,	1612
15: 6	the **v** tree among the trees of the forest,	1612
17: 6	and became a spreading **v** of low stature,	1612
17: 6	so it became a **v**, and brought forth	1612
17: 7	this **v** did bend her roots toward him,	1612
17: 8	bear fruit, that *it* might be a goodly **v**.	1612
19:10	Thy mother *is* like a **v** in thy blood,	1612
Hos 10: 1	Israel *is* an empty **v**, he bringeth forth	1612
14: 7	revive *as* the corn, and grow as the **v**:	1612
Joel 1: 7	He hath laid my **v** waste, and barked my	1612
1:12	The **v** is dried up, and the fig tree	1612
2:22	fig tree and the **v** do yield their strength.	1612
Mic 4: 4	they shall sit every man under his **v** and	1612
Na 2: 2	them out, and marred their **v branches**.	2156
Hag 2:19	as yet the **v**, and the fig tree,	1612
Zec 3:10	under the **v** and under the fig tree.	1612
8:12	the **v** shall give her fruit, and the ground	1612
Mal 3:11	neither shall your **v** cast her fruit before	1612
Mt 26:29	not drink henceforth of this fruit of the **v**,	288
Mk 14:25	I will drink no more of the fruit of the **v**,	288
Lk 22:18	I will not drink of the fruit of the **v**,	288
Jn 15: 1	I am the true **v**, and my Father is	288
15: 4	bear fruit of itself, except it abide in the **v**;	288
15: 5	I am the **v**, ye *are* the branches: He that	288
Jas 3:12	either a **v**, figs? so *can* no fountain *both*	288
Rev 14:18	gather the clusters of the **v** of the earth;	288
14:19	gathered the **v** of the earth, and cast *it*	288

VINE GROWERS See VINEDRESSERS

VINEDRESSERS (5) [VINE]

2Ki 25:12	guard left of the poor of the land to be **v**	3755
2Ch 26:10	*also*, and **v** in the mountains,	3755
Isa 61: 5	alien *shall be* your plowmen and your **v**.	3755
Jer 52:16	left *certain* of the poor of the land for **v**	3755

Joel 1:11	howl, O ye **v**, for the wheat and for	3755

VINEGAR (13)

Nu 6: 3	shall drink no **v** of wine, or vinegar of	2558
6: 3	no vinegar of wine, or **v** of strong drink,	2558
Ru 2:14	of the bread, and dip thy morsel in the **v**.	2558
Ps 69:21	and in my thirst they gave me **v** to drink.	2558
Pr 10:26	As **v** to the teeth, and as smoke to the	2558
25:20	*and as* **v** upon nitre, so *is* he that singeth	2558
Mt 27:34	They gave him **v** to drink mingled with	3690
27:48	and filled *it* with **v**, and put *it* on a reed,	3690
Mk 15:36	And one ran and filled a spunge *full* of **v**,	3690
Lk 23:36	coming to *him*, and offering him **v**,	3690
Jn 19:29	Now there was set a vessel full of **v**:	3690
19:29	and they filled a spunge with **v**, and put *it*	3690
19:30	When Jesus therefore had received the **v**,	3690

VINES (12) [VINE]

Nu 20: 5	or of figs, or **v**, or of pomegranates;	1612
Dt 8: 8	and **v**, and fig trees, and pomegranates;	1612
Ps 78:47	He destroyed their **v** with hail,	1612
105:33	He smote their **v** also and their fig trees;	1612
SS 2:13	the **v** *with* the tender grape give a *good*	1612
2:15	the foxes, the little foxes, that spoil the **v**:	3754
2:15	the vines: for our **v** *have* tender grapes.	3754
Isa 7:23	where there were a thousand **v** at a	1612
Jer 5:17	they shall eat up thy **v** and thy fig trees:	1612
31: 5	shalt yet plant **v** upon the mountains	3754
Hos 2:12	I will destroy her **v** and her fig trees,	1612
Hab 3:17	blossom, neither *shall* fruit *be* in the **v**;	1612

VINEYARD (69) [VINE]

Ge 9:20	*to be* a husbandman, and he planted a **v**:	3754
Ex 22: 5	a man shall cause a field or **v** to be eaten,	3754
22: 5	of the best of his own **v**, shall he make	3754
23:11	In like manner thou shalt deal with thy **v**,	3754
Lev 19:10	thou shalt not glean thy **v**, neither shalt	3754
19:10	shalt thou gather *every* grape of thy **v**;	3754
25: 3	six years thou shalt prune thy **v**,	3754
25: 4	neither sow thy field, nor prune thy **v**.	3754
Dt 20: 6	what man *is he* that hath planted a **v**,	3754
22: 9	shalt not sow thy **v** with divers seeds:	3754
22: 9	sown, and the fruit of thy **v**, be defiled.	3754
23:24	thou comest into thy neighbour's **v**,	3754
24:21	When thou gatherest the grapes of thy **v**,	3754
28:30	thou shalt plant a **v**, and shalt not gather	3754
1Ki 21: 1	*that* Naboth the Jezreelite had a **v**,	3754
21: 2	unto Naboth, saying, Give me thy **v**,	3754
21: 2	I will give thee for it a better **v** than it;	3754
21: 6	said unto him, Give me thy **v** for money;	3754
21: 6	thee, I will give thee *another* **v** for it:	3754
21: 7	he answered, I will not give thee my **v**.	3754
21: 7	I will give thee the **v** of Naboth	3754
21:15	take possession of the **v** of Naboth	3754
21:16	that Ahab rose up to go down to the **v** of	3754
21:18	behold, *he is* in the **v** of Naboth, whither	3754
Ps 80:15	the **v** which thy right hand hath planted,	3657
Pr 24:30	the **v** of the man void of understanding,	3754
31:16	the fruit of her hands she planteth a **v**.	3754
SS 1: 6	*but* mine own **v** have I not kept.	3754
8:11	Solomon had a **v** at Baal-hamon; he let	3754
8:11	he let out the **v** unto keepers;	3754
8:12	My **v**, which *is* mine, *is* before me: thou,	3754
Isa 1: 8	daughter of Zion is left as a cottage in a **v**,	3754
3:14	for ye have eaten up the **v**; the spoil of	3754
5: 1	a song of my beloved touching his **v**.	3754
5: 1	My wellbeloved hath a **v** in a very fruitful	3754
5: 3	judge, I pray you, betwixt me and my **v**.	3754
5: 4	could have been done more to my **v**,	3754
5: 5	I will tell you what I *will* do to my **v**:	3754
5: 7	For the **v** of the LORD of hosts *is*	3754
5:10	ten acres of **v** shall yield one bath,	3754
27: 2	day sing ye unto her, A **v** of red wine.	3754
Jer 12:10	Many pastors have destroyed my **v**,	3754
35: 7	nor plant **v**, nor have *any:* but all your	3754
35: 9	neither have we **v**, nor field, nor seed:	3754
Mic 1: 6	a heap of the field, *and* as plantings of a **v**	3754
Mt 20: 1	in the morning to hire labourers into his **v**.	290
20: 2	for a penny a day, he sent them into his **v**.	290
20: 4	Go ye also into the **v**, and whatsoever is	290
20: 7	He saith unto them, Go ye also into the **v**;	290
20: 8	the lord of the **v** saith unto his steward,	290
21:28	and said, Son, go work to day in my **v**.	290
21:33	which planted a **v**, and hedged it round	290
21:39	and cast *him* out of the **v**, and slew *him*.	290
21:40	When the lord therefore of the **v** cometh,	290
21:41	will let out *his* **v** unto other husbandmen,	290
Mk 12: 1	A *certain* man planted a **v**, and set a hedge	290
12: 2	from the husbandmen of the fruit of the **v**.	290
12: 8	and killed *him*, and cast *him* out of the **v**.	290
12: 9	What shall therefore the lord of the **v** do?	290
12: 9	and will give the **v** unto others.	290
Lk 13: 6	certain *man* had a fig tree planted in his **v**;	290
13: 7	Then said he unto the **dresser of** his **v**,	289
20: 9	A certain man planted a **v**, and let it forth	290
20:10	they should give him of the fruit of the **v**:	290
20:13	said the lord of the **v**, What shall I do?	290
20:15	they cast him out of the **v**, and killed *him*.	290
20:15	shall the lord of the **v** do unto them?	290
20:16	and shall give the **v** to others.	290
1Co 9: 7	planteth a **v**, and eateth not of the fruit	290

VINEYARDS (45) [VINE]

Nu 16:14	or given us inheritance of fields and **v**:	3754
20:17	pass through the fields, or through the **v**,	3754

Nu 21:22	will not turn into the fields, or into the **v**;	3754
22:24	of the LORD stood in a path of the **v**,	3754
Dt 6:11	thou diggedst not, **v** and olive trees,	3754
28:39	Thou shalt plant **v**, and dress *them*, but	3754
Jos 24:13	of the **v** and oliveyards which ye planted	3754
Jdg 9:27	gathered their **v**, and trode the *grapes*,	3754
11:33	twenty cities, and unto the plain of the **v**,	3754
14: 5	Timnath, and came to the **v** of Timnath:	3754
15: 5	the standing corn, with the **v** *and* olives.	3754
21:20	Go and lie in wait in the **v**;	3754
21:21	come ye out of the **v**, and catch you	3754
1Sa 8:14	your **v**, and your oliveyards, *even* the best	3754
8:15	of your **v**, and give to his officers,	3754
22: 7	Jesse give every one of you fields and **v**,	3754
2Ki 5:26	**v**, and sheep, and oxen, and menservants,	3754
18:32	of corn and wine, a land of bread and **v**,	3754
19:29	and plant **v**, and eat the fruits thereof.	3754
1Ch 27:27	over the **v** *was* Shimei the Ramathite:	3754
27:27	over the increase of the **v** for the wine	3754
Ne 5: 3	and houses, that we might buy corn,	3754
5: 4	*and that upon* our lands and **v**.	3754
5: 5	for other men have our lands and **v**.	3754
5:11	them, even *this* day, their lands, their **v**,	3754
9:25	and, oliveyards, and fruit trees in	3754
Job 24:18	he beholdeth not the way of the **v**.	3754
Ps 107:37	sow the fields, and plant **v**, which may	3754
Ecc 2: 4	I builded me houses; I planted me **v**:	3754
SS 1: 6	they made me the keeper of the **v**;	3754
1:14	a cluster of camphire in the **v** of En-gedi.	3754
7:12	Let us get up early to the **v**; let us see if	3754
Isa 16:10	in the **v** there shall be no singing,	3754
36:17	of corn and wine, a land of bread and **v**.	3754
37:30	and plant **v**, and eat the fruit thereof.	3754
65:21	inhabit *them;* and they shall plant **v**,	3754
Jer 32:15	shall be possessed again in this land.	3754
39:10	gave them **v** and fields at the same time.	3754
Eze 28:26	and shall build houses, and plant **v**;	3754
Hos 2:15	I will give her her **v** from thence,	3754
Am 4: 9	and your **v** and your fig trees and	3754
5:11	ye have planted pleasant **v**, but ye shall	3754
5:17	in all **v** *shall be* wailing: for I will pass	3754
9:14	inhabit *them;* and they shall plant **v**,	3754
Zep 1:13	not inhabit *them;* and they shall plant **v**,	3754

VINTAGE (10) [VINE]

Lev 26: 5	your threshing shall reach unto the **v**,	1210
26: 5	the **v** shall reach unto the sowing time:	1210
Jdg 8: 2	of Ephraim better than the **v** of Abi-ezer?	1210
Job 24: 6	and they gather the **v** of the wicked.	1210
Isa 16:10	I have made *their* **v** shouting to cease.	NIH
24:13	the gleaning grapes when the **v** is done.	1210
32:10	ye careless *women:* for the **v** shall fail,	1210
Jer 48:32	upon thy summer fruits and upon thy **v**.	1210
Mic 7: 1	as the grapegleanings of the **v**:	1210
Zec 11: 2	for the forest of the **v** is come down.	1210

VIOL (2) [VIOLS]

Isa 5:12	and the **v**, the tabret, and pipe, and wine,	5035
Am 6: 5	That chant to the sound of the **v**,	5035

VIOLATED (1)

Eze 22:26	Her priests have **v** my law,	2554

VIOLENCE (57) [VIOLENT, VIOLENTLY]

Ge 6:11	God, and the earth was filled with **v**.	2555
6:13	for the earth is filled *with* **v** through them;	2555
Lev 6: 2	or in a **thing taken away by v**.	1498
2Sa 22: 3	my saviour; thou savest me from **v**.	2555
Ps 11: 5	and him that loveth **v** his soul hateth.	2555
55: 9	for I have seen **v** and strife in the city.	2555
58: 2	weigh the **v** of your hands in the earth.	2555
72:14	shall redeem their soul from deceit and **v**:	2555
73: 6	as a chain; **v** covereth them as a garment.	2555
Pr 4:17	of wickedness, and drink the wine of **v**.	2555
10: 6	but **v** covereth the mouth of the wicked.	2555
10:11	but **v** covereth the mouth of the wicked.	2555
13: 2	the soul of the transgressors shall eat **v**.	2555
28:17	A man that **doeth** to the blood of *any*	6231
Isa 53: 9	because he had done no **v**, neither *was*	2555
59: 6	and the act of **v** *is* in their hands.	2555
60:18	**V** shall no more be heard in thy land,	2555
Jer 6: 7	and spoil is heard in her; before me	2555
20: 8	I spake, I cried out, I cried **v** and spoil;	2555
22: 3	do no wrong, **do** no **v**, to the stranger,	2554
22:17	and for oppression, and for **v**, to do *it*.	4835
51:35	The **v** done to me and *to* my flesh *be*	2555
51:46	and **v** in the land, ruler against ruler.	2555
Eze 7:11	**V** is risen up into a rod of wickedness:	2555
7:23	*of* bloody crimes, and the city is full *of* **v**.	2555
8:17	for they have filled the land *with* **v**,	2555
12:19	of the **v** of all them that dwell therein.	2555
18: 7	hath spoiled none by **v**, hath given his	1500
18:12	the poor and needy, hath spoiled by **v**,	1500
18:16	neither hath spoiled by **v**, *but* hath given	1500
18:18	spoiled *his* brother by **v**, and did *that*	1499
28:16	they have filled the midst of thee *with* **v**,	2555
45: 9	remove **v** and spoil, and execute	2555
Joel 3:19	for the **v** against the children of Judah,	2555
Am 3:10	store up **v** and robbery in their palaces.	2555
6: 3	and cause the seat of **v** to come near;	2555
Ob 1:10	For *thy* **v** against thy brother Jacob shame	2555
Jnh 3: 8	and from the **v** that *is* in their hands.	2555
Mic 2: 2	they covet fields, and **take** *them* by **v**:	1497
6:12	For the rich *men* thereof are full of **v**,	2555
Hab 1: 2	*even* cry out unto thee of **v**, and thou wilt	2555

Hab 1: 3 for spoiling and **v** *are* before me: 2555
1: 9 They shall come all for **v**: their faces shall 2555
2: 8 *for* the **v** of the land, *of* the city, and *of* all 2555
2:17 For the **v** of Lebanon shall cover thee, 2555
2:17 *for* the **v** of the land, *of* the city, and *of* all 2555
Zep 1: 9 which fill their masters' houses with **v** 2555
3: 4 sanctuary, they have **done** **v** to the law. 2554
Mal 2:16 for *one* covereth **v** with his garment, 2555
Mt 11:12 now the kingdom of heaven **suffereth v**, 971
Lk 3:14 And he said unto them, Do **v** to no man, 1286
Ac 5:26 the officers, and brought them without **v**: 970
21:35 that he was borne of the soldiers for the **v** 970
24: 7 great **v** took *him* away out of our hands, 970
27:41 the hinder part was broken with the **v** of 970
Heb 11:34 Quenched the **v** of fire, escaped the edge 1411
Rev 18:21 Thus with **v** shall *that* great city Babylon 3731

VIOLENT (10) [VIOLENCE]

2Sa 22:49 thou hast delivered me from the **v** man. 2555
Ps 7:16 his **v** dealing shall come down upon his 2555
18:48 thou hast delivered me from the **v** man. 2555
86:14 the assemblies of **v** *men* have sought after 6184
140: 1 evil man: preserve me from the **v** man; 2555
140: 4 the wicked; preserve me from the **v** man; 2555
140:11 evil shall hunt the **v** man to overthrow 2555
Pr 16:29 A **v** man enticeth his neighbour, 2555
Ecc 5: 8 **v** perverting of judgment and justice in a 1499
Mt 11:12 violence, and the **v** take it by force. 973

VIOLENTLY (10) [VIOLENCE]

Ge 21:25 Abimelech's servants had **v taken away**. 1497
Lev 6: 4 restore that which he **took v away**, 1497+1500
Dt 28:31 thine ass *shall be* **v taken away** from 1497
Job 20:19 he hath **v taken away** a house which he 1497
24: 2 they **v take away** flocks, and feed 1497
Isa 22:18 will **surely v turn and toss** 6801+6801+6802
La 2: 6 he hath **v taken away** his tabernacle, as 2554
Mt 8:32 the whole herd of swine **ran v** down a 3729
Mk 5:13 the herd **ran v** down a steep place into 3729
Lk 8:33 the herd **ran v** down a steep place into 3729

VIOLS (2) [VIOL]

Isa 14:11 down *to* the grave, *and* the noise of thy **v**: 5035
Am 5:23 for I will not hear the melody of thy **v**. 5035

VIPER (3) [VIPER'S, VIPERS]

Isa 30: 6 and old lion, the **v** and fiery flying serpent, 660
59: 5 which is crushed breaketh out *into* a **v**. 660
Ac 28: 3 there came a **v** out of the heat, 2191

VIPER'S (1) [VIPER]

Job 20:16 poison of asps: the **v** tongue shall slay him. 660

VIPERS (4) [VIPER]

Mt 3: 7 he said unto them, O generation of **v**, 2191
12:34 O generation of **v**, how can ye, being evil, 2191
23:33 Ye serpents, ye generation of **v**, how can 2191
Lk 3: 7 O generation of **v**, who have warned you 2191

VIRGIN (33) [VIRGIN'S, VIRGINITY, VIRGINS]

Ge 24:16 a **v**, neither had any man known her: 1330
24:43 *when* the **v** cometh forth to draw *water*, 5959
Lev 21: 3 for his sister a **v**, that is nigh unto him, 1330
21:14 shall take a **v** of his own people to wife. 1330
Dt 22:19 hath brought up an evil name upon a **v** 1330
22:23 If a damsel *that is* a **v** be betrothed unto a 1330
22:28 If a man find a damsel *that is* a **v**, which 1330
32:25 destroy both the young man and the **v**, 1330
2Sa 13: 2 for she *was* a **v**; and Amnon thought it 1330
1Ki 1: 2 be sought for my lord the king a young **v**: 1330
2Ki 19:21 The **v** the daughter of Zion hath despised 1330
Isa 7:14 a **V** shall conceive, and bear a Son, 5959
23:12 O thou oppressed **v**, daughter of Zidon: 1330
37:22 The **v**, the daughter of Zion, hath despised 1330
47: 1 sit in the dust, O **v** daughter of Babylon, 1330
62: 5 For *as* a young man marrieth a **v**, 1330
Jer 14:17 for the **v** daughter of my people is broken 1330
18:13 hath heard such things: the **v** of Israel 1330
31: 4 and thou shalt be built, O **v** of Israel: 1330
31:13 the **v** rejoice in the dance, both young 1330
31:21 again, O **v** of Israel, turn again to these 1330
46:11 Go up *into* Gilead, and take balm, O **v**, 1330
La 1:15 the Lord hath trodden the **v**, the daughter 1330
2:13 I may comfort thee, O **v** daughter of Zion? 1330
Joel 1: 8 Lament like a **v** girded with sackcloth for 1330
Am 5: 2 The **v** of Israel is fallen; she shall no more 1330
Mt 1:23 a **v** shall be with child, and shall bring 3933
Lk 1:27 To a **v** espoused to a man whose name 3933
1Co 7:28 and if a **v** marry, she hath not sinned. 3933
7:34 is difference *also* between a wife and a **v**. 3933
7:36 behaveth himself uncomely toward his **v**, 3933
7:37 in his heart that *he* will keep his **v**, 3933
2Co 11: 2 that *I* may present *you as* a chaste **v** to 3933

VIRGIN'S (1) [VIRGIN]

Lk 1:27 of David; and the **v** name *was* Mary. 3933

VIRGINITY (9) [VIRGIN]

Lev 21:13 And he shall take a wife in her **v**. 1331
Dt 22:15 bring forth *the* tokens *of* the damsel's **v** 1331
22:17 these *are* the tokens *of* my daughter's **v**. 1331
22:20 *tokens of* **v** be not found for the damsel: 1331
Jdg 11:37 and bewail my **v**, I and my fellows. 1331
11:38 and bewailed her **v** upon the mountains. 1331
Eze 23: 3 and there they bruised the teats of their **v**. 1331
23: 8 they bruised the breasts of her **v**. 1331

Lk 2:36 with a husband seven years from her **v**; 3932

VIRGINS (22) [VIRGIN]

Ex 22:17 pay money according to the dowry of **v**. 1330
Jdg 21:12 of Jabesh-gilead four hundred young **v**, 1330
2Sa 13:18 king's daughters *that were* **v** apparelled. 1330
Est 2: 2 Let there be fair young **v** sought for 1330
2: 3 the fair young **v** unto Shushan the palace, 1330
2:17 favour in his sight more than all the **v**; 1330
2:19 when the **v** were gathered together 1330
Ps 45:14 the **v** her companions that follow her 1330
SS 1: 3 poured forth, therefore do the **v** love thee. 5959
6: 8 and **v** without number. 5959
Isa 23: 4 I nourish up young men, *nor* bring up **v**. 1330
La 1: 4 her **v** *are* afflicted, and she is in bitterness. 1330
1:18 my **v** and my young men are gone into 1330
2:10 the **v** of Jerusalem hang down their heads 1330
2:21 my **v** and my young men are fallen by 1330
Am 8:13 In that day shall the fair **v** and young men 1330
Mt 25: 1 kingdom of heaven be likened unto ten **v**, 3933
25: 7 Then all those **v** arose, and trimmed their 3933
25:11 Afterward came also the other **v**, saying, 3933
Ac 21: 9 four daughters, **v**, which did prophesy. 3933
1Co 7:25 concerning **v** I have no commandment 3933
Rev 14: 4 not defiled with women; for they are **v**. 3933

VIRTUE (7) [VIRTUOUS, VIRTUOUSLY]

Mk 5:30 in himself that **v** had gone out of him, 1411
Lk 6:19 for there went **v** out of him, and healed 1411
8:46 for I perceive that **v** is gone out of me. 1411
Php 4: 8 *there be* any **v**, and if *there be* any praise, 703
2Pe 1: 3 of him that hath called us to glory and **v**: 703
1: 5 giving all diligence, add to your faith **v**; 703
1: 5 to your faith virtue; and to **v** knowledge; 703

VIRTUOUS (3) [VIRTUE]

Ru 3:11 doth know that thou *art* a **v** woman. 2428
Pr 12: 4 A **v** woman *is* a crown to her husband: 2428
31:10 Who can find a **v** woman? for her price *is* 2428

VIRTUOUSLY (1) [VIRTUE]

Pr 31:29 Many daughters have done **v**, 2428

VISAGE (3) [VISION]

Isa 52:14 his **v** *was* so marred more than *any* man, 4758
La 4: 8 Their **v** is blacker than a coal; they are 8389
Da 3:19 the form of his **v** was changed against 600

VISIBLE (1) [VISION]

Col 1:16 and that are in earth, **v** and invisible, 3707

VISION (79) [VISAGE, VISIBLE, VISIONS]

Ge 15: 1 of the LORD came unto Abram in a **v**, 4236
Nu 12: 6 will make myself known unto him in a **v**, 4759
24: 4 which saw the **v** of the Almighty, 4236
24:16 *which* saw the **v** of the Almighty, 4236
1Sa 3: 1 in those days; *there was* no open **v**. 2377
3:15 And Samuel feared to shew Eli the **v**. 4759
2Sa 7:17 according to all this **v**, so did Nathan 2384
1Ch 17:15 according to all this **v**, so did Nathan 2377
2Ch 32:32 they *are* written in the **v** of Isaiah 2377
Job 20: 8 shall be chased away as a **v** of the night. 2384
33:15 In a dream, *in* a **v** of the night, when 2384
Ps 89:19 thou spakest in **v** to thy holy one, 2377
Pr 29:18 Where *there is* no **v**, the people perish: 2377
Isa 1: 1 The **v** of Isaiah the son of Amoz, which 2377
21: 2 A grievous **v** is declared unto me; 2380
22: 1 The burden of the valley of **v**. What aileth 2384
22: 5 the Lord GOD of hosts in the valley of **v**, 2384
28: 7 they err in **v**, they stumble *in* judgment. 7203
29: 7 shall be as a dream of a night **v**. 2377
29:11 the **v** of all is become unto you as 2380
Jer 14:14 they prophesy unto you a false **v** and 2377
23:16 they speak a **v** of their own heart, 2377
La 2: 9 prophets also find no **v** from the LORD. 2377
Eze 7:13 for the **v** *is* touching the whole multitude 2377
7:26 shall they seek a **v** of the prophet; 2377
8: 4 according to the **v** that I saw in the plain. 4758
11:24 brought me in **v** by the Spirit of God into 4758
11:24 the **v** that I had seen went up from me. 4758
12:22 days are prolonged, and every **v** faileth? 2377
12:23 are at hand, and the effect of every **v**. 2377
12:24 For there shall be no more any vain **v** nor 2377
12:27 The **v** that he seeth *is* for many days *to* 2377
13: 7 Have ye not seen a vain **v**, and have ye 4236
43: 3 *was* according to the appearance of the **v** 4758
43: 3 *even* according to the **v** that I saw when I 4758
43: 3 the visions *were* like the **v** that I saw by 4758
Da 2:19 secret revealed unto Daniel in a night **v**. 2376
7: 2 said, I saw in my **v** by night, and behold, 2376
8: 1 of king Belshazzar a **v** appeared unto me, 2377
8: 1 I saw in a **v**; and it came to pass, when I 2377
8: 2 saw in a **v**, and I was by the river of Ulai. 2377
8:13 How long *shall be* the **v** concerning 2377
8:15 seen the **v**, and sought for the meaning, 2377
8:16 make this man to understand the **v**. 4758
8:17 for at the time of the end *shall be* the **v**. 2377
8:26 the **v** of the evening and the morning 4758
8:26 wherefore shut thou up the **v**; for *it shall* 2377
8:27 I was astonished at the **v**, 4758
9:21 I had seen in the **v** at the beginning, 2377
9:23 the matter, and consider the **v**. 4758
9:24 seal up the **v** and prophecy, and to anoint 2377
10: 1 thing, and had understanding of the **v**. 4758
10: 7 I Daniel alone saw the **v**: for the men that 4759

Da 10: 7 men that were with me saw not the **v**; 4759
10: 8 saw this great **v**, and there remained no 4759
10:14 latter days: for yet the **v** *is* for *many* days. 2377
10:16 by the **v** my sorrows are turned upon me, 4759
11:14 shall exalt themselves to establish the **v**; 2377
Ob 1: 1 The **v** of Obadiah. Thus saith the Lord 2377
Mic 3: 6 *be* unto you, that *ye* shall not have a **v**; 2377
Na 1: 1 book of the **v** of Nahum the Elkoshite. 2377
Hab 2: 2 Write the **v**, and make *it* plain upon 2377
2: 3 For the **v** *is* yet for an appointed time, 2377
Zec 13: 4 shall be ashamed every one of his **v** 2377
Mt 17: 9 Tell the **v** to no *man*, until the Son of man 3705
Lk 1:22 they perceived that he had seen a **v** in 3701
24:23 that *they* had also seen a **v** of angels, 3701
Ac 9:10 and to him said the Lord in a **v**, Ananias. 3705
9:12 hath seen in a **v** a man named Ananias 3705
10: 3 He saw in a **v** evidently, about the ninth 3705
10:17 *this* **v** which he had seen should mean, 3705
10:19 Peter thought on the **v**, the Spirit 3705
11: 5 and in a trance I saw a **v**, A certain vessel 3705
12: 9 by the angel; but thought he saw a **v**. 3705
16: 9 And a **v** appeared to Paul in the night; 3705
16:10 And after he had seen the **v**, 3705
18: 9 spake the Lord to Paul in the night by a **v**, 3705
26:19 was not disobedient unto the heavenly **v**: 3701
Rev 9:17 And thus I saw the horses in the **v**, 3706

VISIONS (24) [VISION]

Ge 46: 2 spake unto Israel in the **v** of the night, 4759
2Ch 9:29 in the **v** of Iddo the seer against Jeroboam 2378
26: 5 who had understanding in the **v** of God: 7200
Job 4:13 In thoughts from the **v** of the night, 2384
7:14 with dreams, and terrifiest me through **v**: 2384
Eze 1: 1 were opened, and I saw **v** of God. 4759
8: 3 brought me in the **v** of God to Jerusalem, 4759
13:16 which see **v** of peace for her, and *there is* 2377
40: 2 In the **v** of God brought he me into the 4759
43: 3 the **v** *were* like the vision that I saw by 4759
Da 1:17 Daniel had understanding in all **v** and 2377
2:28 the **v** of thy head upon thy bed, *are* these; 2376
4: 5 bed and the **v** of my head troubled me. 2376
4: 9 *me* the **v** of my dream that I have seen, 2376
4:10 Thus *were* the **v** of mine head in my bed; 2376
4:13 I saw in the **v** of my head upon my bed, 2376
7: 1 a dream and **v** of his head upon his bed: 2376
7: 7 After this I saw in the night **v**, 2376
7:13 I saw in the night **v**, and behold, *one* like 2376
7:15 and the **v** of my head troubled me. 2376
Hos 12:10 I have multiplied **v**, and used similitudes 2377
Joel 2:28 dreams, your young men shall see **v**: 2384
Ac 2:17 and your young men shall see **v**, 3706
2Co 12: 1 I will come to **v** and revelations of 3701

VISIT (38) [VISITATION, VISITED, VISITEST, VISITETH, VISITING]

Ge 50:24 God will **surely v** you, and bring 6485+6485
50:25 God will **surely v** you, and ye shall 6485+6485
Ex 13:19 saying, God will **surely v** you; 6485+6485
32:34 nevertheless in the day when I **v**, I will 6485
32:34 when I visit, I will **v** their sin upon them. 6485
Lev 18:25 I do **v** the iniquity thereof upon it, 6485
Job 5:24 thou shalt **v** thy habitation, and shalt not 6485
7:18 *that* thou shouldest **v** him every morning, 6485
Ps 59: 5 God of Israel, awake to **v** all the heathen: 6485
80: 14 from heaven, and behold, and **v** this vine; 6485
89:32 will I **v** their transgression with the rod, 6485
106: 4 thy people: O **v** me with thy salvation; 6485
Isa 23:17 *that* the LORD will **v** Tyre, and she shall 6485
Jer 3:16 neither shall they **v** *it*; neither shall *that* 6485
5: 9 Shall I not **v** for these *things?* saith 6485
5:29 Shall I not **v** for these *things?* saith 6485
6:15 at the time *that* I **v** them they shall be cast 6485
9: 9 Shall I not **v** them for these *things?* saith 6485
14:10 remember their iniquity, and **v** their sins. 6485
15:15 **v** me, and revenge me of my persecutors, 6485
23: 2 I will **v** upon you the evil of your doings, 6485
27:22 there shall they be until the day that I **v** 6485
29:10 be accomplished at Babylon I will **v** you, 6485
32: 5 there shall he be until I **v** him, saith 6485
49: 8 Esau upon him, the time *that* I will **v** him. 6485
50:31 day is come, the time *that* I will **v** thee. 6485
La 4:22 he will **v** thine iniquity, O daughter of 6485
Hos 2:13 I will **v** upon her the days of Baalim, 6485
8:13 remember their iniquity, and **v** their sins: 6485
9: 9 their iniquity, he will **v** their sins. 6485
Am 3:14 That in the day that I shall **v** 6485
3:14 upon him I will also **v** the altars of Beth-el: 6485
Zep 2: 7 for the LORD their God shall **v** them, 6485
Zec 11:16 *which* shall not **v** those that be cut off, 6485
Ac 7:23 it came into his heart to **v** his brethren 1980
15:14 how God at the first did **v** the Gentiles, 1980
15:36 **v** our brethren in every city where we 1980
Jas 1:27 To **v** the fatherless and widows in their 1980

VISITATION (15) [VISIT]

Nu 16:29 or if they be visited after the **v** of all men; 6486
Job 10:12 and thy **v** hath preserved my spirit. 6486
Isa 10: 3 what will ye do in the day of **v**, and in 6486
Jer 8:12 in the time of their **v** they shall be cast 6486
10:15 in the time of their **v** they shall perish. 6486
11:23 men of Anathoth, *even* the year of their **v**. 6486
23:12 *even* the year of their **v**, saith the LORD. 6486
46:21 come upon them, *and* the time of their **v**. 6486
48:44 *even* upon Moab, the year of their **v**, 6486
50:27 for their day is come, the time of their **v**. 6486

Jer	51:18 in the time of their **v** they shall perish.	6486
Hos	9: 7 The days of **v** are come, the days of	6486
Mic	7: 4 day of thy watchmen *and* thy **v** cometh;	6486
Lk	19:44 thou knewest not the time of thy **v**.	1984
1Pe	2:12 that behold, glorify God in the day of **v**.	1984

VISITED (23) [VISIT]

Ge	21: 1 the Lord **v** Sarah as he had said,	6485
Ex	3:16 I have **surely v** you, and *seen* that	6485+6485
	4:31 when they heard that the Lord had **v**	6485
Nu	16:29 if they be **v** after the visitation of all men;	6485
Jdg	15: 1 that Samson **v** his wife with a kid;	6485
Ru	1: 6 had **v** his people in giving them bread.	6485
1Sa	2:21 the Lord **v** Hannah, so that she	6485
Job	35:15 *it is* not so, he hath **v** *in* his anger;	6485
Ps	17: 3 hast **v** *me* in the night; thou hast tried	6485
Pr	19:23 abide satisfied; he shall not be **v** *with* evil.	6485
Isa	24:22 and after many days shall they be **v**.	6485
	26:14 therefore hast thou **v** and destroyed them,	6485
	26:16 Lord, in trouble have they **v** thee,	6485
	29: 6 Thou shalt be **v** of the Lord of hosts	6485
Jer	6: 6 this is the city to be **v**; she *is* wholly	6485
	23: 2 driven them away, and have not **v** them:	6485
Eze	38: 8 After many days thou shalt be **v**:	6485
Zec	10: 3 for the Lord of hosts hath **v** his flock	6485
Mt	25:36 I was sick, and ye **v** me: I was in prison,	1980
	25:43 sick, and in prison, and ye **v** me not.	1980
Lk	1:68 for he hath **v** and redeemed his people,	1980
	1:78 the dayspring from on high hath **v**	1980
	7:16 and, That God hath **v** his people.	1980

VISITEST (3) [VISIT]

Ps	8: 4 and the son of man, that thou **v** him?	6485
	65: 9 Thou **v** the earth, and waterest it:	6485
Heb	2: 6 or the son of man, that thou **v** him?	1980

VISITETH (1) [VISIT]

Job	31:14 and when he **v**, what shall I answer him?	6485

VISITING (4) [VISIT]

Ex	20: 5 **v** the iniquity of the fathers upon the	6485
	34: 7 **v** the iniquity of the fathers upon the	6485
Nu	14:18 **v** the iniquity of the fathers upon the	6485
Dt	5: 9 **v** the iniquity of the fathers upon the	6485

VOCATION (1)

Eph	4: 1 beseech you that *ye* walk worthy of the **v**	2821

VOICE (505) [VOICES]

Ge	3: 8 they heard the **v** of the Lord God	6963
	3:10 I heard thy **v** in the garden, and I was	6963
	3:17 Because thou hast hearkened unto the **v**	6963
	4:10 the **v** of thy brother's blood crieth unto	6963
	4:23 his wives, Adah and Zillah, Hear my **v**;	6963
	16: 2 And Abram hearkened to the **v** of Sarai.	6963
	21:12 hath said unto thee, hearken unto her **v**;	6963
	21:16 she sat over against *him*, and lift up her **v**,	6963
	21:17 God heard the **v** of the lad; and the angel	6963
	21:17 for God hath heard the **v** of the lad where	6963
	22:18 blessed; because thou hast obeyed my **v**.	6963
	26: 5 Because that Abraham obeyed my **v**,	6963
	27: 8 obey my **v** according to *that* which I	6963
	27:13 only obey my **v**, and go fetch me *them*.	6963
	27:22 The **v** *is* Jacob's voice, but the hands *are*	6963
	27:22 The voice *is* Jacob's **v**, but the hands *are*	6963
	27:38 And Esau lift up his **v**, and wept.	6963
	27:43 Now therefore, my son, obey my **v**;	6963
	29:11 and lifted up his **v**, and wept.	6963
	30: 6 hath also heard my **v**, and hath given me	6963
	39:14 to lie with me, and I cried with a loud **v**:	6963
	39:15 when he heard that I lifted up my **v** and	6963
	39:18 it came to pass, as I lift up my **v** and cried,	6963
Ex	3:18 they shall hearken to thy **v**: and thou shalt	6963
	4: 1 not believe me, nor hearken unto my **v**:	6963
	4: 8 neither hearken to the **v** of the first sign,	6963
	4: 8 that they will believe the **v** of the latter	6963
	4: 9 two signs, neither hearken unto thy **v**,	6963
	5: 2 that I should obey his **v** to let Israel go?	6963
	15:26 If thou wilt diligently hearken to the **v** of	6963
	18:19 Hearken now unto my **v**, I will give thee	6963
	18:24 So Moses hearkened to the **v** of his father	6963
	19: 5 if ye will obey my **v** indeed, and keep my	6963
	19:16 and the **v** of the trumpet exceeding loud;	6963
	19:19 when the **v** of the trumpet sounded long,	6963
	19:19 and God answered him by a **v**.	6963
	23:21 Beware of him, and obey his **v**,	6963
	23:22 if thou shalt indeed obey his **v**, and do all	6963
	24: 3 and all the people answered *with* one **v**,	6963
	32:18 *It is* not the **v** of *them that* shout for	6963
	32:18 neither *is it* the **v** of *them that* cry for	6963
Lev	5: 1 hear the **v** of swearing, and *is* a witness,	6963
Nu	7:89 he heard the **v** of one speaking unto him	6963
	14: 1 all the congregation lifted up their **v**,	6963
	14:22 times, and have not hearkened to my **v**;	6963
	20:16 he heard our **v**, and sent an angel,	6963
	21: 3 the Lord hearkened to the **v** of Israel,	6963
Dt	1:34 the Lord heard the **v** of your words,	6963
	1:45 the Lord would not hearken to your **v**,	6963
	4:12 ye heard the **v** of the words, but saw no	6963
	4:12 but saw no similitude; only *ye heard* a **v**.	6963
	4:30 thy God, and shalt be obedient unto his **v**;	6963
	4:33 Did *ever* people hear the **v** of God	6963
	4:36 Out of heaven he made thee to hear his **v**,	6963
	5:22 and of the thick darkness, *with* a great **v**:	6963
	5:23 when ye heard the **v** out of the midst of	6963

Dt	5:24 we have heard his **v** out of the midst of	6963
	5:25 if we hear the **v** of the Lord our God any	6963
	5:26 that hath heard the **v** of the living God	6963
	5:28 the Lord heard the **v** of your words,	6963
	5:28 I have heard the **v** of the words of this	6963
	8:20 ye would not be obedient unto the **v** of	6963
	9:23 believed him not, nor hearkened to his **v**.	6963
	13: 4 obey his **v**, and you shall serve him,	6963
	13:18 When thou shalt hearken to the **v** of	6963
	15: 5 Only if thou carefully hearken to the **v**	6963
	18:16 Let me not hear again the **v** of the Lord	6963
	21:18 which will not obey the **v** of his father,	6963
	21:18 or the **v** of his mother, and *that*, when	6963
	21:20 and rebellious, he will not obey our **v**;	6963
	26: 7 the Lord heard our **v**, and looked on our	6963
	26:14 I have hearkened to the **v** of the Lord thy	6963
	26:17 his judgments, and to hearken unto his **v**:	6963
	27:10 obey the **v** of the Lord thy God,	6963
	27:14 unto all the men of Israel *with* a loud **v**,	6963
	28: 1 if thou shalt hearken diligently unto the **v**	6963
	28: 2 if thou shalt hearken unto the **v** of	6963
	28:15 if thou wilt not hearken to the **v** of	6963
	28:45 thou hearkenedst not unto the **v** of	6963
	28:62 thou wouldest not obey the **v** of	6963
	30: 2 shalt obey his **v** according to all that	6963
	30: 8 shalt return and obey the **v** of the Lord,	6963
	30:10 If thou shalt hearken unto the **v** of	6963
	30:20 *and* that thou mayest obey his **v**,	6963
	33: 7 the **v** of Judah, and bring him unto his	6963
Jos	5: 6 they obeyed not the **v** of the Lord:	6963
	6:10 shout, nor make any noise with your **v**,	6963
	10:14 that the Lord hearkened unto the **v** of a	6963
	22: 2 obeyed my **v** in all that I commanded	6963
	24:24 will we serve, and his **v** will we obey.	6963
Jdg	2: 2 ye have not obeyed my **v**: why have ye	6963
	2: 4 that the people lift up their **v**, and wept.	6963
	2:20 and have not hearkened unto my **v**;	6963
	6:10 ye dwell: but ye have not obeyed my **v**.	6963
	9: 7 lift up his **v**, and cried, and said unto	6963
	13: 9 God hearkened to the **v** of Manoah;	6963
	18: 3 they knew the **v** of the young man	6963
	18:25 Let not thy **v** be heard among us, lest	6963
	20:13 of their brethren the children of Israel:	6963
Ru	1: 9 and they lift up their **v**, and wept.	6963
	1:14 they lift up their **v**, and wept again:	6963
1Sa	1:13 her lips moved, but her **v** was not heard:	6963
	2:25 hearkened not unto the **v** of their father,	6963
	8: 7 Hearken unto the **v** of the people in all	6963
	8: 9 Now therefore hearken unto their **v**:	6963
	8:19 people refused to obey the **v** of Samuel;	6963
	8:22 Hearken unto their **v**, and make them a	6963
	12: 1 I have hearkened unto your **v** in all that	6963
	12:14 obey his **v**, and not rebel against	6963
	12:15 But if ye will not obey the **v** of the Lord,	6963
	15: 1 hearken thou unto the **v** of the words of	6963
	15:19 didst thou not obey the **v** of the Lord,	6963
	15:20 I have obeyed the **v** of the Lord,	6963
	15:22 as in obeying the **v** of the Lord?	6963
	15:24 I feared the people, and obeyed their **v**.	6963
	24: 16 Saul lifted up his **v**, and wept.	6963
	24:16 that Saul said, *Is* this thy **v**, my son David?	6963
	24:16 And Saul lift up his **v**, and wept.	6963
	25:35 I have hearkened to thy **v**,	6963
	26:17 Saul knew David's **v**, and said, *Is* this thy	6963
	26:17 and said, *Is* this thy **v**, my son David?	6963
	26:17 David said, It *is* my **v**, my lord, O king.	6963
	28:12 saw Samuel, she cried with a loud **v**:	6963
	28:18 Because thou obeyedst not the **v** of	6963
	28:21 thine handmaid hath obeyed thy **v**,	6963
	28:22 hearken thou also unto the **v** of thine	6963
	28:23 and he hearkened unto their **v**.	6963
	30: 4 people that *were* with him lift up their **v**	6963
2Sa	3:32 king lift up his **v**, and wept at the grave	6963
	12:18 and he would not hearken unto our **v**:	6963
	13:14 he would not hearken unto her **v**:	6963
	13:36 sons came, and lift up their **v** and wept:	6963
	15:23 all the country wept *with* a loud **v**,	6963
	19: 4 the king cried *with* a loud **v**, O my son	6963
	19:35 can I hear any more the **v** of singing *men*	6963
	22: 7 he did hear my **v** out of his temple,	6963
	22:14 and the most High uttered his **v**.	6963
1Ki	8:55 the congregation of Israel *with* a loud **v**,	6963
	17:22 the Lord heard the **v** of Elijah;	6963
	18:26 *there was* no **v**, nor any that answered.	6963
	18:29 *there was* neither **v**, nor any to answer,	6963
	19:12 in the fire: and after the fire a still small **v**.	6963
	19:13 *there came* a **v** unto him, and said,	6963
	20:25 he hearkened unto their **v**, and did so.	6963
	20:36 Because thou hast not obeyed the **v** of	6963
2Ki	4:31 but *there was* neither **v**, nor hearing.	6963
	7:10 neither **v** of man, but horses tied,	6963
	10: 6 mine, and *if* ye will hearken unto my **v**,	6963
	18:12 Because they obeyed not the **v** of	6963
	18:28 cried with a loud **v** in the Jews' language,	6963
	19:22 against whom hast thou exalted *thy* **v**,	6963
1Ch	15:16 sounding, by lifting up the **v** with joy.	6963
2Ch	5:13 *they* lift up *their* **v** with the trumpets	6963
	15:14 they sware unto the Lord with a loud **v**,	6963
	20:19 God of Israel with a loud **v** on high.	6963
	30:27 their **v** was heard, and their prayer came	6963
	32:18 cried with a loud **v** in the Jews' speech	6963
Ezr	3:12 laid before their eyes, wept with a loud **v**;	6963
	10:12 and said *with* a loud **v**,	6963
Ne	9: 4 cried with a loud **v** unto the Lord their	6963
Job	2:12 him not, they lifted up their **v**, and wept;	6963

Job	3: 7 be solitary, let no **joyful v** come therein.	7445
	3:18 they hear not the **v** of the oppressor.	6963
	4:10 the **v** of the fierce lion, and the teeth of	6963
	4:16 *there was* silence, and I heard a **v**, *saying*,	6963
	9:16 believe that he had hearkened unto my **v**.	6963
	30:31 my organ into the **v** of them that weep.	6963
	33: 8 I have heard the **v** of *thy* words,	6963
	34:16 hear this: hearken to the **v** of my words.	6963
	37: 2 Hear attentively the noise of his **v**,	6963
	37: 4 After it a **v** roareth: he thundereth with	6963
	37: 4 thundereth with the **v** of his excellency;	6963
	37: 4 will not stay them when his **v** is heard.	6963
	37: 5 God thundereth marvellously with his **v**;	6963
	38:34 Canst thou lift up thy **v** to the clouds,	6963
	40: 9 or, canst thou thunder with a **v** like him?	6963
Ps	3: 4 I cried unto the Lord with my **v**,	6963
	5: 2 Hearken unto the **v** of my cry, my King,	6963
	5: 3 My **v** shalt thou hear *in* the morning,	6963
	6: 8 for the Lord hath heard the **v** of my	6963
	18: 6 he heard my **v** out of his temple,	6963
	18:13 the heavens, and the Highest gave his **v**;	6963
	19: 3 nor language, *where* their **v** is not heard.	6963
	26: 7 That *I* may publish with thy **v**,	6963
	27: 7 Hear, O Lord, *when* I cry *with* my **v**:	6963
	28: 2 Hear the **v** of my supplications, when I	6963
	28: 6 he hath heard the **v** of my supplications.	6963
	29: 3 The **v** of the Lord *is* upon the waters:	6963
	29: 4 The **v** of the Lord *is* powerful; the voice	6963
	29: 4 The **v** of the Lord *is* full of majesty.	6963
	29: 5 The **v** of the Lord breaketh the cedars;	6963
	29: 7 The **v** of the Lord divideth the flames of	6963
	29: 8 The **v** of the Lord shaketh	6963
	29: 9 The **v** of the Lord maketh the hinds to	6963
	31:22 nevertheless thou heardest the **v** of my	6963
	42: 4 with the **v** of joy and praise, *with* a	6963
	44:16 For the **v** of him that reproacheth and	6963
	46: 6 he uttered his **v**, the earth melted.	6963
	47: 1 shout unto God with the **v** of triumph.	6963
	55: 3 Because of the **v** of the enemy, because	6963
	55:17 and cry aloud: and he shall hear my **v**.	6963
	58: 5 Which will not hearken to the **v** of	6963
	64: 1 Hear my **v**, O God, in my prayer:	6963
	66: 8 and make the **v** of his praise to be heard:	6963
	66:19 he hath attended to the **v** of my prayer.	6963
	68:33 he doth send out his **v**, *and that* a mighty	6963
	68:33 send out his voice, *and that* a mighty **v**.	6963
	74:23 Forget not the **v** of thine enemies:	6963
	77: 1 I cried unto God *with* my **v**, *even* unto	6963
	77: 1 *with* my voice, *even* unto God *with* my **v**;	6963
	77:18 The **v** of thy thunder *was* in the heaven:	6963
	81:11 my people would not hearken to my **v**;	6963
	86: 6 and attend to the **v** of my supplications.	6963
	93: 3 O Lord, the floods have lifted up their **v**;	6963
	95: 7 of his hand. To day if ye will hear his **v**,	6963
	98: 5 with the harp, and the **v** of a psalm.	6963
	102: 5 By reason of the **v** of my groaning my	6963
	103:20 hearkening unto the **v** of his word.	6963
	104: 7 at the **v** of thy thunder they hasted away.	6963
	106:25 hearkened not unto the **v** of the Lord.	6963
	116: 1 because he hath heard my **v** and	6963
	118:15 The **v** of rejoicing and salvation *is* in	6963
	119:149 Hear my **v** according unto thy	6963
	130: 2 hear my **v**: let thine ears be attentive	6963
	130: 2 let thine ears be attentive to the **v** of my	6963
	140: 6 hear the **v** of my supplications, O Lord.	6963
	141: 1 give ear unto my **v**, when I cry unto thee.	6963
	142: 1 I cried unto the Lord *with* my **v**;	6963
	142: 1 *with* my **v** unto the Lord did I make my	6963
Pr	1:20 she uttereth her **v** in the streets:	6963
	2: 3 *and* liftest up thy **v** for understanding;	6963
	5:13 have not obeyed the **v** of my teachers,	6963
	8: 1 and understanding put forth her **v**?	6963
	8: 4 I call; and my **v** *is* to the sons of man.	6963
	27:14 He that blesseth his friend with a loud **v**,	6963
Ecc	5: 3 fool's **v** *is known* by multitude of words.	6963
	5: 6 wherefore should God be angry at thy **v**,	6963
	10:20 for a bird of the air shall carry the **v**,	6963
	12: 4 he shall rise up at the **v** of the bird,	6963
SS	2: 8 The **v** of my beloved! behold, he cometh	6963
	2:12 the **v** of the turtle is heard in our land;	6963
	2:14 see thy countenance, let me hear thy **v**;	6963
	2:14 for sweet *is* thy **v**, and thy countenance *is*	6963
	5: 2 *it is* the **v** of my beloved that knocketh	6963
	8:13 the companions hearken to thy **v**:	6963
Isa	6: 4 posts of the door moved at the **v** of him	6963
	6: 8 Also I heard the **v** of the Lord, saying,	6963
	10:30 Lift up thy **v**, O daughter of Gallim:	6963
	13: 2 exalt the **v** unto them, shake the hand,	6963
	15: 4 their **v** shall be heard *even* unto Jahaz:	6963
	24:14 They shall lift up their **v**, they shall sing,	6963
	28:23 Give ye ear, and hear my **v**; hearken,	6963
	29: 4 thy **v** shall be, as of one that hath a	6963
	30:19 will be very gracious unto thee at the **v**	6963
	30:30 the Lord shall cause his glorious **v** to be	6963
	30:31 For through the **v** of the Lord shall	6963
	31: 4 he will not be afraid of their **v**, nor abase	6963
	32: 9 ye women that are at ease, hear my **v**;	6963
	36:13 cried with a loud **v** in the Jews' language,	6963
	37:23 against whom hast thou exalted *thy* **v**,	6963
	40: 3 The **v** of him that crieth in the wilderness,	6963
	40: 6 The **v** said, Cry. And he said, What shall I	6963
	40: 9 good tidings, lift up thy **v** with strength;	6963
	42: 2 nor cause his **v** to be heard in the street.	6963
	42:11 the cities thereof lift up *their* **v**, the villages	NIH
	48:20 with a **v** of singing declare ye, tell this,	6963

Isa		
50:10	that obeyeth the v of his servant,	6963
51: 3	thanksgiving, and the v of melody.	6963
52: 8	Thy watchmen shall lift up the v; with	6963
52: 8	with the v together shall they sing:	6963
58: 1	lift up thy v like a trumpet, and shew my	6963
58: 4	to make your v to be heard on high.	6963
65:19	the v of weeping shall be no more heard	6963
65:19	no more heard in her, nor the v of crying.	6963
66: 6	A v of noise from the city, a voice from	6963
66: 6	noise from the city, a v from the temple,	6963
66: 6	a v of the LORD that rendereth	6963
Jer		
3:13	ye have not obeyed my v, saith	6963
3:21	A v was heard upon the high places,	6963
3:25	have not obeyed the v of the LORD our	6963
4:15	For a v declareth from Dan,	6963
4:16	give out their v against the cities of Judah.	6963
4:31	For I have heard a v as of a woman in	6963
4:31	the v of the daughter of Zion,	6963
6:23	their v roareth like the sea; and they ride	6963
7:23	Obey my v, and I will be your God,	6963
7:28	This is a nation that obeyeth not the v of	6963
7:34	the v of mirth, and the voice of gladness,	6963
7:34	the voice of mirth, and the v of gladness,	6963
7:34	the v of the bridegroom, and the voice of	6963
7:34	of the bridegroom, and the v of the bride:	6963
8:19	Behold the v of the cry of the daughter of	6963
9:10	neither can men hear the v of the cattle;	6963
9:13	have not obeyed my v, neither walked	6963
9:19	For a v of wailing is heard out of Zion,	6963
10:13	he uttereth his v, there is a multitude	6963
11: 4	saying, Obey my v, and do them,	6963
11: 7	and protesting, saying, Obey my v.	6963
16: 9	the v of mirth, and the voice of gladness,	6963
16: 9	the voice of mirth, and the v of gladness,	6963
16: 9	the v of the bridegroom, and the voice of	6963
16: 9	of the bridegroom, and the v of the bride.	6963
18:10	that it obey not my v, then I will repent	6963
18:19	hearken to the v of them that contend	6963
22:20	lift up thy v in Bashan, and cry from	6963
22:21	thy youth, that thou obeyedst not my v.	6963
25:10	Moreover I will take from them the v of	6963
25:10	the v of gladness, the voice of	6963
25:10	the v of the bridegroom, and the voice of	6963
25:10	the v of the bride, the sound of	6963
25:30	and utter his v from his holy habitation;	6963
25:36	A v of the cry of the shepherds,	6963
26:13	and obey the v of the LORD your God;	6963
30: 5	We have heard a v of trembling, of fear,	6963
30:19	and the v of them that make merry.	6963
31:15	A v was heard in Ramah, lamentation,	6963
31:16	Refrain thy v from weeping, and thine	6963
32:23	they obeyed not thy v, neither walked in	6963
33:11	The v of joy, and the voice of gladness,	6963
33:11	The voice of joy, and the v of gladness,	6963
33:11	the v of the bridegroom, and the voice of	6963
33:11	of the bridegroom, and the v of the bride,	6963
33:11	of the bride, the v of them that shall say,	6963
35: 8	Thus have we obeyed the v of Jonadab	6963
38:20	I beseech thee, the v of the LORD, which	6963
40: 3	have not obeyed his v, therefore this	6963
42: 6	we will obey the v of the LORD our God,	6963
42: 6	when we obey the v of the LORD our	6963
42:13	neither obey the v of the LORD your God,	6963
42:21	ye have not obeyed the v of the LORD	6963
43: 4	the people, obeyed not the v of the LORD,	6963
43: 7	For they obeyed not the v of the LORD:	6963
44:23	have not obeyed the v of the LORD,	6963
46:22	The v thereof shall go like a serpent;	6963
48: 3	A v of crying shall be from Horonaim,	6963
48:34	unto Jahaz, have they uttered their v,	6963
50:28	The v of them that flee and escape out of	6963
50:42	their v shall roar like the sea, and they	6963
51:16	he uttereth his v, there is a multitude	6963
51:55	and destroyed out of her the great v;	6963
51:55	great waters, a noise of their v is uttered:	6963
La		
3:56	Thou hast heard my v: hide not thine ear	6963
Eze		
1:24	as the v of the Almighty, the voice of	6963
1:24	the v of speech, as the noise of a host:	6963
1:25	there was a v from the firmament that	6963
1:28	face, and I heard a v of one that spake.	6963
3:12	I heard behind me a v of a great rushing,	6963
8:18	they cry in mine ears with a loud v,	6963
9: 1	He cried also in mine ears with a loud v,	6963
10: 5	as the v of the Almighty God when he	6963
11:13	cried with a loud v, and said, Ah Lord	6963
19: 9	that his v should no more be heard upon	6963
21:22	slaughter, to lift up the v with shouting,	6963
23:42	a v of a multitude being at ease was with	6963
27:30	cause their v to be heard against thee,	6963
33:32	lovely song of one that hath a pleasant v,	6963
43: 2	his v was like a noise of many waters:	6963
Da		
4:31	there fell a v from heaven, saying, O king	7032
6:20	he cried with a lamentable v unto Daniel:	7032
7:11	the v of the great words which the horn	7032
8:16	I heard a man's v between the banks of	6963
9:10	Neither have we obeyed the v of the	6963
9:11	that they might not obey thy v;	6963
9:14	which he doeth: for we obeyed not his v.	6963
10: 6	the v of his words like the voice of a	6963
10: 6	the voice of his words like the v of a	6963
10: 9	Yet heard I the v of his words: and when	6963
10: 9	when I heard the v of his words, then	6963
Joel		
2:11	the LORD shall utter his v before his	6963
3:16	of Zion, and utter his v from Jerusalem;	6963
Am		
1: 2	Zion, and utter his v from Jerusalem;	6963

Jnh		
2: 2	of hell cried I, and thou heardest my v.	6963
2: 9	I will sacrifice unto thee with the v of	6963
Mic		
6: 1	mountains, and let the hills hear thy v.	6963
6: 9	The LORD's v crieth unto the city,	6963
Na		
2: 7	her maids shall lead her as with the v of	6963
2:13	the v of thy messengers shall no more be	6963
Hab		
3:10	deep uttered his v, and lift up his hands	6963
3:16	belly trembled; my lips quivered at the v:	6963
Zep		
1:14	even the v of the day of the LORD:	6963
2:14	their v shall sing in the windows;	6963
2: 9	She obeyed not the v; she received not	6963
Hag		
1:12	obeyed the v of the LORD their God,	6963
Zec		
6:15	if ye will diligently obey the v of	6963
11: 3	There is a v of the howling of	6963
11: 3	a v of the roaring of young lions;	6963
Mt		
2:18	In Rama was there a v heard, lamentation,	5456
3: 3	The v of one crying in the wilderness,	5456
3:17	And lo a v from heaven, saying, This is my	5456
12:19	neither shall any man hear his v in	5456
17: 5	behold a v out of the cloud, which said,	5456
27:46	the ninth hour Jesus cried with a loud v,	5456
27:50	when he had cried again with a loud v,	5456
Mk		
1: 3	The v of one crying in the wilderness,	5456
1:11	And there came a v from heaven,	5456
1:26	and cried with a loud v, he came out of	5456
5: 7	And cried with a loud v, and said,	5456
9: 7	and a v came out of the cloud, saying,	5456
15:34	the ninth hour Jesus cried with a loud v,	5456
15:37	Jesus cried with a loud v, and gave up	5456
Lk		
1:42	And she spake out with a loud v,	5456
1:44	as soon as the v of thy salutation sounded	5456
3: 4	The v of one crying in the wilderness,	5456
3:22	and a v came from heaven, which said,	5456
4:33	unclean devil, and cried out with a loud v,	5456
8:28	down before him, and with a loud v said,	5456
9:35	And there came a v out of the cloud,	5456
9:36	And when the v was past, Jesus was found	5456
11:27	woman of the company lift up her v,	5456
17:15	and with a loud v glorified God,	5456
19:37	praise God with a loud v for all the mighty	5456
23:46	And when Jesus had cried with a loud v,	5456
Jn		
1:23	I am the v of one crying in the wilderness,	5456
3:29	because of the bridegroom's v:	5456
5:25	the dead shall hear the v of the Son of	5456
5:28	all that are in the graves shall hear his v,	5456
5:37	Ye have neither heard his v at any time,	5456
10: 3	porter openeth; and the sheep hear his v:	5456
10: 4	the sheep follow him: for they know his v:	5456
10: 5	for they know not the v of strangers.	5456
10:16	I must bring, and they shall hear my v;	5456
10:27	My sheep hear my v, and I know them,	5456
11:43	cried with a loud v, Lazarus, come forth.	5456
12:28	Then came there a v from heaven, saying,	5456
12:30	This v came not because of me,	5456
18:37	one that is of the truth heareth my v.	5456
Ac		
2:14	lift up his v, and said unto them, Ye men	5456
4:24	lift up their v to God with one accord,	5456
7:31	as he drew near to behold it, the v of	5456
7:57	Then they cried out with a loud v,	5456
7:60	and cried with a loud v, Lord,	5456
8: 7	For unclean spirits, crying with loud v,	5456
9: 4	heard a v saying unto him, Saul, Saul,	5456
9: 7	hearing a v, but seeing no man.	5456
10:13	there came a v to him, Rise, Peter; kill,	5456
10:15	the v spake unto him again the second	5456
11: 7	And I heard a v saying unto me, Arise,	5456
11: 9	the v answered me again from heaven,	5456
12:14	when she knew Peter's v, she opened	5456
12:22	saying, It is the v of a god, and not of a	5456
14:10	Said with a loud v, Stand upright on thy	5456
16:28	But Paul cried with a loud v, saying,	5456
19:34	with one v about the space of two hours	5456
22: 7	and heard a v saying unto me, Saul, Saul,	5456
22: 9	they heard not the v of him that spake to	5456
22:14	and shouldest hear the v of his mouth.	5456
24:21	Except it be for this one v, that I cried	5456
26:10	put to death, I gave my v against them.	5586
26:14	I heard a v speaking unto me, and saying	5456
26:24	Festus said with a loud v, Paul, thou art	5456
1Co		
14:11	if I know not the meaning of the v,	5456
14:19	that by my v I might teach others also,	NIG
Gal		
4:20	with you now, and to change my v;	5456
1Th		
4:16	with the v of the archangel, and with	5456
Heb		
3: 7	Ghost saith, To day if ye will hear his v,	5456
3:15	it is said, To day if ye will hear his v,	5456
4: 7	as it is said, To day if ye will hear his v,	5456
12:19	sound of a trumpet, and the v of words;	5456
12:19	which v they that heard intreated that	NIG
12:26	Whose v then shook the earth: but now	5456
2Pe		
1:17	when there came such a v to him from	5456
1:18	And this v which came from heaven we	5456
2:16	dumb ass speaking with man's v forbad	5456
Rev		
1:10	and heard behind me a great v, as of a	5456
1:12	And I turned to see the v that spake with	5456
1:15	and his v as the sound of many waters.	5456
3:20	if any man hear my v, and open the door,	5456
4: 1	the first v which I heard was as it were of	5456
5: 2	a strong angel proclaiming with a loud v,	5456
5:11	I heard the v of many angels round about	5456
5:12	Saying with a loud v, Worthy is the Lamb	5456
6: 1	And I heard a v in the midst of the four	5456
6: 6	And I heard a v in the midst of the four	5456
6: 7	I heard the v of the fourth beast say,	5456
6:10	And they cried with a loud v, saying,	5456
7: 2	he cried with a loud v to the four angels,	5456
7:10	And cried with a loud v, saying, Salvation	5456

Rev		
8:13	saying with a loud v, Woe, woe, woe,	5456
9:13	I heard a v from the four horns of	5456
10: 3	And cried with a loud v, as when a lion	5456
10: 4	I heard a v from heaven saying unto me,	5456
10: 7	But in the days of the v of the seventh	5456
10: 8	the v which I heard from heaven spake	5456
11:12	they heard a great v from heaven	5456
12:10	And I heard a loud v saying in heaven,	5456
14: 2	And I heard a v from heaven, as the voice	5456
14: 2	as the v of many waters, and as the voice	5456
14: 2	and as the v of a great thunder:	5456
14: 2	I heard the v of harpers harping with their	5456
14: 7	Saying with a loud v, Fear God,	5456
14: 9	saying with a loud v, If any man worship	5456
14:13	And I heard a v from heaven saying unto	5456
14:15	crying with a loud v to him that sat on	5456
16: 1	And I heard a great v out of the temple	5456
16:17	there came a great v out of the temple of	5456
18: 2	And he cried mightily with a strong v,	5456
18: 4	I heard another v from heaven, saying,	5456
18:22	And the v of harpers, and musicians,	5456
18:23	and the v of the bridegroom and of	5456
19: 1	And after these things I heard a great v of	5456
19: 5	And a v came out of the throne, saying,	5456
19: 6	And I heard as it were the v of a great	5456
19: 6	and as the v of many waters, and as	5456
19: 6	as the v of mighty thunderings, saying,	5456
19:17	and he cried with a loud v, saying to all	5456
21: 3	I heard a great v out of heaven saying,	5456

VOICES (17) [VOICE]

Jdg	21: 2	and lift up their v, and wept sore;	6963
1Sa	11: 4	all the people lift up their v, and wept.	6963
Lk	17:13	And they lifted up their v, and said, Jesus,	5456
	23:23	And they were instant with loud v,	5456
	23:23	And the v of them and of the chief priests	5456
Ac	13:27	yet the v of the prophets which are read	5456
	14:11	they lift up their v, saying in the speech of	5456
	22:22	and then lift up their v, and said,	5456
1Co	14:10	so many kinds of v in the world,	5456
Rev	4: 5	and thunderings and v:	5456
	8: 5	and there were v, and thunderings,	5456
	8:13	other v of the trumpet of the three angels,	5456
	10: 3	had cried, seven thunders uttered their v.	5456
	10: 4	the seven thunders had uttered their v,	5456
	11:15	and there were great v in heaven, saying,	5456
	11:19	v, and thunderings, and an earthquake,	5456
	16:18	And there were v, and thunders,	5456

VOID (24)

Ge	1: 2	the earth was without form, and v;	922
Nu	30:12	utterly made them v on the day	6565+6565
	30:12	her husband hath made them v;	6565
	30:13	or her husband may make it v.	6565
	30:15	if he made any ways make them v	6565+6565
Dt	32:28	For they are a nation v of counsel, neither	6
1Ki	2:28	in a v place in the entrance of the gate of	1637
2Ch	18: 9	they sat in a v place at the entering in of	1637
Ps	89:39	Thou hast made v the covenant of thy	5010
	119:126	to work: for they have made v thy law.	6565
Pr	7: 7	a young man v of understanding,	2638
	10:13	a rod is for the back of him that is v of	2638
	11:12	He that is v of wisdom despiseth his	2638
	12:11	he that followeth vain persons is v of	2638
	17:18	A man v of understanding striketh hands,	2638
	24:30	by the vineyard of the man v of	2638
Isa	55:11	it shall not return unto me, but it shall	7387
Jer	4:23	earth, and, lo, it was without form, and v;	922
	19: 7	And I will make v the counsel of Judah	1238
Na	2:10	She is empty, and v, and waste:	4003
Ac	24:16	have always a conscience v of offence	677
Ro	3:31	we then make v the law through faith?	2673
	4:14	faith is made v, and the promise made of	2758
1Co	9:15	any man should make my glorying v.	2758

VOLUME (2)

Ps	40: 7	in the v of the book it is written of me,	4039
Heb	10: 7	I come (in the v of the book it is written	2777

VOLUNTARILY (1) [VOLUNTARY]

Eze	46:12	or peace offerings v unto the LORD,	5071

VOLUNTARY (4) [VOLUNTARILY]

Lev	1: 3	he shall offer it of his own v will at	7522
	7:16	of his offering be a vow, or a v offering,	5071
Eze	46:12	Now when the prince shall prepare a v	5071
Col	2:18	beguile you of your reward in a v humility	2309

VOMIT (8) [VOMITED, VOMITETH]

Job	20:15	riches, and he shall v them up again:	6958
Pr	23: 8	which thou hast eaten shalt thou v up,	6958
	25:16	lest thou be filled therewith, and v it.	6958
	26:11	As a dog returneth to his v, so a fool	6892
Isa	19:14	as a drunken man staggereth in his v.	6892
	28: 8	For all tables are full of v and filthiness,	6892
Jer	48:26	Moab also shall wallow in his v,	6892
2Pe	2:22	The dog is turned to his own v again;	1829

VOMITED (1) [VOMIT]

Jnh	2:10	and it v out Jonah upon the dry land.	6958

VOMITETH (1) [VOMIT]

Lev	18:25	and the land itself v out her inhabitants.	6958

VOPHSI (1)

Nu	13:14	the tribe of Naphtali, Nabbi the son of V.	2058

V

VOW (41) [VOWED, VOWEDST, VOWEST, VOWETH, VOWS]

Ge	28:20 Jacob vowed a **v**, saying, If God will be	5088
	31:13 *and* where thou vowedst a **v** unto me:	5088
Lev	7:16 if the sacrifice of his offering *be* a **v**,	5088
	22:21 unto the LORD to accomplish *his* **v**,	5088
	22:23 but for a **v** it shall not be accepted.	5088
	27: 2 a man shall **make a singular v**,	5088+6381
Nu	6: 2 woman shall separate *themselves* to a **v**	5087
	6: 2 *themselves* to vow a **v** of a Nazarite.	5088
	6: 5 All the days of the **v** of his separation	5088
	6:21 according to the **v** which he vowed,	5088
	15: 3 or a sacrifice in performing a **v**, or in a	5088
	15: 8 or *for* a sacrifice in performing a **v**,	5088
	21: 2 Israel vowed a **v** unto the LORD,	5087
	30: 2 If a man **v** a vow unto the LORD,	5087
	30: 2 If a man vow a **v** unto the LORD,	5088
	30: 3 If a woman also **v** a vow unto the LORD,	5087
	30: 3 If a woman also vow a **v** unto the LORD,	5088
	30: 4 her father hear her **v**, and her bond	5088
	30: 8 he shall make her **v** which she vowed,	5088
	30: 9 every **v** of a widow, and of her that is	5088
	30:13 Every **v**, and every binding oath to afflict	5088
Dt	12:11 all your choice vows which ye **v** unto	5087
	23:18 the house of the LORD thy God for any **v:**	5088
	23:21 When thou shalt **v** a vow unto the LORD	5087
	23:21 When thou shalt vow a **v** unto the LORD	5088
	23:22 if thou shalt forbear to **v**, it shall be no sin	5088
Jdg	11:30 Jephthah vowed a **v** unto the LORD,	5088
	11:39 who did with her *according to* his **v**	5088
1Sa	1:11 she vowed a **v**, and said, O LORD of	5087
	1:21 the LORD the yearly sacrifice, and his **v**.	5088
2Sa	15: 7 I pray thee, let me go and pay my **v**,	5088
	15: 8 thy servant vowed a **v** while I abode at	5088
Ps	65: 1 and unto thee shall the **v** be performed.	5087
	76:11 **V**, and pay unto the LORD your God:	5087
Ecc	5: 4 When thou vowest a **v** unto God, defer	5088
	5: 5 Better *is it* that thou shouldest not **v**,	5087
	5: 5 than that thou shouldest **v** and not pay.	5087
Isa	19:21 they shall **v** a vow unto the LORD,	5087
	19:21 they shall vow a **v** unto the LORD,	5088
Ac	18:18 *his* head in Cenchrea: for he had a **v**.	2171
	21:23 have four men which have a **v** on them;	2171

VOWED (18) [VOW]

Ge	28:20 Jacob **v** a vow, saying, If God will be with	5087
Lev	27: 8 according to his ability that **v** shall	5087
Nu	6:21 *is* the law of the Nazarite who hath **v**,	5087
	6:21 according to the vow which he **v**,	5087
	21: 2 Israel **v** a vow unto the LORD, and said,	5087
	30: 6 she **v**, or uttered ought out of her lips,	5087
	30: 8 then he shall make her vow which she **v**,	5921
	30:10 if she **v** *in* her husband's house,	5087
Dt	23:23 according as thou hast **v** unto the LORD	5087
Jdg	11:30 Jephthah **v** a vow unto the LORD,	5087
	11:39 her *according to* his vow which he had **v:**	5087
1Sa	1:11 which I have **v** a vow, and said, O LORD of hosts,	5087
2Sa	15: 7 which I have **v** a vow while I abode at	5087
	15: 8 For thy servant **v** a vow while I abode at	5087
Ps	132: 2 *and* **v** unto the mighty *God* of Jacob;	5087
Ecc	5: 4 in fools: pay that which thou hast **v**.	5087
Jer	44:25 surely perform our vows that we have **v**,	5087
Jnh	2: 9 I will pay *that* that I have **v**.	5087

VOWEDST (1) [VOW]

Ge	31:13 pillar, *and* where thou **v** a vow unto me:	5087

VOWEST (2) [VOW]

Dt	12:17 nor any of thy vows which thou **v**,	5087
Ecc	5: 4 When thou **v** a vow unto God, defer not	5087

VOWETH (1) [VOW]

Mal	1:14 **v**, and sacrificeth unto the Lord a corrupt	5087

VOWS (30) [VOW]

Lev	22:18 that will offer his oblation for all his **v**,	5088
	23:38 beside all your **v**, and beside all your	5088
Nu	29:39 besides your **v**, and your freewill offerings,	5088
	30: 4 all her **v** shall stand, and every bond	5088
	30: 5 not any of her **v**, or of her bonds	5088
	30: 7 that he heard *it*: then her **v** shall stand,	5088
	30:11 all her **v** shall stand, and every bond	5088
	30:12 out of her lips concerning her **v**,	5088
	30:14 he establisheth all her **v**, or all her bonds,	5088
Dt	12: 6 your **v**, and your freewill offerings,	5088
	12:11 all your choice **v** which ye vow unto	5088
	12:17 nor any of thy **v** which thou vowest,	5088
	12:26 thy **v** which thou shalt take, and go unto	5088
Job	22:27 shall hear thee, and thou shalt pay thy **v**.	5088
Ps	22:25 I will pay my **v** before them that fear him.	5088
	50:14 and pay thy **v** unto the most High:	5088
	56:12 Thy **v** *are* upon me, O God: I will render	5088
	61: 5 For thou, O God, hast heard my **v:**	5088
	61: 8 for ever, that I may daily perform my **v**,	5088
	66:13 with burnt offerings: I will pay thee my **v**,	5088
	116:14 I will pay my **v** unto the LORD now in	5088
	116:18 I will pay my **v** unto the LORD now in	5088
Pr	7:14 with me; *this* day have I payed my **v**.	5088
	20:25 *is* holy, and after **v** to make inquiry.	5088
	31: 2 of my womb? and what, the son of my **v?**	5088
Jer	44:25 We will surely perform our **v** that we	5088
	44:25 ye will surely accomplish your **v**,	5088
	44:25 your vows, and surely perform your **v**.	5088
Jnh	1:16 a sacrifice unto the LORD, and made **v**.	5088
Na	1:15 keep thy solemn feasts, perform thy **v:**	5088

VOYAGE (1)

Ac	27:10 I perceive that *this* **v** will be with hurt and	4144

VULTURE (2) [VULTURE'S, VULTURES]

Lev	11:14 And the **v**, and the kite after his kind,	1676
Dt	14:13 and the kite, and the **v** after his kind,	1772

VULTURE'S (1) [VULTURE]

Job	28: 7 and which the **v** eye hath not seen:	344

VULTURES (1) [VULTURE]

Isa	34:15 shall the **v** also be gathered, every one	1772

VULTURE; VULTURES See also EAGLE; EAGLES; OSPRAY; OSSIFRAGE

W

WADI See BROOKS

WAFER (3) [WAFERS]

Ex	29:23 one **w** out of the basket of the unleavened	7550
Lev	8:26 one **w**, and put *them* on the fat,	7550
Nu	6:19 one unleavened **w**, and shall put *them*	7550

WAFERS (4) [WAFER]

Ex	16:31 taste of it *was* like **w** *made* with honey.	6838
	29: 2 and **w** unleavened anointed with oil:	7550
Lev	2: 4 oil, or unleavened **w** anointed with oil.	7550
	7:12 unleavened **w** anointed with oil,	7550
Nu	6:15 **w** of unleavened bread anointed with oil,	7550

WAG (2) [WAGGING]

Jer	18:16 shall be astonished, and **w** his head.	5110
La	2:15 **w** their head at the daughter of Jerusalem,	5128
Zep	2:15 passeth by her shall hiss, *and* **w** his hand.	5128

WAGES (18)

Ge	29:15 for nought? tell me, what *shall* thy **w** be?	4909
	30:28 Appoint me thy **w**, and I will give *it*.	7939
	31: 7 me, and changed my **w** ten times;	4909
	31: 8 he said thus, The speckled shall be thy **w;**	7939
	31:41 and thou hast changed my **w** ten times.	4909
Ex	2: 9 it for me, and I will give *thee* thy **w**.	7939
Lev	19:13 neither rob *him*: the **w** of him that is hired	6468
Jer	22:13 useth his neighbour's service **without w**,	2600
Eze	29:18 yet had he no **w**, nor his army, for Tyrus,	7939
	29:19 prey; and it shall be the **w** for his army.	7939
Hag	1: 6 that **earneth w** earneth wages *to put it*	7936
	1: 6 that earneth wages **earneth** *to put it*	7936
Mal	3: 5 those that oppress the hireling in *his* **w**,	7939
Lk	3:14 *any* falsely; and be content with your **w**.	3800
Jn	4:36 And he that reapeth receiveth **w**,	3408
Ro	6:23 For the **w** of sin *is* death; but the gift of	3800
2Co	11: 8 taking **w** *of them*, to do you service.	3800
2Pe	2:15 who loved the **w** of unrighteousness;	3408

WAGGING (2) [WAG]

Mt	27:39 that passed by, reviled him, **w** their heads,	2795
Mk	15:29 **w** their heads, and saying, Ah, *thou* that	2795

WAGON (1) [WAGONS]

Nu	7: 3 a **w** for two of the princes, and for each	5699

WAGONS (9) [WAGON]

Ge	45:19 take you **w** out of the land of Egypt for	5699
	45:21 Joseph gave them **w**, according to	5699
	45:27 he saw the **w** which Joseph had sent	5699
	46: 5 in the **w** which Pharaoh had sent to carry	5699
Nu	7: 3 six covered **w**, and twelve oxen;	5699
	7: 6 Moses took the **w** and the oxen,	5699
	7: 7 Two **w** and four oxen he gave unto	5699
	7: 8 four **w** and eight oxen he gave unto	5699
Eze	23:24 **w**, and wheels, and with an assembly of	7393

WAIL (3) [WAILED, WAILING]

Eze	32:18 **w** for the multitude of Egypt, and cast	5091
Mic	1: 8 Therefore I will **w** and howl, I will go	5594
Rev	1: 7 and all kindreds of the earth shall **w**	2875

WAILED (1) [WAIL]

Mk	5:38 and them that wept and **w** greatly.	214

WAILING (16) [WAIL]

Est	4: 3 Jews, and fasting, and weeping, and **w;**	4553
Jer	9:10 will I take up a weeping and **w**,	5092
	9:18 let them make haste, and take up a **w** for	5092
	9:19 For a voice of **w** is heard out of Zion,	5092
	9:20 teach your daughters **w**, and every one	5092
Eze	7:11 theirs: neither *shall there be* **w** for them.	5089
	27:31 thee with bitterness of heart *and* bitter **w**.	4553
	27:32 in their **w** they shall take up a lamentation	5204
Am	5:16 **W** *shall be* in all streets; and they shall say	4553
	5:16 such as are skilful of lamentation to **w**.	4553
	5:17 in all vineyards *shall be* **w:** for I will pass	4553
Mic	1: 8 I will make a **w** like the dragons,	4553

WAIT (106) [AWAIT, WAITED, WAITETH, WAITING]

Mt	13:42 there shall be **w** and gnashing of teeth.	2805
	13:50 there shall be **w** and gnashing of teeth.	2805
Rev	18:15 the fear of her torment, weeping and **w**,	3996
	18:19 and cried, weeping and **w**, saying, Alas,	3996

Ex	21:13 if a man **lie** not **in w**, but God deliver	6658
Nu	3:10 and they shall **w** on their priest's office:	8104
	8:24 upward they shall go in to **w** upon	6633+6635
	35:20 or hurl at him by **laying of w**, that he die;	6660
	35:22 upon him any thing without **laying of w**,	6660
Dt	19:11 **lie in w** for him, and rise up against him,	693
Jos	8: 4 Behold, ye shall **lie in w against** the city,	693
	8:13 their **liers in w** on the west of the city,	6119
Jdg	9:25 the men of Shechem set **liers in w** for him	693
	9:32 that *is* with thee, *and* **lie in w** in the field:	693
	9:34 they **laid w** against Shechem in four	693
	9:35 that *were* with him, from **lying in w**.	3993
	9:43 **laid w** in the field, and looked, and behold,	693
	16: 2 **laid w** for him all night in the gate of	693
	16: 9 Now *there were* men **lying in w**	693
	16:12 *were* **liers in w** abiding in the chamber.	693
	20:29 Israel set **liers in w** round about Gibeah.	693
	20:33 the **liers in w** of Israel came forth out of	693
	20:36 they trusted unto the **liers in w** which	693
	20:37 the **liers in w** hasted, and rushed upon	693
	20:37 the **liers in w** drew *themselves* along,	693
	20:38 the men of Israel and the **liers in w**,	693
	21:20 Go and **lie in w** in the vineyards,	693
1Sa	15: 2 how he laid **w** for him in the way, when	NIH
	15: 5 a city of Amalek, and **laid w** in the valley.	7378
	22: 8 against me, to **lie in w**, as at this day?	693
	22:13 rise against me, to **lie in w**, as at this day?	693
2Ki	6:33 what should I **w** for the LORD any	3176
1Ch	23:28 Because their office *was* to **w** on the sons	3027
2Ch	5:11 and all of such as **lay in w** by the way.	8104
	13:10 and the Levites **w** upon *their* business:	NIH
Ezr	8:31 and of such as **lay in w** by the way.	693
Job	14:14 all the days of my appointed time will I **w**,	3176
	17:13 If I **w**, the grave *is* mine house: I have	6960
	31: 9 or *if* I have **laid w** at my neighbour's door;	693
	38:40 *and* abide in the covert to **lie in w?**	695
Ps	10: 9 He lieth in **w** secretly as a lion in his den:	693
	10: 9 he lieth in **w** to catch the poor: he doth	693
	25: 3 Yea, let none that **w** on thee be ashamed:	6960
	25: 5 my salvation; on thee do I **w** all the day.	6960
	25:21 uprightness preserve me; for I **w** on thee.	6960
	27:14 **W** on the LORD: be of good courage,	6960
	27:14 thine heart: **w**, I say, on the LORD.	6960
	37: 7 in the LORD, and **w patiently** for him:	2342
	37: 7 those that **w** upon the LORD, they shall	6960
	37:34 **W** on the LORD, and keep his way,	6960
	39: 7 now, Lord, what **w** I for? my hope *is* in	6960
	52: 9 hast done *it*: and I will **w** on thy name;	6960
	56: 6 mark my steps, when they **w** for my soul.	6960
	59: 3 lo, they **lie in w** for my soul: the mighty	693
	59: 9 *of* his strength will I **w** upon thee:	8104
	62: 5 My soul, **w** thou only upon God; for my	1826
	69: 3 mine eyes fail while *I* **w** for my God.	3176
	69: 6 Let not them that **w** on thee, O Lord GOD	6960
	71:10 they that **lay w** for my soul take counsel	8104
	104:27 These **w** all upon thee; that *thou* mayest	7663
	123: 2 so our eyes *w* upon the LORD our God,	NIH
	130: 5 I **w** for the LORD, my soul doth **w**,	6960
	130: 5 soul doth **w**, and in his word do I hope.	6960
	145:15 The eyes of all **w** upon thee;	7663
Pr	1:11 Come with us, let us **lay w** for blood,	693
	1:18 they **lay w** for their own blood; they lurk	693
	7:12 the streets, and **lieth in w** at every corner.)	693
	12: 6 The words of the wicked *are* to **lie in w**	693
	20:22 *but* **w** on the LORD, and he shall save	6960
	23:28 She also **lieth in w** as *for* a prey,	693
	24:15 Lay not **w**, O wicked *man*, against	693
Isa	8:17 I will **w** upon the LORD, that hideth his	2442
	30:18 therefore will the LORD **w**, that *he* may	2442
	30:18 blessed *are* all they that **w** for him.	2442
	40:31 they that **w** upon the LORD shall renew	6960
	42: 4 the earth: and the isles shall **w** for his law.	3176
	49:23 for they shall not be ashamed that **w for**	6960
	51: 5 the isles shall **w** upon me, and on mine	6960
	59: 9 we **w** for light, but behold obscurity;	6960
	59: 9 Surely the isles shall **w** for me,	6960
Jer	5:26 people are found wicked *men*: they **lay w**,	7789
	9: 8 his mouth, but in heart he layeth his **w**.	696
	14:22 therefore we will **w** upon thee: for thou	6960
La	3:10 He *was* unto me *as* a bear **lying in w**,	693
	3:25 The LORD *is* good unto them that **w for**	6960
	3:26 *quietly* **w** for the salvation of the LORD.	1748
	4:19 they **laid w** for us in the wilderness.	693
Hos	6: 9 as troops *of robbers* **w for** a man,	2442
	7: 6 heart like an oven, whiles they **lie in w:**	693
	12: 6 judgment, and **w** on thy God continually.	6960
Mic	7: 2 they all **lie in w** for blood; they hunt	693
	7: 7 I will **w** for the God of my salvation:	3176
Hab	2: 3 though it tarry, **w** for it; because it will	2442
Zep	3: 8 Therefore **w** ye upon me, saith the LORD,	2442
Mk	3: 9 a small ship should **w** on him because	4342
Lk	11:54 **Laying** in **w** for him, and seeking to catch	1748
	12:36 ye yourselves like unto men that **w for**	4327
Ac	1: 4 **w for** the promise of the Father, which,	4037
	20: 3 and when the Jews **laid w** for him,	1096+1917
	20:19 which befell me by the **lying in w** of	1917
	23:16 sister's son heard of *their* **lying in w**,	1747
	23:21 for there **lie in w for** him of them moe	1748

Ac 23:30 me how that the Jews **laid w** for the man, *1917*
 25: 3 **laying w** in the way to kill him. *1747+4160*
Ro 8:25 see not, *then* do we with patience **w for** *it.* 553
 12: 7 Or ministry, *let us* **w** on *our* ministering: NIG
1Co 9:13 they which **w at** the altar are partakers *4332*
Gal 5: 5 For we through the Spirit **w for** the hope of *553*
Eph 4:14 whereby they **lie in w** to deceive; *3180*
1Th 1:10 to **w for** his Son from heaven, whom he 362

WAITED (35) [WAIT]
Ge 49:18 I have **w** for thy salvation, O Lord. 6960
1Ki 20:38 **w** for the king by the way, 5975
2Ki 5: 2 she **w on** Naaman's wife. *1961+6440+3807.1*
1Ch 6:32 they **w** on their office according to their 5975
 6:33 these *are* they that **w** with their children. 5975
 9:18 hitherto in the king's gate eastward: NIH
2Ch 7: 6 the priests **w** on their offices: the Levites 5975
 17:19 These **w** on the king, besides *those* 8334
 35:15 seer; and the porters **w** at every gate; NIH
Ne 12:44 for the priests and for the Levites that **w.** 5975
Job 6:19 the companies of Sheba **w** for them. 6960
 15:22 of darkness, and he *is* **w** for of the sword. 6822
 29:21 and **w**, and kept silence at my counsel. 3176
 29:23 they **w** for me as for the rain; 3176
 30:26 came *unto* me: and when I **w** for light, 3176
 32: 4 Now Elihu had **w** till Job had spoken, 2442
 32:11 Behold, I **w** for your words; I gave ear to 3176
 32:16 When I had **w**, (for they spake not, 3176
Ps 40: 1 I **w patiently for** the Lord; *6960+6960*
 106:13 his works; they **w** not for his counsel. 2442
 119:95 The wicked have **w** for me to destroy me: 6960
Isa 25: 9 we have **w** for him, and he will save us: 6960
 25: 9 we have **w** for him, we will be glad and 6960
 26: 8 O Lord, have we **w for** thee; 6960
 33: 2 be gracious unto us; we have **w for** thee: 6960
Eze 19: 5 Now when she saw that she had **w**, 3176
Mic 1:12 For the inhabitant of Maroth **w carefully** 2342
Zec 11:11 poor of the flock that **w** upon me knew 8104
Mk 15:43 which also **w** for the kingdom of God, 4327
Lk 1:21 And the people **w** for Zacharias, 4328
 23:51 who also himself **w for** the kingdom of 4327
Ac 10: 7 of them that **w on** him **continually;** 4342
 10:24 Cornelius **w for** them, and had called 4328
 17:16 Now while Paul **w for** them at Athens, 1551
1Pe 3:20 when once the longsuffering of God **w** in 1551

WAITETH (11) [WAIT]
Job 24:15 The eye also of the adulterer **w** for 8104
Ps 33:20 Our soul **w** for the Lord: he *is* our help 2442
 62: 1 Truly my soul **w** upon God: from him 1747
 65: 1 Praise **w** for thee, O God, in Zion: 1747
 130: 6 My soul *w* for the Lord more than they NIH
Pr 27:18 that **w** on his master shall be honoured. 8104
Isa 64: 4 *what* he hath prepared for him that **w** for 2442
Da 12:12 Blessed *is* he that **w**, and cometh to 2442
Mic 5: 7 not for man, nor **w** for the sons of men. 3176
Ro 8:19 **w for** the manifestation of the sons of God. 553
Jas 5: 7 the husbandman **w for** the precious fruit 1551

WAITING (8) [WAIT]
Nu 8:25 they shall cease **w upon** the service 6635
Pr 8:34 at my gates, **w** at the posts of my doors. 8104
Lk 2:25 devout, **w for** the consolation of Israel: 4327
 8:40 received him: for they were all **w** for him. 4328
Jn 5: 3 withered, **w for** the moving of the water. 1551
Ro 8:23 **w for** the adoption, *to wit*, the redemption 553
1Co 1: 7 **w for** the coming of our Lord Jesus Christ: 553
2Th 3: 5 of God, and into the **patient w** for Christ. 5281

WAKE (4) [AWAKE, AWAKED, AWAKEST,
 AWAKETH, AWAKING, AWOKE, WAKED,
 WAKENED, WAKENEST, WAKETH, WAKING]
Jer 51:39 and not **w**, saith the Lord. 6974
 51:57 perpetual sleep, and not **w**, saith the King, 6974
Joel 3: 9 **w** up the mighty *men*, let all the men of 5782
1Th 5:10 died for us, that, whether we **w** or sleep, 1127

WAKED (1) [WAKE]
Zec 4: 1 **w** me, as a man that is wakened out of 5782

WAKENED (2) [WAKE]
Joel 3:12 Let the heathen be **w**, and come up to 5782
Zec 4: 1 as a man that is **w** out of his sleep, 5782

WAKENETH (2) [WAKE]
Isa 50: 4 he **w** morning by morning, he wakeneth 5782
 50: 4 he **w** mine ear to hear as the learned. 5782

WAKETH (2) [WAKE]
Ps 127: 1 the city, the watchman **w** *but* in vain. 8245
SS 5: 2 I sleep, but my heart **w:** *it is* the voice of 5782

WAKING [WAKE]
Ps 77: 4 Thou holdest mine eyes **w:** I am *so* 8109

WALK (212) [WALKED, WALKEDST, WALKEST,
 WALKETH, WALKING]
Ge 13:17 **w** through the land in the length of it and 1980
 17: 1 **w** before me, and be thou perfect. 1980
 24:40 unto me, The Lord, before whom I **w**, 1980
 48:15 my fathers Abraham and Isaac did **w**, 1980
Ex 16: 4 whether they will **w** in my law, or no. 1980
 18:20 shew them the way *wherein* they must **w**, 1980
 21:19 **w** abroad upon his staff, then shall he 1980
Lev 18: 3 neither shall ye **w** in their ordinances. 1980
 18: 4 and keep mine ordinances, to **w** therein: 1980

Lev 20:23 shall not **w** in the manners of the nation, 1980
 26: 3 If ye **w** in my statutes, and keep my 1980
 26:12 will **w** among you, and will be your God, 1980
 26:21 if ye **w** contrary unto me, and will not 1980
 26:23 *things*, but will **w** contrary unto me; 1980
 26:24 will I also **w** contrary unto you, 1980
 26:27 unto me, but **w** contrary unto me; 1980
 26:28 I will **w** contrary unto you also in fury; 1980
Dt 5:33 You shall **w** in all the ways which 1980
 8: 6 God, to **w** in his ways, and to fear him. 1980
 8:19 **w** after other gods, and serve them, 1980
 10:12 to **w** in all his ways, and to love him, 1980
 11:22 to **w** in all his ways, and to cleave unto 1980
 13: 4 Ye shall **w** after the Lord your God, 1980
 13: 5 Lord thy God commanded thee to **w** in. 1980
 19: 9 thy God, and to **w** ever in his ways, 1980
 26:17 in his ways, and to keep his statutes, 1980
 28: 9 of the Lord thy God, and **w** in his ways. 1980
 29:19 though I **w** in the imagination of mine 1980
 30:16 in his ways, and to keep his 1980
Jos 16: 8 and **w** through the land, and describe it, 1980
 22: 5 to **w** in all his ways, and to keep his 1980
Jdg 2:22 keep the way of the Lord to **w** therein, 1980
 5:10 that sit in judgment, and **w** by the way. 1980
1Sa 2:30 thy father, should **w** before me for ever: 1980
 2:35 he shall **w** before mine anointed for ever. 1980
 8: 5 art old, and thy sons **w** not in thy ways: 1980
1Ki 2: 3 to **w** in his ways, to keep his statutes, 1980
 2: 4 to **w** before me in truth with all their 1980
 3:14 if thou wilt **w** in my ways, to keep my 1980
 3:14 as thy father David did **w**, then I will 1980
 6:12 if thou wilt **w** in my statutes, and execute 1980
 6:12 keep all my commandments to **w** in them 1980
 8:23 mercy with thy servants that **w** before 1980
 8:25 they **w** before me as thou hast walked 1980
 8:36 the good way wherein they should **w**, 1980
 8:58 to **w** in all his ways, and to keep his 1980
 8:61 to **w** in his statutes, and to keep his 1980
 9: 4 if thou wilt **w** before me, as David thy 1980
 11:38 wilt **w** in my ways, and do that *is* right in 1980
 16:31 as if it had been a light thing for him to **w** 1980
2Ki 10:31 Jehu took no heed to **w** in the law of 1980
 23: 3 to **w** after the Lord, and to keep his 1980
2Ch 6:14 that **w** before thee with all their hearts; 1980
 6:16 take heed to their way to **w** in my law, 1980
 6:27 the good way, wherein they should **w**; 1980
 6:31 to **w** in thy ways, so long as they live in 1980
 7:17 *as for* thee, if thou wilt **w** before me, 1980
 34:31 to **w** after the Lord, and to keep his 1980
Ne 5: 9 ought ye not to **w** in the fear of our God 1980
 10:29 and into an oath, to **w** in God's law, 1980
Ps 12: 8 The wicked **w** on every side, when 1980
 23: 4 though I **w** through the valley of 1980
 26:11 *as for* me, I will **w** in mine integrity: 1980
 48:12 **W** about Zion, and go round about her: 5437
 56:13 that *I* may **w** before God in the light of 1980
 78:10 of God, and refused to **w** in his law; 1980
 82: 5 they understand; they **w** on in darkness: 1980
 84:11 he withhold from them that **w** uprightly. 1980
 86:11 thy way, O Lord; I will **w** in thy truth: 1980
 89:15 they shall **w**, O Lord, in the light of thy 1980
 89:30 my law, and **w** not in my judgments; 1980
 101: 2 I will **w** within my house with a perfect 1980
 115: 7 feet *have* they, but they **w** not: 1980
 116: 9 I will **w** before the Lord in the land of 1980
 119: 1 the way, who **w** in the law of the Lord. 1980
 119: 3 also do no iniquity: they **w** in his ways. 1980
 119:45 I will **w** at liberty: for I seek thy precepts. 1980
 138: 7 Though I **w** in the midst of trouble, 1980
 143: 8 me to know the way wherein I should **w**; 1980
Pr 1:15 son, **w** not thou in the way with them; 1980
 2: 7 *he is* a buckler to them that **w** uprightly. 1980
 2:13 to **w** in the ways of darkness; 1980
 2:20 That thou mayest **w** in the way of good 1980
 3:23 shalt thou **w** in thy way safely, and thy 1980
Ecc 4:15 I considered all the living which **w** under 1980
 6: 8 that knoweth to **w** before the living? 1980
 11: 9 **w** in the ways of thine heart, and in 1980
Isa 2: 3 us of his ways, and we will **w** in his paths: 1980
 2: 5 and let us **w** in the light of the Lord. 1980
 3:16 **w** with stretched forth necks and 1980
 8:11 me that *I* should not **w** in the way 1980
 30: 2 That **w** to go down *into* Egypt, 1980
 30:21 This *is* the way, **w** ye in it, when ye 1980
 35: 9 but the redeemed shall **w** *there*: 1980
 40:31 be weary; *and* they shall **w**, and not faint. 1980
 42: 5 upon it, and spirit to them that **w** therein: 1980
 42:24 for they would not **w** in his ways, 1980
 50:11 **w** in the light of your fire, and in the 1980
 59: 9 for brightness, *but* we **w** in darkness. 1980
Jer 3:17 neither shall they **w** any more after 1980
 3:18 In those days the house of Judah shall **w** 1980
 6:16 **w** therein, and ye shall find rest for your 1980
 6:16 But they said, We will not **w** *therein*. 1980
 6:25 not forth *into* the field, nor **w** by the way; 1980
 7: 6 neither **w** after other gods to your hurt: 1980
 7: 9 **w** after other gods whom ye know not; 1980
 7:23 **w** ye in all the ways that I have 1980
 9: 4 every neighbour will **w** *with* slanders. 1980
 13:10 which **w** in the imagination of their heart, 1980
 13:10 **w** after other gods, to serve them, 1980
 16:12 ye every one after the imagination of 1980
 18:12 we will **w** after our own devices, 1980
 18:15 to **w** *in* paths, *in* a way not cast up; 1980
 23:14 *they* commit adultery, and **w** in lies: 1980

Jer 26: 4 to **w** in my law, which I have set before 1980
 31: 9 I will **cause** them to **w** by the rivers of 1980
 42: 3 may shew us the way wherein we may **w**, 1980
La 5:18 which is desolate, the foxes **w** upon it. 1980
Eze 11:20 That they may **w** in my statutes, and keep 1980
 20:18 **W** ye not in the statutes of your fathers, 1980
 20:19 **w** in my statutes, and keep my judgments, 1980
 33:15 **w** in the statutes of life, without 1980
 36:12 Yea, I will **cause** men to **w** upon you, 1980
 36:27 cause you to **w** in my statutes, and ye 1980
 37:24 they shall also **w** in my judgments, 1980
 42: 4 the chambers *was* a **w** of ten cubits 4109
Da 4:37 those that **w** in pride he *is* able to abase. 1981
 9:10 to **w** in his laws, which he set before us 1980
Hos 11:10 They shall **w** after the Lord: he shall 1980
 14: 9 *are* right, and the just shall **w** in them: 1980
Joel 2: 8 they shall **w** every one in his path: 1980
Am 3: 3 two **w** together, except they be agreed? 1980
Mic 4: 2 of his ways, and we will **w** in his paths: 1980
 4: 5 all people will **w** every one in the name 1980
 4: 5 we will **w** in the name of the Lord our 1980
 6: 8 and to **w** humbly with thy God? 1980
 6:16 of Ahab, and ye **w** in their counsels; 1980
Na 2: 5 they shall stumble in their **w**; they shall 1979
Hab 3:15 Thou didst **w** through the sea *with* thine 1869
 3:19 he will **make** me to **w** upon mine high 1869
Zep 1:17 that they shall **w** like blind *men*, because 1980
Zec 1:10 the Lord hath sent to **w to and fro** 1980
 3: 7 If thou wilt **w** in my ways, and if thou 1980
 3: 7 I will give thee **places** to **w** among these 4108
 6: 7 to go that *they* might **w to and fro** 1980
 6: 7 Get ye *hence*, **w to and fro** through 1980
 10:12 they shall **w up and down** in his name, 1980
Mt 9: 5 be forgiven thee; or to say, Arise, and **w?** 4043
 11: 5 and the lame **w**, the lepers are cleansed, 4043
 15:31 the lame to **w**, and the blind to see: 4043
Mk 2: 9 say, Arise, and take up thy bed, and **w?** 4043
 7: 5 Why **w** not thy disciples according to 4043
Lk 5:23 forgiven thee; or to say, Rise up and **w?** 4043
 7:22 how that the blind see, the lame **w**, 4043
 11:44 men that **w** over *them* are not aware *of* 4043
 13:33 Nevertheless I must **w** to day, 4198
 20:46 which desire to **w** in long robes, 4043
 24:17 one to another, as ye **w**, and are sad? 4043
Jn 5: 8 unto him, Rise, take up thy bed, and **w**. 4043
 5:11 said unto me, Take up thy bed, and **w**. 4043
 5:12 said unto thee, Take up thy bed, and **w?** 4043
 7: 1 for he would not **w** in Jewry, because 4043
 8:12 he that followeth me shall not **w** in 4043
 11: 9 any *man* **w** in the day, he stumbleth not, 4043
 11:10 But if a man **w** in the night, he stumbleth, 4043
 12:35 while ye have the light, lest darkness 4043
Ac 3: 6 of Jesus Christ of Nazareth rise up and **w**. 4043
 3:12 or holiness we had made this *man* to **w**? 4043
 14:16 in times past suffered all nations to **w** 4198
 21:21 neither to **w** after the customs. 4043
Ro 4:12 who also **w** in the steps of *that* faith of 4748
 6: 4 so we also should **w** in newness of life. 4043
 8: 1 in Christ Jesus who **w** not after the flesh, 4043
 8: 4 who **w** not after the flesh, but after 4043
 13:13 Let us **w** honestly, as in the day; not in 4043
1Co 3: 3 are ye not carnal, and **w** as men? 4043
 7:17 Lord hath called every one, so let him **w**. 4043
2Co 5: 7 (For we **w** by faith, not by sight:) 4043
 6:16 and **w** in *them*; and I will be their God, 1704
 10: 3 For though we **w** in the flesh, we do not 4043
Gal 5:16 **W** in the Spirit, and ye shall not fulfil 4043
 5:25 in the Spirit, let us also **w** in the Spirit. 4748
 6:16 And as many as **w** according to this rule, 4748
Eph 2:10 ordained that we should **w** in them. 4043
 4: 1 beseech you that ye **w** worthy of 4043
 4:17 ye henceforth **w** not as other Gentiles 4043
 4:17 henceforth walk not as other Gentiles **w**, 4043
 5: 2 **w** in love, as Christ also hath loved us, 4043
 5: 8 *ye* light in the Lord: **w** as children of light: 4043
 5:15 See then that ye **w** circumspectly, not as 4748
Php 3:16 let us **w** by the same rule, *let us* mind 4748
 3:17 and mark them which **w** so as ye have us 4043
 3:18 (For many **w**, of whom I have told you 4043
Col 1:10 That ye might **w** worthy of the Lord unto 4043
 2: 6 Christ Jesus the Lord, *so* **w** ye in him: 4043
 4: 5 **W** in wisdom toward them that are 4043
1Th 2:12 That ye would **w** worthy of God, who 4043
 4: 1 ye have received of us how ye ought to **w** 4043
 4:12 That ye may **w** honestly toward them that 4043
2Th 3:11 For we hear that *there are* some which **w** 4043
2Pe 2:10 But chiefly them that **w** after the flesh in 4198
1Jn 1: 6 and **w** in darkness, we lie, and do not 4043
 1: 7 if we **w** in the light, as he is in the light, 4043
 2: 6 abideth in him ought himself also so to **w**, 4043
2Jn 1: 6 love, that we **w** after his commandments. 4043
 1: 6 from the beginning, ye should **w** in it. 4043
3Jn 1: 4 than to hear that my children **w** in truth. 4043
Jude 1:18 who should **w** after their own ungodly 4198
Rev 3: 4 and they shall **w** with me in white: 4043
 9:20 which neither can see, nor hear, nor **w:** 4043
 16:15 lest he **w** naked, and they see his shame. 4043
 21:24 which are saved shall **w** in the light of it: 4043

WALKED (122) [WALK]
Ge 5:22 Enoch **w** with God after he begat 1980
 5:24 Enoch **w** with God: and he *was* not; 1980
 6: 9 in his generations, *and* Noah **w** with God. 1980
Ex 2: 5 her maidens **w** along by the river's side; 1980
 14:29 the children of Israel **w** upon dry *land* in 1980

Lev 26:40 that also they have **w** contrary unto me; 1980
 26:41 that I also have **w** contrary unto them, 1980
Jos 5: 6 For the children of Israel **w** forty years in 1980
Jdg 2:17 out of the way which their fathers **w** in, 1980
 5: 6 and the travellers **w** through byways. 1980
 11:16 **w** through the wilderness unto the Red 1980
1Sa 8: 3 his sons **w** not in his ways, but turned 1980
 12: 2 I have **w** before you from my childhood 1980
2Sa 2:29 men **w** all that night through the plain, 1980
 7: 6 but have **w** in a tent and in a tabernacle. 1980
 7: 7 In all the places wherein I have **w** with 1980
 11: 2 and **w** upon the roof of the king's house: 1980
1Ki 3: 6 according as he **w** before thee in truth, 1980
 8:25 that they walk before me as thou hast **w** 1980
 9: 4 as David thy father **w**, in integrity of heart 1980
 11:33 have not **w** in my ways, to do that which 1980
 15: 3 he **w** in all the sins of his father, which he 1980
 15:26 **w** in the way of his father, and in his sin 1980
 15:34 **w** in the way of Jeroboam and in his sin 1980
 16: 2 thou hast **w** in the way of Jeroboam, 1980
 16:26 he **w** in all the way of Jeroboam the son 1980
 22:43 he **w** in all the ways of Asa his father; 1980
 22:52 **w** in the way of his father, and in the 1980
2Ki 4:35 returned, and **w** in the house to and fro; 1980
 8:18 he **w** in the way of the kings of Israel, 1980
 8:27 he **w** in the way of the house of Ahab, 1980
 13: 6 who made Israel sin, but **w** therein: 1980
 13:11 who made Israel sin: but he **w** therein. 1980
 16: 3 he **w** in the way of the kings of Israel, 1980
 17: 8 **w** in the statutes of the heathen, whom 1980
 17:19 **w** in the statutes of Israel which they 1980
 17:22 the children of Israel **w** in all the sins of 1980
 20: 3 remember now how I have **w** before thee 1980
 21:21 he **w** in all the way that his father walked 1980
 21:21 he walked in all the way that his father **w** 1980
 21:22 and **w** not in the way of the Lord. 1980
 22: 2 **w** in all the way of David his father, 1980
1Ch 7: 6 Wheresoever I have **w** with all Israel, 1980
 17: 8 with thee whithersoever thou hast **w**, 1980
2Ch 6:16 in my law, as thou hast **w** before me. 1980
 7:17 as David thy father **w**, and do according 1980
 11:17 for three years they **w** in the way of David 1980
 17: 3 he **w** in the first ways of his father David, 1980
 17: 4 **w** in his commandments, and not after 1980
 20:32 he **w** in the way of Asa his father, 1980
 21: 6 he **w** in the way of the kings of Israel, 1980
 21:12 Because thou hast not **w** in the ways of 1980
 21:13 hast **w** in the way of the kings of Israel, 1980
 22: 3 He also **w** in the ways of the house of 1980
 22: 5 He **w** also after their counsel, 1980
 28: 2 he **w** in the ways of the kings of Israel, 1980
 34: 2 **w** in the ways of David his father, 1980
Est 2:11 Mordecai **w** every day before the court of 1980
Job 29: 3 when by his light I **w** through darkness; 1980
 31: 5 If I have **w** with vanity, or if my foot hath 1980
 31: 7 mine heart **w** after mine eyes, and if any 1980
 38:16 or hast thou **w** in the search of the depth? 1980
Ps 26: 1 O Lord; for I have **w** in mine integrity: 1980
 26: 3 mine eyes: and I have **w** in thy truth. 1980
 55:14 **w** unto the house of God in company. 1980
 81:12 and they **w** in their own counsels. 1980
 81:13 unto me, and Israel had **w** in my ways! 1980
 142: 3 In the way wherein I **w** have they privily 1980
Isa 9: 2 The people that **w** in darkness have seen 1980
 20: 3 Like as my servant Isaiah hath **w** naked 1980
 38: 3 how I have **w** before thee in truth and 1980
Jer 2: 5 have **w** after vanity, and are become vain? 1980
 2: 8 and **w** after things that do not profit. 1980
 7:24 in the counsels and in the imagination 1980
 8: 2 after whom they have **w**, and whom they 1980
 9:13 not obeyed my voice, neither **w** therein; 1980
 9:14 have **w** after the imagination of their own 1980
 11: 8 **w** every one in the imagination of their 1980
 16:11 have **w** after other gods, and have served 1980
 32:23 not thy voice, neither **w** in thy law; 1980
 44:10 nor **w** in my law, nor in my statutes, that 1980
 44:23 nor **w** in his law, nor in his statutes, nor 1980
Eze 5: 6 my statutes, they have not **w** in them. 1980
 5: 7 have not **w** in my statutes, neither have 1980
 11:12 for ye have not **w** in my statutes, 1980
 16:47 Yet hast thou not **w** after their ways, 1980
 18: 9 Hath **w** in my statutes, and hath kept my 1980
 18:17 my judgments, hath **w** in my statutes; 1980
 20:13 they **w** not in my statutes, and they 1980
 20:16 **w** not in my statutes, but polluted my 1980
 20:21 they **w** not in my statutes, neither kept 1980
 23:31 Thou hast **w** in the way of thy sister; 1980
 28:14 thou hast **w** up and down in the midst 1980
Da 4:29 At the end of twelve months he **w** in 1981
Hos 5:11 he willingly **w** after the commandment. 1980
Am 2: 4 err, after the which their fathers have **w**: 1980
Na 2:11 w, and the lion's whelp, and none made 1980
Zec 1:11 We have **w** to and fro through the earth, 1980
 6: 7 So they **w** to and fro through the earth. 1980
Mal 2: 6 he **w** with me in peace and equity, 1980
 3:14 that we have **w** mournfully before 1980
Mt 14:29 ship, he **w** on the water, to go to Jesus. 4043
Mk 1:16 as he **w** by the sea of Galilee, he saw 4043
 5:42 And straightway the damsel arose, and **w**; 4043
 16:12 as they **w**, and went into the country. 4043
Jn 1:36 And looking upon Jesus as he **w**, he saith, 4043
 5: 9 made whole, and took up his bed, and **w**: 4043
 6:66 went back, and **w** no more with him. 4043
 7: 1 After these things Jesus **w** in Galilee: for 4043
 10:23 And Jesus **w** in the temple in Solomon's 4043

Jn 11:54 **w** no more openly among the Jews; 4043
Ac 3: 8 and **w**, and entered with them into 4043
 14: 8 his mother's womb, who never had **w**: 4043
 14:10 upright on thy feet. And he leaped and **w**. 4043
2Co 10: 2 which think of us as if we **w** according to 4043
 12:18 we **w** not in the same spirit? walked we 4043
 12:18 same spirit? **w** we not in the same steps? NIG
Gal 2:14 when I saw that they **w** not **uprightly** 3716
Eph 2: 2 Wherein in time past ye **w** according to 4043
Col 3: 7 In the which ye also **w** sometime, when 4043
1Pe 4: 3 when we **w** in lasciviousness, lusts, 4198
1Jn 2: 6 himself also so to walk, even as he **w**. 4043

WALKEDST (1) [WALK]
Jn 21:18 and **w** whither thou wouldest: 4043

WALKEST (7) [WALK]
Dt 6: 7 when thou **w** by the way, and when thou 1980
 11:19 when thou **w** by the way, when thou liest 1980
1Ki 2:42 **w** abroad any whither, that thou shalt 1980
Isa 43: 2 thou **w** through the fire, thou shalt not 1980
Ac 21:24 but that thou thyself also **w** **orderly** 4748
Ro 14:15 thy meat, now **w** thou not charitably. 4043
3Jn 1: 3 is in thee, even as thou **w** in the truth. 4043

WALKETH (41) [WALK]
Ge 24:65 What man is this that **w** in the field to 1980
Dt 23:14 For the Lord thy God **w** in the midst of 1980
1Sa 12: 2 now behold, the king **w** before you: 1980
Job 18: 8 by his own feet, and he **w** upon a snare. 1980
 22:14 not; and he **w** in the circuit of heaven. 1980
 34: 8 of iniquity, and **w** with wicked men. 1980
Ps 1: 1 Blessed is the man that **w** not in the 1980
 15: 2 He that **w** uprightly, 1980
 39: 6 Surely every man **w** in a vain shew: 1980
 73: 9 and their tongue **w** through the earth. 1980
 91: 6 Nor for the pestilence that **w** in darkness; 1980
 101: 6 he that **w** in a perfect way, he shall serve 1980
 104: 3 who **w** upon the wings of the wind: 1980
 128: 1 that feareth the Lord; that **w** in his ways. 1980
Pr 6:12 a wicked man, **w** with a froward mouth. 1980
 10: 9 He that **w** uprightly walketh surely: 1980
 10: 9 He that walketh uprightly **w** surely: 1980
 13:20 He that **w** with wise men shall be wise: 1980
 14: 2 He that **w** in his uprightness feareth 1980
 15:21 but a man of understanding **w** uprightly. 1980
 19: 1 Better is the poor that **w** in his integrity, 1980
 20: 7 The just man **w** in his integrity: his 1980
 28: 6 is the poor that **w** in his uprightness, 1980
 28:18 Whoso uprightly **w** shall be saved: 1980
 28:26 whoso **w** wisely, he shall be delivered. 1980
Ecc 2:14 in his head; but the fool **w** in darkness: 1980
 10: 3 when he that is a fool **w** by the way, 1980
Isa 33:15 He that **w** righteously, 1980
 50:10 that **w** in darkness, and hath no light? 1980
 65: 2 which **w** in a way that was not good, 1980
Jer 10:23 it is not in man that **w** to direct his steps. 1980
 23:17 they say unto every one that **w** after 1980
Eze 11:21 as for them whose heart **w** after the heart 1980
Mic 2: 7 do not my words do good to him that **w** 1980
Mt 12:43 he **w through** dry places, 1330
Lk 11:24 **w through** dry places, seeking rest; 1330
Jn 12:35 for he that **w** in darkness knoweth not 4043
2Th 3: 6 from every brother that **w** disorderly, 4043
1Pe 5: 8 the devil, as a roaring lion, **w about**, 4043
1Jn 2:11 and **w** in darkness, and knoweth not 4043
Rev 2: 1 who **w** in the midst of the seven golden 4043

WALKING (30) [WALK]
Ge 3: 8 they heard the voice of the Lord God **w** 1980
Dt 2: 7 he knoweth thy **w** through this great 1980
1Ki 3: 3 **w** in the statutes of David his father: 1980
 16:19 **w** in the way of Jeroboam, and in his sin 1980
Job 1: 7 earth, and from **w up and down** in it. 1980
 2: 2 earth, and from **w up and down** in it. 1980
 31:26 it shined, or the moon **w** in brightness; 1980
Ecc 10: 7 and princes **w** as servants upon the earth. 1980
Isa 3:16 **w** and mincing as they go, and making a 1980
 20: 2 And he did so, **w** naked and barefoot. 1980
 57: 2 their beds, each one **w** in his uprightness. 1980
Jer 6:28 all grievous revolters, **w** with slanders: 1980
Da 3:25 **w** in the midst of the fire, and they have 1981
Mic 2:11 If a man **w** in the spirit and falsehood do 1980
Mt 4:18 Jesus, **w** by the sea of Galilee, saw two 4043
 14:25 Jesus went unto them, **w** on the sea. 4043
 14:26 And when the disciples saw him **w** on 4043
Mk 6:48 **w** upon the sea, and would have passed 4043
 6:49 But when they saw him **w** upon the sea, 4043
 8:24 up, and said, I see men as trees, **w**. 4043
 11:27 as he was **w** in the temple, there come 4043
Lk 1: 6 **w** in all the commandments and 4198
Jn 6:19 they see Jesus **w** on the sea, and drawing 4043
Ac 3: 8 **w**, and leaping, and praising God. 4043
 3: 9 And all the people saw him **w** and 4043
 9:31 and **w** in the fear of the Lord, and in 4198
2Co 4: 2 not **w** in craftiness, nor handling the word 4043
2Pe 3: 3 last days scoffers, **w** after their own lusts, 4198
2Jn 1: 4 that I found of thy children **w** in truth, 4043
Jude 1:16 complainers, **w** after their own lusts; 4198

WALL (179) [UNWALLED, WALLED, WALLS]
Ge 49: 6 in self will they digged down a **w**. 7794
 49:22 a well; whose branches run over the **w**. 7791
Ex 14:22 the waters were a **w** unto them on their 2346
 14:29 the waters were a **w** unto them on their 2346

Lev 14:37 which in sight are lower than the **w**; 7023
 25:31 houses of the villages which have no **w** 2346
Nu 22:24 a **w** being on this side, and a wall on that 1447
 22:24 being on this side, and a **w** on that side. 1447
 22:25 she thrust herself unto the **w**, 7023
 22:25 and crusht Balaam's foot against the **w**: 7023
 35: 4 shall reach from the **w** of the city and 7023
Jos 2:15 for her house was upon the town **w**, 2346
 2:15 town wall, and she dwelt upon the **w**. 2346
 6: 5 the **w** of the city shall fall down flat, 2346
 6:20 the **w** fell down flat, so that the people 2346
1Sa 18:11 I will smite David even to the **w** with it. 7023
 19:10 Saul sought to smite David even to the **w** 7023
 19:10 and he smote the javelin into the **w**: 7023
 20:25 other times, even upon a seat by the **w**: 7023
 25:16 They were a **w** unto us both by night and 2346
 25:22 light any that pisseth against the **w**. 7023
 25:34 light any that pisseth against the **w**. 7023
 31:10 they fastened his body to the **w** of 2346
 31:12 the bodies of his sons from the **w** of 2346
2Sa 11:20 ye not that they would shoot from the **w**? 2346
 11:21 of a millstone upon him from the **w**, 2346
 11:21 why went ye nigh the **w**? then say thou, 2346
 11:24 the shooters shot off the **w** upon thy 2346
 18:24 up to the roof over the gate unto the **w**, 2346
 20:15 that were with Joab battered the **w**, 2346
 20:21 head shall be thrown to thee over the **w**. 2346
 22:30 troop: by my God have I leaped over a **w**. 7791
1Ki 3: 1 of Jerusalem round about. 2346
 4:33 the hyssop that springeth out of the **w**: 7023
 6: 5 against the **w** of the house he built 7023
 6: 6 for without in the **w** of the house he made NIH
 6:27 the wing of the one touched the one **w**, 7023
 6:27 of the other cherub touched the other **w**; 7023
 6:31 and side posts were a fifth part of the **w**. NIH
 6:33 posts of olive tree, a fourth part of the **w**. NIH
 9:15 the **w** of Jerusalem, and Hazor, 2346
 14:10 Jeroboam him that pisseth against the **w**, 7023
 16:11 left him not one that pisseth against a **w**, 7023
 20:30 there a **w** fell upon twenty and 2346
 21:21 from Ahab him that pisseth against the **w**, 7023
 21:23 The dogs shall eat Jezebel by the **w** of 2426
2Ki 3:27 him for a burnt offering upon the **w**. 2346
 4:10 a little chamber, I pray thee, on the **w**; 7023
 6:26 king of Israel was passing by upon the **w**, 2346
 6:30 he passed by upon the **w**, and the people 2346
 9: 8 from Ahab him that pisseth against the **w**, 7023
 9:33 of her blood was sprinkled on the **w**, 7023
 14:13 brake down the **w** of Jerusalem from 2346
 18:26 the ears of the people that are on the **w**. 2346
 18:27 sent me to the men which sit on the **w**, 2346
 20: 2 he turned his face to the **w**, and prayed 7023
2Ch 3:11 cubits, reaching to the **w** of the house: 7023
 3:12 cubits, reaching to the **w** of the house: 7023
 25:23 brake down the **w** of Jerusalem from 2346
 26: 6 brake down the **w** of Gath, and the wall 2346
 26: 6 the **w** of Jabneh, and the wall of Ashdod, 2346
 26: 6 the **w** of Ashdod, and built cities about 2346
 26: 9 the turning of the **w**, and fortified them. NIH
 27: 3 and on the **w** of Ophel he built much. 2346
 32: 5 built up all the **w** that was broken, 2346
 32: 5 another without, and repaired Millo in 2346
 32:18 people of Jerusalem that were on the **w**, 2346
 33:14 after this he built a **w** without the city 2346
 36:19 brake down the **w** of Jerusalem, 2346
Ezr 5: 3 build this house, and to make up this **w**? 846
 9: 9 to give us a **w** in Judah and in Jerusalem. 1447
Ne 1: 3 the **w** of Jerusalem also is broken down, 2346
 2: 8 for the **w** of the city, and for the house 2346
 2:15 viewed the **w**, and turned back, 2346
 2:17 and let us build up the **w** of Jerusalem, 2346
 3: 8 they fortified Jerusalem unto the broad **w**. 2346
 3:13 thousand cubits on the **w** unto the dung 2346
 3:15 the **w** of the pool of Siloah by the king's 2346
 3:19 up to the armoury at the turning of the **w**. NIH
 3:20 from the turning of the **w** unto the door of NIH
 3:24 turning of the **w**, even unto the corner. NIH
 3:25 over against the turning of the **w**, NIH
 3:27 that lieth out, even unto the **w** of Ophel. 2346
 4: 1 Sanballat heard that we builded the **w**, 2346
 4: 3 he shall even break down their stone **w**. 2346
 4: 6 So built we the **w**; and all the wall was 2346
 4: 6 all the **w** was joined together unto the 2346
 4:10 so that we are not able to build the **w**. 2346
 4:13 set I in the lower places behind the **w**, 2346
 4:15 that we returned all of us to the **w**, 2346
 4:17 They which builded on the **w**, and they 2346
 4:19 large, and we are separated upon the **w**, 2346
 5:16 also I continued in the work of this **w**, 2346
 6: 1 heard that I had builded the **w**, 2346
 6: 6 for which cause thou buildest the **w**, 2346
 6:15 So the **w** was finished in the twenty and 2346
 7: 1 when the **w** was built, and I had set up 2346
 12:27 at the dedication of the **w** of Jerusalem 2346
 12:30 the people, and the gates, and the **w**. 2346
 12:31 up the princes of Judah upon the **w**, 2346
 12:31 hand upon the **w** toward the dung gate: 2346
 12:37 at the going up of the **w**, above the house 2346
 12:38 and the half of the people upon the **w**, 2346
 12:38 of the furnaces even unto the broad **w**; 2346
 13:21 unto them, Why lodge ye about the **w**? 2346
Ps 18:29 and by my God have I leaped over a **w**. 7791
 62: 3 as a bowing shall ye be, and as a 7023
Pr 18:11 and as a high **w** in his own conceit. 2346
 24:31 the stone **w** thereof was broken down. 1444

W

SS 2: 9 behold, he standeth behind our **w**, 3796
 8: 9 If she *be* a **w**, we will build upon her a 2346
 8:10 I *am* a **w**, and my breasts like towers: 2346
Isa 2:15 high tower, and upon every fenced **w**, 2346
 5: 5 *and* break down the **w** thereof, and it 1447
 22:10 have ye broken down to fortify the **w**. 2346
 25: 4 terrible ones *is* as a storm *against* the **w**, 7023
 30:13 swelling out in a high **w**, whose breaking 2346
 36:11 the ears of the people that *are* on the **w**, 2346
 36:12 *sent me* to the men that sit upon the **w**, 2346
 38: 2 Hezekiah turned his face toward the **w**, 7023
 59:10 We grope for the **w** like the blind, 7023
Jer 15:20 thee unto this people a fenced brasen **w**: 2346
 49:27 I will kindle a fire in the **w** of Damascus, 2346
 51:44 unto him: yea, the **w** of Babylon shall fall. 2346
La 2: 8 The LORD hath purposed to destroy the **w** 2346
 2: 8 made the rampart and the **w** to lament; 2346
 2:18 the Lord, O **w** of the daughter of Zion, 2346
Eze 4: 3 set it *for* a **w** of iron between thee and 7023
 8: 7 when I looked, behold a hole in the **w**. 7023
 8: 8 unto me, Son of man, dig now in the **w**: 7023
 8: 8 I had digged in the **w**, behold a door. 7023
 8:10 pourtrayed upon the **w** round about. 7023
 12: 5 Dig thou through the **w** in their sight, 7023
 12: 7 in the even I digged through the **w** with 7023
 12:12 they shall dig through the **w** to carry out 7023
 13:10 one built up a **w**, and lo, others daubed it 2434
 13:12 when the **w** is fallen, shall it not be said 7023
 13:14 So will I break down the **w** that ye have 7023
 13:15 will I accomplish my wrath upon the **w**, 7023
 13:15 The **w** *is* no *more*, neither they that 7023
 23:14 she saw men pourtrayed upon the **w**, 7023
 38:20 and every **w** shall fall to the ground. 2346
 40: 5 behold a **w** on the outside of the house 2346
 41: 5 After he measured the **w** of the house, 7023
 41: 6 they entered into the **w** which *was* of 7023
 41: 6 they had not hold in the **w** of the house. 7023
 41: 9 The thickness of the **w**, which *was* for 7023
 41:12 the **w** of the building *was* five cubits thick 7023
 41:17 by all the **w** round about within 7023
 41:20 trees made, and on the **w** of the temple. 7023
 42: 7 the **w** that *was* without over against 1447
 42:10 of the **w** of the court toward the east, 1444
 42:12 the way directly before the **w** toward 1448
 42:20 had a **w** round about, five hundred *reeds* 2346
 43: 8 posts, and the **w** between me and them, 7023
Da 5: 5 the plaister of the **w** of the king's palace: 3797
 9:25 and the **w**, even in troublous times. 2742
Hos 2: 6 **make a w**, that she shall not find 1443+1447
Joel 2: 7 they shall climb the **w** like men of war; 2346
 2: 9 shall run upon the **w**, they shall climb 2346
Am 1: 7 I will send a fire on the **w** of Gaza, 2346
 1:10 I will send a fire in the **w** of Tyrus, 2346
 1:14 I will kindle a fire in the **w** of Rabbah, 2346
 5:19 leaned his hand on the **w**, and a serpent 7023
 7: 7 the Lord stood upon a **w** made by a 2346
Na 2: 5 they shall make haste to the **w** thereof, 2346
 3: 8 *was* the sea, *and* her **w** *was* from the sea? 2346
Hab 2:11 For the stone shall cry out of the **w**, 7023
Zec 2: 5 will be unto her a **w** of fire round about, 2346
Ac 9:25 and let *him* down by the **w** in a basket. 5038
 23: 3 God shall smite thee, *thou* whited **w**: 5109
2Co 11:33 in a basket was I let down by the **w**, 5038
Eph 2:14 hath broken down the **middle w** of 3320
Rev 21:12 And had a **w** great and high, 5038
 21:14 And the **w** of the city had twelve 5038
 21:15 and the gates thereof, and the **w** thereof. 5038
 21:17 he measured the **w** thereof, an hundred 5038
 21:18 And the building of the **w** of it was *of* 5038
 21:19 And the foundations of the **w** of the city 5038

WALLED (4) [WALL]

Lev 25:29 if a man sell a dwelling house in a **w** city, 2346
 25:30 the house that *is* in the **w** city shall be 2346
Nu 13:28 and the cities *are* **w**, *and* very great: 1219
Dt 1:28 the cities *are* great and **w** up to heaven; 1219

WALLOW (4) [WALLOWED, WALLOWING]

Jer 6:26 with sackcloth, and **w** thyself in ashes: 6428
 25:34 **w** yourselves *in the ashes*, ye principal of 6428
 48:26 Moab also shall **w** in his vomit, and he 5606
Eze 27:30 they shall **w** themselves in the ashes: 6428

WALLOWED (2) [WALLOW]

2Sa 20:12 Amasa **w** in blood in the midst of 1556
Mk 9:20 he fell on the ground, and **w** foaming. 2947

WALLOWING (1) [WALLOW]

2Pe 2:22 The sow that was washed to *her* **w** in 2946

WALLS (66) [WALL]

Lev 14:37 if the plague *be* in the **w** of the house 7023
 14:39 if the plague be spread in the **w** of 7023
Dt 3: 5 All these cities *were* fenced with high **w**, 2346
 28:52 until thy high and fenced **w** come down, 2346
1Ki 4:13 threescore great cities with **w** and 2346
 6: 5 *against* the **w** of the house round about, 7023
 6: 6 not be fastened in the **w** of the house. 7023
 6:15 he built the **w** of the house within with 7023
 6:15 of the house, and the **w** of the cieling: 7023
 6:16 the floor and the **w** with boards of cedar: 7023
 6:29 he carved the **w** of the house round 7023
2Ki 25: 4 *by* the way of the gate between **two w**, 2346
 25:10 brake down the **w** of Jerusalem round 2346
1Ch 29: 4 to overlay the **w** of the houses *withal*: 7023

2Ch 3: 7 and the **w** thereof, and the doors thereof, 7023
 3: 7 gold; and graved cherubims on the **w**. 7023
 8: 5 fenced cities, with **w**, gates, and bars; 2346
 14: 7 make about *them* **w**, and towers, gates, 2346
Ezr 4:12 have set up the **w** *thereof*, and joined 7792
 4:13 the **w** set up *again*, *then* will they not 7792
 4:16 builded *again*, and the **w** thereof set up, 7792
 5: 3 timber *is* laid in the **w**, and this work 3797
 5: 9 build this house, and to make up these **w**? 846
Ne 2:13 port, and viewed the **w** of Jerusalem, 2346
 4: 7 heard that the **w** of Jerusalem were made 2346
Job 24:11 *Which* make oil within their **w**, 7791
Ps 51:18 unto Zion: build thou the **w** of Jerusalem. 2346
 55:10 they go about it upon the **w** thereof: 2346
 122: 7 Peace be within thy **w**, 2426
Pr 25:28 city that is broken down, *and* without **w**. 2346
SS 5: 7 the keepers of the **w** took away my vail 2346
Isa 22: 5 breaking down the **w**, and of crying to 7023
 22:11 Ye made also a ditch between the **two w** 2346
 25:12 the fortress of the high fort of thy **w** shall 2346
 26: 1 salvation will *God* appoint *for* **w** and 2346
 49:16 hands; thy **w** *are* continually before me. 2346
 56: 5 within my **w** a place and a name better 2346
 60:10 the sons of strangers shall build up thy **w**, 2346
 60:18 thou shalt call thy **w** Salvation, 2346
 62: 6 I have set watchmen upon thy **w**, 2346
Jer 1:15 against all the **w** thereof round about, 2346
 1:18 and brasen **w** against the whole land, 2346
 5:10 Go ye up upon her **w**, and destroy; 8284
 21: 4 which besiege you without the **w**, and I 2346
 39: 4 by the gate betwixt the **two w**: 2346
 39: 8 and brake down the **w** of Jerusalem. 2346
 50:15 are fallen, her **w** are thrown down: 2346
 51:12 up the standard upon the **w** of Babylon, 2346
 51:58 The broad **w** of Babylon shall be utterly 2346
 52: 7 the way of the gate between the **two w**, 2346
 52:14 brake down all the **w** of Jerusalem round 2346
La 2: 7 hand of the enemy the **w** of her palaces; 2346
Eze 26: 4 they shall destroy the **w** of Tyrus, 2346
 26: 9 he shall set engines of war against thy **w**, 2346
 26:10 thy **w** shall shake at the noise of 2346
 26:12 they shall break down thy **w**, 2346
 27:11 thine army *were* upon thy **w** round about, 2346
 27:11 hanged their shields upon thy **w** round 2346
 33:30 still are talking against thee by the **w** 7023
 38:11 all of them dwelling without **w**, 2346
 41:13 and the building, with the **w** thereof, 7023
 41:22 and the **w** thereof, *were* of wood: 7023
 41:25 trees, like as *were* made upon the **w**; 7023
Mic 7:11 In the day that thy **w** are *to be* built, 1447
Zec 2: 4 **towns without w** for the multitude of 6519
Heb 11:30 By faith the **w** of Jericho fell down, 5038

WANDER (14) [WANDERED, WANDERERS, WANDEREST, WANDERETH, WANDERING, WANDERINGS]

Ge 20:13 when God **caused** me to **w** from my 8582
Nu 14:33 your children shall **w** in the wilderness 7462
 32:13 he **made** them **w** in the wilderness forty 5128
Dt 27:18 Cursed *be* he that **maketh** the blind to **w** 7686
Job 12:24 **causeth** them to **w** in a wilderness 8582
 38:41 cry unto God, they **w** for lack of meat. 8582
Ps 55: 7 Lo, *then* would I **w** far off, and remain in 5074
 59:15 Let them **w** up and down for meat, 5128
 107:40 **causeth** them to **w** in the wilderness, 8582
 119:10 O let me not **w** from thy commandments. 7686
Isa 47:15 they shall **w** every one to his quarter; 5128
Jer 14:10 Thus have they loved to **w**, they have not 5128
 14:10 that shall **cause** them to **w**, and that 6808
Am 8:12 they shall **w** from sea to sea, and from 5128

WANDERED (10) [WANDER]

Ge 21:14 and **w** in the wilderness of Beer-sheba. 8582
Jos 14:10 while *the children of* Israel **w** in 1980
Ps 107: 4 **w** in the wilderness in a solitary way; 8582
Isa 16: 8 Jazer, they **w** through the wilderness: 8582
La 4:14 They have **w** as blind *men* in the streets, 5128
 4:15 touch not, when they fled away and **w**: 5128
Eze 34: 6 My sheep **w** through all the mountains, 7686
Am 4: 8 So two *or* three cities **w** unto one city, 5128
Heb 11:37 they **w** about in sheepskins and goatskins; 4022
 11:38 they **w** in deserts, and *in* mountains, 4105

WANDERERS (2) [WANDER]

Jer 48:12 the LORD, that I will send unto him **w**, 6808
Hos 9:17 and they shall be **w** among the nations. 5074

WANDEREST (1) [WANDER]

Jer 2:20 hill and under every green tree thou **w**, 6808

WANDERETH (6) [WANDER]

Job 15:23 He **w** abroad for bread, *saying*, Where is 5074
Pr 21:16 The man that **w** out of the way of 8582
 27: 8 As a bird that **w** from her nest, so *is* a 5074
 27: 8 nest, so *is* a man that **w** from his place. 5074
Isa 16: 3 hide the outcasts; bewray not him that **w**. 5074
Jer 49: 5 and none shall gather up him that **w**. 5074

WANDERING (6) [WANDER]

Ge 37:15 and, behold, *he was* **w** in the field: 8582
Pr 26: 2 As the bird by **w**, as the swallow by flying 5110
Ecc 6: 9 Better *is* the sight of the eyes than the **w** 1980
Isa 16: 2 *that*, as a **w** bird cast out of the nest, 5074
1Ti 5:13 *to be* idle, **w** about from house to house; 4022
Jude 1:13 **w** stars, to whom is reserved the 4107

WANDERINGS (1) [WANDER]

Ps 56: 8 Thou tellest my **w**: put thou my tears into 5112

WANT (31) [WANTED, WANTETH, WANTING, WANTS]

Dt 28:48 in **w** of all *things*: and he shall put a yoke 2640
 28:57 eat them for **w** of all *things* 2640
Jdg 18:10 a place where *there is* no **w** of any thing 4270
 19:19 thy servants: *there is* no **w** of any thing. 4270
Job 24: 8 embrace the rock *for* **w** of a shelter. 1097+4480
 30: 3 For **w** and famine *they were* solitary; 2639
 31:19 If I have seen *any* perish for **w** of clothing, 1097
Ps 23: 1 The LORD *is* my shepherd; I shall not **w**. 2637
 34: 9 for *there is* no **w** to them that fear him. 4270
 34:10 they that seek the LORD shall not **w** any 2637
Pr 6:11 travelleth, and thy **w** as an armed man. 4270
 10:21 feed many: but fools die for **w** of wisdom. 2638
 13:23 is *that* is destroyed for **w** of judgment. 3808
 13:25 but the belly of the wicked shall **w**. 2637
 14:28 in the **w** of people *is* the destruction of 657
 21: 5 but *of* every one that is hasty only to **w**. 4270
 22:16 giveth to the rich, *shall* surely *come* to **w**. 4270
 24:34 travelleth; and thy **w** as an armed man. 4270
Isa 34:16 of these shall fail, none shall **w** her mate: 6485
Jer 33:17 David shall never **w** a man to sit upon 3772
 33:18 Neither shall the priests the Levites **w** a 3772
 35:19 Jonadab the son of Rechab shall not **w** a 3772
La 4: 9 stricken through for *w* of the fruits of NIH
Eze 4:17 That they may **w** bread and water, 2637
Am 4: 6 and of bread in all your places: 2640
Mk 12:44 she of her **w** did cast in all that she had, 5304
Lk 15:14 in that land; and he began to be in **w**. 5302
2Co 8:14 abundance *may be a supply* for their **w**, 5303
 8:14 also may be *a supply* for your **w**: 5303
 9:12 not only supplieth the **w** of the saints, 5303
Php 4:11 Not that I speak in respect of **w**: for I have 5304

WANTED (3) [WANT]

Jer 44:18 we have **w** all *things*, and have been 2637
Jn 2: 3 when they **w** wine, the mother of Jesus 5302
2Co 11: 9 when I was present with you, and **w**, 5302

WANTETH (7) [WANT]

Dt 15: 8 for his need, *in that* which he **w**. 2637
Pr 9: 4 *as for* him that **w** understanding, she saith 2638
 9:16 *as for* him that **w** understanding, she saith 2638
 10:19 In the multitude of words there **w** not sin: 2308
 28:16 The prince that **w** understanding *is* also a 2638
Ecc 6: 2 that he **w** nothing for his soul of all that 2638
SS 7: 2 *is* like a round goblet, *which* **w** not liquor: 2637

WANTING (8) [WANT]

2Ki 10:19 and all his priests; let none be **w**: 6485
 10:19 whosoever shall be **w**, he shall not live. 6485
Pr 19: 7 *them* with words, *yet* they are **w** to him. 3808
Ecc 1:15 that which is **w** cannot be numbered. 2642
Da 5:27 weighed in the balances, and art found **w**. 2627
Tit 1: 5 set in order the *things* that are **w**, 3007
 3:13 that nothing be **w** unto them. 3007
Jas 1: 4 ye may be perfect and entire, **w** nothing. 3007

WANTON (3) [WANTONNESS]

Isa 3:16 with stretched forth necks and **w** eyes, 8265
1Ti 5:11 when they have *begun to* **wax w** against 2691
Jas 5: 5 in pleasure on the earth, and been **w**; 4684

WANTONNESS (2) [WANTON]

Ro 13:13 not in chambering and **w**, not in strife and 766
2Pe 2:18 the lusts of the flesh, through much **w**, 766

WANTS (2) [WANT]

Jdg 19:20 howsoever *let* all thy **w** *lie* upon me; 4270
Php 2:25 and he that ministered to my **w**. 5532

WAR (225) [WARFARE, WARRED, WARRETH, WARRING, WARRIOR, WARRIORS, WARS]

Ge 14: 2 *That* these made **w** with Bera king of 4421
Ex 1:10 pass, that, when there falleth out any **w**, 4421
 13:17 the people repent when they see **w**, 4421
 15: 3 The LORD *is* a man of **w**: the LORD *is* 4421
 17:16 with Amalek from generation to 4421
 32:17 There *is* a noise of **w** in the camp. 4421
Nu 1: 3 all that *are able to* go forth to **w** in Israel: 6635
 1:20 all that *were able to* go forth to **w**; 6635
 1:22 all that *were able to* go forth to **w**; 6635
 1:24 all that *were able to* go forth to **w**; 6635
 1:26 all that *were able to* go forth to **w**; 6635
 1:28 all that *were able to* go forth to **w**; 6635
 1:30 all that *were able to* go forth to **w**; 6635
 1:32 all that *were able to* go forth to **w**; 6635
 1:34 all that *were able to* go forth to **w**; 6635
 1:36 all that *were able to* go forth to **w**; 6635
 1:38 all that *were able to* go forth to **w**; 6635
 1:40 all that *were able to* go forth to **w**; 6635
 1:42 all that *were able to* go forth to **w**; 6635
 1:45 all that *were able to* go forth to **w** in Israel; 6635
 10: 9 if ye go to **w** in your land against 4421
 26: 2 all that are *able to* go to **w** in Israel. 6635
 31: 3 Arm some of yourselves unto the **w**, 6635
 31: 4 the tribes of Israel, shall ye send to the **w**. 6635
 31: 5 tribe, twelve thousand armed for **w**. 6635
 31: 6 Moses sent them to the **w**, a thousand of 6635
 31: 6 to the **w**, with the holy instruments, 6635
 31:21 Eleazar the priest said unto the men of **w** 6635
 31:27 them that took the **w** upon them, 4421

Nu 31:28 of the men of **w** which went out to battle: 4421
31:32 the prey which the men of **w** had caught, 6635
31:36 the portion of them that went out to **w**, 6635
31:49 men of **w** which *are* under our charge, 4421
31:53 *For* the men of **w** had taken spoil, 6635
32: 6 Shall your brethren go to **w**, and shall ye 4421
32:20 ye will go armed before the LORD to **w**, 6635
32:27 every man armed for **w**, before the LORD 6635
Dt 1:41 girded on every man his weapons of **w**, 4421
2:14 until all the generation of the men of **w** 4421
2:16 when all the men of **w** were consumed 4421
3:18 Israel, all *that are* **meet for the w**. 1121+2428
4:34 by **w**, and by a mighty hand, and by a 4421
20:12 will make **w** against thee, then thou shalt 4421
20:19 time, in **making w** against it to take it, 3898
20:20 against the city that maketh **w** with thee, 4421
21:10 When thou goest forth to **w** against thine 4421
24: 5 a new wife, he shall not go out to **w**, 6635
Jos 4:13 About forty thousand prepared for **w** 6635
5: 4 *that were* males, *even* all the men of **w**, 4421
5: 6 till all the people *that were* men of **w**, 4421
6: 3 all ye men of **w**, *and* go round about 4421
8: 1 take all the people of **w** with thee, 4421
8: 3 So Joshua arose, and all the people of **w**, 4421
8:11 *even* the people of **w** *that were* with him, 4421
10: 5 before Gibeon, and **made w** against it. 3898
10: 7 he, and all the people of **w** with him, 4421
10:24 said unto the captains of the men of **w** 4421
11: 7 and all the people of **w** with him, 4421
11:18 Joshua made **w** a long time with all those 4421
11:23 their tribes. And the land rested from **w**. 4421
14:11 for **w**, both to go out, and to come in. 4421
14:15 Anakims. And the land had rest from **w**. 4421
17: 1 because he was a man of **w**, therefore 4421
22:12 *at* Shiloh, to go up to **w** against them. 6635
Jdg 3: 2 to teach them **w**, at the least such as 4421
3:10 and he judged Israel, and went out to **w**: 4421
5: 8 chose new gods; then *was* **w** in the gates: 3901
11: 4 that the children of Ammon **made w** 3898
11: 5 when the children of Ammon **made w** 3898
11:27 thou doest me wrong to **w** against me: 3898
18:11 men appointed *with* weapons of **w**. 4421
18:16 men appointed *with* their weapons of **w**, 4421
18:17 that were appointed *with* weapons of **w**, 4421
20:17 drew sword: all these *were* men of **w**. 4421
21:22 not to each man his wife in the **w**: 4421
1Sa 8:12 to make his instruments of **w**, 4421
14:52 there was sore **w** against the Philistines 4421
16:18 a mighty valiant *man*, and a man of **w**, 4421
17:33 youth, and he a man of **w** from his youth. 4421
18: 5 Saul set him over the men of **w**, and he 4421
19: 8 there was **w** again: and David went out, 4421
23: 8 Saul called all the people together to **w**, 4421
28:15 for the Philistines **make w** against me, 3898
2Sa 1:27 and the weapons of **w** perished! 4421
3: 1 there was long **w** between the house 4421
3: 6 while there was **w** between the house of 4421
11: 7 the people did, and how the **w** prospered. 4421
11:18 David all the things concerning the **w**; 4421
11:19 telling the matters of the **w** unto the king, 4421
17: 8 father *is* a man of **w**, and will not lodge 4421
21:15 Moreover the Philistines had yet **w** again 4421
22:35 teacheth my hands to **w**; so that a bow 4421
1Ki 2: 5 shed the blood of **w** in peace, and put 4421
2: 5 put the blood of **w** upon his girdle that 4421
9:22 they *were* men of **w**, and his servants, 4421
14:30 there was **w** between Rehoboam and 4421
15: 6 there was **w** between Rehoboam and 4421
15: 7 there was **w** between Abijam and 4421
15:16 there was **w** between Asa and Baasha 4421
15:32 there was **w** between Asa and Baasha 4421
20:18 or whether they be come out for **w**, 4421
22: 1 they continued three years without **w** 4421
2Ki 8:28 war Hazael king of Syria in 4421
13:25 of the hand of Jehoahaz his father by **w**. 4421
14: 7 took Selah by **w**, and called the name of 4421
16: 5 king of Israel came up *to* Jerusalem to **w**: 4421
18:20 *I have* counsel and strength for the **w**. 4421
24:16 all *that were* strong *and* apt for **w**, 4421
25: 4 all the men of **w** *fled* by night *by* the way 4421
25:19 an officer that was set over the men of **w**, 4421
1Ch 5:10 in the days of Saul they made **w** with 4421
5:18 skilful in **w**, *were* four and forty thousand 4421
5:18 and threescore, that went out *to* the **w**. 6635
5:19 made **w** with the Hagarites, with Jetur, 4421
5:22 many slain, because the **w** *was* of God. 4421
7: 4 *were* bands of soldiers for **w**, six and 4421
7:11 two hundred *soldiers*, *fit* to go out *for* **w** 6635
7:40 genealogy of them *that were* apt *to* the **w** 6635
12: 1 among the mighty *men*, helpers of the **w**. 4421
12: 8 *and* men of **w** *fit* for the battle, that could 6635
12:23 bands that were ready armed to the **w**, 6635
12:24 and eight hundred, ready armed to the **w**. 6635
12:25 mighty *men* of valour for the **w**, 6635
12:33 expert in **w**, with all instruments of war, 4421
12:33 expert in war, with all instruments of **w**, 4421
12:35 of the Danites expert in **w** twenty and 4421
12:36 to battle, expert in **w**, forty thousand. 4421
12:37 with all *manner of* instruments of **w** for 6635
12:38 All these men of **w**, that could keep rank, 4421
18:10 (for Hadarezer **had w** with 376+1961+4421
20: 4 that there arose **w** at Gezer with 4421
20: 5 There was **w** again with the Philistines; 4421
20: 6 yet again there was **w** at Gath, where was 4421
28: 3 because thou *hast been* a man of **w**, 4421

2Ch 6:34 If thy people go out to **w** against their 4421
8: 9 *were* men of **w**, and chief of his 4421
13: 2 was **w** between Abijah and Jeroboam. 4421
13: 3 array with an army of valiant *men of* **w**. 4421
14: 6 had rest, and he had no **w** in those years; 4421
15:19 there was no *more* **w** unto the five and 4421
17:10 they **made no w** against Jehoshaphat. 3898
17:13 the men of **w**, mighty *men* of valour. 4421
17:18 thousand ready prepared for the **w**. 6635
18: 3 and *we will* be with thee in the **w**. 4421
22: 5 **w** against Hazael king of Syria at 4421
25: 5 choice *men*, able to go forth *to* **w**, 6635
26:11 *men*, that went out to **w** by bands, 6635
26:13 that made **w** with mighty power, 4421
28:12 up against them that came from the **w**, 6635
32: 6 he set captains of **w** over the people, 4421
33:14 put captains of **w** in all the fenced cities 2428
35:21 against the house wherewith I have **w**: 4421
Job 5:20 and in **w** from the power of the sword. 4421
10:17 upon me; changes and **w** *are* against me. 6635
38:23 trouble, against the day of battle and **w**? 4421
Ps 18:34 teacheth my hands to **w**, so that a bow 4421
27: 3 though **w** should rise against me, in this 4421
55:21 than butter, but **w** *was* in his heart: 7128
68:30 scatter thou the people *that* delight in **w**. 7128
120: 7 peace: but when I speak, they *are* for **w**. 4421
140: 2 are they gathered together *for* **w**. 4421
144: 1 which teacheth my hands to **w**, 7128
Pr 20:18 counsel: and with good advice make **w**. 4421
24: 6 by wise counsel thou shalt make thy **w**: 4421
Ecc 3: 8 to hate; a time of **w**, and a time of peace. 4421
8: 8 *there is* no discharge in *that* **w**; neither 4421
9:18 Wisdom *is* better than weapons of **w**: 7128
SS 3: 8 They all hold swords, *being* expert in **w**: 4421
Isa 2: 4 neither shall they learn **w** any more. 4421
3: 2 The mighty *man*, and the man of **w**, 4421
3:25 by the sword, and thy mighty in the **w**. 4421
7: 1 up *towards* Jerusalem to **w** against it, 4421
21:15 bow, and from the grievousness of **w**. 4421
36: 5 *I have* counsel and strength for **w**: 4421
37: 9 He is come forth to **make w** with thee. 3898
41:12 that **w** against thee shall be as nothing, 4421
42:13 he shall stir up jealousy like a man of **w**: 4421
Jer 4:19 the sound of the trumpet, the alarm of **w**. 4421
6: 4 Prepare ye **w** against her; arise, and let us 4421
6:23 set in array as men for **w** against thee, 4421
21: 2 king of Babylon **maketh w** against us; 3898
21: 4 I *will* turn back the weapons of **w** that 4421
28: 8 of **w**, and of evil, and of pestilence. 4421
38: 4 of the men of **w** that remain in this city, 4421
39: 4 all the men of **w**, then they fled, 4421
41: 3 that were found there, *and* the men of **w**. 4421
41:16 *even* mighty men of **w**, and the women, 4421
42:14 land of Egypt, where we shall see no **w**, 4421
48:14 *are* mighty and strong men for the **w**? 4421
49: 2 I will cause an alarm of **w** to be heard 4421
49:26 the men of **w** shall be cut off in that day, 4421
50:30 her men of **w** shall be cut off in that day, 4421
51:20 *art* my battle axe *and* weapons of **w**: 4421
51:32 with fire, and the men of **w** are affrighted. 4421
52: 7 all the men of **w** fled, and went forth out 4421
52:25 which had the charge of the men of **w**; 4421
Eze 17:17 great company make for him in the **w**, 4421
26: 9 he shall set engines of **w** against thy walls, 6904
27:10 Phut were in thine army, thy men of **w**: 4421
27:27 all thy men of **w**, that *are* in thee, and in 4421
32:27 down to hell with their weapons of **w**: 4421
39:20 with mighty *men*, and *with* all men of **w**, 4421
Da 7:21 the same horn made **w** with the saints, 7129
9:26 unto the end of the **w** desolations *are* 4421
Joel 2: 7 they shall climb the wall like men of **w**; 4421
3: 9 Prepare **w**, wake up the mighty *men*, let 4421
3: 9 men, let all the men of **w** draw near; 4421
Mic 2: 8 pass by securely *as men* averse from **w**. 4421
3: 5 they even prepare **w** against him. 4421
4: 3 neither shall they learn **w** any more. 4421
Lk 14:31 **make w against** another 1519+4171+4820
23:11 And Herod with his men of **w** set him at 4753
2Co 10: 3 in the flesh, we do not **w** after the flesh: 4754
1Ti 1:18 that thou by them mightest war a good 4754
Jas 4: 1 of your lusts that **w** in your members? 4170
4: 2 ye fight and **w**, yet ye have not, because 4170
1Pe 2:11 fleshly lusts, which **w** against the soul; 4754
Rev 11: 7 bottomless *pit* shall make **w** against them, 4171
12: 7 And there was **w** in heaven: Michael and 4171
12:17 went to make **w** with the remnant of her 4171
13: 4 who is able to **make w** with him? 4170
13: 7 it was given unto him to make **w** with 4170
17:14 These shall **make w** with the Lamb, 4170
19:11 righteousness he doth judge and **make w**. 4170
19:19 gathered together to make **w** against him 4171

WARD (22) [WARDS]

Ge 40: 3 he put them in **w** *in* the house of the 4929
40: 4 and they continued a season in **w**. 4929
40: 7 with him in the **w** of his lord's house, 4929
41:10 put me in **w** *in* the captain of the guard's 4929
42:17 put them all together into **w** three days. 4929
Lev 24:12 they put him in **w**, that the mind of 4929
Nu 15:34 they put him in **w**, because it was not 4929
2Sa 20: 3 put them *in* **w**, and fed them, 1004+4931
1Ch 12:29 had kept the **w** of the house of Saul. 4931
25: 8 **w** against ward, as well the small as 4931
25: 8 ward against **w**, as well the small as NIH
26:16 causeway of the going up, against ward. 4929

1Ch 26:16 causeway of the going up, ward against **w**. 4929
Ne 12:24 the man of God, **w** over against ward, 4929
12:24 the man of God, ward over against **w**, 4929
12:25 *were* porters keeping the **w** at 4929
12:45 and the porters kept the **w** of their God, 4931
12:45 their God, and the **w** of the purification, 4931
Isa 21: 8 and I *am* set in my **w** whole nights: 4931
Jer 37:13 captain of the **w** *was* there, whose name 6488
Eze 19: 9 they put him in **w** in chains, 5474
Ac 12:10 they were past the first and the second **w**, 5438

WARDROBE (2)

2Ki 22:14 the son of Harhas, keeper of the **w**; 899
2Ch 34:22 the son of Hasrah, keeper of the **w**; 899

WARDS (3) [WARD]

1Ch 9:23 the house of the tabernacle, by **w**. 4931
26:12 chief men, *having* **w** one against another, 4931
Ne 13:30 appointed the **w** of the priests and 4931

WARE (8) [AWARE, WARES, WEAR]

Ne 10:31 *if* the people of the land bring **w** or 4728
13:16 all *manner of* **w**, and sold on the sabbath 4377
13:20 sellers of all *kind of* **w** lodged without 4465
Mt 24:50 him, and in an hour that he is not **w** of, 1097
Lk 8:27 and **w** no clothes, neither abode in *any* 1737
12:46 *him*, and at an hour when he is not **w**, 1097
Ac 14: 6 They were **w** of *it*, and fled unto Lystra 4894
2Ti 4:15 Of whom **be** thou **w** also; for he hath 5442

WARES (5) [WARE]

Jer 10:17 Gather up thy **w** out of the land, 3666
Eze 27:16 of the multitude of the **w** of thy **making**; 4639
27:18 in the multitude of the **w** of thy **making**, 4639
27:33 When thy **w** went forth out of the seas, 5801
Jnh 1: 5 cast forth the **w** that *were* in the ship into 3627

WARFARE (5) [WAR]

1Sa 28: 1 gathered their armies together for **w**, 6635
Isa 40: 2 cry unto her, that her **w** is accomplished, 6635
1Co 9: 7 Who **goeth a w** any time at his own 4754
2Co 10: 4 (For the weapons of our **w** *are* not carnal, 4752
1Ti 1:18 that thou by them mightest war a good **w**; 4752

WARM (8) [LUKEWARM]

2Ki 4:34 and the flesh of the child **waxed w**. 2552
Job 6:17 What time they **wax w**, they vanish: 2215
37:17 How thy garments *are* **w**, when he 2525
Ecc 4:11 have heat: but how can one be **w** *alone*? 3179
Isa 44:15 for he will take thereof, and **w** himself; 2552
44:16 saith, Aha, I am **w**, I have seen the fire: 2552
47:14 *there shall* not *be* a coal to **w** at, *nor* fire 2552
Hag 1: 6 *ye* clothe you, but there is none **w**; and 2527

WARMED (6) [WARMETH, WARMING]

Job 31:20 *if* he were *not* **w** with the fleece of my 2552
Mk 14:54 the servants, and **w** himself at the fire. 2328
Jn 18:18 and they **w** themselves: and Peter stood 2328
18:18 Peter stood with them, and **w** himself. 2328
18:25 And Simon Peter stood and **w** himself: 2328
Jas 2:16 Depart in peace, be you **w** and filled; 2328

WARMETH (2) [WARMED]

Job 39:14 her eggs in the earth, and **w** them in dust, 2552
Isa 44:16 yea, he **w** himself, and saith, Aha, I am 2552

WARMING (1) [WARMED]

Mk 14:67 And when she saw Peter **w** himself, 2328

WARN (11) [FOREWARN, FOREWARNED, WARNED, WARNING]

2Ch 19:10 that even **w** them that they trespass not 2094
Eze 3:18 nor speakest to **w** the wicked from his 2094
3:19 Yet if thou **w** the wicked, and he turn not 2094
3:21 Nevertheless if thou **w** the righteous *man*, 2094
33: 3 he blow the trumpet, and **w** the people; 2094
33: 7 word at my mouth, and **w** them from me. 2094
33: 8 if thou dost not speak to **w** the wicked 2094
33: 9 if thou **w** the wicked of his way to turn 2094
Ac 20:31 years I ceased not to **w** every one night 3560
1Co 4:14 but as my beloved sons I **w** you. 3560
1Th 5:14 brethren, **w** *them that are* unruly, 3560

WARNED (10) [WARN]

2Ki 6:10 the man of God told him and **w** him of, 2094
Ps 19:11 Moreover by them *is* thy servant **w**: 2094
Eze 3:21 he shall surely live, because he is **w**; 2094
33: 6 the trumpet, and the people be not **w**; 2094
Mt 2:12 being **w** of God in a dream that *they* 5537
2:22 being **w** of God in a dream, 5537
3: 7 who hath **w** you to flee from the wrath to 5263
Lk 3: 7 who hath **w** you to flee from the wrath to 5263
Ac 10:22 was **w** from God by a holy angel to send 5537
Heb 11: 7 being **w** of God *of* *things* not seen as yet, 5537

WARNING (8) [WARN]

Jer 6:10 I speak, and **give w**, that they may hear? 5749
Eze 3:17 at my mouth, and **give w** from me. 2094
3:18 and thou **givest** him not **w**, 2094
3:20 because thou hast not **given** him **w**, he 2094
33: 4 sound of the trumpet, and **taketh** not **w**; 2094
33: 5 sound of the trumpet, and **took** not **w**; 2094
33: 5 he that **taketh w** shall deliver his soul. 2094
Col 1:28 **w** every man, and teaching every man in 3560

WARP (9)

Lev	13:48 Whether *it be* in the **w**, or woof; of linen,	8359
	13:49 either in the **w**, or in the woof, or in a	8359
	13:51 either in the **w**, or in the woof, or in a	8359
	13:52 whether **w** or woof, in woollen or in	8359
	13:53 either in the **w**, or in the woof, or in any	8359
	13:56 the skin, or out of the **w**, or out of the	8359
	13:57 either in the **w**, or in the woof, or in any	8359
	13:58 either in the **w**, or woof, or whatsoever thing of	8359
	13:59 either *in* the **w**, or woof, or any thing of	8359

WARRED (9) [WAR]

Nu	31: 7 they **w** against the Midianites,	6633
	31:42 Moses divided from the men that **w**,	6633
Jos	24: 9 arose and **w** against Israel, and sent and	3898
1Ki	14:19 how he **w**, and how he reigned,	3898
	20: 1 and besieged Samaria, and **w** against it.	3898
	22:45 might that he shewed, and how he **w**,	3898
2Ki	6: 8 the king of Syria **w** against Israel,	3898
	14:28 how he **w**, and how he recovered	3898
2Ch	26: 6 went forth and **w** against the Philistines,	3898

WARRETH (1) [WAR]

2Ti	2: 4 No *man* that **w** entangleth himself with	4754

WARRING (3) [WAR]

2Ki	19: 8 found the king of Assyria **w** against	3898
Isa	37: 8 found the king of Assyria **w** against	3898
Ro	7:23 **w against** the law of my mind,	497

WARRIOR (1) [WAR]

Isa	9: 5 For every battle of the **w** *is* with confused	5431

WARRIORS (2) [WAR]

1Ki	12:21 chosen *men*, which were **w**,	4421+6213
2Ch	11: 1 chosen *men*, which were **w**,	4421+6213

WARS (15) [WAR]

Nu	21:14 Wherefore it is said in the book of the **w**	4421
Jdg	3: 1 as had not known all the **w** of Canaan;	4421
2Sa	8:10 Hadadezer **had w with** Toi.	376+1961+4421
1Ki	5: 3 which were about him on every side,	4421
1Ch	22: 8 blood abundantly, and hast made great **w**:	4421
2Ch	12:15 *there were* **w** between Rehoboam and	4421
	16: 9 from henceforth thou shalt have **w**.	4421
	27: 7 of Jotham, and all his **w**, and his ways,	4421
Ps	46: 9 He maketh **w** to cease unto the end of	4421
Mt	24: 6 And ye shall hear of **w** and rumours of	4171
	24: 6 ye shall hear of wars and rumours of **w**:	4171
Mk	13: 7 And when ye shall hear of **w** and	4171
	13: 7 ye shall hear of wars and rumours of **w**,	4171
Lk	21: 9 But when ye shall hear of **w** and	4171
Jas	4: 1 From whence *come* **w** and fightings	4171

WART See WEN

WAS (4531) [BE] See Index of Articles, Etc.

WASH (89) [UNWASHEN, WASHED, WASHEST, WASHING, WASHINGS, WASHPOT]

Ge	18: 4 **w** your feet, and rest yourselves under	7364
	19: 2 **w** your feet, and ye shall rise up early,	7364
	24:32 water to **w** his feet, and the men's feet	7364
Ex	2: 5 the daughter of Pharaoh came down to **w**	7364
	19:10 to morrow, and let them **w** their clothes,	3526
	29: 4 and shalt **w** them with water.	7364
	29:17 **w** the inwards of him, and his legs,	7364
	30:18 to **w** *withal*: and thou shalt put it	7364
	30:19 and his sons shall **w** their hands and	7364
	30:20 they shall **w** *with* water, that they die not;	7364
	30:21 So they shall **w** their hands and their feet,	7364
	40:12 congregation, and **w** them with water.	7364
	40:30 altar, and put water there, to **w** *withal*.	7364
Lev	1: 9 and his legs shall he **w** in water:	7364
	1:13 he shall **w** the inwards and the legs with	7364
	6:27 shalt **w** that whereon it was sprinkled	3526
	9:14 he did **w** the inwards and the legs,	7364
	11:25 of the carcase of them shall **w** his clothes,	3526
	11:28 that beareth the carcase of them shall **w**	3526
	11:40 that eateth of the carcase of it shall **w** his	3526
	11:40 also that beareth the carcase of it shall **w**	3526
	13: 6 and he shall **w** his clothes, and be clean.	3526
	13:34 and he shall **w** his clothes, and be clean.	3526
	13:54 the priest shall command that they **w**	3526
	13:58 thing of skin *it be*, which thou shalt **w**,	3526
	14: 8 that is to be cleansed shall **w** his clothes,	3526
	14: 8 off all his hair, and **w** *himself* in water,	7364
	14: 9 he shall **w** his clothes, also he shall wash	3526
	14: 9 also he shall **w** his flesh in water,	7364
	14:47 he that lieth in the house shall **w** his	3526
	14:47 he that eateth in the house shall **w** his	3526
	15: 5 whosoever toucheth his bed shall **w**	3526
	15: 6 sat that hath the issue shall **w** his clothes,	3526
	15: 7 that hath the issue shall **w** his clothes,	3526
	15: 8 shall **w** his clothes, and bathe *himself*	3526
	15:10 that beareth *any* of those *things* shall **w**	3526
	15:11 he shall **w** his clothes, and bathe *himself*	3526
	15:13 **w** his clothes, and bathe his flesh in	3526
	15:16 he shall **w** all his flesh in water,	7364
	15:21 whosoever toucheth her bed shall **w** his	3526
	15:22 thing that she sat upon shall **w** his clothes,	3526
	15:27 shall **w** his clothes, and bathe *himself* in	3526
	16: 4 therefore shall he **w** his flesh in water,	7364
	16:24 he shall **w** his flesh with water in the holy	7364
	16:26 goat for the scapegoat shall **w** his clothes,	3526
	16:28 he that burneth them shall **w** his clothes,	3526
Lev	17:15 he shall both **w** his clothes,	3526
	17:16 if he **w** *them* not, nor bathe his flesh; then	3526
	22: 6 not eat of the holy *things*, unless he **w**	7364
Nu	8: 7 let them **w** their clothes, and *so*	3526
	19: 7 the priest shall **w** his clothes, and he shall	3526
	19: 8 he that burneth her shall **w** his clothes in	3526
	19:10 the ashes of the heifer shall **w** his	3526
	19:19 he shall purify him*self*, and **w** his clothes,	3526
	19:21 water of separation shall **w** his clothes;	3526
	31:24 shall **w** your clothes on the seventh day,	3526
Dt	21: 6 *that are* next unto the slain *man*, shall **w**	7364
	23:11 he shall **w** *with* water:	7364
Ru	3: 3 **W** thyself therefore, and anoint thee,	7364
1Sa	25:41 *let* thine handmaid be a servant to **w**	7364
2Sa	11: 8 Go down to thy house, and **w** thy feet.	7364
2Ki	5:10 Go and **w** in Jordan seven times,	7364
	5:12 may I not **w** in them, and be clean?	7364
	5:13 when he saith to thee, **W**, and be clean?	7364
2Ch	4: 6 and five on the left, to **w** in them:	7364
	4: 6 but the sea *was* for the priests to **w** in.	7364
Job	9:30 If I **w** myself with snow water,	7364
Ps	26: 6 I will **w** mine hands in innocency: so will	7364
	51: 2 **W** me throughly from mine iniquity,	3526
	51: 7 **w** me, and I shall be whiter than snow.	3526
	58:10 he shall **w** his feet in the blood of	7364
Isa	1:16 **W** ye, make you clean; put away the evil	7364
Jer	2:22 For though thou **w** thee with nitre,	3526
	4:14 **w** thine heart from wickedness,	3526
Eze	23:40 for whom thou didst **w** thyself, paintedst	7364
Mt	6:17 anoint thine head, and **w** thy face;	3538
	15: 2 for they **w** not their hands when they eat	3538
Mk	7: 3 except they **w** *their* hands oft, eat not,	3538
	7: 4 the market, except they **w**, they eat not.	907
Lk	7:38 and began to **w** his feet with tears,	1026
Jn	9: 7 unto him, Go, **w** in the pool of Siloam,	3538
	9:11 me, Go to the pool of Siloam, and **w**:	3538
	13: 5 and began to **w** the disciples' feet,	3538
	13: 6 unto him, Lord, dost thou **w** my feet?	3538
	13: 8 unto him, Thou shalt never **w** my feet.	3538
	13: 8 Jesus answered him, If I **w** thee not,	3538
	13:10 that is washed needeth not save to **w** *his*	3538
	13:14 ye also ought to **w** one another's feet.	3538
Ac	22:16 and be baptized, and **w** away thy sins,	628

WASHBASIN See WASHPOT

WASHED (45) [WASH]

Ge	43:24 gave *them* water, and they **w** their feet;	7364
	43:31 he **w** his face, and went out,	7364
	49:11 he **w** his garments in wine, and his	3526
Ex	19:14 the people; and they **w** their clothes.	3526
	40:31 and Aaron and his sons **w** their hands and	7364
	40:32 they came near unto the altar, they **w**;	7364
Lev	8: 6 and his sons, and **w** them with water.	7364
	8:21 he **w** the inwards and the legs in water;	7364
	13:55 shall look on the plague, after *that* it is **w**:	3526
	13:58 it shall be **w** the second time, and shall be	3526
	15:17 shall be **w** with water, and be unclean	3526
Nu	8:21 were purified, and they **w** their clothes;	3526
Jdg	19:21 they **w** their feet, and did eat and drink.	7364
2Sa	12:20 **w**, and anointed *himself*, and changed his	7364
	19:24 nor trimmed his beard, nor **w** his clothes,	3526
1Ki	22:38 one **w** the chariot in the pool of Samaria;	7857
	22:38 his blood; and they **w** his armour;	7364
2Ch	4: 6 for the burnt offering they **w** in them;	1740
Job	29: 6 When *I* **w** my steps with butter,	7364
Ps	73:13 *in* vain, and **w** my hands in innocency.	7364
Pr	30:12 and *yet* is not **w** from their filthiness.	7364
SS	5: 3 I have **w** my feet; how shall I defile them?	7364
	5:12 of waters, **w** with milk, *and* fitly set.	7364
Isa	4: 4 the Lord shall have **w** away the filth	7364
Eze	16: 4 neither wast thou **w** in water to supple	7364
	16: 9 Then I **w** thee with water; yea, I throughly	7364
	16: 9 I throughly **w** away thy blood from thee,	7857
	40:38 gates, where they **w** the burnt offering.	1740
Mt	27:24 and **w** his hands before the multitude,	633
Lk	7:44 but she hath **w** my feet with tears,	1026
	7:38 that had not first **w** before dinner.	907
Jn	9: 7 way therefore, and **w**, and came seeing.	3538
	9:11 and I went and **w**, and I received sight.	3538
	9:15 He put clay upon mine eyes, and I **w**,	3538
	13:10 He that is **w** needeth not save to wash *his*	3068
	13:12 after he had **w** their feet, and had taken	3538
	13:14 *your* Lord and Master, have **w** your feet;	3538
Ac	9:37 whom when they had **w**, they laid *her* in	3068
	16:33 hour of the night, and **w** *their* stripes;	3068
1Co	6:11 but ye are **w**, but ye are sanctified, but ye	628
1Ti	5:10 if she have **w** the saints' feet,	3538
Heb	10:22 and *our* bodies **w** with pure water.	3068
2Pe	2:22 The sow that was **w** to *her* wallowing in	3068
Rev	1: 5 and **w** us from our sins in his own blood,	3068
	7:14 and have **w** their robes, and made them	4150

WASHERMAN'S See FULLER'S

WASHEST (1) [WASH]

Job	14:19 thou **w** away the things which grow out	7857

WASHING (10) [WASH]

Lev	13:56 the plague *be* somewhat dark after the **w**	3526
2Sa	11: 2 from the roof he saw a woman **w** herself;	7364
Ne	4:23 *saving* that every one put them off for **w**.	4325
SS	4: 2 even shorn, which came up from the **w**;	7367
	6: 6 a flock of sheep which go up from the **w**,	7367
Mk	7: 4 *as* the **w** of cups, and pots, brasen vessels,	909
	7: 8 tradition of men, *as* the **w** of pots and cups:	909

Lk	5: 2 gone out of them, and were **w** *their* nets.	637
Eph	5:26 *it* with the **w** of water by the word,	3067
Tit	3: 5 by the **w** of regeneration, and renewing of	3067

WASHINGS (1) [WASH]

Heb	9:10 drinks, and divers **w**, and carnal ordinances,	909

WASHPOT (2) [POT, WASH]

Ps	60: 8 Moab *is* my **w**; over Edom will I	5518+7366
	108: 9 Moab *is* my **w**; over Edom will I	5518+7366

WAST (66) [BE]

Ge	3:11 he said, Who told thee that thou **w** naked?	NIH
	3:19 the ground; for out of it **w** thou taken:	NIH
	33:10 face of God, and thou **w** pleased with me.	NIH
	40:13 after the former manner when thou **w** his	1961
Dt	5:15 remember that thou **w** a servant in the	1961
	15:15 thou shalt remember that thou **w** a	1961
	16:12 thou shalt remember that thou **w** a	1961
	23: 7 because thou **w** a stranger in his land.	1961
	24:18 thou shalt remember that thou **w** a	1961
	24:22 thou shalt remember that thou **w** a	1961
	25:18 thee, when thou **w** faint and weary;	NIH
	28:60 diseases of Egypt, which thou **w** afraid of;	NIH
Ru	3: 2 kindred, with whose maidens thou **w**?	1961
1Sa	15:17 When thou **w** little in thine own sight,	NIH
	15:17 **w** thou not made the head of the tribes of	NIH
2Sa	1:14 How **w** thou not afraid to stretch forth	NIH
	1:25 thou **w** slain in thine high places.	NIH
	5: 2 thou **w** he that leddest out and broughtest	1961
1Ch	11: 2 thou **w** he that leddest out and broughtest	1110
Job	15: 7 born? or **w** thou made before the hills?	NIH
	38: 4 **w** thou when I laid the foundations	1961
	38:21 thou *it*, because thou **w** then born?	NIH
Ps	99: 8 thou **w** a God that forgavest them,	1961
	114: 5 thou Jordan, *that* thou **w** driven back?	NIH
Isa	12: 1 though thou **w** angry with me, thine anger	NIH
	14: 3 from the hard bondage wherein thou **w**	NIH
	33: 1 thee that spoilest, and thou **w** not spoiled;	NIH
	43: 4 Since thou **w** precious in my sight, thou	NIH
	48: 8 **w** called a transgressor from the womb.	NIH
	54: 6 when thou **w** refused, saith thy God.	NIH
	57:10 thine hand; therefore thou **w** not grieved.	NIH
Jer	2:36 of Egypt, as thou **w** ashamed of Assyria.	NIH
	50:24 O Babylon, and thou **w** not aware:	NIH
Eze	16: 4 in the day thou **w** born thy navel was not	NIH
	16: 4 neither **w** thou washed in water to supple	NIH
	16: 4 to supple *thee*; thou **w** not salted at all,	NIH
	16: 5 thou **w** cast out in the open field,	NIH
	16: 5 of thy person, in the day that thou **w** born.	NIH
	16: 6 I said unto thee *when thou* **w** in thy blood,	NIH
	16: 6 I said unto thee *when thou* **w** in thy blood,	NIH
	16: 7 is grown, whereas thou **w** naked and bare.	NIH
	16:13 Thus **w** thou decked *with* gold and silver;	NIH
	16:13 thou **w** exceeding beautiful, and thou	NIH
	16:22 when thou **w** naked and bare,	1961
	16:22 and bare, *and* **w** polluted in thy blood.	NIH
	16:28 the Assyrians, because thou **w** unsatiable;	NIH
	16:29 and yet thou **w** not satisfied herewith.	NIH
	16:47 as *if that were* a very little *thing*, thou **w**	NIH
	21:30 will judge thee in the place where thou **w**	NIH
	24:13 have purged thee, and thou **w** not purged,	NIH
	26:17 *that* inhabited of seafaring men,	NIH
	26:17 which **w** strong in the sea, she and	1961
	27:25 **w** replenished, and made very glorious	NIH
	28:13 in thee in the day that thou **w** created;	NIH
	28:14 thou **w** upon the holy mountain of God;	1961
	28:15 Thou **w** perfect in thy ways from the day	NIH
	28:15 ways from the day that thou **w** created,	NIH
Ob	1:11 even thou **w** as one of them.	NIH
Mt	26:69 saying, Thou also **w** with Jesus of Galilee.	1510
Mk	14:67 *And* thou also **w** with Jesus of Nazareth.	1510
Jn	1:48 thou **w** under the fig tree, I saw thee.	1510
	9:34 thou **w** altogether born in sins,	NIG
	21:18 I say unto thee, When thou **w** young,	1510
Rev	5: 9 for thou **w** slain, and hast redeemed us to	NIG
	11:17 which art, and **w**, and art to come;	1510
	16: 5 O Lord, which art, and **w**, and shalt be,	1510

WASTE (64) [WASTED, WASTENESS, WASTER, WASTES, WASTETH, WASTING]

Lev	26:31 I will make your cities **w**, and bring your	2723
	26:33 land shall be desolate, and your cities **w**.	2723
Nu	21:30 we have **laid** *them* even unto Nophah,	8074
Dt	32:10 and in the **w** howling wilderness;	8414
1Ki	17:14 The barrel of meal shall not **w**, neither	3615
2Ki	19:25 thou shouldest be to **lay w** fenced cities	7582
1Ch	17: 9 shall the children of wickedness **w**	1086
Ne	2: 3 **w**, and the gates thereof are consumed	2720
	2:17 how Jerusalem *lieth* **w**, and the gates	2720
Job	30: 3 wilderness in former time desolate and **w**.	4875
	38:27 To satisfy the desolate and **w** *ground*; and	4875
Ps	79: 7 and **laid w** his dwelling place.	8074
	80:13 The boar out of the wood doth **w** it,	3765
Isa	5: 6 I will lay it **w**: it shall not be pruned,	1326
	5:17 **w places** of the fat ones shall strangers	2723
	15: 1 in the night Ar of Moab is **laid w**,	7703
	15: 1 in the night Kir of Moab is **laid w**,	7703
	23: 1 for it is **laid w**, so that *there is* no house,	7703
	23:14 of Tarshish: for your strength is **laid w**.	7703
	24: 1 **maketh** it **w**, and turneth it upside down,	1110
	33: 8 The highways **lie w**, the wayfaring man	8074
	34:10 generation to generation it shall **lie w**;	2717
	37:18 the kings of Assyria have **laid w** all	2717
	37:26 that thou shouldest be to **lay w** defenced	7582

Isa	42:15 I will **make** w mountains and hills,	2717
	49:17 they that **made** thee w shall go forth of	2717
	49:19 For thy w and thy desolate places,	2723
	51: 3 he will comfort all her w **places**;	2723
	52: 9 sing together, ye w **places** of Jerusalem:	2723
	58:12 be of thee shall build the old w **places**;	2723
	61: 4 they shall repair the w cities,	2721
	64:11 and all our pleasant things are **laid** w.	2723
Jer	2:15 *and* yelled, and they made his land w	8047
	4: 7 *and* thy cities shall be **laid** w, without an	5327
	27:17 wherefore should this city be **laid** w?	2723
	46:19 Noph shall be w and desolate without	8047
	49:13 desolation, a reproach, a w, and a curse;	2721
	50:21 w and utterly destroy after them, saith	2717
Eze	5:14 Moreover I will make thee w,	2723
	6: 6 dwelling places the cities shall be **laid** w,	2717
	6: 6 that your altars may be **laid** w and	2717
	12:20 cities that are inhabited shall be **laid** w,	2717
	19: 7 palaces, and he **laid** w their cities;	2717
	26: 2 I shall be replenished, *now* she is **laid** w:	2717
	29: 9 the land of Egypt shall be desolate and w,	2723
	29:10 make the land of Egypt **utterly** w	2721+2723
	29:12 her cities among the cities *that are* **laid** w	2723
	30:12 I will **make** the land w, and all that is	8074
	35: 4 I will lay thy cities w, and thou shalt be	2723
	36:35 the w and desolate and ruined cities *are*	2720
	36:38 shall the w cities be filled *with* flocks of	2720
	38: 8 of Israel, which have been always w:	2723
Joel	1: 7 He hath laid my vine w, and barked my	8047
Am	7: 9 the sanctuaries of Israel shall be **laid** w;	2717
	9:14 they shall build the w cities,	8074
Mic	5: 6 they shall the land of Assyria with	7462
Na	2:10 She *is* empty, and void, and w:	1110
	3: 7 from thee, and say, Nineveh is **laid** w:	7703
Zep	3: 6 I **made** their streets w, that none passeth	2717
Hag	1: 4 your cieled houses, and this house **lie** w?	2720
	1: 9 Because of mine house that *is* w,	2720
Mal	1: 3 his heritage w for the dragons of	8077
Mt	26: 8 saying, To what purpose *is* this w?	684
Mk	14: 4 Why was this w of the ointment made?	684

WASTED (16) [WASTE]

Nu	14:33 your carcases be w in the wilderness.	8552
	24:22 Nevertheless the Kenite shall be w,	1197
Dt	2:14 of war were w out from among the host,	8552
1Ki	17:16 *And* the barrel of meal w not, neither did	3615
1Ch	20: 1 the country of the children of Ammon,	7843
Ps	137: 3 they that w us *required of us* mirth,	8437
Isa	6:11 Until the cities be w without inhabitant,	7582
	19: 5 and the river shall be w and dried up,	2717
	60:12 *those* nations shall be **utterly** w.	2717+2717
Jer	44: 7 they are w *and* desolate, as *at* this day.	2723
Eze	30: 7 be in the midst of the cities *that are* w.	2717
Joel	1:10 The field is w, the land mourneth;	7703
	1:10 the corn is w, the new wine is dried up,	7703
Lk	15:13 there w his substance with riotous living.	1287
	16: 1 unto him that he had w his goods.	1287
Gal	1:13 I persecuted the church of God, and w it:	4199

WASTENESS (1) [WASTE]

Zep	1:15 and distress, a day of w and desolation,	7722

WASTER (2) [WASTE]

Pr	18: 9 work *is* brother to him that is a great w.	7843
Isa	54:16 and I have created the w to destroy.	7843

WASTES (7) [WASTE]

Isa	61: 4 they shall build the old w, they shall raise	2723
Jer	49:13 all the cities thereof shall be perpetual w.	2723
Eze	33:24 they that inhabit those w of the land of	2723
	33:27 surely *they* that *are* in the w shall fall by	2723
	36: 4 to the desolate, and to the cities that	2723
	36:10 be inhabited, and the w shall be builded:	2723
	36:33 in the cities, and the w shall be builded.	2723

WASTETH (3) [WASTE]

Job	14:10 dieth, **and away**: yea, man giveth up	2522
Ps	91: 6 *nor* for the destruction *that* w at noonday.	7736
Pr	19:26 He that w *his* father, *and* chaseth away	7703

WASTING (2) [WASTE]

Isa	59: 7 w and destruction are in their paths.	7701
	60:18 w nor destruction within thy borders;	7701

WATCH (61) [WATCHED, WATCHER, WATCHERS,
WATCHES, WATCHETH, WATCHFUL,
WATCHING, WATCHINGS, WATCHMAN,
WATCHMAN'S, WATCHMEN, WATCHT,
WATCHTOWER]

Ge	31:49 The LORD w between me and thee,	6822
Ex	14:24 that in the morning w the LORD looked	821
Jdg	7:19 camp *in* the beginning of the middle w;	821
	7:19 *and* they had but newly set the w:	8104
1Sa	11:11 the midst of the host in the morning w,	821
	19:11 him, and to slay him in the morning:	8104
2Sa	13:34 the young man that **kept** the w went up	6822
2Ki	11: 5 be keepers of the w of the king's house;	4931
	11: 6 so shall ye keep the w of the house, that	4931
	11: 7 even they shall keep the w of the house	4931
2Ch	20:24 when Judah came toward the w **tower** in	4707
	23: 6 all the people shall keep the w of	4931
Ezr	8:29 **W** ye, and keep *them*, until ye weigh	8245
Ne	4: 9 set a w against them day and night,	4929
	7: 3 every one in his w, and every one *to be*	4929
Job	7:12 a whale, that thou settest a w over me?	4929

Job	14:16 my steps: dost thou not w over my sin?	8104
Ps	90: 4 when it is past, and *as* a w in the night.	821
	102: 7 I w, and am as a sparrow alone upon	8245
	130: 6 more than they that w for the morning:	8104
	130: 6 I *say, more* than they that w for	8104
	141: 3 Set a w, O LORD, before my mouth;	8108
Isa	21: 5 table, w in the watchtower, eat, drink:	6822
	29:20 and all that w for iniquity are cut off:	8245
Jer	5: 6 a leopard shall w over their cities:	8245
	31:28 will I w over them, to build, and to plant,	8245
	44:27 I *will* w over them for evil, and not for	8245
	51:12 make the w strong, set up the watchmen,	4929
Na	2: 1 keep the munition, w the way, make *thy*	6822
Hab	2: 1 I will stand upon my w, and set me upon	4931
	2: 1 will w to see what he will say unto me,	6822
Mt	24:42 W therefore: for ye know not what hour	1127
	24:43 known in what w the thief would come,	5438
	25:13 W therefore, for ye know neither the day	1127
	26:38 unto death: tarry ye here, and w with me.	1127
	26:40 What, could ye not w with me one hour?	1127
	26:41 W and pray, that ye enter not into	1127
	27:65 Pilate said unto them, Ye have a w: go	2892
	27:66 sealing the stone, and setting a w.	2892
	28:11 some of the w came into the city,	2892
Mk	6:48 about the fourth w of the night he cometh	5438
	13:33 Take ye heed, w and pray: for ye know not	69
	13:34 work, and commanded the porter to w.	1127
	13:35 W ye therefore: for ye know not when	1127
	13:37 what I say unto you I say unto all, W.	1127
	14:34 unto death: tarry ye here, and w.	1127
	14:37 couldest not thou w one hour?	1127
	14:38 W ye and pray, lest ye enter into	1127
Lk	2: 8 **keeping** w over their flock by	5438+5442
	12:38 And if he shall come in the second w,	5438
	12:38 or come in the third w, and find *them* so,	5438
	21:36 W ye therefore, and pray always, that ye	69
Ac	20:31 Therefore w, and remember, that *by*	1127
1Co	16:13 W ye, stand fast in the faith, quit you like	1127
Col	4: 2 in the same with thanksgiving;	1127
1Th	5: 6 as *do* others; but let us w and be sober.	1127
2Ti	4: 5 w thou in all *things*, endure afflictions,	3525
Heb	13:17 for they w for your souls, as they that must	69
1Pe	4: 7 therefore be sober, and w unto prayer.	3525
Rev	3: 3 If therefore thou shalt not w, I will come	1127

WATCHED (12) [WATCH]

Jer	20:10 All my familiars w for my halting,	8104
	31:28 like as I have w over them, to pluck up,	8245
La	4:17 in our watching we have w for a nation	6822
Da	9:14 Therefore hath the LORD w upon the evil,	8245
Mt	24:43 he would have w, and would not have	1127
	27:36 And sitting down they w him there;	5083
Mk	3: 2 And they w him, whether he would heal	3906
Lk	6: 7 And the scribes and Pharisees w him,	3906
	12:39 he would have w, and not have suffered	1127
	14: 1 on the sabbath day, that they w him.	3906
	20:20 And they w *him*, and sent forth spies,	3906
Ac	9:24 And they w the gates day and night to kill	3906

WATCHER (2) [WATCH]

Da	4:13 a w and a holy one came down from	5894
	4:23 whereas the king saw a w and a holy one	5894

WATCHERS (2) [WATCH]

Jer	4:16 that w come from a far country,	5341
Da	4:17 This matter *is* by the decree of the w,	5894

WATCHES (3) [WATCH]

Ne	7: 3 appoint w of the inhabitants of Jerusalem,	4931
	12: 9 *were* over against them in the w.	4931
Ps	63: 6 *and* meditate on thee in the *night* w.	821
	119:148 Mine eyes prevent the *night* w, that I	821
La	2:19 in the beginning of the w, pour out thine	821

WATCHETH (3) [WATCH]

Ps	37:32 The wicked w the righteous, and seeketh	6822
Eze	7: 6 is come: it w for thee; behold, it is come.	6974
Rev	16:15 Blessed *is* he that w, and keepeth his	1127

WATCHFUL (1) [WATCH]

Rev	3: 2 Be w, and strengthen the *things* which	1127

WATCHING (6) [WATCH]

1Sa	4:13 Eli sat upon a seat *by* the wayside w:	6822
Pr	8:34 daily at my gates, waiting at the posts	8245
La	4:17 in our w we have watched for a nation	6836
Mt	27:54 Jesus, saw the earthquake,	5083
Lk	12:37 the lord when he cometh shall find w:	1127
Eph	6:18 and w thereunto with all perseverance and	69

WATCHINGS (2) [WATCH]

2Co	6: 5 in tumults, in labours, in w, in fastings;	70
	11:27 painfulness, in w often, in hunger and thirst,	70

WATCHMAN (18) [WATCH]

2Sa	18:24 the w went *up* to the roof over the gate	6822
	18:25 he cried, and told the king.	6822
	18:26 the w saw another man running:	6822
	18:26 the w called unto the porter, and said,	6822
	18:27 the w said, Me thinketh the running of	6822
2Ki	9:17 there stood a w on the tower in Jezreel,	6822
	9:18 the w told, saying, The messenger came	6822
	9:20 the w told, saying, He came even unto	6822
Ps	127: 1 keep the city, the w waketh *but* in vain.	8104
Isa	21: 6 set a w, let him declare what he seeth.	6822

Isa	21:11 to me out of Seir, **W**, what of the night?	8104
	21:11 what of the night? **W**, what of the night?	8104
	21:12 The w said, The morning cometh,	8104
Eze	3:17 I have made thee a w unto the house of	6822
	33: 2 of their coasts, and set him for their w:	6822
	33: 6 if the w see the sword come, and blow	6822
	33: 7 have set thee a w unto the house of Israel;	6822
Hos	9: 8 The w of Ephraim *was* with my God:	6822

WATCHMAN'S (1) [WATCH]

Eze	33: 6 but his blood will I require at the w hand.	6822

WATCHMEN (12) [WATCH]

1Sa	14:16 of Saul in Gibeah of Benjamin	6822
2Ki	17: 9 the tower of the w to the fenced city.	5341
	18: 8 the tower of the w to the fenced city.	5341
SS	3: 3 The w that go about the city found me:	8104
	5: 7 The w that went about the city found me,	8104
Isa	52: 8 Thy w shall lift up the voice; *with the*	6822
	56:10 His w *are* blind: they are all ignorant,	6822
	62: 6 I have set w upon thy walls, O Jerusalem,	8104
Jer	6:17 Also I set w over you, *saying*, Hearken to	6822
	31: 6 *that* the w upon the mount Ephraim shall	5341
	51:12 set up the w, prepare the ambushes;	8104
Mic	7: 4 day of thy w *and* thy visitation cometh;	6822

WATCHT (1) [WATCH]

Ps	59: T sent, and they w the house to kill him.	8104

WATCHTOWER (2) [TOWER, WATCH]

Isa	21: 5 the table, watch *in* the w, eat, drink:	6844
	21: 8 I stand continually upon the w in	4707

WATER (396) [WATERCOURSE, WATERED,
WATEREDST, WATEREST, WATERETH,
WATERFLOOD, WATERING, WATERPOT,
WATERPOTS, WATERS, WATERSPOUTS,
WATERSPRINGS]

Ge	2:10 a river went out of Eden to w the garden;	8248
	16: 7 her by a fountain of w in the wilderness,	4325
	18: 4 Let a little w, I pray you, be fetched,	4325
	21:14 and a bottle of w, and gave *it* unto Hagar,	4325
	21:15 the w was spent in the bottle, and she	4325
	21:19 opened her eyes, and she saw a well of w;	4325
	21:19 filled the bottle *with* w, and gave the lad	4325
	21:25 because of a well of w,	4325
	24:11 by a well of w at the time of the evening,	4325
	24:11 the time that *women* go out to draw w.	NIH
	24:13 Behold, I stand *here* by the well of w;	4325
	24:13 the men of the city come out to draw w:	4325
	24:17 I pray thee, drink a little w of thy pitcher.	4325
	24:19 she said, I will draw w for thy camels also,	NIH
	24:20 ran again unto the well to draw w,	NIH
	24:32 w to wash his feet, and the men's feet	4325
	24:43 Behold, I stand by the well of w;	4325
	24:43 *when* the virgin cometh forth to draw w,	NIH
	24:43 pray thee, a little w of thy pitcher to drink;	4325
	24:45 drew w: and I said unto her, Let me drink,	NIH
	26:18 Isaac digged again the wells of w,	4325
	26:19 and found there a well of springing w.	4325
	26:20 Isaac's herdmen, saying, The w *is* ours:	4325
	26:32 and said unto him, We have found w	4325
	29: 7 ye the sheep, and go *and* feed *them*.	8248
	29: 8 the well's mouth; then we w the sheep.	8248
	37:24 the pit *was* empty, *there was* no w in it.	4325
	43:24 gave *them* w, and they washed their feet;	4325
	49: 4 Unstable as w, thou shalt not excel;	4325
Ex	2:10 said, Because I drew him out of the w.	4325
	2:16 they came and **drew** w, and filled	1802
	2:16 filled the troughs to w their father's flock.	8248
	2:19 also **drew** w enough for us,	1802+1802
	4: 9 that thou shalt take of the w of the river,	4325
	4: 9 the w which thou takest out of the river	4325
	7:15 he goeth out unto the w; and thou shalt	4325
	7:18 Egyptians shall lothe to drink of the w of	4325
	7:19 their ponds, and upon all their pools of w,	4325
	7:21 the Egyptians could not drink of the w of	4325
	7:24 round about the river *for* w to drink;	4325
	7:24 for they could not drink of the w of the	4325
	8:20 he cometh forth to the w; and say unto	4325
	12: 9 sodden at all with w, but roast with fire;	4325
	15:22 days in the wilderness, and found no w.	4325
	15:27 where *were* twelve wells of w,	4325
	17: 1 *there was* no w for the people to drink.	4325
	17: 2 and said, Give us w that we may drink.	4325
	17: 3 the people thirsted there for w;	4325
	17: 6 rock, and there shall come w out of it,	4325
	20: 4 or that *is* in the w under the earth:	4325
	23:25 and shall bless thy bread, and thy w;	4325
	29: 4 and shalt wash them with w.	4325
	30:18 the altar, and thou shalt put w therein.	4325
	30:20 they shall wash *with* w, that they die not;	4325
	32:20 strawed *it* upon the w, and made	4325
	34:28 he did neither eat bread, nor drink w.	4325
	40: 7 the altar, and shalt put w therein.	4325
	40:12 the congregation, and wash them with w	4325
	40:30 the altar, and put w there,	4325
Lev	1: 9 inwards and his legs shall he wash in w:	4325
	1:13 wash the inwards and the legs with w:	4325
	6:28 it shall be both scoured, and rinsed in w.	4325
	8: 6 and his sons, and washed them with w.	4325
	8:21 he washed the inwards and the legs in w;	4325
	11:32 it must be put into w, and it shall be	4325
	11:34 *that* on which such w cometh shall be	4325
	11:36 or pit, *wherein* there is plenty of w,	4325

Lev 11:38 if *any* **w** be put upon the seed, and *any* 4325
14: 5 in an earthen vessel over running **w**: 4325
14: 6 bird *that was* killed over the running **w**: 4325
14: 8 off all his hair, and wash *himself* in **w**, 4325
14: 9 also he shall wash his flesh in **w**, 4325
14:50 in an earthen vessel over running **w**: 4325
14:51 in the running **w**, and sprinkle the house 4325
14:52 with the running **w**, and with the living 4325
15: 5 bathe *himself* in **w**, and be unclean until 4325
15: 6 bathe *himself* in **w**, and be unclean until 4325
15: 7 bathe *himself* in **w**, and be unclean until 4325
15: 8 bathe *himself* in **w**, and be unclean until 4325
15:10 bathe *himself* in **w**, and be unclean until 4325
15:11 hath not rinsed his hands in **w**, he shall 4325
15:11 bathe *himself* in **w**, and be unclean until 4325
15:12 every vessel of wood shall be rinsed in **w**. 4325
15:13 bathe his flesh in running **w**, and shall be 4325
15:16 he shall wash all his flesh in **w**, 4325
15:17 be washed with **w**, and be unclean 4325
15:18 they shall *both* bathe *themselves* in **w**, 4325
15:21 bathe *himself* in **w**, and be unclean until 4325
15:22 bathe *himself* in **w**, and be unclean until 4325
15:27 bathe *himself* in **w**, and be unclean until 4325
16: 4 therefore shall he wash his flesh in **w**, 4325
16:24 he shall wash his flesh with **w** in the holy 4325
16:26 bathe his flesh in **w**, and afterward come 4325
16:28 bathe his flesh in **w**, and afterward he 4325
17:15 bathe *himself* in **w**, and be unclean until 4325
22: 6 *things*, unless he wash his flesh with **w**. 4325
Nu 5:17 the priest shall take holy **w** in an earthen 4325
5:17 the priest shall take, and put *it* into the **w**: 4325
5:18 priest shall have in his hand the bitter **w** 4325
5:19 be thou free from this bitter **w** that 4325
5:22 this **w** that causeth the curse shall go into 4325
5:23 he shall blot *them* out with the bitter **w**: 4325
5:24 drink the bitter **w** that causeth the curse: 4325
5:24 the **w** that causeth the curse shall enter 4325
5:26 shall cause the woman to drink the **w**. 4325
5:27 when he hath made her to drink the **w**, 4325
5:27 the **w** that causeth the curse shall enter 4325
8: 7 Sprinkle **w** of purifying upon them, 4325
19: 7 he shall bathe his flesh in **w**, 4325
19: 8 burneth shall wash his clothes in **w**, 4325
19: 8 bathe his flesh in **w**, and shall be unclean 4325
19: 9 children of Israel for a **w** of separation: 4325
19:13 the **w** of separation was not sprinkled 4325
19:17 running **w** shall be put thereto in a vessel: 4325
19:18 dip *it* in the **w**, and sprinkle *it* upon the 4325
19:19 bathe *himself* in **w**, and be clean at 4325
19:20 **w** of separation hath not been sprinkled 4325
19:21 that he that sprinkleth the **w** of separation 4325
19:21 he that toucheth the **w** of separation shall 4325
20: 2 there was no **w** for the congregation: 4325
20: 5 neither *is there any* **w** to drink. 4325
20: 8 it shall give forth his **w**, and thou shalt 4325
20: 8 thou shalt bring forth to them **w** out of 4325
20:10 must we fetch you **w** out of this rock? 4325
20:11 the **w** came out abundantly, 4325
20:13 This *is* the **w** of Meribah; because 4325
20:17 will we drink of the **w** of the wells: 4325
20:19 if I and my cattle drink *of* thy **w**, then I 4325
20:24 ye rebelled against my word at the **w** of 4325
21: 5 *there is* no bread, neither *is there any* **w**; 4325
21:16 people together, and I will give them **w**. 4325
24: 7 He shall pour the **w** out of his buckets, 4325
27:14 to sanctify me at the **w** before their eyes: 4325
27:14 that *is* the **w** of Meribah in Kadesh *in* 4325
31:23 it shall be purified with the **w** 4325
31:23 the fire ye shall make go through the **w**. 4325
33: 9 in Elim *were* twelve fountains of **w**, 4325
33:14 where was no **w** for the people to drink. 4325
Dt 2: 6 ye shall also buy **w** of them for money, 4325
2:28 give me **w** for money, that I may drink: 4325
8: 7 a land of brooks of **w**, of fountains and 4325
8:15 and drought, where *there was* no **w**; 4325
8:15 brought thee forth **w** out of the rock of 4325
9: 9 I neither did eat bread nor drink **w**, 4325
9:18 nor drink **w**, because of all your sins 4325
11: 4 how he made the **w** of the Red sea to 4325
11:11 *and* drinketh **w** of the rain of heaven: 4325
12:16 ye shall pour it upon the earth as **w**. 4325
12:24 thou shalt pour it upon the earth as **w**. 4325
15:23 thou shalt pour it upon the ground as **w**. 4325
23: 4 not with bread and with **w** in the way, 4325
23:11 cometh on, he shall wash *himself* with **w**: 4325
29:11 of thy wood unto the drawer of thy **w**: 4325
Jos 2:10 dried up the **w** of the Red sea for you, 4325
3: 8 When ye are come to the brink of the **w** 4325
3:15 the ark were dipped in the brim of the **w** 4325
7: 5 of the people melted, and became as **w**. 4325
9:21 drawers of **w** unto all the congregation; 4325
9:23 drawers of **w** for the house of my God. 4325
9:27 and drawers of **w** for the congregation, 4325
15: 9 unto the fountain of the **w** of Nephtoah, 4325
15:19 a south land; give me also springs of **w**. 4325
16: 1 unto the **w** of Jericho on the east, 4325
Jdg 1:15 a south land; give me also springs of **w**. 4325
4:19 Give me, I pray thee, a little **w** to drink; 4325
5: 4 the clouds also dropped **w**. 4325
5:11 **w**, there shall they rehearse the righteous NIH
5:25 He asked **w**, *and* she gave *him* milk; 4325
6:38 dew out of the fleece, a bowl full *of* **w**. 4325
7: 4 bring them down unto the **w**, and I will 4325
7: 5 he brought down the people unto the **w**: 4325
7: 5 Every one that lappeth of the **w** with his 4325

Jdg 7: 6 down upon their knees to drink **w**. 4325
7:15 in the jaw, and there came **w** thereout; 4325
1Sa 7: 6 drew **w**, and poured *it* out before 4325
9:11 young maidens going out to draw **w**, 4325
25:11 my **w**, and my flesh that I have killed for 4325
26:11 and the cruse of **w**, and let us go. 4325
26:12 and the cruse of **w** from Saul's bolster; 4325
26:16 and the cruse of **w** that *was* at his bolster. 4325
30:11 he did eat; and they made him drink **w**; 4325
30:12 nor drunk *any* **w**, three days and 4325
2Sa 14:14 die, and *are* as **w** spilt on the ground, 4325
17:20 They be gone over the brook of **w**. 4325
17:21 Arise, and pass quickly over the **w**: 4325
21:10 from the beginning of harvest until **w** 4325
23:15 that one would give me drink of the **w** 4325
23:16 drew **w** out of the well of Beth-lehem, 4325
1Ki 13: 8 neither will I eat bread nor drink **w** in 4325
13: 9 saying, Eat no bread, nor drink **w**, 4325
13:16 neither will I eat bread nor drink **w** with 4325
13:17 shalt eat no bread nor drink **w** there, 4325
13:18 that he may eat bread and drink **w**. 4325
13:19 did eat bread in his house, and drank **w**. 4325
13:22 eaten bread and drunk **w** in the place, 4325
13:22 to thee, Eat no bread, and drink no **w**; 4325
14:15 as a reed is shaken in the **w**, and he shall 4325
17:10 me, I pray thee, a little **w** in a vessel, 4325
18: 4 a cave, and fed them *with* bread and **w**.) 4325
18: 5 all fountains of **w**, and unto all brooks: 4325
18:13 a cave, and fed them *with* bread and **w**? 4325
18:33 Fill four barrels *with* **w**, and pour *it* on 4325
18:35 the **w** ran round about the altar; 4325
18:35 and he filled the trench also *with* **w**. 4325
18:38 licked up the **w** that *was* in the trench. 4325
19: 6 the coals, and a cruse of **w** at his head. 4325
22:27 bread of affliction and with **w** of affliction, 4325
2Ki 2:19 the **w** *is* naught, and the ground barren. 4325
3: 9 there was no **w** for the host, and for 4325
3:11 which poured **w** on the hands of Elijah. 4325
3:17 yet that valley shall be filled *with* **w**, that 4325
3:19 stop all wells of **w**, and mar every good 4325
3:20 there came **w** by the way of Edom, 4325
3:20 and the country was filled with **w**. 4325
3:22 sun shone upon the **w**, and the Moabites 4325
3:22 the Moabites saw the **w** on the other side 4325
3:25 they stopped all the wells of **w**, 4325
6: 5 a beam, the axe head fell into the **w**: 4325
6:22 set bread and **w** before them, that they 4325
8:15 dipt *it* in **w**, and spread *it* on his face, 4325
20:20 a conduit, and brought **w** into the city, 4325
1Ch 11:17 that one would give me drink *of* the **w** 4325
11:18 drew **w** out of the well of Beth-lehem, 4325
2Ch 18:26 bread of affliction and with **w** of affliction, 4325
32: 4 kings of Assyria come, and find much **w**? 4325
Ezr 10: 6 he did eat no bread, nor drink **w**: 4325
Ne 3:26 unto *the place* over against the **w** gate 4325
8: 1 into the street that *was* before the **w** gate; 4325
8: 3 **w** gate from the morning until midday, 4325
8:16 in the street of the **w** gate, and in the 4325
9:15 forth **w** for them out of the rock 4325
9:20 and gavest them **w** for their thirst. 4325
12:37 of David, even unto the **w** gate eastward. 4325
13: 2 children of Israel with bread and with **w**, 4325
Job 8:11 mire? can the flag grow without **w**? 4325
9:30 If I wash myself with snow **w**, 4325
14: 9 *Yet* through the sent of **w** it will bud, 4325
15:16 *is* man, which drinketh iniquity like **w**? 4325
22: 7 Thou hast not given **w** to the weary to 4325
34: 7 Job, *who* drinketh up scorning like **w**? 4325
36:27 For he maketh small the drops of **w**: 4325
Ps 1: 3 be like a tree planted by the rivers of **w**, 4325
6: 6 to swim; I **w** my couch with my tears. 4529
22:14 I am poured out like **w**, and all my bones 4325
42: 1 As the hart panteth after the **w** brooks, 4325
63: 1 in a dry and thirsty land, where no **w** is; 4325
65: 9 *with* the river of God, *which* is full *of* **w**: 4325
66:12 we went through fire and through **w**: 4325
72: 6 mown grass: as showers that **w** the earth. 2222
77:17 The clouds poured out **w**: the skies sent 4325
79: 3 Their blood have they shed like **w** round 4325
88:17 They came round about me daily like **w**; 4325
107:35 turneth the wilderness into a standing **w**, 4325
109:18 so let it come into his bowels like **w**, 4325
114: 8 Which turned the rock *into* a standing **w**, 4325
Pr 8:24 *were* no fountains abounding with **w**. 4325
17:14 of strife *is as* when one letteth out **w**: 4325
20: 5 in the heart of man *is like* deep **w**; 4325
21: 1 the hand of the LORD, *as* the rivers of **w**: 4325
25:21 and if he *be* thirsty, give him **w** to drink: 4325
27:19 As in **w** face *answereth* to face, so the 4325
30:16 the earth *that* is not filled with **w**: 4325
Ecc 2: 6 I made me pools of **w**, to water therewith 4325
2: 6 to **w** therewith the wood *that* bringeth 8248
Isa 1:22 is become dross, thy wine mixt with **w**: 4325
1:30 fadeth, and as a garden that hath no **w**. 4325
3: 1 stay of bread, and the whole stay of **w**, 4325
12: 3 Therefore with joy shall ye draw **w** out of 4325
14:23 possession for the bittern, and pools of **w**: 4325
16: 9 I will **w** thee *with* my tears, O Heshbon, 7301
21:14 Tema brought **w** to him that was thirsty, 4325
22:11 the two walls for the **w** of the old pool: 4325
27: 3 do keep it; I will **w** it every moment: 8248
30:14 or to take **w** *withal* out of the pit. 4325
30:20 bread of adversity, and the **w** of affliction, 4325
32: 2 as rivers of **w** in a dry place, as the 4325
35: 7 a pool, and the thirsty land springs of **w**: 4325

Isa 37:25 I have digged, and drunk **w**; and with 4325
41:17 *When* the poor and needy seek **w**, 4325
41:18 I will make the wilderness a pool of **w**, 4325
41:18 of water, and the dry land springs of **w**. 4325
44: 3 For I will pour **w** upon *him that is* thirsty, 4325
44: 4 the grass, as willows by the **w** courses. 4325
44:12 he drinketh no **w**, and is faint. 4325
49:10 even by the springs of **w** shall he guide 4325
50: 2 because *there is* no **w**, and dieth for thirst. 4325
58:11 like a spring of **w**, whose waters fail not. 4325
63:12 dividing the **w** before them, to make 4325
Jer 2:13 broken cisterns, that can hold no **w**. 4325
8:14 given us **w** of gall to drink, because 4325
9:15 and give them **w** of gall to drink. 4325
13: 1 I put it upon thy loins, and put it not in **w**. 4325
14: 3 they came to the pits, *and* found no **w**; 4325
23:15 and make them drink the **w** of gall: 4325
38: 6 in the dungeon *there was* no **w**, but mire: 4325
La 1:16 mine eye runneth down *with* **w**, because 4325
2:19 pour out thine heart like **w** before the face 4325
3:48 eye runneth down *with* rivers of **w** for 4325
4: 4 We have drunken our **w** for money; 4325
Eze 4:11 Thou shalt drink also **w** by measure, 4325
4:16 they shall drink **w** by measure, 4325
4:17 That they may want bread and **w**, 4325
7:17 feeble, and all knees shall be weak *as* **w**. 4325
12:18 drink thy **w** with trembling and 4325
12:19 and drink their **w** with astonishment, 4325
16: 4 neither wast thou washed in **w** to supple 4325
16: 9 washed I thee with **w**; yea, I throughly 4325
17: 7 that *he might* water it by the furrows of her 8248
21: 7 and all knees shall be weak *as* **w**. 4325
24: 3 on a pot, set *it* on, and also pour **w** into it: 4325
26:12 and thy dust in the midst of the **w**. 4325
31:14 stand up in their height, all that drink **w**: 4325
31:16 and best of Lebanon, all that drink **w**, 4325
32: 6 I will also **w** with thy blood the land 8248
36:25 will I sprinkle clean **w** upon you, 4325
Da 1:12 them give us pulse to eat, and **w** to drink. 4325
Hos 2: 5 give *me* my bread and my **w**, my wool 4325
5:10 will pour out my wrath upon them like **w**. 4325
10: 7 her king is cut off as the foam upon the **w**. 4325
Joel 3:18 and shall **w** the valley of Shittim. 8248
Am 4: 8 cities wandered unto one city, to drink **w**; 4325
8:11 not a thirst for **w**, but of hearing the 4325
Jnh 3: 7 any thing: let them not feed, nor drink **w**: 4325
Na 2: 8 Nineveh *is* of old like a pool of **w**: yet 4325
Hab 3:10 the overflowing of the **w** passed by: 4325
Zec 9:11 prisoners out of the pit wherein *is* no **w**. 4325
Mt 3:11 I indeed baptize you with **w** unto 5204
3:16 went up straightway out of the **w**: 5204
10:42 of cold **w** only in the name of a disciple, NIG
14:28 bid me come unto thee on the **w**. 5204
14:29 ship, he walked on the **w**, to go to Jesus. 5204
17:15 he falleth into the fire, and oft into the **w**. 5204
27:24 he took **w**, and washed *his* hands before 5204
Mk 1: 8 I indeed have baptized you with **w**: 5204
1:10 And straightway coming up out of the **w**, 5204
9:41 whosoever shall give you a cup of **w** to 5204
14:13 meet you a man bearing a pitcher of **w**: 5204
Lk 3:16 them all, I indeed baptize you with **w**; 5204
7:44 thou gavest me no **w** for my feet: 5204
8:23 and they were filled *with* **w**, and were in NIG
8:24 rebuked the wind and the raging of the **w**: 5204
8:25 he commandeth even the winds and **w**, 5204
16:24 that he may dip the tip of his finger in **w**, 5204
22:10 a man meet you, bearing a pitcher of **w**; 5204
Jn 1:26 answered them, saying, I baptize with **w**: 5204
1:31 therefore am I come baptizing with **w**. 5204
1:33 but he that sent me to baptize with **w**, 5204
2: 7 unto them, Fill the waterpots with **w**. 5204
2: 9 the ruler of the feast had tasted the **w** 5204
2: 9 the servants which drew the **w** knew;) 5204
3: 5 Except a man be born of **w** and *of* 5204
3:23 Salim, because there was much **w** there: 5204
4: 7 cometh a woman of Samaria to draw **w**: 5204
4:10 he would have given thee living **w**. 5204
4:11 whence then hast thou *that* living **w**? 5204
4:13 Whosoever drinketh of this **w** shall thirst 5204
4:14 But whosoever drinketh of the **w** that I 5204
4:14 the **w** that I shall give him shall be in him 5204
4:14 well of **w** springing up into everlasting life 5204
4:15 Sir, give me this **w**, that I thirst not, 5204
4:46 of Galilee, where he made the **w** wine. 5204
5: 3 waiting for the moving of the **w**. 5204
5: 4 season into the pool, and troubled the **w**: 5204
5: 4 after the troubling of the **w** stepped in, 5204
5: 7 I have no man, when the **w** is troubled, 5204
7:38 of his belly shall flow rivers of living **w**. 5204
13: 5 he poureth **w** into a bason, and began to 5204
19:34 forthwith came there out blood and **w**. 5204
Ac 1: 5 John truly baptized with **w**; but ye shall 5204
8:36 *their* way, they came unto a certain **w**: 5204
8:36 and the eunuch said, See, *here is* **w**; 5204
8:38 and they went down both into the **w**, 5204
8:39 when they were come up out of the **w**, 5204
10:47 Can any *man* forbid **w**, that these should 5204
11:16 he said, John indeed baptized with **w**; 5204
Eph 5:26 cleanse *it* with the washing of **w** by 5204
1Ti 5:23 **Drink** no longer **w**, but use a little wine 5202
Heb 9:19 with **w**, and scarlet wool, and hyssop, 5204
10:22 and *our* bodies washed with pure **w**. 5204
Jas 3:11 send forth at the same place sweet **w** NIG
3:12 so *can* no fountain *both* yield salt **w** and 5204
1Pe 3:20 that is, eight souls were saved by **w**. 5204

2Pe	2:17 These are wells **without w**, clouds that	504
	3: 5 and the earth standing out of the **w** and	5204
	3: 5 standing out of the water and in the **w**:	5204
	3: 6 then was, being overflowed with **w**,	5204
1Jn	5: 6 This is he that came by **w** and blood,	5204
	5: 6 not by **w** only, but by water and blood.	5204
	5: 6 not by water only, but by **w** and blood.	5204
	5: 8 the Spirit, and the **w**, and the blood:	5204
Jude	1:12 clouds *they are* without **w**, carried about	504
Rev	12:15 the serpent cast out of his mouth as **w**	5204
	16:12 and the **w** thereof was dried up, that	5204
	21: 6 of the fountain of the **w** of life freely.	5204
	22: 1 he shewed me a pure river of **w** of life,	5204
	22:17 let him take the river of **w** of life freely.	5204

WATERCOURSE (2) [WATER]
2Ch	32:30 also stopped the upper **w** of Gihon,	4161+4325
Job	38:25 hath divided a **w** for the overflowing	8585

WATERED (11) [WATER]
Ge	2: 6 and **w** the whole face of the ground.	8248
	13:10 Jordan, that it *was* **well w** every where,	4945
	29: 2 for out of that well they **w** the flocks:	8248
	29: 3 **w** the sheep, and put the stone again	8248
	29:10 **w** the flock of Laban his mother's brother.	8248
Ex	2:17 and helped them, and **w** their flock.	8248
	2:19 water enough for us, and **w** the flock.	8248
Pr	11:25 he that watereth shall be **w** also himself.	3384
Isa	58:11 thou shalt be like a **w** garden, and like a	7302
Jer	31:12 their soul shall be as a **w** garden;	7302
1Co	3: 6 I have planted, Apollos **w**; but God gave	4222

WATEREDST (1) [WATER]
Dt	11:10 **w** *it* with thy foot, as a garden of herbs:	8248

WATEREST (2) [WATER]
Ps	65: 9 Thou visitest the earth, and **w** it:	7783
	65:10 *Thou* **w** the ridges thereof **abundantly**:	7301

WATERETH (5) [WATER]
Ps	104:13 He **w** the hills from his chambers;	8248
Pr	11:25 he that **w** shall be watered also himself.	7301
Isa	55:10 **w** the earth, and maketh it bring forth	7301
1Co	3: 7 planteth any *thing*, neither he that **w**;	4222
	3: 8 he that planteth and he that **w** are one:	4222

WATERFALLS See WATERSPOUTS

WATERFLOOD (1) [FLOOD, WATER]
Ps	69:15 Let not the **w** overflow me,	4325+7641

WATERING (3) [WATER]
Ge	30:38 **w** troughs when the flocks came to drink,	4325
Job	37:11 Also by **w** he wearieth the thick cloud:	7377
Lk	13:15 from the stall, and lead *him* away to **w**?	4222

WATERPOT (1) [POT, WATER]
Jn	4:28 The woman then left her **w**, and went her	5201

WATERPOTS (2) [POT, WATER]
Jn	2: 6 And there were set there six **w** of stone,	5201
	2: 7 saith unto them, Fill the **w** with water.	5201

WATERS (287) [WATER]
Ge	1: 2 of God moved upon the face of the **w**.	4325
	1: 6 be a firmament in the midst of the **w**,	4325
	1: 6 let it divide the **w** from the waters.	4325
	1: 6 let it divide the waters from the **w**.	4325
	1: 7 divided the **w** which *were* under	4325
	1: 7 the **w** which *were* above the firmament:	4325
	1: 9 Let the **w** under the heaven be gathered	4325
	1:10 the gathering together of the **w** called he	4325
	1:20 Let the **w** bring forth abundantly	4325
	1:21 which the **w** brought forth abundantly,	4325
	1:22 fill the **w** in the seas, and let fowl multiply	4325
	6:17 do bring a flood of **w** upon the earth,	4325
	7: 6 when the flood of **w** was upon the earth.	4325
	7: 7 the ark, because of the **w** of the flood.	4325
	7:10 the **w** of the flood were upon the earth,	4325
	7:17 the **w** increased, and bare up the ark,	4325
	7:18 the **w** prevailed, and were increased	4325
	7:18 and the ark went upon the face of the **w**.	4325
	7:19 **w** prevailed exceedingly upon the earth;	4325
	7:20 Fifteen cubits upward did the **w** prevail;	4325
	7:24 the **w** prevailed upon the earth an	4325
	8: 1 pass over the earth, and the **w** assuaged;	4325
	8: 3 the **w** returned from off the earth	4325
	8: 3 and fifty days the **w** were abated.	4325
	8: 5 the **w** decreased continually until the	4325
	8: 7 until the **w** were dried up from off	4325
	8: 8 to see if the **w** were abated from off	4325
	8: 9 for the **w** *were* on the face of the whole	4325
	8:11 Noah knew that the **w** were abated from	4325
	8:13 the **w** were dried up from off the earth:	4325
	9:11 be cut off any more by the **w** of a flood;	4325
	9:15 the **w** shall no more become a flood to	4325
Ex	7:17 and the **w** which *are* in the river,	4325
	7:19 out thine hand upon the **w** of Egypt,	4325
	7:20 and smote the **w** that *were* in the river,	4325
	7:20 all the **w** that *were* in the river were	4325
	8: 6 Aaron stretched out his hand over the **w**	4325
	14:21 the sea dry *land*, and the **w** were divided.	4325
	14:22 *were* a wall unto them on their right	4325
	14:26 that the **w** may come again upon	4325
	14:28 the **w** returned, and covered the chariots,	4325
	14:29 **w** *were* a wall unto them on their right	4325

Ex	15: 8 with the blast of thy nostrils the **w** were	4325
	15:10 they sank as lead in the mighty **w**.	4325
	15:19 the Lord brought again the **w** of the sea	4325
	15:23 they could not drink of the **w** of Marah,	4325
	15:25 *which* when he had cast into the **w**,	4325
	15:25 into the waters, the **w** were made sweet:	4325
	15:27 and they encamped there by the **w**.	4325
Lev	11: 9 These ye shall eat of all that *are* in the **w**:	4325
	11: 9 whatsoever hath fins and scales in the **w**,	4325
	11:10 all that move in the **w**, and of any living	4325
	11:10 and of any living thing which *is* in the **w**,	4325
	11:12 hath no fins nor scales in the **w**,	4325
	11:46 living creature that moveth in the **w**,	4325
Nu	21:22 we will not drink *of* the **w** of the well:	4325
	24: 6 *and* as cedar trees beside the **w**.	4325
	24: 7 his seed *shall be* in many **w**, and his king	4325
Dt	4:18 the likeness of any fish that *is* in the **w**	4325
	5: 8 or that *is* in the **w** beneath the earth:	4325
	10: 7 to Jotbath, a land of rivers of **w**.	4325
	14: 9 These ye shall eat of all that *are* in the **w**:	4325
	32:51 of Israel at the **w** of Meribah-Kadesh,	4325
	33: 8 *with* whom thou didst strive at the **w** of	4325
Jos	3:13 all the earth, shall rest in the **w** of Jordan,	4325
	3:13 *that* the **w** of Jordan shall be cut off *from*	4325
	3:13 *from* the **w** that come down from above;	4325
	3:16 That the **w** which came down from above	4325
	4: 7 That the **w** of Jordan were cut off before	4325
	4: 7 over Jordan, the **w** of Jordan were cut off:	4325
	4:18 the **w** of Jordan returned unto their place,	4325
	4:23 For the Lord your God dried up the **w** of	4325
	5: 1 heard that the Lord had dried up the **w**	4325
	11: 5 and pitched together at the **w** of Merom,	4325
	11: 7 against them by the **w** of Merom	4325
	15: 7 the border passed towards the **w** of	4325
	18:15 went out to the well of the **w** of Nephtoah:	4325
Jdg	5:19 Canaan in Taanach by the **w** of Megiddo;	4325
	7:24 take before them the **w** unto Beth-barah	4325
	7:24 took the **w** unto Beth-barah and Jordan.	4325
2Sa	5:20 enemies before me, as the breach of **w**.	4325
	12:27 and have taken the city of **w**.	4325
	22:12 dark **w**, *and* thick clouds of the skies.	4325
	22:17 he took me; he drew me out of many **w**;	4325
2Ki	2: 8 smote the **w**, and they were divided	4325
	2:14 smote the **w**, and said, Where *is*	4325
	2:14 he also had smitten the **w**, they parted	4325
	2:21 he went forth unto the spring of the **w**,	4325
	2:21 saith the Lord, I have healed these **w**;	4325
	2:22 So the **w** were healed unto this day,	4325
	5:12 better than all the **w** of Israel?	4325
	18:31 drink ye every one the **w** of his cistern:	4325
	19:24 I have digged and drunk strange **w**,	4325
1Ch	14:11 mine hand like the breaking forth of **w**:	4325
2Ch	32: 3 his mighty *men* to stop the **w** of	4325
Ne	9:11 the deeps, as a stone into the mighty **w**.	4325
Job	3:24 my roarings are poured out like the **w**.	4325
	5:10 the earth, and sendeth **w** upon the fields:	4325
	11:16 *and* remember *it* as **w** *that* pass away:	4325
	12:15 he withholdeth the **w**, and they dry up:	4325
	14:11 *As* the **w** fail from the sea, and the flood	4325
	14:19 The **w** wear the stones: thou washest	4325
	22:11 not see; and abundance of **w** cover thee.	4325
	24:18 He *is* swift as the **w**; their portion *is*	4325
	24:19 Drought and heat consume the snow **w**:	4325
	26: 5 *things* are formed from under the **w**,	4325
	26: 8 He bindeth up the **w** in his thick clouds;	4325
	26:10 He hath compassed the **w** with bounds,	4325
	27:20 Terrors take hold on him as **w**, a tempest	4325
	28: 4 *even the* **w** forgotten of the foot:	NIH
	28:25 and he weigheth the **w** by measure.	4325
	29:19 My root *was* spread out by the **w**,	NIH
	30:14 came *upon* me as a wide breaking in *of* **w**:	NIH
	37:10 and the breadth of the **w** is straitened.	4325
	38:25 a watercourse for the **overflowing of w**,	7858
	38:30 The **w** are hid as *with* a stone, and the	4325
	38:34 that abundance of **w** may cover thee?	4325
Ps	18:11 his pavilion round about him *were* dark **w**	4325
	18:15 the channels of **w** were seen,	4325
	18:16 he took me, he drew me out of many **w**.	4325
	23: 2 he leadeth me beside the still **w**.	4325
	29: 3 The voice of the Lord *is* upon the **w**:	4325
	29: 3 the Lord *is* upon many **w**.	4325
	32: 6 surely in the floods of great **w** they shall	4325
	33: 7 He gathereth the **w** of the sea together as	4325
	46: 3 the **w** thereof roar *and* be troubled,	4325
	58: 7 Let them melt away as **w** *which* run	4325
	69: 1 God; for the **w** are come in unto *my* soul.	4325
	69: 2 I am come into deep **w**, where the floods	4325
	69:14 that hate me, and out of the deep **w**.	4325
	73:10 **w** of a full *cup* are wrung out to them.	4325
	74:13 brakest the heads of the dragons in the **w**.	4325
	77:16 The **w** saw thee, O God, the waters saw	4325
	77:16 waters saw thee, O God, the **w** saw thee;	4325
	77:19 thy path in the great **w**, and thy footsteps	4325
	78:13 and he made the **w** to stand as a heap.	4325
	78:16 and caused **w** to run down like rivers.	4325
	78:20 that the **w** gushed out, and the streams	4325
	81: 7 I proved thee at the **w** of Meribah. Selah.	4325
	93: 4 *is* mightier than the noise of many **w**,	4325
	104: 3 the beams of his chambers in the **w**:	4325
	104: 6 the **w** stood above the mountains.	4325
	105:29 He turned their **w** into blood, and slew	4325
	105:41 opened the rock, and the **w** gushed out;	4325
	106:11 the **w** covered their enemies: there was	4325
	106:32 They angered *him* also at the **w** of strife,	4325
	107:23 sea in ships, that do business in great **w**;	4325

Ps	114: 8 the flint into a fountain of **w**.	4325
	119:136 Rivers of **w** run down mine eyes, because	4325
	124: 4 the **w** had overwhelmed us, the stream	4325
	124: 5 the proud **w** had gone over our soul.	4325
	136: 6 that stretched out the earth above the **w**:	4325
	144: 7 rid me, and deliver me out of great **w**,	4325
	147:18 his wind to blow, *and* the **w** flow.	4325
	148: 4 and ye **w** that *be* above the heavens.	4325
Pr	5:15 Drink **w** out of thine own cistern,	4325
	5:15 and **running** out of thine own well.	5140
	5:16 *and* rivers of **w** in the streets.	4325
	8:29 that the **w** should not pass his	4325
	9:17 Stolen **w** are sweet, and bread *eaten* in	4325
	18: 4 words of a man's mouth *are as* deep **w**,	4325
	25:25 cold **w** to a thirsty soul, so *is* good news	4325
	30: 4 who hath bound the **w** in a garment?	4325
Ecc	11: 1 Cast thy bread upon the **w**: for thou shalt	4325
SS	4:15 a well of living **w**, and streams from	4325
	5:12 as *the eyes of* doves by the rivers of **w**,	4325
	8: 7 Many **w** cannot quench love, neither can	4325
Isa	8: 6 Forsomuch as this people refuseth the **w**	4325
	8: 7 the Lord bringeth up upon them the **w** of	4325
	11: 9 of the Lord, as the **w** cover the sea.	4325
	15: 6 For the **w** of Nimrim shall be desolate:	4325
	15: 9 For the **w** of Dimon shall be full *of* blood:	4325
	17:12 a rushing like the rushing of mighty **w**.	4325
	17:13 shall rush like the rushing of many **w**:	4325
	18: 2 even in vessels of bulrushes upon the **w**,	4325
	19: 5 the **w** shall fail from the sea, and the river	4325
	19: 8 they that spread nets upon the **w** shall	4325
	22: 9 ye gathered together the **w** of the lower	4325
	23: 3 by great **w** the seed of Sihor, the harvest	4325
	28: 2 as a flood of mighty **w** overflowing,	4325
	28:17 and the **w** shall overflow the hiding place.	4325
	30:25 streams of **w** in the day of the great	4325
	32:20 Blessed *are* ye that sow beside all **w**,	4325
	33:16 *shall be* given him; his **w** *shall be* sure.	4325
	35: 6 for in the wilderness shall **w** break out,	4325
	36:16 ye every one of **w** of his own cistern;	4325
	40:12 Who hath measured the **w** in the hollow	4325
	43: 2 When thou passest through the **w**, I *will*	4325
	43:16 in the sea, and a path in the mighty **w**;	4325
	43:20 because I give **w** in the wilderness,	4325
	48: 1 and are come forth out of the **w** of Judah,	4325
	48:21 he caused the **w** to flow out of the rock	4325
	48:21 clave the rock also, and the **w** gushed out.	4325
	51:10 dried the sea, the **w** of the great deep;	4325
	54: 9 For this *is as* the **w** of Noah unto me:	4325
	54: 9 for *as* I have sworn that the **w** of Noah	4325
	55: 1 come ye to the **w**, and he that hath no	4325
	57:20 rest, whose **w** cast up mire and dirt.	4325
	58:11 like a spring of water, whose **w** fail not.	4325
	64: 2 burneth, the fire causeth the **w** to boil,	4325
Jer	2:13 have forsaken me the fountain of living **w**,	4325
	2:18 the way of Egypt, to drink the **w** of Sihor?	4325
	2:18 of Assyria, to drink the **w** of the river?	4325
	6: 7 As a fountain casteth out her **w**,	4325
	9: 1 O that my head were **w**, and mine eyes a	4325
	9:18 tears, and our eyelids gush out with **w**.	4325
	10:13 *there is* a multitude of **w** in the heavens,	4325
	14: 3 nobles have sent their little ones to the **w**:	4325
	15:18 unto me as a liar, *and as* **w** *that* fail?	4325
	17: 8 For he shall be as a tree planted by the **w**,	4325
	17:13 the Lord, the fountain of living **w**.	4325
	18:14 shall the cold flowing **w** that come from	4325
	31: 9 will cause them to walk by the rivers of **w**	4325
	41:12 found him by the great **w** that *are* in	4325
	46: 7 a flood, whose **w** are moved as the rivers?	4325
	46: 8 and *his* **w** are moved like the rivers;	4325
	47: 2 **w** rise up out of the north, and shall be an	4325
	48:34 for the **w** also of Nimrim shall be desolate.	4325
	50:38 A drought *is* upon her **w**; and they shall	4325
	51:13 O thou that dwellest upon many **w**,	4325
	51:16 *there is* a multitude of **w** in the heavens;	4325
	51:55 when her waves do roar like great **w**,	4325
La	3:54 **W** flowed over mine head; *then* I said,	4325
Eze	1:24 like the noise of great **w**, as the voice of	4325
	17: 5 he placed *it* by great **w**, *and* set it *as* a	4325
	17: 8 It *was* planted in a good soil by great **w**,	4325
	19:10 like a vine in thy blood, planted by the **w**:	4325
	19:10 and full of branches by reason of many **w**.	4325
	26:19 upon thee, and great **w** shall cover thee;	4325
	27:26 rowers have brought thee into great **w**:	4325
	27:34 broken by the seas in the depths of the **w**,	4325
	31: 4 The **w** made him great, the deep set him	4325
	31: 5 long because of the multitude of **w**,	4325
	31: 7 his branches: for his root was by great **w**.	4325
	31:14 by the **w** exalt themselves for their height,	4325
	31:15 thereof, and the great **w** were stayed:	4325
	32: 2 troublest the **w** with thy feet,	4325
	32:13 beasts thereof from besides the great **w**;	4325
	32:14 will I make their **w** deep, and cause their	4325
	34:18 to have drunk of the deep **w**, but ye must	4325
	43: 2 his voice *was* like a noise of many **w**:	4325
	47: 1 **w** issued out from under the threshold of	4325
	47: 1 **w** came down from under from the right	4325
	47: 2 behold, there ran out **w** on the right side.	4325
	47: 3 and he brought me through the **w**;	4325
	47: 3 the waters; the **w** *were* to the ankles.	4325
	47: 4 thousand, and brought me through the **w**;	4325
	47: 4 waters; the **w** *were* to the knees.	4325
	47: 4 me through; the **w** *were* to the loins.	4325
	47: 5 for the **w** were risen, waters to swim in,	4325
	47: 5 for the waters were risen, **w** to swim in,	4325
	47: 8 **w** issue out toward the east country,	4325

W

Eze 47: 8 forth into the sea, the **w** shall be healed. 4325
47: 9 fish, because these **w** shall come thither: 4325
47:12 their **w** they issued out of the sanctuary: 4325
47:19 from Tamar *even* to the **w** of strife *in* 4325
48:28 Tamar *unto* the **w** of strife *in* Kadesh, 4325
Da 12: 6 linen, which *was* upon the **w** of the river, 4325
12: 7 which *was* upon the **w** of the river, when 4325
Joel 1:20 the rivers of **w** are dried up, and the fire 4325
3:18 all the rivers of Judah shall flow *with* **w**, 4325
Am 5: 8 that calleth for the **w** of the sea, 4325
5:24 let judgment run down as **w**, 4325
9: 6 he that calleth for the **w** of the sea, 4325
Jnh 2: 5 The **w** compassed me about, *even* to 4325
Mic 1: 4 as the **w** *that are* poured down a steep 4325
Na 3: 8 *that had* the **w** round about it, 4325
3:14 Draw thee **w** for the siege, fortify thy 4325
Hab 2:14 of the LORD, as the **w** cover the sea. 4325
3:15 thine horses, *through* the heap of great **w**. 4325
Zec 14: 8 *that* living **w** shall go out from Jerusalem: 4325
Mt 8:32 place into the sea, and perished in the **w**. 5204
Mk 5:13 the fire, and into the **w**, to destroy him: 5204
2Co 11:26 *in* perils of **w**, *in* perils of robbers, 4215
Rev 1:15 and his voice as the sound of many **w**. 5204
7:17 shall lead them unto living fountains of **w**: 5204
8:10 of the rivers, and upon the fountains of **w**; 5204
8:11 third *part* of the **w** became wormwood; 5204
8:11 and many men died of the **w**, because 5204
11: 6 have power over **w** to turn them to blood, 5204
14: 2 as the voice of many **w**, and as the voice 5204
14: 7 and the sea, and the fountains of **w**. 5204
16: 4 vial upon the rivers and fountains of **w**; 5204
16: 5 And I heard the angel of the **w** say, 5204
17: 1 great whore that sitteth upon many **w**: 5204
17:15 saith unto me, The **w** which thou sawest, 5204
19: 6 and as the voice of many **w**, and as 5204

WATERSPOUTS (1) [WATER]
Ps 42: 7 calleth unto deep at the noise of thy **w**: 6794

WATERSPRINGS (2) [SPRING, WATER]
Ps 107:33 and the **w** into dry ground; 4161+4325
107:35 and dry ground into **w**; 4161+4325

WAVE (32) [WAVED, WAVES]
Ex 29:24 shalt **w** them *for* a wave offering before 5130
29:24 shalt wave them *for* a **w** offering before 8573
29:26 **w** it *for* a wave offering before the LORD: 5130
29:26 wave it *for* a **w** offering before 8573
29:27 shalt sanctify the breast of the **w** offering, 8573
Lev 7:30 waved *for* a **w** offering before the LORD. 8573
7:34 For the breast and the heave shoulder 8573
8:27 waved them *for* a **w** offering before 8573
8:29 waved it *for* a **w** offering before the LORD; 8573
9:21 waved *for* a **w** offering before the LORD; 8573
10:14 the **w** breast and heave shoulder shall ye 8573
10:15 the **w** breast shall they bring with 8573
10:15 to **w** *it for* a wave offering before 5130
10:15 to wave *it for* a **w** offering before 8573
14:12 **w** them *for* a wave offering before 5130
14:12 wave them *for* a **w** offering before 8573
14:24 priest shall **w** them *for* a wave offering 5130
14:24 priest shall wave them *for* a **w** offering 8573
23:11 he shall **w** the sheaf before the LORD, 5130
23:11 after the sabbath the priest shall **w** it. 5130
23:12 shall offer that day when ye **w** the sheaf 5130
23:15 ye brought the sheaf of the **w** offering, 8573
23:17 habitations two **w** loaves of two tenth 8573
23:20 the priest shall **w** them with the bread of 5130
23:20 *for* a **w** offering before the LORD, 8573
Nu 5:25 and shall **w** the offering before the LORD, 5130
6:20 priest shall **w** them *for* a wave offering 5130
6:20 priest shall wave them *for* a **w** offering 8573
6:20 with the **w** breast and heave shoulder: 8573
18:11 with all the **w** offerings of the children of 8573
18:18 as the **w** breast and as the right shoulder 8573
Jas 1: 6 for he that wavereth is like a **w** of the sea 2830

WAVED (6) [WAVE]
Ex 29:27 which is **w**, and which is heaved up, 5130
Lev 7:30 that the breast may be **w** *for* a wave 5130
8:27 **w** them *for* a wave offering before 5130
8:29 **w** it *for* a wave offering before the LORD: 5130
9:21 the right shoulder Aaron **w** *for* a wave 5130
14:21 one lamb *for* a trespass offering to be **w**, 8573

WAVERETH (1) [WAVERING]
Jas 1: 6 for he that **w** is like a wave of the sea 1252

WAVERING (2) [WAVERETH]
Heb 10:23 fast the profession of *our* hope **without w**; 186
Jas 1: 6 But let him ask in faith, nothing **w**: for he 1252

WAVES (26) [WAVE]
2Sa 22: 5 When the **w** of death compassed me, 4867
Job 9: 8 and treadeth upon the **w** of the sea. 1116
38:11 and here shall thy proud **w** be stayed? 1530
Ps 42: 7 thy **w** and thy billows are gone over me. 4867
65: 7 the noise of their **w**, and the tumult of 1530
88: 7 and thou hast afflicted *me with* all thy **w**. 4867
89: 9 the **w** thereof arise, thou stillest them. 1530
93: 3 up their voice; the floods lift up their **w**. 1796
93: 4 *yea, than* the mighty **w** of the sea. 4867
107:25 which lifteth up the **w** thereof. 1530
107:29 a calm, so that the **w** thereof are still. 1530
Isa 48:18 and thy righteousness as the **w** of the sea: 1530

Isa 51:15 that divided the sea, whose **w** roared: 1530
Jer 5:22 though the **w** thereof toss themselves, 1530
31:35 divideth the sea when the **w** thereof 1530
51:42 is covered with the multitude of the **w** 1530
51:55 when her **w** do roar like great waters, 1530
Eze 26: 3 as the sea causeth his **w** to come up. 1530
Jnh 2: 3 thy billows and thy **w** passed over me. 1530
Zec 10:11 shall smite the **w** in the sea, and all 1530
Mt 8:24 that the ship was covered with the **w**: 2949
14:24 in the midst of the sea, tossed with **w**: 2949
Mk 4: 37 the **w** beat into the ship, so that it was 2949
Lk 21:25 perplexity; the sea and the **w** roaring; 4535
Ac 27:41 was broken with the violence of the **w**. 2949
Jude 1:13 Raging **w** of the sea, foaming out their 2949

WAVY See BUSHY

WAX (24) [WAXED, WAXEN, WAXETH, WAXING]
Ex 22:24 my wrath shall **w** hot, and I will kill you 2734
32:10 that my wrath may **w** hot against them, 2734
32:11 why doth thy wrath **w** hot against thy 2734
32:22 Let not the anger of my lord **w** hot: 2734
Lev 25:47 or stranger **w** rich by thee, 3027+5381
25:47 thy brother *that dwelleth* by him **w** poor, 4134
1Sa 3: 2 his eyes began *to* **w** dim, *that* he could not NIH
14: 8 the root thereof **w** old in the earth, 2204
Job 6:17 What time they **w** warm, they vanish: 2215
Ps 22:14 my heart is like **w**; it is melted in the 1749
68: 2 as **w** melteth before the fire, *so* let 1749
97: 5 The hills melted like **w** at the presence of 1749
102:26 all of them shall **w** old like a garment; 1086
Isa 17: 4 and the fatness of his flesh shall **w** lean. 7329
29:22 neither shall his face now **w** pale. 2357
50: 9 lo, they all shall **w** old as a garment; 1086
51: 6 the earth shall **w** old like a garment, 1086
Jer 6:24 our hands **w** feeble: anguish hath taken 7503
Mic 1: 4 as before the fire, *and* as the waters 1749
Mt 24:12 the love of many shall **w** cold. 5594
Lk 12:33 provide yourselves bags which **w** not old, 3822
1Ti 5:11 have *begun to* **w** wanton against Christ, 2691
2Ti 3:13 and seducers shall **w** worse and worse, 4298
Heb 1:11 they all shall **w** old as *doth* a garment; 3822

WAXED (38) [WAX]
Ge 18:12 After I am **w** old shall I have pleasure, 1086
26:13 the man **w** great, and went forward, 1431
41:56 the famine **w** sore in the land of Egypt. 2388
Ex 1: 7 and multiplied, and **w** exceeding mighty; 6105
1:20 people multiplied, and **w** very mighty. 6105
16:21 and when the sun **w** hot, it melted. 2552
19:19 **w** louder and louder, Moses 2390+3966
32:19 Moses' anger **w** hot, and he cast the 2734
Nu 11:23 Is the LORD's hand **w** short? 7114
Dt 8: 4 Thy raiment **w** not old upon thee, 1086
32:15 Jeshurun **w** fat, and kicked: thou art 8080
32:15 thou art **w** fat, thou art grown thick, 8080
Jos 23: 1 that Joshua **w** old *and* stricken in age. 2204
1Sa 2: 5 she that hath many children is **w** feeble. 535
2Sa 3: 1 David **w** stronger and stronger, 1980
3: 1 the house of Saul **w** weaker and weaker. 1980
21:15 against the Philistines: and David **w** faint. 5774
2Ki 4:34 and the flesh of the child **w** warm. 2552
1Ch 11: 9 So David **w** greater and greater: 1980+1980
2Ch 13:21 Abijah **w** mighty, and married fourteen 2388
17:12 Jehoshaphat **w** great exceedingly; 1980
24:15 Jehoiada **w** old, and was full *of* days 2204
Ne 9:21 their clothes **w** not old, and their feet 1086
Est 9: 4 for *this* man Mordecai **w** greater and 1980
Ps 32: 3 my bones **w** old through my roaring all 1086
Jer 49:24 Damascus is **w** feeble, *and* turneth 7503
50:43 report of them, and his hands **w** feeble: 7503
Da 8: 8 Therefore the he goat **w** very great: 1431
8: 9 exceeding great, toward the south, 4480
8:10 it **w** great, *even* to the host of heaven; 1431
Mt 13:15 For this people's heart is **w** gross, and 3975
Lk 1:80 and **w** strong in spirit, and was in 2901
2:40 and **w** strong in spirit, filled with wisdom: 2901
13:19 and it grew, and **w** a great tree; 1096+1519
Ac 13:46 Then Paul and Barnabas **w** bold, and said, 3955
28:27 For the heart of this people is **w** gross, 3975
Heb 11:34 were made strong, **w** valiant in fight, 1096
Rev 18: 3 the merchants of the earth are **w** rich 4147

WAXEN (11) [WAX]
Ge 19:13 the cry of them is **w** great before the face 1431
Lev 25:25 If thy brother be **w** poor, and hath sold 4134
25:35 if thy brother be **w** poor, and fallen in 4134
25:39 brother *that dwelleth* by thee be **w** poor, 4134
Dt 29: 5 your clothes are not **w** old upon you, 1086
29: 5 and thy shoe is not **w** old upon thy foot. 1086
31:20 and filled *themselves*, and **w** fat; 1878
Jos 17:13 the children of Israel were **w** strong, 2388
Jer 5:27 they are become great, and **w** rich. 6238
5:28 They are **w** fat, they shine: yea, 8080
Eze 16: 7 thou hast increased and **w** great, 1431

WAXETH (2) [WAX]
Ps 6: 7 it **w** old because of all mine enemies. 6275
Heb 8:13 and **w** old *is* ready to vanish away. 1095

WAXING (1) [WAX]
Php 1:14 in the Lord, **w** confident by my bonds, 3982

WAY (665) [BYWAYS, HIGHWAY, HIGHWAYS, WAYFARING, WAYMARKS, WAYS, WAYSIDE]
Ge 3:24 a flaming sword which **turned every w**, 2015

Ge 3:24 way, to keep the **w** of the tree of life. 1870
6:12 for all flesh had corrupted his **w** upon 1870
12:19 behold thy wife, take *her*, and go thy **w**. NIH
14:11 and all their victuals, and went their **w**. NIH
16: 7 by the fountain in the **w** to Shur. 1870
18:16 went with them to **bring** them **on** the **w**. 7971
18:19 they shall keep the **w** of the LORD, to do NIH
18:33 the LORD went his **w**, as soon as he had NIH
21:16 her down over against *him* a **good w** off, 7368
24:27 I *being* in the **w**, the LORD led me to 1870
24:40 his angel with thee, and prosper thy **w**; 1870
24:42 if now thou do prosper my **w** which I go: 1870
24:48 which had led me in the right **w** to take 1870
24:56 seeing the LORD hath prospered my **w**; 1870
24:61 servant took Rebekah, and went his **w**. NIH
24:62 Isaac came from the **w** of the well 935
25:34 and drink, and rose up, and went his **w**: NIH
28:20 will keep me in this **w** that I go, 1870
32: 1 Jacob went on his **w**, and the angels of 1870
33:16 So Esau returned that day on his **w** unto 1870
35: 3 and was with me in the **w** which I went. 1870
35:16 little **w** to come to Ephrath: 776+3530+1886.1
35:19 and was buried in the **w** to Ephrath, 1870
38:14 place, which *is* by the **w** to Timnath; 1870
38:16 he turned unto her by the **w**, and said, 1870
38:21 the harlot, that *was* openly by the **w** side? 1870
42:25 and to give them provision for the **w**: 1870
42:38 if mischief befall him by the **w** in the 1870
45:21 and gave them provision for the **w**. 1870
45:23 bread and meat for his father by the **w**. 1870
45:24 them, See that ye fall not out by the **w**. 1870
48: 7 by me in the land of Canaan in the **w**, 1870
48: 7 but a little **w** to come unto Ephrath: 776
48: 7 I buried her there in the **w** of Ephrath; 1870
49:17 Dan shall be a serpent by the **w**, an adder 1870
Ex 2:12 he looked **this w** and that way, 3541
2:12 he looked this way and **that w**, 3541
4:24 it came to pass by the **w** in the inn, that 1870
5:20 and Aaron, who stood in the **w**, 7125+3807.1
13:17 that God led them not *through* the **w** of 1870
13:18 *through* the **w** of the wilderness of the 1870
13:21 in a pillar of a cloud, to lead them the **w**; 1870
18: 8 that had come upon them by the **w**, 1870
18:20 shew them the **w** *wherein* they must 1870
18:27 and he **went** his **w** into his own land. 1980
23:20 to keep thee in the **w**, and to bring thee 1870
32: 8 out of the **w** which I commanded them: 1870
33: 3 lest I consume thee in the **w**. 1870
33:13 shew me now thy **w**, that I may know 1870
Nu 13:17 Get you up this **w** southward, and go up NIH
14:25 get you *into* the wilderness by the **w** of 1870
20:17 we will go *by* the king's **high w**, we will 1870
20:19 said unto him, We will go by the **high w**: 4546
21: 1 heard *tell* that Israel came *by* the **w** of 1870
21: 4 journeyed from mount Hor *by* the **w** of 1870
21: 4 was much discouraged because of the **w**. 1870
21:22 *but* we will go along by the king's **high w**, 1870
21:33 and went up *by* the **w** of Bashan: 1870
22:22 the angel of the LORD stood in the **w** for 1870
22:23 the angel of the LORD standing in the **w**, 1870
22:23 the ass turned aside out of the **w**, 1870
22:23 smote the ass, to turn her *into* the **w**. 1870
22:26 *was* no **w** to turn *either* to the right 1870
22:31 the angel of the LORD standing in the **w**, 1870
22:32 because *thy* **w** is perverse before me: 1870
22:34 I knew not that thou stoodest in the **w** 1870
24:25 to his place: and Balak also went his **w**. 1870
Dt 1: 2 the **w** of mount Seir unto Kadesh-barnea.) 1870
1:19 you saw *by* the **w** of the mountain of 1870
1:22 bring us word again by what **w** we must 1870
1:31 bear his son, in all the **w** that ye went, 1870
1:33 Who went in the **w** before you, to search 1870
1:33 to shew you by what **w** ye should go, 1870
1:40 the wilderness *by* the **w** of the Red sea. 1870
2: 1 the wilderness *by* the **w** of the Red sea: 1870
2: 8 through the **w** of the plain from Elath, 1870
2: 8 *by* the **w** of the wilderness of Moab. 1870
2:27 I will go along by the **high w**, I will 1870
3: 1 we turned, and went up the **w** to Bashan: 1870
6: 7 when thou walkest by the **w**, and when 1870
8: 2 thou shalt remember all the **w** which 1870
9:12 out of the **w** which I commanded them; 1870
9:16 ye had turned aside quickly out of the **w** 1870
11:19 when thou walkest by the **w**, when thou 1870
11:28 turn aside out of the **w** which I command 1870
11:30 by the **w** where the sun goeth down, 1870
13: 5 to thrust thee out of the **w** which 1870
14:24 if the **w** be too long for thee, so that thou 1870
17:16 shall henceforth return no more that **w**. 1870
19: 3 Thou shalt prepare thee a **w**, and divide 1870
19: 6 because the **w** is long, and slay him; 1870
22: 4 brother's ass or his ox fall down by the **w**, 1870
22: 6 to be before thee in the **w** in any tree, 1870
23: 4 not with bread and with water in the **w**, 1870
24: 9 LORD thy God did unto Miriam by the **w**, 1870
25:17 what Amalek did unto thee by the **w**, 1870
25:18 How he met thee by the **w**, and smote 1870
27:18 maketh the blind to wander out of the **w**. 1870
28: 7 they shall come out against thee one **w**, 1870
28:25 thou shalt go out one **w** against them, 1870
28:68 by the **w** where *of* I spake unto thee, 1870
31:29 turn aside from the **w** which I have 1870
Jos 1: 8 then thou shalt make thy **w** prosperous, 1870
2: 7 men pursued after them the **w** to Jordan 1870
2:16 and afterward may ye go your **w**. 1870

Jos
2:22 sought *them* throughout all the **w**, 1870
3: 4 ye may know the **w** by which ye must 1870
3: 4 for ye have not passed *this* **w** heretofore. 1870
5: 4 of war, died in the wilderness by the **w**, 1870
5: 5 by the **w** as they came forth out of Egypt, 1870
5: 7 they had not circumcised them by the **w**. 1870
8:15 and fled by the **w** of the wilderness. 1870
8:20 they had no power to flee **this** **w** or 2008
8:20 had no power to flee this way or **that w**: 2008
10:10 chased them *along* the **w** that goeth up to 1870
12: 3 sea on the east, the **w** to Beth-jeshimoth; 1870
23:14 *this* day I am going the **w** of all the earth: 1870
24:17 us in all the **w** wherein we went, 1870

Jdg
2:17 they turned quickly out of the **w** which 1870
2:19 own doings, nor from their stubborn **w**. 1870
2:22 whether they will keep the **w** of 1870
5:10 that sit in judgment, and walk by the **w**. 1870
8:11 Gideon went up *by* the **w** of them that 1870
9:25 they robbed all that came along *that* **w** by 1870
18: 5 we may know whether our **w** which we 1870
18: 6 before the Lord *is* your **w** wherein ye 1870
18:22 *And* when they were a **good w** from 7368
18:26 the children of Dan went their **w**: 1870
19: 5 morsel of bread, and afterward go your **w**. NIH
19: 9 to morrow get you early on your **w**, that 1870
19:14 they passed on and went *their* **w**; NIH
19:27 of the house, and went out to go his **w**: 1870
20:42 of Israel unto the **w** of the wilderness. 1870

Ru
1: 7 went on the **w** to return unto the land 1870
1:12 go your **w**, for I am too old to have a NIH

1Sa
1:18 So the woman went her **w**, and did eat, 1870
6: 9 if it goeth up *by* the **w** of his own coast to 1870
6:12 the kine took the straight **w** to the way of 1870
6:12 the kine took the straight way to the **w** of 1870
9: 6 peradventure he can shew us our **w** that 1870
9: 8 I give to the man of God, to tell us our **w**: 1870
12:23 I will teach you the good and the right **w**: 1870
13:17 company turned unto the **w** that leadeth 1870
13:18 another company turned the **w** to 1870
13:18 another company turned *to* the **w** of 1870
15: 2 how he laid *wait* for him in the **w**, when 1870
15:20 have gone the **w** which the Lord sent 1870
17:52 Philistines fell down by the **w** to Shaaraim, 1870
20:22 go thy **w**: for the Lord hath sent thee NIH
24: 3 he came to the sheepcotes by the **w**, 1870
24: 7 out of the cave, and went on *his* **w**. 1870
25:12 So David's young men turned their **w**, 1870
26: 3 which *is* before Jeshimon, by the **w**. 1870
26:25 David went on his **w**, and Saul returned 1870
28:22 have strength, when thou goest on *thy* **w**. 1870
30: 2 carried *them* away, and went on their **w**. 1870

2Sa
2:24 that *lieth* before Giah by the **w** of 1870
13:30 it came to pass, while they *were* in the **w**, 1870
13:34 came much people by the **w** of the hill 1870
15: 2 and stood beside the **w** of the gate: 1870
15:23 toward the **w** of the wilderness. 1870
16:13 as David and his men went by the **w**, 1870
18:23 Ahimaaz ran *by* the **w** of the plain, 1870
19:36 Thy servant will go a little *w* over Jordan NIH
22:31 *As for* God, his **w** *is* perfect; the word of 1870
22:33 *and* power: and he maketh my **w** perfect. 1870

1Ki
1:49 and rose up, and went every man his **w**. 1870
2: 2 I go the **w** of all the earth: be thou strong 1870
2: 4 If thy children take heed to their **w**, 1870
8:25 so that thy children take heed to their **w**, 1870
8:32 the wicked, to bring his **w** upon his head; 1870
8:36 that thou teach them the good **w** wherein 1870
11:29 Ahijah the Shilonite found him in the **w**; 1870
13: 9 nor turn again by the *same* **w** that thou 1870
13:10 he went another **w**, and returned not by 1870
13:10 returned not by the **w** that he came to 1870
13:12 father said unto them, What **w** went he? 1870
13:12 For his sons had seen what **w** the man of 1870
13:17 nor turn again to go by the **w** that thou 1870
13:24 a lion met him by the **w**, and slew him: 1870
13:24 his carcase was cast in the **w**, and the ass 1870
13:25 the carcase cast in the **w**, and the lion 1870
13:26 back from the **w** heard *thereof*, he said, 1870
13:28 went and found his carcase cast in the **w**, 1870
13:33 Jeroboam returned not from his evil **w**, 1870
15:26 walked in the **w** of his father, and in his 1870
15:34 walked in the **w** of Jeroboam and in his 1870
16: 2 thou hast walked in the **w** of Jeroboam, 1870
16:19 in walking in the **w** of Jeroboam, and in 1870
16:26 For he walked in all the **w** of Jeroboam 1870
18: 6 Ahab went one **w** by himself, 1870
18: 6 Obadiah went another **w** by himself. 1870
18: 7 Obadiah was in the **w**, behold Elijah met 1870
19:15 return on thy **w** to the wilderness of 1870
20:38 waited for the king by the **w**, 1870
22:24 **Which w** went the spirit of 335+2088
22:52 walked in the **w** of his father, and in 1870
22:52 in the **w** of his mother, and in the way of 1870
22:52 in the **w** of Jeroboam the son of Nebat, 1870

2Ki
2:23 as he was going up by the **w**, there came 1870
3: 8 he said, Which **w** shall we go up? And he 1870
3: 8 The **w** through the wilderness of Edom. 1870
3:20 there came water by the **w** of Edom, 1870
4:29 go thy **w**: if thou meet any man, salute him NIH
5:19 So he departed from him a little **w**. 776
6:19 This *is* not the **w**, neither *is* this the city: 1870
7:15 all the **w** *was* full *of* garments and vessels, 1870
8:18 he walked in the **w** of the kings of Israel, 1870
8:27 he walked in the **w** of the house of Ahab, 1870
9:27 he fled *by* the **w** of the garden house. 1870

2Ki
10:12 as he *was at* the shearing house in the **w**, 1870
11:16 went *by* the **w** by the which the horses 1870
11:19 came *by* the **w** of the gate of the guard *to* 1870
16: 3 he walked in the **w** of the kings of Israel, 1870
19:28 I will turn thee back by the **w** by which 1870
19:33 By the **w** that he came, *by the same* shall 1870
21:21 he walked in all the **w** that his father 1870
21:22 and walked not in the **w** of the Lord. 1870
22: 2 walked in all the **w** of David his father, 1870
25: 4 the men of war *fled* by night *by* the **w** of 1870
25: 4 the **king** went the **w** toward the plain. 1870

2Ch
6:16 that thy children take heed to their **w** to 1870
6:23 recompensing his **w** upon his own head; 1870
6:27 when thou hast taught them the good **w**, 1870
6:34 enemies by the **w** that thou shalt send 1870
11:17 for three years they walked in the **w** of 1870
18:23 Which **w** went the spirit of the Lord 1870
20:32 he walked in the **w** of Asa his father, 1870
21: 6 he walked in the **w** of the kings of Israel, 1870
21:13 walked in the **w** of the kings of Israel, 1870

Ezr
8:21 to seek of him a right **w** for us, and for 1870
8:22 to help us against the enemy in the **w**: 1870
8:31 and of such as lay in wait by the **w**. 1870

Ne
8:10 Go your **w**, eat the fat, and drink the sweet NIH
8:12 all the people went *their* **w** to eat, NIH
9:12 to give them light in the **w** wherein they 1870
9:19 from them by day, to lead them in the **w**; 1870
9:19 and the **w** wherein they should go. 1870

Est
4:17 Mordecai went his **w**, and did according NIH

Job
3:23 *is* light given to a man whose **w** is hid, 1870
6:18 The paths of their **w** are turned aside; 1870
8:19 is the joy of his **w**, and out of the earth 1870
12:24 in a wilderness *where there is* no **w**. 1870
16:22 I shall go the **w** *whence* I shall not return. 734
17: 9 The righteous also shall hold on his **w**, 1870
18:10 the ground, and a trap for him in the **w**. 5410
19: 8 hath fenced up my **w** that I cannot pass, 734
19:12 raise up their **w** against me, 1870
21:29 Have ye not asked them that go by the **w**? 1870
21:31 Who shall declare his **w** to his face? 1870
22:15 Hast thou marked the old **w** which wicked 734
23:10 he knoweth the **w** that I take: *when he* 1870
23:11 his **w** have I kept, and not declined. 1870
24: 4 They turn the needy out of the **w**: 1870
24:18 he beholdeth not the **w** of the vineyards. 1870
24:24 they are **taken out of the w** as all *other*, 7092
28:23 God understandeth the **w** thereof, 1870
28:26 and a **w** for the lightning of the thunder; 1870
29:25 I chose out their **w**, and sat chief, 1870
31: 7 If my step hath turned out of the **w**, 1870
36:23 Who hath enjoined him his **w**? or who 1870
38:19 Where *is* the **w** *where* light dwelleth? 1870
38:24 By what **w** is the light parted, 1870
38:25 or a **w** for the lightning of thunder; 1870

Ps
1: 1 nor standeth in the **w** of sinners, nor 1870
1: 6 For the Lord knoweth the **w** of 1870
1: 6 but the **w** of the ungodly shall perish. 1870
2:12 he be angry, and ye perish *from* the **w**, 1870
5: 8 make thy **w** straight before my face. 1870
18:30 *As for* God, his **w** *is* perfect: the word of 1870
18:32 *with* strength, and maketh my **w** perfect. 1870
25: 8 will he teach sinners in the **w**. 1870
25: 9 and the meek will he teach his **w**. 1870
25:12 him shall he teach in the **w** *that* he shall 1870
27:11 Teach me thy **w**, O Lord, and lead me in 1870
32: 8 teach thee in the **w** which thou shalt go: 1870
35: 3 stop the *w* against them that persecute NIH
35: 6 Let their **w** be dark and slippery: and let 1870
36: 4 he setteth himself in a **w** *that is* not good; 1870
37: 5 Commit thy **w** unto the Lord; trust also 1870
37: 7 because of him who prospereth *in* his **w**, 1870
37:23 by the Lord: and he delighteth in his **w**. 1870
37:34 keep his **w**, and he shall exalt thee to 1870
44:18 have our steps declined from thy **w**; 734
49:13 their **w** *is* their folly: yet their posterity 1870
67: 2 That thy **w** may be known upon earth, 1870
77:13 Thy **w**, O God, *is* in the sanctuary: who 1870
77:19 Thy **w** *is* in the sea, and thy path in 1870
78:50 He made a **w** to his anger; he spared not 5410
80:12 that all *thou* which pass by the **w** do pluck 1870
85:13 and shall set *us* in the **w** of his steps. 1870
86:11 Teach me thy **w**, O Lord; I will walk in 1870
89:41 All that pass by the **w** spoil him: he is a 1870
101: 2 I will behave myself wisely in a perfect **w**. 1870
101: 6 he that walketh in a perfect **w**, he shall 1870
102:23 He weakened my strength in the **w**; 1870
107: 4 in the wilderness in a solitary **w**; 1870
107: 7 he led them forth by the right **w**, 1870
107:40 in the wilderness, *where there is* no **w**. 1870
110: 7 He shall drink of the brook in the **w**: 1870
119: 1 Blessed *are* the undefiled in the **w**, 1870
119: 9 shall a young man cleanse his **w**? 734
119:14 have rejoiced in the **w** of thy testimonies, 1870
119:27 Make me to understand the **w** of thy 1870
119:29 Remove from me the **w** of lying: 1870
119:30 I have chosen the **w** of truth: 1870
119:32 I will run the **w** of thy commandments, 1870
119:33 Teach me, O Lord, the **w** of thy statutes; 1870
119:37 *and* quicken thou me in thy **w**. 1870
119:101 I have refrained my feet from every evil **w**, 734
119:104 I hate every false **w**. 734
119:128 *things* to be right; *and* I hate every false **w**. 734
139:24 see if *there be any* wicked **w** in me, 1870
139:24 in me, and lead me in the **w** everlasting. 1870
140: 5 have spread a net by the **w side**; 3027+4570

Ps
142: 3 In the **w** wherein I walked have they 734
143: 8 cause me to know the **w** wherein I 1870
146: 9 the **w** of the wicked he turneth upside 1870

Pr
1:15 son, walk not thou in the **w** with them; 1870
1:31 shall they eat of the fruit of their own **w**, 1870
2: 8 and preserveth the **w** of his saints. 1870
2:12 deliver thee from the **w** of the evil *man*, 1870
2:20 That thou mayest walk in the **w** of good 1870
3:23 shalt thou walk in *thy* **w** safely, 1870
4:11 I have taught thee in the **w** of wisdom; 1870
4:14 and go not in the **w** of evil *men*. 1870
4:19 The **w** of the wicked *is* as darkness: 1870
5: 8 Remove thy **w** far from her, and come not 1870
6:23 reproofs of instruction *are* the **w** of life: 1870
7: 8 corner; and he went the **w** to her house, 1870
7:27 Her house *is* the **w** to hell, going down to 1870
8: 2 in the top of high places by the **w**, 1870
8:13 the evil **w**, and the froward mouth, do I 1870
8:20 I lead in the **w** of righteousness, in the 734
8:22 possessed me in the beginning of his **w**, 1870
9: 6 live; and go in the **w** of understanding. 1870
10:17 He *is* in the **w** of life that keepeth 734
10:29 The **w** of the Lord *is* strength to 1870
11: 5 of the perfect shall direct his **w**: 1870
11:20 *such as are* upright in *their* **w** *are* his 1870
12:15 The **w** of a fool *is* right in his own eyes: 1870
12:26 but the **w** of the wicked seduceth them. 1870
12:28 In the **w** of righteousness *is* life; and *in* 734
13: 6 keepeth *him that is* upright in the **w**: 1870
13:15 but the **w** of transgressors *is* hard. 1870
14: 8 of the prudent *is* to understand his **w**: 1870
14:12 There is a **w** which seemeth right unto a 1870
15: 9 The **w** of the wicked *is* an abomination 1870
15:10 *is* grievous unto him that forsaketh the **w**: 734
15:19 The **w** of the slothful *man is* as a hedge of 1870
15:19 but the **w** of the righteous *is* made plain. 734
15:24 The **w** of life *is* above to the wise, that *he* 734
16: 9 A man's heart deviseth his **w**: 1870
16:17 he that keepeth his **w** preserveth his soul. 1870
16:25 is a **w** that seemeth right unto a man, 1870
16:29 leadeth him into the **w** *that is* not good. 1870
16:31 *if* it be found in the **w** of righteousness. 1870
19: 3 The foolishness of man perverteth his **w**: 1870
20:14 when he is **gone** his **w**, then he boasteth. 235
20:24 can a man then understand his own **w**? 1870
21: 2 Every **w** of a man *is* right in his own eyes: 1870
21: 8 The **w** of man *is* froward and strange: 1870
21:16 The man that wandereth out of the **w** of 1870
21:29 but *as for* the upright, he directeth his **w**. 1870
22: 5 and snares *are* in the **w** of the froward: 1870
22: 6 child **in the w** he should go: 1870+5921+6310
23:19 be wise, and guide thine heart in the **w**. 1870
26:13 *man* saith, There *is* a lion in the **w**; 1870
28:10 the righteous to go astray in an evil **w**, 1870
29:27 *he that is* upright in the **w** *is* abomination 1870
30:19 The **w** of an eagle in the air; the way of a 1870
30:19 in the air; the **w** of a serpent upon a rock; 1870
30:19 the **w** of a ship in the midst of the sea; 1870
30:19 the sea; and the **w** of a man with a maid. 1870
30:20 Such *is* the **w** of an adulterous woman; 1870

Ecc
9: 7 Go thy **w**, eat thy bread with joy, NIH
10: 3 when he that is a fool walketh by the **w**, 1870
11: 5 As thou knowest not what *is* the **w** of 1870
12: 5 fears *shall be* in the **w**, and the almond 1870

SS
1: 8 go thy **w** forth by the footsteps of 3318

Isa
3:12 to err, and destroy the **w** of thy paths. 1870
8:11 *I* should not walk in the **w** of this people, 1870
9: 1 grievously afflict *her by* the **w** of the sea, 1870
15: 5 *in* the **w** of Horonaim they shall raise up 1870
26: 7 The **w** of the just *is* uprightness: thou, 734
26: 8 Yea, *in* the **w** of thy judgments, O Lord, 734
28: 7 through strong drink are **out of the w**; 8582
28: 7 are **out of the w** through strong drink; 8582
30:11 Get ye out of the **w**, turn aside out of 1870
30:21 saying, This *is* the **w**, walk ye in it, when 1870
35: 8 a **w**, and it shall be called The way of 1870
35: 8 and it shall be called The **w** of holiness; 1870
37:29 I will turn thee back by the **w** by which 1870
37:34 By the **w** that he came, *by the same* shall 1870
40: 3 Prepare ye the **w** of the Lord, 1870
40:14 shewed to him the **w** of understanding? 1870
40:27 My **w** is hid from the Lord, 1870
41: 3 *even by* the **w** *that* he had not gone with 734
42:16 I will bring the blind by a **w** *that they* 1870
43:16 which maketh a **w** in the sea, and a path 1870
43:19 I will even make a **w** in the wilderness, 1870
48:15 and he shall make his **w** prosperous. 1870
48:17 which leadeth thee by the **w** *that* thou 1870
49:11 I will make all my mountains a **w**, 1870
51:10 hath made the depths of the sea a **w** for 1870
53: 6 we have turned every one to his own **w**; 1870
55: 7 Let the wicked forsake his **w**, 1870
56:11 they all look to their own **w**, every one for 1870
57:10 art wearied in the greatness of thy **w**; 1870
57:14 Cast ye up, cast ye up, prepare the **w**, 1870
57:14 take up the stumblingblock out of the **w** 1870
57:17 went on frowardly in the **w** of his heart. 1870
59: 8 The **w** of peace they know not; and *there* 1870
62:10 prepare you the **w** of the people; cast up, 1870
65: 2 which walketh in a **w** *that was* not good, 1870

Jer
2:17 thy God, when he led thee by the **w**? 1870
2:18 what hast thou to do in the **w** of Egypt, 1870
2:18 what hast thou to do in the **w** of Assyria, 1870
2:23 see thy **w** in the valley, know what thou 1870
2:33 Why trimmest thou thy **w** to seek love? 1870

Jer	2:36 thou about *so* much to change thy **w**?	1870
	3:21 for they have perverted their **w**,	1870
	4: 7 the destroyer of the Gentiles is **on** his **w**;	5265
	4:18 Thy **w** and thy doings have procured these	1870
	5: 4 for they know not the **w** of the LORD,	1870
	5: 5 for they have known the **w** of the LORD,	1870
	6:16 where *is* the good **w**, and walk therein,	1870
	6:25 forth *into* the field, nor walk by the **w**;	1870
	6:27 that thou mayest know and try their **w**.	1870
	10: 2 Learn not the **w** of the heathen, and be	1870
	10:23 know that the **w** of man *is* not in himself:	1870
	12: 1 Wherefore doth the **w** of the wicked	1870
	18:11 return ye now every one from his evil **w**,	1870
	18:15 to walk in paths, in a **w** not cast up;	1870
	21: 8 I set before you the **w** of life, and the way	1870
	21: 8 you the way of life, and the **w** of death.	1870
	23:12 Wherefore their **w** shall be unto them as	1870
	23:22 have turned them from their evil **w**,	1870
	25: 5 ye again now every one from his evil **w**,	1870
	25:35 the shepherds shall have no **w to flee**,	4498
	26: 3 and turn every man from his evil **w**,	1870
	28:11 And the prophet Jeremiah went his **w**.	1870
	31: 9 by the rivers of waters in a straight **w**,	1870
	31:21 *even* the **w** which thou wentest:	1870
	32:39 one **w**, that *they* may fear me for ever,	1870
	35:15 Return ye now every man from his evil **w**,	1870
	36: 3 may return every man from his evil **w**;	1870
	36: 7 and will return every one from his evil **w**:	1870
	39: 4 *by* the **w** of the king's garden, by the gate	1870
	39: 4 and he went out the **w** of the plain.	1870
	42: 3 shew us the **w** wherein we may walk,	1870
	48:19 of Aroer, stand by the **w** and espy;	1870
	50: 5 They shall ask the **w** *to* Zion with their	1870
	52: 7 forth out of the city by night *by* the **w**	1870
	52: 7 and they went *by* the **w** of the plain.	1870
Eze	3:18 to warn the wicked from his wicked **w**,	1870
	3:19 nor from his wicked **w**, he shall die in his	1870
	7:27 I will do unto them after their **w**,	1870
	8: 5 lift up thine eyes now the **w** towards	1870
	8: 5 So I lift up mine eyes the **w** toward	1870
	9: 2 six men came from the **w** of the higher	1870
	9:10 will recompense their **w** upon their head.	1870
	11:21 I will recompense their **w** upon their own	1870
	13:22 *he* should not return from his wicked **w**,	1870
	14:22 and ye shall see their **w** and their doings:	1870
	16:25 thy high place at every head of the **w**,	1870
	16:27 which are ashamed of thy lewd **w**.	1870
	16:31 eminent place in the head of every **w**,	1870
	16:43 I also will recompense thy **w** upon *thine*	1870
	18:25 Yet ye say, The **w** of the Lord is not equal.	1870
	18:25 O house of Israel; Is not my **w** equal?	1870
	18:29 of Israel, The **w** of the Lord is not equal.	1870
	21:16 **Go** thee **one w or other**, *either* on the	258
	21:19 choose *it*, at the head of the **w** to the city.	1870
	21:20 Appoint a **w**, that the sword may come to	1870
	21:21 of Babylon stood at the parting of the **w**,	1870
	22:31 their own **w** have I recompensed upon	1870
	23:13 was defiled, *that* they took both one **w**,	1870
	23:31 Thou hast walked in the **w** of thy sister;	1870
	33: 8 speak to warn the wicked from his **w**,	1870
	33: 9 if thou warn the wicked of his **w** to turn	1870
	33: 9 if he do not turn from his **w**, he shall die	1870
	33:11 that the wicked turn from his **w** and live:	1870
	33:17 say, The **w** of the Lord is not equal:	1870
	33:17 but *as for* them, their **w** is not equal.	1870
	33:20 ye say, The **w** of the Lord is not equal.	1870
	36:17 they defiled it by their own **w** and by	1870
	36:17 their **w** was before me as the uncleanness	1870
	36:19 according to their **w** and according to	1870
	42: 1 the utter court, the **w** toward the north:	1870
	42: 4 cubits breadth inward, a **w** of one cubit;	1870
	42:11 **w** before them *was* like the appearance	1870
	42:12 south *was* a door in the head of the **w**,	1870
	42:12 the **w** directly before the wall toward	1870
	43: 2 God of Israel came from the **w** of the east:	1870
	43: 4 **w** of the gate whose prospect *is* toward	1870
	44: 1 he brought me back the **w** of the gate of	1870
	44: 3 he shall enter by the **w** of the porch of	1870
	44: 3 and shall go out by the **w** of the same.	1870
	44: 4 brought he me the **w** of the north gate	1870
	46: 2 prince shall enter by the **w** of the porch	1870
	46: 8 he shall go in *by* the **w** of the porch of	1870
	46: 8 and he shall go forth by the **w** thereof.	1870
	46: 9 he that entereth in *by* the **w** of the north	1870
	46: 9 shall go out *by* the **w** of the south gate:	1870
	46: 9 that entereth *by* the **w** of the south gate	1870
	46: 9 shall go forth *by* the **w** of the north gate:	1870
	46: 9 he shall not return *by* the **w** of the gate	1870
	47: 2 brought he me out *of* the **w** of the gate	1870
	47: 2 led me about the **w** without unto the	1870
	47: 2 utter gate *by* the **w** that looketh east*ward;*	1870
	47:15 from the great sea, the **w** of Hethlon,	1870
	48: 1 From the north end to the coast of the **w**	1870
Da	12: 9 he said, Go thy **w**, Daniel: for the words	NIH
	12:13 go thou thy **w** till the end *be:* for thou	NIH
Hos	2: 6 I will hedge up thy **w** with thorns,	1870
	6: 9 the company of priests murder *in* the **w**	1870
	10:13 because thou didst trust in thy **w**,	1870
	13: 7 as a leopard by the **w** will I observe *them:*	1870
Am	2: 7 poor, and turn aside the **w** of the meek:	1870
Jnh	3: 8 let them turn every one from his evil **w**,	1870
	3:10 that they turned from their evil **w**;	1870
Na	1: 3 the LORD *hath* his **w** in the whirlwind	1870
	2: 1 keep the munition, watch the **w**, make	1870
Zec	10: 2 therefore they went their **w** as a flock,	NIH

W

Mal	2: 8 ye are departed out of the **w**; ye have	1870
	3: 1 he shall prepare the **w** before me:	1870
Mt	2:12 into their own country another **w**.	3598
	3: 3 Prepare ye the **w** of the Lord, make his	3598
	4:15 *by* the **w** of the sea, beyond Jordan,	3598
	5:24 thy gift before the altar, and go thy **w**;	NIG
	5:25 whiles thou art in the **w** with him;	3598
	7:13 for wide *is* the gate, and broad *is* the **w**,	3598
	7:14 and narrow *is* the **w**, which leadeth unto	3598
	8: 4 See thou tell no *man;* but go thy **w**,	NIG
	8:13 Jesus said unto the centurion, Go thy **w**;	NIG
	8:28 so that no *man* might pass by that **w**.	3598
	8:30 And there was a **good w off** from them a	3112
	10: 5 Go not into the **w** of the Gentiles,	3598
	11:10 which shall prepare thy **w** before thee.	3598
	13: 4 some *seeds* fell by the **w** side, and the	3598
	13:19 This is he which received seed by the **w**	3598
	13:25 tares among the wheat, and went his **w**.	565
	15:32 them away fasting, lest they faint in the **w**.	3598
	18: 4 I will give you. And they went their **w**.	565
	20:14 Take *that* thine is, and go thy **w**: I will give	NIG
	20:17 took the twelve disciples apart in the **w**,	3598
	20:30 two blind men sitting by the **w** side,	3598
	21: 8 multitude spread their garments in the **w**;	3598
	21: 8 the trees, and strawed *them* in the **w**.	3598
	21:19 And when he saw a fig tree in the **w**,	3598
	21:32 For John came unto you in the **w** of	3598
	22:16 true, and teachest the **w** of God in truth,	3598
	22:22 and left him, and went their **w**.	NIG
	27:65 go your **w**, make *it* as sure as you can.	NIG
Mk	1: 2 which shall prepare thy **w** before thee.	3598
	1: 3 Prepare ye the **w** of the Lord, make his	3598
	1:44 say nothing to any *man:* but go thy **w**,	NIG
	2:11 thy bed, and go thy **w** into thine house.	NIG
	4: 4 some fell by the **w** side, and the fowls of	3598
	4:15 And these are they by the **w side**, where	3598
	7:29 he said unto her, For this saying go thy **w**;	NIG
	8: 3 their own houses, they will faint by the **w**:	3598
	8:27 and by the **w** he asked his disciples,	3598
	9:33 ye disputed among yourselves by the **w**?	3598
	9:34 for by the **w** they had disputed among	3598
	10:17 And when he was gone forth into the **w**,	3598
	10:21 go thy **w**, sell whatsoever thou hast,	NIG
	10:32 And they were in the **w** going up to	3598
	10:52 And Jesus said unto him, Go thy **w**;	NIG
	10:52 his sight, and followed Jesus in the **w**.	3598
	11: 2 Go your **w** into the village over against	NIG
	11: 4 where their **w** met, and found the colt	NIG
	11: 8 And many spread their garments in the **w**:	3598
	11: 8 off the trees, and strawed *them* in the **w**.	3598
	12:12 and they left him, and went their **w**.	NIG
	12:14 men, but teachest the **w** of God in truth:	3598
	16: 7 But go your **w**, tell his disciples and Peter	NIG
Lk	1:79 to guide our feet into the **w** of peace.	3598
	3: 4 Prepare ye the **w** of the Lord, make his	3598
	4:30 through the midst of them went his **w**,	NIG
	5:19 And when they could not find by what **w**	NIG
	7:22 Go your **w**, and tell John what *things* ye	NIG
	7:27 which shall prepare thy **w** before thee.	3598
	8: 5 and as he sowed, some fell by the **w side**;	3598
	8:12 Those by the **w side** are they that hear;	3598
	8:39 And he went his **w**,	NIG
	9:57 came to pass *that*, as they went in the **w**,	3598
	10: 4 nor shoes: and salute no *man* by the **w**.	3598
	10:31 there came down a certain priest that **w**:	3598
	12:58 *as thou* art in the **w**, give diligence that	3598
	14:32 else, while the other is yet a **great w** off,	4206
	15:20 But when he was yet a **great w** off,	3112
	17:19 go thy **w**: thy faith hath made thee whole.	NIG
	18:35 a certain blind man sat by the **w side**	3598
	19: 4 tree to see him: for he was to pass that **w**.	NIG
	19:32 And they that were sent went their **w**,	NIG
	19:36 went, they spread their clothes in the **w**.	3598
	20:21 *of any*, but teachest the **w** of God truly:	3598
	22: 4 And he went his **w**, and communed with	NIG
	24:32 while he talked with us by the **w**,	3598
	24:35 told what *things were* done in the **w**,	3598
Jn	1:23 Make straight the **w** of the Lord, as said	3598
	4:28 and went her **w** into the city, and saith to	NIG
	4:50 saith unto him, Go thy **w**; thy son liveth.	NIG
	4:50 had spoken unto him, and he went his **w**.	NIG
	8:21 I go my **w**, and ye shall seek me,	NIG
	9: 7 He went his **w** therefore, and washed,	NIG
	10: 1 climbeth up **some other w**, the same is a	237
	11:28 she went her **w**, and called Mary her sister	NIG
	14: 4 I go ye know, and the **w** ye know.	3598
	14: 5 thou goest; and how can we know the **w**?	3598
	14: 6 him, I am the **w**, the truth, and the life:	3598
	16: 5 But now I go my **w** to him that sent me;	NIG
	18: 8 therefore ye seek me, let these go their **w**:	NIG
Ac	8:26 toward the south unto the **w** that goeth	3598
	8:36 And as they went on *their* **w**, they came	3598
	8:39 no more: and he went on his **w** rejoicing.	3598
	9: 2 if he found any of *this* **w**, whether they	3598
	9:15 Go thy **w**: for he is a chosen vessel unto	NIG
	9:17 And Ananias went his **w**, and entered into	NIG
	9:17 that appeared unto thee in the **w** as thou	3598
	9:27 them how he had seen the Lord in the **w**,	3598
	15: 3 And being **brought on** their **w** by	4311
	16:17 which shew unto us the **w** of salvation.	3598
	18:25 This *man* was instructed in the **w** of	3598
	18:26 expounded unto him the **w** of God more	3598
	19: 9 spake evil of *that* **w** before the multitude,	3598
	19:23 there arose no small stir about *that* **w**.	3598
	21: 5 we departed and went our **w**; and *they* all	NIG

Ac	21: 5 our *way;* and *they* all brought us on our **w**,	NIG
	22: 4 And I persecuted this **w** unto the death,	3598
	24:14 that after the **w** which they call heresy,	3598
	24:22 having more perfect knowledge of *that* **w**,	3598
	24:25 and answered, Go thy **w** for *this* time;	NIG
	25: 3 laying wait in the **w** to kill him.	3598
	26:13 king, I saw in the **w** a light from heaven,	3598
Ro	3: 2 Much every **w**: chiefly, because that unto	5158
	3:12 They are all **gone out of the w**, they are	1578
	3:17 And the **w** of peace have they not known:	3598
	14:13 **put** a stumblingblock or an occasion	
	to fall in *his* brother's **w**.	5087
	15:24 be **brought on** my **w** thitherward by you,	4311
1Co	10:13 the temptation also make a **w to escape**,	1545
	12:31 yet shew I unto you a more excellent **w**.	3598
	16: 7 For I will not see you now by the **w**; but I	3938
2Co	1:16 of you to be **brought on** *my* **w** toward	4311
Php	1:18 notwithstanding, every **w**, whether in	5158
Col	2:14 and took it out of the **w**, nailing it to *his*	3319
1Th	3:11 Lord Jesus Christ, direct our **w** unto you.	3598
2Th	2: 7 *will let*, until he be taken out of the **w**.	3319
Heb	5: 2 and on them that are **out of the w**,	4105
	9: 8 that the **w** into the holiest *of all* was not	3598
	10:20 *By* a new and living **w**, which he hath	3598
	12:13 *which is* lame be **turned out of the w**;	1624
Jas	1:24 **goeth** his **w**, and straightway forgetteth	565
	2:25 and had sent *them* out another **w**?	3598
	5:20 error of his **w** shall save a soul from death,	3598
2Pe	2: 2 by reason of whom the **w** of truth shall be	3598
	2:15 Which have forsaken the right **w**,	3598
	2:15 following the **w** of Balaam *the son* of	3598
	2:21 to have known the **w** of righteousness,	3598
	3: 1 your pure minds **by w** of remembrance:	1722
Jude	11 for they have gone in the **w** of Cain,	3598
Rev	16:12 that the **w** of the kings of the east might	3598

WAYFARING (6) [FARE, WAY]

Jdg	19:17 he saw a **w** man in the street of the city:	732
2Sa	12: 4 to dress for the **w man** that was come unto	732
Isa	33: 8 lie waste, the **w man** ceaseth:	734+5674
	35: 8 the **w men**, though fools, shall not	1870+1980
Jer	9: 2 the wilderness a lodging place of **w men**;	732
	14: 8 as a **w man** *that* turneth aside to tarry for	732

WAYMARKS (1) [MARK, WAY]

Jer	31:21 Set thee up **w**, make thee high heaps:	6725

WAYS (205) [WAY]

Ge	19: 2 ye shall rise up early, and go on your **w**.	1870
Lev	20: 4 **any w** hide their eyes from the	5956+5956
	26:22 and your **high w** shall be desolate.	1870
Nu	30:15 if he shall **any w make** them void	6565+6565
Dt	5:33 You shall walk in all the **w** which	1870
	8: 6 God, to walk in his **w**, and to fear him.	1870
	10:12 to walk in all his **w**, and to love him,	1870
	11:22 to walk in all his **w**, and to cleave unto	1870
	19: 9 LORD thy God, and to walk ever in his **w**,	1870
	26:17 to walk in his **w**, and to keep his statutes,	1870
	28: 7 one way, and flee before thee seven **w**.	1870
	28: 9 of the LORD thy God, and walk in his **w**.	1870
	28:25 and flee seven **w** before them:	1870
	28:29 and thou shalt not prosper in thy **w**:	1870
	30:16 to walk in his **w**, and to keep his	1870
	32: 4 for all his **w** *are* judgment: a God of truth	1870
Jos	22: 5 to walk in all his **w**, and to keep his	1870
1Sa	8: 3 his sons walked not in his **w**,	1870
	8: 5 art old, and thy sons walk not in thy **w**;	1870
	18:14 David behaved himself wisely in all his **w**;	1870
2Sa	22:22 For I have kept the **w** of the LORD,	1870
1Ki	2: 3 to walk in his **w**, to keep his statutes,	1870
	3:14 if thou wilt walk in my **w**, to keep my	1870
	8:39 and give to every man according to his **w**,	1870
	8:58 to walk in all his **w**, and to keep his	1870
	11:33 not walked in my **w**, to do *that* which	1870
	11:38 wilt walk in my **w**, and do that *is* right in	1870
	22:43 walked in all the **w** of Asa his father;	1870
2Ki	17:13 Turn ye from your evil **w**, and keep my	1870
2Ch	6:30 unto every man according unto all his **w**,	1870
	6:31 to walk in thy **w**, so long as they live in	1870
	7:14 my face, and turn from their wicked **w**;	1870
	13:22 acts of Abijah, and his **w**, and his sayings,	1870
	17: 3 walked in the first **w** of his father David,	1870
	17: 6 his heart was lift up in the **w** of	1870
	21:12 Because thou hast not walked in the **w** of	1870
	21:12 nor in the **w** of Asa king of Judah,	1870
	22: 3 He also walked in the **w** of the house of	1870
	27: 6 he prepared his **w** before the LORD his	1870
	27: 7 of Jotham, and all his wars, and his **w**,	1870
	28: 2 For he walked in the **w** of the kings of	1870
	28:26 Now the rest of his acts and of all his **w**,	1870
	32:13 **any w** able to deliver their lands	3201+3201
	34: 2 walked in the **w** of David his father,	1870
Job	4: 6 thy hope; and the uprightness of thy **w**?	1870
	13:15 I will maintain mine own **w** before him.	1870
	21:14 for we desire not the knowledge of thy **w**.	1870
	22: 3 *is it* gain *to him*, that thou makest thy **w**	1870
	22:28 and the light shall shine upon thy **w**.	1870
	24:13 they know not the **w** thereof, nor abide in	1870
	24:23 he resteth; yet his eyes *are* upon their **w**.	1870
	26:14 these *are* parts of his **w**: but how little a	1870
	30:12 they raise up against me the **w** of their	734
	31: 4 Doth not he see my **w**, and count all my	1870
	34:11 every man shall he render according to his **w**.	734
	34:21 For his eyes *are* upon the **w** of man,	1870
	34:27 and would not consider any of his **w**:	1870

Job	40:19 He *is* the chief of the **w** of God: he that	1870
Ps	10: 5 His **w** are always grievous; thy judgments	1870
	18:21 For I have kept the **w** of the LORD,	1870
	25: 4 Shew me thy **w**, O LORD; teach me thy	1870
	39: 1 I said, I will take heed to my **w**, that /sin	1870
	51:13 *Then* will I teach transgressors thy **w**;	1870
	81:13 unto me, *and* Israel had walked in my **w**!	1870
	84: 5 thee; in whose heart *are* the **w** *of them*.	4546
	91:11 over thee, to keep thee in all thy **w**.	1870
	95:10 heart, and they have not known my **w**:	1870
	103: 7 He made known his **w** unto Moses, his	1870
	119: 3 also do no iniquity: they walk in his **w**.	1870
	119: 5 O that my **w** were directed to keep thy	1870
	119:15 thy precepts, and have respect unto thy **w**.	734
	119:26 I have declared my **w**, and thou heardest	1870
	119:59 I thought on my **w**, and turned my feet	1870
	119:168 for all my **w** *are* before thee.	1870
	125: 5 such as turn aside *unto* their **crooked w**,	6128
	128: 1 feareth the LORD; that walketh in his **w**.	1870
	138: 5 they shall sing in the **w** of the LORD:	1870
	139: 3 and art acquainted *with* all my **w**.	1870
	145:17 The LORD *is* righteous in all his **w**,	1870
Pr	1:19 So *are* the **w** of every one that is greedy of	734
	2:13 to walk in the **w** of darkness;	1870
	2:15 Whose **w** *are* crooked, and *they* froward	734
	3: 6 In all thy **w** acknowledge him, and he	1870
	3:17 Her **w** *are* ways of pleasantness, and all	1870
	3:17 Her ways *are* **w** of pleasantness, and all	1870
	3:31 the oppressor, and choose none of his **w**.	1870
	4:26 thy feet, and let all thy **w** be established.	1870
	5: 6 her **w** are moveable, *that* thou canst not	4570
	5:21 For the **w** of man *are* before the eyes of	1870
	6: 6 sluggard; consider her **w**, and be wise:	1870
	7:25 not thine heart decline to her **w**, go not	1870
	8:32 for blessed *are they that* keep my **w**.	1870
	9:15 call passengers who go right *on* their **w**:	734
	10: 9 he that perverteth his **w** shall be known.	1870
	14: 2 he that is perverse in his **w** despiseth him.	1870
	14:12 but the end thereof *are* the **w** of death.	1870
	14:14 in heart shall be filled with his own **w**:	1870
	16: 2 All the **w** of a man *are* clean in his own	1870
	16: 7 When a man's **w** please the LORD,	1870
	16:25 but the end thereof *are* the **w** of death.	1870
	17:23 the bosom to pervert the **w** of judgment.	734
	19:16 *but* he that despiseth his **w** shall die.	1870
	22:25 Lest thou learn his **w**, and get a snare to	734
	23:26 and let thine eyes observe my **w**.	1870
	28: 6 than *he that is* perverse in *his* **w**, though	1870
	28:18 *he that is* perverse in *his* **w** shall fall at	1870
	31: 3 nor thy **w** to *that which* destroyeth kings.	1870
	31:27 looketh well to the **w** of her household,	1979
Ecc	11: 9 walk in the **w** of thine heart, and in	1870
SS	3: 2 the city in the streets and in the **broad w**,	7339
Isa	2: 3 will teach us of his **w**, and we will walk	1870
	42:24 for they would not walk in his **w**,	1870
	45:13 righteousness, and I will direct all his **w**:	1870
	49: 9 shall feed in the **w**, and their pastures	1870
	55: 8 neither *are* your **w** my ways, saith	1870
	55: 8 neither *are* your ways my **w**, saith	1870
	55: 9 so are my **w** higher than your ways,	1870
	55: 9 so are my ways higher than your **w**,	1870
	57:18 I have seen his **w**, and will heal him:	1870
	58: 2 seek me daily, and delight to know my **w**,	1870
	58:13 shalt honour him, not doing thine own **w**,	1870
	63:17 why hast thou made us to err from thy **w**,	1870
	64: 5 *those that* remember thee in thy **w**:	1870
	66: 3 they have chosen their own **w**,	1870
Jer	2:23 *art* a swift dromedary traversing her **w**;	1870
	2:33 thou also taught the wicked ones thy **w**.	1870
	3: 2 In the **w** hast thou sat for them,	1870
	3:13 hast scattered thy **w** to the strangers	1870
	6:16 Stand ye in the **w**, and see, and ask for	1870
	7: 3 Amend your **w** and your doings, and I	1870
	7: 5 For if you throughly amend your **w** and	1870
	7:23 walk ye in all the **w** that I have	1870
	12:16 if they will diligently learn the **w** of my	1870
	15: 7 *sith* they return not from their **w**.	1870
	16:17 For mine eyes *are* upon all their **w**: they	1870
	17:10 to give every man according to his **w**,	1870
	18:11 and make your **w** and your doings good.	1870
	18:15 stumble in their **w** *from* the ancient paths,	1870
	23:12 unto them as slippery **w** in the darkness;	NIH
	26:13 Therefore now amend your **w** and	1870
	32:19 for thine eyes *are* open upon all the **w** of	1870
	32:19 to give every one according to his **w**,	1870
La	1: 4 The **w** of Zion do mourn, because	1870
	3: 9 He hath inclosed my **w** with hewn stone,	1870
	3:11 He hath turned aside my **w**, and pulled	1870
	3:40 Let us search and try our **w**, and turn	1870
Eze	7: 3 will judge thee according to thy **w**,	1870
	7: 4 I will recompense thy **w** upon thee,	1870
	7: 8 I will judge thee according to thy **w**	1870
	7: 9 will recompense thee according to thy **w**	1870
	14:23 when ye see their **w** and their doings:	1870
	16:47 Yet hast thou not walked after their **w**,	1870
	16:47 corrupted more than they in all thy **w**.	1870
	16:61 thou shalt remember thy **w**,	1870
	18:23 *and* not that he should return from his **w**?	1870
	18:25 my way equal? *are* not your **w** unequal?	1870
	18:29 O house of Israel, are not my **w** equal?	1870
	18:29 my ways equal? are not your **w** unequal?	1870
	18:30 of Israel, every one according to his **w**,	1870
	20:43 there shall ye remember your **w**, and all	1870
	20:44 not according to your wicked **w**,	1870
	21:19 thou son of man, appoint thee two **w**,	1870

Eze	21:21 the head of the two **w**, to use divination;	1870
	24:14 according to thy **w**, and according to thy	1870
	28:15 Thou *wast* perfect in thy **w** from the day	1870
	33:11 turn ye, turn ye from your evil **w**; for why	1870
	33:20 I will judge you every one after his **w**.	1870
	36:31 shall ye remember your own evil **w**,	1870
	36:32 and confounded for your own **w**,	1870
Da	4:37 works *are* truth, and his **w** judgment:	735
	5:23 thy breath *is*, and whose *are* all thy **w**,	735
Hos	4: 9 I will punish them for their **w**,	1870
	9: 8 prophet *is* a snare of a fowler in all his **w**,	1870
	12: 2 and *will* punish Jacob according to his **w**;	1870
	14: 9 for the **w** of the LORD *are* right,	1870
Joel	2: 7 they shall march every one on his **w**,	1870
Mic	4: 2 will teach us of his **w**, and we will walk	1870
Na	2: 1 justle one against another in the **broad w**:	7339
Hab	3: 6 hills did bow: his **w** *are* everlasting.	1979
Hag	1: 5 the LORD of hosts; Consider your **w**.	1870
	1: 7 the LORD of hosts; Consider your **w**.	1870
Zec	1: 6 according to our **w**, and according to our	1870
	3: 7 If thou wilt walk in my **w**, and if thou	1870
Mal	2: 9 according as ye have not kept my **w**,	1870
Mt	8:33 and went their **w** into the city,	NIG
	22: 5 they made light of *it*, and went their **w**,	NIG
Mk	11: 4 door without in a place where two **w** met;	NIG
Lk	1:76 the face of the Lord to prepare his **w**;	3598
	3: 5 and the rough **w** *shall be* made smooth;	3598
	10: 3 Go your **w**: behold, I send you forth as	NIG
	10:10 go your **w** out into the streets of the same,	NIG
Jn	11:46 But some of them went their **w** to	NIG
Ac	2:28 hast made known to me the **w** of life;	3598
	13:10 thou not cease to pervert the right **w** of	3598
	14:16 all nations to walk in their own **w**.	3598
Ro	3:16 Destruction and misery *are* in their **w**:	3598
	11:33 his judgments, and his **w** past finding out!	3598
1Co	4:17 remembrance of my **w** which be in Christ,	3598
Heb	3:10 heart; and they have not known my **w**.	3598
Jas	1: 8 minded man *is* unstable in all his **w**.	1870
	1:11 shall the rich *man* fade away in his **w**.	4197
2Pe	2: 2 many shall follow their **pernicious w**;	684
Rev	15: 3 and true *are* thy **w**, thou King of saints.	3598
	16: 1 Go your **w**, and pour out the vials of	NIG

WAYSIDE (1) [SIDE, WAYSIDE]

1Sa	4:13 sat upon a seat *by* the **w** watching:	1870+3027

WAYWARDNESS See BACKSLIDERS; BACKSLIDING

WE (1844) [OUR, OURS, OURSELVES, US, US-WARD] See Index of Articles, Etc.

WEAK (46) [WEAKEN, WEAKENED, WEAKENETH, WEAKER, WEAKNESS]

Nu	13:18 they be strong or **w**, few or many;	7504
Jdg	16: 7 then shall I be **w**, and be as another man.	2470
	16:11 shall I be **w**, and be as another man.	2470
	16:17 I shall become **w**, and be like any *other*	2470
2Sa	3:39 I *am* this day **w**, though anointed king;	7390
	17: 2 him while he *is* **w** and handed,	7504
2Ch	15: 7 and let not your hands be **w**:	7503
Job	4: 3 and thou hast strengthened the **w** hands.	7504
Ps	6: 2 mercy upon me, O LORD; for I *am* **w**:	536
	109:24 My knees are **w** through fasting;	3782
Isa	14:10 thee, Art thou also **become w** as we?	2470
	35: 3 Strengthen ye the **w** hands, and confirm	7504
Eze	7:17 feeble, and all knees shall be **w** as water.	1980
	16:30 How **w** is thine heart, saith the Lord GOD,	535
	21: 7 and all knees shall be **w** *as* water:	1980
Joel	3:10 into spears: let the **w** say, I *am* strong.	2523
Mt	26:41 spirit indeed *is* willing, but the flesh *is* **w**.	772
Mk	14:38 The spirit truly *is* ready, but the flesh *is* **w**.	772
Ac	20:35 so labouring ye ought to support the **w**,	770
Ro	4:19 being not **w** in faith, he considered not	770
	8: 3 not do, in that it was **w** through the flesh,	770
	14: 1 Him that is **w** in the faith receive you,	770
	14: 2 all *things*: another, who is **w**, eateth herbs.	770
	14:21 or is offended, or is made **w**.	770
	15: 1 ought to bear the infirmities of the **w**,	102
1Co	1:27 God hath chosen the **w** *things* of the world	772
	4:10 we *are* **w**, but ye are strong; ye *are*	772
	8: 7 and their conscience being **w** is defiled.	772
	8: 9 a stumblingblock to them that are **w**.	772
	8:10 shall not the conscience of him which is **w**	770
	8:11 And through thy knowledge shall the **w**	770
	8:12 brethren, and wound their **w** conscience,	772
	9:22 To the **w** became I as weak, that I might	772
	9:22 To the weak became I as **w**, that I might	772
	9:22 became I as weak, that I might gain the **w**:	772
	11:30 For this cause many *are* **w** and sickly	772
2Co	10:10 *his* bodily presence *is* **w**, and *his* speech	770
	11:21 as though we had been **w**.	770
	11:29 Who is **w**, and I am not weak? who is	770
	11:29 Who is weak, and I am not **w**? who is	770
	12:10 for when I am **w**, then am I strong.	772
	13: 3 which to you-ward is not **w**, but is mighty	770
	13: 4 For we also are **w** in him, but we shall live	770
	13: 9 glad, when we are **w**, and ye are strong:	770
Gal	4: 9 how turn ye again to the **w** and	772
1Th	5:14 comfort the feebleminded, support the **w**,	772

WEAK-WILLED See SILLY

WEAKEN (1) [WEAK]

Isa	14:12 to the ground, which didst **w** the nations!	2522

WEAKENED (3) [WEAK]

Ezr	4: 4 the people of the land **w** the hands of	7503
Ne	6: 9 Their hands shall be **w** from the work,	7503
Ps	102:23 He **w** my strength in the way;	6031

WEAKENETH (2) [WEAK]

Job	12:21 and the strength of the mighty.	7503
Jer	38: 4 for thus he **w** the hands of the men of war	7503

WEAKER (3) [WEAK]

2Sa	3: 1 the house of Saul **waxed w** and weaker.	1980
	3: 1 the house of Saul waxed weaker and **w**.	1800
1Pe	3: 7 as unto the **w** vessel, and as *being* heirs	772

WEAKNESS (7) [WEAK]

1Co	1:25 and the **w** of God is stronger than men.	772
	2: 3 And I was with you in **w**, and in fear,	769
	15:43 it is sown in **w**; it is raised in power:	769
2Co	12: 9 for my strength is made perfect in **w**.	769
	13: 4 For though he was crucified through **w**,	769
Heb	7:18 the commandment going before for the **w**	772
	11:34 out of **w** were made strong, waxed valiant	769

WEALTH (27) [WEALTHY]

Ge	34:29 all their **w**, and all their little ones,	2428
Dt	8:17 of mine hand hath gotten me this **w**.	2428
	8:18 *it is* he that giveth thee power to get **w**,	2428
Ru	2: 1 a mighty man of **w**, of the family of	2428
1Sa	2:32 in all the **w** which *God* shall give Israel:	NIH
2Ki	15:20 *even* of all the mighty *men* of **w**, of each	2428
2Ch	1:11 thou hast not asked riches, **w**, or honour,	5233
	1:12 will give thee riches, and **w**, and honour,	5233
Ezr	9:12 nor seek their peace or their **w** for ever:	2896
Est	10: 3 seeking the **w** of his people,	2896
Job	21:13 They spend their days in **w**, and in a	2896
	31:25 If I rejoiced because my **w** was great,	2428
Ps	44:12 and dost not increase *thy* **w** by their price.	NIH
	49: 6 They that trust in their **w**,	2428
	49:10 person perish, and leave their **w** to others.	2428
	112: 3 **W** and riches *shall be* in his house:	1952
Pr	5:10 Lest strangers be filled *with* thy **w**;	3581
	10:15 The rich *man's* **w** *is* his strong city:	1952
	13:11 **W** *gotten* by vanity shall be diminished:	1952
	13:22 the **w** of the sinner *is* laid up for the just.	2428
	18:11 The rich man's **w** *is* his strong city, and as	1952
	19: 4 **W** maketh many friends; but the poor is	1952
Ecc	5:19 to whom God hath given riches and **w**,	5233
	6: 2 **w**, and honour, so that he wanteth	5233
Zec	14:14 the **w** of all the heathen round about shall	2428
Ac	19:25 ye know that by this craft we have our **w**.	2142
1Co	10:24 seek his own, but every man another's **w**.	NIG

WEALTHY (2) [WEALTH]

Ps	66:12 but thou broughtest us out into a **w** place.	7310
Jer	49:31 Arise, get you up unto the **w** nation,	7961

WEANED (12)

Ge	21: 8 the child grew, and was **w**:	1580
	21: 8 great feast the *same* day that Isaac was **w**.	1580
1Sa	1:22 *I will not go up* until the child be **w**,	1580
	1:23 thee good; tarry until thou have **w** him;	1580
	1:23 and gave her son suck until she had **w** him.	1580
	1:24 when she had **w** him, she took him up	1580
1Ki	11:20 whom Tahpenes **w** in Pharaoh's house:	1580
Ps	131: 2 as a **child** that is **w** of his mother:	1580
	131: 2 his mother: my soul *is even* as a **w child**.	1580
Isa	11: 8 the **w child** shall put his hand on	1580
	28: 9 them that are **w** from the milk,	1580
Hos	1: 8 Now when she had **w** Lo-ruhamah,	1580

WEAPON (8) [WEAPONS]

Nu	35:18 *if* he smite him with a hand **w** of wood,	3627
Dt	23:13 thou shalt have a paddle upon thy **w**;	240
2Ch	23:10 every man having his **w** in his hand,	7973
Ne	4:17 work, and with the other *hand* held a **w**.	7973
Job	20:24 shall flee from the iron **w**, *and* the bow	5402
Isa	54:17 No **w** *that is* formed against thee shall	3627
Eze	9: 1 even every man *with* his destroying **w** in	3627
	9: 2 and every man a slaughter **w** in his hand;	3627

WEAPONS (21) [WEAPON]

Ge	27: 3 thy **w**, thy quiver and thy bow, and go	3627
Dt	1:41 when ye had girded on every man his **w**	3627
Jdg	18:11 hundred men appointed *with* **w** of war.	3627
	18:16 six hundred men appointed *with* their **w**	3627
	18:17 men that were appointed *with* **w** of war.	3627
1Sa	21: 8 brought my sword nor my **w** with me,	3627
2Sa	1:27 mighty fallen, and the **w** of war perished!	3627
2Ki	11: 8 every man with his **w** in his hand,	3627
	11:11 every man with his **w** in his hand,	3627
2Ch	23: 7 every man with his **w** in his hand,	3627
Ecc	9:18 Wisdom *is* better than **w** of war:	3627
Isa	13: 5 the LORD, and the **w** of his indignation,	3627
Jer	21: 4 I *will* turn back the **w** of war that *are* in	3627
	22: 7 against thee, every one with his **w**:	3627
	50:25 brought forth the **w** of his indignation:	3627
	51:20 Thou *art* my battle axe *and* **w** of war:	3627
Eze	32:27 are gone down *to* hell with their **w** of	3627
	39: 9 shall set on fire and burn the **w**, both	5402
	39:10 for they shall burn the **w** with fire:	5402
Jn	18: 3 thither with lanterns and torches and **w**.	3696
2Co	10: 4 (For the **w** of our warfare *are* not carnal,	3696

WEAR (12) [WARE, WEARETH, WEARING]

Ex	18:18 Thou wilt **surely w** away, both	5034+5034

Dt 22: 5 The woman shall not **w** that which 1961+5921
 22:11 Thou shalt not **w** a garment of divers 3847
1Sa 2:28 burn incense, to **w** an ephod before me? 5375
 22:18 and five persons that did **w** a linen ephod. 5375
Est 6: 8 be brought which the king *useth* to **w**, 3847
Job 14:19 The waters **w** the stones; thou washest 3847
Isa 4: 1 our own bread, and **w** our own apparel: 3847
Da 7:25 shall **w** out the saints of the most High, 1080
Zec 13: 4 neither shall they **w** a rough garment to 3847
Mt 11: 8 they that **w** soft *clothing* are in kings' 5409
Lk 9:12 And *when* the day began to **w** away, 2827

WEARETH (1) [WEAR]
Jas 2: 3 ye have respect to him that **w** the gay 5409

WEARIED (14) [WEARY]
Ge 19:11 that they **w** themselves to find the door. 3811
Isa 43:23 with an offering, nor **w** thee with incense. 3021
 43:24 thou hast **w** me with thine iniquities. 3021
 47:13 art **w** in the multitude of thy counsels. 3811
 57:10 Thou art **w** in the greatness of thy way; 3021
Jer 4:31 for my soul is **w** because of murderers. 5888
 12: 5 they have **w** thee, then how canst thou 3811
 12: 5 *they* **w** thee, then how wilt thou do in NIH
Eze 24:12 She hath **w** *herself* with lies, and her great 3811
Mic 6: 3 wherein have I **w** thee? testify against me. 3811
Mal 2:17 Ye have **w** the Lᴏʀᴅ with your words. 3021
 2:17 Wherein have we **w** *him?* When ye say, 3021
Jn 4: 6 Jesus therefore, being **w** with *his* journey, 2872
Heb 12: 3 lest ye be **w** and faint in your minds. 2577

WEARIETH (2) [WEARY]
Job 37:11 Also by watering he **w** the thick cloud: 2959
Ecc 10:15 The labour of the foolish **w** every one of 3021

WEARINESS (3) [WEARY]
Ecc 12:12 end; and much study *is* a **w** of the flesh. 3024
Mal 1:13 what a **w** *is it!* and ye have snuffed at it, 4972
2Co 11:27 In **w** and painfulness, in watchings often, 2873

WEARING (3) [WEAR]
1Sa 14: 3 the Lᴏʀᴅ's priest in Shiloh, **w** an ephod. 5375
Jn 19: 5 **w** the crown of thorns, and the purple 5409
1Pe 3: 3 and of gold, or of putting on of 4025

WEARISOME (1) [WEARY]
Job 7: 3 and nights are appointed to me. 5999

WEARY (42) [WEARIED, WEARIETH, WEARINESS, WEARISOME]
Ge 27:46 I am **w** of my life because of the daughters 6973
Dt 25:18 behind thee, when thou *wast* faint and **w**; 3023
Jdg 4:21 for he was fast asleep and **w**. So he died. 5774
 8:15 give bread unto thy men *that are* **w**? 3287
2Sa 16:14 came **w**, and refreshed themselves there. 5889
 17: 2 I will come upon him while he *is* **w** and 3023
 17:29 and **w**, and thirsty, in the wilderness. 5889
 23:10 the Philistines until his hand was **w**, 3021
Job 3:17 and there the **w** be at rest. 3019+3581
 10: 1 My soul is **w** of my life; I will leave my 5354
 16: 7 now he hath **made** me **w**: thou hast made 3811
 22: 7 hast not given water to the **w** to drink, 5889
Ps 6: 6 I am **w** with my groaning; all the night 3021
 68: 9 thine inheritance, when it was **w**. 3811
 69: 3 I am **w** of my crying: my throat is dried: 3021
Pr 3:11 the Lᴏʀᴅ; neither be **w** of his correction: 6973
 25:17 lest he be **w** of thee, and *so* hate thee. 7646
Isa 1:14 a trouble unto me; I am **w** to bear *them*. 3811
 5:27 None *shall be* **w** nor stumble amongst 5889
 7:13 *Is it* a small thing for you to **w** men, 3811
 7:13 weary men, but will ye **w** my God also? 3811
 16:12 it is seen that Moab is **w** on the high 3811
 28:12 *wherewith* ye may cause the **w** to rest; 5889
 32: 2 as the shadow of a great rock in a **w** land. 5889
 40:28 of the earth, fainteth not, neither is **w**? 3021
 40:30 Even the youths shall faint and be **w**, 3021
 40:31 they shall run, and not be **w**; *and* they 3021
 43:22 but thou hast been **w** of me, O Israel. 3021
 46: 1 *they are* a burden to the **w** *beast.* 5889
 50: 4 speak a word in season to *him that is* **w**: 3287
Jer 2:24 they that seek her will not **w** themselves; 3286
 6:11 of the Lᴏʀᴅ; I am **w** with holding in: 3811
 9: 5 *and* **w** themselves to commit iniquity. 3811
 15: 6 and destroy thee; I am **w** with repenting. 3811
 20: 9 I was **w** with forbearing, and I could not 3811
 31:25 For I have satiated the **w** soul, and I have 5889
 51:58 the folk in the fire, and they shall be **w**. 3286
 51:64 they shall be **w**. Thus far *are* the words of 3286
Hab 2:13 the people shall **w** themselves for very 3286
Lk 18: 5 lest by her continual coming she **w** me. 5299
Gal 6: 9 And let us not be **w** in well doing: for in 1573
2Th 3:13 But ye, brethren, be not **w** in well doing. 1573

WEASEL (1)
Lev 11:29 the **w**, and the mouse, and the tortoise 2467

WEATHER (4)
Job 37:22 Fair **w** cometh out of the north: with God 2091
Pr 25:20 he that taketh away a garment in cold **w**, 3117
Mt 16: 2 it is evening, ye say, It will be **fair w**: 2105
 16: 3 in the morning, It will be **foul w** to day: 5494

WEAVE (3) [WEAVER, WEAVER'S, WEAVEST, WOVE, WOVEN]
Isa 19: 9 they that **w** networks, shall be confounded. 707
 59: 5 cockatrice' eggs, and **w** the spider's web: 707

WEAVER (2) [WEAVE]
Ex 35:35 in scarlet, and in fine linen, and of the **w**, 707
Isa 38:12 I have cut off like a **w** my life: he will cut 707

WEAVER'S (5) [WEAVE]
1Sa 17: 7 The staff of his spear *was* like a **w** beam; 707
2Sa 21:19 the staff of whose spear *was* like a **w** beam. 707
1Ch 11:23 in the Egyptian's hand *was* a spear like a **w** 707
 20: 5 whose spear staff *was* like a **w** beam. 707
Job 7: 6 My days are swifter than a **w** **shuttle**, 708

WEAVEST (1) [WEAVE]
Jdg 16:13 If thou **w** the seven locks of my head with 707

WEB (4) [WEBS]
Jdg 16:13 the seven locks of my head with the **w**. 4545
 16:14 the pin of the beam, and with the **w**. 4545
Job 8:14 and whose trust *shall be* a spider's **w**. 1004
Isa 59: 5 eggs, and weave the spider's **w**: 6980

WEBS (1) [WEB]
Isa 59: 6 Their **w** shall not become garments, 6980

WEDDING (7) [WEDLOCK]
Mt 22: 3 to call them that were bidden to the **w**: 1062
 22: 8 The **w** is ready, but they which were 1062
 22:10 and the **w** was furnished with guests. 1062
 22:11 saw there a man which had not on a **w** 1062
 22:12 camest thou in hither not having a **w** 1062
Lk 12:36 lord, when he will return from the **w**; 1062
 14: 8 When thou art bidden of any *man* to a **w**, 1062

WEDGE (3)
Jos 7:21 a **w** of gold of fifty shekels weight, then 3956
 7:24 the **w** of gold, and his sons, and his 3956
Isa 13:12 even a man than the **golden w** of Ophir. 3800

WEDLOCK (1) [WEDDING]
Eze 16:38 as *women* that **break** **w** and shed blood 5003

WEED See COCKLE

WEEDS (1)
Jnh 2: 5 the **w** were wrapt about my head. 5488

WEEK (13) [WEEKS]
Ge 29:27 Fulfil her **w**, and we will give thee this 7620
 29:28 Jacob did so, and fulfilled her **w**: 7620
Da 9:27 the covenant with many *for* one **w**: 7620
 9:27 *in* the midst of the **w** he shall cause 7620
Mt 28: 1 to dawn towards the first *day* of the **w**, 4521
Mk 16: 2 in the morning the first *day* of the **w**, 4521
 16: 9 Jesus was risen early the first *day* of the **w**, 4521
Lk 18:12 I fast twice in the **w**, I give tithes of all 4521
 24: 1 upon the first *day* of the **w**, very early 4521
Jn 20: 1 first *day* of the **w** cometh Mary 4521
 20:19 at evening, being the first *day* of the **w**, 4521
Ac 20: 7 And upon the first *day* of the **w**, when 4521
1Co 16: 2 Upon the first *day* of the **w** let every one 4521

WEEKS (15) [WEEK]
Ex 34:22 thou shalt observe the feast of **w**, 7620
Lev 12: 5 shall be unclean two **w**, as *in* her 7620
Nu 28:26 after your **w** *be out*, ye shall have a holy 7620
Dt 16: 9 Seven **w** shalt thou number unto thee: 7620
 16: 9 begin to number the seven **w** from *such* 7620
 16:10 thou shalt keep the feast of **w** unto 7620
 16:16 in the feast of **w**, and in the feast of 7620
2Ch 8:13 in the feast of **w**, and in the feast of 7620
Jer 5:24 he reserveth unto us the appointed **w** of 7620
Da 9:24 Seventy **w** are determined upon thy 7620
 9:25 the Messiah the Prince *shall be* seven **w**, 7620
 9:25 seven weeks, and threescore and two **w**, 7620
 9:26 and two **w** shall Messiah be cut off, 7620
 10: 2 Daniel was mourning three **full w**. 3117+7620
 10: 3 till three **whole w** were fulfilled. 3117+7620

WEEP (49) [WEEPEST, WEEPETH, WEEPING, WEPT]
Ge 2: 2 to mourn for Sarah, and to **w** for her. 1058
 43:30 he sought *where* to **w**; and he entered 1058
Nu 11:10 Moses heard the people **w** throughout 1058
 11:13 for they **w** unto me, saying, Give us flesh, 1058
1Sa 11: 5 What aileth the people that they **w**? 1058
 30: 4 wept, until they had no more power to **w**. 1058
2Sa 1:24 Ye daughters of Israel, **w** over Saul, 1058
 12:21 thou didst fast and **w** for the child, *while* 1058
2Ch 34:27 didst rend thy clothes, and **w** before me; 1058
Ne 8: 9 the Lᴏʀᴅ your God; mourn not, nor **w**. 1058
Job 27:15 in death: and his widows shall not **w**. 1058
 30:25 Did not I **w** for him that was in trouble? 1058
 30:31 my organ into the voice of them that **w**. 1058
Ecc 3: 4 A time to **w**, and a time to laugh; a time 1058
Isa 15: 2 and *to* Dibon, the high places, to **w**: 1065
 22: 4 I will **w** bitterly, labour not to comfort me, 1065
 30:19 thou shalt **w** no **more**: he will be 1058+1058
 33: 7 the ambassadors of peace shall **w** bitterly. 1058
Jer 9: 1 that I might **w** day and night for the slain 1058
 13:17 my soul shall **w** in secret places for *your* 1058
 13:17 mine eye shall **w** **sore**, and run 1830+1830
 22:10 **W** ye not for the dead, neither bemoan 1058
 22:10 **w** sore for him that goeth away: 1058+1058
 48:32 will **w** for thee with the weeping of Jazer: 1058
La 1:16 For these *things* I **w**; mine eye, mine eye 1058
Eze 24:16 yet neither shalt thou mourn nor **w**, 1058
 24:23 shall not mourn nor **w**; but ye shall pine 1058
 27:31 they shall **w** for thee with bitterness of 1058

Joel 1: 5 Awake, ye drunkards, and **w**; and howl, 1058
 2:17 between the porch and the altar, 1058
Mic 1:10 ye *it* not at Gath, **w** ye not **at all**: 1058+1058
Zec 7: 3 Should I **w** in the fifth month, 1058
Mk 5:39 them, Why make ye *this* ado, and **w**? 2799
Lk 6:21 Blessed *are ye* that **w** now: for ye shall 2799
 6:25 laugh now: for ye shall mourn and **w**. 2799
 7:13 on her, and said unto her, **W** not. 2799
 8:52 but he said, **W** not; she is not dead, 2799
 23:28 **w** not for me, but weep for yourselves, 2799
 23:28 **w** for yourselves, and for your children. 2799
Jn 11:31 She goeth unto the grave to **w** there. 2799
 16:20 That ye shall **w** and lament, but the world 2799
Ac 21:13 What mean ye to **w** and to break 2799+4160
Ro 12:15 do rejoice, and **w** with them that weep. 2799
 12:15 do rejoice, and weep with them that **w**. 2799
1Co 7:30 And they that **w**, as though they wept not; 2799
Jas 4: 9 Be afflicted, and mourn, and **w**: let your 2799
 5: 1 ye rich *men*, **w** and howl for your miseries 2799
Rev 5: 5 one of the elders saith unto me, **W** not: 2799
 18:11 the merchants of the earth *shall* **w** and 2799

WEEPEST (3) [WEEP]
1Sa 1: 8 husband to her, Hannah, why **w** thou? 1058
Jn 20:13 they say unto her, Woman, why **w** thou? 2799
 20:15 saith unto her, Woman, why **w** thou? 2799

WEEPETH (4) [WEEP]
2Sa 19: 1 the king **w** and mourneth for Absalom. 1058
2Ki 8:12 Hazael said, Why **w** my lord? And he 1058
Ps 126: 6 that goeth forth and **w**, bearing precious 1058
La 1: 2 **w** sore in the night, and her tears 1058+1058

WEEPING (44) [WEEP]
Nu 25: 6 who *were* **w** *before* the door of 1058
Dt 34: 8 so the days of **w** *and* mourning for Moses 1065
2Sa 3:16 husband went with her along **w** behind 1058
 15:30 and they went up, **w** as they went up. 1058
Ezr 3:13 joy from the noise of the **w** of the people: 1065
 10: 1 **w** and casting himself down before 1058
Est 4: 3 the Jews, and fasting, and **w**, and wailing; 1065
Job 16:16 My face is foul with **w**, and on mine 1065
Ps 6: 8 the Lᴏʀᴅ hath heard the voice of my **w**. 1065
 30: 5 **w** may endure for a night, but joy *cometh* 1065
 102: 9 like bread, and mingled my drink with **w**, 1065
Isa 15: 3 every one shall howl, **w** abundantly. 1065
 15: 5 for *by* the mounting up of Luhith with **w** 1065
 16: 9 Therefore I will bewail with the **w** of Jazer 1065
 22:12 day did the Lord Gᴏᴅ of hosts call to **w**, 1065
 65:19 the voice of **w** shall be no more heard in 1065
Jer 3:21 **w** *and* supplications of the children of 1065
 9:10 For the mountains will I take up a **w** and 1065
 31: 9 They shall come with **w**, 1065
 31:15 in Ramah, lamentation, *and* bitter **w**; 1065
 31:15 Rahel **w** for her children refused to be 1058
 31:16 Refrain thy voice from **w**, and thine eyes 1065
 41: 6 to meet them, **w** all along as he went: 1058
 48: 5 of Luhith **continual w** shall go up; 1065+1065
 48:32 I will weep for thee with the **w** of Jazer: 1065
 50: 4 children of Judah together, going and **w**: 1058
Eze 8:14 behold, there sat women **w** for Tammuz. 1058
Joel 2:12 and with **w**, and with mourning: 1065
Mal 2:13 *with* tears, *with* **w**, and with crying out, 1065
Mt 2:18 lamentation, and **w**, and great mourning, 2805
 2:18 Rachel **w** for her children, and would not 2799
 8:12 there shall be **w** and gnashing of teeth. 2805
 22:13 there shall be **w** and gnashing of teeth. 2805
 24:51 there shall be **w** and gnashing of teeth. 2805
 25:30 there shall be **w** and gnashing of teeth. 2805
Lk 7:38 And stood at his feet behind *him* **w**, 2799
 13:28 There shall be **w** and gnashing of teeth, 2805
Jn 11:33 When Jesus therefore saw her **w**, 2799
 11:33 the Jews also **w** which came with her, 2799
 20:11 Mary stood without at the sepulchre **w**: 2799
Ac 9:39 and all the widows stood by him **w**, 2799
Php 3:18 told you often, and now tell *you* even **w**, 2799
Rev 18:15 for the fear of her torment, **w** and wailing, 2799
 18:19 and cried, **w** and wailing, saying, Alas, 2799

WEIGH (6) [UNWEIGHED, WEIGHED, WEIGHETH, WEIGHING, WEIGHT, WEIGHTIER, WEIGHTS, WEIGHTY]
1Ch 20: 2 found it to **w** a talent of gold, 4948
Ezr 8:29 *them*, until ye **w** *them* before the chief 8254
Ps 58: 2 you the violence of your hands in 6424
Isa 26: 7 most upright, dost **w** the path of the just. 6424
 46: 6 silver in the balance, *and* hire a 8254
Eze 5: 1 take thee balances to **w**, and divide 4948

WEIGHED (17) [WEIGH]
Ge 23:16 Abraham **w** to Ephron the silver, which 8254
Nu 7:85 all the silver vessels **w** two thousand and NIH
1Sa 2: 3 of knowledge, and by him actions are **w**. 8505
 17: 7 his spear's head **w** six hundred shekels *of* NIH
2Sa 14:26 he **w** the hair of his head *at* two hundred 8254
 21:16 weight of whose spear **w** three hundred NIH
Ezr 8:25 **w** unto them the silver, and the gold, 8254
 8:26 I even **w** unto their hand six hundred and 8254
 8:33 the vessels **w** in the house of our God by 8254
Job 6: 2 that my grief were **throughly w**, 8254+8254
 28:15 neither shall silver be **w** *for* the price 8254
 31: 6 Let me be **w** in an even balance, that God 8254
Isa 40:12 the mountains in scales, and the hills in 8254
Jer 32: 9 *was* in Anathoth, and **w** him the money, 8254
 32:10 **w** *him* the money in the balances. 8254

Da	5:27 Thou art **w** in the balances, and art found	8625
Zec	11:12 So they **w** *for* my price thirty *pieces* of	8254

WEIGHETH (2) [WEIGH]

Job	28:25 winds; and he **w** the waters by measure.	8505
Pr	16: 2 his own eyes; but the LORD **w** the spirits.	8505

WEIGHING (2) [WEIGH]

Nu	7:85 Each charger of silver **w** an hundred and	NIH
	7:86 full *of* incense, **w** ten *shekels* apiece,	NIH

WEIGHT (58) [WEIGH]

Ge	24:22 took a golden earring of half a shekel **w**,	4948
	24:22 bracelets for her hands of ten *shekels* **w**	4948
	43:21 mouth of his sack, our money in **full w**:	4948
Ex	30:34 of each shall there be a like **w**:	NIH
Lev	19:35 in meteyard, in **w**, or in measure.	4948
	26:26 shall deliver *you* your bread again by **w**:	4948
Nu	7:13 **w** thereof *was* an hundred and	4948
	7:19 the **w** whereof *was* an hundred and	4948
	7:25 the **w** whereof *was* an hundred and	4948
	7:31 one silver charger of the **w** of an hundred	4948
	7:37 the **w** whereof *was* an hundred and	4948
	7:43 one silver charger of the **w** of an hundred	4948
	7:49 the **w** whereof *was* an hundred and	4948
	7:55 one silver charger of the **w** of an hundred	4948
	7:61 the **w** whereof *was* an hundred and	4948
	7:67 the **w** whereof *was* an hundred and	4948
	7:73 the **w** whereof *was* an hundred and	4948
	7:79 the **w** whereof *was* an hundred and	4948
Dt	25:15 *But* thou shalt have a perfect and just **w**,	68
Jos	7:21 and a wedge of gold of fifty shekels **w**,	4948
Jdg	8:26 the **w** of the golden earrings that he	4948
1Sa	17: 5 **w** of the coat *was* five thousand shekels	4948
2Sa	12:30 the whereof *was* a talent of gold with **w**	4948
	14:26 *at* two hundred shekels after the king's **w**.	68
	21:16 the **w** of whose *spear weighed* three	4948
	21:16 three hundred *shekels* of brass in **w**,	4948
1Ki	7:47 neither was the **w** of the brass found out.	4948
	10:14 the **w** of gold that came to Solomon in	4948
2Ki	25:16 brass of all these vessels was without **w**.	4948
1Ch	21:25 place six hundred shekels of gold *by* **w**	4948
	22: 3 and brass in abundance without **w**;	4948
	22:14 of brass and iron without **w**; for it is in	4948
	28:14 *He* gave of gold by **w** for *things of* gold,	4948
	28:14 *also* for all instruments of silver by **w**,	4948
	28:15 Even the **w** for the candlesticks of gold,	4948
	28:15 by **w** for every candlestick, and *for*	4948
	28:15 for the candlesticks of silver by **w**, *both*	4948
	28:16 *by* **w** he gave gold for the tables of	4948
	28:17 for the golden basons he gave *gold* by **w**	4948
	28:17 *likewise* silver by **w** for every bason of	4948
	28:18 for the altar of incense refined gold by **w**;	4948
2Ch	3: 9 the **w** of the nails *was* fifty shekels of gold.	4948
	4:18 for the **w** of the brass could not be found	4948
	9:13 the **w** of gold that came to Solomon in	4948
Ezr	8:30 and the Levites the **w** of the silver,	4948
	8:34 By number *and* by **w** of every one:	4948
	8:34 and all the **w** was written at that time.	4948
Job	28:25 To make the **w** for the winds;	4948
Pr	11: 1 to the LORD: but a just **w** *is* his delight.	68
	16:11 A just **w** and balance *are* the LORD'S:	6425
Jer	52:20 brass of all these vessels was without **w**.	4948
Eze	4:10 meat which thou shalt eat *shall be* by **w**,	4946
	4:16 they shall eat bread by **w**, and with care;	4948
Zec	5: 8 cast the **w** of lead upon the mouth thereof.	68
Jn	19:39 and aloes, about an hundred pound **w**.	NIG
2Co	4:17 far more exceeding *and* eternal **w** of glory;	922
Heb	12: 1 let us lay aside every **w**, and the sin which	3591
Rev	16:21 *every stone* about the **w of a talent**:	5006

WEIGHTIER (1) [WEIGH]

Mt	23:23 and have omitted the **w** *matters* of the law,	926

WEIGHTS (6) [WEIGH]

Lev	19:36 just **w**, a just ephah, and a just hin, shall ye	68
Dt	25:13 not have in thy bag **divers w**,	68+68+2050.1
Pr	11: all the **w** of the bag *are* his work.	68
	20:10 **Divers w**, *and* divers measures,	68+68+2050.1
	20:23 **Divers w** are an abomination	68+68+2050.1
Mic	6:11 and with the bag of deceitful **w**?	68

WEIGHTY (2) [WEIGH]

Pr	27: 3 A stone *is* heavy, and the sand **w**;	5192
2Co	10:10 *his* letters, say they, *are* **w** and powerful;	926

WELDING See SODERING

WELFARE (7) [WELL]

Ge	43:27 he asked them of *their* **w**, and said, *Is*	7965
Ex	18: 7 they asked each other of *their* **w**;	7965
1Ch	18:10 inquire of his **w**, and to congratulate him,	7965
Ne	2:10 to seek the **w** of the children of Israel.	2896
Job	30:15 and my **w** passeth away as a cloud.	3444
Ps	69:22 *that* which should have been for *their* **w**,	7965
Jer	38: 4 for this man seeketh not the **w** of this	7965

WELL (258) [BEER-LAHAI-ROI, WELFARE, WELL'S, WELLBELOVED, WELL-BELOVED, WELLFAVOURED, WELLS, WELLSPRING]

Ge	4: 7 thou doest **w**, *shalt* thou not be accepted?	3190
	4: 7 if thou doest not **w**, sin lieth at the door.	3190
	12:13 that it may be **w** with me for thy sake;	3190
	12:16 he **entreated** Abram for her sake;	3190
	13:10 that it *was* **w** watered every where,	4945
	16:14 Wherefore the **w** was called Beer-lahai-roi;	875

Ge	18:11 Sarah *were* old *and* **w** stricken in age;	935
	21:19 her eyes, and she saw a **w** of water;	875
	21:25 because of a **w** of water,	875
	21:30 witness unto me, that I have digged this **w**.	875
	24: 1 Abraham was old, *and* **w** stricken in age:	935
	24:11 by a **w** of water at the time of the evening,	875
	24:13 Behold, I stand *here* by the **w** of water;	5869
	24:16 she went down to the **w**, and filled her	5869
	24:20 and ran again unto the **w** to draw *water*,	875
	24:29 Laban ran out unto the man, unto the **w**.	5869
	24:30 behold, he stood by the camels at the **w**.	5869
	24:42 I came this day unto the **w**, and said,	5869
	24:43 Behold, I stand by the **w** of water;	5869
	24:45 she went down unto the **w**, and drew	5869
	24:62 came from the way of the **w Lahai-roi**;	883
	25:11 and Isaac dwelt by the **w Lahai-roi**.	883
	26:19 and found there a **w** of springing water.	875
	26:20 he called the name of the **w Esek**; because	875
	26:21 they digged another **w**, and strove for that	875
	26:22 from thence, and digged another **w**;	875
	26:25 and there Isaac's servants digged a **w**.	875
	26:32 told him concerning the **w** which they had	875
	29: 2 and behold a **w** in the field, and lo,	875
	29: 2 for out of that **w** they watered the flocks:	875
	29: 6 said unto them, *Is* he **w**? And they said,	7965
	29: 6 they said, *He is* **w**: and behold, Rachel his	7965
	29:17 but Rachel was beautiful and **w** favoured.	3303
	32: 9 thy kindred, and I will **deal w** with thee:	3190
	37:14 see whether it be **w** with thy brethren,	7965
	37:14 with thy brethren, and **w** with the flocks;	7965
	39: 6 was a goodly *person*, and **w** favoured.	3303
	40:14 think on me when it shall be **w** with thee,	3190
	41: 2 there came up out of the river seven **w**	3303
	41: 4 leanfleshed kine did eat up the seven **w**	3303
	41:18 seven kine, fatfleshed and **w** favoured;	3303
	43:27 Is your father **w**, the old man of whom	7965
	45:16 and it **pleased** Pharaoh well,	3190+5869+871.1
	49:22 *even* a fruitful bough by a **w**;	5869
Ex	1:20 God **dealt w** with the midwives;	3190
	2:15 land of Midian: and he sat down by a **w**.	875
	4:14 I know that he can **speak w**.	1696+1696
	10:29 Moses said, Thou hast spoken **w**, I will	3651
Lev	24:16 **as w** the stranger, as he is born in	3509.1
	24:22 **as w for** the stranger, as for one of your	3509.1
Nu	11:18 for *it was* **w** with us in Egypt: therefore	2895
	13:30 for we are **w able to overcome** it.	3201+3201
	21:16 that *is* the **w** whereof the LORD spake unto	875
	21:17 Israel sang this song, Spring up, O **w**;	875
	21:18 The princes digged the **w**, the nobles of	875
	21:22 we will not drink of the waters of the **w**:	875
	36: tribe of the sons of Joseph hath said **w**.	3651
Dt	1:17 shall hear the small **as w** as the great;	3509.1
	1:23 the saying **pleased** me **w**:	3190+5869+871.1
	3:20 **as w as** *unto* you, and *until* they also	3509.1
	4:40 that it may go **w** with thee, and *that* thou	3190
	5:14 thy maidservant may rest **as w as** thou.	3644
	5:16 and that it may go **w** with thee,	3190
	5:28 have **w** said all that they have spoken.	3190
	5:29 that it might be **w** with them, and with	3190
	5:33 that it may be **w** with you, and *that* ye	2895
	6: 3 to do it; that it may be **w** with thee,	3190
	6:18 that it may be **w** with thee, and *that* thou	3190
	7:18 shalt **w remember** what the LORD	2142+2142
	12:25 that it may go **w** with thee, and with thy	3190
	12:28 that it may go **w** with thee, and with thy	3190
	15:16 thine house, because he is **w** with thee;	2895
	18:17 They have **w** spoken that which they	3190
	19:13 from Israel, that *it may go* **w** with thee.	3190
	20: 8 lest his brethren's heart faint **as w** as his	3509.1
	22: 7 that it may be **w** with thee, and *that* thou	3190
Jos	8:33 **as w** the stranger, as he that was born	3509.1
	18:15 went out to the **w** of waters of Nephtoah.	4599
Jdg	7: 1 and pitched beside the **w** of Harod:	5869
	9:16 if ye have dealt **w** with Jerubbaal and his	2896
	14: 3 her for me; for she **pleaseth** me **w**.	3474+5869+871.1
	14: 7 she **pleased** Samson **w**.	3474+5869+871.1
	20:48 **as w** the men of *every* city, as the beast,	4480
Ru	3: 1 rest for thee, that it may be **w** with thee?	3190
	3:13 unto thee the part of a kinsman, **w**;	2896
1Sa	9:10 said Saul to his servant, **W** said; come,	2896
	16:16 play with his hand, and thou shalt be **w**.	2895
	16:17 Provide me now a man that can play **w**,	3190
	16:23 was **w**, and the evil spirit departed from	2895
	18:26 it **pleased** David **w** to be	3474+5869+871.1
	19:22 and came to a great **w** that *is* in Sechu;	953
	20: 7 If he say thus, *It is* **w**; thy servant shall	2896
	24:18 day how that thou hast dealt **w** with me:	2896
	24:19 his enemy, will he let him go **w** away?	2896
	24:20 I **know** that thou shalt surely be king,	3045
	25:31 when the LORD shall have **dealt w** with	3190
2Sa	3:13 said, **W**; I will make a league with thee:	2896
	3:26 which brought him again from the **w** of	953
	6:19 **as w** to the women as men,	4480+3807.1
	11:25 for the sword devoureth one **as w** as	3541
	17: 4 saying **pleased** Absalom **w**,	3474+5869+871.1
	17:18 in Bahurim, which had a **w** in his court;	875
	17:21 that they came up out of the **w**, and went	875
	18:28 and said unto the king, **All is w**.	7965
	19: 6 then it had **pleased** thee **w**.	3477+5869+871.1
	23:15 drink *of* the water of the **w** of Beth-lehem,	953
	23:16 drew water out of the **w** of Beth-lehem,	953
1Ki	2:18 Bath-sheba said, **W**; I will speak for thee	2896
	8:18 thou **didst w** that it was in thine heart.	2895
	18:24 people answered and said, It is **w** spoken.	3190
2Ki	4:23 nor sabbath. And she said, *It shall be* **w**.	7965

2Ki	4:26 and say unto her, *Is it* **w** with thee?	7965
	4:26 *is it* **w** with thy husband? *is it* well with	7965
	4:26 *is it* **w** with the child? And she answered,	7965
	4:26 with the child? And she answered, *It is* **w**.	7965
	5:21 chariot to meet him, and said, *Is all* **w**?	7965
	5:22 he said, *All is* **w**. My master hath sent me,	7965
	7: 9 they said one to another, We do not **w**:	3651
	9:11 *one* said unto him, *Is all* **w**?	7965
	10:30 Because thou hast **done w** in executing	2895
	25:24 of Babylon; and it shall be **w** with you.	3190
1Ch	11:17 drink *of* the water of the **w** of Beth-lehem,	953
	11:18 drew water out of the **w** of Beth-lehem,	953
	25: 8 **w**ard against *ward*, as **w** the small as	3509.1
	26:13 cast lots, **as w** the small as the great,	3509.1
2Ch	6: 8 thou **didst w** in that it was in thine heart:	2895
	12:12 and also in Judah things went **w**.	2896
	31:15 **as w** to the great as to the small:	3509.1
Ne	2:13 before the dragon **w**, and to the dung	5869
Job	12: 3 I have understanding **as w as** you; *I am*	3644
	33:31 **Mark w**, O Job, hearken unto me: hold	7181
Ps	48:13 **Mark** ye **w** her bulwarks, consider her	3820
	49:18 praise thee, when thou **doest w** to thyself.	3190
	73: 2 my steps had **w** nigh slipt.	369+3509.1
	78:29 So they did eat, and were **w** filled: for he	3966
	84: 6 through the valley of Baca make it a **w**;	4599
	87: 7 **As w** the singers as the players on	2050.1
	119:65 Thou hast dealt **w** with thy servant,	2896
	128: 2 *shalt* thou be, and *it shall be* **w** with thee.	2896
	139:14 and *that* my soul knoweth **right w**.	3966
Pr	5:15 and running waters out of thine own **w**.	875
	10:11 The mouth of a righteous *man is* a **w** of	4726
	11:10 When it **goeth w** with the righteous,	2898
	13:10 but with the **w** advised *is* wisdom.	3289
	14:15 the prudent *man* **looketh w** to his going.	995
	24:32 *and* considered *it* **w**: I looked upon *it*,	NIH
	27:23 of thy flocks, *and* look **w** to thy herds.	3820
	30:29 There be three *things* which go **w**, yea,	2895
	31:27 She **looketh w** to the ways of her	6822
Ecc	8:12 yet surely I know that it shall be **w** with	2896
	8:13 it shall not be **w** with the wicked,	2896
SS	4:15 a **w** of living waters, and streams from	875
Isa	1:17 Learn to **do w**; seek judgment, relieve	3190
	3:10 that *it shall be* **w** *with him*: for they shall	2896
	3:24 instead of **w** set hair baldness;	4639+4748
	25: 6 marrow, of wines on the lees **w** refined.	2212
	33:23 they could not **w** strengthen their mast,	3653
	42:21 The LORD is **w** pleased for his	2654
Jer	1:12 the LORD unto me, Thou hast **w** seen:	3190
	7:23 that it may be **w** unto you.	3190
	15:11 Verily it shall be **w** with thy remnant;	2896
	15:11 to entreat thee **w** in the time of evil,	NIH
	22:15 and justice, and then *it was* **w** with him?	2896
	22:16 *it was* **w** with him: was not this to know	2896
	38:20 it shall be **w** unto thee, and thy soul shall	3190
	39:12 **look w** to him, and do him no	5869+7760
	40: 4 come; and I will **look w** unto thee:	5869+7760
	40: 9 of Babylon, and it shall be **w** with you.	3190
	42: 6 that it may be **w** with us, when we obey	3190
	42:17 of victuals, and were **w**, and saw no evil.	3190
Eze	24: 5 *and* **make** it **boil w**, and let them	7570+7571
	24:10 and spice it **w**, and let the bones be burnt.	4841
	33:32 and can play **w** on an instrument:	2895
	44: 5 **mark w**, and behold with thine	3820+7760
	44: 5 **mark w** the entering in of the	3820+7760
	47:14 ye shall inherit it, one **as w as** another:	3509.1
Da	1: 4 **w** favoured, and skilful in all wisdom,	2896
	3:15 **w**: but if ye worship not, ye shall be cast	NIH
Jnh	4: 4 said the LORD, Doest thou **w** to be angry?	3190
	4: 9 Doest thou **w** to be angry for the gourd?	3190
	4: 9 he said, I **do w** to be angry, *even* unto	3190
Zec	8:15 in these days to **do w** unto Jerusalem	3190
Mt	3:17 beloved Son, in whom I am **w** pleased.	2106
	12:12 Wherefore it is lawful to do **w** on	2573
	12:18 in whom my soul is **w** pleased:	2106
	15: 7 **w** did Esaias prophesy of you, saying,	2573
	17: 5 beloved Son, in whom I am **w** pleased;	2106
	25:21 **W** done, thou good and faithful servant:	2095
	25:23 **W** done, good and faithful servant;	2095
Mk	1:11 beloved Son, in whom I am **w** pleased.	2106
	7: 6 **W** hath Esaias prophesied of you	2573
	7: 9 **Full w** ye reject the commandment of	2573
	7:37 saying, He hath done all *things* **w**:	2573
	12:28 perceiving that he had answered them **w**,	2573
	12:32 **W**, Master, thou hast said the truth:	2573
Lk	1: 7 they both were *now* **w** stricken in years.	4260
	1:18 man, and my wife **w** stricken in years.	4260
	3:22 my beloved Son; in thee I am **w** pleased.	2106
	6:26 when all men shall speak **w** of you:	2573
	13: 9 And if it bear fruit, *w*. and if not,	NIG
	19:17 he said unto him, **W**, *thou* good servant:	2095
	20:39 answering said, Master, thou hast **w** said.	2573
Jn	2:10 and when *men* have **w** drunk, then	3182
	4: 6 Now Jacob's **w** was there. Jesus therefore,	4077
	4: 6 with *his* journey, sat thus on the **w**:	4077
	4:11 nothing to draw with, and the **w** is deep:	5421
	4:12 which gave us the **w**, and drank thereof	4077
	4:14 **w** of water springing up into everlasting	4077
	4:17 Thou hast **w** said, I have no husband:	2573
	8:48 Say we not that thou art a Samaritan,	4982
	11:12 Lord, if he sleep, he shall **do w**.	2573
	13:13 and Lord: and ye say **w**; for *so* I am.	2573
	18:23 the evil: but if **w**, why smitest thou me?	2573
Ac	10:33 and thou hast **w** done that thou art come.	2573
	10:47 have received the Holy Ghost **as w** as	2531
	15:29 if ye keep yourselves, ye shall **do w**.	2095

Ac	15:29	ye shall do well. **Fare** ye *w.*	4517
	16: 2	was *w* **reported of** by the brethren	3140
	25:10	done no wrong, as thou **very** *w* knowest.	2573
	28:25	spake the Holy Ghost by Esaias	2573
Ro	2: 7	To them who by patient continuance in *w*	18
	11:20	*W;* because of unbelief they were broken	2573
1Co	7:37	that *he* will keep his virgin, doeth *w.*	2573
	7:38	he that giveth *her* in marriage doeth *w;*	2573
	9: 5	**as** *w* as other apostles, and *as the*	2532
	10: 5	many of them God was not *w* **pleased.**	2106
	14:17	For thou verily givest thanks *w,*	2573
2Co	6: 9	As unknown, and *yet* *w* **known;** as dying,	1921
	11: 4	not accepted, ye might *w* bear with *him.*	2573
Gal	4:17	They zealously affect you, *but* not *w;* yea,	2573
	4:17	Ye did run *w;* who did hinder you that ye	2573
	6: 9	And let us not be weary in *w* doing: for in	2570
Eph	6: 3	That it may be *w* with thee,	2095
Php	4:14	Notwithstanding ye have *w* done, that ye	2573
	4:18	a sacrifice acceptable, *w* **pleasing** to God.	2101
Col	3:20	for this is *w* **pleasing** unto the Lord.	2101
2Th	3:13	ye, brethren, be not weary in *w* **doing.**	2569
1Ti	3: 4	One that ruleth *w* his own house, having	2573
	3:12	*their* children and their own houses *w.*	2573
	3:13	*w* purchase to themselves a good degree,	2573
	5:10	*W* **reported** of for good works; if she	3140
	5:17	Let the elders that rule *w* be counted	2573
2Ti	1:18	*me* at Ephesus, thou knowest **very** *w.*	957
Tit	2: 9	to **please** *them* *w* in all *things;* not	1510+2101
Heb	4: 2	The gospel preached, **as** *w* as unto them:	2509
	13:16	for with such sacrifices God is *w* **pleased.**	2100
	13:21	working in you *that which is* *w* **pleasing**	2101
Jas	2: 8	love thy neighbour as thyself, ye do *w:*	2573
	2:19	that there is one God; thou doest *w:*	2573
1Pe	2:14	and *for* the praise of them that do *w.*	17
	2:15	that with *w* **doing** ye may put to silence	15
	2:20	But if, when ye **do** *w,* and suffer for it,	15
	3: 6	as long as ye **do** *w,* and are not afraid *with*	15
	3:17	ye suffer for *w* **doing,** than for evil doing.	15
	4:19	keeping of their souls *to him* in *w* **doing,**	16
2Pe	1:17	beloved Son, in whom I am *w* **pleased.**	2106
	1:19	whereunto ye do *w* that ye take heed,	2573
3Jn	1: 6	after a godly sort, thou shalt do *w:*	2573

WELL'S (6) [WELL]

Ge	29: 2	and a great stone *was* upon the *w* mouth.	875
	29: 3	they rolled the stone from the *w* mouth	875
	29: 3	put the stone again upon the *w* mouth in	875
	29: 8	*till* they roll the stone from the *w* mouth,	875
	29:10	rolled the stone from the *w* mouth,	875
2Sa	17:19	and spread a covering over the *w* mouth.	875

WELL-BUILT See GOODLIER; GOODLIEST; GOODLY

WELLBELOVED, WELL-BELOVED (6) [LOVE, WELL]

SS	1:13	A bundle of myrrh *is* my *w* unto me;	1730
Isa	5: 1	Now will I sing to my *w* a song of my	3039
	5: 1	My *w* hath a vineyard in a very fruitful	3039
Mk	12: 6	Having yet therefore one son, his *w,* he sent	27
Ro	16: 5	Salute my *w* Epenetus, who is the firstfruits	27
3Jn	1: 1	The elder unto the *w* Gaius, whom I love in	27

WELLFAVOURED (1) [FAVOUR, WELL]

| Na | 3: 4 | of the whoredoms of the *w* harlot, | 2580+2896 |

WELLS (11) [WELL]

Ge	26:15	all the *w* which his father's servants had	875
	26:18	Isaac digged again the *w* of water,	875
Ex	15:27	where *were* twelve *w* of water,	5869
Nu	20:17	will we drink *of* the water of the *w:*	875
Dt	6:11	digged, which thou diggedst not,	953
2Ki	3:19	stop all *w* of water, and mar every good	4599
	3:25	they stopped all the *w* of water,	4599
2Ch	26:10	towers in the desert, and digged many *w:*	953
Ne	9:25	*w* digged, vineyards, and oliveyards,	953
Isa	12: 3	ye draw water out of the *w* of salvation.	4599
2Pe	2:17	These are *w* without water, clouds that	4077

WELLSPRING (2) [SPRING, WELL]

| Pr | 16:22 | Understanding *is a* *w* of life unto him that | 4726 |
| | 18: 4 | *and* the *w* of wisdom *as* a flowing brook. | 4726 |

WEN (1)

| Lev | 22:22 | or **having a** *w,* or scurvy, or scabbed, | 2990 |

WENCH (1)

| 2Sa | 17:17 | a *w* went and told them; and they went | 8198 |

WENT (1400) [GO]

Ge	2: 6	there *w* up a mist from the earth,	5927
	2:10	river *w* out of Eden to water the garden;	3318
	4:16	Cain *w* out from the presence of	3318
	7: 7	Noah and his sons, and his wife,	935
	7: 9	There *w* in two and two unto Noah into	935
	7:15	they *w* in unto Noah into the ark, two and	935
	7:16	they that *w* in, went in male and female of	935
	7:16	went in, *w* in male and female of all flesh,	935
	7:18	and the ark *w* upon the face of the waters.	1980
	8: 7	forth a raven, which *w* **forth** to and fro,	3318
	8:18	Noah *w* **forth,** and his sons, and his wife,	3318
	8:19	after their kinds, *w* **forth** out of the ark.	3318
	9:18	that *w* **forth** of the ark, were Shem,	3318
	9:23	backward, and covered the nakedness	1980
	10:11	Out of that land *w* **forth** Asshur,	3318
	11:31	they *w* **forth** with them from Ur of	3318

Ge	12: 4	spoken unto him; and Lot *w* with him:	1980
	12: 5	*w* **forth** to go into the land of Canaan;	3318
	12:10	Abram *w* **down** into Egypt to sojourn	3381
	13: 1	Abram *w* **up** out of Egypt, he, and his	5927
	13: 3	he *w* on his journeys from the south even	1980
	13: 5	which *w* with Abram, had flocks,	1980
	14: 8	there *w* **out** the king of Sodom,	3318
	14:11	and all their victuals, and *w* their way.	1980
	14:17	the king of Sodom *w* out to meet him	3318
	14:24	the portion of the men which *w* with me,	1980
	15:17	when the sun *w* **down,** and it was dark,	935
	16: 4	he *w* in unto Hagar, and she conceived:	935
	17:22	with him, and God *w* up from Abraham.	5927
	18:16	Abraham *w* with them to bring them on	1980
	18:22	faces from thence, and *w* toward Sodom:	1980
	18:33	the LORD *w* his way, as soon as he had	1980
	19: 6	Lot *w* **out** at the door unto them,	3318
	19:14	Lot *w* **out,** and spake unto his sons in law	3318
	19:28	the smoke of the country *w* **up** as	5927
	19:30	Lot *w* **up** out of Zoar, and dwelt in	5927
	19:33	the firstborn *w* **in,** and lay with her father;	935
	21:16	she *w,* and sat her down over against *him*	1980
	21:19	she *w,* and filled the bottle *with* water,	1980
	22: 3	*w* unto the place of which God had told	1980
	22: 6	a knife; and they *w* both of them together.	1980
	22: 8	so they *w* both of them together.	1980
	22:13	Abraham *w* and took the ram,	1980
	22:19	rose up and *w* together to Beer-sheba;	1980
	23:10	*even* of all that *w* **in** *at* the gate of his city,	935
	23:18	before all that *w* **in** *at* the gate of his city.	935
	24:10	he arose, and *w* to Mesopotamia, unto	1980
	24:16	she *w* **down** to the well, and filled her	3381
	24:45	she *w* **down** unto the well, and drew	3381
	24:61	the servant took Rebekah, and *w* his way.	1980
	24:63	Isaac *w* **out** to meditate in the field at	3318
	25:22	And she *w* to inquire of the LORD.	1980
	25:34	and drink, and rose up, and *w* his way:	1980
	26: 1	Isaac *w* unto Abimelech king of	1980
	26:13	*w* **forward,** and grew until he	1980+1980
	26:23	And he *w* **up** from thence to Beer-sheba.	5927
	26:26	Abimelech *w* to him from Gerar,	1980
	27: 5	Esau *w* to the field to hunt for venison,	1980
	27:14	he *w,* and fetched, and brought *them* to	1980
	27:22	Jacob *w* **near** unto Isaac his father;	5066
	28: 5	he *w* to Padan-aram unto Laban, son of	1980
	28: 9	Esau *w* unto Ishmael, and took unto	1980
	28:10	Jacob *w* **out** from Beer-sheba,	3318
	28:10	from Beer-sheba, and *w* toward Haran.	1980
	29: 1	Jacob *w* **on** his journey,	5375+7272
	29:10	that Jacob *w* **near,** and rolled the stone	5066
	29:23	brought her to him; and he *w* **in** unto her.	935
	29:30	he *w* **in** also unto Rachel, and he loved	935
	30: 4	to wife: and Jacob *w* **in** unto her.	935
	30:14	Reuben *w* in the days of wheat harvest,	1980
	30:16	Leah *w* **out** to meet him, and said,	3318
	31:19	Laban *w* to shear his sheep; and Rachel	1980
	31:33	Laban *w* **into** Jacob's tent, and into Leah's	935
	31:33	he *w* **out** of Leah's tent, and entered into	3318
	32: 1	Jacob *w* **on** his way, and the angels of God	1980
	32:21	So *w* the present **over** before him:	5674
	34: 1	*w* **out** to see the daughters of the land.	3318
	34: 6	Hamor the father of Shechem *w* **out** unto	3318
	34:24	all that *w* **out** of the gate of his city;	3318
	34:24	all that *w* **out** of the gate of his city.	3318
	34:26	out of Shechem's house, and *w* **out.**	3318
	35: 3	and was with me in the way which I *w.*	1980
	35:13	God *w* **up** from him in the place where	5927
	35:22	that Reuben *w* and lay with Bilhah his	1980
	36: 6	*w* into the country from the face of his	1980
	37:12	his brethren *w* to feed their father's flock	1980
	37:17	Joseph *w* after his brethren, and found	1980
	38: 1	that Judah *w* **down** from his brethren,	3381
	38: 2	and he took her, and *w* **in** unto her.	935
	38: 9	when he *w* **in** unto his brother's wife,	935
	38:11	as his brethren *did.* And Tamar *w* and	1980
	38:12	*w* **up** unto his sheepshearers to Timnath,	5927
	38:19	*w* **away,** and laid by her vail from her,	1980
	39:11	that *Joseph* *w* into the house to do his	935
	41:45	Joseph *w* **out** over *all* the land of Egypt.	3318
	41:46	Joseph *w* **out** from the presence of	3318
	41:46	*w* **throughout** all the land of	5674+871.1
	42: 3	Joseph's ten brethren *w* **down** to buy	3381
	43:15	*w* **down** *to* Egypt, and stood before	3381
	43:31	*w* **out,** and refrained himself, and said,	3318
	44:28	the one *w* **out** from me, and I said,	3318
	45:25	they *w* **up** out of Egypt, and came *into*	5927
	46:29	*w* **up** to meet Israel his father, to Goshen,	5927
	47:10	and *w* **out** from before Pharaoh.	3318
	49: 4	defiledst thou *it:* he *w* **up** to my couch.	5927
	50: 7	Joseph *w* **up** to bury his father:	5927
	50: 7	him *w* **up** all the servants of Pharaoh,	5927
	50: 9	there *w* **up** with him both chariots and	5927
	50:14	all that *w* **up** with him to bury his father,	5927
	50:18	brethren also *w* and fell down before his	1980
Ex	2: 1	there *w* a man of the house of Levi,	1980
	2: 8	the maid *w* and called the child's mother.	1980
	2:11	that he *w* **out** unto his brethren,	3318
	2:13	when he *w* **out** the second day, behold,	3318
	4:18	Moses *w* and returned to Jethro his father	1980
	4:27	he *w,* and met him in the mount of God,	3318
	4:29	Moses and Aaron *w* and gathered together	1980
	5: 1	afterward Moses and Aaron *w* **in,**	935
	5:10	the taskmasters of the people *w* **out,**	3318
	7:10	Moses and Aaron *w* **in** unto Pharaoh,	935
	7:23	Pharaoh turned and *w* into his house,	935

Ex	8:12	and Aaron *w* **out** from Pharaoh:	3318
	8:30	Moses *w* **out** from Pharaoh,	3318
	9:33	Moses *w* **out** of the city from Pharaoh,	3318
	10: 6	turned himself, and *w* **out** from Pharaoh.	3318
	10:14	locusts *w* **up** over all the land of Egypt,	5927
	10:18	he *w* **out** from Pharaoh, and intreated	3318
	11: 8	*w* **out** from Pharaoh in a great anger.	3318
	12:28	the children of Israel *w* **away,** and did as	1980
	12:38	a mixed multitude *w* **up** also with them;	5927
	12:41	*that* all the hosts of the LORD *w* **out** from	3318
	13:18	the children of Israel *w* **up** harnessed out	5927
	13:21	the LORD *w* before them by day in a	1980
	14: 8	the children of Israel *w* **out** with a high	3318
	14:19	which *w* before the camp of Israel,	1980
	14:19	of Israel, removed and *w* behind them;	1980
	14:19	the pillar of the cloud *w* from before their	5265
	14:22	the children of Israel *w* **into** the midst of	935
	14:23	*w* **in** after them to the midst of the sea,	935
	15:19	For the horse of Pharaoh *w* **in** with his	935
	15:19	the children of Israel *w* on dry *land* in	1980
	15:20	the women *w* **out** after her with timbrels	3318
	15:22	they *w* **out** into the wilderness of Shur;	3318
	15:22	they *w* three days in the wilderness,	1980
	16:27	that there *w* **out** *some* of the people on	3318
	17:10	and Hur *w* **up** to the top of the hill.	5927
	18: 7	Moses *w* **out** to meet his father in law,	3318
	18:27	and he *w* his way into his own land.	1980
	19: 3	Moses *w* **up** unto God, and the LORD	5927
	19:14	Moses *w* **down** from the mount unto	3381
	19:20	to the top of the mount; and Moses *w* **up.**	5927
	19:25	So Moses *w* **down** unto the people,	3381
	24: 9	*w* **up** Moses, and Aaron, Nadab,	5927
	24:13	and Moses *w* **up** into the mount of God.	5927
	24:15	Moses *w* **up** into the mount, and a cloud	5927
	24:18	Moses *w* into the midst of the cloud,	935
	32:15	*w* **down** from the mount, and the two	3381
	33: 7	*w* **out** unto the Tabernacle of	3318
	33: 8	when Moses *w* **out** unto the tabernacle,	3318
	34: 4	in the morning, and *w* **up** unto mount	5927
	34:34	when Moses *w* **in** before the LORD to	935
	34:35	again, until he *w* **in** to speak with him.	935
	38:26	for every one that *w* to be numbered,	5674
	40:32	When they *w* **into** the tent of	935
	40:36	the children of Israel *w* **onward** in all	5265
Lev	9: 8	Aaron therefore *w* unto the altar,	7126
	9:23	Aaron *w* **into** the tabernacle of	935
	10: 2	there *w* **out** fire from the LORD,	3318
	10: 5	So they *w* **near,** and carried them in their	7126
	16:23	which he put on when he *w* **into** the holy	935
	24:10	*w* **out** among the children of Israel:	3318
Nu	8:22	that the Levites *w* **in** to do their service	935
	10:14	the first *place* *w* the standard of the camp	5265
	10:33	the ark of the covenant of the LORD *w*	5265
	10:34	by day, when they *w* **out** of the camp.	5265
	11: 8	*And* the people *w* **about,** and gathered *it,*	7751
	11:24	Moses *w* **out,** and told the people the	3318
	11:26	but *w* not **out** unto the tabernacle:	3318
	11:31	there *w* **forth** a wind from the LORD,	5265
	13:21	So they *w* **up,** and searched the land from	5927
	13:26	they *w* and came to Moses, and to Aaron,	1980
	13:31	the men that *w* **up** with him said, We be	5927
	14:24	will I bring into the land whereinto he *w;*	935
	14:38	*which were* of the men that *w* to search	1980
	16:25	rose up and *w* unto Dathan and Abiram;	1980
	16:33	they *w* **down** alive into the pit, and the earth	3381
	17: 8	that on the morrow Moses *w* **into**	935
	20: 6	Aaron *w* from the presence of the	935
	20:15	How our fathers *w* **down** into Egypt,	3381
	20:27	they *w* **up** into mount Hor in the sight of	5927
	21:16	thence *they* *w* to Beer: that *is* the well	NIH
	21:18	from the wilderness *they* *w* to Mattanah:	NIH
	21:23	*w* **out** against Israel into the wilderness:	3318
	21:33	and *w* **up** *by* the way of Bashan.	5927
	21:33	Og the king of Bashan *w* **out** against	3318
	22:14	they *w* unto Balak, and said,	935
	22:21	his ass, and *w* with the princes of Moab.	1980
	22:22	God's anger was kindled because he *w:*	1980
	22:23	aside out of the way, and *w* into the field:	1980
	22:26	And the angel of the LORD *w* further,	5674
	22:32	I *w* **out** to withstand thee, because	3318
	22:35	So Balaam *w* with the princes of Balak.	1980
	22:36	*w* **out** to meet him unto a city of Moab,	3318
	22:39	Balaam *w* with Balak, and they came	1980
	23: 3	I will tell thee. And he *w* to a high place.	1980
	24: 1	he *w* **not,** as at other times, to seek for	1980
	24:25	rose up, and *w* and returned to his place:	1980
	24:25	to his place: and Balak also *w* his way.	1980
	25: 8	he *w* after the man of Israel into the tent,	935
	26: 4	which *w* **forth** out of the land of Egypt.	3318
	31:13	*w* **forth** to meet them without the camp.	3318
	31:21	the men of war which *w* to the battle,	935
	31:27	who *w* **out** to battle, and between all	3318
	31:28	of the men of war which *w* **out** to battle:	3318
	31:36	*was* the portion of them that *w* **out** to	3318
	32: 9	For when they *w* **up** unto the valley of	5927
	32:39	Machir the son of Manasseh *w* to Gilead,	1980
	32:41	Jair the son of Manasseh *w* and took	1980
	32:42	Nobah *w* and took Kenath, and the	1980
	33: 1	which *w* **forth** out of the land of Egypt	3318
	33: 3	*w* **out** with a high hand in the sight of all	3318
	33: 8	*w* three days' journey in the wilderness	1980
	33:23	they *w* from Kehelathah, and pitched in	5265
	33:29	they *w* from Mithcah, and pitched in	5265
	33:33	they *w* from Hor-hagidgad, and pitched in	5265
	33:38	Aaron the priest *w* **up** into mount Hor at	5927

Dt	1:19 we w *through* all that great and terrible	1980
	1:24 they turned and w up into the mountain,	5927
	1:31 bear his son, in all the way that ye w,	1980
	1:33 Who w in the way before you, to search	1980
	1:43 we w presumptuously up into the hill.	5927
	2:13 And we w over the brook Zered.	5674
	3: 1 we turned, and w up the way to Bashan:	5927
	5: 5 of the fire, and w not up into the mount;)	5927
	10: 3 w up unto the mount, having the two	5927
	10:22 Thy fathers w down into Egypt with	3381
	26: 5 he w down into Egypt, and sojourned	3381
	29:26 For they w and served other gods,	1980
	31: 1 Moses w and spake these words unto all	1980
	31:14 Moses and Joshua w,	1980
	33: 2 from his right hand w *a* fiery law for them.	NIH
	34: 1 Moses w up from the plains of Moab unto	5927
Jos	2: 1 they w, and came *into* a harlot's house,	1980
	2: 5 when it was dark, that the men w out:	3318
	2: 5 whither the men w I wot not: pursue after	1980
	2:22 they w, and came unto the mountain,	1980
	3: 2 that the officers w through the host;	5674
	3: 6 of the covenant, and w before the people.	1980
	5:13 Joshua w unto him, and said unto him,	1980
	6: 1 of Israel: none w out, and none came in.	3318
	6: 9 the armed men w before the priests that	1980
	6:13 ark of the LORD w on continually,	1980+1980
	6:13 the armed men w before them;	1980
	6:20 so that the people w up into the city,	5927
	6:23 the young men that were spies w in,	935
	7: 2 And the men w up and viewed Ai.	5927
	7: 4 So there w up thither of the people about	5927
	8: 9 they w to lie in ambush, and abode	1980
	8:10 and w up, he and the elders of Israel,	5927
	8:11 w up, and drew nigh, and came before	5927
	8:13 Joshua w that night into the midst of	1980
	8:14 the men of the city w out against Israel to	3318
	8:17 Ai or Beth-el, that w not out after Israel:	3318
	9: 4 w and made as if they had been	1980
	9: 6 they w to Joshua unto the camp *at* Gilgal,	1980
	10: 5 w up, they and all their hosts,	5927
	10: 9 and w up from Gilgal all night.	5927
	10:24 of the men of war which w with him,	1980
	10:36 Joshua w up from Eglon, and all Israel	5927
	11: 4 they w out, they and all their hosts with	3318
	14: 8 Nevertheless my brethren that w up with	5927
	15: 3 it w out to the south side to	3318
	15: 3 w up to Adar, and fetched a compass to	5927
	15: 4 and w out *unto* the river of Egypt;	3318
	15: 6 the border w up *to* Beth-hogla,	5927
	15: 6 the border w up *to* the stone of Bohan	5927
	15: 7 the border w up toward Debir from	5927
	15: 8 the border w up *by* the valley of the son	5927
	15: 8 border w up to the top of the mountain	5927
	15: 9 and w out to the cities of mount Ephron;	3318
	15:10 w down *to* Beth-shemesh, and passed on	3381
	15:11 the border w out unto the side of Ekron	3318
	15:11 *to* mount Baalah, and w out *to* Jabneel;	3318
	15:15 w up thence to the inhabitants of Debir:	5927
	16: 6 the border w out toward the sea *to*	3318
	16: 6 the border w about eastward *unto*	5437
	16: 7 it w down from Janohah to Ataroth,	3381
	16: 7 and came to Jericho, and w out *at* Jordan.	3318
	16: 8 The border w out from Tappuah	1980
	17: 7 the border w along on the right hand	1980
	18: 8 the men arose, and w away:	1980
	18: 8 Joshua charged them that w to describe	1980
	18: 9 the men w and passed through the land,	1980
	18:12 the border w up to the side of Jericho on	5927
	18:12 w up through the mountains westward;	5927
	18:13 border w over from thence toward Luz,	5674
	18:15 border w out on the west, and went out	3318
	18:15 w out to the well of waters of Nephtoah;	3318
	18:17 w forth *to* En-shemesh, and went forth	3318
	18:17 and w forth toward Geliloth,	3318
	18:18 and w down unto Arabah:	3381
	19:11 their border w up toward the sea,	5927
	19:47 the coast of the children of Dan w out	3318
	19:47 the children of Dan w up to fight against	5927
	22: 6 them away: and they w unto their tents.	1980
	24: 4 and his children w down *into* Egypt.	3381
	24:11 ye w over Jordan, and came unto Jericho:	5674
	24:17 preserved us in all the way wherein we w	1980
Jdg	1: 3 them into thy lot. So Simeon w with him.	1980
	1: 4 Judah w up; and the LORD delivered	5927
	1: 9 afterward the children of Judah w down	3381
	1:10 Judah w against the Canaanites that dwelt	1980
	1:11 thence he w against the inhabitants of	1980
	1:16 w up out of the city of palm trees with	5927
	1:16 and they w and dwelt among the people.	1980
	1:17 Judah w with Simeon his brother,	1980
	1:22 of Joseph, they also w up *against* Beth-el:	5927
	1:26 the man w *into* the land of the Hittites,	1980
	2: 6 the children of Israel w every man unto	1980
	2:15 Whithersoever they w out, the hand of	3318
	2:17 they w a whoring after other gods,	2181
	3:10 and he judged Israel, and w out to war:	3318
	3:13 w and smote Israel, and possessed the city	1980
	3:19 all that stood by him w out from him.	3318
	3:22 the haft also w in after the blade; and the	935
	3:23 Ehud w forth through the porch,	3318
	3:27 the children of Israel w down with him	3381
	3:28 w down after him, and took the fords	3381
	4: 9 and w with Barak to Kedesh.	1980
	4:10 w up with ten thousand men at his feet:	5927
	4:10 at his feet: and Deborah w up with him.	5927

Jdg	4:14 So Barak w down from mount Tabor,	3381
	4:18 Jael w out to meet Sisera, and said unto	3318
	4:21 w softly unto him, and smote the nail into	935
	6:19 And Gideon w in, and made ready a kid,	935
	6:33 w over, and pitched in the valley of	5674
	7:11 w he down with Phurah his servant unto	3381
	8: 8 he w up thence *to* Penuel, and spake	5927
	8:11 Gideon w up *by* the way of them that	5927
	8:27 all Israel w thither a whoring after it:	2181
	8:29 Jerubbaal the son of Joash w and dwelt in	1980
	8:33 w a whoring after Baalim,	2181
	9: 1 Abimelech the son of Jerubbaal w to	1980
	9: 5 he w unto his father's house at Ophrah,	935
	9: 6 Millo, and w, and made Abimelech king,	1980
	9: 7 he w and stood in the top of mount	1980
	9: 8 The trees w forth on a time to	1980+1980
	9:21 and fled, and w to Beer, and dwelt there,	1980
	9:26 his brethren, and w over to Shechem:	5674
	9:27 they w out *into* the fields,	3318
	9:27 w *into* the house of their god, and did eat	935
	9:35 Gaal the son of Ebed w out, and stood *in*	3318
	9:39 Gaal w out before the men of Shechem,	3318
	9:42 the people w out *into* the field;	3318
	9:50 w Abimelech to Thebez,	1980
	9:52 w hard unto the door of the tower to	5066
	11: 3 men to Jephthah, and w out with him.	3318
	11: 5 the elders of Gilead w to fetch Jephthah	1980
	11:11 Jephthah w with the elders of Gilead,	1980
	11:18 they w along through the wilderness,	1980
	11:38 she w with her companions,	1980
	11:40 *That* the daughters of Israel w yearly to	1980
	12: 1 w northward, and said unto Jephthah,	5674
	13:11 w after his wife, and came to the man,	1980
	13:20 when the flame w up toward heaven	5927
	14: 1 Samson w down *to* Timnath, and saw a	3381
	14: 5 w Samson down, and his father and	3381
	14: 7 he w down, and talked with the woman,	3381
	14: 9 w on eating, and came to his father	1980+1980
	14:10 So his father w down unto the woman:	3381
	14:18 the seventh day before the sun w down,	935
	14:19 he w down *to* Ashkelon, and slew thirty	3381
	14:19 and he w up *to* his father's house.	5927
	15: 4 Samson w and caught three hundred	1980
	15: 8 w down and dwelt in the top of the rock	3381
	15: 9 Philistines w up, and pitched in Judah,	5927
	15:11 three thousand men of Judah w to the top	3381
	16: 1 w Samson to Gaza, and saw there a	1980
	16: 1 and saw there a harlot, and w in unto her.	935
	16: 3 w away with them, bar and all,	5265
	16:14 w away with the pin of the beam,	5265
	16:19 afflict him, and his strength w from him.	5493
	17:10 and thy victuals. So the Levite w in.	1980
	18:11 there w from thence of the family of	5265
	18:12 they w up, and pitched in Kirjath-jearim,	5927
	18:14 answered the five men that w to spy out	1980
	18:17 the five men that w to spy out the land	1980
	18:17 men that went to spy out the land w up,	5927
	18:18 these w *into* Micah's house, and fetched	935
	18:20 and w in the midst of the people.	935
	18:26 the children of Dan w their way:	1980
	18:26 he turned and w back unto his house.	7725
	19: 2 w away from him unto her father's house	1980
	19: 3 husband arose, and w after her, to speak	1980
	19:14 they passed on and w *their way;* and	1980
	19:14 the sun w down upon them when *they*	1980
	19:15 when he w in, he sat him down in a street	935
	19:18 I w to Beth-lehem-judah, but I am *now*	1980
	19:23 w out unto them, and said unto them,	3318
	19:27 of the house, and w out to go his way:	3318
	20: 1 all the children of Israel w out,	3318
	20:18 w up *to* the house of God,	5927
	20:20 the men of Israel w out to battle against	3318
	20:23 (And the children of Israel w up and	5927
	20:25 Benjamin w forth against them out of	3318
	20:26 w up, and came *unto* the house of God,	5927
	20:30 the children of Israel w up against	5927
	20:31 the children of Benjamin w out against	3318
	21:23 w and returned unto their inheritance,	1980
	21:24 they w out from thence every man to his	1980
Ru	1: 1 a *certain* man of Beth-lehem-judah w to	1980
	1: 7 Wherefore she w forth out of the place	3318
	1: 7 they w on the way to return unto the land	1980
	1:19 So they two w until they came *to*	1980
	1:21 I w out full, and the LORD hath brought	1980
	2: 3 she w, and came, and gleaned in the field	1980
	2:18 she took *it* up, and w *into* the city:	935
	3: 6 she w down *unto* the floor,	3381
	3: 7 he w to lie down at the end of the heap *of*	935
	3:15 and laid *it* on her: and he w *into* the city.	935
	4: 1 w Boaz up *to* the gate, and sat him down	5927
	4:13 when he w in unto her, the LORD gave her	935
1Sa	1: 3 this man w up out of his city yearly to	1980
	1: 7 when she w up to the house of the LORD,	5927
	1:18 So the woman w her way, and did eat,	1980
	1:21 w up to offer unto the LORD the yearly	5927
	1:22 Hannah w not up; for she said unto her	5927
	2:11 Elkanah w to Ramah to his house.	1980
	2:20 And they w unto their own home.	1980
	3: 3 ere the lamp of God w out in the temple	3518
	3: 5 lie down again. And he w and lay down.	1980
	3: 6 Samuel arose and w to Eli, and said,	1980
	3: 8 arose and w to Eli, and said, Here *am* I;	1980
	3: 9 So Samuel w and lay down in his place.	1980
	4: 1 Israel w out against the Philistines to	3318
	5:12 and the cry of the city w up *to* heaven.	5927

1Sa	6:12 *and* w along the highway, lowing as they	1980
	6:12 lowing as they w, and turned not aside *to*	1980
	6:12 the lords of the Philistines w after them	1980
	7: 7 the lords of the Philistines w up against	5927
	7:11 the men of Israel w out of Mizpeh,	3318
	7:16 w from year to year in circuit *to* Beth-el,	1980
	9: 9 when a man w to inquire of God, thus he	1980
	9:10 So they w unto the city where the man of	1980
	9:11 *And* as they w up the hill to the city, they	5927
	9:14 they w up *into* the city: *and* when they	5927
	9:26 they w out both of them, he and Samuel,	3318
	10:14 him and to his servant, Whither ye?	1980
	10:26 Saul also w home to Gibeah;	1980
	10:26 there w with him a band of men,	1980
	11:15 all the people w *to* Gilgal; and there they	1980
	13: 7 *some of* the Hebrews w over Jordan to	5674
	13:10 Saul w out to meet him, that he might	3318
	13:20 the Israelites w down *to* the Philistines,	3381
	13:23 the garrison of the Philistines w out *to*	3318
	14:16 they w on beating down *one another.*	1980
	14:19 in the host of the Philistines w on	1980+1980
	14:21 which w up with them into the camp	5927
	14:46 Saul w up from following the Philistines:	5927
	14:46 the Philistines w to their own place.	5927
	15:34 Samuel w to Ramah; and Saul went up to	1980
	15:34 Saul w up to his house to Gibeah of Saul.	5927
	16:13 So Samuel rose up, and w to Ramah.	1980
	17: 4 there w out a champion out of the camp	3318
	17: 7 and one bearing a shield w before him.	1980
	17:12 the man w among men *for* an old man in	935
	17:13 the three eldest sons of Jesse w *and*	1980
	17:13 the names of his three sons that w to	1980
	17:15 David w and returned from Saul to feed	1980
	17:20 sheep with a keeper, and took, and w,	1980
	17:35 I w out after him, and smote him,	3318
	17:41 man that bare the shield w before him.	NIH
	18: 5 David w out whithersoever Saul sent him,	3318
	18:13 he w out and came in before the people.	3318
	18:16 he w out and came in before them.	3318
	18:27 Wherefore David arose and w, he and	1980
	18:30 the princes of the Philistines w forth:	3318
	18:30 it came to pass, after they w forth,	3318
	19: 8 David w out, and fought with	3318
	19:12 window: and he w, and fled, and escaped.	1980
	19:18 he and Samuel w and dwelt in Naioth.	1980
	19:22 w he also to Ramah, and came to a great	1980
	19:23 he w thither to Naioth in Ramah:	1980
	19:23 he w on, and prophesied, until he	1980+1980
	20:11 they w both of them *into* the field.	3318
	20:35 that Jonathan w out *into* the field at	3318
	20:42 departed: and Jonathan w *into* the city.	935
	21:10 of Saul, and w to Achish the king of Gath.	935
	22: 1 his father's house heard *it,* they w down	3381
	22: 3 David w thence *to* Mizpeh of Moab:	1980
	23: 5 So David and his men w to Keilah,	1980
	23:13 and w whithersoever they could go.	1980
	23:16 w to David *into* the wood,	1980
	23:18 the wood, and Jonathan w to his house.	1980
	23:24 they arose, and w to Ziph before Saul:	1980
	23:25 his men w to seek *him.* And they told	1980
	23:26 Saul w on this side of the mountain,	1980
	23:28 after David, and w against the Philistines:	1980
	23:29 David w up from thence, and dwelt in	5927
	24: 2 w to seek David and his men upon	1980
	24: 3 a cave; and Saul w in to cover his feet:	935
	24: 7 up out of the cave, and w on *his* way.	1980
	24: 8 w out of the cave, and cried after Saul,	3318
	24:22 Saul w home; but David and his men gat	1980
	25: 1 and w down to the wilderness of Paran.	3381
	25:12 w again, and came and told him all those	7725
	25:13 w up after David about four hundred	5927
	25:42 with five damsels of hers that w after her;	1980
	25:42 she w after the messengers of David,	1980
	26: 2 and w down to the wilderness of Ziph,	3381
	26:13 David w over to the *other* side,	5674
	26:25 So David w on his way, and Saul returned	1980
	27: 8 David and his men w up, and invaded	5927
	28: 8 he w, and two men with him,	1980
	28:25 they arose up, and w away that night.	1980
	29:11 And the Philistines w up *to* Jezreel.	5927
	30: 2 carried *them* away, and w on their way.	1980
	30: 9 So David w, he and the six hundred men	1980
	30:21 they w forth to meet David, and to meet	3318
	30:22 of those that w with David, and said,	1980
	30:22 and said, Because they w not with us,	1980
	31: 3 the battle w sore against Saul,	3513
	31:12 w all night, and took the body of Saul and	1980
2Sa	1: 4 David said unto him, How w the matter?	1961
	2: 2 So David w up thither, and his two wives	5927
	2:12 of Saul, w out from Mahanaim to Gibeon.	3318
	2:13 w out, and met together by the pool of	3318
	2:15 w over by number twelve of Benjamin,	5674
	2:24 the sun w down when they were come	935
	2:29 w *through* all Bithron, and they came to	1980
	2:32 Joab and his men w all night, and they	1980
	3:16 her husband w with her along weeping	1980
	3:19 Abner w also to speak in the ears of	1980
	3:21 sent Abner away; and he w in peace.	1980
	4: 5 w, and came about the heat of the day to	1980
	5: 6 men w *to* Jerusalem unto the Jebusites,	1980
	5:10 David w on, and grew great,	1980+1980
	5:17 heard *of it,* and w down to the hold.	3381
	6: 2 w with all the people that *were* with him	1980
	6: 4 ark of God: and Ahio w before the ark.	1980
	6:12 David w and brought up the ark of God	1980

2Sa
7:18 **w** king David **in**, and sat before the LORD, 935
7:23 whom God **w** to redeem for a people to 1980
8: 3 as he **w** to recover his border at the river 935
8: 6 preserved David whithersoever he **w**. NIH
8:14 preserved David whithersoever he **w**. NIH
10:16 of the host of Hadarezer **w** before them. NIH
11: 9 **w** his lord, and **w** not **down** to his house. 3381
11:10 Uriah **w** not **down** unto his house, 3381
11:13 at even he **w** out to lie on his bed with 3318
11:13 in his lord, but **w** not **down** to his house. 3381
11:17 the men of the city **w** out, and fought 3318
11:21 why **w** ye **nigh** the wall? then say 5066
11:22 So the messenger **w**, and came and 1980
12:16 and **w** in, and lay all night upon the earth. 935
12:17 *and* **w** to him, to raise him up from NIH
12:24 wife, and **w** in unto her, and lay with her: 935
12:29 **w** to Rabbah, and fought against it, 1980
13: 8 Tamar **w** *to her* brother Amnon's house; 1980
13: 9 And they **w** out every man from him. 3318
13:19 on her head, and **w** on crying. 1980+1980
13:37 Absalom fled, and **w** to Talmai, the son of 1980
13:38 **w** to Geshur, and was there three years. 1980
14:23 So Joab arose and **w** to Geshur, 1980
15: 9 in peace. So he arose, and **w** to Hebron. 1980
15:11 with Absalom **w** two hundred men out of 1980
15:11 they **w** in their simplicity, and they knew 1980
15:16 the king **w** forth, and all his household 3318
15:17 the king **w** forth, and all the people after 3318
15:24 Abiathar **w** up, until all the people had 5927
15:30 David **w** up by the ascent of *mount* 5927
15:30 wept as he **w** up, and had his head 5927
15:30 had his head covered, and he **w** barefoot: 1980
15:30 and they **w** up, weeping as they went up. 5927
15:30 they **w** up, weeping as they **w** up. 5927
16:13 as David and his men **w** by the way, 1980
16:13 Shimei **w** along on the hill's side over 1980
16:13 cursed as he **w**, and threw stones at him, 1980
16:22 Absalom **w** in unto his father's concubines 935
17:17 a wench **w** and told them; and they went 1980
17:17 them; and they **w** and told king David. 1980
17:18 they **w** both of them **away** quickly, 1980
17:18 well in his court; whither they **w down**. 3381
17:21 **w** and told king David, and said unto 1980
17:25 **w** in to Abigail the daughter of Nahash, 935
18: 6 So the people **w** out *into* the field against 3318
18: 9 the mule **w** under the thick boughs of a 935
18: 9 the mule that *was* under him **w away**. 5674
18:24 the watchman **w** up to the roof over 1980
18:33 **w** up to the chamber over the gate, 5927
18:33 as he **w**, thus he said, O my son Absalom, 1980
19:17 and they **w** over Jordan before the king. 6743
19:18 there **w** over a ferry boat to carry over 5674
19:19 that my lord the king **w** out of Jerusalem, 3318
19:31 **w** over Jordan with the king, to conduct 5674
19:39 all the people **w** over Jordan. And when 5674
19:40 the king **w** on to Gilgal, 5674
19:40 to Gilgal, and Chimham **w** on with him: 5674
20: 2 So every man of Israel **w** up from after 5927
20: 3 and fed them, but **w** not **in** unto them. 935
20: 5 Amasa **w** to assemble the *men of* Judah: 1980
20: 7 there **w** out after him Joab's men, 3318
20: 7 mighty *men*: and they **w** out of Jerusalem, 3318
20: 8 which *is* in Gibeon, Amasa **w** before them. 935
20: 8 thereof; and as he **w forth** it fell out. 3318
20:13 all the people **w** on after Joab, to pursue 5674
20:14 he **w through** all the tribes of Israel unto 5674
20:14 gathered together, and **w** also after him. 935
20:22 the woman **w** unto all the people in her 935
21:12 David **w** and took the bones of Saul and 1980
21:15 David **w down**, and his servants with 3381
22: 9 There **w** up a smoke out of his nostrils, 5927
23:13 three of the thirty chief **w down**, 3381
23:17 *is not this* the blood of the men that **w** in 1980
23:20 he **w down** also and slew a lion in a 3381
23:21 he **w down** to him with a staff, 3381
24: 4 the captains of the host **w** out from 3318
24: 7 they **w** out to the south of Judah, *even to* 3318
24:19 of Gad, **w** up as the LORD commanded. 5927
24:20 Araunah **w** out, and bowed himself before 3318

1Ki
1:15 Bath-sheba **w** in unto the king into 935
1:38 **w down**, and caused Solomon to ride 3381
1:49 and rose up, and **w** every man his way. 1980
1:50 **w**, and caught hold on the horns of 1980
2: 8 curse in the day when I **w** to Mahanaim: 1980
2:19 Bath-sheba therefore **w** unto king Solomon, 935
2:34 So Benaiah the son of Jehoiada **w** up, 5927
2:40 **w** to Gath to Achish to seek his servants: 1980
2:40 Shimei **w**, and brought his servants from 1980
2:46 which **w** out, and fell upon him, that he 3318
3: 4 the king **w** to Gibeon to sacrifice there; 1980
6: 8 they **w** up with winding stairs into 5927
8:66 **w** unto their tents joyful and glad of heart 1980
10: 5 ascent *by* which he **w** up *unto* the house 5927
10:13 So she turned and **w** to her own country, 1980
10:16 **w** into *it*: six hundred *shekels* of gold 5927
10:17 three pound *of* gold to one shield: 5927
10:29 **w** out of Egypt for six hundred *shekels* of 3318
11: 5 Solomon **w** after Ashtoreth the goddess 1980
11: 6 **w** not **fully** after the LORD, as *did* David 4390
11:24 them *of Zobah*: and they **w** to Damascus, 1980
11:29 time when Jeroboam **w** out of Jerusalem, 3318
12: 1 Rehoboam **w** to Shechem: for all Israel 1980
12:25 **w** out from thence, and built Penuel. 3318
12:30 the people **w** *to worship* before the one, 1980
13:10 he **w** another way, and returned not by 1980

1Ki
13:12 father said unto them, What way **w** he? 1980
13:12 had seen what way the man of God **w**, 1980
13:14 after the man of God, and found him 1980
13:19 he **w back** with him, and did eat bread 7725
13:28 **w** and found his carcase cast in the way, 1980
14: 4 **w** *to* Shiloh, and came *to* the house of 1980
14:28 when the king **w** into the house of 935
15:17 Baasha king of Israel **w** up against Judah, 5927
16:10 Zimri **w** in and smote him, and killed him, 1980
16:17 Omri **w** up from Gibbethon, and all Israel 5927
16:18 he **w** into the palace of the king's house, 935
16:31 **w** and served Baal, and worshipped him. 1980
17: 5 So he **w** and did according unto the word 1980
17: 5 for he **w** and dwelt by the brook Cherith, 1980
17:10 So he arose and **w** to Zarephath. 1980
17:15 she **w** and did according to the saying of 1980
18: 2 Elijah **w** to shew himself unto Ahab. 1980
18: 6 Ahab **w** one way by himself, 1980
18: 6 Obadiah **w** another way by himself. 1980
18:16 Obadiah **w** to meet Ahab, and told him: 1980
18:16 and told him: and Ahab **w** to meet Elijah. 1980
18:42 So Ahab **w** up to eat and to drink. 5927
18:42 Elijah **w** up to the top of Carmel, 5927
18:43 he **w** up, and looked, and said, *There is* 5927
18:45 And Ahab rode, and **w** to Jezreel. 1980
19: 3 **w** for his life, and came *to* Beer-sheba, 1980
19: 4 he himself **w** a day's journey into 1980
19: 8 in the strength of that meat forty days 1980
19:13 **w** out, and stood *in* the entering in of 3318
19:21 **w** after Elijah, and ministered unto him. 1980
20: 1 he **w** up and besieged Samaria, 5927
20:16 they **w** out at noon. But Ben-hadad *was* 1980
20:17 the princes of the provinces **w** out first; 3318
20:21 the king of Israel **w** out, and smote 3318
20:26 **w** up to Aphek, to fight against Israel. 5927
20:27 and were all present, and **w** against them: 1980
20:39 Thy servant **w** out into the midst of 3318
20:43 king of Israel **w** to his house heavy 1980
21:27 fasted, and lay in sackcloth, and **w** softly. 1980
22:24 Zedekiah the son of Chenaanah **w** near, 5066
22:24 Which way **w** the spirit of the LORD from 5674
22:29 Jehoshaphat the king of Judah **w** up *to* 5927
22:30 disguised himself, and **w** into the battle. 935
22:36 there **w** a proclamation throughout the 5674
22:48 they **w** not; for the ships were broken at 1980

2Ki
1: 4 he **w** up to him: and behold, he sat on 5927
1:13 the third captain of fifty **w** up, and came 5927
1:15 and **w down** with him unto the king. 3381
2: 1 that Elijah **w** with Elisha from Gilgal. 1980
2: 2 leave thee. So they **w down** *to* Beth-el. 3381
2: 6 I will not leave thee. And they two **w** on. 1980
2: 7 fifty men of the sons of the prophets **w**, 1980
2: 8 so that they two **w** over on dry *ground*. 5674
2:11 still **w** on, and talked, that behold, 1980+1980
2:11 Elijah **w** up by a whirlwind *into* heaven. 5927
2:13 **w back**, and stood by the bank of Jordan; 7725
2:14 and thither: and Elisha **w** over. 5674
2:21 he **w forth** unto the spring of the waters, 3318
2:23 And he **w** up from thence *unto* Beth-el: 5927
2:25 he **w** from thence to mount Carmel, 1980
3: 6 king Jehoram **w** out of Samaria the same 3318
3: 7 he **w** and sent to Jehoshaphat the king of 1980
3: 9 So the king of Israel **w**, and the king of 1980
3:12 and the king of Edom **w down** to him. 3381
3:24 they **w** forward smiting the Moabites, 935
3:25 howbeit the slingers **w** about *it*, and 5437
4: 5 she **w** from him, and shut the door upon 1980
4:18 that he **w** out to his father to the reapers. 3318
4:21 she **w** up, and laid him on the bed of 5927
4:21 and shut *the door* upon him, and **w** out. 3318
4:25 So she **w** and came unto the man of God 1980
4:31 Wherefore he **w** again to meet him, 7725
4:33 He **w** in therefore, and shut the door upon 935
4:34 **w** up, and lay upon the child, and put 5927
4:35 **w** up, and stretched himself upon him: 5927
4:37 she **w** in, and fell at his feet, 935
4:37 ground, and took up her son, and **w** out. 3318
4:39 one **w** out into the field to gather herbs, 3318
5: 4 *one* **w** in, and told his lord, saying, Thus 935
5:11 and **w away**, and said, Behold, I thought, 1980
5:12 So he turned and **w away** in a rage. 1980
5:14 he **w down**, and dipped *himself* seven 3381
5:25 he **w** in, and stood before his master. 935
5:25 And he said, Thy servant **w** no whither. 1980
5:26 **W** not mine heart *with thee*, when the 1980
5:27 he **w** out from his presence a leper *as* 3318
6: 4 So he **w** with them. And when they came 1980
6:23 them away, and they **w** to their master. 1980
6:24 his host, and **w** up, and besieged Samaria. 5927
7: 8 who **w** into one tent, and did eat and drink, 935
7: 8 **w** and hid *it*; and came again, 1980
7: 8 and carried thence *also*, and **w** and hid *it*. 1980
7:15 they **w** after them unto Jordan: and lo, 1980
7:16 the people **w** out, and spoiled the tents of 3318
8: 2 she **w** with her household, and sojourned 1980
8: 3 she **w forth** to cry unto the king for her 3318
8: 9 So Hazael **w** to meet him, and took a 1980
8:21 So Joram **w** over to Zair, and all 5674
8:28 he **w** with Joram the son of Ahab to the 1980
8:29 king Joram **w back** to be healed in Jezreel 7725
8:29 **w down** to see Joram the son of Ahab in 3381
9: 4 man the prophet, **w** to Ramoth-gilead. 1980
9: 6 he arose, and **w** into the house; 935
9:16 Jehu rode *in a chariot*, and **w** to Jezreel; 1980
9:18 there **w** one on horseback to meet him, 1980

2Ki
9:21 Israel and Ahaziah king of Judah **w** out, 3318
9:21 they **w** out against Jehu, and met him in 3318
9:24 the arrow **w** out at his heart, and he sunk 3318
9:35 they **w** to bury her: but they found no 1980
10: 9 that he **w** out, and stood, and said to all 3318
10:23 Jehu **w**, and Jehonadab the son of Rechab, 935
10:24 when they **w** in to offer sacrifices and 935
10:25 and **w** to the city of the house of Baal. 1980
11:16 she **w** *by* the way by the which the horses 935
11:18 all the people of the land **w** *into* the house 935
12:17 Hazael king of Syria **w** up, 5927
12:18 of Syria: and he **w away** from Jerusalem. 5927
13: 5 that they **w** out from under the hand of 3318
14:11 Therefore Jehoash king of Israel **w** up; 5927
15:14 For Menahem the son of Gadi **w** up from 5927
16: 9 for the king of Assyria **w** up against 5927
16:10 king Ahaz **w** to Damascus to meet 1980
17: 5 **w** up *to* Samaria, and besieged it three 5927
17:15 **w** after the heathen that *were* round about NIH
18: 7 he prospered whithersoever he **w forth**: 3318
18:17 they **w** up and came *to* Jerusalem, 5927
19: 1 and **w** into the house of the LORD, 935
19:14 Hezekiah **w** up *into* the house of 5927
19:35 that the angel of the LORD **w** out, 3318
19:36 and returned, and dwelt at Nineveh. 1980
22:14 Asahiah **w**, unto Huldah the prophetess, 1980
23: 2 the king **w** up *into* the house of 5927
23:29 **w** up against the king of Assyria to 5927
23:29 Josiah **w** against him; and he slew him 1980
24:12 Jehoiachin the king of Judah **w** out 3318
25: 4 and *the king* **w** the way toward the plain. 1980

1Ch
2:21 afterward Hezron **w in** to the daughter of 935
4:39 they **w** to the entrance of Gedor, *even* 1980
4:42 five hundred men, **w** to mount Seir, 1980
5:18 and threescore, that **w** out *to* the war. 3318
5:25 **w** a whoring after the gods of the people 2181
6:15 Jehozadak **w** *into captivity*, when 1980
7:23 when he **w** in to his wife, she conceived, 935
7:23 because it **w** evil with his house. 1961
10: 3 the battle **w** sore against Saul, 3513
11: 4 David and all Israel **w** to Jerusalem, 1980
11: 6 So Joab the son of Zeruiah **w** first **up**, 5927
11:15 three of the thirty captains **w down** to 3381
11:22 he **w down** and slew a lion in a pit in a 3381
11:23 he **w down** to him with a staff, 3381
12:15 These *are* they that **w** over Jordan in 5674
12:17 David **w** out to meet them, and answered 3318
12:20 As he **w** to Ziklag, there fell to him of 1980
12:33 Of Zebulun, such as **w forth** to battle, 3318
12:36 such as **w forth** to battle, expert in war, 3318
13: 6 David **w** up, and all Israel, to Baalah, 5927
14: 8 all the Philistines **w** up to seek David. 5927
14:17 the fame of David **w** out into all lands; 3318
15:25 **w** to bring up the ark of the covenant of 1980
16:20 *when* they **w** from nation to nation, 1980
17:21 whom God **w** to redeem *to be* his own 1980
18: 3 as he **w** to stablish his dominion by 1980
18: 6 preserved David whithersoever he **w**. NIH
18:13 preserved David whithersoever he **w**. NIH
19: 5 there **w** *certain*, and told David how 1980
19:16 of the host of Hadarezer **w** before them. NIH
21: 4 **w** throughout all Israel, and came *to* 1980
21:19 David **w** up at the saying of Gad, which 5927
21:21 he **w** out of the threshingfloor, 3318
27: 1 **w** out month by month throughout all 3318
29:30 times that **w** over him, and over Israel, 5674

2Ch
1: 3 **w** to the high place that *was* at Gibeon; 1980
1: 6 Solomon **w** up thither to the brasen altar 5927
8: 3 Solomon **w** *to* Hamath-zobah, 1980
8:17 **w** Solomon to Ezion-geber, and to Eloth, 1980
8:18 they **w** with the servants of Solomon *to* 935
9: 4 ascent *by* which he **w** up *into* the house 5927
9:12 **w away** to her own land, she and 1980
9:15 six hundred *shekels* of beaten gold **w** to 5927
9:16 three hundred *shekels* of gold **w** to one 5927
9:21 For the king's ships **w** *to* Tarshish with 1980
10: 1 Rehoboam **w** to Shechem: for *to* Shechem 1980
10:16 own house. So all Israel **w** to their tents. 1980
12:12 and also in Judah things **w** well. 1961
14:10 Asa **w** out against him, and they set 3318
15: 2 he **w** out to meet Asa, and said unto him, 3318
15: 5 *there was* no peace to him that **w** out, 3318
17: 9 **w** about throughout all the cities of 5437
18: 2 after *certain* years he **w down** to Ahab 3381
18:12 messenger that **w** to call Micaiah spake 1980
18:23 Which way **w** the spirit of the LORD from 5674
18:28 Jehoshaphat the king of Judah **w** up *to* 5927
18:29 disguised himself; and they **w** to the battle. 935
19: 2 Jehu the son of Hanani the seer **w** out to 3318
19: 4 he **w** out again through the people from 1980
20:20 and **w forth** into the wilderness of Tekoa: 3318
20:20 as they **w forth**, Jehoshaphat stood and 3318
20:21 as *they* **w** out before the army, and to say, 3318
21: 9 Jehoram **w forth** with his princes, 5674
22: 5 **w** with Jehoram the son of Ahab king of 1980
22: 6 **w down** to see Jehoram the son of Ahab 3381
22: 7 **w** out with Jehoram against Jehu the son 3318
23: 2 they **w** about in Judah, and gathered 5437
23:17 all the people **w** to the house of Baal, 1980
25:11 **w** to the valley of salt, and smote *of* 1980
25:21 So Joash the king of Israel **w** up; 5927
26: 6 he **w forth** and warred against 3318
26:11 fighting *men*, that **w** out to war by bands, 3318
26:16 **w** into the temple of the LORD to burn 935

2Ch 26:17 Azariah the priest **w in** after him,	935	
28: 9 he **w out** before the host that came to	3318	
29:16 the priests **w** into the inner part *of* the	935	
29:18 they **w in** to Hezekiah the king, and said,	935	
29:20 and **w up** *to* the house of the LORD.	5927	
30: 6 So the posts **w** with the letters from	1980	
31: 1 all Israel that were present **w out** to	3318	
34:22 *they* that the king *had* appointed, **w** to	1980	
34:30 the king **w up** *into* the house of	5927	
35:20 and Josiah **w out** against him.	3318	
Ezr 2: 1 province that **w up** out of the captivity,	5927	
2:59 these *were* they which **w up** from	5927	
4:23 they **w up** in haste to Jerusalem unto	236	
5: 8 that we **w** into the province of Judea,	236	
7: 6 This Ezra **w up** from Babylon; and he	5927	
7: 7 there **w up** *some* of the children of Israel,	5927	
8: 1 *this is* the genealogy of them that **w up**	5927	
10: 6 **w** into the chamber of Johanan the son of	1980	
Ne 2:13 I **w out** by night by the gate of the valley,	3318	
2:14 I **w** on to the gate of the fountain,	5674	
2:15 **w** I **up** in the night by the brook,	5927	
2:16 the rulers knew not whither I **w**, or what	1980	
7: 6 that **w up** out of the captivity, *of* those	5927	
7:61 these *were* they which **w up** *also* from	5927	
8:12 all the people **w** *their way* to eat,	1980	
8:16 So the people **w forth**, and brought *them*,	3318	
9:11 they **w through** the midst of the sea on	5674	
9:24 the children **w in** and possessed the land,	935	
12: 1 the Levites that **w up** with Zerubbabel	5927	
12:31 whereof *one* **w** on the right hand upon	8418	
12:32 after them **w** Hoshaiah, and half of	1980	
12:37 **w up** by the stairs of the city of David,	5927	
12:38 *that gave* thanks **w** over against *them*,	1980	
Est 2:14 In the evening she **w**, and on the morrow	935	
3:15 The posts **w out**, being hastened by	3318	
4: 1 **w out** into the midst of the city,	3318	
4: 6 So Hatach **w forth** to Mordecai unto	3318	
4:17 Mordecai **w** his way, and did according	5674	
5: 9 **w** Haman **forth** that day joyful and with a	3318	
7: 7 in his wrath **w** into the palace garden:	NIH	
7: 8 As the word **w out** of the king's mouth,	3318	
8:14 that rode upon mules *and* camels **w out**,	3318	
8:15 Mordecai **w** from the presence of	3318	
9: 4 his fame **w out** throughout all	1980	
Job 1: 4 his sons and feasted *in their* houses,	1980	
1:12 So Satan **w forth** from the presence of	3318	
2: 7 So **w** Satan **forth** from the presence of	3318	
18:20 as **they** that **w before** were affrighted.	6931	
29: 7 **w** out *to* the gate through the city,	1980	
30:28 I **w** mourning without the sun: I stood up,	1980	
31:34 I kept silence, *and* **w** not *out of* the door?	3318	
42: 9 Shuhite *and* Zophar the Naamathite **w**,	1980	
Ps 18: 8 There **w up** a smoke out of his nostrils,	5927	
42: 4 I **w** with them to the house of God, with	1718	
66: 6 He turned the sea into dry *land*: they **w**	5674	
66:12 we **w** through fire and through water:	935	
68:25 The singers **w before**, the players on	6923	
73:17 Until I **w** into the sanctuary of God; *then*	935	
77:17 out a sound: thine arrows also **w abroad**.	1980	
81: 5 he **w out** through the land of Egypt:	3318	
105:13 When they **w** from one nation to another,	1980	
106:32 so that it **w** ill with Moses for their sakes:	NIH	
106:39 **w** a **whoring** with their own inventions.	2181	
114: 1 When Israel **w out** of Egypt, the house of	3318	
119:67 Before I was afflicted I **w astray**:	7683	
133: 2 **w down** to the skirts of his garments:	3381	
Pr 7: 8 corner; and he **w** the way to her house,	6805	
24:30 I **w** by the field of the slothful, and by	5674	
Ecc 2:20 Therefore I **w about** to cause my heart to	5437	
SS 5: 7 The watchmen that **w about** the city	5437	
6:11 I **w down** into the garden of nuts to see	3381	
Isa 7: 1 **w up** *towards* Jerusalem to war against it,	5927	
8: 3 I **w** unto the prophetess; and she	7126	
37: 1 and **w** *into* the house of the LORD.	935	
37:14 Hezekiah **w up** *unto* the house of	5927	
37:36 the angel of the LORD **w forth**,	3318	
37:37 **w** and returned, and dwelt at Nineveh.	1980	
48: 3 they **w forth** out of my mouth,	3318	
51:23 and as the street, to them that **w over**.	5674	
52: 4 My people **w down** aforetime *into* Egypt	3381	
57:17 he **w** on frowardly in the way of his heart.	1980	
60:15 that no man **w through** *thee*, I will make	5674	
Jer 3: 8 feared not, but **w** and played the harlot	1980	
7:24 and **w** backward, and not forward.	1961	
11:10 they **w** after other gods to serve them:	1980	
13: 5 So I **w**, and hid it by Euphrates,	1980	
13: 7 I **w** to Euphrates, and digged, and took	1980	
18: 3 I **w down** to the potter's house, and,	3381	
22:11 father, which **w forth** out of this place;	3318	
26:21 he was afraid, and fled, and **w** *into* Egypt;	935	
28: 4 that **w** into Babylon, saith the LORD:	935	
28:11 And the prophet Jeremiah **w** his way.	1980	
31: 2 *even* Israel when *I* **w** to cause him to rest.	1980	
36:12 he **w down** into the king's house, into	3381	
36:20 And they **w in** to the king into the court,	935	
37: 4 came in and **w out** among the people:	3318	
37:12 Jeremiah **w forth** out of Jerusalem to go	3318	
38: 8 Ebed-melech **w forth** out of the king's	3318	
38:11 **w** *into* the house of the king under	935	
39: 4 and **w forth** out of the city by night,	3318	
39: 4 and he **w out** the way of the plain.	3318	
40: 6 **w** Jeremiah unto Gedaliah the son of	935	
41: 6 Ishmael the son of Nethaniah **w forth**	3318	
41: 6 weeping **all along as** he **w**:	1980+1980	
41:12 **w** to fight with Ishmael the son of	1980	

Jer 41:14 and **w** unto Johanan the son of Kareah.	1980	
41:15 with eight men, and **w** to the Ammonites.	1980	
44: 3 that *they* **w** to burn incense, *and* to serve	1980	
51:59 he **w** with Zedekiah the king of Judah	1980	
52: 7 **w forth** out of the city by night *by* the	3318	
52: 7 and they **w** *by* the way of the plain.	1980	
Eze 1: 9 they turned not when they **w**; they went	1980	
1: 9 they **w** every one straight forward.	1980	
1:12 they **w** every one straight forward.	1980	
1:12 whither the spirit was to go, they **w**;	1980	
1:12 *and* they turned not when they **w**.	1980	
1:13 it **w up and down** among the living	1980	
1:13 and out of the fire **w forth** lightning.	3318	
1:17 When they **w**, they went upon their four	1980	
1:17 they went, they upon their four sides;	1980	
1:17 *and* they turned not when they **w**.	1980	
1:19 when the living creatures **w**, the wheels	1980	
1:19 creatures went, the wheels **w** by them:	1980	
1:20 they **w**, thither *was their* spirit to go;	1980	
1:21 When those **w**, *these* went; and when	1980	
1:21 When those went, *these* **w**; and when	1980	
1:24 when they **w**, I heard the noise of their	1980	
3:14 took me away, and I **w** in bitterness,	1980	
3:23 I arose, and **w forth** into the plain:	3318	
8:10 So I **w in** and saw; and behold every form	935	
8:11 and a thick cloud of incense **w up**.	5927	
9: 2 **w in**, and stood beside the brasen altar.	935	
9: 7 And they **w forth**, and slew in the city.	3318	
10: 2 over the city. And he **w in** in my sight.	935	
10: 3 side of the house, when the man **w in**;	935	
10: 4 the glory of the LORD **w up** from	7311	
10: 6 he **w in**, and stood beside the wheels.	935	
10: 7 with linen: who took *it*, and **w** out.	3318	
10:11 When they **w**, they went upon their four	1980	
10:11 they went, they **w** upon their four sides;	1980	
10:11 turned not as they **w**, but *to* the place	1980	
10:11 followed it; they turned not as they **w**.	1980	
10:16 when the cherubims **w**, the wheels went	1980	
10:16 cherubims went, the wheels **w** by them:	1980	
10:19 when they **w out**, the wheels also *were*	3318	
10:22 they **w** every one straight forward.	1980	
11:23 the glory of the LORD **w up** from	5927	
11:24 the vision that I had seen **w up** from me.	5927	
16:14 thy renown **w forth** among the heathen	3318	
19: 6 he **w up and down** among the lions,	1980	
20:16 for their heart **w** after their idols.	1980	
23:44 Yet they **w** in unto her, as *they* go in unto	935	
23:44 they **w in** unto Aholah and unto Aholibah,	935	
24:12 her great scum **w** not **forth** out of her:	3318	
25: 3 of Judah, when they **w** into captivity;	1980	
27:33 When thy wares **w forth** out of the seas,	3318	
31:15 In the day when he **w down** to the grave	3381	
31:17 They also **w down** into hell with him	3381	
36:20 whither they **w**, they profaned my holy	935	
36:21 among the heathen, whither they **w**.	935	
36:22 among the heathen, whither ye **w**.	935	
39:23 Israel **w into captivity** for their iniquity:	1540	
40: 6 **w up** the stairs thereof, and measured	5927	
40:22 they **w up** unto it by seven steps;	5927	
40:49 *me* by the steps whereby they **w up** to it:	5927	
41: 3 he **w** inward, and measured the post of	935	
41: 7 for the winding about of the house **w** still	NIH	
44:10 away far from me, when Israel **w astray**,	8582	
44:10 which **w astray** away from me after their	8582	
44:15 the children of Israel **w astray** from me,	8582	
47: 3 **w forth** east*ward*, he measured a	3318	
48:11 which **w** not **astray** when the children of	8582	
48:11 when the children of Israel **w astray**,	8582	
48:11 went astray, as the Levites **w astray**.	8582	
Da 2:13 the decree **w forth** that the wise *men*	5312	
2:16 Daniel **w in**, and desired of the king that	5954	
2:17 Daniel **w** to his house, and made the thing	236	
2:24 Therefore Daniel **w in** unto Arioch,	5954	
2:24 he **w** and said thus unto him; Destroy not	236	
6:10 writing *was* signed, he **w** into his house;	5954	
6:18 the king **w** to his palace, and passed	236	
6:18 before him: and his sleep **w** from him.	5075	
6:19 and **w** in haste unto the den of lions.	236	
Hos 1: 3 So he **w** and took Gomer the daughter of	1980	
2:13 and she **w** after her lovers, and forgat me,	1980	
5:13 **w** Ephraim to the Assyrian, and sent to	1980	
9:10 *but* they **w** to Baal-peor,	935	
11: 2 they called them, so they **w** from them:	1980	
Am 5: 3 The city that **w out** *by* a thousand shall	3318	
5: 3 that which **w forth** *by* an hundred shall	3318	
5:19 **w** *into* the house, and leaned his hand on	935	
Jnh 1: 3 of the LORD, and **w down** *to* Joppa;	3381	
1: 3 paid the fare thereof, and **w down** into it,	3381	
2: 6 **w down** to the bottoms of the mountains;	3381	
3: 3 So Jonah arose, and **w** unto Nineveh,	1980	
4: 5 So Jonah **w out** of the city, and sat on	3318	
Na 3:10 she carried away, she **w** into captivity:	1980	
Hab 3: 5 Before him **w** the pestilence,	1980	
3: 5 and burning coals **w forth** at his feet.	3318	
3:11 at the light of thine arrows they **w**,	1980	
Zec 2: 3 the angel that talked with me **w forth**,	3318	
2: 3 and another angel **w out** to meet him,	3318	
5: 5 the angel that talked with me **w forth**,	3318	
6: 7 the bay **w forth**, and sought to go that	3318	
8:10 *was* there *any* peace to him that **w out**	3318	
10: 2 therefore they **w** their way as a flock,	5265	
Mt 2: 9 **w before** them, till it came and stood over	4254	
3: 5 Then **w out** to him Jerusalem,	1607	
3:16 **w up** straightway out of the water:	305	
4:23 And Jesus **w about** all Galilee, teaching in	4013	

Mt 4:24 And his fame **w** throughout all Syria:	565	
5: 1 the multitudes, he **w up** into a mountain:	305	
8:32 come out, they **w** into the herd of swine:	565	
8:33 **w** their ways into the city, and told every	565	
9:25 he **w in**, and took her by the hand,	1525	
9:26 And the fame hereof **w abroad** into all	1831	
9:32 As they **w out**, behold, they brought to	1831	
9:35 And Jesus **w about** all the cities and	4013	
11: 7 What **w** ye **out** into the wilderness to see?	1831	
11: 8 But what **w** ye **out** for to see? A man	1831	
11: 9 But what **w** ye **out** for to see? A prophet?	1831	
12: 1 At that time Jesus **w** on the sabbath day	4198	
12: 9 thence, he **w** into their synagogue:	2064	
12:14 Then the Pharisees **w out**, and held a	1831	
13: 1 The same day **w** Jesus **out** of the house,	1831	
13: 2 saying, he **w** into a ship, and sat;	1684	
13: 3 saying, Behold, a sower **w forth** to sow;	1831	
13:25 tares among the wheat, and **w** his way.	565	
13:36 multitude away, and **w** into the house:	2064	
13:46 **w** and sold all that he had, and bought it.	565	
14:12 and buried it, and **w** and told Jesus.	2064	
14:14 And Jesus **w forth**, and saw a great	1831	
14:23 he **w up** into a mountain apart to pray:	305	
14:25 in the fourth watch of the night Jesus **w**	565	
15:21 Then Jesus **w** thence, and departed into	1831	
15:29 and **w up** into a mountain, and sat down	305	
18:13 the ninety and nine which **w** not **astray**.	4105	
18:28 But the same servant **w out**, and found	1831	
18:30 and **w** and cast him into prison, till he should	565	
19:22 heard *that* saying, he **w away** sorrowful:	565	
20: 1 which **w out** early in the morning to hire	1831	
20: 3 And he **w out** about the third hour,	1831	
20: 4 I will give you. And they **w** their way.	565	
20: 5 Again he **w out** about the sixth and	1831	
20: 6 And about the eleventh hour he **w out**,	1831	
21: 6 And the disciples **w**, and did as Jesus	4198	
21: 9 And the multitudes that **w before**,	4254	
21:12 And Jesus **w into** the temple of God,	1525	
21:17 and **w out** of the city into Bethany;	1831	
21:29 will not: but afterward he repented, and **w**.	565	
21:30 he answered and said, I *go*, sir: and **w** not.	565	
21:33 to husbandmen, and **w into a far country**:	589	
22: 5 But they made light of *it*, and **w** their ways,	565	
22:10 those servants **w out** into the *high*ways,	1831	
22:15 Then **w** the Pharisees, and took counsel	4198	
22:22 and left him, and **w** their way.	565	
24: 1 And Jesus **w out**, and departed from	1831	
25: 1 and **w forth** to meet the bridegroom.	1831	
25:10 And while they **w** to buy, the bridegroom	565	
25:10 they *that were* ready **w in** with him to	1525	
25:16 he that had received the five talents **w**	4198	
25:18 he that had received one **w** and digged in	565	
25:25 and **w** and hid thy talent in the earth:	565	
26:14 Judas Iscariot, **w** unto the chief priests,	4198	
26:30 they **w out** into the mount of Olives.	1831	
26:39 And he **w** a little **further**, and fell on his	4281	
26:42 He **w away** again the second time,	565	
26:44 and he **w away** again, and prayed the third	565	
26:58 off unto the high priest's palace, and **w in**,	1525	
26:75 And he **w out**, and wept bitterly.	1831	
27: 5 and departed, and **w** and hanged himself.	565	
27:53 and **w into** the holy city,	1525	
27:58 he **w** to Pilate, and begged the body of	4334	
27:66 So they **w**, and made the sepulchre sure,	4198	
28: 9 And as they **w** to tell his disciples, behold,	4198	
28:16 Then the eleven disciples **w** *away* into	4198	
Mk 1: 5 And there **w out** unto him all the land of	1607	
1:20 with the hired servants, and **w** after him.	565	
1:21 And they **w into** Capernaum;	1531	
1:35 **w out**, and departed into a solitary place,	1831	
1:45 he **w out**, and began to publish *it* much,	1831	
2:12 up the bed, and **w forth** before *them* all;	1715	
2:13 he **w forth** again by the sea side;	1831	
2:23 that he **w** through the corn fields on	3899	
2:23 and his disciples began, as they **w**,	3598+4160	
2:26 How he **w into** the house of God in	1525	
3: 6 And the Pharisees **w forth**,	1831	
3:19 betrayed him. And they **w into** a house.	2064	
3:21 heard *of it*, they **w out** to lay hold on him:	1831	
4: 3 Behold, there **w out** a sower to sow:	1831	
5:13 And the unclean spirits **w out**,	1831	
5:14 they **w out** to see what it was that was	1831	
5:24 And *Jesus* **w** with him; and much people	565	
6: 1 And he **w out** from thence, and came into	1831	
6: 6 And he **w** round about the villages,	4013	
6:12 And they **w out**, and preached that *men*	1831	
6:24 she **w forth**, and said unto her mother,	1831	
6:27 and he **w** and beheaded him in the prison,	565	
6:51 And he **w up** unto them into the ship;	305	
7:24 and **w** into the borders of Tyre and Sidon,	565	
8:27 And Jesus **w out**, and his disciples, into	1831	
10:22 sad at *that* saying, and **w away** grieved:	565	
10:32 to Jerusalem; and Jesus **w before** them:	4254	
10:46 as he **w** out of Jericho with his disciples	1607	
11: 4 And they **w** their way, and found the colt	565	
11: 9 And they that **w before**, and they that	4254	
11:11 he **w out** unto Bethany with the twelve.	1831	
11:15 Jesus **w** into the temple, and began to	1525	
11:19 even was come, he **w out** of the city.	1607	
12: 1 to husbandmen, and **w into a far country**.	589	
12:12 and they left him, and **w** their way.	565	
13: 1 And as he **w out** of the temple, one of his	1607	
14:10 one of the twelve, **w** unto the chief priests,	565	
14:16 And his disciples **w forth**, and came into	1831	
14:26 they **w out** into the mount of Olives.	1831	

Mk	14:35 And he **w forward** a little, and fell on	4281
	14:39 And again he **w away**, and prayed,	565
	14:68 he **w out** into the porch; and *the* cock	1831
	15:43 and **w in** boldly unto Pilate, and craved	1525
	16: 8 And they **w** quickly, and fled from	1831
	16:10 *And* she **w** and told them that had been	4198
	16:12 as they walked, and **w** into the country.	4198
	16:13 And they **w** and told *it* unto the residue:	565
	16:20 And they **w forth**, and preached every	1831
Lk	1: 9 he **w into** the temple of the Lord.	1525
	1:39 and **w** into the hill country with haste,	4198
	2: 1 *that* there **w** out a decree from Cesar	1831
	2: 3 And all **w** to be taxed, every one into his	4198
	2: 4 And Joseph also **w up** from Galilee, out of	305
	2:41 his parents **w** to Jerusalem every year	4198
	2:42 they **w up** to Jerusalem after the custom	305
	2:44 been in the company, **w** a day's journey;	2064
	2:51 And he **w down** with them, and came to	2597
	4:14 there **w** out a fame of him through all	1831
	4:16 he **w into** the synagogue on	1525
	4:30 through the midst of them **w** *his way*,	4198
	4:37 the fame of him **w** out into every place	1607
	4:42 he departed and **w** into a desert place:	4198
	5:15 *much* the more there **w** a fame **abroad** of	1330
	5:19 **w upon** the housetop, and let him down	305
	5:27 And after these *things* **w forth**,	1831
	6: 1 that he **w through** the corn fields;	1279
	6: 4 How he **w into** the house of God,	1525
	6:12 *that* he **w** out into a mountain to pray,	1831
	6:19 for there **w** virtue out of him,	1831
	7: 6 Jesus **w** with them. And when he was	4198
	7:11 after, *that* he **w** into a city called Nain;	4198
	7:11 and many of his disciples **w** with him,	4848
	7:17 this rumour of him **w forth** throughout	1831
	7:24 What **w** ye out into the wilderness for to	1831
	7:25 But what **w** ye **out** for to see? A man	1831
	7:26 But what **w** ye **out** for to see? A prophet?	1831
	7:36 And he **w into** the Pharisee's house,	1525
	8: 1 that he **w throughout** every city and	1353
	8: 2 out of whom **w** seven devils,	1831
	8: 5 A sower **w out** to sow his seed: and as he	1831
	8:22 that he **w** into a ship with his disciples:	1684
	8:27 And when he **w forth** to land, there met	1831
	8:33 Then **w** the devils **out** of the man,	1831
	8:34 And **w** and told *it* in the city and in	565
	8:35 Then they **w out** to see what was done;	1831
	8:37 and he **w up** into the ship,	1684
	8:39 he **w** his way, and published throughout	565
	8:42 (But as he **w** the people thronged him.	5217
	9: 6 they departed, and **w through** the towns,	1330
	9:10 **w aside** privately into a desert place	5298
	9:28 James, and **w up** into a mountain to pray.	305
	9:52 and they **w**, and entered into a village of	4198
	9:56 to save *them*. And they **w** to another	4198
	9:57 And it came to pass *that*, as they **w** in	4198
	10:30 A certain man **w down** from Jerusalem to	2597
	10:34 And **w to** *him*, and bound up his wounds,	4334
	10:38 Now it came to pass, as they **w**, that he	4198
	11:37 and he **w in**, and sat down to meat.	1525
	13:22 And he **w through** the cities and villages,	1279
	14: 1 as he **w** into the house of one of the chief	2064
	14:25 And there **w** great multitudes **with** him:	4848
	15:15 he **w** and joined himself to a citizen of	4198
	16:30 but if one **w** unto them from the dead,	4198
	17:11 And it came to pass, as he **w** to Jerusalem,	4198
	17:14 And it came to pass *that*, as they **w**,	5217
	17:29 the *same* day that Lot **w out** of Sodom	1831
	18:10 Two men **w up** into the temple to pray;	305
	18:14 this man **w down** to his house justified	2597
	18:39 And they which **w before** rebuked him,	4254
	19:12 A certain nobleman **w** into a far country	4198
	19:28 he **w** before, ascending up to Jerusalem.	
	19:32 And they that were sent **w** their way,	565
	19:36 And as he **w**, they spread their clothes in	4198
	19:45 And he **w into** the temple,	1525
	20: 9 and **w into** a far country for a long time.	589
	21:37 and at night he **w out**, and abode in	1831
	22: 4 And he **w** his way, and communed with	565
	22:13 And they **w**, and found as he had said unto	565
	22:39 And he came out, and **w**, as he was wont,	4198
	22:47 **w before** them, and drew near unto Jesus	4281
	22:62 And Peter **w out**,	1831
	23:52 This *man* **w unto** Pilate, and begged	4334
	24:13 two of them **w** *that* same day to a village	4198
	24:15 himself drew near, and **w with** them.	4848
	24:24 certain of them which were with us **w** to	565
	24:28 nigh unto the village, whither they **w**:	4198
	24:29 And he **w in** to tarry with them.	1525
Jn	2:12 After this he **w down** to Capernaum,	2597
	2:13 was at hand, and Jesus **w up** to Jerusalem,	305
	4:28 and her way into the city, and saith to	565
	4:30 Then they **w out** of the city, and came	1831
	4:43 he departed thence, and **w** into Galilee.	565
	4:45 at the feast: for they also **w** unto the feast.	2064
	4:47 he **w** unto him, and besought him that he	565
	4:50 had spoken unto him, and he **w** *his way*.	4198
	5: 1 of the Jews; and Jesus **w up** to Jerusalem.	305
	5: 4 For an angel **w down** at a *certain* season	2597
	6: 1 After these *things* Jesus **w** over the sea of	565
	6: 3 And Jesus **w up** into a mountain,	424
	6:16 his disciples **w down** unto the sea,	2597
	6:17 and **w** over the sea towards Capernaum.	2064
	6:21 the ship was at the land whither they **w**.	5217
	6:22 that Jesus **w** not **with** his disciples into	4897
	6:66 his disciples **w back**, 565+1519+3588+3694	

Jn	7:10 **w** he also **up** unto the feast, not openly,	305
	7:14 about the midst of the feast Jesus **w up**	305
	7:53 And every man **w** unto his own house.	4198
	8: 1 Jesus **w** unto the mount of Olives.	4198
	8: 9 **w out** one by one, beginning at the eldest,	1831
	8:59 hid himself, and **w out** of the temple,	1831
	9: 7 He **w** his way therefore, and washed,	565
	9:11 and I **w** and washed, and I received sight.	565
	10:40 And **w away** again beyond Jordan into	565
	11:20 that Jesus was coming, **w** and met him:	5221
	11:28 she **w** her way, and called Mary her sister	565
	11:31 that she rose up hastily and **w out**,	1831
	11:46 But some of them **w** their ways to	565
	11:54 **w** thence unto a country near to	565
	11:55 many **w** out of the country **up** to Jerusalem	305
	12:11 reason of him many of the Jews **w away**,	5217
	12:13 and **w forth** to meet him, and cried,	1831
	13: 3 he was come from God, and **w** to God;	5217
	13:30 received the sop **w** immediately **out**:	1831
	18: 1 **w forth** with his disciples over the brook	1831
	18: 4 **w forth**, and said unto them, Whom seek	1831
	18: 6 unto them, I am *he*, they **w** backward,	565
	18:15 **w in** with Jesus into the palace of the	4897
	18:16 Then **w out** *that* other disciple, which	1831
	18:28 they themselves **w** not into the judgment	1525
	18:29 Pilate then **w out** unto them, and said,	1831
	18:38 he **w out** again unto the Jews,	1831
	19: 4 Pilate therefore **w forth** again,	1831
	19: 9 And **w** again **into** the judgment hall,	1525
	19:17 And he bearing his cross **w forth** into a	1831
	20: 3 Peter therefore **w forth**, and *that* other	1831
	20: 5 the linen clothes lying; yet **w** he not **in**.	1525
	20: 6 and **w into** the sepulchre, and seeth	1525
	20: 8 Then **w in** also *that* other disciple,	1525
	20:10 Then the disciples **w away** again unto	565
	21: 3 They **w forth**, and entered into a ship	1831
	21:11 Simon Peter **w up**, and drew the net to	305
	21:23 Then **w** this saying **abroad** among	1831
Ac	1:10 toward heaven as he **w** *up*, behold,	4198
	1:13 they **w up** into an upper room, where	305
	1:21 all the time that the Lord Jesus **w in**	1525
	3: 1 John **w up** together into the temple at	305
	4:23 they **w** to their own *company*, and	2064
	5:26 Then **w** the captain with the officers,	565
	7:15 So Jacob **w down** into Egypt, and died,	2597
	8: 4 **w** every where preaching the word.	1330
	8: 5 Philip **w down** to the city of Samaria,	2718
	8:27 And he arose and **w**: and behold, a man	4198
	8:36 And as they **w** on *their* way, they came	4198
	8:38 and they **w down** both into the water,	2597
	8:39 no more: and he **w** *on* his way rejoicing.	4198
	9: 1 of the Lord, **w** unto the high priest,	4334
	9:17 And Ananias **w** his way, and entered into	565
	9:29 Grecians: but they **w** about to slay him.	2021
	9:39 Then Peter arose and **w with** them.	4905
	10: 9 as they **w** on *their* journey, and drew	3596
	10: 9 Peter **w up** upon the house to pray about	305
	10:21 Then Peter **w down** to the men which	2597
	10:23 on the morrow Peter **w away** with them,	1831
	10:27 he **w in**, and found many *that were* come	1525
	10:38 who **w about** doing good, and healing all	1330
	12: 9 And he **w out**, and followed him;	1831
	12:10 they **w out**, and passed on through one	1831
	12:17 he departed, and **w** into another place.	4198
	12:19 And he **w down** from Judea to Cesarea,	2718
	13:11 he **w about** seeking some to lead him by	4013
	13:14 **w into** the synagogue on the sabbath	1525
	14: 1 that they **w** *both* together **into**	
	14:25 word in Perga, they **w down** into Attalia:	2597
	15:24 that certain which **w out** from us have	1831
	15:38 and **w** not **with** them to the work.	4905
	15:41 And he **w through** Syria and Cilicia,	1330
	16: 4 And as they **w through** the cities,	1279
	16:13 on the sabbath we **w out** of the city by	1831
	16:16 And it came to pass, as we **w** to prayer,	4198
	16:40 And they **w out** of the prison,	1831
	17: 2 **w in** unto them, and three sabbath days	1525
	17:10 who coming *thither* **w** into the synagogue	549
	18:22 the church, he **w down** to Antioch,	2597
	18:23 And **w** over *all* the country of Galatia and	1330
	19: 8 And he **w into** the synagogue,	1525
	19:12 and the evil spirits **w out** of them.	1831
	20:10 And Paul **w down**, and fell on him,	2597
	20:13 And we **w before** to ship, and sailed unto	4281
	21: 5 we departed and **w** *our way*; and *they* all	4198
	21:15 up our carriages, and **w up** to Jerusalem.	305
	21:16 There **w with** us also *certain* of	4905
	21:18 And the *day* following Paul **w in** with us	1524
	21:31 And as *they* **w** about to kill him,	2212
	22: 5 and **w** to Damascus, to bring them which	4198
	22:26 When the centurion *heard* *that*, he **w** and	4334
	23:16 he **w** and entered into the castle,	3854
	23:19 the hand, and **w** *with him* **aside** privately,	402
	24:11 twelve days since I **w up** to Jerusalem for	305
	25: 6 than ten days, he **w down** unto Cesarea;	2597
	26:12 Whereupon as I **w** to Damascus with	4198
	26:21 in the temple, and **w about** to kill *me*.	3987
	28:14 seven days: and so we **w** toward Rome.	2064
Ro	10:18 their sound **w** into all the earth,	1831
2Co	2:13 them, I **w** from *thence* into Macedonia.	1831
	8:17 of his own accord he **w** unto you.	1831
Gal	1:17 Neither **w** I up to Jerusalem to them which	424
	1:17 I **w** into Arabia, and returned again unto	565
	1:18 Then after three years I **w up** to Jerusalem	424

Gal	2: 1 Then fourteen years after I **w up** again to	305
	2: 2 And I **w up** by revelation.	305
1Ti	1: 3 at Ephesus, when I **w** into Macedonia,	4198
	1:18 the prophecies which **w before** on thee,	4254
Heb	9: 6 the priests **w** always into the first	1524
	9: 7 into the second **w** the high priest alone	NIG
	11: 8 and he **w** out, not knowing whither he	1831
	11: 8 he went out, not knowing whither he **w**.	2064
1Pe	3:19 By which also he **w** and preached unto	4198
1Jn	2:19 They **w** from us, but they were not of	1831
	2:19 *they* **w out**, that they might be made	NIG
3Jn	1: 7 for his name's sake they **w forth**,	1831
Rev	1:16 out of his mouth **w** a sharp twoedged	1607
	6: 2 he **w forth** conquering, and to conquer.	1831
	6: 4 And there **w out** another horse *that was*	1831
	10: 9 And I **w** unto the angel, and said unto him,	565
	12:17 **w** to make war with the remnant of her	565
	16: 2 the first **w**, and poured out his vial upon	565
	20: 9 they **w up** on the breadth of the earth,	305

WENTEST (14) [GO]

Ge	49: 4 because thou **w up** to thy father's bed;	5927
Jdg	5: 4 Lord, when thou **w out** of Seir,	3318
	8: 1 thou **w** to fight with the Midianites?	1980
1Sa	10: 2 asses which thou **w** to seek are found:	1980
2Sa	7: 9 I was with thee whithersoever thou **w**,	1980
	16:17 why **w** thou not with thy friend?	1980
	19:25 Wherefore **w** not thou with me,	1980
Ps	68: 7 when thou **w forth** before thy people,	3318
Isa	57: 7 even thither **w** thou **up** to offer sacrifice.	5927
	57: 9 thou **w** to the king with ointment,	7788
Jer	2: 2 when thou **w** after me in the wilderness,	1980
	31:21 highway, *even* the way *which* thou **w**:	1980
Hab	3:13 Thou **w forth** for the salvation of thy	3318
Ac	11: 3 Saying, Thou **w in** to men uncircumcised,	1525

WEPT (71) [WEEP]

Ge	21:16 against *him*, and lift up her voice, and **w**.	1058
	27:38 And Esau lift up his voice, and **w**.	1058
	29:11 and lifted up his voice, and **w**.	1058
	33: 4 on his neck, and kissed him: and they **w**.	1058
	37:35 son mourning. Thus his father **w** for him.	1058
	42:24 turned himself about from them, and **w**;	1058
	43:30 he entered into *his* chamber, and **w** there.	1058
	45: 2 he **w aloud**: 1065+5414+6963+871.1	
	45:14 upon his brother Benjamin's neck, and **w**;	1058
	45:14 and wept; and Benjamin **w** upon his neck.	1058
	45:15 kissed all his brethren, and **w** upon them:	1058
	46:29 his neck, and **w** on his neck a good while.	1058
	50: 1 and **w** upon him, and kissed him.	1058
	50:17 And Joseph **w** when they spake unto him.	1058
Ex	2: 6 behold, the babe **w**. And she had	1058
Nu	11: 4 the children of Israel also **w** again,	1058
	11:18 for you have **w** in the ears of the Lord,	1058
	11:20 have **w** before him, saying, Why came we	1058
	14: 1 and cried; and the people **w** that night.	1058
Dt	1:45 ye returned and **w** before the Lord;	1058
	34: 8 the children of Israel **w** for Moses in	1058
Jdg	2: 4 that the people lift up their voice, and **w**.	1058
	14:16 Samson's wife **w** before him, and said,	1058
	14:17 she **w** before him the seven days,	1058
	20:23 and **w** before the Lord until even,	1058
	20:26 **w**, and sat there before the Lord,	1058
	21: 2 up their voices, and **w sore**; 1058+1065+1419	
Ru	1: 9 and they lift up their voice, and **w**.	1058
	1:14 They lift up their voice, and **w** again:	1058
1Sa	1: 7 therefore she **w**, and did not eat.	1058
	1:10 prayed unto the Lord, and **w sore**. 1058+1058	
	11: 4 all the people lift up their voices, and **w**.	1058
	20:41 **w** one with another, until David	1058
	24:16 And Saul lift up his voice, and **w**.	1058
	30: 4 *were* with him lift up their voice and **w**,	1058
2Sa	1:12 w, and fasted until even, for Saul,	1058
	3:32 up his voice, and **w** at the grave of Abner;	1058
	3:32 the grave of Abner; and all the people **w**.	1058
	3:34 And all the people **w** again over him.	1058
	12:22 the child *was* yet alive, I fasted and **w**:	1058
	13:36 sons came, and lift up their voice and **w**:	1058
	13:36 and all his servants **w** very sore. 1058+1065	
	15:23 all the country **w** with a loud voice,	1058
	15:30 as he went up, and had his head	1058
	18:33 up to the chamber over the gate, and **w**:	1058
2Ki	8:11 *he* was ashamed: and the man of God **w**.	1058
	13:14 **w** over his face, and said, O my father,	1058
	20: 3 And Hezekiah **w sore**. 1058+1065+1419	
	22:19 hast rent thy clothes, and **w** before me;	1058
Ezr	3:12 before their eyes, **w** with a loud voice;	1058
	10: 1 for the people **w** very **sore**. 1058+1059	
Ne	1: 4 *that* I sat down and **w**, and mourned	1058
	8: 9 For all the people **w**, when they heard	1058
Job	2:12 him not, they lifted up their voice, and **w**;	1058
Ps	69:10 When I **w**, *and* chastened my soul with	1058
	137: 1 of Babylon, there we sat down, yea, we **w**,	1058
Isa	38: 3 And Hezekiah **w sore**. 1058+1065+1419	
Hos	12: 4 he **w**, and made supplication unto him:	1058
Mt	26:75 And he went out, and **w** bitterly:	2799
Mk	5:38 that we and wailed greatly.	2799
	14:72 And when he thought thereon, he **w**.	2799
	16:10 been with him, as they mourned and **w**.	2799
Lk	7:32 have mourned to you, and ye have not **w**.	2799
	8:52 And all **w**, and bewailed her: but he said,	2799
	19:41 he beheld the city, and **w** over it,	2799
	22:62 And Peter went out, and **w** bitterly.	2799
Jn	11:35 Jesus **w**.	1145
	20:11 and as she **w**, she stooped down,	2799

Ac 20:37 And *they* all **w** sore, and fell on 1096+2805
1Co 7:30 they that weep, as though they **w** not; 2799
Rev 5: 4 I **w** much, because no *man* was found 2799

WERE (2776) [BE] See Index of Articles, Etc.

WERT (6) [BE]
Job 8: 6 If thou **w** pure and upright; surely now he NIH
SS 8: 1 O that thou **w** as my brother, that sucked NIH
Ro 11:17 **w** graffed in amongst them, and with NIG
 11:24 For if thou **w** cut out of the olive tree NIG
 11:24 **w** graffed contrary to nature into a good NIG
Rev 3:15 cold nor hot: I would thou **w** cold or hot. 1510

WEST (69) [WESTERN, WESTWARD]
Ge 12: 8 *having* Beth-el on the **w**, and Hai on 3220
 28:14 thou shalt spread abroad to the **w**, 3220
Ex 10:19 the LORD turned a mighty strong **w** wind, 3220
 27:12 for the breadth of the court on the **w** side 3220
 38:12 the **w** side *were* hangings of fifty cubits, 3220
Nu 2:18 On the **w** side *shall be* the standard of 3220
 34: 6 for a border: this shall be your **w** border. 3220
 35: 5 on the **w** side two thousand cubits, 3220
Dt 33:23 possess thou the **w** and the south. 3220
Jos 8: 9 and Ai, on the **w side** of Ai: 3220
 8:12 and Ai, on the **w side** of the city. 3220
 8:13 their liers in wait on the **w** of the city, 3220
 11: 2 and in the borders of Dor on the **w**, 3220
 11: 3 the Canaanite on the east and on the **w**, 3220
 12: 7 Israel smote on this side Jordan on the **w**, 3220
 15:12 the border *was* to the great sea, 3220
 18:14 children of Judah: this *was* the **w** quarter. 3220
 18:15 the border went out on the **w**, and went 3220
 19:34 reacheth to Asher on the **w** side, 3220
1Ki 7:25 three looking toward the **w**, 3220
1Ch 9:24 toward the east, **w**, north, and south. 3220
 12:15 *both* toward the east, and toward the **w**. 4628
2Ch 4: 4 three looking toward the **w** *side* of 3220
 32:30 brought it straight down to the **w** *side* of 4628
 33:14 on the **w** *side* of Gihon, in the valley, 4628
Ps 75: 6 nor from the **w**, nor from the south. 4628
 103:12 As far as the east is from the **w**, *so far* 4628
 107: 3 from the east, and from the **w**, from 4628
Isa 11:14 shoulders of the Philistines toward the **w**; 3220
 43: 5 the east, and gather thee from the **w**; 4628
 45: 6 the **w**, that *there is* none besides me. 4628
 49:12 lo, these from the north and from the **w**; 3220
 59:19 fear the name of the LORD from the **w**, 4628
Eze 41:12 toward the **w** *was* seventy cubits broad; 3220
 42:19 He turned about to the **w** side, 3220
 45: 7 from the **w** side westward, and from 3220
 45: 7 from the **w** border unto the east border. 3220
 47:20 The **w** side also *shall be* the great sea 3220
 47:20 over against Hamath. This *is* the **w** side. 3220
 48: 1 for these are his sides east *and* **w**; 3220
 48: 2 the east side unto the **w** side, 3220+1886.5
 48: 3 the east side even unto the **w** 3220+1886.5
 48: 4 the east side unto the **w** side, 3220+1886.5
 48: 5 the east side unto the **w** side, 3220+1886.5
 48: 6 the east side even unto the **w** 3220+1886.5
 48: 7 the east side unto the **w** side, 3220+1886.5
 48: 8 the east side unto the **w** side, 3220+1886.5
 48: 8 the east side unto the **w** side: 3220+1886.5
 48:10 toward the **w** ten thousand *in* breadth, 3220
 48:16 the **w** side four thousand and 3220+1886.5
 48:17 and toward the **w** two hundred and fifty. 3220
 48:21 thousand toward the **w** border, 3220+1886.5
 48:23 the east side unto the **w** side, 3220+1886.5
 48:24 the east side unto the **w** side, 3220+1886.5
 48:25 the east side unto the **w** side, 3220+1886.5
 48:26 the east side unto the **w** side, 3220+1886.5
 48:27 the east side unto the **w** side, 3220+1886.5
 48:34 *At* the **w** side four thousand and 3220
Da 8: 5 the goat came from the **w** on the face of 4628
Hos 11:10 the children shall tremble from the **w**. 3220
Zec 8: 7 and from **the w** country; 3996+8121+1886.1
 14: 4 toward the east and toward the **w**, 3220
Mt 8:11 many shall come from the east and **w**, 1424
 24:27 of the east, and shineth *even* unto the **w**; 1424
Lk 12:54 When ye see a cloud rise out of the **w**, 1424
 13:29 and *from* the **w**, and from the north, 1424
Ac 27:12 and lieth toward the **south w** and 3047
 27:12 lieth toward the south west and **north w**. 5566
Rev 21:13 three gates; and on the **w** three gates. 1424

WESTERN (1) [WEST]
Nu 34: 6 *as for* the **w** border, you shall even have 3220

WESTWARD (26) [WEST]
Ge 13:14 southward, and eastward, and **w**: 3220+1886.5
Ex 26:22 for the sides of the tabernacle **w** 3220+1886.5
 26:27 tabernacle, for the two sides **w**. 3220+1886.5
 36:27 for the sides of the tabernacle **w** 3220+1886.5
 36:32 of the tabernacle for the sides **w**. 3220+1886.5
Nu 3:23 pitch behind the tabernacle **w**. 3220+1886.5
Dt 3:27 thine eyes **w**, and northward, 3220+1886.5
Jos 5: 1 *were* on the side of Jordan **w**, 3220+1886.5
 15: 8 before the valley of Hinnom **w**, 3220+1886.5
 15:10 from Baalah **w** unto mount Seir, 3220+1886.5
 16: 3 goeth down to the coast of 3220+1886.5
 16: 8 Tappuah **w** *unto* the river Kanah; 3220+1886.5
 18:12 up through the mountains **w**; 3220+1886.5
 19:26 reacheth to Carmel **w**, 3220+1886.5
 19:34 coast turneth **w** *to* Aznoth-tabor, 3220+1886.5
 22: 7 brethren on *this* side Jordan **w**. 3220+1886.5

Jos 23: 4 even *unto* the great sea **w**. 3996+8121+1886.1
1Ch 7:28 and **w** Gezer, 4628+1886.1+3807.1
 26:16 and Hosah *the* lot came forth **w**, 4628
 26:18 At Parbar **w**, four at the causeway, 4628
 26:30 **w** in all the business of 4628+1886.5
Eze 45: 7 from the west side **w**, and from 3220+1886.5
 46:19 *was* a place on the two sides **w**. 3220+1886.5
 48:18 and ten thousand **w**: 3220+1886.5
 48:21 **w** over against the five and 3220+1886.5
Da 8: 4 I saw the ram pushing **w**, 3220+1886.5

WET (6)
Job 24: 8 They are **w** with the showers of 7372
Da 4:15 let it be **w** with the dew of heaven, 6647
 4:23 let it be **w** with the dew of heaven, 6647
 4:25 *shall* **w** with the dew of heaven, 6647
 4:33 his body was **w** with the dew of heaven, 6647
 5:21 his body was **w** with the dew of heaven; 6647

WHALE (2) [WHALE'S, WHALES]
Job 7:12 *Am* I a sea, or a **w**, that thou settest a 8577
Eze 32: 2 nations, and thou *art* as a **w** in the seas: 8577

WHALE'S (1) [WHALE]
Mt 12:40 three days and three nights in the **w** belly; 2785

WHALES (1) [WHALE]
Ge 1:21 God created great **w**, and every living 8577

WHAT (984) [SOMEWHAT, WHATSOEVER]
Ge 2:19 brought *them* unto Adam to see **w** he 4100
 3:13 woman, **W** *is* this *that* thou hast done? 4100
 4:10 he said, **W** hast thou done? the voice of 4100
 9:24 **w** his younger son had done unto him. 834
 12:18 **W** *is* this *that* thou hast done unto me? 4100
 15: 2 Lord GOD, **w** wilt thou give me, 4100
 20: 9 said unto him, **W** hast thou done unto us? 4100
 20: 9 have I offended thee, that thou hast 4100
 20:10 **W** sawest thou, that thou hast done this 4100
 21:17 unto her, **W** aileth thee, Hagar? 4100+3807.1
 21:29 **W** *mean* these seven ewe lambs which 4100
 23:15 of silver; **w** *is* that betwixt me and thee? 4100
 24:65 **W** man *is* this that walketh in the field 4310
 25:32 **w** *profit* shall this birthright do 4100+3807.1
 26:10 **W** *is* this thou hast done unto us? 4100
 27:37 and **w** I do now unto thee, my son? 4100
 27:46 daughters of the land, **w good** 4100+3807.1
 29:15 tell me, **w** *shall* my wages *be?* 4100
 29:25 **W** *is* this thou hast done unto me? 4100
 30:31 he said, **W** shall I give thee? And Jacob 4100
 31:26 Laban said to Jacob, **W** hast thou done, 4100
 31:32 our brethren discern thou **w** *is* thine 4100
 31:36 and said to Laban, **W** *is* my trespass? 4100
 31:36 **w** *is* my sin, that thou hast *so* hotly 4100
 31:37 **w** hast thou found of all thy household 4100
 31:43 **w** can I do *this* day unto these my 4100
 32:27 he said unto him, **W** *is* thy name? And he 4100
 33: 8 **W** meanest thou by all this drove which I 4310
 33:15 said, **W** needeth it? let me find 4100+3807.1
 34:11 and **w** ye shall say unto me I will give. 834
 37:10 **W** *is* this dream that thou hast dreamed? 4100
 37:15 man asked him, saying, **W** seekest thou? 4100
 37:20 we shall see **w** will become of his dreams. 4100
 37:26 **W** profit *is it* if we slay our brother, 4100
 38:16 she said, **W** wilt thou give me, that thou 4100
 38:18 he said, **W** pledge shall I give thee? 4100
 39: 8 my master wotteth not **w** *is* with me in 4100
 41:25 God hath shewed Pharaoh **w** *is* about 834
 41:28 **W** God *is* about to do he sheweth unto 834
 41:55 Go unto Joseph; **w** he saith to you, 834
 42:28 saying one to another, **W** *is* this 4100+3807.1
 44:15 **W** deed *is* this that ye have done? 4100
 44:16 Judah said, **W** shall we say unto my lord? 4100
 44:16 **w** shall we speak? or how shall we clear 4100
 46:33 and shall say, **W** *is* your occupation? 4100
 47: 3 unto his brethren, **W** *is* your occupation? 4100
Ex 2: 4 afar off, to wit **w** would be done to him. 4100
 3:13 and they shall say to me, **W** *is* his name? 4100
 3:13 *is* his name? **w** shall I say unto them? 4100
 4: 2 said unto him, **W** *is* that in thine hand? 4100
 4:12 mouth, and teach thee **w** thou shalt say. 834
 4:15 mouth, and will teach you **w** ye shall do. 834
 6: 1 Now shalt thou see **w** I will do to Pharaoh: 834
 10: 2 **w** things I have wrought in Egypt, and my 834
 10:26 we know not with **w** we must serve 4100
 12:26 say unto you, **W** mean you by this service? 4100
 13:14 thee in time to come, saying, **W** *is* this? 4100
 15:24 against Moses, saying, **W** shall we drink? 4100
 16: 7 and **w** *are* we, that ye murmur against us? 4100
 16: 8 **w** *are* we? your murmurings *are* not 4100
 16:15 they wist not **w** it *was*. And Moses said 4100
 16:15 **W** shall I do unto this people? 4100
 18:14 **W** *is* this thing that thou doest to 4100
 19: 4 Ye have seen **w** I did unto the Egyptians, 834
 23:11 **w** they leave the beasts of the field shall NIH
 32: 1 of Egypt, we wot not **w** is become of him. 4100
 32:21 **W** did this people unto thee, that thou 4100
 32:23 of Egypt, we wot not **w** is become of him. 4100
 33: 5 that I may know **w** to do unto thee. 4100
Lev 15: 9 **w** saddle **soever** he rideth upon that 834+3605
 17: 3 **W man soever** *there be* of the house 376+376
 22: 4 **W man soever** of the seed of Aaron 376+376
 25:20 shall say, **W** shall we eat the seventh year? 4100
Nu 9: 8 I will hear **w** the LORD will command 4100
 10:32 *that* **w** goodness the LORD shall do 834+1931

Nu 13:18 **w** it *is;* and the people that dwelleth 4100
 13:19 **w** the land *is* that they dwell in, whether 4100
 13:19 **w** cities they *be* that they dwell in, 4100
 13:20 **w** the land *is*, whether it *be* fat or lean, 4100
 15:34 it was not declared **w** should be done to 4100
 16:11 **w** *is* Aaron, that ye murmur against him? 4100
 21:14 **W** he did in the Red sea, and *in* the 2052
 22: 9 and said, **W** men *are* these with thee? 4310
 22:19 that I may know **w** the LORD will say 4100
 22:28 unto Balaam, **W** have I done unto thee, 4100
 23:11 unto Balaam, **W** hast thou done unto me? 4100
 23:17 said unto him, **W** hath the LORD spoken? 4100
 23:23 and of Israel, **W** hath God wrought! 4100
 24:13 *but* **w** the LORD saith, that will I speak? 834
 24:14 I will advertise thee **w** this people shall do 834
 26:10 **w time** the fire devoured two hundred 871.1
 31:50 **w** every man hath gotten, *of* jewels of gold, 834
Dt 1:22 bring us word again by **w** way we must go 834
 1:22 go up, and into **w** cities we shall come. 1886.3
 1:33 to shew you by **w** way ye should go, and in 834
 3:24 for **w** God *is there* in heaven or in earth, 4310
 4: 3 Your eyes have seen **w** the LORD did 834
 4: 7 For **w** nation *is there* so great, who hath 4310
 4: 8 **w** nation *is there* so great, that hath 4310
 6:20 **W** *mean* the testimonies, and the statutes, 4100
 7:18 shalt well remember **w** the LORD thy God 834
 8: 2 prove thee, to know **w** *was* in thine heart, 834
 10:12 **w** doth the LORD thy God require of thee, 4100
 11: 4 **w** he did unto the army of Egypt, unto 834
 11: 5 **w** he did unto you in the wilderness, until 834
 11: 6 **w** he did unto Dathan and Abiram, 834
 12:32 **W** thing **soever** I command you, 834+3605
 20: 5 **W** man *is there* that hath built a new 4310
 20: 6 **w** man *is he* that hath planted a vineyard, 4310
 20: 7 **w** man *is there* that hath betrothed a wife, 4310
 20: 8 **W** man *is there* that *is* fearful and 4310
 24: Remember **w** the LORD thy God did unto 834
 25:17 Remember **w** Amalek did unto thee by 834
 29:24 **w** *meaneth* the heat of this great anger? 4100
 32:20 I will see **w** their end *shall be:* for they 4100
Jos 2:10 **w** you did unto the two kings of 834
 4: 6 **W** mean you by these stones? 4100
 4:21 to come, saying, **W** *mean* these stones? 4100
 5:14 **w** saith my lord unto his servant? 4100
 7: 8 O Lord, **w** shall I say, when Israel turneth 4100
 7: 9 and **w** wilt thou do unto thy great name? 4100
 7:19 tell me now **w** thou hast done; hide *it* not 4100
 9: 3 when the inhabitants of Gibeon heard **w** 834
 15:18 Caleb said unto her, **W** wouldest thou? 4100
 22:16 **W** trespass *is* this that ye have committed 4100
 22:24 have you to do with the LORD God of 4100
 24: 7 eyes have seen **w** I have done in Egypt: 834
Jdg 1:14 and Caleb said unto her, **W** wilt thou? 4100
 7:11 thou shalt hear **w** they say; 4100
 8: 2 **W** have I done now in comparison of you? 4100
 8: 3 **w** was I able to do in comparison of you? 4100
 8:18 **W manner** of men *were they* whom ye 375
 9:48 **W** ye have seen me do, make haste, 4100
 10:18 **W** man *is he* that will begin to fight 4310
 11:12 saying, **W** hast thou to do with me, 4100
 13: 8 teach us **w** we shall do unto the child that 4100
 13:17 the angel of the LORD, **W** *is* thy name, 4310
 14: 6 his father or his mother **w** he had done. 834
 14:18 went down, **W** *is* sweeter than honey? 4100
 14:18 **w** *is* stronger than a lion? And he said 4100
 15:11 **w** *is* this *that* thou hast done unto us? 4100
 16: 5 by **w** *means* we may prevail against him, 4100
 18: 3 **w** makest thou in this *place?* and what 4100
 18: 3 thou in this *place?* and **w** hast thou here? 4100
 18: 8 their brethren said unto them, **W** *say* ye? 4100
 18:14 now therefore consider **w** ye have to do. 4100
 18:18 Then said the priest unto them, **W** do ye? 4100
 18:23 and said unto Micah, **W** aileth thee, 4100
 18:24 **w** have I more? and what is this *that* ye 4100
 18:24 **w** is this *that* ye say unto me, What aileth 4100
 18:24 is this *that* ye say unto me, **W** aileth thee? 4100
 19:24 with them **w** seemeth good unto you: 1886.1
 20:12 **W** wickedness *is* this that is done among 4100
 21: 8 **W** one *is there* of the tribes of Israel that 4310
Ru 2:18 her mother in law saw **w** she had gleaned: 834
 3: 4 and he will tell thee **w** thou shalt do. 834
 3: 4 **w** day thou buyest the field of the hand of NIH
1Sa 1:23 said unto her, Do **w** seemeth thee good; 1886.1
 3:17 **W** *is* the thing that *the* LORD hath said 4100
 3:18 let him do **w** seemeth him good. 1886.1
 4: 6 **W** *meaneth* the noise of this great shout 4100
 4:14 **W** *meaneth* the noise of this tumult? 4100
 4:16 **W** is there done, my son? 1697+4100+1886.1
 5: 8 **W** shall we do with the ark of the God of 4100
 6: 2 **W** shall we do to the ark of the LORD? 4100
 6: 4 **W** *shall be* the trespass offering which we 4100
 9: 7 if we go, **w** shall we bring the man? 4100
 9: 7 to bring to the man of God: **w** have we? 4100
 10: 2 for you, saying, **W** shall I do for my son? 4100
 10: 8 to thee, and shew thee **w** thou shalt do. 834
 10:11 **W** *is* this *that* is come unto the son of 4100
 10:15 I pray thee, **w** Samuel said unto you. 4100
 11: 5 **W** aileth the people that they weep? 4100
 13:11 Samuel said, **W** hast thou done? And Saul 4100
 14:40 Saul, Do **w** seemeth good unto thee. 1886.1
 14:43 to Jonathan, Tell me **w** thou hast done. 4100
 15:14 **W** *meaneth* then this bleating of the 4100
 15:16 I will tell thee **w** the LORD hath said to me 834
 16: 3 and I will shew thee **w** thou shalt do: 834
 17:26 **W** shall be done to the man that killeth 4100

W

1Sa 17:29 David said, **W** have I now done? *Is there* 4100
18: 8 and **w** can he have more but the kingdom? NIH
18:18 **w** is my life, *or* my father's family in 4310
19: 3 of thee; and **w** I see, that I will tell thee. 4100
20: 1 and said before Jonathan, **W** have I done? 4100
20: 1 **w** *is* mine iniquity? and what *is* my sin 4100
20: 1 **w** is my sin before thy father, that he 4100
20:10 or **w** *if* thy father answer thee roughly? 4100
20:32 shall he be slain? **w** hath he done? 4100
21: 2 send thee, and **w** I have commanded thee: 834
21: 3 Now therefore **w** is under thine hand? 4100
21: 3 in mine hand, or **w** there is present. 1886.1
22: 3 you, till I know **w** God will do for me. 4100
25:17 know and consider **w** thou wilt do; 4100
26:18 for **w** have I done? or what evil *is* in mine 4100
26:18 have I done? or **w** evil *is* in mine hand? 4100
28: 2 thou shalt know **w** thy servant can do. 834
28: 9 Behold, thou knowest **w** Saul hath done, 834
28:13 for **w** sawest thou? And the woman said 4100
28:14 he said unto her, **W** form is he of? 4100
28:15 *thou* mayest make known unto me **w** I 4100
29: 3 **W** *do* these Hebrews *here?* And Achish 4100
29: 8 said unto Achish, But **w** have I done? 4100
29: 8 **w** hast thou found in thy servant so long 4100
2Sa 3:24 to the king, and said, **W** hast thou done? 4100
7:18 **w** is my house, that thou hast brought me 4310
7:20 **w** can David say more unto thee? 4100
7:23 **w** one nation in the earth *is* like thy 4310
9: 8 bowed himself, and said, **W** *is* thy servant, 4100
12:21 **W** thing *is* this that thou hast done? 4100
14: 5 the king said unto her, **W** aileth thee? 4100
15: 2 and said, Of **w** city *art* thou? 335+2088+4480
15:21 surely in **w** place my lord the king shall be, 834
15:35 *that* **w** thing **soever** thou shalt hear 834+3605
16: 2 said unto Ziba, **W** meanest thou by these? 4100
16:10 the king said, **W** have I to do with you, 4100
16:20 Give counsel among you **w** we shall do. 4100
17: 5 and let us hear likewise **w** he saith. 4100
18: 4 unto them, **W** seemeth you best I will do. 834
18:21 Cushi, Go tell the king **w** thou hast seen. 834
18:29 a great tumult, but I knew not **w** *it was.* 4100
19:18 and to do **w** he thought good. 1886.1
19:22 David said, **W** have I to do with you, 4100
19:27 do therefore **w** *is* good in thine eyes. 1886.1
19:28 **W** right therefore have I yet to cry any 4100
19:35 thy servant taste **w** I eat or what I drink? 834
19:35 thy servant taste what I eat or **w** I drink? 834
19:37 do to him **w** shall seem good unto thee. 834
21: 3 unto the Gibeonites, **W** shall I do for you? 4100
21: 4 he said, **W** you shall say, *that* will I do for 4100
21:11 it was told David **w** Rizpah the daughter of 834
24:13 see **w** answer I shall return *to* him that 4100
24:17 these sheep, **w** have they done? let thine 4100
24:22 and offer up **w** seemeth good unto thee: 1886.1
1Ki 1:16 And the king said, **W** wouldest thou? 4100
2: 5 Moreover thou knowest also **w** Joab did 834
2: 5 **w** he did to the two captains of the hosts of 834
2: 9 knowest **w** thou oughtest to do unto him; 834
3: 5 God said, Ask **w** I shall give thee. 4100
8:38 **W** prayer and supplication soever be 3605
9:13 **W** cities *are* these which thou hast given 4100
11:22 **w** *hast* thou lacked with me, that behold, 4100
12: 9 **W** counsel give ye that we may answer 4100
12:16 saying, **W** portion have we in David? 4100
13:12 said unto them, **W** way went he? 335+2088
13:12 For his sons had seen **w** way the man of 1886.1
14: 3 he shall tell thee **w** shall become of 4100
14:14 of Jeroboam that day: but **w**? even now. 4100
16: 5 of Baasha, and **w** he did, and his might, 834
17:18 **W** have I to do with thee, O thou man of 4100
18: 9 he said, **W** have I sinned, that thou 4100
18:13 Was it not told my lord **w** I did when 834
19: 9 said unto him, **W** doest thou here, Elijah? 4100
19:13 and said, **W** doest thou here, Elijah? 4100
19:20 Go back again: for **w** have I done to thee? 4100
20:22 and mark, and see **w** thou doest: 834
22:14 the LORD saith unto me, that will I 834
2Ki 1: 7 **W** manner of man *was* he which came up 4100
2: 9 said unto Elisha, Ask **w** I shall do for thee, 4100
3:13 king of Israel, **W** have I to do with thee? 4100
4: 2 Elisha said unto her, **W** shall I do for thee? 4100
4: 2 tell me, **w** hast thou in the house? 4100
4:13 all this care; **w** *is* to be done for thee? 4100
4:14 he said, **W** then *is* to be done for her? 4100
4:43 servitor said, **W**, should I set this before 4100
6:28 the king said unto her, **W** aileth thee? 4100
6:33 **w** should I wait for the LORD any longer? 4100
7:12 I will now shew you **w** the Syrians have 834
8:13 Hazael said, But **w**, *is* thy servant a dog, 4100
8:14 who said to him, **w** said Elisha to thee? 4100
9:18 Jehu said, **W** hast thou to do with peace? 4100
9:19 **W** hast thou to do with peace? 4100
9:22 **w** peace, so long as the whoredoms of 4100
18:19 **W** confidence *is* this where*in* thou 4100
19:11 thou hast heard **w** the kings of Assyria 834
20: 8 **W** *shall be* the sign that the LORD will 4100
20:14 and said unto him, **W** said these men? 4100
20:15 said, **W** have they seen in thine house? 4100
22:19 when thou heardest **w** I spake against this 834
23:17 he said, **W** title *is* that that I see? 4100
1Ch 12:32 the times, to know **w** Israel ought to do; 4100
17:16 am I, O LORD God, and **w** *is* mine house, 4310
17:18 for thine honour, **w** can David *speak* more to thee for 4100
17:21 **w** one nation in the earth *is* like thy 4310
21:12 advise thyself **w** word I shall bring again 4100

1Ch 21:17 *as for* these sheep, **w** have they done? 4100
29:14 who *am* I, and **w** *is* my people, that we 4310
2Ch 1: 7 said unto him, Ask **w** I shall give thee. 4100
6:29 *Then* **w** prayer *or* what supplication 3605
6:29 **w** supplication soever shall be *made* of 3605
10: 6 **W** counsel give ye *me* to return answer to 349
10: 9 **W** advice give ye that we may return 4100
10:16 saying, **W** portion have we in David? 4100
18:13 even **w** my God saith, that will I speak. 834
19: 6 said to the judges, Take heed **w** ye do: 4100
19:10 **w** cause **soever** shall come to you of 834+3605
20:12 against us; neither know we **w** to do: 4100
24:11 that at **w** time the chest was brought unto NIH
25: 9 **w** *shall we* do for the hundred talents 4100
32:13 Know ye not **w** I and my fathers have 4100
35:21 **w** have I to do with thee, thou king 4100
Ezr 5: 4 **W** are the names of the men that make 4479
6: 8 I make a decree **w** ye shall 1768+3964+3807.2
8:17 I told them **w** they should say unto Iddo, 1697
9:10 O our God, **w** shall we say after this? 4100
Ne 2: 4 For **w** dost thou make request? 4100+4100
2:12 neither told I *any* man **w** my God had put 4100
2:16 knew not whither I went, or **w** I did; 4100
2:19 and said, **W** is this thing that ye do? 4100
4: 2 and said, **W** do *these* feeble Jews? 4100
4:20 In **w** place *therefore* ye hear the sound of 834
13:17 **W** evil thing *is* this that ye do, 4100
Est 1:15 **W** shall *we* do unto the queen Vashti 4100
2: 1 **w** she had done, and what was decreed 834
2: 1 had done, and **w** was decreed against her. 834
2:11 Esther did, and **w** should become of her. 4100
2:15 but **w** Hegai the king's chamberlain, 834
4: 5 to know **w** it was, and why it was. 4100
5: 3 unto her, **W** wilt thou, queen Esther? 4100
5: 3 **w** *is* thy request? it shall be even given 4100
5: 6 at the banquet of wine, **W** *is* thy petition? 4100
6: 3 **w** honour and dignity hath been done to 4100
6: 6 **W** shall be done unto the man whom 4100
7: 2 of wine, **W** *is* thy petition, queen Esther? 4100
7: 2 **w** *is* thy request? and it shall be 4100
8: 1 for Esther had told **w** he *was* unto her. 4100
9: 5 did **w** they would unto those that hated 3509.1
9:12 **w** have they done in the rest of the king's 4100
9:12 now **w** *is* thy petition? and it shall be 4100
9:12 or **w** *is* thy request further? and it shall be 4100
Job 2:10 **W**? shall we receive good at the hand of 1571
6:11 **W** *is* my strength, that I should hope? 4100
6:11 **w** *is* mine end, that I should prolong my 4100
6:17 **W** time they wax warm, they vanish: 871.1
6:25 but **w** doth your arguing reprove? 4100
7:17 **W** *is* man, that thou shouldest magnify 4100
7:20 **w** shall I do unto thee, O thou preserver 4100
9:12 who will say unto him, **W** doest thou? 4100
11: 8 *It is* as high as heaven; **w** canst thou do? 4100
11: 8 deeper than hell; **w** canst thou know? 4100
13: 2 **W** ye know, *the same* do I know also. 3509.1
13:13 I may speak, and let come on me **w** *will.* 4100
15: 9 **W** knowest thou, that we know not? 4100
15: 9 **w** understandest thou, which *is* not in us? NIH
15:12 thee away? and **w** do thine eyes wink at, 4100
15:14 **W** *is* man, that he should be clean? 4100
16: 3 **w** emboldeneth thee that thou answerest? 4100
16: 6 and *though* I forbear, **w** am I eased? 4100
21:15 **W** *is* the Almighty, that we should serve 4100
21:15 **w** profit should we have, if we pray unto 4100
21:21 For **w** pleasure hath he in his house after 4100
21:31 and who shall repay him **w** he hath done? NIH
22:17 and **w** can the Almighty do for them? 4100
23: 5 and understand **w** he would say unto me. 4100
23:13 **w** his soul desireth, even *that* he doeth. NIH
27: 8 For **w** *is* the hope of the hypocrite, 4100
31: 2 For **w** portion of God *is there* from above? 4100
31: 2 **w** inheritance of the Almighty from on NIH
31:14 **W** then shall I do when God riseth up? 4100
31:14 when he visiteth, **w** shall I answer him? 4100
32:11 whilst you searched out **w** to say. 4405
34: 4 let us know among ourselves **w** *is* good. 4100
34: 7 **W** man *is* like Job, *who* drinketh up 4310
34:33 not I: therefore speak **w** thou knowest. 4100
35: 3 **W** advantage will it be unto thee? 4100
35: 3 **W** profit shall I have, *if I be cleansed* 4100
35: 6 If thou sinnest, **w** doest thou against him? 4100
35: 6 be multiplied, **w** doest thou unto him? 4100
35: 7 If thou be righteous, **w** givest thou him? 4100
35: 7 or **w** receiveth he of thine hand? 4100
37:19 Teach us **w** we shall say unto him; *for* **w** 4100
38:24 **By** **w** way is the light parted, 335+2088
39:18 **W** time she lifteth up herself on high, 3509.1
40: 8 Behold, I am vile; **w** shall I answer thee? 4100
Ps 8: 4 **W** *is* man, that thou art mindful of him? 4100
11: 3 be destroyed, **w** can the righteous do? 4100
25:12 **W** man *is* he that feareth 2088+4310
30: 9 **W** profit *is there* in my blood, when I go 4100
34:12 **W** man *is* he that desireth life, 4310
39: 4 **w** it *is; that* I may know how frail I *am.* 4100
39: 7 now, Lord, **w** wait I for? my hope *is* in 4100
44: 1 **w** work thou didst in their days, in the NIH
46: 8 **w** desolations he hath made in the earth. 834
50:16 **W** hast thou to do to declare my statutes, 4100
56: 3 **W** time I am afraid, I will trust in thee. NIH
56: 4 I will not fear **w** flesh can do unto me. 4100
56:11 will not be afraid **w** man can do unto me. 4100
66:16 I will declare **w** he hath done for my soul. 834
85: 8 I will hear **w** God the LORD will speak: 4100

Ps 89:48 **W** man *is he that* liveth, and shall not see 4310
114: 5 **W** ailed thee, O thou sea, that thou 4100
116:12 **W** shall I render unto the LORD *for* all his 4100
118: 6 I will not fear: **w** can man do unto me? 4100
120: 3 **W** shall be given unto thee? or what shall 4100
120: 3 or **w** shall be done unto thee, thou false 4100
144: 3 LORD, **w** *is* man, that thou takest 4100
Pr 4:19 they know not at **w** they stumble. 4100
10:32 The lips of the righteous know **w** is NIH
23: 1 ruler, consider diligently **w** *is* before thee: 834
25: 8 lest *thou know not* **w** to do in the end 4100
27: 1 for thou knowest not **w** a day may bring 4100
30: 4 **w** *is* his name, and what *is* his son's 4100
30: 4 **w** *is* his son's name, if thou canst tell? 4100
31: 2 **W**, my son? and what, the son of my 4100
31: 2 **w**, the son of my womb? and what, the 4100
31: 2 my womb? and **w**, the son of my vows? 4100
Ecc 1: 3 **W** profit hath a man of all his labour 4100
2: 2 *It is* mad: and of mirth, **W** doeth it? 4100
2: 3 I might see **w** *was* that good for the sons 335
2:12 for **w** can the man *do* that cometh after 4100
2:22 For **w** hath man of all his labour, and of 4100
3: 9 **W** profit *hath* he that worketh in *that* 4100
3:22 for who shall bring him to see **w** shall be 4100
5:11 **w** good *is there* to the owners thereof, 4100
5:16 **w** profit hath he that hath laboured for 4100
6: 8 For **w** hath the wise more than the fool? 4100
6: 8 **w** hath the poor, that knoweth to walk 4100
6:11 that increase vanity, **w** *is* man the better? 4100
6:12 For who knoweth **w** *is* good for man in 4100
6:12 who can tell a man **w** shall be after him 4100
7:10 **W** is *the cause* that the former days were 4100
8: 4 who may say unto him, **W** doest thou? 4100
10:14 a man cannot tell **w** shall be; and what 4100
10:14 shall be after him, who can tell him? 834
11: 2 for thou knowest not **w** evil shall be upon 4100
11: 5 As thou knowest not **w** *is* the way of 4100
SS 5: 9 **W** *is* thy beloved more than *another* 4100
5: 9 **w** *is* thy beloved more than *another* 4100
6:13 **W** will ye see in the Shulamite? As it were 4100
8: 8 **w** shall we do for our sister in the day 4100
Isa 1:11 To **w** purpose *is* the multitude of your 4100
3:15 **W** mean ye *that* ye beat my people to 4100
5: 4 **W** could have been done more to my 4100
5: 5 I will tell you **w** I *will* do to my vineyard? 834
10: 3 **w** will ye do in the day of visitation, 4100
14:32 **W** shall *one* then answer the messengers 4100
19:12 let them know **w** the LORD of hosts hath 4100
21: 6 a watchman, let him declare **w** he seeth. 834
21:11 out of Seir, Watchman, **w** of the night? 4100
21:11 of the night? Watchman, **w** of the night? 4100
22: 1 **W** aileth thee now, that thou art wholly 4100
22:16 **W** hast thou here? and whom hast thou 4100
33:13 Hear, ye *that are* far off, **w** I have done; 834
36: 4 **W** confidence *is* this where*in* thou 834
37:11 thou hast heard **w** the kings of Assyria 834
38:15 **W** shall I say? he hath both spoken unto 4100
38:22 **W** *is* the sign that I shall go up *to* the 4100
39: 3 and said unto him, **W** said these men? 4100
39: 4 said he, **W** have they seen in thine house? 4100
40: 6 he said, **W** shall I cry? All flesh *is* grass, 4100
40:18 or **w** likeness will ye compare unto him? 4100
41:22 *them* forth, and shew us **w** shall happen: 834
41:22 them shew the former *things,* **w** they *be,* 4100
45: 9 to him that fashioneth it, **W** makest thou? 4100
45:10 saith unto *his* father, **W** begettest thou? 4100
45:10 the woman, **W** hast thou brought forth? 4100
52: 5 Now therefore, **w** have I here, saith 4100
64: 4 *w* he hath prepared for him that waiteth NIH
Jer 1:11 unto me, saying, Jeremiah, **w** seest thou? 4100
1:13 the second time, saying, **W** seest thou? 4100
2: 5 **W** iniquity have your fathers found in me, 4100
2:18 **w** hast thou to do in the way of Egypt, 4100
2:18 or **w** hast thou to do in the way of Assyria, 4100
2:23 in the valley, know **w** thou hast done: 4100
4:30 when thou art spoiled, **w** wilt thou do? 4100
5:15 neither understandest **w** they say. 4100
5:31 *it* so: and will ye do in the end thereof? 4100
6:18 know, O congregation, **w** *is* among them. 834
6:20 To **w** purpose cometh there to me incense 4100
7:12 see **w** I did to it for the wickedness of my 834
7:17 Seest thou not **w** they do in the cities of 4100
8: 6 of his wickedness, saying, **W** have I done? 4100
8: 9 of the LORD; and **w** wisdom *is* in them? 4100
9:12 **w** the land perisheth *and* is burnt up like 4100
11:15 **W** hath my beloved to do in mine house, 4100
13:21 **W** wilt thou say when he shall punish 4100
16:10 or **w** *is* our iniquity? or what *is* our sin 4100
16:10 **w** *is* our sin that we have committed 4100
18: 7 *At* **w** instant I shall speak concerning a NIH
18: 9 *at* **w** instant I shall speak concerning a NIH
23:25 I have heard **w** the prophets said, 834
23:28 **W** *is* the chaff to the wheat? saith 4100
23:33 **W** *is* the burden of the LORD? 4100
23:33 thou shalt then say unto them, **W** burden? 4100
23:35 his brother, **W** hath the LORD answered? 4100
23:35 and, **W** hath the LORD spoken? 4100
23:37 **W** hath the LORD answered thee? 4100
23:37 and, **w** hath the LORD spoken? 4100
24: 3 LORD unto me, **W** seest thou, Jeremiah? 4100
32:24 and **w** thou hast spoken is come to pass; 834
33:24 Considerest thou not **w** this people have 4100
37:18 **W** have I offended against thee, 4100
38:25 Declare unto us now **w** thou hast said 4100
38:25 to death; also **w** the king said unto thee: 4100

Jer	48:19 her that escapeth, *and* say, **W** is done?	4100
La	2:13 **W** thing shall I take to witness for thee?	4100
	2:13 w thing shall I liken to thee, O daughter	4100
	2:13 w shall I equal to thee, that I may comfort	4100
	5: 1 Remember, O LORD, **w** is come upon us:	4100
Eze	2: 8 thou, son of man, hear **w** I say unto thee;	834
	8: 6 me, Son of man, seest thou **w** they do?	4100
	8:12 hast thou seen **w** the ancients of the house	834
	12: 9 said unto thee, **W** doest thou?	4100
	12:22 **w** is that proverb *that* ye have in the land	4100
	15: 2 **W** is the vine tree more than any tree,	4100
	17:12 Know ye not **w** these *things* mean? tell	4100
	18: 2 **W** mean ye, that ye use this proverb	4100
	19: 2 say, **W** is thy mother? A lioness: she lay	4100
	20:29 **W** is the high place whereunto ye go?	4100
	21:13 **w** if the *sword* contemn even the rod?	4100
	24:19 Wilt thou not tell us **w** these *things are* to	4100
	27:32 over thee, *saying,* **W** city is like Tyrus,	4310
	33:30 hear **w** is the word that cometh forth	4100
	37:18 Wilt thou not shew us **w** thou meanest by	4100
	47:23 *that* in **w** tribe the stranger sojourneth,	834
Da	2:22 secret *things:* he knoweth **w** is in	4101
	2:23 hast made known unto me now **w** we	1768
	2:28 w shall be in the latter days.	4101
	2:29 thy bed, **w** should come to pass hereafter:	4101
	2:29 known to thee **w** shall come to pass.	4101
	2:45 the king **w** shall come to pass hereafter:	4101
	3: 5 **at w time** ye hear 0.2+1768+5732+871.2	
	3:15 Now if ye be ready that at **w** time ye hear	1768
	4:35 his hand, or say unto him, **W** doest thou?	4101
	8:19 I *will* make thee know **w** shall be in the	834
	10:14 I am come to make thee understand **w**	834
	12: 8 **w** *shall be* the end of these *things?*	4100
Hos	6: 4 O Ephraim, **w** shall I do unto thee?	4100
	6: 4 O Judah, **w** shall I do unto thee? for your	4100
	9: 5 **W** will ye do in the solemn day, and in	4100
	9:14 w wilt thou give? give them a miscarrying	4100
	10: 3 the LORD; **w** then should a king do to us?	4100
	14: 8 Ephraim *shall say,* **W** have I to do any	4100
Joel	3: 4 and **w** have ye to do with me, O Tyre,	4100
Am	4:13 and declareth unto man **w** *is* his thought,	4100
	5:18 to **w end** *is* it for you? the day of 4100+3807.1	
	7: 8 LORD said unto me, Amos, **w** seest thou?	4100
	8: 2 he said, Amos, **w** seest thou? And I said,	4100
Jnh	1: 6 unto him, **W** meanest thou, O sleeper?	4100
	1: 8 evil *is* upon us; **W** *is* thine occupation?	4100
	1: 8 **w** *is* thy country? and of what people *art*	4100
	1: 8 *is* thy country? and of **w** people *art* thou?	2088
	1:11 they unto him, **W** shall we do unto thee,	4100
	4: 5 till he might see **w** would become of	4100
Mic	1: 5 **W** *is* the transgression of Jacob? *is it* not	4310
	1: 5 **w** *are* the high places of Judah? *are they*	4310
	6: 1 Hear ye now **w** the LORD saith; Arise,	834
	6: 3 O my people, **w** have I done unto thee?	4100
	6: 5 remember now **w** Balak king of Moab	4100
	6: 5 w Balaam the son of Beor answered him;	4100
	6: 8 He hath shewed thee, O man, **w** *is* good;	4100
	6: 8 **w** doth the LORD require of thee, but to	4100
Na	1: 9 **W** do ye imagine against the LORD?	4100
Hab	2: 1 will watch to see **w** he will say unto me,	4100
	2: 1 and **w** I shall answer when I am reproved.	4100
	2:18 **W** profiteth the graven image that	4100
Zec	1: 9 said I, O my lord, **w** *are* these?	4100
	1: 9 unto me, I will shew thee **w** these *be.*	4100
	1:19 angel that talked with me, **W** *be* these?	4100
	1:21 said I, **W** come these to do? And he spake,	4100
	2: 2 to see **w** *is* the breadth thereof, 4100+3509.1	
	2: 2 and **w** *is* the length thereof. 4100+3509.1	
	4: 2 said unto me, **W** seest thou? And I said,	4100
	4: 4 with me, saying, **W** *are* these, my lord?	4100
	4: 5 Knowest thou not **w** these *be?* And I said,	4100
	4:11 **W** *are* these two olive trees upon the right	4100
	4:12 **W** *be* these two olive branches which	4100
	4:13 Knowest thou not **w** these *be?* And I said,	4100
	5: 2 he said unto me, **W** seest thou? And I	4100
	5: 5 and see **w** *is* this that goeth forth.	4100
	5: 6 I said, **W** *is* it? And he said, This *is* an	4100
	6: 4 talked with me, **W** *are* these, my lord?	4100
	13: 6 **W** *are* these wounds in thine hands?	4100
Mal	1:13 **w** a weariness *is it!* and ye have snuffed	4100
	3:13 **W** have we spoken so much against thee?	4100
	3:14 **w** profit *is it* that we have kept his	4100
Mt	2: 7 inquired of them diligently **w** time the star	3588
	5:46 them which love you, **w** reward have ye?	5101
	5:47 **w** do ye more *than others?* do not even	5101
	6: 3 let not thy left hand know **w** thy right	5101
	6: 8 for your Father knoweth **w** *things* ye have	3739
	6:25 **w** ye shall eat, or **w** ye shall drink;	5101
	6:25 what ye shall eat, or **w** ye shall drink;	5101
	6:25 nor yet for your body, **w** ye shall put on.	5101
	6:31 take no thought, saying, **W** shall we eat?	5101
	6:31 **W** shall we drink? or, Wherewithal shall	5101
	7: 2 For with **w** judgment ye judge, ye shall be	3739
	7: 2 and with **w** measure ye mete, it shall be	3739
	7: 9 **w** man is there of you, whom if his son	5101
	8:27 saying, **W manner of man** is this,	4217
	8:29 **W** have we to do with thee, Jesus,	5101
	8:33 **w** was befallen to the possessed of	3588
	9:13 But go ye and learn **w** *that* meaneth, I will	5101
	10:19 take no thought how or **w** ye shall speak:	5101
	10:19 you in that *same* hour **w** ye shall speak.	5101
	10:27 **W** I tell you in darkness, *that* speak ye in	3739
	10:27 and **w** ye hear in the ear, *that* preach ye	3739
	11: 7 went ye out into the wilderness to see?	5101
	11: 8 But **w** went ye out for to see? A man	5101

Mt	11: 9 But **w** went ye out for to see? A prophet?	5101
	12: 3 unto them, Have ye not read **w** David did,	5101
	12: 7 if ye had known **w** *this* meaneth, I will	5101
	12:11 **W** man shall there be among you,	5101
	16:26 For **w** is a man profited, if he shall gain	5101
	16:26 **w** shall a man give in exchange for his	5101
	17:25 saying, **W** thinkest thou, Simon?	5101
	18:31 So when his fellowservants saw **w** was	3588
	19: 6 **W** therefore God hath joined together,	3739
	19:16 Good Master, **w** good *thing* shall I do,	5101
	19:20 I kept from my youth up: **w** lack I yet?	5101
	19:27 followed thee; **w** shall we have therefore?	5101
	20:15 Is it not lawful for me to do **w** I will with	3739
	20:21 And he said unto her, **W** wilt thou?	5101
	20:22 and said, Ye know not **w** ye ask.	5101
	20:32 said, **W** will ye *that* I shall do unto you?	5101
	21:16 said unto him, Hearest thou, **w** these say?	5101
	21:23 By **w** authority doest thou these *things?*	4169
	21:24 I in like wise will tell you by **w** authority I	4169
	21:27 Neither tell I you by **w** authority I do	4169
	21:28 But **w** think you? A *certain* man had two	5101
	21:40 **w** will he do unto those husbandmen?	5101
	22:17 Tell us therefore, **W** thinkest thou? Is it	5101
	22:42 **W** think ye of Christ? whose son is	5101
	24: 3 and **w** *shall be* the sign of thy coming,	5101
	24:42 for ye know not **w** hour your Lord doth	5101
	24:43 known in **w** watch the thief would come,	4169
	26: 8 saying, To **w purpose** *is* this waste?	5101
	26:15 And said *unto them,* **W** will ye give me,	5101
	26:40 them asleep, and saith unto Peter, **W,**	3779
	26:62 **w** *is it which* these witness against thee?	5101
	26:65 **w** further need have we of witnesses?	5101
	26:66 **w** think ye? They answered and said,	5101
	26:70 all, saying, I know not **w** thou sayest.	5101
	27: 4 they said, **W** *is that* to us? see thou to	5101
	27:22 **W** shall I do then with Jesus which is	5101
	27:23 governor said, Why, **w** evil hath he done?	5101
Mk	1:24 **w** have we to do with thee, *thou* Jesus of	5101
	1:27 themselves, saying, **W** thing is this?	5101
	1:27 **w** new doctrine *is* this? for with authority	5101
	2:25 Have ye never read **w** David did, when he	5101
	3: 8 they had heard **w great** things he did,	3745
	4:24 said unto them, Take heed **w** you hear:	5101
	4:24 with **w** measure ye mete, it shall	3739
	4:30 with **w** comparison shall we compare it?	4169
	4:41 **W** *manner of* **man** is this, that even 687+5101	
	5: 7 and said, **W** have I to do with thee, Jesus,	5101
	5: 9 And he asked him, **W** is thy name?	5101
	5:14 they went out to see **w** it was that was	5101
	5:33 knowing **w** was done in her, came and	3739
	6: 2 **w** wisdom *is* this which is given unto him,	5101
	6:10 In **w** place soever ye enter into a 1437+3699	
	6:24 and said unto her mother, **W** shall I ask?	5101
	6:30 told him all *things,* both **w** they had done,	3745
	6:30 they had done, and **w** they had taught.	3745
	8:36 For **w** shall it profit a man, if he shall gain	5101
	8:37 Or **w** shall a man give in exchange for his	5101
	9: 6 he wist not **w** to say; for they were sore	5101
	9: 9 tell no *man* **w** things they had seen,	3739
	9:10 questioning *one* with *another* **w** the rising	5101
	9:16 the scribes, **W** question ye with them?	5101
	9:33 **W** *was it that* ye disputed among	5101
	10: 3 unto them, **W** did Moses command you?	5101
	10: 9 **W** therefore God hath joined together,	3739
	10:17 **w** shall I do that I may inherit eternal life?	5101
	10:32 began to tell them **w** things should happen	3588
	10:36 **W** would ye that I should do for you?	5101
	10:38 said unto them, Ye know not **w** ye ask:	5101
	10:51 **W** wilt thou *that* I should do unto thee?	5101
	11: 5 said unto them, **W** do ye, loosing the colt?	5101
	11:24 **W** things soever ye desire, when ye pray,	3745
	11:28 By **w** authority doest thou these *things?*	4169
	11:29 I will tell you by **w** authority I do these	4169
	11:33 Neither do I tell you by **w** authority I do	4169
	12: 9 **W** shall therefore the lord of the vineyard	5101
	13: 1 see **w manner** of stones and	4217
	13: 1 of stones and **w** buildings *are* here.	4217
	13: 4 **w** *shall be* the sign when all these *things*	5101
	13:11 take no thought beforehand **w** ye shall	5101
	13:37 I say unto you I say unto all, Watch.	3739
	14: 8 She hath done **w** she could: she is come	3739
	14:36 not that I will, but **w** thou wilt.	5101
	14:40 neither wist they **w** to answer him.	5101
	14:60 **w** *is it which* these witness against thee?	5101
	14:63 saith, **W** need we any further witnesses?	5101
	14:64 **w** think ye? And they all condemned him	5101
	14:68 neither understand I **w** thou sayest.	5101
	15:12 **W** will ye then *that* I shall do *unto* him	5101
	15:14 unto them, Why, **w** evil hath he done?	5101
	15:24 lots upon them, **w** every *man* should take.	5101
Lk	1:29 cast in her mind **w manner** of salutation	4217
	1:66 **W** *manner of* child shall this be! 687+5101	
	3:10 asked him, saying, **W** shall we do then?	5101
	3:12 and said unto him, Master, **w** shall we do?	5101
	3:14 of him, saying, And **w** shall we do?	5101
	4:34 have we to do with thee, *thou* Jesus of	5101
	4:36 saying, **W** a word is this!	5101
	5:19 And when they could not find by **w** *way*	4169
	5:22 unto them, **W** reason ye in your hearts?	5101
	6: 3 ye not read so much as this, **w** David did,	3739
	6:11 communed one with another **w** they	5101
	6:32 them which love you, **w** thank have ye?	4169
	6:33 which do good to you, **w** thank have ye?	4169
	6:34 ye hope to receive, **w** thank have ye?	4169
	7:22 and tell John **w** *things* ye have seen and	3739

Lk	7:24 **W** went ye out into the wilderness for to	5101
	7:25 But **w** went ye out for to see? A man	5101
	7:26 But **w** went ye out for to see? a prophet?	5101
	7:31 of this generation? and to **w** are they like?	5101
	7:39 **w manner** of woman *this is* that toucheth	4217
	8: 9 saying, **W** might this parable be?	5101
	8:25 another, **W** *manner of man* is this? 687+5101	
	8:28 said, **W** have I to do with thee, Jesus,	5101
	8:30 Jesus asked him, saying, **W** is thy name?	5101
	8:34 they that fed *them* saw **w** was done,	3588
	8:35 Then they went out to see **w** was done;	3588
	8:36 **by w means** he that was possessed of	4459
	8:47 people for **w** cause she had touched him,	3739
	8:56 that they should tell no *man* **w** was done.	3588
	9:25 For **w** is a man advantaged, if he gain	5101
	9:33 and one for Elias: not knowing **w** he said.	5101
	9:55 Ye know not **w manner** of spirit ye are of.	3634
	10:25 Master, **w** shall I do to inherit eternal life?	5101
	10:26 said unto him, **W** is written in the law?	5101
	12:11 thought how or **w** *thing* ye shall answer,	5101
	12:11 *thing* ye shall answer, or **w** ye shall say:	5101
	12:12 you in the same hour **w** ye ought to say.	3739
	12:17 saying, **W** shall I do, because I have no	5101
	12:22 no thought for your life, **w** ye shall eat;	5101
	12:22 neither for the body, **w** ye shall put on.	5101
	12:29 seek not ye **w** ye shall eat, or what ye	5101
	12:29 or **w** ye shall drink, neither be ye of	5101
	12:39 had known **w** hour the thief would come,	4169
	12:49 and will I, if it be already kindled?	5101
	12:57 why even of yourselves judge ye not **w** is	3588
	13:18 Unto **w** is the kingdom of God like?	5101
	14:31 Or **w** king, going to make war against	5101
	15: 4 **W** man of you, having an hundred sheep,	5101
	15: 8 Either **w** woman having ten pieces of	5101
	15:26 and asked **w** these *things* meant.	5101
	16: 3 steward said within himself, **W** shall I do?	5101
	16: 4 I am resolved **w** to do, that, when I am	5101
	18: 6 Lord said, Hear **w** the unjust judge saith.	5101
	18:18 **w** shall I do to inherit eternal life?	5101
	18:36 multitude pass by, he asked **w** it meant.	5101
	18:41 **W** wilt thou *that* I shall do unto thee?	5101
	19:48 could not find **w** they might do: for all	5101
	20: 2 by **w** authority doest thou these *things?*	4169
	20: 8 Neither tell I you by **w** authority I do	4169
	20:13 said the lord of the vineyard, **W** shall I do?	5101
	20:15 and killed *him.* **W** therefore shall the lord	5101
	20:17 and said, **W** is this then that is written,	5101
	21: 7 **w** sign *will there be* when these *things*	5101
	21:14 not to meditate before **w** ye shall answer:	NIG
	22:49 When they which were about him saw **w**	3588
	22:60 said, Man, I know not **w** thou sayest.	3739
	22:71 they said, **W** need we any further witness?	5101
	23:22 the third time, Why, **w** evil hath he done?	5101
	23:31 a green tree, **w** shall be done in the dry?	5101
	23:34 them; for they know not **w** they do.	5101
	23:47 when the centurion saw **w** was done,	3588
	24:17 **W** *manner of* communications *are* these	5101
	24:19 **W** *things?* And they said unto him,	4169
	24:35 And they told **w** things were done in	3588
Jn	1:21 And they asked him, **W** then? Art thou	5101
	1:22 that sent us. **W** sayest thou of thyself?	5101
	1:38 and saith unto them, **W** seek ye?	5101
	2: 4 her, Woman, **w** have I to do with thee?	5101
	2:18 unto him, **W** sign shewest thou unto us,	5101
	2:25 of man: for he knew **w** was in man.	5101
	3:32 And **w** he hath seen and heard, that he	3739
	4:22 Ye worship ye know not **w:** we know	3739
	4:22 we know **w** we worship: for salvation is	3739
	4:27 yet no *man* said, **W** seekest thou?	5101
	5:12 **W** man is that which said unto thee,	5101
	5:19 of himself, but **w** he seeth the Father do:	5100
	5:19 for **w** things soever he doeth, these also	5100
	6: 6 for he himself knew **w** he would do.	5101
	6: 9 but **w** are they among so many?	5101
	6:28 Then said they unto him, **W** shall we do,	5101
	6:30 unto him, **W** sign shewest thou then,	5101
	6:30 and believe thee? **w** dost thou work?	5101
	6:62 **W** and if ye shall see the Son of man	NIG
	7:36 **W** *manner of* saying is this that he said,	5101
	7:51 before it hear him, and know **w** he doeth?	5101
	8: 5 such should be stoned: but **w** sayest thou?	5101
	9:17 **W** sayest thou of him, that he hath opened	5101
	9:21 But **by w means** he now seeth, we know	4459
	9:26 said they to him again, **W** did he to thee?	5101
	10: 6 they understood not **w** things they were	5101
	10:32 and told them **w** things Jesus had done.	5101
	11:47 Pharisees a council, and said, **W** do we?	3739
	11:56 as they stood in the temple, **W** think ye,	5101
	12: 6 had the bag, and bare **w** was put *therein.*	3588
	12:27 is my soul troubled; and **w** shall I say?	5101
	12:33 he said, signifying **w** death he should die.	4169
	12:49 **w** I should say, and what I should speak.	5101
	12:49 what I should say, and **w** I should speak.	5101
	13: 7 unto him, **W** I do thou knowest not now;	3739
	13:12 them, Know ye **w** I have done to you?	5101
	13:28 no *man* at the table knew for **w** intent	5101
	15: 7 ye shall ask **w** ye will, and it shall 1437+3739	
	15:15 for the servant knoweth not **w** his lord	5101
	16:17 **W** is this that he saith unto us, A little	5101
	16:18 **W** is this A little while? A little while?	5101
	16:18 A little while? we cannot tell **w** he saith.	5101
	18:21 ask them which heard *me,* **w** I have said	3739
	18:21 unto them: behold, they know **w** I said.	3739
	18:29 **W** accusation bring you against this man?	5101
	18:32 spake, signifying **w** death he should die.	4169

Jn
18:35 thee unto me: w hast thou done? 5101
18:38 Pilate saith unto him, W is truth? 5101
19:22 W I have written I have written. 3739
21:19 signifying by w death he should glorify 4169
21:21 to Jesus, Lord, and w shall this man do? 5101
21:22 that he tarry till I come, w is that to thee? 5101
21:23 that he tarry till I come, w is that to thee? 5101
Ac
2:12 saying one to another, W meaneth this? 5101
2:37 Men and brethren, w shall we do? 5101
4: 7 asked, By w power, or by what name, 4169
4: 7 asked, By what power, or by w name, 4169
4: 9 by w means he is made whole; 5101
4:16 Saying, W shall we do to these men? 5101
5: 7 wife, not knowing w was done, came in. 3588
5:35 take heed to yourselves w ye intend to do 5101
7:40 of Egypt, we wot not w is become of him. 5101
7:49 w house will ye build me? saith the Lord: 4169
7:49 the Lord: or w is the place of my rest? 5101
8:30 said, Understandest thou w thou readest? 3739
8:36 water; w doth hinder me to be baptized? 5101
9: 6 Lord, w wilt thou have me to do? 5101
9: 6 it shall be told thee w thou must do. 3739+5101
10: 4 he was afraid, and said, W is it, Lord? 5101
10: 6 he shall tell thee w thou oughtest to do. 5101
10:15 W God hath cleansed, that call not thou 3739
10:17 while Peter doubted in himself w 302+5101
10:21 w is the cause wherefore ye are come? 5101
10:29 therefore w intent ye have sent for me? 5101
11: 9 W God hath cleansed, that call not thou 3739
11:17 w was I, that I could withstand God? 5101
12:18 the soldiers, w was become of Peter. 5101
13:12 when he saw w was done, believed, 3588
14:11 when the people saw w Paul had done, 3739
15:12 declaring w miracles and wonders God 3745
16:30 and said, Sirs, w must I do to be saved? 5101
17:18 And some said, W will this babbler 302+5101
17:19 May we know w this new doctrine, 5101
17:20 therefore w these things mean. 302+5101
19: 3 them, Unto w then were ye baptized? 5101
19:35 w man is there that knoweth not how 5101
20:18 after w manner I have been with you at 4459
21:13 W mean ye to weep and to break mine 5101
21:19 he declared particularly w things God had 3739
21:22 W is it therefore? the multitude must 5101
21:33 who he was, and w he had done. 5101
22:10 And I said, W shall I do, Lord? 5101
22:15 witness unto all men of w thou hast seen 3739
22:26 saying, Take heed w thou doest: 5101
23:19 asked him, W is that thou hast to tell me? 5101
23:30 to say before thee w they had against him. 3588
23:34 the letter, he asked of w province he was: 4169
28:22 But we desire to hear of thee w thou 3739
Ro
3: 1 W advantage then hath the Jew? 5101
3: 1 or w profit is there of circumcision? 5101
3: 3 For w if some did not believe? shall their 5101
3: 5 the righteousness of God, w shall we say? 5101
3: 9 W then? are we better than they? 5101
3:19 we know that w things soever the law 3745
3:27 By w law? of works? Nay: but by the law 4169
4: 1 W shall we say then that Abraham our 5101
4: 3 For w saith the scripture? 5101
4:21 w he had promised, he was able also to 3739
6: 1 W shall we say then? Shall we continue in 5101
6:15 W then? shall we sin, because we are not 5101
6:21 W fruit had ye then in those things 5101
7: 7 W shall we say then? Is the law sin? 5101
7:15 w I would, that do I not; but what I hate, 3739
7:15 that do I not; but w I hate, that do I. 5101
8: 3 For w the law could not do, in that it was NIG
8:24 for w a man seeth, why doth he yet hope 3739
8:26 for we know not w we should pray for as 5101
8:27 he that searcheth the hearts knoweth w 5101
8:31 W shall we then say to these things? 5101
9:14 W shall we say then? Is there 5101
9:22 W if God, willing to shew his wrath, 1487
9:30 W shall we say then? That the Gentiles, 5101
10: 8 But w saith it? The word is nigh thee, 5101
11: 2 Wot ye not w the scripture saith of Elias? 5101
11: 4 But w saith the answer of God unto him? 5101
11: 7 W then? Israel hath not obtained that 5101
11:15 w shall the receiving of them be, but life 5101
12: 2 that ye may prove w is that good, 5101
1Co
2:11 For w man knoweth the things of a man, 5101
3:13 try every man's work of w sort it is. 3697
4: 7 w hast thou that thou didst not receive? 5101
4:21 W will ye? shall I come unto you with a 5101
5:12 For w have I to do to judge them 1473+5101
6:16 W? know ye not that he which is joined to 2228
6:19 W? know ye not that your body is 2228
7:16 For w knowest thou, O wife, whether 5101
7:36 and need so require, let him do w he will, 3739
9:18 W is my reward then? Verily that, when I 5101
10:15 I speak as to wise men; judge ye w I say. 5101
10:19 W say I then? that the idol is any thing, or 5101
11:22 W? have ye not houses to eat and to drink NIG
11:22 W shall I say to you? shall I praise you in 5101
14: 6 with tongues, w shall I profit you, 5101
14: 7 how shall it be known w is piped or 3588
14: 9 how shall it be known w is spoken? 3588
14:15 W is it then? I will pray with the spirit, 5101
14:16 he understandeth not w thou sayest? 5101
14:36 W? came the word of God out from you? 2228
15: 2 if ye keep in memory w I preached unto 5101
15:10 But by the grace of God I am w I am: 3739
15:29 Else w shall they do which are baptized 5101

1Co
15:32 w advantageth it me, if the dead rise not? 5101
15:35 and with w body do they come? 4169
2Co
1:13 you, than w you read or acknowledge; 3739
6:14 for w fellowship hath righteousness with 5101
6:14 w communion hath light with darkness? 5101
6:15 And w concord hath Christ with Belial? 5101
6:15 w part hath he that believeth with an 5101
6:16 And w agreement hath the temple of God 5101
7:11 w carefulness it wrought in you, yea, 4214
7:11 yea, w clearing of yourselves, yea, NIG
7:11 yea, w indignation, yea, what fear, yea, NIG
7:11 yea, what indignation, yea, w fear, yea, NIG
7:11 yea, what fear, yea, w vehement desire, NIG
7:11 yea, w zeal, yea, what revenge! NIG
7:11 yea, what zeal, yea, w revenge! NIG
11:12 But w I do, that I will do, that I may cut 3739
12:13 For w is it wherein ye were inferior to 5101
Gal
4:30 Nevertheless w saith the scripture? 5101
Eph
1:18 that ye may know w is the hope of his 5101
1:18 w the riches of the glory of his inheritance 5101
1:19 And w is the exceeding greatness of his 5101
3: 9 And to make all men see w is 5101
3:18 with all saints w is the breadth, 5101
4: 9 w is it but that he also descended first into 5101
5:10 Proving w is acceptable unto the Lord. 5101
5:17 understanding w the will of the Lord is. 5101
Php
1:18 W then? notwithstanding, every way, 5101
1:22 my labour: yet w I shall choose I wot not. 5101
3: 7 But w things were gain to me, those I 3748
Col
1:27 To whom God would make known w is 5101
2: 1 I would that ye knew w great conflict 2245
1Th
1: 5 as ye know w manner of men we were 3634
1: 9 w manner of entering in we had unto 3697
2:19 For w is our hope, or joy, or crown of 5101
3: 9 For w thanks can we render to God again 5101
4: 2 For ye know w commandments we gave 5101
2Th
2: 6 And now ye know w withholdeth that he 3588
1Ti
2: 7 understanding neither w they say, 3739
2Ti
2: 7 Consider w I say; and the Lord give thee 3739
3:11 at Lystra; w persecutions I endured: 3634
Heb
2: 6 saying, W is man, that thou art mindful of 5101
7:11 w further need was there that another 5101
11:32 w shall I more say? for the time would 5101
12: 7 w son is he whom the father chasteneth 5101
13: 6 I will not fear w man shall do unto me. 5101
Jas
1:24 straightway forgetteth w manner of man 3697
2:14 W doth it profit, my brethren, though a 5101
2:16 are needful to the body; w doth it profit? 5101
4:14 Whereas ye know not w shall be on 3588
4:14 for w is your life? It is even a vapour, 4169
1Pe
1:11 Searching w, or what manner of time 5101
1:11 w manner of time the Spirit of Christ 4169
2:20 For w glory is it, if, when ye be buffeted 4169
4:17 w shall the end be of them that obey not 5101
2Pe
3:11 w manner of persons ought ye to be in 4217
1Jn
3: 1 w manner of love the Father hath 4217
3: 2 and it doth not yet appear w we shall be: 5101
Jude
1:10 they know naturally, as brute beasts, 3745
Rev
1:11 and, W thou seest, write in a book, 3739
2: 7 let him hear w the Spirit saith unto 5101
2:11 let him hear w the Spirit saith unto 5101
2:17 let him hear w the Spirit saith unto 5101
2:29 let him hear w the Spirit saith unto 5101
3: 3 thou shalt not know w hour I will come 4169
3: 6 let him hear w the Spirit saith unto 5101
3:13 let him hear w the Spirit saith unto 5101
3:22 let him hear w the Spirit saith unto 5101
7:13 W are these which are arrayed in white 5101
18:18 saying, W city is like unto this great city? 5101

WHATSOEVER (152) [EVER, SO, WHAT]

Ge
2:19 w Adam called every living creature, 834+3605
8:19 fowl, and w creepeth upon the earth, 3605
19:12 w thou hast in the city, 834+3605
31:16 w God hath said unto thee, 834+3605
39:22 w they did there, he was the doer of 834+3605
Ex
13: 2 openeth the womb among the children 3605
21:30 his life w is laid upon him. 834+3605+3509.1
29:37 w toucheth the altar shall be holy. 3605
30:29 most holy: w toucheth them shall be holy. 3605
Lev
5: 3 w uncleanness it be that a man 3605+3807.1
5: 4 w it be that a man shall 3605+3807.1
6:27 W shall touch the flesh thereof shall 834+3605
7:27 W soul it be that eateth any manner of 3605
11: 3 W parteth the hoof, and is clovenfooted, 3605
11: 9 w hath fins and scales in the waters, 834+3605
11:12 W hath no fins nor scales in 834+3605
11:27 w goeth upon his paws, among all 3605
11:32 upon w any of them, when they are 834+3605
11:32 w vessel it be, wherein any work is 834+3605
11:33 w is in it shall be unclean; 834+3605
11:42 W goeth upon the belly, 3605
11:42 w goeth upon all four, or whatsoever 3605
11:42 w hath more feet among all creeping 3605
13:58 w thing of skin it be, which thou shalt 3605
15:26 w she sitteth upon shall be 3605+3627+1886.1
17: 8 W man there be of the house of Israel 376+376
17:10 w man there be of the house of Israel 376+376
17:13 w man there be of the children of 376+376
21:18 w man he be that hath a blemish, 834+3605
22: 5 take uncleanness, w uncleanness he hath; 3605
22:18 W he be of the house of Israel, or of 376
22:20 w hath a blemish, that shall ye not 834+3605
23:29 For w soul it be that shall not be afflicted 3605
23:30 w soul it be that doeth any work in that 3605

Lev
27:32 even of w passeth under the rod, 834+3605
Nu
18:13 And w is first ripe in the land, 834+3605
19:22 w the unclean person toucheth shall 834+3605
22:17 I will do w thou sayest unto me: 834+3605
23: 3 w he sheweth me I will tell thee. 1697+4100
30:12 w proceeded out of her lips concerning 3605
Dt
2:37 w the LORD our God forbad us. 834+3605
12: 8 every man w is right in his own eyes. 3605
12:15 thy gates, w thy soul lusteth after, 3605+871.1
12:20 eat flesh, w thy soul lusteth after. 3605+871.1
12:21 shalt eat in thy gates w thy soul 3605+871.1
14:10 w hath not fins and scales ye may 834+3605
14:26 thou shalt bestow that money for w 834+3605
14:26 or for w thy soul desireth: 834+3605
Jdg
10:15 do thou unto us w seemeth good 3605+3509.1
11:31 w cometh forth of the doors of my house 834
11:31 they said, Do w seemeth good unto thee, 834
1Sa
14:36 they said, W thy soul desireth, I will even do it for 4100
20: 4 w thy soul desireth, I will even do it for 4100
25: 8 w cometh to thine hand unto thy servants, 834
2Sa
3:36 w the king did, pleased all the 834+3605
15:15 servants are ready to do w 834+3605+3509.1
19:38 w thou shalt require of me, that will 834+3605
1Ki
8:37 w plague, whatsoever sickness there be; 3605
8:37 whatsoever plague, w sickness there be; 3605
10:13 w she asked, besides that which 834
2Ch
6:28 w sore or whatsoever sickness there be: 3605
6:28 whatsoever sore or w sickness there be; 3605
9:12 w she asked, besides that which she 834
Ezr
7:18 w shall seem good to thee, and to 1768+4101
7:20 w more shall be needful for the house of NIH
7:21 that w Ezra the priest, 1768+1768+3606
7:23 W is commanded by the God of 1768+3606
Est
2:13 w she desired was given her to go 834+3605
Job
37:12 that they may do w he commandeth 834+3605
41:11 that I should repay him? w is under NIH
Ps
1: 3 and w he doeth shall prosper. 834+3605
8: 8 w passeth through the paths of the seas. NIH
115: 3 he hath done w he pleased. 834+3605
135: 6 W the LORD pleased, that did he in 834+3605
Ecc
2:10 w mine eyes desired I kept not from 3605
3:14 I know that, w God doeth, it shall 834+3605
8: 3 for he doeth w pleaseth him. 834+3605
9:10 W thy hand findeth to do, do it with 834+3605
Jer
1: 7 w I command thee thou shalt speak. 834+3605
42: 4 w thing the LORD shall answer you, 3605
44:17 we will certainly do w thing goeth 834+3605
Mt
5:37 for w is more than these cometh of evil. 3588
7:12 Therefore all things w ye would that 302+3745
10:11 into w city or town ye shall enter, 302+3739
14: 7 oath to give her w she would ask. 1437+3739
15: 5 w thou mightest be profited by me; 1437+3739
15:17 that w entereth in at the mouth goeth into 3956
16:19 w thou shalt bind on earth shall be 1437+3739
16:19 w thou shalt loose on earth shall be 1437+3739
17:12 but have done unto him w they listed. 3745
18:18 W ye shall bind on earth shall 1437+3745
18:18 w ye shall loose on earth shall be 1437+3745
20: 4 and w is right I will give you. 1437+3739
20: 7 and w is right, that shall ye receive. 1437+3739
21:22 And all things, w ye shall ask in 302+3745
23: 3 All therefore w they bid you observe, 302+3745
28:20 Teaching them to observe all things w I 3745
Mk
6:22 Ask of me w thou wilt, and I will 1437+3739
6:23 W thou shalt ask of me, I will give 1437+3739
7:11 w thou mightest be profited by me; 1437+3739
7:18 that w thing from without entereth into 3956
9:13 they have done unto him w they listed, 3745
10:21 sell w thou hast, and give to the poor, 3745
10:35 do for us w we shall desire. 1437+3739
11:23 to pass; he shall have w he saith. 1437+3739
13:11 w shall be given you in that hour, 1437+3739
Lk
4:23 w we have heard done in Capernaum, 3745
9: 4 And w house ye enter into, 302+3739
10: 5 And into w house ye enter, first say, 302+3739
10: 8 And into w city ye enter, 302+3739
10:10 But into w city ye enter, 302+3739
10:35 and w thou spendest more, when I 302+3748
12: 3 Therefore w ye have spoken in darkness 3745
Jn
2: 5 He saith unto you, do it. 302+3739+5100
5: 4 was made whole of w disease he had. 3739
11:22 even now, w thou wilt ask of God, 302+3745
12:50 w I speak therefore, even as the Father 3739
14:13 w ye shall ask in my name, 302+3739+5100
14:26 I have said unto you. 3739
15:14 my friends, if ye do w I command you. 3739
15:16 w ye shall ask of the Father 302+3739+5100
16:13 but w he shall hear, that shall he speak: 3739
16:23 W ye shall ask the Father in my 302+3739
17: 7 Now they have known that all things w 3745
Ac
3:22 him w he shall say unto all things w he 302+3745
4:28 For to do w thy hand and thy counsel 3745
Ro
15: 4 For w things were written aforetime were 3745
16: 2 that ye assist her in w business she 302+3739
1Co
10:25 W is sold in the shambles, that eat, 3956
10:27 w is set before you, eat, asking no 3956
10:31 therefore ye eat, or drink, or w ye do, 5100
Gal
2: 6 (w they were, it maketh no matter to me: 3697
2: 6 w a man soweth, that shall he also 1437+3739
Eph
5:13 light: for w doth make manifest is light. 3956
6: 8 Knowing that w good thing 1437+3739+5100
Php
4: 8 Finally, brethren, w things are true, 3745
4: 8 w things are honest, whatsoever things 3745

Php	4: 8 *w* things *are* just, whatsoever *things are*	3745
	4: 8 *things are* just, *w things are* pure,	3745
	4: 8 *things are* pure, *w things are* lovely,	3745
	4: 8 *are* lovely, *w things are* of good report;	3745
	4:11 for I have learned, in *w* state I am,	3739
Col	3:17 And *w* ye do in word or	302+302+3739+5100
	3:23 And *w* ye do, do *it*	1437+3748+3956+5100
1Jn	3:22 And *w* we ask, we receive of him,	1437+3739
	5: 4 For *w* is born of God overcometh	3956
	5:15 if we know that he hear us, *w* we	302+3739
3Jn	1: 5 thou doest faithfully *w* thou doest	1437+3739
Rev	18:22 *w* craft *he be,* shall be found any more	3956
	21:27 neither *w* worketh abomination,	NIG

WHEAT (51) [WHEATEN]

Ge	30:14 Reuben in the days of *w* harvest,	2406
Ex	9:32 the *w* and the rye were not smitten: for	2406
	34:22 the firstfruits of *w* harvest, and the feast	2406
Nu	18:12 and all the best of the wine, and of the *w,*	1715
Dt	8: 8 A land of *w,* and barley, and vines,	2406
	32:14 and goats, with the fat of kidneys of *w;*	2406
Jdg	6:11 his son Gideon threshed *w* by	2406
	15: 1 in the time of *w* harvest, that Samson	2406
Ru	2:23 end of barley harvest and of *w* harvest;	2406
1Sa	6:13 *of* Beth-shemesh *were* reaping *their w*	2406
	12:17 *Is it* not *w* harvest to day? I will call unto	2406
2Sa	4: 6 *as though* they would have fetched *w;*	2406
	17:28 *w,* and barley, and flour, and parched	2406
1Ki	5:11 measures of *w* for food to his household,	2406
1Ch	21:20 Now Ornan was threshing *w.*	2406
	21:23 for wood, and the *w* for the meat offering;	2406
2Ch	2:10 twenty thousand measures of beaten *w,*	2406
	2:15 Now therefore the *w,* and the barley,	2406
	27: 5 ten thousand measures of *w,*	2406
Ezr	6: 9 the God of heaven, *w,* salt, wine, and oil,	2591
	7:22 to an hundred measures *of w,* and to an	2591
Job	31:40 Let thistles grow instead of *w,*	2406
Ps	81:16 fed them also with the finest of the *w:*	2406
	147:14 *and* filleth thee *with* the finest of the *w.*	2406
Pr	27:22 a fool in a mortar among *w* with a pestle,	7383
SS	7: 2 thy belly *is like* a heap of *w* set about	2406
Isa	28:25 cast in the principal *w* and the appointed	2406
Jer	12:13 They have sown *w,* but shall reap thorns:	2406
	23:28 What *is* the chaff to the *w?* saith	1250
	31:12 for *w,* and for wine, and for oil, and for	1715
	41: 8 *of w,* and *of* barley, and *of* oil,	2406
Eze	4: 9 Take thou also unto thee *w,* and barley,	2406
	27:17 they traded in thy market *w* of Minnith,	2406
	45:13 sixth *part* of an ephah of a homer of *w,*	2406
Joel	1:11 for the *w* and for the barley;	2406
	2:24 The floors shall be full *of w,* and the fats	1250
Am	5:11 and ye take from him burdens of *w:*	1250
	8: 5 the sabbath, that we may set forth *w,*	1250
	8: 6 of shoes; *yea,* sell the refuse of the *w?*	1250
Mt	3:12 his floor, and gather his *w* into the garner;	4621
	13:25 came and sowed tares among the *w,*	4621
	13:29 tares, ye root up also the *w* with them.	4621
	13:30 them: but gather the *w* into my barn.	4621
Lk	3:17 and will gather the *w* into his garner;	4621
	16: 7 And he said, An hundred measures of *w.*	4621
	22:31 to have you, that he may sift *you* as *w:*	4621
Jn	12:24 Except a corn of *w* fall into the ground	4621
Ac	27:38 the ship, and cast out the *w* into the sea.	4621
1Co	15:37 may chance of *w,* or of some other *grain:*	4621
Rev	6: 6 A measure of *w* for a penny,	4621
	18:13 and *w,* and beasts, and sheep, and horses,	4621

WHEATEN (1) [WHEAT]

Ex	29: 2 with oil: *of w* flour shalt thou make them.	2406

WHEEL (15) [WHEELS]

1Ki	7:32 the height of a *w was* a cubit and half a	212
	7:33 wheels *was* like the work of a chariot *w:*	212
Ps	83:13 O my God, make them like a *w;*	1534
Pr	20:26 wicked, and bringeth the *w* over them.	212
Ecc	12: 6 fountain, or the *w* broken at the cistern.	1534
Isa	28:27 a cart *w* turned about upon the cummin;	212
	28:28 nor break *it with* the *w* of his cart,	1536
Eze	1:15 behold one *w* upon the earth by the living	212
	1:16 work *was* as it were a *w* in the middle	212
	1:16 as it were a wheel in the middle of a *w.*	212
	10: 9 one *w* by one cherub, and another wheel	212
	10: 9 and another *w* by another cherub:	212
	10:10 as if a *w* had been in the midst of a wheel.	212
	10:10 as if a wheel had been in the midst of a *w.*	212
	10:13 was cried unto them in my hearing, O *w.*	1534

WHEELS (33) [WHEEL]

Ex	14:25 took off their chariot *w,* that they drave	212
Jdg	5:28 coming? why tarry the *w* of his chariots?	6471
1Ki	7:30 every base had four brasen *w,* and plates	212
	7:32 under the borders *were* four *w;*	212
	7:32 the axletrees of the *w were* joined to	212
	7:33 the work of the *w was* like the work of a	212
Isa	5:28 like flint, and their *w* like a whirlwind:	1534
Jer	18: 3 and behold, he wrought a work on the *w.*	70
	47: 3 *and* at the rumbling of his *w,* the fathers	1534
Eze	1:16 The appearance of the *w* and their work	212
	1:19 living creatures went, the *w* went by them:	212
	1:19 lift up from the earth, the *w* were lift up.	212
	1:20 the *w* were lifted up over against them:	212
	1:20 spirit of the living creature *was* in the *w.*	212
	1:21 the *w* were lifted up over against them:	212
	1:21 spirit of the living creature *was* in the *w.*	212
	3:13 the noise of the *w* over against them,	212

Eze	10: 2 said, Go in between the *w, even* under	1534
	10: 6 saying, Take fire from between the *w,*	1534
	10: 6 then he went in, and stood beside the *w.*	212
	10: 9 behold the four *w* by the cherubims,	212
	10: 9 the appearance of the *w* was as the colour	212
	10:12 their hands, and their wings, and the *w,*	212
	10:12 about, or *even* that they four had.	212
	10:13 As for the *w,* it was cried unto them in my	212
	10:16 the cherubims went, the *w* went by them:	212
	10:16 the same *w* also turned not from beside	212
	10:19 the *w* also *were* beside them, and *every*	212
	11:22 lift up their wings, and the *w* besides them;	212
	23:24 and *w,* and with an assembly of people,	1534
	26:10 of the *w,* and of the chariots, when he	1534
Da	7: 9 the fiery flame, *and* his *w* as burning fire.	1535
Na	3: 2 the noise of the rattling of the *w,* and of	212

WHELP (3) [WHELPS]

Ge	49: 9 Judah *is* a lion's *w:* from the prey, my son,	1482
Dt	33:22 of Dan he said, Dan *is* a lion's *w:* he shall	1482
Na	2:11 *and* the lion's *w,* and none made *them*	1482

WHELPS (10) [WHELP]

2Sa	17: 8 as a bear **robbed of** her *w* in the field:	7909
Job	4:11 the stout lion's *w* are scattered abroad.	1121
	28: 8 The lion's *w* have not trodden it,	1121
Pr	17:12 *Let* a bear robbed of her *w* meet a man,	NIH
Jer	51:38 like lions: they shall yell as lions' *w,*	1484
Eze	19: 2 she nourished her *w* among young lions.	1482
	19: 3 she brought up one of her *w:* it became a	1482
	19: 5 she took another of her *w, and* made him	1482
Hos	13: 8 them as a bear *that is* bereaved of her *w,*	7909
Na	2:12 lion did tear in pieces enough for his *w,*	1484

WHEN (2848) [WHENSOEVER]

Ge	2: 4 and of the earth *w* they were created,	871.1
	3: 6 And *w* the woman saw that the tree	2050.1
	4: 8 it came to pass, *w* they were in the field,	871.1
	4:12 *W* thou tillest the ground, it shall not	3588
	5: 2 in the day *w* they were created.	NIH
	6: 1 *w* men began to multiply on the face of	3588
	6: 4 *w* the sons of God came in unto	834
	7: 6 Noah *was* six hundred years old *w*	2050.1
	9:14 to pass, *w* I bring a cloud over the earth,	871.1
	12: 4 years old *w* he departed out of Haran.	871.1
	12:11 *w* he was come near to enter into	834+3509.1
	12:12 *w* the Egyptians shall see thee, that they	3588
	12:14 that, *w* Abram was come into Egypt,	3509.1
	14:14 And *w* Abram heard that his brother	2050.1
	15:11 And *w* the fowls came down upon	2050.1
	15:12 And *w* the sun was going down, a deep	2050.1
	15:17 *w* the sun went down, and it was dark,	NIH
	16: 4 And *w* she saw that she had conceived,	2050.1
	16: 5 and *w* she saw that she had conceived,	2050.1
	16: 6 And *w* Sarai dealt hardly with her,	2050.1
	16:16 old, *w* Hagar bare Ishmael to Abram.	871.1
	17: 1 And *w* Abram was ninety years old and	2050.1
	17:24 *w* he was circumcised *in* the flesh of his	871.1
	17:25 *w* he was circumcised in the flesh of his	871.1
	18: 2 and *w* he saw *them,* he ran to meet	2050.1
	19:15 *w* the morning arose, then the angels	3644
	19:17 *w* they had brought them forth abroad,	3509.1
	19:23 The sun was risen upon the earth *w* Lot	2050.1
	19:29 *w* God destroyed the cities of the plain,	871.1
	19:29 *w* he overthrew the cities in the which	871.1
	19:33 he perceived not *w* she lay down,	871.1
	19:33 not when she lay down, nor *w* she arose.	871.1
	19:35 he perceived not *w* she lay down,	871.1
	19:35 not when she lay down, nor *w* she arose.	871.1
	20:13 *w* God caused me to wander from	834+3509.1
	21: 5 his son Isaac was born unto him.	871.1
	24:19 And *w* she had done giving him drink,	2050.1
	24:30 *w* he saw the earring and bracelets upon	3509.1
	24:30 *w* he heard the words of Rebekah his	3509.1
	24:36 bare a son to my master *w* she was old:	310
	24:41 my oath, *w* thou comest to my kindred;	3588
	24:43 that *w* the virgin cometh forth to draw	NIH
	24:52 *w* Abraham's servant heard their	834+3509.1
	24:64 and *w* she saw Isaac, she lighted off	2050.1
	25:20 Isaac was forty years old *w* he took	871.1
	25:24 And *w* her days to be delivered were	2050.1
	25:26 Isaac *was* threescore years old *w* she bare	871.1
	26: 8 to pass, *w* he had been there a long time,	3588
	26:34 Esau was forty years old *w* he took to	2050.1
	27: 1 *w* Isaac was old, and his eyes were dim,	NIH
	27: 5 Rebekah heard *w* Isaac spake to Esau his	871.1
	27:34 Esau heard the words of his father,	3509.1
	27:40 it shall come to pass *w* thou shalt	834+3509.1
	28: 6 *W* Esau saw that Isaac had blessed	2050.1
	29:10 *w* Jacob saw Rachel the daughter	834+3509.1
	29:13 *w* Laban heard the tidings of Jacob his	3509.1
	29:31 And *w* the Lord saw that Leah *was*	2050.1
	30: 1 And *w* Rachel saw that she bare Jacob	2050.1
	30: 9 *W* Leah saw that she had left bearing,	2050.1
	30:25 to pass, *w* Rachel had born Joseph,	834+3509.1
	30:30 was small *w* I provide for mine own house	4970
	30:33 *w* it shall come for my hire before thy	3588
	30:38 troughs *w* the flocks came to drink,	834
	30:38 that they should conceive *w* they came	871.1
	30:42 *w* the cattle were feeble, he put *them* not	871.1
	31:49 *w* we are absent one from another.	3588
	32: 2 *w* Jacob saw them, he said, This *is*	834+3509.1
	32:17 *W* Esau my brother meeteth thee,	3588
	32:19 you speak unto Esau, *w* you find him.	871.1
	32:25 And *w* he saw that he prevailed not	2050.1

Ge	33:18 of Canaan, *w* he came from Padan-aram;	871.1
	34: 2 And *w* Shechem the son of Hamor	2050.1
	34: 7 sons of Jacob came out of the field *w*	3509.1
	34:25 *w* they were sore, that two of the sons of	871.1
	35: 1 that appeared unto thee *w* thou fleddest	871.1
	35: 7 *w* he fled from the face of his brother.	871.1
	35: 9 *w* he came out of Padan-aram,	871.1
	35:17 came to pass, *w* she was in hard labour,	871.1
	35:22 *w* Israel dwelt in that land, that Reuben	871.1
	37: 4 And *w* his brethren saw that their	2050.1
	37:18 And *w* they saw him afar off, even	2050.1
	37:23 *w* Joseph was come unto his	834+3509.1
	38: 5 and he was at Chezib, *w* she bare him.	871.1
	38: 9 pass, *w* he went in unto his brother's wife,	518
	38:15 *W* Judah saw her, he thought her to be	2050.1
	38:25 *W* she *was* brought forth, she sent to	2050.1
	38:28 it came to pass, *w* she travailed, that	871.1
	39:13 *w* she saw that he had left his garment	3509.1
	39:15 *w* he heard that I lifted up my voice and	3509.1
	39:19 *w* his master heard the words of his	3509.1
	40:13 after the former manner *w* thou wast his	834
	40:14 think on me *w* it shall be well	834+3509.1
	40:16 *W* the chief baker saw that	2050.1
	41:21 And *w* they had eaten them up, it	2050.1
	41:46 Joseph *was* thirty years old *w* he stood	871.1
	41:55 And *w* all the land of Egypt was	2050.1
	42: 1 Now *w* Jacob saw that there was corn	2050.1
	42:21 *w* he besought us, and we would not	871.1
	42:35 and *w both* they and their father saw	2050.1
	43: 2 *w* they had eaten up the corn	834+3509.1
	43:16 And *w* Joseph saw Benjamin with	2050.1
	43:21 it came to pass, *w* we came to the inn,	3588
	43:26 And *w* Joseph came home, they	2050.1
	44: 4 *And w* they were gone out of the city,	NIH
	44: 4 and *w* thou dost overtake them, say	2050.1
	44:24 it came to pass *w* we came up unto thy	3588
	44:30 *w* I come to thy servant my father,	2050.1
	44:31 *w* he seeth that the lad *is* not *with us,*	2050.1
	45:27 and *w* he saw the wagons which	2050.1
	46:33 *w* Pharaoh shall call you, and shall say,	3588
	47:15 And *w* money failed in the land of	2050.1
	47:18 *W* that year was ended, they came unto	2050.1
	48: 2 as for me, *w* I came from Padan,	871.1
	48: 7 *w* yet *there was* but a little way to come	871.1
	48:17 And *w* Joseph saw that his father laid	2050.1
	49:33 And *w* Jacob had made an end of	2050.1
	50: 4 And the days of his mourning were	2050.1
	50:11 And *w* the inhabitants of the land,	2050.1
	50:15 And *w* Joseph's brethren saw that their	2050.1
	50:17 Joseph wept *w* they spake unto him.	871.1
Ex	1:10 pass, that, *w* there falleth out any war,	2050.1
	1:16 *W* ye do the office of a midwife to	871.1
	2: 2 and *w* she saw him that he *was* a	2050.1
	2: 3 And *w* she could not longer hide him,	2050.1
	2: 5 And *w* she saw the ark among the flags,	2050.1
	2: 6 And *w* she had opened *it,* she saw	2050.1
	2:11 in those days, *w* Moses was grown,	2050.1
	2:12 and *w* he saw that *there was* no man,	2050.1
	2:13 And *w* he went out the second day,	2050.1
	2:15 Now *w* Pharaoh heard this thing,	2050.1
	2:18 And *w* they came to Reuel their father,	2050.1
	3: 4 And *w* the Lord saw that he turned	2050.1
	3:12 *W* thou hast brought forth the people	871.1
	3:13 *w* I come unto the children of Israel,	NIH
	3:21 it shall come to pass, that, *w* ye go, ye	3588
	4: 6 he took it out, behold, his hand	2050.1
	4:14 and *w* he seeth thee, he will be glad in	2050.1
	4:21 *W* thou goest to return into Egypt,	871.1
	4:31 and *w* they heard that the Lord had	2050.1
	5:13 *your* daily tasks, as *w* there was straw.	871.1
	6:28 it came to pass on the day *w* the Lord	NIH
	7: 5 *w* I stretch forth mine hand upon Egypt,	871.1
	7: 7 years old, *w* they spake unto Pharaoh.	871.1
	7: 9 *W* Pharaoh shall speak unto you, saying,	3588
	8: 9 Glory over me: *w* shall I intreat	4970+3807.1
	8:15 But *w* Pharaoh saw that there was	2050.1
	9:34 And *w* Pharaoh saw that the rain and	2050.1
	10:13 *and w* it was morning, the east wind	2050.1
	11: 1 *w* he shall let *you* go, he shall surely	3509.1
	12:13 where you *are:* and *w* I see the blood,	2050.1
	12:13 destroy *you, w* I smite the land of Egypt.	871.1
	12:23 and *w* he seeth the blood upon the	2050.1
	12:25 *w* ye be come to the land which	3588
	12:26 pass, *w* your children shall say unto you,	3588
	12:27 *w* he smote the Egyptians, and delivered	871.1
	12:44 thou hast circumcised him, then	2050.1
	12:48 *w* a stranger shall sojourn with thee,	3588
	13: 5 it shall be *w* the Lord shall bring thee	3588
	13: 8 of that *which* the Lord did unto me *w* I	871.1
	13:11 it shall be *w* the Lord shall bring thee	3588
	13:14 it shall be *w* thy son asketh thee in time	3588
	13:15 pass, *w* Pharaoh would hardly let us go,	871.1
	13:17 to pass, *w* Pharaoh had let the people go,	871.1
	13:17 Lest peradventure the people repent *w*	871.1
	14:10 And *w* Pharaoh drew nigh, the children	2050.1
	14:18 *w* I have gotten me honour upon	2050.1
	14:27 *w* the morning **appeared;**	6437+3807.1
	15:23 And *w* they came to Marah, they could	2050.1
	15:25 *which w* he had cast into the waters,	2050.1
	16: 3 *w* we sat by the flesh pots, *and* when we	871.1
	16: 3 and *w* we did eat bread to the full;	2050.1
	16: 8 *This shall be,* w the Lord shall give you	871.1
	16:14 the dew that lay was gone up,	2050.1
	16:15 And *w* the children of Israel saw *it,*	2050.1
	16:18 And *w* they did mete *it* with an omer,	2050.1

Ex	16:21 **and** w the sun waxed hot, it melted.	2050.1
	16:32 w I brought you forth from the land of	871.1
	17:11 pass, w Moses held up his hand,	834+3509.1
	17:11 w he let down his hand,	834+3509.1
	18: 1 W Jethro, the priest of Midian,	2050.1
	18:14 **And** w Moses' father in law saw all that	2050.1
	18:16 W they have a matter, they come unto	3588
	19: 1 w the children of Israel were gone forth	NIH
	19: 9 that the people may hear w I speak with	871.1
	19:13 w the trumpet soundeth long, they shall	871.1
	19:19 w the voice of the trumpet sounded long,	NIH
	20:18 **and** w the people saw *it*, they removed,	2050.1
	22:27 w he crieth unto me, that I will hear;	3588
	23:16 w thou hast gathered in thy labours out	871.1
	28:29 w he goeth in unto the holy *place*, for a	871.1
	28:30 w he goeth in before the LORD:	871.1
	28:35 sound shall be heard w he goeth in unto	871.1
	28:35 and w he cometh out, that he die not.	871.1
	28:43 w they come in unto the tabernacle of	871.1
	28:43 w they come near unto the altar to	871.1
	29:30 w he cometh into the tabernacle of	834
	29:36 w thou hast made an atonement for it,	871.1
	30: 7 w he dresseth the lamps, he shall burn	871.1
	30: 8 w Aaron lighteth the lamps at even,	871.1
	30:12 W thou takest the sum of the children of	3588
	30:12 unto the LORD, w *thou* numberest them;	871.1
	30:12 amongst them, w *thou* numberest them.	871.1
	30:15 w *they* give an offering unto the LORD,	3807.1
	30:20 W they go into the tabernacle of	871.1
	30:20 w they come near to the altar to minister	871.1
	31:18 w he had made an end of communing	3509.1
	32: 1 **And** w the people saw that Moses	2050.1
	32: 5 **And** w Aaron saw *it*, he built an altar	2050.1
	32:17 **And** w Joshua heard the noise of	2050.1
	32:25 **And** w Moses saw that the people *were*	2050.1
	32:34 nevertheless in the day w I visit, I will	2050.1
	33: 4 **And** w the people heard these evil	2050.1
	33: 8 w Moses went out unto the tabernacle,	3509.1
	34:24 w thou shalt go up to appear before	871.1
	34:29 w Moses came down from mount Sinai	871.1
	34:29 w he came down from the mount,	871.1
	34:30 **And** w Aaron and all the children of	2050.1
	34:34 w Moses went in before the LORD to	871.1
	40:32 W they went into the tent of	871.1
	40:32 w they came near unto the altar,	871.1
	40:36 w the cloud was taken up from over	871.1
Lev	2: 1 w any will offer a meat offering unto	3588
	2: 8 **And** w it is presented unto the priest,	2050.1
	4:14 W the sin, which they have sinned	2050.1
	4:22 W a ruler hath sinned, and done	834
	5: 3 w he knoweth *of it*, then he shall be	2050.1
	5: 4 w he knoweth *of it*, then he shall be	2050.1
	5: 5 w he shall be guilty in one of these *things*,	3588
	6:20 the LORD in the day w he is anointed,	NIH
	6:21 *and* w it is baken, thou shalt bring it in:	NIH
	6:27 **and** w there is sprinkled of the blood	2050.1
	7:35 the day w he presented them to minister	NIH
	9:24 w all the people saw, they shouted,	2050.1
	10: 9 w ye go into the tabernacle of	871.1
	10:20 **And** w Moses heard *that*, he was	2050.1
	11:31 doth touch them, w they be dead,	871.1
	11:32 w they are dead, doth fall, it shall be	871.1
	12: 6 w the days of her purifying are fulfilled,	871.1
	13: 2 W a man shall have in the skin of his flesh	3588
	13: 3 *w* the hair in the plague is turned white,	NIH
	13: 9 W the plague of leprosy is in a man, then	3588
	13:14 w raw flesh appeareth in him,	3117+871.1
	13:20 W the priest seeth it, behold, it *be* in sight	NIH
	14:34 W ye be come into the land of Canaan,	3588
	14:57 To teach w *it is* unclean, and when	3117+871.1
	14:57 *it is* unclean, and w *it is* clean:	3117+871.1
	15: 2 W any man hath a running issue out of	3588
	15:13 w he that hath an issue is cleansed of his	3588
	15:23 whereon she sitteth, w he toucheth it,	871.1
	15:31 w they defile my tabernacle that *is*	871.1
	16: 1 w they offered before the LORD,	871.1
	16:17 w he goeth in to make an atonement in	871.1
	16:20 **And** w he hath made an end of	2050.1
	16:23 which he put on w he went into the holy	871.1
	18:28 land spue not you out also, w ye defile it,	871.1
	19: 9 w ye reap the harvest of your land,	871.1
	19:23 w ye shall come into the land,	3588
	20: 4 w the giveth of his seed unto Molech,	871.1
	22: 7 **And** w the sun is down, he shall be	2050.1
	22:16 w they eat their holy *things*: for I	871.1
	22:27 W a bullock, or a sheep, or a goat,	3588
	22:29 w ye will offer a sacrifice of thanksgiving	3588
	23:10 W ye be come into the land which I give	3588
	23:12 shall offer that day w ye wave the sheaf	871.1
	23:22 w ye reap the harvest of your land,	871.1
	23:22 the corners of thy field w thou reapest,	871.1
	23:39 w ye have gathered in the fruit of the	871.1
	23:43 w I brought them out of the land of	871.1
	24:16 w he blasphemeth the name *of*	871.1
	25: 2 W ye come into the land which I give you,	3588
	26:17 and ye shall flee w none pursueth you.	2050.1
	26:25 **and** w ye are gathered together within	2050.1
	26:26 **And** w I have broken the staff of your	871.1
	26:35 rest in your sabbaths, w ye dwelt upon it.	871.1
	26:36 and they shall fall w none pursueth.	2050.1
	26:37 were before a sword, w none pursueth:	2050.1
	26:44 w they be in the land of their enemies,	871.1
	27: 2 W a man shall make a singular vow,	3588
	27:14 w a man shall sanctify his house *to be*	3588
	27:21 the field, w it goeth out in the jubile,	871.1

Nu	1:51 w the tabernacle setteth forward,	871.1
	1:51 w the tabernacle is to be pitched,	871.1
	3: 4 w they offered strange fire before	871.1
	4: 5 w the camp setteth forward, Aaron shall	871.1
	4:15 **And** w Aaron and his sons have made	2050.1
	4:19 w they approach unto the most holy	871.1
	4:20 they shall not go in to see w the holy	3509.1
	5: 6 W a man or woman shall commit any sin	3588
	5:21 w the LORD doth make thy thigh to rot,	871.1
	5:27 **And** w he hath made her to drink	2050.1
	5:29 w a wife goeth aside *to another* instead of	834
	5:30 w the spirit of jealousy cometh upon him,	834
	6: 2 W either man or woman shall separate	3588
	6: 7 his brother, or for his sister, w they die:	871.1
	6:13 w the days of his separation are	3117+871.1
	7:84 the day w it was anointed, by the princes	NIH
	7:89 w Moses was gone into the tabernacle of	871.1
	8: 2 say unto him, W thou lightest the lamps,	871.1
	8:19 w the children of Israel come nigh unto	871.1
	9:17 w the cloud was taken up from	6310+3807.1
	9:19 w the cloud tarried long upon	871.1
	9:20 w the cloud was a few days upon	834
	9:21 w the cloud abode from even unto	NIH
	9:22 but w it was taken up, they journeyed.	871.1
	10: 3 **And** w they shall blow with them,	2050.1
	10: 5 W ye blow an alarm, then the camps	2050.1
	10: 6 W you blow an alarm the second time,	2050.1
	10: 7 w the congregation is to be gathered	871.1
	10:28 to their armies, w they set forward.	2050.1
	10:34 by day, w they went out of the camp.	871.1
	10:35 w the ark set forward, that Moses said,	871.1
	10:36 w it rested, he said, Return, O LORD,	871.1
	11: 1 *and* w the people complained, it displeased	NIH
	11: 2 **and** w Moses prayed unto the LORD,	2050.1
	11: 9 w the dew fell upon the camp in the	871.1
	11:25 that w the spirit rested upon them,	3509.1
	12:12 of whom the flesh is half consumed w he	871.1
	15: 2 W ye be come into the land of your	3588
	15: 8 w thou preparest a bullock *for* a burnt	3588
	15:18 W ye come into the land whither I bring	871.1
	15:19 *that* w ye eat of the bread of the land,	871.1
	15:28 w he sinneth by ignorance before	871.1
	16: 4 **And** w Moses heard *it*, he fell upon his	2050.1
	16:42 w the congregation was gathered against	871.1
	18:26 W ye take of the children of Israel	3588
	18:30 W ye have heaved the best thereof from	871.1
	18:32 w ye have heaved from it the best of it:	871.1
	19:14 This *is* the law, w a man dieth in a tent:	3588
	20: 3 Would God that we had died w our	871.1
	20:16 **And** w we cried unto the LORD,	2050.1
	20:29 **And** w all the congregation saw that	2050.1
	21: 1 w king Arad the Canaanite, which dwelt	NIH
	21: 8 bitten, w he looketh upon it, shall live.	2050.1
	21: 9 w he beheld the serpent of brass,	2050.1
	22:25 **And** w the ass saw the angel of	2050.1
	22:27 **And** w the ass saw the angel of	2050.1
	22:36 **And** w Balak heard that Balaam was	2050.1
	23:17 **And** w he came to him, behold,	2050.1
	24: 1 **And** w Balaam saw that it pleased	2050.1
	24:20 **And** w he looked on Amalek, he took	2050.1
	24:23 Alas, who shall live w God doeth this!	4480
	25: 7 w Phinehas, the son of Eleazar,	2050.1
	26: 9 w they strove against the LORD:	871.1
	26:10 w that company died, what time the fire	871.1
	26:61 w they offered strange fire before	871.1
	26:64 w they numbered the children of Israel in	834
	27:13 w thou hast seen it, thou also shalt	2050.1
	28:26 w ye bring a new meat offering unto	871.1
	30: 9 w she vowed, or uttered ought out of	2050.1
	32: 1 **and** w they saw the land of Jazer,	871.1
	32: 8 w I sent them from Kadesh-barnea to see	871.1
	32: 9 **For** w they went up unto the valley of	2050.1
	33:39 three years old w he died in mount Hor.	871.1
	33:51 W ye are passed over Jordan into the land	3588
	34: 2 W ye come into the land of Canaan;	3588
	35:10 W ye be come over Jordan into the land	3588
	35:19 w he meeteth him, he shall slay him.	871.1
	35:21 slay the murderer, w he meeteth him.	871.1
	36: 4 w the jubile of the children of Israel shall	518
Dt	1:19 **And** w we departed from Horeb, we	2050.1
	1:41 **And** w ye had girded on every man his	2050.1
	2: 8 **And** w we passed by from our brethren	2050.1
	2:12 w they had destroyed them from before	2050.1
	2:16 w all the men of war were	834+3509.1
	2:19 *w* thou comest nigh over against	NIH
	2:22 w he destroyed the Horims from before	834
	4:10 w the LORD said unto me, Gather me	871.1
	4:19 **and** w thou seest the sun, and the	2050.1
	4:25 W thou shalt beget children,	3588
	4:30 W thou art in tribulation, and all these	3807.1
	5:23 w ye heard the voice out of the midst of	3509.1
	5:28 of your words, w ye spake unto me;	871.1
	6: 7 shalt talk of them w thou sittest in thine	871.1
	6: 7 w thou walkest by the way, and when	871.1
	6: 7 w thou liest down, and when thou risest	871.1
	6: 7 thou liest down, and w thou risest up.	871.1
	6:10 w the LORD thy God hath brought	3588
	6:11 w thou shalt have eaten and be full;	2050.1
	6:20 w thy son asketh thee in time to come,	3588
	7: 1 W the LORD thy God shall bring thee	3588
	7: 2 **And** w the LORD thy God shall deliver	2050.1
	8:10 W thou hast eaten and art full, then	2050.1
	8:12 Lest *w* thou hast eaten and art full,	NIH
	8:13 *w* thy herds and thy flocks multiply,	NIH
	9: 9 W I was gone up into the mount to	871.1

Dt	9:23 Likewise **w** the LORD sent you from	871.1
	11:19 speaking of them w thou sittest in thine	871.1
	11:19 w thou walkest by the way, when thou	871.1
	11:19 w thou liest down, and when thou risest	871.1
	11:19 thou liest down, and w thou risest up.	871.1
	11:29 w the LORD thy God hath brought thee in	3588
	12:10 *w* ye go over Jordan and dwell in the land	NIH
	12:10 *w* he giveth you rest from all your enemies	NIH
	12:20 W the LORD thy God shall enlarge thy	3588
	12:25 w thou shalt do *that which is* right in	3588
	12:28 w thou doest *that which is* good and right	3588
	12:29 W the LORD thy God shall cut off	3588
	13:18 W thou shalt hearken to the voice of	3588
	14:24 w the LORD thy God hath blessed thee:	3588
	15: 4 Save w there shall be no poor among you;	3588
	15:10 thine heart shall not be grieved w thou	871.1
	15:13 w thou sendest him out free from thee,	3588
	15:18 w thou sendest him away free from thee;	871.1
	16: 3 thou mayest remember the day w thou	NIH
	17:14 W thou art come unto the land which	3588
	17:18 w he sitteth upon the throne of his	3509.1
	18: 9 W thou art come into the land which	3588
	18:22 W a prophet speaketh in the name of	834
	19: 1 W the LORD thy God hath cut off	3588
	19: 5 **As** *w a man* goeth into the wood with	2050.1
	20: 1 W thou goest out to battle against thine	3588
	20: 2 w ye are come nigh unto the battle,	3509.1
	20: 9 w the officers have made an end of	3509.1
	20:10 W thou comest nigh unto a city to fight	3588
	20:13 **And** w the LORD thy God hath	2050.1
	20:19 W thou shalt besiege a city a long time,	3588
	21: 9 w thou shalt do *that which is* right in	3588
	21:10 W thou goest forth to war against thine	3588
	21:16 w he maketh his sons to inherit	3117+871.1
	21:18 and *that*, w they have chastened him,	NIH
	22: 8 W thou buildest a new house, then	3588
	22:14 took this woman, **and** w I came to her,	2050.1
	22:26 for **as** w a man riseth against his	834+3509.1
	23: 4 in the way, w ye came forth out of Egypt;	871.1
	23: 9 W the host goeth forth against thine	3588
	23:11 it shall be, w evening cometh on, he shall	NIH
	23:11 w the sun is down, he shall come into	3509.1
	23:13 shall be, w thou wilt ease thyself abroad,	871.1
	23:21 W thou shalt vow a vow unto the LORD	3588
	23:24 W thou comest into thy neighbour's	3588
	23:25 W thou comest into the standing corn of	3588
	24: 1 W a man hath taken a wife,	3588
	24: 2 **And** w she is departed out of his house,	2050.1
	24: 5 W a man hath taken a new wife, he shall	3588
	24:10 W thou dost lend thy brother any thing,	3588
	24:13 the pledge again w the sun goeth down,	3509.1
	24:19 W thou cuttest down thine harvest in thy	3588
	24:20 W thou beatest thine olive tree, thou shalt	3588
	24:21 W thou gatherest the grapes of thy	3588
	25: 4 Thou shalt not muzzle the ox w he	871.1
	25:11 W men strive together one with another,	3588
	25:17 w ye were come forth out of Egypt;	871.1
	25:18 thee, w thou *wast* faint and weary;	2050.1
	25:19 w the LORD thy God hath given thee rest	871.1
	26: 1 w thou art come in unto the land which	3588
	26: 7 **And** w we cried unto the LORD God of	2050.1
	26:12 W thou hast made an end of tithing all	3588
	27: 2 shall be on the day w you shall pass over	834
	27: 3 of this law, w thou art passed over,	871.1
	27: 4 Therefore it shall be w ye be gone over	871.1
	27:12 the people, w ye are come over Jordan;	871.1
	28: 6 Blessed *shalt* thou *be* w thou comest in,	871.1
	28: 6 blessed *shalt* thou *be* w thou goest out.	871.1
	28:19 Cursed *shalt* thou *be* w thou comest in,	871.1
	28:19 cursed *shalt* thou *be* w thou goest out.	871.1
	29: 7 **And** w ye came unto this place, Sihon	2050.1
	29:19 w he heareth the words of this curse,	871.1
	29:22 w they see the plagues of that land,	2050.1
	29:25 which he made with them w he brought	871.1
	30: 1 w all these things are come upon thee,	3588
	31:11 W all Israel is come to appear before	871.1
	31:20 *For* w I shall have brought them into	3588
	31:21 w many evils and troubles are befallen	3588
	31:24 w Moses had made an end of writing	3509.1
	32: 8 W the most High divided to the nations	871.1
	32: 8 w he separated the sons of Adam,	871.1
	32:19 **And** w the LORD saw *it*, he abhorred	2050.1
	32:36 w he seeth that *their* power is gone,	3588
	33: 5 w the heads of the people *and* the tribes	871.1
	34: 7 and twenty years old w he died:	871.1
Jos	2: 5 w it was dark, that the men went out:	871.1
	2:10 sea for you, w ye came out of Egypt;	871.1
	2:14 w the LORD hath given us the land,	871.1
	2:18 *w* we come into the land, thou shalt	NIH
	3: 3 W ye see the ark of the covenant of	3588
	3: 8 W ye are come to the brink of the water	3509.1
	3:14 w the people removed from their tents,	871.1
	4: 1 w all the people were clean passed	834+3509.1
	4: 6 *that* w your children ask *their fathers* in	3588
	4: 7 w it passed over Jordan, the waters of	871.1
	4:11 w all the people were clean passed	834+3509.1
	4:18 w the priests that bare the ark of	3509.1
	4:21 W your children shall ask their fathers in	834
	5: 1 to pass, w all the kings of the Amorites,	871.1
	5: 8 w they had done circumcising all	834+3509.1
	5:13 it came to pass, w Joshua was by Jericho,	871.1
	6: 5 *that* w they make a long blast with	NIH
	6: 5 *and* w ye hear the sound of the trumpet,	3509.1
	6: 8 w Joshua had spoken unto the people,	3509.1
	6:16 w the priests blew with the trumpets,	NIH

Jos	6:18 **w** ye take of the accursed thing,	2050.1
	6:20 the people shouted **w** *the priests* blew	2050.1
	6:20 **w** the people heard the sound of	3509.1
	7: 8 **w** Israel turneth *their* backs before	310+834
	7:21 **W** I saw among the spoils a goodly	2050.1
	8: 5 **w** they come out against us, as at the first,	3588
	8: 8 it shall be, **w** ye have taken the city,	3509.1
	8:13 **And w** they had set the people, *even* all	2050.1
	8:14 **w** the king of Ai saw *it*, that they hasted	3509.1
	8:20 **And w** the men of Ai looked behind	2050.1
	8:21 **And w** Joshua and all Israel saw that	3509.1
	8:24 **w** Israel had made an end of slaying all	3509.1
	8:24 *w* they were all fallen on the edge of	NIH
	9: 1 **w** all the kings which *were* on *this* side	3509.1
	9: 3 **w** the inhabitants of Gibeon heard what	NIH
	9:22 far from you; **w** ye dwell among us?	2050.1
	10: 1 **w** Adoni-zedek king of Jerusalem had	3509.1
	10:12 spake Joshua to the LORD in the day **w**	NIH
	10:20 **w** Joshua and the children of Israel had	3509.1
	10:24 **w** they brought out those kings unto	3509.1
	11: 1 **w** Jabin king of Hazor had heard *those*	3509.1
	11: 5 **And w** all these kings were met	2050.1
	14: 7 Forty years old *was* I **w** Moses the	871.1
	17:13 the children of Israel were waxen	3588
	19:49 **W** they had made an end of dividing	2050.1
	20: 4 **And w** he that doth flee unto one of	2050.1
	22: 7 Joshua sent them away also unto their	3588
	22:10 **And w** they came unto the borders of	2050.1
	22:12 **And w** the children of Israel heard *of it*,	2050.1
	22:28 **w** they should *say* to us or to our	3588
	22:30 **And w** Phinehas the priest,	2050.1
	23:16 **W** ye have transgressed the covenant of	871.1
	24: 7 **And w** they cried unto the LORD,	2050.1
Jdg	1:14 **w** she came *to him*, that she moved him	871.1
	1:25 **And w** he shewed them the entrance	2050.1
	1:28 it came to pass, **w** Israel was strong,	3588
	2: 4 **w** the angel of the LORD spake these	3509.1
	2: 6 **And w** Joshua had let the people go,	2050.1
	2:18 the LORD raised them up judges, then	3588
	2:19 the judge was dead, *that* they returned	871.1
	2:21 nations which Joshua left **w** he died:	2050.1
	3: 9 **And w** the children of Israel cried unto	2050.1
	3:15 **But w** the children of Israel cried unto	2050.1
	3:18 **w** he had made an end to offer	834+3509.1
	3:24 **W** he was gone out, his servants came;	2050.1
	3:24 **and w** they saw that behold, the doors	2050.1
	3:27 it came to pass, **w** he was come, that he	871.1
	4: 1 sight of the LORD, **w** Ehud was dead.	2050.1
	4:18 **And w** he had turned in unto her into	2050.1
	4:20 **w** any man doth come and inquire of thee,	518
	4:22 **And w** he came into her *tent,* behold,	2050.1
	5: 2 **w** the people willingly offered	871.1
	5: 4 LORD, **w** thou wentest out of Seir,	871.1
	5: 4 **w** thou marchedst out of the field of	871.1
	5:26 **w** she had pierced and stricken through	2050.1
	5:31 *let* them that love him *be* as the sun **w** he	NIH
	6: 3 *so* it was, **w** Israel had sown, that	518
	6: 7 **w** the children of Israel cried unto	3588
	6:22 **And w** Gideon perceived that he *was*	2050.1
	6:28 **And w** the men of the city arose early	2050.1
	6:29 **And w** they inquired and asked, they	2050.1
	7:13 **And w** Gideon was come, behold,	2050.1
	7:15 **w** Gideon heard the telling of the dream,	3509.1
	7:17 **w** I come to the outside of the camp,	NIH
	7:18 **W** I blow with a trumpet, I and all that	2050.1
	8: 1 **w** thou wentest to fight with	3588
	8: 3 abated toward him, **w** he had said that.	871.1
	8: 7 Therefore **w** the LORD hath delivered	871.1
	8: 9 saying, **W** I come again in peace, I will	871.1
	8:12 **And w** Zebah and Zalmunna fled,	2050.1
	9: 7 **And w** they told *it* to Jotham, he went	2050.1
	9:22 **W** Abimelech had reigned three years	2050.1
	9:30 **And w** Zebul the ruler of the city heard	2050.1
	9:33 *w* he and the people that *is* with him	NIH
	9:36 **And w** Gaal saw the people, he said to	2050.1
	9:46 **And w** all the men of the tower of	2050.1
	9:55 **And w** the men of Israel saw that	2050.1
	11: 5 **that w** the children of Ammon	834+3509.1
	11: 7 why are ye come unto me now **w**	834+3509.1
	11:13 **w** they came up out of Egypt, from Arnon	871.1
	11:16 **w** Israel came up from Egypt,	871.1
	11:31 **w** I return in peace from the children of	871.1
	11:35 came to pass, **w** he saw her, that he rent	3509.1
	12: 2 **and w** I called you, ye delivered me not	2050.1
	12: 3 **w** I saw that ye delivered me not,	2050.1
	12: 5 that **w** those Ephraimites which were	NIH
	13:17 that **w** thy sayings come to pass we may do	NIH
	13:20 the flame went up toward heaven	871.1
	14:11 came to pass, **w** they saw him, that they	3509.1
	15: 5 **And w** he had set the brands on fire,	2050.1
	15:14 *And* **w** he came unto Lehi, the Philistines	NIH
	15:17 **w** he had made an end of speaking,	3509.1
	15:19 **and w** he had drunk, his spirit came	2050.1
	16: 2 saying, In the morning, **w** it is day,	2050.1
	16: 9 a thread of tow is broken **w** it toucheth	871.1
	16:15 love thee, **w** thine heart *is* not with me?	2050.1
	16:16 she pressed him daily with her words,	3588
	16:18 **And w** Delilah saw that he had told her	2050.1
	16:24 **And w** the people saw him, they	2050.1
	16:25 **w** their hearts were merry, that they	3509.1
	17: 3 **And w** he had restored the eleven	2050.1
	18: 2 who **w** they came *to* mount Ephraim,	2050.1
	18: 3 **W** they *were* by the house of Micah, they	NIH
	18:10 **W** ye go, ye shall come unto a people	3509.1
	18:22 *And* **w** they were a good way from	NIH

Jdg	18:26 **and w** Micah saw that they *were* too	2050.1
	19: 1 days, **w** *there* was no king in Israel,	2050.1
	19: 3 **and w** the father of the damsel saw	2050.1
	19: 5 **w** they arose early in the morning, that	2050.1
	19: 7 **And w** the man rose up to depart,	2050.1
	19: 9 **And w** the man rose up to depart, he,	2050.1
	19:11 **w** they *were* by Jebus, the day was far	NIH
	19:14 sun went down upon them *w* they were	NIH
	19:15 **and w** he went in, he sat him down in	2050.1
	19:17 **And w** he had lift up his eyes, he saw a	2050.1
	19:25 **w** the day began to spring, they let her	3509.1
	19:29 **And w** he was come into his house,	2050.1
	20:10 **w** they come to Gibeah of Benjamin,	3807.1
	20:39 **And w** the men of Israel retired in	2050.1
	20:40 **But w** the flame began to arise up out	2050.1
	20:41 **And w** the men of Israel turned *again*,	2050.1
	21:22 **w** their fathers or their brethren come	3588
Ru	1: 1 Now it came to pass in the days **w**	NIH
	1:18 **W** she saw that she *was* stedfastly	2050.1
	1:19 pass, **w** they were come *to* Beth-lehem,	3509.1
	2: 9 **and w** thou art athirst, go unto	2050.1
	2:15 **And w** she was risen up to glean, Boaz	2050.1
	3: 4 shall be, **w** he lieth down, that thou shalt	871.1
	3: 7 **And w** Boaz had eaten and drunk,	2050.1
	3:15 **And w** she held it, he measured six	2050.1
	3:16 **And w** she came to her mother in law,	2050.1
	4:13 **and w** he went in unto her, the LORD	2050.1
1Sa	1: 4 **And w** the time was that Elkanah	2050.1
	1: 7 **w** she went up to the house of	1767+4480
	1:20 the time was come about after Hannah	871.1
	1:24 **w** she had weaned him, she took	834+3509.1
	2:13 *was, that* **w** any man offered sacrifice,	NIH
	2:19 **w** she came up with her husband to offer	871.1
	2:27 **w** they were in Egypt in Pharaoh's	871.1
	3: 2 **w** Eli *was* laid down in his place,	2050.1
	3:12 **w** I begin, I will also make an end.	NIH
	4: 2 **and w** they joined battle, Israel was	2050.1
	4: 3 **And w** the people were come into	2050.1
	4: 3 **w** it cometh among us, it may save us	2050.1
	4: 5 **w** the ark of the covenant of the LORD	3509.1
	4: 6 **And w** the Philistines heard the noise of	2050.1
	4:13 **And w** he came, lo, Eli sat upon a seat	2050.1
	4:13 **And w** the man came into the city,	2050.1
	4:14 **And w** Eli heard the noise of the crying,	2050.1
	4:18 **w** he made mention of the ark of God,	3509.1
	4:19 **and w** she heard the tidings that the ark	2050.1
	5: 2 **W** the Philistines took the ark of God,	2050.1
	5: 3 **And w** they of Ashdod arose early on	2050.1
	5: 4 **And w** they arose early on the morrow	2050.1
	5: 7 **And w** the men of Ashdod saw that *it*	2050.1
	6: 6 **w** he had wrought wonderfully	834+3509.1
	6:16 **And w** the five lords of the Philistines	2050.1
	7: 7 **And w** the Philistines heard that	2050.1
	7: 7 **And w** the children of Israel heard *it*,	2050.1
	8: 1 it came to pass, **w** Samuel was old,	834+3509.1
	8: 6 **w** they said, Give us a king to	834+3509.1
	9: 5 they were come to the land of Zuph,	NIH
	9: 9 **w** a man went to inquire of God, thus he	NIH
	9:14 *and* **w** they were come into the city,	2050.1
	9:17 **and w** Samuel saw Saul, the LORD	2050.1
	9:25 **And w** they were come down from	2050.1
	10: 2 **W** thou art departed from me to day,	871.1
	10: 5 **w** thou art come thither *to* the city,	3509.1
	10: 7 it be, **w** these signs are come unto thee,	3588
	10: 9 **w** he had turned his back to go from	3509.1
	10:10 **And w** they came thither to the hill,	2050.1
	10:11 **w** all that knew him beforetime saw	2050.1
	10:13 **And w** he had made an end of	2050.1
	10:14 **and w** we saw that *they were* no	2050.1
	10:20 **And w** Samuel had caused all the tribes	2050.1
	10:21 **W** he had caused the tribe of Benjamin	2050.1
	10:21 **and w** they sought him, he could not be	2050.1
	10:23 **and w** he stood among the people, he	2050.1
	11: 6 the spirit of God came upon Saul **w** he	3509.1
	11: 8 **And w** he numbered them in Bezek,	2050.1
	12: 8 **W** Jacob was come *into* Egypt,	834+3509.1
	12: 9 **And w** they forgat the LORD their God,	2050.1
	12:12 **And w** ye saw that Nahash the king of	2050.1
	12:12 **w** the LORD your God *was* your king.	2050.1
	13: 1 **w** he had reigned two years over Israel,	871.1
	13: 6 **W** the men of Israel saw that they were	2050.1
	14:17 **And w** they had numbered, behold,	2050.1
	14:22 *w* they heard that the Philistines fled,	NIH
	14:26 **And w** the people were come into	2050.1
	14:27 Jonathan heard not **w** his father charged	871.1
	14:52 **and w** Saul saw any strong man,	2050.1
	15: 2 in the way, **w** they came up from Egypt.	871.1
	15: 6 of Israel, **w** they came up out of Egypt.	871.1
	15:12 **And w** Samuel rose early to meet Saul	2050.1
	15:17 **W** thou *wast* little in thine own sight,	518
	16: 6 came to pass, **w** they were come, that he	871.1
	16:16 **w** the evil spirit from God is upon thee,	871.1
	16:23 **w** the *evil* spirit from God was upon Saul,	871.1
	17:11 **W** Saul and all Israel heard those words	2050.1
	17:24 **w** they saw the man, fled from him,	871.1
	17:28 Eliab his eldest brother heard **w** he spake	871.1
	17:31 **And w** the words were heard which	2050.1
	17:35 **w** he arose against me, I caught *him* by	2050.1
	17:42 **And w** the Philistine looked about,	2050.1
	17:48 **w** the Philistine arose, and came and	3588
	17:51 **And w** the Philistines saw their	2050.1
	17:55 **w** Saul saw David go forth against	3509.1
	18: 1 **w** he made an end of speaking unto	3509.1
	18: 6 **w** David was returned from the slaughter	871.1
	18:15 **Wherefore w** Saul saw that he behaved	2050.1

1Sa	18:19 it came to pass at the time **w** Merab Saul's	NIH
	18:26 **And w** his servants told David these	2050.1
	19:14 **And w** Saul sent messengers to take	2050.1
	19:16 **And w** the messengers were come in,	2050.1
	19:20 **and w** they saw the company of	2050.1
	19:21 **And w** it was told Saul, he sent other	2050.1
	20:12 **w** I have sounded my father about to	3588
	20:15 not **w** the LORD hath cut off the enemies	871.1
	20:19 *w* thou hast stayed three days, then	NIH
	20:19 **w** the business was *in hand,*	3117+871.1
	20:24 **and w** the new moon was come,	2050.1
	20:37 **And w** the lad was come to the place of	2050.1
	21: 6 to put hot bread in the day **w** it was taken	NIH
	22: 1 **and w** his brethren and all his father's	2050.1
	22: 6 **W** Saul heard that David was	2050.1
	22:17 because they knew **w** he fled, and did not	3588
	22:22 that day, **w** Doeg the Edomite *was* there,	3588
	23: 6 **w** Abiathar the son of Ahimelech fled to	871.1
	23:25 **And w** Saul heard *that,* he pursued after	2050.1
	24: 1 **w** Saul was returned from	834+3509.1
	24: 8 **And w** Saul looked behind him, David	2050.1
	24:16 **w** David had made an end of speaking	3509.1
	24:18 **forasmuch as w** the LORD had delivered	834
	25: 9 **And w** David's young men came, they	2050.1
	25:15 with them, **w** we were in the fields:	871.1
	25:23 **And w** Abigail saw David, she hasted,	2050.1
	25:30 **w** the LORD shall have done to my lord	3588
	25:31 **but w** the LORD shall have dealt well	2050.1
	25:37 **w** the wine was gone out of Nabal,	871.1
	25:39 **And w** David heard that Nabal was	2050.1
	25:40 **And w** the servants of David were	2050.1
	26:20 **as w** *one* doth hunt a partridge in	834+3509.1
	28: 5 **And w** Saul saw the host of	2050.1
	28: 6 **And w** Saul inquired of the LORD,	2050.1
	28:12 **And w** the woman saw Samuel, she	2050.1
	28:22 have strength, **w** thou goest on *thy* way.	3588
	30: 1 **w** David and his men were come *to*	871.1
	30:12 **and w** he had eaten, his spirit came	2050.1
	30:16 **And w** he had brought him down,	2050.1
	30:21 **and w** David came near to the people,	2050.1
	30:26 **And w** David came to Ziklag, he sent of	2050.1
	31: 5 **And w** his armourbearer saw that Saul	2050.1
	31: 7 **And w** the men of Israel that *were* on	2050.1
	31: 8 **w** the Philistines came to strip the slain,	2050.1
	31:11 **And w** the inhabitants of Jabesh-gilead	2050.1
2Sa	1: 1 **w** David was returned from the	2050.1
	1: 2 *so* it was, **w** he came to David, that he	871.1
	1: 7 **And w** he looked behind him, he saw	2050.1
	2:10 years old **w** he *began* to reign over Israel,	871.1
	2:24 the sun went down **w** they were come	2050.1
	2:30 **and w** he had gathered all the people	2050.1
	3:13 **w** thou comest to see my face.	871.1
	3:23 **W** Joab and all the host that *was* with	2050.1
	3:26 **And w** Joab was come out from David,	2050.1
	3:27 **And w** Abner was returned *to* Hebron,	2050.1
	3:28 **w** David heard *it,* he said, I and	2050.1
	3:35 **And w** all the people came to cause	2050.1
	4: 1 **w** Saul's son heard that Abner was	2050.1
	4: 4 was five years old **w** the tidings came of	871.1
	4: 7 **For w** they came *into* the house, he lay	2050.1
	4:10 **W** one told me, saying, Behold, Saul is	3588
	4:11 **w** wicked men have slain a righteous	3588
	5: 2 in time past, **w** Saul was king over us,	2050.1
	5: 4 David *was* thirty years old **w** he *began* to	871.1
	5:17 **But w** the Philistines heard that they	2050.1
	5:23 **And w** David inquired of the LORD,	2050.1
	5:24 **w** thou hearest the sound of a going in	3509.1
	6: 6 **And w** they came to Nachon's,	2050.1
	6:13 that **w** they that bare the ark of the LORD	3588
	7: 1 **w** the king sat in his house, and the LORD	3588
	7:12 **And w** thy days be fulfilled, and thou	3588
	8: 5 **And w** the Syrians of Damascus came	2050.1
	8: 9 **W** Toi king of Hamath heard that David	2050.1
	8:13 David gat *him* a name **w** he returned	871.1
	9: 2 **and w** they had called him unto David,	2050.1
	9: 6 **Now w** Mephibosheth, the son of	2050.1
	10: 5 **W** they told *it* unto David, he sent to	2050.1
	10: 6 **And w** the children of Ammon saw that	2050.1
	10: 7 **And w** David heard *of it,* he sent Joab,	2050.1
	10: 9 **W** Joab saw that the front of the battle	2050.1
	10:14 **And w** the children of Ammon saw that	2050.1
	10:15 **And w** the Syrians saw that they were	2050.1
	10:17 **And w** it was told David, he gathered	2050.1
	10:19 **And w** all the kings *that were* servants	2050.1
	11: 1 at the time **w** kings go forth *to* battle, that	NIH
	11: 7 **And w** Uriah was come unto him,	2050.1
	11:10 **And w** they had told David, saying,	2050.1
	11:13 **And w** David had called him, he did eat	2050.1
	11:16 came to pass, **w** Joab observed the city,	871.1
	11:19 **W** thou hast made an end of telling	3509.1
	11:20 *so* nigh unto the city **w** *ye* did fight?	3807.1
	11:26 **And w** the wife of Uriah heard that	2050.1
	11:27 **And w** the mourning was past,	2050.1
	12:19 **But w** David saw that his servants	2050.1
	12:20 **and w** he required, they set bread	2050.1
	12:21 **w** the child was dead, thou didst	834+3509.1
	13: 5 **and w** thy father cometh to see thee,	2050.1
	13: 6 **and w** the king was come to see him,	2050.1
	13:11 **And w** she had brought *them* unto him	2050.1
	13:21 **But w** king David heard of all these	2050.1
	13:28 Mark ye now **w** Amnon's heart is merry	3509.1
	13:28 **w** I say unto you, Smite Amnon;	2050.1
	14: 4 **And w** the woman of Tekoah spake to	2050.1
	14:26 **w** he polled his head, (for it was at every	871.1
	14:29 **And w** he sent again the second time,	2050.1

2Sa 14:33 and **w** he had called for Absalom,	2050.1	
15: 2 **w** any man that had a controversy came	NIH	
15: 5 that **w** any man came nigh *to him* to do	871.1	
15:32 that **w** David was come to the top *of*	NIH	
16: 1 **And w** David was a little past the top	2050.1	
16: 5 **And w** king David came to Bahurim,	2050.1	
16: 7 thus said Shimei **w** he cursed, Come out,	871.1	
16:16 **w** Hushai the Archite,	834+3509.1	
17: 6 **And w** Hushai was come to Absalom,	2050.1	
17: 9 **w** *some* of them be overthrown at	3509.1	
17:20 **And w** Absalom's servants came to	2050.1	
17:20 **And w** they had sought and could not	2050.1	
17:23 **And w** Ahithophel saw that his counsel	2050.1	
17:27 pass, **w** David was come to Mahanaim,	871.1	
18: 5 all the people heard **w** the king gave all	871.1	
18:29 **W** Joab sent the king's servant, and *me*	NIH	
19: 3 as people being ashamed steal away **w**	871.1	
19:25 **w** he was come *to* Jerusalem to meet	3588	
19:39 **And w** the king was come over,	2050.1	
20: 8 **W** they *were* at the great stone which *is* in	NIH	
20:12 **And** the man saw that all the people	2050.1	
20:12 **w** he saw that every one that	834+3509.1	
20:13 **W** he was removed out of	834+3509.1	
20:17 **And w** he was come near unto her,	2050.1	
21:12 **w** the Philistines had slain Saul in	3117+871.1	
21:21 **And w** he defied Israel, Jonathan the	2050.1	
22: 5 **W** the waves of death compassed me,	3588	
23: 4 **w** the sun riseth, *even* a morning without	NIH	
23: 9 **w** they defied the Philistines *that* were	871.1	
24: 8 So **w** they had gone through all the	2050.1	
24:11 For **w** David was up in the morning,	2050.1	
24:16 **And w** the angel stretched out his hand	2050.1	
24:17 David spake unto the Lord **w** he saw	871.1	
1Ki 1:21 **w** my lord the king shall sleep with his	3509.1	
1:23 **And w** he was come in before the king,	2050.1	
1:41 **And w** Joab heard the sound of	2050.1	
2: 7 for so they came to me **w** I fled because	871.1	
2: 8 curse in the day **w** I went *to* Mahanaim:	NIH	
3:21 **And w** I rose in the morning to give my	2050.1	
3:21 but **w** I had considered it in the	2050.1	
5: 7 **w** Hiram heard the words of Solomon,	3509.1	
6: 7 the house, **w** it was in building, was built	871.1	
7:24 *were* cast *in* two rows, **w** it was cast.	871.1	
8: 9 **w** the Lord made a covenant with	834	
8: 9 **w** they came out of the land of Egypt.	871.1	
8:10 **w** the priests were come out of the holy	871.1	
8:21 **w** I brought them out of the land of	871.1	
8:30 **w** they shall pray towards this place:	834	
8:30 and **w** thou hearest, forgive.	2050.1	
8:33 **W** thy people Israel be smitten down	871.1	
8:35 **W** heaven is shut up, and there is no	871.1	
8:35 from their sin, **w** thou afflictest them:	3588	
8:42 **w** he shall come and pray towards this	2050.1	
8:53 **w** thou broughtest our fathers out of	871.1	
8:54 *that* **w** Solomon had made an end of	3509.1	
9: 1 **w** Solomon had finished the building of	3509.1	
9:10 **w** Solomon had built the two houses,	834	
10: 1 **And w** the queen of Sheba heard of	2050.1	
10: 2 and **w** she was come to Solomon,	2050.1	
10: 4 **And w** the queen of Sheba had seen all	2050.1	
11: 4 For it came to pass, **w** Solomon	6256+3807.1	
11:15 **w** David was in Edom, and Joab	871.1	
11:21 **And w** Hadad heard in Egypt that	2050.1	
11:24 **w** David slew them *of Zobah:* and	871.1	
11:29 it came to pass at that time **w** Jeroboam	2050.1	
12: 2 to pass, **w** Jeroboam the son of Nebat,	3509.1	
12:16 **So w** all Israel saw that the king	2050.1	
12:20 **w** all Israel heard that Jeroboam was	3509.1	
12:21 **And w** Rehoboam was come to	2050.1	
13: 4 **w** king Jeroboam heard the saying of	3509.1	
13:24 **And w** he was gone, a lion met him by	2050.1	
13:26 **And w** the prophet that brought him	2050.1	
13:31 **W** I am dead, then bury me in	871.1	
14: 5 it shall be, **w** she cometh in, that she	3509.1	
14: 6 **w** Ahijah heard the sound of her feet,	3509.1	
14:12 **w** thy feet enter into the city, the child	871.1	
14:17 **w** she came to the threshold of the door,	NIH	
14:21 and one years old **w** he *began* to reign,	871.1	
14:28 **w** the king went *into* the house of	1767+4480	
15:21 **w** Baasha heard *thereof,* that he left off	3509.1	
15:29 it came to pass, **w** he reigned, *that he*	3509.1	
16:11 it came to pass, **w** he *began* to reign,	871.1	
16:18 **w** Zimri saw that the city was taken,	3509.1	
17:10 **And w** he came to the gate of the city,	2050.1	
18: 4 **w** Jezebel cut off the prophets of	871.1	
18:10 and **w** they said, *He is* not there; he	2050.1	
18:12 and *so* **w** I come and tell Ahab,	2050.1	
18:13 Was it not told my lord what I did **w**	871.1	
18:17 it came to pass, **w** Ahab saw Elijah,	3509.1	
18:29 **w** midday was past, and they prophesied	3509.1	
18:39 **And w** all the people saw *it,* they fell on	2050.1	
19: 3 **And w** he saw *that,* he arose,	2050.1	
19:13 **w** Elijah heard *it,* that he wrapped his	3509.1	
19:15 and **w** thou comest, anoint Hazael to	2050.1	
20:12 **w** Ben-hadad heard this message, as he	3509.1	
21:15 **w** Jezebel heard that Naboth was	3509.1	
21:16 **w** Ahab heard that Naboth was dead,	3509.1	
21:27 to pass, **w** Ahab heard those words,	3509.1	
22:25 **w** thou shalt go into an inner chamber to	834	
22:32 **w** the captains of the chariots saw	3509.1	
22:33 **w** the captains of the chariots perceived	3509.1	
22:42 and five years old **w** he *began* to reign;	871.1	
2Ki 1: 5 **And w** the messengers turned back	2050.1	
2: 1 **w** the Lord would take up Elijah *into*	871.1	
2: 9 it came to pass, **w** they were gone over,	3509.1	

2Ki 2:10 if thou see me **w** *I am* taken	NIH	
2:14 and **w** he also had smitten the waters,	637	
2:15 **And w** the sons of the prophets which	2050.1	
2:17 **And w** they urged him till *he* was	2050.1	
2:18 **And w** they came again to him, (for he	2050.1	
3: 5 it came to pass, **w** Ahab was dead,	3509.1	
3:15 it came to pass, **w** the minstrel played,	3509.1	
3:20 **w** the meat offering was offered,	3509.1	
3:21 **And w** all the Moabites heard that	2050.1	
3:24 **And w** they came to the camp of Israel,	2050.1	
3:26 **And w** the king of Moab saw that	2050.1	
4: 4 **And w** thou art come in, thou shalt	2050.1	
4: 6 it came to pass, **w** the vessels were full,	3509.1	
4:10 shall be, **w** he cometh to us, that he shall	871.1	
4:12 **And w** he had called her, she stood	2050.1	
4:15 **And w** he had called her, she stood in	2050.1	
4:18 **And w** the child was grown, it fell on a	2050.1	
4:20 **And w** he had taken him,	2050.1	
4:25 the man of God saw her afar off,	3509.1	
4:27 **And w** she came to the man of God to	2050.1	
4:32 **And w** Elisha was come into the house,	2050.1	
4:36 **And w** she was come in unto him,	2050.1	
5: 6 Now **w** this letter is come unto thee,	3509.1	
5: 7 **w** the king of Israel had read the letter,	3509.1	
5: 8 **w** Elisha the man of God had heard that	3509.1	
5:13 **w** he saith to thee, Wash, and be clean?	3588	
5:18 *that* **w** my master goeth *into* the house	871.1	
5:18 **w** I bow down myself in the house of	871.1	
5:21 **w** Naaman saw *him* running after	2050.1	
5:24 **And w** he came to the tower, he took	2050.1	
5:26 Went not mine heart *with thee,* **w**	834+3509.1	
6: 4 **And w** they came to Jordan, they cut	2050.1	
6:15 **And w** the servant of the man of God	2050.1	
6:18 **And w** they came down to him, Elisha	2050.1	
6:20 **w** they were come *into* Samaria,	3509.1	
6:21 unto Elisha, **w** he saw them, My father,	3509.1	
6:23 **And w** they had eaten and drunk, he	2050.1	
6:30 **w** the king heard the words of	3509.1	
6:32 look, **w** the messenger cometh, shut	3509.1	
7: 5 and **w** they were come to the uttermost	2050.1	
7: 8 **And w** these lepers came to the	2050.1	
7:12 saying, **W** they come out of the city,	3588	
7:17 spake the king came down to him.	871.1	
8: 6 **And w** the king asked the woman,	2050.1	
8:17 years old was he **w** he *began* to reign;	871.1	
8:26 years old *was* Ahaziah **w** he *began*	871.1	
8:29 **w** he fought against Hazael king of Syria.	871.1	
9: 2 **And w** thou comest thither, look out	2050.1	
9: 5 **And w** he came, behold, the captains of	2050.1	
9:15 **w** he fought with Hazael king of Syria.)	871.1	
9:22 **w** Joram saw Jehu, that he said, *Is it*	2050.1	
9:25 **w** I and thou rode together after Ahab his	NIH	
9:27 **But w** Ahaziah the king of Judah saw	2050.1	
9:30 **And w** Jehu was come to Jezreel,	2050.1	
9:34 **And w** he was come in, he did eat and	2050.1	
10: 7 came to pass, **w** the letter came to them,	3509.1	
10:15 **And w** he was departed thence, he	2050.1	
10:17 **And w** he came *to* Samaria, he slew all	2050.1	
10:24 **And w** they went in to offer sacrifices	2050.1	
11: 1 **And w** Athaliah the mother of Ahaziah	2050.1	
11:13 **And w** Athaliah heard the noise of	2050.1	
11:14 **And w** she looked, behold, the king	2050.1	
11:21 Seven years old *was* Jehoash **w** he *began*	871.1	
12:10 **w** they saw that *there was* much money	3509.1	
13:21 and **w** the man was let down,	2050.1	
14: 2 and five years old **w** he *began* to reign,	871.1	
14: 5 Sixteen years old *was* he **w** he *began* to	871.1	
15:33 twenty years old *was* he **w** he *began* to	871.1	
16: 2 Twenty years old *was* Ahaz **w** he *began*	871.1	
16:12 **And w** the king was come from	2050.1	
18: 2 years old *was* he **w** he *began* to reign;	871.1	
18:17 **And w** they were come up, they came	2050.1	
18:18 **And w** they had called to the king,	2050.1	
18:32 **w** he persuadeth you, saying,	3588	
19: 1 **w** king Hezekiah heard *it,* that he rent	3509.1	
19: 9 **And w** he heard say of Tirhakah king of	2050.1	
19:35 and **w** they arose early in the morning,	871.1	
21: 1 Manasseh *was* twelve years old **w** he	871.1	
21:19 and two years old **w** he *began* to reign,	871.1	
22: 1 Josiah *was* eight years old **w** he *began* to	871.1	
22:11 **w** the king had heard the words of	871.1	
22:19 **w** thou heardest what I spake against	871.1	
23:29 him at Megiddo, **w** he had seen him.	3509.1	
23:31 and three years old **w** he *began* to reign;	871.1	
23:36 and five year old **w** he *began* to reign;	871.1	
24: 8 Jehoiachin *was* eighteen years old **w** he	871.1	
24:18 and one years old **w** he *began* to reign,	871.1	
25:23 **And w** all the captains of the armies,	2050.1	
1Ch 1:44 **And w** Bela was dead, Jobab the son of	2050.1	
1:45 **And w** Jobab was dead, Husham of	2050.1	
1:46 **And w** Husham was dead, Hadad the	2050.1	
1:47 **And w** Hadad was dead, Samlah of	2050.1	
1:48 **And w** Samlah was dead, Shaul of	2050.1	
1:49 **And w** Shaul was dead, Baal-hanan	2050.1	
1:50 **And w** Baal-hanan was dead,	2050.1	
2:19 **And w** Azubah was dead, Caleb took	2050.1	
2:21 whom he married **w** he *was* threescore	2050.1	
5: 7 the genealogy of their generations was	871.1	
6:15 Jehozadak went *into* captivity, **w**	871.1	
7:23 **And w** he went in to his wife,	2050.1	
10: 5 **And w** his armourbearer saw that Saul	2050.1	
10: 7 **And w** all the men of Israel that *were* in	2050.1	
10: 8 **w** the Philistines came to strip the slain,	2050.1	
10: 9 **And w** they had stripped him, they	2050.1	
10:11 **And w** all Jabesh-gilead heard all that	2050.1	

1Ch 11: 2 in time past, even **w** Saul was king,	871.1	
12:15 **w** it had overflown all his banks;	2050.1	
12:19 **w** he came with the Philistines against	2050.1	
13: 9 **And w** they came unto the	2050.1	
14: 8 **And w** the Philistines heard that David	2050.1	
14:12 **And w** they had left their gods there,	2050.1	
14:15 **w** thou shalt hear a sound of going in	3509.1	
15:26 **w** God helped the Levites that bare the	871.1	
16: 2 **And** David had made an end of	2050.1	
16:19 **W** ye were *but* few, even a few,	871.1	
16:20 And **w** they went from nation to nation,	NIH	
17:11 **w** thy days be expired that *thou* must go	3588	
18: 5 **w** the Syrians of Damascus came	2050.1	
18: 9 Now **w** Tou king of Hamath heard how	2050.1	
19: 6 **w** the children of Ammon saw that	2050.1	
19: 8 **And w** David heard *of it,* he sent Joab,	2050.1	
19:10 Now **w** Joab saw that the battle was set	2050.1	
19:15 **And w** the children of Ammon saw that	2050.1	
19:16 **And w** the Syrians saw that they were	2050.1	
19:17 **So w** David had put the battle in array	2050.1	
19:19 **And w** the servants of Hadarezer saw	2050.1	
20: 7 **But w** he defied Israel, Jonathan the son	2050.1	
21:28 At that time **w** David saw that the Lord	871.1	
23: 1 **So w** David was old and full *of* days,	2050.1	
2Ch 4: 3 rows *of* oxen *were* cast, **w** it was cast.	871.1	
5:10 **w** the Lord made a covenant with	834	
5:10 of Israel, **w** they came out of Egypt.	871.1	
5:11 **w** the priests were come out of the holy	871.1	
5:13 **w** *they* lift up *their* voice with	3509.1	
6:21 and **w** thou hearest, forgive.	2050.1	
6:26 **W** the heaven is shut up, and there is no	871.1	
6:26 from their sin, **w** thou dost afflict them;	3588	
6:27 **w** thou hast taught them the good way,	3588	
6:29 **w** every one shall know his own sore and	834	
7: 1 Now **w** Solomon had made an end of	3509.1	
7: 3 **And w** all the children of Israel saw	2050.1	
7: 6 **w** David praised by their ministry;	871.1	
9: 1 **And w** the queen of Sheba heard of	2050.1	
9: 1 and **w** she was come to Solomon,	2050.1	
9: 3 **And w** the queen of Sheba had seen	2050.1	
10: 2 **w** Jeroboam the son of Nebat, who *was*	3509.1	
10:16 **And w** all Israel saw that the king	2050.1	
11: 1 **And w** Rehoboam was come *to*	2050.1	
12: 1 **w** Rehoboam had established	3509.1	
12: 7 **w** the Lord saw that they humbled	871.1	
12:11 **w** the king entered *into* the house	1767+4480	
12:12 **w** he humbled himself, the wrath of	871.1	
12:13 and forty years old **w** he *began* to reign,	871.1	
13: 7 **w** Rehoboam was young and	2050.1	
13:14 **And w** Judah looked back, behold,	2050.1	
15: 4 **But w** they in their trouble did turn	2050.1	
15: 8 **w** Asa heard these words,	3509.1	
15: 9 **w** they saw that the Lord his God *was*	871.1	
16: 5 **w** Baasha heard *it,* that he left off	3509.1	
18:14 **And w** he was come to the king,	2050.1	
18:24 thou shalt see on that day **w** thou shalt go	834	
18:31 **w** the captains of the chariots saw	3509.1	
18:32 that **w** the captains of the chariots	3509.1	
19: 8 **w** they returned *to* Jerusalem.	2050.1	
20: 9 If, **w** evil cometh upon us, *as* the sword,	NIH	
20:10 **w** they came out of the land of Egypt,	871.1	
20:21 **And w** he had consulted with the	2050.1	
20:22 **w** they began to sing and to praise,	6256+871.1	
20:23 **w** they had made an end of	3509.1	
20:24 **And w** Judah came toward the watch	2050.1	
20:25 **And w** Jehoshaphat and his people	2050.1	
20:29 **w** they had heard that the Lord fought	871.1	
20:31 and five years old **w** he *began* to reign,	871.1	
21: 4 Now **w** Jehoram was risen up to	2050.1	
21: 5 and two years old **w** he *began* to reign,	871.1	
21:20 *years* old was he **w** he *began* to reign,	871.1	
22: 2 years old *was* Ahaziah **w** he *began* to	871.1	
22: 6 **w** he fought with Hazael king of Syria.	871.1	
22: 7 for **w** he was come, he went out with	871.1	
22: 8 **w** Jehu was executing judgment upon	3509.1	
22: 9 **w** they had slain him, they buried	871.1	
22:10 **But w** Athaliah the mother of Ahaziah	2050.1	
23: 7 be you with the king **w** he cometh in,	871.1	
23: 7 when he cometh in, and **w** he goeth out.	871.1	
23:12 Now **w** Athaliah heard the noise of	2050.1	
23:15 and **w** she was come to the entering of	2050.1	
24: 1 Joash *was* seven years old **w** he *began* to	871.1	
24:11 **w** they saw that *there was* much	3509.1	
24:14 **w** they had finished *it,* they brought	3509.1	
24:15 and was full *of* days **w** he died;	2050.1	
24:15 and thirty years old *was* he **w** he died.	871.1	
24:22 he died, he said, The Lord look	3509.1	
24:25 **w** they were departed from him, (for	871.1	
25: 1 and five years old **w** he *began* to reign,	NIH	
25: 3 **w** the kingdom was established to	834+3509.1	
26: 3 Sixteen years old *was* Uzziah **w** he	871.1	
26:16 **w** he was strong, his heart was lifted up	3509.1	
27: 1 and five years old **w** he *began* to reign,	871.1	
27: 8 twenty years old **w** he *began* to reign,	871.1	
28: 1 Ahaz *was* twenty years old **w** he *began*	871.1	
29: 1 Hezekiah *began* to reign **w** he *was* five	NIH	
29:22 **likewise,** **w** they had killed the rams,	2050.1	
29:27 **w** the burnt offering began,	6256+871.1	
29:29 **w** *they* had made an end of offering,	3509.1	
31: 1 Now **w** all this was finished, all Israel	3509.1	
31: 8 **And w** Hezekiah and the princes came	2050.1	
32: 2 **And w** Hezekiah saw that Sennacherib	2050.1	
32:21 **And w** he was come *into* the house of	2050.1	
33: 1 Manasseh *was* twelve years old **w** he	871.1	
33:12 **And w** he was in affliction, he besought	2050.1	

2Ch 33:21	twenty years old **w** he *began* to reign,	871.1
34: 1	Josiah *was* eight years old **w** he *began* to	871.1
34: 7	**And w** he had broken down the altars	2050.1
34: 8	**w** he had purged the land, and the	3807.1
34: 9	**And w** they came to Hilkiah the high	2050.1
34:14	**w** they brought out the money that was	3509.1
34:19	**w** the king had heard the words of	834
34:27	**w** thou heardest his words against this	871.1
35:20	all this, **w** Josiah had prepared the temple,	834
36: 2	and three years old **w** he *began* to reign,	871.1
36: 5	and five years old **w** he *began* to reign,	871.1
36: 9	Jehoiachin *was* eight years old **w** he	871.1
36:10	**And w** the year was expired, king	2050.1
36:11	twenty years old **w** he *began* to reign,	871.1
Ezr 2:68	**w** they came to the house of the Lᴏʀᴅ	871.1
3: 1	**And w** the seventh month was come,	2050.1
3:10	**w** the builders laid the foundation	2050.1
3:11	**w** they praised the Lᴏʀᴅ, because	871.1
3:12	**w** the foundation of this house was laid	871.1
4: 1	Now **w** the adversaries of Judah and	NIH
4:23	Now **w** the copy of king Artaxerxes' letter	4481
9: 1	Now **w** these *things* were done,	3509.1
9: 3	**w** I heard this thing, I rent my garment	3509.1
10: 1	Now **w** Ezra had prayed, and when he	3509.1
10: 1	he had confessed, weeping and	3509.1
10: 6	**w** he came thither, he did eat no bread,	NIH
Ne 1: 4	**w** I heard these words, *that* I sat down	3509.1
2: 3	**w** the city, the place of my fathers'	834
2: 6	**w** wilt thou return? So it pleased the king	4970
2:10	**W** Sanballat the Horonite, and Tobiah	2050.1
2:19	**But w** Sanballat the Horonite,	2050.1
4: 1	**that w** Sanballat heard that we	834+3509.1
4: 7	*that* **w** Sanballat, and Tobiah,	834+3509.1
4:12	**that w** the Jews which dwelt by	834+3509.1
4:15	**w** our enemies heard that it was	834+3509.1
5: 6	was very angry **w** I heard their cry	834+3509.1
6: 1	**w** Sanballat, and Tobiah,	834+3509.1
6:16	**that w** all our enemies heard	834+3509.1
7: 1	**w** the wall was built, *and* I had set	834+3509.1
7:73	**w** the seventh month came, the children	2050.1
8: 5	**w** he opened *it*, all the people stood *up:*	3509.1
8: 9	**w** they heard the words of the law.	3509.1
9:18	**w** they had made them a molten calf,	3588
9:27	of their trouble, **w** they cried unto thee,	NIH
9:28	**yet w** they returned, and cried unto	2050.1
10:38	the Levites, **w** the Levites take tithes;	871.1
13: 3	came to pass, **w** they had heard the law,	3509.1
13:19	that **w** the gates of Jerusalem began to be	834
Est 1: 2	**w** the king Ahasuerus sat on the throne	3509.1
1: 4	**W** he shewed the riches of his glorious	871.1
1: 5	**w** these days were expired, the king	871.1
1:10	**w** the heart of the king was merry with	3509.1
1:17	in their eyes, **w** it shall be reported,	871.1
1:20	**And w** the king's decree which he shall	2050.1
2: 1	**w** the wrath of king Ahasuerus was	3509.1
2: 7	**w** her father and mother were dead,	871.1
2: 8	**w** the king's commandment and his	871.1
2: 8	**w** many maidens were gathered together	871.1
2:12	**w** every maid's turn was come to go	871.1
2:15	**w** the turn of Esther, the daughter of	871.1
2:19	**w** the virgins were gathered together	871.1
2:20	**like as w** she was brought up	834+3509.1
2:23	**And w** inquisition was made of	2050.1
3: 4	**w** they spake daily unto him,	3509.1
3: 5	**And w** Haman saw that Mordecai	2050.1
4: 1	**W** Mordecai perceived all that was	2050.1
5: 2	**w** the king saw Esther the queen	3509.1
5: 9	**w** Haman saw Mordecai in the king's	3509.1
5:10	**and w** he came home, he sent and	2050.1
9: 1	**w** the king's commandment and his	834
9:25	**w** Esther came before the king,	871.1
Job 1: 5	**w** the days of *their* feasting were gone	NIH
1: 6	there was a day **w** the sons of God	2050.1
1:13	there was a day **w** his sons and	2050.1
2: 1	there was a day **w** the sons of God	2050.1
2:11	Now **w** Job's three friends heard of all	2050.1
2:12	**And w** they lift up their eyes afar off,	2050.1
3:11	did I *not* give up the ghost **w** I came	2050.1
3:22	are glad, **w** they can find the grave?	3588
4:13	the night, **w** deep sleep falleth on men.	871.1
5:21	shalt thou be afraid of destruction **w**	3588
6: 5	Doth the wild ass bray **w** he hath grass?	5921
6:17	it is hot, they are consumed out of	871.1
7: 4	**W** I lie down, I say, When shall I arise,	518
7: 4	**W** shall I arise, and the night be gone?	4970
7:13	**W** I say, My bed shall comfort me,	3588
11: 3	**and w** thou mockest, shall no man	2050.1
16:22	**W** a few years are come, then I shall go	3588
17:16	the pit, **w** *our* rest together *is* in the dust.	871.1
20:23	**W** he is about to fill his belly, *God* shall	NIH
21: 6	Even **w** I remember I am afraid,	518
21:21	**w** the number of his months is cut off	2050.1
22:29	**W** *men* are cast down, then thou shalt	3588
23:10	**w** he hath tried me, I shall come forth as	NIH
23:15	**w** I consider, I am afraid of him.	NIH
27: 8	hath gained, **w** God taketh away his soul?	3588
27: 9	Will God hear his cry **w** trouble cometh	3588
28:26	**W** he made a decree for the rain,	871.1
29: 2	as *in* the days **w** God preserved me;	NIH
29: 3	**W** his candle shined upon my head,	871.1
29: 3	**w** by his light I walked *through* darkness;	NIH
29: 4	**w** the secret of God *was* upon my	871.1
29: 5	**W** the Almighty *was* yet with me,	NIH
29: 5	with me, **w** my children *were* about me;	NIH
29: 6	**W** I washed my steps with butter,	871.1

Job 29: 7	**W** I went out *to* the gate through the	871.1
29: 7	city, **w** I prepared my seat in the street;	NIH
29:11	**W** the ear heard *me*, then it blessed me;	3588
29:11	and **w** the eye saw *me*, it gave witness	2050.1
30:26	**W** I looked for good, then evil came *unto*	3588
30:26	*unto* me: **and w** I waited for light,	2050.1
31:13	**w** they contended with me;	871.1
31:14	What then shall I do **w** God riseth up?	3588
31:14	**w** he visiteth, what shall I answer him?	3588
31:21	fatherless, **w** I saw my help in the gate:	3588
31:26	I beheld the sun **w** it shined, or the moon	3588
31:29	or lift up myself **w** evil found him:	3588
32: 5	**W** Elihu saw that *there* was no answer	2050.1
32:16	**W** I had waited, (for they spake not,	2050.1
33:15	night, **w** deep sleep falleth upon men,	871.1
34:29	**W** he giveth quietness, who then	2050.1
34:29	**and w** he hideth *his* face, who then	2050.1
36:13	wrath: they cry not **w** he bindeth them.	3588
36:20	**w** people are cut off in their place.	3807.1
37: 4	will not stay them **w** his voice is heard.	3588
37:15	Dost thou know **w** God disposed them,	871.1
37:17	**w** he quieteth the earth by the south	871.1
38: 4	wast thou **w** I laid the foundations	871.1
38: 7	**W** the morning stars sang together,	871.1
38: 8	**w** up the sea with doors, **w** it brake forth,	871.1
38: 9	**W** I made the cloud the garment thereof,	871.1
38:38	**W** the dust groweth into hardness,	871.1
38:40	**W** they couch in *their* dens, *and* abide in	3588
38:41	**w** his young ones cry unto God,	3588
39: 1	Knowest thou the time **w** the wild goats	NIH
39: 1	*or* canst thou mark **w** the hinds do calve?	NIH
39: 2	knowest thou the time **w** they bring forth?	NIH
41:25	**W** he raiseth up *himself*, the mighty are	4480
42:10	of Job, **w** he prayed for his friends:	871.1
Ps 2:12	way, **w** his wrath is kindled but a little:	3588
3: T	**W** David, **w** he fled from Absalom his son.	871.1
4: 1	I Hear me **w** I call, O God of my	871.1
4: 1	hast enlarged me **w** I was in distress;	NIH
4: 3	the Lᴏʀᴅ will hear **w** I call unto him.	871.1
8: 3	**W** I consider thy heavens, the work of	3588
9: 3	**W** mine enemies are turned back,	3588
9:12	**W** he maketh inquisition for blood,	3588
10: 9	the poor, **w** he draweth him into his net.	871.1
12: 8	every side, **w** the vilest men are exalted.	3509.1
13: 4	those that trouble me rejoice **w** I am	3588
14: 7	**w** the Lᴏʀᴅ bringeth back the captivity	871.1
17:15	satisfied, **w** I awake, with thy likeness.	871.1
20: 9	let the king hear us **w** we call.	3117+871.1
21:12	**w** thou shalt make ready *thine arrows*	NIH
22: 9	thou didst make me hope **w** I was upon	871.1
22:24	but **w** he cried unto him, he heard.	871.1
27: 2	**W** the wicked, *even* mine enemies and	871.1
27: 7	Hear, O Lᴏʀᴅ, **w** I cry *with* my voice:	NIH
27: 8	**W** thou saidst, Seek ye my face; my heart	NIH
27:10	**W** my father and my mother forsake me,	3588
28: 2	of my supplications, **w** I cry unto thee,	871.1
28: 2	**w** I lift up my hands toward thy holy	871.1
30: 9	in my blood, **w** I go down to the pit?	871.1
31:22	of my supplications, **w** I cried unto thee.	871.1
32: 3	**W** I kept silence, my bones waxed old	3588
32: 6	thee in a time **w** thou mayest be found:	NIH
34: T	**w** he changed his behaviour before	871.1
35:13	*as for* me, **w** they were sick, my clothing	871.1
37:33	hand, nor condemn him **w** he is judged.	871.1
37:34	**w** the wicked are cut off, thou shalt see	871.1
38:16	**w** my foot slippeth, they magnify	871.1
39:11	**W** thou with rebukes dost correct man	871.1
41: 5	me, **W** shall he die, and his name perish?	4970
41: 6	to itself; **w** he goeth abroad, he telleth *it.*	NIH
42: 2	**w** shall I come and appear before God?	4970
42: 4	**W** I remember these *things*, I pour out	2050.1
49: 5	**w** the iniquity of my heels shall compass	NIH
49:16	Be not thou afraid **w** one is made rich,	3588
49:16	**w** the glory of his house is increased;	3588
49:17	For **w** he dieth he shall carry nothing	871.1
49:18	praise thee, **w** thou doest well to thyself.	3588
50:18	**W** thou sawest a thief, then thou	518
51: T	**w** Nathan the prophet came unto him,	871.1
51: 4	that thou mightest be justified **w** thou	871.1
51: 4	speakest, *and* be clear **w** thou judgest.	871.1
52: T	**w** Doeg the Edomite came and told Saul,	871.1
53: 6	**W** God bringeth back the captivity of his	871.1
54: T	**w** the Ziphims came and said to Saul,	871.1
56: T	**w** the Philistines took him in Gath.	871.1
56: 6	my steps, **w** they wait for my soul.	834+3509.1
56: 9	**W** I cry *unto thee*, then shall mine	3117+871.1
57: T	of David, **w** he fled from Saul in the cave.	871.1
58: 7	**w** he bendeth *his* bow *to shoot* his arrows,	NIH
58:10	The righteous shall rejoice **w** he seeth	3588
59: T	**w** Saul sent, and they watcht the house	871.1
60: T	**w** he strove with Aram-naharaim and	871.1
60: T	**w** Joab returned, and smote of Edom in	2050.1
61: 2	unto thee, **w** my heart is overwhelmed:	871.1
63: T	**w** he was in the wilderness of Judah.	871.1
63: 6	**W** I remember thee upon my bed,	518
65: 3	corn, **w** thou hast so provided for it.	3588
66:14	mouth hath spoken, **w** I was in trouble.	3807.1
68: 7	**W** thou wentest forth before thy people,	871.1
68: 7	**w** thou didst march through the	871.1
68: 9	thine inheritance, **w** it was weary.	2050.1
68:14	**W** the Almighty scattered kings in it,	871.1
69:10	**W** I wept, *and chastened* my soul with	2050.1
71: 9	forsake me not **w** my strength faileth.	3509.1
71:18	Now also **w** I am old and grayheaded,	5704
71:23	My lips shall greatly rejoice **w** I sing unto	3588

Ps 72:12	For he shall deliver the needy **w** he crieth;	NIH
73: 3	**w** I saw the prosperity of the wicked.	NIH
73:16	**W** I thought to know this, it *was* too	2050.1
73:20	As a dream **w** one awaketh; *so*, O Lord,	4480
73:20	*so*, O Lord, **w** thou awakest, thou shalt	871.1
75: 2	**W** I shall receive the congregation I will	3588
76: 7	who may stand in thy sight **w** once	227+4480
76: 9	**W** God arose to judgment, to save all	871.1
78:34	**W** he slew them, then they sought him:	518
78:42	*nor* the day **w** he delivered them from	834
78:59	**W** God heard *this*, he was wroth,	2050.1
81: 5	**w** he went out through the land of Egypt	871.1
87: 6	shall count, **w** he writeth *up* the people,	871.1
89: 9	**w** the waves thereof arise, thou stillest	871.1
90: 4	thy sight *are but* as yesterday **w** it is past,	3588
92: 7	The wicked spring as the grass,	871.1
92: 7	**and w** all the workers of iniquity do	2050.1
94: 8	people: and ye fools, **w** will ye be wise?	4970
94:18	**W** I said, My foot slippeth; thy mercy,	518
95: 9	**W** your fathers tempted me, proved me,	834
101: 2	O **w** wilt thou come unto me? I will walk	4970
102: T	**w** he is overwhelmed, and poureth out	3588
102: 2	Hide not thy face from me in the day **w** I	NIH
102: 2	in the day **w** I call answer me speedily.	NIH
102:16	**W** the Lᴏʀᴅ shall build up Zion, he shall	3588
102:22	**W** the people are gathered together,	871.1
105:12	**W** they were *but a few* men in number;	871.1
105:13	**W** they went from one nation to	2050.1
105:38	Egypt was glad **w** they departed:	871.1
106:44	their affliction, **w** he heard their cry:	871.1
109: 7	**W** he shall be judged, let him be	871.1
109:23	am gone like the shadow **w** it declineth:	3509.1
109:25	**w** they looked upon me they shaked their	NIH
109:28	**w** they arise, let them be ashamed:	NIH
114: 1	**W** Israel went out of Egypt, the house of	871.1
119: 6	**w** I have respect unto all thy	871.1
119: 7	**w** I shall have learned thy righteous	871.1
119:32	**w** thou shalt enlarge my heart.	3588
119:74	They that fear thee will be glad **w** they see	NIH
119:82	word, saying, **W** wilt thou comfort me?	4970
119:84	**w** wilt thou execute judgment on them	4970
119:171	**w** thou hast taught me thy statutes.	3588
120: 7	*for* peace: but **w** I speak, they *are* for war.	3588
122: 1	I was glad **w** they said unto me, Let us go	871.1
124: 2	on our side, **w** men rose up against us:	871.1
124: 3	**w** their wrath was kindled against us:	871.1
126: 1	**W** the Lᴏʀᴅ turned again the captivity	871.1
137: 1	yea, we wept, **w** we remembered Zion.	871.1
138: 3	In the day **w** I cried thou answeredst me,	NIH
138: 4	**w** they hear the words of thy mouth.	3588
139:15	**w** I was made in secret,	834
139:16	**w** *as yet there* was none of them.	2050.1
139:18	the sand: **w** I awake, I am still with thee.	NIH
141: 1	ear unto my voice, **w** I cry unto thee.	871.1
141: 6	**W** their judges are overthrown in stony	NIH
141: 7	as **w** one cutteth and cleaveth *wood* upon	NIH
142: T	of David; A Prayer **w** he was in the cave.	871.1
142: 3	**W** my spirit was overwhelmed within	871.1
Pr 1:26	I will mock **w** your fear cometh;	871.1
1:27	**W** your fear cometh as desolation,	871.1
1:27	**w** distress and anguish cometh upon you:	871.1
2:10	**W** wisdom entereth into thine heart,	3588
3:24	**W** thou liest down, thou shalt not be	518
3:25	desolation of the wicked, **w** it cometh.	3588
3:27	**w** it is in the power of thine hand to do	871.1
3:28	I will give; **w** thou hast it by thee.	2050.1
4: 8	to honour, **w** thou dost embrace her.	3588
4:12	**W** thou goest thy steps shall not be	871.1
4:12	**w** thou runnest, thou shalt not stumble.	518
5:11	**w** thy flesh and thy body are consumed,	871.1
6: 3	**w** thou art come into the hand of thy	3588
6: 9	**w** wilt thou arise out of thy sleep?	4970
6:22	**W** thou goest, it shall lead thee; when	871.1
6:22	**w** thou sleepest, it shall keep thee;	871.1
6:22	**w** thou awakest, it shall talk *with* thee.	NIH
6:30	he steal to satisfy his soul **w** he is hungry;	3588
8:24	**W** *there were* no depths, I was brought	871.1
8:24	**w** *there were* no fountains abounding	871.1
8:27	**W** he prepared the heavens, I *was* there:	871.1
8:27	**w** he set a compass upon the face of	871.1
8:28	**W** he established the clouds above:	871.1
8:28	**w** he strengthened the fountains of	871.1
8:29	**W** he gave to the sea his decree, that	871.1
8:29	**w** he appointed the foundations of	871.1
11: 2	**W** pride cometh, then cometh shame:	NIH
11: 7	**W** a wicked man dieth, *his* expectation	871.1
11:10	**W** it goeth well with the righteous, the	871.1
11:10	**w** the wicked perish, *there* is shouting.	871.1
13:12	but **w** the desire cometh, *it is* a tree of life.	NIH
14: 7	**w** thou perceivest not *in* him the lips of	2050.1
16: 7	**W** a man's ways please the Lᴏʀᴅ,	871.1
17:14	The beginning of strife *is as* **w** one letteth	NIH
17:28	Even a fool, **w** he holdeth his peace,	NIH
18: 3	**W** the wicked cometh, *then* cometh also	871.1
20:14	but **w** he is gone his way, then	2050.1
21:11	**W** the scorner is punished, the simple is	871.1
21:11	**w** the wise is instructed, he receiveth	871.1
21:27	**w** he bringeth it with a wicked mind?	NIH
22: 6	**w** he is old, he will not depart from it.	3588
23: 1	**W** thou sittest to eat with a ruler,	3588
23:16	rejoice, **w** thy lips speak right things.	871.1
23:22	and despise not thy mother **w** she is old.	3588
23:31	Look not thou upon the wine **w** it is red,	3588
23:31	**w** it giveth his colour in the cup, *when* it	3588
23:31	in the cup, **w** it moveth itself aright.	NIH

Pr 23:35 **w** shall I awake? I will seek it yet again. 4970
24:14 **w** hast found *it,* then there shall be a 518
24:17 Rejoice not **w** thine enemy falleth, 871.1
24:17 not thine heart be glad **w** he stumbleth: 871.1
25: 8 **w** thy neighbour hath put thee to shame. 871.1
26:25 **W** he speaketh fair, believe him not: 3588
28: 1 The wicked flee **w** no man pursueth: 2050.1
28:12 **W** righteous *men* do rejoice, *there is* 871.1
28:12 but **w** the wicked rise, a man is hidden. 871.1
28:28 **W** the wicked rise, men hide themselves: 871.1
28:28 but **w** they perish, the righteous increase. 871.1
29: 2 **W** the righteous are in authority, 871.1
29: 2 **w** the wicked beareth rule, the people 871.1
29:16 **W** the wicked are multiplied, 871.1
30:22 For a servant **w** he reigneth; and a fool 3588
30:22 and a fool **w** he is filled *with* meat; 3588
30:23 For an odious *woman* **w** she is married; 3588
31:23 **w** he sitteth among the elders of the land. 871.1
Ecc 4:10 woe to him *that* is alone **w** he falleth; 7945
5: 1 Keep thy foot **w** thou goest to 834+3509.1
5: 4 **W** thou vowest a vow unto God, 834+3509.1
5:11 **W** goods increase, they are increased that 871.1
8: 7 for who can tell him **w** it shall be? 834+3509.1
8:16 **W** I applied mine heart to know 834+3509.1
9:12 **w** it falleth suddenly upon them. 7945+3509.1
10: 3 **w** he that is a fool walketh by the way, 3509.1
10:16 **w** thy king *is* a child, and thy princes eat 7945
10:17 **w** thy king *is* the son of nobles, 7945
12: 1 nor the years draw nigh, **w** thou shalt say, 834
12: 3 In the day **w** the keepers of the house 7945
12: 4 **w** the sound of the grinding is low, 871.1
12: 5 **w** they shall be afraid of *that which is* NIH
SS 5: 6 my soul failed **w** he spake: I sought him, 871.1
8: 1 **w** I should find thee without, I would kiss NIH
8: 8 shall we do for our sister in the day **w** 7945
Isa 1:12 **W** ye come to appear before me, who 3588
1:15 **w** ye spread forth your hands, I will hide 871.1
1:15 yea, **w** ye make many prayers, I will not 3588
2:19 **w** he ariseth to shake terribly the earth. 871.1
2:21 **w** he ariseth to shake terribly the earth. 871.1
3: 6 **W** a man shall take hold of his brother *of* 3588
4: 4 **W** the Lord shall have washed away the 518
5: 4 **w** I looked that *it* should bring forth NIH
6:13 **w** they cast *their leaves: so* the holy seed 871.1
8:19 **w** they say unto you, Seek unto 3588
8:21 to pass, **that w** they shall be hungry, 3588
9: 1 **w** at the first he lightly afflicted the land 6256
9: 3 as *men* rejoice **w** they divide the spoil. 871.1
10:12 *that* **w** the Lord hath performed his whole 3588
10:18 they shall be as **w** a standard-bearer NIH
13:19 shall be as **w** God overthrew Sodom and NIH
16:12 **w** it is seen that Moab is weary on the 3588
17: 5 it shall be as **w** the harvestman gathereth NIH
18: 3 **w** *he* lifteth up an ensign *on* 871.1
18: 3 and **w** *he* bloweth a trumpet, hear ye. 3509.1
18: 5 **w** the bud is perfect, and the sour grape 3509.1
20: 1 (**w** Sargon the king of Assyria sent him,) 871.1
24:13 **W** thus it shall be in the midst of the land 3588
24:13 the gleaning grapes **w** the vintage is done. 518
24:23 **w** the LORD of hosts shall reign in mount 3588
25: 4 **w** the blast of the terrible ones *is* as a 3588
26: 9 **w** thy judgments *are* in the earth, 834+3509.1
26:11 LORD, **w** thy hand is lifted up, they will NIH
26:16 they poured out a prayer **w** thy chastening NIH
27: 8 In measure, **w** it shooteth forth, thou wilt 871.1
27: 9 **w** he maketh all the stones of the altar as 871.1
27:11 the boughs thereof are withered, 871.1
28: 4 which **w** he that looketh upon it seeth, NIH
28:15 **w** the overflowing scourge shall pass 3588
28:18 **w** the overflowing scourge shall pass 3588
28:25 **W** he hath made plain the face thereof, 518
29: 8 shall even be **as w** a hungry *man* 834+3509.1
29: 8 or **as w** a thirsty *man* dreameth, 834+3509.1
29:23 **w** he seeth his children, the work of 871.1
30:19 **w** he shall hear it, he will answer thee. 3509.1
30:21 **w** ye turn to the right hand, and when ye 3588
30:21 the right hand, and **w** ye turn to the left. 3588
30:25 of the great slaughter, **w** the towers fall. 871.1
30:29 as *in* the night **w** a holy solemnity is kept; NIH
30:29 as **w** one goeth with a pipe to come into NIH
31: 3 **W** the LORD shall stretch out his hand, 2050.1
31: 4 **w** a multitude of shepherds is called forth 834
32: 7 even **w** the needy speaketh right. 871.1
32:19 **W** it shall hail, coming down *on* 2050.1
33: 1 **w** thou shalt cease to spoil, thou shalt 3509.1
33: 1 **w** thou shalt make an end to deal 3509.1
37: 1 **w** king Hezekiah heard *it,* that he rent 3509.1
37: 9 **And w** he heard *it,* he sent messengers 2050.1
37:36 **and w** they arose early in the morning, 2050.1
38: 9 **w** he had been sick, and was recovered 871.1
41:17 **W** the poor and needy seek water, NIH
41:28 that, **w** I asked of them, could answer a NIH
43: 2 **W** thou passest through the waters, I *will* 3588
43: 2 **w** thou walkest through the fire, thou 3588
43:12 **w** *there was* no strange *god* among you: 2050.1
48: 7 before the day **w** thou heardest them 2050.1
48:13 **w** I call unto them, they stand *up* together. NIH
48:21 they thirsted not **w** he led them through NIH
50: 2 Wherefore, **w** I came, *was there* no man? NIH
50: 2 **w** I called, *was there* none to answer? NIH
52: 8 **w** the LORD shall bring again Zion. NIH
53: 2 **and w** we shall see him, *there is* no 2050.1
53:10 **w** thou shalt make his soul an offering for 518
54: 6 **w** thou wast refused, saith thy God. 3588
57:13 **W** thou criest, let thy companies deliver 871.1

Isa 57:20 **w** it cannot rest, whose waters cast up 3588
58: 7 **w** thou seest the naked, that thou cover 3588
59:19 **W** the enemy shall come in like a flood, 3588
64: 2 As **w** the melting fire burneth, the fire NIH
64: 3 **W** thou didst terrible things *which* we 871.1
65:12 because **w** I called, ye did not answer; NIH
65:12 **w** I spake, ye did not hear; but did evil NIH
66: 4 because **w** I called, none did answer; NIH
66: 4 did answer; **w** I spake, they did not hear: NIH
66:14 **And w** ye see *this,* your heart shall 2050.1
Jer 2: 2 **w** thou wentest after me in the wilderness, NIH
2: 7 **but w** ye entered, ye defiled my land, 2050.1
2:17 God, **w** he led thee by the way? 6256+871.1
2:20 **w** upon every high hill and under every 3588
2:26 As the thief is ashamed **w** he is found, 3588
3: 8 **w** for all the causes whereby backsliding 3588
3:16 **w** ye be multiplied and increased in 3588
4:30 **w** thou art spoiled, what wilt thou do? NIH
5: 7 **w** I had fed them to the full, then 2050.1
5:19 it shall come to pass, **w** ye shall say, 3588
6:14 Peace, peace; **w** *there is* no peace. 2050.1
6:15 they ashamed **w** they had committed 3588
8:11 Peace, peace; **w** *there is* no peace. 2050.1
8:12 they ashamed **w** they had committed 3588
8:18 **W** I would comfort myself against sorrow, NIH
10:13 **W** he uttereth his voice, *there is* a 3807.1
11:15 **w** thou doest evil, then thou rejoicest. 3588
12: 1 art thou, O LORD, **w** I plead with thee: 3588
13:21 wilt thou say **w** he shall punish thee? 3588
13:27 be made clean? **w** *shall it* once *be?* 310+490
14:12 **W** they fast, I will not hear their cry; 3588
14:12 **w** they offer burnt offering and an 3588
16:10 **w** thou shalt shew this people all these 3588
17: 6 and shall not see **w** good cometh; 3588
17: 8 shall not see **w** heat cometh, but her leaf 3588
18:22 **w** thou shalt bring a troop suddenly upon 3588
21: 1 **w** king Zedekiah sent unto him Pashur 871.1
22:23 how gracious shalt thou be **w** pangs 871.1
23:33 **w** this people, or the prophet, or a priest, 3588
25:12 **w** seventy years are accomplished, 3509.1
26: 8 **w** Jeremiah had made an end of 3509.1
26:10 **W** the princes of Judah heard these 2050.1
26:21 **And w** Jehoiakim the king, with all his 2050.1
26:21 **but w** Urijah heard *it,* he was afraid, 2050.1
27:20 **w** he carried away captive Jeconiah the 871.1
28: 9 **w** the word of the prophet shall come to 871.1
29:13 find *me,* **w** ye shall search for me with all 3588
31: 2 *even* Israel **w** *I* went to cause him to rest. NIH
31:23 **w** I shall bring again their captivity; 871.1
31:35 which divideth the sea **w** the waves 2050.1
32:16 Now **w** I had delivered the evidence of 310
34: 1 **w** Nebuchadnezzar king of Babylon, 2050.1
34: 7 **W** the king of Babylon's army fought 2050.1
34:10 **w** all the princes, and all the people, 2050.1
34:14 **and w** he hath served thee six years, 2050.1
34:18 **w** they cut the calf in twain, 834
35:11 **w** Nebuchadrezzar king of Babylon came 871.1
36:11 **W** Michaiah the son of Gemariah, 2050.1
36:13 **w** Baruch read the book in the ears of 871.1
36:16 it came to pass **w** they had heard all 3509.1
36:23 **w** Jehudi had read three or four leaves, 3509.1
37: 5 **and w** the Chaldeans that besieged 2050.1
37:11 *that* **w** the army of the Chaldeans was 871.1
37:13 **And w** he was in the gate of Benjamin, 2050.1
37:16 **W** Jeremiah was entered into the 3588
38: 7 Now **w** Ebed-melech the Ethiopian, 2050.1
38:28 was *there* **w** Jerusalem was taken. 834+3509.1
39: 4 *that* **w** Zedekiah the king of Judah 834+3509.1
39: 5 **and w** they had taken him, they 2050.1
40: 1 **w** he had taken him being bound in 871.1
40: 7 Now **w** all the captains of the forces 2050.1
40:11 Likewise **w** all the Jews that *were* in 2050.1
41: 7 **w** they came into the midst of the city, 3509.1
41:11 **But w** Johanan the son of Kareah, 2050.1
41:13 *that* **w** all the people which *were* with 3509.1
42: 6 **w** we obey the voice of the LORD our 3588
42:18 upon you, **w** ye shall enter *into* Egypt: 871.1
42:20 **w** ye sent me unto the LORD your God, 3588
43: 1 *that* Jeremiah had made an end of 3509.1
43:11 **And w** he cometh, he shall smite the 2050.1
44:19 **w** we burnt incense to the queen of 3588
45: 1 **w** he had written these words in a book 871.1
51:16 **W** he uttereth *his* voice, *there is* a 3807.1
51:55 **w** her waves do roar like great waters, 2050.1
51:59 **w** he went with Zedekiah the king of 871.1
51:61 **W** thou comest *to* Babylon, and shalt 3509.1
51:63 **w** thou hast made an end of reading this 3509.1
52: 1 and twenty year old **w** he *began* to reign, 871.1
La 1: 7 **w** her people fell into the hand of 871.1
2:12 **w** they swooned as the wounded in 871.1
2:12 **w** their soul was poured out into their 871.1
3: 8 **w** I cry and shout, he shutteth out my 3588
3:37 to pass, **w** the Lord commandeth *it* not? NIH
4:15 not, **w** they fled away and wandered: 3588
Eze 1: 9 they turned not **w** they went; they went 871.1
1:12 *and* they turned not **w** they went. 871.1
1:17 **W** they went, they went upon their four 871.1
1:17 *and* they turned not **w** they went. 871.1
1:19 **w** the living creatures went, the wheels 871.1
1:19 **w** the living creatures were lift up from 871.1
1:21 **W** those went, *these* went; and when 871.1
1:21 **w** those stood, *these* stood; and when 871.1
1:21 **w** those were lifted up from the earth, 871.1
1:24 **w** they went, I heard the noise of their 871.1
1:24 **w** they stood, they let down their wings. 871.1

Eze 1:25 **w** they stood, *and* had let down their 871.1
1:28 **And w** I saw *it,* I fell upon my face, 2050.1
2: 2 spirit entered into me **w** he spake 834+3509.1
2: 9 **And w** I looked, behold, a hand *was* 2050.1
3:18 **W** I say unto the wicked, Thou shalt 871.1
3:20 **W** a righteous *man* doth turn from his 871.1
3:27 **w** I speak with thee, I will open thy 871.1
4: 6 **And w** thou hast accomplished them, 2050.1
5: 2 **w** the days of the siege are fulfilled: 3509.1
5:13 **w** I have accomplished my fury in them. 871.1
5:15 **w** I shall execute judgments in thee in 871.1
5:16 **W** I shall send upon them the evil arrows 871.1
6: 8 **w** ye shall be scattered through 871.1
6:13 **w** their slain *men* shall be among their 871.1
8: 7 **and w** I looked, behold a hole in the 2050.1
8: 8 **and w** I had digged in the wall, behold 2050.1
10: 3 side of the house, **w** the man went in; 871.1
10: 5 as the voice of the Almighty God **w** he 871.1
10: 6 **w** he had commanded the man clothed 871.1
10: 9 **And w** I looked, behold the four wheels 2050.1
10:11 **W** they went, they went upon their four 871.1
10:16 **w** the cherubims went, the wheels went 871.1
10:16 **w** the cherubims lift up their wings to 871.1
10:17 **W** they stood, *these* stood; and when 871.1
10:17 **w** they were lifted up, *these* lift up 871.1
10:19 **w** they went out, the wheels also *were* 871.1
11:13 it came to pass, **w** I prophesied, 3509.1
12:15 **w** I shall scatter them among the nations, 871.1
13:12 Lo, **w** the wall is fallen, shall it not be 2050.1
14: 9 if the prophet be deceived **w** he hath 2050.1
14:13 the land sinneth against me by 3588
14:21 How much more **w** I send my four sore NIH
14:23 **w** ye see their ways and their doings: 3588
15: 5 **w** it was whole, it was meet for no 871.1
15: 5 **w** the fire hath devoured it, and it is 2050.1
15: 7 the LORD, **w** I set my face against them. 871.1
16: 6 **And w** I passed by thee, and saw thee 2050.1
16: 6 I said unto thee **w** *thou wast* in thy blood, NIH
16: 6 I said unto thee **w** *thou wast* in thy blood, NIH
16: 8 **Now w** I passed by thee, and looked 2050.1
16:22 **w** thou wast naked and bare, 871.1
16:53 **W** I shall bring again their captivity, 2050.1
16:55 **W** thy sisters, Sodom and her daughters, 2050.1
16:61 **w** thou shalt receive thy sisters, thine 871.1
16:63 **w** I am pacified toward thee for all that 871.1
17:10 **w** the east wind toucheth it? 3509.1
17:18 **w** lo, he had given his hand, 2050.1
18:19 **W** the son hath done that which is 2050.1
18:24 **But w** the righteous turneth away from 2050.1
18:26 **W** a righteous *man* turneth away from 871.1
18:27 **w** the wicked *man* turneth away from 871.1
19: 5 **Now w** she saw that she had waited, 871.1
20: 5 In the day **w** I chose Israel, and lifted up 871.1
20: 5 **w** I lifted up mine hand unto them, 871.1
20:28 *For* **w** I had brought them into the land, 2050.1
20:31 For **w** ye offer your gifts, when *ye* make 871.1
20:31 **w** *ye* make your sons to pass through 871.1
20:41 **w** I bring you out from the people, 871.1
20:42 **w** I shall bring you into the land of Israel, 871.1
20:44 **w** I have wrought with you for my 871.1
21: 7 shall be, **w** they say unto thee, Wherefore 3588
21:25 iniquity *shall have* an end, 6256+871.1
21:29 **w** *their* iniquity *shall have* an end. 6256+871.1
22:28 the LORD hath not spoken. 2050.1
23: 5 Aholah played the harlot **w** she was mine; NIH
23:11 **And w** her sister Aholibah saw *this,* she 2050.1
23:14 **for w** she saw men pourtrayed upon 2050.1
23:39 **For w** they had slain their children to 871.1
24:24 **w** this cometh, ye shall know that I *am* 871.1
24:25 not *be* in the day **w** I take from them NIH
25: 3 against my sanctuary, **w** it was profaned; 3588
25: 3 the land of Israel, **w** it was desolate; 3588
25: 3 of Judah, **w** they went into captivity; 3588
25:17 **w** I shall lay my vengeance upon them. 871.1
26:10 chariots, **w** he shall enter into thy gates, 871.1
26:15 sound of thy fall, **w** the wounded cry, 871.1
26:15 **w** the slaughter is made in the midst of 871.1
26:19 **W** I shall make thee a desolate city, 871.1
26:19 **w** *I* shall bring up the deep upon thee, 871.1
26:20 **W** I shall bring thee down with them 2050.1
27:33 **W** thy wares went forth out of the seas, 871.1
27:34 *In the* time **w** *thou shalt be* broken by NIH
28:22 **w** I shall have executed judgments in 871.1
28:25 **W** I shall have gathered the house of 871.1
28:26 **w** I have executed judgments upon all 871.1
29: 7 **w** they took hold of thee by thy hand, 871.1
29: 7 **w** they leaned upon thee, thou brakest, 871.1
29:16 **w** they shall look after them: 871.1
30: 4 **w** the slain shall fall in Egypt, 871.1
30: 8 **w** I have set a fire in Egypt, and *when* all 871.1
30: 8 and **w** all her helpers shall be destroyed. NIH
30:18 **w** I shall break there the yokes of Egypt: 871.1
30:25 **w** I shall put my sword into the hand of 871.1
31: 5 the multitude of waters, **w** he shot forth. 871.1
31:15 In the day **w** he went down to the grave I NIH
31:16 **w** I cast him down to hell with them that 871.1
32: 7 **w** *I* shall put thee out, I will cover 871.1
32: 9 **w** I shall bring thy destruction among 871.1
32:10 **w** I shall brandish my sword before 871.1
32:15 **W** I shall make the land of Egypt desolate 871.1
32:15 **w** I shall smite all them that dwell 871.1
33: 2 **W** I bring the sword upon a land, 3588
33: 3 *If* **w** he seeth the sword come upon 2050.1
33: 8 **W** I say unto the wicked, O wicked *man,* 871.1
33:13 **W** I shall say to the righteous, *that* he 871.1

Eze	33:14 **w** I say unto the wicked, Thou shalt	871.1
	33:18 **W** the righteous turneth from his	871.1
	33:29 **w** I have laid the land most desolate	871.1
	33:33 **w** this cometh to pass, (lo, it will come)	871.1
	34: 5 of the field, **w** they were scattered,	2050.1
	34:27 **w** I have broken the bands of their yoke,	871.1
	35:11 them, **w** I have judged them.	834+3509.1
	35:14 **W** the whole earth rejoiceth, I will	3509.1
	36:17 the house of Israel dwelt in their own	NIH
	36:20 **And w** they entered unto the heathen,	2050.1
	36:20 my holy name, **w** they said to them,	871.1
	36:23 **w** I shall be sanctified in you before their	871.1
	37: 8 **And w** I beheld, lo, the sinews and	2050.1
	37:13 **w** I have opened your graves, O my	871.1
	37:18 **w** the children of thy people shall	834+3509.1
	37:28 **w** my sanctuary shall be in the midst of	871.1
	38:14 In that day **w** my people of Israel	871.1
	38:16 **w** I shall be sanctified in thee, O Gog,	871.1
	38:18 **w** Gog shall come against the land	3117+871.1
	39:15 **w** *any* seeth a man's bone, then shall he	2050.1
	39:26 **w** they dwelt safely in their land,	871.1
	39:27 **W** I have brought them again from	871.1
	42:14 the priests enter *therein,* then shall	871.1
	42:15 **Now w** he had made an end of	2050.1
	43: 3 according to the vision that I saw **w** I	871.1
	43:18 the altar in the day **w** *they* shall make it,	NIH
	43:23 **W** thou hast made an end of cleansing *it,*	871.1
	43:27 **W** *these* days are expired, it shall	2050.1
	44: 7 **w** ye offer my bread, the fat and the	871.1
	44:10 away far from me, **w** Israel went astray,	871.1
	44:15 that kept the charge of my sanctuary **w**	871.1
	44:17 **w** they enter in at the gates of the inner	871.1
	44:19 **w** they go forth into the utter court,	871.1
	44:21 **w** they enter into the inner court.	871.1
	45: 1 **w** ye shall divide *by lot* the land for	871.1
	46: 8 **w** the prince shall enter, he shall go in	871.1
	46: 9 **w** the people of the land shall come	871.1
	46:10 midst of them, **w** they go in, shall go in;	871.1
	46:10 go in; and **w** they go forth, shall go forth.	871.1
	46:12 the prince shall prepare a voluntary	3588
	47: 3 **w** the man that had the line in his hand	871.1
	47: 7 **w** I had returned, behold, at the bank	871.1
	48:11 which went not astray **w** the children of	871.1
Da	3: 7 at all the people heard the sound	1768+3509.4
	5:20 **w** his heart was lifted up,	1768+3509.4
	6:10 **Now w** Daniel knew that	1768+3509.4
	6:14 king, **w** he heard *these* words,	1768+3509.4
	6:20 **w** he came to the den, he cried with a	3509.4
	8: 2 it came to pass, I saw, that I *was* at	871.1
	8: 8 **w** he was strong, the great horn was	3509.1
	8:15 **w** I, *even* I Daniel, had seen the vision,	871.1
	8:17 **w** he came, I was afraid, and fell upon	871.1
	8:23 the transgressors are come to the full,	3509.1
	10: 9 **w** I heard the voice of his words, then	3509.1
	10:11 he had spoken this word unto me,	871.1
	10:15 **w** he had spoken such words unto me,	3509.1
	10:19 **w** he had spoken unto me, I was	3509.1
	10:20 **and w** I am gone forth, lo, the prince of	2050.1
	11: 4 **w** he shall stand up, his kingdom shall	3509.1
	11:12 **w** he hath taken away the multitude,	2050.1
	11:34 **w** they shall fall, they shall be holpen	871.1
	12: 7 **w** he held up his right hand and his left	2050.1
	12: 7 **w** *he* shall have accomplished to scatter	3509.1
Hos	1: 2 **Now w** the LORD began to speak by Hosea,	871.1
	1: 2 **Now w** she had weaned Lo-ruhamah,	2050.1
	2:15 *in* the day **w** she came up out of the land	NIH
	4:14 I will not punish your daughters **w** they	3588
	4:14 nor your spouses **w** they commit adultery:	3588
	5:13 **W** Ephraim saw his sickness,	2050.1
	6:11 **w** I returned the captivity of my people.	871.1
	7: 1 **W** I *would* have healed Israel, then	3509.1
	7:12 **W** they go, I will spread my	834+3509.1
	7:14 heart, **w** they howled upon their beds:	3588
	9:12 woe also to them **w** I depart from them!	871.1
	10:10 **w** *they* shall bind themselves in their two	871.1
	11: 1 **W** Israel *was* a child, then I loved him,	3588
	11:10 **w** he shall roar, then the children shall	3509.1
	13: 1 **W** Ephraim spake trembling, he exalted	3509.1
	13: 1 but **w** he offended in Baal, he died.	2050.1
Joel	2: 8 **w** they fall upon the sword, they shall not	NIH
	3: 1 **w** I shall bring again the captivity of Judah	834
Am	3: 4 roar in the forest, **w** he hath no prey?	2050.1
	4: 7 **w** *there were* yet three months to	871.1
	4: 9 **w** your gardens and your vineyards and	871.1
	7: 2 *that* **w** they had made an end of eating	518
	8: 5 Saying, **W** will the new moon be gone,	4970
Jnh	2: 7 **W** my soul fainted within me I	871.1
	4: 2 my saying, **w** I was yet in my country?	NIH
	4: 7 God prepared a worm **w** the morning	871.1
	4: 8 it came to pass, **w** the sun did arise,	3509.1
Mic	2: 1 **w** the morning is light, they practise it,	871.1
	5: 5 **w** the Assyrian shall come into our land:	3588
	5: 5 **w** he shall tread in our palaces, then	3588
	5: 6 **w** he cometh into our land, and when he	3588
	5: 6 and **w** he treadeth within our borders.	NIH
	7: 1 for I am as **w** they have gathered	NIH
	7: 8 **w** I fall, I shall arise; when I sit in	3588
	7: 8 **w** I sit in darkness, the LORD *shall be* a	3588
Na	1:12 be cut down, **w** he shall pass through.	2050.1
	3:17 *but* **w** the sun ariseth they flee away,	2050.1
Hab	1:13 thy tongue **w** the wicked devoureth	871.1
	2: 1 what shall I answer **w** I am reproved.	5921
	3:16 **W** I heard, my belly trembled; my lips	2050.1
	3:16 **w** *he* cometh up unto the people, he	3807.1
Zep	3:20 **w** I turn back your captivity before your	871.1
Hag	1: 9 **and w** ye brought *it* home, I did blow	2050.1

Hag	2: 5 with you **w** ye came out of Egypt,	871.1
	2:16 **w** *one* came to a heap of twenty	NIH
	2:16 **w** *one* came to the pressfat for to draw out	NIH
Zec	7: 2 **W** they had sent *unto* the house of God	2050.1
	7: 3 **W** ye fasted and mourned in the fifth and	3588
	7: 6 **w** ye did eat, and when ye did drink,	3588
	7: 6 when ye did eat, and **w** ye did drink,	3588
	7: 7 Jerusalem was inhabited and	871.1
	7: 7 **w** *men* inhabited the south and the	2050.1
	8:14 your fathers provoked me to wrath,	871.1
	9: 1 **w** the eyes of man, as of all the tribes of	3588
	9:13 **W** I have bent Judah for me, filled the	3588
	12: 2 **w** they shall be in the siege both against	NIH
	13: 3 *that* **w** any shall yet prophesy, then	3588
	13: 3 thrust him through **w** he prophesieth.	871.1
	13: 4 one of his vision, **w** he hath prophesied;	871.1
	14: 3 as **w** he fought in the day of battle.	3117
Mal	2:17 have we wearied *him?* **W** ye say,	871.1
	3: 2 who *shall* stand **w** he appeareth? for he	871.1
	3:17 hosts, in that day **w** I make *up my* jewels;	834
Mt	1:18 **W** as his mother Mary was espoused to	NIG
	2: 1 Now **w** Jesus was born in Bethlehem of	NIG
	2: 3 **W** Herod the king had heard *these things,*	1161
	2: 4 **w** he had gathered all the chief priests	NIG
	2: 7 **w** he had privily called the wise men,	NIG
	2: 8 **w** ye have found *him,* bring me word	1875
	2: 9 **W** they had heard the king, they departed;	1161
	2:10 **W** they saw the star, they rejoiced *with*	1161
	2:11 And **w** they were come into the house,	NIG
	2:11 and **w** they had opened their treasures,	NIG
	2:13 And **w** they were departed, behold,	NIG
	2:14 **W** he arose, he took the young child and	1161
	2:16 **w** he saw that he was mocked of the wise	NIG
	2:19 But **w** Herod was dead, behold, an angel	NIG
	2:22 But **w** he heard that Archelaus did reign in	NIG
	3: 7 But **w** he saw many of the Pharisees and	NIG
	3:16 And Jesus, **w** he was baptized, went up	NIG
	4: 2 And **w** he had fasted forty days and	NIG
	4: 3 And **w** the tempter came to him, he said,	NIG
	4:12 Now **w** Jesus had heard that John was cast	NIG
	5: 1 and **w** he was set, his disciples came unto	NIG
	5:11 **w** *men* shall revile you, and persecute	3752
	6: 2 **w** thou doest *thine* alms, do not	3752
	6: 3 **w** thou doest alms, let not thy left hand	NIG
	6: 5 And **w** thou prayest, thou shalt not be as	3752
	6: 6 But thou, **w** thou prayest, enter into thy	3752
	6: 6 thy closet, and **w** thou hast shut thy door,	NIG
	6: 7 But **w** ye pray, use not vain repetitions,	NIG
	6:16 Moreover **w** ye fast, be not as	3752
	6:17 thou, **w** thou fastest, anoint thine head,	NIG
	7:28 to pass, **w** Jesus had ended these sayings,	3753
	8: 1 **W** he was come down from the mountain,	1161
	8: 5 And **w** Jesus was entered into Capernaum,	NIG
	8:10 **W** Jesus heard *it,* he marvelled, and said to	1161
	8:14 And **w** Jesus was come into Peter's house,	NIG
	8:16 **W** the even was come, they brought unto	1161
	8:18 Now **w** Jesus saw great multitudes about	NIG
	8:23 And **w** he was entered into a ship,	NIG
	8:28 And **w** he was come to the other side into	NIG
	8:32 **w** they were come out, they went into	NIG
	8:34 **w** they saw him, they besought *him* that	NIG
	9: 8 **w** the multitudes saw *it,* they marvelled,	NIG
	9:11 And **w** the Pharisees saw *it,* they said unto	NIG
	9:12 But **w** Jesus heard *that,* he said unto them,	NIG
	9:15 **w** the bridegroom shall be taken from	3752
	9:22 he saw her, he said, Daughter, be of	NIG
	9:23 And **w** Jesus came into the ruler's house,	NIG
	9:25 But **w** the people were put forth, he went	3753
	9:27 And **w** Jesus departed thence, two blind	NIG
	9:28 And **w** he was come into the house,	NIG
	9:31 But they, **w** they were departed,	NIG
	9:33 And **w** the devil was cast out, the dumb	NIG
	9:36 **w** he saw the multitudes, he was moved	NIG
	10: 1 And **w** he had called unto *him* his twelve	NIG
	10:12 And **w** ye come into a house salute it.	NIG
	10:14 **w** ye depart out of that house or city,	NIG
	10:19 **w** they deliver you up, take no thought	3752
	10:23 But **w** they persecute you in this city,	3752
	11: 1 **w** Jesus had made an end of commanding	3753
	11: 2 Now **w** John had heard in the prison	NIG
	12: 2 But **w** the Pharisees saw *it,* they said unto	NIG
	12: 3 **w** he was a hungred, and they that were	3753
	12: 9 **w** he was departed thence, he went into	NIG
	12:15 But **w** Jesus knew *it,* he withdrew himself	NIG
	12:24 But **w** the Pharisees heard *it,* they said,	NIG
	12:43 **W** the unclean spirit is gone out of a man,	3752
	12:44 and **w** he is come, he findeth *it* empty,	NIG
	13: 4 **w** he sowed, some *seeds* fell by	1722+3588
	13: 6 **w** the sun was up, they were scorched;	NIG
	13:19 **W** any one heareth the word of	NIG
	13:21 for **w** tribulation or persecution ariseth	NIG
	13:26 But **w** the blade was sprung up,	3753
	13:32 but **w** it is grown, it is the greatest among	3752
	13:44 the which **w** a man hath found, he hideth,	NIG
	13:46 **w** he had found one pearl of great price,	NIG
	13:48 Which, **w** it was full, they drew to shore,	3753
	13:53 *that* **w** Jesus had finished these parables,	3753
	13:54 And **w** he was come into his own country,	NIG
	14: 5 And **w** he would have put him to death,	NIG
	14: 6 But **w** Herod's birthday was kept,	NIG
	14:13 **W** Jesus heard *of it,* he departed thence by	2532
	14:13 **w** the people had heard *thereof,* they	NIG
	14:15 **w** it was evening, his disciples came to	NIG
	14:23 And **w** he had sent the multitudes away,	NIG
	14:23 **w** the evening was come, he was there	NIG

Mt	14:26 And **w** the disciples saw him walking on	NIG
	14:29 And **w** Peter was come down out of	NIG
	14:30 **w** he saw the wind boysterous, he was	NIG
	14:32 And **w** they were come into the ship,	NIG
	14:34 And **w** they were gone over, they came into	NIG
	14:35 **w** the men of that place had knowledge	NIG
	15: 2 for they wash not their hands **w** they eat	3752
	15:31 **w** they saw the dumb to speak,	NIG
	16: 2 said unto them, **W** it is evening, ye say,	NIG
	16: 5 **w** his disciples were come to the other	NIG
	16: 8 *Which* **w** Jesus perceived, he said unto	1161
	16:13 **W** Jesus came into the coasts of Cesarea	1161
	17: 6 And **w** the disciples heard *it,* they fell on	NIG
	17: 8 **w** they had lift up their eyes, they saw	NIG
	17:14 And **w** they were come to the multitude,	NIG
	17:24 And **w** they were come to Capernaum,	NIG
	17:25 And **w** he was come into the house,	3753
	17:27 and **w** thou hast opened his mouth,	NIG
	18:24 And **w** he had begun to reckon, one was	NIG
	18:31 So **w** his fellowservants saw what was	3767
	19: 1 *that* **w** Jesus had finished these sayings,	3753
	19:22 But **w** the young man heard *that* saying,	NIG
	19:25 **W** his disciples heard *it,* they were	1161
	19:28 **w** the Son of man shall sit in the throne	3752
	20: 2 **w** he had agreed with the labourers for	NIG
	20: 8 So **w** even was come, the lord of	NIG
	20: 9 And **w** they came that *were hired* about	NIG
	20:10 But **w** the first came, they supposed that	NIG
	20:11 **w** they had received *it,* they murmured	NIG
	20:24 And **w** the ten heard *it,* they were moved	NIG
	20:30 **w** they heard that Jesus passed by, cried	NIG
	21: 1 And **w** they drew nigh unto Jerusalem,	3753
	21:10 And **w** he was come into Jerusalem,	NIG
	21:15 And **w** the chief priests and scribes saw	NIG
	21:19 **w** he saw a fig tree in the way, he came	NIG
	21:20 **w** the disciples saw *it,* they marvelled,	NIG
	21:23 And **w** he was come into the temple,	NIG
	21:32 **w** ye had seen *it,* repented not afterward,	NIG
	21:34 And **w** the time of the fruit drew near,	3753
	21:38 But **w** the husbandmen saw the son,	NIG
	21:40 **W** the lord therefore of the vineyard	3752
	21:45 And **w** the chief priests and Pharisees had	NIG
	21:46 But **w** they sought to lay hands on him,	NIG
	22: 7 **w** the king heard *thereof,* he was wroth:	NIG
	22:11 And **w** the king came in to see the guests,	NIG
	22:22 **W** they had heard *these words,* they	2532
	22:25 **w** he had married *a* wife, deceased, and,	NIG
	22:33 And **w** the multitude heard *this,* they were	NIG
	22:34 But **w** the Pharisees had heard that he had	NIG
	23:15 to make one proselyte, and **w** he is made,	3752
	24: 3 Tell us, **w** shall these *things* be?	4219
	24:15 **W** ye therefore shall see the abomination	3752
	24:32 **W** his branch is yet tender,	3752
	24:33 **w** ye shall see all these *things,* know that	3752
	24:46 whom his lord **w** he cometh shall find so	NIG
	24:50 come in a day **w** he looketh not for *him,*	3739
	25:31 **W** the Son of man shall come in his glory,	3752
	25:37 **w** saw we thee a hungred, and fed *thee?*	4219
	25:38 **W** saw we thee a stranger, and took *thee*	4219
	25:39 Or **w** saw we thee sick,	4219
	25:44 **w** saw we thee a hungred, or athirst,	4219
	26: 1 **w** Jesus had finished all these sayings,	3753
	26: 6 **w** Jesus was in Bethany, in the house	NIG
	26: 8 But **w** his disciples saw *it,* they had	NIG
	26:10 **W** Jesus understood *it,* he said unto them,	1161
	26:20 Now **w** the even was come, he sat down	NIG
	26:29 until that day **w** I drink it new with you in	3752
	26:30 **w** they had sung a hymn, they went out	NIG
	26:71 And **w** he was gone out into the porch,	NIG
	27: 1 **W** the morning was come, all the chief	1161
	27: 2 And **w** they had bound him, they led him	NIG
	27: 3 **w** he saw that he was condemned,	NIG
	27:12 And **w** he was accused of the chief	1722+3588
	27:17 Therefore **w** they were gathered together,	NIG
	27:19 **W** he was set down on the judgment seat,	1161
	27:24 **W** Pilate saw that he could prevail	1161
	27:26 and **w** he had scourged Jesus, he delivered	NIG
	27:29 And **w** they had platted a crown of thorns,	NIG
	27:33 **w** they were come unto a place called	NIG
	27:34 **w** he had tasted *thereof,* he would not	NIG
	27:47 **w** they heard *that,* said, This *man* calleth	NIG
	27:50 **w** he had cried again with a loud voice,	NIG
	27:54 Now **w** the centurion, and they that were	NIG
	27:57 **W** the even was come, there came a rich	1161
	27:59 And **w** Joseph had taken the body,	NIG
	28:11 Now **w** they were going, behold, some of	NIG
	28:12 **w** they were assembled with the elders,	NIG
	28:17 **w** they saw him, they worshipped him:	NIG
Mk	1:19 And **w** he had gone a little further thence,	NIG
	1:26 And **w** the unclean spirit had torn him,	NIG
	1:29 **w** they were come out of the synagogue,	NIG
	1:32 And at even, **w** the sun did set,	3753
	1:37 **And w** they had found him, they said	2532
	2: 4 **w** they could not come nigh unto him	NIG
	2: 4 **w** they had broken *it* up, they let down	NIG
	2: 5 **W** Jesus saw their faith, he said unto	1161
	2: 8 **w** Jesus perceived in his spirit that they so	NIG
	2:16 And **w** the scribes and Pharisees saw him	NIG
	2:17 **W** Jesus heard *it,* he saith unto them,	2532
	2:20 **w** the bridegroom shall be taken away	3752
	2:25 **w** he had need, and was a hungred, he,	3753
	3: 5 **w** he had looked round about on them	NIG
	3: 8 **w** they had heard what great *things* he	NIG
	3:11 And unclean spirits, **w** they saw him,	3752
	3:21 **w** his friends heard *of it,* they went out	NIG

Mk	4: 6 But **w** the sun was up, it was scorched;	3753

Mk
4: 6 But **w** the sun was up, it was scorched; 3753
4:10 **w** he was alone, they that were about 3753
4:15 but **w** they have heard, Satan cometh 3752
4:16 who, **w** they have heard the word, 3752
4:17 **w** affliction or persecution ariseth for NIG
4:29 But **w** the fruit is brought forth, 3752
4:31 which, **w** it is sown in the earth, 3752
4:32 But **w** it is sown, it groweth up, 3752
4:34 and **w** they were alone, he expounded all NIG
4:35 And the same day, **w** the even was come, NIG
4:36 And **w** they had sent away the multitude, NIG
5: 2 And **w** he was come out of the ship, NIG
5: 6 But **w** he saw Jesus afar off, he ran and NIG
5:18 And **w** he was come into the ship, he that NIG
5:21 And **w** Jesus was passed over again by ship NIG
5:22 and **w** he saw him, he fell at his feet, NIG
5:27 **W** she had heard of Jesus, came in the NIG
5:39 **w** he was come in, he saith unto them, NIG
5:40 But **w** he had put *them* all out, he taketh NIG
6: 2 **w** the sabbath day was come, he began NIG
6:11 nor hear you, **w** ye depart thence, NIG
6:16 But **w** Herod heard *thereof,* he said, It is NIG
6:20 and **w** he heard him, he did many *things,* NIG
6:21 And **w** a convenient day was come, NIG
6:22 And the daughter of the said Herodias 2532
6:29 And **w** his disciples heard *of it,* they came NIG
6:34 And Jesus, **w** he came out, saw much NIG
6:35 And the day was now far spent, NIG
6:38 And **w** they knew, they say, Five, NIG
6:41 And **w** he had taken the five loaves and NIG
6:46 he had sent them away, he departed NIG
6:47 And **w** even was come, the ship was in NIG
6:49 **w** they saw him walking upon the sea, NIG
6:53 **w** they had passed over, they came into NIG
6:54 And **w** they were come out of the ship, NIG
7: 2 And **w** they saw some of his disciples eat NIG
7: 4 And **w** *they come* from the market, NIG
7:14 And he had called all the people unto NIG
7:17 **w** he was entered into *the* house from 3753
7:30 And **w** she was come to her house, NIG
8:17 And **w** Jesus knew *it,* he saith unto them, NIG
8:19 **W** I brake the five loaves among five 3753
8:20 And **w** the seven among four thousand, 3753
8:23 and **w** he had spit on his eyes, and put *his* NIG
8:33 But **w** he had turned about and looked on NIG
8:34 And **w** he had called the people unto *him* NIG
8:38 **w** he cometh in the glory of his Father 3752
9: 8 **w** they had looked round about, NIG
9:14 And **w** he came to *his* disciples, he saw a NIG
9:15 **w** they beheld him, were greatly amazed, NIG
9:20 and **w** he saw him, straightway the spirit NIG
9:25 **W** Jesus saw that the people came 1161
9:28 And **w** he was come into *the* house, his NIG
9:36 he had taken him in his arms, he said NIG
10:14 **w** Jesus saw *it,* he was much displeased, NIG
10:17 And **w** he was gone forth into the way, NIG
10:41 And **w** the ten heard *it,* they began to be NIG
10:47 And **w** he heard that it was Jesus of NIG
11: 1 And **w** they came nigh to Jerusalem, 3753
11:11 **w** he had looked round about upon all NIG
11:12 **w** they were come from Bethany, he was NIG
11:13 **w** he came to it, he found nothing but NIG
11:19 And **w** even was come, he went out of 3753
11:24 **w** ye pray, believe that ye receive *them,* NIG
11:25 **w** ye stand praying, forgive, if have 3752
12:14 **w** they were come, they say unto him, NIG
12:23 resurrection therefore, **w** they shall rise, 3752
12:25 For **w** they shall rise from the dead, 3752
12:34 And **w** Jesus saw that he answered NIG
13: 4 Tell us, **w** shall these *things* be? 4219
13: 4 what *shall* be the sign **w** all these *things* 3752
13: 7 **w** ye shall hear of wars and rumours of 3752
13:11 **w** they shall lead *you,* and deliver you 3752
13:14 But **w** ye shall see the abomination of 3752
13:28 **w** her branch is yet tender, 3752
13:29 **w** ye shall see these *things* come to pass, 3752
13:33 and pray: for ye know not **w** the time is. 4219
13:35 ye know not **w** the master of the house 4219
14:11 And **w** they heard *it,* they were glad, NIG
14:12 **w** they killed the passover, his disciples 3753
14:23 and **w** he had given thanks, he gave *it* to NIG
14:26 **w** they had sung a hymn, they went out NIG
14:40 And **w** he returned, he found them asleep NIG
14:67 And **w** she saw Peter warming himself, NIG
14:72 And **w** he thought thereon, he wept. NIG
15:15 **w** he had scourged *him,* to be crucified. NIG
15:20 And **w** they had mocked him, they took off 3753
15:24 And **w** they had crucified him, they parted NIG
15:33 And **w** the sixth hour was come, there was NIG
15:35 And **w** they heard *it,* said, Behold, he calleth NIG
15:39 And **w** the centurion, which stood over NIG
15:41 (Who also, **w** he was in Galilee, 3753
15:42 And now **w** the even was come, because NIG
15:45 **w** he knew *it* of the centurion, he gave NIG
16: 1 And **w** the sabbath was past, NIG
16: 4 **w** they looked, they saw that the stone NIG
16: 9 **w** *Jesus* was risen early the first *day* of NIG
16:11 **w** they had heard that he was alive, NIG

Lk
1: 9 lot was to burn incense **w** he went into NIG
1:12 **w** Zacharias saw *him,* he was troubled, NIG
1:22 **w** he came out, he could not speak unto NIG
1:29 **w** she saw *him,* she was troubled at his NIG
1:41 it came to pass that, **w** Elisabeth heard 5613
2: 2 this taxing was first made **w** Cyrenius NIG
2:17 And **w** they had seen *it,* they made known NIG

Lk
2:21 And **w** eight days were accomplished for 3753
2:22 And **w** the days of her purification 3753
2:27 **w** the parents brought in the child 1722+3588
2:39 And **w** they had performed all *things* 5613
2:42 And **w** he was twelve years old, they went 3753
2:43 And **w** they had fulfilled the days, as they NIG
2:45 **w** they found him not, they turned back NIG
2:48 And **w** they saw him, they were amazed: NIG
3:21 **w** all the people were baptized, 1722+3588
4: 2 and **w** they were ended, he afterward NIG
4:13 And **w** the devil had ended all NIG
4:17 And **w** he had opened the book, he found NIG
4:25 **w** the heaven was shut up three years and 3753
4:25 **w** great famine was throughout all the 5613
4:28 **w** they heard these *things,* were filled NIG
4:35 And **w** the devil had thrown him in NIG
4:40 **w** the sun was setting, all they that had NIG
4:42 And **w** it was day, he departed and NIG
5: 4 Now **w** he had left speaking, he said unto 5613
5: 6 And **w** they had done this, they inclosed a NIG
5: 8 **W** Simon Peter saw *it,* he fell down at 1161
5:11 they had brought *their* ships to land, NIG
5:12 to pass, **w** he was in a certain city, 1722+3588
5:19 And **w** they could not find by what *way* NIG
5:20 **w** he saw their faith, he said unto him, NIG
5:22 But **w** Jesus perceived their thoughts, NIG
5:35 **w** the bridegroom shall be taken away 3752
6: 3 **w** himself was a hungred, and they which 3698
6:13 And **w** it was day, he called unto *him* his 3753
6:22 **w** men shall hate you, and when they 3752
6:22 **w** they shall separate you *from their* 3752
6:26 **w** all men shall speak well of you: 3752
6:42 **w** thou thyself beholdest not the beam NIG
6:48 and **w** the flood arose, the stream beat NIG
7: 1 Now **w** he had ended all his sayings in 1893
7: 3 **w** he heard of Jesus, he sent unto him NIG
7: 4 And **w** they came to Jesus, they besought NIG
7: 6 **w** he was now not far from the house, NIG
7: 9 **W** Jesus heard these *things,* he marvelled 1161
7:12 **w** he came nigh to the gate of the city, 5613
7:13 And **w** the Lord saw her, he had compassion NIG
7:20 **W** the men were come unto him, they 1161
7:24 And **w** the messengers of John were NIG
7:37 **w** she knew that *Jesus* sat at meat in NIG
7:39 **w** the Pharisee which had bidden him NIG
7:42 And **w** they had nothing to pay, he frankly NIG
8: 4 **w** much people were gathered together, NIG
8: 8 And **w** he had said these *things,* he cried, NIG
8:13 **w** they hear, receive the word with joy; 3752
8:14 which, **w** they have heard, go forth, and NIG
8:16 No *man,* **w** he hath lighted a candle, NIG
8:27 **w** he went forth to land, there met him NIG
8:28 **w** he saw Jesus, he cried out, and fell 1161
8:34 **W** they that fed *them* saw what was done, 1161
8:40 to pass that, **w** Jesus was returned, 1722+3588
8:45 **W** all denied, Peter and they that were 1161
8:47 **w** the woman saw that she was not hid, NIG
8:50 But **w** Jesus heard *it,* he answered him, NIG
8:51 **w** he came into the house, he suffered NIG
9: 5 not receive you, **w** ye go out of that city, NIG
9:10 And the apostles, **w** they were returned, NIG
9:11 the people, **w** they knew *it,* followed him: NIG
9:12 And **w** the day began to wear away, then NIG
9:26 **w** he shall come in his own glory, and *in* 3752
9:32 **w** they were awake, they saw his glory, NIG
9:36 **w** the voice was past, Jesus was 1722+3588
9:37 **w** they were come down from the hill, NIG
9:51 **w** the time was come that he 1722+3588
9:54 And **w** his disciples James and John saw NIG
10:31 and **w** he saw him, he passed by on NIG
10:32 **w** he was at the place, came and looked NIG
10:33 and **w** he saw him, he had compassion *on* NIG
10:35 on the morrow **w** he departed, he took NIG
10:35 **w** I come again, I will repay thee. 1722+3588
11: 1 **w** he ceased, one of his disciples said unto 5613
11: 2 And he said unto them, **W** ye pray, say, 3752
11:14 the devil was gone out, the dumb NIG
11:21 **W** a strong *man* armed keepeth his 3752
11:22 But **w** a stronger than he shall come upon 1875
11:24 **W** the unclean spirit is gone out of a man, 3752
11:25 **w** he cometh, he findeth *it* swept and NIG
11:29 And the people were gathered thick NIG
11:33 No *man,* **w** he hath lighted a candle, NIG
11:34 therefore **w** thine eye is single, thy whole 3752
11:34 But **w** *thine eye* is evil, thy body also *is* full 1875
11:36 as **w** the bright shining of a candle doth 3752
11:38 And **w** the Pharisee saw *it,* he marvelled NIG
12: 1 **w** there were gathered together an NIG
12:11 **w** they bring you unto the synagogues, 3752
12:36 **w** he will return from the wedding; 4219
12:36 **w** he cometh and knocketh, they may NIG
12:37 whom the lord **w** he cometh shall find NIG
12:40 the Son of man cometh at an hour **w** ye 3739
12:43 whom his lord **w** he cometh shall find so NIG
12:46 come in a day **w** he looketh not for *him,* 3739
12:46 for *him,* and at an hour **w** he is not ware, 3739
12:54 **W** ye see a cloud rise out of the west, 3752
12:55 **w** *ye see* the south wind blow, ye say, 3752
12:58 **W** thou goest with thine adversary 1063+5613
13:12 **w** Jesus saw her, he called *her* to him, NIG
13:17 And **w** he had said these *things,* all his NIG
13:25 **W** once the master of the house is risen NIG
13:28 **W** ye shall see Abraham, and Isaac, 3752
13:35 me, until *the time* come **w** ye shall say, 3753
14: 7 **w** he marked how they chose out the NIG

Lk
14: 8 **W** thou art bidden of any *man* to a 3752
14:10 But **w** thou art bidden, go and sit down in 3752
14:10 that **w** he that bade thee cometh, he may 3752
14:12 **W** thou makest a dinner or a supper, 3752
14:13 But **w** thou makest a feast, call the poor, 3752
14:15 And **w** one of them that sat at meat with NIG
15: 5 And **w** he hath found *it,* he layeth it on his NIG
15: 6 **w** he cometh home, he calleth together NIG
15: 9 And **w** she hath found *it,* she calleth *her* NIG
15:14 And **w** he had spent all, there arose a NIG
15:17 And **w** he came to himself, he said, NIG
15:20 **w** he was yet a great way off, his father NIG
16: 4 that, **w** I am put out of the stewardship, 3752
16: 9 that, **w** ye fail, they may receive you into 3752
17: 7 **w** he is come from the field, Go and NIG
17:10 **w** ye shall have done all those *things* 3752
17:14 And **w** he saw *them,* he said unto them, NIG
17:15 **w** he saw that he was healed, turned back, NIG
17:20 And **w** he was demanded of the Pharisees, NIG
17:20 the kingdom of God should come, 4219
17:22 **w** ye shall desire to see one of the days of 3753
17:30 Even thus shall it be in the day **w** the Son NIG
18: 8 Nevertheless **w** the Son of man cometh, NIG
18:15 **w** *his* disciples saw *it,* they rebuked them. NIG
18:22 Now **w** Jesus heard these *things,* he said NIG
18:23 **w** he heard this, he was very sorrowful: NIG
18:24 And **w** Jesus saw that he was very NIG
18:40 and **w** he was come near, he asked him, NIG
18:43 they saw *it,* gave praise unto God. NIG
19: 5 And **w** Jesus came to the place, he looked 5613
19: 7 And **w** they saw *it,* they all murmured, NIG
19:15 to pass, that **w** he was returned, 1722+3588
19:28 **w** he had thus spoken, he went before, NIG
19:29 **w** he was come nigh to Bethphage and 5613
19:37 And **w** he was come nigh, *even* now at NIG
19:41 And **w** he was come near, he beheld 5613
20:13 it may be they will reverence *him* **w** they NIG
20:14 But **w** the husbandmen saw him, NIG
20:16 **w** they heard *it,* they said, God forbid. NIG
20:37 **w** he calleth the Lord the God of Abraham 5613
21: 7 Master, but **w** shall these *things* be? 4219
21: 7 what sign *will there be* **w** these *things* 3752
21: 9 But **w** ye shall hear of wars and 3752
21:20 And **w** ye shall see Jerusalem compassed 3752
21:28 And **w** these *things* begin to come to pass, NIG
21:30 **W** they now shoot forth, ye see and NIG
21:31 **w** ye see these *things* come to pass, 3752
22: 7 the passover must be killed. 1722+3739
22:10 Behold, **w** ye are entered into the city, NIG
22:14 And **w** the hour was come, he sat down, NIG
22:32 and **w** thou art converted, strengthen thy 4218
22:35 **W** I sent you without purse, and scrip, 3753
22:40 And **w** he was at the place, he said unto NIG
22:45 And **w** he rose up from prayer, NIG
22:49 **W** they which were about him saw what 1161
22:53 **W** I was daily with you in the temple, NIG
22:55 And **w** they had kindled a fire in the midst NIG
22:64 And **w** they had blindfolded him, NIG
23: 6 **W** Pilate heard of Galilee, he asked 1161
23: 8 And **w** Herod saw Jesus, he was exceeding NIG
23:13 he had called together the chief priests NIG
23:33 And **w** they were come to the place, 3753
23:42 remember me **w** thou comest into thy 3752
23:46 And **w** Jesus had cried with a loud voice, NIG
23:47 Now **w** the centurion saw what was done, NIG
24: 6 remember how he spake unto you **w** he NIG
24:23 **w** they found not his body, they came, NIG
24:40 **w** he had thus spoken, he shewed them NIG

Jn
1:19 **w** the Jews sent priests and Levites from 3753
1:42 **w** Jesus beheld him, he said, Thou art NIG
1:48 **w** thou wast under the fig tree, I saw thee. NIG
2: 3 And **w** they wanted wine, the mother of NIG
2: 9 **W** the ruler of the feast had tasted 1161+5613
2:10 and **w** *men* have well drunk, then 3752
2:15 And **w** he had made a scourge of small NIG
2:22 **W** therefore he was risen from the dead, 3753
2:23 Now **w** he was in Jerusalem at 5613
2:23 **w** they saw the miracles which he did. NIG
3: 4 How can a man be born **w** he is old? NIG
4: 1 **W** therefore the Lord knew 5613
4:21 **w** ye shall neither in this mountain, 3753
4:23 **w** the true worshippers shall worship 3753
4:25 **w** he is come, he will tell us all *things.* 3752
4:40 **w** the Samaritans were come unto him, 5613
4:45 Then **w** he was come into Galilee, 3753
4:47 **W** he heard that Jesus was come out of NIG
4:52 inquired he of them the hour **w** 1722+3739
4:54 **w** he was come out of Judea into Galilee. NIG
5: 6 **W** Jesus saw him lie, and knew that he NIG
5: 7 I have no man, **w** the water is troubled, 3752
5:25 **w** the dead shall hear the voice of the Son 3753
6: 5 **W** Jesus then lift up *his* eyes, NIG
6:11 **w** he had given thanks, he distributed to NIG
6:12 **W** they were filled, he said unto his 5613
6:14 **w** they had seen the miracle that Jesus did, NIG
6:15 **W** Jesus therefore perceived that they NIG
6:16 And **w** even was *now* come, his disciples 5613
6:19 **w** they had rowed about five and twenty 5613
6:22 **w** the people which stood on the other NIG
6:24 **W** the people therefore saw that Jesus was 3753
6:25 **w** they had found him on the other side NIG
6:25 unto him, Rabbi, **w** camest thou hither? 4219
6:60 his disciples, **w** they had heard *this,* said, NIG
6:61 **W** Jesus knew in himself that his disciples 1161
7: 9 **W** he had said these *words* unto them, 1161

Jn	7:10 But **w** his brethren were gone up, then	5613
	7:27 but **w** Christ cometh, no *man* knoweth	3752
	7:31 on him, and said, **W** Christ cometh,	3752
	7:40 they heard *this* saying, said, Of a truth	NIG
	8: 3 and **w** they had set her in the midst,	NIG
	8: 7 **w** they continued asking him, he lift up	5613
	8:10 **W** Jesus said lift up *himself,* and saw none	1161
	8:28 **W** ye have lift up the Son of man, then	3752
	8:44 **W** he speaketh a lie, he speaketh of his	3752
	9: 4 the night cometh, **w** no *man* can work.	3753
	9: 6 **w** he had thus spoken, he spat on	NIG
	9:14 And it was the sabbath day **w** Jesus made	3753
	9:35 **w** he had found him, he said unto him,	NIG
	10: 4 And **w** he putteth forth his own sheep,	3752
	11: 4 **W** Jesus heard *that,* he said, This sickness	1161
	11: 6 **W** he had heard therefore that he was sick	5613
	11:17 Then **w** Jesus came, he found that he had	NIG
	11:28 And **w** she had so said, she went her way,	NIG
	11:31 and comforted her, **w** they saw Mary,	NIG
	11:32 Then **w** Mary was come where Jesus was,	5613
	11:33 **W** Jesus therefore saw her weeping,	5613
	11:43 And **w** he thus had spoken, he cried with	NIG
	12:12 **w** they heard that Jesus was coming to	NIG
	12:14 And Jesus, **w** he had found a young ass,	NIG
	12:16 but **w** Jesus was glorified, then	3753
	12:17 was with him **w** he called Lazarus out	3753
	12:41 **w** he saw his glory, and spake of him.	3753
	13: 1 **w** Jesus knew that his hour was come	NIG
	13:19 that, **w** it is come to pass, ye may believe	3752
	13:21 **W** Jesus had thus said, he was troubled in	NIG
	13:26 **w** I have dipped *it.* And when he had	NIG
	13:26 I have dipped *it.* And **w** he had dipped	NIG
	13:31 Therefore, **w** he was gone out, Jesus said,	3753
	14:29 **w** it is come to pass, ye might believe.	3752
	15:26 But **w** the Comforter is come, whom I	3752
	16: 4 I told you, that **w** the time shall come,	3752
	16: 8 And **w** he is come, he will reprove	NIG
	16:13 **w** he, the Spirit of truth, is come,	3752
	16:21 A woman **w** she is in travail hath sorrow,	3752
	16:25 **w** I shall no more speak unto you in	3753
	18: 1 **W** Jesus had spoken these *words,* he went	NIG
	18:22 And **w** he had thus spoken, one of	NIG
	18:38 And **w** he had said this, he went out again	NIG
	19: 6 **W** the chief priests therefore and officers	3753
	19: 8 **W** Pilate therefore heard that saying,	3753
	19:13 **W** Pilate therefore heard that saying,	NIG
	19:23 the soldiers, **w** they had crucified Jesus,	3753
	19:26 **W** Jesus therefore saw *his* mother,	NIG
	19:30 **W** Jesus therefore had received the	3753
	19:33 But **w** they came to Jesus, and saw that	NIG
	20: 1 **w** it was yet dark, unto the sepulchre.	NIG
	20:14 she had thus said, she turned herself	NIG
	20:19 **w** the doors were shut where the disciples	NIG
	20:20 **w** he had so said, he shewed unto them	NIG
	20:20 the disciples glad, **w** they saw the Lord.	NIG
	20:22 And **w** he had said this, he breathed on	NIG
	20:24 was not with them **w** Jesus came.	3753
	21: 4 But **w** the morning was now come,	NIG
	21: 7 Now **w** Simon Peter heard that it was	NIG
	21:15 So **w** they had dined, Jesus saith to Simon	3753
	21:18 I say unto thee, **W** thou wast young,	3753
	21:18 **w** thou shalt be old, thou shalt stretch	3752
	21:19 And **w** he had spoken this, he saith unto	NIG
Ac	1: 6 **W** they therefore were come together,	NIG
	1: 9 And **w** he had spoken these *things,* while	NIG
	1:13 And **w** they were come in, they went up	3753
	2: 1 **w** the day of Pentecost was fully	1722+3588
	2: 6 Now **w** this was noised abroad,	NIG
	2:37 **w** they heard *this,* they were pricked in	NIG
	3:12 And **w** Peter saw *it,* he answered unto	NIG
	3:13 **w** he was determined to let *him* go.	NIG
	3:19 **w** *the* times of refreshing shall come	302+3704
	4: 7 And **w** they had set them in the midst,	NIG
	4:13 Now **w** they saw the boldness of Peter and	NIG
	4:15 But **w** they had commanded them to go	NIG
	4:21 So **w** they had further threatened *them,*	NIG
	4:24 And **w** they heard *that,* they lift up their	NIG
	4:31 And **w** they had prayed, the place was	NIG
	5: 7 **w** his wife, not knowing what was done,	2532
	5:21 And **w** they heard *that,* they entered into	NIG
	5:22 But **w** the officers came, and found them	NIG
	5:23 but **w** we had opened, we found no *man*	NIG
	5:24 Now **w** the *high* priest and the captain of	5613
	5:27 **w** they had brought them, they set *them*	NIG
	5:33 **W** they heard *that,* they were cut *to*	1161
	5:40 and **w** they had called the apostles,	NIG
	6: 1 **w** the number of the disciples was	NIG
	6: 6 **w** they had prayed, they laid *their* hands	NIG
	7: 2 **w** he was in Mesopotamia, before he	NIG
	7: 4 and from thence, **w** his father was dead,	3326
	7: 5 seed after him, **w** *as yet* he had no child.	NIG
	7:12 But **w** Jacob heard that there was corn in	NIG
	7:17 But **w** the time of the promise drew nigh,	2531
	7:21 **w** he was cast out, Pharaoh's daughter	NIG
	7:23 And **w** he was full forty years old, it came	5613
	7:30 And **w** forty years were expired,	NIG
	7:31 **W** Moses saw *it,* he wondered at the sight	1161
	7:54 **W** they heard these *things,* they were cut	1161
	7:60 And **w** he had said this, he fell asleep.	NIG
	8:12 But **w** they believed Philip preaching	3753
	8:13 and **w** he was baptized, he continued with	NIG
	8:14 Now **w** the apostles which were at	NIG
	8:15 Who, **w** they were come down, prayed for	NIG
	8:18 **w** Simon saw that through laying on of	NIG
	8:25 **w** they had testified and preached the	3767
Ac	8:39 **w** they were come up out of the water,	3753
	9: 8 and **w** his eyes were opened, he saw no	NIG
	9:19 And **w** he had received meat, he was	NIG
	9:26 And **w** Saul was come to Jerusalem,	NIG
	9:30 **w** the brethren knew, they brought	NIG
	9:37 **w** they had washed, they laid *her* in	1161
	9:39 **W** he was come, they brought him into	NIG
	9:40 her eyes: and **w** she saw Peter, she sat up.	NIG
	9:41 **w** he had called the saints and widows,	NIG
	10: 4 **w** he looked on him, he was afraid,	NIG
	10: 7 And **w** the angel which spake unto	5613
	10: 8 **w** he had declared all *these* things unto	NIG
	10:32 who, **w** he cometh, shall speak unto thee.	NIG
	11: 2 And **w** Peter was come up to Jerusalem,	3753
	11: 6 the which **w** I had fastened mine eyes,	NIG
	11:18 **W** they heard these *things,* they held their	1161
	11:20 which, **w** they were come to Antioch,	NIG
	11:23 **w** he came, and had seen the grace of God	NIG
	11:26 And **w** he had found him, he brought him	NIG
	12: 4 **w** he had apprehended him, he put *him*	NIG
	12: 6 And **w** Herod would have brought him	3753
	12:10 **W** they were past the first and the second	1161
	12:11 **w** Peter was come to himself, he said,	NIG
	12:12 **w** he had considered *the thing,* he came	NIG
	12:14 And **w** she knew Peter's voice, she opened	NIG
	12:16 And **w** they had opened *the door,* and	NIG
	12:19 And **w** Herod had sought for him,	NIG
	12:25 **w** they had fulfilled *their* ministry,	NIG
	13: 3 And **w** they had fasted and prayed,	5119
	13: 5 **w** they were at Salamis, they preached	NIG
	13: 6 And **w** they had gone through the isle unto	NIG
	13:12 **w** he saw what was done, believed,	NIG
	13:13 Now **w** Paul and his company loosed from	NIG
	13:14 **w** they departed from Perga, they came	NIG
	13:17 exalted the people **w** *they* dwelt as	1722
	13:19 And **w** he had destroyed seven nations in	NIG
	13:22 And **w** he had removed him, he raised up	NIG
	13:24 **W** John had first preached before his	NIG
	13:29 And **w** they had fulfilled all that was	5613
	13:42 And **w** the Jews were gone out of	NIG
	13:43 Now **w** the congregation was broken up,	NIG
	13:45 But **w** the Jews saw the multitudes,	NIG
	13:48 And **w** the Gentiles heard *this,* they were	NIG
	14: 5 And **w** there was an assault made both of	5613
	14:11 **w** the people saw what Paul had done,	NIG
	14:14 *Which* **w** the apostles, Barnabas and Paul,	1161
	14:21 **w** they had preached the gospel to that	NIG
	14:23 And **w** they had ordained them elders in	NIG
	14:25 And **w** they had preached the word in Perga,	NIG
	14:27 And **w** they were come, and had gathered	NIG
	15: 2 **W** therefore Paul and Barnabas had no	NIG
	15: 4 And **w** they were come to Jerusalem,	NIG
	15: 7 And **w** there had been much disputing,	NIG
	15:30 So **w** they were dismissed, they came to	NIG
	15:30 **w** they had gathered the multitude	NIG
	15:31 *Which* **w** they had read, they rejoiced for	1161
	16: 6 Now **w** they had gone throughout Phrygia	NIG
	16:15 And **w** she was baptized,	5613
	16:19 And **w** her masters saw that the hope of	NIG
	16:23 And **w** they had laid many stripes upon	NIG
	16:34 **w** he had brought them into his house,	NIG
	16:35 And **w** it was day, the magistrates sent	NIG
	16:38 **w** they heard that they were Romans,	NIG
	16:40 and **w** they had seen the brethren,	NIG
	17: 1 Now **w** they had passed through	NIG
	17: 6 And **w** they found them not, they drew	NIG
	17: 8 of the city, **w** they heard these *things.*	NIG
	17: 9 And **w** they had taken security of Jason,	NIG
	17:13 But **w** the Jews of Thessalonica had	5613
	17:16 **w** he saw the city wholly given to idolatry.	NIG
	17:32 And **w** they heard of the resurrection of	NIG
	18: 5 And **w** Silas and Timotheus were come	5613
	18: 6 And **w** they opposed themselves,	NIG
	18:12 And **w** Gallio was the deputy of Achaia,	NIG
	18:14 And **w** Paul was *now* about to open *his*	NIG
	18:20 **W** they desired *him* to tarry longer time	1161
	18:22 And **w** he had landed at Cesarea,	NIG
	18:26 whom **w** Aquila and Priscilla had heard,	NIG
	18:27 **w** he was disposed to pass into Achaia,	NIG
	18:27 who, **w** he was come, helped them much	NIG
	19: 5 **W** they heard *this,* they were baptized in	1161
	19: 6 **w** Paul had laid *his* hands upon them,	NIG
	19: 9 But **w** divers were hardened,	5613
	19:21 **w** he had passed through Macedonia and	NIG
	19:28 **w** they heard *these sayings,* they were	NIG
	19:30 And **w** Paul would have entered in unto	NIG
	19:34 **w** *they* knew that he was a Jew, all with	NIG
	19:35 And **w** the townclerk had appeased	NIG
	19:41 And **w** he had thus spoken, he dismissed	NIG
	20: 2 And **w** he had gone over those parts,	NIG
	20: 3 **w** the Jews laid wait for him, as he was	NIG
	20: 7 **w** the disciples came together to break	NIG
	20:11 **W** he therefore was come up *again,* and	NIG
	20:14 And **w** he met with us at Assos, we took	NIG
	20:18 **w** they were come to him, he said unto	NIG
	20:36 And **w** he had thus spoken, he kneeled	NIG
	21: 3 **w** we had discovered Cyprus, we left it	NIG
	21: 5 And **w** we had accomplished *those* days,	3753
	21: 6 And **w** we had taken our leave one of	NIG
	21: 7 And **w** we had finished *our* course from	NIG
	21:11 **w** he was come unto us, he took Paul's	NIG
	21:12 And **w** we heard these *things,* both we,	5613
	21:14 And **w** he would not be persuaded,	NIG
	21:17 And **w** we were come to Jerusalem,	NIG
	21:19 And **w** he had saluted them, he declared	NIG
Ac	21:20 **w** they heard *it,* they glorified the Lord,	NIG
	21:27 And **w** the seven days were almost ended,	5613
	21:27 **w** they saw him in the temple, stirred up	NIG
	21:32 And **w** they saw the chief captain and	NIG
	21:34 **w** he could not know the certainty for	NIG
	21:35 And **w** he came upon the stairs, so it was,	3753
	21:40 **w** he had given *him* licence, Paul stood	NIG
	21:40 And **w** there was made a great silence,	NIG
	22: 2 (And **w** they heard that he spake in	NIG
	22:11 And **w** I could not see for the glory of that	5613
	22:17 that, **w** I was come again to Jerusalem,	NIG
	22:20 the blood of thy martyr Stephen was	3753
	22:26 **W** the centurion heard *that,* he went and	NIG
	23: 6 **w** Paul perceived that the one part were	NIG
	23: 7 And **w** he had so said, there arose a	NIG
	23:10 And **w** there arose a great dissension,	NIG
	23:12 And **w** it was day, certain of the Jews	NIG
	23:16 And **w** Paul's sister's son heard of *their*	NIG
	23:28 And **w** I would have known the cause	NIG
	23:30 **w** it was told me how that the Jews laid	NIG
	23:33 **w** they came to Cesarea, and delivered	NIG
	23:34 And **w** the governor had read *the letter,*	NIG
	23:34 **w** he understood that *he was* of Cilicia;	NIG
	23:35 said he, **w** thine accusers are also come.	3752
	24: 2 **w** he was called *forth,* Tertullus began	NIG
	24:22 And **w** Felix heard these *things,* having	NIG
	24:22 **W** Lysias the chief captain shall come	3752
	24:24 **W** Felix came with his wife Drusilla,	NIG
	24:25 **w** I have a convenient season, I will call	1161
	25: 1 Now **w** Festus was come into the province,	NIG
	25: 6 And **w** he had tarried among them more	NIG
	25: 7 **w** he was come, the Jews which came	NIG
	25:12 **w** he had conferred with the council,	NIG
	25:14 And **w** they had been there many days,	5613
	25:15 About whom, **w** I was at Jerusalem,	NIG
	25:17 Therefore, **w** they were come hither,	NIG
	25:18 Against whom **w** the accusers stood *up,*	NIG
	25:21 But **w** Paul had appealed to be reserved	NIG
	25:23 **w** Agrippa was come, and Bernice,	NIG
	25:25 But **w** I found that he had committed	NIG
	26:10 and **w** they were put to death, I gave my	NIG
	26:14 And **w** we were all fallen to the earth,	NIG
	26:30 **w** he had thus spoken, the king rose up,	NIG
	26:31 And **w** they were gone aside, they talked	NIG
	27: 1 And **w** it was determined that we should	5613
	27: 4 And **w** we had launched from thence,	NIG
	27: 5 **w** we had sailed over the sea of Cilicia	NIG
	27: 7 And **w** we had sailed slowly many days,	NIG
	27: 9 Now **w** much time was spent,	NIG
	27: 9 and **w** sailing was now dangerous,	NIG
	27:13 And **w** the south wind blew softly,	NIG
	27:15 And **w** the ship was caught, and could not	NIG
	27:17 Which **w** they had taken up, they used	NIG
	27:20 And **w** neither sun nor stars in many days	NIG
	27:27 But **w** the fourteenth night was come, as	5613
	27:28 And **w** they had gone a little further,	NIG
	27:30 **w** they had let down the boat into the sea,	2532
	27:35 And **w** he had thus spoken, he took bread,	NIG
	27:35 And **w** he had broken *it,* he began to eat.	NIG
	27:38 And **w** they had eaten enough,	NIG
	27:39 **w** it was day, they knew not the land:	3753
	27:40 And **w** they had taken up the anchors,	NIG
	28: 1 And **w** they were escaped, then they knew	NIG
	28: 3 **w** Paul had gathered a bundle of sticks,	NIG
	28: 4 And **w** the barbarians saw the *venomous*	5613
	28: 6 Howbeit they looked **w** he should have	NIG
	28: 9 **w** this was done, others also, which had	NIG
	28:10 **w** we departed, they laded *us* with such	NIG
	28:15 from thence, **w** the brethren heard of us,	NIG
	28:15 whom **w** Paul saw, he thanked God,	NIG
	28:16 And **w** we came to Rome, the centurion	3753
	28:17 and **w** they were come together, he said	NIG
	28:18 **w** they had examined me, would have	NIG
	28:19 But **w** the Jews spake against *it,* I was	NIG
	28:23 And **w** they had appointed him a day,	NIG
	28:25 And **w** they agreed not among themselves,	NIG
	28:29 And **w** he had said these *words,* the Jews	NIG
Ro	1:21 Because that, **w** they knew God,	NIG
	2:14 **w** *the* Gentiles, which have not the law,	3752
	2:16 In the day **w** God shall judge the secrets of	3753
	3: 4 overcome **w** thou art judged.	1722+3588
	4:10 **w** he was in circumcision,	NIG
	4:19 **w** he was about an hundred year old,	NIG
	5: 6 **w** we were yet without strength, in due	NIG
	5:10 For if, **w** we were enemies, we were	NIG
	5:13 but sin is not imputed **w** there is no law.	NIG
	6:20 **w** ye were the servants of sin, ye were	3753
	7: 5 **w** we were in the flesh, the motions of	3753
	7: 9 **w** the commandment came, sin revived,	NIG
	7:21 find then a law, that, **w** I would do good,	NIG
	9:10 but **w** Rebecca also had conceived by one,	NIG
	11:27 unto them, **w** I shall take away their sins.	3752
	13:11 for now *is* our salvation nearer than **w** we	3753
	15:28 **W** therefore I have performed this,	NIG
	15:29 And I am sure that, **w** I come unto you,	NIG
1Co	2: 1 I, brethren, **w** I came to you, came not	NIG
	5: 4 **w** ye are gathered together, and my spirit,	NIG
	8:12 But **w** ye sin so against the brethren,	NIG
	9:18 *Verily* that, **w** I preach the gospel, I may	NIG
	9:27 any means, **w** I have preached to others,	NIG
	11:18 of all, **w** ye come together in the church,	NIG
	11:20 **W** ye come together therefore into one	NIG
	11:24 And **w** he had given thanks, he brake it,	NIG
	11:25 **w** *he* had supped, saying, This cup	3326+3588
	11:32 But **w** we are judged, we are chastened of	NIG

1Co 11:33 my brethren, **w** ye come together to eat, NIG
11:34 the rest will I set in order **w** I come. 302+5613
13:10 But *that which is* perfect is come, then 3752
13:11 **W** I was a child, I spake as a child, 3753
13:11 **w** I became a man, I put away childish 3753
14:16 Else **w** thou shalt bless with the spirit, 1437
14:26 **w** ye come together, every one of you 3752
15:24 **w** he shall have delivered up the kingdom 3752
15:24 **w** he shall have put down all rule and 3752
15:27 **w** he saith, all *things* are put under *him*, 3752
15:28 And **w** all *things* shall be subdued unto 3752
15:54 So **w** this corruptible shall have put on 3752
16: 2 that there be no gatherings **w** I come. 3752
16: 3 And **w** I come, whomsoever ye shall 3752
16: 5 **w** I shall pass through Macedonia: 3752
16:12 he will come **w** he shall have convenient 3752

2Co 1:17 **W** I therefore was thus minded, did I use NIG
2: 3 wrote this same unto you, lest, **w** I came, NIG
2:12 **w** I came to Troas to *preach* Christ's NIG
3:15 But *even* unto this day, **w** Moses is 302+2259
3:16 Nevertheless **w** *it* shall turn to 302+2259
7: 5 For, **w** we were come into Macedonia, NIG
7: 7 **w** he told you your earnest desire, your NIG
10: 2 I beseech *you*, that I may not be bold **w** NIG
10: 6 **w** your obedience is fulfilled. 3752
10:11 such as we are in word by letters **w** we NIG
10:11 such *will we be* also in deed **w** we are NIG
10:15 but having hope, **w** your faith is increased, NIG
11: 9 **w** I was present with you, and wanted, NIG
12:10 for **w** I am weak, then am I strong. 3752
12:20 For I fear, lest, **w** I come, I shall not find NIG
12:21 *And* lest, **w** I come again, my God will NIG
13: 9 glad, **w** we are weak, and ye are strong: 3752

Gal 1:15 But **w** it pleased God, who separated me 3753
2: 7 **w** they saw that the gospel of NIG
2: 9 And **w** James, Cephas, and John, NIG
2:11 But **w** Peter was come to Antioch, 3753
2:12 but **w** they were come, he withdrew and 3753
2:14 I saw that they walked not uprightly 3753
4: 3 Even so we, **w** we were children, were in 3753
4: 4 But **w** the fulness of the time was come, 3753
4: 8 Howbeit then, **w** ye knew not God, ye did 1722
4:18 and not only **w** I am present with you. 1722
6: 3 **w** he is nothing, he deceiveth himself. NIG

Eph 1:20 **w** he raised him from the dead, and set NIG
2: 5 Even **w** we were dead in sins, NIG
3: 4 Whereby, **w** ye read, ye may understand NIG
4: 8 *he* saith, **W** he ascended up on high, NIG

Php 2:19 be of good comfort, **w** I know your state. NIG
2:28 that, **w** ye see him again, ye may rejoice, NIG
4:15 the gospel, **w** I departed from Macedonia, 3753

Col 3: 4 **W** Christ, *who is* our life, shall appear, 3752
3: 7 walked sometime, **w** ye lived in them. 3753
4:16 And **w** *this* epistle is read amongst you, 3752

1Th 2: 6 **w** we might have been burdensome, NIG
2:13 **w** ye received the word of God which *ye* NIG
3: 1 Wherefore **w** we could no longer forbear, NIG
3: 4 For verily, **w** we were with you, we told 3753
3: 5 this cause, **w** I could no longer forbear, 2504
3: 6 now **w** Timotheus came from you unto NIG
5: 3 For **w** they shall say, Peace and safety; 3752

2Th 1: 7 **w** the Lord Jesus shall be revealed from 1722
1:10 **W** he shall come to be glorified in his 3752
2: 5 ye not, that, **w** I was yet with you, NIG
3:10 For even **w** we were with you, this we 3753

1Ti 1: 3 *still* at Ephesus, **w** I went into Macedonia, NIG
5:11 for **w** they have *begun to* wax wanton 3752

2Ti 1: 5 **W** I call to remembrance the unfeigned NIG
1:17 But, **w** he was in Rome, he sought me out NIG
4: 3 For the time will come **w** they will not 3753
4:13 **w** thou comest, bring *with thee*, and NIG
4: S **w** Paul was brought before Nero the 3753

Tit 3:12 **W** I shall send Artemas unto thee, 3752

Heb 1: 3 he had by himself purged our sins, NIG
1: 6 **w** he bringeth in the firstbegotten into 3752
3: 9 **W** your fathers tempted me, proved me, 3757
3:16 For some, **w** they had heard, did provoke: NIG
5: 7 **w** he had offered up prayers and NIG
5:12 **w** for the time ye ought to be teachers, 2532
6:13 For **w** God made promise to Abraham, NIG
7:10 of his father, **w** Melchisedec met him. 3753
7:27 this he did once, **w** he offered up himself. NIG
8: 5 God **w** he was about to make the NIG
8: 8 **w** I will make a new covenant with 2532
8: 9 **w** I took them by the hand to lead them NIG
9: 6 Now **w** these *things* were thus ordained, NIG
9:19 For **w** Moses had spoken every precept to NIG
10: 8 Above **w** he said, Sacrifice and offering and NIG
11: 8 **w** he was called to go out into a place NIG
11:11 delivered of a child **w** *she* was past age, NIG
11:17 **w** he was tried, offered up Isaac: NIG
11:21 By faith Jacob, **w** he was a dying, NIG
11:22 By faith Joseph, **w** he died, made mention NIG
11:23 By faith Moses, **w** he was born, was hid NIG
11:24 By faith Moses, **w** he was come to years, NIG
11:31 **w** she had received the spies with peace. NIG
12: 5 nor faint **w** thou art rebuked of him: NIG
12:17 **w** he would have inherited the blessing, NIG

Jas 1: 2 count *it* all joy **w** ye fall into divers 3752
1:12 **w** he is tried, he shall receive the crown NIG
1:13 Let no *man* say **w** he is tempted, I am NIG
1:14 **w** he is drawn away of his own lust, NIG
1:15 Then **w** lust hath conceived, it bringeth NIG
1:15 and sin, **w** it is finished, bringeth forth NIG

Jas 2:21 **w** he had offered Isaac his son upon NIG
2:25 **w** she had received the messengers, NIG
1Pe 1:11 **w** it testified beforehand the sufferings of NIG
2:20 *is it*, if, **w** ye be buffeted for your faults, 2532
2:20 but if, **w** ye do well, and suffer *for it*, ye NIG
2:23 Who, **w** he was reviled, reviled not again; NIG
2:23 **w** he suffered, he threatened not; NIG
3:20 **w** once the longsuffering of God waited in 3753
4: 3 **w** we walked in lasciviousness, lusts, NIG
4:13 that, **w** his glory shall be revealed, ye may 1722
2Pe 5: 4 And **w** the chief Shepherd shall appear, NIG
1:16 **w** we made known unto you the power NIG
1:17 **w** there came such a voice to him from NIG
1:18 **w** we were with him in the holy mount. NIG
2:18 For **w** they speak great swelling *words* of NIG
1Jn 2:28 that, **w** he shall appear, we may have 3752
3: 2 but we know that, **w** he shall appear, 1437
5: 2 **w** we love God, and keep his 3752
3Jn 1: 3 **w** the brethren came and testified of NIG
Jude 1: 3 **w** I gave all diligence to write unto you of NIG
1: 9 **w** contending with the devil he disputed 3753
1:12 These are spots in your feasts of charity **w** NIG
Rev 1:17 And **w** I saw him, I fell at his feet as dead. 3753
4: 9 And **w** *those* beasts give glory and honour 3752
5: 8 And **w** he had taken the book, the four 3753
6: 1 And I saw **w** the Lamb opened one of 3753
6: 3 And **w** he had opened the second seal, 3753
6: 5 And **w** he had opened the third seal, 3753
6: 7 And **w** he had opened the fourth seal, 3753
6: 9 And **w** he had opened the fifth seal, I saw 3753
6:12 And I beheld **w** he had opened the sixth 3753
6:13 **w** she is shaken of a mighty wind. NIG
6:14 the heaven departed as a scroll **w** it is NIG
8: 1 And **w** he had opened the seventh seal, 3753
9: 5 of a scorpion, **w** he striketh a man. 3752
10: 3 with a loud voice, as **w** a lion roareth: NIG
10: 3 **w** he had cried, seven thunders uttered 3753
10: 4 **w** the seven thunders had uttered their 3753
10: 7 **w** he shall begin to sound, the mystery of 3752
11: 7 And **w** they shall have finished their 3752
12:13 the dragon saw that he was cast unto 3753
17: 6 and **w** I saw her, I wondered *with* great NIG
17: 8 **w** they behold the beast that was, and is NIG
17:10 **w** he cometh, he must continue a short 3752
18: 9 **w** they shall see the smoke of her burning, 3752
18:18 And cried **w** they saw the smoke of her NIG
20: 7 And **w** the thousand years are expired, 3752
22: 8 and heard *them*. And **w** I had heard and 3753

WHENCE (72)

Ge 3:23 till the ground from **w** he was taken. 834+8033
16: 8 Sarai's maid, **w** camest thou? 335+2088+4480
24: 5 again unto the land from **w** thou camest? 8033
29: 4 unto them, My brethren, **w** *be* ye? 370+4480
42: 7 and he said unto them, **W** come ye? 370+4480
Nu 11:13 **W** should I have flesh to give unto all 370+4480
23:13 from **w** thou mayest see them: 8033
Dt 9:28 the land **w** thou broughtest 834+4480+8033
11:10 land of Egypt, from **w** ye came out, 834+4480
Jos 2: 4 me, but I wist not **w** they *were:* 370+4480
9: 8 Who *are* ye? and from **w** come ye? 370
20: 6 own house, unto the city from **w** he fled. 8033
Jdg 13: 6 I asked him not **w** he *was*, 335+2088+4480
17: 9 said unto him, **W** comest thou? 370+4480
19:17 goest thou? and **w** comest thou? 370+4480
1Sa 25:11 whom I know not **w** they *be?* 335+2088+4480
30:13 **w** *art* thou? And he said, 335+2088+4480
2Sa 1: 3 **From w** comest thou? 335+2088+4480
1:13 that told him, **W** *art* thou? 335+2088+4480
2Ki 5:25 unto him, **W** *comest thou*, Gehazi? 370+4480
6:27 *If* the LORD do not help thee, **w** 370+4480
20:14 from **w** came they unto thee? 370
Ne 4:12 From all places **w** ye shall return unto us 834
Job 1: 7 said unto Satan, **W** comest thou? 370+4480
2: 2 **From w** comest thou? 335+2088+4480
10:21 Before I go **w** I shall not return, *even* to NIH
16:22 I shall go the way *w* I shall not return. NIH
28:20 **W** then cometh wisdom? and where 370+4480
Ps 121: 1 unto the hills, from **w** cometh my help. 370
Ecc 1: 7 unto the place from **w** the rivers come, 7945
Isa 30: 6 from **w** *come* the young and old lion, 1992.1
39: 3 from **w** came they unto thee? 370
47:11 thou shalt not know from **w** it riseth: NIH
51: 1 look unto the rock *w* ye are hewn, and to NIH
51: 1 and to the hole of the pit *w* ye are digged. NIH
Jer 29:14 **w** I caused you to be carried 834+4480+8033
Jnh 1: 8 **w** comest thou? what *is* thy country? 370+4480
Na 3: 7 **w** shall I seek comforters for thee? 370+4480
Mt 12:44 will return into my house **from w** I came 3606
13:27 in thy field? **from w** then hath it tares? 4159
13:54 **w** hath this *man* this wisdom, 4159
13:56 Then hath this *man* all these *things?* 4159
15:33 **W** should we have so much bread in 4159
21:25 The baptism of John, **w** was it? 4159
Mk 6: 2 **From w** hath this *man* these *things?* and 4159
8: 4 **From w** can a man satisfy these *men* 4159
12:37 him Lord; and **w** is he *then* his son? 4159
Lk 1:43 **w** *is* this to me, that the mother of my 4159
11:24 will return unto my house **w** I came out; 3606
13:25 say unto you, I know you not **w** you are: 4159
13:27 I tell you, I know you not **w** you are; 4159
20: 7 that *they* could not tell **w** it was. 4159
Jn 1:48 saith unto him, **W** knowest thou me? 4159
2: 9 *was* made wine, and knew not **w** it was: 4159
3: 8 but canst not tell **w** it cometh, 4159

Jn 4:11 **from w** then hast thou *that* living water? 4159
6: 5 **W** shall we buy bread, that these may eat? 4159
7:27 Howbeit we know this *man* **w** he is: 4159
7:27 Christ cometh, no *man* knoweth **w** he is. 4159
7:28 Ye both know me, and ye know **w** I am: 4159
8:14 for I know **w** I came, and whither I go; 4159
8:14 but ye cannot tell **w** I come, and whither 4159
9:29 *as for* this *fellow*, we know not **from w** 4159
9:30 thing, that ye know not **from w** he is, 4159
19: 9 and saith unto Jesus, **W** art thou? 4159
Ac 14:26 **from w** they had been recommended to 3606
Php 3:20 from **w** also we look for the Saviour, 3757
Heb 11:15 of that *country* from **w** they came out, 3739
11:19 from **w** also he received him in a figure. 3606
Jas 4: 1 **From w** come wars and fightings among 4159
Rev 2: 5 therefore **from w** thou art fallen, 4159
7:13 arrayed in white robes? and **w** came they? 4159

WHENSOEVER (3) [EVER, SO, WHEN]

Ge 30:41 **w** the stronger cattle did conceive, 3605+871.1
Mk 14: 7 and **w** ye will ye may do them good: 3752
Ro 15:24 **w** I take my journey into Spain, 1437+5613

WHERE (401)

Ge 2:11 land of Havilah, **w** *there is* gold; 834+8033
3: 9 Adam, and said unto him, **W** *art* thou? 335
4: 9 said unto Cain, **W** *is* Abel thy brother? 335
13: 3 unto the place **w** his tent had been at 8033
13:10 Jordan, that it *was* well watered every **w**, 3605
13:14 the place **w** thou *art* northward, 834+8033
18: 9 They said unto him, **W** *is* Sarah thy wife? 346
19: 5 **W** *are* the men which came in to thee this 346
19:27 place **w** he stood before the LORD: 834+8033
20:15 *is* before thee: dwell **w** it pleaseth thee. 871.1
21:17 the voice of the lad **w** he *is*. 834+8033+871.1
22: 7 but **w** *is* the lamb for a burnt offering? 346
27:33 **w** *is* he that hath taken venison, 645
31:13 **w** thou anointedst the pillar, 834+8033
31:13 **w** thou vowedst a vow unto me: 834+8033
33:19 of a field, **w** he had spread his tent, 834+8033
35:13 God went up from him in the place **w** he 834
35:14 Jacob set up a pillar in the place **w** he 834
35:15 Jacob called the name of the place **w** 834+8033
35:27 **w** Abraham and Isaac sojourned. 834+8033
37:16 me, I pray thee, **w** they feed *their* flocks. 375
38:21 saying, **W** *is* the harlot, that *was* openly by 346
39:20 place **w** the king's prisoners *were* bound: 834
40: 3 the place **w** Joseph *was* bound. 834+8033
43:30 he sought **w** to weep; and he entered into NIH
Ex 2:20 he said unto his daughters, And **w** *is* he? 335
5:11 get you straw **w** you can find *it:* yet 834+4480
9:26 the children of Israel *were*, was 834+8033
12:13 for a token upon the houses **w** you 834+8033
12:30 *there was* not a house **w** *there was* 834+8033
15:27 **w** *were* twelve wells of water, 8033
18: S **w** he encamped *at* the mount of God: 834
20:21 unto the thick darkness **w** God *was.* 834+8033
20:24 in all places **w** I record my name I will 834
27:18 fifty every **w**, 2572+2572+871.1+1886.1
29:42 **w** I will meet you, to speak 834+8033+1886.5
30: 6 **w** I will meet with thee. 834+8033+1886.5
30:36 **w** I will meet with thee: 834+8033+1886.5
Lev 4:12 **w** the ashes are poured out, and burn him NIH
4:12 **w** the ashes are poured out shall he be 5921
4:24 kill it in the place **w** they kill the burnt 834
4:33 slay it for a sin offering in the place **w** they 834
6:25 In the place **w** the burnt offering is killed 834
7: 2 In the place **w** they kill the burnt offering 834
14:13 shall slay the lamb in the place **w** he shall 834
Nu 9:17 in the place **w** the cloud abode, 834+8033
13:22 **w** Ahiman, Sheshai, and Talmai, 8033
17: 4 **w** I will meet with you. 834+8033+1886.5
22:26 **w** *was* no way to turn *either* to the right 834
33:14 **w** was no water for the people to drink. 8033
33:54 shall be in the **place w** his lot falleth; 8033
Dt 1:31 **w** thou hast seen how that the LORD thy 834
8:15 and drought, **w** *there was* no water; 834
11:10 **w** thou sowedst thy seed, and wateredst *it* 834
11:30 by the way **w** the sun goeth down, NIH
18: 6 **w** he sojourned, and come with all 834+8033
23:16 in one of thy gates, **w** it liketh him best: NIH
32:37 he shall say, **W** *are* their gods, *their* rock in 335
Jos 3: 4 out of the place **w** the priests' feet stood NIH
4: 3 lodging place, **w** you shall lodge *this* night. 834
4: 8 with them unto the **place w** they lodged, 4411
4: 9 in the place **w** the feet of the priests which NIH
Jdg 5:27 he bowed, there he fell down 834+871.1
6:13 **w** be all his miracles which our fathers told 346
9:38 **W** *is* now thy mouth, wherewith thou 346
17: 8 to sojourn **w** he could find *a place:* 834+871.1
17: 9 I go to sojourn **w** I may find *a place.* 834+871.1
18:10 **w** *there is* no want of any thing 834+8033
19:26 her lord *was*, till it was light. 834+8033
20:22 **w** they put *themselves* in array 834+8033
Ru 1: 7 out of the place **w** she was, 834+8033+1886.5
1:16 and **w** thou lodgest, I will lodge: 834+871.1
1:17 **W** thou diest, will I die, 834+871.1
2:19 unto her, **W** hast thou gleaned to day? 375
2:19 wroughtest thou? blessed be he 575+1886.5
3: 4 that thou shalt mark the place **w** 834+8033
1Sa 3: 3 **w** the ark of God *was*, and 834+8033
6:14 stood there, **w** *there was* a great stone. 8033
9:10 they went unto the city **w** the man 834+8033
9:18 I pray thee, **w** the seer's house *is.* 335+2088
10: 5 **w** *is* the garrison of the Philistines: 834+8033

W

1Sa 10:14 we saw that *they were* no **w**, we came	369
14:11 holes **w** they had hid themselves.	834+8033
19: 3 beside my father in the field **w**	834+8033
19:22 asked and said, **W** are Samuel and David?	375
20:19 come to the place **w** thou didst hide	834+8033
23:22 know and see his place **w** his haunt is,	834
23:23 lurking places **w** he hideth himself,	834+8033
24: 3 the sheepcotes by the way, **w** *was* a cave;	8033
26: 5 to the place **w** Saul had pitched:	834+8033
26: 5 David beheld the place **w** Saul lay,	834+8033
26:16 saw the king's spear *is*, and the cruse	335
30: 9 **w** those that were left behind stayed.	2050.1
30:31 to all the places **w** David himself and	834+8033
2Sa 2:23 that as many as came to the place **w**	834+8033
9: 4 the king said unto him, **W** *is* he? And Ziba	375
11:16 he assigned Uriah unto a place **w**	834+8033
15:32 *the mount*, **w** he worshipped God,	834+8033
16: 3 the king said, And **w** *is* thy master's son?	346
17:12 in some place **w** he shall be found,	834+8033
17:20 they said, **W** *is* Ahimaaz and Jonathan?	346
18: 7 **W** the people of Israel were slain before	8033
21:12 **w** the Philistines had hanged them,	834+8033
21:19 Elhanan the son of Jaare-oregim, **w**	834+8033
21:20 **w** was a man of *great* stature, that had on	NIH
23:11 was a piece of ground full *of* lentiles.	NIH
1Ki 4:28 unto the place **w** *the officers* were,	834+8033
7: 7 he made a porch for the throne **w** he	834+8033
7: 8 his house **w** he dwelt *had* another	834+8033
13:25 told *it* in the city **w** the old prophet dwelt.	834
17:19 he abode, and laid him upon his	834+8033
21:19 In the place **w** dogs licked the blood of	834
2Ki 2:14 and said, **W** *is* the LORD God of Elijah?	346
4: 8 to Shunem, **w** *was* a great woman;	8033
6: 1 place **w** we dwell with thee is too	834+8033
6: 2 make us a place there, **w** we may dwell.	8033
6: 6 the man of God said, **W** fell it?	575+1886.5
6:13 Go and spy **w** he *is*, that I may send and	351
18:34 **W** *are* the gods of Hamath, and of Arpad?	346
18:34 *are* the gods of Sepharvaim, Hena,	346
19:13 **W** *is* the king of Hamath, and the king of	335
23: 7 the women wove hangings for	834+8033
23: 8 defiled the high places **w**	834+8033+1886.5
1Ch 11: 4 **w** the Jebusites *were*, the inhabitants of	8033
11:13 **w** was a parcel of ground full *of* barley,	NIH
13: 2 send **abroad** unto our brethren **every w**,	6555
20: 6 **w** was a man of *great* stature, whose	NIH
2Ch 3: 1 **w** *the* LORD appeared unto David his	834
25: 4 **w** the LORD commanded, saying,	834
36:20 they were servants to him and his sons	NIH
Ezr 1: 4 whosoever remaineth in any place **w**	834+8033
6: 1 **w** the treasures were laid up in Babylon.	8536
6: 3 the place **w** they offered sacrifices,	1768
Ne 10:39 **w** *are* the vessels of the sanctuary,	8033
13: 5 **w** aforetime they laid the meat offerings,	8033
Est 1: 6 **W** *were* white, green, and blue *hangings*,	NIH
7: 5 the queen, Who *is* he, and **w** *is* he,	335+2088
Job 4: 7 or **w** were the righteous cut off?	375
9:24 judges thereof; if not, **w**, *and* who *is* he?	645
10:22 any order, and **w** the light is as darkness.	NIH
12:24 causeth them to wander in a wilderness **w**	NIH
14:10 yea, man giveth up the ghost, and **w** *is* he?	335
15:23 *saying*, **W** *is it?* he knoweth that the day of	346
17:15 **w** is now my hope? as for my hope,	346
20: 7 which have seen him shall say, **W** *is* he?	335
21:28 For ye say, **W** *is* the house of the prince?	346
21:28 **w** *are* the dwelling places of the wicked?	346
23: 3 O that I knew **w** I might find him! that I	871.1
23: 9 **w** he doth work, but I cannot behold	871.1
28: 1 and a place for gold **w** they fine *it*.	NIH
28:12 **w** shall wisdom be found?	370+4480
28:12 and **w** *is* the place of understanding?	335+2088
28:20 and **w** *is* the place of understanding?	335+2088
34:22 **w** the workers of iniquity may hide	8033
35:10 saith, **W** *is* God my Maker, who giveth	346
36:16 **w** *there is* no straitness;	8478+1886.3
38: 4 **W** wast thou when I laid the foundations	375
38:19 **W** *is* the way *where* light dwelleth?	335+2088
38:19 Where *is* the way **w** light dwelleth?	NIH
38:19 *for* darkness, **w** *is* the place thereof,	335+2088
38:26 **w** no man *is*; on the wilderness,	NIH
39:30 and **w** the slain *are*, there *is* she.	834+871.1
40:20 food, **w** all the beasts of the field play.	8033
Ps 19: 3 *nor* language, **w** their voice is not heard.	NIH
26: 8 and the place **w** thine honour **dwelleth**,	4908
42: 3 continually say unto me, **W** *is* thy God?	346
42:10 they say daily unto me, **W** *is* thy God?	346
53: 5 were they in great fear, **w** no fear was:	NIH
63: 1 in a dry and thirsty land, **w** no water is;	NIH
69: 2 sink in deep mire, **w** *there is* no standing:	NIH
69: 2 deep waters, **w** the floods overflow me.	NIH
79:10 should the heathen say, **W** *is* their God?	346
81: 5 **w** I heard a language *that* I understood not.	NIH
84: 3 she may lay her young, *even* thine altars,	834
89:49 Lord, **w** *are* thy former lovingkindnesses,	346
104:17 **W** the birds make their nests: *as for*	834+8033
107:40 in the wilderness, **w** *there is* no way.	NIH
115: 2 the heathen say, **W** *is* now their God?	346
Pr 11:14 **W** no counsel *is*, the people fall: but in	871.1
14: 4 **W** no oxen *are*, the crib *is* clean:	871.1
15:17 Better *is* a dinner of herbs **w** love is, than	8033
26:20 **W** no wood is, *there* the fire goeth out:	871.1
26:20 so **w** *there is* no talebearer, the strife	871.1
29:18 **W** *there is* no vision, the people perish:	871.1
Ecc 1: 5 and hasteth to his place **w** he arose.	8033
8: 4 **W** the word of a king *is*, there is	834+871.1
Ecc 8:10 they were forgotten in the city **w** they had	834
11: 3 *in* the place **w** the tree falleth, there it	7945
SS 1: 7 whom my soul loveth, **w** thou feedest,	349
1: 7 **w** thou makest *thy flock* to rest at noon:	349
Isa 7:23 **w** there were a thousand vines at a	834+8033
10: 3 and **w** will ye leave your glory?	575+1886.5
19:12 **W** *are* they? where *are* thy wise **men**?	335
19:12 **W** *are* thy wise **men**? and let them tell thee	645
29: 1 to Ariel, to Ariel, the city **w** David dwelt!	NIH
30:32 *in* every *place* **w** the grounded staff shall	NIH
33:18 **W** *is* the scribe? where *is* the receiver?	346
33:18 **w** *is* the receiver? where *is* he that counted	346
33:18 **w** *is* he that counted the towers?	346
35: 7 **w** each *lay, shall be* grass with reeds and	7258
36:19 **W** *are* the gods of Hamath and Arphad?	346
36:19 **w** *are* the gods of Sepharvaim? and have	346
37:13 **W** *is* the king of Hamath, and the king of	346
49:21 I was left alone; these, **w** *had they been?*	375
50: 1 **W** *is* the bill of your mother's	335+2088
51:13 and **w** *is* the fury of the oppressor?	346
57: 8 thou lovedst their bed **w** thou sawest *it*.	3027
63:11 **w** *is* he that brought them up out of	346
63:11 **w** *is* he that put his holy Spirit within him?	346
63:15 **w** *is* thy zeal and thy strength,	346
64:11 beautiful house, **w** our fathers praised thee,	834
66: 1 *is* the house that ye build unto	335+2088
66: 1 and **w** *is* the place of my rest?	335+2088
Jer 2: 6 **W** *is* the LORD that brought us up out of	346
2: 6 passed through, and **w** no man dwelt?	8033
2: 8 The priests said not, **W** *is* the LORD?	346
2:28 **w** *are* thy gods that thou hast made thee?	346
3: 2 and see **w** thou hast not been lien with.	375
6:16 **w** *is* the good way, and walk therein	335+2088
7:12 **w** I set my name at the first,	834+8033
13: 7 from the place **w** I had hid	834+8033+1886.5
13:20 **w** *is* the flock *that* was given thee,	346
16:13 and night; **w** I will not shew you favour.	834
17:15 say unto me, **W** *is* the word of the LORD?	346
22:26 country, **w** ye were not born;	834+8033
35: 7 days in the land **w** ye *be* strangers.	834+8033
36:19 Jeremiah; and let no man know **w** ye *be*.	375
37:19 **W** *are* now your prophets which	346
38: 9 is like to die for hunger **in the place w**	8478
39: 5 Hamath, **w** he gave judgment upon him.	834
42:14 the land of Egypt, **w** we shall see no war,	834
52: 9 Hamath; **w** he gave judgment upon him.	834
La 2:12 say to their mothers, **W** *is* corn and wine?	346
Eze 3:15 I sat **w** they sat, and remained there	8033
6:13 the place **w** they did offer sweet	834+8033
8: 3 **w** *was* the seat of the image of	834+8033
11:16 in the countries **w** they shall come.	834+8033
11:17 **w** ye have been scattered,	834+871.1+1992.1
13:12 **W** *is* the daubing where **with** ye have	346
17:10 it shall wither in the furrows **w** it grew.	NIH
17:16 surely in the place **w** the king *dwelleth*	NIH
20:38 will bring them forth out of the country **w**	NIH
21:30 I will judge thee in the place **w** thou wast	834
34:12 will deliver them out of all places **w**	834+8033
40:38 gates, **w** they washed the burnt offering.	8033
42:13 the priests that approach unto	834+8033
43: 7 **w** I will dwell in the midst of	834+8033
46:20 This *is* the place **w** the priests shall	834+8033
46:20 **w** they shall bake the meat offering;	834
46:24 the ministers of the house shall	834+8033
Da 8:17 So he came near **w** I **stood**: and when he	5977
Hos 1:10 *that* in the place **w** it was said unto them,	834
13:10 **w** *is any other* that may save thee *from*	165+645
Joel 2:17 say among the people, **W** *is* their God?	346
Am 5: 2 upon the earth, **w** no gin *is* for him?	2050.1
Mic 7:10 said unto me, **W** *is* the LORD thy God?	335
Na 2:11 **W** *is* the dwelling of the lions,	346
2:11 the lion, *even* the old lion, walked,	8033
3:17 and their place is not known **w** they *are*.	335
Zep 3: 8 fame in every land **w** they have been put	NIH
Zec 1: 5 Your fathers, **w** *are* they? and the prophets,	346
Mal 1: 6 if then I *be* a father, **w** *is* mine honour?	346
1: 6 if I *be* a master, **w** *is* my fear? saith	346
2:17 in them; or, **W** *is* the God of judgment?	346
Mt 2: 2 **W** is he that is born King of the Jews?	4226
2: 4 he demanded of them **w** Christ should be	4226
2: 9 and stood over **w** the young child was.	3757
6:19 **w** moth and rust doth corrupt,	3699
6:19 and **w** thieves break through and steal:	3699
6:20 **w** neither moth nor rust doth corrupt,	3699
6:20 **w** thieves do not break through nor steal:	3699
6:21 **w** your treasure is, there will your heart	3699
8:20 Son of man hath not **w** to lay *his* head.	4226
13: 5 Some fell upon stony *places*, **w** they had	3699
18:20 **w** two or three are gathered together in	3757
25:24 reaping **w** thou hast not sown,	3699
25:24 and gathering **w** thou hast not strawed:	3606
25:26 thou knewest that I reap **w** I sowed not,	3699
25:26 and gather **w** I have not strawed?	3606
26:17 **W** wilt thou *that* we prepare for thee to	4226
26:57 the scribes and the elders were	4226
28: 6 Come, see the place **w** the Lord lay.	3699
28:16 into a mountain **w** Jesus had appointed	3757
Mk 2: 4 they uncovered the roof **w** he was:	3699
4: 5 stony *ground*, **w** it had not much earth;	3699
4:15 they by the way side, **w** the word is sown;	3699
5:40 and entereth in **w** the damsel was lying.	3699
6:55 that were sick, **w** they heard he was.	3699
9:44 **W** their worm dieth not, and the fire is	3699
9:46 **W** their worm dieth not, and the fire is	3699
9:48 **W** their worm dieth not, and the fire is	3699
Mk 11: 4 door without in a place **w** two ways met;	NIG
13:14 the prophet, standing **w** it ought not,	3699
14:12 **w** wilt thou *that* we go and prepare that	4226
14:14 The Master saith, **W** is the guestchamber,	4226
14:14 **w** I shall eat the passover with my	3699
15:47 Mary *the mother* of Joses beheld the place **w**	4226
16: 6 here: behold the place **w** they laid him.	3699
16:20 they went forth, and preached **every w**,	3837
Lk 4:16 to Nazareth, **w** he had been brought up:	3757
4:17 he found the place **w** it was written,	3757
8:25 And he said unto them, **W** is your faith?	4226
9: 6 the gospel, and healing **every w**.	3837
9:58 Son of man hath not **w** to lay *his* head.	4226
10:33 as he journeyed, came **w** he was:	2596
12:17 I have no room **w** to bestow my fruits?	4226
12:33 **w** no thief approacheth, neither moth	3699
12:34 **w** your treasure is, there will your heart	3699
12:17 not ten cleansed? but **w** *are* the nine?	4226
17:37 answered and said unto him, **W**, Lord?	4226
22: 9 unto him, **W** wilt thou *that* we prepare?	4226
22:10 him into the house **w** he entereth in.	3757
22:11 saith unto thee, **W** is the guestchamber,	4226
22:11 **w** I shall eat the passover with my	3699
Jn 1:28 beyond Jordan, **w** John was baptizing.	3699
1:38 Master,) **w** dwellest thou?	4226
1:39 They came and saw **w** he dwelt,	4226
3: 8 The wind bloweth **w** it listeth,	3699
4:20 in Jerusalem is the place **w** *men* ought	3699
4:46 of Galilee, **w** he made the water wine.	3699
6:23 nigh unto the place **w** they did eat bread,	3699
6:62 ye shall see the Son of man ascend up **w**	3699
7:11 sought him at the feast, and said, **W** is he?	4226
7:36 and shall not find *me*: and **w** I am,	3699
7:36 and shall not find *me*: and **w** I am,	3699
7:42 of the town of Bethlehem, **w** David was?	3699
8:10 Woman, **w** are those thine accusers?	4226
8:19 Then said they unto him, **W** is thy Father?	4226
9:12 Then said they unto him, **W** is he?	4226
10:40 into the place **w** John at first baptized:	3699
11: 6 abode two days *still* in the *same* place **w**	3739
11:30 but was in *that* place **w** Martha met him.	3699
11:32 Then when Mary was come **w** Jesus was,	3699
11:34 And said, **W** have ye laid him? They say	3699
11:41 stone *from the place* **w** the dead was laid.	3757
11:57 that, if any *man* knew **w** he were,	4226
12: 1 **w** Lazarus was which had been dead,	3699
12:26 **w** I am, there shall also my servant be:	3699
14: 3 that **w** I am, *there* ye may be also.	3699
17:24 thou hast given me, be with me **w** I am;	3699
18: 1 **w** was a garden, into the which he	3699
19:18 **W** they crucified him, and two other with	3699
19:20 for the place **w** Jesus was crucified was	3699
19:41 Now in the place **w** he was crucified	3699
20: 2 and we know not **w** they have laid him.	4226
20:12 at the feet, **w** the body of Jesus had lain.	3699
20:13 and I know not **w** they have laid him.	4226
20:15 if thou have borne him *hence*, tell me **w**	4226
20:19 when the doors were shut **w** the disciples	3699
Ac 1:13 abode both Peter, and James, and John,	3757
2: 2 it filled all the house **w** they were sitting.	3757
4:31 the place was shaken **w** they were	1722+3739
7:29 the land of Madian, **w** he begat two sons.	3757
7:33 the place **w** thou standest is holy	1722+3739
8: 4 **w** *every* **w** preaching the word.	1330
11:11 come unto the house **w** I was,	1722+3739
12:12 many were gathered together praying,	3757
15:36 visit our brethren in every city **w**	1722+3739
16:13 river side, **w** prayer was wont to be made;	3757
17: 1 was a synagogue of the Jews:	3699
17:30 now commandeth all men **every** to	3837
20: 6 in five days; **w** we abode seven days.	3757
20: 8 **w** they were gathered together.	3757
21:28 that teacheth all *men* **every w** against	3837
25:10 judgment seat, **w** I ought to be judged:	3757
27:41 And falling into a place **w** two seas met,	1337
28:14 We found brethren, and were desired	3757
28:22 know that **every w** it is spoken against.	3837
Ro 3:27 **W** is boasting then? It is excluded.	4226
4:15 for **w** no law is, *there is* no transgression.	3757
5:20 sin abounded, grace did much more	3757
9:26 *that* in the place **w** it was said unto them,	3699
15:20 the gospel, not **w** Christ was named,	3699
1Co 1:20 **W** is the wise? where is the scribe?	4226
1:20 **w** is the scribe? where is the disputer of	4226
1:20 **w** is the disputer of this world? hath not	4226
4:17 as I teach **every w** in every church.	3837
12:17 body *were* an eye, **w** *were* the hearing?	4226
12:17 *were* hearing, **w** *were* the smelling?	4226
12:19 were all one member, **w** *were* the body?	4226
15:55 death, **w** *is* thy sting? O grave, where *is*	4226
15:55 thy sting? O grave, **w** *is* thy victory?	4226
2Co 3:17 the Spirit of the Lord *is*, there *is* liberty.	4226
Gal 4:15 **W** is then the blessedness you spake of?	5101
Php 4:12 every w, and in all *things* I am instructed	3956
Col 3: 1 **w** Christ sitteth on the right hand of God.	3757
3:11 **W** there is neither Greek nor Jew,	3699
1Ti 2: 8 I will therefore that men pray every **w**,	5117
Heb 9:16 For **w** *a* testament *is*, there must also of	3699
10:18 Now remission of these *is*, there is no	3699
Jas 3:16 For *w* envying and strife *is*, there *is*	3699
1Pe 4:18 shall the ungodly and the sinner appear?	4226
2Pe 3: 4 **W** is the promise of his coming?	4226
Rev 2:13 I know thy works, and **w** thou dwellest,	4226
2:13 *even* **w** Satan's seat *is*: and thou holdest	3699
2:13 was slain among you, **w** Satan dwelleth.	3699

W

Rev 11: 8 and Egypt, **w** also our Lord was crucified. 3699
12: 6 **w** she hath a place prepared of God, 3699
12:14 **w** she is nourished for a time, and times, 3699
17:15 **w** the whore sitteth, are peoples, 3757
20:10 **w** the beast and the false prophet *are*, and 3699

WHEREABOUT (1) [ABOUT]
1Sa 21: 2 any thing of the business **w** I send thee, 834

WHEREAS (33) [AS]
Ge 31:37 **W** thou hast searched all my stuff, 3588
Dt 19: 6 **w** he *was* not worthy of death, 2050.1
28:62 **w** ye were as the stars of heaven for 834
1Sa 24:17 me good, **w** I have rewarded thee evil. 2050.1
2Sa 7: 6 **W** I have not dwelt in *any* house since 3588
15:20 **W** thou camest *but* yesterday, should I *this* NIH
1Ki 8:18 **W** it was in thine heart to build a 834+3282
12:11 now **w** my father did lade you with a 2050.1
2Ki 13:19 *it*: **w** now thou shalt smite Syria 2050.1
2Ch 10:11 For **w** my father put a heavy yoke upon 6258
28:13 for **w** we have offended against 3807.1
Job 22:20 **W** our substance is not cut down, 518
Ecc 4:14 **w** also *he that is* born in his kingdom 3588
Isa 37:21 **W** thou hast prayed to me against 834
60:15 **W** thou hast been forsaken and hated, 8478
Jer 4:10 **w** the sword reacheth unto the soul). 2050.1
Eze 13: 7 not spoken a lying divination, **w** ye say, 2050.1
16: 7 is grown, **w** thou *wast* naked and bare. 2050.1
16:34 **w** none followeth thee to commit 2050.1
35:10 will possess it; **w** the Lord was there: 2050.1
36:34 **w** it lay desolate in the sight of all 834+8478
Da 2:41 **w** thou sawest the feet and toes, part of 1768
2:43 **w** thou sawest iron mixt with miry clay, 1768
4:23 **w** the king saw a watcher and a holy one 1768
4:26 **w** they commanded to leave the stump of 1768
8:22 being broken, **w** four stood up for it, 2050.1
Mal 1: 4 **W** Edom saith, We are impoverished, 3588
Jn 9:25 I know, that, **w** I was blind, now I see. NIG
1Co 3: 3 for **w** *there is* among you envying, 3699
Jas 4:14 **W** ye know not what *shall* be on 3748
1Pe 2:12 that, **w** they speak against you as 1722+3739
3:16 that, **w** they speak evil of you, as of 1722+3739
2Pe 2:11 **W** angels, which are greater in power and 3699

WHEREBY (39) [BY]
Ge 15: 8 Lord God, **w** shall I know that I 4100+871.1
44: 5 and **w** indeed he divineth? 871.1+2050.2
Lev 22: 5 **w** he may be made unclean, or a man of 834
Nu 5: 8 **w** an atonement shall be 834+871.1+2050.2
17: 5 Israel, **w** they murmur against you. 834+1992
Dt 7:19 **w** the Lord thy God brought thee out: 834
28:20 of thy doings, **w** thou hast forsaken me. 834
1Sa 20:33 Jonathan knew that it was 2050.1
Ps 45: 5 **w** the people fall under thee. NIH
45: 8 **w** by they have made thee glad. 4482
68: 9 **w** thou didst confirm thine inheritance, 1886.3
Jer 3: 8 for all the causes **w** backsliding Israel 834
17:19 **w** the kings of Judah come 834+871.1+2050.2
23: 6 this *is* his name **w** he shall be called, 834
33: 8 **w** they have sinned against me, and I will 834
33: 8 **w** they have sinned, and whereby they 834
33: 8 **w** they have transgressed against me. 834
Eze 18:31 **w** ye have transgressed; 834+871.1
20:25 **w** they should not live; 871.1+1992.1
39:26 all their trespasses **w** they have trespassed 834
40:49 he brought me by the steps **w** they went 834
46: 9 of the gate **w** he came in, 834+871.1+2050.2
47:13 **w** ye shall inherit the land according to 834
Zep 2: 8 **w** they have reproached my people, 834
Lk 1:18 the angel, **W** shall I know this? 2596+5101
1:78 **w** the dayspring from on high hath 1722+3739
Ac 4:12 among men, **w** we must be saved. 1722+3739
11:14 **w** thou and all thy house shall be 1722+3739
19:40 being no cause **w** we may give 3739+4012
Ro 8:15 adoption, **w** we cry, Abba, Father. 1722+3739
14:21 nor *any thing* **w** thy brother 1722+3739
Eph 3: 4 **W**, when ye read, ye may 3739+4314
4:14 **w** they lie in wait to deceive; 4314
4:30 **w** ye are sealed unto the day of 1722+3739
Php 3:21 according to the working **w** he is able NIG
Heb 12:28 we may serve God acceptably 1223+3739
2Pe 1: 4 **W** are given unto us exceeding 1223+3739
3: 6 **W** the world that then was, 1223+3739
1Jn 2:18 we know that it is the last time. 3606

WHEREFORE (348)
Ge 10: 9 mighty hunter before the Lord: **w** 3651+5921
16:14 The well was called 3651+5921
18:13 said unto Abraham, **W** 2088+4100+3807.1
21:10 **W** she said unto Abraham, Cast out this 3651+3807.1
21:31 **W** he called that place Beer-sheba, 3651+5921
24:31 thou blessed of the Lord; **w** 4100+3807.1
26:27 **W** come ye to me, seeing ye hate me, 4069
29:25 I serve with thee for Rachel? **w** 4100+3807.1
31:27 **W** didst thou flee away secretly, 4100+3807.1
31:30 after thy father's house, *yet* **w** 4100+3807.1
32:29 he said, **W** *is it* that thou dost ask 4100+3807.1
38:10 the Lord: **w** he slew him also. 2050.1
40: 7 saying, **W** look ye so sadly to day? 4069
43: 6 Israel said, **W** dealt ye *so* ill with 4100+3807.1
44: 4 say unto them, **W** have ye 4100+3807.1
44: 7 they said unto him, **W** saith my 4100+3807.1
47:19 **W** shall we die before thine eyes, 4100+3807.1
47:22 which Pharaoh gave them: **w** 3651+5921
50:11 mourning to the Egyptians: **w** 3651+5921

Ex 2:13 to him that did the wrong, **W** 4100+3807.1
5: 4 king of Egypt said unto them, **W** 4100+3807.1
5:14 **W** have ye not fulfilled your task in 4069
5:15 saying, **W** dealest thou thus with 4100+3807.1
5:22 **W** hast thou *so* evil entreated 4100+3807.1
6: 6 **W** say unto the children of Israel, 3651+3807.1
14:11 **w** hast thou dealt thus with us, to carry 4100
14:15 said unto Moses, **W** criest thou unto me? 4100
17: 2 **W** the people did chide with Moses, 4100
17: 2 you with me? **w** do ye tempt the Lord? 4100
17: 3 said, **W** *is* this that thou hast 4100+3807.1
20:11 **w** the Lord blessed the sabbath 3651+5921
32:12 **W** should the Egyptians speak, 4100+3807.1
Lev 10:17 **W** have ye not eaten the sin offering in 4069
13:25 **w** the priest shall pronounce him 2050.1
25:18 **W** ye shall do my statutes, and keep my 2050.1
Nu 9: 7 by the dead body of a man: **w** 4100+3807.1
11:11 Moses said unto the Lord, **W** 4100+3807.1
11:11 **w** have I not found favour in thy 4100+3807.1
12: 8 **w** then were ye not afraid to speak against 4069
14: 3 **w** *hath* the Lord brought us unto 4100+3807.1
14:41 Moses said, **W** now do ye 4100+3807.1
16: 3 **w** then lift you up yourselves above 4069
20: 5 **w** have ye made us to come up 4100+3807.1
20:21 **w** Israel turned away from him. 2050.1
21: 5 Moses, **W** have ye brought 4100+3807.1
21:14 **W** it is said in the book of the wars 3651+5921
21:27 **W** they that speak in proverbs say, 3651+5921
22:32 of the Lord said unto him, **W** 4100
22:37 send unto thee to call thee? **w** 4100+3807.1
25:12 **W** say, Behold, I give unto him 3651+3807.1
32: 5 **W**, said they, if we have found grace in 2050.1
32: 7 **w** discourage ye the heart of 4100+3807.1
Dt 7:12 it shall come to pass, if ye hearken to 2050.1
10: 9 **W** Levi hath no part nor inheritance 3651+5921
19: 7 **W** I command thee, saying, 3651+5921
29:24 Even all nations shall say, **W** hath 4100+5921
Jos 5: 9 **W** the name of the place is called Gilgal 2050.1
7: 5 **w** the hearts of the people melted, 2050.1
7: 7 **w** hast thou at all brought this 4100+3807.1
7:10 **w** liest thou thus upon thy face? 4100+3807.1
7:26 **W** the name of that place was 3651+5921
9:11 **W** our elders and all the inhabitants of 2050.1
9:22 **W** have ye beguiled us, saying, 4100+3807.1
10: 3 **W** Adoni-zedek king of Jerusalem sent 2050.1
10:13 **w** I will deliver you no more. 3651+3807.1
11:27 **W** I have not sinned against thee, 2050.1
Jdg 2: 3 **W** I also said, I will not drive them out 2050.1
12: 1 **W** passedst thou over to fight against 4069
12: 3 **w** then are ye come up unto me 4100+3807.1
15:19 **w** he called the name thereof 3651+5921
18:12 **w** they called that place 3651+5921
Ru 1: 7 **W** she went forth out of the place 2050.1
1Sa 1:20 **W** it came to pass, when the time was 2050.1
2:17 **W** the sin of the young men was very 2050.1
2:29 **W** kick ye at my sacrifice and 4100+3807.1
2:30 **W** the Lord God of Israel saith, 3651+3807.1
4: 3 the elders of Israel said, **W** hath 4100+3807.1
6: 5 **W** ye shall make images of your 2050.1
6: 6 **W** then do ye harden your hearts, 4100+3807.1
9:21 of the tribe of Benjamin? **w** 4100+3807.1
14:27 **w** he put forth the end of the rod that 2050.1
15:19 **W** then didst thou not obey 4100+3807.1
16:19 **W** Saul sent messengers unto Jesse, 2050.1
18:15 **W** when Saul saw that he behaved 2050.1
18:21 **W** Saul said to David, Thou shalt *this* 2050.1
18:27 **W** David arose and went, he and his 2050.1
19: 5 sawest *it*, and didst rejoice: **w** 4100+3807.1
19:24 **W** they say, *Is* Saul also among 3651+5921
20:27 **W** cometh not the son of Jesse to meat, 4069
20:31 **W** now send and fetch him unto me, 2050.1
20:32 unto him, **W** shall he be slain? 4100+3807.1
21:14 you see the man *is* mad: **w** then 4100+3807.1
23:25 **w** he came down *into* a rock, 2050.1
23:28 **W** Saul returned from pursuing after 2050.1
24: 9 David said to Saul, **W** hearest 4100+3807.1
24:19 **w** the Lord reward thee good for that 2050.1
25: 8 **W** let the young men find favour in 2050.1
25:36 **w** she told him nothing, less or more, 2050.1
26:15 *is* like to thee in Israel? **w** then 4100+3807.1
26:18 **W** doth my lord thus pursue after 4100+3807.1
27: 6 gave him Ziklag that day: **w** 3651+5921
28: 9 of the land: **w** then layest thou 4100+3807.1
28:16 Samuel, **W** then dost thou ask 4100+3807.1
29: 7 **W** now return, and go in peace, that 2050.1
29:10 **W** now rise up early in the morning 2050.1
2Sa 2:16 **w** that place was called 3651+5921
2:22 thee aside from following me: **w** 4100+3807.1
2:23 **w** Abner with the hinder end of the 2050.1
3: 7 **W** hast thou gone in unto my father's 4069
5: 8 **W** they said, The blind and the 3651+5921
7:22 **W** thou art great, O Lord God: 3651+5921
10: 4 **W** Hanun took David's servants, 2050.1
11:20 **W** approached ye *so* nigh unto the city 4069
12: 9 **W** hast thou despised the commandment 4069
12:23 now he is dead, **w** should I fast? 4100+3807.1
14:13 woman said, **W** then hast thou 4100+3807.1
14:31 unto him, **W** have thy servants 4069
14:32 say, **W** am I come from Geshur? 4100+3807.1
15:19 the king to Ittai the Gittite, **W** 4100+3807.1
16:10 then say, **W** hast thou done so? 4069
18:22 said, **W** wilt thou run, 2088+4100+3807.1
19:12 ye *are* my bones and my flesh: **w** 4100+3807.1
19:25 that the king said unto him, **W** 4100+3807.1

2Sa 19:35 and singing *women?* **w** then 4100+3807.1
19:42 the king *is* near of kin to us: **w** 4100+3807.1
21: 3 **W** David said unto the Gibeonites, 2050.1
24:21 **W** is my lord the king come to his 4069
1Ki 1: 2 **W** his servants said unto him, Let there 2050.1
1:11 **W** Nathan spake unto Bath-sheba 2050.1
1:41 **W** *is* this noise of the city being in an 4069
11:11 **W** the Lord said unto Solomon, 2050.1
12:15 **W** the king hearkened not unto 2050.1
16:16 **w** all Israel made Omri, the captain of 2050.1
20: 9 **W** he said unto the messengers of 2050.1
22:34 **w** he said unto the driver of his chariot, 2050.1
2Ki 4:23 he said, **W** wilt thou go to him to day? 4069
4:31 **W** he went again to meet him, 2050.1
5: 7 **w** consider, I pray you, and see how 389+3588
5: 8 **W** hast thou rent thy clothes? 4100+3807.1
7: 7 **W** they arose and fled in the twilight, 2050.1
9:11 **w** came this mad *fellow* to thee? And he 4069
9:36 **W** they came again, and told him. 2050.1
17:26 **W** they spake to the king of Assyria, 2050.1
19: 4 **w** lift up *thy* prayer for the remnant that 2050.1
1Ch 13:11 **w** that place is called Perez-uzza to this 2050.1
19: 4 **W** Hanun took David's servants, 2050.1
21: 4 **W** Joab departed, and went throughout 2050.1
29:10 **W** David blessed the Lord before all 2050.1
2Ch 5: 3 **W** all the men of Israel assembled 2050.1
19: 7 **W** now let the fear of the Lord be 2050.1
22: 4 **W** he did evil in the sight of the Lord, 2050.1
25:10 to go home *again:* **w** their anger was 2050.1
25:15 **W** the anger of the Lord was kindled 2050.1
28: 5 **W** the Lord his God delivered him 2050.1
29: 8 **W** the wrath of the Lord was upon 2050.1
29:34 **W** their brethren the Levites did help 2050.1
33:11 **W** the Lord brought upon them 2050.1
Ne 2: 2 **W** the king said unto me, Why *is* thy 4069
Est 3: 6 **w** Haman sought to destroy all the Jews 2050.1
9:26 **W** they called these days Purim 3651+5921
Job 3:20 **W** is light given to him that is in 4100+3807.1
10: 2 me **w** Thou contendest with me. 4100+3807.1
10:18 **W** then hast thou brought me 4100+3807.1
13:14 **W** do I take my flesh in my teeth, 4100+5921
13:24 **W** hidest thou thy face, 4100+3807.1
18: 3 **W** are we counted as beasts, 4069
21: 7 **W** do the wicked live, become old, yea, 4069
32: 6 **w** I was afraid, and durst not shew 3651+5921
33: 1 **W**, Job, I pray thee, hear my 199+2050.1
42: 6 **W** I abhor *myself*, and repent in 3651+5921
Ps 10:13 **W** doth the wicked contemn God? 4100+5921
44:24 **W** hidest thou thy face, 4100+3807.1
49: 5 **W** should I fear in the days of 4100+3807.1
79:10 **W** should the heathen say, 4100+3807.1
89:47 **w** hast thou made all men in vain? 4100+3807.1
115: 2 **W** should the heathen say, 4100+3807.1
Pr 17:16 **W** *is there* a price in 2088+4100+3807.1
Ecc 3:22 **W** I perceive that *there is* nothing 2050.1
4: 2 **W** I praised the dead which are already 2050.1
5: 6 it *was* an error: **w** should God 4100+3807.1
Isa 1: 4, when I looked that *it* should bring 4069
10:12 **W** it shall come to pass, *that* when 2050.1
16:11 my bowels shall sound like a 3651+5921
24:15 **W** glorify ye the Lord in the fires, 3651+5921
28:14 **W** hear the word of the Lord, 3651+3807.1
29:13 the Lord said, Forasmuch as this 2050.1
30:12 **W** thus saith the Holy One of 3651+3807.1
37: 4 **w** lift up *thy* prayer for the remnant that 2050.1
50: 2 **W**, when I came, *was there* no man? 4069
55: 2 **W** do ye spend money for *that* 4100+3807.1
58: 3 **W** have we fasted, *say they*, and 4100+3807.1
58: 3 **w** have we afflicted our soul, NIH
63: 2 **W** *art thou* red in thine apparel, 4069
Jer 2: 9 **W** I will yet plead with you, 3651+3807.1
2:29 **W** will ye plead with me? ye all 4100+3807.1
2:31 **w** say my people, We are lords; we will 4069
5: 6 a lion out of the forest shall slay 3651+5921
5:14 **W** thus saith the Lord God of 3651+3807.1
5:19 **W** doth the Lord our God all 4100+8478
12: 1 **W** doth the way of the wicked prosper? 4069
12: 1 **w** are all they happy that deal very NIH
13:22 heart, **W** come these *things* upon me? 4100+5921
16:10 they shall say unto thee, **W** hath 4100+5921
20:18 **W** came I forth out of 2088+4100+3807.1
22: 8 say every man to his neighbour, **W** 4100+5921
22:28 **w** are they cast out, he and his seed, 4069
23:12 **W** their way shall be unto them 3651+3807.1
27:17 **w** should this city be laid waste? 4100+3807.1
30: 6 **w** do I see every man *with* his hands on 4069
32: 3 saying, **W** dost thou prophesy, and say, 4069
37:15 **W** the princes were wroth with 2050.1
40:15 man shall know *it:* **w** should he 4100+3807.1
44: 6 **W** my fury and mine anger was poured 2050.1
44: 7 The God of Israel; **W** commit ye 4100+3807.1
46: 5 **W** have I seen them dismayed and 4069
49: 4 **W** gloriest thou in the valleys, thy flowing 4100
51:52 **W** behold, the days come, saith 3651+3807.1
La 3:39 **W** doth a living man complain, a man for 4100
5:20 **W** dost thou forget us for ever, 4100+3807.1
Eze 5:11 **W**, *as* I live, saith the Lord God; 3651+3807.1
7:24 **W** I will bring the worst of the heathen, 2050.1
13:20 **W** thus saith the Lord God; 3651+3807.1
16:35 **W**, O harlot, hear the word of 3651+3807.1
18:32 **w** turn *yourselves*, and live ye. 2050.1
20:10 **W** I caused them to go forth out of 2050.1
20:25 **W** I gave them also statutes *that were* 2050.1
20:30 **W** say unto the house of Israel, 3651+3807.1
21: 7 they say unto thee, **W** sighest thou? 4100+5921

Eze 23: 9 W I have delivered her into 3651+3807.1
24: 6 W thus saith the Lord God; 3651+3807.1
33:25 W say unto them, Thus saith 3651+3807.1
36:18 W I poured my fury upon them for 2050.1
43: 8 w I have consumed them in mine anger 2050.1
Da 3: 8 W at that time certain 1836+3606+6903
4:27 W, O king, let my counsel be acceptable 3861
6: 9 W king Darius signed 1836+3606+6903
8:26 w shut thou up the vision; for *it shall* 2050.1
10:20 thou w I come unto thee? 4100+3807.1
Joel 2:17 w should they say among 4100+3807.1
Jnh 1:14 W they cried unto the Lord, and said, 2050.1
Hab 1:13 w lookest thou upon them that 4100+3807.1
Mal 2:14 Yet ye say, W? Because the Lord 4100+5921
2:15 w one? That he might seek a godly seed. 4100
Mt 6:30 W, if God so clothe the grass of the field, 1161
7:20 W by their fruits ye shall know 686+1065
9: 4 W think ye evil in your hearts? 2444
12:12 W it is lawful to do well on the sabbath 5620
12:31 W I say unto you, All *manner of* sin 1223+3778
13:41 of little faith, w didst thou doubt? 1519+5101
18: 8 W if thy hand or thy foot offend thee, 1161
19: 6 W they are no more twain, but one flesh. 5620
23:31 W ye be witnesses unto yourselves, that 5620
23:34 W behold, I send unto you 1223+3778
24:26 W if they shall say unto you, Behold, he 3767
26:50 unto him, Friend, w art thou come? 1909+3739
27: 8 W that field was called, The field of blood, 1352
Lk 7: 7 W neither thought I myself worthy to 1352
7:47 W I say unto thee, Her sins, 3739+5484
19:23 W then gavest not thou my money into 1302
Jn 9:27 w would you hear *it* again? will ye also 5101
Ac 1:21 W of these men which have companied 3767
6: 3 W, brethren, look ye out among you 3767
10:21 what *is* the cause w ye are come? 1223+3739
13:35 W he saith also in another *psalm,* Thou 1352
15:19 W my sentence is, that *we* trouble not 1352
19:32 more part knew not w they were 1752+5101
19:38 W if Demetrius, and the craftsmen which 3767
20:26 W I take you to record this day, that I *am* 1352
22:24 he might know w they cried 156+1223+3739
22:30 he would have known the certainty w he 5101
23:28 the cause w they accused him, 1223+3739
24:26 w he sent for him the oftener, 1352+2532
25:26 W I have brought him forth before you, 1352
26: 3 w I beseech thee to hear me patiently. 1352
27:25 W, sirs, be of good cheer: for I believe 1352
27:34 W I pray you to take *some* meat: for this 1352
Ro 1:24 W God also gave them up to uncleanness 1352
5:12 W, as by one man sin entered into 1223+3778
7: 4 W, my brethren, ye also are become dead 5620
7:12 W the law *is* holy, and the commandment 5620
9:32 W? Because they *sought it* not by faith, 1302
13: 5 W *ye* must needs be subject, not only for 1352
15: 7 W receive ye one another, as Christ also 1352
1Co 4:16 W I beseech you, be ye followers of me. 3767
8:13 W, if meat make my brother to offend, 1355
10:12 W let him that thinketh he standeth take 5620
10:14 W, my dearly beloved, flee from idolatry. 1355
11:27 W whosoever shall eat this bread, 5620
11:33 W, my brethren, when ye come together 5620
12: 3 W I give you to understand, that no *man* 1352
14:13 W let him that speaketh in an *unknown* 1355
14:22 W tongues are for a sign, not to them that 5620
14:39 W, brethren, covet to prophesy, 5620
2Co 2: 8 W I beseech you that *you* would confirm 1352
5: 9 W we labour, that, whether present or 1352
5:16 W henceforth know we no *man* after 5620
6:17 W come out from among them, and be ye 1352
7:12 W, though I wrote unto you, *I did it* not, 686
8:24 W shew ye to them, and before 3767
11:11 W? because I love you not? God knoweth. 1302
Gal 3:19 W then *serveth* the law? It was added 5101
3:24 W the law was our schoolmaster *to bring* 5620
4: 7 W thou art no more a servant, but a son; 5620
Eph 1:15 W I also, after I heard of your faith 1223+3778
2:11 W remember, that ye *being* in time passed 1352
3:13 W I desire that *ye* faint not at my 1352
4: 8 W *he* saith, When he ascended up on 1352
4:25 W putting away lying, speak every man 5620
5:14 W *he* saith, Awake thou that sleepest, 1352
5:17 W be ye not unwise, 1223+3778
6:13 W take unto *you* the whole armour 1223+3778
Php 2: 9 W God also hath highly exalted him, 1352
2:12 W, my beloved, as ye have always obeyed, 5620
Col 2:20 W if ye be dead with Christ from 3767
1Th 2:18 W we would have come unto you, even I 1352
3: 1 W when we could no longer forbear, 1352
4:18 W comfort one another with these words. 5620
5:11 W comfort yourselves together, 1352
2Th 1:11 W also we pray always for you, 1519+3739
2Ti 1: 6 W I put thee in remembrance 156+1223+3739
Tit 1:13 W rebuke them sharply, 156+1223+3739
Phm 1: 8 W, though I might be much bold in Christ 1352
Heb 2:17 W in all *things* it behoved him to be made 3606
3: 1 W, holy brethren, partakers of the 3606
3: 7 W, as the Holy Ghost saith, To day if ye 1352
3:10 W I was grieved with that generation, 1352
7:25 W he is able also to save them to 3606
8: 3 w *it is* of necessity that this *man* have 3606
10: 5 W when he cometh into the world, 1352
11:16 W God is not ashamed to be called their 1352
12: 1 W **seeing** we also are compassed about 5105
12:12 W lift up the hands which hang down, 1352
12:28 W we receiving a kingdom which cannot 1352

Heb 13:12 W Jesus also, that he might sanctify 1352
Jas 1:19 W, my beloved brethren, let every man be 5620
1:21 W lay apart all filthiness and superfluity of 1352
4: 6 W *he* saith, God resisteth the proud, 1352
1Pe 1:13 W gird up the loins of your mind, be 1352
2: 1 W laying aside all malice, and all guile, 3767
2: 6 W also it is contained in the scripture, 1352
4:19 W let them that suffer according to 2532+5620
2Pe 1:10 W the rather, brethren, give diligence to 1352
1:12 W I will not be negligent to put you 1352
3:14 W, beloved, **seeing that** ye look for such 1352
1Jn 3:12 And w slew he him? Because his 5101+5484
3Jn 1:10 W, if I come, I will remember his 1223+3778
Rev 17: 7 W angel said unto me, Wherefore 1302

WHEREIN (167) [IN]
Ge 1:30 w *there is* life, I have given every 834+871.1
6:17 destroy all flesh, w *is* the breath of 834+871.1
7:15 of all flesh, w *is* the breath of life. 834+871.1
17: 8 after thee, the land w thou art a stranger, NIH
21:23 w thou hast sojourned. 834+871.1+1886.3
28: 4 that thou mayest inherit the land w thou NIH
36: 7 the land w they were strangers could not NIH
37: 1 Jacob dwelt in the land w his father was a NIH
Ex 1:14 all their service, w they made them 834+871.1
6: 4 w they were strangers. 834+871.1+1886.3
12: 7 of the houses, w they shall eat it. 834+871.1
18:11 for in the thing w they dealt proudly 834
18:20 shew them the way w they must walk, NIH
22:27 w shall he sleep? and it 4100+871.1+1886.1
33:16 For w shall it be known here that 4100+871.1
Lev 4:23 Or if his sin, w he hath 834+871.1+1886.3
5:18 him concerning his ignorance w he erred 834
6:28 earthen vessel w it is sodden shall 834+871.1
11:32 whatsoever vessel *it be,* w any 871.1+1992.1
11:36 fountain or pit, w *there is* plenty of water, NIH
13:46 All the days w the plague *shall be* in him 834
13:52 of skin, w the plague *is:* 834+871.1+2050.2
13:54 *the thing* w the plague *is,* 834+871.1+2050.2
13:57 that w the plague *is* with fire. 834+871.1
18: 3 w ye dwelt, shall ye not do 834+871.1+1886.3
Nu 12:11 we have done foolishly, and wherein 834
12:11 done foolishly, and w we have sinned. 834
19: 2 w *is* no blemish, 834+871.1+1886.3
31:10 they burnt all their cities w they dwelt, 871.1
33:55 you in the land w ye dwell. 834+871.1+1886.3
35:33 ye shall not pollute the land w ye 834+871.1
35:34 ye shall inhabit, w I dwell: 834+8432+871.1
Dt 8: 9 land w thou shalt eat bread without 834+871.1
8:15 w *were* fiery serpents, and scorpions, NIH
12: 2 w the nations which ye shall possess 834+8033
12: 7 w the Lord thy God hath blessed thee. 834
17: 1 w is blemish, *or* any evil 834+871.1
28:52 w thou trustedst, throughout all thy 834+871.1
Jos 8:24 in the wilderness w they 834+871.1+2050.2
10:27 cast them into the cave w they had 834+8033
22:19 w the Lord's tabernacle dwelleth, 834+8033
22:33 destroy the land w the children of Reuben 834
24:17 in all the way w 834+871.1+1886.3
Jdg 16: 5 see w his great strength *lieth,* and 4100+871.1
16: 6 w thy great strength *lieth,* and 4100+871.1
16:15 told me w thy great strength *lieth.* 4100+871.1
18: 6 Lord *is* your way w ye go. 834+871.1+1886.3
1Sa 6:15 w the jewels of gold *were,* 834+871.1+2050.2
14:38 see w this sin *hath* been *this* day. 4100+871.1
2Sa 7: 7 In all *the places* w I have walked with all 834
1Ki 2:26 thou hast been afflicted in all w my father 834
8:21 w *is* the covenant of the Lord, 834+8033
8:36 thou teach them the good way w 834+871.1
8:50 all their transgressions w they have 834
13:31 bury me in the sepulchre w the man 834+871.1
2Ki 12: 2 days w the priest instructed him. 834
14: 6 w the Lord commanded, saying, 834
17:29 nation in their cities w they dwelt. 834+8033
18:19 What confidence *is this* w thou trustest? 834
23:23 w this passover was holden to the Lord NIH
2Ch 3: 3 Now these *are the things* w Solomon NIH
6:11 w *is* the covenant of the Lord, 834+8033
6:27 w they should walk; 834+871.1+1886.3
8: 1 w Solomon had built the house of 834
33:19 the places w he built high 834+871.1+1992.1
Ezr 5: 7 unto him, w *was* written thus: 1459+871.2
Ne 6: 6 w *was* written, It is reported 871.1+1886.3
9:12 the way w they should go. 834+871.1+1886.3
9:19 the way w they should go. 834+871.1+1886.3
13:15 I testified *against them* in the day w 3963.1
Est 5:11 all *the things* w the king had promoted 834
8:11 W the king granted the Jews which *were* 834
9:22 As the days w the Jews rested from their 834
Job 3: 3 Let the day perish w I was born, 871.1+2050.2
6:16 of the ice, *and* w the snow is hid: 5921+4123.1
6:24 cause me to understand w I have erred. 4100
38:26 wilderness, w *there is* no man; 871.1+2050.2
Ps 74: 2 mount Zion, w thou hast dwelt. 871.1+2050.2
90:15 Make us glad according to the days w thou NIH
90:15 *and* the years w we have seen evil. NIH
104:20 w all the beasts of the forest do 871.1+2050.2
104:25 w *are* things creeping innumerable, 8033
142: 3 In the way w I walked have they privily 2098
143: 8 me to know the way w I should walk; 2098
Ecc 2:19 over all my labour w I have laboured, 7945
2:19 I have shewed myself wise under 7945
2:22 w he *hath* laboured under the sun? 7945
3: 9 What profit *hath* he that worketh in *that* w 834
8: 9 *there* is a time w one man ruleth over 834

Isa 2:22 for w is he *to be* accounted of? 4100+871.1
14: 3 from the hard bondage w thou wast made 834
33:21 w shall go no galley with oars, 871.1+2050.2
36: 4 What confidence *is this* w thou trustest? 834
47:12 w thou hast laboured from thy 834+871.1
65:12 and did choose *that* w I delighted not. 871.1
Jer 5:17 w thou trustedst, with 834+2007+871.1
7:14 w ye trust, and unto the place 834+871.1
12: 5 w thou trustedst, *they wearied thee,* then NIH
16:19 and *things* w *there is* no profit. 871.1+3963.1
20:14 Cursed *be* the day w I was born: 834+871.1
20:14 let not the day w my mother bare me be 834
22:28 *is he* a vessel w *is* no pleasure? 871.1+2050.2
31: 9 w they shall not stumble: 871.1+1886.3
36:14 in thine hand the roll w 834+871.1+1886.3
41: 9 Now the pit w Ishmael had cast all 834+8033
42: 3 the way w we may walk, 834+871.1+1886.3
48:38 like a vessel w *is* no pleasure, 871.1+2050.2
51:43 a land w no man dwelleth. 871.1+2006.1
Eze 20:34 w ye are scattered, 834+871.1+3963.1
20:41 w ye have been scattered; 834+871.1+3963.1
20:43 w ye have been defiled; 834+871.1+3963.1
23:19 w she had played the harlot in the land of 834
26:10 men enter into a city w is made a breach. NIH
32: 6 will also water with thy blood the land w NIH
37:23 w they have sinned, 834+871.1+1992.1
37:25 w your fathers have dwelt; 834+871.1+1886.3
42:14 garments w they minister; 834+871.1+2006.1
44:19 w they ministered, 834+871.1+3963.1
Hos 2:13 w she burnt incense to them, 834
8: 8 as a vessel w *is* no pleasure. 871.1+2050.2
Jnh 4:11 w are more than sixscore 871.1+1886.3
Mic 6: 3 w have I wearied thee? testify against me. 4100
Zep 3:11 w thou hast transgressed against me: 834
Zec 9:11 out of the pit w *is* no water. 871.1+2050.2
Mal 1: 2 Yet ye say, W hast thou loved us? 4100+871.1
1: 6 W have we despised thy name? 4100+871.1
1: 7 ye say, W have we polluted thee? 4100+871.1
2:17 W have we wearied *him?* When 4100+871.1
3: 7 But ye said, W shall we return? 4100+871.1
3: 8 ye say, W have we robbed thee? 4100+871.1
Mt 11:20 began he to upbraid the cities w 1722+3739
25:13 hour w the Son of man cometh. 1722+3739
Mk 2: 4 they let down the bed w the sick of 1909+3739
Lk 1: 4 w thou hast been instructed. 3739+4012
1:25 he looked on *me,* to take away my 3739
11:22 taketh *from him* all his armour 1909+3739
23:53 in stone, w never man before was laid. 3757
Jn 19:41 w was never man yet laid. 1722+3739
Ac 2: 8 our own tongue, w we were born? 1722+3739
7: 4 into this land, w ye now dwell. 1519+3739
10:12 W were all *manner of* fourfooted 1722+3739
Ro 2: 1 for w thou judgest another, 1722+3739
5: 2 by faith into this grace w we stand, 1722+3739
7: 6 *that* being dead w we were held; 1722+3739
1Co 7:20 calling w he was called. 1722+3739+3778
7:24 Brethren, let every man, w he is 1722+3739
15: 1 you have received, and w ye stand; 1722+3739
2Co 11:12 w they glory, they may be found 1722+3739
12:13 For what is it w ye were inferior to other 3739
Eph 1: 6 w he hath made us accepted in 1722+3739
1: 8 W he hath abounded toward us in all 3739
2: 2 In time past ye walked according 1722+3739
5:18 And be not drunk with wine, w is 1722+3739
Php 4:10 w ye were also careful, but ye 1909+3739
Col 2:12 w also you are risen with *him* 1722+3739
2Ti 2: 9 W I suffer trouble, as an evil doer, 1722+3739
Heb 6:17 W God, willing more abundantly to 1722+3739
9: 2 *was* the candlestick, and the table, 1722
9: 4 *was* the golden pot that had 1722+3739
1Pe 1: 6 W ye greatly rejoice, though now 1722+3739
3:20 ark was a preparing, w few, that is, 1519+3739
4: 4 W they think it strange that you run 1722+3739
5:12 is the true grace of God w ye stand. 1519+3739
2Pe 3:12 w the heavens being on fire shall be 1223+3739
3:13 earth, w dwelleth righteousness. 1722+3739
Rev 2:13 even in *those* days w Antipas *was* 1722+3739
18:19 w were made rich all that had ships 1722+3739

WHEREINSOEVER (1) [EVER, IN, SO]
2Co 11:21 Howbeit w any is 302+1161+1722+3739

WHEREINTO (4) [INTO]
Lev 11:33 vessel, w *any* of them falleth, 413+8432
Nu 14:24 into the land w he went; 834+8033+1886.5
36: 3 be put to the inheritance of the tribe w 834
Jn 6:22 save that one w his disciples were 1519+3739

WHEREOF (71) [OF]
Ge 3:11 w I commanded thee that thou shouldest 834
Lev 6:30 w *any* of the blood is brought into 834
13:24 in the skin w *there is* a hot burning, 2050.2
27: 9 *men* bring an offering unto the Lord, 834
Nu 5: 3 camps, in the midst w I dwell. 834+3963.1
7:19 the weight w *was* an hundred and 1886.3
7:25 the weight w *was* an hundred and 1886.3
7:37 the weight w *was* an hundred and 1886.3
7:49 the weight w *was* an hundred and 1886.3
7:61 the weight w *was* an hundred and 1886.3
7:67 the weight w *was* an hundred and 1886.3
7:73 the weight w *was* an hundred and 1886.3
7:79 the weight w *was* an hundred and 1886.3
21:16 that *is* the well w the Lord spake unto 834
Dt 13: 2 come to pass, w he spake unto thee, 834
28:27 with the itch, w thou canst not be healed. 834

Dt 28:68 the way **w** I spake unto thee, Thou shalt 834
Jos 14:12 **w** the LORD spake in that day; 834
 20: 2 **w** I spake unto you by the hand of Moses: 834
 22: 9 of their possession, **w** they were possessed, 834
1Sa 10:16 **w** Samuel spake, he told him not. 834
 13: 2 **w** two thousand were with Saul in NIH
2Sa 12:30 the weight **w** *was* a talent of gold with 1886.3
2Ki 13:14 of his sickness **w** he died. 834+871.1+2050.2
 17:12 the LORD had said unto them, 834
2Ch 3: 8 length **w** *was* according to the breadth 2050.2
 6:20 upon the place **w** thou hast said that *thou* 834
 24:14 were made vessels for the house of 1930.2
 33: 4 **w** the LORD had said, In Jerusalem shall 834
Ne 12:31 **w** *one* went on the right hand upon the 834
Job 6: 4 the poison **w** drinketh up my spirit: 3963.1
Ps 46: 4 the streams **w** shall make glad the city 2050.2
 57: 6 into the midst **w** they are fallen 1886.3
 126: 3 done great things for us; **w** we are glad. NIH
Ecc 1:10 Is there *any* thing **w** it may be said, See, 7945
SS 4: 2 every one beareth twins, and none *is* 7945
 6: 6 every one beareth twins, and *there is* 7945
Jer 32:36 of Israel, concerning this city, **w** ye say, 834
 32:43 **w** ye say, It *is* desolate without man or 834
 42:16 the famine, **w** ye were afraid, 834+4480
Eze 32:15 the country shall be destitute of that **w** it 4480
 39: 8 Lord GOD; this *is* the day **w** I have spoken. 834
Da 9: 2 **w** the word of the LORD came to 834
Hos 2:12 vines and her fig trees, **w** she hath said, 834
Lk 23:14 *touching those things* **w** ye accuse him: 3739
Ac 2:32 God raised up, **w** we all are witnesses. 3739
 3:15 raised from the dead; **w** we are witnesses. 3739
 17:19 this new doctrine, **w** thou speakest, 5259
 17:31 **w** he hath given assurance unto all *men*, NIG
 21:24 all may know that *those things*, **w** they 3739
 24: 8 of all these *things*, **w** we accuse him. 3739
 24:13 can they prove *the things* **w** 3739+4012
 25:11 if there be none *of these things* **w** these 3739
 26: 2 all *the things* **w** I am accused of the Jews: 3739
Ro 4: 2 justified by works, he hath **w** to glory; NIG
 6:21 *in those things* **w** ye are now ashamed? 3739
 15:17 **w** *I* may glory through Jesus Christ *in* NIG
1Co 7: 1 concerning *the things* **w** ye wrote unto 3739
2Co 9: 5 **w** ye had notice before, that the same NIG
Eph 3: 7 **W** I was made a minister, according to 3739
Php 3: 4 If any other *man* thinketh that *he hath* **w** NIG
Col 1: 5 **w** ye heard before in the word of the truth 3739
 1:23 **w** I Paul am made a minister; 3739
 1:25 **W** I am made a minister, according to 3739
1Ti 1: 7 what they say, nor **w** they affirm. 4012+5101
 6: 4 **w** cometh envy, strife, railings, 1537
Heb 2: 5 the world to come, **w** we speak: 3739+4012
 10:15 **W** the Holy Ghost also is a witness to us: NIG
 12: 8 **w** all are partakers, then are ye bastards, 3739
 13:10 **w** they have no right to eat which 1537+3739
1Jn 4: 3 **w** you have heard that it should come; 3739

WHEREON (27) [ON]

Ge 28:13 the land **w** thou liest, to thee will I give it, 834
Ex 3: 5 the place **w** thou standest *is* holy ground. 834
 8:21 also the ground **w** they *are*. 834+5921+1886.3
Lev 6:27 thou shalt wash that **w** it was 834+5921
 15: 4 **w** he lieth that hath the issue, 834+5921
 15: 4 every thing, **w** he sitteth, shall be 834+5921
 15: 6 he that sitteth on *any* thing **w** he sat 834+5921
 15:17 **w** is the seed of copulation, 834+5921
 15:23 on *any* thing **w** she sitteth, when he 834+5921
 15:24 the bed **w** he lieth shall be unclean. 834+5921
 15:26 Every bed **w** she lieth all the days of 834+5921
Dt 11:24 Every place **w** the soles of your feet 834+871.1
Jos 5:15 for the place **w** thou standest *is* holy. 834+5921
 14: 9 Surely the land **w** thy feet have trodden 834
1Sa 6:18 **w** they set down the ark of 834+5921+1886.3
2Ch 4:19 tables **w** the shewbread *was set*; 5921+1992.1
 32:10 **W** do ye trust, that ye abide in 4100+5921
Est 7: 8 **w** Esther *was*. Then said 834+5921+1886.3
Job 24:23 given him *to be* in safety, **w** he resteth; 2050.1
SS 4: 4 **w** there hang a thousand bucklers 5921+2050.2
Isa 36: 6 **w** if a man lean, it will go into his 834+5921
Eze 37:20 the sticks **w** thou writest 834+5921+1992.1
Mk 11: 2 find a colt tied, **w** never man sat: 1909+3739
Lk 4:29 led him unto the brow of the hill **w** 1909+3739
 5:25 and took up *that* **w** he lay, 1909+3739
 19:30 find a colt tied, **w** yet never man sat: 1909+3739
Jn 4:38 I sent you to reap *that* **w** ye bestowed no 3739

WHERESOEVER (12) [EVER, SO]

Lev 13:12 from his head even to his foot, **w** 3605+3807.1
2Ki 8: 1 and sojourn **w** thou canst sojourn: 834+871.1
 12: 5 **w any** breach shall be found. 834+3605+8033
1Ch 17: 6 **W** I have walked with all 834+3605+871.1
Jer 40: 5 **w** it seemeth convenient unto thee 413+3605
Da 2:38 w the children of men dwell 1768+4480+871.2
Mt 24:28 For **w** the carcase is, there will 1437+3699
 26:13 **W** this gospel shall be preached in 1437+3699
Mk 9:18 he taketh him, he teareth him: 302+3699
 14: 9 **W** this gospel shall be preached 302+3699
 14:14 And **w** he shall go in, say ye to 1437+3699
Lk 17:37 **W** the body *is*, thither will the eagles be 3699

WHERETO (3) [TO]

Job 30: 2 Yea, **w** *might* the strength of their 4100+3807.1
Isa 55:11 it shall prosper *in the thing* **w** I sent it. 834
Php 3:16 Nevertheless, **w** we have *already* 1519+3739

WHEREUNTO (26) [UNTO]

Nu 36: 4 inheritance of the tribe **w** they are 834
Dt 4:26 **w** you go over Jordan to 834+8033+1886.5
2Ch 8:11 the ark of the LORD hath come. 413+834
Est 10: 2 of Mordecai, **w** the king advanced him, 834
Ps 7: 1 **w** *I* may continually resort: NIH
Jer 22:27 to the land **w** they desire to return, 834+8033
Eze 5: 9 **w** I will not do any more the like, because 834
 20:29 What *is* the high place **w** ye go? 834+8033
Mt 11:16 But **w** shall I liken this generation? 5101
Mk 4:30 **W** shall we liken the kingdom of God? 5101
Lk 7:31 **W** then shall I liken the men of this 5101
 13:18 of God like? and **w** shall I resemble it? 5101
 13:20 **W** shall I liken the kingdom of God? 5101
Ac 5:24 doubted of them **w** this would grow. 302+5101
 13: 2 Saul for the work **w** I have called them. 3739
 27: 8 fair havens; nigh **w** was the city *of* Lasea. 3739
Gal 4: 9 ye desire again to be in bondage? 3739+3825
Col 1:29 **W** I also labour, striving according 1519+3739
2Th 2:14 **W** he called you by our gospel, 1519+3739
1Ti 2: 7 **W** I am ordained a preacher, 1519+3739
 4: 6 of good doctrine, **w** thou hast attained. 3739
 6:12 **w** thou art also called, 1519+3739
2Ti 1:11 **W** I am appointed a preacher, 1519+3739
1Pe 2: 8 also they were appointed. 1519+3739
 3:21 The like figure **w** *even* baptism doth also 3739
2Pe 1:19 ye do well that ye take heed, as unto a 3739

WHEREUPON (17) [UPON]

Lev 11:35 every *thing* **w** *any part* of their carcase 834
Jdg 16:26 Suffer me that I may feel the pillars **w** 834
1Ki 7:48 table *of* gold, **w** the shewbread *was*, 834+5921
 12:28 **W** the king took counsel, and made two 2050.1
2Ch 12: 6 the princes of Israel and the king 2050.1
Job 38: 6 **w** are the foundations thereof 4100+5921
Eze 9: 3 **w** he was, to the threshold of 834+5921
 23:41 **w** thou hast set mine incense and 5921+1886.3
 24:25 that **w** they set their minds, their sons and NIH
 40:41 **w** they slew *their sacrifices*. 413+1992.1
 40:42 also they laid the instruments 413+1992.1
Am 4: 7 and the piece **w** it rained not withered. 834
Mt 14: 7 **W** he promised with an oath to give her 3606
Ac 24:18 **w** certain Jews from Asia found me 1722+3739
 26:12 as I went to Damascus with 1722+3739
 26:19 **W**, O king Agrippa, I was not disobedient 3606
Heb 9:18 **W** neither the first *testament* was 3606

WHEREWITH (110) [WITH]

Ge 27:41 of the blessing **w** his father blessed him: 834
Ex 3: 9 I have also seen the oppression **w** 834
 4:17 **w** thou shalt do signs. 834+871.1+2050.2
 16:32 they may see the bread **w** I have fed you 834
 17: 5 thy rod, **w** thou smotest 834+871.1+2050.2
 29:33 shall eat those *things* **w** 834+871.1+1992.1
Nu 3:31 the vessels of the sanctuary **w** they 834+871.1
 3:48 **w** the odd number of them is *to be* NIH
 4: 9 **w** they minister unto it: 834+871.1
 4:12 **w** they minister in the sanctuary, 834+871.1
 4:14 **w** they minister about it, even 834+871.1
 16:39 **w** they that were burnt had offered; 834
 25:18 **w** they have beguiled you in the matter of 834
 30: 4 her bond **w** she hath bound her soul, 834+5921
 30: 4 bond **w** she hath bound her soul 834+5921
 30: 5 of her bonds **w** she hath bound her 834+5921
 30: 6 of her lips, **w** she bound her soul; 834+5921
 30: 7 the bond **w** she bound her soul shall stand. 834+5921
 30: 8 **w** she bound her soul, of none effect: 834+5921
 30: 9 **w** they have bound their souls, 834+5921
 30:11 bond **w** she bound her soul shall 834+5921
 35:17 **w** he may die, and he die, he *is* a 834+871.1
 35:18 **w** he may die, and he die, he *is* a 834+871.1
 35:23 *a man* may die, seeing *him* not, 834+871.1
Dt 9:19 **w** the LORD was wroth against you to 834
 15:14 *of that* **w** the LORD thy God hath 834
 22:12 vesture, **w** thou coverest *thyself*. 834+871.1
 28:53 **w** thine enemies shall distress thee: 834
 28:55 **w** thine enemies shall distress thee in all 834
 28:57 **w** thine enemy shall distress thee in thy 834
 28:67 for the fear of thine heart **w** thou shalt 834
 33: 1 **w** Moses the man of God blessed 834
Jos 8:26 he stretched out the spear, 834+871.1
Jdg 6:15 O my Lord, **w** shall I save Israel? 4100+871.1
 9: 4 Abimelech hired vain 871.1+1992.1+2050.1
 9: 9 **w** by me they honour God and man, 871.1
 9:38 thou saidst, Who *is* Abimelech, 834
 16: 6 **w** thou mightest be bound 4100
 16:10 **w** thou mightest be bound. 4100+871.1
 16:13 tell me **w** thou mightest be bound. 4100+871.1
1Sa 6: 2 us **w** we shall send it to his place. 4100
 8: 8 they have forsaken me, 2050.1
 29: 4 for **w** should he reconcile himself 4100+871.1
2Sa 13:15 the hatred **w** he hated her *was* greater 834
 13:15 greater than the love **w** he had loved her. 834
 21: 3 **w** shall I make the atonement, 4100+871.1
1Ki 8:59 **w** I have made supplication before 834
 15:22 timber thereof, **w** Baasha had builded: 834
 15:26 and in his sin **w** he made Israel to sin. 834
 15:30 by his provocation **w** he provoked 834
 15:34 and in his sin **w** he made Israel to sin. 834
 16:26 and in his sin **w** he made Israel to sin, 834
 21:22 the provocation **w** thou hast provoked *me* 834
 22:22 the LORD said unto him, **W**? 4100+871.1
2Ki 13:12 his might **w** he fought against Amaziah 834
 21:16 beside his sin **w** he made Judah to sin, 834
 23:26 his anger was kindled against Judah, 834

2Ki 25:14 vessels of brass **w** they ministered, 834+871.1
1Ch 18: 8 **w** Solomon made the brasen sea, 871.1+1886.3
2Ch 2:17 after the numbering **w** David his father 834
 16: 6 Baasha was a building; 834
 18:20 And the LORD said unto him, **W**? 4100+871.1
 35:21 day, but against the house **w** I have war: NIH
Ne 9:34 **w** thou didst testify against them. 834
Job 15: 3 speeches **w** he can do no good? 871.1+3963.1
Ps 79:12 **w** they have reproached thee, O Lord. 834
 89:51 **W** thine enemies have reproached, 834
 89:51 **w** they have reproached the footsteps of 834
 93: 1 with strength, **w** he hath girded himself; NIH
 109:19 a girdle **w** he is girded continually. 1886.3
 119:42 So shall I have to answer him that 1697
 129: 7 **W** the mower filleth not his hand; 7945
SS 3:11 king Solomon with the crown **w** 7945
Isa 28:12 This *is* the rest **w** ye may cause the weary NIH
 37: 6 **w** the servants of the king of Assyria 834
Jer 18:10 of the good, **w** I said *I* would benefit them. 834
 19: 9 **w** their enemies, and they that seek their 834
 21: 4 **w** ye fight against the king of 834+871.1
 33:16 this *is the name* **w** she shall be called, 834
 52:18 of brass **w** they ministered, 834+871.1+1992.1
La 1:12 **w** the LORD hath afflicted *me* in the day of 834
Eze 13:12 Where *is* the daubing **w** ye have daubed 834
 13:20 **w** ye there hunt the souls to make *them* 834
 16:19 fine flour, and oil, and honey, **w** I fed thee, NIH
 29:20 Egypt *for* his labour **w** he served against it, 834
 32:16 This *is* the lamentation **w** they shall 2050.1
 36:18 and for their idols **w** they had polluted it: NIH
 40:42 **w** they slew the burnt 834+871.1+3963.1
Da 2: 1 his spirit was troubled, and his sleep 2050.1
Mic 6: 6 **W** shall I come before the LORD, 4100+871.1
Zec 14:12 this shall be the plague **w** the LORD 834
 14:18 the LORD will smite the heathen 834
Mal 2: 5 I gave them to him *for* the fear **w** he 2050.1
Mt 5:13 lost his savour, **w** shall it be salted? 1722+5101
Mk 3:28 blasphemies **w soever** they shall 302+3745
 9:50 his saltness, **w** will you season it? 1722+5101
Lk 14:34 his savour, **w** shall it be seasoned? 1722+5101
 17: 8 Make ready **w** I may sup, and gird thyself, 5101
Jn 13: 5 to wipe *them* with the towel **w** he was 3739
 17:26 will declare *it*; that the love **w** thou 3739
Ro 14:19 and *things* **w** one may edify another. 1519
2Co 1: 4 by the comfort **w** we ourselves are 3739
 7: 7 by the consolation **w** he was comforted in 3739
 10: 2 **w** I think to be bold against some, 3739
Gal 5: 1 the liberty **w** Christ hath made us free, 3739
Eph 2: 4 in mercy, for his great love **w** he loved us, 3739
 4: 1 worthy of the vocation **w** ye are called, 3739
 6:16 **w** ye shall be able to quench all 1722+3739
1Th 3: 9 for all the joy **w** we joy for your sakes 3739
Heb 10:29 **w** he was sanctified, an unholy 1722+3739

WHEREWITHAL (2) [WITHAL]

Ps 119: 9 Shall a young man cleanse his 4100+871.1
Mt 6:31 shall we drink? or, **W** shall we be clothed? 5101

WHET (4)

Dt 32:41 If I **w** my glittering sword, and mine hand 8150
Ps 7:12 If he turn not, he will **w** his sword; 3913
 64: 3 Who **w** their tongue like a sword, 8150
Ecc 10:10 he do not **w** the edge, then must he put 7043

WHETHER (171)

Ge 18:21 see **w** they have done altogether 1886.2
 24:21 to wit **w** the LORD had made his 1886.2
 27:21 **w** thou *be* my very son Esau or not. 1886.2
 31:39 **w** stolen by day, or stolen by night. NIH
 37:14 see **w** it be well with thy brethren, NIH
 37:32 know now **w** it *be* thy son's coat **or** no. 518
 42:16 be proved, **w** *there be any* truth in you: 1886.2
 43: 6 to tell the man **w** ye had yet a brother? 1886.2
Ex 4:18 in Egypt, and see **w** they be yet alive. 1886.2
 12:19 **w** he be a stranger, or born in the land. 871.1
 16: 4 **w** they will walk in my law, or no. 1886.2
 19:13 **w** *it be* beast or man, it shall not live: 518
 21:31 **W** he have gored a son, or have gored a 176
 22: 4 hand alive, **w** it be ox, or ass, or sheep; 4480
 22: 8 *see* **w** he have put his hand unto his 518+3808
 22: 9 **w** it be for ox, for ass, for sheep, NIH
 34:19 thy cattle, **w** *ox* or sheep, *that is* male. NIH
Lev 3: 1 **w** *it be* a male or female, he shall offer it 518
 5: 1 **w** he hath seen or known *of it*; if he do not 176
 5: 2 **w** *it be* a carcase of an unclean beast, or a 176
 7:26 **w** *it be* of fowl or of beast, in any of your NIH
 11:32 **w** *it be* any vessel of wood, or raiment, 4480
 11:35 **w** *it be* oven, or ranges for pots, they shall NIH
 13:47 **w** *it be* a woollen garment, or a linen 176
 13:48 **W** *it be* in the warp, or woof; of linen, 176
 13:48 **w** in a skin, or in any thing made of skin; 176
 13:52 **w** warp or woof, in woollen or in linen, 176
 13:55 inward, **w** *it be* bare within or without. NIH
 15: 3 **w** his flesh run with his issue, or his flesh NIH
 16:29 do no work *at all*, **w** *it be* one of your own NIH
 17:15 which was torn *with beasts*, **w** *it be* one NIH
 18: 9 **w** *she* be born at home, or born abroad, NIH
 22:28 **w** *it be* cow or ewe, ye shall not kill it and NIH
 27:12 priest shall value it, **w** it be good or bad: 996
 27:14 priest shall estimate it, **w** it be good or bad: 996
 27:26 man shall sanctify it; **w** *it be* ox, or sheep: 518
 27:30 **w** of the seed of the land, *or* of the fruit of NIH
 27:33 He shall not search **w** it be good or bad, 996
Nu 9:21 *it was* by day or by night that the cloud 176
 9:22 Or **w** *it were* two days, or a month, NIH

Nu	11:23 shalt see now **w** my word shall come	1886.2
	13:18 **w** they be strong or weak, few or many;	1886.2
	13:19 that they dwell in, **w** it *be* good or bad;	1886.2
	13:19 dwell in, **w** in tents, or in strong holds;	1886.2
	13:20 what the land *is,* **w** it *be* fat or lean,	1886.2
	13:20 lean, **w** there be wood therein, or not.	1886.2
	15:30 **w** *he be* born in the land, or a stranger,	NIH
	18:15 **w** it *be* of men or beasts, shall be thine:	NIH
Dt	4:32 there hath been *any such thing* as	1886.2
	8: 2 **w** thou wouldest keep his	1886.2
	13: 3 to know **w** you love the LORD your	1886.2
	18: 3 that offer a sacrifice, **w** it *be* ox or sheep;	518
	22: 6 **w** they be young ones, or eggs, and the	NIH
	24:14 **w** *he be* of thy brethren, or of thy strangers	NIH
Jos	24:15 **w** the gods which your fathers served that	518
Jdg	2:22 **w** they will keep the way of the LORD	1886.2
	3: 4 to know **w** they would hearken unto	1886.2
	9: 2 **W** *is* better for you, either that all the sons	4100
	18: 5 that we may know **w** our way which we	1886.2
Ru	3:10 followedst not young men, **w** poor or rich.	518
2Sa	12:22 Who can tell **w** GOD will be gracious to	NIH
	15:21 in death or life, even there also will thy	518
1Ki	20:18 he said, **W** they be come out for peace,	518
	20:18 or **w** they be come out for war, take them	518
	20:33 Now the men did diligently observe **w**	1886.2
2Ki	1: 2 of Baal-zebub the god of Ekron **w** I	518
2Ch	14:11 **w** with many, *or* with *them that have* no	NIH
	15:13 small or great, whether man or	4480+3807.1
	15:13 or great, **w** man or woman.	4480+3807.1
Ezr	2:59 their seed, **w** they *were* of Israel:	518+4480
	5:17 **w** it be *so,* that a decree *was* made of	2006
	7:26 **w** it *be* unto death, or to banishment,	2006
Ne	7:61 nor their seed, **w** they *were* of Israel.	518
Est	3: 4 see **w** Mordecai's matters would stand:	1886.2
	4:11 know, that whosoever, **w** man or woman,	NIH
	4:14 who knoweth **w** thou art come to	518
Job	34:29 **w** *it be done* against a nation, or against	2050.1
	34:33 thou refuse, or whether thou choose;	3588
	34:33 whether thou refuse, or **w** thou choose;	3588
	37:13 **w** for correction, or for his land,	518
Pr	20:11 **w** his work *be* pure, and whether *it be*	518
	20:11 his work *be* pure, and **w** *it be* right.	518
	29: 9 **w** he rage or laugh, *there is* no rest.	2050.1
Ecc	2:19 knoweth **w** he shall be a wise *man*	1886.2
	5:12 *man* is sweet, **w** he eat little or much:	518
	11: 6 thou knowest not **w** shall prosper,	335+2088
	11: 6 or that, or **w** they both *shall be* alike good.	518
	12:14 with every secret *thing,* **w** it *be* good,	518
	12:14 *thing,* whether *it be* good, or **w** *it be* evil.	518
SS	6:11 *and* to see **w** the vine flourished,	1886.2
	7:12 **w** the tender grape appear,	NIH
Jer	30: 6 and see **w** a man doth travail with child?	518
	42: 6 **W** *it be* good, or whether *it be* evil, we will	518
	42: 6 Whether *it be* good, or **w** *it be* evil, we will	518
Eze	2: 5 they will hear, or whether they will	518
	2: 5 they will hear, or **w** they will forbear,	518
	2: 7 they will hear, or whether they will	518
	2: 7 they will hear, or **w** they will forbear:	518
	3:11 they will hear, or whether they will	518
	3:11 they will hear, or **w** they will forbear.	518
	44:31 of itself, or torn, **w** it *be* fowl or beast.	4480
Mt	9: 5 **w** is easier, to say, *Thy* sins be forgiven	5101
	21:31 **W** of *them* twain did the will of *his* father?	5101
	23:17 **w** is greater, the gold, or the temple that	5101
	23:19 **w** *is* greater, the gift, or the altar that	5101
	26:63 that thou tell us **w** thou be the Christ,	1487
	27:21 **W** of the twain will ye *that* I release unto	5101
	27:49 let us see **w** Elias will come to save him.	1487
Mk	2: 9 **W** is it easier to say to the sick of the	5101
	3: 2 **w** he would heal him on the sabbath day;	1487
	15:36 let us see **w** Elias will come to take him	1487
	15:44 he asked him **w** he had been any while	1487
Lk	3:15 of John, **w** he were the Christ, **or not;**	3379
	5:23 **W** is easier, to say, Thy sins be forgiven	5101
	6: 7 **w** he would heal on the sabbath day;	1487
	14:28 the cost, **w** he have sufficient to finish it?	1487
	14:31 **w** he be able with ten thousand	1487
	22:27 For **w** *is* greater, he that sitteth at meat,	5101
	23: 6 he asked **w** the man were a Galilean.	1487
Jn	7:17 **w** it be of God, or *whether* I speak of	4220
	7:17 it be of God, or **w** I speak of myself.	NIG
	9:25 said, **W** he be a sinner *or no,* I know not:	1487
Ac	1:24 **w** of these two thou hast chosen,	1520+3739
	4:19 **W** it be right in the sight of God to	1487
	5: 8 Tell me **w** ye sold the land for so much?	1487
	9: 2 of *this* way, **w** they were men or women,	5037
	10:18 called, and asked **w** Simon, which was	1487
	17:11 scriptures daily, **w** those *things* were so.	1487
	19: 2 as heard **w** there be *any* Holy Ghost.	1487
	25:20 I asked *him* **w** he would go to Jerusalem,	1487
Ro	6:16 **w** of sin unto death, or of obedience unto	2273
	12: 6 **w** prophecy, *let us prophesy* according to	1535
	14: 8 we live, we live unto the Lord;	1437+5037
	14: 8 **and w** we die, we die unto the	1437+5037
	14: 8 we live therefore, or die, we are	1437+5037
1Co	1:16 I know not **w** I baptized **any** other.	1536
	3:22 **W** Paul, or Apollos, or Cephas,	1535
	7:16 O wife, **w** thou shalt save *thy* husband?	1487
	7:16 O man, **w** thou shalt save *thy* wife?	1487
	8: 5 **w** in heaven or in earth, (as there be gods	1535
	12:13 **w** *we be* Jews or Gentiles, whether *we be*	1535
	12:13 Jews or Gentiles, **w** *we be* bond or free;	1535
	12:26 **w** one member suffer, all the members	1535
	13: 8 but **w** *there be* prophecies, they shall fail;	1535

1Co	13: 8 **w** *there be* tongues, they shall cease;	1535
	13: 8 **w** *there be* knowledge, it shall vanish	1535
	14: 7 without life giving sound, **w** pipe or harp,	1535
	15:11 **w** *it were* I or they, so we preach,	1535
2Co	1: 6 And we **w** be afflicted, *it is* for your	1535
	1: 6 **or w** we be comforted, *it is* for your	1535
	2: 9 of you, **w** ye be obedient in all *things.*	1487
	5: 9 we labour, that, **w** present or absent,	1535
	5:10 to that he hath done, **w** *it be* good or bad.	1535
	5:13 we be besides ourselves, *it is* to God:	1535
	5:13 **or w** we be sober, *it is* for your cause.	1535
	8:23 **W** *any do inquire* of Titus, *he is* my	1535
	12: 2 years ago, (**w** in the body, I cannot tell;	1535
	12: 2 or out of the body, I cannot tell:	1535
	12: 3 (**w** in the body, or out of the body,	1535
	13: 5 Examine yourselves, **w** ye be in the faith;	1487
Eph	6: 8 receive of the Lord, **w** *he be* bond or free.	1535
Php	1:18 every way, **w** in pretence, or in truth,	1535
	1:20 in my body, **w** *it be* by life, or by death.	1535
	1:27 that **w** I come and see you, or *else* be	1535
Col	1:16 **w** *they be* thrones, or dominions,	1535
	1:20 **w** *they be* things in earth, or *things* in	1535
1Th	5:10 died for us, that, **w** we wake or sleep,	1535
2Th	2:15 been taught, **w** by word, or by our epistle.	1535
1Pe	2:13 **w** *it be* to the king, as supreme;	1535
1Jn	4: 1 but try the spirits **w** they are of God:	1487

WHICH (4419)

Ge	1: 7 divided the waters **w** *were* under	834
	1: 7 the waters **w** *were* above the firmament:	834
	1:21 the waters brought forth abundantly,	834
	1:29 **w** *is* upon the face of all the earth,	834
	1:29 in the **w** *is* the fruit of a tree yielding seed;	834
	2: 2 the seventh day God ended his work **w** he	834
	2: 2 day from all his work **w** he had made.	834
	2: 3 that in it had rested from all his work **w**	834
	2:11 that *is it* **w** compasseth the whole land	1886.1
	2:14 that *is it* **w** goeth toward the east of	1886.1
	2:22 **w** the LORD God had taken from man,	834
	3: 1 of the field **w** the LORD God had made.	834
	3: 3 of the fruit of the tree **w** *is* in the midst of	834
	3:17 the tree, of **w** I commanded thee, saying,	834
	3:24 a flaming sword **w** turned every way,	1886.1
	4:11 **w** hath opened her mouth to receive thy	834
	5:29 of the ground **w** the LORD hath cursed.	834
	6: 2 they took them wives of all **w** they chose.	834
	6: 4 same *became* mighty *men* **w** *were* of old,	834
	6:15 this *is the fashion* **w** thou shalt make it *of:*	834
	7:23 living substance was destroyed **w** *was*	834
	8: 6 Noah opened the window of the ark **w**	834
	8: 7 forth a raven, **w** went forth to and fro,	2050.1
	8:12 **w** returned not again unto him any	2050.1
	9: 4 **w** *is* the blood thereof, shall you not eat.	NIH
	9:12 *is* the token of the covenant **w** I make	834
	9:15 **w** *is* between me and you and every living	834
	9:17 **w** I have established between me and all	834
	11: 5 the tower, **w** the children of men builded.	834
	11: 6 from them, **w** they have imagined to do.	834
	13: 4 the altar, **w** he had made there at the first:	834
	13: 5 went with Abram, had flocks,	1886.1
	13:15 For all the land **w** thou seest, to thee will I	834
	13:18 **w** *is* in Hebron, and built there an altar	834
	14: 2 and the king of Bela, **w** *is* Zoar.	1931
	14: 3 in the vale of Siddim, **w** *is* the salt sea.	1931
	14: 6 unto El-paran, **w** *is* by the wilderness.	834
	14: 7 **w** *is* Kadesh, and smote all the country of	1931
	14:15 **w** *is* on the left hand of Damascus.	834
	14:17 the valley of Shaveh, **w** *is* the king's dale.	1931
	14:20 **w** hath delivered thine enemies into thy	834
	14:24 only that **w** the young men have eaten,	834
	14:24 the portion of the men **w** went with me,	834
	16:15 his son's name, **w** Hagar bare, Ishmael.	834
	17:10 **w** ye shall keep, between me and you and	834
	17:12 of any stranger, **w** *is* not of thy seed.	834
	17:21 **w** Sarah shall bear unto thee at this set	834
	18: 8 the calf **w** he had dressed, and set *it* before	834
	18:10 *it in* the tent door, **w** *was* behind him.	1931
	18:13 Shall I of a surety bear *a child,* **w** am old?	NIH
	18:17 I hide from Abraham *that thing* **w** I do;	834
	18:19 Abraham that **w** he hath spoken of him.	834
	18:21 to the cry of it, **w** is come unto me;	1886.1
	18:27 the Lord, **w** *am but* dust and ashes;	2050.1
	19: 5 Where *are* the men **w** came in to thee this	834
	19: 8 I have two daughters **w** have not known	834
	19:14 **w** married his daughters, and said,	NIH
	19:15 and thy two daughters, **w** are here;	1886.1
	19:19 **w** thou hast shewed unto me in saving my	834
	19:21 *this* city, for the **w** thou hast spoken.	834
	19:25 and that **w** grew upon the ground.	6780
	19:29 when he overthrew the cities in the **w** Lot	834
	20: 3 man, for the woman **w** thou hast taken;	834
	20:13 *is* thy kindness **w** thou shalt shew unto	834
	21: 2 the set time of **w** God had spoken to him.	834
	21: 9 **w** she had born unto Abraham, mocking.	834
	21:25 **w** Abimelech's servants had violently	834
	21:29 What *mean* these seven ewe lambs **w** thou	834
	22: 2 one of the mountains **w** I will tell thee of.	834
	22: 3 unto the place of **w** God had told him	834
	22: 9 came to the place **w** God had told him	834
	22:17 and as the sand **w** *is* upon the sea shore;	834
	23: 9 **w** he hath, which, **w** *is* in the end of his field;	834
	23: 9 which he hath, **w** *is* in the end of his field;	834
	23:16 **w** he had named in the audience of the	834
	23:17 the field of Ephron, **w** *was* in Machpelah,	834
	23:17 **w** *was* before Mamre, the field, and the	834

Ge	23:17 the cave **w** *was* therein, and all the trees	834
	24: 7 **w** took me from my father's house,	834
	24: 7 **w** spake unto me, and that sware unto me,	834
	24:24 the son of Milcah, **w** she bare unto Nahor.	834
	24:42 if now thou do prosper my way **w** I go:	834
	24:48 **w** had led me in the right way to take my	834
	24:60 thy seed possess the gate of those **w** hate	NIH
	25: 6 Abraham had, Abraham gave gifts,	834
	25: 7 of the years of Abraham's life **w** he lived,	834
	25: 9 of Zohar the Hittite, **w** *is* before Mamre;	834
	25:10 The field **w** Abraham purchased of the	834
	26: 2 dwell in the land **w** I shall tell thee of:	834
	26: 3 I will perform the oath **w** I sware unto	834
	26:15 For all the wells **w** his father's servants had	834
	26:18 **w** they had digged in the days of Abraham	834
	26:18 he called their names after the names by **w**	834
	26:32 told him concerning the well **w** they had	834
	26:35 **W** were a grief of mind unto Isaac and	2050.1
	27: 8 obey my voice according to *that* **w** I	834
	27:15 **w** *were* with her in the house, and put	834
	27:17 and the bread, **w** she had prepared,	834
	27:27 smell of a field **w** the LORD hath blessed:	834
	27:45 he forget *that* **w** thou hast done to him:	834
	27:46 such as these **w** *are* of the daughters of	NIH
	28: 4 art a stranger, **w** God gave unto Abraham.	834
	28: 9 took unto the wives **w** he had Mahalath	NIH
	28:15 until I have done *that* **w** I have spoken to	834
	28:22 this stone, **w** I have set *for a* pillar, shall be	834
	29:27 will give thee this also for the service **w**	834
	30:26 thou knowest my service **w** I have done	834
	30:30 *it was* little **w** thou hadst before I *came,*	834
	30:37 made the white appear **w** *was* in the rods.	834
	30:38 he set the rods **w** he had pilled before	834
	31: 1 *that* **w** *was* of our father's hath he gotten	834
	31:10 the rams **w** leaped upon the cattle *were*	1886.1
	31:12 all the rams **w** leap upon the cattle *are*	1886.1
	31:16 all the riches **w** God hath taken from our	834
	31:18 all his goods **w** he had gotten, the cattle of	834
	31:18 getting, **w** he had gotten in Padan-aram,	834
	31:39 **That w** was torn *of beasts* I brought not	2966
	31:43 or unto their children **w** they have born?	834
	31:51 **w** I have cast betwixt me and thee;	834
	32: 8 *other* company **w** is left shall escape.	1886.1
	32: 9 the LORD **w** saidst unto me,	1886.1
	32:10 **w** thou hast shewed unto thy servant;	834
	32:12 sea, **w** cannot be numbered for multitude.	834
	32:13 took of that **w** came to his hand a present	NIH
	32:32 of Israel eat not *of* the sinew **w** shrank,	834
	32:32 **w** *is* upon the hollow of the thigh, unto	NIH
	33: 5 The children **w** God hath graciously given	834
	33: 8 What meanest thou by all this drove **w** I	834
	33:18 of Shechem, **w** *is* in the land of Canaan,	834
	34: 1 daughter of Leah, **w** she bare unto Jacob,	834
	34: 7 **w** thing ought not to be done.	3651
	34:28 that **w** *was* in the city, and that which *was*	834
	34:28 *was* in the city, and that **w** *was* in the field,	834
	35: 3 and was with me in the way **w** I went.	834
	35: 4 they gave unto Jacob all the strange gods **w**	834
	35: 4 and *all their* earrings **w** *were* in their ears;	834
	35: 4 Jacob hid them under the oak **w** *was* by	834
	35: 6 **w** *is* in the land of Canaan, that *is,* Beth-el,	834
	35:12 the land **w** I gave Abraham and Isaac,	834
	35:19 in the way to Ephrath, **w** *is* Beth-lehem.	1931
	35:26 Jacob, **w** were born to him in Padan-aram.	834
	35:27 **w** *is* Hebron, where Abraham and	1931
	36: 5 **w** were born unto him in the land of	834
	36: 6 he had got in the land of Canaan;	834
	37: 6 I pray you, this dream **w** I have dreamed:	834
	38:10 the *thing* **w** he did displeased the LORD:	834
	38:14 an open place, **w** *is* by the way to Timnath;	834
	39: 1 **w** had brought him down thither.	834
	39: 6 ought he had, save the bread **w** he did eat.	834
	39:17 **w** thou hast brought unto us,	834
	39:19 she spake unto him, saying, After this	834
	39:23 the LORD *was* with him, and *that* **w** he did,	834
	40: 5 king of Egypt, **w** *were* bound in the prison.	834
	40:20 the third day, **w** *was* Pharaoh's birthday,	NIH
	41:28 This *is* the thing **w** I have spoken unto	834
	41:36 of famine, **w** shall be in the land of Egypt;	834
	41:43 made him to ride in the second chariot **w**	834
	41:48 **w** were in the land of Egypt, and laid up	834
	41:48 of the field, **w** *was* round about every city,	834
	41:50 **w** Asenath the daughter of Poti-pherah	834
	42: 9 Joseph remembered the dreams **w**	834
	42:38 if mischief befall him by the way in the **w**	834
	43: 2 they had eaten up the corn **w** they had	834
	43:26 brought him the present **w** *was* in their	834
	43:32 w did eat with him, by themselves:	1886.1
	44: 5 *Is* not this *it* in **w** my lord drinketh,	834
	44: 8 we found in our sacks' mouths,	834
	45: 6 in the **w** there *shall* neither *be* earing nor	834
	45:27 words of Joseph, **w** he had said unto them:	834
	45:27 he saw the wagons **w** Joseph had sent	834
	46: 5 in the wagons **w** Pharaoh had sent to carry	834
	46: 6 they had gotten in the land of Canaan,	834
	46: 8 **w** came into Egypt, Jacob and his sons:	1886.1
	46:15 **w** she bare unto Jacob in Padan-aram,	834
	46:20 Asenath the daughter of Poti-pherah	834
	46:22 the sons of Rachel, **w** were born to Jacob:	834
	46:25 w Laban gave unto Rachel his daughter,	834
	46:26 **w** came out of his loins, besides Jacob's	NIH
	46:27 **w** were born him in Egypt, *were* two souls:	834
	46:27 **w** came into Egypt, *were* threescore and	1886.1
	46:31 **w** *were* in the land of Canaan, are come	834
	47:14 of Canaan, for the corn **w** they bought:	834

Ge 47:22 did eat their portion **w** Pharaoh gave them: 834
47:26 the priests only, **w** became not Pharaoh's. NIH
48: 5 **w** were born unto thee in the land of 1886.1
48: 6 **w** thou begettest after them, shall be thine, 834
48:15 the God **w** fed me all my life long unto 1886.1
48:16 The Angel **w** redeemed me from all evil, 1886.1
48:22 **w** I took out of the hand of the Amorite 834
49: 1 that I may tell you *that* **w** shall befall you 834
49:30 **w** *is* before Mamre, in the land of Canaan, 834
49:30 **w** Abraham bought with the field of 834
50: 3 are fulfilled the days of those **w** are NIH
50: 5 in my grave **w** I have digged for me in 834
50:10 **w** *is* beyond Jordan, and there they 834
50:11 called Abel-mizraim, **w** *is* beyond Jordan. 834
50:13 **w** Abraham bought with the field for a 834
50:15 certainly requite us all the evil **w** we did 834
50:24 you out of this land unto the land **w** he 834
Ex 1: 1 children of Israel, **w** came into Egypt; 1886.1
1: 8 new king over Egypt, **w** knew not Joseph. 834
1:15 **w** the name of the one *was* Shiphrah, 834
3: 7 the affliction of my people **w** *are* in Egypt, 834
3:16 and *seen* that **w** is done to you in Egypt: NIH
3:20 smite Egypt with all my wonders **w** I will 834
4: 9 the water **w** thou takest out of the river 834
4:18 return unto my brethren **w** *are* in Egypt, 834
4:19 all the men are dead **w** sought thy life. 1886.1
4:21 Pharaoh, **w** I have put in thine hand: 834
4:28 all the signs **w** he had commanded him. 834
4:30 Aaron spake all the words **w** the Lord had 834
5: 8 **w** they did make heretofore, you shall lay 834
5:14 **w** Pharaoh's taskmasters had set over 834
6: 7 **w** bringeth you out from under 1886.1
6: 8 *concerning* the **w** I did swear to give it to 834
6:27 *These are* they **w** spake to Pharaoh king 1886.1
7:15 the rod **w** was turned to a serpent shalt 834
7:17 hand upon the waters **w** *are* in the river, 834
8: 3 **w** shall go up and come into thine 2050.1
8:12 of the frogs **w** he had brought against 834
8:22 in **w** my people dwell, that no swarms 1886.3
9: 3 the hand of the Lord is upon thy cattle **w** 834
9:19 and beast **w** shall be found in the field, 834
10: 2 my signs **w** I have done amongst them; 834
10: 5 **w** *is* escaped which remaineth unto you 6413
10: 5 **w** remaineth unto you from the hail, 1886.1
10: 5 shall eat every tree **w** groweth for you 1886.1
10: 6 **w** neither thy fathers, nor thy fathers' 834
10:15 all the fruit of the trees **w** the hail had left: 834
10:19 **w** took away the locusts, and cast them 2050.1
10:21 of Egypt, even darkness **w** may be felt. NIH
12:10 that **w** remaineth of it until the morning NIH
12:16 save *that* **w** every man must eat, that only 834
12:19 for whosoever eateth **that w is leavened,** 2556
12:25 when ye be come to the land **w** the Lord 834
12:39 baked unleavened cakes of the dough **w** 834
13: 3 this day, *in* **w** ye came out from Egypt, 834
13: 5 **w** he sware unto thy fathers to give thee, 834
13: 8 of that **w** the Lord did unto me when I NIH
13:12 firstling that cometh of a beast **w** thou 834
14:13 of the Lord, **w** he will shew to you to day: 834
14:19 **w** went before the camp of Israel, 1886.1
14:31 Israel saw *that* great work **w** the Lord did 834
15: 7 thy wrath, **w** consumed them as stubble. NIH
15:13 forth the people **w** thou hast redeemed: NIH
15:16 people pass over, **w** thou hast purchased. NIH
15:17 **w** thou hast made for thee to dwell in, NIH
15:17 O Lord, **w** thy hands have established. NIH
15:25 **w** when he had cast into the waters, NIH
15:26 wilt do that **w** is right in his sight, NIH
15:26 **w** I have brought upon the Egyptians: 834
16: 1 of Sin, **w** *is* between Elim and Sinai, 834
16: 5 they shall prepare *that* **w** they bring in; 834
16: 8 murmurings **w** ye murmur against him: 834
16:15 This *is* the bread **w** the Lord hath given 834
16:16 This *is* the thing **w** the Lord hath 834
16:16 take ye every man for *them* **w** are in his 834
16:23 This *is that* **w** the Lord hath said, 834
16:23 bake *that* **w** you will bake to day, 834
16:23 that **w** remaineth over lay up for you to 1886.1
16:26 on the seventh day, **w** *is* the sabbath, in it NIH
16:32 This *is* the thing **w** the Lord commandeth, 834
18: 3 of **w** the name of the one *was* Gershom; 834
18: 9 Jethro rejoiced for all the goodness **w** 834
19: 6 These *are* the words **w** thou shalt speak 834
19: 7 laid before their faces all these words **w** 834
19:22 **w** come near to the Lord, 1886.1
20: 2 **w** have brought thee out of the land of 834
20:12 that thy days may be long upon the land **w** 834
21: 1 Now these *are* the judgments **w** thou shalt 834
22: 9 for any manner of lost *thing,* **w** *another* 834
22:13 he shall not make good that **w** was torn. NIH
23:16 thy labours, **w** thou hast sown in the field: 834
23:16 of ingathering, **w** *is* in the end of the year, NIH
23:20 to bring thee into the place **w** I have 834
23:28 **w** shall drive out the Hivite, 2050.1
24: 3 All the words **w** the Lord hath said will 834
24: 5 **w** offered burnt offerings, 2050.1
24: 8 **w** the Lord hath made with you 834
24:12 and commandments **w** I have written; 834
25: 3 this *is* the offering **w** ye shall take of them; 834
25:16 shalt put into the ark the Testimony **w** I 834
25:22 between the two cherubims **w** *are* upon 834
25:22 of all *things* **w** I will give thee in 834
25:40 **w** was shewed thee in the mount. 834
26:10 fifty loops in the edge of the curtain **w** 1886.1
26:13 a cubit on the other side of **that w** 1886.1

Ex 26:30 thereof **w** was shewed thee in the mount. 834
27:21 **w** *is* before the Testimony, Aaron and 834
28: 4 these *are* the garments **w** they shall make; 834
28: 8 **w** *is* upon it, shall be of the same, 834
28:24 rings **w** *are* on the ends of the breastplate. NIH
28:26 **w** *is* in the side of the ephod inward. 834
28:38 **w** the children of Israel shall hallow in all 834
29:27 **w** is waved, and which is heaved up, 834
29:27 which is waved, and **w** is heaved up, 834
29:27 *even of that* **w** is for Aaron, and of *that* 834
29:27 *is* for Aaron, and of *that* **w** is for his sons: 834
29:35 to all *things* **w** I have commanded 834
29:38 Now this *is that* **w** thou shalt offer upon 834
30:37 *as for* the perfume **w** thou shalt make, 834
32: 1 Up, make us gods, **w** shall go before us; 834
32: 2 **w** *are* in the ears of your wives, of your 834
32: 3 the golden earrings **w** *were* in their ears, 834
32: 4 **w** brought thee up out of the land of Egypt. 834
32: 7 **w** thou broughtest out of the land of Egypt, 834
32: 8 out of the way **w** I commanded them: 834
32: 8 **w** have brought thee up out of the land of 834
32:11 **w** thou hast brought forth out of the land 834
32:14 the Lord repented of the evil **w** he 834
32:20 he took the calf **w** they had made, 834
32:23 Make us gods, **w** shall go before us: 834
32:32 out of thy book **w** thou hast written. 834
32:34 lead the people unto *the place* of **w** I have 834
32:35 they made the calf, **w** Aaron made. 834
33: 1 the people **w** thou hast brought up out of 834
33: 1 unto the land **w** I sware unto Abraham, 834
33: 7 *that* every one **w** sought the Lord went NIH
33: 7 Congregation, **w** *was* without the camp. 834
34: 1 were in the first tables, **w** thou brakest. 834
34:10 all the people among **w** thou *art* shall see 834
34:11 Observe thou that **w** I command thee *this* 834
34:34 spake unto the children of Israel *that* **w** he 834
35: 1 These *are* the words **w** the Lord hath 834
35: 4 This *is* the thing, **w** the Lord commanded, 834
35:25 that **w** they had spun, *both* of blue, NIH
35:29 the Lord had commanded to be made 834
36: 3 **w** the children of Israel had brought for 834
36: 4 came every man from his work **w** they 834
36: 5 **w** the Lord commanded to make. 834
36:12 curtain **w** *was* in the coupling of the 834
36:17 of the curtain **w** coupleth the second. 1886.1
36:25 **w** *is* toward the north corner, he made NIH
37:16 made the vessels **w** *were* upon the table, 834
38: 8 **w** assembled *at* the door of the tabernacle 834
39:19 **w** *was* on the side of the ephod inward. 834
Lev 1: 8 order upon the wood that *is* on the fire **w** 834
1:12 that *is* on the fire **w** *is* upon the altar: 834
2:10 that **w** is left of the meat offering *shall be* NIH
2:11 ye shall bring unto the Lord, 834
3: 4 **w** *is* by the flanks, and the caul above 834
3: 5 **w** *is* upon the wood that *is* on the fire: 834
3:10 **w** *is* by the flanks, and the caul above 834
3:15 **w** *is* by the flanks, and the caul above 834
4: 2 *things* **w** ought not to be done), 834
4: 3 let him bring for his sin, **w** he hath sinned, 834
4: 7 **w** is in the tabernacle of the congregation; 834
4: 7 **w** *is* at the door of the tabernacle of 834
4: 9 **w** *is* by the flanks, and the caul above 834
4:13 *concerning things* **w** should not be done, 834
4:14 **w** they have sinned against it, is known, 834
4:18 horns of the altar **w** *is* before the Lord, 834
4:18 **w** *is* at the door of the tabernacle of 834
4:22 *concerning things* **w** should not be done, 834
4:27 *concerning things* **w** ought not to be done, 834
4:28 if his sin, **w** he hath sinned, come to his 834
4:28 for his sin **w** he hath sinned. 834
5: 6 the Lord for his sin **w** he hath sinned, 834
5: 7 **w** he hath committed, two turtledoves, 834
5: 8 shall offer *that* **w** *is* for the sin offering 834
5:10 for him for his sin **w** he had sinned, 834
5:17 any *of these things* **w** are forbidden 834
6: 2 in *that* **w was delivered him to keep,** 6487
6: 3 Or have found **that w was lost,** 9
6: 4 he shall restore *that* **w** he took violently 834
6: 4 of the thing **w** he hath deceitfully gotten, 834
6: 4 or *that* **w** was delivered him to keep, 834
6: 4 him to keep, or the lost *thing* **w** he found, 834
6: 5 Or all *that* about **w** he hath sworn falsely; 834
6:10 the ashes **w** the fire hath consumed 834
6:15 all the frankincense **w** *is* upon the meat 834
6:20 **w** they shall offer unto the Lord in 834
7: 4 **w** *is* by the flanks, and the caul *that is* 834
7: 8 of the burnt offering **w** he hath offered. 834
7:11 he shall offer unto the Lord. 834
7:21 **w** *pertain* unto the Lord, even that soul 834
7:24 the fat of that **w is torn** *with beasts,* may 2966
7:25 of **w** *men* offer an offering made by fire 834
7:36 the Lord commanded to be given them 834
7:38 **w** the Lord commanded Moses in mount 834
8: 5 This *is* the thing **w** the Lord commanded 834
8:30 of the blood **w** *was* upon the altar, 834
8:32 that **w** remaineth of the flesh and of NIH
8:36 his sons did all things **w** the Lord 834
9: 5 they brought *that* **w** Moses commanded 834
9: 6 This *is* the thing **w** the Lord commanded 834
9: 8 calf of the sin offering, **w** *was* for himself. 834
9:12 **w** he sprinkled round about upon 2050.1
9:15 **w** *was* the sin offering for the people, 834
9:18 of peace offerings, **w** *was* for the people: 834
9:18 **w** he sprinkled upon the altar round 1930.2
9:19 that **w** covereth *the* inwards, and NIH

Lev 9:24 **w** when all the people saw, they shouted, NIH
10: 1 the Lord, **w** he commanded them not. 834
10: 6 bewail the burning **w** the Lord hath 834
10:11 **w** the Lord hath spoken unto them by 834
10:14 **w** are given out of the sacrifices of peace 834
10:16 Ithamar the sons of Aaron **w** were left 1886.1
11: 2 These *are* the beasts **w** ye shall eat among 834
11:10 and of any living thing **w** *is* in the waters, 834
11:13 these *are they* **w** ye shall have in NIH
11:21 **w** have legs above their feet, to leap withal 834
11:23 **w** have four feet, *shall be* an abomination 834
11:26 The carcases of every beast **w** divideth 834
11:34 Of all meat **w** may be eaten, *that* on which 834
11:34 *that* on **w** such water cometh shall be 834
11:36 that **w** toucheth their carcase shall be NIH
11:37 fall upon any sowing seed **w** is to be sown, 834
11:39 if any beast, of **w** ye may eat, die; he that 834
13:18 The flesh also, in **w,** *even* in the skin 2050.2
13:58 whatsoever thing of skin *it be,* **w** thou shalt 834
14:32 whose hand is not able to get *that* **w** NIH
14:34 **w** I give to you for a possession, and I put 834
14:37 in sight *are* lower than the wall; 2050.1
14:40 take away the stones in **w** the plague *is,* 834
15:12 that he toucheth **w** hath the issue, 2050.2
15:33 of him that lieth with her **w** is unclean. NIH
16: 2 before the mercy seat, **w** *is* upon the ark; 834
16: 6 **w** *is* for himself, and make an atonement 834
16: 9 Aaron shall bring the goat upon **w** 834
16:10 on **w** the lot fell to be the scapegoat, 834
16:11 **w** *is* for himself, and shall make an 834
16:11 kill the bullock of the sin offering **w** *is* 834
16:23 he put on when he went into the holy 834
17: 2 This *is* the thing **w** the Lord hath 834
17: 5 **w** they offer in the open field, even that 834
17: 8 or of the strangers **w** sojourn among you, 834
17:13 **w** hunteth and catcheth *any* beast or 834
17:15 soul that eateth **that w** died of itself, 5038
17:15 **that w is torn** *with beasts,* 2966
18: 5 **w** if a man do, he shall live in them: I *am* 834
18:24 nations are defiled **w** I cast out before you: 834
18:27 **w** *were* before you, and the land is defiled; 834
18:30 **w** were committed before you, and that ye 834
19:22 the Lord for his sin **w** he hath done: 834
19:22 sin **w** he hath done shall be forgiven him. 834
19:36 **w** brought you out of the land of Egypt. 834
20: 8 do them: I *am* the Lord **w** sanctify you. NIH
20:23 of the nation, **w** I cast out before you: 834
20:24 **w** have separated you from *other* people. 834
20:25 **w** I have separated from you as unclean. 834
21: 3 is nigh unto him, **w** hath had no husband; 834
21: 8 for I the Lord, **w** sanctify you, *am* holy. NIH
22: 2 *in those things* **w** they hallow unto me: 834
22: 3 that goeth unto the holy *things* **w** 834
22: 6 The soul **w** hath touched *any* such shall be 834
22: 8 **That w dieth of itself,** or is torn *with* 5038
22:15 of Israel, **w** they offer unto the Lord; 834
22:18 **w** they will offer unto the Lord for a 834
22:24 Ye shall not offer unto the Lord that **w** is NIH
22:32 of Israel: I *am* the Lord **w** hallow you, NIH
23: 2 **w** ye shall proclaim *to be* holy 834
23: 4 **w** ye shall proclaim in their seasons. 834
23:10 ye be come into the land **w** I give unto 834
23:37 **w** ye shall proclaim *to be* holy 834
23:38 **w** ye give unto the Lord. 834
25: 2 When ye come into the land **w** I give you, 834
25: 5 **That growth of it own accord** of 5599
25:11 neither reap **that w** growth of itself in 5599
25:25 shall he redeem **that w** his brother **sold.** 4465
25:28 **that w is sold** shall remain in the hand of 4465
25:31 the houses of the villages **w** have no wall 834
25:38 **w** brought you forth out of the land of 834
25:42 **w** I brought forth out of the land of Egypt: 834
25:44 and thy bondmaids, **w** thou shalt have, 834
25:45 *are* with you, **w** they begat in your land: 834
26:13 **w** brought you forth out of the land of 834
26:22 **w** shall rob you of your children, 2050.1
26:32 your enemies **w** dwell therein shall be 1886.1
26:40 their trespass **w** they trespassed against 834
26:46 the Lord made between him and 834
27:11 of **w** they do not offer a sacrifice unto 834
27:22 if *a man* sanctify unto the Lord a field **w** NIH
27:22 **w** *is* not of the fields of his possession; 834
27:26 **w** should be the Lord's firstling, no man 834
27:29 None devoted, **w** shall be devoted of men, 834
27:34 **w** the Lord commanded Moses for 834
Nu 1:17 Aaron took these men **w** are expressed by 834
1:44 **w** Moses and Aaron numbered, 834
2:12 those **w** pitch by him *shall be* the tribe of NIH
2:32 These *are* those **w** were numbered of NIH
3: 3 of Aaron, the priests **w** were anointed, 1886.1
3:26 **w** *is* by the tabernacle, and by the altar 834
3:39 **w** Moses and Aaron numbered at 834
3:46 of Israel, **w** are more than the Levites; 1886.1
4:26 **w** *is* by the tabernacle and by the altar 834
4:37 **w** Moses and Aaron did number according 834
5: 7 they shall confess their sin **w** they have 834
5: 9 **w** they bring unto the priest, shall be his. 834
5:18 in her hands, **w** *is* the jealousy offering: 1931
6: 5 in the **w** he separateth *himself* unto 834
6:18 put *it* in the fire **w** *is* under the sacrifice of 834
6:21 according to the vow **w** he vowed, 834
8: 4 according unto the pattern **w** the Lord had 834
10: 4 **w** *are* heads of the thousands of Israel, NIH
10:25 **w** *was* the rereward of all the camps NIH
10:29 We *are* journeying unto the place of **w** 834

Nu 11: 5 the fish, **w** we did eat in Egypt freely;	834
11:12 unto the land **w** thou swarest unto their	834
11:17 I will take of the spirit **w** *is* upon thee,	834
11:20 that ye have despised the Lord **w** *is*	834
12: 3 above all the men **w** *were* upon the face of	834
13: 2 **w** I give unto the children of Israel:	834
13:16 These *are* the names of the men **w** Moses	834
13:24 of the cluster of grapes **w** the children of	834
13:32 brought up an evil report of the land **w**	834
13:32 through **w** we have gone to search it,	834
13:33 the sons of Anak, **w** *come* of the giants:	NIH
14: 6 **w** *were* of them that searched the land,	NIH
14: 7 The land, **w** we passed through to search	834
14: 8 a land **w** floweth with milk and honey.	834
14:11 for all the signs **w** I have shewed among	834
14:15 the nations **w** have heard the fame of thee	834
14:16 into the land **w** he sware unto them,	834
14:22 Because all *those* men **w** have seen my	1886.1
14:22 **w** I did in Egypt and in the wilderness,	834
14:23 they shall not see the land **w** I sware	834
14:27 evil congregation, **w** murmur against me?	834
14:27 of Israel, **w** they murmur against me.	834
14:29 upward, **w** have murmured against me,	834
14:30 *concerning* **w** I sware to make you dwell	834
14:31 little ones, **w** ye said should be a prey,	834
14:31 shall know the land **w** ye have despised.	834
14:34 After the number of the days *in* **w** ye	834
14:36 the men, **w** Moses sent to search the land,	834
14:38 **w** *were* of the men that went to search	NIH
14:40 will go up unto the place **w** the Lord hath	834
14:45 the Canaanites **w** dwelt in that hill,	1886.1
15: 2 land of your habitations, **w** I give unto you,	834
15:22 **w** the Lord hath spoken unto Moses,	834
15:39 own eyes, after **w** ye use to go a whoring:	834
15:41 **w** brought you out of the land of Egypt,	834
16:11 For **w** cause *both* thou and all	3651+3807.1
16:12 of Eliab: **w** said, We will not come up:	2050.1
16:40 no stranger, **w** *is* not of the seed of Aaron,	834
18: 9 **w** they shall render unto me, *shall be* most	834
18:12 firstfruits of them **w** they shall offer unto	834
18:13 **w** they shall bring unto the Lord, shall be	834
18:15 **w** they bring unto the Lord, *whether it be*	834
18:16 of the sanctuary, **w** *is* twenty gerahs.	1931
18:19 the heave offerings of the holy *things,* **w**	834
18:21 for their service **w** they serve, *even*	834
18:24 **w** they offer *as* a heave offering unto	834
18:26 **w** I have given you from them for your	834
18:28 **w** ye receive of the children of Israel;	834
19: 2 This *is* the ordinance of the law **w**	834
19: 2 no blemish, *and* upon **w** never came yoke:	834
19:15 **w** hath no covering bound upon it,	834
20:12 into the land **w** I have given them.	834
20:24 he shall not enter into the land **w** I have	834
21: 1 Arad the Canaanite, **w** dwelt *in* the south,	NIH
21:11 in the wilderness **w** *is* before Moab,	834
21:13 **w** *is* in the wilderness that cometh out of	834
21:20 of Pisgah, **w** looketh toward Jeshimon.	2050.1
21:30 unto Nophah, **w** *reacheth* unto Medeba.	834
21:34 king of the Amorites, **w** dwelt at Heshbon.	834
22: 5 **w** *is* by the river *of* the land of the children	834
22:11 **w** covereth the face of the earth:	2050.1
22:20 yet the word **w** I shall say unto thee,	834
22:30 upon **w** thou hast ridden ever since *I was*	834
22:36 **w** *is* in the border of Arnon, which *is* in	834
22:36 border of Arnon, **w** *is* in the utmost coast.	834
23:12 Must I not take heed to speak that **w**	834
24: 4 He hath said, **w** heard the words of God,	NIH
24: 4 **w** saw the vision of the Almighty,	834
24: 6 as the trees of lign aloes **w** the Lord hath	NIH
24:12 Spake I not also to thy messengers **w** thou	834
24:16 **w** heard the words of God, and knew	NIH
24:16 **w** saw the vision of the Almighty,	NIH
25:18 **w** was slain in the day of the plague for	1886.1
26: 4 **w** went forth out of the land of Egypt.	1886.1
26: 9 **w** *were* famous in the congregation,	NIH
27:12 the land **w** I have given unto the children	834
27:17 **W** may go out before them, and which	834
27:17 **w** may go in before them, and which may	834
27:17 **w** may lead them out, and which may	834
27:17 lead them out, and **w** may bring them in;	834
27:17 Lord be not as sheep **w** have no shepherd.	834
28: 3 This *is* the offering made by fire **w** ye shall	834
28: 6 **w** was ordained in mount Sinai for a	1886.1
28:23 **w** *is* for a continual burnt offering.	834
30: 1 This *is* the thing **w** the Lord hath	834
30: 8 then he shall make her vow **w** she vowed,	834
30: 8 that **w** she uttered with her lips,	4008
30:14 vows, or all her bonds, **w** *are* upon her:	834
30:16 **w** the Lord commanded Moses,	834
31:12 of Moab, **w** *are* by Jordan *near* Jericho.	834
31:14 over hundreds, **w** came from the battle.	1886.1
31:21 the men of war **w** went to the battle,	1886.1
31:21 This *is* the ordinance of the law **w**	834
31:28 of the men of war **w** went out to battle:	1886.1
31:30 **w** keep the charge of the tabernacle of	NIH
31:32 the rest of the prey **w** the men of war	834
31:36 **w** *was* the portion of them that went out	834
31:38 of **w** the Lord's tribute *was* threescore	3963.1
31:39 of **w** the Lord's tribute *was* threescore	3963.1
31:40 of **w** the Lord's tribute *was* thirty and	3963.1
31:41 **w** was the Lord's heave offering,	NIH
31:42 **w** Moses divided from the men that	834
31:47 **w** kept the charge of the tabernacle of	NIH
31:48 the officers **w** *were* over thousands of	834
31:49 of the men of war **w** *are* under our charge,	834

Nu 32: 4 *Even* the country **w** the Lord smote	834
32: 7 into the land **w** the Lord hath given them?	834
32: 9 that *they* should not go into the land **w**	834
32:11 see the land **w** I sware unto Abraham,	834
32:24 that **w** hath proceeded out of your mouth.	NIH
32:38 gave other names unto the cities **w** they	834
32:39 and dispossessed the Amorite **w** *was* in it.	834
33: 1 **w** went forth out of the land of Egypt with	834
33: 4 **w** the Lord had smitten among them:	834
33: 6 Etham, **w** *is* in the edge of the wilderness.	834
33: 7 unto Pi-hahiroth, **w** *is* before Baal-zephon:	834
33:36 in the wilderness of Zin, **w** *is* Kadesh.	1931
33:40 **w** dwelt in the south in the land of	1931
33:55 *those* **w** ye let remain of them *shall be*	834
34:13 This *is* the land **w** ye shall inherit by lot,	834
34:13 **w** the Lord commanded to give unto	834
34:17 These *are* the names of the men **w** shall	834
35: 4 the cities, **w** ye shall give unto the Levites,	834
35: 6 *among* the cities **w** ye shall give unto	834
35: 6 **w** ye shall appoint for the manslayer,	834
35: 7 So all the cities **w** ye shall give	834
35: 8 the cities **w** ye shall give *shall be* of	834
35: 8 to his inheritance **w** he inheriteth.	834
35:11 **w** killeth *any* person at unawares.	NIH
35:13 *these* cities **w** ye shall give six cities shall	834
35:14 land of Canaan, **w** shall be cities of refuge.	NIH
35:25 priest, **w** was anointed with the holy oil.	834
35:31 the life of a murderer, **w** *is* guilty of death:	834
35:34 therefore the land **w** ye shall inhabit,	834
36: 6 This *is* the thing **w** the Lord doth	834
36:13 **w** the Lord commanded by the hand of	834
Dt 1: 1 These *be* the words **w** Moses spake unto	834
1: 4 **w** dwelt in Heshbon, and Og the king of	834
1: 4 of Bashan, **w** dwelt at Astaroth in Edrei:	834
1: 8 possess the land **w** the Lord sware unto	834
1:14 **w** thou hast spoken *is* good *for us*	834
1:18 at that time all the things **w** ye should do.	834
1:19 **w** you saw *by* the way of the mountain of	834
1:20 **w** the Lord our God doth give unto us.	834
1:25 *It is* a good land **w** the Lord our God doth	834
1:30 The Lord your God **w** goeth before	1886.1
1:35 **w** I sware to give unto your fathers,	834
1:38 **w** standeth before thee, he shall go in	1886.1
1:39 **w** ye said should be a prey,	834
1:39 **w** *in* that day had no knowledge between	834
1:44 the Amorites, **w** dwelt in that mountain,	1886.1
2: 4 the children of Esau, **w** dwell in Seir;	1886.1
2: 8 **w** dwelt in Seir, through the way of	1886.1
2:11 **W** also were accounted giants,	1992
2:12 **w** the Lord gave unto them.)	834
2:14 the space in **w** we came from	834
2:22 to the children of Esau, **w** dwelt in Seir,	1886.1
2:23 Avims **w** dwelt in Hazerim, *even* unto	1886.1
2:23 **w** came forth out of Caphtor,	1886.1
2:29 (As the children of Esau **w** dwell in Seir,	1886.1
2:29 the Moabites **w** dwell in Ar, did unto	1886.1
2:29 I shall pass over Jordan into the land **w**	834
2:35 and the spoil of the cities **w** we took.	834
2:36 **w** *is* by the brink of the river of Arnon,	834
3: 2 king of the Amorites, **w** dwelt at Heshbon.	834
3: 4 there was not a city **w** we took not from	834
3: 9 (**W** Hermon the Sidonians call Sirion;	NIH
3:12 **w** we possessed at that time, from Aroer,	NIH
3:12 **w** *is* by the river Arnon, and half mount	834
3:13 Bashan, **w** was called the land of giants.	1931
3:16 **w** *is* the border of the children of Ammon;	NIH
3:19 abide in your cities **w** I have given you;	834
3:20 *until* ye also possess the land **w**	834
3:20 unto his possession, **w** I have given you.	834
3:28 he shall cause them to inherit the land **w**	834
4: 1 and unto the judgments, **w** I teach you,	834
4: 1 possess the land **w** the Lord God of your	834
4: 2 shall not add unto the word **w** I command	834
4: 2 of the Lord your God **w** I command you.	834
4: 6 **w** shall hear all these statutes, and say,	834
4: 8 as all this law, **w** I set before you *this* day?	834
4: 9 lest thou forget the things **w** thine eyes	834
4:13 **w** he commanded you to perform, *even*	834
4:19 **w** the Lord thy God hath divided unto all	834
4:21 **w** the Lord thy God giveth thee *for* an	834
4:23 **w** he made with you, and make you a	834
4:23 the likeness of any *thing,* **w** the Lord thy	834
4:28 wood and stone, **w** neither see, nor hear,	834
4:31 nor forget the covenant of thy fathers **w** he	834
4:32 the days that are past, **w** were before thee,	834
4:40 **w** I command thee *this* day,	834
4:40 **w** the Lord thy God giveth thee, for ever.	834
4:42 **w** should kill his neighbour unawares,	834
4:44 this *is* the law **w** Moses set before	834
4:45 **w** Moses spake unto the children of Israel,	834
4:47 **w** *were* on *this* side Jordan *toward*	834
4:48 **w** *is* by the bank of the river Arnon,	834
4:48 even unto mount Sion, **w** *is* Hermon,	1931
5: 1 judgments **w** I speak in your ears *this* day,	834
5: 6 **w** brought thee out of the land of Egypt,	834
5:16 in the land **w** the Lord thy God giveth	834
5:28 this people, **w** they have spoken unto thee:	834
5:31 the judgments, **w** thou shalt teach them,	834
5:31 that they may do *them* in the land **w** I give	834
5:33 You shall walk in all the ways **w** the Lord	834
5:33 ye may prolong *your* days in the land **w**	834
6: 1 the Lord your God commanded to	834
6: 2 **w** I command thee, thou, and thy son,	834
6: 6 these words, **w** I command thee *this* day,	834
6:10 into the land **w** he sware unto thy fathers,	834

Dt 6:10 and goodly cities, **w** thou buildedst not,	834
6:11 full *of* all good *things,* **w** thou filledst	834
6:11 **w** thou diggedst not, vineyards and	834
6:11 and olive trees, **w** thou plantedst not;	834
6:12 **w** brought thee forth out of the land of	834
6:14 the gods of the people **w** *are* round about	834
6:17 his statutes, **w** he hath commanded thee.	834
6:18 thou shalt do *that* **w** *is* right and good in	NIH
6:18 possess the good land **w** the Lord sware	834
6:20 **w** the Lord our God hath commanded	834
6:23 to give us the land **w** he sware unto our	834
7: 8 would keep the oath **w** he had sworn unto	834
7: 9 keepeth covenant and mercy with them	NIH
7:11 **w** I command thee *this* day, to do them.	834
7:12 the mercy **w** he sware unto thy fathers:	834
7:13 in the land **w** he sware unto thy fathers to	834
7:15 of Egypt, **w** thou knowest, upon thee;	834
7:16 thou shalt consume all the people **w**	834
7:19 The great temptations **w** thine eyes saw,	834
8: 1 All the commandments **w** I command thee	834
8: 1 possess the land **w** the Lord sware unto	834
8: 2 thou shalt remember all the way **w**	834
8: 3 fed thee with manna, **w** thou knewest not,	834
8:10 for the good land **w** he hath given thee.	834
8:11 his statutes, **w** I command thee *this* day:	834
8:14 brought thee forth out of the land of	1886.1
8:16 **w** thy fathers knew not, that he might	834
8:18 that he may establish his covenant **w** he	834
8:20 As the nations **w** the Lord destroyeth	834
9: 3 that the Lord thy God *is* he **w** goeth	1886.1
9: 5 that he may perform the word **w** the Lord	834
9: 9 *even* the tables of the covenant **w**	834
9:10 **w** the Lord spake with you in the mount	834
9:12 thy people **w** thou hast brought forth out	834
9:12 out of the way **w** I commanded them;	834
9:16 had turned aside quickly out of the way **w**	834
9:18 because of all your sins **w** ye sinned,	834
9:21 the calf **w** ye had made, and burnt it with	834
9:23 and possess the land **w** I have given you;	834
9:26 **w** thou hast redeemed through thy	834
9:26 **w** thou hast brought forth out of Egypt	834
9:28 them into the land **w** he promised them,	834
9:29 **w** thou broughtest out by thy mighty	834
10: 2 were in the first tables **w** thou brakest,	834
10: 4 **w** the Lord spake unto you in the mount	834
10: 5 put the tables in the ark **w** I had made;	834
10:11 **w** I sware unto their fathers to give unto	834
10:13 **w** I command *thee* this day for thy good?	834
10:17 and a terrible, **w** regardeth not persons,	834
10:21 terrible *things,* **w** thine eyes have seen.	834
11: 2 *I speak* not with your children **w** have not	834
11: 2 **w** have not seen the chastisement of	834
11: 3 he did in the midst of Egypt unto	834
11: 7 all the great acts of the Lord **w** he did.	834
11: 8 commandments **w** I command you *this*	834
11: 9 the Lord sware unto your fathers to	834
11:12 A land **w** the Lord thy God careth for:	834
11:13 commandments **w** I command you *this*	834
11:17 off the good land **w** the Lord giveth you.	834
11:21 in the land **w** the Lord sware unto your	834
11:22 these commandments **w** I command you,	834
11:27 your God, **w** I command you *this* day:	834
11:28 aside out of the way **w** I command you	834
11:28 go after other gods, **w** ye have not known.	834
11:30 **w** dwell in the champaign over against	1886.1
11:31 the land **w** the Lord your God giveth you,	834
11:32 and judgments **w** I set before you *this* day.	834
12: 1 ye shall observe to do in the land,	834
12: 1 **w** the Lord God of thy fathers giveth thee	834
12: 2 wherein the nations **w** ye shall possess	834
12: 5 unto the place **w** the Lord your God shall	834
12: 9 **w** the Lord your God giveth you.	834
12:10 dwell in the land **w** the Lord your God	834
12:11 there shall be a place **w** the Lord your	834
12:11 all your choice vows **w** ye vow unto	834
12:14 in the place **w** the Lord shall choose in	834
12:15 of the Lord thy God **w** he hath given thee:	834
12:17 nor any of thy vows **w** thou vowest,	834
12:18 place **w** the Lord thy God shall choose,	834
12:21 If the place **w** the Lord thy God hath	834
12:21 of thy flock, **w** the Lord hath given thee,	834
12:25 when thou shalt do *that* **w** *is* right in	NIH
12:26 Only thy holy *things* **w** thou hast,	834
12:26 go unto the place **w** the Lord shall	834
12:28 hear all these words **w** I command thee,	834
12:28 when thou doest *that* **w** *is* good and right	NIH
12:31 **w** he hateth, have they done unto their	834
13: 2 **w** thou hast not known, and let us serve	834
13: 5 **w** brought you out of the land of Egypt,	1886.1
13: 5 to thrust thee out of the way **w** the Lord	834
13: 6 or thy friend, **w** *is* as thine own soul,	834
13: 6 **w** thou hast not known, thou, nor thy	834
13: 7 *Namely,* of the gods of the people **w** *are*	834
13:10 brought thee out of the land of Egypt,	1886.1
13:12 the Lord thy God hath given thee to	834
13:13 serve other gods, **w** ye have not known;	834
13:18 keep all his commandments **w** I command	834
13:18 to do *that* **w** *is* right in the eyes of	NIH
14: 4 These *are* the beasts ye shall eat: the ox,	834
14:12 these *are they* **w** ye shall not eat:	834
14:23 in the place **w** he shall choose to place his	834
14:24 the Lord thy God shall choose to set	834
14:25 shalt go unto the place **w** the Lord thy	834
14:29 the widow, **w** *are* within thy gates,	834
14:29 in all the work of thine hand **w** thou doest.	834

Dt 15: 3 *that* **w** is thine with thy brother thine hand 834
15: 4 **w** the Lord thy God giveth thee *for* an 834
15: 5 observe to do all these commandments **w** 834
15: 7 thy land **w** the Lord thy God giveth thee, 834
15: 8 for his need, *in that* **w** he wanteth. 834
15:20 year in the place **w** the Lord shall choose, 834
16: 2 in the place **w** the Lord shall choose to 834
16: 4 thou sacrificedst the first day at even, 834
16: 5 **w** the Lord thy God giveth thee: 834
16: 6 at the place **w** the Lord thy God shall 834
16: 7 eat *it* in the place **w** the Lord thy God 834
16:10 thou shalt give *unto the Lord thy God,* 834
16:11 in the place **w** the Lord thy God hath 834
16:15 the place **w** the Lord shall choose: 834
16:16 thy God in the place **w** he shall choose; 834
16:17 of the Lord thy God **w** he hath given thee. 834
16:18 **w** the Lord thy God giveth thee, 834
16:20 That **w** is altogether just shalt thou follow, NIH
16:20 inherit the land **w** the Lord thy God 834
16:21 Lord thy God, **w** thou shalt make thee. 834
16:22 up *any* image; **w** the Lord thy God hateth. 834
17: 2 within any of thy gates **w** the Lord thy 834
17: 3 host of heaven, **w** I have not commanded; 834
17: 5 **w** have committed that wicked thing, 834
17: 8 get thee up into the place **w** the Lord thy 834
17:10 **w** *they* of that place which the Lord shall 834
17:10 which *they* of that place **w** the Lord shall 834
17:11 According to the sentence of the law **w** 834
17:11 according to the judgment **w** they shall tell 834
17:11 thou shalt not decline from the sentence **w** 834
17:14 When thou art come unto the land **w** 834
17:15 a stranger over thee, **w** is not thy brother. 834
17:18 of *that* **w** is before the priests the Levites: NIH
18: 6 unto the place **w** the Lord shall choose; 834
18: 7 as all his brethren the Levites *do,* **w** stand NIH
18: 8 beside **that w cometh** of the **sale** of his 4465
18: 9 When thou art come into the land **w** 834
18:14 For these nations, **w** thou shalt possess, 834
18:17 They have well *spoken that* **w** they have 834
18:19 my words **w** he shall speak in my name, 834
18:20 **w** shall presume to speak a word in my 834
18:20 **w** I have not commanded him to speak, 834
18:21 How shall we know the word **w** the Lord 834
18:22 that *is* the thing **w** the Lord hath not 834
19: 2 **w** the Lord thy God giveth thee to 834
19: 3 **w** the Lord thy God giveth thee to inherit, 834
19: 4 shall flee thither, that he may live: 834
19: 8 thee all the land **w** he promised to give 834
19: 9 **w** I command thee *this* day, to love 834
19:10 **w** the Lord thy God giveth thee *for* an 834
19:14 they of old time have set in thine 834
19:14 thou shalt inherit in the land that 834
19:16 to testify against him *that* **w** is wrong; NIH
19:17 and the judges, **w** shall be in those days; 834
19:20 those **w** remain shall hear, and fear, NIH
20: 1 **w** brought thee up out of the land of 1886.1
20:14 **w** the Lord thy God hath given thee. 834
20:15 Thus shalt thou do unto all the cities **w** *are* NIH
20:15 **w** *are* not of the cities of these nations. 834
20:16 **w** the Lord thy God doth give thee *for* an 834
20:18 **w** they have done unto their gods; 834
20:20 Only the trees **w** thou knowest that they 834
21: 1 If *one* be found slain in the land **w** 834
21: 2 they shall measure unto the cities **w** *are* 834
21: 3 *that* the city **w** is next unto the slain *man,* NIH
21: 3 **w** hath not been wrought with, 834
21: 3 *and* **w** hath not drawn in the yoke; 834
21: 4 **w** is neither eared nor sown, and shall 834
21: 9 when thou shalt do *that* **w** is right in NIH
21:16 he maketh his sons to inherit *that* **w** he 834
21:16 of the hated, **w** is *indeed* the firstborn: NIH
21:18 **w** will not obey the voice of his father, 5105.2
21:23 **w** the Lord thy God giveth thee *for* an 834
22: 3 **w** he hath lost, and thou hast found, shalt 834
22: 5 not wear **that w pertaineth** unto a man, 3627
22: 9 lest the fruit of *thy* seed **w** thou hast sown, 834
22:28 **w** is not betrothed, and lay hold on her, 834
23:13 and cover that **w** cometh from thee: NIH
23:15 **w** is escaped from his master unto thee: 834
23:16 in *that* place **w** he shall choose in one of 834
23:23 That **w is gone out** of thy lips thou shalt 4161
23:23 thou hast promised with thy mouth. 834
24: 3 husband die, **w** took her *to be* his wife; 834
24: 4 Her former husband, **w** sent her away, 834
24: 4 **w** the Lord thy God giveth thee *for* an 834
24: 5 shall cheer up his wife **w** he hath taken. 834
25: 6 the firstborn **w** she beareth shall succeed 834
25: 6 in the name of his brother **w** is dead, 1886.1
25:15 the land **w** the Lord thy God giveth thee. 834
25:19 in the land **w** the Lord thy God giveth 834
26: 1 when thou art come in unto the land **w** 834
26: 2 **w** thou shalt bring of thy land that 834
26: 2 shalt go unto the place **w** the Lord thy 834
26: 3 that I am come unto the country **w** 834
26:10 the land, **w** thou, O Lord, hast given me. 834
26:11 thou shalt rejoice in every good thing **w** 834
26:12 **w** *is* the year of tithing, and hast given *it* NIH
26:13 according to all thy commandments **w** 834
26:15 and the land **w** thou hast given us, 834
26:19 to make thee high above all nations **w** he 834
27: 1 Keep all the commandments **w** I command 834
27: 2 the land **w** the Lord thy God giveth thee, 834
27: 3 that thou mayest go in unto the land **w** 834
27: 4 **w** I command you *this* day, in mount Ebal, 834
27:10 his statutes, **w** I command thee *this* day. 834

Dt 28: 1 to do all his commandments **w** I command 834
28: 8 he shall bless thee in the land **w** the Lord 834
28:11 in the land **w** the Lord sware unto thy 834
28:13 **w** I command thee *this* day, to observe and 834
28:14 of the words **w** I command thee *this* day, 834
28:15 his statutes **w** I command thee *this* day; 834
28:33 shall a nation **w** thou knowest not eat up; 834
28:34 for the sight of thine eyes **w** thou shalt see. 834
28:36 and thy king **w** thou shalt set over thee, 834
28:36 a nation **w** neither thou nor thy fathers 834
28:45 and his statutes **w** he commanded thee: 834
28:48 shalt thou serve thine enemies **w** 834
28:50 **w** shall not regard the person of the old, 834
28:51 **w** *also* shall not leave thee *either* corn, 834
28:52 **w** the Lord thy God hath given thee. 834
28:53 **w** the Lord thy God hath given thee. 834
28:54 towards the remnant of his children **w** he 834
28:56 **w** would not adventure to set the sole of 834
28:57 and towards her children **w** she shall bear: 834
28:60 diseases of Egypt, **w** thou wast afraid of; 834
28:61 **w** *is* not written in the book of this law, 834
28:64 neither thou nor thy fathers have 834
28:67 for the sight of thine eyes **w** thou shalt see. 834
29: 1 **w** the Lord commanded Moses to make 834
29: 1 the covenant **w** he made with them in 834
29: 3 The great temptations **w** thine eyes have 834
29:12 **w** the Lord thy God maketh with thee *this* 834
29:16 how we came through the nations **w** ye 834
29:17 silver and gold, **w** *were* among them;) 834
29:22 the sicknesses **w** the Lord hath laid upon 834
29:23 **w** the Lord overthrew in his anger, 834
29:25 **w** he made with them when he brought 834
29:29 *things* **w** are revealed *belong* unto us 1886.1
30: 1 **w** I have set before thee, and thou shalt 834
30: 5 thee into the land **w** thy fathers possessed, 834
30: 7 on them that hate thee, **w** persecuted thee. 834
30: 8 do all his commandments **w** I command 834
30:10 his statutes **w** are written in this book of 1886.1
30:11 For this commandment **w** I command thee 834
30:20 that thou mayest dwell in the land **w** 834
31: 5 commandments **w** I have commanded you. 834
31: 7 **w** the Lord hath sworn unto their fathers 834
31: 9 **w** bare the ark of the covenant of 1886.1
31:11 thy God in the place **w** he shall choose, 834
31:13 **w** have not known *any thing,* may hear, 834
31:16 break my covenant **w** I have made with 834
31:18 for all the evils **w** they shall have wrought, 834
31:20 into the land **w** I sware unto their fathers, 834
31:21 for I know their imagination **w** they go 834
31:21 I have brought them into the land **w** I 834
31:23 Israel into the land **w** I sware unto them: 834
31:25 **w** bare the ark of the covenant of NIH
31:29 turn aside from the way **w** I have 834
32:15 then he forsook God **w** made him, NIH
32:21 me to jealousy with *that* **w** *is* not God; NIH
32:21 will move them to jealousy with *those* **w** NIH
32:38 **W** did eat the fat of their sacrifices, 834
32:46 Set your hearts unto all the words **w** I 834
32:46 ye shall command your children to 834
32:49 mount Nebo, **w** *is* in the land of Moab, 834
32:49 **w** I give unto the children of Israel for a 834
32:52 thou shalt not go thither unto the land **w** I 834
34: 4 This *is* the land **w** I sware unto Abraham, 834
34:11 **w** the Lord sent him to do in the land of 834
34:12 in all the great terror **w** Moses shewed in 834
Jos 1: 2 unto the land **w** I do give to them, 834
1: 6 **w** I sware unto their fathers to give them. 834
1: 7 **w** Moses my servant commanded thee: 834
1:11 **w** the Lord your God giveth you to 834
1:13 Remember the word **w** Moses the servant 834
1:14 shall remain in the land **w** Moses gave you 834
1:15 they also have possessed the land **w** 834
1:15 **w** Moses the Lord's servant gave you on 834
2: 3 to thee, **w** are entered into thine house: 834
2: 6 she had laid in order upon the roof. NIH
2: 7 as soon as they **w** pursued after them were NIH
2:17 We *will be* blameless of this thine oath **w** 834
2:18 the window **w** thou didst let us down by: 834
2:20 we will be quit of thine oath **w** thou hast 834
3: 4 ye may know the way by **w** ye must go: 834
3:16 That the waters **w** came down from 1886.1
4: 9 the place where the feet of the priests **w** NIH
4:10 For the priests **w** bare the ark stood in NIH
4:20 twelve stones, **w** they took out of Jordan, 834
4:23 he dried up from before us, 834+3509.1
5: 1 **w** *were* on the side of Jordan westward, 834
5: 1 kings of the Canaanites, **w** *were* by the sea, 834
5: 6 **w** came out of Egypt, were consumed, 1886.1
5: 6 **w** the Lord sware unto their fathers that 834
6:25 **w** Joshua sent to spy out Jericho. 834
7: 2 **w** *is* beside Beth-aven, on the east side of 834
7:11 they have also transgressed my covenant **w** 834
7:14 *that* the tribe **w** the Lord taketh shall 834
7:14 the family **w** the Lord shall take shall 834
7:14 the household **w** the Lord shall take shall 834
8:27 according unto the word of the Lord **w** he 834
8:31 over **w** no *man* hath lift up *any* iron: 834
8:32 **w** he wrote in the presence of the children 834
8:33 **w** bare the ark of the covenant of NIH
8:35 **w** Joshua read not before all 834
9: 1 when all the kings **w** *were* on *this* side 834
9:10 to Og king of Bashan, **w** *was* at Ashtaroth. 834
9:13 bottles of wine, **w** we filled, *were* new; 834
9:20 of the oath **w** we sware unto them. 834
9:27 this day, in the place **w** he should choose. 834

Jos 10:11 *were* moe **w** died with hailstones than 834
10:20 that the rest **w** remained of them entered NIH
10:24 of the men of war **w** went with him, 1886.1
10:27 mouth, **w** remain until this very day. NIH
10:32 **w** took it on the second day, and smote 2050.1
12: 1 **w** the children of Israel smote, 834
12: 2 **w** *is* upon the bank of the river of Arnon, 834
12: 2 **w** *is* the border of the children of Ammon; NIH
12: 4 **w** *was* of the remnant of the giants, NIH
12: 7 *are* the kings of the country **w** Joshua 834
12: 7 Joshua gave unto the tribes of Israel 2050.1
12: 9 the king of Ai, **w** *is* beside Beth-el, one; 834
13: 3 From Sihor, **w** *is* before Egypt, even unto 834
13: 3 **w** is counted to the Canaanite: NIH
13: 8 **w** Moses gave them, beyond Jordan 834
13:10 **w** reigned in Heshbon, unto the border of 834
13:12 **w** reigned in Ashtaroth and in Edrei, 834
13:21 of the Amorites, **w** reigned in Heshbon, 834
13:21 Hur, and Reba, **w** *were* dukes of Sihon, NIH
13:30 of Jair, **w** *are* in Bashan, threescore cities: 834
13:32 These *are the countries* **w** Moses did 834
14: 1 these *are the countries* **w** the children of 834
14: 1 **w** Eleazar the priest, and Joshua the son of 834
14:15 **w** *Arba was* a great man among NIH
15: 7 **w** is on the south side of the river: 834
15: 8 **w** *is* at the end of the valley of the giants 834
15: 9 was drawn *to* Baalah, **w** *is* Kirjath-jearim: 1931
15:10 **w** *is* Chesalon, on the north side, 1931
15:13 Arba the father of Anak, **w** *city is* Hebron. 1931
15:25 and Kerioth, *and* Hezron, **w** *is* Hazor, 1931
15:49 and Kirjath-sannah, **w** *is* Debir, 1931
15:54 and Kirjath-arba, **w** *is* Hebron, and Zior; 1931
15:60 **w** *is* Kirjath-jearim, and Rabbah; 1931
17: 5 **w** *were* on the *other* side Jordan; 834
18: 2 **w** had not *yet* received their inheritance. 834
18: 3 **w** the Lord God of your fathers hath 834
18: 7 **w** Moses the servant of the Lord gave 834
18:13 the side of Luz, **w** *is* Beth-el, southward; 1931
18:14 **w** *is* Kirjath-jearim, a city of the children 1931
18:16 **w** *is* in the valley of the giants on the 834
18:17 **w** *is* over against the going up of 834
18:28 and Jebusi, **w** *is* Jerusalem, Gibeath, 1931
19:50 Lord they gave him the city **w** he asked, 834
19:51 **w** Eleazar the priest, and Joshua the son of 834
20: 7 Kirjath-arba, **w** *is* Hebron, in the mountain 1931
21: 4 of Aaron the priest, **w** *were* of the Levites, NIH
21: 9 cities **w** are *here* mentioned by name, 834
21:10 **W** the children of Aaron, *being* of 2050.1
21:11 **w** *city is* Hebron, in the hill *country* of 1931
21:20 Levites **w** remained of the children of 1886.1
21:40 were remaining of the families of 1886.1
21:43 the Lord gave unto Israel all the land **w** 834
21:45 There failed not ought of any good thing **w** 834
22: 4 **w** Moses the servant of the Lord gave 834
22: 5 **w** Moses the servant of the Lord charged 834
22: 9 **w** *is* in the land of Canaan, to go unto 834
22:17 from **w** we are not cleansed until this day, 834
22:28 **w** our fathers made, not for burnt offerings, 834
22:30 of the thousands of Israel **w** *were* with 834
23:13 until ye perish from off this good land **w** 834
23:14 **w** the Lord your God spake concerning 834
23:15 **w** the Lord your God promised you; 834
23:15 **w** the Lord your God hath given you. 834
23:16 he commanded you, and have gone and 834
23:16 the good land **w** he hath given unto you. 834
24: 5 according to *that* **w** I did amongst them: 834
24: 8 **w** dwelt on the *other* side Jordan; 1886.1
24:12 **w** drave them out from before you, 2050.1
24:13 I have given you a land for **w** ye did not 834
24:13 cities **w** ye built not, and ye dwell in them; 834
24:13 and oliveyards **w** ye planted not do ye eat. 834
24:14 put away the gods **w** your fathers served 834
24:15 whether the gods **w** your fathers served 834
24:17 and **w** did those great signs in our sight, 834
24:18 even the Amorites **w** dwelt in the land: NIH
24:23 the strange gods **w** *are* among you, 834
24:27 words of the Lord **w** he spake unto us: 834
24:30 **w** *is* in mount Ephraim, on the north side 834
24:31 **w** had known all the works of the Lord, 834
24:32 **w** the children of Israel brought up out of 834
24:32 in a parcel of ground **w** Jacob bought of 834
24:33 son, **w** was given him in mount Ephraim. 834
Jdg 1:16 of Judah, **w** *lieth* in the south of Arad; 834
1:26 **w** *is* the name thereof unto this day. 1931
2: 1 I have brought you unto the land **w** I sware 834
2:10 after them, **w** knew not the Lord, 834
2:10 yet the works **w** he had done for Israel. 834
2:12 brought them out of the land of Egypt, 1886.1
2:16 **w** delivered them out of the hand of 2050.1
2:17 they turned quickly out of the way **w** their 834
2:20 my covenant **w** I commanded their fathers, 834
2:21 of the nations **w** Joshua left when he died: 834
3: 1 Now these *are* the nations **w** the Lord left, 834
3: 4 he commanded their fathers by the hand 834
3:16 Ehud made him a dagger **w** had two 2050.1
3:20 parlour, **w** he had for himself alone. 834
3:31 he slew *of* the Philistines six hundred 2050.1
4: 2 **w** dwelt in Harosheth of the Gentiles. 1931
4:11 **w** *was* of the children of Hobab the father NIH
4:11 unto the plain of Zaanaim, **w** *is* by Kedesh. 834
4:14 for this *is* the day in **w** the Lord hath 834
6: 2 them the dens **w** *are* in the mountains, 834
6: 8 **w** said unto them, Thus saith the Lord 2050.1
6:11 sat under an oak **w** *was* in Ophrah, 834
6:13 *be* all his miracles **w** our fathers told 834

Jdg	6:26 wood of the grove **w** thou shalt cut down.	834
	8:27 **w** thing became a snare unto Gideon,	NIH
	8:35 according to all the goodness **w** he had	834
	9: 2 *w* are threescore and ten persons, reign	NIH
	9: 4 and light persons, **w** followed him.	2050.1
	9:13 **w** cheereth God and man, and go to be	1886.1
	9:24 Abimelech their brother, **w** slew them;	834
	9:24 **w** aided him in the killing of his brethren.	834
	9:56 **w** he did unto his father, in slaying his	834
	10: 4 **w** are called Havoth-jair unto this day,	NIH
	10: 4 unto this day, **w** are in the land of Gilead.	834
	10: 8 in the land of the Amorites, **w** is in Gilead.	834
	10:14 and cry unto the gods **w** ye have chosen;	834
	11:24 Wilt not thou possess that **w** Chemosh thy	834
	11:28 unto the words of Jephthah **w** he sent him.	834
	11:36 to me according to that **w** hath proceeded	834
	11:39 who did with her *according to* his vow **w**	834
	12: 5 that when those Ephraimites **w** were	NIH
	13: 8 the man of God **w** thou didst send come	834
	14:19 gave change *of garments* unto them **w**	NIH
	15:19 **w** is in Lehi unto this day.	834
	16: 8 seven green withs **w** had not been dried,	834
	16:24 destroyer of our country, **w** slew many of	834
	16:29 middle pillars upon **w** the house stood,	834
	16:29 on **w** it was borne up, of the one with	1992.1
	16:30 the dead **w** he slew at his death were moe	834
	16:30 were moe than *they* **w** he slew in his life.	834
	17: 2 about **w** thou cursedst, and spakest of also	NIH
	17: 6 every man did *that* **w** was right in his	1886.1
	18: 5 we may know whether our way **w** we go	834
	18:16 **w** were of the children of Dan, stood *by*	834
	18:24 Ye have taken away my gods **w** I made,	834
	18:27 they took *the things* **w** Micah had made,	834
	18:27 the priest **w** he had, and came unto Laish,	834
	18:31 Micah's graven image, **w** he made,	834
	19:10 came over against Jebus, **w** is Jerusalem;	1931
	19:14 by Gibeah, **w** belongeth to Benjamin.	834
	19:16 at even, **w** was also of mount Ephraim;	2050.1
	19:19 for the young man **w** is with thy servants:	NIH
	20: 9 now this *shall be* the thing **w** we will do to	834
	20:13 the children of Belial, **w** are in Gibeah,	834
	20:15 **w** were numbered seven hundred chosen	NIH
	20:18 **W** of us shall go up first to the battle	4310
	20:31 *of* **w** one goeth up *to* the house of God,	834
	20:36 they trusted unto the liers in wait **w** they	834
	20:42 **w** came out of the cities they destroyed	834
	20:46 So that all **w** fell that day of Benjamin	1886.1
	21:12 *to* Shiloh, **w** is in the land of Canaan.	834
	21:14 gave them wives **w** they had saved alive	834
	21:19 *a place* **w** is on the north side of Beth-el,	834
	21:25 every man did *that* **w** was right in his	1886.1
Ru	1:22 **w** returned out of the country of Moab:	1886.1
	2: 9 of that **w** the young men have drawn.	834
	2:11 come unto a people **w** thou knewest not	834
	4: 3 of land, **w** was our brother Elimelech's:	834
	4:11 **w** two did build the house of Israel:	834
	4:12 of the seed **w** the LORD shall give thee of	834
	4:14 **w** hath not left thee *this* day without a	834
	4:15 for thy daughter in law, **w** loveth thee,	834
	4:15 **w** is better to thee than seven sons, hath	834
1Sa	1:27 the LORD hath given me my petition **w** I	834
	2:20 woman for the loan **w** is lent to the LORD.	834
	2:29 **w** I have commanded *in my* habitation;	834
	2:32 in all *the wealth* **w** God shall give Israel:	834
	2:35 *that* shall do according to *that* **w** is in my	834
	3:11 **w** both the ears of every one that heareth	834
	3:12 for I have spoken concerning his house:	834
	3:13 for ever for the iniquity **w** he knoweth;	834
	4: 4 hosts, **w** dwelleth *between* the cherubims:	NIH
	6: 4 What *shall be* the trespass offering **w** we	834
	6: 7 on **w** there hath come no yoke, and tie	1992.1
	6: 8 **w** ye return him *for a* trespass offering,	834
	6:17 these *are* the golden emerods **w**	834
	6:18 **w** stone remaineth unto this day in the	NIH
	7:14 the cities the Philistines had taken from	834
	8: 8 According to all the works **w** they have	834
	8:18 of your king **w** ye shall have chosen you;	834
	9:22 bidden, **w** were about thirty persons.	834
	9:23 Bring the portion **w** I gave thee, of which I	834
	9:23 of **w** I said unto thee, Set it by thee.	834
	9:24 **w** was upon it, and set *it* before Saul.	1886.1
	9:24 *Samuel* said, Behold that **w** is left; set *it*	NIH
	10: 2 asses **w** thou wentest to seek are found:	834
	10: 4 **w** thou shalt receive of their hands.	2050.1
	11:11 that they **w** remained were scattered,	NIH
	12: 7 he did to you and to your fathers.	834
	12: 8 **w** brought forth your fathers out of Egypt,	NIH
	12:16 **w** the LORD will do before your eyes.	834
	12:17 **w** ye have done in the sight of the LORD,	834
	12:21 *should ye go* after vain *things,* **w** cannot	834
	13: 5 people as the sand **w** is on the sea shore in	834
	13:13 the LORD thy God, **w** he commanded thee:	834
	13:14 thou hast not kept *that* **w** the LORD	834
	14: 2 under a pomegranate tree **w** is in Migron:	834
	14: 4 *by* **w** Jonathan sought to go over unto	834
	14:14 Jonathan and his armourbearer made,	834
	14:14 of land, **w** a yoke of oxen might plow.	NIH
	14:21 **w** went up with them into the camp *from*	834
	14:22 Likewise all the men of Israel **w** had hid	1886.1
	14:30 of the spoil of their enemies **w** they found?	834
	14:39 For, *as* the LORD liveth, **w** saveth	1886.1
	15: 2 I remember *that* **w** Amalek did to Israel,	834
	15:14 and the lowing of the oxen **w** I hear?	834
	15:20 have gone the way **w** the LORD sent me,	834
	15:21 the chief of the things **w** should have been	NIH

1Sa	16: 4 Samuel did *that* **w** the LORD spake,	834
	16:16 our lord now command thy servants **w**	NIH
	16:19 me David thy son, **w** is with the sheep.	834
	17: 1 **w** belongeth to Judah, and pitched	834
	17:31 the words were heard **w** David spake,	834
	17:40 put them in a shepherd's bag **w** he had,	834
	20:23 *as touching* the matter **w** thou and I have	834
	20:27 **w** was the second *day* of the month,	NIH
	20:36 Run, find out now the arrows **w** I shoot.	834
	20:37 place of the arrow **w** Jonathan had shot,	834
	22: 9 **w** was set over the servants of Saul,	1931
	22:14 **w** is the king's son in law, and goeth at	2050.1
	23:13 **w** were about six hundred, arose and	NIH
	23:19 Hachilah, **w** is on the south of Jeshimon?	834
	24: 4 Behold the day of **w** the LORD said unto	834
	25: 7 thy shepherds **w** were with us, we hurt	834
	25:27 now this blessing **w** thine handmaid hath	834
	25:32 of Israel, **w** sent thee this day to meet me;	834
	25:33 **w** hast kept me this day from coming to	834
	25:34 **w** hath kept me back from hurting thee,	834
	25:35 So David received of her hand *that* **w** she	834
	25:44 to Phalti the son of Laish, **w** was of Gallim.	834
	26: 1 the hill of Hachilah, *w* is before Jeshimon?	NIH
	26: 1 before Jeshimon, by the way.	834
	28:21 have hearkened unto thy words **w** thou	834
	29: 1 the Israelites pitched by a fountain **w** is in	834
	29: 3 **w** hath been with me these days,	834
	29: 4 **w** thou hast appointed him, and let him	834
	30:10 for two hundred abode *behind,* **w** were so	834
	30:14 upon *the coast* **w** belongeth to Judah,	834
	30:17 young men, **w** rode upon camels, and fled.	834
	30:20 **w** they drave before those *other* cattle,	NIH
	30:21 **w** were so faint that they could not follow	834
	30:23 with *that* **w** the LORD hath given us,	834
	30:27 To *them* **w** were in Beth-el, and to *them*	834
	30:27 to *them* **w** were in south Ramoth,	834
	30:27 Ramoth, and to *them* **w** were in Jattir,	834
	30:28 *them* **w** were in Aroer, and to *them* which	834
	30:28 to *them* **w** were in Siphmoth, and to *them*	834
	30:28 and to *them* **w** were in Eshtemoa,	834
	30:29 to *them* **w** were in Rachal, and to *them*	834
	30:29 to *them* **w** were in the cities of	834
	30:29 to *them* **w** were in the cities of the Kenites,	834
	30:30 to *them* **w** were in Hormah, and to *them*	834
	30:30 to *them* **w** were in Chor-ashan, and to	834
	30:30 and to *them* **w** were in Athach,	834
	30:31 to *them* **w** were in Hebron, and to all	834
	31:11 of that **w** the Philistines had done to Saul,	834
2Sa	2:15 **w** pertained to Ish-bosheth the son of	2050.1
	2:16 called Helkath-hazzurim, **w** is in Gibeon.	834
	2:32 of his father, **w** was in Beth-lehem.	834
	3: 8 against Judah do shew kindness *this* day	834
	3:14 **w** I espoused to me for an hundred	834
	3:26 brought him again from the well of	NIH
	4: 8 son of Saul thine enemy, **w** sought thy life;	834
	5: 6 **w** spake unto David, saying, Except thou	NIH
	6: 4 of the house of Abinadab **w** was at Gibeah,	834
	6:21 chose me before thy father, and before	834
	6:22 of the maidservants **w** thou hast spoken of,	834
	7:12 **w** shall proceed out of thy bowels, and I	834
	7:23 thou redeemedst to thee from Egypt,	834
	8:11 **W** also king David did dedicate unto	3963.1
	8:11 gold that he had dedicated of all nations	834
	9: 3 hath yet a son, *w* is lame on *his* feet.	NIH
	10:12 the LORD do that **w** seemeth him good.	NIH
	12: 3 **w** he had bought and nourished up:	834
	13:10 Tamar took the cakes **w** she had made,	834
	13:23 in Baal-hazor, **w** is beside Ephraim:	834
	14: 7 *so* they shall quench my coal **w** is left,	834
	14:13 doth speak this thing as one **w** is faulty,	818
	14:14 cannot be gathered up *again;* neither	834
	15: 4 that every man **w** hath *any* suit or	834
	15: 7 **w** I have vowed unto the LORD,	834
	15:16 **w** were concubines, to keep the house.	NIH
	15:18 six hundred men **w** came after him from	834
	16:11 my son, **w** came forth of my bowels,	834
	16:21 **w** he hath left to keep the house;	834
	16:23 **w** he counselled in those days,	834
	17:10 and *they* **w** be with him *are* valiant men.	834
	17:18 in Bahurim, **w** had a well in his court;	2050.2
	17:25 Amasa *was* a man's son, whose name	2050.1
	18:18 for himself a pillar, **w** is in the king's dale:	834
	18:28 **w** hath delivered up the men that lift up	834
	19: 5 **w** this day have saved thy life, and the	NIH
	19:16 **w** was of Bahurim, hasted and came down	834
	19:19 do thou remember *that* **w** thy servant	834
	19:38 I will do to him *that* **w** shall seem good	1886.1
	20: 5 tarried longer than the set time **w** he had	834
	20: 8 When they *were* at the great stone **w** is in	834
	21:12 **w** had stolen them from the street of	834
	21:16 **w** was of the sons of the giant,	834
	21:18 slew Saph, **w** was of the sons of the giant.	834
	22:44 a people **w** I knew not shall serve me.	NIH
	23:15 of the well of Beth-lehem, **w** is by the gate.	834
	24: 2 **w** was with him, Go now through all	NIH
	24:24 my God of that **w** doth cost me nothing.	NIH
1Ki	1: 8 and the mighty *men* **w** belonged to David,	834
	1: 9 **w** is by En-rogel, and called all his brethren	834
	1:48 **w** hath given *one* to sit on my throne *this*	834
	2: 4 That the LORD may continue his word **w**	834
	2: 8 **w** cursed me *with* a grievous curse in	1931
	2:24 **w** hath established me, and set me on	834
	2:27 he spake concerning the house of Eli in	834
	2:31 **w** Joab shed, from me, and from the house	834
	2:44 Thou knowest all the wickedness **w** thine	834

1Ki	2:46 **w** went out, and fell upon him, that he	2050.1
	3: 8 thy servant *is* in the midst of thy people **w**	834
	3:13 I have also given thee *that* **w** thou hast not	834
	3:21 it was not my son, **w** I did bear.	834
	3:28 all Israel heard of the judgment **w** the king	834
	4: 2 these *were* the princes **w** he had; Azariah	834
	4: 7 **w** provided victuals for the king and his	NIH
	4:11 **w** had Taphath the daughter of Solomon to	NIH
	4:12 **w** is by Zartanah beneath Jezreel,	834
	4:13 Jair the son of Manasseh, **w** are in Gilead;	834
	4:13 **w** is in Bashan, threescore great cities *with*	834
	4:19 *he was* the only officer **w** was in the land.	834
	4:20 as the sand **w** is by the sea in multitude,	834
	4:34 of the earth, **w** had heard of his wisdom.	834
	5: 3 the wars **w** were about him on every side,	834
	5: 7 **w** hath given unto David a wise son over	834
	5: 8 have considered *the things* **w** thou sentest	834
	5:16 Besides the chief of Solomon's officers **w**	834
	5:16 **w** ruled over the people that wrought in	1886.1
	6: 1 in the month Zif, **w** is the second month,	1931
	6: 2 the house **w** king Solomon built for	834
	6:12 *Concerning* this house **w** thou art in	834
	6:12 with thee, **w** I spake unto David thy father:	834
	6:20 and *so* covered the altar **w** *was* of cedar.	NIH
	6:38 in the month Bul, **w** is the eighth month,	1931
	7: 8 within the porch, *w* was of the like work.	NIH
	7:17 for the chapiters **w** *were* upon the top of	834
	7:20 against the belly **w** *was* by the network:	834
	7:41 to cover the two bowls of the chapiters **w**	834
	7:45 Hiram made to king Solomon *for*	834
	7:51 Solomon brought in the *things* **w** David	NIH
	8: 1 LORD out of the city of David, **w** *is* Zion.	1931
	8: 2 month Ethanim, **w** *is* the seventh month.	1931
	8: 9 of stone, **w** Moses put there at Horeb,	834
	8:15 spake with his mouth unto David my	834
	8:21 of the LORD, **w** he made with our fathers,	834
	8:26 **w** thou spakest unto thy servant David my	834
	8:28 **w** thy servant prayeth before thee to day:	834
	8:29 *even* toward the place of **w** thou hast said,	834
	8:29 *thou* mayest hearken unto the prayer **w**	834
	8:34 them again unto the land **w** thou gavest	834
	8:36 **w** thou hast given to thy people for an	834
	8:38 **w** shall know every man the plague of his	834
	8:40 in the land **w** thou gavest unto our fathers.	834
	8:43 **w** I have builded, is called by thy name.	834
	8:44 LORD toward the city **w** thou hast chosen,	834
	8:48 **w** led them away captive, and pray unto	834
	8:48 **w** thou gavest unto their fathers, the city	834
	8:48 the city **w** thou hast chosen, and the house	834
	8:48 and the house **w** I have built for thy name:	834
	8:51 **w** thou broughtest forth out of Egypt,	834
	8:56 he promised by the hand of Moses his	834
	8:58 judgments, **w** he commanded our fathers.	834
	8:63 **w** he offered unto the LORD, two and	834
	9: 1 Solomon's desire **w** he was pleased to do,	834
	9: 3 hallowed this house, **w** thou hast built,	834
	9: 6 *and* my statutes **w** I have set before you,	834
	9: 7 will I cut off Israel out of the land **w** I have	834
	9: 7 house, **w** I have hallowed for my name,	834
	9: 8 *at* this house, **w** is high, every one that	NIH
	9:12 came out from Tyre to see the cities **w**	834
	9:13 cities *are* these **w** thou hast given me,	834
	9:15 is the reason of the levy **w** king Solomon	834
	9:19 that **w** Solomon desired to build in	834
	9:20 **w** *were* not of the children of Israel,	834
	9:23 **w** bare rule over the people that	1886.1
	9:24 her house *Solomon* had built for her:	834
	9:25 peace offerings upon the altar **w** he built	834
	9:26 **w** is beside Eloth, on the shore of the Red	834
	10: 3 thing hid from the king, **w** he told her not.	834
	10: 5 his ascent *by* **w** he went up *unto* the house	834
	10: 7 prosperity exceedeth the fame **w** I heard.	834
	10: 8 **w** stand continually before thee,	1886.1
	10: 9 be the LORD thy God, **w** delighted in thee,	834
	10:10 **w** the queen of Sheba gave to king	834
	10:13 *that* **w** Solomon gave her of his royal	834
	10:24 his wisdom, **w** God had put in his heart.	834
	11: 2 Of the nations *concerning* **w** the LORD	834
	11: 8 **w** burnt incense and sacrificed unto their	NIH
	11: 9 Israel, **w** had appeared unto him twice,	1886.1
	11:10 he kept not *that* **w** the LORD commanded.	834
	11:11 my statutes, **w** I have commanded thee,	834
	11:13 and for Jerusalem's sake, **w** I have chosen.	834
	11:18 **w** gave him a house, and appointed him	NIH
	11:23 **w** fled from his lord Hadadezer king of	834
	11:32 city **w** I have chosen out of all the tribes	834
	11:33 to do *that* **w** is right in mine eyes,	1886.1
	11:36 city **w** I have chosen me to put my name	834
	12: 4 his heavy yoke **w** he put upon us, lighter,	834
	12: 8 **w** they had given him, and consulted with	834
	12: 8 with him, *and* **w** stood before him:	834
	12: 9 Make the yoke **w** thy father did put upon	834
	12:15 the LORD spake by Ahijah the Shilonite	834
	12:17 *as for* the children of Israel **w** dwelt in	1886.1
	12:21 fourscore thousand chosen *men,* were	NIH
	12:28 **w** brought thee up out of the land of Egypt	834
	12:31 the people, **w** were not of the sons of Levi.	834
	12:32 priests of the high places **w** he had made.	834
	12:33 he offered upon the altar **w** he had made	834
	12:33 *even* in the month **w** he had devised of his	834
	13: 3 This *is* the sign **w** the LORD hath spoken;	834
	13: 4 **w** had cried against the altar in Beth-el,	834
	13: 4 he put forth against him, dried up,	834
	13: 5 according to the sign **w** the man of God	834
	13:11 the words **w** he had spoken unto the king,	834

1Ki 13:12 the man of God went, **w** came from Judah. 834
13:21 hast not kept the commandment **w** 834
13:22 of the **w** *the* LORD did say to thee, Eat no 834
13:26 **w** hath torn him, and slain him, according NIH
13:26 word of the LORD, **w** he spake unto him. 834
13:32 For the saying **w** he cried by the word of 834
13:32 against all the houses of the high places **w** 834
14: 2 **w** told me that I should be king over this 1931
14: 8 do *that* only **w** *was* right in mine eyes; 1886.1
14:15 he gave to their fathers, and shall scatter 834
14:18 **w** he spake by the hand of his servant 834
14:20 the days **w** Jeroboam reigned *were* two 834
14:21 the city **w** the LORD did choose out of all 834
14:22 with their sins **w** they had committed, 834
14:24 the LORD cast out before the children of 834
14:26 he took away all the shields of gold **w** 834
14:27 **w** kept the door of the king's house. 1886.1
15: 3 of his father, **w** he had done before him: 834
15: 5 Because David did *that* **w** *was* right in 1886.1
15:11 Asa did *that* **w** *was* right in the eyes of 1886.1
15:15 he brought in the things **w** his father had NIH
15:15 *the things* **w** himself had dedicated, *into* NIH
15:20 sent the captains of the hosts **w** he had 834
15:23 all that he did, and the cities **w** he built, 834
15:27 Gibbethon, **w** *belongeth* to the Philistines; 834
15:29 **w** he spake by his servant Ahijah 834
15:30 Because of the sins of Jeroboam **w** he 834
15:30 he sinned, and **w** he made Israel sin, 834
16:12 **w** he spake against Baasha by Jehu 834
16:13 *by* **w** they sinned, and *by* which they made 834
16:13 and *by* **w** they made Israel to sin, 834
16:15 **w** *belonged* to the Philistines. 834
16:19 For his sins **w** he sinned in doing evil in 834
16:19 and in his sin **w** he did, to make Israel sin. 834
16:24 and called the name of the city **w** he built, 834
16:27 Now the rest of the acts of Omri **w** he did, 834
16:32 house of Baal, **w** he had built in Samaria. 834
16:34 **w** he spake by Joshua the son of Nun. 834
17: 9 **w** *belongeth* to Zidon, and dwell there: 834
17:16 word of the LORD, **w** he spake by Elijah. 834
18: 3 **w** *was* the governor of *his* house. 834
18:19 four hundred, **w** eat *at* Jezebel's table. NIH
18:26 they took the bullock **w** was given them, 834
18:26 they leapt upon the altar **w** was made. 834
19: 3 **w** *belongeth* to Judah, and left his servant 834
19:18 all the knees **w** have not bowed unto Baal, 834
19:18 and every mouth **w** hath not kissed him. 834
20:19 of the city, and the army **w** followed them. 834
20:34 cities, **w** my father took from thy father, 834
21: 1 Jezreelite had a vineyard, **w** *was* in Jezreel, 834
21: 4 of the word **w** Naboth the Jezreelite had 834
21:11 *it was* written in the letters **w** she had sent 834
21:15 **w** he refused to give thee for money: 834
21:18 meet Ahab king of Israel, **w** *is* in Samaria. 834
21:25 **w** did sell himself to work wickedness in 834
22:13 of one of them, and speak *that* **w** *is* good. NIH
22:16 *that* **w** is true in the name of the LORD? NIH
22:24 **W** way went the spirit of the LORD 335+2088
22:38 according unto the word of the LORD **w** he 834
22:39 ivory house **w** he made, and all the cities 834
22:43 doing *that* **w** *was* right in the eyes of 1886.1
22:46 remained in the days of his father Asa, 834

2Ki 1: 4 from *that* bed on **w** thou art gone up, 834
1: 6 shalt not come down from *that* bed on **w** 834
1: 7 What manner of man *was he* **w** came up 834
1:16 shalt not come down off *that* bed on **w** 834
1:17 word of the LORD **w** Elijah had spoken. 834
1:18 the rest of the acts of Ahaziah **w** he did, 834
2:15 when the sons of the prophets **w** *were* to 834
2:22 to the saying of Elisha **w** he spake. 834
3: 3 the son of Nebat, **w** made Israel to sin; 834
3: 8 he said, **W** way shall we go up? 335+2088
3:11 **w** poured water on the hands of Elijah. 834
4: 4 and thou shalt set aside *that* **w** is full. 1886.1
4: 9 man of God, **w** *passeth* by us continually. NIH
5:20 in not receiving at his hands *that* **w** he 834
6:10 king of Israel sent to the place **w** the man 834
6:11 ye not shew me **w** of us *is* for the king 4310
7:13 that remain, **w** are left in the city, (behold, 834
7:15 the Syrians had cast away in their haste. 834
8:21 smote the Edomites **w** compassed him 1886.1
8:29 the Syrians had given him at Ramah, 834
9: 5 Jehu said, Unto **w** of all us? And he said, 4310
9:15 the wounds **w** the Syrians had given him, 834
9:19 **w** came to them, and said, Thus saith NIH
9:27 *so* at the going up to Gur, **w** *is* by Ibleam. 834
9:36 **w** he spake by his servant Elijah 834
10: 5 do thou *that* **w** *is* good in thine eyes. 1886.1
10: 6 great *men* of the city, **w** brought them up. NIH
10:10 the LORD spake concerning the house of 834
10:10 for the LORD hath done *that* **w** he spake by 834
10:17 saying of the LORD, **w** he spake to Elijah. 834
10:30 executing *that* **w** is right in mine eyes, 1886.1
10:31 the sins of Jeroboam, **w** made Israel to sin. 834
10:33 from Aroer, **w** *is* by the river Arnon, 834
11: 2 stale him from among the king's sons **w** 1886.1
11:16 she went *by* the way **w** the horses NIH
12: 2 Jehoash did *that* **w** *was* right in the sight 1886.1
12:20 house of Millo, **w** goeth down *to* Silla. 1886.1
13: 2 he did *that* **w** *was* evil in the sight of 1886.1
13: 2 the son of Nebat, **w** made Israel to sin; 834
13:11 he did *that* **w** *was* evil in the sight of 1886.1
13:25 **w** he had taken out of the hand of 834
14: 3 he did *that* **w** *was* right in the sight of 1886.1
14: 5 that he slew his servants **w** had slain 1886.1

2Ki 14: 6 according unto that **w** is written in the NIH
14:11 at Beth-shemesh, **w** *belongeth* to Judah. 834
14:15 the rest of the acts of Jehoash **w** he did, 834
14:21 **w** *was* sixteen years old, and made him 1931
14:24 he did *that* **w** *was* evil in the sight of 1886.1
14:25 **w** he spake by the hand of his servant 834
14:25 the prophet, **w** *was* of Gath-hepher. 834
14:28 Hamath, **w** *belonged* to Judah, for Israel, NIH
15: 3 he did *that* **w** *was* right in the sight of 1886.1
15: 9 he did *that* **w** *was* evil in the sight of 1886.1
15:12 This *was* the word of the LORD **w** he spake 834
15:15 and his conspiracy **w** he made, behold, 834
15:18 he did *that* **w** *was* evil in the sight of 1886.1
15:24 he did *that* **w** *was* evil in the sight of 1886.1
15:28 he did *that* **w** *was* evil in the sight of 1886.1
15:34 he did *that* **w** *was* right in the sight of 1886.1
16: 2 did not *that* **w** *was* right in the sight of 1886.1
16: 7 the king of Israel, **w** rise up against me. 1886.1
16:14 **w** *was* before the LORD, from the forefront 834
16:19 Now the rest of the acts of Ahaz **w** he did, 834
17: 2 he did *that* **w** *was* evil in the sight of 1886.1
17: 7 **w** had brought them up out of the land 1886.1
17: 8 of the kings of Israel, **w** they had made. 834
17:13 according to all the law **w** I commanded 834
17:13 **w** I sent to you by my servants the 834
17:15 testimonies **w** he testified against them; 834
17:19 in the statutes of Israel **w** they made. 834
17:22 in all the sins of Jeroboam **w** he did; 834
17:25 lions among them, **w** slew *some* of them. NIH
17:26 The nations **w** thou hast removed, 834
17:29 *them* in the houses of the high places **w** 834
17:32 **w** sacrificed for them in the houses of NIH
17:34 commandment **w** the LORD commanded 834
17:37 the commandment, **w** he wrote for you, 834
18: 3 he did *that* **w** *was* right in the sight of 1886.1
18: 6 **w** the LORD commanded Moses. 834
18: 9 **w** *was* the seventh year of Hoshea son of 1931
18:14 *that* **w** thou puttest on me will I bear. 834
18:16 *from* the pillars **w** Hezekiah king of Judah 834
18:17 **w** *is* in the highway of the fuller's field. 834
18:18 **w** *was* over the household, and Shebna 834
18:21 *even* upon Egypt, on **w** if a man lean, 834
18:27 *hath* he not *sent me* to the men **w** sit 1886.1
18:37 **w** *was* over the household, and Shebna 834
19: 2 **w** *was* over the household, and Shebna 834
19: 4 will reprove the words **w** the LORD thy 834
19: 6 not afraid of the words **w** thou hast heard, 834
19: 6 *with* **w** the servants of the king of Assyria 834
19:12 them **w** my fathers have destroyed; 834
19:12 the children of Eden **w** *were* in Thelasar? 834
19:15 **w** dwellest *between* the cherubims, thou NIH
19:16 **w** hath sent him to reproach the living 834
19:20 *That* **w** thou hast prayed to me against 834
19:28 I will turn thee back by the way by **w** thou 834
19:29 year that **w** springeth of the same; 7823
20: 3 have done *that* **w** *is* good in thy sight. 1886.1
20:11 by **w** it had gone down in the dial of Ahaz. 834
20:17 *that* **w** thy fathers have laid up in store 834
20:18 **w** thou shalt beget, shall they take *away;* 834
20:19 Good *is* the word of the LORD **w** thou hast 834
21: 2 he did *that* **w** *was* evil in the sight of 1886.1
21: 3 For he built *up* again the high places **w** 834
21: 4 of **w** the LORD said, In Jerusalem will I 834
21: 7 of **w** the LORD said to David, 834
21: 7 **w** I have chosen out of all tribes of Israel, 834
21: 8 out of the land **w** I gave their fathers; 834
21:11 **w** *were* before him, and hath made Judah 834
21:15 Because they have done *that* **w** *was* evil 1886.1
21:16 in doing *that* **w** *was* evil in the sight of 1886.1
21:20 he did *that* **w** *was* evil in the sight of 1886.1
21:25 the rest of the acts of Amon **w** he did, 834
22: 2 he did *that* **w** *was* right in the sight of 1886.1
22: 4 that he may sum the silver **w** is brought 1886.1
22: 4 the keepers of the door have gathered 834
22: 5 let them give it to the doers of the work **w** 834
22:13 to do according unto all that **w** is written NIH
22:16 *even* all the words of the book **w** the king 834
22:18 king of Judah **w** sent you to inquire 1886.1
22:18 *As touching* the words **w** thou hast heard; 834
22:20 thine eyes shall not see all the evil **w** I will 834
23: 2 **w** *was* found in the house of the LORD. 1886.1
23: 8 **w** *were* on a man's left hand at the gate of 834
23:10 **w** *is* in the valley of the children of 834
23:11 **w** *was* in the suburbs, and burnt the 834
23:12 the kings of Judah had made, 834
23:12 altars **w** Manasseh had made in the two 834
23:13 **w** *were* on the right hand of the mount of 834
23:13 **w** Solomon the king of Israel had builded 834
23:15 high place **w** Jeroboam the son of Nebat, 834
23:16 according to the word of the LORD **w** 834
23:17 **w** came from Judah, and proclaimed these 834
23:19 the kings of Israel had made to provoke 834
23:24 **w** were written in the book that Hilkiah 1886.1
23:27 will cast off this city Jerusalem **w** I have 834
23:27 the house of **w** I said, My name shall be 834
23:32 he did *that* **w** *was* evil in the sight of 1886.1
23:37 he did *that* **w** *was* evil in the sight of 1886.1
24: 2 **w** he spake by his servants the prophets. 834
24: 4 the LORD would not pardon. NIH
24: 9 he did *that* **w** *was* evil in the sight of 1886.1
24:13 cut in pieces all the vessels of gold **w** 834
24:19 he did *that* **w** *was* evil in the sight of 1886.1
25: 4 two walls, **w** *is* by the king's garden: 834
25: 8 **w** *is* the nineteenth year of king 1931
25:16 bases **w** Solomon had made for the house 834

2Ki 25:19 **w** were found in the city, and the principal 834
25:19 **w** mustered the people of the land, 1886.1
1Ch 1:46 **w** smote Midian in the field of Moab, 1886.1
2: 3 **w** three were born unto him of the NIH
2:19 took unto him Ephrath, **w** bare him Hur. NIH
2:42 his firstborn, **w** *was* the father of Ziph; 1931
2:55 families of the scribes **w** dwelt at Jabez; NIH
3: 1 David, **w** were born unto him in Hebron; 834
4:10 God granted *him that* **w** he requested. 834
4:11 begat Mehir, **w** *was* the father of Eshton. 1931
4:18 the daughter of Pharaoh, **w** Mered took. 834
6:61 were left of the family of *that* tribe, 1886.1
6:65 these cities, **w** are called by *their* names. 834
9:22 All these **w** were chosen to be porters 1886.1
9:25 their brethren, **w** *were* in their villages, NIH
10:13 So Saul died for his transgression **w** he 834
10:13 he kept not, and also for asking *counsel* 834
11: 4 all Israel went *to* Jerusalem, **w** *is* Jebus; 1931
11: 5 the castle of Zion, **w** *is* the city of David. 1931
12:31 were expressed by name, to come and 834
12:32 **w** were men that had understanding of NIH
12:33 of war, fifty thousand, **w** could keep rank: NIH
13: 2 Levites **w** *are* in their cities *and* suburbs, NIH
13: 6 *is,* to Kirjath-jearim, **w** *belonged* to Judah, 834
14: 4 Now these *are* the names of *his* children **w** 834
15: 3 unto his place, **w** he had prepared for it. 834
16:15 the word **w** he commanded to a thousand NIH
16:16 *Even of the covenant* **w** he made with 834
16:40 law of the LORD, **w** he commanded Israel; 834
17:11 thy seed after thee, **w** shall be of thy sons; 834
19:13 let the LORD do *that* **w** is good in his 1886.1
19:18 seven thousand *men* **w** fought in chariots, NIH
20: 4 **at w** time Sibbechai the Hushathite slew 227
21:19 **w** he spake in the name of the LORD. 834
21:23 let my lord the king do *that* **w** is good in 1886.1
21:24 for I will not take *that* **w** is thine for 834
21:29 **w** Moses made in the wilderness, 834
22:13 judgments **w** the LORD charged Moses 834
23: 4 **w**, twenty and four thousand were to set 428
23: 5 the LORD with the instruments **w** I made, 834
23:29 for *that* **w** is baked in the pan, and for *that* NIH
23:29 for that **w** is fried, and for all *manner of* NIH
25: 2 **w** prophesied according to the order of 1886.1
26:22 **w** were over the treasures of the house of NIH
26:26 **W** Shelomith and his brethren *were* over 1931
26:26 of the dedicate *things,* **w** David the king, 834
27: 1 **w** came in and went out month by 1886.1
27:31 these **w** were the rulers of the substance **w** 834
29: 3 **w** I have given to the house of my God, NIH
29:17 **w** are present here, to offer willingly 1886.1
29:19 palace, *for* the **w** I have made provision. 834
2Ch 1: 3 **w** Moses the servant of the LORD had 834
1: 4 to the place **w** David had prepared for it: NIH
1: 6 **w** *was* at the tabernacle of the 834
1:14 he placed in the chariot cities, 3963.1
2: 5 house **w** I build *is* great: for great *is* our 834
2: 9 the house **w** I am about to build *shall be* 834
2:11 he sent to Solomon, Because the LORD NIH
2:14 to find out every device **w** shall be put to 834
2:15 and the wine, **w** my lord hath spoken of, 834
3: 5 he overlaid with fine gold, 1930.2
4: 3 of oxen, **w** did compass it round about: NIH
4:12 the chapiters **w** *were* on the top of the two NIH
4:12 chapiters **w** *were* on the top of the pillars; 834
4:13 cover the two pommels of the chapiters **w** 834
5: 2 LORD out of the city of David, **w** *is* Zion. 1931
5: 3 in the feast **w** *was in* the seventh month. 1931
5: 6 could not be told nor numbered for 834
5:10 two tables **w** Moses put *therein* at Horeb, 834
5:12 the Levites **w** *were* the singers, all of NIH
6: 4 hath with his hands fulfilled *that* **w** he 834
6: 9 son **w** shall come forth out of thy loins, 1886.1
6:14 keepest covenant, and *shewest* mercy NIH
6:15 Thou **w** hast kept with thy servant David 834
6:15 my father *that* **w** thou hast promised him; 834
6:16 with thy servant David my father *that* **w** 834
6:17 **w** thou hast spoken unto thy servant 834
6:18 how much less this house **w** I have built? 834
6:19 prayer **w** thy servant prayeth before thee: 834
6:20 to hearken unto the prayer **w** thy servant 834
6:21 **w** they shall make towards this place: 834
6:25 them again unto the land **w** thou gavest 834
6:27 **w** thou hast given unto thy people for an 834
6:31 long as they live in the land **w** thou gavest 834
6:32 **w** *is* not of thy people Israel, but is come 834
6:33 may know that this house **w** I have built is 834
6:34 they pray unto thee toward this city **w** thou 834
6:34 the house **w** I have built for thy name; 834
6:36 (for *there is* no man **w** sinneth not,) 834
6:38 **w** thou gavest unto their fathers, 834
6:38 and *toward* the city **w** thou hast chosen, 834
6:38 toward the house **w** I have built for the 834
6:39 forgive thy people **w** have sinned against 834
7: 6 David the king had made to praise 834
7: 7 the brasen altar **w** Solomon had made was 834
7:14 If my people, **w** are called by my name, 834
7:19 **w** I have set before you, and shall go and 834
7:20 roots out of my land **w** I have given them; 834
7:20 house, **w** I have sanctified for my name, 834
7:21 this house, **w** is high, shall be an 834
7:22 brought them forth out of the land of 834
8: 2 That the cities **w** Huram had restored to 834
8: 4 all the store cities, **w** he built in Hamath. 834
8: 7 and the Jebusites, **w** *were* not of Israel, 834
8:12 the LORD, **w** he had built before the porch, 834

2Ch	9: 2 there was nothing hid from Solomon **w** he	834
	9: 4 his ascent *by* **w** he went up *into* the house	834
	9: 5 *It was* a true report **w** I heard in mine own	834
	9: 7 **w** stand continually before thee,	1886.1
	9: 8 **w** delighted in thee to set thee on his	834
	9:10 **w** brought gold from Ophir, brought algum	834
	9:12 *that* **w** she had brought unto the king.	834
	9:14 Besides *that* **w** chapmen and merchants	NIH
	9:18 **w** were fastened to the throne, and stays	NIH
	10: 8 he forsook the counsel **w** the old men gave	834
	10: 9 **w** have spoken to me, saying,	834
	10:15 **w** he spake by the hand of Ahijah	834
	11: 1 fourscore thousand chosen *men,* **w** were	NIH
	11:10 **w** *are* in Judah and in Benjamin,	834
	11:15 devils, and for the calves **w** he had made.	834
	11:19 **W** bare him children; Jeush,	NIH
	11:20 **w** bare him Abijah, and Attai, and Ziza,	2050.1
	12: 4 he took the fenced cities **w** *pertained* to	834
	12: 9 he carried away also the shields of gold **w**	834
	12:10 Instead of **w** king Rehoboam made	1992.1
	12:13 the city **w** the LORD had chosen out of all	834
	13: 4 **w** *is* in mount Ephraim, and said, Hear me,	834
	13: 8 **w** Jeroboam made you for gods.	834
	13:10 and the priests, **w** minister unto the LORD,	834
	14: 2 Asa did *that* **w** was good and right in	1886.1
	15: 8 out of the cities **w** he had taken from	834
	15:11 of the spoil **w** they had brought,	NIH
	16:14 **w** he had made for himself in the city of	834
	16:14 laid him in the bed **w** was filled *with* sweet	834
	17: 2 of Ephraim, **w** Asa his father had taken.	834
	18:23 **W** way went the spirit of the LORD	335+2088
	20: 2 they *be* in Hazazon-tamar, *is* En-gedi.	1931
	20:11 **w** thou hast given us to inherit.	834
	20:22 mount Seir, **w** were come against Judah;	1886.1
	20:25 **w** they stript off for themselves,	2050.1
	20:32 doing *that* **w** was right in the sight of	1886.1
	21: 6 wrought *that* **w** was evil in the eyes of	1886.1
	21: 9 smote the Edomites **w** compassed him	1886.1
	21:13 father's house, *w* were better than thyself:	NIH
	22: 6 the wounds **w** were given him at Ramah,	834
	23: 9 king David's, **w** were in the house of God.	834
	23:19 that none *w* was unclean in any thing	NIH
	24: 2 Joash did *that* **w** was right in the sight	1886.1
	24:20 **w** stood above the people, and said unto	NIH
	24:22 **w** Jehoiada his father had done to him,	834
	25: 2 he did *that* **w** was right in the sight of	1886.1
	25: 9 *shall* we do for the hundred talents **w** I	834
	25:13 the soldiers of the army **w** Amaziah sent	834
	25:15 sent unto him a prophet, **w** said unto him,	NIH
	25:15 **w** could not deliver their own people out	834
	25:21 at Beth-shemesh, **w** *belongeth* to Judah.	834
	26: 4 he did *that* **w** *belonged* to the kings;	1886.1
	26:23 field of the burial **w** *belonged* to the kings;	834
	27: 2 he did *that* **w** was right in the sight of	1886.1
	28: 1 he did not *that* **w** was right in the sight	1886.1
	28: 6 in one day, *w* were all valiant men;	NIH
	28:11 ye have taken captive of your brethren:	834
	28:15 men **w** were expressed by name rose up,	NIH
	28:23 the gods of Damascus, **w** smote him:	1886.1
	29: 2 he did *that* **w** was right in the sight of	1886.1
	29: 6 done *that* **w** was evil in the eyes of	1886.1
	29:19 king Ahaz in his reign did cast away in	834
	29:32 **w** the congregation brought,	834
	30: 7 **w** trespassed against the LORD God of	834
	30: 8 sanctuary, **w** he hath sanctified for ever:	834
	30:16 *w* they received of the hand of the Levites.	NIH
	31: 6 the tithe of holy *things* **w** were	1886.1
	31:10 and that **w** is left *is* this great store.	NIH
	31:12 over **w** Cononiah the Levite *was* ruler,	1992.1
	31:19 **w** were in the fields of the suburbs of	NIH
	31:20 wrought *that* **w** was good and right and	1886.1
	32: 3 of the fountains **w** *were* without the city:	834
	32:19 *w* were the work of the hands of man.	NIH
	32:21 **w** cut off all the mighty *men* of valour,	NIH
	33: 2 did *that* **w** was evil in the sight of	1886.1
	33: 3 For he built again the high places **w**	834
	33: 7 idol **w** he had made, in the house of God,	834
	33: 7 God had said to David and to Solomon	834
	33: 7 **w** I have chosen before all the tribes of	834
	33: 8 land **w** I have appointed for your fathers;	834
	33:11 **w** took Manasseh among the thorns,	834
	33:22 he did *that* **w** was evil in the sight of	1886.1
	33:22 images **w** Manasseh his father had made,	834
	34: 2 he did *that* **w** was right in the sight of	1886.1
	34: 9 **w** the Levites that kept the doors had	834
	34:11 to floor the houses **w** the kings of Judah	834
	34:24 **w** they have read before the king of Judah:	834
	34:26 *concerning* the words **w** thou hast heard;	834
	34:31 to perform the words of the covenant **w**	1886.1
	35: 3 all Israel, **w** were holy unto the LORD,	1886.1
	35: 3 Put the holy ark in the house **w** Solomon	834
	35:26 to that **w** was written in the law	1886.1
	36: 5 he did *that* **w** was evil in the sight of	1886.1
	36: 8 his abominations **w** he did, and that which	834
	36: 8 and that **w** was found in him, behold,	NIH
	36: 9 he did *that* **w** was evil in the sight of	1886.1
	36:12 he did *that* **w** was evil in the sight of	1886.1
	36:14 polluted the house of the LORD **w** he had	834
	36:23 him a house in Jerusalem, **w** *is* in Judah.	834
Ezr	1: 2 him a house at Jerusalem, **w** *is* in Judah.	834
	1: 3 **w** *is* in Judah, and build the house of	834
	1: 3 Israel, (he *is* the God,) **w** *is* in Jerusalem.	834
	1: 5 to go up to build the house of the LORD **w**	834
	1: 7 Nebuchadnezzar had brought forth out	834
	2: 1 *of* those **w** had been carried away,	1886.1

Ezr	2: 2 **W** came with Zerubbabel: Jeshua,	834
	2:59 these *were* they **w** went up from	1886.1
	2:61 **w** took a wife of the daughters of Barzillai	834
	2:68 the house of the LORD **w** *is* at Jerusalem,	834
	4: 2 king of Assur, **w** brought us up hither.	1886.1
	4:12 the Jews **w** came up from thee to us are	1768
	4:15 for **w** *cause* was this city destroyed.	1836
	4:18 The letter **w** ye sent unto us *hath* been	1768
	4:20 have ruled over all *countries* beyond	NIH
	4:24 the work of the house of the God **w**	1768
	5: 2 began to build the house of God **w** *is* at	1768
	5: 6 **w** *were* on *this* side the river, sent unto	1768
	5: 8 **w** *is* builded *with* great stones,	2050.3
	5:11 **w** a great king of Israel builded and	1958.2
	5:14 Nebuchadnezzar took out of the temple	1768
	5:16 laid the foundation of the house of God **w**	1768
	5:17 **w** *is* there at Babylon, whether it be so,	1768
	6: 5 Nebuchadnezzar took forth out of	1768
	6: 5 forth out of the temple **w** *is* at Jerusalem,	1768
	6: 5 brought *again* unto the temple **w** *is* at	1768
	6: 6 **w** *are* beyond the river, be ye far from	1768
	6: 9 *that* **w** *they* have need of, both young	4101
	6: 9 of the priests **w** *are* at Jerusalem,	1768
	6:12 to destroy this house of God **w** *is* at	1768
	6:13 according to **that w** Darius the king had	1768
	6:15 **w** *was* in the sixth year of the reign of	1768
	6:18 for the service of God, **w** *is* at Jerusalem;	1768
	6:21 **w** were come again out of captivity,	1886.1
	7: 6 **w** the LORD God of Israel had given:	834
	7: 8 **w** *was* in the seventh year of the king.	1931
	7:13 **w** *are* minded of their own freewill to go	NIH
	7:14 according to the law of thy God **w** *is* in	1768
	7:15 the king and his counsellers have freely	1768
	7:16 the house of their God **w** *is* in Jerusalem:	1768
	7:17 the house of your God **w** *is* in Jerusalem.	1768
	7:20 **w** thou shalt have occasion to bestow,	1768
	7:21 make a decree to all the treasurers **w** *are*	1768
	7:25 **w** may judge all the people that *are*	1768
	7:27 hath put *such a thing* as this in the	834
	7:27 to beautify the house of the LORD **w** *is* in	834
	8:25 the king, and his counsellers,	NIH
	8:35 **w** were come out of the captivity,	1886.1
	9:11 **W** thou hast commanded by thy servants	834
	9:11 The land, *unto* **w** ye go to possess it,	834
	9:11 **w** have filled it from one end to another	834
	10:14 let all *them* **w** have taken strange wives in	834
Ne	1: 2 **w** were left of the captivity,	834
	1: 6 **w** I pray before thee now, day and night,	834
	1: 6 of Israel, **w** we have sinned against thee:	834
	1: 7 **w** thou commandedst thy servant Moses.	834
	2: 8 of the palace **w** *appertained* to the house,	834
	2:13 **w** were broken down, and the gates	834
	2:18 I told them of the hand of my God **w** was	834
	3:25 the tower **w** lieth out from the king's	1886.1
	4: 2 of the heaps of the rubbish **w** are burnt?	1992
	4: 3 he said, Even *that* **w** they build, if a fox go	834
	4:12 when the Jews **w** dwelt by them came,	1886.1
	4:14 **w** *is* great and terrible, and fight for your	NIH
	4:17 They **w** builded on the wall, and they	1886.1
	4:23 nor the men of the guard **w** followed me,	834
	5: 8 Jews, **w** were sold unto the heathen;	1886.1
	5:18 Now *that* **w** was prepared *for me* daily *was*	834
	6: 6 for **w** *cause* thou buildest the wall	3651+5921
	7: 5 of them **w** came up at the first,	1886.1
	7:61 these *were* they **w** went up *also* from	1886.1
	7:63 **w** took *one* of the daughters of Barzillai	834
	7:72 the rest of the people gave *was* twenty	834
	8: 1 **w** the LORD had commanded to Israel.	834
	8: 4 wood, **w** they had made for the purpose;	834
	8: 9 **w** *is* the Tirshatha, and Ezra the priest	1931
	8:14 they found written in the law **w** the LORD	834
	9: 5 **w** *is* exalted above all blessing and	2050.1
	9:15 the land **w** thou hadst sworn to give them.	834
	9:23 *concerning* **w** thou hadst promised to their	834
	9:26 slew thy prophets **w** testified against them	834
	9:29 (**w** if a man do, he shall live in them;)	834
	9:35 and fat land **w** thou gavest before them,	834
	10:29 was given by Moses the servant of God,	834
	12: 8 **w** *was* over the thanksgiving, he and	NIH
	12:37 fountain gate, **w** *was* over against them,	2050.1
	13: 5 **w** was commanded *to be given* to	NIH
	13:15 **w** they brought *into* Jerusalem on	2050.1
	13:16 brought fish, and all *manner of* ware,	NIH
Est	1: 1 (this *is* Ahasuerus **w** reigned, from India	1886.1
	1: 2 his kingdom, **w** *was* in Shushan the palace,	834
	1: 9 royal house **w** *belonged* to king Ahasuerus.	834
	1:13 the king said to the wise *men,* **w** knew	NIH
	1:14 **w** saw the king's face, *and* which sat	NIH
	1:14 *and* **w** sat the first in the kingdom;)	1886.1
	1:18 have heard of the deed of the queen.	834
	1:20 when the king's decree **w** he shall make	834
	2: 4 let the maiden **w** pleaseth the king be	834
	2: 6 **w** had been carried away with Jeconiah	834
	2: 9 **w** *were* meet to be given her,	834
	2:14 chamberlain, **w** kept the concubines:	834
	2:16 **w** *is* the month Tebeth, in the seventh	1931
	2:21 and Teresh, of those **w** kept the door,	NIH
	3: 3 **w** *were* in the king's gate, said unto	834
	3:13 **w** *is* the month Adar, and *to take* the spoil	1931
	4: 6 of the city, **w** *was* before the king's gate.	834
	4:16 the king, **w** *is* not according to the law:	834
	6: 8 Let the royal apparel be brought **w** the	834
	6: 8 the crown royal **w** is set upon his head:	834
	7: 9 **w** Haman had made for Mordecai,	834
	8: 2 **w** he had taken from Haman, and gave it	834

Est	8: 5 **w** he wrote to destroy the Jews which *are*	834
	8: 5 which he wrote to destroy the Jews **w** are	834
	8: 8 for the writing **w** *is* written in the king's	834
	8: 9 rulers of the provinces **w** *are* from India	834
	8:11 Where*in* the king granted the Jews **w** were	834
	8:12 the twelfth month, **w** *is* the month Adar.	1931
	9:13 be granted to the Jews **w** *are* in Shushan	834
	9:22 the month **w** was turned unto them from	834
	9:25 **w** he devised against the Jews, should	834
	9:26 *of that* **w** they had seen concerning this	4100
	9:26 this *matter,* and **w** had come unto them,	4100
Job	3: 3 the night *in* **w** it was said, There is a man	NIH
	3:14 **w** built desolate places for themselves;	1886.1
	3:16 not been; as infants **w** never saw light.	NIH
	3:21 **W** long for death, but it *cometh* not;	1886.1
	3:22 **W** rejoice exceedingly, *and are* glad,	1886.1
	3:25 For the thing **w** I greatly feared is come	NIH
	3:25 *that* **w** I was afraid of is come unto me.	834
	4:14 **w** made all my bones to shake.	2050.1
	4:19 dust, **w** are crushed before the moth?	3963.1
	4:21 Doth not their excellency **w** is in them go	NIH
	5: 1 and to **w** of the saints wilt thou turn?	4310
	5: 9 **W** doeth great *things* and unsearchable;	NIH
	5:11 that those **w** mourn may be exalted *to*	NIH
	6: 6 Can *that* **w** is unsavoury be eaten	8602
	6:16 **W** are blackish by reason of the ice,	1886.1
	6:26 of one that is desperate, **w** are as wind?	NIH
	9: 5 **W** removeth the mountains,	1886.1
	9: 5 **w** overturneth them in his anger.	834
	9: 6 **W** shaketh the earth out of her place,	1886.1
	9: 7 **W** commandeth the sun, and it riseth	1886.1
	9: 8 **W** alone spreadeth out the heavens,	NIH
	9: 9 **W** maketh Arcturus, Orion, and Pleiades,	NIH
	9:10 **W** doeth great *things* past finding out; yea,	NIH
	11: 6 that *they are* double to *that* **w** is.	8454
	14:19 washest away the **things w** grow out	5599
	15: 9 understandest thou, **w** *is* not in us?	2050.1
	15:14 *he is* born of a woman, that he should	NIH
	15:16 *is* man, **w** drinketh iniquity like water?	NIH
	15:17 and that **w** I have seen I will declare;	NIH
	15:18 **W** wise *men* have told from their fathers,	834
	15:28 *and* in houses **w** no man	3807.1+4123.1
	15:28 are ready to become heaps.	834
	16: 8 *w* is a witness *against* me: and my	NIH
	20: 7 They **w** have seen him shall say, Where *is*	NIH
	20: 9 The eye also **w** saw him shall *see him* no	NIH
	20:11 **w** shall lie down with him in the dust.	2050.1
	20:18 That **w** he **laboured for** shall he restore,	3022
	20:19 hath violently taken away a house **w**	2050.1
	20:20 he shall not save of that **w** he desired.	NIH
	21:27 the devices **w** ye wrongfully imagine	NIH
	22:15 Hast thou marked the old way **w** wicked	834
	22:16 **W** were cut down out of time,	834
	22:17 **W** said unto God, Depart from us:	1886.1
	23: 5 know the words **w** he would answer	NIH
	24:11 **W** make oil within their walls,	NIH
	24:16 **w** they had marked for themselves in	NIH
	24:19 *so doth* the grave *those* **w** have sinned.	NIH
	25: 6 and the son of man, **w** *is* a worm?	NIH
	27:11 *that* **w** *is* with the Almighty will I not	834
	27:13 **w** they shall receive of the Almighty.	NIH
	28: 7 *There is* a path **w** no fowl knoweth,	2050.2
	28: 7 and the vulture's eye hath not seen:	2050.2
	29:16 the cause **w** I knew not I searched out.	NIH
	32:19 my belly *is* as wine **w** hath no vent;	NIH
	33:27 perverted *that* **w** was right, and it profited	NIH
	34: 8 **W** goeth in company with the workers	2050.1
	34:32 *That* **w** I see not teach thou me: if I have	NIH
	35: 5 behold the clouds **w** are higher than thou.	NIH
	36:16 that **w** should **be set on** thy table	5183
	36:24 thou magnify his work, **w** men behold.	834
	36:28 **W** the clouds do drop *and* distil upon man	834
	37: 5 doeth he, **w** we cannot comprehend.	2050.1
	37:16 the wondrous works of *him* **w** is perfect in	NIH
	37:18 **w** is strong, *and* as a molten looking glass?	NIH
	37:21 now *men* see not the bright light **w** *is* in	1931
	38:23 **W** I have reserved against the time of	834
	38:24 **w** scattereth the east wind upon the earth?	NIH
	39:14 **W** leaveth her eggs in the earth,	3588
	40:15 now behemoth, **w** I made with thee;	834
	41: 1 tongue with a cord **w** thou lettest down?	NIH
	42: 3 too wonderful for me, **w** I knew not.	2050.1
	42: 8 ye have not spoken of me *the thing* **w**	NIH
Ps	1: 4 like the chaff **w** the wind driveth away.	834
	3: 2 Many there *be* **w** say of my soul, *There is*	NIH
	5: 7 T of David, **w** he sang unto the LORD,	NIH
	7:10 *is* of God, **w** saveth the upright in heart.	NIH
	7:15 and is fallen into the ditch **w** he made.	NIH
	8: 3 and the stars, **w** thou hast ordained;	834
	9:11 *praises* to the LORD, **w** dwelleth in Zion:	NIH
	9:13 consider my trouble **w** *I suffer* of them	NIH
	9:15 in the net **w** they hid is their own foot	2098
	9:16 The LORD is known *by* the judgment **w**	NIH
	17: 7 thou that savest by thy right hand them **w**	NIH
	17:13 thy soul from the wicked, **w** *is* thy sword:	NIH
	17:14 From men **w** *are* thy hand, O LORD,	NIH
	17:14 **w** *have* their portion in *this* life,	NIH
	18:17 enemy, and from them **w** hated me:	NIH
	19: 5 **W** is as a bridegroom coming out of his	1931
	21:11 **w** they are not able *to perform.*	NIH
	25: 3 let them be ashamed **w** transgress	1886.1
	28: 3 **w** speak peace to their neighbours,	NIH
	31:18 **w** speak grievous things proudly and	1886.1
	31:19 **w** thou hast laid up for them that fear	834
	31:19 *w* thou hast wrought for them that trust	NIH

Ps 32: 8 teach thee in the way **w** thou shalt go: 2098
32: 9 *or* as the mule, **w** *have* no understanding: NIH
35: 7 **w** without cause they have digged for my NIH
35:10 **w** deliverest the poor from him that is too NIH
35:27 **w** hath pleasure in the prosperity of his 1886.1
40: 5 thy wonderful works **w** thou hast done, NIH
40: 5 and thy thoughts **w** *are* to us-ward: NIH
41: 9 whom I trusted, **w** did eat *of* my bread, 2050.2
44:10 and they **w** hate us spoil for themselves. NIH
45: 1 I speak of the things **w** I have made NIH
51: 8 *that* the bones **w** thou hast broken may NIH
58: 5 **W** will not hearken to the voice of 834
58: 7 Let them melt away as waters **w** run NIH
58: 8 As a snail **w** melteth, let *every one* of NIH
59:12 and for cursing and lying **w** they speak. NIH
60:10 *Wilt* not thou, O God, **w** hadst cast us off? NIH
60:10 God, **w** didst not go out with our armies? NIH
61: 7 and truth, **w** may preserve him. NIH
65: 6 **W** by his strength setteth fast NIH
65: 7 **W** stilleth the noise of the seas, the noise NIH
65: 9 it *with* the river of God, **w** is full *of* water: NIH
66: 9 **W** holdeth our soul in life, 1886.1
66:14 **W** my lips have uttered, and my mouth 834
66:20 God, **w** hath not turned away my prayer, 834
68: 6 he bringeth out those **w** are bound with NIH
68:16 *this is* the hill *w* God desireth to dwell in; NIH
68:28 O God, **that** *w* thou hast wrought for us. 2098
68:33 the heavens of heavens, **w** were of old; NIH
69: 4 then I restored *that* **w** I took not away. 834
69:22 *that* **w** should have been for *their* welfare, 834
71:20 *Thou,* **w** hast shewed me great and 834
71:23 and my soul, **w** thou hast redeemed. 834
74: 2 **w** thou hast purchased of old; NIH
74: 2 thine inheritance, **w** thou hast redeemed; NIH
78: 3 **W** we have heard and known, 834
78: 5 in Israel, **w** he commanded our fathers, 834
78: 6 *even* the children **w** should be born; NIH
78:45 *of flies* among them, **w** devoured them; 2050.1
78:45 and frogs, **w** destroyed them. 2050.1
78:54 **w** his right hand had purchased. NIH
78:60 Shiloh, the tent **w** he placed among men; NIH
78:68 tribe of Judah, the mount Zion **w** he loved. 834
78:69 the earth **w** he hath established for ever. 1886.3
79:10 of the blood of thy servants **w** is shed. 1886.1
80:12 that all they **w** pass by the way do pluck NIH
80:15 vineyard **w** thy right hand hath planted, 834
81:10 **w** brought thee out of the land of Egypt: 1886.1
83:10 **W** perished at En-dor: they became *as* NIH
85:12 Yea, the LORD shall give *that* **w** is good; NIH
86:17 that they **w** hate me may see *it,* and NIH
89:49 **w** thou swarest unto David in thy truth? NIH
90: 5 in the morning *they are* like grass **w** NIH
91: 9 **w** is my refuge, *even* the most High, NIH
94:20 *with* thee, **w** frameth mischief by a law? NIH
102:18 the people **w** *shall be* created shall praise NIH
104: 8 the place **w** thou hast founded for them. 2088
104:10 into the valleys, **w** run among the hills. NIH
104:12 habitation, **w** sing among the branches. NIH
104:15 and bread **w** strengtheneth man's heart. NIH
104:16 the cedars of Lebanon, **w** he hath planted; 834
105: 8 the word **w** he commanded to a thousand NIH
105: 9 **W** *covenant* he made with Abraham, 834
106:21 **w** had done great *things* in Egypt; NIH
106:36 their idols: **w** were a snare unto them. NIH
107:25 wind, **w** lifteth up the waves thereof. NIH
107:37 **w** may yield fruits of increase. NIH
109:19 Let it be unto him as the garment **w** NIH
114: 8 **W** turned the rock *into* a standing water 1886.1
115:15 You *are* blessed of the LORD **w** made NIH
118:20 into **w** the righteous shall enter. 2050.2
118:22 The stone **w** the builders refused is NIH
118:24 This *is* the day **w** the LORD hath made; NIH
118:27 *is* the LORD, **w** hath shewed us light: 2050.1
119:21 **w** do err from thy commandments. 1886.1
119:39 Turn away my reproach **w** I fear: for thy 834
119:47 in thy commandments, **w** I have loved. 834
119:48 unto thy commandments, **w** I have loved; 834
119:49 upon **w** thou hast caused me to hope. 834
119:85 pits for me, **w** *are* not after thy law. NIH
119:165 Great peace have they **w** love thy law: NIH
121: 2 from the LORD, **w** made heaven and earth. NIH
125: 1 **w** cannot be removed, *but* abideth for NIH
129: 6 **w** withereth afore it groweth up: 7945
129: 8 Neither do they **w** go by say, 1886.1
134: 1 **w** by night stand in the house of 1886.1
135:21 out of Zion, **w** dwelleth *at* Jerusalem. NIH
136:13 To him **w** divided the Red sea into parts: NIH
136:16 To him **w** led his people through NIH
136:17 To him **w** smote great kings: for his NIH
138: 8 The LORD will perfect *that* **w** concerneth NIH
139:16 *w* in continuance were fashioned, when NIH
140: 2 **W** imagine mischiefs in *their* heart; 834
141: 5 excellent oil, **w** shall not break my head: NIH
141: 9 Keep me from the snare **w** they have laid NIH
144: 1 **w** teacheth my hands to war, 1886.1
146: 6 **W** made heaven, and earth, the sea, and NIH
146: 6 therein is: **w** keepeth truth for ever: 1886.1
146: 7 **W** executeth judgment for the oppressed: NIH
146: 7 **w** giveth food to the hungry. The LORD NIH
147: 9 his food, *and* to the young ravens **w** cry. 834
148: 6 he hath made a decree **w** shall not pass. 2050.1

Pr 1:19 **w** taketh away the life of the owners NIH
2:16 from the stranger **w** flattereth with her NIH
2:17 **W** forsaketh the guide of her youth, 1886.1
6: 7 **W** having no guide, overseer, or ruler, 834

Pr 7: 5 from the stranger **w** flattereth with her NIH
9: 5 and drink of the wine **w** I have mingled. NIH
11:22 *so is* a fair woman **w** is without discretion. NIH
12:27 slothful *man* roasteth not that **w** he took NIH
14:12 is a way **w** seemeth right unto a man, NIH
14:33 *that* **w** is in the midst of fools is made NIH
19:17 he **w** he hath given will he pay him again. NIH
20:25 to the man *who* devoureth *that* **w** *is* holy, NIH
22:28 ancient landmark, **w** thy fathers have set. 834
23: 5 Wilt thou set thine eyes upon that **w** is 2050.1
23: 8 The morsel **w** thou hast eaten shalt thou NIH
24:13 the honeycomb, **w** *is* sweet to thy taste: NIH
25: 1 **w** the men of Hezekiah king of Judah 834
27:16 of his right hand, **w** bewrayeth *itself.* NIH
28: 3 *like* a sweeping rain **w** leaveth no food. 2050.1
30:18 be three *things* **w** are too wonderful NIH
30:18 for me, yea, four **w** I know not: NIH
30:21 disquieted, and for four **w** it cannot bear: NIH
30:24 There be four *things* **w** are little upon NIH
30:29 There be three *things* **w** go well, yea, NIH
30:30 A lion **w** *is* strongest among beasts, NIH
31: 3 nor thy ways to *that* **w** destroyeth kings. NIH

Ecc 1: 3 What profit hath a man of all his labour **w** 7945
1: 9 thing that hath been, *it is* that **w** shall be; 7945
1: 9 is done *is* that which shall be done: 7945
1: 9 which is done *is* that shall be done: 7945
1:10 been already of old time, **w** was before us. 834
1:15 **w** *is* crooked cannot be made straight: NIH
1:15 **that** *w* is wanting cannot be numbered. 2642
2: 3 **w** they should do under the heaven all NIH
2:12 *even* that **w** hath been already done. 1930.2
2:16 seeing *that* **w** now is, *in* the days to come 7945
2:18 I hated all my labour **w** I *had* taken under 7945
2:20 of all the labour **w** I took under the sun. 7945
3: 2 and a time to pluck up *that* **w** is planted; NIH
3:10 **w** God hath given to the sons of men to be 834
3:15 That **w** hath been, *is* now; and *that* which 7945
3:15 *that* **w** is to be hath already been; and God 834
3:15 and God requireth that **w** is past. NIH
3:19 For that **w** befalleth the sons of men NIH
4: 2 Wherefore I praised the dead **w** are 7945
4: 2 dead more than the living **w** are yet alive. 834
4: 3 *is he* than both they, **w** hath not yet been, 834
4:15 I considered all the living **w** walk under 1886.1
5: 4 in fools: pay that **w** thou hast vowed. 834
5:13 There is a sore evil **w** I have seen under NIH
5:15 **w** he may carry away in his hand. 7945
5:18 Behold *that* **w** I have seen: *it is* good and 834
5:18 all the days of his life, **w** God giveth him: 834
6: 1 is an evil **w** I have seen under the sun, 834
6:10 That **w** hath been is named already, 7945
6:12 the days of his vain life **w** he spendeth 2050.1
7:13 *that* straight, **w** he hath made crooked? 834
7:19 than ten mighty *men* **w** are in the city. 834
7:24 That **w** is far off, and exceeding deep, 7945
7:28 **W** yet my soul seeketh, but I find not: 834
8: 7 For he knoweth not that **w** shall be: for 7945
8:12 them that fear God, **w** fear before him: 834
8:13 he prolong *his* days, **w** *are* as a shadow; NIH
8:14 There is a vanity **w** is done upon the earth; 834
8:15 his life, **w** God giveth him under the sun. 834
9: 9 **w** he hath given thee under the sun, 834
9: 9 in thy labour **w** thou takest under the sun. 834
10: 5 is an evil **w** I have seen under the sun, NIH
10: 5 as an error **w** proceedeth from the ruler: NIH
10:20 **that** **w** hath wings shall tell the matter. 1167
12: 5 Also *when* they shall be afraid of *that* **w** is NIH
12:10 **w** was written *was* upright, *even* words NIH
12:11 **w** are given from one shepherd. NIH

SS 1: 1 The song of songs, **w** *is* Solomon's. 834
3: 7 Behold his bed, **w** *is* Solomon's; 7945
4: 2 shorn, **w** came up from the washing; 7945
4: 5 *that* are twins, **w** feed among the lilies. 1886.1
4: 9 Thy teeth *are* as a flock of sheep **w** go up 7945
7: 2 *like* a round goblet, **w** wanteth not liquor: NIH
7: 4 thy nose *is* as the tower of Lebanon **w** NIH
7:13 and old, **w** I have laid up for thee, NIH
8: 6 of fire, **w** *hath* a most vehement flame. NIH
8:12 My vineyard, **w** *is* mine, *is* before me: 7945

Isa 1: 1 the saw concerning Judah and Jerusalem 834
1:29 For they shall be ashamed of the oaks **w** ye 834
2: 8 *that* **w** their own fingers have made: 834
2:20 **w** they made *each one* for himself to 834
3:12 they **w** lead thee cause *thee* to err, NIH
5:23 **W** justify the wicked for reward, NIH
6: 6 **w** he had taken with the tongs from off NIH
8:18 of hosts, **w** dwelleth in mount Zion. 1886.1
10: 1 that write grievousness *that* **w** have NIH
10: 3 in the desolation **w** shall come from far? NIH
11:10 **w** shall stand for an ensign of the people; 834
11:11 **w** shall be left from Assyria, 834
11:16 of his people, **w** shall be left from Assyria; 834
13: 1 **w** Isaiah the son of Amoz did see. NIH
13:17 against them, **w** shall not regard silver; 834
14:12 the ground, **w** didst weaken the nations! NIH
15: 7 have gotten, and that **w** they have laid up, NIH
17: 2 **w** shall lie down, and none shall make NIH
17: 8 neither shall respect *that* **w** his fingers 834
17: 9 **w** they left because of the children of 834
17:12 **w** make a noise like the noise of the seas; NIH
18: 1 **w** is beyond the rivers of Ethiopia: 834
19:15 **w** the head or tail, branch or rush, may do. NIH
19:16 of the LORD of hosts, **w** he shaketh over it. 834
19:17 of hosts, **w** he hath determined against it. 834
21:10 that **w** I have heard of the LORD of hosts, 834

Isa 22: 3 are bound together, **w** have fled from far. NIH
22:15 Shebna, **w** *is* over the house, *and say,* 834
26: 2 the righteous nation **w** keepeth the truth NIH
27:13 shall come **w** were ready to perish in 1886.1
28: 1 **w** *are* on the head of the fat valleys of 834
28: 2 **w** as a tempest of hail *and* a destroying NIH
28: 4 **w** *is* on the head of the fat valley, shall be 834
28: 4 **w** when he that looketh upon it seeth, 834
28:14 that rule this people **w** *is* in Jerusalem. 834
28:29 **w** is wonderful in counsel, *and* excellent NIH
29:11 **w** *men* deliver to one that is learned, 834
30:10 **W** say to the seers, See not; and to 834
30:24 **w** hath been winnowed with the shovel 834
30:31 be beaten down, **w** smote with a rod. 834
30:32 **w** the LORD shall lay upon him, *it* shall be 834
31: 7 **w** your own hands have made unto you 834
36: 3 **w** *was* over the house, and Shebna 834
37: 4 will reprove the words **w** the LORD thy 834
37:12 them **w** my fathers have destroyed, 834
37:12 the children of Eden **w** *were* in Telassar? 834
37:17 **w** hath sent to reproach the living God. 834
37:22 This *is* the word **w** the LORD hath spoken 834
37:29 I will turn thee back by the way by **w** thou 834
37:30 year *that* **w** springeth of the same: 7823
38: 3 have done *that* **w** is good in thy sight. 1886.1
38: 8 **w** is gone down in the sun dial of Ahaz, 834
38: 8 degrees, by **w** degrees it was gone down. 834
39: 6 *that* **w** thy fathers have laid up in store 834
39: 7 **w** thou shalt beget, shall they take away; 834
39: 8 Good *is* the word of the LORD **w** thou hast 1886.1
42: 5 the earth, and **that** **w** **cometh out** of it; 6631
43:16 **w** maketh a way in the sea, and a path 1886.1
43:17 **W** bringeth forth the chariot and horse, 1886.1
44: 2 thee from the womb, **w** will help thee; NIH
44:14 **w** he strengtheneth for himself among 2050.1
45: 3 the LORD, **w** call *thee* by thy name, 1886.1
46: 3 **w** are borne *by me* from the belly, 1886.1
46: 3 the belly, **w** are carried from the womb: 1886.1
47:11 thee suddenly, **w** thou shalt not know. NIH
48: 1 **w** are called by the name of Israel, 1886.1
48: 1 **w** swear by the name of the LORD, 1886.1
48:14 **w** among them hath declared these 4310
48:17 I *am* the LORD thy God **w** teacheth thee to NIH
48:17 **w** leadeth thee by the way *that* thou NIH
49:20 The children **w** thou shalt have, after thou NIH
50: 1 **w** of my creditors *is it* to whom I have 4310
51:10 *Art* thou not it **w** hath dried the sea, 1886.1
51:12 the son of man **w** shall be made *as* grass; NIH
51:17 **w** hast drunk at the hand of the LORD 834
51:23 **w** have said to thy soul, Bow down, that 834
52:15 *that* **w** had not been told them shall they 834
52:15 *that* **w** they had not heard shall they NIH
55: 2 Wherefore do ye spend money for *that* **w** NIH
55: 2 your labour for *that* **w** satisfieth not? NIH
55: 2 eat ye *that* **w** is good, and let your soul NIH
55:11 it shall accomplish that **w** I please, 834
56: 8 The Lord GOD **w** gathereth the outcasts of NIH
56:11 *they are* greedy dogs **w** can never have NIH
57:16 before me, and the souls **w** I have made. NIH
59: 5 **w** is crushed breaketh out *into* a viper. NIH
59:21 and my words **w** I have put in thy mouth, 834
61: 9 that they *are* the seed **w** the LORD hath NIH
62: 2 **w** the mouth of the LORD shall name. 834
62: 6 **w** shall never hold their peace day nor NIH
62: 8 thy wine, for the **w** thou hast laboured: 834
63: 7 **w** he hath bestowed on them according to 834
64: 3 thou didst terrible things **w** we looked NIH
65: 2 **w** walketh *in* a way *that was* not good, 1886.1
65: 4 **W** remain among the graves, and lodge 1886.1
65: 4 **w** eat swine's flesh, and broth of 1886.1
65: 5 **W** say, Stand by thyself, come not near 1886.1
65: 7 **w** have burnt incense upon the mountains, 834
65:18 and rejoice for ever *in that* **w** I create: 834
66: 4 and chose *that* in **w** I delighted not. 834
66:22 and the new earth, **w** I will make, 834

Jer 2:11 changed *their* gods, **w** *are* yet no gods? 1992
2:11 their glory for *that* **w** doth not profit. NIH
3: 6 Hast thou seen *that* **w** backsliding Israel 834
3:15 **w** shall feed you with knowledge and NIH
5:17 **w** thy sons and thy daughters should eat: NIH
5:21 **w** have eyes, and see not; which have 1992.1
5:21 and see not; **w** have ears, and hear not: 1992.1
5:22 **w** have placed the sand *for* the bound of 834
7:10 house, **w** is called by my name, and say, 834
7:11 Is this house, **w** is called by my name, 834
7:12 go ye now unto my place **w** *was* in Shiloh, 834
7:14 **w** is called by my name, wherein ye trust, 834
7:14 unto the place **w** I gave to you and to your 834
7:30 in the house **w** is called by my name, 834
7:31 **w** *is* in the valley of the son of Hinnom, 834
7:31 **w** I commanded *them* not, neither came it 834
8: 3 **w** remain in all the places whither I have 834
8:17 **w** *will* not *be* charmed, and they shall bite 834
9:13 Because they have forsaken my law **w** I set 834
9:14 after Baalim, **w** their fathers taught them: 834
9:24 that I *am* the LORD **w** exercise NIH
9:25 that I will punish *all them* **w** are NIH
10: 1 Hear ye the word **w** the LORD speaketh 834
11: 4 **W** I commanded your fathers in the day 834
11: 4 them, according to all **w** I command you: 834
11: 5 *That* I may perform the oath **w** I have sworn 834
11: 8 covenant, **w** I commanded *them* to do; 834
11:10 **w** refused to hear my words; 834
11:10 my covenant **w** I made with their fathers. 834
11:11 **w** they shall not be able to escape; 834

Jer	11:17 **w** they have done against themselves to	834
	12:14 that touch the inheritance **w** I have caused	834
	13: 4 **w** is upon thy loins, and arise, go to	834
	13: 6 **w** I commanded thee to hide there.	834
	13:10 evil people, **w** refuse to hear my words,	834
	13:10 walk in the imagination of their heart,	1886.1
	13:10 be as this girdle, **w** is good for nothing.	834
	15: 4 of Judah, for *that* **w** he did in Jerusalem.	834
	15:14 enemies into a land *w* thou knowest not:	NIH
	15:14 in mine anger, **w** shall burn upon you.	NIH
	15:18 wound incurable, *w* refuseth to be healed?	NIH
	17: 4 enemies in the land **w** thou knowest not:	834
	17: 4 a fire in mine anger, *w* shall burn for ever.	NIH
	17:16 that **w** came out of my lips was right	4161
	17:19 by the **w** they go out, and in all the gates	834
	18: 1 The word **w** came to Jeremiah from	834
	18:14 Will *a man* leave the snow of Lebanon **w**	NIH
	19: 2 **w** is by the entry of the east gate,	834
	19: 3 the **w** whosoever heareth, his ears shall	834
	19: 5 **w** I commanded not, nor spake *it*, neither	834
	20: 2 **w** *was* by the house of the LORD.	834
	20: 5 **w** shall spoil them, and take them,	2050.1
	20:16 let that man be as the cities **w** the LORD	834
	21: 1 The word **w** came unto Jeremiah from	834
	21: 4 **w** besiege you without the walls,	1886.1
	21:13 **w** say, Who shall come down against	1886.1
	22: 6 wilderness *and* cities **w** are not inhabited.	834
	22:11 **w** reigned instead of Josiah his father,	1886.1
	22:11 his father, **w** went forth out of this place,	834
	22:28 and are cast into a land **w** they know not?	834
	23: 4 I will set up shepherds over them **w** shall	NIH
	23: 7 **w** brought up the children of Israel out of	834
	23: 8 **w** brought up and which led the seed of	834
	23: 8 **w** led the seed of the house of Israel out of	834
	23:27 **w** think to cause my people to forget	1886.1
	23:27 **w** they tell every man to his neighbour,	834
	23:40 perpetual shame, **w** shall not be forgotten.	834
	24: 2 **w** could not be eaten, they were so bad.	834
	24: 8 figs, **w** cannot be eaten, they are so evil;	834
	25: 2 The **w** Jeremiah the prophet spake unto all	834
	25:13 I will bring upon that land all my words **w**	834
	25:13 Jeremiah hath prophesied against all	834
	25:22 kings of the isles **w** *are* beyond the sea,	834
	25:26 world, **w** *are* upon the face of the earth:	834
	25:27 of the sword **w** I will send among you.	834
	25:29 I begin to bring evil on the city **w** is called	834
	26: 2 **w** come to worship *in* the LORD'S	1886.1
	26: 3 **w** I purpose to do unto them because of	834
	26: 4 walk in my law, **w** I have set before you,	834
	26:19 the LORD repented him of the evil **w** he	834
	27: 3 by the hand of the messengers **w** come	1886.1
	27: 8 kingdom **w** will not serve the same	834
	27: 9 to your sorcerers, **w** speak unto you,	834
	27:18 that the vessels **w** are left in the house	1886.1
	27:20 **W** Nebuchadnezzar king of Babylon took	834
	28: 1 son of Azur the prophet, **w** *was* of Gibeon,	834
	28: 6 the LORD perform thy words **w** thou hast	834
	28: 9 The prophet **w** prophesieth of peace,	834
	29: 1 the elders were carried away captives,	1886.1
	29: 8 neither hearken to your dreams **w** ye	834
	29:19 **w** I sent unto them by my servants	834
	29:21 **w** prophesy a lie unto you in my name;	1886.1
	29:22 all the captivity of Judah **w** *are* in Babylon,	834
	29:23 my name, **w** I have not commanded them;	834
	29:27 **w** maketh himself a prophet to you?	1886.1
	31: 2 people **w** were left of the sword found	NIH
	31:21 highway, *even* the way *w* thou wentest:	NIH
	31:32 **w** my covenant they brake, although I was	834
	31:35 **w** giveth the sun for a light by day,	NIH
	31:35 **w** divideth the sea when the waves	NIH
	32: 1 **w** *was* the eighteenth year of	1931
	32: 2 **w** *was in* the king of Judah's house.	834
	32: 8 **w** *is* in the country of Benjamin:	834
	32:11 that **w** was sealed *according to* the law	NIH
	32:11 the law and custom, and that **w** was open:	NIH
	32:14 both **w** is sealed, and this evidence	1886.1
	32:14 is sealed, and this evidence **w** is open;	1886.1
	32:20 **W** hast set signs and wonders in the land	834
	32:22 **w** thou didst swear to their fathers to give	834
	32:32 **w** they have done to provoke me to anger,	834
	32:34 **w** is called by my name, to defile it.	834
	32:35 **w** *are* in the valley of the son of Hinnom,	834
	32:35 **w** I commanded them not, neither came it	834
	33: 3 and mighty *things*, **w** thou knowest not.	NIH
	33: 4 **w** are thrown down by the mounts,	1886.1
	33: 9 **w** shall hear all the good that I do unto	834
	33:10 ye say *shall* be desolate without man	834
	33:12 **w** is desolate without man and	NIH
	33:14 I will perform *that* good thing **w** I have	834
	33:24 The two families **w** the LORD hath chosen,	834
	34: 1 The word **w** came unto Jeremiah from	834
	34: 5 the former kings **w** were before thee,	834
	34: 8 with all the people **w** *were* at Jerusalem,	834
	34:10 people, **w** had entered into the covenant,	834
	34:14 a Hebrew, **w** hath been sold unto thee;	834
	34:15 me in the house **w** is called by my name.	834
	34:18 have not performed the words of	834
	34:18 the covenant **w** they had made before me,	834
	34:19 **w** passed between the parts of the calf;	1886.1
	34:21 Babylon's army, **w** are gone up from	1886.1
	35: 1 The word **w** came unto Jeremiah from	834
	35: 4 **w** by the chamber of the princes,	834
	35: 4 **w** *was* above the chamber of Maaseiah	834
	35:15 ye shall dwell in the land **w** I have given to	834
	35:16 of their father, **w** he commanded them;	834

Jer	36: 3 all the evil **w** I purpose to do unto them;	834
	36: 4 **w** he had spoken unto him, upon a roll of	834
	36: 6 roll, **w** thou hast written from my mouth,	834
	36:21 in the ears of all the princes **w** stood	1886.1
	36:27 the words **w** Baruch wrote at the mouth of	834
	36:28 **w** Jehoiakim the king of Judah hath burnt.	834
	36:32 **w** Jehoiakim king of Judah had burnt in	834
	37: 2 **w** he spake by the prophet Jeremiah.	834
	37: 7 **w** is come forth to help you,	1886.1
	37:19 *are* now your prophets **w** prophesied	834
	38: 3 king of Babylon's army, **w** shall take it.	2050.1
	38: 7 one of the eunuchs **w** *was* in the king's	1931
	38:20 voice of the LORD, **w** I speak unto thee:	834
	39:10 **w** had nothing, in the land of Judah,	834
	40: 1 The word **w** came to Jeremiah from	834
	40: 1 **w** were carried away captive unto	1886.1
	40: 4 I loose thee *this* day from the chains **w**	834
	40: 7 *Now* when all the captains of the forces **w**	834
	40:10 serve the Chaldeans, **w** will come unto us:	834
	40:15 all the Jews **w** are gathered unto thee	1886.1
	41: 9 *was* it **w** Asa the king had made for fear of	834
	41:13 *that* when all the people **w** *were* with	834
	41:17 **w** *is* by Beth-lehem, to go to enter *into*	834
	42: 5 the LORD thy God shall send thee to us.	834
	42: 8 all the captains of the forces **w** *were* with	834
	42:16 come to pass, *that* the sword, **w** ye feared,	834
	42:21 any *thing* for the **w** he hath sent me unto	834
	43: 1 *for* **w** the LORD their God had sent him to	834
	43: 9 **w** *is* at the entry of Pharaoh's house in	834
	44: 1 the Jews **w** dwell in the land of Egypt,	1886.1
	44: 1 **w** dwell at Migdol, and at Tahpanhes,	1886.1
	44: 3 Because of their wickedness **w** they have	834
	44: 9 **w** they have committed in the land of	834
	44:14 **w** are gone into the land of Egypt to	1886.1
	44:14 the **w** they have a desire to return to dwell	834
	44:15 the men **w** knew that their wives had	1886.1
	44:20 to all the people **w** had given him *that*	1886.1
	44:22 of the abominations **w** ye have committed;	834
	45: 4 *that* **w** I have built *will* I break down,	834
	45: 4 *that* **w** I have planted I *will* pluck up,	834
	46: 1 The word of the LORD **w** came to	834
	46: 2 **w** *was* by the river Euphrates in	834
	46: 2 **w** Nebuchadrezzar king of Babylon smote	834
	49:28 **w** Nebuchadrezzar king of Babylon shall	834
	49:31 **w** have neither gates nor bars,	2050.2
	49:31 have neither gates nor bars, *w* dwell alone.	NIH
	50: 3 **w** shall make her land desolate,	1931
	51:12 that **w** he spake against the inhabitants	834
	51:25 the LORD, **w** destroyest all the earth:	1886.1
	51:44 I will bring forth out of his mouth that **w**	NIH
	51:59 The word **w** Jeremiah the prophet	834
	52: 2 he did *that* **w** *was* evil in the eyes of	1886.1
	52: 7 two walls, **w** *was* by the king's garden;	834
	52:12 **w** *was* the nineteenth year of	1931
	52:12 *w* served the king of Babylon,	NIH
	52:19 *that* **w** *was of* gold in gold, and *that* which	834
	52:19 in gold, and *that* **w** *was of* silver *in* silver,	834
	52:20 **w** king Solomon had made in the house of	834
	52:25 **w** had the charge of the men of war;	834
	52:25 king's person, **w** were found in the city;	834
La	1:12 like unto my sorrow, **w** is done unto me,	834
	2: 3 a flaming fire, *w* devoureth round about.	NIH
	2:17 The LORD hath done *that* **w** he had	834
	5:18 **w** is desolate, the foxes walk upon it.	7945
Eze	1: 2 **w** *was* the fifth year of king Jehoiachin's	1931
	1:23 **w** covered on this *side*, and every one had	NIH
	1:23 **w** covered on that *side*, their bodies.	NIH
	3:20 righteousness **w** he hath done shall not be	834
	3:23 the glory **w** I saw by the river of Chebar:	834
	4:10 meat **w** thou shalt eat *shall be* by weight,	834
	4:14 have I not eaten *of* that **w** dieth of itself,	NIH
	5: 9 I will do in thee that **w** I have not done,	834
	5:16 **w** shall be for *their* destruction, *and* which	834
	5:16 *and* **w** I will send to destroy you:	834
	6: 9 **w** hath departed from me, and with their	834
	6: 9 **w** go a whoring after their idols:	1886.1
	6: 9 they shall lothe themselves for the evils **w**	834
	7:13 For the seller shall not return to that **w** is	NIH
	7:13 multitude thereof, *w* shall not return;	NIH
	8: 3 of jealousy, **w** provoketh to jealousy.	1886.1
	8:14 LORD's house **w** *was* towards the north;	834
	8:17 the abominations **w** they commit here?	834
	9: 2 **w** lieth toward the north, and every man a	834
	9: 3 **w** *had* the writer's inkhorn by his side;	834
	9: 6 they began at the ancient men **w** *were*	834
	9:11 **w** *had* the inkhorn by his side, reported	834
	10:22 same faces **w** I saw by the river of Chebar,	834
	11: 1 the LORD's house, **w** looketh eastward:	1886.1
	11: 3 **W** say, It is not near; *let us* build houses	1886.1
	11:23 stood upon the mountain **w** is on the east	834
	12: 2 **w** have eyes to see, and see not;	834
	12:28 the word **w** I have spoken shall be done,	834
	13:11 unto them **w** daub *it with* untempered	NIH
	13:16 the prophets of Israel **w** prophesy	1886.1
	13:16 see visions of peace for her,	1886.1
	13:17 **w** prophesy out of their own heart;	834
	14: 7 separateth himself from me,	NIH
	15: 2 *than* a branch **w** is among the trees of	834
	15: 6 **w** I have given to the fire for fuel, so will I	834
	16:14 I had put upon thee, saith the Lord GOD.	834
	16:17 **w** I had given thee, and madest to thyself	834
	16:19 My meat also **w** I gave thee, fine flour,	834
	16:27 **w** are ashamed of thy lewd way.	1886.1
	16:32 *w* taketh strangers instead of her husband.	NIH
	16:36 thy children, **w** thou didst give unto them;	834

Eze	16:45 **w** lothed their husbands and their children:	834
	16:51 all thine abominations **w** thou hast done.	834
	16:52 Thou also, **w** hast judged thy sisters,	834
	16:57 **w** despise thee round about.	1886.1
	16:59 **w** hast despised the oath in breaking	834
	17: 3 full *of* feathers, **w** had divers colours,	834
	18: 5 just, and do **that w is lawful**	4941
	18:14 that seeth all his father's sins **w** he hath	834
	18:18 did *that* **w** *is* not good among his people,	834
	18:19 the son hath done **that w is lawful**	4941
	18:21 do **that w is lawful** and right, he shall	4941
	18:27 doeth **that w is lawful** and right, he shall	4941
	19:14 **w** hath devoured her fruit, so that she	NIH
	20: 6 and honey, **w** *is* the glory of all lands;	1931
	20:11 **w** *if* a man do, he shall even live in them.	834
	20:13 **w** *if* a man do, he shall even live in them;	834
	20:15 *I* would not bring them into the land **w** I	834
	20:15 and honey, **w** *is* the glory of all lands;	1931
	20:21 **w** *if* a man do, he shall even live in them;	834
	20:28 *for* the **w** I lifted up mine hand to give it to	834
	20:32 that **w** cometh into your mind shall not be	NIH
	20:42 into the country *for* the **w** I lifted up mine	834
	21:14 entereth into their privy chambers.	1886.1
	22: 4 defiled *thyself* in thine idols **w** thou hast	834
	22: 5 thee, *w* art infamous *and* much vexed.	NIH
	22:13 at thy dishonest gain **w** thou hast made,	834
	22:13 at thy blood **w** hath been in the midst of	834
	23: 6 **W** *were* clothed with blue, captains and	NIH
	23:24 **w** shall set against thee buckler and shield	NIH
	23:42 **w** put bracelets upon their hands,	2050.1
	24:21 of your eyes, and that **w** your soul pitieth;	NIH
	24:27 thy mouth be opened to him **w** is escaped,	NIH
	25: 9 from his cities *w* are on his frontiers,	NIH
	26: 6 daughters **w** *are* in the field shall be slain	834
	26:17 **w** wast strong in the sea, she and	834
	26:17 wast their terror *to be* on all that haunt	NIH
	27: 3 *w* art a merchant of the people for many	NIH
	27: 7 **w** thou **spreadest forth** to be thy sail;	4666
	27: 7 purple from the isles of Elishah was that **w**	NIH
	27:27 all thy company **w** *is* in the midst of thee,	834
	29: 3 **w** hath said, My river *is* mine own,	834
	29:16 **w** bringeth *their* iniquity to remembrance,	NIH
	30:22 arms, the strong, and that **w** was broken;	NIH
	32: 9 into the countries **w** thou hast not known.	834
	32:23 **w** caused terror in the land of the living.	834
	32:24 **w** are gone down uncircumcised into	834
	32:24 **w** caused their terror in the land of	834
	32:27 **w** are gone down to hell with their	834
	32:29 **w** with their might are laid by *them that*	834
	32:30 **w** are gone down with the slain;	834
	33:14 sin, and do **that w is lawful** and right;	4941
	33:16 he hath done **that w is lawful** and right;	4941
	33:19 do **that w is lawful** and right, he shall	4941
	33:29 of all their abominations **w** they have	834
	34: 4 neither have ye healed that **w** was sick,	NIH
	34: 4 neither have ye bound up that **w** was	NIH
	34: 4 neither have ye brought again that **w** was	NIH
	34: 4 neither have ye sought that **w** was lost;	NIH
	34:16 I will seek that **w** was lost, and bring again	NIH
	34:16 bring again that **w** was driven away,	NIH
	34:16 will bind up that **w** was broken,	NIH
	34:16 and will strengthen that **w** was sick:	NIH
	34:19 eat **that w** ye have **trodden** with your	4823
	34:19 drink **that w** ye have **fouled** with your	4833
	35:11 according to thine envy **w** thou hast used	834
	35:12 I have heard all thy blasphemies **w** thou	834
	36: 4 became a prey and derision to the	834
	36: 5 **w** have appointed my land into their	834
	36:21 **w** the house of Israel had profaned among	834
	36:22 **w** ye have profaned among the heathen,	834
	36:23 **w** was profaned among the heathen,	1886.1
	36:23 **w** ye have profaned in the midst of them;	834
	37: 1 set me down in the midst of the valley **w**	1931
	37:19 **w** *is* in the hand of Ephraim, and the tribes	834
	38: 8 of Israel, **w** have been always waste:	834
	38:12 **w** have gotten cattle and goods, that dwell	NIH
	38:17 prophesied in those days *many* years,	1886.1
	39:19 of my sacrifice **w** I have sacrificed for you,	834
	39:28 **w** caused them to be led into captivity	NIH
	40: 2 by **w** *was* as the frame of a city on	2050.2
	40: 6 came he unto the gate **w** looketh toward	834
	40: 6 of the gate, **w** *was* one reed broad;	NIH
	40: 6 the other threshold *of the gate*, **w** *was* one	NIH
	40:40 **w** *was* at the porch of the gate, *were* two	834
	40:44 **w** *was* at the side of the north gate;	834
	40:46 **w** come near to the LORD to minister	1886.1
	41: 1 **w** *was* the breadth of the tabernacle.	NIH
	41: 6 entered into the wall **w** *was* of the house	834
	41: 9 **w** *was* for the side chamber without,	834
	41: 9 *that* **w** *was* left *was* the place of the side	834
	41:15 against the separate place **w** *was* behind it,	834
	42: 1 **w** *was* before the building toward the	834
	42: 3 Over against the twenty *cubits* **w** *were* for	834
	42: 3 over against the pavement **w** *was* for	834
	42:11 of the chambers **w** *were* toward the north,	834
	42:13 **w** *are* before the separate place,	834
	42:14 shall approach to *those things* **w** *are* for	834
	43: 3 to the appearance of the vision **w** I saw,	834
	43:19 **w** approach unto me, to minister unto	1886.1
	44: 1 sanctuary **w** looketh *toward* the east;	1886.1
	44:10 **w** went astray away from me after their	834
	44:13 abominations **w** they have committed.	834
	45: 4 **w** shall come near to minister unto	1886.1
	45:14 out of the cor, **w** *is* a homer of ten baths;	NIH
	46:19 the entry, **w** *was* at the side of the gate,	834

Eze 46:19 the priests, **w** looked toward the north: 1886.1
47: 8 **w** being brought forth into the sea, NIH
47: 9 *that* every thing that liveth, **w** moveth, 834
47:14 *concerning* the **w** I lifted up mine hand to 834
47:16 **w** *is* between the border of Damascus and 834
47:16 Hazar-hatticon, **w** *is* by the coast of 834
47:22 **w** shall beget children among you: 834
48: 8 shall be the offering ye **w** shall offer *of* five 834
48:11 **w** have kept my charge, which went not 834
48:11 **w** went not astray when the children of 834
48:22 in the midst *of that* **w** is the prince's, 834
48:29 This *is* the land **w** ye shall divide *by lot* 834

Da 1: 2 **w** he carried *into* the land of Shinar *to* 2050.1
1: 5 king's meat, and of the wine **w** he drank: NIH
1: 8 meat, nor with the wine **w** he drank: NIH
1:10 than the children **w** *are* of your sort? 834
1:15 fatter in flesh than all the children **w** did 1886.1
2:14 **w** was gone forth to slay the wise *men* of 1768
2:26 known unto me the dream **w** I have seen, 1768
2:27 The secret the king hath demanded 1768
2:34 **w** smote the image upon his feet *that* 2050.3
2:39 brass, **w** shall bear rule over all the earth. 1768
2:44 a kingdom, **w** shall never be destroyed: 1768
3: 2 to come to the dedication of the image **w** 1768
3:12 worship the golden image **w** thou hast 1768
3:14 worship the golden image **w** I have set 1768
3:15 and worship the image **w** I have made; 1768
3:18 worship the golden image **w** thou hast 1768
3:29 **w** speak any thing amiss against the God 1768
4: 5 I saw a dream **w** made me afraid, 2050.3
4:20 thou sawest, **w** grew, and was strong, 1768
4:21 under **w** the beasts of the field dwelt, 1958.2
4:24 **w** is come upon my lord the king: 1768
5: 2 vessels **w** his father Nebuchadnezzar 1768
5: 2 out of the temple **w** *was* in Jerusalem; 1768
5: 3 of the house of God **w** *was* at Jerusalem; 1768
5:13 **w** *art* of the children of the captivity of 1768
5:23 brass, iron, wood, and stone, **w** see not, 1768
6: 1 should be over the whole kingdom; 1768
6: 8 the Medes and Persians, **w** altereth not. 1768
6:12 the Medes and Persians, **w** altereth not. 1768
6:13 **w** *is* of the children of the captivity of 1768
6:15 Persians *is*, That no decree nor statute **w** 1768
6:24 they brought those men **w** had accused 1768
6:26 kingdom *that* **w** shall not be destroyed, 1768
7: 6 **w** had upon the back of it four wings of 2050.3
7:11 the voice of the great words **w** the horn 1768
7:14 **w** shall not pass away, and his kingdom 1768
7:14 kingdom *that* **w** shall not be destroyed. 1768
7:17 great beasts, **w** *are* four kings, 581
7:17 four kings, **w** shall arise out of the earth. NIH
7:19 **w** was diverse from all the others, 1768
7:19 **w** devoured, brake in pieces, NIH
7:20 the other **w** came up, and before whom 1768
7:23 **w** shall be diverse from all kingdoms, 1768
8: 1 after that **w** appeared unto me at the first. NIH
8: 2 the palace, **w** *is* in the province of Elam; 834
8: 3 stood before the river a ram **w** had 2050.1
8: 6 **w** I had seen standing before the river, 834
8: 9 **w** waxed exceeding great, toward 2050.1
8:13 said unto that certain *saint* **w** spake, 1886.1
8:16 **w** called, and said, Gabriel, make this 2050.1
8:20 The ram **w** thou sawest having two horns 834
8:26 and the morning **w** was told *is* true: 834
9: 1 **w** was made king over the realm of 834
9: 6 **w** spake in thy name to our kings, 834
9:10 **w** he set before us by his servants 834
9:12 **w** he spake against us, and against our 834
9:14 *is* righteous in all his works **w** he doeth: 834
9:18 and the city **w** is called by thy name: 834
10: 4 the side of the great river, **w** *is* Hiddekel; 1931
10:10 **w** set me upon my knees and *upon* 2050.1
10:21 I will shew thee that **w** is noted in NIH
11: 4 nor according to his dominion **w** he ruled: 834
11: 7 **w** shall come with an army, 2050.1
11:16 by his hand shall be consumed. 2050.1
11:24 shall do *that* **w** his fathers have not done, 834
12: 1 the great prince **w** standeth for 1886.1
12: 6 linen, **w** *was* upon the waters of the river, 834
12: 7 **w** *was* upon the waters of the river, when 834

Hos 1: 3 **w** conceived, and bare him a son. 2050.1
1:10 **w** cannot be measured nor numbered; 834
2: 8 and gold, **w** they prepared for Baal. NIH
2:23 I will say to *them* **w** *were* not my people, NIH
5 have I made known that **w** shall surely be. NIH

Joel 1: 4 That **w** the palmerworm hath left hath NIH
1: 4 that **w** the locust hath left hath NIH
1: 4 that **w** the cankerworm hath left hath NIH
2:25 my great army **w** I sent among you. 834

Am 1: 1 **w** he saw concerning Israel in the days of 834
1: 4 **w** shall devour the palaces of 2050.1
1: 7 **w** shall devour the palaces thereof: 2050.1
1:10 **w** shall devour the palaces thereof. 2050.1
1:12 **w** shall devour the palaces of Bozrah. 2050.1
2: 4 err, after the which their fathers have walked: 834
3: 1 against the whole family **w** I brought up 834
4: 1 **w** oppress the poor, which crush 1886.1
4: 1 which oppress the poor, which crush 1886.1
4: 1 **w** say to their masters, Bring, and let us 1886.1
4: 3 every *cow at that* **w** *is* before her; NIH
5: 1 Hear ye this word **w** I take up against you, 834
5: 3 that went forth *by* an hundred shall NIH
5:26 star of your god, **w** ye made to yourselves. 834
6: 1 **w** *are* named chief of the nations, NIH
6:13 Ye **w** rejoice in a thing of nought, 1886.1

Am 6:13 rejoice in a thing of nought, **w** say, 1886.1
9:10 **w** say, The evil shall not overtake nor 1886.1
9:12 all the heathen, **w** are called by my name, 834
9:15 up out of their land **w** I have given them, 834

Ob 1:20 captivity of Jerusalem, **w** *is* in Sepharad, 834

Jnh 1: 9 **w** hath made the sea and the dry *land.* 834
4:10 for the **w** thou hast not laboured, neither 834
4:10 **w** came up in a night, and perished in a 7945

Mic 1: 1 **w** he saw concerning Samaria and 834
2: 3 from **w**^s ye shall not remove your necks; 8033
5: 3 until the time *that* she **w** travaileth hath NIH
6:14 *that* **w** thou deliverest will I give up to NIH
7:10 shame shall cover her **w** said unto me, 1886.1
7:14 **w** dwell solitarily *in* the wood, in the NIH
7:20 **w** thou hast sworn unto our fathers from 834

Na 3:17 **w** camp in the hedges in the cold day, 1886.1

Hab 1: 1 The burden **w** Habakkuk the prophet did 834
1: 5 **w** ye will not believe, though it be told NIH
1: 6 **w** *shall* march through the breadth of 1886.1
2: 4 soul **w** is lifted up is not upright in him: NIH
2: 6 Woe to him that increaseth *that* **w** is not NIH
2:17 **w** made them afraid, because of men's NIH

Zep 1: 1 The word of the LORD **w** came unto 834
1: 9 **w** fill their masters' houses *with* violence 1886.1
2: 3 the earth, **w** have wrought his judgment; 834

Hag 1:11 upon *that* **w** the ground bringeth forth, 834
2:14 and *that* **w** they offer there *is* unclean. 834

Zec 1: 6 **w** I commanded my servants the prophets, 834
1: 7 **w** is the month Sebat, in the second year 1931
1:12 *against* **w** thou hast had indignation these 834
1:19 *are* the horns **w** have scattered Judah, 834
1:21 *are* the horns **w** have scattered Judah, 834
1:21 **w** lift up *their* horn over the land of 1886.1
2: 8 me unto the nations **w** spoiled you: 1886.1
4: 2 seven lamps, **w** *were* upon the top thereof: 834
4:10 **w** run to and fro through the whole earth. NIH
4:12 What *be* these two olive branches **w** 834
5: 4 **w** go forth from standing before the Lord NIH
6: 6 The black horses **w** *are* therein go forth 834
6:10 **w** are come from Babylon, and come thou 834
7: 3 *And* to speak unto the priests **w** *were* in 834
7: 7 *Should* ye not *hear* the words **w** the LORD 834
7:12 the words **w** the LORD of hosts hath sent 834
8: 9 **w** *were* in the day *that* the foundation of 834
10: 5 shall be as mighty *men*, **w** tread down NIH
11:10 that *I* might break my covenant **w** I had 834
11:16 **w** shall not visit those that be cut off, NIH
12: 1 **w** stretcheth forth the heavens, NIH
13: 6 *Those with* **w** I was wounded *in* the house 834
14: 4 **w** *is* before Jerusalem on the east, 834
14: 7 it shall be one day **w** shall be known to NIH
14:16 **w** came against Jerusalem shall even go 1886.1

Mal 1:13 ye brought *that* **w** *was* torn, and the lame, NIH
1:14 **w** hath in his flock a male, and voweth, 2050.1
2:11 the holiness of the LORD **w** he loved, 834
4: 4 **w** I commanded him in Horeb for all 834

Mt 1:20 that **w** is conceived in her is of the Holy 834
1:22 that it might be fulfilled **w** was spoken of 3588
1:23 **w** being interpreted is, God with us. 3739
2: 9 and lo, the star, **w** they saw in the east, 3739
2:15 that it might be fulfilled **w** was spoken of 3588
2:16 according to the time **w** he had diligently 3739
2:17 Then was fulfilled that **w** was spoken by NIG
2:20 for they are dead **w** sought the young 3588
2:23 that it might be fulfilled **w** was spoken by 3588
3:10 every tree **w** bringeth not forth good fruit NIG
4:13 in Capernaum, **w** is upon the sea coast, 3588
4:14 That it might be fulfilled **w** was spoken by 3588
4:16 The people **w** sat in darkness saw great 3588
4:16 and to them **w** sat in the region and NIG
4:24 and those **w** were possessed with devils, NIG
4:24 and those **w** were lunatick, and those that NIG
5: 6 Blessed *are* they **w** do hunger and NIG
5:10 Blessed *are* they **w** are persecuted for NIG
5:12 persecuted they the prophets **w** were 3588
5:16 and glorify your Father **w** is in heaven. 3588
5:44 and pray for them **w** despitefully use you, 3588
5:45 children of your Father **w** is in heaven: 3588
5:46 For if ye love them **w** love you, NIG
5:48 even as your Father **w** is in heaven is 3588
6: 1 no reward of your Father **w** is in heaven. 3588
6: 4 thy Father **w** seeth in secret himself shall 3588
6: 6 door, pray to thy Father **w** is in secret; 3588
6: 6 thy Father **w** seeth in secret shall reward 3588
6: 9 Our Father **w** art in heaven, Hallowed be 3588
6:18 to fast, but unto thy Father **w** is in secret: 3588
6:18 and thy Father, **w** seeth in secret, 3588
6:27 **W** of you by taking thought can add one 5101
6:30 **w** to day is, and to morrow is cast into NIG
7: 6 Give not that **w** is holy unto the dogs, NIG
7:11 how much more shall your Father **w** is in 3588
7:13 and many there be **w** go in thereat: 3588
7:14 **w** leadeth unto life, and few there be that 3588
7:15 **w** come to you in sheep's clothing, 3748
7:21 that doeth the will of my Father **w** is in 3588
7:24 wise man, **w** built his house upon a rock: 3748
7:26 **w** built his house upon the sand: 3748
8:17 That it might be fulfilled **w** was spoken 3588
9: 8 **w** had given such power unto men. 3588
9: 16 for that **w** is put in to fill it up taketh from NIG
9:20 **w** was diseased with an issue of blood NIG
10:20 Spirit of your Father **w** speaketh in you. 3588
10:28 And fear not them **w** kill the body, NIG
10:28 rather fear him **w** is able to destroy both NIG
10:32 will I confess also before my Father **w** 3588

Mt 10:33 will I also deny before my Father **w** is 3588
11: 4 John again *those things* ye do hear 3739
11:10 **w** shall prepare thy way before thee. 3739
11:14 receive *it*, this is Elias, **w** was for to come. 3588
11:21 for if the mighty works **w** were done in 3588
11:23 Capernaum, **w** art exalted unto heaven, NIG
11:23 mighty works, **w** have been done in thee, 3588
12: 2 thy disciples do *that* **w** is not lawful to do 3739
12: 4 **w** was not lawful for him to eat, 3739
12: 4 neither for them **w** were with him, but NIG
12:10 was a man **w** had *his* hand withered. NIG
12:17 That it might be fulfilled **w** was spoken by 3588
12:50 do the will of my Father **w** is in heaven, 3588
13:14 **w** saith, By hearing ye shall hear, 3588
13:17 have desired to see *those things* **w** ye see, 3739
13:17 and to hear *those things* **w** ye hear, 3739
13:19 away that **w** was sown in his heart. NIG
13:19 is he **w** received seed by the way side. NIG
13:23 understandeth *it*; **w** also beareth fruit, 3739
13:24 a man **w** sowed good seed in his field: NIG
13:31 **w** a man took, and sowed in his field: 3739
13:32 **W** indeed is the least of all seeds: 3739
13:33 **w** a woman took, and hid in three 3739
13:35 That it might be fulfilled **w** was spoken by 3588
13:35 will utter *things* **w** have been kept secret NIG
13:41 that offend, and them **w** do iniquity; NIG
13:44 the **w** when a man hath found, he hideth, 3739
13:48 **W**, when it was full, they drew to shore, 3739
13:52 Therefore every scribe **w** is instructed NIG
13:52 **w** bringeth forth out of his treasure *things* 3748
14: 9 and them **w** sat with him at meat, NIG
15: 1 Pharisees, **w** were of Jerusalem, saying, 3588
15:11 Not that **w** goeth into the mouth defileth NIG
15:11 but that **w** cometh out of the mouth, NIG
15:13 **w** my heavenly Father hath not planted, 3739
15:18 those *things* **w** proceed out of the mouth NIG
15:20 These are *the things* **w** defile a man: 3588
15:27 yet the dogs eat of the crumbs **w** fall from 3588
16: 8 **W** when Jesus perceived, he said unto NIG
16:17 unto thee, but my Father **w** is in heaven. 3588
16:28 standing here, **w** shall not taste of death, 3748
17: 5 **w** said, This is my beloved Son, in whom 3739
18: 6 one of these little ones **w** believe in me, 3588
18:10 the face of my Father **w** is in heaven. 3588
18:11 the Son of man is come to save that **w** NIG
18:12 and seeketh that **w** is gone astray? NIG
18:13 of the ninety and nine **w** went not astray. 3588
18:14 it is not the will of your Father **w** is in 3588
18:19 shall be done for them of my Father **w** is 3588
18:23 **w** would take account of his servants. 3739
18:24 him, **w** ought him ten thousand talents. NIG
18:28 **w** ought him an hundred pence: 3739
19: 4 that he **w** made *them* at the beginning NIG
19: 9 whoso marrieth her **w** is put away doth 3739
19:12 **w** were so born from *their* mother's 3748
19:12 **w** were made eunuchs of men: 3748
19:12 **w** have made themselves eunuchs for 3748
19:18 He saith unto him, **W**? Jesus said, 4169
19:28 That ye **w** have followed me, 3588
20: 1 **w** went out early in the morning to hire 3748
20:12 **w** have borne the burden and heat of 3588
21: 4 that it might be fulfilled **w** was spoken by 3588
21:21 shall not only do this **w** is done to the fig NIG
21:24 will ask you one thing, **w** if ye tell me, 3739
21:33 **w** planted a vineyard, and hedged it 3748
21:41 **w** shall render him the fruits in their 3748
21:42 The stone **w** the builders rejected, 3739
22: 2 **w** made a marriage for his son, 3748
22: 4 saying, Tell them **w** are bidden, Behold, NIG
22: 8 they **w** were bidden were not worthy. NIG
22:11 saw there a man **w** had not on a wedding NIG
22:21 unto Cesar the *things* **w** are Cesar's; NIG
22:23 **w** say that there is no resurrection, NIG
22:31 have ye not read that **w** was spoken unto NIG
22:35 Then one of them, **w** *was* a lawyer, NIG
22:36 **w** is the great commandment in the law? 4169
23: 9 for one is your Father, **w** is in heaven. 3588
23:16 Woe unto you, *ye* blind guides, **w** say, 3588
23:24 **w** strain out a gnat, and swallow a camel. 3588
23:26 cleanse first that **w** *is* within the cup and NIG
23:27 and indeed appear beautiful outward, 3748
23:31 that ye are the children of them **w** killed NIG
23:37 and stonest them **w** are sent unto thee, NIG
24:16 Then let them **w** be in Judea flee into NIG
24:17 Let him **w** is on the housetop not come NIG
24:18 let him **w** is in the field return back NIG
25: 1 **w** took their lamps, and went forth to 3748
25:24 he **w** had received the one talent came NIG
25:28 and give *it* unto him **w** hath ten talents. NIG
25:29 shall be taken away even *that* **w** he hath. 3739
26:25 betrayed him, answered and said, 3588
26:28 **w** is shed for many for the remission of 3588
26:51 of them **w** were with Jesus stretched out NIG
26:62 what *is it* **w** these witness against thee? NIG
26:75 **w** said unto him, Before *the* cock crow, NIG
27: 3 Judas, **w** had betrayed him, when he 3588
27: 9 Then was fulfilled that **w** was spoken by NIG
27:17 Barabbas, or Jesus **w** is called Christ? 3588
27:22 I do then with Jesus **w** is called Christ? 3588
27:35 that it might be fulfilled **w** was spoken by NIG
27:44 thieves also, **w** were crucified with him, 3588
27:52 and many bodies of saints **w** slept arose, 3588
27:55 **w** followed Jesus from Galilee, 3748
27:56 Among **w** was Mary Magdalene, 3739
27:60 tomb, **w** he had hewn out in the rock: 3739

Mt 28: 5	know that ye seek Jesus, **w** was crucified.	3588
Mk 1: 2	**w** shall prepare thy way before thee.	3739
1:44	offer for thy cleansing *those things* **w**	3739
2: 3	sick of the palsy, **w** was borne of four.	NIG
2:24	why do they on the sabbath day *that* **w** is	3739
2:26	**w** is not lawful to eat but for the priests,	3739
2:26	and gave also to them **w** were with him?	NIG
3: 1	there was a man there **w** had a withered	NIG
3: 3	And he saith unto the man **w** had	3588
3:17	**w** is, The sons of thunder:)	3739
3:19	And Judas Iscariot, **w** also betrayed him.	3739
3:22	And the scribes **w** came down from	3588
3:34	he looked round about on them **w** sat	NIG
4:16	these are they likewise **w** are sown on	NIG
4:18	And these are they **w** are sown among	NIG
4:20	And these are they **w** are sown on good	NIG
4:22	is nothing hid, **w** shall not be manifested;	3739
4:25	from him shall be taken even *that* **w** he	3739
4:31	**w**, when it is sown in the earth,	3739
5:25	**w** had an issue of blood twelve years,	NIG
5:35	of the synagogue's *house certain* **w** said,	NIG
5:41	**w** is, being interpreted, Damsel (I say unto	3739
6: 2	what wisdom *is this* **w** is given unto him,	3588
6:26	their sakes **w** sat with *him*, he would not	NIG
7: 1	of the scribes, **w** came from Jerusalem.	NIG
7: 4	**w** they have received to hold,	3739
7:13	your tradition, **w** ye have delivered:	3739
7:15	the *things* **w** come out of him, those are	NIG
7:20	he said, That **w** cometh out of the man,	NIG
9: 1	that stand here, **w** shall not taste of death,	3748
9:17	unto thee my son, **w** hath a dumb spirit:	NIG
9:39	for there is no *man* **w** shall do a miracle in	3739
10:42	know that they **w** are accounted to rule	NIG
11:21	the fig tree **w** thou cursedst is withered	3739
11:23	shall believe that *those things* **w** he saith	3739
11:25	that your Father also **w** is in heaven may	3588
11:26	neither will your Father **w** is in heaven	3588
12:10	The stone **w** the builders rejected is	3739
12:18	**w** say there is no resurrection;	3748
12:25	but are as *the* angels **w** are in heaven.	NIG
12:28	**W** is the first commandment of all?	4169
12:38	**w** love to go in long clothing,	3588
12:40	**W** devour widows' houses, and for a	3588
12:42	threw in two mites, **w** make a farthing.	3739
12:43	all they **w** have cast into the treasury:	NIG
13:19	creation **w** God created unto this time,	3739
13:32	not the angels **w** are in heaven, neither	3588
14:18	One of you **w** eateth with me shall betray	3588
14:24	of the new testament, **w** is shed for many.	3588
14:32	And they came to a place **w** was named	3739
14:60	what *is it* **w** these witness against thee?	NIG
15: 7	**w** lay bound with them that had made	NIG
15:22	**w** is, being interpreted, The place of a	3739
15:28	And the scripture was fulfilled, **w** saith,	3588
15:34	**w** is, being interpreted, My God, my God,	3739
15:39	**w** stood over against him, saw that he so	3588
15:41	many other *women* **w** came up with him	3739
15:43	who also waited for the kingdom of God,	3739
15:46	laid him in a sepulchre **w** was hewn out	3739
16: 6	seek Jesus of Nazareth, **w** was crucified:	3588
16:14	they believed not them **w** had seen him	NIG
Lk 1: 1	**w** are most surely believed among us,	NIG
1: 2	**w** from the beginning were eyewitnesses,	3588
1:20	**w** shall be fulfilled in their season.	3748
1:35	*that* holy thing **w** shall be born of thee	NIG
1:45	*things* **w** were told her from the Lord.	NIG
1:70	**w** have been since the world began:)	NIG
1:73	The oath he sware to our father	3739
2: 4	the city of David, **w** is called Bethlehem;	3748
2:10	of great joy, **w** shall be to all people.	3748
2:11	of David a Saviour, **w** is Christ the Lord.	3739
2:15	and see this thing **w** is come to pass,	3588
2:15	the Lord hath made known unto us.	3739
2:17	**w** was told them concerning this child.	3588
2:18	**w** were told them by the shepherds.	NIG
2:21	**w** was *so* named of the angel before he	3588
2:24	to offer a sacrifice according to that **w**	NIG
2:31	**W** thou hast prepared before the face of	3739
2:33	mother marvelled at those *things* **w** were	NIG
2:34	and for a sign **w** shall be spoken against;	NIG
2:37	**w** departed not from the temple,	3739
2:50	And they understood not the saying **w** he	3739
3: 9	bringeth not forth good fruit is hewn	NIG
3:13	Exact no more than that **w** is appointed	NIG
3:19	and for all the evils **w** Herod had done,	3739
3:22	**w** said, Thou art my beloved Son;	NIG
3:23	the son of Joseph, **w** was *the son* of Heli,	NIG
3:24	**W** was *the son* of Matthat, which was	NIG
3:24	**w** was *the son* of Levi, which was *the son*	NIG
3:24	*the son* of Levi, **w** was *the son* of Melchi,	NIG
3:24	**w** was *the son* of Janna, which was *the*	NIG
3:24	*son* of Janna, **w** was *the son* of Joseph,	NIG
3:25	**W** was *the son* of Mattathias, which was	NIG
3:25	**w** was *the son* of Amos, which was *the*	NIG
3:25	**w** was *the son* of Naum, which was *the*	NIG
3:25	*the son* of Naum, **w** was *the son* of Esli,	NIG
3:25	*the son* of Esli, **w** was *the son* of Nagge,	NIG
3:26	**W** was *the son* of Maath, which was *the*	NIG
3:26	**w** was *the son* of Mattathias, which was	NIG
3:26	**w** was *the son* of Semei, which was *the*	NIG
3:26	**w** was *the son* of Joseph, which was *the*	NIG
3:26	*the son* of Joseph, **w** was *the son* of Juda,	NIG
3:27	**W** was *the son* of Joanna, which was	NIG
3:27	*son* of Joanna, **w** was *the son* of Rhesa,	NIG
3:27	*of Rhesa*, **w** was *the son* of Zorobabel,	NIG

Lk 3:27	**w** was *the son* of Salathiel, which was	NIG
3:27	*son* of Salathiel, **w** was *the son* of Neri,	NIG
3:28	**W** was *the son* of Melchi, which was	NIG
3:28	**w** was *the son* of Addi, which was *the*	NIG
3:28	*the son* of Addi, **w** was *the son* of Cosam,	NIG
3:28	**w** was *the son* of Elmodam, which was	NIG
3:28	*son* of Elmodam, **w** was *the son* of Er,	NIG
3:29	**W** was *the son* of Jose, which was *the*	NIG
3:29	*the son* of Jose, **w** was *the son* of Eliezer,	NIG
3:29	*the son* of Eliezer, **w** was *the son* of Jorim,	NIG
3:29	**w** was *the son* of Matthat, which was	NIG
3:29	*son* of Matthat, **w** was *the son* of Levi,	NIG
3:30	**W** was *the son* of Simeon, which was	NIG
3:30	**w** was *the son* of Juda, which was *the*	NIG
3:30	*the son* of Juda, **w** was *the son* of Joseph,	NIG
3:30	*of Joseph*, **w** was *the son* of Jonan,	NIG
3:30	*the son* of Jonan, **w** was *the son* of Eliakim,	NIG
3:31	**W** was *the son* of Melea, which was *the*	NIG
3:31	*the son* of Melea, **w** was *the son* of Menan,	NIG
3:31	*of Menan*, **w** was *the son* of Mattatha,	NIG
3:31	**w** was *the son* of Nathan, which was *the*	NIG
3:31	*son* of Nathan, **w** was *the son* of David,	NIG
3:32	**W** was *the son* of Jesse, which was *the*	NIG
3:32	**w** was *the son* of Obed, which was *the*	NIG
3:32	*the son* of Obed, **w** was *the son* of Booz,	NIG
3:32	*son* of Booz, **w** was *the son* of Salmon,	NIG
3:32	*son* of Salmon, **w** was *the son* of Naasson,	NIG
3:33	**w** was *the son* of Aminadab, which was	NIG
3:33	**w** was *the son* of Aram, which was *the*	NIG
3:33	*the son* of Aram, **w** was *the son* of Esrom,	NIG
3:33	**w** was *the son* of Phares, which was *the*	NIG
3:33	*the son* of Phares, **w** was *the son* of Juda,	NIG
3:34	**W** was *the son* of Jacob, which was *the*	NIG
3:34	*the son* of Jacob, **w** was *the son* of Isaac,	NIG
3:34	*son* of Isaac, **w** was *the son* of Abraham,	NIG
3:34	**w** was *the son* of Thara, which was *the*	NIG
3:34	*son* of Thara, **w** was *the son* of Nachor,	NIG
3:35	**W** was *the son* of Saruch, which was	NIG
3:35	**w** was *the son* of Ragau, which was *the*	NIG
3:35	*the son* of Ragau, **w** was *the son* of Phalec,	NIG
3:35	**w** was *the son* of Heber, which was *the*	NIG
3:35	*the son* of Heber, **w** was *the son* of Sala,	NIG
3:36	**W** was *the son* of Cainan, which was	NIG
3:36	**w** was *the son* of Arphaxad, which was	NIG
3:36	**w** was *the son* of Sem, which was *the son*	NIG
3:36	*the son* of Sem, **w** was *the son* of Noe,	NIG
3:36	*the son* of Noe, **w** was *the son* of Lamech,	NIG
3:37	**W** was *the son* of Mathusala, which was	NIG
3:37	**w** was *the son* of Enoch, which was *the*	NIG
3:37	*the son* of Enoch, **w** was *the son* of Jared,	NIG
3:37	*son* of Jared, **w** was *the son* of Maleleel,	NIG
3:37	*son* of Maleleel, **w** was *the son* of Cainan,	NIG
3:38	**W** was *the son* of Enos, which was *the*	NIG
3:38	*the son* of Enos, **w** was *the son* of Seth,	NIG
3:38	*the son* of Adam, which was *the son*	NIG
3:38	*the son* of Adam, **w** was *the son* of God.	NIG
4:22	wondered at the gracious words **w**	3588
4:33	**w** had a spirit of an unclean devil,	NIG
5: 3	**w** was Simon's, and prayed him that *he*	3739
5: 7	**w** were in the other ship, that *they* should	NIG
5: 9	at the draught of the fishes **w** they had	3739
5:10	of Zebedee, **w** were partners with Simon.	3739
5:17	doctors of the law sitting *by*, **w** were	3739
5:18	men brought in a bed a man **w** was taken	3739
5:21	Who is this **w** speaketh blasphemies?	3739
6: 2	Why do ye *that* **w** is not lawful to do on	3739
6: 3	a hungred, and they **w** were with him;	NIG
6: 4	**w** it is not lawful to eat but for the priests	3739
6: 8	said to the man **w** had the withered hand,	NIG
6:16	and Judas Iscariot, **w** also was the traitor.	3739
6:17	**w** came to hear him, and to be healed of	3739
6:27	But I say unto you **w** hear, Love your	3588
6:27	enemies, do good to them **w** hate you,	NIG
6:28	and pray for them **w** despitefully use you.	NIG
6:32	if ye love them **w** love you, what thank	NIG
6:33	And if ye do good to them **w** do good to	NIG
6:45	of his heart bringeth forth that **w** is good;	NIG
6:45	of his heart bringeth forth that **w** is evil:	NIG
6:46	Lord, and do not the *things* **w** I say?	3739
6:48	He is like a man **w** built a house,	3739
6:49	against **w** the stream did beat vehemently,	3739
7:25	they **w** are gorgeously apparelled,	NIG
7:27	**w** shall prepare thy way before thee.	3739
7:37	a woman in the city, **w** was a sinner,	3748
7:39	when the Pharisee **w** had bidden him	3588
7:41	There was a certain creditor **w** had two	NIG
7:42	**w** of them will love him most?	5101
7:47	Her sins, **w** are many, are forgiven;	3588
8: 2	**w** had been healed of evil spirits and	3739
8: 3	**w** ministered unto him of their substance.	3748
8:13	They on the rock *are they*, **w**, when they	3739
8:13	**w** for a while believe, and in time of	3739
8:14	And that **w** fell among thorns are they,	NIG
8:14	**w**, when they have heard, go *forth*, and	NIG
8:15	**w** in an honest and good heart,	3748
8:16	that they **w** enter in may see the light.	NIG
8:18	from him shall be taken even *that* **w** he	3739
8:20	And it was told him by *certain* **w** said,	NIG
8:21	my brethren are these **w** hear the word of	3588
8:26	the Gadarenes, **w** is over against Galilee.	3748
8:27	**w** had devils long time, and ware no	3739
8:36	also **w** saw *it* told them by what means	NIG
8:43	**w** had spent all *her* living upon physicians	3748
9:27	standing here, **w** shall not taste of death,	3739
9:30	him two men, **w** were Moses and Elias:	3748

Lk 9:31	spake of his decease **w** he should	3739
9:36	days any of *those things* **w** they had seen.	3739
9:43	every one at all *things* **w** Jesus did,	3739
9:46	**w** of them should be greatest.	302+5101
9:61	farewell, **w** are *at home* in my house.	NIG
10:11	**w** cleaveth on us, we do wipe off against	3588
10:13	and Sidon, **w** have been done in you,	NIG
10:15	Capernaum, **w** art exalted to heaven,	NIG
10:23	Blessed *are* the eyes **w** see *the things* that	3588
10:24	kings have desired to see *those things* **w**	3739
10:24	and to hear *those things* **w** ye hear,	3739
10:30	**w** stripped him of his raiment,	3739
10:36	**W** now of these three, thinkest thou,	5101
10:39	**w** also sat at Jesus' feet, and heard his	3739
10:42	**w** shall not be taken away from her.	3748
11: 2	ye pray, say, Our Father **w** art in heaven,	3588
11: 5	**W** of you shall have a friend, and shall go	5101
11:27	thee, and the paps **w** thou hast sucked.	3739
11:33	that they **w** come in may see the light.	NIG
11:35	that the light **w** is in thee be not darkness.	3588
11:40	not he that made that **w** is without make	NIG
11:40	*is* without make that **w** is within also?	NIG
11:44	for ye are as graves **w** appear not,	3588
11:50	**w** was shed from the foundation of	3588
11:51	**w** perished between the altar and	3588
12: 1	leaven of the Pharisees, **w** is hypocrisy.	3748
12: 3	**w** ye have spoken in the ear in closets	3739
12: 5	after *he* hath killed hath power to cast	NIG
12:15	abundance of the *things* **w** he possesseth.	3588
12:20	*those things* be, **w** thou hast provided?	3739
12:24	**w** neither have storehouse nor barn;	3739
12:25	**w** of you with taking thought can add	5101
12:26	be not able *to do that thing* **w** is least,	NIG
12:28	**w** is to day in the field, and to morrow is	NIG
12:33	provide yourselves bags **w** wax not old,	NIG
12:47	**w** knew his lord's will, and prepared not	3588
13:11	there was a woman **w** had a spirit of	NIG
13:14	are six days in **w** *men* ought to work:	3739
13:19	**w** a man took, and cast into his garden;	3739
13:21	**w** a woman took and hid in three	3739
13:30	there are last **w** shall be first, and there	3739
13:30	be first, and there are first **w** shall be last.	3739
13:34	**w** killest the prophets, and stonest them	3588
14: 2	certain man before him, **w** had the dropsy.	NIG
14: 5	**W** of you shall have an ass or an ox fallen	5101
14: 7	he put forth a parable to those **w** were	NIG
14:24	That none of those men **w** were bidden	3588
14:28	For **w** of you, intending to build a tower,	5101
15: 4	and go after that **w** is lost, until he find it?	3588
15: 6	for I have found my sheep **w** was lost.	3588
15: 7	nine just *persons* **w** need no repentance.	3748
15: 9	for I have found the piece **w** I had lost.	3739
15:30	**w** hath devoured thy living with harlots,	3588
16: 1	was a certain rich man, **w** had a steward;	3739
16:10	He that is faithful in *that* **w** is least is	NIG
16:12	if ye have not been faithful in that **w** is	NIG
16:12	who shall give you that **w** is your own?	NIG
16:15	Ye are they **w** justify yourselves before	NIG
16:15	that **w** is highly esteemed amongst men	NIG
16:19	**w** was clothed in purple and fine linen,	2532
16:20	**w** was laid at his gate, full of sores,	3739
16:21	desiring to be fed with the crumbs **w**	3588
16:26	that they **w** would pass from hence to you	NIG
17: 7	But **w** of you, having a servant plowing or	5101
17:10	ye shall have done all those *things* **w**	3739
17:10	we have done that **w** was our duty to do.	3739
17:12	men that *were* lepers, **w** stood afar off:	3739
17:31	he **w** shall be upon the housetop,	3739
18: 2	**w** feared not God, neither regarded man:	NIG
18: 7	**w** cry day and night unto him, though he	3588
18: 9	And he spake this parable unto certain **w**	3588
18:27	The *things* **w** are unpossible with men are	NIG
18:34	neither knew they the *things* **w** were	NIG
18:39	And they **w** went before rebuked him,	NIG
19: 2	**w** was the chief among the publicans,	846
19:10	come to seek and to save that **w** was lost.	NIG
19:20	**w** I have kept laid up in a napkin:	3739
19:26	unto every one **w** hath shall be given;	3588
19:27	**w** would not that I should reign over	3588
19:30	**w** at your entering ye shall find a colt tied,	3739
19:42	day, the *things* **w** belong unto thy peace!	3739
20:17	The stone **w** the builders rejected,	3739
20:20	**w** *should* feign themselves just *men*, that	NIG
20:25	unto Cesar the *things* **w** be Cesar's,	NIG
20:25	and unto God the *things* **w** be God's.	NIG
20:27	**w** deny that there is any resurrection;	3588
20:35	But they **w** shall be accounted worthy to	NIG
20:46	**w** desire to walk in long robes,	3588
20:47	**W** devour widows' houses, and for a	3739
21: 6	*As for these things* **w** ye behold, the days	3739
21: 6	in the **w** there shall not be left one stone	3739
21:15	**w** all your adversaries shall not be able to	3739
21:21	Then let them **w** are in Judea flee to	NIG
21:21	them **w** are in the midst of it depart out;	NIG
21:22	that all *things* **w** are written may be	3588
21:26	looking after those *things* **w** are coming	NIG
22: 1	bread drew nigh, **w** is called the Passover.	3588
22:19	This is my body **w** is given for you:	3588
22:20	testament in my blood, **w** is shed for you.	3588
22:23	**w** of them it was that should do this	5101
22:24	**w** of them should be accounted the	5101
22:28	Ye are they **w** have continued with me in	NIG
22:49	When they **w** were about him saw what	NIG
22:52	and the elders, **w** were come to him,	NIG
23:27	**w** also bewailed and lamented him.	3739

Lk 23:29 days are coming, in the **w** they shall say, 3739
23:29 and the paps **w** never gave suck. 3739
23:33 **w** is called Calvary, there they crucified 3588
23:39 one of the malefactors **w** were hanged NIG
23:48 beholding the *things* **w** were done, NIG
23:55 **w** came with him from Galilee, 3748
24: 1 bringing the spices **w** they had prepared, 3739
24:10 **w** told these *things* unto the apostles. 3739
24:12 wondering in himself at that **w** was come NIG
24:13 **w** was from Jerusalem *about* threescore 3739
24:14 of all these *things* **w** had happened. 3588
24:18 hast not known the *things* **w** are come to NIG
24:19 **w** was a prophet mighty in deed and 3739
24:21 we trusted that it had been he **w** should 3588
24:22 **w** were early at the sepulchre; NIG
24:23 vision of angels, **w** said that he was alive. 3739
24:24 certain of them **w** were with us went to NIG
24:44 These *are* the words **w** I spake unto you, 3739
24:44 **w** were written in the law of Moses, 3588

Jn 1: 9 **w** lighteth every man *that* cometh into 3739
1:13 **W** were born, not of blood, nor of the will 3739
1:18 is in the bosom of the Father, he hath 3588
1:24 they **w** were sent were of the Pharisees. NIG
1:29 God, **w** taketh away the sin of the world. 3588
1:30 After me cometh a man **w** is preferred 3739
1:33 the same is he **w** baptizeth with the Holy NIG
1:38 Rabbi, (**w** is to say, being interpreted, 3739
1:40 One of the two **w** heard John speak, 3588
1:41 **w** is, being interpreted, the Christ. 3739
1:42 **w** is by interpretation, A stone. 3739
2: 9 the servants **w** drew the water knew;) 3588
2:10 have well drunk, then that **w** is worse: NIG
2:22 and the word **w** Jesus had said. 3739
2:23 when they saw the miracles **w** he did. 3739
3: 6 That **w** is born of the flesh is flesh; NIG
3: 6 and that **w** is born of the Spirit is spirit. NIG
3:13 *even* the Son of man **w** is in heaven. 3588
3:29 standeth and heareth him, 3588
4: 5 he to a city of Samaria, **w** is called Sychar, 3739
4: 9 drink of me, **w** am a woman of Samaria? 3739
4:12 **w** gave us the well, and drank thereof 3739
4:25 that Messias cometh, **w** is called Christ: 3588
4:29 man, **w** told me all *things* that ever I did: 3739
4:39 **w** testified, He told me all *things* that ever I did: NIG
4:53 in the **w** Jesus said unto him, Thy son 3739
5: 2 **w** is called in the Hebrew tongue 3588
5: 5 **w** had an infirmity thirty *and* eight years. NIG
5:12 What man is that **w** said unto thee, 3588
5:15 it was Jesus, **w** had made him whole. 3588
5:23 honoureth not the Father **w** hath sent 3588
5:28 the **w** all that are in the graves shall hear 3739
5:30 but the will of the Father **w** hath sent me. 3588
5:32 I know that the witness **w** he witnesseth 3739
5:36 the works **w** the Father hath given me to 3739
5:37 And the Father himself, **w** hath sent me, NIG
5:39 and they are they **w** testify of me. NIG
5:44 **w** receive honour one of another, NIG
6: 1 sea of Galilee, **w** is the *sea* of Tiberias. NIG
6: 2 they saw his miracles **w** he did on them 3739
6: 9 **w** hath five barley loaves, and two small 3739
6:13 remained over and above unto them 3739
6:22 the people **w** stood on the other side 3588
6:27 Labour not for the meat **w** perisheth, 3588
6:27 *that* meat **w** endureth unto everlasting 3588
6:27 the Son of man shall give unto you: 3739
6:33 the bread of God is he **w** cometh down 3588
6:39 And this is the Father's will **w** hath sent 3588
6:39 of all **w** he hath given me I should lose 3739
6:40 that every one **w** seeth the Son, 3588
6:41 the bread **w** came down from heaven. 3588
6:44 the Father **w** hath sent me draw him: 3588
6:46 save he **w** is of God, he hath seen NIG
6:50 This is the bread **w** cometh down from 3588
6:51 I am the living bread **w** came down from 3588
6:51 I will give for the life of the world. 3739
6:58 This is *that* bread **w** came down from 3588
7:31 he do moe miracles than these **w** this 3739
7:39 **w** they that believe on him should receive 3739
8: 9 And they **w** heard *it*, being convicted by NIG
8:26 speak to the world those *things* **w** I have 3739
8:31 said Jesus to those Jews **w** believed on NIG
8:38 speak *that* **w** I have seen with my Father: 3739
8:38 do *that* **w** ye have seen with your father. 3739
8:40 you the truth, **w** I have heard of God: 3739
8:46 **W** of you convinceth me of sin? And if I 5101
8:53 than our father Abraham, **w** is dead? 3748
9: 1 he saw a man *w* was blind from *his* birth. NIG
9: 7 of Siloam, (**w** is by interpretation, Sent.) 3739
9: 8 they **w** before had seen him that he was 3588
9:39 this world, that they **w** see not might see; NIG
9:39 and that they **w** see might be made blind. NIG
9:40 And *some* of the Pharisees **w** were with 3588
10: 6 *things* they were **w** he spake unto them. 3739
10:16 other sheep I have, **w** are not of this fold: 3739
10:29 My Father, **w** gave *them* me, is greater 3739
10:32 for **w** of those works do ye stone me? 4169
11: 2 (It was *that* Mary **w** anointed the Lord 3588
11:16 Then said Thomas, **w** is called Didymus, 3588
11:27 of God, **w** should come into the world. 3588
11:31 then **w** were with her in the house, 3588
11:33 the Jews also weeping **w** came with her, NIG
11:37 Could not this *man*, **w** opened the eyes of 3588
11:42 the people **w** stand by I said *it*, that they 3588
11:45 Then many of the Jews **w** came to Mary, 3588
11:45 and had seen the *things* **w** Jesus did, 3739

Jn 12: 1 where Lazarus was **w** had been dead, 3588
12: 4 Simon's *son*, **w** should betray him, 3588
12:21 **w** was of Bethsaida of Galilee, 3588
12:38 he spake, Lord, who hath believed our 3739
12:49 but the Father **w** sent me, he gave me a 3588
13: 1 loved his own **w** were in the world, 3588
14:24 and the word **w** you hear is not mine, 3739
14:24 is not mine, but the Father's **w** sent me. NIG
14:26 But the Comforter, **w** *is* the Holy Ghost, 3588
15: 3 Now ye are clean through the word **w** I 3739
15:24 I had not done among them the works **w** 3739
15:26 proceedeth from the Father, he shall 3739
17: 4 I have finished the work **w** thou gavest 3739
17: 5 **w** I had with thee before the world was. 3739
17: 6 manifested thy name unto the men **w** 3739
17: 8 For I have given unto them the words **w** 3739
17: 9 but for *them* **w** thou hast given me; 3739
17:20 them also **w** shall believe on me through NIG
17:22 And the glory **w** thou gavest me I have 3739
17:24 behold my glory, **w** thou hast given me: 3739
18: 1 into the **w** he entered, and his disciples. 3739
18: 2 Judas also, **w** betrayed him, knew the 3588
18: 5 betrayed him, stood with them. 3588
18: 9 the saying might be fulfilled, **w** he spake, 3739
18: 9 them **w** thou gavest me have I lost none. 3739
18:11 the cup **w** my Father hath given me, shall 3588
18:13 was the high priest that *same* year. 3739
18:14 was he, **w** gave counsel to the Jews, 3588
18:16 was known unto the high priest, 3739
18:21 ask them **w** heard *me*, what I have said NIG
18:22 one of the officers **w** stood by stroke Jesus NIG
18:32 he spake, signifying what death he 3739
19:17 skull, **w** is called in the Hebrew Golgotha: 3739
19:24 the scripture might be fulfilled, **w** saith, 3588
19:32 of the other **w** was crucified with him. 3588
19:39 **w** at the first came to Jesus by night, 3588
20: 8 **w** came first to the sepulchre, and he saw, 3588
20:16 unto him, Rabboni; **w** is to say, Master. 3739
20:30 disciples, **w** are not written in this book: 3739
21:10 Bring of the fish **w** ye have now caught. 3739
21:20 also leaned on his breast at supper, 3739
21:20 said, Lord, **w** is he that betrayeth thee? 5101
21:24 This is the disciple **w** testifieth of these 3588
21:25 And there are also many other *things* **w** 3745
21:25 **w**, if they should be written every one, 3748

Ac 1: 2 Until the day *in* **w** he was taken up, 3739
1: 4 **w**, *saith he*, ye have heard of me. 3739
1: 7 **w**, the Father hath put in his own power. 3588
1:11 **W** also said, Ye men of Galilee, why stand 3739
1:11 is taken up from you into heaven, shall 3588
1:12 **w** is from Jerusalem a sabbath day's 3739
1:16 the Holy Ghost by the mouth of David 3739
1:16 **w** was guide to them that took Jesus. 3588
1:21 of these men **w** have companied 3588
1:24 knowest the hearts of all *men*, shew NIG
1:25 from **w** Judas by transgression fell, 3739
2: 7 are not all these **w** speak Galileans? 3588
2:16 this is that **w** was spoken by the prophet NIG
2:22 God did by him in the midst of you, 3739
2:33 shed forth this, **w** ye now see and hear. 3739
3: 2 gate of the temple **w** is called Beautiful, 3588
3:10 they knew that it was he **w** sat for alms 3588
3:10 amazement at that **w** had happened unto NIG
3:11 And as the lame *man* **w** was healed held NIG
3:16 the faith **w** is by him hath given him this 3588
3:18 *those things*, **w** God before had shewed 3739
3:20 **w** before was preached unto you: NIG
3:21 **w** God hath spoken by the mouth of all 3739
3:23 **w** will not hear that prophet, 302+3748
3:25 of the covenant **w** God made with our 3739
4: 4 Howbeit many of them **w** heard the word NIG
4:11 is the stone **w** was set at nought of you 3588
4:11 is become the head of the corner. 3588
4:14 And beholding the man **w** was healed 3588
4:20 but speak *the things* **w** we have seen and 3739
4:21 for all *men* glorified God for that **w** was 3588
4:24 **w** hast made heaven, and earth, and the 3588
4:32 of the *things* **w** he possessed was his own; NIG
4:36 (**w** is, being interpreted, The son of 3739
5: 9 feet of them **w** have buried thy husband NIG
5:16 *them* **w** were vexed with unclean spirits: NIG
5:17 him, (**w** is the sect of the Sadducees,) 3588
6: 9 is called the synagogue **w** he spake. 3588
6:10 the wisdom and the spirit by **w** he spake. 3739
6:11 they suborned men, **w** said, We have NIG
6:13 And set up false witnesses, **w** said, NIG
6:14 shall change the customs **w** Moses 3739
7: 3 come into the land **w** I shall shew thee. 3739
7:17 God had sworn to Abraham, the people 3739
7:18 another king arose, **w** knew not Joseph. 3739
7:20 In **w** time Moses was born, 3739
7:34 I have seen the affliction of my people **w** 3588
7:35 a deliverer by the hand of the angel **w** 3588
7:37 **w** said unto the children of Israel, 3588
7:38 angel **w** spake to him in the mount Sina, 3588
7:40 **w** brought us out of the land of Egypt, 3739
7:43 figures **w** ye made to worship them: 3739
7:45 **W** also our fathers that came after brought 3739
7:52 **W** of the prophets have not your fathers 5101
7:52 they have slain them **w** shewed before of 3739
8: 1 against the church **w** was at Jerusalem; 3588
8: 6 heed unto those *things* **w** Philip spake, NIG
8: 6 hearing and seeing the miracles **w** he did. 3739
8: 9 beforetime in the *same* city used NIG
8:13 the miracles and signs **w** were done. NIG

Ac 8:14 when the apostles **w** were at Jerusalem NIG
8:24 none of *these things* **w** ye have spoken 3739
8:26 from Jerusalem unto Gaza, **w** is desert. 3778
8:32 The place of the scripture **w** he read was 3739
9: 7 the men **w** journeyed with him stood NIG
9:11 and go into the street **w** is called Straight, 3739
9:19 with the disciples **w** were at Damascus. 3588
9:21 not this he that destroyed them **w** called NIG
9:22 the Jews **w** dwelt at Damascus. 3588
9:30 **W** when the brethren knew, they brought NIG
9:32 down also to the saints **w** dwelt at Lydda. 3588
9:33 **w** had kept his bed eight years, and was NIG
9:36 **w** by interpretation is called Dorcas: 3739
9:36 of good works and almsdeeds **w** she did. 3739
9:39 the coats and garments **w** Dorcas made, 3745
10: 2 **w** gave much alms to the people, NIG
10: 7 And when the angel **w** spake unto 3588
10:17 *this* vision **w** he had seen should mean, 3739
10:17 the men **w** were sent from Cornelius had 3588
10:18 **w** was surnamed Peter, were lodged 3588
10:21 Peter went down to the men **w** were NIG
10:36 The word **w** *God* sent unto the children 3739
10:37 **w** was published throughout all Judea, 3739
10:37 after the baptism **w** John preached; 3739
10:39 we are witnesses of all *things* **w** he did 3739
10:42 to testify that it is he **w** was ordained of 3588
10:44 the Holy Ghost fell on all them **w** heard NIG
10:45 And they of the circumcision **w** believed 3739
10:47 **w** have received the Holy Ghost as well as 3748
11: 6 Upon the **w** when I had fastened mine 3739
11:13 **w** stood and said unto him, Send men to NIG
11:19 Now they **w** were scattered abroad upon NIG
11:20 were men of Cyprus and Cyrene, **w**, 3748
11:22 ears of the church **w** was in Jerusalem: 3588
11:28 **w** came to pass in the days of Claudius 3748
11:29 to send relief unto the brethren **w** NIG
11:30 **W** also they did, and sent it to the elders 3739
12: 9 wist not that it was true **w** was done by 3588
12:10 **w** opened to them of his own accord: 3748
13: 1 **w** had been brought up with Herod 3739
13: 7 **W** was with the deputy *of the country*, 3739
13:22 mine own heart, **w** shall fulfil all my will. 3739
13:27 nor *yet* the voices of the prophets **w** are 3588
13:31 And he was seen many days of them **w** NIG
13:32 how that the promise **w** was made unto 3739
13:39 **w** ye could not be justified by the law of 3739
13:40 upon you, **w** is spoken of in the prophets; 3739
13:41 a work **w** you shall in no wise believe, 3739
13:45 spake against those *things* **w** were spoken NIG
14: 3 **w** gave testimony unto the word of his 3588
14:13 was before their city, brought oxen 3588
14:14 **W** when the apostles, Barnabas and Paul, NIG
14:15 **w** made heaven, and earth, and the sea, 3739
14:26 grace of God for the work **w** they fulfilled. 3739
15: 1 certain *men* **w** came down from Judea NIG
15: 5 of the sect of the Pharisees **w** believed, 3588
15: 8 God, **w** knoweth the hearts, bare them NIG
15:10 neither our fathers nor we were able to 3739
15:16 the tabernacle of David, **w** is fallen down; 3588
15:19 **w** from among the Gentiles are turned to NIG
15:23 *send* greeting unto the brethren **w** 3588
15:24 that certain **w** went out from us have NIG
15:29 from **w** if ye keep yourselves, ye shall do 3739
15:31 **W** when they had read, they rejoiced for NIG
16: 1 **w** was a Jewess, and believed; NIG
16: 2 **W** was well reported of by the brethren 3739
16: 3 of the Jews **w** were in those quarters: 3588
16: 4 and elders **w** were at Jerusalem. 3588
16:12 **w** is the chief city of *that* part of 3748
16:13 spake unto the women **w** resorted *thither*. NIG
16:14 of the city of Thyatira, **w** worshipped God, NIG
16:14 that *she* attended unto the *things* **w** were NIG
16:16 **w** brought her masters much gain by 3748
16:17 **w** shew unto us the way of salvation. 3748
16:21 we are not lawful for us to receive, neither NIG
17: 5 But the Jews **w** believed not, moved with NIG
17:12 of honourable women **w** were Greeks, 3588
17:21 strangers **w** were there spent their time in 3588
17:31 in the **w** he will judge the world in 3739
17:34 among the **w** *was* Dionysius 3739
18:27 helped them much **w** had believed NIG
19: 4 that they should believe on him **w** should NIG
19:10 all they **w** dwelt in Asia heard the word NIG
19:13 upon them to call over them **w** had evil NIG
19:14 a Jew, *and* chief of the priests, **w** did so. NIG
19:19 Many also of them **w** used curious arts NIG
19:24 **w** made silver shrines for Diana, NIG
19:26 they be no gods, **w** are made with hands: NIG
19:31 of Asia, **w** his friends, sent unto him, NIG
19:35 of the *image* **w** fell down from Jupiter? NIG
19:37 **w** *are* neither robbers of churches, nor yet NIG
19:38 and the craftsmen **w** are with him, NIG
20:19 befell me by the lying in wait of 3588
20:24 **w** I have received of the Lord Jesus, 3739
20:28 the **w** the Holy Ghost hath made you 3739
20:28 **w** he hath purchased with his own blood. 3739
20:32 **w** is able to build *you* up, and to give you 3588
20:32 among all them **w** are sanctified. NIG
20:38 Sorrowing most *of all* for the words **w** he 3739
21: 8 the evangelist, **w** was *one* of the seven, NIG
21: 9 four daughters, virgins, **w** did prophesy. NIG
21:20 how many thousands of Jews there are **w** 3588
21:21 thou teachest all the Jews **w** are among 3588
21:23 have four men **w** have a vow on them; NIG
21:25 As touching the Gentiles **w** believe, NIG

Ac
21:27 the Jews **w** were of Asia, when they saw	NIG
21:38 **w** before these days madest an uproar,	3588
21:39 said, I am a man *w am* a Jew of Tarsus,	NIG
22: 1 ye my defence *w I make* now unto you.	NIG
22: 3 I am verily a man *w am* a Jew, born in	NIG
22: 5 to Damascus, to bring them **w** were there,	NIG
22:10 it shall be told thee of all *things* **w** are	3739
22:12 having a good report of all the Jews **w**	NIG
22:29 from him **w** should have examined him:	3588
23:13 they were more *than* forty **w** had made	3588
23:21 **w** have bound themselves with an oath,	3748
24:14 that after the way **w** they call heresy,	3739
24:14 all *things* **w** are written in the law	3588
24:15 **w** they themselves also allow,	3739
24:24 **w** was a Jewess, he sent for Paul,	NIG
25: 5 said he, **w** among you are able, go down	NIG
25: 7 the Jews **w** came down from Jerusalem	NIG
25: 7 against Paul, **w** they could not prove.	3739
25:16 before that he **w** is accused have	NIG
25:19 and of one Jesus, *w was* dead, whom Paul	NIG
25:24 and all men **w** are here present with us,	3588
26: 3 and questions **w** are among the Jews:	NIG
26: 4 **w** was at the first among mine own nation	3588
26: 5 **W** knew me from the beginning, if they	NIG
26: 7 Unto **w** *promise* our twelve tribes,	3739
26: 7 hope's sake, king Agrippa, I am	3739
26:10 **W** *thing* I also did in Jerusalem:	3739
26:13 about me and them **w** journeyed with me.	NIG
26:16 witness both of *these things* **w** thou hast	3739
26:16 *those things* in the **w** I will appear unto	3739
26:18 inheritance among them **w** are sanctified	NIG
26:22 saying none other *things* than those **w**	3739
27: 8 came unto a place *w is* called The fair	NIG
27:11 more than those *things* **w** were spoken by	NIG
27:12 *w is* a haven of Crete, and lieth toward	NIG
27:16 And running under a certain island *w is*	NIG
27:17 **W** when they had taken up, they used	3739
27:39 into the **w** they were minded, if it were	3739
27:43 commanded that they **w** could swim	NIG
28: 9 **w** had diseases in the island, came,	3588
28:11 **w** had wintered in the isle, *whose* sign	NIG
28:24 And some believed the *things* **w** were	NIG
28:31 teaching those *things* **w** concern the Lord	NIG

Ro
1: 2 (**W** he had promised afore by his prophets	3739
1: 3 **w** was made of the seed of David	3588
1:19 Because that **w** may be known of God is	NIG
1:26 natural use into that **w** is against nature:	NIG
1:27 with men working that **w** is unseemly,	NIG
1:27 recompence of their error **w** was meet.	3739
1:28 to do those *things* **w** are not convenient;	NIG
1:32 they **w** commit such *things* are worthy	NIG
2: 2 truth against them **w** commit such *things*.	NIG
2: 3 that judgest them **w** do such *things*, and	NIG
2:14 when *the* Gentiles, **w** have not the law,	3588
2:15 **W** shew the work of the law written in	3748
2:19 blind, a light of them **w** are in darkness,	NIG
2:20 **w** hast the form of knowledge and of	NIG
2:21 Thou therefore **w** teachest another,	3588
2:27 And shall not uncircumcision **w** is by	3588
2:28 For he is not a Jew, **w** is one outwardly;	3588
2:28 circumcision, **w** is outward in the flesh:	NIG
2:29 But he *is* a Jew, **w** is one inwardly;	NIG
3:22 the righteousness of God *w is* by faith	NIG
3:26 the justifier of him **w** believeth in Jesus.	NIG
3:30 **w** shall justify the circumcision by faith	3739
4:11 seal of the righteousness of the faith **w** he	3588
4:12 **w** he had being *yet* uncircumcised.	NIG
4:14 if they **w** are of the law *be* heirs, faith is	NIG
4:16 not to that only **w** is of the law, but to	NIG
4:16 to that also **w** is of the faith of Abraham;	NIG
4:17 calleth those *things* **w** be not as though	NIG
4:18 according to that **w** was spoken, So shall	NIG
5: 5 by the Holy Ghost **w** is given unto us.	3588
5:15 by grace, **w** is by one man, Jesus Christ,	NIG
5:17 much more they **w** receive abundance of	NIG
6:17 form of doctrine **w** was delivered you.	3739
7: 2 the woman **w** hath a husband is bound	NIG
7: 5 the motions of sins, **w** were by the law,	3588
7:10 commandment, **w** was *ordained* to life,	3588
7:13 that **w** is good made death unto me?	3588
7:13 working death in me by that **w** is good;	3588
7:15 For *that* **w** I do I allow not: for what I	3739
7:16 If then I do that **w** I would not, I consent	3739
7:18 *how* to perform that **w** is good I find not.	3588
7:19 but the evil **w** I would not, that I do.	3739
7:23 to the law of sin **w** is in my members.	3588
8: 1 now no condemnation to them *w are* in	NIG
8:18 with the glory **w** shall be revealed in us.	NIG
8:23 **w** have the firstfruits of the Spirit,	NIG
8:26 us with groanings **w** cannot be uttered.	NIG
8:39 love of God, **w** is in Christ Jesus our Lord.	3588
9: 6 For they *are* not all Israel, **w** are of Israel:	3588
9: 8 is, They **w** *are* the children of the flesh,	NIG
9:23 we he had afore prepared unto glory,	3739
9:25 *them* my people, **w** were not my people;	3588
9:25 and her beloved, **w** was not beloved.	NIG
9:30 **w** followed not *after* righteousness,	3588
9:30 even the righteousness **w** is of faith.	3588
9:31 **w** followed *after* the law of righteousness,	NIG
10: 5 For Moses describeth the righteousness **w**	3588
10: 5 the man **w** doeth those *things* shall live	NIG
10: 6 the righteousness **w** is of faith speaketh	NIG
10: 8 that is, the word of faith, **w** we preach;	3739
11: 2 God hath not cast away his people **w** he	3739
11: 7 Israel hath not obtained that **w** he seeketh	3739

Ro
11:14 to emulation *them* **w** are my flesh,	NIG
11:20 on them **w** fell, severity; but toward thee,	NIG
11:24 out of the **olive tree w is wild** by nature,	65
11:24 be the natural branches, be graffed into	NIG
12: 1 unto God, **w** is your reasonable service.	NIG
12: 9 Abhor that **w** is evil; cleave to *that which*	NIG
12: 9 **w** is evil; cleave to *that* **w** is good.	NIG
12:14 Bless them **w** persecute you: bless,	NIG
13: 3 that **w** is good, and thou shalt have praise	NIG
13: 4 But if thou do that **w** is evil, be afraid;	NIG
14: 3 let not him **w** eateth not judge him that	NIG
14:19 follow *after the things* **w** make for peace,	3739
14:22 not himself in *that thing* **w** he alloweth.	3739
15:17 Christ *in those things* **w** pertain to God.	NIG
15:18 *things* **w** Christ hath not wrought by me,	3739
15:22 **For w cause** also I have been much	1352
15:26 for the poor saints **w** are at Jerusalem.	NIG
15:31 that my service **w** I have for Jerusalem	3588
16: 1 **w** is a servant of the church which is at	NIG
16: 1 which is a servant of the church **w** is at	3588
16:10 Salute them **w** are of Aristobulus'	NIG
16:11 of Narcissus, **w** are in the Lord.	3588
16:12 **w** laboured much in the Lord.	3748
16:14 and the brethren **w** are with them.	NIG
16:15 and all the saints **w** are with them.	NIG
16:17 mark them **w** cause divisions and offences	3588
16:17 offences contrary to the doctrine **w** ye	3739
16:19 *yet* I would have you wise unto *that* **w** is	NIG
16:25 **w** was kept secret since the world began,	NIG

1Co
1: 2 Unto the church of God **w** is at Corinth,	NIG
1: 4 for the grace of God **w** is given you by	3588
1:11 by them **w** are of the *house* of Chloe,	NIG
1:18 us **w** are saved it is the power of God.	3588
1:24 unto them **w** are called, both Jews and	3588
1:27 to confound the *things* **w** *are* mighty;	NIG
1:28 *things* **w** are despised, hath God chosen,	NIG
1:28 God chosen, *yea*, and *things* **w** are not,	NIG
2: 7 the hidden *wisdom*, **w** God ordained	3739
2: 8 **W** none of the princes of this world	3739
2: 9 *the things* **w** God hath prepared for them	3739
2:11 a man, save the spirit of man **w** is in him?	3588
2:12 of the world, but the Spirit **w** is of God;	3588
2:13 **W** *things* also we speak, not in the words	3739
2:13 in the words **w** man's wisdom teacheth,	NIG
2:13 but **w** the Holy Ghost teacheth;	NIG
3:10 According to the grace of God **w** is given	3588
3:11 lay than that is laid, **w** is Jesus Christ.	3739
3:14 If any *man's* work abide **w** he hath built	3739
3:17 temple of God is holy, **w** *temple* ye are.	3748
4: 6 to think *of men* above that **w** is written,	3739
4:17 remembrance of my ways **w** be in Christ,	3588
4:19 not the speech of them **w** are puffed up,	NIG
6:16 know ye not that he **w** is joined to a harlot	NIG
6:19 the temple of the Holy Ghost **w** is in you,	NIG
6:19 ye have of God, and ye are not your	3739
6:20 body, and in your spirit, **w** are God's.	3748
7:13 And the woman **w** hath a husband that	3748
7:35 for that **w** is comely, and that you may	NIG
8:10 if any *man* see thee **w** hast knowledge	3588
8:10 shall not the conscience of him **w** is weak	NIG
8:10 to eat those things **w** are offered to idols;	NIG
9:13 Do ye not know that they **w** minister	NIG
9:13 they **w** wait at the altar are partakers with	NIG
9:14 hath the Lord ordained that they **w** preach	NIG
9:24 Know ye not that they **w** run in a race run	NIG
10:16 The cup of blessing **w** we bless, is it not	3739
10:16 The bread **w** we break, is it not	3739
10:18 not they **w** eat *of* the sacrifices partakers	NIG
10:19 that **w** is offered in sacrifice to idols is any	NIG
10:20 But *I say*, that the *things* **w** the Gentiles	3739
10:30 why am I evil spoken of for *that for* **w** I	3739
11:19 that they *w are* approved may be made	NIG
11:23 I have received of the Lord that **w** also	3739
11:23 the Lord Jesus the *same* night in **w** he:	3739
11:24 this is my body, **w** is broken for you:	3588
12: 6 it is the same God **w** worketh all in all.	3588
12:22 seem to be more feeble, are necessary:	3588
12:23 body, **w** we think to be less honourable,	NIG
12:24 abundant honour to that *part* **w** lacked:	NIG
13:10 But when *that* **w** is perfect is come, then	NIG
13:10 then that **w** is in part shall be done away.	NIG
14:22 that believe not, but for them **w** believe.	NIG
15: 1 declare unto you the gospel **w** I preached	3739
15: 1 **w** also you have received, and wherein ye	3739
15: 2 By **w** also ye are saved, if ye keep in	3739
15: 3 I delivered unto you first *of all* that **w** I	3739
15:10 grace **w** was *bestowed* upon me was not	3588
15:10 but the grace of God **w** was with me.	3588
15:18 they also **w** are fallen asleep in Christ	NIG
15:27 excepted, **w** did put all *things* under him.	3588
15:29 Else what shall they do **w** are baptized for	NIG
15:31 I protest by your rejoicing **w** I have in	3739
15:36 *that* **w** thou sowest is not quickened,	3739
15:37 And *that* **w** thou sowest, thou sowest not	3739
15:46 Howbeit *that* was not first *w is* spiritual,	NIG
15:46 *which is* spiritual, but *that* **w** *is* natural;	NIG
15:46 natural; *and afterward that* **w** *is* spiritual.	NIG
15:57 giveth us the victory through our Lord	3588
16:17 for that **w** was lacking on your part they	NIG

2Co
1: 1 unto the church of God **w** is at Corinth,	3588
1: 1 with all the saints **w** are in all Achaia:	3588
1: 4 we may be able to comfort them **w** are	NIG
1: 6 **w** is effectual in the enduring of the same	3588
1: 6 of the same sufferings **w** we also suffer:	3739
1: 8 have you ignorant of our trouble **w** came	3588

2Co
1: 9 ourselves, but in God **w** raiseth the dead:	3588
1:21 he **w** stablisheth us with you in Christ,	NIG
2: 2 but *the same* **w** is made sorry by me?	NIG
2: 4 ye might know the love **w** I have more	3739
2: 6 this punishment, **w** *was inflicted* of many.	3588
2:14 **w** always causeth us to triumph in Christ,	3588
2:17 not as many, **w** corrupt the word of God:	NIG
3: 7 **w** *glory* was to be done away:	3588
3:10 even that **w** was made glorious had no	NIG
3:11 For if that **w** is done away *was* glorious,	NIG
3:11 much more that **w** remaineth *is* glorious.	NIG
3:13 not as Moses, *w* put a vail over his face,	NIG
3:13 look to the end of that **w** is abolished:	NIG
3:14 **w** *vail* is done away in Christ.	3748
4: 4 blinded the minds of them **w** believe not,	NIG
4:11 For we **w** live are alway delivered unto	3588
4:14 Knowing that he **w** raised up the Lord	NIG
4:16 **For w cause** we faint not; but though	1352
4:17 our light affliction, **w** is but for a moment,	NIG
4:18 we look not at the *things* **w** are seen,	NIG
4:18 seen, but at the *things* **w** are not seen:	NIG
4:18 for the *things* **w** are seen *are* temporal;	NIG
4:18 but the *things* **w** are not seen *are* eternal.	NIG
5: 2 upon with our house **w** is from heaven:	3588
5:12 to *answer* them **w** glory in appearance,	NIG
5:15 that they **w** live should not henceforth live	NIG
5:15 but unto him **w** died for them,	NIG
7:14 so our boasting, **w** *I made* before Titus,	3588
8:11 performance also out of that **w** you have.	NIG
8:16 **w** put the same earnest care into the heart	3588
8:19 **w** is administered by us to the glory of	3588
8:20 this abundance **w** is administered by us:	3588
8:22 the great confidence **w** *I have* in you.	3588
9: 2 I boast of you to them of Macedonia,	3739
9: 6 this *I say*, He **w** soweth sparingly shall	3588
9: 6 he **w** soweth bountifully shall reap also	NIG
9:11 **w** causeth through us thanksgiving to	3748
9:14 long after you for the exceeding grace	NIG
10: 2 think of us as if we walked according	3588
10: 8 the Lord hath given us for edification,	3739
10:13 to the measure of the rule **w** God	3739
11: 4 ye have not received, or another gospel,	3739
11: 4 another gospel, **w** ye have not received,	3739
11: 9 I was chargeable to no *man:* for that **w**	NIG
11: 9 brethren **w** came from Macedonia	NIG
11:12 that I may cut off occasion from them **w**	NIG
11:17 *That* **w** I speak, I speak *it* not after	3739
11:28 that **w** cometh upon me daily, the care of	NIG
11:30 I will glory of the *things* **w** concern mine	3588
11:31 **w** is blessed for evermore, knoweth that I	3588
12: 4 *w it is* not lawful for a man to utter.	3739
12: 6 think of me above *that* **w** he seeth me *to*	3739
12:21 *that* I shall bewail many **w** have sinned	3588
12:21 lasciviousness **w** they have committed.	3739
13: 2 being absent now I write to them **w**	NIG
13: 3 to you-ward is not weak, but is mighty	3739
13: 7 but that ye should do *that* **w** is honest,	NIG
13:10 according to the power **w** the Lord hath	3739

Gal
1: 2 And all the brethren **w** are with me, unto	NIG
1: 7 **W** is not another; but there be some that	3739
1: 8 than *that* **w** we have preached unto you,	3739
1:11 the gospel **w** was preached of me is not	3588
1:17 Neither went I up to Jerusalem to them **w**	NIG
1:20 Now *the things* **w** I write unto you,	3739
1:22 the churches of Judea **w** were in Christ:	3588
1:23 That he **w** persecuted us in times past	NIG
1:23 preacheth the faith **w** once he destroyed.	NIG
2: 2 communicated unto them *that* gospel **w** I	3739
2: 2 privately to them **w** were of reputation,	NIG
2: 4 out our liberty **w** we have in Christ Jesus,	3739
2:10 the same **w** I also was forward to do.	NIG
2:12 fearing them **w** were of the circumcision.	NIG
2:18 For if I build again the *things* **w** I	3739
2:20 *the life* **w** I now live in the flesh I live by	3739
3: 7 Know ye therefore that they **w** are of faith,	NIG
3: 9 they **w** be of faith are blessed with faithful	NIG
3:10 as are written in the book of the law to do	3588
3:16 as of one, And to thy seed, **w** is Christ.	3739
3:17 **w** was four hundred and thirty years after,	NIG
3:21 for if there had been a law given **w** could	3588
3:23 shut up unto the faith **w** should afterwards	NIG
4: 8 did service unto them **w** by nature are no	NIG
4:14 And my temptation **w** was in my flesh ye	NIG
4:24 **W** *things* are an allegory: for these are	3748
4:24 **w** gendereth to bondage, which is Agar.	NIG
4:24 which gendereth to bondage, **w** is Agar.	3748
4:25 and answereth to Jerusalem **w** now is,	3588
4:26 But Jerusalem **w** is above is free, which is	3588
4:26 is above is free, **w** is the mother of us all.	3748
4:27 moe children than she **w** hath a husband.	NIG
5: 6 but faith **w** worketh by love.	NIG
5:12 I would they were even cut off **w** trouble	NIG
5:19 **w** are *these;* Adultery, fornication,	3748
5:21 of the **w** I tell you before, as I have also	3739
5:21 they **w** do such *things* shall not inherit	NIG
6: 1 be overtaken in a fault, ye **w** are spiritual,	3588

Eph
1: 1 to the saints **w** are at Ephesus, and to	3588
1: 9 according to his good pleasure **w** he had	3739
1:10 both **w** are in heaven, and which are on	3588
1:10 which are in heaven, and **w** are on earth;	3588
1:14 **W** is the earnest of our inheritance,	3739
1:20 **W** he wrought in Christ, when he raised	NIG
1:21 this world, but also in that **w** is to come:	3588
1:23 **W** is his body, the fulness of him that	3748
2:10 **w** God hath before ordained that we	3739

Eph 2:11 are called Uncircumcision by that **w** is — NIG
2:17 preached peace to you **w** were afar off, — 3588
3: 2 grace of God **w** is given me to you-ward: — 3588
3: 5 **W** in other ages was not made known — 3739
3: 9 **w** from the beginning of the world hath — 3588
3:11 According to the eternal purpose **w** he — 3739
3:13 my tribulations for you, **w** is your glory. — 3748
3:19 the love of Christ, **w** passeth knowledge, — NIG
4:15 may grow *up* into him in all *things*, **w** is — 3739
4:16 compacted by that **w** every joint supplieth, — 3739
4:22 **w** is corrupt according to the deceitful — 3588
4:24 **w** after God is created in righteousness — 3588
4:28 with *his* hands the *thing* **w** *is* good, — NIG
4:29 but *that* **w** *is* good to the use of edifying, — 1536
5: 4 nor jesting, **w** are not convenient: — 3588
5:12 those *things* **w** are done of them in secret. — NIG
6: 2 (**w** is the first commandment with — 3748
6:17 sword of the Spirit, **w** is the word of God: — 3739
6:20 For **w** I am an ambassador in bonds: — 3739
Php 1: 1 to all the saints in Christ Jesus **w** are at — 3588
1: 6 confident of this very *thing*, that he **w** — NIG
1:11 are by Jesus Christ unto the glory and — 3588
1:12 that the *things* **w** *happened* unto me have — NIG
1:23 and to be with Christ; **w** *is* far better: — NIG
1:28 **w** is to them an evident token of — 3748
1:30 Having the same conflict **w** ye saw in me, — 3634
2: 5 be in you, **w** *was* also in Christ Jesus: — 3739
2: 9 given him a name **w** is above every name: — 3588
2:13 it is God **w** worketh in you both to will — 3588
2:21 not the *things* **w** *are* Jesus Christ's. — NIG
3: 3 **w** worship God in the spirit, and rejoice — 3588
3: 6 the righteousness **w** is in the law, — 3588
3: 9 **w** is of the law, but that which is through — 3588
3: 9 but that **w** is through the faith of Christ, — NIG
3: 9 the righteousness **w** is of God by faith: — 3588
3:12 **w** also I am apprehended of Christ Jesus. — 3739
3:13 one *thing I do*, forgetting those *things* **w** — NIG
3:13 reaching forth unto those *things* **w** are — NIG
3:17 mark them **w** walk so as ye have us for — NIG
4: 3 help those *women* **w** laboured with me — 3748
4: 7 **w** passeth all understanding, shall keep — 3588
4: 9 Those *things*, **w** ye have both learned, — 3739
4:13 I can do all *things* through Christ **w** — 3588
4:18 the *things* **w** *were* sent from you, — NIG
4:21 The brethren **w** are with me greet you. — NIG
Col 1: 2 brethren in Christ **w** are at Colosse: — NIG
1: 4 of the love **w** *ye have* to all the saints, — 3588
1: 5 the hope **w** is laid up for you in heaven, — 3588
1: 6 **W** is come unto you, as *it is* in all — 3588
1:12 **w** hath made us meet to be partakers of — 3588
1:23 **w** ye have heard, *and* which was — 3739
1:23 **w** was preached to every creature which — 3588
1:23 was preached to every creature **w** is — 3588
1:24 fill up that **w** is behind of the afflictions of — NIG
1:24 flesh for his body's sake, **w** is the church: — 3739
1:25 according to the dispensation of God **w** is — 3588
1:26 *Even* the mystery **w** hath been hid from — 3588
1:27 **w** is Christ in you, the hope of glory: — 3739
1:29 his working, **w** worketh in me mightily. — 3588
2:10 **w** is the head of all principality and — 3739
2:14 **w** was contrary to us, and took it out of — 3739
2:17 **W** are a shadow of *things* to come; — 3739
2:18 intruding into those *things* **w** he hath not — 3739
2:19 from **w** all the body by joints and — 3739
2:22 **W** all are to perish with the using;) after — 3739
2:23 **W** *things* have indeed a shew of wisdom — 3748
3: 1 Christ, seek those *things* **w** are above, — NIG
3: 5 your members **w** are upon the earth; — 3588
3: 5 and covetousness, **w** is idolatry: — 3748
3: 6 For **w** *things'* sake the wrath of God — 3739
3: 7 In the **w** ye also walked sometime, when — 3739
3:10 And have put on the new *man*, **w** is — 3588
3:14 charity, **w** is the bond of perfectness. — 3739
3:15 to the **w** also ye are called in one body; — NIG
3:25 receive *for* the wrong **w** he hath done: — 3739
4: 1 give unto *your* servants that **w** is just and — NIG
4: 3 of Christ, for **w** I am also in bonds: — 3739
4: 9 unto you all *things* **w** *are* done here. — 3588
4:11 And Jesus, **w** is called Justus, who are of — 3588
4:11 of God, **w** have been a comfort unto me. — 3748
4:15 Salute the brethren **w** are in Laodicea, — NIG
4:15 and the church **w** is in his house. — NIG
4:17 Take heed to the ministry **w** thou hast — 3739
1Th 1: 1 unto the church of the Thessalonians **w** *is* — NIG
1:10 delivered us from the wrath to come. — 3588
2: 4 men, but God, **w** trieth our hearts. — 3588
2:13 when ye received the word of God **w** ye — NIG
2:13 **w** effectually worketh also in you that — 3739
2:14 followers of the churches of God **w** — NIG
3:10 might perfect that **w** is lacking in your — NIG
4: 5 even as the Gentiles **w** know not God: — 3588
4:10 all the brethren **w** are in all Macedonia: — 3588
4:13 brethren, concerning them **w** are asleep, — NIG
4:13 not, even as others **w** have no hope. — 3588
4:14 them also **w** sleep in Jesus will God bring — 3588
4:15 that we **w** are alive *and* remain unto — 3588
4:15 Lord shall not prevent them **w** are asleep. — NIG
4:17 Then we **w** are alive *and* remain shall be — 3588
5:12 to know them **w** labour among you, — NIG
5:15 any *man*; but ever follow *that* **w** *is* good, — NIG
5:21 Prove all *things*; hold fast *that* **w** *is* good. — NIG
2Th 1: 4 is a manifest token of the righteous — NIG
1: 5 the kingdom of God, for **w** ye also suffer: — 3739
2:15 hold the traditions **w** ye have been taught, — 3739
2:16 **w** hath loved us, and hath given *us* — 3588

2Th 3: 4 will do *the things* **w** we command you. — 3739
3: 6 not after the tradition **w** he received of us. — 3739
3:11 For we hear that *there are* some **w** walk — NIG
3:17 own hand, **w** is the token in every epistle: — 3739
1Ti 1: 1 and Lord Jesus Christ, **w** *is* our hope; — NIG
1: 4 endless genealogies, **w** minister questions, — 3748
1: 4 rather than godly edifying **w** is in faith: — 3588
1: 6 some having swerved have turned — 3739
1:11 God, **w** was committed to my trust. — 3739
1:14 with faith and love **w** is in Christ Jesus. — 3588
1:16 for a pattern to them **w** should hereafter — NIG
1:18 according to the prophecies **w** went — NIG
1:19 some having put away, concerning — 3739
2:10 But (**w** becometh women professing — 3739
3: 7 a good report of them **w** are without; — NIG
3:13 great boldness in the faith **w** is in Christ — 3588
3:15 **w** is the church of the living God, — 3748
4: 3 **w** God hath created to be received with — 3739
4: 3 with thanksgiving of them **w** believe — NIG
4: 8 life that now is, and of that **w** is to come. — 3588
4:14 is in thee, **w** was given thee by prophecy, — 3739
5:13 speaking *things* **w** they ought not. — 3588
6: 3 the doctrine **w** is according to godliness; — 3588
6: 9 **w** drown men in destruction and — 3748
6:10 while some coveted after, they have — 3739
6:15 **W** in his times he shall shew, *who is* — 3739
6:16 the light **w** no *man* **can approach unto**; — 676
6:20 keep that **w** is committed to *thy* trust, — 3588
6:21 **w** some professing have erred concerning — 3739
2Ti 1: 1 according to the promise of life **w** is in — 3588
1: 5 **w** dwelt first in thy grandmother Lois, — 3748
1: 6 **w** is in thee by the putting on of my hands — 3739
1: 9 **w** was given us in Christ Jesus before — 3588
1:12 For **w** cause I also suffer these *things*: — 3739
1:12 persuaded that he is able to keep that **w** — 3588
1:13 **w** thou hast heard of me, in faith and — 3739
1:13 in faith and love **w** is in Christ Jesus. — 3588
1:14 *That* good thing **w** was committed unto — NIG
1:14 keep by the Holy Ghost **w** dwelleth in us. — 3588
1:15 that all they **w** are in Asia be turned away — NIG
2:10 they may also obtain the salvation **w** is — 3588
3: 6 of this sort are they **w** creep into houses, — NIG
3:11 afflictions, **w** came unto me at Antioch, — 3634
3:14 continue thou in *the things* **w** thou hast — 3739
3:15 we are able to make thee wise unto — 3588
3:15 salvation through faith **w** is in Christ — 3588
4: 8 the Lord, the righteous judge, shall give — 3739
Tit 1: 1 the acknowledging of the truth **w** is after — 3588
1: 2 of eternal life, **w** God, that cannot lie, — 3739
1: 3 **w** is committed unto me according to — 3739
1:11 teaching *things* **w** *they* ought not, — 3739
2: 1 speak thou *the things* **w** become sound — 3739
3: 5 Not by works of righteousness **w** we have — 3739
3: 6 **W** he shed on us abundantly through — 3739
3: 8 that they **w** have believed in God might be — NIG
Phm 1: 5 **w** thou hast toward the Lord Jesus, — 3739
1: 6 good *thing* **w** is in you in Christ Jesus. — 3588
1: 8 to enjoin thee that **w** is convenient, — NIG
1:11 **w** in time past was to thee unprofitable, — 3588
Heb 1: 5 For unto **w** of the angels said he at any — 5101
1:13 But to **w** of the angels said he at any time, — 5101
2: 1 heed to *the things* **w** we have heard, — NIG
2: 3 **w** at the first began to be spoken by — 3748
2:11 for **w** cause he is not ashamed to call — 3739
2:13 I, and the children **w** God hath given me. — 3739
3: 5 for a testimony of those *things* **w** were to — NIG
4: 3 For we **w** have believed do enter into rest, — NIG
4:15 For we have not a high priest **w** cannot be — NIG
5: 8 learned he obedience by the *things* **w** he — 3739
5:12 have need that *one* teach you again **w** *be* — 5101
6: 7 For the earth **w** drinketh *in* the rain that — 3588
6: 8 But that **w** beareth thorns and briers *is* — NIG
6:10 **w** ye have shewed toward his name, — 3739
6:18 in **w** *it was* impossible for God to lie, — 3739
6:19 **W** hope we have as an anchor of the soul, — 3739
6:19 and entereth into that within the vail; — NIG
7: 2 also King of Salem, **w** is, King of peace; — 3739
7:13 of **w** no *man* gave attendance at the altar. — 3739
7:14 tribe Moses spake nothing concerning — 3739
7:19 by the **w** we draw nigh unto God. — 3739
7:28 the law maketh men high priests **w** have — NIG
7:28 **w** was since the law, *maketh* the Son, — 3588
8: 1 of the *things* **w** we have spoken *this is* — NIG
8: 2 the **w** the Lord pitched, and not man. — 3739
8: 6 **w** was established upon better promises. — 3748
8:13 Now that **w** decayeth and waxeth old *is* — 3588
9: 2 the shewbread; **w** is called the sanctuary. — 3748
9: 3 tabernacle **w** is called the holiest of all; — 3588
9: 4 **W** had the golden censer, and the ark of — NIG
9: 5 of **w** we cannot now speak particularly. — 3739
9: 7 **w** he offered for himself, and *for* the — 3739
9: 9 **W** *was* a figure for the time *then* present, — 3748
9: 9 were offered both gifts and sacrifices, — 3739
9:10 **W** stood only in meats and drinks, — NIG
9:15 are called might receive the promise — NIG
9:20 This *is* the blood of the testament **w** God — 3739
9:24 with hands, **w** *are* the figures of the true; — NIG
10: 1 can never with those sacrifices **w** they — 3739
10: 8 neither hadst pleasure *therein*: **w** are — 3748
10:10 By the **w** will we are sanctified through — NIG
10:11 **w** can never take away sins: — 3748
10:20 living way, **w** he hath consecrated for us, — NIG
10:27 **w** shall devour the adversaries. — NIG
10:32 **w**, after ye were illuminated, ye endured — 3739

Heb 10:35 **w** hath great recompence of reward. — 3748
11: 3 that *things* **w** are seen were not made of — NIG
11: 3 were not made of *things* **w** do appear. — NIG
11: 4 by **w** he obtained witness that he was — 3739
11: 7 by the **w** he condemned the world, — 3739
11: 7 became heir of the righteousness **w** is by — NIG
11: 8 he was called to go out into a place **w** — 3739
11:10 he looked for a city **w** hath foundations, — NIG
11:12 as the sand **w** is by the sea shore — 3588
11:29 the Egyptians assaying to do were — NIG
12: 1 and the sin **w** doth so easily beset *us*, and — NIG
12: 5 And ye have forgotten the exhortation **w** — 3748
12: 9 had fathers of our flesh **w** corrected *us*, — NIG
12:11 unto them **w** are exercised thereby. — NIG
12:12 Wherefore lift up the hands **w** hang down, — NIG
12:13 *that* **w** *is* lame be turned out of the way; — NIG
12:14 without **w** no *man* shall see the Lord: — 3739
12:19 **w** voice they that heard intreated that — 3739
12:20 (For they could not endure that **w** was — NIG
12:23 **w** are written in heaven, and to God — NIG
12:27 that those *things* **w** cannot be shaken may — NIG
12:28 Wherefore we receiving a kingdom **w** — NIG
13: 3 with *them; and* them **w** suffer adversity, — NIG
13: 7 Remember them **w** have the rule over — NIG
13: 9 **w** have not profited them that have been — 3739
13:10 whereof they have no right to eat **w** serve — NIG
13:21 working in you *that* **w** is well pleasing in — NIG
Jas 1: 1 the twelve tribes **w** are scattered abroad, — 3588
1:12 the Lord hath promised to them that — 3739
1:21 **w** is able to save your souls. — 3588
2: 5 heirs of the kingdom **w** he hath promised — 3739
2: 7 *that* worthy name by the **w** ye are called? — 3739
2:16 those *things* **w** *are* needful to the body; — NIG
2:23 And the scripture was fulfilled **w** saith, — 3588
3: 4 though they be so great, and are driven — NIG
3: 9 are made after the similitude of God. — 3588
5: 4 the hire of the labourers **w** have reaped — 3588
5: 4 **w** is of you kept back by fraud, crieth: — NIG
5: 4 cries of them **w** have reaped are entered — NIG
5:11 Behold, we count them happy **w** endure. — NIG
5:20 that he **w** converteth the sinner from — NIG
1Pe 1: 3 **w** according to his abundant mercy hath — 3588
1:10 Of **w** salvation the prophets have inquired — 3739
1:11 manner of time the Spirit of Christ **w** — 3588
1:12 **w** are now reported unto you by them that — 3739
1:12 **w** *things* the angels desire to look into. — NIG
1:15 as he **w** hath called you is holy, so be ye — NIG
1:23 word of God, **w** liveth and abideth for — NIG
1:25 And this is the word **w** by the gospel is — NIG
2: 7 therefore **w** believe *he is* precious: — 3588
2: 7 unto them **w** be disobedient, the stone — NIG
2: 7 the stone **w** the builders disallowed, — 3739
2: 8 *even to them* **w** stumble at the word, — 3739
2:10 **W** in time past *were* not a people, — 3588
2:10 **w** had not obtained mercy, but now have — 3588
2:11 from fleshly lusts, **w** war against the soul; — 3748
2:12 by *your* good works, **w** they shall behold, — NIG
3: 4 in *that* **w** is not corruptible, *even* — NIG
3: 4 **w** is in the sight of God of great price. — 3739
3:13 if ye be followers of *that* **w** *is* good? — NIG
3:19 By also he went and preached unto — 3739
3:20 **W** sometime were disobedient, when — NIG
4:11 *him do it* as of the ability **w** God giveth: — 3739
4:12 concerning the fiery trial **w** is to try you, — NIG
5: 1 The elders **w** are among you I exhort, — NIG
5: 2 Feed the flock of God **w** is among you, — NIG
2Pe 1:18 And this voice **w** came from heaven we — NIG
2:11 **w** are greater in power and might, — NIG
2:15 **W** have forsaken the right way, — NIG
3: 1 both **w** I stir up your pure minds by way — 3739
3: 2 That *ye* may be mindful of the words **w** — NIG
3: 7 the heavens and the earth, **w** are now, — NIG
3:10 in the **w** the heavens shall pass away with — 3739
3:16 speaking in them of these *things*; in **w** are — 3739
3:16 **w** they that *are* unlearned and — 3739
1Jn 1: 1 *That* **w** was from the beginning, which — 3739
1: 1 **w** we have heard, which we have seen — 3739
1: 1 heard, **w** we have seen with our eyes, — 3739
1: 1 **w** we have looked upon, and our hands — 3739
1: 2 was with the Father, and **w** was — 3748
1: 3 *That* **w** we have seen and heard declare — 3739
1: 5 is the message **w** we have heard of him, — 3739
2: 7 an old commandment **w** ye had from — NIG
2: 7 The old commandment is the word **w** ye — 3739
2: 8 you, **w** thing is true in him and in you: — 3739
2:24 ye have heard from the beginning. — 3739
2:24 *that* **w** ye have heard from the beginning — 3739
2:27 But the anointing **w** ye have received of — 3739
2:29 ye know that every one **w** doeth — 3588
3:24 in us, by the Spirit **w** he hath given us. — 3739
5: 9 for this is the witness of God **w** he hath — 3739
5:16 If any *man* see his brother sin a sin **w** — NIG
2Jn 1: 2 **w** dwelleth in us, and shall be with us for — 3588
1: 5 but *that* **w** we had from the beginning, — 3739
1: 8 that we lose not those *things* **w** we have — 3739
3Jn 1: 6 **W** have borne witness of thy charity — 3739
1:10 I will remember his deeds **w** he doeth, — 3739
1:11 follow not *that* **w** is evil, but *that which is* — NIG
1:11 not *that* **w** is evil, but *that* **w** is good. — NIG
Jude 1: 3 faith **w** was once delivered unto the — NIG
1: 6 the angels **w** kept not their first estate, — NIG
1:10 these speak **w** of those *things* **w** they — 3745
1:15 deeds **w** they have ungodly committed, — NIG
1:15 all *their* hard *speeches* **w** ungodly sinners — 3739
1:17 remember ye the words **w** were spoken — NIG

Rev		
1: 1	of Jesus Christ, **w** God gave unto him,	3739
1: 1	to shew unto his servants *things* **w** must	3739
1: 3	keep those *things* **w** are written therein:	NIG
1: 4	John to the seven churches **w** are in Asia:	3588
1: 4	from him **w** is, and which was,	3588
1: 4	is, and **w** was, and which is to come;	3588
1: 4	is, and which was, and **w** is to come;	3588
1: 4	from the seven spirits **w** are before his	3739
1: 7	see him, and they *also* **w** pierced him:	3748
1: 8	**w** is, and which was, and which is to	3588
1: 8	is, and **w** was, and which is to come,	3588
1: 8	is, and which was, and **w** is to come,	3588
1:11	send *it* unto the seven churches **w** are in	3588
1:19	Write *the things* **w** thou hast seen,	3739
1:19	*the things* **w** are, and *the things* which	3739
1:19	and *the things* **w** shall be hereafter;	3739
1:20	The mystery of the seven stars **w** thou	3739
1:20	the seven candlesticks **w** thou sawest are	3739
2: 2	how thou canst not bear *them* **w** are evil:	NIG
2: 2	hast tried them **w** say *they* are apostles,	NIG
2: 6	deeds of the Nicolaitans, **w** I also hate.	3739
2: 7	**w** is in the midst of the paradise of God.	3739
2: 8	and the last, **w** was dead, and is alive;	3739
2: 9	*I know* the blasphemy of them **w** say they	NIG
2:10	Fear none *of those things* **w** thou shalt	3739
2:12	These *things* saith he **w** hath the sharp	NIG
2:15	of the Nicolaitans, **w** *thing* I hate.	3739
2:17	**w** no *man* knoweth saving he that	3739
2:20	**w** calleth herself a prophetess, to teach	3588
2:23	the churches shall know that I am he **w**	NIG
2:24	**w** have not known the depths of Satan,	3748
2:25	But *that* **w** ye have *already* hold fast till I	3739
3: 2	and strengthen the *things* **w** remain,	NIG
3: 4	**w** have not defiled their garments;	3739
3: 9	**w** say they are Jews, and are not, but do	3588
3:10	**w** shall come upon all the world, to try	3588
3:11	*that* fast **w** thou hast, that no *man* take	3739
3:12	the city of my God, **w** *is* new Jerusalem,	NIG
3:12	**w** cometh down out of heaven from my	3739
4: 1	the first voice **w** I heard *was* as *it were* of	3739
4: 1	**w** said, Come up hither, and I will shew	NIG
4: 1	I shew thee *things* **w** must be hereafter.	3739
4: 5	throne, **w** are the seven spirits of God.	3739
4: 8	**w** was, and is, and is to come.	3588
5: 6	**w** are the seven spirits of God sent forth	3739
5: 8	full of odours, **w** are the prayers of saints.	3739
5:13	And every creature **w** is in heaven,	3739
6: 9	God, and for the testimony **w** they held:	3739
7: 4	And I heard the number of them **w** were	NIG
7: 9	**w** no *man* could number, of all nations,	3739
7:10	Salvation to our God **w** sitteth upon	3588
7:13	What are these **w** are arrayed in white	3588
7:14	These are they **w** came out of great	NIG
7:17	For the Lamb **w** is in the midst of	3588
8: 2	I saw the seven angels **w** stood before	3739
8: 3	the golden altar **w** was before the throne.	3588
8: 4	**w** *came* with the prayers of the saints,	NIG
8: 6	And the seven angels **w** had the seven	3588
8: 9	the third *part* of the creatures **w** were in	NIG
8:13	of the three angels, **w** are yet to sound.	NIG
9: 4	*those* men **w** have not the seal of God	3748
9:11	**w** *is* the angel of the bottomless *pit*,	NIG
9:13	horns of the golden altar **w** is before God,	3588
9:14	Saying to the sixth angel **w** had	3739
9:14	Loose the four angels **w** are bound in	3588
9:15	**w** were prepared for an hour, and a day,	3588
9:18	brimstone, **w** issued out of their mouths.	3588
9:20	the rest of the men **w** were not killed	3739
9:20	**w** neither can see, nor hear, nor walk:	3739
10: 4	Seal *up those things* **w** the seven	3739
10: 5	And the angel **w** I saw stand upon the sea	3739
10: 6	and the sea, and the *things* **w** are therein,	NIG
10: 8	the voice **w** I heard from heaven spake	3739
10: 8	take the little book **w** is open in the hand	3588
10: 8	hand of the angel **w** standeth upon the sea	3588
11: 2	the court **w** is without the temple leave	3588
11: 8	spiritually is called Sodom and Egypt,	3748
11:11	and great fear fell upon them **w** saw them.	NIG
11:16	**w** sat before God on their seats,	3588
11:17	**w** art, and wast, and art to come;	3588
11:18	destroy them **w** destroy the earth.	NIG
12: 4	dragon stood before the woman **w** was	3739
12: 9	and Satan, **w** deceiveth the whole world:	3588
12:10	**w** accused them before our God day and	3588
12:13	persecuted the woman **w** brought forth	3748
12:16	swallowed up the flood **w** the dragon cast	3739
12:17	**w** keep the commandments of God,	3588
13: 2	And the beast **w** I saw was like unto a	3739
13: 4	And they worshipped the dragon **w** gave	3739
13:12	them **w** dwell therein to worship the first	3588
13:14	**w** he had power to do in the sight of	3739
13:14	**w** had the wound by a sword, and did	3739
13: 4	were redeemed from the earth.	3588
14: 4	These are they **w** were not defiled with	3739
14: 4	These are they **w** follow the Lamb	NIG
14:10	**w** is poured out without mixture into	3588
14:13	Blessed *are* the dead **w** die in the Lord	3588
14:17	another angel came out of the temple **w**	3588
14:18	out from the altar, **w** had power over fire;	3588
16: 2	sore upon the men **w** had the mark	NIG
16: 2	and *upon* them **w** worshipped his image.	NIG
16: 5	O Lord, **w** art, and wast, and shalt be,	3588
16: 9	of God, **w** hath power over these plagues:	3588
16:14	**w** go forth unto the kings of the earth and	3739
17: 1	there came one of the seven angels **w**	3588

Rev		
17: 7	**w** hath the seven heads and ten horns.	3588
17: 9	And here *is* the mind **w** hath wisdom.	3588
17: 9	mountains, on **w** the woman sitteth.	846
17:12	And the ten horns **w** thou sawest are ten	3588
17:12	**w** have received no kingdom as yet;	3748
17:15	saith unto me, The waters **w** thou sawest,	3739
17:16	the ten horns **w** thou sawest upon	3739
17:18	the woman **w** thou sawest is *that* great	3739
17:18	**w** reigneth over the kings of the earth.	3588
18: 6	in the cup **w** she hath filled fill to her	3739
18:14	all *things* **w** were dainty and goodly are	NIG
18:15	The merchants of these *things*, **w** were	3588
19: 2	**w** did corrupt the earth with her	3748
19: 9	Blessed *are* they **w** are called unto	NIG
19:14	the armies **w** were in heaven followed	NIG
19:20	with **w** he deceived them that had	3739
19:21	*sword* proceeded out of his mouth:	3588
20: 2	**w** is the devil, and Satan, and bound him	3739
20: 4	and **w** had not worshipped the beast,	3748
20: 8	And shall go out to deceive the nations **w**	3588
20:12	book was opened, **w** is the *book* of life:	3739
20:12	dead were judged out of those *things* **w**	NIG
20:13	the sea gave up the dead **w** were in it;	3588
20:13	delivered up the dead **w** were in them:	3588
21: 8	shall have their part in the lake **w** burneth	3588
21: 8	and brimstone: **w** is the second death.	3739
21: 9	**w** had the seven vials full of the seven last	3588
21:12	**w** are *the names* of the twelve tribes of	3739
21:24	And the nations of them **w** are saved shall	NIG
21:27	they **w** are written in the Lamb's book of	NIG
22: 2	**w** bare twelve *manner of* fruits,	NIG
22: 6	the *things* **w** must shortly be done.	3739
22: 8	of the angel **w** shewed me these *things*.	3588
22: 9	of them **w** keep the sayings of this book:	NIG
22:11	and he **w** is filthy, let him be filthy still:	NIG
22:19	the *things* **w** are written in this book.	NIG
22:20	He **w** testifieth these *things* saith, Surely I	NIG

WHILE (210) [WHILES, WHILST]

Ge		
8:22	**W** the earth remaineth, seedtime	3605+5750
19:16	And **w** he lingered, the men laid hold	2050.1
25: 6	**w** he yet lived, eastward, unto the east	871.1
29: 9	**w** he yet spake with them, Rachel came	5750
45: 1	**w** Joseph made himself known unto his	871.1
46:29	neck, and wept on his neck a **good w**.	5750
Ex 33:22	come to pass, **w** my glory passeth by,	871.1
33:22	cover thee with my hand **w** I pass by:	5704
34:29	of his face shone **w** he talked with him.	871.1
Lev 4:27	**w** he doeth somewhat against *any of*	871.1
14:46	**w** that it is shut up shall be unclean until	3117
26:43	she lieth desolate without them:	871.1
Nu 11:33	the flesh *was yet* between their teeth,	5750
15:32	And **w** the children of Israel were in	2050.1
23:15	I meet the LORD yonder.	2050.1
25:11	**w** he was zealous for my sake among	871.1
Dt 19: 6	**w** his heart is hot, and overtake him,	3588
31:27	**w** I am yet alive with you *this* day,	871.1
Jos 14:10	**w** *the children of* Israel wandered in	834
Jdg 3:26	Ehud escaped **w** they tarried, and passed	5704
11:26	**W** Israel dwelt in Heshbon and her	871.1
14:17	him the seven days, **w** their feast lasted:	834
15: 1	it came to pass **within a w after**,	3117+4480
16:27	that beheld **w** Samson made sport.	871.1
1Sa 2:13	came, **w** the flesh was in seething,	3509.1
7: 2	**w** the ark abode in Kirjath-jearim,	3117+4480
9:27	stand thou still a **w**,	3117+1886.1+3509.1
14:19	to pass, **w** Saul communed with the priest,	5704
20:14	thou shalt not only **w** yet I live shew me	5750
22: 4	they dwelt with him all the **w** that David	3117
25: 7	them, all the **w** they were in Carmel.	3117
25:16	all the **w** we were with them keeping	3117
27:11	*will be* his manner all the **w** he dwelleth	3117
2Sa 3: 6	**w** there was war between the house of	871.1
3:35	David to eat meat **w** it was yet day,	871.1
7:19	house for a **great w to come**.	4480+7350
12:18	Behold, **w** the child was *yet* alive,	871.1
12:21	and weep for the child, **w** *it was* alive;	NIH
12:22	**W** the child *was yet* alive, I fasted and	871.1
13:30	it came to pass, **w** *they were* in the way,	NIH
15: 8	thy servant vowed a vow **w** I abode at	871.1
15:12	from Giloh, **w** he offered sacrifices.	871.1
17: 2	I will come upon him **w** he *is* weary	2050.1
18:14	**w** he *was yet* alive in the midst of the	5750
19:32	had provided the king of sustenance **w**	871.1
24:13	thine enemies, **w** they pursue thee?	2050.1
1Ki 1:14	**w** thou yet talkest there with the king,	5750
1:22	lo, **w** she yet talked with the king,	5750
1:42	**w** he yet spake, behold, Jonathan the son	5750
3:20	**w** thine handmaid slept, and laid it in	2050.1
6: 7	heard in the house, **w** it was in building.	871.1
12: 6	stood before Solomon his father **w** he	871.1
17: 7	it came to pass after a **w**, that the brook	3117
18:45	came to pass **in the mean w**,	
		3541+3541+5704+5704+2050.1
2Ki 6:33	**w** he talked with them, behold,	5750
1Ch 12: 1	**w** he yet kept himself close because of	5750
17:17	house for a **great w to come**,	4480+7350
21:12	**w** that the sword of thine enemies	2050.1
2Ch 10: 6	Solomon **w** he *yet* lived,	871.1+1961
14: 7	and bars, **w** the land *is* yet before us;	NIH
15: 2	The LORD *is* with you, **w** ye be with	871.1
26:19	he was wroth **w** the priests,	871.1
34: 3	year of his reign, **w** he was yet young,	2050.1
Ne 7: 3	**w** they stand by, let them shut the doors,	5704
Est 2:21	**w** Mordecai sat in the king's gate,	2050.1

Est		
6:14	**w** they *were yet* talking with him, came	5750
Job 1:16	**W** he *was yet* speaking, there came also	5750
1:17	**W** he *was yet* speaking, there came also	5750
1:18	**W** he *was yet* speaking, there came also	5704
20:23	and shall rain *it* upon **w** he is eating.	871.1
24:24	are exalted for a **little w**, but are gone	4592
27: 3	All the **w** my breath *is* in me, and the	5750
Ps 7: 2	*it* in pieces, **w** *there is* none to deliver.	2050.1
31:13	**w** they took counsel together against me,	871.1
37:10	yet a **little w**, and the wicked *shall* not	4592
39: 1	keep my mouth with a bridle, **w**	5750+871.1
39: 3	me, **w** I was musing the fire burned:	871.1
42: 3	night, **w** *they* continually say unto me,	871.1
42:10	**w** they say daily unto me, Where *is* thy	871.1
63: 4	Thus will I bless thee **w** I live: I will lift	871.1
69: 3	dried: mine eyes fail **w** *I* wait for my God.	NIH
78:30	But **w** their meat *was yet* in their mouths,	5750
88:15	ready to die from *my* youth *up:* **w** I suffer	NIH
104:33	to my God **w** I have my being.	5750+871.1
146: 2	**W** I live will I praise the LORD: I will	871.1
146: 2	my God **w** I have *any* being.	5750+871.1
Pr 8:26	**W** as yet he had not made the earth,	5704
19:18	Chasten thy son **w** there is hope, and let	3588
31:15	She riseth also **w** *it is* yet night,	871.1
Ecc 9: 3	madness *is* in their heart **w** they live,	834+5704
12: 1	**w** the evil days come not,	834+5704
12: 2	**W** the sun, or the light, or the moon,	834+5704
SS 1:12	**W** the king *sitteth* at his table,	5704+7945
Isa 10:25	For yet a **very little w**,	4213+4592
28: 4	**w** it is yet in his hand he eateth it up.	871.1
29:17	*Is* it not yet a **very little w**,	4213+4592
55: 6	Seek ye the LORD **w** he may be found,	871.1
55: 6	be found, call ye upon him **w** he is near:	871.1
63:18	holiness have possessed *it* but a **little w**:	4705
Jer 13:16	and, **w** ye look for light, he turn it into	NIH
15: 9	her sun is gone down **w** *it was* yet day:	871.1
33: 1	**w** he was yet shut up in the court of	2050.1
39:15	**w** he was shut up in the court of the	871.1
40: 5	Now **w** he was not yet gone back, *he said,*	NIH
51:33	yet a **little w**, and the time of her harvest	4592
La 1:19	**w** they sought their meat, to relieve their	3588
Eze 9: 8	**w** they were slaying them, and I *was*	3509.1
Da 4:31	**W** the word *was* in the king's mouth,	5751
Hos 1: 4	for yet a little **w**, and I will avenge the	NIH
Na 1:10	For **w** *they* be folden together *as* thorns,	NIH
1:10	**w** they be drunken *as* drunkards,	3509.1
Hag 2: 6	*is* a **little w**, and I will shake the heavens,	4592
Zec 14:12	Their flesh *shall* consume away **w** they	2050.1
Mt 1:20	But **w** he thought on these *things*, behold,	NIG
9:18	**W** he spake these *things* unto them,	NIG
12:46	**W** he talked to the people, behold,	2089
13:21	he not root in himself, but dureth **for a w**:	4340
13:25	But **w** men slept, his enemy came	1722+3588
13:29	lest **w** ye gather up the tares, ye root up	NIG
14:22	**w** he sent the multitudes away.	2193+3739
17: 5	**W** he yet spake, behold, a bright cloud	NIG
17:22	And **w** they abode in Galilee, Jesus said	NIG
22:41	the Pharisees were gathered together,	1161
25: 5	**W** the bridegroom tarried, they all	1161
25:10	And **w** they went to buy, the bridegroom	NIG
26:36	Sit ye here, **w** I go and pray yonder.	2193+3739
26:47	And **w** he yet spake, lo, Judas, one of	2089
26:73	And after a **w** came unto *him* they that	3398
27:63	**w** he was yet alive, After three days I will	2089
28:13	by night, and stole him *away* **w** we slept.	NIG
Mk 1:35	a **great w** before day, he went out,	3029
2:19	**w** the bridegroom is with them?	1722+3739
5:35	**W** he yet spake, there came from the	2089
6:31	apart into a desert place, and rest a **w**:	3641
6:45	Bethsaida, **w** he sent away the people.	2193
12:35	and said, **w** he taught in the temple,	NIG
14:32	his disciples, Sit ye here, **w** I shall pray.	2193
14:43	And **w** he yet spake, cometh Judas, one of	2089
15:44	asked him whether he had been any **w**	3819
Lk 1: 8	**w** he executed the priest's office	1722+3588
2: 6	And so it was, that, **w** they	1510+1722+3588
5:34	**w** the bridegroom is with them?	1722+3739
8:13	which for a **w** believe, and in time of	2540
8:49	**W** he yet spake, there cometh one from	NIG
9:34	**W** he thus spake, there came a cloud,	1161
9:43	they wondered every one at all *things*	NIG
10:13	had a **great w ago** repented, sitting in	3819
14:32	Or else, **w** the other is yet a great way off,	NIG
18: 4	he would not for a **w**: but afterward he	5550
22:47	And **w** he yet spake, behold a multitude,	NIG
22:58	And after a **little w** another saw him,	1024
22:60	And **w** he yet spake, the cock crew.	2089
24:15	that **w** they communed *together*	1722+3588
24:32	he talked with us by the way,	5613
24:32	and **w** he opened to us the scriptures?	5613
24:41	And **w** they yet believed not for joy,	2089
24:44	**w** I was yet with you, that all *things* must	NIG
24:51	And it came to pass, **w** he blessed	1722+3588
Jn 4:31	In the **mean w** *his* disciples prayed him,	3342
5: 7	**w** I am coming, another steppeth	1722+3739
7:33	Yet a little **w am** I with you, and *then* I go	5550
9: 4	the works of him that sent me, **w** it is day:	2193
12:35	Yet a little **w** is the light with you.	5550
12:35	Walk **w** ye have the light, lest darkness	2193
12:36	**W** ye have light, believe in the light, that	2193
13:33	children, yet a **little w** I am with you.	3398
14:19	Yet a little **w**, and the world seeth me no	2089
16:16	A **little w**, and ye shall not see me:	3398
16:16	and again, a **little w**, and ye shall see me,	3398
16:17	us, A **little w**, and ye shall not see me:	3398

Jn	16:17	and again, a **little w**, and ye shall see me:	3398
	16:18	What is this that he saith, A **little w**?	3398
	16:19	I said, A **little w**, and ye shall not see me:	3398
	16:19	and again, a **little w**, and ye shall see me?	3398
	17:12	**W** I was with them in the world, I kept	3753
Ac	1: 9	And when he had spoken these *things*, **w**	NIG
	1:10	And **w** they looked stedfastly toward	5613
	9:39	Dorcas made, **w** she was with them.	NIG
	10:10	**w** they made ready, he fell into a trance,	NIG
	10:17	Now **w** Peter doubted in himself what	5613
	10:19	**W** Peter thought on the vision, the Spirit	1161
	10:44	**W** Peter yet spake these words, the Holy	NIG
	15: 7	know how that **a good w** ago	575+744+2250
	17:16	Now **w** Paul waited for them at Athens,	1722+3588
	18:18	*this* tarried *there* yet a **good w**,	2250+2425
	19: 1	pass *that*, **w** Apollos was at Corinth,	1722+3588
	20:11	and eaten, and talked a **long w**,	1909+2425
	22:17	even **w** I prayed in the temple, I was in a	NIG
	24:20	doing in me, **w** I stood before the council,	NIG
	25: 8	**W** he answered for himself, Neither	NIG
	27:33	And **w** the day was coming on, Paul	891+3739
	28: 6	but after they had looked a **great w**,	1909+4183
Ro	2:15	*their* thoughts the mean **w** accusing or	NIG
	5: 8	that, **w** we were yet sinners, Christ died	NIG
	7: 3	So then if, **w** *her* husband liveth, she be	NIG
1Co	3: 4	**w** one saith, I am of Paul; and another,	3752
	8:13	I will eat no flesh **w** the world **standeth**,	1519
	16: 7	I trust to tarry a **w** with you, if the Lord	5550
2Co	4:18	We look not at the *things* which are	NIG
Gal	2:17	But if, **w** we seek to be justified by Christ,	NIG
1Ti	5: 6	she that liveth in pleasure is dead **w** she	NIG
	6:10	which **w** some coveted after, they have	NIG
Heb	3:13	another daily, **w** it is called To day;	891+3739
	9: 8	**w as** the first tabernacle was **yet** standing:	2089
	10:37	For yet a **little w**,	3398+3745+3745
1Pe	3: 2	**W** they behold your chaste conversation	NIG
	3:20	**w** the ark was a preparing, wherein few,	NIG
	5:10	after that ye have suffered a **w**, make you	3641
2Pe	2:13	own deceivings **w** they feast with you;	NIG
	2:19	promise them liberty,	NIG

WHILES (12) [WHILE]

Ps	49:18	Though **w** he lived he blessed his soul:	871.1
Isa	65:24	and **w** they are yet speaking, I will hear.	NIH
Eze	21:29	**W** *they* see vanity unto thee, whiles *they*	871.1
	21:29	unto thee, **w** *they* divine a lie unto thee,	871.1
	44:17	**w** they minister in the gates of the inner	871.1
Da	5: 2	Belshazzar, **w** *he* tasted the wine,	871.2
	9:20	**w** I *was* speaking, and praying,	5750
	9:21	Yea, **w** I *was* speaking in prayer, even	5750
Hos	7: 6	heart like an oven, **w** they lie in wait:	871.1
Mt	5:25	**w** thou art in the way with him;	2193+3748
Ac	5: 4	**W** it remained, was it not thine own?	NIG
2Co	9:13	**W** by the experiment of this ministration	NIG

WHILST (12) [WHILE]

Jdg	6:31	him be put to death **w** *it is yet* morning:	5704
Ne	6: 3	**w** I leave it, and come down to	834+3509.1
Job	8:12	**W** it *is yet* in his greenness, *and* not cut	5750
	32:11	**w** you searched out what to say.	5704
Ps	141:10	their own nets, **w** that I withal escape.	5704
Jer	17: 2	**W** their children remember their altars	3509.1
2Co	5: 6	that, **w** we are at home in the body,	NIG
	7:15	**w** he remembereth the obedience of you	NIG
Heb	3:15	**W** it is said, To day if ye will hear	1722+3588
	9:17	otherwise it is of no strength at all **w**	3753
	10:33	**w** ye were made a gazingstock both by	NIG
	10:33	**w** ye became companions of them that	NIG

WHIP (2) [WHIPS]

| Pr | 26: 3 | A **w** for the horse, a bridle for the ass, | 7752 |
| Na | 3: 2 | The noise of a **w**, and the noise of | 7752 |

WHIPS (4) [WHIP]

1Ki	12:11	my father hath chastised you with **w**,	7752
	12:14	my father *also* chastised you with **w**,	7752
2Ch	10:11	my father chastised you with **w**, but I *will*	7752
	10:14	my father chastised you with **w**, but I *will*	7752

WHIRLETH (1) [WHIRLWIND, WHIRLWINDS]

| Ecc | 1: 6 | it **w** about **continually**, | 1980+5437+5437 |

WHIRLWIND (27) [WHIRLETH, WIND]

2Ki	2: 1	would take up Elijah *into* heaven by a **w**,	5591
	2:11	and Elijah went up by a **w** *into* heaven.	5591
Job	37: 9	Out of the south cometh the **w**: and cold out	5492
	38: 1	the Lord answered Job out of the **w**,	5591
	40: 6	the Lord unto Job out of the **w**,	5591
Ps	58: 9	he shall **take** them **away as with a w**,	8175
Pr	1:27	and your destruction cometh as a **w**;	5492
	10:25	As the **w** passeth, so *is* the wicked no more	5492
Isa	5:28	counted like flint, and their wheels like a **w**	5492
	17:13	and like a rolling thing before the **w**,	5492
	40:24	and the **w** shall take them away as stubble.	5591
	41:16	them away, and the **w** shall scatter them:	5591
	66:15	with his chariots like a **w**, to render his	5492
Jer	4:13	as clouds, and his chariots *shall be* as a **w**:	5492
	23:19	of the Lord is gone forth *in* fury,	5591
	23:19	is gone forth *in* fury, even a grievous **w**:	5591
	25:32	a great **w** shall be raised up from the coasts	5591
	30:23	the **w** of the Lord goeth forth *with* fury,	5591
	30:23	goeth forth *with* fury, a continuing **w**:	5591
Eze	1: 4	behold, a **w** came out of the north,	5591+7307
Da	11:40	the north shall **come** against him **like a w**,	8175
Hos	8: 7	sown the wind, and they shall reap the **w**:	5492

Hos	13: 3	as the chaff *that* is **driven with a w** out of	5590
Am	1:14	with a tempest in the day of the **w**:	5492
Na	1: 3	*wicked:* the Lord *hath* his way in the **w**	5492
Hab	3:14	they **came out as a w** to scatter me:	5590
Zec	7:14	I **scattered** them **with a w** among all	5590

WHIRLWINDS (2) [WHIRLETH, WIND]

| Isa | 21: 1 | As **w** in the south pass through; | 5492 |
| Zec | 9:14 | and shall go with **w** of the south. | 5591 |

WHISPER (2) [WHISPERED, WHISPERER, WHISPERERS, WHISPERINGS]

| Ps | 41: 7 | All that hate me **w** together against me: | 3907 |
| Isa | 29: 4 | and thy speech shall **w** out of the dust. | 6850 |

WHISPERED (1) [WHISPER]

| 2Sa | 12:19 | when David saw that his servants **w**, | 3907 |

WHISPERER (1) [WHISPER]

| Pr | 16:28 | and a **w** separateth chief friends. | 5372 |

WHISPERERS (1) [WHISPER]

| Ro | 1:29 | murder, debate, deceit, malignity; **w**, | 5588 |

WHISPERINGS (1) [WHISPER]

| 2Co | 12:20 | strifes, backbitings, **w**, swellings, tumults: | 5587 |

WHIT (5)

Dt	13:16	all the spoil thereof **every w**,	3632
1Sa	3:18	Samuel told him every **w**, and hid nothing	1697
Jn	7:23	I have made a man **every w** whole on	3650
	13:10	to wash *his* feet, but is clean **every w**:	3650
2Co	11: 5	For I suppose *I* was **not a w** behind	3367

WHITE (75) [WHITED, WHITER]

Ge	30:35	*and* every one that had *some* **w** in it,	3836
	30:37	pilled **w** strakes in them, and made	3836
	30:37	the **w** appear which *was* in the rods.	3836
	40:16	I *had* three **w** baskets on my head:	2751
	49:12	red with wine, and *his* teeth **w** with milk.	3836
Ex	16:31	*was* like coriander seed, **w**; and the taste	3836
Lev	13: 3	*when* the hair in the plague is turned **w**,	3836
	13: 4	If the bright spot *be* **w** in the skin of his	3836
	13: 4	and the hair thereof be not turned **w**;	3836
	13:10	*if* the rising *be* **w** in the skin, and it have	3836
	13:10	it have turned the hair **w**, and *there be*	3836
	13:13	the plague: it is all turned **w**: he *is* clean.	3836
	13:16	be changed unto **w**, he shall come unto	3836
	13:17	behold, *if* the plague be turned into **w**;	3836
	13:19	the place of the boil there be a **w** rising,	3836
	13:19	**w**, *and* somewhat reddish, and it be	3836
	13:20	skin, and the hair thereof be turned **w**;	3836
	13:21	*there be* no **w** hairs therein, and *if* it be	3836
	13:24	quick *flesh* that burneth have a **w** bright	3836
	13:24	bright spot, somewhat reddish, or **w**;	3836
	13:25	*if* the hair in the bright spot be turned **w**,	3836
	13:26	*there be* no **w** hair in the bright spot,	3836
	13:38	flesh bright spots, *even* **w** bright spots;	3836
	13:39	in the skin of their flesh *be* darkish **w**;	3836
	13:42	or bald forehead, a **w** reddish sore;	3836
	13:43	*if* the rising of the sore *be* **w** reddish in his	3836
Nu	12:10	Miriam *became* leprous, **w** as snow:	NIH
Jdg	5:10	Speak, ye that ride on **w** asses, ye that sit	6715
2Ki	5:27	went out from his presence a leper *as* **w**	NIH
2Ch	5:12	their brethren, *being* arrayed in **w** linen,	948
Est	1: 6	*Where were* **w**, green, and blue *hangings*,	2353
	1: 6	of red, and blue, and **w**, and black marble.	1858
	8:15	of the king in royal apparel *of* blue and **w**,	2353
Job	6: 6	or is there *any* taste in the **w** of an egg?	7388
Ps	68:14	kings in it, it was **w** *as* snow in Salmon.	NIH
Ecc	9: 8	Let thy garments be always **w**; and let thy	3836
SS	5:10	My beloved *is* **w** and ruddy, the chiefest	6703
Isa	1:18	be as scarlet, they shall be as **w** as snow;	3835
Eze	27:18	in the wine of Helbon, and **w** wool.	6713
Da	7: 9	garment *was* **w** as snow, and the hair	2358
	11:35	and to purge, and to **make** *them* **w**,	3835
	12:10	shall be purified, and **made w**, and tried;	3835
Joel	1: 7	away; the branches thereof are **made w**.	3835
Zec	1: 8	*were there* red horses, speckled, and **w**.	3836
	6: 3	in the third chariot **w** horses; and in	3836
	6: 6	go forth after them; and the grisled	3836
Mt	5:36	thou canst not make one hair **w** or black.	3022
	17: 2	sun, and his raiment was **w** as the light.	3022
	28: 3	like lightning, and his raiment **w** as snow:	3022
Mk	9: 3	became shining, exceeding **w** as snow;	3022
	9: 3	so as no fuller on earth can **w** them.	3021
	16: 5	right side, clothed in a long **w** *garment*;	3022
Lk	9:29	and his raiment was **w** *and* glistering.	3022
Jn	4:35	fields; for they are **w** already to harvest.	3022
	20:12	And seeth two angels in **w** sitting, the one	3022
Ac	1:10	two men stood by them in **w** apparel;	3022
Rev	1:14	His head and *his* hairs *were* **w** like wool,	3022
	1:14	hairs *were* white like wool, *as* **w** as snow;	3022
	2:17	will give him a **w** stone, and in	3022
	3: 4	and they shall walk with me in **w**:	3022
	3: 5	the same shall be clothed in **w** raiment;	3022
	3:18	**w** raiment, that thou mayest be clothed,	3022
	4: 4	elders sitting, clothed in **w** raiment;	3022
	6: 2	And I saw, and behold a **w** horse:	3022
	6:11	And **w** robes were given unto every one	3022
	7: 9	clothed with **w** robes, and palms in their	3022
	7:13	What are these which are arrayed in **w**	3022
	7:14	**made** them **w** in the blood of the Lamb.	3021
	14:14	and behold a **w** cloud, and upon the cloud	3022
	15: 6	clothed in pure and **w** linen,	2986
	19: 8	be arrayed in fine linen, clean and **w**:	2986

Rev	19:11	heaven opened, and behold a **w** horse;	3022
	19:14	in heaven followed him upon **w** horses,	3022
	19:14	clothed in fine linen, **w**, and clean.	3022
	20:11	And I saw a great **w** throne, and him that	3022

WHITED (2) [WHITE]

| Mt | 23:27 | for ye are like unto **w** sepulchres, | 2867 |
| Ac | 23: 3 | God shall smite thee, *thou* **w** wall: | 2867 |

WHITER (2) [WHITE]

| Ps | 51: 7 | wash me, and I shall be **w** than snow. | 3835 |
| La | 4: 7 | purer than snow, they were **w** than milk, | 6705 |

WHITEWASH See MORTER

WHITHER (124) [WHITHERSOEVER]

Ge	16: 8	**w** wilt thou go? And she said,	575+1886.5
	20:13	at every place **w** we shall	834+8033+1886.5
	28:15	will keep thee in all *places* **w** thou goest,	834
	32:17	**w** goest thou? and whose *are*	575+1886.5
	37:30	child *is* not; and I, **w** shall I go?	575+1886.5
Ex	21:13	thee a place **w** he shall flee.	834+8033+1886.5
	34:12	inhabitants of the land **w** thou goest,	834+5921
Lev	18: 3	**w** I bring you, shall ye not	834+8033+1886.5
	20:22	**w** I bring you to dwell	834+8033+1886.5
Nu	13:27	We came unto the land **w** thou sentest us,	834
	15:18	into the land **w** I bring you,	834+8033+1886.5
	35:25	his refuge, **w** he was fled:	834+8033+1886.5
	35:26	his refuge, **w** he was fled:	834+8033+1886.5
Dt	1:28	**W** shall we go up? our brethren	575+1886.5
	3:21	kingdoms **w** thou passest.	834+8033+1886.5
	4: 5	land **w** ye go to possess it.	834+8033+1886.5
	4:14	**w** ye go over to possess it.	834+8033+1886.5
	4:27	**w** the Lord shall lead you.	834+8033+1886.5
	6: 1	land **w** ye go to possess it,	834+8033+1886.5
	7: 1	**w** thou goest to possess it,	834+8033+1886.5
	11: 8	**w** ye go to possess it;	834+8033+1886.5
	11:10	the land, **w** thou goest in	834+8033+1886.5
	11:11	land, **w** ye go to possess it,	834+8033+1886.5
	11:29	**w** thou goest to possess it,	834+8033+1886.5
	12:29	**w** thou goest to possess	834+8033+1886.5
	21:14	then thou shalt let her go **w** she will;	3807.1
	23:12	**w** thou shalt go forth abroad:	8033+1886.5
	23:20	**w** thou goest to possess it.	834+8033+1886.5
	28:21	**w** thou goest to possess it.	834+8033+1886.5
	28:37	among all nations **w**	834+8033+1886.5
	28:63	**w** thou goest to possess	834+8033+1886.5
	30: 1	**w** the Lord thy God hath	834+8033+1886.5
	30: 3	**w** the Lord thy God hath	834+8033+1886.5
	30:16	**w** thou goest to possess it.	834+8033+1886.5
	30:18	**w** thou passest over Jordan	834+8033+1886.5
	31:13	long as ye live in the land **w**	834+8033+1886.5
	31:16	**w** they go *to be* amongst	834+8033+1886.5
	32:47	**w** ye go over Jordan to	834+8033+1886.5
	32:50	in the mount **w** thou goest	834+8033+1886.5
Jos	2: 5	the men went I wot not:	575+1886.5
Jdg	19:17	the old man said, **W** goest thou?	575+1886.5
Ru	1:16	for **w** thou goest, I will go;	413+834
1Sa	14:47	unto him and his servant, **W** went ye?	575
	27:10	said, **W** have ye made a road to day?	408
2Sa	2: 1	David said, **W** shall I go up?	575+1886.5
	13:13	I, **w** shall I cause my shame to go?	575+1886.5
	15:20	seeing I go **w** I may, return thou,	834+5921
	17:18	**w** and in his court; they went down.	8033
1Ki	2:36	go forth thence **any w**.	575+575+1886.5+1886.5+2050.1
	2:42	and walkest *abroad* **any w**,	575+575+1886.5+1886.5+2050.1
	8:47	land **w** they were carried captives,	834+8033
	18:10	**w** my lord hath not sent to seek	834+8033
	18:12	Lord shall carry thee **w** I know not;	834+5921
	21:18	he is gone down to possess it.	834+8033
2Ki	5:25	Thy servant went no **w**.	575+575+1886.5+1886.5+2050.1
2Ch	6:37	the land **w** they are carried captive,	834+8033
	6:38	**w** they have carried them captives,	834
	10: 2	**w** he had fled from the presence of	834
Ne	2:16	the rulers knew not **w** I went,	575+1886.5
Ps	122: 4	**W** the tribes go up, the tribes of	7945+8033
	139: 7	**W** shall I go from thy spirit?	575+1886.5
	139: 7	**w** shall I flee from thy presence?	575+1886.5
Ecc	9:10	in the grave, **w** thou goest.	834+8033+1886.5
SS	6: 1	**W** is thy beloved gone, O thou	575+1886.5
	6: 1	**w** is thy beloved turned aside?	575+1886.5
Isa	20: 6	**w** we flee for help to be delivered	834+8033
Jer	8: 3	which remain in all the places **w** I have	8033
	15: 2	say unto thee, **W** shall we go forth?	575+1886.5
	16:15	lands **w** he had driven them	834+8033+1886.5
	19:14	**w** the Lord had sent him to	834+8033
	22:12	shall die in the place **w** they have	834+8033
	23: 3	all countries **w** I have driven them,	834+8033
	23: 8	all countries **w** I had driven them;	834+8033
	24: 9	in all places **w** I shall drive them.	834+8033
	29: 7	seek the peace of the city **w**	834+8033+1886.5
	29:14	all the places **w** I have driven you,	834+8033
	29:18	all the nations **w** I have driven	834+8033
	30:11	all nations **w** I have scattered thee,	834+8033
	32:37	**w** I have driven them in mine anger,	834+8033
	40: 4	**w** it seemeth good and convenient for thee	413
	40:12	out of all places **w** they were driven,	834+8033
	42:22	in the place **w** ye desire to go and	834+8033
	43: 5	**w** they had been driven, to dwell in	834+8033
	44: 8	**w** ye be gone to dwell, that ye might	834+8033
	45: 5	for a prey in all places **w** thou goest.	834+8033
	46:28	**w** I have driven thee:	834+8033+1886.5

Jer	49:36 shall be no nation **w** the outcasts	834+8033	
Eze	1:12 **w** the spirit was to go, they went;	8033+1886.5	
	4:13 the Gentiles, **w** I will drive them.	834+8033	
	6: 9 **w** they shall be carried captives,	834+8033	
	10:11 the place **w** the head looked they followed	834	
	12:16 among the heathen **w** they come;	834+8033	
	29:13 **w** they were scattered.	834+8033+1886.5	
	36:20 **w** they went, they profaned my holy	834+8033	
	36:21 the heathen, **w** they went.	834+8033+1886.5	
	36:22 among the heathen, **w** ye went.	834+8033	
	37:21 **w** they be gone, and will gather	834+8033	
	47: 9 live **w** the river cometh.	834+8033+1886.5	
Da	9: 7 through all the countries **w** thou	834+8033	
Joel	3: 7 place **w** ye have sold them,	834+8033+1886.5	
Zec	2: 2 said I, **W** goest thou? And he said	575+1886.5	
	5:10 **W** do these bear the ephah?	575+1886.5	
Lk	10: 1 and place, **w** he himself would come.	3757	
	24:28 drew nigh unto the village, **w** they went:	3757	
Jn	3: 8 not tell whence it cometh, and **w** it goeth:	4226	
	6:21 ship was at the land **w** they went.	1519+3739	
	7:35 **W** will he go, that we shall not find him?	4226	
	8:14 for I know whence I came, and **w** I go;	4226	
	8:14 ye cannot tell whence I come, and **w** I go.	4226	
	8:21 die in your sins: **w** I go, ye cannot come.	3699	
	8:22 because he saith, **W** I go, ye cannot come.	3699	
	12:35 in darkness knoweth not **w** he goeth.	4226	
	13:33 unto the Jews, **W** I go, ye cannot come;	3699	
	13:36 Peter said unto him, Lord, **w** goest thou?	4226	
	13:36 answered him, **W** I go, thou canst not	3699	
	14: 4 **w** I go ye know, and the way ye know.	3699	
	14: 5 him, Lord, we know not **w** thou goest;	4226	
	16: 5 none of you asketh me, **W** goest thou?	4226	
	18:20 in the temple, **w** the Jews always resort;	3699	
	21:18 and walkedst **w** thou wouldest:	3699	
	21:18 and carry **thee w** thou wouldest not.	3699	
Heb	6:20 the forerunner is for us entered,	3699	
	11: 8 he went out, not knowing **w** he went.	4226	
1Jn	2:11 and knoweth not **w** he goeth, because	4226	

WHITHERSOEVER (29) [EVER, SO, WHITHER]

Jos	1: 7 mayest prosper **w** thou goest.	834+3605+871.1	
	1: 9 is with thee **w** thou goest.	834+3605+871.1	
	1:16 **w** thou sendest us, we will go.	413+834+3605	
Jdg	2:15 **W** they went out, the hand	834+3605+871.1	
1Sa	14:47 he turned himself, he	834+3605+871.1	
	18: 5 David went out **w** Saul sent	834+3605+871.1	
	23:13 Keilah, and went **w** they could go.	834+871.1	
2Sa	7: 9 with thee **w** thou wentest,	834+3605+871.1	
	8: 6 the Lord preserved David **w**	834+3605+871.1	
	8:14 the Lord preserved David **w**	834+3605+871.1	
1Ki	2: 3 and **w** thou turnest thyself:	834+3605+8033	
	8:44 thou shalt send	834+1870+871.1+1886.1	
2Ki	18: 7 prospered he **w** he went forth:	834+3605+871.1	
1Ch	17: 8 I have been with thee **w** thou	834+3605+871.1	
	18: 6 preserved David **w** he went.	834+3605+871.1	
	18:13 preserved David **w** he went.	834+3605+871.1	
Est	4: 3 **w** the king's commandment and	834+4725	
	8:17 **w** the king's commandment and	834+4725	
Pr	17: 8 **w** it turneth, it prospereth.	413+834+3605	
	21: 1 he turneth it **w** he will.	834+3605+5921	
Eze	1:20 **w** the spirit was to go,	834+5921+8033	
	21:16 on the left, **w** thy face *is* set.	575+1886.5	
	47: 9 the rivers shall come,	413+834+3605	
Mt	8:19 I will follow thee **w** thou goest.	1437+3699	
Mk	6:56 And **w** he entered, into villages,	302+3699	
Lk	9:57 I will follow thee **w** thou goest.	302+3699	
1Co	16: 6 bring me on my journey **w** I go.	1437+3757	
Jas	3: 4 small helm, the governor listeth.	302+3699	
Rev	14: 4 which follow the Lamb **w** he goeth.	302+3699	

WHO (969) [WHOM, WHOMSOEVER, WHOSE, WHOSO, WHOSOEVER]

Ge	3:11 said, **W** told thee that thou *wast* naked?	4310	
	12: 7 unto the Lord, **w** appeared unto him.	1886.1	
	14:12 **w** dwelt in Sodom, and his goods,	1931	
	21: 7 **W** would have said unto Abraham,	4310	
	21:26 I wot not **w** hath done this thing:	4310	
	24:15 **w** was born to Bethuel, son of Milcah,	834	
	24:27 **w** hath not left destitute my master of his	834	
	27:18 he said, Here *am* I; **w** *art* thou, my son?	4310	
	27:32 Isaac his father said unto him, **W** *art* thou?	4310	
	27:33 trembled very exceedingly, and said, **W?**	4310	
	30: 2 **w** hath withheld from thee the fruit of	834	
	33: 5 and said, **W** *are* those with thee?	4310	
	35: 3 **w** answered me in the day of my	1886.1	
	36: 1 *are* the generations of Esau, **w** *is* Edom.	1931	
	36:19 **w** *is* Edom, and these *are* their dukes.	1931	
	36:20 of Seir the Horite, **w** inhabited the land;	834	
	36:35 **w** smote Midian in the field of Moab,	1886.1	
	42:30 The man, **w** *is* the lord of the land,	NIH	
	43:22 we cannot tell **w** put our money in our	4310	
	48: 8 Joseph's sons, and said, **W** *are* these?	4310	
	48:14 **w** *was* the younger, and his left hand	1931	
	49: 9 and as an old lion; **w** shall rouse him up?	4310	
	49: 9 the God of thy father, **w** shall help thee;	NIH	
	49:25 **w** shall bless thee *with* blessings of heaven	NIH	
Ex	2:14 **W** made thee a prince and a judge over	4310	
	3:11 Moses said unto God, **W** *am* I, that I	4310	
	4:11 unto him, **W** hath made man's mouth?	4310	
	4:11 or **w** maketh the dumb, or deaf,	4310	
	4:28 all the words of the Lord **w** had sent him,	834	
	5: 2 Pharaoh said, **W** *is* the Lord, that I	4310	
	5:20 Moses and Aaron, **w** stood in the way,	NIH	
	6:12 hear me, **w** *am* of uncircumcised lips?	589	
	10: 8 your God: *but* **w** *are* they that shall go?	4310	

Ex	12:27 **w** passed over the houses of the children	834	
	12:40 **w** dwelt in Egypt, *was* four hundred and	834	
	15:11 **W** *is* like unto thee, O Lord, among	4310	
	15:11 **W** *is* like thee, glorious in holiness,	4310	
	18:10 **w** hath delivered you out of the hand of	834	
	18:10 **w** hath delivered the people from under	834	
	21: 8 **w** hath betrothed her to himself, then shall	834	
	32:26 and said, **W** *is* on the Lord's side?	4310	
Lev	5: 8 **w** shall offer *that* which *is* for the sin	2050.1	
	12: 7 **W** shall offer it before the Lord,	NIH	
	27:12 valuest it, **w** *art* the priest, so shall it be.	NIH	
Nu	6:21 This *is* the law of the Nazarite **w** hath	834	
	7: 2 **w** *were* the princes of the tribes, and	1992	
	9: 6 **w** were defiled by the dead body of a man,	834	
	11: 4 and said, **W** shall give us flesh to eat?	4310	
	11:18 **W** shall give us flesh to eat?	4310	
	12: 7 *is* not so, **w** *is* faithful in all mine house.	1931	
	14:36 **w** returned, and made all the congregation	834	
	16: 5 Even to morrow the Lord will shew **w** *are*	834	
	16: 5 will shew who *are* his, and **w** *is* holy;	NIH	
	21:26 **w** had fought against the former king of	1931	
	23:10 **W** can count the dust of Jacob,	4310	
	24: 9 **w** shall stir him up? Blessed *is* he that	4310	
	24:23 Alas, **w** shall live when God doeth this!	4310	
	25: 6 **w** *were* weeping *before* the door of	1992	
	26: 9 **w** strove against Moses and against Aaron	834	
	26:47 **w** *were* fifty and three thousand and	NIH	
	26:63 **w** numbered the children of Israel in	834	
	27:21 **w** shall ask *counsel* for him after	NIH	
	31:27 **w** went out to battle, and between all	1886.1	
Dt	1:33 **w** went in the way before you,	1886.1	
	2:25 **w** shall hear report of thee,	834	
	4: 7 *so* great, **w** hath God *so* nigh unto them,	834	
	4:46 **w** dwelt at Heshbon, whom Moses and	834	
	5: 3 *even* us, **w** *are* all of us here alive *this* day.	428	
	5:26 For **w** *is there* of all flesh, that hath heard	4310	
	8:15 **W** led thee through *that* great and	1886.1	
	8:15 **w** brought thee forth water out of the	1886.1	
	8:16 **W** fed thee in the wilderness with	1886.1	
	9: 2 *whom* thou hast heard *say,* **W** can stand	4310	
	21: 1 *and* it be not known **w** hath slain him:	4310	
	30:12 **W** shall go up for us to heaven, and bring	4310	
	30:13 **W** shall go over the sea for us, and bring	4310	
	33: 9 **W** said unto his father and to his	1886.1	
	33:26 **w** rideth *upon* the heaven in thy help,	NIH	
	33:29 **w** *is* like unto thee, O people saved by	4310	
	33:29 and **w** *is* the sword of thy excellency!	834	
Jos	9: 8 Joshua said unto them, **W** are ye?	4310	
	11: 8 **w** smote them, and chased them unto	NIH	
	12: 2 **w** dwelt in Heshbon, *and* ruled from	1886.1	
	13:12 **w** remained of the remnant of the giants:	NIH	
	15:19 **w** answered, Give me a blessing;	2050.1	
	17:16 both they **w** *are* of Beth-shean and	834	
	17:16 and they **w** *are* of the valley of Jezreel.	834	
	21:10 **w** *were* of the children of Levi, had:	NIH	
Jdg	1: 1 **W** shall go up for us against the	4310	
	2: 7 **w** had seen all the great works of	834	
	3: 9 **w** delivered them, *even* Othniel the son of	NIH	
	3:19 **w** said, Keep silence. And all that stood by	NIH	
	6:29 one to another, **W** hath done this thing?	4310	
	6:35 **w** also was gathered after him:	1931	
	7: 1 **w** *is* Gideon, and all the people that *were*	1931	
	8:34 **w** had delivered them out of the hands	1886.1	
	9:28 **W** *is* Abimelech, and who *is* Shechem,	4310	
	9:28 Who *is* Abimelech, and **w** *is* Shechem,	4310	
	9:38 wherewith thou saidst, **W** *is* Abimelech,	4310	
	11:39 **w** did with her *according* to his vow	NIH	
	15: 6 the Philistines said, **W** hath done this?	4310	
	17: 4 **w** made thereof a graven image and	NIH	
	17: 5 one of his sons, **w** became his priest.	NIH	
	17: 7 **w** *was* a Levite, and he sojourned there.	1931	
	18: 2 when they came to mount Ephraim,	NIH	
	18: 3 said unto him, **W** brought thee thither?	4310	
	18:29 Dan their father, **w** was born unto Israel:	834	
	19: 1 **w** took to him a concubine out of	NIH	
	21: 5 **W** *is there* among all the tribes of Israel	4310	
Ru	2: 3 **w** *was* of the kindred of Elimelech.	834	
	2:20 **w** hath not left off his kindness to the	834	
	3: 9 he said, **W** *art* thou? And she answered,	4310	
	3:16 she said, **W** *art* thou, my daughter?	4310	
1Sa	2: 25 the Lord, **w** shall intreat for him?	4310	
	4: 8 **w** shall deliver us out of the hand of these	4310	
	6:20 **W** is able to stand before this holy Lord	4310	
	10:12 and said, But **w** *is* their father?	4310	
	10:19 **w** himself saved you out of all your	834	
	11:12 **W** *is* he that said, Shall Saul reign over us?	4310	
	14:17 Number now, and see **w** is gone from us.	4310	
	14:45 **w** hath wrought this great salvation in	834	
	16:16 a man, **w** *is* a cunning player on a harp:	NIH	
	17:25 it shall be, *that* the man **w** killeth him,	834	
	17:26 for **w** *is* this uncircumcised Philistine,	4310	
	18:18 David said unto Saul, **W** *am* I? and what	4310	
	20:10 said David to Jonathan, **W** shall tell me?	4310	
	22:14 **w** *is* so faithful among all thy servants as	4310	
	23:22 his haunt is, *and* **w** hath seen him there:	4310	
	25:10 David's servants, and said, **W** *is* David?	4310	
	25:10 **w** *is* the son of Jesse? there be many	4310	
	26: 6 **W** will go down with me to Saul to	4310	
	26: 9 for **w** can stretch forth his hand against	4310	
	26:14 said, **W** *art* thou *that* criest to the king?	4310	
	26:15 **w** *is* like to thee in Israel? wherefore then	4310	
	30:23 **w** hath preserved us, and delivered	4310	
	30:24 **w** will hearken unto you in this matter?	4310	
2Sa	1: 8 he said unto me, **W** *art* thou? And I	4310	
	1:24 over Saul, **w** clothed you in scarlet,	1886.1	

2Sa	1:24 **w** put on ornaments of gold upon your	1886.1	
	4: 5 of Ish-bosheth, **w** lay on a bed at noon.	1931	
	4: 9 **w** hath redeemed my soul out of all	834	
	4:10 **w** *thought* that I would have given him a	834	
	6:20 **w** uncovered himself to day in the eyes of	834	
	7:18 and he said, **W** *am* I, O Lord God?	4310	
	10:18 the captain of their host, **w** died there.	NIH	
	11:21 **w** smote Abimelech the son of	4310	
	12:22 **W** can tell *whether* God will be gracious	4310	
	16:10 **W** shall then say, Wherefore hast thou	4310	
	22: 4 on the Lord, **w** *is worthy* to be praised:	NIH	
	22:32 For **w** *is* God, save the Lord? and who *is*	4310	
	22:32 and **w** *is* a rock, save our God?	4310	
	23: 1 and the man **w** was raised up on high,	NIH	
	23:20 of Kabzeel, **w** had done many acts,	NIH	
1Ki	1:20 *thou* shouldest tell them **w** shall sit on	4310	
	1:27 **w** should sit on the throne of my lord	4310	
	2:24 **w** hath made me a house, as he promised,	834	
	2:32 **w** fell upon two men more righteous and	834	
	3: 9 for **w** is able to judge this thy *so* great a	4310	
	8:23 **w** keepest covenant and mercy with thy	NIH	
	8:24 **W** hast kept with thy servant David my	834	
	8:50 give them compassion before them **w**	NIH	
	9: 9 **w** brought forth their fathers out of the	834	
	12: 2 the son of Nebat, **w** was yet in Egypt,	1931	
	12: 9 this people, **w** have spoken to me, saying,	834	
	12:18 sent Adoram, **w** *was* over the tribute;	834	
	13:26 **w** was disobedient unto the word of	834	
	14: 8 **w** kept my commandments,	834	
	14: 8 and **w** followed me with all his heart,	834	
	14:14 **w** shall cut off the house of Jeroboam that	834	
	14:16 **w** did sin, and who made Israel to sin.	834	
	14:16 who did sin, and **w** made Israel to sin.	834	
	17: 1 **w** *was* of the inhabitants of Gilead,	834	
	19:19 **w** *was* plowing *with* twelve yoke *of* oxen	1931	
	20:14 he said, **W** shall order the battle? And he	4310	
	21:11 nobles **w** *were* the inhabitants in his city,	834	
	22:20 **W** shall persuade Ahab, that he may go	4310	
	22:52 the son of Nebat, **w** made Israel to sin:	834	
2Ki	4: 5 her sons, **w** brought *the vessels* to her;	1992	
	7:17 **w** spake when the king came down to	834	
	8:14 **w** said to him, What said Elisha to thee?	NIH	
	9:31 *Had* Zimri peace, **w** slew his master?	NIH	
	9:32 the window, and said, **W** *is* on my side?	4310	
	9:32 Who *is* on my side? **w?**	4310	
	10: 9 and slew him: but **w** slew all these?	4310	
	10:13 king of Judah, and said, **W** *are* ye?	4310	
	10:29 **w** made Israel to sin, Jehu departed not	834	
	13: 6 **w** made Israel sin, *but* walked therein:	834	
	13:11 the son of Nebat, **w** made Israel to sin:	834	
	14:24 the son of Nebat, **w** made Israel to sin.	834	
	15: 9 the son of Nebat, **w** made Israel to sin.	834	
	15:18 the son of Nebat, **w** made Israel to sin.	834	
	15:24 the son of Nebat, **w** made Israel to sin.	834	
	15:28 the son of Nebat, **w** made Israel to sin.	834	
	17:36 **w** brought you up out of the land of Egypt	834	
	18:35 **W** *are they* among all the gods of	4310	
	23:15 **w** made Israel to sin, had made, both that	834	
	23:16 proclaimed, **w** proclaimed these words.	834	
1Ch	2: 7 **w** transgressed in the thing accursed.	834	
	2:22 **w** had three and twenty cities in the	2050.2	
	4:22 **w** had the dominion in Moab,	834	
	5: 8 the son of Joel, **w** dwelt in Aroer, even	1931	
	5:10 with the Hagarites, **w** fell by their hand:	NIH	
	6:39 Asaph, **w** stood on his right hand,	1886.1	
	7:24 **w** built Beth-horon the nether,	NIH	
	7:31 and Malchiel, **w** *is* the father of Birzavith.	1931	
	8:12 and Shamed, **w** built Ono, and Lod,	1931	
	8:13 **w** *were* heads of the fathers of	1992	
	8:13 **w** drove away the inhabitants of Gath:	1992	
	9: 1 **w** *were* carried away to Babylon for their	NIH	
	9:18 **w** hitherto *waited* in the king's gate	NIH	
	9:31 **w** *was* the firstborn of Shallum	1931	
	9:33 **w** *remaining* in the chambers *were* free:	NIH	
	11:10 **w** strengthened themselves with him in	1886.1	
	11:12 **w** was one of the three mighties.	1931	
	11:22 man of Kabzeel, **w** had done many acts;	NIH	
	12:18 **w** *was* chief of the captains, *and he said,*	NIH	
	16:41 were chosen, **w** were expressed by name,	834	
	17:16 said, **W** *am* I, O Lord God, and what *is*	4310	
	19: 7 **w** came and pitched before Medeba.	NIH	
	21:16 the elders *of Israel,* **w** *were* clothed in	NIH	
	22: 9 be born to thee, **w** shall be a man of rest;	1931	
	24:28 Of Mahli *came* Eleazar, **w** had no sons.	2050.2	
	25: 1 **w** should prophesy with harps,	1886.1	
	25: 3 **w** prophesied with a harp, to give	1886.1	
	25: 9 **w** with his brethren and sons *were*	1931	
	27: 6 **w** *was* mighty among the thirty,	NIH	
	29: 5 **w** *then* is willing to consecrate his service	4310	
	29:14 **w** *am* I, and what *is* my people, that we	4310	
2Ch	1:10 for **w** can judge this people, *that is so*	4310	
	2: 6 **w** is able to build him a house, seeing	4310	
	2: 6 **w** *am* I then, that I should build him a	4310	
	2:12 **w** hath given to David the king a wise son,	834	
	6: 4 **w** hath with his hands fulfilled *that* which	NIH	
	8: 8 **w** were left after them in the land,	834	
	10: 2 the son of Nebat, **w** *was* in Egypt,	NIH	
	17:16 **w** willingly offered himself unto	1886.1	
	18:19 **W** shall entice Ahab king of Israel, that he	4310	
	19: 6 the Lord, **w** *is* with you in the judgment.	NIH	
	20: 7 **w** didst drive out the inhabitants of this	NIH	
	20:34 **w** is mentioned in the book of the kings of	834	
	20:35 king of Israel, **w** did very wickedly:	1931	
	22: 9 **w** sought the Lord with all his heart.	834	
	26: 1 **w** *was* sixteen years old, and made him	1931	

2Ch 26: 5 w had understanding in the visions of 1886.1
28: 5 w smote him *with* a great slaughter. NIH
30: 7 w therefore gave them up to desolation, NIH
32: 4 w stopt all the fountains, and the brook NIH
32:14 W *was* there among all the gods of those 4310
32:31 w sent unto him to inquire of the 1886.1
34:26 w sent you to inquire of the Lord, 1886.1
35:21 w *is* with me, that he destroy thee not. 834
36:13 w had made him swear by God: 834
36:17 w slew their young men with the sword NIH
36:23 W *is there* among you of all his people? 4310

Ezr 1: 3 W *is there* among you of all his people? 4310
3:12 w *were* ancient men that had seen the NIH
5: 3 W hath commanded you to build this 4479
5: 9 W commanded you to build this house, 4479
5:12 w destroyed this house, and carried NIH

Ne 1:11 thy servants, w desire to fear thy name: 1886.1
3: 3 w also laid the beams thereof, and set up 1992
6:10 the son of Mehetabeel, w *was* shut up; 1931
6:11 w *is there*, that, *being* as I *am*, would go 4310
7: 7 w came with Zerubbabel, Jeshua, 1886.1
9: 7 w didst choose Abram, and broughtest him 834
9:27 the hand of their enemies, w vexed them: NIH
9:27 w saved them out of the hand of their NIH
9:32 w keepest covenant and mercy, NIH
13:26 w was beloved of his God, and God 2050.1

Est 2: 6 W had been carried away from Jerusalem 834
2:15 w had taken *her* for his daughter, 834
2:22 w told *it* unto Esther the queen; NIH
4:11 w is not called, *there* is one law of his to 834
4:14 w knoweth whether thou art come to 4310
6: 2 w sought to lay hand on the king 834
6: 4 the king said, W *is* in the court? 4310
7: 5 Esther the queen, W *is* he, and where 4310
7: 9 w had spoken good for the king, standeth 834

Job 3: 8 w are ready to raise up their mourning. 1886.1
3:15 w filled their houses *with* silver: 1886.1
4: 2 w can withhold himself from speaking? 4310
4: 7 Remember, I pray thee, w *ever* perished, 4310
5:10 W giveth rain upon the earth, 1886.1
9: 4 W hath hardened *himself* against him, 4310
9:12 he taketh away, w can hinder him? 4310
9:12 w will say unto him, What doest thou? 4310
9:19 w shall set me a time *to plead*? 4310
9:24 judges thereof; if not, where, *and* w is he? 4310
11:10 gather together, then w can hinder him? 4310
12: 3 yea, w knoweth not such *things* as these? 4310
12: 4 w calleth upon God, and he answereth 4310
12: 9 W knoweth not in all these that the hand 4310
13:19 W *is* he *that* will plead with me? for now, 4310
14: 4 W can bring a clean *thing* out of an 4310
16: 9 He teareth *me* in his wrath, w hateth me: NIH
17: 3 w *is* he *that* will strike hands with me? 4310
17:15 my hope? as for my hope, w shall see it? 4310
21:31 W shall declare his way to his face? 4310
21:31 w shall repay him *what* he hath done? 4310
23:13 he *is* in one *mind*, and w can turn him? 4310
24:25 w will make me a liar, and make my 4310
26:14 thunder of his power w can understand? 4310
27: 2 w hath taken away my judgment; NIH
27: 2 and the Almighty, w hath vexed my soul; NIH
30: 4 W cut up mallows by the bushes, 1886.1
34: 7 Job, w drinketh up scorning like water? NIH
34:13 W hath given him a charge over the earth? 4310
34:13 or w hath disposed the whole world? 4310
34:29 quietness, w can make trouble? 4310
34:29 hideth *his* face, w then can behold him? 4310
35:10 my Maker, w giveth songs in the night; NIH
35:11 W teacheth us more than the beasts of NIH
36:22 by his power: w teacheth like him? 4310
36:23 W hath enjoined him his way? or who 4310
36:23 or w can say, Thou hast wrought iniquity? 4310
38: 2 W *is* this that darkeneth counsel by words 4310
38: 5 W hath laid the measures thereof, if thou 4310
38: 5 or w hath stretched the line upon it? 4310
38: 6 or w laid the corner stone thereof; 4310
38: 8 Or w shut up the sea with doors, when it NIH
38:25 W hath divided a watercourse for 4310
38:28 or w hath begotten the drops of dew? 4310
38:29 hoary frost of heaven, w hath gendered it? 4310
38:36 W hath put wisdom in the inward parts? 4310
38:36 w hath given understanding to the heart? 4310
38:37 W can number the clouds in wisdom? 4310
38:37 or w can stay the bottles of heaven, 4310
38:41 W provideth for the raven his food? 4310
39: 5 W hath sent out the wild ass free? 4310
39: 5 w hath loosed the bands of the wild ass? 4310
41:10 w then is able to stand before me? 4310
41:11 W hath prevented me, that I should repay 4310
41:13 W can discover the face of his garment? 4310
41:13 w can come *to him* with his double 4310
41:14 W can open the doors of his face? 4310
41:33 is not his like, w is made without fear. 1886.1
42: 3 W *is* he that hideth counsel without 4310

Ps 4: 6 many that say, W will shew us *any* good? 4310
4: 6 in the grave w shall give thee thanks? 4310
8: 1 w hast set thy glory above the heavens. 834
12: 4 W have said, With our tongue will we 834
12: 4 our lips *are* our own: w *is* lord over us? 4310
14: 4 w eat up my people *as* they eat bread, NIH
15: 1 Lord, w shall abide in thy tabernacle? 4310
15: 1 w shall dwell in thy holy hill? 4310
16: 7 bless the Lord, w hath given me counsel: 834
17: 9 my deadly enemies, w compass me about. NIH
18: T w spake unto the Lord the words of this 834

Ps 18: 3 upon the Lord, w *is worthy* to be praised: NIH
18:31 For w *is* God save the Lord? or who *is* a 4310
18:31 the Lord? or w *is* a rock save our God? 4310
19:12 W can understand *his* errors? cleanse 4310
24: 3 W shall ascend into the hill of the Lord? 4310
24: 3 and w shall stand in his holy place? 4310
24: 4 w hath not lift up his soul unto vanity, 834
24: 8 W *is* this King of glory? the Lord strong 4310
24:10 W is this King of glory? The Lord of 4310
34: T w drove him away, and he departed. NIH
35:10 shall say, Lord, w *is* like unto thee, 4310
37: 7 because of him w prospereth *in* his way, NIH
37: 7 of the man w bringeth wicked devices to NIH
39: 6 and knoweth not w shall gather them. NIH
42:11 w *is* the health of my countenance, NIH
43: 5 w *is* the health of my countenance, NIH
53: 4 w eat up my people *as* they eat bread: NIH
59: 7 in their lips: for w, *say they*, doth hear? 4310
60: 9 W will bring me *into* the strong city? 4310
60: 9 strong city? w will lead me into Edom? 4310
64: 3 W whet their tongue like a sword, 834
64: 5 snares privily; they say, W shall see them? 4310
65: 5 w *art* the confidence of all the ends of NIH
68:19 w daily loadeth us *with benefits*, *even* NIH
71:19 w hast done great *things*: O God, 834
71:19 great *things*: O God, w *is* like unto thee! 4310
72:18 Israel, w only doeth wondrous *things*. 2050.2
73:12 the ungodly, w prosper in the world; NIH
76: 7 w may stand in thy sight when once thou 4310
77:13 w *is* so great a God as *our* God? 4310
78: 6 w should arise and declare *them* to their NIH
83:12 W said, Let us take to ourselves the 834
84: 6 W passing through the valley of Baca NIH
89: 6 w in the heaven can be compared unto NIH
89: 6 w among the sons of the mighty can be NIH
89: 8 w *is* a strong Lord like unto thee? 4310
90:11 W knoweth the power of thine anger? 4310
94:16 W will rise up for me against the 4310
94:16 w will stand up for me against the 4310
103: 3 W forgiveth all thine iniquities; 1886.1
103: 3 w healeth all thy diseases; 1886.1
103: 4 W redeemeth thy life from destruction; 1886.1
103: 4 w crowneth thee with lovingkindness 1886.1
103: 5 W satisfieth thy mouth with good 1886.1
104: 2 W coverest *thyself* with light as with a NIH
104: 2 w stretchest out the heavens like a curtain: NIH
104: 3 W layeth the beams of his chambers in 1886.1
104: 3 w maketh the clouds his chariot: 1886.1
104: 3 w walketh upon the wings of the wind: 1886.1
104: 4 W maketh his angels spirits; his ministers NIH
104: 5 W laid the foundations of the earth, *that* it NIH
105:17 *even* Joseph, w was sold for a servant: NIH
106: 2 W can utter the mighty acts of the Lord? 4310
106: 2 w can shew forth all his praise? NIH
108:10 W will bring me *into* the strong city? 4310
108:10 strong city? w will lead me into Edom? 4310
108:11 *Wilt* not thou, O God, w hast cast us off? NIH
113: 5 w *is* like unto the Lord our God, 4310
113: 5 the Lord our God, w dwelleth on high, NIH
113: 6 w humbleth *himself* to behold the 1886.1
119: 1 w walk in the law of the Lord. 1886.1
119:38 unto thy servant, w *is* devoted to thy fear. 834
124: 1 If *it had* not *been* the Lord w was on our 7945
124: 2 If *it had* not *been* the Lord w was on our 7945
124: 6 w hath not given us *as* a prey to their 7945
124: 8 of the Lord, w made heaven and earth. 7945
130: 3 mark iniquities, O Lord, w shall stand? 4310
135: 8 W smote the firstborn of Egypt, both of 7945
135: 9 W sent tokens and wonders into the midst NIH
135:10 W smote great nations, and slew mighty 7945
136: 4 To him w alone doeth great wonders: NIH
136:23 W remembered us in our low estate: for 7945
136:25 W giveth food to all flesh: for his mercy NIH
137: 7 w said, Rase *it*, rase *it*, *even* to 1886.1
137: 8 of Babylon, w art *to be* destroyed; 1886.1
140: 4 w have purposed to overthrow my goings. 834
142: 2 w subdueth my people under me. 1886.1
144:10 w deliverest David his servant from 1886.1
147: 8 W covereth the heaven with clouds, 1886.1
147: 8 w prepareth rain for the earth, 1886.1
147: 8 w maketh grass to grow *upon* 1886.1
147:17 morsels: w can stand before his cold? 4310

Pr 2:13 w leave the paths of uprightness, 1886.1
2:14 w rejoice to do evil, *and* delight in 1886.1
9:15 To call passengers w go right *on* their 1886.1
18:14 but a wounded spirit w can bear? 4310
20: 6 but a faithful man w can find? 4310
20: 9 W can say, I have made my heart clean, 4310
20:25 *It is* a snare to the man w devoureth *that* 4310
21:24 *is* his name, w dealeth in proud wrath. NIH
23:29 W hath woe? who hath sorrow? who 4310
23:29 W hath sorrow? who hath contentions? 4310
23:29 w hath contentions? who hath babbling? 4310
23:29 w hath babbling? who hath wounds NIH
23:29 w hath wounds without cause? who hath 4310
23:29 without cause? w hath redness of eyes? 4310
24:22 and w knoweth the ruin of them both? 4310
26:18 As a mad man w casteth firebrands, 1886.1
27: 4 but w is able to stand before envy? 4310
30: 4 W hath ascended up *into* heaven, 4310
30: 4 w hath gathered the wind in his fists? 4310
30: 4 w hath bound the waters in a garment? 4310
30: 4 w hath established all the ends of the 4310
30: 9 and deny *thee*, and say, W *is* the Lord? 4310
31:10 W can find a virtuous woman? for her 4310

Ecc 2:19 w knoweth whether he shall be a wise 4310
2:25 For w can eat, or who else can hasten 4310
2:25 or w else can hasten *hereunto*, more 4310
3:21 W knoweth the spirit of man that goeth 4310
3:22 for w shall bring him to see what shall be 4310
4: 3 w hath not seen the evil work that is done 834
4:13 king, w will no more be admonished. 4310
6:12 For w knoweth what *is* good for man in 4310
6:12 w can tell a man what shall be after him 4310
7:13 w can make *that* straight, which he hath 4310
7:24 and exceeding deep, w can find it out? 4310
8: 1 W *is* as the wise *man*? and who knoweth 4310
8: 1 w knoweth the interpretation of a thing? 4310
8: 4 w may say unto him, What doest thou? 4310
8: 7 for w can tell him when it shall be? 4310
8:10 w had come and gone from the place of 4310
10:14 what shall be after him, w can tell him? 4310
11: 5 thou knowest not the works of God 834
12: 7 the spirit shall return unto God w gave it. 834

SS 3: 6 W *is* this that cometh up out of the 4310
6:10 W *is* she that looketh forth as the 4310
8: 2 my mother's house, w would instruct me: NIH
8: 5 W *is* this that cometh up from 4310

Isa 1:12 w hath required this at your hand, 4310
6: 8 Whom shall I send, and w will go for us? 4310
14: 6 He w smote the people in wrath with a NIH
14:27 w shall disannul *it*? and his hand *is* 4310
14:27 *is* stretched out, and w shall turn it back? 4310
23: 8 W hath taken this counsel against Tyre, 4310
24:18 he w fleeth from the noise of the fear 1886.1
27: 4 w would set the briers *and* thorns against 4310
29:15 are in the dark, and they say, W seeth us? 4310
29:15 say, Who seeth us? and w knoweth us? 4310
29:22 w redeemed Abraham, concerning the 834
33:14 W among us shall dwell *with* the 4310
33:14 w amongst us shall dwell *with* everlasting 4310
36:20 W *are they* amongst all the gods of these 4310
37: 2 w *was* over the household, and Shebna 834
40:12 W hath measured the waters in the 4310
40:13 W hath directed the spirit of the Lord, 4310
40:14 w instructed him, and taught him in the NIH
40:26 behold w hath created these *things*, that 4310
41: 2 W raised up the righteous *man* from 4310
41: 4 W hath wrought and done *it*, calling 4310
41:26 W hath declared from the beginning, 4310
42:19 W *is* blind, but my servant? or deaf, as 4310
42:19 w *is* blind as he that is perfect, and blind 4310
42:23 W among you will give ear to this? 4310
42:23 w will hearken and hear for the time to NIH
42:24 W gave Jacob for a spoil, and Israel to 4310
43: 9 w among them can declare this, 4310
43:13 my hand: I will work, and w shall let it? 4310
44: 7 w, as I, shall call, and shall declare it, 4310
44:10 W hath formed a god, or molten a graven 4310
45:21 w hath declared this from ancient time? 4310
45:21 w hath told it from that time? *have* not I NIH
49:21 W hath begotten me these, seeing I have 4310
49:21 w hath brought up these? Behold, I was 4310
50: 8 justifieth me; w will contend with me? 4310
50: 8 w *is* mine adversary? let him come near 4310
50: 9 help me; w *is* he *that* shall condemn me? 4310
50:10 W *is* among you that feareth the Lord, 4310
51:12 w *art* thou, that thou shouldest be afraid 4310
51:19 come unto thee; w shall be sorry for thee? 4310
53: 1 W hath believed our report? and to whom 4310
53: 8 w shall declare his generation? for he was 4310
60: 8 W *are* these *that* fly as a cloud, and as 4310
63: 1 W *is* this *that* cometh from Edom, 4310
65:16 That he w blesseth himself in the earth 1886.1
66: 8 W hath heard such *a thing*? who hath 4310
66: 8 hath heard such *a thing*? w hath seen 4310

Jer 1:16 w have forsaken me, and have burnt 834
2:24 in *her* occasion w can turn her away? 4310
9:12 W *is* the wise man, that may understand 4310
9:12 w *is* he to whom the mouth of the Lord NIH
10: 7 W would not fear thee, O King of nations? 4310
15: 5 For w shall have pity upon thee, 4310
15: 5 or w shall bemoan thee? or who shall go 4310
15: 5 w shall go aside to ask how thou doest? 4310
17: 9 and desperately wicked: w can know it? 4310
18:13 w hath heard such *things*: the virgin of 4310
20: 1 w was also chief governor in the house of 1931
20:15 Cursed *be* the man w brought tidings to 834
21:13 say, W shall come down against us? 4310
21:13 or w shall enter into our habitations? 4310
23:18 For w hath stood in the counsel of 4310
23:18 w hath marked his word, and heard *it*? 4310
26:20 w prophesied against this city and 1886.1
26:23 w slew him with the sword, and cast his NIH
30:21 for w *is* this that engaged his heart to 4310
36:32 w wrote therein from the mouth of NIH
46: 7 W *is* this *that* cometh up as a flood, 4310
49: 4 *saying*, W shall come unto me? 4310
49:19 w *is* a chosen *man*, *that* I may appoint 4310
49:19 for w *is* like me? and who will appoint 4310
49:19 w will appoint me the time? and who *is* 4310
49:19 w *is that* shepherd that will stand before 4310
50:44 w *is* a chosen *man*, *that* I may appoint 4310
50:44 for w *is* like me? and who will appoint 4310
50:44 w will appoint me the time? and who *is* 4310
50:44 w *is that* shepherd that will stand before 4310
52:25 w mustered the people of the land; 1886.1

La 2:13 *is* great like the sea: w can heal thee? 4310
3:37 W *is* he *that* saith, and it cometh to pass, 4310

Eze 10: 7 with linen: w took *it*, and went out. NIH

Da	1:10	w hath appointed your meat and your	834
	2:23	w hast given me wisdom and might,	1768
	3:15	w is that God that shall deliver you out of	4479
	3:28	w hath sent his angel, and delivered his	1768
	6:27	w hath delivered Daniel from the power	1768
Hos	3: 1	w look to other gods, and love flagons of	1992
	7: 4	w ceaseth from raising after *he* hath	NIH
	14: 9	W *is* wise, and he shall understand these	4310
Joel	2:11	and very terrible; and w can abide it?	4310
	2:14	w knoweth *if* he will return and repent,	4310
Am	1: 1	w was among the herdmen of Tekoa,	834
	3: 8	The lion hath roared, w will not fear?	4310
	3: 8	GOD hath spoken, w can but prophesy?	4310
	3:10	w store up violence and robbery in their	1886.1
	5: 7	*Ye* w turn judgment to wormwood,	1886.1
Ob	1: 3	W shall bring me down to the ground?	4310
Jnh	3: 9	W can tell *if* God will turn and repent,	4310
Mic	3: 2	W hate the good, and love the evil;	NIH
	3: 2	w pluck off their skin from off them,	NIH
	3: 3	W also eat the flesh of my people,	834
	5: 8	w, if he go through, both treadeth down,	834
	6: 9	hear ye the rod, and w hath appointed it.	4310
	7:18	W *is* a God like unto thee, that pardoneth	4310
Na	1: 6	W can stand before his indignation?	4310
	1: 6	w can abide in the fierceness of his anger?	4310
	3: 7	w will bemoan her? whence shall I seek	4310
Hab	2: 5	w enlargeth his desire as hell, and *is* as	834
Zep	3:18	w are of thee, *to whom* the reproach of is	NIH
Hag	2: 3	W *is* left among you that saw this house	4310
Zec	4: 7	W *art* thou, O great mountain?	4310
	4:10	For w hath despised the day of small	4310
Mal	1:10	W *is there* even among you that would	4310
	3: 2	w *may* abide the day of his coming?	4310
	3: 2	w *shall* stand when he appeareth? for he	4310
Mt	1:16	whom was born Jesus, w is called Christ.	3588
	3: 7	w hath warned you to flee from the wrath	5101
	10: 2	w is called Peter, and Andrew his brother;	3588
	10: 4	and Judas Iscariot, w also betrayed him.	3588
	10:11	ye shall enter, inquire w in it is worthy;	5101
	12:48	unto him that told him, W is my mother?	5101
	12:48	is my mother? and w are my brethren?	5101
	13: 9	W hath ears to hear, let him hear.	3588
	13:43	W hath ears to hear, let him hear.	3588
	13:46	W, when he had found one pearl of great	3739
	18: 1	W is the greatest in the kingdom of	5101
	19:25	saying, W then can be saved?	5101
	21:10	all the city was moved, saying, W is this?	5101
	21:23	and w gave thee this authority?	5101
	24:45	W then is a faithful and wise servant,	5101
	25:14	w called his own servants,	NIG
	26: 3	of the high priest, w was called Caiaphas,	3588
	26:68	*thou* Christ, W is he that smote thee?	5101
	27:57	w also himself was Jesus' disciple:	3739
Mk	1:19	w also *were* in the ship mending *their* nets.	846
	1:24	I know thee w thou art, the Holy One of	5101
	2: 7	w can forgive sins but God only?	5101
	3:33	saying, W is my mother, or my brethren?	5101
	4:16	w, when they have heard the word,	3739
	5: 3	W had *his* dwelling among the tombs;	3739
	5:30	press, and said, W touched my clothes?	5101
	5:31	and sayest thou, W touched me?	5101
	9:34	w *should be* the greatest.	5101
	10:26	among themselves, W then can be saved?	5101
	11:28	w gave thee this authority to do these	5101
	13:34	w left his house, and gave authority to his	NIG
	15: 7	w had committed murder in	3748
	15:21	w passed by, coming out of the country,	NIG
	15:41	(W also, when he was in Galilee,	3739
	16: 3	W shall roll us away the stone from	5101
Lk	1:36	month with her, w was called barren.	3588
	3: 7	w hath warned you to flee from the wrath	5101
	4:34	I know thee w thou art, the Holy One of	5101
	5:12	w seeing Jesus fell on *his* face,	NIG
	5:21	W is this which speaketh blasphemies?	5101
	5:21	W can forgive sins, but God alone?	5101
	7: 2	w was dear unto him, was sick,	3739
	7:39	would have known w and what manner	5101
	7:49	W is this that forgiveth sins also?	5101
	8:45	And Jesus said, W touched me? When all	5101
	8:45	and sayest thou, W touched me?	5101
	9: 9	but w is this, of whom I hear such *things*?	5101
	9:31	W appeared in glory, and spake of his	3739
	10:22	and no *man* knoweth w the Son is,	5101
	10:22	the Father is, but the Son, and *he* to	5101
	10:29	said unto Jesus, And w is my neighbour?	5101
	12:14	w made me a judge or a divider over you?	5101
	12:42	W then is *that* faithful and wise steward,	5101
	16:11	w will commit to your trust the true	5101
	16:12	w shall give you that which is your own?	5101
	16:14	w were covetous, heard all these *things:*	NIG
	18:26	that heard *it* said, W then can be saved?	5101
	18:30	W shall not receive manifold more in this	3739
	19: 3	And he sought to see Jesus w he was;	5101
	20: 2	or w is he that gave thee this authority?	5101
	22:64	saying, Prophesy, w is it that smote thee?	5101
	23: 7	w himself also was at Jerusalem at that	NIG
	23:19	(W for a certain sedition made in the city,	3748
	23:51	w also himself waited for the kingdom of	3739
Jn	1:19	from Jerusalem to ask him, W art thou?	5101
	1:22	Then said they unto him, W art thou?	5101
	1:27	w coming after me is preferred before me,	3588
	4:10	and w it is that saith to thee, Give me to	5101
	5:13	And he that was healed wist not w it was:	5101
	6:60	This is a hard saying; w can hear it?	5101
	6:64	Jesus knew from the beginning w they	5101

Jn	6:64	believed not, and w should betray him.	5101
	7:20	hast a devil: w goeth about to kill thee?	5101
	7:49	But this people w knoweth not the law	3588
	8:25	Then said they unto him, W art thou?	5101
	9: 2	saying, Master, w did sin, this *man,* or	5101
	9:19	Is this your son, w ye say was born blind?	3739
	9:21	or w hath opened his eyes, we know not:	5101
	9:36	He answered and said, W is he, Lord, that	5101
	12:34	must be lift up? w is this Son of man?	5101
	12:38	spake, Lord, w hath believed our report?	5101
	13:11	For he knew w should betray him;	5101
	13:24	that *he* should ask w it should be of	302+5101
	13:25	Jesus' breast saith unto him, Lord, w is it?	5101
	18:18	officers stood *there,* w had made a fire of	NIG
	21:12	of the disciples durst ask him, W art thou?	5101
Ac	1:23	w was surnamed Justus, and Matthias,	3739
	3: 3	W seeing Peter and John about to go into	3739
	4:25	By the mouth of thy servant David hast	3588
	4:36	w by the apostles was surnamed Barnabas,	3588
	5:36	w was slain; and all, as many as obeyed	3739
	7:27	W made thee a ruler and a judge over us?	5101
	7:35	saying, W made thee a ruler and a judge?	5101
	7:38	w received *the* lively oracles to give unto	3739
	7:46	W found favour before God, and desired	3739
	7:53	W have received the law by the	3748
	8:15	W, when they were come down, prayed	3748
	8:27	w had the charge of all her treasure,	3739
	8:33	and w shall declare his generation? for his	5101
	8:33	And he said, W art thou, Lord?	5101
	10:32	w, when he cometh, shall speak unto	3739
	10:38	W went about doing good, and healing all	3739
	10:41	w did eat and drink with him after he rose	3748
	11:14	W shall tell thee words, whereby thou	3739
	11:17	w believed on the Lord Jesus Christ;	NIG
	11:23	W, when he came, and had seen the	3739
	13: 7	w called for Barnabas and Saul,	3778
	13: 9	Then Saul, (w also *is called* Paul,)	3588
	13:31	w are his witnesses unto the people.	3748
	13:43	w, speaking to them, persuaded them to	3748
	14: 8	his mother's womb, w never had walked:	3739
	14: 9	w stedfastly beholding him,	3739
	14:16	W in times past suffered all nations to	3739
	14:19	Iconium, w persuaded the people, and,	NIG
	15:17	saith the Lord, w doeth all these *things.*	3588
	15:27	w shall also tell *you* the same *things* by	846
	15:38	w departed from them from Pamphylia,	NIG
	16:24	W, having received such a charge,	3739
	17:10	w coming *thither* went into the	3748
	18:27	w, when he was come, helped them	3739
	19:15	I know, and Paul I know; but w are ye?	5101
	21: 4	w said to Paul through the Spirit, that *he*	3748
	21:32	W immediately took soldiers and	3739
	21:33	demanded w he was, and what he had	5101
	21:37	W said, Canst thou speak Greek?	1161+3588
	22: 8	And I answered, W art thou, Lord?	5101
	23:18	w hath something to say unto thee.	NIG
	23:33	W, when they came to Cesarea,	3748
	24: 1	w informed the governor against Paul.	3748
	24: 6	W also hath gone about to profane	3739
	24:19	W ought to have been here before thee,	3739
	26:15	I said, W art thou, Lord? And he said,	5101
	28: 7	w received us, and lodged *us* three days	3739
	28:10	W also honoured us with many honours;	3739
	28:18	W, when they had examined me,	3748
Ro	1:18	w hold the truth in unrighteousness;	3588
	1:25	W changed the truth of God into a lie,	3748
	1:25	than the Creator, w is blessed for ever.	3739
	1:32	W knowing the judgment of God, that	3748
	2: 6	W will render to every *man* according to	3739
	2: 7	To them w by patient continuance in well	NIG
	2:27	w by the letter and circumcision dost	3588
	3: 5	*Is* God unrighteous w taketh vengeance?	3588
	3:19	it saith to them w are under the law:	NIG
	4:12	And the father of circumcision to them w	NIG
	4:12	who also walk in the steps of *that* faith of	3588
	4:16	faith of Abraham; w is the father of us all,	3739
	4:17	w quickeneth the dead, and calleth those	3739
	4:18	W against hope believed in hope, that he	3739
	4:25	W was delivered for our offences,	3739
	5:14	w is the figure of *him* that was to come.	3739
	7: 4	*even* to him w is raised from the dead,	5101
	7:24	w shall deliver me from the body of this	5101
	8: 1	in Christ Jesus w walk not after the flesh,	NIG
	8: 4	w walk not after the flesh, but after	3588
	8:20	by reason of him w hath subjected *the*	NIG
	8:28	to them w are the called according to *his*	3588
	8:31	If God *be* for us, w *can be* against us?	5101
	8:33	W shall lay any thing to the charge of	5101
	8:34	W *is* he that condemneth? *It is* Christ that	5101
	8:34	that is risen *again,* w is even at the right	3739
	8:34	of God, w also maketh intercession for us.	3739
	8:35	W shall separate us from the love of	5101
	9: 4	are Israelites; to whom pertaineth	3748
	9: 5	the flesh Christ *came,* w is over all,	3588
	9:19	find fault? For w hath resisted his will?	5101
	9:20	w art thou that repliest against God?	5101
	10: 6	thine heart, W shall ascend into heaven?	5101
	10: 7	Or, W shall descend into the deep?	5101
	10:16	Lord, w hath believed our report?	5101
	11: 4	w have not bowed the knee to *the image*	3748
	11:34	For w hath known the mind of the Lord?	5101
	11:34	the Lord? or w hath been his counsellor?	5101
	11:35	Or w hath first given to him, and it shall	5101
	14: 2	*things:* another, w is weak, eateth herbs.	NIG
	14: 4	W art thou that judgest another *man's*	5101

Ro	14:20	*is* evil for *that* man w eateth with offence.	NIG
	16: 4	W have for my life laid down their own	3748
	16: 5	w is the firstfruits of Achaia unto Christ.	3739
	16: 6	w bestowed much labour on us.	3748
	16: 7	w are of note among the apostles,	3748
	16: 7	w also were in Christ before me.	3739
	16:12	and Tryphosa, w labour in the Lord.	3588
	16:22	I Tertius, w wrote *this* epistle, salute you	3588
1Co	1: 8	W shall also confirm you unto the end,	3739
	1:30	w of God is made unto us wisdom,	3739
	2:16	For w hath known the mind of the Lord,	5101
	3: 5	W then is Paul, and who is Apollos,	5101
	3: 5	and w is Apollos, but ministers by whom	5101
	4: 5	w both will bring to light the hidden	3739
	4: 7	w maketh thee to differ *from another?*	5101
	4:17	w is my beloved son, and faithful in	3739
	4:17	w shall bring you into remembrance of	3739
	6: 4	set them to judge w are least esteemed in	3588
	9: 7	W goeth a warfare any time at his own	5101
	9: 7	w planteth a vineyard, and eateth not of	5101
	9: 7	or w feedeth a flock, and eateth not of	5101
	10:13	w will not suffer you to be tempted above	3739
	14: 8	w shall prepare himself to the battle?	5101
2Co	1: 4	W comforteth us in all our tribulation,	3588
	1:10	W delivered us from so great a death,	3739
	1:19	w was preached among you by us, *even*	3588
	1:22	W hath also sealed us, and given	3588
	2: 2	w is then that maketh me glad,	5101
	2:16	And w *is* sufficient for these *things?*	5101
	3: 6	W also hath made us able ministers of	3739
	4: 4	w is the image of God, should shine unto	3739
	4: 6	w commanded the light to shine out of	3588
	5: 5	w also hath given unto us the earnest of	3588
	5:18	w hath reconciled us to himself by Jesus	3588
	5:21	him *to be* sin for us, w knew no sin;	3588
	8:10	w have begun before, not only to do,	3748
	8:19	w was also chosen of the churches to	NIG
	10: 1	w in presence *am* base among you,	3739
	11:29	W is weak, and I am not weak? who is	5101
	11:29	not weak? w is offended, and I burn not?	5101
Gal	1: 1	the Father, w raised him from the dead;)	3588
	1: 4	W gave himself for our sins, that he might	3588
	1:15	w separated me from my mother's womb,	3588
	2: 3	w was with me, being a Greek,	3588
	2: 4	w came in privily to spy out our liberty	3748
	2: 6	But of these w seemed to be somewhat,	NIG
	2: 6	for they w seemed *to be somewhat* in	NIG
	2: 9	Cephas, and John, w seemed to be pillars,	3588
	2:15	We w are Jews by nature, and not sinners	NIG
	2:20	w loved me, and gave himself for me.	3588
	3: 1	foolish Galatians, w hath bewitched you,	5101
	4:23	he w was of the bondwoman was born	NIG
	5: 7	w did hinder you that *ye* should not obey	5101
	6:10	unto them w are of the household of faith.	NIG
	6:13	For neither they themselves w are	NIG
Eph	1: 3	w hath blessed us with all spiritual	3588
	1:11	w worketh all *things* after the counsel of	NIG
	1:12	of his glory, w first trusted in Christ:	3588
	1:19	of his power to us-ward w believe,	3588
	2: 1	you *hath he quickened,* w were dead in	NIG
	2: 4	But God, w is rich in mercy, for his great	NIG
	2:11	w are called Uncircumcision by that	3588
	2:13	But now in Christ Jesus ye w sometimes	3588
	2:14	w hath made both one, and hath broken	3588
	3: 8	w *am* less than the least of all saints,	NIG
	3: 9	w created all *things* by Jesus Christ:	3588
	4: 6	w *is* above all, and through all, and in you	3588
	4:19	W being past feeling have given	3748
	5: 5	unclean *person,* nor covetous man w is	3739
Php	2: 6	W, being in the form of God, thought it	3739
	2:20	w will naturally care for your state.	3748
	3:19	w *is* in their shame, w mind earthly *things.*)	3588
	3:21	W shall change our vile body, that it may	3739
Col	1: 7	w is for you a faithful minister of Christ;	3739
	1: 8	W also declared unto us your love in	3588
	1:13	W hath delivered us from the power of	3739
	1:15	W is the image of the invisible God,	3739
	1:18	w is the beginning, the firstborn from	3739
	1:24	W now rejoice in my sufferings for you,	3739
	2:12	of God, w hath raised him from the dead.	3588
	3: 4	w is our life, shall appear, then shall ye	NIG
	4: 7	w *is* a beloved brother, and a faithful	NIG
	4: 9	and beloved brother, w is *one* of you.	3739
	4:11	called Justus, w are of the circumcision.	3588
	4:12	Epaphras, w is *one* of you, a servant of	3588
1Th	2:12	w hath called you unto his kingdom and	3588
	2:15	W both killed the Lord Jesus, and their	3588
	4: 8	w hath also given unto us his holy Spirit.	3588
	5: 8	But let us, w are of the day, be sober,	NIG
	5:10	W died for us, that, whether we wake or	3588
	5:24	*is* he that calleth you, w also will do *it.*	3739
2Th	1: 7	And to you w are troubled rest with us,	3588
	1: 9	W shall be punished *with* everlasting	3748
	2: 4	W opposeth and exalteth himself above	3588
	2: 7	only he w now letteth *will let,* until he be	NIG
	2:12	That they all might be damned w believed	3588
	3: 3	w stablish you, and keep you from	3739
1Ti	1:12	w hath enabled me, for that he counted	3588
	1:13	W was before a blasphemer,	NIG
	2: 4	W will have all men to be saved,	3739
	2: 6	W gave himself a ransom for all, to be	3588
	4:10	living God, w is the Saviour of all men,	3739
	5:17	especially they w labour in the word and	NIG
	6:13	w quickeneth all *things,* and *before* Christ	3588
	6:13	w before Pontius Pilate witnessed a good	3588

W

1Ti	6:15 **w** is the blessed and only Potentate,	NIG
	6:16 W only hath immortality, dwelling in	3588
	6:17 **w** giveth us richly all *things* to enjoy;	3588
2Ti	1: 9 W hath saved us, and called *us* with a	3588
	1:10 **w** hath abolished death, and hath brought	NIG
	2: 2 **w** shall be able to teach others also.	3748
	2: 4 he may please him **w** hath chosen *him*	3748
	2:18 W concerning the truth have erred,	3748
	2:26 **w** are taken captive by him at his will.	3748
	4: 1 **w** shall judge the quick and the dead at	3588
Tit	1:11 must be stopped, **w** subvert whole houses,	3748
	2:14 W gave himself for us, that he might	3739
Heb	1: 1 **w** at sundry times and in divers manners	NIG
	1: 3 W being the brightness of *his* glory,	3739
	1: 7 W maketh his angels spirits,	3588
	1:14 sent forth to minister for them **w** shall be	3588
	2: 9 **w** was made a little lower than the angels,	3588
	2:11 and they **w** are sanctified *are* all of one:	NIG
	2:15 And deliver them **w** through fear of death	3745
	3: 2 W was faithful to him that appointed him,	NIG
	3: 3 inasmuch as he **w** hath builded the house	NIG
	5: 2 W can have compassion on the ignorant,	NIG
	5: 7 W in the days of his flesh, when he had	3739
	5:14 *even* those **w** by reason of use have their	3588
	6: 4 For *it is* impossible for those **w** were once	NIG
	6:12 but followers of them **w** through faith and	NIG
	6:18 **w** have fled for refuge to lay hold upon	3588
	7: 1 **w** met Abraham returning from	3588
	7: 5 **w** receive the office of the priesthood	3588
	7: 9 *I* may so say, Levi also, **w** receiveth tithes,	3588
	7:16 **w** is made, not after the law of a carnal	3739
	7:26 **w** is holy, harmless, undefiled,	NIG
	7:27 W needeth not daily, as *those* high priests,	3739
	7:28 the Son, **w** is consecrated for evermore.	NIG
	8: 1 **w** is set on the right hand of the throne of	3739
	8: 5 W serve unto the example and shadow of	3748
	9:14 **w** through the eternal Spirit offered	3739
	10:29 **w** hath trodden under foot the Son of	3588
	10:39 But we are not of *them* **w** draw back unto	NIG
	11:11 she judged him faithful **w** had promised.	NIG
	11:27 he endured, as seeing *him* **w** *is* invisible.	NIG
	11:33 W through faith subdued kingdoms,	3739
	12: 2 **w** for the joy that was set before him	3739
	12:16 **w** for one morsel of meat sold his	3739
	12:25 for if they escaped not **w** refused him that	NIG
	13: 7 **w** have spoken unto you the word of God:	3748
Jas	3:13 W *is* a wise *man* and endued with	5101
	4:12 **w** is able to save and to destroy:	3588
	4:12 destroy: **w** art thou that judgest another?	5101
	5:10 **w** have spoken in the name of the Lord,	3739
1Pe	1: 5 W are kept by the power of God through	3588
	1:10 **w** prophesied of the grace *that should*	3588
	1:17 without respect of persons judgeth	3588
	1:20 W verily was foreordained before	NIG
	1:21 W by him do believe in God, that raised	3588
	2: 9 **w** hath called you out of darkness into his	NIG
	2:22 W did no sin, neither was guile found in	3739
	2:23 W, when he was reviled, reviled not	3739
	2:24 W his own self bare our sins in his own	3739
	3: 5 **w** trusted in God, adorned themselves,	3588
	3:13 And **w** *is* he that will harm you, if ye be	5101
	3:22 W is gone into heaven, and is on the right	3739
	4: 5 W shall give account to him that is ready	3739
	5: 1 **w** am also an elder, and a witness of	3588
	5:10 **w** hath called us into his eternal glory by	3588
2Pe	2: 1 **w** privily shall bring in damnable heresies,	3748
	2:15 **w** loved the wages of unrighteousness;	3739
	2:18 that were clean escaped from them **w**	NIG
1Jn	2:22 W is a liar but he that denieth that Jesus	5101
	3:12 **w** was of *that* wicked one, and slew his	NIG
	4:21 he **w** loveth God love his brother also.	NIG
	5: 5 W is he that overcometh the world, but	NIG
2Jn	1: 7 **w** confess not that Jesus Christ is come in	3588
3Jn	1: 9 **w** loveth to have the preeminence among	3588
Jude	1: 4 **w** were before of old ordained to this	3588
	1:18 **w** should walk after their own ungodly	NIG
	1:19 These be they **w** separate themselves,	NIG
Rev	1: 2 W bare record of the word of God,	3739
	1: 5 **w** *is* the faithful witness, *and* the first	NIG
	1: 9 **w** also am your brother, and companion	3588
	2: 1 **w** walketh in the midst of the seven	3588
	2:13 **w** was slain among you, where Satan	3739
	2:14 **w** taught Balac to cast a stumblingblock	3739
	2:18 **w** hath his eyes like unto a flame of fire,	3588
	4: 9 on the throne, **w** liveth for ever and ever,	3588
	5: 2 W is worthy to open the book, and to	5101
	6:17 is come; and **w** shall be able to stand?	5101
	10: 6 **w** created heaven, and the *things* that	3739
	12: 5 **w** was to rule all nations with a rod of	3739
	13: 4 beast, saying, W *is* like unto the beast?	5101
	13: 4 **w** is able to make war with him?	5101
	14:11 **w** worship the beast and his image,	3588
	15: 4 W shall not fear thee, O Lord,	5101
	15: 7 wrath of God, **w** liveth for ever and ever.	3588
	18: 8 for strong is the Lord God **w** judgeth her.	3588
	18: 9 **w** have committed fornication and	3588

WHOLE (250) [WHOLESOME, WHOLLY]

Ge	2: 6 and watered the **w** face of the ground.	3605
	2:11 that *is it* which compasseth the **w** land	3605
	2:13 the same *is it* that compasseth the **w** land	3605
	7:19 that *were* under the **w** heaven,	3605
	8: 9 for the waters *were* on the face of the **w**	3605
	9:19 and of them was the **w** earth overspread.	3605
	11: 1 the **w** earth was *of* one language,	3605

Ge	11: 4 abroad upon the face of the **w** earth.	3605
	13: 9 *Is* not the **w** land before thee?	3605
	47:28 so the **w** age of Jacob was	2416+3117+8141
Ex	10:15 For they covered the face of the **w** earth,	3605
	12: 6 the **w** assembly of the congregation of	3605
	16: 2 **w** congregation of the children of Israel	3605
	16:10 as Aaron spake unto the **w** congregation	3605
	16:10 this **w** assembly with hunger.	3605
	19:18 furnace, and the **w** mount quaked greatly.	3605
	29:18 thou shalt burn the **w** ram upon the altar:	3605
Lev	3: 9 the fat thereof, *and the* **w** rump, it shall	8549
	4:12 Even the **w** bullock shall he carry forth	3605
	4:13 if the **w** congregation of Israel sin through	3605
	7:14 he shall offer one out of the **w** oblation	3605
	8:21 Moses burnt the **w** ram upon the altar:	3605
	10: 6 let your brethren, the **w** house of Israel,	3605
	25:29 he may redeem it within a **w** year after	8552
Nu	3: 7 the charge of the **w** congregation before	3605
	8: 9 thou shalt gather the **w** assembly of	3605
	10: 2 of a **w** **piece** thou shalt make them:	4749
	11:20 But even a **w** month, until it come out at	3117
	11:21 them flesh, that they may eat a **w** month.	3117
	14: 2 the **w** congregation said unto them,	3605
	14:29 according to your **w** number, from	3605
	20: 1 of Israel, *even the* **w** congregation,	3605
	20:22 *even* the **w** congregation, journeyed from	3605
Dt	2:25 the nations *that are* under the **w** heaven,	3605
	4:19 unto all nations under the **w** heaven,	3605
	27: 6 altar of the LORD thy God *of* **w** stones:	8003
	29:23 *And that* the **w** land thereof *is* brimstone,	3605
	33:10 and **w** burnt *sacrifice* upon thine altar.	3632
Jos	5: 8 their places in the camp, till they were **w**.	2421
	8:31 an altar of **w** stones, over which no *man*	8003
	10:13 and hasted not to go down about a **w** day.	8549
	11:23 Joshua took the **w** land, according to all	3605
	18: 1 **w** congregation of the children of Israel	3605
	22:12 **w** congregation of the children of Israel	3605
	22:16 Thus saith the **w** congregation of	3605
	22:18 to morrow he will be wroth with the **w**	3605
Jdg	19: 2 was there four **w** months.	3117
	21:13 the **w** congregation sent *some* to speak to	3605
2Sa	3: 1 upon me, because my life *is yet* **w** in me.	3605
	3:19 that seemed *good* to the **w** house of	3605
	6:19 *even* among the **w** multitude of Israel,	3605
	14: 7 the **w** family is risen against thine	3605
1Ki	6:22 the **w** house he overlaid with gold, until	3605
	6:22 also the **w** altar *that was* by the oracle he	3605
	11:34 Howbeit I will not take the **w** kingdom	3605
2Ki	8: 8 For the **w** house of Ahab shall perish:	3605
2Ch	6: 3 and blessed the **w** congregation of Israel:	3605
	15:15 and sought him with their **w** desire;	3605
	16: 9 run to and fro throughout the **w** earth,	3605
	26:12 The **w** number of the chief of the fathers	3605
	30:23 the **w** assembly took counsel to keep	3605
	33: 8 according to the **w** law and the statutes	3605
Ezr	2:64 The **w** congregation together *was* forty	3605
Ne	7:66 The **w** congregation together *was* forty	3605
Est	3: 6 throughout the **w** kingdom of Ahasuerus,	3605
Job	5:18 he woundeth, and his hands **make w**.	7495
	28:24 the earth, *and* seeth under the **w** heaven;	3605
	34:13 or who hath disposed the **w** world?	3605
	37: 3 He directeth it under the **w** heaven,	3605
	41:11 *is* under the **w** heaven *is* mine.	3605
Ps	9: 1 praise *thee*, O LORD, with my **w** heart;	3605
	48: 2 the joy of the **w** earth, *is* mount Zion,	3605
	51:19 burnt offering and **w** *burnt offering*: then	3632
	72:19 let the **w** earth be filled *with* his glory;	3605
	97: 5 the presence of the Lord of the **w** earth.	3605
	105:16 the land: he brake the **w** staff of bread.	3605
	111: 1 I will praise the LORD with *my* **w** heart,	3605
	119: 2 *and that* seek him with the **w** heart.	3605
	119:10 With my **w** heart have I sought thee:	3605
	119:34 yea, I shall observe it with *my* **w** heart.	3605
	119:58 I intreated thy favour with *my* **w** heart:	3605
	119:69 I will keep thy precepts with *my* **w** heart.	3605
	119:145 I cried with *my* **w** heart; hear me,	3605
	138: 1 I will praise thee with my **w** heart:	3605
Pr	1:12 and **w**, as those that go down into the pit:	8549
	16:33 the **w** disposing thereof *is* of the LORD.	3605
	26:26 be shewed before the **w** congregation.	NIH
Ecc	12:13 us hear the conclusion of the **w** matter:	3605
	12:13 for this *is* the **w** *duty of* man.	3605
Isa	1: 5 the **w** head *is* sick, and the whole heart	3605
	1: 5 whole head *is* sick, and the heart faint.	3605
	3: 1 the **w** stay of bread, and the whole stay	3605
	3: 1 stay of bread, and the **w** stay of water,	3605
	6: 3 of hosts: the **w** earth *is* full of his glory.	3605
	10:12 *that* when the Lord hath performed his **w**	3605
	13: 5 of his indignation, to destroy the **w** land.	3605
	14: 7 The **w** earth is at rest, *and is* quiet:	3605
	14:26 that is purposed upon the **w** earth:	3605
	14:29 **w** Palestina, because the rod of him that	3605
	14:31 O city; thou, **w** Palestina, *art* dissolved:	3605
	21: 8 and I *am* set in my ward **w** nights:	3605
	28:22 even determined upon the **w** earth.	3605
	54: 5 God of the **w** earth shall he be called.	3605
Jer	1:18 and brasen walls against the **w** land,	3605
	3:10 not turned unto me with her **w** heart,	3605
	4:20 is cried; for the **w** land is spoiled:	3605
	4:27 LORD said, The **w** land shall be desolate:	3605
	4:29 The **w** city shall flee for the noise of	3605
	7:15 brethren, the **w** seed of Ephraim.	3605
	8:16 the **w** land trembled at the sound of	3605
	12:11 the **w** land is made desolate, because	3605
	13:11 have I caused to cleave unto me the **w**	3605

Jer	13:11 house of Israel and the **w** house of Judah,	3605
	15:10 and a man of contention to the **w** earth!	3605
	19:11 that cannot be **made w** again:	7495
	24: 7 they shall return unto me with their **w**	3605
	25:11 this **w** land shall be a desolation,	3605
	31:40 the **w** valley of the dead bodies, and of	3605
	32:41 in this land assuredly with my **w** heart	3605
	32:41 my whole heart and with my **w** soul.	3605
	35: 3 and the **w** house of the Rechabites;	3605
	37:10 For though ye had smitten the **w** army of	3605
	45: 4 planted I *will* pluck up, even this **w** land.	3605
	50:23 How is the hammer of the **w** earth cut	3605
	51:41 is the praise of the **w** earth surprised!	3605
	51:47 her **w** land shall be confounded, and all	3605
La	2:15 of beauty, The joy of the **w** earth?	3605
Eze	5:10 the **w** remnant of thee will I scatter into	3605
	7:13 for the vision *is* touching the **w** multitude	3605
	10:12 their **w** body, and their backs,	3605
	15: 5 when it was **w**, it was meet for no	8549
	32: 4 I will fill the beasts of the **w** earth with	3605
	35:14 When the **w** earth rejoiceth, I will make	3605
	37:11 these bones *are* the **w** house of Israel:	3605
	39:25 have mercy upon the **w** house of Israel,	3605
	43:11 that they may keep the **w** form thereof,	3605
	43:12 Upon the top of the mountain the **w** limit	3605
	45: 6 it shall be for the **w** house of Israel.	3605
Da	2:35 a great mountain, and filled the **w** earth.	3606
	2:48 made him ruler over the **w** province of	3606
	6: 1 which should be over the **w** kingdom;	3606
	6: 3 the king thought to set him over the **w**	3606
	7:23 shall devour the **w** earth, and shall tread	3606
	7:27 the greatness of the kingdom under the **w**	3606
	8: 5 from the west on the face of the **w** earth,	3605
	9:12 under the **w** heaven hath not been done	3605
	10: 3 till three **w** weeks were fulfilled.	3117+7620
	11:17 enter with the strength of his **w** kingdom,	3605
Am	1: 6 they carried away captive the **w** captivity,	8003
	1: 9 delivered up the **w** captivity to Edom,	8003
	3: 1 against the **w** family which I brought up	3605
Mic	4:13 their substance unto the Lord of the **w**	3605
Zep	1:18 the **w** land shall be devoured by the fire	3605
Zec	4:10 run to and fro through the **w** earth.	3605
	4:14 that stand by the Lord of the **w** earth.	3605
	5: 3 goeth forth over the face of the **w** earth:	3605
Mal	3: 9 ye *have* robbed me, *even* this **w** nation.	3605
Mt	5:29 *that* thy **w** body should be cast into hell.	3650
	5:30 *that* thy **w** body should be cast into hell.	3650
	6:22 be single, thy **w** body shall be full of light.	3650
	6:23 thy **w** body shall be full of darkness.	3650
	8:32 the **w** herd of swine ran violently down a	3956
	8:34 the **w** city came out to meet Jesus:	3956
	9:12 They that be **w** need not a physician,	2480
	9:21 I may but touch his garment, I shall be **w**.	4982
	9:22 comfort; thy faith hath **made** thee **w**.	4982
	9:22 And the woman was **made w** from that	4982
	12:13 and it was restored **w**, *like* as the other.	5199
	13: 2 and the **w** multitude stood on the shore.	3956
	13:33 measures of meal, till the **w** was leavened.	3650
	14:36 as touched were **made perfectly w**.	1295
	15:28 And her daughter was **made w** from that	2390
	15:31 the maimed *to be* **w**, the lame to walk,	5199
	16:26 if he shall gain the **w** world, and lose his	3650
	26:13 gospel shall be preached in the **w** world,	3650
	27:27 gathered unto him the **w** band *of soldiers*.	3650
Mk	2:17 They that are **w** have no need of	2480
	3: 5 his hand was restored **w** as the other.	5199
	4: 1 **w** multitude was by the sea on the land.	3956
	5:28 I may touch but his clothes, I shall be **w**.	4982
	5:34 Daughter, thy faith hath **made** thee **w**;	4982
	5:34 in peace, and be **w** of thy plague.	5199
	6:55 ran through that **w** region round about,	3650
	6:56 as many as touched him were **made w**.	4982
	8:36 if he shall gain the **w** world, and lose his	3650
	10:52 Go thy way; thy faith hath **made** thee **w**.	4982
	12:33 is more than all **w burnt offerings** and	3646
	14: 9 be preached throughout the **w** world,	3650
	15: 1 the elders and scribes and the **w** council,	3650
	15:16 and they call together the **w** band.	3650
	15:33 there was darkness over the **w** land until	3650
Lk	1:10 And the **w** multitude of the people were	3956
	5:31 They that are **w** need not a physician;	5198
	6:10 and his hand was restored **w** as the other.	5199
	6:19 **w** multitude sought to touch him:	3956
	7:10 found the servant **w** that had been sick.	5198
	8:37 Then the **w** multitude of the country of	537
	8:39 published throughout the **w** city how	3650
	8:48 thy faith hath **made** thee **w**; go in peace.)	4982
	8:50 believe only, and she shall be **made w**.	4982
	9:25 if he gain the **w** world, and lose himself,	3650
	11:34 is single, thy **w** body also is full of light;	3650
	11:36 If thy **w** body therefore *be* full of light,	3650
	11:36 no part dark, the **w** shall be full of light,	3650
	13:21 measures of meal, till the **w** was leavened.	3650
	17:19 go *thy way*: thy faith hath **made** thee **w**.	4982
	19:37 the **w** multitude of the disciples began to	537
	21:35 that dwell on the face of the **w** earth.	3956
	23: 1 And the **w** multitude of them arose,	537
Jn	4:53 and himself believed, and his **w** house.	3650
	5: 4 made **w** of whatsoever disease he had.	5199
	5: 6 he saith unto him, Wilt thou be made **w**?	5199
	5: 9 And immediately the man was made **w**,	5199
	5:11 He answered them, He that made me **w**,	5199
	5:14 said unto him, Behold, thou art made **w**:	5199
	5:15 that it was Jesus, which had made him **w**.	5199
	7:23 I have made a man every whit **w** on	5199

Jn	11:50 people, and *that* the **w** nation perish not.	3650
Ac	4: 9 by what means is **made w**;	4982
	4:10 doth this *man* stand here before you **w**.	5199
	6: 5 And the saying pleased the **w** multitude;	3956
	9:34 Aeneas, Jesus Christ **maketh** thee **w**:	2390
	11:26 that a **w** year they assembled themselves	3650
	13:44 **w** city together to hear the word of God.	3956
	15:22 apostles and elders, with the **w** church,	3650
	19:29 And the **w** city was filled with confusion:	3650
	28:30 And Paul dwelt two **w** years in his own	3650
Ro	1: 8 faith is spoken of throughout the **w** world.	3650
	8:22 For we know that the **w** creation groaneth	3956
	16:23 and of the **w** church, saluteth you.	3650
1Co	5: 6 that a little leaven leaveneth the **w** lump?	3650
	12:17 If the **w** body were an eye, where *were*	3650
	12:17 If the **w** were hearing, where *were*	3650
	14:23 the **w** church be come together into one	3650
Gal	5: 3 that he is a debtor to do the **w** law.	3650
	5: 9 A little leaven leaveneth the **w** lump.	3650
Eph	3:15 whom the **w** family in heaven and earth	3956
	4:16 From whom the **w** body fitly joined	3956
	6:11 Put on the **w armour** of God, that ye	3833
	6:13 Wherefore take unto *you* the **w armour**	3833
1Th	5:23 and *I* pray God your **w** spirit and soul and	3648
Tit	1:11 must be stopped, who subvert **w** houses,	3650
Jas	2:10 For whosoever shall keep the **w** law,	3650
	3: 2 *and* able also to bridle the **w** body.	3650
	3: 3 obey us; and we turn about their **w** body.	3650
	3: 6 that it defileth the **w** body, and setteth on	3650
1Jn	2: 2 but also for *the sins of* the **w** world.	3650
	5:19 and the **w** world lieth in wickedness.	3650
Rev	12: 9 and Satan, which deceiveth the **w** world:	3650
	16:14 the kings of the earth and of the **w** world,	3650

WHOLESOME (2) [WHOLE]

Pr	15: 4 A **w** tongue *is* a tree of life:	4832
1Ti	6: 3 and consent not to **w** words,	5198

WHOLLY (29) [WHOLE]

Lev	6:22 ever unto the LORD; it shall be **w** burnt.	3632
	6:23 priest shall be **w** burnt: it shall not be	3632
	19: 9 thou shalt not **w** reap	3615+3807.1+7114
Nu	3: 9 they *are* **w** given unto him out of	5414+5414
	4: 6 shall spread over *it* a cloth **w** of blue,	3632
	8:16 they *are* **w** given unto me from	5414+5414
	32:11 because they have not **w** followed me:	4390
	32:12 for they have **w** followed the LORD.	4390
Dt	1:36 because he hath **w** followed the LORD.	4390
Jos	14: 8 I **w** followed the LORD my God.	4390
	14: 9 thou hast **w** followed the LORD my God.	4390
	14:14 that he **w** followed the LORD God of	4390
Jdg	17: 3 I had **dedicated** the silver unto	6942+6942
1Sa	7: 9 offered it *for* a burnt offering **w** unto	3632
1Ch	28:21 all the people *will be* **w** at thy	3605
Job	21:23 full strength, *being* **w** at ease and quiet.	3605
Isa	22: 1 that thou art **w** gone up to the housetops?	3605
Jer	2:21 planted thee a noble vine, **w** a right seed:	3605
	6: 6 she *is* **w** oppression in the midst of her.	7965
	13:19 all of it, it shall be **w** carried away captive.	7965
	42:15 If ye **w set** your faces to enter *into*	7760+7760
	46:28 I not **leave** thee **w unpunished**.	5352+5352
	50:13 be inhabited, but it shall be **w** desolate.	3605
Eze	11:15 kindred, and all the house of Israel **w**,	3605
Am	8: 8 it shall rise up **w** as a flood; and it shall be	3605
	9: 5 it shall rise up **w** like a flood; and shall be	3605
Ac	17:16 saw the city **w given to idolatry**.	1510+2712
1Th	5:23 the very God of peace sanctify you **w**;	3651
1Ti	4:15 upon these *things;* give thyself **w to** them;	1722

WHOM (763) [WHO]

Ge	2: 8 there he put the man **w** he had formed.	834
	3:12 The woman **w** thou gavest *to be* with me,	834
	4:25 seed instead of Abel, **w** Cain slew.	3588
	6: 7 I will destroy man **w** I have created from	834
	10:14 and Casluhim, (out of **w**^s came Philistim)	8033
	15:14 nation, **w** they shall serve, will I judge:	834
	21: 3 born unto him, **w** Sarah bare to him, Isaac.	834
	22: 2 **w** thou lovest, and get thee into the land of	834
	24: 3 of the Canaanites, amongst **w** I dwell:	834
	24:14 the damsel to **w** I shall say, Let down	1886.3
	24:40 said unto me, The LORD, before **w** I walk,	834
	24:44 let the same *be* the woman **w** the LORD	834
	24:47 Nahor's son, **w** Milcah bare unto him:	834
	25:12 Abraham's son, **w** Hagar the Egyptian,	834
	30:26 for **w** I have served thee, and let me go:	834
	41:38 *is*, a man in **w** the spirit of God *is?*	834+2050.2
	43:27 father well, the old man of **w** ye spake?	834
	43:29 younger brother, of **w** ye spake unto me?	834
	44:10 with **w** it is found shall be my servant;	2050.2
	44:16 and *he* also with **w** the cup is found.	834
	45: 4 Joseph your brother, **w** ye sold into Egypt.	834
	46:18 **w** Laban gave to Leah his daughter,	834
	48: 9 **w** God hath given me in this *place*.	834+1992
	48:15 before **w** my fathers Abraham and Isaac	834
	49: 8 thou *art he* **w** thy brethren shall praise:	NIH
Ex	4:13 by the hand of *him* **w** thou wilt send.	NIH
	6: 5 of Israel, **w** the Egyptians keep in bondage;	834
	6:26 and Moses, to **w** the LORD said,	1992.1
	14:13 for the Egyptians **w** ye have seen to day,	834
	18: 9 **w** he had delivered out of the hand of	834
	22: 9 **w** the judges shall condemn, he shall pay	834
	23:27 will destroy all the people to **w** thou	1992.1
	28: 3 **w** I have filled with the spirit of wisdom,	834
	32:13 to **w** thou swarest by thine own self,	1992.1
	33:12 hast not let me know **w** thou wilt send	834

Ex	33:19 will be gracious to **w** I will be gracious,	834
	33:19 will shew mercy on **w** I will shew mercy.	834
	35:21 and every one **w** his spirit made willing,	834
	35:23 with **w** was found blue, and purple,	2050.2
	35:24 with **w** was found shittim wood for any	2050.2
	36: 1 in **w** the LORD put wisdom and	1992
Lev	6: 5 *and* give it unto him to **w** it appertaineth,	834
	13:45 the leper in **w** the plague *is*, his clothes	2050.2
	14:32 This *is* the law *of him* in **w** *is* the plague	2050.2
	15:18 The woman also with **w** man shall lie	1886.3
	16:32 **w** he shall anoint, and whom he shall	834
	16:32 **w** he shall consecrate to minister in	834
	17: 7 after **w** they have gone a whoring.	1992.1
	22: 5 or a man of **w** he may take uncleanness,	834
	25:27 restore the overplus unto the man to **w** he	834
	25:55 *are* my servants **w** I brought forth out of	834
	26:45 **w** I brought forth out of the land of	3963.1
	27:24 shall return unto him of **w** it was bought,	834
	27:24 to him to **w** the possession of the land	834
Nu	3: 3 **w** he consecrated to minister in the priest's	834
	4:41 **w** Moses and Aaron did number according	834
	4:45 **w** Moses and Aaron numbered according	834
	4:46 **w** Moses and Aaron and the chief of Israel	834
	5: 7 give *it* unto *him* against **w** he hath	834
	11:16 **w** thou knowest to be the elders of	834+1992
	11:21 amongst **w** I *am, are* six hundred	834+2050.2
	12: 1 the Ethiopian woman **w** he had married:	834
	12:12 of **w** the flesh is half consumed when he	834
	16: 5 *him* **w** he hath chosen	834+871.1+2050.2
	16: 7 it shall be *that* the man **w** the LORD doth	834
	17: 5 **w** I shall choose, shall	834+871.1+2050.2
	22: 6 I wot that *he* **w** thou blessest *is* blessed,	834
	22: 6 blessed, and *he* **w** thou cursest is cursed.	834
	23: 8 How shall I curse, **w** God hath not cursed?	NIH
	23: 8 shall I defy, **w** the LORD hath not defied?	NIH
	26: 5 of **w** *cometh* the family of the Hanochites:	834
	26:59 Levi, **w** her mother bare to Levi in Egypt:	834
	26:64 these there was not a man of them **w**	NIH
	27:18 a man in **w** *is* the spirit,	834+2050.2
	34:29 These *are they* **w** the LORD commanded to	834
	36: 6 Let them marry to **w** they think best;	1886.1
Dt	4:46 **w** Moses and the children of Israel smote,	834
	7:19 do unto all the people of **w** thou afraid.	834
	9: 2 **w** thou knowest, and *of whom* thou hast	834
	9: 2 *of* **w** thou hast heard say, Who can stand	NIH
	17:15 **w** the LORD thy God shall choose:	834
	19: 4 **w** he hated not in time past;	1931
	19:17 between **w** the controversy *is*, shall stand	834
	21: 8 **w** thou hast redeemed, and lay not	834
	24:11 the man to **w** thou dost lend shall bring	834
	28:55 of the flesh of his children **w** he shall eat:	834
	29:26 gods, **w** they knew not, and *whom* he had	NIH
	29:26 and *w* he had not given unto them:	NIH
	31: 4 unto the land of them, **w** he destroyed.	834
	32:17 *to* gods they knew not, *to* new *gods*	3963.1
	32:17 newly up, **w** your fathers feared not.	3963.1
	32:20 children in **w** *is* no faith.	3963.1
	32:37 their gods, *their* rock in **w** they trusted,	2050.2
	33: 8 **w** thou didst prove at Massah,	834
	33: 8 *with* **w** thou didst strive at the waters of	1930.2
	34:10 **w** the LORD knew face to face,	834
Jos	2:10 and Og, **w** ye utterly destroyed.	834
	4: 4 **w** he had prepared of the children of Israel,	834
	5: 6 unto **w** the LORD sware that *he* would not	834
	5: 7 children, *w* he raised up in their stead,	NIH
	10:11 **w** the children of Israel slew with the	834
	10:25 to all your enemies against **w** ye fight.	3963.1
	13: 8 With **w** the Reubenites and the Gadites	2050.2
	13:21 **w** Moses smote with the princes of Midian,	834
	24:15 choose you *this* day **w** you will serve;	4310
	24:17 all the people through **w** we passed:	834
Jdg	4:22 I will shew thee the man **w** thou seekest.	834
	7: 4 it shall be, *that* of **w** I say unto thee,	834
	8:15 with **w** ye did upbraid me, saying,	834
	8:18 What manner of men *were they* **w** ye slew	NIH
	12: 9 **w** he sent abroad, and took in thirty	834
	14:20 companion, **w** he had used as his friend.	834
	21:23 of them that danced, **w** they caught:	834
Ru	2:19 she shewed her mother in law with **w**	2050.2
	2:19 man's name with **w** I wrought to day	2050.2
	4: 1 the kinsman of **w** Boaz spake came by;	834
	4: 1 unto **w** he said, Ho, such a one, turn aside,	NIH
	4:12 house of Pharez, **w** Tamar bare unto Judah,	834
1Sa	2:33 *w* I shall not cut off from mine altar,	NIH
	6:20 unto **w** shall he go up from us?	4310
	9:17 Behold the man **w** I spake to thee of:	834
	9:20 on **w** *is* all the desire of Israel? *Is it* not on	4310
	10:24 See ye him **w** the LORD hath chosen,	834
	12: 3 or have I defrauded? whom have I	4310
	12: 3 **w** have I oppressed? or of whose hand	4310
	12:13 behold the king **w** ye have chosen,	834
	12:13 ye have chosen, *and* **w** ye have desired:	4310
	16: 3 thou shalt anoint unto me *him* **w** I name	834
	17:28 with **w** hast thou left those few sheep in	4310
	17:45 of the armies of Israel, **w** thou hast defied.	834
	21: 9 **w** thou slewest in the valley of Elah,	834
	24:14 After **w** is the king of Israel come out?	4310
	24:14 After **w** dost thou pursue? after a dead	4310
	25:11 unto men, **w** I know not whence they *be?*	4310
	25:25 young men of my lord, **w** thou didst send.	834
	28: 8 *him* up, **w** I shall name unto thee.	834
	28:11 the woman, **w** shall I bring up unto thee?	4310
	29: 5 of **w** they sang one to another in dances,	4310
	30:13 said unto him, To **w** *belongest* thou?	4310
	30:21 **w** they had made also to abide at	3963.1

2Sa	7: 7 **w** I commanded to feed my people Israel,	834
	7:15 from Saul, **w** I put away before thee.	834
	7:23 **w** God went to redeem for a people to	834
	14: 7 for the life of his brother **w** he slew;	834
	15:33 Unto **w** David said, If thou passest on	2050.2
	16:18 **w** the LORD, and this people, and all	834
	16:19 **w** should I serve? *should I* not *serve*	4310
	17: 3 man **w** thou seekest *is* as if all returned:	834
	19:10 Absalom, **w** we anointed over us, is dead	834
	20: 3 **w** he had left to keep the house,	834
	21: 6 Gibeah of Saul, **w** the LORD did choose.	NIH
	21: 8 she bare unto Saul, Armoni and	834
	21: 8 **w** she brought up for Adriel the son of	834
	23: 8 These *be* the names of the mighty *men* **w**	834
	23: 8 eight hundred, **w** he slew at one time.	NIH
1Ki	2: 5 he slew, and shed the blood of war in	3963.1
	5: 5 **w** I will set upon thy throne in thy room,	834
	7: 8 **w** he had taken *to* wife, like unto this	834
	9:21 **w** the children of Israel also were not able	834
	10:26 **w** he bestowed in the cities for chariots,	3963.1
	11:20 **w** Tahpenes weaned in Pharaoh's	1930.2
	11:34 **w** I chose, because he kept my	834
	13:23 *to wit*, for the prophet **w** he had brought	834
	17: 1 God of Israel liveth, before **w** I stand,	834
	17:20 evil upon the widow with **w** I sojourn,	1886.3
	18:15 the LORD of hosts liveth, before **w** I stand,	834
	18:31 unto **w** the word of the LORD came,	834
	20:14 Ahab said, By **w**? And he said, Thus saith	4310
	20:42 a man **w** I appointed to utter destruction,	NIH
	21:25 of the LORD, **w** Jezebel his wife stirred up.	834
	21:26 **w** the LORD cast out before the children of	834
	22: 8 by **w** we may inquire of the LORD:	2050.2
2Ki	3:14 of hosts liveth, before **w** I stand, surely,	834
	5:16 before **w** I stand, I will receive none.	834
	6:19 and I will bring you to the man **w** ye seek.	834
	6:22 **w** thou hast taken captive with thy sword	834
	8: 5 this *is* her son, **w** Elisha restored to life.	834
	10:24 *If* any of the men **w** I have brought into	834
	16: 3 **w** the LORD cast out from before	834
	17: 8 **w** the LORD cast out from before	834
	17:11 as *did* the heathen **w** the LORD carried	834
	17:15 concerning **w** the LORD had charged them,	834
	17:27 Carry thither one of the priests **w** ye	834
	17:28 one of the priests **w** they had carried away	834
	17:33 after the manner of the nations **w** they	834
	17:34 the children of Jacob, **w** he named Israel;	834
	17:35 With **w** the LORD had made a covenant,	3963.1
	18:20 Now on **w** dost thou trust, that thou	4310
	19: 4 **w** the king of Assyria his master hath sent	834
	19:10 Let not thy God in **w** thou trustest deceive	834
	19:22 **W** hast thou reproached and blasphemed?	4310
	19:22 against **w** hast thou exalted *thy* voice,	4310
	21: 2 **w** the LORD cast out before the children of	834
	21: 9 **w** the LORD destroyed before the children	834
	23: 5 **w** the kings of Judah had ordained to burn	834
	25:22 **w** Nebuchadnezzar king of Babylon had	834
1Ch	1:12 (of **w** came the Philistines,)	834+8033
	2:21 **w** he married when he *was* threescore	1886.3
	5: 6 **w** Tilgath-pilneser king of Assyria carried	834
	5:25 of the land, **w** God destroyed before them.	834
	6:31 these *are they* **w** David set over the service	834
	7:14 The sons of Manasseh; Ashriel, **w** she bare:	834
	8: 7 the men of Gath that were born in	3963.1
	9:22 **w** David and Samuel the seer did ordain	1992
	11:10 also *are the* chief of the mighty *men* **w**	834
	11:11 this *is* the number of the mighty *men* **w**	834
	17: 6 **w** I commanded to feed my people, saying,	834
	17:21 **w** God went to redeem *to be* his own	834
	17:21 **w** thou hast redeemed out of Egypt?	834
	26:32 **w** king David made rulers over	3963.1
	29: 1 **w** alone God hath chosen, *is yet* young	2050.2
	29: 8 they with **w** precious stones were found	2050.2
2Ch	1:11 my people, over **w** I have made thee king:	834
	2: 7 **w** David my father did provide.	834
	8: 8 **w** the children of Israel consumed not,	834
	9:25 **w** he bestowed in the chariot cities,	3963.1
	17:19 besides *those* **w** the king put in the fenced	834
	18: 7 by **w** we may inquire of the LORD:	2050.2
	20:10 **w** thou wouldest not let Israel invade,	834
	22: 7 **w** the LORD had anointed to cut off	834
	23:18 **w** David had distributed in the house of	834
	28: 3 **w** the LORD had cast out before	834
	33: 2 **w** the LORD had cast out before	834
	33: 9 **w** the LORD had destroyed before	834
Ezr	2: 1 **w** Nebuchadnezzar the king of Babylon	834
	2:65 of **w** *there were* seven thousand three	428
	4:10 the rest of the nations **w** the great and	1768
	5:14 Sheshbazzar, **w** he had made governor;	1768
	8:20 **w** David and the princes had appointed	7945
	10:44 *some* of them had wives by **w** they had	NIH
Ne	1:10 **w** thou hast redeemed by thy great power,	834
	7: 6 **w** Nebuchadnezzar the king of Babylon	834
	7:67 of **w** *there were* seven thousand three	428
	8:10 send portions unto *them* for **w** nothing	2050.2
	9:37 yieldeth much increase unto the kings **w**	834
Est	2: 6 **w** Nebuchadnezzar the king of Babylon	834
	2: 7 **w** Mordecai, when her father and	NIH
	4: 5 **w** he had appointed to attend upon her,	834
	4:11 except such to **w** the king shall hold out	2050.2
	6: 6 What shall be done unto the man **w**	834
	6: 6 **w** would the king delight to do honour	4310
	6: 6 the man **w** the king delighteth to honour,	834
	6: 9 that they may array the man *withal* **w**	834
	6: 9 Thus shall it be done to the man **w** the	834
	6:11 Thus shall it be done unto the man **w**	834

Est 6:13 before **w** thou hast begun to fall, thou shalt 834
Job 3:23 way is hid, and **w** God hath hedged in? 2050.2
5:17 happy *is* the man **w** God correcteth: 5105.2
9:15 **W**, though I were righteous, *yet* would I 834
15:19 Unto **w** alone the earth was given, 1992.1
19:19 and they **w** I loved are turned against me. NIH
19:27 **W** I shall see for myself, and mine eyes 834
25: 3 and upon **w** doth not his light arise? 4310
26: 4 To **w** hast thou uttered words? 4310
30: 2 profit me, in **w** old age was perished? 4123.1
Ps 10: 3 the covetous, **w** the LORD abhorreth. NIH
16: 3 *to* the excellent, in **w** *is* all my delight. 3963.1
18: 2 my God, my strength, in **w** I will trust; 2050.2
18:43 people **w** I have not known shall serve me. NIH
27: 1 my light and my salvation; **w** shall I fear? 4310
27: 1 strength of my life; of **w** shall I be afraid? 4310
32: 2 Blessed *is* the man unto **w** the LORD 2050.2
33:12 the people **w** he hath chosen for his own NIH
41: 9 mine own familiar friend, in **w** I trusted, 834
45:16 **w** thou mayest make princes in all 4123.1
47: 4 for us, the excellency of Jacob **w** he loved. 834
65: 4 Blessed *is* the man **w** thou choosest, NIH
69:26 they persecute *him* **w** thou hast smitten; 834
69:26 they talk to the grief of those **w** thou hast 4310
73:25 **W** have I in heaven *but thee?* and *there is* 4310
80:17 upon the son of man **w** thou madest strong NIH
86: 9 All nations **w** thou hast made shall come 834
88: 5 the grave, **w** thou rememberest no more: 834
89:21 With **w** my hand shall be established: NIH
94: 1 O LORD God, to **w** vengeance belongeth; NIH
94: 1 O God, to **w** vengeance belongeth, NIH
94:12 Blessed *is* the man **w** thou 834+5105.2
95:11 *Unto* **w** I sware in my wrath that they 834
104:26 **w** thou hast made to play therein. NIH
105:26 his servant; *and* Aaron **w** he had chosen. 834
106:34 *concerning* **w** the LORD commanded them: 834
106:38 **w** they sacrificed unto the idols of Canaan: 834
107: 2 **w** he hath redeemed from the hand of 834
144: 2 my shield, and *he* in **w** I trust; 2050.2
146: 3 in the son of man, in **w** *there is* no help. 7945
Pr 3:12 For **w** the LORD loveth he correcteth; 834
3:12 as a father the son *in* **w** he delighteth. NIH
3:27 not good from **them** to **w** it is due, 1167
25: 7 of the prince **w** thine eyes have seen. 834
30:31 a king, against **w** *there is* no rising up. 2050.2
Ecc 4: 8 neither *saith he*, For **w** do I labour, 4310
5:19 Every man also to **w** God hath given 834
6: 2 man to **w** God hath given riches, wealth, 834
8:14 there be just *men*, unto **w** it happeneth 834
8:14 there be wicked *men*, to **w** it happeneth 1992.1
9: Live joyfully with the wife **w** thou lovest 834
SS 1: 7 Tell me, O thou **w** my soul loveth, 7945
3: 1 By night on my bed I sought *him* **w** my 7945
3: 2 I will seek *him* **w** my soul loveth: 7945
3: 3 *to* **w** *I said*, Saw ye *him* **w** my soul NIH
3: 3 *to whom I said*, Saw ye **w** my soul 7945
3: 4 but I found *him* **w** my soul loveth: 7945
Isa 6: 8 **W** shall I send, and who will go for us? 4310
8:12 to all *them* to **w** this people shall say, 834
8:18 the children *w* the LORD hath given me *are* 834
10: 3 to **w** will ye flee for help? and where will 4310
19:25 the LORD of hosts shall bless, saying, 834
22:16 **w** hast thou here, that thou hast hewed 4310
23: 2 **w** the merchants of Zidon, that pass 3509.3
28: 9 **W** shall he teach knowledge? and whom 4310
28: 9 **w** shall he make to understand doctrine? 4310
28:12 To **w** he said, This *is* the rest **wherewith** ye 834
31: 6 Turn ye unto *him from* **w** the children of 834
36: 5 on **w** dost thou trust, that thou rebellest 4310
37: 4 **w** the king of Assyria his master hath sent 834
37:10 in **w** thou trustest, deceive thee, saying, 4310
37:23 **W** hast thou reproached and blasphemed? 4310
37:23 against **w** hast thou exalted *thy* voice, 4310
40:14 With **w** took he counsel, 4310
40:18 To **w** then will ye liken God? 4310
40:25 To **w** then will ye liken me, or shall I be 4310
41: 8 *art* my servant, Jacob **w** I have chosen, 834
41: 9 *Thou* **w** I have taken from the ends of 834
42: 1 Behold my servant, **w** I uphold; mine 2050.2
42: 1 mine elect, *in* **w** my soul delighteth; NIH
42:24 the LORD, he against **w** we have sinned? 2098
43:10 and my servant **w** I have chosen: 834
44: 1 my servant; and Israel, **w** I have chosen: 2050.2
44: 2 and *thou*, Jeshurun, **w** I have chosen. 2050.2
46: 5 will ye liken me, and make *me* equal, 4310
47:15 Thus shall they be unto thee *with* **w** thou 834
49: 3 servant, O Israel, in **w** I will be glorified. 834
49: 7 his Holy One, to him **w** man despiseth, NIH
49: 7 him **w** the nation abhorreth, to a servant NIH
50: 1 divorcement, **w** I have put away? 834
50: 1 of my creditors *is it* to **w** I have sold 834
51:18 all the sons **w** she hath brought forth; NIH
51:19 and the sword: *by* **w** shall I comfort thee? 4310
53: 1 to **w** is the arm of the LORD revealed? 4310
57: 4 Against **w** do ye sport yourselves? 4310
57: 4 against **w** make ye a wide mouth, 4310
57:11 of **w** hast thou been afraid or feared, 4310
66:13 as one **w** his mother comforteth, so will I 834
Jer 1: 2 To **w** the word of the LORD came in 834
6:10 To **w** shall I speak, and give warning, 4310
7: 9 and walk after other gods **w** ye know not; 834
8: 2 **w** they have loved, and whom 834+3963.1
8: 2 **w** they have served, and after 834+3963.1
8: 2 after **w** they have walked, 834+1992.1
8: 2 **w** they have sought, and whom 834+3963.1

Jer 8: 2 and **w** they have worshipped: 834+1992.1
9:12 *who is he* to **w** the mouth of the LORD 834
9:16 **w** neither they nor their fathers have 834
11:12 unto the gods unto **w** they offer 834+1992.1
14:16 people to **w** they prophesy shall be cast 834
18: 8 that nation, against **w** I have pronounced, 834
19: 4 **w** neither they nor their fathers have 834
20: 6 thy friends, to **w** thou hast prophesied lies. 834
23: 9 like a man **w** wine hath overcome, 2050.2
24: 5 **w** I have sent out of this place *into* the 834
25:15 the nations, to **w** I send thee, to drink it. 834
25:17 to drink, unto **w** the LORD had sent me: 834
27: 5 I sent unto you, both rising up early, 834
27: 5 have given it unto **w** it seemed meet unto 834
29: 1 to all the **w** Nebuchadnezzar had 834
29: 3 **w** Zedekiah king of Judah sent unto 834
29: 4 **w** I have caused to be carried away from 834
29:20 **w** I have sent from Jerusalem to Babylon: 834
29:22 **w** the king of Babylon roasted in the fire; 834
30: 9 their king, **w** I will raise up unto them. 834
30:17 This *is* Zion, **w** no man seeketh after. 1886.3
33: 5 **w** I have slain in mine anger and in my 834
34:11 **w** they had let go free, to return, 834
34:16 **w** ye had set at liberty at their pleasure, 834
37: 1 **w** Nebuchadnezzar king of Babylon made 834
38: 9 **w** they have cast into the dungeon; 834
39:17 the hand of the men of **w** thou *art* afraid. 834
40: 5 **w** the king of Babylon hath made governor 834
41: 2 **w** the king of Babylon made governor 834
41: 9 men, **w** he had slain because of Gedaliah, 834
41:10 **w** Nebuzar-adan the captain of the guard 834
41:16 all the remnant of the people **w** he had 834
41:16 **w** he had brought again from Gibeon, 834
41:18 the king of Babylon made governor in 834
42: 6 of the LORD our God, to **w** we send thee; 834
42: 9 unto **w** ye sent me to present your 834
42:11 of Babylon, of **w** ye *are* afraid; 834+4480+6440
44: 3 **w** they knew not, *neither* they, you, 834
50:20 found: for I will pardon them **w** I reserve. 834
52:28 This *is* the people **w** Nebuchadrezzar 834
La 1:10 **w** thou didst command *that* they should 834
1:14 hands, *from* **w** I am not able to rise up. NIH
2:20 and consider to **w** thou hast done this. 4310
4:20 was taken in their pits, *of* **w** we said, 834
Eze 9: 6 near any man upon **w** *is* the mark; 834
11: 1 among **w** I saw Jaazaniah the son of 3963.1
11: 7 Your slain **w** ye have laid in the midst of it, 834
11:15 they unto **w** the inhabitants of Jerusalem 834
13:22 righteous man, **w** I have not made sad; 2050.2
16:20 **w** thou hast borne unto me, and these hast 834
16:37 with **w** thou hast taken pleasure, and all 834
20: 7 among **w** they *were*, in whose sight I made 834
23: 7 of Assyria, and with all *on* **w** she doted: 834
23: 9 hand of the Assyrians, upon **w** she doted. 834
23:22 from **w** thy mind is alienated, and I will 834
23:28 I *will* deliver thee into the hand *of them* **w** 834
23:28 into the hand *of them* from **w** thy mind is 834
23:37 caused their sons, **w** they bare unto me, 834
23:40 from far, unto **w** a messenger *was* sent; 834
23:40 for **w** thou didst wash *thyself*, paintedst 834
24:21 your daughters **w** ye have left shall fall by 834
28:25 the people among **w** they are scattered, 834
31: 2 **W** art thou like in thy greatness? 4310
31:18 To **w** art thou like in glory and 4310
32:19 **w** dost thou pass in beauty? go down, 4310
38:17 *Art* thou he of **w** I have spoken in old time 834
Da 1: 4 Children in **w** *was* no blemish, 834
1: 4 **w** *they* might teach the learning and NIH
1: 7 Unto **w** the prince of the eunuchs gave 1992.1
1:11 the prince of the eunuchs had set over 834
2:24 the king had ordained to destroy the 1768
3:12 There are certain Jews **w** thou hast set 1768
3:17 our God **w** we serve *is* able to deliver us 1768
4: 8 and in **w** *is* the spirit of the holy gods: 1886.8
5:11 in **w** *is* the spirit of the holy gods; 1886.8
5:11 **w** the king Nebuchadnezzar thy father, NIH
5:12 the king named Belteshazzar: 1768
5:13 the king my father brought out of 1768
5:19 he would he slew; and whom he 1768
5:19 he would he kept alive; and whom he 1768
5:19 he would he set up; and whom he 1768
5:19 he set up; and **w** he would he put down. 1768
6: 2 three presidents; of **w** Daniel *was* first: 1952.1
6:16 Thy God **w** thou servest continually, 1768
6:20 is thy God, **w** thou servest continually, 1768
7: 8 before **w** there were three of the first 1886.9
7:20 which came up, and before **w** three fell; 1886.9
9:21 I had seen in the vision at the beginning, 834
11:21 to **w** they shall not give the honour of 2050.2
11:38 a god **w** his fathers knew not shall he 834
11:39 he shall acknowledge *and* increase *with* 834
Hos 13:10 thy judges *of* **w** thou saidst, Give me a king 834
Joel 2:32 and in the remnant **w** the LORD *shall* call. 834
3: 7 they have scattered among the nations, 834
Am 6: 1 to the house of Israel came! 1992.1
7: 2 *by* **w** shall Jacob arise? for he *is* small. 4310
7: 5 *by* **w** shall Jacob arise? for he *is* small. 4310
Na 3:19 upon **w** hath not thy wickedness passed 4310
Zep 3:18 *to* **w** the reproach of it *was* a burden. NIH
Zec 1: 4 unto **w** the former prophets have cried, 834
1:10 These *are they* **w** the LORD hath sent to 834
7:14 among all the nations **w** they knew not: 834
12:10 they shall look upon me **w** they have 834
Mal 1: 4 The people *against* **w** the LORD hath 834
2:14 against **w** thou hast dealt treacherously: 834

Mal 3: 1 the LORD, **w** ye seek, shall suddenly come 834
3: 1 messenger of the covenant, **w** ye delight 834
Mt 1:16 of **w** was born Jesus, who is called Christ. 3739
3:17 my beloved Son, in **w** I am well pleased. 3739
7: 9 **w** if his son ask bread, will he give him a 3739
11:10 For this is *he*, of **w** it is written, Behold, 3739
12:18 Behold my servant, **w** I have chosen; 3739
12:18 my beloved, in **w** my soul is well pleased: 3739
12:27 by **w** do your children cast *them* out? 5101
16:13 **W** do men say that I the Son of man am? 5101
16:15 saith unto them, But **w** say ye that I am? 5101
17: 5 my beloved Son, in **w** I am well pleased; 3739
17:25 **w** do the kings of the earth take custom 5101
18: 7 woe to that man by **w** the offence cometh 3739
19:11 this saying, save *they* to **w** it is given. 3739
20:23 *be given to them* for **w** it is prepared 3739
23:35 **w** ye slew between the temple and the 3739
24:45 **w** his lord hath made ruler over his 3739
24:46 **w** his lord when he cometh shall find so 3739
26:24 woe unto that man by **w** the Son of man 3739
27: 9 they of the children of Israel did value; 3739
27:15 unto the people a prisoner, **w** they would. 3739
27:17 **W** will ye *that* I release unto you? 5101
Mk 1:11 my beloved Son, in **w** I am well pleased. 3739
3:13 and calleth unto *him* **w** he would: 3739
6:16 *thereof*, he said, It is John, **w** I beheaded: 3739
8:27 unto them, **W** do men say that I am? 5101
8:29 saith unto them, But **w** say ye that I am? 5101
10:40 *it shall be given to them* for **w** it is 3739
13:20 for the elect's sake, **w** he hath chosen, 3739
14:21 woe to that man by **w** the Son of man is 3739
14:71 I know not this man of **w** ye speak. 3739
15:12 I shall do *unto him* **w** ye call the King 5101
15:40 among **w** was Mary Magdalene, 3739
16: 9 out of **w** he had cast seven devils, 3739
Lk 6:13 chose twelve, **w** also he named apostles; 3739
6:14 Simon, (**w** he also named Peter,) and 3739
6:34 And if ye lend *to them* of **w** ye hope to 3739
6:47 them, I will shew you to **w** he is like: 5101
7: 4 That he was worthy for **w** he should do 3739
7:27 This is *he*, of **w** it is written, Behold, 3739
7:43 I suppose that *he*, to **w** he forgave most. 3739
7:47 but to **w** little is forgiven, *the same* loveth 3739
8: 2 out of **w** went seven devils, 3739
8:35 man, out of **w** the devils were departed, 3739
8:38 Now the man out of **w** the devils were 3739
9: 9 of **w** I hear such *things?* And he desired to 3739
9:18 saying, **W** say the people that I am? 5101
9:20 said unto them, But **w** say ye that I am? 5101
10:22 *he* to the Son will reveal *him*. 1437+3739
11:19 by **w** do your sons cast *them* out? 5101
12: 5 But I will forewarn you **w** you shall fear: 5101
12:37 **w** the lord when he cometh shall find 3739
12:42 **w** *his* lord shall make ruler over his 3739
12:43 **w** his lord when he cometh shall find so 3739
12:48 and to **w** *men* have committed much, 3739
13: 4 upon **w** the tower in Siloam fell, 3739
13:16 **w** Satan hath bound, lo *these* eighteen 3739
17: 1 but woe *unto him*, through **w** they come. 3739
19:15 unto him, to **w** he had given the money, 3739
22:22 woe unto that man by **w** he is betrayed. 3739
23:25 was cast into prison, **w** they had desired; 3739
Jn 1:15 cried, saying, This was he of **w** I spake, 3739
1:26 standeth one among you, **w** ye know not; 3739
1:30 This is he of **w** I said, After me cometh a 3739
1:33 Upon **w** thou shalt see the Spirit 302+3739
1:45 of **w** Moses in the law, and the prophets, 3739
1:47 an Israelite indeed, in **w** is no guile. 3739
3:26 to **w** thou barest witness, behold, 3739
3:34 he **w** God hath sent speaketh the words 3739
4:18 he **w** thou now hast is not thy husband. 3739
5:21 so the Son quickeneth **w** he will. 3739
5:38 for he **w** he hath sent, him ye believe not. 3739
5:45 accuseth you, *even* Moses, in **w** ye trust. 3739
6:29 that ye believe on *him* **w** he hath sent. 3739
6:68 answered him, Lord, to **w** shall we go? 5101
7:25 Is not this he, **w** they seek to kill? 3739
7:28 he that sent me is true, **w** ye know not. 3739
8:53 prophets are dead: **w** makest thou thyself? 5101
8:54 of **w** ye say, that he is your God: 3739
10:35 unto **w** the word of God came, 3739
10:36 ye of him, **w** the Father hath sanctified, 3739
11: 3 Lord, behold, he **w** thou lovest is sick. 3739
12: 1 been dead, **w** he raised from the dead. 3739
12: 9 he had raised from the dead. 3739
12:38 to **w** hath the arm of the Lord been 5101
13:18 I know **w** I have chosen: but that 3739
13:22 one on another, doubting of **w** he spake. 5101
13:23 bosom one of his disciples, **w** Jesus loved. 3739
13:24 he should ask who it should be of **w** he 3739
13:26 He it is, to **w** I shall give a sop, 3739
14:17 the world cannot receive, because 3739
14:26 **w** the Father will send in my name, 3739
15:26 **w** I will send unto you from the Father, 3739
17: 3 and Jesus Christ, **w** thou hast sent. 3739
17:11 through thine own name those **w** thou 3739
17:24 will *that* they also, **w** thou hast given me, 3739
18: 4 forth, and said unto them, **W** seek ye? 5101
18: 7 Then asked he them again, **W** seek ye? 5101
19:26 and the disciple standing by, **w** he loved, 3739
19:37 They shall look on *him* **w** they pierced. 3739
20: 2 **w** Jesus loved, and saith unto them, 3739
20:15 **w** seekest thou? She, supposing him to be 5101
21: 7 Therefore that disciple **w** Jesus loved saith 3739
21:20 seeth the disciple **w** Jesus loved following; 3739

Ac	1: 2 unto the Apostles **w** he had chosen:	3739
	1: 3 To **w** also he shewed himself alive after	3739
	2:24 **W** God hath raised up, having loosed	3739
	2:36 w ye have crucified, both Lord and Christ.	3739
	3: 2 **w** they laid daily at the gate of the temple	3739
	3:13 w ye delivered up, and denied him in	3739
	3:15 of life, **w** God hath raised from the dead;	3739
	3:16 this *man* strong, **w** ye see and know:	3739
	3:21 **W** the heaven must receive until the	3739
	4:10 ye crucified, whom God raised from	3739
	4:10 ye crucified, **w** God raised from the dead,	3739
	4:22 on **w** this miracle of healing was shewed.	3739
	4:27 **w** thou hast anointed, both Herod,	3739
	5:25 the men **w** ye put in prison are standing	3739
	5:30 up Jesus, **w** ye slew and hanged on a tree.	3739
	5:32 **w** God hath given to them that obey him.	3739
	5:36 **w** a number of men, about four hundred,	3739
	6: 3 **w** we may appoint over this business.	3739
	6: 6 **W** they set before the apostles:	3739
	7: 7 the nation to **w** they shall be in	1437+3739
	7:35 This Moses **w** they refused, saying,	3739
	7:39 To **w** our fathers would not obey,	3739
	7:45 **w** God drave out before the face of our	3739
	7:52 of ye have been now the betrayers and	3739
	8:10 To **w** they all gave heed, from the least to	3739
	8:34 pray thee, of **w** speaketh the prophet this?	5101
	9: 5 Lord said, I am Jesus **w** thou persecutest:	3739
	9:37 **w** when they had washed, they laid *her* in	NIG
	10:21 and said, Behold, I am he **w** ye seek:	3739
	10:39 **w** they slew and hanged on a tree:	3739
	13:22 to **w** also he gave testimony, and said,	3739
	13:25 *his* course, he said, **W** think ye that I am?	5101
	13:37 **w** God raised *again*, saw no corruption.	3739
	14:23 them to the Lord, on **w** they believed.	3739
	15:17 upon **w** my name is called, saith the Lord,	3739
	15:24 to **w** we gave no *such* commandment:	3739
	17: 3 this Jesus, **w** I preach unto you, is Christ.	3739
	17: 7 **W** Jason hath received: and these all do	3739
	17:23 **W** therefore ye ignorantly worship,	3739
	17:31 by *that* man **w** he hath ordained;	3739
	18:26 **w** when Aquila and Priscilla had heard,	846
	19:13 We adjure you by Jesus **w** Paul preacheth.	3739
	19:16 And the man in **w** the evil spirit was leapt	3739
	19:25 **W** he called together with the workmen	3739
	19:27 **w** all Asia and the world worshippeth.	3739
	20:25 among **w** I have gone preaching	3739
	21:16 an old disciple, with **w** we should lodge.	3739
	21:29 **w** they supposed that Paul had brought	3739
	22: 5 from **w** also I received letters unto	3739
	22: 8 Jesus of Nazareth, **w** thou persecutest.	3739
	23:29 **W** I perceived to be accused of questions	3739
	24: 6 **w** we took, and would have judged	3739
	24: 8 by examining of **w** thyself mayest take	3739
	25:15 About **w**, when I was at Jerusalem,	3739
	25:16 To **w** I answered, It is not the manner of	3739
	25:18 Against **w** when the accusers stood *up*,	3739
	25:19 *was* dead, **w** Paul affirmed to be alive.	3739
	25:24 see this *man*, about **w** all the multitude	3739
	25:26 Of **w** I have no certain *thing* to write unto	3739
	26:15 he said, I am Jesus **w** thou persecutest.	3739
	26:17 the Gentiles, unto **w** now I send thee,	3739
	26:26 these *things*, before **w** also I speak freely:	3739
	27:23 angel of God, whose I am, and **w** I serve,	3739
	28: 4 **w**, though he hath escaped the sea,	3739
	28: 8 to **w** Paul entered in, and prayed,	3739
	28:15 **w** when Paul saw, he thanked God,	3739
	28:23 to **w** he expounded and testified	3739
Ro	1: 5 By **w** we have received grace and	3739
	1: 6 Among **w** are ye also the called of Jesus	3739
	1: 9 I serve with my spirit in the gospel of	3739
	3:25 **W** God hath set forth *to be* a propitiation	3739
	4: 6 **w** God imputeth righteousness without	3739
	4: 8 Blessed *is* the man to **w** the Lord will not	3739
	4:17 before *him* **w** he believed, *even* God,	3739
	4:24 But for us also, to **w** it shall be imputed,	3739
	5: 2 By **w** also we have access by faith into	3739
	5:11 **w** we have now received the atonement.	3739
	6:16 that to **w** ye yield yourselves servants to	3739
	6:16 to obey, *his* servants ye are to **w** ye obey;	3739
	8:29 For **w** he did foreknow, he also did	3739
	8:30 Moreover **w** he did predestinate, them he	3739
	8:30 and **w** he called, them he also justified:	3739
	8:30 and **w** he justified, them he also glorified.	3739
	9: 4 **w** pertaineth the adoption, and the glory,	3739
	9: 5 of **w** as concerning the flesh Christ *came*,	3739
	9:15 I will have mercy on **w** I will have	302+3739
	9:15 I will have compassion on **w** I will	302+3739
	9:18 Therefore hath he mercy on **w** he will	3739
	9:18 have mercy, and **w** he will he hardeneth.	3739
	9:24 Even us, **w** he hath called, not of the Jews	3739
	10:14 they shall call on *him* in **w** they have not	3739
	10:14 how shall they believe *in him* of **w** they	3739
	11:36 him, *are* all *things*: to **w** *be* glory for ever.	846
	13: 7 tribute to **w** tribute *is due*; custom to	3588
	13: 7 to whom tribute *is due*; custom to **w**	3588
	13: 7 fear to **w** fear; honour to whom honour.	3588
	13: 7 fear to whom fear; honour to **w** honour.	3588
	14:15 not him with thy meat, for **w** Christ died.	3739
	15:21 To **w** he was not spoken of, they shall see:	3739
	16: 4 unto **w** not only I give thanks, but also all	3739
1Co	1: 9 by **w** ye were called unto the fellowship	3739
	3: 5 *is* Apollos, but ministers by **w** ye believed,	3739
	7:39 is at liberty to be married to **w** she will;	3739
	8: 6 of **w** *are* all *things*, and we in him;	3739
	8: 6 by **w** *are* all *things*, and we by him.	3739

1Co	8:11 weak brother perish, for **w** Christ died?	3739
	10:11 upon **w** the ends of the world are come.	3739
	15: 6 of **w** the greater part remain unto this	3739
	15:15 we have not raised up, if so be that the dead	3739
2Co	1:10 in **w** we trust that he will yet deliver *us*;	3739
	2: 3 I should have sorrow from *them* of **w** I	3739
	2:10 To **w** ye forgive any *thing*, I *forgive* also:	3739
	2:10 if I forgave any *thing*, to **w** I *forgave it*,	3739
	4: 4 In **w** the god of this world hath blinded	3739
	8:22 **w** we have oftentimes proved diligent in	3739
	10:18 is approved, but **w** the Lord commendeth.	3739
	11: 4 **w** we have not preached, or *if* ye receive	3739
	12:17 I make a gain of you by any of them **w**	3739
Gal	1: 5 To **w** *be* glory for ever and ever. Amen.	3739
	2: 5 To **w** we gave place by subjection,	3739
	3:19 the seed should come to **w** the promise	3739
	4:19 of **w** I travail in birth again until Christ be	3739
	6:14 by **w** the world is crucified unto me, and	3739
Eph	1: 7 In **w** we have redemption through his	3739
	1:11 In **w** also we have obtained an inheritance,	3739
	1:13 In **w** ye also *trusted*, after that ye heard	3739
	1:13 in **w** also after that ye believed, ye were	3739
	2: 3 Among **w** also we all had our	3739
	2:21 In **w** all the building fitly framed together	3739
	2:22 In **w** you also are builded together for a	3739
	3:12 In **w** we have boldness and access with	3739
	3:15 Of **w** the whole family in heaven and	3739
	4:16 From **w** the whole body fitly joined	3739
	6:22 **W** I have sent unto you for the same	3739
Php	2:15 among **w** ye shine as lights in the world;	3739
	3: 8 for **w** I have suffered the loss of all *things*,	3739
	3:18 of **w** I have told you often, and now tell	3739
Col	1:14 In **w** we have redemption through his	3739
	1:27 To **w** God would make known what *is*	3739
	1:28 **W** we preach, warning every man,	3739
	2: 3 In **w** are hid all the treasures of wisdom	3739
	2:11 In **w** also ye are circumcised with	3739
	4: 8 **W** I have sent unto you for the same	3739
	4:10 (touching **w** ye received commandments:	3739
1Th	1:10 **w** he raised from the dead, *even* Jesus,	3739
2Th	2: 8 **w** the Lord shall consume with the spirit	3739
1Ti	1:15 the world to save sinners; of **w** I am chief.	3739
	1:20 Of **w** is Hymeneus and Alexander; whom	3739
	1:20 **w** I have delivered unto Satan, that they	3739
	6:16 **w** no man hath seen, nor can see:	3739
	6:16 to **w** *be* honour and power everlasting.	3739
2Ti	1: 3 **w** I serve from *my* forefathers with pure	3739
	1:12 for I know **w** I have believed, and I am	3739
	1:15 of **w** are Phygellus and Hermogenes.	3739
	2:17 a canker: of **w** is Hymeneus and Philetus;	3739
	3:14 knowing of **w** thou hast learned *them*;	3739
	4:15 Of **w** be thou ware also; for he hath	3739
	4:18 to **w** *be* glory for ever and ever. Amen.	3739
Phm	1:10 **w** I have begotten in my bonds:	3739
	1:12 **W** I have sent again: thou therefore	3739
	1:13 **W** I would have retained with me, that in	3739
Heb	1: 2 **w** he hath appointed heir of all *things*, by	3739
	1: 2 all *things*, by **w** also he made the worlds;	3739
	2:10 for **w** *are* all *things*, and by whom *are* all	3739
	2:10 by **w** *are* all *things*, in bringing many sons	3739
	3:17 But with **w** was he grieved forty years?	5101
	3:18 And to **w** sware he that *they* should not	5101
	4: 6 to **w** it was first preached entered not in	NIG
	4:13 opened unto the eyes of him with **w** we	3739
	5:11 Of **w** we have many things to say,	3739
	6: 7 bringeth forth herbs meet for them by **w**	3739
	7: 2 **w** also Abraham gave a tenth *part* of all;	3739
	7: 4 **w** even the patriarch Abraham gave	3739
	7: 8 he *receiveth them*, of **w** it is witnessed	NIG
	7:13 For he of **w** these *things* are spoken	3739
	11:18 Of **w** it was said, That in Isaac shall thy	3739
	11:38 (Of **w** the world was not worthy:)	3739
	12: 6 For **w** the Lord loveth he chasteneth,	3739
	12: 6 and scourgeth every son **w** he receiveth.	3739
	12: 7 what son is *he* **w** the father chasteneth	3739
	13:21 to **w** *be* glory for ever and ever.	3739
	13:23 with **w**, if he come shortly, I will see you.	3739
Jas	1:17 with **w** is no variableness, neither shadow	3739
1Pe	1: 8 **W** having not seen, ye love; in whom,	3739
	1: 8 in **w**, though now ye see *him* not,	3739
	1:12 Unto **w** it was revealed, that not unto	3739
	2: 4 To **w** coming, *as unto* a living stone,	3739
	4:11 to **w** be praise and dominion for ever and	3739
	5: 8 walketh about, seeking **w** he may devour:	5101
	5: 9 **W** resist stedfast in the faith, knowing	3739
2Pe	1:17 my beloved Son, in **w** I am well pleased.	3739
	2: 2 by reason of **w** the way of truth shall be	3739
	2:17 to **w** the mist of darkness is reserved for	3739
	2:19 of **w** a man is overcome, of the same	3739
1Jn	4:20 he that loveth not his brother **w** he hath	3739
	4:20 can he love God **w** he hath not seen?	3739
2Jn	1: 1 and her children, **w** I love in the truth;	3739
3Jn	1: 1 wellbeloved Gaius, **w** I love in the truth.	3739
	1: 6 if thou bring forward on their journey	3739
Jude	1:13 to **w** is reserved the blackness of darkness	3739
Rev	7: 2 to **w** it was given to hurt the earth and	3739
	17: 2 With **w** the kings of the earth have	3739
	20: 8 the number of **w** *is* as the sand of the sea.	3739

WHOMSOEVER (20) [EVER, SO, WHO]

Ge	31:32 With **w** thou findest thy gods, let him not	834
	44: 9 With **w** of thy servants it be found,	834
Lev	15:11 he toucheth that hath the issue,	834+3605
Jdg	7: 4 I say unto thee, This shall not go	834+3605
	11:24 So **w** the LORD our God shall drive	834+3605

Da	4:17 giveth it to **w** he will, and setteth	1768+4479
	4:25 of men, and giveth it to **w** he will.	1768+4479
	4:32 of men, and giveth it to **w** he will.	1768+4479
	5:21 that he appointeth over **w** he will.	1768+4479
Mt	11:27 he to **w** the Son will reveal *him*.	1437+3739
	21:44 on **w** it shall fall, it will grind him	302+3739
	26:48 **W** I shall kiss, that *same* is he:	302+3739
Mk	14:44 **W** I shall kiss, *that* same is he;	302+3739
	15: 6 unto them one prisoner, **w** they desired.	3746
Lk	4: 6 unto me; and to **w** I will I give it.	1437+3739
	12:48 *stripes*. For unto **w** much is given,	3739+3956
	20:18 on **w** it shall fall, it will grind him	302+3739
Jn	13:20 receiveth **w** I send receiveth me;	1437+5100
Ac	8:19 this power, that on **w** I lay hands,	1437+3739
1Co	16: 3 **w** you shall approve by *your* letters,	1437+3739

WHORE (14) [WHORE'S, WHOREDOM, WHOREDOMS, WHOREMONGER, WHOREMONGERS, WHORES, WHORING, WHORISH]

Lev	19:29 thy daughter, to **cause** her to be a **w**;	2181
	21: 7 They shall not take a wife *that is* a **w**,	2181
	21: 9 if she profane herself by **playing the w**,	2181
Dt	22:21 to **play the w** *in* her father's house:	2181
	23:17 There shall be no **w** of the daughters of	6948
	23:18 Thou shalt not bring the hire of a **w**,	2181
Jdg	19: 2 his concubine **played the w** against him,	2181
Pr	23:27 For a **w** *is* a deep ditch; and a strange	2181
Isa	57: 3 the seed of the adulterer and the **w**.	2181
Eze	16:28 Thou hast **played the w** also in this	2181
Rev	17: 1 great **w** that sitteth upon many waters:	4204
	17:15 where the **w** sitteth, are peoples,	4204
	17:16 these shall hate the **w**, and shall make her	4204
	19: 2 for he hath judged the great **w**, which did	4204

WHORE'S (1) [WHORE]

Jer	3: 3 thou hadst a **w** forehead,	802+2181

WHOREDOM (22) [WHORE]

Ge	38:24 and also, behold, she *is* with child by **w**.	2183
Lev	19:29 lest the land **fall** to **w**, and the land	2181
	20: 5 to commit **w** with Molech, from among	2181
Nu	25: 1 the people begun to **commit w** with	2181
Jer	3: 9 to pass through the lightness of her **w**,	2184
	13:27 the lewdness of thy **w**,	2184
Eze	16:17 of men, and didst **commit w** with them,	2181
	16:33 come unto thee on every side for thy **w**.	8457
	20:30 **commit** ye **w** after their abominations?	2181
	23: 8 virginity, and poured their **w** upon her.	8457
	23:17 they defiled her with their **w**, and she	8457
	23:27 thy **w** *brought* from the land of Egypt:	2184
	43: 7 *neither* they, nor their kings, by their **w**,	2184
	43: 9 Now let them put away their **w**,	2184
Hos	1: 2 the land hath **committed great w**,	2181+2181
	4:10 they shall **commit w**, and shall not	2181
	4:11 **W** and wine and new wine take *away*	2184
	4:13 your daughters shall **commit w**,	2181
	4:14 your daughters when they **commit w**,	2181
	4:18 have **committed w continually**:	2181+2181
	5: 3 thou **committest w**, *and* Israel is defiled.	2181
	6:10 *is* the **w** of Ephraim, Israel is defiled.	2184

WHOREDOMS (32) [WHORE]

Nu	14:33 bear your **w**, until your carcases be	2184
2Ki	9:22 so long as the **w** of thy mother Jezebel	2183
2Ch	21:13 like to the **w** of the house of Ahab,	2181
Jer	3: 2 thou hast polluted the land with thy **w**	2184
Eze	16:20 *Is this* of thy **w** a small matter,	8457
	16:22 thy **w** thou hast not remembered the days	8457
	16:25 one that passed by, and multiplied thy **w**.	8457
	16:26 hast increased thy **w**, to provoke me to	8457
	16:34 is in thee from *other* women in thy **w**,	8457
	16:34 none followeth thee to **commit w**:	2181
	16:36 thy nakedness discovered through thy **w**	8457
	23: 3 they **committed w** in Egypt;	2181
	23: 3 Egypt; they **committed w** in their youth:	2181
	23: 7 Thus she committed her **w** with them,	8457
	23: 8 left she her **w** *brought* from Egypt:	8457
	23:11 in her **w** more than her sister in *her*	8457
	23:11 more than her sister in *her* **w**.	2183
	23:14 *that* she increased her **w**: for when she	8457
	23:18 So she discovered her **w**,	8457
	23:19 Yet she multiplied her **w**, in calling to	8457
	23:29 nakedness of thy **w** shall be discovered,	2183
	23:29 both thy lewdness and thy **w**.	8457
	23:35 bear thou also thy lewdness and thy **w**.	8457
	23:43 Will they now **commit w** with her,	2181+8457
Hos	1: 2 take unto thee a wife of **w** and children	2183
	1: 2 a wife of whoredoms and children of **w**:	2183
	2: 2 therefore put away her **w** out of her sight,	2183
	2: 4 children; for they *be* the children of **w**.	2183
	4:12 the spirit of **w** hath caused *them* to err,	2183
	5: 4 for the spirit of **w** *is* in the midst of them,	2183
Na	3: 4 Because of the multitude of the **w** of	2183
	3: 4 that selleth nations through her **w**,	2183

WHOREMONGER (1) [WHORE]

Eph	5: 5 For this ye know, that no **w**, nor unclean	4205

WHOREMONGERS (4) [WHORE]

1Ti	1:10 For **w**, for them that defile themselves	4205
Heb	13: 4 but **w** and adulterers God will judge.	4205
Rev	21: 8 and **w**, and sorcerers, and idolaters,	4205
	22:15 and **w**, and murderers, and idolaters,	4205

WHORES (2) [WHORE]

Eze 16:33 They give gifts to all **w**: but thou givest 2181
Hos 4:14 for themselves are separated with **w**, 2181

WHORING (19) [WHORE]

Ex 34:15 they **go a w** after their gods, 2181
 34:16 their daughters **go a w** after their gods, 2181
 34:16 **make** thy sons **go a w** after their gods. 2181
Lev 17: 7 after whom they have **gone a w**. 2181
 20: 5 cut him off, and all that **go a w** after him, 2181
 20: 6 after wizards, to **go a w** after them, I will 2181
Nu 15:39 own eyes, after which ye use to **go a w**: 2181
Dt 31:16 **go a w** after the gods of the strangers of 2181
Jdg 2:17 they **went a w** after other gods, 2181
 8:27 all Israel **went** thither **a w** after it: 2181
 8:33 **went a w** after Baalim, 2181
1Ch 5:25 **went a w** after the gods of the people of 2181
2Ch 21:13 **made** Judah and the inhabitants of
 Jerusalem **to go a w**, 2181
Ps 73:27 thou hast destroyed all them that **go a w** 2181
 106:39 and **went a w** with their own inventions. 2181
Eze 6: 9 their eyes, which **go a w** after their idols: 2181
 23:30 thou hast **gone a w** after the heathen, 2181
Hos 4:12 have **gone a w** from under their God. 2181
 9: 1 for thou hast **gone a w** from thy God, 2181

WHORISH (3) [WHORE]

Pr 6:26 For by means of a **w** woman *a man is* 2181
Eze 6: 9 because I am broken with their **w** heart, 2181
 16:30 the work of an imperious **w** woman? 2181

WHOSE (314) [WHO]

Ge 1:11 kind, **w** seed *is* in itself, upon the earth: 834
 1:12 **w** seed *was* in itself, after his kind: 834
 7:22 All in **w** nostrils *was* the breath of life, 2050.2
 11: 4 a tower, **w** top *may reach* unto heaven; 2050.2
 16: 1 an Egyptian, **w** name *was* Hagar. 1886.3
 17:14 the uncircumcised man *child* **w** flesh of 834
 22:24 his concubine, **w** name *was* Reumah, 1886.3
 24:23 said, **W** daughter *art* thou? tell me, I pray 4310
 24:37 of the Canaanites, in **w** land I dwell: 834
 24:47 asked her, and said, **W** daughter *art* thou? 4310
 32:17 asketh thee, saying, **W** *art* thou? 4310+3807.1
 32:17 and **w** *are* these before thee? 4310+3807.1
 38: 1 certain Adullamite, **w** name *was* Hirah. 2050.2
 38: 2 certain Canaanite, **w** name *was* Shuah; 2050.2
 38: 6 Er his firstborn, **w** name *was* Tamar. 1886.3
 38:25 **w** these *are, am* I with 834+2050.2+3807.1
 38:25 Discern, I pray thee, **w** *are* these, 4310+1807.1
 44:17 *but* the man in **w** hand the cup is 834+2050.2
 by a well; **w** branches run over the wall. NIH
Ex 34:14 for the LORD, **w** name *is* Jealous, *is* a 2050.2
 35:21 every one **w** heart stirred him up, 834
 35:26 all the women **w** heart stirred them up in 834
 35:29 **w** heart made them willing to bring for all 834
 36: 2 unto whom the LORD had put wisdom, 2050.2
 36: 2 *even* every one **w** heart stirred him up to 834
Lev 13:40 the man **w** hair is fallen off his head, he *is* 3588
 14:32 **w** hand is not able to get *that which* 2050.2
 15:32 *of him* **w** seed goeth from him, and is 834
 16:27 **w** blood was brought in to make 3963.1
 21:10 upon **w** head the anointing oil was 2050.2
 22: 4 dead, or a man **w** seed goeth from him, 834
 24:10 **w** father *was* an Egyptian, 1931
Nu 24: 3 and the man **w** eyes are open hath said: 1886.1
 24:15 and the man **w** eyes are open hath said: 1886.1
Dt 8: 9 a land **w** stones *are* iron, and out of whose 834
 8: 9 out of **w** hills thou mayest dig brass. 1886.3
 19: 1 **w** land the LORD thy God giveth thee, 834
 28:49 nation **w** tongue thou shalt not understand; 834
 29:18 **w** heart turneth away *this* day from 834
Jos 24:15 gods of the Amorites, in **w** land ye dwell: 834
Jdg 4: 2 the captain of **w** host *was* Sisera, which 2050.2
 6:10 of the Amorites, in **w** land ye dwell: 3963.1
 8:31 a son, **w** name he called Abimelech. 2050.2
 13: 2 of the Danites, **w** name *was* Manoah; 2050.2
 16: 4 valley of Sorek, **w** name *was* Delilah. 1886.3
 17: 1 of mount Ephraim, **w** name *was* Micah. 2050.2
Ru 2: 2 glean ears of corn after *him* in **w** sight 846
 2: 5 that was set over the reapers, **W** 4310+3807.1
 2:12 under **w** wings thou art come to trust. 2050.2
 3: 2 kindred, with **w** maidens thou wast? 2050.2
1Sa 9: 1 **w** name *was* Kish, the son of Abiel, 2050.2
 9: 2 he had a son, **w** name *was* Saul, 2050.2
 10:26 band of men, **w** hearts God had touched. 834
 12: 3 **w** ox have I taken? or whose ass have I 4310
 12: 3 or **w** ass have I taken? or whom have I 4310
 12: 3 of **w** hand have I received *any* bribe to 4310
 17: 4 **w** height *was* six cubits and a span. 2050.2
 17:12 Beth-lehem-judah, **w** name *was* Jesse; 2050.2
 17:55 of the host, Abner, **W** son *is* this youth? 4310
 17:56 Inquire thou **W** son the stripling *is*. 4310
 17:58 to him, **W** son *art* thou, *thou* young man? 4310
 25: 2 Maon, **w** possessions *were* in Carmel; 1930.2
2Sa 3: 7 **w** name *was* Rizpah, the daughter of 1886.3
 3:12 his behalf, saying, **W** *is* the land? 4310+3807.1
 6: 2 **w** name is called *by* the name of the LORD 834
 9: 2 of Saul a servant **w** name *was* Ziba. 2050.2
 9:12 had a young son, **w** name *was* Micha. 2050.2
 13: 1 had a fair sister, **w** name *was* Tamar; 1886.3
 13: 3 had a friend, **w** name *was* Jonadab, 2050.2
 14:27 and one daughter, **w** name *was* Tamar: 1886.3
 16: 5 **w** name *was* Shimei, the son of Gera: 2050.2
 16: 8 of Saul, in **w** stead thou hast reigned; 2050.2
 17:10 **w** heart *is* as the heart of a lion, shall 834

2Sa 17:25 son, **w** name *was* Ithra an Israelite, 2050.2
 20: 1 **w** name *was* Sheba, the son of Bichri, 2050.2
 21:16 the weight of **w** spear *weighed* three 2050.2
 21:19 the staff of **w** spear *was* like a weaver's 2050.2
1Ki 3:26 the woman **w** the living child *was* unto 834
 8:39 to his ways, **w** heart thou knowest; 834+2050.2
 11:26 **w** mother's name *was* Zeruah, a widow 2050.2
2Ki 7: 2 a lord on **w** hand the king leaned answered 834
 7:17 the king appointed the lord on **w** hand he 834
 8: 1 **w** son he had restored to life, saying, Arise, 834
 8: 5 the woman, **w** son he had restored to life, 834
 12:15 into **w** hand they delivered the money to 834
 18:22 **w** high places and whose altars 834+2050.2
 18:22 and **w** altars Hezekiah hath taken away, 2050.2
1Ch 2:16 **W** sisters *were* Zeruiah, and Abigail. 1992.1
 2:26 also another wife, **w** name *was* Atarah; 1886.3
 2:34 an Egyptian, **w** name *was* Jarha. 2050.2
 7: 2 **w** number *was* in the days of David two 3963.1
 7:15 **w** sister's name *was* Maachah;) 2050.2
 8:29 Gibeon; **w** wife's name *was* Maachah: 2050.2
 8:38 **w** names *are* these, Azrikam, Bocheru, 3963.1
 9:35 Jehiel, **w** wife's name *was* Maachah: 2050.2
 9:44 **w** names *are* these, Azrikam, Bocheru, 3963.1
 12: 8 **w** faces *were* like the faces of lions, 1992.1
 13: 6 the cherubims, **w** name is called *on it.* 834
 20: 5 **w** spear staff *was* like a weaver's beam. 2050.2
 20: 6 **w** fingers and toes *were* four and 834
 26: 7 **w** brethren *were* strong men, Elihu, 2050.2
2Ch 6:30 unto all his ways, **w** heart thou knowest; 834
 16: 9 of *them* **w** heart *is* perfect towards him. 3963.1
 28: 9 LORD was there, **w** name *was* Oded: 834
Ezr 1: 5 with all *them* **w** spirit God had raised, 2050.2
 5:14 they *were* delivered unto one, **w** name 1886.8
 7:15 of Israel, **w** habitation *is* in Jerusalem, 1768
 8:13 **w** names *are* these, Eliphelet, Jeiel, 3963.1
Est 2: 5 **w** name *was* Mordecai, the son of Jair, 2050.2
Job 1: 1 in the land of Uz, **w** name *was* Job; 2050.2
 3:23 Why *is* light given to a man **w** way is hid, 834
 4:19 foundation *is* in the dust, which are 834
 5: 5 **W** harvest the hungry eateth up, 834
 8:14 **W** hope shall be cut off, and whose trust 2050.2
 8:14 and **w** trust *shall be* a spider's web. 834
 12: 6 into **w** hand God bringeth *abundantly.* 2050.2
 12:10 In **w** hand *is* the soul of every living 2050.2
 22:16 **w** foundation was overflown with a 3963.1
 26: 4 and **w** spirit came from thee? 4310
 30: 1 **w** fathers I would have disdained to 3963.1
 38:29 Out of **w** womb came the ice? 4310
Ps 15: 4 In **w** eyes a vile *person* is contemned; 2050.2
 17:14 **w** belly thou fillest *with* thy hid 3963.1
 26:10 In **w** hands *is* mischief, and their right 834
 32: 1 Blessed *is he* **w** transgression *is* forgiven, NIH
 32: 1 transgression *is* forgiven, **w** sin *is* covered. NIH
 32: 2 and in **w** spirit *there* is no guile. 2050.2
 32: 9 **w** mouth must be held in with bit and 2050.2
 33:12 Blessed *is* the nation **w** God *is* the LORD; 834
 38:14 and in **w** mouth *are* no reproofs. 2050.2
 57: 4 **w** teeth *are* spears and arrows, 1992.1
 78: 8 and **w** spirit was not stedfast with God. 2050.2
 83:18 that thou, **w** name alone *is* JEHOVAH, 3509.2
 84: 5 Blessed *is* the man **w** strength 2050.2+3807.1
 84: 5 thee; in **w** heart *are* the ways *of them.* 3963.1
 105:18 **W** feet they hurt with fetters: he was 2050.2
 144: 8 **W** mouth speaketh vanity, and their right 834
 144:11 **w** mouth speaketh vanity, and their right 834
 144:15 happy *is* that people, **w** God *is* the LORD. 7945
 146: 5 **w** hope *is* in the LORD his God: 2050.2
Pr 2:15 **W** ways *are* crooked, and *they* froward in 834
 26:26 *W* hatred is covered by deceit, NIH
 30:14 **w** teeth *are as* swords, and their jaw 2050.2
Ecc 2:21 For there is a man **w** labour *is* in 7945+2050.2
 7:26 **w** heart *is* snares and nets, *and* her hands 834
Isa 1:30 For ye shall be as an oak **w** leaf fadeth, 1886.3
 2:22 ye from man, **w** breath *is* in his nostrils: 834
 5:28 **W** arrows *are* sharp, and all their bows 834
 6:13 and as an oak, **w** substance *is* in them, 834
 10:10 **w** graven images did excel *them* of 1992.1
 14: 2 take them captives, **w** captives they were; NIH
 18: 2 **w** land the rivers have spoiled. 834
 18: 7 under foot, **w** land the rivers have spoiled, 834
 23: 7 *Is* this your joyous *city,* **w** antiquity *is* of 1886.3
 23: 8 crowning *city,* **w** merchants *are* princes, 834
 23: 8 **w** traffickers *are* the honourable of 1886.3
 26: 3 **w** mind *is* stayed *on thee:* because NIH
 28: 1 **w** glorious beauty *is* a fading flower, 2050.2
 30:13 **w** breaking cometh suddenly at an instant. 834
 31: 9 **w** fire *is* in Zion, and his 2050.2+3807.1
 36: 7 **w** high places and whose altars Hezekiah 834
 36: 7 and **w** altars Hezekiah hath taken away, 2050.2
 43:14 the Chaldeans, **w** cry *is* in the ships. 3963.1
 45: 1 to Cyrus, **w** right hand I have holden, 834
 51: 7 the people in **w** heart *is* my law; 3963.1
 51:15 that divided the sea, **w** waves roared: 2050.2
 57:15 inhabiteth eternity, **w** name *is* Holy; 834
 57:20 **w** waters cast up mire and dirt. 2050.2
 58:11 like a spring of water, **w** waters fail not. 834
Jer 5:15 a nation **w** language thou knowest not, 2050.2
 17: 5 and **w** heart departeth from the LORD. 2050.2
 17: 7 the LORD, and **w** hope the LORD is. 834
 19:13 of all the houses upon **w** roofs they have 834
 22:25 into the hand *of them* **w** face thou fearest, 834
 32:29 upon **w** roofs they have offered incense 834
 33: 5 for all **w** wickedness I have hid my face 834
 37:13 **w** name *was* Irijah, the son of 2050.2

Jer 44:28 shall know **w** words shall stand, mine, 4310
 46: 7 waters are moved as the rivers? 2050.2
 46:18 the King, **w** name *is* the LORD of hosts, 2050.2
 48:15 the King, **w** name *is* the LORD of hosts. 2050.2
 49:12 **w** judgment *was* not to drink of the cup 834
 51:57 the King, **w** name *is* the LORD of hosts. 2050.2
Eze 3: 6 **w** words thou canst not understand. 834
 11:21 *as for them* **w** heart walketh after 3963.1
 17: 6 **w** branches turned toward him, 2050.2
 17:16 **w** oath he despised, and whose covenant 834
 17:16 he despised, and **w** covenant he brake, 834
 20: 9 among whom they *were*, in **w** sight I made 834
 20:14 heathen, in **w** sight I brought them out. 834
 20:22 heathen, in **w** sight I brought them forth. 834
 21:25 wicked prince of Israel, **w** day is come, 834
 21:27 he come **w** right it is; 834+2050.2+3807.1
 21:29 **w** day is come, when *their* iniquity shall 834
 23:20 **w** flesh *is as* the flesh of asses, 2050.2
 23:20 and **w** issue *is like* the issue of horses. 3963.1
 24: 6 to the pot **w** scum *is* therein, 834
 24: 6 and **w** scum is not gone out of it! 1886.3
 32:23 **W** graves are set in the sides of the pit, 834
 40: 3 **w** appearance *was* like the appearance 1930.2
 40:45 **w** prospect *is* toward the south, 834
 40:46 chamber **w** prospect *is* toward the north 834
 42:15 he brought me forth toward the gate **w** 834
 43: 4 of the gate **w** prospect *is* toward the east. 834
 47:12 all trees for meat, **w** leaf shall not fade, 1930.2
Da 2:11 the gods, **w** dwelling is not with flesh. 1768
 2:26 said to Daniel, **w** name *was* Belteshazzar, 1768
 2:31 great image, **w** brightness *was* excellent, 1886.8
 3: 1 **w** height *was* threescore cubits, 1886.8
 3:27 upon **w** bodies the fire had no power, 1952.1
 4: 8 **w** name *was* Belteshazzar, according to 1768
 4:19 Daniel, **w** name *was* Belteshazzar, 1886.8
 4:20 **w** height reached unto the heaven, 1886.8
 4:21 **W** leaves *were* fair, and the fruit thereof 1886.8
 4:21 **w** branches the fowls of the heaven 1958.2
 4:34 **w** dominion *is* an everlasting dominion, 1886.8
 4:37 all **w** works *are* truth, and his ways 1958.2
 5:23 the God in **w** hand thy breath *is*, and 1886.8
 5:23 thy breath *is*, and **w** *are* all thy ways, 1886.8
 7: 9 **w** garment *was* white as snow, 1886.9
 7:19 **w** teeth *were* of iron, and his nails *of* 1886.9
 7:20 a mouth that spake very great *things*, 1886.9
 7:27 **w** kingdom *is* an everlasting kingdom, 1886.9
 10: 1 name was called Belteshazzar; 834
 10: 5 **w** loins *were* girded with fine gold of 2050.2
 10: 6 **w** teeth *are* the teeth of a lion, 2050.2+3807.1
Joel 1: 6 **w** teeth *are* like the height of the cedars, 834
Am 2: 9 **w** height *was* like the height of the cedars, 834
 5:27 the LORD, **w** name *is* The God of hosts. 2050.2
Ob 1: 3 clefts of the rock, **w** habitation *is* high; 2050.2
Jnh 1: 7 that we may know for **w** cause 4310+3807.1
 1: 8 for **w** cause this evil *is* upon us; 4310+3807.1
Mic 5: 2 **w** goings forth *have been* from of old, 2050.2
Na 3: 4 **w** rampart *was* the sea, 1886.3+3807.1
Zec 6:12 the man **w** name *is* THE BRANCH; 2050.2
 11: 5 **W** possessors slay them, 834
Mt 3:11 than I, **w** shoes I am not worthy to bear: 3739
 3:12 **W** fan *is* in his hand, and he will 3739
 10: 3 and Lebbeus, **w** surname *was* Thaddeus; NIG
 22:20 **W** *is* this image and superscription? 5101
 22:28 Therefore in the resurrection **w** wife *shall* 5101
 22:42 What think ye of Christ? **w** son is he? 5101
Mk 1: 7 the latchet of **w** shoes I am not worthy to 3739
 7:25 **w** young daughter had an unclean spirit, 3739
 12:16 **W** *is* this image and superscription? 5101
 12:23 shall rise, **w** wife shall she be of them? 5101
Lk 1:27 To a virgin espoused to a man **w** name 3739
 2:25 a man in Jerusalem, **w** name *was* Simeon; 3739
 3:16 the latchet of **w** shoes I am not worthy to 3739
 3:17 **W** fan *is* in his hand, and he will 3739
 6: 6 was a man **w** right hand was withered. 846
 12:20 then **w** shall *those things* be, which thou 5101
 13: 1 blood Pilate had mingled with their 3739
 20:24 **W** image and superscription hath it? 5101
 20:33 Therefore in the resurrection **w** wife of 5101
 24:18 the one *of them,* **w** name *was* Cleopas, 3739
Jn 1: 6 a man sent from God, **w** name *was* John. 846
 1:27 **w** shoe's latchet I am not worthy to 3739
 4:46 **w** son was sick at Capernaum. 3739
 6:42 of Joseph, **w** father and mother we know? 3739
 10:12 the shepherd, **w** own the sheep are not, 3739
 11: 2 her hair, **w** brother Lazarus was sick.) 3739
 18:26 *his* kinsman he **w** ear Peter cut off, saith, 3739
 19:24 not rent it, but cast lots for it, **w** it shall be: 5101
 20:23 **W** soever sins ye remit, they are remitted 5100
 20:23 and **w** soever sins ye retain, they are 5100
Ac 7:58 at a young man's feet, **w** name *was* Saul. NIG
 10: 5 call for *one* Simon, **w** surname is Peter: 3739
 10: 6 a tanner, **w** house is by the sea side: 3739
 10:32 call hither Simon, **w** surname is Peter; 3739
 11:13 and call for Simon, **w** surname is Peter; 3739
 12:12 mother of John, **w** surname was Mark; 3588
 12:25 with *them* John, **w** surname was Mark. 3588
 13: 6 a Jew, **w** name *was* Bar-jesus: 3739
 13:25 **w** shoes of *his* feet I am not worthy to 3739
 15:37 with *them* John, **w** surname was Mark. 3588
 16:14 heard *us:* **w** heart the Lord opened, 3739
 18: 7 **w** house joined hard to the synagogue. 3739
 27:23 angel of God, **w** I am, and whom I serve, 3739
 28: 7 *man* of the island, **w** name was Publius; NIG
 28:11 in the isle, **w** sign *was* Castor and Pollux. NIG
Ro 2:29 **w** praise *is* not of men, but of God. 3739
 3: 8 that good may come? **w** damnation is just. 3739

Ro	3:14	**W** mouth is full of cursing and bitterness:	3739
	4: 7	*Saying,* Blessed *are they* **w** iniquities are	3739
	4: 7	are forgiven, and **w** sins are covered.	3739
	9: 5	**W** *are* the fathers, and of whom as	3739
2Co	8:18	**w** praise *is* in the gospel throughout all	3739
	11:15	we end shall be according to their works.	3739
Gal	3: 1	before **w** eyes Jesus Christ hath been	3739
Php	3:19	**W** end *is* destruction, whose God *is their*	3739
	3:19	**w** God *is their* belly, and *whose* glory *is in*	3739
	3:19	*their* belly, and **w** glory *is* in their shame,	NIG
	4: 3	**w** names *are* in the book of life.	3739
2Th	2: 9	*Even him,* **w** coming is after the working	3739
Tit	1:11	**W** mouths must be stopped, who subvert	3739
Heb	3: 6	**w** house are we, if we hold fast	3739
	3:17	**w** carcases fell in the wilderness?	3739
	6: 8	nigh unto cursing; **w** end *is* to be burned.	3739
	7: 6	he **w** descent is not counted from them	3588
	11:10	**w** builder and maker *is* God.	3739
	12:26	**W** voice then shook the earth: but now	3739
	13: 7	**w** faith follow, considering the end of	3739
	13:11	**w** blood is brought into the sanctuary by	3739
1Pe	2:24	by **w** stripes ye were healed.	3739
	3: 3	**W** adorning let it not be that outward	3739
	3: 6	**w** daughters ye are, as long as ye do well,	3739
2Pe	2: 3	**w** judgment now of a long time lingereth	3739
Jude	1:12	trees **w** fruit withereth, without fruit,	NIG
Rev	9:11	*which is* the angel of the bottomless *pit,* **w**	846
	13: 8	**w** names are not written in the book of	3739
	13:12	first beast, **w** deadly wound was healed.	3739
	17: 8	**w** names were not written in the book of	3739
	20:11	from **w** face the earth and the heaven fled	3739

WHOSO (54) [SO, WHO]

Ge	9: 6	**W** sheddeth man's blood, by man shall his	NIH
Lev	11:27	**w** toucheth their carcase shall be unclean	3605
	22: 4	**w** toucheth any *thing that is* unclean by	1886.1
Nu	35:30	**W** killeth *any* person, the murderer shall	3605
Dt	19: 4	**W** killeth his neighbour ignorantly, whom	834
2Ch	23:14	**w** followeth her, let him be slain with	1886.1
Ps	50:23	**W** offereth praise glorifieth me: and to him	NIH
	101: 5	**W** privily slandereth his neighbour,	3605
	107:43	**W** *is* wise, and will observe these *things,*	4310
Pr	1:33	**w** hearkeneth unto me shall dwell safely,	NIH
	6:32	*But* **w** committeth adultery with a woman	NIH
	8:35	For **w** findeth me findeth life,	NIH
	9: 4	**W** *is* simple, let him turn in hither: *as for*	4310
	9:16	**W** *is* simple, let him turn in hither:	4310
	12: 1	**W** loveth instruction loveth knowledge:	NIH
	13:13	**w** despiseth the word shall be destroyed:	NIH
	16:20	and **w** trusteth in the LORD, happy *is* he.	NIH
	17: 5	**W** mocketh the poor reproacheth his	NIH
	17:13	**W** rewardeth evil for good, evil shall not	NIH
	18:22	**W** findeth a wife findeth a good *thing,* and	NIH
	20: 2	**w** provoketh him to anger sinneth *against*	NIH
	20:20	**W** curseth his father or his mother, his	NIH
	21:13	**W** stoppeth his ears at the cry of the poor,	NIH
	21:23	**W** keepeth his mouth and his tongue	NIH
	25:14	**W** boasteth himself of a false gift *is like*	376
	26:27	**W** diggeth a pit shall fall therein:	NIH
	27:18	**W** keepeth the fig tree shall eat the fruit	NIH
	28: 7	**W** keepeth the law *is* a wise son: but he	NIH
	28:10	**W** causeth the righteous to go astray in an	NIH
	28:13	**w** confesseth and forsaketh *them* shall	NIH
	28:18	**W** walketh uprightly shall be saved:	NIH
	28:24	**W** robbeth his father or his mother,	NIH
	28:26	**w** walketh wisely, he shall be delivered.	NIH
	29: 3	**W** loveth wisdom rejoiceth his father:	376
	29:24	**W** is partner with a thief hateth his own	NIH
	29:25	**w** putteth his trust in the LORD shall be	NIH
Ecc	7:26	**w** pleaseth God shall escape from her;	NIH
	8: 5	**W** keepeth the commandment shall feel no	NIH
	10: 8	**w** breaketh a hedge, a serpent shall bite	NIH
	10: 9	**W** removeth stones shall be hurt	NIH
Da	3: 6	**w** falleth not down and	1768+4479
	3:11	**w** falleth not down and	1768+4479
Zec	14:17	*that* **w** will not come up of *all* the families	834
Mt	18: 5	And **w** shall receive one such little	1437+3739
	18: 6	But **w** shall offend one of these little	302+3739
	19: 9	**w** marrieth her *which is* put away doth	3588
	23:20	**W** therefore shall swear by the altar,	3588
	23:21	And **w** shall swear by the temple,	3588
	24:15	place, (**w** readeth, let him understand:)	3588
Mk	7:10	and, **W** curseth father or mother, let him	3588
Jn	6:54	**W** eateth my flesh, and drinketh my blood	3588
Jas	1:25	But **w** looketh into the perfect law of	3588
1Jn	2: 5	**w** keepeth his word, in him verily	302+3739
	3:17	But **w** hath *this* world's good,	302+3739

WHOSOEVER (183) [EVER, SO, WHO]

Ge	4:15	said unto him, Therefore **w** slayeth Cain,	3605
Ex	12:15	for **w** eateth leavened bread from the first	3605
	12:19	for **w** eateth that which is leavened,	3605
	19:12	**w** toucheth the mount shall be surely put	3605
	22:19	**W** lieth with a beast shall surely be put to	3605
	30:33	**W** compoundeth *any* like it,	376+834
	30:33	or **w** putteth *any* of it upon a stranger,	834
	30:38	**W** shall make like unto that, to smell	376+834
	31:14	for **w** doeth *any* work therein, that soul	3605
	31:15	**w** doeth *any* work in the sabbath day,	3605
	32:24	**W** hath *any* gold, let them break *it* off.	4310
	32:33	**W** hath sinned against me, him will I	834+4310
	35: 2	**w** doeth work therein shall be put to	3605
	35: 5	**w** *is* of a willing heart, let him	3605+2050.2
Lev	7:25	For **w** eateth the fat of the beast, of which	3605
	11:24	**w** toucheth the carcase of these shall be	3605

Lev	11:25	**w** beareth *ought* of the carcase of them	3605
	11:31	**w** doth touch them, when they be dead,	3605
	15: 5	**w** toucheth his bed shall wash his	376+834
	15:10	**w** toucheth any *thing* that was under him	3605
	15:19	**w** toucheth her shall be unclean until	3605
	15:21	**w** toucheth her bed shall wash his clothes	3605
	15:22	**w** toucheth any thing that she sat upon	3605
	15:27	**w** toucheth those *things* shall be unclean,	3605
	17:14	blood thereof: **w** eateth it shall be cut off.	3605
	18:29	For **w** shall commit any of these	834+3605
	19:20	**w** lieth carnally with a woman that *is* a	376
	20: 2	**W** *he be* of the children of Israel, or of	376
	21:17	**W** *he be* of thy seed in their generations	376
	22: 3	**W** *he be* of all your seed	376+834+3605
	22: 5	Or **w** toucheth any creeping thing,	376+834
	22:21	**w** offereth a sacrifice of peace offerings	376
	24:15	**W** curseth his God shall bear his sin.	376+376
Nu	5: 2	an issue, and **w** is defiled by the dead:	3605
	15:14	or **w** *be* among you in your generations,	834
	17:13	**w** cometh any thing near unto	1886.1
	19:13	**W** toucheth the dead *body* of *any* man	3605
	19:16	**w** toucheth one that is slain with a	834+3605
	31:19	**w** hath killed *any* person,	3605
	31:19	**w** hath touched *any* slain, purify *both*	3605
Dt	18:19	**w** will not hearken unto my words	376+834
Jos	1:18	**W** *he be* that doth rebel against thy	376+3605
	2:19	**w** shall go out of the doors of thy	834+3605
	2:19	**w** shall be with thee in the house,	834+3605
	20: 9	**w** killeth *any* person at unawares might	3605
Jdg	7: 3	saying, **W** *is* fearful and afraid, let him	4310
1Sa	11: 7	**W** cometh not forth after Saul and	834+5105.2
2Sa	5: 8	**w** getteth up to the gutter, and smiteth	3605
	14:10	**W** saith *ought* unto thee, bring him to	1886.1
	17: 9	at the first, that **w** heareth *it* will say,	1886.1
1Ki	13:33	**w** would, he consecrated him,	1886.1
2Ki	12:12	be wanting, he shall not live.	834+3605
	21:12	and Judah, that **w** heareth of it,	3605
1Ch	11: 6	**W** smiteth the Jebusites first shall be chief	3605
	26:28	**w** had dedicated *anything, it was* under	3605
2Ch	13: 9	**w** cometh to consecrate himself with a	3605
	15:13	That **w** would not seek the LORD	834+3605
	23: 7	**w** *else* cometh into the house, he shall	1886.1
Ezr	1: 4	**w** remaineth in any place where he	3605
	6:11	a decree, that **w** shall alter this word,	606+3606
	7:26	**w** will not do the law of thy God,	1768+3606
	10: 8	*that* **w** would not come within three	834+3605
Est	4:11	know, that **w,** *whether* man or woman,	3605
Pr	6:29	**w** toucheth her shall not be innocent.	3605
	20: 1	and **w** is deceived thereby is not wise.	3605
	27:16	**W** hideth her, hideth the wind,	NIH
Isa	54:15	**w** shall gather together against thee shall	4310
	59: 8	**w** goeth therein shall not know peace.	3605
Jer	19: 3	the which **w** heareth, his ears shall tingle.	3605
Eze	33: 4	**w** heareth the sound of the trumpet,	1886.1
Da	5: 7	**W** shall read this	606+1768+1768+3606
	6: 7	**w** shall ask a petition of any God	1768+3605
Joel	2:32	*that* **w** shall call on the name of	834+3605
Mt	5:19	**W** therefore shall break one of these	1437+3739
	5:19	but **w** shall do and teach *them,*	302+3739
	5:21	**w** shall kill shall be in danger of	302+3739
	5:22	That **w** is angry with his brother without a	3956
	5:22	and **w** shall say to his brother, Raca,	302+3739
	5:22	but **w** shall say, *Thou* fool, shall be in	302+3739
	5:28	That **w** looketh on a woman to lust after	3956
	5:31	been said, **W** shall put away his wife,	302+3739
	5:32	That **w** shall put away his wife,	302+3739
	5:32	**w** shall marry her that is divorced	1437+3739
	5:39	but **w** shall smite thee on thy right cheek,	3748
	5:41	And **w** shall compel thee to go a mile,	3748
	7:24	Therefore **w** heareth these sayings	3748+3956
	10:14	And **w** shall not receive you,	1437+3739
	10:32	**W** therefore shall confess me before	3748+3956
	10:33	But **w** shall deny me before men,	302+3748
	10:42	And **w** shall give to drink unto one	1437+3739
	11: 6	And blessed is *he,* **w** shall not be	1437+3739
	12:32	And **w** speaketh a word against	302+3739
	12:32	but **w** speaketh against the Holy	302+3739
	12:50	For **w** shall do the will of my Father	302+3748
	13:12	For **w** hath, to him shall be given,	3748
	13:12	but **w** hath not, from him shall be taken	3748
	15: 5	**W** shall say to *his* father or	302+3739
	16:25	For **w** will save his life shall lose it:	302+3739
	16:25	**w** will lose his life for my sake shall	302+3739
	18: 4	**W** therefore shall humble himself as this	3588
	19: 9	unto you, **W** shall put away his wife,	302+3739
	20:26	but **w** will be great among you,	1437+3739
	20:27	And **w** will be chief among you,	1437+3739
	21:44	And **w** shall fall on this stone shall be	3588
	23:12	And **w** shall exalt himself shall be abased;	3748
	23:16	which say, **W** shall swear by	302+3739
	23:16	**w** shall swear by the gold of	302+3739
	23:18	And, **W** shall swear by the altar, it is	1437+3739
	23:18	but **w** sweareth by the gift that is	302+3739
Mk	3:35	For **w** shall do the will of God,	302+3739
	6:11	And **w** shall not receive you, nor hear	302+3745
	8:34	he said unto them, **W** will come after me,	3748
	8:35	For **w** will save his life shall lose it;	302+3739
	8:35	but **w** shall lose his life for my sake	302+3739
	8:38	**W** therefore shall be ashamed of me	302+3739
	9:37	**W** shall receive one of such	1437+3739
	9:37	**w** shall receive me, receiveth not	1437+3739
	9:41	**w** shall give you a cup of water to	302+3739
	9:42	**w** shall offend one of these little	302+3739
	10:11	**W** shall put away his wife,	1437+3739
	10:15	**W** shall not receive the kingdom of	1437+3739

Mk	10:43	but **w** will be great among you,	1437+3739
	10:44	And **w** of you will be the chiefest,	302+3739
	11:23	That **w** shall say unto this mountain,	302+3739
Lk	6:47	**W** cometh to me, and heareth my sayings,	3956
	7:23	And blessed is *he,* **w** shall not be	1437+3739
	8:18	for **w** hath, to him shall be given;	302+3739
	8:18	and **w** hath not, from him shall be	302+3739
	9: 5	And **w** will not receive you, when ye	302+3745
	9:24	For **w** will save his life shall lose it:	302+3739
	9:24	but **w** will lose his life for my sake,	302+3739
	9:26	For **w** shall be ashamed of me and	302+3739
	9:48	**W** shall receive this child in my	1437+3739
	9:48	**w** shall receive me receiveth him	1437+3739
	12: 8	**W** shall confess me before	302+3739+3956
	12:10	And **w** shall speak a word against	3739+3956
	14:11	For **w** exalteth himself shall be abased;	3956
	14:27	And **w** doth not bear his cross,	3748
	14:33	**w** *he be* of you that forsaketh not all that	3956
	16:18	**W** putteth away his wife,	3956
	16:18	**w** marrieth her that is put away from *her*	3956
	17:33	**W** shall seek to save his life shall	1437+3739
	17:33	**w** shall lose *his life* shall preserve it.	1437+3739
	18:17	**W** shall not receive the kingdom of	1437+3739
	20:18	**W** shall fall upon that stone shall be	3956
Jn	3:15	**w** believeth in him should not perish,	3956
	3:16	that **w** believeth in him should not perish,	3956
	4:13	**W** drinketh of this water shall thirst again:	3956
	4:14	**w** drinketh of the water that I shall	302+3739
	5: 4	**w** then first after the troubling of the water	NIG
	8:34	**W** committeth sin is the servant of sin.	3956
	11:26	And **w** liveth and believeth in me shall	3956
	12:46	that **w** believeth on me should not abide	3956
	16: 2	that **w** killeth you will think that he doeth	3956
	19:12	**w** maketh himself a king speaketh against	3956
Ac	2:21	*that* **w** shall call on the name	302+3739+3956
	10:43	that through his name **w** believeth in him	3956
	13:26	and **w** among you feareth God,	3588
Ro	2: 1	O man, **w** thou art that judgest:	3956
	9:33	**w** believeth on him shall be not ashamed.	3956
	10:11	**W** believeth on him shall not be ashamed.	3956
	10:13	**w** shall call upon the name	302+3739+3956
	13: 2	**W** therefore resisteth the power,	3588
1Co	11:27	Wherefore **w** shall eat this bread,	302+3739
Gal	5: 4	you, **w** of you are justified by the law;	3748
	5:10	but **w** shall bear *his* judgment, **w** he be.	302+3748
Jas	2:10	For **w** shall keep the whole law,	3748
	4: 4	**w** therefore will be a friend of	302+3739
1Jn	2:23	**W** denieth the Son, the same hath not	3956
	3: 4	**W** committeth sin transgresseth also	3956
	3: 6	**W** abideth in him sinneth not:	3956
	3: 6	**w** sinneth hath not seen him, neither	3956
	3: 9	**W** is born of God doth not commit sin;	3956
	3:10	**w** doeth not righteousness is not of God,	3956
	3:15	**W** hateth his brother is a murderer:	3956
	4:15	**W** shall confess that Jesus is the Son	302+3739
	5: 1	**W** believeth that Jesus is the Christ is	3956
	5:18	know that **w** is born of God sinneth not;	3956
2Jn	1: 9	**W** transgresseth,	3956
Rev	14:11	and **w** receiveth the mark of his name.	1536
	20:15	**w** was not found written in the book of	1536
	22:15	and **w** loveth and maketh a lie.	3588
	22:17	And **w** will, let him take the water of life	3588

WHY (282)

Ge	4: 6	the LORD said unto Cain, **W** art	4100+3807.1
	4: 6	**w** is thy countenance fallen?	4100+3807.1
	12:18	**w** didst thou not tell me that she	4100+3807.1
	12:19	**W** saidst thou, She *is* my sister?	4100+3807.1
	25:22	she said, If *it be* so, **w** *am* I thus?	4100+3807.1
	27:45	fetch thee from thence: **w** should	4100+3807.1
	42: 1	Jacob said unto his sons, **W** do ye	4100+3807.1
	47:15	for **w** should we die in thy	4100+3807.1
Ex	1:18	**W** have ye done this thing, and have	4069
	2:20	where *is* he? **w** *is* it *that* ye have	4100+3807.1
	3: 3	this great sight, **w** the bush is not burnt.	4069
	5:22	evil entreated this people? **w** *is* it	4100+3807.1
	14: 5	they said, **W** have we done this, that we	4100
	17: 2	said unto them, **W** chide you with me?	4100
	18:14	**w** sittest thou thyself alone, and all	4069
	32:11	LORD, **w** doth thy wrath wax hot	4100+3807.1
Nu	11:20	**W** came we forth out of Egypt?	4100+3807.1
	20: 4	**w** have ye brought up	4100+3807.1
	27: 4	**W** should the name of our father	4100+3807.1
Dt	5:25	Now therefore **w** should we die?	4100+3807.1
Jos	5: 4	this *is* the cause **w** Joshua did circumcise:	834
	7:25	Joshua said, **W** hast thou troubled us?	4100
	17:14	hast thou given me *but* one lot and	4069
Jdg	2: 2	obeyed my voice: **w** have ye done this?	4100
	5:16	**W** abodest thou among	4100+3807.1
	5:17	**w** did Dan remain *in ships*?	4100+3807.1
	5:28	**W** is his chariot *so* long in coming?	4069
	5:28	**w** tarry the wheels of his chariots?	4069
	6:13	if the LORD be with us, **w** then	4100+3807.1
	8: 1	**W** hast thou served us thus, that *thou*	4100
	9:28	of Shechem: for **w** should we serve him?	4069
	11: 7	**w** are ye come unto me now when ye are	4069
	11:26	**w** therefore did ye not recover *them*	4069
	13:18	of the LORD said unto him, **W**	4100+3807.1
	15:10	the men of Judah said, **W** are ye	4100+3807.1
	21: 3	**w** is this come to pass in Israel,	4100+3807.1
Ru	1:11	**w** will you go with me?	4100+3807.1
	1:21	**w** *then* call ye me Naomi,	4100+3807.1
	2:10	**w** have I found grace in thine eyes,	4069
1Sa	1: 8	to her, Hannah, **w** weepest thou?	4100+3807.1
	1: 8	**w** eatest thou not? and why is	4100+3807.1

1Sa	1: 8	**w** is thy heart grieved? *am* not I	4100+3807.1
	2:23	he said unto them, **W** do ye such	4100+3807.1
	6: 3	be known to you **w** his hand	4100+3807.1
	17: 8	unto them, **W** are ye come out	4100+3807.1
	17:28	**W** camest thou down hither?	4100+3807.1
	19:17	said unto Michal, **W** hast thou	4100+3807.1
	19:17	Let me go; **w** should I kill thee?	4100+3807.1
	20: 2	**w** should my father hide this thing from	4069
	20: 8	for **w** shouldest thou bring me to	4100+3807.1
	21: 1	**W** *art* thou alone, and no man with thee?	4069
	22:13	Saul said unto me, **W** have ye	4100+3807.1
	27: 5	**w** should thy servant dwell in the royal	4100
	28:12	**w** hast thou deceived me?	4100+3807.1
	28:15	Saul, **W** hast thou disquieted me,	4100+3807.1
2Sa	3:24	came unto thee; **w** *is* it *that*	4100+3807.1
	7: 7	**W** build ye not me a house	4100+3807.1
	11:10	**w** *then* didst thou not go down unto	4069
	11:21	he died in Thebez? **w** went ye	4100+3807.1
	13: 4	**W** *art* thou, *being* the king's son, lean	4069
	13:26	king said unto him, **W** should	4100+3807.1
	16: 9	the king, **W** should this dead dog	4100+3807.1
	16:17	**w** wentest thou not with thy	4069
	18:11	**w** didst thou not smite him there to	4069
	19:10	**w** speak ye not a word of	4100+3807.1
	19:11	saying, **W** are ye the last to bring	4100+3807.1
	19:29	king said unto him, **W** speakest	4100+3807.1
	19:36	**w** should the king recompense *it*	4100+3807.1
	19:41	**W** have our brethren the men of Judah	4069
	19:43	**w** then did ye despise us, that our advice	4069
	20:19	a mother in Israel: **w** wilt thou	4100+3807.1
	24: 3	**w** doth my lord the king delight	4069
1Ki	1: 6	any time in saying, **W** hast thou done so?	4069
	1:13	my throne? **w** then doth Adonijah reign?	4069
	2:22	**w** dost thou ask Abishag	4100+3807.1
	2:43	**W** then hast thou not kept the oath of	4069
	9: 8	they shall say, **W** hath the Lord	4100+5921
	14: 6	thou wife of Jeroboam; **w**	2088+4100+3807.1
2Ki	5: 5	unto them, **W** are ye now turned back?	4100
	7: 3	to another, **W** sit we here until we die?	4100
	8:12	Hazael said, **w** weepeth my lord? And he	4069
	12: 7	**W** repair ye not the breaches of the house?	4069
	14:10	**w** shouldest thou meddle to thy	4100+3807.1
1Ch	17: 6	saying, **W** have ye not built me a	4100+3807.1
	21: 3	**w** *then* doth my lord require this	4100+3807.1
	21: 3	**w** will he be a cause of trespass	4100+3807.1
2Ch	7:21	that he shall say, **W** hath	4100+871.1
	24: 6	**W** hast thou not required of the Levites to	4100
	24:20	Thus saith God, **W** transgress ye	4100+3807.1
	25:15	said unto him, **W** hast thou	4100+3807.1
	25:16	forbear; **w** shouldest thou be	4100+3807.1
	25:19	abide now at home; **w** shouldest	4100+3807.1
	32: 4	saying, **W** should the kings of	4100+3807.1
Ezr	4:22	that ye fail not to do this: **w**	4101+3807.2
	7:23	**w** should there be wrath against	4101+3807.2
Ne	2: 2	**W** *is* thy countenance sad, seeing thou *art*	4069
	2: 3	**w** should not my countenance be sad,	4069
	6: 3	I cannot come down: **w** should	4100+3807.1
	13:11	and said, **W** is the house of God forsaken?	4069
	13:21	unto them, **W** lodge ye about the wall?	4069
Est	3: 3	**W** transgressest thou the king's	4069
	4: 5	to know what it *was*, and **w** it *was*.	4100
Job	3:11	**W** died I not from the womb?	4100+3807.1
	3:11	**w** did I *not* give up the ghost when I came	NIH
	3:12	**W** did the knees prevent me? or why	4069
	3:12	or **w** the breasts that I should suck?	4100
	3:23	**W** *is* light given to a man whose way is	NIH
	7:20	O thou preserver of men? **w** hast	4100+3807.1
	7:21	**w** dost thou not pardon my transgression,	4100
	9:29	*if* I be wicked, **w** then	2088+4100+3807.1
	15:12	**W** doth thine heart carry thee away?	4100
	19:22	**W** do ye persecute me as God,	4100+3807.1
	19:28	ye should say, **W** persecute we him?	4100
	21: 4	*so*, **w** should not my spirit be troubled?	4069
	24: 1	**w**, seeing times are not hidden from	4069
	27:12	all ye yourselves have seen *it;* **w**	4100+3807.1
	31: 1	**w** then should I think upon a maid?	4100
	33:13	**W** dost thou strive against him? for he	4069
Ps	2: 1	**W** do the heathen rage,	4100+3807.1
	10: 1	**W** standest thou afar off,	4100+3807.1
	10: 1	**w** hidest thou *thyself* in times of trouble?	NIH
	22: 1	God, **w** hast thou forsaken me?	4100+3807.1
	22: 1	**w** *art thou so* far from helping me,	NIH
	42: 5	**W** art thou cast down, O my soul?	4100
	42: 5	**w** art thou disquieted in me? hope thou in	NIH
	42: 9	**W** hast thou forgotten me?	4100+3807.1
	42: 9	**w** go I mourning because of	4100+3807.1
	42:11	**W** art thou cast down, O my soul?	4100
	42:11	**w** art thou disquieted within me? hope	4100
	43: 2	**w** dost thou cast me off?	4100+3807.1
	43: 2	**w** go I mourning because of	4100
	43: 5	**W** art thou cast down, O my soul?	4100
	43: 5	**w** art thou disquieted within me? hope in	4100
	44:23	Awake, **w** sleepest thou, O Lord?	4100+3807.1
	52: 1	**W** boastest thou thyself in mischief,	4100
	68:16	**W** leap ye, ye high hills? *this is*	4100+3807.1
	74: 1	God, **w** hast thou cast *us* off for	4100+3807.1
	74: 1	**w** doth thine anger smoke against the	NIH
	74:11	**w** withdrawest thou thy hand,	NIH
	80:12	**W** hast thou *then* broken down	4100
	88:14	Lord, **w** castest thou off my	4100+3807.1
	88:14	soul? **w** hidest thou thy face from me?	NIH
Pr	5:20	**w** wilt thou, my son, be ravish	4100+3807.1
	22:27	**w** should he take away thy bed	4100+3807.1
Ecc	2:15	and **w** was I then more wise?	4100+3807.1

Ecc	7:16	neither make thyself over wise: **w**	4100+3807.1
	7:17	neither be thou foolish: **w**	4100+3807.1
SS	1: 7	for **w** should I be as one that	4100+3807.1
Isa	1: 5	**W** should ye be stricken any more?	4100+5921
	40:27	**W** sayest thou, O Jacob,	4100+3807.1
	63:17	O Lord, **w** hast thou made us to	4100+3807.1
Jer	2:14	*is* he a homeborn *slave?* **w** is he spoiled?	4069
	2:33	**W** trimmest thou thy way to seek love?	4100
	2:36	**W** gaddest thou about *so* much to change	4100
	8: 5	**W** *then* is this people of Jerusalem slidden	4069
	8:14	**W** do we sit still?	4100+5921
	8:19	**W** have they provoked me to anger with	4069
	8:22	**w** then is not the health of the daughter	4069
	14: 8	thereof in time of trouble, **w**	4100+3807.1
	14: 9	**W** shouldest thou be as a man	4100+3807.1
	14:19	**w** hast thou smitten us, and *there is* no	4069
	15:18	**W** is my pain perpetual,	4100+3807.1
	26: 9	**W** hast thou prophesied in the name of	4069
	27:13	**W** will ye die, thou and thy	4100+3807.1
	29:27	**w** hast thou not reproved	4100
	30:15	**W** criest thou for thine affliction?	4100
	36:29	**W** hast thou written therein, saying,	4069
	46:15	**W** are thy valiant *men* swept away?	4069
	49: 1	**w** *then* doth their king inherit Gad,	4069
Eze	18:19	Yet say ye, **W**? doth not the son bear	4069
	18:31	for **w** will ye die, O house of Israel?	4100
	33:11	for **w** will ye die, O house of Israel?	4100
Da	1:10	for **w** should he see your faces	4100+3807.1
	2:15	the king's captain, **W** *is* the decree	4101+5922
Jnh	1:10	said unto him, **W** hast thou done this?	4100
Mic	4: 9	Now **w** dost thou cry out aloud?	4100+3807.1
Hab	1: 3	**W** dost thou shew me iniquity,	4100+3807.1
Hag	1: 9	**W**? saith the Lord of hosts. Because of	4100
Mal	2:10	**w** do we deal treacherously every man	4069
Mt	6:28	And **w** take ye thought for raiment?	5101
	7: 3	And **w** beholdest thou the mote that is in	5101
	8:26	**W** are ye fearful, O ye of little faith?	5101
	9:11	**W** eateth your Master with publicans and	1302
	9:14	**W** do we and the Pharisees fast oft,	1302
	13:10	**W** speakest thou unto them in parables?	1302
	15: 2	**W** do thy disciples transgress the tradition	1302
	15: 3	**W** do you also transgress	1302
	16: 8	**w** reason ye among yourselves, because	5101
	17:10	**W** then say the scribes that Elias must first	5101
	17:19	and said, **W** could not we cast him out?	1302
	19: 7	**W** did Moses then command to give a	5101
	19:17	said unto him, **W** callest thou me good?	5101
	20: 6	**W** stand ye here all the day idle?	5101
	21:25	unto us, **W** did ye not then believe him?	1302
	22:18	and said, **W** tempt ye me, *ye* hypocrites?	5101
	26:10	said unto them, **W** trouble ye the woman?	5101
	27:23	And the governor said, **W**, what evil hath	1063
	27:46	my God, **w** hast thou forsaken me?	2444
Mk	2: 7	**W** doth this *man* thus speak blasphemies?	5101
	2: 8	**W** reason ye these *things* in your hearts?	5101
	2:18	**W** do the disciples of John and of	1302
	2:24	**w** do they on the sabbath day *that* which	1302
	4:40	he said unto them, **W** are ye so fearful?	5101
	5:35	**w** troublest thou the Master any further?	5101
	5:39	them, **W** make ye this ado, and weep?	5101
	7: 5	**W** walk not thy disciples according to	1302
	8:12	**W** doth this generation seek after a sign?	5101
	8:17	**W** reason ye, because ye have no bread?	5101
	9:11	**W** say the scribes that Elias must first	NIG
	9:28	**W** could not we cast him out?	3754
	10:18	said unto him, **W** callest thou me good?	5101
	11: 3	if *any* man say unto you, **W** do ye this?	5101
	11:31	will say, **W** then did ye not believe him?	1302
	12:15	said unto them, **W** tempt ye me?	5101
	14: 4	**W** was this waste of the ointment	1519+5101
	14: 6	Let her alone; **w** trouble you her?	5101
	15:14	unto them, **W**, what evil hath he done?	1063
	15:34	my God, **w** hast thou forsaken me?	1519+5101
Lk	2:48	Son, **w** hast thou thus dealt with us?	5101
	5:30	**W** do ye eat and drink with publicans and	1302
	5:33	**W** do the disciples of John fast often,	1302
	6: 2	**W** do ye *that* which is not lawful to do on	5101
	6:41	And **w** beholdest thou the mote that is in	5101
	6:46	And **w** call ye me, Lord, Lord, and do not	5101
	12:26	*is* least, **w** take ye thought for the rest?	5101
	12:57	**w** even of yourselves judge ye not what *is*	5101
	13: 7	cut it down; **w** cumbereth it the ground?	2444
	18:19	said unto him, **W** callest thou me good?	5101
	19:31	**W** do ye loose *him?* thus shall ye say unto	1302
	19:33	said unto them, **W** loose ye the colt?	5101
	20: 5	he will say, **W** then believed ye him not?	1302
	20:23	and said unto them, **W** tempt ye me?	5101
	22:46	And said unto them, **W** sleep ye? rise and	5101
	23:22	third time, **W**, what evil hath he done?	1063
	24: 5	**W** seek ye the living among the dead?	5101
	24:38	he said unto them, **W** are ye troubled?	5101
	24:38	and **w** do thoughts arise in your hearts?	1302
Jn	1:25	and said unto him, **W** baptizest thou then,	5101
	4:27	or, **W** talkest thou with her?	5101
	7:19	the law? **W** go ye about to kill me?	5101
	7:45	unto them, **W** have ye not brought him?	1302
	8:43	**W** do ye not understand my speech? *even*	1302
	8:46	if I say the truth, **w** do ye not believe me?	1302
	9:30	**W** herein is a marvellous *thing*, that ye	1063
	10:20	hath a devil, and is mad; **w** hear ye him?	1302
	12: 5	**W** was not this ointment sold for three	1302
	13:37	Lord, **w** cannot I follow thee now?	1302
	18:21	**W** askest thou me? ask them which heard	5101
	18:23	the evil: but if well, **w** smitest thou me?	5101
	20:13	say unto her, Woman, **w** weepest thou?	5101

Jn	20:15	saith unto her, Woman, **w** weepest thou?	5101
Ac	1:11	**w** stand ye gazing up into heaven?	5101
	3:12	Ye men of Israel, **w** marvel ye at this?	5101
	3:12	or **w** look ye *so* earnestly on us, as though	5101
	4:25	**W** did the heathen rage, and the people	2444
	5: 3	**w** hath Satan filled thine heart to lie to	1302
	5: 4	**w** hast thou conceived this thing in thine	5101
	7:26	**w** do ye wrong one to another?	2444
	9: 4	Saul, Saul, **w** persecutest thou me?	5101
	14:15	**w** do ye these *things?* We also are men of	5101
	15:10	Now therefore **w** tempt ye God, to put a	5101
	22: 7	Saul, Saul, **w** persecutest thou me?	5101
	26: 8	**W** should it be thought *a* thing incredible	5101
	26:14	Saul, Saul, **w** persecutest thou me?	5101
Ro	3: 7	**w** yet am I also judged as a sinner?	5101
	8:24	a man seeth, **w** doth he yet hope for?	5101
	9:19	then unto me, **W** doth he yet find fault?	5101
	9:20	formed *it*, **W** hast thou made me thus?	5101
	14:10	But **w** dost thou judge thy brother?	5101
	14:10	or **w** dost thou set at nought thy brother?	5101
1Co	4: 7	now if thou didst receive *it*, **w** dost thou	5101
	6: 7	**W** do ye not rather take wrong? why do	1302
	6: 7	**w** do ye not rather *suffer yourselves* to be	1302
	10:29	**w** is my liberty judged of another man's	2444
	10:30	**w** am I evil spoken of for *that for* which I	5101
	15:29	**w** are they then baptized for the dead?	5101
	15:30	And **w** stand we in jeopardy every hour?	5101
Gal	2:14	**w** compellest thou the Gentiles to live as	5101
	5:11	do I yet suffer persecution?	5101
Col	2:20	**w**, as though living in the world, are ye	5101

WICK See TOW

WICK TRIMMERS See SNUFFERS

WICKED (344) [WICKEDLY, WICKEDNESS]

Ge	13:13	the men of Sodom *were* **w** and	7451
	18:23	also destroy the righteous with the **w**?	7563
	18:25	to slay the righteous with the **w**:	7563
	18:25	that the righteous should be as the **w**,	7563
	38: 7	was **w** in the sight of the Lord;	7451
Ex	9:27	*is* righteous, and I and my people *are* **w**.	7563
	23: 1	put not thine hand with the **w** to be an	7563
	23: 7	slay thou not: for I will not justify the **w**.	7563
Lev	20:17	it *is* a **w** thing; and they shall be cut off in	2617
Nu	16:26	from the tents of these **w** men,	7563
Dt	15: 9	that there be not a thought in thy **w**	1100
	17: 5	which have committed that **w** thing,	7451
	23: 9	then keep thee from every **w** thing.	7451
	25: 1	justify the righteous, and condemn the **w**.	7563
	25: 2	if the **w** *man be* worthy to be beaten,	7563
1Sa	2: 9	and the **w** shall be silent in darkness;	7563
	24:13	Wickedness proceedeth from the **w**:	7563
	30:22	all the **w** men and *men* of Belial,	7451
2Sa	3:34	as a *man* falleth before **w** men,	5766
	4:11	**w** men have slain a righteous person	7563
1Ki	8:32	judge thy servants, condemning the **w**,	7563
2Ki	17:11	wrought **w** things to provoke the Lord to	7451
2Ch	6:23	judge thy servants, by requiting the **w**,	7563
	7:14	my face, and turn from their **w** ways;	7451
	24: 7	For the sons of Athaliah, *that* **w** woman,	4849
Ne	9:35	neither turned they from their **w** works.	7451
Est	7: 6	adversary and enemy *is* this **w** Haman.	7451
	9:25	commanded by letters *that* his **w** device,	7451
Job	3:17	There the **w** cease *from* troubling;	7563
	8:22	the dwelling place of the **w** shall come to	7563
	9:22	He destroyeth the perfect and the **w**.	7563
	9:24	The earth is given into the hand of the **w**:	7563
	9:29	*If* I be **w**, why then labour I in vain?	7561
	10: 3	and shine upon the counsel of the **w**?	7563
	10: 7	Thou knowest that I am not **w**; and *there*	7561
	10:15	If I be **w**, woe unto me; and *if* I	7561
	11:20	the eyes of the **w** shall fail, and they shall	7563
	15:20	The **w** *man* travaileth with pain all his	7563
	16:11	turned me over into the hands of the **w**.	7563
	18: 5	the light of the **w** shall be put out,	7563
	18:21	Surely such *are* the dwellings of the **w**,	5767
	20: 5	That the triumphing of the **w** *is* short,	7563
	20:22	hand of the **w** shall come *upon* him.	6001
	20:29	This *is* the portion of a **w** man from God,	7563
	21: 7	Wherefore do the **w** live, become old,	7563
	21:16	the counsel of the **w** is far from me.	7563
	21:17	How oft is the candle of the **w** put out!	7563
	21:28	where *are* the dwelling places of the **w**?	7563
	21:30	That the **w** is reserved to the day of	7451
	22:15	thou marked the old way which **w** men	205
	22:18	but the counsel of the **w** is far from me.	7563
	24: 6	and they gather the vintage of the **w**.	7563
	27: 7	Let mine enemy be as the **w**, and he that	7563
	27:13	This *is* the portion of a **w** man with God,	7563
	29:17	I brake the jaws of the **w**, and pluckt	5767
	31: 3	*Is* not destruction to the **w**? and a strange	5767
	34: 8	of iniquity, and walketh with **w** men.	7562
	34:18	*Is it* fit to say to a king, *Thou art* **w**?	1100
	34:26	He striketh them as **w** *men* in the open	7563
	34:36	the end because of *his* answers for **w** men.	205
	36: 6	He preserveth not the life of the **w**:	7563
	36:17	thou hast fulfilled the judgment of the **w**:	7563
	38:13	that the **w** might be shaken out of it?	7563
	38:15	from the **w** their light is withholden,	7563
	40:12	and tread down the **w** in their place.	7563
Ps	7: 9	O let the wickedness of the **w** come to an	7563
	7:11	and God is angry *with the* **w** every day.	NIH
	9: 5	the heathen, thou hast destroyed the **w**,	7563

Ps 9:16 the **w** is snared in the work of his own | 7563
9:17 The **w** shall be turned into hell, *and* all | 7563
10: 2 **w** in *his* pride doth persecute the poor: | 7563
10: 3 For the **w** boasteth of his heart's desire, | 7563
10: 4 The **w**, through the pride of his | 7563
10:13 Wherefore doth the **w** contemn God? | 7563
10:15 Break thou the arm of the **w** and the evil | 7563
11: 2 For lo, the **w** bend *their* bow, they make | 7563
11: 5 **w** and him that loveth violence his soul | 7563
11: 6 Upon the **w** he shall rain snares, fire and | 7563
11: 2 The **w** walk on every side, when the vilest | 7563
12: 8 The **w** walk on every side, when the vilest | 7563
17: 9 From the **w** that oppress me, *from* my | 7563
17:13 deliver my soul from the **w**, *which is* thy | 7563
22:16 the assembly of the **w** have inclosed me: | 7489
26: 5 of evildoers; and will not sit with the **w**. | 7563
27: 2 When the **w**, *even* mine enemies and | 7489
28: 3 Draw me not away with the **w**, and with | 7563
31:17 the **w** be ashamed, *and* let them be silent | 7563
32:10 Many sorrows *shall be* to the **w**: but he | 7563
34:21 Evil shall slay the **w**: and they that hate | 7563
36: 1 The transgression of the **w** saith within | 7563
36:11 and let not the hand of the **w** remove me. | 7563
37: 7 the man who bringeth **w devices** to pass. | 4209
37:10 a little while, and the **w** *shall* not *be:* yea, | 7563
37:12 The **w** plotteth against the just, | 7563
37:14 The **w** have drawn out the sword, | 7563
37:16 hath *is* better than the riches of many **w**. | 7563
37:17 For the arms of the **w** shall be broken: | 7563
37:20 the **w** shall perish, and the enemies of | 7563
37:21 The **w** borroweth, and payeth not again: | 7563
37:28 but the seed of the **w** shall be cut off. | 7563
37:32 The **w** watcheth the righteous, | 7563
37:34 when the **w** are cut off, thou shalt see *it*. | 7563
37:35 I have seen the **w** in great power, | 7563
37:38 the end of the **w** shall be cut off. | 7563
37:40 he shall deliver them from the **w**, | 7563
39: 1 with a bridle, while the **w** *is* before me. | 7563
50:16 the **w** God saith, What hast thou to do | 7563
55: 3 because of the oppression of the **w**: | 7563
58: 3 The **w** are estranged from the womb: | 7563
58:10 shall wash his feet in the blood of the **w**. | 7563
59: 5 be not merciful to any **w** transgressors. | 205
64: 2 Hide me from the secret counsel of the **w**; | 7489
68: 2 let the **w** perish at the presence of God. | 7563
71: 4 O my God, out of the hand of the **w**, | 7563
73: 3 *when* I saw the prosperity of the **w**. | 7563
74:19 **w**: forget not the congregation of thy poor | NIH
75: 4 and to the **w**, Lift not up the horn: | 7563
75: 8 the **w** of the earth shall wring *them* out, | 7563
75:10 All the horns of the **w** also will I cut off; | 7563
82: 2 and accept the persons of the **w**? | 7563
82: 4 needy: rid *them* out of the hand of the **w**. | 7563
91: 8 thou behold and see the reward of the **w**. | 7563
92: 7 When the **w** spring as the grass, | 7563
92:11 mine ears shall hear *my desire* of the **w** | 7489
94: 3 LORD, how long shall the **w**, how long | 7563
94: 3 wicked, how long shall the **w** triumph? | 7563
94:13 until the pit be digged for the **w**. | 7563
97:10 delivereth them out of the hand of the **w**. | 7563
101: 3 I will set no **w** thing before mine eyes: | 1100
101: 4 from me: I will not know a **w** *person*. | 7451
101: 8 I will early destroy all the **w** of the land; | 7563
101: 8 that *I* may cut off all **w** doers from the city | 205
104:35 of the earth, and let the **w** be no more. | 7563
106:18 their company; the flame burnt up the **w**. | 7563
109: 2 For the mouth of the **w** and the mouth of | 7563
109: 6 Set thou a **w** man over him: and let Satan | 7563
112:10 The **w** shall see *it*, and be grieved; | 7563
112:10 away: the desire of the **w** shall perish. | 7563
119:53 because of the **w** that forsake thy law. | 7563
119:61 The bands of the **w** have robbed me: | 7563
119:95 The **w** have waited for me to destroy me: | 7563
119:110 The **w** have laid a snare for me: yet I | 7563
119:119 Thou puttest away all the **w** of the earth | 7563
119:155 Salvation *is* far from the **w**: for they seek | 7563
125: 3 For the rod of the **w** shall not rest upon | 7562
129: 4 he hath cut asunder the cords of the **w**. | 7563
139:19 Surely thou wilt slay the **w**, O God: | 7563
139:24 see if *there be any* **w** way in me, | 6090
140: 4 O LORD, from the hands of the **w**; | 7563
140: 8 Grant not, O LORD, the desires of the **w**: | 7563
140: 8 further not his **w device**; *lest* they exalt | 7563
141: 4 to practise **w** works with men that work | 7562
141:10 Let the **w** fall into their own nets, | 7563
145:20 love him: but all the **w** will he destroy. | 7563
146: 9 way of the **w** he turneth upside down. | 7563
147: 6 he casteth the **w** down to the ground. | 7563

Pr 2:14 *and* delight in the frowardness of the **w**; | 7451
2:22 the **w** shall be cut off from the earth, | 7563
3:25 neither of the desolation of the **w**, when | 7563
3:33 of the LORD *is* in the house of the **w**: | 7563
4:14 Enter not into the path of the **w**, and go | 7563
4:19 The way of the **w** *is* as darkness: they | 7563
5:22 own iniquities shall take the **w** himself, | 7563
6:12 A naughty person, a **w** man, walketh *with* | 205
6:18 A heart that deviseth **w** imaginations, | 205
9: 7 he that rebuketh a **w** *man* getteth himself | 7563
10: 3 he casteth away the substance of the **w**. | 7563
10: 6 violence covereth the mouth of the **w**. | 7563
10: 7 *is* blessed: but the name of the **w** shall rot. | 7563
10:11 violence covereth the mouth of the **w**. | 7563
10:16 *tendeth* to life: the fruit of the **w** to sin. | 7563
10:20 the heart of the **w** *is* little worth. | 7563
10:24 The fear of the **w**, it shall come *upon* him: | 7563
10:25 so *is* the **w** no *more*: but the righteous *is* | 7563

Pr 10:27 but the years of the **w** shall be shortened. | 7563
10:28 but the expectation of the **w** shall perish. | 7563
10:30 but the **w** shall not inhabit the earth. | 7563
10:32 mouth of the **w** *speaketh* frowardness. | 7563
11: 5 the **w** shall fall by his own wickedness. | 7563
11: 7 When a **w** man dieth, *his* expectation | 7563
11: 8 of trouble, and the **w** cometh in his stead. | 7563
11:10 and when the **w** perish, *there is* shouting. | 7563
11:11 it is overthrown by the mouth of the **w**. | 7563
11:18 The **w** worketh a deceitful work: but *to* | 7563
11:21 in hand, the **w** shall not be unpunished: | 7451
11:23 *but* the expectation of the **w** *is* wrath. | 7563
11:31 earth: much more the **w** and the sinner. | 7563
12: 2 a man of **w devices** will he condemn. | 4209
12: 5 *but* the counsels of the **w** *are* deceit. | 7563
12: 6 The words of the **w** *are* to lie in wait *for* | 7563
12: 7 The **w** are overthrown, and *are* not: | 7563
12:10 but the tender mercies of the **w** *are* cruel. | 7563
12:12 The **w** desireth the net of evil *men:* but | 7563
12:13 The **w** is snared by the transgression of | 7451
12:21 but the **w** shall be filled *with* mischief. | 7563
12:26 but the way of the **w** seduceth them. | 7563
13: 5 a **w** *man* is loathsome, and cometh to | 7563
13: 9 but the lamp of the **w** shall be put out. | 7563
13:17 A **w** messenger falleth into mischief: | 7563
13:25 his soul: but the belly of the **w** shall want. | 7563
14:11 The house of the **w** shall be overthrown: | 7563
14:17 and a man of **w devices** is hated. | 4209
14:19 and the **w** at the gates of the righteous. | 7563
14:32 The **w** is driven away in his wickedness: | 7563
15: 6 but in the revenues of the **w** *is* trouble. | 7563
15: 8 The sacrifice of the **w** *is* an abomination | 7563
15: 9 The way of the **w** *is* an abomination unto | 7563
15:26 The thoughts of the **w** *are* an abomination | 7451
15:28 mouth of the **w** poureth out evil *things*. | 7563
15:29 The LORD *is* far from the **w**: | 7563
16: 4 yea, even the **w** for the day of evil. | 7563
17: 4 A **w doer** giveth heed to false lips; | 7489
17:15 He that justifieth the **w**, and he that | 7563
17:23 A **w** *man* taketh a gift out of the bosom to | 7563
18: 3 When the **w** cometh, *then* cometh also | 7563
18: 5 *is* not good to accept the person of the **w**, | 7563
19:28 the mouth of the **w** devoureth iniquity. | 7563
20:26 A wise king scattereth the **w**, | 7563
21: 4 *and* the plowing of the **w**, *is* sin. | 7563
21: 7 The robbery of the **w** shall destroy them; | 7563
21:10 The soul of the **w** desireth evil: | 7563
21:12 wisely considereth the house of the **w**: | 7563
21:12 *God* overthroweth the **w** for *their* | 7563
21:18 The **w** *shall be* a ransom for the righteous, | 7563
21:27 The sacrifice of the **w** *is* abomination: | 7563
21:27 *when* he bringeth it with a **w mind**? | 2154
21:29 A **w** man hardeneth his face: but *as for* | 7563
24:15 O **w** *man*, against the dwelling of | 7563
24:16 again: but the **w** shall fall into mischief. | 7563
24:19 *men*, neither be thou envious at the **w**; | 7563
24:20 *man*; the candle of the **w** shall be put out. | 7563
24:24 He that saith unto the **w**, Thou *art* | 7563
25: 5 Take away the **w** *from* before the king, | 7563
25:26 righteous *man* falling down before the **w** | 7563
26:23 a **w** heart *are* like a potsherd covered | 7451
28: 1 The **w** flee when no man pursueth: | 7563
28: 4 They that forsake the law praise the **w**: | 7563
28:12 but when the **w** rise, a man is hidden. | 7563
28:15 *so is* a **w** ruler over the poor people. | 7563
28:28 When the **w** rise, men hide themselves: | 7563
29: 2 the **w** beareth rule, the people mourn. | 7563
29: 7 *but* the **w** regardeth not to know *it*. | 7563
29:12 hearken to lies, all his servants *are* **w**. | 7563
29:16 When the **w** are multiplied, | 7563
29:27 in the way *is* abomination to the **w**. | 7563

Ecc 3:17 God shall judge the righteous and the **w**: | 7563
7:15 there is a *just* man that prolongeth *his life* | 7561
7:17 Be not over much **w**, neither be thou | 7561
8:10 so I saw the **w** buried, who had come | 7563
8:13 it shall not be well with the **w**, neither | 7563
8:14 according to the work of the **w**; | 7563
8:14 there be **w** men, to whom it happeneth | 7563
9: 2 one event to the righteous, and to the **w**; | 7563

Isa 3:11 Woe unto the **w**! *it shall be* ill *with him*: | 7563
5:23 Which justify the **w** for reward, | 7563
11: 4 the breath of his lips shall he slay the **w**. | 7563
13:11 for *their* evil, and the **w** for their iniquity; | 7563
14: 5 The LORD hath broken the staff of the **w**, | 7563
26:10 Let favour be shewed to the **w**, *yet* will | 7563
32: 7 deviseth **w devices** to destroy the poor | 2154
48:22 *is* no peace, saith the LORD, unto the **w**. | 7563
53: 9 he made his grave with the **w**, and with | 7563
55: 7 Let the **w** forsake his way, | 7563
57:20 the **w** *are* like the troubled sea, when it | 7563
57:21 *is* no peace, saith my God, to the **w**. | 7563

Jer 2:33 thou also taught the **w ones** thy ways. | 7451
5:26 For among my people are found **w** men: | 7563
5:28 yea, they overpass the deeds of the **w**: | 7451
6:29 in vain: for the **w** are not plucked away. | 7451
12: 1 Wherefore doth the way of the **w** prosper? | 7563
15:21 will deliver thee out of the hand of the **w**, | 7451
17: 9 above all *things*, and **desperately w**: | 605
23:19 fall grievously upon the head of the **w**. | 7563
25:31 will give them *that are* **w** to the sword, | 7563
30:23 fall with pain upon the head of the **w**. | 7563

Eze 3:18 When I say unto the **w**, Thou shalt surely | 7563
3:18 speakest to warn the **w** from his wicked | 7563
3:18 speakest to warn the wicked from his **w** | 7563
3:18 the same **w** *man* shall die in his iniquity; | 7563

Eze 3:19 Yet if thou warn the **w**, and he turn not | 7563
3:19 nor from his **w** way, he shall die in his | 7563
7:21 prey, and to the **w** of the earth for a spoil; | 7563
8: 9 behold the **w** abominations that they do | 7451
11: 2 and give **w** counsel in this city: | 7451
13:22 strengthened the hands of the **w**, that *he* | 7451
13:22 that *he* should not return from his **w** way, | 7563
18:20 wickedness of the **w** shall be upon him. | 7563
18:21 if the **w** will turn from all his sins that he | 7563
18:23 Have I any pleasure at all that the **w** | 7563
18:24 the abominations that the **w** *man* doeth, | 7563
18:27 when the **w** *man* turneth away from his | 7563
20:44 not according to your **w** ways, | 7451
21: 3 cut off from thee the righteous and the **w**. | 7563
21: 4 cut off from thee the righteous and the **w**, | 7563
21:25 profane **w** prince of Israel, whose day | 7563
21:29 the necks of *them that are* slain of the **w**, | 7563
30:12 and sell the land into the hand of the **w**: | 7451
33: 8 When I say unto the **w**, O wicked man, | 7563
33: 8 wicked, O **w** *man*, thou shalt surely die; | 7563
33: 8 if thou dost not speak to warn the **w** from | 7563
33: 8 that **w** *man* shall die in his iniquity; | 7563
33: 9 if thou warn the **w** of his way to turn | 7563
33:11 I have no pleasure in the death of the **w**; | 7563
33:11 but that the **w** turn from his way and live: | 7563
33:12 as for the wickedness of the **w**, he shall | 7563
33:14 Again, when I say unto the **w**, Thou shalt | 7563
33:15 *If* the **w** restore the pledge, give again that | 7563
33:19 if the **w** turn from his wickedness, | 7563

Da 12:10 and tried; but the **w** shall do wickedly: | 7563
12:10 none of the **w** shall understand: | 7563

Mic 6:10 of wickedness *in* the house of the **w**, | 7563
6:11 Shall I count *them* pure with the **w** | 7562

Na 1: 3 will not at all acquit the **w**: the LORD hath | NIH
1:11 evil against the LORD, a **w** counsellor. | 1100
1:15 for the **w** shall no more pass through thee; | 1100

Hab 1: 4 the **w** doth compass about the righteous; | 7563
1:13 holdest thy tongue when the **w** devoureth | 7563
3:13 the head out of the house of the **w**, | 7563

Zep 1: 3 and the stumblingblocks with the **w**; | 7563

Mal 3:18 discern between the righteous and the **w**, | 7563
4: 3 ye shall tread down the **w**; for they shall | 7563

Mt 12:45 seven other spirits **more w than** himself, | 4191
12:45 so shall it be also unto this **w** generation. | 4190
13:19 cometh the **w** one, and catcheth away | 4190
13:38 the tares are the children of the **w** one; | 4190
13:49 and sever the **w** from among the just, | 4190
16: 4 A **w** and adulterous generation seeketh | 4190
18:32 unto him, O thou **w** servant, I forgave | 4190
21:41 He will miserably destroy those **w** men, | 2556
25:26 unto him, Thou **w** and slothful servant, | 4190

Lk 11:26 seven other spirits **more w than** himself; | 4191
19:22 mouth will I judge thee, *thou* **w** servant. | 4190

Ac 2:23 and by **w** hands have crucified and slain: | 459
18:14 it were a matter of wrong or **w** lewdness, | 4190

1Co 5:13 from among yourselves that **w** person. | 4190

Eph 6:16 able to quench all the fiery darts of the **w**. | 4190

Col 1:21 and enemies in *your* mind by **w** works, | 4190

2Th 2: 8 And then shall that **W** be revealed, | 459
2: 2 delivered from unreasonable and **w** men: | 4190

2Pe 2: 7 with the filthy conversation of the **w**: | 113
2:17 being led away with the error of the **w**, | 113

1Jn 2:13 because you have overcome the **w** one. | 4190
2:14 in you, and ye have overcome the **w** one. | 4190
3:12 who was of that **w** one, and slew his | 4190
5:18 and that **w** one toucheth him not. | 4190

WICKEDLY (23) [WICKED]

Ge 19: 7 said, I pray you, brethren, **do** not *so* **w**. | 7489
Dt 9:18 in doing **w** in the sight of the LORD, | 7451
Jdg 19:23 brethren, *nay*, I pray you, do not *so* **w**; | 7489
1Sa 12:25 if ye shall **still do w**, ye shall be 7489+7489
2Sa 22:22 and have not **w departed** from my God. | 7561
24:17 Lo, I have sinned, and I have **done w** | 5753
2Ki 21:11 hath **done w** above all that the Amorites | 7489
2Ch 6:37 we have done amiss, and have **dealt w**; | 7561
20:35 Ahaziah king of Israel, who did **very w**: | 7561
22: 3 his mother was his counseller to **do w**. | 7561
Ne 9:33 hast done right, but we have **done w**: | 7561
Job 34: 7 Will you speak for God? | 5766
34:12 surely God will not do **w**, neither will | 7561
Ps 18:21 and have not **w departed** from my God. | 7561
73: 8 speak **w** *concerning* oppression: | 7451+871.1
74: 3 *even* all *that* the enemy hath **done w** in | 7489
106: 6 committed iniquity, we have **done w**. | 7561
139:20 For they speak against thee **w**, | 4209+3807.1
Da 9: 5 and have **done w**, and have rebelled, | 7561
9:15 day; we have sinned, we have **done w**. | 7561
11:32 such as **do w** against the covenant shall | 7561
12:10 and tried; but the wicked shall **do w**: | 7561
Mal 4: 1 all the proud, yea, and all that **do w**, | 7564

WICKEDNESS (127) [WICKED]

Ge 6: 5 GOD saw that the **w** of man *was* great in | 7451
39: 9 how then can I do this great **w**, and sin | 7451
Lev 18:17 *for* they *are* her near kinswomen: it *is* **w**. | 2154
19:29 and the land become full of **w**. | 2154
20:14 man take a wife and her mother, it *is* **w**: | 2154
20:14 and they; that there be no **w** among you. | 2154
Dt 9: 4 for the **w** of these nations the LORD doth | 7564
9: 5 for the **w** of these nations the LORD thy | 7564
9:27 people, nor to their **w**, nor to their sin: | 7562
13:11 shall do no more any such **w** as this is | 7451
17: 2 that hath wrought **w** in the sight of | 7451
28:20 because of the **w** of thy doings, | 7455

Jdg	9:56 Thus God rendered the **w** of Abimelech,	7451
	20: 3 of Israel, Tell *us*, how was this **w**?	7451
	20:12 What **w** *is* this that is done among you?	7451
1Sa	12:17 perceive and see that your **w** *is* great,	7451
	12:20 ye have done all this **w**: yet turn not aside	7451
	24:13 **W** proceedeth from the wicked:	7562
	25:39 for the Lord hath returned the **w** of	7451
2Sa	3:39 the doer of evil according to his **w**.	7451
	7:10 neither shall the children of **w** afflict them	5766
1Ki	1:52 if **w** shall be found in him, he shall die.	7451
	2:44 Thou knowest all the **w** which thine heart	7451
	2:44 the Lord shall return thy **w** upon thine	7451
	8:47 done perversely, we have **committed w**;	7561
	21:25 which did sell himself to work **w** in	7451
2Ki	21: 6 he wrought much **w** in the sight of	7451
1Ch	17: 9 neither shall the children of **w** waste them	5766
Job	4: 8 plow iniquity, and sow **w**, reap the same.	5999
	11:11 he seeth **w** also; will he not then consider	205
	11:14 and let not **w** dwell in thy tabernacles.	5766
	20:12 Though **w** be sweet in his mouth, *though*	7451
	22: 5 *Is* not thy **w** great? and thine iniquities	7451
	24:20 and **w** shall be broken as a tree.	5766
	27: 4 My lips shall not speak **w**, nor my tongue	5766
	34:10 far be it from God, *that he should do* **w**;	7562
	35: 8 Thy **w** *may hurt* a man as thou *art*; and	7562
Ps	5: 4 *art* not a God that hath pleasure in **w**:	7451
	5: 9 their inward *part is* very **w**; their throat *is*	1942
	7: 9 let the **w** of the wicked come to an end;	7451
	10:15 the evil *man*: seek out his **w** *till* thou find	7562
	28: 4 according to the **w** of their endeavours;	7455
	45: 7 Thou lovest righteousness, and hatest **w**:	7562
	52: 7 *and* strengthened himself in his **w**.	1942
	55:11 **W** *is* in the midst thereof: deceit and	1942
	55:15 for **w** *is* in their dwellings,	7451
	58: 2 Yea, in heart you work **w**; you weigh	5766
	84:10 my God, than to dwell in the tents of **w**.	7562
	89:22 upon him; nor the son of **w** afflict him.	5766
	94:23 and shall cut them off in their own **w**;	7451
	107:34 for the **w** of them that dwell therein.	7451
Pr	4:17 For they eat the bread of **w**, and drink	7562
	8: 7 and **w** *is* an abomination to my lips.	7562
	10: 2 Treasures of **w** profit nothing:	7562
	11: 5 but the wicked shall fall by his own **w**.	7564
	12: 3 A man shall not be established by **w**:	7562
	13: 6 the way: but **w** overthroweth the sinner.	7564
	14:32 The wicked is driven away in his **w**:	7451
	16:12 *is* an abomination to kings to commit **w**:	7562
	21:12 overthroweth the wicked for *their* **w**.	7451
	26:26 his **w** shall be shewed before the *whole*	7451
	30:20 her mouth, and saith, I have done no **w**.	205
Ecc	3:16 the place of judgment, *that* **w** *was* there;	7562
	7:15 *man* that prolongeth *his life* in his **w**.	7451
	7:25 *of things*, and to know the **w** of folly,	7562
	8: 8 neither shall **w** deliver those that are	7562
Isa	9:18 For **w** burneth as the fire: it shall devour	7564
	47:10 For thou hast trusted in thy **w**: thou hast	7451
	58: 4 debate, and to smite with the fist of **w**:	7562
	58: 6 loose the bands of **w**, to undo the heavy	7562
Jer	1:16 against them touching all their **w**,	7451
	2:19 Thine own **w** shall correct thee,	7451
	3: 2 with thy whoredoms and with thy **w**.	7451
	4:14 Jerusalem, wash thine heart from **w**, that	7451
	4:18 this *is* thy **w**, because *it is* bitter, because	7451
	6: 7 out her waters, so she casteth out her **w**:	7451
	7:12 what I did to it for the **w** of my people	7451
	8: 6 no man repented him of his **w**, saying,	7451
	12: 4 for the **w** of them that dwell therein?	7451
	14:16 for I will pour their **w** upon them.	7451
	14:20 our **w**, *and* the iniquity of our fathers:	7562
	22:22 ashamed and confounded for all thy **w**.	7451
	23:11 yea, in my house have I found their **w**,	7451
	23:14 that none doth return from his **w**:	7451
	33: 5 for all whose **w** I have hid my face from	7451
	44: 3 Because of their **w** which they have	7451
	44: 5 inclined their ear to turn from their **w**,	7451
	44: 9 Have ye forgotten the **w** of your fathers,	7451
	44: 9 the **w** of the kings of Judah,	7451
	44: 9 the **w** of their wives, and your own	7451
	44: 9 your own **w**, and the wickedness of your	7451
	44: 9 wickedness, and the **w** of your wives,	7451
La	1:22 Let all their **w** come before thee;	7451
Eze	3:19 turn not from his **w**, nor from his wicked	7562
	5: 6 she hath changed my judgments into **w**	7564
	7:11 Violence is risen up into a rod of **w**:	7562
	16:23 it came to pass after all thy **w**, (woe,	7451
	16:57 Before thy **w** was discovered, as *at the*	7451
	18:20 the **w** of the wicked shall be upon him.	7564
	18:27 away from his **w** that he hath committed,	7564
	31:11 I have driven him out for his **w**.	7562
	33:12 for the **w** of the wicked, he shall not fall	7564
	33:12 in the day that he turneth from his **w**;	7562
	33:19 if the wicked turn from his **w**, and do	7564
Hos	7: 1 was discovered, and the **w** of Samaria:	7451
	7: 2 their hearts *that* I remember all their **w**:	7451
	7: 3 They make the king glad with their **w**,	7451
	9:15 All their **w** *is* in Gilgal, for there I hated	7451
	9:15 for the **w** of their doings I will drive them	7455
	10:13 Ye have plowed, ye have reaped	7562
	10:15 unto you because of your **great w**;	7451+7465
Joel	3:13 the fats overflow; for their **w** *is* great.	7451
Jnh	1: 2 for their **w** is come up before me.	7451
Mic	6:10 Are there yet the treasures of **w** in	7562
Na	3:19 for upon whom hath not thy **w** passed	7451
Zec	5: 8 he said, This *is* **w**. And he cast it into	7564
Mal	1: 4 they shall call them, The border of **w**,	7564

Mal	3:15 yea, they that work **w** are set up; yea,	7564
Mt	22:18 But Jesus perceived their **w**, and said,	4189
Mk	7:22 Thefts, covetousness, **w**, deceit,	4189
Lk	11:39 your inward part is full of ravening and **w**.	4189
Ac	8:22 Repent therefore of this thy **w**,	2549
	25: 5 accuse this man, if there be any **w** in him.	NIG
Ro	1:29 fornication, **w**, covetousness,	4189
1Co	5: 8 neither with the leaven of malice and **w**;	4189
Eph	6:12 against spiritual **w** in high *places*.	4189
1Jn	5:19 of God, and the whole world lieth in **w**.	4190

WIDE (15) [WIDENESS]

Dt	15: 8 thou shalt **open** thine hand **w**	6605+6605
	15:11 Thou shalt **open** thine hand **w**	6605+6605
1Ch	4:40 the land was **w**, and quiet,	3027+7342
Job	29:23 they **opened** their mouth **w** *as* for the	6473
	30:14 They came *upon me* as a **w** breaking in	7342
Ps	35:21 they **opened** their mouth **w** against me,	7337
	81:10 open thy mouth **w**, and I will fill it.	7337
	104:25 *So is* this great and **w** sea,	3027+7342
Pr	13: 3 he that **openeth w** his lips shall have	6589
	21: 9 with a brawling woman in a **w** house.	2267
	25:24 a brawling woman and in a **w** house.	2267
Isa	57: 4 against whom **make** ye a **w** mouth,	7337
Jer	22:14 I will build me a **w** house and	4060
Na	3:13 the gates of thy land shall be **set w** open	6605
Mt	7:13 for **w** *is* the gate, and broad *is* the way,	4116

WIDENESS (1) [WIDE]

Eze	41:10 the chambers *was* the **w** of twenty	7341

WIDOW (50) [WIDOW'S, WIDOWHOOD, WIDOWS, WIDOWS']

Ge	38:11 Remain **w** *at* thy father's house, till	490
Ex	22:22 shall not afflict any **w**, or fatherless child.	490
Lev	21:14 A **w**, or a divorced *woman*, or profane,	490
	22:13 if the priest's daughter be a **w**, or divorced,	490
Nu	30: 9 every vow of a **w**, and of her that is	490
Dt	10:18 the judgment of the fatherless and **w**,	490
	14:29 the stranger, and the fatherless, and the **w**,	490
	16:11 the stranger, and the fatherless, and the **w**,	490
	16:14 the stranger, and the fatherless, and the **w**,	490
	24:19 stranger, for the fatherless, and for the **w**:	490
	24:20 stranger, for the fatherless, and for the **w**.	490
	24:21 stranger, for the fatherless, and for the **w**.	490
	26:12 the stranger, the fatherless, and the **w**,	490
	26:13 stranger, to the fatherless, and to the **w**,	490
	27:19 of the stranger, fatherless, and **w**.	490
2Sa	14: 5 I *am* indeed a **w** woman, and mine	490
1Ki	11:26 mother's name *was* Zeruah, a **w** woman,	490
	17: 9 I have commanded a **w** woman there to	490
	17:10 **w** woman *was* there gathering of sticks:	490
	17:20 hast thou also brought evil upon the **w**	490
Job	24:21 beareth not: and doeth not good to the **w**.	490
	31:16 or have caused the eyes of the **w** to fail;	490
Ps	94: 6 They slay the **w** and the stranger,	490
	109: 9 children be fatherless, and his wife a **w**.	490
	146: 9 he relieveth the fatherless and **w**:	490
Pr	15:25 but he will establish the border of the **w**.	490
Isa	1:17 judge the fatherless, plead for the **w**.	490
	1:23 neither doth the cause of the **w** come unto	490
	47: 8 I shall not sit *as* a **w**, neither shall I know	490
Jer	7: 6 the **w**, and shed not innocent blood in this	490
	22: 3 to the stranger, the fatherless, nor the **w**,	490
La	1: 1 how is she become as a **w**! she *that was*	490
Eze	22: 7 have they vexed the fatherless and the **w**.	490
	44:22 Neither shall they take for their wives a **w**,	490
	44:22 of Israel, or a **w** that had a priest before.	490
Zec	7:10 oppress not the **w**, nor the fatherless,	490
Mal	3: 5 the **w**, and the fatherless, and that turn	490
Mk	12:42 And there came a certain poor **w**,	5503
	12:43 That this poor **w** hath cast more in,	5503
Lk	2:37 And she *was* a **w** of about fourscore and	5503
	4:26 of Sidon, unto a woman *that was* a **w**.	5503
	7:12 only son of his mother, and she was a **w**:	5503
	18: 3 And there was a **w** in that city;	5503
	18: 5 Yet because this **w** troubleth me, I will	5503
	21: 2 he saw also a certain poor **w** casting in	5503
	21: 3 this poor **w** hath cast in more than *they*	5503
1Ti	5: 4 But if any **w** have children or nephews,	5503
	5: 5 Now she that is a **w** indeed, and desolate,	5503
	5: 9 Let not a **w** be taken into the number	5503
Rev	18: 7 and am no **w**, and shall see no sorrow.	5503

WIDOW'S (5) [WIDOW]

Ge	38:14 she put her **w** garments off from her,	491
Dt	24:17 nor take a **w** raiment to pledge;	490
1Ki	7:14 *was* a **w** son of the tribe of Naphtali,	490+802
Job	24: 3 they take the **w** ox for a pledge.	490
	29:13 and I caused the **w** heart to sing for joy.	490

WIDOWHOOD (4) [WIDOW]

Ge	38:19 her, and put on the garments of her **w**.	491
2Sa	20: 3 up unto the day of their death, living in **w**.	491
Isa	47: 9 in one day, the loss of children, and **w**:	489
	54: 4 shalt not remember the reproach of thy **w**	491

WIDOWS (23) [WIDOW]

Ex	22:24 your wives shall be **w**, and your children	490
Job	22: 9 hast sent **w** away empty, and the arms	490
	27:15 buried in death: and his **w** shall not weep.	490
Ps	68: 5 of the fatherless, and a judge of the **w**,	490
	78:64 sword; and their **w** made no lamentation.	490
Isa	9:17 shall have mercy on their fatherless and **w**:	490
	10: 2 that **w** may be their prey, and *that* they	490

Jer	15: 8 Their **w** are increased to me above the	490
	18:21 be bereaved of their children, and *be* **w**;	490
	49:11 *them* alive; and let thy **w** trust in me.	490
La	5: 3 and fatherless, our mothers *are* as **w**.	490
Eze	22:25 they have made her many **w** in the midst	490
Lk	4:25 many **w** were in Israel in the days of Elias,	5503
Ac	6: 1 their **w** were neglected in the daily	5503
	9:39 and all the **w** stood by him weeping,	5503
	9:41 and when he had called the saints and **w**,	5503
1Co	7: 8 I say therefore to the unmarried and **w**,	5503
1Ti	5: 3 Honour **w** that are widows indeed.	5503
	5: 3 Honour widows that are **w** indeed.	5503
	5:11 But the younger **w** refuse: for when they	5503
	5:16 any man or woman that believeth have **w**,	5503
	5:16 it may relieve them that are **w** indeed.	5503
Jas	1:27 the fatherless and **w** in their affliction,	5503

WIDOWS' (3) [WIDOW]

Mt	23:14 ye devour **w** houses, and for a pretence	5503
Mk	12:40 devour **w** houses, and for a pretence	5503
Lk	20:47 Which devour **w** houses, and for a shew	5503

WIFE (396) [WIFE'S, WIVES, WIVES']

Ge	2:24 his mother, and shall cleave unto his **w**:	802
	2:25 man and his **w**, and were not ashamed.	802
	3: 8 his **w** hid themselves from the presence of	802
	3:17 hast hearkened unto the voice of thy **w**,	802
	3:21 to his **w** did the Lord God make coats of	802
	4: 1 Adam knew Eve his **w**; and she conceived,	802
	4:17 Cain knew his **w**; and she conceived,	802
	4:25 Adam knew his **w** again; and she bare a	802
	6:18 and thy **w**, and thy sons' wives with thee.	802
	7: 7 and his **w**, and his sons' wives with him,	802
	7:13 Noah's **w**, and the three wives of his sons	802
	8:16 thy **w**, and thy sons, and thy sons' wives	802
	8:18 and his **w**, and his sons' wives with him:	802
	11:29 the name of Abram's **w** *was* Sarai;	802
	11:29 name of Nahor's **w**, Milcah, the daughter	802
	11:31 his daughter in law, his son Abram's **w**;	802
	12: 5 Abram took Sarai his **w**, and Lot his	802
	12:11 that he said unto Sarai his **w**, Behold now,	802
	12:12 see thee, that they shall say, This *is* his **w**:	802
	12:17 great plagues because of Sarai Abram's **w**.	802
	12:18 didst thou not tell me that she *was* thy **w**?	802
	12:19 so I might have taken her to me to **w**:	802
	12:19 now therefore behold thy **w**, take *her*, and	802
	12:20 him away, and his **w**, and all that he had.	802
	13: 1 he, and his **w**, and all that he had,	802
	16: 1 Sarai Abram's **w** bare him no *children*:	802
	16: 3 Sarai Abram's **w** took Hagar her maid	802
	16: 3 her to her husband Abram to be his **w**.	802
	17:15 said unto Abraham, *As for* Sarai thy **w**,	802
	17:19 Sarah thy **w** shall bear thee a son indeed;	802
	18: 9 they said unto him, Where *is* Sarah thy **w**?	802
	18:10 of life; and lo, Sarah thy **w** shall have a son.	802
	19:15 Arise, take thy **w**, and thy two daughters,	802
	19:16 upon the hand of his **w**, and upon the hand	802
	19:26 But his **w** looked back from behind him,	802
	20: 2 Abraham said of Sarah his **w**, She *is* my	802
	20: 3 thou hast taken; for she *is* a man's **w**.	1166
	20: 7 Now therefore restore the man *his* **w**;	802
	20:12 of my mother; and she became my **w**.	802
	20:14 and restored him Sarah his **w**.	802
	20:17 and his **w**, and his maidservants;	802
	20:18 because of Sarah Abraham's **w**.	802
	21:21 his mother took him a **w** out of the land of	802
	23:19 Abraham buried Sarah his **w** in the cave of	802
	24: 3 thou shalt not take a **w** unto my son of	802
	24: 4 kindred, and take a **w** unto my son Isaac.	802
	24: 7 thou shalt take a **w** unto my son from	802
	24:15 son of Milcah, the **w** of Nahor,	802
	24:36 Sarah my master's **w** bare a son to my	802
	24:37 Thou shalt not take a **w** to my son of	802
	24:38 to my kindred, and take a **w** unto my son.	802
	24:40 thou shalt take a **w** for my son of my	802
	24:51 go, and let her be thy master's son's **w**,	802
	24:67 and took Rebekah, and she became his **w**;	802
	25: 1 again Abraham took a **w**, and her name	802
	25:10 was Abraham buried, and Sarah his **w**.	802
	25:20 years old when he took Rebekah to **w**,	802
	25:21 Isaac intreated the Lord for his **w**,	802
	25:21 of him, and Rebekah his **w** conceived.	802
	26: 7 the men of the place asked *him* of his **w**;	802
	26: 7 for he feared to say, *She is* my **w**; lest,	802
	26: 8 Isaac *was* sporting with Rebekah his **w**.	802
	26: 9 and said, Behold, of a surety she *is* thy **w**:	802
	26:10 people might lightly have lien with thy **w**,	802
	26:11 or his **w** shall surely be put to death.	802
	26:34 was forty years old when he took to **w**	802
	27:46 if Jacob take a **w** of the daughters of Heth,	802
	28: 1 Thou shalt not take a **w** of the daughters	802
	28: 2 take thee a **w** from thence of the daughters	802
	28: 6 Padan-aram, to take him a **w** from thence;	802
	28: 6 Thou shalt not take a **w** of the daughters	802
	28: 9 the sister of Nebajoth, to be his **w**.	802
	29:21 Give *me* my **w**, for my days are fulfilled,	802
	29:28 gave him Rachel his daughter to **w** *also*.	802
	30: 4 she gave him Bilhah her handmaid to **w**:	802
	30: 9 Zilpah her maid, and gave her Jacob to **w**.	802
	34: 4 saying, Get me this damsel to **w**.	802
	34: 8 daughter: I pray you give her him to **w**.	802
	34:12 say unto me: but give me the damsel to **w**.	802
	36:10 Eliphaz the son of Adah the **w** of Esau,	802
	36:10 Reuel the son of Bashemath the **w** of Esau.	802

Ge	36:12 these *were* the sons of Adah Esau's **w.** 802
	36:13 were the sons of Bashemath Esau's **w.** 802
	36:14 of Anah, daughter of Zibeon, Esau's **w:** 802
	36:17 these *are* the sons of Bashemath Esau's **w.** 802
	36:18 *are* the sons of Aholibamah Esau's **w;** 802
	36:18 the daughter of Anah, Esau's **w.** 802
	38: 6 Judah took a **w** for Er his firstborn, 802
	38: 8 Go in unto thy brother's **w**, and marry her, 802
	38: 9 when he went in unto his brother's **w**, 802
	38:12 the daughter of Shuah Judah's **w** died; 802
	38:14 and she was not given unto him to **w**. 802
	39: 7 that his master's **w** cast her eyes upon 802
	39: 8 and said unto his master's **w**, Behold, 802
	39: 9 me but thee, because thou *art* his **w:** 802
	39:19 his master heard the words of his **w**, 802
	41:45 he gave him to **w** Asenath the daughter of 802
	44:27 Ye know that my **w** bare me two *sons:* 802
	46:19 The sons of Rachel Jacob's **w;** Joseph, 802
	49:31 they buried Abraham and Sarah his **w;** 802
	49:31 they buried Isaac and Rebekah his **w;** 802
Ex	2: 1 of Levi, and took a **w** a daughter of Levi. NIH
	4:20 Moses took his **w** and his sons, and set 802
	6:20 took him Jochebed his father's sister to **w**, 802
	6:23 of Amminadab, sister of Naashon, to **w;** 802
	6:25 him *one* of the daughters of Putiel to **w**, 802
	18: 2 father in law, took Zipporah, Moses' **w**, 802
	18: 5 and his **w** unto Moses into the wilderness, 802
	18: 6 and thy **w**, and her two sons with her. 802
	20:17 thou shalt not covet thy neighbour's **w**, 802
	21: 3 then his **w** shall go out with him. 802
	21: 4 If his master have given him a **w**, 802
	21: 4 **w** and her children shall be her master's, 802
	21: 5 I love my master, my **w**, and my children; 802
	21:10 If he take him another **w**; her food, NIH
	22:16 he shall surely endow her to be his **w**. 802
Lev	18: 8 The nakedness of thy father's **w** shalt thou 802
	18:14 thou shalt not approach to his **w**: 802
	18:15 she *is* thy son's **w**; thou shalt not uncover 802
	18:16 uncover the nakedness of thy brother's **w:** 802
	18:18 Neither shalt thou take a **w** to her sister, 802
	18:20 not lie carnally with thy neighbour's **w**, 802
	20:10 adultery with *another* man's **w**, 802
	20:10 adultery with his neighbour's **w**, 802
	20:11 the man that lieth with his father's **w** hath 802
	20:14 if a man take a **w** and her mother, it *is* 802
	20:20 if a man shall lie with his **uncle's w**, 1733
	20:21 if a man take his brother's **w**, it *is* an 802
	21: 7 They shall not take a **w** *that is* a whore, 802
	21:13 And he shall take a **w** in her virginity. 802
	21:14 shall take a virgin of his own people to **w**. 802
Nu	5:12 If any man's **w** go aside, and commit a 802
	5:14 he be jealous of his **w**, and she be defiled: 802
	5:14 he be jealous of his **w**, and she be not 802
	5:15 shall the man bring his **w** unto the priest, 802
	5:29 when a **w** goeth aside *to another* instead 802
	5:30 he be jealous over his **w**, and shall set 802
	26:59 the name of Amram's **w** *was* Jochebed, 802
	30:16 between a man and his **w**, between the 802
	36: 8 shall be **w** unto one of the family 802+3807.1
Dt	5:21 thou shalt thou desire thy neighbour's **w**, 802
	13: 6 or the **w** of thy bosom, or thy friend, 802
	20: 7 man *is there* that hath betrothed a **w**, 802
	21:11 that thou wouldest have *her* to thy **w;** 802
	21:13 be her husband, and she shall be thy **w**. 802
	22:13 If any man take a **w**, and go in unto her, 802
	22:16 I gave my daughter unto this man to **w**, 802
	22:19 she shall be his **w;** he may not put her 802
	22:24 he hath humbled his neighbour's **w:** 802
	22:29 *shekels* of silver, and she shall be his **w;** 802
	22:30 A man shall not take his father's **w**, 802
	24: 1 When a man hath taken a **w**, 802
	24: 2 she may go and be another man's **w**. NIH
	24: 3 husband die, which took her *to be* his **w;** 802
	24: 4 may not take her again to be his **w**, 802
	24: 5 When a man hath taken a new **w**, he shall 802
	24: 5 shall cheer up his **w** which he hath taken. 802
	25: 5 the **w** of the dead shall not marry without 802
	25: 5 take her to him to **w**, and perform the duty 802
	25: 7 the man like not to take his **brother's w**, 2994
	25: 7 let his **brother's w** go up to the gate unto 2994
	25: 9 shall his **brother's w** come unto him in 2994
	25:11 the **w** of the one draweth near for to 802
	27:20 Cursed *be* he that lieth with his father's **w;** 802
	28:30 Thou shalt betroth a **w**, and another man 802
	28:54 toward the **w** of his bosom, and towards 802
Jos	15:16 him will I give Achsah my daughter to **w**. 802
	15:17 he gave him Achsah his daughter to **w**. 802
Jdg	1:12 him will I give Achsah my daughter to **w**. 802
	1:13 he gave him Achsah his daughter to **w**. 802
	4: 4 a prophetess, the **w** of Lapidoth, 802
	4:17 the tent of Jael the **w** of Heber the Kenite: 802
	4:21 Jael Heber's **w** took a nail of the tent, 802
	5:24 Blessed above women shall Jael the **w** of 802
	11: 2 Gilead's **w** bare him sons; and *his* wife's 802
	13: 2 and his **w** *was* barren, and bare not. 802
	13:11 went after his **w**, and came to the man, 802
	13:19 and Manoah and his **w** looked on. 802
	13:20 Manoah and his **w** looked on *it*, and fell 802
	13:21 no more appear to Manoah and to his **w**. 802
	13:22 Manoah said unto his **w**, We shall surely 802
	13:23 his **w** said unto him, If the LORD were 802
	14: 2 therefore get her for me to **w**. 802
	14: 3 that thou goest to take a **w** of 802
	14:15 that they said unto Samson's **w**, Entice 802
	14:16 Samson's **w** wept before him, and said, 802

Jdg	14:20 Samson's **w** was *given* to his companion, 802
	15: 1 that Samson visited his **w** with a kid; 802
	15: 1 I will go in to my **w** into the chamber. 802
	15: 6 because he had taken his **w**, and given her 802
	21: 1 give his daughter unto Benjamin to **w**. 802
	21:18 Cursed *be* he that giveth a **w** to Benjamin. 802
	21:21 catch you every man his **w** of the 802
	21:22 we reserved not to each man his **w** in 802
Ru	1: 2 of Moab, he, and his **w**, and his two sons. 802
	1: 2 the name of his **w** Naomi, and the name of 802
	4: 5 of Ruth the Moabitess, the **w** of the dead, 802
	4:10 Ruth the Moabitess, the **w** of Mahlon, 802
	4:10 of Mahlon, have I purchased to be my **w**, 802
	4:13 So Boaz took Ruth, and she was his **w**: 802
1Sa	1: 4 he gave to Peninnah his **w**, and to all her 802
	1:19 Elkanah knew Hannah his **w**; 802
	2:20 Eli blessed Elkanah and his **w**, and said, 802
	4:19 Phinehas' **w**, was with child, *near* to be 802
	14:50 the name of Saul's **w** *was* Ahinoam, 802
	18:17 daughter Merab, her will I give thee to **w:** 802
	18:19 as given unto Adriel the Meholathite to **w**. 802
	18:27 Saul gave him Michal his daughter to **w**. 802
	19:11 Michal David's **w** told him, saying, If thou 802
	25: 3 *was* Nabal; and the name of his **w** Abigail: 802
	25:14 told Abigail, Nabal's **w**, saying, Behold, 802
	25:37 his **w** had told him these things, that his 802
	25:39 with Abigail, to take her to him to **w**. 802
	25:40 us unto thee, to take thee to him to **w**. 802
	25:42 messengers of David, and became his **w**. 802
	25:44 David's **w**, to Phalti the son of Laish, 802
	27: 3 and Abigail the Carmelitess, Nabal's **w**. 802
	30: 5 and Abigail the **w** of Nabal the Carmelite. 802
	30:22 save *to* every man his **w** and his children, 802
2Sa	2: 2 and Abigail Nabal's **w** the Carmelite. 802
	3: 3 of Abigail the **w** of Nabal the Carmelite; 802
	3: 5 the sixth, Ithream, by Eglah David's **w**. 802
	3:14 son, saying, Deliver *me* my **w** Michal, 802
	11: 3 of Eliam, the **w** of Uriah the Hittite? 802
	11:11 to eat and to drink, and to lie with my **w?** 802
	11:26 when the **w** of Uriah heard that Uriah her 802
	11:27 and she became his **w**, and bare him a son. 802
	12: 9 hast taken his **w** to be thy wife, 802
	12: 9 hast taken his wife to be thy **w**, and hast 802
	12:10 hast taken the **w** of Uriah the Hittite to be 802
	12:10 the wife of Uriah the Hittite to be thy **w**. 802
	12:15 the LORD strake the child that Uriah's **w** 802
	12:24 And David comforted Bath-sheba his **w**, 802
1Ki	2:17 he give me Abishag the Shunammite to **w**. 802
	2:21 be given to Adonijah thy brother to **w**. 802
	4:11 Taphath the daughter of Solomon to **w:** 802
	4:15 Basmath the daughter of Solomon to **w:** 802
	7: 8 whom he had taken *to* **w**, like unto this NIH
	9:16 a present unto his daughter, Solomon's **w**. 802
	11:19 that he gave him *to* **w** the sister of his own 802
	11:19 gave him *to* wife the sister of his own **w**, 802
	14: 2 Jeroboam said to his **w**, Arise, I pray thee, 802
	14: 2 that thou be not known to be the **w** of 802
	14: 4 Jeroboam's **w** did so, and arose, and went 802
	14: 5 the **w** of Jeroboam cometh to ask a thing of 802
	14: 6 that he said, Come in, thou **w** of Jeroboam; 802
	14:17 Jeroboam's **w** arose, and departed, 802
	16:31 that he took to Jezebel the daughter of 802
	21: 5 Jezebel his **w** came to him, and said unto 802
	21: 7 Jezebel his **w** said unto him, Dost thou 802
	21:25 the LORD, whom Jezebel his **w** stirred up. 802
2Ki	5: 2 maid; and she waited on Naaman's **w**. 802
	8:18 for the daughter of Ahab was his **w:** 802
	14: 9 Give thy daughter to my son to **w:** 802
	22:14 the **w** of Shallum the son of Tikvah, 802
1Ch	2:18 of Hezron begat *children* of Azubah *his* **w**, 802
	2:24 Abiah Hezron's **w** bare him Ashur the 802
	2:26 Jerahmeel had also another **w**, whose 802
	2:29 the name of the **w** of Abishur *was* Abihail, 802
	2:35 his daughter to Jarha his servant to **w;** 802
	3: 3 Abital: the sixth, Ithream by Eglah his **w**. 802
	4:18 his **w** Jehudijah bare Jered the father of 802
	4:19 the sons of *his* **w** Hodiah the sister of 802
	7:15 Machir took to **w** the *sister* of Huppim and 802
	7:16 Maachah the **w** of Machir bare a son, 802
	7:23 when he went in to his **w**, she conceived, 802
	8: 9 he begat of Hodesh his **w**, Jobab, and Zibia, 802
2Ch	8:11 My **w** shall not dwell in the house of David 802
	11:18 of Jerimoth the son of David *to* **w**, 802
	21: 6 for he had the daughter of Ahab to **w:** 802
	22:11 king Jehoram, the **w** of Jehoiada the priest, 802
	25:18 Give thy daughter to my son to **w:** 802
	34:22 the **w** of Shallum the son of Tikvah, 802
Ezr	2:61 took a **w** of the daughters of Barzillai 802
Ne	7:63 daughters of Barzillai the Gileadite *to* **w**, 802
Est	5:10 called for his friends, and Zeresh his **w**. 802
	5:14 said Zeresh his **w** and all his friends unto 802
	6:13 told Zeresh his **w** and all his friends 802
	6:13 his wise *men* and Zeresh his **w** unto him, 802
Job	2: 9 said his **w** unto him, Dost thou still retain 802
	19:17 My breath is strange to my **w**, though I 802
	31:10 *Then* let my **w** grind unto another, 802
Ps	109: 9 children be fatherless, and his **w** a widow. 802
	128: 3 Thy **w** *shall be* as a fruitful vine by the 802
Pr	5:18 and rejoice with the **w** of thy youth. 802
	6:29 So he that goeth in to his neighbour's **w;** 802
	18:22 *Whoso* findeth a **w** findeth a good *thing*, 802
	19:13 the contentions of a **w** *are* a continual 802
	19:14 and a prudent **w** *is* from the LORD. 802
Ecc	9: 9 Live joyfully with the **w** whom thou lovest 802
Isa	54: 1 than the children of the **married w**. 1166

Isa	54: 6 and grieved in spirit, and a **w** of youth, 802
Jer	3: 1 If a man put away his **w**, and she go from 802
	3:20 Surely *as* a **w** treacherously departeth from 802
	5: 8 every one neighed after his neighbour's **w**. 802
	6:11 for even the husband with the **w** shall be 802
	16: 2 Thou shalt not take thee a **w**, neither shalt 802
Eze	16:32 *But as* a **w** that committeth adultery, 802
	18: 6 neither hath defiled his neighbour's **w**, 802
	18:11 and defiled his neighbour's **w**, 802
	18:15 Israel, hath not defiled his neighbour's **w**, 802
	22:11 abomination with his neighbour's **w;** 802
	24:18 at even my **w** died; and I did in the 802
	33:26 and ye defile every one his neighbour's **w:** 802
Hos	1: 2 take unto thee a **w** of whoredoms and 802
	2: 2 for she *is* not my **w**, neither *am* I her 802
	12:12 Israel served for a **w**, and for a wife he kept 802
	12:12 for a wife, and for a **w** he kept *sheep*. 802
Am	7:17 Thy **w** shall be a harlot in the city, 802
Mal	2:14 between thee and the **w** of thy youth, 802
	2:14 companion, and the **w** of thy covenant. 802
	2:14 none deal treacherously against the **w** of 802
Mt	1: 6 of *her that had been* the **w** of Urias; NIG
	1:20 fear not to take unto *thee* Mary thy **w**: 1135
	1:24 had bidden him, and took unto *him* his **w:** 1135
	5:31 said, Whosoever shall put away his **w**, 1135
	5:32 That whosoever shall put away his **w**, 1135
	14: 3 for Herodias' sake, his brother Philip's **w**. 1135
	18:25 his **w**, and children, and all that he had, 1135
	19: 3 Is it lawful for a man to put away his **w** 1135
	19: 5 and mother, and shall cleave to his **w:** 1135
	19: 9 you, Whosoever shall put away his **w**, 1135
	19:10 If the case of the man be so with *his* **w**, 1135
	19:29 or mother, or **w**, or children, or lands, 1135
	22:24 his brother shall marry his **w**, and raise up 1135
	22:25 when he had married a **w**, deceased, and, NIG
	22:25 no issue, left his **w** unto his brother: 1135
	22:28 Therefore in the resurrection whose **w** 1135
	27:19 judgment seat, his **w** sent unto him, 1135
Mk	6:17 for Herodias' sake, his brother Philip's **w**. 1135
	6:18 lawful for thee to have thy brother's **w**. 1135
	10: 2 Is it lawful for a man to put away *his* **w?** 1135
	10: 7 father and mother, and cleave to his **w;** 1135
	10:11 Whosoever shall put away his **w**, 1135
	10:29 or mother, or **w**, or children, or lands, 1135
	12:19 and leave *his* **w** *behind him*, and leave no 1135
	12:19 that his brother should take his **w**, 1135
	12:20 and the first took a **w**, and dying left no 1135
	12:23 shall rise, whose **w** shall she be of them? 1135
	12:23 be of them? for the seven had her to **w**. 1135
Lk	1: 5 and his **w** *was* of the daughters of Aaron, 1135
	1:13 and thy **w** Elisabeth shall bear thee a son, 1135
	1:18 old man, and my **w** well stricken in years. 1135
	1:24 And after those days his **w** Elisabeth 1135
	2: 5 To be taxed with Mary his espoused **w**, 1135
	3:19 him for Herodias his brother Philip's **w**, 1135
	8: 3 And Joanna the **w** of Chuza Herod's 1135
	14:20 I have married a **w**, and therefore I cannot 1135
	14:26 and **w**, and children, and brethren, 1135
	16:18 Whosoever putteth away his **w**, 1135
	17:32 Remember Lot's **w**. 1135
	18:29 or parents, or brethren, or **w**, or children, 1135
	20:28 having a **w**, and he die without children, 1135
	20:28 that his brother should take *his* **w**, 1135
	20:29 and the first took a **w**, and died without 1135
	20:30 And the second took her to **w**, and he died 1135
	20:33 Therefore in the resurrection whose **w** of 1135
	20:33 of them is she? for seven had her to **w**. 1135
Jn	19:25 Mary the **w** of Cleophas, NIG
Ac	5: 1 with Sapphira his **w**, sold a possession, 1135
	5: 2 his **w** also being privy *to it*, and brought 1135
	5: 7 when his **w**, not knowing what was done, 1135
	18: 2 come from Italy, with his **w** Priscilla, 1135
	24:24 When Felix came with his **w** Drusilla, 1135
1Co	5: 1 that one should have *his* father's **w**. 1135
	7: 2 let every man have his own **w**, 1135
	7: 3 Let the husband render unto the **w** due 1135
	7: 3 and likewise also the **w** unto the husband. 1135
	7: 4 The **w** hath not power of her own body, 1135
	7: 4 not power of his own body, but the **w**. 1135
	7:10 Let not the **w** depart from *her* husband: 1135
	7:11 and let not the husband put away *his* **w**. 1135
	7:12 If any brother hath a **w** that believeth not, 1135
	7:14 husband is sanctified by the **w**, 1135
	7:14 the unbelieving **w** is sanctified by 1135
	7:16 For what knowest thou, O **w**, whether 1135
	7:16 O man, whether thou shalt save *thy* **w?** 1135
	7:27 Art thou bound unto a **w?** seek not to be 1135
	7:27 thou loosed from a **w?** seek not a wife. 1135
	7:27 thou loosed from a **w**? seek not a **w**. 1135
	7:33 of the world, how he may please *his* **w**. 1135
	7:34 There is difference *also* between a **w** and 1135
	7:39 The **w** is bound by the law as long as her 1135
	9: 5 a **w**, as well as other apostles, and *as* 1135
Eph	5:23 For the husband is the head of the **w**, 1135
	5:28 He that loveth his **w** loveth himself. 1135
	5:31 and shall be joined unto his **w**, 1135
	5:33 in particular so love his **w** even as himself; 1135
	5:33 the **w** *see* that she reverence *her* husband. 1135
1Ti	3: 2 the husband of one **w**, vigilant, sober, 1135
	3:12 the deacons be the husbands of one **w**, 1135
	5: 9 years old, having been the **w** of one man, 1135
Tit	1: 6 any be blameless, the husband of one **w**, 1135
1Pe	3: 7 giving honour unto the **w**, as unto 1134
Rev	19: 7 come, and his **w** hath made herself ready. 1135
	21: 9 I will shew thee the bride, the Lamb's **w**. 1135

WIFE'S (11) [WIFE]

Ge	3:20 Adam called his **w** name Eve; because	802
	20:11 and they will slay me for my **w** sake.	802
	36:39 his **w** name *was* Mehetabel, the daughter	802
Lev	18:11 The nakedness of thy father's **w** daughter,	802
Jdg	11: 2 *his* **w** sons grew up, and they thrust out	802
1Ch	1:50 his **w** name *was* Mehetabel, the daughter	802
	8:29 of Gibeon; whose **w** name *was* Maachah:	802
	9:35 Jehiel, whose **w** name *was* Maachah:	802
Mt	8:14 he saw his **w** mother laid, and sick of a	3994
Mk	1:30 But Simon's **w** mother lay sick of a fever,	3994
Lk	4:38 And Simon's **w** mother was taken with a	3994

WILD (44) [WILDERNESS]

Ge	16:12 he will be a **w** man; his hand *will be*	6501
Lev	26:22 I will also send **w** beasts among you,	7704
Dt	14: 5 **w** goat, and the pygarg, and the wild ox,	689
	14: 5 pygarg, and the **w** ox, and the chamois.	8377
1Sa	17:46 the air, and to the **w** beasts of the earth;	2416
	24: 2 his men upon the rocks of the **w** goats.	3277
2Sa	2:18 *as* light of foot as a **w** roe. 7704+871.1+1886.1	
2Ki	4:39 found a **w** vine, and gathered thereof	7704
	4:39 gathered thereof **w** gourds his lap full,	7704
	14: 9 there passed by a **w** beast that *was* in	7704
2Ch	25:18 there passed by a **w** beast that *was* in	7704
Job	6: 5 Doth the **w** ass bray when he hath grass?	6501
	11:12 though man be born *like* a **w** ass's colt.	6501
	24: 5 Behold, *as* **w** asses in the desert, go they	6501
	39: 1 knowest thou the time when the **w** goats	3277
	39: 5 Who hath sent out the **w** ass free?	6501
	39: 5 who hath loosed the bands of the **w** ass?	6171
	39:15 or *that* the **w** beast may break them.	7704
Ps	50:11 and the **w** beasts of the field *are* mine.	2123
	80:13 the **w** beast of the field doth devour it.	2123
	104:11 the field: the **w** asses quench their thirst.	6501
	104:18 high hills *are* a refuge for the **w** goats;	3277
Isa	5: 2 grapes, and it brought forth **w** grapes.	891
	5: 4 forth grapes, brought it forth **w** grapes?	891
	13:21 **w** beasts of the desert shall lie there;	6728
	13:22 the **w** beasts of the islands shall cry in	338
	32:14 a joy of **w** asses, a pasture of flocks;	6501
	34:14 The **w** beasts of the desert shall also	6728
	34:14 meet with the **w** beasts of the island,	338
	51:20 of all the streets, as a **w** bull *in* a net:	8377
Jer	2:24 A **w** ass used to the wilderness,	6501
	14: 6 the **w** asses did stand in the high places,	6501
	50:39 Therefore the **w** beasts of the desert	6728
	50:39 the **w** beasts of the islands shall dwell	338
Da	5:21 and his dwelling *was* with the **w** asses:	6167
Hos	8: 9 up *to* Assyria, a **w** ass alone by himself:	6501
	13: 8 like a lion; the **w** beast shall tear them.	7704
Mt	3: 4 and his meat was locusts and **w** honey.	66
Mk	1: 6 loins; and he did eat locusts and **w** honey;	66
	1:13 was with the **w** beasts; and the angels	2342
Ac	10:12 and **w** beasts, and creeping things,	2342
	11: 6 and **w** beasts, and creeping things,	2342
Ro	11:17 thou, being a **w** olive tree, wert graffed in	65
	11:24 out of the **olive tree which is w** by nature,	65

WILD GOATS See SATYRS

WILD OX, OXEN See UNICORN; UNICORNS

WILDERNESS (305) [WILD]

Ge	14: 6 unto El-paran, which *is* by the **w**,	4057
	16: 7 found her by a fountain of water in the **w**,	4057
	21:14 and wandered in the **w** of Beer-sheba.	4057
	21:20 dwelt in the **w**, and became an archer.	4057
	21:21 dwelt in the **w** of Paran: and his mother	4057
	36:24 *that* Anah that found the mules in the **w**,	4057
	37:22 *but* cast him into this pit that *is* in the **w**,	4057
Ex	3:18 three days' journey into the **w**,	4057
	4:27 to Aaron, Go into the **w** to meet Moses.	4057
	5: 1 they may hold a feast unto me in the **w**.	4057
	7:16 go, that they may serve me in the **w**:	4057
	8:27 will go three days' journey into the **w**,	4057
	8:28 sacrifice to the Lord your God in the **w**;	4057
	13:18 *through* the way of the **w** of the Red sea:	4057
	13:20 encamped in Etham, in the edge of the **w**.	4057
	14: 3 in the land, the **w** hath shut them in.	4057
	14:11 hast thou taken us away to die in the **w**?	4057
	14:12 than that we should die in the **w**.	4057
	15:22 and they went out into the **w** of Shur;	4057
	15:22 they went three days in the **w**, and found	4057
	16: 1 children of Israel came unto the **w** of Sin,	4057
	16: 2 against Moses and Aaron in the **w**:	4057
	16: 3 for ye have brought us forth into this **w**,	4057
	16:10 they looked toward the **w**, and, behold,	4057
	16:14 upon the face of the **w** *there lay* a small	4057
	16:32 bread wherewith I have fed you in the **w**,	4057
	17: 1 of Israel journeyed from the **w** of Sin,	4057
	18: 5 and his wife unto Moses into the **w**,	4057
	19: 1 same day came they *into* the **w** of Sinai.	4057
	19: 2 desert of Sinai, and had pitched in the **w**;	4057
Lev	7:38 unto the Lord, in the **w** of Sinai.	4057
	16:10 to let him go for a scapegoat into the **w**.	4057
	16:21 away by the hand of a fit man into the **w**:	4057
	16:22 and he shall let go the goat in the **w**.	4057
Nu	1: 1 the Lord spake unto Moses in the **w** of	4057
	1:19 so he numbered them in the **w** of Sinai.	4057
	3: 4 the **w** of Sinai, and they had no children:	4057
	3:14 the Lord spake unto Moses in the **w** of	4057
	9: 1 the Lord spake unto Moses in the **w** of	4057
	9: 5 the first month at even in the **w** of Sinai:	4057
	10:12 took their journeys out of the **w** of Sinai;	4057

Nu	10:12 and the cloud rested in the **w** of Paran.	4057
	10:31 knowest how we are to encamp in the **w**,	4057
	12:16 and pitched in the **w** of Paran.	4057
	13: 3 the Lord sent them from the **w** of Paran:	4057
	13:21 searched the land from the **w** of Zin unto	4057
	13:26 of Israel, unto the **w** of Paran, to Kadesh;	4057
	14: 2 or would God we had died in this **w**!	4057
	14:16 therefore he hath slain them in the **w**.	4057
	14:22 which I did in Egypt and in the **w**,	4057
	14:25 get you *into* the **w** *by* the way of the Red	4057
	14:29 Your carcases shall fall in this **w**;	4057
	14:32 your carcases, they shall fall in this **w**.	4057
	14:33 your children shall wander in the **w** forty	4057
	14:33 until your carcases be wasted in the **w**.	4057
	14:35 in this **w** they shall be consumed,	4057
	15:32 the children of Israel were in the **w**,	4057
	16:13 with milk and honey, to kill us in the **w**,	4057
	20: 4 the congregation of the Lord into this **w**,	4057
	21: 5 us up out of Egypt to die in the **w**?	4057
	21:11 in the **w** which *is* before Moab, toward	4057
	21:13 which *is* in the **w** that cometh out of	4057
	21:18 And from the **w** *they went* to Mattanah:	4057
	21:23 and went out against Israel into the **w**:	4057
	24: 1 but he set his face toward the **w**.	4057
	26:64 the children of Israel in the **w** of Sinai.	4057
	26:65 of them, They shall surely die in the **w**.	4057
	27: 3 Our father died in the **w**, and he was not	4057
	27:14 of Meribah in Kadesh *in* the **w** of Zin.	4057
	32:13 made them wander in the **w** forty years,	4057
	32:15 he will yet again leave them in the **w**;	4057
	33: 6 in Etham, which *is* in the edge of the **w**.	4057
	33: 8 through the midst of the sea into the **w**,	4057
	33: 8 three days' journey in the **w** of Etham,	4057
	33:11 the ed sea, and encamped in the **w** of Sin.	4057
	33:12 took their journey out of the **w** of Sin,	4057
	33:15 and pitched in the **w** of Sinai.	4057
	33:36 pitched in the **w** of Zin, which *is* Kadesh.	4057
	34: 3 your south quarter shall be from the **w** of	4057
Dt	1: 1 all Israel on *this* side Jordan in the **w**,	4057
	1:19 *through* all that great and terrible **w**,	4057
	1:31 in the **w**, where thou hast seen how that	4057
	1:40 take your journey into the **w** *by* the way	4057
	2: 1 took our journey into the **w** *by* the way	4057
	2: 7 thy walking *through* this great **w**:	4057
	2: 8 and passed by the way of the **w** of Moab.	4057
	2:26 I sent messengers out of the **w** of	4057
	4:43 *Namely*, Bezer in the **w**, in the plain	4057
	8: 2 God led thee these forty years in the **w**,	4057
	8:15 thee through *that* great and terrible **w**,	4057
	8:16 Who fed thee in the **w** with manna,	4057
	9: 7 the Lord thy God to wrath in the **w**:	4057
	9:28 brought them out to slay them in the **w**.	4057
	11: 5 what he did unto you in the **w**, until ye	4057
	11:24 from the **w** and Lebanon, from the river,	4057
	29: 5 I have led you forty years in the **w**:	4057
	32:10 desert land, and in the waste howling **w**;	3452
	32:51 of Meribah-Kadesh, *in* the **w** of Zin;	4057
Jos	1: 4 From the **w** and this Lebanon even unto	4057
	5: 4 men of war, died in the **w** by the way,	4057
	5: 5 all the people *that* were born in the **w** by	4057
	5: 6 of Israel walked forty years in the **w**,	4057
	8:15 them, and fled by the way of the **w**.	4057
	8:20 the people that fled *to* the **w** turned back	4057
	8:24 in the **w** wherein they chased them,	4057
	12: 8 in the **w**, and in the south *country*;	4057
	14:10 *the children* of Israel wandered in the **w**:	4057
	15: 1 the **w** of Zin southward *was* the uttermost	4057
	15:61 In the **w**, Beth-arabah, Middin,	4057
	16: 1 *to* the **w** that goeth up from Jericho	4057
	18:12 the goings out thereof were at the **w** of	4057
	20: 8 assigned Bezer in the **w** upon the plain	4057
	24: 7 and ye dwelt in the **w** a long season.	4057
Jdg	1:16 the children of Judah *into* the **w** of Judah,	4057
	8: 7 tear your flesh with the thorns of the **w**	4057
	8:16 thorns of the **w** and briers, and with them	4057
	11:16 walked through the **w** unto the Red sea,	4057
	11:18 they went along through the **w**,	4057
	11:22 and from the **w** even unto Jordan.	4057
	20:42 the men of Israel unto the way of the **w**;	4057
	20:45 fled toward the **w** unto the rock of	4057
	20:47 and fled to the **w** unto the rock Rimmon,	4057
1Sa	4: 8 Egyptians with all the plagues in the **w**.	4057
	13:18 to the valley of Zeboim toward the **w**.	4057
	17:28 hast thou left those few sheep in the **w**?	4057
	23:14 David abode in the **w** in strong holds,	4057
	23:14 remained in a mountain in the **w** of Ziph.	4057
	23:15 David *was* in the **w** of Ziph in a wood.	4057
	23:24 and his men *were* in the **w** of Maon,	4057
	23:25 *into* a rock, and abode in the **w** of Maon.	4057
	23:25 he pursued after David *in* the **w** of Maon.	4057
	24: 1 Behold, David *is* in the **w** of En-gedi.	4057
	25: 1 and went down to the **w** of Paran.	4057
	25: 4 David heard in the **w** that Nabal did shear	4057
	25:14 David sent messengers out of the **w** to	4057
	25:21 I kept all that this *fellow* hath in the **w**,	4057
	26: 2 and went down to the **w** of Ziph,	4057
	26: 2 with him, to seek David in the **w** of Ziph.	4057
	26: 3 David abode in the **w**, and he saw that	4057
	26: 3 saw that Saul came after him into the **w**.	4057
2Sa	2:24 *lieth* before Giah *by* the way of the **w**	4057
	15:23 passed over, toward the way of the **w**.	4057
	15:28 See, I will tarry in the plain of the **w**,	4057
	16: 2 that such as be faint in the **w** may drink.	4057
	17:16 not *this* night in the plains of the **w**,	4057
	17:29 hungry, and weary, and thirsty, in the **w**.	4057

1Ki	2:34 he was buried in his own house in the **w**.	4057
	9:18 and Tadmor in the **w**, in the land,	4057
	19: 4 himself went a day's journey into the **w**,	4057
	19:15 return on thy way to the **w** of Damascus:	4057
2Ki	3: 8 The way through the **w** of Edom.	4057
1Ch	5: 9 in of the **w** from the river Euphrates:	4057
	6:78 Bezer in the **w** with her suburbs,	4057
	12: 8 into the hold to the **w** men of might,	4057
	21:29 Moses made in the **w**, and the altar	4057
2Ch	1: 3 servant of the Lord had made in the **w**.	4057
	8: 4 built Tadmor in the **w**, and all the store	4057
	20:16 end of the brook, before the **w** of Jeruel.	4057
	20:20 and went forth into the **w** of Tekoa:	4057
	20:24 came toward the watch tower in the **w**,	4057
	24: 9 servant of God laid upon Israel in the **w**.	4057
Ne	9:19 mercies forsookest them not in the **w**,	4057
	9:21 years didst thou sustain them in the **w**,	4057
Job	1:19 there came a great wind from the **w**,	4057
	12:24 causeth them to wander in a **w** *where*	8414
	24: 5 the **w** *yieldeth* food for them *and* for	6160
	30: 3 flying *into* the **w** in former time desolate	6723
	38:26 no man *is; on* the **w**, wherein *there is*	4057
	39: 6 Whose house I have made the **w**,	6160
Ps	29: 8 The voice of the Lord shaketh the **w**:	4057
	29: 8 the Lord shaketh the **w** of Kadesh.	4057
	55: 7 I wander far off, *and* remain in the **w**.	4057
	63: 1 T of David, when he was in the **w** of Judah.	4057
	65:12 They drop *upon* the pastures of the **w**:	4057
	68: 7 when thou didst march through the **w**;	3452
	72: 9 They that dwell in the **w** shall bow	6728
	74:14 *be* meat to the people inhabiting the **w**.	6728
	78:15 He clave the rocks in the **w**, and gave	4057
	78:17 him by provoking the most High in the **w**.	6723
	78:19 said, Can God furnish a table in the **w**?	4057
	78:40 How oft did they provoke him in the **w**,	4057
	78:52 and guided them in the **w** like a flock.	4057
	95: 8 and as *in* the day of temptation in the **w**:	4057
	102: 6 I am like a pelican of the **w**: I am like an	4057
	106: 9 through the depths, as *through* the **w**.	4057
	106:14 lusted exceedingly in the **w**,	4057
	106:26 them, to overthrow them in the **w**:	4057
	107: 4 wandered in the **w** in a solitary way;	4057
	107:33 He turneth rivers into a **w**,	4057
	107:35 He turneth the **w** into a standing water,	4057
	107:40 causeth them to wander in the **w**,	8414
	136:16 him which led his people through the **w**:	4057
Pr	21:19 *It is* better to dwell in the **w**, than	776+4057
SS	3: 6 Who *is* this that cometh out of the **w** like	4057
	8: 5 Who *is* this that cometh up from the **w**,	4057
Isa	14:17 *That* made the world as a **w**,	4057
	16: 1 the ruler of the land from Sela to the **w**,	4057
	16: 8 Jazer, they wandered through the **w**:	4057
	23:13 founded it for them that dwell in the **w**:	6728
	27:10 the habitation forsaken, and left like a **w**:	4057
	32:15 the **w** be a fruitful field, and the fruitful	4057
	32:16 judgment shall dwell in the **w**,	4057
	33: 9 Sharon is like a **w**; and Bashan and	6160
	35: 1 The **w** and the solitary place shall be glad	4057
	35: 6 for in the **w** shall waters break out,	4057
	40: 3 The voice of him that crieth in the **w**,	4057
	41:18 I will make the **w** a pool of water,	4057
	41:19 I will plant in the **w** the cedar, the shittah	4057
	42:11 Let the **w** and the cities thereof lift up	4057
	43:19 I will even make a way in the **w**, *and* rivers	4057
	43:20 because I give waters in the **w**, *and* rivers	4057
	50: 2 I dry up the sea, I make the rivers a **w**:	4057
	51: 3 he will make her **w** like Eden,	4057
	63:13 as a horse in the **w**, *that* they should not	4057
	64:10 Thy holy cities are a **w**, Zion is a	4057
	64:10 Zion is a **w**, Jerusalem a desolation.	4057
Jer	2: 2 when thou wentest after me in the **w**,	4057
	2: 6 led us through the **w**, through a land of	4057
	2:24 A wild ass used to the **w**, *that* snuffeth up	4057
	2:31 Have I been a **w** unto Israel? a land of	4057
	3: 2 sat for them, as the Arabian in the **w**;	4057
	4:11 A dry wind of the high places in the **w**	4057
	4:26 lo, the fruitful place *was* a **w**, and all	4057
	9: 2 O that I had in the **w** a lodging place of	4057
	9:10 for the habitations of the **w** a lamentation,	4057
	9:12 land perisheth *and* is burnt up like a **w**,	4057
	9:26 the utmost corners, that dwell in the **w**,	4057
	12:10 made my pleasant portion a desolate **w**,	4057
	12:12 come upon all high places through the **w**:	4057
	13:24 that passeth away by the wind of the **w**,	4057
	17: 6 shall inhabit the parched places in the **w**,	4057
	22: 6 *yet* surely I will make thee a **w**, *and*	4057
	23:10 the pleasant places of the **w** are dried up,	4057
	31: 2 left of the sword found grace in the **w**;	4057
	48: 6 your lives, and be like the heath in the **w**,	4057
	50:12 hindermost of the nations *shall be* a **w**,	4057
	51:43 are a desolation, a dry land, and a **w**,	6160
La	4: 3 become cruel, like the ostriches in the **w**.	4057
	4:19 they laid wait for us in the **w**.	4057
	5: 9 our lives because of the sword of the **w**.	4057
Eze	6:14 more desolate than the **w** toward Diblath,	4057
	19:13 now she *is* planted in the **w**, in a dry and	4057
	20:10 of Egypt, and brought them into the **w**.	4057
	20:13 of Israel rebelled against me in the **w**:	4057
	20:13 pour out my fury upon them in the **w**,	4057
	20:15 I lifted up my hand unto them in the **w**,	4057
	20:17 did I make an end of them in the **w**.	4057
	20:18 I said unto their children in the **w**, Walk	4057
	20:21 my anger against them in the **w**.	4057
	20:23 up mine hand unto them also in the **w**,	4057
	20:35 I will bring you into the **w** of the people,	4057

Eze	20:36 as I pleaded with your fathers in the **w**,	4057
	23:42 sort *were* brought Sabeans from the **w**,	4057
	29: 5 I will leave thee *thrown* into the **w**, thee	4057
	34:25 they shall dwell safely in the **w**,	4057
Hos	2: 3 her as a **w**, and set her like a dry land,	4057
	2:14 bring her *into* the **w**, and speak	4057
	9:10 I found Israel like grapes in the **w**; I saw	4057
	13: 5 I did know thee in the **w**, in the land of	4057
	13:15 of the LORD *shall* come up from the **w**,	4057
Joel	1:19 fire hath devoured the pastures of the **w**,	4057
	1:20 fire hath devoured the pastures of the **w**,	4057
	2: 3 them, and behind them a desolate **w**;	4057
	2:22 for the pastures of the **w** do spring,	4057
	3:19 and Edom shall be a desolate **w**,	4057
Am	2:10 led you forty years through the **w**,	4057
	5:25 and offerings in the **w** forty years,	4057
	6:14 in of Hemath unto the river of the **w**.	6160
Zep	2:13 Nineveh a desolation, *and* dry like a **w**.	4057
Mal	1: 3 heritage waste for the dragons of the **w**.	4057
Mt	3: 1 the Baptist, preaching in the **w** of Judea,	2048
	3: 3 saying, The voice of one crying in the **w**,	2048
	4: 1 into the **w** to be tempted of the devil.	2048
	11: 7 What went ye out into the **w** to see?	2048
	15:33 should we have so much bread in the **w**,	2047
Mk	1: 3 The voice of one crying in the **w**,	2048
	1: 4 John did baptize in the **w**, and preach	2048
	1:12 the Spirit driveth him into the **w**.	2048
	1:13 And he was there in the **w** forty days,	2048
	8: 4 these *men* with bread here in the **w**?	2047
Lk	3: 2 unto John the son of Zacharias in the **w**.	2048
	3: 4 saying, The voice of one crying in the **w**,	2048
	4: 1 and was led by the Spirit into the **w**,	2048
	5:16 And he withdrew himself into the **w**,	2048
	7:24 What went ye out into the **w** for to see?	2048
	8:29 and was driven of the devil into the **w**.)	2048
	15: 4 not leave the ninety and nine in the **w**,	2048
Jn	1:23 I *am* the voice of one crying in the **w**,	2048
	3:14 as Moses lifted up the serpent in the **w**,	2048
	6:49 Your fathers did eat manna in the **w**,	2048
	11:54 thence unto a country near to the **w**,	2048
Ac	7:30 there appeared to him in the **w** of mount	2048
	7:36 in the Red sea, and in the **w** forty years.	2048
	7:38 that was in the church in the **w** with	2048
	7:42 *by the space of* forty years in the **w**?	2048
	7:44 had the tabernacle of Witness in the **w**,	2048
	13:18 years suffered he their manners in the **w**.	2048
	21:38 leddest out into the **w** four thousand men	2048
1Co	10: 5 for they were overthrown in the **w**.	2048
2Co	11:26 *in* perils in the **w**, *in* perils in the sea,	2047
Heb	3: 8 in the day of temptation in the **w**:	2048
	3:17 had sinned, whose carcases fell in the **w**?	2048
Rev	12: 6 the woman fled into the **w**, where she	2048
	12:14 she might fly into the **w**, into her place,	2048
	17: 3 carried me away in the spirit into the **w**:	2048

WILES (2) [WILILY]

Nu	25:18 For they vex you with their **w**,	5231
Eph	6:11 that ye may be able to stand against the **w**	3180

WILFULLY (1) [WILL]

Heb	10:26 if we sin **w** after that *we* have received	1596

WILILY (1) [WILES]

Jos	9: 4 They did work **w**, and went and	6195+871.1

WILL (3837) [FREEWILL, SELFWILL, SELFWILLED, WILFULLY, WILLETH, WILLING, WILLINGLY, WILT, WOULD]

Ge	2:18 alone; I **w** make him a help meet for him.	NIH
	3:15 I **w** put enmity between thee and	NIH
	3:16 I **w** greatly multiply thy sorrow and	NIH
	6: 7 I **w** destroy man whom I have created	NIH
	6:13 behold, I **w** destroy them with the earth.	NIH
	6:18 with thee **w** I establish my covenant;	NIH
	7: 4 I **w** cause it to rain upon the earth forty	NIH
	7: 4 every living substance that I have made **w**	NIH
	8:21 I **w** not again curse the ground any more	NIH
	8:21 neither **w** I again smite any more every	NIH
	9: 5 surely your blood of your lives **w** I require;	NIH
	9: 5 at the hand of every beast **w** I require it,	NIH
	9: 5 at the hand of every man's brother **w** I	NIH
	9:11 I **w** establish my covenant with you;	NIH
	9:15 I **w** remember my covenant, which *is*	NIH
	9:16 I **w** look upon it, that I may remember	NIH
	11: 6 now nothing **w** be restrained from them,	NIH
	12: 1 unto a land that I **w** shew thee:	NIH
	12: 2 I **w** make of thee a great nation, and I will	NIH
	12: 2 I **w** bless thee, and make thy name great;	NIH
	12: 3 I **w** bless them that bless thee,	NIH
	12: 7 and said, Unto thy seed **w** I give this land:	NIH
	12:12 **w** kill me, but they will save thee alive.	NIH
	12:12 will kill me, but they **w** save thee alive.	NIH
	13: 9 the left hand, then I **w** go to the right;	NIH
	13: 9 *to* the right hand, then I **w** go to the left.	NIH
	13:15 thee **w** I give it, and to thy seed for ever.	NIH
	13:16 I **w** make thy seed as the dust of the earth:	NIH
	13:17 the breadth of it; for I **w** give it unto thee.	NIH
	14:23 That I **w** not *take* from a thread even to a	NIH
	14:23 that I **w** not take any thing that *is* thine,	NIH
	15:14 whom they shall serve, **w** I judge:	NIH
	16:10 I **w** multiply thy seed exceedingly, that it	NIH
	16:12 he **w** be a wild man; his hand *will be*	NIH
	16:12 his hand *w* be against every man,	NIH
	17: 2 I **w** make my covenant between me and	NIH
	17: 2 thee, and **w** multiply thee exceedingly.	NIH

Ge	17: 6 I **w** make thee exceeding fruitful, and I	NIH
	17: 6 I **w** make nations of thee, and kings shall	NIH
	17: 7 I **w** establish my covenant between me	NIH
	17: 8 I **w** give unto thee, and to thy seed after	NIH
	17: 8 and I **w** be their God.	NIH
	17:16 I **w** bless her, and give thee a son also of	NIH
	17:16 I **w** bless her, and she shall be *a mother* of	NIH
	17:19 I **w** establish my covenant with him for an	NIH
	17:20 **w** make him fruitful, and will multiply	NIH
	17:20 and **w** multiply him exceedingly;	NIH
	17:20 beget, and I **w** make him a great nation.	NIH
	17:21 my covenant **w** I establish with Isaac,	NIH
	18: 5 I **w** fetch a morsel of bread, and comfort	NIH
	18:10 I **w** certainly return unto thee according to	NIH
	18:14 At the time appointed I **w** return unto	NIH
	18:19 that he **w** command his children and his	NIH
	18:21 I **w** go down now, and see whether they	NIH
	18:21 is come unto me; and if not, I **w** know.	NIH
	18:26 then I **w** spare all the place for their sakes.	NIH
	18:28 there and five, I **w** not destroy *it*.	NIH
	18:29 And he said, I **w** not do *it* for forty's sake.	NIH
	18:30 let not the Lord be angry, and I **w** speak:	NIH
	18:30 he said, I **w** not do *it*, if I find thirty there.	NIH
	18:31 said, I **w** not destroy *it* for twenty's sake.	NIH
	18:32 angry, and I **w** speak yet but *this* once:	NIH
	18:32 he said, I **w** not destroy *it* for ten's sake.	NIH
	19: 2 but we **w** abide in the street all night.	NIH
	19: 9 to sojourn, and he **w** needs be a judge:	NIH
	19: 9 now we **w** deal worse with thee, than	NIH
	19:13 we **w** destroy this place, because the cry	NIH
	19:14 for the LORD **w** destroy this city.	NIH
	19:21 that I **w** not overthrow *this* city,	NIH
	19:32 father drink wine, and we **w** lie with him,	NIH
	20:11 and they **w** slay me for my wife's sake.	NIH
	21: 6 *so that* all that hear **w** laugh with me.	NIH
	21:13 of the son of the bondwoman **w** I make	NIH
	21:18 hand; for I **w** make him a great nation.	NIH
	21:24 And Abraham said, I **w** swear.	NIH
	22: 2 of the mountains which I **w** tell thee of.	NIH
	22: 5 I and the lad **w** go yonder and worship,	NIH
	22: 8 God **w** provide himself a lamb for a burnt	NIH
	22:17 That in blessing I **w** bless thee,	NIH
	22:17 in multiplying I **w** multiply thy seed as	NIH
	23:13 I **w** give *thee* money for the field; take *it* of	NIH
	23:13 take *it* of me, and I **w** bury my dead there.	NIH
	24: 3 I **w** make thee swear by the LORD,	NIH
	24: 5 Peradventure the woman **w** not be willing	NIH
	24: 7 Unto thy seed **w** I give this land;	NIH
	24: 8 if the woman **w** not be willing to follow	NIH
	24:14 Drink, and I **w** give thy camels drink also:	NIH
	24:19 she said, I **w** draw *water* for thy camels	NIH
	24:33 he said, I **w** not eat, until I have told mine	NIH
	24:39 Peradventure the woman **w** not follow	NIH
	24:40 **w** send his angel with thee, and prosper	NIH
	24:44 and I **w** also draw for thy camels:	NIH
	24:46 Drink, and I **w** give thy camels drink also:	NIH
	24:49 now if ye **w** deal kindly and truly with my	3426
	24:57 We **w** call the damsel, and inquire at her	NIH
	24:58 go with this man? And she said, I **w** go.	NIH
	26: 3 I **w** be with thee, and will bless thee;	NIH
	26: 3 I will be with thee, and **w** bless thee;	NIH
	26: 3 I **w** give all these countries, and I will	NIH
	26: 3 I **w** perform the oath which I sware unto	NIH
	26: 4 I **w** make thy seed to multiply as the stars	NIH
	26: 4 I **w** give unto thy seed all these countries;	NIH
	26:24 **w** bless thee, and multiply thy seed for my	NIH
	27: 9 I **w** make them savoury meat for thy	NIH
	27:12 My father peradventure **w** feel me,	NIH
	27:25 to me, and I **w** eat of my son's venison,	NIH
	27:41 at hand; then **w** I slay my brother Jacob.	NIH
	27:45 sent and, fetch thee from thence:	NIH
	28:13 to thee **w** I give it, and to thy seed;	NIH
	28:15 **w** keep thee in all *places* whither thou	NIH
	28:15 and **w** bring thee again into this land;	NIH
	28:15 for I **w** not leave thee, until I have done	NIH
	28:20 If God **w** be with me, and will keep me in	NIH
	28:20 **w** keep me in this way that I go,	NIH
	28:20 give me bread to eat, and raiment to put	NIH
	28:22 all that thou shalt give me I **w** surely give	NIH
	29:18 I **w** serve thee seven years for Rachel thy	NIH
	29:27 we **w** give thee this also for the service	NIH
	29:32 now therefore my husband **w** love me.	NIH
	29:34 Now *this* time **w** my husband be joined	NIH
	29:35 she said, Now **w** I praise the LORD:	NIH
	30:13 am I, for the daughters **w** call me blessed:	NIH
	30:20 now **w** my husband dwell with me,	NIH
	30:28 Appoint me thy wages, and I **w** give *it*.	NIH
	30:31 for me, I **w** again feed *and* keep thy flock:	NIH
	30:32 I **w** pass through all thy flock to day,	NIH
	31: 3 and to thy kindred; and I **w** be with thee.	NIH
	31:52 that I **w** not pass over this heap to thee,	NIH
	32: 9 thy kindred, and I **w** deal well with thee:	NIH
	32:11 lest he **w** come and smite me,	NIH
	32:12 I **w** surely do thee good, and make thy	NIH
	32:20 I **w** appease him with the present that	NIH
	32:20 before me, and afterward I **w** see his face;	NIH
	32:20 his face; peradventure he **w** accept of me.	NIH
	32:26 he said, I **w** not let thee go, except thou	NIH
	33:12 and let us go, and I **w** go before thee.	NIH
	33:13 them one day, all the flock **w** die.	NIH
	33:14 I **w** lead on softly, according as the cattle	NIH
	34:11 and what ye shall say unto me **w** I give	NIH
	34:12 I **w** give according as ye shall say unto me:	NIH
	34:15 in this **w** we consent unto you: If ye will	NIH
	34:15 If ye **w** be as we *be*, that every male of	NIH

Ge	34:16 **w** we give our daughters unto you,	NIH
	34:16 we **w** take your daughters to us, and we	NIH
	34:16 we **w** dwell with you, and we will	NIH
	34:16 with you, and we **w** become one people.	NIH
	34:17 if ye **w** not hearken unto us, to be	NIH
	34:17 we **w** take our daughter, and we will be	NIH
	34:17 we take our daughter, and we **w** be gone.	NIH
	34:22 Only herein **w** the men consent unto us	NIH
	34:23 unto them, and they **w** dwell with us.	NIH
	35: 3 I **w** make there an altar unto God,	NIH
	35:12 to thee I **w** give it, and to thy seed after	NIH
	35:12 to thy seed after thee **w** I give the land.	NIH
	37:13 come, and I **w** send thee unto them.	NIH
	37:20 and cast him into some pit, and we **w** say,	NIH
	37:20 shall see what **w** become of his dreams.	NIH
	37:35 For I **w** go down into the grave unto my	NIH
	38:17 said, I **w** send *thee* a kid from the flock.	NIH
	41:32 God, and God **w** shortly bring it to pass.	NIH
	41:40 *in* the throne **w** I be greater than thou.	NIH
	42:34 true *men: so* **w** I deliver you your brother,	NIH
	42:36 ye **w** take Benjamin *away*: all these things	NIH
	42:37 my hand, and I **w** bring him to thee again.	NIH
	43: 4 we **w** go down and buy thee food:	NIH
	43: 5 if thou wilt not send *him*, we **w** not go	NIH
	43: 8 the lad with me, and we **w** arise and go;	NIH
	43: 9 I **w** be surety for him; of my hand shalt	NIH
	43: 9 and we also **w** be my lord's bondmen.	NIH
	44:26 brother be with us, then **w** we go down:	NIH
	44:31 that the lad *is* not *with us*, that he **w** die:	NIH
	45:11 there **w** I nourish thee; for yet *there are*	NIH
	45:18 I **w** give you the good of the land of Egypt,	NIH
	45:28 yet alive: I **w** go and see him before I die.	NIH
	46: 3 for I **w** there make of thee a great nation.	NIH
	46: 4 I **w** go down with thee into Egypt; and I	NIH
	46: 4 I **w** also surely bring thee up *again*: and	NIH
	46:31 I **w** go up, and shew Pharaoh, and say	NIH
	47:16 I **w** give you for your cattle, if money fail.	NIH
	47:18 unto him, We **w** not hide *it* from my lord,	NIH
	47:19 and our land **w** be servants unto Pharaoh:	NIH
	47:25 my lord, and we **w** be Pharaoh's servants.	NIH
	47:30 I **w** lie with my fathers, and thou shalt	NIH
	47:30 And he said, I **w** do as thou hast said.	NIH
	48: 4 I **w** make thee fruitful, and multiply thee,	NIH
	48: 4 **w** make of thee a multitude of people;	NIH
	48: 4 **w** give this land to thy seed after thee *for*	NIH
	48: 9 I pray thee, unto me, and I **w** bless them.	NIH
	49: 7 I **w** divide them in Jacob, and scatter them	NIH
	50: 5 and bury my father, and I **w** come again.	NIH
	50:15 Joseph **w** peradventure hate us,	NIH
	50:15 **w** certainly requite us all the evil which	NIH
	50:21 I **w** nourish you and your little ones.	NIH
	50:24 God **w** surely visit you, and bring you out	NIH
	50:25 God **w** surely visit you, and ye shall carry	NIH
Ex	2: 9 it for me, and I **w** give *thee* thy wages.	NIH
	3: 1 now turn aside, and see this great	NIH
	3:10 and I **w** send thee unto Pharaoh,	NIH
	3:12 And he said, Certainly I **w** be with thee;	NIH
	3:17 I **w** bring you up out of the affliction of	NIH
	3:19 I am sure that the king of Egypt **w** not let	NIH
	3:20 I **w** stretch out my hand, and smite Egypt	NIH
	3:20 Egypt with all my wonders which I **w**	NIH
	3:20 thereof: and after that he **w** let you go.	NIH
	3:21 I **w** give this people favour in the sight of	NIH
	4: 1 said, But behold, they **w** not believe me,	NIH
	4: 1 for they **w** say, The LORD hath not	NIH
	4: 8 come to pass, if they **w** not believe thee,	NIH
	4: 8 that they **w** believe the voice of the latter	NIH
	4: 9 if they **w** not believe also these two signs,	NIH
	4:12 therefore go, and I **w** be with thy mouth,	NIH
	4:14 he seeth thee, he **w** be glad in his heart.	NIH
	4:15 I **w** be with thy mouth, and with his	NIH
	4:15 and **w** teach you what ye shall do.	NIH
	4:21 I **w** harden his heart, that he shall not let	NIH
	4:23 I **w** slay thy son, *even* thy firstborn.	NIH
	5: 2 not the LORD, neither **w** I let Israel go.	NIH
	5:10 saith Pharaoh, I **w** not give you straw.	NIH
	6: 1 shalt thou see what I **w** do to Pharaoh:	NIH
	6: 6 I **w** bring you out from under the burdens	NIH
	6: 6 I **w** rid you out of their bondage, and I will	NIH
	6: 6 I **w** redeem you with a stretched out arm,	NIH
	6: 7 I **w** take you to me for a people, and I will	NIH
	6: 7 me for a people, and I **w** be to you a God:	NIH
	6: 8 I **w** bring you in unto the land,	NIH
	6: 8 Jacob; and I **w** give it you *for* an heritage:	NIH
	7: 3 I **w** harden Pharaoh's heart,	NIH
	7:17 I **w** smite with the rod that *is* in mine	NIH
	8: 2 I **w** smite all thy borders with frogs:	NIH
	8: 8 I **w** let the people go, that they may do	NIH
	8:21 I **w** send swarms *of flies* upon thee,	NIH
	8:22 I **w** sever in that day the land of Goshen,	NIH
	8:23 I **w** put a division between my people and	NIH
	8:26 their eyes, and **w** they not stone us?	NIH
	8:27 We **w** go three days' journey into	NIH
	8:28 Pharaoh said, I **w** let you go, that ye may	NIH
	8:29 I intreat thee I **w** that the swarms *of*	NIH
	9:14 For I **w** at this time send all my plagues	NIH
	9:15 now I **w** stretch out my hand, that I may	NIH
	9:18 to morrow about *this* time I **w** cause it to	NIH
	9:28 I **w** let you go, and ye shall stay no longer.	NIH
	9:29 I **w** spread abroad my hands unto	NIH
	9:30 I know that ye **w** not yet fear the LORD	NIH
	10: 4 to morrow **w** I bring the locusts into thy	NIH
	10: 9 We **w** go with our young and with our	NIH
	10: 9 our flocks and with our herds **w** we go;	NIH
	10:10 as I **w** let you go, and your little ones:	NIH

Ex 10:29 well, I **w** see thy face again no more.	NIH
11: 1 Yet I **w** bring one plague *more* upon	NIH
11: 1 afterwards he **w** let you go hence:	NIH
11: 4 About midnight I **w** go out into the midst	NIH
11: 8 after that I **w** go out. And he went out	NIH
12:12 For I **w** pass through the land of Egypt this	NIH
12:12 **w** smite all the firstborn in the land of	NIH
12:12 against all the gods of Egypt I **w** execute	NIH
12:13 I **w** pass over you, and the plague shall not	NIH
12:23 For the LORD **w** pass through to smite	NIH
12:23 the LORD **w** pass over the door,	NIH
12:23 **w** not suffer the destroyer to come in unto	NIH
12:25 to the land which the LORD **w** give you,	NIH
12:48 **w** keep the passover to the LORD, let all	NIH
13:19 of Israel, saying, God **w** surely visit you;	NIH
14: 3 Pharaoh **w** say of the children of Israel,	NIH
14: 4 I **w** harden Pharaoh's heart, that he shall	NIH
14: 4 I **w** be honoured upon Pharaoh, and upon	NIH
14:13 which he **w** shew to you to day:	NIH
14:17 I **w** harden the hearts of the Egyptians,	NIH
14:17 I **w** get me honour upon Pharaoh,	NIH
15: 1 spake, saying, I **w** sing unto the LORD,	NIH
15: 2 God, and I **w** prepare him a habitation;	NIH
15: 2 my father's God, and I **w** exalt him.	NIH
15: 9 enemy said, I **w** pursue, I will overtake,	NIH
15: 9 enemy said, I will pursue, I **w** overtake,	NIH
15: 9 I will overtake, I **w** divide the spoil;	NIH
15: 9 I **w** draw my sword, my hand shall	NIH
15:26 I **w** put none of *these* diseases upon thee,	NIH
16: 4 I **w** rain bread from heaven for you;	NIH
16: 4 whether they **w** walk in my law, or no.	NIH
16:23 bake *that* which you **w** bake *to* day, and	NIH
16:23 bake *to* day, and seethe that ye **w** seethe;	NIH
17: 6 I **w** stand before thee there upon the rock	NIH
17: 9 to morrow I **w** stand on the top of the hill	NIH
17:14 for I **w** utterly put out the remembrance of	NIH
17:16 **w** *have* war with Amalek from generation	NIH
18:19 I **w** give thee counsel, and God shall be	NIH
19: 5 if ye **w** obey my voice indeed, and keep	NIH
19: 8 All that the LORD hath spoken we **w** do.	NIH
19:11 for the third day the LORD **w** come down	NIH
20: 7 for the LORD **w** not hold him guiltless that	NIH
20:19 Speak thou with us, and we **w** hear:	NIH
20:24 in all places where I record my name I **w**	NIH
20:24 I **w** come unto thee, and I **w** bless thee.	NIH
21: 5 and my children; I **w** not go out free:	NIH
21:13 I **w** appoint thee a place whither he shall	NIH
21:22 according as the woman's husband **w** lay	NIH
22:23 at all unto me, I **w** surely hear their cry;	NIH
22:24 wax hot, and I **w** kill you with the sword;	NIH
22:27 when he crieth unto me, that I **w** hear;	NIH
23: 7 thou not: for I **w** not justify the wicked.	NIH
23:21 for he **w** not pardon your transgressions:	NIH
23:22 I **w** be an enemy unto thine enemies,	NIH
23:23 and the Jebusites: and I **w** cut them off.	NIH
23:25 I **w** take sickness away from the midst of	NIH
23:26 thy land: the number of thy days I **w** fulfil.	NIH
23:27 I **w** send my fear before thee,	NIH
23:27 **w** destroy all the people to whom thou	NIH
23:27 I **w** make all thine enemies turn their	NIH
23:28 I **w** send hornets before thee, which shall	NIH
23:29 I **w** not drive them out from before thee	NIH
23:30 little I **w** drive them out from before thee,	NIH
23:31 I **w** set thy bounds from the Red sea even	NIH
23:31 for I **w** deliver the inhabitants of the land	NIH
23:33 gods, it **w** surely be a snare unto thee.	NIH
24: 3 words which the LORD hath said **w** we do.	NIH
24: 7 All that the LORD hath said we **w** do,	NIH
24:12 I **w** give thee tables of stone, and a law,	NIH
25:22 there I **w** meet with thee, and I will	NIH
25:22 I **w** commune with thee from above	NIH
25:22 of all *things* which I **w** give thee in	NIH
29:42 where I **w** meet you, to speak there unto	NIH
29:43 there I **w** meet with the children of Israel,	NIH
29:44 I **w** sanctify the tabernacle of	NIH
29:44 I **w** sanctify also both Aaron and his sons,	NIH
29:45 I **w** dwell amongst the children of Israel,	NIH
29:45 the children of Israel, and **w** be their God.	NIH
30: 6 the Testimony, where I **w** meet with thee.	NIH
30:36 congregation, where I **w** meet with thee:	NIH
32:10 and I **w** make of thee a great nation.	NIH
32:13 I **w** multiply your seed as the stars of	NIH
32:13 all this land that I have spoken of **w** I give	NIH
32:30 now I **w** go up unto the LORD;	NIH
32:33 against me, him **w** I blot out of my book.	NIH
32:34 when I visit, I **w** visit their sin upon them.	NIH
33: 1 to Jacob, saying, Unto thy seed **w** I give it:	NIH
33: 2 I **w** send an angel before thee; and I will	NIH
33: 2 I **w** drive out the Canaanite, the Amorite,	NIH
33: 3 for I **w** not go up in the midst of thee;	NIH
33: 5 I **w** come up into the midst of thee in a	NIH
33:14 shall go *with thee,* and I **w** give thee rest.	NIH
33:17 I **w** do this thing also that thou hast	NIH
33:19 I **w** make all my goodness pass before	NIH
33:19 I **w** proclaim the name of the LORD	NIH
33:19 **w** be gracious to whom I will be gracious,	NIH
33:19 will be gracious to whom I **w** be gracious,	NIH
33:19 **w** shew mercy on whom I will shew	NIH
33:19 shew mercy on whom I **w** shew mercy.	NIH
33:22 that I **w** put thee in a clift of the rock,	NIH
33:22 **w** cover thee with my hand while I pass	NIH
33:23 I **w** take away mine hand, and thou shalt	NIH
34: 1 I **w** write upon *these* tables the words that	NIH
34: 7 *that* **w** by no means clear *the guilty;*	NIH
34:10 before all thy people I **w** do marvels,	NIH

Ex 34:10 it *is* a terrible thing that I **w** do with thee.	NIH
34:24 For I **w** cast out the nations before thee,	NIH
Lev 1: 3 he shall offer it of his own **voluntary w**	7522
2: 1 when any **w** offer a meat offering unto	NIH
9: 4 for to day the LORD **w** appear unto you.	NIH
10: 3 I **w** be sanctified in them that come nigh	NIH
10: 3 and before all the people I **w** be glorified.	NIH
16: 2 I **w** appear in the cloud upon the mercy	NIH
17:10 I **w** even set my face against *that* soul that	NIH
17:10 and **w** cut him off from among his people.	NIH
19: 5 the LORD, ye shall offer it at your own **w**.	7522
20: 3 I **w** set my face against that man,	NIH
20: 3 and **w** cut him off from among his people;	NIH
20: 5 I **w** set my face against that soul,	NIH
20: 5 **w** cut him off, and all that go a whoring	NIH
20: 6 I **w** even set my face against that soul,	NIH
20: 6 and **w** cut him off from among his people.	NIH
20:24 and I **w** give it unto you to possess it,	NIH
22:18 that **w** offer his oblation for all his vows,	NIH
22:18 which they **w** offer unto the LORD for a	NIH
22:19 *Ye shall offer* at your own **w** a male	7522
22:29 ye **w** offer a sacrifice of thanksgiving	NIH
22:29 unto the LORD, offer *it* at your own **w**.	7522
22:32 I **w** be hallowed among the children of	NIH
23:30 the same soul **w** I destroy from among his	NIH
25:21 I **w** command my blessing upon you in	NIH
26: 4 I **w** give you rain in due season,	NIH
26: 6 I **w** give peace in the land, and ye shall lie	NIH
26: 6 I **w** rid evil beasts out of the land,	NIH
26: 9 For I **w** have respect unto you,	NIH
26:11 I **w** set my tabernacle amongst you:	NIH
26:12 **w** walk among you, and will be your God,	NIH
26:12 **w** be your God, and ye shall be my people.	NIH
26:14 if ye **w** not hearken unto me, and will not	NIH
26:14 and **w** not do all these commandments;	NIH
26:15 that *ye* **w** not do all my commandments,	NIH
26:16 I also **w** do this unto you; I will even	NIH
26:16 I **w** even appoint over you terror,	NIH
26:17 I **w** set my face against you, and ye shall	NIH
26:18 ye **w** not yet for *all* this hearken unto me,	NIH
26:18 I **w** punish you seven *times* more for your	NIH
26:19 I **w** break the pride of your power;	NIH
26:19 I **w** make your heaven as iron, and your	NIH
26:21 unto me, and **w** not hearken unto me;	14
26:21 I **w** bring seven *times* moe plagues upon	NIH
26:22 I **w** also send wild beasts among you,	NIH
26:23 if ye **w** not be reformed by me by these	NIH
26:23 *things,* but **w** walk contrary unto me;	NIH
26:24 **w** I also walk contrary unto you,	NIH
26:24 I **w** punish you yet seven *times* for your	NIH
26:25 I **w** bring a sword upon you, that shall	NIH
26:25 I **w** send the pestilence among you;	NIH
26:27 if ye **w** not for *all* this hearken unto me,	NIH
26:28 I **w** walk contrary unto you also in fury;	NIH
26:28 I **w** chastise you seven *times* for your sins.	NIH
26:30 I **w** destroy your high places, and cut	NIH
26:31 I **w** make your cities waste, and bring your	NIH
26:31 I **w** not smell the savour of your sweet	NIH
26:32 I **w** bring the land into desolation:	NIH
26:33 And I **w** scatter you among the heathen,	NIH
26:33 and **w** draw out a sword after you:	NIH
26:36 them that are left *alive* of you I **w** send	NIH
26:42 **w** I remember my covenant with Jacob,	NIH
26:42 also my covenant with Abraham **w** I	NIH
26:42 I remember; and I **w** remember the land.	NIH
26:44 I **w** not cast them away, neither will I	NIH
26:44 neither **w** I abhor them, to destroy them	NIH
26:45 I **w** for their sakes remember the covenant	NIH
27:13 if he **w** at all redeem it, then he shall add	NIH
27:15 if he that sanctified *it* **w** redeem his house,	NIH
27:19 if he that sanctified the field **w** in any wise	NIH
27:20 if he **w** not redeem the field, or if he have	NIH
27:31 if a man **w** at all redeem *ought* of his	NIH
Nu 6:27 the children of Israel; and I **w** bless them.	NIH
9: 8 I **w** hear what the LORD will command	NIH
9: 8 I will hear what the LORD **w** command	NIH
9:14 and **w** keep the passover unto the LORD;	NIH
10:29 of which the LORD said, I **w** give it you:	NIH
10:29 thou with us, and we **w** do thee good:	NIH
10:30 he said unto him, I **w** not go; but I will	NIH
10:30 I **w** depart to mine own land, and to my	NIH
10:32 do unto us, the same **w** we do unto thee.	NIH
11:17 I **w** come down and talk with thee there:	NIH
11:17 I **w** take of the spirit which *is* upon thee,	NIH
11:17 *is* upon thee, and **w** put *it* upon them;	NIH
11:18 therefore the LORD **w** give you flesh,	NIH
11:21 hast said, I **w** give them flesh, that they	NIH
12: 6 *I* the LORD **w** make myself known unto	NIH
12: 6 vision, *and* **w** speak unto him in a dream.	NIH
12: 8 With him **w** I speak mouth to mouth,	NIH
14: 8 he **w** bring us into this land, and give it	NIH
14:11 How long **w** this people provoke me?	NIH
14:11 how long **w** it be ere they believe me, for	NIH
14:12 I **w** smite them with the pestilence,	NIH
14:12 **w** make of thee a greater nation and	NIH
14:14 **w** tell *it* to the inhabitants of this land:	NIH
14:15 have heard the fame of thee **w** speak,	NIH
14:24 him **w** I bring into the land whereinto he	NIH
14:28 spoken in mine ears, so **w** I do to you:	NIH
14:31 them **w** I bring in, and they shall know	NIH
14:35 I **w** surely do it unto all this evil	NIH
14:40 **w** go up unto the place which the LORD	NIH
14:43 therefore the LORD **w** not be with you.	NIH
15: 3 **w** make an offering by fire unto	NIH
15:14 **w** offer an offering made by fire, of a	NIH

Nu 16: 5 Even to morrow the LORD **w** shew who	NIH
16: 5 and cause *him* to come near unto him:	NIH
16: 5 *him* whom he hath chosen **w** he cause	NIH
16:12 of Eliab: which said, We **w** not come up:	NIH
16:14 eyes of these men? we **w** not come up.	NIH
17: 4 the Testimony, where I **w** meet with you.	NIH
17: 5 I **w** make to cease from me the	NIH
20:17 we **w** not pass through the fields,	NIH
20:17 we drink *of* the water of the wells:	NIH
20:17 we **w** go *by* the king's *high* way, we will	NIH
20:17 we **w** not turn *to* the right hand nor *to*	NIH
20:19 said unto him, We **w** go by the high way:	NIH
20:19 drink *of* thy water, then I **w** pay for it:	NIH
20:19 I **w** only, without *doing any* thing else, go	NIH
21: 2 then I **w** utterly destroy their cities.	NIH
21:16 people together, and I **w** give them water.	NIH
21:22 we **w** not turn into the fields, or into	NIH
21:22 we **w** not drink *of* the waters of the well:	NIH
21:22 *but* we **w** go along by the king's *high* way,	NIH
22: 8 *this* night, and I **w** bring you word again,	NIH
22:17 For I **w** promote thee unto very great	NIH
22:17 I **w** do whatsoever thou sayest unto me:	NIH
22:19 that I may know what the LORD **w** say	NIH
22:34 if it displease thee, I **w** get me back again.	NIH
23: 3 Stand by thy burnt offering, and I **w** go:	NIH
23: 3 peradventure the LORD **w** come to meet	NIH
23: 3 whatsoever he sheweth me I **w** tell thee.	NIH
23:27 thee, I **w** bring thee unto another place;	NIH
23:27 peradventure it **w** please God that thou	NIH
24:13 *but* what the LORD saith, that **w** I speak?	NIH
24:14 I **w** advertise thee what this people shall	NIH
32:15 **w** yet again leave them in the wilderness;	NIH
32:16 We **w** build sheepfolds here for our cattle,	NIH
32:17 ourselves **w** go ready armed before	NIH
32:18 We **w** not return unto our houses, until	NIH
32:19 we **w** not inherit with them on *yonder*	NIH
32:20 said unto them, If ye **w** do this thing,	NIH
32:20 if ye **w** go armed before the LORD to war,	NIH
32:21 **w** go all of you armed over Jordan before	NIH
32:23 if ye **w** not do so, behold, ye have sinned	NIH
32:23 and be sure your sin **w** find you out.	NIH
32:25 servants **w** do as my lord commandeth.	NIH
32:27 servants **w** pass over, every man armed	NIH
32:29 the children of Reuben **w** pass with you	NIH
32:30 if they **w** not pass over with you armed,	NIH
32:31 hath said unto thy servants, so **w** we do.	NIH
32:32 We **w** pass over armed before the LORD	NIH
33:55 if ye **w** not drive out the inhabitants of	NIH
Dt 1:13 and I **w** make them rulers over you.	NIH
1:17 for you, bring *it* unto me, and I **w** hear it.	NIH
1:22 We **w** send men before us, and they shall	NIH
1:36 him **w** I give the land that he hath trodden	NIH
1:39 them **w** I give it, and they shall possess	NIH
1:41 against the LORD, we **w** go up and fight,	NIH
2: 5 for I **w** not give you of their land, no, not	NIH
2: 9 for I **w** not give thee of their land *for* a	NIH
2:19 for I **w** not give thee of the land of	NIH
2:25 This day **w** I begin to put the dread of	NIH
2:27 I **w** go along by the high way, I will	NIH
2:27 I **w** neither turn *unto* the right hand nor	NIH
2:28 only I **w** pass through on my feet;	NIH
3: 2 for I **w** deliver him, and all his people,	NIH
4:10 and I **w** make them hear my words,	NIH
4:31 he **w** not forsake thee, neither destroy	NIH
5:11 for the LORD **w** not hold *him* guiltless that	NIH
5:25 this great fire **w** consume us: if we hear	NIH
5:27 unto thee; and we **w** hear *it,* and do *it.*	NIH
5:31 I **w** speak unto thee all the	NIH
7: 4 For they **w** turn away thy son from	NIH
7: 4 **w** the anger of the LORD be kindled	NIH
7:10 he **w** not be slack to him that hateth him,	NIH
7:10 hateth him, he **w** repay him to his face.	NIH
7:13 he **w** love thee, and bless thee,	NIH
7:13 he **w** also bless the fruit of thy womb,	NIH
7:15 the LORD **w** take away from thee all	NIH
7:15 **w** put none of the evil diseases of Egypt,	NIH
7:15 **w** lay them upon all *them* that hate thee.	NIH
7:16 their gods; for that **w** be a snare unto thee.	NIH
7:20 Moreover the LORD thy God **w** send	NIH
7:22 the LORD thy God **w** put out those nations	NIH
9:14 I **w** make of thee a nation mightier and	NIH
10: 2 I **w** write on the tables the words that	NIH
11:14 That I **w** give *you* the rain of your land in	NIH
11:15 I **w** send grass in thy fields for thy cattle,	NIH
11:23 **w** the LORD drive out all these nations	NIH
11:28 if ye **w** not obey the commandments of	NIH
12:20 I **w** eat flesh, because thy soul longeth to	NIH
12:30 serve their gods? even so **w** I do likewise.	NIH
15:16 say unto thee, I **w** not go away from thee;	NIH
17:12 And the man that **w** do presumptuously,	NIH
17:12 **w** not hearken unto the priest that	NIH
17:14 shalt say, I **w** set a king over me,	NIH
18:15 The LORD thy God **w** raise up unto thee a	NIH
18:18 I **w** raise them up a Prophet from among	NIH
18:18 and **w** put my words in his mouth;	NIH
18:19 *that* whosoever **w** not hearken unto my	NIH
18:19 speak in my name, I **w** require *it* of him.	NIH
20:12 if it **w** make no peace with thee,	NIH
20:12 **w** make war against thee, then thou shalt	NIH
21:14 then thou shalt let her go whither she **w;**	5315
21:18 which **w** not obey the voice of his father,	NIH
21:18 chastened him, **w** not hearken unto them:	NIH
21:20 and rebellious, he **w** not obey our voice;	NIH
23:21 for the LORD thy God **w** surely require it	NIH
25: 7 he **w** not perform the duty of my	14

Dt 25: 9 shall it be done unto *that* man that **w** not NIH
28: 1 that the Lord thy God **w** set thee on high NIH
28:27 The Lord **w** smite thee with the botch of NIH
28:55 So that *he* **w** not give to any of them of NIH
28:59 the Lord **w** make thy plagues wonderful, NIH
28:60 Moreover he **w** bring upon thee all NIH
28:61 them **w** the Lord bring upon thee, NIH
28:63 the Lord **w** rejoice over you to destroy NIH
29:20 The Lord **w** not spare him, but then 14
30: 3 the Lord thy God **w** turn thy captivity, NIH
30: 3 **w** return and gather thee from all NIH
30: 4 from thence the Lord thy God gather NIH
30: 4 and from thence **w** he fetch thee: NIH
30: 5 the Lord thy God **w** bring thee into NIH
30: 5 he **w** do thee good, and multiply thee NIH
30: 6 the Lord thy God **w** circumcise thine NIH
30: 7 the Lord thy God **w** put all these curses NIH
30: 9 the Lord thy God **w** make thee plenteous NIH
30: 9 for the Lord **w** again rejoice over thee NIH
31: 3 he **w** go over before thee, *and* he will NIH
31: 3 he **w** destroy these nations from before NIH
31: 6 he **w** not fail thee, nor forsake thee. NIH
31: 8 he **w** be with thee, he will not fail thee, NIH
31: 8 he will be with thee, he **w** not fail thee, NIH
31:16 this people **w** rise up, and go a whoring NIH
31:16 **w** forsake me, and break my covenant NIH
31:17 I **w** forsake them, and I will hide my face NIH
31:17 I **w** hide my face from them, and they NIH
31:17 so that they **w** say in that day, Are not NIH
31:18 I **w** surely hide my face in that day for all NIH
31:20 they turn unto other gods, NIH
31:23 I sware unto them: and I **w** be with thee. NIH
31:29 I know that after my death ye **w** utterly NIH
31:29 evil **w** befall you in the latter days; NIH
31:29 ye **w** do evil in the sight of the Lord, NIH
32: 1 Give ear, O ye heavens, and I **w** speak; NIH
32: 3 Because I **w** publish the name of NIH
32: 7 ask thy father, and he **w** shew thee; NIH
32: 7 thy elders, and they **w** tell thee. NIH
32:20 he said, I **w** hide my face from them, NIH
32:20 I **w** see what their end *shall be:* for they NIH
32:21 I **w** move them to jealousy with *those* NIH
32:21 I **w** provoke them to anger with a foolish NIH
32:23 I **w** heap mischiefs upon them; I will NIH
32:23 I **w** spend mine arrows upon them. NIH
32:24 I **w** also send the teeth of beasts upon NIH
32:41 I **w** render vengeance to mine enemies, NIH
32:41 and **w** reward them that hate me. NIH
32:42 I **w** make mine arrows drunk with blood, NIH
32:43 for he **w** avenge the blood of his servants, NIH
32:43 I **w** render vengeance to his adversaries, NIH
32:43 **w** be merciful *unto* his land, *and to* his NIH
33:16 *for the* **good w** of him that dwelt in 7522
34: 4 saying, I **w** give it unto thy seed: NIH
Jos 1: 5 as I was with Moses, *so* I **w** be with thee: NIH
1: 5 I **w** not fail thee, nor forsake thee. NIH
1:16 All that thou commandest us we **w** do, NIH
1:16 whithersoever thou sendest us, we **w** go. NIH
1:17 in all *things,* so **w** we hearken unto thee: NIH
1:18 **w** not hearken unto thy words in all that NIH
2:12 that ye **w** also shew kindness unto my NIH
2:13 *that* ye **w** save alive my father, NIH
2:14 that we **w** deal kindly and truly with thee. NIH
2:17 We **w** *be* blameless of this thine oath NIH
2:19 *be* upon his head, and we **w** *be* guiltless: NIH
2:20 we **w** be quit of thine oath which thou NIH
3: 5 for to morrow the Lord **w** do wonders NIH
3: 7 This day **w** I begin to magnify thee in NIH
3: 7 as I was with Moses, *so* I **w** be with thee. NIH
3:10 *that* he **w** without fail drive out from NIH
7:12 neither **w** I be with you any more, except NIH
8: 5 *are* with me, we approach unto the city: NIH
8: 5 as at the first, that we **w** flee before them, NIH
8: 6 (For they **w** come out after us) till we have NIH
8: 6 for they **w** say, *They* flee before us, as at NIH
8: 6 the first: therefore we **w** flee before them. NIH
8: 7 for the Lord your God deliver it into NIH
8:18 toward Ai; for I **w** give it into thine hand. NIH
9:20 This we **w** do to them, we will even let NIH
9:20 we **w** even let them live, lest wrath be NIH
11: 6 for to morrow about this time **w** I deliver NIH
13: 6 **w** I drive out from before the children NIH
14:12 if so be the Lord **w** *be* with me, then NIH
15:16 to him **w** I give Achsah my daughter to NIH
18: 4 I **w** send them, and they shall rise, NIH
22:18 it **w** be, *seeing* ye rebel to day against NIH
22:18 that to morrow he **w** be wroth with NIH
23:13 **w** no more drive out *any of* these nations NIH
24:15 choose you *this* day whom you **w** serve; NIH
24:15 and my house, we **w** serve the Lord. NIH
24:18 *therefore* we **w** also serve the Lord; NIH
24:19 he **w** not forgive your transgressions nor NIH
24:20 he **w** turn and do you hurt, NIH
24:21 Nay; but we **w** serve the Lord. NIH
24:24 The Lord our God **w** we serve, and his NIH
24:24 will we serve, and his voice **w** we obey. NIH
Jdg 1: 3 and I likewise **w** go with thee into thy lot. NIH
1:12 to him **w** I give Achsah my daughter to NIH
1:24 into the city, and we **w** shew thee mercy. NIH
2: 1 I **w** never break my covenant with you. NIH
2: 3 I **w** not drive them out from before you; NIH
2:21 I also **w** not henceforth drive out any from NIH
2:22 whether they **w** keep the way of the Lord NIH
4: 7 I **w** draw unto thee to the river Kishon NIH
4: 7 and I **w** deliver him into thine hand. NIH

Jdg 4: 8 If thou wilt go with me, then I **w** go: NIH
4: 8 wilt not go with me, *then* I **w** not go. NIH
4: 9 she said, I **w** surely go with thee: NIH
4:22 I **w** shew thee the man whom thou NIH
5: 3 I, *even* I, **w** sing unto the Lord; NIH
5: 3 I **w** sing *praise* to the Lord God of Israel. NIH
6:16 Surely I **w** be with thee, and thou shalt NIH
6:18 he said, I **w** tarry until thou come again. NIH
6:31 stood against him, **W** ye plead for Baal? NIH
6:31 **w** ye save him? he that will plead for him, NIH
6:31 he that **w** plead for him, let him be put to NIH
6:37 I **w** put a fleece of wool in the floor; NIH
6:39 against me, and I **w** speak but *this* once: NIH
7: 4 the water, and I **w** try them for thee there: NIH
7: 7 By the three hundred men that lapped **w** I NIH
8: 7 I **w** tear your flesh with the thorns of NIH
8: 9 again in peace, I **w** break down this tower. NIH
8:23 said unto them, I **w** not rule over you, NIH
8:25 We **w** willingly give *them.* NIH
10:13 wherefore I **w** deliver you no more. NIH
10:18 What man *is he* that **w** begin to fight NIH
11:24 out from before us, them **w** we possess. NIH
11:31 and I **w** offer it up *for* a burnt offering. NIH
12: 1 **w** burn thine house upon thee with fire. NIH
13:16 thou detain me, I **w** not eat of thy bread: NIH
14:12 I **w** now put forth a riddle unto you: NIH
14:12 I **w** give you thirty sheets and thirty NIH
15: 1 I **w** go in to my wife into the chamber. NIH
15: 7 yet **w** I be avenged of you, and after *that* I NIH
15: 7 avenged of you, and after *that* I **w** cease. NIH
15:12 that ye **w** not fall upon me yourselves. NIH
15:13 we **w** bind thee fast, and deliver thee into NIH
15:13 surely we **w** not kill thee. And they bound NIH
16: 5 we **w** give thee every one *of us* eleven NIH
16:20 I **w** go out as at other times *before,* and NIH
17: 3 now therefore I **w** restore it unto thee. NIH
17:10 I **w** give thee ten *shekels* of silver by NIH
17:13 Now know I that the Lord **w** do me NIH
19:12 We **w** not turn aside hither into the city NIH
19:12 of Israel; we **w** pass over to Gibeah. NIH
19:24 them I **w** bring out now, and humble ye NIH
20: 8 We **w** not any *of us* go to his tent, NIH
20: 8 we **w** any *of us* turn into his house. NIH
20: 9 this *shall be* the thing which we **w** do NIH
20: 9 to Gibeah; *we* **w** go by lot against it; NIH
20:10 we **w** take ten men of an hundred NIH
20:28 for to morrow I **w** deliver them into thine NIH
21: 7 **w** not give them of our daughters to NIH
21:22 that we **w** say unto them, Be favourable NIH
Ru 1:10 Surely we **w** return with thee unto thy NIH
1:11 why **w** you go with me? *are there* yet *any* NIH
1:16 for whither thou goest, I **w** go; NIH
1:16 and where thou lodgest, I **w** lodge: NIH
1:17 **w** I die, and there will I be buried: NIH
1:17 will I die, and there **w** I be buried: NIH
3: 4 and he **w** tell thee what thou shalt do. NIH
3: 5 All that thou sayest unto me I **w** do. NIH
3:11 I **w** do to thee all that thou requirest: NIH
3:13 *that* if he **w** perform unto thee the part of NIH
3:13 if he **w** not do the part of a kinsman to 2654
3:13 **w** I do the part of a kinsman to thee, NIH
3:18 until thou know how the matter **w** fall: NIH
3:18 for the man **w** not be in rest, until he have NIH
4: 4 after thee. And he said, I **w** redeem *it.* NIH
1Sa 1:11 I **w** give him unto the Lord all the days NIH
1:22 I **w** *not go up* until the child be weaned, NIH
1:22 *then* I **w** bring him, that he may appear NIH
2: 9 He **w** keep the feet of his saints, NIH
2:15 for he **w** not have sodden flesh of thee, NIH
2:16 *it me* now: and if not, I **w** take *it* by force. NIH
2:30 for them that honour me I **w** honour, NIH
2:31 that I **w** cut off thine arm, and the arm of NIH
2:35 I **w** raise me up a faithful priest, *that* shall NIH
2:35 I **w** build him a sure house; and he shall NIH
3:11 to Samuel, Behold, I **w** do a thing in Israel, NIH
3:12 In that day I **w** perform against Eli all NIH
3:12 when I begin, I **w** also make an end. NIH
3:13 I have told him that I **w** judge his house NIH
6: 5 peradventure he **w** lighten his hand from NIH
7: 3 he **w** deliver you out of the hand of NIH
7: 5 and I **w** pray for you unto the Lord. NIH
7: 8 that he **w** save us out of the hand of NIH
8:11 This **w** be the manner of the king that NIH
8:11 He **w** take your sons, and appoint *them* for NIH
8:12 he **w** appoint him captains over thousands, NIH
8:12 **w** *set them* to ear his ground, and to reap NIH
8:13 he **w** take your daughters to be NIH
8:14 he **w** take your fields, and your vineyards, NIH
8:15 he **w** take the tenth of your seed, NIH
8:16 he **w** take your menservants, and your NIH
8:17 He **w** take the tenth of your sheep: NIH
8:18 and the Lord **w** not hear you in that day. NIH
8:19 Nay, but we **w** have a king over us; NIH
9: 8 *that* I **w** give to the man of God, to tell us NIH
9:13 for the people **w** not eat until he come, NIH
9:16 To morrow about *this* time I **w** send thee NIH
9:19 to morrow I **w** let thee go, and will tell NIH
9:19 and **w** tell thee all that *is* in thine heart. NIH
10: 2 they **w** say unto thee, The asses which NIH
10: 4 they **w** salute thee, and give thee two NIH
10: 6 the spirit of the Lord **w** come upon thee, NIH
10: 8 behold, I **w** come down unto thee, to offer NIH
11: 1 a covenant with us, and we **w** serve thee. NIH
11: 2 On this *condition* **w** I make *a covenant* NIH

1Sa 11: 3 no man to save us, we **w** come out to NIH
11:10 To morrow we **w** come out unto you, NIH
12: 3 eyes therewith? and I **w** restore *it* you. NIH
12:10 of our enemies, and we **w** serve thee. NIH
12:14 If ye **w** fear the Lord, and serve him, NIH
12:15 if ye **w** not obey the voice of the Lord, NIH
12:16 which the Lord **w** do before your eyes. NIH
12:17 I **w** call unto the Lord, and he shall send NIH
12:22 For the Lord **w** not forsake his people for NIH
12:23 I teach you the good and the right way: NIH
13:12 The Philistines **w** come down now upon NIH
14: 6 it may be that the Lord **w** work for us: NIH
14: 8 we **w** pass over unto *these* men, and we NIH
14: 8 and we **w** discover ourselves unto them. NIH
14: 9 we **w** stand still in our place, and will not NIH
14: 9 in our place, and **w** not go up unto them. NIH
14:10 Come up unto us; then we **w** go up: NIH
14:12 up to us, and we **w** shew you a thing. NIH
14:40 Jonathan my son **w** be on the other side. NIH
15:16 I **w** tell thee what the Lord hath said to NIH
15:26 said unto Saul, I **w** not return with thee: NIH
15:29 also the Strength of Israel **w** not lie nor NIH
16: 1 I **w** send thee to Jesse the Beth-lehemite: NIH
16: 2 if Saul hear *it,* he **w** kill me. NIH
16: 3 and I **w** shew thee what thou shalt do: NIH
16:11 for we **w** not sit down till he come hither. NIH
17: 9 *to* kill me, then **w** we be your servants; NIH
17:25 the king **w** enrich him *with* great riches, NIH
17:25 **w** give him his daughter, and make his NIH
17:32 thy servant **w** go and fight with this NIH
17:37 he **w** deliver me out of the hand of this NIH
17:44 I **w** give thy flesh unto the fowls of the air, NIH
17:46 This day **w** the Lord deliver thee into NIH
17:46 I **w** smite thee, and take thine head from NIH
17:46 I **w** give the carcases of the host of NIH
17:47 and he **w** give you into our hands. NIH
18:11 I **w** smite David even to the wall *with it.* NIH
18:17 daughter Merab, her **w** I give thee to wife: NIH
18:21 Saul said, I **w** give him her, that she may NIH
19: 3 I **w** go out and stand beside my father in NIH
19: 3 and I **w** commune with my father of thee; NIH
19: 3 of thee; and what I see, that I **w** tell thee. NIH
20: 2 my father **w** do nothing *either* great or NIH
20: 2 or small, but that he **w** shew it me: NIH
20: 4 thy soul desireth, I **w** even do *it* for thee. NIH
20:13 I **w** shew it thee, and send thee away, NIH
20:18 be missed, because thy seat **w** be empty. NIH
20:20 I **w** shoot three arrows on the side *thereof,* NIH
20:21 I **w** send a lad, *saying,* Go, find out NIH
22: 3 till I know what God **w** do for me. NIH
22: 7 **w** the son of Jesse give every one of you NIH
23: 4 for I **w** deliver the Philistines into thine NIH
23:11 W be his manner all the while he dwelleth NIH
23:11 **W** Saul come down, as thy servant hath NIH
23:11 And the Lord said, He **w** come down. NIH
23:12 **W** the men of Keilah deliver me and my NIH
23:12 the Lord said, They **w** deliver *thee* up. NIH
23:23 with the certainty, and I **w** go with you: NIH
23:23 that I **w** search him out throughout all NIH
24: 4 I **w** deliver thine enemy into thine hand, NIH
24:10 I **w** not put forth mine hand against my NIH
24:19 his enemy, he **w** let him go well away? NIH
25: 8 thy young men, and they **w** shew thee. NIH
25:28 for the Lord **w** certainly make my lord a NIH
26: 6 Who **w** go down with me to Saul to NIH
26: 6 And Abishai said, I **w** go down with thee. NIH
26: 8 I **w** not *smite* him the second time. NIH
26:21 for I **w** no more do thee harm, because NIH
27:11 *w* be his manner all the while he dwelleth NIH
28: 2 Therefore **w** I make thee keeper of mine NIH
28:19 Moreover the Lord **w** also deliver Israel NIH
28:23 he refused, and said, I **w** not eat. But his NIH
30:15 and I **w** bring thee down to this company. NIH
30:22 we **w** not give them *ought* of the spoil NIH
30:24 who **w** hearken unto you in this matter? NIH
2Sa 2: 6 I also **w** requite you this kindness, because NIH
2:26 knowest thou not that it **w** be bitterness in NIH
3:13 said, Well; I **w** make a league with thee: NIH
3:18 By the hand of my servant David I **w** save NIH
3:21 I **w** arise and go, and will gather all Israel NIH
3:21 **w** gather all Israel unto my lord the king, NIH
5:19 for I **w** doubtless deliver the Philistines NIH
6:21 therefore **w** I play before the Lord. NIH
6:22 I **w** yet be more vile than thus, and will be NIH
6:22 thus, and **w** be base in mine own sight: NIH
7:10 I **w** appoint a place for my people NIH
7:10 **w** plant them, that they may dwell in a NIH
7:11 Also the Lord telleth thee that he **w** NIH
7:12 thy fathers, I **w** set up thy seed after thee, NIH
7:12 thy bowels, and I **w** establish his kingdom. NIH
7:13 I **w** stablish the throne of his kingdom for NIH
7:14 I **w** be his father, and he shall be my son. NIH
7:14 I **w** chasten him with the rod of men, NIH
7:27 thy servant, saying, I **w** build thee a house: NIH
9: 7 for I **w** surely shew thee kindness for NIH
9: 7 **w** restore thee all the land of Saul thy NIH
10: 2 I **w** shew kindness unto Hanun the son of NIH
10:11 for thee, then I **w** come and help thee. NIH
11:11 *as* thy soul liveth, I **w** not do this thing. NIH
11:12 also, and to morrow I **w** let thee depart. NIH
12:11 I **w** raise up evil against thee out of thine NIH
12:11 I **w** take thy wives before thine eyes, NIH
12:12 I **w** do this thing before all Israel, NIH
12:18 how **w** he then vex himself, if we tell him NIH
12:22 Who can tell *whether* God **w** be gracious NIH

2Sa 13:13 for he **w** not withhold me from thee.	**1Ki** 14:10 I **w** bring evil upon the house of Jeroboam	**1Ch** 17:13 I **w** not take my mercy away from him,
14: 7 he slew; and we **w** destroy the heir also:	14:10 **w** cut off from Jeroboam *him that* pisseth	17:14 I **w** settle him in mine house and in my
14: 8 and I **w** give charge concerning thee.	14:10 **w** take away the remnant of the house of	19: 2 I **w** shew kindness unto Hanun the son of
14:15 I **w** now speak unto the king;	16: 3 I **w** take away the posterity of Baasha,	19:12 be too strong for thee, then I **w** help thee.
14:15 it may be that the king **w** perform	16: 3 **w** make thy house like the house of	21: 3 my lord require this *thing?* why **w** he
14:16 the king **w** hear, to deliver his handmaid	18: 1 and I **w** send rain upon the earth.	21:24 but I **w** verily buy *it* for the full price:
14:17 the LORD thy God **w** be with thee.	18:15 I **w** surely shew myself unto him to day.	21:24 for I **w** not take *that* which *is* thine for
15: 8 *to* Jerusalem, then I **w** serve the LORD.	18:23 and I **w** dress the other bullock,	22: 5 I **w** *therefore* now make preparation for it.
15:21 or life, even there *also* **w** thy servant be.	18:24 and I **w** call on the name of the LORD:	22: 9 I **w** give him rest from all his enemies
15:25 he **w** bring me again, and shew me *both*	19:20 and my mother, and *then* I **w** follow thee.	22: 9 I **w** give peace and quietness unto Israel in
15:28 I **w** tarry in the plain of the wilderness,	20: 6 Yet I **w** send my servants unto thee to	22:10 he shall be my son, and I **w** be his father;
15:34 unto Absalom, I **w** be thy servant, O king;	20: 9 send for to thy servant at the first I **w** do:	22:10 I **w** establish the throne of his kingdom
15:34 so *w* I now also *be* thy servant;	20:13 I **w** deliver it into thine hand *this* day;	28: 6 him to be my son, and I **w** be his father.
16:12 It may be that the LORD **w** look on mine	20:22 the king of Syria **w** come up against thee.	28: 7 Moreover I **w** establish his kingdom for
16:12 that the LORD **w** requite me good for his	20:25 we **w** fight against them in the plain,	28: 9 if thou seek him, he **w** be found of thee;
16:18 his **w** I be, and with him will I abide.	20:28 **w** I deliver all this great multitude into	28: 9 forsake him, he **w** cast thee off for ever.
16:18 his will I be, and with him **w** I abide.	20:31 of Israel: peradventure he **w** save thy life.	28:20 LORD God, *even* my God, **w** be with thee;
16:19 presence, so **w** I be in thy presence.	20:34 father took from thy father, I **w** restore;	28:20 he **w** not fail thee, nor forsake thee,
17: 1 I **w** arise and pursue after David *this* night:	20:34 *said* Ahab, So **w** I send thee away with *this*	28:21 all the people **w** be wholly at thy
17: 2 I **w** come upon him while he *is* weary and	21: 2 I **w** give thee for it a better vineyard than	**2Ch** 1:12 I **w** give thee riches, and wealth,
17: 2 weak handed, and **w** make him afraid:	21: 2 I **w** give thee the worth of it *in* money.	2:10 I **w** give to thy servants, the hewers
17: 3 I **w** bring back all the people unto thee:	21: 4 I **w** not give thee the inheritance of	2:16 we **w** cut wood out of Lebanon, as much
17: 8 of war, and **w** not lodge with the people.	21: 6 I **w** give thee *another* vineyard for it:	2:16 we **w** bring it to thee *in* flotes by sea *to*
17: 9 it **w** come to pass, when *some* of them be	21: 6 answered, I **w** not give thee my vineyard.	6:18 **w** God in very deed dwell with men on
17: 9 the first, that whosoever heareth *it* **w** say,	21: 7 I **w** give thee the vineyard of Naboth	7:14 **w** I hear from heaven, and will forgive
17:12 we **w** *light* upon him as the dew falleth	21:21 I **w** bring evil upon thee, and will take	7:14 **w** forgive their sin, and will heal their land.
17:13 that city, and we **w** draw it into the river,	21:21 **w** take away thy posterity, and will cut off	7:14 **w** forgive their sin, and **w** heal their land.
18: 2 I **w** surely go forth with you myself also.	21:21 **w** cut off from Ahab *him that* pisseth	7:18 I **w** stablish the throne of thy kingdom,
18: 3 for if we flee away, they **w** not care for us;	21:22 **w** make thine house like the house of	7:20 **w** I pluck them up by the roots out of my
18: 3 neither if half of us die, **w** they care for us:	21:29 I **w** not bring the evil in his days:	7:20 **w** I cast out of my sight, and will make it
18: 4 unto them, What seemeth you best I **w** do.	21:29 in his son's day's I **w** bring the evil upon	7:20 **w** make it to be a proverb and a byword
19: 7 there **w** not tarry one with thee *this* night:	22:14 the LORD saith unto me, that **w** I speak.	10: 4 that he put upon us, and we **w** serve thee.
19: 7 that **w** be worse unto thee than all the evil	22:21 the LORD, and said, I **w** persuade him.	10: 7 to them, they **w** be thy servants for ever.
19:26 for thy servant said, I **w** saddle me an ass,	22:22 I **w** go forth, and I will be a lying spirit in	10:11 upon you, I **w** put more to your yoke:
19:33 and I **w** feed thee with me in Jerusalem.	22:22 I **w** be a lying spirit in the mouth of all his	10:11 but I **w** *chastise you* with scorpions.
19:36 Thy servant **w** go a little *way* over Jordan	22:30 I **w** disguise myself, and enter into	10:14 your yoke heavy, but I **w** add thereto:
19:38 I **w** do to him *that* which shall seem good	**2Ki** 2: 2 and *as* thy soul liveth, I **w** not leave thee.	10:14 but I **w** *chastise you* with scorpions.
19:38 shalt require of me, *that* **w** I do for thee.	2: 3 Knowest thou that the LORD **w** take away	12: 7 *therefore* I **w** not destroy them, but I will
20:21 him only, and I **w** depart from the city.	2: 4 and *as* thy soul liveth, I **w** not leave thee.	12: 7 but I **w** grant them some deliverance;
21: 4 We **w** have no silver nor gold of Saul,	2: 5 Knowest thou that the LORD **w** take away	15: 2 if ye seek him, he **w** be found of you;
21: 4 What you shall say, *that* **w** I do for you.	2: 6 and *as* thy soul liveth, I **w** not leave thee.	15: 2 but if ye forsake him, he **w** forsake you.
21: 6 we **w** hang them up unto the LORD in	3: 7 he said, I **w** go up: I *am* as thou *art,* my	18: 3 and *we* **w** be with thee in the war.
21: 6 And the king said, I **w** give *them.*	3:18 he **w** deliver the Moabites also into your	18: 5 for God **w** deliver *it* into the king's hand.
22: 3 The God of my rock; in him **w** I trust:	4:30 and *as* thy soul liveth, I **w** not leave thee.	18:13 even what my God saith, that **w** I speak.
22: 4 I **w** call on the LORD, who is *worthy* to be	5: 5 I **w** send a letter unto the king of Israel.	18:20 before the LORD, and said, I **w** entice him.
22:29 and the LORD **w** lighten my darkness.	5:11 He **w** surely come out to me, and stand,	18:21 I **w** go out, and be a lying spirit in
22:50 Therefore I **w** give thanks unto thee,	5:16 before whom I stand, I **w** receive none.	18:29 I **w** disguise myself, and will go to
22:50 and I **w** sing praises unto thy name.	5:17 for thy servant **w** henceforth offer neither	18:29 disguise myself, and **w** go to the battle;
24:24 but I **w** surely buy *it* of thee at a price:	5:20 I **w** run after him, and take somewhat of	20:17 for the LORD **w** be with you.
24:24 neither **w** I offer burnt offerings unto	6: 3 thy servants. And he answered, I **w** go.	21:14 *with* a great plague **w** the LORD smite thy
1Ki 1: 5 exalted himself, saying, I **w** be king:	6:11 **W** ye not shew me which of us *is* for	28:23 *therefore* I **w** sacrifice to them, that they
1:14 I also **w** come in after thee, and confirm	6:19 I **w** bring you to the man whom ye seek.	30: 6 and he **w** return to the remnant of you,
1:30 stead; even so **w** I certainly do this day.	6:28 to day, and we **w** eat my son to morrow.	30: 9 and **w** not turn away *his* face from you,
1:51 he **w** not slay his servant with the sword.	7: 4 We **w** enter *into* the city, then the famine	33: 7 tribes of Israel, **w** I put my name for ever:
1:52 If he **w** shew himself a worthy man,	7: 9 *some* mischief **w** come upon us:	33: 8 Neither **w** I any more remove the foot of
2: 8 I **w** not put thee to death with the sword.	7:12 I **w** now shew you what the Syrians have	33: 8 that they **w** take heed to do all that I have
2:17 the king, (for he **w** not say thee nay,)	8: 1 I **w** cut off from Ahab *him that* pisseth	34:24 I **w** bring evil upon this place, and upon
2:18 Well; I **w** speak for thee unto the king.	9: 9 I **w** make the house of Ahab like the	34:28 I **w** gather thee to thy fathers, and thou
2:20 my mother: for I **w** not say thee nay.	9:26 I **w** requite thee in this plat, saith	34:28 all the evil that I **w** bring upon this place,
2:26 I **w** not at this time put thee to death,	10: 5 and **w** do all that thou shalt bid us;	**Ezr** 4: 3 we ourselves together **w** build unto
2:30 he said, Nay; but I **w** die here.	10: 5 shalt bid us; we **w** not make any king:	4:13 set up *again, then* **w** they not pay toll,
2:38 the king hath said, so **w** thy servant do.	10: 6 mine, and *if* ye **w** hearken unto my voice,	7:18 gold, *that* do after the **w** of your God. 7470
3:14 did walk, then I **w** lengthen thy days.	18:14 *that* which thou puttest on me **w** I bear.	7:26 whosoever **w** not do the law of thy God,
5: 5 I **w** set upon thy throne in thy room,	18:21 it **w** go into his hand, and pierce it:	10: 4 also **w** be with thee: be of good courage,
5: 6 unto thee **w** I give hire for thy servants	18:23 and I **w** deliver thee two thousand horses,	**Ne** 1: 8 I **w** scatter you abroad among the nations:
5: 8 I **w** do all thy desire concerning timber of	18:30 The LORD **w** surely deliver us,	1: 9 *yet* **w** I gather them from thence,
5: 9 I **w** convey them by sea *in* flotes unto	18:32 saying, The LORD **w** deliver us.	1: 9 **w** bring them unto the place that I have
5: 9 we cause them to be discharged there,	19: 4 It may be the LORD thy God **w** hear all	2:19 that ye do? **w** ye rebel against the king?
6:12 **w** I perform my word with thee, which I	19: 4 reprove the words which the LORD thy	2:20 The God of heaven, he **w** prosper us;
6:13 I **w** dwell among the children of Israel,	19: 7 I **w** send a blast upon him, and he shall	2:20 we his servants **w** arise and build:
6:13 and **w** not forsake my people Israel.	19: 7 I **w** cause him to fall by the sword in his	4: 2 **w** they fortify themselves? will they
8:27 **w** God indeed dwell on the earth? behold,	19:23 cut down the tall cedar trees thereof,	4: 2 **w** they sacrifice? will they make an end in
9: 5 I **w** establish the throne of thy kingdom	19:23 I **w** enter *into* the lodgings of his borders,	4: 2 **w** they make an end in a day? will they
9: 6 **w** not keep my commandments *and*	19:28 therefore I **w** put my hook in thy nose,	4: 2 **w** they revive the stones out of the heaps
9: 7 **w** I cut off Israel out of the land which I	19:28 I **w** turn thee back by the way by which	4:12 shall return unto us *they* **w** be *upon* you.
9: 7 for my name, **w** I cast out of my sight;	19:34 I **w** defend this city, to save it, for mine	5: 8 and **w** you even sell your brethren?
11: 2 *for* surely they **w** turn away your heart	20: 5 I **w** heal thee: on the third day thou	5:12 We **w** restore *them,* and will require
11:11 I **w** surely rend the kingdom from thee,	20: 6 And I **w** add unto thy days fifteen years;	5:12 and **w** require nothing of them;
11:11 from thee, and **w** give it to thy servant.	20: 6 I **w** deliver thee and this city out of the	5:12 of them; so **w** we do as thou sayest.
11:12 Notwithstanding in thy days I **w** not do it	20: 6 I **w** defend this city for mine own sake,	6:10 for they **w** come to slay thee; yea,
11:12 *but* I **w** rend it out of the hand of thy son.	20: 8 What *shall* be the sign that the LORD **w**	6:10 in the night **w** they come to slay thee.
11:13 I **w** not rend away all the kingdom;	20: 9 that the LORD **w** do the thing that he hath	6:11 the temple to save his life? I **w** not go in.
11:13 **w** give one tribe to thy son for David my	21: 4 In Jerusalem **w** I put my name.	10:39 we **w** not forsake the house of our God.
11:31 I **w** rent the kingdom out of the hand of	21: 7 tribes of Israel, **w** I put my name for ever:	13:21 if ye do so again, I **w** lay hands on you.
11:31 of Solomon, and **w** give ten tribes to thee:	21: 8 Neither **w** I make the feet of Israel move	**Est** 3: 9 I **w** pay ten thousand talents of silver to
11:34 Howbeit I **w** not take the whole kingdom	21: 8 only if they **w** observe to do according to	4:16 I also and my maidens **w** fast likewise;
11:34 we make him prince all the days of his life	21:13 I **w** stretch over Jerusalem the line of	4:16 so **w** I go in unto the king, which *is* not
11:35 I **w** take the kingdom out of his son's	21:13 I **w** wipe Jerusalem as *a man* wipeth a	5: 8 I **w** do to morrow as the king hath said.
11:35 and **w** give it unto thee, *even* ten tribes.	21:14 I **w** forsake the remnant of mine	7: 8 **W** he force the queen also before me in
11:36 unto his son **w** I give one tribe, that David	22:16 I **w** bring evil upon this place, and upon	**Job** 1:11 and he **w** curse thee to thy face. 518+3808
11:37 I **w** take thee, and thou shalt reign	22:20 I **w** gather thee unto thy fathers,	2: 4 all that a man hath **w** he give for his life.
11:38 I **w** be with thee, and build thee a sure	22:20 eyes shall not see all the evil which I **w**	2: 5 and he **w** curse thee to thy face. 518+3808
11:38 for David, and **w** give Israel unto thee.	23:27 I **w** remove Judah also out of my sight,	5: 1 if there be *any* that **w** answer thee;
11:39 I **w** for this afflict the seed of David,	23:27 **w** cast off this city Jerusalem which I have	6:24 Teach me, and I **w** hold my tongue:
12: 4 upon us, lighter, and we **w** serve thee.	**1Ch** 12:19 He **w** fall to his master Saul to	7:11 Therefore I **w** not refrain my mouth; I will
12: 7 then they **w** be thy servants for ever.	14:10 for I **w** deliver them into thine hand.	7:11 I **w** speak in the anguish of my spirit;
12:11 with a heavy yoke, I **w** add to your yoke:	16:18 Unto thee **w** I give the land of Canaan,	7:11 I **w** complain in the bitterness of my soul.
12:11 but I **w** *chastise you* with scorpions.	17: 9 Also I **w** ordain a place for my people	8:20 God **w** not cast away a perfect *man,*
12:14 yoke heavy, and I **w** add to your yoke:	17: 9 **w** plant them, and they shall dwell in	8:20 *man,* neither **w** he help the evil doers:
12:14 but I **w** *chastise you* with scorpions.	17:10 Moreover I **w** subdue all thine enemies.	9: 3 If he **w** contend with him, he cannot 2654
13: 7 refresh *thyself,* and I **w** give thee a reward.	17:10 Furthermore I tell thee that the LORD **w**	9:12 who **w** say unto him, What doest thou?
13: 8 Half thine house, I **w** not go in with thee,	17:11 that I **w** raise up thy seed after thee,	9:13 *If* God **w** not withdraw his anger,
13: 8 neither **w** I eat bread nor drink water in	17:11 of thy sons; and I **w** stablish his kingdom.	9:18 He **w** not suffer me to take my breath,
13:16 neither **w** I eat bread nor drink water with	17:12 and I **w** stablish his throne for ever.	9:23 he **w** laugh at the trial of the innocent.
	17:13 I **w** be his father, and he shall be my son:	9:27 If I say, I **w** forget my complaint, I will

Job	9:27 I **w** leave off my heaviness,	NIH
	10: 1 I **w** leave my complaint upon myself;	NIH
	10: 1 I **w** speak in the bitterness of my soul.	NIH
	10: 2 I **w** say unto God, Do not condemn me;	NIH
	10:15 be righteous, *yet* **w** I not lift up my head.	NIH
	11:11 also; **w** he not then consider *it*?	NIH
	13: 7 **W** you speak wickedly for God?	NIH
	13: 8 **W** ye accept his person? will ye contend	NIH
	13: 8 accept his person? **w** ye contend for God?	NIH
	13:10 He **w** surely reprove you, if ye do secretly	NIH
	13:13 I may speak, and let come on me what **w**.	NIH
	13:15 Though he slay me, *yet* **w** I trust in him:	NIH
	13:15 I **w** maintain mine own ways before him.	NIH
	13:19 Who *is* he *that* **w** plead with me? for now,	NIH
	13:20 then **w** I not hide myself from thee.	NIH
	13:22 call thou, and I **w** answer: or let me speak,	NIH
	14: 7 that it **w** sprout again, and that the tender	NIH
	14: 7 the tender branch thereof **w** not cease.	NIH
	14: 9 *Yet* through the sent of water it **w** bud,	NIH
	14:14 the days of my appointed time **w** I wait,	NIH
	14:15 Thou shalt call, and I **w** answer thee:	NIH
	15:17 I **w** shew thee, hear me; and that which I	NIH
	15:17 and that which I have seen I **w** declare;	NIH
	17: 3 who *is* he *that* **w** strike hands with me?	NIH
	18: 2 How long **w** *it* be *ere* you make an end of	NIH
	18: 2 mark, and afterwards we **w** speak.	NIH
	19: 2 How long **w** ye vex my soul, and break	NIH
	19: 5 If indeed ye **w** magnify *yourselves* against	NIH
	22: 4 **W** he reprove thee for fear of thee? will he	NIH
	22: 4 **w** he enter with thee into judgment?	NIH
	23: 6 **W** he plead against me with *his* great	NIH
	24:25 who **w** make me a liar, and make my	NIH
	27: 5 till I die I **w** not remove my integrity from	NIH
	27: 6 I hold fast, and **w** not let it go:	NIH
	27: 9 **W** God hear his cry when trouble cometh	NIH
	27:10 **W** he delight himself in the Almighty?	NIH
	27:10 Almighty? **w** he always call upon God?	NIH
	27:11 I **w** teach you by the hand of God:	NIH
	27:11 *that* which *is* with the Almighty **w** I not	NIH
	30:24 Howbeit *he* **w** not stretch out *his* hand to	NIH
	32:10 to me; I also **w** shew mine opinion.	NIH
	32:14 I **w** answer him with your speeches.	NIH
	32:17 *I said,* I **w** answer also my part, I also will	NIH
	32:17 also my part, I also **w** shew mine opinion.	NIH
	32:20 I **w** speak, that I may be refreshed: I will	NIH
	32:20 be refreshed: I **w** open my lips and answer.	NIH
	33:12 I **w** answer thee, that God is greater than	NIH
	33:26 God, and he **w** be favourable unto him:	NIH
	33:26 he **w** render unto man his righteousness.	NIH
	33:28 He **w** deliver his soul from going into	NIH
	33:31 unto me: hold thy peace, and I **w** speak.	NIH
	34:12 Yea, surely God **w** not do wickedly,	NIH
	34:12 neither **w** the Almighty pervert judgment.	NIH
	34:23 he **w** not lay upon man more *than right;*	NIH
	34:31 I have borne *chastisement,* I **w** not offend	NIH
	34:32 if I have done iniquity, I **w** do no more.	NIH
	34:33 he **w** recompense it, whether thou refuse,	NIH
	35: 3 What advantage **w** it be unto thee?	NIH
	35: 4 I **w** answer thee, and thy companions with	NIH
	35:13 Surely God **w** not hear vanity, neither will	NIH
	35:13 neither **w** the Almighty regard it.	NIH
	36: 2 I **w** shew thee that *I have* yet to speak on	NIH
	36: 3 I **w** fetch my knowledge from afar,	NIH
	36: 3 and **w** ascribe righteousness to my Maker.	NIH
	36:19 He esteem thy riches? *no,* not gold,	NIH
	37: 4 **w** not stay them when his voice is heard.	NIH
	37:23 and *in* plenty of justice: he **w** not afflict.	NIH
	38: 3 for I **w** demand of thee, and answer thou	NIH
	39: 9 **W** the unicorn be willing to serve thee,	NIH
	39:10 or **w** he harrow the valleys after thee?	NIH
	39:12 he **w** bring home thy seed, and gather *it*	NIH
	40: 4 I **w** lay my hand upon my mouth.	NIH
	40: 5 Once have I spoken; but I **w** not answer:	NIH
	40: 5 yea, twice; but I **w** proceed no further.	NIH
	40: 7 I **w** demand of thee, and declare thou	NIH
	40:14 I also confess unto thee that thine own	NIH
	41: 3 **W** he make many supplications unto thee?	NIH
	41: 3 **w** he speak soft *words* unto thee?	NIH
	41: 4 **W** he make a covenant with thee?	NIH
	41:12 I **w** not conceal his parts, nor *his* power,	NIH
	42: 4 Hear, I beseech thee, and I **w** speak: I will	NIH
	42: 4 I **w** demand of thee, and declare thou unto	NIH
	42: 8 for him **w** I accept: lest *I* deal with you	NIH
Ps	2: 7 I **w** declare the decree: the LORD hath	NIH
	3: 6 I **w** not be afraid of ten thousands of	NIH
	4: 2 how long **w** ye turn my glory into shame?	NIH
	4: 2 *how long* **w** ye love vanity, *and* seek after	NIH
	4: 3 the LORD **w** hear when I call unto him.	NIH
	4: 6 many that say, Who **w** shew us *any* good?	NIH
	4: 8 I **w** both lay me down in peace, and sleep:	NIH
	5: 2 and my God: for unto thee **w** I pray.	NIH
	5: 3 *in* the morning **w** I direct *my prayer* unto	NIH
	5: 3 *my prayer* unto thee, and **w** look up.	NIH
	5: 6 the LORD **w** abhor the bloody and	NIH
	5: 7 I **w** come *into* thy house in the multitude	NIH
	5: 7 in thy fear **w** I worship toward thy holy	NIH
	6: 9 the LORD **w** receive my prayer.	NIH
	7:12 If he turn not, he **w** whet his sword;	NIH
	7:17 **w** praise the LORD according to his	NIH
	7:17 **w** sing *praise* to the name of the LORD	NIH
	9: 1 I **w** praise *thee,* O LORD, with my whole	NIH
	9: 1 I **w** shew forth all thy marvellous works.	NIH
	9: 2 I **w** be glad and rejoice in thee: I will sing	NIH
	9: 2 I **w** sing *praise* to thy name, O thou most	NIH
	9: 9 The LORD also **w** be a refuge for	NIH

Ps	9:10 they that know thy name **w** put their trust	NIH
	9:14 of Zion: I **w** rejoice in thy salvation.	NIH
	10: 4 **w** not seek *after God:* God is not *in* all his	NIH
	10:11 he hideth his face; he **w** never see *it.*	NIH
	12: 4 have said, With our tongue **w** we prevail;	NIH
	12: 5 the needy, now **w** I arise, saith the LORD;	NIH
	12: 5 I **w** set *him* in safety *from him that* puffeth	NIH
	13: 6 I **w** sing unto the LORD, because he hath	NIH
	16: 4 their drink offerings of blood **w** I not offer,	NIH
	16: 7 I **w** bless the LORD, who hath given me	NIH
	17:15 I **w** behold thy face in righteousness:	NIH
	18: 1 I **w** love thee, O LORD, my strength.	NIH
	18: 2 my God, my strength, in whom I **w** trust;	NIH
	18: 3 I **w** call upon the LORD, who is *worthy* to	NIH
	18:28 the LORD my God **w** enlighten my	NIH
	18:49 Therefore **w** I give thanks unto thee,	NIH
	20: 5 We **w** rejoice in thy salvation, and in	NIH
	20: 5 in the name of our God we **w** set up *our*	NIH
	20: 6 he **w** hear him from his holy heaven with	NIH
	20: 7 we **w** remember the name of the LORD	NIH
	21:13 so **w** we sing and praise thy power.	NIH
	22:22 I **w** declare thy name unto my brethren:	NIH
	22:22 in the midst of the congregation **w** I praise	NIH
	22:25 I **w** pay my vows before them that fear	NIH
	23: 4 of the shadow of death, I **w** fear no evil:	NIH
	23: 6 I **w** dwell in the house of the LORD for	NIH
	25: 8 **w** he teach sinners in the way.	NIH
	25: 9 The meek **w** he guide in judgment:	NIH
	25: 9 and the meek **w** he teach his way.	NIH
	25:14 and he **w** shew them his covenant.	NIH
	26: 4 neither **w** I go in with dissemblers.	NIH
	26: 5 evildoers; and **w** not sit with the wicked.	NIH
	26: 6 I **w** wash mine hands in innocency: so	NIH
	26: 6 so **w** I compass thine altar, O LORD:	NIH
	26:11 *as for* me, I **w** walk in mine integrity:	NIH
	26:12 in the congregations **w** I bless the LORD.	NIH
	27: 3 rise against me, in this **w** I be confident.	NIH
	27: 4 I desired of the LORD, that **w** I seek after;	NIH
	27: 6 I offer in his tabernacle sacrifices of joy;	NIH
	27: 6 I **w** sing, yea, I will sing *praises* unto	NIH
	27: 6 yea, I **w** sing *praises* unto the LORD.	NIH
	27: 8 said unto thee, Thy face, LORD, **w** I seek.	NIH
	27:10 forsake me, then the LORD **w** take me up.	NIH
	27:12 Deliver me not over unto the **w** of mine	5315
	28: 1 Unto thee **w** I cry, O LORD, my rock;	NIH
	28: 7 and with my song **w** I praise him.	NIH
	29:11 The LORD **w** give strength unto his	NIH
	29:11 the LORD **w** bless his people with peace.	NIH
	30: 1 I **w** extol thee, O LORD; for thou hast	NIH
	30:12 God, I **w** give thanks unto thee for ever.	NIH
	31: 7 I **w** be glad and rejoice in thy mercy:	NIH
	32: 5 I **w** confess my transgressions unto	NIH
	32: 8 I **w** instruct thee and teach thee in the	NIH
	32: 8 shalt go: I **w** guide thee with mine eye.	NIH
	34: 1 I **w** bless the LORD at all times: his praise	NIH
	34:11 I **w** teach you the fear of the LORD.	NIH
	35:18 I **w** give thee thanks in the great	NIH
	35:18 I **w** praise thee among much people.	NIH
	37:33 The LORD **w** not leave him in his hand,	NIH
	38:18 For I **w** declare mine iniquity; I will be	NIH
	38:18 mine iniquity; I **w** be sorry for my sin.	NIH
	39: 1 I **w** take heed to my ways, that *I* sin	NIH
	39: 1 I **w** keep my mouth with a bridle, while	NIH
	40: 8 I delight to do thy **w**, O my God: yea,	7522
	41: 1 the LORD **w** deliver him in time of	NIH
	41: 2 The LORD **w** preserve him, and keep him	NIH
	41: 2 wilt not deliver him unto the **w** of his	5315
	41: 3 The LORD **w** strengthen him upon the bed	NIH
	42: 6 I **w** remember thee from the land of	NIH
	42: 8 *Yet* the LORD **w** command his	NIH
	42: 9 I **w** say unto God my rock, Why hast thou	NIH
	43: 4 I go unto the altar of God, unto God	NIH
	43: 4 upon the harp **w** I praise thee, O God	NIH
	44: 5 Through thee **w** we push down our	NIH
	44: 5 through thy name **w** we tread them under	NIH
	44: 6 For I **w** not trust in my bow, neither shall	NIH
	45:17 I **w** make thy name to be remembered in	NIH
	46: 2 Therefore **w** not we fear, though the earth	NIH
	46:10 I **w** be exalted among the heathen, I will	NIH
	46:10 the heathen, I **w** be exalted in the earth.	NIH
	48: 8 God **w** establish it for ever. Selah.	NIH
	48:14 ever: he **w** be our guide *even* unto death.	NIH
	49: 4 I **w** incline mine ear to a parable: I will	NIH
	49: 4 I **w** open my dark saying upon the harp.	NIH
	49:15 God **w** redeem my soul from the power of	NIH
	49:18 *men* **w** praise thee, when thou doest well	NIH
	50: 7 Hear, O my people, and I **w** speak;	NIH
	50: 7 O Israel, and I **w** testify against thee:	NIH
	50: 8 I **w** not reprove thee for thy sacrifices or	NIH
	50: 9 I **w** take no bullock out of thy house,	NIH
	50:13 **W** I eat the flesh of bulls, or drink	NIH
	50:15 I **w** deliver thee, and thou shalt glorify me.	NIH
	50:21 I **w** reprove thee, and set *them* in order	NIH
	50:23 *aright* **w** I shew the salvation of God.	NIH
	51:13 *Then* **w** I teach transgressors thy ways;	NIH
	52: 9 I **w** praise thee for ever, because thou hast	NIH
	52: 9 hast done *it:* and I **w** wait on thy name;	NIH
	54: 6 I **w** freely sacrifice unto thee: I will praise	NIH
	54: 6 I **w** praise thy name, O LORD; for *it is*	NIH
	55:16 *As for* me, I **w** call upon God;	NIH
	55:17 and at noon, **w** I pray, and cry aloud:	NIH
	55:23 half their days; but I **w** trust in thee.	NIH
	56: 3 *What* time I am afraid, I **w** trust in thee.	NIH
	56: 4 In God I **w** praise his word, in God I have	NIH
	56: 4 I **w** not fear what flesh can do unto me.	NIH

Ps	56:10 In God **w** I praise *his* word: in the LORD	NIH
	56:10 in the LORD **w** I praise *his* word.	NIH
	56:11 I **w** not be afraid what man can do unto	NIH
	56:12 O God: I **w** render praises unto thee.	NIH
	57: 1 in the shadow of thy wings **w** I make my	NIH
	57: 2 I **w** cry unto God most High; unto God	NIH
	57: 7 my heart is fixed: I **w** sing and give praise.	NIH
	57: 8 and harp: I *myself* **w** awake early.	NIH
	57: 9 I **w** praise thee, O Lord, among the people:	NIH
	57: 9 I **w** sing unto thee among the nations.	NIH
	58: 5 Which **w** not hearken to the voice of	NIH
	59: 9 *Because* of his strength **w** I wait upon	NIH
	59:16 I **w** sing of thy power; yea, I will sing	NIH
	59:16 I **w** sing aloud of thy mercy in the	NIH
	59:17 Unto thee, O my strength, **w** I sing:	NIH
	60: 6 I **w** rejoice, I will divide Shechem,	NIH
	60: 6 I **w** divide Shechem, and mete out the	NIH
	60: 8 over Edom **w** I cast out my shoe:	NIH
	60: 9 Who **w** bring me *into* the strong city?	NIH
	60: 9 strong city? who **w** lead me into Edom?	NIH
	61: 2 From the end of the earth **w** I cry unto	NIH
	61: 4 I **w** abide in thy tabernacle for ever: I will	NIH
	61: 4 I **w** trust in the covert of thy wings. Selah.	NIH
	61: 8 So **w** I sing *praise* unto thy name for ever,	NIH
	62: 3 How long **w** ye imagine mischief against a	NIH
	63: 1 thou *art* my God; early **w** I seek thee:	NIH
	63: 4 Thus **w** I bless thee while I live: I will lift	NIH
	63: 4 I live: I **w** lift up my hands in thy name.	NIH
	63: 7 in the shadow of thy wings **w** I rejoice.	NIH
	66:13 I **w** go *into* thy house with burnt offerings:	NIH
	66:13 burnt offerings: I **w** pay thee my vows,	NIH
	66:15 I **w** offer unto thee burnt sacrifices of	NIH
	66:15 of rams; I **w** offer bullocks with goats.	NIH
	66:16 I **w** declare what he hath done for my	NIH
	66:18 in my heart, the Lord **w** not hear *me:*	NIH
	68:16 yea, the LORD **w** dwell *in it* for ever.	NIH
	68:22 Lord said, I **w** bring again from Bashan,	NIH
	68:22 **w** bring *my people* again from the	NIH
	69:30 I **w** praise the name of God with a song;	NIH
	69:30 and **w** magnify him with thanksgiving.	NIH
	69:35 For God **w** save Zion, and will build	NIH
	69:35 save Zion, and **w** build the cities of Judah:	NIH
	71:14 I **w** hope continually, and will yet praise	NIH
	71:14 and **w** yet praise thee more and more.	NIH
	71:16 I **w** go in the strength of the Lord GOD:	NIH
	71:16 I **w** make mention of thy righteousness,	NIH
	71:22 I **w** also praise thee with the psaltery,	NIH
	71:22 unto thee **w** I sing with the harp, O thou	NIH
	73:15 If I say, I **w** speak thus; behold, I should	NIH
	75: 2 When I shall receive the congregation I **w**	NIH
	75: 9 I **w** declare for ever; I will sing *praises* to	NIH
	75: 9 I **w** sing *praises* to the God of Jacob.	NIH
	75:10 the horns of the wicked also **w** I cut off;	NIH
	77: 7 **W** the Lord cast off for ever? and will he	NIH
	77: 7 and **w** he be favourable no more?	NIH
	77:10 *I* **w** *remember* the years of the right hand	NIH
	77:11 I **w** remember the works of the LORD:	NIH
	77:11 surely I **w** remember thy wonders of old.	NIH
	77:12 I **w** meditate also of all thy work, and talk	NIH
	78: 2 I **w** open my mouth in a parable: I will	NIH
	78: 2 in a parable: I **w** utter dark sayings of old:	NIH
	78: 4 We **w** not hide *them* from their children,	NIH
	79:13 sheep of thy pasture **w** give thee thanks	NIH
	79:13 we **w** shew forth thy praise to all	NIH
	80:18 **w** not we go *back* from thee: quicken us,	NIH
	80:18 quicken us, and we **w** call upon thy name.	NIH
	81: 8 O my people, and I **w** testify unto thee:	NIH
	81:10 open thy mouth wide, and I **w** fill it.	NIH
	82: 2 How long **w** ye judge unjustly,	NIH
	82: 5 know not, neither **w** they understand;	NIH
	84: 4 they **w** be still praising thee. Selah.	NIH
	84:11 the LORD **w** give grace and glory:	NIH
	84:11 no good *thing* **w** he withhold from them	NIH
	85: 8 I **w** hear what God the LORD will speak:	NIH
	85: 8 I will hear what God the LORD will speak:	NIH
	85: 8 for he **w** speak peace unto his people,	NIH
	86: 7 In the day of my trouble I **w** call upon	NIH
	86:11 thy way, O LORD; I **w** walk in thy truth:	NIH
	86:12 I **w** praise thee, O Lord my God, with all	NIH
	86:12 and I **w** glorify thy name for evermore.	NIH
	87: 4 I **w** make mention of Rahab and Babylon	NIH
	89: 1 I **w** sing of the mercies of the LORD for	NIH
	89: 1 with my mouth **w** I make known thy	NIH
	89: 4 Thy seed **w** I stablish for ever, and build	NIH
	89:23 I **w** beat down his foes before his face,	NIH
	89:25 I **w** set his hand also in the sea, and his	NIH
	89:27 Also I **w** make him *my* firstborn,	NIH
	89:28 My mercy **w** I keep for him for evermore,	NIH
	89:29 His seed also **w** I make *to endure* for ever,	NIH
	89:32 **w** I visit their transgression with the rod,	NIH
	89:33 Nevertheless my lovingkindness **w** I not	NIH
	89:34 My covenant **w** I not break, nor alter	NIH
	89:35 Once have I sworn by my holiness that I **w**	NIH
	91: 2 I **w** say of the LORD, *He is* my refuge and	NIH
	91: 2 and my fortress: my God; in him I trust.	NIH
	91:14 love upon me, therefore **w** I deliver him:	NIH
	91:14 I **w** set him on high, because he hath	NIH
	91:15 shall call upon me, and I **w** answer him:	NIH
	91:15 I **w** be with him in trouble; I will deliver	NIH
	91:15 trouble; I **w** deliver him, and honour him.	NIH
	91:16 *With* long life **w** I satisfy him,	NIH
	92: 4 I **w** triumph in the works of thy hands.	NIH
	94: 8 and ye fools, when **w** ye be wise?	NIH
	94:14 For the LORD **w** not cast off his people,	NIH
	94:14 neither **w** he forsake his inheritance.	NIH

Ps 94:16 **w** rise up for me against the evildoers? NIH
 94:16 **w** stand up for me against the workers NIH
 95: 7 of his hand. To day if ye **w** hear his voice, NIH
 101: 1 **w** sing of mercy and judgment: unto thee, NIH
 101: 1 judgment: unto thee, O LORD, **w** I sing. NIH
 101: 2 I **w** behave myself wisely in a perfect way. NIH
 101: 2 I **w** walk within my house with a perfect NIH
 101: 3 I **w** set no wicked thing before mine eyes: NIH
 101: 4 from me: I **w** not know a wicked *person.* NIH
 101: 5 slandereth his neighbour, him **w** I cut off: NIH
 101: 5 high look and a proud heart **w** not I suffer. NIH
 101: 8 I **w** early destroy all the wicked of the NIH
 102:17 He **w** regard the prayer of the destitute, NIH
 103: 9 He **w** not always chide: neither will he NIH
 103: 9 neither **w** he keep *his anger* for ever. NIH
 104:33 I **w** sing unto the LORD as long as I live: NIH
 104:33 I **w** sing *praise* to my God while I have my NIH
 104:34 shall be sweet: I **w** be glad in the LORD. NIH
 105:11 Unto thee **w** I give the land of Canaan, NIH
 107:43 **w** observe these *things,* even they shall NIH
 108: 1 I **w** sing and give praise, even *with* my NIH
 108: 2 and harp: I *myself* **w** awake early. NIH
 108: 3 I **w** praise thee, O LORD, among NIH
 108: 3 I **w** sing *praises* unto thee among NIH
 108: 7 I **w** rejoice, I will divide Shechem, NIH
 108: 7 I **w** divide Shechem, and mete out the NIH
 108: 9 over Edom **w** I cast out my shoe; NIH
 108: 9 my shoe; over Philistia **w** I triumph. NIH
 108:10 Who **w** bring me *into* the strong city? NIH
 108:10 strong city? who **w** lead me into Edom? NIH
 109:30 I **w** greatly praise the LORD with my NIH
 109:30 yea, I **w** praise him among the multitude. NIH
 110: 4 The LORD hath sworn, and **w** not repent, NIH
 111: 1 I **w** praise the LORD with *my* whole heart, NIH
 111: 5 he **w** ever be mindful of his covenant. NIH
 112: 5 he **w** guide his affairs with discretion. NIH
 115:12 he **w** bless *us;* he will bless the house of NIH
 115:12 he will bless *us;* he **w** bless the house of NIH
 115:12 of Israel; he **w** bless the house of Aaron. NIH
 115:13 He **w** bless them that fear the LORD, *both* NIH
 115:18 we **w** bless the LORD from this time forth NIH
 116: 2 **w** I call upon *him* as long as I live. NIH
 116: 9 I **w** walk before the LORD in the land of NIH
 116:13 I **w** take the cup of salvation, and call NIH
 116:14 I **w** pay my vows unto the LORD now in NIH
 116:17 and **w** call upon the name of the LORD. NIH
 116:17 and **w** call upon the name of the LORD. NIH
 116:18 I **w** pay my vows unto the LORD now in NIH
 118: 6 The LORD *is* on my side; I **w** not fear: NIH
 118:10 in the name of the LORD I **w** destroy NIH
 118:11 in the name of the LORD I **w** destroy NIH
 118:12 for in the name of the LORD I **w** destroy NIH
 118:19 I **w** go into them, *and* I will praise NIH
 118:19 go into them, *and* **w** praise the LORD: NIH
 118:21 I **w** praise thee: for thou hast heard me, NIH
 118:24 hath made; we **w** rejoice and be glad in it. NIH
 118:28 Thou *art* my God, and I **w** praise thee: NIH
 118:28 *thou art* my God, I **w** exalt thee. NIH
 119: 7 I **w** praise thee with uprightness of heart, NIH
 119: 8 I **w** keep thy statutes: O forsake me not NIH
 119:15 I **w** meditate in thy precepts, NIH
 119:16 I **w** delight myself in thy statutes: I will NIH
 119:16 in thy statutes: I **w** not forget thy word. NIH
 119:32 I **w** run the way of thy commandments, NIH
 119:45 I **w** walk at liberty: for I seek thy precepts. NIH
 119:46 I **w** speak of thy testimonies also before NIH
 119:46 also before kings, and **w** not be ashamed. NIH
 119:47 I **w** delight myself in thy commandments, NIH
 119:48 My hands also **w** I lift up unto thy NIH
 119:48 loved; and I **w** meditate in thy statutes. NIH
 119:62 At midnight I **w** rise to give thanks unto NIH
 119:69 I **w** keep thy precepts with *my* whole NIH
 119:74 They that fear thee **w** be glad when they NIH
 119:78 a cause: *but* I **w** meditate in thy precepts. NIH
 119:93 I **w** never forget thy precepts: for with NIH
 119:95 *but* I **w** consider thy testimonies. NIH
 119:106 I **w** perform *it,* that *I* will keep thy NIH
 119:106 perform *it,* that *I* **w** keep thy righteous NIH
 119:115 I **w** keep the commandments of my God. NIH
 119:117 I **w** have respect unto thy statutes NIH
 119:134 of man: so **w** I keep thy precepts. NIH
 119:145 hear me, O LORD: I **w** keep thy statutes. NIH
 121: 1 I **w** lift up mine eyes unto the hills, NIH
 121: 3 He **w** not suffer thy foot to be moved: NIH
 121: 3 he that keepeth thee **w** not slumber. NIH
 122: 8 and companions' sakes, I **w** now say, NIH
 122: 9 of the LORD our God I **w** seek thy good. NIH
 132: 3 Surely I **w** not come into the tabernacle of NIH
 132: 4 I **w** not give sleep to mine eyes, NIH
 132: 7 We **w** go into his tabernacles: we will NIH
 132: 7 we **w** worship at his footstool. NIH
 132:11 truth unto David; he **w** not turn from it; NIH
 132:11 Of the fruit of thy body **w** I set upon thy NIH
 132:12 If thy children **w** keep my covenant and NIH
 132:14 here **w** I dwell; for I have desired it. NIH
 132:15 I **w** abundantly bless her provision: I will NIH
 132:15 I **w** satisfy her poor *with* bread. NIH
 132:16 I **w** also clothe her priests with salvation: NIH
 132:17 There **w** I make the horn of David to bud: NIH
 132:18 His enemies **w** I clothe with shame: NIH
 135:14 For the LORD **w** judge his people, NIH
 135:14 he **w** repent himself concerning his NIH
 138: 1 I **w** praise thee with my whole heart: NIH
 138: 1 before the gods **w** I sing *praise* unto thee. NIH
 138: 2 I **w** worship toward thy holy temple, NIH

Ps 138: 8 The LORD **w** perfect that which NIH
 139:14 I **w** praise thee; for I am fearfully and NIH
 140:12 I know that the LORD **w** maintain NIH
 143:10 Teach me to do thy **w**; for thou *art* my 7522
 144: 9 I **w** sing a new song unto thee, O God: NIH
 144: 9 an instrument of ten strings **w** I sing NIH
 145: 1 I **w** extol thee, my God, O king; and I will NIH
 145: 1 and I **w** bless thy name for ever and ever. NIH
 145: 2 Every day **w** I bless thee; and I will praise NIH
 145: 2 and I **w** praise thy name for ever and ever. NIH
 145: 5 I **w** speak of the glorious honour of thy NIH
 145: 6 terrible acts: and I **w** declare thy greatness. NIH
 145:19 He **w** fulfil the desire of them that fear NIH
 145:19 he also **w** hear their cry, and will save NIH
 145:19 also will hear their cry, and **w** save them. NIH
 145:20 him: but all the wicked **w** he destroy. NIH
 146: 2 While I live **w** I praise the LORD: I will NIH
 146: 2 I **w** sing *praises* unto my God while I have NIH
 149: 4 he **w** beautify the meek with salvation. NIH

Pr 1: 5 A wise *man* **w** hear, and will increase NIH
 1: 5 *man* will hear, and **w** increase learning; NIH
 1:22 ye simple ones, **w** ye love simplicity? NIH
 1:23 behold, I **w** pour out my spirit unto you, NIH
 1:23 I **w** make known my words unto you. NIH
 1:26 I also **w** laugh at your calamity; I will NIH
 1:26 I **w** mock when your fear cometh; NIH
 1:28 they call upon me, but I **w** not answer; NIH
 3:28 and come again, and to morrow I **w** give; NIH
 6:26 the adulteress **w** hunt for the precious life. NIH
 6:34 he **w** not spare in the day of vengeance. NIH
 6:35 He **w** not regard any ransom; neither will NIH
 6:35 neither **w** he rest content, though thou NIH
 7:20 w come home at the day appointed. NIH
 8: 6 Hear, for I **w** speak of excellent things; NIH
 8:21 and I **w** fill their treasures. NIH
 9: 8 rebuke a wise *man,* and he **w** love thee. NIH
 9: 9 to a wise *man,* and he **w** be yet wiser: NIH
 9: 9 a just *man,* and he **w** increase in learning. NIH
 10: 3 The LORD **w** not suffer the soul of NIH
 10: 8 The wise in heart **w** receive NIH
 12: 2 a man of wicked devices **w** he condemn. NIH
 14: 5 A faithful witness **w** not lie: but a false NIH
 14: 5 not lie: but a false witness **w** utter lies. NIH
 15:12 neither **w** he go unto the wise. NIH
 15:25 The LORD **w** destroy the house of NIH
 15:25 he **w** establish the border of the widow. NIH
 16:14 of death: but a wise man **w** pacify it. NIH
 18:14 spirit of a man **w** sustain his infirmity; NIH
 19: 6 Many **w** intreat the favour of the prince: NIH
 19:17 that which he hath given **w** he pay him NIH
 19:24 so much as bring it to his mouth NIH
 19:25 Smite a scorner, and the simple **w** beware: NIH
 19:25 *and* he **w** understand knowledge. NIH
 20: 3 from strife: but every fool **w** be meddling. NIH
 20: 4 The sluggard **w** not plow by reason of NIH
 20: 5 a man of understanding **w** draw it out. NIH
 20: 6 Most men **w** proclaim every one his own NIH
 20:22 Say not thou, I **w** recompense evil; NIH
 21: 1 he turneth it whithersoever he **w.** 2654
 22: 6 when he is old, he **w** not depart from it. NIH
 22:23 For the LORD **w** plead their cause, NIH
 23: 9 he **w** despise the wisdom of thy words. NIH
 23:35 when shall I awake? I **w** seek it yet again. NIH
 24:29 I **w** do so to him as he hath done to me: NIH
 24:29 I **w** render to the man according to his NIH
 26:27 that rolleth a stone, it **w** return upon him. NIH
 27:22 *yet* **w** not his foolishness depart from him. NIH
 28: 8 he shall gather it for him that **w** pity NIH
 28:21 for for a piece of bread *that* man **w** NIH
 29:19 A servant **w** not be corrected by words: NIH
 29:19 though he understand he **w** not answer. NIH
 31:12 She **w** do him good and not evil all the NIH

Ec 2: 1 I **w** prove thee with mirth, therefore NIH
 4:10 if they fall, the one **w** lift up his fellow: NIH
 4:13 who **w** no more be admonished. 3045
 5:12 the abundance of the rich **w** not suffer NIH
 7: 2 men; and the living **w** lay *it* to his heart. NIH
 7:23 said, I **w** be wise; but it *was* far from me. NIH
 10:11 Surely the serpent **w** bite without NIH
 10:12 the lips of a fool **w** swallow up himself. NIH
 11: 9 that for all these *things* God **w** bring thee NIH

SS 1: 4 Draw me, we **w** run after thee: the king NIH
 1: 4 we **w** be glad and rejoice in thee, we will NIH
 1: 4 we **w** remember thy love more than wine: NIH
 1:11 We **w** make thee borders of gold with NIH
 3: 2 I **w** rise now, and go about the city in NIH
 3: 2 I **w** seek *him* whom my soul loveth: NIH
 4: 6 I **w** get me to the mountain of myrrh, NIH
 6:13 What **w** ye see in the Shulamite? NIH
 7: 8 I said, I **w** go up to the palm tree, I will NIH
 7: 8 I **w** take hold of the boughs thereof: NIH
 7:12 bud forth: there **w** I give thee my loves. NIH
 8: 9 we **w** build upon her a palace of silver: NIH
 8: 9 we **w** inclose her with boards of cedar. NIH

Isa 1: 5 ye **w** revolt more and more: the whole NIH
 1:15 your hands, I **w** hide mine eyes from you: NIH
 1:15 ye make many prayers, I **w** not hear: NIH
 1:24 I **w** ease me of mine adversaries, NIH
 1:25 I **w** turn my hand upon thee, and purely NIH
 1:26 I **w** restore thy judges as at the first, NIH
 2: 3 he **w** teach us of his ways, and we will NIH
 2: 3 his ways, and we **w** walk in his paths: NIH
 3: 4 I **w** give children *to be* their princes, NIH
 3: 7 shall he swear, saying, I **w** not be a healer; NIH
 3:14 The LORD **w** enter into judgment with NIH

Isa 3:17 Therefore the Lord **w** smite with a scab NIH
 3:17 the LORD **w** discover their secret parts. NIH
 3:18 In that day the Lord **w** take away NIH
 4: 1 We **w** eat our own bread, and wear our NIH
 4: 5 the LORD **w** create upon every dwelling NIH
 5: 1 Now **w** I sing to my wellbeloved a song of NIH
 5: 5 I **w** tell you what I *will* do to my vineyard: NIH
 5: 5 I will tell you what I ***w*** do to my vineyard: NIH
 5: 5 I ***w*** take away the hedge thereof, and it NIH
 5: 6 I **w** lay it waste: it shall not be pruned, NIH
 5: 6 I **w** also command the clouds that they NIH
 5:26 he **w** lift up an ensign to the nations from NIH
 5:26 **w** hiss unto them from the end of the NIH
 6: 8 Whom shall I send, and who **w** go for us? NIH
 7: 9 If ye **w** not believe, surely ye shall not be NIH
 7:12 Ahaz said, I **w** not ask, neither will I tempt NIH
 7:12 I will not ask, neither **w** I tempt the LORD. NIH
 7:13 weary men, but **w** ye weary my God also? NIH
 8:17 I **w** wait upon the LORD, that hideth his NIH
 8:17 the house of Jacob, and I **w** look for him. NIH
 9: 7 The zeal of the LORD of hosts **w** perform NIH
 9:10 but we **w** build *with* hewn stones; NIH
 9:10 but we **w** change *them into* cedars. NIH
 9:14 Therefore the LORD **w** cut off from Israel NIH
 10: 3 what **w** ye do in the day of visitation, NIH
 10: 3 to whom **w** ye flee for help? and where NIH
 10: 3 and where **w** ye leave your glory? NIH
 10: 6 I **w** send him against a hypocritical nation, NIH
 10: 6 against the people of my wrath **w** I give NIH
 10:12 I **w** punish the fruit of the stout heart of NIH
 12: 1 thou shalt say, O LORD, I **w** praise thee: NIH
 12: 2 my salvation; I **w** trust, and not be afraid: NIH
 13:11 I **w** punish the world for *their* evil, NIH
 13:11 I **w** cause the arrogancy of the proud to NIH
 13:11 I **w** lay low the haughtiness of the terrible. NIH
 13:12 I **w** make a man more precious than fine NIH
 13:13 Therefore I **w** shake the heavens, NIH
 13:17 I **w** stir up the Medes against them, NIH
 14: 1 For the LORD **w** have mercy on Jacob, NIH
 14: 1 **w** yet choose Israel, and set them in their NIH
 14:13 in thine heart, I **w** ascend *into* heaven, NIH
 14:13 I **w** exalt my throne above the stars of NIH
 14:13 I **w** sit also upon the mount of NIH
 14:14 I **w** ascend above the heights of the NIH
 14:14 of the clouds; I **w** be like the most High. NIH
 14:22 For I **w** rise up against them, saith NIH
 14:23 I **w** also make it a possession for the NIH
 14:23 I **w** sweep it with the besom of NIH
 14:25 That I **w** break the Assyrian in my land, NIH
 14:30 I **w** kill thy root with famine, and he shall NIH
 15: 9 for I **w** bring more upon Dimon, lions NIH
 16: 9 Therefore I **w** bewail with the weeping of NIH
 16: 9 I **w** water thee *with* my tears, O Heshbon, NIH
 18: 4 I **w** take my rest, and I will consider in my NIH
 18: 4 I **w** consider in my dwelling place like a NIH
 19: 2 I **w** set the Egyptians against the NIH
 19: 3 and I **w** destroy the counsel thereof: NIH
 19: 4 the Egyptians **w** I give over into the hand NIH
 21:12 if ye **w** inquire, inquire ye: return, come. NIH
 22: 4 I **w** weep bitterly, labour not to comfort NIH
 22:17 the LORD **w** carry thee away with a NIH
 22:17 mighty captivity, and **w** surely cover thee. NIH
 22:18 He **w** surely violently turn and toss thee NIH
 22:19 I **w** drive thee from thy station, NIH
 22:20 that I **w** call my servant Eliakim the son of NIH
 22:21 I **w** clothe him with thy robe, NIH
 22:21 I **w** commit thy government into his hand: NIH
 22:22 key of the house of David **w** I lay upon NIH
 22:23 I **w** fasten him *as* a nail in a sure place; NIH
 23:17 *that* the LORD **w** visit Tyre, and she shall NIH
 25: 1 I **w** exalt thee, I will praise thy name; NIH
 25: 1 I will exalt thee, I **w** praise thy name; NIH
 25: 7 he **w** destroy in this mountain the face of NIH
 25: 8 He **w** swallow up death in victory; NIH
 25: 8 the Lord GOD **w** wipe away tears from off NIH
 25: 9 have waited for him, and he **w** save us: NIH
 25: 9 we **w** be glad and rejoice in his salvation. NIH
 26: 1 salvation **w** God appoint *for* walls and NIH
 26: 9 *with* my spirit within me **w** I seek thee NIH
 26: 9 the inhabitants of the world **w** learn NIH
 26:10 *yet* **w** he not learn righteousness: NIH
 26:10 in the land of uprightness **w** he deal NIH
 26:10 **w** not behold the majesty of the LORD. NIH
 26:11 thy hand is lifted up, they **w** not see: NIH
 26:13 by thee only **w** we make mention of thy NIH
 27: 3 do keep it; I **w** water it every moment: NIH
 27: 3 lest *any* hurt it, I **w** keep it night and day. NIH
 27:11 he that made them **w** not have mercy on NIH
 27:11 he that formed them **w** shew them no NIH
 28:11 another tongue **w** he speak to this people. NIH
 28:17 Judgment also **w** I lay to the line, NIH
 28:28 because he **w** not ever be threshing it, NIH
 29: 2 Yet I **w** distress Ariel, and there shall be NIH
 29: 3 And I **w** camp against thee round about, NIH
 29: 3 **w** lay siege against thee *with* a mount, NIH
 29: 3 a mount, and I **w** raise forts against thee. NIH
 29:14 I **w** proceed to do a marvellous work NIH
 30: 6 **w** carry their riches upon the shoulders NIH
 30: 9 children *that* **w** not hear the law of 14
 30:16 ye said, No; for we **w** flee upon horses; NIH
 30:16 and, We **w** ride upon the swift; therefore NIH
 30:18 therefore **w** the LORD wait, that he may NIH
 30:18 unto you, and therefore **w** he be exalted, NIH
 30:19 he **w** be very gracious unto thee at the NIH
 30:19 when *he* shall hear it, he **w** answer thee. NIH

Isa 30:32 in battles of shaking w he fight with it. — NIH
31: 2 w bring evil, and will not call back his — NIH
31: 2 bring evil, and w not call back his words: — NIH
31: 2 w arise against the house of the evildoers, — NIH
31: 4 he w not be afraid of their voice, nor — NIH
31: 5 so the LORD of hosts defend Jerusalem; — NIH
31: 5 defending also he w deliver *it;* and — NIH
31: 5 and passing over he w preserve *it.* — NIH
32: 6 For the vile person w speak villany, — NIH
32: 6 his heart w work iniquity, to practise — NIH
32: 6 he w cause the drink of the thirsty to fail. — NIH
33:10 Now w I rise, saith the LORD; now will I — NIH
33:10 I rise, saith the LORD; now w I be exalted; — NIH
33:10 will I be exalted; now w I lift up myself. — NIH
33:21 there the glorious LORD *w be* unto us a — NIH
33:22 the LORD *is* our king; he w save us. — NIH
35: 4 your God w come *with* vengeance, — NIH
35: 4 a recompence; he w come and save you. — NIH
36: 6 w go into his hand, and pierce it: — NIH
36: 8 and I w give thee two thousand horses, — NIH
36:15 The LORD w surely deliver us. — NIH
36:18 saying, The LORD w deliver us. — NIH
37: 4 It may be the LORD thy God w hear — NIH
37: 4 w reprove the words which the LORD thy — NIH
37: 7 I w send a blast upon him, and he shall — NIH
37: 7 I w cause him to fall by the sword in his — NIH
37:24 and I w cut down the tall cedars thereof, — NIH
37:24 I w enter *into* the height of his border, — NIH
37:29 therefore w I put my hook in thy nose, — NIH
37:29 I w turn thee back by the way by which — NIH
37:35 w defend this city to save it for mine — NIH
38: 5 I w add unto thy days fifteen years. — NIH
38: 6 I w deliver thee and this city out of the — NIH
38: 6 king of Assyria: and I w defend this city. — NIH
38: 7 that the LORD w do this thing that he hath — NIH
38: 8 I w bring again the shadow of the degrees, — NIH
38:12 he w cut me off with pining sickness: — NIH
38:13 *that,* as a lion, so w he break all my bones: — NIH
38:20 we w sing my songs *to* the stringed — NIH
40:10 the Lord GOD w come with strong *hand,* — NIH
40:18 To whom then w ye liken God? — NIH
40:18 or what likeness w ye compare unto him? — NIH
40:20 no oblation chooseth a tree *that* w not rot; — NIH
40:25 To whom then w ye liken me, or shall I — NIH
41:10 I w strengthen thee; yea, I will help thee; — NIH
41:10 yea, I w help thee; yea, I will uphold thee — NIH
41:10 I w uphold thee with the right hand of my — NIH
41:13 For I the LORD thy God w hold thy right — NIH
41:13 saying unto thee, Fear not; I w help thee. — NIH
41:14 I w help thee, saith the LORD, — NIH
41:15 I w make thee a new sharp threshing — NIH
41:17 faileth for thirst, I the LORD w hear them, — NIH
41:17 *I* the God of Israel w not forsake them. — NIH
41:18 I w open rivers in high places, — NIH
41:18 I w make the wilderness a pool of water, — NIH
41:19 I w plant in the wilderness the cedar, — NIH
41:19 I w set in the desert the fir tree, — NIH
41:27 I w give to Jerusalem one that bringeth — NIH
42: 6 w hold thine hand, and will keep thee, — NIH
42: 6 w keep thee, and give thee for a covenant — NIH
42: 8 my glory w I not give to another, neither — NIH
42:14 *now* w I cry like a travailing woman; I will — NIH
42:14 I w destroy and devour at once. — NIH
42:15 I w make waste mountains and hills, — NIH
42:15 I w make the rivers islands, and I will dry — NIH
42:15 rivers islands, and I w dry up the pools. — NIH
42:16 I w bring the blind by a way *that* they — NIH
42:16 I w lead them in paths *that* they have not — NIH
42:16 I w make darkness light before them, — NIH
42:16 These things w I do unto them, — NIH
42:21 he w magnify the law, and make *it* — NIH
42:23 Who among you w give ear to this? — NIH
42:23 *who* w hearken and hear for the time to — NIH
43: 2 through the waters, I *w be* with thee; — NIH
43: 4 therefore w I give men for thee, — NIH
43: 5 I w bring thy seed from the east, — NIH
43: 6 I w say to the north, Give *up;* and to — NIH
43:13 my hand: I w work, and who shall let it? — NIH
43:19 I w do a new *thing;* now it shall spring — NIH
43:19 I w even make a way in the wilderness, — NIH
43:25 own sake, and w not remember thy sins. — NIH
44: 2 thee from the womb, *which* w help thee; — NIH
44: 3 I w pour water upon *him that is* thirsty, — NIH
44: 3 floods upon the dry *ground:* I w pour my — NIH
44:15 for he w take thereof, and warm himself; — NIH
44:26 I w raise up the decayed places thereof: — NIH
44:27 deep, Be dry, and I w dry up thy rivers: — NIH
45: 1 I w loose the loins of kings, to open before — NIH
45: 2 I w go before thee, and make the crooked — NIH
45: 2 I w break in pieces the gates of brass, — NIH
45: 3 I w give thee the treasures of darkness, — NIH
45:13 righteousness, and I w direct all his ways: — NIH
46: 4 *even* to hoar hairs w I carry *you:* I have — NIH
46: 4 I carry *you:* I have made, and I w bear; — NIH
46: 4 even I w carry, and will deliver *you.* — NIH
46: 4 even I will carry, and w deliver *you.* — NIH
46: 5 To whom w ye liken me, and make *me* — NIH
46:10 shall stand, and I w do all my pleasure: — NIH
46:11 I have spoken *it,* I w also bring it to pass; — NIH
46:11 to pass; I have purposed *it,* I w also do it. — NIH
46:13 I w place salvation in Zion for Israel my — NIH
47: 3 I w take vengeance, and I will not meet — NIH
47: 3 and I w not meet *thee as* a man. — NIH
48: 6 w not ye declare *it?* I have shewed thee — NIH
48: 9 For my name's sake w I defer mine anger, — NIH

Isa 48: 9 *for* my praise w I refrain for thee, that *I* cut — NIH
48:11 w I do *it:* for how should *my name* be — NIH
48:11 and I w not give my glory unto another. — NIH
48:14 he w do his pleasure on Babylon, — NIH
49: 3 O Israel, in whom I w be glorified. — NIH
49: 6 I w also give thee for a light to the — NIH
49: 8 I w preserve thee, and give thee for a — NIH
49:11 I w make all my mountains a way, — NIH
49:13 and w have mercy upon his afflicted. — NIH
49:15 they may forget, yet w I not forget thee. — NIH
49:22 I w lift up mine hand to the Gentiles, — NIH
49:25 for I w contend with him that contendeth — NIH
49:25 with thee, and I w save thy children. — NIH
49:26 I w feed them that oppress thee with their — NIH
50: 7 For the Lord GOD w help me; therefore — NIH
50: 8 justifieth me; who w contend with me? — NIH
50: 9 Behold, the Lord GOD w help me; who *is* — NIH
51: 3 he w comfort all her waste places; — NIH
51: 3 he w make her wilderness like Eden, — NIH
51: 4 I w make my judgment to rest for a light — NIH
51:23 I w put it into the hand of them that afflict — NIH
52:12 for the LORD w go before you; — NIH
52:12 and the God of Israel *w be* your rereward. — NIH
53:12 Therefore w I divide him *a portion* with — NIH
54: 7 but with great mercies w I gather thee. — NIH
54: 8 with everlasting kindness w I have mercy — NIH
54:11 I w lay thy stones with fair colours, — NIH
54:12 I w make thy windows *of* agates, — NIH
55: 3 I w make an everlasting covenant with — NIH
55: 7 and he w have mercy upon him; — NIH
55: 7 to our God, for he w abundantly pardon. — NIH
56: 5 Even unto them w I give in mine house — NIH
56: 5 I w give them an everlasting name, — NIH
56: 7 them w I bring to my holy mountain, — NIH
56: 8 Yet w I gather *others* to him, besides — NIH
56:12 *say they,* I w fetch wine, and we will fill — NIH
56:12 and we w fill ourselves with strong drink; — NIH
57:12 I w declare thy righteousness, and thy — NIH
57:16 For I w not contend for ever, neither will — NIH
57:16 for ever, neither w I be always wroth: — NIH
57:18 I have seen his ways, and w heal him: — NIH
57:18 I w lead him also, and restore comforts — NIH
57:19 *is* near, saith the LORD; and I w heal him. — NIH
58:14 w I cause thee to ride upon the high — NIH
59: 2 hid *his* face from you, that he w not hear. — NIH
59:18 accordingly he w repay, fury to his — NIH
59:18 to the islands he w repay recompence. — NIH
60: 7 and I w glorify the house of my glory. — NIH
60:12 that w not serve thee shall perish; — NIH
60:13 I w make the place of my feet glorious. — NIH
60:15 that no man went through *thee,* I w make — NIH
60:17 brass I w bring gold, and for iron I will — NIH
60:17 iron I w bring silver, and for wood brass, — NIH
60:17 I w also make thy officers peace, — NIH
60:22 I the LORD w hasten it in his time. — NIH
61: 8 I w direct their work in truth, and I will — NIH
61: 8 I w make an everlasting covenant with — NIH
61:10 I w greatly rejoice in the LORD, my soul — NIH
61:11 so the Lord GOD w cause righteousness — NIH
62: 1 For Zion's sake w I not hold my peace, — NIH
62: 1 and for Jerusalem's sake I w not rest, — NIH
62: 8 I w no more give thy corn *to be* meat — NIH
63: 3 for I w tread down in mine anger, — NIH
63: 3 garments, and I w stain all my raiment. — NIH
63: 6 I w tread down the people in mine anger, — NIH
63: 6 I w bring down their strength to the earth. — NIH
63: 7 I w mention the lovingkindnesses of — NIH
63: 8 *are* my people, children *that* w not lie: — NIH
65: 6 I w not keep silence, but will recompense, — NIH
65: 6 I will not keep silence, but w recompense, — NIH
65: 7 w I measure their former work into their — NIH
65: 8 so w I do for my servants' sakes, that *I* — NIH
65: 9 And I w bring forth a seed out of Jacob, — NIH
65:12 Therefore w I number you to the sword, — NIH
65:19 w rejoice in Jerusalem, and joy in my — NIH
65:24 to pass, that before they call, I w answer; — NIH
65:24 whiles they are yet speaking, I w hear. — NIH
66: 2 to this *man* w I look, *even to him that is* — NIH
66: 4 I also w choose their delusions, — NIH
66: 4 and w bring their fears upon them; — NIH
66:12 I w extend peace to her like a river, — NIH
66:13 mother comforteth, so w I comfort you; — NIH
66:15 the LORD w come with fire, and with his — NIH
66:16 by his sword w the LORD plead with all — NIH
66:18 that *I* w gather all nations and tongues; — NIH
66:19 I w set a sign among them, and I will — NIH
66:19 I w send those that escape of them unto — NIH
66:21 I w also take of them for priests *and* — NIH
66:22 and the new earth, which I w make, — NIH
Jer 1:12 for I w hasten my word to perform it. — NIH
1:15 I w call all the families of the kingdoms of — NIH
1:16 I w utter my judgments against them — NIH
2: 9 Wherefore I w yet plead with you, saith — NIH
2: 9 with your children's children w I plead. — NIH
2:20 and thou saidst, I w not transgress; — NIH
2:24 all they that seek her w not weary — NIH
2:25 loved strangers, and after them w I go. — NIH
2:27 in the time of their trouble they w say, — NIH
2:29 Wherefore w ye plead with me? ye all — NIH
2:31 are lords; we w come no more unto thee? — NIH
2:35 Behold, I *w* plead with thee, because — NIH
3: 5 W he reserve *his* anger for ever? will he — NIH
3: 5 w he keep *it* to the end? Behold, thou hast — NIH
3:12 I w not cause mine anger to fall upon you: — NIH
3:12 *and* I w not keep *anger* for ever. — NIH

Jer 3:14 I w take you one of a city, and two of a — NIH
3:14 two of a family, and I w bring you *to* Zion: — NIH
3:15 I w give you pastors according to mine — NIH
3:22 *and* I w heal your backslidings. — NIH
4: 6 I w bring evil from the north, and a great — NIH
4:12 now also w I give sentence against them. — NIH
4:27 be desolate; yet w I not make a full end. — NIH
4:28 *it,* I have purposed *it,* and w not repent, — NIH
4:28 not repent, neither w I turn back from it. — NIH
4:30 *thy* lovers w despise thee, they will seek — NIH
4:30 will despise thee, they w seek thy life. — NIH
5: 1 that seeketh the truth; and I w pardon it. — NIH
5: 5 I w get me unto the great men, — NIH
5: 5 the great men, and w speak unto them; — NIH
5:14 I w make my words in thy mouth fire, — NIH
5:15 Lo, I w bring a nation upon you from far, — NIH
5:18 I w not make a full end with you. — NIH
5:22 w ye not tremble at my presence, — NIH
5:31 and what w ye do in the end thereof? — NIH
6:11 *w* pour *it* out upon the children abroad, — NIH
6:12 for I w stretch out my hand upon — NIH
6:16 But they said, We w not walk *therein.* — NIH
6:17 But they said, We w not hearken. — NIH
6:19 behold, I w bring evil upon this people, — NIH
6:21 I w lay stumblingblocks before this people, — NIH
7: 3 and I w cause you to dwell in this place. — NIH
7: 7 w I cause you to dwell in this place, — NIH
7: 9 W ye steal, murder, and commit adultery, — NIH
7:14 Therefore w I do unto *this* house, which — NIH
7:15 w cast you out of my sight, as I have cast — NIH
7:16 intercession to me: for I *w* not hear thee. — NIH
7:23 I w be your God, and ye shall be my — NIH
7:27 them; but they w not hearken to thee: — NIH
7:27 unto them; but they w not answer thee. — NIH
7:34 w I cause to cease from the cities of Judah, — NIH
8:10 Therefore w I give their wives unto others, — NIH
8:13 I w surely consume them, saith the LORD: — NIH
8:17 For behold, I w send serpents, cockatrices, — NIH
8:17 *w* not be charmed, and they shall bite — NIH
9: 4 for every brother w utterly supplant, — NIH
9: 4 every neighbour w walk *with* slanders. — NIH
9: 5 they w deceive every one his neighbour, — NIH
9: 5 his neighbour, and w not speak the truth: — NIH
9: 7 Behold, I w melt them, and try them; — NIH
9:10 For the mountains w I take up a weeping — NIH
9:11 w make Jerusalem heaps, *and* a den of — NIH
9:11 w make the cities of Judah desolate, — NIH
9:15 Behold, I *w* feed them, *even* this people, — NIH
9:16 I w scatter them also among the heathen, — NIH
9:16 I w send a sword after them, till I have — NIH
9:25 that I w punish all *them* which are — NIH
10:18 I w sling out the inhabitants of the land at — NIH
10:18 w distress them, that they may find *it so.* — NIH
11: 4 ye be my people, and I w be your God: — NIH
11: 8 I w bring upon them all the words of this — NIH
11:11 Behold, I *w* bring evil upon them, — NIH
11:11 cry unto me, I w not hearken unto them. — NIH
11:14 w not hear *them* in the time that they — NIH
11:22 LORD of hosts, Behold, I w punish them: — NIH
11:23 for I w bring evil upon the men of — NIH
12:14 I w pluck them out of their land, — NIH
12:15 I w return, and have compassion on them, — NIH
12:15 w bring them again, every man to his — NIH
12:16 if they w diligently learn the ways of my — NIH
12:17 if they w not obey, I will utterly pluck up — NIH
12:17 I w utterly pluck up and destroy that — NIH
13: 9 After this manner w I mar the pride of — NIH
13:13 I *w* fill all the inhabitants of this land, — NIH
13:14 I w dash them one against another, even — NIH
13:14 I w not pity, nor spare, nor have mercy, — NIH
13:17 if ye w not hear it, my soul shall weep in — NIH
13:24 Therefore w I scatter them as the stubble — NIH
13:26 Therefore w I discover thy skirts upon thy — NIH
14:10 he w now remember their iniquity, — NIH
14:12 When they fast, I w not hear their cry; — NIH
14:12 and an oblation, I w not accept them: — NIH
14:12 w consume them by the sword, and by — NIH
14:13 I w give you assured peace in this place. — NIH
14:16 for I w pour their wickedness upon them. — NIH
14:22 therefore we w wait upon thee: for thou — NIH
15: 1 w appoint over them four kinds, saith — NIH
15: 4 I w cause them to be removed into all — NIH
15: 6 w I stretch out my hand against thee, — NIH
15: 7 I w fan them with a fan in the gates of — NIH
15: 7 I w bereave *them* of children, I will — NIH
15: 7 *them* of children, I w destroy my people, — NIH
15: 9 residue of them w I deliver to the sword — NIH
15:11 verily I w cause the enemy to entreat thee — NIH
15:13 thy treasures w I give to the spoil without — NIH
15:14 I w make *thee* to pass with thine enemies — NIH
15:19 w I bring thee again, *and* thou shalt stand — NIH
15:20 I w make thee unto this people a fenced — NIH
15:21 I w deliver thee out of the hand of — NIH
15:21 I w redeem thee out of the hand of — NIH
16: 9 I w cause to cease out of this place in your — NIH
16:13 Therefore w I cast you out of this land into — NIH
16:13 and night; where I w not shew you favour. — NIH
16:15 I w bring them again into their land that I — NIH
16:16 Behold, I w send for many fishers, saith — NIH
16:16 after w I send for many hunters, — NIH
16:18 first I w recompense their iniquity and — NIH
16:21 I *w* this once cause them to know, — NIH
16:21 I w cause them to know mine hand — NIH
17: 3 I w give thy substance *and* all thy — NIH
17: 4 I w cause thee to serve thine enemies in — NIH

Jer 17:27 if you **w** not hearken unto me to hallow	NIH	
17:27 **w** I kindle a fire in the gates thereof,	NIH	
18: 2 there I **w** cause thee to hear my words.	NIH	
18: 8 I **w** repent of the evil that I thought to do	NIH	
18:10 not my voice, then I **w** repent of the good,	NIH	
18:12 we **w** walk after our own devices,	NIH	
18:12 we **w** every one do the imagination of his	NIH	
18:14 **W** *a* man leave the snow of Lebanon	NIH	
18:17 I **w** scatter them as *with* an east wind	NIH	
18:17 I **w** shew them the back, and not the face,	NIH	
19: 3 Behold, I **w** bring evil upon this place,	NIH	
19: 7 I **w** make void the counsel of Judah and	NIH	
19: 7 I **w** cause them to fall by the sword before	NIH	
19: 7 their carcases **w** I give to be meat for	NIH	
19: 8 I **w** make this city desolate, and a hissing;	NIH	
19: 9 I **w** cause them to eat the flesh of their	NIH	
19:11 so **w** I break this people and this city,	NIH	
19:12 Thus **w** I do unto this place, saith	NIH	
19:15 I **w** bring upon this city and upon all her	NIH	
20: 4 I **w** make thee a terror to thyself, and to	NIH	
20: 4 I **w** give all Judah into the hand of the king	NIH	
20: 5 Moreover I **w** deliver all the strength of	NIH	
20: 5 all the treasures of the kings of Judah **w** I	NIH	
20: 9 I said, I **w** not make mention of him,	NIH	
20:10 Report, *say they,* and we **w** report it.	NIH	
20:10 *saying,* Peradventure he **w** be enticed,	NIH	
21: 2 be that the Lᴏʀᴅ **w** deal with us	NIH	
21: 4 I **w** turn back the weapons of war that *are*	NIH	
21: 4 I **w** assemble them into the midst of this	NIH	
21: 5 I myself **w** fight against you with an	NIH	
21: 6 I **w** smite the inhabitants of this city, both	NIH	
21: 7 I **w** deliver Zedekiah king of Judah, and	NIH	
21:14 I **w** punish you according to the fruit of	NIH	
21:14 I **w** kindle a fire in the forest thereof,	NIH	
22: 5 if ye **w** not hear these words, I swear by	NIH	
22: 6 *yet* surely I **w** make thee a wilderness *and*	NIH	
22: 7 I **w** prepare destroyers against thee,	NIH	
22:14 I **w** build me a wide house and	NIH	
22:21 prosperity; *but* thou saidst, I **w** not hear.	NIH	
22:25 I **w** give thee into the hand of them that	NIH	
22:26 I **w** cast thee out, and thy mother that bare	NIH	
23: 2 I **w** visit upon you the evil of your doings,	NIH	
23: 3 I **w** gather the remnant of my flock out of	NIH	
23: 3 and **w** bring them again to their folds;	NIH	
23: 4 I **w** set up shepherds over them which	NIH	
23: 5 that I **w** raise unto David a righteous	NIH	
23:12 I **w** bring evil upon them, *even* the year	NIH	
23:15 I **w** feed them with wormwood,	NIH	
23:33 I **w** even forsake you, saith the Lᴏʀᴅ.	NIH	
23:34 I **w** even punish that man and his house.	NIH	
23:39 **w** utterly forget you, and I will forsake you,	NIH	
23:39 I **w** forsake you, and the city that I gave	NIH	
23:40 I **w** bring an everlasting reproach upon	NIH	
24: 5 **w** I acknowledge them that are carried	NIH	
24: 6 For I **w** set mine eyes upon them for good,	NIH	
24: 6 and I **w** bring them again to this land:	NIH	
24: 6 I **w** build them, and not pull *them* down;	NIH	
24: 6 I **w** plant them, and not pluck *them* up.	NIH	
24: 7 I **w** give them a heart to know me, that	NIH	
24: 7 shall be my people, and I **w** be their God:	NIH	
24: 8 So **w** I give Zedekiah the king of Judah,	NIH	
24: 9 I **w** deliver them to be removed into all	NIH	
24:10 I **w** send the sword, the famine,	NIH	
25: 6 of your hands; and I **w** do you no hurt.	NIH	
25: 9 I **w** send and take all the families of	NIH	
25: 9 I **w** bring them against this land,	NIH	
25: 9 **w** utterly destroy them, and make them an	NIH	
25:10 Moreover I **w** take from them the voice of	NIH	
25:12 *that* I **w** punish the king of Babylon,	NIH	
25:12 and **w** make it perpetual desolations.	NIH	
25:13 I **w** bring upon that land all my words	NIH	
25:14 I **w** recompense them according to their	NIH	
25:16 of the sword that I **w** send among them.	NIH	
25:27 of the sword which I **w** send among you.	NIH	
25:29 for I **w** call for a sword upon all	NIH	
25:31 with the nations, he **w** plead with all flesh;	NIH	
25:31 he **w** give them *that are* wicked to	NIH	
26: 3 If so be they **w** hearken, and turn every	NIH	
26: 4 If ye **w** not hearken to me, to walk in my	NIH	
26: 6 I **w** make this house like Shiloh, and will	NIH	
26: 6 **w** make this city a curse to all the nations	NIH	
26:13 the Lᴏʀᴅ **w** repent him of the evil that he	NIH	
27: 8 kingdom which **w** not serve the same	NIH	
27: 8 that **w** not put their neck under the yoke	NIH	
27: 8 that nation **w** I punish, saith the Lᴏʀᴅ,	NIH	
27:11 those **w** I remain still in their own land,	NIH	
27:13 Why **w** ye die, thou and thy people,	NIH	
27:13 that **w** not serve the king of Babylon?	NIH	
27:22 **w** I bring them up, and restore them to	NIH	
28: 3 Within two full years **w** I bring again into	NIH	
28: 4 I **w** bring again to this place Jeconiah	NIH	
28: 4 for I **w** break the yoke of the king of	NIH	
28:11 I **w** break the yoke of Nebuchadnezzar	NIH	
28:16 I **w** cast thee from off the face of the earth:	NIH	
29:10 be accomplished at Babylon I **w** visit you,	NIH	
29:12 pray unto me, and I **w** hearken unto you.	NIH	
29:14 And I **w** be found of you, saith the Lᴏʀᴅ:	NIH	
29:14 I **w** turn away your captivity, and I will	NIH	
29:14 and I **w** gather you from all the nations,	NIH	
29:14 I **w** bring you again into the place whence	NIH	
29:17 Behold, I **w** send upon them the sword,	NIH	
29:17 and **w** make them like vile figs,	NIH	
29:18 I **w** persecute them with the sword, with	NIH	
29:18 **w** deliver them to be removed to all	NIH	
29:21 I **w** deliver them into the hand of	NIH	

Jer 29:32 I **w** punish Shemaiah the Nehelamite,	NIH	
29:32 neither shall he behold the good that I **w**	NIH	
30: 3 that I **w** bring again the captivity of my	NIH	
30: 3 I **w** cause them to return to the land that I	NIH	
30: 8 *that* I **w** break his yoke from off thy neck,	NIH	
30: 8 **w** burst thy bonds, and strangers shall no	NIH	
30: 9 their king, whom I **w** raise up unto them.	NIH	
30:10 I **w** save thee from afar, and thy seed from	NIH	
30:11 yet **w** I not make a full end of thee:	NIH	
30:11 I **w** correct thee in measure, and will not	NIH	
30:11 **w** not leave thee altogether unpunished.	NIH	
30:16 all that prey upon thee **w** I give for a prey.	NIH	
30:17 For I **w** restore health unto thee, and I will	NIH	
30:17 I **w** heal thee of thy wounds, saith	NIH	
30:18 I **w** bring again the captivity of Jacob's	NIH	
30:19 I **w** multiply them, and they shall not be	NIH	
30:19 I **w** also glorify them, and they shall not be	NIH	
30:20 and I **w** punish all that oppress them.	NIH	
30:21 I **w** cause him to draw near, and he shall	NIH	
30:22 shall be my people, and I **w** be your God.	NIH	
31: 1 **w** I be the God of all the families of Israel,	NIH	
31: 4 Again I **w** build thee, and thou shalt be	NIH	
31: 8 I **w** bring them from the north country,	NIH	
31: 9 and with supplications **w** I lead them:	NIH	
31: 9 I **w** cause them to walk by the rivers of	NIH	
31:10 He that scattered Israel **w** gather him,	NIH	
31:13 for I **w** turn their mourning into joy,	NIH	
31:13 **w** comfort them, and make them rejoice	NIH	
31:14 I **w** satiate the soul of the priests with	NIH	
31:20 I **w** surely have mercy upon him, saith	NIH	
31:27 that I **w** sow the house of Israel and	NIH	
31:28 so **w** I watch over them, to build,	NIH	
31:31 that I **w** make a new covenant with	NIH	
31:33 this *shall be* the covenant that I **w** make	NIH	
31:33 I **w** put my law in their inward parts,	NIH	
31:33 **w** be their God, and they shall be my	NIH	
31:34 for I **w** forgive their iniquity, and I will	NIH	
31:34 and I **w** remember their sin no more.	NIH	
31:37 I **w** also cast off all the seed of Israel for all	NIH	
32: 3 I **w** give this city into the hand of the king	NIH	
32:28 I **w** give this city into the hand of	NIH	
32:37 I **w** gather them out of all countries,	NIH	
32:37 I **w** bring them again unto this place,	NIH	
32:37 and I **w** cause them to dwell safely:	NIH	
32:38 shall be my people, and I **w** be their God:	NIH	
32:39 I **w** give them one heart, and one way,	NIH	
32:40 I **w** make an everlasting covenant with	NIH	
32:40 that I **w** not turn away from them, to do	NIH	
32:40 I **w** put my fear in their hearts, that *they*	NIH	
32:41 I **w** rejoice over them to do them good,	NIH	
32:41 I **w** plant them in this land assuredly with	NIH	
32:42 **w** I bring upon them all the good that I	NIH	
32:44 for I **w** cause their captivity to return,	NIH	
33: 3 I **w** answer thee, and shew thee great and	NIH	
33: 6 I **w** bring it health and cure, and I will	NIH	
33: 6 I **w** cure them, and will reveal unto them	NIH	
33: 6 **w** reveal unto them the abundance of	NIH	
33: 7 I **w** cause the captivity of Judah and	NIH	
33: 7 return, and **w** build them, as at the first.	NIH	
33: 8 I **w** cleanse them from all their iniquity,	NIH	
33: 8 I **w** pardon all their iniquities, whereby	NIH	
33:11 For I **w** cause to return the captivity of	NIH	
33:14 that I **w** perform *that* good thing which I	NIH	
33:15 **w** I cause the Branch of righteousness to	NIH	
33:22 **w** I multiply the seed of David my servant,	NIH	
33:26 **w** I cast away the seed of Jacob,	NIH	
33:26 I **w** not take *any* of his seed *to be* rulers	NIH	
33:26 for I **w** cause their captivity to return,	NIH	
34: 2 I **w** give this city into the hand of the king	NIH	
34: 5 and they **w** lament thee, *saying,* Ah lord!	NIH	
34:17 I **w** make you to be removed into all	NIH	
34:18 I **w** give the men that have transgressed	NIH	
34:20 I **w** even give them into the hand of their	NIH	
34:21 his princes **w** I give into the hand of their	NIH	
34:22 Behold, I **w** command, saith the Lᴏʀᴅ,	NIH	
34:22 I **w** make the cities of Judah a desolation	NIH	
35: 6 said, We **w** drink no wine: for Jonadab	NIH	
35:13 **W** ye not receive instruction to hearken to	NIH	
35:17 I **w** bring upon Judah and upon all	NIH	
36: 3 It may be that the house of Judah **w** hear	NIH	
36: 7 It may be they **w** present their supplication	NIH	
36: 7 and **w** return every one from his evil way:	NIH	
36:16 **w** surely tell the king of all these words.	NIH	
36:31 I **w** punish him and his seed and his	NIH	
36:31 I **w** bring upon them, and upon	NIH	
38:14 said unto Jeremiah, I **w** ask thee a thing;	NIH	
38:16 us this soul, I **w** not put thee to death,	NIH	
38:16 **w** I give thee into the hand of these	NIH	
38:25 from us, and we **w** not put thee to death;	NIH	
39:16 I **w** bring my words upon this city for evil,	NIH	
39:17 **w** deliver thee in that day, saith	NIH	
39:18 For I **w** surely deliver thee, and thou shalt	NIH	
40: 4 come; and I **w** look well unto thee:	NIH	
40:10 **w** dwell at Mizpah to serve the Chaldeans,	NIH	
40:10 the Chaldeans, which **w** come unto us:	NIH	
40:15 I **w** slay Ishmael the son of Nethaniah,	NIH	
42: 4 I **w** pray unto the Lᴏʀᴅ your God	NIH	
42: 4 shall answer you, I **w** declare *it* unto you;	NIH	
42: 4 I **w** keep nothing back from you.	NIH	
42: 6 we **w** obey the voice of the Lᴏʀᴅ our	NIH	
42:10 If ye **w** still abide in this land, then will I	NIH	
42:10 I **w** build you, and not pull *you* down,	NIH	
42:10 and I **w** plant you, and not pluck *you* up:	NIH	
42:12 I **w** shew mercies unto you, that he may	NIH	
42:13 if ye say, We **w** not dwell in this land,	NIH	

Jer 42:14 we **w** go *into* the land of Egypt, where we	NIH	
42:14 hunger of bread; and there **w** we dwell:	NIH	
42:17 escape from the evil that I **w** bring upon	NIH	
42:20 so declare unto us, and we **w** do *it.*	NIH	
43:10 I **w** send and take Nebuchadrezzar the	NIH	
43:10 **w** set his throne upon these stones that I	NIH	
43:12 I **w** kindle a fire in the houses of the gods	NIH	
44:11 I **w** set my face against you for evil,	NIH	
44:12 I **w** take the remnant of Judah, that have	NIH	
44:13 For I **w** punish them that dwell in the land	NIH	
44:16 of the Lᴏʀᴅ, we **w** not hearken unto thee.	NIH	
44:17 we **w** certainly do whatsoever thing goeth	NIH	
44:25 We **w** surely perform our vows that we	NIH	
44:25 ye **w** surely accomplish your vows,	NIH	
44:27 I **w** watch over them for evil, and not for	NIH	
44:29 that I **w** punish you in this place,	NIH	
44:30 I **w** give Pharaoh-hophra king of Egypt into	NIH	
45: 4 *that* which I have built **w** I break down,	NIH	
45: 4 *that* which I have planted I **w** pluck up,	NIH	
45: 5 for behold, I **w** bring evil upon all flesh,	NIH	
45: 5 thy life **w** I give unto thee for a prey in all	NIH	
46: 8 saith, I **w** go up, *and* will cover the earth;	NIH	
46: 8 saith, I **w** go up, *and* **w** cover the earth;	NIH	
46: 8 I **w** destroy the city and the inhabitants	NIH	
46:25 I **w** punish the multitude of No,	NIH	
46:26 I **w** deliver them into the hand of those	NIH	
46:27 I **w** save thee from afar off, and thy seed	NIH	
46:28 for I **w** make a full end of all the nations	NIH	
46:28 I **w** not make a full end of thee,	NIH	
46:28 yet **w** I not leave thee wholly unpunished.	NIH	
47: 4 for the Lᴏʀᴅ **w** spoil the Philistines,	NIH	
47: 6 how long **w** it be ere thou be quiet?	NIH	
48:12 that I **w** send unto him wanderers,	NIH	
48:31 Therefore **w** I howl for Moab, and I will	NIH	
48:31 for Moab, and I **w** cry out for all Moab;	NIH	
48:32 I **w** weep for thee with the weeping of	NIH	
48:35 Moreover I **w** cause to cease in Moab,	NIH	
48:44 for I **w** bring upon it, *even* upon Moab,	NIH	
48:47 Yet **w** I bring again the captivity of Moab	NIH	
49: 2 I **w** cause an alarm of war to be heard in	NIH	
49: 5 Behold, I **w** bring a fear upon thee, saith	NIH	
49: 6 afterward I **w** bring again the captivity of	NIH	
49: 8 for I **w** bring the calamity of Esau upon	NIH	
49: 8 upon him, the time *that* I **w** visit him.	NIH	
49: 9 they **w** destroy till they have enough.	NIH	
49:11 children, I **w** preserve *them* alive;	NIH	
49:15 I **w** make thee small among the heathen,	NIH	
49:16 I **w** bring thee down from thence, saith	NIH	
49:19 I **w** suddenly make him run away from	NIH	
49:19 who **w** appoint me the time? and who *is*	NIH	
49:19 who *is* that shepherd that **w** stand before	NIH	
49:27 I **w** kindle a fire in the wall of Damascus,	NIH	
49:32 I **w** scatter into all winds *that are* in	NIH	
49:32 I **w** bring their calamity from all sides	NIH	
49:35 Behold, I **w** break the bow of Elam,	NIH	
49:36 upon Elam **w** I bring the four winds from	NIH	
49:36 **w** scatter them towards all those winds;	NIH	
49:37 For I **w** cause Elam to be dismayed before	NIH	
49:37 I **w** bring evil upon them, *even* my fierce	NIH	
49:37 and **w** send the sword after them, till I have	NIH	
49:38 I **w** set my throne in Elam, and will	NIH	
49:38 **w** destroy from thence the king and	NIH	
49:39 *that* I **w** bring again the captivity of Elam,	NIH	
50: 9 I **w** raise and cause to come up against	NIH	
50:18 I **w** punish the king of Babylon and his	NIH	
50:19 I **w** bring Israel again to his habitation,	NIH	
50:20 for I **w** pardon them whom I reserve.	NIH	
50:31 day is come, the time *that* I **w** visit thee.	NIH	
50:32 I **w** kindle a fire in his cities, and it shall	NIH	
50:42 they *are* cruel, and **w** not shew mercy:	NIH	
50:44 I **w** make them suddenly run away from	NIH	
50:44 who **w** appoint me the time? and who *is*	NIH	
50:44 who *is* that shepherd that **w** stand before	NIH	
51: 1 I **w** raise up against Babylon,	NIH	
51: 2 **w** send unto Babylon fanners, that shall	NIH	
51: 6 he **w** render unto her a recompence.	NIH	
51:14 *saying,* Surely I **w** fill thee *with* men,	NIH	
51:20 with thee **w** I break in pieces the nations,	NIH	
51:20 and with thee **w** I destroy kingdoms;	NIH	
51:21 with thee **w** I break in pieces the horse	NIH	
51:21 with thee **w** I break in pieces the chariot	NIH	
51:22 With thee also **w** I break in pieces man	NIH	
51:22 with thee **w** I break in pieces old and	NIH	
51:22 with thee **w** I break in pieces the young	NIH	
51:23 I **w** also break in pieces with thee	NIH	
51:23 with thee **w** I break in pieces	NIH	
51:23 with thee **w** I break in pieces captains and	NIH	
51:24 I **w** render unto Babylon and to all	NIH	
51:25 I **w** stretch out mine hand upon thee,	NIH	
51:25 and **w** make thee a burnt mountain.	NIH	
51:36 **w** plead thy cause, and take vengeance	NIH	
51:36 I **w** dry up her sea, and make her springs	NIH	
51:39 In their heat I **w** make their feasts, and I	NIH	
51:39 I **w** make them drunken, that they may	NIH	
51:40 I **w** bring them down like lambs to	NIH	
51:44 I **w** punish Bel in Babylon, and I will bring	NIH	
51:44 I **w** bring forth out of his mouth that	NIH	
51:47 that I **w** do judgment upon the graven	NIH	
51:52 that I **w** do judgment upon her graven	NIH	
51:57 I **w** make drunk her princes, and her wise	NIH	
51:64 shall not rise from the evil that I **w** bring	NIH	
La 3:24 saith my soul; therefore **w** I hope in him.	NIH	
3:31 For the Lord **w** not cast off for ever:	NIH	
3:32 yet **w** he have compassion according to	NIH	
4:16 divided them; he **w** no more regard them:	NIH	

La	4:22 he **w** no more carry thee away into	NIH
	4:22 he **w** visit thine iniquity, O daughter of	NIH
	4:22 daughter of Edom; he **w** discover thy sins.	NIH
Eze	2: 1 upon thy feet, and I **w** speak unto thee.	NIH
	2: 5 whether they **w** hear, or whether they	NIH
	2: 5 they will hear, or whether they **w** forbear,	NIH
	2: 7 whether they **w** hear, or whether they	NIH
	2: 7 they will hear, or whether they **w** forbear:	NIH
	3: 7 house of Israel **w** not hearken unto thee;	14
	3: 7 thee; for they **w** not hearken unto me:	14
	3:11 whether they **w** hear, or whether they	NIH
	3:11 they will hear, or whether they **w** forbear.	NIH
	3:18 but his blood **w** I require at thine hand.	NIH
	3:20 but his blood **w** I require at thine hand.	NIH
	3:22 the plain, and I **w** there talk with thee.	NIH
	3:26 I **w** make thy tongue cleave to the roof of	NIH
	3:27 I **w** open thy mouth, and thou shalt say	NIH
	4: 8 I **w** lay bands upon thee, and thou shalt	NIH
	4:13 the Gentiles, whither I **w** drive them.	NIH
	4:16 I **w** break the staff of bread in Jerusalem:	NIH
	5: 2 and I **w** draw out a sword after them.	NIH
	5: 8 **w** execute judgments in the midst of thee	NIH
	5: 9 I **w** do in thee that which I have not done,	NIH
	5: 9 whereunto I **w** not do any more the like,	NIH
	5:10 I **w** execute judgments in thee,	NIH
	5:10 the whole remnant of thee **w** I scatter into	NIH
	5:11 **w** I also diminish *thee;* neither shall mine	NIH
	5:11 mine eye spare, neither **w** I have any pity.	NIH
	5:12 I **w** scatter a third *part* into all the winds,	NIH
	5:12 and I **w** draw out a sword after them.	NIH
	5:13 I **w** cause my fury to rest upon them,	NIH
	5:13 to rest upon them, and I **w** be comforted:	NIH
	5:14 Moreover I **w** make thee waste,	NIH
	5:16 *and* which I **w** send to destroy you:	NIH
	5:16 I **w** increase the famine upon you,	NIH
	5:16 upon you, and **w** break your staff of bread:	NIH
	5:17 So **w** I send upon you famine and	NIH
	5:17 and I **w** bring the sword upon thee.	NIH
	6: 3 **w** bring a sword upon you, and I will	NIH
	6: 3 you, and I **w** destroy your high places.	NIH
	6: 4 I **w** cast down your slain *men* before your	NIH
	6: 5 I **w** lay the dead carcases of the children	NIH
	6: 5 I **w** scatter your bones round about your	NIH
	6: 8 Yet **w** I leave a remnant, that ye may have	NIH
	6:12 thus **w** I accomplish my fury upon them.	NIH
	6:14 So **w** I stretch out mine hand upon them,	NIH
	7: 3 **w** send mine anger upon thee,	NIH
	7: 3 and **w** judge thee according to thy ways,	NIH
	7: 3 **w** recompense upon thee all thine	NIH
	7: 4 shall not spare thee, neither **w** I have pity:	NIH
	7: 4 but I **w** recompense thy ways upon thee,	NIH
	7: 8 Now **w** I shortly pour out my fury upon	NIH
	7: 8 I **w** judge thee according to thy ways,	NIH
	7: 8 **w** recompense thee for all thine	NIH
	7: 9 eye shall not spare, neither **w** I have pity:	NIH
	7: 9 I **w** recompense thee according to thy	NIH
	7:21 I **w** give it into the hands of the strangers	NIH
	7:22 My face **w** I turn also from them,	NIH
	7:24 Wherefore I **w** bring the worst of	NIH
	7:24 I **w** also make the pomp of the strong to	NIH
	7:27 I **w** do unto them after their way,	NIH
	7:27 according to their deserts **w** I judge them;	NIH
	8:18 Therefore **w** I also deal in fury: mine eye	NIH
	8:18 eye shall not spare, neither **w** I have pity:	NIH
	8:18 *with* a loud voice, *yet* **w** I not hear them.	NIH
	9:10 I have pity, *but* I **w**ill recompense	NIH
	9:10 I **w** recompense their way upon their	NIH
	11: 7 I **w** bring you forth out of the midst of it.	NIH
	11: 8 I **w** bring a sword upon you, saith the	NIH
	11: 9 I **w** bring you out of the midst thereof,	NIH
	11: 9 and **w** execute judgments among you.	NIH
	11:10 I **w** judge you in the border of Israel;	NIH
	11:11 *but* I **w** judge you in the border of Israel:	NIH
	11:16 yet **w** I be to them as a little sanctuary in	NIH
	11:17 I **w** even gather you from the people,	NIH
	11:17 and I **w** give you the land of Israel.	NIH
	11:19 I **w** give them one heart, and I will put a	NIH
	11:19 and I **w** put a new spirit within you;	NIH
	11:19 I **w** take the stony heart out of their flesh,	NIH
	11:19 and **w** give them a heart of flesh:	NIH
	11:20 shall be my people, and I **w** be their God.	NIH
	11:21 I **w** recompense their way upon their own	NIH
	12: 3 it may be they **w** consider, though they *be*	NIH
	12:13 My net also **w** I spread upon him,	NIH
	12:13 I **w** bring him to Babylon *to* the land of	NIH
	12:14 I **w** scatter toward every wind all that *are*	NIH
	12:14 and I **w** draw out the sword after them.	NIH
	12:16 I **w** leave a few men of them from	NIH
	12:23 I **w** make this proverb to cease,	NIH
	12:25 I **w** speak, and the word that I shall speak	NIH
	12:25 I **w** say the word, and will perform it,	NIH
	12:25 will I say the word, and **w** perform it,	NIH
	13:13 I **w** even rent *it with* a stormy wind in my	NIH
	13:14 So **w** I break down the wall that ye have	NIH
	13:15 Thus **w** I accomplish my wrath upon	NIH
	13:15 untempered *morter,* and **w** say unto you,	NIH
	13:18 **W** ye hunt the souls of my people,	NIH
	13:18 **w** ye save the souls alive *that* come unto	NIH
	13:19 **w** ye pollute me among my people for	NIH
	13:20 I **w** tear them from your arms, and will let	NIH
	13:20 from your arms, and **w** let the souls go,	NIH
	13:21 Your kerchiefs also **w** I tear, and deliver	NIH
	13:23 I **w** deliver my people out of your hand:	NIH
	14: 4 I the LORD **w** answer him that cometh	NIH
	14: 7 I the LORD **w** answer him by myself:	NIH

Eze	14: 8 I **w** set my face against that man,	NIH
	14: 8 **w** make him a sign and a proverb, and I	NIH
	14: 8 I **w** cut him off from the midst of my	NIH
	14: 9 I **w** stretch out my hand upon him,	NIH
	14: 9 **w** destroy him from the midst of my	NIH
	14:13 **w** I stretch out mine hand upon it,	NIH
	14:13 **w** break the staff of the bread thereof,	NIH
	14:13 **w** send famine upon it, and will cut off	NIH
	14:13 and **w** cut off man and beast from it:	NIH
	15: 3 **w** *men* take a pin of it to hang any vessel	NIH
	15: 6 so **w** I give the inhabitants of Jerusalem.	NIH
	15: 7 I **w** set my face against them; they shall go	NIH
	15: 8 I **w** make the land desolate, because	NIH
	16:27 thee unto the **w** of them that hate	5315
	16:37 Behold therefore, I **w** gather all thy lovers,	NIH
	16:37 I **w** even gather them round about against	NIH
	16:37 I **w** discover thy nakedness unto them,	NIH
	16:38 I **w** judge thee, as *women* that break	NIH
	16:38 I **w** give thee blood in fury and jealousy.	NIH
	16:39 I **w** also give thee into their hand,	NIH
	16:41 I **w** cause thee to cease from playing	NIH
	16:42 So **w** I make my fury towards thee to rest,	NIH
	16:42 I **w** be quiet, and **w** be no more angry.	NIH
	16:42 I will be quiet, and **w** be no more angry.	NIH
	16:43 I also **w** recompense thy way upon *thine*	NIH
	16:53 **w** I bring again the captivity of thy	NIH
	16:59 I **w** even deal with thee as thou hast done,	NIH
	16:60 Nevertheless I **w** remember my covenant	NIH
	16:60 I **w** establish unto thee an everlasting	NIH
	16:61 I **w** give them unto thee for daughters,	NIH
	16:62 I **w** establish my covenant with thee;	NIH
	17:19 it **w** I recompense upon his own head.	NIH
	17:20 I **w** spread my net upon him, and he shall	NIH
	17:20 I **w** bring him to Babylon, and will plead	NIH
	17:20 **w** plead with him there *for* his trespass	NIH
	17:22 I **w** also take of the highest branch of	NIH
	17:22 **w** set *it;* I will crop off from the top of his	NIH
	17:22 will set *it;* I **w** crop off from the top of his	NIH
	17:22 **w** plant *it* upon a high mountain and	NIH
	17:23 In the mountain of the height of Israel **w** I	NIH
	18:21 if the wicked **w** turn from all his sins that	NIH
	18:30 I **w** judge you, O house of Israel,	NIH
	18:31 for why **w** ye die, O house of Israel?	NIH
	20: 3 Lord GOD, I **w** not be inquired of by you.	NIH
	20: 8 I said, *I* **w** pour out my fury upon them,	NIH
	20:31 Lord GOD, I **w** not be inquired of by you.	NIH
	20:32 that ye say, We **w** be as the heathen,	NIH
	20:33 with fury poured out, **w** I rule over you:	NIH
	20:34 I **w** bring you out from the people,	NIH
	20:34 **w** gather you out of the countries wherein	NIH
	20:35 I **w** bring you into the wilderness of	NIH
	20:35 and there **w** I plead with you face to face.	NIH
	20:36 so **w** I plead with you, saith the Lord	NIH
	20:37 I **w** cause you to pass under the rod,	NIH
	20:37 I **w** bring you into the bond of the	NIH
	20:38 I **w** purge out from among you the rebels,	NIH
	20:38 I **w** bring them forth out of the country	NIH
	20:39 *also,* if ye **w** not hearken unto me:	NIH
	20:40 there **w** I accept them, and there will I	NIH
	20:40 there **w** I require your offerings,	NIH
	20:41 I **w** accept you with *your* sweet savour,	NIH
	20:41 **w** be sanctified in you before the heathen.	NIH
	20:47 I **w** kindle a fire in thee, and it shall	NIH
	21: 3 **w** draw forth my sword out of his sheath,	NIH
	21: 3 **w** cut off from thee the righteous and	NIH
	21: 4 that I **w** cut off from thee the righteous	NIH
	21:17 I **w** also smite mine hands together,	NIH
	21:17 and I **w** cause my fury to rest:	NIH
	21:23 he **w** call to remembrance the iniquity,	NIH
	21:27 I **w**^s overturn, overturn, overturn it:	7760
	21:27 whose right it is; and I **w** give it *him.*	NIH
	21:30 I **w** judge thee in the place where thou	NIH
	21:31 I **w** pour out mine indignation upon thee,	NIH
	21:31 I **w** blow against thee in the fire of my	NIH
	22:14 the LORD have spoken *it,* and **w** do *it.*	NIH
	22:15 And I **w** scatter thee among the heathen,	NIH
	22:15 and **w** consume thy filthiness out of thee.	NIH
	22:19 I **w** gather you into the midst of Jerusalem.	NIH
	22:20 so **w** I gather *you* in mine anger and	NIH
	22:20 and I **w** leave *you there,* and melt you.	NIH
	22:21 I **w** gather you, and blow upon you in	NIH
	23:22 I **w** raise up thy lovers against thee,	NIH
	23:22 I **w** bring them against thee on every side;	NIH
	23:24 I **w** set judgment before them, and they	NIH
	23:25 I **w** set my jealousy against thee,	NIH
	23:27 Thus **w** I make thy lewdness to cease from	NIH
	23:28 I **w** deliver thee into the hand *of them*	NIH
	23:30 I **w** do these *things* unto thee, because	NIH
	23:31 therefore **w** I give her cup into thine hand.	NIH
	23:43 **W** they now commit whoredoms with her,	NIH
	23:46 I **w** bring up a company upon them,	NIH
	23:46 **w** give them to be removed and spoiled.	NIH
	23:48 Thus **w** I cause lewdness to cease out of	NIH
	24: 9 I **w** even make the pile for fire great.	NIH
	24:14 I **w** do *it;* I will not go back, neither will I	NIH
	24:14 I will do *it;* I **w** not go back, neither will I	NIH
	24:14 neither **w** I spare, neither will I repent;	NIH
	24:14 neither will I spare, neither **w** I repent;	NIH
	24:21 Behold, I **w** profane my sanctuary,	NIH
	25: 4 I **w** deliver thee to the men of the east for	NIH
	25: 5 I **w** make Rabbah a stable for camels,	NIH
	25: 7 I **w** stretch out mine hand upon thee,	NIH
	25: 7 **w** deliver thee for a spoil to the heathen;	NIH
	25: 7 I **w** cut thee off from the people, and I will	NIH
	25: 7 I **w** cause thee to perish out of the	NIH

Eze	25: 7 I **w** destroy thee; and thou shalt know that	NIH
	25: 9 I **w** open the side of Moab from the cities,	NIH
	25:10 and **w** give them in possession,	NIH
	25:11 And I **w** execute judgments upon Moab;	NIH
	25:13 I **w** also stretch out mine hand upon	NIH
	25:13 and **w** cut off man and beast from it;	NIH
	25:13 I **w** make it desolate from Teman;	NIH
	25:14 I **w** lay my vengeance upon Edom by	NIH
	25:16 I **w** stretch out mine hand upon	NIH
	25:16 I **w** cut off the Cherethims, and destroy	NIH
	25:17 I **w** execute great vengeance upon them	NIH
	26: 3 **w** cause many nations to come up against	NIH
	26: 4 I **w** also scrape her dust from her,	NIH
	26: 7 I **w** bring upon Tyrus Nebuchadrezzar	NIH
	26:13 I **w** cause the noise of thy songs to cease;	NIH
	26:14 I **w** make thee like the top of a rock:	NIH
	26:21 I **w** make thee a terror, and thou *shalt be*	NIH
	28: 7 I **w** bring strangers upon thee,	NIH
	28:16 I **w** cast thee as profane out of the	NIH
	28:16 I **w** destroy thee, O covering cherub,	NIH
	28:17 I **w** cast thee to the ground, I will lay thee	NIH
	28:17 I **w** lay thee before kings, that *they* may	NIH
	28:18 I **w** bring forth a fire from the midst of	NIH
	28:18 I **w** bring thee to ashes upon the earth in	NIH
	28:22 and I **w** be glorified in the midst of thee:	NIH
	28:23 For I **w** send into her pestilence,	NIH
	29: 4 I **w** put hooks in thy jaws, and I will cause	NIH
	29: 4 I **w** cause the fish of thy rivers to stick	NIH
	29: 4 I **w** bring thee up out of the midst of thy	NIH
	29: 5 I **w** leave thee *thrown* into the wilderness,	NIH
	29: 8 I **w** bring a sword upon thee, and cut off	NIH
	29:10 I **w** make the land of Egypt utterly waste	NIH
	29:12 I **w** make the land of Egypt desolate in	NIH
	29:12 I **w** scatter the Egyptians among the	NIH
	29:12 **w** disperse them through the countries.	NIH
	29:13 At the end of forty years **w** I gather	NIH
	29:14 I **w** bring again the captivity of Egypt,	NIH
	29:14 **w** cause them to return *into* the land of	NIH
	29:15 for I **w** diminish them, that *they* shall no	NIH
	29:19 I **w** give the land of Egypt unto	NIH
	29:21 In that day **w** I cause the horn of the house	NIH
	29:21 I **w** give thee the opening of the mouth in	NIH
	30:10 I **w** also make the multitude of Egypt to	NIH
	30:12 I **w** make the rivers dry, and sell the land	NIH
	30:12 I **w** make the land waste, and all that is	NIH
	30:13 I **w** also destroy the idols, and I will cause	NIH
	30:13 I **w** cause *their* images to cease out of	NIH
	30:13 and I **w** put a fear in the land of Egypt.	NIH
	30:14 I **w** make Pathros desolate, and will set fire	NIH
	30:14 **w** set fire in Zoan, and will execute	NIH
	30:14 in Zoan, and **w** execute judgments in No.	NIH
	30:15 I **w** pour my fury upon Sin, the strength of	NIH
	30:15 and I **w** cut off the multitude of No.	NIH
	30:16 I **w** set fire in Egypt: Sin shall have great	NIH
	30:19 Thus **w** I execute judgments in Egypt:	NIH
	30:22 I **w** break his arms, the strong, and that	NIH
	30:22 I **w** cause the sword to fall out of his hand.	NIH
	30:23 I **w** scatter the Egyptians among the	NIH
	30:23 **w** disperse them through the countries.	NIH
	30:24 I **w** strengthen the arms of the king of	NIH
	30:24 I **w** break Pharaoh's arms, and he shall	NIH
	30:25 I **w** strengthen the arms of the king of	NIH
	30:26 I **w** scatter the Egyptians among the	NIH
	32: 3 I **w** therefore spread out my net over thee	NIH
	32: 4 I **w** leave thee upon the land, I will cast	NIH
	32: 4 I **w** cast thee forth upon the open field,	NIH
	32: 4 **w** cause all the fowls of the heaven to	NIH
	32: 4 I **w** fill the beasts of the whole earth with	NIH
	32: 5 I **w** lay thy flesh upon the mountains,	NIH
	32: 6 I **w** also water with thy blood the land	NIH
	32: 7 I **w** cover the heaven, and make the stars	NIH
	32: 7 I **w** cover the sun with a cloud,	NIH
	32: 8 All the bright lights of heaven **w** I make	NIH
	32: 9 I **w** also vex the hearts of many people,	NIH
	32:10 I **w** make many people amazed at thee,	NIH
	32:12 By the swords of the mighty **w** I cause thy	NIH
	32:13 I **w** destroy also all the beasts thereof from	NIH
	32:14 **w** I make their waters deep, and cause	NIH
	33: 6 his blood **w** I require at the watchman's	NIH
	33: 8 but his blood **w** I require at thine hand.	NIH
	33:11 for why **w** ye die, O house of Israel?	NIH
	33:20 I **w** judge you every one after his ways.	NIH
	33:27 him that *is* in the open field **w** I give to	NIH
	33:28 For I **w** lay the land most desolate,	NIH
	33:31 hear thy words, but they **w** not do them:	NIH
	33:33 when this cometh to pass, (lo, it **w** come)	NIH
	34:10 I **w** require my flock at their hand,	NIH
	34:10 for I **w** deliver my flock from their mouth,	NIH
	34:11 I **w** both search my sheep, and seek them	NIH
	34:12 so **w** I seek out my sheep, and will deliver	NIH
	34:12 **w** deliver them out of all places where	NIH
	34:13 I **w** bring them out from the people,	NIH
	34:13 **w** bring them to their own land,	NIH
	34:14 I **w** feed them in a good pasture,	NIH
	34:15 I **w** feed my flock, and I will cause them	NIH
	34:15 my flock, and I **w** cause them to lie down,	NIH
	34:16 I **w** seek that which was lost, and bring	NIH
	34:16 and **w** bind up that which was broken,	NIH
	34:16 and **w** strengthen that which was sick:	NIH
	34:16 I **w** destroy the fat and the strong; I will	NIH
	34:16 the strong; I **w** feed them with judgment.	NIH
	34:20 **w** judge between the fat cattle and	NIH
	34:22 Therefore **w** I save my flock, and they	NIH
	34:22 and I **w** judge between cattle and cattle.	NIH
	34:23 And I **w** set up one shepherd over them,	NIH

Eze 34:24 I the Lord **w** be their God, NIH
34:25 I **w** make with them a covenant of peace, NIH
34:25 **w** cause the evil beasts to cease out of NIH
34:26 I **w** make them and the places round NIH
34:26 I **w** cause the shower to come down in NIH
34:29 I **w** raise up for them a plant of renown, NIH
35: 3 I **w** stretch out mine hand against thee, NIH
35: 3 and I **w** make thee most desolate. NIH
35: 4 I **w** lay thy cities waste, and thou shalt be NIH
35: 6 I **w** prepare thee unto blood, and blood NIH
35: 7 Thus **w** I make mount Seir most desolate, NIH
35: 8 I **w** fill his mountains *with* his slain *men:* NIH
35: 9 I **w** make thee perpetual desolations, NIH
35:10 shall be mine, and we **w** possess it; NIH
35:11 I **w** even do according to thine anger, NIH
35:11 I **w** make myself known amongst them, NIH
35:14 earth rejoiceth, I **w** make thee desolate. NIH
35:15 it was desolate, so **w** I do unto thee: NIH
36: 9 I **w** turn unto you, and ye shall be tilled NIH
36:10 I **w** multiply men upon you, all the house NIH
36:11 I **w** multiply upon you man and beast; NIH
36:11 and I **w** settle you after your old estates, NIH
36:11 **w** do better *unto* you than at your NIH
36:12 Yea, I **w** cause men to walk upon you, NIH
36:15 Neither **w** I cause *men* to hear in thee NIH
36:23 I **w** sanctify my great name, which was NIH
36:24 I **w** take you from among the heathen, NIH
36:24 and **w** bring you into your own land. NIH
36:25 **w** I sprinkle clean water upon you, NIH
36:25 and from all your idols, **w** I cleanse you. NIH
36:26 A new heart also **w** I give you, and a new NIH
36:26 and a new spirit **w** I put within you: NIH
36:26 I **w** take away the stony heart out of your NIH
36:26 flesh, and I **w** give you a heart of flesh. NIH
36:27 I **w** put my spirit within you, and cause NIH
36:28 shall be my people, and I **w** be your God. NIH
36:29 I **w** also save you from all your NIH
36:29 I **w** call for the corn, and will increase it, NIH
36:29 **w** increase it, and lay no famine upon you. NIH
36:30 I **w** multiply the fruit of the tree, NIH
36:33 I **w** also cause *you* to dwell in the cities, NIH
36:36 I the Lord have spoken *it*, and I **w** do *it.* NIH
36:37 I **w** yet *for* this be inquired of by the house NIH
36:37 I **w** increase them *with* men like a flock. NIH
37: 5 I **w** cause breath to enter into you, NIH
37: 6 I **w** lay sinews upon you, and will bring up NIH
37: 6 **w** bring up flesh upon you, and cover you NIH
37:12 I **w** open your graves, and cause you to NIH
37:19 Behold, I **w** take the stick of Joseph, NIH
37:19 **w** put them with him, *even* with the stick NIH
37:21 I **w** take the children of Israel from among NIH
37:21 **w** gather them on every side, NIH
37:22 I **w** make them one nation in the land NIH
37:23 I **w** save them out of all their dwelling NIH
37:23 they have sinned, and **w** cleanse them: NIH
37:23 they be my people, and I **w** be their God. NIH
37:26 Moreover I **w** make a covenant of peace NIH
37:26 I **w** place them, and multiply them, NIH
37:26 **w** set my sanctuary in the midst of them NIH
37:27 I **w** be their God, and they shall be my NIH
38: 4 I **w** turn thee back, and put hooks into NIH
38: 4 I **w** bring thee forth, and all thine army, NIH
38:11 I **w** go up to the land of unwalled villages; NIH
38:11 I **w** go *to* them that are at rest, that dwell NIH
38:16 and I **w** bring thee against my land, NIH
38:21 I **w** call *for* a sword against him NIH
38:22 I **w** plead against him with pestilence and NIH
38:22 I **w** rain upon him, and upon his bands, NIH
38:23 Thus **w** I magnify myself, NIH
38:23 I **w** be known in the eyes of many nations, NIH
39: 2 I **w** turn thee back, and leave but the sixth NIH
39: 2 **w** cause thee to come up from the north NIH
39: 2 **w** bring thee upon the mountains of Israel: NIH
39: 3 I **w** smite thy bow out of thy left hand, NIH
39: 3 **w** cause thine arrows to fall out of thy NIH
39: 4 I **w** give thee unto the ravenous birds of NIH
39: 6 I **w** send a fire on Magog, and among NIH
39: 7 So **w** I make my holy name known in NIH
39: 7 I **w** not let *them* pollute my holy name NIH
39:11 *that* I **w** give unto Gog a place there of NIH
39:21 I **w** set my glory among the heathen, NIH
39:25 Now **w** I bring again the captivity of Jacob, NIH
39:25 and **w** be jealous for my holy name; NIH
39:29 Neither **w** I hide my face any more from NIH
43: 7 I **w** dwell in the midst of the children NIH
43: 9 I **w** dwell in the midst of them for ever. NIH
43:27 and I **w** accept you, saith the Lord God. NIH
44:14 I **w** make them keepers of the charge of NIH
Da 2: 4 and we **w** shew the interpretation. NIH
2: 5 if ye **w** not make known unto me the NIH
2: 7 and we **w** shew the interpretation of it. NIH
2: 9 if ye **w** not make known unto me the NIH
2:24 I **w** shew unto the king the interpretation. NIH
2:25 that **w** make known unto the king NIH
2:36 we **w** tell the interpretation thereof before NIH
3:17 he **w** deliver *us* out of thine hand, O king. NIH
3:18 O king, that we **w** not serve thy gods, 383
4:17 giveth it to whomsoever he **w**, 6634
4:25 men, and giveth it to whomsoever he **w**. 6634
4:32 men, and giveth it to whomsoever he **w**. 6634
4:35 he doeth according to his **w** in the army 6634
5:12 called, and he **w** shew the interpretation. NIH
5:17 yet I **w** read the writing unto the king, NIH
5:21 he appointeth over it whomsoever he **w**. 6634
6:16 servest continually, he **w** deliver thee. NIH

Da 8: 4 he did according to his **w**, 7522
8:19 I **w** make thee know what shall be in the NIH
10:20 now **w** I return to fight with the prince of NIH
10:21 I **w** shew thee that which is noted in NIH
11: 2 now **w** I shew thee the truth. Behold, NIH
11: 3 dominion, and do according to his **w**. 7522
11:16 him shall do according to his own **w**, 7522
11:36 the king shall do according to his **w**; 7522
Hos 1: 4 I **w** avenge the blood of Jezreel upon NIH
1: 4 **w** cause to cease the kingdom of the NIH
1: 5 I **w** break the bow of Israel in the valley NIH
1: 6 I **w** no more have mercy upon the house NIH
1: 6 of Israel; but I **w** utterly take them away. NIH
1: 7 I **w** have mercy upon the house of Judah, NIH
1: 7 I **w** save them by the Lord their God, NIH
1: 7 **w** not save them by bow, nor by sword, NIH
1: 9 not my people, and I **w** not be your *God.* NIH
2: 4 I **w** not have mercy upon her children; NIH
2: 5 for she said, I **w** go after my lovers, NIH
2: 6 I **w** hedge up thy way with thorns, NIH
2: 7 I **w** go and return to my first husband; NIH
2: 9 Therefore **w** I return, and take *away* my NIH
2: 9 **w** recover my wool and my flax *given* to NIH
2:10 **w** I discover her lewdness in the sight NIH
2:11 I **w** also cause all her mirth to cease, NIH
2:12 I **w** destroy her vines and her fig trees, NIH
2:12 I **w** make them a forest, and the beasts of NIH
2:13 I **w** visit upon her the days of Baalim, NIH
2:14 I **w** allure her, and bring her *into* NIH
2:15 I **w** give her her vineyards from thence, NIH
2:17 I **w** take away the names of Baalim out NIH
2:18 in that day **w** I make a covenant for them NIH
2:18 I **w** break the bow and the sword and NIH
2:18 and **w** make them to lie down safely. NIH
2:19 I **w** betroth thee unto me for ever; yea, NIH
2:19 I **w** betroth thee unto me in righteousness, NIH
2:20 I **w** even betroth thee unto me in NIH
2:21 I **w** hear, saith the Lord, I will hear NIH
2:21 I **w** hear the heavens, and they shall hear NIH
2:23 I **w** sow her unto me in the earth; and I NIH
2:23 I **w** have mercy upon her that had not NIH
2:23 I **w** say to *them which were* not my NIH
3: 3 for *another* man: so **w** I also *be* for thee. NIH
4: 5 *in* the night, and I **w** destroy thy mother. NIH
4: 6 rejected knowledge, I **w** also reject thee, NIH
4: 6 of thy God, I **w** also forget thy children. NIH
4: 7 **w** I change their glory into shame. NIH
4: 9 I **w** punish them for their ways, NIH
4:14 I **w** not punish your daughters when they NIH
4:16 now the Lord **w** feed them as a lamb in a NIH
5: 4 They **w** not frame their doings to turn NIH
5:10 I **w** pour out my wrath upon them like NIH
5:12 Therefore **w** I *be* unto Ephraim as a moth, NIH
5:14 I **w** *be* unto Ephraim as a lion, and as a NIH
5:14 I, *even* I, **w** tear and go away; I will take NIH
5:14 **w** take away, and none shall rescue *him.* NIH
5:15 I **w** go *and* return to my place, till they NIH
5:15 in their affliction they **w** seek me early. NIH
6: 1 he hath torn, and he **w** heal us; he hath NIH
6: 1 he hath smitten, and he **w** bind us up. NIH
6: 2 After two days he **w** revive us: in the NIH
6: 2 in the third day he **w** raise us up, NIH
7:12 shall go, I **w** spread my net upon them; NIH
7:12 I **w** bring them down as the fowls of NIH
7:12 I **w** chastise them, as their congregation NIH
8: 5 how long **w** it *be* ere they attain to NIH
8:10 Now **w** I gather them, and they shall sorrow NIH
8:13 now **w** he remember their iniquity, NIH
8:14 I **w** send a fire upon his cities, and it shall NIH
9: 5 What **w** ye do in the solemn day, and in NIH
9: 9 *therefore* he **w** remember their iniquity, NIH
9: 9 their iniquity, he **w** visit their sins. NIH
9:12 up their children, yet **w** I bereave them, NIH
9:15 the wickedness of their doings I **w** drive NIH
9:15 of mine house, I **w** love them no more: NIH
9:16 yet **w** I slay *even* the beloved *fruit* of their NIH
9:17 My God **w** cast them away, because NIH
10:11 I **w** make Ephraim to ride; Judah shall NIH
11: 9 I **w** not execute the fierceness of mine NIH
11: 9 I **w** not return to destroy Ephraim: NIH
11: 9 of thee: and I **w** not enter into the city. NIH
11:11 I **w** place them in their houses, saith NIH
12: 2 and **w** punish Jacob according to his ways; NIH
12: 2 according to his doings **w** he recompense NIH
12: 9 yet **w** make thee to dwell in tabernacles, NIH
13: 7 Therefore I **w** be unto them as a lion: as a NIH
13: 7 as a leopard by the way **w** I observe *them:* NIH
13: 8 I **w** meet them as a bear *that is* bereaved NIH
13: 8 **w** rent the caul of their heart, and there NIH
13: 8 and there **w** I devour them like a lion: NIH
13:10 I **w** be thy king: where *is any other* that NIH
13:14 I **w** ransom them from the power of NIH
13:14 of the grave; I **w** redeem them from death: NIH
13:14 death, I **w** be thy plagues; O grave, I will NIH
13:14 plagues; O grave, I **w** be thy destruction: NIH
14: 2 so **w** we render the calves of our lips. NIH
14: 3 we **w** not ride upon horses: neither will NIH
14: 3 neither **w** we say any more to the work of NIH
14: 4 I **w** heal their backsliding, I will love them NIH
14: 4 their backsliding, I **w** love them freely: NIH
14: 5 I **w** be as the dew unto Israel: he shall NIH
Joel 1:19 O Lord, to thee **w** I cry: for the fire hath NIH
2:14 Who knoweth *if* he **w** return and repent, NIH
2:18 **w** the Lord be jealous for his land, NIH
2:19 the Lord **w** answer and say unto his NIH

Joel 2:19 I **w** send you corn, and wine, and oil, NIH
2:19 I **w** no more make you a reproach among NIH
2:20 I **w** remove far off from you the northern NIH
2:20 **w** drive him into a land barren and NIH
2:21 rejoice: for the Lord **w** do great things. NIH
2:23 **w** cause to come down for you the rain, NIH
2:25 I **w** restore to you the years that the locust NIH
2:28 that I **w** pour out my spirit upon all flesh; NIH
2:29 the handmaids in those days **w** I pour NIH
2:30 I **w** shew wonders in the heavens and in NIH
3: 2 I **w** also gather all nations, and will bring NIH
3: 2 **w** bring them down into the valley of NIH
3: 2 **w** plead with them there for my people NIH
3: 4 **w** ye render me a recompence? and if ye NIH
3: 4 speedily **w** I return your recompence upon NIH
3: 7 I **w** raise them out of the place whither ye NIH
3: 7 **w** return your recompence upon your own NIH
3: 8 I **w** sell your sons and your daughters into NIH
3:12 for there **w** I sit to judge all the heathen NIH
3:16 but the Lord **w** be the hope of his people, NIH
3:21 For I **w** cleanse their blood *that* I have not NIH
Am 1: 2 The Lord **w** roar from Zion, and utter his NIH
1: 3 I **w** not turn away *the punishment* NIH
1: 4 I **w** send a fire into the house of Hazael, NIH
1: 5 I **w** break also the bar of Damascus, NIH
1: 6 I **w** not turn away *the punishment* NIH
1: 7 I **w** send a fire on the wall of Gaza, NIH
1: 8 I **w** cut off the inhabitant from Ashdod, NIH
1: 8 and I **w** turn mine hand against Ekron: NIH
1: 9 I **w** not turn away *the punishment* NIH
1:10 I **w** send a fire on the wall of Tyrus, NIH
1:11 I **w** not turn away *the punishment* NIH
1:12 I **w** send a fire upon the Teman, which NIH
1:13 I **w** not turn away *the punishment* NIH
1:14 I **w** kindle a fire in the wall of Rabbah, NIH
2: 1 I **w** not turn away *the punishment* NIH
2: 2 I **w** send a fire upon Moab, and it shall NIH
2: 3 I **w** cut off the judge from the midst NIH
2: 3 **w** slay all the princes thereof with him, NIH
2: 4 I **w** not turn away *the punishment* NIH
2: 5 I **w** send a fire upon Judah, and it shall NIH
2: 6 I **w** not turn away *the punishment* NIH
2: 7 his father **w** go in unto the *same* maid, NIH
3: 2 I **w** punish you for all your iniquities. NIH
3: 4 **W** a lion roar in the forest, when he hath NIH
3: 4 **w** a young lion cry out of his den, if he NIH
3: 7 Surely the Lord God **w** do nothing, but he NIH
3: 8 The lion hath roared, who **w** not fear? NIH
3:14 him I **w** also visit the altars of Beth-el: NIH
3:15 I **w** smite the winter house with the NIH
4: 2 that he **w** take you away with hooks, NIH
4:12 Therefore thus **w** I do unto thee, O Israel: NIH
4:12 *and* because I **w** do this unto thee, NIH
5:15 it may be that the Lord God of hosts **w** NIH
5:17 for I **w** pass through thee, saith the Lord. NIH
5:21 I **w** not smell in your solemn assemblies. NIH
5:22 I **w** not accept *them:* neither will I regard NIH
5:22 I **w** not accept *them:* neither **w** I regard NIH
5:23 for I **w** not hear the melody of thy viols. NIH
5:27 **w** I cause you to go into captivity NIH
6: 8 I **w** deliver up the city with all that is NIH
6:11 he **w** smite the great house *with* breaches, NIH
6:12 **w** *one* plow *there* with oxen? for ye have NIH
6:14 I **w** raise up against you a nation, NIH
7: 8 I **w** set a plumbline in the midst of my NIH
7: 8 I **w** not again pass by them any more: NIH
7: 9 I **w** rise against the house of Jeroboam NIH
8: 2 I **w** not again pass by them any more. NIH
8: 5 Saying, When **w** the new moon be gone, NIH
8: 7 Surely I **w** never forget any of their works. NIH
8: 9 I **w** cause the sun to go down at noon, NIH
8: 9 and I **w** darken the earth in the clear day: NIH
8:10 And I **w** turn your feasts into mourning, NIH
8:10 I **w** bring up sackcloth upon all loins, NIH
8:10 I **w** make it as the mourning of an only NIH
8:11 that I **w** send a famine in the land, NIH
9: 1 I **w** slay the last of them with the sword: NIH
9: 2 *to* heaven, thence **w** I bring them down: NIH
9: 3 I **w** search and take them out thence; NIH
9: 3 thence **w** I command the serpent, NIH
9: 4 thence **w** I command the sword, and it NIH
9: 4 I **w** set mine eyes upon them for evil, NIH
9: 8 I **w** destroy it from off the face of the NIH
9: 8 that I **w** not utterly destroy the house NIH
9: 9 I **w** command, and I will sift the house of NIH
9: 9 I **w** sift the house of Israel among all NIH
9:11 In that day **w** I raise up the tabernacle of NIH
9:11 I **w** raise up his ruins, and I will build it as NIH
9:11 and I **w** build it as *in* the days of old: NIH
9:14 I **w** bring again the captivity of my people NIH
9:15 I **w** plant them upon their land, NIH
Ob 1: 4 thence **w** I bring thee down, saith NIH
Jnh 1: 6 if so be that God **w** think upon us, that we NIH
2: 4 yet I **w** look again toward thy holy temple. NIH
2: 9 I **w** sacrifice unto thee with the voice of NIH
2: 9 I **w** pay *that* that I have vowed. NIH
3: 9 Who can tell *if* God **w** turn and repent, NIH
Mic 1: 3 **w** come down and tread upon the high NIH
1: 6 Therefore I **w** make Samaria as a heap of NIH
1: 6 I **w** pour down the stones thereof into NIH
1: 6 and I **w** discover the foundations thereof. NIH
1: 7 and all the idols thereof **w** I lay desolate: NIH
1: 8 I **w** wail and howl, I will go stript NIH
1: 8 wail and howl, I **w** go stript and naked: NIH
1: 8 I **w** make a wailing like the dragons, NIH

Mic	1:15 Yet **w** I bring an heir unto thee,	NIH
	2:11 *saying,* I **w** prophesy unto thee of wine	NIH
	2:12 I **w** surely assemble, O Jacob, all of thee;	NIH
	2:12 I **w** surely gather the remnant of Israel;	NIH
	2:12 I **w** put them together as the sheep of	NIH
	3: 4 unto the Lord, but he **w** not hear them:	NIH
	3: 4 he **w** even hide his face from them at that	NIH
	3:11 yet **w** they lean upon the Lord, and say,	NIH
	4: 2 he **w** teach us of his ways, and we will	NIH
	4: 2 of his ways, and we **w** walk in his paths:	NIH
	4: 5 all people **w** walk every one in the name	NIH
	4: 5 we **w** walk in the name of the Lord our	NIH
	4: 6 I **w** assemble her that halteth, and I will	NIH
	4: 6 I **w** gather her that is driven out, and *her*	NIH
	4: 7 I **w** make her that halted a remnant,	NIH
	4:13 for I **w** make thine horn iron, and I will	NIH
	4:13 horn iron, and I **w** make thy hoofs brass:	NIH
	4:13 I **w** consecrate their gain unto the Lord,	NIH
	5: 3 Therefore **w** he give them up, until the	NIH
	5:10 that I **w** cut off thy horses out of the midst	NIH
	5:10 of thee, and I **w** destroy thy chariots:	NIH
	5:11 I **w** cut off the cities of thy land,	NIH
	5:12 I **w** cut off witchcrafts out of thine hand;	NIH
	5:13 Thy graven images also **w** I cut off,	NIH
	5:14 I **w** pluck up thy groves out of the midst	NIH
	5:14 the midst of thee: so **w** I destroy thy cities.	NIH
	5:15 I **w** execute vengeance in anger and fury	NIH
	6: 2 his people, and he **w** plead with Israel.	NIH
	6: 7 **W** the Lord be pleased with thousands of	NIH
	6:13 Therefore also **w** I make *thee* sick in	NIH
	6:14 *that* which thou deliverest **w** I give up to	NIH
	7: 7 Therefore I **w** look unto the Lord; I will	NIH
	7: 7 I **w** wait for the God of my salvation:	NIH
	7: 7 God of my salvation: my God **w** hear me.	NIH
	7: 9 I **w** bear the indignation of the Lord,	NIH
	7: 9 he **w** bring me forth to the light, *and* I	NIH
	7:15 **w** I shew unto him marvellous *things.*	NIH
	7:19 He **w** turn again, he will have compassion	NIH
	7:19 he **w** have compassion upon us;	NIH
	7:19 he **w** subdue our iniquities; and thou wilt	NIH
Na	1: 2 the Lord **w** take vengeance on his	NIH
	1: 3 **w** not at all acquit *the wicked:* the Lord	NIH
	1: 8 with an overrunning flood he **w** make an	NIH
	1: 9 he **w** make an utter end: affliction shall	NIH
	1:12 afflicted thee, I **w** afflict thee no more.	NIH
	1:13 For now **w** I break his yoke from off thee,	NIH
	1:13 off thee, and **w** burst thy bonds in sunder.	NIH
	1:14 out of the house of thy gods **w** I cut off	NIH
	1:14 I **w** make thy grave; for thou art vile.	NIH
	2:13 I **w** burn her chariots in the smoke,	NIH
	2:13 I **w** cut off thy prey from the earth,	NIH
	3: 5 I **w** discover thy skirts upon thy face,	NIH
	3: 5 and I **w** shew the nations thy nakedness,	NIH
	3: 6 I **w** cast abominable filth upon thee,	NIH
	3: 6 vile, and **w** set thee as a gazing-stock.	NIH
	3: 7 who **w** bemoan her? whence shall I seek	NIH
Hab	1: 5 for *I* **w** work a work in your days, *which*	NIH
	1: 5 *which* ye **w** not believe, though it be told	NIH
	2: 1 I **w** stand upon my watch, and set me	NIH
	2: 1 I **w** watch to see what he will say unto me,	NIH
	2: 1 I will watch to see what he **w** say unto me,	NIH
	2: 3 because it **w** surely come, it will not tarry.	NIH
	2: 3 because it will surely come, it **w** not tarry.	NIH
	3:16 he **w** invade them with his troops.	NIH
	3:18 Yet I **w** rejoice in the Lord, I will joy in	NIH
	3:18 I **w** joy in the God of my salvation.	NIH
	3:19 and he **w** make my feet like hinds' *feet,*	NIH
	3:19 he **w** make me to walk upon mine high	NIH
Zep	1: 2 I **w** utterly consume all *things* from off	NIH
	1: 3 I **w** consume man and beast; I will	NIH
	1: 3 I **w** consume the fowls of the heaven,	NIH
	1: 3 I **w** cut off man from off the land, saith	NIH
	1: 4 I **w** also stretch out mine hand upon	NIH
	1: 4 I **w** cut off the remnant of Baal from this	NIH
	1: 8 that I **w** punish the princes, and the king's	NIH
	1:12 *that* I **w** search Jerusalem with candles,	NIH
	1:12 in their heart, The Lord **w** not do good,	NIH
	1:12 will not do good, neither **w** he do evil.	NIH
	1:17 I **w** bring distress upon men, that they	NIH
	2: 5 of the Philistines, I **w** even destroy thee,	NIH
	2:11 The Lord **w** be terrible unto them: for he	NIH
	2:11 for he **w** famish all the gods of the earth;	NIH
	2:13 **w** stretch out his hand against the north,	NIH
	2:13 **w** make Nineveh a desolation, *and* dry	NIH
	3: 5 the midst thereof; he **w** not do iniquity:	NIH
	3: 9 **w** I turn to the people a pure language,	NIH
	3:11 I **w** take away out of the midst of thee	NIH
	3:12 I **w** also leave in the midst of thee an	NIH
	3:17 he **w** save, he will rejoice over thee with	NIH
	3:17 will save, he **w** rejoice over thee with joy;	NIH
	3:17 he **w** rest in his love, he will joy over thee	NIH
	3:17 his love, he **w** joy over thee with singing.	NIH
	3:18 I **w** gather *them that are* sorrowful for	NIH
	3:19 at that time I **w** undo all that afflict thee:	NIH
	3:19 I **w** save that halteth, and gather her	NIH
	3:19 I **w** get them praise and fame in every land	NIH
	3:20 At that time I **w** bring you *again,* even in	NIH
	3:20 for I **w** make you a name and a praise	NIH
Hag	1: 8 I **w** take pleasure in it, and I will be	NIH
	1: 8 in it, and I **w** be glorified, saith the Lord.	NIH
	2: 6 I **w** shake the heavens, and the earth,	NIH
	2: 7 I **w** shake all nations, and the desire of all	NIH
	2: 7 I **w** fill this house *with* glory, saith	NIH
	2: 9 in this place **w** I give peace, saith	NIH

Hag	2:19 brought forth: from this day **w** I bless *you.*	NIH
	2:21 I **w** shake the heavens and the earth;	NIH
	2:22 I **w** overthrow the throne of kingdoms,	NIH
	2:22 I **w** destroy the strength of the kingdoms	NIH
	2:22 I **w** overthrow the chariots, and those that	NIH
	2:23 **w** I take thee, O Zerubbabel, my servant,	NIH
	2:23 the Lord, and **w** make thee as a signet:	NIH
Zec	1: 3 I **w** turn unto you, saith the Lord of	NIH
	1: 9 unto me, I **w** shew thee what these *be.*	NIH
	2: 5 **w** be unto her a wall of fire round about,	NIH
	2: 5 and **w** be the glory in the midst of her.	NIH
	2: 9 I **w** shake mine hand upon them,	NIH
	2:10 come, and I **w** dwell in the midst of thee,	NIH
	2:11 I **w** dwell in the midst of thee,	NIH
	3: 4 *I* **w** clothe thee with change of raiment.	NIH
	3: 7 I **w** give thee places to walk among these	NIH
	3: 8 I **w** bring forth my servant the BRANCH.	NIH
	3: 9 behold, I **w** engrave the graving thereof,	NIH
	3: 9 I **w** remove the iniquity of that land in one	NIH
	5: 4 I **w** bring it forth, saith the Lord of hosts,	NIH
	6:15 if ye **w** diligently obey the voice of	NIH
	8: 3 and **w** dwell in the midst of Jerusalem:	NIH
	8: 7 I **w** save my people from the east country,	NIH
	8: 8 I **w** bring them, and they shall dwell in	NIH
	8: 8 I **w** be their God, in truth and	NIH
	8:11 now I **w** not *be* unto the residue of this	NIH
	8:12 I **w** cause the remnant of this people to	NIH
	8:13 so **w** I save you, and ye shall be a blessing:	NIH
	8:21 to seek the Lord of hosts: I **w** go also.	NIH
	8:23 that is a Jew, saying, We **w** go with you:	NIH
	9: 4 the Lord **w** cast her out, and he will smite	NIH
	9: 4 and he **w** smite her power in the sea;	NIH
	9: 6 and I **w** cut off the pride of the Philistines.	NIH
	9: 7 I **w** take away his blood out of his mouth,	NIH
	9: 8 I **w** encamp about mine house because	NIH
	9:10 I **w** cut off the chariot from Ephraim,	NIH
	9:12 even to day do I declare *that* I **w** render	NIH
	10: 6 I **w** strengthen the house of Judah, and I	NIH
	10: 6 I **w** save the house of Joseph, and I will	NIH
	10: 6 and **w** bring them *again* to place them;	NIH
	10: 6 *am* the Lord their God, and **w** hear them.	NIH
	10: 8 I **w** hiss for them, and gather them; for I	NIH
	10: 9 I **w** sow them among the people: and they	NIH
	10:10 I **w** bring them again also out of the land	NIH
	10:10 I **w** bring them into the land of Gilead and	NIH
	10:12 I **w** strengthen them in the Lord;	NIH
	11: 6 For I **w** no more pity the inhabitants of	NIH
	11: 6 I **w** deliver the men every one into his	NIH
	11: 6 out of their hand I **w** not deliver *them.*	NIH
	11: 7 I **w** feed the flock of slaughter, *even* you,	NIH
	11: 9 said I, I **w** not feed you: that that dieth,	NIH
	11:16 lo, I **w** raise up a shepherd in the land,	NIH
	12: 2 I **w** make Jerusalem a cup of trembling	NIH
	12: 3 in that day **w** I make Jerusalem a	1961
	12: 4 I **w** smite every horse with astonishment,	NIH
	12: 4 I **w** open mine eyes upon the house of	NIH
	12: 4 **w** smite every horse of the people with	NIH
	12: 6 In that day **w** I make the governors of	NIH
	12: 9 I **w** seek to destroy all the nations that	NIH
	12:10 I **w** pour upon the house of David,	NIH
	13: 2 I **w** cut off the names of the idols out of	NIH
	13: 2 I **w** cause the prophets and the unclean	NIH
	13: 7 I **w** turn mine hand upon the little ones.	NIH
	13: 9 I **w** bring the third *part* through the fire,	NIH
	13: 9 refine them as silver is refined,	NIH
	13: 9 refined, and **w** try them as gold is tried:	NIH
	13: 9 shall call on my name, and I **w** hear them:	NIH
	13: 9 I **w** say, It *is* my people: and they shall say,	NIH
	14: 2 I **w** gather all nations against Jerusalem	NIH
	14:12 **w** smite all the people that have fought	NIH
	14:17 whoso **w** not come up of *all* the families	NIH
	14:18 where*with* the Lord **w** smite the heathen	NIH
Mal	1: 4 we **w** return and build the desolate places;	NIH
	1: 4 They shall build, but I **w** throw down;	NIH
	1: 5 The Lord **w** be magnified from	NIH
	1: 8 **w** he be pleased with thee, or accept thy	NIH
	1: 9 God that he **w** be gracious unto us:	NIH
	1: 9 **w** he regard your persons? saith the Lord	NIH
	1:10 **w** I accept an offering at your hand.	NIH
	2: 2 If ye **w** not hear, and if ye **w** not lay *it*	NIH
	2: 2 not hear, and if ye **w** not lay *it* to heart,	NIH
	2: 2 I **w** even send a curse upon you,	NIH
	2: 2 upon you, and **w** curse your blessings:	NIH
	2: 3 I **w** corrupt your seed, and spread dung	NIH
	2:12 The Lord **w** cut off the man that doth	NIH
	2:13 or receiveth *it with* **good** at your hand.	7522
	3: 1 I **w** send my messenger, and he shall	NIH
	3: 5 I **w** come near to you to judgment;	NIH
	3: 5 I **w** be a swift witness against the	NIH
	3: 7 I **w** return unto you, saith the Lord of	NIH
	3: 8 **W** a man rob God? Yet ye *have* robbed	NIH
	3:10 if I **w** not open you the windows of	NIH
	3:11 I **w** rebuke the devourer for your sakes,	NIH
	3:17 **w** spare them, as a man spareth his own	NIH
	4: 5 I **w** send you Elijah the prophet before	NIH
Mt	2:13 for Herod **w** seek the young child to	3195
	3:12 and he **w** throughly purge his floor,	NIG
	3:12 **w** burn up the chaff with unquenchable	NIG
	4: 9 unto him, All these *things* **w** I give thee,	NIG
	4:19 and I **w** make you fishers of men.	NIG
	5:40 And if any man **w** sue thee at the law,	2309
	6:10 Thy **w** be done in earth, as *it is* in heaven.	2307
	6:14 your heavenly Father **w** also forgive you:	NIG
	6:15 neither **w** your Father forgive your	NIG
	6:21 treasure is, there **w** your heart be also.	NIG

Mt	6:24 for either he **w** hate the one, and love	NIG
	6:24 or else he **w** hold to the one, and despise	NIG
	7: 9 his son ask bread, **w** he give him a stone?	NIG
	7:10 if he ask a fish, **w** he give him a serpent?	NIG
	7:21 he that doeth the **w** of my Father which	2307
	7:22 Many **w** say to me in that day, Lord, Lord,	NIG
	7:23 And then **w** I profess unto them, I never	NIG
	7:24 I **w** liken him unto a wise man,	NIG
	8: 3 *his* hand, and touched him, saying, I **w**;	2309
	8: 7 saith unto him, I **w** come and heal him.	NIG
	8:19 I **w** follow thee whithersoever thou goest.	NIG
	9:13 I **w** have mercy, and not sacrifice:	NIG
	9:15 the days **w** come, when the bridegroom	NIG
	9:38 that he **w** send forth labourers into his	NIG
	10:17 for they **w** deliver you up to the councils,	NIG
	10:17 they **w** scourge you in their synagogues;	NIG
	10:32 him **w** I confess also before my Father	NIG
	10:33 him **w** I also deny before my Father which	NIG
	11:14 And if ye **w** receive *it,* this is Elias,	2309
	11:27 he to whomsoever the Son **w** reveal *him.*	1014
	11:28 are heavy laden, and I **w** give you rest.	NIG
	12: 7 I **w** have mercy, and not sacrifice,	NIG
	12:11 he not lay hold on it, and lift *it* out?	NIG
	12:18 I **w** put my spirit upon him, and he shall	NIG
	12:29 and then he **w** spoil his house.	NIG
	12:44 I **w** return into my house from whence I	NIG
	12:50 whosoever shall do the **w** of my Father	2307
	13:30 the time of harvest I **w** say to the reapers,	NIG
	13:35 saying, I **w** open my mouth in parables;	NIG
	13:35 I **w** utter *things which have been* kept	NIG
	15:32 and I **w** not send them away fasting,	2309
	16: 2 it is evening, ye say, *It* **w** be fair weather:	NIG
	16: 3 the morning, *It* **w** be foul weather to day:	NIG
	16:18 and upon this rock I **w** build my church;	NIG
	16:19 And I **w** give unto thee the keys of	NIG
	16:24 If any *man* **w** come after me, let him deny	2309
	16:25 For whosoever **w** save his life shall lose it:	2309
	16:25 whosoever **w** lose his life for my sake shall	NIG
	18:14 it is not the **w** of your Father which is in	2307
	18:16 But if he **w** not hear *thee, then* take with	NIG
	18:26 patience with me, and I **w** pay thee all.	NIG
	18:29 patience with me, and I **w** pay thee all.	NIG
	20: 4 and whatsoever is right I **w** give you.	NIG
	20:14 I **w** give unto this last, even as unto thee.	2309
	20:15 Is it not lawful for me to do what I **w**	2309
	20:26 but whosoever **w** be great among you,	2309
	20:27 And whosoever **w** be chief among you,	2309
	20:32 said, What **w** ye *that* I shall do unto you?	2309
	21: 3 of them; and straightway he **w** send them.	NIG
	21:24 unto them, I also **w** ask you one thing,	NIG
	21:24 I in like wise **w** tell you by what authority	NIG
	21:25 he **w** say unto us, Why did ye not then	NIG
	21:29 He answered and said, I **w** not:	2309
	21:31 Whether of *them* twain did the **w** of *his*	2307
	21:37 his son, saying, They **w** reverence my son.	NIG
	21:40 what **w** he do unto those husbandmen?	NIG
	21:41 He **w** miserably destroy those wicked	NIG
	21:41 **w** let out *his* vineyard unto other	NIG
	21:44 it shall fall, it **w** grind him to powder.	NIG
	23: 4 they *themselves* **w** not move them with	2309
	24:28 there **w** the eagles be gathered together.	NIG
	25:21 hast been faithful over a few *things,* I **w**	NIG
	25:23 hast been faithful over a few *things,* I **w**	NIG
	26:15 And said *unto them,* What **w** ye give me,	2309
	26:15 ye give me, and I **w** deliver him unto you?	NIG
	26:18 I **w** keep the passover at thy house with	NIG
	26:29 I **w** not drink henceforth of this fruit of	NIG
	26:31 I **w** smite the shepherd, and the sheep of	NIG
	26:32 after I am risen *again,* I **w** go before you	NIG
	26:33 of thee, *yet* **w** I never be offended.	NIG
	26:35 die with thee, *yet* **w** I not deny thee.	NIG
	26:39 nevertheless not as I **w**, but as thou *wilt.*	2309
	26:42 except I drink it, thy **w** be done.	2307
	27:17 Whom **w** ye *that* I release unto you?	2309
	27:21 Whether of the twain **w** ye *that* I release	2309
	27:42 from the cross, and we **w** believe him.	NIG
	27:43 him deliver him now, if he **w** have him:	2309
	27:49 let us see whether Elias **w** come to save	NIG
	27:63 yet alive, After three days I **w** rise *again.*	NIG
	28:14 we **w** persuade him, and secure you.	NIG
Mk	1:17 I **w** make you to become fishers of men.	NIG
	1:41 touched him, and saith unto him, I **w**;	2309
	2:20 the days **w** come, when the bridegroom	NIG
	2:22 is spilled, and the bottles **w** be marred:	NIG
	3:27 except he **w** first bind the strong *man;*	NIG
	3:27 *man;* and then he **w** spoil his house.	NIG
	3:35 For whosoever shall do the **w** of God,	2307
	4:13 and how *then* **w** ye know all parables?	NIG
	6:22 whatsoever thou wilt, and I **w** give *it* thee.	NIG
	6:23 I **w** give *it* thee, unto the half of my	NIG
	6:25 I **w** that thou give me by and by in a	2309
	8: 3 own houses, they **w** faint by the way:	NIG
	8:34 unto them, Whosoever **w** come after me,	2309
	8:35 whosoever **w** save his life shall lose it;	2309
	9:50 his saltness, wherewith **w** ye season it?	NIG
	10:43 but whosoever **w** be great among you,	2309
	10:44 And whosoever of you **w** be the chiefest,	2309
	11: 3 and straightway he **w** send him hither.	NIG
	11:26 neither **w** your Father which is in heaven	NIG
	11:29 I **w** also ask you one question,	NIG
	11:29 I **w** tell you by what authority I do these	NIG
	11:31 **w** say, Why then did ye not believe him?	NIG
	12: 6 saying, They **w** reverence my son.	NIG
	12: 9 he **w** come and destroy the husbandmen,	NIG
	12: 9 and **w** give the vineyard unto others.	NIG

Mk 14: 7 whensoever ye **w** may do them good: 2309
14:15 And he **w** shew you a large upper room NIG
14:25 I **w** drink no more of the fruit of the vine, NIG
14:27 I **w** smite the shepherd, and the sheep NIG
14:28 I am risen, I **w** go before you into Galilee. NIG
14:29 all shall be offended, yet **w** not I. NIG
14:31 with thee, I **w** not deny thee in any wise. NIG
14:36 nevertheless not that I **w**, but what thou 2309
14:58 I **w** destroy this temple that is made with NIG
14:58 within three days I **w** build another made NIG
15: 9 **W** ye *that* I release unto you the King of 2309
15:12 What **w** ye then *that* I shall do *unto him* 2309
15:36 let us see whether Elias **w** come to take NIG
Lk 2:14 on earth peace, **good** w towards men. 2107
3:17 and he **w** throughly purge his floor, NIG
3:17 and **w** gather the wheat into his garner; NIG
3:17 chaff he **w** burn with fire unquenchable. NIG
4: 6 All this power **w** I give thee, and the glory NIG
4: 6 me; and to whomsoever I **w** I give it. 2309
4:23 Ye **w** surely say unto me this proverb, NIG
5: 5 nevertheless at thy word I **w** let down NIG
5:13 *his* hand, and touched him, saying, I **w**: 2309
5:35 the days **w** come, when the bridegroom NIG
5:37 else the new wine **w** burst the bottles, NIG
6: 9 I **w** ask you one *thing*; Is it lawful on NIG
6:47 I **w** shew you to whom he is like: NIG
7:42 which of them **w** love him most? NIG
9: 5 whosoever **w** not receive you, when ye NIG
9:23 If any *man* **w** come after me, let him deny 2309
9:24 For whosoever **w** save his life shall lose it: 2309
9:24 but whosoever **w** lose his life for my sake, NIG
9:57 I **w** follow thee whithersoever thou goest. NIG
9:61 another also said, Lord, I **w** follow thee; NIG
10:22 and *he* to whom the Son **w** reveal *him*. 1014
10:35 when I come again, I **w** repay thee. NIG
11: 2 Thy **w** be done, as in heaven, so in earth. 2307
11: 8 Though he **w** not rise and give him, NIG
11: 8 because of his importunity he **w** rise and NIG
11:11 that is a father, he **w** give him a stone? NIG
11:11 a fish, he **w** for a fish give him a serpent? NIG
11:12 ask an egg, he **w** offer him a scorpion? NIG
11:24 I **w** return unto my house whence I came NIG
11:49 I **w** send them prophets and apostles, NIG
12: 5 I **w** *forewarn* you whom you shall fear: NIG
12:18 And he said, This **w** I do: I will pull down NIG
12:18 I **w** pull down my barns, and build greater; NIG
12:18 and there **w** I bestow all my fruits and NIG
12:19 And I **w** say to my soul, Soul, thou hast NIG
12:28 how much more **w** *he* clothe you, O ye of NIG
12:34 treasure is, there **w** your heart be also. NIG
12:36 when he **w** return from the wedding; NIG
12:37 meat, and **w** come forth and serve them. NIG
12:44 that he **w** make him ruler over all that he NIG
12:46 The lord of that servant **w** come in a day NIG
12:46 and **w** cut him in sunder, and will appoint NIG
12:46 **w** appoint *him* his portion with NIG
12:47 knew his lord's **w**, and prepared not 2307
12:47 *himself*, neither did according to his **w**, 2307
12:48 of him they **w** ask the more. NIG
12:49 and what **w** I, if it be already kindled? 2309
12:55 wind blow, ye say, There **w** be heat; NIG
13:24 **w** seek to enter in, and shall not be able. NIG
13:31 and depart hence: for Herod **w** kill thee. 2309
14: 5 **w** not straightway pull him out on NIG
15:18 I **w** arise and go to my father, and will say NIG
15:18 go to my father, and **w** say unto him, NIG
16:11 **w** commit to your trust the true *riches*? NIG
16:13 for either he **w** hate the one, and love NIG
16:13 or else he **w** hold to the one, and despise NIG
16:30 unto them from the dead, they **w** repent. NIG
16:31 prophets, neither **w** they be persuaded, NIG
17: 1 It is impossible but that offences **w** come: NIG
17: 7 feeding cattle, **w** say *unto him* by and by, NIG
17: 8 **w** not *rather* say unto him, Make ready NIG
17:22 said unto the disciples, The days **w** come, NIG
17:37 Wheresoever the body *is*, thither **w** NIG
18: 5 this widow troubleth me, I **w** avenge her, NIG
18: 8 I tell you that he **w** avenge them speedily. 4160
19:14 We **w** not have this *man* to reign over us. 2309
19:22 Out of thine own mouth **w** I judge thee, NIG
20: 3 unto them, I **w** also ask you one thing; NIG
20: 5 he **w** say, Why then believed ye him not? NIG
20: 6 we say, Of men; all the people **w** stone us: NIG
20:13 I **w** send my beloved son: it may be they NIG
20:13 it may be they **w** reverence *him* when NIG
20:18 it shall fall, it **w** grind him to powder. NIG
21: 6 *things* which ye behold, the days **w** come, NIG
21: 7 what sign **w** *there* be when these *things* NIG
21:15 For I **w** give you a mouth and wisdom, NIG
22:16 I say unto you, I **w** not any more eat NIG
22:18 I **w** not drink of the fruit of the vine, NIG
22:42 not my **w**, but thine, be done. 2307
22:67 them, If I tell you, you **w** not believe: NIG
22:68 if I also ask *you*, you **w** not answer me, NIG
23:16 I **w** therefore chastise him, and release NIG
23:22 I **w** therefore chastise him, and let *him* go. NIG
23:25 but he delivered Jesus to their **w**. 2307
Jn 1:13 not of blood, nor of the **w** of the flesh, 2307
1:13 flesh, nor of the **w** of man, but of God. 2307
2:19 temple, and in three days I **w** raise it up. NIG
4:25 when he is come, he **w** tell us all *things*. NIG
4:34 meat is to do the **w** of him that sent me, 2307
4:48 see signs and wonders, ye **w** not believe. NIG
5:20 he **w** shew him greater works than these, NIG
5:21 so the Son quickeneth whom he **w**. 2309

Jn 5:30 is just; because I seek not mine own **w**, 2307
5:30 the **w** of the Father which hath sent me. 2307
5:40 And ye **w** not come to me, that ye might 2309
5:43 come in his own name, him ye **w** receive. NIG
5:45 Do not think that I **w** accuse you to NIG
6:37 that cometh to me I **w** in no wise cast NIG
6:38 to do mine own own **w**, but the will of 2307
6:38 own will, but the **w** of him that sent me. 2307
6:39 this is the Father's **w** which hath sent 2307
6:40 And this is the **w** of him that sent me, 2307
6:40 and I **w** raise him up *at* the last day. NIG
6:44 and I **w** raise him up *at* the last day. NIG
6:51 and the bread that I **w** give is my flesh, NIG
6:51 which I **w** give for the life of the world. NIG
6:54 and I **w** raise him up *at* the last day. NIG
6:67 unto the twelve, **W** ye also go away? 2309
7:17 If any *man* **w** do his will, he shall know 2309
7:17 If any *man* will do his **w**, he shall know 2307
7:31 he do moe miracles than these which NIG
7:35 Whither he go, that we shall not find 3195
7:35 he go unto the dispersed among 3195
8:22 Then said the Jews, **W** he kill himself? NIG
8:44 and the lusts of your father ye **w** do. 2309
9:27 hear *it* again? **w** ye also be his disciples? 2309
9:31 of God, and doeth his **w**, him he heareth. 2307
10: 5 And a stranger **w** they not follow, NIG
10: 5 will they not follow, but **w** flee from him: NIG
11:22 thou wilt ask of God, God **w** give *it* thee. NIG
11:48 him thus alone, all *men* **w** believe on him: NIG
11:56 think ye, that he **w** not come to the feast? NIG
12:26 *man* serve me, him **w** *my* Father honour. NIG
12:28 both glorified *it*, and **w** glorify *it* again. NIG
12:32 from the earth, **w** draw all *men* unto me. NIG
13:37 I **w** lay down my life for thy sake. NIG
14: 3 I **w** come again, and receive you unto NIG
14:13 ye shall ask in my name, that **w** I do, NIG
14:14 shall ask any *thing* in my name, I **w** do *it*. NIG
14:16 And I **w** pray the Father, and he shall give NIG
14:18 I **w** not leave you comfortless: I will come NIG
14:18 leave you comfortless: I **w** come to you. NIG
14:21 I **w** love him, and will manifest myself NIG
14:21 love him, and **w** manifest myself to him. NIG
14:23 If a man love me, he **w** keep my words: NIG
14:23 and my Father **w** love him, and we will NIG
14:23 and we **w** come unto him, and make *our* NIG
14:26 whom the Father **w** send in my name, NIG
14:30 Hereafter I **w** not talk much with you: NIG
15: 7 shall ask what ye **w**, and it shall be done 2309
15:20 persecuted me, they **w** also persecute you; NIG
15:20 kept my saying, they **w** keep yours also. NIG
15:21 all these *things* **w** they do unto you for NIG
15:26 whom I **w** send unto you from the Father, NIG
16: 2 whosoever killeth you **w** think that he NIG
16: 3 And these *things* **w** they do unto you, NIG
16: 7 the Comforter **w** not come unto you; NIG
16: 7 but if I depart, I **w** send him unto you. NIG
16: 8 he **w** reprove the world of sin, NIG
16:13 is come, he **w** guide you into all truth: NIG
16:13 and he **w** shew you *things* to come. NIG
16:22 I **w** see you again, and your heart shall NIG
16:23 the Father in my name, he **w** give *it* you. NIG
16:26 you, that I **w** pray the Father for you: NIG
17:24 Father, I **w** that they also, whom thou 2309
17:26 **w** declare *it*: that the love where*with* thou 2309
18:39 **w** ye therefore *that* I release unto you 1014
20:15 hast laid him, and I **w** take him away. NIG
20:25 my hand into his side, I **w** not believe. NIG
21:22 If I **w** that he tarry till I come, what *is* 2309
21:23 If I **w** that he tarry till I come, what *is* 2309
Ac 2:17 I **w** pour out of my Spirit upon all flesh: NIG
2:18 on my handmaidens I **w** pour out in NIG
2:19 And I **w** shew wonders in heaven above, NIG
3:23 soul, which **w** not hear that prophet, NIG
5:38 work be of men, it **w** come to nought: NIG
6: 4 But we **w** give ourselves continually to NIG
7: 7 whom they shall be in bondage **w** I judge, NIG
7:34 And now come, I **w** send thee into Egypt. NIG
7:43 and I **w** carry you away beyond Babylon. NIG
7:49 what house **w** ye build me? saith the Lord: NIG
9:16 I **w** shew him how great *things* he must NIG
13:22 own heart, which shall fulfil all my **w**. 2307
13:34 I **w** give you the sure mercies of David. NIG
13:36 his own generation by the **w** of God, 1012
15:16 After this I **w** return, and will build again NIG
15:16 **w** build again the tabernacle of David, NIG
15:16 and I **w** build again the ruins thereof, NIG
15:16 again the ruins thereof, and I **w** set it up: NIG
17:18 And some said, What **w** this babbler say? 2309
17:31 in the which he **w** judge the world in 3195
17:32 We hear these again of this *matter*. NIG
18: 6 from henceforth I **w** go unto the Gentiles. NIG
18:15 look ye *to it*; for I **w** be no judge of such 1014
18:21 but I **w** return again unto you, if God will. 2309
18:21 but I will return again unto you, if God **w**. 2309
21:14 saying, The **w** of the Lord be done. 2307
21:22 for they **w** hear that thou art come. NIG
22:14 that *thou* shouldest know his **w**, 2307
22:18 for they **w** not receive thy testimony NIG
22:21 for I **w** send thee far hence unto NIG
23:14 that we **w** eat nothing until we have slain NIG
23:21 that *they* **w** neither eat nor drink till they NIG
23:35 I **w** hear thee, said he, when thine NIG
24:22 I **w** know the uttermost of your matter. NIG
24:25 a convenient season, I **w** call for thee. NIG
26:16 *those things* in the which I **w** appear unto NIG

Ac 27:10 I perceive that *this* voyage **w** be with hurt 3195
28:28 unto the Gentiles, and *that* they **w** hear it. NIG
Ro 1:10 journey by the **w** of God to come unto 2307
2: 6 Who **w** render to every *man* according to NIG
2:18 And knowest *his* **w**, and approvest 2307
4: 8 Blessed *is* the man to whom the Lord **w** NIG
5: 7 scarcely for a righteous *man* **w** one die: NIG
7:18 no good *thing*: for to **w** is present 2309
8:27 for the saints according to *the* **w** *of* God. NIG
9: 9 At this time **w** I come, and Sara shall have NIG
9:15 I **w** have mercy on whom I will have NIG
9:15 have mercy on whom I **w** have mercy, NIG
9:15 I **w** have compassion on whom I will have NIG
9:15 I will have compassion on whom I **w** have NIG
9:18 Therefore hath he mercy on whom he **w** 2309
9:18 *mercy*, and whom he **w** he hardeneth. 2309
9:19 find fault? For who hath resisted his **w**? 1013
9:25 also in Osee, I **w** call *them* my people, NIG
9:28 For he **w** finish the work, and cut *it* short NIG
9:28 a short work **w** the Lord make upon NIG
10:19 I **w** provoke you to jealousy by *them that* NIG
10:19 *and* by a foolish nation I **w** anger you. NIG
12: 2 and acceptable, and perfect, **w** of God. 2307
12:19 *is* mine; I **w** repay, saith the Lord. NIG
15: 9 For this cause I **w** confess to thee among NIG
15:18 For I **w** not dare to speak of any of *those* NIG
15:24 my journey into Spain, I **w** come to you: NIG
15:28 this fruit, I **w** come by you into Spain. NIG
15:32 come unto you with joy by the **w** of God, 2307
1Co 1: 1 of Jesus Christ through the **w** of God, 2307
1:19 I **w** destroy the wisdom of the wise, NIG
1:19 **w** bring to nothing the understanding of NIG
4: 5 both **w** bring to light the hidden *things* NIG
4: 5 **w** make manifest the counsels of the NIG
4:19 But I **w** come to you shortly, if the Lord NIG
4:19 you shortly, if the Lord **w**, and will know, 2309
4:19 you shortly, if the Lord will, and **w** know, 2309
4:21 What **w** ye? shall I come unto you with a 2309
6:12 **w** not be brought under the power of NIG
6:14 and **w** *also* raise up us by his own power. NIG
7:36 need so require, let him do what he **w**, 2309
7:37 hath power over his own **w**, and hath so 2307
7:37 decreed in his heart that *he* **w** keep his NIG
7:39 is at liberty to be married to whom she **w**; 2309
8:13 I **w** eat no flesh while the world standeth, NIG
9:17 but if **against** my **w**, a dispensation *of* 210
10:13 who **w** not suffer you to be tempted above NIG
10:13 with the temptation also make a way to NIG
11:34 And the rest **w** I set in order when I come. NIG
12:11 dividing to every man severally as he **w**. 1014
14:15 I **w** pray with the spirit, and will pray with NIG
14:15 and **w** pray with the understanding also: NIG
14:15 I **w** sing with the spirit, and I will sing NIG
14:15 and I **w** sing with the understanding also. NIG
14:21 and other lips **w** I speak unto this people; NIG
14:21 and yet for all that **w** they not hear me, NIG
14:23 **w** they not say that ye are mad? NIG
14:25 down on *his* face he **w** worship God, NIG
14:35 if they **w** learn any *thing*, let them ask 2309
15:35 But some *man* **w** say, How are the dead NIG
16: 3 them **w** I send to bring your liberality unto NIG
16: 5 Now I **w** come unto you, when I shall pass NIG
16: 6 And it may be that I **w** abide, yea, NIG
16: 7 For I **w** not see you now by the way; but 2309
16: 8 But I **w** tarry at Ephesus until Pentecost. 2307
16:12 *his* **w** was not at all to come at this time; 2307
16:12 he **w** come when he shall have convenient NIG
2Co 1: 1 an apostle of Jesus Christ by the **w** of God, 2307
1:10 whom we trust that he **w** yet deliver *us*; NIG
6:16 I **w** dwell in them, and walk in *them*; and NIG
6:16 and walk in *them*; and I **w** be their God, NIG
6:17 not the unclean *thing*; and I **w** receive you, NIG
6:18 **w** be a Father unto you, and ye shall be NIG
8: 5 to the Lord, and unto us by the **w** of God. 2307
8:11 *of it*; that as *there was* a readiness to **w**, 2309
10:11 such **w** *we be* also in deed when we are NIG
10:13 But we **w** not boast of *things* without *our* NIG
11: 9 to you, and *so* **w** I keep *myself*. NIG
11:12 what I do, that I **w** do, that I may cut off NIG
11:18 many glory after the flesh, I **w** glory also. NIG
11:30 If I **w** glory of the *things* which concern NIG
12: 1 I **w** come to visions and revelations of NIG
12: 5 such a one **w** I glory: yet of myself I will NIG
12: 5 yet of myself I **w** not glory, but in mine NIG
12: 6 I shall not be a fool; for I **w** say the truth: NIG
12: 9 **w** I rather glory in my infirmities, NIG
12:14 and I **w** not be burdensome to you: NIG
12:15 I **w** very gladly spend and be spent for NIG
12:21 my God **w** humble *me* among you, NIG
13: 2 other, that, if I come again, I **w** not spare: NIG
Gal 1: 4 according to the **w** of God and our Father: 2307
5:10 that you **w** be none otherwise minded: NIG
Eph 1: 1 apostle of Jesus Christ by the **w** of God, 2307
1: 5 according to the good pleasure of his **w**, 2307
1: 9 known unto us the mystery of his **w**, 2307
1:11 all *things* after the counsel of his own **w**: 2307
5:17 understanding what the **w** of the Lord *is*. 2307
6: 6 doing the **w** of God from the heart; NIG
6: 7 **good w** doing service, as to the Lord, 2133
Php 1: 6 **w** perform *it* until the day of Jesus Christ: NIG
1:15 and strife; and some also of **good w**: 2107
1:18 I therein do rejoice, yea, and **w** rejoice. NIG
2:13 God which worketh in you both to **w** 2309
2:20 who **w** naturally care for your state. NIG
2:23 I shall see **how it w** go with me. 3588+4012

Col	1: 1 apostle of Jesus Christ by the **w** of God,	2307
	1: 9 the knowledge of his **w** in all wisdom	2307
	2:23 indeed a shew of wisdom in **w** worship,	1479
	4:12 and complete in all the **w** of God,	2307
1Th	4: 3 For this is the **w** of God, *even* your	2307
	4:14 also which sleep in Jesus **w** God bring	NIG
	5:18 for this *is* the **w** of God in Christ Jesus	2307
	5:24 *is* he that calleth you, who also **w** do *it*.	NIG
2Th	2: 7 he who now letteth **w** *let*, until he be	NIG
	3: 4 **w** do *the things* which we command you.	NIG
1Ti	2: 4 Who **w** have all men to be saved,	2309
	2: 8 I **w** therefore that men pray every where,	1014
	5:11 wax wanton against Christ, they **w** marry;	2309
	5:14 I **w** therefore that the younger *women*	1014
	6: 9 they that **w** be rich fall into temptation	1014
2Ti	1: 1 apostle of Jesus Christ by the **w** of God,	2307
	2:12 if we deny *him*, he also **w** deny us:	NIG
	2:16 they **w** increase unto more ungodliness.	NIG
	2:17 And their word **w** eat as *doth* a canker:	NIG
	2:25 if God peradventure **w** give them	NIG
	2:26 *who are* taken captive by him at his **w**.	2307
	3:12 all that **w** live godly in Christ Jesus shall	2309
	4: 3 For the time **w** come when they **w**ill not	NIG
	4: 3 For the time will come when they **w** not	NIG
	4:18 **w** preserve *me* unto his heavenly	NIG
Tit	3: 8 *things* I **w** that thou affirm constantly,	1014
Phm	1:19 I **w** repay *it*: albeit I do not say to thee how	NIG
Heb	1: 5 I **w** be to him a Father, and he shall be to	NIG
	2: 4 the Holy Ghost, according to his own **w**?	2308
	2:12 I **w** declare thy name unto my brethren,	NIG
	2:12 in the midst of the church **w** I sing praise	NIG
	2:13 And again, I **w** put my trust in him.	1510
	7: 7 God saith, To day if ye **w** hear his voice,	NIG
	3:15 it is said, To day if ye **w** hear his voice,	NIG
	4: 7 as it is said, To day if ye **w** hear his voice,	NIG
	6: 3 And this **w** we do, if God permit.	NIG
	6:14 Surely blessing I **w** bless thee,	NIG
	6:14 and multiplying I **w** multiply thee.	NIG
	7:21 him, The Lord sware and **w** not repent,	NIG
	8: 8 when I **w** make a new covenant with	NIG
	8:10 For this *is* the covenant that I **w** make	NIG
	8:10 I **w** put my laws into their mind,	2307
	8:10 I **w** be to them a God, and they shall be	NIG
	8:12 For I **w** be merciful to their	NIG
	8:12 their iniquities will I remember no more.	NIG
	10: 7 it is written of me,) to do thy **w**, O God.	2307
	10: 9 said he, Lo, I come to do thy **w**, O God.	2307
	10:10 By the which **w** we are sanctified through	2307
	10:16 This *is* the covenant that I **w** make with	NIG
	10:16 I **w** put my laws into their hearts,	NIG
	10:16 and in their minds **w** I write them;	NIG
	10:17 and iniquities **w** I remember no more.	NIG
	10:30 unto me, I **w** recompense, saith the Lord.	NIG
	10:36 that, after ye have done the **w** of God,	2307
	10:37 *and* he that shall come **w** come,	NIG
	10:37 shall come will come, and **w** not tarry.	NIG
	13: 4 and adulterers God **w** judge.	NIG
	13: 5 for he hath said, I **w** never leave thee,	NIG
	13: 6 I **w** not fear what man shall do unto me.	NIG
	13:21 perfect in every good work to do his **w**,	2307
	13:23 whom, if he come shortly, I **w** see you.	2309
Jas	1:18 Of his **own w** begat he us with the word	1014
	2:18 and I **w** shew thee my faith by my works.	NIG
	4: 4 **w** be a friend of the world is the enemy of	1014
	4: 7 Resist the devil, and he **w** flee from you.	NIG
	4: 8 nigh to God, and he **w** draw nigh to you.	NIG
	4:13 or to morrow we **w** go into such a city,	NIG
	4:15 If the Lord **w**, we shall live, and do this,	2309
1Pe	2:15 so is the **w** of God, that with well doing	2307
	3:10 he that **w** love life, and see good days,	2309
	3:13 And who *is* he that **w** harm you, if ye be	NIG
	3:17 For *it is* better, if the **w** of God be so,	2307
	4: 2 to the lusts of men, but to the **w** of God.	2307
	4: 3 us to have wrought the **w** of the Gentiles,	2307
	4:19 of God commit the keeping of their	2307
2Pe	1:12 Wherefore I **w** not be negligent to put you	3195
	1:15 Moreover I **w** endeavour that you may be	NIG
	1:21 came not in old time by the **w** of man:	2307
	3:10 the day of the Lord **w** come as a thief in	NIG
1Jn	2:17 that doeth the **w** of God abideth for ever.	2307
	5:14 if we ask any *thing* according to his **w**,	2307
3Jn	1:10 I **w** remember his deeds which he doeth,	NIG
	1:13 but I **w** not with ink and pen write unto	2309
Jude	1: 5 I **w** therefore put you in remembrance,	1014
Rev	2: 5 or else I **w** come unto thee quickly,	NIG
	2: 5 remove thy candlestick out of his place,	NIG
	2: 7 To him that overcometh **w** I give to eat of	NIG
	2:10 and I **w** give thee a crown of life.	NIG
	2:16 or else I **w** come unto thee quickly,	NIG
	2:16 **w** fight against them with the sword of my	NIG
	2:17 To him that overcometh **w** I give to eat of	NIG
	2:17 and **w** give him a white stone, and in	NIG
	2:22 I **w** cast her into a bed, and them that	NIG
	2:23 And I **w** kill her children with death;	NIG
	2:23 I **w** give unto every one of you according	NIG
	2:24 I **w** put upon you none other burden.	NIG
	2:26 to him **w** I give power over the nations:	NIG
	2:28 And I **w** give him the morning star.	NIG
	3: 3 I **w** come on thee as a thief, and thou shalt	NIG
	3: 3 thou shalt not know what hour I **w** come	NIG
	3: 5 I **w** not blot out his name out of the book	NIG
	3: 5 but I **w** confess his name before my Father,	NIG
	3: 9 I **w** make *them* of the synagogue of Satan,	NIG
	3: 9 I **w** make them to come and worship	NIG
	3:10 I also **w** keep thee from the hour of	NIG

Rev	3:12 Him that overcometh **w** I make a pillar in	NIG
	3:12 I **w** write upon him the name of my God,	NIG
	3:12 and *I* **w** write upon him my new name.	NIG
	3:16 nor hot, I **w** spue thee out of my mouth.	3195
	3:20 I **w** come in to him, and will sup with	NIG
	3:20 and **w** sup with him, and he with me.	NIG
	3:21 To him that overcometh **w** I grant to sit	NIG
	4: 1 I **w** shew thee *things* which must be	NIG
	11: 3 I **w** give *power* unto my two witnesses,	NIG
	11: 5 And if any *man* **w** hurt them,	2309
	11: 5 if any *man* **w** hurt them, he must in this	2309
	11: 6 earth with all plagues, as often as they **w**.	2309
	17: 1 I **w** shew unto thee the judgment of	NIG
	17: 7 I **w** tell thee the mystery of the woman,	NIG
	17:17 God hath put in their hearts to fulfil his **w**,	1106
	21: 3 he **w** dwell with them, and they shall be	NIG
	21: 6 I **w** give unto him that is athirst of	NIG
	21: 7 shall inherit all *things;* and I **w** be his God,	NIG
	21: 9 *Come* hither, I **w** shew thee the bride,	NIG
	22:17 whosoever **w**, let him take the water of	2309

WILLETH (1) [WILL]
Ro	9:16 So then *it is* not of him that **w**, nor of him	2309

WILLING (32) [WILL]
Ge	24: 5 Peradventure the woman will not be **w** to	14
	24: 8 if the woman will not be **w** to follow thee,	14
Ex	35: 5 whosoever *is* of a **w** heart, let him bring	5081
	35:21 and every one whom his spirit **made w**,	5068
	35:22 as many as were **w** hearted,	5081
	35:29 children of Israel brought a **w** offering	5071
	35:29 whose heart **made** them **w** to bring for	5068
1Ch	28: 9 with a perfect heart and with a **w** mind:	2655
	28:21 **w** skilful *man*, for any *manner of* service:	5081
	29: 5 is **w** to consecrate his service *this* day	5068
Job	39: 9 the unicorn **w** to serve thee,	14
Ps	110: 3 Thy people *shall be* **w** in the day of thy	5071
Isa	1:19 If ye be **w** and obedient, ye shall eat the	14
Mt	1:19 not **w** to make her a publick example,	2309
	26:41 spirit indeed *is* **w**, but the flesh *is* weak.	4289
Mk	15:15 And *so* Pilate, **w** to content the people,	1014
Lk	10:29 But he, **w** to justify himself, said unto	2309
	22:42 Saying, Father, if thou be **w**, remove this	1014
Jn	23:20 Pilate therefore, **w** to release Jesus, spake	2309
	5:35 ye were **w** for a season to rejoice in his	2309
Ac	24:27 and Felix, **w** to shew the Jews a pleasure,	2309
	25: 9 But Festus, **w** to do the Jews a pleasure,	2309
	27:43 But the centurion, **w** to save Paul,	1014
Ro	9:22 **w** to shew *his* wrath, and to make his	2309
2Co	5: 8 and **w** rather to be absent from the body,	2106
	8: 3 *their* power *they were* **w** of themselves,	830
	8:12 if there be first a **w** mind, *it is* accepted	4288
1Th	2: 8 we were **w** to have imparted unto you,	2106
1Ti	6:18 ready to distribute, **w to communicate;**	2843
Heb	6:17 more abundantly to shew unto the	1014
	13:18 in all *things* **w** to live honestly,	2309
2Pe	3: 9 not **w** that any should perish, but that all	1014

WILLINGLY (25) [WILL]
Ex	25: 2 every man that **giveth** it **w** with his heart	5068
Jdg	5: 2 when the people **w offered** themselves.	5068
	5: 9 that **offered** themselves among	5068
	8:25 We will **w give** *them*. And they	5414+5414
1Ch	29: 6 rulers over the king's work, **offered w**,	5068
	29: 9 for that they **offered w**, because	5068
	29: 9 with perfect heart they **offered w** to	5068
	29:14 that we should be able to **offer** *so* **w**	5068
	29:17 heart I have **w offered** all these *things:*	5068
	29:17 are present here, to **offer w** unto thee.	5068
2Ch	17:16 who **w offered** himself unto the LORD;	5068
	35: 8 princes gave **w** unto the people,	5071+3807.1
Ezr	1: 6 beside all *that* was **w offered**.	5068
	3: 5 of every one that **w offered** a freewill	5068
	7:16 **w offered** for the house of their God	5069
Ne	11: 2 that **w offered** themselves to dwell at	5068
Pr	31:13 and worketh **w** with her hands.	2656+871.1
La	3:33 For he doth not afflict **w** nor grieve	3820+4480
Hos	5:11 he **w** walked after the commandment.	2974
Jn	6:21 Then they **w** received him into the ship:	2309
Ro	8:20 not **w**, but by reason of him who hath	1635
1Co	9:17 For if I do this *thing* **w**, I have a reward:	1635
Phm	1:14 be as *it were* of necessity, but **w**.	1595+2596
1Pe	5: 2 *thereof*, not by constraint, but **w**;	1596
2Pe	3: 5 For this they **w** are ignorant of, that by	2309

WILLOW (1) [WILLOWS]
Eze	17: 5 *it* by great waters, *and* set it *as* a **w** tree.	6851

WILLOWS (5) [WILLOW]
Lev	23:40 boughs of thick trees, and **w** of the brook;	6155
Job	40:22 the **w** of the brook compass him about.	6155
Ps	137: 2 We hanged our harps upon the **w** in	6155
Isa	15: 7 they carry away to the brook of the **w**.	6155
	44: 4 the grass, as **w** by the water courses.	6155

WILT (245) [WILL]
Ge	13: 9 if *thou* **w** take the left hand, then I will go	NIH
	15: 2 Lord GOD, what **w** thou give me,	NIH
	16: 8 whither **w** thou go? And she said, I flee	NIH
	18:23 **W** thou also destroy the righteous with	NIH
	18:24 **w** thou also destroy and not spare the	NIH
	18:28 **w** thou destroy all the city for *lack* of five?	NIH
	20: 4 Lord, **w** thou slay also a righteous nation?	NIH
	21:23 swear unto me here by God that thou **w**	NIH
	23:13 saying, But if thou **w** *give it*, I pray thee,	NIH

Ge	24:58 said unto her, **W** thou go with this man?	NIH
	26:29 That thou **w** do us no hurt, as we have	NIH
	30:31 if thou **w** do this thing for me, I will again	NIH
	38:16 she said, What **w** thou give me, that thou	NIH
	38:17 she said, **W** thou give *me* a pledge, till	NIH
	43: 4 If thou **w** send our brother with us, we	3426
	43: 5 If thou **w** not send *him*, we will not go	NIH
Ex	4:13 by the hand *of him whom* thou **w** send.	NIH
	8:21 if thou **w** not let my people go, behold,	NIH
	9: 2 to let *them* go, and **w** hold them still,	NIH
	9:17 my people, that *thou* **w** not let them go?	NIH
	10: 3 How long **w** thou refuse to humble	NIH
	13:13 if thou **w** not redeem *it*, then thou shalt	NIH
	15:26 If thou **w** diligently hearken to the voice	NIH
	15:26 and **w** do that which is right in his sight,	NIH
	15:26 **w** give ear to his commandments,	NIH
	18:18 Thou **w** surely wear away, both thou,	NIH
	20:25 if thou **w** make me an altar of stone,	NIH
	32:32 Yet now, if thou **w** forgive their sin;	NIH
	33:12 thou hast not let me know whom thou **w**	NIH
Nu	16:14 **w** thou put out the eyes of these men?	NIH
	16:22 **w** thou be wroth with all the	NIH
	21: 2 If thou **w** indeed deliver this people into	NIH
Dt	23:13 shall be, when thou **w** ease thyself abroad,	NIH
	28:15 if thou **w** not hearken unto the voice of	NIH
	28:58 If thou **w** not observe to do all the words	NIH
	30:17 that thou **w** not hear, but shalt be drawn	NIH
Jos	7: 9 and what **w** thou do unto thy great name?	NIH
Jdg	1:14 and Caleb said unto her, What **w** thou?	NIH
	4: 8 If thou **w** go with me, then I will go:	NIH
	4: 8 if thou **w** not go with me, *then* I will not	NIH
	6:36 If thou **w** save Israel by mine hand,	3426
	6:37 know that thou **w** save Israel by mine	NIH
	11:24 **W** not thou possess that which Chemosh	NIH
	13:16 if thou **w** offer a burnt offering, thou must	NIH
Ru	4: 4 If thou **w** redeem *it*, redeem *it*: but if thou	NIH
	4: 4 but if thou **w** not redeem *it*, *then* tell me,	NIH
1Sa	1:11 if thou **w** indeed look on the affliction of	NIH
	1:11 **w** give unto thine handmaid a man child,	NIH
	1:14 unto her, How long **w** thou be drunken?	NIH
	14:37 **w** thou deliver them into the hand of	NIH
	16: 1 How long **w** thou mourn for Saul,	NIH
	19: 5 then **w** thou sin against innocent blood,	NIH
	21: 9 If thou **w** take that, take *it*: for *there is* no	NIH
	24:21 that thou **w** not cut off my seed after me,	NIH
	24:21 that thou **w** not destroy my name out of	NIH
	25:17 know and consider what thou **w** do;	NIH
	30:15 by God, that thou **w** neither kill me,	NIH
2Sa	5:19 **W** thou deliver them into mine hand?	NIH
	13: 4 **w** thou not tell me? And Amnon said unto	NIH
	18:22 Joab said, Wherefore **w** thou run, my son,	NIH
	20:19 why **w** thou swallow up the inheritance	NIH
	22:26 With the merciful thou **w** shew thyself	NIH
	22:26 with the upright man thou **w** shew thyself	NIH
	22:27 With the pure thou **w** shew thyself pure;	NIH
	22:27 with the froward thou **w** shew thyself	NIH
	22:28 the afflicted people thou **w** save:	NIH
	24:13 **w** thou flee three months before thine	NIH
1Ki	3:14 if thou **w** walk in my ways, to keep my	NIH
	6:12 if thou **w** walk in my statutes, and	NIH
	9: 4 if thou **w** walk before me, as David thy	NIH
	9: 4 **w** keep my statutes and my judgments:	NIH
	11:38 if thou **w** hearken unto all that I command	NIH
	11:38 **w** walk in my ways, and do that *is* right in	NIH
	12: 7 If thou **w** be a servant unto this people	NIH
	12: 7 **w** serve them, and answer them,	NIH
	13: 8 If thou **w** give me half thine house, I will	NIH
	22: 4 And **W** thou go with me to battle *to*	NIH
2Ki	3: 7 **w** thou go with me against Moab to	NIH
	4:23 Wherefore **w** thou go to him to day?	NIH
	8:12 Because I know the evil that thou **w** do	NIH
	8:12 their strong holds **w** thou set on fire,	NIH
	8:12 their young *men* **w** thou slay with	NIH
	8:12 **w** dash their children, and rip up their	NIH
	18:24 **w** thou turn away the face of one captain	NIH
1Ch	14:10 **w** thou deliver them into mine hand?	NIH
	17:25 hast told thy servant that *thou* **w** build him	NIH
2Ch	7:17 *as for* thee, if thou **w** walk before me,	NIH
	18: 3 **W** thou go with me *to* Ramoth-gilead?	NIH
	20: 9 our affliction, then thou **w** hear and help.	NIH
	20:12 O our God, **w** thou not judge them?	NIH
	25: 8 if thou **w** go, do *it*, be strong for the battle:	NIH
Ne	2: 6 when **w** thou return? So it pleased	NIH
Est	5: 3 unto her, What **w** thou, queen Esther?	NIH
Job	4: 2 commune with thee, **w** thou be grieved?	NIH
	5: 1 and to which of the saints **w** thou turn?	NIH
	7:19 How long **w** thou not depart from me,	NIH
	8: 2 How long **w** thou speak these *things?*	NIH
	9:28 I know that thou **w** not hold me innocent.	NIH
	10: 9 and **w** thou bring me into dust again?	NIH
	10:14 thou **w** not acquit me from mine iniquity.	NIH
	13:25 **W** thou break a leaf driven to and fro?	NIH
	13:25 and **w** thou pursue the dry stubble?	NIH
	14:15 thou **w** have a desire to the work of thine	NIH
	30:23 For I know *that* thou **w** bring me *to* death,	NIH
	34:17 **w** thou condemn him that is most just?	NIH
	38:39 **W** thou hunt the prey for the lion? or fill	NIH
	39:11 **W** thou trust him, because his strength *is*	NIH
	39:11 or **w** thou leave thy labour to him?	NIH
	39:12 **W** thou believe him, that he will bring	NIH
	40: 8 **W** thou also disannul my judgment?	NIH
	40: 8 **w** thou condemn me, that thou mayest be	NIH
	41: 4 **w** thou take him for a servant for ever?	NIH
	41: 5 **W** thou play with him as *with* a bird?	NIH
	41: 5 or **w** thou bind him for thy maidens?	NIH

Ps	5:12 For thou, LORD, **w** bless the righteous;	NIH
	5:12 *with* favour **w** thou compass him as *with*	NIH
	10:13 said in his heart, Thou **w** not require *it*.	NIH
	10:17 thou **w** prepare their heart, thou wilt	NIH
	10:17 thou **w** cause thine ear to hear:	NIH
	13: 1 How long **w** thou forget me, O LORD?	NIH
	13: 1 how long **w** thou hide thy face from me?	NIH
	16:10 For thou **w** not leave my soul in hell;	NIH
	16:10 neither **w** thou suffer thine Holy One to	NIH
	16:11 Thou **w** shew me the path of life: in thy	NIH
	17: 6 upon thee, for thou **w** hear me, O God:	NIH
	18:25 With the merciful thou **w** shew thyself	NIH
	18:25 with an upright man thou **w** shew thyself	NIH
	18:26 With the pure thou **w** shew thyself pure;	NIH
	18:26 with the froward thou **w** shew thyself	NIH
	18:27 For thou **w** save the afflicted people;	NIH
	18:27 but **w** bring down high looks.	NIH
	18:28 For thou **w** light my candle: the LORD my	NIH
	35:17 Lord, how long **w** thou look on? rescue	NIH
	38:15 do I hope: thou **w** hear, O Lord my God.	NIH
	41: 2 thou **w** not deliver him unto the will of	NIH
	41: 3 thou **w** make all his bed in his sickness.	NIH
	51:17 contrite heart, O God, thou **w** not despise.	NIH
	56:13 **w**not *deliver* my feet from falling,	NIH
	60:10 **W** not thou, O God, *which* hadst cast us	NIH
	61: 6 Thou **w** prolong the king's life:	NIH
	65: 5 *By* terrible *things* in righteousness **w** thou	NIH
	79: 5 **w** thou be angry, for ever? shall thy	NIH
	80: 4 how long **w** thou be angry against	NIH
	81: 8 O Israel, if thou **w** hearken unto me;	NIH
	85: 5 **W** thou be angry with us for ever?	NIH
	85: 5 **w** thou draw out thine anger to all	NIH
	85: 6 **W** thou not revive us again: that thy	NIH
	86: 7 I will call upon thee: for thou **w** answer	NIH
	88:10 **W** thou shew wonders to the dead? shall	NIH
	89:46 **w** thou hide thyself, for ever? shall thy	NIH
	101: 2 when **w** thou come unto me? I will walk	NIH
	108:11 **W** not *thou*, O God, *which* hast cast us off?	NIH
	108:11 **w** not thou, O God, go forth with our	NIH
	119:82 saying, When **w** thou comfort me?	NIH
	119:84 when **w** thou execute judgment on them	NIH
	138: 7 in the midst of trouble, thou **w** revive me:	NIH
	139:19 Surely thou **w** slay the wicked, O God:	NIH
Pr	2: 1 if thou **w** receive my words, and hide my	NIH
	5:20 why **w** thou, my son, be ravisht with a	NIH
	6: 9 How long **w** thou sleep, O sluggard?	NIH
	6: 9 when **w** thou arise out of thy sleep?	NIH
	23: 5 **W** thou set thine eyes upon that which is	NIH
Isa	26: 3 Thou **w** keep *him* in perfect peace, *whose*	NIH
	26:12 LORD, thou **w** ordain peace for us:	NIH
	27: 8 it shooteth forth, thou **w** debate with it:	NIH
	36: 9 **w** thou turn away the face of one captain	NIH
	38:12 day *even* to night **w** thou make an end	NIH
	38:13 day *even* to night **w** thou make an end	NIH
	38:16 thou recover me, and make me to live.	NIH
	58: 5 ashes *under him*? **w** thou call this a fast,	NIH
	64:12 **W** thou refrain thyself for these *things*,	NIH
	64:12 **w** thou hold thy peace, and afflict us very	NIH
Jer	3: 4 **W** thou not from this time cry unto me,	NIH
	4: 1 If thou **w** return, O Israel, saith the LORD,	NIH
	4: 1 if thou **w** put away thine abominations	NIH
	4:30 when thou art spoiled, what **w** thou do?	NIH
	12: 5 how **w** thou do in the swelling of Jordan?	NIH
	13:21 **w** thou say when he shall punish thee?	NIH
	13:27 **w** thou not be made clean? when *shall it*	NIH
	15:18 **w** thou be altogether unto me as a liar,	NIH
	31:22 How long **w** thou go about, O thou	NIH
	38:15 **w** thou not surely put me to death?	NIH
	38:15 counsel, **w** thou not hearken unto me?	NIH
	38:17 If thou **w** assuredly go forth unto the king	NIH
	38:18 if thou **w** not go forth to the king of	NIH
	47: 5 their valley: how long **w** thou cut thyself?	NIH
La	1:21 are glad that thou hast done *it*: thou **w**	NIH
Eze	9: 8 *w*thou destroy all the residue of Israel in	NIH
	11:13 **w** thou make a full end of the remnant of	NIH
	20: 4 **W** thou judge them, son of man, wilt thou	NIH
	20: 4 **w** thou judge *them?* cause them to know	NIH
	22: 2 Now, thou son of man, **w** thou judge, wilt	NIH
	22: 2 thou judge, **w** thou judge the bloody city?	NIH
	23:36 **w** thou judge Aholah and Aholibah?	NIH
	24:19 **W** thou not tell us what these *things* are	NIH
	28: 9 **W** thou yet say before him that slayeth	NIH
	37:18 **W** thou not shew us what thou meanest	NIH
Hos	9:14 what **w** thou give? give them a	NIH
Mic	7:19 thou **w** cast all their sins into the depths	NIH
	7:20 Thou **w** perform the truth to Jacob,	NIH
Hab	1: 2 how long shall I cry, and thou **w** not hear?	NIH
	1: 2 thee *of* violence, and thou **w** not save?	NIH
Zep	3: 7 I said, Surely thou **w** fear me, thou wilt	NIH
	3: 7 wilt fear me, thou **w** receive instruction;	NIH
Zec	1:12 how long **w** thou not have mercy on	NIH
	3: 7 If thou **w** walk in my ways, and if thou	NIH
	3: 7 if thou **w** keep my charge, then thou shalt	NIH
Mt	4: 9 if thou **w** fall down and worship me.	NIG
	7: 4 Or how **w** thou say to thy brother, Let me	NIG
	8: 2 worshipped him, saying, Lord, if thou,	2309
	13:28 **W** thou then *that* we go and gather them	2309
	15:28 be it unto thee *even* as thou **W**. And her	2309
	17: 4 if thou **w**, let us make here three	2309
	19:17 but if thou **w** enter into life, keep	2309
	19:21 If thou **w** be perfect, go *and* sell that thou	2309
	20:21 And he said unto her, What **w** thou?	2309
	26:17 Where **w** thou that we prepare for thee to	2309
	26:39 nevertheless not as I will, but as thou **w**.	NIG
Mk	1:40 to him, and saying, If thou **w**,	2309

Mk	6:22 Ask of me whatsoever thou **w**, and I will	2309
	10:51 What **w** thou *that* I should do unto thee?	2309
	14:12 Where **w** thou *that* we go and prepare	2309
	14:36 not that I will, but what thou **w**.	NIG
Lk	4: 7 If thou therefore **w** worship me, all shall	NIG
	5:12 besought him, saying, Lord, if thou **w**,	2309
	9:54 **w** thou *that* we command fire to come	2309
	18:41 What **w** thou *that* I shall do unto thee?	2309
	22: 9 him, Where **w** thou *that* we prepare?	2309
Jn	2:20 and **w** thou rear it up in three days?	NIG
	5: 6 saith unto him, **W** thou be made whole?	2309
	11:22 now, whatsoever thou **w** ask of God,	NIG
	13:38 **W** thou lay down thy life for my sake?	NIG
	14:22 how is it that thou **w** manifest thyself	3195
Ac	1: 6 **w** thou at this time restore again	NIG
	2:27 Because thou **w** not leave my soul in hell,	NIG
	2:27 neither **w** thou suffer thine Holy One to	NIG
	7:28 **W** thou kill me, as thou didst the Egyptian	2309
	9: 6 Lord, what **w** thou have me to do?	NIG
	13:10 **w** thou not cease to pervert the right ways	NIG
	25: 9 **W** thou go up to Jerusalem, and there be	2309
Ro	9:19 Thou **w** say then unto me, Why doth he	NIG
	11:19 Thou **w** say then, The branches were	NIG
	13: 3 **W** thou then not be afraid of the power?	2309
Phm	1:21 knowing that thou **w** also do more than	NIG
Jas	2:20 But **w** thou know, O vain man, that faith	2309

WILY See FROWARD

WIMPLES (1)
Isa	3:22 and the **w**, and the crisping pins,	4304

WIN (2) [WINNETH, WON]
2Ch	32: 1 and thought to **w** them for himself.	1234
Php	3: 8 *them but* dung, that I may **w** Christ,	2770

WIND (123) [WHIRLWIND, WHIRLWINDS, WINDING, WINDS, WINDY, WOUND]
Ge	8: 1 God made a **w** to pass over the earth,	7307
	41: 6 blasted with the **east w** sprang up after	6921
	41:23 thin, *and* blasted with the **east w**,	6921
	41:27 the **east w** shall be seven years of famine.	6921
Ex	10:13 the LORD brought an east **w** upon	7307
	10:13 the east **w** brought the locusts.	7307
	10:19 the LORD turned a mighty strong west **w**,	7307
	14:21 go *back* by a strong east **w** all *that* night,	7307
	15:10 Thou didst blow with thy **w**, the sea	7307
Nu	11:31 there went forth a **w** from the LORD,	7307
2Sa	22:11 he was seen upon the wings of the **w**.	7307
1Ki	18:45 the heaven was black *with* clouds and **w**,	7307
	19:11 a great and strong **w** rent the mountains,	7307
	19:11 *but* the LORD *was* not in the **w**:	7307
	19:11 after the **w** an earthquake; *but* the LORD	7307
2Ki	3:17 shall not see **w**, neither shall ye see rain;	7307
Job	1:19 came a great **w** from the wilderness,	7307
	6:26 of one that is desperate, *which are* as **w**?	7307
	7: 7 O remember that my life *is* **w**: mine eye	7307
	8: 2 words of thy mouth *be like* a strong **w**?	7307
	15: 2 and fill his belly *with* the **east w**?	6921
	21:18 They are as stubble before the **w**,	7307
	27:21 The **east w** carrieth him away,	6921
	30:15 they pursue my soul as the **w**:	7307
	30:22 Thou liftest me up to the **w**; thou causest	7307
	37:17 he quieteth the earth by the south **w**?	NIH
	37:21 but the **w** passeth, and cleanseth them.	7307
	38:24 scattereth the **east w** upon the earth?	6921
Ps	1: 4 like the chaff which the **w** driveth away.	7307
	18:10 yea, he did fly upon the wings of the **w**.	7307
	18:42 beat them small as the dust before the **w**:	7307
	35: 5 Let them be as chaff before the **w**:	7307
	48: 7 the ships of Tarshish with an east **w**.	7307
	78:26 caused an east **w** to blow in the heaven:	6921
	78:26 by his power he brought in the **south w**.	8486
	78:39 a **w** that passeth away, and cometh not	7307
	83:13 like a wheel; as the stubble before the **w**.	7307
	103:16 For the **w** passeth over it, and it is gone;	7307
	104: 3 who walketh upon the wings of the **w**:	7307
	107:25 commandeth, and raiseth the stormy **w**,	7307
	135: 7 he bringeth the **w** out of his treasures.	7307
	147:18 he causeth his **w** to blow, *and* the waters	7307
	148: 8 and vapour; stormy **w** fulfilling his word:	7307
Pr	11:29 his own house shall inherit the **w**:	7307
	25:14 gift *is like* clouds and **w** without rain.	7307
	25:23 The north **w** driveth away rain: so *doth*	7307
	27:16 hideth the **w**, and the ointment of his	7307
	30: 4 who hath gathered the **w** in his fists?	7307
Ecc	1: 6 The **w** goeth toward the south,	7307
	1: 6 the **w** returneth *again* according to his	7307
	5:16 hath he that hath laboured for the **w**?	7307
	11: 4 He that observeth the **w** shall not sow;	7307
SS	4:16 O **north w**; and come thou south;	6828
Isa	7: 2 trees of the wood are moved with the **w**.	7307
	11:15 with his mighty **w** shall he shake his hand	7307
	17:13 the chaff of the mountains before the **w**,	7307
	26:18 pain, we have as it were brought forth **w**;	7307
	27: 8 he stayeth his rough **w** in the day of the	7307
	27: 8 his rough wind in the day of the **east w**.	6921
	32: 2 shall be as a hiding place from the **w**,	7307
	41:16 the **w** shall carry them away,	7307
	41:29 their molten images *are* **w** and confusion.	7307
	57:13 the **w** shall carry them all away;	7307
	64: 6 our iniquities, like the **w**, have taken us	7307
Jer	2:24 *that* snuffeth up the **w** at her pleasure;	7307
	4:11 A dry **w** of the high places in	7307
	4:12 a full **w** from those *places* shall come	7307

Jer	5:13 prophets shall become **w**, and the word	7307
	10:13 bringeth forth the **w** out of his treasures.	7307
	13:24 passeth away by the **w** of the wilderness.	7307
	14: 6 they snuffed up the **w** like dragons;	7307
	18:17 I will scatter them as *with* an east **w**	7307
	22:22 The **w** shall eat up all thy pastors,	7307
	51: 1 that rise up against me, a destroying **w**;	7307
	51:16 bringeth forth the **w** out of his treasures.	7307
Eze	5: 2 a third *part* thou shalt scatter in the **w**;	7307
	12:14 I will scatter toward every **w** all that *are*	7307
	13:11 shall fall; and a stormy **w** shall rent *it*.	7307
	13:13 I will even rent *it* with a stormy **w** in my	7307
	17:10 wither, when the east **w** toucheth it?	7307
	19:12 and the east **w** dried up her fruit:	7307
	27:26 the east **w** hath broken thee in the midst	7307
	37: 9 Prophesy unto the **w**, prophesy, son of	7307
	37: 9 prophesy, son of man, and say to the **w**,	7307
Da	2:35 the **w** carried them away, that no place	7308
Hos	4:19 The **w** hath bound her up in her wings,	7307
	8: 7 For they have sown the **w**, and they shall	7307
	12: 1 Ephraim feedeth on **w**, and followeth	7307
	12: 1 on wind, and followeth after the **east w**:	6921
	13:15 among *his* brethren, an east **w** shall come,	7307
	13:15 the **w** of the LORD *shall* come up from	NIH
Am	4:13 createth the **w**, and declareth unto man	7307
Jnh	1: 4 the LORD sent out a great **w** into the sea,	7307
	4: 8 that God prepared a vehement east **w**;	6921
Hab	1: 9 their faces shall sup up *as the* **east w**,	6921
Zec	5: 9 women, and the **w** *was* in their wings;	7307
Mt	11: 7 to see? A reed shaken with the **w**?	417
	14:24 tossed with waves: for the **w** was contrary.	417
	14:30 when he saw the **w** boysterous, he was	417
	14:32 were come into the ship, the **w** ceased.	417
Mk	4:37 And there arose a great storm of **w**,	417
	4:39 and rebuked the **w**, and said unto the sea,	417
	4:39 And the **w** ceased, and there was a great	417
	4:41 that even the **w** and the sea obey him?	417
	6:48 rowing; for the **w** was contrary unto them:	417
	6:51 unto them into the ship; and the **w** ceased:	417
Lk	7:24 for to see? A reed shaken with the **w**?	417
	8:23 there came down a storm of **w** on the lake;	417
	8:24 and rebuked the **w** and the raging of	417
	12:55 when *ye see* the **south w** blow, ye say,	3558
Jn	3: 8 The **w** bloweth where it listeth,	4151
	6:18 the sea arose by reason of a great **w** that	417
Ac	2: 2 from heaven as of a rushing mighty **w**,	4157
	27: 7 the **w** not suffering us, we sailed under	417
	27:13 And when the **w** blew softly,	3558
	27:14 there arose against it a tempestuous **w**,	417
	27:15 could not bear up into the **w**, we let *her*	417
	27:40 and hoised up the mainsail to the **w**,	4154
	28:13 and after one day the **south w** blew,	3558
Eph	4:14 carried about with every **w** of doctrine,	417
Jas	1: 6 like a wave of the sea **driven with the w**	416
Rev	6:13 when she is shaken of a mighty **w**.	417
	7: 1 that the **w** should not blow on the earth,	417

WINDING (3) [WIND]
1Ki	6: 8 went up with **w** stairs into the middle	3883
Eze	41: 7 a **w** about still upward to the side	5437
	41: 7 for the **w** about of the house *went* still	5437

WINDOW (16) [WINDOWS]
Ge	6:16 A **w** shalt thou make to the ark, and in a	6672
	8: 6 Noah opened the **w** of the ark which he	2474
	26: 8 king of the Philistins looked out at a **w**,	2474
Jos	2:15 let them down by a cord through the **w**:	2474
	2:18 in the **w** which thou didst let us down by:	2474
	2:21 and she bound the scarlet line in the **w**.	2474
Jdg	5:28 The mother of Sisera looked out at a **w**,	2474
1Sa	19:12 So Michal let David down through a **w**:	2474
2Sa	6:16 Saul's daughter looked through a **w**,	2474
2Ki	9:30 tired her head, and looked out at a **w**.	2474
	9:32 he lift up his face to the **w**, and said,	2474
	13:17 he said, Open the **w** eastward. And he	2474
1Ch	15:29 looking out at a **w** saw king David	2474
Pr	7: 6 at the **w** of my house I looked through	2474
Ac	20: 9 And there sat in a **w** a certain young man	2376
2Co	11:33 through a **w** in a basket was I let down	2376

WINDOWS (30) [WINDOW]
Ge	7:11 and the **w** of heaven were opened.	699
	8: 2 deep and the **w** of heaven were stopped,	699
1Ki	6: 4 for the house he made **w** of narrow lights.	699
	7: 4 *there were* **w** in three rows, and light	8261
	7: 5 and posts *were* square, *with the* **w**:	8260
2Ki	7: 2 *if* the LORD would make **w** in heaven,	699
	7:19 *if* the LORD should make **w** in heaven,	699
Ecc	12: 3 those that look out of the **w** be darkened,	2474
SS	2: 9 our wall, he looketh forth at the **w**,	2474
Isa	24:18 for the **w** from on high are open,	699
	54:12 I will make thy **w** of agates, and thy gates	8121
	60: 8 fly as a cloud, and as the doves to their **w**?	699
Jer	9:21 For death is come up into our **w**,	2474
	22:14 large chambers, and cutteth him out **w**;	2474
Eze	40:16 *were* narrow **w** to the little chambers,	2474
	40:16 **w** *were* round about inward: and upon	2474
	40:22 their **w**, and their arches, and their palm	2474
	40:25 *were* **w** in it and in the arches thereof	2474
	40:25 arches thereof round about, like those **w**:	2474
	40:29 *were* **w** in it and in the arches thereof	2474
	40:33 *there were* **w** therein and in the arches	2474
	40:36 thereof, and the **w** to it round about:	2474
	41:16 narrow **w**, and the galleries round about	2474
	41:16 *from* the ground up to the **w**,	2474

Eze	41:16 to the windows, and the **w** *were* covered;	2474
	41:26 *there were* narrow **w** and palm trees on	2474
Da	6:10 his **w** being open in his chamber toward	3551
Joel	2: 9 they shall enter in at the **w** like a thief.	2474
Zep	2:14 *their* voice shall sing in the **w**;	2474
Mal	3:10 if I will not open you the **w** of heaven,	699

WINDS (23) [WINDY]

Job	28:25 To make the weight for the **w**;	7307
Jer	49:32 I will scatter into all **w** them *that are* in	7307
	49:36 upon Elam will I bring the four **w** from	7307
	49:36 scatter them towards all those **w**;	7307
Eze	5:10 of thee will I scatter into all the **w**.	7307
	5:12 I will scatter a third *part* into all the **w**,	7307
	17:21 remain shall be scattered towards all **w**:	7307
	37: 9 Come from the four **w**, O breath,	7307
Da	7: 2 the four **w** of the heaven strove upon	7308
	8: 8 ones toward the four **w** of heaven.	7307
	11: 4 shall be divided toward the four **w** of	7307
Zec	2: 6 I have spread you abroad as the four **w**	7307
Mt	7:25 the **w** blew, and beat upon that house;	417
	7:27 the **w** blew, and beat upon that house,	417
	8:26 he arose, and rebuked the **w** and the sea;	417
	8:27 this, that even the **w** and the sea obey him?	417
	24:31 gather together his elect from the four **w**,	417
Mk	13:27 gather together his elect from the four **w**,	417
Lk	8:25 for he commandeth even the **w** and water,	417
Ac	27: 4 Cyprus, because the **w** were contrary.	417
Jas	3: 4 they be so great, and are driven of fierce **w**,	417
Jude	1:12 *they are* without water, carried about of **w**;	417
Rev	7: 1 holding the four **w** of the earth, that the	417

WINDY (1) [WINDS]

Ps	55: 8 hasten my escape from the **w** storm	7307

WINE (232) [WINEBIBBER, WINEBIBBERS, WINEFAT, WINEPRESS, WINEPRESSES, WINES]

Ge	9:21 he drank of the **w**, and was drunken;	3196
	9:24 Noah awoke from his **w**, and knew what	3196
	14:18 king of Salem brought forth bread and **w**:	3196
	19:32 let us make our father drink **w**, and we	3196
	19:33 they made their father drink **w** that night:	3196
	19:34 let us make him drink **w** this night also;	3196
	19:35 they made their father drink **w** that night	3196
	27:25 and he brought him **w**, and he drank.	3196
	27:28 of the earth, and plenty of corn and **w**:	8492
	27:37 with corn and **w** have I sustained him:	8492
	49:11 he washed his garments in **w**,	3196
	49:12 eyes *shall be* red with **w**, and *his* teeth	3196
Ex	29:40 the fourth *part* of a hin of **w** *for* a drink	3196
Lev	10: 9 Do not drink **w** nor strong drink, thou,	3196
	23:13 the drink offering thereof *shall be* of **w**,	3196
Nu	6: 3 He shall separate *himself* from and	3196
	6: 3 *and* shall drink no vinegar of **w**,	3196
	6:20 and after *that* the Nazarite may drink **w**.	3196
	15: 5 the fourth *part* of a hin of **w** for a drink	3196
	15: 7 shalt offer the third *part* of a hin of **w**,	3196
	15:10 bring for a drink offering half a hin *of* **w**,	3196
	18:12 all the best of the **w**, and of the wheat,	8492
	28: 7 **strong w** to be poured unto the Lᴏʀᴅ *for*	7941
	28:14 drink offerings shall be half a hin of **w**	3196
Dt	7:13 land, thy corn, and thy **w**, and thine oil,	8492
	11:14 in thy corn, and thy **w**, and thine oil.	8492
	12:17 or of thy **w**, or of thy oil, or the firstlings	8492
	14:23 thy **w**, and of thine oil, and the firstlings	8492
	14:26 or for **w**, or for strong drink,	3196
	16:13 thou hast gathered in thy corn and thy **w**:	3342
	18: 4 of thy **w**, and of thy oil, and the first of	8492
	28:39 but shalt neither drink of the **w**,	3196
	28:51 **w**, or oil, *or* the increase of thy kine,	8492
	29: 6 have you drunk **w** or strong drink:	3196
	32:33 Their **w** *is* the poison of dragons,	3196
	32:38 *and* drank the **w** of their drink offerings?	3196
	33:28 Jacob *shall be* upon a land of corn and **w**;	8492
Jos	9: 4 bottles, old, and rent, and bound up;	3196
	9:13 these bottles of **w**, which we filled,	3196
Jdg	9:13 Should I leave my **w**, which cheereth	8492
	13: 4 drink not **w** nor strong drink, and eat not	3196
	13: 7 now drink no **w** nor strong drink,	3196
	13:14 neither let her drink **w** or strong drink,	3196
	19:19 there is bread and **w** also for me,	3196
1Sa	1:14 be drunken? put away thy **w** from thee.	3196
	1:15 I have drunk neither **w** nor strong drink,	3196
	1:24 a bottle of **w**, and brought him *unto*	3196
	10: 3 and another carrying a bottle of **w**:	3196
	16:20 a bottle of **w**, and a kid, and sent *them* by	3196
	25:18 two bottles of **w**, and five sheep ready	3196
	25:37 when the **w** was gone out of Nabal,	3196
2Sa	6:19 a flagon *of* **w**. So all the people departed	NIH
	13:28 when Amnon's heart is merry with **w**,	3196
	16: 1 of summer fruits, and a bottle of **w**.	3196
	16: 2 the **w**, that such as be faint in	3196
2Ki	18:32 a land of corn and **w**, a land of bread and	8492
1Ch	9:29 the **w**, and the oil, and the frankincense,	3196
	12:40 **w**, and oil, and oxen, and sheep	3196
	16: 3 a good piece *of flesh*, and a flagon *of* **w**.	NIH
	27:27 the increase of the vineyards for the **w**	3196
2Ch	2:10 twenty thousand baths of **w**,	3196
	2:15 and the barley, the oil, and the **w**,	3196
	11:11 and store of victual, and of oil and **w**.	3196
	31: 5 **w**, and oil, and honey, and of all	8492
	32:28 for the increase of corn, and **w**, and oil;	3196
Ezr	6: 9 God of heaven, wheat, salt, **w**, and oil,	2562
	7:22 to an hundred baths of **w**, and to an	2562
Ne	2: 1 Artaxerxes the king, *that* **w** *was* before	3196

Ne	2: 1 took up the **w**, and gave *it* unto the king.	3196
	5:11 the corn, the **w**, and the oil, that ye exact	8492
	5:15 taken of them bread and **w**, beside forty	3196
	5:18 once in ten days store of all *sorts of* **w**:	3196
	10:37 *of* trees, of **w** and of oil, unto the priests,	8492
	10:39 of the **new w**, and the oil, unto	8492
	13: 5 tithes of the corn, the **new w**, and the oil,	8492
	13:12 **new w** and the oil unto the treasuries.	8492
	13:15 *some* treading **w presses** on the sabbath,	1660
	13:15 also **w**, grapes, and figs, and all *manner*	3196
Est	1: 7 royal **w** in abundance, according to	3196
	1:10 the heart of the king was merry with **w**,	3196
	5: 6 said unto Esther at the banquet of **w**,	3196
	7: 2 on the second day at the banquet of **w**,	3196
	7: 7 the king arising from the banquet of **w** in	3196
	7: 8 into the place of the banquet of **w**;	3196
Job	1:13 drinking **w** in their eldest brother's house:	3196
	1:18 drinking **w** in their eldest brother's house:	3196
	32:19 my belly *is* as **w** *which* hath no vent;	3196
Ps	4: 7 *that* their corn and their **w** increased.	8492
	60: 3 made us to drink the **w** *of* astonishment.	3196
	75: 8 the Lᴏʀᴅ *there is* a cup, and the **w** is red;	3196
	78:65 mighty *man* that shouteth by reason of **w**.	3196
	104:15 **w** that maketh glad the heart of man,	3196
Pr	3:10 thy presses shall burst out with **new w**.	8492
	4:17 wickedness, and drink the **w** of violence.	3196
	9: 2 killed her beasts; she hath mingled her **w**;	3196
	9: 5 and drink of the **w** *which* I have mingled.	3196
	20: 1 **W** *is* a mocker, strong drink *is* raging:	3196
	21:17 he that loveth **w** and oil shall not be rich.	3196
	23:30 They that tarry long at the **w**; they that go	3196
	23:30 at the wine; they that go to seek **mixt w**	4469
	23:31 Look not thou upon the **w** when it is red,	3196
	31: 4 O Lemuel, *it is* not for kings to drink **w**;	3196
	31: 6 and **w** unto those that be of heavy hearts.	3196
Ecc	2: 3 in mine heart to give myself unto **w**,	3196
	9: 7 and drink thy **w** with a merry heart;	3196
	10:19 made for laughter, and **w** maketh merry:	3196
SS	1: 2 his mouth: for thy love *is* better than **w**.	3196
	1: 4 we will remember thy love more than **w**:	3196
	4:10 how much better is thy love than **w**! and	3196
	5: 1 I have drunk my **w** with my milk:	3196
	7: 9 the roof of thy mouth like the best **w**,	3196
	8: 2 I would cause thee to drink of spiced **w**,	3196
Isa	1:22 is become dross, thy **w** mixt with water:	5435
	5:11 continue until night, *till* **w** inflame them!	3196
	5:12 and the viol, the tabret, and pipe, and **w**,	3196
	5:22 unto *them that are* mighty to drink **w**,	3196
	16:10 the treaders shall tread out no **w** in *their*	3196
	22:13 killing sheep, eating flesh, and drinking **w**:	8492
	24: 7 The **new w** mourneth, the vine	8492
	24: 9 They shall not drink **w** with a song;	3196
	24:11 *There is* a crying for **w** in the streets;	3196
	27: 2 sing ye unto her, A vineyard of **red w**.	2561
	28: 1 of them that are overcome with **w**.	3196
	28: 7 they also have erred through **w**,	3196
	28: 7 strong drink, they are swallowed up of **w**,	3196
	29: 9 they are drunken, but not *with* **w**;	3196
	36:17 a land of corn and **w**, a land of bread and	8492
	49:26 with their own blood, as with **sweet w**:	6071
	51:21 afflicted, and drunken, but not with **w**:	3196
	55: 1 buy **w** and milk without money and	3196
	56:12 *say they*, I will fetch **w**, and we will fill	3196
	62: 8 sons of the stranger shall not drink thy **w**,	8492
	65: 8 As the **new w** is found in the cluster,	8492
Jer	13:12 Every bottle shall be filled *with* **w**:	3196
	13:12 that every bottle shall be filled *with* **w**?	3196
	23: 9 like a man whom **w** hath overcome,	3196
	25:15 Take the **w** cup of this fury at mine hand,	3196
	31:12 for **w**, and for oil, and for the young of	8492
	35: 2 the chambers, and give them **w** to drink.	3196
	35: 5 the house of the Rechabites pots full *of* **w**,	3196
	35: 5 cups, and I said unto them, Drink ye **w**.	3196
	35: 6 said, We will drink no **w**: for Jonadab	3196
	35: 6 saying, Ye shall drink no **w**, *neither* ye,	3196
	35: 8 to drink no **w** all our days, we, our wives,	3196
	35:14 he commanded his sons not to drink **w**;	3196
	40:10 gather ye **w**, and summer fruits, and oil;	3196
	40:12 gathered **w** and summer fruits very much.	3196
	48:33 I have caused **w** to fail from the **w**	3196
	48:33 caused wine to fail from the **w presses**;	3342
	51: 7 the nations have drunken of her **w**;	3196
La	2:12 to their mothers, Where *is* corn and **w**?	3196
Eze	27:18 in the **w** of Helbon, and white wool.	3196
	44:21 Neither shall any priest drink **w**, when	3196
Da	1: 5 meat, and of the **w** which he drank:	3196
	1: 8 nor with the **w** which he drank:	3196
	1:16 and the **w** that they should drink;	3196
	5: 1 lords, and drank **w** before the thousand.	2562
	5: 2 Belshazzar, whiles *he* tasted the **w**,	2562
	5: 4 They drank **w**, and praised the gods of	2562
	5:23 thy concubines, *have* drunk **w** in them;	2562
	10: 3 neither came flesh nor **w** in my mouth,	3196
Hos	2: 8 **w**, and oil, and multiplied her silver and	8492
	2: 9 my **w** in the season thereof,	8492
	2:22 hear the corn, and the **w**, and the oil;	8492
	3: 1 look to other gods, and love flagons of **w**.	6025
	4:11 Whoredom and **w** and new wine take	3196
	4:11 wine and **new w** take away the heart.	8492
	7: 5 have made *him* sick *with* bottles of **w**;	3196
	7:14 assemble themselves for corn and **w**,	8492
	9: 2 them, and the **new w** shall fail in her.	8492
	9: 4 They shall not offer **w** *offerings* to	3196
	14: 7 the scent thereof *shall be* as the **w** of	3196
Joel	1: 5 howl, all ye drinkers of **w**, because of	3196

Joel	1: 5 drinkers of wine, because of the **new w**,	6071
	1:10 **new w** is dried up, the oil languisheth.	8492
	2:19 **w**, and oil, and ye shall be satisfied	8492
	2:24 the fats shall overflow *with* **w** and oil.	8492
Am	3: 3 sold a girl for **w**, that they might drink.	3196
	3:18 the mountains shall drop down **new w**,	6071
	2: 8 they drink the **w** of the condemned *in*	3196
	2:12 ye gave the Nazarites **w** to drink;	3196
	5:11 but ye shall not drink **w** of them.	3196
	6: 6 That drink **w** in bowls,	3196
	9:13 the mountains shall drop **sweet w**,	6071
	9:14 plant vineyards, and drink the **w** thereof;	3196
Mic	2:11 I will prophesy unto thee of **w** and	3196
	6:15 and **sweet w**, but shalt not drink wine.	8492
	6:15 and sweet wine, but shalt not drink **w**.	3196
Hab	2: 5 Yea also, because he transgresseth *by* **w**,	3196
Zep	1:13 vineyards, but not drink the **w** thereof.	3196
Hag	1:11 upon the **new w**, and upon the oil,	8492
	2:12 pottage, or **w**, or oil, or any meat, shall it	3196
Zec	9:15 drink, *and* make a noise as *through* **w**;	3196
	9:17 men cheerful, and **new w** the maids.	8492
	10: 7 and their heart shall rejoice as *through* **w**:	3196
Mt	9:17 do *men* put new **w** into old bottles:	3631
	9:17 **w** runneth out, and the bottles	3631
	9:17 but they put new **w** into new bottles,	3631
Mk	2:22 no *man* putteth new **w** into old bottles:	3631
	2:22 else the new **w** doth burst the bottles,	3631
	2:22 the **w** is spilled, and the bottles will be	3631
	2:22 but new **w** must be put into new bottles.	3631
	15:23 they gave him to drink **w** mingled with	3631
Lk	1:15 shall drink neither **w** nor strong drink;	3631
	5:37 no *man* putteth new **w** into old bottles;	3631
	5:37 else the new **w** will burst the bottles,	3631
	5:38 But new **w** must be put into new bottles;	3631
	5:39 No *man* also having drunk old **w**	NIG
	7:33 came neither eating bread nor drinking **w**;	3631
	10:34 pouring in oil and **w**, and set him on his	3631
Jn	2: 3 And when they wanted **w**, the mother of	3631
	2: 3 of Jesus saith unto him, They have no **w**.	3631
	2: 9 had tasted the water *that was* made **w**,	3631
	2:10 at the beginning doth set forth good **w**;	3631
	2:10 *but* thou hast kept the good **w** until now.	3631
	4:46 of Galilee, where he made the water **w**.	3631
Ac	2:13 *These men* are full of **new w**.	1098
Ro	14:21 good neither to eat flesh, nor to drink **w**,	3631
Eph	5:18 And be not drunk with **w**, wherein is	3631
1Ti	3: 3 Not **given to w**, no striker, not greedy of	3943
	3: 8 not doubletongued, not given to much **w**,	3631
	5:23 but use a little **w** for thy stomach's sake	3631
Tit	1: 7 soon angry, not **given to w**, no striker,	3943
	2: 3 not false accusers, not given to much **w**,	3631
1Pe	4: 3 **excess of w**, revellings, banquetings,	3632
Rev	6: 6 and *see* thou hurt not the oil and the **w**.	3631
	14: 8 she made all nations drink of the **w** of	3631
	14:10 same shall drink of the **w** of the wrath	3631
	16:19 to give unto her the cup of the **w** of	3631
	17: 2 made drunk with the **w** of her fornication.	3631
	18: 3 For all nations have drunk of the **w** of	3631
	18:13 and **w**, and oil, and fine flour, and wheat,	3631

WINEBIBBER (2) [WINE]

Mt	11:19 a **w**, a friend of publicans and sinners.	3630
Lk	7:34 a **w**, a friend of publicans and sinners.	3630

WINEBIBBERS (1) [WINE]

Pr	23:20 Be not amongst **w**; amongst riotous	3196+5433

WINEFAT (2) [WINE]

Isa	63: 2 garments like him that treadeth in the **w**?	1660
Mk	12: 1 about *it*, and digged *a place for* the **w**,	5276

WINEPRESS (15) [PRESS, WINE]

Nu	18:27 as the fulness of the **w**.	3342
	18:30 and as the increase of the **w**.	3342
Dt	15:14 and out of thy floor, and out of thy **w**:	3342
Jdg	6:11 his son Gideon threshed wheat by the **w**,	1660
	7:25 Zeeb they slew at the **w** of Zeeb,	3342
2Ki	6:27 out of the barnfloor, or out of the **w**?	3342
Isa	5: 2 midst of it, and also made a **w** therein:	6333
	63: 3 have I trodden the **w** alone; and of	6333
La	1:15 virgin, the daughter of Judah, *as in* a **w**.	1660
Hos	9: 2 The floor and the **w** shall not feed them,	3342
Mt	21:33 and digged a **w** in it, and built a tower,	3025
Rev	14:19 *it* into the great **w** of the wrath of God.	3025
	14:20 And the **w** was trodden without the city,	3025
	14:20 and blood came out of the **w**, *even* unto	3025
	19:15 and he treadeth the **w** of	3025+3631

WINEPRESSES (2) [PRESS, WINE]

Job	24:11 *and* tread *their* **w**, and suffer thirst.	3342
Zec	14:10 the tower of Hananeel unto the king's **w**.	3342

WINES (2) [WINE]

Isa	25: 6 a feast of **w on the lees**, of fat things full	8105
	25: 6 marrow, of **w on the lees** well refined.	8105

WING (13) [LONGWINGED, WINGED, WINGS]

1Ki	6:24 five cubits *was* the one **w** of the cherub,	3671
	6:24 and five cubits the other **w** of the cherub:	3671
	6:24 from the uttermost part of the one **w** unto	3671
	6:27 the **w** of the one touched the *one* wall,	3671
	6:27 the **w** of the other cherub touched the	3671
2Ch	3:11 *one* **w** of the one *cherub was* five cubits,	3671
	3:11 the other **w** was *likewise* five cubits,	3671
	3:11 reaching to the **w** of the other cherub.	3671

W

2Ch	3:12 **w** of the other cherub *was* five cubits,	3671
	3:12 the other **w** *was* five cubits *also,* joining	3671
	3:12 *also,* joining to the **w** of the other cherub.	3671
Isa	10:14 there was none that moved the **w,**	3671
Eze	17:23 under it shall dwell all fowl of every **w;**	3671

WINGED (2) [WING]

Ge	1:21 kind, and every **w** fowl after his kind:	3671
Dt	4:17 the likeness of any **w** fowl that flieth in	3671

WINGS (76) [WING]

Ex	19: 4 *how* I bare you on eagles' **w,**	3671
	25:20 the cherubims shall stretch forth *their* **w**	3671
	25:20 covering the mercy seat with their **w,**	3671
	37: 9 the cherubims spread out *their* **w** on high,	3671
	37: 9 covered with their **w** over the mercy seat,	3671
Lev	1:17 he shall cleave it with the **w** thereof,	3671
Dt	32:11 spreadeth abroad her **w,** taketh them,	3671
	32:11 taketh them, beareth them on her **w:**	84
Ru	2:12 under whose **w** thou art come to trust.	3671
2Sa	22:11 and he was seen upon the **w** of the wind.	3671
1Ki	6:27 stretched forth the **w** of the cherubims,	3671
	6:27 their **w** touched one another in the midst	3671
	8: 6 the most holy *place,* even under the **w** of	3671
	8: 7 the cherubims spread forth *their* **two w**	3671
1Ch	28:18 spread out *their* **w,** and covered the ark	NIH
2Ch	3:11 **w** of the cherubims *were* twenty cubits	3671
	3:13 The **w** of these cherubims spread	3671
	5: 7 the most holy *place,* even under the **w**	3671
	5: 8 the cherubims spread forth *their* **w** over	3671
Job	39:13 *Gavest* thou the goodly **w** unto	3671
	39:13 or **w** and feathers *unto* the ostrich?	84
	39:26 *and* stretch her **w** toward the south?	3671
Ps	17: 8 hide me under the shadow of thy **w,**	3671
	18:10 yea, he did fly upon the **w** of the wind.	3671
	36: 7 put their trust under the shadow of thy **w.**	3671
	55: 6 O that I had **w** like a dove, *for then* would	83
	57: 1 in the shadow of thy **w** will I make my	3671
	61: 4 I will trust in the covert of thy **w.** Selah.	3671
	63: 7 in the shadow of thy **w** will I rejoice.	3671
	68:13 *yet shall ye be* as the **w** of a dove covered	3671
	91: 4 and under his **w** shalt thou trust:	3671
	104: 3 who walketh upon the **w** of the wind:	3671
	139: 9 *If* I take the **w** of the morning, *and* dwell	3671
Pr	23: 5 for *riches* certainly make themselves **w;**	3671
Ecc	10:20 that which hath **w** shall tell the matter.	3671
Isa	6: 2 one had six **w;** with twain he covered	3671
	8: 8 the stretching out of his **w** shall fill	3671
	18: 1 Woe to the land shadowing with **w,**	3671
	40:31 they shall mount up *with* **w** as eagles;	83
Jer	48: 9 Give **w** unto Moab, that it may flee and	6731
	48:40 eagle, and shall spread his **w** over Moab.	3671
	49:22 the eagle, and spread his **w** over Bozrah:	3671
Eze	1: 6 had four faces, and every one had four **w.**	3671
	1: 8 *had* the hands of a man under their **w**	3671
	1: 8 and they four had their faces and their **w.**	3671
	1: 9 Their **w** *were* joined one to another; they	3671
	1:11 their **w** *were* stretched upward; two	3671
	1:11 two **w** of every one *were* joined one to	NIH
	1:23 the firmament *were* their **w** straight,	3671
	1:24 they went, I heard the noise of their **w,**	3671
	1:24 when they stood, they let down their **w.**	3671
	1:25 they stood, *and* had let down their **w.**	3671
	3:13 *I heard* also the noise of the **w** of those	3671
	10: 5 the sound of the cherubims' **w** was heard	3671
	10: 8 the form of a man's hand under their **w.**	3671
	10:12 their hands, and their **w,** and the wheels,	3671
	10:16 when the cherubims lift up their **w** to	3671
	10:19 the cherubims lift up their **w,**	3671
	10:21 four faces apiece, and every one four **w;**	3671
	10:21 of the hands of a man *was* under their **w.**	3671
	11:22 did the cherubims lift up their **w,**	3671
	17: 3 A great eagle with great **w,** longwinged,	3671
	17: 7 was also another great eagle with great **w**	3671
Da	7: 4 first *was* like a lion, and had eagle's **w:**	1611
	7: 4 I beheld till the **w** thereof were pluckt,	1611
	7: 6 which had upon the back of it four **w** of a	1611
Hos	4:19 The wind hath bound her up in her **w,**	3671
Zec	5: 9 women, and the wind *was* in their **w;**	3671
	5: 9 for they had **w** like the wings of a stork:	3671
	5: 9 for they had wings like the **w** of a stork:	3671
Mal	4: 2 righteousness arise with healing in his **w;**	3671
Mt	23:37 hen gathereth her chickens under *her* **w,**	4420
Lk	13:34 a hen *doth gather* her brood under *her* **w,**	4420
Rev	4: 8 the four beasts had each of them six **w**	4420
	9: 9 the sound of their **w** *was* as the sound of	4420
	12:14 And to the woman were given two **w** of	4420

WINK (2) [WINKED, WINKETH]

Job	15:12 thee away? and what do thine eyes **w** at,	7335
Ps	35:19 let them **w** *with* the eye that hate me	7169

WINKED (1) [WINK]

Ac	17:30 And the times of *this* ignorance God **w** at;	5237

WINKETH (2) [WINK]

Pr	6:13 He **w** with his eyes, he speaketh with his	7169
	10:10 He that **w** with the eye causeth sorrow:	7169

WINNETH (1) [WIN]

Pr	11:30 a tree of life; and he that **w** souls *is* wise.	3947

WINNOWED (1) [WINNOWETH]

Isa	30:24 which hath been **w** with the shovel and	2219

WINNOWETH (1) [WINNOWED]

Ru	3: 2 he **w** barley to night in the threshingfloor.	2219

WINTER (14) [WINTERED, WINTERHOUSE]

Ge	8:22 summer and **w,** and day and night shall	2779
Ps	74:17 earth: thou hast made summer and **w.**	2779
SS	2:11 For lo, the **w** is past, the rain is over *and*	5638
Isa	18: 6 all the beasts of the earth shall **w** upon	2778
Am	3:15 I will smite the **w** house with the summer	2779
Zec	14: 8 sea: in summer and in **w** shall it be.	2779
Mt	24:20 pray ye that your flight be not in the **w,**	5494
Mk	13:18 pray ye that your flight be not in the **w.**	5494
Jn	10:22 *the feast of* the dedication, and it was **w.**	5494
Ac	27:12 the haven was not commodious to **w in,**	3915
	27:12 might attain to Phenice, *and there* to **w;**	3914
1Co	16: 6 be that I will abide, yea, and **w** with you,	3914
2Ti	4:21 Do thy diligence to come before **w.**	5494
Tit	3:12 for I have determined there to **w.**	3914

WINTERED (1) [WINTER]

Ac	28:11 which had **w** in the isle, *whose* sign *was*	3914

WINTERHOUSE (1) [HOUSE, WINTER]

Jer	36:22 Now the king sat *in* the **w** in	1004+2779

WIPE (8) [WIPED, WIPETH, WIPING]

2Ki	21:13 will **w** Jerusalem as *a man* wipeth a dish,	4229
Ne	13:14 **w** not out my good deeds that I have	4229
Isa	25: 8 the Lord God will **w away** tears from off	4229
Lk	7:38 did **w** *them* with the hairs of her head,	1591
	10:11 cleaveth on us, we do **w off against** you:	631
Jn	13: 5 to **w** *them* with the towel wherewith he	1591
Rev	7:17 God shall **w away** all tears from their	1813
	21: 4 God shall **w away** all tears from their	1813

WIPED (4) [WIPE]

Pr	6:33 and his reproach shall not be **w away.**	4229
Lk	7:44 and **w** *them* with the hairs of her head.	1591
Jn	11: 2 **w** his feet with her hair, whose brother	1591
	12: 3 feet of Jesus, and **w** his feet with her hair:	1591

WIPETH (2) [WIPE]

2Ki	21:13 will wipe Jerusalem as *a man* **w** a dish,	4229
Pr	30:20 she eateth, and **w** her mouth, and saith,	4229

WIPING (1) [WIPE]

2Ki	21:13 a dish, **w** *it,* and turning *it* upside down.	4229

WIRES (1)

Ex	39: 3 cut *it into* **w,** to work *it* in the blue,	6616

WISDOM (234) [UNWISE]

Ex	28: 3 whom I have filled with the spirit of **w,**	2451
	31: 3 in **w,** and in understanding,	2451
	31: 6 of all that are wise hearted I have put **w,**	2451
	35:26 stirred them up in **w** spun goats' *hair.*	2451
	35:31 **w,** in understanding, and in knowledge,	2451
	35:35 Them hath he filled *with* **w** of heart,	2451
	36: 1 in whom the Lord put **w** and	2451
	36: 2 in whose heart the Lord had put **w,**	2451
Dt	4: 6 and do *them;* for this *is* your **w** and	2451
	34: 9 the son of Nun was full *of* the spirit of **w;**	2451
2Sa	14:20 according to the **w** of an angel of God,	2451
	20:22 went unto all the people in her **w.**	2451
1Ki	2: 6 therefore according to thy **w,** and let not	2451
	3:28 they saw that the **w** of God *was* in him,	2451
	4:29 God gave Solomon **w** and	2451
	4:30 Solomon's **w** excelled the wisdom of all	2451
	4:30 Solomon's wisdom excelled the **w** of all	2451
	4:30 the east country, and all the **w** of Egypt.	2451
	4:34 there came of all people to hear the **w** of	2451
	4:34 of the earth, which had heard of his **w.**	2451
	5:12 the Lord gave Solomon **w,** as he	2451
	7:14 he was filled *with* **w,** and understanding,	2451
	10: 4 of Sheba had seen all Solomon's **w,**	2451
	10: 6 mine own land of thy acts and of thy **w.**	2451
	10: 7 thy **w** and prosperity exceedeth the fame	2451
	10: 8 before thee, *and* that hear thy **w.**	2451
	10:23 kings of the earth for riches and for **w.**	2451
	10:24 to hear his **w,** which God had put in his	2451
	11:41 Solomon, and all that he did, and his **w,**	2451
1Ch	22:12 Only the Lord give thee **w** and	7922
2Ch	1:10 Give me now **w** and knowledge, that I	2451
	1:11 hast asked **w** and knowledge for thyself,	2451
	1:12 **W** and knowledge *is* granted unto thee;	2451
	9: 3 the queen of Sheba had seen the **w** of	2451
	9: 5 own land of thine acts, and of thy **w:**	2451
	9: 6 *the one* half of the greatness of thy **w**	2451
	9: 7 continually before thee, and hear thy **w.**	2451
	9:22 all the kings of the earth in riches and **w.**	2451
	9:23 hear his **w,** that God had put in his heart.	2451
Ezr	7:25 Ezra, after the **w** of thy God, that *is* in	2452
Job	4:21 them go away? they die, even without **w.**	2451
	6:13 in me? and is **w** driven *quite* from me?	8454
	11: 6 he would shew thee the secrets of **w,**	2451
	12: 2 *are* the people, and **w** shall die with you.	2451
	12:12 the ancient *is* **w;** and *in* length of days	2451
	12:13 With him *is* **w** and strength, he hath	2451
	12:16 With him *is* strength and **w:** the deceived	8454
	13: 5 hold your peace, and it should be your **w.**	2451
	15: 8 and dost thou restrain **w** to thyself?	2451
	26: 3 thou counselled *him that hath* no **w?**	2451
	28:12 where shall **w** be found? and where *is*	2451
	28:18 pearls: for the price of **w** *is* above rubies.	2451
	28:20 Whence then cometh **w?** and where *is*	2451

Job	28:28 Behold, the fear of the Lord, that *is* **w;**	2451
	32: 7 and multitude of years should teach **w.**	2451
	32:13 ye should say, We have found out **w:**	2451
	33:33 hold thy peace, and I shall teach thee **w.**	2451
	34:35 and his words *were* without **w.**	7919
	36: 5 not *any: he is* mighty in strength *and* **w.**	3820
	38:36 Who hath put **w** in the inward parts?	2451
	38:37 Who can number the clouds in **w?**	2451
	39:17 Because God hath deprived her of **w,**	2451
	39:26 Doth the hawk fly by thy **w,** *and* stretch	998
Ps	37:30 The mouth of the righteous speaketh **w,**	2451
	49: 3 My mouth shall speak of **w;**	2454
	51: 6 *part* thou shalt make me to know **w.**	2451
	90:12 that we may apply our hearts unto **w.**	2451
	104:24 in **w** hast thou made them all: the earth	2449
	105:22 at his pleasure; and **teach** his senators **w.**	2449
	111:10 fear of the Lord *is* the beginning of **w:**	2451
	136: 5 To him that by **w** made the heavens: for	8394
Pr	1: 2 To know **w** and instruction; to perceive	2451
	1: 3 To receive the instruction of **w,** justice,	7919
	1: 7 *but* fools despise **w** and instruction.	2451
	1:20 **W** crieth without; she uttereth her voice	2454
	2: 2 So that *thou* incline thine ear unto **w,**	2451
	2: 6 For the Lord giveth **w:** out of his mouth	2451
	2: 7 He layeth up **sound w** for the righteous:	8454
	2:10 When **w** entereth into thine heart,	2451
	3:13 Happy *is* the man that findeth **w,**	2451
	3:19 The Lord by **w** hath founded the earth;	2451
	3:21 thine eyes: keep **sound w** and discretion:	8454
	4: 5 Get **w,** get understanding: forget *it not;*	2451
	4: 7 **W** *is* the principal thing; *therefore*	2451
	4: 7 *is* the principal thing; *therefore* get **w:**	2451
	4:11 I have taught thee in the way of **w;** I have	2451
	5: 1 attend unto my **w,** *and* bow thine ear to	2451
	7: 4 Say unto **w,** Thou *art* my sister;	2451
	8: 1 Doth not **w** cry? and understanding put	2451
	8: 5 O ye simple, understand **w:** and, ye fools,	6195
	8:11 For **w** *is* better than rubies; and all	2451
	8:12 I **w** dwell *with* prudence, and find out	2451
	8:14 Counsel *is* mine, and **sound w:** I *am*	8454
	9: 1 **W** hath builded her house, she hath hewn	2454
	9:10 fear of the Lord *is* the beginning of **w:**	2451
	10:13 the lips of him that hath understanding **w**	2451
	10:21 feed many: but fools die for want of **w.**	3820
	10:23 but a man of understanding hath **w.**	2451
	10:31 The mouth of the just bringeth forth **w:**	2451
	11: 2 cometh shame: but with the lowly *is* **w.**	2451
	11:12 He that is void of **w** despiseth his	3820
	12: 8 shall be commended according to his **w:**	7922
	13:10 but with the well advised *is* **w.**	2451
	14: 6 A scorner seeketh **w,** and *findeth* it not:	2451
	14: 8 The **w** of the prudent *is* to understand his	2451
	14:33 **W** resteth in the heart of him that hath	2451
	15:21 Folly *is* joy to *him that is* destitute of **w:**	3820
	15:33 fear of the Lord *is* the instruction of **w;**	2451
	16:16 How much better *is it* to get **w** than gold!	2451
	17:16 a price in the hand of a fool to get **w,**	2451
	17:24 **W** *is* before him that hath understanding;	2451
	18: 1 seeketh *and* intermeddleth with all **w.**	8454
	18: 4 the wellspring of **w** *as a* flowing brook.	2451
	19: 8 He that getteth **w** loveth his own soul:	3820
	21:30 *There is* no **w** nor understanding nor	2451
	23: 4 not to be rich: cease from thine own **w.**	998
	23: 9 for he will despise the **w** of thy words.	7922
	23:23 **w,** and instruction, and understanding.	2451
	24: 3 Through **w** is a house builded;	2451
	24: 7 **W** *is too* high for a fool: he openeth not	2454
	24:14 So shall the knowledge of **w** be unto thy	2451
	29: 3 Whoso loveth **w** rejoiceth his father:	2451
	29:15 The rod and reproof give **w:** but a child	2451
	30: 3 I neither learned **w,** nor have	2451
	31:26 She openeth her mouth with **w;** and in	2451
Ecc	1:13 search out by **w** concerning all	2451+2050.2
	1:16 gotten more **w** than all *they* that have	2451
	1:16 my heart had great experience of **w** and	2451
	1:17 I gave my heart to know **w,** and to know	2451
	1:18 For in much **w** *is* much grief: and he that	2451
	2: 3 (yet acquainting mine heart with **w)**	2451
	2: 9 Jerusalem: also my **w** remained with me.	2451
	2:12 turned myself to behold **w,** and madness,	2451
	2:13 I saw that **w** excelleth folly, as far as light	2451
	2:21 For there is a man whose labour *is* in **w,**	2451
	2:26 to a man that *is* good in his sight, **w,**	2451
	7:11 **W** *is* good with an inheritance: and *by it*	2451
	7:12 **w** is a defence, *and* money *is* a defence:	2451
	7:12 the excellency of knowledge *is, that* **w**	2451
	7:19 **W** strengtheneth the wise more than ten	2451
	7:23 All this have I proved by **w:** I said, I will	2451
	7:25 to seek out **w,** and the reason *of things,*	2451
	8: 1 a man's **w** maketh his face to shine,	2451
	8:16 When I applied mine heart to know **w,**	2451
	9:10 nor knowledge, nor **w,** in the grave,	2451
	9:13 This **w** have I seen also under the sun,	2451
	9:15 and he by his **w** delivered the city;	2451
	9:16 said I, **W** *is* better than strength:	2451
	9:16 the poor *man's* **w** *is* despised,	2451
	9:18 **W** *is* better than weapons of war:	2451
	10: 1 little folly *him that is* in reputation for **w**	2451
	10: 3 his **w** faileth *him,* and he saith to every	3820
	10:10 strength: but **w** *is* profitable to direct.	2451
Isa	10:13 of my hand I have done *it,* and by my **w;**	2451
	11: 2 spirit of **w** and understanding, the spirit	2451
	29:14 for the **w** of their wise *men* shall perish,	2451
	33: 6 **w** and knowledge shall be the stability of	2451
	47:10 Thy **w** and thy knowledge, it hath	2451

Jer	8: 9 of the LORD; and what **w** *is* in them?	2451
	9:23 Let not the wise *man* glory in his **w**,	2451
	10:12 he hath established the world by his **w**,	2451
	49: 7 LORD of hosts; *Is* **w** no more in Teman?	2451
	49: 7 from the prudent? is their **w** vanished?	2451
	51:15 he hath established the world by his **w**,	2451
Eze	28: 4 With thy **w** and with thine understanding	2451
	28: 5 By thy great **w** *and* by thy traffick hast	2451
	28: 7 their swords against the beauty of thy **w**,	2451
	28:12 the sum, full *of* **w**, and perfect in beauty.	2451
	28:17 thou hast corrupted thy **w** by reason of	2451
Da	1: 4 skilful in all **w**, and cunning in knowledge	2451
	1:17 and skill in all learning and **w**:	2451
	1:20 *in* all matters of **w** *and* understanding,	2451
	2:14 **w** to Arioch the captain of the king's	2942
	2:20 ever and ever: for **w** and might are his:	2452
	2:21 he giveth **w** unto the wise,	2452
	2:23 who hast given me **w** and might,	2452
	2:30 secret *is* not revealed to me for *any* **w**	2452
	5:11 light and understanding and **w**,	2452
	5:11 and wisdom, like the **w** of the gods,	2452
	5:14 and excellent **w** is found in thee.	2452
Mic	6: 9 and *the man of* **w** shall see thy name:	8454
Mt	11:19 But **w** is justified of her children.	4678
	12:42 of the earth to hear the **w** of Solomon;	4678
	13:54 Whence hath this *man* this **w**,	4678
Mk	6: 2 what **w** *is* this which is given unto him,	4678
Lk	1:17 and the disobedient to the **w** of the just;	5428
	2:40 and waxed strong in spirit, filled with **w**:	4678
	2:52 And Jesus increased in **w** and stature,	4678
	7:35 But **w** is justified of all her children.	4678
	11:31 of the earth to hear the **w** of Solomon;	4678
	11:49 Therefore also said the **w** of God, I will	4678
	21:15 For I will give you a mouth and **w**,	4678
Ac	6: 3 full of the Holy Ghost and **w**, whom we	4678
	6:10 they were not able to resist the **w** and	4678
	7:10 **w** in the sight of Pharaoh king of Egypt;	4678
	7:22 And Moses was learned in all the **w** of	4678
Ro	11:33 the depth of the riches both of the **w** and	4678
1Co	1:17 not with **w** of words, lest the cross of	4678
	1:19 I will destroy the **w** of the wise,	4678
	1:20 hath not God made foolish the **w** of this	4678
	1:21 after that in the **w** of God the world by	4678
	1:21 of God the world by **w** knew not God,	4678
	1:22 a sign, and the Greeks seek after **w**:	4678
	1:24 the power of God, and the **w** of God.	4678
	1:30 who of God is made unto us **w**,	4678
	2: 1 not with excellency of speech or of **w**,	4678
	2: 4 *was* not with enticing words of man's **w**,	4678
	2: 5 your faith should not stand in the **w** of	4678
	2: 6 Howbeit we speak **w** among *them that*	4678
	2: 6 yet not the **w** of this world, nor of	4678
	2: 7 But we speak the **w** of God in a mystery,	4678
	2: 7 *even* the hidden **w**, which God ordained	NIG
	2:13 in the words which man's **w** teacheth,	4678
	3:19 the **w** of this world is foolishness with	4678
	12: 8 one is given by the Spirit the word of **w**;	4678
2Co	1:12 with fleshly **w**, but by the grace of God,	4678
Eph	1: 8 he hath abounded toward us in all **w**	4678
	1:17 may give unto you the spirit of **w** and	4678
	3:10 by the church the manifold **w** of God,	4678
Col	1: 9 *with* the knowledge of his will in all **w**	4678
	1:28 and teaching every man in all **w**;	4678
	2: 3 In whom are hid all the treasures of **w**	4678
	2:23 Which *things* have indeed a shew of **w** in	4678
	3:16 of Christ dwell in you richly in all **w**;	4678
	4: 5 Walk in **w** toward them that are without,	4678
Jas	1: 5 If any of you lack **w**, let him ask of God,	4678
	3:13 his works with meekness of **w**.	4678
	3:15 This **w** descendeth not from above,	4678
	3:17 But the **w** that is from above is first pure,	4678
2Pe	3:15 **w** given unto him hath written unto you;	4678
Rev	5:12 **w**, and strength, and honour, and glory,	4678
	7:12 and **w**, and thanksgiving, and honour,	4678
	13:18 Here is **w**. Let him that hath	4678
	17: 9 *And* here *is* the mind which hath **w**.	4678

WISE (247) [WISELY, WISER]

Ge	3: 6 a tree to be desired to **make** *one* **w**,	7919
	41: 8 of Egypt, and all the **w** men thereof:	2450
	41:33 Pharaoh look out a man discreet and **w**,	2450
	41:39 *there* is none so discreet and **w** as thou	2450
Ex	7:11 Pharaoh also called the **w** men and	2450
	22:23 If thou **afflict** them **in any w**,	6031+6031
	23: 8 for the gift blindeth the **w**,	6493
	28: 3 shalt speak unto all *that are* **w** hearted,	2450
	31: 6 in the hearts of all that are **w** hearted	2450
	35:10 every **w** hearted among you shall come,	2450
	35:25 the women that were **w** hearted did spin	2450
	36: 1 and Aholiab, and every **w** hearted man,	2450
	36: 2 and Aholiab, and every **w** hearted man,	2450
	36: 4 all the **w** men, that wrought all the work	2450
	36: 8 every **w** hearted *man* among them that	2450
Lev	7:24 nor any **w**, **in no w** eat of it.	398+398+3808
	19:17 thou shalt **in any w** rebuke thy	3198+3198
	27:19 the field will **in any w** redeem it,	1350+1350
Nu	6:23 **On this w** ye shall bless the children of	3541
Dt	1:13 Take ye **w** men, and understanding,	2450
	1:15 **w** men, and known, and made them	2450
	4: 6 Surely this great nation *is a* **w** and	2450
	16:19 for a gift doth blind the eyes of the **w**,	2450
	17:15 Thou shalt **in any w** set *him* king	7760+7760
	21:23 shalt **in any w** bury him that day;	6912+6912
	22: 7 shalt **in any w** let the dam **go**,	7971+7971
	32:29 that they were **w**, *that* they understood	2449

Jos	6:18 **in any w** keep *yourselves* from	7535
	23:12 Else if ye do **in any w go back**,	7725+7725
Jdg	5:29 Her **w** ladies answered *her*, yea,	2450
1Sa	6: 3 **in any w return** send a trespass	7725+7725
2Sa	14: 2 fetch thence a **w** woman, and said unto	2450
	14:20 my lord *is* **w**, according to the wisdom of	2450
	20:16 cried a **w** woman out of the city, Hear,	2450
1Ki	2: 9 for thou *art* a **w** man, and knowest what	2450
	3:12 given thee a **w** and an understanding	2450
	3:26 living child, and **in no w** slay it.	4191+4191
	3:27 living child, and **in no w** slay it:	4191+4191
	5: 7 which hath given unto David a **w** son	2450
	11:22 howbeit **let me go in any w**.	7971+7971
1Ch	26:14 his son, a **w** counseller, they cast lots;	7922
	27:32 *was* a counseller, a **w** man, and a scribe:	995
2Ch	2:12 hath given to David the king a **w** son,	2450
Est	1:13 the king said to the **w** men, which knew	2450
	6:13 said his **w** men and Zeresh his wife unto	2450
Job	5:13 He taketh the **w** in their own craftiness:	2450
	9: 4 *He is* **w** in heart, and mighty in strength:	2450
	11:12 For vain man would be **w**, though man	3823
	15: 2 Should a **w** *man* utter vain knowledge,	2450
	15:18 **w** men have told from their fathers,	2450
	17:10 for I cannot find one **w** man among you.	2450
	22: 2 as he that is **w** may be profitable unto	7919
	32: 9 Great men are not *always* **w**: neither do	2449
	34: 2 O ye **w** men; and give ear unto me,	2450
	34:34 and let a **w** man hearken unto me.	2450
	37:24 respecteth not any *that are* **w** of heart.	2450
Ps	2:10 Be **w** now therefore, O ye kings:	7919
	19: 7 the LORD *is* sure, **making** **w** the simple.	2449
	36: 3 he hath left off to be **w**, *and* to do good.	7919
	37: 8 fret not thyself **in any w** to do evil.	389
	49:10 For he seeth that **w** men die, likewise	2450
	94: 8 and ye fools, when will ye be **w**?	7919
	107:43 Whoso *is* **w**, and will observe these	2450
Pr	1: 5 A **w** *man* will hear, and will increase	2450
	1: 5 shall attain unto **w counsels**:	8458
	1: 6 words of the **w**, and their dark sayings.	2450
	3: 7 Be not **w** in thine own eyes: fear	2450
	3:35 The **w** shall inherit glory: but shame shall	2450
	6: 6 consider her ways, and be **w**:	2449
	8:33 be **w**, and refuse *it* not.	2449
	9: 8 rebuke a **w** *man*, and he will love thee.	2450
	9: 9 Give *instruction* to a **w** *man*, and he will	2450
	9:12 If thou be **w**, thou shalt be wise for	2449
	9:12 thou be wise, thou shalt be **w** for thyself:	2449
	10: 1 A **w** son maketh a glad father: but a	2450
	10: 5 He that gathereth in summer *is* a **w** son:	7919
	10: 8 The **w** in heart will receive	2450
	10:14 **w** *men* lay up knowledge: but the mouth	2450
	10:19 but he that refraineth his lips *is* **w**.	7919
	11:29 the fool shall be servant to the **w** of heart.	2450
	11:30 of life; and he that winneth souls *is* **w**.	2450
	12:15 he that hearkeneth unto counsel *is* **w**.	2450
	12:18 sword: but the tongue of the **w** *is* health.	2450
	13: 1 A **w** son *heareth his* father's instruction:	2450
	13:14 The law of the **w** *is* a fountain of life,	2450
	13:20 that walketh with **w** *men* shall be wise:	2450
	13:20 that walketh with wise *men* shall be **w**:	2449
	14: 1 Every **w** woman buildeth her house:	2450
	14: 3 but the lips of the **w** shall preserve them.	2450
	14:16 A **w** *man* feareth, and departeth from evil:	2450
	14:24 The crown of the **w** *is* their riches:	2450
	14:35 The king's favour *is* toward a **w** servant:	7919
	15: 2 The tongue of the **w** useth knowledge	2450
	15: 7 The lips of the **w** disperse knowledge:	2450
	15:12 neither will he go unto the **w**.	2450
	15:20 A **w** son maketh a glad father: but a	2450
	15:24 The way of life *is* above to the **w**, that *he*	7919
	15:31 the reproof of life abideth among the **w**.	2450
	16:14 of death: but a **w** man will pacify it.	2450
	16:21 The **w** in heart shall be called prudent:	2450
	16:23 The heart of the **w** teacheth his mouth,	2450
	17: 2 A **w** servant shall have rule over a son	7919
	17:10 A reproof entereth more into a **w** *man*	995
	17:28 when he holdeth his peace, is counted **w**:	2450
	18:15 and the ear of the **w** seeketh knowledge.	2450
	19:20 that thou mayest be **w** in thy latter end.	2449
	20: 1 whosoever is deceived thereby is not **w**.	2449
	20:26 A **w** king scattereth the wicked,	2450
	21:11 is punished, the simple is **made w**:	2449
	21:11 when the **w** is instructed, he receiveth	2450
	21:20 desired and oil in the dwelling of the **w**;	2450
	21:22 A **w** *man* scaleth the city of the mighty,	2450
	22:17 hear the words of the **w**, and apply thine	2450
	23:15 My son, if thine heart be **w**, my heart	2449
	23:19 be **w**, and guide thine heart in the way.	2449
	23:24 he that begetteth a **w** *child* shall have joy	2450
	24: 5 A **w** man *is* strong; yea, a man of	2450
	24: 6 by **w counsel** thou shalt make thy war:	8458
	24:23 These *things* also **belong** to the **w**.	2450
	25:12 *so is* a **w** reprover upon an obedient ear.	2450
	26: 5 his folly, lest he be **w** in his own conceit.	2450
	26:12 Seest thou a man **w** in his own conceit?	2450
	27:11 My son, be **w**, and make my heart glad,	2449
	28: 7 Whoso keepeth the law *is* a **w** son:	995
	28:11 The rich man *is* **w** in his own conceit;	2450
	29: 8 into a snare: but **w** *men* turn away wrath.	2450
	29: 9 If a **w** man contendeth with a foolish	2450
	29:11 but a **w** *man* keepeth it in *till* afterwards.	2450
	30:24 earth, but they *are* **exceeding w**:	2449+2450
Ecc	2:14 The **w** *man's* eyes *are* in his head;	2450
	2:15 even to me; and why was I then more **w**?	2449
	2:16 *there is* no remembrance of the **w** more	2450

Ecc	2:16 And how dieth the **w** *man*? as the fool.	2450
	2:19 knoweth whether he shall be a **w** *man*	2450
	2:19 wherein I have **shewed** myself **w** under	2449
	4:13 a **w** child than an old and foolish king,	2450
	6: 8 For what hath the **w** more than the fool?	2450
	7: 4 The heart of the **w** *is* in the house of	2450
	7: 5 *It is* better to hear the rebuke of the **w**,	2450
	7: 7 Surely oppression maketh a **w** *man* mad;	2450
	7:16 over much; neither **make** thyself over **w**:	2449
	7:19 Wisdom strengtheneth the **w** more than	2450
	7:23 I said, I will be **w**; but it *was* far from me.	2449
	8: 1 Who *is* as the **w** *man*? and who knoweth	2450
	8: 5 a **w** man's heart discerneth *both* time and	2450
	8:17 though a **w** man think to know *it*, yet	2450
	9: 1 the righteous, and the **w**, and their works,	2450
	9:11 to the strong, neither yet bread to the **w**,	2450
	9:15 Now there was found in it a poor **w** man,	2450
	9:17 The words of **w** *men* are heard in quiet,	2450
	10: 2 A **w** *man's* heart *is* at his right hand;	2450
	10:12 The words of a **w** *man's* mouth *are*	2450
	12: 9 because the Preacher was **w**,	2450
	12:11 The words of the **w** *are* as goads,	2450
Isa	5:21 Woe unto *them that are* **w** in their own	2450
	19:11 counsel of the **w** counsellers of Pharaoh	2450
	19:11 I *am* the son of the **w**, the son of ancient	2450
	19:12 where *are* thy **w** *men*? and let them tell	2450
	29:14 the wisdom of their **w** *men* shall perish,	2450
	31: 2 Yet he also *is* **w**, and will bring evil,	2450
	44:25 that turneth **w** *men* backward,	2450
Jer	4:22 they *are* **w** to do evil, but to do good they	2450
	8: 8 We *are* **w**, and the law of the LORD *is*	2450
	8: 9 The **w** *men* are ashamed, they are	2450
	9:12 Who *is* the **w** man, that may understand	2450
	9:23 Let not the **w** *man* glory in his wisdom,	2450
	10: 7 forasmuch as among all the **w** *men* of	2450
	18:18 nor counsel from the **w**, nor the word	2450
	50:35 upon her princes, and upon her **w** *men*.	2450
	51:57 her **w** men, her captains, and her rulers,	2450
Eze	27: 8 thy **w** *men*, O Tyrus, *that* were in thee,	2450
	27: 9 the **w** *men* thereof were in thee thy	2450
Da	2:12 commanded to destroy all the **w** *men* of	2445
	2:13 the decree went forth that the **w** *men*	2445
	2:14 which was gone forth to slay the **w** *men*	2445
	2:18 with the rest of the **w** *men* of Babylon.	2445
	2:21 he giveth wisdom unto the **w**,	2445
	2:24 to destroy the **w** *men* of Babylon:	2445
	2:24 Destroy not the **w** *men* of Babylon:	2445
	2:27 cannot the **w** *men*, the astrologians,	2445
	2:48 chief of the governors over all the **w** *men*	2445
	4: 6 in all the **w** *men* of Babylon before me,	2445
	4:18 as all the **w** *men* of my kingdom	2445
	5: 7 and said to the **w** *men* of Babylon,	2445
	5: 8 came in all the king's **w** *men*: but	2445
	5:15 now the **w** *men*, the astrologers, have	2445
	12: 3 that be **w** shall shine as the brightness	7919
	12:10 but the **w** shall understand.	7919
Hos	14: 9 Who *is* **w**, and he shall understand these	2450
Ob	1: 8 even destroy the **w** *men* out of Edom,	2450
Zec	9: 2 and Zidon, though it be very **w**.	2449
Mt	1:18 the birth of Jesus Christ was **on this w**:	3779
	2: 1 there came **w men** from the east to	3097
	2: 7 when he had privily called the **w men**,	3097
	2:16 saw that he was mocked of the **w men**,	3097
	2:16 he had diligently inquired of the **w men**.	3097
	5:18 one tittle shall **in no w** pass from the law,	3364
	7:24 them, I will liken him unto a **w** man,	5429
	10:16 be ye therefore **w** as serpents,	5429
	10:42 you, he shall **in no w** lose his reward.	3364
	11:25 hast hid these *things* from the **w** and	4680
	21:24 I **in like w** will tell you by what authority	2504
	23:34 you prophets, and **w** *men*, and scribes:	4680
	24:45 Who then is a faithful and **w** servant,	5429
	25: 2 And five of them were **w**, and five *were*	5429
	25: 4 the **w** took oil in their vessels with their	5429
	25: 8 the foolish said unto the **w**, Give us of	5429
	25: 9 But the **w** answered, saying, *Not so*;	5429
Mk	14:31 with thee, I will **not** deny thee **in any w**.	3364
Lk	10:21 thou hast hid these *things* from the **w**	4680
	12:42 Who is *that* faithful and **w** steward,	5429
	13:11 **in no w** lift up	1519+3361+3588+3838
	18:17 as a little child shall **in no w** enter therein	3364
Jn	6:37 that cometh to me I will **in no w** cast	3364
	21: 1 and **on this w** shewed he *himself*.	3779
Ac	7: 6 And God spake **on this w**, That his seed	3779
	13:34 to return to corruption, he said **on this w**,	3779
	13:41 a work which you shall **in no w** believe,	3364
Ro	1:14 both to the **w**, and to the unwise.	4680
	1:22 Professing *themselves* to be **w**,	4680
	3: 9 are we better *than they*? No, **in no w**:	3843
	10: 6 which is of faith speaketh **on this w**,	3779
	11:25 lest ye should be **w** in your own conceits;	5429
	12:16 Be not **w** in your own conceits.	5429
	16:19 I would have you **w** unto *that which is*	4680
	16:27 To God only **w**, *be* glory through Jesus	4680
1Co	1:19 I will destroy the wisdom of the **w**,	4680
	1:20 Where *is* the **w**? where *is* the scribe?	4680
	1:26 how that not many **w** *men* after the flesh,	4680
	1:27 *things* of the world to confound the **w**;	4680
	3:10 as a **w** masterbuilder, I have laid	4680
	3:18 *If any* man among you seemeth to be **w** in	4680
	3:18 let him become a fool, that he may be **w**.	4680
	3:19 He taketh the **w** in their own craftiness.	4680
	3:20 The Lord knoweth the thoughts of the **w**,	4680
	4:10 for Christ's sake, but ye *are* **w** in Christ;	5429
	6: 5 that there is not a **w** *man* amongst you?	4680

1Co 10:15 I speak as to **w** men; judge ye what I say. 5429
2Co 10:12 amongst themselves, are not **w**. 4920
 11:19 fools gladly, seeing ye yourselves are **w**. 5429
Eph 5:15 circumspectly, not as fools, but as **w**, 4680
1Ti 1:17 immortal, invisible, the only **w** God, 4680
2Ti 3:15 which are able to **make** thee **w** unto 4679
Heb 4: 4 place of the seventh day on this **w**, 3779
Jas 3:13 Who is a **w** man and endued with 4680
Jude 1:25 To the only **w** God our Saviour, be glory 4680
Rev 21:27 And there shall **in no w** enter into it any 3364

WISELY (14) [WISE]
Ex 1:10 Come on, let us **deal w** with them; lest 2449
1Sa 18: 5 Saul sent him, and **behaved** himself **w**: 7919
 18:14 David **behaved** himself **w** in all his ways; 7919
 18:15 saw that he **behaved** himself very **w**, 7919
 18:30 that David **behaved** himself more **w** than 7919
2Ch 11:23 he **dealt w**, and dispersed of all his 995
Ps 58: 5 voice of charmers, charming never so **w**. 2449
 64: 9 for they shall **w consider** of his doing. 7919
 101: 2 I will **behave** myself **w** in a perfect way. 7919
Pr 16:20 He that **handleth** a matter **w** shall find 7919
 21:12 The righteous man **w considereth** 7919
 28:26 whoso walketh **w**, he shall be 2451+871.1
Ecc 7:10 dost not inquire **w** concerning this. 2451+4480
Lk 16: 8 unjust steward, because he had done **w**: 5430

WISER (8) [WISE]
1Ki 4:31 For he was **w** than all men; than Ethan 2449
Job 35:11 **maketh** us **w** than the fowls of heaven? 2449
Ps 119:98 hast **made** me **w** than mine enemies: 2449
Pr 9: 9 to a wise man, and he will be yet **w**: 2449
 26:16 The sluggard is **w** in his own conceit than 2450
Eze 28: 3 thou art **w** than Daniel; there is no 2450
Lk 16: 8 generation **w** than the children of light. 5429
1Co 1:25 Because the foolishness of God is **w** than 4680

WISH (6) [WISHED, WISHING]
Job 33: 6 I am according to thy **w** in God's stead: 6310
Ps 40:14 and put to shame that **w** me evil. 2655
 73: 7 they have more than heart could **w**. 4906
Ro 9: 3 For I could **w** that myself were accursed 2172
2Co 13: 9 and this also we **w**, even your perfection. 2172
3Jn 1: 2 I **w** above all things that thou mayest 2172

WISHED (2) [WISH]
Jnh 4: 8 and **w** in himself to die, and said, 7592
Ac 27:29 out of the stern, and **w for** the day. 2172

WISHING (1) [WISH]
Job 31:30 my mouth to sin by **w** a curse to his soul.) 7592

WIST (13) [WIT]
Ex 16:15 for they **w** not what it was. And Moses 3045
 34:29 that Moses **w** not that the skin of his face 3045
Lev 5:17 though he **w** it not, yet is he guilty, 3045
 5:18 ignorance wherein he erred and **w** it not, 3045
Jos 2: 4 unto me, but I **w** not whence they were: 3045
 8:14 he **w** not that there were liers in ambush 3045
Jdg 16:20 he **w** not that the LORD was departed 3045
Mk 9: 6 For he **w** not what to say; for they were 1492
 14:40 neither **w** they what to answer him. 1492
Lk 2:49 **w** ye not that I must be about my Father's 1492
Jn 5:13 And he that was healed **w** not who it was: 1492
Ac 12: 9 **w** not that it was true which was done by 1492
 23: 5 Then said Paul, I **w** not, brethren, that he 1492

WIT (21) [UNWITTINGLY, WIST, WIT'S, WITTINGLY, WITTY, WOT, WOTTETH]
Ge 24:21 to **w** whether the LORD had made his 3045
Ex 2: 4 afar off, to **w** what would be done to him. 3045
Jos 17: 1 to **w**, for Machir the firstborn of Manasseh, NIH
1Ki 2:32 father David not knowing thereof, to **w**, NIH
 7:50 doors of the house, to **w**, of the temple. NIH
 13:23 to **w**, for the prophet whom he had NIH
2Ki 10:29 to **w**, the golden calves that were in NIH
1Ch 7: 2 of their fathers' house, to **w**, of Tola: NIH
 27: 1 to **w**, the chief fathers and captains of NIH
2Ch 4:12 To **w**, the two pillars, and the pommels, NIH
 25: 7 to **w**, with all the children of Ephraim. NIH
 25:10 separated them, to **w**, the army 3807.1
 31: 3 to **w**, for the morning and evening burnt NIH
Ne 11: 3 to **w**, Israel, the priests, and the Levites, NIH
Est 2:12 to **w**, six months with oil of myrrh, NIH
Jer 25:18 To **w**, Jerusalem, and the cities of Judah, NIH
 34: 9 himself of them, to **w**, of a Jew his brother. NIH
Eze 13:16 To **w**, the prophets of Israel which NIH
Ro 8:23 to **w**, the redemption of our body. NIG
2Co 5:19 To **w**, that God was in Christ reconciling 5613
 8: 1 we do you to **w** of the grace of God 1107

WIT'S (1) [WIT]
Ps 107:27 and are **at** their **w** end. 1104+2451+3605

WITCH (2) [WITCHCRAFT, WITCHCRAFTS]
Ex 22:18 Thou shalt not suffer a **w** to live. 3784
Dt 18:10 observer of times, or an enchanter, or a **w**, 3784

WITCHCRAFT (3) [CRAFT, WITCH]
1Sa 15:23 For rebellion is as the sin of **w**, 7081
2Ch 33: 6 **used w**, and dealt with a familiar spirit, 3784
Gal 5:20 Idolatry, **w**, hatred, variance, emulations, 5331

WITCHCRAFTS (4) [CRAFT, WITCH]
2Ki 9:22 mother Jezebel and her **w** are so many? 3785
Mic 5:12 I will cut off **w** out of thine hand; 3785

Na 3: 4 the mistress of **w**, that selleth nations 3785
 3: 4 and families through her **w**. 3785

WITH (6016) [HEREWITH, THEREWITH, WHEREWITH] See Index of Articles, Etc.

WITHAL (33) [WHEREWITHAL]
Ex 25:29 bowls thereof, to cover **w**: 834+871.1+2006.1
 30: 4 places for the staves to bear it **w**. 1992+871.1
 30:18 to wash **w**: and thou shalt put it between NIH
 36: 3 to make it **w**. And they brought yet unto NIH
 37:16 and his covers to cover **w**, 871.1+2006.1
 37:27 places for the staves to bear it **w**. 871.1+1992.1
 38: 7 sides of the altar, to bear it **w**; 871.1+1992.1
 40:30 altar, and put water there, to wash **w**. NIH
Lev 5: 3 that a man shall be defiled **w**, 871.1+1886.3
 6:30 reconcile **w** in the holy place, shall be NIH
 11:21 feet, to leap **w** upon the earth; 871.1+2006.1
 19:24 shall be holy to praise the LORD **w**. NIH
Nu 4: 7 and the bowls, and covers to cover **w**: 5262
Jdg 7:20 trumpets in their right hands to blow **w**: NIH
1Sa 16:12 and **w** of a beautiful countenance, 5973
1Ki 19: 1 **w** how he had slain all the prophets with 3605
2Ki 23:26 that Manasseh had provoked him **w**. NIH
1Ch 29: 4 to overlay the walls of the houses **w**: NIH
2Ch 24:14 to offer **w**, and spoons, and vessels of gold NIH
 26:15 to shoot arrows and great stones **w**. 871.1
Est 6: 9 that they may array the man **w** whom NIH
Job 2: 8 a potsherd to scrape himself **w**; 871.1+2050.2
Ps 141:10 their own nets, whilst that I **w** escape. 3162
Pr 22:18 they shall **w** be fitted in thy lips. 3162
Isa 30:14 hearth, or to take water **w** out of the pit. NIH
 30:23 seed, that thou shalt sow the ground **w**; NIH
Mk 10:39 with the baptism that I am baptized **w** NIG
Lk 6:38 with the same measure that ye mete **w** it NIG
Ac 25:27 not **w** to signify the crimes laid against 3361
1Co 12: 7 Spirit is given to every man to **profit w**. 4851
Col 4: 3 **W** praying also for us, that God would open 260
1Ti 5:13 and **w** they learn to be idle, wandering about 260
Phm 1:22 But **w** prepare me also a lodging: for I trust 260

WITHDRAW (11) [WITHDRAWEST, WITHDRAWETH, WITHDRAWN, WITHDREW]
1Sa 14:19 Saul said unto the priest, **W** thine hand. 622
Job 9:13 If God will not **w** his anger, the proud 7725
 13:21 **W** thine hand far from me: and let not 7368
 33:17 That he may **w** man from his purpose, 5493
Pr 25:17 **W** thy foot from thy neighbour's house; 3365
Ecc 7:18 yea, also from this **w** not thine hand: 3240
Isa 60:20 go down; neither shall thy moon **w** itself: 622
Joel 2:10 dark, and the stars shall **w** their shining. 622
 3:15 and the stars shall **w** their shining. 622
2Th 3: 6 that ye yourselves from every brother 4724
1Ti 6: 5 that gain is godliness: from such **w** thyself. 868

WITHDRAWEST (1) [WITHDRAW]
Ps 74:11 Why **w** thou thy hand, even thy right 7725

WITHDRAWETH (1) [WITHDRAW]
Job 36: 7 He **w** not his eyes from the righteous: 1639

WITHDRAWN (6) [WITHDRAW]
Dt 13:13 have **w** the inhabitants of their city, 5080
SS 5: 6 beloved had **w** himself, and was gone: 2559
La 2: 8 he hath not **w** his hand from destroying; 7725
Eze 18: 8 that hath **w** his hand from iniquity, 7725
Hos 5: 6 they shall not find him; he hath **w** himself 2502
Lk 22:41 And he was **w** from them about a stone's 645

WITHDREW (6) [WITHDRAW]
Ne 9:29 **w** the shoulder, and hardened their 5414+5637
Eze 20:22 Nevertheless I **w** mine hand, 7725
Mt 12:15 But when Jesus knew it, he **w** himself from 402
Mk 3: 7 But Jesus **w** himself with his disciples to 402
Lk 5:16 And he **w** himself into the wilderness, 5298
Gal 2:12 were come, he **w** and separated himself, 5288

WITHER (11) [WITHERED, WITHERETH]
Ps 1: 3 his leaf also shall not **w**; and whatsoever 5034
 37: 2 like the grass, and **w** as the green herb. 5034
Isa 19: 6 and dried up: the reeds and flags shall **w**. 7060
 19: 7 shall **w**, be driven away, and be no more. 3001
 40:24 they shall **w**, and the whirlwind shall take 3001
Jer 12: 4 mourn, and the herbs of every field **w**, 3001
Eze 17: 9 and cut off the fruit thereof, that it **w**? 3001
 17: 9 it shall **w** in all the leaves of her spring, 3001
 17:10 it not utterly **w**, when the east 3001+3001
 17:10 it shall **w** in the furrows where it grew. 3001
Am 1: 2 mourn, and the top of Carmel shall **w**. 3001

WITHERED (25) [WITHER]
Ge 41:23 **w**, thin, and blasted with the east wind, 6798
Ps 102: 4 My heart is smitten, and **w** like grass; 3001
 102:11 that declineth; and I am **w** like grass. 3001
Isa 15: 6 for the hay is **w** away, the grass faileth, 3001
 27:11 When the boughs thereof are **w**, they 3001
La 4: 8 bones; it is **w**, it is become like a stick. 3001
Eze 19:12 her strong rods were broken and **w**, 3001
Joel 1:12 even all the trees of the field, are **w**: 3001
 1:12 joy is **w** away from the sons of men. 3001
 1:17 barns are broken down; for the corn is **w**. 3001
Am 4: 7 and the piece whereupon it rained not **w**. 3001
Jnh 4: 7 day, and it smote the gourd, that it **w**. 3001
Mt 12:10 there was a man which had his hand **w**. 3584
 13: 6 because they had not root, they **w** away. 3583
 21:19 And presently the fig tree **w** away. 3583

Mt 21:20 saying, How soon is the fig tree **w** away! 3583
Mk 3: 1 was a man there which had a **w** hand. 3583
 3: 3 he saith unto the man which had the **w** 3583
 4: 6 and because it had no root, it **w** away. 3583
 11:21 fig tree which thou cursedst is **w** away. 3583
Lk 6: 6 was a man whose right hand was **w**. 3584
 6: 8 said to the man which had the **w** hand, 3584
 8: 6 it **w** away, because it lacked moisture. 3583
Jn 5: 3 halt, **w**, waiting for the moving of 3584
 15: 6 he is cast forth as a branch, and is **w**; 3583

WITHERETH (8) [WITHER]
Job 8:12 not cut down, it **w** before any other herb. 3001
Ps 90: 6 in the evening it is cut down, and **w**. 3001
 129: 6 housetops, which afore it groweth up: 3001
Isa 40: 7 The grass **w**, the flower fadeth: because 3001
 40: 8 The grass **w**, the flower fadeth: 3001
Jas 1:11 but it **w** the grass, and the flower thereof 3583
1Pe 1:24 The grass **w**, and the flower falleth 3583
Jude 1:12 trees whose fruit **w**, without fruit, 5352

WITHHELD (6) [WITHHOLD]
Ge 20: 6 for I also **w** thee from sinning against me: 2820
 22:12 seeing thou hast not **w** thy son, thine only 2820
 22:16 hast not **w** thy son, thine only son: 2820
 30: 2 who hath **w** from thee the fruit of 4513
Job 31:16 If I have **w** the poor from their desire, 4513
Ecc 2:10 them, I **w** not my heart from any joy; 4513

WITHHELDEST (1) [WITHHOLD]
Ne 9:20 **w** not thy manna from their mouth, 4513

WITHHOLD (9) [WITHHELD, WITHHELDEST, WITHHOLDEN, WITHHOLDETH]
Ge 23: 6 of us shall **w** from thee his sepulchre, 3607
2Sa 13:13 the king; for he will not **w** me from thee. 4513
Job 4: 2 but who can **w** himself from speaking? 6113
Ps 40:11 **W** not thou thy tender mercies from me, 3607
 84:11 no good thing will he **w** from them that 4513
Pr 3:27 **W** not good from them to whom it is due, 4513
 23:13 **W** not correction from the child: for 4513
Ecc 11: 6 and in the evening **w** not thine hand: 3240
Jer 2:25 **W** thy foot from being unshod, 4513

WITHHOLDEN (10) [WITHHOLD]
1Sa 25:26 seeing the LORD hath **w** thee from 4513
Job 22: 7 and thou hast **w** bread from the hungry. 4513
 38:15 from the wicked their light is **w**, 4513
 42: 2 and that no thought can be **w** from thee. 1219
Ps 21: 2 and hast not **w** the request of his lips. 4513
Jer 3: 3 Therefore the showers have been **w**, 4513
 5:25 your sins have **w** good things from you. 4513
Eze 18:16 hath not **w** the pledge, 2254+2258
Joel 1:13 the drink offering is **w** from the house of 4513
Am 4: 7 I have **w** the rain from you, when there 4513

WITHHOLDETH (4) [WITHHOLD]
Job 12:15 Behold, he **w** the waters, and they dry up: 6113
Pr 11:24 there is that **w** more than is meet, 2820
 11:26 that **w** corn, the people shall curse him: 4513
2Th 2: 6 now ye know what **w** that he might be 2722

WITHIN (186) [IN]
Ge 6:14 pitch it **w** and without with pitch. 1004+4480
 9:21 and he was uncovered **w** his tent. 8432+871.1
 18:12 Therefore Sarah laughed **w** herself, 7130+871.1
 18:24 there be fifty righteous **w** the city: 8432+871.1
 18:26 If I find in Sodom fifty righteous **w** 8432+871.1
 25:22 the children struggled together **w** 7130+871.1
 39:11 none of the men of the house there **w**. 871.1
 40:13 Yet **w** three days shall Pharaoh lift up 871.1
 40:19 Yet **w** three days shall Pharaoh lift 5750+871.1
Ex 20:10 nor thy stranger that is **w** thy gates: 871.1
 25:11 shalt overlay it with pure gold, **w** 1004+4480
 26:33 that thou mayest bring in thither **w** 1004+4480
 37: 2 he overlaid it with pure gold **w** 1004+4480
Lev 10:18 the blood of it was not brought in **w** 413+6441
 13:55 whether it be bare **w** or without. 7146
 14:41 house to be scraped **w** round about 1004+4480
 16: 2 place **w** the vail before the mercy 1004+4480
 16:12 small, and bring it **w** the vail: 1004+4480
 16:15 bring his blood **w** the vail, 1004+4480
 25:29 he may redeem it **w** a whole year after it NIH
 25:29 it is sold; **w** a full year may he redeem it. NIH
 25:30 If it be not redeemed **w** the space of a full 5704
 26:25 ye are gathered together **w** your cities, 413
Nu 4:10 all the vessels thereof **w** a covering of 413
 18: 7 of the altar, and **w** the vail; 1004+4480+3807.1
Dt 5:14 nor thy stranger that is **w** thy gates; 871.1
 12:12 and the Levite that is **w** your gates; 871.1
 12:17 Thou mayest not eat **w** thy gates the tithe 871.1
 12:18 and the Levite that is **w** thy gates: 871.1
 14:27 The Levite that is **w** thy gates; thou shalt 871.1
 14:28 same year, and shalt lay it up **w** thy gates: 871.1
 14:29 the widow, which are **w** thy gates, 871.1
 15: 7 **w** any of thy gates in thy land which 871.1
 15:22 Thou shalt eat it **w** thy gates: the unclean 871.1
 16: 5 Thou mayest not sacrifice the passover **w** 871.1
 16:11 the Levite that is **w** thy gates, 871.1
 16:14 and the widow, that are **w** thy gates. 871.1
 17: 2 **w** any of thy gates which the LORD thy 871.1
 17: 8 being matters of controversy **w** thy gates: 871.1
 23:10 the camp, he shall not come **w** the camp: 8432
 24:14 thy strangers that are in thy land **w** thy 871.1
 26:12 they may eat **w** thy gates, and be filled; 871.1

Dt
28:43 The stranger that *is* w thee shall 7130+871.1
31:12 and thy stranger that *is* w thy gates, 871.1
32:25 The sword without, and terror w, 2315+4480
Jos
1:11 for w three days ye shall pass over 5750+871.1
19: 1 their inheritance was w 8432+871.1
19: 9 w the inheritance of them. 8432+871.1
21:41 All the cities of the Levites w 8432+871.1
Jdg
7:16 and lamps w the pitchers. 8432+871.1
9:51 was a strong tower w the city, 8432+871.1
11:18 but came not w the border of Moab 871.1
11:26 did ye not recover *them* w that time? 871.1
14:12 if you can certainly declare it me *w* NIH
15: 1 it came to pass w a while after, 3117+4480
1Sa
13:11 thou camest not w the days appointed, 3807.1
14:14 w as it were a half acre of land, 871.1
25:36 Nabal's heart *was* merry w him, for he 5921
25:37 that his heart died w him, 7130+871.1
26: 7 Saul lay sleeping w the trench, 871.1
2Sa
7: 2 ark of God dwelleth w curtains. 8432+871.1
20: 4 Assemble me the men of Judah w three NIH
1Ki
6:15 w with boards of cedar, 1004+4480+1886.5
6:16 he even built therefor it w, 1004+4480
6:18 the cedar of the house w *was* carved 6441
6:19 oracle he prepared in the house w, 4480+6441
6:21 So Solomon overlaid the house w 4480+6441
6:23 the oracle he made two cherubims *of* 871.1
6:27 he set the cherubims w the inner 8432+871.1
6:29 flowers, and without. 4480+6440+3807.1
6:30 house he overlaid with gold, w 6441+3807.1
7: 8 *had* another court by the porch, 1004+4480
7: 9 sawed with saws, w and without, 1004+4480
7:31 the mouth of it w the chapiter and 1004+4480
2Ki
4:27 her alone; for her soul *is* vexed w her: 3807.1
6:30 *he had* sackcloth w upon his flesh. 1004+4480
7:11 and they told it *to* the king's house w. 6441
11: 8 he that cometh w the ranges, let him be 413
2Ch
3: 4 he overlaid it w with pure gold. 4480+6441
Ezr
4:15 they have moved sedition w the same 871.2
10: 8 whosoever would not come w three 3807.1
10: 9 together *unto* Jerusalem w three days. 3807.1
Ne
4:22 his servant lodge w Jerusalem, 8432+871.1
6:10 the temple, and let us shut the 413+8432
Job
6: 4 For the arrows of the Almighty *are* w me, 5978
14:22 pain, and his soul w him shall mourn. 5921
19:27 my reins be consumed w me. 2436+871.1
20:13 but keep it still w his mouth: 8432+871.1
20:14 turned, *it is* the gall of asps w him. 7130+871.1
24:11 *Which* make oil w their walls, *and* tread 996
32:18 matter, the spirit w me constraineth me. 990
Ps
36: 1 of the wicked saith w my heart, 7130+871.1
39: 3 My heart was hot w me, while I 7130+871.1
40: 8 God: yea, thy law *is* w my heart. 8432+871.1
40:10 I have not hid thy righteousness w 8432+871.1
42: 6 O my God, my soul is cast down w me: 5921
42:11 why art thou disquieted w me? hope thou 5921
43: 5 why art thou disquieted w me? hope in 5921
45:13 The king's daughter *is* all glorious w: 6441
51:10 and renew a right spirit w me. 7130+871.1
55: 4 My heart is sore pained w me: 7130+871.1
94:19 In the multitude of my thoughts w 7130+871.1
101: 2 I will walk w my house with a 7130+871.1
101: 7 deceit shall not dwell w my house: 7130+871.1
103: 1 and all that is w me, *bless* his holy name. 7130
109:22 and my heart is wounded w me. 7130+871.1
122: 2 Our feet shall stand w thy gates, 871.1
122: 7 Peace be w thy walls, 871.1
122: 7 thy walls, *and* prosperity w thy palaces. 871.1
122: 8 I will now say, Peace *be* w thee. 871.1
142: 3 When my spirit was overwhelmed w me, 5921
143: 4 Therefore is my spirit overwhelmed w me; 5921
143: 4 my heart w me is desolate. 8432+871.1
147:13 hath blessed thy children w thee. 7130+871.1
Pr
22:18 *thing* if thou keep them w thee; 990+871.1
26:24 lips, and layeth up deceit w him; 7130+871.1
Ecc
9:14 *was* a little city, and few men w it; 871.1
SS
4: 1 thou hast doves' eyes w thy locks: 1157+4480
4: 3 of a pomegranate w thy locks. 1157+4480
6: 7 *are* thy temples w thy locks. 1157+4480
Isa
7: 8 w threescore and five years shall 5750+871.1
16:14 saying, W three years, as the years of a 871.1
21:16 W a year, according to the years of 5750+871.1
26: 9 spirit w me will I seek thee early: 7130+871.1
56: 5 w my walls a place and a name better 871.1
60:18 wasting nor destruction w thy borders; 871.1
63:11 he that put his holy Spirit w him? 7130+871.1
Jer
4:14 thy vain thoughts lodge w thee? 7130+871.1
23: 9 Mine heart w me is broken 7130+871.1
28: 3 W two full years *will* I bring again 5750+871.1
28:11 w the space of two full years. 5750+871.1
La
1:20 mine heart is turned w me; 7130+871.1
Eze
1:27 the appearance of fire round about w it, 1004
2:10 and it *was* written w and without: 6440
3:24 Go, shut thyself w thine house. 8432+871.1
7:15 the pestilence and the famine w. 1004+4480
11:19 and I will put a new spirit w you; 7130+871.1
12:24 divination w the house of Israel. 8432+871.1
36:26 and a new spirit will I put w you: 7130+871.1
36:27 I will put my spirit w you, 7130+871.1
40: 7 the gate w *was* one reed. 1004+4480+1886.1
40: 8 the porch of the gate w, 1004+4480+1886.1
40:16 to their posts w the gate round 6441+3807.1
40:43 w *were* hooks, a hand 1004+871.1+1886.1
41: 9 chambers that *were* w. 1004+1886.1+3807.1
41:17 the wall round about w 6442+871.1+1886.1
44:17 gates of the inner court, and w. 1004+1886.5

Da
6:12 *petition* of any God or man w thirty days, 5705
11:20 w few days he shall be destroyed, 871.1
Hos
11: 8 mine heart is turned w me, my repentings 5921
Jnh
2: 7 my soul fainted w me I remembered 5921
Mic
3: 3 the pot, and as flesh w the caldron. 8432+871.1
5: 6 and when he treadeth w our borders. 871.1
Zep
3: 3 princes w her *are* roaring lions; 7130+871.1
Zec
12: 1 formeth the spirit of man w him. 7130+871.1
Mt
3: 9 And think not to say w yourselves, 1722
9: 3 certain of the scribes said w themselves, 1722
9:21 For she said w herself, If I may but 1722
23:25 w they are full of extortion and excess. 2081
23:26 cleanse first that which is w the cup and 1787
23:27 but are w full of dead *men's* bones, 2081
23:28 but w ye are full of hypocrisy and iniquity. 2081
Mk
2: 8 spirit that they so reasoned w themselves, 1722
7:21 For from w, out of the heart of men, 2081
7:23 All these evil *things* come from w, 2081
14: 4 some that had indignation w themselves, 4314
14:58 w three days I will build another made 1223
Lk
3: 8 and begin not to say w yourselves, 1722
7:39 bidden him saw *it*, he spake w himself, 1722
7:49 with *him* began to say w themselves, 1722
11: 7 And he from w shall answer and say, 2081
11:40 is without make that *which* is w also? 2081
12:17 And he thought w himself, saying, 1722
16: 3 Then the steward said w himself, 1722
17:21 for behold, the kingdom of God is w you. 1787
18: 4 but afterward he said w himself, Though 1722
19:44 with the ground, and thy children w thee: 1722
24:32 to another, Did not our heart burn w us, 1722
Jn
20:26 eight days again his disciples were w, 2080
Ac
5:23 we had opened, we found no *man* w. 2080
Ro
8:23 even we ourselves groan w ourselves, 1722
1Co
5:12 do not ye judge them that are w? 2080
2Co
7: 5 without *were* fightings, w *were* fears. 2081
Heb
6:19 and which entereth into that w the vail; 2082
Rev
4: 8 about *him;* and *they were* full of eyes w: 2081
5: 1 that sat on the throne a book written w 2081

WITHOUT (426) [, OUT]

Ge
1: 2 the earth was w form, and void; 8414
6:14 pitch it within and w with pitch. 2351+4480
9:22 told his two brethren w. 2351+871.1+1886.1
19:16 him forth, and set him w the city. 2351+4480
24:11 made *his* camels to kneel down w 2351+4480
24:31 standest thou w? 2351+871.1+1886.1
37:33 Joseph is w doubt rent in pieces. 2963+2963
41:44 w thee shall no man lift up his hand or 1107
41:49 he left numbering; for *it was* w number. 369
Ex
5: 2 Your lamb shall be w blemish, a male of 8549
21:11 then shall she go out free w money. 369
25:11 within and w shalt thou overlay it, 2351+4480
26:35 thou shalt set the table w the vail, 2351+4480
27:21 of the congregation w the vail, 2351+4480
29: 1 young bullock, and two rams w blemish, 8549
29:14 thou burn with fire w the camp: 2351+4480
33: 7 pitched it w the camp, afar off from 2351+4480
33: 7 which *was* w the camp. 2351+4480
37: 2 it with pure gold within and w, 2351+4480
40:22 of the tabernacle northward, w 2351+4480
Lev
1: 3 the herd, let him offer a male w blemish: 8549
1:10 he shall bring it a male w blemish. 8549
3: 1 he shall offer it w blemish before 8549
3: 6 or female, he shall offer it w blemish. 8549
4: 3 a young bullock w blemish unto 8549
4:12 w the camp unto a clean place, 2351+4480
4:21 he shall carry forth the bullock w 2351+4480
4:23 a kid of the goats, a male w blemish; 8549
4:28 a kid of the goats, a female w blemish, 8549
4:32 he shall bring it a female w blemish. 8549
5:15 LORD a ram w blemish out of the flocks, 8549
5:18 he shall bring a ram w blemish out of 8549
6: 6 a ram w blemish out of the flock, with 8549
6:11 carry forth the ashes w the camp 2351+4480
8:17 he burnt with fire w the camp; 2351+4480
9: 2 w blemish, and offer *them* before 8549
9: 3 first year, w blemish, for a burnt offering; 8549
9:11 hide he burnt with fire w the camp. 2351+4480
10:12 fire, and eat it w leaven beside the altar: 4682
13:46 he shall dwell alone; w the camp 2351+4480
13:55 inward, whether it *be* bare within or w. 1372
14:10 he shall take two he lambs w blemish, 8549
14:10 ewe lamb of the first year w blemish, 8549
14:40 into an unclean place w the city: 2351+4480
14:41 off w the city into an unclean place: 2351+4480
16:27 shall *one* carry forth w the camp; 2351+4480
22:19 *offer* at your own will a male w blemish, 8549
23:12 w blemish of the first year for a burnt 8549
23:18 seven lambs w blemish of the first year, 8549
24: 3 W the vail of the Testimony, 2351+4480
24:14 Bring forth him that hath cursed w 2351+4480
26:43 while she lieth desolate w them: 4480
Nu
5: 3 female shall ye put out, w the camp 2351+4480
5: 4 so, and put them out w the camp: 2351+4480
6:14 one he lamb of the first year w blemish 8549
6:14 one ewe lamb of the first year w blemish 8549
6:14 one ram w blemish for peace offerings, 8549
15:24 the knowledge of 4480+5869
15:35 stone him with stones w the camp. 2351+4480
15:36 all the congregation brought him w 2351+4480
19: 2 that they bring thee a red heifer w spot, 8549
19: 3 that he may bring her forth w 2351+4480
19: 9 up w the camp in a clean place, 2351+4480
20:19 w doing *any* thing else, go through on my 369

Nu
28: 3 two lambs of the first year w spot day by 8549
28: 9 day two lambs of the first year w spot, 8549
28:11 seven lambs of the first year w spot; 8549
28:19 they shall be unto you w blemish: 8549
28:31 (they shall be unto you w blemish) 8549
29: 2 seven lambs of the first year w blemish: 8549
29: 8 they shall be unto you w blemish: 8549
29:13 of the first year; they shall be w blemish: 8549
29:17 fourteen lambs of the first year w spot: 8549
29:20 lambs of the first year w blemish: 8549
29:23 lambs of the first year w blemish: 8549
29:26 fourteen lambs of the first year w spot: 8549
29:29 lambs of the first year w blemish: 8549
29:32 lambs of the first year w blemish: 8549
29:36 seven lambs of the first year w blemish: 8549
31:13 forth to meet them w the camp. 2351+4480
31:19 ye abide w the camp seven days: 2351+4480
35: 5 shall measure from w the city *on* the east 2351
35:22 he thrust him suddenly w enmity, 3808+871.1
35:22 have cast upon him any thing w 3808+871.1
35:26 if the slayer shall at any time come *w* NIH
35:27 the revenger of blood find him w 2351+4480
Dt
8: 9 A land wherein thou shalt eat bread w 3808
23:12 Thou shalt have a place also w 2351+4480
25: 5 marry w unto a stranger: 2351+1886.1+1886.5
32: 4 a God of truth and w iniquity, just and 369
32:25 The sword w, and terror within, 2351+4480
Jos
3:10 *that* he will w fail drive out from 3423+3423
6:23 and left them w the camp of Israel. 2351+4480
Jdg
2:23 those nations, w driving them out hastily; 1115
6: 5 they and their camels were w number: 369
7:12 their camels *were* w number, as the sand 369
11:30 If thou shalt w fail deliver 5414+5414
Ru
4:14 which hath not left thee *this* day w a 7673
1Sa
19: 5 innocent blood, to slay David w a cause? 2600
30: 8 and w fail recover *all*. 5337+5337
2Sa
23: 4 the sun riseth, *even* a morning w clouds; 3808
1Ki
6: 6 for w *in the wall* of the house he 2351+1886.5
6:29 trees and open flowers, within and w. 2435
6:30 he overlaid with gold, within and w. 2435
7: 9 sawed with saws, within and w, 2351+4480
8: 8 and they were not seen w: 2351+1886.5
22: 1 they continued three years w war between 369
2Ki
10:24 fourscore men w, and 2351+871.1+1886.1
11:15 Have her forth w the ranges: 413+1004+4480
16:18 house, and the king's entry w, 2435+1886.5
18:25 Am I now come up w the LORD 1107+4480
23: 4 he burnt them w Jerusalem in 2351+4480
23: 6 from the house of the LORD, w 2351+4480
25:16 brass of all these vessels was w weight. 3808
1Ch
2:30 and Appaim: but Seled died w children. 3808
2:32 and Jonathan: and Jether died w children. 3808
21:24 nor offer burnt offerings w cost. 2600
22: 3 and brass in abundance w weight; 369
22:14 of brass and iron w weight; for it is in 369
2Ch
5: 9 but they were not seen w. 2351+1886.5
12: 3 the people *were* w number that came with 369
15: 3 Israel hath been w the true God, 3808+3807.1
15: 3 w a teaching priest, and without 3808+3807.1
15: 3 a teaching priest, and w law. 3808+3807.1
21:20 and departed w being desired. 3808+871.1
24: 8 set it w at the gate of the house 2351+1886.5
32: 3 fountains which were w the city: 2351+4480
32: 5 wall w, and repaired Millo 2351+1886.5
33:14 Now after this he built a wall w the city 2435
Ezr
6: 9 let *it* be given them day by day w fail: 3809
7:22 of oil, and salt w prescribing *how much.* 3809
10:13 *are* not able to stand w, 2351+871.1+1886.1
Ne
13:20 sellers of all *kind of* ware lodged w 2351+4480
Job
2: 3 against him, to destroy him w cause. 2600
4:20 perish for ever w *any* regarding *it.* 1097+4480
4:21 they die, even w wisdom. 3808+871.1
5: 9 marvellous *things* w number: 369+5704
6: 6 which is unsavoury be eaten w salt? 1097+4480
7: 6 and are spent w hope. 657+871.1
8:11 Can the rush grow up w mire? 3808+871.1
8:11 without mire? can the flag grow w water? 1097
9:10 yea, and wonders w number. 369+5704
9:17 and multiplieth my wounds w cause. 2600
10:22 w *any* order, and *where* the light 3808+2050.1
11:15 then shalt thou lift up thy face w spot; 4480
12:25 They grope in the dark w light, 3808+2050.1
24: 7 They cause the naked to lodge w 1097+4480
24:10 They cause *him* to go naked w clothing, 1097
26: 2 hast thou helped *him that is* w power? 3808
30:28 I went mourning w the sun: 3808+871.1
31:19 want of clothing, or *any* poor w covering; 369
31:39 If I have eaten the fruits thereof w money, 1097
33: 9 I am clean w transgression, *I am* innocent; 1097
34: 6 my wound *is* incurable w transgression. 1097
34:20 the mighty shall be taken away w hand. 3808
34:24 He shall break in pieces mighty *men* w 3808
34:35 Job hath spoken w knowledge, 3808+871.1
34:35 and his words *were* w wisdom. 3808+871.1
35:16 he multiplieth words w knowledge. 1097+871.1
36:12 and they shall die w knowledge. 1097+3509.1
38: 2 counsel by words w knowledge? 1097
39:16 not hers: her labour is in vain w fear; 1097
41:33 not his like, who is made w fear. 1097+3807.1
42: 3 Who *is he* that hideth counsel w 1097
Ps
7: 4 I have delivered him that w cause is mine 7387
25: 3 be ashamed which transgress w much. 7387
31:11 see me w fled from me. 2351+871.1+4480
35: 7 For w cause have they hid for me their 2600
35: 7 which w cause they have digged for my 2600

Ps	35:19	*with* the eye that hate me **w a cause.** 2600
	59: 4	and prepare themselves **w** *my* fault: 1097
	69: 4	They that hate me **w a cause** are moe 2600
	105:34	and caterpillars, and that **w** number, 369
	109: 3	hatred; and fought against me **w a cause.** 2600
	119:78	they dealt perversely with me **w a cause.** 8267
	119:161	Princes have persecuted me **w a cause:** 2600
Pr	1:11	lurk privily for the innocent **w cause:** 2600
	1:20	Wisdom crieth **w;** 2351+871.1+1886.1
	3:30	Strive not with a man **w cause,** if he 2600
	5:23	He shall die **w** instruction; and in 369+871.1
	6:15	suddenly shall he be broken **w** remedy. 369
	7:12	Now *is she* **w,** now in 2351+871.1+1886.1
	11:22	*so is* a fair woman which is **w** discretion. 5493
	15:22	**W** counsel purposes *are* 369+871.1
	16: 8	than great revenues **w** right. 3808+871.1
	19: 2	*that* the soul *be* **w** knowledge, 3808+871.1
	22:13	saith, There is a lion **w,** 2351+871.1+1886.1
	23:29	who hath wounds **w cause?** who hath 2600
	24:27	Prepare thy work **w** 2351+871.1+1886.1
	24:28	a witness against thy neighbour **w** cause; 2600
	25:14	a false gift *is like* clouds and wind **w** rain. 369
	25:28	a city *that is* broken down, *and* **w** walls. 369
	29: 1	be destroyed, and that **w** remedy. 369
Ecc	10:11	Surely the serpent will bite **w** 3808+871.1
SS	6: 8	concubines, and virgins **w** number. 369
	8: 1	I should find thee **w,** 2351+871.1+1886.1
Isa	5: 9	*even* great and fair, **w** inhabitant. 369
	5:14	opened her mouth **w** measure: 1097+3807.1
	6:11	Until the cities be wasted **w** 369+4480
	6:11	the houses **w** man, and the land be 369+4480
	10: 4	**W** me they shall bow down under 1115
	33: 7	their valiant ones shall cry **w:** 2351+1886.5
	36:10	am I now come up **w** the LORD 1107+4480
	45:17	confounded **world w** end. 5703+5704+5769
	52: 3	ye shall be redeemed **w** money. 3808+871.1
	52: 4	Assyrian oppressed them **w cause.** 657+871.1
	55: 1	I buy wine and milk **w** money and 3808+871.1
	55: 1	milk without money and **w** price. 3808+871.1
Jer	2:15	his cities are burnt **w** inhabitant. 1097+4480
	2:32	yet my people have forgotten me days **w** 369
	4: 7	thy cities shall be laid waste, **w** an 369+4480
	4:23	the earth, and lo, *it was* **w** form, and void; 8414
	5:21	O foolish people, and **w** understanding: 369
	9:11	of Judah desolate, **w** an inhabitant. 1097+4480
	9:21	to cut off the children from **w,** 2351
	15:13	will I give to the spoil **w** price, 3808+871.1
	21: 4	which besiege you **w** the walls, 2351+4480
	22:13	useth his neighbour's service **w wages,** 2351+4480
	26: 9	shall be desolate **w** an inhabitant? 369+4480
	32:43	say, It is desolate **w** man or beast; 369+4480
	33:10	ye say *shall be* desolate **w** man 369+4480
	33:10	desolate without man and **w** beast, 369+4480
	33:10	are desolate, **w** man, and without 369+4480
	33:10	**w** inhabitant, and without beast, 369+4480
	33:10	without inhabitant, and **w** beast, 369+4480
	33:12	*which is* desolate **w** man and 369+4480
	33:12	*is* desolate without man and **w** beast, 5704
	34:22	Judah a desolation **w** an inhabitant. 369+4480
	44:19	out drink offerings unto her, **w** 1107+4480
	44:22	**w** an inhabitant, as *at* this day. 369+4480
	46:19	waste and desolate **w** an inhabitant. 369+4480
	48: 9	cities thereof shall be desolate, **w** 369+4480
	49:31	that dwelleth **w** care, saith the LORD, 983
	51:29	a desolation **w** an inhabitant. 369+4480
	51:37	and a hissing, **w** an inhabitant. 369+4480
	52:20	brass of all these vessels was **w** weight. 3808
La	1: 6	they are gone **w** strength before 3808+871.1
	3:49	ceaseth not, **w** any intermission, 369+4480
	3:52	chased me sore, like a bird, **w** cause. 2600
Eze	2:10	me; and it *was* written within and **w:** 268
	7:15	The sword *is* **w,** 2351+871.1+1886.1
	14:23	shall know that I have not done **w** cause 2600
	17: 9	**w** great power or many people 3808+871.1
	33:15	of life, **w** committing iniquity; 1115+3807.1
	38:11	all of them dwelling **w** walls, 369+871.1
	40:19	the forefront of the inner court **w,** 2351+4480
	40:40	at the side **w,** as one goeth 2351+4480+1886.5
	40:44	**w** the inner gate *were* 2351+4480+1886.5
	41: 9	for the side chamber **w,** 413+2351+3807.1
	41:17	**w,** and by all the wall 2351+1886.1+3807.1
	41:17	about within and **w,** 2435+871.1+1886.1
	41:25	the face of the porch **w.** 2351+4480+1886.1
	42: 7	the wall that was **w** over 2351+1886.1+3807.1
	43:21	appointed place of the house, **w** 2351+4480
	43:22	of the goats **w blemish** for a sin offering; 8549
	43:23	shall offer a young bullock **w blemish,** 8549
	43:23	and a ram out of the flock **w blemish.** 8549
	43:25	and a ram out of the flock, **w blemish.** 8549
	45:18	shalt take a young bullock **w blemish,** 8549
	45:23	seven rams **w blemish** daily the seven 8549
	46: 2	way of the porch of *that* gate **w,** 2351+4480
	46: 4	day *shall be* six lambs **w blemish,** 8549
	46: 4	without blemish, and a ram **w blemish.** 8549
	46: 6	*it shall be* a young bullock **w blemish,** 8549
	46: 6	and a ram: they shall be **w blemish.** 8549
	46:13	*of* a lamb of the first year **w blemish:** 8549
	47: 2	me about the way **w** unto the utter gate 2351
Da	2:34	that a stone was cut out **w** hands, 3809+871.2
	2:45	cut out of the mountain **w** hands, 3809+871.2
	8:25	but he shall be broken **w** hand. 657+871.1
	11:18	**w** his own reproach he shall cause *it* to 1115
Hos	3: 4	of Israel shall abide many days **w** a king, 369
	3: 4	**w** a prince, and without a sacrifice, 369
	3: 4	and **w** a sacrifice, and without an image, 369

Hos	3: 4	**w** an image, and without an ephod, 369
	3: 4	and **w** an ephod, and *without* teraphim: 369
	3: 4	and without an ephod, and *w* teraphim: NIH
	7: 1	*of robbers* spoileth **w.** 2351+871.1+1886.1
	7:11	Ephraim also is like a silly dove, **w** heart: 369
Joel	1: 6	strong, and **w** number, whose teeth *are* 369
Zec	2: 4	**towns w walls** for the multitude of men 6519
Mt	5:22	**w a cause** shall be in danger of 1500
	10:29	one of them shall not fall on the ground **w** 427
	12:46	*his* mother and his brethren stood **w,** 1854
	12:47	thy mother and thy brethren stand **w,** 1854
	13:34	and **w** a parable spake he not unto them: 5565
	13:57	A prophet is not **w honour,** save in his 820
	15:16	Are ye so yet **w understanding?** 801
	26:69	Now Peter sat **w** in the palace: 1854
Mk	1:45	into the city, but was **w** in desert places: 1854
	3:31	brethren and his mother, and, standing **w,** 1854
	3:32	and thy brethren **w** seek for thee. 1854
	4:11	unto them that are **w,** all *these things* 1854
	4:34	But **w** a parable spake he not unto them: 5565
	6: 4	A prophet is not **w honour,** but in his 820
	7:15	There is nothing **from w** a man, 1855
	7:18	Are ye so **w understanding** also? 801
	7:18	whatsoever *thing* **from w** entereth into 1855
	11: 4	the colt tied by the door **w** in a place 1854
	14:58	days I will build another **made w hands.** 886
Lk	1:10	were praying **w** at the time of incense. 1854
	1:74	of our enemies might serve him **w fear,** 870
	6:49	is like a man that **w** a foundation built a 5565
	8:20	Thy mother and thy brethren stand **w,** 1854
	11:40	not he that made that *which is* **w** make 1855
	13:25	and ye begin to stand **w,** and to knock at 1854
	20:28	having a wife, and he die **w children,** 815
	20:29	the first took a wife, and died **w children.** 815
	22:35	When I sent you **w** purse, and scrip, 817
Jn	1: 3	**w** him was not any *thing* made that was 5565
	8: 7	unto them, He that is **w sin** among you, 361
	15: 5	much fruit: for **w** me ye can do nothing. 5565
	15:25	in their law, They hated me **w a cause.** 1432
	18:16	But Peter stood at the door **w.** Then went 1854
	19:23	now the coat was **w seam,** woven from 729
	20:11	But Mary stood **w** at the sepulchre 1854
Ac	5:23	the keepers standing **w** before the doors: 1854
	5:26	and brought them **w** violence; 3326+3756
	9: 9	And he was three days **w** sight, 3361
	10:29	Therefore came I *unto you* **w gainsaying,** 369
	12: 5	prayer was made **w** ceasing of the church 1618
	14:17	he left not himself **w witness,** 267
	25:17	they were come hither, **w** any delay, 3367
Ro	1: 9	that **w** ceasing I make mention of you, 89
	1:20	and Godhead; so that they are **w excuse:** 379
	1:31	**W understanding,** covenant-breakers, 801
	1:31	**w natural affection,** implacable, 794
	2:12	For as many as have sinned **w** law shall 460
	2:12	without law shall also perish **w law:** 460
	3: 3	unbelief **make** the faith of God **w effect?** 2673
	3:21	But now the righteousness of God **w** 5565
	3:28	justified by faith **w** the deeds of the law. 5565
	4: 6	whom God imputeth righteousness **w** 5565
	5: 6	For when we were yet **w strength,** in due 772
	7: 8	For the law sin **w** dead. 5565
	7: 9	For I was alive **w** the law once: 5565
	10:14	and how shall they hear **w** a preacher? 5565
	11:29	and calling of God *are* **w repentance.** 278
	12: 9	*Let* love *be* **w dissimulation.** 505
1Co	4: 8	are rich, ye have reigned as kings **w** us: 5565
	5:12	I to do to judge them also that are **w?** 1854
	5:13	But them that are **w** God judgeth. 1854
	6:18	Every sin that a man doeth is **w** the body; 1622
	7:32	But I would have you **w carelessness.** 275
	7:35	may attend upon the Lord **w distraction.** 563
	9:18	I may make the gospel of Christ **w charge,** 77
	9:21	To them *that are* **w** law, as without law, 459
	9:21	To them *that are* without law, as **w** law, 459
	9:21	not **w** law to God, but under the law 459
	9:21	that I might gain them *that are* **w** law. 459
	11:11	Nevertheless neither *is* the man **w** 5565
	11:11	the woman **w** the man, in the Lord. 5565
	14: 7	*And* even *things* **w** life giving sound, 895
	14:10	and none of them *is* **w** signification. 880
	16:10	see that he may be with you **w fear:** 870
2Co	7: 5	*we were* troubled on every *side;* **w** were 1855
	10:13	will not boast of *things* **w** our **measure,** 280
	10:15	Not boasting of *things* **w** our **measure,** 280
	11:28	Besides those *things* that are **w,** that 3924
Eph	1: 4	be holy and **w blame** before him in love: 299
	2:12	That at that time ye were **w** Christ, 5565
	2:12	having no hope, and **w God** in the world: 112
	3:21	all ages, **world w** end. 165+165+3588+3588
	5:27	but that it should be holy and **w blemish.** 299
Php	1:10	and **w** offence till the day of Christ; 677
	1:14	much more bold to speak the word **w fear.** 870
	2:14	Do all *things* **w** murmurings and 5565
	2:15	and harmless, the sons of God **w rebuke,** 298
Col	2:11	with the circumcision **made w hands,** 886
	4: 5	Walk in wisdom toward them that are **w,** 1854
1Th	1: 3	Remembering **w** ceasing your work of faith, 89
	2:13	this cause also thank we God **w ceasing,** 89
	4:12	walk honestly toward them that are **w,** 1854
	5:17	Pray **w ceasing.** 89
1Ti	2: 8	up holy hands, **w** wrath and doubting. 5565
	3: 7	have a good report of them which are **w;** 1855
	3:16	And **w controversy** great is the mystery 3672
	5:21	thou observe these *things* **w** preferring 5565
	6:14	thou keep *this* commandment **w spot,** 784

2Ti	1: 3	that **w** ceasing I have remembrance of 88
	3: 3	**W natural affection,** trucebreakers, 794
Phm	1:14	But **w** thy mind would I do nothing; 5565
Heb	4:15	*points* tempted like as *we are, yet* **w** sin. 5565
	7: 3	**W father,** without mother, without 540
	7: 3	father, **w mother,** without descent, 282
	7: 3	father, without mother, **w descent,** 35
	7: 7	And **w** all contradiction the less is blessed 5565
	7:20	And inasmuch as not **w** an oath *he was* 5565
	7:21	(For those priests were made **w** an oath; 5565
	9: 7	not **w** blood, which he offered for himself, 5565
	9:14	Spirit offered himself **w spot** to God, 299
	9:18	first *testament* was dedicated **w** blood. 5565
	9:22	and **w** shedding of blood is no remission. 5565
	9:28	the second time **w** sin unto salvation. 5565
	10:23	the profession of *our* hope **w** wavering; 186
	10:28	that despised Moses' law died **w** mercy 5565
	11: 6	But **w** faith *it is* impossible to please *him:* 5565
	11:40	they **w** us should not be made perfect. 5565
	12: 8	if ye be **w** chastisement, whereof all are 5565
	12:14	**w** which no *man* shall see the Lord: 5565
	13: 5	*your* conversation *be* **w covetousness;** 866
	13:11	high priest for sin, are burnt **w** the camp. 1854
	13:12	with his own blood, suffered **w** the gate. 1854
	13:13	go forth therefore unto him **w** the camp, 1854
Jas	2:13	For he shall have judgment **w mercy,** 448
	2:18	shew me thy faith **w** thy works, and I will 5565
	2:20	O vain man, that faith **w** works is dead? 5565
	2:26	as the body **w** the spirit is dead, so faith 5565
	2:26	is dead, so faith **w** works is dead also. 5565
	3:17	**w partiality,** and without hypocrisy. 87
	3:17	without partiality, and **w hypocrisy.** 505
1Pe	1:17	who **w respect of persons** judgeth 678
	1:19	as of a lamb **w blemish** and without spot: 299
	1:19	as of a lamb without blemish and **w spot:** 784
	3: 1	they also may **w** the word be won by 427
	4: 9	Use hospitality one to another **w** grudging. 427
2Pe	2:17	These are wells **w water,** clouds that are 504
	3:14	of him in peace, **w spot,** and blameless. 784
Jude	1:12	feast with *you,* feeding themselves **w fear:** 870
	1:12	clouds *they are* **w water,** carried about of 504
	1:12	**w fruit,** twice dead, plucked up by the 175
Rev	11: 2	But the court which is **w** the temple leave 1855
	14: 5	for they are **w fault** before the throne of 299
	14:10	is poured out **w mixture** into the cup 194
	14:20	the winepress was trodden **w** the city, 1854
	22:15	For **w** *are* dogs, and sorcerers, 1854

WITHS (3)

Jdg	16: 7	If they bind me with seven green **w** that 3499
	16: 8	seven green **w** which had not been dried, 3499
	16: 9	brake the **w,** as a thread of tow is broken 3499

WITHSTAND (10) [WITHSTOOD]

Nu	22:32	behold, I went out to **w** thee, because 7854
2Ch	13: 7	and could not **w** them. 2388+6440+3807.1
	13: 8	now ye think to **w** the 2388+6440+3807.1
	20: 6	so that none is **able to w** thee? 3320+5973
Est	9: 2	no man could **w** them; 5975+6440+3807.1
Ecc	4:12	against him, two shall **w** him; 5048+5975
Da	11:15	the arms of the south shall not **w,** 5975
	11:15	neither *shall there be any* strength to **w.** 5975
Ac	11:17	what was I, that I could **w** God? 2967
Eph	6:13	that ye may be able to **w** in the evil day, 436

WITHSTOOD (6) [WITHSTAND]

2Ch	26:18	they **w** Uzziah the king, 5921+5975
Da	10:13	kingdom of Persia **w** me 5048+5975+3807.1
Ac	13: 8	**w** them, seeking to turn away the deputy 436
Gal	2:11	I **w** him to the face, because he was *to be* 436
2Ti	3: 8	Now as Jannes and Jambres **w** Moses, 436
	4:15	ware also; for he hath greatly **w** our words. 436

WITNESS (135) [EYEWITNESSES, WITNESSED, WITNESSES, WITNESSETH, WITNESSING]

Ge	21:30	they may be a **w** unto me, that I have 5713
	31:44	let it be for a **w** between me and thee. 5707
	31:48	This heap *is* a **w** between me and thee 5707
	31:50	see, God *is* **w** betwixt me and thee. 5707
	31:52	This heap *be* **w,** and *this* pillar *be* witness, 5707
	31:52	This heap *be* witness, and *this* pillar *be* **w,** 5713
Ex	20:16	Thou shalt not bear false **w** against thy 5707
	22:13	*then* let him bring it *for* **w,** *and* he shall 5707
	23: 1	with the wicked to be an unrighteous **w.** 5707
Lev	5: 1	*is* a **w,** whether he hath seen or known 5707
Nu	5:13	be defiled, and *there be* no **w** against her, 5707
	17: 7	before the LORD in the tabernacle of **W.** 5715
	17: 8	Moses went into the tabernacle of **W;** 5715
	18: 2	*shall minister* before the tabernacle of **W.** 5715
	35:30	one **w** shall not testify against *any* person 5707
Dt	4:26	I **call** heaven and earth **to w** against you 5749
	5:20	Neither shalt thou bear false **w** against thy 5707
	17: 6	at the mouth of one **w** he shall not be put 5707
	19:15	One **w** shall not rise up against a man for 5707
	19:15	If a false **w** rise up against any man to 5707
	19:18	*if* the **w** *be* a false witness, 5707
	19:18	*if* the witness *be* a false **w,** 5707
	31:19	that this song may be a **w** for me against 5707
	31:21	this song shall testify against them as a **w;** 5707
	31:26	that it may be there for a **w** against thee. 5707
Jos	22:27	*that it may* be a **w** between us, and you, 5707
	22:28	but it *is* a **w** between us and you. 5707
	22:34	*be* a **w** between us that the LORD *is* God. 5707
	24:27	Behold, this stone shall be a **w** unto us; 5713
	24:27	it shall be therefore a **w** unto you, lest ye 5713

Jdg	11:10 The Lord be **w** between us, if we do not	8085
1Sa	12: 3 here I *am*: **w** against me before the Lord,	6030
	12: 5 The Lord *is* **w** against you,	5707
	12: 5 and his anointed *is* **w** this day,	5707
	12: 5 my hand. And they answered, *He is* **w**.	5707
1Ki	21:10 before him, to **bear w** against him,	5749
2Ch	24: 6 of Israel, for the tabernacle of **W**?	5715
Job	16: 8 is a **w** *against me*: and my leanness	
	16: 8 my leanness rising up in me **beareth w** to	6030
	16:19 my **w** *is* in heaven, and my record *is*	5707
	29:11 when the eye saw *me*, it **gave w** to me:	5749
Ps	89:37 the moon, and *as* a faithful **w** in heaven.	5707
Pr	6:19 A false **w** *that* speaketh lies, and he that	5707
	12:17 forth righteousness: but a false **w** deceit.	5707
	14: 5 faithful **w** will not lie: but a false witness	5707
	14: 5 will not lie: but a false **w** will utter lies.	5707
	14:25 A true **w** delivereth souls: but a deceitful	5707
	14:25 but a deceitful **w** speaketh lies.	NIH
	19: 5 A false **w** shall not be unpunished,	5707
	19: 9 A false **w** shall not be unpunished,	5707
	19:28 An ungodly **w** scorneth judgment:	5707
	21:28 A false **w** shall perish: but the man that	5707
	24:28 Be not a **w** against thy neighbour without	5707
	25:18 A man that beareth false **w** against his	5707
Isa	3: 9 The shew of their countenance doth **w**	6030
	19:20 for a **w** unto the Lord of hosts in	5707
	55: 4 I have given him *for* a **w** to the people,	5707
Jer	29:23 even I know, and *am* a **w**, saith	5707
	42: 5 be a true and faithful **w** between us,	5707
La	2:13 What *thing* shall I **take to w** for thee?	5749
Mic	1: 2 let the Lord God be **w** against you,	5707
Mal	2:14 Because the Lord hath been **w** between	5749
	3: 5 I will be a swift **w** against the sorcerers,	5707
Mt	15:19 adulteries, fornications, thefts, **false w**,	5577
	19:18 not steal, Thou shalt not **bear false w**,	5576
	24:14 in all the world for a **w** unto all nations;	3142
	26:59 the council, sought **false w** against Jesus,	5577
	26:62 what *is it which* these **w** against thee?	2649
	27:13 how many *things* they **w against** thee?	2649
Mk	10:19 Do not **bear false w**, Defraud not,	5576
	14:55 all the council sought for **w** against Jesus	3141
	14:56 For many **bare false w** against him,	5576
	14:56 but *their* **w** agreed not together.	3141
	14:57 and **bare false w** against him, saying,	5576
	14:59 But neither so did their **w** agree together.	3141
	14:60 what *is it which* these **w** against thee?	2649
	15: 4 behold how many *things* they **w against**	2649
Lk	4:22 And all **bare** him **w**, and wondered at	3140
	11:48 Truly ye **bear w** that ye allow the deeds	3140
	18:20 Do not steal, Do not **bear false w**,	5576
	22:71 they said, What need we any further **w**?	3141
Jn	1: 7 The same came for a **w**, to bear witness	3141
	1: 7 for a witness, to **bear w** of the Light,	3140
	1: 8 but *was sent* to **bear w** of *that* Light.	3140
	1:15 John **bare w** of him, and cried, saying,	3140
	3:11 we have seen; and ye receive not our **w**	3141
	3:26 whom thou **barest w**, behold, the same	3140
	3:28 Ye yourselves **bear** me **w**, that I said,	3140
	5:31 If I **bear w** of myself, my witness is not	3140
	5:31 bear witness of myself, my **w** is not true.	3141
	5:32 There is another that **beareth w** of me;	3140
	5:32 I know that the **w** which he **witnesseth**	3141
	5:33 unto John, and he **bare w** unto the truth.	3140
	5:36 But I have greater **w** than *that of* John:	3141
	5:36 the same works that I do, **bear w** of me,	3140
	5:37 hath sent me, hath **borne w** of me.	3140
	8:18 I am *one* that **bear w** of myself,	3140
	8:18 Father that sent me **beareth w** of me.	3140
	10:25 in my Father's name, they **bear w** of me.	3140
	15:27 ye also shall **bear w**, because ye have	3140
	18:23 If I have spoken evil, **bear w** of the evil:	3140
	18:37 that I should **bear w** unto the truth.	3140
Ac	1:22 must one be ordained *to be* a **w** with us	3144
	4:33 with great power gave the apostles **w**	3142
	7:44 Our fathers had the tabernacle of **W** in	3142
	10:43 To him **give** all the prophets **w**,	3140
	14:17 he left not himself **without w**,	267
	15: 8 which knoweth the hearts, **bare** them **w**,	3140
	22: 5 As also the high priest doth **bear** me **w**,	3140
	22:15 For thou shalt be his **w** unto all men of	3144
	23:11 so thou **bear w** also at Rome.	3140
	26:16 a **w** both of *these things* which thou hast	3144
Ro	1: 9 For God is my **w**, whom I serve with my	3144
	2:15 their conscience **also bearing w**,	4828
	8:16 Spirit itself **beareth w** with our spirit,	4828
	9: 1 my conscience **also bearing** me **w** in	4828
	13: 9 not steal, Thou shalt not **bear false w**,	5576
1Th	2: 5 nor a cloke of covetousness; God *is* **w**:	3144
Tit	1:13 This **w** is true. Wherefore rebuke them	3141
Heb	2: 4 God **also bearing** *them* **w**, both with	4901
	10:15 *Whereof* the Holy Ghost also is a **w** to us:	3140
	11: 4 by which he **obtained** **w** that he was	3140
Jas	5: 3 the rust of them shall be a **w** against you,	3142
1Pe	5: 1 and a **w** of the sufferings of Christ,	3144
1Jn	1: 2 and we have seen *it*, and **bear w**,	3140
	5: 6 And it is the Spirit that **beareth w**,	3140
	5: 8 And there are three that **bear w** in earth,	3140
	5: 9 If we receive the **w** of men, the witness of	3141
	5: 9 witness of men, the **w** of God is greater:	3141
	5: 9 for this is the **w** of God which he hath	3141
	5:10 on the Son of God hath the **w** in himself:	3141
3Jn	1: 6 Which have **borne w** of thy charity	3140
Rev	1: 5 *is* the faithful **w**, *and* the first begotten	3144
	3:14 saith the Amen, the faithful and true **w**,	3144
	20: 4 that were beheaded for the **w** of Jesus,	3141

WITNESSED (4) [WITNESS]

1Ki	21:13 the men of Belial **w against** him,	5749
Ro	3:21 being **w** by the law and the prophets;	3140
1Ti	6:13 who before Pontius Pilate **w** a good	3140
Heb	7: 8 there he *receiveth them*, of whom it is **w**	3140

WITNESSES (49) [WITNESS]

Nu	35:30 shall be put to death by the mouth of **w**:	5707
Dt	17: 6 At the mouth of two **w**, or three	5707
	17: 6 the mouth of two witnesses, or three **w**,	5707
	17: 7 The hands of the **w** shall be first upon	5707
	19:15 at the mouth of two **w**, or at the mouth	5707
	19:15 at the mouth of three **w**, shall the matter	5707
Jos	24:22 Ye *are* **w** against yourselves that ye have	5707
	24:22 to serve him. And they said, *We are* **w**.	5707
Ru	4: 9 *unto* all the people, Ye *are* **w** this day,	5707
	4:10 the gate of his place: ye *are* **w** this day.	5707
	4:11 the gate, and the elders, said, *We are* **w**.	5707
Job	10:17 Thou renewest thy **w** against me,	5707
Ps	27:12 for false **w** are risen up against me,	5707
	35:11 False **w** did rise up; they laid to my	5707
Isa	8: 2 I took unto me faithful **w** to record, Uriah	5707
	43: 9 let them bring forth their **w**,	5707
	43:10 Ye *are* my **w**, saith the Lord,	5707
	43:12 therefore ye *are* my **w**, saith the Lord,	5707
	44: 8 and have declared *it?* ye *are* even my **w**.	5707
	44: 9 they *are* their own **w**; they see not,	5707
Jer	32:10 sealed *it*, and **took w**,	5707+5749
	32:12 in the presence of the **w** that subscribed	5707
	32:25 the field for money, and **take w**;	5707+5749
	32:44 **take w** in the land of Benjamin,	5707+5749
Mt	18:16 three **w** every word may be established.	3144
	23:31 Wherefore ye be **w** unto yourselves, that	3140
	26:60 though many **false w** came, *yet* found	5575
	26:60 they none. At the last came two **false w**,	5575
	26:65 what further need have we of **w**?	3144
Mk	14:63 and saith, What need we any further **w**?	3144
Lk	24:48 And ye are **w** of these *things*.	3144
Ac	1: 8 ye shall be **w** unto me both in Jerusalem,	3144
	2:32 God raised up, whereof we all are **w**.	3144
	3:15 raised from the dead; whereof we are **w**.	3144
	5:32 And we are his **w** of these things; and *so*	3144
	6:13 And set up false **w**, which said, This man	3144
	7:58 the **w** laid down their clothes at a young	3144
	10:39 And we are **w** of all *things* which he did	3144
	10:41 but unto **w** chosen before of God, *even* to	3144
	13:31 who are his **w** unto the people.	3144
1Co	15:15 Yea, and we are found **false w** of God;	5575
2Co	13: 1 three **w** shall every word be established.	3144
1Th	2:10 Ye *are* **w**, and God *also*, how holily and	3144
1Ti	5:19 an accusation, but before two or three **w**.	3144
	6:12 a good profession before many **w**.	3144
2Ti	2: 2 thou hast heard of me among many **w**,	3144
Heb	10:28 died without mercy under two or three **w**:	3144
	12: 1 about with so great a cloud of **w**,	3144
Rev	11: 3 And I will give *power* unto my two **w**,	3144

WITNESSETH (2) [WITNESS]

Jn	5:32 know that the witness which he **w** of me	3140
Ac	20:23 Save that the Holy Ghost **w** in every city,	1263

WITNESSING (1) [WITNESS]

Ac	26:22 unto this day, **w** both to small and great,	3140

WITTINGLY (1) [WIT]

Ge	48:14 Manasseh's head, **guiding** his hands **w**;	7919

WITTY (1) [WIT]

Pr	8:12 and find out knowledge of **w inventions**.	4209

WIVES (132) [WIFE]

Ge	4:19 Lamech took unto him two **w**: the name	802
	4:23 Lamech said unto his **w**, Adah and Zillah,	802
	4:23 ye **w** of Lamech, hearken unto my speech:	802
	6: 2 they took them **w** of all which they chose.	802
	6:18 and thy wife, and thy sons' **w** with thee.	802
	7: 7 and his wife, and his sons' **w** with him,	802
	7:13 the three **w** of his sons with them, into	802
	8:16 and thy sons, and thy sons' **w** with thee.	802
	8:18 and his wife, and his sons' **w** with him:	802
	11:29 Abram and Nahor took them **w**: the name	802
	28: 9 took unto the **w** which he had Mahalath	802
	30:26 Give *me* my **w** and my children, for whom	802
	31:17 and set his sons and his **w** upon camels;	802
	31:50 If thou shalt take *other* **w** beside my	802
	32:22 his two **w**, and his two womenservants,	802
	34:21 let us take their daughters to us for **w**,	802
	34:29 their **w** took they captive, and spoiled	802
	36: 2 Esau took his **w** of the daughters of	802
	36: 6 Esau took his **w**, and his sons, and his	802
	37: 2 with the sons of Zilpah, his father's **w**:	802
	45:19 your **w**, and bring your father, and come.	802
	46: 5 father, their little ones, and their **w**,	802
	46:26 out of his loins, besides Jacob's sons' **w**,	802
Ex	19:15 against the third day: come not at *your* **w**.	802
	22:24 your **w** shall be widows, and your children	802
	32: 2 which *are* in the ears of your **w**, of your	802
Nu	14: 3 *that* our **w** and our children should be a	802
	16:27 their **w**, and their sons, and their little	802
	32:26 our **w**, our flocks, and all our cattle,	802
Dt	3:19 **w**, and your little ones, and your cattle,	802
	17:17 Neither shall he multiply **w** to himself,	802
	21:15 If a man have two **w**, one beloved,	802
	29:11 **w**, and thy stranger that *is* in thy camp,	802
Jos	1:14 Your **w**, your little ones, and your cattle,	802

Jdg	3: 6 they took their daughters to be their **w**,	802
	8:30 of his body begotten: for he had many **w**.	802
	21: 7 shall we do for **w** for them that remain,	802
	21: 7 not give them of our daughters to **w**?	802
	21:14 they gave them **w** which they had saved	802
	21:16 How shall we do for **w** for them that	802
	21:18 Howbeit we may not give them **w** of our	802
	21:23 took *them* **w**, according to their number,	802
Ru	4: 1 they took them **w** of the women of Moab;	802
1Sa	1: 2 he had two **w**; the name of the one *was*	802
	25:43 and they were also both of them his **w**.	802
	27: 3 *even* David with his two **w**, Ahinoam	802
	30: 3 **w**, and their sons, and their daughters,	802
	30: 5 David's two **w** were taken captives,	802
	30:18 away: and David rescued his two **w**.	802
2Sa	2: 2 his two **w** also, Ahinoam the Jezreelitess,	802
	5:13 mo concubines and **w** out of Jerusalem,	802
	12: 8 thy master's **w** into thy bosom,	802
	12:11 I will take thy **w** before thine eyes,	802
	12:11 he shall lie with thy **w** in the sight of this	802
	19: 5 the lives of thy **w**, and the lives of thy	802
1Ki	11: 3 he had seven hundred **w**, princesses,	802
	11: 3 and his **w** turned away his heart.	802
	11: 4 his **w** turned away his heart after other	802
	11: 8 likewise did he for all his strange **w**,	802
	20: 3 thy **w** also and thy children, *even*	802
	20: 5 thy gold, and thy **w**, and thy children;	802
	20: 7 for he sent unto me for my **w**, and for my	802
2Ki	2: 1 there cried a certain woman of the **w** of	802
	24:15 the king's **w**, and his officers,	802
1Ch	4: 5 Ashur the father of Tekoa had two **w**,	802
	7: 4 thirty thousand *men*: for they had many **w**	802
	8: 8 them away; Hushim and Baara *were* his **w**.	802
	14: 3 David took moe **w** at Jerusalem:	802
2Ch	11:21 the daughter of Absalom above all his **w**	802
	11:21 (for he took eighteen **w**,	802
	11:23 in abundance. And he desired many **w**.	802
	13:21 married fourteen **w**, and begat twenty and	802
	20:13 little ones, their **w**, and their children.	802
	21:14 thy children, and thy **w**, and all thy goods:	802
	21:17 king's house, and his sons also, and his **w**;	802
	24: 3 Jehoiada took for him two **w**; and he begat	802
	29: 9 and our **w** *are* in captivity for this.	802
	31:18 **w**, and their sons, and their daughters,	802
Ezr	10: 2 have taken strange **w** of the people of	802
	10: 3 with our God to put away all the **w**,	802
	10:10 transgressed, and have taken strange **w**,	802
	10:11 of the land, and from the strange **w**.	802
	10:14 let all *them* which have taken strange **w** in	802
	10:17 strange **w** by the first day of the first	802
	10:18 were found that had taken strange **w**:	802
	10:19 hands that *they* would put away their **w**;	802
	10:44 All these had taken strange **w**: and *some*	802
	10:44 *some* of them had **w** by *whom* they had	802
Ne	4:14 your daughters, your **w**, and your houses.	802
	5: 1 of their **w** against their brethren the Jews.	802
	10:28 their **w**, their sons, and their daughters,	802
	12:43 the **w** also and the children rejoiced:	802
	13:23 saw I Jews *that* had married **w** of Ashdod,	802
	13:27 against our God in marrying strange **w**?	802
Est	1:20 the **w** shall give to their husbands honour,	802
Isa	13:16 shall be spoiled, and their **w** ravished.	802
Jer	6:12 others, *with their* fields and **w** together;	802
	8:10 Therefore will I give their **w** unto others,	802
	14:16 them, their **w**, nor their sons, nor their	802
	18:21 let their **w** be bereaved of their children,	802
	29: 6 Take ye **w**, and beget sons and daughters;	802
	29: 6 take **w** for your sons, and give your	802
	29:23 adultery with their neighbours' **w**,	802
	35: 8 we, our **w**, our sons, nor our daughters;	802
	38:23 So they *shall* bring out all thy **w** and thy	802
	44: 9 the wickedness of their **w**, and your own	802
	44: 9 and the wickedness of your **w**,	802
	44:15 all the men which knew that their **w** had	802
	44:25 **w** have both spoken with your mouths,	802
Eze	44:22 shall they take for their **w** a widow,	802
Da	5: 2 his princes, his **w**, and his concubines,	7695
	5: 3 his princes, his **w**, and his concubines,	7695
	5:23 thy lords, thy **w**, and thy concubines,	7695
	6:24 lions, them, their children, and their **w**;	5389
Zec	12:12 house of David apart, and their **w** apart;	802
	12:12 house of Nathan apart, and their **w** apart;	802
	12:13 the house of Levi apart, and their **w** apart;	802
	12:13 family of Shimei apart, and their **w** apart;	802
	12:14 every family apart, and their **w** apart.	802
Mt	19: 8 hearts suffered you to put away your **w**:	1135
Lk	17:27 they married **w**, they were given in	NIG
Ac	21: 5 with **w** and children, till we were out of	1135
1Co	7:29 that both they that have **w** be as though	1135
Eph	5:22 **W**, submit yourselves unto your own	1135
	5:24 *let the* **w** *be* to their own husbands in	1135
	5:25 Husbands, love your **w**, even as Christ	1135
	5:28 So ought men to love their **w** as their own	1135
Col	3:18 **W**, submit yourselves unto your own	1135
	3:19 love your **w**, and be not bitter against	1135
1Ti	3:11 Even so *must their* **w** be grave,	1135
1Pe	3: 1 Likewise, ye **w**, *be* in subjection to your	1135
	3: 1 be won by the conversation of the **w**;	1135

WIVES' (1) [WIFE]

1Ti	4: 7 But refuse profane and **old w** fables,	1126

WIZARD (2) [WIZARDS]

Lev	20:27 that is a **w**, shall surely be put to death:	3049
Dt	18:11 familiar spirits, or a **w**, or a necromancer.	3049

WIZARDS (9) [WIZARD]

Lev 19:31 seek after w, to be defiled by them: 3049
20: 6 after w, to go a whoring after them, I will 3049
1Sa 28: 3 familiar spirits, and the w, out of the land. 3049
28: 9 familiar spirits, and the w, out of the land: 3049
2Ki 21: 6 and dealt with familiar spirits and w: 3049
23:24 the w, and the images, and the idols, 3049
2Ch 33: 6 dealt with a familiar spirit, and with w: 3049
Isa 8:19 and unto w that peep, and that mutter: 3049
19: 3 that have familiar spirits, and to the w. 3049

WOE (106) [WOEFUL, WOES]

Nu 21:29 W to thee, Moab! thou art undone, 188
1Sa 4: 7 they said, W unto us: for there hath not 188
4: 8 unto us: who shall deliver us out of 188
Job 10:15 If I be wicked, w unto me; and if I be 480
Ps 120: 5 W is me, that I sojourn in Mesech, that I 190
Pr 23:29 Who hath w? who hath sorrow? who hath 188
Ecc 4:10 w to him that is alone when he falleth; 337
10:16 w to thee, O land, when thy king is a 337
Isa 3: 9 W unto their soul! for they have rewarded 188
3:11 W unto the wicked! it shall be ill with 188
5: 8 W unto them that join house to house, 1945
5:11 W unto them that rise up early in 1945
5:18 W unto them that draw iniquity with 1945
5:20 W unto them that call evil good, and 1945
5:21 W unto them that are wise in their own 1945
5:22 W unto them that are mighty to drink 1945
6: 5 said I, W is me! for I am undone; because 188
10: 1 W unto them that decree unrighteous 1945
17:12 W to the multitude of many people, 1945
18: 1 W to the land shadowing with wings, 1945
24:16 My leanness, my leanness, w unto 188
28: 1 W to the crown of pride, to the drunkards 1945
29: 1 W to Ariel, to Ariel, the city where David 1945
29:15 W unto them that seek deep to hide their 1945
30: 1 W to the rebellious children, saith 1945
31: 1 W to them that go down to Egypt for 1945
33: 1 W to thee that spoilest, and thou wast 1945
45: 9 W unto him that striveth with his maker! 1945
45:10 W unto him that saith unto his father, 1945
Jer 4:13 than eagles. W unto us! for we are spoiled. 188
4:31 her hands, saying, W is me now! 188
6: 4 W unto us! for the day goeth away, 188
10:19 W is me for my hurt! my wound is 188
13:27 W unto thee, O Jerusalem! wilt thou not 188
15:10 W is me, my mother, that thou hast borne 188
22:13 W unto him that buildeth his house by 1945
23: 1 W be unto the pastors that destroy and 1945
45: 3 Thou didst say, W is me now! for 188
48: 1 of hosts, the God of Israel; W unto Nebo! 1945
48:46 W be unto thee, O Moab! the people of 188
50:27 W unto them! for their day is come, 1945
La 5:16 head: w unto us, that we have sinned! 188
Eze 2:10 lamentations, and mourning, and w. 1958
13: 3 W unto the foolish prophets, that follow 1945
13:18 W to the women that sew pillows to all 1945
16:23 all thy wickedness, (w, woe unto thee! 188
16:23 all thy wickedness, (woe, w unto thee! 188
24: 6 to the bloody city, to the pot whose 188
24: 9 saith the Lord God; W to the bloody city! 188
30: 2 Lord God; Howl ye, W worth the day! 1929
34: 2 W be to the shepherds of Israel that do 1945
Hos 7:13 W unto them! for they have fled from me: 188
9:12 w also to them when I depart from them! 188
Am 5:18 W unto you that desire the day of 1945
6: 1 W to them that are at ease in Zion, 1945
Mic 2: 1 W to them that devise iniquity, 1945
2: 1 W is me! for I am as when they have 480
Na 3: 1 W to the bloody city! it is all full of lies 1945
Hab 2: 6 W to him that increaseth that which is 1945
2: 9 W to him that coveteth an evil 1945
2:12 W to him that buildeth a town with 1945
2:15 W unto him that giveth his neighbour 1945
2:19 W unto him that saith to the wood, 1945
Zep 2: 5 W unto the inhabitants of the sea coast, 1945
3: 1 W to her that is filthy and polluted, 1945
Zec 11:17 W to the idol shepherd that leaveth 1945
Mt 11:21 W unto thee, Chorazin, woe unto thee, 3759
11:21 Chorazin, w unto thee, Bethsaida: 3759
18: 7 W unto the world because of offences! 3759
18: 7 w to that man by whom the offence 3759
23:13 But w unto you, scribes and Pharisees, 3759
23:14 W unto you, scribes and Pharisees, 3759
23:15 W unto you, scribes and Pharisees, 3759
23:16 W unto you, ye blind guides, which say, 3759
23:23 W unto you, scribes and Pharisees, 3759
23:25 W unto you, scribes and Pharisees, 3759
23:27 W unto you, scribes and Pharisees, 3759
23:29 W unto you, scribes and Pharisees, 3759
24:19 And w unto them that are with child, 3759
26:24 w unto that man by whom the Son of 3759
Mk 13:17 But w to them that are with child, 3759
14:21 w to that man by whom the Son of man 3759
Lk 6:24 But w unto you that are rich! for ye have 3759
6:25 W unto you that are full: for ye shall 3759
6:25 W unto you that laugh now: for ye shall 3759
6:26 W unto you, when all men shall speak 3759
10:13 W unto thee, Chorazin, woe unto thee, 3759
10:13 Chorazin, w unto thee, Bethsaida: 3759
11:42 W unto you, Pharisees! for ye tithe mint 3759
11:43 W unto you, Pharisees! for ye love 3759
11:44 W unto you, scribes and Pharisees, 3759
11:46 he said, W unto you also, ye lawyers! 3759
11:47 W unto you! for ye build the sepulchres 3759

Lk 11:52 W unto you, lawyers! for ye have taken 3759
17: 1 w unto him, through whom they come. 3759
21:23 But w unto them that are with child, 3759
22:22 w unto that man by whom he is betrayed. 3759
1Co 9:16 yea, w is unto me, if I preach not 3759
Jude 1:11 W unto them! for they have gone in 3759
Rev 8:13 saying with a loud voice, W, woe, woe, 3759
8:13 saying with a loud voice, Woe, w, woe, 3759
8:13 saying with a loud voice, Woe, woe, w, 3759
9:12 One w is past; and behold, there come 3759
11:14 The second w is past; and behold, 3759
11:14 and behold, the third w cometh quickly. 3759
12:12 W to the inhabiters of the earth and of 3759

WOEFUL (1) [WOE]

Jer 17:16 neither have I desired the w day; 605

WOES (1) [WOE]

Rev 9:12 there come two w more hereafter. 3759

WOLF (6) [WOLVES]

Ge 49:27 Benjamin shall ravin as a w: 2061
Isa 11: 6 The w also shall dwell with the lamb, 2061
65:25 The w and the lamb shall feed together, 2061
Jer 5: 6 and a w of the evenings shall spoil them, 2061
Jn 10:12 the w coming, and leaveth the sheep, 3074
10:12 and the w catcheth them, and scattereth 3074

WOLVES (7) [WOLF]

Eze 22:27 princes in the midst thereof are like w 2061
Hab 1: 8 and are more fierce than the evening w: 2061
Zep 3: 3 roaring lions; her judges are evening w; 2061
Mt 7:15 but inwardly they are ravening w. 3074
10:16 send you forth as sheep in the midst of w: 3074
Lk 10: 3 I send you forth as lambs among w. 3074
Ac 20:29 that after my departing shall grievous w 3074

WOMAN (360) [BONDWOMAN, BONDWOMEN, FREEWOMAN, KINSWOMAN, KINSWOMEN, WOMAN'S, WOMANKIND, WOMEN, WOMEN'S, WOMENSERVANTS]

Ge 2:22 made he a w, and brought her unto the 802
2:23 she shall be called W, because she was 802
3: 1 he said unto the w, Yea, hath God said, 802
3: 2 the w said unto the serpent, We may eat 802
3: 4 the serpent said unto the w, Ye shall not 802
3: 6 when the w saw that the tree was good 802
3:12 The w whom thou gavest to be with me, 802
3:13 the Lord God said unto the w, What is 802
3:13 the w said, The serpent beguiled me, 802
3:15 I will put enmity between thee and the w, 802
3:16 Unto the w he said, I will greatly multiply 802
12:11 I know that thou art a fair w to look upon: 802
12:14 Egyptians beheld the w that she was very 802
12:15 and the w was taken into Pharaoh's house. 802
20: 3 man, for the w which thou hast taken; 802
24: 5 Peradventure the w will not be willing to 802
24: 8 if the w will not be willing to follow thee, 802
24:39 Peradventure the w will not follow me. 802
24:44 let the same be the w whom the Lord 802
46:10 and Shaul the son of a Canaanitish w. NIH
Ex 2: 2 the w conceived, and bare a son: 802
2: 9 And the w took the child, and nursed it. 802
3:22 every w shall borrow of her neighbour, 802
6:15 and Shaul the son of a Canaanitish w: 3669
11: 2 every w of her neighbour, jewels of silver, 802
21:22 hurt a w with child, so that her fruit 802
21:28 If an ox gore a man or a w, that they die: 802
21:29 but that he hath killed a man or a w; 802
35:29 every man and w, whose heart made 802
36: 6 Let neither man nor w make any more 802
Lev 12: 2 If a w have conceived seed, and born a 802
13:29 If a man or w hath a plague upon the head 802
13:38 a w have in the skin of their flesh bright 802
15:18 The w also with whom man shall lie with 802
15:19 if a w have an issue, and her issue in her 802
15:25 if a w have an issue of her blood many 802
15:33 of the w, and of him that lieth with her 5347
18:17 shalt not uncover the nakedness of a w 802
18:19 Also thou shalt not approach unto a w to 802
18:23 shall any w stand before a beast to lie 802
19:20 whosoever lieth carnally with a w that is a 802
20:13 lie with mankind, as with a w, it is 802
20:16 if a w approach unto any beast, and lie 802
20:16 thou shalt kill the w and the beast: 802
20:18 if a man shall lie with a w having her 802
20:27 A man also or w that hath a familiar spirit, 802
21: 7 neither shall they take a w put away from 802
21:14 or a divorced w, or profane, or a harlot, NIH
24:10 the son of an Israelitish w, whose father 802
24:10 this son of the Israelitish w and a man of NIH
Nu 5: 6 w shall commit any sin that men commit, 802
5:18 the priest shall set the w before the Lord, 802
5:19 say unto the w, If no man have lain with 802
5:21 the priest shall charge the w with an oath 802
5:21 the priest shall say unto the w, The Lord 802
5:22 to rot: And the w shall say, Amen, amen. 802
5:24 shall cause the w to drink the bitter water 802
5:26 afterward shall cause the w to drink 802
5:27 the w shall be a curse among her people. 802
5:28 if the w be not defiled, and be clean; then 802
5:30 shall set the w before the Lord, 802
5:31 and this w shall bear her iniquity. 802
6: 2 w shall separate themselves to vow a vow 802
12: 1 of the Ethiopian w whom he had married: 802

Nu 12: 1 for he had married an Ethiopian w. 802
25: 6 brought unto his brethren a Midianitish w NIH
25: 8 man of Israel, and the w through her belly. 802
25:14 that was slain with the Midianitish w, 4084
25:15 name of the Midianitish w that was slain 802
30: 3 If a w also vow a vow unto the Lord, 802
31:17 kill every w that hath known man by lying 802
Dt 15:12 a Hebrew man, or a Hebrew w, be sold 5680
17: 2 the Lord thy God giveth thee, man or w, 802
17: 5 shalt thou bring forth that man or that w, 802
17: 5 even that man or that w, and shalt stone 802
21:11 seest among the captives a beautiful w, 802
22: 5 The w shall not wear that which 802
22:14 say, I took this w, and when I came to her, 802
22:22 If a man be found lying with a w married 802
22:22 both the man that lay with the w, 802
22:22 man that lay with the woman, and the w: 802
28:56 The tender and delicate w among you, NIH
29:18 among you man, or w, or family, or tribe, 802
Jos 2: 4 the w took the two men, and hid them, 802
6:21 both man and w, young and old, and ox, 802
6:22 out thence the w, and all that she hath, 802
Jdg 4: 9 sell Sisera into the hand of a w. 802
9:53 a certain w cast a piece of a millstone upon 802
9:54 that men say not of me, A w slew him. 802
11: 2 for thou art the son of a strange w. 802
13: 3 angel of the Lord appeared unto the w, 802
13: 6 the w came and told her husband, saying, 802
13: 9 the angel of God came again unto the w as 802
13:10 the w made haste, and ran, and shewed 802
13:11 Art thou the man that spakest unto the w? 802
13:13 all that I said unto the w let her beware. 802
13:24 the w bare a son, and called his name 802
14: 1 saw a w in Timnath of the daughters of 802
14: 2 I have seen a w in Timnath of the 802
14: 3 Is there never a w among the daughters 802
14: 7 he went down, and talked with the w; 802
14:10 So his father went down unto the w: 802
16: 4 that he loved a w in the valley of Sorek, 802
19:26 came the w in the dawning of the day, 802
19:27 the w his concubine was fallen down at 802
20: 4 The husband of the w that was slain, 802
21:11 and every w that hath lien by man. 802
Ru 1: 5 the w was left of her two sons and 802
3: 8 and behold, a w lay at his feet. 802
3:11 doth know that thou art a virtuous w. 802
3:14 Let it not be known that a w came into 802
4:11 The Lord make the w that is come into 802
4:12 shall the Lord give thee of this young w. 5291
1Sa 1:15 my lord, I am a w of a sorrowful spirit: 802
1:18 So the w went her way, and did eat, 802
1:23 the w abode, and gave her son suck until 802
1:26 lord, I am the w that stood by thee here, 802
2:20 The Lord give thee seed of this w for 802
15: 3 slay both man and w, infant and suckling, 802
20:30 Thou son of the perverse rebellious w, NIH
25: 3 and she was a w of good understanding, 802
27: 9 left neither man nor w alive, and took 802
27:11 David saved neither man nor w alive, 802
28: 7 Seek me a w that hath a familiar spirit, 802
28: 7 there is a w that hath a familiar spirit at 802
28: 8 him, and they came to the w by night: 802
28: 9 w said unto him, Behold, thou knowest 802
28:11 the w, Whom shall I bring up unto thee? 802
28:12 when the w saw Samuel, she cried with a 802
28:13 the w said unto Saul, I saw gods ascending 802
28:21 the w came unto Saul, and saw that he 802
28:23 together with the w, compelled him; 802
28:24 the w had a fat calf in the house; 802
2Sa 3: 8 to day with a fault concerning this w? 802
11: 2 from the roof he saw a w washing herself; 802
11: 2 the w was very beautiful to look upon. 802
11: 3 David sent and inquired after the w. 802
11: 5 the w conceived, and sent and told David, 802
11:21 did not a w cast a piece of a millstone 802
13:17 Put now this w out from me, and bolt NIH
14: 2 fetch thence a wise w, and said unto her, 802
14: 2 be as a w that had a long time mourned for 802
14: 4 when the w of Tekoah spake to the king, 802
14: 5 I am indeed a widow w, and mine 802
14: 8 king said unto the w, Go to thine house, 802
14: 9 the w of Tekoah said unto the king, 802
14:12 the w said, Let thine handmaid, I pray 802
14:13 the w said, Wherefore then hast thou 802
14:18 the king answered and said unto the w, 802
14:18 w said, Let my lord the king now speak. 802
14:19 and answered and said, As thy soul liveth, 802
14:27 she was a w of a fair countenance. 802
17:19 the w took and spread a covering over 802
17:20 when Absalom's servants came to the w to 802
17:20 the w said unto them, They be gone over 802
20:16 cried a wise w out of the city, Hear, hear; 802
20:17 near unto her, the w said, Art thou Joab? 802
20:21 the w said unto Joab, Behold, his head 802
20:22 the w went unto all the people in her 802
1Ki 3:17 one w and I, O my lord, I and this woman 802
3:17 my lord, I and this w dwell in one house; 802
3:18 that this w was delivered also: 802
3:22 the other w said, Nay; but the living is my 802
3:26 spake the w whose living child was 802
11:26 mother's name was Zeruah, a widow w, 802
14: 5 she shall feign herself to be another w. NIH
17: 9 I have commanded a widow w there to 802
17:10 widow w was there gathering of sticks: 802

1Ki	17:17 *that* the son of the **w**, the mistress of	802
	17:24 the **w** said to Elijah, Now *by* this I know	802
2Ki	4: 1 there cried a certain **w** of the wives of	802
	4: 8 passed to Shunem, where *was* a great **w**;	802
	4:17 the **w** conceived, and bare a son at that	802
	4:26 there cried a **w** unto him, saying, Help,	802
	6:28 This **w** said unto me, Give thy son,	802
	6:30 when the king heard the words of the **w**,	802
	8: 1 spake Elisha unto the **w**, whose son he	802
	8: 2 the **w** arose, and did after the saying of	802
	8: 3 that the **w** returned out of the land of	802
	8: 3 that behold, the **w**, whose son he had	802
	8: 5 O king, this *is* the **w**, and this *is* her son,	802
	8: 6 when the king asked the **w**, she told him.	802
	9:34 Go, see now this cursed **w**, and bury her:	NIH
1Ch	16: 3 both man and **w**, to every one a loaf of	802
2Ch	2:14 The son of a **w** of the daughters of Dan,	802
	15:13 small or great, whether man or **w**.	802
	24: 7 For the sons of Athaliah, *that* **wicked w**,	4849
Est	4:11 that whosoever, *whether* man or **w**,	802
Job	14: 1 Man *that is* born of a **w** *is* of few days,	802
	15:14 *he which is* born of a **w**, that he should be	802
	25: 4 how can he be clean *that is* born of a **w**?	802
	31: 9 If mine heart have been deceived by a **w**,	802
Ps	48: 6 There, *and* pain, as of a **w** in travail.	NIH
	58: 8 *like* the untimely birth of a **w**, *that* they	NIH
	113: 9 He maketh the barren **w** to keep house,	NIH
Pr	2:16 To deliver thee from the strange **w**,	802
	5: 3 For the lips of a strange **w** drop *as a*	NIH
	5:20 be ravisht with a strange **w**, and embrace	NIH
	6:24 To keep thee from the evil **w**, from	802
	6:24 the flattery of the tongue of a strange **w**.	NIH
	6:26 For by means of a whorish **w** *a man is*	NIH
	6:32 *But* whoso committeth adultery with a **w**	802
	7: 5 *they* may keep thee from the strange **w**,	NIH
	7:10 met him a **w** *with* the attire of a harlot,	802
	9:13 A foolish **w** *is* clamorous: *she is* simple,	802
	11:16 A gracious **w** retaineth honour:	802
	11:22 *so is* a fair **w** which is without discretion.	802
	12: 4 A virtuous **w** *is* a crown to her husband:	802
	14: 1 Every wise **w** buildeth her house:	802
	20:16 and take a pledge of him for a strange **w**.	NIH
	21: 9 than with a brawling **w** in a wide house.	802
	21:19 than with a contentious and an angry **w**.	802
	23:27 and a strange **w** *is* a narrow pit.	NIH
	25:24 with a brawling **w** and in a wide house.	802
	27:13 and take a pledge of him for a strange **w**.	NIH
	27:15 rainy day and a contentious **w** are alike.	802
	30:20 Such *is* the way of an adulterous **w**;	802
	30:23 For an odious **w** when she is married;	NIH
	31:10 Who can find a virtuous **w**? for her price	802
	31:30 *but* a **w** that feareth the LORD, she shall be	802
Ecc	7:26 I find more bitter than death the **w**,	802
	7:28 but a **w** among all those have I not found.	802
Isa	13: 8 they shall be in pain as a **w** that travaileth:	NIH
	21: 3 as the pangs of a **w** that travaileth:	NIH
	26:17 Like as a **w** with child, *that* draweth near	NIH
	42:14 *now* will I cry like a **travailing w**; I will	3205
	45:10 to the **w**, What hast thou brought forth?	802
	49:15 Can a **w** forget her sucking child, *that she*	802
	54: 6 For the LORD hath called thee as a **w**	802
Jer	4:31 I have heard a voice as of a **w** in travail,	NIH
	6: 2 of Zion *to* a comely and delicate **w**.	NIH
	6:24 hold of us, *and* pain, as of a **w** in travail.	NIH
	13:21 not sorrows take thee, as a **w** in travail?	802
	22:23 upon thee, the pain as of a **w** in travail.	NIH
	30: 6 as a **w** in travail, and all faces are turned	NIH
	31: 8 the **w** with child and her that travaileth	NIH
	31:22 in the earth, A **w** shall compass a man.	5347
	44: 7 to cut off from you man and **w**, child and	802
	48:41 shall be as the heart of a **w** in her pangs.	802
	49:22 Edom be as the heart of a **w** in her pangs.	802
	49:24 sorrows have taken her as a **w** in travail.	NIH
	50:43 hold of him, *and* pangs as of a **w** in travail.	NIH
	51:22 thee also will I break in pieces man and **w**;	802
La	1:17 Jerusalem is as a menstruous **w** among	NIH
Eze	16:30 the work of an imperious whorish **w**;	802
	18: 6 hath come near to a menstruous **w**,	NIH
	23:44 they go in unto a **w** that playeth the harlot:	802
	36:17 me as the uncleanness of a **removed w**.	5079
Hos	3: 1 Go yet, love a **w** beloved of *her* friend,	802
	13:13 The sorrows of a travailing **w** shall come	NIH
Mic	4: 9 for pangs have taken thee as a **w** in travail.	NIH
	4:10 O daughter of Zion, like a **w** in travail:	NIH
Zec	5: 7 this *is* a **w** that sitteth in the midst of	802
Mt	5:28 whosoever looketh on a **w** to lust after	1135
	9:20 behold, a **w**, which was diseased with	1135
	9:22 And the **w** was made whole from that	1135
	13:33 a **w** took, and hid in three measures	1135
	15:22 a **w** of Canaan came out of the same	1135
	15:28 Jesus answered and said unto her, O **w**,	1135
	22:27 And last of all the **w** died also.	1135
	26: 7 There came unto him a **w** having an	1135
	26:10 said unto them, Why trouble ye the **w**?	1135
	26:13 shall also *this*, that this **w** hath done,	NIG
Mk	5:25 And a certain **w**, which had an issue of	1135
	5:33 But the **w** fearing and trembling,	1135
	7:25 a *certain* **w**, whose young daughter had	1135
	7:26 The **w** was a Greek, a Syrophenician by	1135
	10:12 And if a **w** shall put away her husband,	1135
	12:22 left no seed: last of all the **w** died also.	1135
	14: 3 there came a **w** having an alabaster box	1135
Lk	4:26 *city* of Sidon, unto a **w** *that was* a widow,	1135
	7:37 And behold, a **w** in the city, which was a	1135
	7:39 manner of **w** *this is* that toucheth him:	1135

Lk	7:44 And he turned to the **w**, and said unto	1135
	7:44 and said unto Simon, Seest thou this **w**?	1135
	7:45 this **w** since the time I came in hath not	NIG
	7:46 **w** hath anointed my feet with ointment.	NIG
	7:50 he said to the **w**, Thy faith hath saved	1135
	8:43 And a **w** having an issue of blood twelve	1135
	8:47 when the **w** saw that she was not hid,	1135
	10:38 a certain **w** named Martha received him	1135
	11:27 as he spake these *things*, a certain **w** of	1135
	13:11 there was a **w** which had a spirit of	1135
	13:12 called *her* to *him*, and said unto her, **W**,	1135
	13:16 ought not this **w**, being a daughter of	NIG
	13:21 a **w** took and hid in three measures	1135
	15: 8 Either what **w** having ten pieces of silver,	1135
	20:32 Last of all the **w** died also.	1135
	22:57 denied him, saying, **W**, I know him not.	1135
Jn	2: 4 Jesus saith unto her, **W**, what have I to do	1135
	4: 7 There cometh a **w** of Samaria to draw	1135
	4: 9 Then saith the **w** of Samaria unto him,	1135
	4: 9 drink of me, which am a **w** of Samaria?	1135
	4:11 The **w** saith unto him, Sir, thou hast	1135
	4:15 The **w** saith unto him, Sir, give me this	1135
	4:17 The **w** answered and said, I have no	1135
	4:19 The **w** saith unto him, Sir, I perceive that	1135
	4:21 her, **W**, believe me, the hour cometh,	1135
	4:25 The **w** saith unto him, I know that	1135
	4:27 and marvelled that he talked with the **w**:	1135
	4:28 The **w** then left her waterpot, and went	1135
	4:39 believed on him for the saying of the **w**,	1135
	4:42 And said unto the **w**, Now we believe,	1135
	8: 3 Pharisees brought unto him a **w** taken in	1135
	8: 4 Master, this **w** was taken in adultery,	1135
	8: 9 left alone, and the **w** standing in the midst.	1135
	8:10 lift up *himself*, and saw none but the **w**,	1135
	8:10 but the woman, he said unto her, **W**,	1135
	16:21 A **w** when she is in travail hath sorrow,	1135
	19:26 saith unto his mother, **W**, behold thy son.	1135
	20:13 they say unto her, **W**, why weepest thou?	1135
	20:15 saith unto her, **W**, why weepest thou?	1135
Ac	9:36 this **w** was full of good works and	NIG
	16: 1 named Timotheus, the son of a certain **w**,	1135
	16:14 And a certain **w** named Lydia, a seller of	1135
	17:34 and a **w** named Damaris, and others with	1135
Ro	1:27 the men, leaving the natural use of the **w**,	2338
	7: 2 For the **w** which hath a husband is bound	1135
1Co	7: 1 *It is* good for a man not to touch a **w**.	1135
	7: 2 and let **every w** have her own husband.	1538
	7:13 And the **w** which hath a husband that	1135
	7:34 The unmarried **w** careth for the *things* of	NIG
	11: 3 and the head of the **w** *is* the man;	1135
	11: 5 But every **w** that prayeth or	1135
	11: 6 For if the **w** be not covered, let her also	1135
	11: 6 but *if it* be a shame for a **w** to be shorn or	1135
	11: 7 of God: but the **w** is the glory of the man.	1135
	11: 8 the man is not of the **w**; but the woman	1135
	11: 8 not of the woman; but the **w** of the man.	1135
	11: 9 Neither was the man created for the **w**;	1135
	11: 9 for the woman; but the **w** for the man.	1135
	11:10 For this cause ought the **w** to have power	1135
	11:11 neither *is* the man without the **w**,	1135
	11:11 the **w** without the man, in the Lord.	1135
	11:12 For as the **w** *is* of the man, *even so is*	1135
	11:12 man, *even so is* the man also by the **w**;	1135
	11:13 is it comely that a **w** pray unto God	1135
	11:15 But if a **w** have long hair, it is a glory to	1135
Gal	4: 4 Son, made of a **w**, made under the law,	1135
1Th	5: 3 them, as travail upon a **w** with child,	NIG
1Ti	2:11 Let the **w** learn in silence with all	1135
	2:12 But I suffer not a **w** to teach, nor to usurp	1135
	2:14 the **w** being deceived was in	1135
	5:16 man or **w** **that believeth** have widows,	4103
Rev	2:20 because thou sufferest *that* **w** Jezebel,	1135
	12: 1 a **w** clothed with the sun, and the moon	1135
	12: 4 the dragon stood before the **w** which was	1135
	12: 6 And the **w** fled into the wilderness,	1135
	12:13 he persecuted the **w** which brought forth	1135
	12:14 And to the **w** were given two wings of a	1135
	12:15 of his mouth water as a flood after the **w**,	1135
	12:16 And the earth helped the **w**, and the earth	1135
	12:17 And the dragon was wroth with the **w**,	1135
	17: 3 I saw a **w** sit upon a scarlet coloured beast,	1135
	17: 4 And the **w** was arrayed in purple and	1135
	17: 6 And I saw the **w** drunken with the blood	1135
	17: 7 I will tell thee the mystery of the **w**,	1135
	17: 9 seven mountains, on which the **w** sitteth.	1135
	17:18 And the **w** which thou sawest is *that* great	1135

WOMAN'S (7) [WOMAN]

Ge	38:20 to receive *his* pledge from the **w** hand:	802
Ex	21:22 according as the **w** husband will lay upon	802
Lev	24:11 the Israelitish **w** son blasphemed the name	802
Nu	5:18 uncover the **w** head, and put the offering	802
	5:25 the jealousy offering out of the **w** hand,	802
Dt	22: 5 neither shall a man put on a **w** garment:	802
1Ki	3:19 this **w** child died in the night; because	802

WOMANKIND (1) [WOMAN]

Lev	18:22 shalt not lie with mankind, as with **w**:	802

WOMB (71) [WOMBS]

Ge	25:23 Two nations *are* in thy **w**, and two manner	990
	25:24 behold, *there were* twins in her **w**.	990
	29:31 that Leah *was* hated, he opened her **w**:	7358
	30: 2 hath withheld from thee the fruit of the **w**?	990
	30:22 God hearkened to her, and opened her **w**.	7358

Ge	38:27 travail, that, behold, twins *were* in her **w**.	990
	49:25 blessings of the breasts, and of the **w**:	7356
Ex	13: 2 whatsoever openeth the **w** among	7358
Nu	8:16 instead of such as open every **w**,	7358
	12:12 when he cometh out of his mother's **w**.	7358
Dt	7:13 he will also bless the fruit of thy **w**,	990
Jdg	13: 5 shall be a Nazarite unto God from the **w**:	990
	13: 7 to God from the **w** to the day of his death.	990
	16:17 a Nazarite unto God from my mother's **w**:	990
Ru	1:11 *are there* yet *any* moe sons in my **w**,	4578
1Sa	1: 5 but the LORD had shut up her **w**.	7358
	1: 6 because the LORD had shut up her **w**.	7358
Job	1:21 Naked came I out of my mother's **w**,	990
	3:10 it shut not up the doors of my *mother's* **w**,	990
	3:11 Why died I not from the **w**? why did I	7358
	10:18 hast thou brought me forth out of the **w**?	7358
	10:19 I should have been carried from the **w** to	990
	24:20 The **w** shall forget him; the worm shall	7358
	31:15 not he that made me in the **w** make him?	990
	31:15 and did not one fashion us in the **w**?	7358
	31:18 I have guided him from my mother's **w**;)	990
	38: 8 forth, *as if* it had issued out of the **w**?	7358
	38:29 Out of whose **w** came the ice?	990
Ps	22: 9 thou *art* he that took me out of the **w**:	990
	22:10 I was cast upon thee from the **w**: thou *art*	7358
	58: 3 The wicked are estranged from the **w**:	7358
	71: 6 thee have I been holden up from the **w**:	990
	110: 3 in the beauties of holiness from the **w** of	7358
	127: 3 *and* the fruit of the **w** *is his* reward.	990
	139:13 thou hast covered me in my mother's **w**.	990
Pr	30:16 The grave; and the barren **w**; the earth	7356
	31: 2 what, the son of my **w**? and what, the son	990
Ecc	5:15 As he came forth of his mother's **w**,	990
	11: 5 how the bones *do grow* in the **w** of her	990
Isa	13:18 shall have no pity on the fruit of the **w**;	990
	44: 2 formed thee from the **w**, *which* will help	990
	44:24 and he that formed thee from the **w**,	990
	46: 3 the belly, which are carried from the **w**:	7356
	48: 8 wast called a transgressor from the **w**.	990
	49: 1 The LORD hath called me from the **w**;	990
	49: 5 saith the LORD that formed me from the **w**	990
	49:15 not have compassion on the son of her **w**?	990
	66: 9 bring forth, and shut the **w**? saith thy God.	NIH
Jer	1: 5 before thou camest forth out of the **w** I	7358
	20:17 Because he slew me not from the **w**;	7358
	20:17 and her **w** *to be* always great *with* me.	7358
	20:18 came I forth out of the **w** to see	7358
Eze	20:26 through *the fire* all that openeth the **w**,	7356
Hos	9:11 and from the **w**, and from the conception.	990
	9:14 them a miscarrying **w** and dry breasts.	7358
	9:16 I slay *even* the beloved *fruit* of their **w**.	990
	12: 3 He took his brother by the heel in the **w**,	990
Mt	19:12 were so born from *their* mother's **w**:	2836
Lk	1:15 Holy Ghost, even from his mother's **w**.	2836
	1:31 thou shalt conceive in thy **w**,	1064
	1:41 of Mary, the babe leaped in her **w**;	2836
	1:42 and blessed *is* the fruit of thy **w**.	2836
	1:44 ears, the babe leaped in my **w** for joy.	2836
	2:21 angel before he was conceived in the **w**.	2836
	2:23 Every male that openeth the **w** shall be	3388
	11:27 Blessed *is* the **w** that bare thee,	2836
Jn	3: 4 the second time into his mother's **w**,	2836
Ac	3: 2 lame from his mother's **w** was carried,	2836
	14: 8 being a cripple from his mother's **w**,	2836
Ro	4:19 neither *yet* the deadness of Sara's **w**:	3388
Gal	1:15 who separated me from my mother's **w**,	2836

WOMBS (2) [WOMB]

Ge	20:18 For the LORD had fast closed up all the **w**	7358
Lk	23:29 the **w** that never bare, and the paps	2836

WOMEN (178) [WOMAN]

Ge	14:16 his goods, and the **w** also, and the people.	802
	18:11 to be with Sarah after the manner of **w**.	802
	24:11 the time that **w** go out to draw *water*.	NIH
	31:35 thee; for the custom of **w** *is* upon me.	802
	33: 5 his eyes, and saw the **w** and the children;	802
Ex	1:16 the office of a midwife to the **Hebrew w**,	5680
	1:19 Because the **Hebrew w** *are* not as	5680
	1:19 Hebrew women *are* not as the Egyptian **w**;	802
	2: 7 and call to thee a nurse of the Hebrew **w**,	802
	15:20 all the **w** went out after her with timbrels	802
	35:22 came, both men and **w**, as many as were	802
	35:25 all the **w** that were wise hearted did spin	802
	35:26 all the **w** whose heart stirred them up in	802
	38: 8 of the lookingglasses of the **w** assembling,	NIH
Lev	26:26 ten **w** shall bake your bread in one oven,	802
Nu	31: 9 the children of Israel took all the **w** of	802
	31:15 unto them, Have ye saved all the **w** alive?	5347
	31:18 all the **w** children, that have not known a	802
	31:35 of **w** that had not known man by lying	802
Dt	2:34 the **w**, and the little ones, of every city,	802
	3: 6 the men, **w**, and children, of every city.	802
	20:14 the **w**, and the little ones, and the cattle,	802
	31:12 **w**, and children, and thy stranger that *is*	802
Jos	8:25 of men and **w**, *were* twelve thousand,	802
	8:35 with the **w**, and the little ones,	802
Jdg	5:24 Blessed *above* **w** shall Jael the wife of	802
	5:24 blessed shall she be above **w** in the tent.	802
	9:49 died also, about a thousand men and **w**.	802
	9:51 thither fled all the men and **w**, and all they	802
	16:27 Now the house was full of men and **w**;	802
	16:27 the roof about three thousand men and **w**,	802
	21:10 of the sword, with the **w** and the children.	802
	21:14 had saved alive of the **w** of Jabesh-gilead:	802

Jdg 21:16 the **w** are destroyed out of Benjamin? 802
Ru 1: 4 they took them wives of the **w of Moab**; 4125
 4:14 the **w** said unto Naomi, Blessed *be* 802
 4:17 the **w** *her* neighbours gave it a name, 802
1Sa 2:22 how they lay with the **w** that assembled *at* 802
 4:20 about the time for her death the **w** that NIH
 15:33 As thy sword hath made **w** childless, 802
 15:33 so shall thy mother be childless among **w.** 802
 18: 6 that the **w** came out of all cities of Israel, 802
 18: 7 **w** answered *one another* as they played, 802
 21: 4 have kept themselves at least from **w** 802
 21: 5 Of a truth *have been* kept from us about 802
 22:19 both men and **w**, children and sucklings, 802
 30: 2 taken the **w** captives, that *were* therein: 802
2Sa 1:26 was wonderful, passing the love of **w.** 802
 6:19 as well to the **w** as men, to every one a 802
 15:16 king left ten **w**, *which were* concubines, 802
 19:35 singing *men* and singing **w**, wherefore NIH
 20: 3 the king took the ten **w** *his* concubines, 802
1Ki 3:16 came there two **w**, *that were* harlots, unto 802
 11: 1 king Solomon loved many strange **w**, 802
 11: 1 **w** *of the* Moabites, Ammonites, Edomites, NIH
2Ki 8:12 and rip up their **w with child**. 2030
 15:16 all the **w** therein that were **with child** he 2030
 23: 7 where the **w** wove hangings for the grove. 802
2Ch 28: 8 **w**, sons, and daughters, and took also 802
 35:25 the singing **w** spake of Josiah in their NIH
Ezr 2:65 two hundred singing *men* and singing **w.** NIH
 10: 1 congregation *of* men and **w** and children: 802
Ne 7:67 and five singing *men* and singing **w**. NIH
 8: 2 the congregation both of men and **w**, 802
 8: 3 before the men and the **w**, and those that 802
 13:26 *nevertheless* even him did outlandish **w** 802
Est 1: 9 Vashti the queen made a feast for the **w** 802
 1:17 of the queen shall come abroad unto all **w**, 802
 2: 3 to the house of the **w**, unto the custody of 802
 2: 3 the king's chamberlain, keeper of the **w**; 802
 2: 8 to the custody of Hegai, keeper of the **w**, 802
 2: 9 unto the best *place* of the house of the **w.** 802
 2:12 according to the manner of the **w**, (for so 802
 2:12 *other* things for the purifying of the **w**;) 802
 2:13 the house of the **w** unto the king's house. 802
 2:14 returned into the second house of the **w**, 802
 2:15 the keeper of the **w**, appointed. 802
 2:17 the king loved Esther above all the **w**, 802
 3:13 both young and old, little children and **w**, 802
 8:11 little ones and **w**, and *to take* the spoil 802
Job 2:10 Thou speakest as one of the foolish **w** NIH
 42:15 in all the land were no **w** found *so* fair as NIH
Ps 45: 9 daughters *were* among thy honourable **w**: NIH
Pr 22:14 The mouth of strange **w** *is* a deep pit: NIH
 23:33 Thine eyes shall behold strange **w**, NIH
 31: 3 Give not thy strength unto **w**, nor thy 802
Ecc 2: 8 I gat me *men* singers and **w** singers, NIH
SS 1: 8 If thou know not, O thou fairest among **w**, 802
 5: 9 *another* beloved, O thou fairest among **w**? 802
 6: 1 thy beloved gone, O thou fairest among **w**? 802
Isa 3:12 *are* their oppressors, and **w** rule over them. 802
 4: 1 in that day seven **w** shall take hold of one 802
 19:16 In that day shall Egypt be like unto **w**: 802
 27:11 the **w** come, *and* set them on fire: for it *is* 802
 32: 9 Rise up, ye **w** that are at ease, hear my 802
 32:10 ye careless **w**: for the vintage shall fail, NIH
 32:11 ye **w** that are at ease; be troubled, NIH
Jer 7:18 the fire, and the **w** knead *their* dough, 802
 9:17 call for the mourning **w**, that they may NIH
 9:17 send for cunning **w**, that they may come: NIH
 9:20 ye **w**, and let your ear receive the word of 802
 38:22 all the **w** that are left in the king of Judah's 802
 38:22 those **w** *shall* say, Thy friends have set NIH
 40: 7 **w**, and children, and of the poor of the 802
 41:16 the **w**, and the children, and the eunuchs, 802
 43: 6 **w**, and children, and the king's daughters, 802
 44:15 all the **w** that stood *by*, a great multitude, 802
 44:20 to the **w**, and to all the people which had 802
 44:24 to all the **w**, Hear the word of the LORD, 802
 50:37 midst of her; and they shall become as **w**: 802
 51:30 their might hath failed; they became as **w**: 802
La 2:20 Shall the **w** eat their fruit, *and* children of 802
 4:10 The hands of the pitiful **w** have sodden 802
 5:11 They ravished the **w** in Zion, 802
Eze 8:14 behold, there sat **w** weeping for Tammuz, 802
 9: 6 both maids, and little children, and **w**: 802
 13:18 Woe to the **w** that sew pillows to all NIH
 16:34 the contrary is in thee from *other* **w** in thy 802
 16:38 as **w** that break wedlock and shed blood NIH
 16:41 upon thee in the sight of many **w**: 802
 23: 2 Son of man, there were two **w**, 802
 23:10 she became famous among **w**; for they 802
 23:44 Aholah and unto Aholibah, the lewd **w**. 802
 23:45 and after the manner of **w** that shed blood; NIH
 23:48 all **w** may be taught not to do after your 802
Da 11:17 he shall give him the daughter of **w**, 802
 11:37 nor the desire of **w**, nor regard any god: 802
Hos 13:16 and their **w with child** shall be ript up. 2030
Am 1:13 they have ript up the **w with child** at 2030
Mic 2: 9 The **w** of my people have ye cast out from 802
Na 3: 13 thy people in the midst of thee *are* **w**: 802
Zec 5: 9 there came out two **w**, and the wind *was* 802
 8: 4 **old w** dwell in the streets of Jerusalem, 2205
 14: 2 and the houses rifled, and the **w** ravished; 802
Mt 11:11 Among *them that are* born of **w** there hath 1135
 14:21 five thousand men, beside **w** and children. 1135
 15:38 four thousand men, beside **w** and children. 1135
 24:41 Two **w** *shall be* grinding at the mill; NIG

Mt 27:55 many **w** were there beholding afar off, *1135*
 28: 5 the angel answered and said unto the **w**, *1135*
Mk 15:40 There were also **w** looking on afar off: *1135*
 15:41 many other **w** which came up with him NIG
Lk 1:28 *is* with thee: blessed *art* thou among **w**. *1135*
 1:42 Blessed *art* thou among **w**, and blessed *is* *1135*
 7:28 Among *those that are* born of **w** there is *1135*
 8: 2 And certain **w**, which had been healed of *1135*
 17:35 Two **w** shall be grinding together; the one NIG
 23:27 and of **w**, which also bewailed and *1135*
 23:49 and the **w** that followed him from Galilee, *1135*
 23:55 the **w** also, which came with him from *1135*
 24:10 James, and other **w** *that were* with them, NIG
 24:22 certain **w** *also* of our company made us *1135*
 24:24 and found *it* even so as the **w** had said: *1135*
Ac 1:14 with the **w**, and Mary the mother of Jesus, *1135*
 5:14 the Lord, multitudes both of men and **w**.) *1135*
 8: 3 and **w** committed *them* to prison. *1135*
 8:12 they were baptized, both men and **w**. *1135*
 9: 2 *this* way, whether they were men or **w**, *1135*
 13:50 stirred up the devout and honourable **w**, *1135*
 16:13 spake unto the **w** which resorted *thither*. *1135*
 17: 4 and of the **w** not a few. *1135*
 17:12 also of honourable **w** which were Greeks, *1135*
 22: 4 delivering into prisons both men and **w**. *1135*
Ro 1:26 for even their **w** did change the natural *2338*
1Co 14:34 Let your **w** keep silence in the churches: *1135*
 14:35 for it is a shame for **w** to speak in *1135*
Php 4: 3 help those **w** which laboured with me in NIG
1Ti 2: 9 **w** adorn themselves in modest apparel, *1135*
 2:10 But (which becometh **w** professing *1135*
 5: 2 The elder **w** as mothers; the younger as NIG
 5:14 I will therefore that the younger **w** marry, NIG
2Ti 3: 6 and lead captive **silly w** laden with sins, *1133*
Tit 2: 3 The **aged w** likewise, *that they be* in *4247*
 2: 4 That they may teach the young **w** to be NIG
Heb 11:35 received their dead raised to life again: *1135*
1Pe 3: 5 this manner in the old time the holy **w** *1135*
Rev 9: 8 And they had hair as the hair of **w**, *1135*
 14: 4 are they which were not defiled with **w**; *1135*

WOMEN'S (1) [WOMAN]

Est 2:11 every day before the court of the **w** house, 802

WOMENSERVANTS (3) [SERVE, WOMAN]

Ge 20:14 **w**, and gave *them* unto Abraham, 8198
 32: 5 asses, flocks, and menservants, and **w**: 8198
 32:22 his two **w**, and his eleven sons, 8198

WON (3) [WIN]

1Ch 26:27 Out of the **spoils** won in battles did they 7998
Pr 18:19 A brother offended *is* harder to be **w** than a NIH
1Pe 3: 1 they also may without the word be **w** by 2770

WONDER (15) [WONDERED, WONDERFUL, WONDERFULLY, WONDERING, WONDERS, WONDROUS, WONDROUSLY]

Dt 13: 1 of dreams, and giveth thee a sign or a **w**, 4159
 13: 2 the sign or the **w** come to pass, whereof 4159
 28:46 shall be upon thee for a sign and for a **w**, 4159
2Ch 32:31 sent unto him to inquire of the **w** that 4159
Ps 71: 7 I am as a **w** unto many; but thou *art* my 4159
Isa 20: 3 and **w** upon Egypt and upon Ethiopia; 4159
 29: 9 Stay yourselves, and **w**; cry ye out, 8539
 29:14 *even* a marvellous work and a **w**: 6382
Jer 4: 9 be astonished, and the prophets shall **w**. 8539
Hab 1: 5 and regard, and **w** marvellously: 8539
Ac 3:10 and they were filled with **w** and 2285
 13:41 Behold *ye* despisers, and **w**, and perish: 2296
Rev 12: 1 And there appeared a great **w** in heaven; 4592
 12: 3 And there appeared another **w** in heaven; 4592
 17: 8 and they that dwell on the earth shall **w**, 2296

WONDERED (15) [WONDER]

Isa 59:16 and **w** that *there was* no intercessor: 8074
 63: 5 and I **w** that *there was* none to uphold: 8074
Zec 3: 8 for they *are* men **w at**: for behold, I *will* 4159
Mt 15:31 Insomuch that the multitude **w**, 2296
Mk 6:51 in themselves beyond measure, and **w**. 2296
Lk 2:18 all they that heard *it* **w** at those *things* 2296
 4:22 **w** at the gracious words which proceeded 2296
 8:25 And they **w**, saying *one to* 2296
 9:43 But while they **w** every one at all *things* 2296
 11:14 the dumb spake; and the people **w**. 2296
 24:41 and **w**, he said unto them, Have ye here 2296
Ac 7:31 When Moses saw *it*, he **w** at the sight: 2296
 8:13 and **w**, beholding the miracles and 1839
Rev 13: 3 and all the world **w** after the beast. 2296
 17: 6 I saw her, I **w** *with* great admiration. 2296

WONDERFUL (21) [WONDER]

Dt 28:59 the LORD will **make** thy plagues **w**, 6381
2Sa 1:26 thy love to me was **w**, passing the love of 6381
2Ch 2: 9 I am about to build *shall be* **w** great. 6381
Job 42: 3 *things* too **w** for me, which I knew not. 6381
Ps 40: 5 *are* thy **works** which thou hast done, 6381
 78: 4 and his **w works** that he hath done. 6381
 107: 8 *for* his **w works** to the children of men! 6381
 107:15 *for* his **w works** to the children of men! 6381
 107:21 *for* his **w works** to the children of men! 6381
 107:31 *for* his **w works** to the children of men! 6381
 111: 4 He hath made his **w works** to be 6381
 119:129 Thy testimonies *are* **w**: therefore doth my 6382
 139: 6 knowledge *is* too **w** for me; it is high, 6383
Pr 30:18 There be three *things* which are too **w** 6381

Isa 9: 6 his name shall be called **W**, Counseller, 6382
 25: 1 thy name; for thou hast done **w things**; 6382
 28:29 which is **w** in counsel, *and* excellent in 6381
Jer 5:30 A **w** and horrible thing is committed in 8047
Mt 7:22 and in thy name done many **w works**? *1411*
 21:15 and scribes saw the **w** *things* that he did, *2297*
Ac 2:11 in our tongues the **w works** of God. *3167*

WONDERFULLY (4) [WONDER]

1Sa 6: 6 when he had **wrought w** among them, 5953
Ps 139:14 for I am fearfully and **w made**: 6381
La 1: 9 her last end; therefore she came down **w**: 6382
Da 8:24 he shall destroy **w**, and shall prosper, 6381

WONDERING (3) [WONDER]

Ge 24:21 the man **w** at her held his peace, to wit 7583
Lk 24:12 **w** in himself at that which was come to 2296
Ac 3:11 porch that is called Solomon's, **greatly w**. *1569*

WONDERS (55) [WONDER]

Ex 3:20 smite Egypt with all my **w** which I will do 6381
 4:21 that thou do all *those* **w** before Pharaoh, 4159
 7: 3 my signs and my **w** in the land of Egypt. 4159
 11: 9 that my **w** may be multiplied in the land 4159
 11:10 and Aaron did all these **w** before Pharaoh: 4159
 15:11 in holiness, fearful *in* praises, doing **w**? 6382
Dt 4:34 by **w**, and by war, and by a mighty hand, 4159
 6:22 the LORD shewed signs and **w**, great and 4159
 7:19 the **w**, and the mighty hand, 4159
 26: 8 and with signs, and with **w**: 4159
 34:11 In all the signs and the **w**, which 4159
Jos 3: 5 for to morrow the LORD will do **w** among 6381
1Ch 16:12 his **w**, and the judgments of his mouth; 4159
Ne 9:10 shewedst signs and **w** upon Pharaoh, 4159
 9:17 neither were mindful of thy **w** that thou 6381
Job 9:10 finding out; yea, and **w** without number. 6381
Ps 77:11 surely I will remember thy **w** of old. 6382
 77:14 Thou *art* the God that doest **w**: thou hast 6382
 78:11 and his **w** that he had shewed them. 6381
 78:43 in Egypt, and his **w** in the field of Zoan: 4159
 88:10 Wilt thou shew **w** to the dead? shall 6382
 88:12 Shall thy **w** be known in the dark? 6382
 89: 5 the heavens shall praise thy **w**, O LORD: 6382
 96: 3 the heathen, his **w** among all people. 6381
 105: 5 his **w**, and the judgments of his mouth; 4159
 105:27 among them, and **w** in the land of Ham. 4159
 106: 7 fathers understood not thy **w** in Egypt; 6381
 107:24 of the LORD, and his **w** in the deep. 6381
 135: 9 sent tokens and **w** into the midst of thee, 6381
 136: 4 To him who alone doeth great **w**: for his 6381
Isa 8:18 for **w** in Israel from the LORD of hosts, 4159
Jer 32:20 hast set signs and **w** in the land of Egypt, 4159
 32:21 with **w**, and with a strong hand, and with 4159
Da 4: 2 **w** that the high God hath wrought toward 8540
 4: 3 how mighty *are* his **w**! his kingdom *is* an 8540
 6:27 signs and **w** in heaven and in earth, 8540
 12: 6 long *shall it be* to the end of *these* **w**? 6382
Joel 2:30 I will shew **w** in the heavens and in 4159
Mt 24:24 and shall shew great signs and **w**; *5059*
Mk 13:22 shall shew signs and **w**, to seduce, if *it* *5059*
Jn 4:48 Except ye see signs and **w**, ye will not *5059*
Ac 2:19 And I will shew **w** in heaven above, *5059*
 2:22 among you by miracles and **w** and signs, *5059*
 2:43 and many **w** and signs were done by *5059*
 4:30 **w** may be done by the name of thy holy *5059*
 5:12 and **w** wrought among the people; *5059*
 6: 8 great **w** and miracles among the people. *5059*
 7:36 after that he had shewed **w** and signs in *5059*
 14: 3 and **w** to be done by their hands. *5059*
 15:12 **w** God had wrought among the Gentiles *5059*
Ro 15:19 Through mighty signs and **w**, by the *5059*
2Co 12:12 in signs, and **w**, and mighty deeds. *5059*
2Th 2: 9 with all power and signs and lying **w**, *5059*
Heb 2: 4 both with signs and **w**, and with divers *5059*
Rev 13:13 And he doeth great **w**, so that he maketh *4592*

WONDROUS (15) [WONDER]

1Ch 16: 9 unto him, talk you of all his **w works**. 6381
Job 37:14 and consider the **w works** of God. 6381
 37:16 the **w works** of him which is perfect in 4652
Ps 26: 7 and tell of all thy **w works**. 6381
 71:17 hitherto have I declared thy **w works**. 6381
 72:18 God of Israel, who only doeth **w things**. 6381
 75: 1 for *that* thy name *is* near thy **w works** 6381
 78:32 and believed not for his **w works**. 6381
 86:10 and doest **w things**: thou *art* God alone. 6381
 105: 2 unto him: talk ye of all his **w works**. 6381
 106:22 **W works** in the land of Ham, 6381
 119:18 that I may behold **w** *things* out of thy law. 6381
 119:27 precepts: so shall I talk of thy **w works**. 6381
 145: 5 of thy majesty, and of thy **w works**. 6381
Jer 21: 2 with us according to all his **w works**, 6381

WONDROUSLY (2) [WONDER]

Jdg 13:19 the angel did **w**; and Manoah and his 6381
Joel 2:26 that hath dealt **w** with you: 6381+3807.1

WONT (9)

Ex 21:29 if the ox *were* **w to push with his horn** 5056
Nu 22:30 was I **ever w** to do so unto thee? 5532+5532
1Sa 30:31 and his men were **w to haunt**. 1980
2Sa 20:18 were **w to speak** in old time, 1696+1696
Da 3:19 *times* more than it *was* **w** to be heat. 2370
Mt 27:15 Now at *that* feast the governor was **w** to *1486*
Mk 10: 1 and, as he was **w**, he taught them again. *1486*

Lk	22:39 and went, **as** he was **w,**	1485+2596+3588
Ac	16:13 where prayer was **w** to be made;	3543

WOOD (140) [WOODS, WORMWOOD]

Ge	6:14 Make thee an ark of gopher **w;** rooms	6086
	22: 3 clave the **w** for the burnt offering,	6086
	22: 6 Abraham took the **w** of the burnt offering,	6086
	22: 7 he said, Behold the fire and the **w:**	6086
	22: 9 laid the **w** in order, and bound Isaac his	6086
	22: 9 and laid him on the altar upon the **w.**	6086
Ex	7:19 both in *vessels of* **w,** and in *vessels of*	6086
	25: 5 and badgers' skins, and shittim **w,**	6086
	25:10 they shall make an ark of shittim **w:**	6086
	25:13 thou shalt make staves of shittim **w,**	6086
	25:23 shalt also make a table *of* shittim **w,**	6086
	25:28 thou shalt make the staves *of* shittim **w,**	6086
	26:15 the tabernacle *of* shittim **w** standing up.	6086
	26:26 thou shalt make bars *of* shittim **w;** five for	6086
	26:32 four pillars of shittim **w** overlaid with gold:	NIH
	26:37 for the hanging five pillars of shittim **w,**	NIH
	27: 1 thou shalt make an altar *of* shittim **w,**	6086
	27: 6 staves of shittim **w,** and overlay them	6086
	30: 1 *of* shittim **w** shalt thou make it.	6086
	30: 5 thou shalt make the staves *of* shittim **w,**	6086
	35: 7 and badgers' skins, and shittim **w,**	6086
	35:24 with whom was found shittim **w** for any	6086
	35:33 stones, to set *them,* and in carving of **w,**	6086
	36:20 boards for the tabernacle *of* shittim **w,**	6086
	36:31 he made bars of shittim **w;** five for	6086
	36:36 made thereunto four pillars of shittim **w,**	NIH
	37: 1 Bezaleel made the ark *of* shittim **w:**	6086
	37: 4 he made staves of shittim **w,**	6086
	37:10 made the table *of* shittim **w:** two cubits	6086
	37:15 he made the staves *of* shittim **w,**	6086
	37:25 he made the incense altar *of* shittim **w:**	6086
	37:28 he made the staves *of* shittim **w,**	6086
	38: 1 the altar of burnt offering *of* shittim **w:**	6086
	38: 6 he made the staves *of* shittim **w,**	6086
Lev	1: 7 and lay the **w** in order upon the fire:	6086
	1: 8 in order upon the **w** that *is* on the fire	6086
	1:12 priest shall lay them in order on the **w**	6086
	1:17 altar, upon the **w** that *is* upon the fire:	6086
	3: 5 which *is* upon the **w** that *is* on the fire:	6086
	4:12 and burn him on the **w** with fire:	6086
	6:12 priest shall burn **w** on it every morning,	6086
	14: 4 and cedar **w,** and scarlet, and hyssop:	6086
	14: 6 cedar **w,** and the scarlet, and the hyssop	6086
	14:49 and cedar **w,** and scarlet, and hyssop:	6086
	14:51 shall take the cedar **w,** and the hyssop,	6086
	14:52 with the cedar **w,** and with the hyssop,	6086
	15:12 every vessel of **w** shall be rinsed in water.	6086
Nu	13:20 lean, whether there be **w** therein, or not.	6086
	19: 6 the priest shall take cedar **w,** and hyssop,	6086
	31:20 of goats' *hair,* and all things made of **w.**	6086
	35:18 *if* he smite him with a hand weapon of **w,**	6086
Dt	4:28 **w** and stone, which neither see, nor hear,	6086
	10: 1 the mount, and make thee an ark of **w.**	6086
	10: 3 I made an ark of shittim **w,** and hewed	6086
	19: 5 As when *a man* goeth into the **w** with his	3293
	19: 5 the wood with his neighbour to hew **w,**	6086
	28:36 shalt thou serve other gods, **w** and stone.	6086
	28:64 fathers have known, *even* **w** and stone.	6086
	29:11 the hewer of thy **w** unto the drawer of	6086
	29:17 their idols, **w** and stone, silver and gold,	6086
Jos	9:21 let them be hewers of **w** and drawers of	6086
	9:23 hewers of **w** and drawers of water for	6086
	9:27 Joshua made them that day hewers of **w**	6086
	17:15 *then* get thee up to the **w** *country,* and	3293
	17:18 for it *is* a **w,** and thou shalt cut it down:	3293
Jdg	6:26 offer a burnt sacrifice with the **w** of	6086
1Sa	6:14 they clave the **w** of the cart, and offered	6086
	14:25 all *they* of the land came to a **w;**	3293
	14:26 when the people were come into the **w,**	3293
	23:15 *was* in the wilderness of Ziph in a **w.**	2793
	23:16 went to David *into* the **w,**	2793
	23:18 David abode in the **w,** and Jonathan went	2793
	23:19 himself with us in strong holds in the **w,**	2793
2Sa	6: 5 all *manner of instruments made of* fir **w,**	6086
	18: 6 and the battle was in the **w** of Ephraim;	3293
	18: 8 the **w** devoured more people that day	3293
	18:17 cast him into a great pit in the **w,** and laid	3293
	24:22 and *other* instruments of the oxen for **w.**	6086
1Ki	6:15 he covered *them* on the inside with **w,**	6086
	18:23 lay *it* on **w,** and put no fire *under:*	6086
	18:23 and lay *it* on **w,** and put no fire *under:*	6086
	18:33 put the **w** in order, and cut the bullock in	6086
	18:33 pieces, and laid *him* on the **w,** and said,	6086
	18:33 *it* on the burnt sacrifice, and on the **w.**	6086
	18:38 the **w,** and the stones, and the dust,	6086
2Ki	2:24 came forth two she bears out of the **w,**	3293
	6: 4 they came to Jordan, they cut down **w.**	6086
	19:18 the work of men's hands, **w** and stone:	6086
1Ch	16:33 shall the trees of the **w** sing out at	3293
	21:23 the threshing instruments for **w,**	6086
	22: 4 they of Tyre brought much cedar **w** to	6086
	29: 2 *things of* iron, and **w** for *things of* wood;	6086
	29: 2 *things of* iron, and wood for *things of* **w;**	6086
2Ch	2:16 we will cut **w** out of Lebanon, as much as	6086
Ne	8: 4 Ezra the scribe stood upon a pulpit of **w,**	6086
	10:34 and the people, for the **w** offering,	6086
	13:31 for the **w** offering, at times appointed,	6086
Job	41:27 iron as straw, *and* brass as rotten **w.**	6086
Ps	80:13 The boar out of the **w** doth waste it,	3293
	83:14 As the fire burneth a **w,** and as the flame	3293

Ps	96:12 shall all the trees of the **w** rejoice	3293
	132: 6 we found it in the fields of the **w.**	3293
	141: 7 cutteth and cleaveth *w* upon the earth.	NIH
Pr	26:20 Where no **w** is, *there* the fire goeth out:	6086
	26:21 coals *are* to burning coals, and **w** to fire;	6086
Ecc	2: 6 water therewith the **w** that bringeth forth	3293
	10: 9 he that cleaveth **w** shall be endangered	6086
SS	3: 9 the apple tree among the trees of the **w,**	3293
	3: 9 himself a chariot of the **w** of Lebanon.	6086
Isa	7: 2 as the trees of the **w** are moved with	3293
	10:15 should lift up *itself, as if it were* no **w.**	6086
	30:33 the pile thereof *is* fire and much **w;**	6086
	37:19 the work of men's hands, **w** and stone:	6086
	45:20 have no knowledge that set up the **w**	6086
	60:17 and for **w** brass, and for stones iron:	6086
Jer	5:14 this people **w,** and it shall devour them.	6086
	7:18 The children gather **w,** and the fathers	6086
	28:13 Thou hast broken the yokes of **w;**	6086
	46:22 against her with axes, as hewers of **w.**	6086
La	5: 4 water for money; our **w** is sold *unto us.*	6086
	5:13 grind, and the children fell under the **w.**	6086
Eze	15: 3 Shall **w** be taken thereof to do *any* work?	6086
	20:32 of the countries, to serve **w** and stone.	6086
	24:10 Heap on **w,** kindle the fire, consume	6086
	39:10 that they shall take no **w** out of the field,	6086
	41:16 cieled with **w** round about, and *from*	6086
	41:22 The altar *of* **w** was three cubits high,	6086
	41:22 and the walls thereof, *were of* **w:**	6086
Da	5: 4 silver, of brass, of iron, of **w,** and of stone.	636
	5:23 gold, of brass, iron, **w,** and stone,	636
Mic	7:14 dwell solitarily *in* the **w,** in the midst	3293
Hab	2:19 Woe unto him that saith to the **w,** Awake;	6086
Hag	1: 8 and bring **w,** and build the house;	6086
Zec	12: 6 Judah like a hearth of fire among the **w,**	6086
1Co	3:12 silver, precious stones, **w,** hay, stubble;	3586
2Ti	2:20 of silver, but also of **w** and of earth;	3585
Rev	9:20 silver, and brass, and stone, and of **w:**	3585
	18:12 all thyine **w,** and all *manner* vessels of	3586
	18:12 all *manner* vessels of most precious **w,**	3586

WOODCUTTER See HEWER

WOODS (1) [WOOD]

Eze	34:25 in the wilderness, and sleep in the **w.**	3293

WOOF (9)

Lev	13:48 Whether *it* be in the warp, or **w;** of linen,	6154
	13:49 or in the **w,** or in any thing of skin;	6154
	13:51 or in the **w,** or in a skin, *or* in any work	6154
	13:52 warp or **w,** in woollen or in linen,	6154
	13:53 or in the **w,** or in any thing of skin;	6154
	13:56 skin, or out of the warp, or out of the **w:**	6154
	13:57 or in the **w,** or in any thing of skin;	6154
	13:58 or **w,** or whatsoever thing of skin *it be,*	6154
	13:59 *in* the warp, or **w,** or any thing of skins,	6154

WOOL (14) [WOOLLEN]

Jdg	6:37 I will put a fleece of **w** in the floor;	6785
2Ki	3: 4 an hundred thousand rams, *with* the **w.**	6785
Ps	147:16 He giveth snow like **w:** he scattereth	6785
Pr	31:13 She seeketh **w,** and flax,	6785
Isa	1:18 be red like crimson, they shall be as **w.**	6785
	51: 8 and the worm shall eat them like **w:**	6785
Eze	27:18 in the wine of Helbon, and white **w.**	6785
	34: 3 eat the fat, and ye clothe you with the **w,**	6785
	44:17 no **w** shall come upon them, whiles they	6785
Da	7: 9 and the hair of his head like the pure **w:**	6015
Hos	2: 5 my **w** and my flax, mine oil and my drink.	6785
	2: 9 will recover my **w** and my flax *given* to	6785
Heb	9:19 and scarlet **w,** and hyssop,	2053
Rev	1:14 His head and *his* hairs *were* white like **w,**	2053

WOOLLEN (6) [WOOL]

Lev	13:47 *whether it be* a **w** garment, or a linen	6785
	13:48 in the warp, or woof; of linen, or of **w;**	6785
	13:52 in **w** or in linen, or any thing of skin,	6785
	13:59 of the plague of leprosy in a garment of **w**	6785
	19:19 garment **mingled of linen and w**	3610+8162
Dt	22:11 of divers sorts, *as* of **w** and linen together.	6785

WORD (698) [BYWORD, WORD'S, WORDS]

Ge	15: 1 After these things the **w** of the LORD	1697
	15: 4 the **w** of the LORD *came* unto him,	1697
	30:34 I would it might be according to thy **w.**	1697
	37:14 with the flocks; and bring me **w** again.	1697
	41:40 according unto thy **w** shall all my people	6310
	44: 2 he did according to the **w** that Joseph had	1697
	44:18 speak a **w** in my lord's ears, and let not	1697
Ex	8:10 he said, *Be it* according to thy **w:**	1697
	8:13 the LORD did according to the **w** of	1697
	8:31 the LORD did according to the **w** of	1697
	9:20 He that feared the **w** of the LORD	1697
	9:21 he that regarded not the **w** of the LORD	1697
	12:35 children of Israel did according to the **w**	1697
	14:12 *Is* not this the **w** that we did tell thee in	1697
	32:28 children of Levi did according to the **w**	1697
Lev	10: 7 they did according to the **w** of Moses.	1697
Nu	3:16 numbered them according to the **w**	6310
	3:51 his sons, according to the **w** of the LORD,	6310
	4:45 Aaron numbered according to the **w** of	6310
	11:23 thou shalt see now whether my **w** shall	1697
	13:26 brought back **w** unto them, and unto all	1697
	14:20 I have pardoned according to thy **w:**	1697
	15:31 because he hath despised the **w** of	1697
	20:24 ye rebelled against my **w** at the water of	6310
	22: 8 *this* night, and I will bring you **w** again,	1697

Nu	22:18 I cannot go beyond the **w** of the LORD	6310
	22:20 yet the **w** which I shall say unto thee,	1697
	22:35 only the **w** that I shall speak unto thee,	1697
	22:38 the **w** that God putteth in my mouth,	1697
	23: 5 the LORD put a **w** in Balaam's mouth,	1697
	23:16 put a **w** in his mouth, and said, Go again	1697
	27:21 at his **w** shall they go out, and at his word	6310
	27:21 at his **w** they shall come in, *both* he,	6310
	30: 2 he shall not break his **w,** he shall do	1697
	36: 5 of Israel according to the **w** of the LORD,	6310
Dt	1:22 bring us **w** again, by what way we must	1697
	1:25 and brought us **w** again, and said,	1697
	4: 2 Ye shall not add unto the **w** which I	1697
	5: 5 to shew you the **w** of the LORD:	1697
	8: 3 by every *w* that proceedeth out of the	NIH
	9: 5 that he may perform the **w** which	1697
	18:20 which shall presume to speak a **w** in my	1697
	18:21 How shall we know the **w** which	1697
	21: 5 by their **w** shall every controversy and	6310
	30:14 **w** is very nigh unto thee, in thy mouth,	1697
	33: 9 for they have observed thy **w,** and kept	565
	34: 5 according to the **w** of the LORD.	6310
Jos	1:13 Remember the **w** which Moses the	1697
	6:10 neither shall *any* **w** proceed out of your	1697
	8:27 according unto the **w** of the LORD which	1697
	8:35 There was not a **w** of all that Moses	1697
	14: 7 I brought him **w** again *as it was* in mine	1697
	14:10 *even* since the LORD spake this **w** unto	1697
	19:50 According to the **w** of the LORD they	6310
	22: 9 according to the **w** of the LORD by	6310
	22:32 of Israel, and brought them **w** again.	1697
1Sa	1:23 only the LORD establish his **w.**	1697
	3: 1 the **w** of the LORD was precious in those	1697
	3: 7 neither was the **w** of the LORD yet	1697
	3:21 Samuel in Shiloh by the **w** of the LORD.	1697
	4: 1 the **w** of Samuel came to all Israel.	1697
	9:27 that I may shew thee the **w** of God.	1697
	15:10 came the **w** of the LORD unto Samuel,	1697
	15:23 Because thou hast rejected the **w** of	1697
	15:26 for thou hast rejected the **w** of the LORD,	1697
2Sa	3:11 he could not answer Abner a **w** again,	1697
	7: 4 that the **w** of the LORD came unto	1697
	7: 7 spake I a **w** with any of the tribes of Israel,	1697
	7:25 the **w** that thou hast spoken concerning	1697
	14:12 speak unto my lord the king.	1697
	14:17 The **w** of my lord the king shall now be	1697
	15:28 there come **w** from you to certify me.	1697
	19:10 **speak** ye **not a w** of bringing the king	2790
	19:14 so that they sent *this w* unto the king,	NIH
	22:31 way *is* perfect; the **w** of the LORD *is* tried:	565
	23: 2 by me, and his **w** *was* in my tongue.	4405
	24: 4 Notwithstanding the king's **w** prevailed	1697
	24:11 the **w** of the LORD came unto the prophet	1697
1Ki	2: 4 That the LORD may continue his **w** which	1697
	2:23 Adonijah have not spoken this **w** against	1697
	2:27 that *he* might fulfil the **w** of the LORD,	1697
	2:30 Benaiah brought the king **w** again, saying,	1697
	2:42 me, The **w** *that* I have heard *is* good.	1697
	3:12 Behold, I have done according to thy **w:**	1697
	6:11 the **w** of the LORD came to Solomon,	1697
	6:12 will I perform my **w** with thee, which I	1697
	8:20 the LORD hath performed his **w** that he	1697
	8:26 let thy **w,** I pray thee, be verified,	1697
	8:56 there hath not failed one **w** of all his good	1697
	12:22 the **w** of God came to Shemaiah the	1697
	12:24 therefore to the **w** of the LORD,	1697
	12:24 according to the **w** of the LORD.	1697
	13: 1 Judah by the **w** of the LORD unto Beth-el:	1697
	13: 2 he cried against the altar in the **w** of	1697
	13: 5 of God had given by the **w** of the LORD,	1697
	13: 9 was it charged me by the **w** of the LORD,	1697
	13:17 For it was said to me by the **w** of	1697
	13:18 an angel spake unto me by the **w** of	1697
	13:20 that the **w** of the LORD came unto	1697
	13:26 who was disobedient unto the **w** of	6310
	13:26 according to the **w** of the LORD,	1697
	13:32 For the saying which he cried by the **w** of	1697
	14:18 for him, according to the **w** of the LORD,	1697
	16: 1 the **w** of the LORD came to Jehu the son	1697
	16: 7 came the **w** of the LORD against Baasha,	1697
	16:12 according to the **w** of the LORD,	1697
	16:34 according to the **w** of the LORD, which he	1697
	17: 1 rain these years, but according to my **w.**	1697
	17: 2 the **w** of the LORD came unto him,	1697
	17: 5 did according unto the **w** of the LORD:	1697
	17: 8 the **w** of the LORD came unto him,	1697
	17:16 according to the **w** of the LORD, which he	1697
	17:24 *that* the **w** of the LORD in thy mouth *is*	1697
	18: 1 that the **w** of the LORD came to Elijah in	1697
	18:21 And the people answered him not a **w.**	1697
	18:31 unto whom the **w** of the LORD came,	1697
	18:36 *that* I have done all these things at thy **w.**	1697
	19: 9 the **w** of the LORD *came* to him,	1697
	20: 9 and brought him **w** again.	1697
	20:35 unto his neighbour in the **w** of the LORD,	1697
	21: 4 of the **w** which Naboth the Jezreelite had	1697
	21:17 the **w** of the LORD came to Elijah	1697
	21:28 the **w** of the LORD came to Elijah	1697
	22: 5 I pray thee, at the **w** of the LORD to day.	1697
	22:13 let thy **w,** I pray thee, be like the word of	1697
	22:13 be like the **w** of one of them, and speak	1697
	22:19 Hear thou therefore the **w** of the LORD:	1697
	22:38 according unto the **w** of the LORD which	1697
2Ki	1:16 *is* no God in Israel to inquire of his **w?**	1697
	1:17 So he died according to the **w** of	1697

W

2Ki 3:12 the **w** of the LORD is with him.	1697
4:44 left *thereof,* according to the **w** of	1697
6:18 blindness according to the **w** of Elisha.	1697
7: 1 Elisha said, Hear ye the **w** of the LORD;	1697
7:16 a shekel, according to the **w** of the LORD,	1697
9:26 *ground,* according to the **w** of the LORD.	1697
9:36 he said, This *is* the **w** of the LORD,	1697
10:10 the earth nothing of the **w** of the LORD,	1697
14:25 according to the **w** of the LORD God of	1697
15:12 This *was* the **w** of the LORD which he	1697
18:28 saying, Hear the **w** of the great king,	1697
18:36 their peace, and answered him not a **w:**	1697
19:21 This *is* the **w** that the LORD hath spoken	1697
20: 4 that the **w** of the LORD came to him,	1697
20:16 unto Hezekiah, Hear the **w** of the LORD.	1697
20:19 Good *is* the **w** of the LORD which thou	1697
22: 9 and brought the king **w** again, and said,	1697
22:20 And they brought the king **w** again.	1697
23:16 according to the **w** of the LORD which	1697
24: 2 according to the **w** of the LORD,	1697
1Ch 10:13 *even* against the **w** of the LORD, which he	1697
11: 3 according to the **w** of the LORD by	1697
11:10 according to the **w** of the LORD	1697
12:23 to him, according to the **w** of the LORD.	6310
15:15 Moses commanded according to the **w** of	1697
16:15 **w** *which* he commanded to a thousand	1697
17: 3 the **w** of God came to Nathan, saying,	1697
17: 6 spake I a **w** to any of the judges of Israel,	1697
21: 4 Nevertheless the king's **w** prevailed	1697
21: 6 for the king's **w** was abominable to Joab.	1697
21:12 advise thyself what **w** I shall bring again	1697
22: 8 the **w** of the LORD came to me, saying,	1697
2Ch 6:10 performed his **w** that he hath spoken:	1697
6:17 LORD God of Israel, let thy **w** be verified,	1697
10:15 that the LORD might perform his **w,**	1697
11: 2 the **w** of the LORD came to Shemaiah	1697
12: 7 the **w** of the LORD came to Shemaiah,	1697
18: 4 I pray thee, at the **w** of the LORD to day.	1697
18:12 let thy **w** therefore, I pray thee, be like	1697
18:18 Therefore hear the **w** of the LORD;	1697
30:12 and of the princes, by the **w** of the LORD.	1697
34:16 brought the king **w** back again, saying,	1697
34:21 our fathers have not kept the **w** of	1697
34:28 So they brought the king **w** again.	1697
35: 6 that *they* may do according to the **w** of	1697
36:21 To fulfil the **w** of the LORD by the mouth	1697
36:22 that the **w** of the LORD *spoken* by	1697
Ezr 1: 1 that the **w** of the LORD by the mouth of	1697
6:11 decree, that whosoever shall alter this **w,**	6600
10: 5 that *they* should do according to this **w.**	1697
Ne 1: 8 **w** that thou commandedst thy servant	1697
Est 1:21 the king did according to the **w** of	1697
7: 8 As the **w** went out of the king's mouth,	1697
Job 2:13 nights, and none spake a **w** unto him:	1697
Ps 17: 4 by the **w** of thy lips I have kept *me from*	1697
18:30 the **w** of the LORD is tried: he *is* a buckler	565
33: 4 For the **w** of the LORD *is* right; and all his	1697
33: 6 By the **w** of the LORD were the heavens	1697
56: 4 In God I will praise his **w,** in God I have	1697
56:10 In God will I praise *his* **w:** in the LORD	1697
56:10 *his* word: in the LORD will I praise *his* **w.**	1697
68:11 The Lord gave the **w:** great *was*	562
103:20 hearkening unto the voice of his **w.**	1697
105: 8 the **w** *which* he commanded to a	1697
105:19 Until the time that his **w** came: the word	1697
105:19 word came: the **w** of the LORD tried him.	565
105:28 dark; and they rebelled not against his **w.**	1697
106:24 pleasant land, they believed not his **w:**	1697
107:20 He sent his **w,** and healed them;	1697
119: 9 taking heed *thereto* according to thy **w.**	1697
119:11 Thy **w** have I hid in mine heart, that I	565
119:16 in thy statutes: I will not forget thy **w.**	1697
119:17 servant, *that* I may live, and keep thy **w.**	1697
119:25 quicken thou me according to thy **w.**	1697
119:28 strengthen thou me according unto thy **w.**	1697
119:38 Stablish thy **w** unto thy servant, who *is*	565
119:41 *even* thy salvation, according to thy **w.**	565
119:42 that reproacheth me: for I trust in thy **w.**	1697
119:43 take not the **w** of truth utterly out of my	1697
119:49 Remember the **w** unto thy servant,	1697
119:50 affliction: for thy **w** hath quickened me.	565
119:58 be merciful unto me according to thy **w.**	565
119:65 O LORD, according unto thy **w.**	1697
119:67 I went astray: but now have I kept thy **w.**	565
119:74 see me; because I have hoped in thy **w.**	1697
119:76 according to thy **w** unto thy servant.	565
119:81 for thy salvation: *but* I hope in thy **w.**	1697
119:82 Mine eyes fail for thy **w,** saying, When	565
119:89 O LORD, thy **w** *is* settled in heaven.	1697
119:101 every evil way, that I might keep thy **w.**	1697
119:105 Thy **w** *is* a lamp unto my feet, and a light	1697
119:107 O LORD, according unto thy **w.**	1697
119:114 and my shield: I hope in thy **w.**	1697
119:116 Uphold me according unto thy **w,** that I	565
119:123 and for the **w** of thy righteousness.	565
119:133 Order my steps in thy **w:** and let not any	565
119:140 Thy **w** *is* very pure: therefore thy servant	565
119:147 the morning, and cried: I hoped in thy **w.**	1697
119:148 that *I* might meditate in thy **w.**	565
119:154 quicken me according to thy **w.**	565
119:158 was grieved; because they kept not thy **w.**	565
119:160 Thy **w** *is* true *from* the beginning:	1697
119:161 but my heart standeth in awe of thy **w.**	1697
119:162 I rejoice at thy **w,** as one that findeth	565
119:169 understanding according to thy **w.**	1697

Ps 119:170 thee: deliver me according to thy **w.**	565
119:172 My tongue shall speak of thy **w:** for all thy	565
130: 5 soul doth wait, and in his **w** do I hope.	1697
138: 2 for thou hast magnified thy **w** above all	565
139: 4 For *there is* not a **w** in my tongue, *but* lo,	4405
147:15 *upon* earth: his **w** runneth very swiftly.	1697
147:18 He sendeth out his **w,** and melteth them:	1697
147:19 He sheweth his **w** unto Jacob, his statutes	1697
148: 8 and vapour; stormy wind fulfilling his **w:**	1697
Pr 12:25 it stoop: but a good **w** maketh it glad.	1697
13:13 despiseth the **w** shall be destroyed:	1697
14:15 The simple believeth every **w:**	1697
15:23 a **w** *spoken* in due season, how good *is it!*	1697
25:11 A **w** fitly spoken *is like* apples of gold in	1697
30: 5 Every **w** of God *is* pure: he *is* a shield unto	565
Ecc 8: 4 Where the **w** of a king *is, there is* power:	1697
Isa 1:10 Hear the **w** of the LORD, ye rulers of	1697
2: 1 The **w** that Isaiah the son of Amoz saw	1697
2: 3 and the **w** of the LORD from Jerusalem.	1697
5:24 despised the **w** of the Holy One of Israel.	565
8:10 speak the **w,** and it shall not stand:	1697
8:20 if they speak not according to this **w,** *it is*	1697
9: 8 The Lord sent a **w** into Jacob, and it hath	1697
16:13 This *is* the **w** that the LORD hath spoken	1697
24: 3 for the LORD hath spoken this **w.**	1697
28:13 the **w** of the LORD was unto them precept	1697
28:14 Wherefore hear the **w** of the LORD,	1697
29:21 That make a man an offender for a **w,**	1697
30:12 Because ye despise this **w,** and trust in	1697
30:21 thine ears shall hear a **w** behind thee,	1697
36:21 their peace, and answered him not a **w:**	1697
37:22 This *is* the **w** which the LORD hath	1697
38: 4 came the **w** of the LORD to Isaiah,	1697
39: 5 Hear the **w** of the LORD of hosts:	1697
39: 8 Good *is* the **w** of the LORD which thou	1697
40: 8 but the **w** of our God shall stand for ever.	1697
41:28 when I asked of them, could answer a **w.**	1697
44:26 That confirmeth the **w** of his servant,	1697
45:23 the **w** is gone out of my mouth *in*	1697
50: 4 that *I* should know how to speak a **w** in	1697
55:11 shall my **w** be that goeth forth out of my	1697
66: 2 a contrite spirit, and trembleth at my **w.**	1697
66: 5 Hear the **w** of the LORD, ye that tremble	1697
66: 5 of the LORD, ye that tremble at his **w;**	1697
Jer 1: 2 To whom the **w** of the LORD came in	1697
1: 4 the **w** of the LORD came unto me, saying,	1697
1:11 the **w** of the LORD came unto me, saying,	1697
1:12 for I will hasten my **w** to perform it.	1697
1:13 the **w** of the LORD came unto me	1697
2: 1 Moreover the **w** of the LORD came to me,	1697
2: 4 Hear ye the **w** of the LORD, O house of	1697
2:31 O generation, see ye the **w** of the LORD.	1697
5:13 become wind, and the **w** *is* not in them:	1699'
5:14 Because ye speak this **w,** behold, I will	1697
6:10 the **w** of the LORD is unto them a	1697
7: 1 The **w** that came to Jeremiah from	1697
7: 2 proclaim there this **w,** and say, Hear	1697
7: 2 say, Hear the **w** of the LORD, all *ye of*	1697
8: 9 lo, they have rejected the **w** of the LORD;	1697
9:20 Yet hear the **w** of the LORD, O ye	1697
9:20 let your ear receive the **w** of his mouth,	1697
10: 1 Hear ye the **w** which the LORD speaketh	1697
11: 1 The **w** that came to Jeremiah from	1697
13: 2 according to the **w** of the LORD,	1697
13: 3 the **w** of the LORD came unto me	1697
13: 8 the **w** of the LORD came unto me, saying,	1697
13:12 thou shalt speak unto them this **w;**	1697
14: 1 The **w** of the LORD that came to Jeremiah	1697
14:17 thou shalt say this **w** unto them;	1697
15:16 thy **w** was unto me the joy and rejoicing	1697
16: 1 The **w** of the LORD came also unto me,	1697
17:15 unto me, Where *is* the **w** of the LORD?	1697
17:20 Hear ye the **w** of the LORD, ye kings of	1697
18: 1 The **w** which came to Jeremiah from	1697
18: 5 the **w** of the LORD came to me, saying,	1697
18:18 the wise, nor the **w** from the prophet.	1697
19: 3 say, Hear ye the **w** of the LORD, O kings	1697
20: 8 the **w** of the LORD was made a reproach	1697
20: 9 *his* **w** was in mine heart as a burning fire	NIH
21: 1 The **w** which came unto Jeremiah from	1697
21:11 *say,* Hear ye the **w** of the LORD.	1697
22: 1 the king of Judah, and speak there this **w,**	1697
22: 2 say, Hear the **w** of the LORD, O king of	1697
22:29 earth, earth, hear the **w** of the LORD.	1697
23:18 and hath perceived and heard his **w?**	1697
23:18 who hath marked his **w,** and heard *it?*	1697
23:28 that hath my **w,** let him speak my word	1697
23:28 my word, let him speak my **w** faithfully.	1697
23:29 *Is* not my **w** like as a fire? saith	1697
23:36 for every man's **w** shall be his burden;	1697
23:38 Because you say this **w,** The burden of	1697
24: 4 Again the **w** of the LORD came unto me,	1697
25: 1 The **w** that came to Jeremiah concerning	1697
25: 3 the **w** of the LORD hath come unto me,	1697
26: 1 of Judah came this **w** from the LORD,	1697
26: 2 to speak unto them; diminish not a **w:**	1697
27: 1 this **w** unto Jeremiah from the LORD,	1697
27:18 and if the **w** of the LORD be with them,	1697
28: 7 Nevertheless hear thou now this **w** that I	1697
28: 9 when the **w** of the prophet shall come to	1697
28:12 the **w** of the LORD came unto Jeremiah	1697
29:10 perform my good **w** towards you,	1697
29:20 Hear ye therefore the **w** of the LORD,	1697
29:30 came the **w** of the LORD unto Jeremiah,	1697
30: 1 The **w** that came to Jeremiah from	1697

Jer 31:10 Hear the **w** of the LORD, O ye nations,	1697
32: 1 The **w** that came to Jeremiah from	1697
32: 6 The **w** of the LORD came unto me,	1697
32: 8 prison according to the **w** of the LORD,	1697
32: 8 I knew that this *was* the **w** of the LORD.	1697
32:26 came the **w** of the LORD unto Jeremiah,	1697
33: 1 Moreover the **w** of the LORD came unto	1697
33:19 the **w** of the LORD came unto Jeremiah,	1697
33:23 Moreover the **w** of the LORD came to	1697
34: 1 The **w** which came unto Jeremiah from	1697
34: 4 Yet hear the **w** of the LORD, O Zedekiah	1697
34: 5 for I have pronounced the **w,** saith	1697
34: 8 *This is* the **w** that came unto Jeremiah	1697
34:12 Therefore the **w** of the LORD came to	1697
35: 1 The **w** which came unto Jeremiah from	1697
35:12 came the **w** of the LORD unto Jeremiah,	1697
36: 1 *that* this **w** came unto Jeremiah from	1697
36:27 the **w** of the LORD came to Jeremiah,	1697
37: 6 came the **w** of the LORD unto the prophet	1697
37:17 and said, Is there *any* **w** from the LORD?	1697
38:21 this *is* the **w** that the LORD hath shewed	1697
39:15 Now the **w** of the LORD came unto	1697
40: 1 The **w** which came to Jeremiah from	1697
42: 7 that the **w** of the LORD came unto	1697
42:15 therefore hear the **w** of the LORD,	1697
43: 8 came the **w** of the LORD unto Jeremiah in	1697
44: 1 The **w** that came to Jeremiah concerning	1697
44:16 *As for* the **w** that thou hast spoken unto	1697
44:24 all the women, Hear the **w** of the LORD,	1697
44:26 Therefore hear ye the **w** of the LORD,	1697
45: 1 The **w** that Jeremiah the prophet spake	1697
46: 1 The **w** of the LORD which came to	1697
46:13 The **w** that the LORD spake to Jeremiah	1697
47: 1 The **w** of the LORD that came to Jeremiah	1697
49:34 The **w** of the LORD that came to Jeremiah	1697
50: 1 The **w** that the LORD spake against	1697
51:59 The **w** which Jeremiah the prophet	1697
La 2:17 he hath fulfilled his **w** that he had	565
Eze 1: 3 The **w** of the LORD came expressly unto	1697
3:16 that the **w** of the LORD came unto me,	1697
3:17 therefore hear the **w** at my mouth,	1697
6: 1 the **w** of the LORD came unto me, saying,	1697
6: 3 of Israel, hear the **w** of the Lord GOD;	1697
7: 1 Moreover the **w** of the LORD came unto	1697
11:14 Again the **w** of the LORD came unto me,	1697
12: 1 The **w** of the LORD also came unto me,	1697
12: 8 in the morning came the **w** of the LORD	1697
12:17 Moreover the **w** of the LORD came to me,	1697
12:21 the **w** of the LORD came unto me, saying,	1697
12:25 **w** that I shall speak shall come to pass;	1697
12:25 will I say the **w,** and will perform it,	1697
12:26 Again the **w** of the LORD came to me,	1697
12:28 the **w** which I have spoken shall be done,	1697
13: 1 the **w** of the LORD came unto me, saying,	1697
13: 2 own hearts, Hear ye the **w** of the LORD;	1697
13: 6 to hope that *they* would confirm the **w.**	1697
14: 2 the **w** of the LORD came unto me, saying,	1697
14:12 The **w** of the LORD came again to me,	1697
15: 1 the **w** of the LORD came unto me, saying,	1697
16: 1 Again the **w** of the LORD came unto me,	1697
16:35 O harlot, hear the **w** of the LORD:	1697
17: 1 the **w** of the LORD came unto me, saying,	1697
17:11 Moreover the **w** of the LORD came unto	1697
18: 1 the **w** of the LORD came unto me again,	1697
20: 2 came the **w** of the LORD unto me, saying,	1697
20:45 Moreover the **w** of the LORD came unto	1697
20:46 drop *thy* **w** toward the south,	NIH
20:47 of the south, Hear the **w** of the LORD;	1697
21: 1 the **w** of the LORD came unto me, saying,	1697
21: 2 drop *thy* **w** toward the holy places,	NIH
21: 8 Again the **w** of the LORD came unto me,	1697
21:18 The **w** of the LORD came unto me again,	1697
22: 1 Moreover the **w** of the LORD came unto me,	1697
22:17 the **w** of the LORD came unto me, saying,	1697
22:23 the **w** of the LORD came unto me, saying,	1697
23: 1 The **w** of the LORD came again unto me,	1697
24: 1 the **w** of the LORD came again unto me,	1697
24:15 Also the **w** of the LORD came unto me,	1697
24:20 The **w** of the LORD came unto me,	1697
25: 1 The **w** of the LORD came again unto me,	1697
25: 3 Hear the **w** of the Lord GOD;	1697
26: 1 *that* the **w** of the LORD came unto me,	1697
27: 1 The **w** of the LORD came again unto me,	1697
28: 1 The **w** of the LORD came unto me, saying,	1697
28:11 Moreover the **w** of the LORD came unto	1697
28:20 Again the **w** of the LORD came unto me,	1697
29: 1 the **w** of the LORD came unto me, saying,	1697
29:17 the **w** of the LORD came unto me, saying,	1697
30: 1 The **w** of the LORD came unto me, saying,	1697
30:20 *that* the **w** of the LORD came unto me,	1697
31: 1 *that* the **w** of the LORD came unto me,	1697
32: 1 *that* the **w** of the LORD came unto me,	1697
32:17 *that* the **w** of the LORD came unto me,	1697
33: 1 Again the **w** of the LORD came unto me,	1697
33: 7 thou shalt hear the **w** at my mouth,	1697
33:23 the **w** of the LORD came unto me, saying,	1697
33:30 hear what *is* the **w** that cometh forth from	1697
34: 1 the **w** of the LORD came unto me, saying,	1697
34: 7 ye shepherds, hear the **w** of the LORD;	1697
34: 9 O ye shepherds, hear the **w** of the LORD;	1697
35: 1 Moreover the **w** of the LORD came unto	1697
36: 1 of Israel, hear the **w** of the LORD:	1697
36: 4 Israel, hear the **w** of the Lord GOD;	1697
36:16 Moreover the **w** of the LORD came unto	1697
37: 4 O ye dry bones, hear the **w** of the LORD.	1697

Eze	37:15	The w of the LORD came again unto me,	1697
	38: 1	the w of the LORD came unto me, saying,	1697
Da	3:28	have changed the king's w,	4406
	4:17	the demand by the w of the holy ones:	3983
	4:31	While the w was in the king's mouth,	4406
	9: 2	whereof the w of the LORD came to	1697
	10:11	when he had spoken this w unto me,	1697
Hos	1: 1	The w of the LORD that came unto	1697
	1: 2	The beginning of the w of the LORD by	1699'
	4: 1	Hear the w of the LORD, ye children of	1697
Joel	1: 1	The w of the LORD that came to Joel	1697
	2:11	for he is strong that executeth his w:	1697
Am	3: 1	Hear this w that the LORD hath spoken	1697
	4: 1	Hear this w, ye kine of Bashan, that are	1697
	5: 1	Hear ye this w which I take up against	1697
	7:16	therefore hear thou the w of the LORD:	1697
	7:16	drop not thy w against the house of Isaac.	NIH
	8:12	run to and fro to seek the w of the LORD,	1697
Jnh	1: 1	Now the w of the LORD came unto Jonah	1697
	3: 1	the w of the LORD came unto Jonah	1697
	3: 3	according to the w of the LORD.	1697
	3: 6	For w came unto the king of Nineveh,	1697
Mic	1: 1	The w of the LORD that came to Micah	1697
	4: 2	and the w of the LORD from Jerusalem.	1697
Hab	3: 9	to the oaths of the tribes, even thy w.	562
Zep	1: 1	The w of the LORD which came unto	1697
	2: 5	the w of the LORD is against you;	1697
Hag	1: 1	came the w of the LORD by Haggai	1697
	1: 3	came the w of the LORD by Haggai	1697
	2: 1	came the w of the LORD by the prophet	1697
	2: 5	According to the w that I covenanted	1697
	2:10	came the w of the LORD by Haggai	1697
	2:20	again the w of the LORD came unto	1697
Zec	1: 1	came the w of the LORD unto Zechariah,	1697
	1: 7	came the w of the LORD unto Zechariah,	1697
	4: 6	This is the w of the LORD unto	1697
	4: 8	Moreover the w of the LORD came unto	1697
	6: 9	the w of the LORD came unto me, saying,	1697
	7: 1	that the w of the LORD came unto	1697
	7: 4	came the w of the LORD of hosts unto	1697
	7: 8	the w of the LORD came unto Zechariah,	1697
	8: 1	Again the w of the LORD of hosts came	1697
	8:18	the w of the LORD of hosts came unto	1697
	9: 1	The burden of the w of the LORD	1697
	11:11	me knew that it was the w of the LORD.	1697
	12: 1	The burden of the w of the LORD for	1697
Mal	1: 1	The burden of the w of the LORD to	1697
Mt	2: 8	ye have found him, **bring** me **w again**,	518
	2:13	and be thou there until I **bring** thee **w:**	3004
	4: 4	by every w that proceedeth out of	4487
	8: 8	speak the w only, and my servant shall	3056
	8:16	and he cast out the spirits with his w,	3056
	12:32	And whosoever speaketh a w against	3056
	12:36	That every idle w that men shall speak,	4487
	13:19	When any one heareth the w	3056
	13:20	the same is he that heareth the w,	3056
	13:21	or persecution ariseth because of the w,	3056
	13:22	the thorns is he that heareth the w;	3056
	13:22	choke the w, and he becometh unfruitful.	3056
	13:23	the good ground is he that heareth the w,	3056
	15:23	But he answered her not a w. And his	3056
	18:16	three witnesses every w may be	4487
	22:46	And no man was able to answer him a w,	3056
	26:75	And Peter remembered the w of Jesus,	4487
	27:14	And he answered him to never a w;	4487
	28: 8	and did run to **bring** his disciples **w.**	518
Mk	2: 2	door: and he preached the w unto them.	3056
	4:14	The sower soweth the w.	3056
	4:15	by the way side, where the w is sown;	3056
	4:15	taketh away the w that was sown in their	3056
	4:16	who, when they have heard the w,	3056
	4:18	sown among thorns; such as hear the w,	3056
	4:19	choke the w, and it becometh unfruitful.	3056
	4:20	such as hear the w, and receive it,	3056
	4:33	such parables spake he the w unto them,	3056
	5:36	As soon as Jesus heard the w that was	3056
	7:13	Making the w of God of none effect	3056
	14:72	And Peter called to mind the w that Jesus	4487
	16:20	confirming the w with signs following.	3056
Lk	1: 2	eyewitnesses, and ministers of the w;	3056
	1:38	Lord; be it unto me according to thy w.	4487
	2:29	depart in peace, according to thy w:	4487
	3: 2	the w of God came unto John the son of	4487
	4: 4	by bread alone, but by every w of God.	4487
	4:32	at his doctrine: for his w was with power.	3056
	4:36	saying, What a w is this!	3056
	5: 1	pressed upon him to hear the w of God,	3056
	5: 5	nevertheless at thy w I will let down	4487
	7: 7	but say in a w, and my servant shall be	3056
	8:11	parable is this: The seed is the w of God.	3056
	8:12	taketh away the w out of their hearts,	3056
	8:13	when they hear, receive the w with joy;	3056
	8:15	heard the w, keep it, and bring forth	3056
	8:21	my brethren are these which hear the w	3056
	10:39	also sat at Jesus' feet, and heard his w.	3056
	11:28	blessed are they that hear the w of God,	3056
	12:10	And whosoever shall speak a w against	3056
	22:61	Peter remembered the w of the Lord,	3056
	24:19	and w before God and all the people:	3056
Jn	1: 1	In the beginning was the W, and the	3056
	1: 1	and the W was with God, and the Word	3056
	1: 1	was with God, and the W was God.	3056
	1:14	And the W was made flesh,	3056
	2:22	and the w which Jesus had said.	3056
	4:41	moe believed because of his own w;	3056

Jn	4:50	the man believed the w that Jesus had	3056
	5:24	He that heareth my w, and believeth on	3056
	5:38	And ye have not his w abiding in you:	3056
	8:31	If ye continue in my w, then are ye my	3056
	8:37	because my w hath no place in you.	3056
	8:43	even because ye cannot hear my w.	3056
	10:35	unto whom the w of God came,	3056
	12:48	the w that I have spoken, the same shall	3056
	14:24	and the w which ye hear is not mine,	3056
	15: 3	Now ye are clean through the w which I	3056
	15:20	Remember the w that I said unto you,	3056
	15:25	this cometh to pass, that the w might be	3056
	17: 6	them me; and they have kept thy w.	3056
	17:14	I have given them thy w; and the world	3056
	17:17	them through thy truth: thy w is truth.	3056
	17:20	shall believe on me through their w;	3056
Ac	2:41	Then they that gladly received his w were	3056
	4: 4	many of them which heard the w	3056
	4:29	with all boldness they may speak thy w,	3056
	4:31	they spake the w of God with boldness.	3056
	6: 2	not reason that we should leave the w	3056
	6: 4	to prayer, and to the ministry of the w.	3056
	6: 7	And the w of God increased;	3056
	8: 4	went every where preaching the w.	3056
	8:14	that Samaria had received the w of God,	3056
	8:25	and preached the w of the Lord,	3056
	10:36	The w which God sent unto the children	3056
	10:37	That w, I say, you know, which was	4487
	10:44	Ghost fell on all them which heard the w.	3056
	11: 1	Gentiles had also received the w of God.	3056
	11:16	Then remembered I the w of the Lord,	4487
	11:19	preaching the w to none but unto the Jews	3056
	12:24	But the w of God grew and multiplied.	3056
	13: 5	they preached the w of God in	3056
	13: 7	Saul, and desired to hear the w of God.	3056
	13:15	if ye have any w of exhortation for	3056
	13:26	to you is the w of this salvation sent.	3056
	13:44	whole city together to hear the w of God.	3056
	13:46	It was necessary that the w of God should	3056
	13:48	were glad, and glorified the w of the Lord:	3056
	13:49	And the w of the Lord was published	3056
	14: 3	which gave testimony unto the w of his	3056
	14:25	And when they had preached the w in	3056
	15: 7	mouth should hear the w of the gospel,	3056
	15:35	teaching and preaching the w of the Lord,	3056
	15:36	we have preached the w of the Lord,	3056
	16: 6	the Holy Ghost to preach the w in Asia,	3056
	16:32	they spake unto him the w of the Lord,	3056
	17:11	in that they received the w with all	3056
	17:13	w of God was preached of Paul at Berea,	3056
	18:11	teaching the w of God among them.	3056
	19:10	in Asia heard the w of the Lord Jesus,	3056
	19:20	So mightily grew the w of God and	3056
	20:32	you to God, and to the w of his grace,	3056
	22:22	And they gave him audience unto this w,	3056
	28:25	after that Paul had spoken one w,	4487
Ro	9: 6	Not as though the w of God hath taken	3056
	9: 9	For this is the w of promise, At this time	3056
	10: 8	The w is nigh thee, even in thy mouth,	4487
	10: 8	that is, the w of faith, which we preach;	4487
	10:17	by hearing, and hearing by the w of God.	4487
	15:18	the Gentiles obedient, by w and deed,	3056
1Co	4:20	For the kingdom of God is not in w,	3056
	12: 8	For to one is given by the Spirit the w of	3056
	12: 8	to another the w of knowledge by the	3056
	14:36	came the w of God out from you?	3056
2Co	1:18	our w toward you was not yea and nay.	3056
	2:17	not as many, which corrupt the w of God:	3056
	4: 2	nor handling the w of God deceitfully;	3056
	5:19	hath committed unto us the w of	3056
	6: 7	By the w of truth, by the power of God,	3056
	13: 1	three witnesses shall every w be	4487
Gal	5:14	For all the law is fulfilled in one w, even	3056
	6: 6	Let him that is taught in the w	3056
Eph	1:13	trusted, after that ye heard the w of truth,	3056
	5:26	it with the washing of water by the w,	4487
	6:17	sword of the Spirit, which is the w of God:	4487
Php	1:14	much more bold to speak the w without	3056
	2:16	Holding forth the w of life; that I may	3056
Col	1: 5	whereof ye heard before in the w of	3056
	1:25	given to me for you, to fulfil the w of God;	3056
	3:16	Let the w of Christ dwell in you richly in	3056
	3:17	whatsoever ye do in w or deed, do all	3056
1Th	1: 5	For our gospel came not unto you in w	3056
	1: 6	having received the w in much affliction,	3056
	1: 8	For from you sounded out the w of	3056
	2:13	when ye received the w of God which ye	3056
	2:13	ye received it not as the w of men, but as	3056
	2:13	of men, but as it is in truth, the w of God,	3056
	4:15	For this we say unto you by the w of	3056
2Th	2: 2	be troubled, neither by spirit, nor by w,	3056
	2:15	whether by w, or by our epistle.	3056
	2:17	stablish you in every good w and work.	3056
	3: 1	that the w of the Lord may have free	3056
	3:14	And if any man obey not our w by this	3056
1Ti	4: 5	For it is sanctified by the w of God and	3056
	4:12	in w, in conversation, in charity, in spirit,	3056
	5:17	especially they who labour in the w and	3056
2Ti	2: 9	bonds; but the w of God is not bound.	3056
	2:15	ashamed, rightly dividing the w of truth.	3056
	2:17	And their w will eat as doth a canker:	3056
	4: 2	Preach the w; be instant in season, out of	3056
Tit	1: 3	But hath in due times manifested his w	3056
	1: 9	Holding fast the faithful w as he hath	3056

Tit	2: 5	that the w of God be not blasphemed.	3056
Heb	1: 3	all things by the w of his power,	4487
	2: 2	if the w spoken by angels was stedfast,	3056
	4: 2	but the w preached did not profit them,	3056
	4:12	For the w of God is quick, and powerful,	3056
	5:13	is unskilful in the w of righteousness:	3056
	6: 5	And have tasted the good w of God,	4487
	7:28	but the w of the oath, which was since	3056
	11: 3	the worlds were framed by the w of God,	4487
	12:19	w should not be **spoken** to them	3056
	12:27	And this w, Yet once more, signifieth	NIG
	13: 7	who have spoken unto you the w of God:	3056
	13:22	brethren, suffer the w of exhortation:	3056
Jas	1:18	Of his own will begat he us with the w of	3056
	1:21	receive with meekness the engrafted w,	3056
	1:22	But be ye doers of the w, and not hearers	3056
	1:23	For if any be a hearer of the w, and not a	3056
	3: 2	If any man offend not in w, the same is a	3056
1Pe	1:23	by the w of God, which liveth and	3056
	1:25	But the w of the Lord endureth for ever.	4487
	1:25	And this is the w which by the gospel is	4487
	2: 2	desire the sincere milk of the w,	3050
	2: 8	even to them which stumble at the w,	3056
	3: 1	that, if any obey not the w, they also may	3056
	3: 1	they also may without the w be won by	3056
2Pe	1:19	We have also a more sure w of prophecy;	3056
	3: 5	that by the w of God the heavens were of	3056
	3: 7	are now, by the same w are kept in store,	3056
1Jn	1: 1	our hands have handled, of the W of life;	3056
	1:10	we make him a liar, and his w is not in us.	3056
	2: 5	But whoso keepeth his w, in him verily is	3056
	2: 7	The old commandment is the w which ye	3056
	2:14	and the w of God abideth in you,	3056
	3:18	let us not love in w, neither in tongue;	3056
Rev	1: 2	Who bare record of the w of God,	3056
	1: 9	for the w of God, and for the testimony of	3056
	3: 8	hast kept my w, and hast not denied my	3056
	3:10	Because thou hast kept the w of my	3056
	6: 9	of them that were slain for the w of God,	3056
	12:11	Lamb, and by the w of their testimony;	3056
	19:13	and his name is called The W of God.	3056
	20: 4	and for the w of God, and which had not	3056

WORD'S (2) [WORD]

2Sa	7:21	For thy w sake, and according to thine	1697
Mk	4:17	or persecution ariseth for the w sake,	3056

WORDS (547) [WORD]

Ge	24:30	he heard the w of Rebekah his sister,	1697
	24:52	when Abraham's servant heard their w,	1697
	27:34	when Esau heard the w of his father,	1697
	27:42	these w of Esau her elder son were told	1697
	31: 1	he heard the w of Laban's sons, saying,	1697
	34:18	their w pleased Hamor, and Shechem	1697
	37: 8	the more for his dreams, and for his w.	1697
	39:17	she spake unto him according to these w,	1697
	39:19	when his master heard the w of his wife,	1697
	42:16	in prison, that your w may be proved,	1697
	42:20	shall your w be verified, and ye shall not	1697
	43: 7	him according to the tenor of these w:	1697
	44: 6	and he spake unto them these same w.	1697
	44: 7	Wherefore saith my lord these w?	1697
	44:10	Now also let it be according unto your w:	1697
	44:24	my father, we told him the w of my lord.	1697
	45:27	they told him all the w of Joseph, which	1697
	49:21	is a hind let loose: he giveth goodly w.	561
Ex	4:15	speak unto him, and put w in his mouth:	1697
	4:28	Moses told Aaron all the w of the LORD	1697
	4:30	Aaron spake all the w which the LORD	1697
	5: 9	and let them not regard vain w.	1697
	19: 6	These are the w which thou shalt speak	1697
	19: 7	laid before their faces all these w which	1697
	19: 8	Moses returned the w of the people unto	1697
	19: 9	Moses told the w of the people unto	1697
	20: 1	And God spake all these w, saying,	1697
	23: 8	and perverteth the w of the righteous.	1697
	24: 3	told the people all the w of the LORD,	1697
	24: 3	All the w which the LORD hath said will	1697
	24: 4	Moses wrote all the w of the LORD,	1697
	24: 8	made with you concerning all these w.	1697
	34: 1	I will write upon these tables the w that	1697
	34:27	said unto Moses, Write thou these w:	1697
	34:27	for after the tenor of these w I have made	1697
	34:28	he wrote upon the tables the w of	1697
	35: 1	These are the w which the LORD hath	1697
Nu	11:24	told the people the w of the LORD,	1697
	12: 6	he said, Hear now my w: If there be a	1697
	16:31	had made an end of speaking all these w,	1697
	22: 7	and spake unto him the w of Balak.	1697
	24: 4	He hath said, which heard the w of	561
	24:16	which heard the w of God, and knew	561
Dt	1: 1	These be the w which Moses spake unto	1697
	1:34	The LORD heard the voice of your w,	1697
	2:26	Sihon king of Heshbon with w of peace,	1697
	4:10	and I will make them hear my w,	1697
	4:12	ye heard the voice of the w, but saw no	1697
	4:36	thou heardest his w out of the midst of	1697
	5:22	These w the LORD spake unto all your	1697
	5:28	The LORD heard the voice of your	1697
	5:28	I have heard the voice of the w of this	1697
	6: 6	these w, which I command thee this day,	1697
	9:10	them was written according to all the w,	1697
	10: 2	I will write on the tables the w that were	1697
	11:18	Therefore shall ye lay up these my w in	1697

Dt 12:28 hear all these **w** which I command thee,	1697	
13: 3 Thou shalt not hearken unto the **w** of that	1697	
16:19 wise, and pervert the **w** of the righteous.	1697	
17:19 to keep all the **w** of this law and	1697	
18:18 thee, and will put my **w** in his mouth;	1697	
18:19 whosoever will not hearken unto my **w**	1697	
27: 3 shalt write upon them all the **w** of this	1697	
27: 8 shalt write upon the stones all the **w** of	1697	
27:26 *be* he that confirmeth not *all* the **w**	1697	
28:14 thou shalt not go aside from any of the **w**	1697	
28:58 If thou wilt not observe to do all the **w** of	1697	
29: 1 These *are* the **w** of the covenant, which	1697	
29: 9 Keep therefore the **w** of this covenant,	1697	
29:19 when he heareth the **w** of this curse,	1697	
29:29 that *we* may do all the **w** of this law.	1697	
31: 1 and spake these **w** unto all Israel.	1697	
31:12 and observe to do all the **w** of this law:	1697	
31:24 end of writing the **w** of this law in a book,	1697	
31:28 that I may speak these **w** in their ears,	1697	
31:30 congregation of Israel the **w** of this song,	1697	
32: 1 and hear, O earth, the **w** of my mouth.	561	
32:44 spake all the **w** of this song in the ears of	1697	
32:45 made an end of speaking all these **w**	1697	
32:46 Set your hearts unto all the **w** which I	1697	
32:46 to observe to do, all the **w** of this law.	1697	
33: 3 thy feet; *every one* shall receive of thy **w.**	1703	
Jos 1:18 will not hearken unto thy **w** in all that	1697	
2:21 she said, According unto your **w**, so *be* it.	1697	
3: 9 and hear the **w** of the Lord your God.	1697	
8:34 afterward he read all the **w** of the law,	1697	
22:30 heard the **w** that the children of Reuben	1697	
24:26 wrote these **w** in the book of the law	1697	
24:27 for it hath heard all the **w** of the Lord	561	
Jdg 2: 4 these **w** unto all the children of Israel,	1697	
9: 3 of all the men of Shechem all these **w:**	1697	
9:30 Zebul the ruler of the city heard the **w**	1697	
11:10 if we do not so according to thy **w.**	1697	
11:11 Jephthah uttered all his **w** before	1697	
11:28 the **w** of Jephthah which he sent him.	1697	
13:12 said, Now let thy **w** come to pass.	1697	
16:16 when she pressed him daily with her **w,**	1697	
1Sa 3:19 did let none of his **w** fall to the ground.	1697	
8:10 Samuel told all the **w** of the Lord unto	1697	
8:21 Samuel heard all the **w** of the people,	1697	
15: 1 hearken thou unto the voice of the **w** of	1697	
15:24 commandment of the Lord, and thy **w:**	1697	
17:11 all Israel heard those **w** of the Philistine,	1697	
17:23 and spake according to the same **w:**	1697	
17:31 the **w** were heard which David spake,	1697	
18:23 Saul's servants spake these **w** in the ears	1697	
18:26 when his servants told David these **w,**	1697	
21:12 David laid up these **w** in his heart,	1697	
24: 7 David stayed his servants with *these* **w,**	1697	
24: 9 Wherefore hearest thou men's **w,** saying,	1697	
24:16 an end of speaking these **w** unto Saul,	1697	
25: 9 to all those **w** in the name of David,	1697	
25:24 and hear the **w** of thine handmaid.	1697	
26:19 let my lord the king hear the **w** of his	1697	
28:20 sore afraid, because of the **w** of Samuel:	1697	
28:21 have hearkened unto thy **w** which thou	1697	
2Sa 3: 8 was Abner very wroth for the **w** of	1697	
7:17 According to all these **w,** and according	1697	
7:28 thy **w** be true, and thou hast promised	1697	
14: 3 unto him. So Joab put the **w** in her mouth.	1697	
14:19 he put all these **w** in the mouth of thine	1697	
19:43 the **w** of the men of Judah were fiercer	1697	
19:43 fiercer than the **w** of the men of Israel.	1697	
20:17 unto him, Hear the **w** of thine handmaid.	1697	
22: 1 David spake unto the Lord the **w** of this	1697	
23: 1 Now these *be* the last **w** of David.	1697	
1Ki 1:14 come in after thee, and confirm thy **w.**	1697	
5: 7 when Hiram heard the **w** of Solomon,	1697	
8:59 let these my **w,** wherewith I have made	1697	
10: 7 I believed not the **w,** until I came,	1697	
12: 7 speak good **w** to them, then they will be	1697	
13:11 **w** which he had spoken unto the king,	1697	
21:27 came to pass, when Ahab heard those **w,**	1697	
22:13 the **w** of the prophets *declare* good unto	1697	
2Ki 1: 7 up to meet you, and told you these **w?**	1697	
6:12 telleth the king of Israel the **w** that thou	1697	
6:30 when the king heard the **w** of the woman,	1697	
18:20 Thou sayest, (but *they are but* vain **w,**)	1697	
18:27 thy master, and to thee, to speak these **w?**	1697	
18:37 and told him the **w** of Rab-shakeh.	1697	
19: 4 thy God will hear all the **w** of Rab-shakeh,	1697	
19: 4 will reprove the **w** which the Lord thy	1697	
19: 6 Be not afraid of the **w** which thou hast	1697	
19:16 hear the **w** of Sennacherib, which hath	1697	
22:11 the king had heard the **w** of the book	1697	
22:13 the **w** of this book that is found:	1697	
22:13 fathers have not hearkened unto the **w**	1697	
22:16 *even* all the **w** of the book which the king	1697	
22:18 *As touching* the **w** which thou hast heard;	1697	
23: 2 he read in their ears all the **w** of the book	1697	
23: 3 perform the **w** of this covenant that were	1697	
23:16 proclaimed, who proclaimed these **w.**	1697	
23:24 that he might perform the **w** of the law	1697	
1Ch 17:15 According to all these **w,** and according	1697	
23:27 For by the last **w** of David, the Levites	1697	
25: 5 of Heman the king's seer in the **w** of God,	1697	
2Ch 9: 6 Howbeit I believed not their **w,** until I	1697	
10: 7 please them, and speak good **w** to them,	1697	
10: 7 they obeyed the **w** of the Lord,	1697	
15: 8 Asa heard these **w,** and the prophecy	1697	
18:12 the **w** of the prophets *declare* good to	1697	

2Ch 29:15 by the **w** of the Lord, to cleanse	1697	
29:30 unto the Lord with the **w** of David,	1697	
32: 8 people rested themselves upon the **w** of	1697	
33:18 the **w** of the seers that spake to him in	1697	
34:19 the king had heard the **w** of the law,	1697	
34:21 the **w** of the book that is found:	1697	
34:26 *concerning* the **w** which thou hast heard;	1697	
34:27 thou heardest his **w** against this place,	1697	
34:30 he read in their ears all the **w** of the book	1697	
34:31 to perform the **w** of the covenant which	1697	
35:22 hearkened not unto the **w** of Necho from	1697	
36:16 despised his **w,** and misused his prophets,	1697	
Ezr 7:11 *even* a scribe of the **w** of	1697	
9: 4 trembled at the **w** of the God of Israel,	1697	
Ne 1: 1 The **w** of Nehemiah the son of Hachaliah.	1697	
1: 4 when I heard these **w,** *that* I sat down	1697	
2:18 as also the king's **w** that he had spoken	1697	
5: 6 angry when I heard their cry and these **w.**	1697	
6: 6 be their king, according to these **w.**	1697	
6: 7 reported to the king according to these **w.**	1697	
6:19 before me, and uttered my **w** to him.	1697	
8: 9 when they heard the **w** of the law.	1697	
8:12 they had understood the **w** that were	1697	
8:13 even to understand the **w** of the law.	1697	
9: 8 to his seed, and hast performed thy **w,**	1697	
Est 4: 9 and told Esther the **w** of Mordecai.	1697	
4:12 And they told to Mordecai Esther's **w.**	1697	
9:26 Therefore for all the **w** of this letter,	1697	
9:30 of Ahasuerus, *with* **w** of peace and truth,	1697	
Job 4: 4 have upholden him that was falling,	4405	
6: 3 sea: therefore my **w** are swallowed up.	1697	
6:10 for I have not concealed the **w** of the Holy	561	
6:25 How forcible are right **w!** but what doth	561	
6:26 Do ye imagine to reprove **w,**	4405	
8: 2 *how long shall* the **w** of thy mouth *be like*	561	
8:10 tell thee, and utter **w** out of their heart?	4405	
9:14 choose out my **w** *to reason* with him?	4405	
11: 2 Should not the multitude of **w** be	1697	
12:11 Doth not the ear try **w?** and the mouth	4405	
15:13 and lettest *such* **w** go out of thy mouth?	4405	
16: 3 Shall vain **w** have an end?	4405	
16: 4 I could heap up **w** against you,	4405	
18: 2 long *will it be ere* you make an end of **w?**	4405	
19: 2 my soul, and break me in pieces with **w?**	4405	
19:23 O that my **w** were now written! O that	4405	
22:22 his mouth, and lay up his **w** in thine heart.	561	
23: 5 I would know the **w** *which* he would	4405	
23:12 I have esteemed the **w** of his mouth more	561	
26: 4 To whom hast thou uttered **w?**	4405	
29:22 After my **w** they spake not again;	1697	
31:40 instead of barley. The **w** of Job are ended.	1697	
32:11 Behold, I waited for your **w;** I gave ear to	1697	
32:12 convinced Job, *or* that answered his **w:**	561	
32:14 he hath not directed *his* **w** against me:	4405	
33: 1 my speeches, and hearken to all my **w.**	1697	
33: 3 My **w** *shall be of* the uprightness of my	561	
33: 5 set *thy* **w** in order before me, stand up.	NIH	
33: 8 I have heard the voice of *thy* **w,**	4405	
34: 2 Hear my **w,** O ye wise *men;* and give ear	4405	
34: 3 For the ear trieth **w,** as the mouth tasteth	4405	
34:16 hear this: hearken to the voice of my **w.**	4405	
34:35 and his **w** *were* without wisdom.	1697	
34:37 and multiplieth his **w** against God.	561	
35:16 he multiplieth **w** without knowledge.	4405	
36: 4 truly my **w** *shall* not *be* false: he that *is*	4405	
38: 2 Who *is* this that darkeneth counsel by **w**	4405	
41: 3 unto thee? will he speak soft **w** unto thee?	NIH	
42: 7 that after the Lord had spoken these **w**	1697	
Ps 5: 1 Give ear to my **w,** O Lord, consider my	561	
7: 1 concerning the **w** of Cush the Benjamite.	1697	
12: 6 The **w** of the Lord *are* pure words:	565	
12: 6 The words of the Lord *are* pure **w:**	565	
18: 1 who spake unto the Lord the **w** of this	1697	
19: 4 and their **w** to the end of the world.	4405	
19:14 the **w** of my mouth, and the meditation	561	
22: 1 *and from* the **w** of my roaring?	1697	
36: 3 The **w** of his mouth *are* iniquity and	1697	
50:17 and castest my **w** behind thee.	1697	
52: 4 Thou lovest all devouring **w,** O thou	1697	
54: 2 O God; give ear to the **w** of my mouth.	561	
55:21 The **w** *of his* mouth were smoother than	NIH	
55:21 his **w** were softer than oil, yet *were* they	1697	
56: 5 Every day they wrest my **w:** all their	1697	
59:12 the **w** of their lips let them even be taken	1697	
64: 3 *bows to shoot* their arrows, *even* bitter **w:**	1697	
78: 1 incline your ears to the **w** of my mouth.	561	
106:12 believed they his **w;** they sang his praise.	1697	
107:11 they rebelled against the **w** of God,	561	
109: 3 They compassed me about also *with* **w** of	1697	
119:57 I have said that *I* would keep thy **w.**	1697	
119:103 How sweet are thy **w** unto my taste!	565	
119:130 The entrance of thy **w** giveth light;	1697	
119:139 mine enemies have forgotten thy **w.**	1697	
138: 4 when they hear the **w** of thy mouth.	561	
141: 6 in stony places, they shall hear my **w;**	561	
Pr 1: 2 to perceive the **w** of understanding;	1697	
1: 6 the **w** of the wise, and their dark sayings.	1697	
1:21 in the city she uttereth her **w,** *saying,*	561	
1:23 I will make known my **w** unto you.	1697	
2: 1 if thou wilt receive my **w,** and hide my	561	
2:16 the stranger *which* flattereth with her **w;**	561	
4: 4 unto me, Let thine heart retain my **w:**	1697	
4: 5 neither decline from the **w** of my mouth.	561	
4:20 My son, attend to my **w;** incline thine ear	1697	
5: 7 and depart not from the **w** of my mouth.	561	

Pr 6: 2 Thou art snared with the **w** of thy mouth,	561	
6: 2 thou art taken with the **w** of thy mouth.	561	
7: 1 keep my **w,** and lay up my commandments	561	
7: 5 the stranger *which* flattereth with her **w.**	561	
7:24 and attend to the **w** of my mouth.	561	
8: 8 the **w** of my mouth *are* in righteousness;	561	
10:19 the multitude of **w** there wanteth not sin:	1697	
12: 6 The **w** of the wicked *are* to lie in wait *for*	1697	
15: 1 away wrath: but grievous **w** stir up anger.	1697	
15:26 but *the* **w** *of* the pure *are* pleasant words.	NIH	
15:26 but the *words of* the pure *are* pleasant **w.**	NIH	
16:24 Pleasant **w** *are as* a honeycomb, sweet to	561	
17:27 He that hath knowledge spareth his **w:**	561	
18: 4 The **w** of a man's mouth *are as* deep	1697	
18: 8 The **w** of a talebearer *are as* wounds,	1697	
19: 7 he pursueth *them with* **w,** yet they are	561	
19:27 *causeth* to err from the **w** of knowledge.	561	
22:12 overthroweth the **w** of the transgressor.	1697	
22:17 hear the **w** of the wise, and apply thine	561	
22:21 thee know the certainty of the **w** of truth;	561	
22:21 that *thou* mightest answer the **w** of truth	561	
23: 8 thou vomit up, and lose thy sweet **w.**	1697	
23: 9 for he will despise the wisdom of thy **w.**	4405	
23:12 and thine ears to the **w** of knowledge.	561	
26:22 The **w** of a talebearer *are as* wounds,	1697	
29:19 A servant will not be corrected by **w:**	1697	
29:20 Seest thou a man that is hasty in his **w?**	1697	
30: 1 The **w** of Agur the son of Jakeh, *even*	1697	
30: 6 Add thou not unto his **w,** lest he reprove	1697	
31: 1 The **w** of king Lemuel, the prophecy that	1697	
Ecc 1: 1 The **w** of the Preacher, the son of David,	1697	
5: 2 upon earth: therefore let thy **w** be few.	1697	
5: 3 fool's voice *is known* by multitude of **w.**	1697	
5: 7 many **w** *there are* also *divers* vanities:	1697	
7:21 Also take no heed unto all **w** that are	1697	
9:16 *is* despised, and his **w** are not heard.	1697	
9:17 The **w** of wise *men* are heard in quiet,	1697	
10:12 **w** of a wise *man's* mouth *are* gracious;	1697	
10:13 The beginning of the **w** of his mouth *is*	1697	
10:14 A fool also is full of **w:** a man cannot tell	1697	
12:10 Preacher sought to find out acceptable **w:**	1697	
12:10 *was* written *was* upright, *even* **w** of truth.	1697	
12:11 The **w** of the wise *are* as goads, and as	1697	
Isa 29:11 as the **w** of a book that is sealed,	1697	
29:18 in that day shall the deaf hear the **w** of	1697	
31: 2 bring evil, and will not call back his **w:**	1697	
32: 7 devices to destroy the poor with lying **w,**	561	
36: 5 *sayest* thou, (but *they are but* vain **w,**)	1697	
36:12 thy master and to thee to speak these **w?**	1697	
36:13 said, Hear ye the **w** of the great king,	1697	
36:22 and told him the **w** of Rabshakeh.	1697	
37: 4 thy God will hear the **w** of Rabshakeh,	1697	
37: 4 will reprove the **w** which the Lord thy	1697	
37: 6 not afraid of the **w** that thou hast heard,	1697	
37:17 hear all the **w** of Sennacherib, which hath	1697	
41:26 yea, *there is* none that heareth your **w.**	561	
51:16 I have put my **w** in thy mouth,	1697	
58:13 own pleasure, nor speaking *thine own* **w:**	1697	
59:13 uttering from the heart **w** of falsehood.	1697	
59:21 and my **w** which I have put in thy mouth,	1697	
Jer 1: 1 The **w** of Jeremiah the son of Hilkiah,	1697	
1: 9 Behold, I have put my **w** in thy mouth.	1697	
3:12 and proclaim these **w** toward the north,	1697	
5:14 I will make my **w** in thy mouth fire,	1697	
6:19 they have not hearkened unto my **w,**	1697	
7: 4 Trust ye not in lying **w,** saying, The	1697	
7: 8 Behold, ye trust in lying **w,** that cannot	1697	
7:27 thou shalt speak all these **w** unto	1697	
11: 2 Hear ye the **w** of this covenant,	1697	
11: 3 *be* the man that obeyeth not the **w**	1697	
11: 6 Proclaim all these **w** in the cities of Judah,	1697	
11: 6 Hear ye the **w** of this covenant,	1697	
11: 8 I will bring upon them all the **w** of this	1697	
11:10 which refused to hear my **w;**	1697	
12: 6 though they speak fair **w** unto thee.	NIH	
13:10 evil people, which refuse to hear my **w,**	1697	
15:16 Thy **w** were found, and I did eat them;	1697	
16:10 thou shalt shew this people all these **w,**	1697	
18: 2 and there I will cause thee to hear my **w.**	1697	
18:18 and let us not give heed to any of his **w.**	1697	
19: 2 proclaim there the **w** that I shall tell thee,	1697	
19:15 necks, that *they* might not hear my **w.**	1697	
22: 5 if ye will not hear these **w,** I swear by	1697	
23: 9 and because of the **w** of his holiness.	1697	
23:16 Hearken not unto the **w** of the prophets	1697	
23:22 had caused my people to hear my **w,** then	1697	
23:30 that steal my **w** every one from his	1697	
23:36 for ye have perverted the **w** of the living	1697	
25: 8 hosts; Because ye have not heard my **w,**	1697	
25:13 I will bring upon that land all my **w**	1697	
25:30 prophesy thou against them all these **w,**	1697	
26: 2 all the **w** that I command thee to speak	1697	
26: 5 To hearken to the **w** of my servants	1697	
26: 7 these **w** in the house of the Lord.	1697	
26:12 against this city all the **w** that ye have	1697	
26:15 unto you to speak all these **w** in your ears.	1697	
26:20 against this land according to all the **w** of	1697	
26:21 and all the princes, heard his **w,**	1697	
27:12 king of Judah according to all these **w,**	1697	
27:14 Therefore hearken not unto the **w** of	1697	
27:16 Hearken not to the **w** of your prophets	1697	
28: 6 the Lord perform thy **w** which thou hast	1697	
29: 1 Now these *are* the **w** of the letter that	1697	
29:19 they have not hearkened unto my **w,**	1697	
29:23 have spoken lying **w** in my name, which I	1697	

Jer	30: 2 Write thee all the **w** that I have spoken	1697
	30: 4 these *are* the **w** that the Lᴏʀᴅ spake	1697
	34: 6 Jeremiah the prophet spake all these **w**	1697
	34:18 which have not performed the **w** of	1697
	35:13 receive instruction to hearken to my **w**?	1697
	35:14 The **w** of Jonadab the son of Rechab,	1697
	36: 2 write therein all the **w** that I have spoken	1697
	36: 4 mouth of Jeremiah all the **w** of the Lᴏʀᴅ,	1697
	36: 6 the **w** of the Lᴏʀᴅ in the ears of	1697
	36: 8 reading in the book the **w** of the Lᴏʀᴅ *in*	1697
	36:10 Baruch in the book the **w** of Jeremiah	1697
	36:11 had heard out of the book all the **w** of	1697
	36:13 Michaiah declared unto them all the **w**	1697
	36:16 to pass when they had heard all the **w**,	1697
	36:16 We will surely tell the king of all these **w**	1697
	36:17 How didst thou write all these **w** at his	1697
	36:18 He pronounced all these **w** unto me with	1697
	36:20 and told all the **w** in the ears of the king.	1697
	36:24 any of his servants that heard all these **w**	1697
	36:27 the **w** which Baruch wrote at the mouth	1697
	36:28 write in it all the former **w** that were in	1697
	36:32 **w** of the book which Jehoiakim king of	1697
	36:32 added besides unto them many like **w**.	1697
	37: 2 did hearken unto the **w** of the Lᴏʀᴅ,	1697
	38: 1 heard the **w** that Jeremiah had spoken	1697
	38: 4 people, in speaking such **w** unto them:	1697
	38:24 Let no man know of these **w**, and thou	1697
	38:27 he told them according to all these **w** that	1697
	39:16 I *will* bring my **w** upon this city for evil,	1697
	42: 4 the Lᴏʀᴅ your God according to your **w**;	1697
	43: 1 people all the **w** of the Lᴏʀᴅ their God,	1697
	43: 1 had sent him to them, *even* all these **w**;	1697
	44:28 shall know whose **w** shall stand, mine,	1697
	44:29 that ye may know that my **w** shall surely	1697
	45: 1 when he had written these **w** in a book	1697
	51:60 *even* all these **w** that are written against	1697
	51:61 and shalt see, and shalt read all these **w**;	1697
	51:64 be weary. Thus far *are* the **w** of Jeremiah.	1697
Eze	2: 6 be not afraid of their **w**, though briers	1697
	2: 6 be not afraid of their **w**, nor be dismayed	1697
	2: 7 thou shalt speak my **w** unto them,	1697
	3: 4 of Israel, and speak with my **w** unto them.	1697
	3: 6 whose **w** thou canst not understand.	1697
	3:10 my **w** that I shall speak unto thee receive	1697
	12:28 There shall none of my **w** be prolonged	1697
	33:31 hear thy **w**, but they will not do them:	1697
	33:32 they hear thy **w**, but they do them not.	1697
	35:13 and have multiplied your **w** against me:	1697
Da	2: 9 and corrupt **w** to speak before me,	4406
	5:10 reason of the **w** of the king and his lords,	4406
	6:14 king, when he heard *these* **w**, was sore	4406
	7:11 the voice of the great **w** which the horn	4406
	7:25 he shall speak *great* **w** against the most	4406
	9:12 he hath confirmed his **w**, which he spake	1697
	10: 6 the voice of his **w** like the voice of a	1697
	10: 9 Yet heard I the voice of his **w**: and when	1697
	10: 9 when I heard the voice of his **w**, then	1697
	10:11 understand the **w** that I speak unto thee,	1697
	10:12 thy **w** were heard, and I am come for thy	1697
	10:12 were heard, and I am come for thy **w**.	1697
	10:15 when he had spoken such **w** unto me,	1697
	12: 4 Daniel, shut up the **w**, and seal the book,	1697
	12: 9 for the **w** *are* closed up and sealed till	1697
Hos	6: 5 I have slain them by the **w** of my mouth:	561
	10: 4 They have spoken **w**, swearing falsely in	1697
	14: 2 Take with you **w**, and turn to the Lᴏʀᴅ:	1697
Am	1: 1 The **w** of Amos, who was among	1697
	7:10 the land is not able to bear all his **w**.	1697
	8:11 but of hearing the **w** of the Lᴏʀᴅ:	1697
Mic	2: 7 do not my **w** do good to him that walketh	1697
Hag	1:12 the **w** of Haggai the prophet, as the Lᴏʀᴅ	1697
Zec	1: 6 **w** and my statutes, which I commanded	1697
	1:13 angel that talked with me *with* good **w**	1697
	1:13 me *with* good words *and* comfortable **w**.	1697
	7: 7 *Should ye* not *hear* the **w** which	1697
	7:12 the **w** which the Lᴏʀᴅ of hosts hath sent	1697
	8: 9 ye that hear in these days these **w** by	1697
Mal	2:17 Ye have wearied the Lᴏʀᴅ with your **w**.	1697
	3:13 Your **w** have been stout against me,	1697
Mt	10:14 hear your **w**, when ye depart out of that	3056
	12:37 For by thy **w** thou shalt be justified,	3056
	12:37 and by thy **w** thou shalt be condemned.	3056
	22:22 When they had heard *these* **w**, they	NIG
	24:35 pass away, but my **w** shall not pass away.	3056
	26:44 prayed the third time, saying the same **w**.	3056
Mk	8:38 and of my **w** in this adulterous and	3056
	the disciples were astonished at his **w**.	3056
	12:13 of the Herodians, to catch him in *his* **w**.	3056
	13:31 pass away: but my **w** shall not pass away.	3056
	14:39 and prayed, and spake the same **w**.	3056
Lk	1:20 because thou believest not my **w**,	3056
	3: 4 As it is written in the book of the **w** of	3056
	4:22 wondered at the gracious **w** which	3056
	9:26 shall be ashamed of me and of my **w**,	3056
	20:20 men, that they might take hold of his **w**,	3056
	20:26 And they could not take hold of his **w**	4487
	21:33 pass away: but my **w** shall not pass away.	3056
	23: 9 Then he questioned *with* him in many **w**;	3056
	24: 8 And they remembered his **w**,	4487
	24:11 And their **w** seemed to them as idle tales,	4487
	24:44 These *are* the **w** which I spake unto you,	3056
Jn	3:34 he whom God hath sent speaketh the **w**	4487
	5:47 his writings, how shall ye believe my **w**?	4487
	6:63 **w** that I speak unto you, *they* are spirit,	4487
	6:68 we go? thou hast the **w** of eternal life.	4487

Jn	7: 9 When he had said these **w** unto them,	NIG
	8:20 These **w** spake Jesus in the treasury, as he	4487
	8:30 he spake these **w**, many believed on him.	NIG
	8:47 He that is of God heareth God's **w**:	4487
	9:22 These **w** spake his parents, because	NIG
	9:40 which were with him heard these **w**,	NIG
	10:21 These are not the **w** of him that hath a	4487
	12:47 if any *man* hear my **w**, and believe not,	4487
	12:48 rejecteth me, and receiveth not my **w**,	4487
	14:10 the **w** that I speak unto you, I speak not	4487
	14:23 If a man love me, he will keep my **w**:	3056
	15: 7 If ye abide in me, and my **w** abide in you,	4487
	17: 1 These **w** spake Jesus, and lift up his eyes	NIG
	17: 8 For I have given unto them the **w** which	4487
	18: 1 When Jesus had spoken these **w**, he went	NIG
Ac	2:14 known unto you, and hearken to my **w**:	4487
	2:22 Ye men of Israel, hear these **w**; Jesus of	3056
	2:40 with many other **w** did he testify and	3056
	5: 5 And Ananias hearing these **w** fell down,	3056
	5:20 in the temple to the people all the **w**	4487
	6:11 have heard him speak blasphemous **w**	4487
	6:13 blasphemous **w** against this holy place,	4487
	7:22 and was mighty in **w** and in deeds.	3056
	10:22 into his house, and to hear **w** of thee.	4487
	10:44 While Peter yet spake these **w**, the Holy	4487
	11:14 Who shall tell thee **w**, whereby thou and	4487
	13:42 Gentiles besought that these **w** might be	4487
	15:15 And to this agree the **w** of the prophets;	3056
	15:24 out from us have troubled you with **w**,	3056
	15:32 exhorted the brethren with many **w**,	3056
	16:38 And the sergeants told these **w** unto	4487
	18:15 But if it be a question of **w** and names,	3056
	20:35 and to remember the **w** of the Lord Jesus,	3056
	20:38 Sorrowing most *of all* for the **w** which he	3056
	24: 4 hear us of thy clemency a **few w**.	4935
	26:25 but speak forth the **w** of truth and	4487
	28:29 And when he had said these **w**, the Jews	NIG
Ro	10:18 and their **w** unto the ends of the world.	4487
	16:18 and by **good w** and fair speeches deceive	5542
1Co	1:17 not with wisdom of **w**, lest the cross of	3056
	2: 4 my preaching *was* not with enticing **w** of	3056
	2:13 in the **w** which man's wisdom teacheth,	3056
	14: 9 except ye utter by the tongue **w** easy to	3056
	14:19 in the church I had rather speak five **w**	3056
	14:19 ten thousand **w** in an *unknown* tongue.	3056
2Co	12: 4 and heard unspeakable **w**, which *it is* not	4487
Eph	3: 3 the mystery; (as I wrote afore in few **w**,	NIG
	5: 6 Let no *man* deceive you with vain **w**:	3056
Col	2: 4 *man* should beguile you with **enticing w**.	4086
1Th	2: 5 neither at any time used we flattering **w**,	3056
	4:18 comfort one another with these **w**.	3056
1Ti	6: 3 nourished up in the **w** of faith and of good	3056
	6: 3 and consent not to wholesome **w**,	3056
	6: 3 *even* the **w** of our Lord Jesus Christ,	NIG
	6: 4 doting about questions and **strifes of w**,	3055
2Ti	1:13 Hold fast the form of sound **w**, which	3056
	2:14 that *they* **strive** not *about* **w** to no profit,	3054
	4:15 for he hath greatly withstood our **w**.	3056
Heb	12:19 sound of a trumpet, and the voice of **w**;	4487
	13:22 I have written a letter unto you in few **w**.	NIG
2Pe	2: 3 with feigned **w** make merchandise of you:	3056
	2:18 For when they speak great swelling **w** of	NIG
	3: 2 That *ye* may be mindful of the **w** which	4487
3Jn	1:10 prating against us with malicious **w**:	3056
Jude	1:16 their mouth speaketh great swelling **w**,	NIG
	1:17 remember ye the **w** which were spoken	4487
Rev	1: 3 they that hear the **w** of *this* prophecy,	3056
	17:17 until the **w** of God shall be fulfilled.	4487
	21: 5 Write: for these **w** are true and faithful.	3056
	22:18 the **w** of the prophecy of this book,	3056
	22:19 if any *man* shall take away from the **w**	3056

WORK (419) [FELLOWWORKERS, HANDYWORK, NEEDLEWORK, NETWORK, NETWORKS, WORK'S, WORKER, WORKERS, WORKETH, WORKFELLOW, WORKING, WORKMAN, WORKMANSHIP, WORKMEN, WORKMEN'S, WORKS, WORKS']

Ge	2: 2 on seventh day God ended his **w**	4399
	2: 2 rested on the seventh day from all his **w**	4399
	2: 3 that in it he had rested from all his **w**	4399
	5:29 *same* shall comfort us concerning our **w**	4639
Ex	5: 9 Let there more **w** be laid upon the men,	5656
	5:11 not ought of your **w** *shall be* diminished.	5656
	5:18 Go therefore now, *and* **w**; for there shall	5647
	12:16 no *manner of* **w** shall be done in them,	4399
	14:31 Israel saw *that* great **w** which the Lᴏʀᴅ	3027
	18:20 must walk, and the **w** that they must do.	4639
	20: 9 days shalt thou labour, and do all thy **w**:	4399
	20:10 *in it* thou shalt not do any **w**, thou,	4399
	23:12 Six days thou shalt do thy **w**, and on	4639
	24:10 as it were a paved **w** of a sapphire stone,	4639
	25:18 *of* **beaten w** shalt thou make them;	4749
	25:31 **beaten w** shall the candlestick be made:	4749
	25:36 all it shall be one **beaten w** *of* pure gold.	4749
	26: 1 *with* cherubims *of* **cunning w** shalt thou	4639
	26:31 and fine twined linen *of* **cunning w**:	4639
	28: 6 fine twined linen, *with* **cunning w**.	4639
	28: 8 of the same, according to the **w** thereof;	4639
	28:11 *With* the **w** of an engraver in stone, *like*	4639
	28:14 *of* **wreathen w** shalt thou make them,	4639
	28:15 breastplate of judgment *with* **cunning w**;	4639
	28:15 after the **w** of the ephod thou shalt make	4639
	28:22 at the ends *of* **wreathen w** *of* pure gold.	4639
	28:32 it shall have a binding of woven **w** round	4639

Ex	31: 4 to **w** in gold, and in silver, and in brass,	6213
	31: 5 to **w** in all *manner of* workmanship,	6213
	31:14 for whosoever doeth *any* **w** therein, that	4399
	31:15 Six days may **w** be done; but in the	4399
	31:15 doeth *any* **w** in the sabbath day,	4399
	32:16 the tables *were* the **w** of God,	4639
	34:10 thou *art* shall see the **w** of the Lᴏʀᴅ:	4639
	34:21 Six days thou shalt **w**, but on the seventh	5647
	35: 2 Six days shall **w** be done, but on	4399
	35: 2 whosoever doeth **w** therein shall be put	4399
	35:21 **w** of the tabernacle of the congregation,	4399
	35:24 shittim wood for any **w** of the service,	4399
	35:29 them willing to bring for all *manner of* **w**,	4399
	35:32 to **w** in gold, and in silver, and in brass,	6213
	35:33 to make any *manner of* **cunning w**.	4639
	35:35 to **w** all *manner of* work, of the engraver,	6213
	35:35 to **w** all *manner of* **w**, of the engraver,	4399
	35:35 *even* of them that do any **w**, and of those	4399
	35:35 of **those that devise cunning w**.	2803+4284
	36: 1 understanding to know how to **w** all	6213
	36: 1 *of* **w** for the service of the sanctuary,	4399
	36: 2 him up to come unto the **w** to do it:	4399
	36: 3 for the **w** of the service of the sanctuary,	4399
	36: 4 all the wise *men*, that wrought all the **w**	4399
	36: 4 came every man from his **w** which they	4399
	36: 5 than enough for the service of the **w**,	4399
	36: 6 more **w** for the offering of the sanctuary.	4399
	36: 7 was sufficient for all the **w** to make it,	4399
	36: 8 **w** *of* the tabernacle made ten curtains *of*	4399
	36: 8 *with* cherubims *of* **cunning w** made he	4639
	36:35 *with* cherubims made he it *of* **cunning w**.	4639
	37:17 *of* **beaten w** made he the candlestick;	4749
	37:22 all of it *was* one **beaten w** *of* pure gold.	4749
	37:29 *according to* the **w** of the apothecary.	4639
	38:24 All the gold that was occupied for the **w**	4399
	38:24 **w** of the holy *place*, even the gold of	4399
	39: 3 to **w** *it* in the blue, and in the purple,	6213
	39: 3 in the fine linen, *with* **cunning w**.	4639
	39: 5 of the same, according to the **w** thereof;	4639
	39: 8 he made the breastplate *of* **cunning w**,	4639
	39: 8 *of* **cunning work**, like the **w** of the ephod;	4639
	39:15 at the ends, *of* **wreathen w** of pure gold.	4639
	39:22 made the robe of the ephod *of* **woven w**,	4639
	39:27 they made coats *of* fine linen *of* **woven w**	4639
	39:32 Thus was all the **w** of the tabernacle of	5656
	39:42 so the children of Israel made all the **w**.	5656
	39:43 Moses did look upon all the **w**, and	4399
	40:33 the court gate. So Moses finished the **w**.	4399
Lev	11:32 whatsoever vessel *it be*, wherein *any* **w** is	4399
	13:51 in a skin, *or* in any **w** that is made of skin;	4399
	16:29 do no **w** *at all, whether it be* one of your	4399
	23: 3 Six days shall **w** be done: but the seventh	4399
	23: 3 ye shall do no **w** *therein*: it is the sabbath	4399
	23: 7 ye shall do no servile **w** *therein*.	4399
	23: 8 ye shall do no servile **w** *therein*.	4399
	23:21 ye shall do no servile **w** *therein: it shall*	4399
	23:25 Ye shall do no servile **w** *therein*: but	4399
	23:28 ye shall do no **w** in that same day: for it *is*	4399
	23:30 whatsoever soul *it be* that doeth any **w** in	4399
	23:31 Ye shall do no *manner of* **w**: *it shall be* a	4399
	23:35 ye shall do no servile **w** *therein*.	4399
	23:36 *and* ye shall do no servile **w** *therein*.	4399
Nu	4: 3 to do the **w** in the tabernacle of	4399
	4:23 to do the **w** of the tabernacle of	5656
	4:30 to do the **w** of the tabernacle of	5656
	4:35 for the **w** in the tabernacle of	5656
	4:39 for the **w** in the tabernacle of	5656
	4:43 for the **w** in the tabernacle of	5656
	8: 4 this **w** of the candlestick *was* of beaten	4639
	8: 4 unto the flowers thereof, *was* **beaten w**:	4749
	28:18 do no *manner of* servile **w** *therein*:	4399
	28:25 convocation; ye shall do no servile **w**	4399
	28:26 convocation; ye shall do no servile **w**:	4399
	29: 1 convocation; ye shall do no servile **w**:	4399
	29: 7 your souls: ye shall not do any **w** *therein*:	4399
	29:12 ye shall do no servile **w**, and ye shall keep	4399
	29:35 ye shall do no servile **w**; *therein*:	4399
	31:20 all **w** of goats' *hair*, and all things made of	4639
Dt	4:28 the **w** of men's hands, wood and stone,	4639
	5:13 days thou shalt labour, and do all thy **w**:	4399
	5:14 *in it* thou shalt not do any **w**, thou, nor	4399
	14:29 all the **w** of thine hand which thou doest.	4639
	15:19 thou shalt do no **w** with the firstling of	5647
	16: 8 thy God: thou shalt do no **w** *therein*.	4399
	24:19 bless thee in all the **w** of thine hands.	4639
	27:15 the **w** of the hands of the craftsman,	4639
	28:12 and to bless all the **w** of thine hand:	4639
	30: 9 thee plenteous in every **w** of thine hand,	4639
	31:29 to provoke him to anger through the **w** of	4639
	32: 4 *He is* the Rock, his **w** *is* perfect: for all his	6467
	33:11 and accept the **w** of his hands:	6467
Jos	7: They did **w** wilily, and went and made as	6213
Jdg	19:16 there came an old man from his **w** out of	4639
Ru	2:12 The Lᴏʀᴅ recompense thy **w**, and a full	6467
1Sa	8:16 and your asses, and put *them* to his **w**.	4399
	14: 6 it may be that the Lᴏʀᴅ will **w** for us:	6213
1Ki	5:16 officers which *were* over the **w**,	4399
	5:16 over the people that wrought in the **w**.	4399
	6:35 with gold fitted upon the **carved w**.	2707
	7: 8 the porch, which *was* of the like **w**.	4639
	7:14 and cunning to **w** all works in brass.	6213
	7:14 to king Solomon, and wrought all his **w**.	4399
	7:17 *And* nets of checker, *and* wreaths of	4639
	7:17 of checker work, *and* wreaths of chain **w**,	4639
	7:19 of the pillars *were* of lily **w** in the porch,	4639

1Ki 7:22 upon the top of the pillars *was* lily **w:** 4639
 7:22 so was the **w** of the pillars finished. 4399
 7:28 the **w** of the bases *was on* this *manner:* 4639
 7:29 *were certain* additions made of thin **w.** 4639
 7:31 the mouth thereof *was* round *after* the **w.** 4639
 7:33 the **w** of the wheels *was* like the work of 4639
 7:33 the work of the wheels *was* like the **w** of 4639
 7:40 So Hiram made an end of doing all the **w** 4399
 7:51 was ended all the **w** that king Solomon 4399
 9:23 the officers that *were* over Solomon's **w,** 4399
 9:23 over the people that wrought in the **w.** 4399
 16: 7 in provoking him to anger with the **w** of 4639
 21:20 hast sold thyself to **w** evil in the sight 6213
 21:25 which did sell himself to **w** wickedness in 6213
2Ki 12:11 into the hands of *them* that did the **w,** 4399
 19:18 the **w** of men's hands, wood and stone: 4639
 22: 5 it into the hand of the doers of the **w,** 4399
 22: 5 let them give it to the doers of the **w** 4399
 22: 9 it into the hand of them that do the **w,** 4399
 25:17 the **wreathen w,** and pomegranates upon 7639
 25:17 had the second pillar with **wreathen w** 7639
1Ch 4:23 there they dwelt with the king for his **w.** 4399
 6:49 *were appointed* for all the **w** of the *place* 4399
 9:13 very able men *for* the **w** of the service of 4399
 9:19 *were* over the **w** of the service, 4399
 9:33 for they were employed in *that* **w** day and 4399
 16:37 continually, as every day's **w** required: 1697
 22:15 *of* cunning *men* for every *manner of* **w.** 4399
 23: 4 four thousand *were* to set forward the **w** 4399
 23:24 that did the **w** for the service of the house 4399
 23:28 the **w** of the service of the house of God; 4639
 27:26 over them that did the **w** of the field for 4399
 28:13 for all the **w** of the service of the house of 4399
 28:20 until *thou* hast finished all the **w** for 4399
 29: 1 *yet* young and tender, and the **w** *is* great: 4399
 29: 5 for all *manner of* **w** *to be made* by 4399
 29: 6 with the rulers over the king's **w,** 4399
2Ch 2: 7 therefore a man cunning to **w** in gold, 6213
 2:14 skilful to **w** in gold, and in silver, in brass, 6213
 2:18 hundred overseers to **set** the people **a w.** 5647
 3:10 he made two cherubims of image **w,** 4639
 4: 5 the brim of it like the **w** of the brim of a 4639
 4:11 Huram finished the **w** that he was to 4399
 5: 1 Thus all the **w** that Solomon made for 4399
 8: 9 did Solomon make no servants for his **w;** 4399
 8:16 Now all the **w** of Solomon was prepared 4399
 15: 7 be weak: for your **w** shall be rewarded. 6468
 16: 5 building of Ramah, and let his **w** cease. 4399
 24:12 Jehoiada gave it to such as did the **w** of 4399
 24:13 the **w** was perfected by them, and they 4399
 29:34 till the **w** was ended, and until the *other* 4399
 31:21 in every **w** that he began in the service of 4639
 32:19 *which were* the **w** of the hands of man. 4639
 34:12 the men did the **w** faithfully: 4399
 34:13 overseers of all that wrought the **w** in 4399
Ezr 2:69 unto the treasure of the **w** threescore 4399
 3: 8 to set forward the **w** of the house of 4399
 4:24 ceased the **w** of the house of the God 5673
 5: 8 this **w** goeth fast on, and prospereth in 5673
 6: 7 Let the **w** of this house of God alone; 5673
 6:22 to strengthen their hands in the **w** of 4399
Ne 10:13 neither *is this* a **w** of one day or two: 4399
 2:16 the rulers, nor to the rest that did the **w.** 4399
 2:18 strengthened their hands for *this* good **w.** NIH
 3: 5 their nobles put not their necks to the **w** 5656
 4: 6 for the people had a mind to **w.** 6213
 4:11 and slay them, and cause the **w** to cease. 4399
 4:15 of us to the wall, every one unto his **w.** 4399
 4:16 the half of my servants wrought in the **w,** 4399
 4:17 with one of his hands wrought in the **w,** 4399
 4:19 The **w** *is* great and large, and we *are* 4399
 4:21 we laboured in the **w:** and half of them 4399
 5:16 also I continued in the **w** of this wall, 4399
 5:16 *were* gathered thither unto the **w.** 4399
 6: 3 I *am* doing a great **w,** so that I cannot 4399
 6: 3 why should the **w** cease, whilst I leave it, 4399
 6: 9 hands shall be weakened from the **w,** 4399
 6:16 they perceived that this **w** was wrought 4399
 7:70 the chief of the fathers gave unto the **w.** 4399
 7:71 of the **w** twenty thousand drams *of* gold, 4399
 10:33 and *for* all the **w** of the house of our God. 4399
 11:12 their brethren that did the **w** of the house 4399
 13:10 Levites and the singers, that did the **w,** 4399
Job 1:10 thou hast blessed the **w** of his hands, 4639
 7: 2 hireling looketh for the **reward of** his **w:** 6467
 10: 3 that thou shouldest despise the **w** of thine 3018
 14:15 thou wilt have a desire to the **w** of thine 4639
 23: 9 he doth **w,** but I cannot behold *him:* 6213
 24: 5 in the desert, go they forth to their **w;** 6467
 34:11 For the **w** of a man shall he render unto 6467
 34:19 for they all *are* the **w** of his hands. 4639
 36: 9 he sheweth them their **w,** 6467
 36:24 Remember that thou magnify his **w,** 6467
 37: 7 every man; that all men may know his **w.** 4639
Ps 8: 3 **w** of thy fingers, the moon and the stars, 4639
 9:16 the wicked is snared in the **w** of his own 6467
 28: 4 give them after the **w** of their hands; 4639
 44: 1 **w** thou didst in their days, in the times 6467
 58: 2 in heart you **w** wickedness; you weigh 6466
 62:12 to *every* man according to his **w.** 4639
 64: 9 shall fear, and shall declare the **w** of God; 6467
 74: 6 they break down the **carved w** thereof 6603
 77:12 I will meditate also of all thy **w,** and talk 6467
 90:16 Let thy **w** appear unto thy servants, 6467
 90:17 establish thou the **w** of our hands upon 4639

Ps 90:17 yea, the **w** of our hands establish thou it. 4639
 92: 4 Lord, hast made me glad through thy **w:** 6467
 95: 9 tempted me, proved me, and saw my **w.** 6467
 101: 3 I hate the **w** of them that turn aside; 6213
 102:25 and the heavens *are* the **w** of thy hands. 4639
 104:23 Man goeth forth unto his **w** and to his 6467
 111: 3 His **w** *is* honourable and glorious: 6467
 115: 4 silver and gold, the **w** of men's hands. 4639
 119:126 *It is* time for *thee,* Lord, to **w:** *for* they 6213
 135:15 are silver and gold, the **w** of men's hands. 4639
 141: 4 practise wicked works with men that **w** 6466
 143: 5 thy works; I muse on the **w** of thy hands. 4639
Pr 11:18 The wicked worketh a deceitful **w:** 6468
 16:11 all the weights of the bag *are* his **w.** 4639
 18: 9 He also that is slothful in his **w** *is* brother 4399
 20:11 whether his **w** *be* pure, and whether *it be* 6467
 21: 8 strange: but *as for* the pure, his **w** *is* right. 6467
 24:27 Prepare thy **w** without, and make it fit for 4399
 24:29 will render to the man according to his **w.** 6467
Ecc 2:17 the **w** that is wrought under the sun *is* 4639
 3:11 that no man can find out the **w** that God 4639
 3:17 there for every purpose and for every **w.** 4639
 4: 3 who hath not seen the evil **w** that is done 4639
 4: 4 I considered all travail, and every right **w,** 4639
 5: 6 and destroy the **w** of thine hands? 4639
 7:13 Consider the **w** of God: for who can 4639
 8: 9 applied my heart unto every **w** that is 4639
 8:11 Because sentence *against* an evil **w** is not 4639
 8:14 according to the **w** of the wicked; 4639
 8:14 according to the **w** of the righteous: 4639
 8:17 I beheld all the **w** of God, that a man 4639
 8:17 that a man cannot find out the **w** that is 4639
 9:10 for *there* is no **w,** nor device, 4639
 12:14 God shall bring every **w** into judgment, 4639
SS 7: 1 **w** of the hands of a cunning workman. 4639
Isa 2: 8 they worship the **w** of their own hands, 4639
 5:12 they regard not the **w** of the Lord, 6467
 5:19 *and* hasten his **w,** that we may see *it:* and 4639
 10:12 performed his whole **w** upon mount Zion 4639
 17: 8 not look to the altars, the **w** of his hands, 4639
 19: 9 Moreover they that **w** in fine flax, 5647
 19:14 they have caused Egypt to err in every **w** 4639
 19:15 Neither shall there be any **w** for Egypt, 4639
 19:25 Assyria the **w** of my hands, and Israel 4639
 28:21 that *he* may do his **w,** his strange work: 4639
 28:21 that *he* may do his work, his strange **w;** 4639
 29:14 I will proceed to **do a marvellous w** 6381
 29:14 even a **marvellous w** and a wonder: 6381
 29:16 for shall the **w** say of him that made it, 4639
 29:23 the **w** of mine hands, in the midst of him, 4639
 31: 2 against the help of them that **w** iniquity. 6466
 32: 6 his heart will **w** iniquity, to practise 6213
 32:17 the **w** of righteousness shall be peace; 4639
 37:19 the **w** of men's hands, wood and stone. 4639
 40:10 reward *is* with him, and his **w** before 6468
 41:24 ye *are* of nothing, and your **w** of nought: 6467
 43:13 of my hand: I will **w,** and who shall let it? 6466
 45: 9 or thy **w,** He hath no hands? 6467
 45:11 concerning the **w** of my hands command 6467
 49: 4 with the Lord, and my **w** with my God. 6468
 54:16 bringeth forth an instrument for his **w;** 4639
 60:21 **w** of my hands, that *I* may be glorified. 4639
 61: 8 I will direct their **w** in truth, and I will 6468
 62:11 reward *is* with him, and his **w** before 6468
 64: 8 and we all *are* the **w** of thine hand. 4639
 65: 7 will I measure their former **w** into their 6468
 65:22 mine elect shall long enjoy the **w** of their 4639
Jer 10: 3 the **w** of the hands of the workman, 4639
 10: 9 the **w** of the workman, and of the hands 4639
 10: 9 they *are* all the **w** of cunning *men.* 4639
 10:15 They *are* vanity, *and* the **w** of errors: 4639
 17:22 neither do ye any **w,** but hallow ye 4399
 17:24 the sabbath day, to do no **w** therein; 4399
 18: 3 behold, he wrought a **w** on the wheels. 4399
 22:13 and giveth him not *for* his **w;** 6467
 31:16 for thy **w** shall be rewarded, saith 6468
 32:19 Great in counsel, and mighty in **w:** 5950
 32:30 me to anger with the **w** of their hands, 4639
 48:10 Cursed *be* he that doeth the **w** of 4399
 50:25 for this *is* the **w** of the Lord God of hosts 4399
 50:29 recompense her according to her **w;** 6467
 51:10 let us declare in Zion the **w** of the Lord 4639
 51:18 They *are* vanity, the **w** of errors: 4639
La 3:64 according to the **w** of their hands. 4639
 4: 2 the **w** of the hands of the potter! 4639
Eze 1:16 their **w** was like unto the colour of a 4639
 1:16 their **w** *was* as it were a wheel in the 4639
 15: 3 Shall wood be taken thereof to do *any* **w?** 4399
 15: 4 midst of it is burnt. Is it meet for *any* **w?** 4399
 15: 5 when it was whole, it was meet for no **w:** 4399
 15: 5 much less shall it be meet yet for *any* **w,** 4399
 16:10 I clothed thee also with **broidered w,** 7553
 16:13 *of* fine linen, and silk, and **broidered w;** 7553
 16:30 seeing thou doest all these *things,* the **w** 4639
 27: 7 Fine linen with **broidered w** from Egypt 7553
 27:16 **broidered w,** and fine linen, and coral, 7553
 27:24 **broidered w,** and in chests of rich 7553
 33:26 ye **w** abomination, and ye defile every 6213
Da 11:23 the league *made* with him he shall **w** 6213
Hos 6: 8 Gilead *is* a city of them that **w** iniquity, 6466
 13: 2 all of it the **w** of the craftsmen. 4639
 14: 3 neither will we say any more to the **w** of 4639
Mic 2: 1 iniquity, and **w** evil upon their beds! 6466
 5:13 shalt no more worship the **w** of thine 4639
Hab 1: 5 for *I will* **w** a work in your days, *which* ye 6466

Hab 1: 5 for *I will* work a **w** in your days, *which* ye 6467
 2:18 that the maker of his **w** trusteth therein, 3336
 3: 2 revive thy **w** in the midst of the years, 6467
Zep 2:14 for he shall uncover the **cedar w.** 731
Hag 1:14 did **w** in the house of the Lord of hosts, 4399
 2: 4 of the land, saith the Lord, and **w:** 6213
 2:14 so *is* every **w** of their hands; and *that* 4639
Mal 3:15 they that **w** wickedness are set up; yea, 6213
Mt 7:23 depart from me, ye that **w** iniquity. 2038
 21:28 said, Son, go **w** to day in my vineyard. 2038
 26:10 for she hath wrought a good **w** upon me. 2041
Mk 6: 5 And he could there do no **mighty w,** 1411
 13:34 and to every man his **w,** 2041
 14: 6 she hath wrought a good **w** on me. 2041
Lk 13:14 are six days in which *men* ought to **w:** 2038
Jn 4:34 of him that sent me, and to finish his **w.** 2041
 5:17 My Father worketh hitherto, and I **w.** 2038
 6:28 do, that we might **w** the works of God? 2038
 6:29 and said unto them, This is the **w** of God, 2041
 6:30 and believe thee? what dost thou **w?** 2038
 7:21 I have done one **w,** and ye all marvel. 2041
 9: 4 I must **w** the works of him that sent me, 2038
 9: 4 the night cometh, when no *man* can **w.** 2038
 10:33 saying, For a good **w** we stone thee not; 2041
 17: 4 I finished the **w** which thou gavest me 2041
Ac 5:38 for if this counsel or this **w** be of men, 2041
 13: 2 Saul for the **w** whereunto I have called 2041
 13:41 I **w** a work in your days, a work which 2038
 13:41 I work a **w** in your days, a work which 2041
 13:41 a **w** which you shall in no wise believe, 2041
 14:26 of God for the **w** which they fulfilled. 2041
 15:38 and went not with them to the **w.** 2041
 27:16 had **much w** to come by the boat: 2480+3433
Ro 2:15 Which shew the **w** of the law written in 2041
 7: 5 did **w** in our members to bring forth fruit 1754
 8:28 we know that all *things* **w** together for 4903
 9:28 he will finish the **w,** and cut *it* short in 3056
 9:28 a short **w** will the Lord make upon 3056
 11: 6 grace: otherwise **w** is no more work. 2041
 11: 6 grace: otherwise work is no more **w** 2041
 14:20 For meat destroy not the **w** of God. 2041
1Co 3:13 Every man's **w** shall be made manifest: 2041
 3:13 the fire shall try every man's **w** of what 2041
 3:14 If any *man's* **w** abide which he hath built 2041
 3:15 If any *man's* **w** shall be burnt, he shall 2041
 9: 1 our Lord? are not you my **w** in the Lord? 2041
 15:58 always abounding in the **w** of the Lord, 2041
 16:10 for he worketh the **w** of the Lord, as I 2041
2Co 9: 8 all *things,* may abound to every good **w:** 2041
Gal 6: 4 But let every man prove his own **w,** 2041
Eph 4:12 the perfecting of the saints for the **w** of 2041
 4:19 to **w** all uncleanness with greediness. 2039
Php 1: 6 **w** in you will perform *it* until the day of 2041
 2:12 **w** out your own salvation with fear and 2716
 2:30 Because for the **w** of Christ he was nigh 2041
Col 1:10 being fruitful in every good **w,** 2041
1Th 1: 3 Remembering without ceasing your **w** of 2041
 4:11 and to **w** with your own hands, 2038
2Th 1:11 and the **w** of faith with power: 2041
 2: 7 the mystery of iniquity doth already **w:** 1754
 2:17 stablish you in every good word and **w.** 2041
 3:10 that if any would not **w,** neither should 2038
 3:12 that with quietness they **w,** and eat their 2038
1Ti 3: 1 office of a bishop, he desireth a good **w.** 2041
 5:10 have diligently followed every good **w.** 2041
2Ti 2:21 and prepared unto every good **w.** 2041
 4: 5 do the **w** of an evangelist, make full proof 2041
 4:18 Lord shall deliver me from every evil **w,** 2041
Tit 1:16 unto every good **w** reprobate. 2041
 3: 1 to be ready to every good **w,** 2041
Heb 6:10 God *is* not unrighteous to forget your **w** 2041
 13:21 Make you perfect in every good **w** to do 2041
Jas 1: 4 But let patience have *her* perfect **w,** that 2041
 1:25 but a doer of the **w,** this *man* shall be 2041
 3:16 is, there *is* confusion and every evil **w.** 4229
1Pe 1:17 judgeth according to every man's **w,** 2041
Rev 22:12 to give every man according as his **w** shall 2041

WORK'S (1) [WORK]

1Th 5:13 them very highly in love for their **w** sake. 2041

WORKER (1) [WORK]

1Ki 7:14 father *was* a man of Tyre, a **w** in brass: 2790

WORKERS (27) [WORK]

2Ki 23:24 Moreover the **w** with familiar spirits, NIH
1Ch 22:15 hewers and **w** of stone and timber, 2796
Job 31: 3 strange punishment to the **w** of iniquity? 6466
 34: 8 Which goeth in company with the **w** of 6466
 34:22 where the **w** of iniquity may hide 6466
Ps 5: 5 in thy sight: thou hatest all **w** of iniquity. 6466
 6: 8 Depart from me, all ye **w** of iniquity; 6466
 14: 4 Have all the **w** of iniquity no knowledge? 6466
 28: 3 the wicked, and with the **w** of iniquity, 6466
 36:12 There are the **w** of iniquity fallen: they 6466
 37: 1 neither be thou envious against the **w** of 6213
 53: 4 Have the **w** of iniquity no knowledge? 6466
 59: 2 Deliver me from the **w** of iniquity, 6466
 64: 2 from the insurrection of the **w** of iniquity: 6466
 92: 7 and when all the **w** of iniquity do flourish; 6466
 92: 9 all the **w** of iniquity shall be scattered. 6466
 94: 4 all the **w** of iniquity boast themselves? 6466
 94:16 who will stand up for me against the **w** of 6466
 125: 5 lead them forth with the **w** of iniquity: 6466
 141: 9 for me, and the grins of the **w** of iniquity. 6466

Pr 10:29 destruction *shall be* to the **w** of iniquity. 6466
21:15 destruction *shall be* to the **w** of iniquity. 6466
Lk 13:27 depart from me, all *ye* **w** of iniquity. 2040
1Co 12:29 are all teachers? *are* all **w** of miracles? 1411
2Co 6: 1 *as* **w together** *with* him, beseech you also 4903
11:13 For such *are* false apostles, deceitful **w**, 2040
Php 3: 2 Beware of dogs, beware of evil **w**, 2040

WORKETH (37) [WORK]
Job 33:29 all these *things* **w** God oftentimes with 6466
Ps 15: 2 **w** righteousness, and speaketh the truth 6466
101: 7 He that **w** deceit shall not dwell within 6213
Pr 11:18 The wicked **w** a deceitful work: but *to* 6213
26:28 by it; and a flattering mouth **w** ruin. 6213
31:13 and flax, and **w** willingly with her hands. 6213
Ecc 3: 9 What profit *hath* he that **w** in *that* 6213
Isa 44:12 The smith *with* the tongs both **w** in 6466
44:12 and **w** it with the strength of his arms: 6466
64: 5 him that rejoiceth and **w** righteousness, 6213
Da 6:27 he **w** signs and wonders in heaven and 5648
Jn 5:17 answered them, My Father **w** hitherto, 2038
Ac 10:35 **w** righteousness, is accepted with him. 2038
Ro 2:10 and peace, to every *man* that **w** good, 2038
4: 4 Now to him that **w** is the reward not 2038
4: 5 to him that **w** not, but believeth on him 2038
4:15 the law **w** wrath: for where no law 2716
5: 3 knowing that tribulation **w** patience; 2716
13:10 Love **w** no ill to *his* neighbour: therefore 2038
1Co 12: 6 but it is the same God which **w** all in all. 1754
12:11 But all these **w** *that* one and the selfsame 1754
16:10 he **w** the work of the Lord, as I also *do*. 2038
2Co 4:12 So then death **w** in us, but life in you. 1754
4:17 **w** for us a far more exceeding *and* 2716
7:10 godly sorrow **w** repentance to salvation 2716
7:10 but the sorrow of the world **w** death. 2716
Gal 3: 5 you the Spirit, and miracles among you, 1754
5: 6 but faith which **w** by love. 1754
Eph 1:11 **w** all *things* after the counsel of his own 1754
2: 2 the spirit that now **w** in the children of 1754
3:20 according to the power that **w** in us, 1754
Php 2:13 For it is God which **w** in you both to will 1754
Col 1:29 to his working, which **w** in me mightily. 1754
1Th 2:13 which **effectually w** also in you that 1754
Jas 1: 3 that the trying of your faith **w** patience. 2716
1:20 For the wrath of man **w** not 2716
Rev 21:27 neither *whatsoever* **w** abomination, 4160

WORKFELLOW (1) [FELLOW, WORK]
Ro 16:21 Timotheus my **w**, and Lucius, and Jason, 4904

WORKING (20) [WORK]
Ps 52: 2 like a sharp razor, **w** deceitfully. 6213
74:12 **w** salvation in the midst of the earth. 6466
Isa 28:29 wonderful in counsel, *and* excellent in **w**. 8454
Eze 46: 1 the east shall be shut the six **w** days; 4639
Mk 16:20 the Lord **w** with **them**, and confirming 4903
Ro 1:27 men with men **w** that which is unseemly, 2716
7:13 **w** death in me by that which is good; 2716
1Co 4:12 And labour, **w** with our own hands: 2038
9: 6 have not we power to forbear **w**? 2038
12:10 To another the **w** of miracles; to another 1755
Eph 1:19 according to the **w** of his mighty power, 1753
1:19 unto me by the **effectual w** of his power. 1753
4:16 according to the **effectual w** in the 1753
4:28 with *his* hands the *thing which is* good, 2038
Php 3:21 according to the **w** whereby he is able 1753
Col 1:29 I also labour, striving according to his **w**, 1753
2Th 2: 9 *Even him*, whose coming is after the **w** of 1753
3:11 **w** not at all, but are busybodies. 2038
Heb 13:21 in you *that which is* well pleasing in his 4160
Rev 16:14 they are the spirits of devils, **w** miracles, 4160

WORKMAN (10) [MAN, WORK]
Ex 35:35 the **cunning w**, and of the embroiderer, 2803
38:23 a **cunning w**, and an embroiderer in blue, 2803
SS 7: 1 the work of the hands of a **cunning w**. 542
Isa 40:19 The **w** melteth a graven image, 2796
40:20 seeketh unto him a cunning **w** to prepare 2796
Jer 10: 3 the work of the hands of the **w**, with 2796
10: 9 the work of the **w**, and of the hands of 2796
Hos 8: 6 the **w** made it; therefore it *is not* God: 2796
Mt 10:10 staves: for the **w** is worthy of his meat. 2040
2Ti 2:15 a **w** that needeth not to be ashamed, 2040

WORKMANSHIP (7) [MAN, WORK]
Ex 31: 3 in knowledge, and in all *manner of* **w**, 4399
31: 5 of timber, to work in all *manner of* **w**. 4399
35:31 in knowledge, and in all *manner of* **w**. 4399
2Ki 16:10 of it, according to all the **w** thereof. 4639
1Ch 28:21 *shall be* with thee for all *manner of* **w** 4399
Eze 28:13 the **w** of thy tabrets and of thy pipes was 4399
Eph 2:10 For we are his **w**, created in Christ Jesus 4161

WORKMEN (11) [MAN, WORK]
2Ki 12:14 they gave that to the **w**, 4399+6213
12:15 the money to be bestowed on **w**: 4399+6213
1Ch 22:15 Moreover *there are* **w** with thee in 4399+6213
25: 1 the number of the **w** according to 376+4399
2Ch 24:13 So the **w** wrought, 4399+6213+1886.1
34:10 **w** that had the oversight 4399+6213+1886.1
34:10 they gave it *to* the **w** that 4399+6213+1886.1
34:17 and to the hand of the **w**, 4399+6213+1886.1
Ezr 3: 9 to set forward the **w** in the house of God: 6213
Isa 44:11 the **w**, they *are* of men: let them all be 2796
Ac 19:25 Whom he called together with the **w** of 2040

WORKMEN'S (1) [MAN, WORK]
Jdg 5:26 and her right hand to the **w** hammer; 6001

WORKS (236) [WORK]
Ex 5: 4 and Aaron, let the people from their **w**? 4639
5:13 Fulfil your **w**, *your* daily tasks, as when 4639
23:24 nor serve them, nor do after their **w**: 4639
31: 4 To devise **cunning w**, to work in gold, 4284
35:32 to devise **curious w**, to work in gold, 4284
Nu 16:28 the Lord hath sent me to do all these **w**; 4639
Dt 2: 7 hath blessed thee in all the **w** of thy hand: 4639
3:24 that can do according to thy **w**, 4639
15:10 thy God shall bless thee in all thy **w**, 4639
16:15 in all the **w** of thine hands, therefore 4639
Jos 24:31 which had known all the **w** of the Lord, 4639
Jdg 2: 7 who had seen all the great **w** of 4639
2:10 yet the **w** which he had done for Israel. 4639
1Sa 8: 8 According to all the **w** which they have 4639
19: 4 his **w** *have been* to thee-ward very good: 4639
1Ki 7:14 and cunning to work all the **w** in brass. 4399
13:11 told him all the **w** that the man of God 4639
2Ki 22:17 me to anger with all the **w** of their hands; 4639
1Ch 16: 9 him, talk you of all his **wondrous w**. 6381
16:12 Remember his **marvellous w** that he 6381
16:24 his **marvellous w** among all nations. 6381
28:19 upon me, *even* all the **w** of *this* pattern. 4399
2Ch 20:37 the Lord hath broken thy **w**. 4639
32:30 And Hezekiah prospered in all his **w**. 4639
34:25 to anger with all the **w** of their hands; 4639
Ne 6:14 and Sanballat according to these their **w**, 4639
9:35 neither turned they from their wicked **w**. 4611
Job 34:25 Therefore he knoweth their **w**, 4566
37:14 and consider the **wondrous w** of God. 6381
37:16 the **wondrous w** of *him which is* perfect 4652
Ps 8: 6 have dominion over the **w** of thy hands; 4639
9: 1 I will shew forth all thy **marvellous w**. 6381
14: 1 corrupt, they have done abominable **w**, 5949
17: 4 Concerning the **w** of men, by the word of 6468
26: 7 and tell of all thy **wondrous w**. 6381
28: 5 Because they regard not the **w** of 6468
33: 4 *is* right; and all his **w** *are done* in truth. 4639
33:15 hearts alike; he considereth all their **w**. 4639
40: 5 thy **wonderful w** *which* thou hast done, 6381
46: 8 Come, behold the **w** of the Lord, 4659
66: 3 unto God, How terrible *art thou* in thy **w**! 4639
66: 5 Come and see the **w** of God: *he is* terrible 4659
71:17 have I declared thy **wondrous w**. 6381
73:28 Lord God, that *I* may declare all thy **w**. 4399
75: 1 *that* thy name *is* near thy **wondrous w** 6381
77:11 I will remember the **w** of the Lord: 4611
78: 4 and his **wonderful w** that he hath done. 6381
78: 7 not forget the **w** of God, but keep his 4611
78:11 forgat his **w**, and his wonders that he had 5949
78:32 and believed not for his **wondrous w**. 6381
86: 8 neither *are there any* **w** like unto thy NIH
86: 8 *are there any* works like unto thy **w**. 4639
92: 4 I will triumph in the **w** of thy hands. 4639
92: 5 O Lord, how great are thy **w**! *and* 4639
103:22 all his **w** in all places of his dominion: 4639
104:13 earth is satisfied with the fruit of thy **w**. 4639
104:24 O Lord, how manifold are thy **w**! 4639
104:31 for ever: the Lord shall rejoice in his **w**. 4639
105: 2 unto him: talk ye of all his **wondrous w**. 6381
105: 5 Remember his **marvellous w** that he 6381
106:13 They soon forgat his **w**; they waited not 4639
106:22 **Wondrous w** in the land of Ham, 6381
106:35 among the heathen, and learned their **w**. 4639
106:39 Thus were they defiled with their own **w**, 4639
107: 8 *for* his **wonderful w** to the children of 6381
107:15 *for* his **wonderful w** to the children of 6381
107:21 *for* his **wonderful w** to the children of 6381
107:22 and declare his **w** with rejoicing. 4639
107:24 These see the **w** of the Lord, 4639
107:31 *for* his **wonderful w** to the children of 6381
111: 2 The **w** of the Lord *are* great, sought out 4639
111: 4 He hath made his **wonderful w** to be 6381
111: 6 shewed his people the power of his **w**, 4639
111: 7 The **w** of his hands *are* verity and 4639
118:17 but live, and declare the **w** of the Lord. 4639
119:27 so shall I talk of thy **wondrous w**. 6381
138: 8 forsake not the **w** of thine own hands. 4639
139:14 marvellous *are* thy **w**; and *that* my soul 4639
141: 4 to practise wicked **w** with men that work 5949
143: 5 the days of old; I meditate on all thy **w**; 6467
145: 4 One generation shall praise thy **w** to 4639
145: 5 of thy majesty, and of thy wondrous **w**. 1697
145: 9 and his tender mercies *are* over all his **w**. 4639
145:10 All thy **w** shall praise thee, O Lord; 4639
145:17 in all his ways, and holy in all his **w**. 4639
Pr 7:16 with carved **w**, *with* fine linen of Egypt. NIH
8:22 beginning of his way, before his **w** of old. 4659
16: 3 Commit thy **w** unto the Lord, 4639
24:12 render to *every* man according to his **w**? 6467
31:31 and let her own **w** praise her in the gates. 4639
Ecc 1:14 I have seen all the **w** that are done under 4639
2: 4 I made me great **w**; I builded me houses; 4639
2:11 I looked on all the **w** that my hands had 4639
3:22 that a man should rejoice in his own **w**; 4639
9: 1 the righteous, and the wise, and their **w**, 5652
9: 7 for God now accepteth thy **w**. 4639
11: 5 knowest the **w** of God who maketh 4639
Isa 26:12 thou also hast wrought all our **w** in us. 4639
29:15 we are in the dark, and they say, 4639
41:29 they *are* all vanity; their **w** *are* nothing: 4639
57:12 will declare thy righteousness, and thy **w**; 4639

Isa 59: 6 shall they cover themselves with their **w**: 4639
59: 6 their **w** *are* works of iniquity, and the act 4639
59: 6 their works *are* **w** of iniquity, and the act 4639
66:18 For *I know* their **w** and their thoughts. 4639
Jer 1:16 worshipped the **w** of their own hands. 4639
7:13 because ye have done all these **w**, 4639
21: 2 with us according to all his **wondrous w**, 6381
25: 6 provoke me not to anger with the **w** of 4639
25: 7 the **w** of your hands to your own hurt. 4639
25:14 according to the **w** of their own hands. 4639
44: 8 me unto wrath with the **w** of your hands, 4639
48: 7 For because thou hast trusted in thy **w** 4639
Eze 6: 6 cut down, and your **w** may be abolished. 4639
Da 4:37 all whose *are* truth, and his ways 4639
9:14 *is* righteous in all his **w** which he doeth: 4639
Am 3: 7 Surely I will never forget any of their **w**. 4639
Jnh 3:10 God saw their **w**, that they turned from 4639
Mic 6:16 all the **w** of the house of Ahab, and ye 4639
Mt 5:16 that they may see your good **w**, 2041
7:22 in thy name done many **wonderful w**? 1411
11: 2 had heard in the prison the **w** of Christ, 1411
11:20 wherein most of his **mighty w** were done, 1411
11:21 for if the **mighty w**, which were done in 1411
11:23 if the **mighty w**, which have been done 1411
13:54 *man* this wisdom, and *these* **mighty w**? 1411
13:58 And he did not many **mighty w** there, 1411
14: 2 **mighty w** do shew forth themselves in 1411
16:27 reward every man according to his **w**. 4234
23: 3 and do; but do not ye after their **w**: 2041
23: 5 But all their **w** they do for to be seen of 2041
Mk 6: 2 that even such **mighty w** are wrought by 1411
6:14 **mighty w** do shew forth themselves in 1411
Lk 10:13 if the **mighty w** had been done in Tyre 1411
19:37 for all the **mighty w** that they had seen; 1411
Jn 5:20 he will shew him greater **w** than these, 2041
5:36 for the **w** which the Father hath given me 2041
5:36 the same **w** that I do, bear witness of me, 2041
6:28 we do, that we might work the **w** of God? 2041
7: 3 that thy disciples also may see the **w** that 2041
7: 7 I testify of it, that the **w** thereof are evil. 2041
8:39 ye would do the **w** of Abraham. 2041
9: 3 the **w** of God should be made manifest 2041
9: 4 I must work the **w** of him that sent me, 2041
10:25 the **w** that I do in my Father's name, 2041
10:32 Many good **w** have I shewed you from 2041
10:32 for which of those **w** do ye stone me? 2041
10:37 If I do not the **w** of my Father, believe me 2041
10:38 though ye believe not me, believe the **w**: 2041
14:10 that dwelleth in me, he doeth the **w**. 2041
14:12 on me, the **w** that I do shall he do also; 2041
14:12 and greater **w** than these shall he do; NIG
15:24 If I had not done among them the **w** 2041
Ac 2:11 in our tongues the **wonderful w** of God. 3167
7:41 and rejoiced in the **w** of their own hands. 2041
9:36 this *woman* was full of good **w** and 2041
15:18 Known unto God are all his **w** from 2041
26:20 to God, and do **w** meet for repentance. 2041
Ro 3:27 of **w**? Nay: but by the law of faith. 2041
4: 2 For if Abraham were justified by **w**, 2041
4: 6 God imputeth righteousness without **w**, 2041
9:11 not of **w**, but of him that calleth;) 2041
9:32 faith, but as *it were* by the **w** of the law. 2041
11: 6 And if by grace, *then is it* no more of **w**: 2041
11: 6 But if *it be* of **w**, then is it no more grace: 2041
13: 3 For rulers are not a terror to good **w**, 2041
13:12 let us therefore cast off the **w** of darkness, 2041
2Co 11:15 whose end shall be according to their **w**. 2041
Gal 2:16 a man is not justified by the **w** of the law, 2041
2:16 of Christ, and not by the **w** of the law: 2041
2:16 for by the **w** of the law shall no flesh be 2041
3: 2 Received ye the Spirit by the **w** of the law, 2041
3: 5 *doeth he it* by the **w** of the law, or by 2041
3:10 For as many as are of the **w** of the law are 2041
5:19 Now the **w** of the flesh are manifest, 2041
Eph 2: 9 Not of **w**, lest any *man* should boast. 2041
2:10 created in Christ Jesus unto good **w**, 2041
5:11 with the unfruitful **w** of darkness, 2041
Col 1:21 and enemies in *your* mind by wicked **w**, 2041
1Ti 2:10 professing godliness) with good **w**. 2041
5:10 Well reported of for good **w**; if she have 2041
5:25 Likewise also the good **w** of *some* are 2041
6:18 that *they* be rich in good **w**, ready to 2041
2Ti 1: 9 not according to our **w**, but according to 2041
3:17 throughly furnished unto all good **w**. 2041
4:14 The Lord reward him according to his **w**: 2041
Tit 1:16 in *they* deny *him*, being abominable, 2041
2: 7 shewing thyself a pattern of good **w**: 2041
2:14 a peculiar people, zealous of good **w**. 2041
3: 5 Not by **w** of righteousness which we have 2041
3: 8 God might be careful to maintain good **w**. 2041
3:14 let ours also learn to maintain good **w** 2041
Heb 1:10 the heavens are the **w** of thine hands: 2041
2: 7 didst set him over the **w** of thy hands: 2041
3: 9 proved me, and saw my **w** forty years. 2041
4: 3 although the **w** were finished from 2041
4: 4 did rest the seventh day from all his **w**. 2041
4:10 he also hath ceased from his own **w**, as 2041
6: 1 foundation of repentance from dead **w**, 2041
9:14 purge your conscience from dead **w** to 2041
10:24 to provoke unto love and to good **w**: 2041
Jas 2:14 a man say *he* hath faith, and have not **w**? 2041
2:17 Even so faith, if it hath not **w**, is dead, 2041
2:18 may say, Thou hast faith, and I have **w**: 2041
2:18 shew me thy faith without thy **w**, and I 2041
2:18 and I will shew thee my faith by my **w**. 2041

Jas		
	2:20 O vain man, that faith without **w** is dead?	2041
	2:21 not Abraham our father justified by **w**,	2041
	2:22 Seest thou how faith wrought with his **w**,	2041
	2:22 and by **w** was faith made perfect?	2041
	2:24 then how that by **w** a man is justified,	2041
	2:25 was not Rahab the harlot justified by **w**,	2041
	2:26 is dead, so faith without **w** is dead also.	2041
	3:13 his **w** with meekness of wisdom.	2041
1Pe	2:12 they may by *your good* **w**, *which* they	2041
2Pe	3:10 the **w** that are therein shall be burnt up.	2041
1Jn	3: 8 that he might destroy the **w** of the devil.	2041
	3:12 Because his own **w** were evil, and his	2041
Rev	2: 2 I know thy **w**, and thy labour,	2041
	2: 5 art fallen, and repent, and do the first **w**;	2041
	2: 9 I know thy **w**,	2041
	2:13 I know thy **w**, and where thou dwellest,	2041
	2:19 I know thy **w**, and charity, and service,	2041
	2:19 and faith, and thy patience, and thy **w**;	2041
	2:23 every one of you according to your **w**.	2041
	2:26 and keepeth my **w** unto the end,	2041
	3: 1 I know thy **w**, that thou hast a name that	2041
	3: 2 for I have not found thy **w** perfect before	2041
	3: 8 I know thy **w**: behold, I have set before	2041
	3:15 I know thy **w**, that thou art neither cold	2041
	9:20 *yet* repented not of the **w** of their hands,	2041
	14:13 their labours; and their **w** do follow them.	2041
	15: 3 saying, Great and marvellous *are* thy **w**,	2041
	18: 6 unto her double according to her **w**:	2041
	20:12 written in the books, according to their **w**.	2041
	20:13 judged every man according to their **w**.	2041

WORKS' (1) [WORK]

Jn	14:11 or else believe me for the very **w** sake.	2041

WORLD (287) [WORLD'S, WORLDLY, WORLDS]

1Sa	2: 8 and he hath set the **w** upon them.	8398
2Sa	22:16 foundations of the **w** were discovered,	8398
1Ch	16:30 the **w** also shall be stable, that it be not	8398
Job	18:18 into darkness, and chased out of the **w**.	8398
	34:13 or who hath disposed the whole **w**?	8398
	37:12 them upon the face of the **w** in the earth.	8398
Ps	9: 8 he shall judge the **w** in righteousness,	8398
	17:14 thy hand, O Lord, from men of the **w**,	2465
	18:15 the foundations of the **w** were discovered	8398
	19: 4 and their words to the end of the **w**.	8398
	22:27 All the ends of the **w** shall remember and	776
	24: 1 the **w**, and they that dwell therein.	8398
	33: 8 all the inhabitants of the **w** stand in awe	8398
	49: 1 give ear, all ye inhabitants of the **w**:	2465
	50:12 for the **w** *is* mine, and the fulness thereof.	8398
	73:12 *are* the ungodly, who prosper in the **w**;	5769
	77:18 the lightnings lightened the **w**: the earth	8398
	89:11 *as for* the **w** and the fulness thereof,	8398
	90: 2 thou hadst formed the earth and the **w**,	8398
	93: 1 the **w** also is stablished, *that* it cannot be	8398
	96:10 the **w** also shall be established *that* it shall	8398
	96:13 he shall judge the **w** with righteousness,	8398
	97: 4 lightnings enlightened the **w**: the earth	8398
	98: 7 the **w**, and they that dwell therein.	8398
	98: 9 with righteousness shall he judge the **w**,	8398
Pr	8:26 nor the highest part of the dust of the **w**.	8398
Ecc	3:11 he hath set the **w** in their heart, so that	5769
Isa	13:11 I will punish the **w** for *their* evil,	8398
	14:17 *That* made the **w** as a wilderness,	8398
	14:21 nor fill the face of the **w** *with* cities.	8398
	18: 3 All ye inhabitants of the **w**, and dwellers	8398
	23:17 of the **w** upon the face of the earth.	776
	24: 4 the **w** languisheth *and* fadeth away,	8398
	26: 9 the inhabitants of the **w** will learn	8398
	26:18 have the inhabitants of the **w** fallen.	8398
	27: 6 bud, and fill the face of the **w** *with* fruit.	8398
	34: 1 the **w**, and all things that come forth of it.	8398
	38:11 no more with the inhabitants of the **w**.	2309
	45:17 confounded **w** *without end*.	5703+5704+5769
	62:11 hath proclaimed unto the end of the **w**,	776
	64: 4 For *since the beginning of the* **w**	4480+5769
Jer	10:12 he hath established the **w** by his wisdom,	8398
	25:26 another, and all the kingdoms of the **w**,	776
	51:15 he hath established the **w** by his wisdom,	8398
La	4:12 earth, and all the inhabitants of the **w**,	8398
Na	1: 5 yea, the **w**, and all that dwell therein.	8398
Mt	4: 8 sheweth him all the kingdoms of the **w**,	2889
	5:14 Ye are the light of the **w**. A city that is set	2889
	12:32 shall not be forgiven him, neither in this **w**,	165
	12:32 in this world, neither in the **w** to come.	NIG
	13:22 the care of this **w**, and the deceitfulness	165
	13:35 kept secret from the foundation of the **w**.	2889
	13:38 The field is the **w**; the good seed are	2889
	13:39 the harvest is the end of the **w**;	165
	13:40 the fire; so shall it be in the end of this **w**.	165
	13:49 shall it be at the end of the **w**: the angels	165
	16:26 if he shall gain the whole **w**, and lose his	2889
	18: 7 Woe unto the **w** because of offences! for	2889
	24: 3 of thy coming, and of the end of the **w**?	165
	24:14 in all the **w** for a witness unto all nations;	3625
	24:21 as was not since the beginning of the **w**	2889
	25:34 for you from the foundation of the **w**:	2889
	26:13 gospel shall be preached in the whole **w**,	2889
	28:20 you alway, *even* unto the end of the **w**.	165
Mk	4:19 And the cares of this **w**,	165
	8:36 if he shall gain the whole **w**, and lose his	2889
	10:30 and in the **w** to come eternal life.	165
	14: 9 be preached throughout the whole **w**,	2889
	16:15 Go ye into all the **w**, and preach the	2889
Lk	1:70 which have been since the **w** began:)	165

Lk		
	2: 1 that all the **w** should be taxed.	3625
	4: 5 unto him all the kingdoms of the **w**	2889
	9:25 if he gain the whole **w**, and lose himself,	2889
	11:50 was shed from the foundation of the **w**	2889
	12:30 all these *things* do the nations of the **w**	2889
	16: 8 for the children of this **w** are in their	165
	18:30 and in the **w** to come life everlasting.	165
	20:34 The children of this **w** marry, and are given	165
	20:35 shall be accounted worthy to obtain that **w**,	165
Jn	1: 9 every man *that* cometh into the **w**.	2889
	1:10 He was in the **w**, and the world was	2889
	1:10 the **w** was made by him, and the world	2889
	1:10 made by him, and the **w** knew him not.	2889
	1:29 God, which taketh away the sin of the **w**.	2889
	3:16 For God so loved the **w**, that he gave his	2889
	3:17 For God sent not his Son into the **w** to	2889
	3:17 Son into the world to condemn the **w**;	2889
	3:17 that the **w** through him might be saved.	2889
	3:19 light is come into the **w**, and men loved	2889
	4:42 is indeed the Christ, the Saviour of the **w**.	2889
	6:14 *that* prophet that should come into the **w**.	2889
	6:33 from heaven, and giveth life unto the **w**.	2889
	6:51 which I will give for the life of the **w**.	2889
	7: 4 do these *things*, shew thyself to the **w**.	2889
	7: 7 The **w** cannot hate you; but me it hateth,	2889
	8:12 them, saying, I am the light of the **w**:	2889
	8:23 ye are of this **w**; I am not of this world.	2889
	8:23 ye are of this world; I am not of this **w**.	2889
	8:26 I speak to the **w** those *things* which I	2889
	9: 5 As long as I am in the **w**, I am the light of	2889
	9: 5 I am in the world, I am the light of the **w**.	2889
	9:32 Since the **w** began was it not heard that	165
	9:39 For judgment I am come into this **w**,	2889
	10:36 and sent into the **w**, Thou blasphemest;	2889
	11: 9 because he seeth the light of this **w**.	2889
	11:27 of God, which should come into the **w**.	2889
	12:19 behold, the **w** is gone after him.	2889
	12:25 he that hateth his life in this **w** shall keep	2889
	12:31 Now is the judgment of this **w**: now shall	2889
	12:31 now shall the prince of this **w** be cast out.	2889
	12:46 I am come a light into the **w**,	2889
	12:47 for I came not to judge the **w**, but to save	2889
	12:47 not to judge the world, but to save the **w**.	2889
	13: 1 I depart out of this **w** unto the Father,	2889
	13: 1 loved his own which were in the **w**,	2889
	14:17 whom the **w** cannot receive, because	2889
	14:19 little while, and the **w** seeth me no more;	2889
	14:22 thyself unto us, and not unto the **w**?	2889
	14:27 not as the **w** giveth, give I unto you.	2889
	14:30 for the prince of this **w** cometh,	2889
	14:31 But that the **w** may know that I love	2889
	15:18 If the **w** hate you, ye know that it hated	2889
	15:19 If ye were of the **w**, the world would love	2889
	15:19 of the world, the **w** would love his own:	2889
	15:19 because ye are not of the **w**, but I have	2889
	15:19 but I have chosen you out of the **w**,	2889
	15:19 of the world, therefore the **w** hateth you.	2889
	16: 8 he will reprove the **w** of sin,	2889
	16:11 because the prince of this **w** is judged.	2889
	16:20 and lament, but the **w** shall rejoice:	2889
	16:21 for joy that a man is born into the **w**.	2889
	16:28 from the Father, and am come into the **w**:	2889
	16:28 again, I leave the **w**, and go to the Father.	2889
	16:33 In the **w** ye shall have tribulation: but be	2889
	16:33 be of good cheer; I have overcome the **w**.	2889
	17: 5 which I had with thee before the **w** was.	2889
	17: 6 men which thou gavest me out of the **w**:	2889
	17: 9 I pray not for the **w**, but for *them* which	2889
	17:11 And *now* I am no more in the **w**,	2889
	17:11 these are in the **w**, and I come to thee.	2889
	17:12 While I was with them in the **w**, I kept	2889
	17:13 these *things* I speak in the **w**, that they	2889
	17:14 And the **w** hath hated them, because	2889
	17:14 them, because they are not of the **w**,	2889
	17:14 of the world, even as I am not of the **w**.	2889
	17:15 thou shouldest take them out of the **w**,	2889
	17:16 They are not of the **w**, even as I am not of	2889
	17:16 of the world, even as I am not of the **w**.	2889
	17:18 As thou hast sent me into the **w**, even *so*	2889
	17:18 even *so* have I also sent them into the **w**.	2889
	17:21 the **w** may believe that thou hast sent	2889
	17:23 that the **w** may know that thou hast sent	2889
	17:24 me before the foundation of the **w**.	2889
	17:25 the **w** hath not known thee:	2889
	18:20 answered him, I spake openly to the **w**;	2889
	18:36 My kingdom is not of this **w**:	2889
	18:36 this world: if my kingdom were of this **w**,	2889
	18:37 and for this cause came I into the **w**,	2889
	21:25 I suppose that even the **w** itself could not	2889
Ac	3:21 of all his holy prophets since the **w** began.	165
	11:28 be great dearth throughout all the **w**:	3625
	15:18 all his works from the beginning of the **w**.	165
	17: 6 These that have turned the **w** upside	3625
	17:24 God that made the **w** and all things	2889
	17:31 in the which he will judge the **w** in	3625
	19:27 whom all Asia and the **w** worshippeth.	3625
	24: 5 among all the Jews throughout the **w**,	3625
Ro	1: 8 is spoken of throughout the whole **w**.	2889
	1:20 the creation of the **w** are clearly seen,	2889
	3: 6 for then how shall God judge the **w**?	2889
	3:19 all the **w** may become guilty before God.	2889
	4:13 that he should be the heir of the **w**,	2889
	5:12 as by one man sin entered into the **w**,	2889
	5:13 For until the law sin was in the **w**: but sin	2889
	10:18 and their words unto the ends of the **w**.	3625

Ro		
	11:12 if the fall of them *be* the riches of the **w**,	2889
	11:15 away of them *be* the reconciling of the **w**,	2889
	12: 2 And be not conformed to this **w**: but be ye	165
	16:25 was kept secret **since the world began**,	166+5550
1Co	1:20 where *is* the disputer of this **w**? hath not	165
	1:20 God made foolish the wisdom of this **w**?	2889
	1:21 after that in the wisdom of God the **w**	2889
	1:27 *things* of the **w** to confound the wise;	2889
	1:27 hath chosen the weak *things* of the **w**	2889
	1:28 base *things* of the **w**, and *things* which	2889
	2: 6 yet not the wisdom of this **w**, nor of	165
	2: 6 nor of the princes of this **w**, that come to	165
	2: 7 God ordained before the **w** unto our glory:	165
	2: 8 Which none of the princes of this **w** knew:	165
	2:12 not the spirit of the **w**, but the Spirit	2889
	3:18 among you seemeth to be wise in this **w**,	165
	3:19 For the wisdom of this **w** is foolishness	2889
	3:22 the **w**, or life, or death, or *things* present,	2889
	4: 9 for we are made a spectacle unto the **w**,	2889
	4:13 we are made as the filth of the **w**,	2889
	5:10 altogether with the fornicators of this **w**,	2889
	5:10 for then must ye needs go out of the **w**.	2889
	6: 2 know that the saints shall judge the **w**?	2889
	6: 2 if the **w** shall be judged by you, are ye	2889
	7:31 they that use this **w**, as not abusing *it*:	2889
	7:31 as not abusing *it*: for the fashion of this **w**	2889
	7:33 careth for the *things that are* of the **w**,	2889
	7:34 is married careth for the *things* of the **w**,	2889
	8: 4 we know that an idol *is* nothing in the **w**,	2889
	8:13 I will eat no flesh while the **w** standeth,	165
	10:11 upon whom the ends of the **w** are come.	165
	11:32 should not be condemned with the **w**.	2889
	14:10 so many kinds of voices in the **w**,	2889
2Co	1:12 we have had our conversation in the **w**,	2889
	4: 4 In whom the god of this **w** hath blinded	165
	5:19 that God was in Christ reconciling the **w**	2889
	7:10 but the sorrow of the **w** worketh death.	2889
Gal	1: 4 might deliver us from *this* present evil **w**,	165
	4: 3 in bondage under the elements of the **w**:	2889
	6:14 by whom the **w** is crucified unto me, and	2889
	6:14 is crucified unto me, and I unto the **w**.	2889
Eph	1: 4 us in him before the foundation of the **w**,	2889
	1:21 not only in this **w**, but also in that which	165
	2: 2 walked according to the course of this **w**,	2889
	2:12 no hope, and without God in the **w**:	2889
	3: 9 which from the **beginning of the w** hath	165
	3:21 ages, **w without end**.	165+165+3588+3588
	6:12 against the rulers of the darkness of this **w**,	165
Php	2:15 among whom ye shine as lights in the **w**;	2889
Col	1: 6 is come unto you, as *it is* in all the **w**;	2889
	2: 8 after the rudiments of the **w**, and not after	2889
	2:20 with Christ from the rudiments of the **w**,	2889
	2:20 why, as though living in the **w**, are ye	2889
1Ti	1:15 that Christ Jesus came into the **w** to save	2889
	3:16 believed on in the **w**, received up into	2889
	6: 7 For we brought nothing into *this* **w**,	2889
	6:17 Charge *them that are* rich in this **w**, that	165
2Ti	1: 9 in Christ Jesus before the **w** began,	166+5550
	4:10 loved *this* present **w**, and is departed	165
Tit	1: 2 promised before the **w** began;	166+5550
	2:12 and godly, in *this* present **w**;	165
Heb	1: 6 bringeth in the firstbegotten into the **w**,	3625
	2: 5 he not put in subjection the **w** to come,	3625
	4: 3 finished from the foundation of the **w**.	2889
	6: 5 of God, and the powers of the **w** to come,	165
	9:26 suffered since the foundation of the **w**:	2889
	9:26 now once in the end of the **w** hath he	165
	10: 5 Wherefore when he cometh into the **w**,	2889
	11: 7 by the which he condemned the **w**,	2889
	11:38 (Of whom the **w** was not worthy:)	2889
Jas	1:27 to keep himself unspotted from the **w**.	2889
	2: 5 not God chosen the poor of this **w** rich	2889
	3: 6 and the tongue *is* a fire, a **w** of iniquity:	2889
	4: 4 know ye not that the friendship of the **w**	2889
	4: 4 will be a friend of the **w** is the enemy of	2889
1Pe	1:20 before the foundation of the **w**,	2889
	5: 9 in your brethren that are in the **w**.	2889
2Pe	1: 4 corruption that is in the **w** through lust:	2889
	2: 5 And spared not the old **w**, but saved Noah	2889
	2: 5 bringing in the flood upon the **w** of	2889
	2:20 the **w** through the knowledge of the Lord	2889
	3: 6 Whereby the **w** that then was,	2889
1Jn	2: 2 but also for *the sins of* the whole **w**.	2889
	2:15 Love not the **w**, neither the *things* that	2889
	2:15 neither the *things* that are in the **w**.	2889
	2:15 If any *man* love the **w**, the love of	2889
	2:16 all that is in the **w**, the lust of the flesh,	2889
	2:16 life, is not of the Father, but is of the **w**.	2889
	2:17 And the **w** passeth away, and the lust	2889
	3: 1 therefore the **w** knoweth us not, because	2889
	3:13 my brethren, if the **w** hate you.	2889
	4: 1 false prophets are gone out into the **w**.	2889
	4: 3 and *even* now already is it in the **w**.	2889
	4: 4 he that is in you, than he that is in the **w**.	2889
	4: 5 They are of the **w**, therefore speak they	2889
	4: 5 therefore speak they of the **w**,	2889
	4: 5 of the world, and the **w** heareth them.	2889
	4: 9 sent his only begotten Son into the **w**,	2889
	4:14 sent the Son *to be* the Saviour of the **w**.	2889
	4:17 because as he is, so are we in this **w**.	2889
	5: 4 is born of God overcometh the **w**:	2889
	5: 4 this is the victory that overcometh the **w**,	2889
	5: 5 Who is he that overcometh the **w**, but he	2889
	5:19 and the whole **w** lieth in wickedness.	2889
2Jn	1: 7 many deceivers are entered into the **w**,	2889

W

Rev 3:10 which shall come upon all the **w**, to try 3625
11:15 The kingdoms of *this* **w** are become 2889
12: 9 Satan, which deceiveth the whole **w**: 3625
13: 3 and all the **w** wondered after the beast. 1093
13: 8 Lamb slain from the foundation of the **w**. 2889
16:14 kings of the earth and of the whole **w**, 3625
17: 8 book of life from the foundation of the **w**, 2889

WORLD'S (1) [WORLD]
1Jn 3:17 But whoso hath *this* **w** good, and seeth 2889

WORLDLY (2) [WORLD]
Tit 2:12 and **w** lusts we should live soberly, 2886
Heb 9: 1 of divine service, and a **w** sanctuary. 2886

WORLDS (2) [WORLD]
Heb 1: 2 all *things,* by whom also he made the **w**; 165
11: 3 Through faith we understand that the **w** 165

WORM (14) [CANKERWORM, PALMERWORM, WORMS, WORMWOOD]
Ex 16:24 neither was there any **w** therein. 7415
Job 17:14 to the **w**, Thou art my mother, 7415
24:20 the **w** shall feed sweetly on him; 7415
25: 6 How much less man, *that is* a **w**? 7415
25: 6 and the son of man, *which is* a **w**? 8438
Ps 22: 6 I *am* a **w**, and no man; a reproach of men, 8438
Isa 14:11 the **w** is spread under thee, and the 7415
41:14 thou **w** Jacob, *and* ye men of Israel; 8438
51: 8 and the **w** shall eat them like wool; 5580
66:24 their **w** shall not die, neither shall their 8438
Jnh 4: 7 God prepared a **w** when the morning 8438
Mk 9:44 Where their **w** dieth not, and the fire is 4663
9:46 Where their **w** dieth not, and the fire is 4663
9:48 Where their **w** dieth not, and the fire is 4663

WORMS (8) [WORM]
Ex 16:20 the morning, and it bred **w**, and stank: 8438
Dt 28:39 nor gather *the grapes;* for the **w** shall eat 8438
Job 7: 5 My flesh is clothed with **w** and clods of 7415
19:26 *though* after my skin **w** destroy this *body,* NIH
21:26 in the dust, and the **w** shall cover them. 7415
Isa 14:11 spread under thee, and the **w** cover thee. 8438
Mic 7:17 they shall move out of their holes like **w** 2119
Ac 12:23 and he was **eaten of w**, and gave up 4662

WORMWOOD (9) [WOOD, WORM]
Dt 29:18 among you a root that beareth gall and **w**; 3939
Pr 5: 4 end is bitter as **w**, sharp as a twoedged 3939
Jer 9:15 with **w**, and give them water of gall to 3939
23:15 I will feed them with **w**, and make them 3939
La 3:15 he hath made me drunken *with* **w**. 3939
3:19 and my misery, the **w** and the gall. 3939
Am 5: 7 who turn judgment to **w**, and leave off 3939
Rev 8:11 And the name of the star is called **W**: 894
8:11 the third *part* of the waters became **w**; 894

WORSE (26) [BAD]
Ge 19: 9 now will we **deal w** with thee, than with 7489
2Sa 7 that *will be* **w** unto thee than all the evil 7489
1Ki 16:25 and did **w** than all that *were* before him. 7489
2Ki 14:12 Judah was **put to the w** before Israel; 5062
1Ch 19:16 that they were **put to the w** before Israel, 5062
19:19 that they were **put to the w** before Israel, 5062
2Ch 6:24 if thy people Israel be **put to the w** before 5062
25:22 Judah was **put to the w** before Israel, 5062
33: 9 to err, *and* to do **w** than the heathen, 7451
Jer 7:26 their neck: they **did w** than their fathers. 7489
16:12 ye have done **w** than your fathers; 7489
Da 1:10 why should he see your faces **w liking** 2196
Mt 9:16 the garment, and the rent is made **w**. 5501
12:45 last *state* of that man is **w than** the first. 5501
27:64 so the last error shall be **w than** the first. 5501
Mk 2:21 *from* the old, and the rent is made **w**. 5501
5:26 was nothing bettered, but rather grew **w**, 5501
Lk 11:26 last *state* of that man is **w than** the first. 5501
Jn 2:10 have well drunk, then that which is **w**: 1640
5:14 no more, lest a **w** *thing* come unto thee. 5501
1Co 8: 8 neither, if we eat not, are we the **w**. 5302
11:17 together not for the better, but for the **w**. 2276
1Ti 5: 8 denied the faith, and is **w than** an infidel. 5501
2Ti 3:13 shall wax **w and worse**, 1909+3588+5501
3:13 shall wax **worse and w**, 1909+3588+5501
2Pe 2:20 the latter *end* is **w** with them than 5501

WORSHIP (108) [WORSHIPPED, WORSHIPPER, WORSHIPPERS, WORSHIPPETH, WORSHIPPING]
Ge 22: 5 I and the lad will go yonder and **w**, 7812
Ex 24: 1 of the elders of Israel; and **w** ye afar off. 7812
34:14 For thou shalt **w** no other god: 7812
Dt 4:19 shouldest be driven to **w** them, 7812
8:19 other gods, and serve them, and **w** them, 7812
11:16 and serve other gods, and **w** them; 7812
26:10 and **w** before the LORD thy God: 7812
30:17 and **w** other gods, and serve them; 7812
Jos 5:14 did **w**, and said unto him, What saith my 7812
1Sa 1: 3 man went up out of his city yearly to **w** 7812
15:25 again with me, that I may **w** the LORD. 7812
15:30 with me, that I may **w** the LORD thy God. 7812
1Ki 9: 6 but go and serve other gods, and **w** them: 7812
12:30 for the people went to **w** before the one, NIH
2Ki 5:18 *into* the house of Rimmon to **w** there, 7812
17:36 him shall ye **w**, and to him shall ye do 7812
18:22 Ye shall **w** before this altar in Jerusalem? 7812
1Ch 16:29 **w** the LORD in the beauty of holiness. 7812
2Ch 7:19 go and serve other gods, and **w** them; 7812

2Ch 32:12 Ye shall **w** before one altar, 7812
Ps 5: 7 thy fear will I **w** toward thy holy temple. 7812
22:27 all the kindreds of the nations shall **w** 7812
22:29 *that be* fat upon earth shall eat and **w**: 7812
29: 2 **w** the LORD in the beauty of holiness. 7812
45:11 for he *is* thy Lord; and thou him. 7812
66: 4 All the earth shall **w** thee, and shall sing 7812
81: 9 neither shall thou **w** *any* strange god. 7812
86: 9 hast made shall come and **w** before thee, 7812
95: 6 O come, let us **w** and bow down: let us 7812
96: 9 O **w** the LORD in the beauty of holiness: 7812
97: 7 themselves of idols: **w** him, all ye gods. 7812
99: 5 LORD our God, and **w** at his footstool; 7812
99: 9 the LORD our God, and **w** at his holy hill; 7812
132: 7 his tabernacles: we will **w** at his footstool. 7812
138: 2 I will **w** toward thy holy temple, 7812
Isa 2: 8 they **w** the work of their own hands, 7812
2:20 they made *each one* for himself to **w**, 7812
27:13 shall **w** the LORD in the holy mount at 7812
36: 7 Jerusalem, Ye shall **w** before this altar? 7812
46: 6 it a god: they fall down, yea, they **w**. 7812
49: 7 shall see and arise, princes also shall **w**, 7812
66:23 shall all flesh come to **w** before me, 7812
Jer 7: 2 that enter in at these gates to **w** the LORD. 7812
13:10 other gods, to serve them, and to **w** them, 7812
25: 6 to **w** them, and provoke me not to anger 7812
26: 2 which come to **w** *in* the LORD's house, 7812
44:19 did we make her cakes to **w** her, 6087
Eze 46: 2 he shall **w** at the threshold of the gate: 7812
46: 3 Likewise the people of the land shall **w** *at* 7812
46: 9 **w** shall go out *by* the way of the south 7812
Da 3: 5 **w** the golden image that Nebuchadnezzar 5457
3:10 shall fall down and **w** the golden image: 5457
3:12 nor **w** the golden image which thou hast 5457
3:14 nor **w** the golden image which I have set 5457
3:15 and **w** the image which I have made; 5457
3:15 *well:* but if ye **w** not, ye shall be cast 5457
3:18 nor **w** the golden image which thou hast 5457
3:28 that they might not serve nor **w** any god, 5457
Mic 5:13 thou shalt no more **w** the work of thine 7812
Zep 1: 5 them that **w** the host of heaven upon 7812
1: 5 them that **w** *and* that swear by the LORD, 7812
1: 5 them, every one from his place, 7812
Zec 14:16 go up from year to year to **w** the King, 7812
14:17 the earth unto Jerusalem to **w** the King, 7812
Mt 2: 2 star in the east, and are come to **w** him. 4352
2: 8 that I may come and **w** him also. 4352
4: 9 if thou wilt fall down and **w** me. 4352
4:10 Thou shalt **w** the Lord thy God, 4352
15: 9 But in vain they do **w** me, teaching for 4576
Mk 7: 7 Howbeit in vain do they **w** me, teaching 4576
Lk 4: 7 If thou therefore wilt **w** me, all shall be 4352
4: 8 Thou shalt **w** the Lord thy God, 4352
14:10 shalt thou have **w** in the presence of them 1391
Jn 4:20 is the place where *men* ought to **w**. 4352
4:21 nor *yet* at Jerusalem, **w** the Father. 4352
4:22 Ye **w** ye know not what: we know what 4352
4:22 we know what we **w**: for salvation is of 4352
4:23 when the true worshippers shall **w** 4352
4:23 for the Father seeketh such to **w** him. 4352
4:24 that **w** him must worship *him* in spirit 4352
4:24 that worship him must **w** *him* in spirit 4352
12:20 them that came up to **w** at the feast: 4352
Ac 7:42 gave them up to **w** the host of heaven; 3000
7:43 figures which ye made to **w** them: 4352
8:27 and had come to Jerusalem for to **w**, 4352
17:23 Whom therefore ye ignorantly **w**, 2151
18:13 This *fellow* persuadeth men to **w** God 4576
24:11 since I went up to Jerusalem for to **w**. 4352
24:14 call heresy, so **w** I the God of my fathers, 3000
1Co 14:25 falling down on *his* face he will **w** 4352
Php 3: 3 which **w** God in the spirit, and rejoice in 3000
Col 2:23 have indeed a shew of wisdom in **will w**, 1479
Heb 1: 6 And let all the angels of God **w** him. 4352
Rev 3: 9 them to come and **w** before thy feet, 4352
4:10 and **w** him that liveth for ever and ever, 4352
9:20 that they should not **w** devils, and idols 4352
11: 1 and the altar, and them that **w** therein. 4352
13: 8 And all that dwell upon the earth shall **w** 4352
13:12 them which dwell therein to **w** the first 4352
13:15 cause that as many as would not **w** 4352
14: 7 and **w** him that made heaven, and earth, 4352
14: 9 If any *man* **w** the beast and his image, 4352
14:11 who **w** the beast and his image, 4352
15: 4 all nations shall come and **w** before thee; 4352
19:10 And I fell at his feet to **w** him. And he said 4352
19:10 **w** God: for the testimony of Jesus is 4352
22: 8 I fell down to **w** before the feet of 4352
22: 9 keep the sayings of this book: **w** God. 4352

WORSHIPPED (70) [WORSHIP]
Ge 24:26 bowed down his head, and **w** the LORD. 7812
24:48 the LORD, and blessed the LORD 7812
24:52 he **w** the LORD, *bowing himself* to 7812
Ex 4:31 then they bowed their heads and **w**. 7812
12:27 And the people bowed the head and **w**. 7812
32: 8 have **w** it, and have sacrificed thereunto, 7812
33:10 all the people rose up and **w**, every man 7812
34: 8 bowed his head toward the earth, and **w**. 7812
Dt 17: 3 **w** them, either the sun, or moon, or any 7812
29:26 and served other gods, and **w** them, 7812
Jdg 7:15 that he **w**, and returned into the host of 7812
1Sa 1:19 **w** before the LORD, and returned, 7812
1:28 to the LORD. And he **w** the LORD there. 7812
15:31 again after Saul; and Saul **w** the LORD. 7812

2Sa 12:20 came *into* the house of the LORD, and **w**: 7812
15:32 the top *of the mount,* where he **w** God, 7812
1Ki 9: 9 and have **w** them, and served them: 7812
11:33 have **w** Ashtoreth the goddess of 7812
16:31 and went and served Baal, and **w** him. 7812
22:53 **w** him, and provoked to anger the LORD 7812
2Ki 17:16 **w** all the host of heaven, and served Baal. 7812
21: 3 **w** all the host of heaven, and served 7812
21:21 idols that his father served, and **w** them: 7812
1Ch 29:20 and **w** the LORD, and the king. 7812
2Ch 7: 3 **w**, and praised the LORD, *saying,* For he 7812
7:22 other gods, and **w** them, and served 7812
29:28 all the congregation **w**, and the singers 7812
29:29 with him bowed themselves, and **w**. 7812
29:30 and they bowed their heads and **w**. 7812
33: 3 **w** all the host of heaven, and served 7812
Ne 8: 6 **w** the LORD *with their* faces to 7812
9: 3 and **w** the LORD their God. 7812
Job 1:20 and fell down upon the ground, and **w**, 7812
Ps 106:19 a calf in Horeb, and **w** the molten image. 7812
Jer 1:16 and **w** the works of their own hands, 7812
8: 2 have sought, and whom they have **w**, 7812
16:11 have **w** them, and have forsaken me, 7812
22: 9 and **w** other gods, and served them. 7812
Eze 8:16 and they **w** the sun towards the east. 7812
Da 2:46 **w** Daniel, and commanded that *they* 5457
3: 7 **w** the golden image that Nebuchadnezzar 5457
Mt 2:11 his mother, and fell down, and **w** him: 4352
8: 2 there came a leper and **w** him, saying, 4352
9:18 came a *certain* ruler, and **w** him, saying, 4352
14:33 that were in the ship came and **w** him, 4352
15:25 Then came she and **w** him, saying, Lord, 4352
18:26 fell down, and **w** him, saying, Lord, 4352
28: 9 and held him by the feet, and **w** him. 4352
28:17 And when they saw him, they **w** him: 4352
Mk 5: 6 he saw Jesus afar off, he ran and **w** him, 4352
15:19 and bowing *their* knees **w** him. 4352
Lk 24:52 they **w** him, and returned to Jerusalem 4352
Jn 4:20 fathers **w** in this mountain; and ye say, 4352
9:38 he said, Lord, I believe. And he **w** him. 4352
Ac 10:25 and fell down at *his* feet, and **w** *him*. 4352
16:14 of the city of Thyatira, which **w** God, 4576
17:25 Neither is **w** with men's hands, as though 2323
18: 7 named Justus, one that **w** God, 4576
Ro 1:25 and served the creature more than 4573
2Th 2: 4 above all that is called God, or that is **w**; 4574
Heb 11:21 and **w**, *leaning* upon the top of his staff. 4352
Rev 5:14 and **w** him that liveth for ever and ever. 4352
7:11 the throne on their faces, and **w** God, 4352
11:16 fell upon their faces, and **w** God, 4352
13: 4 And they **w** the dragon which gave power 4352
13: 4 and they **w** the beast, saying, Who *is* like 4352
16: 2 and *upon* them which **w** his image. 4352
19: 4 down and **w** God that sat on the throne, 4352
19:20 of the beast, and them that **w** his image. 4352
20: 4 which had not **w** the beast, neither his 4352

WORSHIPPER (2) [WORSHIP]
Jn 9:31 but if any *man* be a **w of God**, 2318
Ac 19:35 is a **w** of the great goddess Diana, 3511

WORSHIPPERS (7) [WORSHIP]
2Ki 10:19 to the intent that *he* might destroy the **w** 5647
10:21 all the **w** of Baal came, so that there was 5647
10:22 Bring forth vestments for all the **w** of Baal. 5647
10:23 said unto the **w** of Baal, Search, 5647
10:23 of the LORD, but the **w** of Baal only. 5647
Jn 4:23 when the true **w** shall worship the Father 4353
Heb 10: 2 the once purged should have had no 3000

WORSHIPPETH (6) [WORSHIP]
Ne 9: 6 them all; and the host of heaven **w** thee. 7812
Isa 44:15 **w** *it*; he maketh it a graven image, 7812
44:17 **w** *it,* and prayeth unto it, and saith, 7812
Da 3: 6 **w** shall the same hour be cast into the 5457
3:11 whoso falleth not down and **w**, *that he* 5457
Ac 19:27 whom all Asia and the world **w**. 4576

WORSHIPPING (5) [WORSHIP]
2Ki 19:37 as he was **w** *in* the house of Nisroch his 7812
2Ch 20:18 fell before the LORD, **w** the LORD. 7812
Isa 37:38 as he was **w** *in* the house of Nisroch his 7812
Mt 20:20 **w** him, and desiring a certain *thing* of 4352
Col 2:18 in a voluntary humility and **w** of angels, 2356

WORST (1) [BAD]
Eze 7:24 Wherefore I will bring the **w** of 7451

WORTH (9) [THANKWORTHY, UNWORTHILY, UNWORTHY, WORTHIES, WORTHILY, WORTHY]
Ge 23: 9 as much money as it is **w** he shall give it 4392
23:15 land *is* **w** four hundred shekels of silver; NIH
Lev 27:23 the priest shall reckon unto him the **w** of 4373
Dt 15:18 he hath been **w** a double hired servant *to* 7939
2Sa 18: 3 now *thou art* **w** ten thousand of us: 3644
1Ki 21: 2 I will give thee the **w** of it *in* money. 4242
Job 24:25 a liar, and make my speech nothing **w**? 3807.1
Pr 10:20 heart of the wicked *is* **little w**. 4592+3509.1
Eze 30: 2 Lord GOD; Howl ye, Woe **w** the day! 3807.1

WORTHIES (1) [WORTH]
Na 2: 5 He shall recount his **w**: they shall stumble 117

WORTHILY (1) [WORTH]
Ru 4:11 do thou **w** in Ephratah, and be famous in 2428

WORTHLESS See NOUGHT; VANITIES; VANITY

WORTHY (68) [WORTH]

Ge	32:10 I am **not** w of the least of all the mercies,	6994
Dt	17: 6 shall he that is w of death be put to death;	
	19: 6 whereas he *was* not w of death,	4941
	21:22 if a man have committed a sin w of death,	4941
	22:26 *there is* in the damsel no sin w of death;	NIH
	25: 2 if the wicked *man be* w to be beaten,	1121
1Sa	1: 5 unto Hannah he gave a w portion; for he	639
	26:16 *are* w to die, because ye have not	1121+4194
2Sa	22: 4 call on the LORD, who is w to be praised:	NIH
1Ki	1:52 If he will shew himself a w man,	2428
	2:26 thine own fields; for thou *art* w of death:	376
Ps	18: 3 upon the LORD, who is w to be praised:	NIH
Jer	26:11 the people, saying, This man *is* w to die;	4941
	26:16 to the prophets; This man *is* not w to die;	4941
Mt	3:11 than I, whose shoes I am not w to bear:	2425
	8: 8 I am not w that thou shouldest come	2425
	10:10 staves: for the workman is w of his meat.	514
	10:11 town ye shall enter, inquire who in it is w;	514
	10:13 If the house be w, let your peace come	514
	10:13 but if it be not w, let your peace return to	514
	10:37 or mother more than me is not w of me;	514
	10:37 or daughter more than me is not w of me.	514
	10:38 and followeth after me, is not w of me.	514
	22: 8 but they which were bidden were not w.	514
Mk	1: 7 the latchet of whose shoes I am not w to	2425
Lk	3: 8 Bring forth therefore fruits w of repentance,	514
	3:16 the latchet of whose shoes I am not w to	2425
	7: 4 he was w for whom he should do this:	
	7: 6 for I am not w that thou shouldest enter	2425
	7: 7 Wherefore neither **thought** I myself w to	515
	10: 7 for the labourer is w of his hire. Go not	514
	12:48 and did commit *things* w of stripes,	514
	15:19 And am no more w to be called thy son:	514
	15:21 and am no more w to be called thy son.	514
	20:35 But they which shall be **accounted** w to	2661
	21:36 ye may be **accounted** w to escape all	2661
	23:15 lo, nothing is w of death is done unto him.	514
Jn	1:27 shoe's latchet I am not w to unloose.	514
Ac	5:41 rejoicing that they were **counted** w to	2661
	13:25 shoes of *his* feet I am not w to loose.	514
	23:29 have nothing laid to his charge w of death	514
	24: 2 **very w** deeds are done unto this nation	2735
	25:11 or have committed any *thing* w of death,	514
	25:25 that he had committed nothing w of death,	514
	26:31 This man doeth nothing w of death or	514
Ro	1:32 they which commit such *things* are w of	514
	8:18 w to be compared with the glory which	514
Eph	4: 1 beseech you that ye **walk** w of the vocation	516
Col	1:10 That ye might walk w of the Lord unto all	516
1Th	2:12 That ye would walk w of God, who hath	516
2Th	1: 5 ye may be **counted** w of the kingdom	2661
	1:11 that our God would **count** you w of *this*	515
1Ti	1:15 a faithful saying, and w of all acceptation,	514
	4: 9 a faithful saying and w of all acceptation.	514
	5:17 the elders that rule well be **counted** w of	514
	5:18 And, The labourer *is* w of his reward.	514
	6: 1 count their own masters w of all honour,	514
Heb	3: 3 this *man* was **counted** w of more glory	515
	10:29 suppose ye, shall he be **thought** w,	515
	11:38 (Of whom the world was not w:)	514
Jas	2: 7 Do not they blaspheme *that* w name by	2570
Rev	3: 4 walk with me in white; for they are w.	514
	4:11 Thou art w, O Lord, to receive glory and	514
	5: 2 Who is w to open the book, and to loose	514
	5: 4 because no *man* was found w to open and	514
	5: 9 Thou art w to take the book, and to open	514
	5:12 W is the Lamb that was slain to receive	514
	16: 6 given them blood to drink; for they are w.	514

WOT (10) [WIT]

Ge	21:26 I w not who hath done this thing:	3045
	44:15 w ye not that such a man as I can	3045
Ex	32: 1 Egypt, we w not what is become of him.	3045
	32:23 Egypt, we w not what is become of him.	3045
Nu	22: 6 for I w that *he* whom thou blessest *is*	3045
Jos	2: 5 whither the men went I w not: pursue	3045
Ac	3:17 I w that through ignorance ye did *it*, as	1492
	7:40 Egypt, we w not what is become of him.	1492
Ro	11: 2 W ye not what the scripture saith of Elias?	1492
Php	1:22 labour: yet what I shall choose I w not.	1107

WOTTETH (1) [WIT]

Ge	39: 8 my master w not what *is* with me in	3045

WOULD (451) [WILL, WOULDEST]

Ge	2:19 *them* unto Adam to see what he w	NIH
	21: 7 she said, Who w have said unto Abraham,	NIH
	30:34 I w it might be according to thy word.	3863
	42:21 when he besought us, and we w not hear;	NIH
	42:22 sin against the child; and ye w not hear?	NIH
	43: 7 could we certainly know that he w say,	NIH
	44:22 should leave his father, *his* father w die.	NIH
Ex	2: 4 afar off, to wit what w be done to him.	NIH
	8:32 time also, neither w he let the people go.	NIH
	9:35 neither w he let the children of Israel go;	NIH
	10:20 but w not let the children of Israel go.	NIH
	10:27 Pharaoh's heart, and he w not let them go.	14
	11:10 he w not let the children of Israel go out	NIH
	13:15 to pass, when Pharaoh w hardly let us go,	NIH
	16: 3 W to God we had died by the	4310+5414
Nu	11:29 w God that all the LORD's people	4310+5414
	11:29 that the LORD w put his spirit upon them!	NIH

Nu	14: 2 W God that we had died in the land of	3863
	14: 2 or w God we had died in this wilderness!	3863
	20: 3 W God that we had died when our	3863
	21:23 Sihon w not suffer Israel to pass through	NIH
	22:18 If Balak w give me his house full of silver	NIH
	22:29 I w there were a sword in mine hand,	3863
	22:29 sword in mine hand, for now w I kill thee.	NIH
	24:13 If Balak w give me his house full of silver	NIH
Dt	1:26 Notwithstanding ye w not go up,	14
	1:43 you w not hear, but rebelled against	NIH
	1:45 the LORD w not hearken to your voice,	NIH
	2:30 Sihon king of Heshbon w not let us pass by	14
	3:26 me for your sakes, and w not hear me:	NIH
	5:29 that they w fear me, and keep all my	NIH
	7: 8 he w keep the oath which he had sworn	NIH
	8:20 ye w not be obedient unto the voice of	NIH
	9:25 the LORD had said he w destroy you.	NIH
	10:10 time also, *and* the LORD w not destroy thee.	14
	23: 5 Nevertheless the LORD thy God w not	14
	23:21 require it of thee; and it w be sin in thee.	NIH
	28:56 which w not adventure to set the sole of	NIH
	28:67 shalt say, W God it were even!	4310+5414
	28:67 shalt say, W God it were morning!	4310+5414
	32:26 I said, I w scatter them into corners,	NIH
	32:26 I w make the remembrance of them to	NIH
	32:29 that they w consider their latter end!	NIH
Jos	5: 6 unto whom the LORD sware that *he* w not	NIH
	5: 6 sware unto their fathers that he w give us,	NIH
	7: 7 w to God we had been content,	3863+2050.1
	17:12 but the Canaanites w dwell in that land.	2974
	24:10 I w not hearken unto Balaam; therefore	14
Jdg	1:27 but the Canaanites w dwell in that land.	2974
	1:34 they w not suffer them to come down to	NIH
	1:35 the Amorites w dwell in mount Heres in	2974
	2:17 yet they w not hearken unto their judges,	NIH
	3: 4 to know whether they w hearken unto	NIH
	8:19 ye had saved them alive, I w not slay you.	NIH
	8:24 unto them, I w desire a request of you,	NIH
	8:24 you w give me every man the earrings	NIH
	9:29 w to God this people were under	4310+5414
	9:29 my hand; then w I remove Abimelech.	NIH
	11:17 the king of Edom w not hearken *thereto.*	NIH
	11:17 he w not consent: and Israel abode in	NIH
	11:23 he w not have received a burnt offering	NIH
	13:23 neither w he have shewed us all these	NIH
	13:23 w as *at this* time have told us *such things*	NIH
	14: 6 and he rent him as *he* w have rent a kid,	NIH
	15: 1 But her father w not suffer him to go in.	NIH
	19:10 the man w not tarry *that* night, but he rose	14
	19:25 the men w not hearken to him: so the man	14
	20:13 the children of Benjamin w not hearken to	14
Ru	1:13 W ye tarry for them till they were grown?	NIH
	1:13 w ye stay for them from having husbands?	NIH
1Sa	2:16 he w answer him, *Nay;* but thou shalt give	2654
	2:25 because the LORD w slay them.	NIH
	13:13 for now w the LORD have established thy	NIH
	15: 9 *was* good, and w not utterly destroy them:	14
	18: 2 w let him go no more home *to* his father's	NIH
	20: 9 come upon thee, then w not I tell it thee?	NIH
	22:17 servants of the king w not put forth their	14
	22:22 *was* there, that he w surely tell Saul:	NIH
	26:23 I w not stretch forth mine hand against	14
	31: 4 his armourbearer w not; for he was sore	14
2Sa	2:21 Asahel w not turn aside from following of	14
	4: 6 as *though* they w have fetched wheat;	NIH
	4:10 who *thought* that I w have given him a	NIH
	6:10 So David w not remove the ark of the LORD	14
	11:20 knew ye not that they w shoot from	NIH
	12: 8 I w moreover have given unto thee such	NIH
	12:17 he w not, neither did he eat bread with	14
	12:18 and he w not hearken unto our voice:	NIH
	13:14 Howbeit he w not hearken unto her voice:	14
	13:16 But he w not hearken unto her.	14
	13:25 howbeit he w not go, but blessed him.	14
	14:16 of the hand of the man *that* w destroy me	NIH
	14:29 him to the king; but he w not come to him:	14
	14:29 sent again the second time, he w not come.	14
	15: 4 come unto me, and I w do him justice.	NIH
	18:11 I w have given thee ten *shekels* of silver,	NIH
	18:12 *yet* I w not put forth mine hand against	NIH
	18:33 w God I had died for thee, O Absalom,	4310
	23:15 that one w give me drink of the water of	14
	23:16 nevertheless he w not drink thereof,	14
	23:17 therefore he w not drink it. These *things*	14
1Ki	8:12 The LORD said that *he* w dwell in	NIH
	13:33 whosoever w, he consecrated him,	2655
	18:32 great as w contain two measures of seed.	NIH
	20:33 whether *any thing* w come from him,	NIH
	21: 4 turned away his face, and w eat no bread.	NIH
	22:18 Did I not tell thee that w prophesy no	NIH
	22:49 in the ships. But Jehoshaphat w not.	14
2Ki	2: 1 when the LORD w take up Elijah *into*	NIH
	3:14 w not look toward thee, nor see thee.	NIH
	5: 3 W God my lord *were* with the prophet	305
	5: 7 for he w recover him of his leprosy.	NIH
	7: 2 *if* the LORD w make windows in heaven,	NIH
	8:19 Yet the LORD w not destroy Judah for	14
	13:23 Isaac, and Jacob, and w not destroy them,	14
	14:11 Amaziah w not hear. Therefore Jehoash	NIH
	14:27 the LORD said that *he* w blot out	NIH
	17:14 Notwithstanding they w not hear,	NIH
	18:12 and w not hear *them*, nor do *them.*	NIH
	24: 4 which the LORD w not pardon.	14
1Ch	10: 4 his armourbearer w not; for he was sore	14
	11:17 that one w give me drink of the water of	NIH

1Ch	11:18 David w not drink *of* it, but poured it out	14
	11:19 Therefore he w not drink it. These *things*	14
	13: 4 the congregation said that *they* w do so:	NIH
	19:19 neither w the Syrians help the children of	14
	27:23 the LORD had said *he* w increase Israel	NIH
2Ch	6: 1 The LORD hath said that *he* w dwell in	NIH
	10:16 when all Israel saw that the king w not	NIH
	12:12 that *he* w not destroy *him* altogether:	NIH
	15:13 That whosoever w not seek the LORD	NIH
	18:17 Did I not tell thee *that* he w not prophesy	NIH
	21: 7 Howbeit the LORD w not destroy the house	14
	24:19 against them: but they w not give ear.	NIH
	25:20 Amaziah w not hear; for it *came* of God,	NIH
	33:10 and to his people: but they w not hearken.	NIH
	35:22 Nevertheless Josiah w not turn his face	NIH
Ezr	10: 8 *that* whosoever w not come within three	NIH
	10:19 they gave their hands that *they* w put	NIH
Ne	6:11 as I *am*, w go into the temple to save	NIH
	6:14 the prophets, that w have put me in fear.	NIH
	9:24 that *they* might do with them as they w.	7522
	9:29 and hardened their neck, and w not hear.	NIH
	9:30 yet w they not give ear: therefore	NIH
	10:30 that we w not give our daughters unto	NIH
	10:31 we w not buy *it* of them on the sabbath,	NIH
	10:31 *that* we w leave the seventh year,	NIH
Est	3: 4 see whether Mordecai's matters w stand:	NIH
	6: 6 whom the king delight to do honour	NIH
	8:11 people and province that w assault them,	NIH
	9: 5 what they w unto those that hated them,	7522
	9:27 they w keep these two days according	1961
Job	5: 8 I w seek unto God, and unto God would	199
	5: 8 and unto God w I commit my cause:	NIH
	6: 3 For now it w be heavier than the sand of	NIH
	6: 8 *that* God w grant *me* the thing that I long	NIH
	6: 9 Even *that* it w please God to destroy me:	NIH
	6: 9 he w let loose his hand, and cut me off!	NIH
	6:10 yea, I w harden myself in sorrow; let him	NIH
	7:16 loathe *it*; I w not live alway: let me alone;	NIH
	8: 6 surely now he w awake for thee,	NIH
	9:15 yet w I not answer, *but* I would make	NIH
	9:15 *but* I w make supplication to my judge.	NIH
	9:16 yet w I not believe that he had hearkened	NIH
	9:21 *were* perfect, *yet* w I not know my soul:	NIH
	9:21 I not know my soul: I w despise my life.	NIH
	9:35 *Then* w I speak, and not fear him; but *it is*	NIH
	11: 5 O that God w speak, and open his lips	NIH
	11: 6 w he shew thee the secrets of wisdom,	NIH
	11:12 For vain man w be wise, though man be	NIH
	13: 3 Surely I w speak to the Almighty,	NIH
	13: 5 O that you w altogether hold your peace,	NIH
	16: 5 *But* I w strengthen you with my mouth,	NIH
	23: 4 I w order *my* cause before him, and fill my	NIH
	23: 5 I w know the words *which* he would	NIH
	23: 5 know the words *which* he w answer	NIH
	23: 5 and understand what he w say unto me.	NIH
	23: 6 No; but he w put *strength* in me.	NIH
	27:22 he w **fain flee** out of his hand.	1272+1272
	30: 1 whose fathers I w have disdained to have	NIH
	31:12 and w root out all mine increase.	NIH
	31:35 that one w hear me! behold, my desire *is,*	NIH
	31:35 my desire *is, that* the Almighty w answer	NIH
	31:36 Surely I w take it upon my shoulder,	NIH
	31:37 I w declare unto him the number of my	NIH
	31:37 steps; as a prince w I go near unto him.	NIH
	32:22 *doing* my Maker w soon take me away.	NIH
	34:27 and w not consider any of his ways:	NIH
	36:16 w he have removed thee out of the strait	NIH
	41:32 him; *one* w think the deep to be hoary.	NIH
Ps	22: 8 He trusted on the LORD *that* he w deliver	NIH
	35:25 say in their hearts, Ah, so w we have it:	NIH
	40: 5 *if* I w declare and speak *of them,* they are	NIH
	50:12 If I were hungry, I w not tell thee:	NIH
	51:16 else w I give *it*: thou delightest not in	NIH
	55: 6 *for then* w I fly away, and be at rest.	NIH
	55: 7 *then* w I wander far off, *and* remain in	NIH
	55: 8 I w hasten my escape from the windy	NIH
	55:12 then I w have hid myself from him:	NIH
	56: 1 man w swallow me up; he fighting daily	NIH
	56: 2 Mine enemies w daily swallow *me* up:	NIH
	57: 3 save me *from* the reproach of him that w	NIH
	69: 4 that w destroy me, *being* mine enemies	NIH
	81:11 my people w not hearken to my voice;	NIH
	81:11 to my voice; and Israel w none of me.	NIH
	106:23 Therefore he said that *he* w destroy them,	NIH
	107: 8 Oh that *men* w praise the LORD *for* his	NIH
	107:15 Oh that *men* w praise the LORD *for* his	NIH
	107:21 Oh that *men* w praise the LORD *for* his	NIH
	107:31 Oh that *men* w praise the LORD *for* his	NIH
	119:57 I have said that *I* w keep thy words.	NIH
	142: 4 but *there was* no man that w know me:	NIH
Pr	1:25 all my counsel, and w none of my reproof:	14
	1:30 They w none of my counsel: they despised	14
SS	3: 4 I held him, and w not let him go, until I	NIH
	8: 1 I should find thee without, I w kiss thee;	NIH
	8: 2 I w lead thee, *and* bring thee into my	NIH
	8: 2 my mother's house, *who* w instruct me:	NIH
	8: 2 I w cause thee to drink of spiced wine,	NIH
	8: 7 if a man w give all the substance of his	NIH
	8: 7 house for love, it w utterly be contemned.	NIH
Isa	27: 4 who w set the briers *and* thorns against	NIH
	27: 4 I w go through them, I would burn them	NIH
	27: 4 go through them, I w burn them together.	NIH
	28:12 this *is* the refreshing: yet they w not hear.	14
	30:15 shall be your strength: and ye w not.	14
	42:24 for they w not walk in his ways, neither	14

W

Isa	54: 9	have I sworn that *I* **w** not be wroth with	NIH
Jer	8:18	*When* I **w** comfort myself against sorrow,	NIH
	10: 7	Who **w** not fear thee, O King of nations?	NIH
	13:11	and for a glory: but they **w** not hear.	NIH
	18:10	good, wherewith I said *I* **w** benefit them.	NIH
	22:24	my right hand, yet I **w** pluck thee thence;	NIH
	29:19	and sending *them*; but ye **w** not hear,	NIH
	36:25	to the king that *he* **w** not burn the roll:	NIH
	36:25	not burn the roll: but he **w** not hear them.	NIH
	38:26	that *he* **w** no cause me to return to	NIH
	49: 9	they not leave *some* gleaning grapes?	NIH
	51: 9	We **w** have healed Babylon, but she is not	NIH
La	4:12	**w** not have believed that the adversary	NIH
Eze	3: 6	them, they **w** have hearkened unto thee.	NIH
	6:10	I have not said in vain that *I* **w** do this	NIH
	13: 6	have made *others* to hope that *they* **w**	NIH
	20: 8	against me, and **w** not hearken unto me:	14
	20:13	*I* **w** pour out my fury upon them in	NIH
	20:15	that *I* **w** not bring them into the land	NIH
	20:21	I said, *I* **w** pour out my fury upon them,	NIH
	20:23	that *I* **w** scatter them among the heathen,	NIH
	38:17	that *I* **w** bring thee against them?	NIH
Da	1: 8	Daniel purposed in his heart that he **w** not	NIH
	2: 8	know of certainty that ye **w** gain the time,	NIH
	2:16	of the king that he **w** give him time,	NIH
	2:16	*he* **w** shew the king the interpretation.	NIH
	2:18	That *they* **w** desire mercies of the God of	NIH
	5:19	whom he **w** he slew; and whom he	6634
	5:19	whom he **w** he kept alive; and whom he	6634
	5:19	whom he **w** he set up; and whom he	6634
	5:19	he set up; and whom he **w** he put down.	6634
	7:19	I **w** know the truth of the fourth beast,	6634
	9: 2	that *he* **w** accomplish seventy years in	NIH
Hos	7: 1	When I **w** have healed Israel, then	NIH
	11: 7	to the most High, none at all **w** exalt *him.*	NIH
Ob	1: 5	they not have stolen till they had	NIH
	1: 5	to thee, **w** they not leave *some* grapes?	NIH
Jnh	3:10	that he had said that he **w** do unto them;	NIH
	4: 5	he might see what **w** become of the city.	NIH
Zec	7:13	*that* as he cried, and they **w** not hear;	NIH
	7:13	so they cried, and I **w** not hear, saith	NIH
Mal	1:10	Who *is there* even among you that **w** shut	NIH
Mt	2:18	**w** not be comforted, because they are	2309
	5:42	from him that **w** borrow of thee turn not	2309
	7:12	Therefore all *things* whatsoever ye **w** that	2309
	8:34	they besought *him* that he **w** depart out of	NIG
	11:21	Sidon they **w** have repented long ago in	302
	11:23	Sodom, it **w** have remained until this day.	302
	12: 7	ye **w** not **have** condemned the guiltless.	302
	12:38	Master, we **w** see a sign from thee.	2309
	14: 5	And when he **w** have put him to death,	2309
	14: 7	an oath to give her whatsoever she **w** ask.	NIG
	16: 1	tempting desired that *he* **w** shew	NIG
	18:23	which **w** take account of his servants.	2309
	18:30	And he **w** not: but went and cast him into	2309
	22: 3	to the wedding: and they **w** not come.	2309
	23:30	we **w** not **have** been partakers with them	302
	23:37	how often **w** I have gathered thy children	2309
	23:37	chickens under *her* wings, and ye **w** not?	2309
	24:43	known in what watch the thief **w** come,	NIG
	24:43	he **w** have **watched**, and would not have	302
	24:43	**w** not **have** suffered his house to be broken	302
	27:15	the people a prisoner, whom they **w.**	2309
	27:34	he had tasted *thereof*, he **w** not drink.	2309
Mk	3: 2	he **w** heal him on the sabbath day;	NIG
	3:13	and calleth unto *him* whom he **w:**	2309
	5:10	And he besought him much that he **w** not	2309
	6:19	against him, and **w** have killed him;	2309
	6:26	their sakes which sat with *him,* he **w** not	2309
	6:48	the sea, and **w** have passed by them.	2309
	7:24	he **w** no man know *it:* but he could	2309
	7:26	she besought him that he **w** cast forth	NIG
	9:30	he **w** not that any *man* should know *it.*	2309
	10:35	we **w** that thou shouldest do for us	2309
	10:36	What **w** ye that I should do for you?	2309
	11:16	**w** not suffer that any *man* should carry	NIG
Lk	1:62	to his father, how he **w** have him called.	302
	1:74	That he **w** grant unto us, that *we* being	NIG
	5: 3	prayed him that he **w** thrust out a little	NIG
	6: 7	whether he **w** heal on the sabbath day;	NIG
	6:31	And as ye **w** that men should do to you,	2309
	7: 3	beseeching him that he **w** come and heal	NIG
	7:36	desired him that he **w** eat with him.	NIG
	7:39	he **w** have known who and what manner of	302
	8:31	And they besought him that he **w** not	NIG
	8:32	they besought him that he **w** suffer them	NIG
	8:41	besought him that he **w** come into his	NIG
	9:53	his face was *as though he* **w** go to	NIG
	10: 1	and place, whither he himself **w** come.	3195
	10: 2	that he **w** send forth labourers into his	NIG
	12:39	had known what hour the thief **w** come,	NIG
	12:39	he **w** have **watched**, and not have suffered	NIG
	13:34	how often **w** I have gathered thy children	2309
	13:34	brood under *her* wings, and ye **w** not?	2309
	15:16	And he **w** **fain** have filled his belly with	1937
	15:28	And he was angry, and **w** not go in:	2309
	16:26	they which **w** pass from hence to you	NIG
	16:26	they pass to us, that *w come* from thence.	NIG
	18: 4	he **w** not for a while: but afterward he	2309
	18:13	**w** not lift up so much as *his* eyes unto	2309
	18:15	also infants, that he **w** touch them:	NIG
	19:27	**w** not that I should reign over them,	2309
	19:40	the stones **w** immediately cry out.	NIG
	22:49	were about him saw what **w** follow,	NIG
	24:28	made as though he **w** have gone further.	NIG

Jn	1:43	The day following Jesus **w** go forth into	2309
	4:10	and he **w** have given thee living water.	302
	4:40	they besought that he **w** tarry with	NIG
	4:47	and besought him that he **w** come down,	NIG
	5:46	believed Moses, ye **w** have believed me:	NIG
	6: 6	for he himself knew what he **w** do.	3195
	6:11	likewise of the fishes as much as they **w.**	2309
	6:15	therefore perceived that they **w** come	3195
	7: 1	for he **w** not walk in Jewry, because	2309
	7:44	And some of them **w** have taken him;	2309
	8:39	ye **w** do the works of Abraham.	NIG
	8:42	If God were your Father, ye **w** love me:	302
	9:27	wherefore **w** you hear *it* again? will ye	2309
	12:21	desired him, saying, Sir, we **w** see Jesus.	2309
	14: 2	if *it were not so,* I **w have** told you.	302
	14:28	If ye loved me, ye **w** rejoice, because I said,	302
	15:19	of the world, the world **w** love his own:	302
	18:30	**w** not **have** delivered him up into thine.	302
	18:36	of this world, then **w** my servants fight,	302
Ac	2:30	he **w** raise up Christ to sit on his throne;	NIG
	5:24	they doubted of them whereunto this **w**	NIG
	7: 5	yet he promised that he **w** give it to him.	NIG
	7:25	For he supposed his brethren **w** have	NIG
	7:25	that God by his hand **w** deliver them:	NIG
	7:26	**w** have set them at one *again,* saying,	2309
	7:39	To whom our fathers **w** not obey,	2309
	8:31	And he desired Philip that he **w** come up	NIG
	9:38	desiring him that he **w** not delay to come	NIG
	10:10	became very hungry, and **w** have eaten:	2309
	11:23	that with purpose of heart *they* **w** cleave	NIG
	12: 6	And when Herod **w** have brought him	3195
	14:13	**w** have done sacrifice with the people.	2309
	16: 3	Him **w** Paul have to go forth with him;	2309
	16:27	out his sword, and **w** have killed himself,	3195
	17:20	we **w** know therefore what these *things*	1014
	18:14	reason **w** that I should bear with you:	302
	19:30	And when Paul **w** have entered in unto	1014
	19:31	desiring him that he **w** not adventure	NIG
	19:33	**w** have made *his* defence into the people.	2309
	20:16	because he **w** not spend the time in Asia:	NIG
	21:14	And when he **w** not be persuaded,	NIG
	22:30	he **w** have known the certainty wherefore	1014
	23:12	saying that *they* **w** neither eat nor drink	2309
	23:15	as though ye **w** inquire something more	3195
	23:20	as though they **w** inquire somewhat of	3195
	23:28	And when I **w** have known the cause	1014
	24: 6	and **w** have judged according to our law.	2309
	25: 3	that he **w** send for him to Jerusalem,	NIG
	25: 4	that he himself **w** depart shortly *thither.*	3195
	25:20	asked *him* whether he **w** go to Jerusalem,	1014
	25:22	unto Festus, I **w** also hear the man myself.	1014
	26: 5	me from the beginning, if they **w** testify,	2309
	26:29	And Paul said, I **w** to God, that not	302+2172
	27:30	under colour as though they **w** have cast	3195
	28:18	**w have** let *me* go, because there was no	1014
Ro	1:13	Now I **w** not have you ignorant, brethren,	2309
	5: 7	yet peradventure for a good *man* some **w**	NIG
	7:15	what I **w,** that do I not; but what I hate,	2309
	7:16	If then I do that which I **w** not, I consent	2309
	7:19	the good that I **w** do not: but the evil	2309
	7:19	but the evil which I **w** not, that I do.	2309
	7:20	if I do that I **w** not, it is no more I that	2309
	7:21	I find then a law, that, when I **w** do good,	2309
	11:25	For I **w** not, brethren, that ye should be	2309
	16:19	yet I **w** have you wise unto *that which is*	2309
1Co	2: 8	for had they known *it,* they **w** not **have**	302
	4: 8	and I **w** *to God* ye did reign, that we also	3785
	4:18	puffed up, as though I **w** not come to you.	NIG
	7: 1	I **w that** all men were even as I myself.	2309
	7:32	But I **w** have you without carefulness.	2309
	10: 1	I **w** not that ye should be ignorant,	2309
	10:20	I **w** not that ye should have fellowship	2309
	11: 3	But I **w** have you know, that the head of	2309
	11:31	if we **w** judge ourselves, we should not	NIG
	12: 1	brethren, I **w** not have you ignorant.	2309
	14: 5	I **w** that ye all spake with tongues,	2309
2Co	1: 8	we **w** not, brethren, have you ignorant	2309
	2: 1	**w** not come again to you in heaviness.	NIG
	2: 8	Wherefore I beseech you that *you* **w**	2309
	5: 4	not for that we **w** be unclothed,	2309
	8: 6	Praying us with much intreaty that we **w**	NIG
	8: 6	he **w** also finish in you the same grace	NIG
	9: 5	that they **w** go before unto you,	NIG
	10: 9	That I may not seem as if *I* **w** terrify you	NIG
	11: 1	**W** *to God* you could bear with me a little	3785
	12: 6	For though I **w** desire to glory, I shall not	NIG
	12:20	I shall not find you such as I **w,** and *that* I	2309
	12:20	I shall be found unto you such as ye **w**	NIG
Gal	1: 7	and **w** pervert the gospel of Christ.	2309
	2:10	Only *they* **w** that we should remember	NIG
	3: 2	This only **w** I learn of you, Received ye	2309
	3: 8	foreseeing that God **w** justify the heathen	NIG
	4:15	ye **w** have plucked out your own eyes,	NIG
	4:17	yea, they **w** exclude you, that you might	2309
	5:12	I **w** they were even cut off which trouble	3785
	5:17	so that ye cannot do the *things* that ye **w.**	2309
Eph	3:16	he **w** grant you, according to the riches	NIG
Php	1:12	But I **w** ye should understand, brethren,	1014
Col	1:27	To whom God **w** make known what *is*	2309
	2: 1	For I **w** that ye knew what great conflict	2309
	4: 3	that God **w** open unto us a door of	NIG
1Th	2: 9	we **w** not be chargeable unto any of you,	NIG
	2:12	That ye **w** walk worthy of God, who hath	NIG
	2:18	Wherefore we **w** have come unto you,	2309
	4: 1	*so* ye **w** abound more *and more.*	2443

1Th	4:13	But I **w** not have you to be ignorant,	NIG
2Th	1:11	that our God **w** count you worthy of *this*	NIG
	3:10	that if any **w** not work, neither should he	NIG
Phm	1:13	Whom I **w** have retained with me, that in	1014
	1:14	But without thy mind **w** I do nothing;	2309
Heb	4: 8	**w** he not afterward have spoken of another	302
	10: 2	then **w** they not **have** ceased to be offered?	302
	11:32	for the time **w** fail me to tell of Gedeon,	NIG
	12:17	when he **w** have inherited the blessing,	2309
1Jn	2:19	they **w** *no doubt* **have** continued with us:	NIG
2Jn	1:12	I **w** not *write* with paper and ink:	1014
3Jn	1:10	and forbiddeth them that **w,**	1014
Rev	3:15	cold nor hot: I **w** thou wert cold or hot.	3785
	13:15	cause that as many as **w** not worship	302

WOULDEST (38) [WOULD]

Ge	30:15	**w** thou take away my son's mandrakes	NIH
	31:30	*though* thou **w** needs be gone, because	NIH
	31:31	Peradventure thou **w** take by force thy	NIH
Ex	7:16	and behold, hitherto thou **w** not hear.	NIH
	23: 5	**w** forbear to help him, thou shalt surely	NIH
Dt	8: 2	whether thou **w** keep his commandments,	NIH
	21:11	unto her, that thou **w** have her to thy wife;	NIH
	28:62	thou **w** not obey the voice of the LORD	NIH
Jos	15:18	and Caleb said unto her, What **w** thou?	3807.1
2Sa	14:11	that thou **w** not suffer the revengers of	NIH
	18:13	thyself **w** have set thyself against *me.*	NIH
1Ki	1:16	And the king said, What **w** thou?	3807.1
	18: 9	thou **w** deliver thy servant into the hand	NIH
2Ki	4:13	**w** thou be spoken for to the king, or to	3426
	5:13	thou **w** not have done *it?* how much	NIH
	6:22	Thou shalt not smite *them:* **w** thou smite	NIH
1Ch	4:10	Oh that thou **w** bless me indeed,	NIH
	4:10	thou **w** keep *me* from evil, that it	NIH
2Ch	6:20	hast said that *thou* **w** put thy name there;	NIH
	20:10	whom thou **w** not let Israel invade,	NIH
Ezr	9:14	**w** thou not be angry with us till *thou*	NIH
Ne	2: 5	that thou **w** send me unto Judah, unto	NIH
Job	8: 5	If thou **w** seek unto God betimes,	NIH
	14:13	O that thou **w** hide me in the grave,	NIH
	14:13	thou **w** keep me secret, until thy wrath	NIH
	14:13	that thou **w** appoint me a set time,	NIH
Isa	48: 8	for I knew that thou **w** deal very	NIH
	64: 1	thou **w** rend the heavens, that thou	NIH
	64: 1	the heavens, that thou **w** come down,	NIH
Lk	16:27	thou **w** send him to my father's house:	NIG
Jn	4:10	thou **w** have asked of him, and he would	302
	11:40	I not unto thee, that, if thou **w** believe,	NIG
	21:18	and walkedst whither thou **w:**	2309
	21:18	and carry *thee* whither thou **w** not.	2309
Ac	23:20	**w** bring down Paul to morrow into	NIG
	24: 1	I pray *thee* that thou **w** hear us of thy	NIG
Heb	10: 5	Sacrifice and offering thou **w** not,	2309
	10: 8	and *offering* for sin thou **w** not,	2309

WOUND (25) [WIND, WOUNDED, WOUNDEDST, WOUNDETH, WOUNDING, WOUNDS]

Ex	21:25	burning, **w** for wound, stripe for stripe.	6482
	21:25	burning, wound for **w,** stripe for stripe.	6482
Dt	32:39	I kill, and I make alive; I **w,** and I heal:	4272
1Ki	22:35	the blood ran out of the **w** into the midst	4347
Job	34: 6	my **w** *is* incurable without transgression.	2671
Ps	68:21	God shall **w** the head of his enemies,	4272
	110: 6	shall **w** the heads over many countries.	4272
Pr	6:33	A **w** and dishonour shall he get;	5061
	20:30	The blueness of a **w** cleanseth away evil:	6482
Isa	30:26	and healeth the stroke of their **w.**	4347
Jer	10:19	my **w** *is* grievous: but I said, Truly this *is*	4347
	15:18	is my pain perpetual, and my **w** incurable,	4347
	30:12	bruise *is* incurable, *and* thy **w** *is* grievous.	4347
	30:14	for I have wounded thee *with the* **w** of an	4347
Hos	5:13	Judah *saw* his **w,** then went Ephraim to	4205
	5:13	he not heal you nor cure you of your **w.**	4205
Ob	1: 7	*that eat* thy bread have laid a **w** under	4204
Mic	1: 9	her **w** *is* incurable; for it is come unto	4347
Na	3:19	healing of thy bruise; thy **w** *is* grievous:	4347
Jn	19:40	and **w** it in linen clothes with the spices,	1210
Ac	5: 6	**w** him **up,** and carried *him* out,	4958
1Co	8:12	brethren, and **w** their weak conscience,	5180
Rev	13:	to death; and his deadly **w** was healed:	4127
	13:12	first beast, whose deadly **w** was healed.	4127
	13:14	had the **w** by a sword, and did live.	4127

WOUNDED (35) [WOUND]

Dt	23: 1	He that is **w** in the stones, or hath *his*	6481
Jdg	9:40	and many were overthrown *and,*	2491
1Sa	17:52	the **w** of the Philistines fell down by	2491
	31: 3	and he was sore **w** of the archers.	2342
2Sa	22:39	and **w** them, that they could not arise:	4272
1Ki	20:37	smote him, so that in smiting he **w** him.	6481
	22:34	and carry me out of the host; for I am **w.**	2470
2Ki	8:28	Ramoth-gilead; and the Syrians **w** Joram.	5221
1Ch	10: 3	hit him, and he was **w** of the archers.	2342
2Ch	18:33	carry me out of the host; for I am **w.**	2470
	35:23	Have me away; for I am sore **w.**	2470
Job	24:12	the city, and the soul of the **w** crieth out:	2491
Ps	18:38	I have **w** them that they were not able to	4272
	64: 7	*with* an arrow; suddenly shall they be **w.**	4347
	69:26	to the grief of those whom thou hast **w.**	2491
	109:22	and needy, and my heart is **w** within me.	2490
Pr	7:26	For she hath cast down many **w:** yea,	2491
	18:14	his infirmity; but a **w** spirit who can bear?	5218
SS	5: 7	found me, they smote me, they **w** me;	6481
Isa	51: 9	that hath cut Rahab, *and* **w** the dragon?	2490

Isa 53: 5 he *was* **w** for our transgressions, *he was* 2490
Jer 30:14 for I have **w** thee *with* the wound of an 5221
 37:10 there remained *but* **w** men among them, 1856
 51:52 through all her land the **w** shall groan. 2491
La 2:12 they swooned as the **w** in the streets 2491
Eze 26:15 at the sound of thy fall, when the **w** cry, 2491
 28:23 the **w** shall be judged in the midst of her 2491
 30:24 *with* the groanings of a **deadly w** man. 2491
Joel 2: 8 fall upon the sword, they shall not be **w** 1214
Zec 13: 6 *Those with* which I was **w** *in* the house of 5221
Mk 12: 4 **w** *him* **in the head,** and sent *him* away 2007+4127
Lk 10:30 **w** *him,* and departed, *2007+4127*
 20:12 and they **w** him also, and cast *him* out. *5135*
Ac 19:16 *they* fled out of that house naked and **w.** *5135*
Rev 13: 3 And I saw one of his heads as *it were* **w** 4969

WOUNDEDST (1) [WOUND]

Hab 3:13 thou **w** the head out of the house of 4272

WOUNDETH (1) [WOUND]

Job 5:18 he **w,** and his hands make whole. 4272

WOUNDING (1) [WOUND]

Ge 4:23 for I have slain a man to my **w,** 6482

WOUNDS (15) [WOUND]

2Ki 8:29 the **w** which the Syrians had given him at 4347
 9:15 the **w** which the Syrians had given him, 4347
2Ch 22: 6 the **w** which were given him at Ramah, 4347
Job 9:17 and multiplieth my **w** without cause. 6482
Ps 38: 5 My **w** stink *and* are corrupt because of 2250
 147: 3 broken in heart, and bindeth up their **w.** 6094
Pr 18: 8 The words of a talebearer *are as* **w,** 3859
 23:29 who hath **w** without cause? who hath 6482
 26:22 The words of a talebearer *are as* **w,** 3859
 27: 6 Faithful *are* the **w** of a friend; but the 6482
Isa 1: 6 *but* **w,** and bruises, and putrifying sores: 6482
Jer 6: 7 before me continually *is* grief and **w.** 4347
 30:17 I will heal thee of thy **w,** saith the Lord; 4347
Zec 13: 6 then, What *are* these **w** in thine hands? 4347
Lk 10:34 And went to *him,* and bound up his **w,** *5134*

WOVE (1) [WEAVE]

2Ki 23: 7 the women **w** hangings for the grove. 707

WOVEN (4) [WEAVE]

Ex 28:32 it shall have a binding of **w** work round 707
 39:22 he made the robe of the ephod *of* **w** work, 707
 39:27 they made coats *of* fine linen *of* **w** work 707
Jn 19:23 without seam, **w** from the top throughout. *5307*

WRAP (2) [WRAPPED, WRAPT]

Isa 28:20 the covering narrower than that *he* can **w** 3664
Mic 7: 3 his mischievous desire: so they **w** it **up.** 5686

WRAPPED (9) [WRAP]

Ge 38:14 and **w** herself, and sat in an open place, 5968
1Ki 19:13 when Elijah heard *it,* that he **w** his face in 3874
Job 8:17 His roots are **w** about the heap, 5440
Mt 27:59 the body, he **w** it in a clean linen cloth, *1794*
Mk 15:46 and **w** *him* **in** the linen, and laid him in a *1750*
Lk 2: 7 and **w** him **in swaddling clothes,** *4683*
 2:12 him **w** **in swaddling clothes,** *4683*
 23:53 **w** it in linen, and laid it in a sepulchre *1794*
Jn 20: 7 but **w together** in a place by itself. *1794*

WRAPT (5) [WRAP]

1Sa 21: 9 it *is here* **w** in a cloth behind the ephod: 3874
2Ki 2: 8 **w** *it* **together,** and smote the waters, 1563
Job 40:17 the sinews of his stones are **w together.** 8276
Eze 21:15 made bright, *it is* **w up** for the slaughter. 4593
Jnh 2: 5 the weeds *were* **w** about my head. 2280

WRATH (198) [WRATHFUL, WRATHS, WROTH]

Ge 39:19 thy servant to me; that his **w** was kindled. 639
 49: 7 *it was* fierce; and their **w,** for it was cruel: 5678
Ex 15: 7 sentest forth thy **w,** *which* consumed 2740
 22:24 my **w** shall wax hot, and I will kill you 639
 32:10 that my **w** may wax hot against them, 639
 32:11 doth thy **w** wax hot against thy people, 639
 32:12 Turn from thy fierce **w,** and repent of *this* 639
Lev 10: 6 and lest **w** come upon all the people: 7107
Nu 1:53 that there be no **w** upon the congregation 7110
 11:33 the **w** of the Lord was kindled against 639
 16:46 for there is **w** gone out from the Lord; 7110
 18: 5 that there be no **w** any more upon 7110
 25:11 hath turned my **w** away from the children 2534
Dt 9: 7 **provokedst** the Lord thy God **to w** in 7107
 9: 8 in Horeb ye **provoked** the Lord **to w,** 7107
 9:22 ye **provoked** the Lord **to w.** 7107
 11:17 *then* the Lord's **w** be kindled against you, 639
 29:23 overthrew in his anger, and in his **w:** 2534
 29:28 in **w,** and in great indignation, 2534
 32:27 Were it not that I feared the **w** of 3708
Jos 9:20 lest **w** be upon us, because of the oath 7110
 22:20 **w** fell on all the congregation of Israel? 7110
1Sa 28:18 nor executedst his fierce **w** upon Amalek, 639
2Sa 11:20 if so be that the king's **w** arise, and he say 2534
2Ki 22:13 for great *is* the **w** of the Lord that is 2534
 22:17 my **w** shall be kindled against this place, 2534
 23:26 not from the fierceness of his great **w,** 639
1Ch 27:24 because there fell **w** for it against Israel; 7110
2Ch 12: 7 my **w** shall not be poured out upon 2534
 12:12 the **w** of the Lord turned from him, 639
 19: 2 *is* **w** upon thee from before the Lord. 7110
 19:10 *so* **w** come upon you, and upon your 7110

2Ch 24:18 **w** came upon Judah and Jerusalem for 7110
 28:11 for the fierce **w** of the Lord *is* upon you. 639
 28:13 great, and *there is* fierce **w** against Israel. 639
 29: 8 Wherefore the **w** of the Lord was upon 7110
 29:10 that his fierce **w** may turn away from us. 639
 30: 8 that the fierceness of his **w** may turn away 639
 32:25 therefore there was **w** upon him, 7110
 32:26 that the **w** of the Lord came not upon 7110
 34:21 for great *is* the **w** of the Lord that is 2534
 34:25 my **w** shall be poured out upon this place, 2534
 36:16 until the **w** of the Lord arose against his 2534
Ezr 5:12 **provoked** the God of heaven **unto w,** 7265
 7:23 why should there be **w** against the realm 7109
 8:22 his **w** *is* against all them that forsake him. 639
 10:14 until the fierce **w** of our God for this matter 639
Ne 13:18 yet ye bring more **w** upon Israel by 2740
Est 1:18 *there arise* too much contempt and **w.** 7110
 2: 1 when the **w** of king Ahasuerus was 2534
 3: 5 reverence, *then* was Haman full of **w.** 2534
 7: 7 in his **w** *went* into the palace garden: 2534
 7:10 Then was the king's **w** pacified. 2534
Job 5: 2 For **w** killeth the foolish man, 3708
 14:13 keep me secret, until thy **w** be past, 639
 16: 9 He teareth *me* in his **w,** who hateth me: 639
 19:11 He hath also kindled his **w** against me, 639
 19:29 for **w** *bringeth* the punishments of 2534
 20:23 *God* shall cast the fury of his **w** upon him, 639
 20:28 *goods shall* flow away in the day of his **w.** 639
 21:20 he shall drink of the **w** of the Almighty. 2534
 21:30 shall be brought forth to the day of **w.** 5678
 32: 2 was kindled the **w** of Elihu the son of 639
 32: 2 against Job was his **w** kindled, because 639
 32: 3 Also against his three friends was his **w** 639
 32: 5 *these* three men, then his **w** was kindled. 639
 36:13 the hypocrites in heart heap up **w:** 639
 36:18 Because *there is* **w,** *beware* lest he take 2534
 40:11 Cast abroad the rage of thy **w:** 639
 42: 7 My **w** is kindled against thee, and against 639
Ps 2: 5 Then shall he speak unto them in his **w,** 639
 2:12 the way, when his **w** is kindled but a little: 639
 21: 9 the Lord shall swallow them up in his **w,** 639
 37: 8 Cease from anger, and forsake **w:** fret not 2534
 38: 1 O Lord, rebuke me not in thy **w:** 7110
 55: 3 iniquity upon me, and in **w** they hate me. 639
 58: 9 a whirlwind, both living, and in *his* **w.** 2740
 59:13 Consume *them* in **w,** consume *them,* 2534
 76:10 Surely the **w** of man shall praise thee: 2534
 76:10 the remainder of **w** shalt thou restrain. 2534
 78:31 The **w** of God came upon them, and slew 639
 78:38 anger away, and did not stir up all his **w.** 2534
 78:49 **w,** and indignation, and trouble, 5678
 79: 6 Pour out thy **w** upon the heathen that 2534
 85: 3 Thou hast taken away all thy **w:** thou hast 5678
 88: 7 Thy **w** lieth hard upon me, and thou hast 2534
 88:16 Thy **fierce w** goeth over me; thy terrors 2740
 89:46 for ever? shall thy **w** burn like fire? 2534
 90: 7 anger, and by thy **w** are we troubled. 2534
 90: 9 For all our days are passed away in thy **w:** 5678
 90:11 even according to thy fear, *so is* thy **w.** 5678
 95:11 *Unto* whom I sware in my **w** that they 639
 102:10 Because of thine indignation and thy **w:** 7110
 106:23 to turn away his **w,** lest *he* should destroy 2534
 106:40 Therefore was the **w** of the Lord kindled 639
 110: 5 strike through kings in the day of his **w.** 639
 124: 3 when their **w** was kindled against us: 639
 138: 7 thine hand against the **w** of mine enemies, 639
Pr 11: 4 Riches profit not in the day of **w:** 5678
 11:23 *but* the expectation of the wicked *is* **w.** 5678
 12:16 A fool's **w** is presently known: 3708
 14:29 He that is slow to **w** is of great 639
 14:35 his **w** is *against* him that causeth shame. 5678
 15: 1 A soft answer turneth away **w:** 2534
 16:14 The **w** of a king *is as* messengers of death: 2534
 19:12 The king's **w** *is as* the roaring of a lion; 2197
 19:19 *A man* of great **w** *shall* suffer punishment: 2534
 21:14 and a reward in the bosom strong **w.** 2534
 21:24 *is* his name, who dealeth in proud **w.** 5678
 24:18 and he turn away his **w** from him. 639
 27: 3 but a fool's **w** *is* heavier than them both. 3708
 27: 4 **W** *is* cruel, and anger *is* outrageous; 2534
 29: 8 into a snare: but wise *men* turn away **w.** 639
 30:33 so the forcing of **w** bringeth forth strife. 639
Ecc 5:17 much sorrow and **w** with his sickness. 7110
Isa 9:19 Through the **w** of the Lord of hosts is 5678
 10: 6 against the people of my **w** will I give him 5678
 13: 9 cruel both *with* **w** and fierce anger, to lay 5678
 13:13 in the **w** of the Lord of hosts, and in 5678
 14: 6 He who smote the people in **w** with a 5678
 16: 6 his haughtiness, and his pride, and his **w:** 5678
 54: 8 In a little **w** I hid my face from thee for a 7110
 60:10 in my **w** I smote thee, but in my favour 7110
Jer 7:29 and forsaken the generation of his **w.** 5678
 10:10 at his **w** the earth shall tremble, 7110
 18:20 *and* to turn away thy **w** from them. 2534
 21: 5 in anger, and in fury, and in great **w.** 7110
 32:37 anger, and in my fury, and in great **w;** 7110
 44: 8 In that *ye* **provoke** me **unto w** with 3707
 48:30 I know his **w,** saith the Lord; *but it shall* 5678
 50:13 Because of the **w** of the Lord it shall not 7110
La 2: 2 he hath thrown down in his **w** the strong 5678
 3: 1 hath seen affliction by the rod of his **w.** 5678
Eze 7:12 for **w** *is* upon all the multitude thereof. 2740
 7:14 my **w** *is* upon all the multitude thereof. 2740
 7:19 them in the day of the **w** of the Lord: 5678
 13:15 Thus will I accomplish my **w** upon 2534

Eze 21:31 will blow against thee in the fire of my **w,** 5678
 22:21 blow upon you in the fire of my **w,** 5678
 22:31 consumed them with the fire of my **w,** 5678
 38:19 *and* in the fire of my **w** have I spoken, 5678
Hos 5:10 will pour out my **w** upon them like water. 5678
 13:11 mine anger, and took *him* away in my **w.** 5678
Am 1:11 perpetually, and he kept his **w** for ever: 5678
Na 1: 2 and he reserveth **w** for his enemies. NIH
Hab 3: 2 make known; in **w** remember mercy. 7267
 3: 8 *was* thy **w** against the sea, that thou didst 5678
Zep 1:15 That day *is* a day of **w,** a day of trouble 5678
 1:18 deliver them in the day of the Lord's **w;** 5678
Zec 7:12 came a great **w** from the Lord of hosts. 7110
 8:14 when your fathers **provoked** me to **w,** 7107
Mt 3: 7 hath warned you to flee from the **w** to 3709
Lk 3: 7 hath warned you to flee from the **w** to 3709
 4:28 heard these *things,* were filled with **w,** 2372
 21:23 in the land, and **w** upon this people. *3709*
Jn 3:36 see life; but the **w** of God abideth on him. 3709
Ac 19:28 heard *these sayings,* they were full of **w,** 2372
Ro 1:18 For the **w** of God is revealed from heaven 3709
 2: 5 heart treasurest up unto thyself **w** 3709
 2: 5 unto thyself **wrath** against the day of 3709
 2: 8 obey unrighteousness, indignation and **w,** 3709
 4:15 Because the law worketh **w:** for where no 3709
 5: 9 we shall be saved from **w** through him. 3709
 9:22 willing to shew his **w,** and to make his 3709
 9:22 *the* vessels of **w** fitted to destruction: 3709
 12:19 but *rather* give place unto **w:** 3709
 13: 4 a revenger to *execute* **w** upon him that 3709
 13: 5 not only for **w,** but also for conscience 3709
Gal 5:20 emulations, **w,** strife, seditions, heresies, 2372
Eph 2: 3 and were by nature the children of **w,** 3709
 4:26 let not the sun go down upon your **w:** 3950
 4:31 and **w,** and anger, and clamour, 2372
 5: 6 these *things* cometh the **w** of God upon 3709
 6: 4 fathers, **provoke** not your children **to w:** 3949
Col 3: 6 For which *things'* sake the **w** of God 3709
 3: 8 **w,** malice, blasphemy, 2372
1Th 1:10 which delivered us from the **w** to come. 3709
 2:16 for the **w** is come upon them to 3709
 5: 9 For God hath not appointed us to **w,** 3709
1Ti 2: 8 up holy hands, without **w** and doubting. 3709
Heb 3:11 So I sware in my **w,** They shall not enter 3709
 4: 3 as *he* said, As I have sworn in my **w,** 3709
 11:27 not fearing the **w** of the king: 2372
Jas 1:19 swift to hear, slow to speak, slow to **w:** 3709
 1:20 For the **w** of man worketh not 3709
Rev 6:16 the throne, and from the **w** of the Lamb: 3709
 6:17 For the great day of his **w** is come; 3709
 11:18 and thy **w** is come, and the time of 3709
 12:12 having great **w,** because he knoweth that 2372
 14: 8 of the wine of the **w** of her fornication. 2372
 14:10 The same shall drink of the wine of the **w** 2372
 14:19 cast *it* into the great winepress of the **w** of 2372
 15: 1 for in them is filled up the **w** of God. 2372
 15: 7 seven golden vials full of the **w** of God, 2372
 16: 1 pour out the vials of the **w** of God upon 2372
 16:19 cup of the wine of the fierceness of his **w.** 3709
 18: 3 of the wine of the **w** of her fornication, 2372
 19:15 of the fierceness and **w** of Almighty God. 3709

WRATHFUL (2) [WRATH]

Ps 69:24 and let thy **w** anger take hold of them. 2740
Pr 15:18 A **w** man stirreth up strife: but *he that is* 2534

WRATHS (1) [WRATH]

2Co 12:20 envyings, **w,** strifes, backbitings, *2372*

WREATH (1) [WREATHED, WREATHEN, WREATHS]

2Ch 4:13 two rows *of* pomegranates on each **w,** 7639

WREATHED (1) [WREATH]

La 1:14 they are **w,** *and* come up upon my neck: 8276

WREATHEN (10) [WREATH]

Ex 28:14 *of* **w** work shalt thou make them, 5688
 28:14 and fasten the **w** chains to the ouches. 5688
 28:22 chains at the ends *of* **w** work *of* pure gold. 5688
 28:24 thou shalt put the two **w** *chains of* gold in 5688
 28:25 *the other* two ends of the two **w** chains 5688
 39:15 at the ends, *of* **w** work *of* pure gold. 5688
 39:17 they put the two **w** *chains of* gold in 5688
 39:18 the two ends of the two **w** *chains* they 5688
2Ki 25:17 the **w work,** and pomegranates upon 7639
 25:17 these had the second pillar with **w work.** 7639

WREATHS (3) [WREATH]

1Ki 7:17 of checker work, *and* **w** of chain work, 1434
2Ch 4:12 the two **w** to cover the two pommels of 7639
 4:13 hundred pomegranates on the two **w;** 7639

WREST (5) [WRESTLE]

Ex 23: 2 to decline after many to **w** *judgment:* 5186
 23: 6 shalt not **w** the judgment of thy poor 5186
Dt 16:19 Thou shalt not **w** judgment; thou shalt 5186
Ps 56: 5 Every day they **w** my words: all their 6087
2Pe 3:16 *they that are* unlearned and unstable **w,** *4761*

WRESTLE (1) [WREST, WRESTLED, WRESTLINGS]

Eph 6:12 For we **w** not against flesh and *1510+3823*

WRESTLED (3) [WRESTLE]

Ge 30: 8 With great wrestlings have I **w** with my 6617
 32:24 there **w** a man with him until the breaking 79

Ge 32:25 thigh was out of joint, as he **w** with him. 79

WRESTLINGS (1) [WRESTLE]
Ge 30: 8 With great **w** have I wrestled with my 5319

WRETCHED (2) [WRETCHEDNESS]
Ro 7:24 O **w** man that I am! who shall deliver me *5005*
Rev 3:17 and knowest not that thou art **w**, *5005*

WRETCHEDNESS (1) [WRETCHED]
Nu 11:15 in thy sight; and let me not see my **w**. 7451

WRING (3) [WRINGED, WRINGING, WRUNG]
Lev 1:15 **w** off his head, and burn *it* on the altar; 4454
 5: 8 **w** off his head from his neck, but shall 4454
Ps 75: 8 the wicked of the earth shall **w** *them* out, 4680

WRINGED (1) [WRING]
Jdg 6:38 **w** the dew out of the fleece, a bowl full 4680

WRINGING (1) [WRING]
Pr 30:33 the **w** of the nose bringeth forth blood: 4330

WRINKLE (1) [WRINKLES]
Eph 5:27 or **w**, or any such *thing*; but that it should *4512*

WRINKLES (1) [WRINKLE]
Job 16: 8 thou hast **filled** me **with w**, *which* is a 7059

WRITE (91) [HANDWRITING, WRITER, WRITER'S, WRITEST, WRITETH, WRITING, WRITINGS, WRITTEN, WROTE]
Ex 17:14 **W** this *for* a memorial in a book, 3789
 34: 1 I will **w** upon *these* tables the words that 3789
 34:27 said unto Moses, **W** thou these words: 3789
Nu 5:23 the priest shall **w** these curses in a book, 3789
 17: 2 **w** thou every man's name upon his rod. 3789
 17: 3 thou shalt **w** Aaron's name upon the rod 3789
Dt 6: 9 thou shalt **w** them upon the posts of thy 3789
 10: 2 I will **w** on the tables the words that were 3789
 11:20 thou shalt **w** them upon the door posts of 3789
 17:18 that he shall **w** him a copy of this law in a 3789
 24: 1 let him **w** her a bill of divorcement, 3789
 24: 3 **w** her a bill of divorcement, and giveth *it* 3789
 27: 3 shalt **w** upon them all the words of this 3789
 27: 8 shalt **w** upon the stones all the words 3789
 31:19 Now therefore ye this song for you, 3789
2Ch 26:22 Isaiah the prophet, the son of Amoz, **w**. 3789
Ezr 5:10 we might **w** the names of the men that 3790
Ne 9:38 **w** *it*; and our princes, Levites, *and* priests, 3789
Est 8: 8 **W** ye also for the Jews, as it liketh you, 3789
Pr 3: 3 **w** them upon the table of thine heart: 3789
 7: 3 **w** them upon the table of thine heart. 3789
Isa 8: 1 **w** in it with a man's pen concerning 3789
 10: 1 that **w** grievousness *which* they have 3789
 10:19 shall be few, that a child may **w** them. 3789
 30: 8 **w** it before them in a table, and note it in 3789
Jer 22:30 saith the LORD, **W** ye this man childless, 3789
 30: 2 **W** thee all the words that I have spoken 3789
 31:33 inward parts, and **w** it in their hearts; 3789
 36: 2 **w** therein all the words that I have spoken 3789
 36:17 How didst thou **w** all these words at his 3789
 36:28 **w** in it all the former words that were in 3789
Eze 24: 2 Son of man, **w** thee the name of the day, 3789
 37:16 **w** upon it, For Judah, and for the children 3789
 37:16 another stick, and **w** upon it, For Joseph, 3789
 43:11 **w** *it* in their sight, that they may keep 3789
Hab 2: 2 **W** the vision, and make *it* plain upon 3789
Mk 10: 4 Moses suffered to **w** a bill of divorcement, 1125
Lk 1: 3 to **w** unto thee in order, most excellent 1125
 16: 6 thy bill, and sit down quickly, and **w** fifty. 1125
 16: 7 unto him, Take thy bill, and **w** fourscore. 1125
Jn 1:45 the prophets, did **w**, Jesus of Nazareth, 1125
 19:21 to Pilate, **W** not, The King of the Jews; 1125
Ac 15:20 that we **w** unto them, that *they* abstain 1989
 25:26 Of whom I have no certain *thing* to **w** 1125
 25:26 I might have somewhat to **w**. 1125
1Co 4:14 I **w** not these *things* to shame you, 1125
 14:37 him acknowledge that the *things* that I **w** 1125
2Co 1:13 For we **w** none other *things* unto you, 1125
 2: 9 For to this end also did I **w**, that I might 1125
 9: 1 it is superfluous for me to **w** to you: 1125
 13: 2 being absent now I **w** to them which 1125
 13:10 Therefore I **w** these *things* being absent, 1125
Gal 1:20 Now the *things* which I **w** unto you, 1125
Php 3: 1 To **w** the same *things* to you, to me 1125
1Th 4: 9 love ye need not that *I* **w** unto you: 1125
 5: 1 ye have no need that *I* **w** unto you. 1125
2Th 3:17 which is the token in every epistle: so I **w**. 1125
1Ti 3:14 These *things* **w** I unto thee, hoping to 1125
Heb 8:10 their mind, and **w** them in their hearts: 1924
 10:16 and in their minds will I **w** them; 1924
2Pe 3: 1 epistle, beloved, I now **w** unto you; 1125
1Jn 1: 4 these *things* **w** we unto you, that your 1125
 2: 1 these *things* **w** I unto you, that ye sin not. 1125
 2: 7 I **w** no new commandment unto you, 1125
 2: 8 a new commandment I **w** unto you, 1125
 2:12 I **w** unto you, little children, because 1125
 2:13 I **w** unto you, fathers, because ye have 1125
 2:13 I **w** unto you, young men, because 1125
 2:13 I **w** unto you, little children, because 1125
2Jn 1:12 Having many *things* to **w** unto you, 1125
 1:12 you, I would not *with* paper and ink: NIG
3Jn 1:13 I had many *things* to **w**, 1125
 1:13 I will not with ink and pen **w** unto thee: 1125
Jude 1: 3 when I gave all diligence to **w** unto you 1125

Jude 1: 3 it was needful for me to **w** unto you, *1125*
Rev 1:11 **w** in a book, and send *it* unto the seven *1125*
 1:19 **W** *the things* which thou hast seen, *1125*
 2: 1 the angel of the church of Ephesus **w**; *1125*
 2: 8 the angel of the church in Smyrna **w**; *1125*
 2:12 to the angel of the church in Pergamos **w**; *1125*
 2:18 the angel of the church in Thyatira **w**; *1125*
 3: 1 unto the angel of the church in Sardis **w**; *1125*
 3: 7 the angel of the church in Philadelphia **w**; *1125*
 3:12 I will **w** upon him the name of my God, *1125*
 3:12 and *I will* **w** *upon him* my new name. NIG
 3:14 angel of the church of the Laodiceans **w**; *1125*
 10: 4 uttered their voices, I was about to **w**: *1125*
 10: 4 seven thunders uttered, and **w** them not. *1125*
 14:13 a voice from heaven saying unto me, **W**, *1125*
 19: 9 he saith unto me, **W**, Blessed *are* they *1125*
 21: 5 And he said unto me, **W**: for these words *1125*

WRITER (2) [WRITE]
Jdg 5:14 they that handle the pen of the **w**. 5608
Ps 45: 1 king: my tongue *is* the pen of a ready **w**. 5608

WRITER'S (2) [WRITE]
Eze 9: 2 *with* linen, with a **w** inkhorn by his side: 5608
 9: 3 which *had* the **w** inkhorn by his side; 5608

WRITEST (2) [WRITE]
Job 13:26 For thou **w** bitter *things* against me, 3789
Eze 37:20 sticks whereon thou **w** shall be in thine 3789

WRITETH (1) [WRITE]
Ps 87: 6 shall count, when he **w** *up* the people, 3789

WRITING (38) [WRITE]
Ex 32:16 the **w** *was* the writing of God, graven 4385
 32:16 the writing *was* the **w** of God, graven 4385
 39:30 wrote upon it a **w**, *like to* the engravings 4385
Dt 10: 4 according to the first **w**, the ten 4385
 31:24 when Moses had made an end of **w** 3789
1Ch 28:19 understand in **w** by *his* hand upon me, 3791
2Ch 2:11 Huram the king of Tyre answered in **w**, 3791
 21:12 there came a **w** to him from Elijah 4385
 35: 4 according to the **w** of David king of Israel, 3791
 35: 4 according to the **w** of Solomon his son. 4385
 36:22 his kingdom, and *put* also in **w**, saying, 4385
Ezr 1: 1 his kingdom, and *put* also in **w**, saying, 4385
 4: 7 **w** of the letter *was* written in the Syrian 3791
Est 1:22 into every province according to the **w** 3791
 3:12 province according to the **w** thereof, 3791
 3:14 The copy of the **w** for a commandment to 3791
 4: 8 Also he gave him the copy of the **w** of 3791
 8: 8 for the **w** which *is* written in the king's 3791
 8: 9 *unto* every province according to the **w** 3791
 8: 9 to the Jews according to their **w**, 3791
 8:13 The copy of the **w** for a commandment to 3791
 9:27 keep these two days according to their **w**, 3791
Isa 38: 9 The **w** of Hezekiah, king of Judah, when 4385
Eze 13: 9 neither shall they be written in the **w** of 3791
Da 5: 7 Whosoever shall read this **w**, and shew 3792
 5: 8 wise *men*: but they could not read the **w**, 3792
 5:15 that they should read this **w**, 3792
 5:16 now if thou canst read the **w**, 3792
 5:17 yet I will read the **w** unto the king, 3792
 5:24 sent from him; and this **w** was written. 3792
 5:25 this *is* the **w** that *was* written, MENE, 3792
 6: 8 establish the decree, and sign the **w**, 3792
 6: 9 Wherefore king Darius signed the **w** and 3792
 6:10 Now when Daniel knew that the **w** *was* 3792
Mt 5:31 let him give her a **w** of divorcement: 647
 19: 7 then command to give a **w** of divorcement, 975
Lk 1:63 And he asked for a **w table**, and wrote, 4093
Jn 19:19 And the **w** was, JESUS OF NAZARETH 1125

WRITINGS (1) [WRITE]
Jn 5:47 But if ye believe not his **w**, how shall ye 1121

WRITTEN (291) [WRITE]
Ex 24:12 and commandments which I have **w**; 3789
 31:18 tables of stone, **w** with the finger of God. 3789
 32:15 the tables *were* **w** on both their sides; 3789
 32:15 one side and on the other *were* they **w**. 3789
 32:32 out of thy book which thou hast **w**. 3789
Nu 11:26 they *were* of them that **were w**, 3789
Dt 9:10 tables of stone **w** with the finger of God; 3789
 9:10 them *was* **w** according to all the words NIH
 28:58 words of this law that are **w** in this book, 3789
 28:61 which *is* not **w** in the book of this law, 3789
 29:20 all the curses that are **w** in this book shall 3789
 29:21 that are **w** in this book of the law: 3789
 29:27 to bring upon it all the curses that are **w** 3789
 30:10 his statutes which are **w** in this book of 3789
Jos 1: 8 to do according to all that is **w** therein: 3789
 8:31 as it is **w** in the book of the law of Moses, 3789
 8:34 according to all that is **w** in the book of 3789
 10:13 *Is* not this **w** in the book of Jasher? 3789
 23: 6 to do all that is **w** in the book of the law 3789
2Sa 1:18 behold, *it is* **w** in the book of Jasher.) 3789
1Ki 2: 3 as *it is* **w** in the law of Moses, 3789
 11:41 *are* they not **w** in the book of the acts of 3789
 14:19 behold they *are* **w** in the book of the 3789
 14:29 they not **w** in the book of the chronicles 3789
 15: 7 they not **w** in the book of the chronicles 3789
 15:23 they not **w** in the book of the chronicles 3789
 15:31 they not **w** in the book of the chronicles 3789
 16: 5 they not **w** in the book of the chronicles 3789

1Ki 16:14 they not **w** in the book of the chronicles 3789
 16:20 they not **w** in the book of the chronicles 3789
 16:27 they not **w** in the book of the chronicles 3789
 21:11 *it was* **w** in the letters which she had sent 3789
 22:39 they not **w** in the book of the chronicles 3789
 22:45 they not **w** in the book of the chronicles 3789
2Ki 1:18 they not **w** in the book of the chronicles 3789
 8:23 they not **w** in the book of the chronicles 3789
 10:34 they not **w** in the book of the chronicles 3789
 12:19 they not **w** in the book of the chronicles 3789
 13: 8 they not **w** in the book of the chronicles 3789
 13:12 they not **w** in the book of the chronicles 3789
 14: 6 unto that which is **w** in the book 3789
 14:15 they not **w** in the book of the chronicles 3789
 14:18 they not **w** in the book of the chronicles 3789
 14:28 they not **w** in the book of the chronicles 3789
 15: 6 they not **w** in the book of the chronicles 3789
 15:11 they *are* **w** in the book of the chronicles 3789
 15:15 they *are* **w** in the book of the chronicles 3789
 15:21 they *are* **w** in the book of the chronicles 3789
 15:26 they *are* **w** in the book of the chronicles 3789
 15:31 they *are* **w** in the book of the chronicles 3789
 15:36 they not **w** in the book of the chronicles 3789
 16:19 they not **w** in the book of the chronicles 3789
 20:20 they not **w** in the book of the chronicles 3789
 21:17 they not **w** in the book of the chronicles 3789
 21:25 they not **w** in the book of the chronicles 3789
 22:13 to do according unto all that which is **w** 3789
 23: 3 of this covenant that were **w** in this book. 3789
 23:21 as it is **w** in the book of this covenant. 3789
 23:24 **w** in the book that Hilkiah the priest 3789
 23:28 they not **w** in the book of the chronicles 3789
 24: 5 they not **w** in the book of the chronicles 3789
1Ch 4:41 these **w** by name came in the days of 3789
 9: 1 they *were* **w** in the book of the kings of 3789
 16:40 *to do* according to all that is **w** in the law 3789
 29:29 *are* **w** in the book of Samuel the seer, 3789
2Ch 9:29 *are* they not **w** in the book of Nathan 3789
 12:15 *are* they not **w** in the book of Shemaiah 3789
 13:22 *are* **w** in the story of the prophet Iddo. 3789
 16:11 *are* **w** in the book of the kings of Judah 3789
 20:34 behold they *are* **w** in the book of Jehu 3789
 23:18 as it is **w** in the law of Moses, 3789
 24:27 they *are* **w** in the story of the book 3789
 25: 4 *did* as it is **w** in the law in the book of 3789
 25:26 are they not **w** in the book of the kings of 3789
 27: 7 lo they *are* **w** in the book of the kings of 3789
 28:26 are **w** in the book of the kings of Judah 3789
 30: 5 *it* of a long *time in such sort* as it was **w**. 3789
 30:18 eat the passover otherwise than it was **w**. 3789
 31: 3 as it is **w** in the law of the LORD. 3789
 32:32 they *are* **w** in the vision of Isaiah 3789
 33:18 *are* **w** in the book of the kings of Israel. NIH
 33:19 *are* **w** among the sayings of the seers. 3789
 34:21 to do after all that is **w** in this book. 3789
 34:24 *even* all the curses that are **w** in the book 3789
 34:31 of the covenant which are **w** in this book. 3789
 35:12 as it is **w** in the book of Moses. 3789
 35:25 behold, they *are* **w** in the lamentations. 3789
 35:26 according to that which was **w** in the law 3789
 35:27 *are* **w** in the book of the kings of Israel 3789
 36: 8 *are* **w** in the book of the kings of Israel 3789
Ezr 3: 2 as it is **w** in the law of Moses the man of 3789
 3: 4 as it is **w**, and *offered* the daily burnt 3789
 4: 7 writing of the letter *was* **w** in the Syrian 3789
 5: 7 a letter unto him, wherein *was* **w** thus: 3790
 6: 2 a roll, and therein *was* a record thus **w**: 3790
 6:18 as it is **w** in the book of Moses. 3792
 8:34 and all the weight was **w** at that time. 3789
Ne 6: 6 Wherein *was* **w**, It *is* reported among 3789
 7: 5 came up at the first, and found **w** therein, 3789
 8:14 they found **w** in the law which the LORD 3789
 8:15 of thick trees, to make booths, as it is **w**. 3789
 10:34 the LORD our God, as it is **w** in the law: 3789
 10:36 as it is **w** in the law, and the firstlings of 3789
 12:23 *were* **w** in the book of the chronicles, 3789
 13: 1 therein was found **w**, that the Ammonite 3789
Est 1:19 let it be **w** among the laws of the Persians 3789
 2:23 it was **w** in the book of the chronicles 3789
 3: 9 let it be **w** that they may be destroyed: 3789
 3:12 there was **w** according to all that Haman 3789
 3:12 in the name of king Ahasuerus was it **w**, 3789
 6: 2 it was found **w**, that Mordecai had told of 3789
 8: 5 let it be **w** to reverse the letters devised 3789
 8: 8 for the writing which *is* **w** in the king's 3789
 8: 9 it was **w** according to all that Mordecai 3789
 9:23 and as Mordecai had **w** unto them; 3789
 9:32 of Purim; and *it was* **w** in the book. 3789
 10: 2 they not **w** in the book of the chronicles 3789
Job 19:23 O that my words were now **w**! O that 3789
 31:35 and *that* mine adversary had **w** a book. 3789
Ps 40: 7 in the volume of the book *it is* **w** of me, 3789
 69:28 living, and not be **w** with the righteous. 3789
 102:18 shall be **w** for the generation to come: 3789
 139:16 in thy book all *my members* were **w**, 3789
 149: 9 To execute upon them the judgment **w**: 3789
Pr 22:20 Have not I **w** to thee excellent things in 3789
Ecc 12:10 *which was* **w** *was* upright, *even* words 3789
Isa 4: 3 *even* every one that is **w** among the living 3789
 65: 6 Behold, *it is* **w** before me: I will not keep 3789
Jer 17: 1 The sin of Judah *is* **w** with a pen of iron, 3789
 17:13 that depart from me shall be **w** in 3789
 25:13 *even* all that is **w** in this book, which 3789
 36: 6 roll, which thou hast **w** from my mouth, 3789
 36:29 Why hast thou **w** therein, saying, 3789

Jer 45: 1 when he had **w** these words in a book at 3789
 51:60 *even* all these words that are **w** against 3789
Eze 2:10 and it *was* **w** within and without: 3789
 2:10 *there was* **w** therein lamentations, 3789
 13: 9 neither shall they be **w** in the writing of 3789
Da 5:24 sent from him; and this writing *was* **w**. 7560
 5:25 this *is* the writing that *was* **w**, MENE, 7560
 9:11 the oath that *is* **w** in the law of Moses 3789
 9:13 As *it is* **w** in the law of Moses, all this evil 3789
 12: 1 one that *shall* be found **w** in the book. 3789
Hos 8:12 have **w** to him the great things of my law, 3789
Mal 3:16 book of remembrance was **w** before him 3789
Mt 2: 5 of Judea: for thus it is **w** by the prophet, 1125
 4: 4 But he answered and said, It is **w**, 1125
 4: 6 for it is **w**, He shall give his angels charge 1125
 4: 7 Jesus said unto him, It is **w** again, 1125
 4:10 for it is **w**, Thou shalt worship the Lord 1125
 11:10 For this is *he*, of whom it is **w**, Behold, 1125
 21:13 said unto them, It is **w**, My house shall 1125
 26:24 The Son of man goeth as it is **w** of him: 1125
 26:31 for it is **w**, I will smite the shepherd, 1125
 27:37 set up over his head his accusation **w**, 1125
Mk 1: 2 As it is **w** in the prophets, Behold, I send 1125
 7: 6 as it is **w**, This people honoureth me with 1125
 9:12 and how it is **w** of the Son of man, 1125
 9:13 whatsoever they listed, as it is **w** of him. 1125
 11:17 he taught, saying unto them, Is it not **w**, 1125
 14:21 Son of man indeed goeth, as it is **w** of him 1125
 14:27 for it is **w**, I will smite the shepherd, 1125
 15:26 of his accusation was **w** over, 1924
Lk 2:23 (As it is **w** in the law of the Lord, Every 1125
 3: 4 As it is **w** in the book of the words of 1125
 4: 4 And Jesus answered him, saying, It is **w**, 1125
 4: 8 it is **w**, Thou shalt worship the Lord thy 1125
 4:10 For it is **w**, He shall give his angels charge 1125
 4:17 he found the place where it was **w**, 1125
 7:27 This is *he*, of whom it is **w**, Behold, I send 1125
 10:20 because your names are **w** in heaven. 1125
 10:26 He said unto him, What is **w** in the law? 1125
 18:31 all *things* that are **w** by the prophets 1125
 19:46 Saying unto them, It is **w**, My house is 1125
 20:17 and said, What is this then that is **w**, 1125
 21:22 all *things* which are **w** may be fulfilled. 1125
 22:37 this that is **w** must yet be accomplished 1125
 23:38 And a superscription also was **w** over him 1125
 24:44 which were **w** in the law of Moses, 1125
 24:46 Thus it is **w**, and thus it behoved Christ to 1125
Jn 2:17 his disciples remembered that it was **w**, 1125
 6:31 it is **w**, He gave them bread from heaven 1125
 6:45 It is **w** in the prophets, And they shall be 1125
 8:17 It is also **w** in your law, that the testimony 1125
 10:34 Is it not **w** in your law, I said, Ye are gods? 1125
 12:14 found a young ass, sat thereon; as it is **w**, 1125
 12:16 they that these *things* were **w** 1125
 15:25 might be fulfilled that is **w** in their law, 1125
 19:20 and it was **w** in Hebrew, *and* Greek, 1125
 19:22 What I have **w** I have written. 1125
 19:22 What I have written I have **w**. 1125
 20:30 disciples, which are not **w** in this book: 1125
 20:31 these are, that ye might believe that 1125
 21:25 the which, if they should be **w** every one, 1125
 21:25 not contain the books that should be **w**. 1125
Ac 1:20 For it is **w** in the book of Psalms, Let his 1125
 7:42 as it is **w** in the book of the prophets, 1125
 13:29 when they had fulfilled all that was **w** 1125
 13:33 as it is also **w** in the second psalm, Thou 1125
 15:15 agree the words of the prophets; as it is **w**, 1125
 21:25 have **w** and concluded that they observe 1989
 23: 5 for it is **w**, Thou shalt not speak evil of 1125
 24:14 all *things* which are **w** in the law 1125
Ro 1:17 as it is **w**, The just shall live by faith. 1125
 2:15 Which shew the work of the law **w** in 1123
 2:24 the Gentiles through you, as it is **w**. 1125
 3: 4 as it is **w**, That thou mightest be justified 1125
 3:10 As it is **w**, There is none righteous, 1125
 4:17 (As it is **w**, I have made thee a father of 1125
 4:23 Now it was not **w** for his sake alone, that 1125
 8:36 As it is **w**, For thy sake we are killed all 1125
 9:13 As it is **w**, Jacob have I loved, 1125
 9:33 As it is **w**, Behold, I lay in Sion a 1125
 10:15 as it is **w**, How beautiful *are* the feet of 1125
 11: 8 (According as it is **w**, God hath given 1125
 11:26 as it is **w**, There shall come out of Sion 1125
 12:19 it is **w**, Vengeance *is* mine; I will repay, 1125
 14:11 it is **w**, *As* I live, saith the Lord, every 1125
 15: 3 as it is **w**, The reproaches of them that 1125
 15: 4 whatsoever *things* were **w aforetime** 4270
 15: 4 aforetime were **w** for our learning, 4270
 15: 9 as it is **w**, For this cause I will confess to 1125
 15:15 I have **w** the more boldly unto you in 1125
 15:21 as it is **w**, To whom he was not spoken 1125
 16: S **W** to the Romans from Corinthus, 1125
1Co 1:19 For it is **w**, I will destroy the wisdom of 1125
 1:31 according as it is **w**, He that glorieth, 1125
 2: 9 But as it is **w**, Eye hath not seen, nor ear 1125
 3:19 For it is **w**, He taketh the wise in their 1125
 4: 6 to think *of men* above *that* which is **w**, 1125
 5:11 But now I have **w** unto you not to keep 1125
 9: 9 For it is **w** in the law of Moses, Thou shalt 1125
 9:10 For our sakes, no doubt, *this* is **w**: that he 1125
 9:15 have I **w** these *things*, that it should be 1125
 10: 7 as it is **w**, The people sat down to eat and 1125
 10:11 and they are **w** for our admonition, 1125
 14:21 In the law it is **w**, With *men* of other 1125
 15:45 And so it is **w**, The first man Adam was 1125

1Co 15:54 be brought to pass the saying that is **w**, 1125
 16: S The first *epistle* to the Corinthians was **w** 1125
2Co 3: 2 Ye are our epistle **w** in our hearts, known 1449
 3: 3 ye **w** not with ink, but with the Spirit of 1449
 3: 7 **w** *and* engraven in stones, 1121+1722
 4:13 according as it is **w**, I believed, 1125
 8:15 As it is **w**, He that *had* gathered much 1125
 9: 9 (As it is **w**, He hath dispersed abroad; 1125
 13: S to the Corinthians was **w** from Philippi, 1125
Gal 3:10 For it is **w**, Cursed *is* every one that 1125
 3:10 are **w** in the book of the law to do them. 1125
 3:13 it is **w**, Cursed *is* every one that hangeth 1125
 4:22 For it is **w**, that Abraham had two sons, 1125
 4:27 it is **w**, Rejoice, *thou* barren that bearest 1125
 6:11 Ye see how large a letter I have **w** unto 1125
 6: S Unto the Galatians **w** from Rome. 1125
Eph 6: S **W** from Rome unto the Ephesians by 1125
Php 4: S It was **w** to the Philippians from Rome by 1125
Col 4: S **W** from Rome to the Colossians by 1125
1Th 5: S the Thessalonians was **w** from Athens. 1125
2Th 3: S to the Thessalonians was **w** from Athens. 1125
1Ti 6: S The first to Timothy was **w** from Laodicea, 1125
2Ti 4: S **w** from Rome, when Paul was brought 3238
Tit 3: S was **w** to Titus, ordained the first bishop 1125
Phm 1:19 I Paul have **w** *it* with mine own hand, 1125
 1: S **W** from Rome to Philemon, by Onesimus 1125
Heb 10: 7 I come (in the volume of the book it is **w** 1125
 12:23 are **w** in heaven, and to God the Judge 583
 13:22 for I have **a letter** unto you in few 1989
 13: S to the Hebrews from Italy by Timothy. 1125
1Pe 1:16 Because it is **w**, Be ye holy; for I am holy. 1125
 5:12 I have **w** briefly, exhorting, 1125
2Pe 3:15 wisdom given unto him hath **w** unto you; 1125
1Jn 2:14 I have **w** unto you, fathers, because ye 1125
 2:14 I have **w** unto you, young men, because 1125
 2:21 I have not **w** unto you because ye know 1125
 2:26 These *things* have I **w** unto you 1125
 5:13 These *things* have I **w** unto you that 1125
Rev 1: 3 keep those *things* which are **w** therein: 1125
 2:17 and in the stone a new name **w**, 1125
 5: 1 that sat on the throne a book **w** within 1125
 13: 8 whose names are not **w** in the book of life 1125
 14: 1 having his Father's name **w** in their 1125
 17: 5 And upon her forehead *was* a name **w**, 1125
 17: 8 names were not **w** in the book of life 1125
 19:12 and he had a name **w**, that no *man* knew, 1125
 19:16 on *his* vesture and on his thigh a name **w**, 1125
 20:12 those *things* which were **w** in the books, 1125
 20:15 And whosoever was not found **w** in 1125
 21:12 twelve angels, and names **w there**on, 1924
 21:27 they which are **w** in the Lamb's book of 1125
 22:18 him the plagues that are **w** in this book: 1125
 22:19 *from* the *things* which are **w** in this book. 1125

WRONG (26) [WRONGED, WRONGETH, WRONGFULLY]

Ge 16: 5 Sarai said unto Abram, My **w** *be* upon 2555
Ex 2:13 said to **him that did** the **w**, Wherefore 7563
Dt 19:16 to testify against him *that which is* **w**; 5627
Jdg 11:27 but thou doest me **w** to war against me: 7451
1Ch 12:17 seeing *there is* no **w** in mine hands, 2555
 16:21 He suffered no man to **do** them **w**: yea, 6231
Est 1:16 Vashti the queen hath not **done w** to 5753
Job 19: 7 I cry out *of* **w**, but I am not heard: 2555
Ps 105:14 He suffered no man to **do** them **w**: yea, 6231
Jer 22: 3 **do** no **w**, do no violence, to the stranger, 3238
 22:13 his chambers by **w**; 3808+4941
La 3:59 O Lord, thou hast seen my **w** 5792
Hab 1: 4 therefore **w** judgment proceedeth. 6127
Mt 20:13 of them, and said, Friend, I do thee no **w**: 91
Ac 7:24 And seeing one *of them* **suffer w**, 91
 7:26 are brethren; why do ye **w** one to another? 91
 7:27 But he that **did** his neighbour **w** thrust him 91
 18:14 If it were a matter of **w** or wicked lewdness, 92
 25:10 to the Jews have I **done** no **w**, as thou very 91
1Co 6: 7 Why do ye not rather **take w**? why do ye 91
 6: 8 you do **w**, and defraud, and that *your* 91
2Co 7:12 not for his cause that had **done** the **w**, 91
 7:12 nor for his cause that **suffered w**, but that 91
 12:13 not burdensome to you? forgive me this **w**. 93
Col 3:25 But he that **doeth w** shall receive *for* 91
 3:25 shall receive *for* the **w** which he hath **done**: 91

WRONGED (2) [WRONG]

2Co 7: 2 we have **w** no *man*, we have corrupted no 91
Phm 1:18 If he hath **w** thee, or oweth *thee* ought, 91

WRONGETH (1) [WRONG]

Pr 8:36 that sinneth *against* me **w** his own soul: 2554

WRONGFULLY (7) [WRONG]

Job 21:27 the devices *which* ye **w imagine** against 2554
Ps 35:19 Let not them that are mine enemies **w** 8267
 38:19 and they that hate me **w** are multiplied. 8267
 69: 4 *being* mine enemies **w**, are mighty: 8267
 119:86 they persecute me **w**; help thou me. 8267
Eze 22:29 oppressed the stranger **w**, 3808+4941+871.1
1Pe 2:19 toward God endure grief, suffering **w**. 95

WROTE (62) [WRITE]

Ex 24: 4 Moses **w** all the words of the Lord, 3789
 34:28 he **w** upon the tables the words of 3789
 39:30 **w** upon it a writing, *like* to the 3789
Nu 33: 2 Moses **w** their goings out according to 3789
Dt 4:13 he **w** them upon two tables of stone. 3789

Dt 5:22 he **w** them in two tables of stone, 3789
 10: 4 he **w** on the tables, according to the first 3789
 31: 9 Moses **w** this law, and delivered it unto 3789
 31:22 Moses therefore **w** this song the same 3789
Jos 8:32 he **w** there upon the stones a copy of 3789
 8:32 he **w** in the presence of the children 3789
 24:26 Joshua **w** these words in the book of 3789
1Sa 10:25 **w** *it* in a book, and laid *it* up before 3789
2Sa 11:14 David **w** a letter to Joab, and sent *it* by 3789
 11:15 he **w** in the letter, saying, Set ye Uriah in 3789
1Ki 21: 8 So she **w** letters in Ahab's name, 3789
 21: 9 in the letters, saying, Proclaim a fast, 3789
2Ki 10: 1 Jehu **w** letters, and sent *to* Samaria, 3789
 10: 6 he **w** a letter the second time to them, 3789
 17:37 the commandment, which he **w** for you, 3789
1Ch 24: 6 **w** them before the king, and the princes, 3789
2Ch 30: 1 **w** letters also to Ephraim and Manasseh, 3789
 32:17 He **w** also letters to rail on the Lord God 3789
Ezr 4: 6 **w** they *unto him* an accusation against 3789
 4: 7 in the days of Artaxerxes **w** Bishlam, 3789
 4: 8 Shimshai the scribe **w** a letter against 3789
 4: 9 *w* Rehum the chancellor, and Shimshai NIH
Est 8: 5 which he **w** to destroy the Jews which 3789
 8:10 And he **w** in the king Ahasuerus' name, 3789
 9:20 Mordecai **w** these things, and sent letters 3789
 9:29 Mordecai the Jew, **w** with all authority, 3789
Jer 36: 4 Baruch **w** from the mouth of Jeremiah all 3789
 36:18 and I **w** *them* with ink in the book. 3789
 36:27 the words which Baruch **w** at the mouth 3789
 36:32 **w** therein from the mouth of Jeremiah 3789
 51:60 So Jeremiah **w** in a book all the evil that 3789
Da 5: 5 **w** over against the candlestick upon 3790
 5: 5 the king saw the part of the hand that **w**. 3790
 6:25 king Darius **w** unto all people, nations, 3790
 7: 1 he **w** the dream, *and* told the sum of 3790
Mk 10: 5 For the hardness of your heart he **w** you 1125
 12:19 Master, Moses **w** unto us, If a man's 1125
Lk 1:63 and, saying, His name is John. 1125
 20:28 Saying, Master, Moses **w** unto us, If any 1125
Jn 5:46 would have believed me: for he **w** of me. 1125
 8: 6 and with *his* finger **w** on the ground, 1125
 8: 8 he stooped down, and **w** on the ground. 1125
 19:19 Pilate **w** a title, and put *it* on the cross. 1125
 21:24 and **w** these *things*: and we know that his 1125
Ac 15:23 And they **w** *letters* by them after this 1125
 18:27 the brethren **w**, exhorting the disciples to 1125
 23:25 And he **w** a letter after this manner: 1125
Ro 16:22 I Tertius, who **w** *this* epistle, salute you in 1125
1Co 5: 9 I **w** unto you in an epistle not to company 1125
 7: 1 Now concerning *the things* whereof ye **w** 1125
2Co 2: 3 And I **w** this same unto you, lest, when I 1125
 2: 4 anguish of heart I **w** unto you with many 1125
 7:12 Wherefore, though I **w** unto you, *I did it* 1125
Eph 3: 3 the mystery; (as I **w** afore in few *words*, 4270
Phm 1:21 Having confidence in thy obedience I **w** 1125
2Jn 1: 5 not as though I **w** a new commandment 1125
3Jn 1: 9 I **w** unto the church: but Diotrephes, 1125

WROTH (49) [WRATH]

Ge 4: 5 Cain was very **w**, and his countenance 2734
 4: 6 Lord said unto Cain, Why art thou **w**? 2734
 31:36 Jacob was **w**, and chode with Laban: 2734
 34: 7 were very **w**, because he had wrought 2734
 40: 2 Pharaoh was **w** against two *of* his officers, 7107
 41:10 Pharaoh was **w** with his servants, 7107
Ex 16:20 and stank: and Moses was **w** with them. 7107
Nu 16:15 Moses was very **w**, and said unto 2734
 16:22 wilt thou be **w** with all the congregation? 7107
 31:14 Moses was **w** with the officers of the host, 7107
Dt 1:34 your words, and was **w**, and sware, 7107
 3:26 the Lord was **w** with me for your sakes, 5674
 9:19 where*with* the Lord was **w** against you 7107
Jos 22:18 to morrow he will be **w** with the whole 7107
1Sa 18: 8 Saul was very **w**, and the saying 2734
 20: 7 if he be **very w**, *then* be sure that 2734+2734
 29: 4 the princes of the Philistines were **w** with 7107
2Sa 3: 8 was Abner very **w** for the words of 2734
 13:21 heard of all these things, he was very **w**. 2734
 22: 8 and shook, because he was **w**. 2734
2Ki 5:11 Naaman was **w**, and went away, and said, 7107
 13:19 the man of God was **w** with him, 7107
2Ch 16:10 Asa was **w** with the seer, and put him *in* 7107
 26:19 Uzziah was **w**, and *had* a censer in his 2196
 26:19 he was **w** with the priests, the leprosy 2196
 28: 9 the Lord God of your fathers was **w** 2534
Ne 4: 1 he was **w**, and took great indignation, 2734
 4: 7 to be stopped, then they were very **w**, 2734
Est 1:12 therefore was the king very **w**, 7107
 2:21 **w**, and sought to lay hand on the king 7107
Ps 18: 7 and were shaken, because he was **w**. 2734
 78:21 the Lord heard *this*, and was **w**: 5674
 78:59 When God heard *this*, he was **w**, 5674
 78:62 sword; and was **w** with his inheritance. 5674
 89:38 thou hast been **w** with thine anointed. 5674
Isa 28:21 he shall be **w** as *in* the valley of Gibeon, 7264
 47: 6 I was **w** with my people, I have polluted 7107
 54: 9 have I sworn that *I* would not be **w** with 7107
 57:16 for ever, neither will I be always **w**: 7107
 57:17 the iniquity of his covetousness was I **w**, 7107
 57:17 was **w**, and he went on frowardly in 7107
 64: 5 behold, thou art **w**; for we have sinned: 7107
 64: 9 Be not **w** very sore, O Lord, 7107
Jer 37:15 Wherefore the princes were **w** with 7107
La 5:22 rejected us; thou art very **w** against us. 7107
Mt 2:16 was exceeding **w**, and sent forth, 2373

W

Mt	18:34 And his lord was **w**, and delivered him to	3710
	22: 7 when the king heard *thereof*, he was **w**:	3710
Rev	12:17 And the dragon was **w** with the woman,	3710

WROUGHT (100) [WROUGHTEST]

Ge	34: 7 he had **w** folly in Israel in lying with	6213
Ex	10: 2 what things I have **w** in Egypt, and my	5953
	26:36 linen, **w with needlework.**	4639+7551
	27:16 fine twined linen, **w** with needlework.	4639
	36: 1 **w** Bezaleel and Aholiab, and every wise	6213
	36: 4 all the wise *men*, that **w** all the work of	6213
	36: 8 wise hearted *man* among them that **w**	6213
	39: 6 they **w** onyx stones inclosed *in* ouches *of*	6213
Lev	20:12 they have **w** confusion; their blood *shall*	6213
Nu	23:23 of Jacob and of Israel, What hath God **w**!	6466
	31:51 took the gold of them, *even* all **w** jewels.	4639
Dt	13:14 *that* such abomination is **w** among you;	6213
	17: 2 that hath **w** wickedness in the sight of	6213
	17: 4 *that* such abomination is **w** in Israel:	6213
	21: 3 which hath not been **w** with,	5647
	22:21 because she hath **w** folly in Israel, to play	6213
	31:18 for all the evils which they shall have **w**,	6213
Jos	7:15 and because he hath **w** folly in Israel.	6213
Jdg	20:10 according to all the folly that they have **w**	6213
Ru	2:19 her mother in law with whom she had **w**,	6213
	2:19 The man's name with whom I **w** to day	6213
1Sa	6: 6 he had **w wonderfully** among them,	5953
	11:13 for to day the Lord hath **w** salvation in	6213
	14:45 who hath **w** this great salvation in Israel?	6213
	14:45 for he hath **w** with God this day.	6213
	19: 5 the Lord **w** a great salvation for all	6213
2Sa	18:13 Otherwise I should have **w** falsehood	6213
	23:10 the Lord **w** a great victory that day;	6213
	23:12 and the Lord **w** a great victory.	6213
1Ki	5:16 which ruled over the people that **w** in	6213
	7:14 to king Solomon, and **w** all his work.	6213
	7:26 the brim thereof was **w** like the brim of a	4639
	9:23 which bare rule over the people that **w** in	6213
	16:20 acts of Zimri, and his treason that he **w**,	7194
	16:25 Omri **w** evil in the eyes of the Lord,	6213
2Ki	3: 2 he **w** evil in the sight of the Lord;	6213
	12:11 that **w** upon the house of the Lord,	6213
	17:11 **w** wicked things to provoke the Lord to	6213
	21: 6 he **w** much wickedness in the sight of	6213
1Ch	4:21 the families of the house of them that **w**	5656
	22: 2 he set masons to hew **w** stones to build	1496
2Ch	3:14 and fine linen, and **w** cherubims thereon.	5927
	21: 6 he **w** *that* which *was* evil in the eyes of	6213
	24:12 also such as **w** iron and brass to mend	2796
	24:13 So the workmen **w**, and the work was	6213
	31:20 **w** *that* which *was* good and right and	6213
	33: 6 he **w** much evil in the sight of the Lord,	6213
	34:10 they gave it *to* the workmen that **w** in	6213
	34:13 overseers of all that **w** the work in any	6213
Ne	4:16 the half of my servants **w** in the work,	6213
	4:17 *every one* with one of his hands **w** in	6213
	6:16 they perceived that this work was **w** of	6213
	9:18 of Egypt, and had **w** great provocations;	6213
	9:26 to thee, and they **w** great provocations.	6213
Job	12: 9 that the hand of the Lord hath **w** this?	6466
	36:23 or who can say, Thou hast **w** iniquity?	6466
Ps	31:19 *which* thou hast **w** for them that trust in	6466
	45:13 glorious within: her clothing *is* of **w** gold.	4865
	68:28 O God, that which thou hast **w** for us.	6466
	78:43 How he had **w** his signs in Egypt,	7760
	139:15 **curiously w** in the lowest parts of the	7551
Ecc	2:11 on all the works that my hands had **w**,	6213
	2:17 work that is **w** under the sun *is* grievous	6213
Isa	26:12 for thou also hast **w** all our works in us.	6466
	26:18 have not **w** any deliverance *in* the earth;	6213
	41: 4 Who hath **w** and done *it*, calling	6466
Jer	11:15 *seeing* she hath **w** lewdness *with* many,	6213
	18: 3 and behold, he **w** a work on the wheels.	6213
Eze	20: 9 I **w** for my name's sake, that *it* should not	6213
	20:14 I **w** for my name's sake, that *it* should not	6213
	20:22 mine hand, and **w** for my name's sake,	6213
	20:44 when I have **w** with you for my name's	6213
	29:20 because they **w** for me, saith the Lord	5647
Da	4: 2 wonders that the high God hath **w** toward	5648
Jnh	1:11 for the sea **w**, and was tempestuous.	1980
	1:13 for the sea **w**, and was tempestuous.	1980
Zep	2: 3 of the earth, which have **w** his judgment;	6466
Mt	20:12 These last have **w** *but* one hour,	4160
	26:10 for she hath **w** a good work upon me.	2038
Mk	6: 2 that even such mighty works are **w** by his	1096
	14: 6 you her? she hath **w** a good work on me.	2038
Jn	3:21 be made manifest, that they are **w** in God.	2038
Ac	5:12 and wonders **w** among the people;	1096
	15:12 wonders God had **w** among the Gentiles	4160
	18: 3 same craft, he abode with them, and **w**:	2038
	19:11 And God **w** special miracles by the hands	4160
	21:19 had **w** among the Gentiles by his ministry.	4160
Ro	7: 8 **w** in me all *manner of* concupiscence.	2716
	15:18 *things* which Christ hath not **w** by me,	2716
2Co	5: 5 Now he that hath **w** us for the selfsame	2716
	7:11 what carefulness it **w** in you, yea,	2716
	12:12 Truly the signs of an apostle were **w**	2716
Gal	2: 8 (For he that **w effectually** in Peter to	1754
Eph	1:20 Which he **w** in Christ, when he raised	1754
2Th	3: 8 with labour and travail night and day,	2038
Heb	11:33 **w** righteousness, obtained promises,	2038
Jas	2:22 Seest thou how faith **w with** his works,	4903
1Pe	4: 3 us to have **w** the will of the Gentiles,	2716
2Jn	1: 8 lose not *those things* which we have **w**,	2038
Rev	19:20 the false prophet that **w** miracles	4160

WROUGHTEST (1) [WROUGHT]

Ru	2:19 where **w** thou? blessed be he that did	6213

WRUNG (4) [WRING]

Lev	1:15 blood thereof shall be **w out** at the side	4680
	5: 9 the rest of the blood shall be **w out** at	4680
Ps	73:10 waters of a full *cup* are **w out** to them.	4680
Isa	51:17 the cup of trembling, *and* **w** *them* **out.**	4680

X

XERXES See AHASUERUS

Y

YARN (4)

1Ki	10:28 horses brought out of Egypt, and **linen y:**	4723
	10:28 the king's merchants received the **linen y**	4723
2Ch	1:16 horses brought out of Egypt, and **linen y:**	4723
	1:16 the king's merchants received the **linen y**	4723

YE (3796) [YOU] See Index of Articles, Etc.

YEA (340)

Ge	3: 1 unto the woman, **Y**, hath God said,	637+3588
	17:16 **y**, I will bless her, and she shall be *a*	2050.1
	20: 6 God said unto him in a dream, **Y**, I know	1571
	27:33 blessed him? **y**, *and* he shall be blessed.	1571
Lev	25:35 **y**, *though he be* a stranger, or a sojourner;	NIH
Nu	10:32 shall be, if thou go with us, **y**, it shall be,	2050.1
Dt	33: 3 **Y**, he loved the people; all his saints *are* in	637
Jdg	5:29 Her wise ladies answered *her*, **y**,	637
1Sa	15:20 Saul said unto Samuel, **Y**, I have obeyed	834
	21: 5 the bread is in *a* manner common, **y**,	2050.1
	24:11 see, **y** see the skirt of thy robe in my hand:	1571
2Sa	19:30 said unto the king, **Y**, let him take all,	1571
	22:39 arise: **y**, they are fallen under my feet.	2050.1
2Ki	2: 3 **Y**, I know *it*; hold you your peace.	1571
	2: 5 he answered, **Y**, I know *it*; hold you your	1571
	3: 3 **y**, and made his son to pass through	1571
1Ch	16:21 **y**, he reproved kings for their sakes,	2050.1
2Ch	26:20 **y**, himself hasted also to go out, because	1571
Ezr	9: 2 **y**, the hand of the princes and rulers	2050.1
Ne	5:15 **y**, even their servants bare rule over	NIH
	5:16 **Y** also I continued in the work of this wall,	1571
	6:10 **y**, in the night will they come to slay	2050.1
	9:18 **Y**, when they had made them a molten calf,	637
	9:21 **Y**, forty years didst thou sustain them in	2050.1
Est	5:12 Haman said moreover, **Y**, Esther the queen	637
Job	1:15 **y**, they have slain the servants with	2050.1
	1:17 **y**, and slain the servants with the edge	2050.1
	2: 4 the Lord, and said, Skin for skin, **y**,	2050.1
	5:19 **y**, in seven there shall no evil touch	2050.1
	6:10 **y**, I would harden myself in sorrow;	2050.1
	6:27 **Y**, ye overwhelm the fatherless, and you	637
	6:29 **y**, return again, my righteousness *is* in	2050.1
	9:10 **y**, and wonders without number.	NIH
	11:15 **y**, thou shalt be stedfast, and shalt not	2050.1
	11:18 **y**, thou shalt dig *about thee*, and	2050.1
	11:19 **y**, many shall make suit unto thee.	2050.1
	12: 3 **y**, who knoweth not such *things* as	2050.1
	14:10 **y**, man giveth up the ghost, and where	2050.1
	15: 4 **Y**, thou castest off fear,	637
	15: 6 **y**, thine own lips testify against thee.	2050.1
	15:15 **y**, the heavens are not clean in his sight.	2050.1
	18: 5 **Y**, the light of the wicked shall be put out,	1571
	19:18 **y**, young children despised me; I arose,	1571
	20: 8 **y**, he shall be chased away as a vision of	2050.1
	20:25 **y**, the glistering sword cometh out of his	2050.1
	21: 7 become old, **y**, are mighty *in* power?	1571
	22:25 **Y**, the Almighty shall be thy defence,	2050.1
	25: 5 **y**, the stars are not pure in his sight.	2050.1
	28:27 he prepared it, **y**, and searched it out.	2050.1
	30: 2 **Y**, whereto *might* the strength of their	1571
	30: 8 children of fools, **y**, children of base men:	1571
	30: 9 am I their song, **y**, I am their byword.	2050.1
	31: 8 **y**, let my offspring be rooted out.	2050.1
	31:11 **y**, it *is* an iniquity *to be punished by*	2050.1
	32:12 **Y**, I attended unto you, and behold,	2050.1
	33:14 God speaketh once, **y** twice, *yet man*	2050.1
	33:22 **Y**, his soul draweth near unto the grave,	2050.1
	34:12 **y**, surely God will not do wickedly,	637
	36: 7 **y**, he doth establish them for ever,	2050.1
	40: 5 **y**, twice; but I will proceed no further.	2050.1
	41:24 **y**, as hard as a piece of the nether	2050.1
Ps	7: 4 (**y**, I have delivered him that without	2050.1

Ps	7: 5 enemy persecute my soul, and take *it*; **y**,	2050.1
	8: 7 and oxen, **y**, and the beasts of the field;	2050.1
	16: 6 are fallen unto me in pleasant *places*; **y**,	637
	18:10 he did fly upon the wings of the	2050.1
	18:14 **Y**, he sent out his arrows,	2050.1
	18:48 **y**, thou liftest me up above those that rise	637
	19:10 *they* than gold, **y**, than much fine gold:	2050.1
	23: 4 **Y**, though I walk through the valley of	1571
	25: 3 **Y**, let none that wait on thee be ashamed:	1571
	27: 6 I will sing, **y**, I will sing *praises* unto	2050.1
	29: 5 **y**, the Lord breaketh the cedars of	2050.1
	29:10 **y**, the Lord sitteth King for ever.	2050.1
	31: 9 with grief, *y*, my soul and my belly.	NIH
	35:10 **y**, the poor and the needy from him that	2050.1
	35:15 **y**, the abjects gathered themselves together	NIH
	35:21 **Y**, they opened their mouth wide against	2050.1
	35:27 **y**, let them say continually,	2050.1
	37:10 and the wicked *shall* not be: **y**,	2050.1
	37:36 **y**, I sought him, but he could not be	2050.1
	40: 8 my God: **y**, thy law *is* within my heart.	2050.1
	41: 9 **Y**, mine own familiar friend, in whom I	1571
	43: 4 **y**, upon the harp will I praise thee,	2050.1
	44:22 **Y**, for thy sake are we killed all the day	3588
	57: 1 **y**, in the shadow of thy wings will I	2050.1
	58: 2 **Y**, in heart you work wickedness;	637
	59:16 **y**, I will sing aloud of thy mercy in	2050.1
	68: 3 **y**, let them exceedingly rejoice.	2050.1
	68:16 **y**, the Lord will dwell *in it* for ever.	637
	68:18 **y**, *for* the rebellious also, that the Lord	637
	72:11 **Y**, all kings shall fall down before him:	2050.1
	78:19 **y**, they spake against God; they said,	2050.1
	78:38 **y**, many a time turned he his anger	2050.1
	78:41 **Y**, they turned *back* and tempted God,	2050.1
	83:11 **y**, all their princes as Zebah,	2050.1
	83:17 **y**, let them be put to shame, and perish:	2050.1
	84: 2 My soul longeth, **y**, even fainteth for	2050.1
	84: 3 **Y**, the sparrow hath found a house,	1571
	85:12 **Y**, the Lord shall give *that which is*	1571
	90:17 **y**, the work of our hands establish thou	2050.1
	93: 4 **y**, than the mighty waves of the sea.	NIH
	94:23 *y*, the Lord our God shall cut them off.	NIH
	102:13 to favour her, **y**, the set time, is come.	3588
	102:26 **y**, all of them shall wax old like a	2050.1
	105:12 **y**, *very* few, and strangers in it.	3509.1
	105:14 **y**, he reproved kings for their sakes;	2050.1
	106:24 **Y**, they despised the pleasant land,	2050.1
	106:37 **Y**, they sacrificed their sons and their	2050.1
	109:30 **y**, I will praise him among the	2050.1
	116: 5 and righteous; **y**, our God *is* merciful.	2050.1
	118:11 me about; **y**, they compassed me about:	1571
	119:34 **y**, I shall observe it with *my* whole	2050.1
	119:103 *y*, *sweeter* than honey to my mouth!	NIH
	119:127 above gold; **y**, above fine gold.	2050.1
	128: 6 **Y**, thou shalt see thy children's children,	2050.1
	137: 1 Babylon, there we sat down, **y**, we wept,	1571
	138: 5 **Y**, they shall sing in the ways of	2050.1
	139:12 **y**, the darkness hideth not from thee;	1571
	144:15 *y*, happy *is that* people, whose God *is*	NIH
Pr	2: 3 **Y**, if thou criest after knowledge,	3588
	2: 9 judgment, and equity; **y**, every good path.	NIH
	3:24 **y**, thou shalt lie down, and thy sleep	2050.1
	6:16 **y**, seven *are* an abomination unto him:	2050.1
	7:26 **y**, many strong *men have been* slain by	2050.1
	8:18 *y*, durable riches and righteousness.	2050.1
	8:19 *is* better than gold, **y**, than fine gold;	2050.1
	16: 4 **y**, even the wicked for the day of evil.	2050.1
	22:10 go out; **y**, strife and reproach shall cease.	2050.1
	23:16 **Y**, my reins shall rejoice, when thy lips	2050.1
	23:34 **y**, thou shalt be as he that lieth down in	2050.1
	24: 5 **y**, a man of knowledge increaseth	2050.1
	29:17 **y**, he shall give delight unto thy soul.	2050.1
	30:15 *y*, four *things* say not, *It is* enough:	NIH
	30:18 for me, **y**, four which I know not:	2050.1
	30:29 go well, **y**, four are comely in going:	2050.1
	31:20 **y**, she reacheth forth her hands to	2050.1
Ecc	1:16 **y**, my heart had great experience of	2050.1
	2:18 **Y**, I hated all my labour which I *had*	2050.1
	2:23 **y**, his heart taketh not rest in the night.	1571
	3:19 **y**, they have all one breath; so that a	2050.1
	4: 3 **Y**, better *is he* than both they, which	2050.1
	4: 8 **y**, he hath neither child nor brother:	1571
	4: 8 This *is* also vanity, **y**, it *is* a sore travail.	2050.1
	6: 4 **Y**, though he live a thousand years	2050.1
	7:18 **y**, also from this withdraw not thine	2050.1
	8:17 **y** out, yet he shall not find *it*; **y** further,	2050.1
	9: 3 **y**, also the heart of the sons of men is	2050.1
	10: 3 **Y** also, when he that is a fool walketh	2050.1
	12: 9 **y**, he gave good heed, and sought out,	2050.1
SS	1:16 thou *art* fair, my beloved, **y**, pleasant:	637
	5: 1 drink, **y**, drink abundantly, O beloved.	2050.1
	5:16 **y**, he *is* altogether lovely. This *is* my	2050.1
	6: 9 **y**, the queens and the concubines,	NIH
	8: 1 kiss thee; **y**, I should not be despised.	1571
Isa	1:15 **y**, when ye make many prayers, I will not	1571
	5:10 **Y**, ten acres of vineyard shall yield one	3588
	5:29 **y**, they shall roar, and lay hold of	2050.1
	14: 8 **Y**, the fir trees rejoice at thee,	1571
	19:21 **y**, they shall vow a vow unto the Lord,	2050.1
	24:16 **y**, the treacherous dealers have dealt	2050.1
	26: 8 **Y**, in the way of thy judgments, O Lord,	637
	26: 9 **y**, *with* my spirit within me will I seek thee	637
	26:11 **y**, the fire of thine enemies shall devour	637
	29: 5 **y**, it shall be at an instant suddenly.	2050.1
	30:33 **y**, for the king it is prepared; he hath made	1571
	32:13 **y**, upon all the houses of joy *in* the joyous	3588

Isa 40:24 **Y**, they shall not be planted; yea, they shall 637
40:24 not be planted; **y**, they shall not be sown: 637
40:24 their stock shall not take root in the 637
41:10 **y**, I will help thee; yea, I will uphold thee 637
41:10 **y**, I will uphold thee with the right hand of 637
41:23 **y**, do good, or do evil, that we may be 637
41:26 **y**, *there is* none that sheweth, yea, *there is* 637
41:26 yea, *there is* none that sheweth, **y**, *there is* 637
41:26 yea, *there is* none that declareth, **y**, 637
42:13 he shall cry, **y**, roar; he shall prevail against 637
43: 7 I have formed him; **y**, I have made him. 637
43:13 **Y**, before the day *was* I *am* he; and *there* 1571
44: 8 **y**, *there is* no God; I know not *any*. 2050.1
44:12 **y**, he is hungry, and his strength faileth: 1571
44:15 he kindleth *it*, and baketh bread; yea, 637
44:15 he maketh a god, and worshippeth *it*; he 637
44:16 he warmeth himself, and saith, Aha, I am 637
44:19 **y**, also I have baked bread upon the coals 637
45:21 **y**, let them take counsel together: 637
46: 6 it a god: they fall down, **y**, they worship. 637
46: 7 **y**, *one* shall cry unto him, yet can he not 637
46:11 **y**, I have spoken *it*, I will also bring it to 637
47: 3 be uncovered, **y**, thy shame shall be seen: 1571
48: 8 **Y**, thou heardest not; yea, thou knewest 1571
48: 8 **y**, thou knewest not; yea, from that time 1571
48: 8 **y**, from that time *that* thine ear was not 1571
48:15 *even* I, have spoken; **y**, I have called him: 637
49:15 yea, they may forget, yet will I not forget 1571
55: 1 **y**, come, buy wine and milk without 2050.1
56: 9 to devour, **y**, all ye beasts in the forest. NIH
56:11 **Y**, *they are* greedy dogs *which* can never 2050.1
59:15 **Y**, truth faileth; and he *that* departeth 2050.1
60:12 **y**, *those* nations shall be utterly wasted. 2050.1
66: 3 **Y**, they have chosen their own ways, 1571
Jer 2:37 **Y**, thou shalt go forth from him, 1571
5:28 **y**, they overpass the deeds of the wicked: 1571
8: 7 **Y**, the stork in the heaven knoweth her 1571
12: 2 planted them, **y**, they have taken root: 1571
12: 2 grow, **y**, they bring forth fruit: thou *art* 1571
12: 6 **y**, they have called a multitude after thee: 1571
14: 5 **Y**, the hind also calved in the field, 3588
14:18 **y**, both the prophet and the priest go 3588
23:11 **y**, in my house have I found their 1571
23:26 **y**, *they are* prophets of the deceit of 2050.1
27:21 **Y**, thus saith the LORD of hosts, the God 3588
31: 3 *saying*, **Y**, I have loved thee *with* an 2050.1
31:19 I was ashamed, **y**, even confounded, 1571
32:41 **Y**, I will rejoice over them to do them 2050.1
46:16 many to fall, **y**, one fell upon another: 1571
51:44 not flow *together* any **more** unto him: **y**, 1571
La 1: 8 **y**, she sigheth, and turneth backward. 1571
Eze 6:14 them, and make the land desolate, **y**, 2050.1
16: 6 **y**, I said unto thee *when thou wast* in 2050.1
16: 8 **y**, I sware unto thee, and entered into a 2050.1
16: 9 **y**, I throughly washed away thy blood 2050.1
16:28 **y**, thou hast played the harlot with 2050.1
16:52 **y**, be thou confounded also, and bear 2050.1
17:10 **Y** behold, *being* planted, shall it prosper? 2050.1
22: 2 **y**, thou shalt shew her all her 2050.1
22:21 **Y**, I will gather you, and blow upon you 2050.1
22:29 **y**, they have oppressed the stranger 2050.1
23:36 **y**, declare unto them their abominations 2050.1
26:18 **y**, the isles that *are* in the sea shall be 2050.1
28:26 **y**, they shall dwell with confidence, 2050.1
32:10 **Y**, I will make many people amazed at 2050.1
32:28 **Y**, thou shalt be broken in the midst of 2050.1
34: 6 **y**, my flock was scattered upon all 2050.1
36:12 **Y**, I will cause men to walk upon you, 2050.1
37:27 **y**, I will be their God, and they shall be 2050.1
39:13 **Y**, all the people of the land shall bury 2050.1
Da 8:11 **Y**, he magnified *himself even* to 2050.1
9:11 **Y**, all Israel have transgressed thy law, 2050.1
9:21 **Y**, whiles I *was* speaking in prayer, 2050.1
10:19 peace *be* unto thee, be strong, **y**, 2050.1
11:22 **y** also, the prince of the covenant. 2050.1
11:24 **y**, and he shall forecast his devices against NIH
11:26 **Y**, they that feed of the portion of his 2050.1
Hos 2:19 **y**, I will betroth thee unto me in 2050.1
4: 3 **y**, the fishes of the sea also shall be 2050.1
7: 9 **y**, gray hairs are here and there upon him, 1571
8:10 **Y**, though they have hired among 1571
9:12 *that there shall* not *be* a man *left*: **y**, 3588
9:16 **y**, though they bring forth, yet will I slay 1571
12: 4 **Y**, he had power over the angel, 2050.1
12:11 **y**, their altars *are* as heaps in the furrows 1571
Joel 1:12 **y**, joy and gladness from the house of our NIH
1:18 **y**, the flocks of sheep are made desolate, 1571
2: 3 them a desolate wilderness; **y**, 1571+2050.1
2:19 **Y**, the LORD will answer and say unto 2050.1
4: 3 **Y**, and what have ye to do with me, 1571
Am 8: 6 **y**, and sell the refuse of the wheat? NIH
Ob 1:13 **y**, thou shouldest not have looked on 1571
1:16 **y**, they shall drink, and they shall 2050.1
Jnh 3: 8 **y**, let them turn every one from his evil 2050.1
Mic 3: 7 **y**, they shall all cover their lips; for 2050.1
Na 1: 5 **y**, the world, and all that dwell therein. 2050.1
Hab 2: 5 **Y** also, because he transgresseth *by* 2050.1
Zep 2: 1 **y**, gather together, O nation not desired; 2050.1
Hag 2:19 **y**, as yet the vine, and the fig tree, 2050.1
Zec 7:12 **Y**, they made their hearts *as* an adamant 2050.1
8:22 **Y**, many people and strong nations shall 2050.1
10: 7 **y**, their children shall see *it*, and be glad; 2050.1
14: 5 **y**, ye shall flee, like as ye fled from 2050.1
14:21 **Y**, every pot in Jerusalem and in Judah 2050.1
Mal 2: 2 **y**, I have cursed them already, 1571+2050.1

Mal 3:15 **y**, they that work wickedness are set up; 1571
3:15 **y**, *they that* tempt God are even delivered. 1571
4: 1 all the proud, **y**, and all that do wickedly, NIH
Mt 5:37 But let your communication be, **Y**, yea; 3483
5:37 But let your communication be, Yea, **y**; 3483
9:28 to do this? They said unto him, **Y**, Lord. 3483
11: 9 **y**, I say unto you, and more than a 3483
13:51 these *things*? They say unto him, **Y**, Lord. 3483
21:16 And Jesus saith unto them, **Y**; have ye 3483
26:60 **y**, though many false witnesses came, NIG
Lk 2:35 (**Y**, a sword shall pierce through thy own 1161
7:26 **Y**, I say unto you, and much more than a 3483
11:28 he said, **Y** rather, blessed *are* they that 3304
12: 5 cast into hell; **y**, I say unto you, Fear him. 3483
12:57 **Y**, and why even of yourselves judge ye NIG
14:26 and brethren, and sisters, **y**, 2089+5037
24:22 **Y**, and certain women *also* of our company 235
Jn 11:27 She saith unto him, **Y**, Lord: I believe that 3483
16: 2 **y**, the time cometh, that whosoever killeth 235
16:32 Behold, the hour cometh, **y**, is now come, 2532
21:15 He saith unto him, **Y**, Lord; thou knowest 3483
21:16 He saith unto him, **Y**, Lord; thou knowest 3483
Ac 3:16 **y**, the faith which is by him hath given 2532
3:24 **Y**, and all the prophets from Samuel and 2532
5: 8 so much? And she said, **Y**, for so much. 3483
7:43 **Y**, ye took up the tabernacle of Moloch, 2532
20:34 **Y**, ye yourselves know, that these hands 1161
22:27 Tell me, art thou a Roman? He said, **Y**. 3483
Ro 3: 4 let God be true, but every man a liar; NIG
3:31 God forbid: **y**, we establish the law. 235
8:34 *It is* Christ that died, **y**, rather, that is risen 1161
14: 4 **Y**, he shall be holden up: for God is able to 1161
15:20 **Y**, so have I strived to preach the gospel, 1161
1Co 1:28 God chosen, **y**, and *things* which are not, NIG
2:10 for the Spirit searcheth all *things*, **y**, 2532
4: 3 **y**, I judge not mine own self. 235
9:16 **y**, woe is unto me, if I preach not 1161
15:15 **Y**, and we are found false witnesses of 1161
16: 6 that I will abide, **y**, and winter with you, 2228
2Co 1:17 with me there should be **y** yea, and nay 3483
1:17 with me there should be yea **y**, and nay 3483
1:18 our word toward you was not **y** and nay. 3483
1:19 was not **y** and nay, but in him was yea. 3483
1:19 was not yea and nay, but in him was **y**. 3483
1:20 For all the promises of God in him *are* **y**, 3483
5:16 **y**, though we have known Christ after 1161
7:11 **y**, *what* clearing of yourselves, yea, 235
7:11 **y**, *what* indignation, yea, *what* fear, yea, 235
7:11 yea, *what* indignation, **y**, *what* fear, yea, 235
7:11 yea, *what* indignation, yea, *what* fear, **y**, 235
7:11 **y**, *what* zeal, yea, *what* revenge! 235
7:11 yea, *what* zeal, **y**, *what* revenge! 235
7:13 **y**, and exceedingly the more joyed we for NIG
8: 3 **y**, and beyond *their* power *they were* NIG
Gal 4:17 **y**, they would exclude you, that you might 235
Php 1:18 and I therein do rejoice, **y**, and will rejoice. 235
2:17 **y**, and if I be offered upon the sacrifice and 235
3: 8 **Y** doubtless, and I count all *things* but 235
2Ti 3:12 **Y**, and all that will live godly in Christ 1161
Phm 1:20 **Y**, brother, let me have joy of thee in 3483
Heb 11:36 trial of *cruel* mockings and scourgings, **y**, NIG
Jas 2:18 **Y**, a man may say, Thou hast faith, and I 235
5:12 but let your **y** be yea; and *your* nay, nay; 3483
5:12 but let your yea be **y**; and *your* nay, nay; 3483
1Pe 5: 5 **Y**, all *of you* be subject one to another, NIG
2Pe 1:13 **Y**, I think it meet, as long as I am in this NIG
3Jn 1:12 **y**, and we also bear record; and ye know 1161
Rev 14:13 **Y**, saith the Spirit, that they may rest from 3483

YEAR (372) [YEAR'S, YEARLY, YEARS, YEARS']

Ge 7:11 In the six hundredth **y** of Noah's life, 8141
8:13 to pass in the six hundredth and first **y**, 8141
14: 4 and *in* the thirteenth **y** they rebelled. 8141
14: 5 in the fourteenth **y** came Chedorlaomer, 8141
17:21 unto thee at this set time in the next **y**. 8141
26:12 received in the same **y** an hundredfold: 8141
47:17 with bread for all their cattle for that **y**. 8141
47:18 When that **y** was ended, they came unto 8141
47:18 they came unto him the second **y**, 8141
Ex 12: 2 it *shall be* the first month of the **y** to you. 8141
12: 5 be without blemish, a male of the first **y**: 8141
13:10 keep this ordinance in his season from **y** 3117
13:10 ordinance in his season from year to **y**. 3117
23:11 the seventh *y* thou shalt let it rest and NIH
23:14 thou shalt keep a feast unto me in the **y**. 8141
23:16 ingathering, *which is* in the end of the **y**, 8141
23:17 Three times in the **y** all thy males shall 8141
23:29 drive them out from before thee in one **y**; 8141
29:38 two lambs of the first **y** day by day 8141
30:10 **y** with the blood of the sin offering of 8141
30:10 once in the **y** shall he make atonement 8141
34:23 Thrice in the **y** shall all your men children 8141
34:24 before the LORD thy God thrice in the **y**. 8141
40:17 to pass in the first month in the second **y**, 8141
Lev 9: 3 a calf and a lamb, both of the first **y**, 8141
12: 6 she shall bring a lamb of the first **y** for a 8141
14:10 one ewe lamb of the first **y** without 8141
16:34 of Israel for all their sins once a **y**. 8141
19:24 in the fourth **y** all the fruit thereof shall be 8141
19:25 the fifth **y** shall ye eat of the fruit thereof, 8141
23:12 first **y** for a burnt offering unto the LORD. 8141
23:18 lambs without blemish of the first **y**, 8141
23:19 two lambs of the first **y** for a sacrifice of 8141
23:41 feast unto the LORD seven days in the **y**. 8141
25: 4 in the seventh **y** shall be a sabbath of rest 8141

Lev 25: 5 *for* it is a **y** of rest unto the land. 8141
25:10 ye shall hallow the fiftieth **y**, 8141
25:11 A jubile shall that fiftieth **y** be unto you: 8141
25:13 In the **y** of this jubile ye shall return every 8141
25:20 say, What shall we eat the seventh **y**? 8141
25:21 my blessing upon you in the sixth **y**, 8141
25:22 shall sow the eighth **y**, and eat *yet of* 8141
25:22 and eat *yet* of old fruit until the ninth **y**; 8141
25:28 that hath bought it until the **y** of jubile: 8141
25:29 may redeem it within a whole **y** after it 8141
25:29 is sold; *within* a **full y** may he redeem it. 3117
25:30 not redeemed within the space of a full **y**, 8141
25:33 shall go out in the **y** *of* jubile: NIH
25:40 *and* shall serve thee unto the **y** of jubile: 8141
25:50 **y** that he was sold to him unto the year of 8141
25:50 he was sold to him unto the **y** of jubile: 8141
25:52 but few years unto the **y** of jubile, 8141
25:54 then he shall go out in the **y** of jubile, 8141
27:17 If he sanctify his field from the **y** of jubile, 8141
27:18 *even* unto the **y** of the jubile, and it shall 8141
27:23 *even* unto the **y** of the jubile: 8141
27:24 In the **y** of the jubile the field shall return 8141
Nu 1: 1 in the second **y** after they were come out 8141
6:12 shall bring a lamb of the **first y** 1121+8141
6:14 one he lamb of the **first y** without 1121+8141
6:14 one ewe lamb of the **first y** without 1323+8141
7:15 one ram, one lamb of the **first y**, 1121+8141
7:17 he goats, five lambs of the **first y**: 1121+8141
7:21 one ram, one lamb of the **first y**, 1121+8141
7:23 he goats, five lambs of the **first y**: 1121+8141
7:27 one ram, one lamb of the **first y**, 1121+8141
7:29 he goats, five lambs of the **first y**: 1121+8141
7:33 one ram, one lamb of the **first y**, 1121+8141
7:35 he goats, five lambs of the **first y**, 1121+8141
7:39 one ram, one lamb of the **first y**, 1121+8141
7:41 he goats, five lambs of the **first y**, 1121+8141
7:45 one ram, one lamb of the **first y**, 1121+8141
7:47 he goats, five lambs of the **first y**, 1121+8141
7:51 one ram, one lamb of the **first y**, 1121+8141
7:53 he goats, five lambs of the **first y**, 1121+8141
7:57 one ram, one lamb of the **first y**, 1121+8141
7:59 he goats, five lambs of the **first y**, 1121+8141
7:63 one ram, one lamb of the **first y**, 1121+8141
7:65 he goats, five lambs of the **first y**, 1121+8141
7:69 one ram, one lamb of the **first y**, 1121+8141
7:71 he goats, five lambs of the **first y**, 1121+8141
7:75 one ram, one lamb of the **first y**, 1121+8141
7:77 he goats, five lambs of the **first y**, 1121+8141
7:81 one ram, one lamb of the **first y**, 1121+8141
7:83 he goats, five lambs of the **first y**, 1121+8141
7:87 the lambs of the **first y** twelve, 1121+8141
7:88 the lambs of the **first y** sixty. 1121+8141
9: 1 in the first month of the second **y** after 8141
9:22 *it were* two days, or a month, or a **y**, 3117
10:11 of the second month, in the second **y**, 8141
14:34 *even* forty days, each day for a **y**, shall ye 8141
15:27 he shall bring a she goat of the first **y** for a 8141
28: 3 lambs of the **first y** without spot 1121+8141
28: 9 the sabbath day two lambs of the first **y** 8141
28:11 lambs of the **first y** without spot; 1121+8141
28:14 month throughout the months of the **y**. 8141
28:19 and seven lambs of the **first y**: 1121+8141
28:27 one ram, seven lambs of the **first y**; 1121+8141
29: 2 of the **first y** without blemish: 1121+8141
29: 8 *and* seven lambs of the **first y**; 1121+8141
29:13 and fourteen lambs of the **first y**; 1121+8141
29:17 lambs of the **first y** without spot: 1121+8141
29:20 lambs of the **first y** without 1121+8141
29:23 lambs of the **first y** without 1121+8141
29:26 lambs of the **first y** without spot: 1121+8141
29:29 lambs of the **first y** without 1121+8141
29:32 lambs of the **first y** without 1121+8141
29:36 lambs of the **first y** without 1121+8141
33:38 in the fortieth **y** after the children of Israel 8141
Dt 1: 3 it came to pass in the fortieth **y**, 8141
11:12 from the beginning of the **y** even unto 8141
11:12 of the year even unto the end of the **y**. 8141
14:22 the field bringeth forth **y by year**. 8141+8141
14:22 the field bringeth forth **year by y**. 8141+8141
14:28 all the tithe of thine increase the same **y**, 8141
15: 9 saying, The seventh **y**, the year of release, 8141
15: 9 seventh year, the **y** of release, is at hand; 8141
15:12 in the seventh **y** thou shalt let him go free 8141
15:20 **y by year** in the place 8141+8141+871.1
15:20 **year by y** in the place 8141+8141+871.1
16:16 Three times in a **y** shall all thy males 8141
24: 5 *but* he shall be free at home one **y**, 8141
26:12 all the tithes of thine increase the third **y**, 8141
26:12 *which is* the **y** of tithing, and hast given 8141
31:10 in the solemnity of the **y** of release, 8141
Jos 5:12 of the fruit of the land of Canaan that **y**. 8141
Jdg 10: 8 that **y** they vexed and oppressed 8141
11:40 of Jephthah the Gileadite four days in a **y**. 8141
17:10 give thee ten *shekels* of silver by the **y**, 3117
1Sa 1: 7 *as* he did so **y** by year, when she went up 8141
1: 7 *as* he did so year by **y**, when she went up 8141
2:19 and brought *it* to him from **y** to year, 3117
2:19 and brought *it* to him from year to **y**, 3117
7:16 went from **y** to year in circuit *to* Beth-el, 8141
7:16 went from year to **y** in circuit *to* Beth-el, 8141
13: 1 Saul reigned one **y**; and when he had 8141
27: 7 the country of the Philistines was a **full y** 3117
2Sa 11: 1 it came to pass, after the **y** was expired, 8141
21: 1 the days of David three years, **y** after year; 8141
21: 1 the days of David three years, year after **y**; 8141

1Ki 4: 7	man *his* month in a **y** made provision. 8141
5:11	thus gave Solomon to Hiram **y** by year. 8141
5:11	thus gave Solomon to Hiram year by **y**. 8141
6: 1	eightieth **y** after the children of Israel 8141
6: 1	in the fourth **y** of Solomon's reign over 8141
6:37	In the fourth **y** was the foundation of 8141
6:38	in the eleventh **y**, in the month Bul, 8141
9:25	three times in a **y** did Solomon offer burnt 8141
10:14	in one **y** was six hundred threescore 8141
10:25	horses, and mules, a rate **y** by year. 8141
10:25	horses, and mules, a rate year by **y**. 8141
14:25	it came to pass in the fifth **y** of king 8141
15: 1	in the eighteenth **y** of king Jeroboam 8141
15: 9	in the twentieth **y** of Jeroboam king of 8141
15:25	in the second **y** of Asa king of Judah, 8141
15:28	in the third **y** of Asa king of Judah did 8141
15:33	In the third **y** of Asa king of Judah *began* 8141
16: 8	sixth **y** of Asa king of Judah *began* Elah 8141
16:10	and seventh **y** of Asa king of Judah, 8141
16:15	seventh **y** of Asa king of Judah did Zimri 8141
16:23	first **y** of Asa king of Judah *began* Omri to 8141
16:29	eighth **y** of Asa king of Judah *began* Ahab 8141
18: 1	of the LORD came to Elijah in the third **y**, 8141
20:22	for at the return of the **y** the king of Syria 8141
20:26	it came to pass at the return of the **y**, 8141
22: 2	it came to pass on the third **y**, that 8141
22:41	in the fourth **y** of Ahab king of Israel. 8141
22:51	**y** of Jehoshaphat king of Judah, 8141
2Ki 1:17	**y** of Jehoram the son of Jehoshaphat king 8141
3: 1	eighteenth **y** of Jehoshaphat king of 8141
8:16	in the fifth **y** of Joram the son of Ahab 8141
8:25	In the twelfth **y** of Joram the son of Ahab 8141
8:26	reign; and he reigned one **y** in Jerusalem. 8141
9:29	the eleventh **y** of Joram the son of Ahab 8141
11: 4	the seventh **y** Jehoiada sent and fet 8141
12: 1	In the seventh **y** of Jehu Jehoash *began* to 8141
12: 6	twentieth **y** of king Jehoash the priests 8141
13: 1	twentieth **y** of Joash the son of Ahaziah 8141
13:10	seventh **y** of Joash king of Judah *began* 8141
13:20	the land *at* the coming in of the **y**. 8141
14: 1	In the second **y** of Joash son of Jehoahaz 8141
14:23	In the fifteenth **y** of Amaziah the son of 8141
15: 1	seventh **y** of Jeroboam king of Israel 8141
15: 8	eighth **y** of Azariah king of Judah did 8141
15:13	thirtieth **y** of Uzziah king of Judah; 8141
15:17	thirtieth **y** of Azariah king of Judah *began* 8141
15:23	In the fiftieth **y** of Azariah king of Judah 8141
15:27	fiftieth **y** of Azariah king of Judah Pekah 8141
15:30	in the twentieth **y** of Jotham the son of 8141
15:32	In the second **y** of Pekah the son of 8141
16: 1	In the seventeenth **y** of Pekah the son of 8141
17: 1	In the twelfth **y** of Ahaz king of Judah 8141
17: 4	king of Assyria, as *he had done* **y** by year: 8141
17: 4	king of Assyria, as *he had done* year by **y**: 8141
17: 6	In the ninth **y** of Hoshea, the king of 8141
18: 1	Now it came to pass in the third **y** of 8141
18: 9	it came to pass in the fourth **y** of king 8141
18: 9	which *was* the seventh **y** of Hoshea son 8141
18:10	*even* in the sixth **y** of Hezekiah, that *is* 8141
18:10	*is* the ninth **y** of Hoshea king of Israel, 8141
18:13	Now in the fourteenth **y** of king Hezekiah 8141
19:29	Ye shall eat *this* **y** such things as grow of 8141
19:29	in the second **y** that which springeth of 8141
19:29	in the third **y** sow ye, and reap, 8141
22: 3	it came to pass in the eighteenth **y** of king 8141
23:23	in the eighteenth **y** of king Josiah, 8141
23:36	and five **y** old when he *began* to reign; 8141
24:12	king of Babylon took him in the eighth **y** 8141
25: 1	it came to pass in the ninth **y** of his reign, 8141
25: 2	city was besieged unto the eleventh **y** of 8141
25: 8	which *is* the nineteenth **y** of king 8141
25:27	thirtieth **y** of the captivity of Jehoiachin 8141
25:27	Babylon, in the **y** that he *began* to reign, 8141
1Ch 20: 1	came to pass, that after the **y** was expired, 8141
26:31	In the fortieth **y** of the reign of David 8141
27: 1	throughout all the months of the **y**, 8141
2Ch 3: 2	month, in the fourth **y** of his reign. 8141
8:13	the solemn feasts, three times in the **y**, 8141
9:13	to Solomon in one **y** was six hundred 8141
9:24	horses, and mules, a rate **y** by year. 8141
9:24	horses, and mules, a rate year by **y**. 8141
12: 2	*that* in the fifth **y** of king Rehoboam 8141
13: 1	in the eighteenth **y** of king Jeroboam 8141
15:10	in the fifteenth **y** of the reign of Asa. 8141
15:19	five and thirtieth **y** of the reign of Asa. 8141
16: 1	thirtieth **y** of the reign of Asa Baasha king 8141
16:12	**y** of his reign was diseased in his feet, 8141
16:13	died in the one and fortieth **y** of his reign. 8141
17: 7	in the third **y** of his reign he sent to his 8141
22: 2	reign, and he reigned one **y** in Jerusalem. 8141
23: 1	in the seventh **y** Jehoiada strengthened 8141
24: 5	the house of your God from **y** to year, 8141
24: 5	the house of your God from year to **y**, 8141
24:23	it came to pass at the end of the **y**, *that* 8141
27: 5	the same **y** an hundred talents of silver, 8141
27: 5	him, both the second **y**, and the third. 8141
29: 3	He in the first **y** of his reign, in the first 8141
34: 3	For in the eighth **y** of his reign, while he 8141
34: 3	in the twelfth **y** he began to purge Judah 8141
34: 8	Now in the eighteenth **y** of his reign, 8141
35:19	In the eighteenth **y** of the reign of Josiah 8141
36:10	when the **y** was expired, king 8141
36:22	Now in the first **y** of Cyrus king of Persia, 8141
Ezr 1: 1	Now in the first **y** of Cyrus king of Persia, 8141
3: 8	Now in the second **y** of their coming unto 8141

Ezr 4:24	it ceased unto the second **y** of the reign 8140
5:13	in the first **y** of Cyrus the king of Babylon 8140
6: 3	In the first **y** of Cyrus the king *the same* 8140
6:15	which *was* in the sixth **y** of the reign of 8140
7: 7	in the seventh **y** of Artaxerxes the king. 8141
7: 8	which *was* in the seventh **y** of the king. 8141
Ne 1: 1	*in* the twentieth **y**, as I was in Shushan 8141
2: 1	in the twentieth **y** of Artaxerxes the king, 8141
5:14	from the twentieth **y** even unto the two 8141
5:14	and thirtieth **y** of Artaxerxes the king, 8141
10:31	*that* we would leave the seventh **y**, 8141
10:34	our fathers, at times appointed **y** by year, 8141
10:34	our fathers, at times appointed year by **y**, 8141
10:35	**y** by year, unto the house of the LORD: 8141
10:35	year by **y**, unto the house of the LORD: 8141
13: 6	thirtieth **y** of Artaxerxes king of Babylon 8141
Est 1: 3	In the third **y** of his reign, he made a feast 8141
2:16	Tebeth, in the seventh **y** of his reign. 8141
3: 7	in the twelfth **y** of king Ahasuerus, 8141
9:27	time every **y**, 3605+8141+8141+2050.1
Job 3: 6	let it not be joined unto the days of the **y**, 8141
Ps 65:11	Thou crownest the **y** with thy goodness; 8141
Isa 14:28	In the **y** that king Uzziah died I saw also 8141
14:28	In the **y** that king Ahaz died was this 8141
20: 1	In the **y** that Tartan came unto Ashdod, 8141
21:16	Within a **y**, according to the years of a 8141
29: 1	add ye **y** to year; let them kill sacrifices. 8141
29: 1	add year to **y**; let them kill sacrifices. 8141
34: 8	the **y** of recompenses for the controversy 8141
36: 1	Now it came to pass in the fourteenth **y** 8141
37:30	shall eat *this* **y** such as groweth of itself; 8141
37:30	the second **y** that which springeth of 8141
37:30	in the third **y** sow ye, and reap, 8141
61: 2	To proclaim the acceptable **y** of 8141
63: 4	and the **y** of my redeemed is come. 8141
Jer 1: 2	of Judah, in the thirteenth **y** of his reign. 8141
1: 3	the end of the eleventh **y** of Zedekiah 8141
11:23	Anathoth, *even* the **y** of their visitation. 8141
17: 8	shall not be careful in the **y** of drought, 8141
23:12	*even* the **y** of their visitation, saith 8141
25: 1	**y** of Jehoiakim the son of Josiah king of 8141
25: 1	*was* the first **y** of Nebuchadrezzar king 8141
25: 3	From the thirteenth **y** of Josiah the son of 8141
25: 3	this day, that *is* the three and twentieth **y**, 8141
28: 1	came to pass the same **y**, in the beginning 8141
28: 1	in the fourth **y**, *and* in the fifth month, 8141
28:16	*this* **y** thou *shalt* die, because thou hast 8141
28:17	Hananiah the prophet died the same **y** in 8141
32: 1	in the tenth **y** of Zedekiah king of Judah, 8141
32: 1	which *was* the eighteenth **y** of 8141
36: 1	came to pass in the fourth **y** of Jehoiakim 8141
36: 9	it came to pass in the fifth **y** of Jehoiakim 8141
39: 1	In the ninth **y** of Zedekiah king of Judah, 8141
39: 2	*And* in the eleventh **y** of Zedekiah, 8141
45: 1	in the fourth **y** of Jehoiakim the son of 8141
46: 2	of Jehoiakim the son of Josiah king of 8141
48:44	*even* upon Moab, the **y** of their visitation, 8141
51:46	a rumour shall both come one **y**, 8141
51:46	that in *another* **y** *shall* come a rumour, 8141
51:59	*into* Babylon in the fourth **y** of his reign. 8141
52: 1	twenty **y** old when he *began* to reign, 8141
52: 4	it came to pass in the ninth **y** of his reign, 8141
52: 5	the city was besieged unto the eleventh **y** 8141
52:12	which *was* the nineteenth **y** of 8141
52:28	in the seventh **y** three thousand Jews and 8141
52:29	In the eighteenth **y** of Nebuchadrezzar he 8141
52:30	twentieth **y** of Nebuchadrezzar 8141
52:31	thirtieth **y** of the captivity of Jehoiachin 8141
52:31	of his reign lifted up the head of 8141
Eze 1: 1	Now it came to pass in the thirtieth **y**, 8141
1: 2	which *was* the fifth **y** of king Jehoiachin's 8141
4: 6	I have appointed thee each day for a **y**. 8141
8: 1	it came to pass in the sixth **y**, in the sixth 8141
20: 1	came to pass in the seventh **y**, in the fifth 8141
24: 1	Again in the ninth **y**, in the tenth month, 8141
26: 1	came to pass in the eleventh **y**, in the first 8141
29: 1	In the tenth **y**, in the tenth *month*, in 8141
29:17	to pass in the seven and twentieth **y**, 8141
30:20	it came to pass in the eleventh **y**, 8141
31: 1	it came to pass in the eleventh **y**, 8141
32: 1	it came to pass in the twelfth **y**, 8141
32:17	It came to pass also in the twelfth **y**, 8141
33:21	came to pass in the twelfth **y** of our 8141
40: 1	the five and twentieth **y** of our captivity, 8141
40: 1	the beginning of the **y**, in the tenth *day* of 8141
40: 1	in the fourteenth **y** after that the city was 8141
46:13	of a lamb of the first **y** without blemish: 8141
46:17	then it shall be his to the **y** of liberty: 8141
Da 1: 1	In the third **y** of the reign of Jehoiakim 8141
1:21	Daniel continued *even* unto the first **y** of 8141
2: 1	in the second **y** of the reign of 8141
5:31	*being* about threescore and two **y** old. 8140
7: 1	the first **y** of Belshazzar king of Babylon 8140
8: 1	In the third **y** of the reign of king 8141
9: 1	In the first **y** of Darius the son of 8141
9: 2	In the first **y** of his reign I Daniel 8141
10: 1	In the third **y** of Cyrus king of Persia a 8141
11: 1	Also I in the first **y** of Darius the Mede, 8141
Am 1: 1	of Israel, two **y** before the earthquake. 8141
Mic 6: 6	burnt offerings, with calves of a **y** old? 8141
Hag 1: 1	In the second **y** of Darius the king, 8141
1:15	in the second **y** of Darius the king. 8141
2:10	ninth *month*, in the second **y** of Darius, 8141
Zec 1: 1	eighth month, in the second **y** of Darius, 8141
1: 7	month Sebat, in the second **y** of Darius, 8141

Zec 7: 1	it came to pass in the fourth **y** of king 8141
14:16	go up from **y** to year to worship the King, 8141
14:16	go up from year to **y** to worship the King, 8141
Lk 2:41	his parents went to Jerusalem every **y** 2094
3: 1	Now in the fifteenth **y** of the reign of 2094
4:19	To preach the acceptable **y** of the Lord. 1763
13: 8	Lord, let it alone this **y** also, till I shall dig 2094
Jn 11:49	being the high priest that *same* **y**, said 1763
11:51	but being high priest that **y**, he prophesied 1763
18:13	which was the high priest that *same* **y**. 1763
Ac 11:26	that a whole **y** they assembled themselves 1763
18:11	he continued *there* a **y** and six months, 1763
Ro 4:19	when he was about an hundred **y** old, 1541
2Co 8:10	to do, but also to be forward a **y** ago. 575+4070
9: 2	that Achaia was ready a **y** ago; 575+4070
Heb 9: 7	*went* the high priest alone once every **y**, 1763
9:25	holy *place* every **y** with blood of others; 1763
10: 1	**y** by year continually make 1763+2596
10: 1	**year** by **y** continually make 1763+2596
10: 3	remembrance *again made* of sins every **y**. 1763
Jas 4:13	and continue there a **y**, and buy and sell, 1763
Rev 9:15	a day, and a month, and a **y**, for to slay 1763

YEAR'S (2) [YEAR]

Ex 34:22	and the feast of ingathering *at* the **y** end. 8141
2Sa 14:26	(for it was at *every* **y** end 3117+3117+3807.1

YEARLING See FATLING

YEARLY (9) [YEAR]

Lev 25:53	*And* as a **y** hired servant 8141+8141+871.1
Jdg 11:40	**y** to lament 3117+3117+4480+1886.5
21:19	*in a place* which 3117+3117+4480+1886.5
1Sa 1: 3	his city **y** to worship 3117+3117+4480+1886.5
1:21	went up to offer unto the LORD the **y** 3117
2:19	with her husband to offer the **y** sacrifice. 3117
20: 6	for *there is* a **y** sacrifice there for all 3117
Ne 10:32	to charge ourselves **y** with the third *part* 8141
Est 9:21	the same, **y**, 3605+8141+8141+871.1+2050.1

YEARN, YEARNED See YERN, YERNED

YEARS (532) [YEAR]

Ge 1:14	and for seasons, and for days, and **y**: 8141
5: 3	Adam lived an hundred and thirty **y**, 8141
5: 4	had begotten Seth were eight hundred **y**: 8141
5: 5	lived were nine hundred and thirty **y**. 8141
5: 6	Seth lived an hundred and five **y**, 8141
5: 7	he begat Enos eight hundred and seven **y**, 8141
5: 8	of Seth were nine hundred and twelve **y**: 8141
5: 9	Enos lived ninety **y**, and begat Cainan: 8141
5:10	begat Cainan eight hundred and fifteen **y**, 8141
5:11	of Enos were nine hundred and five **y**: 8141
5:12	Cainan lived seventy **y**, 8141
5:13	Mahalaleel eight hundred and forty **y**, 8141
5:14	of Cainan were nine hundred and ten **y**: 8141
5:15	Mahalaleel lived sixty and five **y**, 8141
5:16	he begat Jared eight hundred and thirty **y**, 8141
5:17	were eight hundred ninety and five **y**, 8141
5:18	Jared lived an hundred sixty and two **y**, 8141
5:19	after he begat Enoch eight hundred **y**, 8141
5:20	Jared were nine hundred sixty and two **y**: 8141
5:21	Enoch lived sixty and five **y**, 8141
5:22	he begat Methuselah three hundred **y**, 8141
5:23	were three hundred sixty and five **y**: 8141
5:25	lived an hundred eighty and seven **y**, 8141
5:26	Lamech seven hundred eighty and two **y**, 8141
5:27	were nine hundred sixty and nine **y**: 8141
5:28	lived an hundred eighty and two **y**, 8141
5:30	Noah five hundred ninety and five **y**, 8141
5:31	were seven hundred seventy and seven **y**: 8141
5:32	Noah was five hundred **y** old: 8141
6: 3	days shall be an hundred and twenty **y**. 8141
7: 6	Noah *was* six hundred **y** old when the 8141
9:28	after the flood three hundred and fifty **y**. 8141
9:29	of Noah were nine hundred and fifty **y**: 8141
11:10	Shem *was* an hundred **y** old, 8141
11:10	and begat Arphaxad **two y** after the flood: 8141
11:11	after he begat Arphaxad five hundred **y**, 8141
11:12	Arphaxad lived five and thirty **y**, 8141
11:13	he begat Salah four hundred and three **y**, 8141
11:14	And Salah lived thirty **y**, and begat Eber: 8141
11:15	he begat Eber four hundred and three **y**, 8141
11:16	Eber lived four and thirty **y**, 8141
11:17	he begat Peleg four hundred and thirty **y**, 8141
11:18	And Peleg lived thirty **y**, and begat Reu: 1541
11:19	he begat Reu two hundred and nine **y**, 8141
11:20	Reu lived two and thirty **y**, 8141
11:21	he begat Serug two hundred and seven **y**, 8141
11:22	And Serug lived thirty **y**, and begat Nahor: 8141
11:23	lived after he begat Nahor two hundred **y**, 8141
11:24	Nahor lived nine and twenty **y**, 8141
11:25	begat Terah an hundred and nineteen **y**, 8141
11:26	Terah lived seventy **y**, and begat Abram, 8141
11:32	of Terah were two hundred and five **y**: 8141
12: 4	**y** old when he departed out of Haran. 8141
14: 4	Twelve **y** they served Chedorlaomer, 8141
15: 9	Take me a heifer of **three y** old, and a 8027
15: 9	a she goat of **three y** old, and a ram of 8027
15: 9	a ram of **three y** old, and a turtle-dove, 8027
15:13	they shall afflict them four hundred **y**; 8141
16: 3	Abram had dwelt ten **y** in the land of 8141
16:16	Abram *was* fourscore and six **y** old, 8141
17: 1	when Abram was ninety **y** old and nine, 8141
17:17	born unto him that is an hundred **y** old? 8141
17:17	and shall Sarah, that is ninety **y** old, bear? 8141

Ge	17:24 Abraham *was* ninety **y** old and nine,	8141
	17:25 Ishmael his son *was* thirteen **y** old, when	8141
	21: 5 Abraham *was* an hundred **y** old, when his	8141
	23: 1 an hundred and seven and twenty **y old:**	8141
	23: 1 *these were* the **y** of the life of Sarah.	8141
	25: 7 these *are* the days of the **y** of Abraham's	8141
	25: 7 an hundred threescore and fifteen **y.**	8141
	25: 8 full *of* **y**, and was gathered to his people.	NIH
	25:17 these *are* the **y** of the life of Ishmael,	8141
	25:17 an hundred and thirty and seven **y:**	8141
	25:20 Isaac was forty **y** old when he took	8141
	25:26 Isaac was threescore **y** old when she bare	8141
	26:34 Esau was forty **y** old when he took to wife	8141
	29:18 I will serve thee seven **y** for Rachel thy	8141
	29:20 Jacob served seven **y** for Rachel;	8141
	29:27 shalt serve with me yet seven other **y.**	8141
	29:30 and served with him yet seven other **y.**	8141
	31:38 This twenty **y** have I *been* with thee;	8141
	31:41 Thus have I been twenty **y** in thy house;	8141
	31:41 I served thee fourteen **y** for thy two	8141
	31:41 two daughters, and six **y** for thy cattle:	8141
	35:28 Isaac were an hundred and fourscore **y.**	8141
	37: 2 Joseph, *being* seventeen **y** old, was	8141
	41: 1 to pass at the end of **two full y**,	3117+8141
	41:26 The seven good kine *are* seven **y;**	8141
	41:26 and the seven good ears *are* seven **y:**	8141
	41:27 kine that came up after them *are* seven **y;**	8141
	41:27 the east wind shall be seven **y** of famine.	8141
	41:29 there come seven **y** of great plenty	8141
	41:30 there shall arise after them seven **y** of	8141
	41:34 land of Egypt in the seven plenteous **y.**	8141
	41:35 them gather all the food of those good **y**	8141
	41:36 to the land against the seven **y** of famine,	8141
	41:46 Joseph *was* thirty **y** old when he stood	8141
	41:47 the seven plenteous **y** the earth brought	8141
	41:48 gathered up all the food of the seven **y,**	8141
	41:50 two sons before the **y** of famine came,	8141
	41:53 the seven **y** of plenteousness, that was in	8141
	41:54 the seven **y** of dearth began to come,	8141
	45: 6 For these **two y** *hath* the famine *been* in	8141
	45: 6 yet *there are* five **y**, *in* the which *there*	8141
	45:11 yet *there are* five **y** of famine; lest thou,	8141
	47: 9 The days of the **y** of my pilgrimage *are* an	8141
	47: 9 pilgrimage *are* an hundred and thirty **y**	8141
	47: 9 evil have the days of the **y** of my life been,	8141
	47: 9 have not attained unto the days of the **y**	8141
	47:28 lived in the land of Egypt seventeen **y:**	8141
	47:28 Jacob was an hundred forty and seven **y.**	8141
	50:22 and Joseph lived an hundred and ten **y.**	8141
	50:26 *being* an hundred and ten **y** old:	8141
Ex	6:16 the **y** of the life of Levi *were* an hundred	8141
	6:16 Levi *were* an hundred thirty and seven **y.**	8141
	6:18 **y** of the life of Kohath *were* an hundred	8141
	6:18 *were* an hundred thirty and three **y.**	8141
	6:20 **y** of the life of Amram *were* an hundred	8141
	6:20 *were* an hundred and thirty and seven **y.**	8141
	7: 7 Moses *was* fourscore **y** old,	8141
	7: 7 Aaron fourscore and three **y** old, when	8141
	12:40 in Egypt, *was* four hundred and thirty **y.**	8141
	12:41 the end of the four hundred and thirty **y,**	8141
	16:35 children of Israel did eat manna forty **y,**	8141
	21: 2 a Hebrew servant, six **y** he shall serve:	8141
	23:10 six **y** thou shalt sow thy land,	8141
	30:14 from twenty **y** old and above, shall give	8141
	38:26 from twenty **y** old and upward, for six	8141
Lev	19:23 three **y** shall it be as uncircumcised unto	8141
	25: 3 Six **y** thou shalt sow thy field, and six	8141
	25: 3 and six **y** thou shalt prune thy vineyard,	8141
	25: 8 shalt number seven sabbaths of **y** unto	8141
	25: 8 of years unto thee, seven times seven **y;**	8141
	25: 8 the space of the seven sabbaths of **y** shall	8141
	25: 8 years shall be unto thee forty and nine **y.**	8141
	25:15 According to the number of **y** after	8141
	25:15 according unto the number of **y** of the	8141
	25:16 According to the multitude of **y** thou shalt	8141
	25:16 according to the fewness of **y** thou shalt	8141
	25:16 for *according to* the number *of the* **y** of	NIH
	25:21 it shall bring forth fruit for three **y.**	8141
	25:27 let him count the **y** of the sale thereof,	8141
	25:50 shall be according unto the number of **y,**	8141
	25:51 If *there be* many **y** *behind*, according	8141
	25:52 but few **y** unto the year of jubile,	8141
	25:52 according unto his **y** shall he give *him*	8141
	25:54 if he be not redeemed in these **y**, then	NIH
	27: 3 of the male from twenty **y** old even unto	8141
	27: 3 twenty years old even unto sixty **y** old,	8141
	27: 5 if *it be* from five **y** old even unto twenty	8141
	27: 5 five years old even unto twenty **y** old,	8141
	27: 6 if *it be* from a month old even unto five **y**	8141
	27: 7 if *it be* from sixty **y** old and above; if *it be*	8141
	27:18 the money according to the **y** that remain,	8141
Nu	1: 3 From twenty **y** old and upward, all that	8141
	1:18 from twenty **y** old and upward, by their	8141
	1:20 male from twenty **y** old and upward,	8141
	1:22 male from twenty **y** old and upward,	8141
	1:24 from twenty **y** old and upward, all that	8141
	1:26 from twenty **y** old and upward, all that	8141
	1:28 from twenty **y** old and upward, all that	8141
	1:30 from twenty **y** old and upward, all that	8141
	1:32 from twenty **y** old and upward, all that	8141
	1:34 from twenty **y** old and upward, all that	8141
	1:36 from twenty **y** old and upward, all that	8141
	1:38 from twenty **y** old and upward, all that	8141
	1:40 from twenty **y** old and upward, all that	8141
	1:42 from twenty **y** old and upward, all that	8141

Nu	1:45 from twenty **y** old and upward,	8141
	4: 3 From thirty **y** old and upward even until	8141
	4: 3 old and upward even until fifty **y** old,	8141
	4:23 From thirty **y** old and upward until fifty	8141
	4:23 until fifty **y** old shalt thou number	8141
	4:30 From thirty **y** old and upward even unto	8141
	4:30 upward even unto fifty **y** old shalt thou	8141
	4:35 From thirty **y** old and upward even unto	8141
	4:35 old and upward even unto fifty **y** old,	8141
	4:39 From thirty **y** old and upward even unto	8141
	4:39 old and upward even unto fifty **y** old,	8141
	4:43 From thirty **y** old and upward even unto	8141
	4:43 old and upward even unto fifty **y** old,	8141
	4:47 From thirty **y** old and upward even unto	8141
	4:47 old and upward even unto fifty **y** old,	8141
	8:24 from twenty and five **y** old and	8141
	8:25 from the age of fifty **y** they shall cease	8141
	13:22 *were*. (Now Hebron was built seven **y**	8141
	14:29 from twenty **y** old and upward,	8141
	14:33 shall wander in the wilderness forty **y,**	8141
	14:34 forty **y**, and ye shall know my breach	8141
	26: 2 twenty **y** old and upward, throughout	8141
	26: 2 *the sum of the people*, from twenty **y**	8141
	32:11 from twenty **y** old and upward, shall see	8141
	32:13 them wander in the wilderness forty **y,**	8141
	33:39 three **y** old when he died in mount Hor.	8141
Dt	2: 7 these forty **y** the LORD thy God *hath* been	8141
	2:14 the brook Zered, *was* thirty and eight **y;**	8141
	8: 2 led thee these forty **y** in the wilderness,	8141
	8: 4 neither did thy foot swell, these forty **y.**	8141
	14:28 At the end of three **y** thou shalt bring	8141
	15: 1 At the end of *every* seven **y** thou shalt	8141
	15:12 be sold unto thee, and serve thee six **y;**	8141
	15:18 servant *to thee*, in serving thee six **y:**	8141
	29: 5 I have led you forty **y** in the wilderness:	8141
	31: 2 an hundred and twenty **y** old *this* day;	8141
	31:10 saying, At the end of *every* seven **y,**	8141
	32: 7 old, consider the **y** of many generations:	8141
	34: 7 hundred and twenty **y** old when he died:	8141
Jos	5: 6 the children of Israel walked forty **y** in	8141
	13: 1 Now Joshua was old *and* stricken in **y;**	3117
	13: 1 Thou art old *and* stricken in **y.**	3117
	14: 7 Forty **y** old *was* I when Moses the servant	8141
	14:10 alive, as he said, these forty and five **y,**	8141
	14:10 *am this* day fourscore and five **y** old.	8141
	24:29 died, *being* an hundred and ten **y** old.	8141
Jdg	2: 8 died, *being* an hundred and ten **y** old.	8141
	3: 8 Israel served Chushan-rishathaim eight **y.**	8141
	3:11 the land had rest forty **y.** And Othniel	8141
	3:14 Eglon the king of Moab eighteen **y.**	8141
	3:30 And the land had rest fourscore **y.**	8141
	4: 3 twenty **y** he mightily oppressed the	8141
	5:31 his might. And the land had rest forty **y.**	8141
	6: 1 them into the hand of Midian seven **y.**	8141
	6:25 even the second bullock of seven **y** old,	8141
	8:28 the country was in quietness forty **y** in	8141
	9:22 Abimelech had reigned three **y** over	8141
	10: 2 he judged Israel twenty and three **y,**	8141
	10: 3 and judged Israel twenty and two **y.**	8141
	10: 8 eighteen **y**, all the children of Israel that	8141
	11:26 by the coasts of Arnon, three hundred **y?**	8141
	12: 7 Jephthah judged Israel six **y.** Then died	8141
	12: 9 his sons. And he judged Israel seven **y.**	8141
	12:11 judged Israel; and he judged Israel ten **y.**	8141
	12:14 ten ass colts: and he judged Israel eight **y.**	8141
	13: 1 into the hand of the Philistines forty **y.**	8141
	15:20 in the days of the Philistines twenty **y.**	8141
	16:31 his father. And he judged Israel twenty **y.**	8141
Ru	1: 4 and they dwelled there about ten **y.**	8141
1Sa	4:15 Now Eli *was* ninety and eight **y** old;	8141
	4:18 heavy. And he had judged Israel forty **y.**	8141
	7: 2 for it was twenty **y:** and all the house of	8141
	13: 1 when he had reigned two **y** over Israel,	8141
	29: 3 these **y**, and I have found no *fault* in him	8141
2Sa	2:10 Ish-bosheth Saul's son *was* forty **y** old	8141
	2:10 to reign over Israel, and reigned two **y.**	8141
	2:11 over the house of Judah was seven **y**	8141
	4: 4 was five **y** old when the tidings came of	8141
	5: 4 David *was* thirty **y** old when he *began* to	8141
	5: 4 he *began* to reign, *and* he reigned forty **y.**	8141
	5: 5 In Hebron he reigned over Judah seven **y**	8141
	5: 5 and three **y** over all Israel and Judah.	8141
	13:23 it came to pass after **two full y,**	3117+8141
	13:38 went to Geshur, and was there three **y.**	8141
	14:28 So Absalom dwelt **two full y** in	3117+8141
	15: 7 it came to pass after forty **y**, that Absalom	8141
	19:32 a very aged man, *even* fourscore **y** old:	8141
	19:35 I *am this* day fourscore **y** old: and can I	8141
	21: 1 a famine in the days of David three **y,**	8141
	24:13 Shall seven **y** of famine come unto thee in	8141
1Ki	1: 1 king David was old *and* stricken in **y;**	3117
	2:11 David reigned over Israel *were* forty **y:**	8141
	2:11 seven **y** reigned he in Hebron, and thirty	8141
	2:11 thirty and three **y** reigned he in Jerusalem.	8141
	2:39 it came to pass at the end of three **y,**	8141
	6:38 of it. So was he seven **y** in building it.	8141
	7: 1 was building his own house thirteen **y,**	8141
	9:10 it came to pass at the end of twenty **y,**	8141
	10:22 in three **y** came the navy of Tharshish,	8141
	11:42 in Jerusalem over all Israel *was* forty **y.**	8141
	14:20 Jeroboam reigned *were* two and twenty **y:**	8141
	14:21 and one **y** old when he *began* to reign,	8141
	14:21 and he reigned seventeen **y** in Jerusalem,	8141
	15: 2 Three **y** reigned he in Jerusalem. And his	8141
	15:10 and one **y** reigned he in Jerusalem.	8141

1Ki	15:25 of Judah, and reigned over Israel **two y.**	8141
	15:33 all Israel in Tirzah, twenty and four **y.**	8141
	16: 8 to reign over Israel in Tirzah, **two y.**	8141
	16:23 Omri to reign over Israel, twelve **y:**	8141
	16:23 twelve years: six **y** reigned he in Tirzah.	8141
	16:29 over Israel in Samaria twenty and two **y.**	8141
	17: 1 there shall not be dew nor rain these **y,**	8141
	22: 1 continued three **y** without war between	8141
	22:42 and five **y** old when he *began* to reign;	8141
	22:42 reigned twenty and five **y** in Jerusalem.	8141
	22:51 of Judah, and reigned **two y** over Israel.	8141
2Ki	3: 1 king of Judah, and reigned twelve **y.**	8141
	8: 1 it shall also come upon the land seven **y.**	8141
	8: 2 in the land of the Philistines seven **y.**	8141
	8:17 two **y** old was he when he *began* to reign	8141
	8:17 and he reigned eight **y** in Jerusalem.	8141
	8:26 twenty **y** old *was* Ahaziah when he	8141
	10:36 Israel in Samaria *was* twenty and eight **y.**	8141
	11: 3 her hid *in* the house of the LORD six **y.**	8141
	11:21 Seven **y** old *was* Jehoash when he *began*	8141
	12: 1 and forty **y** reigned he in Jerusalem.	8141
	13: 1 in Samaria, *and reigned* seventeen **y.**	8141
	13:10 Israel in Samaria, *and reigned* sixteen **y.**	8141
	14: 2 and five **y** old when he *began* to reign,	8141
	14: 2 reigned twenty and nine **y** in Jerusalem.	8141
	14:17 son of Jehoahaz king of Israel fifteen **y.**	8141
	14:21 which *was* sixteen **y** old, and made him	8141
	14:23 in Samaria, *and reigned* forty and one **y.**	8141
	15: 2 Sixteen **y** old *was* he when he *began* to	8141
	15: 2 he reigned two and fifty **y** in Jerusalem.	8141
	15:17 over Israel, *and reigned* ten **y** in Samaria.	8141
	15:23 Israel in Samaria, *and reigned* **two y.**	8141
	15:27 Israel in Samaria, *and reigned* twenty **y.**	8141
	15:33 twenty **y** old *was* he when he *began* to	8141
	15:33 and he reigned sixteen **y** in Jerusalem.	8141
	16: 2 Twenty **y** old *was* Ahaz when he *began*	8141
	16: 2 reigned sixteen **y** in Jerusalem, and did	8141
	17: 1 to reign in Samaria over Israel nine **y.**	8141
	17: 5 up *to* Samaria, and besieged it three **y.**	8141
	18: 2 five **y** old *was* he when he *began* to reign;	8141
	18: 2 reigned twenty and nine **y** in Jerusalem.	8141
	18:10 at the end of three **y** they took it: *even* in	8141
	20: 6 I will add unto thy days fifteen **y;**	8141
	21: 1 Manasseh *was* twelve **y** old when he	8141
	21: 1 and reigned fifty and five **y** in Jerusalem.	8141
	21:19 and two **y** old when he *began* to reign.	8141
	21:19 reign, and he reigned two **y** in Jerusalem.	8141
	22: 1 Josiah *was* eight **y** old when he *began* to	8141
	22: 1 he reigned thirty and one **y** in Jerusalem.	8141
	23:31 and three **y** old when he *began* to reign;	8141
	23:36 and he reigned eleven **y** in Jerusalem.	8141
	24: 1 Jehoiakim became his servant three **y:**	8141
	24: 8 Jehoiachin *was* eighteen **y** old when he	8141
	24:18 and one **y** old when he *began* to reign,	8141
	24:18 and he reigned eleven **y** in Jerusalem.	8141
1Ch	2:21 he married when he *was* threescore **y**	8141
	3: 4 there he reigned seven and six months:	8141
	3: 4 Jerusalem he reigned thirty and three **y.**	8141
	23: 3 were numbered from the age of thirty **y**	8141
	23:24 from the age of twenty **y** and upward,	8141
	23:27 Levites *were* numbered from twenty **y**	8141
	27:23 the number of them from twenty **y** old	8141
	29:27 that he reigned over Israel *was* forty **y;**	8141
	29:27 seven **y** reigned he in Hebron, and thirty	8141
	29:27 thirty and three **y** reigned he in Jerusalem.	NIH
2Ch	8: 1 it came to pass at the end of twenty **y,**	8141
	9:21 every three **y** once came the ships of	8141
	9:30 in Jerusalem over all Israel forty **y.**	8141
	11:17 the son of Solomon strong, three **y:**	8141
	11:17 three **y** they walked in the way of David	8141
	12:13 and forty **y** old when he *began* to reign,	8141
	12:13 and he reigned seventeen **y** in Jerusalem,	8141
	13: 2 He reigned three **y** in Jerusalem.	8141
	14: 1 In his days the land was quiet ten **y.**	8141
	14: 6 had rest, and he had no war in those **y;**	8141
	18: 2 after *certain* **y** he went down to Ahab to	8141
	20:31 and five **y** old when he *began* to reign,	8141
	20:31 reigned twenty and five **y** in Jerusalem.	8141
	21: 5 and two **y** old when he *began* to reign,	8141
	21: 5 and he reigned eight **y** in Jerusalem.	8141
	21:19 in process of time, after the end of two **y,**	3117
	21:20 two **y** old was he when he *began* to reign,	NIH
	21:20 he reigned in Jerusalem eight **y,**	8141
	22: 2 two **y** old *was* Ahaziah when he *began* to	8141
	22:12 with them hid in the house of God six **y:**	8141
	24: 1 Joash *was* seven **y** old when he *began* to	8141
	24: 1 and he reigned forty **y** in Jerusalem.	8141
	24:15 and thirty **y** old *was* he when he died.	8141
	25: 1 and five **y** old *when* he *began* to reign,	8141
	25: 1 reigned twenty and nine **y** in Jerusalem.	8141
	25: 5 he numbered them from twenty **y** old	8141
	25:25 son of Jehoahaz king of Israel fifteen **y.**	8141
	26: 1 *was* sixteen **y** old, and made him king	8141
	26: 3 Sixteen **y** old *was* Uzziah when he	8141
	26: 3 he reigned fifty and two **y** in Jerusalem.	8141
	27: 1 and five **y** old when he *began* to reign,	8141
	27: 1 and he reigned sixteen **y** in Jerusalem.	8141
	27: 8 twenty **y** old when he *began* to reign,	8141
	27: 8 and reigned sixteen **y** in Jerusalem.	8141
	28: 1 Ahaz *was* twenty **y** old when he *began* to	8141
	28: 1 and he reigned sixteen **y** in Jerusalem:	8141
	29: 1 reign when he *was* five and twenty **y** old,	8141
	29: 1 reigned nine and twenty **y** in Jerusalem.	8141
	31:16 of males, from three **y** old and upward,	8141
	31:17 the Levites from twenty **y** old and upward,	8141

Y

2Ch 33: 1 Manasseh was twelve **y** old when he — 8141
33: 1 he reigned fifty and five **y** in Jerusalem: — 8141
33:21 and twenty **y** old when he *began* to reign, — 8141
33:21 to reign, and reigned two **y** in Jerusalem. — 8141
34: 1 Josiah *was* eight **y** old when he *began* to — 8141
34: 1 he reigned in Jerusalem one and thirty **y**. — 8141
36: 2 and three **y** old when he *began* to reign, — 8141
36: 5 and five **y** old when he *began* to reign, — 8141
36: 5 and he reigned eleven **y** in Jerusalem: — 8141
36: 9 Jehoiachin *was* eight **y** old when he — 8141
36:11 and twenty **y** old when he *began* to reign, — 8141
36:11 reign, and reigned eleven **y** in Jerusalem. — 8141
36:21 sabbath, to fulfil threescore and ten **y**. — 8141
Ezr 3: 8 appointed the Levites from twenty **y** old — 8141
5:11 house that was builded these many **y** ago, — 8140
Ne 5:14 *that is,* twelve **y**, I and my brethren have — 8141
9:21 forty **y** didst thou sustain them in — 8141
9:30 Yet many **y** didst thou forbear them, — 8141
Job 10: 5 the days of man? *are* thy **y** as man's days, — 8141
15:20 number of **y** is hidden to the oppressor. — 8141
16:22 When a few **y** are come, then I shall go — 8141
32: 7 and multitude of **y** should teach wisdom. — 8141
36:11 in prosperity, and their **y** in pleasures. — 8141
36:26 can the number of his **y** be searched — 8141
42:16 this lived Job an hundred and forty **y**, — 8141
Ps 31:10 spent with grief, and my **y** with sighing: — 8141
61: 6 king's life: *and* his **y** as many generations. — 8141
77: 5 the days of old, the **y** of ancient times. — 8141
77:10 I will remember the **y** of the right hand of — 8141
78:33 consume in vanity, and their **y** in trouble. — 8141
90: 4 For a thousand **y** in thy sight *are but* — 8141
90: 9 we spend our **y** as a tale *that is told.* — 8141
90:10 The days of our **y** *are* threescore years and — 8141
90:10 The days of our **y** *are* threescore and — 8141
90:10 by reason of strength *they be* fourscore **y**, — 8141
90:15 *and the* **y** *wherein* we have seen evil. — 8141
95:10 Forty **y** long was I grieved with *this* — 8141
102:24 thy **y** *are* throughout all generations. — 8141
102:27 the same, and thy **y** shall have no end. — 8141
Pr 4:10 and the **y** of thy life shall be many. — 8141
5: 9 unto others, and thy **y** unto the cruel: — 8141
9:11 and the **y** of thy life shall be increased. — 8141
10:27 the **y** of the wicked shall be shortened. — 8141
Ecc 6: 3 an hundred *children*, and live many **y**, — 8141
6: 3 so that the days of his **y** be many, — 8141
6: 6 though he live a thousand **y** twice *told,* — 8141
11: 8 if a man live many **y**, *and* rejoice in them — 8141
12: 1 nor the **y** draw nigh, when thou shalt say, — 8141
Isa 7: 8 and five **y** shall Ephraim be broken, — 8141
15: 5 *flee* unto Zoar, a heifer of **three y old**: — 7992
16:14 saying, Within three **y**, as the years of a — 8141
16:14 as the **y** of a hireling, and the glory of — 8141
20: 3 barefoot three **y** *for* a sign and wonder — 8141
21:16 according to the **y** of a hireling, and all — 8141
23:15 that Tyre shall be forgotten seventy **y**, — 8141
23:15 after the end of seventy **y** shall Tyre sing — 8141
23:17 come to pass after the end of seventy **y**, — 8141
32:10 Many days and **y** shall ye be troubled, — 8141
38: 5 behold, I will add unto thy days fifteen **y**. — 8141
38:10 I am deprived of the residue of my **y**. — 8141
38:15 softly all my **y** in the bitterness of my soul. — 8141
65:20 for the child shall die an hundred **y** old; — 8141
65:20 the sinner *being* an hundred **y** old shall — 8141
Jer 25:11 shall serve the king of Babylon seventy **y**. — 8141
25:12 pass, when seventy **y** are accomplished, — 8141
28: 3 Within **two full y** *will* I bring again — 3117+8141
28:11 within the space of **two full y**. — 3117+8141
29:10 That after seventy **y** be accomplished at — 8141
34:14 At the end of seven **y** let ye go every man — 8141
34:14 when he hath served thee six **y**, thou — 8141
48:34 Horonaim, *as a heifer of* **three y old**: — 7992
52: 1 and he reigned eleven **y** in Jerusalem. — 8141
Eze 4: 5 For I have laid upon thee the **y** of their — 8141
22: 4 draw near, and art come *even* unto thy **y**: — 8141
29:11 neither shall it be inhabited forty **y**. — 8141
29:12 *are* laid waste shall be desolate forty **y**: — 8141
29:13 At the end of forty **y** I will gather — 8141
38: 8 the latter **y** thou shalt come into the land — 8141
38:17 which prophesied in those days *many* **y**, — 8141
39: 9 they shall burn them with fire seven **y**: — 8141
Da 1: 5 nourishing them three **y**, that at the end — 8141
9: 2 by books the number of the **y**, — 8141
9: 2 that *he* would accomplish seventy **y** in — 8141
11: 6 in the end of **y** they shall join themselves — 8141
11: 8 he shall continue *more* **y** than the king of — 8141
11:13 shall certainly come after certain **y** with a — 8141
Joel 2: 2 *even* to the **y** of many generations. — 8141
2:25 I will restore to you the **y** that the locust — 8141
Am 2:10 led you forty **y** through the wilderness, — 8141
4: 4 *and* your tithes after three **y**: — 3117
5:25 and offerings in the wilderness forty **y**, — 8141
Hab 3: 2 revive thy work in the midst of the **y**, — 8141
3: 2 in the midst of the **y** make known; — 8141
Zec 1:12 indignation these threescore and ten **y**? — 8141
7: 3 as I have done these so many **y**? — 8141
7: 5 seventh *month*, *even* those seventy **y**, — 8141
Mal 3: 4 as *in* the days of old, and as *in* former **y**. — 8141
Mt 2:16 coasts thereof, from **two y** old and under, — 1332
9:20 diseased with an issue of blood twelve **y**, — 2094
Mk 5:25 which had an issue of blood twelve **y**, — 2094
5:42 for she was *of the age of* twelve **y**. — 2094
Lk 1: 7 they both were *now* well stricken in **y**. — 2250
1:18 old man, and my wife well stricken in **y**. — 2250
2:36 had lived with a husband seven **y** from — 2094
2:37 a widow of about fourscore and four **y**, — 2094

Lk 2:42 when he was twelve **y old**, they went — 2094
3:23 himself began *to be* about thirty **y of age**, — 2094
4:25 when the heaven was shut up three **y** and — 2094
4:42 twelve **y of age**, and she lay a dying. — 2094
8:43 woman having an issue of blood twelve **y**, — 2094
12:19 thou hast much goods laid up for many **y**; — 2094
13: 7 these three **y** I come seeking fruit on this — 2094
13:11 which had a spirit of infirmity eighteen **y**, — 2094
13:16 Satan hath bound, lo these eighteen **y**, — 2094
15:29 father, Lo, these many **y** do I serve thee, — 2094
Jn 2:20 Forty and six **y** was this temple in — 2094
5: 5 which had an infirmity thirty *and* eight **y**. — 2094
8:57 Thou art not yet fifty **y** old, and hast thou — 2094
Ac 4:22 For the man was above forty **y old**, — 2094
7: 6 and entreat *them* evil four hundred **y**. — 2094
7:23 And when he was full **forty y** old, it came — 5063
7:30 And when forty **y** were expired, — 2094
7:36 the Red sea, and in the wilderness forty **y**. — 2094
7:42 sacrifices *by the space of* forty **y** in — 2094
9:33 which had kept his bed eight **y**, and was — 2094
13:18 And about the time of **forty y** suffered he — 5063
13:20 *the space of* four hundred and fifty **y**, — 2094
13:21 tribe of Benjamin, *by the space of* forty **y**. — 2094
19:10 And this continued by the space of two **y**; — 2094
20:31 *by the space of* **three y** I ceased not to — 5148
24:10 been of many **y** a judge unto this nation, — 2094
24:17 Now after many **y** I came to bring alms to — 2094
24:27 But after **two y** Porcius Festus came into — 1333
28:30 And Paul dwelt **two** whole **y** in his own — 1333
Ro 15:23 a great desire these many **y** to come — 2094
2Co 12: 2 I knew a man in Christ above fourteen **y** — 2094
Gal 1:18 after three **y** I went up to Jerusalem to — 2094
2: 1 Then fourteen **y** after I went up again to — 2094
3:17 was four hundred and thirty **y** after, — 2094
4:10 and months, and times, and **y**. — 1763
1Ti 5: 9 into the number under threescore **y**, — 2094
Heb 1:12 thou art the same, and thy **y** shall not fail. — 2094
3: 9 proved me, and saw my works forty **y**. — 2094
3:17 But with whom was he grieved forty **y**? — 2094
11:24 By faith Moses, when he was **come to y**, — 3173
Jas 5:17 not on the earth *by the space of* **three y** — 1763
2Pe 3: 8 one day *is* with the Lord as a thousand **y**, — 2094
3: 8 and a thousand **y** as one day. — 2094
Rev 20: 2 and Satan, and bound him a thousand **y**, — 2094
20: 3 till the thousand **y** should be fulfilled: — 2094
20: 4 and reigned with Christ a thousand **y**. — 2094
20: 5 again until the thousand **y** were finished. — 2094
20: 6 and shall reign with him a thousand **y**. — 2094
20: 7 And when the thousand **y** are expired, — 2094

YEARS' (2) [YEAR]
2Ki 8: 3 it came to pass at the seven **y** end, that — 8141
1Ch 21:12 three **y** famine; or three months to be — 8141

YELL (1) [YELLED]
Jer 51:38 like lions: they shall **y** as lions' whelps, — 5286

YELLED (1) [YELL]
Jer 2:15 **y**, and they made his land waste: — 5414+6963

YELLOW (4)
Lev 13:30 *there be* in it a **y** thin hair; then the priest — 6669
13:32 be in it no **y** hair, and the scall *be* not — 6669
13:36 skin, the priest shall not seek for **y** hair; — 6669
Ps 68:13 with silver, and her feathers with **y** gold. — 3422

YERN (1) [YERNED]
Ge 43:30 for his bowels did **y** upon his brother: — 3648

YERNED (1) [YERN]
1Ki 3:26 her bowels **y** upon her son, and she said, — 3648

YES (4)
Mt 17:25 He saith, **Y**. And when he was come into — 3483
Mk 7:28 she answered and said unto him, **Y**, Lord: — 3483
Ro 3:29 of the Gentiles? **Y**, of the Gentiles also: — 3483
10:18 **Y verily**, their sound went into all — 3304

YESTERDAY (9) [DAY]
Ex 5:14 fulfilled your task in making brick both **y** — 8543
1Sa 20:27 of Jesse to meat, neither **y**, nor to day? — 8543
2Sa 15:20 *Whereas* thou camest *but* **y**, should I *this* — 8543
2Ki 9:26 Surely I have seen **y** the blood of Naboth, — 570
Job 8: 9 (For we *are but of* **y**, and know nothing, — 8543
Ps 90: 4 thy sight *are but* as **y** when it is past, — 865+3117
Jn 4:52 **Y** at the seventh hour the fever left him. — 5504
Ac 7:28 thou kill me, as thou didst the Egyptian **y**? — 5504
Heb 13: 8 Jesus Christ the same, and to day, — 5504

YESTERNIGHT (3) [NIGHT]
Ge 19:34 younger, Behold, I lay **y** with my father: — 570
31:29 The God of your father spake unto me **y**, — 570
31:42 labour of my hands, and rebuked *thee* **y**. — 570

YET (683)
Ge 6: 3 **y** his days shall be an hundred and — 2050.1
7: 4 **y** seven days, *and* I will cause — 5750+3807.1
8:10 stayed **y** other seven days; and again he — 5750
8:12 stayed **y** other seven days; and sent forth — 5750
15:16 of the Amorites is not **y** full. — 2008+5704
18:22 but Abraham stood **y** before the LORD. — 5750
18:29 spake unto him **y again**, and said, — 3254+5750
18:32 be angry, and I will speak **y** *but this* once: — 389
20:12 **y** indeed *she is* my sister; she *is* — 1571
21:26 **neither y** heard I *of it,* — 1571+3808+2050.1
25: 6 while he **y** lived, eastward, unto the east — 5750

Ge 27:30 Jacob was **y** scarce gone out from — 389
29: 7 he said, Lo, *it is* **y** high day, neither *is it* — 5750
29: 9 **while** he **y** spake with them, Rachel came — 5750
29:27 shalt serve with me **y** seven other years. — 5750
29:30 and served with him **y** seven other years. — 5750
31:14 *there* **y** any portion or inheritance for us — 5750
31:30 **y** wherefore hast thou stolen my gods? — NIH
37: 5 and they hated him **y the more**. — 3254+5750
37: 8 they hated him **y the more** for his — 3254+5750
37: 9 dreamed **y** another dream, and told it his — 5750
38: 5 she **y again** conceived, and bare a — 3254+5750
40:13 **Y** within three days shall Pharaoh lift up — 5750
40:19 **Y** within three days shall Pharaoh lift up — NIH
40:23 **Y** did not the chief butler remember — 2050.1
43: 6 *as* to tell the man whether ye had **y** a — 5750
43: 7 kindred, saying, *Is* your father **y** alive? — 5750
43:27 old man of whom ye spake? *Is he* **y** alive? — 5750
43:28 our father is in good health, he *is* **y** alive. — 5750
44: 4 *and* not **y** far off, Joseph said unto his — NIH
44:14 to Joseph's house; for he *was* **y** there: — 5750
45: 3 I *am* Joseph; doth my father **y** live? — 5750
45: 6 **y** there *are* five years, in the which *there* — 5750
45:11 for **y** *there are* five years of famine; — 5750
45:26 Joseph *is* **y** alive, and he *is* governor over — 5750
45:28 *It is* enough; Joseph my son *is* **y** alive: — 5750
46:30 seen thy face, because thou *art* **y** alive. — 5750
48: 7 when **y** *there* was but a little way to come — 5750
Ex 4:18 in Egypt, and see whether they be **y** alive. — 5750
5:11 get you straw where you can find *it*: **y** not — 3588
5:18 **y** shall ye deliver the tale of bricks. — 2050.1
9:17 **As y** exaltest thou thyself against my — 5750
9:30 I know that ye will **not y** fear the LORD — 2962
9:34 sinned **y** more, and hardened his heart, — 2962
10: 7 knowest thou **not y** that Egypt is — 2962
11: 1 I will bring one plague *more* upon — 5750
21:22 *from her*, **and y** no mischief follow: — 2050.1
32:32 **Y** now, if thou wilt forgive their sin; — 2050.1
33:12 **Y** thou hast said, I know thee by name, — 2050.1
36: 3 make it *withal*. And they brought **y** unto — 5750
Lev 5:17 *is* he guilty, and shall bear his iniquity. — 2050.1
11: 7 he cheweth not the cud; — 2050.1
11:21 **Y** these may ye eat of every flying creeping — 389
13:40 fallen off his head, he is bald: **y** *is* he clean. — NIH
13:41 his face, he *is* forehead bald: **y** *is* he clean. — NIH
25:22 and eat **y** of old fruit until the ninth year; — NIH
25:51 *If there be* **y** many years *behind,* — 5750
26:18 if ye will **not y** for *all* this hearken unto — 5704
26:24 punish you **y** seven *times* for your sins. — 1571
26:44 **y** for all that, when they be in the land of — 637
Nu 9:10 **y** he shall keep the passover unto — 2050.1
11:33 **while** the flesh *was* **y** between their teeth — 5750
19:13 unclean; his uncleanness *is* **y** upon him. — 5750
22:20 Balak sent **y** again princes, more, — 5750
22:20 the word which I shall say unto thee, — 389
30:16 *being* **y** in her youth in her father's house. — NIH
32:14 to augment **y** the fierce anger of — 5750
32:15 he will **y** again leave them in — 5750
Dt 1:32 **Y** in this thing ye did not believe — 2050.1
9:29 **Y** they *are* thy people and — 2050.1
12: 9 For ye are not as **y** come to the rest — 5704+6258
14: 8 the hoof, **y** *cheweth* not the cud, — 2050.1
20: 6 a vineyard, and hath not **y** eaten of it? — NIH
22:17 **y** these *are* the tokens of my daughter's — NIH
29: 4 **Y** the LORD hath not given you a heart — 2050.1
31:27 while I am **y** alive with you *this* day, — 5750
32:52 **Y** thou shalt see the land before *thee*; but — 3588
Jos 3: 4 **Y** there shall be a space between you and — 389
13: 1 there remaineth **y** very much land to be — NIH
13: 2 This is the land that **y** remaineth: — NIH
14:11 **As y** I *am as* strong *this* day as *I was* in — 5750
17:12 **Y** the children of Manasseh could not — 2050.1
17:13 **Y** it came to pass, when the children of — 2050.1
18: 2 had not **y** received their inheritance. — NIH
Jdg 1:35 **y** the hand of the house of Joseph — 2050.1
2:10 nor **y** the works which he had done for — 1571
2:17 **y** they would not hearken unto their — 1571
6:24 unto this day it is **y** in Ophrah of — 5750
6:31 let him be put to death whilst it *is* **y** — NIH
7: 4 unto Gideon, The people *are* **y** too many; — 5750
8: 4 were with him, faint, **y** pursuing *them.* — 2050.1
8:20 for he feared, because he was **y** a youth. — 5750
9: 5 **notwithstanding y** Jotham the — 2050.1
10:13 **Y** ye have forsaken me, and served other — 2050.1
15: 7 **y** will I be avenged of you, — 518+3588
17: 4 **Y** he restored the money unto his — 2050.1
19:19 **Y** there is both straw and provender for — 5750
20:28 Shall I **y again** go out to battle — 3254+5750
21:14 and **y** so they sufficed them not. — 2050.1
Ru 1:11 *are there* **y** any moe sons in my womb, — 5750
1Sa 3: 6 the LORD called **y again**, Samuel. — 5750
3: 7 Now Samuel did **not y** know the LORD, — 2962
3: 7 **neither** was the word of
the LORD revealed unto him. — 2962+2050.1
8: 9 **howbeit y** protest solemnly unto — 389+3588
10:22 if the man should **y** come thither. — 5750
12:20 **y** turn not aside from following the LORD, — 389
13: 7 he was **y** in Gilgal, and all the people — 5750
13:21 **Y** they had a file for the mattocks, — 2050.1
15:30 **y** honour me now, I pray thee, before — NIH
16:11 There remaineth **y** the youngest, — 5750
18:29 Saul was **y** the more afraid of David; — 5750
20:14 thou shalt not only **while y** I live shew — 5750
23: 4 David inquired of the LORD **y again**. — 5750
23:22 prepare **y**, and know and see his place — 5750
24:11 **y** thou huntest my soul to take it. — 2050.1

1Sa 25:29 **Y** a man is risen to pursue thee, 2050.1
2Sa 1: 9 because my life *is* **y** whole in me. 5750
3:35 David to eat meat while it was **y** day, 5750
5:13 there were **y** sons and daughters born to 5750
5:22 the Philistines came up **y** again, 5750
6:22 I will **y** be more vile than thus, and will 5750
7:19 this was **y** a small thing in thy sight, 5750
9: 1 Is there **y** *any* that is left of the house of 5750
9: 3 *Is there* not **y** any of the house of Saul, 5750
9: 3 Jonathan hath **y** a son, *which is* lame on 5750
12:18 Behold, while the child was **y** alive, NIH
12:22 While the child *was* **y** alive, I fasted and 5750
14:14 **y** doth he devise means, that *his* 2050.1
18:12 **y** would I not put forth mine hand against NIH
18:14 **while** he *was* **y** alive in the midst of 5750
18:22 the son of Zadok **y** again to Joab, 3254+5750
19:28 **y** didst thou set thy servant among them 2050.1
19:28 have I **y** to cry any more unto the king? 5750
19:35 should thy servant be **y** a burden unto my 5750
21:15 Moreover the Philistines had **y** war **again** 5750
21:20 there was **y** a battle in Gath, where was a 5750
23: 5 **y** he hath made with me an everlasting 3588
1Ki 1:14 **while** thou **y** talkest there with the king, 5750
1:22 lo, **while** she **y** talked with the king, 5750
1:42 **while y** spake, behold, Jonathan the 5750
8:28 **Y** have thou respect unto the prayer of 2050.1
8:47 **Y** if they shall bethink themselves in NIH
11:17 go *into* Egypt; Hadad *being* **y** a little child. NIH
12: 2 the son of Nebat, who was **y** in Egypt, 5750
12: 5 Depart **y** for three days, then come again 5750
12: 6 before Solomon his father while he **y** lived, NIH
14: 8 **y** thou hast not been as my servant David, 5750
19:18 **Y** I have left *me* seven thousand in 2050.1
20: 6 **Y** I will send my servants unto thee 518+3588
20:32 he said, *Is* he **y** alive? he is my brother. 5750
22: 8 *There is* **y** one man, Micaiah the son of 5750
22:43 and burnt incense **y** in the high places. 5750
2Ki 3:17 **y** that valley shall be filled *with* water, 2050.1
4: 6 said unto her son, Bring me **y** a vessel. 5750
6:33 **while** he **y** talked with them, behold, 5750
8:19 **y** the LORD would not destroy Judah 2050.1
8:22 **Y** Edom revolted from under the hand 2050.1
13:23 he them from his presence as **y.** 5704+6258
14: 3 of the LORD, **y** not like David his father: 7535
14: 4 as **y** the people did sacrifice and 5750
17:13 the LORD testified against Israel, 2050.1
19:30 Judah shall **y** again take root downward, NIH
1Ch 12: 1 while he **y** kept himself close because NIH
14:13 the Philistines **y** again spread themselves 2050.1
17:17 **y** this was a small thing in thine eyes, NIH
20: 6 **And y** again there was war at Gath, 2050.1
26:10 **y** his father made him the chief;) 2050.1
29: 1 is **y** young and tender, and the work *is* NIH
2Ch 1:11 neither **y** hast asked long life; 1571
6:16 **y** so that thy children take heed to their 7535
6:26 **y** if they pray towards this place, NIH
6:37 **Y** if they bethink themselves in the land NIH
10: 6 before Solomon his father while he **y** lived, NIH
13: 6 **Y** Jeroboam the son of Nebat, 2050.1
14: 7 and bars, *while* the land *is* **y** before us; 5750
16: 8 **y**, because thou didst rely on the LORD, 2050.1
16:12 **y** in his disease he sought not to 1571+2050.1
18: 7 *There is* **y** one man, by whom *we* may 5750
20:33 for as **y** the people had not prepared their 5750
24:19 **Y** he sent prophets to them, to bring 2050.1
27: 2 And the people did **y** corruptly. 5750
28:22 he trespass **y** more against the LORD: 2050.1
30:18 **y** did they eat the passover otherwise 3588
32:15 manner, **neither y** believe him: 408+2050.1
32:16 his servants spake **y** *more* against 5750
33:17 **y** unto the LORD their God only. NIH
34: 3 year of his reign, while he was **y** young, 5750
Ezr 3: 6 of the temple of the LORD was not **y** laid. NIH
5:16 it been in building, and **y** it is not finished. NIH
9: 9 **y** our God hath not forsaken us in our 2050.1
9:15 for we remain **y** escaped, as *it is* this day: NIH
10: 2 **y** now there is hope in Israel concerning 2050.1
Ne 1: 9 **y** will I gather them from thence, NIH
2:16 had I **as y** told *it* to the Jews, 3651+5704
5: 5 **Y** now our flesh *is* as the flesh of our 2050.1
5:18 **y** for *all* this required not I the bread of 2050.1
6: 4 **Y** they sent unto me four times after this 2050.1
9:19 **Y** thou in thy manifold mercies 2050.1
9:28 **y when** they returned, and cried unto 5750
9:29 **y** they dealt proudly, and hearkened not 2050.1
9:30 **Y** many years didst thou forbear them, 2050.1
9:30 **y** wouldest thou not give ear: therefore 5750
13:18 ye bring more wrath upon Israel by 2050.1
13:26 **y** among many nations was there no 2050.1
Est 2:20 Esther had not **y** shewed her kindred nor NIH
5:13 **Y** all this availeth me nothing, so long as 2050.1
6:14 **while** they *were* **y** talking with him, 5750
8: 3 Esther spake **y** again before the king, 5750
Job 1:16 **While** he *was* **y** speaking, there came also 5750
1:17 **While** he *was* **y** speaking, there came also 5750
1:18 **While** he *was* **y** speaking, there came also 5704
3:26 neither was I quiet; **y** trouble came. 2050.1
5: 7 **Y** man is born unto trouble, as the sparks 3588
6:10 should I **y** have comfort; yea, I would 5750
8: 7 **y** thy latter end should greatly increase. 2050.1
8:12 **Whilst** it *is* **y** in his greenness, *and* not 2050.1
9:15 **y** would I not answer, *but* I would make NIH
9:16 **y** would I not believe that he had NIH
9:21 *were* perfect, **y** would I not know my soul: NIH
9:31 **Y** shalt thou plunge me in the ditch, 227

Job 10: 8 round about; **y** thou dost destroy me. 2050.1
10:15 Be righteous, **y** will I not lift up my head. NIH
13:15 Though he slay me, **y** will I trust in him: NIH
14: 9 **Y** through the scent of water it will bud, NIH
19:26 this *body*, **y** in my flesh shall I see God: 2050.1
20: 7 **Y** he shall perish for ever like his own NIH
20:14 **Y** his meat in his bowels is turned, *it is* NIH
21:32 **Y** shall he be brought to the grave, 2050.1
22:18 **Y** he filled their houses *with* good 2050.1
24:12 **y** God layeth not folly *to them*. NIH
24:23 resteth; **y** his eyes *are* upon their ways. 2050.1
29: 5 When the Almighty *was* **y** with me, 5750
32: 3 no answer, and **y** had condemned Job. NIH
33:14 yea twice, **y** man perceiveth it not. NIH
35:14 not see him, **y** judgment *is* before him; NIH
35:15 **y** he knoweth *it* not in great extremity: NIH
36: 2 I will shew thee that I *have* **y** to speak on 5750
Ps 2: 6 **Y** have I set my king upon my holy hill 5750
37:10 For **y** a little while, and the wicked *shall* 5750
37:25 **y** have I not seen the righteous forsaken, 2050.1
37:36 **Y** he passed away, and, lo, he *was* not: 5750
40:17 and needy; **y** the Lord thinketh upon me: NIH
42: 5 for I shall **y** praise him *for* the help of his 5750
42: 8 **Y** the LORD will command his NIH
42:11 I shall **y** praise him, *who is* the health of 5750
43: 5 I shall **y** praise him, *who is* the health of 5750
44:17 **y** have we not forgotten thee, neither 2050.1
49:13 **y** their posterity approve their sayings. 2050.1
55:21 than oil, **y** *were* they drawn swords. 2050.1
68:13 **y** shall ye be as the wings of a dove NIH
71:14 **and** will **y** praise thee more and more. 2050.1
78:17 they sinned **y more** against him by 3254+5750
78:30 **while** their meat *was* **y** in their mouths, 5750
78:56 **Y** they tempted and provoked the most 2050.1
90:10 **y** *is* their strength labour and sorrow; 2050.1
94: 7 **Y** they say, The LORD shall not see, 2050.1
107:41 **Y** setteth he the poor on high from 2050.1
119:51 **y** have I not declined from thy law. NIH
119:83 the smoke; **y** do I not forget thy statutes. NIH
119:109 in my hand: **y** do I not forget thy law. 2050.1
119:110 for me: **y** I erred not from thy precepts. 2050.1
119:141 despised: **y** do not I forget thy precepts. NIH
119:143 **y** thy commandments *are* my delights. NIH
119:157 **y** do I not decline from thy testimonies. NIH
129: 2 **y** they have not prevailed against me. 1571
138: 6 high, **y** hath he respect unto the lowly: 2050.1
139:16 see my **substance, y being unperfect;** 1564
139:16 when as **y** there *was* none of them. NIH
141: 5 for **y** my prayer also *shall be* in their 5750
Pr 6:10 **Y** a little sleep, a little slumber, a little NIH
8:26 **While as y** he had not made the earth, 5704
9: 9 to a wise *man*, and he will be **y** wiser: 5750
11:24 There is that scattereth, and **y** increaseth; 5750
13: 7 is that maketh himself rich, **y** *hath* 2050.1
13: 7 himself poor, **y** *hath* great riches. 2050.1
19: 7 *with* words, **y** they are wanting *to him*. NIH
19:19 if thou deliver *him*, **y** thou must do *it* 2050.1
23:35 I awake? I will seek it **y again.** 3254+5750
24:33 **Y** a little sleep, a little slumber, a little 5750
27:22 **y** will not his foolishness depart from him. NIH
30:12 and **y** is not washed from their filthiness. NIH
30:25 **y** they prepare their meat in the summer; 2050.1
30:26 **y** make they their houses in the rocks; 2050.1
30:27 **y** go they forth all of them by bands; 2050.1
31:15 She riseth also while *it is* **y** night, 5750
Ecc 1: 7 run into the sea; **y** the sea *is* not full; 2050.1
2: 3 (**y** acquainting mine heart with wisdom) 2050.1
2:19 **y** shall he have rule over all my labour 2050.1
2:21 **y** to a man that hath not laboured 2050.1
4: 2 more than the living which are **y** alive. 5728
4: 3 *he* than both they, which hath not **y** been, 5728
4: 8 **y** *is there* no end of all his labour; 2050.1
6: 2 God giveth him not power to eat 2050.1
6: 6 twice *told*, **y** hath he seen no good: NIH
6: 7 his mouth, and **y** the appetite is not filled. 1571
7:28 Which **y** my soul seeketh, but I find not: 5750
8:12 **y** surely I know that it shall be well with 1571
8:17 it out, **y** he shall not find *it*; yea further, 2050.1
8:17 a wise man think to know it, **y** shall NIH
9:11 to the strong, neither **y** bread to the wise, 1571
9:11 nor **y** riches to men of understanding, 1571
9:11 nor **y** favour to men of skill; 1571
9:15 **y** no man remembered that *same* poor 2050.1
11: 8 let him remember the days of 2050.1
Isa 6:13 **y** in it *shall be* a tenth, and *it* shall return, 5750
10:22 the sea, **y** a remnant of them shall return: NIH
10:25 For **y** a very little while, 2050.1
10:32 As **y** shall *he* remain at Nob that day: 5750
14: 1 will **y** choose Israel, and set them in their 5750
14:15 **Y** thou shalt be brought down to hell, 389
17: 6 gleaning grapes shall be left in it, 5750
26:10 **y** will he not learn righteousness: NIH
27:10 **Y** the defenced city *shall be* desolate, 3588
28: 4 while it is **y** in his hand he eateth it up. 5750
28:12 is the refreshing: **y** they would not hear. NIH
29: 1 **Y** I will distress Ariel, and there shall be 2050.1
29:17 *Is it* not **y** a very little while, 5750
30:20 **y** shall not thy teachers be removed into 2050.1
31: 2 **Y** he also *is* wise, and will bring evil, 2050.1
42:25 on fire round about, **y** he knew not; 2050.1
42:25 it burned him, **y** he laid *it* not to heart. 2050.1
47: 1 Now hear, O Jacob my servant; 2050.1
44:11 let them stand *up;* **y** they shall fear, NIH
46: 7 shall cry unto him, **y** can he not answer, 2050.1
46:10 ancient times *the* things that are not **y** NIH

Isa 49: 4 **y** surely my judgment *is* with the Lord, NIH
49: 5 **y** shall I be glorious in the eyes of 2050.1
49:15 they may forget, **y** will I not forget thee. 2050.1
53: 4 **y** we did esteem him stricken, smitten 2050.1
53: 7 afflicted, **y** he opened not his mouth: NIH
53:10 **Y** it pleased the LORD to bruise him; 2050.1
56: 8 **Y** will I gather *others* to him, besides 5750
57:10 way; **y** saidst thou not, There is no hope: NIH
58: 2 **Y** they seek me daily, and delight to 2050.1
65:24 whiles they are **y** speaking, I will hear. 5750
Jer 2: 9 Wherefore I will **y** plead with you, saith 2050.1
2:11 *their* gods, which *are* **y** no gods? 2050.1
2:21 **Y** I had planted thee a noble vine, 2050.1
2:22 **y** thine iniquity *is* marked before me, NIH
2:32 **y** my people have forgotten me days 2050.1
2:35 **Y** thou sayest, Because I am innocent, 2050.1
3: 1 return again to me, saith the LORD. 2050.1
3: 8 **y** her treacherous sister Judah feared NIH
3:10 **y** for all this her treacherous sister Judah 1571
4:27 be desolate; **y** will I not make a full end. 2050.1
5:22 toss themselves, **y** can they not prevail; 2050.1
5:22 **y** they roar, **y** can they not pass over it? 2050.1
5:28 cause of the fatherless, **y** they prosper; 2050.1
7:26 **y** they hearkened not unto me, 2050.1
9:20 **Y** hear the word of the LORD, O ye 3588
11: 8 **y** they obeyed not, nor inclined their 2050.1
12: 1 **y** let me talk with thee of *thy* judgments. 389
14: 9 **y** thou, O LORD, *art* in the midst of us, 2050.1
14:15 **y** they say, Sword and famine shall not 2050.1
15: 1 **y** my mind could not *be* toward this NIH
15: 9 her sun is gone down while *it was* **y** day: 5750
15:10 **y** every one of them doth curse me. NIH
18:23 **Y**, LORD, thou knowest all their 2050.1
22: 6 **y** surely I will make thee a wilderness *and* NIH
22:24 right hand, **y** would I pluck thee thence; 3588
23:21 not sent *these* prophets, **y** they ran: 2050.1
23:21 not spoken to them, **y** they prophesied. 2050.1
23:32 **y** I sent them not, nor commanded 2050.1
25: 7 **Y** ye have not hearkened unto me, 2050.1
27:15 **y** they prophesy a lie in my name; 2050.1
30:11 **y** will I not make a full end of thee: 389
31: 5 Thou shalt **y** plant vines upon 5750
31:23 **As y** they shall use this speech in the land 5750
31:39 the measuring line shall **y** go forth over 5750
32:33 *them*, **y** they have not hearkened 2050.1
33: 1 while he was **y** shut up in the court of 5750
34: 4 **y** hear the word of the LORD, O Zedekiah 389
36:24 **Y** they were not afraid, nor rent their 2050.1
37:10 **y** should they rise up every man in his NIH
40: 5 while he was not **y** gone back, *he said*, 5750
44:28 **Y** a small number that escape the sword 2050.1
46:28 **y** will I not leave thee wholly 2050.1
48:47 **Y** will I bring again the captivity of 2050.1
51:33 a little while, and the time of her harvest 5750
51:53 **y** from me shall spoilers come unto her, NIH
La 3:32 **y** will he have compassion according to 2050.1
4:17 our eyes **as y** failed for our vain help: 5750
Eze 2: 5 **y** shall know that there hath been a 2050.1
3:19 If thou warn the wicked, and he turn 2050.1
6: 8 **Y** will I leave a remnant, that ye may 2050.1
7:13 which is sold, although they were **y** alive: 5750
8: 6 turn thee **y** again, *and* thou shalt see 5750
8:13 Turn thee **y** again, *and* thou shalt see 5750
8:15 turn thee **y** again, *and* thou shalt see 5750
8:18 with a loud voice, **y** will I not hear them. NIH
11:16 **y** will I be to them as a little sanctuary 2050.1
12:13 **y** shall he not see it, though he shall die 2050.1
14:22 **y** behold, therein shall be left a remnant 2050.1
15: 5 how much less shall it be meet **y** for *any* 5750
16:28 them, **and y** couldest not be satisfied. 1571
16:29 and **y** thou wast not satisfied herewith. 1571
16:47 **Y** hast thou not walked after their ways, 2050.1
18:19 **Y** say ye, Why? doth not the son bear 2050.1
18:25 **Y** ye say, The way of the Lord is not 2050.1
18:29 **Y** saith the house of Israel, The way of 2050.1
20:15 **Y** also I lifted up mine hand unto them in 2050.1
20:27 **Y** in this your fathers have blasphemed 5750
23:19 **Y** she multiplied her whoredoms, 2050.1
23:44 **Y** they went in unto her, as *they* go in 2050.1
24:16 **y** neither shalt thou mourn nor 3808+2050.1
26:21 **y** shalt thou never be found again, 2050.1
28: 2 **y** thou *art* a man, and not God, 2050.1
28: 9 thou **y** say before him that slayeth 559+559
29:13 **Y** thus saith the Lord GOD; At the end of 3588
29:18 **y** had he no wages, nor his army, 2050.1
31:18 **y** shalt thou be brought down with 2050.1
32:24 **y** have they borne their shame with 2050.1
32:25 **y** have they borne their shame with 2050.1
33:17 **Y** the children of thy people say, The 2050.1
33:20 **Y** ye say, The way of the Lord is not 2050.1
36:37 will **y** *for* this be inquired of by the house 5750
44:11 **Y** they shall be ministers in my 2050.1
Da 4:23 **y** leave the stump of the roots thereof in 1297
5:17 I will read the writing unto the king, 1297
7:12 **y** their lives were prolonged for a season 2050.3
9:13 **y** made we not our prayer before 2050.1
10: 9 **Y** heard I the voice of his words: 2050.1
10:14 for **y** the vision *is* for *many* days. 5750
11: 2 *shall* stand up **y** three kings in Persia; 5750
11:27 **y** the end *shall be* at the time appointed. 5750
11:33 **y** they shall fall by the sword, 5750
11:35 because *it is* **y** for a time appointed. 5750
11:45 **y** he shall come to his end, and none 2050.1
Hos 1: 4 for **y** a little *while*, and I will avenge 5750
1:10 **Y** the number of the children of Israel 2050.1

Hos	3: 1 said the LORD unto me, Go **y**, love a	5750
	3: 1 beloved of *her* friend, **y** an adulteress,	2050.1
	4: 4 let no man strive, nor reprove another:	389
	4:15 play the harlot, **y** let not Judah offend;	NIH
	5:13 could he not heal you nor cure you of	2050.1
	7: 9 and there upon him, **y** he knoweth not.	2050.1
	7:13 **y** they have spoken lies against me.	2050.1
	7:15 **y** do they imagine mischief against me.	2050.1
	9:12 up their children, **y** will I bereave them,	2050.1
	9:16 **y** will I slay *even* the beloved *fruit* of	2050.1
	11:12 Judah **y** ruleth with God, and is faithful	5750
	12: 8 Ephraim said, **Y** I am become rich, I have	389
	12: 9 will **y** make thee to dwell in tabernacles,	5750
	13: 4 **Y** I *am* the LORD thy God from	2050.1
Am	2: 9 **Y** destroyed I the Amorite before them,	2050.1
	2: 9 I destroyed his fruit from above,	2050.1
	4: 6 **y** have ye not returned unto me, saith	5750
	4: 7 when *there were* **y** three months to	5750
	4: 8 **y** have ye not returned unto me, saith	2050.1
	4: 9 palmerworm devoured *them:* **y** have	2050.1
	4:10 **y** have ye not returned unto me, saith	2050.1
	4:11 **y** have ye not returned unto me, saith	2050.1
	6:10 of the house, *Is there* **y** *any* with thee?	5750
	9: 9 **y** shall not the least grain fall *upon*	2050.1
Jnh	2: 4 **y** I will look again toward thy holy temple.	389
	2: 6 **y** hast thou brought up my life from	2050.1
	3: 4 **Y** forty days, and Nineveh *shall be*	5750
	4: 2 my saying, when I was **y** in my country?	5704
Mic	1:15 **Y** will I bring an heir unto thee,	5750
	3:11 **y** will they lean upon the LORD,	2050.1
	5: 2 **y** out of thee shall he come forth unto me	NIH
	6:10 Are there **y** the treasures of wickedness *in*	5750
Na	1:12 **y** thus shall they be cut down,	2050.1
	2: 8 **y** they *shall* flee away. Stand, stand,	2050.1
	3:10 **Y** was she carried away, she went into	1571
Hab	2: 3 For the vision *is* **y** for an appointed time,	5750
	3:18 **Y** I will rejoice in the LORD, I will joy	2050.1
Hag	2: 4 **Y** now be strong, O Zerubbabel, saith	5750
	2: 6 **Y** once, *it is* a little while, and I *will* shake	2050.1
	2:17 **y** turned not to me, saith the LORD.	2050.1
	2:19 *Is* the seed **y** in the barn? yea, as yet	5750
	2:19 **as y** the vine, and the fig tree,	5704
Zec	1:17 Cry **y**, saying, Thus saith the LORD of	5750
	1:17 My cities through prosperity shall **y** be	5750
	1:17 the LORD shall **y** comfort Zion,	5750
	1:17 and shall **y** choose Jerusalem.	5750
	8: 4 There shall **y** old men and old women	5750
	8:20 *It shall* **y** *come to pass*, that there shall	5750
	11:15 Take unto thee **y** the instruments of a	5750
	13: 3 *that* when any shall **y** prophesy, then	5750
Mal	1: 2 **Y** ye say, Wherein hast thou loved us?	2050.1
	1: 2 saith the LORD: **y** I loved Jacob,	2050.1
	2:14 **Y** ye say, Wherefore? Because	2050.1
	2:14 **y** *is* she thy companion, and the wife of	2050.1
	2:15 **Y** had he the residue of the spirit.	2050.1
	2:17 **Y** ye say, Wherein have we wearied	2050.1
	3: 8 **Y** ye *have* robbed me. But ye say, Wherein	3588
	3:13 **Y** ye say, What have we spoken so	2050.1
Mt	6:25 **nor y** for your body, what ye shall put on.	3366
	6:26 **y** your heavenly Father feedeth them.	2532
	6:29 **And y** I say unto you, That even Solomon	1161
	10:10 two coats, neither shoes, **nor y** staves:	3366
	12:46 **While** he **y** talked to the people, behold,	2089
	13:21 **Y** hath he not root in himself, but dureth	1161
	15:16 Are ye also **y** without understanding?	188
	15:17 **Do not** ye **y** understand, that whatsoever	3768
	15:27 **y** the dogs eat of the crumbs which	1063+2532
	16: 9 ye **not y** understand, neither remember	3768
	17: 5 While he **y** spake, behold, a bright cloud	2089
	19:20 I kept from my youth up: what lack I **y**?	2089
	24: 6 must come to pass, but the end is **not y**.	2089
	24:32 When his branch is **y** tender,	2235
	26:33 because of thee, **y** will I never be offended.	NIG
	26:35 die with thee, **y** will I not deny thee.	NIG
	26:47 And **while** he **y** spake, lo, Judas, one of	2089
	26:60 false witnesses came, **y** found they none.	NIG
	27:63 **while** he was **y** alive, After three days I	2089
Mk	5:35 **While** he **y** spake, there came from	2089
	6:26 **y** for his oath's sake, and for their sakes	NIG
	7:28 **y** the dogs under the table eat of	1063+2532
	8:17 perceive ye **not y**, neither understand?	3768
	8:17 have ye your heart **y** hardened?	2089
	11:13 but leaves; for the time of figs was not **y**.	NIH
	12: 6 Having **y** therefore one son,	2089
	13: 7 needs be; but the end *shall* **not** be **y**.	3768
	13:28 When her branch is **y** tender,	2235
	14:29 Although all shall be offended, **y** *will* not I.	235
	14:43 **while** he **y** spake, cometh Judas, one of	2089
	15: 5 Jesus **y** answered nothing; so that Pilate	3765
Lk	3:20 Added **y** this above all, that he shut up	2532
	8:49 While he **y** spake, there cometh one from	2089
	9:42 **as** he was **y** a coming, the devil threw	2089
	11: 8 **y** because of his importunity he will rise	1065
	12:27 **and y** I say unto you, *that* Solomon in all	1161
	14:22 hast commanded, and **y** there is room.	2089
	14:32 else, while the other is **y** a great way off,	2089
	14:35 fit for the land, **nor y** for the dunghill;	3777
	15:20 But when he was **y** a great way off,	2089
	15:29 *and* **y** thou never gavest me a kid, that I	2532
	18: 5 **Y** because this widow troubleth me, I will	1065
	18:22 **Y** lackest thou one *thing:* sell all that thou	2089
	19:30 tied, whereon **y** never man sat:	3762+4455
	22:37 that this that is written must **y** be	2089
	22:47 while he **y** spake, behold a multitude,	2089
	22:60 **while** he **y** spake, the cock crew.	2089

Lk	23:15 No, **nor y** Herod: for I sent you to him;	3761
	24: 6 spake unto you when he was in Galilee,	2089
	24:41 And **while** they **y** believed not for joy,	2089
	24:44 while I was **y** with you, that all *things*	2089
Jn	2: 4 do with thee? mine hour is **not y** come.	3768
	3:24 For John was **not y** cast into prison.	3768
	4:21 nor **y** at Jerusalem, worship the Father.	NIG
	4:27 **y** no *man* said, What seekest thou?	3305
	4:35 are **y** four months, and *then* cometh	2089
	7: 6 said unto them, My time is **not y** come:	3768
	7: 8 I go **not up y** unto this feast; for my time	3768
	7: 8 this feast; for my time is **not y** full come.	3768
	7:19 law, and **y** none of you keepeth the law?	NIG
	7:30 him, because his hour was **not y** come.	3768
	7:33 **Y** a little while am I with you, and *then* I	2089
	7:39 for the Holy Ghost was **not y** given;	3768
	7:39 because that Jesus was **not y** glorified.)	3764
	8:14 bear record of myself, **y** my record is true:	NIG
	8:16 **And y** if I judge, my judgment is true: for	2532
	8:20 on him; for his hour was **not y** come.	3768
	8:55 **Y** ye have not known him; but I know	2532
	8:57 Thou art **not y** fifty years old, and hast	3768
	9:30 he is, and **y** he hath opened mine eyes.	NIG
	11:25 though he were dead, **y** shall he live:	NIG
	11:30 Now Jesus was **not y** come into the town,	3768
	12:35 **Y** a little while is the light with you.	2089
	12:37 before them, **y** they believed not on him:	NIG
	13:33 **y** a little while I am with you.	2089
	14: 9 and **y** hast thou not known me, Philip?	NIG
	14:19 **Y** a little **while**, and the world seeth me	2089
	14:25 unto you, being **y** present with you.	NIG
	16:12 I have **y** many *things* to say unto you,	2089
	16:32 **y** I am not alone, because the Father is	NIG
	19:41 wherein was **never** man **y** laid.	3764
	20: 1 when it was **y** dark, unto the sepulchre,	2089
	20: 5 the linen clothes lying; **y** went he not in.	3305
	20: 9 For **as y** they knew **not** the scripture,	NIG
	20:17 for I am **not y** ascended to my Father:	3768
	20:29 that have **not** seen, and **y** have believed.	NIG
	21:11 so many, **y** was not the net broken.	NIG
	21:23 Jesus said not unto him, He shall not	2532
Ac	7: 5 **y** he promised that *he* would give it to	2532
	7: 5 seed after him, when *as* **y** he had no child.	NIG
	8:16 as **y** he was fallen upon none of them:	3768
	9: 1 breathing out threatenings and	2089
	10:44 While Peter **y** spake these words, the	2089
	13:27 nor **y** the voices of the prophets which are	NIG
	13:28 **y** desired they Pilate that he should be	NIG
	18:18 And Paul *after this* tarried *there* **y** a good	2089
	19:37 **nor y** blasphemers of your goddess.	3777
	22: 3 **y** brought up in this city at the feet of	1161
	24:11 that there are **y** but twelve days since I	NIG
	25: 8 against the temple, nor **y** against Cesar,	NIG
	28: 4 the sea, Vengeance suffereth not to live.	NIG
	28:17 **y** was I delivered prisoner from Jerusalem	NIG
Ro	3: 7 why am I also judged as a sinner?	2089
	4:11 faith which he had **y** being uncircumcised:	NIG
	4:12 which he had being uncircumcised.	NIG
	4:19 neither **y** the deadness of Sara's womb:	NIG
	5: 6 For when we were **y** without strength,	2089
	5: 7 peradventure for a good *man* some	1063
	5: 8 in that, while we were **y** sinners,	2089
	8:24 a man seeth, why doth he **y** hope for?	2532
	9:11 (For *the children* being **not y** born,	3380
	9:19 then unto me, Why doth he **y** find fault?	2089
	11:30 **y** have now obtained mercy through their	1161
	11:30 **y** I would have you wise unto *that which*	NIG
1Co	2: 6 **y** not the wisdom of this world, nor of	1161
	2:15 he that is spiritual judgeth all *things,* **y**	1161
	3: 2 able to *bear it*, neither **y** now are ye able.	235
	3: 3 For ye are **y** carnal: for whereas *there is*	2089
	3:15 he himself shall be saved; **y** so as by fire.	1161
	4: 4 by myself; **y** am I not hereby justified:	235
	4:15 in Christ, **y** *have* ye not many fathers:	235
	5:10 **Y** not altogether with the fornicators of	2532
	7:10 married I command, **y** not I, but the Lord,	NIG
	7:25 I give *my* judgment, as one that hath	1161
	8: 2 knoweth nothing **y** as he ought to know.	3764
	9: 2 others, **y** doubtless I am to you:	235+1065
	9:19 though I be free from all *men,* **y** have I	NIG
	12:20 *are* they many members, **y** *but* one body.	1161
	12:31 **y** shew I unto you a more excellent way.	2089
	14:19 **Y** in the church I had rather speak five	235
	14:21 and **y** for all that will they **not** hear me,	3761
	15:10 **y** not I, but the grace of God which was	1161
	15:17 your faith is vain; ye are **y** in your sins.	2089
2Co	1:10 whom we trust that he will **y** deliver *us;*	2089
	1:23 that to spare you I came **not as y** unto	3765
	4: 8 *We are* troubled on every *side,* **y** not	235
	4:16 **y** the inward *man* is renewed day by day.	235
	5:16 **y** now henceforth know we *him* no more.	235
	6: 8 and good report: as deceivers, and **y** true;	NIG
	6: 9 As unknown, and **y** well known; as dying,	NIG
	6:10 As sorrowful, **y** alway rejoicing; as poor,	1161
	6:10 as poor, **y** making many rich; as having	1161
	6:10 nothing, and **y** possessing all *things.*	NIG
	9: 3 rich, **y** for your sakes he became poor,	NIG
	9: 3 I have I sent the brethren, lest our	1161
	11: 6 *I be* rude in speech, **y** not in knowledge;	235
	11:16 if otherwise, **y** as a fool receive me, that I	2579
	12: 5 **y** of myself I will not glory, but in mine	1161
	13: 4 **y** he liveth by the power of God.	235
Gal	1:10 for if I **y** pleased men, I should not be	2089
	2:20 I live; **y** not I, but Christ liveth in me:	NIG
	3: 4 so many *things* in vain? if *it be* **y** in vain.	2532

Gal	3:15 but a man's covenant, **y** *if it be* confirmed,	NIG
	5:11 I, brethren, if I **y** preach circumcision,	2089
	5:11 why do I **y** suffer persecution?	2089
Eph	5:29 For no *man* **ever y** hated his own flesh;	4218
Php	1: 9 that your love may abound **y** more and	2089
	1:22 labour; **y** what I shall choose I wot not.	2532
	2:25 **Y** I supposed it necessary to send to you	1161
Col	1:21 wicked works, **y** now hath he reconciled	1161
	2: 5 **y** am I with you in the spirit, joying and	235
1Th	2: 6 we glory, neither of you, nor **y** of others,	NIG
2Th	2: 5 ye not, that, when I was **y** with you,	2089
	3:15 **Y** count *him* not as an enemy,	2532
2Ti	2: 5 **y** is he not crowned, except he strive	NIG
	2:13 If we believe not, **y** he abideth faithful:	NIG
Phm	1: 9 **Y** for love's sake I rather beseech *thee,*	NIG
Heb	2: 8 now we see **not y** all *things* put under	3768
	4:15 in all *points* tempted like as *we are,* **y**	NIG
	5: 8 **y** learned he obedience by the *things*	NIG
	7:10 For he was **y** in the loins of his father,	2089
	7:15 And it is **y** far more evident: for that after	2089
	9: 8 the holiest *of all* was **not y** made manifest,	3380
	9: 8 **while** as the first tabernacle was **y**	2089
	9:25 **Nor y** that he should offer himself often,	3761
	10:37 For **y** a little while,	2089
	11: 4 and by it he being dead **y** speaketh.	2089
	11: 7 warned of God of *things* **not** seen **as y**,	3369
	12: 4 Ye have **not y** resisted unto blood,	3768
	12:26 **Y** once *more* I shake not the earth only,	2089
	12:27 And this *word,* **Y** once *more,* signifieth	2089
Jas	2:10 **y** offend in one *point,* he is guilty of all.	NIG
	2:11 If thou commit no adultery, **y** *if* thou kill,	1161
	3: 4 **y** are they turned about with a very small	NIG
	4: 2 ye fight and war, **y** ye have not, because	1161
1Pe	1: 8 though now ye see *him* not, **y** believing,	1161
	4:16 **Y** if *any man suffer* as a Christian, let him	1161
1Jn	3: 2 it doth **not y** appear what we shall be:	3768
Jude	1: 9 **Y** Michael the archangel, when	1161
Rev	6:11 that they should rest **y** for a little season,	2089
	8:13 of the three angels, which are **y** to sound.	3195
	9:20 **y** repented not of the works of their hands,	NIG
	17: 8 the beast that was, and is not, **and y** is.	2539
	17:10 and one is, *and* the other is **not y** come;	2089
	17:12 which have received **no** kingdom **as y**;	3768

YIELD (30) [YIELDED, YIELDETH, YIELDING]

Ge	4:12 it shall not henceforth **y** unto thee her	5414
	49:20 *shall* be fat, and he shall **y** royal dainties.	5414
Lev	19:25 it may **y** unto you the increase thereof:	3254
	25:19 the land shall **y** her fruit, and ye shall eat	5414
	26: 4 land shall **y** her increase, and the trees	5414
	26: 4 the trees of the field shall **y** their fruit.	5414
	26:20 for your land shall not **y** her increase,	5414
	26:20 neither shall the trees of the land **y** their	5414
Dt	11:17 no rain, and *that* the land **y** not her fruit;	5414
2Ch	30: 8 *but* **y** yourselves unto the LORD,	3027+5414
Ps	67: 6 *Then* shall the earth **y** her increase;	5414
	85:12 *is* good; and our land shall **y** her increase.	5414
	107:37 which may **y** fruits of increase.	6213
Pr	7:21 much fair speech she **caused** him to **y**,	5186
Isa	5:10 ten acres of vineyard shall **y** one bath,	6213
	5:10 and the seed of a homer shall **y** an ephah.	6213
Eze	34:27 the tree of the field shall **y** her fruit,	5414
	34:27 the earth shall **y** her increase, and they	5414
	36: 8 and **y** your fruit to my people of Israel;	5375
Hos	8: 7 the bud shall **y** no meal: if so be it yield,	6213
	8: 7 if so be it **y**, *the* strangers shall swallow it	6213
Joel	2:22 fig tree and the vine do **y** their strength.	5414
Hab	3:17 shall fail, and the fields shall **y** no meat;	6213
Mk	4: 8 **y** fruit that sprang up and	1325
Ac	23:21 But do not thou **y unto** them: for there lie	3982
Ro	6:13 Neither **y** ye your members *as* instruments	3936
	6:13 but **y** yourselves unto God, as *those that*	3936
	6:16 that to whom ye **y** yourselves servants to	3936
	6:19 now **y** your members servants to	3936
Jas	3:12 so *can* no fountain *both* **y** salt water and	4160

YIELDED (8) [YIELD]

Ge	49:33 **y** up the ghost, and was gathered unto	1478
Nu	17: 8 and bloomed blossoms, and **y** almonds.	1580
Da	3:28 the king's word, and **y** their bodies,	3052
Mt	27:50 again with a loud voice, **y up** the ghost.	863
Mk	4: 7 grew up, and choked it, and it **y** no fruit.	1325
Ac	5:10 at his feet, and **y up the ghost:**	1634
Ro	6:19 for as ye have **y** your members servants to	3936
Rev	22: 2 of fruits, *and* **y** her fruit every month:	591

YIELDETH (4) [YIELD]

Ne	9:37 It **y** much increase unto the kings whom	8393
Job	24: 5 the wilderness **y** food for them *and* for	NIH
Pr	12:12 but the root of the righteous **y** fruit.	5414
Heb	12:11 nevertheless afterward it **y** the peaceable	591

YIELDING (7) [YIELD]

Ge	1:11 herb **y** seed, *and* the fruit tree yielding	2232
	1:11 and the fruit tree **y** fruit after his kind,	6213
	1:12 herb **y** seed after his kind, and the tree	2232
	1:12 the tree **y** fruit, whose seed *was* in itself,	6213
	1:29 in the which *is* the fruit of a tree **y** seed;	2232
Ecc	10: 4 thy place; for **y** pacifieth great offences.	4832
Jer	17: 8 drought, neither shall cease from **y** fruit.	6213

YOKE (59) [YOKED, YOKEFELLOW, YOKES]

Ge	27:40 that thou shalt break his **y** from off thy	5923
Lev	26:13 I have broken the bands of your **y**,	5923
Nu	19: 2 blemish, *and* upon which never came **y**:	5923

Y

Dt 21: 3 *and* which hath not drawn in the **y**; 5923
28:48 he shall put a **y** of iron upon thy neck, 5923
1Sa 6: 7 on which there hath come no **y**, and tie 5923
11: 7 he took a **y** of oxen, and hewed them in 6776
14:14 of land, which *a* **y** *of oxen might plow*. 6776
1Ki 12: 4 Thy father made our **y** grievous: 5923
12: 4 heavy which he put upon us, lighter, 5923
12: 9 Make the **y** which thy father did put upon 5923
12:10 Thy father made our **y** heavy, 5923
12:11 my father did lade you with a heavy **y**, 5923
12:11 with a heavy yoke, I will add to your **y**: 5923
12:14 My father made your **y** heavy, and I will 5923
12:14 your yoke heavy, and I will add to your **y**: 5923
19:19 who *was* plowing *with* twelve **y** *of oxen* 6776
19:21 took a **y** of oxen, and slew them, and 6776
2Ch 10: 4 Thy father made our **y** grievous: 5923
10: 4 his heavy **y** that he put upon us, and we 5923
10: 9 Ease somewhat the **y** that thy father did 5923
10:10 Thy father made our **y** heavy, 5923
10:11 whereas my father put a heavy **y** upon 5923
10:11 yoke upon you, I will put more to your **y**: 5923
10:14 My father made your **y** heavy, but I will 5923
Job 1: 3 five hundred **y** of oxen, and five hundred 6776
42:12 a thousand **y** of oxen, and a thousand she 6776
Isa 9: 4 For thou hast broken the **y** of his burden, 5923
10:27 his **y** from off thy neck, and the yoke shall 5923
10:27 the **y** shall be destroyed because of 5923
14:25 shall his **y** depart from off them, 5923
47: 6 ancient hast thou very heavily laid thy **y**. 5923
58: 6 go free, and *that* ye break every **y**? 4133
58: 9 take away from the midst of thee the **y**, 4133
Jer 2:20 For of old time I have broken thy **y**, 5923
5: 5 these have altogether broken the **y**, 5923
27: 8 that will not put their neck under the **y** of 5923
27:11 nations that bring their neck under the **y** 5923
27:12 Bring your necks under the **y** of the king 5923
28: 2 have broken the **y** of the king of Babylon. 5923
28: 4 for I will break the **y** of the king of 5923
28:10 Hananiah the prophet took the **y** from off 4133
28:11 will I break the **y** of Nebuchadnezzar king 5923
28:12 **y** from off the neck of the prophet 4133
28:14 I have put a **y** of iron upon the neck of all 5923
30: 8 *that* I will break his **y** from off thy neck, 5923
31:18 as a bullock unaccustomed *to the* **y**; turn NIH
51:23 the husbandman and his **y of oxen**; 6776
La 1:14 The **y** of my transgressions is bound by his 5923
3:27 *It is* good for a man that he bear the **y** in 5923
Eze 34:27 when I have broken the bands of their **y**, 5923
Hos 11: 4 I was to them as they that take off the **y** 5923
Na 1:13 For now will I break his **y** from off thee, 4132
Mt 11:29 Take my **y** upon you, and learn of me; for 2218
11:30 For my **y** is easy, and my burden is light. 2218
Lk 14:19 I have bought five **y** of oxen, and I go to 2201
Ac 15:10 to put a **y** upon the neck of the disciples, 2218
Gal 5: 1 be not entangled again with the **y** of 2218
1Ti 6: 1 Let as many servants as are under the **y** 2218

YOKED (1) [YOKE]
2Co 6:14 Be ye not **unequally y together** with 2086

YOKEFELLOW (1) [FELLOW, YOKE]
Php 4: 3 And I intreat thee also, true **y**, help those 4805

YOKES (4) [YOKE]
Jer 27: 2 Make thee bonds and **y**, and put them 4133
28:13 hast broken the **y** of wood; 4133
28:13 but thou shalt make for them **y** of iron. 4133
Eze 30:18 when I shall break there the **y** of Egypt: 4133

YONDER (7)
Ge 22: 5 I and the lad will go **y** and worship, 3541+5704
Nu 16:37 the burning, and scatter thou the fire **y**; 1973
23:15 burnt offering, while I meet the LORD **y**. 3541
32:19 we will not inherit with them on **y** side NIH
2Ki 4:25 his servant, Behold, **y** *is* that Shunammite: NIH
Mt 17:20 this mountain, Remove hence **to y place**; 1563
26:36 Sit ye here, while I go and pray **y**. 1563

YOU (2802) [YE, YOU-WARD, YOU-WARDS, YOUR, YOURS, YOURSELVES] See Index of Articles, Etc.

YOUNG (300) [YOUTH]
Ge 4:23 my wounding, and a **y man** to my hurt. 3206
14:24 only that which the **y men** have eaten, 5288
15: 9 and a turtle-dove, and a **y pigeon**. 1469
18: 7 and good, and gave *it* unto a **y man**; 5288
19: 4 the house round, both old and **y**, 5288
22: 3 two of his **y men** with him, and Isaac 5288
22: 5 Abraham said unto his **y men**, Abide you 5288
22:19 So Abraham returned unto his **y men**, 5288
31:38 and thy she goats have not **cast** their **y**, 7921
33:13 the flocks and herds with **y** *are* with me: 5763
34:19 the **y man** deferred not to do the thing, 5288
41:12 *was* there with us a **y man**, a Hebrew, 5288
Ex 10: 9 We will go with our **y** and with our old, 5288
23:26 There shall nothing **cast** their **y**, nor be 7921
24: 5 he sent **y men** of the children of Israel, 5288
29: 1 Take one **y** bullock, and two rams 1121
33:11 servant Joshua, the son of Nun, a **y man** 5288
Lev 1:14 his offering of turtledoves, or of **y** pigeons. 1121
4: 3 a **y** bullock without blemish unto 1121
4:14 the congregation shall offer a **y** bullock 1121
5: 7 two turtledoves, or two **y** pigeons, unto 1121
5:11 two **y** pigeons, then he that sinned shall 1121

Lev 9: 2 Take thee a **y** calf for a sin offering, 1121
12: 6 a **y** pigeon, or a turtledove, for a sin 1121
12: 8 shall bring two turtles, or two **y** pigeons; 1121
14:22 two turtledoves, or two **y** pigeons, such 1121
14:30 or of the **y** pigeons, such as he can get; 1121
15:14 or two **y** pigeons, and come before 1121
15:29 or two **y** pigeons, and bring them unto 1121
16: 3 *place*: with a **y** bullock for a sin offering, 1121
22:28 shall not kill it and her **y** both in one day. 1121
23:18 year, and one **y** bullock, and two rams: 1121
Nu 6:10 turtles, or two **y** pigeons, to the priest, 1121
7:15 One **y** bullock, one ram, one lamb of 1121
7:21 One **y** bullock, one ram, one lamb of 1121
7:27 One **y** bullock, one ram, one lamb of 1121
7:33 One **y** bullock, one ram, one lamb of 1121
7:39 One **y** bullock, one ram, one lamb of 1121
7:45 One **y** bullock, one ram, one lamb of 1121
7:51 One **y** bullock, one ram, one lamb of 1121
7:57 One **y** bullock, one ram, one lamb of 1121
7:63 One **y** bullock, one ram, one lamb of 1121
7:69 One **y** bullock, one ram, one lamb of 1121
7:75 One **y** bullock, one ram, one lamb of 1121
7:81 One **y** bullock, one ram, one lamb of 1121
8: 8 let them take a **y** bullock with his meat 1121
8: 8 another **y** bullock shalt thou take for a sin 1121
11:27 there ran a **y man**, and told Moses, 5288
11:28 *one* of his **y men**, answered and said, 979
15:24 that all the congregation shall offer one **y** 1121
23:24 a great lion, and lift up himself as a **y** lion: 738
28:11 two **y** bullocks, and one ram, seven lambs 1121
28:19 two **y** bullocks, and one ram, 1121
28:27 two **y** bullocks, one ram, seven lambs of 1121
29: 2 one **y** bullock, one ram, *and* seven lambs 1121
29: 8 one **y** bullock, one ram, *and* seven lambs 1121
29:13 thirteen **y** bullocks, two rams, 1121
29:17 on the second day *ye shall offer* twelve **y** 1121
Dt 22: 6 *whether they be* **y** ones, or eggs, and the 667
22: 6 dam sitting upon the **y**, or upon the eggs, 667
22: 6 thou shalt not take the dam with the **y**: 1121
22: 7 let the dam go, and take the **y** to thee; 1121
28:50 of the old, nor shew favour to the **y**: 5288
28:57 towards her **y** one that cometh out from 7988
32:11 fluttereth over her **y**, spreadeth abroad 1469
32:25 destroy both the **y man** and the virgin, 970
Jos 6:21 **y** and old, and ox, and sheep, and ass, 5288
6:23 the **y men** that were spies went in, 5288
Jdg 6:25 unto him, Take thy father's **y** bullock, 6499
8:14 caught a **y man** of the men of Succoth, 5288
9:54 he called hastily unto the **y man** his 5288
9:54 **y man** thrust him through, and he died. 3716
14: 5 behold, a **y** lion roared against him. 3715
14:10 there a feast; for so used the **y men** to do. 970
17: 7 was a **y man** out of Beth-lehem-judah 5288
17:11 **y man** was unto him as one of his sons. 5288
17:12 the **y man** became his priest, and was in 5288
18: 3 they knew the voice of the **y man** 5288
18:15 to the house of the **y man** the Levite, 5288
19:19 the **y man** *which is* with thy servants; 5288
21:12 of Jabesh-gilead four hundred **y** virgins, 5291
Ru 2: 9 have I not charged the **y men** that *they* 5288
2: 9 drink of *that* which the **y men** have 5288
2:15 Boaz commanded his **y men**, saying, 5288
2:21 also, Thou shalt keep fast by my **y men**, 5288
3:10 inasmuch as *thou* followedst not **y men**, 970
4:12 LORD shall give thee of this **y woman**. 5291
1Sa 1:24 the LORD *in* Shiloh: and the child *was* **y**. 5288
2:17 Wherefore the sin of the **y men** was very 5288
8:16 your goodliest **y men**, and your asses, 970
9: 2 *was* Saul, a choice **y man**, and a goodly: NIH
9:11 they found **y maidens** going out to draw 5291
14: 1 said unto the **y man** that bare his armour, 5288
14: 6 Jonathan said to the **y man** that bare his 5288
17:58 to him, Whose son *art* thou, thou **y man**? 5288
20:22 if I say thus unto the **y man**, Behold, 5958
21: 4 if the **y men** have kept themselves at least 5288
21: 5 the vessels of the **y men** are holy, 5288
25: 5 David sent out ten **y men**, and David said 5288
25: 5 David said unto the **y men**, Get you up to 5288
25: 8 Ask thy **y men**, and they will shew thee. 5288
25: 8 Wherefore let the **y men** find favour in 5288
25: 9 when David's **y men** came, they spake to 5288
25:12 So David's **y men** turned their way, 5288
25:14 one of the **y men** told Abigail, 5288
25:25 I thine handmaid saw not the **y men** of 5288
25:27 let it even be given unto the **y men** that 5288
26:22 one of the **y men** come over and fetch it. 5288
30:13 he said, I *am* a **y man** of Egypt, servant to 5288
30:17 four hundred **y men**, which rode 376+5288
2Sa 1: 5 David said unto the **y man** that told him, 5288
1: 6 the **y man** that told him said, As I 5288
1:13 David said unto the **y man** that told him, 5288
1:15 David called one of the **y men**, and said, 5288
2:14 Let the **y men** now arise, and play before 5288
2:21 lay thee hold on one of the **y men**, 5288
4:12 David commanded *his* **y men**, 5288
9:12 Mephibosheth had a **y** son, whose name 6996
13:32 have slain all the **y men** the king's sons; 5288
13:34 the **y man** that kept the watch lift up his 5288
14:21 bring the **y man** Absalom again. 5288
16: 2 and summer fruit for the **y men** to eat; 5288
18: 5 *Deal* gently for my sake with the **y man**, 5288
18:12 Beware *that* none touch the **y man** 5288
18:15 ten **y men** that bare Joab's armour 5288
18:29 the king said, *Is* the **y man** Absalom safe? 5288
18:32 unto Cushi, *Is* the **y man** Absalom safe? 5288

2Sa 18:32 thee to do *thee* hurt, be as *that* **y man** *is*. 5288
1Ki 1: 2 there be sought for my lord the king a **y** 5291
1:28 Solomon seeing the **y man** that he was 5288
12: 8 consulted with the **y men** that were 3206
12:10 the **y men** that were grown up with him 3206
12:14 to them after the counsel of the **y men**, 3206
20:14 Even by the **y men** of the princes of 5288
20:15 he numbered the **y men** of the princes of 5288
20:17 the **y men** of the princes of the provinces 5288
20:19 So these **y men** of the princes of 5288
2Ki 4:22 one of the **y men**, and one of the asses, 5288
5:22 two **y men** of the sons of the prophets: 5288
6:17 the LORD opened the eyes of the **y man**; 5288
8:12 their **y men** wilt thou slay with the sword, 970
9: 4 So the **y man**, *even* the young man 5288
9: 4 young man, *even* the **y man** the prophet, 5288
1Ch 12:28 a **y man** mighty of valour, and *of* his 5288
22: 5 Solomon my son *is* **y** and tender, 5288
29: 1 *is* yet **y** and tender, and the work *is* great: 5288
2Ch 10: 8 took counsel with the **y men** that were 3206
10:10 the **y men** that were brought up with him 3206
10:14 them after the advice of the **y men**, 3206
13: 7 Rehoboam was **y** and tender hearted, 5288
13: 9 to consecrate himself with a **y** bullock 1121
34: 3 year of his reign, while he was yet **y**, 5288
36:17 who slew their **y men** with the sword in 970
36:17 no compassion upon **y man** or maiden, 970
Ezr 6: 9 both **y** bullocks, and rams, and lambs, 1123
Est 2: 2 Let there be fair **y** virgins sought for 5291
2: 3 they may gather together all the fair **y** 5291
3:13 all Jews, both **y** and old, little children and 5288
8:10 on mules, camels, *and* **y** dromedaries: 1121
Job 1:19 it fell upon the **y men**, and they are dead; 5288
4:10 and the teeth of the **y lions**, are broken. 3715
19:18 Yea, **y children** despised me; I arose, 5759
29: 8 The **y men** saw me, and hid themselves: 5288
32: 6 *am* **y**, and ye *are* very old; 3117+6810+3807.1
38:39 the lion? or fill the appetite of the **y lions**, 3715
38:41 his **y** ones cry unto God, they wander 3206
39: 3 they bring forth their **y** ones, 3206
39: 4 Their **y** ones are in good liking, they grow 1121
39:16 She is hardened against her **y** ones, 1121
39:30 Her **y** ones also suck up blood: and where 667
Ps 17:12 as it were a **y** lion lurking in secret places. 3715
29: 6 calf; Lebanon and Sirion like a **y** unicorn. 1121
34:10 The **y lions** do lack, and suffer hunger: 3715
37:25 I have been **y**, and *now* am old; yet have 5288
58: 6 break out the great teeth of the **y lions**, 3715
78:63 The fire consumed their **y men**; 970
78:71 From following the ewes **great with y** he 5763
84: 3 where she may lay her **y**, *even* thine altars, 667
91:13 the **y** lion and the dragon shalt thou 3715
104:21 The **y lions** roar after *their* prey, and seek 3715
119: 9 Wherewithal shall a **y man** cleanse his 5288
147: 9 his food, *and* to the **y** ravens which cry. 1121
148:12 Both **y men**, and maidens; old men, 970
Pr 1: 4 to the **y man** knowledge and discretion. 5288
7: 7 youths, a **y man** void of understanding, 5288
20:29 The glory of **y men** *is* their strength: 970
30:17 pick it out, and the **y** eagles shall eat it. 1121
Ecc 11: 9 Rejoice, O **y man**, in thy youth; and let 970
SS 2: 9 My beloved is like a roe or a **y** hart: 6082
2:17 or a **y** hart upon the mountains of Bether. 6082
4: 5 Thy two breasts *are* like two **y** roes *that* 6082
7: 3 Thy two breasts *are* like two **y** roes *that* 6082
8:14 to a **y** hart upon the mountains of spices. 6082
Isa 5:29 be like a lion, they shall roar like **y lions**: 3715
7:21 *that* a man shall nourish a **y cow**, 1241+5697
9:17 the Lord shall have no joy in their **y men**, 970
11: 6 the calf and the **y lion** and the fatling 3715
11: 7 their **y** ones shall lie down together: 3206
13:18 *Their* bows also shall dash the **y men** to 5288
20: 4 **y** and old, naked and barefoot, 5288
23: 4 neither do I nourish up **y men**, *nor* bring 970
30: 6 from whence *come* the **y**s and old lion, 3833
30: 6 their riches upon the shoulders of **y asses**, 5895
30:24 the **y asses** that ear the ground shall eat 5895
31: 4 lion and the **y lion** roaring on his prey, 3715
31: 8 and his **y men** shall be discomfited. 970
40:11 shall gently lead those that are **with y**. 5763
40:30 be weary, and the **y men** shall utterly fall: 970
62: 5 *as* a **y man** marrieth a virgin, *so* shall thy 5763
Jer 2:15 The **y lions** roared upon him, *and* yelled, 3715
6:11 and upon the assembly of **y men** together: 970
9:21 *and* the **y men** from the streets. 970
11:22 **y men** shall die by the sword; their sons 970
15: 8 mother of the **y men** a spoiler at noonday: 970
18:21 *let* their **y men** be slain by the sword in 970
31:12 and for the **y** of the flock and of the herd: 1121
31:13 in the dance, both **y men** and old together: 970
48:15 his chosen **y men** are gone down to 970
49:26 her **y men** shall fall in her streets, 970
50:30 shall her **y men** fall in the streets, 970
51: 3 spare ye not her **y men**; destroy ye utterly 970
51:22 with thee will I break in pieces old and **y**; 5288
51:22 with thee will I break in pieces the **y man** 970
La 1:15 assembly against me to crush my **y men**: 970
1:18 and my **y men** are gone into captivity. 970
2:19 toward him for the life of thy **y children**, 5768
2:21 The **y** and the old lie on the ground in 5288
2:21 and my **y men** are fallen by the sword; 970
4: 3 the breast, they give suck to their **y** ones: 1482
4: 4 the **y children** ask bread, *and* no man 5768
5:13 They took the **y men** to grind, 970
5:14 the gate, the **y men** from their musick. 970

Eze	9: 6	Slay utterly old *and* **y**, both maids,	970
	17: 4	He cropt off the top of his **y twigs**,	3242
	17:22	from the top of his **y** twigs a tender one,	3127
Hos	19: 2	she nourished her whelps among **y lions.**	3715
	19: 3	it became a **y lion**, and it learned to catch	3715
	19: 5	of her whelps, *and* made him a **y lion.**	3715
	19: 6	he became a **y lion**, and learned to catch	3715
	23: 6	and rulers, all of them desirable **y men**,	970
	23:12	upon horses, all of them desirable **y men.**	970
	23:23	all of them desirable **y men**, captains and	970
	30:17	The **y men** of Aven and of Phi-beseth shall	970
	31: 6	the beasts of the field **bring forth** their **y**,	3205
	32: 2	Thou art like a **y lion** of the nations,	3715
	38:13	with all the **y lions** thereof, shall say unto	3715
	41:19	the face of a **y lion** toward the palm tree	3715
	43:19	Lord GOD, a **y bullock** for a sin offering.	1121
	43:23	shalt offer a **y bullock** without blemish.	1121
	43:25	they shall also prepare a **y bullock**,	1121
	45:18	shalt take a **y bullock** without blemish,	1121
	46: 6	in the day of the new moon *it shall be* a **y**	1121
Hos	5:14	and as a **y lion** to the house of Judah:	3715
Joel	2:28	dreams, your **y men** shall see visions:	970
Am	2:11	and of your **y men** for Nazarites.	970
	3: 4	will a **y lion** cry out of his den, if he have	3715
	4:10	your **y men** have I slain with the sword,	970
	8:13	the fair virgins and **y men** faint for thirst.	970
Mic	5: 8	as a **y lion** among the flocks of sheep:	3715
Na	2:11	the feeding place of the **y lions**, where	3715
	2:13	and the sword shall devour thy **y lions.**	3715
	3:10	her **y children** also were dashed in pieces	5768
Zec	2: 4	him, Run, speak to this **y man**, saying,	5288
	9:17	corn shall make the **y men** cheerful,	970
	11: 3	a voice of the roaring of **y lions**,	3715
	11:16	neither shall seek the **y one**, nor heal that	5289
Mt	2: 8	Go and search diligently for the **y child**;	3813
	2: 9	and stood over where the **y child** was.	3813
	2:11	saw the **y child** with Mary his mother,	3813
	2:13	and take the **y child** and his mother,	3813
	2:13	for Herod will seek the **y child** to destroy	3813
	2:14	took the **y child** and his mother by night,	3813
	2:20	and take the **y child** and his mother,	3813
	2:20	they are dead which sought the **y child's**	3813
	2:21	and took the **y child** and his mother,	3813
	19:20	The **y man** saith unto him, All these	3495
	19:22	But when the **y man** heard *that* saying,	3495
Mk	7:25	whose **y daughter** had an unclean spirit,	2365
	10:13	And they brought **y children** to him,	3813
	14:51	And there followed him a certain **y man**,	3495
	14:51	and the **y men** laid hold on him:	3495
	16: 5	they saw a **y man** sitting on the right side,	3495
Lk	2:24	A pair of turtledoves, or two **y** pigeons.	3502
	7:14	he said, **Y man, I say unto thee, Arise.**	3495
Jn	12:14	And Jesus, when he had found a **y ass**,	3678
	21:18	I say unto thee, When thou wast **y**,	3501
Ac	2:17	and your **y men** shall see visions,	3495
	5: 6	And the **y men** arose, wound him up,	3501
	5:10	the **y men** came in, and found her dead,	3495
	7:19	so that *they* cast out their **y children**,	1025
	7:58	laid down their clothes at a **y man's** feet,	3494
	20: 9	there sat in a window a certain **y man**	3494
	20:12	And they brought the **y man** alive,	3816
	23:17	Bring this **y man** unto the chief captain:	3494
	23:18	prayed *me* to bring this **y man** unto thee,	3494
	23:22	chief captain then let the **y man** depart,	3494
Tit	2: 4	That they may teach the **y women** to be	3501
	2: 6	**Y** *men* likewise exhort to be sober	3501
1Jn	2:13	**y men**, because you have overcome	3495
	2:14	**y men**, because ye are strong, and the	3495

YOUNGER (31) [YOUTH]

Ge	9:24	knew what his **y son** had done unto him.	6996
	19:31	the firstborn said unto the **y**, Our father *is*	6810
	19:34	that the firstborn said unto the **y**, Behold,	6810
	19:35	the **y** arose, and lay with him;	6810
	19:38	the **y**, she also bare a son, and called his	6810
	25:23	and the elder shall serve the **y**.	6810
	27:15	and put them upon Jacob her **y** son:	6996
	27:42	she sent and called Jacob her **y** son,	6996
	29:16	and the name of the **y** *was* Rachel.	6996
	29:18	seven years for Rachel thy **y** daughter.	6996
	29:26	to give the **y** before the firstborn.	6810
	43:29	and said, *Is* this your **y** brother,	6996
	48:14	who *was* the **y**, and his left hand upon	6810
	48:19	truly his **y** brother shall be greater than he,	6996
Jdg	1:13	son of Kenaz, Caleb's **y** brother, took it:	6996
	3: 9	the son of Kenaz, Caleb's **y** brother.	6996
	15: 2	not her **y** sister fairer than she? take her,	6996
1Sa	14:49	and the name of the **y** Michal.	6996
1Ch	24:31	fathers over against their **y** brethren.	6996
Job	30: 1	*they that are* **y** than I have me in	3117+6810
Eze	16:46	**y** sister, that dwelleth at thy right hand,	6996
	16:61	receive thy sisters, thine elder and thy **y**.	6996
Lk	15:12	the **y** of them said to *his* father, Father,	3501
	15:13	not many days after the **y** son gathered	3501
	22:26	is greatest among you, let him be as the **y**;	3501
Ro	9:12	said unto her, The elder shall serve the **y**.	1640
1Ti	5: 1	as a father; *and* the **y men** as brethren;	3501
	5: 2	as mothers; the **y** as sisters, with all purity.	3501
	5:11	But the **y** widows refuse: for when they	3501
	5:14	I will therefore that the **y** *women* marry,	3501
1Pe	5: 5	Likewise, ye **y**, submit yourselves unto	3501

YOUNGEST (18) [YOUTH]

Ge	42:13	the **y** *is this* day with our father, and one	6996
	42:15	except your **y** brother come hither.	6996

Ge	42:20	bring your **y** brother unto me; so shall	6996
	42:32	the **y** *is this* day with our father in the	6996
	42:34	bring your **y** brother unto me: then shall	6996
	43:33	and the **y** according to his youth:	6810
	44: 2	in the sack's mouth of the **y**, and his corn	6996
	44:12	*and* began at the eldest, and left at the **y**:	6996
	44:23	Except your **y** brother come down with	6996
	44:26	if our **y** brother be with us, then will we	6996
	44:26	face, except our **y** brother *be* with us.	6996
Jos	6:26	in his **y** *son* shall he set up the gates of it.	6810
Jdg	9: 5	notwithstanding yet Jotham the **y** son of	6996
1Sa	16:11	There remaineth yet the **y**, and, behold,	6996
	17:14	David *was* the **y**: and the three eldest	6996
1Ki	16:34	the gates thereof in his **y** son Segub,	6810
2Ch	21:17	left him, save Jehoahaz, the **y** of his sons.	6996
	22: 1	made Ahaziah his **y** son king in his stead:	6996

YOUR (1776) [YOU]

Ge	3: 5	**y** eyes shall be opened, and ye shall be	3641.1
	9: 2	the sea; into **y** hand are they delivered.	3641.1
	9: 5	**y** blood of your lives will I require;	3641.1
	9: 5	your blood of **y** lives will I require;	3641.1
	9: 9	with you and with **y** seed after you;	3641.1
	17:11	ye shall circumcise the flesh of **y**	3641.1
	17:12	every man *child* in **y** generations, he	3641.1
	17:13	my covenant shall be in **y** flesh for an	3641.1
	18: 4	wash **y** feet, and rest yourselves under	3641.1
	18: 5	of bread, and comfort ye **y** hearts;	3641.1
	18: 5	for therefore are you come to **y** servant.	3641.1
	19: 2	**y** servant's house, and tarry all night,	3641.1
	19: 2	wash **y** feet, and ye shall rise up early,	3641.1
	19: 2	ye shall rise up early, and go on **y** ways.	3641.1
	19: 8	and do ye to them as *is* good in **y** eyes:	3641.1
	23: 8	If it be **y** mind that I should bury my	3641.1
	31: 5	unto them, I see **y** father's countenance,	3654.1
	31: 6	all my power I have served **y** father.	3654.1
	31: 7	**y** father hath deceived me,	3654.1
	31: 9	God hath taken away the cattle of **y**	3641.1
	31:29	the God of **y** father spake unto me	3641.1
	34: 8	son Shechem longeth for **y** daughter:	3641.1
	34: 9	*and* give **y** daughters unto us, and take	3641.1
	34:11	Let me find grace in **y** eyes, and what	3641.1
	34:16	we will take **y** daughters to us,	3641.1
	35: 2	and be clean, and change **y** garments:	3641.1
	37: 7	**y** sheaves stood round about,	3641.1
	42:15	except **y** youngest brother come hither.	3641.1
	42:16	let him fetch **y** brother, and ye shall be	3641.1
	42:16	in prison, that **y** words may be proved,	3641.1
	42:19	If ye *be* true *men*, let one of **y** brethren	3641.1
	42:19	be bound in the house of **y** prison:	3641.1
	42:19	carry corn *for* the famine of **y** houses:	3641.1
	42:20	bring **y** youngest brother unto me;	3641.1
	42:20	shall **y** words be verified, and ye shall	3641.1
	42:33	leave one of **y** brethren *here* with me,	3641.1
	42:33	*food for* the famine of **y** households,	3641.1
	42:34	bring **y** youngest brother unto me: then	3641.1
	42:34	so will I deliver you **y** brother,	3641.1
	43: 3	my face, except **y** brother *be* with you.	3641.1
	43: 5	my face, except **y** brother *be* with you.	3641.1
	43: 7	kindred, saying, *Is* **y** father yet alive?	3641.1
	43: 7	he would say, Bring **y** brother down?	3641.1
	43:11	take of the best fruits in the land in **y**	3641.1
	43:12	take double money in **y** hand;	3641.1
	43:12	brought again in the mouth of **y** sacks,	3641.1
	43:12	of your sacks, carry *it* again in **y** hand;	3641.1
	43:13	Take also **y** brother, and arise, go again	3641.1
	43:14	that he may send away **y** other brother,	3641.1
	43:23	**y** God, and the God of your father,	3641.1
	43:23	your God, and the God of **y** father,	3641.1
	43:23	hath given you treasure in **y** sacks:	3641.1
	43:23	I had **y** money. And he brought Simeon	3641.1
	43:27	said, *Is* **y** father well, the old man of	3641.1
	43:29	and said, *Is* this **y** younger brother,	3641.1
	44:10	also *let* it *be* according unto **y** words:	3641.1
	44:17	you, get you up in peace unto **y** father.	3641.1
	44:23	Except **y** youngest brother come down	3641.1
	45: 4	said, I *am* Joseph **y** brother, whom ye	3641.1
	45: 7	**y** lives by a great deliverance.	3641.1+3807.1
	45:12	**y** eyes see, and the eyes of my brother	3641.1
	45:17	lade **y** beasts, and go, get you unto	3641.1
	45:18	take **y** father and your households,	3641.1
	45:18	take your father and **y** households,	3641.1
	45:19	out of the land of Egypt for **y** little ones,	3641.1
	45:19	for **y** wives, and bring your father,	3641.1
	45:19	wives, and bring **y** father, and come.	3641.1
	45:20	Also regard not **y** stuff; for the good of	3641.1
	46:33	and shall say, What *is* **y** occupation?	3641.1
	47: 3	his brethren, What *is* **y** occupation?	3641.1
	47:16	Joseph said, Give **y** cattle; and I will give	3641.1
	47:16	I will give you for **y** cattle, if money fail.	3641.1
	47:23	you *this* day and **y** land for Pharaoh:	3641.1
	47:24	four parts shall be **y** own, for seed of	3641.1
	47:24	for **y** food, and for them of your	3641.1
	47:24	for them of **y** households, and for food	3641.1
	47:24	and for food for **y** little ones.	3641.1
	48:21	you again unto the land of **y** fathers.	3641.1
	49: 2	Jacob; and hearken unto Israel **y** father.	3641.1
	50: 4	I have found grace in **y** eyes, speak,	3641.1
	50:21	I will nourish you and **y** little ones.	3641.1
Ex	3:13	The God of **y** fathers hath sent me unto	3641.1
	3:15	The God of **y** fathers, the God of	3641.1
	3:16	unto them, The LORD God of **y** fathers,	3641.1
	3:22	ye shall put *them* upon **y** sons,	3641.1
	3:22	upon your sons, and upon **y** daughters;	3641.1
	5: 4	their works? get you unto **y** burdens.	3641.1

Ex	5:11	ought of **y** work *shall be* diminished.	3641.1
	5:13	Fulfil **y** works, *your* daily tasks, as when	3641.1
	5:13	Fulfil **y** works, *your* daily tasks, as when	NIH
	5:14	Wherefore have ye not fulfilled **y** task in	3641.1
	5:19	Ye shall not minish *ought* from **y** bricks	3641.1
	5:19	*ought* from your bricks of **y** daily task.	NIH
	6: 7	shall know that I *am* the LORD **y** God,	3641.1
	8:25	Go ye, sacrifice to **y** God in the land.	3641.1
	8:28	that ye may sacrifice to the LORD **y**	3641.1
	10: 8	unto them, Go, serve the LORD **y** God:	3641.1
	10:10	as I will let you go, and **y** little ones:	3641.1
	10:16	I have sinned against the LORD **y** God,	3641.1
	10:17	*this* once, and intreat the LORD **y** God,	3641.1
	10:24	let **y** flocks and your herds be stayed:	3641.1
	10:24	let your flocks and **y** herds be stayed:	3641.1
	10:24	let **y** little ones also go with you.	3641.1
	12: 4	eating shall make **y** count for the lamb.	NIH
	12: 5	**Y** lamb shall be without	3641.1+3807.1
	12:11	*with* **y** loins girded, your shoes on your	3641.1
	12:11	**y** shoes on your feet, and your staff in	3641.1
	12:11	your shoes on **y** feet, and your staff in	3641.1
	12:11	on your feet, and **y** staff in your hand;	3641.1
	12:11	on your feet, and your staff in **y** hand;	3641.1
	12:14	to the LORD throughout **y** generations;	3641.1
	12:15	shall put away leaven out of **y** houses:	3641.1
	12:17	in this selfsame day have I brought **y**	3641.1
	12:17	ye observe this day in **y** generations	3641.1
	12:19	there be no leaven found in **y** houses:	3641.1
	12:20	in all **y** habitations shall ye eat	3641.1
	12:21	take you a lamb according to **y** families,	3641.1
	12:23	to come in unto **y** houses to smite *you.*	3641.1
	12:26	when **y** children shall say unto you,	3641.1
	12:32	Also take **y** flocks and your herds, as	3641.1
	12:32	Also take your flocks and **y** herds, as ye	3641.1
	14:14	fight for you, and ye shall hold **y** peace.	NIH
	16: 7	that he heareth **y** murmurings against	3641.1
	16: 8	for that the LORD heareth **y**	3641.1
	16: 8	**y** murmurings *are* not against us,	3641.1
	16: 9	for he hath heard **y** murmurings.	3641.1
	16:12	shall know that I *am* the LORD **y** God.	3641.1
	16:16	*according to* the number of **y** persons;	3641.1
	16:32	Fill an omer of it to be kept for **y**	3641.1
	16:33	the LORD, to be kept for **y** generations.	3641.1
	19:15	the third day: come not at **y** wives.	NIH
	20:20	that his fear may be before **y** faces,	3641.1
	22:24	**y** wives shall be widows,	3641.1
	22:24	be widows, and **y** children fatherless.	3641.1
	23:21	for he will not pardon **y** transgressions:	3641.1
	23:25	ye shall serve the LORD **y** God,	3641.1
	23:31	the inhabitants of the land into **y** hand;	3641.1
	29:42	**y** generations *at* the door of the	3641.1
	30: 8	the LORD throughout **y** generations.	3641.1
	30:10	upon it throughout **y** generations:	3641.1
	30:15	to make an atonement for **y** souls.	3641.1
	30:16	to make an atonement for **y** souls.	3641.1
	30:31	oil unto me throughout **y** generations.	3641.1
	31:13	and you throughout **y** generations;	3641.1
	32: 2	*are* in the ears of **y** wives, of your	3641.1
	32: 2	of **y** sons, and of your daughters,	3641.1
	32: 2	**y** daughters, and bring *them* unto me.	3641.1
	32:13	I will multiply **y** seed as the stars of	3641.1
	32:13	I have spoken of will I give unto **y** seed,	3641.1
	32:30	I shall make an atonement for **y** sin.	3641.1
	34:23	Thrice in the year shall all **y** men	3509.2
	35: 3	Ye shall kindle no fire throughout **y**	3641.1
Lev	1: 2	ye shall bring **y** offering of the cattle,	3641.1
	3:17	*It shall be* a perpetual statute for **y**	3641.1
	3:17	generations throughout all **y** dwellings,	3641.1
	6:18	*It shall be* a statute for ever in **y**	3641.1
	7:26	fowl or of beast, in any of **y** dwellings.	3641.1
	7:32	of the sacrifices of **y** peace offerings.	3641.1
	8:33	until the days of **y** consecration be at an	3641.1
	10: 4	carry **y** brethren from before	3641.1
	10: 6	Ithamar his sons, Uncover not **y** heads,	3641.1
	10: 6	not your heads, neither rend **y** clothes;	3641.1
	10: 6	**y** brethren, the whole house of Israel,	3641.1
	10: 6	be a statute for ever throughout **y**	3641.1
	11:44	For I *am* the LORD **y** God: ye shall	3641.1
	11:45	the land of Egypt, to be **y** God:	3641.1+3807.1
	14:34	in a house of the land of **y** possession;	3641.1
	16:29	ye shall afflict **y** souls, and do no work	3641.1
	16:29	*whether it be* one of **y** own country,	249
	16:30	that ye may be clean from all **y** sins	3641.1
	16:31	ye shall afflict **y** souls, *by* a statute for	3641.1
	17:11	altar to make an atonement for **y** souls:	3641.1
	17:15	*whether it be* one of **y** own country,	249
	18: 2	say unto them, I *am* the LORD **y** God.	3641.1
	18: 4	to walk therein: I *am* the LORD **y** God.	3641.1
	18:26	*neither* any of **y** own nation, nor any	249
	18:30	I *am* the LORD **y** God.	3641.1
	19: 2	be holy: for I the LORD **y** God *am* holy.	3641.1
	19: 3	my sabbaths: I *am* the LORD **y** God.	3641.1
	19: 4	molten gods: I *am* the LORD **y** God.	3641.1
	19: 5	ye shall offer it at **y** own will.	3641.1
	19: 9	when ye reap the harvest of **y** land,	3641.1
	19:10	and stranger: I *am* the LORD **y** God.	3641.1
	19:25	increase thereof: I *am* the LORD **y** God.	3641.1
	19:27	shall not round the corners of **y** heads,	3641.1
	19:28	shall not make any cuttings in **y** flesh	3641.1
	19:31	defiled by them: I *am* the LORD **y** God.	3641.1
	19:33	if a stranger sojourn with thee in **y** land,	3641.1
	19:34	land of Egypt: I *am* the LORD **y** God.	3641.1
	19:36	I *am* the LORD **y** God, which brought	3641.1
	20: 7	be ye holy: for I *am* the LORD **y** God.	3641.1
	20:24	I *am* the LORD **y** God, which have	3641.1

Y

Lev	20:25 ye shall not make **y** souls abominable	3641.1
	22: 3 Whosoever *he be* of all **y** seed among	3641.1
	22: 3 *be* of all your seed among **y** generations,	3641.1
	22:19 *Ye shall offer* at **y own** will a male	3641.1
	22:24 you make *any offering thereof* in **y** land.	3641.1
	22:25 offer the bread of **y** God of any of these;	3641.1
	22:29 unto the Lord, offer *it* at **y own** will.	3641.1
	22:33 the land of Egypt, to be **y** God:	3641.1+3807.1
	23: 3 sabbath of the Lord in all **y** dwellings.	3641.1
	23:10 firstfruits of **y** harvest unto the priest:	3641.1
	23:14 ye have brought an offering unto **y** God:	3641.1
	23:14 *shall be* a statute for ever throughout **y**	3641.1
	23:14 your generations in all **y** dwellings.	3641.1
	23:17 Ye shall bring out of **y** habitations two	3641.1
	23:21 **y** dwellings throughout your	3641.1
	23:21 dwellings throughout **y** generations.	3641.1
	23:22 when ye reap the harvest of **y** land,	3641.1
	23:22 to the stranger: I *am* the Lord **y** God.	3641.1
	23:27 ye shall afflict **y** souls, and offer an	3641.1
	23:28 for you before the Lord **y** God.	3641.1
	23:31 *shall be* a statute for ever throughout **y**	3641.1
	23:31 your generations in all **y** dwellings.	3641.1
	23:32 of rest, and ye shall afflict **y** souls:	3641.1
	23:32 unto even, shall ye celebrate **y** sabbath.	3641.1
	23:38 beside **y** gifts, and beside all your vows,	3641.1
	23:38 beside all **y** vows, and beside all your	3641.1
	23:38 and beside all **y** freewill offerings,	3641.1
	23:40 ye shall rejoice before the Lord **y** God	3641.1
	23:41 *It shall be* a statute for ever in **y**	3641.1
	23:43 **y** generations may know that I made	3641.1
	23:43 land of Egypt: I *am* the Lord **y** God.	3641.1
	24: 3 *it shall be* a statute for ever in **y**	3641.1
	24:22 the stranger, as for one of **y** own country:	NIH
	24:22 own country: for I *am* the Lord **y** God.	3641.1
	25: 9 trumpet sound throughout all **y** land.	3641.1
	25:17 fear thy God: for I *am* the Lord **y** God.	3641.1
	25:19 ye shall eat **y** fill, and dwell therein in	NIH
	25:24 in all the land of **y** possession ye shall	3641.1
	25:38 I *am* the Lord **y** God, which brought	3641.1
	25:38 of Canaan, *and* to be **y** God.	3641.1+3807.1
	25:45 with you, which they begat in **y** land:	3641.1
	25:45 and they shall be **y** possession.	3641.1+3807.1
	25:46 shall take them as an inheritance for **y**	3641.1
	25:46 they shall be **y** bondmen for ever:	NIH
	25:46 over **y** brethren the children of Israel,	3641.1
	25:55 land of Egypt: I *am* the Lord **y** God.	3641.1
	26: 1 ye set up *any* image of stone in **y** land,	3641.1
	26: 1 down unto it: for I *am* the Lord **y** God.	3641.1
	26: 5 **y** threshing shall reach unto	3641.1+3807.1
	26: 5 ye shall eat **y** bread to the full,	3641.1
	26: 5 to the full, and dwell in **y** land safely.	3641.1
	26: 6 shall the sword go through **y** land.	3641.1
	26: 7 ye shall chase **y** enemies, and they shall	3641.1
	26: 8 **y** enemies shall fall before you by	3641.1
	26:12 will be **y** God, and ye shall be	3641.1+3807.1
	26:13 I *am* the Lord **y** God, which brought	3641.1
	26:13 I have broken the bands of **y** yoke,	3641.1
	26:15 or if **y** soul abhor my judgments,	3641.1
	26:16 ye shall sow **y** seed in vain, for your	3641.1
	26:16 seed in vain, for **y** enemies shall eat it.	3641.1
	26:17 and ye shall be slain before **y** enemies;	3641.1
	26:18 will punish you seven *times* more for **y**	3641.1
	26:19 I will break the pride of **y** power;	3641.1
	26:19 I will make **y** heaven as iron, and your	3641.1
	26:19 heaven as iron, and **y** earth as brass:	3641.1
	26:20 **y** strength shall be spent in vain: for	3641.1
	26:20 for **y** land shall not yield her increase,	3641.1
	26:21 plagues upon you according to **y** sins.	3641.1
	26:22 which shall rob you of **y** children,	NIH
	26:22 destroy **y** cattle, and make you few in	3641.1
	26:22 **y** high ways shall be desolate.	3641.1
	26:24 punish you yet seven *times* for **y** sins.	3641.1
	26:25 when ye are gathered together within **y**	3641.1
	26:26 broken the staff of **y** bread,	3641.1+3807.1
	26:26 ten women shall bake **y** bread in one	3641.1
	26:26 they shall deliver *you* **y** bread again by	3641.1
	26:28 will chastise you seven *times* for **y** sins.	3641.1
	26:29 ye shall eat the flesh of **y** sons,	3641.1
	26:29 and the flesh of **y** daughters shall ye eat.	3641.1
	26:30 I will destroy **y** high places, and cut	3641.1
	26:30 cut down **y** images, and cast your	3641.1
	26:30 cast **y** carcases upon the carcases of	3641.1
	26:30 your carcases upon the carcases of **y**	3641.1
	26:31 I will make **y** cities waste, and bring	3641.1
	26:31 bring **y** sanctuaries unto desolation,	3641.1
	26:31 I will not smell the savour of **y** sweet	3641.1
	26:32 **y** enemies which dwell therein shall be	3641.1
	26:33 **y** land shall be desolate, and your cities	3641.1
	26:33 shall be desolate, and **y** cities waste.	3641.1
	26:34 and ye *be* in **y** enemies' land;	3641.1
	26:35 because it did not rest in **y** sabbaths,	3641.1
	26:37 shall have no power to stand before **y**	3641.1
	26:38 the land of **y** enemies shall eat you up.	3641.1
	26:39 in their iniquity in **y** enemies' lands;	3641.1
Nu	9:10 **y** posterity shall be unclean by reason	3641.1
	10: 8 for ever throughout **y** generations.	3641.1
	10: 9 if ye go *to* war in **y** land against	3641.1
	10: 9 remembered before the Lord **y** God,	3641.1
	10: 9 and ye shall be saved from **y** enemies.	3641.1
	10:10 in the day of **y** gladness, and in your	3641.1
	10:10 in **y** solemn days, and in the beginnings	3641.1
	10:10 and in the beginnings of **y** months,	3641.1
	10:10 ye shall blow with the trumpets over **y**	3641.1
	10:10 over the sacrifices of **y** peace offerings;	3641.1
	10:10 be to you for a memorial before **y** God:	3641.1

Nu	10:10 your God: I *am* the Lord **y** God.	3641.1
	11:20 until it come out at **y** nostrils, and it be	3641.1
	14:29 **Y** carcases shall fall in this wilderness;	3641.1
	14:29 according to **y** whole number,	3641.1
	14:31 **y** little ones, which ye said should be a	3641.1
	14:32 *as for* you, **y** carcases, they shall fall in	3641.1
	14:33 **y** children shall wander in the	3641.1
	14:33 bear **y** whoredoms, until your carcases	3641.1
	14:33 until **y** carcases be wasted in	3641.1
	14:34 shall ye bear **y** iniquities, *even* forty	3641.1
	14:42 that ye be not smitten before **y** enemies.	3641.1
	15: 2 When ye be come into the land of **y**	3641.1
	15: 3 a freewill offering, or in **y** solemn feasts,	3641.1
	15:14 *be* among you in **y** generations,	3641.1
	15:15 an ordinance for ever in **y** generations:	3641.1
	15:20 Ye shall offer up a cake *of* the first of **y**	3641.1
	15:21 Of the first of **y** dough ye shall give unto	3641.1
	15:21 a heave offering in **y** generations.	3641.1
	15:23 henceforward among **y** generations;	3641.1
	15:39 that ye seek not after **y own** heart and	3641.1
	15:39 after your own heart and **y own** eyes,	3641.1
	15:40 and be holy unto **y** God.	3641.1
	15:41 I *am* the Lord **y** God, which brought	3641.1
	15:41 the land of Egypt, to be **y** God:	3641.1+3807.1
	15:41 to be your God: I *am* the Lord **y** God.	3641.1
	18: 1 shall bear the iniquity of **y** priesthood.	3641.1
	18: 6 I have taken **y** brethren the Levites from	3641.1
	18: 7 thy sons with thee shall keep **y** priest's	3641.1
	18: 7 I have given **y** priest's office *unto you as*	3641.1
	18:23 *shall be* a statute for ever throughout **y**	3641.1
	18:26 given you from them for **y** inheritance,	3641.1
	18:27 *this* **y** heave offering shall be reckoned	3641.1
	18:28 offering unto the Lord of all **y** tithes,	3641.1
	18:29 Out of all **y** gifts ye shall offer every	3641.1
	18:31 it in every place, ye and **y** households;	3641.1
	18:31 it *is* a reward for your service	3641.1+3807.1
	18:31 for it *is* your reward for **y** service in	3641.1
	22:13 princes of Balak, Get you into **y** land:	3641.1
	28:11 in the beginnings of **y** months ye shall	3641.1
	28:26 after **y** weeks *be out,* ye shall have a	3641.1
	29: 7 and ye shall afflict **y** souls:	3641.1
	29:39 shall do unto the Lord in **y** set feasts,	3641.1
	29:39 besides **y** vows, and your freewill	3641.1
	29:39 your vows, and **y** freewill offerings,	3641.1
	29:39 for **y** burnt offerings, and for your meat	3641.1
	29:39 for **y** meat offerings, and for your drink	3641.1
	29:39 for **y** drink offerings, and for your peace	3641.1
	29:39 drink offerings, and for **y** peace offerings.	3641.1
	31:19 and **y** captives on the third day,	3641.1
	31:20 purify all **y** raiment, and all that is made of	NIH
	31:24 ye shall wash **y** clothes on the seventh	3641.1
	32: 6 Shall **y** brethren go to war, and shall ye	3641.1
	32: 8 Thus did **y** fathers, when I sent them	3641.1
	32:14 ye are risen up in **y** fathers' stead,	3641.1
	32:22 this land shall be **y** possession	3641.1+3807.1
	32:23 and be sure **y** sin will find you out.	3641.1
	32:24 Build ye cities for **y** little ones,	3641.1
	32:24 your little ones, and folds for **y** sheep;	3641.1
	32:24 do that which hath proceeded out of **y**	3641.1
	33:54 lot for an inheritance among **y** families:	3641.1
	33:54 according to the tribes of **y** fathers ye	3641.1
	33:55 remain of them *shall be* pricks in **y** eyes,	3641.1
	33:55 thorns in **y** sides, and shall vex you in	3641.1
	34: 3 **y** south quarter shall be from	3641.1+3807.1
	34: 3 **y** south border shall be	3641.1+3807.1
	34: 4 **y** border shall turn from the	3641.1+3807.1
	34: 6 this shall be **y** west border.	3641.1+3807.1
	34: 7 this shall be **y** north border:	3641.1+3807.1
	34: 8 mount Hor ye shall point out **y** *border*	NIH
	34: 9 this shall be **y** north border.	3641.1+3807.1
	34:10 ye shall point out **y** east border	3641.1+3807.1
	34:12 this shall be **y** land with	3641.1+3807.1
	35:29 **y** generations in all your dwellings.	3641.1
	35:29 your generations in all **y** dwellings.	3641.1
Dt	1: 7 take **y** journey, and go *to* the mount of	3641.1
	1: 8 which the Lord sware unto **y** fathers,	3641.1
	1:10 The Lord **y** God hath multiplied you,	3641.1
	1:11 (The Lord God of **y** fathers make you	3641.1
	1:12 How can I myself alone bear **y**	3641.1
	1:12 and **y** burden, and your strife?	3641.1
	1:12 and your burden, and **y** strife?	3641.1
	1:13 known among **y** tribes, and I will make	3641.1
	1:15 So I took the chief of **y** tribes, wise men,	3641.1
	1:15 over tens, and officers among **y** tribes.	3641.1
	1:16 I charged **y** judges at that time, saying,	3641.1
	1:16 Hear the *causes* between **y** brethren,	3641.1
	1:26 the commandment of the Lord **y** God:	3641.1
	1:27 ye murmured in **y** tents, and said,	3641.1
	1:30 The Lord **y** God which goeth before	3641.1
	1:30 he did for you in Egypt before **y** eyes;	3641.1
	1:32 ye did not believe the Lord **y** God,	3641.1
	1:33 search you out a place to pitch **y** tents	3641.1
	1:34 the Lord heard the voice of **y** words,	3641.1
	1:35 which I sware to give unto **y** fathers,	3641.1
	1:37 Also the Lord was angry with me for **y**	3641.1
	1:39 Moreover **y** little ones, which ye said	3641.1
	1:39 ye said should be a prey, and **y** children,	3641.1
	1:40 take **y** journey into the wilderness *by*	NIH
	1:42 lest ye be smitten before **y** enemies.	3641.1
	1:45 the Lord would not hearken to **y** voice,	3641.1
	2: 4 Ye are to pass through the coast of **y**	3641.1
	2:24 take **y** journey, and pass over the river	NIH
	3:18 The Lord **y** God hath given you this	3641.1
	3:18 ye shall pass over armed before **y**	3641.1
	3:19 **y** wives, and your little ones,	3641.1

Dt	3:19 and **y** little ones, and your cattle,	3641.1
	3:19 and your little ones, and **y** cattle,	3641.1
	3:19 abide in **y** cities which I have given	3641.1
	3:20 Until the Lord have given rest unto **y**	3641.1
	3:20 **y** God hath given them beyond Jordan:	3641.1
	3:21 **y** God hath done unto these two kings:	3641.1
	3:22 for the Lord **y** God he shall fight for	3641.1
	3:26 the Lord was wroth with me for **y**	3641.1
	4: 1 the Lord God of **y** fathers giveth you.	3641.1
	4: 2 Lord **y** God which I command you.	3641.1
	4: 3 **Y** eyes have seen what the Lord did	3641.1
	4: 4 ye that did cleave unto the Lord **y** God	3641.1
	4: 6 and do *them;* for this *is* **y** wisdom and	3641.1
	4: 6 **y** understanding in the sight of	3641.1
	4:21 Lord was angry with me for **y** sakes,	3641.1
	4:23 forget the covenant of the Lord **y** God,	3641.1
	4:26 ye shall not prolong **y** days upon it,	NIH
	4:34 according to all that the Lord **y** God	3641.1
	4:34 God did for you in Egypt before **y** eyes?	3509.2
	5: 1 which I speak in **y** ears *this* day,	3641.1
	5:22 These words the Lord spake unto all **y**	3641.1
	5:23 *even* all the heads of **y** tribes,	3641.1
	5:23 the heads of your tribes, and **y** elders;	3641.1
	5:28 the Lord heard the voice of **y** words,	3641.1
	5:30 say to them, Get you into **y** tents again.	3641.1
	5:32 as the Lord **y** God hath commanded	3641.1
	5:33 the Lord **y** God hath commanded you,	3641.1
	5:33 *that* ye may prolong **y** days in the land	NIH
	6: 1 which the Lord **y** God commanded to	3641.1
	6:16 Ye shall not tempt the Lord **y** God,	3641.1
	6:17 the commandments of the Lord **y** God,	3641.1
	7: 8 which he had sworn unto **y** fathers,	3641.1
	7:14 barren among you, or among **y** cattle.	3509.2
	8: 1 which the Lord sware unto **y** fathers.	3641.1
	8:20 the Lord destroyeth before **y** face,	3641.1
	8:20 unto the voice of the Lord **y** God.	3641.1
	9:16 ye had sinned against the Lord **y** God,	3641.1
	9:17 hands, and brake them before **y** eyes.	3641.1
	9:18 because of all **y** sins which ye sinned,	3641.1
	9:21 I took **y** sin, the calf which ye had made,	3641.1
	9:23 the commandment of the Lord **y** God,	3641.1
	10:16 therefore the foreskin of **y** heart,	3641.1
	10:17 For the Lord **y** God *is* God of gods,	3641.1
	11: 2 for *I speak* not with **y** children which	3641.1
	11: 2 the chastisement of the Lord **y** God,	3641.1
	11: 7 **y** eyes have seen all the great acts of	3641.1
	11: 9 that ye may prolong **y** days in the land,	NIH
	11: 9 which the Lord sware unto **y** fathers to	3641.1
	11:13 to love the Lord **y** God, and to serve	3641.1
	11:13 to serve him with all **y** heart and with	3641.1
	11:13 with all your heart and with all **y** soul,	3641.1
	11:14 That I will give *you* the rain of **y** land in	3641.1
	11:16 **y** heart be not deceived, and ye turn	3641.1
	11:18 ye lay up these my words in **y** heart	3641.1
	11:18 my words in your heart and in **y** soul,	3641.1
	11:18 and bind them for a sign upon **y** hand,	3641.1
	11:18 that they may be as frontlets between **y**	3641.1
	11:19 ye shall teach them **y** children, speaking	3641.1
	11:21 That **y** days may be multiplied,	3641.1
	11:21 multiplied, and the days of **y** children,	3641.1
	11:21 sware unto **y** fathers to give them,	3641.1
	11:22 to do them, to love the Lord **y** God,	3641.1
	11:24 Every place whereon the soles of **y** feet	3641.1
	11:24 unto the uttermost sea shall **y** coast	3641.1
	11:25 *for* the Lord **y** God shall lay the fear of	3641.1
	11:27 the commandments of the Lord **y** God,	3641.1
	11:28 the commandments of the Lord **y** God,	3641.1
	11:31 land which the Lord **y** God giveth you,	3641.1
	12: 4 shall not do so unto the Lord **y** God.	3641.1
	12: 5 unto the place which the Lord **y** God	3641.1
	12: 5 out of all **y** tribes to put his name there,	3641.1
	12: 6 thither ye shall bring **y** burnt offerings,	3641.1
	12: 6 **y** sacrifices, and your tithes, and heave	3641.1
	12: 6 **y** tithes, and heave offerings of your	3641.1
	12: 6 heave offerings of **y** hand,	3641.1
	12: 6 **y** vows, and your freewill offerings,	3641.1
	12: 6 **y** freewill offerings, and the firstlings of	3641.1
	12: 6 the firstlings of **y** herds and of your	3641.1
	12: 6 firstlings of your herds and of **y** flocks:	3641.1
	12: 7 there ye shall eat before the Lord **y**	3641.1
	12: 7 shall rejoice in all that you put **y** hand	3641.1
	12: 7 ye and **y** households, wherein the Lord	3641.1
	12: 9 which the Lord **y** God giveth you.	3509.2
	12:10 dwell in the land which the Lord **y**	3641.1
	12:10 *when* he giveth you rest from all **y**	3641.1
	12:11 there shall be a place which the Lord **y**	3641.1
	12:11 **y** burnt offerings, and your sacrifices,	3641.1
	12:11 **y** sacrifices, your tithes, and the heave	3641.1
	12:11 **y** tithes, and the heave offering of your	3641.1
	12:11 heave offering of **y** hand, and all your	3641.1
	12:11 all **y** choice vows which ye vow unto	3641.1
	12:12 ye shall rejoice before the Lord **y** God,	3641.1
	12:12 ye, and **y** sons, and your daughters,	3641.1
	12:12 **y** daughters, and your menservants,	3641.1
	12:12 **y** menservants, and your maidservants,	3641.1
	12:12 **y** maidservants, and the Levite that *is*	3641.1
	12:12 and the Levite that *is* within **y** gates;	3641.1
	13: 3 for the Lord **y** God proveth you,	3641.1
	13: 3 to know whether ye love the Lord **y**	3641.1
	13: 3 the Lord your God with all **y** heart	3641.1
	13: 3 with all your heart and with all **y** soul.	3641.1
	13: 4 Ye shall walk after the Lord **y** God,	3641.1
	13: 5 turn *you* away from the Lord **y** God,	3641.1
	14: 1 Ye *are* the children of the Lord **y** God:	3641.1
	14: 1 nor make *any* baldness between **y** eyes	3641.1

Y

Dt	20: 3 *this* day unto battle against **y** enemies:	3641.1	
	20: 3 let not **y** hearts faint, fear not, and do	3641.1	
	20: 4 For the Lord **y** God *is* he that goeth	3641.1	
	20: 4 fight for you against **y** enemies, to save	3641.1	
	20:18 should ye sin against the Lord **y** God.	3641.1	
	28:68 there ye shall be sold unto **y** enemies	3509.2	
	29: 2 **y** eyes in the land of Egypt unto	3641.1	
	29: 5 **y** clothes are not waxen old upon you,	3641.1	
	29: 6 might know that I *am* the Lord **y** God.	3641.1	
	29:10 day all of you before the Lord **y** God;	3641.1	
	29:10 **y** captains of your tribes, your elders,	3641.1	
	29:10 your captains of your tribes, your elders,	3641.1	
	29:10 **y** elders, and your officers, *with* all	3641.1	
	29:10 your elders, and **y** officers, *with* all	3641.1	
	29:11 **Y** little ones, your wives, and thy	3641.1	
	29:11 **y** wives, and thy stranger *that is* in thy	3641.1	
	29:22 So that the generation to come of **y**	3641.1	
	30:18 *that* ye shall not prolong **y** days upon	NIH	
	31: 5 the Lord shall give them up before **y**	3641.1	
	31:12 fear the Lord **y** God, and observe to do	3641.1	
	31:13 and learn to fear the Lord **y** God,	3641.1	
	31:26 ark of the covenant of the Lord **y** God,	3641.1	
	31:28 Gather unto me all the elders of **y** tribes,	3641.1	
	31:28 **y** officers, that I may speak these words	3641.1	
	31:29 to anger through the work of **y** hands.	3641.1	
	32:17 newly up, whom **y** fathers feared not.	3641.1	
	32:38 up and help you, *and* be **y** protection.	3641.1	
	32:46 Set **y** hearts unto all the words which I	3641.1	
	32:46 which ye shall command **y** children to	3641.1	
	32:47 a vain thing for you; because it *is* **y** life:	3641.1	
	32:47 through this thing ye shall prolong **y** days	NIH	
Jos	1: 3 Every place that the sole of **y** foot shall	3641.1	
	1: 4 going down of the sun, shall be **y** coast.	3641.1	
	1:11 which the Lord **y** God giveth you to	3641.1	
	1:13 The Lord **y** God hath given you rest,	3641.1	
	1:14 **Y** wives, your little ones, and your	3641.1	
	1:14 your wives, **y** little ones, and your	3641.1	
	1:14 your wives, your little ones, and **y** cattle,	3641.1	
	1:14 ye shall pass before **y** brethren armed,	3641.1	
	1:15 Until the Lord have given **y** brethren	3641.1	
	1:15 which the Lord **y** God giveth them:	3641.1	
	1:15 ye shall return unto the land of **y**	3641.1	
	2: 9 **y** terror is fallen upon us, and that all	3641.1	
	2:11 for the Lord **y** God, he *is* God in	3641.1	
	2:16 and afterward may ye go **y** way.	3641.1	
	2:21 According unto **y** words, so be it.	3641.1	
	3: 3 ark of the covenant of the Lord **y** God,	3641.1	
	3: 3 ye shall remove from **y** place,	3641.1	
	3: 9 and hear the words of the Lord **y** God.	3641.1	
	4: 5 Pass over before the ark of the Lord **y**	3641.1	
	4: 6 *that* when **y** children ask *their fathers*	3641.1	
	4:21 **y** children shall ask their fathers in	3641.1	
	4:22 ye shall let **y** children know, saying,	3641.1	
	4:23 For the Lord **y** God dried up	3641.1	
	4:23 as the Lord **y** God did to the Red sea,	3641.1	
	4:24 that ye might fear the Lord **y** God for	3641.1	
	6:10 nor make any noise with **y** voice,	3641.1	
	6:10 neither shall *any* word proceed out of **y**	3641.1	
	7:14 shall be brought according to **y** tribes:	3641.1	
	8: 7 for the Lord **y** God will deliver it into	3641.1	
	8: 7 your God will deliver it into **y** hand.	3641.1	
	9:11 and say unto them, We *are* **y** servants:	3641.1	
	10:19 *but* pursue after **y** enemies, and smite	3641.1	
	10:19 for the Lord **y** God hath delivered	3641.1	
	10:19 God hath delivered them into **y** hand.	3641.1	
	10:24 **y** feet upon the necks of these kings.	3641.1	
	10:25 for thus shall the Lord do to all **y**	3641.1	
	15: 4 this shall be **y** south coast.	3641.1+3807.1	
	18: 3 which the Lord God of **y** fathers hath	3641.1	
	20: 3 they shall be **y** refuge from	3641.1+3807.1	
	22: 3 Ye have not left **y** brethren these many	3641.1	
	22: 3 the commandment of the Lord **y** God.	3641.1	
	22: 4 now the Lord **y** God hath given rest	3641.1	
	22: 4 God hath given rest unto **y** brethren,	3641.1	
	22: 4 get ye unto **y** tents, *and* unto the land	3641.1	
	22: 4 *and* unto the land of **y** possession,	3641.1	
	22: 5 to love the Lord **y** God, and to walk in	3641.1	
	22: 5 serve him with all **y** heart and with all	3641.1	
	22: 5 with all your heart and with all **y** soul.	3641.1	
	22: 8 Return with much riches unto **y** tents,	3641.1	
	22: 8 divide the spoil of **y** enemies with your	3641.1	
	22: 8 divide the spoil of your enemies with **y**	3641.1	
	22:19 if the land of **y** possession *be* unclean,	3641.1	
	22:24 In time to come **y** children might speak	3641.1	
	22:25 shall **y** children make our children	3641.1	
	22:27 that **y** children may not say to our	3641.1	
	23: 3 ye have seen all that the Lord **y** God	3641.1	
	23: 3 for the Lord **y** God *is* he that hath	3641.1	
	23: 4 to be an inheritance for **y** tribes,	3641.1	
	23: 5 the Lord **y** God, he shall expel them	3641.1	
	23: 5 and drive them from out of **y** sight;	3641.1	
	23: 5 as the Lord **y** God hath promised unto	3641.1	
	23: 8 cleave unto the Lord **y** God, as ye	3641.1	
	23:10 For the Lord **y** God, he *it is* that	3641.1	
	23:11 that ye love the Lord **y** God.	3641.1	
	23:13 Know for a certainty that the Lord **y**	3641.1	
	23:13 scourges in **y** sides, and thorns in your	3641.1	
	23:13 in your sides, and thorns in **y** eyes,	3641.1	
	23:13 which the Lord **y** God hath given you.	3641.1	
	23:14 ye know in all **y** hearts and in all your	3641.1	
	23:14 in all your hearts and in all **y** souls,	3641.1	
	23:14 the Lord **y** God spake concerning you;	3641.1	
	23:15 which the Lord **y** God promised you;	3641.1	
	23:15 which the Lord **y** God hath given you.	3641.1	
	23:16 the covenant of the Lord **y** God,	3641.1	

Jos	24: 2 **Y** fathers dwelt on the *other* side of	3641.1	
	24: 3 took **y** father Abraham from the *other*	3641.1	
	24: 6 I brought **y** fathers out of Egypt:	3641.1	
	24: 6 the Egyptians pursued after **y** fathers	3641.1	
	24: 7 **y** eyes have seen what I have done in	3641.1	
	24: 8 I gave them into **y** hand, that ye might	3641.1	
	24:11 and I delivered them into **y** hand.	3641.1	
	24:14 put away the gods which **y** fathers	3641.1	
	24:15 the gods which **y** fathers served	3641.1	
	24:19 he will not forgive **y** transgressions nor	3641.1	
	24:19 forgive your transgressions nor **y** sins.	3641.1	
	24:23 incline **y** heart unto the Lord God of	3641.1	
	24:27 a witness unto you, lest ye deny **y** God.	3641.1	
Jdg	2: 1 the land which I sware unto **y** fathers;	3641.1	
	2: 3 they shall be *as* thorns in **y** sides,	3641.1	
	3:28 for the Lord hath delivered **y** enemies	3641.1	
	3:28 your enemies the Moabites into **y** hand.	3641.1	
	6:10 I said unto you, I *am* the Lord **y** God;	3641.1	
	7:15 the Lord hath delivered into **y** hand	3641.1	
	8: 3 God hath delivered into **y** hands	3641.1	
	8: 7 I will tear **y** flesh with the thorns of	3641.1	
	9: 2 remember also that I *am* **y** bone and	3641.1	
	9: 2 also that I *am* your bone and **y** flesh.	3641.1	
	9:15 *then* come *and* put **y** trust in my shadow:	NIH	
	9:18 of Shechem, because he *is* **y** brother;)	3641.1	
	10:14 let them deliver you in the time of **y**	3641.1	
	11: 9 before me, shall **y** be head?	3641.1+3807.1	
	18: 6 the Lord *is* **y** way wherein ye go.	3641.1	
	18:10 for God hath given it into **y** hands;	3641.1	
	19: 5 morsel of bread, and afterward go **y** way.	NIH	
	19: 9 to morrow get you early on **y** way, that	3641.1	
	19:30 of it, take advice, and speak **y** minds.	NIH	
	20: 7 give here **y** advice and counsel.	3641.1+3807.1	
Ru	1:11 that they may be **y** husbands?	3641.1+3807.1	
	1:12 go **y** way; for I am too old to have a	NIH	
	1:13 for it grieveth me much for **y** sakes that	3641.1	
1Sa	2: 3 let *not* arrogancy come out of **y** mouth:	3641.1	
	2:23 for I hear of **y** evil dealings by all this	3641.1	
	6: 4 plague *was* on you all, and on **y** lords.	3641.1	
	6: 5 Wherefore ye shall make images of **y**	3641.1	
	6: 5 and images of **y** mice that mar the land;	3641.1	
	6: 5 from off **y** gods, and from off your land.	3641.1	
	6: 5 from off your gods, and from off **y** land.	3641.1	
	6: 6 Wherefore then do ye harden **y** hearts,	3641.1	
	7: 3 If ye do return unto the Lord with all **y**	3641.1	
	7: 3 prepare **y** hearts unto the Lord,	3641.1	
	8:11 He will take **y** sons, and appoint *them*	3641.1	
	8:13 he will take **y** daughters to be	3641.1	
	8:14 he will take **y** fields, and your vineyards,	3641.1	
	8:14 your vineyards, and **y** oliveyards,	3641.1	
	8:14 your vineyards, and **y** oliveyards,	3641.1	
	8:15 he will take the tenth of **y** seed,	3641.1	
	8:15 of **y** vineyards, and give to his officers,	3641.1	
	8:16 he will take **y** menservants, and your	3641.1	
	8:16 **y** maidservants, and your goodliest	3641.1	
	8:16 **y** goodliest young men, and your asses,	3641.1	
	8:16 and **y** asses, and put *them* to his work.	3641.1	
	8:17 He will take the tenth of **y** sheep:	3641.1	
	8:18 **y** king which ye shall have chosen you;	3641.1	
	10:19 ye have *this* day rejected **y** God,	3641.1	
	10:19 who himself saved you out of all **y**	3641.1	
	10:19 of all your adversities and **y** tribulations;	3641.1	
	10:19 yourselves before the Lord by **y** tribes,	3641.1	
	10:19 by your tribes, and by **y** thousands.	3641.1	
	11: 2 that *I* may thrust out all **y** right	3641.1+3807.1	
	12: 1 I have hearkened unto **y** voice in all that	3641.1	
	12: 6 that brought **y** fathers up out of the land	3641.1	
	12: 7 which he did to you and to **y** fathers.	3641.1	
	12: 8 **y** fathers cried unto the Lord, then	3641.1	
	12: 8 which brought forth **y** fathers out of	3641.1	
	12:11 delivered you out of the hand of **y**	3641.1	
	12:12 when the Lord **y** God *was* your king.	3641.1	
	12:12 when the Lord your God *was* **y** king.	3641.1	
	12:14 continue following the Lord **y** God:	3641.1	
	12:15 against you, as *it was* against **y** fathers.	3641.1	
	12:16 which the Lord will do before **y** eyes.	3641.1	
	12:17 and see that **y** wickedness *is* great,	3641.1	
	12:20 but serve the Lord with all **y** heart;	3641.1	
	12:24 and serve him in truth with all **y** heart:	3641.1	
	12:25 shall be consumed, both ye and **y** king.	3641.1	
	17: 8 Why are ye come out to set **y** battle in	NIH	
	17: 9 then will we be **y** servants:	3641.1+3807.1	
	26:16 die, because ye have not kept **y** master,	3641.1	
2Sa	1:24 who put on ornaments of gold upon **y**	3654.1	
	2: 5 ye have shewed this kindness unto **y**	3641.1	
	2: 7 Therefore now let **y** hands be	3641.1	
	2: 7 for **y** master Saul is dead, and also	3641.1	
	3:31 Rent **y** clothes, and gird you with	3641.1	
	4:11 now require his blood of **y** hand,	3641.1	
	10: 5 Tarry at Jericho until **y** beards be grown,	3641.1	
	15:27 **y** two sons with you, Ahimaaz thy son,	3509.2	
1Ki	1:33 Take with you the servants of **y** lord,	3641.1	
	8:61 Let **y** heart therefore be perfect with	3641.1	
	9: 6 you or **y** children, and will not keep my	3641.1	
	11: 2 for surely they will turn away **y** heart	3641.1	
	12:11 with a heavy yoke, I will add to **y** yoke:	3641.1	
	12:14 My father made **y** yoke heavy, and I will	3641.1	
	12:14 yoke heavy, and I will add to **y** yoke:	3641.1	
	12:16 to **y** tents, O Israel: now see to thine	3509.2	
	12:24 nor fight against **y** brethren the children	3641.1	
	18:24 call ye on the name of **y** gods, and I will	3641.1	
	18:25 call on the name of **y** gods, but put no	3641.1	
2Ki	2: 3 he said, Yea, I know *it*; hold you **y** peace.	NIH	
	2: 5 Yea, I know *it*; hold you **y** peace.	NIH	
	3:17 *both* ye, and **y** cattle, and your beasts.	3641.1	

2Ki	3:17 *both* ye, and your cattle, and **y** beasts.	3641.1	
	3:18 he will deliver the Moabites also into **y**	3641.1	
	9:15 If it be **y** minds, *then* let none go forth	3641.1	
	10: 2 seeing **y** master's sons *are* with you,	3641.1	
	10: 3 the best and meetest of **y** master's sons,	3641.1	
	10: 3 and fight for **y** master's house.	3641.1	
	10: 6 take ye the heads of the men **y** master's	3641.1	
	10:24 I *have* brought into **y** hands escape,	3641.1	
	12: 7 no *more* money of **y** acquaintance,	3641.1	
	17:13 Turn ye from **y** evil ways, and keep my	3641.1	
	17:13 the law which I commanded **y** fathers,	3641.1	
	17:39 the Lord **y** God ye shall fear;	3641.1	
	17:39 you out of the hand of all **y** enemies.	3641.1	
	18:32 you away to a land like **y** own land,	3641.1	
	19: 6 Thus shall ye say to **y** master, Thus saith	3641.1	
	23:21 the passover unto the Lord **y** God,	3641.1	
1Ch	15:12 sanctify yourselves, *both* ye and **y**	3641.1	
	16:18 land of Canaan, the lot of **y** inheritance.	3641.1	
	19: 5 Tarry at Jericho until **y** beards be grown,	3641.1	
	22:18 *Is* not the Lord **y** God with you?	3641.1	
	22:19 Now set **y** heart and your soul to seek	3641.1	
	22:19 and **y** soul to seek the Lord your God;	3641.1	
	22:19 and your soul to seek the Lord **y** God;	3641.1	
	28: 8 the commandments of the Lord **y** God:	3641.1	
	28: 8 leave *it* for an inheritance for **y** children	3641.1	
	29:20 Now bless the Lord **y** God.	3641.1	
2Ch	10:11 upon you, I will put more to **y** yoke:	3641.1	
	10:14 My father made **y** yoke heavy, but I will	3641.1	
	10:16 every man to **y** tents, O Israel: and now,	3509.2	
	11: 4 not go up, nor fight against **y** brethren:	3641.1	
	13:12 fight ye not against the Lord God of **y**	3641.1	
	15: 7 and let not **y** hands be weak:	3641.1	
	15: 7 be weak: for **y** work shall be rewarded.	3641.1	
	18:14 and they shall be delivered into **y** hand.	3641.1	
	19:10 cause soever shall come to you of **y**	3641.1	
	19:10 come upon you, and upon **y** brethren:	3641.1	
	20:20 Believe in the Lord **y** God,	3641.1	
	24: 5 the house of **y** God from year to year,	3641.1	
	28: 9 the Lord God of **y** fathers was wroth	3641.1	
	28: 9 he hath delivered them into **y** hand,	3641.1	
	28:10 with you, sins against the Lord **y** God?	3641.1	
	28:11 ye have taken captive of **y** brethren:	3641.1	
	29: 5 house of the Lord God of **y** fathers,	3641.1	
	29: 8 and to hissing, as ye see with **y** eyes.	3641.1	
	30: 7 be not ye like **y** fathers, and like your	3641.1	
	30: 7 ye like your fathers, and like **y** brethren,	3641.1	
	30: 8 as **y** fathers *were, but* yield yourselves	3641.1	
	30: 8 serve the Lord **y** God, that	3641.1	
	30: 9 **y** brethren and your children *shall find*	3641.1	
	30: 9 **y** children *shall find* compassion before	3641.1	
	30: 9 for the Lord **y** God *is* gracious and	3641.1	
	32:14 that **y** God should be able to deliver you	3641.1	
	32:15 how much less shall **y** God deliver you	3641.1	
	33: 8 which I have appointed for **y** fathers;	3641.1	
	35: 3 *be* a burden upon **y** shoulders:	3641.1+3807.1	
	35: 3 serve now the Lord **y** God, and his	3641.1	
	35: 4 prepare *yourselves* by the houses of **y**	3641.1	
	35: 4 after **y** courses, according to the writing	3641.1	
	35: 5 of the fathers of **y** brethren the people,	3641.1	
	35: 6 and prepare **y** brethren,	3641.1	
Ezr	4: 2 for we seek **y** God, as ye *do*; and we do	3641.1	
	6: 6 and **y** companions the Apharsachites,	1952.1	
	7:17 house of **y** God which *is* in Jerusalem.	3641.2	
	7:18 gold, *that* do after the will of **y** God.	3641.2	
	8:28 unto the Lord God of **y** fathers.	3641.1	
	9:12 give not **y** daughters unto their sons,	3641.1	
	9:12 neither take their daughters unto **y** sons,	3641.1	
	9:12 leave *it* for an inheritance to **y** children	3641.1	
	10:11 unto the Lord God of **y** fathers,	3641.1	
Ne	4:14 and terrible, and fight for **y** brethren,	3641.1	
	4:14 **y** sons, and your daughters, your wives,	3641.1	
	4:14 your sons, and **y** daughters, your wives,	3641.1	
	4:14 daughters, **y** wives, and your houses.	3641.1	
	4:14 daughters, your wives, and **y** houses.	3641.1	
	5: 8 and will you even sell **y** brethren?	3641.1	
	8: 9 *This* day *is* holy unto the Lord **y** God;	3641.1	
	8:10 Go **y** way, eat the fat, and drink the sweet,	NIH	
	8:10 for the joy of the Lord *is* **y** strength.	3641.1	
	8:11 Hold **y** peace, for the day *is* holy;	NIH	
	9: 5 *and* bless the Lord **y** God for ever and	3641.1	
	13:18 Did not **y** fathers thus, and *did not* our	NIH	
	13:25 Ye shall not give **y** daughters unto	3641.1	
	13:25 nor take their daughters unto **y** sons,	3641.1	
Job	6:22 Give a reward for me of **y** substance?	3641.1	
	6:25 but what doth **y** arguing reprove?	4480+3641.1	
	6:27 and you dig a *pit* for **y** friend.	3641.1	
	13: 5 that you would altogether hold **y** peace,	NIH	
	13: 5 it should be **y** wisdom.	3641.1+3807.1	
	13:12 **Y** remembrances *are* like unto ashes,	NIH	
	13:12 unto ashes, **y** bodies to bodies of clay.	3641.1	
	13:13 Hold **y** peace, let me alone, that I may	NIH	
	13:17 and my declaration with **y** ears.	3641.1	
	16: 4 also could speak as ye *do*: if **y** soul were	NIH	
	16: 5 the moving of my lips should assuage **y**	NIH	
	18: 3 as beasts, *and* reputed vile in **y** sight?	3641.1	
	21: 2 speech, and let this be **y** consolations.	3641.1	
	21: 5 and lay **y** hand upon *your* mouth.	NIH	
	21: 5 and lay *your* hand upon **y** mouth.	NIH	
	21:27 I know **y** thoughts, and the devices	3641.1	
	21:34 seeing *in* **y** answers there remaineth	3641.1	
	32:11 Behold, I waited for **y** words; I gave ear	3641.1	
	32:11 I gave ear to **y** reasons, whilst you	3641.1	
	32:14 will I answer him with **y** speeches.	3641.1	
	42: 8 lest *I* deal with you *after* **y** folly, in that	NIH	
Ps	4: 4 commune with **y** own heart upon your	3641.1	

Ps
4: 4 commune with your own heart upon **y** 3641.1
4: 5 and put **y** trust in the LORD. NIH
11: 1 my soul, Flee *as a* bird *to* **y** mountain? 3641.1
22:26 that seek him: **y** heart shall live for ever. 3641.1
24: 7 Lift up **y** heads, O ye gates; and be ye 3641.1
24: 9 Lift up **y** heads, O ye gates; even lift 3641.1
31:24 and he shall strengthen **y** heart, 3641.1
47: 1 O clap **y** hands, all ye people; shout unto NIH
58: 2 you weigh the violence of **y** hands in 3641.1
58: 9 Before **y** pots can feel the thorns, 3641.1
62: 8 ye people, pour out **y** heart before him: 3641.1
62:10 increase, set not **y** heart *upon* them. NIH
69:32 and **y** heart shall live that seek God. 3641.1
75: 5 Lift not up **y** horn on high: speak *not* 3641.1
76:11 Vow, and pay unto the LORD **y** God: 3641.1
78: 1 **y** ears to the words of my mouth. 3641.1
95: 8 Harden not **y** heart, as *in the* 3641.1
95: 9 **y** fathers tempted me, proved me, 3641.1
105:11 land of Canaan, the lot of **y** inheritance: 3641.1
115:14 you more and more, you and **y** children. 3641.1
134: 2 Lift up **y** hands *in* the sanctuary, 3641.1
146: 3 Put not **y** trust in princes, *nor* in the son NIH
Pr
1:26 I also will laugh at **y** calamity; I will 3641.1
1:26 I will mock when **y** fear cometh; 3641.1
1:27 When **y** fear cometh as desolation, 3641.1
1:27 destruction cometh as a whirlwind; 3641.1
Isa
1: 7 **Y** country *is* desolate, your cities *are* 3641.1
1: 7 *is* desolate, **y** cities *are* burnt *with* fire: 3641.1
1: 7 **y** land, strangers devour it in your 3641.1
1: 7 strangers devour it in **y** presence, 3641.1
1:11 To what purpose *is* the multitude of **y** 3641.1
1:12 hath required this at **y** hand, to tread 3641.1
1:14 **Y** new moons and your appointed feasts 3641.1
1:14 and **y** appointed feasts my soul hateth: 3641.1
1:15 ye spread forth **y** hands, I will hide 3641.1
1:15 will not hear: **y** hands are full *of* blood. 3641.1
1:16 put away the evil of **y** doings from 3641.1
1:18 though **y** sins be as scarlet, they shall be 3641.1
3:14 the spoil of the poor *is* in **y** houses. 3641.1
8:13 *let* him *be* **y** fear, and *let* him *be* your 3641.1
8:13 *be* your fear, and *let* him *be* **y** dread. 3641.1
10: 3 and where will ye leave **y** glory? 3641.1
23: 7 *Is* this **y** joyous *city,* whose 3641.1+3807.1
23:14 of Tarshish: for **y** strength is laid waste. 3654.1
28:18 **y** covenant with death shall be 3641.1
28:18 **y** agreement with hell shall not stand; 3641.1
28:22 mockers, lest **y** bands be made strong; 3641.1
29:10 of deep sleep, and hath closed **y** eyes: 3641.1
29:10 the prophets and **y** rulers, the seers hath 3641.1
29:16 Surely **y** turning *of things* upside down 3641.1
30: 3 strength of Pharaoh *be* **y** shame, 3641.1+3807.1
30: 3 the trust in the shadow of Egypt **y** NIH
30:15 and in confidence shall be **y** strength: 3641.1
31: 7 **y** own hands have made unto you 3641.1
32:11 ye bare, and gird *sackcloth* upon **y** loins. NIH
33: 4 **y** spoil shall be gathered *like* 3641.1
33:11 **y** breath, *as* fire, shall devour you. 3641.1
35: 4 **y** God will come *with* vengeance, 3641.1
36:17 you away to a land like **y own** land, 3641.1
37: 6 Thus shall ye say unto **y** master, 3641.1
40: 1 comfort ye my people, saith **y** God. 3641.1
40: 9 unto the cities of Judah, Behold **y** God. 3641.1
40:26 Lift up **y** eyes on high, and behold who 3641.1
41:21 Produce **y** cause, saith the LORD; 3641.1
41:21 bring forth **y** strong *reasons,* saith 3641.1
41:24 *are* of nothing, and **y** work of nought: 3641.1
41:26 yea, *there is* none that heareth **y** words. 3641.1
43:14 For **y** sake I have sent to Babylon, 3641.1
43:14 **y** redeemer, the Holy One of Israel; 3641.1
43:15 I *am* the LORD, **y** Holy One, the creator 3641.1
43:15 Holy One, the creator of Israel, **y** King. 3641.1
46: 1 **y** carriages *were* heavy loaden; *they are* 3641.1
46: 4 to **y** old age *I am* he; and *even* to hoar NIH
50: 1 Where *is* the bill of **y** mother's 3641.1
50: 1 **y** iniquities have you sold yourselves, 3641.1
50: 1 for **y** transgressions *is* your mother put 3641.1
50: 1 for your transgressions *is* **y** mother put 3641.1
50:11 walk in the light of **y** fire, and in 3641.1
51: 2 Look unto Abraham **y** father, 3641.1
51: 6 Lift up **y** eyes to the heavens, 3641.1
52:12 the God of Israel *will be* **y** rereward. 3641.1
55: 2 **y** labour for *that which* satisfieth not? 3641.1
55: 2 and let **y** soul delight itself in fatness. 3641.1
55: 3 Incline **y** ear, and come unto me: hear, 3641.1
55: 3 hear, and **y** soul shall live; and I will 3641.1
55: 8 For my thoughts *are* not **y** thoughts, 3641.1
55: 8 neither *are* **y** ways my ways, saith 3641.1
55: 9 so are my ways higher than **y** ways, 3641.1
55: 9 and my thoughts than **y** thoughts. 3641.1
58: 3 in the day of **y** fast you find pleasure, 3641.1
58: 3 find pleasure, and exact all **y** labours. 3641.1
58: 4 to make **y** voice to be heard on high. 3641.1
59: 2 **y** iniquities have separated between you 3641.1
59: 2 have separated between you and **y** God, 3641.1
59: 2 and **y** sins have hid *his* face from you, 3641.1
59: 3 For **y** hands are defiled with blood, 3641.1
59: 3 with blood, and **y** fingers with iniquity; 3641.1
59: 3 **y** lips have spoken lies, your tongue 3641.1
59: 3 **y** tongue hath muttered perverseness. 3641.1
61: 5 strangers shall stand and feed **y** flocks, 3641.1
61: 5 the sons of the alien *shall be* **y** plowmen 3641.1
61: 5 *be* your plowmen and **y** vinedressers. 3641.1
61: 7 For **y** shame *you shall have* double; 3641.1
65: 7 **Y** iniquities, and the iniquities of your 3641.1
65: 7 and the iniquities of **y** fathers together, 3641.1

Isa
65:15 shall leave **y** name for a curse unto my 3641.1
66: 5 **Y** brethren that hated you, that cast you 3641.1
66: 5 he *shall* appear to **y** joy, and they shall 3641.1
66:14 when ye see *this,* **y** heart shall rejoice, 3641.1
66:14 and **y** bones shall flourish like an herb: 3641.1
66:20 they shall bring all **y** brethren *for* an 3641.1
66:22 so shall **y** seed and your name remain. 3641.1
66:22 so shall your seed and **y** name remain. 3641.1
Jer
2: 5 What iniquity have **y** fathers found in 3641.1
2: 9 with **y** children's children will I plead. 3641.1
2:30 In vain have I smitten **y** children; 3641.1
2:30 **y own** sword hath devoured your 3641.1
2:30 your own sword hath devoured **y** 3641.1
3:18 given for an inheritance unto **y** fathers. 3641.1
3:22 *and* I will heal **y** backslidings. 3641.1
4: 3 Break up **y** fallow ground, 3641.1+3807.1
4: 4 take away the foreskins of **y** heart, 3641.1
4: 4 because of the evil of **y** doings. 3641.1
5:19 served strange gods in **y** land, so shall ye 3641.1
5:25 **Y** iniquities have turned away these 3641.1
5:25 **y** sins have withholden good *things* 3641.1
6:16 and ye shall find rest for **y** souls. 3641.1
6:20 **y** burnt offerings *are* not acceptable, 3641.1
6:20 nor **y** sacrifices sweet unto me. 3641.1
7: 3 Amend **y** ways and your doings, 3641.1
7: 3 Amend your ways and **y** doings, 3641.1
7: 5 For if you throughly amend **y** ways and 3641.1
7: 5 amend your ways and **y** doings; 3641.1
7: 6 walk after other gods to **y** hurt: 3641.1+3807.1
7: 7 in the land that I gave to **y** fathers, 3641.1
7:11 become a den of robbers in **y** eyes? 3641.1
7:14 which I gave to you and to **y** fathers, 3641.1
7:15 as I have cast out all **y** brethren, *even* 3641.1
7:21 **y** burnt offerings unto your sacrifices, 3641.1
7:21 your burnt offerings unto **y** sacrifices, 3641.1
7:22 For I spake not unto **y** fathers, 3641.1
7:23 I will be **y** God, and ye shall be 3641.1+3807.1
7:25 Since the day that **y** fathers came forth 3641.1
9:20 let **y** ear receive the word of his mouth, 3641.1
9:20 teach **y** daughters wailing, and every 3641.1
11: 4 Which I commanded **y** fathers in the 3641.1
11: 4 my people, and I will be **y** God: 3641.1+3807.1
11: 5 oath which I have sworn unto **y** fathers, 3641.1
11: 7 I earnestly protested unto **y** fathers in 3641.1
12:13 they shall be ashamed of **y** revenues 3641.1
13:16 Give glory to the LORD **y** God, before 3641.1
13:16 before **y** feet stumble upon the dark 3641.1
13:17 my soul shall weep in secret places for **y** NIH
13:18 for **y** principalities shall come down, 3641.1
13:18 come down, *even* the crown of **y** glory. 3641.1
13:20 Lift up **y** eyes, and behold them that 3641.1
16: 9 will cause to cease out of this place in **y** 3641.1
16: 9 in **y** days, the voice of mirth, 3641.1
16:11 Because **y** fathers have forsaken me, 3641.1
16:12 ye have done worse than **y** fathers; 3641.1
16:13 ye know not, *neither* ye nor **y** fathers; 3641.1
17: 1 heart, and upon the horns of **y** altars; 3641.1
17:22 Neither carry forth a burden out of **y** 3641.1
17:22 sabbath day, as I commanded **y** fathers. 3641.1
18:11 make **y** ways and your doings good. 3641.1
18:11 make your ways and **y** doings good. 3641.1
21: 4 the weapons of war that *are* in **y** hands, 3641.1
21:12 because of the evil of **y** doings. 3641.1
21:14 you according to the fruit of **y** doings, 3641.1
23: 2 will visit upon you the evil of **y** doings, 3641.1
23:39 the city that I gave you and **y** fathers, 3641.1
25: 4 hearkened, nor inclined **y** ear to hear. 3641.1
25: 5 from the evil of **y** doings, and dwell in 3641.1
25: 5 and to **y** fathers for ever and ever: 3641.1
25: 6 not to anger with the works of **y** hands; 3641.1
25: 7 the works of **y** hands to your own hurt. 3641.1
25: 7 the works of your hands to **y own** hurt. 3641.1
25:34 for the days of **y** slaughter and of your 3641.1
25:34 and of **y** dispersions are accomplished. 3641.1
26:11 this city, as ye have heard with **y** ears. 3641.1
26:13 Therefore now amend **y** ways and 3641.1
26:13 now amend your ways and **y** doings, 3641.1
26:13 and obey the voice of the LORD **y** God; 3641.1
26:14 As for me, behold, I *am* in **y** hand: 3641.1
26:15 you to speak all these words in **y** ears. 3641.1
27: 4 Thus shall ye say unto **y** masters; 3641.1
27: 9 Therefore hearken not ye to **y** prophets, 3641.1
27: 9 nor to **y** diviners, nor to your dreamers, 3641.1
27: 9 nor to your diviners, nor to **y** dreamers, 3641.1
27: 9 to **y** enchanters, nor to your sorcerers, 3641.1
27: 9 to **y** sorcerers, which speak unto you, 3641.1
27:10 you, to remove you far from **y** land; 3641.1
27:12 Bring **y** necks under the yoke of the 3641.1
27:16 Hearken not to the words of **y** prophets 3641.1
29: 6 take wives for **y** sons, and give your 3641.1
29: 6 give **y** daughters to husbands, that they 3641.1
29: 8 Let not **y** prophets and your diviners, 3641.1
29: 8 Let not your prophets and **y** diviners, 3641.1
29: 8 neither hearken to **y** dreams which ye 3641.1
29:13 ye shall search for me with all **y** heart. 3641.1
29:14 I will turn away **y** captivity, and I will 3641.1
29:16 of **y** brethren that are not gone forth 3641.1
29:21 and he shall slay them before **y** eyes; 3641.1
30:22 my people, and I will be **y** God. 3641.1+3807.1
34:13 I made a covenant with **y** fathers in 3641.1
34:14 **y** fathers hearkened not unto me, 3641.1
35: 6 no wine, *neither* ye, nor **y** sons for ever: 3641.1
35: 7 but all **y** days ye shall dwell in tents; 3641.1
35:15 amend **y** doings, and go not after other 3641.1
35:15 I have given to you and to **y** fathers: 3641.1

Jer
35:15 have not inclined **y** ear, nor hearkened 3641.1
35:18 the commandment of Jonadab **y** father, 3641.1
37:19 Where *are* now **y** prophets which 3641.1
38: 5 the king said, Behold, he *is* in **y** hand: 3641.1
40:10 oil, and put *them* in **y** vessels, 3641.1
40:10 and dwell in **y** cities that ye have taken. 3641.1
42: 4 I *will* pray unto the LORD **y** God 3641.1
42: 4 LORD your God according to **y** words; 3641.1
42: 9 unto whom ye sent me to present **y** 3641.1
42:12 and cause you to return to **y own** land. 3641.1
42:13 neither obey the voice of the LORD **y** 3641.1
42:15 If ye wholly set **y** faces to enter *into* 3641.1
42:20 For ye dissembled in **y** hearts, when ye 3641.1
42:20 when ye sent me unto the LORD **y** God, 3641.1
42:21 obeyed the voice of the LORD **y** God, 3641.1
44: 3 not, *neither* they, you, nor **y** fathers. 3641.1
44: 7 ye *this* great evil against **y** souls, 3641.1
44: 8 unto wrath with the works of **y** hands, 3641.1
44: 9 Have ye forgotten the wickedness of **y** 3641.1
44: 9 **y own** wickedness, and the wickedness 3641.1
44: 9 and the wickedness of **y** wives, 3641.1
44:10 I set before you and before **y** fathers. 3641.1
44:21 ye, and **y** fathers, your kings, 3641.1
44:21 **y** kings, and your princes, and the 3641.1
44:21 **y** princes, and the people of the land, 3641.1
44:22 because of the evil of **y** doings, 3641.1
44:22 therefore is **y** land a desolation, and an 3641.1
44:25 **y** wives have both spoken with your 3641.1
44:25 and fulfilled with **y** hand, saying, 3641.1
44:25 ye will surely accomplish **y** vows, 3641.1
44:25 your vows, and surely perform **y** vows. 3641.1
46: 4 and stand forth with **y** helmets; NIH
48: 6 save **y** lives, and be like the heath in 3641.1
50:12 **Y** mother shall be sore confounded; 3641.1
51:24 that they have done in Zion in **y** sight, 3641.1
51:46 lest **y** heart faint, and ye fear for 3641.1
51:50 and let Jerusalem come into **y** mind. 3641.1
Eze
5:16 and will break **y** staff of bread: 3641.1+3807.1
6: 3 and I will destroy **y** high places. 3641.1
6: 4 **y** altars shall be desolate, 3641.1
6: 4 and **y** images shall be broken: 3641.1
6: 4 I will cast down **y** slain *men* before your 3641.1
6: 4 I will cast down your slain *men* before **y** 3641.1
6: 5 I will scatter **y** bones round about your 3641.1
6: 5 I will scatter your bones round about **y** 3641.1
6: 6 In all **y** dwelling places the cities shall 3641.1
6: 6 that **y** altars may be laid waste and 3641.1
6: 6 **y** idols may be broken and cease, 3641.1
6: 6 **y** images may be cut down, 3641.1
6: 6 down, and **y** works may be abolished. 3641.1
9: 5 let not **y** eye spare, neither have ye pity: 3641.1
11: 5 for I know the things that come into **y** 3641.1
11: 6 Ye have multiplied **y** slain in this city, 3641.1
11: 7 **Y** slain whom ye have laid in the midst 3641.1
11:11 This *city* shall not be **y** caldron, 3641.1+3807.1
12:11 Say, I *am* **y** sign: like as I have done, 3641.1
12:25 for in **y** days, O rebellious house, will I 3641.1
13:19 **y** lying to my people that hear *your* lies? 3641.1
13:19 your lying to my people that hear **y** lies? NIH
13:20 Behold, I *am* against **y** pillows, 3654.1
13:20 I will tear them from **y** arms, and will 3641.1
13:21 **Y** kerchiefs also will I tear, 3641.1
13:21 deliver my people out of **y** hand, 3641.1
13:21 they shall be no more in **y** hand to be 3654.1
13:23 for I will deliver my people out of **y** 3654.1
14: 6 and turn *yourselves* from **y** idols; 3641.1
14: 6 turn away **y** faces from all your 3641.1
14: 6 turn away your faces from all **y** 3641.1
16:45 **y** mother *was* a Hittite, and your father 3654.1
16:45 *was* a Hittite, and **y** father an Amorite. 3654.1
16:55 thy daughters shall return to **y** former 3641.1
18:25 way equal? are not **y** ways unequal? 3641.1
18:29 ways equal? are not **y** ways unequal? 3641.1
18:30 *yourselves* from all **y** transgressions; 3641.1
18:30 so iniquity shall not be **y** ruin. 3641.1+3807.1
18:31 Cast away from you all **y** transgressions, 3641.1
20: 5 saying, I *am* the LORD **y** God; 3641.1
20: 7 idols of Egypt: I *am* the LORD **y** God. 3641.1
20:18 Walk ye not in the statutes of **y** fathers, 3641.1
20:19 I *am* the LORD **y** God; walk in my 3641.1
20:20 that *ye* may know that I *am* the LORD **y** 3641.1
20:27 *in* this **y** fathers have blasphemed me, 3641.1
20:30 Are ye polluted after the manner of **y** 3641.1
20:31 when *ye* offer **y** gifts, when *ye* make 3641.1
20:31 when *ye* make **y** sons to pass through 3641.1
20:31 ye pollute yourselves with all **y** idols, 3641.1
20:32 which cometh into **y** mind shall not 3641.1
20:36 Like as I pleaded with **y** fathers in 3641.1
20:39 ye my holy name no more with **y** 3641.1
20:39 more with your gifts, and **y** idols. 3641.1
20:40 there will I require **y** offerings, 3641.1
20:40 the firstfruits of **y** oblations, with all 3641.1
20:40 of your oblations, with all **y** holy *things.* 3641.1
20:41 I will accept you with **y** sweet savour, NIH
20:42 up mine hand to give it to **y** fathers. 3641.1
20:43 there shall ye remember **y** ways, and all 3641.1
20:43 all **y** doings, wherein ye have been 3641.1
20:43 ye shall lothe yourselves in **y own** sight 3641.1
20:43 for all **y** evils that ye have committed. 3641.1
20:44 not according to **y** wicked ways, 3641.1
20:44 nor according to **y** corrupt doings, O ye 3641.1
21:24 Because ye have made **y** iniquity to be 3641.1
21:24 in that **y** transgressions are discovered, 3641.1
21:24 that in all **y** doings your sins do appear; 3641.1

Y

Eze
21:24 that in all your doings **y** sins do appear; 3641.1
23:48 be taught not to do after **y** lewdness. 3654.1
23:49 they shall recompense **y** lewdness upon 3654.1
23:49 and ye shall bear the sins of **y** idols: 3654.1
24:21 the excellency of **y** strength, the desire 3641.1
24:21 the desire of **y** eyes, and that which 3641.1
24:21 your sons, and that which **y** soul pitieth; 3641.1
24:21 **y** sons and your daughters whom ye 3641.1
24:21 **y** daughters whom ye have left shall fall 3641.1
24:22 ye shall not cover **y** lips, nor eat the bread NIH
24:23 **y** tires *shall be* upon your heads, 3641.1
24:23 your tires *shall be* upon **y** heads, 3641.1
24:23 **y** heads, and **y** shoes upon your feet: 3641.1
24:23 your heads, and your shoes upon **y** feet: 3641.1
24:23 ye shall pine away for **y** iniquities. 3641.1
33:11 turn ye, turn ye from **y** evil ways; 3641.1
33:25 lift up **y** eyes toward your idols, 3641.1
33:25 lift up your eyes toward **y** idols, 3641.1
33:26 Ye stand upon **y** sword, ye work 3641.1
34:18 ye must tread down with **y** feet 3641.1
34:18 with your feet the residue of **y** pastures? 3641.1
34:18 ye must foul the residue with **y** feet? 3641.1
34:19 that which ye have trodden with **y** feet; 3641.1
34:19 that which ye have fouled with **y** feet. 3641.1
34:21 and pusht all the diseased with **y** horns, 3641.1
34:31 men, *and* I *am* **y** God, saith the Lord 3641.1
35:13 Thus with **y** mouth ye have boasted 3641.1
35:13 have multiplied **y** words against me: 3641.1
36: 8 ye shall shoot forth **y** branches, 3641.1
36: 8 and yield **y** fruit to my people of Israel; 3641.1
36:11 I will settle you after **y** old estates, 3641.1
36:22 I do not *this* for **y** sakes, O house of 3641.1
36:24 and will bring you into **y** own land. 3641.1
36:25 from all **y** filthiness, and from all your 3641.1
36:25 and from all **y** idols, will I cleanse you. 3641.1
36:26 will take away the stony heart out of **y** 3641.1
36:28 shall dwell in the land that I gave to **y** 3641.1
36:28 my people, and I will be **y** God. 3641.1+3807.1
36:29 I will also save you from all **y** 3641.1
36:31 shall ye remember **y** own evil ways, 3641.1
36:31 **y** doings that *were* not good, 3641.1
36:31 shall lothe yourselves in **y** own sight for 3641.1
36:31 in your own sight for **y** iniquities 3641.1
36:31 your iniquities and for **y** abominations. 3641.1
36:32 Not for **y** sakes do I *this,* saith the Lord 3641.1
36:32 and confounded for **y** own ways, 3641.1
36:33 have cleansed you from all **y** iniquities, 3641.1
37:12 I *will* open **y** graves, and cause you to 3641.1
37:12 cause you to come up out of **y** graves, 3641.1
37:13 when I have opened **y** graves, O my 3641.1
37:13 and brought you up out of **y** graves, 3641.1
37:14 and I shall place you in **y** own land: 3641.1
37:25 servant, wherein **y** fathers have dwelt; 3641.1
43:27 the priests shall make **y** burnt offerings 3641.1
43:27 on the altar, and **y** peace offerings; 3641.1
44: 6 let it suffice you of all **y** abominations, 3641.1
44: 7 because of all **y** abominations. 3641.1
44:30 of every *sort* of **y** oblations, shall be 3641.1
44:30 give unto the priest the first of **y** dough, 3641.1
45: 9 take away **y** exactions from my people, 3641.1
45:12 shekels, shall be **y** maneh. 3641.1+3807.1
47:14 up mine hand to give it unto **y** fathers: 3641.1

Da
1:10 hath appointed **y** meat and your drink: 3641.1
1:10 hath appointed your meat and **y** drink: 3641.1
1:10 for why should he see **y** faces worse 3641.1
1:10 than the children which *are* of **y** sort? 3641.1
2: 5 and **y** houses shall be made a dunghill. 3561.1
2:47 Of a truth *it is,* that **y** God *is* a God of 3561.1
10:21 in these *things,* but Michael **y** prince. 3641.1

Hos
1: 9 and I will not be **y** *God.* 3641.1+3807.1
2: 1 Say ye unto **y** brethren, Ammi; 3641.1
2: 1 Ammi; and to **y** sisters, Ruhamah. 3641.1
2: 2 Plead with **y** mother, plead: for she *is* 3641.1
4:13 **y** daughters shall commit whoredom, 3641.1
4:13 and **y** spouses shall commit adultery. 3641.1
4:14 I will not punish **y** daughters when 3641.1
4:14 **y** spouses when they commit adultery: 3641.1
5:13 not heal you nor cure you of **y** wound. 3641.1
6: 4 for **y** goodness *is* as a morning cloud, 3641.1
9:10 I saw **y** fathers as the firstripe in the fig 3641.1
10:12 break up **y** fallow ground: 3641.1+3807.1
10:15 you because of **y** great wickedness: 3641.1

Joel
1: 2 Hath this been in **y** days, or even in 3641.1
1: 2 or even in the days of **y** fathers? 3641.1
1: 3 Tell ye **y** children of it, and *let* your 3641.1
1: 3 *let* **y** children *tell* their children, 3641.1
1: 5 wine, for it is cut off from **y** mouth. 3641.1
1:13 is withholden from the house of **y** God, 3641.1
1:14 land *into* the house of the LORD **y** God, 3641.1
2:12 turn ye *even* to me with all **y** heart, 3641.1
2:13 rent **y** heart, and not your garments, 3641.1
2:13 not **y** garments, and turn unto the LORD 3641.1
2:13 and turn unto the LORD **y** God: 3641.1
2:14 a drink offering unto the LORD **y** God? 3641.1
2:23 and rejoice in the LORD **y** God: 3641.1
2:26 praise the name of the LORD **y** God, 3641.1
2:27 *that* I *am* the LORD **y** God, 3641.1
2:28 **y** sons and your daughters shall 3641.1
2:28 sons and **y** daughters shall prophesy, 3641.1
2:28 **y** old men shall dream dreams, 3641.1
2:28 **y** young men shall see visions: 3641.1
3: 4 speedily will I return **y** recompence 3641.1
3: 4 your recompence upon **y** own head; 3641.1
3: 5 have carried into **y** temples my goodly 3641.1

Joel
3: 7 return **y** recompence upon your own 3641.1
3: 7 return your recompence upon **y** own 3641.1
3: 8 I will sell **y** sons and your daughters into 3641.1
3: 8 **y** daughters into the hand of the 3641.1
3:10 Beat **y** plowshares into swords, 3641.1
3:10 and **y** pruninghooks into spears: 3641.1
3:17 So shall ye know that I *am* the LORD **y** 3641.1

Am
2:11 I raised up of **y** sons for prophets, 3641.1
2:11 and of **y** young men for Nazarites. 3641.1
3: 2 I will punish you for all **y** iniquities. 3641.1
4: 2 and **y** posterity with fishhooks. 3654.1
4: 4 bring **y** sacrifices *every* morning, 3641.1
4: 4 *and* **y** tithes after three years: 3641.1
4: 6 you cleanness of teeth in all **y** cities, 3641.1
4: 6 and want of bread in all **y** places: 3641.1
4: 9 when **y** gardens and your vineyards and 3641.1
4: 9 **y** vineyards and your fig trees and 3641.1
4: 9 your vineyards and **y** fig trees and 3641.1
4: 9 fig trees and **y** olive trees increased, 3641.1
4:10 **y** young men have I slain with the 3641.1
4:10 sword, and have taken away **y** horses; 3641.1
4:10 I have made the stink of **y** camps to 3641.1
4:10 your camps to come up unto **y** nostrils: 3641.1
5:11 as **y** treading *is* upon the poor, 3641.1
5:12 For I know **y** manifold transgressions 3641.1
5:12 and **y** mighty sins: 3641.1
5:21 I despise **y** feast *days,* and I will not 3641.1
5:21 I will not smell in **y** solemn assemblies. 3641.1
5:22 me burnt offerings and **y** meat offerings, 3641.1
5:22 the peace offerings of **y** fat beasts. 3641.1
5:26 have borne the tabernacle of **y** Moloch 3641.1
5:26 of your Moloch and Chiun **y** images, 3641.1
5:26 Chiun your images, the star of **y** god, 3641.1
6: 2 or their border greater than **y** border? 3641.1
8:10 I will turn **y** feasts into mourning, 3641.1
8:10 and all **y** songs into lamentation: 3641.1

Mic
2: 3 which ye shall not remove **y** necks; 3641.1
2:10 Arise ye, and depart; for this *is* not **y** rest: NIH
3:12 shall Zion for **y** sake be plowed 3641.1

Hab
1: 5 For I *will* work a work in **y** days, 3641.1

Zep
3:20 I turn back **y** captivity before your 3641.1
3:20 I turn back your captivity before **y** 3641.1

Hag
1: 4 to dwell in **y** cieled houses, and this 3641.1
1: 5 the LORD of hosts; Consider **y** ways. 3641.1
1: 7 the LORD of hosts; Consider **y** ways. 3641.1
2: 3 *is it* not in **y** eyes in comparison of it as 3641.1
2:17 with hail *in* all the labours of **y** hands; 3641.1

Zec
1: 2 been sore displeased with **y** fathers. 3641.1
1: 4 Be ye not as **y** fathers, unto whom 3641.1
1: 4 Turn ye now from **y** evil ways, 3641.1
1: 4 your evil ways, and *from* **y** evil doings: 3641.1
1: 5 **Y** fathers, where *are* they? 3641.1
1: 6 did they not take hold of **y** fathers? 3641.1
6:15 obey the voice of the LORD **y** God. 3641.1
7:10 evil against his brother in **y** heart. 3641.1
8: 9 Let **y** hands be strong, ye that hear in 3641.1
8:13 fear not, *but* let **y** hands be strong. 3641.1
8:14 when **y** fathers provoked me to wrath, 3641.1
8:16 judgment of truth and peace in **y** gates: 3641.1
8:17 let none of you imagine evil in **y** hearts 3641.1

Mal
1: 9 **y** eyes shall see, and ye shall say, 3641.1
1: 9 this hath been by **y** means: will he 3641.1
1: 9 will he regard **y** persons? saith 3641.1
1:10 will I accept an offering at **y** hand. 3641.1
1:13 should I accept this of **y** hand? saith 3641.1
2: 2 upon you, and will curse **y** blessings: 3641.1
2: 3 I *will* corrupt **y**ˢ seed, and spread dung 1886.1
2: 3 seed, and spread dung upon **y** faces, 3641.1
2: 3 *even* the dung of **y** solemn feasts; 3641.1
2:13 or receiveth *it* with good will at **y** hand. 3641.1
2:15 Therefore take heed to **y** spirit, 3641.1
2:16 therefore take heed to **y** spirit, that ye 3641.1
2:17 Ye have wearied the LORD with **y** 3641.1
3: 7 Even from the days of **y** fathers ye are 3641.1
3:11 I will rebuke the devourer for **y** sakes, 3641.1
3:11 shall not destroy the fruits of **y** ground; 3641.1
3:11 neither shall **y** vine cast her 3641.1+3807.1
3:13 **Y** words have been stout against me, 3641.1
3: 3 **y** feet in the day that I *shall* do *this,* 3641.1

Mt
5:12 for great *is* **y** reward in heaven: for so 4771
5:16 Let **y** light so shine before men, that they 4771
5:16 that they may see **y** good works, 4771
5:16 and glorify **y** Father which is in heaven. 4771
5:20 That except **y** righteousness shall exceed 4771
5:37 let **y** communication be, Yea, yea; Nay, 4771
5:44 But I say unto you, Love **y** enemies, 4771
5:45 That ye may be the children of **y** Father 4771
5:47 And if ye salute **y** brethren only, what do 4771
5:48 even as **y** Father which is in heaven is 4771
6: 1 Take heed that *ye* do not **y** alms before 4771
6: 1 otherwise ye have no reward of **y** Father 4771
6: 8 for **y** Father knoweth what *things* ye have 4771
6:14 **y** heavenly Father will also forgive you: 4771
6:15 neither will **y** Father forgive your 4771
6:15 neither will your Father forgive **y** 4771
6:21 For where **y** treasure is, there will your 4771
6:21 your treasure is, there will **y** heart be also. 4771
6:25 Take no thought for **y** life, what ye shall 4771
6:25 nor yet for **y** body, what ye shall put on. 4771
6:26 yet **y** heavenly Father feedeth them. 4771
6:32 for **y** heavenly Father knoweth that ye 4771
7: 6 neither cast ye **y** pearls before swine, 4771
7:11 know how to give good gifts unto **y** 4771
7:11 how much more shall **y** Father which is 4771
9: 4 Wherefore think ye evil in **y** hearts? 4771

Mt
9:11 Why eateth **y** Master with publicans and 4771
9:29 According to **y** faith be it unto you. 4771
10: 9 nor silver, nor brass in **y** purses; 4771
10:10 Nor scrip for **y** journey, neither two coats, NIG
10:13 be worthy, let **y** peace come upon it: 4771
10:13 be not worthy, let **y** peace return to you. 4771
10:14 nor hear **y** words, when ye depart out of 4771
10:14 or city, shake off the dust of **y** feet. 4771
10:20 the Spirit of **y** Father which speaketh in 4771
10:29 not fall on the ground without **y** Father. 4771
10:30 But the very hairs of **y** head are all 4771
11:29 heart: and ye shall find rest unto **y** souls. 4771
12:27 by whom do **y** children cast *them* out? 4771
12:27 therefore they shall be **y** judges. 4771
13:16 But blessed *are* **y** eyes, for they see: 4771
13:16 for they see: and **y** ears, for they hear. 4771
15: 3 the commandment of God by **y** tradition? 4771
15: 6 of God of none effect by **y** tradition. 4771
17:20 said unto them, Because of **y** unbelief; 4771
17:24 and said, Doth not **y** master pay tribute? 4771
18:14 it is not the will of **y** Father which is in 4771
18:35 if ye from **y** hearts forgive not every one 4771
19: 8 of the hardness of **y** hearts suffered you to 4771
19: 8 hearts suffered you to put away **y** wives: 4771
20:26 great among you, let him be **y** minister; 4771
20:27 be chief among you, let him be **y** servant: 4771
23: 8 for one is **y** Master, *even* Christ; 4771
23: 9 And call no *man* **y** father upon the earth: 4771
23: 9 for one is **y** Father, which is in heaven. 4771
23:10 for one is **y** Master, *even* Christ. 4771
23:11 he that is greatest among you shall be **y** 4771
23:32 Fill ye up then the measure of **y** fathers. 4771
23:34 *some* of them shall ye scourge in **y** 4771
23:38 Behold, **y** house is left unto you desolate. 4771
24:20 But pray ye that **y** flight be not in 4771
24:42 ye know not what hour **y** Lord doth 4771
25: 8 said unto the wise, Give us of **y** oil; 4771
26:45 unto them, Sleep on now, and take **y** rest: NIG
27:65 go **y** way, make *it* as sure as you can. NIG

Mk
2: 8 Why reason ye these *things* in **y** hearts? 4771
6:11 shake off the dust under **y** feet for a 4771
7: 9 God, that ye may keep **y** own tradition. 4771
7:13 of God of none effect through **y** tradition, 4771
8:17 have ye **y** heart yet hardened? 4771
10: 5 For the hardness of **y** heart he wrote you 4771
10:43 be great among you, shall be **y** minister: 4771
11: 2 Go **y** way into the village over against you: NIG
11:25 that **y** Father also which is in heaven may 4771
11:25 in heaven may forgive you **y** trespasses. 4771
11:26 neither will **y** Father which is in heaven 4771
11:26 which is in heaven forgive **y** trespasses. 4771
13:18 And pray ye that **y** flight be not in 4771
14:41 unto them, Sleep on now, and take **y** rest: NIG
16: 7 But go **y** way, tell his disciples and Peter NIG

Lk
3:14 *any* falsely; and be content with **y** wages. 4771
4:21 This day is this scripture fulfilled in **y** ears. 4771
5: 4 deep, and let down **y** nets for a draught. 4771
5:22 unto them, What reason ye in **y** hearts? 4771
6:22 reproach *you,* and cast out **y** name as evil, 4771
6:23 for behold, **y** reward *is* great in heaven: 4771
6:24 rich: for ye have received **y** consolation. 4771
6:27 say unto you which hear, Love **y** enemies, 4771
6:35 But love ye **y** enemies, and do good, 4771
6:35 **y** reward shall be great, and ye shall be 4771
6:36 merciful, as **y** Father also is merciful. 4771
6:38 over, shall *men* give into **y** bosom. 4771
7:22 Go **y** way, and tell John what *things* ye 4771
8:25 And he said unto them, Where is **y** faith? 4771
9: 3 Take nothing for **y** journey, neither staves, NIG
9: 5 shake off the very dust from **y** feet for a 4771
9:44 Let these sayings sink down into **y** ears: 4771
10: 3 Go **y** ways: behold, I send you forth as NIG
10: 6 peace be there, **y** peace shall rest upon it: 4771
10:10 go **y** ways out into the streets of the same, NIG
10:11 the *very* dust of **y** city, which cleaveth 4771
10:20 because **y** names are written in heaven. 4771
11:13 know how to give good gifts unto **y** 4771
11:13 how much more shall **y** heavenly Father NIG
11:19 by whom do **y** sons cast *them* out? 4771
11:19 therefore shall they be **y** judges. 4771
11:39 but **y** inward part is full of ravening and 4771
11:46 not the burdens with one of **y** fingers. 4771
11:47 of the prophets, and **y** fathers killed them. 4771
11:48 that ye allow the deeds of **y** fathers: 4771
12: 7 But even the *very* hairs of **y** head are all 4771
12:22 Take no thought for **y** life, what ye shall 4771
12:30 **y** Father knoweth that ye have need of 4771
12:32 for it is **y** Father's good pleasure to give 4771
12:34 For where **y** treasure is, there will your 4771
12:34 your treasure is, there will **y** heart be also. 4771
12:35 Let **y** loins be girded about, and *your* 4771
12:35 be girded about, and **y** lights burning; NIG
13:35 Behold, **y** house is left unto you desolate: 4771
16:11 will commit to **y** trust the true *riches?* 4771
16:12 who shall give you that which is **y** own? 5212
16:15 before men; but God knoweth **y** hearts: 4771
19:30 at **y** entering ye shall find a colt tied, NIG
21:14 Settle *it* therefore in **y** hearts, not to 4771
21:15 all **y** adversaries shall not be able to 4771
21:18 there shall not a hair of **y** head perish. 4771
21:19 In **y** patience possess ye your souls. 4771
21:19 In your patience possess ye **y** souls. 4771
21:28 to pass; *then* look up, and lift up **y** heads; 4771
21:28 heads; for **y** redemption draweth nigh. 4771
21:30 know of **y** own selves that summer is 1438

Y

Lk
21:34 lest at any time **y** hearts be overcharged — 4771
22:53 but this is **y** hour, and the power of — 4771
23:28 weep for yourselves, and for **y** children. — 4771
24:38 and why do thoughts arise in **y** hearts? — 4771

Jn
4:35 Lift up **y** eyes, and look on the fields; — 4771
6:49 **Y** fathers did eat manna in the wilderness, — 4771
6:58 not as **y** fathers did eat manna, — 4771
7: 6 is not yet come: but **y** time is alway ready. — 5212
8:17 It is also written in **y** law, that — 5212
8:21 ye shall seek me, and shall die in **y** sins: — 4771
8:24 unto you, that ye shall die in **y** sins: — 4771
8:24 not that I am *he*, ye shall die in **y** sins. — 4771
8:38 ye do *that* which ye have seen with **y** — 4771
8:41 Ye do the deeds of **y** father. Then said — 4771
8:42 If God were **y** Father, ye would love me: — 4771
8:44 Ye are of **y** father the devil, and the lusts — NIG
8:44 and the lusts of **y** father ye will do. — 4771
8:54 of whom ye say, that he is **y** God: — 4771
8:56 **Y** father Abraham rejoiced to see my day: — 4771
9:19 they asked them, saying, Is this **y** son, — 4771
9:41 ye say, We see; therefore **y** sin remaineth. — 4771
10:34 Is it not written in **y** law, I said, Ye are — 4771
11:15 And I am glad for **y** sakes that I was not — 4771
12:30 came not because of me, but for **y** sakes. — 4771
13:14 If I then, **y** Lord and Master, have washed — NIG
13:14 Lord and Master, have washed **y** feet; — 4771
14: 1 Let not **y** heart be troubled: ye believe in — 4771
14:26 and bring all *things* to **y** remembrance, — 4771
14:27 Let not **y** heart be troubled, neither let it — 4771
15:11 in you, and that **y** joy might be full. — 4771
15:16 forth fruit, and that **y** fruit should remain: — 4771
16: 6 unto you, sorrow hath filled **y** heart. — 4771
16:20 but **y** sorrow shall be turned into joy. — 4771
16:22 and **y** heart shall rejoice, and your joy no — 4771
16:22 **y** joy no *man* taketh from you. — 4771
16:24 ye shall receive, that **y** joy may be full. — 4771
18:31 him, and judge him according to **y** law. — 4771
19:14 he saith unto the Jews, Behold **y** King? — 4771
19:15 saith unto them, Shall I crucify **y** King? — 4771
20:17 I ascend unto my Father, and **y** Father; — 4771
20:17 your Father; and to my God, and **y** God. — 4771

Ac
2:17 and **y** sons and your daughters shall — 4771
2:17 your sons and **y** daughters shall prophesy, — 4771
2:17 and **y** young men shall see visions, — 4771
2:17 and **y** old men shall dream dreams: — 4771
2:39 and to **y** children, and to all that are afar — 4771
3:17 ignorance ye did *it*, as *did* also **y** rulers. — 4771
3:19 that **y** sins may be blotted out, — 4771
3:22 A prophet shall the Lord **y** God raise up — 4771
3:22 your God raise up unto you of **y** brethren, — 4771
5:28 ye have filled Jerusalem with **y** doctrine, — 4771
7:37 A prophet shall the Lord **y** God raise up — 4771
7:37 your God raise up unto you of **y** brethren, — 4771
7:43 Moloch, and the star of **y** god Remphan, — 4771
7:51 the Holy Ghost: as **y** fathers *did*, so do ye. — 4771
7:52 Which of the prophets have not **y** fathers — 4771
13:41 for I work a work in **y** days, a work which — 4771
15:24 subverting **y** souls, saying, *Ye must be* — 4771
17:23 as I passed by, and beheld **y** devotions, — 4771
17:28 as certain also of **y** own poets have — 2596+4771
18: 6 **Y** blood *be* upon your own heads; — 4771
18: 6 Your blood *be* upon **y** own heads; — 4771
18:15 of words and names, and *of* **y** law, — 2596+4771
19:37 nor yet blasphemers of **y** goddess. — 4771
20:30 Also of **y** own selves shall men arise, — 4771
24:22 I will know the uttermost of **y** matters. — 4771
27:34 for this is for **y** health: for there shall not — 5212

Ro
1: 8 that **y** faith is spoken of throughout — 4771
6:12 not sin therefore reign in **y** mortal body, — 4771
6:13 Neither yield ye **y** members *as* — 4771
6:13 **y** members *as* instruments of — 4771
6:19 of men because of the infirmity of **y** flesh: — 4771
6:19 as ye have yielded **y** members servants — 4771
6:19 now yield **y** members servants to — 4771
6:22 ye have **y** fruit unto holiness, and the end — 4771
8:11 **y** mortal bodies by his Spirit that dwelleth — 4771
11:25 lest ye should be wise in **y** own conceits; — 1438
11:28 the gospel, *they are* enemies for **y** sakes; — 1438
11:31 that through **y** mercy they also may obtain — 5212
12: 1 that ye present **y** bodies a living sacrifice, — 4771
12: 1 unto God, which *is* **y** reasonable service. — 4771
12: 2 be ye transformed by the renewing of **y** — 4771
12:16 low estate. Be not wise in **y** own conceits. — 1438
14:16 Let not then **y** good be evil spoken of: — 4771
15:24 if first I be somewhat filled with **y** — 4771
15:30 ye strive together with me in **y** prayers — NIG
16:19 For **y** obedience is come abroad unto all — 4771
16:19 all *men*. I am glad therefore on **y** behalf: — 4771
16:20 shall bruise Satan under **y** feet shortly. — 4771

1Co
1: 4 I thank my God always on **y** behalf, — 4771
1:26 ye see **y** calling, brethren, how that not — 4771
2: 5 **y** faith should not stand in the wisdom — 4771
4: 6 to myself and *to* Apollos for **y** sakes; — 4771
5: 6 **Y** glorying *is* not good. Know ye not that — 4771
6: 5 I speak to **y** shame. Is it so, that there is — 4771
6: 8 wrong, and defraud, and that **y** brethren. — NIG
6:15 Know ye not that **y** bodies are the — 4771
6:19 know ye not that **y** body is the temple of — 4771
6:19 ye have of God, and ye are not **y** own? — 1438
6:20 therefore glorify God in **y** body, — 4771
6:20 body, and in **y** spirit, which are God's. — 4771
7: 5 that Satan tempt you not for **y** — 4771
7:14 else were **y** children unclean; but now — 4771
7:35 this I speak for **y** own profit; not that I — 4771
9:11 *thing* if we shall reap **y** carnal *things*? — 4771

1Co
14:34 **y** women keep silence in the churches: — 4771
15:14 preaching vain, and **y** faith *is* also vain. — 4771
15:17 And if Christ be not raised, **y** faith *is* vain; — 4771
15:17 your faith *is* vain; ye are yet in **y** sins. — 4771
15:31 I protest by **y** rejoicing which I have in — 5212
15:34 of God: I speak *this* to **y** shame. — 4771
15:58 as you know that **y** labour is not — NIG
16: 3 you shall approve by **y** letters, — NIG
16: 3 them will I send to bring **y** liberality unto — 4771
16:14 Let all **y** things be done with charity. — 4771
16:17 for that which was lacking on **y** part they — 4771

2Co
1: 6 *it is* for **y** consolation and salvation, — 4771
1: 6 *it is* for **y** consolation and salvation. — 4771
1:14 us in part, that we are **y** rejoicing, — 4771
1:24 for that we have dominion over **y** faith, — 4771
1:24 over your faith, but are helpers of **y** joy: — 4771
2: 8 *you* would confirm **y** love towards him. — NIG
2:10 **y** sakes *forgave I it* in the person of Christ; — 4771
4: 5 and ourselves **y** servants for Jesus' sake. — 4771
4:15 For all things *are* for **y** sakes, that — 4771
5:11 I trust also are made manifest in **y** — 4771
5:13 or whether we be sober, *it is* for **y** cause. — 4771
6:12 but ye are straitened in **y** own bowels. — 4771
7: 7 when he told us **y** earnest desire, your — 4771
7: 7 **y** mourning, your fervent mind toward — 4771
7: 7 your mourning, **y** fervent mind toward — 4771
7:13 we were comforted in **y** comfort: — 4771
8: 7 *in all* diligence, and *in* **y** love to us, — 1537+4771
8: 8 and to prove the sincerity of **y** love. — 5212
8: 9 was rich, *yet* for **y** sakes he became poor, — 4771
8:14 now at *this* time **y** abundance *may be a* — 4771
8:14 also may be a *supply* for **y** want: — 4771
8:19 and *declaration of* **y** ready mind: — 4771
8:24 the proof of **y** love, and of our boasting on — 4771
8:24 your love, and of our boasting on **y** behalf. — 4771
9: 2 For I know the forwardness of **y** mind, — 4771
9: 2 **y** zeal hath provoked very many. — 4771
9: 5 and make up beforehand **y** bounty, — 4771
9:10 the sower both minister bread for **y** food, — NIG
9:10 and multiply **y** seed sown, and increase — 4771
9:10 and increase the fruits of **y** righteousness;) — 4771
9:13 **y** professed subjection unto the gospel of — 4771
9:13 and *for* **y** liberal distribution unto them, — NIG
10: 6 when **y** obedience is fulfilled. — 4771
10: 8 and not for **y** destruction, I should not be — 4771
10:15 having hope, when **y** faith is increased, — 4771
11: 3 **y** minds should be corrupted from — 4771
12:19 all *things*, dearly beloved, for **y** edifying. — 4771
13: 5 ye be in the faith; prove **y** own selves. — 1438
13: 5 Know ye not **y** own selves, how that — 1438
13: 9 and this also we wish, *even* **y** perfection. — 4771

Gal
4: 6 forth the Spirit of his Son into **y** hearts, — 4771
4:15 ye would have plucked out **y** own eyes, — 4771
4:16 Am I therefore become **y** enemy, because — 4771
6:13 that they may glory in **y** flesh. — 5212
6:18 grace of our Lord Jesus Christ *be* with **y** — 4771

Eph
1:13 word of truth, the gospel of **y** salvation: — 4771
1:15 after I heard of **y** faith in the Lord Jesus, — 4771
1:18 The eyes of **y** understanding being — 4771
3:13 my tribulations for you, which is **y** glory. — 4771
3:17 That Christ may dwell in **y** hearts by faith; — 4771
4: 4 even as ye are called in one hope of **y** — 4771
4:23 And be renewed in the spirit of **y** mind; — 4771
4:26 let not the sun go down upon **y** wrath: — 4771
4:29 communication proceed out of **y** mouth, — 4771
5:19 and making melody in **y** heart to the Lord; — 4771
5:22 submit yourselves unto **y** own husbands, — 2398
5:25 Husbands, love **y** wives, even as Christ — 1438
6: 1 Children, obey **y** parents in the Lord: — 4771
6: 4 fathers, provoke not **y** children to wrath: — 4771
6: 5 be obedient to *them that are* **y** masters — NIG
6: 5 and trembling, in singleness of **y** heart, — 4771
6: 9 knowing that **y** Master also is in heaven; — 4771
6:14 having **y** loins girt about with truth, — 4771
6:15 And **y** feet shod with the preparation of — NIG
6:22 and *that* he might comfort **y** hearts. — 4771

Php
1: 5 **y** fellowship in the gospel from the first — 4771
1: 9 that **y** love may abound yet more and — 4771
1:19 turn to my salvation through **y** prayer, — 4771
1:25 continue with you all for **y** furtherance — 4771
1:26 That **y** rejoicing may be *more* abundant in — 4771
1:27 Only let **y** conversation be as it becometh — NIG
1:27 or *else* be absent, I may hear of **y** affairs, — 4771
1:28 And in nothing terrified by **y** adversaries: — NIG
2:12 work out **y** own salvation with fear and — 1438
2:17 upon the sacrifice and service of **y** faith, — 4771
2:19 be of good comfort, when I know **y** state. — 4771
2:20 who will naturally care for **y** state. — 4771
2:25 but **y** messenger, and he that ministered — 4771
2:30 to supply **y** lack of service toward me. — 4771
4: 5 Let **y** moderation be known unto all men. — 4771
4: 6 supplication with thanksgiving let **y** — 4771
4: 7 shall keep **y** hearts and minds through — 4771
4:10 that now at the last **y** care of me hath — 3588
4:17 desire fruit that *may* abound to **y** account. — 4771
4:19 But my God shall supply all **y** need — 4771

Col
1: 4 Since we heard of **y** faith in Christ Jesus, — 4771
1: 8 Who also declared unto us **y** love in — 4771
1:21 and enemies in **y** mind by wicked works, — NIG
2: 5 joying and beholding **y** order, — 4771
2: 5 and the stedfastness of **y** faith in Christ. — 4771
2:13 dead in **y** sins and the uncircumcision — NIG
2:13 sins and the uncircumcision of **y** flesh, — 4771
2:18 Let no *man* beguile you of **y** reward in a — NIG
3: 2 Set **y** affection on *things* above, not on — NIG

Col
3: 3 and **y** life is hid with Christ in God. — 4771
3: 5 **y** members which are upon the earth; — 4771
3: 8 filthy communication out of **y** mouth. — 4771
3:15 And let the peace of God rule in **y** hearts, — 4771
3:16 singing with grace in **y** hearts to the Lord. — 4771
3:18 submit yourselves unto **y** own husbands, — 2398
3:19 love **y** wives, and be not bitter against — NIG
3:20 obey **y** parents in all *things*: for this is well — NIG
3:21 provoke not **y** children *to anger*, lest they — 4771
3:22 obey in all *things* **y** masters according to — NIG
4: 1 give unto **y** servants that which is just and — NIG
4: 6 Let **y** speech *be* alway with grace, — 4771
4: 8 that he might know **y** estate, — 4771
4: 8 know your estate, and comfort **y** hearts; — 4771

1Th
1: 3 Remembering without ceasing **y** work of — 4771
1: 4 brethren beloved, **y** election of God. — 4771
1: 5 of *men* we were among you for **y** sake. — 4771
1: 8 also in every place **y** faith to God-ward is — 4771
2:14 suffered like *things* of **y** own countrymen, — 2398
2:17 endeavoured the more abundantly to see **y** — 4771
3: 2 and to comfort you concerning **y** faith: — 4771
3: 5 no longer forbear, I sent to know **y** faith, — 4771
3: 6 and brought us good tidings of **y** faith and — 4771
3: 7 in all our affliction and distress, by **y** faith: — 4771
3: 9 all the joy wherewith we joy for **y** sakes — 4771
3:10 exceedingly that *we* might see **y** face, — 4771
3:10 might perfect that which is lacking in **y** — 4771
3:13 To the end *he* may stablish **y** hearts — 4771
4: 3 is the will of God, *even* **y** sanctification, — 4771
4:11 to do **y** own business, and to work with — 2398
4:11 and to work with **y** own hands, — 4771
5:23 *I pray God* **y** whole spirit and soul and — 4771

2Th
1: 3 because that **y** faith groweth exceedingly, — 4771
1: 4 you in the churches of God for **y** patience — 4771
1: 4 and faith in all **y** persecutions and — 4771
2:17 Comfort **y** hearts, and stablish you in — 4771
3: 5 And the Lord direct **y** hearts into the love — 4771

Phm
1:22 for I trust that through **y** prayers I shall be — 4771
1:25 of our Lord Jesus Christ *be* with **y** spirit. — 4771

Heb
3: 8 Harden not **y** hearts, as in the — 4771
3: 9 When **y** fathers tempted me, proved me, — 4771
3:15 harden not **y** hearts, as in the provocation. — 4771
4: 7 will hear his voice, harden not **y** hearts. — 4771
6:10 God *is* not unrighteous to forget **y** work — 4771
9:14 purge **y** conscience from dead works to — 4771
10:34 and took joyfully the spoiling of **y** goods, — 4771
10:35 Cast not away therefore **y** confidence, — 4771
12: 3 lest ye be wearied and faint in **y** minds. — 4771
12:13 And make straight paths for **y** feet, lest — 4771
13: 5 *Let* **y** conversation *be* without — NIG
13:17 they watch for **y** souls, as they that must — 4771

Jas
1: 3 Knowing *this,* that the trying of **y** faith — 4771
1:21 which is able to save **y** souls. — 4771
1:22 not hearers only, deceiving **y** own selves. — 1438
2: 2 For if there come unto **y** assembly a man — 4771
3:14 have bitter envying and strife in **y** hearts, — 4771
4: 1 *even* of **y** lusts that war in your members? — 4771
4: 1 *even* of your lusts that war in **y** members? — 4771
4: 3 that ye may consume *it* upon **y** lusts. — 4771
4: 8 Cleanse **y** hands, ye sinners; and purify — NIG
4: 8 and purify **y** hearts, *ye* double minded. — NIG
4: 9 let **y** laughter be turned to mourning, — 4771
4: 9 to mourning, and **y** joy to heaviness. — NIG
4:14 for what *is* **y** life? It is even a vapour, — 4771
4:16 But now ye rejoice in **y** boastings: all such — 4771
5: 1 howl for **y** miseries that shall come upon — 4771
5: 2 **Y** riches are corrupted, and your garments — 4771
5: 2 and **y** garments are motheaten. — 4771
5: 3 **Y** gold and silver is cankered; and the rust — 4771
5: 3 and shall eat **y** flesh as *it were* fire: — 4771
5: 4 which have reaped *down* **y** fields, — 4771
5: 5 ye have nourished **y** hearts, as in a day of — 4771
5: 8 Be ye also patient; stablish **y** hearts: — 4771
5:12 but let **y** yea be yea; and *your* nay, nay; — 4771
5:12 but let your yea be yea; and **y** nay, nay; — NIG
5:16 Confess **y** faults one to another, — NIG

1Pe
1: 7 That the trial of **y** faith, *being* much more — 4771
1: 9 Receiving the end of **y** faith, *even* — 4771
1: 9 of your faith, *even* the salvation of **y** souls. — NIG
1:13 Wherefore gird up the loins of **y** mind, — 4771
1:14 to the former lusts in **y** ignorance: — 4771
1:17 pass the time of **y** sojourning *here* in fear: — 4771
1:18 from **y** vain conversation received by — 4771
1:18 received by tradition from **y** fathers; — NIG
1:21 that **y** faith and hope might be in God. — 4771
1:22 Seeing ye have purified **y** souls in obeying — 4771
2:12 Having **y** conversation honest among — 4771
2:12 they may by **y** good works, *which* they — NIG
2:16 not using **y** liberty for a cloke of — NIG
2:18 *be* subject to **y** masters with all fear; — NIG
2:20 is it, if, when ye be buffeted for **y** faults, — NIG
2:25 unto the Shepherd and Bishop of **y** souls. — 4771
3: 1 *be* in subjection to **y** own husbands; — 2398
3: 2 While they behold **y** chaste conversation — 4771
3: 7 of life; that **y** prayers be not hindered. — 4771
3:15 But sanctify the Lord God in **y** hearts: — 4771
3:16 they may be ashamed that falsely accuse **y** — 4771
4:14 evil spoken of, but on **y** part he is glorified. — 4771
5: 2 Casting all **y** care upon him; for he careth — 4771
5: 8 **y** adversary the devil, as a roaring — 4771
5: 9 **y** brethren that are in the world. — 4771

2Pe
1: 5 giving all diligence, add to **y** faith virtue; — 4771
1:10 give diligence to make **y** calling and — 4771
1:19 dawn, and the day star arise in **y** hearts: — 4771
3: 1 both which I stir up **y** pure minds by way — 4771

Y

2Pe 3:17 the wicked, fall from **y** own stedfastness. *2398*
1Jn 1: 4 write we unto you, that **y** joy may be full. *4771*
 2:12 **y** sins are forgiven you for his name's sake. NIG
2Jn 1:10 doctrine, receive him not into **y** house, *4771*
Jude 1:12 These are spots in **y** feasts of charity when *4771*
 1:20 building up yourselves on **y** most holy *4771*
Rev 1: 9 who also am **y** brother, and companion in *4771*
 2:23 every one of you according to **y** works. *4771*
 16: 1 Go **y** ways, and pour out the vials of NIG

YOURS (12) [YOU]

Ge 45:20 of all the land of Egypt *is* **y**. *3641.1+3807.1*
Dt 11:24 your feet shall tread shall be **y**: *3641.1+3807.1*
Jos 2:14 the men answered her, Our life for **y**, *3641.1*
2Ch 20:15 the battle *is not* **y**, but God's. *3641.1+3807.1*
Jer 5:19 strangers in a land *that is* not **y**. *3641.1+3807.1*
Lk 6:20 *be ye* poor: for **y** is the kingdom of God. *5212*
Jn 15:20 kept my saying, they will keep **y** also. *5212*
1Co 3:21 man glory in men. For all *things* are **y**; *4771*
 3:22 present, or *things* to come; all are **y**; *4771*
 8: 9 **y** become a stumblingblock to them that *4771*
 16:18 For they have refreshed my spirit and **y**: *4771*
2Co 12:14 to you: for I seek not **y**, *3588+4771*

YOURSELVES (191) [SELF, YOU]

Ge 18: 4 wash your feet, and rest **y** under the tree: NIH
 45: 5 be not grieved, nor angry with **y**, *3641.1*
 49: 1 unto his sons, and said, Gather **y** together, NIH
 49: 2 Gather **y** together, and hear, ye sons of NIH
Ex 19:12 Take heed to **y**, *that ye* go not up *3641.1*
 30:37 you shall not make to **y** according to *3641.1*
 32:29 Consecrate **y** to day to the Lord, *3641.1*
Lev 11:43 Ye shall not make **y** abominable *5315+3641.1*
 11:43 shall ye make **y** unclean with them, NIH
 11:44 ye shall therefore sanctify **y**, and ye shall NIH
 11:44 neither shall ye defile **y** with any *5315+3641.1*
 18:24 Defile not you **y** in any of these *things*: for NIH
 18:30 you, and that ye **defile** not **y** therein: *2930*
 19: 4 unto idols, nor make to **y** molten gods: NIH
 20: 7 Sanctify **y** therefore, and be ye holy: for I NIH
Nu 11:18 Sanctify **y** against to morrow, and ye shall NIH
 16: 3 lift you up **y** above the congregation of NIH
 16:21 Separate **y** from among this congregation, NIH
 31: 3 Arm some of **y** unto the war, and let *3641.1*
 31:18 man by lying with him, keep alive for **y**. *3641.1*
 31:19 purify *both* **y** and your captives on the *859*
Dt 2: 4 you: take ye good heed unto **y** therefore: NIH
 4:15 therefore good heed unto **y**; *5315+3641.1*
 4:16 Lest ye corrupt **y**, and make you a graven NIH
 4:23 Take heed unto **y**, lest ye forget *3641.1*
 4:25 shall corrupt **y**, and make a graven image, NIH
 11:16 Take heed to **y**, that your heart be not *3641.1*
 11:23 greater nations and mightier than **y**. *3641.1*
 14: 1 ye shall not cut **y**, nor make *any* baldness NIH
 31:14 present in the tabernacle of NIH
 31:29 after my death ye will utterly corrupt **y**, NIH
Jos 2:16 hide ye there three days, until the pursuers NIH
 3: 5 Joshua said unto the people, Sanctify **y**: NIH
 6:18 any wise keep **y** from the accursed thing, NIH
 6:18 lest ye make **y** accursed, when ye take of NIH
 7:13 and say, Sanctify **y** against to morrow: NIH
 8: 2 shall ye take for a prey unto **y**: *3641.1*
 23: 7 neither serve them, nor bow **y** unto them. NIH
 23:11 Take good heed therefore unto **y**, *5315+3641.1*
 23:16 served other gods, and bowed **y** to them; NIH
 24:22 Ye *are* witnesses against **y** that ye have *3641.1*
Jdg 15:12 unto me, that ye will not fall upon me **y**. *859*
1Sa 2:29 to make **y** fat with the chiefest of all *3641.1*
 4: 9 Be strong, and quit **y** like men, O ye NIH
 4: 9 been to you: quit **y** like men, and fight. NIH
 10:19 present **y** before the Lord by your tribes, NIH
 14:34 Disperse **y** among the people, and say unto NIH
 16: 5 sanctify **y**, and come with me to NIH
1Ki 18:25 Choose you one bullock for **y**, and dress *it* NIH
 20:12 Set **y** in array. And they set *themselves in* NIH
2Ki 17:35 nor bow **y** to them, nor serve them, *859*
1Ch 15:12 sanctify **y**, *both* ye and your brethren, NIH
2Ch 20:17 shall not need to fight in this *battle*: set **y**, NIH
 29: 5 sanctify now **y**, and sanctify the house of *3641.1*
 29:31 Now ye have consecrated **y** unto NIH
 30: 8 fathers *were, but* yield **y** unto the Lord, NIH
 32:11 you to give over **y** to die by famine *3641.1*
 35: 4 prepare **y** by the houses of your fathers, NIH
 35: 6 and sanctify **y**, and prepare your brethren, NIH
Ezr 10:11 separate **y** from the people of the land, NIH
Ne 13:25 their daughters unto your sons, or for **y**. *3641.1*
Job 19: 3 you are not ashamed *that* you make **y** NIH
 19: 5 If indeed you will magnify **y** against me, NIH
 27:12 all ye have seen *it*; why then are ye thus *859*
 42: 8 and offer up for **y** a burnt offering; *3641.1*
Isa 8: 9 Associate **y**, O ye people, and ye shall be NIH
 8: 9 gird **y**, and ye shall be broken in pieces; NIH
 8: 9 gird **y**, and ye shall be broken in pieces. NIH
 29: 9 Stay **y**, and wonder; cry ye out, and cry: NIH
 45:20 Assemble **y** and come; draw near together, NIH
 46: 8 Remember this, and **shew y** men: bring *it* *377*
 48:14 All ye, assemble **y**, and hear; which NIH
 49: 9 to *them that are* in darkness, Shew **y**. NIH
 50: 1 for your iniquities have you sold **y**, NIH
 50:11 a fire, that compass **y** about with sparks: NIH
 52: 3 the Lord, Ye have sold **y** for nought; NIH
 57: 4 Against whom do ye sport **y**? against NIH
 57: 5 Inflaming **y** with idols under every green NIH
 61: 6 and in their glory shall you boast **y**. NIH
Jer 4: 4 Circumcise **y** to the Lord, and take away NIH

Jer 4: 5 Assemble **y**, and let us go into the NIH
 6: 1 gather **y** to flee out of the midst of NIH
 8:14 assemble **y**, and let us enter into NIH
 13:18 and to the queen, Humble **y**, sit down: NIH
 17:21 Take heed to **y**, and bear no *5315+3641.1*
 25:34 wallow **y** *in the ashes*, ye principal of NIH
 26:15 surely bring innocent blood upon **y**, *3641.1*
 37: 9 Deceive not **y**, saying, *5315+3641.1*
 44: 8 ye might cut **y** off, and that ye might *3641.1*
 50:14 Put **y** in array against Babylon round NIH
Eze 14: 6 Repent, and turn **y** from your idols; NIH
 18:30 and turn **y** from all your transgressions; NIH
 18:32 Lord God: wherefore turn **y**, and live ye. NIH
 20: 7 and defile not **y** with the idols of Egypt: NIH
 20:18 nor defile **y** with their idols: NIH
 20:31 ye pollute **y** with all your idols, *even* unto NIH
 20:43 ye shall lothe **y** in your own sight for all NIH
 36:31 shall lothe **y** in your own sight for your NIH
 39:17 beast of the field, Assemble **y**, and come; NIH
 39:17 gather on every side to my sacrifice that NIH
 44: 8 of my charge in my sanctuary for **y**. *3641.1*
Hos 10:12 Sow to **y** in righteousness, reap in *3641.1*
Joel 1:13 Gird **y**, and lament, ye priests: howl, NIH
 3:11 Assemble **y**, and come, all ye heathen, NIH
 3:11 and gather **y** together round about: NIH
Am 3: 9 Assemble **y** upon the mountains of NIH
 5:26 star of your god, which ye made to **y**. *3641.1*
Zep 2: 1 Gather **y** together, yea, gather together, NIH
Zec 7: 6 did not ye eat for **y**, and drink for NIH
 7: 6 not ye eat *for yourselves*, and drink *for* **y**? NIH
Mt 3: 9 And think not to say within **y**, We have *1438*
 6:19 Lay not up for **y** treasures upon earth, *4771*
 6:20 But lay up for **y** treasures in heaven, *4771*
 16: 8 why reason ye among **y**, because ye have *1438*
 23:13 for ye neither go in **y**, neither suffer ye *4771*
 23:15 him twofold more *the child of hell than* **y**. *4771*
 23:31 Wherefore ye be witnesses unto **y**, that ye *1438*
 25: 9 ye rather to them that sell, and buy for **y**. *1438*
Mk 6:31 Come ye **y** apart into a desert place, *846*
 9:33 What *was it that* ye disputed among **y** by *1438*
 9:50 Have salt in **y**, and have peace one with *1438*
 13: 9 But take heed to **y**: for they shall deliver *1438*
Lk 3: 8 and begin not to say within **y**, *1438*
 11:46 ye **y** touch not the burdens with one of *846*
 11:52 ye entered not in **y**, and them that were *846*
 12:33 provide **y** bags which wax not old, *1438*
 12:36 And ye **y** like unto men that wait for their NIG
 12:57 why even of **y** judge ye not what *is right*? *4771*
 13:28 kingdom of God, and you **y** thrust out. *1438*
 16: 9 Make to **y** friends of the mammon of *1438*
 16:15 Ye are they which justify **y** before men; *1438*
 17: 3 Take heed to **y**: If thy brother trespass *1438*
 17:14 unto them, Go shew **y** unto the priests. *1438*
 21:34 And take heed to **y**, lest at any time your *1438*
 22:17 said, Take this, and divide *it* among **y**: *1438*
 23:28 but weep for **y**, and for your children. *1438*
Jn 3:28 Ye **y** bear me witness, that I said, I am not *846*
 6:43 said unto them, Murmur not among **y**. *240*
 16:19 Do ye inquire among **y** of that I said, *240*
Ac 2:22 him in the midst of you, as ye **y** also know: *846*
 2:40 Save **y** from this untoward generation. NIG
 5:35 take heed to **y** what ye intend to do as *1438*
 13:46 and judge **y** unworthy of everlasting life, *1438*
 15:29 from which if ye keep **y**, ye shall do well. *1438*
 20:10 and embracing *him* said, Trouble not **y**; NIG
 20:28 Take heed therefore unto **y**, and to all *1438*
 20:34 Yea, ye **y** know, that these hands have *846*
Ro 6:11 Likewise reckon ye also **y** to be dead *1438*
 6:13 yield **y** unto God, as *those that are* alive *1438*
 6:16 that to whom ye yield **y** servants to obey, *1438*
 12:19 avenge not **y**, but *rather* give place unto *1438*
1Co 5:13 Therefore put away from among **y** *that* *4771*
 6: 7 why do ye not rather *suffer* **y** to be NIG
 7: 5 that ye may give **y** to fasting and prayer, *4771*
 11:13 Judge in **y**: is it comely that a woman pray *1438*
 16:16 That ye submit **y** unto such, and to every *846*
2Co 7:11 yea, *what* clearing of **y**, yea, NIG
 11: 1 all *things* ye have approved **y** to be clear *1438*
 11:19 ye suffer fools gladly, seeing ye **y** are wise. NIG
 13: 5 Examine **y**, whether ye be in the faith; *1438*
Eph 2: 8 ye are saved through faith; and that not of **y**: *4771*
 5:19 Speaking to **y** in psalms and hymns and *1438*
 5:21 Submitting **y** one to another in the fear of NIG
 5:22 Wives, submit **y** unto your own husbands, NIG
Col 3:18 Wives, submit **y** unto your own husbands, NIG
1Th 2: 1 For **y**, brethren, know our entrance in unto *846*
 3: 3 ye know that we are appointed thereunto. *846*
 4: 9 for ye **y** are taught of God to love one *846*
 5: 2 ye know perfectly that the day of the Lord *846*
 5:11 Wherefore comfort **y together**, *240*
 5:13 work's sake. And be at peace among **y**. *1438*
 5:15 is good, both among **y**, and to all *men*. *240*
2Th 3: 6 ye withdraw **y** from every brother that NIG
 3: 7 For ye know how ye ought to follow us: *846*
Heb 10:34 knowing in **y** that *ye* have in heaven a *1438*
 13: 3 adversity, as being **y** also in the body. *846*
 13:17 that have the rule over you, and submit **y**: NIG
Jas 2: 4 Are ye not then partial in **y**, and are *1438*
 4: 7 Submit **y** therefore to God. Resist the devil, NIG
 4:10 Humble **y** in the sight of the Lord, NIG
1Pe 1:14 not fashioning **y** according to the former NIG
 2:13 Submit **y** to every ordinance of man for *4771*
 4: 1 arm **y** likewise with the same mind: *1438*
 4: 8 all *things* have fervent charity among **y**: *1438*
 5: 5 *ye* younger, submit **y** unto the elder. NIG

1Pe 5: 6 Humble **y** therefore under the mighty NIG
1Jn 5:21 Little children, keep **y** from idols. Amen. *1438*
2Jn 1: 8 Look to **y**, that we lose not *those things* *1438*
Jude 1:20 building up **y** on your most holy faith, *1438*
 1:21 Keep **y** in the love of God, looking for *1438*
Rev 19:17 gather **y** together unto the supper of NIG

YOUTH (70) [YOUNG, YOUNGER, YOUNGEST, YOUTHFUL, YOUTHS]

Ge 8:21 of man's heart *is* evil from his **y**; *5271*
 43:33 and the youngest according to his **y**: *6812*
 46:34 about cattle from our **y** even until now, *5271*
Lev 22:13 as *in her* **y**, she shall eat of her father's *5271*
Nu 30: 3 *being* in her father's house in her **y**; *5271*
 30:16 *being yet* in her father's house. *5271*
Jdg 8:20 the **y** drew not his sword: for he feared, *5288*
 8:20 for he feared, because he *was* yet a **y**. *5288*
1Sa 17:33 for thou *art but* a **y**, and he a man of war *5271*
 17:33 a youth, and he a man of war from his **y**. *5271*
 17:42 he was *but* a **y**, and ruddy, and of a fair *5288*
 17:55 the host, Abner, whose son *is* this **y**? *5288*
2Sa 19: 7 evil that befell thee from thy **y** until now. *5271*
1Ki 18:12 *I* thy servant fear the Lord from my **y**. *5271*
Job 13:26 me to possess the iniquities of my **y**. *5271*
 20:11 His bones are full *of the sin of* his **y**, *5934*
 29: 4 As I was in the days of my **y**, when *2779*
 30:12 Upon *my* right hand rise the **y**; they push *6526*
 31:18 from my **y** he was brought up *with* me, *5271*
 33:25 he shall return to the days of his **y**: *5934*
 36:14 They die in **y**, and their life *is* among *5290*
Ps 25: 7 Remember not the sins of my **y**, nor my *5271*
 71: 5 Lord God: thou *art* my trust from my **y**. *5271*
 71:17 O God, thou hast taught me from my **y**: *5271*
 88:15 ready to die from my **y** *up: while* I suffer *5290*
 89:45 The days of his **y** hast thou shortened: *5934*
 103: 5 *so that* thy **y** is renewed like the eagle's. *5271*
 110: 3 the morning: thou hast the dew of thy **y**. *3208*
 127: 4 of a mighty *man; so are* children of the **y**. *5271*
 129: 1 a time have they afflicted me from my **y**, *5271*
 129: 2 a time have they afflicted me from my **y**: *5271*
 144:12 *may be* as plants grown up in their **y**; *5271*
Pr 2:17 Which forsaketh the guide of her **y**, *5271*
 5:18 and rejoice with the wife of thy **y**. *5271*
Ecc 11: 9 Rejoice, O young man, in thy **y**; and let *3208*
 11: 9 thy heart cheer thee in the days of thy **y**, *979*
 11:10 thy flesh: for childhood and **y** *are* vanity. *7839*
 12: 1 now thy Creator in the days of thy **y**, *979*
Isa 47:12 wherein thou hast laboured from thy **y**; *5271*
 47:15 *even* thy merchants, from thy **y**: *5271*
 54: 4 for thou shalt forget the shame of thy **y**, *5934*
 54: 6 and grieved in spirit, and a wife of **y**, *5271*
Jer 2: 2 I remember thee, the kindness of thy **y**, *5271*
 3: 4 My father, thou *art* the guide of my **y**? *5271*
 3:24 the labour of our fathers from our **y**; *5271*
 3:25 from our **y** even unto this day, and have *5271*
 22:21 This *hath been* thy manner from thy **y**, *5271*
 31:19 because I did bear the reproach of my **y**. *5271*
 32:30 only done evil before me from their **y**: *5271*
 48:11 Moab hath been at ease from his **y**, *5271*
La 3:27 for a man that he bear the yoke in his **y**. *5271*
Eze 4:14 for from my **y** up even till now have I not *5271*
 16:22 hast not remembered the days of thy **y**, *5271*
 16:43 hast not remembered the days of thy **y**, *5271*
 16:60 covenant with thee in the days of thy **y**, *5271*
 23: 3 they committed whoredoms in their **y**: *5271*
 23: 8 for in her **y** they lay with her, *5271*
 23:19 calling to remembrance the days of her **y**, *5271*
 23:21 to remembrance the lewdness of thy **y**, *5271*
 23:21 by the Egyptians for the paps of thy **y**. *5271*
Hos 2:15 as *in* the days of her **y**, and as *in* the day *5271*
Joel 1: 8 with sackcloth for the husband of her **y**. *5271*
Zec 13: 5 man taught me to keep cattle from my **y**. *5271*
Mal 2:14 between thee and the wife of thy **y**, *5271*
 2:15 treacherously against the wife of his **y**. *5271*
Mt 19:20 these *things* have I kept from my **y** up: *3503*
Mk 10:20 all these have I observed from my **y**. *3503*
Lk 18:21 said, All these have I kept from my **y** up. *3503*
Ac 26: 4 My manner of life from *my* **y**, which was *3503*
1Ti 4:12 Let no *man* despise thy **y**; but be thou an *3503*

YOUTHFUL (1) [YOUTH]

2Ti 2:22 Flee also **y** lusts: but follow righteousness, *3512*

YOUTHS (2) [YOUTH]

Pr 7: 7 the simple ones, I discerned among the **y**, *1121*
Isa 40:30 Even the **y** shall faint and be weary, *5288*

YOU-WARD (2) [YOU]

2Co 13: 3 which to **y** is not weak, but is mighty in *4771*
Eph 3: 2 the grace of God which is given me to **y**: *4771*

YOU-WARDS (1) [YOU]

2Co 1:12 in the world, and more abundantly to **y**. *4771*

Z

ZAANAIM (1)

Jdg 4:11 pitched his tent unto the plain of **Z**, *6815*

ZAANAN (1)
Mic 1:11 the inhabitant of Z came not forth *in* 6630

ZAANANNIM (1)
Jos 19:33 from Allon to Z, and Adami, Nekeb, 6815

ZAAVAN (1)
Ge 36:27 Ezer *are* these; Bilhan, and Z, and Akan. 2190

ZABAD (8)
1Ch 2:36 Attai begat Nathan, and Nathan begat Z, 2066
 2:37 begat Ephlal, and Ephlal begat Obed, 2066
 7:21 his son, and Shuthelah his son, and 2066
 11:41 Uriah the Hittite, Z the son of Ahlai, 2066
2Ch 24:26 Z the son of Shimeath an Ammonitess, 2066
Ezr 10:27 and Jeremoth, and Z, and Aziza. 2066
 10:33 Eliphelet, Jeremai, Manasseh, 2066
 10:43 Z, Zebina, Jadau, and Joel, Benaiah: 2066

ZABBAI (2)
Ezr 10:28 Jehohanan, Hananiah, Z, *and* Athlai. 2079
Ne 3:20 After him Baruch the son of Z earnestly 2079

ZABBUD (1)
Ezr 8:14 and Z, and with them seventy males. 2072

ZABDI (6)
Jos 7: 1 of Carmi, the son of Z, the son of Zerah, 2067
 7:17 Zarhites man by man; and Z was taken: 2067
 7:18 of Carmi, the son of Z, the son of Zerah, 2067
1Ch 8:19 And Jakim, and Zichri, and Z, 2067
 27:27 for the wine cellars *was* Z the Shiphmite 2067
Ne 11:17 the son of Micha, the son of Z, the son of Asaph, 2067

ZABDIEL (2)
1Ch 27: 2 first month *was* Jashobeam the son of Z: 2068
Ne 11:14 their overseer *was* Z, the son of *one* of 2068

ZABUD (1)
1Ki 4: 5 the son of Nathan *was* principal officer, 2071

ZABULON (3) [ZEBULUN]
Mt 4:13 in the borders of Z and Nephthalim: 2194
 4:15 land of Z, and the land of Nephthalim, 2194
Rev 7: 8 Of the tribe of Z *were* sealed twelve 2194

ZACCAI (2)
Ezr 2: 9 The children of Z, seven hundred and 2140
Ne 7:14 The children of Z, seven hundred and 2140

ZACCHEUS (3)
Lk 19: 2 And behold, *there* was a man named Z, *2195*
 19: 5 Z, make haste, and come down; *2195*
 19: 8 And Z stood, and said unto the Lord; *2195*

ZACCHUR (1)
1Ch 4:26 his son, Z his son, Shimei his son. 2139

ZACCUR (8)
Nu 13: 4 tribe of Reuben, Shammua the son of Z. 2139
1Ch 24:27 Beno, and Shoham, and Z, and Ibri. 2139
 25: 2 Z, and Joseph, and Nethaniah, 2139
 25:10 The third to Z, *he,* his sons, 2139
Ne 3: 2 next to them builded Z the son of Imri. 2139
 10:12 Z, Sherebiah, Shebaniah, 2139
 12:35 the son of Z, the son of Asaph: 2139
 13:13 next to them *was* Hanan the son of Z, 2139

ZACHARIAH (4) [ZACHARIAS, ZECHARIAH]
2Ki 14:29 Israel; and Z his son reigned in his stead. 2148
 15: 8 eighth year of Azariah king of Judah did Z 2148
 15:11 the rest of the acts of Z, behold, they *are* 2148
 18: 2 name also *was* Abi, the daughter of Z. 2148

ZACHARIAS (11) [ZACHARIAH]
Mt 23:35 Abel unto the blood of Z son of Barachias, *2197*
Lk 1: 5 king of Judea, a certain priest named Z, *2197*
 1:12 And when Z saw *him,* he was troubled, *2197*
 1:13 But the angel said unto him, Fear not, Z: *2197*
 1:18 Z said unto the angel, Whereby shall I *2197*
 1:21 And the people waited for Z, *2197*
 1:40 And entered into the house of Z, *2197*
 1:59 they called him Z, after the name of his *2197*
 1:67 And his father Z was filled with the Holy *2197*
 3: 2 unto John the son of Z in the wilderness, *2197*
 11:51 the blood of Abel unto the blood of Z, *2197*

ZACHER (1)
1Ch 8:31 And Gedor, and Ahio, and Z. 2144

ZADOK (52) [ZADOK'S]
2Sa 8:17 Z the son of Ahitub, and Ahimelech the 6659
 15:24 lo Z also, and all the Levites *were* with 6659
 15:25 the king said unto Z, Carry back the ark of 6659
 15:27 The king said also unto Z the priest, *Art* 6659
 15:29 Z therefore and Abiathar carried the ark 6659
 15:35 *hast thou* not there with thee Z and Abiathar 6659
 15:35 thou shalt tell *it* to Z and Abiathar 6659
 17:15 said Hushai unto Z and to Abiathar 6659
 18:19 said Ahimaaz the son of Z, Let me now 6659
 18:22 said Ahimaaz the son of Z yet again to 6659
 18:27 like the running of Ahimaaz the son of Z. 6659
 19:11 king David sent to Z and to Abiathar 6659
 20:25 and Z and Abiathar *were* the priests: 6659
1Ki 1: 8 Z the priest, and Benaiah the son of 6659
 1:26 Z the priest, and Benaiah the son of 6659

1Ki 1:32 Call me Z the priest, and Nathan 6659
 1:34 let Z the priest and Nathan the prophet 6659
 1:38 So Z the priest, and Nathan the prophet, 6659
 1:39 Z the priest took a horn of oil out of 6659
 1:44 the king hath sent with him Z the priest, 6659
 1:45 Z the priest and Nathan the prophet have 6659
 2:35 Z the priest did the king put in the room 6659
 4: 2 he had; Azariah the son of Z the priest, 6659
 4: 4 and Z and Abiathar *were* the priests: 6659
2Ki 15:33 name *was* Jerusha, the daughter of Z. 6659
1Ch 6: 8 Ahitub begat Z, and Zadok begat 6659
 6: 8 begat Zadok, and Z begat Ahimaaz, 6659
 6:12 Ahitub begat Z, and Zadok begat Shallum, 6659
 6:12 Ahitub begat Zadok, and Z begat Shallum, 6659
 6:53 his son, Ahimaaz his son. 6659
 9:11 the son of Z, the son of Meraioth, the son 6659
 12:28 Z, a young man mighty of valour, 6659
 15:11 David called for Z and Abiathar the 6659
 16:39 Z the priest, and his brethren the priests, 6659
 18:16 Z the son of Ahitub, and Abimelech the 6659
 24: 3 both Z of the sons of Eleazar, 6659
 24: 6 Z the priest, and Ahimelech the son of 6659
 24:31 Z, and Ahimelech, and the chief of 6659
 27:17 the son of Kemuel: of the Aaronites, Z: 6659
 29:22 be the chief governor, and Z to be priest. 6659
2Ch 27: 1 also *was* Jerushah, the daughter of Z 6659
 31:10 Azariah the chief priest of the house of Z 6659
Ezr 7: 2 Shallum, the son of Z, the son of Ahitub, 6659
Ne 3: 4 next unto them repaired Z the son of 6659
 3:29 After them repaired Z the son of Immer 6659
 10:21 Meshezabeel, Z, Jaddua, 6659
 11:11 the son of Z, the son of Meraioth, the son 6659
 13:13 Z the scribe, and of the Levites, Pedaiah: 6659
Eze 40:46 these *are* the sons of Z among the sons of 6659
 43:19 priests the Levites that *be* of the seed of Z, 6659
 44:15 priests the Levites, the sons of Z, 6659
 48:11 priests that are sanctified of the sons of Z; 6659

ZADOK'S (1) [ZADOK]
2Sa 15:36 Ahimaaz Z *son,* and 6659+3807.1

ZAHAM (1)
2Ch 11:19 children; Jeush, and Shamariah, and Z. 2093

ZAIR (1)
2Ki 8:21 So Joram went over to Z, and all 6811

ZALAPH (1)
Ne 3:30 Hanun the sixth son of Z, another piece. 6764

ZALMON (2)
Jdg 9:48 Abimelech gat him up *to* mount Z, 6756
2Sa 23:28 Z the Ahohite, Maharai the Netophathite, 6756

ZALMONAH (2)
Nu 33:41 from mount Hor, and pitched in Z. 6758
 33:42 they departed from Z, and pitched in 6758

ZALMUNNA (12)
Jdg 8: 5 I am pursuing after Zebah and Z, kings of 6759
 8: 6 hands of Zebah and Z now in thine hand, 6759
 8: 7 delivered Zebah and Z into mine hand, 6759
 8:10 Now Zebah and Z *were* in Karkor, 6759
 8:12 when Zebah and Z fled, he pursued after 6759
 8:12 and Z, and discomfited all the host. 6759
 8:15 said, Behold Zebah and Z, with whom ye 6759
 8:15 hands of Zebah and Z now in thine hand, 6759
 8:18 said he unto Zebah and Z, What manner 6759
 8:21 Zebah and Z said, Rise thou, and fall upon 6759
 8:21 slew Zebah and Z, and took away 6759
Ps 83:11 yea, all their princes as Zebah, and as Z: 6759

ZAMZUMMIMS (1)
Dt 2:20 old time; and the Ammonites call them Z; 2157

ZAMZUMMITES See ZAMZUMMIMS

ZANOAH (5)
Jos 15:34 Z, and En-gannim, Tappuah, and Enam, 2182
 15:56 And Jezreel, and Jokdeam, and Z, 2182
1Ch 4:18 of Socho, and Jekuthiel the father of Z. 2182
Ne 3:13 repaired Hanun, and the inhabitants of Z; 2182
 11:30 Z, Adullam, and *in* their villages, 2182

ZAPHENATH-PANEAH See
 ZAPHNATH-PAANEAH

ZAPHNATH-PAANEAH (1)
Ge 41:45 Pharaoh called Joseph's name Z; 6847

ZAPHON (1)
Jos 13:27 and Beth-nimrah, and Succoth, and Z, 6829

ZARA (1) [ZARAH]
Mt 1: 3 And Judas begat Phares and Z of Thamar; *2196*

ZARAH (1) [ZARA]
Ge 38:30 his hand: and his name was called Z. 2226

ZAREAH (1)
Ne 11:29 at En-rimmon, and at Z, and at Jarmuth, 6881

ZAREATHITES (1)
1Ch 2:53 of them came the Z, and the Eshtaulites. 6882

ZARED (1)
Nu 21:12 and pitched in the valley of Z. 2218

ZAREPHATH (3) [SAREPTA]
1Ki 17: 9 Arise, get thee to Z, which *belongeth* to 6886
 17:10 So he arose and went to Z. And when he 6886
Ob 1:20 that of the Canaanites, *even* unto Z; 6886

ZARETAN (1)
Jos 3:16 from the city Adam, that *is* beside Z: 6891

ZARETHAN See ZARETAN; ZARTANAH;
 ZARTHAN; ZEREDATHAH

ZARETH-SHAHAR (1)
Jos 13:19 Sibmah, and Z in the mount of the valley, 6890

ZARHITES (6)
Nu 26:13 Of Zerah, the family of the Z: of Shaul, 2227
 26:20 Pharzites: of Zerah, the family of the Z. 2227
Jos 7:17 of Judah; and he took the family of the Z: 2227
 7:17 brought the family of the Z man by man; 2227
1Ch 27:11 *was* Sibbecai the Hushathite, of the Z: 2227
 27:13 *was* Maharai the Netophathite, of the Z: 2227

ZARTANAH (1)
1Ki 4:12 which *is* by Z beneath Jezreel, 6891

ZARTHAN (1)
1Ki 7:46 the clay ground between Succoth and Z. 6891

ZATTHU (1)
Ne 10:14 Parosh, Pahath-moab, Elam, Z, Bani, 2240

ZATTU (3)
Ezr 2: 8 The children of Z, nine hundred forty 2240
 10:27 of the sons of Z; Elioenai, Eliashib, 2240
Ne 7:13 The children of Z, eight hundred forty 2240

ZAVAN (1)
1Ch 1:42 sons of Ezer; Bilhan, and Z, *and* Jakan. 2190

ZAZA (1)
1Ch 2:33 the sons of Jonathan; Peleth, and Z. 2117

ZEAL (16) [ZEALOUS, ZEALOUSLY]
2Sa 21: 2 Saul sought to slay them in his z to 7065
2Ki 10:16 with me, and see my z for the LORD. 7068
 19:31 the z of the LORD *of hosts* shall do this. 7068
Ps 69: 9 the z of thine house hath eaten me up; 7068
 119:139 My z hath consumed me, because 7068
Isa 9: 7 The z of the LORD of hosts will perform 7068
 37:32 the z of the LORD of hosts shall do this. 7068
 59:17 clothing, and was clad with z as a cloke. 7068
 63:15 where *is* thy z and thy strength, 7068
Eze 5:13 that I the LORD have spoken *it* in my z, 7068
Jn 2:17 The z of thine house hath eaten me up. *2205*
Ro 10: 2 I bear them record that they have a z of *2205*
2Co 7:11 yea, *what* z, yea, *what* revenge! *2205*
 9: 2 and your z hath provoked very many. *2205*
Php 3: 6 Concerning z, persecuting the church; *2205*
Col 4:13 that he hath a great z for you, and them *2205*

ZEALOT See ZELOTES

ZEALOUS (8) [ZEAL]
Nu 25:11 he was z for my sake among them, 7065+7068
 25:13 because he was z for his God, and made 7065
Ac 21:20 believe; and they are all z of the law: *2207*
 22: 3 and was z towards God, as ye all are this *2207*
1Co 14:12 as ye are z of spiritual *gifts,* seek *2207*
Gal 1:14 more exceedingly z of the traditions *2207*
Tit 2:14 a peculiar people, z of good works. *2207*
Rev 3:19 and chasten: be z therefore, and repent. *2206*

ZEALOUSLY (2) [ZEAL]
Gal 4:17 They z affect you, *but* not well; yea, *2206*
 4:18 But *it is* good to be z affected always in a *2206*

ZEBADIAH (9)
1Ch 8:15 And Z, and Arad, and Ader, 2069
 8:17 Z, and Meshullam, and Hezeki, and 2069
 12: 7 Joelah, and Z, the sons of Jeroham of 2069
 26: 2 Jediael the second, Z the third, Jathniel 2069
 27: 7 brother of Joab, and Z his son after him: 2069
2Ch 17: 8 Z, and Asahel, and Shemiramoth, 2069
 19:11 Z the son of Ishmael, the ruler of the 2069
Ezr 8: 8 Z the son of Michael, and with him 2069
 10:20 of the sons of Immer; Hanani, and Z. 2069

ZEBAH (12)
Jdg 8: 5 I am pursuing after Z and Zalmunna, 2078
 8: 6 Are the hands of Z and Zalmunna now in 2078
 8: 7 when the LORD hath delivered Z 2078
 8:10 Now Z and Zalmunna *were* in Karkor, 2078
 8:12 when Z and Zalmunna fled, he pursued 2078
 8:12 Z and Zalmunna, and discomfited all 2078
 8:15 said, Behold Z and Zalmunna, with whom 2078
 8:15 Are the hands of Z and Zalmunna now in 2078
 8:18 said he unto Z and Zalmunna, 2078
 8:21 Z and Zalmunna said, Rise thou, 2078
 8:21 slew Z and Zalmunna, and took away 2078
Ps 83:11 all their princes as Z, and as Zalmunna: 2078

ZEBAIM See POCHERETH OF ZEBAIM,
 POCHERETH ZEBAIM

ZEBEDEE (10) [ZEBEDEE'S]
Mt 4:21 James the *son* of Z, and John his brother, *2199*
 4:21 his brother, in a ship with Z their father, *2199*

Z

Mt	10: 2 the *son* of **Z**, and John his brother;	2199
	26:37 with *him* Peter and the two sons of **Z**,	2199
Mk	1:19 he saw James the *son* of **Z**, and John his	2199
	1:20 they left their father **Z** in the ship with	2199
	3:17 And James the *son* of **Z**, and John	2199
	10:35 And James and John, the sons of **Z**,	2199
Lk	5:10 *was* also James, and John, *the* sons of **Z**,	2199
Jn	21: 2 and the *sons* of **Z**, and two other of his	2199

ZEBEDEE'S (2) [ZEBEDEE]

Mt	20:20 came to him the mother of **Z** children	2199
	27:56 and Joses, and the mother of **Z** children.	2199

ZEBIDAH See ZEBUDAH

ZEBINA (1)

Ezr	10:43 Zabad, **Z**, Jadau, and Joel, Benaiah.	2081

ZEBOIIM (2) [ZEBOIM]

Ge	14: 2 Shemeber king of **Z**, and the king of Bela,	6636
	14: 8 the king of **Z**, and the king of Bela	6636

ZEBOIM (5) [ZEBOIIM]

Ge	10:19 Gomorrah, and Admah, and **Z**, even unto	6636
Dt	29:23 of Sodom, and Gomorrah, Admah, and **Z**,	6636
1Sa	13:18 to the valley of **Z** toward the wilderness.	6650
Ne	11:34 Hadid, **Z**, Neballat,	6650
Hos	11: 8 *how* shall I set thee as **Z**? mine heart is	6636

ZEBUDAH (1)

2Ki	23:36 his mother's name *was* **Z**, the daughter of	2080

ZEBUL (1)

Jdg	9:28 **Z** his officer? serve the men of Hamor	2083
	9:30 when **Z** the ruler of the city heard	2083
	9:36 Gaal saw the people, he said to **Z**, Behold,	2083
	9:36 **Z** said unto him, Thou seest the shadow	2083
	9:38 **Z** unto him, Where *is* now thy mouth,	2083
	9:41 thrust out Gaal and his brethren, that	2083

ZEBULONITE (2) [ZEBULUN]

Jdg	12:11 after him Elon, a **Z**, judged Israel;	2075
	12:12 Elon the **Z** died, and was buried in Aijalon	2075

ZEBULUN (45) [ZABULON, ZEBULONITE, ZEBULUNITES]

Ge	30:20 him six sons: and she called his name **Z**.	2074
	35:23 and Levi, and Judah, and Issachar, and **Z**:	2074
	46:14 sons of **Z**; Sered, and Elon, and Jahleel.	2074
	49:13 **Z** shall dwell at the haven of the sea;	2074
Ex	1: 3 Issachar, **Z**, and Benjamin,	2074
Nu	1: 9 Of **Z**; Eliab the son of Helon.	2074
	1:30 Of the children of **Z**, *by* their generations,	2074
	1:31 *even* of the tribe of **Z**, *were* fifty and	2074
	2: 7 *Then* the tribe of **Z**: and Eliab the son of	2074
	2: 7 *shall be* captain of the children of **Z**.	2074
	7:24 prince of the children of **Z**, *did offer:*	2074
	10:16 children of **Z** *was* Eliab the son of Helon.	2074
	13:10 Of the tribe of **Z**, Gaddiel the son of Sodi.	2074
	26:26 *Of* the sons of **Z** after their families:	2074
	34:25 prince of the tribe of the children of **Z**,	2074
Dt	27:13 and Asher, and **Z**, and Dan, and Naphtali.	2074
	33:18 he said, Rejoice, Zebulun, in thy going	2074
	33:18 he said, Rejoice, **Z**, in thy going out;	2074
Jos	19:10 third lot came up for the children of **Z**	2074
	19:16 *is* the inheritance of the children of **Z**	2074
	19:27 reacheth to **Z**, and to the valley of	2074
	19:34 reacheth to **Z** on the south side,	2074
	21: 7 and out of the tribe of **Z**, twelve cities.	2074
	21:34 rest of the Levites, out of the tribe of **Z**,	2074
Jdg	1:30 Neither did **Z** drive out the inhabitants of	2074
	4: 6 of Naphtali and of the children of **Z**?	2074
	4:10 Barak called **Z** and Naphtali to Kedesh;	2074
	5:14 out of **Z** they that handle the pen of	2074
	5:18 **Z** and Naphtali *were* a people *that*	2074
	6:35 Asher, and unto **Z**, and unto Naphtali;	2074
	12:12 was buried in Aijalon in the country of **Z**.	2074
1Ch	2: 1 Simeon, Levi, and Judah, Issachar, and **Z**,	2074
	6:63 and out of the tribe of **Z**, twelve cities.	2074
	6:77 of Merari *were* given out of the tribe of **Z**,	2074
	12:33 Of **Z**, such as went forth to battle, expert	2074
	12:40 *even* unto Issachar and **Z** and Naphtali,	2074
	27:19 Of **Z**, Ishmaiah the son of Obadiah.	2074
2Ch	30:10 of Ephraim and Manasseh even unto **Z**:	2074
	30:11 Manasseh and of **Z** humbled themselves,	2074
	30:18 and Manasseh, Issachar, and **Z**,	2074
Ps	68:27 the princes of **Z**, *and* the princes of	2074
Isa	9: 1 the first he lightly afflicted the land of **Z**	2074
Eze	48:26 east side unto the west side, **Z** a *portion*.	2074
	48:27 by the border of **Z**, from the east side unto	2074
	48:33 one gate of Issachar, one gate of **Z**.	2074

ZEBULUNITES (1) [ZEBULUN]

Nu	26:27 These *are* the families of the **Z** according	2075

ZECHARIAH (39) [ZACHARIAH]

1Ch	5: 7 reckoned, *were* the chief, Jeiel, and **Z**,	2148
	9:21 **Z** the son of Meshelemiah *was* porter.	2148
	9:37 Gedor, and Ahio, and **Z**, and Mikloth.	2148
	15:18 **Z**, Ben, and Jaaziel, and Shemiramoth,	2148
	15:20 **Z**, and Aziel, and Shemiramoth, and	2148
	15:24 Amasai, and **Z**, and Benaiah, and Eliezer,	2148
	16: 5 next to him **Z**, Jeiel, and Shemiramoth,	2148
	24:25 *was* Isshiah: the son of Isshiah; **Z**.	2148
	26: 2 the sons of Meshelemiah *were*, **Z**	2148
	26:11 second, Tebaliah the third, **Z** the fourth:	2148

1Ch	26:14 *for* **Z** his son, a wise counseller, they cast	2148
	27:21 of Manasseh in Gilead, Iddo the son of **Z**:	2148
2Ch	17: 7 to **Z**, and to Nethaneel, and to Michaiah,	2148
	20:14 upon Jahaziel the son of **Z**, the son of	2148
	21: 2 **Z**, and Azariah, and Michael,	2148
	24:20 the spirit of God came upon **Z** the son of	2148
	26: 5 he sought God in the days of **Z**, who had	2148
	29: 1 name *was* Abijah, the daughter of **Z**.	2148
	29:13 of the sons of Asaph; **Z**, and Mattaniah:	2148
	34:12 **Z** and Meshullam, of the sons of	2148
	35: 8 Hilkiah and **Z** and Jehiel, rulers of	2148
Ezr	5: 1 Haggai the prophet, and **Z** the son of Iddo	2148
	6:14 Haggai the prophet and **Z** the son of Iddo.	2148
	8: 3 of Shechaniah, of the sons of Pharosh; **Z**:	2148
	8:11 **Z** the son of Bebai, and with him twenty	2148
	8:16 for Nathan, and for **Z**, and for Meshullam,	2148
	10:26 **Z**, and Jehiel, and Abdi, and Jeremoth,	2148
Ne	8: 4 and Hashbadana, **Z**, *and* Meshullam.	2148
	11: 4 the son of **Z**, the son of Amariah, the son	2148
	11: 5 of Adaiah, the son of Joiarib, the son of **Z**,	2148
	11:12 the son of Amzi, the son of **Z**, the son of	2148
	12:16 Of Iddo, **Z**; of Ginnethon, Meshullam;	2148
	12:35 *namely*, **Z** the son of Jonathan, the son of	2148
	12:41 Michaiah, Elioenai, **Z**, and Hananiah,	2148
Isa	8: 2 the priest, and **Z** the son of Jeberechiah.	2148
Zec	1: 1 came the word of the Lord unto **Z**,	2148
	1: 7 came the word of the Lord unto **Z**,	2148
	7: 1 *that* the word of the Lord came unto **Z**	2148
	7: 8 the word of the Lord came unto **Z**,	2148

ZEDAD (2)

Nu	34: 8 goings forth of the border shall be to **Z**:	6657
Eze	47:15 the way of Hethlon, as *men* go to **Z**;	6657

ZEDEKIAH (61) [ZEDEKIAH'S]

1Ki	22:11 **Z** the son of Chenaanah made him horns	6667
	22:24 **Z** the son of Chenaanah went near,	6667
2Ki	24:17 in his stead, and changed his name *to* **Z**.	6667
	24:18 **Z** *was* twenty and one years old when he	6667
	24:20 rebelled against the king of Babylon.	6667
	25: 2 besieged unto the eleventh year of king **Z**.	6667
	25: 7 they slew the sons of **Z** before his eyes,	6667
	25: 7 put out the eyes of **Z**, and bound him	6667
1Ch	3:15 the third **Z**, the fourth Shallum.	6667
	3:16 of Jehoiakim: Jeconiah his son, **Z** his son.	6667
2Ch	18:10 **Z** the son of Chenaanah had made him	6667
	18:23 the son of Chenaanah came near,	6667
	36:10 made **Z** his brother king over Judah and	6667
	36:11 **Z** *was* one and twenty years old when he	6667
Jer	1: 3 unto the end of the eleventh year of **Z**	6667
	21: 1 when king **Z** sent unto him Pashur and	6667
	21: 3 unto them, Thus shall ye say to **Z**:	6667
	21: 7 I will deliver **Z** king of Judah, and his	6667
	24: 8 So will I give **Z** the king of Judah, and his	6667
	27: 3 come *to* Jerusalem unto **Z** king of Judah;	6667
	27:12 I spake also to **Z** king of Judah according	6667
	28: 1 in the beginning of the reign of **Z** king of	6667
	29: 3 whom **Z** king of Judah sent unto Babylon	6667
	29:21 of Kolaiah, and of **Z**, the son of Maaseiah,	6667
	29:22 The Lord make thee like **Z** and	6667
	32: 1 in the tenth year of **Z** king of Judah,	6667
	32: 3 For **Z** king of Judah had shut him up,	6667
	32: 4 **Z** king of Judah shall not escape out of	6667
	32: 5 he shall lead **Z** *to* Babylon, and there	6667
	34: 2 Go and speak to **Z** king of Judah,	6667
	34: 4 word of the Lord, O **Z** king of Judah;	6667
	34: 6 words unto **Z** king of Judah in Jerusalem,	6667
	34: 8 after that the king **Z** had made a covenant	6667
	34:21 **Z** king of Judah and his princes will I give	6667
	36:12 The son of Hananiah, and all the princes.	6667
	37: 1 king **Z** the son of Josiah reigned instead of	6667
	37: 3 **Z** the king sent Jehucal the son of	6667
	37:17 **Z** the king sent, and took him out: and	6667
	37:18 Moreover Jeremiah said unto king **Z**,	6667
	37:21 **Z** the king commanded that they should	6667
	38: 5 **Z** the king said, Behold, he *is* in your	6667
	38:14 **Z** the king sent, and took Jeremiah	6667
	38:15 Jeremiah said unto **Z**, If I declare *it* unto	6667
	38:16 the king sware secretly unto Jeremiah,	6667
	38:17 said Jeremiah unto **Z**, Thus saith	6667
	38:19 the king said unto Jeremiah, I am afraid	6667
	38:24 said **Z** unto Jeremiah, Let no man know	6667
	39: 1 In the ninth year of **Z** king of Judah,	6667
	39: 2 in the eleventh year of **Z**, in the fourth	6667
	39: 4 when **Z** the king of Judah saw them,	6667
	39: 5 and overtook **Z** in the plains of Jericho:	6667
	39: 6 the king of Babylon slew the sons of **Z** in	6667
	44:30 as I gave **Z** king of Judah into the hand of	6667
	49:34 beginning of the reign of **Z** king of Judah,	6667
	51:59 when he went with **Z** the king of Judah	6667
	52: 1 **Z** *was* one and twenty year old when he	6667
	52: 3 **Z** rebelled against the king of Babylon.	6667
	52: 5 besieged unto the eleventh year of king **Z**.	6667
	52: 8 and overtook **Z** in the plains of Jericho;	6667
	52:10 the king of Babylon slew the sons of **Z**	6667
	52:11 he put out the eyes of **Z**; and the king	6667

ZEDEKIAH'S (1) [ZEDEKIAH]

Jer	39: 7 Moreover he put out **Z** eyes,	6667

ZEEB (6)

Jdg	7:25 princes of the Midianites, Oreb and **Z**;	2062
	7:25 they slew at the winepress of Zeeb,	2062
	7:25 Zeeb they slew at the winepress of **Z**,	2062
	7:25 and **Z** to Gideon on the *other* side Jordan.	2062

Jdg	8: 3 hands the princes of Midian, Oreb and **Z**:	2062
Ps	83:11 Make their nobles like Oreb, and like **Z**:	2062

ZEKER See ZACHER

ZELAH (2)

Jos	18:28 **Z**, Eleph, and Jebusi, which *is* Jerusalem,	6762
2Sa	21:14 they in the country of Benjamin in **Z**,	6762

ZELEK (2)

2Sa	23:37 **Z** the Ammonite, Naharai the Beerothite,	6768
1Ch	11:39 **Z** the Ammonite, Naharai the Berothite,	6768

ZELOPHEHAD (11)

Nu	26:33 **Z** the son of Hepher had no sons,	6765
	26:33 the names of the daughters of **Z** *were*	6765
	27: 1 came the daughters of **Z**, the son of	6765
	27: 7 The daughters of **Z** speak right: thou shalt	6765
	36: 2 of **Z** our brother unto his daughters.	6765
	36: 6 command concerning the daughters of **Z**,	6765
	36:10 so did the daughters of **Z**:	6765
	36:11 Milcah, and Noah, the daughters of **Z**,	6765
Jos	17: 3 **Z**, the son of Hepher, the son of Gilead,	6765
1Ch	7:15 and the name of the second *was* **Z**:	6765
	7:15 *was* Zelophehad: and **Z** had daughters.	6765

ZELOTES (2)

Lk	6:15 the *son* of Alpheus, and Simon called **Z**,	2208
Ac	1:13 and Simon **Z**, and Judas *the* brother of	2208

ZELZAH (1)

1Sa	10: 2 sepulchre in the border of Benjamin at **Z**;	6766

ZEMARAIM (2)

Jos	18:22 And Beth-arabah, and **Z**, and Beth-el,	6787
2Ch	13: 4 Abijah stood up upon mount **Z**, which *is*	6787

ZEMARITE (2)

Ge	10:18 Arvadite, and the **Z**, and the Hamathite:	6786
1Ch	1:16 Arvadite, and the **Z**, and the Hamathite.	6786

ZEMIRA (1)

1Ch	7: 8 **Z**, and Joash, and Eliezer, and Elioenai,	2160

ZENAN (1)

Jos	15:37 **Z**, and Hadashah, and Migdal-gad,	6799

ZENAS (1)

Tit	3:13 Bring **Z** the lawyer and Apollos on their	2211

ZEPHANIAH (10)

2Ki	25:18 **Z** the second priest, and the three keepers	6846
1Ch	6:36 of Joel, the son of Azariah, the son of **Z**,	6846
Jer	21: 1 **Z** the son of Maaseiah the priest, saying,	6846
	29:25 and to **Z** the son of Maaseiah the priest,	6846
	29:29 the priest read this letter in the ears of	6846
	37: 3 **Z** the son of Maaseiah the priest to	6846
	52:24 **Z** the second priest, and the three keepers	6846
Zep	1: 1 which came unto **Z** the son of Cushi,	6846
Zec	6:10 go *into* the house of Josiah the son of **Z**;	6846
	6:14 and to Jedaiah, and to Hen the son of **Z**,	6846

ZEPHATH (1)

Jdg	1:17 they slew the Canaanites that inhabited **Z**,	6857

ZEPHATHAH (1)

2Ch	14:10 set the battle in array in the valley of **Z**	6859

ZEPHI (1) [ZEPHO]

1Ch	1:36 Omar, **Z**, and Gatam, Kenaz, and Timna,	6825

ZEPHO (2) [ZEPHI]

Ge	36:11 Omar, **Z**, and Gatam, and Kenaz.	6825
	36:15 duke Omar, duke **Z**, duke Kenaz,	6825

ZEPHON (1) [BAAL-ZEPHON, ZEPHONITES]

Nu	26:15 of **Z**, the family of the Zephonites:	6827

ZEPHONITES (1) [ZEPHON]

Nu	26:15 of Zephon, the family of the **Z**: of Haggi,	6831

ZER (1)

Jos	19:35 **Z**, and Hammath, Rakkath, and	6863

ZERAH (20)

Ge	36:13 Nahath, and **Z**, Shammah, and Mizzah:	2226
	36:17 duke Nahath, duke **Z**, duke Shammah,	2226
	36:33 Jobab the son of **Z** of Bozrah reigned in	2226
	46:12 Onan, and Shelah, and Pharez, and **Z**:	2226
Nu	26:13 Of **Z**, the family of the Zarhites: of Shaul,	2226
	26:20 **Z**, the family of the Zarhites.	2226
Jos	7: 1 of Carmi, the son of Zabdi, the son of **Z**,	2226
	7:18 of Carmi, the son of Zabdi, the son of **Z**,	2226
	7:24 took Achan the son of **Z**, and the silver,	2226
	22:20 Did not Achan the son of **Z** commit a	2226
1Ch	1:37 Nahath, **Z**, Shammah, and Mizzah.	2226
	1:44 Jobab the son of **Z** of Bozrah reigned in	2226
	2: 4 daughter in law bare him Pharez and **Z**.	2226
	2: 6 the sons of **Z**; Zimri, and Ethan, and	2226
	4:24 of Jamin, Jarib, **Z**, *and* Shaul:	2226
	6:21 Joah his son, Iddo his son, **Z** his son,	2226
	6:41 The son of Ethni, the son of **Z**, the son of	2226
	9: 6 of the sons of **Z**; Jeuel, and their brethren,	2226
2Ch	14: 9 there came out against them **Z**	2226
Ne	11:24 of the children of **Z** the son of Judah,	2226

ZERAHIAH (5)
1Ch	6: 6 Uzzi begat **Z**, and Zerahiah begat	2228
	6: 6 begat Zerahiah, and **Z** begat Meraioth,	2228
	6:51 Bukki his son, Uzzi his son, **Z** his son,	2228
Ezr	7: 4 The son of **Z**, the son of Uzzi, the son of	2228
	8: 4 Elihoenai the son of **Z**, and with him two	2228

ZERAHITE See ZARHITES

ZERED (3)
Dt	2:13 *said I*, and get you over the brook **Z**.	2218
	2:13 And we went over the brook **Z**.	2218
	2:14 until we were come over the brook **Z**,,	2218

ZEREDA (1)
1Ki	11:26 an Ephrathite of **Z**, Solomon's servant,	6868

ZEREDATHAH (1)
2Ch	4:17 the clay ground between Succoth and **Z**.	6868

ZERERATH (1)
Jdg	7:22 the host fled to Beth-shittah in **Z**, *and* to	6888

ZERESH (4)
Est	5:10 and called for his friends, and **Z** his wife.	2238
	5:14 said **Z** his wife and all his friends unto	2238
	6:13 Haman told **Z** his wife and all his friends	2238
	6:13 said his wise *men* and **Z** his wife unto	2238

ZERETH (1)
1Ch	4: 7 the sons of Helah *were*, **Z**, and Jezoar,	6889

ZERETH SHAHAR See ZARETHSHAHAR

ZERI (1)
1Ch	25: 3 Gedaliah, and **Z**, and Jeshaiah, Hashabiah,	6874

ZEROR (1)
1Sa	9: 1 the son of Abiel, the son of **Z**, the son of	6872

ZERUAH (1)
1Ki	11:26 whose mother's name *was* **Z**, a widow	6871

ZERUBBABEL (22) [ZOROBABEL]
1Ch	3:19 the sons of Pedaiah *were*, **Z**, and Shimei:	2216
	3:19 the son of **Z**; Meshullam, and Hananiah,	2216
Ezr	2: 2 Which came with **Z**: Jeshua, Nehemiah,	2216
	3: 2 **Z** the son of Shealtiel, and his brethren,	2216
	3: 8 began **Z** the son of Shealtiel, and Jeshua	2216
	4: 2 they came to **Z**, and to the chief of	2216
	4: 3 **Z**, and Jeshua, and the rest of the chief of	2216
	5: 2 rose up **Z** the son of Shealtiel,	2217
Ne	7: 7 Who came with **Z**, Jeshua, Nehemiah,	2216
	12: 1 the Levites that went up with **Z** the son	2216
	12:47 all Israel in the days of **Z**, and in the days	2216
Hag	1: 1 the prophet unto **Z** the son of Shealtiel,	2216
	1:12 **Z** the son of Shealtiel, and Joshua the son	2216
	1:14 the LORD stirred up the spirit of **Z**	2216
	2: 2 Speak now to **Z** the son of Shealtiel,	2216
	2: 4 Yet now be strong, O **Z**, saith the LORD,	2216
	2:21 Speak to **Z**, governor of Judah, saying,	2216
	2:23 will I take thee, O **Z**, my servant, the son	2216
Zec	4: 6 This *is* the word of the LORD unto **Z**,	2216
	4: 7 before **Z** *thou shalt* become a plain:	2216
	4: 9 The hands of **Z** have laid the foundation	2216
	4:10 see the plummet in the hand of **Z** *with*	2216

ZERUIAH (26)
1Sa	26: 6 to Abishai the son of **Z**, brother to Joab,	6870
2Sa	2:13 Joab the son of **Z**, and the servants of	6870
	2:18 there were three sons of **Z** there, Joab,	6870
	3:39 men the sons of **Z** be too hard for me:	6870
	8:16 Joab the son of **Z** *was* over the host;	6870
	14: 1 Now Joab the son of **Z** perceived that	6870
	16: 9 said Abishai the son of **Z** unto the king,	6870
	16:10 What have I to do with you, ye sons of **Z**?	6870
	17:25 of Nahash, sister to **Z** Joab's mother.	6870
	18: 2 under the hand of Abishai the son of **Z**,	6870
	19:21 Abishai the son of **Z** answered and said,	6870
	19:22 What have I to do with you, ye sons of **Z**,	6870
	21:17 Abishai the son of **Z** succoured him,	6870
	23:18 the brother of Joab, the son of **Z**,	6870
	23:37 armourbearer to Joab the son of **Z**,	6870
1Ki	1: 7 he conferred with Joab the son of **Z**,	6870
	2: 5 also what Joab the son of **Z** did to me,	6870
	2:22 the priest, and for Joab the son of **Z**,	6870
1Ch	2:16 Whose sisters *were* **Z**, and Abigail.	6870
	2:16 the sons of **Z**; Abishai, and Joab,	6870
	11: 6 So Joab the son of **Z** went first up,	6870
	11:39 the armourbearer of Joab the son of **Z**,	6870
	18:12 Moreover Abishai the son of **Z** slew of	6870
	18:15 Joab the son of **Z** *was* over the host;	6870
	26:28 and Joab the son of **Z**, had dedicated;	6870
	27:24 Joab the son of **Z** began to number,	6870

ZETHAM (2)
1Ch	23: 8 chief *was* Jehiel, and **Z**, and Joel, three.	2241
	26:22 and Joel his brother, *which* were over	2241

ZETHAN (1)
1Ch	7:10 and **Z**, and Tharshish, and Ahishahar.	2133

ZETHAR (1)
Est	1:10 Bigtha, and Abagtha, **Z**, and Carcas,	2242

ZEUS See JUPITER

ZIA (1)
1Ch	5:13 and Jachan, and **Z**, and Heber, seven.	2127

ZIBA (16)
2Sa	9: 2 of Saul a servant whose name *was* **Z**.	6717
	9: 2 the king said unto him, *Art* thou **Z**?	6717
	9: 3 **Z** said unto the king, Jonathan hath yet a	6717
	9: 4 the king said unto the king, Behold, he *is in*	6717
	9: 9 the king called to **Z**, Saul's servant,	6717
	9:10 Now **Z** had fifteen sons and	6717
	9:11 said **Z** unto the king, According to all that	6717
	9:12 all that dwelt in the house of **Z** *were*	6717
	16: 1 **Z** the servant of Mephibosheth met him,	6717
	16: 2 king said unto **Z**, What meanest thou by	6717
	16: 2 **Z** said, The asses *be* for the king's	6717
	16: 3 **Z** said unto the king, Behold, he abideth	6717
	16: 4 said he to **Z**, Behold, thine *are* all	6717
	16: 4 **Z** said, I humbly beseech thee *that* I may	6717
	19:17 **Z** the servant of the house of Saul,	6717
	19:29 I have said, Thou and **Z** divide the land.	6717

ZIBEON (8)
Ge	36: 2 of Anah the daughter of **Z** the Hivite;	6649
	36:14 of Anah, daughter of **Z**, Esau's wife:	6649
	36:20 Lotan, and Shobal, and **Z**, and Anah,	6649
	36:24 these *are* the children of **Z**; both Aiah,	6649
	36:24 as he fed the asses of **Z** his father.	6649
	36:29 duke Shobal, duke **Z**, duke Anah,	6649
1Ch	1:38 **Z**, and Anah, and Dishon, and Ezer,	6649
	1:40 And the sons of **Z**; Aiah, and Anah.	6649

ZIBIA (1)
1Ch	8: 9 and **Z**, and Mesha, and Malcham,	6644

ZIBIAH (2)
2Ki	12: 1 his mother's name *was* **Z** of Beer-sheba.	6645
2Ch	24: 1 His mother's name also *was* **Z** of	6645

ZICHRI (12)
Ex	6:21 sons of Izhar; Korah, and Nepheg, and **Z**.	2147
1Ch	8:19 And Jakim, and **Z**, and Zabdi,	2147
	8:23 And Abdon, and **Z**, and Hanan,	2147
	8:27 Jaresiah, and Eliah, and **Z**, the sons of	2147
	9:15 of Micah, the son of **Z**, the son of Asaph,	2147
	26:25 and **Z** his son, and Shelomith his son.	2147
	27:16 the Reubenites *was* Eliezer the son of **Z**:	2147
2Ch	17:16 next him *was* Amasiah the son of **Z**,	2147
	23: 1 Elishaphat the son of **Z**, into covenant	2147
	28: 7 **Z**, a mighty *man* of Ephraim, slew	2147
Ne	11: 9 Joel the son of **Z** *was* their overseer;	2147
	12:17 Of Abijah, **Z**; of Miniamin, of Moadiah,	2147

ZICRI See ZICHRI

ZIDDIM (1)
Jos	19:35 fenced cities *are* **Z**, Zer, and Hammath,	6661

ZIDKIJAH (1)
Ne	10: 1 Tirshatha, the son of Hachaliah, and **Z**,	6667

ZIDON (21) [SIDON, ZIDONIANS]
Ge	49:13 of ships; and his border *shall be* unto **Z**.	6721
Jos	11: 8 chased them unto great **Z**,	6721
	19:28 Hammon, and Kanah, *even* unto great **Z**;	6721
Jdg	1:31 nor the inhabitants of **Z**, nor of Ahlab,	6721
	10: 6 the gods of **Z**, and the gods of Moab,	6721
	18:28 because it *was* far from **Z**, and they had	6721
2Sa	24: 6 they came to Dan-jaan, and about to **Z**,	6721
1Ki	17: 9 which *belongeth* to **Z**, and dwell there:	6721
1Ch	1:13 Canaan begat **Z** his firstborn, and Heth,	6721
Ezr	3: 7 oil, unto them of **Z**, and to them of Tyre,	6722
Isa	23: 2 thou whom the merchants of **Z**, that pass	6721
	23: 4 Be thou ashamed, O **Z**: for the sea hath	6721
	23:12 O thou oppressed virgin, daughter of **Z**:	6721
Jer	25:22 the kings of **Z**, and the kings of the isles	6721
	27: 3 to the king of Tyrus, and to the king of **Z**,	6721
	47: 4 and every helper that remaineth:	6721
Eze	27: 8 The inhabitants of **Z** and Arvad were thy	6721
	28:21 set thy face against **Z**, and prophesy	6721
	28:22 Behold, I *am* against thee, O **Z**; and I will	6721
Joel	3: 4 and **Z**, and all the coasts of Palestine?	6721
Zec	9: 2 and **Z**, though it be very wise.	6721

ZIDONIANS (10) [ZIDON]
Jdg	10:12 The **Z** also, and the Amalekites,	6722
	18: 7 the manner of the **Z**, quiet and secure;	6722
	18: 7 they were far from the **Z**, and had no	6722
1Ki	11: 1 Ammonites, Edomites, **Z**, *and* Hittites;	6722
	11: 5 after Ashtoreth the goddess of the **Z**,	6722
	11:33 Ashtoreth the goddess of the **Z**,	6722
	16:31 the daughter of Ethbaal king of the **Z**,	6722
2Ki	23:13 for Ashtoreth the abomination of the **Z**,	6722
1Ch	22: 4 for the **Z** and they of Tyre brought much	6722
Eze	32:30 of the north, all of them, and all the **Z**,	6722

ZIF (1)
1Ki	6: 1 the month **Z**, which *is* the second month,	2099
	6:37 house of the LORD laid, in the month **Z**:	2099

ZIHA (3)
Ezr	2:43 children of **Z**, the children of Hasupha,	6727
Ne	7:46 children of **Z**, the children of Hashupha,	6727
	11:21 **Z** and Gispa *were* over the Nethinims.	6727

ZIKLAG (15)
Jos	15:31 And **Z**, and Madmannah, and Sansannah,	6860

Jos	19: 5 And, and Beth-marcaboth, and Hazar-susah,	6860
1Sa	27: 6 Achish gave him **Z** that day: wherefore	6860
	27: 6 wherefore **Z** pertaineth unto the kings of	6860
	30: 1 his men were come *to* **Z** on the third day,	6860
	30: 1 **Z**, and smitten Ziklag, and burnt it with	6860
	30: 1 and smitten Ziklag, and burnt it with fire;	6860
	30:14 south of Caleb; and we burnt **Z** with fire.	6860
	30:26 David came to **Z**, he sent of the spoil	6860
2Sa	1: 1 and David had abode two days in **Z**;	6860
	4:10 I took hold of him, and slew him in **Z**,	6860
1Ch	4:30 And at Bethuel, and at Hormah, and at **Z**,	6860
	12: 1 these *are* they that came to David to **Z**,	6860
	12:20 As he went to **Z**, there fell to him of	6860
Ne	11:28 at **Z**, and at Mekonah, and in the villages	6860

ZILLAH (3)
Ge	4:19 *was* Adah, and the name of the other **Z**.	6741
	4:22 she also bare Tubal-cain, an instructor	6741
	4:23 his wives, Adah and **Z**, Hear my voice;	6741

ZILLETHAI See ZILTHAI

ZILPAH (7)
Ge	29:24 Laban gave unto Leah **Z** his	2153
	30: 9 she took **Z** her maid, and gave her Jacob	2153
	30:10 And **Z** Leah's maid bare Jacob a son.	2153
	30:12 **Z** Leah's maid bare Jacob a second son.	2153
	35:26 the sons of **Z**, Leah's handmaid; Gad,	2153
	37: 2 and with the sons of **Z**, his father's wives:	2153
	46:18 These *are* the sons of **Z**, whom Laban	2153

ZILTHAI (2)
1Ch	8:20 And Elienai, and **Z**, and Eliel,	6769
	12:20 Michael, and Jozabad, and Elihu, and **Z**,	6769

ZIMMAH (3)
1Ch	6:20 Libni his son, Jahath his son, **Z** his son,	2155
	6:42 The son of Ethan, the son of **Z**, the son	2155
2Ch	29:12 Joah the son of **Z**, and Eden the son of	2155

ZIMRAN (2)
Ge	25: 2 she bare him **Z**, and Jokshan, and Medan,	2175
1Ch	1:32 she bare **Z**, and Jokshan, and Medan,	2175

ZIMRI (15)
Nu	25:14 *was* **Z**, the son of Salu, a prince of a chief	2174
1Ki	16: 9 his servant **Z**, captain of half *his* chariots,	2174
	16:10 **Z** went in and smote him, and killed him,	2174
	16:12 did **Z** destroy all the house of Baasha,	2174
	16:15 seventh year of Asa king of Judah did **Z**	2174
	16:16 **Z** hath conspired, and hath also slain	2174
	16:18 pass, when **Z** saw that the city was taken,	2174
	16:20 Now the rest of the acts of **Z**,	2174
2Ki	9:31 she said, *Had* **Z** peace, who slew his	2174
1Ch	2: 6 and Ethan, and Heman, and Calcol,	2174
	8:36 begat Alemeth, and Azmaveth, and **Z**;	2174
	8:36 and Zimri; and **Z** begat Moza,	2174
	9:42 begat Alemeth, and Azmaveth, and **Z**;	2174
	9:42 and Zimri; and **Z** begat Moza;	2174
Jer	25:25 all the kings of **Z**, and all the kings of	2174

ZIN (7)
Nu	13:21 the land from the wilderness of **Z**	6790
	20: 1 *into* the desert of **Z** in the first month:	6790
	27:14 my commandment in the desert of **Z**,	6790
	27:14 Meribah in Kadesh *in* the wilderness of **Z**.	6790
	33:36 pitched in the wilderness of **Z**, which *is*	6790
	34: 3 of **Z** along by the coast of Edom,	6790
	34: 4 the ascent of Akrabbim, and pass on to **Z**:	6790
Dt	32:51 Meribah-Kadesh, *in* the wilderness of **Z**;	6790
Jos	15: 1 the wilderness of **Z** southward *was*	6790
	15: 3 passed along to **Z**, and ascended up on	6790

ZINA (1) [ZIZAH]
1Ch	23:10 *were*, Jahath, **Z**, and Jeush, and Beriah.	2126

ZION (153) [SION, ZION'S]
2Sa	5: 7 David took the strong hold of **Z**:	6726
1Ki	8: 1 out of the city of David, which *is* **Z**.	6726
2Ki	19:21 virgin the daughter of **Z** hath despised	6726
	19:31 and they that escape out of mount **Z**:	6726
1Ch	11: 5 Nevertheless David took the castle of **Z**,	6726
2Ch	5: 2 out of the city of David, which *is* **Z**.	6726
Ps	2: 6 I set my king upon my holy hill of **Z**.	6726
	9:11 to the LORD, which dwelleth in **Z**:	6726
	9:14 praise in the gates of the daughter of **Z**:	6726
	14: 7 the salvation of Israel *were* come out of **Z**!	6726
	20: 2 sanctuary, and strengthen thee out of **Z**;	6726
	48: 2 *is* mount **Z**, *on* the sides of the north,	6726
	48:11 Let mount **Z** rejoice, let the daughters of	6726
	48:12 Walk about **Z**, and go round about her:	6726
	50: 2 Out of **Z**, the perfection of beauty,	6726
	51:18 Do good in thy good pleasure unto **Z**:	6726
	53: 6 the salvation of Israel *were* come out of **Z**!	6726
	65: 1 Praise waiteth for thee, O God, in **Z**:	6726
	69:35 For God will save **Z**, and will build	6726
	74: 2 this mount **Z**, wherein thou hast dwelt.	6726
	76: 2 tabernacle, and his dwelling place in **Z**.	6726
	78:68 of Judah, the mount **Z** which he loved.	6726
	84: 7 *every one of them* in **Z** appeareth before	6726
	87: 2 The LORD loveth the gates of **Z** more	6726
	87: 5 of **Z** it shall be said, This and that man	6726
	97: 8 **Z** heard, and was glad, and the daughters	6726
	99: 2 The LORD *is* great in **Z**; and he *is* high	6726
	102:13 Thou shalt arise, *and* have mercy upon **Z**:	6726
	102:16 When the LORD shall build up **Z**, he shall	6726

Z

Ref	Text	Strong's
Ps 102:21	To declare the name of the LORD in **Z**,	6726
110: 2	shall send the rod of thy strength out of **Z**:	6726
125: 1	trust in the LORD *shall be* as mount **Z**,	6726
126: 1	the LORD turned again the captivity of **Z**,	6726
128: 5	The LORD shall bless thee out of **Z**:	6726
129: 5	confounded and turned back that hate **Z**.	6726
132:13	For the LORD hath chosen **Z**; he hath	6726
133: 3	that descended upon the mountains of **Z**:	6726
134: 3	heaven and earth bless thee out of **Z**.	6726
135:21	Blessed *be* the LORD out of **Z**,	6726
137: 1	yea, we wept, when we remembered **Z**.	6726
137: 3	*saying,* Sing us *one* of the songs of **Z**.	6726
146:10	*even* thy God, O **Z**, unto all generations.	6726
147:12	O Jerusalem; praise thy God, O **Z**.	6726
149: 2	the children of **Z** be joyful in their King.	6726
SS 3:11	O ye daughters of **Z**, and behold king	6726
Isa 1: 8	the daughter of **Z** is left as a cottage in a	6726
1:27	**Z** shall be redeemed with judgment,	6726
2: 3	for out of **Z** shall go forth the law,	6726
3:16	Because the daughters of **Z** are haughty,	6726
3:17	crown of the head of the daughters of **Z**,	6726
4: 3	*that* he that is left in **Z**, and he that	6726
4: 4	away the filth of the daughters of **Z**,	6726
4: 5	upon every dwelling place of mount **Z**,	6726
8:18	of hosts, which dwelleth in mount **Z**.	6726
10:12	performed his whole work upon mount **Z**	6726
10:24	O my people that dwellest in **Z**, be not	6726
10:32	*against* the mount of the daughter of **Z**:	6726
12: 6	Cry out and shout, thou inhabitant of **Z**:	6726
14:32	That the LORD hath founded **Z**,	6726
16: 1	unto the mount of the daughter of **Z**.	6726
18: 7	name of the LORD of hosts, the mount **Z**.	6726
24:23	the LORD of hosts shall reign in mount **Z**,	6726
28:16	Behold, I lay in **Z** for a foundation a stone,	6726
29: 8	the nations be, that fight against mount **Z**.	6726
30:19	For the people shall dwell in **Z** at	6726
31: 4	of hosts come down to fight for mount **Z**,	6726
31: 9	whose fire *is* in **Z**, and his furnace in	6726
33: 5	he hath filled **Z** *with* judgment and	6726
33:14	The sinners in **Z** are afraid; fearfulness	6726
33:20	Look upon **Z**, the city of our solemnities:	6726
34: 8	of recompences for the controversy of **Z**.	6726
35:10	come *to* **Z** with songs and everlasting joy	6726
37:22	virgin, the daughter of **Z**, hath despised	6726
37:32	and they that escape out of mount **Z**:	6726
40: 9	**Z**, that bringest good tidings, get thee up	6726
41:27	The first *shall say* to **Z**, Behold,	6726
46:13	I will place salvation in **Z** for Israel my	6726
49:14	said, The LORD hath forsaken me,	6726
51: 3	For the LORD shall comfort **Z**: he will	6726
51:11	return, and come with singing *unto* **Z**;	6726
51:16	and say unto **Z**, Thou *art* my people.	6726
52: 1	Awake, awake; put on thy strength, O **Z**;	6726
52: 2	of thy neck, O captive daughter of **Z**.	6726
52: 7	that saith unto **Z**, Thy God reigneth!	6726
52: 8	when the LORD shall bring again **Z**.	6726
59:20	the redeemer shall come to **Z**,	6726
60:14	The **Z** of the Holy One of Israel.	6726
61: 3	To appoint unto them that mourn in **Z**,	6726
62:11	Say ye to the daughter of **Z**, Behold,	6726
64:10	**Z** is a wilderness, Jerusalem a desolation.	6726
66: 8	as soon as **Z** travailed, she brought forth	6726
Jer 3:14	two of a family, and I will bring you to **Z**:	6726
4: 6	Set up the standard toward **Z**: retire,	6726
4:31	the voice of the daughter of **Z**,	6726
6: 2	I have likened the daughter of **Z** *to* a	6726
6:23	for war against thee, O daughter of **Z**.	6726
8:19	*Is* not the LORD in **Z**? *is* not her king in	6726
9:19	For a voice of wailing is heard out of **Z**,	6726
14:19	hath thy soul lothed **Z**? why hast thou	6726
26:18	**Z** shall be plowed *like* a field,	6726
30:17	called thee an Outcast, *saying,* This *is* **Z**,	6726
31: 6	let us go up *to* **Z** unto the LORD our God.	6726
31:12	shall come and sing in the height of **Z**,	6726
50: 5	shall ask the way *to* **Z** with their faces	6726
50:28	to declare in **Z** the vengeance of the LORD	6726
51:10	let us declare in **Z** the work of the LORD	6726
51:24	that they have done in **Z** in your sight,	6726
51:35	shall the inhabitant of **Z** say;	6726
La 1: 4	The ways of **Z** do mourn, because	6726
1: 6	from the daughter of **Z** all her beauty is	6726
1:17	**Z** spreadeth forth her hands, *and there is*	6726
2: 1	daughter of **Z** with a cloud in his anger,	6726
2: 4	in the tabernacle of the daughter of **Z**:	6726
2: 6	and sabbaths to be forgotten in **Z**,	6726
2: 8	to destroy the wall of the daughter of **Z**:	6726
2:10	The elders of the daughter of **Z** sit upon	6726
2:13	comfort thee, O virgin daughter of **Z**?	6726
2:18	the Lord, O wall of the daughter of **Z**,	6726
4: 2	The precious sons of **Z**, comparable to fine	6726
4:11	hath kindled a fire in **Z**, and it hath	6726
4:22	iniquity is accomplished, O daughter of **Z**;	6726
5:11	They ravished the women in **Z**,	6726
5:18	Because of the mountain of **Z**, which is	6726
Joel 2: 1	Blow ye the trumpet in **Z**, and sound an	6726
2:15	Blow the trumpet in **Z**, sanctify a fast,	6726
2:23	ye children of **Z**, and rejoice in the LORD	6726
2:32	for in mount **Z** and in Jerusalem shall be	6726
3:16	The LORD also shall roar out of **Z**,	6726
3:17	I *am* the LORD your God dwelling in **Z**,	6726
3:21	not cleansed: for the LORD dwelleth in **Z**.	6726
Am 1: 2	The LORD will roar from **Z**, and utter his	6726
6: 1	Woe to them *that are* at ease in **Z**, and	6726
Ob 1:17	But upon mount **Z** shall be deliverance,	6726
1:21	saviours shall come up on mount **Z** to	6726

Ref	Text	Strong's
Mic 1:13	beginning of the sin to the daughter of **Z**:	6726
3:10	They build up **Z** with blood,	6726
3:12	Therefore shall **Z** for your sake be plowed	6726
4: 2	for the law shall go forth of **Z**,	6726
4: 7	over them in mount **Z** from henceforth,	6726
4: 8	the strong hold of the daughter of **Z**,	6726
4:10	and labour to bring forth, O daughter of **Z**,	6726
4:11	be defiled, and let our eye look upon **Z**.	6726
4:13	Arise and thresh, O daughter of **Z**: for I	6726
Zep 3:14	Sing, O daughter of **Z**; shout, O Israel;	6726
3:16	*and to* **Z**, Let not thine hands be slack.	6726
Zec 1:14	and for **Z** with a great jealousy.	6726
1:17	the LORD shall yet comfort **Z**,	6726
2: 7	Deliver thyself, O **Z**, that dwellest *with*	6726
2:10	Sing and rejoice, O daughter of **Z**: for lo,	6726
8: 2	I was jealous for **Z** *with* great jealousy,	6726
8: 3	I am returned unto **Z**, and will dwell in	6726
9: 9	Rejoice greatly, O daughter of **Z**; shout,	6726
9:13	O **Z**, against thy sons, O Greece.	6726

ZION'S (1) [ZION]

Ref	Text	Strong's
Isa 62: 1	For **Z** sake will I not hold my peace,	6726

ZIOR (1)

Ref	Text	Strong's
Jos 15:54	and Kirjath-arba, which *is* Hebron, and **Z**;	6730

ZIPH (10) [ZIPHIMS, ZIPHITES]

Ref	Text	Strong's
Jos 15:24	**Z**, and Telem, and Bealoth,	2128
15:55	Maon, Carmel, and **Z**, and Juttah,	2128
1Sa 23:14	in a mountain in the wilderness of **Z**.	2128
23:15	David *was* in the wilderness of **Z** in a	2128
23:24	they arose, and went to **Z** before Saul:	2128
26: 2	and went down to the wilderness of **Z**,	2128
26: 2	to seek David in the wilderness of **Z**.	2128
1Ch 2:42	his firstborn, which *was* the father of **Z**;	2128
4:16	**Z**, and Ziphah, Tiria, and Asareel.	2128
2Ch 11: 8	And Gath, and Mareshah, and **Z**,	2128

ZIPHAH (1)

Ref	Text	Strong's
1Ch 4:16	Ziph, and **Z**, Tiria, and Asareel.	2129

ZIPHIMS (1) [ZIPH]

Ref	Text	Strong's
Ps 54: T	when the **Z** came and said to Saul,	2130

ZIPHION (1)

Ref	Text	Strong's
Ge 46:16	**Z**, and Haggi, Shuni, and Ezbon, Eri,	6837

ZIPHITES (2) [ZIPH]

Ref	Text	Strong's
1Sa 23:19	came up the **Z** to Saul to Gibeah, saying,	2130
26: 1	the **Z** came unto Saul to Gibeah, saying,	2130

ZIPHRON (1)

Ref	Text	Strong's
Nu 34: 9	border shall go on to **Z**, and the goings	2202

ZIPPOR (7)

Ref	Text	Strong's
Nu 22: 2	Balak the son of **Z** saw all that Israel had	6834
22: 4	Balak the son of **Z** *was* king of	6834
22:10	Balak the son of **Z**, king of Moab, hath	6834
22:16	said to him, Thus saith Balak the son of **Z**,	6834
23:18	hear; hearken unto me, thou son of **Z**:	6834
Jos 24: 9	Balak the son of **Z**, king of Moab, arose	6834
Jdg 11:25	any thing better than Balak the son of **Z**,	6834

ZIPPORAH (3)

Ref	Text	Strong's
Ex 2:21	and he gave Moses **Z** his daughter.	6855
4:25	**Z** took a sharp stone, and cut off	6855
18: 2	Moses' father in law, took **Z**, Moses' wife,	6855

ZITHRI (1)

Ref	Text	Strong's
Ex 6:22	of Uzziel; Mishael, and Elzaphan, and **Z**.	5644

ZIV See ZIF

ZIZ (1)

Ref	Text	Strong's
2Ch 20:16	behold, they come up by the cliff of **Z**;	6732

ZIZA (2)

Ref	Text	Strong's
1Ch 4:37	**Z** the son of Shiphi, the son of Allon,	2124
2Ch 11:20	and Attai, and **Z**, and Shelomith.	2124

ZIZAH (1) [ZINA]

Ref	Text	Strong's
1Ch 23:11	Jahath was the chief, and **Z** the second:	2125

ZOAN (7)

Ref	Text	Strong's
Nu 13:22	was built seven years before **Z** in Egypt.)	6814
Ps 78:12	in the land of Egypt, *in* the field of **Z**.	6814
78:43	Egypt, and his wonders in the field of **Z**:	6814
Isa 19:11	Surely the princes of **Z** *are* fools,	6814
19:13	The princes of **Z** are become fools,	6814
30: 4	For his princes were at **Z**,	6814
Eze 30:14	will set fire in **Z**, and will execute	6814

ZOAR (10)

Ref	Text	Strong's
Ge 13:10	the land of Egypt, as thou comest unto **Z**.	6820
14: 2	and the king of Bela, which *is* **Z**.	6820
14: 8	and the king of Bela (the same *is* **Z**);	6820
19:22	the name of the city was called **Z**.	6820
19:23	upon the earth when Lot entered into **Z**.	6820
19:30	Lot went up out of **Z**, and dwelt in	6820
19:30	with him; for he feared to dwell in **Z**:	6820
Dt 34: 3	of Jericho, the city of palm trees, unto **Z**.	6820
Isa 15: 5	his fugitives *shall flee* unto **Z**, a heifer of	6820
Jer 48:34	from **Z** *even* unto Horonaim, *as* a heifer	6820

ZOBA (2) [ZOBAH]

Ref	Text	Strong's
2Sa 10: 6	Syrians of **Z**, twenty thousand footmen,	6678
10: 8	the Syrians of **Z**, and of Rehob,	6678

ZOBAH (11) [ARAM-ZOBAH, HAMATH-ZOBAH, ZOBA]

Ref	Text	Strong's
1Sa 14:47	against the kings of **Z**, and against	6678
2Sa 8: 3	the son of Rehob, king of **Z**,	6678
8: 5	came to succour Hadadezer king of **Z**,	6678
8:12	of Hadadezer, son of Rehob, king of **Z**.	6678
23:36	Igal the son of Nathan of **Z**, Bani	6678
1Ki 11:23	fled from his lord Hadadezer king of **Z**:	6678
11:24	when David slew them *of* **Z**: and they	NIH
1Ch 18: 3	David smote Hadarezer king of **Z** unto	6678
18: 5	came to help Hadarezer king of **Z**,	6678
18: 9	all the host of Hadarezer king of **Z**;	6678
19: 6	and out of Syria-maachah, and out of **Z**.	6678

ZOBEBAH (1)

Ref	Text	Strong's
1Ch 4: 8	**Z**, and the families of Aharhel the son of	6637

ZOHAR (4)

Ref	Text	Strong's
Ge 23: 8	and intreat for me to Ephron the son of **Z**,	6714
25: 9	in the field of Ephron the son of **Z**	6714
46:10	**Z**, and Shaul the son of a Canaanitish	6714
Ex 6:15	**Z**, and Shaul the son of a Canaanitish	6714

ZOHELETH (1)

Ref	Text	Strong's
1Ki 1: 9	and oxen and fat cattle by the stone of **Z**,	2120

ZOHETH (1)

Ref	Text	Strong's
1Ch 4:20	the sons of Ishi *were*, **Z**, and Ben-zoheth.	2105

ZOPHAH (2)

Ref	Text	Strong's
1Ch 7:35	**Z**, and Imna, and Shelesh, and Amal.	6690
7:36	The sons of **Z**; Suah, and Harnepher,	6690

ZOPHAI (1)

Ref	Text	Strong's
1Ch 6:26	of Elkanah; **Z** his son, and Nahath his son,	6689

ZOPHAR (4)

Ref	Text	Strong's
Job 2:11	Bildad the Shuhite, and **Z** the Naamathite:	6691
11: 1	answered **Z** the Naamathite, and said,	6691
20: 1	answered **Z** the Naamathite, and said,	6691
42: 9	the Shuhite *and* **Z** the Naamathite went,	6691

ZOPHIM (1) [RAMATHAIM-ZOPHIM]

Ref	Text	Strong's
Nu 23:14	he brought him *into* the field of **Z**,	6839

ZORAH (8)

Ref	Text	Strong's
Jos 19:41	the coast of their inheritance was **Z**,	6881
Jdg 13: 2	was a certain man of **Z**, of the family	6881
13:25	the camp of Dan, between **Z** and Eshtaol.	6881
16:31	buried him between **Z** and Eshtaol in	6881
18: 2	men of valour, from **Z** and from Eshtaol,	6881
18: 8	they came unto their brethren *to* **Z** and	6881
18:11	out of **Z** and out of Eshtaol, six hundred	6881
2Ch 11:10	**Z**, and Aijalon, and Hebron, which *are* in	6881

ZORATHITES (1)

Ref	Text	Strong's
1Ch 4: 2	Lahad. These *are* the families of the **Z**.	6882

ZOREAH (1)

Ref	Text	Strong's
Jos 15:33	in the valley, Eshtaol, and **Z**, and Ashnah,	6881

ZORITES (1)

Ref	Text	Strong's
1Ch 2:54	and half of the Manahethites, the **Z**.	6882

ZOROBABEL (3) [ZERUBBABEL]

Ref	Text	Strong's
Mt 1:12	begat Salathiel; and Salathiel begat **Z**;	*2216*
1:13	And **Z** begat Abiud; and Abiud begat	*2216*
Lk 3:27	*the son* of Rhesa, which was *the son* of **Z**,	*2216*

ZUAR (5)

Ref	Text	Strong's
Nu 1: 8	Of Issachar; Nethaneel the son of **Z**.	6686
2: 5	Nethaneel the son of **Z** *shall be* captain of	6686
7:18	the second day Nethaneel the son of **Z**,	6686
7:23	the offering of Nethaneel the son of **Z**.	6686
10:15	of Issachar *was* Nethaneel the son of **Z**.	6686

ZUPH (3)

Ref	Text	Strong's
1Sa 1: 1	son of Tohu, the son of **Z**, an Ephrathite:	6689
9: 5	when they were come to the land of **Z**,	6689
1Ch 6:35	The son of **Z**, the son of Elkanah, the son	6689

ZUPHITE See RAMATHAIM-ZOPHIM

ZUR (5) [BETH-ZUR]

Ref	Text	Strong's
Nu 25:15	was slain *was* Cozbi, the daughter of **Z**;	6698
31: 8	and Rekem, and **Z**, and Hur, and Reba,	6698
Jos 13:21	and Rekem, and **Z**, and Hur, and Reba,	6698
1Ch 8:30	and **Z**, and Kish, and Baal, and Nadab,	6698
9:36	and **Z**, and Kish, and Baal, and Ner, and	6698

ZURIEL (1)

Ref	Text	Strong's
Nu 3:35	of Merari *was* **Z** the son of Abihail:	6700

ZURISHADDAI (5)

Ref	Text	Strong's
Nu 1: 6	Of Simeon; Shelumiel the son of **Z**.	6701
2:12	Simeon *shall be* Shelumiel the son of **Z**.	6701
7:36	On the fifth day Shelumiel the son of **Z**,	6701
7:41	the offering of Shelumiel the son of **Z**.	6701
10:19	of Simeon *was* Shelumiel the son of **Z**.	6701

ZUZIMS (1)

Ref	Text	Strong's
Ge 14: 5	the **Z** in Ham, and the Emims in Shaveh	2104

ZUZITES See ZUZIMS

Z

INDEX OF ARTICLES, CONJUNCTIONS, PARTICLES, PREPOSITIONS AND PRONOUNS

INDEX OF ARTICLES, CONJUNCTIONS, PARTICLES, PREPOSITIONS AND PRONOUNS

A (8718)

Ge 1:6, 29; 2:5, 6, 7, 8, 10, 18, 20, 21, 22, 24; 3:6, 24; 4:1, 2, 2, 12, 12, 14, 14, 15, 17, 23, 23, 25, 26; 5:3, 28; 6:9, 16, 16, 17; 8:1, 7, 8, 21; 9:11, 11, 13, 13, 14, 15, 20, 20, 23, 25; 10:8, 9, 12, 30; 11:2, 4, 4, 4; 12:1, 2, 2, 8, 10, 11; 13:7, 16; 14:23, 23; 15:1, 9, 9, 9, 9, 12, 12, 13, 13, 15, 17, 17, 18; 16:1, 7, 11, 12, 15; 17:4, 5, 7, 8, 11, 16, 16, 17, 19, 20; 18:4, 5, 7, 7, 10, 13, 13, 14, 18; 19:3, 9, 20, 20, 26, 28, 30, 31, 37, 38; 20:3, 3, 3, 4, 6, 7, 9, 16, 16; 21:2, 7, 8, 13, 14, 16, 16, 18, 19, 21, 25, 27, 30, 32, 33; 22:2, 6, 7, 8, 8, 13, 13, 13; 23:4, 4, 4, 4, 6, 9, 9, 18, 20, 20; 24:3, 4, 7, 11, 16, 17, 22, 22, 29, 36, 37, 38, 40, 43, 55, 65; 25:1, 8, 25, 27, 27, 27; 26:1, 8, 8, 9, 19, 25, 28, 30, 35; 27:11, 11, 12, 12, 12, 27, 34, 36, 44, 46; 28:1, 2, 3, 4, 6, 6, 11, 12, 18, 20, 22; 29:2, 2, 14, 20, 22, 24, 32, 33, 34, 35; 30:5, 6, 7, 10, 11, 12, 15, 20, 21, 23, 30; 31:10, 11, 13, 24, 44, 44, 45, 45, 46, 48; 32:13, 16, 18, 24, 28; 33:17, 18, 19, 19; 34:14, 31; 35:11, 11, 14, 14, 14, 16, 20; 37:1, 3, 5, 9, 15, 24, 25, 31; 38:1, 2, 2, 3, 4, 5, 6, 11, 14, 15, 17, 17, 28; 39:2, 6, 14, 14, 20; 40:4, 5, 8, 9, 19, 20; 41:2, 7, 11, 12, 12, 15, 15, 18, 33, 38, 38, 42; 43:2, 6, 11, 11, 11; 44:15, 18, 19, 19, 20, 20, 20, 25, 33; 45:7, 7, 8, 8; 46:3, 10, 29; 47:11, 22, 26; 48:4, 7, 16, 19, 19; 49:6, 6, 9, 9, 10, 13, 14, 15, 17, 19, 21, 22, 22, 27; 50:9, 10, 10, 11, 13, 13, 16, 26

Ex 1:8, 16, 16, 16; 2:1, 1, 2, 2, 7, 11, 14, 14, 15, 22, 22, 22; 3:2, 2, 8, 8, 8, 12, 17, 19; 4:2, 3, 4, 10, 16, 25, 25, 26; 5:1, 21; 6:1, 1, 6, 7, 7, 13, 15; 7:1, 9, 9, 10, 19, 22; 8:23, 24; 9:3, 5, 9, 10, 18, 24; 10:7, 9, 19, 22, 26; 11:6, 7, 7, 8; 12:3, 3, 3, 5, 13, 14, 14, 14, 16, 16, 19, 21, 22, 30, 30, 38, 42, 45, 45, 46, 48; 13:5, 6, 9, 19, 21, 21, 21; 14:8, 20, 21, 22, 29; 15:2, 3, 5, 8, 16, 20, 25, 25; 16:4, 14, 23, 33; 17:2, 14, 14; 18:3, 12, 16, 19:5, 6, 6, 9, 13, 16, 18, 19; 20:5, 21:2, 4, 4, 7, 7, 7, 8, 12, 13, 13, 14, 16, 16, 16, 19, 22, 30, 30, 34, 35; 22:1, 1, 1, 2, 5, 5, 7, 10, 10, 14, 15, 16, 16, 18, 19; 23:1, 2, 2, 3, 7, 9, 14, 19, 33; 24:10, 10, 12, 15; 25:8, 10, 10, 10, 10, 16, 17, 17, 17, 23, 23, 23, 24, 25, 26, 29, 31, 31, 33, 33, 33, 33; 22:1, 1, 1, 2, 5, 5, 7, 10, 10, 14, 15, 16, 16, 16, 19; 23:1, 2, 3, 7, 9, 14, 16, 16, 16, 16, 31; 26:7, 13, 13, 14, 14, 16, 16, 16, 31, 36; 27:4, 16, 21; 28:4, 4, 4, 4, 11, 22, 23, 32, 34, 34, 34, 34, 36, 36, 37, 43; 29:9, 10, 14, 16, 18, 22, 24, 25, 25, 26, 28, 29, 30, 31, 31, 32, 32, 33, 33, 37, 43; 29:9, 18, 32, 34; 30:2, 2, 3, 3, 8, 10, 12, 13, 13, 15, 16, 16, 17; 32:4, 4, 5, 8, 9, 10, 11, 17, 21, 29, 30, 31; 33:3, 3, 5, 5, 11, 11, 11, 21, 22; 34:9, 10, 10, 12, 12, 14, 15, 15, 16, 16, 19, 20, 26, 27, 33; 35:5, 2, 2, 5, 29; 36:19, 19, 21, 21, 23, 35, 37; 37:1, 1, 1, 1, 2, 6, 6, 10, 10, 10, 11, 12, 12, 19, 19, 19, 19, 21, 24, 25, 25, 26; 38:4, 23, 25, 26, 26, 27, 27; 39:7, 9, 9, 10, 10, 10, 11, 11, 13, 14, 21, 23, 23, 26, 26, 26, 28, 29, 30, 30, 31; 40:34

Lev 1:3, 3, 4, 5, 5, 6, 7, 9, 9, 10, 12, 14, 15; 3:1, 1, 5, 6, 7, 12, 14, 16, 17; 4:2, 3, 3, 12, 14, 20, 21, 22, 23, 23, 24, 28, 28, 31, 32, 32, 32, 33; 5:1, 1, 2, 2, 2, 3, 4, 4, 6, 6, 6, 6, 7, 7, 9, 10, 11, 11, 12, 13, 15, 15, 15, 15, 17, 18, 18, 19; 6:2, 2, 2, 3, 6, 6, 6, 7, 7, 9, 10, 11, 12, 12, 13, 15, 15, 15, 17, 18, 18, 19; 6:2, 2, 3, 6, 6, 7, 12, 14, 16, 16, 30, 32, 34, 36; 8:2, 2, 21, 21, 26, 27, 28, 29; 9:2, 2, 2, 2, 3, 3, 3, 3, 4, 4, 4, 17, 18, 21, 24; 10:9, 14, 15, 15; 11:36, 47; 12:2, 2, 5, 6, 6, 6, 6, 6, 6, 6, 7, 7, 8, 8; 13:2, 2, 3, 3, 5, 6, 8, 9, 12, 15, 18, 19, 20, 22, 23, 24, 24, 25, 25, 26, 28, 29, 29, 30, 30, 37, 38, 38, 39, 42, 42, 44, 45, 47, 47, 48, 49, 51, 52, 57, 59; 14:10, 12, 12, 21, 21, 21, 22, 24, 31, 34, 34, 35, 44, 55, 55, 56, 56, 56; 15:2, 15, 15, 19, 25, 30, 30; 16:3, 3, 3, 4, 5, 9, 12, 13, 13:2, 3, 5, 5, 6, 9, 12, 13, 13, 14, 14, 18, 18, 19; 19:5, 5, 5, 8, 12, 13, 13, 16, 18, 19, 23, 24, 25, 28, 30, 30; 20:5, 6, 12, 13, 13, 14, 14, 14, 18, 18, 18, 19, 20, 20, 21, 22, 23, 22:4, 4, 4, 5, 10, 10, 11, 12, 14, 14, 14, 14, 14, 14, 14, 18, 18, 18, 18, 20, 20, 21, 21, 23; 23:7, 8, 10, 12, 13, 13, 14, 15, 15, 18, 18, 19, 20, 20, 21, 21, 24, 24, 27, 27, 28, 30, 31, 35, 36, 36, 37, 37, 37, 39, 39, 39, 41, 41; 24:3, 6, 7, 9, 10, 18, 19, 20, 21; 25:2, 4, 4, 5, 10, 11, 24, 29, 29, 29, 29, 30, 33, 35, 35, 35, 39, 40, 40, 46, 47, 50, 53; 26:1, 25, 33, 36, 36, 36, 37; 27:2, 2, 4, 6, 6, 7, 9, 10, 10, 10, 11, 11, 14, 16, 16, 16, 21, 22, 22, 23, 27, 28, 31

Nu 1:4; 3:15, 22, 28, 34, 39, 40, 43, 50; 4:6, 7, 8, 8, 9, 10, 11, 11, 12, 12, 13, 14; 5:6, 6, 12, 13, 21, 23, 26, 27, 29; 6:2, 2, 11, 11, 12, 12, 14, 14, 15, 17, 20; 7:3,

13, 15, 16, 17, 19, 21, 22, 23, 25, 27, 28, 29, 31, 33, 34, 35, 37, 39, 40, 41, 43, 43, 45, 46, 47, 49, 51, 52, 53, 55, 57, 58, 59, 61, 63, 64, 65, 67, 69, 70, 71, 73, 75, 76, 77, 79, 81, 82, 83; 8:8, 8, 12, 14; 9:6, 7, 10, 10, 13, 14, 20, 22, 22; 10:2, 10, 33; 11:4, 8, 12, 20, 21, 25, 27, 31, 31, 33; 12:6, 6, 6; 13:2, 2, 23, 23, 32, 32; 14:3, 4, 8, 12, 14, 14, 14, 31, 34, 36; 15:3, 3, 3, 3, 4, 4, 4, 5, 5, 6, 6, 6, 7, 7, 7, 8, 8, 8, 9, 9, 10, 10, 10, 11, 14, 14, 14, 15, 15, 18; 16:30, 31, 32, 32, 41; 17:8; 18:3, 6, 10, 11, 11, 11, 11, 15, 18, 20:3, 3, 4, 4, 5, 6, 11, 22:5, 5, 6, 6, 7, 7, 7, 7, 7, 8, 8, 8, 8; 9, 9, 9, 10, 10, 10, 17, 17, 17, 18; 21:3, 4, 11, 11, 13, 15, 17, 18, 18, 19, 26; 22:5, 5, 6, 8, 11, 14, 17, 22, 28, 28, 28, 30; 23:2, 2, 4, 4, 14, 17, 22; 24:1, 1, 1, 3, 5, 5, 6, 7, 14, 17; 25:1, 1, 3, 27, 28, 34, 47, 49; 33:2, 4, 7, 20, 21, 22, 28; 34:6, 10

Dt 1:11, 23, 25, 31, 33, 33, 39; 2:5, 5, 9, 9, 10, 19, 20, 21, 35; 3:4, 5, 7, 11, 11; 4:6, 12, 16, 20, 23, 24, 24, 25, 31, 34, 34, 34; 5:2, 9, 15, 15, 15, 22, 29; 6:8, 15, 21; 7:6, 8, 8, 9, 16, 21, 23, 26, 26; 8:5, 7, 7, 8, 8, 9, 9:2, 3, 6, 12, 13, 14, 16, 26; 10:7, 15, 17, 17; 11:9, 10, 11, 12, 18, 20, 26, 27, 28; 12:11, 13:1, 1, 1, 1, 16; 14:2, 2, 21, 21; 15:1, 3, 7, 9, 12, 12, 15, 18; 16:8, 10, 10, 12, 16, 16, 19, 21; 17:8, 14, 15, 18, 18; 18:3, 6, 10, 11, 11, 11, 11, 15, 18, 20:1, 5, 6, 7, 10, 10, 19, 19; 21:3, 4, 11, 11, 13, 15, 17, 18, 18, 22:5, 5, 6, 8, 11, 14, 17, 22, 28, 28, 28, 30; 23:2, 2, 4, 4, 14, 17, 22; 24:1, 1, 1, 3, 5, 5, 6, 7, 14, 17; 25:2, 26:2, 5, 5, 8, 9, 14; 27:3, 15; 28:12, 15, 27, 27, 30, 30, 30, 36, 37, 46, 48, 49, 50, 65; 29:4, 18, 21, 22; 30:2, 2, 3, 8, 10, 12; 31:16, 17, 19, 21, 23, 27, 28; 32:2, 4, 7, 20, 25, 26, 27, 28, 34; 23:1, 10, 13; 24:7, 22:10, 14, 19, 21, 21, 23, 25, 27, 28, 34; 23:1, 10, 13; 24:7, 33

Jos 1:6, 9, 18; 2:1, 12, 15; 3:4, 12, 13, 16; 4:2, 4, 5, 6, 7; 5:6, 13; 6:5, 5, 18, 20; 7:1, 21, 21, 26; 8:2, 11, 14, 17, 27, 28, 28, 29, 29, 32, 35; 9:6, 6, 7, 9, 11, 11, 15, 16; 10:2, 8, 10, 13, 14, 16, 17, 20; 11:14, 18, 19; 12:6, 7; 14:3, 15; 15:3, 13, 18, 19, 19; 17:1, 1, 2, 14, 15, 17, 18; 18:9, 14; 20:4; 21:13, 21, 27, 32, 38, 44; 22:10, 14, 14, 17, 20, 25, 27, 28, 34; 23:1, 10, 13; 24:7, 33

Jdg 1:14, 15, 15, 24, 26; 2:3; 17; 3:9, 15, 15, 15, 16, 16, 17, 19, 20, 20, 25; 4:7, 8, 14, 18, 25, 28, 30, 30; 6:8, 17, 19, 19, 19, 26, 31, 34, 37, 38; 7:5, 13, 13, 13, 13, 13, 14, 16, 18; 8:14, 18, 20, 24, 26, 27, 31, 32; 9:8, 8, 46, 48, 49, 51, 53, 53, 54; 10:1, 3; 11:1, 1, 2, 30, 31, 33, 39, 40; 12:11, 13:2, 3, 5, 5, 6, 10, 16; 14:1, 8, 8, 8, 8, 9, 12, 12, 19; 15:15, 17, 19; 16:1, 4, 4, 7, 7, 8, 13, 13, 13, 14, 16, 18; 17:3, 3, 3, 4, 4, 5, 7, 7, 8, 9, 9, 10, 10, 10, 13; 18:10, 10, 14, 14, 15, 17, 18, 19, 20, 20, 27, 28; 19:1, 1, 3, 5, 12, 15, 17, 24; 20:10, 10, 16, 38, 40; 21:5, 15, 17, 18, 19, 19

Ru 1:1, 1, 1, 12, 12; 2:1, 1, 3, 7, 10, 11, 12; 3:8, 9, 11, 12, 13, 13, 13, 14; 4:1, 3, 7, 7, 13, 14, 15, 15, 17, 17

1Sa 1:1, 5, 9, 9, 11, 15, 15, 16, 20, 24, 36, 36, 36; 3:11; 20; 4:5, 7, 10, 12, 13, 17, 20; 5:9, 11; 6:3, 7, 8, 8, 9, 14, 14, 14, 17, 19; 7:9, 9, 10, 12; 8:5, 6, 10, 19, 22; 9:1, 1, 1, 2, 2, 2, 6, 7, 8, 9, 9, 12, 15, 16, 21, 27; 10:1, 3, 5, 5, 5, 5, 10, 12, 16, 21, 27; 11:1, 2, 2, 7, 12; 12:1, 12, 13, 17, 19; 13:2, 4, 6, 9, 12, 14, 21; 14:1, 4, 14, 14, 14, 14, 18, 18, 18, 19, 20, 20, 21, 21, 23; 22:4, 4, 4, 5, 10, 12, 13, 14, 14, 15, 16, 25, 26, 29, 31, 34, 34, 34; 17:6, 7, 7, 8, 15; 18:5, 17, 18, 19, 23; 19:5, 14, 16, 19; 20, 20, 20, 20, 21, 21, 23; 22:4, 4, 5, 10, 10, 12, 13, 14, 14, 15, 16; 26:7, 7, 7, 9, 12, 14, 22, 24; 29:1; 30:12, 12, 13, 17, 25, 26; 31:4, 13

2Sa 1:2, 13; 2:17, 18, 25, 28; 3:7, 8, 8, 11,

13, 20, 21, 22, 22, 29, 29, 33, 34, 38, 38; 4:2, 4, 5, 10, 11; 5:2, 3, 11, 23, 24; 6:3, 8, 14, 16, 19, 19, 19; 7:2, 5, 6, 6, 7, 7, 9, 10, 10, 11, 13, 19, 19, 23, 23, 24, 27; 8:2, 4, 13; 9:2, 3, 8, 12; 10:6; 11:2, 8, 14, 16, 21, 21, 27; 12:3, 4, 24, 30; 13:1, 2, 3, 3, 6, 9, 8, 13, 14, 16, 17, 17, 18, 18, 19, 25; 14:2, 2, 2, 11, 17, 19, 19, 25, 26; 15:2, 7, 8, 13, 32; 16:1, 1, 5, 5; 17:8, 8, 9, 10, 10, 11, 13, 14, 17, 17, 18, 19, 25, 25; 18:2, 8, 18, 24, 25, 26, 27, 29, 30, 31; 19:1, 10, 11, 24, 32, 32, 35, 42; 20:3, 9, 11, 11, 12, 12, 14, 20, 20, 20, 21, 22; 21:9, 11, 20, 20, 21:1, 8, 8; 22:5, 11, 24, 24, 24, 26, 27, 29, 36; 23:2, 3, 4, 4, 4, 4, 7, 8, 9, 11, 16, 18, 20, 20, 21, 21; 24:14, 15, 16, 16, 20, 20, 20, 21, 21, 24, 24

1Ki 1:2, 3, 3, 6, 39, 42, 52, 52; 2:2, 4, 8, 8, 9, 19, 24, 36, 42; 3:4, 5, 6, 7, 9, 12, 15, 17, 24, 24; 4:7, 32; 5:1, 3, 5, 5, 7, 12, 13, 14, 14; 6:21, 31, 33, 36; 7:3, 6, 7, 8, 12, 14, 14, 14, 14, 15, 23, 23, 24, 26, 29, 31, 31, 31, 32, 32, 33, 35, 35; 8:9, 13, 13, 16, 17, 18, 20, 27, 31, 41, 55, 63, 65; 9:5, 7, 7, 16, 21, 26; 10:2, 6, 18, 22, 25, 26, 28, 29; 11:7, 17, 18, 24, 26, 28, 29, 36, 38; 12:7, 11, 30, 31, 32, 33; 13:1, 2, 3, 7, 18, 24; 14:3, 5, 10, 15; 15:4, 13, 19, 19, 22; 16:11, 31, 33; 17:7, 9, 10, 10, 11, 12, 12, 12, 12, 19, 24; 18:2, 4, 32, 35; 19:2, 4, 5, 6, 6, 9, 9, 11, 12, 12, 13, 13, 19, 20:13, 20, 21, 28, 30, 34; 35, 35, 36, 39, 39, 42; 21:1, 2, 2, 9; 22:7, 10, 17, 21, 22, 23, 24, 34, 34, 36, 47

2Ki 1:2, 3, 6, 6, 8, 8, 9, 9, 10, 12, 13; 2:1, 9, 10, 11, 11, 20; 3:4, 9, 11, 15, 18, 27; 4:1, 2, 3, 6, 6, 8, 8, 9, 10, 10, 10, 10, 11, 16, 17, 18, 19, 38, 39, 42; 5:1, 1, 1, 2, 5, 7, 7, 8, 10, 12, 14, 15, 19, 22, 26, 27; 6:2, 2, 5, 6, 8, 9, 14, 15, 25, 25, 26, 32; 7:1, 1, 1, 2, 6, 6, 6, 9, 16, 16, 16, 18, 18, 19; 8:1, 5, 6, 8, 9, 13, 19, 20; 9:16, 17, 17, 17, 19, 24, 28, 30, 34; 10:2, 6, 8, 18, 19, 20, 21, 27; 11:4, 5, 6, 6, 14; 14:9, 19; 15:5, 5, 13, 19, 25, 30; 16:8, 17; 17:16, 21, 35, 36; 18:17, 21, 28, 31, 32, 32, 32; 32:36; 19:3, 7, 7, 17, 29, 31, 32; 20:3, 7, 7, 10, 12, 14, 14; 22:10, 12, 19, 19; 23:3, 8, 22, 30, 33, 33; 24:16; 25:8, 23, 30, 30

1Ch 2:34; 5:25; 6:33; 7:16, 23; 9:13; 10:4, 11; 11:3, 11, 13, 14, 20, 22, 22, 22, 22, 22, 23, 23, 23, 42; 12:2, 4, 14, 22, 28, 28, 34, 38; 13:7; 14:1, 12, 15; 15:1, 1, 3, 27, 28, 29; 16:3, 3, 5, 15, 17, 19, 42; 17:1, 4, 5, 9, 10, 12, 17, 17, 17, 21, 24; 18:4; 19:6; 20:2, 5, 6; 21:3, 5, 13, 16; 22:6, 7, 8, 8, 9, 10, 14, 25:3, 6; 26:14, 25; 28:4, 11, 20; 29:15, 16, 19, 21, 21, 23, 28

2Ch 1:4, 6, 9, 14, 16, 17, 17; 2:1, 1, 3, 4, 6, 6, 7, 7, 12, 12, 14, 14, 14, 18; 4:2, 2, 3, 5, 5; 5:10, 13; 6:2, 2, 5, 5, 7, 8, 13, 16, 22, 32, 36; 7:5, 8, 8, 9, 12, 18, 20, 20; 8:13; 9:1, 5, 17, 18, 24; 10:11; 13:5, 8, 9, 9, 15, 17; 14:9; 15:3, 12, 14, 16; 16:3, 6, 8, 10, 10, 14; 17:17; 18:6, 9, 20, 21, 21, 22, 33, 33, 33; 19:9; 20:2, 3, 8, 14, 19; 21:7, 8, 24:8, 9, 24, 24, 26; 25:2, 7, 15, 18, 27; 26:11, 19, 21, 21, 21, 23; 28:5, 5, 7, 9, 9; 29:10, 21, 31, 32; 30:5, 5, 13, 18, 24; 32:18, 24; 33:6, 7, 14, 14, 34:14, 18, 20, 31; 35:1, 3, 18; 36:3, 22, 23

Ezr 1:1, 2, 9, 10, 10; 2:7, 12, 31, 37, 38, 39, 61, 63; 3:5, 11, 12; 4:3, 8, 10, 11, 15, 17; 5:7, 11, 13, 17; 6:1, 2, 2, 3, 4, 8, 11, 11, 12, 17; 7:6, 11, 12, 12, 21, 21, 27; 8:18, 21, 22, 27, 28, 35, 35; 9:7, 7, 8, 8, 8, 9; 10:1, 3, 12, 13, 19

Ne 2:6, 8, 10, 17; 3:13; 4:2, 3, 4, 6, 9, 17, 22; 5:1, 7; 6:3, 7, 11; 7:2, 5, 12, 34, 40, 41, 42, 65, 70; 8:4; 9:4, 8, 10, 11, 12, 11:23; 13:2, 5, 7

Est 1:3, 5, 6, 9, 19; 2:5, 5, 18, 18, 23; 3:4, 8, 13, 14; 4:1; 5, 14; 5:9, 14; 8:11, 13, 15, 15, 17, 17; 9:17, 18, 19, 19, 22; 10:1

Job 1:1, 3, 6, 8, 10, 13, 14, 19; 2:1, 3, 4, 8; 3:3, 5, 16, 23; 4:12, 12, 15, 16, 17; 5:26, 26; 6:15, 22, 27; 7:1, 2, 2, 6, 12, 12, 20, 20; 8:2, 9, 14, 20; 9:2, 3, 17, 19, 25, 32; 10:16, 20, 22; 11:2, 12; 12:5, 14, 18, 24, 25; 13:16, 25, 27, 28, 28; 14:1, 2, 3, 4, 4, 7, 9, 13, 14, 15, 16, 19, 21, 21; 17:3, 6, 6, 7; 18:8, 8, 10, 19:10, 11, 23, 29; 20:5, 8, 8; 24:3, 5, 8, 9, 14, 20, 24, 24; 25:4, 4, 6; 26:14; 27:13, 18, 18, 20, 20; 28:1, 1, 28; 31:18, 20, 22; 22:0; 29:18; 30:5, 14, 15; 29:29; 31:1, 1, 3, 9, 11, 12, 18, 23, 30, 34, 35, 36, 37; 32:8; 33:15, 15, 23, 23, 24, 25; 34:9, 11, 13, 20, 29, 29, 34; 35:8; 36:2, 16, 18; 37:4, 18, 20, 38:3, 9, 14, 25, 28, 28, 30; 39:20, 40:7, 9, 17, 23, 41:1, 1, 2, 2, 24, 29, 31, 31, 32, 34; 42:8, 11, 12, 12

Ps 1:3; 2:1, 9, 9; 3:T, 3; 4:T; 5:T, 4, 12; 6:T; 7:2, 15; 8:T; 5; 9:T, 6, 9, 9; 10:9; 11:T, 1, 6; 12:T, 2, 6; 13:T; 14:T; 15:T, 3, 4; 16:6; 17:T, 12, 12; 18:T, 8, 10, 19, 29,

29, 30, 31, 34, 43; 19:T, 4, 5, 5, 5; 20:T; 21:T, 3, 9, 11; 22:T, 6, 6, 13, 13, 15, 30, 30, 31; 23:T, 5; 24:T, 4; 25:T; 26:T; 27:T, 3, 5, 11; 28:T; 29:T, 6, 6; 30:T, 5, 5; 31:T, 2, 8, 11, 11, 12, 12, 20, 21; 32:T, 6; 33:3, 3, 7, 16, 16, 17, 17; 34:T, 18, 18; 35:T, 7, 19; 36:T, 4, 6; 37:T, 10, 16, 16, 23, 35; 38:T, 4, 7, 13, 13, 14; 39:T, 1, 5, 6, 11, 12, 12; 40:T, 2, 2, 3, 15; 41:T; 42:4, 10; 44:3, 13, 13, 13, 14, 14, 20; 45:T, 1, 1, 6, 12; 46:T, 1, 4; 47:T, 2, 5, 5; 48:T, 3, 6; 49:T, 4, 7; 50:T, 3, 5, 10, 18, 21; 51:T, 10, 10, 17, 17; 52:T, 2, 8; 53:T; 54:T; 55:T, 2, 6, 13; 57:4, 6, 6; 58:4, 8, 8, 9, 11, 11, 11; 59:6, 6, 14; 60:4; 61:T, 3, 3; 62:T, 3, 3, 8, 9; 63:T, 1, 10; 64:T, 3, 6; 65:T; 66:T, 1, 12; 67:T; 68:T, 5, 5, 6, 9, 13, 15, 21, 33; 69:T, 4, 8, 11, 22, 22, 30; 70:T, 3; 71:T; 72:T, 16; 73:T, 1, 6, 6, 10, 19, 20, 22, 27, 74:5; 75:T, 5, 8; 76:T, 6; 77:T, 13, 17, 20; 78:2, 5, 5, 8, 8, 13, 14, 14, 19, 21, 38, 39, 50, 52, 57, 65, 66; 79:T, 4, 4; 80:T, 1, 6, 8; 81:T, 1, 2, 4, 4, 5, 5; 82:T; 83:T, 2, 4, 13, 14; 84:T, 3, 3, 6, 10, 10, 10, 11; 85:T; 86:T, 15, 17; 87:T; 88:T, 4; 89:3, 8, 13, 37, 41; 90:T, 4, 4, 5, 5, 9; 91:T, 12; 92:T, 1, 3, 6, 6, 12; 94:2, 20; 95:1, 2, 3, 3, 10; 96:1; 97:3; 98:T, 1, 4, 4, 5, 6; 99:8; 100:T, 1; 101:T, 2, 2, 4, 4, 5, 5, 6; 102:T, 3, 6, 7, 11, 26, 26; 103:T, 13, 15; 104:2, 2, 4, 6, 9, 18; 105:8, 10, 12, 16, 17, 17, 39, 39, 41; 106:18, 19, 36, 39; 107:4, 7, 27, 29, 33, 34, 35, 36, 41; 108:T; 109:T, 2, 3, 6, 9, 19, 25, 29; 110:T, 4; 111:10; 112:5; 113:9; 114:1, 8, 8; 118:5; 119:9, 19, 63, 69, 78, 83, 105, 105, 110, 161, 164, 176; 120:T, 2; 121:T; 122:T, 3; 123:T, 2; 124:T, 6, 7; 125:T; 126:T; 127:T, 4; 128:T, 3; 129:T, 1, 2; 130:T; 131:T, 2, 2; 132:T, 5, 5, 17; 133:T; 134:T; 136:12, 12; 137:3, 4; 138:T; 139:T, 4; 140:T, 3, 5, 5; 141:T, 3, 5; 142:T, 3; 143:T, 6; 144:T, 4, 8, 9, 9, 11, 12, 15; 147:10; 148:6, 14; 149:1, 6

Pr 1:5, 5, 6, 27; 2:7; 3:12, 18, 30; 4:1, 9, 24; 5:3, 3, 4, 10, 20, 20; 6:1, 5, 5, 10, 10, 10, 12, 12, 12, 12, 17, 19, 23, 24, 26, 26, 27, 30, 32, 33, 34; 7:7, 10, 10, 19, 20, 22, 23, 23; 8:27; 9:7, 7, 7, 8, 8, 9, 9, 13, 14; 10:1, 1, 1, 4, 5, 5, 8, 10, 11, 11, 13, 18, 18, 23, 23; 11:1, 1, 7, 9, 12, 13, 13, 15, 16, 18, 18, 20, 22, 22, 22, 28, 30; 12:2, 2, 3, 4, 4, 8, 9, 10, 14, 14, 15, 16, 16, 18, 18, 19, 19, 23, 25, 27; 13:1, 1, 2, 5, 6, 7, 9, 10, 14, 14, 16, 17, 20, 22; 14:1, 5, 7, 9, 10, 11, 14, 15, 15, 17, 18, 19, 20, 22, 22, 24, 24, 24; 19:1, 5, 6, 9, 10, 10, 11, 12, 12, 14, 15, 15, 15, 17, 18, 19, 20, 20, 20; 16:2, 7, 8, 9, 9, 10, 11, 14, 15, 18, 18, 20, 21, 22, 22, 23, 24, 25, 27, 28; 18:1, 2, 4, 4, 6, 7, 8, 9, 10, 11, 16, 17, 18, 18, 20, 21, 21, 22, 22, 23, 24, 24, 25, 25, 27, 28, 28; 18:1, 2, 4, 6, 7, 8, 9, 10, 11, 13, 14, 14, 16, 19, 19, 20, 20, 22, 24, 24, 24; 19:1, 5, 6, 9, 10, 10, 11, 12, 12, 14, 15, 15, 15, 17, 18, 19, 20, 20, 20; 20:1, 2, 3, 5, 6, 8, 11, 15, 16, 16, 17, 19; 21:2, 9, 9, 9, 9, 11, 14, 14, 15, 18, 19, 20, 20, 22, 23, 24, 24, 24, 24, 24, 25, 25, 26, 26, 26, 28; 26:1, 3, 3, 3, 4, 5, 6, 7, 7, 8, 8, 8, 9, 9, 11, 11, 12, 12, 13, 13, 14, 16, 17, 21, 22, 23, 23, 27, 27, 28, 28; 27:1, 2, 3, 3, 6, 7, 8, 8, 9, 10, 10, 12, 13, 13, 14, 14, 15, 15, 15, 17, 21, 22, 22, 22; 28:1, 2, 2, 3, 3, 7, 7, 12, 15, 15, 15, 17, 20, 21, 23, 24, 26, 27; 29:5, 5, 6, 8, 8, 9, 11, 11, 12, 15, 19, 20, 20, 23, 29, 29; 23:1, 2, 2, 4, 9, 11, 12, 13, 14, 24, 24, 24, 24, 25, 25, 26, 26, 28; 26:1, 3, 3, 3, 4, 5, 6, 6, 7, 7, 8, 8, 9, 9, 11, 11, 12, 13, 13, 14, 16, 17, 21, 22, 23, 24, 27, 28; 27:1, 2, 3, 3, 6, 7, 7, 8, 9, 10, 10, 12, 13, 13, 14, 15, 15, 15; 28:1, 2, 2, 3, 3, 7, 7, 12, 15, 15, 15, 17, 20, 21, 23, 24, 26, 27; 29:5, 5, 6, 8, 8, 9, 11, 11, 12, 15, 19, 20, 20, 23, 30:2, 4, 6, 8, 8, 9, 12, 13, 13; 5:3, 3, 4, 8, 12, 13, 14, 16; 6:2, 2, 3, 6, 12, 12; 7:1, 5, 6, 7, 7, 8, 12, 12, 15, 15, 16, 17, 17; 9:4, 4, 4, 5, 7, 14, 14, 15; 10:1, 1, 2, 2, 3, 3, 8, 8, 8, 9, 14, 14, 16, 19, 20; 11:2, 7, 8; 12:5, 12

SS 1:9, 13, 14; 2:9, 9, 13, 17; 3:4, 9; 4:1, 2, 3, 3, 3, 4, 12, 12, 12, 15, 15; 5:11, 13; 6:5, 6, 7, 7; 7:1, 2, 2, 4, 7, 13; 8:6, 6, 6, 7, 8, 9, 9, 9, 10, 11, 11, 12, 14, 14

Isa 1:4, 8, 8, 8, 8, 8, 9, 14, 21, 30, 31; 2:20; 3:6, 7, 7, 16, 17, 24, 24, 24, 24; 4:5, 5, 5, 6, 6, 6, 6; 5:1, 1, 1, 2, 2, 7, 9, 10, 18, 28, 29; 6:1, 5, 5, 6, 12, 13, 13; 7:6, 6, 8, 11, 13, 14, 14, 14, 20, 20, 21, 21, 23, 23; 8:1, 1, 3, 11, 12, 14, 14, 14, 19; 9:2, 6, 6, 8, 17; 10:6, 6, 7, 13, 14, 16, 16, 17, 17, 18, 19, 22, 23, 24, 25, 26, 34; 11:1, 1, 6, 10, 10; 13:2, 4, 4, 4, 5, 6, 8, 12, 14, 14; 14:6, 11, 12, 14; 16:2, 4, 11, 14; 17:1, 7, 9, 11, 12, 12, 18:2, 2, 2, 3, 4, 4, 7, 7; 19:1, 4, 4, 14, 14, 17, 19, 20, 20, 20, 20,

21, 23, 24; 20:3; 21:1, 2, 3, 6, 7, 7, 7,
8, 9, 9, 16, 16; 22:2, 2, 5, 11, 16, 16, 16,
16, 17, 18, 18, 21, 23, 23, 23; 23:3, 10,
11, 15, 16; 24:9, 11, 20, 20; 25:2, 2, 2, 2,
2, 4, 4, 4, 4, 4, 5, 5, 6, 6; 26:1, 16, 17, 20;
27:2, 10, 11; 28:1, 2, 2, 2, 2, 4, 5, 6,
10, 10, 13, 13, 15, 16, 16, 16, 16, 16, 19,
20, 22, 27, 27, 27, 27, 27; 29:3, 4, 7, 7, 8, 8,
11, 14, 14, 14, 17, 17, 17, 21, 21, 21, 21;
30:1, 5, 5, 5, 5, 6, 8, 8, 9, 13, 13, 14, 17,
17, 17, 18, 20, 21, 22, 27, 28, 29, 29, 29,
30, 31, 33; 31:4, 7, 8, 8; 32:1, 2, 2, 2, 2,
2, 2, 14, 14, 15, 15, 18, 19; 33:9, 19, 19,
19, 19, 20, 20, 21, 23; 34:4, 4, 6, 6, 13,
13, 14; 35:4, 4, 6, 7, 8, 8; 36:2, 6, 13, 16,
17, 17, 17, 21; 37:3, 7, 7, 18, 30, 32, 33;
38:3, 7, 12, 12, 13, 14, 14, 14, 21, 21;
39:1, 3; 40:3, 11, 12, 12, 15, 15, 15, 16,
19, 20, 20, 20, 20, 22, 22; 41:12, 15, 18, 28;
42:3, 6, 6, 10, 13, 13, 14, 16, 22, 22, 22,
24; 43:16, 16, 19, 19; 44:8, 9, 10, 10, 13,
13, 13, 15, 15, 15, 17, 19, 20, 20, 22, 22;
45:15, 19, 20, 21, 21; 46:1, 6, 6, 11, 11;
47:3, 7, 8, 9, 14; 48:8, 18, 20; 49:2, 2, 6,
6, 7, 8, 8, 11, 15, 18, 21; 50:2, 4, 7, 9, 11;
51:4, 4, 6, 8, 10, 12, 20, 20; 53:2, 2, 2, 3,
7, 7, 12; 54:6, 6, 7, 8, 8; 55:4, 4, 5, 13;
56:3, 5, 5, 7; 57:4, 4, 6, 6, 7, 8, 15; 58:1,
2, 5, 5, 5, 5, 11, 11, 13; 59:5, 15, 17,
17, 17, 19, 19; 60:8, 15, 22, 22, 22, 22;
61:10, 10; 62:1, 2, 3, 3, 5, 5, 7, 10, 12;
63:13, 14, 14, 18; 64:6, 10, 10, 11, 15, 17, 18,
18, 22; 66:2, 3, 3, 3, 6, 6, 6, 7, 8, 8, 12, 12,
12, 15, 19, 20

Jer 1:5, 8, 11, 13, 18; 2:2, 6, 6, 6, 7, 10,
11, 14, 14, 21, 21, 21, 23, 24, 27, 27, 30,
31, 31, 32, 32; 3:1, 3, 8, 14, 14, 19, 19,
20, 21; 4:6, 11, 12, 13, 15, 16, 17, 19, 20,
26, 27, 29, 31, 31; 5:1, 3, 6, 6, 6, 9, 10,
15, 15, 15, 18, 23, 23, 26, 27, 29,
30; 6:1, 2, 6, 7, 8, 13, 15, 20, 22, 22, 24,
27, 27; 7:5, 11, 28, 29; 8:5, 15, 19; 9:1, 2,
9, 10, 10, 11, 12, 16, 18, 19; 10:3, 8, 13,
19, 22, 22; 11:5, 9, 14, 16, 16, 19; 12:6,
8, 9, 10; 13:1, 2, 4, 11, 11, 11, 11, 11, 21;
14:8, 8, 8, 9, 9, 14, 14, 17, 17, 18; 15:7,
8, 10, 10, 14, 14, 18, 20; 16:2, 13, 20;
17:1, 1, 4, 6, 8, 11, 12, 16, 17, 22, 27, 27;
18:3, 7, 7, 9, 9, 11, 13, 14, 15, 16, 20, 22,
22, 22; 19:1, 8, 11; 20:4, 8, 8, 9, 11, 15;
21:5, 6, 9, 14; 22:5, 6, 14, 23, 28, 28, 28,
30; 23:5, 5, 9, 9, 14, 16, 19, 19, 23, 23,
28, 28, 29, 29, 33, 40; 24:7, 9, 9, 9;
25:9, 11, 18, 18, 18, 19, 29, 30, 31, 31, 32,
34, 36, 36; 26:2, 6, 15, 18, 18, 20; 27:10,
14, 15, 16; 28:14, 15; 29:18, 18, 18, 21,
22, 23, 26, 27, 31, 32; 30:2, 5, 5, 9, 10,
12, 12, 12, 17, 22, 23, 24, 32, 35, 36, 36,
37, 37, 38, 41, 41, 42, 43, 44, 44; 51:1, 6,
7, 14, 16, 25, 26, 26, 26, 27, 27, 29, 33,
33, 34, 37, 37, 39, 43, 43, 43, 43, 46, 46,
54, 54, 55, 57, 59, 60, 63; 52:21, 22, 23,
34, 34

La 1:1, 13, 15, 17; 2:1, 3, 6, 7, 7, 8, 18, 20,
22; 3:10, 10, 12, 14, 26, 27, 35, 36, 39,
39, 44, 47, 52, 53, 64; 4:6, 8, 8, 11, 17

Eze 1:4, 4, 4, 4, 5, 6, 8, 10, 10, 14, 16, 16,
16, 24, 25, 26, 26, 26, 28; 2:3, 5, 5, 6, 6,
9, 9; 3:5, 5, 5, 6, 6, 9, 12, 12, 13, 13, 17,
20, 20, 26, 26, 27; 4:1, 2, 2, 3, 3, 6, 10,
11; 5:1, 1, 2, 2, 2, 3, 4, 12, 12, 12,
12, 14, 15, 15; 6:3, 8, 9; 7:11, 21, 21, 23,
26; 8:2, 3, 3, 7, 8, 11, 17, 18; 9:1, 2, 2, 4;
10:1, 1, 8, 9, 10, 10, 14, 14, 14, 21; 11:8,
13, 13, 16, 19, 19; 12:6, 2, 3, 6, 16, 23;
13:7, 7, 10, 11, 13; 14:7, 8, 8, 9, 17, 19,
22; 15:2, 3, 8; 16:3, 8, 11, 12, 13, 19, 19,
20, 24, 31, 32, 34, 40, 45, 47, 54; 17:2, 2,
3, 4, 4, 5, 5, 6, 6, 8, 8, 13, 22, 22, 23;
18:5, 6, 7, 10, 10, 10, 14, 14, 14, 16, 31;
19:1, 2, 3, 5, 6, 10, 13, 14, 14, 14, 14;
20:6, 11, 12, 13, 20, 21, 27, 33, 33, 34,
34, 47; 21:9, 9, 10, 13, 19, 20, 22, 22, 23,
29; 22:4, 4, 25, 25, 30; 23:30, 40, 41, 41,
42, 42, 44, 46; 24:3, 3, 7, 8, 16, 24, 27;
25:4, 5, 5, 7, 15; 26:4, 5, 5, 7, 8, 8, 10,
10, 12, 12, 14, 14, 17, 19, 19; 27:2, 3, 5,
32, 36; 28:2, 2, 9, 12, 18, 19, 24; 29:6, 7,
8, 14, 18; 30:3, 8, 13, 13, 18, 21, 24;
31:3, 3, 15; 32:2, 2, 2, 2, 7, 25; 33:2, 2,
7, 32, 32, 33; 34:8, 12, 14, 14, 14, 18, 22,
24, 25, 26, 28; 29:9, 35:6; 36:3, 4, 5, 17,
26, 26, 26, 37; 37:7, 7, 26; 38:4, 7, 9, 9,
12, 12, 13, 13, 15, 15, 16, 16, 19, 21;
39:6, 11, 13, 15, 15, 17; 40:2, 2, 3, 3,
5, 5, 5, 17, 24, 27, 42, 42, 42, 42, 43;
41:7, 8, 18, 18, 18, 19; 42:4, 4, 12,
20, 20; 43:2, 13, 13, 13, 13, 17, 17, 17,
19, 19, 22, 22, 23; 44:5, 4, 4, 5, 7, 10, 10,
11, 11, 13, 13, 14, 14, 15, 15, 18, 21,
22, 22, 23, 23, 24, 24, 24; 46:4, 5,

5, 6, 6, 7, 7, 7, 7, 11, 11, 11, 12, 13, 13,
14, 14, 14, 15, 15, 16, 17, 19, 21, 23;
47:3, 4, 4, 5, 5, 5, 9, 10, 20; 48:1, 2, 3, 4,
5, 6, 7, 15, 23, 24, 25, 26, 27

Da 1:5; 2:3, 5, 10, 11, 19, 25, 28, 31, 34, 35,
37, 37, 44, 47, 47, 47, 47, 48; 3:4, 6, 10,
11, 15, 27, 29, 29; 4:5, 6, 10, 13, 13, 15,
16, 23, 23, 23, 27, 31; 5:1, 1, 5, 7, 11, 16,
18, 29, 29; 6:7, 7, 7, 10, 12, 12, 13, 17,
20, 26; 7:1, 4, 4, 5, 5, 6, 6, 7, 8, 10, 12,
14, 20; 8:1, 2, 2, 3, 5, 9, 12, 15, 16,
18, 23; 9:12, 15, 16, 26; 10:1, 5, 6, 7, 9,
10, 11, 18; 11:3, 5, 7, 10, 11, 13, 13, 15,
18, 20, 21, 22, 23, 24, 25, 34, 35, 38,
39, 40; 12:1, 1, 7, 7, 11

Hos 1:2, 3, 4, 6, 8; 2:3, 3, 6, 12, 15, 18; 3:1,
2, 2, 4, 4, 4; 4:1, 12, 16, 16, 16; 5:1, 1, 2,
7, 12, 14, 14; 6:4, 8, 9, 10, 11; 7:6, 8, 11,
12, 13, 14; 10:3, 4, 6, 11, 14; 11:1, 4,
10, 11, 11; 12:1, 2, 7, 12, 12, 13, 13;
13:3, 7, 7, 8, 8, 10, 11, 13; 14:8

Joel 1:6, 6, 6, 8, 14, 14, 15; 2:2, 2, 2, 2, 3, 3,
3:4, 4, 5, 5, 5, 6, 6, 12, 12, 12; 4:5, 11;
5:1, 3, 12, 19, 19, 19, 19, 24; 6:10, 13,
14; 7:4, 7, 7, 7, 8, 8, 14, 14, 14, 17, 17;
8:1, 2, 6, 8, 10, 11, 11, 11; 9:5, 9

Ob 1:1, 7, 12, 18, 18

Jnh 1:3, 4, 4, 9, 16, 17; 3:4, 5; 4:2, 5, 6, 6, 7,
8, 10, 10

Mic 1:4, 6, 6, 7, 7, 8, 14; 2:2, 2, 4, 4, 5, 10,
11; 3:6, 12; 4:3, 7, 7, 9, 10; 5:1, 7, 8, 8;
6:2, 6, 16, 16; 7:2, 3, 4, 4, 5, 5, 6, 6, 8,
17, 18

Na 1:7, 11, 14; 2:8; 3:2, 3, 3, 6

Hab 1:5, 10; 2:5, 6, 6, 12, 12, 18; 3:1, 14
15, 15, 18; 2:4, 9, 13, 13, 15, 15; 3:9, 13,
18, 20, 20

Hag 1:6, 11; 2:6, 13, 15, 15, 16, 23

Zec 1:8, 8, 14, 15, 16; 2:1, 1, 5, 9; 3:2, 5, 5;
4:1, 2, 2, 7; 5:1, 2, 7, 7, 9, 11; 6:13, 14;
7:12, 14; 8:3, 13, 13, 23; 9:3, 6, 7, 7, 9,
13, 15, 16; 10:2, 2, 7; 11:3, 3, 13, 15, 16;
12:2, 3, 6, 6, 6, 11; 13:1, 4, 5; 14:4, 10, 13
15; 3:2, 3, 5, 8, 9, 10, 12, 16, 17; 4:6

Mal 1:6, 6, 6, 6, 11, 13, 14, 14, 14; 2:2, 11,
15; 3:2, 3, 5, 8, 9, 10, 12, 16, 17; 4:6

Mt 1:19, 19, 20, 21, 23, 23; 2:6, 12, 13, 18,
19, 22, 23, 23; 3:4, 16, 17; 4:2, 5, 6, 18,
38, 41; 6:2, 16; 7:4, 9, 10, 10, 17, 18, 18,
24, 24, 25, 26, 30, 32; 8:2, 4, 5, 9, 14, 19, 23, 24,
26, 30, 30, 32; 9:1, 2, 2, 9, 12, 16, 18, 20,
23, 32, 32; 10:12, 18, 29, 34, 35, 36, 41,
41, 41, 41, 41, 41, 42, 42; 11:7, 8, 9, 9,
11, 18, 19, 19, 19; 12:1, 3, 10, 11, 12, 12,
14, 20, 22, 29, 32, 35, 38, 39, 41, 42, 43;
13:2, 3, 21, 24, 31, 31, 32, 33, 34, 42, 44,
44, 45, 47, 52, 52, 57; 14:5, 8, 11, 13, 14,
15, 22, 23, 26, 33; 15:5, 11, 11, 20, 20,
22, 22, 23, 26, 27; 16:1, 4, 26, 26;
17:1, 5, 5, 14, 20, 27, 27; 18:2, 6, 12, 17,
17, 23; 19:3, 5, 7, 23, 24, 24, 24; 20:1, 1,
2, 2, 9, 10, 13, 20, 28, 29; 21:2, 5, 8, 13,
19, 26, 28, 33, 33, 33, 33, 43, 46;
22:2, 2, 11, 11, 12, 19, 24, 24, 24, 25, 36, 40;
23:14, 16, 24, 24, 37; 24:14, 31, 31, 32,
45, 50; 25:6, 14, 14, 19, 21, 23, 24, 32,
35, 35, 37, 38, 42, 43, 44, 44; 26:7, 10,
13, 18, 30, 36, 39, 47, 48, 55, 59, 69, 73;
27:14, 15, 16, 19, 24, 28, 29, 29, 32, 33,
33, 33, 46, 48, 48, 50, 57, 59, 60, 64, 66;
28:2, 16

Mk 1:6, 6, 10, 11, 16, 19, 23, 26, 30, 35, 35,
40, 44; 2:21, 25; 3:1, 1, 7, 8, 9, 13, 19,
24, 25, 27; 4:1, 1, 3, 17, 21, 21, 21, 21,
26, 31, 34, 37, 38, 39; 5:2, 7, 11, 13, 25,
42; 6:4, 5, 8, 10, 11, 15, 19, 20, 20, 21,
21, 25, 28, 29, 31, 31, 32, 34, 35, 44, 49;
7:11, 11, 15, 24, 25, 26, 26, 30; 8:4, 7,
10, 11, 12, 22, 36, 37; 9:2, 7, 7, 14, 17,
21, 36, 39, 41, 42; 10:2, 4, 7, 12, 15, 25,
25, 25, 45, 46, 48; 11:2, 4, 13, 17, 22;
12:1, 1, 1, 1, 1, 1, 25, 19, 20, 40, 42,
42; 13:9, 28, 34, 34; 14:3, 6, 9, 13, 13,
15, 26, 32, 35, 43, 44, 47, 47, 48, 51, 51,
69, 70, 70; 15:1, 17, 19, 21, 22, 34, 36,
36, 37, 46, 46, 46; 16:5, 5

Lk 1:1, 5, 13, 17, 22, 26, 27, 27, 31, 34, 36,
39, 42, 45, 57, 63, 69; 2:1, 7, 11, 12, 12,
13, 16, 24, 24, 25, 32, 34, 35, 36, 36, 36,
37, 44; 3:22, 22, 22; 4:5, 5, 9, 11, 13, 14,
25, 26, 26, 26, 31, 33, 33, 33, 36, 38, 42;
5:3, 4, 6, 8, 12, 12, 14, 15, 17, 18, 18, 18,
27, 29, 29, 31, 36, 36, 36, 36; 6:3, 6, 12,
17, 39, 43, 43, 44, 45, 48, 48, 48, 48, 49;
49, 49; 7:2, 5, 7, 8, 11, 12, 12, 16, 16, 24,
25, 26, 26, 28, 33, 34, 34, 34, 37, 37, 39,
39, 41; 8:4, 5, 6, 11, 16, 16, 16, 16, 22,
22, 23, 24, 27, 28, 32, 33, 41, 41, 42;
9:5, 10, 12, 24, 25, 27, 28, 34, 35, 38, 39,
42, 46, 47, 52; 10:7, 10:13, 25, 30, 31, 32,
33, 38, 38, 39; 11:1, 5, 6, 6, 11, 11, 11, 11,
11, 11, 12, 14, 16, 17, 17, 21, 22, 24, 24,
29, 30, 31, 32, 33, 33, 33, 33, 36, 37;
12:10, 14, 14, 15, 16, 16, 33, 44, 46, 50,
54, 54; 13:6, 6, 11, 11, 16, 19, 19, 21, 21,
33, 34; 14:2, 5, 7, 8, 8, 12, 12, 16, 16, 16,
16, 18, 20, 28, 32; 15:8; 15:11, 13, 14, 15,
20, 22, 29; 16:1, 1, 19, 20, 20; 17:2, 4, 4,
6, 7, 12, 15, 16; 18:1, 2, 2, 3, 4, 4, 10, 10,
13, 17, 18, 25, 25, 35; 19:2, 4, 7, 7, 9,

5, 6, 6, 7, 7, 7, 7, 11, 11, 11, 12, 13, 13,
14, 14, 14, 15, 16, 17, 19, 29; 48:1, 2, 3, 4,
47:3, 4, 4, 5, 5, 5, 9, 10, 20; 48:1, 2, 3, 4,
5, 6, 7, 15, 23, 24, 25, 26, 27

11, 12, 12, 12, 14, 17, 20, 30, 37, 43, 46;
20:6, 9, 9, 9, 9, 10, 12, 24, 28, 29, 38, 47;
21:2, 3, 13, 15, 18, 27, 29, 35; 22:10, 10,
12, 24, 29, 36, 41, 47, 48, 52, 55, 56, 58,
59, 59; 23:2, 6, 8, 11, 19, 26, 27, 31, 38,
44, 46, 47, 50, 50, 50, 50, 51, 53; 24:13,
18, 19, 23, 37, 39, 42, 42, 42

Jn 1:6, 7, 30, 32, 42; 2:1, 15, 16; 3:1, 1, 2, 3,
4, 5, 10, 25, 27; 4:5, 7, 9, 9, 14, 19, 24,
29, 44, 46; 5:1, 2, 3, 4, 5, 6, 13, 14, 35,
35, 35; 6:2, 3, 4, 5, 7, 9, 14, 15, 15, 17,
18, 50, 60, 70; 7:12, 20, 22, 23, 23, 33,
40, 43; 8:3, 7, 40, 44, 44, 44, 48, 48, 49,
51, 52, 52, 55; 9:1, 11, 16, 16, 16, 16, 24,
25, 30, 31; 10:1, 1, 5, 12, 13, 19, 20, 21,
21, 33, 33; 11:1, 10, 38, 38, 43, 44, 47,
54, 54, 57; 12:2, 3, 6, 14, 24, 28, 35, 46,
49; 13:4, 5, 26, 33, 34; 14:2, 3, 19, 23;
15:6, 6, 13, 25; 16:16, 16, 17, 17, 18, 19,
19, 21, 21; 18:1, 3, 10, 18, 30, 35, 37, 37,
39, 40; 19:2, 2, 7, 12, 13, 17, 23, 25, 26,
27, 29, 31, 34, 35, 39, 41, 41; 20:7;
21:3, 8, 9

Ac 1:9, 12, 18, 22; 2:2, 2, 22, 30; 3:2, 14,
34, 34, 34, 36; 6:1, 5, 5, 7; 7:5, 6, 11, 16,
27, 27, 29, 30, 30, 35, 35, 35, 35, 37, 41,
46, 47, 57, 58, 60; 8:1, 9, 27, 32, 32, 36;
9:3, 4, 7, 10, 10, 12, 12, 15, 25, 26, 33,
36, 43; 10:1, 1, 2, 3, 4, 6, 7, 10, 11, 11,
13, 22, 22, 26, 28, 28, 30, 32, 34, 39;
11:5, 5, 5, 5, 7, 21, 24, 26; 12:7, 9, 11,
13, 21, 22, 22, 22; 13:6, 6, 6, 7, 11, 11,
11, 17, 21, 21, 22, 23, 29, 41, 41, 41, 47;
14:1, 8, 8, 10; 15:7, 10, 14, 16, 16, 24,
26, 28, 29; 17:1, 4, 14, 16, 16, 16, 34,
34; 18:2, 7, 9, 11, 14, 15, 18, 24, 27, 28;
19:14, 22, 24, 34, 35, 38, 39; 20:9, 9,
9, 11, 12; 21:1, 2, 10, 23, 39, 39, 39;
40; 22:3, 3, 3, 6, 12, 17, 22, 25, 25, 28,
26, 27, 28, 29; 23:6, 6, 7, 9, 10, 12, 14,
17, 21, 25, 27; 24:1, 4, 5, 5, 5, 10, 15, 16,
23, 24, 25, 27; 25:9, 14, 27; 26:5, 8, 13,
14, 16, 16, 24, 26, 28, 34, 39, 39, 41;
28:2, 3, 3, 4, 6, 6, 8, 8, 11, 19, 23, 26

Ro 1:1, 10, 25, 28; 2:14, 17, 19, 19, 20, 21,
25, 25, 28, 29; 3:4, 5, 7, 25, 28; 4:11, 17;
5:7, 7; 7:1, 2, 21; 8:24; 9:9, 27, 28, 29,
33; 10:2, 14, 19, 21; 11:5, 9, 9, 9, 17,
24; 12:1; 13:3, 4; 14:13; 15:8, 12, 23, 26;
16:1, 2, 16, 23

1Co 1:22, 23; 2:7, 11; 3:10, 14, 18; 4:1, 2, 3,
6, 9, 21; 5:5, 6, 7, 11, 11, 11, 11, 11; 6:1,
5, 7, 15, 16, 18, 20; 7:1, 1, 5, 12, 13, 15,
15, 21, 22, 23, 26, 27, 27, 27, 28, 34, 34,
35; 8:7, 9; 9:5, 5, 7, 7, 7, 27, 28; 10:14, 17,
20, 24, 25, 27; 10:13, 27, 30; 11:6, 6, 6, 7,
13, 14, 14, 15, 15, 15, 28; 12:31; 13:1,
11, 11, 11, 11, 11, 11, 12; 14:7, 11, 11, 22,
25, 26, 26, 26, 26, 35, 37; 15:38, 44, 44,
44, 44, 45, 45, 51, 52; 16:7, 9, 20

2Co 1:10, 15, 23; 2:6, 7, 12, 15; 3:13, 18;
4:17, 17; 5:1, 1, 17; 6:2, 13, 18; 7:8, 8, 9,
11, 14; 8:2, 10, 11, 11, 12, 12, 14, 14;
9:2, 5, 7; 10:6, 11, 13; 11:1, 2, 5, 16, 16,
16, 20, 20, 20, 20, 20, 23, 25, 25, 32, 33,
33; 12:2, 2, 3, 4, 5, 6, 7, 11, 17, 18, 18;
13:3, 12, 99

Gal 2:3, 14, 16, 18; 3:13, 13, 15, 19, 20, 20,
21, 25; 4:1, 1, 4, 7, 7, 7, 18, 22, 22, 27;
5:3, 9; 6:1, 1, 3, 4, 5, 7, 7, 12, 12, 15

Eph 2:21, 22; 3:7; 4:13; 5:2, 2, 12, 27, 31,
32; 6:21

Php 1:6, 23, 23; 2:7, 8, 9, 15, 22; 3:5, 5;
4:17, 18, 18

Col 1:7, 23, 25; 2:15, 16, 17, 18, 23; 3:13;
4:1, 3, 7, 7, 9, 11, 12, 13

1Th 2:5, 7, 11, 17; 4:16; 5:2, 3, 4, 8, 26

2Th 1:5, 6; 2:3, 11; 3:15

1Ti 1:5, 5, 8, 9, 13, 13, 15, 16, 18, 19; 2:2,
6, 17; 3:1, 1, 1, 2, 3, 5, 6, 7, 9, 9, 10,
13, 13; 4:2, 6, 9; 5:1, 5, 9, 23; 6:9, 12,
13, 19

2Ti 1:7, 9, 11, 11; 2:3, 4, 5, 11, 15, 17, 20,
24, 26; 3:2, 3:5, 15; 4:7, 8

Tit 1:1, 7, 8, 8, 12; 2:7, 14; 3:8, 10, 10

Phm 1:1, 9, 9, 15, 16, 16, 16, 17, 22, 99

Heb 1:4, 5, 5, 7, 8, 11, 12; 2:2, 6, 7, 9, 17;
3:5, 5, 6; 4:1, 4, 7, 7, 9, 12, 14, 15; 5:5, 6,
8, 10, 13; 6:18, 20; 7:2, 3, 5, 12, 16, 17,
18, 19, 21, 22, 22, 26; 8:1, 2, 4, 6, 6, 8,
10, 10, 13; 9:1, 2, 9, 11, 11, 13, 16, 17;
10:1, 3, 5, 5, 20, 21, 22, 27, 31, 32, 33,
34, 37; 11:2, 4, 6, 8, 9, 11, 14, 16, 16, 16,
16, 19, 21, 23, 25, 35, 39; 12:1, 10, 19,
20, 20, 28, 29; 13:9, 18, 22

Jas 1:1, 6, 8, 11, 18, 23, 23, 23, 23, 25, 25;
2:2, 2, 2, 3, 11, 14, 15, 18, 24; 3:2, 4, 5,
5, 6, 6, 11, 12, 13, 13; 4:4, 11, 11, 13,
13, 14, 14; 5:3, 5, 16, 17, 20, 20

1Pe 1:3, 6, 19, 22; 2:4, 5, 5, 6, 8, 9, 9, 9,
9, 10, 16, 19; 3:4, 9, 15, 16, 20, 21; 4:15,
15, 15, 16, 19; 5:1, 1, 2, 4, 8, 10, 12, 14

2Pe 1:1, 17, 19, 19, 19; 2:3, 5, 14, 17, 19;
3:8, 8, 10, 10, 13

1Jn 1:10; 2:4, 8, 22; 3:15; 4:20, 20; 5:10, 16,
16, 17

2Jn 1:4, 5, 7, 8

3Jn 1:6

Jude 1:9, 22

Rev 1:10, 10, 11, 13, 13, 14, 16; 2:10,
14, 14, 17, 18, 20, 20, 22, 27, 27; 3:1,
3, 4, 8, 12; 4:1, 1, 2, 3, 3, 3, 6, 7, 7, 7, 7,

7; 5:1, 2, 2, 6, 9, 12; 6:2, 2, 2, 4, 5, 5, 6,
6, 6, 6, 8, 10, 11, 12, 13, 13, 14; 7:2, 9,
10; 8:3, 8, 10, 10, 12, 13; 9:1, 2, 2, 5, 5,
11, 13, 15, 15, 15; 10:1, 1, 2, 3, 3, 4;
11:1, 3, 9, 11, 12, 12, 14, 15; 12:1, 1, 1, 3,
5, 5, 6, 6, 10, 12, 14, 14, 14, 15; 13:1, 2,
2, 2, 5, 11, 11, 14, 16, 16, 18; 14:1, 2, 2, 3,
9, 13, 14, 14, 14, 15, 17, 18, 20; 15:2;
16:1, 2, 3, 15, 16, 17, 18, 21, 21; 17:3, 3, 4,
4, 5, 10; 18:2, 2, 7, 21, 21, 21, 21, 22, 23;
19:1, 5, 6, 11, 12, 13, 14, 15, 15, 16, 17,
20; 20:1, 2, 3, 3, 4, 6, 11; 21:1, 1, 2, 3,
10, 11, 11, 12, 15, 17, 19, 20, 20, 20, 27;
22:1, 15

21:19; 22:24; 23:5, 6, 18, 32; 24:9, 34;
25:12, 12, 19, 23; 27:6; 28:10, 22;
29:6, 22, 27, 27; 30:19, 20, 23
Ecc 4:13; 5:6; 6:1, 2, 3, 3; 7:11; 8:3, 11, 12;
9:2, 3, 12, 12; 10:5, 5
SS 4:4; 13; 6:4, 10
Isa 1:13; 30; 5:10, 26; 6:13; 9:17; 11:10, 12;
14:19; 16:4; 17:6, 9; 18:3; 19:19; 24:13;
29:5, 21; 30:13, 17, 28; 33:1; 36:16;
37:33, 36; 38:12, 13; 41:24; 43:23; 44:14,
19; 45:17; 48:4; 49:8, 18; 53:10; 54:16;
55:3, 13; 56:5; 58:5; 60:15, 19; 61:8;
63:12; 64:6; 65:9, 20, 20, 20, 20; 66:3, 3,
3, 14, 20, 20, 24
Jer 1:11, 14, 18; 2:7, 19; 3:18; 4:7; 5:15, 16;
6:26; 9:2, 8, 11; 10:10; 11:19; 14:12;
18:17; 20:17; 21:25, 29; 23:24; 25:9, 11, 18;
26:8, 9; 29:11, 18; 30:14, 17; 31:3; 32:14,
40; 33:9; 34:22; 42:18, 18; 43:1; 44:12,
12, 22, 22, 27; 46:19, 22; 47:2; 48:40;
49:2, 14; 50:9; 51:29, 34, 37, 37, 41, 63;
52:23, 25
La 1:15; 2:4, 4, 5; 5:10
Eze 1:10; 10; 3:9; 4:3; 5:15, 15; 7:2, 5, 5, 6;
10:14; 13:11, 13; 16:3, 24, 30, 45, 60;
17:13; 20:17; 21:25, 29; 23:24; 33:32;
35:5; 36:3; 37:10, 26; 38:10, 22; 40:19,
23, 27, 47, 47; 41:7, 13, 13, 14, 15; 42:2,
8, 15; 43:23; 44:28; 45:1, 13, 13, 24, 24,
24; 46:5, 5, 7, 7, 7, 11, 11, 11, 14; 47:22
Da 2:46; 3:1; 4:3, 34; 5:12; 6:1, 3; 7:14, 27;
9:24; 11:6, 7
Hos 3:1, 4, 4; 7:4, 6, 7; 8:1; 10:1; 13:13, 15
Joel 2:1;
Am 3:11, 12, 15; 5:3, 3, 13; 7:2; 8:10
Ob 1:1;
Jnh 3:3;
Mic 1:15; 2:3, 8
Na 1:8, 8, 9
Hab 2:3, 9
Zep 3:12;
Zec 5:6; 7:12; 9:9, 9, 16
Mal 1:10; 13; 2:11, 12; 3:3; 4:1
Mt 2:19; 4:8; 5:38, 38; 9:16, 20; 11:1; 12:35,
39; 13:8, 23, 28; 14:7; 16:23; 18:12, 28;
19:29; 21:2, 5, 5; 24:44, 50; 26:5, 7, 72
Mk 1:23; 2:21; 3:26, 30; 4:8, 20; 5:2, 25;
6:27; 7:22, 25, 32; 10:30; 14:2, 3; 15:43
Lk 1:11, 18; 4:33; 5:36; 6:7, 45; 7:37; 8:8,
15, 43; 9:28; 10:34; 11:12, 29; 12:1, 40,
46; 14:5, 5, 32; 15:4; 16:2, 6, 7; 19:21,
22; 22:37, 43, 44
Jn 1:22, 47; 5:4, 5; 12:15, 29; 13:15; 19:39;
21:11
Ac 1:13, 15; 2:30; 3:3; 6:15; 7:30; 8:27;
9:37; 10:3, 28; 11:13; 12:21; 14:5; 17:5,
23; 18:24; 19:40; 20:32; 21:16, 26, 29,
31, 38; 23:9, 21, 27; 25:11
Ro 1:1, 23; 2:20; 3:13; 4:19; 7:3; 11:1; 14:13
1Co 1:1; 5:9, 11, 11; 8:4, 7; 9:1, 2, 25;
12:17; 14:2, 4, 8, 13, 14, 19, 26, 27;
15:9, 52
2Co 1:1; 2:11; 6:15; 8:14; 11:7, 14; 12:12
Gal 1:1, 8; 2:5; 4:7, 14, 24; 5:13
Eph 1:1, 11; 5:2, 5; 6:20
Php 1:28; 3:17; 4:18
Col 1:1;
2Th 3:9, 15
1Ti 1:1; 2:7; 4:12; 5:1, 8, 19, 19
2Ti 1:1, 11; 2:9; 4:5
Tit 1:1;
Heb 3:12; 6:6, 16, 16, 17, 19; 7:16, 20, 21,
21, 24; 10:22, 29, 34; 11:7, 8; 12:22;
13:10
Jas 3:8; 5:10
1Pe 1:1, 4; 2:21; 3:15; 4:15; 5:1
2Pe 1:1, 11; 2:6, 6
1Jn 2:1, 7, 20; 5:20
2Jn 1:7;
Jude 1:7;
Rev 2:7, 11, 17, 29; 3:6, 8, 13, 22; 4:3; 7:4;
8:1, 5, 13; 9:15; 11:19; 13:9, 14; 14:1;
16:18; 19:17; 20:1; 21:17, 19, 20

AND (51713)

Ge 1:1, 2, 2, 2, 2, 3, 3, 4, 4, 5, 5, 5, 6, 6,
7, 7, 7, 8, 8, 8, 9, 9, 9, 10, 10, 10, 11,
11, 11, 12, 12, 12, 13, 13, 14, 14, 14, 14,
14, 15, 15, 15, 16, 16, 17, 17, 18, 18, 18,
19, 20, 20, 21, 21, 21, 21, 22, 22, 22,
23, 23, 24, 24, 24, 25, 25, 25, 26, 26,
26, 26, 26, 26, 27, 28, 28, 28, 28, 28,
28, 28, 28, 29, 29, 30, 30, 30, 30, 31, 31,
31, 31; 2:1, 1, 2, 2, 3, 3, 3, 4, 4, 5, 5, 5, 6,
7, 7, 7, 8, 9, 9, 9, 10, 11, 11, 12, 12,
13, 14, 14, 14, 14, 15, 15, 16, 16, 17,
18, 18, 18, 19, 19, 20, 20, 21, 21, 22,
22, 23, 23, 24, 24, 24, 25; 3:1, 1, 2, 3,
3, 4, 4, 4, 4, 5, 5, 5, 6, 6, 7, 7, 8, 8, 9, 9,
10, 10, 11, 12, 12, 13, 13, 13, 14, 15, 15,
15, 15, 16, 17, 18, 18, 18, 18, 19, 19,
20, 20, 21, 22, 22, 22, 23, 23, 24; 4:1, 1,
2, 3, 4, 4, 4, 5, 5, 5, 5, 6, 6, 7, 7, 8, 8, 8,
9, 9, 10, 11, 12, 12, 13, 13, 13, 13, 13,
14, 14, 14, 14, 15, 15, 15, 16, 16, 17, 17,
18, 18, 18, 18, 19, 19, 20, 20, 20,
22, 22, 23, 23, 24, 24, 24, 25, 25, 25, 26,
26; 5:2, 3, 4, 5, 7, 8, 9, 10, 11, 12, 13, 14,
15, 16, 17, 18, 19, 20, 20, 21, 22, 22,
23, 23, 24, 24, 24, 25, 25, 26, 26, 27, 27,
28, 28, 28, 29, 29, 30, 30, 30, 31, 31,
31, 31; 2:1, 1, 2, 2, 2, 3, 3, 3, 4, 4, 5, 5, 6,
7, 7, 7, 8, 8, 8, 9, 9, 10, 10, 11, 11, 11,
12, 12, 12, 12, 13, 13, 14, 14, 14, 14, 14,
15, 15, 15, 16, 16, 17, 17, 17, 17, 18, 18,
19, 19, 19, 20, 20, 21, 22, 22, 23, 23, 23,
24, 25, 26; 5:2, 2, 3, 3, 3, 3, 3, 4, 4, 4, 5,
5, 5, 6, 6, 6, 7, 7, 7, 7, 8, 8, 9, 9, 10, 11,
11, 12, 12, 13, 13, 13, 13, 13,
14, 14, 15, 15, 15, 15, 16, 16, 17, 17,
18, 18, 19, 19, 19, 20, 20, 21, 22, 22, 22,
22, 24; 23:1, 1, 1, 2, 2, 5, 5, 7, 7, 7, 8, 8, 9,
9, 10, 10, 11, 11, 11, 12, 12, 13, 13, 14, 15,
15, 15, 16, 16, 16, 16, 17, 17, 18, 18, 18,
19, 20, 20; 24:1, 1, 1, 2, 3,
3, 4, 4, 5, 6, 7, 7, 7, 7, 8, 9, 9, 10, 10,
10, 11, 12, 12, 13, 14, 14, 14, 15, 16,
16, 16, 16, 17, 17, 18, 18, 18, 19, 20,
20, 20, 21, 22, 22, 22, 22, 23, 24, 24,
24; 23:1, 1, 1, 2, 2, 3, 3, 3, 4, 4, 4, 5,
5, 6, 6, 7, 7, 7, 8, 8, 8, 8, 9, 9, 10, 11,
12, 12, 14, 14, 14, 14, 14, 15, 16,
17, 17, 17, 17, 19, 19, 20, 20; 24:1, 1, 1, 3,
3, 4, 4, 4, 4, 4, 5, 6, 7, 7, 8, 8, 9, 10, 10,
10, 11, 12, 12, 13, 14, 14, 14, 15, 16,
16, 16, 17, 18, 18, 18, 19, 20, 20, 21, 21,
22, 22, 23, 23, 23, 24, 25, 26; 5:2, 2, 3,
3, 4, 5, 6, 7, 7, 7, 8, 8, 8, 9, 9, 9, 9, 10, 11,
11, 11, 12, 12, 13, 14, 15, 15, 16,
17, 17, 17, 18, 18, 18, 19, 19, 20, 20,
21, 21, 22, 22, 23, 23, 23, 24, 25,
25, 26, 26, 26, 27, 27, 27, 28,
28, 28, 29, 29, 29, 30, 31, 31, 32, 33,
33, 33, 34, 34, 34, 35, 35, 36, 36, 36, 37,
37, 37, 37, 37, 38, 38, 38, 39, 39, 39, 40,
40, 40, 40, 41, 42, 42, 42, 42, 43, 44, 45,
45, 46; 28:1, 1, 1, 2, 3, 3, 3, 4, 4, 5, 6, 6,
7, 7, 8, 9, 10, 11, 11, 11, 11, 11, 12,
12, 12, 13, 13, 13, 13, 14, 14, 14, 14,
14, 15, 15, 16, 16, 17, 17, 18, 18, 19, 19,
20, 22; 29:1, 2, 2, 3, 3, 3, 3, 4, 4, 5, 5, 6,
6, 6, 7, 7, 8, 9, 9, 10, 10, 10, 11, 11, 12,
12, 13, 13, 13, 13, 14, 14, 15, 16, 16, 17,
17, 18, 18, 19, 19, 20, 21, 21, 22, 23,
23, 23, 24, 24, 24, 25, 25, 26, 27, 27, 27,
28, 28, 29, 29, 29, 30, 30, 30, 31; 35:1, 1, 1,
2, 2, 2, 3, 3, 3, 4, 4, 4, 5, 5, 6, 7, 7, 7,
8, 8, 9, 9, 10, 11, 11, 11, 11, 12, 12,
12, 13, 14, 14, 14, 14, 14, 14, 16, 16, 16, 17,
18, 19, 19, 20, 21, 21, 22, 22, 23, 23,
23, 23, 23, 24, 25, 25, 26, 26, 27, 27,
28, 29, 29, 29, 30, 30; 36:2, 3, 3, 3, 4, 5,
5, 6, 6, 7, 7, 7, 8, 9, 9, 10, 10, 10, 10, 10,
11, 11, 11, 12, 12, 13, 13, 13, 14, 14,
14, 15, 15, 16, 16, 17, 17, 18, 18, 19;
37:1, 2, 2, 2, 3, 3, 3, 4, 4, 5, 5, 6, 7,
7, 7, 7, 7, 8, 8, 8, 9, 9, 9, 10, 10, 10, 10,
11, 11, 12, 13, 13, 14, 14, 14, 15, 16, 17,
18, 18, 19, 19, 19, 20, 20, 21, 21, 22,
23, 23, 23, 24, 24, 24, 25, 25, 26, 27,
27, 27, 28, 28, 28, 28, 28, 29, 29, 30,
30; 38:1, 2, 3, 4, 5, 6, 7, 8, 9, 10, 10, 10,
11, 11, 12, 12, 13, 13, 14, 14, 14, 16,
16, 17, 18, 18, 18, 19, 19, 20, 20, 20,
22, 23, 23, 23, 24, 24, 25, 25, 26, 27,
27, 27, 28, 28, 29, 29, 30; 30:31, 31,
31, 31; 9:1, 2, 3, 4, 4, 4, 5, 6, 6, 7, 7, 7,
7, 7, 8, 8, 9, 9, 10, 10, 10, 11, 11, 11,
12, 12, 13, 13, 14, 14, 15, 16, 16, 16,
19, 19, 19, 19, 20, 21, 21, 22, 22, 22,
23, 23, 23, 23, 24, 24, 24, 25, 25, 25, 26,
27, 27, 27, 27, 28, 28, 29, 29, 30,
31, 31, 31, 31, 31, 31, 32, 32, 32, 33,
33, 33, 34, 34, 34, 35; 10:1, 1, 2, 2, 3, 3, 5,
5, 5, 6, 6, 6, 7, 7, 8, 8, 9, 9, 9, 9, 10, 10,
10, 11, 11, 12, 12, 13, 13, 13, 14, 14,
15, 15, 15, 16, 17, 18, 18, 19, 19, 19,
21, 22, 24, 24, 24, 25, 25, 26, 27, 28,
29; 8:1, 1, 1, 2, 3, 3, 3, 3, 3, 3, 4, 4,
5, 5, 5, 6, 6, 6, 7, 7, 8, 8, 8, 9, 9, 9, 9,
10, 10, 11, 11, 11, 11, 12, 12, 13, 14, 14,
15, 15, 16, 16, 16, 17, 17, 18, 19, 19,
21, 22; 29:1, 1, 2, 2, 2, 3, 3, 3, 4, 4, 5, 5,
6, 6, 7, 7, 8, 9, 9, 10, 10, 10, 11, 11, 11,
12, 12, 13, 13, 14, 14, 14, 15, 16, 16,
16, 17, 17, 17, 18, 18, 18, 19, 19, 19,
20, 20, 21, 22; 49:1, 1, 2, 2, 3, 3, 3, 4,
4, 5, 5, 6, 6, 7, 7, 9, 10, 11, 11, 12, 13,
13, 15, 15, 15, 20, 23, 23, 24, 25, 25,
26, 27, 28, 28, 29, 29, 31, 31, 31, 32, 33,
33, 33; 50:1, 1, 2, 2, 3, 3, 4, 4, 5, 5, 6,
6, 7, 7, 7, 8, 8, 9, 10, 10, 11, 11, 12,
13, 13, 14, 14, 14, 15, 15, 16, 17,
17, 17, 18, 18, 18, 19, 21, 21, 21, 22, 22,
22, 22, 23, 24, 24, 24, 24, 25, 25, 26, 26,
26;

Ex 1:1, 2, 3, 4, 5, 6, 6, 7, 7, 7, 7, 9,
9, 10, 10, 10, 11, 11, 12, 12, 13, 14, 14,
15, 15, 16, 16, 17, 18, 18, 18, 19, 19,
20, 20, 21, 22, 22; 2:1, 1, 2, 2, 3, 3, 3,
3, 4, 5, 5, 6, 6, 6, 7, 8, 8, 9, 9, 10, 11, 12,
12, 12, 13, 13, 14, 14, 14, 14, 15, 16,
16, 16, 17, 17, 17, 17, 17, 18, 19, 19, 19,
20, 20, 21, 22, 22, 22, 22, 22; 4:1, 1, 2,
3, 3, 4, 4, 4, 5, 5, 6, 6, 6, 7, 7, 7, 7, 7,
8, 9, 10, 11, 11, 12, 12, 12, 13, 13, 14,
14, 15, 15, 16, 16, 16, 17, 17, 18, 18, 19,
20, 20, 20, 20, 21, 22, 22, 22, 22, 23,
23, 24, 24, 24, 25, 25, 25, 26, 27, 27,
27, 28, 29, 29, 30, 30, 31, 31, 31; 5:1, 1, 2, 3,
4, 5, 5, 6, 7, 8, 8, 9, 10, 10, 11, 12, 13, 14, 14,
15, 16, 16, 17, 18, 19, 20, 20, 21, 21,
22; 6:1, 2, 3, 4, 5, 5, 6, 6, 6, 7,
7, 7, 8, 8, 8, 9, 10, 12, 13, 13, 14, 14, 14,
14, 14, 15, 15, 15, 15, 15, 16, 16, 16,
17, 18, 18, 18, 18, 19, 19, 20, 20, 20, 22,
22, 23, 23, 23, 24, 24, 24, 25, 25, 26,
27, 28, 30, 30; 7:1, 2, 3, 3, 3, 4, 4, 5,
6, 6, 7, 7, 7, 8, 9, 10, 10, 10, 10, 10, 11,
11, 12, 12, 13, 14, 15, 15, 15, 16, 16, 17,
17, 18, 18, 19, 19, 19, 19, 20, 20, 20, 21, 21,
21, 22, 22, 22, 23; 8:1, 1, 2, 3, 3, 3, 3, 4,
5, 5, 5, 6, 7, 8, 8, 8, 9, 10, 10, 11, 11, 11,
12, 12, 12, 13, 13, 14, 15, 16, 16, 16, 16,
17, 17, 17, 18, 18, 19, 19, 20, 21, 21, 21,
21, 22, 22, 23, 23, 24, 24, 24, 25, 25, 25,
26, 27, 28, 29, 29, 29, 30, 30, 31, 31, 31;
9:1, 2, 3, 4, 4, 4, 5, 6, 6, 7, 7, 7, 7, 7, 8,
8, 8, 9, 9, 10, 10, 11, 11,
12, 12, 13, 13, 13, 14, 14, 15, 15, 16, 16,
19, 19, 19, 19, 20, 21, 21, 22, 22, 22,
23, 23, 23, 23, 24, 24, 24, 25, 25, 25, 26,
27, 27, 27, 27, 28, 28, 29, 29, 30,
31, 31, 31, 31, 31, 31, 32, 32, 32, 33,
33, 33, 34, 34, 34, 35; 10:1, 1, 2, 2, 3, 3, 5,
5, 5, 6, 6, 6, 7, 7, 8, 8, 9, 9, 9, 9, 10, 10,
10, 11, 11, 12, 12, 13, 13, 13, 14, 14,
15, 15, 15, 16, 17, 18, 18, 19, 19, 19,
21, 22, 24, 24, 24, 25, 25, 26, 27, 28,
29; 11:1, 1, 2, 2, 3, 3, 4, 5, 5, 6, 7, 8;
12:1, 1, 4, 4, 6, 7, 7, 8, 8, 8, 9, 9, 10, 11,
11, 12, 13, 13, 14, 15, 16, 16, 17, 18, 21,
21, 22, 22, 22, 22, 23, 23, 23, 24,
25, 26, 27, 29, 29, 29, 30, 30, 30, 31, 31,
31, 32, 32, 32, 33, 34, 35, 35, 36, 36, 37,
38, 38, 38, 39, 39, 40, 41, 41, 43, 43, 45,
48, 48, 48, 48, 48, 49, 50, 51; 13:1, 2, 3,
5, 5, 5, 5, 5, 5, 6, 7, 8, 9, 9, 11, 11, 11,

25, 25, 25, 26, 26, 26, 26, 27, 27, 27, 28,
28, 28, 29, 29, 30, 30, 30, 30, 31, 31, 31,
32, 32, 32; 6:1, 1, 2, 3, 3, 4, 4, 5, 5, 6, 6,
7, 7, 7, 7, 8, 8, 9, 9, 10, 11, 12, 12, 13, 13,
14, 14, 15, 15, 16, 16, 16, 17, 17, 18, 18,
18, 18, 19, 19, 20, 21, 21, 21, 21; 7:1, 1,
2, 2, 3, 3, 4, 4, 4, 5, 6, 7, 7, 7, 7, 8, 8, 8,
9, 9, 10, 11, 12, 12, 13, 13, 13, 13, 13,
14, 14, 14, 14, 15, 15, 16, 16, 16, 17, 17,
17, 17, 18, 18, 18, 19, 19, 20, 20, 21, 21,
21, 21, 23, 23, 23, 23, 23, 23, 24, 24,
8:1, 1, 1, 1, 2, 2, 3, 3, 3, 4, 5, 6, 7, 7, 9,
9, 9, 10, 11, 12, 12, 13, 13, 13, 13, 13,
14, 14, 14, 14, 15, 15, 16, 16, 16, 17, 17,
17, 17, 21, 23, 23, 23, 24, 24, 24;
9:1, 1,
1, 1, 1, 1, 2, 2, 2, 2, 5, 5, 7, 7, 7, 7, 8, 8, 8,
10, 10, 11, 11, 12, 13, 13, 13, 14, 15, 15,
16, 17, 17, 17, 18, 18, 19, 19, 20, 20,
21, 21, 23, 24, 24, 25, 26, 26, 26, 27,
28, 28, 29, 29, 29, 30, 30, 31, 31;
10:1, 1, 1, 1, 2, 2, 2, 2, 2, 3, 3, 4, 4, 5,
5, 6, 7, 7, 8, 8, 9, 10, 10, 10, 10, 10, 11,
12, 13, 13, 13, 14, 14, 14, 15, 15, 15,
16, 16, 16, 17, 17, 17, 18, 18, 19,
19, 19, 20, 20, 21, 22, 22, 23, 24, 24, 24,
15:1, 2, 2, 3, 3, 4, 5, 5, 5, 6, 6, 7, 8, 9,
9, 9, 9, 10, 10, 11, 11, 12, 12, 13, 13,
13, 14, 14, 15, 17, 17, 17, 19, 19, 20, 20,
20, 21, 21, 21, 21; 16:1, 2, 2, 3, 3, 4, 4, 4,
5, 5, 6, 7, 8, 8, 9, 9, 10, 11, 11, 11,
12, 12, 13, 14, 15, 15, 16, 16, 17:1, 1,
1, 1, 2, 2, 2, 2, 3, 3, 4, 4, 5, 6, 7, 7, 7, 8,
8, 9, 10, 11, 11, 11, 11, 12, 13, 13,
14, 15, 16, 16, 16, 16, 17, 17, 18, 19,
19, 19, 20, 20, 21, 21, 22, 22, 22, 23, 23,
23, 24, 24, 25, 25, 26, 26, 27, 27, 28, 28,
28, 29, 29, 29, 30, 30, 31; 33:1,
1, 1, 1, 1, 2, 2, 2, 2, 3, 3, 3, 4, 4, 4,
4, 4, 4, 4, 5, 5, 5, 5, 5, 6, 6, 6, 7, 7, 7, 8,
8, 9, 10, 10, 11, 11, 11, 11, 12, 12, 12, 13,
13, 13, 13, 14, 14, 14, 15, 17, 17, 17, 18,
18, 19, 20, 20; 34:1, 1, 2, 2, 2, 2, 3, 3, 3, 4,
5, 6, 7, 7, 7, 8, 8, 9, 9, 9, 10, 10, 10, 11,
11, 11, 12, 13, 13, 14, 14, 16, 16, 16,
17, 18, 18, 18, 19, 20, 21, 21, 22, 22, 23,
23, 23, 24, 24, 25, 25, 25, 26, 26, 27,
27, 28, 28, 28, 29, 29, 30, 30, 31; 35:1, 1, 1,
2, 2, 2, 3, 3, 3, 3, 4, 4, 5, 5, 5, 6, 6, 7, 7,
8, 8, 9, 10, 10, 11, 11, 11, 11, 12, 12,
12, 13, 14, 14, 14, 15, 16, 16, 16, 17,
17, 18, 18, 18, 19, 19, 19, 19, 21, 21,
22, 23, 23, 23, 24, 24, 25, 25, 26, 26,
26, 27, 27, 28, 28, 28, 29, 29, 29; 36:2, 2,
3, 3, 3, 4, 4, 5, 5, 5, 6, 6, 7, 7, 8, 8, 8, 8,
9, 9, 10, 10, 11, 12, 12, 12, 13, 13, 14,
14, 14, 14, 14, 16, 16, 17, 17, 18, 18,
18, 18, 18, 19, 19, 19, 19, 20, 21, 21,
22, 22, 23, 23, 24, 24, 24, 25, 25,
25, 26, 26, 27, 28, 28, 29, 29, 30;
39:1, 1, 2, 2, 3, 3, 3, 4, 4, 4, 5, 5, 5,
5, 6, 6, 6, 6, 7, 7, 8, 9, 10, 11, 11, 11, 12,
12, 12, 13, 13, 14, 14, 15, 15, 15, 15,
16, 17, 18, 18, 19, 20, 20, 20, 21, 21,
22, 22, 23; 40:1, 2, 3, 4, 4, 4, 5, 5, 5,
6, 6, 7, 7, 8, 8, 8, 9, 9, 10, 10, 14, 15, 16,
17, 17, 18, 18, 19, 19, 20, 20, 21, 21;
41:1, 1, 2, 2, 3, 3, 3, 4, 4, 4, 4, 5, 5,
6, 6, 7, 7, 7, 7, 8, 8, 8, 8, 9, 10, 10, 11,
12, 12, 12, 12, 13, 14, 14, 14, 14,
15, 15, 16, 17, 18, 18, 19, 19, 19,
20, 20, 21, 22, 22, 23, 23, 23, 24, 25,
26, 27, 27, 28, 28, 30, 30, 31, 32, 33,
33, 34, 34, 35, 35, 36, 37, 37, 38, 39,
39, 40, 41, 42, 42, 42, 42, 43, 43, 44,
44, 45, 45, 45, 46, 46, 47, 48, 48, 49,
50, 51, 51, 52, 53, 54, 54, 55, 55, 56,
56, 56, 57; 42:2, 2, 2, 3, 5, 6, 6, 6, 6, 7,
7, 7, 8, 9, 9, 11, 12, 13, 13, 14, 16,
16, 17, 18, 20, 20, 21, 22, 22, 23,
24, 24, 24, 24, 24, 25, 25, 26, 26,

12, 12, 13, 13, 13, 14, 14, 14, 15, 16, 17,
17, 17, 18, 18, 19, 19, 20, 20, 21, 21, 21,
22, 22, 22, 22, 22, 23, 24, 24, 24, 24,
25, 25, 25, 25, 26, 26, 27, 27, 27, 28,
28, 29, 29, 30, 30, 31, 31, 31, 31, 32,
32, 33, 34, 34, 34, 35; 27:1, 1, 1, 1, 2, 3,
3, 3, 4, 4, 5, 5, 5, 6, 6, 7, 7, 9, 9, 10, 10, 11,
11, 12, 12, 12, 12, 13, 13, 14, 14, 14, 14,
15, 15, 16, 16, 17, 17, 18, 18, 19, 19, 20,
20, 21, 22, 22, 22, 23, 24, 24, 24, 25,
25, 25, 25, 26, 26, 27, 27, 27, 27, 28,
28, 28, 29, 29, 29, 30, 30, 31, 31, 31, 31,
32, 33, 33, 33, 33, 33, 34, 34, 34, 34,
35, 35, 36, 36, 36, 37, 37, 37, 37, 37,
38, 38, 39, 39, 39, 40, 40, 40, 41, 41,
42, 42, 42, 42, 43, 44, 45, 45, 46; 28:1, 1,
1, 2, 3, 3, 3, 4, 4, 5, 6, 6, 6, 6, 7, 7, 7, 12,
8, 9, 10, 10, 11, 11, 11, 11, 11, 12,
12, 12, 13, 13, 13, 14, 14, 14, 14,
14, 15, 15, 16, 16, 17, 17, 18, 18, 19, 19,
19, 20, 22, 22, 22, 22, 22, 23, 24, 24, 24,
25, 25, 25, 25, 26, 26, 27, 27, 27, 27, 28,
28, 29, 29, 29, 30, 30, 31, 31, 31, 31, 32,
32, 33, 33, 33, 33, 34, 34, 34, 35, 35, 35;
30:1, 1, 2, 2, 2, 3, 3, 4, 4, 5, 5, 6, 6, 6, 7,
6, 6, 7, 7, 7, 8, 8, 9, 10, 10, 11, 12, 13, 14,
14, 14, 15, 15, 15, 16, 16, 16, 16, 16, 17,
17, 18, 18, 19, 19, 20, 20, 21, 21, 22, 22,
22, 23, 23, 23, 24, 24, 25, 25, 26, 26,
27, 28, 28, 29, 29, 29, 30, 30, 31, 31;
33:1,
1, 1, 1, 1, 1, 1, 2, 2, 2, 2, 2, 3, 3, 4, 4,
4, 4, 4, 4, 5, 5, 5, 6, 6, 7, 7, 7, 7, 8, 8,
8, 9, 10, 10, 11, 11, 11, 11, 12, 12, 12, 13,
13, 13, 13, 14, 14, 14, 15, 17, 17, 17, 18,
18, 19, 20, 20; 34:1, 1, 2, 2, 2, 2, 3, 3, 3, 4,
5, 6, 7, 7, 7, 8, 8, 9, 9, 9, 10, 10, 10, 11,
11, 11, 12, 13, 13, 14, 14, 16, 16, 16,
17, 18, 18, 18, 19, 20, 21, 21, 22, 22, 23,
23, 23, 24, 24, 25, 25, 25, 26, 26, 27,
27, 28, 28, 28, 29, 29, 30, 30, 31; 35:1, 1, 1,
2, 2, 2, 3, 3, 3, 3, 4, 4, 5, 5, 5, 6, 6, 7, 7,
8, 8, 9, 10, 10, 11, 11, 11, 11, 12, 12,
12, 13, 14, 14, 14, 15, 16, 16, 16, 17,
17, 18, 18, 18, 19, 19, 19, 19, 21, 21,
22, 23, 23, 23, 24, 24, 25, 25, 26, 26,
26, 27, 27, 28, 28, 28, 29, 29, 29; 36:2, 2,
3, 3, 3, 4, 4, 5, 5, 5, 6, 6, 7, 7, 8, 8, 8, 8,
9, 9, 10, 10, 11, 12, 12, 12, 13, 13, 14,
14, 14, 14, 14, 16, 16, 17, 17, 18, 18,
18, 18, 18, 19, 19, 19, 19, 20, 21, 21,
22, 22, 23, 23, 24, 24, 24, 25, 25,
25, 26, 26, 27, 28, 28, 29, 29, 30;
39:1, 1, 2, 2, 3, 3, 3, 4, 4, 4, 5, 5, 5,
5, 6, 6, 6, 6, 7, 7, 8, 9, 10, 11, 11, 11, 12,
12, 12, 13, 13, 14, 14, 15, 15, 15, 15,
16, 17, 18, 18, 19, 20, 20, 20, 21, 21,
22, 22, 23; 40:1, 2, 3, 4, 4, 4, 5, 5, 5,
6, 6, 7, 7, 8, 8, 8, 9, 9, 10, 10, 14, 15, 16,
17, 17, 18, 18, 19, 19, 20, 20, 21, 21;
41:1, 1, 2, 2, 3, 3, 3, 4, 4, 4, 4, 5, 5,
6, 6, 7, 7, 7, 7, 8, 8, 8, 8, 9, 10, 10, 11,
12, 12, 12, 12, 13, 14, 14, 14, 14,
15, 15, 16, 17, 18, 18, 19, 19, 19,
20, 20, 21, 22, 22, 23, 23, 23, 24, 25,
26, 27, 27, 28, 28, 30, 30, 31, 32, 33,
33, 34, 34, 35, 35, 36, 37, 37, 38, 39,
39, 40, 41, 42, 42, 42, 42, 43, 43, 44,
44, 45, 45, 45, 46, 46, 47, 48, 48, 49,
50, 51, 51, 52, 53, 54, 54, 55, 55, 56,
56, 56, 57; 42:2, 2, 2, 3, 5, 6, 6, 6, 6, 7,
7, 7, 8, 9, 9, 11, 12, 13, 13, 14, 16,
16, 17, 18, 20, 20, 21, 22, 22, 23,
24, 24, 24, 24, 24, 25, 25, 26, 26,

27, 28, 28, 28, 28, 29, 29, 30, 31, 32, 33,
33, 33, 34, 34, 35, 35, 35, 36, 36, 36, 37,
37, 38, 38; 43:1, 2, 3, 4, 6, 7, 7, 8, 8, 8,
8, 8, 9, 11, 11, 11, 11, 11, 12, 12, 13, 13,
14, 14, 15, 15, 15, 15, 15, 15, 16, 16, 16,
17, 17, 18, 18, 19, 20, 21, 21, 21, 21,
21, 22, 23, 23, 23, 24, 24, 24, 24, 25,
26, 27, 27, 28, 28, 29, 29, 30; 44:1, 1,
2, 2, 3, 3, 3, 4, 4, 4, 5, 5, 6, 7, 9, 10, 11,
12, 12, 13, 13, 13, 14, 14, 15, 16, 16, 16,
17, 18, 18, 19, 20, 20, 21, 22, 23, 23, 24,
25, 25, 26, 27, 28, 28, 29, 29, 30, 30,
31, 31, 32, 32, 33, 33, 34, 34, 34, 34;
45:1, 1, 2, 2, 3, 3, 3, 4, 4, 5, 6, 7, 7, 7, 8, 8,
9, 9, 10, 11, 11, 13, 13, 14, 14, 15, 16, 16,
17, 18, 19, 19, 20, 21, 23, 24, 24, 25, 26,
27, 27, 28; 46:1, 1, 1, 2, 2, 2, 3, 3, 4, 4, 5,
5, 6, 6, 7, 7, 8, 9, 9, 9, 10, 10, 10, 10, 11,
12, 13, 14, 15, 15, 16, 16, 16, 16, 17,
17, 18, 18, 19, 20, 20, 21, 21, 21, 22,
23, 23, 23, 24, 24, 24, 25, 25, 25, 26, 27,
27, 28, 28; 47:1, 1, 1, 1, 1, 2, 2, 3, 3, 5, 6,
6, 7, 7, 8, 9, 9, 9, 10, 10, 11, 11, 12, 12,
12, 13, 14, 14, 15, 15, 15, 15, 16, 16,
16, 17, 17, 17, 17, 17, 18, 18, 19, 19,
20, 20, 21, 22, 23, 23, 24, 24, 24, 25, 26,
27, 27, 27, 27, 28, 28, 29, 29, 30, 30, 31;
48:1, 1, 1, 2, 2, 2, 3, 3, 4, 4, 5, 5, 6, 7,
7, 7, 8, 9, 9, 10, 10, 11, 11, 12, 13, 13,
14, 14, 15, 15, 15, 16, 16, 16, 17, 17, 18,
19, 19, 19, 20, 20, 21, 22; 49:1, 1, 1, 2, 2, 3,
3, 4, 4, 4, 5, 5, 6, 6, 6, 7, 7, 7, 7, 8, 8, 9,
9, 10, 10, 11, 11, 11, 12, 13, 14, 15, 15,
16, 16, 17, 17, 17, 18, 19, 19, 21, 22;
49:1, 1,
2, 3, 3, 3, 3, 3, 4, 4, 4, 4, 5, 5, 5, 6, 6, 6,
7, 7, 7, 8, 8, 9, 9, 10, 10, 11, 11, 11, 12,
12, 13, 14, 14, 14, 15, 15, 16, 17, 17, 17,
18, 18, 19, 20, 20, 20, 20, 21, 21, 21,
21, 22, 22, 23, 23, 23, 23, 24, 24, 24, 25,
26, 26, 27, 27, 27, 27, 27, 28, 28, 29,
29, 29, 29, 29, 30, 30, 30, 31,
31, 31; 48:1, 1, 1, 2, 2, 2, 3, 3, 4, 4,
4, 5, 5, 6, 6, 7, 7, 7, 8, 8, 9, 9, 9, 10, 11,
11, 11, 12, 13, 13, 13, 14, 14, 14,
15, 15, 15, 15, 16, 16, 16, 17, 17, 18, 18,
19, 19, 19, 20, 20, 20, 21, 22; 49:1, 1,
1, 2, 3, 13, 15, 20, 23, 23, 23, 24, 25, 25,
26, 27, 28, 28, 29, 29, 31, 31, 31, 32, 33,
33, 33; 50:1, 1, 2, 2, 3, 3, 4, 4, 5, 5, 6,
6, 7, 7, 7, 8, 8, 9, 10, 10, 11, 11, 12,
13, 13, 14, 14, 14, 15, 15, 16, 17,
17, 17, 18, 18, 18, 19, 21, 21, 21, 22, 22,
22, 22, 23, 24, 24, 24, 24, 25, 25, 26, 26,
26;

Ex 1:1, 2, 3, 4, 5, 6, 6, 7, 7, 7, 7, 9,
9, 10, 10, 10, 11, 11, 12, 12, 13, 14, 14,
15, 15, 16, 16, 17, 18, 18, 18, 19, 19,
20, 20, 21, 22, 22; 2:1, 1, 2, 2, 3, 3, 3,
3, 4, 5, 5, 6, 6, 6, 7, 8, 8, 9, 9, 10, 11, 12,
12, 12, 13, 13, 14, 14, 14, 14, 15, 16,
16, 16, 17, 17, 17, 17, 17, 18, 19, 19, 19,
20, 20, 21, 22, 22, 22, 22, 22; 4:1, 1, 2,
3, 3, 4, 4, 4, 5, 5, 6, 6, 6, 7, 7, 7, 7, 7,
8, 9, 10, 11, 11, 12, 12, 12, 13, 13, 14,
14, 15, 15, 16, 16, 16, 17, 17, 18, 18, 19,
20, 20, 20, 20, 21, 22, 22, 22, 22, 23,
23, 24, 24, 24, 25, 25, 25, 26, 27, 27,
27, 28, 29, 29, 30, 30, 31, 31, 31; 5:1, 1, 2, 3,
4, 5, 5, 6, 7, 8, 8, 9, 10, 10, 11, 12, 13, 14, 14,
15, 16, 16, 17, 18, 19, 20, 20, 21, 21,
22; 6:1, 2, 3, 4, 5, 5, 6, 6, 6, 7,
7, 7, 8, 8, 8, 9, 10, 12, 13, 13, 14, 14, 14,
14, 14, 15, 15, 15, 15, 15, 16, 16, 16,
17, 18, 18, 18, 18, 19, 19, 20, 20, 20, 22,
22, 23, 23, 23, 24, 24, 24, 25, 25, 26,
27, 28, 30, 30; 7:1, 2, 3, 3, 3, 4, 4, 5,
6, 6, 7, 7, 7, 8, 9, 10, 10, 10, 10, 10, 11,
11, 12, 12, 13, 14, 15, 15, 15, 16, 16, 17,
17, 18, 18, 19, 19, 19, 19, 20, 20, 20, 21, 21,
21, 22, 22, 22, 23; 8:1, 1, 2, 3, 3, 3, 3, 4,
5, 5, 5, 6, 7, 8, 8, 8, 9, 10, 10, 11, 11, 11,
12, 12, 12, 13, 13, 14, 15, 16, 16, 16, 16,
17, 17, 17, 18, 18, 19, 19, 20, 21, 21, 21,
21, 22, 22, 23, 23, 24, 24, 24, 25, 25, 25,
26, 27, 28, 29, 29, 29, 30, 30, 31, 31, 31;
9:1, 2, 3, 4, 4, 4, 5, 6, 6, 7, 7, 7, 7, 7, 8,
8, 8, 9, 9, 10, 10, 11, 11, 11, 11, 11,

12, 13, 13, 13, 14, 14, 15, 15, 16, 16, 17, 17, 18, 19, 19, 20, 20, 20, 21, 21, 21; 14:1, 2, 2, 4, 4, 4, 4, 5, 5, 5, 5, 6, 6, 7, 7, 7, 8, 8, 8, 9, 9, 9, 9, 10, 10, 10, 10, 11, 13, 13, 14, 15, 16, 16, 16, 17, 17, 17, 17, 17, 18, 18, 19, 19, 19, 19, 20, 20, 20, 20, 21, 21, 21, 21, 22, 22, 22, 23, 23, 23, 24, 24, 25, 26, 26, 27, 27, 27, 27, 28, 28, 28, 29, 29, 30, 31, 31, 31, 31; 15:1, 1, 1, 2, 2, 2, 2, 4, 7, 8, 8, 14, 16, 17, 18, 19, 19, 19, 20, 20, 20, 21, 21, 22, 22, 23, 24, 25, 25, 25, 25, 26, 26, 26, 26, 26, 27, 27, 27, 27; 16:1, 1, 1, 2, 2, 3, 3, 4, 4, 5, 5, 6, 6, 7, 7, 8, 8, 8, 9, 10, 10, 11, 12, 12, 13, 13, 14, 15, 15, 17, 17, 18, 18, 19, 20, 20, 20, 21, 21, 22, 22, 22, 23, 23, 23, 24, 24, 25, 27, 27, 28, 28, 31, 31, 32, 33, 33, 33, 35; 17:1, 1, 1, 2, 2, 3, 3, 3, 3, 4, 4, 5, 5, 5, 5, 6, 6, 6, 6, 7, 7, 7, 7, 8, 9, 9, 10, 10, 11, 12, 12, 12, 12, 12, 13, 13, 14, 14, 15, 15; 18:1, 1, 3, 4, 4, 5, 5, 6, 6, 6, 7, 7, 7, 7, 7, 8, 8, 8, 9, 9, 10, 10, 12, 12, 12, 12, 13, 13, 14, 14, 15, 16, 16, 16, 16, 16, 17, 18, 19, 20, 20, 20, 21, 21, 21, 22, 22, 22, 23, 23, 24, 25, 25, 25, 26, 27, 27; 19:2, 2, 3, 3, 3, 4, 4, 5, 6, 6, 7, 7, 7, 8, 8, 8, 9, 9, 10, 10, 10, 10, 10, 11, 12, 14, 14, 14, 15, 16, 16, 16, 16, 17, 17, 18, 18, 18, 19, 19, 19, 19, 20, 20, 21, 21, 22, 23, 23, 24, 24, 24, 24, 25; 20:1, 5, 6, 6, 9, 11, 11, 11, 11, 12, 18, 18, 18, 18, 18, 19, 19, 20, 20, 21, 21, 22, 22, 24, 24, 24, 24, 25; 21:2, 4, 4, 4, 5, 5, 6, 6, 7, 9, 10, 11, 13, 13, 16, 16, 17, 17, 18, 18, 18, 19, 20, 20, 22, 22, 22, 23, 23, 26, 27, 28, 29, 29, 29, 32, 33, 33, 33, 34, 34, 34, 35, 35, 35, 36, 36; 22:1, 1, 2, 5, 5, 5, 6, 6, 7, 9, 10, 11, 12, 13, 14, 14, 16, 16, 23, 24, 24, 24, 27, 29, 30, 31; 23:5, 7, 7, 8, 8, 10, 10, 11, 11, 11, 12, 12, 12, 12, 13, 13, 16, 16, 20, 21, 22, 22, 23, 23, 23, 23, 24, 25, 25, 25, 27, 28, 29, 30, 30, 31, 31, 31; 24:1, 1, 1, 1, 1, 2, 3, 3, 3, 3, 4, 4, 4, 4, 5, 5, 6, 6, 7, 7, 7, 8, 8, 9, 9, 10, 10, 10, 11, 11, 11, 12, 12, 12, 12, 12, 13, 13, 14, 14, 14, 15, 15, 16, 16, 16, 17, 18, 18, 18, 18, 25:1, 3, 3, 3, 4, 4, 4, 4, 5, 5, 5, 7, 8, 9, 9, 10, 10, 10, 10, 10, 11, 11, 11, 11, 12, 12, 12, 13, 13, 14, 16, 16, 17, 17, 18, 18, 18, 18 25:1, 3, 3, 3, 4, 4, 4, 5, 5, 6, 7, 8, 9, 9, 10, 10, 10, 11, 11, 12, 12, 13, 14, 16, 17, 17, 17, 17, 18, 19, 20, 20, 21, 21, 22, 22, 22, 23, 23, 24, 24, 24, 25, 25, 26, 26, 28, 28, 29, 29, 29, 30, 31, 31, 32, 32, 33, 33, 33, 34, 34, 35, 35, 35, 36, 37, 37, 38, 38, 38, 40; 26:1, 1, 1, 2, 2, 3, 3, 4, 4, 5, 6, 6, 7, 7, 8, 9, 9, 10, 10, 11, 11, 12, 13, 13, 14, 14, 15, 16, 16, 18, 19, 19, 20, 21, 21, 22, 23, 24, 24, 25, 25, 25, 26, 26, 26, 27, 27, 28, 28, 29, 29, 29, 30, 31, 31, 32, 33, 33, 33, 34, 34, 35, 35, 35, 36, 36, 36, 37, 37, 37; 27:1, 1, 1, 2, 2, 3, 3, 3, 3, 4, 4, 5, 6, 6, 7, 7, 9, 10, 10, 10, 11, 11, 11, 12, 12, 13, 14, 15, 15, 16, 16, 16, 16, 16, 17, 17; 18, 18, 18, 19, 19, 19, 20, 21; 28:1, 1, 1, 1, 2, 2, 3, 4, 4, 4, 4, 4, 4, 5, 5, 5, 5, 6, 6, 6, 7, 8, 8, 8, 8, 8, 9, 9, 10, 12, 12, 13, 14, 14, 15, 15, 15, 15, 16, 16, 17, 17, 18, 18, 19, 19, 20, 20, 22, 23, 23, 24, 25, 25, 26, 26, 27, 27, 28, 28, 29, 30, 30, 30, 31, 32, 33, 33, 33, 34, 34, 35, 35, 35, 36, 36, 36, 36, 37, 37, 37, 38, 38, 39, 39, 39, 40, 40, 40, 40, 41, 41, 41, 41, 41, 41, 42, 42, 43, 43, 43, 43; 29:1, 1, 2, 2, 3, 3, 3, 4, 4, 4, 5, 5, 5, 5, 5, 6, 6, 7, 7, 8, 8, 9, 9, 9, 9, 9, 10, 10, 10, 11, 12, 12, 12, 13, 13, 13, 13, 14, 14, 15, 15, 16, 16, 16, 17, 17, 17, 17, 18, 19, 19, 19, 20, 20, 20, 20, 20, 21, 21, 21, 21, 21, 21, 21, 21, 21, 22, 22, 22, 22, 22, 23, 23, 23, 24, 24, 24, 24, 25, 25, 25, 26, 26, 26, 27, 27, 27, 27, 28, 28, 28, 29, 30, 30, 31, 32, 32, 32, 33, 34, 34, 34, 35, 35, 35, 36, 36, 36, 37, 37, 37, 40, 41, 41, 41, 41, 41, 41, 42, 42, 43, 43, 43, 43; 30:1, 2, 2, 3, 3, 3, 3, 4, 4, 5, 5, 6, 7, 8, 10, 11, 14, 15, 16, 16, 17, 18, 18, 18, 18, 19, 19, 21, 21, 21, 23, 23, 23, 23, 24, 24, 25, 26, 26, 27, 27, 27, 27, 28, 28, 28, 29, 30, 30, 31, 32, 34, 34, 34, 35, 35, 36, 36, 37; 31:1, 3, 3, 3, 3, 4, 4, 5, 5, 6, 6, 7, 7, 8, 8, 8, 8, 9, 9, 10, 10, 10, 11, 11, 12, 13, 17, 17, 17, 18; 32:1, 1, 2, 2, 2, 3, 3, 4, 4, 4, 5, 5, 5, 6, 6, 6, 6, 6, 6, 7, 8, 8, 9, 9, 10, 10, 11, 11, 11, 12, 12, 12, 13, 13, 13, 14, 14, 14, 15, 15, 15, 15, 16, 16, 17, 18, 19, 19, 19, 19, 19, 20, 20, 20, 20, 21, 22, 22, 24, 24, 24, 25, 26, 26, 27, 27, 27; 33:1, 1, 1, 1, 2, 2, 2, 2, 3, 4, 4, 5, 6, 7, 7, 7, 7, 8, 8, 8, 9, 9, 9, 10, 10, 11, 11, 12, 12, 13, 14, 14, 15, 16, 16, 17, 17, 18, 19, 19, 19, 20, 20, 21, 21, 22, 22, 23, 23; 34:1, 1, 2, 2, 2, 3, 4, 4, 4, 4, 5, 5, 5, 6, 6, 6, 6, 6, 7, 7, 7, 7, 8, 8, 9, 9, 9, 10, 10, 11, 11, 11, 11, 13, 15, 15, 15, 15, 15, 16, 16, 17, 17, 18, 18, 19, 20, 20, 21, 21, 22, 22, 23; 35:1, 1, 4, 4, 5, 5, 6, 6, 6, 6, 6, 6, 7, 7, 8, 8, 8, 9, 9, 9, 10, 10, 10, 11, 11, 11, 12, 12, 13, 13, 14, 14, 15, 15, 15, 15, 16, 16, 17, 17, 18, 18, 19, 20, 20, 21, 21, 21, 21, 21, 22, 22, 22, 22, 23, 23, 23, 23, 23, 24, 24, 25, 25, 25, 25, 26, 27, 27, 28, 28, 28, 29, 30, 30, 31, 31, 32, 32, 33, 33, 34, 34, 35,

35, 35, 35, 35, 35; 36:1, 1, 1, 2, 2, 2, 3, 3, 4, 5, 6, 6, 7, 8, 8, 8, 8, 9, 9, 10, 10, 11, 12, 13, 13, 14, 15, 16, 16, 17, 17, 17, 18, 19, 19, 20, 20, 21, 23, 24, 24, 24, 26, 26, 27, 28, 29, 29, 30, 30, 31, 32, 32, 33, 34, 34, 34, 35, 35, 35, 35, 36, 36, 36, 37, 37, 37, 37, 38, 38, 38; 37:1, 1, 1, 1, 1, 1, 2, 2, 2, 3, 3, 4, 4, 5, 5, 6, 6, 6, 6, 7, 8, 9, 9, 10, 10, 10, 11, 11, 12, 13, 13, 15, 15, 16, 16, 16, 16, 17, 17, 17, 18, 18, 19, 19, 19, 20, 20, 20, 21, 21, 21, 21, 22, 23, 23, 23, 24, 24, 25, 25, 25, 25, 26, 26, 26, 26, 27, 28, 28, 29; 38:1, 1, 1, 2, 2, 3, 3, 4, 4, 5, 5, 6, 6, 7, 7, 8, 8, 9, 10, 10, 11, 11, 11, 12, 12, 12, 13, 14, 15, 15, 15, 17, 17, 17, 17, 17, 18, 18, 18, 18, 19, 19, 19, 19, 20, 20, 20, 22, 23, 23, 24, 24, 24, 24, 24, 25, 25, 26, 26, 27, 27, 28, 28, 28, 29, 29, 29, 30, 30, 30, 31, 31, 31, 31; 39:1, 1, 1, 1, 2, 2, 2, 2, 3, 3, 3, 3, 5, 5, 5, 5, 6, 7, 8, 8, 8, 8, 9, 9, 10, 10, 11, 11, 12, 12, 13, 14, 16, 16, 16, 16, 17, 17, 18, 18, 19, 20, 20, 21, 21, 22, 23, 24, 24, 24, 25, 25, 26, 26, 27, 27, 28, 28, 29, 29, 29, 29, 30, 30, 31, 31, 31, 31; 40:1, 3, 3, 4, 4, 4, 4, 5, 5, 6, 7, 7, 7, 8, 9, 11, 12, 12, 12, 13, 13, 13, 14, 14, 15, 17, 18, 18, 18, 18, 19, 19, 20, 20, 21, 21, 21, 22, 23, 24, 25, 26, 26, 27, 27, 28, 29, 29, 30, 30, 30, 31, 31, 31, 32, 33, 33, 34, 35, 35, 36, 38;

Lev 1:1, 1, 2, 2, 4, 4, 5, 5, 6, 6, 7, 7, 8, 8, 9, 9, 10, 11, 11, 12, 12, 13, 13, 13, 14, 15, 15, 15, 16, 16, 16, 17, 17; 2:1, 1, 1, 2, 2, 2, 2, 3, 3, 4, 5, 6, 7, 8, 9, 9, 10, 3:1, 2, 2, 2, 3, 3, 4, 4, 4, 4, 5, 6, 8, 8, 8, 9, 9, 9, 10, 11; 4:1, 2, 4, 4, 4, 5, 5, 6, 6, 7, 7, 8, 9, 9, 9, 10, 11, 11, 11, 11, 11, 12, 13, 13, 13, 13, 14, 15, 15, 16, 17, 17, 18, 18, 19, 19, 20, 20, 20, 21, 21, 22, 24, 24, 25, 25, 25, 26, 26, 27, 27, 29, 29, 30, 30, 30, 31, 31, 32, 33, 35, 35, 35; 5:1, 1, 2, 2, 3, 4, 5, 6, 6, 7, 7, 8, 8, 9, 9, 10, 10, 10, 12, 12, 13, 13, 13, 14, 15, 16, 16, 16, 17, 17, 18, 18; 6:1, 2, 2, 3, 3, 4, 5, 5, 6, 7, 7, 8, 9, 9, 10, 10, 11, 11, 12, 12, 13, 14, 15, 15, 15, 16, 16, 16, 17, 17, 18, 19, 20, 20, 21, 22, 24, 24, 28, 31, 31, 32, 33, 34, 35, 37, 37; 8:1, 2, 2, 2, 2, 2, 3, 4, 4, 5, 6, 6, 6, 7, 7, 7, 7, 7, 8, 8, 9, 10, 10, 10, 10, 11, 11, 11, 11, 12, 13, 13, 13, 14, 14, 14, 14, 15, 15, 15, 16, 16, 16, 17, 18, 18, 18; 6:1, 2, 2, 3, 3, 4, 4, 5, 5, 6, 7, 7, 8, 9, 9, 10, 10, 11, 11, 12, 12, 14, 14, 15, 15, 15, 16, 16, 16, 17, 17, 18, 19, 20, 20, 21, 21, 22, 24, 24, 28, 31, 31, 34, 35, 37, 37, 8:1, 8, 2, 2, 2, 2, 3, 4, 4, 5, 6, 6, 6, 7, 7, 7, 7, 8, 8, 9, 10, 10, 10, 11, 11, 11, 12, 13, 13, 14, 14, 14, 15, 15, 15, 16, 16, 16, 17, 18, 18, 18; 9:1, 1, 1, 2, 2, 3, 3, 4, 4, 5, 8, 9, 9, 10, 10, 11, 12, 12, 14, 14, 14, 15, 16, 18, 18, 19, 19, 20, 21, 22, 23, 24; 10:1, 1, 1, 1, 3, 4, 5, 6, 6, 6, 7, 8, 8, 9, 10, 10, 11, 12, 12, 12, 13, 13, 14, 14, 14, 14, 15, 15, 16, 16, 16, 17, 18, 19, 19, 20; 11:1, 1, 3, 3, 5, 6, 7, 8, 9, 9, 10, 12, 13, 14, 14, 16, 17, 18, 19, 20, 21, 24, 25, 26, 27, 28, 28, 28, 30, 31, 32, 33, 34, 34, 35, 35, 36, 9:1, 1, 1, 2, 2, 2, 3, 3, 4, 4, 5, 5, 6, 6, 6, 7, 7, 7, 7, 8, 8, 9, 9, 9, 10, 10, 11, 11, 11, 12, 13, 13, 14, 14, 14, 15, 15, 16, 16, 17, 18, 19, 20; 13:1, 3, 4, 16, 17, 17, 17, 18, 18, 19, 19, 20, 20, 20, 21, 22, 22, 22, 23, 23, 23, 23, 25, 26, 26, 26, 26, 26, 27, 27, 27, 27, 28, 28, 28, 29, 29, 29,

17, 17, 17, 17, 18, 18, 18, 18, 18, 19, 19, 19, 20, 20, 20, 20, 21, 21, 21, 21, 22, 22, 23, 23, 23, 24, 24, 24, 24, 24, 24, 24, 25, 26, 26, 26, 27, 27, 27, 27, 27, 27, 28, 28, 28, 29, 29, 31, 32, 32, 32, 32, 33, 33, 33, 33, 33, 34, 34; 17:1, 2, 2, 2, 2, 4, 4, 5, 6, 6, 7, 8, 9, 10, 10, 11, 13, 13, 13, 15, 15, 15; 18:1, 2, 3, 4, 5, 17, 21, 25, 25, 26, 26, 26, 27, 30; 19:1, 2, 3, 3, 5, 6, 6, 7, 8, 9, 10, 16, 16, 17, 19, 20, 20, 21, 22, 23, 25, 29, 30, 32, 32, 33, 34, 36, 37; 20:1, 3, 3, 4, 4, 5, 5, 5, 6, 6, 7, 8, 8, 9, 10, 10, 11, 11, 12, 12, 13, 14, 14, 14, 15, 15, 16, 16, 16, 17, 17, 17, 17, 18, 18, 19, 20, 21; 21:1, 1, 2, 2, 2, 2, 3, 6, 9, 10, 10, 13, 16, 22, 24, 24, 24; 22:1, 2, 2, 4, 5, 6, 7, 9, 11, 13, 13, 14, 14, 15, 17, 18, 18, 21, 25, 26, 27, 27, 28, 28, 29, 31; 23:1, 2, 6, 9, 10, 10, 11, 11, 12, 13, 14, 15, 16, 16, 18, 18, 18, 19, 20, 21, 22, 23, 26, 27, 28, 28, 29, 31; 23:1, 2, 6, 9, 10, 10, 11, 11, 12, 13, 14, 15, 16, 16, 18, 18, 18, 19, 20, 21, 22, 23, 24:1, 5, 5, 6, 7, 9, 9, 9, 10, 10, 11, 11, 11, 12, 12, 13, 14, 14, 15, 16, 16, 17, 18, 19, 21, 21, 23; 25:1, 2, 3, 3, 6, 6, 6, 6, 7, 7, 8, 8, 10, 10, 10, 14, 15, 16, 18, 18, 19, 19, 19, 20, 21, 22, 23, 24, 24, 28, 29, 30, 31, 32, 33, 33, 35, 35, 38, 39, 39, 40, 40, 41, 41, 42, 44, 44, 45, 45, 46, 46, 47, 47, 47, 47, 48, 48, 52, 52, 53, 53, 54, 54; 26:2, 3, 3, 4, 4, 5, 5, 5, 6, 6, 6, 6, 7, 8, 9, 9, 10, 10, 11, 11, 12, 12, 12, 13, 13, 14, 15, 16, 16, 16, 17, 17, 17, 18, 19, 19, 19, 20, 21, 21, 22, 22, 22, 23, 24, 25, 25, 26, 26, 26, 27, 28, 29, 29, 30, 30, 30, 31, 31, 31, 32, 32, 33, 33, 33, 34, 34, 36, 36, 36, 37, 37, 38, 38, 39, 39, 40, 41, 41, 41, 42, 42, 42, 43, 43, 43, 44, 44, 46, 46, 46; 27:1, 2, 3, 4, 5, 5, 6, 7, 7, 7, 8, 9, 10, 10, 10, 12, 14, 15, 15, 16, 18, 18, 19, 19, 20, 21, 22, 23, 23, 25:1, 2, 3, 3, 6, 6, 6, 6, 7, 7, 8, 8, 9, 10, 10, 10, 14, 15, 16, 18, 18, 19, 19, 19, 20, 21, 21, 22, 22, 23, 23, 24, 24, 25, 25, 26, 26, 26, 27, 28, 29, 30, 30, 30, 31, 31, 32, 32, 33, 33, 33, 34, 34, 36, 36, 36, 37, 37, 38, 38, 39, 39, 40, 41, 41, 41, 42, 42, 42, 43, 43, 43, 44, 44, 44, 45, 45, 46, 46, 47, 47, 47, 47, 48, 48, 49, 50, 50, 50, 51, 51, 51; 4:1, 1, 3, 5, 5, 5, 5, 5, 6, 6, 6, 7, 7, 7, 7, 7, 8, 8, 9, 9, 9, 9, 10, 10, 10, 10, 14, 14, 15, 15, 16, 18, 18, 19, 19, 19, 19, 20, 21, 22, 23, 23; 25:1, 2, 3, 3, 6, 6, 6, 6, 7, 7, 8, 8, 9, 10, 10, 10, 14, 15, 16, 18, 18, 19, 19, 19, 20, 21, 21, 22, 22, 23, 24:1, 2, 2, 3, 3, 3, 5, 6, 7, 7, 9, 10, 11, 11, 14, 15, 15, 16, 17, 17, 17, 18, 19, 19, 20, 20, 21, 22, 23, 23, 25:1, 2, 3, 3, 3, 4, 4, 5, 6, 7, 8, 9, 9, 10, 11, 11, 12, 13, 14, 15, 15, 16, 16, 17, 18, 18, 18, 19, 20, 20, 21, 21, 22, 22, 23, 24, 24, 25, 26, 26, 27, 27, 27, 28, 28, 29, 29, 30, 30, 31, 31, 32, 32, 33, 33, 33;

Nu 1:1, 3, 3, 4, 5, 17, 17, 18, 18, 18, 20, 20, 21, 21, 22, 22, 23, 23, 24, 25, 25, 26, 26, 27, 27, 28, 29, 29, 30, 31, 31, 32, 33, 34, 35, 35, 36, 37, 37, 38, 39, 39, 40, 41, 41, 42, 43, 43, 44, 44, 45, 45, 46, 46, 46, 50, 50, 50, 50, 50, 51, 51, 51, 52, 52, 53, 54; 2:1, 1, 3, 3, 4, 4, 4, 4, 5, 5, 6, 7, 8, 8, 8, 9, 9, 9, 9, 10, 11, 11, 11, 12, 12, 13, 13, 13, 14, 15, 15, 15, 16, 16, 16, 16, 18, 19, 19, 20, 20, 21, 21, 21, 22, 22, 23, 23, 23, 23, 24, 24, 24, 25, 26, 26, 26, 27, 28, 28, 29, 30, 30, 30, 31, 31, 31, 32, 32, 32, 34, 34; 3:1, 2, 2, 2, 4, 4, 4, 4, 4, 6, 7, 8, 8, 9, 9, 10, 10, 10, 10, 11, 12, 13, 14, 15, 16, 17, 17, 18, 18, 19, 19, 19, 20, 20, 21, 22, 22, 24, 25, 25, 25, 26, 26, 26, 27, 27, 27, 28, 30, 31, 31, 31, 32, 32, 33, 33, 34, 34, 35, 35, 36, 36, 36, 36, 36, 37, 37, 37, 37, 38, 38, 38, 39, 39, 39, 40, 40, 41, 41, 42, 43, 43, 43, 43, 43, 44, 44, 45, 45, 46, 46, 46, 48, 48, 49, 49, 50, 50, 51, 51, 51; 4:1, 1, 3, 5, 5, 5, 5, 6, 6, 7, 7, 7, 7, 7, 8, 8, 9, 9, 9, 10, 10, 11, 11, 11, 11, 12, 13, 13, 14, 14, 14, 14, 15, 15, 16, 16, 16, 17, 19, 19, 20, 20, 21, 21, 22, 23, 23, 24, 24, 24, 25, 25, 25, 26, 26, 26, 27, 27, 27, 28, 30, 31, 31, 31, 32, 32, 32, 34, 34; 5:1, 2, 2, 3, 4, 5, 6, 7, 7, 9, 10, 11, 12, 12, 13, 13, 13, 13, 14, 14, 14, 15, 16, 16, 17, 17, 18, 18, 18, 19, 19, 19, 20, 20, 21, 21, 22, 23, 23, 24, 24, 25, 25, 26, 26, 27, 27, 27, 28, 28, 29, 30, 30, 31; 6:1, 2, 3, 3, 5, 9, 9, 10, 11, 11, 11, 11, 12, 12, 13, 14, 14, 14, 14, 15, 15, 15, 16, 16, 16, 16, 17, 17, 18, 18, 18, 19, 19, 20, 20, 20, 21, 21, 22, 23, 24, 25, 26, 27; 7:1, 1, 1, 1, 1, 2, 3, 3, 3, 3, 4, 5, 6, 6, 6, 7, 8, 8, 8, 10, 10, 11, 11, 12, 13, 13, 14, 14, 19, 23, 25, 29, 31, 35, 37, 41, 43, 47, 49, 53, 55, 59, 61, 65, 67, 71, 73, 77, 79, 83, 85, 85, 86, 87, 88, 88, 89, 89; 8:1, 2, 3, 4, 5, 6, 7, 7, 7, 7, 7, 8, 9, 9, 10, 10, 11, 12, 12, 13, 13, 13, 14, 15, 15, 15, 17, 18, 19, 19, 20, 20, 20, 21, 21, 21, 22, 24, 25, 26; 9:1, 3, 4, 5, 6, 6, 6, 7, 8, 8, 9, 11, 11, 13, 13, 14, 14, 14, 15, 16, 16, 17, 18, 19, 19, 20, 20, 21, 22, 23; 10:1, 2, 3, 4, 8, 8, 9, 9, 10, 10, 11, 12, 13, 14, 15, 16, 17, 17, 18, 18, 19, 20, 21, 21, 22, 22, 23, 24, 25, 25, 26, 27, 28, 29, 29, 30, 31, 31, 32, 32, 33, 33, 34, 35, 35, 35, 36; 11:1, 1, 1, 1, 2, 3, 4, 4, 5, 5, 7, 7, 8, 8, 8, 9, 10, 11, 15, 15, 16, 16, 17, 17, 18, 18, 20, 20, 20, 21, 21, 22, 23, 24, 24, 25, 25, 25, 25, 26, 26, 26, 27, 27, 27, 28, 28, 29, 29, 30, 30, 31, 31, 31, 32, 32, 32, 33, 33, 34, 34, 35; 12:1, 1, 2, 2, 4, 4, 4, 4, 5, 5, 6, 8, 9, 10, 10, 10, 10, 11, 13, 14, 13, 14, 15, 15, 16:1, 3, 4, 16, 17, 17, 17, 18, 19, 19, 20, 20, 20, 21, 21, 22, 22, 23, 23, 23, 25, 26, 26, 26, 26, 27, 27, 27, 28, 28, 28, 29, 29,

29, 29, 30, 30, 30, 32, 32, 33, 33, 33; 14:1, 1, 1, 2, 2, 2, 3, 3, 4, 6, 7, 8, 9, 10, 11, 11, 12, 12, 12, 13, 14, 14, 14, 14, 17, 18, 18, 18, 18, 19, 20, 22, 22, 22, 24, 24, 24, 24, 25, 25, 26, 26, 27, 27, 27, 28, 28, 29, 30, 31, 32, 32, 32, 33, 33, 33, 33, 33, 34, 34:17:1, 2, 2, 2, 4, 4, 5, 6, 7, 8, 9, 10, 10, 11, 13, 13, 13, 15, 15, 15; 18:1, 2, 3, 4, 5, 17, 21, 25, 25, 26, 26, 26, 27, 30; 19:1, 2, 3, 5, 6, 6, 7, 8, 9, 10, 16, 16, 17, 19, 20, 20, 21, 22, 23, 25, 29, 30, 32, 32, 33, 34, 35, 36, 36, 36, 37, 38, 38, 39, 39, 39, 40, 40; 16:1, 1, 1, 2, 2, 3, 3, 3, 3, 4, 5, 5, 5, 5, 6, 7, 7, 8, 9, 10, 10, 11, 11, 12, 12, 13, 14, 14, 14, 14, 15, 16, 16, 16, 16, 17, 17, 17, 18, 18, 18, 18, 18, 19, 19, 20, 20, 20, 22, 22, 22, 22, 22, 23, 24, 24, 24, 24, 24, 25, 25, 25, 25, 25, 25, 26, 26; 21:1, 1, 2, 2, 2, 2, 3, 6, 9, 10, 10, 13, 16, 22, 24, 24, 24; 22:1, 2, 2, 4, 5, 6, 7, 9, 11, 13, 13, 14, 14, 15, 17, 18, 18, 21, 25, 26, 27, 27, 28, 28, 29, 31; 23:1, 2, 6, 9, 10, 10, 11, 11, 12, 13, 14, 15, 16, 16, 18, 18, 18, 19, 20, 21, 22, 23, 24, 24, 25, 25, 26; 24:1, 2, 2, 2, 3, 3, 3, 5, 6, 7, 7, 9, 10, 11, 11, 14, 15, 15, 16, 17, 17, 17, 18, 19, 19, 20, 20, 21, 22, 23, 23; 25:1, 2, 3, 3, 3, 4, 4, 5, 6, 7, 8, 9, 9, 10, 11, 11, 12, 13, 13, 14, 15, 16, 17, 18, 18, 18; 26:1, 1, 2, 3, 4, 7, 7, 8, 8, 9, 10, 10, 11, 12, 13, 14, 15, 16, 16, 17, 18, 19, 19, 20, 21, 22, 22, 22, 22, 23, 24, 25, 26, 26, 27, 28, 29, 30, 30, 31, 32, 32, 33, 33, 34, 35, 36, 37, 38, 38, 39, 39, 40, 40, 41, 41, 42, 42, 42, 43, 43, 44, 44, 44, 45, 45, 46, 46, 47, 47, 48, 48, 49, 50, 50, 51, 51, 52, 52, 53, 53, 54, 54, 54, 54, 55; 27:1, 1, 1, 1, 1, 2, 2, 3, 3, 3, 4, 4, 4, 4, 5, 5, 6, 7, 8, 9, 10, 11, 12, 13, 13, 13, 14, 15, 16, 16, 18, 18, 19, 19, 20, 21, 22, 23, 23, 23; 28:1, 2, 2, 3, 4, 5, 7, 8, 9, 9, 10, 11, 11, 12, 12, 13, 14, 14, 14, 15, 16, 17, 19, 20, 22, 24, 24, 25, 26, 26, 27, 28, 29, 31; 29:1, 2, 2, 3, 3, 4, 5, 6, 6, 6, 6, 7, 8, 9, 9, 11, 11, 11, 12, 13, 13, 14, 15, 16, 16, 17, 18, 18, 18, 18, 19, 19, 20, 21, 22, 22, 23, 24, 24, 25, 25, 26, 27, 27, 28, 28, 29, 30, 31, 32, 32, 33, 33, 34, 34, 37, 37, 38, 38, 38, 39, 39, 39; 30:1, 3, 4, 4, 4, 5, 6, 7, 7, 8, 8, 9, 9, 10, 11, 11, 11, 11, 12, 13; 16, 16:31:1, 3, 3, 5, 6, 6, 7, 7, 8, 8, 8, 9, 9, 9, 9, 10, 10, 11, 11, 11, 12, 12, 12, 12, 13, 13, 13, 14, 14, 15, 16, 17, 19, 19, 19, 20, 20, 20, 21, 22, 22, 23, 23, 24, 24, 25, 26, 26, 27, 27, 28, 28, 28, 29, 30, 30, 31, 32, 32, 33, 33, 34, 34, 35, 35, 36, 36, 37, 37, 38, 38, 38, 39, 39, 39, 40, 40, 40, 41, 41, 42, 42, 43, 43, 44, 44, 44, 45, 45, 46, 46, 47, 47, 48, 48, 49, 50, 50, 51, 52, 52, 52, 53, 53, 54, 54, 54, 54, 55, 55; 34:1, 2, 3, 4, 4, 4, 5, 5, 6, 7, 9, 10, 11, 11, 12, 12, 13, 13, 14, 14, 15, 16, 17, 18, 19, 20, 22, 24, 25, 26, 27, 28; 35:1, 2, 3, 3, 3,

Idx

12, 13, 14, 14, 15, 15, 15, 15, 15; 12:1, 1, 2, 2, 2, 2, 2, 3, 3, 4, 5, 5, 5, 6, 6, 6, 7, 8, 8, 9, 9, 9, 9, 10, 10, 10, 10, 11, 11, 11, 11, 11, 11, 12, 12, 13, 13, 14, 14, 14, 14, 16, 17, 17, 17, 18, 18, 18, 18, 19, 20, 21, 23, 24, 25; 13:1, 2, 2, 3, 3, 3, 4, 4, 4, 5, 5, 5, 5, 6, 6, 6, 6, 6, 7, 7, 7, 8, 8, 9, 9, 9, 10, 10, 11, 11, 11, 11, 12, 12, 12, 13, 14, 15, 15, 16, 16, 16, 17, 18, 18, 20, 20, 20, 21, 21, 21, 21, 22, 22, 23, 23; 14:1, 2, 2, 3, 3, 4, 4, 4, 4, 5, 6, 6, 7, 8, 9, 10, 11, 12, 12, 12, 12, 12, 12, 13, 13, 13, 13, 13, 14, 14, 14, 15, 15, 15, 15, 16, 16, 16, 17, 17, 17, 18, 19, 19, 20, 20, 20, 20, 20, 21, 23, 24, 25, 26, 27, 27, 27, 28, 28, 31, 31, 32, 32, 32, 32, 32, 32, 33, 34, 34, 34, 34, 34, 34, 34, 35, 36, 36, 36, 36, 37, 38, 38, 38, 40, 40, 40, 40, 41, 41, 42, 42, 42, 43, 43, 43, 44, 44, 45, 46, 47, 47, 47, 47, 47, 47, 48, 48, 48, 49, 49, 49, 49, 50, 50, 51, 51, 52, 52; 15:3, 3, 3, 3, 3, 3, 4, 4, 4, 5, 5, 6, 7, 8, 8, 9, 9, 9, 9, 9, 11, 11, 11, 12, 12, 12, 12, 12, 12, 13, 13, 14, 14, 15, 15, 15, 16, 16, 16, 17, 17, 18, 18, 19, 20, 20, 20, 20, 20, 21, 22, 22, 22, 23, 23, 24, 24, 24, 25, 25, 26, 26, 27, 27, 28, 28, 29, 30, 30, 31, 32, 32, 32, 33, 33, 34, 34, 35, 35; 16:1, 1, 2, 2, 2, 3, 3, 3, 4, 4, 4, 4, 4, 5, 5, 5, 6, 6, 8, 8, 9, 10, 11, 11, 11, 12, 12, 12, 12, 12, 13, 13, 13, 14, 14, 15, 16, 16, 17, 17, 17, 18, 18, 18, 18, 18, 18, 19, 19, 19, 20, 20, 20, 20, 20, 21, 22, 23, 24, 25, 26, 27, 27, 27, 28, 28, 31, 31, 32, 32, 32, 32, 32, 33, 33, 33, 34, 34, 35, 35; 16:1, 1, 2, 2, 2, 2, 2, 3, 3, 3, 4, 4, 5, 5, 5, 5, 6, 6, 6, 7, 8, 8, 9, 9, 10, 11, 11, 11, 12, 12, 12, 12, 13, 13, 13, 14, 15, 16, 16, 17, 17, 17, 18, 18, 18, 18, 18, 18, 19, 20, 21, 21, 21, 21, 22, 23, 23, 23; 17:1, 1, 1, 2, 2, 2, 2, 2, 3, 3, 4, 4, 5, 5, 5, 6, 6, 6, 7, 7, 7, 8, 8, 8, 9, 9, 10, 11, 11, 12, 12, 13, 13, 13, 13, 14, 14, 15, 16, 16, 16, 16, 17, 17, 17, 18, 18, 18, 18, 18, 18, 18, 19, 19, 20, 20, 20, 21, 21, 21, 22, 22, 22, 22, 22, 23, 23, 23, 23, 23, 23; 17:1, 1, 2, 2, 2, 2, 2, 3, 3, 3, 4, 4, 4, 5, 5, 5, 5, 5, 6, 6, 7, 7, 7, 7, 7, 8, 8, 8, 8, 9, 9, 9, 10, 11, 11, 12, 12, 13, 13, 13, 13, 13, 14, 14, 15, 16, 16, 16, 16, 17, 17, 17, 17, 18, 18, 18, 18, 18, 19, 19, 20, 20, 20, 20, 20, 20, 21, 22, 22, 22, 23, 23, 23, 23, 24, 24, 24, 25, 25, 25, 25, 26, 26, 26, 27, 27, 28, 28, 28, 29, 29, 30; 19:1, 1, 2, 2, 2, 3, 3, 3, 3, 4, 4, 4, 5, 5, 5, 5, 6, 6, 7, 7, 7, 7, 8, 8, 8, 8, 9, 9, 10, 10, 10, 10, 11, 11, 12, 12, 12, 13, 13, 13, 13, 14, 15, 16, 17, 17, 17, 18, 18, 18, 18, 18, 19, 20, 20, 20, 20, 21, 21, 21, 21, 22, 22, 22, 22, 22, 23, 23, 23, 24, 24, 24, 24; 20:1, 1, 1, 1, 2, 2, 3, 3, 3, 3, 3, 5, 5, 9, 11, 11, 12, 12, 13, 13, 13, 14, 17, 18, 19, 19, 19, 20, 20, 21, 21, 23, 23, 23, 24, 25, 25, 25, 27, 28, 29, 29, 29, 29, 30, 30, 31, 32, 32, 32, 33, 34, 36, 36, 37, 37, 38, 38, 38, 39, 40, 40, 41, 41, 41, 41, 41, 42, 42, 42, 42, 42, 42; 21:1, 1, 1, 2, 2, 2, 2, 2, 4, 4, 4, 5, 5, 5, 7, 8, 8, 9, 10, 10, 10, 11, 11, 12, 12, 13, 13; 22:1, 1, 1, 2, 2, 2, 2, 3, 3, 3, 4, 4, 4, 5, 5, 6, 6, 7, 7, 7, 8, 8, 9, 10, 10, 10, 11, 11, 12, 12, 13, 13, 14, 14, 14, 16, 16, 17, 17, 17, 17, 18, 18, 18, 18, 19, 19, 19, 19, 20, 20, 21, 22; 23:1, 1, 2, 2, 3, 3, 3, 4, 4, 5, 5, 5, 6, 6, 7, 7, 8, 8, 9, 10, 10, 11, 12, 13, 13, 13, 14, 14, 14, 16, 16, 17, 17, 17, 18, 18, 18, 18, 19, 19, 19, 19, 19, 20, 20, 21; 22:1, 2, 2, 2, 3,

2Sa 1:1, 2, 2, 2, 3, 3, 4, 4, 4, 4, 4, 4, 5, 5, 6, 6, 7, 7, 7, 8, 8, 9, 10, 10, 10, 10, 11, 11, 12, 12, 12, 12, 12, 12, 13, 13, 14, 15, 15, 15, 16, 17, 17, 22, 23, 23, 27; 2:1, 1, 1, 1, 2, 2, 3, 4, 4, 4, 5, 5, 5, 6, 6, 7, 7, 8, 9, 9, 9, 9, 9, 10, 11, 11, 12, 12, 12, 13, 13, 13, 14, 14, 15, 15, 16, 16, 16, 16, 17, 17, 17, 18, 18, 18, 19, 20, 20, 21, 21, 21, 22, 23, 23, 23, 24, 24, 25, 25, 25, 26, 26, 27, 27, 28, 28, 29, 29, 29, 29, 30, 30, 30, 31, 31, 32, 32, 32, 32; 3:1, 1, 1, 1, 2, 2, 3, 3, 4, 4, 5, 6, 6, 7, 7, 8, 8, 9, 10, 10, 11, 12, 13, 14, 15, 15, 16, 16, 17, 18, 19, 19, 19, 19, 20, 20, 21, 21, 21, 21, 21, 21, 22, 22, 22, 23, 23, 23, 24, 24, 25, 25, 25, 25, 26, 27, 27, 28, 28, 29, 29, 30, 31, 31, 31, 31, 31, 32, 32, 32, 33, 33, 33, 34, 34, 34, 35, 35, 35, 36, 36, 36, 36, 37, 38, 38, 38, 38, 39, 39; 4:1, 1, 2, 2, 3, 3, 4, 4, 4, 4, 4, 4, 5, 5, 5, 6, 6, 6, 6, 7, 7, 7, 7, 7, 8, 8, 8, 8, 9, 9, 10, 11, 12, 12, 12, 12, 12; 5:1, 1, 2, 2, 2, 3, 3, 4, 5, 5, 5, 5, 6, 6, 6, 8, 8, 8, 8, 9, 9, 9, 10, 10, 10, 11, 11, 11, 11, 12, 12, 13, 13, 13, 13, 13, 13, 14, 14, 14, 14, 15, 15, 15, 16, 16, 16, 17, 17, 18, 19, 19, 20, 20, 20, 21, 21, 21, 22, 22, 23, 23, 23, 24, 25, 25; 6:2, 2, 3, 3, 3, 3, 4, 4, 5, 5, 5, 5, 5, 6, 7, 7, 7, 8, 8, 9, 9, 11, 11, 12, 12, 12, 13, 13, 14, 14, 15, 15, 16, 16, 16, 17, 17, 17, 18, 18, 19, 19, 20, 20, 21, 21, 21, 22, 22; 7:1, 1, 3, 4, 5, 6, 9, 10, 11, 12, 12, 13, 14, 14, 14, 14, 15, 15, 16, 16, 17, 18, 18, 18; 9:1, 2, 2, 2, 3, 3, 4, 4, 5, 6, 6, 7, 7, 8, 8, 9, 9, 10, 10, 10, 10, 12, 12, 12, 13; 10:1, 1, 2, 2, 3, 3, 3, 4, 4, 5, 5, 6, 6, 6, 7, 7, 8, 8, 8, 9, 10, 11, 11, 12, 12, 13, 13, 13, 14, 14, 14, 15, 16, 16, 16, 16, 17, 17, 18, 18; 11:1, 1, 1, 1, 2, 2, 3, 3, 3, 4, 4, 4, 4, 5, 5, 6, 6, 7, 7, 7, 8, 8, 8, 9, 9, 10, 11, 11, 11, 11, 11, 11, 11, 11, 12, 13, 13, 14, 15, 15, 15, 16, 16, 17, 17, 18, 19, 20, 20, 21, 21, 21, 22, 22, 23, 23, 23, 24, 24, 25, 25, 25, 26, 26, 26, 27, 27; 12:1, 1, 1, 2, 2, 3, 3, 3, 3, 4, 4, 4, 4, 5, 6, 7, 7, 8, 8, 8, 8, 8, 9, 9, 10, 11, 11, 11, 12, 13, 13, 13, 14, 14, 15, 15, 16, 16, 16, 17, 17, 18, 18, 18, 18, 18, 19, 20, 20, 20, 21, 22, 23, 23, 24, 24, 24, 24, 25, 25, 26, 26, 27, 28, 29, 30, 30, 30, 31, 31, 31; 13:1, 1, 2, 2, 3, 4, 4, 5, 5, 5, 5, 6, 6, 6, 6, 7, 7, 8, 8, 9, 10, 11, 11, 11, 12, 13, 13, 13, 13, 14, 14, 14, 15, 15, 16, 17, 17, 18, 18, 19, 19, 20, 20, 21, 22, 23, 23, 23; 14:2, 2, 2, 3, 3, 3, 3, 4, 4, 5, 6, 6, 7, 7, 7, 7, 8, 9, 9, 10, 10, 11, 11, 12, 12, 12, 13, 13, 14, 15, 16, 16, 17, 17, 17, 18, 19, 19, 19, 20, 20, 20, 21, 22; 15:1, 1, 2, 2, 2, 2, 2, 3, 4, 4, 4, 5, 5, 6, 6, 7, 7, 8, 8, 9, 10, 10, 11, 11, 12, 13, 14; 16:1, 1, 1, 1, 2, 2, 2, 2, 2, 3, 3, 4, 4, 5, 5, 5, 6, 6, 7, 8, 9, 10, 11, 11, 11, 12, 12, 13, 13, 13, 13, 14, 14, 14, 15, 15, 16, 17, 17, 17, 18, 19, 21, 21, 22, 23; 17:1, 1, 2, 2, 2, 2, 3, 4, 4, 5, 6, 7, 8, 8, 8, 9, 10, 11, 11, 12, 12, 13, 14, 14, 15, 15, 15, 15, 16, 16, 17, 17, 17, 18, 18, 19, 19, 19, 19, 19, 20, 20, 20, 21, 21, 21, 21, 22, 22, 23, 23, 23, 23, 24, 25, 26, 27, 27, 27, 27, 28, 28, 28, 28, 28, 29; 18:1, 1, 1, 2, 2, 2, 2, 4, 4, 4, 4, 5, 5, 5, 6, 6, 7, 7, 8, 8, 9, 10, 11, 11, 11, 11, 12, 12, 12, 14, 14, 14, 14, 14, 15, 15, 15, 17, 17, 17, 18, 18, 19, 21, 22, 22, 23, 23, 24, 24, 24, 25, 25, 25, 26; 21:1, 1, 1, 2, 2, 2, 2, 3, 4, 4, 5, 5, 6, 6, 7, 8, 9, 9, 9, 9, 9, 9, 10, 10, 10, 11, 12, 12, 12, 13, 13, 13, 14, 14, 14, 15, 15, 15, 15, 16, 17, 17, 17, 18, 19, 20, 20, 20, 21, 22, 22; 22:1, 1, 2, 2, 2, 3,

3, 7, 7, 8, 8, 9, 10, 10, 11, 11, 11, 12, 12, 14, 15, 15, 15, 16, 18, 22, 23, 24, 26, 27, 28, 29, 32, 33, 33, 34, 36, 38, 38, 39, 39, 43, 46, 47, 47, 48, 49, 50, 51, 51; 23:1, 1, 2, 4, 5, 5, 7, 7, 9, 9, 10, 10, 10, 11, 11, 11, 12, 12, 12, 13, 13, 13, 14, 14, 15, 15, 16, 16, 16, 16, 17, 18, 18, 18, 20, 20, 20, 21, 21, 21, 21, 22, 23, 39; 24:1, 1, 1, 2, 3, 3, 4, 4, 4, 4, 5, 5, 5, 6, 6, 7, 7, 7, 7, 8, 9, 10, 10, 10, 11, 11, 12, 13, 13, 14, 15, 16, 16, 16, 16, 17, 17, 17, 18, 20, 20, 20, 20, 20, 21, 21, 22; 1Ki 1:1, 1, 2, 2, 3, 3, 4, 4, 5, 5, 6, 6, 6, 7, 7, 8, 8, 8, 9, 9, 9, 9, 10, 10, 11, 12, 13, 13, 13, 14, 15, 15, 15, 16, 16, 16, 17, 17, 18, 18, 19, 19, 19, 19, 19, 20, 21, 21, 22, 23, 23, 24, 24, 25, 25, 25, 25, 25, 25, 26, 27, 28, 28, 29, 30, 31, 31, 32, 32, 32, 33, 33, 34, 34, 34, 34, 34, 35, 35, 35, 36, 36, 37, 38, 38, 38, 38, 39, 39, 39, 40, 40, 40, 41, 41, 41, 42, 42, 43, 43, 44, 44, 44, 44, 44, 45, 45, 45, 46, 47, 47, 47, 48, 49, 49, 49, 50, 50, 50, 51, 52, 53, 53, 53, 53; 2:1, 2, 3, 3, 3, 3, 4, 5, 5, 5, 5, 6, 7, 7, 8, 8, 9, 9, 10, 10, 11, 12, 13, 13, 14, 15, 15, 16, 16, 17, 18, 19, 19, 19, 20, 21, 22, 22, 23, 24, 24, 25, 26, 26, 28, 28, 29, 29, 30, 31, 31, 31, 31, 32, 32, 32, 32, 33, 33, 34, 34, 34, 35, 35, 36, 37, 38, 38, 39, 39, 39, 40, 40, 40, 40, 41, 41, 42, 42, 42, 43, 43, 44, 44, 44, 44, 44, 45, 45, 45, 46, 47, 47, 48, 49, 49, 49, 50, 50, 50, 51, 52, 53, 53, 53, 53; 2:1, 2, 3, 3, 3, 3, 4, 5, 5, 5, 6, 7, 7, 8, 9, 9, 11, 12, 13, 13, 13, 14, 15, 15, 15, 16, 16, 17, 18, 19, 19, 19, 20, 21, 22, 22, 23, 24, 24, 25, 25, 26, 27, 27, 28; 4:2, 3, 4, 4, 4, 5, 5, 5, 6, 6, 7, 7, 8, 9, 9, 10, 12, 12, 13, 16, 19, 19, 20, 20, 20, 21, 21, 21, 22, 22, 23, 23, 23, 23, 23, 24, 25, 25, 26, 26, 26, 27, 27, 28; 5:1, 2, 5, 6, 6, 6, 7, 8, 8, 9, 9, 9, 9, 11, 11, 12, 12, 12, 13, 13, 14, 14, 14, 15, 15, 16, 16, 17, 17, 18, 18; 6:1, 1, 2, 2, 2, 3, 3, 4, 5, 5, 5, 6, 6, 7, 8, 8, 9, 9, 9, 10, 11, 12, 13, 14, 15, 15, 15, 15, 16, 16, 17, 18, 18, 19, 20, 20, 20, 21, 21, 21, 22, 22, 23, 23, 24, 24, 25, 25, 25, 26, 27, 27, 27, 27, 28, 29, 29, 29, 30, 30, 31, 31, 32, 32, 34, 35, 35, 35, 36, 36, 38; 7:1, 2, 2, 3, 3, 4, 4, 5, 5, 5, 6, 6, 6, 6, 7, 8, 9, 10, 11, 12, 12, 12, 13, 14, 14, 14, 14, 14, 15, 16, 16, 17, 17, 18, 19, 20, 20, 21, 21, 21, 21, 22, 23, 23, 23, 24, 25, 25, 25, 26, 26, 27, 28, 29, 29, 30, 30, 30, 30, 31, 31, 32, 32, 33, 33, 33, 33, 34, 34, 35, 35, 35, 36, 36, 36, 37, 38, 38, 38, 39, 39, 40, 40, 40, 41, 41, 42, 42, 43, 43, 44, 44, 45, 45, 45, 46, 47, 47, 48, 48, 49, 49, 49, 50, 50, 50, 51, 51; 8:1, 2, 3, 4, 4, 4, 5, 6, 7, 8, 9, 10, 14, 14, 15, 15, 17, 18, 20, 20, 20, 21, 22, 22, 23, 23, 24, 26, 27, 28, 28, 29, 30, 30, 30, 31, 31, 32, 32, 33, 33, 34, 34, 35, 35, 36, 36, 36, 37, 37, 38, 39, 39, 40, 40, 41, 41, 42, 43, 43, 44, 44, 45, 45, 46, 46, 47, 47, 48, 49, 49, 49, 50, 50, 50, 51, 51; 8:1, 2, 3, 4, 4, 14, 14, 15, 15, 17, 18, 20, 20, 20, 21, 22, 22, 23, 24, 26, 27, 28, 28, 29, 29, 30, 30, 30, 31, 31, 32, 32, 33, 33, 34, 34, 35, 35, 36, 36, 36, 37, 37, 38, 39, 39, 40, 40, 41, 41, 42, 43, 43, 44, 45, 45, 46, 46, 47, 47, 48, 49, 49, 49, 50, 50, 51; 9:1, 1, 1, 3, 3, 4, 4, 4, 5, 6, 6, 6, 7, 7, 8, 8, 8, 9, 9, 9, 10, 10, 11, 12, 13, 14, 15, 15, 15, 15, 16, 16, 16, 17, 18, 19, 19, 19, 19, 20, 22, 22, 23, 25, 25, 26, 27, 27, 28, 28; 10:1, 2, 2, 2, 3, 4, 4, 5, 5, 5, 5, 6, 6, 7, 7, 7, 8, 8, 8, 9, 10, 11, 12, 12, 12, 13, 13, 14, 15, 15, 16, 17, 17, 18, 19, 19, 20, 20, 21, 22, 22, 23, 24, 25, 25, 25, 25, 26, 26, 26, 26, 26, 26, 27; 6:1, 1, 2, 2, 3, 3, 4, 5, 5, 6, 6, 6, 6, 7, 7, 8, 8, 9, 10, 10, 11, 11, 12, 13, 13, 13, 14, 14, 14, 14, 15, 15, 15, 15, 16, 16, 17, 18, 18, 19, 20, 20, 20, 20, 21, 22, 22, 22, 22, 23, 23, 23, 24, 24, 25, 25, 25, 26, 27; 6:1, 2, 2, 2, 3, 3, 3, 4, 4, 4, 5, 6, 6, 7, 7, 8, 8, 8, 8, 9, 9, 10, 10, 10, 11, 11, 12, 12, 13, 13, 14, 14, 15, 16, 17; 7:1, 2, 2, 3, 4, 4, 5, 5, 6, 6, 6, 6, 8, 8, 8, 8, 8, 8, 9, 9, 10, 10, 10, 11, 11, 12, 12, 13, 13, 13, 14, 15, 15, 16, 16, 17, 17, 17, 17, 17, 17, 18, 18, 18, 19, 19, 20, 20, 20, 21,

13, 13, 15, 15, 15, 15, 16, 16, 17, 17, 18, 18, 18, 18, 19, 19, 19, 19, 19, 20, 20, 20, 20, 20, 21, 22, 22, 22, 22, 23, 23, 23, 24, 24, 24, 24, 25, 25, 25, 26, 27, 28, 28, 29, 29, 32, 32, 33, 34, 34, 34; 16:2, 2, 2, 3, 3, 4, 5, 5, 6, 6, 7, 7, 7, 8, 8, 9, 10, 10, 10, 11, 13, 13, 14, 15, 15, 16, 16, 16, 17, 17, 17, 18, 18, 18, 19, 19, 20, 20, 20, 21, 21, 22, 23, 23, 24, 24, 25, 25, 26, 27, 27, 28, 28, 29, 29, 29, 29, 29, 31, 31, 31, 31, 32, 33, 33, 34; 17:1, 2, 3, 3, 4, 4, 4, 4, 5, 5, 6, 6, 6, 6, 6, 7, 7, 8, 9, 10, 10, 10, 11, 11, 12, 12, 12, 12, 15, 15, 15, 15, 15, 15, 15, 15, 16, 16, 17, 17, 17, 18, 18, 18, 18, 18, 19, 20, 20, 20, 20, 21, 21, 22, 22, 22, 22, 23, 23, 23, 23, 24; 18:1, 1, 2, 2, 2, 2, 3, 4, 4, 5, 5, 5, 6, 7, 7, 8, 9, 10, 10, 11, 12, 12, 12, 12, 13, 13, 14, 14, 15, 16, 16, 16, 17, 18, 18, 19, 19, 19, 19, 19, 20, 22, 23, 23, 23, 24, 24, 25, 25, 26, 26, 26, 27, 27, 27, 28, 28, 29, 30, 30, 31, 32, 32, 33, 34, 34, 35, 35; 19:1, 1, 2, 3, 4, 4, 4, 4, 5, 5, 6, 6, 6, 6, 7, 7, 8, 8, 9, 10, 10, 11, 11, 11, 11, 12, 13, 13, 13, 13, 14, 15, 15, 16, 16, 16, 17, 17, 17, 18, 18, 18, 19, 19, 20, 20, 20, 21, 21, 21, 21, 22, 22, 22, 23, 23, 24, 24, 25, 25, 25, 26, 26, 26, 27, 27, 28, 29; 20:1, 1, 1, 1, 1, 1, 2, 2, 3, 3, 4, 4, 4, 5, 5, 5, 6, 6, 6, 6, 7, 7, 7, 7, 7, 7, 8, 9, 9, 10, 10, 11, 11, 12, 13, 13, 14, 14, 15, 15, 16, 16, 16, 17, 17, 18, 19, 20, 20, 20, 21, 21, 21, 22, 22, 22, 23, 23, 24, 24, 24, 25, 25, 25, 26, 26, 26, 27, 27, 28, 28, 29, 29, 30, 30, 30, 31, 31, 32, 32, 32, 33, 33, 34, 34, 34, 35, 35, 36, 37, 37, 38, 38, 39, 39, 39, 40, 40, 41, 41, 41, 42, 42, 42, 42, 43; 21:1, 2, 2, 3, 4, 4, 4, 4, 4, 5, 6, 7, 7, 8, 9, 9, 9, 10, 10, 10, 11, 11, 11, 11, 12, 13, 13, 13, 13, 13, 13, 14, 15, 15, 16, 16, 17, 18, 18, 19, 19, 20, 20, 21, 21, 22, 22, 22, 22, 23, 24, 25, 25, 25, 26, 26, 27, 27, 27, 27, 28; 22:1, 1, 2, 3, 3, 4, 4, 5, 6, 6, 6, 7, 8, 8, 9, 9, 10, 11, 12, 13, 13, 14, 15, 15, 16, 16, 17, 17, 18, 19, 19, 20, 20, 21, 21, 21, 22, 22, 22, 23, 23, 23, 24, 24, 25, 25, 26, 26, 26, 26, 27, 27, 28, 29, 30, 30, 30, 31, 32, 32, 33, 34, 35, 35, 35, 36, 36, 36, 37, 37, 38, 38, 38, 39, 39, 40, 41, 42, 42, 42, 42, 43, 43, 43; 21:1, 2, 2, 3, 4, 4, 4, 4, 4, 5, 6, 9, 10, 10, 10, 10, 11, 11, 11, 12, 12, 13, 13, 13, 13, 13, 14, 15, 15, 15, 15, 16, 17, 17, 18, 19, 19, 20, 20, 20, 21, 21, 21, 21, 21, 21, 22, 22, 23, 24, 24, 25, 25, 25, 25, 26, 26, 26, 27, 27, 27, 28; 22:1, 1, 2, 3, 3, 4, 4, 5, 6, 6, 7, 7, 8, 8, 9, 10, 11, 11, 12, 13, 13, 14, 15, 15, 15, 16, 16, 17, 18, 19, 19, 20, 20, 21, 22, 22, 22, 22, 23, 23, 24, 24, 25, 25, 26, 26, 26, 26, 27, 27, 28, 29, 30, 30, 30, 31, 32, 32, 32, 33, 33, 34, 34, 35, 35, 36, 37, 37, 38, 38, 38, 39, 39, 40, 41, 42, 42, 42, 43, 43, 44; 5:1, 2, 2, 2, 3, 4, 4, 4, 5, 5, 5, 6, 6, 7, 7, 7, 8, 9, 9, 10, 10, 11, 11, 12, 13, 13, 13, 14, 14, 15, 15, 16, 17, 18, 19, 20, 21, 22, 22, 23, 23, 24, 24, 25, 25, 25, 26, 26, 26, 26, 27; 6:1, 2, 2, 3, 3, 3, 5, 5, 6, 6, 6, 6, 6, 7, 7, 8, 8, 9, 10, 10, 11, 11, 12, 13, 13, 14, 14, 14, 15, 15, 15, 16, 16, 17, 17, 17, 17, 18, 18, 19, 19, 20, 20, 20, 20, 21, 22, 22, 22, 23, 23, 23, 24, 24, 25, 26, 26, 27, 28, 28, 29, 30, 30, 31, 32, 32, 32, 33, 33; 7:1, 2, 2, 3, 3, 3, 4, 4, 4, 8, 8, 8, 8, 8, 8, 9, 9, 10, 10, 10, 10, 11, 11, 12, 12, 13, 13, 13, 14, 17, 17, 17, 17, 18, 18, 18, 19, 19, 19, 20, 20; 8:1, 1, 1, 1, 2, 2, 2, 3, 3, 3, 4, 5, 5, 5, 5, 6, 6, 7, 7, 8, 8, 8, 8, 9, 9, 10, 11, 12, 12, 13, 14, 15, 15, 15, 15, 16, 17, 17, 17, 17, 18, 19, 19, 20, 20, 20, 21; 9:1, 1, 1, 1, 2, 2, 2, 2, 3, 3, 3, 5, 5, 5, 5, 6, 6, 6, 6, 6, 7, 7, 7, 8, 8, 8,

21, 21, 21, 21, 21, 22, 22, 22, 22, 23, 23, 23, 24, 24, 24, 24, 25, 25, 26, 26, 26, 27, 27, 27, 27, 27, 28, 28, 29, 30, 30, 30, 30, 31, 32, 32, 32, 33, 33, 33, 33, 34, 34, 34, 34, 35, 35, 35, 36, 36, 37; 10:1, 1, 1, 1, 2, 2, 2, 3, 3, 3, 4, 5, 5, 5, 5, 5, 6, 6, 7, 7, 7, 7, 8, 8, 8, 9, 9, 9, 9, 9, 11, 11, 11, 12, 12, 12, 12, 13, 13, 13, 13, 14, 14, 14, 14, 15, 15, 15, 15, 15, 15, 16, 16, 17, 18, 18, 19, 20, 20, 21, 21, 21, 21, 22, 22, 22, 23, 23, 23, 24, 24, 24, 24, 25, 25, 25, 25, 25, 25, 25, 26, 26, 27, 27, 27, 29, 30, 30, 32, 33, 33, 34, 34, 35, 35, 35, 36, 36; 11:1, 1, 2, 2, 2, 3, 3, 4, 4, 4, 4, 4, 5, 6, 6, 7, 8, 8, 8, 8, 8, 9, 9, 9, 10, 11, 11, 12, 12, 12, 12, 12, 12, 12, 13, 13, 14, 14, 14, 14, 14, 14, 14, 15, 15, 15, 16, 16, 17, 17, 17, 17, 17, 18, 18, 18, 18, 19, 19, 19, 19, 19, 19, 19, 20, 20, 20; 12:1, 1, 2, 3, 4, 5, 6, 7, 7, 8, 9, 9, 9, 10, 10, 10, 10, 11, 11, 11, 12, 12, 12, 12, 12, 14, 16, 17, 17, 17, 18, 18, 18, 18, 18, 18, 18, 19, 19, 19, 19, 19, 19, 20, 20; 12:1, 1, 2, 3, 4, 5, 7, 7, 9, 9, 9, 10, 10, 11, 11, 12, 12, 13, 13, 13, 14, 14, 14, 14, 14, 14, 15, 15, 16, 16, 16, 16, 17, 18, 19, 19, 20, 20, 21, 21, 22, 23, 24, 27, 28, 28, 28, 28, 29, 29; 15:1, 2, 2, 2, 3, 4, 5, 7, 7, 9, 9, 9, 10, 10, 11, 11, 12, 12, 13, 13, 13, 14, 14, 14, 14, 14, 14, 15, 15, 16, 16, 16, 16, 16, 17, 17, 18, 19, 19, 20, 20, 21, 21, 22, 23, 24, 25, 27, 28, 28, 29, 29; 15:1, 2, 2, 2, 3, 4, 5, 5, 5, 6, 6, 7, 7, 7, 8, 9, 10, 10, 10, 10, 11, 12, 13, 13, 14, 14, 14, 14, 14, 16, 16, 16, 16, 17, 17, 18, 19, 19, 20, 20, 20, 21, 21, 22, 23, 24, 25, 25, 25, 25, 25, 26, 26, 27, 28, 29, 29, 29, 29, 29, 29, 29, 30, 30, 30, 30, 31, 31, 32, 33, 33, 34, 35, 36, 37, 38, 38, 38; 16:2, 2, 3, 4, 4, 4, 4, 5, 5, 6, 6, 7, 7, 7, 8, 8, 8, 8, 9, 9, 9, 10, 10, 10, 10, 11, 12, 12, 13, 13, 13, 13, 14, 14, 14, 15, 15, 15, 15, 15, 15, 15, 15, 17, 17, 17, 17, 18, 20, 20, 20; 17:2, 3, 3, 4, 4, 4, 5, 5, 6, 6, 6, 6, 7, 8, 8, 9, 10, 10, 10, 11, 11, 13, 13, 13, 15, 15, 15, 15, 15, 16, 16, 16, 16, 16, 17, 17, 17, 17, 17, 18, 20, 20, 20; 17:2, 3, 3, 4, 4, 4, 5, 6, 6, 6, 7, 8, 8, 9, 9, 10, 10, 10, 11, 11, 13, 13, 13, 15, 15, 15, 16, 16, 16, 16, 16, 17, 17, 17, 17, 18, 20, 20, 20, 21, 21, 21, 24, 24, 24, 24, 24, 24, 24, 25, 25, 26, 27, 28, 29, 30, 30, 30, 31, 31, 31, 31, 32, 33, 33, 34, 35, 36, 36, 37, 37, 37, 37, 37, 38, 39, 41, 41; 18:2, 2, 3, 4, 4, 4, 4, 6, 7, 7, 7, 7, 8, 9, 9, 10, 11, 11, 11, 11, 12, 12, 13, 14, 14, 14, 15, 15, 16, 16, 17, 17, 17, 17, 17, 17, 17, 17, 19, 20, 21, 22, 23, 24, 24, 25, 26, 26, 26, 27, 27, 28, 28, 30, 31, 31, 31, 31, 32, 32, 32, 32, 32, 32, 34, 34, 36, 37, 37; 19:1, 1, 1, 2, 2, 2, 3, 3, 3, 3, 4, 4, 6, 7, 7, 7, 8, 9, 11, 12, 12, 12, 12, 13, 13, 13, 14, 14, 14; 20:1, 1, 1, 2, 3, 3, 3, 3, 3, 4, 5, 6, 6, 6, 6, 6, 7, 7, 7, 7, 7, 8, 9, 10, 11, 11, 12, 13, 13, 13, 13, 14, 14, 14, 14, 14, 15, 15, 15, 16, 16, 16, 16, 18, 18, 18, 18, 18, 19, 19, 20, 20, 20, 20, 20, 20, 21, 21; 21:1, 1, 1, 2, 3, 3, 3, 4, 5, 6, 6, 6, 6, 7, 7, 7, 8, 9, 10, 11, 11, 12, 13, 13, 13, 14, 14, 14, 14, 14, 15, 15, 17, 17, 17, 18, 18, 18, 18, 19, 19, 19, 20, 21, 21, 21, 22, 22, 23, 23, 24, 24, 26, 26; 22:1, 1, 1, 2, 2, 2, 3, 5, 6, 6, 6, 6, 9, 9, 9, 9, 10, 11, 12, 12, 12, 12, 12, 12, 14, 14, 15, 16, 17, 17, 19, 19, 19, 19, 19, 20; 23:1, 1, 1, 1, 2, 2, 2, 2, 2, 3, 3, 3, 3, 3, 3, 4, 4, 4, 4, 4, 4, 5, 5, 5, 5, 6, 6, 6, 7, 8, 8, 8, 8, 8, 9, 9, 10, 10, 11, 11, 12, 12, 12, 12, 12, 13, 13, 14, 14, 14, 14, 14, 14, 14, 15, 15, 16, 17, 17, 19, 19, 19, 19, 19, 20, 20; 23:1, 1, 1, 2, 3, 3, 4, 4, 4, 4, 4, 4, 5, 5, 5, 5, 6, 6, 6, 7, 8, 8, 8, 9, 9, 10, 11, 11, 11, 12, 12, 12, 12, 13, 13, 14, 14, 14, 14, 14, 15, 15, 15, 16, 16, 16, 16, 17, 17, 18, 18, 18, 19, 20; 25:1, 1, 1, 1, 2, 3, 3, 4, 4, 5, 5, 6, 6, 7, 7, 7, 7, 8, 9, 10, 11, 12, 13, 13, 13, 13, 14, 14, 14, 14, 14, 15, 15, 15, 15, 16, 17, 17, 17, 17, 18, 18, 19, 19, 20, 20, 20, 21, 22, 23, 23, 23, 23, 23, 23, 24, 24, 24, 24, 25, 25, 25, 26, 26, 26, 27, 27, 27, 28, 28, 29, 29, 30;

1Ch 1:4, 5, 5, 5, 5, 5, 6, 6, 7, 7, 7, 8, 8, 9, 9, 9, 9, 9, 9, 10, 11, 11, 11, 12, 12, 12, 13, 13, 14, 14, 14, 15, 15, 16, 16, 17, 17, 17, 17, 17, 17, 18, 18, 19, 19, 20, 20, 20, 20, 21, 21, 22, 22, 22, 23, 23, 23, 29, 29, 30, 30, 31, 31, 32, 32, 32, 32, 32, 32, 33, 33, 33, 33, 34, 34, 35, 35, 35, 36, 36, 36, 36, 37, 38, 38, 38, 38, 38, 39, 39, 39, 40, 40, 40, 40, 41, 41, 41, 41, 42, 42, 42, 43, 44, 45, 46, 46, 47, 48, 49, 50, 50, 50, 51; 2:1, 1, 2, 2, 3, 3, 3, 3, 4, 4, 6, 6, 6, 6, 7, 8, 9, 9, 10, 11, 11, 12, 12, 13, 13, 16, 16, 16, 16, 17, 17, 18, 18, 18, 19, 20, 20, 21, 21, 22, 22, 23, 23, 24, 25, 25, 25, 25, 27, 28, 28, 28, 29, 29, 29, 30, 30, 31, 31, 31, 31, 32, 32, 32,

33, 33, 34, 35, 35, 36, 36, 37, 37, 38, 38, 39, 39, 40, 40, 41, 41, 42, 43, 43, 43, 43, 44, 44, 45, 45, 46, 46, 46, 46, 47, 47, 47, 47, 47, 48, 49, 49, 52, 52, 52, 53, 53, 53, 54, 54, 54, 55, 55; 3:4, 4, 4, 4, 5, 5, 5, 6, 6, 6, 7, 7, 7, 8, 8, 9, 10, 15, 16, 17, 18, 18, 18, 19, 19, 19, 19, 20, 20, 20, 20, 21, 22, 22, 22, 22, 22, 23, 23, 23, 24, 24, 24, 24, 24, 24; 4:1, 1, 1, 2, 2, 2, 3, 3, 3, 4, 4, 5, 6, 6, 6, 7, 7, 8, 9, 9, 10, 10, 10, 10, 11, 12, 12, 12, 13, 13, 14, 14, 14, 15, 15, 16, 16, 16, 16, 17, 17, 17, 17, 17, 18, 18, 18, 19, 19, 20, 20, 20, 21, 21; 13:1, 1, 2, 2, 2, 3; 4:4, 4, 4, 4, 4, 4, 5, 6, 6, 7, 7, 8, 8, 8, 8, 8, 9, 9, 9, 10, 11, 11, 12, 12, 12, 12, 12, 13, 13, 14, 14, 14, 14, 14, 15, 15, 16, 17, 17, 17, 17, 17, 18, 18, 18, 18, 19, 19, 19, 19, 19, 20, 20, 20, 20, 20, 21, 21, 21, 21, 22, 22, 22, 23, 23, 24, 24, 24, 24, 24, 25, 25, 25, 25, 26, 26, 26, 27, 27, 27, 28, 28, 28, 29, 29; 16:1, 1, 1, 2, 2, 3, 3, 3, 3, 3, 4, 4, 4, 4, 5, 5, 5, 5, 5, 5, 6, 7, 11, 12, 16, 16, 17, 17, 18, 19, 20, 20, 20, 20, 20, 20, 20, 20, 21, 21, 21, 21, 22, 23, 23, 23, 24, 24, 26, 26, 26, 29, 29; 16:1, 1, 1, 2, 2, 3, 3, 3, 3, 4, 4, 4, 5, 5, 5, 5, 5, 6, 7, 11, 12, 16, 16, 17, 17, 18, 19, 19, 19; 19:1, 2, 2, 3, 3, 4, 4, 4, 5, 5, 5, 6, 6, 6, 6, 6, 7, 7, 7, 7, 7, 8, 8, 9, 9, 9, 10, 10, 11, 11, 12, 13, 13, 13, 14, 14, 15, 15, 15, 16, 16, 16, 16, 17, 17, 17, 18, 18, 18, 19; 20:1, 1, 1, 1, 1, 1, 2, 2, 2, 2, 2, 3, 3, 4, 4, 4, 5, 5, 5, 5, 5, 6, 6, 8, 8; 21:1, 1, 2, 2, 2, 3, 3, 4, 4, 5, 5, 5, 5, 5, 6, 7, 7, 8, 8, 8, 8, 8; 11, 12, 13, 14, 15, 15, 15, 15, 16, 16, 16, 16, 17, 17, 17, 18, 18, 19, 20, 20, 20, 21, 21, 21, 21, 23, 23, 23, 24, 24, 26, 26,

33, 33, 34, 35, 35, 36, 36, 37, 37, 38, 38, 39, 39, 40, 40, 41, 41, 41, 42, 43, 43, 43, 43, 44, 45, 45, 45, 46, 46, 46, 47, 47, 48, 49, 52, 52, 52, 53, 53, 53, 54, 54, 54, 55, 55; 3:4, 4, 4, 4, 5, 6, 6, 6, 6, 6, 7, 7, 7, 7, 8, 8, 8, 8, 9, 9, 9, 11, 11, 11, 12, 12, 12, 12, 13, 13, 13, 13, 14, 15, 16, 17, 18, 18, 18, 18, 18, 19, 19, 19, 20, 21, 21, 21, 22, 22, 23, 23, 23, 24, 24, 24, 24, 24; 4:1, 1, 1, 2, 2, 2, 3, 3, 3, 3, 4, 4, 4, 4, 5, 5, 6, 6, 6, 7, 8, 8, 8, 8, 9, 10, 11, 11, 11, 11, 12, 12, 12, 12, 12, 13, 13, 13, 14, 14, 14, 15, 15, 15, 16, 16, 17, 18, 18, 18, 18, 18, 19, 20, 20, 20, 21, 21, 21, 21, 21, 21, 22, 23, 23, 24, 24, 24, 24, 24, 25, 25, 26; 6:1, 1, 2, 3, 3, 3, 4, 5, 5, 6, 7, 8, 8, 9, 10, 10, 11, 11, 11, 11, 11, 12, 12, 13, 13, 13, 13, 14, 14, 14, 14, 15, 16, 17, 17, 17, 18, 19, 23, 24, 25, 25, 25, 26, 26, 26, 26, 26; 6:1, 2, 2, 3, 3, 3, 3, 3, 5, 5, 6, 6, 7, 8, 8, 8, 8, 9, 10, 11, 12, 13, 13, 14, 14, 14, 14, 14, 15, 15, 16, 16, 16, 16, 17, 18, 18, 18, 19, 23, 24, 25, 25, 25, 25, 26, 26, 26, 26; 7:1, 1, 2, 2, 2, 2, 2, 2, 2, 3, 3, 3, 3, 5, 5, 6, 6, 7, 8, 8, 14, 15, 15, 16, 16, 17, 17, 17, 17, 17, 17, 18, 18, 18, 19, 20, 20, 20, 20, 20, 24, 25, 26, 27, 27, 28, 28, 29, 30, 30, 31, 32, 34, 34, 35, 35, 35, 36, 37, 37, 37, 37, 38, 38, 39, 39, 39, 40, 40, 40, 40, 40; 8:1, 2, 8, 9, 9, 9, 10, 11, 11, 11, 11, 12, 13, 13, 14, 14, 14, 14, 14, 15, 15, 15, 16, 16, 16, 16, 17, 17, 17; 4:1, 1, 2, 2, 3, 4, 4, 4, 4, 4, 4, 4, 5, 5, 5, 6, 6, 7, 7, 7, 7, 7, 8, 8, 9, 9, 9, 10, 10, 10, 10, 11, 11, 12, 12, 12, 12, 13, 13, 14, 14, 15, 15, 15, 16, 16, 16, 17, 17, 17, 17, 18, 18, 19, 19, 20, 20, 20, 21; 8:1, 2, 3, 3, 4, 4, 5, 6, 7, 7, 7, 7, 8, 8; 9:1, 1, 2, 3, 3, 3, 5, 5, 6, 6, 7, 8, 8, 10, 11, 11, 11, 12, 12, 13, 13, 13, 14, 14, 15, 15, 15, 15, 16, 16, 17, 17, 18, 18, 18, 18, 18; 9:1, 2, 3, 3, 3, 5, 5, 6, 6, 7, 7, 8, 8, 8, 8, 8, 9, 10, 10, 10, 11, 11, 11, 11, 11, 12, 12, 12, 12, 13, 13, 13,

26, 26, 27, 27, 29; 22:1, 2, 3, 3, 3, 4, 5, 5, 5, 6, 7, 8, 9, 9, 10, 10, 10, 11, 11, 12, 12, 13, 13, 14, 14, 14, 14, 14, 15, 15, 16, 16, 16, 16, 18, 18, 18, 19, 19, 19; 23:1, 2, 2, 3, 3, 3, 4, 4, 4, 5, 6, 6, 7, 7, 8, 9, 9, 10, 10, 11, 11, 12, 13, 13, 13, 13, 14, 15, 16, 17, 17, 19, 20, 20, 21, 22, 22, 23, 23, 23, 23, 24, 24, 24, 24, 24, 24, 24; 4:1, 1, 1, 2, 2, 3, 3, 3, 4, 4, 5, 5, 6, 6, 6, 6, 6, 7, 7, 8, 8, 8, 9, 9, 9, 10, 11, 11, 11, 11, 11, 11, 12, 12, 13, 13, 13, 15, 15, 23, 25, 25, 25, 25, 26, 26, 27, 28, 28, 28, 28, 29, 29, 30, 30, 31, 31, 32, 32, 33, 33, 34, 34, 34; 28:1, 1, 1, 1, 1, 1, 1, 1, 2, 2, 2, 3, 4, 4, 4, 5, 6, 6, 6, 6, 7, 8, 8, 9, 9, 9, 9, 10, 11, 11, 11, 11, 11, 12, 12, 13, 13, 13, 15, 15, 15, 15, 16, 17, 17, 17, 17, 17, 18, 18, 18, 20, 20, 20, 21, 21, 21; 29:1, 1, 2, 2, 2, 3, 3, 4, 5, 5, 5, 6, 7, 7, 7, 7, 7, 7, 8, 9, 10, 11, 11, 11, 11, 11, 12, 12, 12, 13, 13, 13, 15, 15, 15, 15, 16, 16, 17, 18, 18, 19, 19, 20, 20, 20, 20, 20, 21, 21, 21, 22, 22, 22; 5:1, 1, 1, 1, 4, 4, 5, 5, 5, 5, 6, 7, 9, 10, 11, 11, 12, 12, 12, 12, 13, 13, 13, 13, 13; 6:2, 3, 3, 3, 4, 6, 10, 10, 11, 12, 12, 13, 13, 13, 13, 14, 14, 15, 15, 16, 16, 18, 19, 20, 20, 24, 24, 24, 24, 24, 25, 25, 25, 25, 26, 26, 26, 26, 27, 27, 28, 28, 29, 29, 30, 30, 30, 31, 32, 32; 5:1, 1, 1, 2, 3, 3, 4, 4, 5; 7:1, 1, 1, 2, 2, 3, 3, 3, 3, 3, 3, 4, 5, 5, 5, 5, 5, 6, 7, 7, 7, 7, 7, 8, 9; 9:1, 1, 1, 1, 1, 1, 1, 1, 10, 11, 11, 11, 12, 12, 14, 14, 14, 15, 16, 16, 16, 17, 17, 18, 19; 10:1, 1, 1, 1, 3, 3, 3, 3, 4, 5, 5, 6, 6, 7, 7, 7, 8, 8, 8, 9, 9, 9, 10, 11, 11, 11, 12, 12, 13, 14; 11:1, 1, 1, 2, 2, 3, 4, 5, 6, 6, 6, 7, 7, 7, 8, 8, 8, 8, 9, 9, 10, 10, 11, 11, 11, 11, 11, 12, 13, 13, 14, 14, 15, 15, 16, 16, 17; 2:1, 1, 2, 2, 2, 2, 3, 4, 7, 7, 7, 7, 7, 8, 10, 10, 10, 11, 11, 12, 12, 13, 13, 13, 14, 14, 14, 14, 15, 15, 16, 17, 17, 18, 18, 18, 18, 18; 3:2, 3, 4, 4, 4, 5, 6, 7, 7, 7, 8, 8, 9, 9, 10, 11, 11, 12, 12, 13, 13, 14, 14, 14, 14, 15, 15, 16, 16, 16, 17, 17, 17; 4:1, 1, 2, 2, 3, 4, 4, 4, 4, 4, 4, 5, 5, 5, 6, 6, 7, 7, 7, 8, 8, 9, 9, 10, 11, 11, 11, 12, 12, 12, 13, 13, 14, 14, 14, 15, 15, 16, 16, 16, 17, 17, 18, 19, 20, 21, 21, 22; 8:1, 1, 2, 3, 3, 4, 4, 5, 5, 6, 7, 7, 7, 7, 9, 9, 10, 10, 11, 11, 12, 12, 12; 5:1, 1, 1, 1, 1, 1, 2, 4, 6, 6, 6, 7, 7, 7, 7, 8, 8, 9, 9, 10, 11, 12, 12; 6:2, 3, 3, 3, 4, 4, 4, 5, 6, 6, 6, 7, 7, 7, 8, 8, 8, 9, 9, 9, 9, 10, 11, 11, 11, 11, 11, 12, 12, 13, 13, 14;

15, 15, 16, 17, 17, 18, 18, 19, 19, 20, 20, 20, 20, 20, 21, 21, 21, 22, 22, 22, 22, 23, 23, 23, 24, 24, 24, 25, 26, 26, 26, 27, 27, 28, 28, 28, 29, 31, 31, 31, 31, 31, 32, 32, 34, 35, 36, 36, 37; 21:1, 1, 2, 2, 2, 2, 3, 3, 3, 4, 5, 5, 5, 6, 6, 7, 7, 8, 9, 9, 9, 11, 11, 12, 13, 13, 14, 14, 14, 14, 15, 16, 17, 17, 17, 17, 17, 18, 19, 19, 20, 20, 20; 22:1, 2, 2, 5, 5, 6, 6, 7, 8, 8, 9, 9, 9, 9, 9, 11, 11, 11, 12, 12; 23:1, 1, 1, 1, 1, 2, 2, 2, 2, 3, 3, 4, 5, 5, 6, 7, 7, 7, 8, 8, 9, 9, 10, 10, 11, 11, 11, 11, 11, 11, 14, 14, 15, 15, 16, 16, 16, 17, 17, 17, 17, 17, 18, 19, 20, 20, 20, 20, 20, 21; 24:1, 2, 3, 3, 3, 4, 5, 5, 5, 5, 6, 6, 6, 6, 8, 8, 9, 9, 10, 10, 10, 10, 11, 11, 11, 11, 11, 12, 12, 12, 12, 12, 12, 13, 13, 14, 14, 15, 16, 16, 17, 18, 18, 18, 19, 20, 20, 21, 21, 22; 24:1, 2, 3, 3, 4, 5, 5, 5, 5, 5, 6, 6, 6, 8, 8, 8, 8, 8, 9, 9, 10, 10, 10, 10, 11, 11, 11, 11, 11, 11, 11, 12, 12, 12, 12, 13, 13, 14, 14, 14, 14, 14, 15, 15, 16, 16, 17, 18, 18, 18, 19, 20, 20, 20, 21, 21, 21, 22, 22, 22, 22, 23, 23, 24, 24, 24, 25, 25, 25, 26, 26, 26, 27, 27, 27; 25:1, 1, 1, 1, 2, 5, 5, 12, 12, 13, 13, 14, 14, 14, 15, 16, 16, 16, 16, 17, 18, 18, 19, 19, 21, 22, 22, 23, 23, 24, 24, 24, 25, 25, 26, 26; 26:1, 2, 3, 3, 4, 5, 6, 6, 6, 6, 6, 6, 6, 6, 7, 7, 7, 7, 8, 8, 9, 9, 9, 10, 10, 10, 11, 12, 12, 13, 13, 14, 14, 14, 14, 14, 15, 15, 15, 15, 15, 16, 16, 16, 17, 17, 18, 18, 19, 20, 20, 20, 21, 21, 22, 23, 23; 27:1, 1, 2, 3, 4, 4, 5, 5, 5, 6, 7, 7, 7, 8, 8, 8, 9, 9, 9, 9, 9, 10, 10, 11, 12, 12; 23:1, 1, 1, 1, 1, 2, 2, 2, 2, 3, 3, 3, 4, 5, 5, 6, 7, 7, 7, 8, 8, 9, 9, 9, 10, 10, 10, 11, 11, 11, 11, 11, 11, 11, 12, 13, 13, 13, 13, 13, 13, 14, 14, 15, 15, 16, 16, 16, 17, 17, 17, 17, 18, 18, 19, 20, 20, 20, 20, 20, 20, 21; 24:1, 2, 3, 3, 4, 4, 5, 5, 5, 5, 6, 6, 6, 8, 8, 8, 9, 9, 10, 10, 10, 10, 11, 11, 11, 11, 11, 12, 12, 12, 12, 12, 13, 14, 14, 14, 14, 14, 16, 17, 18, 18, 19, 20, 20, 21, 21, 22; 22:23, 23, 23, 23, 24, 25, 25, 25, 26, 26, 26, 27, 27, 27; 25:1, 1, 1, 1, 2, 5, 5, 5, 8, 9, 9, 10, 11, 11, 11, 11, 12, 12, 13, 13, 14, 14, 14, 15, 15, 16, 16, 16, 17, 18, 18, 18, 19, 19, 21, 22, 22, 23, 23, 24, 24, 24, 25, 25, 26, 26, 27; 27:1, 2, 3, 4, 5, 5, 6, 6, 6, 7, 8, 8, 9, 9, 9, 10, 10, 11, 11, 12, 12, 13; 13:1, 3, 3, 3, 5, 6, 6, 6, 6, 6, 7, 8, 8, 9, 9, 10, 10, 11, 11, 12, 12, 13, 13, 13, 14, 14, 14, 15, 15, 15, 15, 16, 16, 16, 16, 18, 18, 19, 19, 19, 19, 19, 20, 20, 21, 21, 22, 23, 23, 24, 24, 25; 34:1, 1, 2, 2, 2, 3, 3, 3, 3, 4, 4, 4, 4, 4, 4, 4, 5, 5, 5, 6, 6, 6, 7, 7, 7, 7, 8, 8, 8, 9, 9, 9, 9, 9, 10, 10, 11, 11, 11, 12, 12, 12, 12, 12, 13, 13, 14, 14, 15, 15, 16, 16, 17, 17, 18, 19, 20, 20, 20, 21, 22, 22, 23, 24, 24, 25, 25, 26, 27, 27, 27, 28, 28, 28, 28, 29, 29, 30, 30, 32, 32, 32, 33, 33, 33, 33; 33:1, 1, 3, 3, 3, 3, 5, 6, 6, 6, 6, 6, 7, 7, 8, 8, 9, 9, 10, 10, 11, 11, 12, 12, 13, 13, 13, 13, 14, 14, 14, 15, 15, 15, 15, 16, 16, 16, 16, 18, 18, 19, 19, 19, 19, 20, 20, 21, 21, 22, 23, 23, 24, 24, 25; 35:1, 2, 2, 3, 3, 4, 4, 5, 5, 6, 6, 7, 7, 7, 8, 8, 8, 8, 8, 9, 9, 10, 11, 11, 11, 12, 12, 13, 13, 13, 14, 14, 14, 14, 14, 15, 15, 15, 16, 17, 17, 18, 18, 18, 18, 20, 22, 22, 23, 23, 25, 25, 26, 27, 27; 36:1, 2, 2, 3, 3, 3, 4, 4, 4, 4, 5, 5, 5, 6, 7, 8, 8, 9, 9, 10, 10, 10, 11, 12, 12, 13, 13, 13, 14, 14, 15, 15, 15, 16, 16, 17, 17, 18, 18, 18, 19, 19, 19, 19, 20, 20, 21, 22, 23;

Ezr 1:1, 2, 3, 3, 4, 4, 4, 4, 5, 5, 5, 6, 6, 7, 8, 9, 10, 11, 11; 2:1, 1, 3, 4, 5, 6, 6, 7, 8, 9, 10, 11, 12, 13, 14, 15, 16, 17, 18, 19, 20, 21, 22, 23, 24, 25, 25, 26, 26, 27, 28, 28, 29, 30, 30, 31, 31, 32, 33, 34, 35, 35, 36, 37, 38, 39, 40, 40, 41, 42, 58, 58, 59, 59, 60, 60, 61, 61, 63, 63, 64, 64, 65, 65, 65, 66, 66, 67, 67, 68, 69, 69, 69, 70, 70, 70, 70, 70, 70; 3:1, 1, 2, 2, 2, 3, 3, 3, 4, 5, 5, 5, 7, 7, 7, 7, 8, 8, 8, 8, 9, 9, 9, 10, 10, 10, 10, 11, 11, 11, 12, 12, 13; 4:1, 2, 2, 2, 3, 3, 4, 5, 6, 6, 7, 7, 7, 8, 9, 9, 10, 10, 10, 11, 12, 12, 12, 13, 13, 13, 14, 14, 15, 15, 15, 16, 16, 17, 17, 18, 18, 18, 19, 20, 21, 23, 23, 23; 5:1, 1, 2, 2, 3, 3, 3, 3, 4, 4, 5, 6, 6, 7, 7, 7, 8, 9, 11, 11, 11, 11, 11, 11, 12, 12, 14, 14, 14, 14, 15, 15, 16, 16, 16, 16, 17; 6:1, 2, 3, 3, 3, 4, 4, 5, 5, 5, 5, 5, 6, 7, 9, 9, 10, 10, 11, 11, 12, 12, 12, 13, 14, 14, 14, 15, 15, 16, 16, 16, 17, 18, 19, 20, 20, 20, 21, 22; 7:6, 6, 7, 7, 7, 7, 7, 7, 8, 9, 10, 10, 10, 12, 13, 13, 14, 14, 15, 15, 15, 16, 16, 16, 17, 17, 18, 18, 18, 20, 21, 22, 22, 22,

Idx

21, 21, 21, 21, 22, 22, 22, 22, 22, 23, 23, 23, 24, 25, 25; 20:1, 1, 2, 2, 2, 2, 3, 3, 3, 4, 4, 4, 4, 5, 5, 5, 6, 6; 21:2, 5, 7, 7, 7, 8, 8, 9, 9, 9, 10, 12, 15, 15, 16, 17; 22:5, 5, 5, 6, 6, 6, 7, 7, 8, 8, 9, 10, 10, 12, 12, 12, 12, 13, 13, 13, 13, 14, 15, 16, 16, 17, 18, 18, 19, 19, 20, 21, 21, 21, 21, 22, 22, 22, 22, 23, 23, 24, 24, 25, 25, 25; 23:3, 3, 9, 12, 13, 15, 17, 17, 17, 18, 18, 18; 24:1, 1, 1, 2, 3, 4, 4, 6, 6, 12, 13, 17, 17, 18, 18, 18, 20, 20, 20, 20, 20, 20, 21, 21, 22, 22, 22, 22, 23, 23, 23; 25:1, 6, 7, 7, 8, 8, 9, 9, 9, 10, 11, 11, 12, 12; 26:1, 6, 8, 10, 11, 14, 14, 14, 19, 19, 20, 21; 27:1, 1, 1, 3, 4, 5, 6, 6, 9, 9, 10, 10, 11, 11, 12, 12, 13, 13, 13, 13; 28:2, 2, 4, 4, 5, 6, 6, 7, 7, 8, 8, 9, 9, 10, 11, 12, 13, 13, 13, 13, 15, 15, 17, 17, 18, 18, 19, 19, 20, 21, 23, 23, 24, 25, 25, 25, 25, 26, 27, 29; 29:2, 2, 3, 3, 3, 4, 4, 4, 4, 5, 6, 6, 6, 6, 7, 7, 7, 8, 8, 8, 8, 9, 9, 10, 10, 11, 11, 12, 12, 12, 13, 13, 14, 15, 15, 15, 17, 17, 18, 18, 18, 19, 20, 20, 21, 21, 23, 23, 24; 30:1, 2, 2, 3, 4, 5, 6, 6, 8, 10, 12, 12, 12, 14, 15, 15, 15, 16, 17, 18, 18, 20, 20, 21, 21, 22, 22, 23, 23, 24, 24, 25, 25, 25, 26, 26, 27, 27, 28, 28, 29, 30, 30, 30, 30, 30, 32, 32, 32, 33, 33; 31:1, 1, 1, 2, 2, 3, 3, 3, 3, 4, 4, 7, 8, 8, 9, 9; 32:1, 2, 2, 3, 3, 3, 4, 6, 6, 6, 8, 11, 13, 14, 14, 15, 16, 17, 17, 17, 18, 18, 18, 19, 20; 33:1, 1, 1, 1, 4, 4, 5, 6, 6, 9, 9, 9, 9, 9, 12, 13, 13, 14, 14, 15, 15, 15, 16, 16, 17, 17; 34:1, 1, 1, 2, 3, 3, 4, 4, 4, 4, 5, 6, 6, 6, 7, 7, 7, 8, 8, 9, 9, 9, 10, 11, 11, 11, 11, 12, 13, 13, 13, 13, 14, 14, 14, 15, 15, 15, 16, 16, 17, 17; 35:1, 1, 1, 2, 2, 2, 3, 4, 5, 6, 6, 7, 7, 7, 8, 8, 8, 10, 10, 10, 10, 10, 10; 36:1, 2, 2, 3, 3, 4, 5, 6, 7, 7, 7, 8, 9, 9, 10, 10, 11, 11, 12, 12, 13, 13, 16, 16, 16, 16, 17, 17, 17, 19, 19, 21, 22, 22, 22; 37:1, 1, 1, 2, 2, 2, 3, 3, 3, 4, 6, 7, 7, 7, 8, 9, 9, 11, 12, 12, 12, 13, 13, 14, 14, 15, 16, 17, 17, 17, 18, 19, 19, 22, 23, 23, 23, 24, 24, 24, 24, 24, 25, 25, 26, 27, 27, 27, 28, 28, 28, 28, 28, 29, 29, 29, 30, 30, 30, 30, 31, 31, 32, 34, 35, 36, 36, 36, 37, 37, 37, 37, 37, 38, 38, 38, 38; 38:1, 1, 1, 2, 3, 3, 5, 6, 6, 6, 6, 7, 9, 12, 15, 16, 16, 21; 39:1, 1, 2, 2, 2, 2, 2, 2, 3, 3, 3, 4, 6, 7, 7, 8; 40:2, 4, 4, 4, 4, 5, 5, 6, 6, 10, 10, 11, 11, 12, 12, 12, 14, 14, 14, 15, 16, 17, 17, 19, 19, 22, 22, 24, 24, 24, 26, 27, 27, 29, 30, 30, 31, 31, 31; 41:1, 2, 3, 4, 4, 5, 5, 6, 7, 7, 9, 9, 9, 11, 11, 12, 12, 14, 14, 15, 15, 16, 16, 16, 16, 17, 17, 17, 18, 18, 19, 19, 19, 20, 20, 20, 20, 22, 22, 23, 24, 25, 25, 25, 26, 27, 28, 28, 29; 42:3, 4, 5, 5, 5, 6, 6, 6, 7, 8, 9, 10, 10, 10, 11, 12, 14, 14, 14, 15, 15, 15, 16, 16, 16, 18, 19, 21, 22, 22, 22, 22, 23, 24, 25, 25, 25; 43:1, 2, 3, 4, 4, 5, 6, 6, 8, 9, 9, 9, 10, 10, 10, 11, 12, 12, 13, 13, 14, 14, 16, 17, 17, 19, 20, 20, 25, 27, 28, 28; 44:1, 2, 9, 9, 11, 11, 12, 12, 12, 12, 13, 13, 14, 14, 14, 14, 15, 15, 15, 15, 16, 16, 17, 17, 17, 18, 18, 19, 19, 21, 22, 23, 24, 25, 25, 26, 26, 27, 28, 28; 45:1, 1, 2, 2, 3, 4, 5, 6, 6, 7, 7, 8, 8, 8, 11, 11, 12, 12, 12, 13, 13, 14, 14, 14, 14, 16, 18, 20, 20, 21, 21, 22, 23, 24, 24, 25, 25, 26, 26, 27, 28, 28; 46:1, 3, 4, 4, 4, 4, 5, 5, 6, 6, 6, 7, 7, 8, 9, 9, 10, 10, 13, 13; 47:1, 1, 2, 3, 5, 6, 7, 8, 9, 9, 10, 10, 10, 11, 11, 12, 13; 48:1, 1, 2, 3, 3, 3, 4, 4, 5, 5, 6, 6, 7, 8, 9, 11, 12, 13, 14, 14, 15, 16, 16, 18, 19, 21, 21; 49:1, 2, 2, 3, 4, 4, 5, 6, 6, 7, 7, 7, 8, 8, 8, 9, 11, 11, 12, 12, 12, 13, 13, 14, 17, 18, 18, 18, 19, 19, 21, 21, 21, 21, 22, 22, 23, 23, 23, 23, 25, 25, 26, 26, 26; 50:1, 2, 3, 5, 6, 6, 9, 10, 11; 51:1, 2, 2, 2, 3, 3, 3, 3, 4, 4, 5, 5, 6, 6, 6, 6, 8, 8, 9, 11, 11, 11, 11, 11, 12, 13, 13, 13, 14, 16, 16, 16, 16, 17, 17, 19, 19, 19, 21, 22, 23, 23; 52:1, 2, 3, 4, 5, 10, 12, 13, 13, 14, 15; 53:1, 2, 2, 3, 3, 3, 4, 4, 4, 5, 7, 7, 8, 8, 9, 9, 10, 10, 12, 12, 12, 12; 54:1, 2, 2, 3, 3, 4, 5, 6, 6, 10, 11, 13, 14, 16, 16, 17, 17; 55:1, 1, 1, 1, 2, 2, 2, 3, 3, 3, 4, 5, 5, 7, 7, 7, 7, 9, 9, 10, 10, 10, 10, 11, 12, 12, 12, 13, 13; 56:1, 1, 2, 2, 4, 4, 4, 5, 5, 6, 6, 6, 7, 7, 11, 12, 12, 12; 57:1, 1, 3, 4, 7, 8, 8, 8, 9, 9, 9, 9, 11, 11, 12, 13, 14, 15, 15, 15, 15, 16, 17, 17, 17, 18, 18, 18, 19, 19, 19, 20; 58:1, 1, 2, 2, 3, 3, 3, 4, 4, 5, 5, 6, 6, 7, 7, 8, 8, 9, 9, 9, 10, 10, 10, 11, 11, 11, 11, 12, 12; 59:2, 3, 4, 4, 5, 5, 6, 7, 7, 8, 8, 10, 11, 12, 12, 12, 13, 13, 13, 14, 14, 14, 15, 15, 16, 16, 16, 17, 17, 17, 19, 20, 20, 21, 21; 60:1, 2, 2, 3, 3, 4, 4, 5, 5, 5, 6, 6, 6, 7, 9, 9, 9, 10, 10, 11, 12, 13, 13, 14, 14, 16, 16, 16, 16, 17, 17, 17, 17, 18, 19, 20, 22; 61:1, 2, 4, 4, 5, 5, 5, 5, 6, 7, 8, 8, 9, 9, 10, 11, 11; 62:1, 1, 2, 2, 3, 4, 4, 5, 7, 7, 8, 8, 9, 9, 11, 12, 12; 63:2, 3, 3, 3, 3, 4, 5, 5, 5, 6, 6, 6, 7, 7, 7, 9, 9, 9, 10, 10, 11, 15, 15, 15, 16, 16, 17; 64:5, 5, 6, 6, 6, 7, 8, 8, 11, 11, 12; 65:3, 4, 4, 7, 7, 8, 9, 9, 9, 10, 10, 11, 12, 12, 14, 15, 15, 16, 16, 17, 17, 18, 18, 19, 19, 19, 21, 21, 21, 21, 22, 22, 23, 24, 24, 25, 25, 25; 66:1, 1, 2, 2, 2, 3, 4, 4, 5, 9, 9, 10, 11, 11, 12, 12, 13, 14, 14, 14,

14, 15, 15, 16, 16, 17, 17, 17, 18, 18, 18, 18, 19, 19, 19, 19, 20, 20, 20, 20, 21, 21, 22, 22, 23, 23, 24, 24, 24;

Jer 1:5, 5, 7, 9, 9, 10, 10, 10, 10, 11, 13, 13, 13, 15, 15, 15, 16, 16, 16, 17, 17, 18, 18, 18, 19; 2:2, 3, 4, 5, 5, 6, 6, 7, 7, 8, 8, 8, 9, 10, 10, 10, 10, 12, 13, 15, 15, 16, 18, 19, 19, 19, 19, 20, 20, 20, 22, 25, 25, 26, 26, 27, 27, 27, 37, 37; 3:1, 1, 2, 2, 2, 3, 3, 5, 6, 6, 6, 7, 7, 8, 8, 9, 9, 9, 10, 11, 12, 12, 12, 12, 13, 13, 14, 14, 14, 15, 15, 16, 16, 17, 18, 19, 19, 19, 21, 21, 22, 23, 24, 24, 25, 25, 25; 4:1, 2, 2, 2, 2, 3, 3, 4, 4, 5, 5, 5, 6, 7, 7, 8, 8, 9, 9, 9, 10, 11, 13, 15, 16, 18, 20, 21, 21, 22, 23, 23, 24, 25, 25, 25; 4:1, 2, 2, 2, 3, 3, 4, 4, 5, 5, 5, 6, 7, 7, 8, 8, 9, 9, 9, 10, 11, 13, 15, 16, 18, 20, 21, 21; 5:1, 1, 1, 1, 2, 5, 5, 5, 6, 6, 7, 7, 9, 9, 10, 10, 11, 13, 14, 14, 17, 17, 17, 17, 17, 19, 19, 20, 21, 21, 21, 22, 23, 23, 24, 24, 25, 27, 28, 30, 31, 31; 6:1, 1, 1, 2, 4, 5, 5, 6, 7, 7, 10, 10, 10, 11, 11, 12, 12, 13, 16, 16, 16, 18, 20, 21, 21, 21, 22, 23, 23, 23, 24, 25, 26, 27, 27, 28; 7:2, 2, 3, 3, 5, 5, 6, 6, 7, 9, 9, 10, 10, 12, 13, 13, 13, 14, 14, 15, 17, 18, 18, 18, 20, 20, 20, 20, 20, 21, 22, 23, 23, 24, 24, 24, 28, 29, 29, 29, 31, 31, 33, 33, 33, 34, 34, 34; 8:1, 1, 1, 1, 2, 2, 2, 2, 2, 2, 2, 3, 4, 4, 6, 7, 7, 8, 8, 9, 10, 13, 14, 14, 14, 15, 15, 16, 16, 17, 19, 20; 9:1, 1, 2, 3, 3, 4, 4, 5, 5, 5, 7, 10, 10, 10, 11, 11, 11, 12, 12, 13, 13, 14, 14, 15, 16, 17, 17, 18, 18, 18, 20, 20, 20, 21, 21, 22, 22, 24, 24, 26, 26, 26, 26, 26; 10:2, 4, 4, 6, 7, 8, 9, 9, 9, 10, 10, 11, 11, 12, 13, 13, 14, 15, 16, 18, 19, 20, 20, 20, 21, 21, 22, 22, 25, 25, 25, 25; 11:2, 2, 3, 4, 4, 5, 5, 6, 6, 7, 9, 9, 10, 10, 11, 12, 12, 13, 15, 16, 16, 17, 18, 18, 19, 19, 20, 22, 23; 12:2, 3, 3, 4, 4, 5, 5, 6, 11, 13, 14, 15, 15, 15, 15, 16, 17; 13:1, 1, 2, 3, 4, 4, 5, 6, 6, 7, 7, 9, 10, 10, 11, 11, 11, 11, 12, 13, 13, 14, 14, 15, 16, 16, 16, 17, 17, 18, 19, 20, 21, 22, 25, 27, 27; 14:2, 2, 3, 3, 3, 5, 6, 8, 9, 10, 12, 12, 12, 12, 14, 14, 14, 15, 15, 16, 16, 16, 17, 17, 18, 19, 19, 19, 19, 20; 15:1, 1, 2, 2, 2, 2, 3, 3, 3, 3, 3, 4, 6, 7, 8, 9, 9, 10, 11, 12, 12, 13, 13, 14, 14, 14, 16, 16, 16, 16, 17, 18, 18, 19, 19, 20, 20, 21, 21; 16:3, 3, 3, 4, 4, 5, 5, 6, 8, 9, 9, 9, 10, 11, 11, 11, 11, 12, 13, 13, 14, 14, 14; 17:1, 1, 2, 3, 3, 4, 4, 5, 5, 6, 6, 7, 8, 8, 8, 9, 10, 10, 11, 11, 13, 13, 15, 15, 16, 16, 16, 16, 18, 18, 18, 19, 19, 19, 19, 20, 21, 21; 17:1, 2, 3, 4, 4, 5, 6, 6, 7, 7, 8, 8, 8, 9, 10, 11, 11, 13, 13, 14, 14, 14, 18, 19, 19; 19, 20, 20, 20, 21, 24, 25, 25, 25, 26, 26, 26, 26, 26, 26, 26, 26, 26, 27; 18:2, 2, 3, 4, 7, 7, 7, 9, 9, 11, 11, 11, 12, 12, 15, 16, 16, 17, 18, 18, 18, 19, 20, 21, 21, 21, 22; 19:1, 1, 1, 2, 2, 3, 3, 4, 4, 4, 7, 7, 7, 7, 7, 8, 8, 9, 9, 9, 9, 11, 11, 12, 12, 13, 13, 13, 14, 14, 15; 20:2, 3, 4, 4, 4, 4, 4, 5, 5, 5, 5, 5, 6, 6, 6, 6, 6, 7, 7, 8, 8, 9, 9, 10, 10, 10, 11, 12, 12, 16, 16, 16, 17, 18; 21:1, 4, 4, 5, 5, 5, 5, 6, 6, 7, 7, 7, 7, 7, 8, 8, 9, 9, 9, 9, 10, 10, 11, 12, 12, 13, 14, 14; 22:1, 2, 2, 3, 3, 3, 4, 4, 6, 6, 7, 7, 7, 8, 8, 9, 9, 12, 13, 13, 14, 14, 14, 15, 15, 15, 15, 16, 17, 17, 17, 19, 20, 20, 20, 22, 25, 25, 25, 26, 28, 30; 23:1, 2, 2, 3, 3, 3, 3, 4, 4, 5, 5, 5, 5, 6, 6, 6, 8, 8, 9, 9, 10, 10, 11, 12, 13, 14, 14, 15, 16, 17, 18, 18, 20, 22, 22, 23, 24, 28, 29, 31, 32, 32, 33, 34, 34, 34, 34, 35, 35, 36, 37, 38, 39, 39, 39, 40, 40; 24:1, 1, 1, 2, 3, 3, 6, 6, 6, 6, 7, 7, 7, 8, 8, 8, 8, 9, 9, 9, 10; 25:2, 3, 3, 3, 4, 4, 4, 5, 5, 5, 6, 6, 8, 9, 9, 9, 9, 10, 10, 10, 11, 11, 12, 12, 12, 12, 13, 14, 14, 15, 15, 16, 16, 17, 18, 19, 20, 20, 21, 21, 22, 22, 23, 23, 23, 23; 27:2, 2, 3, 3, 3, 3, 4, 5, 5, 5, 6, 6, 6, 7, 7, 7, 7, 8, 8, 8, 8, 10, 10, 10, 11, 11, 11, 12, 13, 13, 13, 14, 15, 15, 15, 16, 16, 17, 18, 18, 18, 19, 20, 20, 21, 22, 22, 22; 28:1, 1, 1, 3, 4, 5, 6, 7, 8, 8, 8, 8, 10, 11, 11, 13, 14, 14; 29:1, 1, 1, 2, 2, 2, 2, 3, 5, 5, 5, 6, 6, 6, 6, 6, 7, 7, 8, 10, 11, 12, 12, 13, 13, 14, 14, 14, 14, 14, 14, 16, 17, 18, 18, 18, 18, 18, 19, 21, 21, 22, 23, 23, 23, 25, 25, 26, 26, 26, 28, 28, 28, 29, 31, 31, 32; 30:3, 3, 4, 4, 5, 6, 6, 8, 9, 9, 10, 10, 11, 12, 16, 16, 16, 17, 18, 18, 18, 19, 19, 19, 19, 20, 20, 21, 21, 21, 22, 22, 24; 31:1, 4, 4, 5, 6, 7, 7, 8, 8, 8, 9, 9, 9, 10, 11, 12, 12, 12, 12, 12, 12, 13, 13, 13, 14, 14, 15, 16, 17, 18, 18, 19, 21, 21, 22, 23, 23, 23, 25, 26, 26, 28, 28, 28, 29, 31, 31, 32; 32:1, 1, 4, 5, 6, 7, 8, 8, 8, 8, 10, 10, 12, 16, 16, 16, 17, 18, 18, 18, 19, 19, 19, 19, 20, 20, 20, 21, 21, 21, 22, 24; 31:1, 4, 4, 5, 6, 7, 8, 8, 8, 8, 10, 11, 12, 12, 12, 13, 13, 14, 16, 17, 18, 19, 23, 23, 24, 24, 24, 25, 26, 26, 27, 28, 28, 28, 28, 29, 31, 31, 32; 30:3, 3, 4, 4, 5, 6, 6, 8, 9, 9, 9, 10, 10, 11, 11, 12, 13, 14, 15, 15, 17, 17, 17, 18, 19, 19, 20, 20, 20, 20, 21, 21, 22, 22, 23; 33:3, 4, 4, 4, 5, 6, 6, 6, 7, 10, 10, 11, 13, 14, 14, 16, 18, 19, 20, 20, 20, 21, 21, 21, 22, 22, 23, 24, 24, 24, 25, 28, 28, 29, 29, 29, 29, 29, 30, 31, 32, 32, 32, 32, 33, 33, 33,

33, 35, 35, 36, 36, 36, 37, 37, 37, 37, 38, 38, 39, 39, 39, 40, 41, 41, 43, 44, 44, 44, 44, 44, 44, 44, 44; 33:3, 3, 4, 6, 6, 6, 7, 7, 7, 8, 8, 9, 9, 9, 10, 10, 10, 10, 10, 11, 11, 11, 12, 12, 13, 13, 13, 14, 14, 15, 15, 15, 16, 16, 18, 18, 19, 20, 20, 20, 20, 21, 22, 25, 25, 25, 26, 26, 26; 34:1, 1, 1, 2, 2, 2, 3, 3, 3, 3, 5, 5, 7, 7, 9, 10, 10, 10, 11, 11, 11, 11, 14, 14, 15, 15, 15, 16, 16, 16, 16, 17, 17, 17, 18, 18, 19, 19, 19, 20, 20, 20, 21, 22; 35:2, 2, 2, 3, 3, 3, 4, 5, 5, 10, 10, 10, 11, 11, 13, 13, 14, 15, 15, 15, 15, 15, 17, 18, 18, 18; 36:1, 2, 2, 3, 3, 4, 5, 5, 6, 6, 6, 7, 7, 8, 8, 9, 9, 10, 11, 13, 13, 14, 16, 17, 18, 18, 19, 20, 20, 20, 21, 21, 21, 22, 23, 23, 25, 26, 27, 28, 29, 29, 29, 30, 30, 31, 31, 31, 31, 32, 32; 37:1, 3, 3, 4, 5, 5, 6, 8, 10, 11, 13, 14, 15, 15, 15, 16, 18, 18, 19, 20; 38:1, 1, 1, 2, 2, 4, 6, 6, 6, 8, 9, 10, 12, 13, 14, 14, 14, 15, 16, 17, 17, 17, 17, 18, 18, 19, 20, 22, 22, 22, 22, 23, 23, 24, 25, 25, 26, 27, 27, 28; 39:1, 1, 2, 3, 3, 4, 4, 4, 5, 5, 6, 7, 7, 8, 8, 9, 10, 11, 11, 11, 12, 12, 13, 14, 14, 15, 15, 15; 41:1, 1, 2, 2, 3, 3, 4, 4, 5, 5, 6, 7, 7, 7, 8, 9, 10, 11, 12, 12, 13, 14, 15, 15, 15, 17; 42:1, 1, 2, 3, 4, 5, 5, 7, 7, 9, 10, 10, 10, 11, 11, 11, 12, 12, 13, 14, 14, 14, 15, 15, 16, 16, 17, 17, 17, 18; 43:1, 2, 2, 3, 4, 5, 5, 6, 6, 6, 6, 9, 9, 10, 10, 11, 11, 12, 12, 12, 12, 13; 44:1, 1, 1, 1, 2, 2, 3, 4, 6, 6, 6, 6, 7, 7, 8, 8, 9, 9, 9, 10, 11, 12, 12, 12, 13, 14, 15, 17, 17, 17, 18, 18, 18, 19, 19, 20, 22, 23, 25, 25, 26, 27, 27, 27, 28, 29, 30, 30, 30, 30, 30; 45:3, 4, 5; 46:3, 3, 4, 4, 5, 5, 6, 7, 7, 8, 9, 9, 9, 9, 9, 10, 10, 11, 12, 12, 13, 14, 14, 14, 16, 16, 18, 19, 21, 21, 22, 23, 25, 25, 25, 26, 26, 26, 27, 27, 27, 27, 27, 27, 28; 47:2, 2, 2, 2, 2, 3, 4, 4, 4, 6, 7; 48:1, 1, 2, 3, 6, 7, 7, 7, 8, 8, 9, 9, 10, 11, 11, 11, 11, 12, 12, 13, 14, 15, 15, 16, 17, 18, 18, 19, 19, 20, 20, 20, 21, 21, 22, 22, 23, 23, 24, 24, 25, 26, 28, 28, 29, 29, 31, 32, 32, 32, 33, 33, 33, 35, 36, 36, 36, 37, 37, 37, 38, 38, 39, 40, 41, 41, 42, 42, 43, 43, 44, 44, 44, 45, 45, 46; 49:1, 2, 2, 3, 3, 3, 5, 5, 6, 10, 10, 10, 10, 11, 12, 13, 13, 14, 14, 15, 16, 17, 18, 18, 19, 19, 20, 20, 22, 23, 24, 24, 25, 26, 27, 27, 28, 28, 29, 29, 29, 30, 32, 32, 32, 33, 33, 33, 34, 34, 34, 35, 35, 37, 37, 37, 38, 38, 38, 38; 50:1, 2, 2, 3, 3, 4, 4, 4, 4, 5, 7, 8, 8, 9, 9, 10, 11, 12, 13, 16, 16, 17, 17, 19, 19, 19, 20, 20, 20, 21, 21, 22, 24, 24, 24, 25, 26, 28, 28, 30, 32, 32, 32, 33, 34, 35, 35, 35, 36, 36, 37, 37, 37, 37, 38, 39, 40, 41, 41, 42, 42, 43, 43, 44, 44, 44, 44, 45, 46; 51:1, 2, 2, 3, 3, 4, 6, 8, 9, 9, 10, 12, 13, 14, 15, 16, 16, 17, 19, 20, 21, 21, 21, 22, 22, 22, 23, 23, 23, 23, 24, 24, 25, 25, 26, 27, 28, 28, 29, 29, 31, 32, 32, 33, 35, 35, 36, 36, 36, 37, 37, 39, 39, 41, 43, 44, 44, 44, 45, 46, 46, 46, 47, 47, 48, 50, 52, 53, 54, 54, 55, 57, 57, 57, 57, 57, 58, 58, 58, 58, 59, 61, 61, 61, 63, 63, 64, 64, 64, 64; 52:1, 1, 1, 2, 3, 4, 4, 4, 6, 7, 7, 7, 8, 8, 9, 10, 11, 11, 13, 13, 13, 13, 14, 15, 15, 15, 16, 16, 17, 17, 18, 18, 18, 18, 19, 19, 19, 19, 19, 20, 21, 21, 22, 22, 23, 24, 24, 25, 26, 27, 27, 28, 28, 29, 30, 30, 31, 31, 31, 32, 32, 33, 34;

La 1:1, 2, 3, 4, 6, 6, 7, 7, 8, 11, 12, 13, 14, 17, 18, 18, 19, 21, 22, 22; 2:1, 1, 2, 2, 3, 4, 5, 5, 6, 6, 6, 6, 8, 8, 9, 9, 10, 11, 12, 14, 14, 14, 14, 15, 15, 16, 17, 17, 18, 20, 20, 20, 21, 21, 21, 22; 3:2, 4, 5, 5, 8, 10, 11, 12, 14, 17, 18, 18, 19, 19, 20, 26, 28, 37, 38, 40, 40, 42, 43, 45, 47, 47, 49, 50, 53, 60, 61, 62, 63, 66; 4:4, 6, 11, 11, 12, 12, 13, 15, 21, 21; 5:1, 3, 5, 6, 7, 7, 11, 13, 20, 21

Eze 1:1, 3, 4, 4, 4, 4, 4, 5, 6, 6, 7, 7, 8, 8, 8, 10, 11, 11, 12, 12, 13, 13, 13, 14, 14, 16, 16, 16, 16, 17, 18, 19, 19, 20, 21, 21, 22, 23, 23, 23, 24, 25, 25, 26, 27, 27, 27, 28, 28; 2:1, 1, 2, 2, 3, 3, 4, 4, 5, 6, 6, 6, 7, 8, 9, 9, 10, 10, 10, 10, 10; 3:1, 2, 3, 3, 3, 4, 4, 5, 6, 7, 8, 10, 11, 11, 11, 12, 13, 13, 14, 14, 15, 15, 16, 17, 18, 18, 18, 19, 20, 20, 20, 21, 22, 22, 23, 23, 24, 24, 24, 25, 25, 26, 26, 26, 27, 27; 4:1, 1, 2, 2, 2, 2, 3, 3, 3, 3, 3, 4, 5, 6, 7, 8, 8, 9, 9, 9, 9, 9, 9, 9, 9, 10, 12, 12, 13, 15, 16, 17; 5:1, 1, 1, 1, 2, 2, 3, 4, 4, 5, 6, 6, 6, 6, 8, 9, 9, 10, 10, 11, 12, 12, 13, 13, 14, 15, 15, 15, 16, 16, 16, 17, 17, 17; 6:1, 2, 3, 3, 3, 3, 3, 4, 4, 5, 5, 6, 6, 6, 7, 8, 9, 9, 9, 10, 11, 11, 11, 11, 11, 12, 12, 13, 14, 14; 7:3, 3, 4, 4, 4, 7, 8, 8, 8, 9, 9, 15, 15, 15, 15, 16, 17, 18, 18, 19, 19, 20, 21, 21, 22, 22, 23,

24, 24, 25, 25, 26, 26, 27, 27, 27; 8:1, 1, 2, 2, 3, 3, 3, 3, 4, 5, 6, 7, 8, 9, 9, 10, 10, 10, 10, 11, 11, 11, 13, 14, 15, 16, 16, 16, 16, 16, 16, 16, 17, 17, 18; 9:2, 2, 2, 2, 3, 4, 4, 4, 4, 5, 5, 6, 7, 7, 7, 8, 8, 8, 9, 9, 9, 10; 10:1, 2, 2, 2, 3, 4, 4, 4, 5, 6, 6, 7, 7, 7, 8, 9, 9, 10, 12, 12, 12, 12, 12, 14, 14, 14, 14, 16, 17, 18, 18, 19, 19, 19, 20, 20, 20, 21, 22, 22; 11:1, 1, 1, 1, 2, 3, 5, 5, 6, 7, 8, 9, 9, 9, 10, 12, 13, 13, 13, 15, 16, 17, 17, 18, 19, 19, 19, 20, 20, 20, 20, 20, 21, 22, 22, 23, 23, 24; 12:2, 2, 3, 3, 4, 4, 5, 6, 7, 7, 7, 8, 10, 11, 12, 13, 13, 14, 14, 14, 15, 15, 16, 16, 18, 19, 19, 20, 20, 22, 23, 23, 25, 25, 27; 13:1, 2, 3, 6, 6, 6, 7, 8, 8, 9, 9, 10, 10, 10, 11, 13, 13, 14, 14, 14, 14, 15, 15, 16, 16, 17, 18, 18, 18, 18, 19, 19, 19, 20, 20, 21, 21, 22, 23; 14:1, 2, 3, 4, 4, 4, 6, 6, 7, 7, 7, 8, 8, 8, 8, 9, 9, 9, 10, 11, 13, 13, 13, 14, 15, 17, 17, 19, 19, 20, 21, 21, 21, 21, 22, 22, 22, 23, 23; 15:1, 4, 5, 7, 7, 7, 8; 16:3, 3, 3, 4, 6, 6, 7, 7, 7, 7, 8, 8, 8, 8, 8, 9, 10, 10, 10, 11, 11, 12, 12, 13, 13, 13, 13, 13, 13, 13, 13, 14, 15, 15, 16, 16, 16, 17, 17, 17, 18, 18, 18, 18, 19, 19, 19, 20, 20, 21, 22, 22, 22, 23, 24, 25, 25, 26, 27, 27, 28, 29, 31, 31, 33, 34, 34, 34, 36, 36, 36, 37, 37, 38, 38, 38, 38, 39, 39, 39, 39, 40, 40, 41, 41, 41, 41, 42, 42, 42, 43, 43, 45, 45, 45, 45, 45, 46, 46, 46, 46, 46, 48, 49, 49, 49, 50, 50, 51, 52, 53, 53, 53, 54, 55, 55, 55, 55, 57, 58, 60, 61, 61, 61, 62, 62, 63, 63; 17:1, 2, 3, 3, 4, 5, 5, 6, 6, 6, 6, 7, 7, 7, 7, 8, 9, 10, 12, 13, 13, 15, 15, 16, 17, 17, 18, 19, 20, 20, 20, 20, 21, 21, 22, 22, 22, 23, 23, 23, 23, 24, 24, 24; 18:1, 2, 5, 6, 6, 7, 7, 8, 9, 10, 11, 11, 12, 12, 13, 14, 14, 16, 18, 19, 19, 19, 20, 21, 21, 21, 23, 23, 24, 24, 24, 26, 26, 27, 27, 28, 30, 31, 31, 32; 19:2, 3, 4, 5, 5, 6, 6, 6, 7, 7, 7, 8, 9, 9, 10, 11, 11, 12, 12, 13, 13, 14, 14; 20:1, 1, 3, 5, 5, 5, 6, 7, 8, 9, 10, 11, 12, 13, 13, 14, 15, 16, 17, 17, 18, 19, 20, 20, 21, 21, 22, 23, 24, 24, 25, 26, 27, 28, 28, 29, 30, 32, 32, 33, 33, 34, 34, 34, 34, 35, 37, 37, 38, 38, 39, 39, 40, 40, 41, 41, 42, 42, 42, 43, 44, 45, 45, 45, 46, 46, 47, 47, 47, 49, 49, 49; 24:3, 3, 3, 4, 5, 5, 5, 6, 10, 10, 11, 11, 12, 13, 14, 14, 17, 17, 17, 17, 18, 18, 19, 21, 22, 23, 23, 24, 25, 25, 27, 27, 27, 27; 25:2, 3, 3, 3, 4, 4, 4, 5, 5, 6, 6, 6, 7, 7, 7, 7, 7, 8, 9, 10, 11, 11, 12, 12, 13, 13, 13, 13, 14, 14, 14, 15, 16, 16, 16, 17, 17; 26:1, 3, 4, 4, 4, 4, 5, 6, 6, 7, 7, 7, 7, 8, 8, 8, 9, 9, 10, 11, 12, 12, 12, 16, 17, 17, 19, 20, 20, 21; 27:3, 7, 8, 9, 10, 10, 10, 11, 12, 13, 13, 14, 14, 15, 16, 16, 16, 16, 17, 17, 17, 18, 18, 19, 19, 19, 21, 21, 22, 22, 23, 23, 23, 24, 24, 25, 25, 27, 27, 27, 29, 29, 30, 30, 31, 31, 32, 32, 34, 35, 36; 28:2, 2, 4, 4, 4, 5, 5, 7, 7, 8, 9, 12, 13, 13, 13, 13, 14, 14, 16, 16, 18, 19, 21, 22, 22, 22, 23, 23, 23, 24, 24, 25, 26, 26, 26, 26; 29:2, 2, 3, 3, 4, 4, 4, 5, 5, 5, 6, 7, 7, 7, 8, 8, 9, 9, 10, 10, 12, 12, 14, 14, 14, 16, 17, 18, 18, 19, 19, 19, 20, 21; 30:2, 4, 4, 4, 4, 5, 5, 5, 5, 5, 6, 7, 7, 8, 8, 9, 11, 11, 11, 12, 12, 12, 13, 13, 13, 14, 14, 14, 15, 15, 16, 16, 16, 17, 17, 18, 18, 19, 20, 21, 22, 22, 22, 23, 23, 24, 24, 25, 25, 26, 26; 31:1, 2, 3, 3, 3, 4, 5, 5, 6, 6, 6, 8, 10, 10, 12, 12, 12, 13, 13, 15, 15, 16, 16, 17, 17, 18; 32:1, 2, 2, 2, 2, 2, 3, 3, 4, 4, 4, 5, 5, 6, 6, 7, 7, 7, 7, 8, 8, 9, 9, 10, 10, 10, 10, 11, 13, 13, 14, 14, 16, 18, 19, 20, 22, 22, 23, 24, 26, 26, 27, 27, 28, 29, 30, 30, 31, 31, 32; 33:2, 2, 3, 4, 4, 5, 6, 6, 6, 7, 10, 10, 11, 13, 14, 14, 16, 18, 19, 19, 21, 22, 22, 24, 25, 25, 26, 26, 27, 27, 27, 28, 30, 30, 30, 31, 31, 32, 32, 33; 34:1, 2, 3, 4, 4, 5, 5, 6, 6, 8, 9, 10, 11, 12, 12, 13, 13, 13, 14, 14, 15, 16, 16, 16, 16, 17, 17, 17, 18, 19, 20, 21, 21, 22, 22, 23, 23, 24, 25, 25, 25, 25, 26, 27, 27, 27, 28, 28, 29, 30, 31; 35:2, 3, 3, 3, 4, 4, 5, 6, 7, 7, 8, 8, 9, 9, 10, 11, 11, 12, 13, 15, 15; 36:1, 3, 3, 3, 4, 4, 4, 5, 6, 6, 6, 8, 9, 9, 10, 10, 11, 11, 11, 11, 12, 12, 13, 13, 13, 14, 16, 19, 19, 20, 23, 23, 24, 24, 25, 26, 26, 26, 27, 27, 27, 28, 28, 29, 29, 30, 30, 30, 31, 31, 32,

(entries continue)

Idx

35, 35, 35, 35, 36, 36, 38; 37:1, 1, 2, 2, 2, 3, 4, 5, 6, 6, 6, 6, 6, 6, 7, 7, 7, 8, 8, 8, 9, 9, 10, 10, 10, 11, 12, 12, 13, 13, 14, 14, 14, 14, 16, 16, 16, 16, 17, 17, 18, 19, 19, 19, 19, 20, 21, 21, 22, 22, 22, 23, 23, 24, 24, 24, 24, 25, 25, 25, 25, 26, 26, 26, 27, 28; 38:1, 2, 2, 3, 3, 4, 4, 4, 4, 4, 4, 5, 5, 6, 6, 6, 7, 7, 7, 8, 8, 9, 9, 10, 11, 11, 12, 12, 12, 13, 13, 13, 14, 15, 15, 15, 16, 16, 18, 19, 20, 20, 20, 20, 20, 20, 20, 21, 22, 22, 22, 22, 22, 22, 23, 23, 23; 39:1, 1, 2, 2, 2, 2, 2, 3, 3, 4, 4, 4, 6, 6, 6, 7, 7, 8, 9, 9, 9, 9, 9, 9, 10, 10, 11, 11, 11, 11, 11, 11, 12, 13, 14, 15, 16, 17, 17, 17, 17, 18, 18, 19, 19, 20, 20, 21, 21, 21, 22, 23, 23, 24, 24, 25, 25, 26, 26, 27, 27, 28; 40:1, 1, 2, 3, 3, 3, 4, 4, 5, 5, 5, 6, 6, 6, 7, 7, 7, 7, 9, 9, 10, 10, 10, 16, 16, 17, 17, 18, 19, 20, 20, 21, 21, 21, 21, 21, 21, 22, 22, 22, 22, 23, 23, 24, 24, 24, 25, 25, 25, 25, 26, 26, 26, 27, 27, 28, 28, 29, 29, 29, 29, 30, 30, 30, 31, 31, 31, 32, 32, 33, 33, 33, 33, 33, 33, 33, 34, 34, 34, 34, 35, 35, 36, 36, 36, 36, 37, 37, 37, 38, 38, 39, 39, 39, 40, 40, 41, 42, 42, 42, 42, 42, 42, 43, 43, 44, 44, 45, 46, 47, 47, 48, 48, 48, 48, 48, 49, 49, 49, 49; 41:1, 1, 2, 2, 2, 2, 2, 3, 3, 4, 4, 5, 6, 6, 6, 7, 7, 7, 9, 10, 11, 11, 11, 12, 12, 13, 13, 13, 14, 14, 15, 15, 16, 16, 16, 16, 17, 17, 17, 18, 18, 18, 19, 20, 20, 20, 20, 21, 22, 23, 23, 24, 24, 25, 25, 25, 26, 26, 26, 26, 26; 42:1, 1, 2, 3, 4, 4, 5, 6, 7, 8, 9, 10, 11, 11, 11, 11, 12, 12, 13, 13, 13, 14, 14, 15, 16, 17, 18, 19, 20, 20; 43:2, 2, 2, 3, 3, 4, 5, 5, 6, 6, 7, 7, 7, 8, 8, 8, 9, 9, 10, 11, 11, 11, 11, 11, 11, 11, 11, 11, 11, 11, 11, 13, 13, 13, 13, 14, 14, 14, 14, 15, 16, 17, 17, 17, 17, 17, 18, 18, 18, 19, 20, 20, 20, 20, 20, 21, 22, 22, 23, 24, 24, 24, 24, 25, 25, 25; 44:1, 2, 3, 4, 4, 5, 5, 5, 5, 6, 7, 7, 7, 8, 8, 10, 11, 11, 11, 12, 12, 13, 13, 14, 15, 15, 16, 16, 17, 17, 18, 19, 19, 19, 19, 23, 23, 23, 24, 24, 24, 24, 25, 25, 26, 27, 28, 28, 29, 29, 29, 30, 30; 45:1, 1, 2, 3, 3, 3, 3, 3, 4, 4, 5, 5, 5, 6, 6, 6, 7, 7, 7, 7, 7, 7, 8, 8, 9, 9, 10, 10, 11, 11, 12, 12, 13, 15, 15, 15, 15, 17, 17, 17, 17, 17, 18, 19, 19, 19, 19, 20, 20, 22, 23, 23, 23, 24, 24, 24, 24, 25, 25; 46:1, 2, 2, 2, 2, 2, 3, 4, 4, 5, 5, 6, 6, 6, 7, 7, 7, 8, 8, 9, 10, 10, 11, 11, 11, 11, 12, 14, 14, 15, 15, 19, 20, 21, 21, 22, 23; 47:1, 1, 2, 2, 3, 3, 4, 4, 5, 6, 6, 7, 8, 8, 9, 9, 10, 11, 12, 12, 12, 14, 15, 16, 17, 17, 17, 18, 18, 19, 19, 19, 22, 22, 23; 48:1, 2, 3, 4, 5, 6, 7, 8, 8, 8, 9, 9, 10, 11, 13, 13, 13, 14, 14, 15, 15, 15, 16, 16, 16, 16, 16, 16, 17, 17, 17, 17, 18, 18, 18, 18, 19, 20, 20, 21, 21, 21, 21, 21, 21, 21, 21, 22, 22, 23, 24, 24, 24, 25, 25, 25; 46:1, 2, 2, 2, 3, 4, 4, 5, 5, 6, 6, 7, 7, 7, 8, 9, 9, 10, 10, 11, 11, 11, 11, 11, 12, 12, 14, 14, 15, 15, 19, 20, 21, 21, 22, 23; 47:1, 1, 2, 2, 3, 3, 4, 5, 6, 6, 7, 8, 8, 9, 9, 10, 11, 12, 12, 12, 14, 15, 16, 17, 17, 17, 18, 18, 19, 19, 22, 23; 48:1, 2, 3, 4, 5, 6, 7, 8, 8, 8, 9, 9, 10, 10, 10, 10, 10, 10, 12, 13, 13, 13, 13, 13, 14, 15, 15, 15, 15, 16, 16, 16, 16, 16, 16, 16, 16, 17, 17, 17, 17, 17, 18, 18, 18, 18, 19, 20, 20, 21, 21, 21, 21, 21, 21, 21, 22, 22, 23, 24, 24, 25, 25, 26, 27, 28, 29, 30, 31, 32, 32, 32, 32, 32, 33, 33, 33, 34, 35;

Da 1:1, 2, 2, 2, 3, 3, 4, 4, 4, 4, 5, 5, 6, 7, 7, 7, 9, 10, 10, 11, 12, 12, 13, 13, 14, 15, 15, 16, 16, 17, 17, 19, 19, 19, 19, 20, 20, 20, 21; 2:1, 1, 2, 2, 2, 2, 3, 3, 4, 5, 5, 6, 6, 6, 6, 6, 7, 7, 8, 9, 9, 10, 11, 11, 12, 12, 13, 13, 14, 15, 16, 16, 16, 17, 17, 18, 20, 20, 20, 21, 21, 21, 21, 22, 22, 23, 23, 23, 24, 24, 26, 26, 27, 28, 28, 29, 30, 31, 31, 32, 32, 32, 34, 34, 34, 35, 35, 35, 35, 36, 37, 37, 38, 38, 38, 39, 39, 40, 40, 40, 40, 41, 41, 41, 42, 42, 42, 43, 44, 44, 44, 45, 45, 45, 46, 46, 46, 47, 47, 47, 48, 48, 48, 49, 49; 3:1, 2, 2, 3, 3, 3, 4, 5, 5, 6, 6, 7, 7, 7, 8, 9, 10, 11, 12, 13, 13, 14, 14, 15, 15, 15, 15, 16, 16, 17, 19, 19, 20, 20, 20, 21, 21, 21, 22, 22, 23, 24, 24, 24, 26, 26, 27, 28, 28, 28, 28, 29, 29, 30; 4:1, 2, 3, 3, 4, 5, 5, 7, 7, 8, 8, 8, 9, 9, 10, 10, 11, 11, 11, 12, 12, 12, 12, 13, 13, 14, 14, 14, 14, 15, 15, 15, 16, 16, 16, 16, 17, 17, 17, 17, 18, 18, 18, 19, 20, 20, 20, 21, 21, 21, 22, 22, 23, 24, 24, 24, 25, 25, 25, 26, 26, 26, 26, 27, 28, 28, 29, 30, 31, 32, 32, 33, 33, 33, 34, 35, 35, 35, 35, 35, 36, 36, 36, 37, 37, 37; 5:1, 2, 2, 2, 3, 3, 3, 4, 4, 5, 6, 6, 7, 7, 7, 7, 7, 8, 8, 9, 9, 9, 10, 10, 10, 11, 11, 11, 11, 12, 12, 12, 14, 14, 15, 15, 16, 16, 16, 16, 17, 17, 18, 18, 18, 18, 19, 19, 19, 19, 20, 20, 20, 21, 21, 21, 22, 23, 23, 23, 23, 23, 23, 23, 23, 24, 24, 25, 26, 27, 28, 28, 28, 28, 29, 30; 6:1, 2, 3, 3, 4, 6, 6, 7, 7, 7, 8, 8, 9, 10, 10, 11, 11, 12, 12, 12, 13, 14, 14, 15, 15, 16, 16, 17, 17, 17, 17, 18, 18, 18, 19, 20, 22, 22, 23, 23, 24, 24, 24, 24, 25, 25, 26, 26, 26, 27, 27, 27, 27, 28; 7:1, 1, 2, 2, 3, 4, 4, 4, 4, 5, 5, 5, 6, 6, 7, 7, 7, 7, 7, 7, 7, 8, 8, 9, 9, 10, 10, 10, 10, 11, 11, 12, 12, 13, 13, 13, 14, 14, 14, 15, 16, 16, 18, 19, 19, 19, 20, 20, 21, 21, 22, 23, 23, 23, 24, 24, 25, 25, 26, 26, 27, 27, 27, 27, 27, 28; 8:2, 2, 2, 2, 3, 3, 3, 3, 4, 4, 4, 5, 5, 5, 6, 6, 7, 7, 7, 7, 7, 7, 7, 8, 8, 9, 9, 9, 10, 10, 10, 10, 11, 11, 12, 12, 13, 13, 14, 15, 15, 16, 16, 16, 16, 16, 17, 17, 17, 17, 18, 18, 18, 19, 19, 19, 19, 22, 23, 23, 23, 23, 23, 23, 23, 23, 24, 24, 25, 26, 27, 28, 28, 29, 29, 29, 31, 31; 6:1, 2, 2, 3, 3, 4, 6, 6, 7, 7, 7, 8, 8, 9, 10, 10, 11, 11, 12, 12, 12, 13, 14, 14, 15, 16, 16, 17, 17, 17, 17, 18, 18, 19, 20, 20, 22, 22, 23, 24, 24, 24, 24, 25, 25, 26, 26, 26, 26, 27, 27, 27, 28; 7:1, 1, 2, 2, 3, 4, 4, 4, 4, 5, 5, 5, 6, 6, 7, 7, 7, 7, 7, 7, 7, 7, 7, 8, 8, 9, 9, 10, 10, 10, 10, 10, 11, 12, 13, 13, 13, 14, 14, 14, 15, 16, 16, 18, 19, 19, 19, 20, 20, 21, 21, 22, 23, 23, 23, 24, 24, 25, 25, 26, 26, 27, 27, 27, 27, 27, 28; 8:2, 2, 2, 2, 3, 3, 3, 4, 4, 4, 5, 5, 5, 6, 6, 7, 7, 7, 7, 7, 7, 7, 8, 8, 9, 9, 10, 10, 10, 11, 11, 12, 12, 12, 14, 14, 15, 15, 16, 16, 16, 16, 16, 16, 17, 17, 17, 18, 19, 20, 20, 20, 24, 24, 24, 24, 25, 25, 25, 25, 26, 26, 26, 26, 27, 27, 27, 27, 28; 7:1, 1, 2, 2, 2, 3, 3, 4, 4, 4, 4, 4, 4, 5, 5, 5, 6, 6, 7, 7, 7, 7, 7, 7, 7, 7, 8, 8, 9, 9, 10, 10, 10, 10, 11, 11, 12, 12, 13, 13, 13, 14, 14, 14, 15, 16, 16, 18, 19, 19, 19, 20, 20, 21, 21, 22, 23, 23, 23, 24, 24, 25, 25, 26, 26, 27, 27, 27, 27, 27, 28;

16, 17, 17, 18, 19, 20, 21, 21, 23, 23, 24, 24, 24, 24, 24, 24, 25, 25, 25, 26, 26, 27, 27, 27, 27; 9:3, 3, 3, 3, 4, 4, 4, 4, 4, 4, 5, 5, 5, 5, 6, 6, 7, 7, 7, 8, 9, 11, 12, 12, 13, 13, 14, 15, 15, 16, 16, 16, 17, 17, 18, 18, 18, 18, 18, 19, 19, 20, 21, 21, 22, 22, 22, 22, 23, 23, 24, 24, 24, 24, 24, 24, 24, 24, 24, 25, 25, 25, 26, 26, 26, 26, 26, 27, 27; 10:1, 1, 1, 4, 4, 5, 5, 6, 6, 6, 6, 7, 8, 8, 8, 9, 9, 10, 10, 11, 11, 11, 12, 12, 13, 13, 15, 15, 16, 16, 16, 16, 18, 19, 19, 19, 20, 20, 21; 11:1, 2, 2, 2, 3, 3, 4, 4, 4, 5, 5, 5, 6, 6, 6, 6, 6, 7, 7, 7, 8, 8, 8, 9, 10, 10, 10, 10, 10, 10, 11, 11, 12, 12, 13, 13, 14, 15, 15, 16, 16, 16, 17, 17, 18, 19, 19, 21, 21, 22, 22, 22, 23, 24, 24, 24, 24, 24, 25, 25, 25, 26, 26, 26, 27, 27, 28, 28, 28, 29, 30, 30, 30, 31, 31, 31, 32, 32, 32, 33, 33, 33, 34, 34, 35, 35, 35, 35, 36, 36, 36, 38, 38, 38, 38, 39, 39, 40, 40, 40, 40, 41, 41, 42, 43, 43, 43, 44, 44, 45, 45; 12:1, 1, 1, 2, 3, 3, 3, 3, 4, 4, 4, 5, 5, 6, 6, 6, 6, 7, 7, 7, 7, 7, 7, 8, 9, 9, 10, 10, 10, 11, 11, 11, 12, 12, 12, 13;

Hos 1:1, 1, 2, 2, 2, 3, 3, 4, 4, 4, 5, 6, 6, 6, 7, 7, 7, 8, 9, 10, 11, 11, 11; 2:1, 2, 3, 3, 3, 3, 4, 5, 5, 5, 6, 7, 7, 7, 8, 8, 8, 9, 9, 9, 9, 10, 11, 12, 12, 12, 12, 13, 13, 13, 14, 14, 15, 15, 15, 15, 16, 16, 17, 18, 18, 18, 18, 18, 19, 19, 19, 20, 21, 21, 22, 22, 22, 23, 23, 23, 23; 3:1, 2, 2, 3, 3, 5, 5, 8, 9, 9, 9, 10, 10, 11, 11, 12, 12, 13, 13, 13, 13, 14, 15, 19; 5:1, 1, 1, 2, 3, 3, 4, 5, 5, 6, 8, 11, 12, 13, 13, 14, 14, 14, 15; 6:1, 1, 1, 2, 3, 3, 4, 5, 6, 6, 8, 9; 7:1, 1, 1, 2, 3, 7, 9, 10, 10, 14, 14, 15; 8:1, 4, 4, 7, 10, 13, 13, 14, 14, 14; 9:2, 2, 3, 5, 7, 8, 10, 10, 11, 14, 17; 10:5, 6, 8, 8, 8, 10, 11, 11, 11, 12, 14; 11:1, 2, 4, 4, 6, 6, 6, 7, 9, 9, 11, 11, 12; 12:1, 1, 1, 1, 2, 3, 4, 4, 4, 6, 9, 9, 10, 10, 12, 12, 12, 13, 13, 14; 13:2, 2, 2, 14:2, 2, 5, 6, 6, 7, 8, 9, 9, 9

Joel 1:2, 3, 3, 4, 4, 5, 5, 6, 6, 7, 7, 9, 11, 12, 12, 13, 13, 14, 14, 15, 16, 19, 20; 2:1, 2, 2, 2, 3, 3, 3, 4, 7, 7, 8, 9, 10, 10, 11, 11, 11, 12, 12, 12, 13, 13, 13, 13, 13, 14, 14, 14, 16, 16, 17, 17, 17, 18, 19, 19, 19, 19, 19, 20, 20, 20, 20, 20, 21, 22, 23, 23, 24, 24, 24, 25, 25, 26, 26, 26, 26, 27, 27, 27, 28, 28, 28, 29, 29, 30, 30, 30, 31, 31, 32, 32; 3:1, 1, 2, 2, 2, 3, 3, 3, 3, 4, 4, 4, 4, 5, 5, 6, 6, 6, 7, 8, 8, 8, 10, 10, 11, 12, 12, 14, 14, 14, 14, 15, 15

Ob 1:1, 1, 4, 7, 8, 9, 10, 11, 11, 16, 16, 17, 17, 18, 18, 18, 18, 18, 19, 19, 19, 19, 19, 20, 20, 21, 21

Jnh 1:2, 3, 3, 3, 4, 5, 5, 5, 6, 7, 7, 8, 8, 9, 9, 9, 10, 11, 12, 12, 13, 14, 14, 15, 15, 16, 16, 17; 2:2, 2, 2, 3, 3, 7, 10, 10; 3:1, 2, 3, 4, 4, 4, 4, 5, 5, 6, 6, 6, 7, 7, 8, 8, 8, 9, 9, 10, 10, 10; 4:1, 2, 2, 2, 2, 2, 5, 5, 5, 6, 6, 7, 8, 8, 8, 8, 9, 9, 9, 10, 11, 11

Mic 1:1, 1, 2, 2, 3, 4, 4, 4, 5, 5, 6, 6, 6, 7, 7, 7, 8, 8, 8, 16; 2:1, 2, 2, 2, 2, 2, 4, 3, 3, 3, 5, 5, 6, 6, 6, 7, 8, 8, 8, 9, 9, 10, 11, 11, 11, 12, 12; 4:1, 1, 2, 2, 2, 2, 2, 3, 3, 3, 3, 4, 4, 5, 5, 6, 6, 7, 7, 8, 10, 10, 10, 13, 13, 13, 13; 5:4, 4, 4, 5, 5, 5, 6, 6, 6, 7, 8, 8, 8, 9, 10, 10, 11, 11, 12, 12, 13, 13, 14, 14, 15, 15; 6:1, 2, 2, 3, 4, 4, 4, 5, 6, 6, 7, 8, 8, 8, 9, 9, 11, 12, 12, 14, 14, 15, 16, 16, 16; 7:2, 3, 3, 4, 9, 9, 9, 10, 10, 10, 11, 12, 13, 15, 15, 15, 15, 16, 16, 17, 18, 19, 20

Na 1:2, 2, 2, 3, 3, 3, 4, 4, 4, 4, 5, 5, 5, 6, 7, 9, 10, 10, 10, 10, 10, 11, 11, 11, 12, 12, 13, 13, 13; 3:1, 2, 2, 2, 3, 3, 3, 4, 4, 5, 5, 5, 6, 6, 9, 9, 10, 10, 14, 16, 17, 17, 18

Hab 1:2, 2, 3, 3, 3, 4, 5, 6, 7, 7, 8, 8, 8, 9, 10, 10, 10, 11, 11, 12, 12, 13, 14, 15, 15, 16, 16, 17; 2:1, 1, 1, 2, 2, 2, 3, 5, 5, 9, 15, 16, 6, 6, 6, 7, 7, 8, 8, 9, 10, 11, 12, 13, 15, 16, 17, 17, 17, 18, 19, 19; 3:2, 3, 3, 4, 4, 5, 6, 6, 6, 8, 10, 10, 11, 11, 16, 17, 17, 19

Zep 1:3, 3, 3, 3, 4, 4, 4, 5, 5, 5, 6, 6, 8, 8, 9, 10, 10, 10, 12, 12, 13, 13, 14, 14, 15, 15, 15, 16, 16, 16, 17, 17; 2:4, 4, 6, 6, 6, 7, 7, 8, 8, 9, 9, 9, 9, 10, 11, 13, 13, 13,

13, 14, 14, 15, 15; 3:1, 4, 7, 11, 12, 12, 13, 13, 14, 16, 19, 19, 19, 19, 20

Hag 1:1, 4, 6, 6, 8, 8, 8, 8, 9, 9, 9, 10, 11, 11, 11, 11, 11, 11, 12, 12, 13, 14, 14, 14, 14, 14, 15; 2:1, 2, 2, 3, 4, 4, 4, 6, 6, 6, 6, 7, 7, 7, 8, 9, 10, 12, 12, 12, 13, 13, 14, 14, 14, 14, 14, 15, 15, 17, 17, 18, 18, 19, 19, 19, 20, 20, 21, 22, 22, 22, 22, 22, 23

Zec 1:3, 4, 5, 6, 6, 6, 6, 7, 8, 8, 8, 9, 10, 10, 10, 11, 11, 11, 11, 12, 12, 12, 13, 13, 14, 15, 15, 16, 17, 17, 18, 18, 19, 19, 20, 21; 2:1, 1, 2, 2, 3, 3, 4, 4, 5, 6, 9, 9, 10, 10, 11, 11, 11, 12, 12, 13; 3:1, 1, 2, 3, 4, 4, 4, 4, 5, 5, 6, 7, 7, 7, 8, 9, 10; 4:1, 1, 2, 2, 2, 2, 2, 3, 3, 4, 5, 5, 6, 6, 7, 9, 10, 10, 11, 11, 12, 12, 13, 13, 13, 13; 5:1, 1, 2, 2, 2, 3, 4, 4, 4, 4, 5, 5, 6, 6, 7, 7, 7, 8, 8, 9, 9, 9, 9, 9, 9, 11, 11; 6:1, 1, 1, 1, 1, 2, 3, 4, 5, 5, 6, 6, 6, 7, 7, 7, 8, 9, 10, 10, 10, 10, 11, 11, 11, 12, 12, 13, 13, 13, 13, 13, 14, 14, 14, 14, 15, 15; 7:1, 2, 2, 3, 3, 5, 5, 6, 6, 6, 7, 7, 8, 9, 9, 10, 11, 11, 13, 13; 8:2, 3, 3, 3, 4, 4, 5, 5, 7, 8, 8, 8, 8, 12, 12, 12, 13, 13, 14, 14, 16, 17, 18, 19, 19, 19, 21, 22, 22; 9:1, 1, 2, 2, 3, 3, 4, 5, 5, 5, 6, 7, 7, 7, 8, 8, 8, 9, 9, 9, 9, 10, 10, 10, 10, 11, 12, 13, 13, 14, 14, 14, 14, 15, 15, 15, 16, 17, 17; 10:1, 2, 2, 3, 3, 5, 5, 5, 6, 6, 6, 6, 7, 7, 7, 7, 8, 9, 9, 10, 10, 11, 11, 11, 12, 12; 11:5, 5, 5, 6, 6, 6, 7, 7, 7, 8, 8, 9, 9, 10, 10, 10, 10, 11, 11, 11, 11, 12, 12, 12; 12:1, 1, 2, 3, 4, 4, 4, 5, 6, 6, 6, 7, 8, 8, 9, 10, 10, 10, 10, 10, 12; 13:1, 2, 2, 2, 2, 3, 3, 3, 4, 6, 7, 7, 7, 8, 8, 8, 9, 9, 9, 9, 9; 14:1, 2, 2, 2, 2, 2, 3, 4, 4, 4, 4, 4, 5, 5, 6, 8, 8, 9, 9, 10, 10, 10, 10, 12, 13, 13, 14, 14, 14, 14, 16, 17, 18, 19, 20, 21, 21, 21, 21

Mal 1:3, 3, 3, 4, 4, 4, 5, 5, 6, 6, 6, 7, 8, 8, 8, 9, 11, 12, 13, 13, 13, 14, 14, 14; 2:1, 2, 2, 3, 3, 4, 5, 5, 5, 6, 6, 6, 6, 7, 9, 11, 11, 12, 12, 12, 13, 13, 14, 14, 15, 15, 15, 16, 17; 3:1, 1, 2, 2, 3, 3, 3, 3, 4, 4, 5, 5, 5, 5, 5, 5, 7, 7, 8, 8, 10, 11, 12, 14, 14, 14, 15, 15, 16, 16, 16, 17, 18, 18; 4:1, 1, 1, 2, 2, 3, 4, 5, 6, 6, 6

Mt 1:2, 2, 2, 3, 3, 3, 4, 4, 4, 5, 5, 5, 6, 7, 7, 8, 8, 9, 9, 10, 10, 10, 11, 11, 12, 12, 13, 13, 14, 14, 14, 15, 15, 15, 16, 17, 17, 19, 21, 21, 23, 23, 24, 25; 2:2, 3, 4, 4, 5, 6, 8, 8, 8, 9, 9, 11, 11, 11, 11, 11, 12, 13, 13, 13, 13, 14, 15, 16, 16, 16, 16, 18, 18, 20, 20, 20, 21, 21, 21, 21, 23, 23; 3:2, 4, 4, 4, 4, 5, 5, 6, 7, 9, 10, 11, 12, 12, 14, 15, 16, 16, 16, 16, 17; 4:2, 2, 3, 4, 5, 6, 6, 6, 8, 9, 9, 10, 11, 11, 13, 13, 13, 15, 16, 16, 18, 18, 19, 19, 20, 20, 21, 21, 21, 22, 22, 23, 23, 23, 24, 24, 24, 24, 24, 25, 25, 25, 25; 5:1, 1, 2, 6, 8, 11, 12, 13, 14, 15, 15, 15; 7:1, 2, 2, 3, 3, 5, 5, 5, 6, 6, 6, 7, 7, 8, 8, 9, 9, 9, 10, 11, 11, 12, 12, 13, 13, 14, 14, 15, 15, 15, 16, 16, 17, 18, 19, 20, 20, 21, 21, 21, 22, 22, 22, 23, 23, 23, 23, 24, 24, 24, 24, 25, 25, 26, 26, 26, 26, 27, 27, 27, 28, 29; 8:2, 2, 3, 3, 4, 5, 6, 7, 7, 7, 8, 9, 9, 9, 9, 10, 11, 11, 11, 11, 12, 13, 13, 14, 14, 15, 15, 15, 16, 16, 17, 19, 20, 20, 21, 21, 22, 22, 23, 23, 24, 24, 24, 24, 25, 25, 25, 25; 5:1, 1, 2, 6, 8, 9, 18, 19, 19, 20, 20, 21, 21, 21, 23, 24, 25, 25, 26, 26, 26, 27, 28, 29, 30, 32, 32, 32, 33, 33, 34; 9:1, 1, 2, 2, 3, 4, 5, 6, 7, 7, 8, 9, 9, 9, 9, 10, 10, 11, 13, 14, 14, 15, 15, 16, 17, 17, 17, 18, 18, 19, 19, 19, 20, 22, 22, 23, 23, 24, 25, 25, 26, 27, 27, 27, 28, 28, 29, 30, 30, 33, 33, 35, 35, 35, 36, 10:1, 1, 2, 2, 3, 3, 4, 5, 7, 11, 11, 12, 14, 16, 16, 17, 18, 18, 19, 19, 19, 20, 22, 22, 23, 23, 24, 25, 25, 26, 27, 28, 28, 29, 29, 30, 30, 12:1, 1, 1, 3, 4, 5, 7, 9, 10, 10, 11, 11, 13, 13, 14, 15, 16, 18, 20, 21, 22, 22, 23, 23, 25, 25, 27, 27, 28, 28, 29, 29, 30, 30, 12:1, 1, 1, 2, 2, 3, 3, 5, 7, 9, 10, 10, 11, 11, 13, 13,

34, 34, 35, 36, 36, 36, 36, 36, 37, 37, 37, 38, 38, 39, 39, 39; 16:1, 2, 3, 3, 4, 4, 4, 4, 5, 6, 6, 7, 7, 9, 10, 11, 12, 14, 14, 16, 16, 17, 17, 17, 18, 18, 18, 19, 19, 19, 21, 21, 21, 21, 21, 22, 23, 24, 24, 25, 26, 27; 17:1, 1, 1, 2, 2, 2, 3, 3, 4, 4, 5, 5, 6, 7, 7, 7, 7, 8, 9, 9, 10, 11, 11, 12, 14, 14, 15, 15, 16, 16, 17, 17, 18, 18, 18, 19, 19, 19, 20, 20, 20, 21, 22, 23, 23, 24, 24, 25, 24, 25, 26, 27; 18:2, 2, 3, 3, 5, 6, 8, 9, 9, 12, 12, 12, 12, 13, 13, 15, 15, 17, 17, 17, 18, 21, 21, 24, 25, 25, 26, 27, 27, 28, 28, 28, 29, 29, 30, 30, 31, 31, 34; 34; 19:1, 1, 2, 2, 3, 4, 4, 5, 5, 5, 7, 9, 9, 9, 12, 12, 13, 13, 14, 15, 15, 16, 16, 17, 19, 19, 21, 21, 21, 24, 26, 27, 28, 28, 29, 29, 30; 20:2, 3, 3, 4, 4, 4, 5, 5, 6, 6, 6, 7, 8, 8, 10, 11, 11, 12, 13, 14, 16, 17, 17, 18, 18, 19, 19, 19, 19, 20, 20, 21, 22, 22, 23, 23, 24, 25, 25, 27, 28, 29, 30, 31, 32, 32, 32, 34, 34, 34; 21:1, 1, 2, 2, 2, 3, 5, 5, 6, 7, 7, 7, 8, 8, 8, 9, 9, 11, 12, 12, 13, 13, 15, 15, 16, 16, 17, 17, 19, 19, 19, 20, 21, 21, 23, 23, 24, 24, 25, 27, 28, 29, 30, 31, 32, 32, 32, 34, 34, 34; 22:1, 1, 1, 3, 3, 4, 4, 5, 6, 6, 6, 7, 7, 9, 10, 10, 11, 12, 13, 13, 13, 15, 16, 16, 18, 19, 20, 20, 21, 22, 22, 24, 25, 25, 26, 27, 29, 32, 32, 33, 35, 37, 38, 39, 40, 40, 46; 23:1, 2, 3, 3, 4, 4, 5, 6, 6, 7, 8, 9, 12, 13, 14, 14, 15, 15, 15, 17, 18, 19, 20, 21, 22, 23, 23, 24, 25, 25, 26, 27, 27, 28, 29, 29, 30, 30, 31, 32, 34, 34, 34, 35, 37; 24:1, 1, 1, 2, 3, 3, 3, 4, 4, 4, 5, 6, 7, 9, 9, 10, 10, 11, 11, 12, 14, 14, 19, 19, 22, 24, 24, 27, 29, 29, 29, 30, 30, 31, 31, 32, 35, 36, 38, 38, 40, 41, 43, 45, 48, 49, 49, 49, 50, 51, 51, 51; 25:1, 2, 2, 3, 5, 6, 7, 8, 9, 9, 10, 12, 14, 15, 15, 16, 16, 17, 18, 18, 20, 20, 21, 22, 23, 24, 24, 25, 25, 26, 26, 27, 28, 29, 30, 30, 31, 31, 32, 33, 35, 35, 35, 35, 36, 36, 36, 37, 37, 38, 39, 40, 40, 40, 41, 42, 42, 43, 43, 43, 43, 44, 46; 26:1, 2, 3, 3, 4, 4, 7, 9, 15, 15, 15, 16, 18, 19, 19, 21, 22, 22, 23, 23, 25, 26, 26, 26, 26, 27, 27, 30, 31, 33, 36, 37, 37, 37, 38, 39, 39, 40, 40, 41, 42, 43, 43, 43, 43, 44, 44, 45, 45, 47, 47, 47, 49, 49, 49, 50, 50, 50, 51, 51, 51, 51, 53, 55, 56, 57, 57, 58, 58, 59, 59, 61, 61, 62, 62, 63, 63, 64, 66, 67, 67, 69, 71, 71, 72, 73, 73, 74, 74, 75, 75; 27:1, 2, 2, 3, 4, 5, 5, 5, 6, 6, 7, 9, 10, 11, 11, 11, 12, 14, 16, 20, 20, 21, 23, 24, 25, 25, 26, 26, 27, 28, 28, 29, 29, 30, 30, 31, 31, 32, 33, 34, 35, 35, 35, 36, 37, 38, 39, 40, 40, 41, 42, 46, 48, 48, 48, 48, 48, 51, 51, 51, 52, 52, 53, 53, 53, 54, 54, 55, 56, 56, 57; 7:1, 2, 3, 4, 4, 4, 5, 6, 9, 11, 13, 14, 17, 18, 19, 20, 23, 24, 24, 24, 24, 25, 25, 26, 27, 28,

11, 12, 13, 13, 13, 15, 15, 15, 16, 17, 17, 18, 18, 19, 19, 20, 20, 20, 21, 21, 22, 22, 23, 23, 25, 25, 26, 26, 26, 27, 27, 28, 28, 29, 29, 30, 31, 31, 31, 31, 31, 32, 32, 33, 34, 34, 34, 35, 35, 35, 36, 36, 37, 38, 39, 39, 40, 40, 41, 41, 41, 41, 42, 42, 43, 43, 44, 44, 45, 45, 45; 2:1, 1, 2, 2, 3, 4, 4, 6, 8, 9, 9, 11, 11, 12, 12, 12, 13, 13, 13, 14, 14, 14, 14, 15, 15, 15, 16, 16, 18, 18, 18, 19, 20, 21, 22, 22, 23, 23, 24, 24, 25, 25, 26, 26, 26, 26, 27, 27; 3:1, 1, 2, 3, 4, 5, 5, 5, 6, 6, 7, 7, 8, 8, 9, 11, 11, 12, 13, 13, 14, 14, 15, 15, 16, 17, 17, 18, 18, 18, 18, 18, 19, 20, 20, 21, 21, 22, 23, 24, 25, 26, 26, 26, 27, 27, 27, 28, 28; 4:1, 1, 1, 1, 2, 2, 4, 4, 4, 5, 5, 6, 7, 7, 7, 7, 8, 8, 8, 8, 8, 8, 9, 9, 10, 11, 12, 12, 13, 13, 15, 15, 16, 17, 17, 18, 18, 18, 18, 19, 20, 21, 21, 24, 24, 25, 26, 27, 27, 27, 27, 30, 32, 32, 33, 34, 34, 36, 36, 37, 37, 38, 38, 38, 39, 39, 39, 40, 40, 41, 41; 5:1, 2, 3, 4, 4, 4, 5, 5, 5, 6, 7, 9, 10, 13, 13, 13, 13, 13, 14, 14, 15, 15, 15, 16, 16, 17, 18, 19, 20, 20, 20, 21, 21, 22, 22, 23, 23, 25, 26, 26, 26, 27, 29, 29, 30, 30, 31, 31, 32, 32, 37, 38, 38, 38, 39, 39, 40, 40, 40, 41, 41, 42, 42, 42, 43, 43, 43; 6:1, 1, 1, 2, 3, 3, 3, 3, 4, 4, 5, 5, 6, 7, 7, 7, 8, 9, 10, 11, 12, 13, 14, 17, 17, 19, 20, 20, 21, 21, 22, 22, 23, 24, 24, 25, 26, 26, 26, 27, 29, 29, 30, 30, 31, 31, 31, 32, 32, 33, 33, 33, 33, 34, 34, 34, 35, 35, 36, 37, 37, 38, 39, 40, 40, 40, 40, 41, 41, 42, 42, 43, 43, 44, 45, 45, 46, 47, 47, 48, 48, 48, 49, 50, 50, 50, 51, 51, 51, 51, 51, 53, 53, 54, 55, 55, 56, 56; 7:1, 2, 3, 4, 4, 4, 5, 6, 8, 9, 10, 10, 13, 14, 17, 18, 19, 20, 23, 24, 24, 24, 24, 25, 25, 26, 27, 28,

28, 29, 30, 30, 31, 31, 32, 32, 32, 33, 33, 33, 33, 34, 34, 35, 35, 35, 36, 37, 37; 8:1, 1, 2, 3, 4, 5, 5, 6, 6, 6, 6, 7, 7, 7, 8, 9, 9, 10, 10, 11, 11, 12, 12, 13, 13, 15, 15, 16, 17, 18, 18, 20, 20, 21, 22, 22, 23, 23, 23, 23, 24, 24, 25, 25, 25, 26, 27, 27, 27, 28, 28, 29, 29, 29, 30, 31, 31, 31, 31, 31, 32, 32, 32, 33, 34, 34, 34, 35, 36, 38, 38; 9:1, 2, 2, 2, 2, 2, 3, 4, 4, 5, 5, 5, 5, 7, 7, 8, 8, 9, 10, 11, 12, 12, 12, 12, 12, 13, 13, 14, 14, 15, 15, 16, 17, 17, 18, 18, 18, 18, 18, 18, 19, 20, 20, 20, 20, 21, 21, 22, 22, 22, 24, 24, 25, 25, 26, 26, 26, 26, 27, 27, 28, 29, 29, 30, 30, 30, 31, 31, 31, 32, 33, 33, 35, 35, 35, 36, 36, 36, 37, 38, 38, 38, 42, 42, 43, 44, 45, 46, 47, 48, 49, 50; 10:1, 1, 1, 1, 2, 2, 3, 3, 4, 4, 5, 6, 7, 7, 8, 10, 11, 11, 11, 12, 12, 13, 13, 14, 14, 16, 16, 17, 17, 17, 18, 19, 20, 20, 21, 21, 21, 21, 22, 22, 23, 23, 24, 24, 26, 27, 28, 29, 29, 29, 30, 30, 30, 30, 30, 31, 32, 32, 32, 32, 32, 33, 33, 33, 34, 34, 34, 34, 35, 35, 35, 36, 36, 36, 37, 39, 39, 40, 41, 41, 42, 42, 44, 45, 46, 46, 46, 47, 47, 48, 49, 49, 49, 50, 50, 51, 51, 52, 52, 52; 11:1, 1, 2, 2, 2, 3, 3, 4, 4, 4, 5, 6, 6, 7, 7, 7, 8, 8, 8, 9, 9, 11, 11, 11, 11, 12, 13, 13, 14, 14, 14, 15, 15, 15, 15, 15, 16, 17, 18, 18, 18, 19, 20, 21, 22, 23, 23, 24, 25, 27, 27, 27, 28, 29, 29, 29, 29, 29, 31, 33, 33; 12:1, 1, 1, 1, 1, 1, 2, 3, 3, 4, 4, 4, 4, 5, 5, 5, 5, 7, 7, 8, 8, 8, 8, 9, 9, 9, 10, 11, 12, 12, 13, 13, 14, 14, 16, 16, 16, 16, 17, 17, 17, 18, 18, 19, 19, 19, 20, 20, 21, 21, 21, 22, 22, 24, 24, 24, 25, 25, 26, 26, 26, 28, 28, 28, 29, 30, 30, 30, 30, 31, 32, 33, 33, 33, 34, 34, 34, 35, 35, 35, 36, 37, 37, 38, 38, 39, 39, 40, 41, 41, 41, 42, 42, 43; 13:1, 1, 2, 3, 3, 3, 3, 3, 4, 5, 6, 7, 7, 8, 8, 8, 8, 9, 9, 10, 11, 12, 12, 12, 13, 15, 16, 17, 18, 20, 21, 22, 22, 22, 24, 25, 25, 26, 26, 27, 27, 28, 31, 32, 33, 34, 34, 34, 37; 14:1, 1, 1, 1, 3, 3, 3, 4, 4, 5, 5, 6, 7, 10, 11, 11, 11, 12, 12, 13, 13, 13, 14, 15, 15, 16, 16, 16, 16, 16, 17, 17, 18, 18, 19, 19, 19, 20, 20, 20, 22, 22, 22, 22, 22, 23, 23, 23, 24, 26, 27, 27, 30, 32, 32, 33, 33, 33, 34, 34, 35, 35, 35, 36, 37, 37, 37, 38, 39, 39, 39, 40, 41, 41, 41, 43, 43, 43, 43, 44, 44, 45, 45, 45, 46, 46, 46, 47, 47, 47, 48, 48, 48, 49, 50, 50, 51, 51, 52, 52, 53, 53, 53, 54, 54, 54, 55, 55, 55, 57, 57, 58, 60, 60, 61, 61, 62, 62, 62, 63, 64, 65, 65, 65, 65, 66, 66, 67, 67, 67, 68, 68, 69, 69, 70, 70, 70, 71, 72, 72, 72; 15:1, 1, 1, 1, 1, 2, 2, 3, 4, 7, 8, 9, 12, 13, 14, 14, 15, 15, 16, 16, 17, 17, 17, 18, 19, 19, 19, 20, 20, 20, 21, 21, 22, 23, 24, 25, 25, 27, 27, 28, 29, 29, 29, 30, 32, 32, 33, 34, 35, 36, 36, 36, 37, 37, 37, 38, 40, 40, 41, 41, 42, 43, 43, 43, 44, 44, 45, 45, 46, 46, 46, 47, 47, 47, 48, 48, 49, 50, 50, 51, 51, 52, 52, 53, 53, 54, 54, 54, 55, 55, 55, 57, 57, 58, 60, 60, 61, 61, 62, 62, 62, 63, 64, 65, 65, 65, 65, 66, 66, 67, 67, 67, 68, 68, 69, 69, 70, 70, 70, 71, 72, 72, 72; 15:1, 1, 1, 1, 1, 2, 2, 3, 4, 7, 8, 9, 12, 13, 14, 14, 15, 15, 16, 16, 17, 17, 17, 18, 19, 19, 19, 20, 20, 20, 21, 21, 22, 23, 24, 25, 25, 27, 27, 28, 29, 29, 29, 30, 32, 32, 33, 34, 35, 36, 36, 36, 37, 37, 37, 38, 40, 40, 41, 41, 42, 43, 43, 43, 44, 44, 45, 45, 46, 46, 46, 47, 47, 47, 48, 48, 49, 50, 50, 51, 51, 52, 52, 53, 53, 54, 54, 54, 55, 55, 55, 57, 57, 58, 58, 60, 60, 61, 61, 62, 62, 62, 63, 64, 65, 65, 65, 65, 66, 66, 67, 67, 67, 68, 68, 69, 69, 70, 70, 70, 71, 72, 72, 72; 15:1, 1, 1, 2, 3, 4, 7, 8, 9, 10, 10, 11, 11, 12, 13, 14, 14, 15, 15, 16, 16, 17, 17, 17, 18, 18, 19, 19, 19, 20, 20, 20, 21, 21, 22, 22, 23, 23, 24, 24, 26, 27, 27, 28, 29, 29, 29, 30, 32, 32, 33, 33, 34, 34, 34, 35, 35, 36, 36, 36, 37, 37, 37, 38, 39, 39, 40, 40, 41, 41, 42, 43, 43, 43, 43, 44, 44, 45, 45, 45, 46, 46, 46, 47, 47, 47, 48, 48, 48, 49, 50, 50, 51, 51, 52, 52, 53, 53, 53, 54, 54, 54, 55, 55, 55, 57, 57, 58, 60, 60, 61, 61, 62, 62, 62, 63, 64, 65, 65, 65, 65, 66, 66, 67, 67, 67, 68, 68, 69, 69, 70, 70, 70, 71, 72, 72, 72; 15:1, 1, 1, 1, 1, 2, 2, 3, 4, 7, 8, 9, 12, 13, 14, 15, 16, 16, 17, 17, 17, 18, 19, 19, 19, 20, 20, 20, 21, 22, 23, 23, 23, 24, 24, 26, 27, 28, 29, 29, 29, 30, 32, 32, 33, 34, 35, 35, 36, 36, 36, 37, 37, 37, 38, 39, 39, 40, 40, 41, 41, 42, 43, 43, 43, 43, 44, 44, 45, 45, 45, 46, 46, 46, 47, 47, 47, 48, 48, 48, 49, 50, 50, 51, 51, 52, 52, 53, 53, 53, 54, 54, 54, 55, 55, 55, 57, 58, 60, 60, 61, 61, 62, 62, 62, 63, 64, 65, 65, 65, 65, 66, 66, 67, 67, 67, 68, 68, 69, 69, 70, 70, 70, 71, 72, 72, 72; 15:1, 1, 1, 1, 1, 2, 2, 3, 4, 5, 6, 6, 7, 7, 8, 8, 10, 10, 11, 11, 12, 13, 13, 14, 14, 15, 15, 16, 17, 17, 17, 18, 19, 19, 19, 20, 20, 20, 21, 21, 22, 22, 23, 23, 24, 25, 26, 27, 27, 27, 28, 29, 29, 30, 32, 33, 33, 34, 34, 35, 36, 36, 36, 37, 37, 37, 38, 39, 39, 40, 40, 41, 41, 42, 43, 43, 43, 44, 44, 45, 45, 46, 46, 46, 47, 47, 47, 48, 48, 49, 50, 50, 51, 51, 52, 52, 53, 53, 54, 55, 55, 57, 58, 60, 60, 61, 61, 62, 62, 63, 64, 65, 65, 66, 66, 67, 67, 68, 68, 69, 69, 70, 70, 70, 71, 72, 72, 72; 15:1, 1, 1, 1, 1, 2, 2, 3, 4, 4, 5, 6, 6, 7, 7, 7, 8, 8, 8, 10, 10, 11, 11, 2, 13, 13, 14, 14, 14, 15, 15, 16, 17, 18, 18, 18, 19, 20, 20, 20;

Lk 1:2, 5, 5, 5, 6, 6, 7, 7, 8, 10, 11, 12, 12, 13, 13, 14, 14, 14, 15, 15, 16, 17, 17, 17, 18, 18, 19, 19, 19, 20, 20, 21, 21, 22, 22, 22, 23, 24, 24, 26, 27, 28, 28, 29, 29, 30, 31, 31, 31, 32, 32, 33, 33, 35, 35, 35, 36, 36, 38, 38, 39, 39, 40, 40, 41, 41, 42, 42, 42, 43, 45, 45, 46, 47, 49, 50, 52, 53, 55, 56, 57, 58, 58, 58, 59, 59, 60, 60, 60, 61, 62, 63, 63, 63, 64, 64, 64, 64, 65, 65, 66, 66, 67, 67, 68, 69, 71, 72, 75, 76, 79, 80, 80, 80; 2:1, 2, 3, 4, 4, 6, 6, 7, 7, 8, 9, 9, 9, 10, 12, 13, 13, 14, 15, 15, 16, 16, 16, 16, 17, 18, 19, 20, 20, 20, 21, 21, 22, 24, 24, 25, 25, 25, 25, 26, 27, 27, 28, 28, 32, 33, 33, 34, 34, 34, 34, 36, 36, 37, 37, 37, 37, 38, 38, 39, 40, 40, 42, 43, 43, 43, 44, 44, 45, 46, 46, 47, 47, 48, 48, 48, 49, 50, 51, 51, 51, 52, 52, 52; 3:1, 1, 1, 1, 2, 3, 5, 5, 5, 5, 6, 8, 9, 9, 10, 11, 12, 13, 14, 14, 14, 14, 14, 15, 15, 16, 16, 17, 17, 18, 19, 21, 22, 22, 23; 4:1, 1, 2, 2, 3, 4, 5, 6, 6, 6, 8, 8, 8, 9, 9, 9, 11, 13, 13, 14, 14, 15, 15, 16, 16, 16, 17, 17, 17, 18, 20, 20, 20, 20, 21, 22, 22, 22, 23, 24, 25, 27, 27, 28, 29, 29, 29, 31, 31, 32, 33, 33, 33, 35, 35, 35, 36, 36, 36, 37, 38, 38, 38, 38, 39, 39, 39, 39, 40, 40, 41, 41, 42, 42, 42, 42, 42, 43, 44; 5:1, 2, 2, 3, 3, 3, 3, 4, 5, 5, 6, 6, 7, 7, 7, 9, 10, 10, 10, 11, 11, 12, 12, 12, 13, 13, 14, 14, 14, 15, 15, 16, 16, 17, 17, 17, 17, 18, 18, 18, 19, 19, 20, 21, 23, 24, 24, 25, 25, 25, 26, 26, 26, 27, 27, 28, 28, 29, 29, 30, 31, 33, 33, 34, 34, 34, 35, 36, 37, 37, 38; 6:1, 1, 1, 2, 3, 3, 4, 4, 4, 5, 6, 6, 6, 7, 7, 8, 8, 8, 10, 10, 10, 11, 12, 12, 13, 13, 14, 14, 14, 15, 16, 17, 17, 17, 17, 17, 17, 18, 18, 19, 19, 20, 20, 21, 21, 23, 24, 24, 25, 25, 26, 26, 26, 27, 27, 27, 28, 28, 29, 29, 30, 31, 33, 33, 33, 34, 35, 35, 35, 35, 36, 37, 37, 38; 6:1, 1, 1, 2, 3, 3, 4, 5, 5, 6, 6, 6, 7, 7, 8, 8, 8, 8, 9, 9, 10, 10, 10, 11, 11, 12, 12, 13, 13, 14, 14, 14, 15, 15, 16, 16, 17, 17, 17, 17, 17, 18, 18, 19, 19, 20, 20, 21, 21, 23, 24, 24, 25, 26, 26, 27, 29, 29, 30, 31, 31, 32, 32, 33, 34, 34, 34, 35, 36, 36, 37, 37, 37, 38; 6:1, 1, 1, 2, 2, 3, 3, 4, 4, 4, 5, 5, 6, 6, 6, 7, 7, 7, 7, 8, 8, 9, 10, 10, 10, 11, 11, 12, 12, 13, 13, 13, 14, 14, 15, 15, 16, 17, 17, 17, 17, 18, 18, 19, 21, 21, 21, 21, 22, 23, 23, 24, 24, 25, 25, 26, 26, 27, 28, 29, 29, 30, 31, 33, 34, 34, 35, 36, 36, 37, 37, 37, 38; 6:1, 1, 1, 2, 3, 3, 4, 5, 6, 6, 7, 8, 8, 8, 8, 9, 10, 11, 11, 11, 12, 12, 13, 14, 14, 15, 16, 17, 27, 28, 29, 30, 31, 31, 34, 34, 35, 36, 37, 37, 40, 41, 42, 46, 46, 46, 47; 21:1, 1, 2, 3, 5, 5, 5, 7, 7, 8, 8, 9, 9, 10, 11, 11, 11, 11, 11, 12, 12, 12, 13, 15, 15, 16, 16, 16, 16, 17, 20, 20, 21, 21, 23, 24, 24, 24, 25, 25, 25, 26, 27, 28, 28, 29, 29, 30, 33, 34, 34, 35, 36, 37, 37, 40, 41, 42, 46, 46, 46, 47; 21:1, 1, 2, 3, 5, 5, 5, 7, 7, 8, 8, 9, 9, 10, 11, 11, 11, 11, 11, 12, 12, 12, 13, 15, 15, 16, 16, 16, 16, 17, 20, 20, 21, 21, 23, 24, 24, 24, 25, 25, 25, 26, 27, 27, 27, 27, 28, 28, 29, 29, 30, 31, 31, 34, 34, 35, 36, 37, 37, 38; 22:1, 2, 2, 4, 4, 4, 5, 5, 6, 6, 6, 8, 8, 9, 10, 11, 12, 13, 13, 13, 14, 14, 14, 15, 17, 17, 17, 17, 19, 19, 19, 19, 22, 23, 23, 24, 25, 26, 29, 30, 30, 31, 32, 33, 33, 33, 34, 35, 35, 35, 35, 36, 36, 37, 37, 38, 38, 38, 39, 39, 40, 40, 41, 41, 41, 43, 44, 44, 44, 45, 45, 46, 46, 47, 47, 47, 50, 51, 51, 51, 52, 52, 52, 54, 54, 54, 55, 55, 56, 56, 57, 58, 58, 59, 60, 60, 61, 61, 62, 62, 62, 63, 63, 64, 64, 64, 65, 66, 66, 66, 67, 68, 70, 71; 23:1, 1, 2, 2, 3, 3, 4, 5, 5, 7, 8, 8, 8, 8, 10, 10, 11, 11, 11, 11, 12, 12, 12, 13, 13, 13, 14, 14, 15, 15, 18, 18, 19, 22, 22, 23, 23, 23, 24, 25, 25, 26, 26, 27, 27, 28, 29, 29, 30, 30, 31, 31, 31, 32, 32, 33, 33, 34, 34, 35, 35, 36, 36, 37, 37, 38, 38, 39, 39, 39, 40, 40, 41, 41, 42, 42, 42, 43, 43; 24:1, 1, 1, 2, 2, 3, 5, 5, 6, 7, 7, 8, 8, 9, 10, 11, 11, 12, 12, 13, 14, 14, 15, 15, 15, 16, 16, 16, 17, 17, 18, 18, 19, 19, 20, 20, 21, 21, 22, 23, 24, 24, 25, 26, 29, 30, 30, 31, 31, 31, 31, 32, 33, 33, 33, 33, 34, 35, 35, 36, 36, 37, 37, 38, 38, 39, 39, 40, 40, 41, 41, 42, 42, 43, 43,

10, 12, 12, 13, 13, 14, 14, 14, 14, 14, 15, 15, 17, 18, 19, 19, 20, 20, 21, 21, 21, 21, 22, 22, 22, 23, 23, 23, 24, 24, 24, 24, 24, 25, 25, 25, 25, 26, 27, 27, 28, 28, 29, 29, 29, 30, 30, 30, 31, 32, 32, 33, 33, 33, 34, 34, 34, 35, 35, 35, 35, 37, 37, 39, 39, 40, 40, 41, 41, 41, 41, 42, 42, 43, 44, 44, 45, 45, 45, 46, 47, 47, 48, 50, 51, 51, 51, 51, 51, 51, 51, 51, 52, 53, 54, 54, 54, 55, 55, 55, 55, 56; 9:1, 1, 1, 2, 2, 3, 4, 4, 5, 6, 6, 6, 6, 7, 8, 8, 9, 9, 10, 10, 10, 11, 11, 11, 11, 12, 12, 12, 12, 12, 13, 13, 13, 14, 14, 15, 15, 16, 16, 16, 16, 17, 17, 17, 18, 18, 18, 19, 21, 21, 22, 22, 22, 22, 23, 23, 23, 23, 25, 25, 26, 26, 26, 26, 28, 28, 28, 28, 28, 29, 29, 30, 30, 31, 31, 32, 32, 32, 33, 33, 34, 34, 35, 36, 36, 37, 37, 38, 38, 39, 39, 40, 40, 41, 41, 41, 41, 41, 42, 42, 42, 42, 43, 45, 45, 47, 47, 48, 49, 50, 51, 51, 53, 54, 54, 54, 55, 55, 55, 55, 55, 59, 60, 61, 62, 62; 10:1, 1, 1, 4, 5, 6, 7, 7, 8, 8, 9, 9, 10, 13, 13, 14, 15, 15, 16, 16, 17, 18, 19, 19, 19, 21, 21, 21, 21, 22, 22, 23, 23, 23, 24, 24, 24, 24, 25, 25, 25, 26, 27, 27, 28, 28, 29, 29, 30, 30, 31, 31, 32, 32, 32, 33, 33, 34, 34, 34, 34, 34, 35, 35, 35, 35, 37, 37, 39, 39, 40, 40, 41, 41, 42; 11:1, 2, 4, 4, 4, 5, 5, 5, 6, 7, 7, 7, 7, 8, 8, 8, 8, 9, 9, 9, 9, 10, 10, 14, 14, 14, 16, 17, 19, 22, 22, 23, 24, 24, 25, 25, 26, 26, 26, 26, 27, 27, 27, 27, 28, 29, 29, 31, 31, 31, 32, 32, 33, 34, 34, 34, 34, 34, 35, 35, 35, 35, 37, 37, 38, 39, 39, 40, 40, 41, 41, 41, 42; 11:1, 2, 4, 4, 5, 5, 6, 7, 7, 8, 9, 9, 10, 14, 14, 14, 16, 17, 17, 19, 19, 20, 21, 22, 22, 23, 24, 24, 25, 25, 26, 26, 26, 27, 27, 28, 29, 29, 31, 31, 31, 32, 32, 32, 33, 34, 34, 34, 35, 35, 35, 35, 37, 38, 39, 39, 40, 40, 40, 41; 11:1, 2, 4, 5, 5, 6, 6, 7, 7, 8, 8, 8, 9, 9, 10, 11, 11, 12, 12, 13, 13, 14, 14, 14, 15, 16, 16, 17, 17, 18, 18, 19, 20, 20, 20, 20, 20, 21, 21, 22, 23, 23, 23, 24, 24, 24, 24, 25, 25, 25, 26, 26, 26, 27, 27, 27, 28, 28, 28, 29, 29, 31, 31, 32, 33, 33, 33, 34, 34, 35; 14:1, 2, 3, 4, 4, 5, 5, 6, 6, 7, 8, 8, 8, 8, 9, 11, 11, 12, 14, 15, 16, 16, 16, 16, 17, 18, 18, 18, 19, 19, 20, 20, 21, 21, 21, 21, 21, 22, 23, 23, 24, 24, 24, 25, 25, 25, 26, 26, 26, 27, 27, 27, 28, 28, 29, 29, 30, 30, 31, 32, 32, 32, 32, 32; 15:1, 2, 2, 2, 3, 4, 4, 5, 6, 6, 7, 8, 8, 8, 8, 8, 9, 10, 11, 13, 13, 14, 14, 14, 15, 16, 16, 16, 17, 17, 17, 18, 18, 19, 20, 20, 20, 20, 22, 22, 22, 23, 23, 25, 26, 27, 29, 29, 31, 31, 33, 34, 34, 35, 37; 18:1, 1, 3, 3, 4, 6, 6, 7, 7, 9, 10, 11, 13, 14, 15, 15, 16, 16, 18, 19, 20, 20, 21, 11, 13, 14, 15, 16, 16, 18, 19, 20, 20, 21, 22, 22, 23, 24, 26, 27, 28, 30, 31, 31, 32, 32, 32, 33, 33, 33, 33, 34, 34, 35, 35, 37, 38, 39, 40, 40, 40, 40, 41, 41, 42, 43, 43, 43; 19:1, 1, 2, 2, 3, 4, 4, 5, 5, 6, 6, 6, 7, 8, 9, 10, 11, 11, 11, 12, 13, 13, 14, 15, 17, 17, 20, 21, 21, 22, 22, 23, 23, 24, 24, 25, 27, 28, 28, 29, 29, 30, 30, 31, 31, 31, 31, 34, 34, 36, 37, 37, 40, 41, 46, 46, 46, 47; 21:1, 1, 2, 3, 5, 5, 5, 7, 7, 8, 8, 9, 10, 11, 11, 11, 11, 11, 12, 12, 12, 13, 15, 15, 16, 16, 16, 16, 17, 20, 20, 21, 21, 23, 24, 24, 24, 25, 25, 25, 26, 27, 27, 27, 27, 28, 28, 29, 29, 30, 31, 31, 34, 34, 35, 36, 37, 37; 22:1, 2, 2, 4, 4, 4, 5, 5, 6, 6, 6, 8, 8, 9, 10, 11, 12, 13, 13, 13, 14, 14, 14, 15, 17, 17, 17, 17, 19, 19, 19, 19, 22, 23, 23, 24, 24, 25, 25, 26, 26, 26, 26, 27;

Column 3 (Jn):

44, 44, 44, 46, 46, 46, 47, 47, 48, 49, 50, 50, 50, 51, 51, 52, 52, 53, 53;

Jn 1:1, 1, 3, 4, 5, 5, 10, 10, 11, 14, 14, 14, 14, 15, 16, 16, 17, 19, 19, 20, 20, 21, 21, 24, 25, 25, 29, 31, 32, 32, 33, 33, 34, 34, 35, 36, 37, 38, 38, 39, 39, 40, 41, 42, 42, 43, 43, 44, 45, 45, 46, 46, 47, 48, 49, 50, 51, 51, 51; 2:1, 1, 2, 2, 3, 6, 7, 8, 8, 9, 10, 11, 11, 12, 12, 12, 12, 13, 13, 14, 14, 14, 14, 15, 15, 15, 15, 15, 16, 17, 18, 19, 19, 20, 22, 22, 25; 3:2, 3, 4, 5, 6, 8, 8, 8, 9, 11, 11, 12, 13, 14, 19, 19, 22, 22, 22, 23, 23, 25, 26, 26, 26, 27, 29, 31, 32, 32, 36; 4:1, 3, 4, 6, 10, 10, 11, 12, 12, 13, 16, 17, 18, 20, 23, 24, 27, 27, 28, 28, 30, 34, 35, 35, 36, 36, 36, 37, 37, 38, 39, 40, 41, 42, 43, 45, 47, 48, 50, 50, 51, 52, 53; 5:1, 4, 5, 5, 6, 8, 9, 9, 11, 12, 13, 14, 15, 16, 16, 17, 19, 20, 20, 21, 24, 24, 25, 27, 29, 29, 30, 32, 33, 35, 37, 38, 39, 40, 43, 44; 6:2, 3, 4, 5, 9, 11, 11, 11, 13, 13, 15, 15, 16, 17, 17, 17, 17, 18, 19, 19, 21, 22, 23, 24, 24, 27, 27, 28, 30, 30, 33, 35, 35, 37, 39, 40, 40, 42, 42, 43, 44, 45, 45, 49, 50, 51, 53, 54, 54, 55, 56, 56, 57, 58, 62, 63, 64, 65, 66, 69, 69, 70; 7:3, 4, 11, 12, 14, 15, 16, 18, 19, 20, 21, 21, 22, 26, 28, 28, 29, 31, 31, 32, 32, 33, 34, 34, 35, 36, 36, 37, 42, 44, 45, 45, 51, 52, 52, 53; 8:2, 2, 2, 2, 3, 3, 3, 6, 7, 8, 8, 9, 9, 9, 10, 11, 11, 14, 14, 14, 16, 16, 18, 20, 21, 21, 23, 25, 26, 26, 28, 29, 32, 33, 35, 38, 39, 42, 44, 44, 44, 45, 46, 48, 48, 49, 50, 50, 52, 52, 53, 55, 55, 56, 56, 57, 59; 9:1, 2, 6, 6, 7, 7, 8, 8, 11, 11, 11, 11, 14, 14, 14, 14, 15, 15, 16, 18, 19, 20, 21, 21, 22, 22, 23, 25, 26, 27, 27, 28, 31, 34, 35, 36, 37, 38, 38, 39, 40, 40; 10:1, 3, 3, 3, 4, 4, 5, 8, 9, 9, 10, 10, 10, 12, 12, 12, 12, 12, 13, 14, 14, 15, 16, 16, 16, 17, 18, 18, 20, 22, 23, 24, 25, 26, 26, 28, 28, 29, 31, 31, 33, 35, 36, 38, 38, 40; 11:1, 2, 5, 5, 8, 11, 15, 19, 19, 20, 24, 25, 26, 28, 28, 28, 29, 31, 32, 33, 34, 34, 35, 41, 41, 42, 44, 44, 44, 44, 45, 46, 47, 47, 48, 48, 49, 50, 51, 52, 54, 55, 55, 56, 57; 12:2, 3, 3, 5, 6, 6, 9, 11, 13, 14, 15, 16, 16, 17, 20, 21, 22, 24, 27, 30, 32, 34, 36, 36, 38, 40, 40, 40, 41, 44, 45, 47, 48, 49, 50; 13:2, 3, 4, 4, 5, 6, 7, 9, 10, 11, 12, 13, 16, 17, 18, 22, 24, 24, 27, 28, 28, 29, 30, 32, 32; 14:1, 3, 3, 3, 4, 4, 5, 6, 7, 8, 9, 9, 10, 11, 12, 13, 14, 15, 16, 18, 18, 19, 19, 19, 20, 22, 23, 23, 23, 25, 26, 27, 27, 28, 28, 29, 30, 31; 15:1, 2, 4, 6, 7, 7, 10, 11, 16, 16, 16, 18, 19, 21, 22, 23, 23, 23, 25, 26, 26, 27; 16:1, 4, 5, 5, 7, 10, 12, 13, 14, 15, 16, 16, 16, 17, 17, 17, 17, 17, 19, 19, 19, 20, 20, 20, 22, 22, 23, 24, 25, 26, 27; 28, 28, 29, 30, 32; 17:1, 1, 3, 3, 5, 6, 6, 8, 8, 8, 10, 10, 10, 11, 11, 12, 13, 14, 19, 21, 22, 23, 23, 23, 25, 26, 26; 18:1, 2, 3, 3, 3, 4, 5, 6, 10, 10, 12, 13, 15, 16, 17, 18, 18, 18, 18, 19, 21, 22, 23, 24, 25, 26, 27, 27, 27, 28, 28, 29, 30, 31; 19:1, 2, 2, 2, 3, 4, 5, 6, 6, 7, 9, 9, 10, 12, 13, 14, 14, 14, 15, 16, 17, 18, 18, 19, 20, 20, 21, 23, 23, 23, 24, 24, 25, 26, 27, 27, 27, 28, 28, 29, 30, 31; 20:1, 1, 2, 2, 2, 3, 3, 4, 4, 5, 6, 6, 7, 8, 11, 11, 12, 12, 13, 13, 14, 14, 15, 16, 16, 17, 17, 17, 18, 18, 19, 20, 20, 22, 23, 23, 25, 26, 27, 27, 27, 28, 28, 29, 30, 31; 21:1, 1, 2, 3, 3, 6, 6, 7, 8, 9, 10, 11, 11, 12, 13, 13, 17, 18, 18, 18, 19, 21, 22, 23, 23, 24, 25;

Ac 1:1, 3, 4, 7, 8, 8, 8, 9, 9, 10, 13, 13, 13, 13, 13, 13, 14, 14, 14, 15, 15, 16, 17, 18, 18, 19, 19, 20, 20, 21, 23, 24, 24, 25, 26, 26, 26; 2:1, 2, 2, 3, 3, 4, 4, 5, 6, 7, 7, 8, 9, 9, 9, 10, 10, 10, 11, 11, 12, 12, 14, 14, 14, 17, 17, 17, 18, 18, 18, 19, 19, 19, 20, 20, 21, 22, 22, 23, 23, 23, 26, 29, 29, 29, 30, 30, 31, 32, 33, 33, 34, 37, 37, 37, 38, 38, 39, 39, 40, 40, 41, 42, 42, 42, 42, 43, 43, 44, 44, 45, 45, 46, 46, 47, 47; 3:1, 2, 3, 4, 4, 5, 6, 6, 7, 7, 7, 8, 8, 8, 8, 9, 9, 10, 11, 12, 13, 13, 13, 14, 14, 15, 16, 16, 17, 19, 20, 23, 24, 24, 25, 25; 4:1, 1, 2, 3, 3, 3, 5, 5, 6, 6, 6, 8, 10, 13, 13, 13, 14, 14, 16, 18, 19, 21, 22, 23, 23, 24, 24, 24, 25, 26, 26, 27, 27, 28, 29, 29, 30, 30, 31, 31, 31, 32, 33, 33, 34, 35, 35, 36, 36, 37; 5:2, 2, 3, 3, 4, 5, 5, 6, 6, 7, 8, 8, 9, 10, 10, 11, 11, 12, 12, 12, 13, 14, 14, 14, 15, 15, 16, 16, 17, 18, 18, 19, 20, 21, 21, 21, 21, 22, 22, 23, 24, 24, 24, 24, 25, 26, 26, 27, 27, 28, 29, 29, 30, 30, 31, 31, 31, 32, 32, 33, 33, 34, 35, 35, 36, 36, 37, 37, 38, 38, 39, 39, 40, 40, 41, 41, 42, 42, 43, 43,

29, 30, 31, 32, 32, 32, 34, 34, 34, 35, 35, 36, 36, 36, 38, 39, 41, 41, 41, 42, 42, 43, 43, 46, 49, 51, 51, 51, 52, 52, 53, 54, 55, 55, 56, 56, 57, 57, 58, 58, 58, 59, 59, 60, 60, 60; 8:1, 1, 1, 1, 2, 2, 3, 5, 6, 6, 7, 7, 8, 9, 11, 12, 12, 13, 13, 13, 14, 17, 18, 22, 23, 23, 25, 25, 25, 26, 26, 27, 27, 27, 28, 29, 30, 30, 30, 31, 31, 31, 32, 33, 34, 34, 35, 35, 35, 36, 36, 37, 37, 37, 38, 38, 38, 38, 39, 39, 40; 9:1, 1, 2, 3, 3, 4, 4, 4, 5, 5, 6, 6, 6, 6, 7, 8, 8, 9, 9, 10, 10, 10, 11, 11, 11, 12, 12, 14, 15, 15, 17, 17, 17, 17, 17, 17, 18, 18, 18, 18, 19, 20, 20, 21, 21, 21, 23, 24, 24, 25, 25, 26, 26, 27, 27, 28, 28, 29, 30, 31, 31, 31, 31, 31, 32, 33, 33, 34, 34, 34, 35, 35, 35, 36, 37, 37, 38, 38, 38, 39, 39, 40, 40, 40, 40, 41, 41, 41, 41, 42, 42, 42, 43; 10:2, 2, 3, 4, 4, 4, 4, 5, 5, 6, 6, 6, 6, 7, 7, 7, 7, 7, 8, 8, 8, 8, 9, 9, 10, 10, 11, 11, 11, 12, 13, 13, 14, 14, 14, 15, 16, 16, 16, 17, 17, 19, 19, 19, 19, 19, 20, 20, 20, 21, 22, 22, 23, 23, 23, 24, 25, 25, 25; 13:1, 1, 1, 1, 1, 1, 2, 2, 5, 5, 6, 7, 7, 7, 10, 10, 10, 11, 11, 11, 11, 11, 13, 13, 14, 14, 15, 15, 15, 15, 16, 16, 17, 17, 17, 17, 17, 19, 19, 20, 20, 21, 22, 22, 23, 23, 24, 25, 26, 26, 27, 27, 28, 29, 29, 30, 30, 31, 31, 31, 32, 33, 35, 36, 36, 37, 38, 38, 39, 39, 40, 40; 10:1, 3, 3, 3, 4, 4, 5, 8, 9, 9, 10, 10, 10, 12, 12, 12, 13, 14, 14, 15, 16, 16, 16, 17, 18, 18, 20, 22, 23, 24, 25, 26, 26, 28, 28, 29, 31, 31, 33, 35, 36, 38, 38, 40; 14:1, 1, 1, 1, 2, 3, 3, 4, 4, 5, 5, 6, 6, 7, 8, 9, 9, 10, 11, 12, 13, 13, 14, 14, 15, 15, 15, 15, 15, 17, 17, 18, 19, 19, 19, 20, 20, 20, 21, 21, 21, 21, 22, 23, 23, 24, 25, 25, 25, 26, 26, 26, 27, 28, 28, 29, 29, 30, 30, 30; 15:1, 2, 2, 2, 2, 3, 3, 3, 4, 4, 4, 4, 5, 6, 6, 7, 7, 7, 7, 7, 8, 8, 8, 9, 9, 10, 11, 12, 12, 12, 12, 13, 13, 14, 14, 15, 15, 16, 16, 16, 17, 17, 17, 18, 18, 19, 19, 20, 20, 21, 21, 22, 22, 22, 22, 23, 24, 24, 25, 25, 25, 26, 26, 27, 28, 29, 30, 30, 31; 16:1, 1, 1, 2, 3, 3, 3, 4, 4, 5, 5, 6, 6, 8, 9, 10, 11, 11, 12, 12, 14, 14, 15, 15, 16, 17, 17, 18, 18, 18, 19, 19, 21, 22, 22, 23, 23, 24, 24, 25, 25, 26, 26, 26, 27, 27, 27, 28, 28, 30, 30, 31; 16:1, 1, 1, 2, 3, 3, 4, 5, 6, 6, 6, 7, 8, 8, 8, 9, 10, 11, 12, 13, 14, 14, 15, 16, 16, 16, 17, 18, 18, 19, 19, 20, 20, 21, 21, 23, 24, 25, 26, 26, 27, 29, 29, 30, 30, 30, 31, 31, 32, 32, 33, 34, 34, 34, 35; 21:1, 1, 1, 2, 3, 3, 4, 5, 6, 6, 7, 8, 8, 11, 12, 12, 13, 14, 14, 15, 16, 16, 17, 17, 18, 19, 19, 20, 20, 21, 22, 22, 23, 23, 24, 24, 24, 25, 27, 27; 25:2, 2, 3, 4, 4, 5, 6, 6, 7, 7, 7, 9, 13, 13, 14, 15, 16, 17, 19, 20, 20, 23, 23, 23, 23, 24, 24, 24, 25, 26, 27; 26:1, 3, 6, 6, 7, 10, 10, 11, 11, 11, 12, 13, 14, 15, 15, 16, 16, 17, 18, 18, 20, 20, 20, 20, 20, 30, 30, 30, 31; 27:1, 1, 2, 3, 3, 4, 5, 5, 6, 7, 9, 10, 11, 12, 12, 12, 13, 15, 15, 16, 17, 18, 18, 19, 20, 21, 21, 23, 24, 27, 28, 28, 28, 29, 30, 30, 33, 35, 35, 36, 37, 37, 38, 38, 39, 40, 40, 40, 41, 41, 42, 42, 43, 43, 44, 44, 44; 28:1, 2, 2, 2, 3, 3, 3, 4, 5, 5, 6, 6, 7, 8, 8, 8, 9, 9, 10, 11, 11, 11, 13, 13, 13, 13, 14, 14, 15, 15, 16, 16, 16, 17, 17, 17, 19, 20, 21, 23, 23, 23, 24, 24, 25, 25, 26, 26, 26, 27, 27, 27, 27, 27, 28, 29, 29, 30, 30, 31;

Ro 1:4, 5, 7, 7, 12, 14, 14, 16, 18, 20, 21, 23, 23, 23, 23, 25, 25, 27, 27, 28; 2:3, 3, 4, 4, 5, 5, 7, 7, 8, 8, 9, 9, 10, 10, 12, 15, 17, 17, 18, 18, 19, 20, 27, 27, 29, 29; 3:4, 8, 8, 9, 14, 14, 16, 17, 19, 21, 22, 26, 30; 4:3, 7, 11, 12, 14, 17, 19, 21, 22, 25; 5:2, 3, 4, 4, 5, 11, 12, 12, 15, 16, 17; 6:13, 19, 22, 22; 7:6, 9, 10, 11, 12, 12, 23; 8:2, 3, 6, 10, 17, 17, 22, 23, 27, 28, 30, 30; 9:2, 4, 4, 4, 4, 4, 5, 9, 10, 15, 17, 18, 21, 22, 23, 25, 26, 28, 29, 29, 33, 33; 10:1, 3, 8, 9, 10, 12, 14, 14, 15, 15, 17, 18, 19, 20, 21; 11:3, 3, 6, 7, 8, 9, 9, 9, 10, 12, 14, 16, 17, 17, 17, 17, 20, 22, 23, 24, 26, 26, 29, 33, 33, 35, 36, 36; 12:2, 2, 2, 4, 5, 14, 15; 13:2, 3, 9, 11, 12, 13, 13, 14; 14:3, 6, 6, 6, 7, 8, 9, 9, 9, 11, 14, 17, 17, 17, 18, 19, 23; 15:1, 4, 5, 6, 9, 10, 11, 11, 12, 13, 14, 18, 19, 21, 23, 24, 26, 27, 28, 29, 30, 31, 32; 16:2, 2, 3, 7, 7, 9, 12, 12, 13, 14, 15, 15, 15, 17, 18, 18, 18, 19, 20, 21, 21, 21, 23, 23, 25, 26, 99

1Co 1:1, 2, 3, 3, 5, 10, 10, 12, 12, 14, 19, 22, 23, 24, 24, 25, 27, 28, 28, 28, 30, 30, 30; 2:1, 2, 3, 3, 3, 4, 4, 4; 3:1, 2, 3, 3, 3, 4, 5, 8, 8, 10, 13, 16, 20, 20, 23; 4:1, 5, 5, 6, 6, 7, 8, 8, 9, 9, 11, 11, 11, 11, 12, 13, 17, 19, 21; 5:1, 2, 2, 4, 8, 8; 6:1, 2, 6, 8, 8, 11, 11, 13, 13, 13, 14, 14, 15, 19, 20; 7:2, 3, 4, 5, 5, 6, 7, 8, 10, 11, 11, 12, 13, 14, 17, 19, 28, 28, 30, 30, 31, 34, 34, 35, 35, 36, 37, 40; 8:2, 4, 5, 6, 6, 6, 7, 11, 12; 9:4, 5, 6, 6, 7; 10:1, 2, 2, 3, 4, 4, 7, 7, 8, 8, 9, 10, 11, 17, 20, 20, 21, 21, 26, 27, 28; 11:2, 3, 7, 18, 21, 22, 22, 24, 24, 26, 27, 28, 28, 29, 30, 30, 34, 34; 12:3, 5, 6, 11, 12, 12, 13, 16, 19, 21, 23, 23, 26, 28, 31; 13:1, 1, 2, 2, 2, 2, 3, 3, 3, 4, 9, 13; 14:1, 3, 3, 7, 10, 11, 15, 15, 15, 17, 21, 23, 24, 24, 25, 25, 27, 27, 28, 28, 29, 31, 32, 35, 39, 40; 15:1, 4, 4, 5, 8, 10, 10, 11, 14, 15, 16, 17, 20, 24, 24, 28, 30, 32, 34, 34, 35, 37, 38, 39, 40, 40, 41, 41, 44, 45, 46, 48, 49, 50, 52, 52, 53, 54, 56; 16:3, 4, 6, 10, 10, 15, 17, 17, 18, 19, 20, 99, 99, 99

2Co 1:1, 2, 2, 3, 4, 6, 6, 7, 10, 12, 12, 13, 15, 16, 16, 16, 17, 18, 19, 19, 19, 20, 20, 21; 2:3, 4, 7, 12, 14, 15, 16, 16; 3:2, 4, 7, 13, 17; 4:5, 7, 13, 13, 14; 5:8, 8, 11, 12, 15, 15, 18, 18, 19; 6:2, 7, 8, 8, 9, 9, 9, 10, 14, 15, 16, 16, 16, 16, 17, 17, 17, 18, 18; 7:1, 3, 7, 13, 15, 19; 8:2, 3, 4, 5, 5, 7, 7, 7, 8, 10, 12, 13, 15, 18, 19, 19, 22, 23, 23, 24, 24; 9:2, 4, 4, 5, 6, 8, 10, 10, 13, 14; 10:1, 5, 5, 6, 8, 10, 10, 12, 16; 11:1, 9, 9, 9, 14, 15, 27, 27, 27, 29, 29, 31, 33, 33; 12:1, 3, 4, 7, 9, 12, 14, 15, 15, 18, 20, 21, 21, 21, 21; 13:2, 2, 2, 9, 10, 11, 11, 14, 14, 99

Gal 1:1, 2, 3, 3, 4, 5, 7, 13, 14, 15, 16, 17, 18, 21, 22, 24; 2:1, 2, 2, 4, 9, 9, 9, 9, 12, 13, 14, 15, 16, 20, 20; 3:5, 6, 8, 12, 16, 16, 16, 17, 17, 19, 29, 29; 4:2, 6, 7, 9, 10, 10, 14, 15, 18, 20, 25, 25, 27, 30; 5:1, 11, 15, 16, 17, 17, 21, 24, 24; 6:2, 4, 4, 9, 14, 16, 16, 16, 16

Eph 1:1, 2, 2, 3, 4, 8, 10, 15, 17, 18, 19, 20, 21, 21, 21, 21, 22, 22; 2:1, 1, 3, 3, 6, 6, 8, 12, 12, 14, 16, 16, 17, 17, 17, 19, 19, 20, 20; 3:5, 6, 6, 9, 10, 12, 15, 17, 18, 18, 18, 19; 4:2, 4, 6, 6, 6, 8, 11, 11, 11, 11, 13, 14, 14, 14, 18, 19, 21, 23, 24, 24, 26, 30, 31, 31, 31, 31, 32; 5:2, 2, 2, 3, 5, 9, 9, 11, 14, 14, 18, 19, 19, 20, 23, 25, 26, 27, 29, 30, 31, 31, 31, 32, 33; 6:2, 3, 4, 4, 5, 7, 9, 10, 12, 14, 15, 17, 17, 18, 18, 18, 19; 7, 9, 10, 12, 14, 15, 17, 17, 18, 18, 23, 23, 23

Php 1:1, 1, 2, 2, 7, 7, 9, 9, 10, 11, 13, 14, 15, 15, 18, 18, 19, 20, 21, 23, 25, 25, 25, 27, 28, 28, 30; 2:1, 7, 7, 8, 8, 9, 10, 10, 11, 12, 13, 14, 15, 17, 17, 17, 18, 25, 25, 25, 26, 27, 28, 29; 3:3, 8, 8, 9, 10, 10, 13, 15, 17, 18, 19; 4:1, 1, 2, 3, 3, 4, 6, 7, 7, 8, 9, 9, 9, 9, 12, 12, 12, 12, 15, 16, 18, 20, 20

Col 1:1, 2, 2, 3, 4, 6, 6, 9, 9, 10, 11, 13, 16, 16, 16, 17, 17, 18, 20, 21, 21, 22, 23, 23, 23, 24, 26, 28; 2:1, 1, 2, 2, 2, 3, 4, 5, 5, 7, 7, 8, 8, 10, 13, 14, 15, 15, 18, 19, 19, 19, 22, 23, 23, 23; 3:3, 5, 10, 11, 12, 13, 14, 15, 16, 16, 16, 17, 17, 19, 23, 23, 25; 4:1, 2, 7, 7, 8, 9, 10, 11, 12, 13, 13, 14, 15, 15, 16, 16, 17, 99

1Th 1:1, 1, 1, 1, 3, 3, 3, 5, 5, 6, 6, 7, 8, 9, 9, 10; 2:2, 9, 9, 10, 10, 11, 11, 12, 15, 15, 15, 18, 20; 3:2, 2, 2, 2, 4, 5, 6, 6, 6, 7, 10, 10, 10, 11, 11, 12, 12, 12; 4:1, 1, 1, 4, 6, 6, 10, 10, 11, 11, 12, 14, 15, 16, 17, 17; 5:1, 3, 3, 3, 9, 14, 16, 16, 17, 17; 5:1, 2, 3, 3, 12, 12, 13, 15, 23, 23, 23, 23

2Th 1:1, 1, 1, 2, 3, 4, 4, 7, 8, 9, 9, 10, 11, 13, 15, 16, 16, 16, 17, 17; 3:1, 2, 2, 3, 4, 4, 5, 5, 6, 8, 8, 12, 12, 14, 14

1Ti 1:1, 2, 4, 4, 5, 7, 9, 9, 9, 9, 10, 12, 13, 13, 14, 14, 15, 17, 17, 19, 20; 2:1, 2, 2, 3, 4, 5, 5, 7, 7, 7, 8, 9, 14, 15, 15; 3:7, 10, 12, 13, 15, 16; 4:1, 3, 4, 4, 5, 5, 5, 7, 7, 8, 8, 10, 11, 16; 5:1, 4, 4, 5, 5, 5, 7, 8, 8, 13, 13, 13, 16, 17, 18, 21, 21, 23, 24, 25; 6:1, 2, 2, 3, 3, 4, 5, 7, 8, 8, 9, 9, 9, 10, 11, 12, 13, 15, 15, 16, 20, 20

2Ti 1:2, 2, 3, 5, 5, 7, 7, 9, 9, 10, 10, 11, 12, 13, 15, 16, 17, 18; 2:2, 5, 7, 16, 17, 17, 18, 19, 20, 20, 20, 20, 21, 21, 23, 24, 26; 3:6, 7, 8, 12, 13, 13, 14, 15, 16; 4:1, 1, 1, 2, 4, 4, 6, 8, 10, 12, 13, 17, 17, 17, 18, 18, 18, 19, 19, 21, 21, 21

Tit 1:1, 1, 4, 4, 5, 9, 10, 10, 14, 15, 15, 16, 16; 2:9, 12, 12, 13, 13, 14, 15, 15; 3:1, 3, 3, 3, 4, 5, 8, 8, 9, 9, 9, 9, 10, 11, 13, 14

Phm 1:1, 1, 2, 2, 3, 3, 5, 7, 9, 11, 16

Heb 1:1, 3, 3, 5, 5, 6, 6, 7, 7, 8, 9, 10, 10, 10, 11, 13, 13, 13, 14, 14, 4, 4, 4, 7, 7, 9, 10, 10, 18; 4:4, 5, 6, 12, 12, 12, 12, 12, 12, 12, 13, 16; 5:1, 2, 3, 4, 7, 7, 7, 9, 11, 12, 12, 14; 6:1, 2, 2, 2, 3, 4, 4, 5, 6, 7, 8, 8, 9, 10, 10, 11, 12, 14, 15, 16, 19, 19; 7:1, 2, 5, 6, 7, 8, 9, 11, 15, 18, 20, 21, 23, 26, 27; 8:2, 2, 3, 5, 8, 9, 10, 10, 10, 11, 12, 12, 13; 9:1, 2, 2, 3, 4, 4, 4, 5, 7, 9, 10, 10, 10, 11, 12, 13, 13, 15, 19, 19, 19, 22, 27, 28; 10:1, 4, 5, 6, 8, 8, 11, 11, 16, 17, 19, 21, 22, 24, 24, 25, 25, 27, 29, 30, 33, 34, 37, 37; 11:4, 5, 6, 7, 7, 8, 8, 8, 9, 10, 10, 10, 10, 11, 11, 11, 12, 13, 13, 14, 14, 14, 16, 16, 16, 16, 17, 17, 18; 18:1, 1, 2, 2, 2, 2, 3, 3, 3, 4, 5, 6, 7, 7, 7, 7, 8, 8, 8, 9, 9, 9, 9, 9, 9, 11, 11, 12, 12, 12, 12, 12, 12, 12, 13, 13, 13, 13, 13, 13, 13, 14, 14, 14, 14, 15, 16, 16, 16, 16, 16, 17, 18; 18:1, 1, 2, 2, 2, 2, 2, 3, 3, 3, 3, 4, 4, 4, 5, 5, 6, 6, 7, 7, 7, 7, 8, 8, 8, 8, 8, 8, 9, 9, 9, 10, 11, 11, 11, 12, 12, 13, 13, 13, 13, 14, 15, 16, 16, 16, 17, 17, 17, 17, 17, 19, 19, 19

ARE (2946)

Ge 2:4; 6:9; 7:2, 8; 9:2, 19; 10:1, 20, 31, 32; 11:10, 27; 18:5, 24; 19:5, 15; 20:7, 16; 25:7, 12, 13, 16, 16, 17, 19, 23; 27:22, 41, 46; 29:4, 21; 31:12, 15, 43, 43, 43, 49; 32:17; 33:5, 8, 13, 13, 15; 34:21, 22; 35:2, 26; 36:1, 5, 9, 10, 13, 16, 17, 17, 18, 19, 19, 20, 21, 24, 26, 27, 28, 29, 30, 31, 40, 41; 41:26, 26, 27; 42:9, 9, 10, 11, 11, 11, 12, 13, 14, 16, 21, 31, 31, 33, 34, 34, 36; 43:18; 44:16; 45:6, 11, 16; 46:8, 18, 22, 25, 31, 32; 47:1, 1, 3, 4, 5, 9; 48:5, 8, 9; 49:5, 5, 28; 50:3, 3

Ex 1:1, 9, 19, 19, 19; 2:18; 3:7; 4:18, 19; 5:5, 16, 17, 17; 6:15, 16, 19, 24, 25, 26, 27, 27; 7:17; 8:21; 9:27; 10:8, 11; 12:13; 14:3; 15:4; 16:7, 8, 8, 16; 19:6; 21:1; 24:14; 25:22, 26; 28:3, 4, 24; 29:33; 30:13, 14; 31:6; 32:2, 22; 33:5, 16; 35:1; 39:6; 40:4

Lev 4:12, 12, 13; 5:17; 10:14; 11:2, 2, 8, 9, 13, 13, 26, 27, 28, 31, 32, 35, 42; 12:6; 14:37; 16:4; 18:17, 24; 23:2, 4, 17, 37, 42; 25:7, 33, 42, 44, 45, 55, 55; 26:25, 36, 39, 46; 27:34

Nu 1:3, 5, 17, 44; 2:32; 3:1, 2, 3, 9, 13, 18, 20, 21, 27, 33, 46, 46; 4:15, 20, 41; 6:13; 8:16, 17; 9:7, 7; 10:4, 29, 31; 11:21; 13:16, 28, 30, 31, 32; 14:9, 35, 43, 43; 15:13, 15; 16:3, 5, 11, 37, 38; 18:6, 16, 17, 18; 20:16; 22:4, 6, 9; 24:3, 5, 6, 15; 26:2, 7, 14, 18, 22, 25, 27, 30, 34, 35, 36, 37, 37, 41, 42, 42, 47, 50, 57, 58, 63; 27:1; 30:14, 16; 31:12, 49; 32:14; 33:1, 2, 51; 34:17, 19, 29; 35:33; 36:3, 4, 13

Dt 1:2, 10, 11, 20, 28; 2:4, 25; 3:18; 4:4, 20, 49; 5:3; 6:1, 14; 7:6, 17, 20; 8:9; 9:12, 29; 11:12, 30; 12:1, 9; 13:7, 13; 14:1, 2, 4, 7, 9, 12, 29; 16:11, 14; 17:14; 18:12; 20:2, 15, 15; 21:2, 6; 22:5, 17; 23:8, 18; 24:14; 25:16; 27:12; 28:58; 29:1, 5, 20, 21, 27, 29; 30:1, 10; 31:17, 18, 21; 32:4, 5, 20, 21, 28, 32, 32, 37; 33:3, 17, 17, 27

Jos 2:3; 3:8; 4:9; 6:17, 17, 19; 7:3, 21; 8:5; 9:8, 8, 9, 11, 13, 22, 23, 25; 10:6, 17; 12:1, 7; 13:14, 17, 30, 32; 14:1; 15:32; 16:3; 17:3, 9, 16, 16; 18:3; 19:14, 29, 35, 51; 21:9; 22:10, 17; 23:14, 15; 24:22, 22, 23

Jdg 3:1; 5:11; 6:2; 7:2, 2, 4, 18; 8:6, 15, 15; 9:2, 18; 10:4, 4; 11:7, 7; 12:3, 4; 15:10, 10, 11, 12; 18:9, 24; 19:18; 20:7, 13, 32, 39; 21:16

Ru 1:11; 4:9, 10, 11, 18

1Sa 2:3, 4, 4, 8; 4:8, 17; 6:17; 9:20; 10:2, 7; 12:2, 21; 16:11, 16; 17:8; 19:22; 20:21, 22; 21:5; 26:16; 29:10

2Sa 1:4, 4, 4, 19, 25, 27; 3:28; 5:1, 8; 7:9; 11:11; 13:33; 14:14, 20; 15:3, 13, 15; 16:4, 21; 17:2, 10, 12, 16; 19:11, 12, 12, 22; 20:19; 22:28, 39; 24:14

1Ki 1:20, 45; 4:8, 13; 8:8; 9:13; 10:8, 8, 27; 11:41; 13:3, 32; 14:19, 29; 15:7, 23, 31; 16:5, 14, 20, 27; 18:22, 25; 20:3, 17, 23, 31; 22:39, 45

2Ki 1:5, 18; 3:23; 5:12; 6:9, 16; 7:12, 13, 13, 34; 12:19; 13:8, 12; 14:15, 18, 28; 15:6, 11, 15, 21, 26, 31, 36; 16:19; 18:20, 26, 34, 34, 35; 19:3, 4; 20:14, 15, 20; 21:17, 25; 23:28; 24:5

1Ch 1:29, 31, 33, 43, 54; 2:1, 18, 55; 4:2, 4, 12, 18, 22; 5:14; 6:19, 31, 33, 50, 54, 65; 7:8, 33; 8:6, 6, 38, 40; 9:33, 44; 11:1, 10; 12:1, 15, 18, 23; 13:2, 2; 14:4; 15:12; 16:14, 26, 27, 27; 17:8; 19:3; 21:3, 13; 22:15; 24:1; 26:19; 29:15, 15, 17, 29

2Ch 1:15; 2:7; 3:3; 6:37; 7:14; 8:11; 9:7, 7, 27, 29; 11:10; 12:15; 13:7, 8, 9, 10, 22; 16:11; 17:14; 19:3; 20:12, 34, 23:6; 24:26, 27; 25:26; 26:18; 27:7; 28:10, 26; 29:9, 19; 30:6; 32:32; 33:18, 19; 34:21, 24, 31; 35:25, 27; 36:8

Ezr 2:1; 4:10, 12; 5:4, 11; 6:6, 9; 7:13, 19, 21, 25; 8:1, 13, 28, 28; 9:6, 15; 10:3, 13, 13, 13

Ne 1:3, 3, 3, 10; 2:3, 17, 17; 4:2, 9, 19; 5:2, 5, 17; 6:8; 7:6; 9:6, 36, 36, 37; 10:39; 11:3, 7; 12:1

Est 1:16; 3:8; 4:16; 7:4; 8:5, 9; 9:13; 10:2

Job 1:19; 3:8, 19, 22, 24; 4:9, 10, 11, 19, 20; 5:4, 4; 6:3, 4, 7, 16, 17, 18, 21, 21, 25, 26; 7:1, 3, 6, 6, 8, 16; 8:9, 9, 13, 17; 9:25, 26; 10:5, 5, 17, 20; 11:6; 12:2, 6, 16; 13:4, 4, 12, 23; 14:5, 5, 21; 15:10, 11, 15, 28; 16:2, 22; 17:1, 1, 2, 7, 11; 18:3, 21; 19:3, 13, 19, 22; 20:11, 25; 21:7, 9, 18, 22, 24, 24, 28, 33; 22:10, 12, 14, 19, 29; 23:14; 24:1, 8, 13, 17, 23, 24, 24; 25:2, 5; 26:5, 11, 14; 27:12; 28:4, 4, 6; 30:1, 15, 17, 30; 31:40; 32:6, 9; 34:18, 19, 21, 25; 35:5; 36:7, 7, 20; 37:17, 24; 38:6, 30, 35; 39:4, 30; 40:17, 18, 18; 41:14, 15, 17, 18, 23, 23, 25, 28, 29, 30

Ps 1:4, 4; 2:12; 3:1, 1; 6:2; 9:3, 6, 15; 10:5, 5, 8, 16; 12:4, 6, 8; 14:1, 3, 3; 16:3, 6, 11; 17:2, 10, 14, 14; 18:38; 19:8, 9, 10; 20:8, 8; 21:11; 22:14; 25:10, 15, 17, 19; 27:12; 31:10, 15; 32:11; 33:4; 34:15, 15, 18, 19; 35:19, 20; 36:3, 6, 12, 12; 37:23, 28, 34; 38:4, 4, 5, 7, 14, 19, 19, 19, 20; 39:6; 40:5, 5, 5, 12; 42:7; 44:13, 22, 22; 45:5; 47:9; 49:14; 50:11; 51:17; 53:1, 3; 54:3; 55:4, 5, 10; 56:5, 8, 12; 57:4, 4, 6; 58:3, 4; 59:3, 7; 62:9, 9, 9; 65:5, 8, 13; 68:6, 17; 69:1, 4, 4, 5, 9, 19; 71:13, 24, 24; 72:20; 73:1, 4, 5, 5, 8, 10, 12, 19, 27; 74:20; 75:3; 76:5, 6; 77:19; 79:1, 4, 4, 8, 11; 82:5, 6, 6; 83:5; 84:1, 4, 5; 85:10; 86:8, 14; 87:3, 7; 88:5; 89:7, 11, 14, 49; 90:4, 5, 5, 7, 7, 9, 10; 92:5, 5; 93:5; 94:11; 95:4, 7; 96:5, 6, 6; 97:2, 2; 100:3, 14, 15; 104:16, 17, 18, 24, 25, 28, 29, 30; 105:7; 106:3; 107:17, 27, 29, 30, 38, 39; 109:2, 4, 24; 111:2, 7, 7, 8; 113:6; 115:4, 8, 15, 16; 116:11; 118:12; 119:1, 2, 21, 24, 39, 75, 84, 85, 86, 91, 98, 99, 103, 111, 129, 137, 138, 143, 150, 151, 156, 157, 168, 172; 120:7; 122:5; 123:3, 4; 124:7; 125:2, 4; 126:3; 127:3, 4, 4; 135:15, 18; 139:12, 14, 17, 18; 140:2; 141:6, 6, 7, 8; 142:6; 144:4; 145:9; 146:8

Pr 1:19; 2:15; 3:15, 17, 17, 20; 4:22, 23; 5:6, 11, 21; 6:16, 23; 8:8, 9, 11, 18, 32; 9:17, 18, 18; 10:6; 11:20, 20, 20, 20; 12:5, 5, 6, 7, 7, 10, 22, 22; 13:8; 14:4, 12, 18; 15:3, 11, 15, 22, 22, 26, 26; 16:2, 11, 11, 13, 24, 25; 17:6, 6, 15, 24; 18:4, 7, 8, 19, 21; 19:7, 13, 14, 21, 29; 20:7, 10, 15, 23, 24; 22:3, 4, 5, 26; 23:3; 24:11, 11, 21; 25:1; 26:7, 21, 23, 25, 26, 26, 28:1, 2; 29:2, 12, 16; 30:12, 13, 15, 18, 24, 24, 25, 26, 29; 31:8, 21, 25

Ecc 1:8, 11, 13, 14; 2:14, 23; 3:18, 20; 4:1, 2, 2, 9; 5:7, 11; 7:19, 21; 8:8, 13; 9:1, 3, 12, 12, 12, 16, 17; 10:12; 11:10; 12:3, 11, 11

SS 1:10, 17; 3:7; 4:2, 2, 3, 5, 13; 5:11, 13, 14, 15; 6:6, 7, 8; 7:1, 1, 3, 3, 9, 13; 8:6

Isa 1:4, 4, 7, 14, 15, 23; 2:6, 13, 14; 3:8, 12, 16; 4:2; 5:12, 13, 13, 21, 22, 28; 7:2; 8:18; 9:10, 10, 16, 16; 10:8, 14, 20, 29; 14:19; 16:4, 7, 8, 8; 17:2; 19:11, 12, 12, 13, 13, 21; 21:3; 22:2, 3, 3, 3, 9; 23:8, 8; 24:6, 6, 17, 18, 21, 22; 25:1; 26:9, 14, 14; 27:7, 9, 11; 28:1, 1, 7, 7, 7, 8, 9, 15, 27, 27; 29:9, 15, 20; 30:18, 27; 31:1, 1, 3; 32:7, 9, 11, 20; 33:13, 13, 14, 23; 35:4; 36:5, 11, 19, 19, 20; 37:3; 39:3; 40:11, 15, 15, 17, 18, 22; 41:23, 23, 24, 29, 29, 29; 42:9, 17, 22, 22; 43:10, 12, 17, 17, 44:7; 45:16, 19, 20, 24; 46:1, 2, 3, 10, 12; 48:1, 1, 7; 49:9, 16; 51:1, 1, 19, 20; 52:7; 53:5; 54:1; 55:8, 8, 9, 9; 56:8, 10, 10, 10, 11, 11; 57:1, 4, 6, 20; 58:7; 59:3, 6, 7, 9, 10, 12; 60:8; 61:1, 9, 11; 63:8, 15, 19; 64:6, 6, 8, 8, 9, 10, 11; 65:5, 11, 16, 16, 22, 23, 24

Jer 2:5, 5, 11, 15, 28, 28, 31; 4:13, 13, 17, 20, 22, 22; 5:3, 4, 4, 6, 8; 6:4, 20, 23, 28, 28, 28, 29; 7:4, 10; 8:8, 9, 10, 19, 19, 25, 26, 26, 26; 10:2, 3, 5, 8, 9, 15, 20, 20, 20, 21; 11:10, 16; 12:1, 4, 9; 13:22, 23; 14:2, 7, 9, 18, 22; 15:2, 2, 2, 8, 16; 16:3, 17, 17, 20; 18:6; 21:4, 7;

22:6, 17, 20, 28, 28; 23:10, 11, 14, 26;
24:2, 3, 5, 8; 25:12, 22, 23, 26, 31, 34,
37; 27:5, 18; 29:1, 4, 16, 17, 22, 25; 30:4,
6; 31:20, 29; 32:19, 24, 35; 33:4, 10;
34:21; 35:14; 37:19; 38:19, 22, 22, 22;
40:15; 41:2; 42:2, 11; 43:11, 11, 11;
44:2, 6, 10, 14, 24, 27, 28; 46:5, 5, 7, 8,
12, 15, 21, 21, 23, 23; 48:14, 15, 17,
32, 36, 41, 46; 49:23, 32; 50:2, 2, 11, 15,
15, 37, 38, 42; 51:4, 7, 18, 30, 32, 32, 43,
51, 51, 56, 60, 64
La 1:2, 2, 4, 4, 5, 5, 6, 6, 14, 16, 18, 20, 21,
22; 2:9, 9, 11, 21; 3:22, 23; 4:1, 2, 5, 8, 9,
18, 19; 5:3, 3, 5, 7, 12, 17
Eze 2:4, 5, 7; 3:7, 26, 27; 5:2, 5, 6, 7, 7, 14,
15; 7:9; 11:2, 7, 12, 15; 12:2, 10, 14, 20,
22, 23, 27; 13:4; 14:5; 16:7, 27, 38, 52,
57; 18:2, 4, 25, 29, 29; 20:3, 30, 34;
21:14, 24, 24, 29; 22:9, 18, 18, 19, 27;
23:45; 24:19; 25:9; 26:6, 18, 19; 27:4, 27;
28:8, 24, 25; 29:12, 12; 30:7, 7; 31:12,
12, 12, 14; 32:20, 21, 22, 23, 24, 25, 26,
27, 27, 28, 29, 30, 30, 32; 33:24, 27, 30;
34:3, 12, 30, 31; 35:8, 12, 12; 36:2, 3, 3,
4, 4, 7, 8, 20, 20, 35, 35, 36; 37:11, 11,
11; 38:7, 11, 12, 12, 20, 22; 40:46; 42:13,
14, 14; 43:13, 18, 27; 44:10; 45:14;
46:24; 48:1, 1, 11, 15, 29, 30
Da 1:10; 2:20, 28; 3:12, 16; 4:3, 3, 18, 35,
37; 5:23; 7:17, 17, 24; 8:20, 23; 9:7, 7,
16, 16, 19, 24, 26; 10:16; 12:9
Hos 1:9, 10, 10; 2:12; 4:4, 6, 14; 5:2; 6:5;
7:2, 4, 7, 7, 9, 16; 8:9; 9:6, 7, 7, 15; 11:7,
8; 12:7, 11, 11; 14:3, 9
Joel 1:6, 7, 12, 17, 17, 18, 18, 20
Am 4:1; 5:16; 6:1, 1, 6; 9:7, 8, 12
Ob 1:6, 6
Jnh 4:11;
Mic 1:4, 5, 5, 16; 2:7, 13; 4:11; 6:10, 12, 16;
7:6, 11
Na 1:3, 6; 2:3; 3:13, 17, 17
Hab 1:3, 3, 6, 7, 8, 8, 15; 3:6
Zep 1:6, 11, 11, 12; 3:3, 3, 4, 6, 6, 18, 18
Hag 1:6;
Zec 1:5, 9, 10, 15, 19, 21, 21; 3:8; 4:4, 10,
11, 14; 6:4, 5, 6, 10, 15; 8:16, 17; 11:2;
13:6
Mal 1:4; 2:8; 3:6, 7, 9, 9, 15, 15
Mt 1:17, 17, 17; 2:2, 18, 20; 5:3, 4, 5, 6, 7,
8, 9, 10, 10, 11, 13, 14, 15; 6:5, 26; 7:15;
8:26; 9:12, 17, 37; 10:2, 28, 29, 30, 31;
11:5, 5, 8, 11, 22; 12:5, 48; 13:15, 16,
38, 38, 39, 40, 56; 15:16, 20; 17:26;
18:20; 19:6, 12, 12, 26, 30; 20:22, 22, 25;
22:4, 4, 4, 14, 14, 21, 21, 30, 30; 23:8,
13, 25, 27, 27, 28, 31, 37; 24:8, 19; 25:8;
26:55
Mk 2:17, 17; 4:11, 11, 15, 16, 16, 17, 18,
20, 20, 40; 5:9; 6:2, 3; 7:15, 18; 9:23;
10:8, 27, 31, 42; 12:17, 17, 25, 25, 25;
13:1, 8, 17, 25, 32; 14:36, 48
Lk 1:1; 4:18; 5:20, 31, 31, 38; 6:21, 21, 22,
25; 7:22, 22, 25, 25, 28, 31, 32, 47,
47, 48; 8:12, 13, 14, 14, 15, 21; 9:12, 55,
61; 10:2, 8, 9, 17, 20, 20, 22, 23; 11:7,
21, 28, 41, 44, 44; 12:6, 7, 7, 24, 37, 38;
13:14, 23, 25, 27, 30, 30, 34; 14:17; 16:8,
15; 17:10, 10, 17, 18; 18:11, 27, 27, 31;
19:42; 20:34, 35, 36, 36, 37; 21:21, 21,
21, 22, 23, 26; 22:10, 25, 28, 38; 23:29,
29; 24:17, 17, 18, 38, 44, 48
Jn 3:21; 4:35, 35, 38; 5:28, 39; 6:9, 49, 58,
63, 63, 64, 69; 7:7, 23, 47, 49; 8:10, 23,
23, 31, 37, 44, 47, 53; 9:28, 40; 10:8, 12,
16, 21, 26, 30, 34; 11:9; 13:10, 11, 17,
35; 14:2; 15:3, 5, 6, 14, 19; 16:15; 30;
17:7, 9, 10, 10, 11, 11, 14, 16, 22; 20:23,
23, 29, 30, 31; 21:25
Ac 2:7, 13, 15, 32, 39; 3:15, 25; 5:9, 25, 32;
7:1, 26; 10:4, 21, 31, 33, 33, 39; 13:27,
31, 39; 14:11, 15, 15; 15:18, 19, 23;
16:17, 21, 28; 17:6, 22, 28, 29; 19:15, 26,
37, 38, 38, 40; 20:32; 21:20, 20, 21, 21,
24; 22:3, 10; 23:15, 21, 35; 24:2, 11, 14;
25:5, 24; 26:3, 18, 26; 28:27
Ro 1:6, 15, 20, 20, 20, 28, 32; 2:2, 8, 13, 14,
18, 19; 3:9, 9, 12, 12, 15, 16, 19, 25; 4:7,
7, 7, 12, 14; 6:2, 4, 13, 14, 15, 16, 21;
7:4; 6; 8:1, 5, 5, 8, 9, 12, 14, 14, 16, 18,
24, 28, 36, 36, 37; 9:4, 5, 6, 6, 7, 7, 8, 8,
8, 26; 10:15, 19; 11:14, 16, 18, 28, 29,
33, 36; 12:5; 13:1, 3, 6; 14:8, 20; 15:1,
14, 26, 27; 16:7, 10, 11, 14, 15, 18
1Co 1:2, 5, 11, 11, 18, 24, 26, 27, 28, 28,
28, 30; 2:6, 12, 14, 14; 3:2, 3, 3, 4, 8, 9,
9, 9, 16, 17, 20, 21, 22, 23; 4:8, 8, 9, 10,
10, 10, 10, 10, 10, 11, 11, 13, 13, 18, 19;
5:2, 4, 7, 12, 12, 13; 6:2; 4, 11, 11, 11,
12, 12, 12, 15, 19, 20, 20; 7:14, 23, 33;
8:4, 5, 6, 6, 8, 8, 9, 10; 9:1, 2, 12, 13, 20,
20, 21, 21; 10:11, 11, 13, 17, 17, 18, 22,
23, 23, 23; 11:19, 30, 32, 32; 12:4, 5, 6,
12, 22, 23, 23, 25, 32, 34, 37; 15:2, 6, 15,
17, 18, 18, 19, 23, 27, 29, 29, 35, 40, 48,
48, 48, 48; 16:9, 18
2Co 1:1, 4, 4, 7, 14, 14, 20, 24; 2:11, 15, 15,
18, 18, 18, 18, 18; 5:4, 6, 6, 6, 8, 11, 11,
17, 17, 18, 20; 6:12, 12, 16; 7:3, 6; 8:23;
10:4, 7, 10, 11, 11, 11, 11, 12, 14; 11:13, 19,
22, 22, 22, 23, 28; 13:4, 6, 9, 9, 9
Gal 1:2, 6; 2:15, 17; 3:3, 3, 7, 7, 9, 10, 10,
10, 25, 26, 28, 29; 4:6, 8, 9, 12, 24, 24,

28, 31; 5:4, 4, 17, 18, 19, 19, 24; 6:1,
10, 13
Eph 1:1, 10, 10; 2:5, 8, 10, 11, 13, 19, 20,
22; 4:1, 4, 25, 30; 5:4, 8, 12, 13, 13, 16,
30; 6:5
Php 1:1, 7, 10, 11, 13, 14; 2:21; 3:3, 13, 13,
18; 4:3, 8, 8, 8, 8, 8, 8, 21, 22
Col 1:2, 16, 16; 2:3, 10, 11, 12, 17, 20, 22;
3:1, 3, 5, 15; 4:5, 9, 11, 11, 13, 15
1Th 2:10, 14, 15, 19, 20; 3:3; 4:9, 10, 12,
13, 15, 15, 17; 5:5, 5, 5, 7, 8, 12, 14
2Th 1:3, 7; 2:13; 3:11, 11, 12
1Ti 2:2; 3:7; 5:3, 15, 16, 24, 25, 25; 6:1, 2,
2, 17
2Ti 1:15; 15; 2:19, 20, 26; 3:3, 6, 15
Tit 1:5, 10, 12, 15, 15; 3:8, 9, 15
Phm 1:7;
Heb 1:10, 14; 2:10, 10, 11, 11, 14, 18; 3:6,
14; 4:13, 15; 5:2, 11, 12, 14; 6:9; 7:5, 13;
8:4; 9:15, 17, 22, 24; 10:8, 10, 14, 39;
11:3; 12:1, 8, 8, 11, 18, 22, 23, 27, 27;
13:3, 11
Jas 1:1; 2:4, 4, 7, 9, 16; 3:4, 4, 9; 5:2, 2, 4, 17
1Pe 1:5, 6, 12; 2:5, 9, 10, 14, 25; 3:6, 6, 9,
12, 12, 14; 4:6, 13, 14; 5:1, 9, 9, 14
2Pe 1:4; 2:10, 10, 11, 13, 15, 17, 17, 19, 20;
3:5, 7, 7, 10, 10, 16, 16
1Jn 2:5, 12, 14, 15, 18; 3:2, 10, 19, 22; 4:1,
1, 4, 5, 6, 6, 17; 5:3, 7, 7, 8, 19, 20
2Jn 1:7;
Jude 1:1, 4, 7, 12, 12, 15, 16
Rev 1:3, 4, 4, 11, 19, 20, 20; 2:2, 2, 2, 9, 9,
9, 18; 3:2, 4, 9, 9; 4:5, 11; 5:6, 8, 13, 13;
7:13, 13, 14, 15; 8:13; 9:14; 10:6, 6, 6;
11:4, 15; 13:8; 14:4, 4, 4, 5, 12, 13, 18;
15:3, 3, 4; 16:6, 7, 14; 17:9, 10, 10, 12,
14, 14, 15; 18:3, 14, 14; 19:2, 9, 9, 9;
20:7, 8, 10; 21:4, 5, 12, 16, 22, 24, 27;
22:6, 14, 15, 18, 19

AS (3520)

Ge 3:5, 22; 4:20, 20, 21; 7:9, 16; 8:21; 9:3;
10:9, 19, 19, 30; 11:2; 12:4; 13:10, 10,
16; 16:6; 17:4, 15, 20, 23; 18:5, 25, 33,
33; 19:8, 14, 28; 21:1, 1, 4, 16; 22:14, 17,
17; 23:9, 9; 24:22, 51; 25:18; 26:4, 29,
29; 27:4, 9, 12, 14, 19, 23, 27, 30, 30, 42,
46; 28:6, 14; 31:2, 5, 26; 32:12, 25, 28,
31; 33:10, 14; 34:12, 15, 22, 31; 35:18;
36:24; 38:11, 29; 39:10, 18; 40:10, 22;
41:13, 19, 21, 38, 38, 39, 39, 49, 54; 42:27,
35; 43:6, 17, 34; 44:1, 1, 3, 3, 15, 17, 18;
47:11, 21, 30; 48:5, 7, 20, 20; 49:4, 9, 9,
16, 27; 50:6, 12, 20, 20
Ex 1:17, 19; 2:14; 4:6, 7; 5:7, 13, 14, 20;
7:6, 10, 13, 20, 22; 8:15, 19, 27; 9:12, 17,
18, 24, 29, 29, 30, 35; 10:10, 14; 11:6;
12:25, 28, 31, 32, 36, 48, 50; 13:11;
14:28; 15:5, 7, 8, 10, 16, 16; 16:5, 5, 10,
14, 14, 22, 34, 34; 17:10; 18:21; 19:18;
21:7, 22, 22; 22:23, 25; 24:10, 10, 10;
27:8; 28:32; 30:37; 32:1, 13, 17, 19, 19,
23; 33:9, 11; 34:4, 10, 18; 35:22, 22;
38:21; 39:1, 5, 6, 7, 21, 23, 26, 29, 31,
43; 40:15, 19, 21, 23, 25, 27, 29, 32
Nu 1:19; 2:17, 33; 3:16, 42, 51; 4:15, 29, 49;
5:4; 8:3, 16, 19, 21, 22; 9:15, 18, 18;
10:31; 11:7, 7, 8, 12, 31, 31, 31; 12:10,
12; 13:21, 33; 14:15, 17, 19, 21, 21, 28,
28, 28, 32; 15:14, 15, 20, 36; 16:31, 40,
40, 40, 45, 47; 17:11; 18:6, 7, 18, 18, 24,
27, 27, 30, 30; 20:9, 27; 21:34; 22:4, 8;
23:2, 22, 24, 24, 30; 24:1, 6, 6, 6, 6, 8, 9,
9; 26:4; 27:11, 13, 17, 22, 23; 28:8, 8;
31:7, 31, 41, 47; 32:25, 27, 31, 33:56;
34:6; 36:10
Dt 1:10, 11, 11, 17, 17, 19, 21, 31, 40, 44;
2:1, 5, 10, 11, 12, 14, 21, 22, 29, 30; 3:2,
6, 20, 20; 4:5, 7, 8, 20, 32, 33, 38; 5:12,
14, 14, 16, 26, 31, 32; 6:3, 8, 16, 19, 24,
25; 8:5, 18, 20; 9:3, 3, 18, 21, 21, 25;
10:5, 9, 15, 22; 11:4, 10, 10, 18, 21, 25;
12:9, 12, 15, 15, 16, 19, 19, 20, 21, 22,
24; 13:6, 11, 17; 14:7; 15:6, 21, 22, 22,
23; 16:9, 10, 17; 17:14, 16; 18:2, 7, 14;
19:5, 6, 8, 19; 20:8, 8, 17; 22:11, 26;
23:23; 24:8; 26:15, 18, 19; 27:3; 28:9, 29,
49, 49, 62, 63; 29:13, 13, 28; 30:9; 31:3,
4, 13, 13, 21; 32:2, 2, 2, 2, 10, 11, 31, 50;
33:20, 25; 34:9
Jos 1:3, 5, 15, 17, 17; 2:7, 7, 11, 11; 3:7, 13,
13, 15; 4:8, 8, 12, 14, 18, 23; 5:5, 14;
6:22; 7:5; 8:2, 5, 6, 15, 19, 29, 29, 31, 31,
33, 33, 33; 9:4, 21, 25; 10:1, 2, 11,
28, 30, 39, 39, 40; 11:4, 9, 12, 13, 15, 20;
13:6, 8, 14, 33; 14:2, 5, 7, 10, 11, 11, 11,
11, 12; 15:18; 63; 17:14; 21:8; 22:4; 23:5,
6, 7, 10, 10, 10, 10, 13; 7:4, 4, 8; 8:1, 6, 6,
6, 6, 10
Jdg 1:7, 20; 2:3, 15, 15, 22; 3:1, 1, 2; 4:22;
5:31; 6:5, 16, 27, 30, 37, 7:5, 12, 17; 8:8,
18, 19, 21, 33, 33; 9:33, 33, 33, 36, 48;
11:36; 13:9, 23, 23; 14:6, 20; 15:10, 11,

14; 16:7, 9, 11, 20; 17:8, 11; 19:22; 20:1,
8, 11, 30, 31, 32, 39, 48, 48
Ru 1:8; 3:10, 13
1Sa 1:7, 12, 26, 28, 28; 2:2, 16, 16; 3:10;
4:9; 5:10; 6:6, 12; 7:10; 9:11, 13, 13, 20,
27; 10:7; 12:15, 23; 13:5, 7, 10, 10;
14:14, 39, 45; 15:22, 22, 23, 23, 27, 33;
16:7; 17:20, 20, 23, 36, 55, 57; 18:1, 3, 6,
7, 10; 19:6, 7, 9, 20; 20:3, 3, 13, 17, 20,
21, 23, 25, 31, 31, 36, 41, 41, 42; 22:8,
13, 14; 23:11; 24:4, 13, 18; 25:15, 15, 20,
25, 26, 26, 29, 34, 37; 26:10, 16, 20,
24; 27:8; 28:10, 17; 29:6, 8, 9, 10, 10;
30:24
2Sa 1:6, 21; 2:18, 18, 23, 23, 27; 3:9, 33, 34,
36; 4:4, 6, 9; 5:20, 25; 6:16, 18, 18, 19,
19, 20; 7:10, 11, 15, 25; 8:3; 9:8, 11, 11;
10:2; 11:11, 11, 25, 25; 12:3, 5; 13:13,
13, 29, 35, 36, 36; 14:2, 11, 13, 14, 17,
19, 25; 15:10, 10, 21, 21, 26, 30, 30, 34;
16:2, 5, 13, 13, 19, 23; 17:3, 8, 10, 11,
12, 12; 18:32, 33; 19:3, 14, 28, 37; 20:8;
20:8; 22:23, 31, 43, 43, 43, 45, 45; 23:4,
4; 24:8, 15; 24:19, 23
1Ki 1:29, 30, 37, 41; 2:3, 24, 24, 31, 38; 3:6,
6, 14; 4:20, 29; 5:5, 12; 8:20, 24, 25, 43,
53, 57, 59, 61; 9:2, 4, 5; 10:10, 27, 27;
11:4, 6, 11, 33, 38, 38; 12:12, 17; 13:6;
16:2, 9, 11, 11, 31; 17:1, 11, 12, 13; 18:7,
10, 12, 12, 15, 32, 32; 19:2, 5; 20:11, 12,
34, 36, 36, 36, 36, 39, 40; 21:11, 11, 26;
22:4, 4, 4, 14, 17
2Ki 1:16; 2:2, 2, 4, 4, 6, 6, 11, 19, 23; 3:7, 7,
7, 14, 22, 22; 4:8, 8, 30, 30, 40; 5:16, 20,
27, 27; 6:5, 26; 7:7, 10, 13, 13, 17, 18;
8:5, 18, 19, 27; 9:17, 22, 31, 37; 10:2, 2,
12, 15, 25, 25; 11:8, 8, 14; 12:9; 13:5, 21,
23; 14:3, 4, 5, 5; 15:9; 17:2, 4, 11, 23, 41;
19:12, 26, 26, 26, 26, 29, 37; 21:3, 13,
20; 22:18; 23:16, 21, 27; 24:13; 25:15, 22
1Ch 5:1; 6:26; 12:8, 8, 20, 33, 36; 14:16;
15:15, 29; 16:37; 17:11, 9, 23; 18:3;
21:3, 15, 17; 22:7, 11; 23:24; 24:19;
25:8, 8, 8; 26:13, 13, 21; 28:2, 7; 29:11,
15, 15, 17, 23, 25
2Ch 1:12, 15, 15, 15; 2:3, 16, 16; 3:16; 4:6;
5:13, 13; 6:8, 10, 15, 16, 16, 33; 7:17, 17,
18; 8:7, 14; 9:9, 27, 27; 10:12, 17; 11:16;
13:10, 15; 16:3; 18:3, 3, 13, 16; 20:9, 20,
21, 33; 21:6, 7; 23:3, 13, 18, 18; 24:12,
12; 25:4; 26:10; 26:5, 5; 29:8, 31, 31; 30:5,
7, 8; 31:3, 5, 5, 15, 15; 32:17, 19; 33:22,
23; 34:26; 35:12, 18; 36:21, 21
Ezr 2:62; 3:1, 2, 4, 4; 4:2, 3; 6:18, 21; 7:14,
25, 27, 28; 8:27, 31; 9:7, 13, 15; 10:3, 12
Ne 1:1; 2:16, 18; 5:5, 5, 12; 6:8, 11, 11;
7:64; 8:1, 15; 9:10, 11, 23, 24; 10:34, 36;
13:15
Est 2:9, 20, 20; 3:11; 4:14; 5:5, 8, 13; 6:10;
7:8; 8:8; 9:2, 22, 23, 23, 27, 27, 31, 31
Job 2:10; 3:6, 16, 16; 4:8; 5:7, 14, 25, 26;
6:7, 15, 15, 26; 7:2, 2, 9, 9; 9:26, 26, 32;
10:4, 5, 5, 9, 10, 16, 19, 22, 22; 11:8, 8,
16, 17, 20; 12:3, 3, 3, 4, 5; 13:9, 28, 28;
14:2, 6, 11; 15:24, 33, 33; 16:4, 21; 17:6,
7, 10, 15; 18:3, 20; 19:11, 22; 20:8, 8;
21:4, 18, 18, 33; 22:2, 8, 24, 24; 23:10;
24:5, 14, 17, 18, 20, 24, 24; 26:3; 27:2, 6,
7, 7, 16, 16, 18, 18, 20, 21; 28:5; 29:2, 2,
2, 4, 14, 18, 23, 23, 25; 30:5, 14, 15,
15, 18; 31:18, 33, 36, 37; 32:19 and 34; 36;
35:8; 37:18; 38:8, 14, 14, 19, 30; 39:16,
20; 40:15, 18; 41:5, 15, 20, 24, 24, 24,
24, 27, 29; 42:7, 9, 10, 10, 15
Ps 5:7, 12; 10:5, 9; 11:1; 12:6; 14:4; 17:8,
12, 12, 15; 18:30, 42, 42, 44, 44; 19:5, 5;
21:9; 22:13; 25:10; 26:11; 27:12; 31:12;
32:9, 9; 33:7, 22; 34:18; 35:5, 13, 14, 14;
37:2, 6, 6, 14, 20, 22; 38:4, 10, 13, 13,
14; 39:5, 5, 12; 40:4, 16; 41:12; 42:1, 10;
44:22; 48:6, 8; 50:21; 53:4; 55:16, 20;
58:3, 3, 7, 7, 8, 9; 61:6; 62:3, 3; 63:2, 5;
65:3; 66:10; 68:2, 2, 13, 14, 15, 15, 17,
21; 69:13; 70:4; 71:7; 72:5, 5, 6, 7, 17,
17; 73:1, 2, 6, 19, 20, 22; 74:5;
77:13; 78:8, 13, 15, 27, 27, 65; 83:9, 9, 9,
10, 11, 11, 13, 14, 14; 87:7, 7; 88:4;
89:10, 11, 29, 36, 37; 90:4, 4, 5, 5, 9;
92:7; 95:8, 8; 102:3, 7, 26; 103:11, 12,
12, 13, 15, 15, 15, 18; 104:2, 6, 17, 33,
33; 106:9; 107:10; 109:17, 17, 18, 19, 19,
23, 29; 116:2, 2; 118:12; 119:14, 14, 70,
70, 111, 132, 162; 122:3; 123:2, 2; 124:6,
7; 125:1, 2, 5, 5; 126:4; 127:4; 128:3;
129:6; 131:2, 2; 133:3, 3; 137:8; 139:12,
16; 140:9; 141:2, 2, 7; 143:3, 6; 144:4,
12; 147:20
Pr 1:12, 12, 27, 27; 2:4, 4; 3:12; 4:18, 19;
5:3, 4, 4, 19; 6:5, 5, 11, 11; 7:2, 22, 22,
23; 8:26, 30; 9:4, 16; 10:20, 23, 25, 26,
26; 11:19, 20, 22, 28; 12:4; 15:19; 16:14,
15, 24, 27; 17:8, 14; 18:4, 4, 8, 11; 19:12,
12, 24; 20:2, 19; 21:1, 8, 29; 23:5, 7, 28,
34, 34; 24:29, 34, 34; 25:12, 13, 16, 20,
20, 25, 26; 26:1, 1, 2, 2, 8, 9, 11, 14, 18,
18; 27:8, 19, 21; 28:1, 4, 15; 30:14;
14; 31:8
Ecc 2:8, 13, 13, 15, 16; 3:19; 4:1; 5:15, 15,
16; 6:12; 7:6, 26; 8:1, 13; 9:2, 2, 12, 12;
10:5, 7; 11:5; 12:7, 11, 11
SS 1:3, 5, 5, 7, 14; 2:2, 3; 4:1, 11; 5:11, 11,
6, 7, 10, 10, 10, 10, 13; 7:4, 4, 8; 8:1, 6,
6, 6, 6, 10

Isa 1:7, 8, 8, 8, 9, 18, 18, 18, 18, 26, 26, 30,
30, 31, 31; 3:9, 12, 16; 5:18, 24, 24, 24;
6:13, 13; 7:2; 8:6; 9:1, 3, 4, 18, 19; 10:9,
9, 9, 10, 11, 14, 15, 15, 15, 15, 18, 20,
22, 26, 32; 11:9, 16; 13:4, 6, 8, 8, 14, 14,
14; 14:10, 17, 19, 19, 24, 24; 16:2, 3,
14; 17:3, 5, 5, 6, 9, 13, 19:14; 20:3; 21:1;
3; 22:16, 23; 23:5, 10, 15; 24:2, 2, 2, 2, 2,
2, 13, 13, 22; 25:4, 5, 10, 11; 26:17, 18,
19, 20; 27:7, 9; 28:2, 2, 4, 21, 21; 29:2, 4,
5, 7, 8, 8, 11, 13, 16, 17; 30:13, 14, 17,
17, 22, 26, 26, 27, 28, 29, 29; 31:4, 5;
32:2, 2, 2; 33:4, 11, 12, 12; 34:4, 4, 4;
35:1, 6; 37:12, 27, 27, 27, 27, 30, 38;
38:12, 13, 14, 19; 40:6, 15, 15, 15, 17,
22, 22, 22, 23, 24, 31; 41:2, 2, 11, 12, 12,
15, 25, 25; 42:13, 19, 19, 19; 43:17; 44:4,
4, 7, 22, 22; 47:3, 4, 8, 14; 48:18, 18, 19;
49:18, 18, 18, 26; 50:4, 9; 51:9, 12, 13,
20, 23, 23; 52:14; 53:2, 2, 3, 7, 7; 54:6, 9,
9; 55:9, 10; 56:12; 58:2, 4, 5, 8, 10;
59:10, 10, 10, 12, 17, 17, 21; 60:8, 8;
61:10, 10, 11, 11; 62:1, 1, 5, 5; 63:13, 14;
64:2, 6, 6, 6; 65:8, 22; 66:3, 3, 3, 8, 8,
13, 20, 22
Jer 2:26, 36; 3:2, 5, 20; 4:13, 13, 17, 31, 31;
5:8, 9, 16, 19, 26, 27, 29; 6:7, 9, 9, 23,
24, 26; 7:14, 15; 8:6; 9:8, 9, 22, 22; 10:5,
6, 7; 11:5; 12:8, 9, 16; 13:5, 10, 11, 21,
21, 24; 14:8, 8, 9; 15:2, 2, 2, 2, 18, 18,
19; 16:4; 17:8, 11, 16, 22; 18:4, 6, 6, 17;
19:11, 12, 13; 20:9, 11, 16; 21:7; 22:23,
24; 23:12, 14, 14, 27, 29, 34; 24:8; 25:18,
30, 38; 26:11, 14, 14, 18; 27:13; 30:6, 20;
31:5, 10, 18, 23, 28; 32:20, 31, 42;
33:7, 11, 22; 38:16; 39:12; 40:3, 10; 41:6,
6; 42:2, 18; 43:11, 11, 11, 12; 44:6, 13,
14, 16, 17, 22, 23, 30; 46:7, 7, 18, 18, 18,
22, 26; 48:8, 13, 34, 40, 41; 49:16, 16,
18, 22, 22, 24; 50:8, 9, 11, 11, 15, 18, 26,
37, 40, 43; 51:14, 27, 30, 38, 49
La 1:1, 1, 10, 12, 13, 14, 15, 16, 18, 22, 24,
3:6, 10, 10, 12, 45; 4:2, 6, 14, 17, 17;
5:3, 21
Eze 1:1, 4, 13, 14, 14, 15, 16, 22, 24, 24,
26, 26, 27, 27, 27, 28; 3:3, 9, 23; 4:12;
5:11; 7:17, 20; 8:1, 2, 2, 2; 9:10, 11; 10:1,
1, 5, 9, 10, 10, 11, 11, 13; 11:16, 21;
12:4, 4, 7, 7, 11, 23; 14:10, 16, 18, 20;
15:6; 16:4, 7, 31, 32, 38, 44, 47, 48, 48,
50, 57, 59; 17:5, 16, 19; 18:3, 4, 18; 20:3,
31, 32, 32, 33, 36, 39; 21:7, 10, 23;
22:20, 22; 23:16, 16, 18, 20, 44; 24:18,
22; 26:3, 10; 28:2, 6, 16; 30:9, 18; 32:2;
33:11, 12, 17, 27, 31, 31, 32; 34:8, 12,
17, 19; 35:6, 15; 36:17, 38, 38; 37:7,
7, 10; 38:16; 40:2, 40; 41:21, 25; 42:6, 9,
11, 11, 11, 11, 12; 43:22; 46:5, 7, 11, 12;
47:10, 14, 14, 15, 22; 48:1, 8, 11, 23
Da 1:4, 13, 17; 2:29, 30, 40, 40, 40, 41, 42,
43, 45; 4:18, 25, 32, 33, 35; 5:12; 6:4, 10,
22; 7:4, 9, 9, 12, 28; 8:3, 18; 9:7, 12,
13, 15; 10:4, 6, 6, 17; 11:29, 29, 32; 12:1,
3, 3
Hos 1:10, 10, 10; 2:2, 7; 3:6, 15, 15, 17, 17,
12, 14, 14; 6:3, 3, 3, 4, 4, 5, 9; 7:4, 6, 7,
12, 12; 8:1, 8, 12; 9:1, 4, 9, 10, 10, 11,
13; 10:4, 7, 7, 11, 14; 11:2, 4, 8, 8, 11,
11; 12:9, 11; 13:3, 3, 3, 3, 7, 7, 8; 14:5, 5,
5, 6, 6, 7, 7, 7
Joel 1:15; 2:2, 3, 4, 4, 5, 32
Am 2:9; 3:12; 4:11, 11; 5:11, 14, 16, 19,
24, 24; 7:15; 8:8, 8, 10, 10; 9:5, 7, 9, 11
Ob 1:4, 11, 15, 16, 16
Jnh 1:14;
Mic 1:4, 4, 6, 6, 8, 16; 2:8, 8, 12, 12; 3:3, 3,
4, 12, 12; 4:9, 12; 5:7, 7, 8, 8, 15; 7:1, 1,
4, 10, 14
Na 1:10, 10, 10; 2:2, 7; 3:6, 15, 15, 17, 17
Hab 1:8, 9, 9, 14, 14; 2:5, 5, 14; 3:4, 14, 14
Zep 1:8, 17, 17; 2:2, 9, 9, 9
Hag 1:12; 2:3, 19, 23
Zec 1:4, 6; 2:4, 6; 4:1; 5:3, 3; 7:3, 12, 13;
8:11, 13, 14; 9:1, 3, 3, 7, 7, 11, 13, 14,
15, 15, 16, 16, 16; 10:2, 3, 5, 6, 7, 8;
12:8, 8, 8, 10, 10, 10; 13:9; 14:3, 5,
10, 15
Mal 2:9; 3:3, 3, 4, 4, 17; 4:1, 2
Mt 1:18, 24; 5:48; 6:2, 5, 7, 10, 12, 16; 7:29,
29; 8:13; 9:9, 10, 15, 15, 32, 36; 10:7, 16,
16, 16, 25, 25; 11:7; 12:13, 40; 13:40, 43;
14:5, 36, 36; 15:28, 33; 17:2, 2, 9, 20;
18:3, 4, 17, 19, 25, 33; 19:19; 20:14, 28,
29; 21:6, 18, 23, 26; 22:9, 9, 10, 10, 30,
31, 39; 23:37; 24:3, 21, 27, 37, 38, 44;
25:14, 32, 40, 45; 26:7, 19, 21, 24, 26,
39, 39, 55; 27:10, 32, 65, 65; 28:1, 3, 4,
6, 9, 15
Mk 1:2, 16, 22, 22, 42, 42; 2:2, 14, 15, 19,
19, 23; 3:5, 10, 10, 20; 4:4, 18, 20, 26,
33, 36; 5:36, 36; 6:15, 31, 34, 56, 56; 7:4,
6, 8; 8:24; 9:3, 3, 9, 13, 26; 10:1, 15, 32,
46; 11:2, 2, 6, 20, 27; 12:25, 26, 31, 33;
13:1, 3, 19, 34; 14:3, 16, 18, 21, 22, 45,
45, 48, 66; 15:8; 16:7, 10, 12, 14
Lk 1:1, 2, 23, 23, 44, 44, 55, 70; 2:15, 20,
23, 43; 3:4, 15, 23; 4:16; 5:1, 14, 17; 6:3,
10, 22, 31, 34, 36, 40; 8:5, 6, 6, 23, 42;
9:18, 29, 33, 34, 42, 53, 54, 57; 10:3, 7,
18, 18, 27, 33, 38; 11:1, 1, 2, 8, 8, 27, 30,
36, 37, 41, 44, 53; 12:58; 13:34; 14:1, 22;
15:19, 25, 30, 30; 17:6, 11, 12, 14, 24,
26, 28; 18:11, 13, 13, 17, 35; 19:9, 11,
32, 33, 36; 20:1; 21:5, 6, 35; 22:13, 22,
26, 26, 27, 29, 31, 39, 44, 52, 56, 66, 66;

21, 24; 34:3, 3, 4, 4, 5, 7, 9, 10, 12, 12,
13, 15; 35:1, 2, 4, 5, 5, 7, 8, 8, 8, 9, 9;
36:8, 14, 15; 37:4, 6, 10, 11, 26, 27, 30;
38:7; 39:6, 6, 7, 8; 40:4, 4, 4, 5, 9, 20, 24,
24, 25, 30, 31; 41:6, 7, 10, 11, 11, 12, 22,
23; 42:2, 4, 17, 17; 43:2, 2, 9, 9, 9, 10,
26; 44:8, 9, 11, 11, 11, 15, 24, 26, 27, 27,
28, 28; 45:1, 14, 16, 17, 17, 18, 22, 24,
25; 46:5, 13; 47:1, 3, 3, 5, 7, 11, 12, 12,
12, 14, 14, 15; 48:11, 14; 49:3, 5, 5, 5, 5,
6, 6, 9, 11, 13, 19, 19, 22, 23, 23, 24, 25,
25, 26; 50:7, 7; 51:3, 6, 6, 7, 8, 11, 12,
12, 14, 19; 52:3, 11, 12, 13, 13; 53:11;
54:3, 4, 4, 4, 5, 9, 9, 10, 13, 13, 14, 14;
55:6, 11, 12, 13, 13; 56:1, 5, 6, 7, 7, 12;
57:16; 58:4, 8, 10, 11, 12, 12; 60:2, 4, 5,
5, 7, 11, 11, 11, 12, 18, 19, 19, 20, 20,
21, 21; 61:3, 3, 5, 6, 7, 9, 10; 62:2, 3, 4,
4, 4, 4, 8, 12; 63:3, 10, 16; 64:5, 9; 65:10,
13, 13, 13, 17, 18, 19, 20, 20, 25; 66:5, 5,
8, 8, 10, 11, 11, 12, 12, 13, 14, 16, 17,
24, 24
Jer 1:8, 17; 2:10, 12, 12, 12, 36; 3:1, 3, 16,
16, 17; 4:7, 9, 11, 13, 14, 27, 28, 29; 5:1,
6, 9, 13, 29; 6:6, 8, 11, 12, 15, 22; 7:20,
20, 23, 23, 23, 32, 32, 33, 34; 8:2, 2, 2, 3,
12, 13, 14, 17; 9:2, 9; 10:2, 5, 5, 10, 21;
11:3, 4, 4, 5, 11, 19, 23; 12:13, 16; 13:10,
11, 12, 12, 15, 19, 19, 19, 21, 27, 27;
14:8, 9, 15, 15, 16; 15:1, 4, 11, 18, 18,
19; 16:4, 4, 4, 4, 4, 14; 17:5, 6, 8, 8, 8,
11, 13, 13, 14, 14, 17, 18, 18, 18, 18, 27;
18:14, 16, 20, 21, 21, 21, 21, 22, 23;
19:6, 7, 8, 11, 11, 13; 20:6, 10, 11, 11,
14, 14, 15, 16, 17, 18; 21:2, 9, 10; 22:19,
22, 23; 23:1, 3, 4, 4, 6, 6, 12, 12, 26, 36,
40; 24:2, 3, 7, 7, 8, 9, 9, 10; 25:1, 11, 16,
16, 27, 28, 29, 29, 32, 33, 33, 33, 36;
26:3, 9, 9, 18; 27:16, 17, 18, 18, 22, 22;
28:9; 29:4, 6, 7, 8, 8, 10, 14, 14, 17, 18,
18, 22, 26; 30:7, 10, 10, 10, 16, 16, 16,
18, 19, 19, 20, 20, 21, 22, 22; 31:1, 1, 4,
4, 6, 12, 14, 15, 16, 18, 30, 33, 33, 33,
37, 38, 40, 40; 32:4, 5, 15, 36, 38, 38, 43;
33:9, 10, 10, 12, 16, 16, 20, 21, 22, 24,
25, 26; 34:3, 16, 17, 20; 35:7; 36:3, 7, 19,
30; 37:17, 20; 38:3, 4, 17, 18, 20, 22, 23,
23; 39:16, 17, 18; 40:9, 15; 42:2, 5, 6, 6,
6, 11, 11, 17, 18, 18; 44:8, 8, 12, 12, 12,
26, 27, 27, 29; 46:10, 11, 19, 23, 24, 24,
26, 27, 27; 47:2, 6, 6, 6, 7; 48:2, 2, 3, 4,
6, 7, 8, 9, 10, 13, 26, 28, 30, 33, 34,
37, 37, 38, 39, 41, 42, 43, 44, 46; 49:2, 2,
2, 2, 5, 5, 10, 17, 17, 22, 23, 26, 32,
33, 36, 37; 50:5, 8, 9, 9, 10, 10, 12, 12,
12, 13, 13, 19, 20, 20, 20, 26, 30, 36,
37, 38, 39, 39, 41; 51:2, 6, 8, 8, 26, 29,
35, 46, 47, 58, 58, 58, 62, 63, 64
La 1:12, 17, 21; 2:6, 20; 3:6, 29, 29; 4:9, 9,
21, 21; 5:6, 21
Eze 2:6, 6, 6, 6, 6, 6, 8; 3:9, 9, 12, 20, 26,
26; 4:3, 3, 7, 10, 17; 5:12, 13, 13, 16, 16;
6:4, 4, 6, 6, 6, 6, 6, 8, 9, 13; 7:4, 11,
16, 17, 17, 18, 19, 19, 24, 25, 26, 27, 27;
9:4; 11:3, 11, 11, 16, 20, 20; 12:3, 3, 11,
13, 19, 20, 20, 24, 25, 28, 28; 13:9, 9, 9,
11, 12, 13, 14, 14, 21, 21; 14:3, 9, 10, 11,
11, 11, 15, 16, 16, 18, 22, 23; 15:3, 5;
16:16, 16, 25, 28, 42, 42, 52, 54, 61, 63;
17:8, 14, 15, 20, 21, 23; 18:5, 13, 20, 20,
22, 24, 30; 19:9, 14, 14; 20:3, 9, 12, 14,
20, 22, 31, 31, 32, 32, 41, 47, 47, 48;
21:7, 7, 7, 11, 11, 12, 12, 13, 14,
15, 23, 23, 24, 24, 26, 27, 32, 32, 32;
22:5, 5, 14, 21, 22; 23:25, 29, 32, 33, 46,
48; 24:8, 10, 11, 11, 11, 12, 13, 23, 25,
27, 27, 27; 25:10; 26:2, 5, 6, 13, 14, 14,
16, 17, 18, 21, 21, 21; 27:7, 30, 34,
35, 35, 35, 36, 36; 28:9, 19, 19, 19, 22,
22, 23, 24, 25; 29:5, 7, 9, 11, 12, 14, 15,
16, 19; 30:3, 4, 4, 7, 7, 8, 11, 13, 16, 18,
21, 21; 31:13, 16, 17, 18, 18; 32:6, 10,
12, 15, 19, 25, 27, 28, 30, 30, 31, 32;
33:4, 5, 6, 10, 12, 13, 16, 27, 27, 28;
34:2, 10, 14, 22, 23, 24, 26, 27, 28, 29;
35:4, 10, 15; 36:3, 9, 10, 12, 23, 25,
28, 28, 32, 32, 33, 34, 37, 38; 37:19, 20,
21, 22, 22, 22, 23, 23, 24, 25, 26, 27, 27,
27, 28; 38:7, 7, 8, 9, 16, 16, 19, 20, 21,
23; 39:4, 12, 13, 13, 16, 19, 19, 20, 25,
28; 42:13; 43:10, 11, 12, 13, 13, 14, 14,
14, 15, 15, 16, 17, 17, 17, 19, 27; 44:2, 2,
2, 7, 11, 14, 17, 28, 29, 30, 31; 45:1, 1, 1,
2, 3, 4, 4, 4, 6, 7, 8, 9, 11, 11, 12, 17,
21; 46:1, 1, 1, 2, 4, 5, 5, 6, 6, 11, 16, 16,
17, 17, 18; 47:5, 8, 9, 9, 9, 10, 10, 11, 11,
12, 12, 13, 15, 17, 20, 22; 48:8, 8, 9, 10,
20, 21, 21, 21, 22, 28, 31, 35
Da 1:13; 2:5, 5, 9, 13, 13, 20, 28, 40, 41, 41,
42, 44, 44; 3:6, 11, 15, 15, 17, 18, 19, 28,
29, 29; 4:1, 15, 15, 16, 16, 19, 23, 23, 25,
26, 27, 27, 32; 5:7, 7, 10, 12, 16, 16, 17,
29; 6:1, 7, 8, 12, 15, 17, 25, 26, 26; 7:14,
23, 23, 24, 25, 27; 8:13, 13, 14, 17, 19,
19, 24, 25, 26; 9:16, 25, 25, 26, 26, 27;
10:19, 19, 19; 11:2, 4, 4, 4, 5, 5, 6, 6, 10,
10, 11, 11, 12, 12, 16, 17, 18, 19, 20, 22,
22, 25, 27, 27, 28, 29, 30, 32, 34, 36, 36,
41, 43; 12:1, 1, 1, 3, 4, 6, 7, 7, 8, 10, 11,
11, 13
Hos 1:9, 10, 10, 10, 11, 11; 2:4, 16, 17; 3:3,
3; 4:3, 6, 9, 19; 5:9, 9, 12, 14; 7:4, 16;
8:4, 5, 6, 7, 8, 11, 9; 9:4, 4, 4, 6, 12, 17;

10:2, 6, 6, 8, 10, 14, 15; 11:5; 13:3, 7, 10,
14, 14, 14, 15, 15, 16, 16; 14:5, 6, 7
Joel 1:11; 2:2, 6, 8, 10, 18, 19, 21, 22, 23,
24, 26, 26, 27, 31, 32, 32; 3:12, 15, 16,
17, 19, 19
Am 3:3, 6, 6, 6, 11, 11, 12, 14; 5:6, 14, 15,
15, 16, 17, 20, 20; 6:2, 7; 7:3, 6, 9, 9, 11, 17,
17; 8:3, 3, 5, 8; 9:1, 3, 5, 15
Ob 1:9, 10, 10, 15, 16, 17, 17, 18, 18, 21
Jnh 1:4, 6, 11, 12; 3:4, 7, 8; 4:4, 6, 9, 9
Mic 1:2, 4, 4, 7, 7, 14; 2:4, 11; 3:6, 6, 6, 7,
9; 4:1, 1, 10, 10, 11; 5:2, 2, 4, 5, 7, 8, 9,
9; 6:7, 14, 14; 7:4, 8, 10, 11, 11, 13, 16,
16, 17
Na 1:10, 10, 10, 12, 12, 14; 2:3, 3, 5, 6, 6, 7,
7, 13; 3:11, 11, 12, 12, 13
Hab 1:5; 10; 2:5, 7, 9, 14, 14, 16, 16; 3:17,
17, 17
Zep 1:10, 17, 18, 18; 2:3, 3, 4, 4, 5, 6, 6, 7, 9,
12, 14; 3:7, 8, 11, 11, 13, 14, 16, 16
Hag 1:2, 8; 2:4, 4, 4, 9, 12, 13, 13
Zec 1:4, 9, 16, 16, 17, 19; 2:4, 5, 5, 9, 11,
11, 13; 3:9; 4:5, 12, 13; 5:3, 3, 11; 6:13,
13, 13, 13; 7:3, 5, 6, 6, 8, 8, 9, 9, 11, 12, 13,
13, 19; 9:1, 1, 2, 4, 5, 5, 7, 7, 10, 10,
14, 15, 16; 10:5, 5, 6, 7, 7, 10, 11; 11:5,
9, 9, 16, 17, 17, 17; 12:2, 3, 3, 5, 6, 8, 8,
10, 11; 13:1, 2, 4, 7, 8, 8; 14:1, 2, 2, 4, 9,
7, 7, 7, 8, 8, 9, 9, 10, 10, 11, 11, 12, 13,
14, 15, 15, 17, 17, 18, 19, 20, 20, 20, 21, 21,
21
Mal 1:5, 6, 6, 8, 9, 11, 11, 11, 14; 2:4; 3:4;
5, 10, 10, 12, 17; 4:1, 3
Mt 1:22, 23; 2:4, 13, 15, 18, 23, 23; 3:13,
14, 15; 4:1, 3, 3, 6, 14; 5:4, 6, 9, 12, 13,
13, 13, 14, 18, 19, 19, 21, 22, 22, 24,
25, 29, 30, 37, 45, 48; 6:1, 4, 5, 7, 8, 9,
10, 16, 21, 22, 22, 30, 33; 7:1,
2, 2, 7, 7, 8, 13, 14, 26; 8:3, 8, 12, 12, 13,
17; 9:2, 2, 5, 12, 15, 21, 22, 29; 10:13,
13, 15, 16, 18, 19, 21, 22, 23, 25, 26,
31, 31, 32, 32, 37, 37, 39, 40, 40; 11:6, 9,
18, 22, 22, 26; 30:7, 10, 10, 10, 16, 16, 16,
18, 19, 19, 20, 20, 21, 22, 22; 31:1, 1, 4,
4, 6, 12, 14, 15, 16, 18, 30, 33, 33, 33,
37, 38, 40, 40; 32:4, 5, 15, 36, 38, 38, 43;
28:5:5, 6, 13, 14, 28, 31; 16:2, 3, 4, 19,
19, 21, 21, 22, 22, 23, 23, 28; 17:4, 7, 9,
17, 20, 22, 23; 18:3, 7, 8, 9, 12, 13, 16,
17, 18, 18, 19, 25, 19:5, 9, 10, 12, 21,
25, 30; 20:10, 16, 18, 22, 23, 23, 26,
26, 26, 27, 27, 28; 21:4, 13, 21, 31,
21, 43, 44; 22:13, 28; 23:4, 5, 7, 8, 10,
11, 12, 12, 26, 31; 24:2, 2, 3, 3, 6, 7, 9,
28, 29, 29, 34, 37, 39, 40, 40, 41, 41, 43,
44, 51; 25:1, 9, 29, 29, 30, 32; 26:2, 5,
5, 13, 31, 31, 33, 33, 37, 39, 42, 46, 54,
54, 56, 63; 27:22, 23, 25, 26, 35, 40, 42,
49, 58, 64, 64; 28:10
Mk 1:41; 2:5, 9, 20, 22; 3:14, 24, 25, 26,
28; 4:12, 12, 21, 21, 22, 24, 25, 26, 27, 5,
31, 39; 5:18, 23, 28, 34, 36, 43; 6:9, 11,
27, 50, 50; 7:4, 11, 11, 24, 27, 34; 8:12,
31, 31, 33, 33, 38, 38; 9:1, 5, 12, 19, 34,
35, 35, 43, 45, 45, 47, 49, 49; 10:8, 12,
26, 31, 33, 38, 38, 40, 40, 43, 43, 43, 44,
44, 45, 49, 49; 11:2, 10, 17, 23, 23, 23, 26; 12:7,
23; 13:2, 2, 4, 4, 4, 7, 7, 8, 8, 9, 9, 10,
11, 12, 13, 12, 14, 19, 19, 20, 24, 25,
30; 14:2, 9, 19, 27, 29, 33, 33, 49,
64; 15:15; 16:6, 16, 16
Lk 1:15, 15, 20, 20, 20, 29, 32, 33, 34,
35, 35, 37, 38, 45, 57, 60, 66, 68, 71, 76;
2:1, 3, 5, 6, 10, 12, 23, 34, 35, 49; 3:5, 5,
5, 5, 7, 12, 14, 14, 23; 4:3, 3, 7, 9; 5:13, 15,
23, 35, 37, 38; 6:17, 20, 21, 35, 35, 36,
37, 37, 37, 38, 38, 40; 7:7, 23; 8:9, 12,
17, 17, 18, 18, 18, 43, 48, 50; 9:22, 22,
22, 25, 26, 26, 27, 33, 41, 44, 46, 48, 51;
10:5, 6, 11, 12, 14, 15, 42; 11:2, 2, 9, 9,
10, 18, 19, 29, 30, 35, 36, 36, 46, 50, 51;
12:2, 2, 3, 3, 4, 9, 10, 10, 19, 20, 20, 26,
29, 31, 34, 35, 36, 40, 45, 47, 48, 48, 49,
50, 50, 52, 52, 53, 55, 58; 13:14, 16, 23, 24,
28, 30, 30, 32, 33; 14:8, 11, 11, 12, 14,
14, 23, 24, 27; 15:7, 14,
19, 21, 23, 24, 32; 16:2, 21, 31; 17:6, 6,
24, 25, 26, 30, 31, 34, 34, 34, 35, 35, 36,
36, 37; 18:13, 14, 14, 26, 31, 32, 32, 40;
19:7, 15, 19, 26, 26, 38; 20:6, 13, 14, 18,
25, 25, 35; 21:6, 6, 7, 7, 8, 9, 11, 11, 15,
16, 16, 17, 20, 22, 24, 24, 24, 25, 26,
32, 34, 36; 22:7, 16, 26, 26, 32, 35, 37, 39, 43;
24:7, 20, 36, 44, 47, 49
Jn 1:25, 31, 42; 3:2, 3, 4, 4, 5, 7, 9, 14, 17,
20, 21, 27; 4:14; 5:6, 34; 6:12, 20, 49;
7:4, 17, 23; 8:5, 33, 33, 36, 41, 55; 9:3,
22, 27, 31, 39; 10:9, 16, 24, 35; 11:4:
12:23, 26, 31, 32, 34, 36, 38, 40, 42:
13:18, 24, 32; 14:1, 3, 19, 21, 27, 27;
15:7, 8, 11, 25; 16:1, 20, 20, 24, 32, 33;
17:11, 12, 19, 21, 21, 22, 23, 24, 26;
18:9, 28, 32, 36; 19:16, 24, 28, 37;
31, 36, 36; 20:15, 19, 21, 26, 27; 21:18,
25, 25
Ac 1:5, 8, 20, 22, 22; 2:14, 20, 21, 24, 25,
38, 47; 3:14, 19, 19, 23, 25; 4:9, 10, 12,
19, 28, 30; 5:31, 36, 38, 39, 39; 7:7, 35;
8:20, 22, 36; 9:6, 17; 10:42, 47, 48;
11:14, 16, 28; 12:19; 13:11, 22, 28, 38,
39, 42, 47, 47; 14:3, 9; 15:1, 1, 11, 24;
16:13, 15, 30, 31; 17:18, 27; 18:6, 9, 15,
15; 19:2, 26, 27, 27, 27, 36, 36, 39, 40;
20:16, 21:13, 14, 14, 24, 26, 33, 34, 37;
22:5, 10, 15, 16, 24, 24, 25, 25; 23:3, 11,
31, 36, 36; 20:15, 19, 21, 26, 27; 21:18,
25, 25
Da 1:13; 2:5, 5, 9, 13, 13, 20, 28, 40, 41, 41,

19, 20, 21, 21; 26:3, 8, 23, 28; 27:10, 20,
22, 22, 24, 25, 25, 26, 31; 28:27, 28
Ro 1:1, 4, 7, 7, 11, 12, 19, 22; 2:12, 13, 25,
26; 3:4, 4, 8, 19, 20, 25, 26; 4:11, 11, 11,
13, 14, 16, 16, 17, 18, 24; 5:9, 10, 15, 19;
6:5, 6, 8, 11, 17; 7:2, 3, 3, 3, 3, 4, 10; 8:4,
6, 6, 7, 9, 10, 17, 17, 18, 18, 21, 26, 29,
29, 31, 31, 39; 9:7, 17, 26, 27, 27, 33;
10:1, 9, 11, 13, 15; 11:6, 9, 10, 12, 15,
15, 16, 16, 17, 19, 20, 22, 23, 24, 24, 25,
25, 26, 35, 36; 12:2, 2, 9, 10, 16, 16,
18, 21; 13:1, 1, 3, 4, 5, 9, 14:4, 5, 9, 14,
15, 16; 15:5, 12, 16, 16, 24, 24, 31, 31,
32, 33; 16:11, 20, 24, 27
1Co 1:8, 1, 2, 3, 8, 10, 10, 17; 3:13, 13, 15, 15,
18; 4:2, 3, 6, 16, 17; 5:2, 5, 7, 11; 6:2,
5, 7, 9, 12, 16; 7:9, 11, 18, 21, 23,
25, 26, 27, 29, 34, 39, 39; 8:5, 5, 10; 9:2,
12, 12, 15, 19, 23, 27; 10:1, 7, 13, 13, 21,
27, 30, 33; 11:1, 6, 6, 6, 6, 16, 18, 19,
19, 27, 31, 32; 12:13, 13, 22, 23, 25, 26;
13:3, 8, 8, 8, 10; 14:7, 9, 10, 11, 11,
20, 20, 20, 23, 26, 27, 28, 30, 31, 34, 37,
38, 38, 40; 15:9, 12, 13, 14, 19, 20, 24, 37,
58; 16:2, 4, 6, 10, 13, 14, 22, 23, 24
2Co 1:2, 3, 4, 6, 6, 7, 11, 16, 17; 2:4, 7, 9,
14; 3:3, 7, 8, 9, 16; 4:3, 7, 10, 11; 5:2, 3,
3, 4, 4, 8, 8, 9, 10, 13, 13, 17, 20, 21, 21;
6:3, 13, 14, 16, 16, 17, 18, 18; 7:10, 11,
8:9, 10, 11, 12, 13, 14, 14, 14, 16, 23;
9:3, 3, 4, 5, 15; 10:2, 2, 8, 11, 11; 11:3, 6,
7, 12, 15; 12:6, 6, 7, 7, 11, 13, 14, 15,
11, 14
Gal 1:3, 5, 7, 8, 9, 10; 2:3, 6, 6, 9, 11, 16,
16, 17; 3:4, 8, 9, 15, 15, 18, 22, 23, 24,
29; 4:1, 9, 12, 18, 19, 20, 21, 30; 5:1, 2,
10, 10, 15, 18, 26; 6:1, 1, 3, 7, 9, 12,
16, 18
Eph 1:2, 3, 4, 12, 22; 3:6, 10, 16, 18, 19, 21;
4:14, 21, 23, 26, 31, 32; 5:1, 3, 7, 17, 18,
18, 24, 27, 31, 31; 6:3, 5, 8, 10, 11, 13,
16, 19, 23, 24
Php 1:2, 10, 20, 20, 23, 26, 27, 27, 30;
2:1, 2, 3, 6, 15, 17, 19, 28; 3:9, 15, 15,
15, 17, 21; 4:2, 5, 6, 6, 8, 8, 9, 11, 12, 12,
12, 20, 23
Col 1:2, 9, 12, 16, 20, 23; 2:2, 5, 20; 3:1, 15,
19, 21; 4:6, 16, 18
1Th 1:1; 2:4, 9, 16; 3:1, 3, 5; 4:11, 13, 17,
17; 5:6, 7, 8, 13, 14, 23, 27, 28
2Th 1:5, 7, 9, 10, 10, 12; 2:2, 2, 3, 6, 7, 8,
10, 12; 3:1, 2, 8, 13, 14, 16, 18
1Ti 1:7, 10, 17; 2:1, 4, 6, 12, 15; 3:2, 8, 10,
12; 4:3, 4, 4, 6, 12; 5:7, 9, 13, 16, 17,
22, 25; 6:1, 8, 9, 16, 17, 18, 21
2Ti 1:4, 8, 8, 15; 2:1, 2, 4, 6, 11, 15, 21, 24;
3:2, 9, 17; 4:2, 4, 6, 15, 16, 17, 18, 22, 22
Tit 1:6, 7, 9, 11, 13; 2:2, 3, 4, 5, 5, 6, 8, 8, 9;
3:1, 1, 2, 7, 8, 12, 13, 14, 15
Phm 1:8, 14, 22, 25
Heb 1:5, 5, 12, 14; 2:3, 17, 17; 3:5, 12, 13;
4:15; 5:5, 11, 12; 6:8, 12; 7:11; 8:4,
10, 10, 12; 9:16, 23; 10:2, 13, 29; 11:16,
16, 18, 40; 12:3, 8, 9, 10, 11, 13, 15, 19,
16, 18, 19, 20, 27, 28; 13:2, 5, 5, 9, 9, 19,
21, 25
Jas 1:4, 5, 13, 18, 19, 22, 23, 25, 26; 2:12,
15, 16; 3:1, 4, 10, 17; 4:4, 9, 9, 14; 5:3, 7,
8, 9, 12, 15, 16
1Pe 1:2, 3, 5, 6, 7, 7, 13, 13, 15, 16, 21; 2:3;
6, 7, 13, 18, 20; 3:1, 1, 3, 4, 7, 8, 8, 13,
14, 14, 15, 16, 17; 4:6, 7, 11, 11, 13, 14,
14, 16, 17, 18; 5:1, 5, 5, 8, 8, 11, 14
2Pe 1:2, 4, 8, 11, 12, 12, 15; 2:1, 2, 4, 9,
12; 3:2, 8, 10, 11, 11, 12, 14, 14, 16, 18
1Jn 1:4; 2:19, 28; 3:1, 2, 2; 4:10, 14
2Jn 1:2, 3, 12
3Jn 1:2, 8, 14
Jude 1:2, 18, 19, 25
Rev 1:4, 6, 19; 2:10, 10, 11, 19, 27; 3:2, 5,
18, 18, 19; 4:1; 5:13; 6:11, 11, 17; 7:12;
9:5; 10:6, 7, 9; 11:5, 9, 18; 12:2, 4, 15;
13:10, 15; 14:10; 16:5, 12; 17:17; 18:4, 8,
21, 21, 22, 22, 22, 22, 23; 19:7, 8; 20:3,
3, 6, 10; 21:3, 3, 4, 4, 7, 7, 25, 25;
22:3, 3, 4, 5, 6, 11, 11, 11, 11, 12, 21

BUT (3994)

Ge 2:6, 17, 20, 20; 3:3; 4:2, 5; 6:8, 18; 8:9; 9:4;
11:30; 12:12; 13:13; 15:4, 10, 16; 16:6;
17:5, 5, 21; 18:15, 22, 27, 32; 19:2, 4,
10, 14, 26; 20:3, 3, 4, 12; 21:23, 26; 22:7;
23:6, 13; 24:4, 33, 38; 25:6, 28; 26:29;
27:22, 38; 28:17, 19; 29:17, 20, 31;
30:42; 31:5, 7, 29, 33, 34, 35, 47; 32:28;
34:12, 15, 17; 35:8, 10, 16, 18; 37:11, 22,
35; 38:20; 39:8, 9, 21; 40:14, 22, 23;
41:8, 21, 24, 54; 42:4, 7, 8, 10, 12, 20,
34; 43:5, 34; 44:17; 45:8; 42; 46:12;
47:18, 30; 48:7, 19, 21; 49:19, 24;
50:20, 20
Ex 1:12, 16, 17, 17; 2:15, 17; 3:22; 4:1, 10;
5:16, 17; 6:3, 9; 7:4, 12; 8:15, 18, 29;
9:6, 30, 32; 10:8, 20, 23, 27; 11:7; 12:9;
44; 13:15, 18; 14:9, 16, 20, 29; 15:19;
16:8, 20, 26; 17:12; 18:22, 26; 19:13, 24;
20:10, 19; 21:13, 14, 18, 28, 29, 29;
22:15; 23:11, 22, 24; 24:2; 29:14, 33;
31:15; 32:18; 33:11, 20; 34:13, 20, 21,
34; 35:2; 36:38; 40:37
Lev 1:9, 13, 17; 2:12; 5:8, 11; 6:28; 7:16, 17,

20, 24, 31; 8:17; 9:10; 10:6; 11:4, 5, 6,
11, 23, 36, 38; 12:5; 13:6, 7, 14, 21, 21,
23, 26, 26, 28, 33, 35, 37; 14:9, 53;
15:28; 16:10; 17:16; 19:14, 15, 18, 24,
34; 20:24; 21:2, 4, 14; 22:11, 13, 13, 20,
23, 32; 23:3, 8, 25; 25:4, 17, 28, 31, 34,
36, 40, 43, 46, 52; 26:14, 15, 23, 27, 45;
27:8, 13, 18, 21, 29
Nu 1:47, 50, 53; 2:33; 3:38; 4:15, 19, 20;
5:8, 20, 28; 6:12; 7:9; 8:26; 9:13, 22;
10:4, 7, 7, 30; 11:6, 20, 26, 26; 12:14;
13:31; 14:10, 21, 24, 31, 32, 38, 41, 44;
15:30; 16:9, 30, 41; 18:2, 17, 23, 24;
19:12, 20; 21:22, 23; 22:20, 24, 35;
23:13, 26; 24:1, 4, 11, 13, 16, 17, 17, 20;
26:33, 64; 27:3; 28:19, 27; 29:8, 36; 30:5,
8, 9, 12, 14, 15; 31:18; 32:17, 23, 27, 30;
33:55; 35:8, 20, 22, 26, 28, 30, 31, 33;
36:9
Dt 6:17, 26, 38, 40, 43, 45; 2:11, 12, 21, 30;
3:7, 19, 26, 28; 4:4, 9, 12, 20, 22, 22, 30;
29; 5:3, 14, 31; 7:5, 8, 15, 18, 23, 26; 8:3,
18; 9:4, 5, 19; 10:12; 11:7, 11, 28; 12:5,
10, 14, 18; 13:9; 14:7, 12, 20; 15:3, 6, 6,
8; 16:6; 17:6, 16; 18:14, 20, 22; 19:11,
13, 21; 20:12, 14, 16, 17; 21:14, 17, 23;
22:7, 20, 25, 26; 23:5, 11, 20, 22, 24, 25;
24:5, 18; 25:15; 26:14; 28:15, 38, 39, 40,
41, 65; 29:15, 20, 29; 30:14, 17, 17;
32:15, 52; 34:4, 6
Jos 1:8, 14; 2:4, 6, 22; 5:5, 12, 14; 6:13, 19,
22; 7:1, 3, 3, 12; 8:4, 9, 14; 9:12, 19, 21;
10:16, 19, 30, 37, 40; 11:13, 14, 20;
13:13, 33; 14:3, 8; 15:63; 16:10; 17:3, 3,
8, 12, 13, 14, 18; 18:7; 21:12; 22:3, 5, 7,
18, 19, 27, 28; 23:8, 9, 13; 24:4, 10, 12,
15, 21
Jdg 1:6, 19, 21, 25, 27, 29, 30, 32, 33, 35;
2:2, 3, 17, 17; 3:15, 16, 19; 4:8, 16; 5:31;
6:10, 13, 34, 39; 7:6, 10, 19; 8:20;
9:9, 19, 20, 51; 11:16, 17, 17, 18, 20, 20,
27; 13:3, 6, 7, 9, 21, 23; 14:4, 6, 9, 13,
16, 20; 15:1, 1, 13, 13, 19; 16:21; 17:6;
19:10, 10, 10, 16, 24, 25, 28; 20:9, 13,
14, 32, 34, 40, 42, 47
Ru 1:14, 17; 2:8; 3:3, 13; 4:4
1Sa 1:2, 5, 5, 11, 13, 15, 22; 2:15, 16, 18,
25, 30; 4:20; 5:6; 6:3, 9; 7:10; 8:3, 6, 7,
19; 9:4, 4, 7, 27; 10:12, 16, 19, 27, 27;
12:10, 12, 15, 15, 20, 23, 25; 13:8, 14,
16, 20, 22; 14:1, 10, 26, 27, 37, 39, 41,
43; 15:3, 9, 19, 21; 16:7, 7, 14; 17:9,
15, 33, 42, 45, 50, 54; 18:8, 8, 16, 17, 19,
25, 25; 19:2; 20:2, 3, 5, 7, 13, 15,
22, 39; 21:4, 6; 22:17, 23; 23:14, 24, 27;
24:7, 10, 12, 12; 25:3, 14, 15, 19, 25,
29, 31, 37, 44; 26:3, 7, 11, 19, 23; 28:23,
23; 29:2, 8; 30:2, 6, 10, 24; 31:4
2Sa 2:8, 10, 21, 31; 3:1, 13, 22, 26; 4:12;
5:17, 23; 6:10; 7:2, 6, 15, 19; 8:4; 9:10;
10:11; 11:1, 9, 13, 27; 12:3, 4, 12, 17, 19,
21, 23, 23; 13:3, 9, 14, 16, 20, 21, 25, 27,
34, 37; 14:2, 6, 25, 29; 15:3, 10, 20, 26,
34; 16:18; 17:16, 18; 18:3, 3, 20, 20, 22,
23, 29; 19:4, 21, 27, 28, 37; 20:2, 3, 5,
10, 21; 21:2, 7, 8, 17; 22:19, 28, 42, 42;
23:6, 7, 12, 16, 21, 23; 24:3, 17, 24
1Ki 1:1, 4, 8, 10, 19, 26, 52; 2:7, 8, 9, 26,
30, 33; 3:7, 11, 21, 22, 22, 23, 26, 26;
5:4; 7:1, 31; 8:16, 19, 27, 41; 9:6, 6, 22,
22, 24; 11:1, 10, 13, 27, 40; 14:5, 24, 35,
39; 12:8, 10, 11, 14, 27, 22; 13:18,
22, 33; 14:4, 9, 14; 15:14; 16:22, 25;
17:1, 12, 13; 18:12, 18, 21, 22, 25, 26;
19:4, 11, 11, 12; 20:9, 16, 23, 27, 28, 30;
21:5, 15, 25, 29; 22:8, 8, 16, 18, 24, 30,
31, 48, 49
2Ki 3, 4, 6, 16; 2:10, 17, 19; 3:2, 5, 15, 15,
18, 24, 26; 4:27, 31, 41; 5:1, 11, 15, 16,
16, 17, 20, 20, 25; 6:5, 12, 19, 32, 32;
7:2, 4, 10, 19; 8:13; 9:15, 18, 27, 35;
10:4, 9, 18, 19, 23, 31; 11:2, 15; 12:3, 6,
7, 9, 14; 13:6, 7, 11, 19, 22; 14:6, 6, 11,
19, 27; 15:25; 16:3, 5; 17:2, 14, 18, 19,
36, 39, 40; 18:6, 12, 20, 22, 27, 36;
19:18, 27; 20:10; 21:9; 22:18; 23:9, 23,
35; 25:12, 25
1Ch 2:30, 34; 4:27; 5:1, 2; 6:49, 56; 7:14:
10:4; 11:18, 18, 25; 12:17, 19; 13:13;
15:2; 16:5; 18, 26; 17:1, 5, 14; 18:4; 19:3,
12, 18; 20:1, 7; 21:3, 6, 8, 13, 17, 17, 24,
30; 22:8; 23:11, 17, 22; 24:2; 27:23, 24;
28:3, 9; 29:1, 14
2Ch 1:4, 11; 2:6; 4:6; 5:9; 6:2, 6, 8, 9, 18,
32; 7:19; 8:8, 9, 9; 10:8, 10, 11, 14, 14,
17, 18; 11:2; 12:7; 13:10, 11, 13, 21;
15:2, 4, 5, 17; 16:12; 17:4; 18:6, 7, 7, 15,
17, 29, 31; 19:6; 20:10, 12, 15; 21:13, 13,
20; 22:10, 11; 23:6, 6, 7; 24:15, 19, 22,
25; 25:2, 4, 4, 4, 7, 8, 9, 13, 20, 27;
26:16, 18; 28:1, 9, 10, 20, 21, 23, 27;
29:34; 30:8, 10, 18; 32:8, 9, 25; 33:2, 10,
22, 23, 25; 35:13, 21, 21, 22; 36:13, 16
Ezr 2:59, 62; 3:6, 12; 4:3, 3; 5:5, 12, 13;
8:22; 9:9; 10:13
Ne 1:9; 2:2, 14, 19, 20; 3:3, 5, 14, 15; 4:1, 7;
5:15, 15; 6:2, 8, 12; 7:4, 61, 64; 9:16, 17,
17, 28, 29, 33; 11:3, 21; 13:2, 6, 24
Est 1:12, 16, 17; 2:15; 3:2, 15; 4:4, 11, 14;
5:9, 12; 6:12, 13; 7:4; 9:10, 15, 16, 16,
18, 25
Job 1:11; 2:5, 6, 10; 3:9, 21; 4:2, 5, 16; 5:3;
6:1, 14, 25; 7:21; 8:9, 15, 15; 9:2, 11,
15, 18, 35; 11:5, 20; 12:2, 3, 7; 13:4, 15;
14:10, 21, 22; 16:5, 7, 12, 20; 17:10;

La 1:13; 2:5, 5, 9, 13, 13, 20, 28, 40, 41, 41,
42, 44, 44; 3:6, 11, 15, 15, 17, 18, 19, 28,
29, 29; 4:1, 15, 15, 16, 16, 19, 23, 23, 25,
26, 27, 27, 32; 5:7, 7, 10, 12, 16, 16, 17,
29; 6:1, 7, 8, 12, 15, 17, 25, 26, 26; 7:14,
23, 23, 24, 25, 27; 8:13, 13, 14, 17, 19,
19, 24, 25, 26; 9:16, 25, 25, 26, 26, 27;
10:19, 19, 19; 11:2, 4, 4, 4, 5, 5, 6, 6, 10,
10, 11, 11, 12, 12, 16, 17, 18, 19, 20, 22,
22, 25, 27, 27, 28, 29, 30, 32, 34, 36, 36,
41, 43; 12:1, 1, 1, 3, 4, 6, 7, 7, 8, 10, 11,
11, 13

Idx

62:2, 8, 8; 63:12, 19; 64:4; 65:1, 5, 15, 16; 66:16, 16

Jer 2:8, 17, 34; 4:26; 5:7, 7, 22, 31; 6:5, 25; 7:10, 11, 14, 30; 8:3, 5; 10:12, 12, 12, 14; 11:21, 22, 22; 12:16, 16; 13:5, 24; 14:9, 12, 12, 12, 15; 15:16; 16:4, 4; 17:2, 8, 8, 11, 19, 20, 21; 18:21, 21; 19:2, 7, 7; 20:2, 4; 21:9, 9, 9; 22:2, 4, 5, 8, 13, 13; 23:27, 32, 32; 25:29; 27:3, 5, 5, 8, 13, 13, 13; 29:3, 19, 22; 31:9, 32, 35, 35; 32:17, 34, 36, 36, 36; 33:4, 4; 34:4, 15; 35:4; 37:2; 38:2, 2, 2, 11, 23; 39:4, 4, 4, 18; 41:12, 17; 42:17, 17, 17, 22, 22, 22; 44:12, 12, 12, 13, 13, 13, 15, 18, 18, 26, 27, 27; 46:2, 6, 10, 18; 48:19; 49:3, 9, 13, 17; 50:1, 13; 51:14, 15, 15, 15, 17, 17; 52:7, 7, 7, 7, 7

La 1:12, 14; 2:15, 21; 3:1; 5:12

Eze 1:1, 3, 15, 19; 3:15, 23; 4:10, 11, 16, 16; 5:12, 14; 6:11, 11, 11, 12, 12; 8:3; 9:2, 3, 11; 10:9, 9, 9, 15, 16, 20, 22; 11:10, 24; 12:3, 4, 7; 13:19, 22; 14:3, 7, 13, 14, 20; 16:6, 8, 15, 25, 36, 56, 61; 17:5, 7, 8, 9, 14, 17, 18, 21; 18:7, 12, 16, 18; 19:7, 10, 10; 20:3, 31, 31; 21:12; 22:7, 7, 12; 23:21, 25, 25; 24:6, 21; 25:12, 13, 14, 15; 26:6, 10, 11; 27:12, 16, 34; 28:5, 5, 10, 16, 17, 18, 18, 23; 29:7; 30:5, 6, 10, 12, 17; 31:7, 9, 12, 14; 32:12, 20, 21, 22, 23, 24, 25, 26, 29, 29, 30, 31; 33:27, 30; 34:13; 35:5; 36:17, 17, 34, 37; 37:2, 18; 38:17; 39:15, 23; 40:2, 5, 7, 18, 22, 38, 41, 49, 49; 41:7, 17, 17; 42:20; 43:3, 4, 6, 7, 7, 8, 8, 8, 13; 44:2, 2, 3, 3; 45:1; 46:2, 2, 8, 8, 9, 9, 9, 9, 9, 14, 16, 18, 21; 47:2, 12, 16, 18; 48:2, 3, 4, 5, 6, 7, 8, 12, 20, 24, 25, 26, 27, 28, 29

Da 4:17, 17, 27, 27, 30; 5:10; 7:2, 8, 16; 8:2, 11, 12, 24, 25; 9:2, 3, 5, 10, 11, 12, 18, 19; 10:4, 16; 11:2, 12, 16, 18, 21, 32, 33, 33, 33; 12:7

Hos 1:2, 7, 7, 7, 7, 7; 2:17; 4:2; 6:5, 5, 9; 7:4, 16; 8:4, 9; 11:3; 12:3, 3, 10, 10, 13, 13; 13:7, 16; 14:1

Am 2:8; 4:2; 5:3, 3; 6:8, 10, 13; 7:2, 4, 5, 7, 8, 11, 17, 17; 8:2, 5, 7, 8, 14; 9:5, 10, 12

Ob 1:5, 9

Jnh 2:2; 3:7

Mic 2:2, 5, 8, 12, 13; 3:8; 7:18

Na 1:6;

Hab 1:16; 2:4, 5, 10, 12; 3:10, 13

Zep 1:5, 18; 2:12, 15; 3:6

Hag 1:1, 3; 2:1, 10, 13, 22

Zec 1:8; 3:5, 7; 4:3, 6, 6, 6, 14; 5:4; 7:7, 12; 8:9; 9:8, 11

Mal 1:1, 9; 2:10

Mt 1:22; 2:5, 14, 15, 17, 23; 3:3, 4, 4, 14, 15, 18; 5:12, 12, 20, 22, 33, 34, 35, 35, 36; 6:27; 7:16, 20; 8:17, 28; 9:25; 11:12; 12:17, 24, 27, 27, 28, 33, 37, 37; 13:1, 4, 14, 19, 21, 21, 35; 14:13; 15:3, 5, 5, 6; 17:21; 18:7, 28; 20:30, 30; 21:4, 23, 24, 27; 22:1, 31; 23:16, 16, 18, 18, 20, 20, 20, 21, 21, 21, 22, 22, 22; 24:15; 26:4, 24, 63, 73; 27:9, 32, 35, 39, 64; 28:9, 13

Mk 1:16, 31; 2:13, 14; 3:22; 4:1, 1, 2, 4, 15; 5:4, 7, 21, 22, 41; 6:2, 7, 25, 25, 32, 39, 40, 40, 48; 7:11, 11, 26; 8:3, 23, 27; 9:2, 27, 29, 29, 33, 34; 10:1, 46; 11:4, 20, 28, 29, 33; 12:1, 36; 13:14; 14:1, 19, 21, 47, 69, 70; 15:21, 29, 35

Lk 1:61, 70, 77; 2:8, 18, 26, 27; 3:19; 4:1, 4, 4; 5:1, 2, 15, 17, 19; 6:44; 8:4, 5, 12, 20, 36, 54; 9:7, 14, 47; 10:4, 19, 31, 31, 32; 11:3, 19, 19; 13:17; 16:22; 17:6, 7, 7; 18:5, 31, 35, 36, 37; 19:8, 15, 24; 20:2, 8; 21:9, 9, 16, 24; 22:22, 56; 23:28; 24:4, 12, 32

Jn 1:3, 10, 17, 17, 42; 3:2, 34; 5:2; 6:15, 18, 57, 57; 7:50; 8:9, 9, 59; 9:1, 7, 21; 10:1, 2, 3, 9; 11:39, 42; 12:11, 29; 13:35; 14:6; 16:30; 18:22; 19:7, 25, 26, 39; 20:7; 21:19

Ac 1:3, 10, 16, 25; 2:16, 22, 22, 23, 33, 43; 3:7, 12, 16, 18, 21; 4:7, 7, 9, 10, 10, 16, 25, 30, 30, 36; 5:10, 12, 15, 19; 6:10; 7:25, 35, 42, 53; 9:8, 13, 25, 25, 36, 39; 10:6, 22, 32, 36; 11:4, 5, 28, 30; 12:9, 20; 13:4, 8, 11, 19, 21, 36, 39, 45; 14:3; 15:3, 7, 9, 12, 23, 27, 40; 16:2, 8, 13, 16; 17:10, 23, 29, 31; 18:3, 9, 21, 28; 19:10, 11, 13, 25; 20:16, 19, 31; 21:19; 22:11, 20, 24, 25; 23:2, 4; 25:14; 26:18; 27:2, 11, 12, 13, 16, 23; 28:16, 25

Ro 1:2, 4, 5, 10, 12, 17, 20; 2:7, 12, 14, 16, 27, 27; 3:20, 20, 21, 22, 24, 27, 27, 28, 30; 4:2; 5:1, 2, 2, 5, 9, 10, 10, 11, 12, 12, 15, 15, 16, 16, 17, 17, 17, 18, 18, 19, 19, 21; 6:4; 7:2, 4, 5, 7, 8, 11, 11, 13, 13; 8:11, 14, 20, 24; 9:10, 10, 32, 32; 10:5, 17, 17, 19, 19; 11:6, 14, 20, 24; 12:1, 2; 14:14; 15:16, 18, 19, 24, 28, 32; 16:18, 99

1Co 1:4, 5, 9, 10, 11, 21, 21; 2:10; 3:5, 13, 15; 4:4; 6:2, 11, 14; 7:6, 14, 14, 39; 8:6, 6, 9; 9:22, 27; 10:30; 11:12; 12:3, 3, 8, 8, 9, 9, 13; 14:6, 6, 6, 6, 9, 19, 27, 27, 30, 31; 15:2, 10, 21, 21, 31; 16:2, 3, 7, 99

2Co 1:1, 4, 5, 11, 11, 12, 16, 19, 19, 20; 2:2, 14; 3:3, 10, 18; 4:2, 14, 16; 5:7, 7, 18, 20; 6:6, 6, 6, 6, 6, 6, 7, 7, 7, 8, 9; 7:6, 7, 7, 9, 13; 8:5, 8, 14, 19, 20; 9:12, 13, 14; 10:1, 9, 11, 12, 15; 11:3, 26, 26, 33; 12:17; 13:4, 4, 99

Gal 1:1, 1, 12, 15, 22; 2:2, 2, 5, 15, 16, 16,

16, 16, 16, 17, 20, 21; 3:2, 2, 3, 5, 5, 11, 11, 18, 19, 21, 22, 24, 26; 4:8, 22, 22, 23; 5:4, 5, 6, 13; 6:14

Eph 1:1, 5; 2:3, 5, 8, 11, 11, 13, 16, 18; 3:3, 5, 6, 7, 9, 10, 12, 16, 17, 21; 4:14, 16, 21; 5:13, 26; 6:99

Php 1:11, 14, 20, 20, 26, 28; 3:9, 11, 16; 4:6, 19, 99

Col 1:1, 16, 16, 17, 20, 20, 21; 2:11, 18, 19; 3:17; 4:18, 99

1Th 3:3, 5, 7; 4:1, 2, 15; 5:9, 27

2Th 2:1, 1, 2, 2, 2, 2, 3, 14, 15, 15; 3:12, 14, 16

1Ti 1:1, 18; 4:5, 14; 5:21

2Ti 1:1, 6, 10, 14; 2:26; 3:16; 4:17

Tit 1:9; 3:5, 5, 7

Phm 1:6, 7, 99

Heb 1:1, 2, 2, 3, 3, 4; 2:2, 3, 3, 9, 10; 3:4, 16; 5:3, 8, 14; 6:7, 13, 13, 16, 17, 18; 7:2, 11, 19, 21, 22, 23, 25; 8:6, 9; 9:11, 12, 12, 15, 22, 26; 10:1, 8, 10, 14, 19, 20, 33, 38; 11:2, 3, 4, 4, 4, 5, 7, 7, 7, 8, 9, 12, 17, 20, 21, 22, 23, 24, 27, 29, 29, 30, 31; 13:11, 15, 99

Jas 2:7, 12, 18, 21, 22, 24, 24, 25; 5:4, 12, 12, 12, 17

1Pe 1:3, 5, 12, 18, 21, 23, 25; 2:5, 12, 14, 24; 3:1, 18, 19, 20, 21; 5:2, 10, 12

2Pe 1:4, 13, 21, 21; 2:2; 3:1, 2, 5, 7

1Jn 3:24; 5:2, 6, 6, 6

3Jn 1:14;

Jude 1:1, 12, 23

Rev 1:1; 5:9; 8:13; 9:2, 18, 18, 18, 20; 10:6; 12:11, 11; 13:14, 14; 14:20; 18:15, 17, 19, 23; 21:25

FOR (8985)

Ge 1:14, 14, 14, 15, 29, 30; 2:5, 9, 17, 18, 20, 20; 3:5, 6, 17, 19, 19, 22; 4:23, 25; 5:24; 6:3, 7, 12, 13, 21, 21, 21; 7:1, 4; 8:9, 9, 21, 21; 9:3, 6, 12, 13; 10:25; 11:3, 3; 12:10, 13, 16; 13:6, 8, 15, 15, 17; 14:13; 15:6, 16; 16:10, 13; 17:4, 5, 7, 8, 13, 15, 19, 20; 18:5, 14, 15, 19, 24, 24, 26, 28, 29, 31, 32; 19:8, 13, 14, 17, 21, 22, 30; 20:3, 3, 6, 7, 7, 11, 18; 21:2, 7, 10, 12, 16, 17, 18, 30; 22:2, 3, 8, 12, 13, 16; 23:2, 2, 8, 9, 9, 13, 18, 20; 24:10, 14, 19, 20, 22, 23, 40, 44, 62, 65; 25:21, 30; 26:3, 7, 7, 9, 14, 15, 16, 18, 21, 22, 22, 24, 24; 27:5, 9, 36, 36, 37, 41; 28:11, 15, 18, 18, 20; 29:2, 9, 15, 18, 20, 20, 21, 24, 25, 27, 32; 30:13, 15, 16, 26, 26, 27, 27, 30, 30, 31, 33, 41, 41, 44, 45, 49, 52; 32:10, 11, 12, 13, 20, 26, 28, 30; 33:10, 17, 19; 34:8, 14, 14, 16, 21, 21, 22, 30, 30, 31, 32, 40, 44, 44, 44, 62, 65; 35:21, 30; 36:3, 7, 7, 9, 14, 15, 16, 18, 20; 37:4, 27, 30; 39:2, 3, 3, 5, 5, 9, 10, 16, 18, 18, 20, 23; 41:8, 13, 14, 14, 14, 19, 21, 31, 33, 34, 35, 37, 39, 40, 41, 43, 45, 46, 47, 49, 51, 57, 57, 61; 42:4, 5, 18, 19, 23, 25, 27, 30, 33, 38; 43:5, 9, 9, 9, 16, 18, 25, 30, 32, 32, 32; 44:4, 14, 17, 18, 22, 26, 32, 32, 34; 45:3, 5, 6, 11, 19, 19, 20, 21, 23; 46:3, 32, 34; 47:4, 4, 4, 4, 13, 14, 15, 15, 16, 17, 17, 17, 19, 20; 48:4, 7, 10, 14, 18; 49:6, 7, 7, 13, 18, 30; 50:3, 3

Ex 1:5, 11, 18, 19; 2:3, 7, 9, 19, 22; 3:5, 6, 7, 15; 4:1, 19; 5:7, 8, 18, 23; 6:1, 7, 8, 9; 7:9; 8:9, 24, 26, 28; 9:2, 11, 14, 15, 16, 16, 19, 27, 28, 30, 31, 32; 10:1, 5, 9, 10, 11, 12, 15, 16, 23, 26, 28; 12:3, 4, 4, 12, 13, 14, 14, 15, 17, 17, 19, 21, 23, 26, 28; 12:3, 4, 4, 12, 13, 14, 14, 15, 17, 17, 19, 21, 23, 25, 25; 15:1, 17, 18, 19, 21, 23, 25, 26; 16:3, 4, 7, 8, 9, 15, 16, 16, 22, 23, 25; 17:1, 3, 14, 14, 16; 18:1, 1, 3, 4, 8, 9, 11, 12, 18, 18, 19, 22; 19:2, 5, 7, 9, 11, 23; 20:5, 7, 11, 20, 25; 21:2, 6, 19, 21, 23, 24, 24, 24, 24, 24, 25, 25, 26, 27, 30; 22:1, 1, 2, 3, 3, 3, 9, 9, 9, 9, 9, 13, 15, 21, 27, 27; 23:7, 8, 9, 15, 21, 21, 23, 31, 33; 24:1, 1, 1, 1; 25:6, 6, 6, 12, 26, 29; 26:14, 15, 17, 18, 19, 20, 22, 23, 24, 26, 26, 27, 27, 27, 29, 30, 36, 37, 37; 27:4, 6, 9, 9, 9, 11, 12, 16, 20; 28:2, 2, 4, 12, 29, 40, 40, 40, 40, 43; 29:9, 22, 24, 25, 25, 26, 27, 27, 28, 28, 36, 36, 36, 37, 40, 41; 30:4, 4, 12, 15, 16, 16, 16, 19, 21, 32; 31:10, 11, 13, 14, 14, 16, 17, 17; 32:1, 1, 1, 1; 34:7, 9, 9, 10, 12, 14, 18, 24, 27; 35:8, 8, 8, 9, 14, 14, 15, 17, 19, 21, 21, 24, 27, 27, 28, 28, 28, 29; 36:1, 3, 5, 6, 7, 14, 19, 20, 22, 23, 23, 24, 25, 27, 28, 31, 32, 32, 33, 34, 34, 36; 37:3, 12, 13, 14, 14, 27, 27; 38:4, 5, 5, 11, 12, 13, 14, 14, 17, 27, 27, 27, 28, 30; 39:1, 4, 7, 27, 27, 37, 38, 40, 40, 41; 40:5, 15, 38

Lev 1:4, 4, 10, 14; 2:11, 12, 14; 3:6, 7, 16, 17; 4:3, 3, 8, 14, 20, 20, 21, 26, 28, 31, 31, 32, 33, 35; 5:6, 6, 6, 6, 7, 7, 8, 10, 10, 10, 11, 11, 11, 13, 15, 15, 16, 16, 18; 6:6, 6, 7, 7, 15, 17, 18, 20, 21, 22, 23, 23, 26, 30; 7:5, 7, 12, 13, 14, 15, 19, 25, 30, 32, 33, 34, 34, 36; 8:2, 14, 14, 18, 21, 27, 32, 33, 34, 35; 9:2, 2, 3, 3, 4, 4, 7, 7, 8, 15, 16, 17, 18, 21; 10:7, 9, 12, 13,

14, 15, 17; 11:24, 35, 35, 42, 44, 44, 45, 45; 12:2, 6, 6, 6, 6, 7, 7, 8, 8, 8; 13:7, 11, 15, 28, 36, 52; 14:4, 6, 10, 12, 12, 13, 31, 34, 53, 54, 55, 56, 56; 15:13, 15, 15, 15, 15, 30, 30, 30, 30; 16:2, 3, 3, 5, 15, 15, 15, 16, 16, 17, 17, 17, 18, 24, 24, 24, 26, 27, 27, 29, 30, 30, 31, 33, 33, 33, 33, 33, 34, 34; 17:5, 6, 7, 11, 11, 11, 11, 11, 14, 14, 14; 18:10, 13, 17, 19, 24, 24, 29; 19:2, 10, 21, 22, 23, 24, 28, 29, 31, 34; 20:18, 19, 20, 20, 20, 21, 28, 28, 29, 31, 34, 41; 24:2, 3, 7, 9, 18, 20, 20, 20, 22, 22; 25:4, 5, 6, 6, 6, 6, 6, 7, 7, 12, 16, 17, 21, 23, 23, 23, 34, 37, 42, 46, 46, 46, 51, 55; 26:1, 9, 16, 18, 18, 20, 24, 27, 28, 44, 44, 45; 27:2, 5, 6, 7, 10, 10, 34

Nu 1:44, 48; 3:13, 25, 26, 26, 38, 41, 46; 4:16, 24, 25, 26, 26, 29, 35, 39, 43; 5:8, 15, 15; 6:7, 7, 7, 7, 11, 11, 11, 12, 14, 14, 14, 14, 17, 20; 7:3, 3, 10, 11, 13, 15, 16, 17, 19, 19, 21, 22, 23, 25, 27, 28, 29, 31, 33, 34, 35, 37, 39, 40, 41, 43, 45, 46, 47, 49, 51, 52, 53, 55, 57, 59, 61, 63, 64, 65, 67, 69, 70, 71, 73, 75, 76, 77, 79, 81, 82, 83, 87, 87, 88; 8:8, 11, 12, 12, 13, 13, 15, 16, 17, 17, 18, 19, 21; 9:14, 14; 10:2, 2, 6, 8, 8, 10, 29, 33; 11:13, 14, 18, 18, 22, 32, 32; 12:1, 1; 13:30, 31; 14:3, 9, 9, 11, 13, 14, 32, 34, 40, 42, 43; 15:5, 5, 6, 6, 7, 8, 8, 10, 10, 11, 11, 14, 15, 15, 15, 16, 16, 20, 24, 24, 24, 25, 25, 27, 28, 28, 38, 39, 40, 46, 46, 47; 16:3, 6, 9, 16, 38, 38, 40; 17:3, 3, 6, 8, 10; 18:4, 6, 7, 7, 7, 8, 8, 9, 10, 11, 11, 13, 24, 26, 28, 34; 22:6, 6, 6, 12, 12, 17, 22, 29, 34; 23:9; 24:1, 18, 20, 24; 25:11, 13, 13, 18, 18; 26:53, 62, 65; 27:14, 21; 28:2, 2, 3, 5, 6, 7, 7, 9, 12, 12, 13, 13, 15, 19, 20, 20, 21, 22, 23, 28, 31; 29:2, 3, 3, 4, 5, 5, 6, 8, 10, 11, 13, 13, 14, 14, 14, 15, 16, 19, 21; 34:8, 9

Dt 1:10, 14, 17, 17, 30, 30, 37, 38, 40, 42; 2:5, 5, 6, 6, 7, 9, 9, 9, 15, 19, 19, 28, 28, 30, 35, 36; 3:2, 7, 11, 18, 19, 22, 22, 24, 26, 27, 28; 4:1, 3, 6, 7, 7, 15, 21, 21, 24, 31, 32, 34, 38, 40; 5:5, 9, 11, 23, 25, 26, 29, 31; 6:8, 15, 24; 7:4, 6, 7, 16, 21, 25, 26; 8:7, 10, 18; 9:4, 4, 5, 5, 5, 6, 6, 12, 19, 20; 10:13, 17, 19, 21, 22; 11:2, 10, 12, 15, 18, 22, 25, 31; 12:9, 23, 23, 31; 13:1, 2, 16, 16, 18; 14:1, 2, 7, 21, 24, 24, 26, 26, 26, 26, 27; 15:4, 6, 8, 10, 11, 11, 15, 21; 16:1, 3, 19, 17:1, 3, 9, 10, 11, 15, 15, 21, 21, 21, 21; 20:1, 1, 18, 19, 19, 20; 21:5, 14, 17, 17, 23; 22:5, 8, 20, 26, 27; 23:3, 6, 7, 14, 18, 18, 21; 24:4, 4, 6, 15, 16, 16, 16, 16, 19, 19, 20, 20, 21; 25:11, 16, 19; 26:1, 3, 14, 14, 28:20, 32, 34, 38, 39, 40, 41, 46, 46, 46, 47, 56, 57, 57, 62, 67, 67, 68; 29:8, 13, 16, 20, 29; 30:9, 9, 9, 11, 12, 13, 20; 31:6, 7, 18, 19, 19, 20, 21, 21, 23, 26, 27, 29; 32:4, 9, 20, 22, 28, 31, 32, 35, 36, 36, 40, 40, 43, 47, 47, 49; 33:2, 7, 9, 13, 13, 14, 14, 14, 15, 15, 16, 19, 21; 34:8, 9

Jos 1:6, 8, 9, 11; 2:3, 5, 10, 10, 11, 14, 15, 24; 3:4, 5, 15; 6:16; 7:1, 3, 5, 9, 11, 13; 8:2, 2, 6, 6, 7, 18, 26, 27, 28; 9:9, 11, 12, 22, 23, 27, 27; 10:4, 6, 8, 14, 14, 18, 19, 24, 25, 42; 11:6, 10, 13, 14, 20, 23; 12:6, 7; 13:6, 7, 12, 32; 14:1, 2, 2, 3, 4, 4, 4, 9, 11, 12, 13; 15:19; 16:3; 17:1, 1, 1, 2, 2, 2, 2, 2, 2, 15, 16, 18, 18; 18:6; 19:47, 51; 20:2, 4, 10, 12, 13; 21:2, 12, 26, 27, 32, 38, 40; 22:2, 24, 25, 26, 26, 28, 29, 29, 29, 34; 23:2, 2, 2, 3, 4, 9, 9, 10, 13; 24:1, 1, 1, 1, 13, 15, 17, 18, 19, 32

Jdg 1:1, 15, 32, 34; 2:7, 10, 15, 18; 3:20, 28; 4:3, 5, 9, 14, 17, 19, 21; 5:2, 15, 16, 30; 6:4, 5, 5, 5, 22, 31, 31, 31, 38, 40; 7:2, 4, 9, 12, 12, 14, 15; 8:5, 10, 11, 20, 22, 24, 30; 9:2, 3, 5, 17, 17, 21, 25, 28; 10:16; 11:2, 18, 31, 35, 36, 37, 38; 12:6, 9; 13:5, 5, 7, 15, 16, 20; 14:2, 3, 3, 4, 10; 15:18; 16:2, 7, 18, 18, 19, 23, 23, 24, 25, 25, 28; 17:3; 18:1, 9, 10, 19, 26; 19:6, 15, 19, 19, 19, 20:6, 10, 17, 27, 28; 21:5, 6, 7, 7, 9, 15, 16, 16, 17, 18, 20

Ru 1:6, 12, 13, 13, 13, 16, 20; 2:13, 13, 16; 3:1, 9, 10, 11, 17, 18; 4:4, 6, 6, 7, 8, 15

1Sa 1:5, 6, 16, 16, 22, 22, 27; 2:2, 3, 5, 8, 9, 14, 15, 15, 17, 20, 23, 25, 30, 30, 32; 3:5, 6, 8, 9, 10, 13, 13, 14, 21;

4:7, 7, 10, 13, 13, 18, 19, 20, 22; 5:7, 11; 6:2, 4, 8, 17, 17, 17, 17, 17, 17; 7:2, 5, 8, 9, 9, 17; 8:7, 11, 11, 9:5, 7, 7, 9, 10, 20, 20, 24, 24; 10:2, 2, 7; 11:2, 13, 14, 16, 19, 21, 21, 22, 22, 23, 24, 24; 13:6, 7, 13, 19, 21, 21, 22, 22, 23, 23, 24; 14:6, 45; 15:2, 4, 7, 11, 12, 22; 17:8, 12, 20, 21, 26, 26, 26, 29, 35; 16:1, 1, 7, 7, 11, 12, 22; 17:8, 7, 20, 21, 26, 26, 29, 35; 19:5, 19:5, 19, 21, 22, 32; 20:4, 6, 8, 8, 9, 15, 17, 21, 21, 22, 22, 23, 29, 31, 34, 34; 21:6; 21:6, 8, 9, 10; 22:3, 8, 12, 15, 34, 43, 48, 48, 53

2Sa 1:9, 12, 12, 12, 12, 16, 21, 26; 2:7, 26; 3:6, 8, 14, 17, 18, 22, 26, 27, 37, 39; 4:2, 7, 10; 5:12; 6:6, 7, 17; 7:3, 5, 10, 13, 13, 16, 16, 19, 19, 20, 21, 22, 23, 23, 24, 24, 25, 26, 27, 29, 29; 8:4, 10; 9:1, 7, 7, 10, 11, 13; 10:2, 11, 11, 12, 12; 11:4, 22, 25, 26; 12:4, 4, 12, 16, 18, 21; 22:3, 2, 2, 12, 13, 16, 18, 22, 32, 32, 33, 37, 39; 14:2, 7, 14, 16, 19, 25, 26, 29, 32, 33; 15:2, 3, 11, 13, 16, 17, 18, 34; 16:2, 3, 11, 12, 17; 17:8, 10, 11, 14, 17, 21, 29, 29, 29; 18:3, 3, 3, 5, 8, 12, 13, 16, 18, 18, 31, 33; 19:1, 2, 2, 6, 7, 8, 9, 20, 21, 22, 26, 28, 32, 38, 42; 20:11; 21:1, 1, 3, 4, 4, 8; 22:18, 22, 23, 23, 29, 30, 31, 32, 40, 51, 51; 23:5; 24:2, 10, 11, 14, 22, 24, 25

1Ki 1:2, 3, 25, 31, 35, 42, 51; 2:7, 9, 15, 17, 18, 19, 19, 20, 22, 22, 22, 22, 22, 24, 26, 28, 33, 33, 36, 37, 37, 42, 42, 45; 3:4, 6, 8, 9, 11, 11, 11, 26, 28; 4:7, 22, 24, 26, 27, 29, 31, 31, 33; 5:1, 1, 3, 6, 6, 8, 9, 11; 6:2, 4, 6, 8, 16, 16, 36, 40, 42, 42, 45, 50, 50, 51; 8:5, 7, 11, 13, 17, 27, 30, 31, 33, 35, 36, 39, 41, 42, 43, 44, 46, 48, 52, 53, 64, 66, 66, 66; 9:3, 5, 7, 15, 16, 16, 19, 24; 10:9, 12, 12, 12, 22, 23, 26, 27, 29, 29, 29, 29; 11:2, 4, 5, 7, 7, 8, 12, 13, 13, 15, 16, 17, 22, 32, 33, 34, 38, 39, 39; 12:1, 2, 5, 7, 15, 17, 24, 28, 30; 13:6, 9, 12, 17, 23, 23, 32; 14:4, 5, 5, 5, 6, 9, 11, 13, 13, 15, 15:4, 20; 15:4, 17, 18, 23; 25, 25, 27, 41; 19:3, 4, 4, 7, 10, 10, 14, 20; 20:7, 7, 7, 7, 7, 9, 36; 21:3, 5, 7, 19; 22:3, 13, 15; 24:3, 4, 4, 4, 7, 13, 19, 20, 21, 22, 26, 30

2Ki 2:2, 4, 6, 9, 18; 3:2, 9, 9, 13, 17, 26; 4:2, 10, 13, 13, 13, 14, 24, 27, 38, 39, 40, 41, 43; 5:3, 17, 27; 6:1, 5, 9, 11, 11, 16, 23, 25, 25, 33; 7:1, 1, 6, 7, 16, 16, 18, 18, 20; 8:1, 1, 3, 5, 5, 18, 19, 27; 9:8, 16, 20, 25, 34; 10:3, 10, 16, 19, 20, 22, 24, 31; 11:15; 12:7, 7, 12, 12, 13, 15, 21; 13:4, 4, 7, 17; 14:6, 6, 6, 10, 26, 28; 15:14; 16:8, 9, 15, 18, 18; 17:4, 7, 12, 21, 22, 32, 37, 37; 18:4, 6, 24, 26, 26, 29; 31, 36; 19:3, 4, 8, 11, 31, 34, 34, 34; 20:1, 6, 6, 10, 12; 21:3, 3, 5, 7; 22:13, 13, 13; 23:4, 4, 4, 7, 13, 25; 24:3, 4, 4, 7, 13, 20; 25:3, 16, 22, 26, 30

1Ch 4:14, 23, 39, 40, 41, 42; 5:1, 2, 20, 22; 6:26, 49, 49, 54, 70; 7:4, 4, 11; 9:1, 13, 26, 33; 10:4, 13, 13; 11:9, 19, 20, 40; 13:3, 4, 9; 14:2, 10, 15; 15:1, 1, 2, 2, 3, 11, 11, 11, 12, 13, 22, 23, 24, 34, 34, 34, 36, 41, 42; 17:2, 5, 9, 12, 14, 14, 17, 17, 18, 18, 19, 22, 22, 23, 24, 24, 25, 29, 30; 18:10; 19:3, 5, 12, 12, 13, 13; 21:6, 8, 13, 17, 22, 23, 23, 24, 24, 24, 25, 29, 30; 22:1, 3, 3, 3, 3, 3, 5, 5, 6, 7, 9, 10, 10, 14, 14, 14, 14, 14, 14, 15, 15, 15, 15, 16, 16, 16, 17, 17, 17, 17, 18, 20, 20, 21, 21; 29:1, 1, 1, 2, 2, 2, 2, 3, 5, 5, 5, 7, 9, 10, 11, 14, 15, 15, 19, 21

2Ch 1:3, 4, 4, 4, 9, 10, 11, 15, 17, 17; 2:1, 1, 4, 4, 4, 5, 8, 9, 12, 12; 3:3, 6; 4:6, 6, 9, 11, 11, 16, 18, 19, 22; 5:1, 6, 8, 11, 13, 13, 14; 6:2, 2, 2, 7, 8, 9, 10, 13, 27, 30, 32, 33, 34, 36, 38; 7:3, 3, 3, 6, 7, 9, 10, 11, 14, 14; 9:6, 8, 11, 11, 14; 9:6, 8, 11, 11, 14; 10:7; 11:4, 5, 14, 14, 15, 15, 15, 17, 21, 22; 12:13; 13:5, 8, 10, 11, 12, 12; 14:3, 6, 11, 13, 14, 14; 15:3, 6, 7, 9; 16:9, 10, 14, 14; 17:18; 18:2, 2, 5, 7, 8, 9, 11, 32, 33; 19:6, 7; 20:6, 9, 11, 13, 21, 23, 25, 26, 27; 30:33; 21:6, 7, 19; 22:1, 3, 4, 7, 9, 11; 23:6, 8, 14; 24:3, 6, 7, 14, 18, 24, 25, 25; 25:4, 4, 4, 4, 6, 7, 8, 8, 9, 20, 26, 28; 28:2, 2, 6, 10, 10, 10, 11, 13, 13, 17, 17, 19, 19, 21, 23; 29:6, 9, 9, 11, 21, 21, 21, 24, 24, 24, 25, 32, 34, 35, 36; 30:2, 3, 5, 8, 9, 9, 14, 17, 17,

24, 24; 2:2, 4, 9, 10, 10, 11, 15, 16, 17;
3:6, 7, 9, 10, 11, 14; 4:5, 5, 6, 11, 11, 15,
15, 16, 17, 17, 17, 18; 5:1, 2, 4, 4, 5, 7,
10, 12, 13, 13, 14, 14, 15, 15, 20, 21, 21;
6:2, 13, 14, 16; 7:3, 5, 8, 8, 8, 9, 10, 11,
12, 12, 13, 14; 8:3, 9, 9, 10, 12,
13, 14, 14, 16, 17, 17, 21; 9:1, 1, 2, 2, 7, 9,
10, 12, 13, 13, 14, 14, 15; 10:3, 4, 8, 8, 8,
10, 12, 14, 14, 18; 11:2, 2, 4, 5, 9, 13, 14,
19, 20, 31; 12:1, 4, 6, 6, 8, 14, 14, 15, 19, 20;
11, 11, 13, 14, 14, 14, 14, 15, 19, 20;
13:4, 4, 8, 8, 8, 9
Gal 1:4, 5, 10, 10, 12, 13; 2:5, 6, 8, 12, 16,
18, 19, 20, 21; 3:6, 10, 10, 11, 13, 13, 18,
21, 26, 27, 28; 4:12, 15, 20, 22, 24, 25,
27, 27, 30; 5:3, 5, 5, 6, 13, 13, 14, 17;
6:3, 5, 7, 8, 9, 12, 13, 15, 17
Eph 1:16; 2:4, 8, 10, 14, 15, 18, 22; 3:1, 1,
13, 14; 4:12, 12, 12, 15, 32; 5:2, 2, 5, 6,
8, 9, 12, 13, 20, 23, 25, 29, 30, 31; 6:1,
12, 18, 19, 20, 22
Php 1:4, 5, 7, 8, 17, 19, 21, 23, 24, 25, 26,
27, 29, 29; 2:13, 18, 20, 20, 21, 26, 27,
30; 3:1, 3, 7, 8, 8, 12, 14, 17, 18, 20, 20;
4:1, 6, 11, 16, 20
Col 1:3, 5, 5, 7, 9, 9, 16, 19, 24, 24, 25;
2:1, 1, 1, 1, 5, 9; 3:3, 6, 20, 24, 25; 4:3, 3,
8, 12, 13, 13
1Th 1:2, 5, 5, 8, 9, 10; 2:1, 3, 5, 9, 13, 14,
14, 16, 17, 19, 20; 3:3, 4, 5, 8, 9, 9, 9, 9;
4:2, 3, 7, 9, 14, 15, 16; 5:2, 3, 7, 8, 9, 10,
13, 15, 18, 25
2Th 1:3, 4, 5, 11; 2:3, 7, 11, 13; 3:1, 2, 5, 7,
7, 8, 10, 11
1Ti 1:9, 9, 9, 9, 9, 9, 9, 10, 10, 10, 10, 10,
12, 14, 16, 16, 17; 2:1, 2, 2, 3, 5, 6, 13; 3:5,
13; 4:4, 5, 8, 10, 16; 5:4, 8, 8, 10, 11, 15,
18, 23; 6:7, 10, 19
2Ti 1:7, 12, 12, 16; 2:5, 10, 11, 16, 21; 3:2,
6, 9, 16, 16, 16, 16; 4:3, 6, 8, 10, 11, 11,
15, 18
Tit 1:5, 7, 10, 11; 2:11, 13, 14; 3:3, 9, 12, 14
Phm 1:1, 5, 9, 15, 15, 15, 22
Heb 1:5, 8, 14; 2:2, 5, 8, 9, 9, 10, 10, 11, 11,
16, 17, 18; 3:3, 4, 5, 14, 16; 4:2, 3, 4, 8,
10, 12, 15; 5:1, 1, 1, 2, 3, 3, 3, 6, 12, 12,
13, 13; 6:4, 4, 7, 7, 10, 13, 16, 16, 18, 18,
20, 20; 7:1, 10, 11, 12, 13, 14, 15, 17, 17,
18, 18, 19, 21, 21, 25, 26, 27, 27, 27, 28,
28; 8:3, 4, 5, 7, 7, 8, 10, 11, 12; 9:2, 7, 7,
9, 12, 13, 15, 15, 16, 17, 19, 24, 24, 26,
28; 10:1, 2, 4, 6, 8, 10, 12, 14, 14, 15,
18, 20, 23, 26, 26, 27, 30, 34, 36, 37;
11:1, 2, 5, 6, 8, 10, 10, 14, 16, 16, 25, 26,
27, 32, 40; 12:2, 3, 6, 7, 10, 10, 10, 11,
13, 16, 17, 17, 18, 20, 25, 29; 13:2, 5, 8,
11, 11, 14, 16, 17, 17, 17, 17, 18, 18,
21, 22
Jas 1:6, 7, 11, 12, 13, 20, 23, 24; 2:2, 10, 11,
13, 23, 26; 3:2, 7, 10; 4:14, 14, 15; 5:1, 3,
7, 7, 8, 10, 14, 16
1Pe 1:4, 6, 13, 16, 20, 23, 24, 25; 2:13, 14,
14, 15, 16, 19, 20, 20, 20, 20, 21, 21, 25;
3:5, 9, 9, 10, 12, 14, 17, 17, 17, 18, 18,
18; 4:1, 1, 3, 6, 6, 8, 11, 14, 14, 17; 5:2,
5, 7, 7, 11
2Pe 1:8, 10, 11, 16, 17, 21; 2:4, 8, 16, 17,
18, 19, 20, 21, 21; 3:4, 5, 12, 13, 14, 18
1Jn 1:2; 2:2, 2, 2, 16, 17, 19; 3:2, 4, 8, 8,
9, 11, 16, 16, 20; 4:7, 8, 10, 20; 5:3, 4, 7,
9, 16, 16
2Jn 1:2, 2, 7, 11
3Jn 1:3, 7
Jude 1:3, 3, 4, 7, 11, 11, 13, 21
Rev 1:3, 6, 9, 9, 18; 2:3; 3:2, 4, 8; 4:9, 10,
11; 5:9, 13, 14; 6:6, 6, 9, 9, 11, 17;
7:12, 17; 8:12; 9:15, 15, 19, 19; 10:6;
11:2, 15; 12:4, 10, 12, 14; 13:8, 18; 14:4, 5,
7, 11, 15, 15, 18; 15:1, 4, 4, 4, 7;
16:6, 6, 10, 14, 21; 17:14, 17; 18:3, 5, 7,
8, 9, 10, 10, 11, 15, 17, 19, 20, 23, 23;
19:2, 2, 3, 6, 7, 8, 10; 20:4, 4, 10, 11;
21:1, 2, 4, 5, 22, 23, 25; 22:2, 5, 5, 9, 10,
15, 18

FROM (3660)

Ge 1:4, 6, 7, 14, 18; 2:2, 3, 6, 10, 22; 3:8,
23, 23; 4:1, 10, 11, 11, 14, 14, 16; 6:7,
17; 7:4, 23; 8:2, 7, 8, 8, 11, 13, 21;
9:10, 24; 10:19, 30; 11:2, 6, 8, 9, 31;
12:1, 1, 8; 13:3, 9, 11, 14, 14; 14:17, 23;
15:18; 16:2, 6, 8; 17:14, 22; 18:2, 3, 16,
17, 22, 25, 25; 19:4, 24, 26; 20:1, 6, 13,
22:12; 23:3, 6; 24:5, 7, 7, 7, 8, 41, 41, 46,
50, 62; 25:6, 18, 23, 29; 26:16, 22, 23,
26, 27, 31; 27:9, 30, 30, 39, 40, 45, 45;
28:2, 6, 10; 29:3, 8, 10; 30:2, 32; 31:13,
7, 13, 16; 36:6; 37:25; 38:1, 14, 17, 19,
20; 39:5, 9; 40:19, 19; 41:42, 46; 42:2, 7,
24, 24; 43:34; 44:28, 29; 45:1; 46:5, 34;
47:10, 18, 21; 48:7, 12, 16, 17; 49:9, 10,
10, 24, 26, 32; 50:25
Ex 2:15; 3:5; 4:3; 5:4, 5, 19, 20; 6:6, 7, 26,
27; 7:5; 8:8, 8, 9, 11, 11, 11, 11, 12, 29,
29, 29, 29, 30, 31, 31, 31; 9:15, 33; 10:5,
6, 11, 17, 18, 23, 28; 11:5, 8; 12:5, 5, 15,
15, 19, 29, 31, 37, 41, 42; 13:3, 3, 10, 14,
14, 20, 22; 14:5, 19, 25; 15:22; 16:1, 4, 6,
32; 17:1, 14, 16; 18:4, 10, 13, 14; 19:2,
14; 20:22; 21:14, 22; 22:12; 23:7, 15, 25,
28, 29, 30, 31, 31; 25:15, 22, 22; 26:4,
28; 27:21; 28:1, 28, 42; 29:28, 28; 30:14,

33, 38; 31:14; 32:12, 12, 15, 27; 33:5, 7,
16; 34:18, 29, 29; 35:5, 20; 36:4, 6, 11,
22, 33; 38:26; 39:21; 40:36
Lev 2:9, 13; 4:8, 10, 13, 19, 31, 35; 5:2, 3, 4,
6, 8; 7:20, 21, 25, 27, 34, 34; 8:28; 9:22,
24; 10:2, 4, 7; 12:7; 13:12, 41, 58; 14:7,
19; 15:3, 16, 31, 32; 16:12, 19, 30; 17:4,
9, 10; 18:29; 19:8; 20:3, 4, 5, 6, 18, 24,
25, 26; 21:7; 22:2, 3, 4, 25, 27; 23:15, 15,
29, 30, 32; 24:3, 8; 25:41, 50; 26:36;
27:3, 5, 6, 7, 17, 18
Nu 1:3, 18, 20, 22, 24, 26, 28, 30, 32, 34,
36, 38, 40, 42, 45; 3:12, 15, 22, 28, 34,
39, 40, 43; 4:2, 3, 13, 18, 23, 30, 35, 39,
43, 47; 5:13, 19, 31; 6:3, 4; 7:89, 89; 8:6,
14, 16, 19, 24, 25; 9:13, 17, 21; 10:9, 11,
33; 11:31, 31, 35; 12:10, 14, 15, 16; 13:3,
21, 23, 24, 25; 14:9, 13, 19, 29, 43;
15:23, 30; 16:9, 15, 21, 24, 26, 27, 33,
35, 45, 46, 46; 17:5, 9, 10; 18:6, 9, 16,
26, 30, 32; 19:13, 20; 20:6, 9, 14, 21, 22,
28; 21:4, 7, 11, 12, 13, 16, 18, 19, 19, 26,
28, 34; 22:5, 16, 33, 33; 23:7, 9, 9, 13,
13, 27; 24:11, 24; 25:4, 7, 8, 11; 26:2, 4,
62; 27:4; 30:14; 31:14, 42; 32:7, 8, 11,
15, 21; 33:3, 5, 6, 7, 8, 9, 10, 11, 13, 14,
15, 16, 17, 18, 19, 20, 21, 22, 23, 24, 25,
26, 27, 28, 29, 30, 31, 32, 33, 34, 35, 36,
37, 41, 42, 43, 44, 45, 46, 47, 48, 49, 52,
55; 34:3, 4, 4, 5, 7, 8, 10, 11; 35:4, 5, 8,
8, 12; 36:3, 3, 4, 7, 9
Dt 1:2, 19; 2:8, 8, 8, 12, 14, 14, 15, 16, 22,
36, 36; 3:4, 8, 12, 16, 17; 4:2, 3, 9, 26,
29, 32, 34, 38, 48; 5:6; 6:12, 15, 19, 23;
7:4, 8, 15, 20, 24; 8:14; 9:4, 4, 5, 7, 12,
14, 15, 23, 24; 10:5, 6, 7, 7; 11:10, 12,
17, 23, 24, 24; 12:10, 21, 29, 30, 32;
13:5, 5, 7, 7, 10, 10, 13, 17; 14:24; 15:7,
12, 13, 16, 18; 16:9; 17:7, 11, 12, 15, 20;
18:3, 3, 6, 12, 15, 18; 19:5, 13, 19; 20:15;
21:9, 13, 21; 22:1, 4, 8, 21, 22, 24; 23:9,
13, 14, 15; 24:7; 25:9, 19, 19; 26:15, 15;
28:14, 21, 24, 31, 35, 49, 49, 57, 63, 64;
29:11, 18, 20, 22; 30:3, 4, 4, 11; 31:3, 17,
29; 32:20, 26, 42; 33:2, 2, 2, 2, 7, 16, 22,
27; 34:1
Jos 1:4, 7; 2:13, 23; 3:1, 3, 10, 13, 13, 14,
14, 16; 4:23, 23; 5:1, 9, 15; 6:18; 7:2, 5,
9, 12, 13, 19, 26; 8:4, 6, 7, 16, 29; 9:6, 8,
9, 22, 23, 24; 10:6, 7, 9, 11, 11, 29, 31,
34, 36, 41; 11:17, 21, 21, 21, 21, 21, 21,
23; 12:1, 2, 2, 2, 3, 7; 13:3, 4, 5, 6, 6,
9, 16, 26, 30, 30; 14:7, 15; 15:2, 2, 4, 5,
7, 9, 10, 46; 16:1, 1, 2, 7, 8; 17:7; 18:4,
12, 13, 14, 15, 17; 19:12, 13, 29, 33, 33,
34; 20:3, 6; 22:9, 16, 17, 18, 23, 25, 29,
32, 32; 23:1, 4, 5, 5, 9, 13, 13, 15, 16;
24:3, 8, 12, 17, 18
Jdg 1:11, 14, 36, 36; 2:1, 3, 19, 19, 21; 3:3,
11, 20; 6:8, 9, 11, 13, 14; 7:3; 8:13, 22;
9:20, 20, 20, 35, 36, 48; 10:11, 11, 11,
11, 16; 11:3, 13, 16, 22, 22, 23, 24, 29,
31, 33; 12:9; 13:5, 7, 20; 15:13, 14;
16:12, 17, 17, 19, 20; 17:2, 3, 8; 18:2, 2,
2, 7, 11, 22, 28; 19:2, 10, 18, 18, 30;
20:1, 13, 31, 32; 21:6, 8, 19, 24
Ru 1:6, 13, 16; 2:4, 7, 8; 4:10, 10
1Sa 1:14; 2:8, 19, 30, 33; 3:17, 17, 18, 20;
4:4, 18, 21, 22; 5:1; 6:3, 5, 5, 5, 7, 20;
7:3, 14, 14, 16; 9:2, 25; 10:2, 3, 5, 9, 23;
12:2, 20; 13:5, 8, 11, 15; 14:17, 21, 31,
46; 15:2, 6, 6, 7, 11, 15, 23, 26, 28; 16:1,
13, 14, 14, 16, 16, 23, 23; 17:15, 24, 26,
30, 33, 46, 53, 57; 18:6, 9, 10, 12, 13;
19:8, 9; 20:1, 9, 15, 15, 34; 21:4, 5, 6;
22:15; 23:13, 28, 29; 24:1; 25:10, 26,
26, 33, 33, 34, 39; 26:12, 19; 27:1; 28:15, 16, 23; 30:17, 25; 31:1, 12
2Sa 1:1, 2, 3, 4, 22, 22; 2:12, 19, 21, 22, 24,
27, 30; 3:10, 10, 15, 15, 22, 26, 26, 28,
29; 4:11; 5:9, 13, 25; 6:2, 2, 12; 7:1, 8, 8,
11, 15, 15, 23; 8:4, 8, 8, 13; 9:5;
10:14; 11:2, 4; 12:10, 17, 20, 31; 13:9, 5;
14:7, 9, 13, 25; 15:5, 34; 16:2, 9; 17:29,
22:15; 23:13, 28, 29; 24:1, 13; 25:10, 26,
26, 33, 33, 34, 39; 26:12, 19; 27:1; 28:15, 16, 23; 30:17, 25; 31:1, 12
2Sa 1:1, 2, 3, 4, 22, 22; 2:12, 19, 21, 22, 24,
27, 30; 3:10, 10, 15, 15, 22, 26, 26, 28,
29; 4:11; 5:9, 13, 25; 6:2, 2, 12; 7:1, 8, 8,
11, 15, 15, 23; 8:4, 8, 8, 13; 9:5;
10:14; 11:2, 4; 12:10, 17, 20, 31; 13:9, 5;
14:7, 9, 13, 25; 15:5, 34; 16:2, 9; 17:29,
22; 2, 20, 21, 22; 21:5, 10, 12, 12, 13; 23:3,
4, 14, 17, 18, 18, 22, 23, 24, 44, 49, 49;
23:11, 17; 24:2, 4, 15, 15, 21, 25
1Ki 1:45, 53; 2:15, 27, 31, 31, 33, 40, 41;
3:20; 4:12, 21, 24, 25, 33, 34; 5:9; 6:24;
7:7, 9, 23; 8:35, 51, 53, 54, 54, 65; 9:6,
12, 28; 10:3, 11, 11; 11:9, 11, 23; 12:2,
15, 24, 25; 13:4, 5, 12, 14, 21, 26, 33, 34;
14:7, 8, 10; 15:5, 13, 19; 16:17; 18:12,
12, 26; 19:17, 21; 20:33, 34, 36, 36, 41;
21:21; 22:24, 33, 43
2Ki 1:4, 6, 10, 10, 12, 12, 14; 2:1, 3, 5, 9,
10, 13, 14, 16, 21, 23, 25; 3:27; 4:5, 27,
42; 5:19, 21, 22, 24, 26, 27; 6:32; 8:14,
20, 22; 9:2, 8; 10:21, 29, 29, 31, 33, 33;
11:2, 2, 11, 19; 12:18; 13:5, 6, 11, 17, 23;
14:13, 24, 25, 27; 15:9, 14, 16, 18, 24,
28; 16:3, 6, 11, 11, 12, 14, 14, 17, 17, 18;
17:7, 8, 9, 13, 21, 21, 22, 24, 24, 24, 24,
24, 27, 28, 33; 18:6, 8, 14, 16, 16, 17;
19:8; 20:14, 14, 14, 18; 21:16; 23:6, 8,
15, 18, 19, 27, 29; 24:7, 14, 20; 25:5;
1Ch 2:23; 4:10; 5:9, 23; 9:25; 10:1; 11:8, 13;
13:5, 5; 14:14, 16; 16:20, 20, 23, 35;
17:5, 5, 7, 7, 8, 13, 13, 21; 18:4, 8, 8, 11,
11, 11, 11, 11, 11; 19:7; 20:2; 21:2, 22,
22, 28, 30; 23:3, 24, 27; 27:23
2Ch 1:4, 13, 13; 4:2; 5:9; 6:21, 21, 23, 25,

26, 27, 30, 32, 33, 33, 35, 39, 39; 7:1, 8,
14, 14; 8:15; 9:2, 10, 26; 10:2; 11:4, 14;
12:12; 13:19; 15:8, 16; 16:3, 9; 18:23, 31,
32; 19:2, 4; 20:2, 10, 32; 21:8, 10, 10, 12;
22:11, 11; 23:10, 20; 24:5, 23, 25; 25:5,
12, 13, 14, 13, 27; 26:18, 19, 20, 21;
28:8, 12; 29:6, 10; 30:5, 6, 8, 9, 10;
31:16, 17; 32:22, 22, 23; 33:8; 34:3, 33;
35:11, 15, 18, 21, 22, 22; 36:12, 13, 20
Ezr 1:11; 2:59, 62; 3:6, 7, 8, 13; 4:12, 14,
21; 6:6, 11, 21; 7:6, 9; 8:1, 31, 31; 9:1, 5,
8, 11; 10:6, 8, 11, 11, 14
Ne 1:9; 3:15, 20, 21, 24, 25, 28; 4:5, 14, 16,
19, 21; 5:13, 13, 14, 14, 17; 6:9; 7:61, 64;
8:3, 18; 9:2, 13, 15, 19, 20, 27, 28, 35;
10:28; 11:30, 31; 12:28, 29, 38, 39; 13:3,
21, 28, 30
Est 1:1, 7, 19; 2:6; 3:7, 7, 8, 10; 4:4, 14; 7:7;
8:2, 9, 15; 9:16, 22, 22, 22, 28, 28
Job 1:7, 7, 12, 16, 19; 2:2, 2, 2, 7, 7, 11; 3:4,
10, 11, 17, 19; 4:2, 13, 20; 5:4, 15, 15,
15, 20, 20, 21; 6:13, 14, 23, 23; 7:19;
8:18; 9:34; 10:14, 19; 13:20, 21; 14:6, 11;
15:18; 17:4; 18:17, 18; 19:9, 13, 13;
20:24, 29; 21:9, 14, 16; 22:6, 7, 17, 18;
22, 23; 23:7, 12, 17; 24:1, 9, 10, 12; 26:4,
5; 27:5; 28:4, 4, 11, 21, 21, 28; 30:5, 10;
31:2, 2, 16, 18, 18, 22, 22, 23; 33:17, 17,
18, 18, 24, 28, 30; 34:10, 10, 27; 35:3;
36:3, 7, 10, 30; 37:21; 38:15; 39:4; 42:2
Ps 2:3, 12; 3:T; 6:8; 7:1; 9:13; 12:1, 5, 7;
13:1; 14:2; 17:2, 4, 7, 9, 9, 13, 14, 14;
18:T, T, 3, 16, 17, 17, 21, 22, 23, 43, 48;
48; 19:6, 6, 12, 13, 13; 20:2, 6; 21:10, 10;
22:1, 1, 10, 11, 19, 20, 20, 20, 21, 21, 24;
24:5, 5; 27:9; 30:3; 31:11, 15, 15, 20, 20,
22; 32:7; 33:13, 14, 19; 34:4, 13, 13, 14,
16; 35:10, 10, 17, 17, 22; 37:8, 27, 40, 40;
38:9, 10, 11, 14; 39:2, 8, 10; 40:10, 11,
41:13; 42:6, 6; 43:1; 44:7, 10, 18; 49:14,
15; 50:1, 4; 51:2, 2, 9, 11, 14, 14; 53:2;
55:1, 8, 11, 12, 18; 56:13, 13; 57:T, 3, 3;
58:3; 59:1, 1, 2, 2; 60:11; 61:2, 3; 62:1, 4,
5; 64:1, 2, 2; 66:20; 68:20, 22, 22, 26;
69:5, 14, 17; 71:5, 6, 12, 17, 20; 72:8, 8,
14; 73:27, 27; 75:6, 6, 6; 76:8; 78:4, 23,
30, 42, 50, 70, 71; 80:14, 18; 81:6, 6;
83:4; 84:7, 11; 85:3, 11; 86:13; 88:5, 8,
14, 15, 18; 89:33, 48; 90:2; 91:3, 3; 93:2;
94:13; 96:2; 101:4, 8; 102:2, 19, 19;
103:4, 12, 12, 17; 104:13, 21; 105:13, 13;
106:10, 10, 47, 48; 107:2, 3, 3, 3, 20,
41; 108:12; 109:15, 17, 20, 31; 110:3;
113:2, 3; 114:1; 115:18; 116:8, 8, 8;
119:10, 19, 21, 22, 29, 37, 51, 101, 102,
110, 115, 118, 134, 150, 155, 157, 160;
120:2, 2; 121:1, 2, 7, 8; 125:2; 129:1, 2;
130:8; 131:3; 132:11; 135:7; 136:11, 24;
139:7, 7, 12, 15, 19; 140:1, 1, 4, 4; 141:9;
142:6; 143:7, 9; 144:7, 7, 10, 11; 148:1, 7
Pr 1:15; 3:7; 3:12, 12, 16, 16, 22; 3:7, 21, 26,
27; 4:5, 15, 21, 24, 24, 27; 5:7, 8; 6:5, 5,
24, 24; 7:5, 5; 8:23, 23; 10:2; 11:4; 13:14,
19; 14:7, 14, 16, 27; 15:24, 29; 16:1, 6,
17; 17:13; 19:4, 7, 14, 27; 20:3, 9; 21:23;
22:5, 6, 15, 25; 24:18; 25:4, 24; 28:18; 25:4,
5, 17, 25; 27:8, 8, 22; 28:9; 29:21, 26;
30:8, 12, 14, 14; 31:14
Ecc 1:7; 2:10, 10, 24; 3:5, 11, 14; 7:18, 23,
26; 8:10; 10:5; 11:10, 10; 12:11
SS 3:4; 4:1, 2, 8, 8, 8, 8, 8, 15; 5:7; 6:5, 5,
6; 8:5
Isa 1:6, 15, 16; 2:3, 6, 22; 3:1, 1; 4:4, 6, 6, 6;
5:23, 26, 26; 6:6; 7:17, 17; 8:17, 18; 9:7,
14; 10:2, 3, 27, 27; 11:11, 11, 11, 11,
11, 11, 11, 11, 12, 16, 13:5, 5, 6, 20;
14:3, 3, 3, 3; 18:2, 7, 7; 19:5; 20:2, 2, 6;
21:1, 1, 15, 15, 15, 15; 22:3, 4, 14, 19,
19, 24; 23:1; 24:14, 16, 18, 18; 25:4, 4, 8,
8; 27:12; 28:9, 13, 15; 30:6, 11, 14, 19,
19, 24, 23:11; 24:14, 16, 18, 18; 25:4, 4, 8,
8; 27:12; 28:9, 13, 15; 30:6, 11, 14, 19,
29; 18:21, 34; 19:8, 24, 26, 26, 39, 42;
20:4, 5, 35; 21:11; 22:41, 42, 43, 45;
23:5, 49, 55; 24:2, 9, 13, 46, 49, 51
Jn 1:6, 19, 32; 2:22; 3:2, 13, 27, 31, 31;
4:11; 5:24, 34, 41, 44; 6:23, 31, 32, 32,
33, 38, 41, 42, 50, 58; 7:17, 28, 28, 42;
8:23, 23, 25, 42, 44; 9:1, 29, 30; 10:5, 18,
32; 11:41, 53; 12:1, 9, 17, 27, 28, 32, 36;
13:3, 4; 14:7; 15:26, 26, 27; 16:22, 27, 28,
28, 30; 17:8, 15; 18:3, 28, 36; 19:11, 12,
23, 27; 20:1, 9; 21:8, 14
Ac 1:4, 11, 12, 12, 22, 22, 25, 2:2, 40, 46;
3:2, 15, 19, 23, 24, 26; 4:2, 10; 5:38, 41;
7:3, 4, 33, 39; 8:10, 26, 33; 9:3, 8, 14, 18;
10:17, 21, 22, 23, 37, 41; 11:4, 5, 9, 11,
27; 12:7, 10, 11, 19, 25; 13:4, 8, 13, 13,
14, 29, 30, 31, 34, 39, 39, 46; 14:8, 15,
17, 19, 26; 15:1, 18, 19, 20, 20, 20, 20,
24, 29, 29, 29; 16:24, 33, 38, 38, 39;
16:11, 12; 17:3, 27, 31, 33; 18:1, 2, 2, 5,
6, 16, 21; 19:9; 20:9, 17, 18, 20:6, 9, 17,
18, 20, 26; 21:1, 1, 7, 10, 25, 25, 25;
22:5, 6, 22, 29, 30; 23:10, 21; 24:18;
25:1, 7; 26:4, 5, 10, 12, 13, 17, 17, 18,
18, 23, 26; 27:4, 21, 34, 43; 28:13, 15,
17, 23
Ro 1:4, 7, 17, 18, 20; 4:24; 5:9, 14; 6:4, 7, 9,
13, 17, 18, 20, 22; 7:2, 3, 4, 6, 24; 8:2,
11, 21, 21, 35, 39; 9:3, 10; 10:6, 7, 9; 11:15,
26; 15:19, 23, 31; 16:99
1Co 1:3; 3; 4:7; 5:2, 13; 7:10, 27; 9:19;
10:14; 14:36; 15:12, 20, 41, 47; 16:99
2Co 1:2, 2, 10, 10; 2:3, 13; 3:1, 18; 5:2, 6, 8;
6:17; 7:1; 11:3, 9, 19, 12; 12:8; 13:99
Gal 1:1, 3, 3, 4, 6, 8, 15; 2:12; 3:13; 4:1, 24;
5:4; 6:17, 99

Eph 1:2, 2, 20; 2:12, 12; 3:9; 4:16, 18, 31; 5:14; 6:6, 23, 99
Php 1:2, 2, 5; 3:20; 4:15, 18, 99
Col 1:2, 13, 18, 23, 26, 26; 2:12, 19, 20; 4:16, 99
1Th 1:1, 8, 9, 10, 10; 2:17; 3:6; 4:3, 16; 5:22, 99
2Th 1:2, 7, 9, 9; 2:2, 13; 3:2, 3, 6, 99
1Ti 1:2, 6; 4:1, 3; 5:13; 6:5, 10, 99
2Ti 1:2, 3, 15; 2:8, 19, 21; 3:5, 15; 4:4, 18, 99
Tit 1:4, 14; 2:14; 3:99
Phm 1:3, 99
Heb 3:12; 4:3, 4, 10, 10; 5:1, 7; 6:1, 7; 7:1, 6, 26; 8:11; 9:14; 10:13, 22; 11:15, 19, 19; 12:25, 25; 13:20, 99
Jas 1:17, 17, 27; 3:15, 17; 4:1, 7; 5:19, 20, 20
1Pe 1:3, 12, 18, 18, 21; 2:11; 3:10; 4:1
2Pe 1:9, 17, 17, 18; 2:8, 14, 18, 21; 3:4, 17
1Jn 1:1, 7, 9; 2:7, 7, 13, 14, 19, 20, 24, 24; 3:8, 11, 14, 17; 4:21; 5:21
2Jn 1:3, 3, 4, 5, 6
Jude 1:14, 24
Rev 1:4, 4, 5, 5; 2:5; 3:10, 12; 6:4, 16, 16; 7:2, 17; 8:10; 9:1, 6, 13; 10:1, 4, 8; 11:11, 12; 12:14; 13:8, 13; 14:2, 3, 4, 13, 13, 18; 15:8, 8; 16:17; 17:8; 18:1, 4, 14, 14; 20:1, 9, 11; 21:2, 4, 10; 22:19, 19

HE (10430)

Ge 1:5, 10, 16, 20, 27, 27, 31; 2:2, 2, 2, 3, 8, 8, 19, 21, 22; 3:1, 6, 10, 11, 16, 16, 17, 22, 23, 24, 24; 4:4, 5, 9, 10, 17, 20, 21, 26; 5:1, 2, 4, 4, 5, 7, 8, 10, 11, 13, 14, 16, 17, 18, 19, 20, 22, 24, 26, 27, 29, 30, 31; 6:3, 6, 22; 8:6, 7, 8, 9, 10, 10, 12; 9:6, 20, 21, 21, 25, 25, 26, 27, 29; 10:8, 9; 11:11, 13, 15, 17, 19, 21, 23, 25; 12:4, 7, 8, 8, 11, 11, 16, 16, 16, 20; 13:1, 1, 3, 4; 14:13, 14, 15, 15, 16, 18, 19, 20; 15:4, 5, 5, 6, 7, 8, 9, 10, 10, 13; 16:4, 8, 12, 12; 17:12, 12, 13, 13, 14, 20, 22, 24, 25; 18:1, 2, 2, 2, 7, 8, 8, 9, 10, 15, 19, 19, 28, 29, 29, 30, 30, 31, 31, 32, 32, 33; 19:1, 2, 3, 3, 9, 14, 16, 17, 21, 25, 27, 28, 29, 30, 30, 33, 35; 20:4, 5, 5, 7, 7, 13, 16; 21:1, 1, 13, 17, 20, 21, 30, 31; 22:1, 2, 6, 7, 7, 11, 12; 23:8, 9, 9, 9, 13, 16; 24:2, 7, 10, 11, 12, 15, 27, 30, 30, 30, 31, 32, 33, 33, 34, 35, 35, 36, 36, 40, 52, 53, 54, 54, 56, 62, 63, 66; 67; 25:5, 6, 7, 17, 18, 20, 28, 29, 33, 33, 34; 26:7, 7, 7, 8, 11, 13, 14, 18, 20, 21, 22, 22, 23, 25, 30, 33, 34; 27:1, 1, 1, 2, 9, 10, 10, 14, 18, 18, 20, 22, 23, 23, 24, 24, 25, 25, 25, 27, 27, 29, 31, 32, 33, 33, 34, 35, 36, 36, 36, 36, 45; 28:5, 6, 6, 9, 11, 11, 12, 16, 17, 18, 19; 29:2, 5, 6, 6, 6, 7, 9, 12, 12, 13, 13, 13, 14, 21, 25, 28, 30, 31, 33; 30:2, 15, 16, 28, 29, 31, 35, 35, 36, 38, 38, 40, 42; 31:1, 1, 8, 8, 12, 15, 18, 18, 18, 20, 20, 21, 21, 21, 23, 33, 35, 49; 32:2, 2, 4, 6, 7, 11, 13, 14, 16, 17, 18, 19, 20, 21, 23, 23, 25, 25, 25, 26, 26, 27, 27, 28, 29, 29, 31, 31, 32; 33:1, 2, 3, 3, 5, 5, 8, 8, 11, 11, 12, 13, 15, 18, 19, 19, 19, 20; 34:2, 3, 5, 7, 13, 19, 19, 31; 35:6, 7, 7, 9, 10, 13, 14, 14; 36:6, 24, 43; 37:3, 3, 5, 6, 9, 10, 13, 14, 14, 14, 14, 43; 38:2, 3, 5, 9, 9, 9, 10, 10, 11, 12, 15, 15, 16, 16, 17, 18, 18, 20, 21, 22, 26, 29; 39:2, 2, 3, 4, 4, 4, 4, 5, 5, 5, 6, 6, 6, 6, 6, 8, 8, 9, 10, 12, 13, 14, 14, 15, 15, 18, 20, 22, 23; 40:3, 4, 7, 16, 20, 20, 21, 21, 22; 41:1, 5, 8, 11, 12, 12, 13, 13, 13, 14, 25, 28, 43, 43, 43, 45, 46, 48, 48, 49, 51, 52, 55; 42:2, 4, 6, 7, 7, 9, 12, 17, 21, 23, 24, 25, 27, 28, 38, 38; 43:7, 14, 16, 18, 23, 23, 24, 27, 27, 28, 29, 29, 30, 30, 31, 34; 44:1, 2, 5, 6, 6, 10, 10, 12, 14, 16, 17, 17, 20, 22, 28, 34, 31; 45:1, 2, 4, 8, 14, 15, 22, 23, 24, 24, 26, 26, 27; 46:1, 2, 3, 7, 28, 29; 47:2, 17, 21, 22, 29, 30, 31, 31; 48:1, 9, 10, 10, 12, 15, 17, 19, 19, 20, 20; 49:4, 8, 9, 9, 11, 13, 15, 19, 20, 21, 27, 27, 28, 29, 33; 50:6, 10, 12, 14, 14, 16, 21, 22, 24, 26;

Ex 1:9, 16, 21; 2:2, 10, 11, 11, 12, 12, 12, 22; 3:1, 2, 4, 4, 5, 6, 6, 12, 14, 20; 4:2, 3, 3, 4, 6, 6, 7, 7, 13, 14, 14, 14, 14, 16, 16, 20, 20, 21, 23, 26, 27, 28, 31; 5:3, 17, 23; 6:1, 1, 11; 7:2, 13, 13, 14, 15, 15, 20, 22, 23; 8:8, 10, 10, 12, 13, 19, 25, 26; 9:7, 12, 20, 21, 34, 34, 35; 10:6, 8, 10, 16, 17, 18, 19; 12:19, 23, 25, 27, 30, 31, 44, 48; 13:5, 11, 19, 22; 14:4, 6, 7, 8, 17; 15:1, 1, 2, 2, 4, 21, 21, 25, 25, 25; 16:7, 9, 18, 18, 23, 29; 17:7, 11, 12, 16; 18:2, 3, 4, 5, 6, 9, 11, 14, 14, 24, 27; 19:13, 15, 24; 21:2, 2, 3, 3, 4, 6, 6, 8, 8, 8, 9, 9, 10, 11, 12, 12, 13, 14, 15, 16, 16, 17, 18, 19, 19, 20, 20, 21, 21, 21, 22, 26, 27, 29, 29, 30, 30, 31, 32, 34, 34, 35, 36; 22:1, 2, 3, 3, 4, 4, 5, 6, 7, 8, 9, 11, 12, 14, 15, 16, 17, 20, 27, 27; 23:18, 25; 24:1, 5, 6, 7, 11, 14, 16; 25:39; 28:1, 3, 4, 29, 30; 30:7, 7, 8, 10; 31:15, 17, 18, 18; 32:4, 4, 4, 5, 12, 14, 17, 18, 19, 19, 19, 20, 27, 29; 33:8, 11, 14, 15, 18, 19, 20; 34:4, 9, 10, 28, 28, 28, 29,

Lev 1:3, 4, 5, 6, 9, 10, 11, 12, 13, 14, 16, 17; 2:1, 2, 2, 8; 3:1, 1, 2, 3, 4, 6, 7, 7, 8, 9, 9, 10, 12, 13, 14, 15; 4:3, 4, 8, 9, 12, 12, 18, 19, 20, 20, 20, 21, 24, 24, 25, 26, 27, 28, 28, 28, 29, 31, 32, 32, 33, 35, 35; 5:1, 1, 2, 3, 3, 3, 3, 4, 4, 4, 5, 6, 6, 7, 7, 7, 8, 9, 10, 10, 11, 11, 11, 12, 13, 15, 16, 16, 17, 17, 18, 18, 19; 6:4, 4, 4, 4, 4, 5, 5, 6, 7, 10, 10, 11, 12, 15, 16, 29, 30, 33, 35, 36, 38; 8:7, 7, 8, 8, 9, 9, 11, 12, 14, 15, 16, 17, 18, 19, 20, 21, 21, 22, 23, 24, 25, 26, 27, 33, 34; 9:2, 9, 10, 11, 12, 14, 15, 16, 17, 18, 19, 20, 21; 10:1, 16, 20; 10:1, 16, 20; 11:4, 4, 5, 5, 6, 6, 7, 7, 7, 28, 39, 40, 40; 13:2, 6, 7, 7, 9, 11, 13, 13, 14, 16, 17, 33, 34, 34, 36, 37, 39, 40, 40, 41, 41, 41, 44, 44, 45, 46, 46, 46, 51, 52, 54, 56; 14:2, 6, 7, 8, 8, 8, 8, 9, 9, 9, 9, 10, 12, 13, 13, 18, 19, 20, 21, 22, 23, 25, 29, 30, 30, 31, 35, 37, 41, 42, 43, 43, 45, 45, 46, 47, 47, 49, 50, 51, 52, 53; 15:2, 4, 4, 6, 6, 7, 8, 8, 9, 10, 11, 11, 12, 13, 13, 14, 16, 23, 24, 24; 16:2, 4, 4, 4, 4, 5, 7, 12, 13, 13, 14, 15, 16, 16, 17, 18, 19, 20, 22, 23, 24, 24, 25, 26, 28, 28, 32; 17:4, 13, 15, 16, 16; 18:5; 19:8, 19, 21, 22, 22; 20:2, 2, 3, 4, 9, 10, 13, 14, 15, 17, 18, 18, 18, 19, 20, 21; 21:3, 4, 7, 8, 8, 10, 11, 12, 13, 14, 14, 15, 17, 18, 18, 18, 21, 21, 23, 23; 22:3, 4, 4, 5, 5, 6, 7, 8, 11, 11, 14, 18, 19, 20, 21, 21, 21, 21, 25; 15, 16, 25, 27, 27, 28, 28, 29, 29, 35, 40, 41, 41, 48, 48, 49, 49, 50, 50, 51, 51, 52, 52, 53, 54, 54, 54; 27:8, 8, 10, 10, 11, 13, 13, 15, 17, 18, 19, 19, 20, 20, 22, 23, 27, 28, 31, 33, 33, 33

Nu 1:19; 3:3, 16, 50; 5:7, 7, 14, 14, 15, 15, 23, 24, 27, 30; 6:3, 3, 4, 5, 5, 6, 6, 7, 8, 9, 9, 10, 11, 12, 13, 14, 14, 17, 21; 7:7, 8, 9, 12, 17, 19, 23, 24, 34, 47; 53, 59, 65, 71, 77, 83, 88, 89, 89; 8:3, 4; 9:10, 13, 14; 10:30, 31, 36; 11:3, 30, 32, 34; 12:1, 1, 2, 6, 8, 9, 12; 14:8, 16, 16, 24, 24; 15:4, 9, 14, 27, 28, 30, 31, 36; 16:4, 5, 5, 5, 7, 10, 26, 30, 31, 37, 40, 47, 48; 17:11; 19:3, 5, 7, 7, 8, 10, 11, 12, 12, 13, 19, 20, 20, 21; 20:9, 10, 11, 13, 16, 20, 24; 21:1, 3, 7, 8, 9, 9, 14, 23, 29, 33; 22:5, 6, 6, 8, 22, 22, 25, 27, 30, 31, 34, 41; 23:3, 4, 6, 6, 6, 7, 12, 14, 15, 17, 18, 19, 19, 19, 19, 19, 20, 21, 21, 22, 24, 24; 24:1, 1, 2, 3, 4, 7, 8, 9, 9, 9, 9, 16, 17; 25:7, 8, 11, 13, 13, 15; 27:3, 8, 8, 12, 14, 14, 14, 14, 15, 15, 15; 32:10, 13, 15, 21, 40; 33:39; 35:6, 8, 12, 16, 16, 16, 17, 17, 17, 17, 18, 18, 18, 18, 19, 19, 20, 20, 21, 21, 21, 21, 22, 23, 24, 25, 26, 28, 31, 32

Dt 1:4, 11, 27, 30, 30, 36, 36, 36, 38, 38; 2:7, 22, 27, 30, 32; 3:1, 22, 28, 28; 4:13, 13, 13, 23, 31, 31, 35, 36, 36, 36, 37, 37, 39, 42; 5:22, 22, 24; 6:10, 17, 23, 23, 23, 24, 25; 7:8, 8, 9, 10, 10, 12, 13, 13, 13, 24; 8:3, 3, 10, 16, 16, 18, 18, 18; 9:3, 3, 3, 5, 28, 28, 28; 10:4, 6, 15, 18, 21; 11:3, 4, 4, 5, 6, 7, 17, 25; 12:10, 12, 15, 20, 31; 13:2, 5, 10, 10, 17; 14:21; 15:2, 6, 6, 8, 9, 10, 11, 11, 11, 18; 16:16, 17, 17; 17:6, 6, 16, 16, 17, 17, 18, 18, 19, 19, 19, 19; 18:2, 6, 7, 18, 19; 19:4, 4, 5, 5, 6, 6, 8, 11, 12, 15, 19; 20:4, 5, 6, 6, 7; 21:16, 16, 16, 17, 17, 17, 20, 20, 21, 22, 22; 22:3, 16, 17, 19, 19, 24, 27, 27, 29; 23:1, 2, 7, 10, 10, 11, 11, 14, 16, 16; 24:1, 5, 5, 5, 5, 6, 13, 14, 15, 15; 25:3, 3, 4, 7, 8, 18, 18; 26:5, 9, 18, 19, 19; 27:16, 17, 18, 19, 20, 20, 21, 22, 23, 24, 25, 26; 28:8, 9, 11, 44, 44, 45, 48, 48, 51, 51, 52, 52, 54, 55, 55, 55, 60; 29:1, 13, 13, 13, 13, 19, 19, 25, 25, 26; 30:4, 5, 9; 31:2, 3, 3, 3, 4, 4, 6, 6, 8, 10, 10, 13, 13, 16, 19, 30, 36, 37, 39, 43, 44, 46; 33:2, 2, 2, 3, 5, 7, 8, 9, 12, 12, 13, 17, 20, 21, 28, 29; 34:6, 7

Jos 1:15, 17, 18, 18; 2:11; 3:1, 10; 4:4, 21, 23; 5:6, 6, 7, 13, 14; 6:7, 26, 26; 7:6, 15, 15, 15, 15, 15, 17, 17, 17, 18, 24; 8:4, 10, 12, 14, 14, 18, 19, 22, 26, 27, 29, 29, 32, 32, 33, 34; 9:9, 10, 22, 26, 27; 10:1, 1, 7, 12, 15, 17, 20, 20; 13:14, 14, 33; 14:3, 10, 14, 15:13, 15, 16, 17, 19; 17:1, 1, 1, 4; 19:50, 50; 20:4, 4, 5, 6, 6, 6, 9; 21:43, 44; 22:4, 7, 8, 18, 22, 22; 23:3, 5, 10, 10, 15, 16, 16; 24:7, 10, 17, 18, 19, 19, 19, 20, 20, 23, 27, 31

Jdg 1:7, 11, 12, 13, 19, 20, 25, 33; 2:7, 10,

Ru 1:1; 2:14, 19, 20, 21; 3:2, 3, 4, 4, 4, 7, 9, 10, 13, 14, 15, 15, 15, 17, 17, 18; 4:1, 1, 2, 3, 4, 5, 8, 13, 15, 17

1Sa 1:2, 4, 5, 5, 7, 22, 28, 28, 28; 2:6, 7, 8, 8, 9, 10, 10, 14, 15, 16, 23, 35; 3:2, 4, 5, 5, 5, 6, 8, 9, 13, 13, 16, 17; 4:13, 14, 15, 16, 16, 18, 18, 18; 5:6, 9; 6:5, 6, 9, 19, 19, 20; 7:3, 8, 16, 17; 8:7; 8:1, 11, 11, 12, 13, 14, 15, 16, 16, 17, 21; 9:2, 2, 2, 4, 4, 6, 6, 6, 9, 12, 12, 13, 13, 13, 16, 26, 27; 10:9, 10, 11, 13, 13, 14, 16, 16, 21, 21, 22, 23, 23, 25; 11:6, 7, 8, 12; 12:5, 5, 7, 9, 17, 24; 13:1, 2, 7, 8, 9, 10, 10, 13; 14:1, 27, 36, 39, 39, 40, 45, 45, 47, 47, 48, 52; 15:2, 2, 8, 11, 11, 12, 16, 23, 27, 29, 30, 35; 16:2, 5, 6, 8, 9, 11, 11, 11, 12, 12, 12, 16, 21, 22; 17:5, 6, 8, 9, 9, 12, 20, 23, 25, 26, 28, 28, 30, 31, 33, 35, 36, 37, 38, 39, 40, 40, 42, 42, 49, 54, 55; 18:1, 3, 5, 8, 8, 10, 11, 13, 15, 15, 16, 23; 19:4, 4, 5, 6, 7, 17, 18, 18, 19, 22, 23; 20:1, 2, 3, 5, 6, 7, 13, 17, 17, 17, 26, 26, 26, 29, 29, 30, 31, 32, 32, 34, 36, 42; 21:3, 10; 22:2, 3, 4, 10, 12, 13, 17, 18; 23:6, 7, 7, 13, 13, 18; 24:3, 5, 6, 6, 10, 17, 19; 25:2, 2, 3, 14, 17, 21, 25, 29, 30, 31, 32, 34, 36, 36, 42; 26:1, 2, 3, 4, 8, 11; 27:7, 10; 28:5, 8, 8, 9, 11, 14, 14, 14, 17, 20, 21, 25, 26; 29:3, 4, 4, 4, 9; 30:8, 9, 10, 11, 12, 12, 13, 15, 16, 21, 25, 26; 31:3, 4, 5

2Sa 1:2, 2, 3, 4, 7, 7, 8, 9, 10, 10, 13, 15, 15, 18, 21; 2:1, 9, 10, 19, 20, 23, 23, 30; 3:11, 11, 13, 16, 21, 22, 22, 23, 23, 24, 25, 26, 27, 28, 30; 4:4; 5:2, 4, 4, 4, 5, 8, 12, 13, 20, 23; 6:7, 8, 13, 18, 19; 7:11, 13, 14, 14, 18, 2; 8:2, 13, 18, 19; 9:1, 7, 11:1, 2, 4, 13, 13, 15, 15, 16, 16, 20, 21; 12:1, 3, 4, 13, 15, 15, 16, 16, 20, 21, 22; 12:1, 3, 4, 5, 6, 6, 6, 11, 17, 17, 18, 18, 19, 20, 20, 22, 22, 23, 23, 24, 25, 25, 30, 30, 31, 31; 13:2, 4, 8, 9, 11, 13, 14, 15, 15, 16, 17; 20, 21, 22, 25, 25, 26, 27, 32, 36, 39, 39; 14:7, 10, 11, 32; 15:2, 4, 5, 9, 12, 14, 25, 26, 30, 32, 32, 32; 16:3, 3, 5, 5, 6, 7, 13, 21, 23; 17:2, 5, 9, 10, 12, 13, 23, 24; 18:9, 14, 14, 18, 18, 23, 25, 25, 26, 27, 28, 30, 33, 33; 19:9, 9, 15, 2, 9, 14, 18, 18, 21, 24, 24, 25, 26, 27, 32, 32, 39, 42; 20:1, 3, 5, 5, 6, 8, 8, 9, 10, 11, 12, 12, 13, 15, 16, 21, 25, 26; 21:1, 10, 17; 22:3, 7, 9, 10, 11, 12, 13, 15, 16, 17, 18, 19, 20, 20; 24:1, 10, 17

1Ki 1:1, 5, 6, 7, 10, 13, 19, 23, 23, 24, 24, 24, 30, 30, 35, 35, 37, 41, 42, 51, 51, 52, 52, 53; 2:1, 1, 4, 4, 5, 5, 8, 11, 11, 13, 14, 15, 17, 17, 17, 22, 24, 25, 27, 27, 28, 29, 30, 30, 31, 32, 34, 46; 3:1, 3, 6, 15; 4:2, 15, 19, 24, 24, 31, 33, 33, 33; 5:1, 5, 7, 12, 14; 6:1, 4, 5, 5, 6, 9, 10, 15, 27, 28, 29, 30, 31, 32, 33, 35, 35, 36, 38; 7:1, 2, 6, 7, 7, 8, 8, 14, 14, 14, 15, 16, 18, 21, 21, 21, 23, 27, 36, 37, 38, 39, 39, 40, 51; 8:12, 15, 19, 20, 21, 21, 23, 42, 54, 55, 56, 56, 57, 58, 58, 59, 63, 64, 66; 9:1, 2, 13, 13, 24, 25, 25, 25; 10:3, 4, 5, 9, 15, 17, 19, 26, 27; 11:3, 8, 10, 10, 14, 15, 16, 16, 17, 19, 22, 24, 25, 25, 26, 27, 28, 28, 29, 31, 32, 34, 41; 12:2, 4, 5, 6, 8, 9, 15, 18, 33, 33; 13:2, 3, 4, 4, 4, 4, 10, 10, 12, 13, 13, 14, 14, 16, 18, 18, 19, 21, 23, 23, 24, 26, 26, 27, 30, 31, 31, 31, 33; 14:3, 5, 13, 15, 16, 18, 19, 21; 15:2, 3, 3, 23, 23, 23, 24, 26, 26, 27, 28, 30, 31, 32, 33, 33; 14:3, 5, 16, 18, 18, 19, 21, 23, 25, 26, 27, 28, 29, 29, 29, 30, 30, 31, 34, 34, 41; 16:5, 7, 7, 7, 10, 19, 20, 26, 26, 26, 29, 30, 30, 31, 32, 32, 32, 33, 33; 17:5, 6, 10, 10, 10, 11, 15, 16, 16, 17, 19, 20, 21, 22, 24, 24; 18:7, 8, 9, 10, 14, 19, 21, 32, 34, 41; 12:2, 3, 4, 5, 6, 8, 9, 15, 17, 19, 20, 21, 21, 31, 31, 31, 32, 36; 21:2, 3, 4, 4, 5, 6, 6, 6, 6, 7, 8, 9, 9, 11, 20, 22, 23, 24, 25, 27, 29; 22:8, 9, 20

2Ki 1:2, 5, 7, 7, 8, 8, 9, 9, 11, 11, 13, 15, 16, 17, 17, 18, 18, 20, 21, 22, 13, 14, 14, 16, 17, 17, 18, 18, 20, 21, 22, 23, 23, 24, 25, 25; 3:2, 2, 3, 3, 7, 8, 8, 16, 18, 26, 27; 4:3, 6, 7, 8, 8, 10, 10, 11, 12, 12, 13, 14, 15, 15, 16, 16, 18, 20, 23, 25, 25, 29, 30, 31, 33, 34, 34, 35, 36, 36, 38, 41, 41, 42, 42, 43, 44; 5:1, 1, 3, 5, 6, 7, 8, 9, 10, 11, 12, 14, 15, 15, 16, 16, 18, 19, 19, 20, 21, 22, 23, 24, 24, 25, 25, 26; 6:2, 3, 4, 5, 6, 7, 7, 9, 11, 13, 14, 17, 18, 19, 20, 22, 25, 29, 30, 31, 33; 7:2, 11, 17, 17, 19, 20, 8:1, 5, 5, 5, 10, 11, 11, 13, 14, 14, 14, 15, 15, 17, 17, 18, 18, 19, 19, 23, 26, 27, 28, 29; 9:5, 5, 6, 6, 10, 11, 12, 12, 13, 14, 15, 17, 27, 32, 33, 33, 34, 34, 36; 10:5, 9, 10, 10, 11, 12, 14, 15, 15, 17, 17, 17, 19, 21, 23, 25, 29, 30, 31, 33, 34, 34, 35; 36, 36, 36, 38, 41, 41, 41, 42, 43, 44; 5:1, 1, 3, 5, 6, 16, 16, 16, 18, 19, 19, 20, 20, 21, 22, 23, 24, 24, 25, 25, 26; 6:2, 3, 4, 5, 6, 17, 18, 19, 20, 22, 23, 25, 26, 27, 30, 30, 31, 32, 33, 33; 7:2, 1, 11, 17, 17, 19, 20; 8:1, 5, 5, 5, 11, 11, 12, 14, 14, 14, 15, 15, 17, 17, 18, 19, 20; 9:5, 5, 6, 6, 25:1, 9, 9, 19, 22, 25, 27, 28, 29

1Ch 1:10; 2:3, 21, 21, 23; 3:4, 4; 4:10; 5:1, 1, 6, 9, 20, 26; 6:10; 7:23, 23; 8:7, 8, 9, 11; 10:3, 4, 5, 13, 14; 11:2, 8, 11, 13, 19, 20, 20, 21, 21, 21, 22, 22, 23, 23, 25; 12:1, 18, 19, 19, 20; 13:10, 10, 10, 14; 14:4; 15:3, 22, 22; 16:2, 3, 4, 12, 14, 16; 16, 21, 21, 23, 33, 34, 37, 40; 17:12, 13; 18:2, 3, 6, 10, 10, 11, 13, 13; 19:3, 5, 8, 10, 11, 13, 16, 17; 20:2, 3, 6, 7; 21:3, 6, 7, 11, 18, 18; 23:1, 2, 13, 13; 25:10, 11, 12, 13, 14, 15, 16, 16, 17, 18, 19, 20, 21, 22, 23, 24, 25, 26, 27, 28, 29, 30, 31; 26:10; 27:23, 24; 28:4, 4, 5, 6, 6, 7, 9, 9, 12, 14, 20, 21; 29:27, 27, 27, 28

2Ch 1:4, 5, 14, 14, 15; 2:11, 11, 18; 3:2, 4, 5, 5, 6, 7, 8, 8, 9, 10, 14, 15, 16, 17; 4:1; 2, 6, 7, 8, 8, 9, 10, 11, 14, 14, 21; 5:1, 13; 6:1, 4, 4, 9, 10, 11, 12, 13; 7:3, 7, 10, 11, 21, 22; 8:4, 4, 5, 11, 11, 12, 14; 9:2, 3, 4, 8, 16, 25, 26, 27, 31; 10:2, 4, 5, 6, 8, 19; 11:1, 1, 6, 11, 12, 15, 15, 20, 21, 22, 23, 23, 23; 12:1, 4, 9, 9, 12, 12, 13, 13, 14, 14; 13:2, 20; 14:3, 5, 6, 6, 7, 7; 15:2, 2, 2, 4, 8, 8, 9, 15, 16, 18, 18; 16:1, 3, 5, 6, 8, 10, 12, 14; 17:2, 3, 5, 6, 7, 17, 18, 19, 21, 23, 33; 18:1, 2, 23, 24, 24, 26, 27, 29; 33:1, 1, 3, 3, 4, 4, 5, 6, 6, 6, 7, 7, 12, 12, 13, 13, 14, 15, 16, 19; 19:2, 2, 3, 4, 5, 6, 6, 6, 7, 7, 8, 9, 9, 9; 20:1, 3, 5, 7, 14, 18, 20, 22, 22:2, 3, 4, 4, 5, 6, 6, 7, 8, 9, 9, 9, 10; 23:3, 7, 7, 7, 10, 19; 20; 24:1, 1, 3, 5, 3, 4, 5, 6, 14, 15, 16, 20, 20, 21, 24, 27; 26:2, 3, 3, 4, 5, 6, 8, 10, 10, 10, 15, 15, 16, 16, 19, 20, 21, 21, 23; 27:1, 1, 2, 2, 3, 3, 4, 4, 5, 5, 6, 8, 8; 28:1, 1, 1, 2, 3, 4, 5, 9, 9, 19, 21, 22, 23, 23, 24, 25; 29:1, 1, 2, 3, 4, 8, 21, 23, 33; 30:6, 8, 19; 31:3, 4, 21, 21; 32:2, 3, 5, 6, 9, 17, 21, 21, 23, 24, 24, 26, 27, 29; 33:1, 1, 3, 3, 4, 5, 6, 6, 6, 7, 7, 12, 12, 13, 13, 14, 15, 16, 19; 34:1, 2, 3, 3, 3, 4, 4, 4, 5, 6, 7, 7, 8, 19, 22; 34:1, 2, 7, 8, 9, 11, 12, 13, 13, 14, 15, 16, 19, 22; 36:2, 2, 5, 5, 8, 9, 9, 9, 11, 12, 13, 14, 13, 15, 17, 17, 18, 20, 22, 23

Ezr 1:1, 2, 3, 4; 3:11; 5:12, 14; 6:17; 7:6, 8, 9, 9; 8:23, 31, 35; 10:1, 6, 6, 6

Ne 1:2; 2:8, 18, 20; 3:12, 14, 15; 4:1, 2, 3, 3, 18; 5:13; 6:10, 12, 13, 18; 7:2; 8:3, 5, 5, 10, 18; 9:29; 12:8; 13:2, 5

Est 1:3, 4, 10, 20, 22; 2:1, 4, 7, 9, 9, 17, 18; 3:4, 4, 4, 6; 4:4, 5, 8, 11; 5:5, 9, 9, 10, 10, 11, 14; 6:1, 4; 7:5, 5, 7, 8, 10; 8:1, 2, 3, 5, 7, 10; 9:25, 25, 25, 30

Job 1:10, 11, 12, 12, 16, 17, 18; 2:3, 4, 5, 6, 6, 10; 4:18, 18; 5:12, 13, 15, 18, 18, 19, 20; 6:5, 9, 14; 7:9, 10; 8:4, 6, 15, 15, 16, 17, 18, 19, 22, 23, 24, 24, 32; 11:6, 10, 11, 11, 11; 12:4, 5, 13, 14, 14, 15; 11:6, 17, 18, 19, 20, 23, 28; 14:2, 2, 5, 6, 6, 10, 14, 20, 21, 21; 15:3, 3, 14, 14, 14, 15,

Idx

11, 11, 12, 13, 17, 18, 19, 19, 20, 21, 21; 6:7, 10, 10, 10, 10; 7:1, 2; 8:9, 11, 24, 27, 27, 29, 29, 29, 30, 30, 30, 30, 30, 32, 32, 34; 9:15, 18, 18, 18, 19, 23, 23, 24, 25, 28; 10:21; 11:2, 2, 7, 21, 32; 12:3, 7, 8, 8, 8, 8, 20; 13:4, 4, 4, 8; 14:2, 4, 4, 6, 6, 6, 6, 6, 6, 6, 9, 18, 22, 22, 23, 23, 23; 15:10, 12, 21

1Co 1:31; 2:14, 15, 15, 16; 3:7, 7, 8, 8, 10, 17, 18; 7:13, 20, 22, 22, 24, 32, 32, 33, 33, 36, 36, 36, 37, 37, 38, 38; 8:2, 2, 2; 9:10, 10, 10; 10:12, 12, 22; 11:7, 23, 24, 24, 25, 25, 26, 29; 12:11; 14:2, 2, 3, 4, 4, 5, 5, 5, 11, 13, 16, 16, 24, 24, 25, 15:4, 4, 5, 6, 7, 8, 12, 15, 15, 24, 24, 25, 25, 27, 27, 27; 16:10, 16, 16, 18

2Co 1:10, 21; 2:2, 5; 4:14; 5:5, 10, 15, 17, 21; 6:2, 15; 7:7, 7, 15; 8:6, 6, 9, 9, 12, 15, 15, 17, 23; 9:6, 6, 7, 9, 9, 10; 10:7, 7, 17, 18; 11:4; 12:4, 6, 6, 9; 13:4, 4

Gal 1:4, 23, 23; 2:8, 11, 12; 3:5, 5, 16; 4:1, 1, 23, 23, 29; 5:3, 10, 10; 6:3, 3, 4, 7, 8, 8

Eph 1:4, 6, 8, 9, 10, 20, 20; 2:1, 4, 7, 14, 16; 3:3, 11, 16; 4:8, 8, 8, 9, 9, 10, 10, 11, 28; 5:14, 23, 26, 27, 28; 6:8, 8, 22

Php 1:6; 2:8, 22, 25, 26, 26, 27, 30; 3:4, 4, 21

Col 1:17, 18, 18, 21; 2:13, 15, 18; 3:25, 25; 4:8, 10, 13

1Th 1:10; 3:13; 4:8; 5:24

2Th 1:10; 2:4, 4, 6, 7, 7, 14; 3:6, 10, 14

1Ti 1:12; 3:1, 5, 6, 7, 7; 5:8; 6:4, 15

2Ti 1:12, 16, 17, 17, 18, 18; 2:4, 5, 5, 12, 13, 13, 21; 4:11, 15

Tit 1:9, 9; 2:8, 14; 3:5, 6, 11

Phm 1:13, 15, 18

Heb 1:2, 2, 3, 5, 6, 6, 7, 8, 13; 2:5, 8, 8, 9, 11, 11, 14, 14, 16, 16, 17, 18, 18; 3:3, 4, 17, 18; 4:3, 4, 7, 8, 10, 10; 5:1, 2, 3, 4, 5, 6, 7, 7, 8, 8, 8, 9, 13; 6:13, 13, 13, 15, 15; 7:6, 8, 8, 10, 13, 17, 20, 24, 25, 25, 27, 27; 8:4, 4, 5, 5, 6, 8, 13, 13; 9:7, 12, 15, 19, 21, 25, 26, 26, 28; 10:5, 5, 8, 9, 9, 12, 14, 15, 20, 23, 28, 29, 29, 37; 11:4, 4, 4, 5, 5, 5, 6, 6, 6, 6, 8, 8, 8, 9, 10, 16, 17, 17, 19, 21, 22, 23, 23, 24, 26, 27, 27, 28, 28; 12:6, 6, 7, 10, 17, 17, 17, 17, 26; 13:5, 12, 23

Jas 1:6, 7, 9, 10, 10, 12, 12, 13, 13, 14, 18, 23, 24, 24, 25; 2:5, 10, 11, 13, 14, 23; 4:6, 6, 7, 8, 10, 11; 5:6, 7, 15, 17, 18, 19; 4:1, 2, 14, 14; 5:6, 7, 8

1Pe 1:15; 2:6, 7, 23, 23, 23; 3:10, 13, 18, 19; 4:1, 2, 14, 14; 5:6, 7, 8

2Pe 1:9, 9, 17; 2:19

1Jn 1:7, 9; 2:2, 4, 6, 6, 6, 9, 9, 10, 11, 11, 17, 22, 22, 23, 23, 25, 28, 29; 3:2, 2, 3, 5, 7, 7, 8, 8, 9, 9, 10, 12, 14, 16, 23, 24, 24, 24, 24; 4:4, 4, 6, 6, 8, 10, 13, 13, 15, 16, 17, 18, 19, 20, 20, 20, 21; 5:5, 5, 6, 9, 9, 10, 10, 10, 12, 14, 15, 16, 16, 18

2Jn 1:9, 9, 11

3Jn 1:10, 10, 11, 11

Jude 1:6, 9

Rev 1:1, 2, 3, 7, 16, 17, 18; 2:1, 7, 11, 11, 12, 17, 17, 23, 26, 27, 29; 3:1, 5, 6, 7, 7, 7, 7, 12, 12, 12, 21; 4:3; 5:7, 8; 6:2, 2, 3, 5, 5, 7, 9, 12; 7:2, 14, 15; 8:1, 3; 9:2, 5; 10:2, 3, 7, 7, 9, 9, 11; 11:5, 15; 12:9, 12, 12, 13, 13, 13; 13:6, 10, 10, 10, 11, 11, 12, 13, 13, 14, 14, 16, 16, 17; 14:4, 10, 16, 17; 16:15, 15, 16; 17:3, 10, 10, 10, 11, 14, 15; 18:2, 22; 19:2, 9, 10, 11, 11, 12, 13, 15, 15, 15, 16, 17, 20; 20:2, 3, 3, 6; 21:3, 5, 5, 6, 7, 7, 10, 15, 16, 17; 22:1, 6, 7, 9, 10, 11, 11, 11, 20

HER (1993)

Ge 2:22; 3:6, 6, 15; 4:11, 12; 8:9, 9, 9, 11; 12:15, 15, 16, 19, 19; 16:2, 3, 3, 3, 4, 4, 5, 6, 6, 6, 7, 9, 9, 9, 9, 11, 15, 15, 15, 16, 16, 16, 16; 19:33; 20:4, 6, 7, 13; 21:10, 12, 14, 14, 16, 16, 17, 19; 23:2; 24:15, 15, 16, 16, 17, 18, 18, 20, 21, 22, 28, 43, 45, 45, 45, 46, 46, 47, 47, 47, 51, 51, 53, 53, 55, 55, 57, 58, 59, 60, 61, 64, 67, 67; 25:1, 22, 23, 24, 24; 26:9; 27:6, 15, 15, 15, 17, 42, 42; 29:9, 12, 12, 19, 19, 20, 21, 23, 23, 27, 28, 28, 29, 30, 31; 30:1, 3, 3, 4, 4, 5, 6, 7, 9, 9, 9, 15, 16, 21, 22; 31:19; 33:2, 7; 34:2, 2, 2, 2, 8, 11, 11; 35:17, 18, 20; 38:2, 2, 8, 11, 14, 14, 14, 15, 15, 16, 18, 19, 19, 19, 20, 25, 25, 23, 23, 24, 24, 25, 26, 26, 27; 39:7, 10, 10, 10, 12, 13, 14, 14, 16; 40:10; 48:7

Ex 2:5, 5, 8, 9, 10; 3:22, 22, 22; 4:25; 11:2; 15:20, 20; 18:2, 3, 6, 6; 21:4, 4, 8, 8, 8, 8, 9, 9, 10, 10, 10, 10, 11, 22, 22; 22:16, 16, 17, 17

Lev 11:19; 12:2, 4, 4, 5, 5, 6, 7, 7, 7, 8; 15:19, 19, 19, 20, 21, 23, 24, 25, 25, 25, 25, 25, 26, 26, 26, 26, 28, 29, 29, 30, 30, 33, 33, 33; 18:7, 11, 15, 17, 17, 17, 17, 17, 18, 18, 18, 18, 19, 19, 19, 20, 25; 19:20, 29; 20:14, 17, 18, 18, 18, 18; 21:3, 7, 9, 13; 22:13, 13, 13, 28; 25:19, 22; 26:4, 20, 20, 34, 34, 43

Nu 5:13, 13, 13, 15, 15, 16, 16, 18, 19, 24, 27, 27, 27, 27, 27, 27, 29, 30, 30, 31; 12:12, 13, 14, 14, 14, 14; 16:30, 32; 19:3, 3, 3, 4, 4, 5, 5, 5, 8; 22:23, 25, 33; 25:8;

26:10, 59; 30:3, 3, 4, 4, 4, 4, 4, 4, 4, 5, 5, 5, 5, 5, 5, 5, 6, 6, 7, 7, 7, 7, 7, 8, 8, 8, 8, 8, 8, 9, 9, 10, 10, 11, 11, 11, 11, 11, 12, 12, 12, 12, 12, 12, 13, 13, 14, 14, 14, 14, 14, 14, 14, 15, 15, 16, 16; 36:8

Dt 11:6, 17; 14:18; 20:7, 7; 21:11, 11, 12, 12, 12, 13, 13, 13, 13, 13, 13, 14, 14, 14, 14, 14; 22:13, 13, 14, 14, 14, 14, 15, 16, 17, 19, 19, 21, 21, 21, 21, 23, 23, 24, 25, 25, 25, 27, 27, 28, 28, 29, 29, 29; 24:1, 1, 1, 1, 1, 3, 3, 3, 3, 4, 4, 4; 25:5, 5, 5, 5, 5, 8; 11, 11, 12; 28:30, 56, 56, 56, 56, 56, 57, 57, 57; 32:11, 11, 11, 11, 22

Jos 2:14, 15, 17; 6:17, 22, 23, 23, 23, 23, 25; 8:2, 2; 10:1, 1, 39; 13:17; 15:18, 18, 19, 45, 45, 47, 47, 47, 47; 17:11, 11, 11, 11, 11, 11, 16; 21:13, 13, 14, 14, 15, 15, 16, 16, 16, 17, 17, 18, 18, 21, 21, 22, 22, 23, 23, 24, 24, 25, 25, 27, 27, 28, 28, 29, 30, 30, 31, 31, 32, 32, 32, 34, 34, 35, 35, 36, 36, 37, 37, 38, 38, 39, 39

Jdg 1:14, 14, 14, 15, 27, 27, 27, 27, 27; 4:5, 8, 18, 19, 20, 21, 22; 5:26, 26, 27, 27, 29, 29; 11:26, 26, 34, 35, 37, 38, 38, 38, 39; 13:3, 6, 9, 10, 13, 14, 14, 14; 14:2, 3, 8, 16, 17, 17, 17; 15:1, 2, 2, 2, 2, 2, 6, 6, 6; 16:1, 5, 5, 7, 8, 9, 11, 13, 16, 17, 17, 18, 19; 19:2, 3, 3, 3, 3, 25, 25, 25, 26, 27, 27, 28, 28, 29, 29; 20:6, 6

Ru 1:3, 5, 5, 6, 7, 7, 8, 8, 9, 10, 14, 14, 15, 15, 15, 16, 16, 16, 18, 18, 19, 19, 19, 20, 20, 22, 23; 3:1, 1, 5, 6, 6, 7, 15, 16, 16, 16; 4:13, 13, 16, 17

1Sa 1:4, 4, 5, 6, 6, 6, 6, 7, 8, 8, 12, 13, 13, 14, 14, 18, 18, 19, 22, 23, 23, 23, 24; 2:19; 4:19, 19, 19, 19, 20, 20, 20, 21, 21; 18:17, 21; 25:19, 19, 20, 23, 35, 35, 39, 40, 41, 42; 28:7, 7, 10, 13, 14

2Sa 3:15, 15, 16, 16, 16; 6:16, 23; 11:4, 4, 4, 26, 26, 27; 12:24, 24; 13:1, 2, 5, 6, 8, 10, 11, 11, 14, 14, 14, 14, 15, 15, 15, 16, 17, 18, 18, 18, 19, 19, 19, 19, 20, 20, 20; 14:2, 3, 4, 5; 17:8; 20:17, 22; 21:10

1Ki 1:2, 2, 2, 3, 4, 4, 31; 2:19, 19, 20; 3:1, 17, 20, 20, 26, 26, 26, 27; 9:24, 24; 10:2, 3, 3, 5, 13, 13, 13, 13, 13; 14:5, 5, 6; 15:13, 13; 17:10, 11, 13, 15, 19, 19, 20; 21:6

2Ki 4:2, 5, 5, 5, 6, 6, 9, 12, 13, 14, 14, 15, 16, 16, 16, 20, 22, 24, 25, 26, 26, 27, 27, 27, 30, 36, 37; 5:3; 6:28, 29, 29; 8:2, 3, 3, 5, 5, 5, 6; 9:10, 22, 30, 30, 33, 33, 33, 34, 34, 35, 35, 35; 11:1, 3, 14, 15, 15, 15, 16; 19:21; 22:14

1Ch 2:18; 5:16; 6:57, 58, 58, 59, 59, 60, 60, 60, 67, 67, 68, 68, 69, 69, 70, 70, 71, 71, 72, 72, 73, 73, 74, 74, 75, 75, 76, 76, 76, 77, 77, 78, 78, 79, 79, 80, 80, 81, 81; 7:29, 29, 29, 29; 15:29; 18:1

2Ch 8:11; 9:1, 2, 2, 2, 4, 12, 12, 12; 11:20; 15:16, 16; 22:10; 23:13, 14, 14, 14, 15, 15; 34:22; 36:21

Est 1:11, 19; 2:1, 7, 9, 9, 9, 9, 9, 10, 10, 10, 11, 13, 13, 14, 14, 15, 15, 17, 17, 20, 20, 20; 4:4, 4, 5, 8, 8, 8; 5:1, 3, 12; 8:1

Job 2:10; 5:16; 9:6; 21:10; 31:10, 18; 39:14, 16, 16, 17, 17, 26, 27, 29, 30

Ps 34:2; 45:13, 14, 14; 46:5, 5; 48:3, 12, 13; 55:11; 58:4; 67:6; 68:13, 31; 69:15; 80:11, 11, 12, 12; 84:3; 85:12; 87:5, 5; 102:13, 14; 104:17; 107:42; 123:2; 132:15, 15, 16, 16; 137:5

Pr 1:20, 21; 2:4, 4, 16, 17, 18, 18; 4:6, 6, 8, 8, 13, 13; 5:3, 4, 4, 5, 6, 8, 8, 19, 19, 19; 6:6, 8, 8, 25, 25, 25, 29; 7:5, 8, 8, 11, 11, 21, 21, 22, 25, 25, 25, 26, 27; 8:1; 9:1, 1, 2, 2, 2, 3, 14, 18; 12:4; 14:1, 1; 17:12, 25; 27:8, 16; 30:20, 23, 28; 31:10, 11, 11, 19, 20, 20, 21, 21, 22, 24, 25, 25, 26, 26, 27, 28, 28, 28, 31, 31, 31, 31

Ecc 7:26, 26, 26; 11:5

SS 2:13; 3:4; 6:9, 9, 9, 9, 9; 8:5, 9, 9

Isa 1:27; 3:26; 4:5; 5:14; 7:16; 9:1, 1; 10:11, 11; 13:10, 13, 22, 22; 16:8; 21:9; 23:3, 7, 7, 17, 18, 18, 18; 24:2; 26:17, 17, 21, 21; 27:2; 29:7, 7, 7; 34:12, 13, 15, 15, 16; 37:22; 40:2, 2, 2, 2; 49:15, 15; 51:3, 3, 3, 18, 18; 52:1; 53:7; 61:10, 11; 65:18, 19; 66:7, 8, 10, 10, 10, 10, 11, 11, 12, 12, 12

Jer 2:23, 24, 24, 24, 24, 24, 24, 32, 32; 3:1, 7, 8, 8, 9, 10, 10, 10; 4:17, 31, 31, 31; 5:10, 10; 6:3, 3, 4, 5, 6, 7, 7; 8:7, 19, 19; 9:20; 12:7, 9; 15:9; 17:8, 8; 19:15; 20:17; 30:18; 31:8, 15, 15; 44:17, 18, 19, 19, 19, 19, 25; 46:21, 21, 22, 23; 48:4, 15, 19, 28, 41; 49:2, 4, 14, 19, 19, 22, 24, 24, 26, 26; 50:2, 2, 3, 9, 10, 14, 14, 15, 15, 15, 15, 15, 15, 26, 26, 26, 26, 35, 36, 37, 37, 38, 44, 44; 51:2, 2, 2, 3, 3, 4, 4, 5, 5, 5, 5, 6, 6, 7, 7, 7, 7, 7, 7, 7, 9, 27, 27, 27, 28, 30, 30, 33, 33, 36, 36, 43, 45, 47, 47, 47, 47, 48, 52, 52; 52:1, 55, 56, 56, 56, 57, 57, 57, 57, 57, 58, 64

La 1:2, 2, 2, 2, 2, 2, 2, 2, 3, 3, 4, 4, 4, 5, 5, 5, 5, 5, 6, 6, 6, 7, 7, 7, 7, 7, 7, 7, 17, 17; 2:5, 7, 9, 9, 9, 9, 9, 9, 16; 4:6, 7, 13, 13, 13

Eze 5:5, 6; 12:13; 16:2, 32, 44, 45, 45, 46, 46, 48, 49, 49, 53, 53, 55, 55, 57; 17:7, 7, 9; 19:2, 3, 5, 5, 11, 11, 11, 12, 12, 14, 14, 14; 22:2, 2, 3, 10, 24, 25, 25, 26, 27, 28; 23:4, 5, 5, 7, 8, 8, 8, 8, 8, 9, 9, 10, 10, 11, 11, 11, 11, 12, 14,

16, 17, 17, 17, 18, 18, 18, 18, 19, 19, 31, 42, 43, 43, 44; 24:7, 7, 8, 12, 12; 26:4, 4, 4, 4, 4, 6; 27:28; 22, 23, 23, 23, 23; 29:12, 19, 19, 19; 30:4, 4, 6, 7, 8, 18, 18, 18, 18, 18; 31:4, 4; 32:7, 16, 16, 16, 16, 18, 20, 20, 22, 23, 24, 24, 25, 25, 25, 26, 26, 29, 29; 33:28; 34:27, 27; 36:38; 44:22

Da 11:6, 6, 6, 7, 17

Hos 1:6; 2:2, 2, 2, 2, 2, 2, 2, 3, 3, 3, 3, 3, 4, 6, 7, 8, 8, 9, 10, 10, 10, 11, 11, 11, 11, 11, 12, 12, 13, 13, 13, 14, 14, 14, 14, 15, 15, 17, 23, 23; 3:1, 2, 3; 4:18, 19, 19; 9:2, 10; 10:7, 11, 14; 13:8, 16

Joel 1:8; 2:16, 22; 3:17

Am 4:3; 5:2, 2

Ob 1:1;

Jnh 1:15; 2:6

Mic 1:9; 4:6, 6, 6, 7, 7, 11; 7:5, 6, 6, 10, 10

Na 2:7; 3:4, 4, 7, 8, 9, 10, 10, 10

Zep 2:14, 15, 15; 3:1, 2, 3, 3, 3, 4, 4, 19, 19

Hag 1:10; 2:3

Zec 2:5, 5; 5:11; 7:7; 8:2, 12, 12; 9:4, 4, 5; 12:6; 14:10

Mal 3:11;

Mt 1:6, 19, 19, 19, 20, 25, 25; 2:18; 5:28, 28, 31, 32, 32; 8:15, 15; 9:18, 22, 25; 10:35, 35; 11:19; 14:4, 7, 8, 9, 11; 15:23, 23, 28, 28; 19:7, 9; 20:20, 21; 21:2; 22:28; 23:37, 37; 24:29; 26:13

Mk 1:30, 31, 31, 31; 5:23, 29, 29, 32, 33, 34, 41, 43; 6:17, 23, 24, 26, 28; 7:26, 27, 29, 30, 30; 10:4, 11, 12; 12:21, 22, 23, 44, 44; 13:24, 28; 14:5, 6, 6, 9; 16:11

Lk 1:5, 28, 29, 30, 35, 36, 36, 38, 41, 45, 56, 56, 58, 58, 58, 61; 2:7, 19, 22, 36, 51; 4:38, 39, 39; 7:12, 13, 13, 13, 35, 38, 44, 47, 48; 8:43, 44, 48, 52, 54, 55, 55, 56; 10:38, 40, 41, 42; 11:27; 12:53, 53; 13:12, 12, 12, 13, 34, 34; 15:9, 9; 16:18, 18; 18:5, 5; 20:30, 31, 33; 21:4

Jn 2:4; 4:7, 10, 13, 16, 17, 21, 26, 27, 28, 28; 8:3, 7, 10, 11; 11:1, 2, 5, 23, 25, 28, 28, 31, 31, 31, 33, 33, 40; 12:3, 7; 16:21; 18:16; 19:27; 20:13, 15, 16, 17, 18

Ac 5:8, 9, 10, 10, 10, 10; 7:21; 8:27; 9:37, 40, 41, 41, 41; 12:15; 16:15, 16, 18, 19; 19:27; 21:3; 27:15, 32

Ro 7:2, 3, 3; 9:12, 25; 16:2, 2

1Co 7:2, 4, 10, 11, 11, 12, 13, 13, 34, 36, 38, 38, 39, 39; 11:5, 5, 6, 6, 10, 15, 15, 15; 13:5

Gal 4:25, 30

Eph 5:33;

1Th 2:7;

Jas 1:4; 5:18

2Pe 2:22;

2Jn 1:1;

Rev 2:21, 21, 22, 22, 23; 6:13; 12:1, 1, 4, 5, 6, 14, 15, 16, 17; 14:8, 18; 16:19; 17:2, 4, 4, 5, 6, 7, 16, 16, 16; 18:3, 3, 3, 4, 4, 5, 5, 6, 6, 6, 6, 7, 7, 8, 8, 9, 9, 9, 10, 11, 15, 15, 18, 19, 19, 20, 20, 24; 19:2, 2, 3, 8; 21:2, 11; 22:2

HIM (6667)

Ge 1:27; 2:15, 18, 18, 20; 3:9, 23; 4:7, 8, 15, 15, 15, 15, 19, 26; 5:1, 24; 6:6, 22; 7:5, 7, 16, 16, 23; 8:1, 8, 9, 9, 11, 12, 18; 9:8, 24; 10:21; 12:3, 4, 4, 7, 20, 20; 13:1, 11, 14; 14:5, 17, 17, 19, 20; 15:4, 5, 5, 6, 7, 9, 9, 10, 12; 16:1, 12, 13; 17:1, 3, 17, 19, 19, 20, 20, 20, 20, 22, 23, 27; 18:1, 2, 9, 10, 18, 19, 19, 29, 30; 19:3, 5, 6, 16, 16, 16, 21, 26, 30, 32, 34, 34, 35; 20:3, 6, 9, 14; 21:2, 3, 3, 4, 5, 7, 16, 16, 18, 18, 21; 22:1, 3, 3, 9, 11, 12; 23:5, 14; 24:5, 6, 9, 18, 19, 24, 25, 32, 33, 33, 36, 47, 54; 25:2, 9, 21, 33; 26:2, 7, 9, 12, 14, 20, 24, 26, 31, 32, 32; 27:1, 1, 12, 13, 22, 23, 23, 25, 25, 26, 30, 31, 32, 33, 37, 37, 39, 41, 42, 44, 45; 28:1, 1, 1, 6, 6, 6, 6; 29:5, 13, 13, 13, 13, 13, 20, 28, 30, 34; 30:4, 16, 20, 27, 29, 37; 31:2, 2, 7, 16, 20, 21, 23, 23, 24, 24, 25, 25, 27, 29, 29, 31; 33:1, 4, 4, 4, 11, 13, 17; 34:6, 9, 14, 16, 16, 26, 30, 34, 35; 35:3, 6, 6, 9, 14, 14, 15, 19; 36:5; 37:3, 4, 4, 4, 5, 8, 8, 10, 10, 11, 13, 14, 18, 20, 21, 22, 22, 23, 27, 33, 35, 36; 38:5, 7, 10, 14, 18; 39:1, 1, 3, 4, 4, 5, 12, 15, 19, 20, 20, 21, 21, 21, 22, 22, 22, 23, 23, 24, 24, 27, 27, 33, 35, 35, 36; 38:5, 7, 10, 14, 18; 39:1, 1, 3, 4, 4, 5, 12, 15, 19, 20, 20, 21, 21, 21, 22, 22, 22, 23, 41:12, 13, 14, 33, 34, 42, 43, 43, 43, 45, 50; 42:4, 6, 8, 10, 16, 24, 29, 31, 37, 37, 38; 43:3, 5, 7, 9, 9, 9, 9, 19, 26, 26, 32, 32, 33, 34, 34, 44:7, 9, 14, 18, 20, 21, 22, 28, 28, 29, 30; 45:1, 1, 3, 9, 15, 26, 27, 27, 28; 46:5, 6, 7, 7, 10, 27, 28, 29, 31; 47:7, 18, 19, 31; 48:1, 10, 13; 17; 49:9, 10, 19, 23, 23, 23, 26; 50:1, 1, 3, 3, 7, 9, 12, 13, 13, 14, 15, 17, 26

Ex 1:16; 2:2, 2, 3, 3, 4, 6, 10, 10, 12, 13, 20, 22; 3:2, 4, 18; 4:2, 6, 11, 13, 15, 18, 18, 23, 24, 24, 26, 27, 27, 28, 28; 6:2, 20, 20, 23, 23, 25, 25, 7:10; 8:1, 20; 9:1, 13, 14, 14, 19, 21, 23, 27; 10:1, 3, 7, 28; 12:4, 44, 48, 49; 13:14, 19; 14:6; 15:2, 2, 25; 16:8; 17:10, 12; 18:7, 17; 19:3, 7, 19, 24; 20:7, 21:3, 3, 4, 4, 6, 6, 6, 6, 10, 10, 14, 26, 27, 35, 36; 22:2, 2, 3, 3, 7, 12, 13, 17, 21, 25, 25, 26; 23:4, 5, 5, 5, 21, 21, 31:3, 5

Lev 1:1, 3, 4, 4; 4:3, 12, 14, 19, 21, 26, 26, 31, 31, 35; 5:2, 3, 4, 4, 6, 6, 10, 13, 13, 16, 16, 18, 6:2, 4, 5, 7, 7; 7:18, 20; 8:2, 4, 7, 7, 7, 7, 7, 8, 12, 12, 30, 30; 9:9, 12, 13, 18; 13:3, 3, 4, 5, 5, 6, 6, 8, 10, 11, 11, 12, 13, 14, 15, 17, 17, 20, 21, 22, 23, 25, 26, 27, 27, 30, 33, 34, 36, 36, 37, 44, 46; 14:4, 7, 7, 11, 12, 14, 18, 18, 19, 20, 21, 25, 28, 29, 29, 31, 32; 15:7, 8, 10, 14, 15, 24, 32, 33; 16:9, 10, 10, 21, 21, 24, 32, 32, 32, 33; 17:10; 18:6; 19:13, 13, 17, 22, 22, 33; 20:2, 3, 4, 4, 5, 5, 6, 9; 21:2, 3, 8, 12, 15, 17; 22:3, 4; 24:9, 11, 12, 14, 14, 14, 16, 16, 16, 16, 17, 17, 20, 20, 23; 25:27, 28, 30, 35, 36, 37, 37, 39, 41, 43, 47, 48, 49, 49, 49, 50, 50, 50, 50, 52, 52, 53, 53, 54; 26:46; 27:8, 8, 18, 19, 23, 24, 24

Nu 2:5, 12, 20, 27; 3:6, 9, 42; 4:49; 5:7, 8, 12, 14, 14, 30; 6:9, 11; 7:89, 89, 89; 8:2; 9:7, 14; 10:30; 11:20, 25, 29, 30; 12:6, 6, 8; 13:27, 31; 14:24, 24, 36, 36; 15:28, 28, 29, 29, 31, 33, 34, 34, 35, 36, 36; 16:5, 5, 5, 5, 10, 11, 25, 40; 17:6, 11; 19:13, 13, 18, 19, 20; 20:9, 18, 19, 20, 21; 21:24, 34, 34, 34, 35; 22:5, 7, 16, 20, 22, 22, 32, 36, 40, 41; 23:4, 6, 9, 9, 13, 14, 17, 17, 17, 21; 24:2, 8, 9, 17, 19; 25:12, 13; 26:54; 27:11, 18, 19, 19, 20, 20, 21, 21, 21, 22, 22, 23, 23, 25, 27, 30, 32, 33

Dt 1:3, 16, 36, 38; 2:24, 30, 30, 33, 33; 3:2, 2, 3, 3, 28, 28; 4:7, 20, 25, 29, 29, 34, 34, 35, 42; 5:11; 6:13, 16; 7:9, 10, 10, 10, 10; 8:6; 9:18, 20, 23; 10:8, 9, 12, 18, 20, 20; 11:13, 22; 13:4, 4, 4, 8, 8, 9, 9, 9, 10; 14:27; 15:8, 8, 9, 10, 10, 10, 12, 13, 13, 14, 14, 18; 17:7, 7, 15, 18, 19; 18:4, 5, 5, 5, 18, 19, 20, 20, 22; 19:6, 6, 6, 11, 11, 11, 12, 13, 13, 16, 19; 20:5, 6, 7, 8; 21:1, 2, 5, 15, 17, 18, 19, 19, 21, 22, 23; 22:2, 2, 4, 18, 19, 26, 29; 23:10, 10, 16; 24:1, 7, 7, 13; 25:2, 3, 3, 5, 8, 9, 10, 10, 11; 26:3; 28:44, 55; 29:15, 15, 20, 20, 21; 30:20; 31:7, 14, 29; 32:10, 10, 10, 10, 12; 12, 13, 13, 15, 16, 16; 33:7, 7, 7, 9, 11, 11, 12, 12, 16, 16, 24, 24; 34:1, 4, 6, 9, 9, 11

Jos 1:18; 2:19, 23; 4:14; 5:3, 13, 13, 13, 14; 6:5, 7, 20; 7:3, 19, 24, 25, 26; 8:11, 14, 23; 9:6, 9, 9; 10:7, 15, 23, 24, 29, 31, 33, 33, 34, 36, 38, 43; 11:7, 9; 13:1; 14:6, 7, 13; 15:16, 17, 18, 18; 19:50; 20:4, 4, 5, 5; 22:5, 5, 14, 27, 30; 24:3, 3, 14, 22, 30, 33, 33

Jdg 1:3, 5, 6, 6, 7, 12, 13, 14, 14, 15, 24; 2:9; 3:10, 13, 15, 16, 19, 19, 19, 20, 23, 27, 28, 31; 4:6, 7, 10, 13, 14, 18, 18, 18, 19, 19, 21, 22, 22; 5:13, 25, 31; 6:12, 12, 13, 14, 15, 16, 17, 19, 20, 20, 23, 25, 27, 31, 31, 31, 31, 31, 32, 34, 34, 35; 7:1, 3, 5, 8, 9, 19; 8:1, 3, 4, 4, 8, 14, 14, 31; 9:3, 4, 4, 16, 19, 24, 25, 26, 28, 28, 33, 34, 35, 36, 38, 38, 40, 40, 44, 48, 48, 54, 54, 54, 54; 10:3, 6, 11:2, 3, 11, 15, 29, 34, 36; 11:2, 2, 3, 11, 15, 29, 34, 36; 12:5, 6, 6, 8, 11, 11, 11, 11, 13, 14; 14:2, 5, 11, 15, 18, 18, 19, 19, 24, 25, 26, 28, 28, 33, 34, 36, 38, 38, 40, 40, 44, 48, 48, 54, 54, 54, 54; 14:16:2, 2, 5, 5, 5, 5, 8, 9, 12, 14, 15, 16, 16, 19, 19, 20, 21, 21, 21, 24, 25, 26, 31, 31, 31; 17:9, 9, 10, 11; 18:3, 5, 15, 19, 25, 26; 19:1, 2, 2, 3, 3, 3, 4, 4, 7, 9, 9, 10, 12, 15, 18, 22, 25, 28; 20:23; 21:5

Ru 2:2, 4, 10; 3:13; 4:1, 15

1Sa 1:11, 17, 20, 22, 23, 23, 24, 24, 24, 27, 28; 2:3, 16, 16, 19, 19, 25, 25, 27, 28, 35, 36; 3:7, 13, 18, 18, 18, 18, 19; 5:3, 4; 6:3, 4, 8; 7:3, 9; 8:5, 10, 12; 9:5, 6, 13, 13, 16, 17; 10:1, 9, 10, 10, 11, 14, 16, 19, 21, 23, 24, 24, 26, 27, 27; 11:3, 5; 12:14, 24; 13:2, 7, 8, 10, 10, 14, 14, 15, 15; 14:2, 7, 13, 13, 19, 20, 34, 39, 43, 52, 52; 15:2, 12, 13, 16, 28, 32; 16:1, 3, 6, 7, 8, 11, 12, 13, 14, 15, 17, 18, 20, 21, 21, 21, 23; 17:7, 8, 9, 9, 19, 20, 24, 25, 25, 25, 27, 28, 28; 19:4, 7, 8, 11, 11, 11, 15, 15, 18, 18, 23; 20:2, 7, 17, 17, 24, 26, 30, 31, 32, 33, 33, 34, 35, 36, 40; 21:1, 5, 6, 11, 14, 14; 22:1, 2, 4, 6, 6, 7, 10, 10, 10, 13, 13, 15, 17; 23:3, 4, 7, 9, 14, 14, 17, 20, 22, 23; 24:1, 4, 4, 5, 6, 8, 19; 25:1, 1, 5, 6, 12, 17, 21, 22, 25, 35, 36, 36, 37, 39, 39, 40; 26:2, 3, 5, 7, 8, 8, 9, 10, 19, 24; 27:2, 4, 6, 12; 28:3, 3, 6, 7, 7, 8, 8, 9, 17, 20, 21, 23; 29:3, 4, 4, 4, 4, 6; 30:4, 6, 8, 9, 11, 11, 15, 16, 21; 31:3, 5

2Sa 1:3, 3, 4, 5, 6, 6, 7, 8, 10, 10, 11, 13, 14, 15, 15, 16; 2:1, 3, 5, 8, 9, 20, 21, 21, 23, 23, 32; 3:9, 11, 10, 20, 30, 20, 22, 23, 23, 24, 26, 27, 27, 27, 31, 34; 4:4, 6, 7, 7, 10, 10; 5:10, 12; 6:2, 7, 10, 12, 16; 7:1, 14, 15, 23; 8:4, 10, 10, 10, 13; 9:1, 2, 2, 3, 4, 5, 7, 9, 10; 10:2, 9,

12, 13, 13, 17; 11:1, 4, 7, 7, 8, 13, 13, 13, 15, 21, 22, 25, 27; 12:1, 1, 3, 3, 4, 4, 9, 17, 17, 18, 18, 18, 20, 21, 23, 23, 24; 13:2, 4, 4, 5, 5, 6, 7, 9, 9, 11, 12, 16, 17, 25, 25, 26, 27, 28, 29, 31, 32, 33; 15:1, 1, 2, 3, 4, 5, 9, 13, 14, 16, 17, 17, 18, 18, 22, 24, 26, 26, 30, 32; 16:1, 10, 10, 11, 11, 11, 13, 13, 14, 18; 17:2, 2, 2, 6, 10, 12, 12, 12, 12, 16, 22, 23, 24, 29; 18:1, 9, 11, 11, 15, 17, 17, 19, 20, 23, 30; 19:17, 17, 23, 25, 29, 30, 31, 37, 37, 38, 39, 40, 41; 20:5, 6, 6, 7, 8, 9, 10, 10, 11, 11, 12, 12, 14, 15, 17, 21; 21:4, 15, 17, 17, 17, 21; 22:1, 3, 12, 13, 24, 31; 23:9, 10, 11, 21, 21, 23; 24:2, 10, 13, 13, 13, 16, 18, 20, 22

1Ki 1:1, 2, 2, 4, 5, 5, 6, 6, 7, 13, 17, 20, 25, 33, 34, 35, 35, 38, 40, 41, 42, 44, 44, 45, 52, 52, 53, 53; 2:8, 9, 9, 16, 19, 22, 22, 25, 29, 30, 31, 31, 31, 34, 34, 36, 42, 46; 3:6, 6, 11, 16, 28; 4:10, 12, 13, 13, 24; 5:1, 3, 12; 8:5, 5, 24, 25, 31, 31, 32, 57, 58, 62, 65; 9:2, 3, 12, 12; 10:1, 2; 11:9, 10, 11, 18, 18, 19, 20, 20, 23, 24, 28, 29, 30, 34; 12:1, 3, 7, 8, 8, 8, 10, 10, 13, 14, 14, 15, 15, 18, 18, 18, 20, 20; 13:4, 4, 4, 6, 11, 13, 14, 14, 15, 15, 18, 18, 18, 19, 24, 24, 24, 26, 26, 26, 27, 29, 30, 31, 33; 14:3, 3, 10, 10, 11, 11, 13, 13, 13, 14, 18, 18, 22; 15:3, 4, 4, 5, 8, 27, 27, 28, 29; 16:4, 4, 4, 7, 7, 9, 10, 10, 11, 17, 18, 17, 17; 17:2, 6, 8, 17, 19, 19, 19, 21, 22, 23, 23; 18:7, 7, 8, 15, 16, 17, 21, 21, 21, 24, 30, 30; 19:5, 5, 6, 7, 9, 9, 13, 15, 17, 17, 18, 19, 19, 19, 20, 21, 21; 20:1, 2, 7, 8, 8, 9, 10, 11, 11, 16, 17, 22, 23, 31, 33, 33, 34, 34, 34, 35, 36, 36, 36, 36, 37, 37, 40, 41, 42; 21:4, 4, 5, 5, 6, 7, 10, 10, 10, 10, 13, 13, 13, 19, 19, 21; 22:7, 8, 11, 13, 15, 19, 19, 21, 22, 22, 22, 26, 27, 32, 32, 53

2Ki 1:5, 6, 6, 8, 9, 9, 10, 11, 11, 12, 13, 13, 15, 15, 15, 16; 2:2, 3, 4, 5, 6, 12, 13, 14, 15, 15, 15, 16, 16, 16, 17, 17, 18, 23, 23; 3:11, 12, 12, 13, 15, 26, 26, 27, 27; 4:1, 5, 8, 10, 12, 13, 19, 20, 20, 21, 21, 21, 27, 29, 29, 31, 31, 35, 36, 38; 5:1, 3, 5, 6, 8, 10, 13, 15, 16, 19, 19, 20, 21, 24, 24, 25, 26; 6:6, 10, 10, 13, 13, 15, 18, 20, 28, 28, 29, 30, 31, 32, 32, 32, 33; 7:17, 17, 20, 20; 8:6, 7, 8, 9, 9, 9, 10, 10, 14, 14, 19, 19, 21, 21, 29; 9:1, 2, 2, 6, 8, 8, 11, 13, 15, 15, 17, 18, 21, 25, 25, 26, 27, 27, 28, 28, 32, 36; 10:3, 4, 7, 8, 9, 11, 15, 15, 15, 15, 16, 16, 17, 18, 22, 24, 24, 25; 11:2, 2, 2, 4, 8, 12, 12, 12, 12, 15; 12:2, 21, 21; 13:4, 9, 14, 15, 15, 19, 20, 25; 14:19, 19, 19, 20, 21; 15:7, 10, 10, 10, 14, 16, 19, 25, 25, 30, 30; 16:5, 9; 17:2, 3, 3, 4, 4, 17, 27, 36, 36, 36; 18:5, 5, 6, 7, 7, 15, 21, 30, 36, 36, 37; 19:3, 7, 7, 16, 21, 37; 20:1, 1, 4, 14; 21:6, 11, 23; 22:18; 23:1, 2, 17, 18, 25, 25, 25, 26, 29, 29, 30, 30, 30, 30; 24:1, 2, 12; 25:5, 5, 6, 6, 7, 7, 25, 25, 28, 28, 29, 30

1Ch 2:3, 3, 4, 9, 19, 19, 21, 24, 29, 35; 3:1, 4, 5; 4:6, 9, 10; 5:2, 20; 7:22; 9:20; 10:3, 9, 14; 11:9, 10, 10, 11, 12, 23, 23, 25, 42; 12:19, 20, 22, 23, 27; 13:10; 14:1, 2, 10, 14, 16, 17; 15:1, 2, 13, 27, 29; 16:5, 9, 9, 29, 30; 17:13, 13, 14, 25; 18:4, 10, 10, 10; 19:2, 2, 10, 14, 14, 17; 20:7; 21:11, 12, 15, 20, 26, 28; 22:6, 9; 23:13; 24:19; 26:5, 27:7; 28:6, 9, 9, 9; 29:22, 23, 25, 25, 30

2Ch 1:1, 1, 3, 7; 2:3, 3, 4, 4, 6, 6, 6, 6, 14, 15; 5:6; 6:15, 16, 22, 22, 23; 7:8, 12; 8:18; 9:1; 10:1, 3, 7, 8, 8, 8, 10, 10, 18, 18; 11:13, 15, 18, 19, 20, 22; 12:1, 3, 12, 12; 13:3, 5, 7, 10, 11, 19, 20; 14:1, 5, 6, 7, 10, 13; 15:2, 2, 2, 2, 4, 5, 5, 9, 9, 15; 16:7, 9, 10, 10, 14, 14, 14; 17:11, 14, 14, 17:11, 11, 11; 18:2, 2, 2, 3, 6, 7, 9, 12, 14, 15, 20, 20, 20, 21, 25, 26, 30, 31, 31, 31, 32; 19:2, 20:30, 30; 21:7, 9, 9, 11, 11, 14, 16; 24:3, 6, 16, 21, 21, 22, 22, 25, 25, 25, 26, 26, 27, 27, 28, 28; 26:1, 5, 7, 7, 17, 17, 17, 20, 20, 20, 23; 27:5, 5, 9; 28:5, 5, 5, 16, 20, 20, 20, 21, 23, 23, 24, 27, 27; 29:6, 11, 11, 11, 29; 30:9; 31:10, 15; 32:3, 6, 7, 7, 8, 9, 15, 17, 21, 24, 24, 25, 25, 29, 29, 29, 31, 31, 31, 33, 33; 33:6, 11, 11, 13, 13, 18, 19, 20, 20; 34:26; 35:20, 21, 22, 22, 24, 24, 24; 36:1, 3, 4, 6, 6, 6, 8, 10, 13, 17, 20, 23, 23, 23

Ezr 1:2, 3, 3, 4; 4:2, 6; 5:1; 5:7, 15; 6:11; 7:6, 6, 9, 26; 8:3, 4, 5, 6, 7, 9, 10, 11, 12, 19, 21, 22, 22, 33; 10:1

Ne 1:5, 11; 2:1, 6, 6; 3:2, 8, 8, 10, 12, 16, 17, 17, 18, 19, 20, 21, 22, 23, 23, 24, 25, 29, 30, 30, 31; 4:3; 6:8, 12, 12, 18, 19; 8:4; 9:7, 7, 8; 11:8; 13:5, 7, 26, 26, 26, 28

Est 1:3, 12, 14, 17, 19; 2:2, 9, 9, 20; 3:1, 1, 2, 2, 4, 5, 6; 4:4, 5, 5, 7, 7, 8, 8, 10, 11; 5:4, 9, 11, 11, 14; 6:3, 3, 4, 5, 5, 6, 9, 11, 11, 13, 13, 13, 14; 7:7, 9; 8:3, 7; 9:3, 24; 7:15; 8:3

Job 1:2, 8, 10; 2:3, 3, 3, 8, 9, 11, 11, 11, 12, 13, 13; 3:20; 4:4; 6:10, 14; 7:8, 10, 17, 17, 18, 18; 8:4, 18, 18; 9:3, 3, 4, 11, 11,

12, 12, 13, 14, 14, 32, 34, 35; 11:10, 13; 12:4, 5, 13, 16; 13:7, 9, 15, 15, 16; 14:6, 20, 20, 22, 22; 15:21, 24, 24, 26, 31; 18:6, 7, 9, 9, 10, 10, 11, 11, 14, 20, 21; 19:11, 16, 28; 20:7, 9, 9, 9, 11, 14, 16, 22, 23, 23, 24, 25, 26, 26, 27, 29; 21:15, 15, 19, 21, 27; 23:3, 4, 7, 8, 8, 9, 13, 14, 15; 24:1, 10, 20, 20, 23; 25:2; 26:2, 3, 6, 14; 27:9, 15, 20, 20, 23; 29:12, 12, 13; 30:25; 31:14, 15, 19, 24, 37, 37; 32:13, 14; 33:13, 23, 24, 24, 26; 34:11, 13, 17, 19, 27, 28, 29; 35:6, 6, 7, 14, 14, 14; 36:11, 22, 23, 26; 37:16, 18, 19, 20, 23, 24; 39:11, 11, 12, 20, 23; 40:2, 2, 9, 11, 12, 19, 19, 20, 22, 22; 41:4, 5, 5, 6, 6, 6, 8, 9, 9, 10, 11, 13, 12, 22, 26, 34; 42:8, 11, 11, 11, 11, 11, 11

Ps 2:12; 3:2; 4:3, 3; 5:12; 7:4, 4, 5, 13; 8:4, 4, 5, 5, 6; 10:9; 11:5; 12:5, 5, 5; 13:4; 17:13, 13; 18:T, 6, 11, 12, 23, 30; 20:6; 21:2, 3, 4, 5, 6, 6; 22:8, 8, 8, 8, 23, 23, 23, 24, 24, 25, 26, 29; 24:6; 25:12, 14; 28:7, 7; 32:6, 10; 33:2, 3, 8, 18, 21; 34:T, 5, 6, 6, 7, 8, 9, 19, 22; 35:8, 8, 10, 10, 10, 10, 25; 37:5, 7, 7, 12, 13, 22, 22, 24, 32, 33, 33, 36, 40; 41:1, 2, 2, 3, 8; 42:5, 11; 43:5; 44:16; 45:11; 49:7, 17; 50:3, 3, 18, 23; 51:T; 52:T, 6; 53:5; 55:12, 20; 56:T; 57:3; 59:T; 61:7; 62:1, 4, 5, 8, 8; 63:11; 64:4, 10; 66:6, 17; 67:7; 68:1, 1, 4, 4, 33; 69:26, 30, 34; 71:11, 11, 11; 72:9, 11, 11, 12, 15, 15, 17, 17; 74:14; 76:11, 11; 78:17, 34, 36, 36, 37, 40, 40, 58, 58, 70, 71; 79:10; 81:15; 85:9, 13; 89:7, 20, 21, 22, 22, 23, 24, 27, 28, 28, 33, 41, 43, 45; 91:2, 14, 14, 15, 15, 15, 15, 16, 16; 92:15; 94:12, 13; 95:2; 96:6, 9; 97:2, 3, 7; 98:1; 100:4; 101:5, 5; 103:11, 13, 17; 104:34; 105:2, 2, 19, 20, 20, 21; 106:7, 10, 23, 29, 31, 32, 43; 107:32, 32, 41; 109:6, 7, 12, 17, 17, 19, 19, 30, 31; 111:5; 113:8; 116:2; 117:1; 119:2, 42; 120:6; 126:6; 130:7; 135:1; 136:4, 5, 6, 7, 10, 13, 16, 17; 140:11; 141:5; 142:2, 2; 144:3, 3; 145:18, 18, 19, 20; 147:11; 148:1, 2, 2, 3, 3, 4, 14; 149:2, 2, 3; 150:1, 2, 2, 3, 3, 4, 4, 5, 5

Pr 3:6; 6:16; 7:10, 13, 13, 13, 20, 21, 21; 8:9, 30, 30, 30; 9:4, 4, 4, 16, 16, 16; 10:13, 13, 24, 26; 11:18, 26, 26, 27; 12:14; 13:6, 18, 24, 24; 14:2, 6, 7, 31, 33, 35; 15:9, 10, 12, 14, 21; 16:7, 13, 22, 26, 29; 17:8, 11, 24, 25; 18:9, 13, 16, 16, 17; 19:6, 7, 7, 7, 17, 19; 20:2, 7, 16, 19; 21:25; 22:15; 23:6, 13, 14, 24; 24:18, 18, 24, 24, 25, 29; 25:13, 21, 21; 26:4, 12, 15, 17, 24, 25, 27; 27:11, 13, 14, 22; 28:8, 11, 17, 22; 29:20, 21, 23; 30:5; 31:1, 6, 7, 12

Ecc 2:26; 3:14, 22, 22; 4:10, 10, 12, 12, 16; 5:12, 18, 19, 20; 6:2, 10, 12; 7:14; 8:3, 4, 6, 7, 12, 15, 15; 9:2, 2, 4, 17; 10:1, 3, 8, 14, 14; 11:8

SS 1:2; 3:1, 1, 1, 2, 2, 3, 4, 4, 4, 11; 5:4, 6, 6, 6, 8; 6:1

Isa 3:10, 11, 11; 5:19, 23; 6:4; 7:4; 8:13, 13, 17; 9:11, 13; 10:6, 6, 15, 23, 26; 11:2, 3; 14:25, 29; 15:4, 9; 16:3; 20:1; 21:6, 14, 14; 22:11, 16, 21, 21, 23, 24; 24:2; 25:9, 9, 10; 26:3; 27:5, 7, 7, 7; 28:6, 26, 26; 29:12, 16, 16, 16, 21, 23; 30:18, 32; 31:4, 6, 8; 33:16; 36:3, 6, 21, 21, 22; 37:3, 7, 7, 22, 38; 38:1, 1; 39:3; 40:3, 10, 10, 10, 13, 14, 14, 14, 14, 17, 17, 18, 20; 41:2, 2, 2, 7; 42:1, 25, 25, 25; 43:7, 7, 7; 44:3, 14, 20; 45:1, 1, 9, 9, 10, 13, 24, 24; 46:7, 7, 7, 7; 48:14, 15, 15; 49:5, 7, 7, 25; 50:4, 8, 10; 51:2, 2, 2; 52:7, 15; 53:2, 2, 3, 3, 4, 5, 6, 10, 10, 12; 55:4, 4; 57:15, 17, 18, 18, 18, 19, 19, 19; 58:5, 7, 13; 59:15, 16, 16, 19; 62:7, 11, 11; 63:2, 11, 14; 64:4, 4, 5; 66:2

Jer 2:3, 15, 37; 3:1; 4:2, 2; 6:11; 8:6; 9:24; 10:25, 25; 11:19; 15:8; 18:18; 19:14; 20:2, 3, 9, 10, 10, 15, 16; 21:1, 9, 12; 22:10, 10, 12, 13, 13, 14, 15, 16, 18, 18; 23:24, 28, 28; 26:8, 8, 13, 19, 19, 21, 22, 23, 23, 24, 24; 27:6, 6, 6, 7, 7, 11, 12; 28:9, 14, 14; 29:26, 31; 30:8, 10, 10, 21; 31:2, 10, 10, 11, 11, 11, 20, 20, 20; 32:3, 3, 4, 5, 9, 10; 33:13; 34:2, 14; 36:4, 8, 15, 22, 31; 37:4, 14, 14, 15, 15, 17, 17, 21; 38:6, 11, 13, 14, 27, 27; 39:5, 5, 5, 7, 7, 9, 12, 14, 14; 40:1, 2, 5, 5, 5, 9, 9, 14; 41:1, 2, 2, 3, 7, 11, 12, 13, 16; 42:8, 9, 11; 44:20; 45:4; 46:10, 25, 27; 48:11, 12, 17, 17, 19, 26, 27, 35, 35, 39; 49:5, 8, 8, 19; 50:16, 17, 17, 32, 32, 43; 51:3, 3, 44; 52:8, 9, 9, 11, 11, 11, 31, 32, 33, 34

La 1:17; 2:19; 3:24, 25, 25, 28, 30, 30

Eze 1:3; 2:2; 3:18, 20, 20, 27, 27; 7:15; 9:4; 5; 10:7; 12:13, 13, 14, 14; 13:22; 14:4, 7, 7, 8, 8, 9, 9, 10, 10; 17:6, 6, 7, 7, 12, 13, 13, 15, 15, 16, 16, 17, 20, 20, 20, 20; 18:13, 20, 20, 22; 19:4, 4, 5, 8, 8, 9, 9, 9; 21:26, 26, 27; 24:27; 28:9, 9, 12; 29:2, 20; 30:11, 24; 31:4, 4, 4, 8, 8, 9, 9, 11, 11, 11, 12, 12, 12, 13, 16, 16, 17; 32:2, 21, 21, 22, 22, 22, 25, 32; 33:3, 32, 33; 34:10, 10, 10, 14, 17, 19, 23, 34, 35; 5:6, 9, 11, 17, 19,

Da 2:1, 16, 22, 24, 25, 46, 48, 48; 3:28; 4:8, 16, 16, 19, 23, 34, 35; 5:6, 9, 11, 17, 17, 19,

19, 20, 21, 24, 29; 6:3, 3, 4, 5, 6, 14, 16, 18, 18, 22, 23, 23; 7:10, 10, 10, 13, 13, 14, 14, 16, 27; 8:4, 6, 7, 7, 7, 7, 7, 11, 16, 17, 17, 17, 18, 18, 22, 23, 23, 25, 26, 30, 40, 40, 44, 45; 12:7

Hos 1:3, 4, 6; 4:17; 5:6, 14; 7:5, 9, 10; 8:3, 11, 12; 9:4, 17; 11:1, 7; 12:2, 4, 4, 14, 14, 14; 13:11, 13; 14:2, 4, 8, 8

Joel 2:13, 14, 20

Am 1:5, 8; 2:3; 3:5, 14; 5:8, 10, 10, 11, 19, 19; 6:10, 10, 10; 9:13

Ob 1:7

Jnh 1:6, 6, 8, 10, 11, 15; 3:6, 6; 4:5, 6

Mic 1:4; 2:7; 3:5; 5:5; 6:5; 7:9, 15

Na 1:5, 6, 7, 15

Hab 2:4, 5, 5, 6, 6, 6, 9, 12, 15, 15, 15, 19, 20; 3:5

Zep 1:6; 2:11; 3:9

Hag 1:12;

Zec 2:3, 4; 3:1, 4, 4, 4, 5; 4:11, 12; 5:4; 6:12; 8:10, 23; 9:8, 8; 10:4, 4, 4, 4; 12:1, 10, 10; 13:3, 3, 3, 6

Mal 2:5, 5, 12, 17; 3:16, 17, 18, 18, 18; 4:4

Mt 1:20, 24, 24; 2:2, 3, 5, 8, 8, 11, 11, 13; 3:5, 6, 13, 14, 15, 15, 15, 16, 16; 4:3, 5, 5, 6, 7, 8, 8, 9, 10, 11, 24; 8:1, 2, 3, 4, 5, 5, 7, 7, 16, 18, 19, 20, 22, 23, 25, 25, 27, 28, 31, 34, 34; 9:2, 9, 9, 10, 14, 14, 15, 16, 18, 19, 20, 22, 24, 27, 28, 28, 32; 10:1, 4, 28, 32, 33, 40; 11:3, 15, 27; 12:2, 3, 4, 4, 10, 10, 14, 14, 15, 16, 18, 22, 22, 22, 32, 32, 46, 47, 48, 48; 13:2, 9, 10, 12, 12, 27, 28, 36, 43, 51, 57; 14:2, 3, 3, 4, 5, 5, 9, 9, 13, 15, 15, 19, 22, 24, 26, 28, 31, 31, 35, 35, 36; 15:4, 12, 15, 22, 23, 25, 30, 32, 32, 36; 16:1, 22, 26; 17:3, 9, 10, 14, 14, 16, 17, 22, 22; 18:2, 6, 15, 15, 17, 18, 21, 25, 26, 26, 27, 28, 28, 29, 30, 32, 34; 19:2, 3, 3, 7, 10, 13, 16, 16, 17, 20, 20, 22, 24, 25; 20:7, 18, 19, 19, 20, 20, 20, 21, 22, 23, 23, 25, 27, 27, 28; 21:7, 16, 21, 21, 21, 28, 28, 28; 22:2, 4, 5, 6, 9, 10, 14, 16, 18, 19, 24, 24, 34, 35, 37, 37, 42; 23:3, 3, 4, 4, 4, 18, 18, 21, 35, 37, 38, 40, 43, 44, 45, 46, 46, 49, 54, 55, 56, 57; 24:2, 3, 3, 3, 7, 10, 13, 16, 16, 20, 20, 20, 21, 22, 25, 26, 27, 27, 28, 29, 30, 32, 34, 34, 34, 38; 9:2, 7, 11, 13, 13, 15, 15, 18, 18, 18, 19, 19, 20, 20, 20, 21, 22, 22, 23, 23, 25, 25, 26, 26, 27, 27, 28, 28, 31, 32, 36, 37, 38, 38; 42; 10:1, 2, 2, 10, 13, 17, 18, 20, 21, 21, 21, 24, 28, 32, 32, 34, 34, 34, 35, 37, 39, 42, 48, 49, 49, 51, 51; 11:2, 2, 3, 3, 4, 7, 7, 18, 21, 27, 28, 31; 12:3, 3, 3, 4, 4, 4, 5, 6, 7, 8, 8, 8, 12, 12, 13, 13, 14, 14, 14, 19, 24, 28, 29, 32, 32, 34, 34, 37, 43; 13:1, 2, 3, 14, 15, 16, 21; 14:1, 1, 10, 11, 11, 12, 13, 19, 21, 29, 30, 33, 35, 40, 41, 42, 43, 44, 44, 45, 45, 46, 46, 49, 50, 51, 51, 52; 15:1, 1, 2, 2, 3, 4, 7, 8, 10, 12, 13, 14, 15, 16, 17, 18, 19, 19, 20, 20, 20, 20, 22, 23, 24, 25, 27, 29, 32, 32, 36, 36, 39, 41, 41, 41, 44, 46, 46, 46, 46, 47; 16:1, 6, 7, 10, 14

Lk 1:11, 12, 12, 13, 17, 19, 29, 32, 50, 59, 62, 66, 74, 75; 2:7, 7, 22, 22, 25, 26, 27, 28, 33, 38, 40, 40, 44, 44, 45, 45, 47, 48; 3:7, 10, 11, 11, 11, 12, 14, 19, 22; 4:3, 5, 5, 6, 8, 8, 9, 9, 9, 12, 13, 14, 17, 20, 22, 29, 29, 35, 35, 35, 37, 38, 40, 42, 42, 42; 5:1, 3, 5, 9, 11, 12, 18, 19, 20, 27, 28, 28, 29, 30; 6:3, 4, 4, 7, 7, 13, 17, 19, 19, 29, 30; 7:2, 3, 3, 4, 6, 6, 9, 9, 9, 11, 14, 15, 17, 19, 19, 20, 20, 36, 36, 38, 38, 39, 40, 40, 43, 49; 8:1, 3, 8, 9, 18, 19, 19, 20, 24, 28, 28, 30, 31, 32, 33, 34, 35, 37, 37, 38, 38, 39, 41, 41, 42, 44, 44, 46, 46, 47, 47, 48, 49, 50, 51, 51, 52; 9:2, 4, 13, 18, 20, 20, 21, 22, 25, 26, 27, 28, 29, 29, 30, 30, 31, 32, 32, 33, 34, 34, 34, 35, 36, 37, 37, 38; 10:16, 22, 25, 26, 27, 28, 30, 30, 31, 31, 32, 33, 34, 34, 36, 36, 36, 37, 37, 38; 11:1, 5, 5, 6, 8, 8, 8, 11, 17, 19,

12, 13, 16, 16, 22, 22, 22, 26, 27, 37, 37, 39, 45, 53, 53, 54, 54; 12:5, 5, 8, 10, 10, 13, 14; 14:1, 2, 4, 4, 4, 5, 6, 18, 25, 29, 31; 16:1, 2, 5, 7, 8, 10, 10, 11, 16, 18, 19, 20, 22, 23, 23; 17:2, 2; 18:3, 7, 15, 16, 18, 19, 19, 22, 31, 33, 33, 37, 39, 40, 40, 40, 42, 43; 19:2, 4, 4, 5, 5, 6, 6, 7, 8, 9, 14, 14, 15, 15, 16, 17, 22, 24, 27, 29, 30, 32, 34, 35, 35, 37, 41, 47, 48; 20:1, 2, 5, 10, 10, 11, 11, 11, 12, 13, 13, 14, 14, 15, 18, 19, 20, 21, 27, 27, 28; 21:3, 5, 7, 12, 15, 15, 16, 16, 16, 17, 17, 17, 19, 21, 22, 23

Jn 1:3, 3, 4, 7, 10, 10, 11, 12, 15, 18, 19, 21, 22, 25, 29, 31, 32, 33, 33, 37, 38, 39, 40, 41, 42, 42, 43, 45, 45, 46, 46, 47, 47, 48, 48, 49, 50, 51, 51; 2:3, 10, 11, 18; 3:2, 2, 3, 4, 9, 10, 11, 15, 15, 16, 17, 17, 18, 26, 27, 31, 34, 36; 4:9, 10, 11, 14, 14, 15, 16, 18, 26, 27, 28, 29, 30, 31, 32, 33, 36, 40, 40, 41, 42, 45, 47, 47, 48, 49, 50, 50, 51, 51, 52, 53; 5:6, 6, 7, 8, 10, 12, 14, 14, 15, 16, 18, 20, 20, 23, 24, 27, 38; 6:2, 5, 6, 7, 8, 15, 15, 16, 17, 22, 24, 25, 27, 28, 29, 31, 32, 32, 34, 36, 37, 38, 40, 40, 44, 54, 56, 64, 65, 65, 66, 66, 67, 7, 8, 9; 7:1, 3, 5, 11, 12, 15, 18, 19, 21, 25, 25, 27, 28, 29, 30, 34; 8:7, 8, 9, 11, 12, 15, 16, 20, 24, 28, 29, 30, 34, 37, 38, 40, 40, 41, 44, 48, 54, 56, 57, 59; 9:2, 3, 4, 7, 8, 10, 11, 12, 14, 14, 15, 16, 17, 19, 24, 26, 27, 29, 30, 32, 34, 34, 35, 35, 35, 36, 37, 38, 38; 10:3, 3, 4, 4, 18, 20, 24, 25, 25, 27, 28, 29, 30, 31, 31, 31, 33, 34, 37, 38, 38; 11:3, 4, 6, 6, 6, 7, 9, 10, 12, 15, 15, 15, 16, 16, 16, 17, 20, 24, 27, 28, 29, 29, 30, 32, 34, 35, 35, 37, 38, 41, 44, 45, 47; 12:2, 3, 9, 10, 14, 14, 15, 16, 17, 18, 20, 22, 23, 24, 28, 32, 32, 34, 34, 38; 13:1, 2, 3, 4, 4, 6, 6, 6, 7, 7, 8, 9, 17; 14:5, 7, 9, 9, 11, 14, 15, 16, 20, 21, 21, 23; 15:5, 21; 16:5, 7, 19, 29; 17:2; 18:2, 4, 5, 5, 12, 13, 18, 20, 22, 23, 24, 25, 26, 28, 29, 30, 30, 30, 31, 31, 31, 33, 33, 33, 34, 37, 38; 19:1, 2, 3, 4, 4, 6, 6, 6, 6, 6, 7, 9, 12, 13, 14, 15, 16, 16, 16, 17, 18, 21, 26, 28, 29, 30, 30, 30, 31, 31, 31, 33, 34, 37, 38; 20:2, 6, 13, 15, 15, 16, 16, 25, 28, 29; 21:3, 5, 7, 12, 15, 15, 16, 16, 17, 17, 17, 19, 21, 22, 23

Ac 1:6, 9, 11; 2:22, 23, 25, 30; 3:4, 7, 7, 9, 10, 13, 13, 16, 16, 22, 26; 4:10; 5:6, 6, 6, 11, 21, 31, 32, 36, 37, 37, 40; 6:11, 12, 12, 14, 15; 7:3, 4, 5, 5, 5, 8, 8, 9, 10, 10, 18, 21, 21, 24, 24, 27, 30, 31, 33, 35, 37, 38, 39, 40, 47, 54, 57, 58, 58; 8:2, 11, 20, 30, 30, 31, 35, 38, 38, 39, 40; 9:3, 4, 4, 7, 11, 13, 13, 14, 15, 15, 16, 17, 21, 22, 24, 25, 25, 26, 27, 27, 29, 30, 34, 35, 38; 10:3, 3, 4, 4, 7, 11, 13, 15, 16, 17, 19, 20, 22, 24, 25, 27, 30, 31, 33; 34, 35, 37, 38, 39, 40; 10:3, 4, 4, 7, 11, 11, 15, 19, 22, 25, 26; 12:4, 4, 7, 17, 19, 20, 23; 13:9, 13, 13, 17, 17, 20, 20, 22, 27, 28, 30, 31, 33; 34, 35, 36, 37, 38, 47; 14:9; 15:21, 38; 16:3, 3, 17, 27, 28, 28, 31; 17:15, 15, 18, 19, 19, 21, 22, 28, 28, 30, 31; 18:7, 7, 8, 10, 11, 12, 14, 15, 17; 7:3, 4, 5, 5, 5, 8, 10, 11, 13, 17, 20, 22, 26, 26; 19:2, 3, 3, 4, 5, 9, 13; 11, 12, 26, 26; 12:4, 7, 8, 8, 9, 10, 12, 13; 13:9, 11, 22, 22; 14:9; 15:21, 38; 16:3, 3, 3, 9, 32; 17:15, 15, 16, 17, 18, 19, 19, 23, 27, 27, 31; 34; 18:12, 17, 18, 20, 26, 26, 27; 19:2, 4, 4, 22, 30, 31, 31, 33, 34; 18:12, 17, 18, 20, 26, 26, 27; 19:2, 4, 22, 30, 31, 31, 33, 34; 20:1, 3, 4, 10, 10, 10, 14; 21:8, 11, 11, 12, 20, 27, 27, 29, 30, 31, 33, 33, 34, 36, 40; 22:9, 13, 18, 20, 20, 22, 24, 25, 27, 28, 29, 30, 31; 23:2, 3, 3, 9, 10, 10, 15, 15, 16, 16, 17, 18, 18, 18, 19, 19, 20, 23, 24, 24, 27; 19:2, 4, 4, 4, 10, 34; 18:12, 17, 18, 20, 26, 26, 27; 19:2, 4, 4, 10, 34; 20:1, 3, 4, 10, 10, 10, 10, 14, 18, 37; 21:8, 11, 11, 12, 20, 27, 27, 30, 31, 33, 33, 34, 36, 40; 22:9, 13, 18, 19, 19, 20, 20, 21, 22, 24, 24, 27, 28, 29, 30, 30, 31; 23:2, 3, 3, 9, 10, 10, 11, 12, 14, 15, 19, 19; 24:2, 7, 8, 10, 23, 23, 24, 26, 26, 26, 26; 25:2, 2, 2, 3, 3, 3, 5, 16, 16, 19, 20, 21, 21, 21, 22, 26, 26, 26; 27:3; 28:6, 8, 16, 21, 23, 23, 30, 31

Ro 1:20, 21; 3:26; 4:3, 4, 5, 5, 17, 22, 23, 24; 5:9, 14; 6:4, 6, 8, 9; 7:4; 8:11, 17, 20, 32, 32, 37; 9:11, 16, 16, 20, 33; 10:9, 11, 12, 14, 14; 11:4, 35, 35, 36, 36, 36; 12:8; 13:4, 14; 14:1, 3, 3, 3, 3, 4, 14, 14, 15; 15:11, 12; 16:25

1Co 1:5, 30, 31; 2:2, 9, 11, 14, 16; 3:17, 18; 5:3; 7:12, 12, 13, 15, 17, 18, 18, 36; 8:3, 6, 6, 10; 10:12; 11:14, 28, 34; 12:18; 14:2, 11, 13, 28, 28, 37, 38; 15:27, 27, 28, 28, 28, 38; 16:2, 2, 11, 11, 11, 12, 22

2Co 1:19, 20, 20; 2:7, 7, 8; 5:9, 15, 16, 21, 21; 6:1; 7:14, 15; 8:18; 9:7; 10:7, 17; 11:4; 12:18; 13:4, 4

Gal 1:1, 8, 9, 16, 18; 2:11, 13; 3:6; 4:29; 5:8; 6:6, 6

Eph 1:4, 10, 11, 17, 20, 20, 22, 23; 2:18; 3:12, 20, 21; 4:15, 21, 21, 28, 28, 28; 6:9

Php 1:29; 2:7, 9, 9, 22, 23, 27, 27, 28, 28, 29; 3:9, 10

Col 1:16, 16, 16, 17, 19, 20, 20; 2:6, 7, 9, 10, 12, 12, 12, 13; 3:4, 10, 10, 17; 4:10, 13

1Th 4:14; 5:10

2Th 1:12; 2:1, 9; 3:14, 15, 15

1Ti 1:16; 5:1
2Ti 1:12, 18; 2:4, 4, 11, 11, 12, 12, 26; 4:11, 14
Tit 1:16;
Phm 1:12, 15, 17
Heb 1:5, 6; 2:3, 6, 6, 7, 7, 7, 8, 8, 8, 10, 13, 14, 16, 16, 17; 3:2, 2; 4:13; 5:5, 7, 7, 9; 6:6; 7:1, 6, 10, 21, 21, 22; 9:9, 28; 10:30, 38; 11:5,6, 6, 9, 11, 12, 19, 19, 27; 12:2, 3, 5, 25, 25, 25; 13:13, 15
Jas 1:5, 5, 6, 12; 2:3, 3, 5, 14, 23; 3:13; 4:17, 17; 5:13, 13, 14, 14, 14, 15, 15, 19, 20
1Pe 1:8, 21, 21, 21; 2:6, 9, 14, 23; 3:6, 10, 11, 11, 22; 4:5, 11, 11, 16, 16, 16, 19; 5:7, 11
2Pe 1:3, 17, 18; 3:14, 15, 18
1Jn 1:5, 5, 6, 10; 2:3, 4, 4, 5, 5, 6, 8, 10, 13, 14, 15, 27, 27, 28, 28, 29; 3:1, 2, 2, 3, 5, 6, 6, 6, 9, 12, 15, 17, 17, 19, 22, 24, 24; 4:9, 13, 15, 16, 19, 21; 5:1, 1, 1, 10, 14, 15, 16, 18, 20, 20
2Jn 1:10, 10, 11
Jude 1:9, 15, 24
Rev 1:1, 4, 5, 6, 7, 7, 17; 2:7, 7, 11, 17, 17, 17, 26, 28, 29; 3:6, 12, 12, 12, 13, 20, 20, 21, 22; 4:8, 9, 10, 10; 5:1, 7, 13, 14; 6:2, 2, 4, 4, 5, 8, 8, 16; 7:14, 15; 8:3; 9:1; 10:6, 9; 12:9, 11; 13:2, 4, 5, 5, 7, 7, 8, 9, 12, 18; 14:1, 7, 7, 15, 18; 16:8, 9; 17:14; 19:5, 7, 10, 11, 14, 19, 20, 20, 21; 20:2, 3, 3, 3, 6, 11; 21:6; 22:3, 11, 11, 11, 11, 17, 17, 17, 18

HIS (8478)

Ge 1:11, 12, 12, 21, 24, 24, 25, 25, 27; 2:2, 2, 3, 7, 21, 24, 24, 24, 25; 3:8, 15, 20, 21, 22; 4:1, 2, 4, 4, 5, 5, 7, 8, 8, 17, 17, 21, 23, 25, 25, 26; 5:3, 3, 3, 29; 6:3, 5, 6, 9, 12, 20; 7:2, 2, 7, 7, 7, 13, 14, 14, 14; 8:9, 18, 18, 18, 21, 21; 9:1, 6, 8, 21, 22, 22, 24, 24, 25, 26, 27; 10:5, 10, 15, 25, 25; 11:28, 28, 31, 31, 31, 31; 12:5, 5, 8, 11, 12, 17, 20, 20; 13:1, 3, 3, 10, 12, 18; 14:12, 14, 14, 14, 15, 16, 16, 17; 16:3, 11, 12, 12, 15; 17:3, 14, 14, 17, 17, 19, 19, 23, 23, 23, 24, 24, 25, 25, 26, 27; 18:2, 19, 19, 33, 33; 19:1, 3, 14, 14, 16, 16, 16, 26, 30, 30, 37, 38; 20:2, 7, 8, 14, 17, 17; 21:2, 3, 4, 5, 5, 7, 11, 21, 22, 32; 22:3, 3, 3, 4, 5, 6, 6, 7, 9, 10, 10, 13, 13, 13, 17, 19, 21, 24; 23:3, 6, 9, 10, 18, 19; 24:2, 2, 7, 9, 9, 10, 10, 10, 11, 20, 21, 21, 26, 27, 27, 29, 30, 30, 32, 32, 40, 48, 59, 61, 63, 67, 67, 67; 25:6, 8, 9, 10, 11, 17, 18, 21, 21, 25, 26, 26, 26, 28, 30, 33, 34, 34; 26:7, 8, 11, 11, 15, 17, 18, 18, 25, 26, 26; 27:1, 1, 5, 10, 11, 13, 14, 14, 14, 16, 16, 18, 19, 20, 22, 23, 23, 26, 27, 30, 30, 30, 31, 31, 32, 34, 34, 37, 38, 38, 39, 40, 41, 41; 28:7, 7, 8, 9, 11, 16, 18; 29:1, 3, 6, 10, 10, 10, 11, 13, 13, 23, 24, 24, 28, 29, 29, 32, 33, 34, 35; 30:6, 8, 11, 13, 14, 18, 20, 24, 35, 40; 31:4, 17, 17, 18, 18, 18, 19, 21, 23, 25, 25, 46, 53, 54, 55, 55, 55; 32:1, 3, 13, 13, 16, 16, 20, 22, 22, 22, 25, 31; 33:1, 3, 4, 5, 14, 16, 17, 18, 19; 34:3, 4, 5, 5, 5, 5, 13, 16, 20, 24, 24, 24, 25, 26; 35:2, 7, 10, 18, 18, 21, 22, 27, 29, 29; 36:2, 6, 6, 6, 6, 6, 24, 32, 33, 34, 34, 35, 35, 39; 37:1, 2, 2, 2, 3, 3, 4, 4, 5, 8, 8, 8, 9, 10, 10, 11, 11, 12, 17, 20, 22, 23, 23, 26, 26, 27, 29, 30, 34, 34, 34, 35, 35, 35; 38:1, 3, 4, 5, 6, 9, 9, 9, 11, 11, 12, 12, 13, 16, 20, 28, 29, 29, 30, 30, 30; 39:2, 3, 3, 4, 4, 4, 5, 7, 8, 9, 9, 12, 12, 13, 15, 16, 16, 18, 19, 19, 19, 23; 40:1, 2, 5, 5, 7, 9, 13, 13, 20, 20, 21; 41:8, 8, 10, 11, 12, 14, 37, 38, 42, 42, 42, 44; 42:1, 4, 7, 8, 21, 22, 25, 27, 27, 27, 28, 35, 37, 38; 43:8 16, 21, 29, 29, 29, 30, 30, 33, 33; 45:1, 3, 3, 4, 8, 15, 16, 23, 24; 46:1, 1, 4, 6, 7, 7, 7, 7, 7, 8, 8, 15, 15, 18, 25, 26, 28, 28, 29, 29, 29, 31, 31; 47:2, 3, 7, 11, 11, 12, 12, 20, 29; 48:1, 9, 12, 12, 13, 13, 14, 14, 14, 17, 17, 17, 18, 18, 19, 19, 19; 49:1, 10, 11, 11, 11, 11, 11, 12, 12, 20, 24, 28, 31, 31, 33, 33, 33, 33; 50:1, 2, 2, 4, 7, 7, 8, 8, 10, 12, 13, 14, 14, 14, 18, 18, 22, 24

Ex 1:1, 6, 9, 22; 2:4, 7, 10, 11, 11, 20, 21, 22, 24; 3:1, 6, 13; 4:4, 4, 6, 6, 6, 7, 7, 7, 14, 14, 15, 18, 20, 20, 21, 25; 5:2, 21; 6:1, 11, 20; 7:2, 10, 10, 12, 20, 23, 23; 8:6, 15, 17, 17, 24, 29, 31, 31, 32; 9:20, 20, 21, 21, 33, 34, 34; 10:1, 1, 13, 22, 23; 11:2, 5, 7, 10; 12:4, 4, 4, 9, 9, 9, 17, 17, 17, 18, 18, 21, 23, 23, 27, 27, 31; 15:1, 3, 4, 4, 19, 19, 21, 26, 26; 16:16, 16, 18, 21, 29, 29; 17:11, 11, 12, 12, 13; 18:1, 5, 5, 7, 8, 15, 16, 17, 17, 17, 20; 20:7, 17, 17, 17, 17, 20; 21:3, 4, 6, 6, 6, 7, 9, 13, 14, 15, 15, 16, 19, 20, 20, 21, 26, 26, 26, 27, 27, 28, 29, 29, 29, 30, 34, 34, 36, 36; 22:3, 4, 5, 6, 10, 11, 12, 14, 16, 17, 27, 27, 30; 23:3, 4, 4, 5, 6, 19, 22; 24:10, 10, 11, 13, 25:2, 31, 31, 31, 31; 26:19, 19; 27:2, 3, 3, 3, 3, 3, 3, 3, 11, 21; 28:1, 4, 12, 21, 29, 30, 35, 38, 41,

Lev 1:3, 3, 4, 6, 9, 9, 10, 11, 12, 12, 12, 14, 15, 15, 16; 2:1, 2, 3, 10; 3:1, 2, 2, 6, 7, 8, 8, 12, 13, 14; 4:3, 4, 6, 11, 11, 11, 11, 17, 19, 22, 23, 23, 23, 24, 25, 25, 26, 26, 28, 28, 28, 29, 30, 33, 34, 35; 5:1, 4, 6, 6, 6, 7, 8, 8, 10, 11, 12, 13, 15, 16, 20, 22, 22, 25; 7:13, 13, 15, 16, 16, 18, 18, 20, 20, 21, 25, 27, 29, 29, 30, 30, 31, 33, 34, 35; 8:2, 6, 9, 9, 11, 14, 14, 15, 17, 17, 18, 22, 23, 23, 27, 30, 30, 30, 31, 31, 36; 9:1, 9, 22; 10:1, 3, 6; 12:1; 11:14, 15, 16, 22, 22, 22, 22, 25, 27, 28, 29, 40, 40; 12:3; 13:2, 2, 3, 4, 5, 6, 7, 11, 12, 12, 13, 23, 28, 34, 35, 37, 40, 41, 41, 41, 42, 42, 43, 43, 44, 44, 45, 45, 45, 46, 55; 14:2, 8, 8, 9, 9, 9, 9, 9, 9, 14, 14, 15, 16, 16, 16, 17, 17, 17, 19, 23, 25, 25, 26, 27, 27, 27, 28, 28, 32, 47, 47; 15:2, 2, 3, 3, 3, 3, 3, 5, 6, 7, 8, 10, 10, 11, 13, 13, 13, 16, 21, 22, 27; 16:4, 4, 6, 6, 11, 12, 14, 14, 15, 17, 19, 21, 24, 24, 24, 24, 32; 17:2, 4, 9, 10, 14, 16; 18:14; 19:3, 8, 8, 8, 21, 22; 20:2, 3, 3, 4, 5, 6, 9, 9, 9, 9, 10, 11, 11, 12, 17, 17, 17, 17, 17, 17, 18, 19, 20, 20, 21, 21; 21:2, 2, 2, 2, 2, 3, 4, 7, 10, 10, 11, 11, 14, 15, 15, 17, 19, 21, 22, 23, 23, 27, 30, 37; 24:9, 11, 14, 15, 15; 25:10, 10, 14, 25, 25, 27, 28, 30, 33, 41, 41, 41, 48, 49, 49, 49, 50, 51, 52, 52, 54; 27:8, 14, 15, 15, 16, 17, 18, 22, 28, 31

Nu 1:4, 44, 52, 52; 2:2, 4, 6, 8, 11, 13, 17, 19, 21, 23, 26, 28, 30; 3:7, 9, 10, 38, 48, 51; 4:5, 9, 9, 9, 15, 19, 19, 19, 25, 27, 49, 49; 5:7, 9, 10, 10, 14, 14, 15, 18, 30; 6:4, 5, 5, 5, 7, 7, 7, 7, 7, 8, 9, 9, 9, 11, 12, 13, 14, 16, 16, 17, 17, 18, 18, 19, 21, 21, 21, 21, 25, 26; 7:5, 11, 12, 13, 19, 25, 31, 37, 43, 49, 55, 61, 67, 73, 79; 8:8, 13, 19, 22; 9:2, 3, 7, 13, 13; 10:14, 18, 22, 25; 11:1, 10, 28, 29; 12:12; 14:24; 15:4, 24, 30, 31, 36; 16:4, 5, 5, 6, 7, 17, 17, 18, 40; 17:2, 9; 19:3, 4, 5, 6, 17, 17, 18, 18, 40; 17:2, 9; 20:8, 11, 11, 21, 24, 25, 26, 26, 26, 28, 28, 28; 21:23, 23, 24, 26, 26, 29, 29, 33, 34, 34, 35; 22:5, 18, 21, 22, 22, 23, 23, 31, 31, 31, 31; 23:6, 7, 10, 16, 17, 18, 21; 24:1, 2, 2, 3, 4, 7, 7, 7, 7, 8, 8, 10, 11, 21, 23, 25, 25; 25:5, 6, 7, 13, 13; 26:54; 27:1, 1, 21, 23; 28:10, 15, 24, 31; 29:6, 6, 16, 16, 22, 22, 25, 25, 28, 28, 31, 31, 34, 34, 38, 38; 30:2, 2, 2, 4, 7, 11, 14, 14, 16, 16; 31:6; 32:18, 21, 42; 33:54; 35:8, 8, 21, 23, 23, 25, 27, 28, 28, 32; 36:2, 7, 8, 9

Dt 1:16, 31, 36, 41; 2:12, 24, 30, 30, 31, 31, 32, 33, 33, 34; 3:1, 2, 2, 3, 4, 14, 20; 4:13, 30, 36, 36, 36, 37, 37, 40, 40, 42; 5:11, 21, 21, 21, 21, 21, 24, 24, 24; 6:2, 2, 13, 17, 17, 22; 7:3, 3, 7, 9, 10; 8:2, 5, 6, 11, 11, 11, 18; 9:23; 10:6, 6, 8, 9, 12, 13, 20; 11:1, 1, 1, 1, 2, 2, 3, 3, 14, 22; 12:5, 5, 8, 11, 11; 13:4, 4, 17, 18; 14:13, 14, 15, 21, 23, 24; 15:2, 2, 2, 8, 17; 16:2, 6, 11; 17:2, 17, 18, 19, 19, 20, 20, 20, 20; 18:1, 5, 6, 7, 8, 10, 10, 18; 19:4, 5, 6, 7, 8, 8; 21:16, 17, 17, 18, 18, 19, 20:5, 6, 7, 8, 8, 8; 21:16, 17, 17, 18, 18, 19, 19, 19, 19, 21, 23; 22:1, 3, 3, 4, 19, 19, 24, 24, 26, 29, 30; 23:1, 2, 7, 15, 15, 15, 15, 16; 25:2, 2, 6, 6, 7, 7, 7, 8, 9, 9, 9, 9, 10; 26:2, 7, 17, 17, 17, 17, 18, 18; 27:10, 10, 16, 16, 17, 20, 20, 22, 22, 22, 23, 24; 28:1, 9, 12, 12, 15, 40, 45, 45, 54, 54, 54, 54, 55; 29:2, 2, 12, 19, 20, 20, 23; 30:2, 8, 10, 10, 16, 16, 16, 20; 32:4, 4, 5, 9, 9, 10, 15, 19, 19, 36, 36, 43, 43, 43, 43, 43, 50; 33:1, 2, 3, 6, 7, 7, 7, 9, 9, 9, 11, 11, 16, 17, 17, 17, 24, 26, 28; 34:6, 7, 7, 9, 10, 11

Jos 2:19, 19, 19; 3:15; 4:5, 14, 18; 5:13, 13, 14, 14, 14; 6:26, 26, 27; 7:6, 6, 18, 22, 24, 24, 24, 24, 24, 24, 24, 26; 8:1, 1, 14, 18, 19, 26, 29; 9:24; 10:21, 33; 11:15; 13:27; 15:17; 17:3, 6, 10; 20:4, 5, 5, 6, 6; 21:12; 22:5, 5, 20, 29; 24:3, 4, 10, 24, 28, 30

Jdg 1:2, 3, 6, 6, 13, 17, 25; 2:6, 9; 3:10, 16, 16, 20, 21, 21, 21, 22, 24, 24, 24, 24; 4:7, 7, 10, 11, 13, 15, 15, 15, 15, 17, 21, 21; 5:11, 17, 26, 28, 28, 31; 6:11, 13, 21, 21, 27, 27, 31, 32; 7:5, 5, 7, 8, 11, 13, 14, 14, 21, 22; 8:20, 20, 21, 24, 25, 27, 29, 30, 31, 32; 9:1, 1, 3, 5, 5, 7, 16, 16,

43, 43; 29:4, 6, 7, 8, 9, 9, 10, 14, 14, 15, 16, 17, 17, 17, 19, 20, 20, 20, 21, 21, 21, 21, 24, 27, 28, 29, 30, 31, 32, 35, 44; 30:12, 18, 19, 21, 27, 28, 28, 30, 33, 38; 31:8, 8, 9, 9, 10, 14; 32:11, 14, 15, 19, 27, 27, 27, 27, 29, 29; 33:4, 8, 10, 11, 11; 34:4, 8, 15, 20, 26, 29, 30, 33, 35; 35:11, 11, 11, 11, 11, 11, 13, 14, 14, 15, 16, 16, 16, 16, 16, 17, 19, 21, 21, 34; 36:4, 24, 24; 37:16, 16, 16, 16, 17, 17, 20, 20, 23, 23, 23; 39:5, 14, 17, 17, 20, 20, 23, 23, 23; 39, 39, 39, 39, 40, 40, 40, 40, 41; 40:10, 11, 12, 14, 18, 18, 31

Lev 1:3, 3, 4, 6, 9, 9, 10, 11, 12, 12, 12, 14, 15, 15, 16; 2:1, 2, 3, 10; 3:1, 2, 2, 6, 7, 8, 8, 12, 13, 14; 4:3, 4, 6, 11, 11, 11, 11, 17, 19, 22, 23, 23, 23, 24, 25, 25, 26, 26, 28, 28, 28, 29, 30, 33, 34, 35; 5:1, 4, 6, 6, 6, 7, 8, 8, 10, 11, 12, 13, 15, 16, 20, 22, 22, 25; 7:13, 13, 15, 16, 16, 18, 18, 20, 20, 21, 25, 27, 29, 29, 30, 30, 31, 33, 34, 35; 8:2, 6, 9, 9, 11, 14, 14, 15, 17, 17, 18, 22, 23, 23, 27, 30, 30, 30, 31, 31, 36; 9:1, 9, 22; 10:1, 3, 6; 12:1; 11:14, 15, 16, 22, 22, 22, 22, 25, 27, 28, 29, 40, 40; 12:3; 13:2, 2, 3, 4, 5, 6, 7, 11, 12, 12, 13, 23, 28, 34, 35, 37, 40, 41, 41, 41, 42, 42, 43, 43, 44, 44, 45, 45, 45, 46, 55; 14:2, 8, 8, 9, 9, 9, 9, 9, 9, 14, 14, 15, 16, 16, 16, 17, 17, 17, 19, 23, 25, 25, 26, 27, 27, 27, 28, 28, 32, 47, 47; 15:2, 2, 3, 3, 3, 3, 3, 5, 6, 7, 8, 10, 10, 11, 13, 13, 13, 16, 21, 22, 27; 16:4, 4, 6, 6, 11, 12, 14, 14, 15, 17, 19, 21, 24, 24, 24, 24, 32; 17:2, 4, 9, 10, 14, 16; 18:14; 19:3, 8, 8, 8, 21, 22; 20:2, 3, 3, 4, 5, 6, 9, 9, 9, 9, 10, 11, 11, 12, 17, 17, 17, 17, 17, 17, 18, 19, 20, 20, 21, 21; 21:2, 2, 2, 2, 2, 3, 4, 7, 10, 10, 11, 11, 14, 15, 15, 17, 19, 21, 22, 23, 23; 22:1, 6, 6, 6, 7, 11, 15; 23:5, 6, 8, 11, 13, 14, 14, 15, 16, 18, 22, 22, 24, 25, 26, 26, 26; 24:2, 3, 6, 7, 9, 18, 19, 22; 25:1, 2, 3, 4, 10, 13, 13, 13, 17, 20, 22, 25, 25, 25, 36, 37, 37, 39, 39, 42, 43, 44; 26:5, 7, 7, 9, 10, 16, 18, 19, 23, 23, 25, 25, 27; 27:1, 1, 3, 3, 3, 8, 11, 12; 28:3, 5, 7, 7, 14, 18, 23, 25; 29:2, 4, 4, 5, 5, 11; 30:1, 3, 6, 6, 6, 12, 18, 22, 22, 24, 24, 31; 31:2, 4, 4, 4, 5, 5, 6, 6, 6, 7, 8, 9, 9, 10, 10, 12

2Sa 1:2, 2, 4, 5, 6, 10, 10, 11, 12, 17; 2:2, 3, 3, 16, 16, 21, 27, 29, 32, 38, 39; 4:1, 4, 4, 4, 6, 7, 7, 7, 8, 9, 10, 11, 11, 11, 11, 12; 5:6, 12, 21; 6:6, 7, 11, 14, 17, 19, 20, 20, 21; 7:1, 1, 12, 13, 14, 25, 27; 8:3, 10, 15; 9:3, 6, 9, 11, 13; 10:1, 1, 2, 2, 3, 10, 11:1, 2, 9, 9, 10, 13, 13, 13, 17, 21, 23; 12:3, 3, 3, 5, 11, 16, 17, 18, 18, 18, 20, 20, 21, 24, 24, 24, 25, 25, 25, 30, 30, 32; 13:1, 3, 5, 8, 8, 22, 28, 31, 32, 33, 34, 36, 37; 14:7, 7, 9, 11, 14, 16, 16, 22, 22, 24, 24, 25, 26, 28, 30, 31, 33; 15:5, 12, 14, 16, 18, 22, 23, 30, 30, 32, 32, 36; 16:6, 6, 9, 11, 11, 11, 21, 22, 22, 22, 23; 17:8; 18:9, 14, 17, 18, 18, 19, 24, 24, 24, 30, 39, 41; 20:1, 3, 3, 8, 8, 10, 10, 21, 21, 22; 21:1, 2, 4, 6, 10, 12, 13, 14, 14, 21, 22; 22:1, 7, 7, 9, 10, 16, 30, 31, 31, 47, 48, 49, 51, 51, 51; 23:2, 8, 10, 10, 18, 21, 25, 31, 51, 51, 51; 23:2, 8, 10, 10, 18, 21, 23; 24:14, 16, 20, 20, 21

1Ki 1:2, 6, 6, 9, 10, 21, 23, 37, 47, 49, 51; 2:1, 3, 3, 3, 3, 4, 5, 5, 5, 5, 6, 9, 10, 12, 15, 19, 22, 23, 32, 32, 33, 33, 33, 34, 35, 40, 40, 40; 3:1, 3, 6, 15; 4:7, 21, 25, 26, 27, 28, 31, 32, 34; 5:1, 1, 3, 3, 10, 11; 7:1, 1, 8, 14, 14, 23, 51; 8:6, 14, 15, 15, 20, 22, 28, 31, 32, 32, 38, 38, 39, 54, 54, 56, 56, 56, 58, 58, 58, 58, 59, 59, 61, 61, 66, 66; 9:11, 15, 16, 19, 19, 19, 22, 22, 22, 27; 10:5, 9, 19, 19, 22, 29, 29; 11:3, 3, 4, 4, 4, 4, 4, 6, 9, 17, 26, 27, 27, 33, 34, 34, 35, 36, 41, 43; 12:4, 6, 15, 16, 21, 23, 26, 27, 27, 33, 34, 34, 34, 34; 13:3, 4, 4, 4, 6, 6, 9, 11, 24, 24, 25; 14:2, 4, 4, 11, 12, 19, 24, 27, 28, 30, 31, 31, 31; 15:2, 3, 3, 3, 3, 4, 4, 4, 5, 5, 6, 7, 9, 14, 20, 24, 24, 26, 28, 29, 30; 16:3, 4, 5, 5, 6, 6, 7, 7, 9, 9, 10, 11, 11, 12, 13, 13, 18, 25, 26, 28, 29, 30, 34; 17:17, 19, 23; 18:3, 7, 42, 42, 43, 46; 19:3, 3, 6, 13, 19; 20:1, 1, 9, 10, 14, 15, 15, 16, 16, 17, 21, 22, 29, 31, 31, 31, 31, 32, 34, 34; 5:1, 1, 3, 3, 10, 10, 11; 7:1, 7:1, 1, 8, 14, 14, 23, 51; 22:2, 22:2; 35:3, 4, 5, 7, 8, 8, 8, 10, 12, 13, 13, 15, 15, 16, 16, 17, 18, 20, 22, 23, 23

2Ki 1:2, 8, 9, 10, 11, 12, 13, 13, 16, 17; 2:8, 12; 3:2, 2, 2, 25, 27, 27; 4:12, 18, 19, 19, 20, 25, 32, 34, 34, 34, 34, 34, 34, 35, 37, 38, 39, 43; 5:1, 3, 4, 6, 7, 8, 9, 9, 11, 11, 13, 14, 15, 20, 23, 25, 26, 27; 6:7, 8, 11, 12, 14, 15, 20, 23, 25, 26, 28, 28, 32, 33; 7:12, 13; 8:11, 14, 15, 15, 18, 19, 19, 20, 24, 24, 24, 26; 9:2, 3, 6, 11, 11, 13, 21, 24, 24, 24, 24, 24, 25, 25, 26, 28, 28; 10:3, 10, 11, 14, 15, 15, 17, 23, 24, 30, 33, 34, 35; 11:2, 8, 8, 9, 11, 11, 18, 18; 12:1, 2, 5, 17, 18, 18, 18, 21, 21, 21, 21, 21; 13:8, 9, 13, 14, 14, 16, 16, 20, 23, 24, 25; 14:3, 3, 5, 5, 5, 6, 9, 16, 16, 19, 20, 27, 28, 29, 29; 15:2, 5, 7, 7, 7, 9, 10, 14, 18, 19, 22, 22, 25, 25, 30, 33, 34, 34, 34, 38, 38;

17, 18, 18, 19, 21, 24, 26, 28, 30, 31, 41, 48, 48, 49, 53, 54, 54, 55, 56, 56; 10:16; 11:2, 3, 11, 20, 20, 22, 32, 34, 34, 34, 35, 39; 12:9; 13:2, 5, 6, 6, 7, 11, 19, 20, 21, 22, 23, 24; 14:2, 2, 3, 3, 4, 4, 5, 5, 6, 6, 6, 6, 9, 9, 10, 19, 19, 20; 15:1, 6, 6, 14, 14, 14, 15, 17, 19; 16:3, 5, 9, 12, 14, 16, 17, 18, 18, 19, 19, 20, 21; 17:2, 2, 3, 3, 4, 4, 5, 5, 6, 11, 12; 18:4, 6, 14; 19:2, 3, 4, 4, 5, 7, 9, 9, 9, 10, 11, 12, 13, 15, 16, 17, 21, 21, 25, 27, 27, 28, 29, 29; 20:8; 8; 21:1, 21, 22, 24, 24, 24, 25

Ru 1:1, 1, 2, 2, 6; 2:1, 5, 15, 20, 22; 3:4, 7, 7, 8, 14; 4:5, 7, 7, 8, 10, 10, 10, 13, 14, 17

1Sa 1:1, 3, 4, 11, 11, 19, 20, 21, 21, 23; 2:9, 10, 10, 11, 13, 19, 20, 22; 3:2, 2, 9, 12, 13, 13, 19; 4:10, 12, 12, 13, 13, 18, 19; 5:3, 3, 4, 4, 7, 11; 6:2, 3, 5, 9, 9; 7:1, 15, 17, 17; 8:1, 2, 2, 3, 3, 11, 11, 11, 12, 12, 12, 14, 15, 15, 16, 17, 22; 9:2, 3, 5, 7, 10, 15, 22; 10:1, 1, 9, 14, 16, 23, 25, 27; 11:6, 7; 12:3, 5, 14, 22, 22, 22, 23; 13:2, 14, 14, 16, 20, 20, 20, 20, 22; 14:1, 1, 6, 7, 12, 12, 13, 13, 13, 14, 17, 20, 26, 27, 27, 27, 27, 34, 34, 35, 41, 41, 47, 49, 50; 15:1, 27, 34, 35; 16:1, 4, 5, 7, 7, 10, 13, 16, 17, 20, 20, 23; 17:5, 6, 6, 7, 7, 13, 15, 17, 22, 40, 42, 43, 43, 44, 44, 45, 49, 49, 51, 51, 54, 54, 57; 18:1, 2, 3, 4, 4, 4, 4, 7, 7, 10, 11, 13, 14, 22, 22, 26, 27, 27, 30, 30; 19:1, 1, 4, 4, 4, 5, 7, 10, 11, 11, 13, 15; 20:6, 10, 17, 25, 27, 32, 33, 34; 21:8, 8, 9, 13, 13; 22:1, 1, 6, 6, 6, 7, 11, 15; 23:5, 6, 8, 11, 13, 14, 14, 15, 16, 18, 22, 22, 24, 25, 26, 26, 26; 24:2, 3, 6, 7, 9, 18, 19, 22; 25:1, 2, 3, 4, 10, 13, 13, 13, 17, 20, 22, 25, 25, 25, 36, 37, 37, 39, 39, 42, 43, 44; 26:5, 7, 7, 9, 10, 16, 18, 19, 23, 23, 25, 25, 27; 27:1, 1, 3, 3, 3, 8, 11, 12; 28:3, 5, 7, 7, 14, 18, 23, 25; 29:2, 4, 4, 5, 5, 11; 30:1, 3, 6, 6, 6, 12, 18, 22, 22, 24, 24, 31; 31:2, 4, 4, 4, 5, 5, 6, 6, 6, 7, 8, 9, 9, 10, 10, 12

2Sa 1:2, 2, 4, 5, 6, 10, 10, 11, 12, 17; 2:2, 3, 3, 16, 16, 21, 27, 29, 32, 38, 39; 4:1, 4, 4, 4, 6, 7, 7, 7, 8, 9, 10, 11, 11, 11, 11, 12; 5:6, 12, 21; 6:6, 7, 11, 14, 17, 19, 20, 20, 21; 7:1, 1, 12, 13, 14, 25, 27; 8:3, 10, 15; 9:3, 6, 9, 11, 13; 10:1, 1, 2, 2, 3, 10, 11:1, 2, 9, 9, 10, 13, 13, 13, 17, 21, 23; 12:3, 3, 3, 5, 11, 16, 17, 18, 18, 18, 20, 20, 21, 24, 24, 24, 25, 25, 25, 30, 30, 32; 13:1, 3, 5, 8, 8, 22, 28, 31, 32, 33, 34, 36, 37; 14:7, 7, 9, 11, 14, 16, 16, 22, 22, 24, 24, 25, 26, 28, 30, 31, 33; 15:5, 12, 14, 16, 18, 22, 23, 30, 30, 32, 32, 36; 16:6, 6, 9, 11, 11, 11, 21, 22, 22, 22, 23; 17:8; 18:9, 14, 17, 18, 18, 19, 24, 24, 24, 30, 39, 41; 20:1, 3, 3, 8, 8, 10, 10, 21, 21, 22; 21:1, 2, 4, 6, 10, 12, 13, 14, 14, 21, 22; 22:1, 7, 7, 9, 10, 16, 30, 31, 31, 47, 48, 49, 51, 51, 51; 23:2, 8, 10, 10, 18, 21, 23; 24:14, 16, 20, 20, 21

1Ki 1:2, 6, 6, 9, 10, 21, 23, 37, 47, 49, 51; 2:1, 3, 3, 3, 3, 4, 5, 5, 5, 5, 6, 9, 10, 12, 15, 19, 22, 23, 32, 32, 33, 33, 33, 34, 35, 40, 40, 40; 3:1, 3, 6, 15; 4:7, 21, 25, 26, 27, 28, 31, 32, 34; 5:1, 1, 3, 3, 10, 11; 7:1, 1, 8, 14, 14, 23, 51; 8:6, 14, 15, 15, 20, 22, 28, 31, 32, 32, 38, 38, 39, 54, 54, 56, 56, 56, 58, 58, 58, 58, 59, 59, 61, 61, 66, 66; 9:11, 15, 16, 19, 19, 19, 22, 22, 22, 27; 10:5, 9, 19, 19, 22, 29, 29; 11:3, 3, 4, 4, 4, 4, 4, 6, 9, 17, 26, 27, 27, 33, 34, 34, 35, 36, 41, 43; 12:4, 6, 15, 16, 21, 23, 26, 27, 27, 33, 34, 34, 34, 34; 13:3, 4, 4, 4, 6, 6, 9, 11, 24, 24, 25; 14:2, 4, 4, 11, 12, 19, 24, 27, 28, 30, 31, 31, 31; 15:2, 3, 3, 3, 3, 4, 4, 4, 5, 5, 6, 7, 9, 14, 20, 24, 24, 26, 28, 29, 30; 16:3, 4, 5, 5, 6, 6, 7, 7, 9, 9, 10, 11, 11, 12, 13, 13, 18, 25, 26, 28, 29, 30, 34; 17:17, 19, 23; 18:3, 7, 42, 42, 43, 46; 19:3, 3, 6, 13, 19; 20:1, 1, 9, 10, 14, 15, 15, 16, 16, 17, 21, 22, 29, 31, 31, 31, 31, 32, 34, 34, 34; 21:4, 15, 19, 22, 22; 22:1, 4, 11, 12, 13, 31, 31, 31, 31, 33; 35:3, 4, 5, 7, 8, 8, 8, 10, 12, 13, 13, 15, 15, 16, 16, 17, 18, 20, 22, 23, 23

2Ki 1:2, 8, 9, 10, 11, 12, 13, 13, 16, 17; 2:8, 12; 3:2, 2, 2, 25, 27, 27; 4:12, 18, 19, 19, 20, 25, 32, 34, 34, 34, 34, 34, 34, 35, 37, 38, 39, 43; 5:1, 3, 4, 6, 7, 8, 9, 9, 11, 11, 13, 14, 15, 20, 23, 25, 26, 27; 6:7, 8, 11, 12, 14, 15, 20, 23, 25, 26, 28, 28, 32, 33; 7:12, 13; 8:11, 14, 15, 15, 18, 19, 19, 20, 24, 24, 24, 26; 9:2, 3, 6, 11, 11, 13, 21, 24, 24, 24, 24, 24, 25, 25, 26, 28, 28; 10:3, 10, 11, 14, 15, 15, 17, 23, 24, 30, 33, 34, 35; 11:2, 8, 8, 9, 11, 11, 18, 18; 12:1, 2, 5, 17, 18, 18, 18, 21, 21, 21, 21, 21; 13:8, 9, 13, 14, 14, 16, 16, 20, 23, 24, 25; 14:3, 3, 5, 5, 5, 6, 9, 16, 16, 19, 20, 27, 28, 29, 29; 15:2, 5, 7, 7, 7, 9, 10, 14, 18, 19, 22, 22, 25, 25, 30, 33, 34, 34, 34, 38, 38;

16:2, 2, 3, 13, 13, 13, 13, 15, 20, 20, 20, 20; 17:3, 15, 15, 15, 18, 20, 20, 23; 18:2, 3, 6, 12, 21, 29, 31, 31, 33; 19:1, 4, 7, 7, 19, 23, 23, 37, 37, 37, 37; 20:2, 13, 13, 13, 13, 13, 20, 21, 21; 21:1, 3, 6, 7, 10, 11, 12, 16, 17, 18, 18, 18, 22, 26; 22:1, 2, 11; 23:3, 3, 3, 10, 18, 18, 33, 34, 34, 35, 36, 37; 24:1, 1, 2, 3, 3, 6, 6, 6, 7, 8, 9, 11, 12, 12, 12, 12, 12, 15, 15, 17, 17, 17, 18, 20, 20, 21; 25:1, 1, 5, 7, 28, 29, 29, 30, 30

1Ch 1:19, 19, 43, 44, 45, 46, 46, 47, 48, 49, 50, 50, 50; 2:4, 13, 18, 35, 35, 42; 3:3, 10, 10, 10, 11, 13, 13, 13, 13, 13, 13, 14, 14, 16, 16, 17; 4:9, 9, 9, 18, 19, 23, 25, 25, 26, 26, 26, 27; 5:1, 1, 2, 4, 4, 4, 5, 5, 5, 6, 7, 6:20, 20, 21, 21, 21, 22, 22, 22, 22, 23, 23, 24, 24, 24, 26, 26, 26, 27, 27, 29, 29, 30, 30, 30, 39, 39, 49, 50, 50, 51, 51, 51, 52, 52, 52, 53, 53; 7:14, 16, 16, 16, 20, 20, 20, 20, 21, 21, 21, 23, 23, 23, 23, 24, 25, 25, 25, 26, 26, 26, 27, 27, 35; 8:1, 8, 9, 10, 30, 37, 37, 37, 39, 39; 9:5, 19, 19, 36, 43, 43, 43; 10:2, 4, 4, 5, 6, 8, 9, 9, 10, 10, 12, 13, 13:10, 14; 14:2, 2, 4; 15:3, 5, 6, 7, 8, 9, 10, 17; 16:7, 8, 8, 9, 9, 10, 11, 11, 12, 12, 12, 14, 15, 16, 17, 19; 17:1, 11, 13, 14, 21, 23, 19, 20, 21, 22, 23, 23, 24; 18:3, 10, 10, 14; 19:1, 1, 2, 2, 3, 7, 11, 13, 15, 19; 20:2, 8; 21:3, 13, 16, 16, 20, 21, 23; 27:22; 5:9, 19, 24, 25; 25:9, 10, 10, 11, 11, 12, 12, 13, 13, 14, 14, 15, 15, 16, 16, 17, 17, 18, 18, 19, 19, 20, 20, 21, 21, 22, 22, 23, 23, 24, 24, 25, 25, 26, 27, 27, 28, 28, 29, 29, 30, 30, 30, 31, 31, 32; 26:2, 4, 4, 6, 7, 10, 11, 31; 27:2, 4, 4, 5, 12; 28:1, 2, 6, 7, 11, 10, 11, 12, 13, 14, 15; 28:1, 2, 6, 7, 11, 19, 20; 29:5, 23, 28, 28, 30, 30

2Ch 1:1, 1, 8, 13; 2:1, 11, 12, 14, 15, 17; 3:1, 2; 4:16; 5:1, 7, 13; 6:3, 4, 4, 10, 12, 13, 13, 19, 22, 23, 23, 23, 29, 29, 30; 7:3, 6, 10, 11; 8:1, 6, 9, 9, 14, 18; 9:4, 4, 4, 4, 8, 15, 18; 11:4, 12, 14, 21, 21, 22; 12:8; 13:3, 14, 14, 16, 16; 13:2, 5, 6, 12, 17, 22, 22; 14:1, 1, 1, 1, 2, 11, 13; 15:9, 17, 18; 16:4, 5, 12, 12, 13, 14; 17:1, 2, 3, 4, 4, 5, 5, 6, 7, 18:8; 9, 16, 18, 18, 18, 31, 33, 34; 19:1; 20:18, 20, 20, 21, 25, 30, 31, 32; 21:1, 1, 1, 1, 4, 4, 7, 8, 9, 9, 9, 10, 17, 17, 17, 17, 19; 22:1, 1, 2, 3, 3, 4, 4, 4, 9, 9, 11; 23:7, 7, 8, 10, 10, 11, 13, 17, 17; 24:1, 11, 13, 16, 22, 22, 25, 25, 27, 27, 27; 25:1, 3, 3, 4, 11, 14, 22, 28; 26:1, 2, 3, 4, 8, 15, 16, 16, 16, 19, 19, 21, 21, 21, 23, 23, 23; 27:1, 2, 6, 6, 7, 7, 9, 9, 9; 28:1, 3, 5, 22, 25, 26, 26, 27, 27, 27; 29:1, 2, 3, 10, 19, 19, 25; 30:2, 6, 8, 8, 9, 19, 19, 27; 31:1, 2, 3, 8, 10, 12, 13, 14, 16, 16, 17, 21, 21, 21, 21, 24, 26, 30, 31, 32, 33, 33, 33, 33, 33:3, 6, 7, 10, 12, 12, 13, 18, 18, 19, 20, 21, 22, 23, 24, 24, 24, 25, 25; 34:2, 2, 3, 3, 3, 4, 4, 4, 5, 7, 8, 8, 8, 10, 12, 13, 13, 15, 15, 15, 16, 16, 16, 18, 22, 23; 23

Ezr 1:1, 3, 3, 4, 7; 2:1, 68; 3:2, 2, 3, 9, 9, 9, 11; 4:6; 5:6, 15, 17; 6:5, 7, 10, 11, 12; 7:6, 6, 9, 10, 11, 13, 14, 15, 23, 28; 8:17, 18, 18, 19, 20, 22, 25, 25, 25; 9:8; 10:8, 11, 18

Ne 1:5; 2:1, 20; 3:1, 10, 12, 17, 23, 28, 29, 30; 4:2, 15, 17, 18, 18, 22; 5:7, 13, 13; 6:5, 5, 11, 18, 19; 7:3, 3, 6; 8:4, 4, 16; 9:8, 8, 10, 10; 10:29, 29; 11:3, 13, 17, 20; 12:8, 36, 45, 47; 13:10, 26, 30

Est 1:2, 3, 3, 3, 4, 4, 8, 12, 12, 20, 22; 2:3, 7, 9, 15, 16, 16, 17, 18, 18; 3:1, 10, 10; 4:1, 3, 4, 11, 17; 5:1, 2, 2, 10, 10, 11, 11, 14, 14; 6:6, 8, 12, 12, 13, 13, 13, 13; 7:5, 7, 7; 8:2, 3, 3, 5, 5, 7, 17; 9:1, 4, 25, 25, 25; 10:2, 2, 3, 3

Job 1:3, 4, 4, 10, 10, 13, 13, 20, 20; 2:3, 4, 5, 5, 6, 7, 7, 8, 9, 10, 11, 12, 13; 3:1, 1, 19; 4:9; 17, 18, 18; 5:3, 4, 18, 26; 6:5, 9, 14; 7:1, 2, 10, 10; 8:12, 15, 16, 16, 17, 18, 19; 9:5, 13, 33, 34, 34; 11:5; 12:4, 5, 11, 16; 13:8, 11, 11; 14:5, 5, 5, 6, 18, 20, 21, 22, 22; 15:2, 15, 15, 20, 20, 21, 23, 25, 26, 27, 27, 30, 30, 31, 32, 33; 16:9, 9, 9, 9, 12, 13, 21; 17:5, 5, 9; 18:4, 4, 4, 5, 6, 7, 7, 8, 11, 11, 12, 12, 13, 13, 14, 14, 15, 16, 16, 17, 19, 19, 20; 19:6, 11, 11, 12; 20:6, 6, 9, 11, 11, 12, 12, 13, 14, 14, 15, 18, 20, 21, 21, 22, 23, 23, 25, 25, 26, 26, 27, 28, 28, 28; 21:17, 19, 19, 20, 21, 21, 23, 24, 24, 25, 31, 31; 22:22, 22; 23:3, 6, 11, 11, 12, 12, 13, 15; 24:1, 6, 15, 22, 23; 25:2, 3, 3; 5; 26:8, 9, 9, 13, 14, 14, 14; 27:1, 8, 9, 14, 14, 15, 18, 19, 22; 28:9, 10; 29:1, 3, 3, 17; 30:24, 24; 31:20, 23, 30, 31; 32:1, 2, 3, 3, 5, 12, 14; 33:10, 13, 17, 18, 19, 20, 21, 21, 27, 30; 34:11, 14, 14, 14, 19, 21, 21, 27, 29, 35, 36, 37,

37, 37; 35:15, 16; 36:7, 15, 18, 22, 23, 24, 26, 29, 30; 37:1, 2, 2, 3, 4, 4, 5, 6, 7, 11, 12, 13, 15; 38:12, 32, 32, 41, 41; 39:6, 8, 10, 11, 18, 19, 20, 21; 40:16, 16, 16, 16, 16, 17, 18, 18, 19, 23, 24, 24; 41:1, 2, 2, 7, 7, 12, 12, 12, 13, 13, 14, 14, 15, 15, 18, 18, 19, 20, 21, 21, 22, 23, 24, 33; 42:10, 11, 11, 11, 11, 12, 12, 16, 16

Ps 1:2, 2, 3, 3, 3; 2:2, 5, 5, 12; 3:T, 4; 7:12, 13, 13, 16, 16, 16, 16, 17; 8:6; 9:7, 11, 16; 10:2, 3, 4, 4, 5, 5, 6, 7, 7, 8, 9, 9, 10, 11, 11, 11, 13, 15, 16; 11:4, 4, 4, 5, 7; 12:2; 14:1, 6, 7; 15:2, 3, 3, 4, 4, 5; 17:12; 18:T, 6, 6, 8, 9, 11, 11, 13, 14, 22, 22, 24, 30, 50, 50, 50; 19:1, 5, 6, 6, 12; 20:6, 6, 6; 21:2, 2, 3, 5, 9; 22:24, 29, 31; 23:3; 24:3, 4, 5; 25:9, 10, 10, 13, 13, 14, 22; 27:4, 5, 5, 6; 28:5, 8; 29:2, 9, 9, 11, 11; 30:4, 4, 5; 31:21, 23; 33:4, 6, 11, 12, 14, 17, 18, 21; 34:T, 1, 3, 6, 9, 15, 20, 22; 35:8, 9, 14, 27; 36:1, 2, 2, 3, 4; 37:7, 10, 12, 13, 23, 24, 25, 26, 28, 30, 31, 31, 33, 34; 38:13; 39:5, 11; 40:4; 41:2, 3, 3, 5, 6, 9; 42:5, 8, 8; 46:6; 47:8; 48:1; 49:7, 16, 17, 18, 19; 50:4, 6, 23; 52:7, 7, 7; 53:1, 6; 54:7; 55:20, 20, 21, 21, 21; 56:4, 10, 10; 57:3, 3; 58:7, 7, 9, 10; 59:9; 60:6; 61:6; 62:4, 12; 64:9; 65:6; 66:2, 2, 5, 7, 7, 8, 20; 67:1; 68:1, 4, 4, 5, 21, 21, 33, 34, 34, 35; 69:33, 36, 36; 72:7, 9, 14, 17, 17, 19; 73:10; 76:1, 2, 2; 77:8, 8, 9; 78:4, 4, 7, 10, 11, 20, 22, 26, 32, 37, 38, 38, 42, 43, 43, 49, 50, 52, 54, 54, 56, 61, 61, 62, 62, 66, 69, 70, 71, 71, 72, 72; 79:7; 81:6, 6; 85:8, 8, 9, 13; 87:1; 89:23, 23, 24, 25, 25, 29, 30, 36, 36, 39, 40, 40, 41, 42, 42, 43, 44, 44, 45, 48; 91:4, 4, 11, 14; 94:14, 14; 95:2, 4, 4, 5, 5, 7, 7, 7; 96:2, 2, 3, 3, 6, 8, 8, 13; 97:2, 3, 4, 6, 6, 10, 12; 98:1, 1, 2, 2, 3, 3; 99:5, 6, 6, 7, 9; 100:2, 3, 3, 4, 4, 4, 5, 5; 101:5; 102:T, 16, 19, 21; 103:1, 2, 7, 7, 9, 11, 13, 15, 17, 18, 18, 19, 19, 20, 20, 21, 21, 21, 22, 22; 104:3, 3, 4, 13, 15, 19, 23, 23, 31; 105:1, 1, 2, 3, 4, 4, 5, 6, 7, 8, 9, 19, 21, 21, 22, 22, 24, 25, 25, 26, 27, 28, 42, 42, 43, 43, 45, 45; 106:1, 2, 8, 12, 12, 13, 23, 23, 24, 26, 33, 33, 40, 40, 45, 45; 107:1, 8, 8, 15, 15, 20, 21, 21, 24, 31, 31; 108:7; 109:6, 7, 8, 8, 9, 9, 10, 11, 12, 13, 14, 14, 18, 18, 18, 31; 110:5; 111:3, 3, 4, 5, 6, 7, 7, 9, 9, 9, 10, 10; 112:1, 2, 3, 5, 7, 8, 8, 8, 9, 9, 10; 113:4, 8; 114:2, 2; 116:2, 12, 14, 15, 18; 117:2; 118:1, 3, 4, 29; 119:2, 3, 9; 125:2; 126:6; 127:2, 3, 5; 128:1; 129:7, 7; 130:5, 8; 131:2; 132:1, 7, 7, 13, 18, 18; 133:2; 135:3, 4, 7, 9, 12, 14, 14; 136:1, 2, 3, 4, 6, 7, 8, 9, 10, 11, 12, 13, 14, 15, 15, 16, 16, 17, 18, 19, 20, 21, 21, 22, 22; 143:2, 3, 9, 9, 12, 12, 17, 17, 21; 146:4, 4, 4, 5, 5; 147:5, 9, 11, 15, 15, 17, 17, 18, 18, 19, 19, 19, 20; 148:2, 2, 8, 13, 13, 14, 14; 149:1, 3, 4, 9; 150:1, 1, 2, 2

Pr 2:6, 8; 3:11, 20, 31, 32; 5:21, 22, 22, 23; 6:13, 13, 13, 14, 15, 27, 27, 28, 29, 30, 31, 36; 10:1, 9, 15, 19; 11:1, 5, 5, 7, 8, 9, 12, 12, 17, 17, 19, 20, 28, 29; 12:4, 8, 10, 11, 13, 14, 15, 22, 26; 13:1, 2, 3, 3, 3, 8, 16, 22, 24, 24, 25; 14:2, 2, 8, 10, 10, 14, 15, 20, 21, 26, 31, 32, 32, 35; 15:5, 8, 20, 23, 27, 32; 16:2, 7, 9, 9, 10, 11, 15, 17, 17, 23, 23, 26, 27, 29, 30, 30, 32; 17:5, 13, 18, 19, 21, 25, 27, 28, 28; 18:2, 6, 7, 7, 7, 9, 11, 11, 14, 17, 17, 20, 20; 19:1, 2, 3, 3, 4, 7, 8, 11, 11, 12, 13, 16, 16, 18, 22, 24, 24, 24, 26, 26; 20:2, 6, 7, 7, 8, 11, 11, 14, 16, 17, 19, 20, 20, 20, 24, 28; 21:2, 8, 10, 10, 18, 23, 23, 23, 24, 25, 29, 29; 22:5, 8, 9, 11, 16, 25, 29; 23:3, 6, 7, 7, 14, 31; 24:7, 12, 15, 18, 26, 29; 25:5, 13, 18, 24, 26; 26:4, 5, 5, 11, 11, 22, 24, 14, 15, 15, 16, 19, 24, 25, 26; 27:8, 13, 14, 14, 16, 17, 18, 22, 28:6, 6, 7, 8, 9, 9, 10, 11, 13, 15, 20, 20, 24, 28; 21:2, 8, 10, 20; 30:4, 4, 4, 6, 10, 17, 17; 31:1, 7, 7

Ecc 1:3, 5, 6; 2:14, 21, 22, 22, 23, 23, 24, 24, 26; 3:11, 12, 13, 22, 22; 4:4, 5, 5, 8, 8, 10, 14, 15; 5:14, 15, 15, 17, 17, 18, 18, 19, 19, 20, 20; 6:2, 3, 3, 4, 7, 12; 7:2, 15, 15, 15; 8:1, 1, 3, 9, 12, 15, 16, 16; 9:12, 15, 15, 16; 10:2, 2, 3, 13, 13; 12:5, 13

SS 1:2, 4, 12; 2:3, 3, 4, 6, 6, 16; 3:7, 8, 8, 11, 11, 11; 4:16, 16; 5:4, 11, 11, 12, 13, 13, 11, 11; 4:16, 16; 6:2; 7:10; 8:3, 3, 7, 10

Isa 1:3, 3; 2:3, 3, 10, 19, 20, 20, 21; 3:5, 25; 6:1, 2, 2, 3, 6; 7:2, 2, 14; 8:3, 7, 7, 7, 8, 17; 9:4, 4, 4, 6, 6, 7, 7, 11, 12, 12, 17, 17, 19, 20, 21; 10:4, 4, 7, 7, 12, 12, 17, 17, 17, 18, 18, 19, 24, 24, 26, 27, 27, 28, 32; 11:1, 3, 3, 4, 4, 5, 8, 10, 11, 14, 14; 14:17, 18, 21, 25, 25, 27, 29, 31, 32; 15:4; 16:6, 6, 6, 6, 6; 17:4, 5, 7, 7, 8, 8, 9; 19:1, 2, 2, 14; 22:21, 22, 23, 24; 23:11; 24:2, 23; 25:4; 8, 9, 11, 11; 26:21; 27:1, 8, 9; 28:4, 5, 21, 21, 21, 21, 24, 26, 28, 29:8, 8, 22, 23; 30:4, 4, 26, 27, 27, 27, 28, 30, 30, 30; 31:2, 3, 4, 7, 7, 8,

9, 9, 9; 32:6; 33:6, 15, 15, 15, 16, 16, 17; 34:2, 14, 16, 17; 36:6, 16, 16, 16, 18; 37:1, 4, 7, 7, 20, 24, 24, 38, 38, 38, 38; 38:2, 9; 39:2, 2, 2, 2; 40:10, 10, 10, 11, 11, 11, 12, 13, 26, 28; 41:2, 2, 2, 3, 6, 6; 42:2, 4, 10, 12, 13, 21, 24, 24, 25; 44:5, 6, 11, 12, 12, 13, 17, 19, 20, 20, 26, 26; 45:1, 9, 10, 11, 13; 46:7, 7, 7; 47:4, 15; 48:2, 14, 14, 15, 16, 19, 20; 49:2, 2, 5, 7, 13, 13; 50:10, 10; 51:14, 15, 17, 22; 52:9, 10, 14, 14; 53:5, 6; 59:1, 2, 16, 16, 16; 55:7, 7; 56:2, 3, 6, 10, 11, 11; 57:2, 13, 17, 17, 18, 18; 58:5, 5; 59:1, 2, 16, 16, 17, 18, 18, 19; 60:2, 22; 62:8, 8, 11, 11; 63:1, 1, 7, 7, 9, 9, 9, 10, 11, 11, 11, 12; 65:15, 20; 66:5, 6, 13, 14, 14, 14, 15, 15, 15, 16

Jer 1:2, 9, 15; 2:3, 15, 15, 35; 3:1, 5; 4:7, 7, 7, 13, 13, 26; 5:8, 24; 6:3, 21; 7:5, 29; 8:1, 6, 6, 16, 16; 9:4, 5, 8, 8, 8, 20, 23, 23; 10:10, 10, 12, 12, 12, 13, 13, 14, 14, 16, 16, 23, 25; 11:19; 12:15, 15; 13:23, 23; 16:12; 17:5, 10, 10, 11, 11; 18:11, 12, 16, 18; 19:3, 9; 20:9, 9; 21:2, 7, 9; 22:4, 4, 7, 8, 10, 10, 13, 13, 13, 13, 18, 28, 30; 23:6, 9, 14, 24; 24:8; 25:4, 9; 24, 34, 35, 35; 29:23; 30:6, 6, 8, 18, 21, 24; 31:10, 30, 30, 34, 34, 35; 32:4, 4, 18, 19, 19; 33:2, 11, 21, 26; 34:1, 1, 3, 3, 9, 9, 10, 14, 15, 16, 16, 17, 17, 21; 35:3, 14, 15, 18; 36:3, 7, 14, 17, 18, 24, 30, 31, 31; 37:2, 10, 17; 38:2; 39:1, 6; 40:3; 42:11; 43:10, 10, 12; 44:21, 23, 23, 30, 30, 30; 46:8, 10, 16; 47:3, 3, 3; 48:7, 7, 10, 11, 11, 11, 11, 12, 15, 16, 17, 25, 26, 29, 29, 29, 30, 30, 35, 40; 49:1, 1, 2, 3, 3, 10, 10, 10, 10, 20, 22; 50:16, 16, 17, 18, 19, 19, 25, 25, 28, 32, 34, 43, 45; 51:3, 3, 5, 6, 9, 11, 11, 15, 15, 16, 16, 16, 17, 17, 19, 19, 23, 23, 28, 31, 34, 45, 57; 52:1, 3, 4, 5, 34, 34

La 1:10, 12, 14, 17, 18; 2:1, 1, 1, 2, 3, 3, 4, 4, 4, 5, 6, 6, 6, 7, 7, 8, 7, 13; 3:1, 12, 13, 22, 27, 29, 30, 32, 34, 36, 39; 4:4, 11, 11, 20

Eze 1:15, 27, 27; 3:12, 18, 18, 18, 19, 19, 19, 20, 20, 20, 20; 7:13, 16, 20; 8:2, 2, 11, 11, 12; 9:1, 1, 2, 3, 11; 10:7; 12:12, 12, 12, 14; 13:22; 14:4, 4, 4, 4, 7, 7, 7, 7; 16:15; 17:4, 14, 15, 17, 18, 19, 20, 21, 21, 22; 18:6, 6, 7, 7, 8, 11, 12, 13, 14, 15, 15, 16, 17, 17, 18, 18, 18, 21, 22, 23, 24, 24, 24, 24, 26, 26, 27, 27, 28, 30; 19:7, 9; 20:7, 39; 21:3, 4, 5, 21, 22, 30; 22:11, 11, 11, 11; 25:9, 9; 26:3, 9, 10, 11; 29:3, 18, 19, 20; 30:11, 22, 22, 24; 31:2, 3, 4, 4, 5, 5, 6, 6, 6, 7, 7; 32:10, 22, 31, 31, 32; 33:4, 4, 5, 6, 6, 8, 8, 9, 9, 9, 11, 12, 13, 16, 16, 17, 17, 18; 32:10, 22, 31, 31, 32; 33:4, 4, 5, 6, 6, 8, 8, 9, 9, 9, 11, 12, 13, 13, 13, 14, 14, 16, 16, 17, 18; 34:12, 12, 26; 35:8, 8; 36:20; 37:7, 16, 16, 19; 38:6, 6, 21, 22; 39:11; 40:3; 43:2, 2, 17; 44:27; 45:8; 46:2, 2, 7, 12, 12, 12, 16, 16, 17, 17, 17, 17, 18, 18, 18; 47:3, 12, 23; 48:1

Da 1:2, 2, 2, 3, 8, 20; 2:1, 1, 2, 7, 13, 17, 17, 17, 19, 20, 24, 28, 28; 3:13, 19, 20, 24, 28, 28; 4:3, 3, 3, 3, 14, 14, 14, 14, 15, 16, 16, 19, 23, 33, 33, 33, 34, 35, 35, 37; 5:1, 2, 2, 2, 2, 3, 3, 6, 6, 7, 7, 9, 9, 10, 20, 20, 20, 21, 21, 21, 22, 23; 6:5, 10, 10, 10, 10, 10, 10, 11, 13, 14, 17, 17, 18, 18, 22, 23, 24, 26; 7:1, 1, 9, 9, 9, 11, 14, 14, 19, 19, 20, 20, 25, 26; 8:4, 4, 5, 6, 7, 7, 11, 21, 22, 24, 24, 24, 25, 25, 25; 9:2, 4, 10, 10, 12, 14, 14, 17; 10:6, 6, 6, 6, 6, 6, 9; 11:2, 3, 4, 4, 4, 5, 5, 6, 7, 9, 9, 10, 10, 11, 12, 15, 16, 17, 17, 18, 18, 18, 19, 20, 21, 24, 24, 24, 24, 25, 25, 26, 26, 28, 28, 28; 12:7, 7, 36, 37, 38, 38, 41, 42, 43, 45, 45; 12:7, 7

Hos 1:4, 9; 3:5; 5:5, 13, 13; 6:2, 3; 7:5, 9, 10; 8:14, 14; 9:8, 8, 13; 10:1, 1, 6, 11; 11:5, 6, 6; 12:2, 2, 3, 3, 5, 7, 14, 14, 14, 14; 13:12, 15, 15, 15; 14:5, 6, 6, 6, 7

Joel 2:7, 8, 11, 11, 11, 11, 16, 18, 18, 19, 20, 20, 20, 20; 3:16, 16

Am 1:2, 11, 11, 11, 15; 2:4, 7, 9, 9, 14; 3:4, 7, 7; 4:2, 13, 13; 5:8, 19; 6:8; 7:7, 10, 17; 9:6, 6, 6, 11

Ob 1:3, 6, 11, 11, 14, 14

Jnh 1:5, 7; 2:1; 3:6, 6, 7, 8, 9; 4:6, 6

Mic 1:2, 3, 11; 2:2, 2, 7; 3:4, 8; 4:2, 2, 4, 4, 5; 12; 5:3, 4; 6:2; 7:2, 3, 6, 9, 18, 18

Na 1:2, 2, 3, 3, 6, 6, 6, 6, 8, 13; 2:3, 3, 5, 12, 12, 12, 12

Hab 1:11, 11, 11; 2:4, 4, 5, 6, 9, 9, 15, 18, 20; 3:3, 3, 4, 4, 4, 5, 6, 10, 10, 14, 14, 16

Zep 1:7, 18; 2:11, 13, 13, 15; 3:5, 17

Hag 1:9; 2:12, 12, 22

Zec 1:21; 2:1, 8, 12, 13; 3:1, 5, 5, 10; 4:1, 2, 9; 5:4; 6:12, 13, 13; 7:9, 10, 12; 8:4, 4, 10, 16, 17; 9:7, 7, 7, 7, 10, 14, 16, 16, 17; 10:3, 3, 12; 11:6, 6, 17, 17, 17, 17; 12:4, 10, 10, 10; 13:3, 3, 3, 4; 14:4, 9, 13, 13

Mal 1:3, 3, 6, 10, 14; 2:6, 6, 7, 10, 15, 16; 3:1, 2, 5, 5, 14, 16, 17; 4:2

Mt 1:2, 11, 18, 21, 21, 23, 24, 25; 2:2, 11, 13, 14, 20, 21, 22; 3:3, 4, 4, 4, 7, 12, 12,

12; 4:6, 18, 21, 24; 5:1, 2, 13, 22, 22, 28, 31, 32, 35, 45; 6:27, 29, 33; 7:9, 24, 26, 28; 8:3, 3, 13, 14, 16, 20, 21, 23, 25; 9:1, 7, 10, 11, 19, 20, 21, 31, 37, 38; 10:1, 2, 2, 10, 24, 24, 24, 25, 25, 25, 35, 36, 38, 39, 39, 42; 11:1, 2, 20; 12:1, 10, 19, 21, 26, 29, 29, 33, 33, 33, 46, 46, 49, 49; 13:19, 24, 25, 25, 31, 34, 41, 41, 52, 54, 55, 55, 56, 57, 57; 14:2, 3, 11, 12, 19, 22, 31, 36; 15:5, 5, 6, 6, 12, 23, 32, 33, 36; 16:5, 13, 20, 21, 24, 24, 25, 26, 26, 27, 27, 28; 17:1, 2, 2, 10, 27; 18:6, 15, 23, 25, 25, 28, 29, 29, 31, 34; 19:3, 5, 9, 10, 10, 13, 16, 21, 22; 20:1, 2, 8, 28; 21:31, 34, 35, 37, 38, 41, 45; 22:2, 3, 5, 5, 6, 7, 8, 15, 24, 24, 24, 33, 35, 45; 23:1; 24:1, 17, 18, 31, 31, 32, 43, 45, 45, 46, 47, 48, 48, 49, 51; 25:14, 14, 15, 18, 21, 23, 26, 31, 32, 33, 34, 41; 26:1, 7, 8, 23, 39, 45, 51, 51, 51, 52, 63, 65, 65, 67; 27:19, 24, 25, 29, 29, 31, 32, 35, 37, 37, 44, 53, 60, 64; 28:3, 3, 7, 8, 9, 13

Mk 1:3, 6, 16, 19, 22, 28, 41; 2:8, 15, 15, 16; 3:5; 7, 9, 21, 27, 27, 31, 31; 4:2, 34; 5:3, 15, 22, 27, 28, 41, 42; 6:1, 1, 2, 3, 4, 4, 4, 5, 14, 17, 21, 21, 26, 27, 28, 29, 35, 41, 45, 56; 7:2, 11, 12, 12, 17, 19, 25, 32, 32, 33, 33, 35, 35; 8:1, 4, 6, 10, 12, 23, 23, 25, 26, 26, 27, 27, 33, 34, 34, 35, 36, 37, 38; 9:3, 14, 18, 21, 28, 31, 36, 41, 42, 50; 10:2, 7, 7, 10, 10, 13, 14, 16, 23, 24, 45, 46, 48, 50, 52; 11:1, 14, 16, 23, 23; 12:6, 13, 19, 19, 19, 19, 33, 34; 13:1, 15, 16, 27, 34, 34, 34; 14:3, 13, 16, 22, 36, 42, 50; 15:17, 20, 21, 24, 26, 27, 27; 16:7

Lk 1:5, 8, 9, 13, 14, 15, 23, 23, 24, 29, 31, 32, 33, 48, 49, 50, 51, 54, 54, 55, 59, 60, 62, 63, 64, 64, 67, 68, 69, 70, 72, 76, 77, 80; 2:3, 5, 21, 28, 33, 34, 41, 43, 47, 48, 51; 3:1, 4, 17, 17, 17, 18, 19; 4:10, 16, 22, 24, 30, 32, 32, 40; 5:12, 13, 19, 25, 29, 30; 6:1, 10, 13, 14, 17, 20, 24, 40, 40, 40, 45, 45, 45; 7:1, 3, 11, 12, 13, 14, 17, 20, 24, 40, 40, 44; 9:1, 14, 18, 23, 24, 24, 24, 26, 26, 29, 29, 31, 32, 42, 43, 51, 52, 53, 54, 58, 62; 10:1, 2, 7, 23, 30, 34, 34, 39; 11:1, 1, 6, 8, 8, 8, 21, 21, 22, 22, 54; 12:1, 22, 25, 27, 39, 42, 42, 43, 45, 45, 46, 47, 47; 13:6, 7, 13, 15, 15, 17, 19; 14:17:21, 21, 26, 26, 27, 34; 15:5, 6, 6, 12, 12, 13, 15, 16, 16, 20, 20, 26, 26, 27, 29, 30, 31, 32, 33; 18:7, 13, 13, 33; 18:7, 13, 15, 39, 43; 19:13, 14, 29; 20:20, 26, 26, 28, 28, 28, 44, 45; 22:4, 36, 36, 39, 44, 50, 51, 71; 23:11, 34, 45, 50; 24:8, 23, 26, 40, 40, 47

Jn 1:11, 11, 12, 14, 16, 35, 41; 2:2, 5, 11, 11, 12, 12, 17, 21, 22, 23; 3:4, 16, 17, 20, 21, 22, 32, 33, 33, 35; 4:2, 5, 6, 8, 12, 12, 27, 31, 34, 41, 44, 47, 50, 51, 53; 5:9, 18, 28, 35, 37, 37, 38, 43, 47; 6:2, 3, 5, 8, 12, 16, 22, 22, 24, 52, 53, 60, 61, 66; 7:3, 5, 10, 16, 17, 18, 18, 30, 38, 53; 8:6, 20, 44, 55; 9:1, 2, 2, 3, 7, 14, 15, 18, 18, 20, 21, 22, 22, 23, 25, 41, 50; 10:3, 3, 4, 4, 11; 11:2, 3, 7, 8, 12, 13, 16, 32, 41, 44, 54; 12:3, 4, 16, 17, 25, 25, 41, 50; 13:1, 1, 3, 4, 10, 12, 16, 23, 25; 15:10, 13, 13, 15, 19, 19; 16:17, 29, 32; 17:1; 18:1, 1, 2, 10, 19, 19; 19:2, 3, 23, 26, 27, 32, 38, 38, 39, 39, 40; 20:7, 20, 20, 25, 25, 26, 30; 21:2, 7, 14, 20, 24

Ac 1:3, 7, 14, 18, 20, 20, 22, 25; 2:6, 14, 29, 30, 30, 31, 31, 41; 3:2, 4, 7, 13, 16, 16, 18, 21, 26, 26; 4:26; 5:1, 2, 7, 10, 31, 32, 41; 6:15; 7:4, 5, 5, 6, 10, 10, 13, 14, 14, 20, 23, 23, 25, 25, 27; 8:1, 2, 28, 32, 32, 33, 33, 33, 35, 39, 39; 9:8, 12, 12, 17, 18, 18, 41; 10:2, 7, 22, 24, 30, 41, 45; 11:13, 29; 12:1, 7, 7, 10, 11, 15, 21; 13:8, 9, 13, 16, 23, 24, 25, 31, 36, 36; 14:3, 8, 15:14, 18; 16:1, 3, 27, 27, 32, 33, 34, 34; 17:2, 16, 28; 18:2, 6, 8, 14, 18, 18; 19:6, 12, 31, 33; 20:7, 10, 28, 32, 38; 21:11, 19; 22:14, 14, 15, 20, 30; 23:29; 30; 24:8, 23, 24; 27:3; 28:3, 4, 8, 23, 30

Ro 1:2, 3, 5, 9, 20; 2:4, 6, 18, 20; 7:10, 24, 25, 25, 26; 4:5, 13, 19, 23; 5:8, 9, 10, 10; 6:3, 5, 5, 16; 8:3, 9, 11, 28, 29, 32; 9:19, 22, 22, 23; 11:1, 2, 22, 33, 33, 34; 12:20; 13:10; 14:4, 5, 13; 15:2, 2, 10; 16:13, 15

1Co 1:9, 29; 2:10; 3:8, 8; 5:1; 6:5, 14, 18; 7:2, 4, 7, 11, 33, 36, 37, 37, 37, 37; 9:7, 10; 10:24, 28; 11:4, 4, 7, 21; 14:25, 25; 30; 15:10, 23, 23, 25, 27, 38; 16:12

2Co 2:11, 14; 3:7, 13; 5:10; 7:7, 12, 12, 13, 15; 8:9, 17; 9:7, 9, 15; 10:10, 10, 10; 11:3, 15, 33

Gal 1:15, 16; 3:16; 4:4, 6; 5:10; 6:4, 5, 8

Eph 1:5, 6, 7, 7, 9, 9, 11, 12, 14, 18, 18, 19, 20, 22; 2:3; 2:4, 7, 7, 10, 15; 3:5, 6, 7, 16, 16; 4:25, 28; 5:28, 29, 30, 30, 31, 31, 33; 6:10

Php 1:29; 2:4, 13, 30; 3:10, 10, 10, 21; 4:19

Col 1:9, 11, 13, 14, 20, 22, 22, 24, 26, 29; 2:1, 14; 3:8; 4:15

1Th 1:10; 2:11, 12, 19; 3:13; 4:4, 6, 8

2Th 1:7, 9, 10, 11; 2:6, 8, 8

1Ti 3:4, 4, 5; 5:8, 8, 18; 6:1, 15

2Ti 1:8, 9; 2:19, 26; 4:1, 1, 8, 14, 18

Tit 1:3; 3:5, 7

Heb 1:2, 3, 3, 3, 7, 7; 2:4, 8, 17; 3:2, 5, 6, 7, 15, 18; 4:1, 4, 12, 13, 13; 5:7; 6:10, 17; 7:10, 27; 8:11, 11; 9:12; 10:13, 13, 20, 30; 11:4, 5, 7, 17, 17, 22, 23; 12:10, 16; 13:12, 13, 15, 21, 21

Jas 1:8, 11, 14, 18, 18, 23, 24, 25, 26, 26; 2:21, 22; 3:13; 4:11, 11; 5:20

1Pe 1:3; 2:9, 21, 22, 24, 24; 3:10, 10, 12; 4:2, 13; 5:10

2Pe 1:3, 9, 16; 2:8, 16, 22; 3:4, 9, 13, 16

1Jn 1:3, 7, 10; 2:3, 4, 5, 9, 10, 11, 11, 12, 28; 3:9, 10, 12, 12, 14, 15, 16, 17, 17, 22, 22, 23, 23, 24; 4:9, 10, 12, 13, 20, 20, 21; 5:2, 3, 3, 9, 10, 11, 14, 16, 20

2Jn 1:6, 11

3Jn 1:7, 10

Jude 1:14, 24

Rev 1:1, 1, 1, 4, 5, 6, 14, 14, 14, 15, 15, 16, 16, 16, 17, 17; 2:1, 5, 18, 18; 3:5, 5, 5, 21; 6:5, 8, 17; 7:15; 9:11; 10:1, 1, 1, 2, 2, 2, 5, 7; 11:15, 19, 19; 12:3, 4, 5, 7, 7, 9, 10, 15, 16; 13:1, 1, 2, 2, 2, 3, 3, 6, 6, 6, 17, 18; 14:1, 7, 9, 9, 9, 10, 11, 11, 14, 14, 16, 19; 15:2, 2, 2, 8; 16:2, 2, 3, 4, 8, 10, 10, 12, 12, 13, 15, 16, 16, 19, 20, 21; 17:17; 18:1; 19:2, 2, 5, 7, 7, 10, 12, 12, 13, 15, 16, 16, 19, 20, 21; 20:1, 4, 4, 7; 21:3, 7; 22:3, 4, 4, 6, 6, 12, 14, 19

I (8851)

Ge 1:29, 30; 2:18; 3:10, 10, 10, 10, 11, 12, 13, 15, 16, 17; 4:1, 9, 9, 13, 14, 14, 23; 6:7, 7, 13, 17, 17, 18; 7:1, 4, 4, 4; 8:21, 21, 21; 9:3, 5, 5, 5, 9, 12, 13, 14, 15, 15, 16, 16, 17; 12:1, 2, 2, 3, 7, 11, 13, 19; 13:8, 9, 9, 9, 15, 16, 17; 14:22, 23, 23, 23; 15:1, 2, 7, 8, 8, 14, 18; 16:2, 2, 5, 5, 8, 10, 13; 17:1, 2, 5, 6, 8, 9, 16, 16, 19, 20, 20, 20, 21; 18:3, 3, 4, 5, 10, 12, 12, 13, 14, 15, 17, 17, 19, 21, 21, 26, 26, 27, 28, 28, 29, 30, 30, 30, 30, 31, 31, 32, 32; 19:2, 7, 8, 8, 19, 19, 21, 21, 22, 34; 20:5, 6, 6, 6, 9, 11, 13, 16; 21:7, 13, 18, 23, 24, 26, 30; 22:1, 2, 5, 7, 11, 12, 16, 17; 23:4, 4, 8, 11, 11, 11, 13, 13, 13; 24:2, 3, 3, 5, 7, 12, 13, 14, 14, 14, 14, 17, 19, 23, 24, 27, 31, 33, 33, 34, 34, 37, 39, 40, 42, 42, 43, 43, 44, 45, 45, 45, 46, 46, 47, 47, 48, 49, 56, 58; 25:22, 30, 30, 32; 26:2, 3, 3, 3, 3, 4, 9, 24, 24; 27:1, 2, 2, 3, 4, 4, 6, 7, 8, 9, 11, 12, 12, 18, 19, 19, 19, 21, 21, 24, 25, 32, 33, 33, 37, 37, 37, 41, 45, 45, 46; 28:13, 13, 15, 15, 15, 16, 20, 21, 22; 29:18, 19, 19, 21, 25, 33, 34, 35; 30:1, 2, 3, 8, 8, 13, 14, 15, 16, 18, 23, 25, 26, 26, 27, 27, 27, 28, 28; 31:3, 5, 6, 10, 11, 12, 13, 29, 31, 31, 35, 38, 38, 39, 39, 40, 41, 41, 43, 44, 51, 52; 32:4, 5, 5, 9, 10, 10, 10, 11, 11, 11, 12, 20, 20, 26, 29, 30; 33:8, 9, 10, 10, 10, 10, 11, 12, 14, 14, 14:4:8, 11, 12, 30, 30, 30; 35:3, 3, 11, 12, 12, 12; 37:6, 9, 10, 10, 13, 13, 16, 16, 17, 30, 30, 35; 38:16, 17, 18, 22, 23, 25, 25, 26, 26; 39:9, 9, 14, 15, 18; 40:8, 11, 11, 14, 14, 15, 15, 16, 16; 41:9, 11, 15, 15, 17, 19, 21, 22, 24, 28, 40, 41, 44; 42:2, 14, 18, 22, 34, 34, 37, 37; 43:9, 9, 14, 14, 23; 44:15, 17, 18, 21, 28, 28, 30, 32, 32, 33, 34, 34; 45:3, 4, 4, 11, 11, 18, 28, 28; 46:2, 3, 3, 4, 4, 30; 47:16, 23, 29, 29, 29, 30; 48:4, 4, 5, 7, 9, 9, 11, 19, 19, 21, 22; 49:1, 7, 18, 29, 31; 50:4, 4, 4, 5, 5, 5, 17, 19, 21, 24

Ex 2:7, 9, 10, 22; 3:3, 4, 6, 7, 7, 8, 9, 10, 11, 11, 11, 12, 12, 13, 13, 14, 14, 14, 16, 16, 17, 17, 19, 20, 20, 21; 4:10, 10, 11, 12, 13, 14, 15, 18, 21, 21, 23, 23; 5:2, 2, 2, 10, 23; 6:1, 2, 3, 3, 4, 4, 5, 5, 6, 6, 6, 7, 7, 7, 8, 8, 8, 8, 29, 29, 30; 7:1, 2, 3, 4, 4, 5, 5, 17, 17; 8:2, 8, 9, 21, 22, 23, 28, 29, 29; 9:14, 15, 15, 16, 18, 27, 27, 28, 29, 29; 10:1, 1, 2, 2, 2, 4, 10, 16, 17, 29, 29; 11:1, 4, 8; 12:12, 12, 12, 13, 13, 13, 17; 13:8, 15, 15; 14:4, 4, 4, 17, 17, 17, 18, 18; 15:1, 1, 2, 2, 9, 9, 9, 26, 26, 26; 16:4, 4, 12, 12, 32; 17:4, 6, 6, 9, 14; 18:3, 6, 11, 16, 16, 19; 19:4, 4, 9, 9; 20:2, 5, 22, 24, 24, 24; 21:5, 5, 13; 22:23, 24, 27; 23:7, 15, 20, 20, 22, 22, 23, 25, 26, 27, 27, 28, 29, 30, 31, 31; 24:12; 25:8, 9, 16, 21, 22, 22; 28:3; 29:35, 42, 43, 44, 44, 45, 45, 46, 46; 30:6, 36; 31:2, 3, 6, 6, 6, 6, 13; 32:8, 9, 10, 10, 13, 13, 13, 18, 24, 30, 30, 32, 33, 34, 34; 33:1, 1, 2, 2, 3, 3, 5, 5, 12, 13, 13, 14, 17, 19, 19, 22, 23; 34:1, 4, 10, 10, 11, 16, 16, 19, 4:4, 9, 9; 20:2, 5, 22, 24, 24, 24; 21:5, 5; 32:8, 9, 10, 10, 13, 13, 13; 34:1, 4, 10, 10, 11, 11, 24, 24, 24; 21:5, 5, 13, 13, 22, 23, 23, 25, 26, 27, 27, 29, 30, 31, 31, 32, 33; 23:10, 22, 30, 43, 43; 24:22; 25:2, 17, 21, 38, 42, 55, 55; 26:1, 2, 4, 6, 9, 11, 12, 13, 13, 16, 16, 17, 18, 19, 19, 21, 22, 24, 25, 25, 26, 28, 28, 30, 30, 31, 31, 32,

Lev 6:17; 7:34; 8:31, 35; 10:3, 13, 18, 19; 11:44, 44, 45, 45; 14:34, 34; 16:2; 17:10; 19:2, 3, 4, 10, 12, 14, 16, 18, 25, 28, 30; 31, 32, 34, 36, 37; 20:3, 5, 6, 7, 24, 24, 25, 26, 26; 21:8, 12, 15, 23; 22:2, 3, 8, 9, 16, 30, 31, 32, 32, 33; 23:10, 22, 30, 43, 43; 24:22; 25:2, 17, 21, 38, 42, 55, 55; 26:1, 2, 4, 6, 9, 11, 12, 13, 13, 16, 16, 17, 18, 19, 19, 21, 22, 24, 25, 25, 26, 28, 28, 30, 30, 31, 31, 32,

Idx

18, 19, 19, 21, 22, 23, 23, 23, 24, 25, 25, 26, 26, 26, 26, 27, 28, 28, 29, 29, 30, 32, 33, 33, 36, 36, 36, 37, 37, 38; 37:3, 5, 6, 6, 7, 7, 7, 8, 10, 12, 13, 13, 14, 14, 19, 21, 22, 23, 23, 25, 26, 26, 27, 28; 38:3, 4, 4, 11, 11, 16, 16, 17, 17, 19, 21, 22, 22, 23, 23, 23; 39:1, 2, 7, 3, 4, 5, 6, 7, 7, 7, 8, 11, 13, 17, 19, 21, 21, 21, 21, 22, 22, 23, 25, 27, 28, 28, 29, 29; 40:4, 4; 41:8; 43:3, 3, 3, 3, 3, 6, 7, 8, 9, 27; 44:4, 4, 5, 12, 14, 28, 28; 47:5, 7, 14

Da 1:10, 12; 2:3, 8, 9, 23, 24, 25, 26, 30; 3:14, 15, 25, 29; 4:2, 4, 5, 6, 7, 8, 9, 9, 10, 13, 18, 30, 34, 34, 34, 36, 37; 5:11, 14, 16, 17; 6:22, 26; 7:2, 4, 6, 7, 8, 9, 11, 11, 13, 15, 16, 19, 21, 28; 8:2, 2, 2, 2, 3, 4, 5, 6, 7, 13, 15, 15, 16, 17, 17, 18, 19, 27, 27, 27; 9:2, 3, 4, 16, 20, 21, 21, 22, 23; 10:2, 3, 3, 4, 5, 7, 8, 8, 9, 10, 11, 11, 11, 12, 13, 14, 15, 15, 16, 16, 19, 20, 20, 20, 21; 11:1, 1, 2; 12:5, 7, 8, 8, 8

Hos 1:4, 5, 6, 6, 7, 9; 2:2, 3, 4, 5, 6, 7, 8, 9, 10, 11, 12, 12, 13, 14, 14, 15, 16, 17, 18, 19, 19, 20, 21, 21, 23, 23, 23; 3:2, 3, 3; 4:5, 6, 6, 7, 9, 14; 5:2, 3, 9, 10, 12, 14, 14, 14, 14, 15; 6:4, 4, 5, 5, 6, 10, 11; 7:1, 2, 12, 12, 12, 13, 15; 8:4, 10, 12, 14; 9:10, 10, 12, 13, 15, 15, 16, 16; 10:10, 11, 11; 11:1, 3, 3, 4, 4, 4, 8, 8, 9, 9, 9, 9, 11; 12:8, 8, 9, 10, 10; 13:4, 5, 7, 7, 8, 8, 10, 11, 14, 14, 14, 14; 14:4, 4, 5, 8, 8

Joel 1:19; 2:19, 19, 20, 25, 25, 27, 27, 28, 29, 30; 3:1, 2, 4, 7, 8, 10, 10, 17, 21, 21

Am 1:3, 4, 5, 6, 7, 8, 8, 9, 10, 11, 12, 13, 14; 2:1, 2, 3, 4, 5, 6, 9, 9, 10, 11, 13; 3:1, 2, 2, 14, 14, 15; 4:6, 7, 7, 9, 10, 10, 10, 11, 12, 12; 5:1, 12, 17, 21, 21, 21, 22, 22, 23, 27; 6:8, 8, 14; 7:2, 2, 5, 5, 8, 8, 9, 14, 14, 14, 15; 8:2, 2, 7, 9, 9, 10, 10, 10, 11; 9:1, 1, 2, 3, 3, 4, 4, 7, 8, 8, 9, 9, 11, 11, 11, 14, 15, 15

Ob 1:2, 4, 8

Jnh 1:9, 9, 12; 2:2, 2, 4, 4, 4, 6, 7, 9, 9, 9; 3:2; 4:2, 2, 2, 2, 3, 9, 11

Mic 1:6, 6, 6, 7, 8, 8, 8, 15; 2:3, 11, 12, 12, 12; 3:1, 1, 8, 9; 4:6, 6, 6, 7, 13, 13, 13; 5:10, 10, 11, 12, 13, 14, 14, 15; 6:3, 3, 4, 4, 6, 6, 7, 11, 13, 14, 16; 7:1, 7, 7, 8, 8, 8, 9, 9, 9, 15

Na 1:12, 12, 13, 14, 14; 2:13, 13, 13; 3:5, 5, 5, 6, 7

Hab 1:2, 5, 6; 2:1, 1, 1; 3:2, 7, 16, 16, 16, 18, 18

Zep 1:2, 3, 3, 3, 4, 4, 8, 9, 11, 12; 2:5, 8, 9, 15; 3:6, 6, 7, 7, 8, 8, 9, 11, 12, 18, 19, 19, 19, 20, 20, 20, 20

Hag 1:8, 8, 9, 11, 13; 2:4, 5, 6, 7, 7, 9, 15, 17, 19, 21, 22, 22, 22, 23, 23

Zec 1:3, 6, 8, 9, 9, 14, 15, 15, 16, 18, 19, 21; 2:1, 2, 5, 6, 9, 10, 10, 11; 3:4, 4, 5, 7, 8, 9, 9, 9; 4:2, 2, 4, 5, 11, 12, 13; 5:1, 2, 2, 4, 6, 9, 10; 6:1, 4; 7:3, 3, 13, 14; 8:2, 2, 3, 7, 8, 8, 10, 11, 11, 12, 13, 13, 14, 14, 15, 17, 21; 9:6, 7, 8, 8, 10, 11, 12, 12, 13; 10:3, 6, 6, 6, 6, 6, 6, 8, 8, 9, 10, 10, 12; 11:5, 6, 6, 6, 7, 7, 7, 7, 7, 8, 9, 9, 10, 10, 10, 12, 13, 13, 14, 14, 16; 12:2, 3, 4, 4, 6, 9, 10; 13:2, 2, 5, 5, 6, 7, 9, 9, 9; 14:2

Mal 1:2, 2, 3, 4, 6, 6, 9, 10, 10, 13, 14; 2:2, 2, 3, 4, 5, 9; 3:1, 5, 5, 6, 6, 7, 10, 11, 17; 4:7; 4:3, 4, 5, 6

Mt 2:8, 13, 15; 3:9, 11, 11, 11, 14, 17; 4:9, 9; 5:17, 17, 18, 20, 22, 26, 28, 32, 34, 39, 44; 6:2, 5, 16, 25, 29; 7:23, 23, 24; 8:3, 7, 8, 9, 9, 10, 11, 12, 13, 19, 9:13, 13, 21, 21, 28; 10:15, 16, 23, 27, 32, 33, 34, 34, 35, 42; 11:9, 10, 11, 16, 22, 24, 25, 28, 29; 12:6, 7, 18, 18, 27, 28, 31, 36, 44, 44; 13:13, 15, 17, 30, 35, 35; 14:27; 15:24, 32, 32; 16:11, 13, 15, 18; 17:5, 12, 16, 17, 17, 20; 18:3, 10, 13, 18, 19, 20, 21, 22, 26, 29, 32, 33; 19:9, 16, 16, 20, 23, 24, 28; 20:4, 13, 14, 15, 15, 22, 22, 23, 32; 21:21, 24, 24, 24, 27, 27, 29, 30, 31, 43; 22:4, 32, 44; 23:34, 36, 37, 39; 24:2, 5, 25, 34, 47; 25:12, 12, 20, 21, 22, 23, 24, 25, 26, 26, 27, 35, 35, 35, 36, 36, 40, 42, 42, 43, 45; 26:13, 15, 18, 21, 25, 29, 29, 29, 31, 32, 32, 33, 34, 52, 55, 55, 61, 63, 64, 70, 72, 74; 27:4, 4, 17, 19, 21, 22, 24, 43; 28:5, 7, 20, 20

Mk 1:2, 7, 7, 8, 11, 17, 24, 38, 38, 41; 2:11, 17; 3:28; 5:7, 7, 23, 28, 28, 41; 6:11, 16, 22, 23, 24, 25, 50; 8:2, 3, 12, 19, 24, 27, 29; 9:1, 13, 17, 18, 19, 19, 24, 25, 41; 10:15, 17, 17, 20, 29, 30, 38, 39, 39, 51, 51; 11:23, 24, 29, 29, 30, 31, 32; 12:15, 26, 36, 43; 13:6, 23, 30, 37, 37; 14:9, 14, 18, 19, 19, 25, 25, 25, 27, 28, 28, 29, 30, 31, 31, 32, 36, 44, 49, 58, 58, 62, 68, 68, 71; 15:9, 12

Lk 1:18, 18, 19, 34; 2:10, 48, 49; 3:8, 16, 16, 16, 22; 4:6, 6, 6, 24, 25, 34, 43, 43; 5:5, 8, 13, 24, 32; 6:9, 27, 46, 47; 7:6, 7, 8, 8, 9, 9, 14, 26, 27, 28, 31, 40, 43, 44, 45, 47; 8:28, 28, 46; 9:9, 9, 18, 20, 27, 38, 40, 41, 57, 61; 10:3, 12, 18, 19, 21, 24, 25, 35, 35; 11:6, 7, 8, 9, 18, 19, 20, 24, 35, 49, 50, 50, 51, 51, 59; 13:3, 5, 7, 8, 18, 20, 24, 25, 27, 27, 32, 32, 32, 33, 34, 35; 14:18, 18, 18, 19, 19, 19, 20, 20, 24; 15:6, 7, 9, 9, 10, 17, 18, 18, 21, 29, 29, 29, 31; 16:2, 3,

3, 3, 4, 4, 9, 24, 27, 28; 17:4, 8, 8, 9, 34; 18:4, 5, 8, 11, 12, 12, 12, 14, 17, 18, 21, 29, 41, 41; 19:5, 8, 8, 8, 13, 20, 21, 22, 22, 22, 23, 26, 27, 40; 20:3, 8, 8, 13, 13, 43; 21:3, 8, 15, 32; 22:11, 15, 15, 16, 16, 18, 18, 27, 29, 32, 33, 34, 35, 37, 53, 57, 58, 60, 67, 68, 70; 23:4, 14, 15, 16, 22, 22, 43, 46; 24:39, 44, 44, 49

Jn 1:15, 20, 21, 23, 26, 27, 30, 31, 31, 32, 33, 34, 48, 50, 50, 51; 2:4, 19; 3:3, 5, 7, 11, 12, 12, 28, 28, 28, 30; 4:14, 14, 15, 17, 17, 19, 25, 26, 29, 32, 35, 38, 39; 5:7, 7, 17, 19, 24, 25, 30, 30, 30, 30, 31, 32, 34, 34, 36, 36, 41, 42, 43, 45; 6:20, 26, 32, 35, 36, 37, 38, 39, 40, 41, 42, 44, 47, 48, 51, 51, 51, 53, 54, 56, 57, 63, 65, 70; 7:7, 8, 17, 21, 23, 28, 28, 29, 29, 33, 34, 36, 36, 41, 42, 44, 44, 44, 14, 14, 15, 16, 16, 18, 21, 21, 22, 23, 24, 24, 25, 26, 26, 28, 28, 28, 29, 34, 37, 38, 38, 40, 42, 42, 45, 46, 49, 49, 50, 51, 54, 55, 55, 55, 55, 55, 58, 58; 9:4, 5, 5, 9, 11, 11, 11, 12, 15, 25, 25, 25, 27, 36, 38, 39; 10:1, 7, 7, 9, 10, 11, 14, 14, 14, 14, 14, 16, 17, 18, 18, 18, 25, 25, 26, 28, 30, 32, 34, 34, 36, 36, 37, 38, 38; 11:11, 11, 15, 15, 22, 24, 24, 25, 27, 40, 41, 42, 42; 12:24, 26, 27, 27, 28, 32, 32, 40, 46, 47, 47, 48, 49, 49, 49, 50, 50; 13:7, 8, 12, 13, 14, 15, 15, 16, 16, 18, 18, 19, 19, 20, 20, 21, 26, 26, 33, 33, 33, 34, 34, 36, 37, 37, 38; 14:2, 2, 3, 3, 3, 4, 6, 9, 10, 10, 11, 11, 12, 12, 12, 12, 13, 14, 14, 14, 16, 18, 18, 18, 19, 19, 20, 20, 21, 25, 26, 27, 27, 27, 28, 28, 28, 28, 29, 30, 31, 31; 15:1, 3, 4, 4, 5, 5, 9, 10, 11, 12, 12, 13, 14, 14, 15, 15, 16, 16, 17, 19, 20, 20, 22, 24, 26; 16:1, 4, 4, 4, 4, 5, 5, 7, 7, 7, 7, 10, 12, 13, 14, 14, 15, 16, 18, 19, 20, 22, 23, 25, 25, 26, 26, 27, 28, 28, 32, 33, 33; 17:4, 6, 8, 9, 11, 11, 13, 14, 14, 16, 18, 19, 20, 21, 22, 23, 24, 24, 25, 26, 26, 26, 27, 27, 28, 28, 32, 33, 33; 17:4, 6, 8, 9, 11, 13, 14, 14, 16, 18, 19, 20, 21, 22, 23, 24, 24, 25, 26, 26; 18:5, 6, 8, 8, 9, 11, 11, 11, 17, 20, 20, 23, 25, 26, 35, 36, 37, 37, 37, 38, 38, 39; 19:4, 4, 6, 10, 15, 21, 22, 26; 20:13, 15, 17, 17, 21, 25, 25, 26, 35, 37, 37, 38, 38, 39, 39; 19:4, 4, 6, 10, 15, 21, 22, 24; 21:5, 6, 7, 15, 17, 21, 25, 25; 21:3, 15, 16, 17, 18, 22, 22, 23, 23, 25

Ac 1:1; 2:17, 18, 19, 25, 25, 35; 3:6, 6, 6, 17; 5:38; 7:3, 7, 32, 34, 34, 34, 34, 43, 56; 8:19, 23, 31, 34, 37; 9:5, 10, 13, 16; 10:14, 20, 21, 26, 28, 29, 29, 29, 30, 30, 33, 34, 37; 11:5, 5, 6, 6, 7, 8, 11, 15, 16, 17, 17; 12:11; 13:2, 22, 25, 25, 25, 33, 34, 41, 47; 15:16, 16, 16; 16:18, 30; 17:3, 22, 23, 23, 23; 18:6, 6, 10, 10, 14, 15, 21; 19:15, 15, 21, 21; 20:18, 18, 20, 22, 24, 24, 24, 25, 26, 27, 29, 31, 32, 33, 35; 21:13, 37, 39, 39; 22:1, 3, 4, 5, 6, 7, 8, 8, 10, 10, 11, 13, 17, 17, 17, 19, 20, 21, 21, 22, 25, 25, 25, 25:8, 8, 10, 10, 11, 13, 17, 17, 17, 19, 20, 21, 21, 22, 25, 26, 26; 26:2, 2, 2, 3, 3, 5, 6, 7, 9, 9, 10, 10, 10, 11, 12, 13, 14, 15, 16, 16, 17, 19, 22, 25, 26, 26, 27, 29, 27:10, 22, 23, 23, 25, 34; 28:17, 17, 19, 19, 20, 20, 27

Ro 1:8, 9, 9, 10, 11, 11, 12, 13, 13, 14, 14, 15, 16; 3:5, 7, 26; 4:17; 6:19; 7:1, 7, 7, 9, 9, 10, 14, 15, 15, 15, 15, 15, 16, 16, 16, 17, 18, 18, 19, 19, 19, 19, 20, 20, 21, 21, 22, 23, 24, 25, 25; 8:18, 38; 9:1, 1, 2, 3, 9, 13, 13, 15, 15, 15, 16, 16, 17, 25, 33; 10:2, 18, 19, 19, 19, 20, 20, 21, 22, 22, 23, 24, 25, 25; 11:1, 1, 3, 4, 11, 13, 13, 14, 19, 25, 27; 12:1, 3, 19; 14:11, 14; 15:8, 9, 14, 15, 16, 17, 17, 18, 19, 20, 20, 22, 24, 24, 24, 25, 28, 28, 29, 29, 29, 30, 31, 32; 16:1, 4, 17, 19, 19, 22

1Co 1:4, 10, 12, 12, 12, 12, 12, 14, 14, 15, 16, 16, 16, 19; 2:1, 1, 2, 3; 3:1, 2, 4, 4, 6, 10; 4:3, 3, 4, 4, 6, 8, 9, 14, 14, 15, 16, 17, 17, 18, 19, 21; 5:3, 3, 9, 11, 12; 6:5, 12, 15; 7:6, 7, 7, 8, 8, 10, 12, 17, 25, 25, 26, 26, 28, 29, 32, 35, 35, 40, 40; 8:13, 13; 9:1, 1, 2, 2, 6, 8, 15, 16, 16, 16, 17, 18, 18, 18, 19, 19, 19, 20, 20, 20, 21, 22, 22, 22, 23, 23, 24, 34; 12:1, 3, 15, 15, 16, 16, 21, 21, 22, 22, 22, 23, 23, 24, 34; 12:1, 3, 15, 15, 16, 16, 21, 21, 22, 22, 23, 23, 24, 34; 13:1, 2, 3, 17, 17, 18, 18, 22, 22, 23, 23, 23, 34; 12:1, 3, 15, 15, 15, 15, 16; 16:1, 4, 17, 19, 19, 22

2Co 1:13, 15, 17, 17, 17, 17, 23, 23; 2:1, 1, 2, 3, 3, 3, 4, 4, 4, 8, 9, 9, 10, 10, 10, 10, 12, 13, 13, 13, 13; 4:13, 13; 5:8, 11; 6:2, 2, 13, 16, 16, 17; 7:3, 3, 4, 4, 7, 8, 8, 8, 8, 9, 9, 12, 12, 14, 14, 14, 16; 8:3, 8, 10, 13, 22; 9:2, 2, 3, 3, 5, 6; 10:1, 2, 2, 2, 2, 8, 8, 9, 9; 11:2, 2, 3, 5, 5, 6, 7, 7, 8, 9, 9, 9, 9, 11, 12, 12, 12, 16, 16, 16, 16, 18, 21, 21, 21, 22, 22, 23, 23, 24, 24, 25, 25, 25, 25, 29, 29, 30, 30, 31, 31, 33; 12:1, 2, 2, 2, 3, 3, 5, 5, 6, 6, 6, 6, 7, 8, 9, 9, 10, 10, 11, 11, 11, 11, 13, 14, 14, 14, 14, 15, 15, 16, 16, 16, 17, 18, 19, 20, 20, 20, 21; 13:1, 2, 2, 2, 6, 7, 10, 10, 11

Gal 1:6, 9, 10, 10, 10, 10, 11, 12, 12, 13, 16, 16, 17, 17, 18, 19, 20, 20, 20, 21; 2:1, 2, 2, 2,

10, 11, 14, 14, 14, 18, 18, 18, 19, 19, 20, 20, 20, 20, 20, 21; 3:2, 15, 17; 4:1, 11, 11, 12, 12, 12, 12, 13, 15, 16, 16, 18, 19, 20, 20; 5:2, 3, 10, 11, 11, 11, 11, 12, 16, 21, 21; 6:11, 14, 14, 17

Eph 1:15, 15; 3:1, 3, 7, 8, 13, 14; 4:1, 17; 5:32; 6:19, 20, 20, 20, 21, 22

Php 1:3, 7, 8, 9, 12, 17, 18, 19, 20, 22, 22, 23, 25, 25, 27, 27; 2:16, 16, 17, 17, 19, 19, 19, 20, 23, 23, 24, 24, 25, 27, 28; 3:4, 4, 7, 8, 8, 8, 10, 11, 12, 12, 12, 13, 13, 14, 14, 18; 4:2, 3, 4, 10, 11, 11, 11, 12, 13, 14, 14, 18; 4:2, 3, 4, 10, 11, 11, 11, 12, 13, 14, 14, 18

Col 1:20, 23, 25, 29; 2:1, 1, 4, 5, 5; 4:3, 4, 4, 8, 13

1Th 2:18; 3:5, 5; 4:9, 13; 5:1, 23, 27

2Th 2:5, 5; 3:17

1Ti 1:3, 3, 12, 13, 13, 15, 16, 18, 20; 2:1, 7, 7, 8, 12; 3:14, 15; 4:13; 5:14, 21; 6:13

2Ti 1:3, 3, 3, 4, 5, 5, 6, 11, 12, 12, 12, 12, 12, 12; 2:7, 9, 10; 3:11; 4:1, 6, 7, 7, 7, 12, 13, 16, 17, 20

Tit 1:5, 5; 3:8, 12, 12

Phm 1:4, 8, 9, 10, 10, 12, 13, 14, 19, 19, 21, 21, 22, 22

Heb 1:5, 5, 13; 2:12, 12, 13, 13; 3:10, 11; 4:3; 5:5; 6:14, 14; 7:9; 8:8, 9, 9, 9, 10, 10, 10, 12, 12; 10:7, 7, 9, 16, 16, 16, 17, 30; 11:32; 12:21, 26; 13:5, 6, 19, 19, 22, 22, 23

Jas 1:13; 2:18, 18

1Pe 1:16; 2:6, 11; 5:1, 12, 12

2Pe 1:12, 13, 13, 14, 15, 17; 3:1, 1, 26; 4:20; 5:13, 16

1Jn 2:1, 4, 7, 8, 12, 13, 13, 14, 21, 26; 4:20; 5:13, 16

2Jn 1:1, 1, 4, 4, 5, 5, 12, 12

3Jn 1:1, 2, 3, 4, 9, 10, 10, 13, 13, 14, 14

Jude 1:3, 5

Rev 1:8, 9, 10, 11, 12, 12, 17, 17, 18, 18; 2:2, 4, 5, 6, 7, 9, 9, 10, 13, 14, 15, 16, 17, 19, 20, 21, 21, 22, 23, 23, 23, 24, 24, 25, 26, 27, 28; 3:1, 2, 3, 3, 5, 9, 16, 17, 18, 19, 19, 20, 20, 21, 21; 4:1, 1, 1, 2, 4; 5:1, 2, 4, 6, 11, 11, 13; 6:1, 1, 2, 3, 5, 5, 6, 7, 8, 9, 12; 7:1, 2, 4, 9, 14; 8:2; 9:1, 13, 16, 17; 10:1, 4, 4, 5, 8, 9, 10, 10; 11:3; 12:10; 13:1, 2, 3, 11; 14:1, 2, 2, 6, 13, 14; 15:1, 2, 5; 16:1, 5, 7, 13, 15; 17:1, 3, 6, 6, 6, 7; 18:1, 4, 7; 19:1, 6, 10, 10, 11, 17, 19; 20:1, 4, 4, 11, 12; 21:1, 2, 3, 5, 6, 6, 7, 9, 22; 22:7, 8, 8, 8, 9, 12, 13, 16, 16, 18, 20

IN (12674)

Ge 1:1, 6, 11, 12, 14, 15, 17, 20, 22, 22, 26, 27, 27, 29; 2:3, 4, 5, 8, 9, 17; 3:3, 5, 8, 8, 10, 16, 17, 19, 19; 4:3, 8, 12, 14, 16, 20, 22; 5:1, 1, 2, 3; 6:4, 4, 4, 5, 8, 9, 14, 16, 16, 17; 7:1, 7, 9, 11, 13, 13, 15, 16, 16, 16, 22, 22, 23; 8:1, 4, 5, 9, 11, 11, 13, 13, 13, 22, 22, 23; 9:6, 7, 13, 14, 16, 27; 10:5, 5, 8, 10, 20, 20, 25, 31, 32, 32; 11:2, 28, 28, 31, 32; 12:3, 5, 6, 10, 10; 13:2, 2, 7, 7, 12, 12, 17, 18, 18; 14:1, 3, 4, 5, 5, 5, 15, 15, 16, 18; 16:2; 16:2, 3, 4, 5, 6, 7, 7, 12; 17:7, 9, 12, 12, 13, 17, 21, 23, 23, 24, 25, 25, 26, 27; 18:1, 1, 1, 3, 9, 10, 11, 18, 26; 19:1, 2, 2, 3, 5, 8, 9, 12, 12, 14, 14, 15, 17, 19, 27, 29, 30, 30, 31, 33, 34; 20:1, 3, 5, 6, 6, 8, 11; 21:2, 7, 11, 12, 12, 12, 14, 14, 15, 18, 20, 21, 22, 33, 34; 22:3, 6, 9, 13, 13, 14, 17, 17, 18; 23:2, 6, 9, 10, 11, 13, 14, 17, 17, 18; 24:1, 1, 10, 22, 30, 30, 31, 33, 35, 37, 38, 38, 40, 41, 42, 46; 31:10, 11, 14, 18, 18, 20, 23, 24, 25, 25, 28, 29, 34, 40, 41, 54, 55; 32:5, 21, 32; 33:8, 10, 15, 18; 34:5, 7, 7, 11, 15, 19, 21, 28, 28, 30; 35:3, 4, 4, 6, 13, 14, 17, 18, 19; 36:5, 6, 8, 9, 16, 17, 21, 24, 30, 31, 32, 33, 34, 35, 36, 37, 38, 39, 43; 37:1, 1, 7, 22, 13, 15, 17, 22, 24, 24, 33; 38:1, 2, 7, 8, 9, 11, 11, 12, 13, 14, 16, 16, 18, 18, 21, 24, 25, 27; 39:2, 3, 4, 5, 5, 5, 6, 8, 9, 11, 11, 14, 17, 20, 22; 40:3, 4, 5, 5, 6, 8, 9, 10, 14, 16, 17, 19; 41:8, 12, 12, 12, 13, 15, 17, 18, 19, 26, 29, 33, 34; 20:1, 3, 5, 6, 6, 9, 13, 13, 14, 17, 17, 18; 23:2, 2, 6, 9, 13, 13, 14, 17, 17, 18, 18, 19, 24; 41:1, 10, 20, 22, 26, 30; 45:6, 6, 7, 10, 13, 16; 46:2, 5, 6, 12, 15, 20, 27, 31, 34; 47:1, 4, 4, 4, 6, 6, 7, 9, 11, 11, 11, 13, 14, 14, 15, 15, 17, 18, 24, 25, 27, 27, 28, 29, 29, 30; 48:3, 5, 6, 7, 7, 7, 9, 13, 13, 16, 20; 49:1, 5, 6, 6, 7, 7, 8, 11, 11, 17, 24, 27, 29, 30, 30, 50; 50:4, 4, 5, 5, 8, 14, 19; 2:3, 11, 12, 15,

Ex 1:5, 14, 14, 14, 14, 19; 2:3, 11, 12, 15, 22, 23; 3:1, 2, 7, 16, 20, 21, 22; 4:2, 4, 14, 15, 17, 18, 18, 19, 20, 21, 24, 21, 23; 30; 5:1, 1, 14, 16, 19, 20, 21, 21, 23; 6:5, 8, 11, 28; 7:3, 10, 11, 15, 15, 16, 17, 17, 17, 18, 19, 19, 20, 20, 20, 21; 8:9,

11, 17, 17, 20, 22, 22, 22, 25, 29; 9:1, 3, 5, 8, 9, 13, 14, 16, 16, 18, 19, 19, 21, 22, 24, 25, 26, 31; 10:1, 2, 2, 3, 14, 15, 15, 19, 19, 22, 23, 28; 11:2, 3, 3, 3, 5, 5, 7, 8, 9; 12:1, 3, 6, 6, 8, 11, 11, 12, 16, 16, 18, 19, 20, 20; 5:2, 3, 10, 11, 11, 11, 12, 16, 20, 21; 6:11, 14, 14, 17

(second IN block continued)

Lev 1:7, 8, 9, 12; 2:4, 5, 6, 7, 11; 4:6, 7, 17, 18, 24, 29, 33; 5:4, 5, 5, 13, 15, 16; 6:2, 2, 2, 3, 5, 5, 7, 9, 12, 25, 26, 26, 27, 28, 28, 30; 7:2, 6, 9, 9, 24, 24, 26, 35, 35, 36, 38, 38, 38; 8:8, 21, 31, 33; 9:9; 10:3, 5, 13, 14, 17, 18, 18, 19; 11:9, 9, 9, 10, 10, 10, 10, 11, 13, 33, 34, 46; 12:3, 4, 5, 5; 13:2, 2, 3, 3, 4, 4, 5, 6, 7, 8, 9, 10, 10, 12, 14, 18, 18, 19, 20, 22, 23, 24, 25, 25, 25, 28, 28, 30, 30, 31, 31, 32, 34, 34, 34, 34, 35, 36, 37, 38, 39, 39, 42, 42, 43, 43, 44, 45, 46, 47, 48, 48, 48, 49, 49, 49, 49, 51, 51, 51, 51, 52, 52, 52, 53, 53, 53, 55, 57, 57, 57, 59, 59; 14:2, 3, 5, 6, 8, 9, 13, 13, 16, 16, 17, 18, 37, 39, 40, 42, 43, 44, 44, 47, 47, 47, 48, 48, 50, 51, 51; 15:3, 5, 6, 7, 8, 10, 11, 11, 12, 13, 16, 18, 19, 20, 21, 22, 27, 31; 16:2, 4, 16, 16, 17, 17, 17, 21, 22, 24, 24, 26, 27, 27, 28, 29, 32, 33, 34, 34; 17:3, 5, 11, 15; 18:3, 5, 5, 15, 18, 24, 24, 30; 19:6, 15, 15, 15, 17, 18, 23, 25, 26, 29, 33, 35, 35, 35, 36, 1; 20:2, 11, 11, 14, 12, 12; 17, 28, 28; 37:13, 19, 19, 20; 38:18, 23, 23, 23, 24; 39:1, 3, 3, 3, 6, 10, 13, 13, 23, 23, 24; 39:1, 3, 3, 3, 6, 10, 13, 13, 23, 23, 24, 32, 35, 35, 35; 36:1, 2, 11, 11, 11, 12, 12, 17, 28, 28; 37:13, 19, 19, 20; 38:18, 23, 23, 24; 39:1, 3, 3, 3, 6, 10, 13, 13, 26, 29, 30, 32, 34, 35; 35:15, 19, 19, 26, 31, 31, 31, 31, 32, 32, 32, 33, 34, 35, 35, 35, 36:1, 2, 11, 11, 11, 12, 12, 17, 28, 28; 38:1, 3, 4, 11, 11, 17, 20, 20, 24, 25, 26, 26, 29, 29, 30, 30, 32, 32, 35, 38, 41, 43; 29:1, 3, 17, 24, 24, 29, 30, 30, 31, 32, 39, 44; 30:10, 10, 30, 36; 31:3, 3, 3, 3, 4, 4, 4, 5, 5, 5, 6, 10, 15, 15, 17; 32:2, 3, 12, 15, 17, 20, 26, 27, 34; 33:3, 3, 5, 10, 12, 13, 13, 16, 16, 17, 22; 34:1, 2, 2, 2, 4, 4, 5, 6, 9, 10, 10, 12, 18, 18, 21, 21, 23, 24, 26, 29, 32, 34, 35; 35:15, 19, 19, 26, 31, 31, 31, 31, 32, 32, 32, 33, 34, 35, 35, 35, 36:1, 2, 11, 11, 11, 12, 12, 17, 28, 28; 37:13, 19, 19, 20; 38:18, 23, 23, 24; 36, 38

Nu 1:1, 1, 1, 3, 16, 19, 45; 2:9, 16, 16, 17, 17, 24, 31; 3:1, 1, 3, 4, 4, 4, 13, 13, 14, 25, 28; 4:3, 4, 4, 6, 8, 12, 12, 15, 16, 16, 19, 20, 23, 23, 27, 27, 27, 28, 31, 33, 35, 37, 39, 41, 43, 47; 5:3, 17, 17, 18, 18, 23; 6:5, 9, 18; 7:10, 84; 8:15, 17, 19, 22, 22, 24, 26; 9:1, 1, 3, 3, 5, 7, 10, 13, 13, 14, 17, 18, 20, 20, 23; 10:9, 10, 10, 10, 11, 12, 14, 29, 31, 33; 11:1, 5, 8, 8, 8, 9, 10, 11, 12, 15, 18, 18, 25, 26, 26, 27; 12:5, 5, 6, 6, 7, 8, 14, 14, 15, 16; 13:19, 19, 19, 19, 22, 28, 29, 29, 32, 33, 33; 14:2, 2, 8, 10, 13, 14, 14, 16, 22, 22, 25, 28, 29, 31, 32, 33, 33, 34, 35, 40, 45; 15:3, 3, 3, 8, 13, 14, 15, 21, 26, 30, 32, 34, 38; 16:2, 7, 13, 17, 18, 18, 21, 26, 27, 45, 49; 17:4, 7; 18:10, 11, 13, 13, 14, 15, 20, 21, 31; 19:5, 7, 8, 8, 9, 14, 14, 16, 17, 18, 19; 20:1, 1, 5, 12, 13, 13, 16, 21, 22, 22, 23, 24, 26, 29, 31, 31, 34, 36, 38; 23:5, 12, 16, 21, 21; 24:2, 7, 14, 21; 25:1, 6, 6, 7, 9, 11, 15, 18, 18, 18; 26:2, 3, 9, 9, 19, 59, 63, 64, 65; 27:3, 3, 3, 3, 14, 14, 14, 14, 17, 19, 21; 28:2, 4, 6, 7, 11, 16, 17, 18, 23, 26; 29:1, 39; 30:3, 5, 7, 10, 14, 16, 16; 31:6, 16, 35, 36; 32:5, 13, 14, 15, 17, 20, 30, 33, 39; 33:3, 5, 6, 6, 8, 8, 9, 11, 12, 13, 15, 18, 20, 22, 23, 24, 25, 28, 31, 33, 36, 37, 37, 38, 38, 39, 40, 40, 41, 42, 43, 44, 44, 45, 46, 47, 48, 49, 50, 54, 55, 55, 55; 34:29; 35:1, 2, 3, 5, 12, 14, 25, 32, 26, 29, 32; 36:8, 12, 13

Dt 1:1, 1, 3, 3, 3, 4, 4, 5, 6, 6, 7, 7, 7, 7, 8, 17, 25, 27, 30, 31, 31, 32, 33, 33, 33, 33, 37, 38, 39, 39, 44, 44, 46; 2:4, 7, 8, 9, 10, 12, 12, 14, 20, 21, 22, 22, 23, 23, 24, 25, 28, 29, 37; 3:4, 10, 11, 19, 24, 24, 29; 4:1, 5, 6, 7, 10, 14, 15, 17, 18, 21, 22, 25, 25, 27, 30, 30, 34, 37, 38, 39, 39, 42, 43,

Isa 1:1, 6, 7, 8, 8, 11, 21; 2:2, 2, 3, 5, 6, 10, 11, 17, 20, 22; 3:7, 7, 14, 18, 25; 4:1, 2, 3, 3, 3, 6; 5:1, 2, 4, 8, 9, 11, 12, 16, 16, 21, 21, 25, 30, 30; 6:1, 5, 6, 12, 13, 13; 7:1, 3, 6, 11, 11, 18, 18, 18, 19, 19, 20, 21, 22, 23; 8:1, 6, 9, 9, 14, 17, 18; 10:3, 3, 5, 7, 17, 20, 20, 23, 24, 25, 27; 11:3, 9, 10, 11, 15, 16; 12:1, 4, 5, 6; 13:3, 4, 8, 10, 13, 13, 17, 20, 22, 22; 14:1, 3, 3, 6, 13, 13, 18, 18, 20, 25, 28, 30, 31, 32; 15:1, 1, 3, 3, 5; 16:3, 5, 5, 5, 10, 10; 17:4, 5, 6, 6, 6, 9, 11, 11, 11; 18:2, 4, 4, 5, 7; 19:1, 3, 9, 10, 14, 14, 14, 16, 17, 18, 18, 19, 19, 20, 21, 23, 24, 24; 20:1, 6; 21:1, 5, 8, 8, 13, 13; 22:2, 3, 5, 7, 8, 12, 14, 16, 20, 23, 25, 25; 23:1, 13, 15; 24:10, 11, 12, 13, 15, 15, 18, 21, 22, 22, 23, 23; 25:4, 5, 6, 7, 8, 9, 9, 10, 11; 26:1, 1, 2, 3, 3, 4, 4, 8, 9, 9, 10, 12, 16, 17, 17, 17, 18, 18, 19; 27:1, 1, 2, 4, 4, 8, 8, 9, 12, 13, 13, 13, 13; 28:4, 5, 6, 7, 7, 14, 16, 20, 21, 21, 25, 25, 29, 29; 29:15, 18, 19, 19, 21, 23, 24; 30:2, 2, 3, 7, 8, 8, 12, 13, 14, 14, 15, 15, 15, 19, 21, 23, 23, 25, 26, 28, 29, 32, 32; 31:1, 1, 7, 9, 9; 32:1, 1, 2, 2, 13, 16, 18, 18, 18, 19; 33:2, 12, 14, 17; 34:5, 6, 6, 11, 13, 13; 35:6, 6, 7; 36:1, 2, 4, 6, 6, 7, 11, 11, 11, 13, 15; 37:7, 10, 12, 28, 29, 29, 30, 36, 36, 38, 38; 38:1, 1, 3, 3, 8, 10, 11, 15, 16, 17, 20; 39:2, 2, 2, 4, 6, 6, 7, 8; 40:3, 3, 11, 12, 12, 12, 14, 22, 24, 26; 41:16, 16, 18, 18, 19, 19; 42:1, 2, 4, 6, 7, 12, 16, 17, 22, 22, 24; 43:4, 14, 16, 16, 19, 19, 20, 20, 26; 44:7, 12, 13, 16, 19, 19, 23, 24; 45:2, 2, 13, 14, 14, 17, 18, 19, 19, 19, 23, 24, 25; 46:6, 7, 13; 47:1, 8, 9, 9, 10, 10, 13; 48:1, 1, 10, 16; 49:2, 2, 3, 4, 5, 8, 8, 9, 9, 20, 21, 22; 50:4, 10, 10, 11, 11, 11; 51:6, 7, 9, 9, 14, 16, 16, 20; 52:6, 10; 53:9, 10; 54:6, 8, 14, 16, 17; 55:2, 11; 56:5, 7, 9; 57:2, 2, 5, 6, 10, 13, 15, 17; 58:2, 3, 10, 11, 12, 14; 59:4, 6, 7, 8, 9, 10, 10, 13, 14, 19, 20, 21; 60:10, 10, 18, 22; 61:3, 6, 7, 7, 8, 10, 10, 11; 62:3, 3, 4, 7, 9; 63:1, 1, 1, 2, 2, 3, 3, 4, 6, 6, 9, 9, 9, 13; 64:5, 5; 65:2, 3, 4, 4, 5, 8, 8, 10, 16, 16, 18, 19, 19, 23, 25; 66:3, 4, 8, 13, 17, 17, 20, 20, 20

Jer 1:1, 1, 2, 3, 3, 5, 9; 2:2, 2, 2, 5, 17, 18, 18, 19, 23, 24, 24, 27, 28, 30, 34, 37; 3:2, 2, 6, 16, 16, 18, 23, 23, 25; 4:2, 2, 2, 2, 5, 5, 5, 11, 19, 20, 30, 31; 5:1, 6, 7, 8, 13, 14, 18, 19, 19, 20, 20, 20, 24, 24, 30, 31; 6:1, 1, 3, 6, 7, 10, 11, 16, 23, 24, 26, 29; 7:2, 2, 3, 4, 6, 7, 7, 8, 10, 11, 12, 17, 17, 22, 23, 24, 24, 30, 30, 31, 31, 32; 8:2, 7, 8, 8, 9, 12, 12, 13, 18, 19, 19, 19, 20, 21, 24, 25, 27, 27; 18:4, 6, 6, 10, 15, 15, 15, 19, 20, 23, 24, 25, 27; 19:4, 7, 9, 10, 11, 14; 20:1, 2, 2, 6, 7, 9, 9, 9, 16; 21:4, 5, 5, 5, 5, 7, 9, 12, 14; 22:2, 3, 4, 4, 7, 9, 11, 18, 20, 21, 23, 23, 30, 30; 23:5, 6, 8, 11, 12, 13, 13, 14, 14, 15, 17, 18, 21, 21, 21; 38:2, 4, 4, 5, 6, 6, 6, 6, 7, 7, 7, 7, 9, 13, 14, 17, 19, 17:3, 4, 4, 4, 5, 6, 6, 6, 7, 8, 11, 13, 17, 19, 19, 19, 20, 21, 24, 25, 27, 27; 18:4, 6, 6, 6, 10, 15, 15, 16, 20, 21, 24, 25, 27, 27; 19:4, 7, 9, 10, 11, 11, 14; 20:1, 2, 2, 6, 7, 9, 9, 16; 21:4, 5, 5, 5, 5, 7, 9, 12, 14; 22:2, 3, 4, 4, 7, 9; 23:4, 5, 6, 7, 8, 8, 11, 12, 22, 24, 30, 30, 31, 31, 32; 9:2, 4, 6, 8, 23, 23, 23, 24, 24, 24, 24, 26, 26, 26; 10:5, 6, 7, 13, 14, 14, 15, 23, 23, 24; 11:4, 6, 6, 7, 8, 12, 14, 15, 17, 21; 12:2, 5, 5, 8, 16; 13:1, 4, 10, 17, 21, 22, 25, 27; 14:4, 5, 6, 8, 8, 9, 13, 14, 15, 15, 16; 15:4, 7, 11, 11, 13, 14, 15, 17; 16:2, 3, 3, 6, 7, 7, 9, 9, 17:3, 4, 4, 4, 5, 6, 6, 6, 7, 8, 8, 11, 13, 17, 19, 19, 19, 20, 21, 24, 25, 27, 27; 18:4, 6, 6, 10, 15, 15, 15, 19, 19, 20, 21, 24, 25, 25, 27; 14:4, 5, 6, 8, 8, 9, 13, 14, 15, 15, 16; 20:1, 2, 6, 7, 9, 9, 9, 16; 21:4, 5, 5, 5, 7, 9, 12; 12:2, 5, 5, 8, 16, 18, 18, 19, 21, 21, 28:1, 1, 1, 1, 5, 5, 7, 7, 11, 15, 17; 29:5, 7, 8, 9, 10, 15, 16, 21, 22, 22, 23, 23; 26, 26, 26, 26, 28, 28, 29, 31; 30:2, 6, 8, 10, 11, 24; 31:2, 4, 9, 10, 12, 13, 15, 17, 22, 23, 23, 24, 24, 29, 29, 32, 33, 33; 32:1, 2, 2, 7, 8, 8, 8, 9, 10, 12, 12, 14, 15, 19, 19, 20, 22, 23, 34, 35, 37, 37, 40, 41, 43, 44, 44, 44, 44, 44; 33:1, 5, 5, 10, 10, 10, 12, 13, 13, 13, 13, 13, 15, 15, 16, 20; 34:5, 6, 13, 15, 15, 15, 17, 18; 35:1, 7, 7, 8, 9, 10, 15; 36:1, 6, 6, 6, 6, 8, 8, 9, 9, 10, 10, 10, 13, 14, 14, 15, 15, 17, 18, 18, 19, 21, 21; 38:2, 4, 4, 5, 6, 6, 6, 6, 7, 7, 7, 9, 13, 14, 17, 19, 34, 35; 39:1, 1, 5, 7, 8, 11; 40:1, 1, 2, 4, 6, 6, 9, 11, 11, 13, 15, 15, 17; 41:1, 1, 5, 8, 10, 10, 12, 17, 18; 42:10, 13, 16, 16, 20, 22; 43:4, 5, 6, 8, 9, 9, 9, 10, 12, 12, 13, 13; 44:1, 1, 3, 6, 6, 8, 8, 9, 9, 10, 10, 10, 12, 12, 13, 13, 13, 13, 13, 15, 15, 16, 20; 34:5, 6, 13, 15, 15, 15, 17; 18; 35:1, 7, 7, 8, 9, 10, 15; 36:1, 6, 6, 6, 6, 8, 8, 8, 9, 9, 9, 10, 10, 10, 11, 12, 12, 22, 23, 28, 28, 30, 30, 32; 37:1, 4, 10, 12, 13, 15, 15, 17, 18, 21, 21; 38:2, 4, 4, 5, 6, 6, 6, 6, 7, 7, 7, 7, 9, 13, 14, 22, 22, 28; 39:1, 1, 2, 3, 3, 5, 5, 6, 9, 10, 15, 16, 17, 18; 40:1, 6, 7, 7, 9, 10, 10, 11, 11, 11, 13, 15; 41:1, 1, 5, 8, 10, 10, 12, 17, 18; 42:10, 13, 16, 16, 20, 22; 43:4, 5, 6, 8, 9, 9, 9, 9, 10, 12, 12, 13, 13; 44:1, 1, 3, 6, 6, 8, 8, 9, 9, 9, 14, 14, 19, 19, 21, 25, 26, 26, 28, 28, 28, 35, 35, 38, 41, 41, 44, 47; 49:1, 2, 4, 4, 7, 11, 16, 18, 18, 21, 22, 24, 26, 26, 28, 28, 35, 35, 38, 39; 50:2, 2, 4, 4, 5, 9, 9, 14, 16, 20, 22, 25, 28, 30, 30, 32, 37, 39, 42, 43; 51:1, 2, 3, 4, 4, 6, 7, 10, 13, 16, 17, 18, 20, 21, 21, 22, 22, 24, 27, 30, 39, 44, 46, 46, 46, 47, 58, 58, 59, 60, 62; 52:1, 2, 3, 4, 4, 6, 6, 6, 8, 9, 10, 11, 11, 12, 12, 15, 17, 17, 19, 19, 20, 25, 30, 31, 31, 31, 32

La 1:2, 4, 7, 7, 9, 12, 15, 15, 19, 20; 2:1, 1, 2, 3, 3, 4, 5, 6, 7, 7, 11, 12, 17, 19, 19, 19, 19, 20, 21, 22, 22; 3:6, 10, 10, 11, 20, 20, 24, 27, 29, 36, 41, 45, 53, 57, 66; 4:1,

3, 5, 5, 6, 7, 8, 10, 11, 13, 14, 17, 18, 19, 20, 21; 5:11, 11

Eze 1:1, 1, 1, 2, 3, 16, 20, 21, 28, 28; 3:3, 10, 14, 14, 18, 19, 20; 4:9, 12, 14, 16; 5:2, 2, 3, 3, 4, 5, 6, 7, 8, 8, 9, 10, 12, 13, 13, 14, 15, 15, 15; 6:6, 7, 9, 10, 13, 14; 7:4, 7, 9, 13, 15, 15, 19, 19, 20; 8:1, 1, 1, 1, 3, 4, 5, 7, 8, 9, 10, 11, 11, 12, 12, 18, 18; 9:1, 1, 2, 2, 4, 5, 7, 8; 10:1, 2, 2, 2, 3, 6, 8, 10, 13, 17, 19; 11:2, 6, 7, 10, 11, 11, 12, 15, 16, 20, 20, 24; 12:2, 3, 3, 4, 4, 5, 5, 9, 9, 13, 13, 14, 15, 22, 22, 24, 29, 31, 31, 31, 34, 34, 34, 38, 41, 43, 47, 49, 49, 51, 52, 53, 54, 54, 56, 59, 60; 17:4, 5, 8, 9, 10, 15, 16, 16, 17, 20, 23; 18:3, 9, 17, 18, 22, 24, 24, 24, 26, 32; 19:4, 8, 9, 9, 10, 11, 12, 13, 13; 20:1, 1, 5, 6, 8, 9, 11, 13, 13, 14, 15, 16, 16, 17, 18, 18, 19, 21, 22, 22, 23, 26, 26, 27, 27, 36, 40, 40, 40, 41, 43, 47, 47; 21:20, 21, 22, 22, 23, 24, 24, 30, 30, 31, 32; 22:3, 4, 6, 7, 7, 7, 9, 9, 16, 20, 21, 22, 23, 24, 24, 25, 25, 27, 30; 23:3, 3, 8, 11, 16, 21, 31, 31, 32, 37, 38, 39, 43, 44, 44, 44, 45; 24:1, 1, 7, 11, 12, 13, 18, 18, 25, 26, 27; 25:4, 4, 6, 10, 14; 26:1, 1, 5, 6, 8, 12, 15, 17, 18, 18, 20, 20, 20; 27:4, 8, 9, 9, 10, 10, 11, 12, 13, 14, 16, 17, 18, 18, 19, 19, 20, 20, 21, 21, 24, 24, 24, 25, 25, 26, 27, 27, 27, 30, 32, 32, 34, 34, 34, 35; 28:2, 2, 8, 9, 12, 13, 13, 14, 14, 15, 15, 18, 22, 22, 22, 23, 25, 25, 25; 29:1, 1, 1, 3, 4, 12, 17, 17, 17, 17, 21, 21; 30:4, 4, 5, 6, 7, 7, 8, 9, 10, 12, 14, 14, 15, 16, 16, 17, 18, 18, 21, 21, 25, 25, 25, 26, 27, 28; 32, 32; 33:6 8, 9, 10, 11, 12, 12, 15, 21, 21, 22; 34:2, 2, 2, 3, 10, 17, 17, 19, 20, 23, 23; 47:3, 5, 19, 22, 23; 48:8 8, 8, 9, 10, 10, 10, 10, 10, 13, 13, 15, 15, 18, 21, 22, 28

8, 14, 15; 7:1, 1, 1, 3, 3, 5, 7, 10, 12; 8:3, 4, 14, 15; 9:1, 4, 6, 7, 16; 10:1, 1, 2, 3, 5, 5, 7, 9, 11, 11, 12; 12:11, 8, 11, 13, 16, 16; 12:2, 3, 3, 4, 5, 5, 6, 6, 6, 6, 8, 9, 10, 10, 11, 11, 11, 11; 13:1, 2, 3, 4, 6, 6, 8; 14:1, 3, 4, 4, 5, 6, 6, 8, 9, 10, 11, 12, 12, 13, 14, 15, 15, 20, 20, 20, 21, 21, 21

Mal 1:7, 10, 11, 12, 14; 2:6, 6, 6, 9, 11, 11, 17, 17; 3:1, 3, 4, 4, 5, 8, 8, 10, 11, 17; 4:2, 3, 4

Mt 1:20, 20; 2:1, 1, 2, 5, 5, 6, 9, 12, 13, 16, 16, 17; 4:6, 13, 13, 16, 16, 21, 23; 5:3, 8, 12, 15, 16, 18, 19, 19, 20, 21, 22, 22, 22, 25, 28, 45, 48; 6:1, 2, 2, 4, 4, 5, 5, 6, 6, 9, 10, 10, 18, 18, 20, 20, 23, 29; 7:3, 3, 4, 11, 13, 13, 15, 21, 22, 22, 22, 22; 8:10, 11, 13, 24; 9:4, 10, 16, 25, 31, 33, 35; 10:9, 11, 15, 16, 17, 19, 20, 24, 27, 27, 28, 32, 33, 35, 35, 41, 41, 42, 42; 11:1, 2, 6, 8, 8, 11, 16, 21, 21, 23, 23, 24, 26, 29; 12:5, 5, 6, 18, 19, 21, 32, 32, 36, 40, 40, 41, 42, 45, 50; 13:3, 10, 13, 14, 14, 19, 21, 22, 24, 27, 30, 30, 31, 31, 32, 33, 34, 35, 40, 40; 20:6, 8, 9, 10, 13, 14, 16, 19, 22, 23, 29; 21:18, 27, 29, 31, 39, 40; 22:2, 3, 3, 3, 17, 17, 19; 23:1, 6, 6, 9, 10, 11, 16, 21, 35; 24:3, 12, 12, 14, 18, 20, 21, 24; 25:3, 5, 6, 14; 26:3, 20, 21, 27, 31, 35, 37, 37, 39; 28:7, 8, 9, 11, 11, 18, 30, 30

Mk 1:2, 3, 4, 5, 9, 9, 11, 13, 14, 19, 20, 23, 35, 39, 45; 2:1, 6, 8, 8, 15, 20, 26; 3:3, 29; 4:1, 2, 11, 15, 17, 19, 28, 29, 31, 31, 36, 38; 5:4, 5, 5, 13, 14, 15, 20, 27, 29, 30, 30, 33, 34, 34, 40; 6:2, 4, 4, 8, 10, 11, 14, 17, 22, 25, 25, 27, 28, 29, 40, 47, 48, 51, 55, 56; 7:7, 32; 8:1, 4, 12, 14, 26, 37, 38, 38; 9:3, 9, 30, 32, 37, 37, 38, 38, 39; 8:4, 4, 5, 5, 6, 7, 10; 9:1, 2, 9, 10, 10, 20; 7:15, 17, 18, 20, 22, 28, 34, 34, 37, 37, 38, 38, 39; 8:4, 4, 5, 5, 6, 7, 10; 9:1, 2, 9, 10, 10, 24, 25; 10:2, 2, 5, 8, 19, 25, 28, 33; 11:2, 11, 13, 17, 18, 21, 22, 23, 24, 25, 25, 34; 12:6, 18, 25, 27, 28; 13:6, 6, 9, 9, 9, 10, 12; 14:2, 2, 4, 7, 10, 13, 14, 19, 19, 20, 20, 21, 23, 24, 25, 27, 28, 33, 34, 35, 40; 15:2, 10, 17, 18, 19, 22, 22, 23, 28, 30, 31, 41, 49, 60, 62, 66; 15:1, 7, 29, 38, 41, 43, 46, 46, 46; 16:2, 5, 12, 17

Lk 1:1, 1, 3, 5, 6, 7, 8, 15, 17, 18, 19, 20, 21, 22, 25, 26, 28, 36, 39, 41, 44, 44, 47, 51, 54, 66, 69, 75, 79, 79, 80, 80; 2:1, 7, 7, 7, 8, 8, 11, 12, 12, 14, 16, 19, 21, 23, 24, 25, 27, 27, 28, 29, 34, 36, 39, 40, 43, 44, 44, 46, 46, 51, 52; 3:1, 2, 4, 4, 15, 17, 18, 20, 21, 23; 4:2, 5, 11, 14, 15, 15, 17, 18, 20, 20, 21, 23, 24, 25, 27, 27, 28, 33, 35, 44; 5:7, 12, 18, 18, 19, 22, 29, 35; 6:1, 8, 12, 12, 17, 23, 23, 23, 41, 41, 42, 42; 7:1, 7, 9, 21, 23, 25, 25, 28, 32, 37, 37, 45, 50; 8:10, 13, 15, 16, 23, 27, 27, 29, 34, 40, 48, 51; 9:12, 14, 26, 26, 31, 36, 48, 49, 57, 61; 10:7, 12, 13, 13, 20, 26, 30, 34; 11:1, 2, 2, 2, 6, 7, 21, 26, 31, 32, 33, 33, 35, 37, 43, 43, 52, 52; 12:1, 1, 3, 3, 3, 12, 15, 27, 28, 33, 38, 38, 42, 45, 46, 46, 52, 53, 53, 58; 13:4, 4, 6, 10, 11, 14, 14, 19, 21, 24, 24, 26, 26, 28, 29, 35; 14:8, 10, 10, 15, 21, 25, 28; 16:8, 10, 10, 10, 10, 11, 12, 15, 19, 23, 23, 24, 24, 25; 17:4, 6, 24, 24, 26, 27, 30, 31, 31, 34, 34, 34, 34, 36; 18:2, 3, 9, 17, 22, 30, 30; 19:17, 20, 30, 36, 38, 44, 44, 44, 47, 49, 53; 20:4, 9, 11, 14, 19, 22, 29, 31, 33, 38, 40, 43, 45, 53, 53, 53; 24:1, 3, 4, 6, 12, 18, 18, 19, 27, 29, 35, 36, 38, 44, 44, 44, 47, 49, 53

Jn 1:1, 2, 4, 5, 10, 18, 23, 28, 45, 47; 2:1, 11, 14, 19, 20, 20, 23, 23, 23, 25; 3:13, 14, 15, 16, 18, 21, 23; 4:14, 18, 20, 20, 21, 23, 23, 24, 24, 31, 44, 53; 5:2, 3, 4, 6, 13, 14, 26, 26, 28, 28, 35, 38, 39, 42, 43, 43, 45; 6:10, 10, 31, 37, 45, 49, 53, 56, 56, 59, 59, 61; 7:1, 1, 4, 5, 9, 10, 18, 28, 37; 8:2, 3, 3, 4, 4, 4, 5, 9, 12, 12, 16, 18, 19, 20, 21, 23, 23, 23, 34, 35, 36, 44, 44; 9:3, 5, 7, 34; 10:2, 9, 9, 23, 23, 25, 34, 34, 38, 38; 11:6, 11, 31, 34, 38, 38, 52, 56; 12:13, 25, 35, 36, 46, 48; 13:1, 12, 13, 18, 20, 26, 30, 35; 15:2, 4, 4, 4, 4, 5, 5, 6, 7, 9, 10, 11, 16, 20, 21, 23, 23, 24, 25, 25, 26; 16:21, 23, 23, 26, 26, 26, 26, 26, 27, 27, 27, 27, 32, 33; 17:2, 2, 3, 5, 7, 9, 10, 10, 11, 11, 12, 12, 13, 18, 19; 18:1, 1, 3, 3, 4, 5, 5, 11

7, 10, 12, 18, 20, 21, 22, 25, 25, 28, 34, 34, 37, 40, 42, 42; 6:1, 1, 7, 15; 7:2, 2, 4, 5, 6, 7, 7, 10, 12, 16, 17, 20, 20, 22, 22, 22, 29, 30, 30, 34, 35, 36, 36, 36, 38, 38, 38, 39, 41, 41, 42, 42, 44, 45, 48, 51; 8:8, 9, 16, 21, 21, 23, 23, 25, 28, 33, 40; 9:10, 11, 12, 12, 17, 20, 21, 22, 25, 27, 27, 28, 29, 31, 31, 37, 37, 42, 43; 10:1, 3, 3, 17, 23, 25, 27, 30, 30, 31, 31, 32, 35, 39, 39, 43, 48; 11:1, 3, 5, 5, 13, 22, 22, 26, 27, 28, 29; 12:4, 5, 7, 14, 21; 13:1, 5, 13, 14, 17, 18, 19, 27, 28, 29, 33, 35, 35, 36; 16:3, 5, 5, 6, 9, 12, 18, 24, 29, 32, 34, 36; 17:2, 11, 11, 16, 17, 17, 21, 22, 22, 24, 28, 31, 31, 31; 18:2, 4, 5, 9, 10, 18, 21, 23, 24, 25, 25, 26; 19:5, 9, 10, 16, 21, 22, 27, 29, 30, 39, 40, 40; 20:6, 8, 9, 10, 13, 14, 16, 19, 22, 23, 23, 29; 21:18, 27, 29, 31, 39, 40; 22:2, 3, 3, 17, 17, 19; 23:1, 6, 6, 9, 9, 10, 11, 16, 21, 35; 24:3, 12, 12, 14, 18, 20, 21, 24; 25:3, 5, 6, 14; 26:3, 20, 21, 27, 31, 35, 37, 37, 39; 28:7, 8, 9, 11, 11, 18, 30, 30

Ro 1:2, 7, 9, 9, 15, 18, 19, 21, 27, 27, 28, 32; 2:7, 12, 14, 15, 16, 17, 20, 20, 28, 29, 29; 3:4, 9, 16, 20, 24, 25, 26; 4:10, 10, 10, 12, 18, 19, 20; 5:2, 3, 5, 6, 8, 11, 13, 17; 6:1, 4, 5, 5, 10, 10, 12, 12, 21; 7:5, 5, 6, 6, 8, 13, 17, 18, 18, 20, 22, 23, 23; 8:1, 2, 3, 3, 3, 4, 8, 9, 9, 10, 11, 11, 18, 20, 22, 23, 37, 39; 9:1, 1, 2, 7, 17, 25, 26, 28, 33; 10:6, 8, 8, 9, 14, 14; 11:17, 19, 22, 23, 23, 23, 25, 25, 25, 26, 28, 33; 12:4, 5, 6, 9, 14; 13:4, 11, 13; 14:2, 4, 7, 10, 11, 11, 14, 18, 22; 15:12, 13, 13, 15, 15, 17, 23, 24, 29, 30, 31; 16:2, 2, 3, 5, 7, 8, 9, 10, 11, 12, 12, 13, 22

1Co 1:2, 2, 5, 5, 5, 6, 7, 8, 10, 10, 13, 15, 21, 29, 30, 31; 2:3, 3, 3, 4, 5, 5, 7, 11, 13; 3:1, 16, 18, 19, 21; 4:2, 6, 6, 10, 15, 15, 17, 17, 17, 20, 20, 21, 21; 5:3, 3, 4, 5, 9; 6:4, 11, 19, 20, 20; 7:15, 17, 18, 20, 22, 28, 34, 34, 37, 37, 38, 38, 39; 8:4, 4, 5, 5, 6, 7, 10; 9:1, 2, 9, 10, 10, 24, 25; 10:2, 2, 5, 8, 19, 25, 28, 33; 11:2, 11, 13, 12:6, 18, 25, 27, 28; 13:6, 6, 9, 9, 9, 10, 12; 14:2, 2, 4, 7, 10, 13, 14, 19, 19, 20, 20, 21, 23, 24, 25, 27, 28, 33, 34, 35, 40; 15:2, 10, 17, 18, 19, 19, 22, 22, 23, 28, 30, 31, 41, 49, 60, 62, 66; 16:2, 3, 5, 7, 8, 9, 10, 11, 12, 12, 13, 22

2Co 1:1, 4, 4, 5, 6, 8, 9, 9, 10, 12, 12, 14, 14, 14, 15, 15, 17, 17; 3:2, 3, 7, 9, 10, 14, 14, 18; 4:2, 2, 4, 6, 6, 7, 8, 10, 10, 11, 12; 5:1, 2, 4, 6, 10, 11, 12, 17, 19, 20, 21; 6:1, 2, 2, 3, 4, 4, 4, 4, 5, 5, 5, 5, 5, 12, 12, 13, 14, 16, 16; 7:1, 3, 4, 7, 9, 11, 11, 11, 12, 13, 14, 16, 16; 8:2, 6, 7, 7, 7, 7, 7, 18, 20, 21, 21, 22, 22; 9:3, 3, 4, 7, 8, 11, 14; 10:1, 3, 6, 11, 11, 14, 16, 16, 17; 11:1, 3, 6, 6, 6, 9, 9, 10, 10, 17, 23, 23, 23, 23, 25, 26, 26, 26, 26, 26, 27, 27, 27, 27, 32, 33; 12:2, 2, 3, 5, 7, 9, 9, 10, 10, 10, 11, 11, 11, 12, 12, 18, 19, 19; 13:1, 3, 3, 4, 5, 5, 11

Gal 1:13, 13, 14, 14, 16, 22, 23, 24; 2:2, 4, 4, 4, 8, 8, 16, 20, 20, 21; 3:3, 4, 4, 8, 10, 10, 11, 12, 17, 19, 26, 28; 4:3, 9, 11, 14, 18, 19, 19, 20, 25, 25; 5:1, 6, 10, 14, 14, 16, 21, 25, 25; 6:1, 1, 4, 4, 6, 6, 6, 9, 9, 12, 13, 14, 15, 17

Eph 1:1, 3, 3, 4, 4, 6, 7, 8, 9, 10, 10, 10, 10, 11, 13, 13, 13, 15, 16, 17, 18, 20, 20, 21, 21, 23; 2:1, 2, 2, 3, 3, 4, 5, 6, 6, 7, 10, 10, 11, 11, 12, 13, 15, 15, 16, 21, 21, 22; 3:3, 4, 5, 6, 9, 10, 11, 12, 15, 16, 16, 17, 17, 20, 21; 4:2, 3, 4, 6, 13, 14, 15, 16, 16, 16, 17, 17, 18, 21, 23, 24; 5:2, 5, 8, 9, 12, 18, 19, 20, 21, 24

Php 1:1, 4, 5, 6, 7, 7, 8, 9, 9, 13, 13, 14, 18, 18, 20, 20, 22, 23, 24, 26, 27, 28, 29, 30; 2:1, 3, 5, 5, 6, 7, 8, 10, 10, 12, 13, 13, 15, 15, 16, 16, 19, 22, 24, 25, 29, 29; 3:1, 3, 3, 3, 4, 4, 6, 9, 14, 15, 19, 20; 4:1, 2, 3, 3, 4, 6, 9, 10, 11, 11, 12, 15, 16, 19, 21

Col 1:2, 4, 5, 5, 6, 6, 6, 8, 9, 10, 10, 12, 14, 16, 16, 18, 19, 20, 20, 21, 22, 22, 23, 24, 24, 27, 28, 28, 29; 2:1, 2, 3, 5, 5, 6, 6, 7, 9, 10, 10, 11, 13, 13, 14, 15, 16, 16, 18, 20, 23; 3:3, 4, 7, 7, 10, 10, 11, 15, 15, 16, 16, 16, 16, 16, 17, 17, 18, 20, 22, 22; 4:1, 2, 2, 3, 5, 7, 12, 12, 13, 13, 15, 15, 16, 17

1Th 1:1, 1, 2, 3, 3, 5, 5, 5, 6, 7, 8, 8, 9; 2:1, 1, 2, 3, 4, 13, 13, 14, 14, 17, 17, 19; 3:2, 5, 7, 8, 10, 12, 13; 4:4, 5, 6, 10, 14, 16, 17; 5:2, 4, 7, 7, 12, 13, 18, 18

2Th 1:1, 4, 4, 4, 8, 10, 10, 10, 12; 2:2, 4, 6, 10, 12, 17; 3:4, 6, 13, 17

1Ti 1:2, 4, 13, 14, 16; 2:2, 2, 3, 6, 7, 7, 9, 9, 11, 12, 14, 14, 15, 15; 3:4, 9, 11, 13, 13, 15, 15, 16, 16; 4:1, 2, 6, 6, 10, 12, 12, 14, 16; 5:5, 5, 6, 7, 17; 6:9, 13, 15, 16, 17, 17, 18, 19

2Ti 1:1, 3, 5, 5, 5, 6, 6, 9, 13, 13, 14, 15, 17, 18, 18; 2:1, 1, 7, 10, 14, 20, 25; 3:1, 12, 14, 15, 16; 4:2, 5

3, 5, 5, 6, 7, 8, 10, 11, 13, 14, 17, 18, 19, 20, 21; 5:11, 11

Hos 1:1, 1, 5, 10; 2:3, 9, 9, 10, 13, 15, 15, 5, 16, 19; 5:4, 5, 8, 8, 9, 11, 15; 6:2, 2, 9, 10; 7:1, 2, 5, 6, 6, 10; 8:6; 9:2, 3, 3, 5, 5, 6, 8, 8, 9, 10, 10, 13, 15; 10:4, 4, 9, 10, 10, 12, 12, 13, 14, 14, 15; 11:9, 11; 12:3, 4, 7, 8, 8, 9, 9, 11, 11, 11, 13; 13:1, 1, 5, 5, 9, 10, 11, 11, 13, 16; 14:3, 9

Joel 1:2, 2, 13; 2:1, 1, 5, 8, 9, 9, 13, 23, 23, 26, 27, 29, 30, 30, 32, 32, 32; 3:1, 1, 13, 14, 14, 17, 18, 19, 21

Am 1:1, 1, 14, 14, 14; 2:7, 8, 16; 3:4, 5, 6, 6, 9, 9, 9, 9, 9, 10, 12, 12, 12, 13, 14; 4:1, 6, 6; 5:6, 6, 7, 10, 11, 12, 13, 15, 16, 16, 17, 20, 21, 25; 6:1, 1, 6, 9, 13, 14; 7:1, 7, 8, 10, 17, 17; 8:3, 3, 9, 9, 11, 13; 9:1, 3, 3, 6, 6, 9, 11, 11

Ob 1:1, 3, 3, 7, 8, 11, 11, 12, 12, 12, 13, 13, 14, 14, 18, 20

Jnh 1:4, 5, 17; 2:3, 7; 3:6, 8; 4:2, 5, 8, 10, 10

Mic 1:1, 10, 10, 11, 13; 2:1, 4, 5, 11, 12; 3:3, 4; 4:1, 1, 2, 5, 5, 6, 7, 9, 9, 10, 10, 13; 5:1, 2, 4, 4, 5, 6, 7, 8, 8, 10, 15; 6:10, 12, 13, 13, 14, 16; 7:2, 5, 5, 6, 6, 6, 8, 11, 11, 12, 14, 14, 14, 14, 18

Na 1:3, 3, 3, 6, 7, 7, 13; 2:1, 3, 3, 4, 4, 5, 10, 12, 13; 3:10, 10, 13, 17, 17, 18

Hab 1:5, 15, 15; 2:4, 13, 19, 20; 3:2, 2, 7, 14, 14, 14, 15, 15; 3:2, 5, 11, 11, 12, 12, 13, 15, 16, 17, 19, 20

Zep 1:1, 8, 9, 10, 12, 18, 18; 2:3, 7, 7, 14, 14, 14, 15, 15; 3:2, 5, 11, 11, 12, 12, 13, 15, 16, 17, 19, 20

Hag 1:1, 1, 1, 4, 6, 8, 13, 14, 15; 2:1, 1, 3, 3, 3, 9, 10, 10, 12, 15, 17, 19, 20, 22, 23

Zec 1:1, 1, 7, 8, 16, 2:1, 5, 10, 11, 11, 12; 3:7, 9, 10; 4:10; 5:4, 7, 9, 11; 6:2, 2, 3, 3,

19, 20, 21; 2:1, 6, 8, 9, 9, 9, 10, 16, 17, 18, 19, 19, 22, 26, 27, 31, 37, 38, 42, 42, 42, 46; 3:6, 11, 13, 16, 16, 22, 25, 26; 4:3, 7, 12, 16, 17, 18, 19, 24; 5:4, 4,

Idx

IS (6993)

47; 4:1, 1, 3, 6, 8, 8, 8, 15, 18, 18, 22;
5:1, 2, 4, 8, 15, 15, 16, 17, 18
Eze 1:28; 3:21; 4:14; 5:5; 6:12, 12, 12; 7:2,
3, 5, 6, 6, 6, 7, 7, 7, 10, 10, 11, 12,
13, 13, 14, 15, 15, 15, 19, 23, 23; 8:17;
9:6, 9, 9; 10:15, 20; 11:3, 3, 7, 15, 23;
12:12, 19, 22, 27; 13:12, 12, 15, 16; 15:2,
2, 4, 4, 4, 5; 16:3, 7, 20, 30, 34, 34, 44,
44, 46, 46; 17:12; 18:4, 5, 9, 10, 18, 19,
21, 25, 25, 27, 29; 19:2, 10, 13, 14, 14;
20:6, 15, 29, 29; 21:9, 10, 10, 11, 11, 13,
14, 15, 15, 16, 25, 26, 26, 27, 28, 28, 29;
22:18, 22, 24, 25; 23:4, 20, 20, 22, 28,
37, 45; 24:6, 6, 7, 13, 24, 27; 25:8; 26:2,
2, 2, 10, 15; 27:27, 32; 28:2, 3, 5; 29:3, 9;
30:3, 3, 5, 12; 31:10, 18; 32:16, 20, 22,
23, 24, 25, 26, 29; 33:6, 14, 16, 17, 17,
19, 20, 21, 24, 27, 30; 34:5, 12; 36:35;
37:11, 19; 38:8, 8, 8; 39:4, 8, 8, 8; 40:45,
45, 46, 46; 41:4, 22, 22; 42:13, 15; 43:4,
12, 12, 13; 44:3, 9, 22, 26, 31; 45:13, 14,
20; 46:11, 20; 47:16, 16, 17, 18, 19, 20;
48:12, 14, 22, 29, 35
Da 2:5, 8, 9, 10, 10, 11, 11, 11, 15, 22, 28,
30, 36, 43, 45, 47, 47; 3:4, 14, 15, 17, 25,
29; 4:3, 3, 8, 9, 17, 18, 22, 22, 24, 24, 24,
30, 31, 31, 34, 34, 37; 5:11, 11, 14, 14,
23, 25, 26, 28; 6:12, 13, 15, 20, 26; 7:14,
27, 28; 8:2, 21, 21, 21, 26; 9:11, 11, 13,
13, 14, 17, 18; 10:4, 14, 17, 21, 21;
11:35, 36; 12:12
Hos 2:2; 4:1, 13, 17, 18; 5:1, 3, 3, 4, 11; 6:3,
4, 8, 8, 10, 10; 7:7, 8, 11; 8:3, 5, 6, 8, 8;
9:7, 7, 8, 13, 15, 16, 16; 10:1, 2, 5, 7, 10,
11, 11; 11:8; 12:1, 5, 7, 11; 13:3,
4, 8, 9, 10, 12, 12, 13; 14:4, 8, 9
Joel 1:5, 6, 9, 10, 10, 11, 12, 12, 13, 15,
16, 17, 17; 2:1, 3, 4, 11, 11, 11, 13, 17;
3:13, 13, 13, 14
Am 2:11, 13, 13, 15, 16; 3:5; 4:3, 13, 13;
5:2, 2, 8, 11, 13, 18, 18, 27; 6:8, 10,
10; 7:2, 5, 10, 13; 8:2; 9:5, 6, 6, 9, 11
Ob 1:1, 3, 7, 15, 20
Jnh 1:2, 7, 8, 8, 8, 12; 2:9; 3:8; 4:3, 8
Mic 1:2, 5, 5, 5, 9, 9, 9, 13; 2:1, 1, 3, 7, 8,
10, 10, 13; 3:1, 7, 11; 4:6, 9, 9; 5:2; 6:8,
10, 12; 7:1, 1, 2, 2, 4, 4, 10, 10, 18
Na 1:2, 2, 3, 5, 6, 7, 11, 15; 2:1, 3, 8, 9, 10,
10, 11; 3:1, 3, 3, 7, 17, 18, 19, 19
Hab 1:4, 13, 16; 2:3, 4, 4, 5, 5, 6, 13, 19, 19,
20; 3:19
Zep 1:7, 14, 14, 15; 2:5, 15, 15, 15; 3:1, 5,
6, 6, 8, 15, 17
Hag 1:2, 4, 6, 9, 10, 10; 2:3, 3, 6, 8, 8, 13,
14, 14, 14, 14, 19
Zec 1:7, 11; 2:2, 2, 13; 3:2; 4:1, 6; 5:2, 3, 5,
6, 6, 6, 7, 8, 8; 6:12; 7:13; 8:23; 9:9, 11,
17, 17; 10:5; 11:2, 2, 3, 3, 3, 9, 16; 12:8,
10; 13:7, 9, 9, 9, 9; 14:4, 16
Mal 1:6, 6, 7, 8, 8, 10, 12, 12, 13, 14; 2:1, 7,
11, 14, 17, 17; 3:2, 14, 14
Mt 1:16, 20, 20, 23; 2:2, 2, 5; 3:2, 3, 9, 10,
10, 11, 12, 17; 4:4, 6, 7, 10, 13, 16, 17;
5:3, 10, 12, 13, 14, 16, 22, 29, 30, 32, 34,
35, 35, 37, 45, 48, 48; 6:1, 6, 10, 13, 18,
21, 22, 23, 25, 30, 30, 34; 7:3, 3, 4, 6,
9, 11, 12, 13, 13, 14, 14, 19, 21; 8:27;
9:5, 15, 16, 16, 18, 24, 37; 10:2, 7, 10,
11, 20, 24, 25, 26, 28, 32, 33, 37, 37, 38;
11:6, 10, 10, 11, 11, 14, 16, 19, 30;
12:2, 6, 8, 10, 12, 12, 18, 23, 25, 28, 28,
30, 30, 33, 41, 42, 43, 44, 45, 48, 50, 50;
13:11, 11, 14, 15, 19, 20, 21, 22, 23, 24,
31, 32, 32, 33, 37, 38, 39, 39, 44, 45,
47, 52, 52, 52, 55, 55, 57; 14:2, 2, 4, 15,
15, 26, 27; 15:5, 8, 11, 27; 16:2, 16:2;
2, 3, 7, 11, 17, 26; 17:4, 5, 12, 15; 18:1,
4, 8, 9, 10, 11, 12, 14, 14, 19, 23; 19:3, 9,
10, 11, 12, 14, 17, 17, 24, 26; 20:1, 1, 4,
7, 14, 15, 15, 23, 23; 21:9, 10, 11, 13, 20,
21, 38, 42, 42, 42; 22:2, 8, 17, 20, 23, 32,
38, 38, 39, 42, 45; 23:8, 9, 9, 10, 11, 15,
16, 16, 17, 18, 18, 18, 19, 26, 38, 39;
24:6, 17, 18, 23, 26, 26, 28, 32, 32, 33,
45, 46, 50; 25:14, 25; 26:2, 2, 8, 18, 22,
24, 24, 25, 26, 28, 31, 38, 41, 41, 41, 45,
45, 46, 48, 62, 66, 68; 27:4, 6, 6, 17, 22,
33, 37, 46, 64; 28:6, 6, 7, 15, 18
Mk 1:2, 15, 15, 27, 27; 2:9, 16, 19, 21, 22,
24, 26, 28; 3:4, 17, 21, 29, 33, 35; 4:11,
15, 21, 22, 26, 29, 29, 31, 31, 31, 32, 40,
41; 5:9, 9, 35, 39, 41; 6:2, 2, 3, 4, 15, 15,
16, 16, 18, 35, 35, 50; 7:2, 6, 6, 11, 11,
15, 27, 29, 34; 8:16, 21; 9:5, 7, 12, 13,
13, 21, 26, 31, 31, 39, 40, 40, 42, 43, 44,
45, 46, 47, 48, 50; 10:2, 14, 18, 24,
25, 27, 29, 40, 40; 11:9, 17, 21, 25, 26;
12:7, 10, 11, 14, 16, 16, 17, 28, 29, 29,
30, 31, 31, 32, 32, 33, 35, 37; 13:4, 14,
16, 21, 28, 28, 29, 33, 34; 14:8, 14,
19, 19, 20, 21, 21, 22, 24, 24, 27, 34, 38,
38, 41, 41, 41, 42, 44, 58, 60, 69; 15:22,
34, 42; 16:6, 6, 16
Lk 1:13, 28, 36, 42, 43, 45, 49, 49, 50, 61,
61, 63; 2:4, 11, 11, 15, 23, 24, 34, 49;
3:4, 8, 9, 13, 17; 4:4, 6, 8, 10, 12, 18,
21, 22, 24, 36; 5:21, 24, 34, 39; 6:2, 4, 5,
9, 20, 23, 35, 36, 40, 40, 41, 41, 42, 42;
42, 44, 45, 45, 47, 48, 49; 7:16, 22, 23,
27, 27, 28, 28, 28, 34, 35, 39, 39, 47, 49;
8:10, 11, 11, 17, 25, 25, 26, 30, 46, 49;
52; 9:9, 19, 25, 33, 35, 38, 48, 50, 50, 56,
62; 10:2, 7, 9, 11, 22, 22, 26, 29, 42;
11:4, 6, 7, 8, 11, 17, 20, 23, 24, 29, 39,
27, 29, 31, 32, 34, 34, 34, 34, 35, 39,

40, 40; 12:1, 2, 6, 21, 21, 23, 23, 26, 28,
28, 32, 34, 42, 43, 46, 48, 54, 56, 57;
13:18, 19, 21, 25, 35, 35; 14:3, 15, 22,
22, 29, 32, 34, 35; 15:4, 10, 24, 24, 27,
31, 32, 32; 16:2, 10, 10, 10, 10, 10, 12,
12, 15, 15, 16, 17, 18, 25, 26; 17:1, 7, 21,
30, 31, 37; 18:16, 19, 19, 25, 29; 19:7, 9,
9, 10, 20, 46, 46; 20:2, 14, 17, 17, 17, 22,
27, 33, 38, 41, 44; 21:9, 20, 30, 31, 37;
22:1, 11, 19, 19, 20, 20, 21, 22, 26, 26,
27, 27, 37, 38, 53, 59, 64; 23:2, 15, 33,
38; 24:6, 6, 21, 29, 29, 34, 39, 46
Jn 1:15, 18, 19, 27, 27, 30, 30, 33, 34, 38,
41, 42, 47; 2:4, 10; 3:4, 6, 6, 6, 6, 8, 8,
13, 18, 18, 19, 19, 29, 29, 31, 31, 31, 31,
33; 4:5, 9, 10, 11, 18, 20, 22, 23, 24, 25,
25, 29, 34, 37, 42, 54; 5:2, 2, 7, 10, 10,
12, 24, 25, 27, 28, 30, 31, 32, 32, 45;
6:1, 7, 9, 14, 20, 29, 31, 33, 39, 40, 42,
42, 45, 46, 50, 51, 55, 55, 58, 60, 63, 70;
7:4, 6, 6, 8, 11, 12, 16, 18, 18, 22, 25, 26,
27, 27, 28, 36, 40, 41; 8:7, 13, 14, 16, 17,
17, 19, 26, 29, 34, 39, 44, 44, 47, 50, 52,
53, 54, 54, 54; 9:4, 7, 8, 9, 11, 12, 16,
16, 17, 19, 19, 20, 21, 23, 24, 29, 30, 30,
37; 10:1, 2, 12, 13, 20, 29, 29, 34, 38;
11:3, 4, 10, 14, 16, 28, 50; 12:13, 14, 19,
23, 27, 31, 34, 35, 50; 13:10, 10, 16, 16,
19, 25, 26, 31, 31; 14:21, 22, 24, 26, 28,
29; 15:1, 6, 6, 8, 12, 20, 25, 26; 16:7, 8,
11, 13, 17, 18, 21, 21, 21, 21, 32; 17:1,
17:1, 3, 12, 17; 18:31, 36, 36, 37, 38;
19:13, 17, 30, 35, 40; 20:16, 31; 21:7, 14,
20, 22, 23, 24, 24
Ac 1:7, 8, 11, 12, 19, 19, 20; 2:15, 16, 25,
29, 29, 34, 39; 3:2, 11, 16; 4:9, 11, 11,
12, 12, 16, 24, 36; 5:9, 17; 6:2; 7:33, 34,
37, 38, 40, 42, 49, 49, 49; 8:10, 21, 26,
33, 36; 9:5, 11, 15, 20, 21, 22, 36; 10:4, 5,
6, 14, 21, 28, 28, 31, 32, 32, 34, 35, 36,
42; 11:13, 12:15, 22; 13:8, 9, 11, 26, 33,
38, 40; 15:15, 16, 17, 19; 16:12; 17:3, 7,
19, 24, 25, 29; 19:4, 27, 28, 34, 35, 35,
38; 20:10, 32, 35; 21:22, 28; 22:22, 25,
25, 26; 23:5, 8, 19; 25:14, 16, 16; 26:14,
18; 27:8, 12, 16, 33, 34; 28:4, 22, 27, 28
Ro 1:8, 9, 12, 15, 16, 17, 17, 18, 19, 25, 26,
27; 2:2, 11, 24, 24, 25, 27, 28, 28, 28, 28,
29, 29, 29; 3:1, 4, 5, 8, 10, 10, 11, 11,
12, 13, 13, 14, 18, 20, 21, 22, 22, 24, 27,
27, 28, 29, 29, 30; 4:4, 5, 8, 14, 15, 15,
16, 16, 16, 16, 16, 17; 5:5, 5, 13, 13, 14,
15, 16, 16, 16; 6:6, 7, 7, 21, 23, 23; 7:2, 2, 3,
3, 4, 7, 12, 13, 13, 14, 16, 17, 18, 18, 18,
20, 21, 23; 8:1, 6, 6, 7, 7, 9, 10, 10, 24,
24, 27, 33, 34, 34, 34, 34, 36, 39; 9:5, 8,
9, 13, 14, 16, 30, 33; 10:1, 4, 5, 6, 6, 7, 8,
8, 10, 12, 12, 15, 20; 11:5, 6, 6, 6, 6, 8,
11, 16, 23, 24, 25, 26, 27; 12:1, 2, 3, 6, 9,
12, 12; 14:1, 2, 4, 11, 14, 14, 17, 18, 20,
21, 21, 21, 22, 23, 23; 15:3, 9, 15, 21,
27; 16:1, 1, 5, 5, 19, 19, 25, 26
1Co 1:2, 4, 9, 13, 18, 18, 19, 20, 20, 20, 25,
25, 30, 31; 2:9, 11, 12, 15, 15; 3:3, 5, 5,
6, 17, 20; 5:1, 1, 1, 6, 7, 11; 6:5, 5, 7, 13,
16, 16, 17, 17, 18, 19, 19; 7:1, 8, 9, 14,
14, 15, 18, 18, 19, 19, 22, 22, 22, 24,
26, 26, 29, 32, 33, 34, 34, 35, 39, 39, 40;
8:3, 4, 4, 6, 7, 7, 10; 9:3, 9, 10, 11, 16,
16, 17, 18, 25; 10:7, 13, 13, 16, 16, 19,
19, 19, 25, 26, 27, 28, 28, 29; 11:3, 3, 3,
5, 7, 7, 8, 11, 12, 12, 13, 14, 15, 15, 20,
21, 21, 24, 24, 25; 12:3, 6, 7, 8, 12, 12,
14, 15, 16; 13:4, 4, 5, 5, 10, 10, 10, 13;
14:5, 7, 9, 10, 14, 15, 17, 21, 24, 24, 25,
26, 33, 34, 35; 15:12, 13, 14, 14, 16, 17,
20, 26, 27, 27, 36, 39, 39, 40, 40, 41, 42,
42, 42, 43, 43, 43, 44, 44, 44, 44, 45,
46, 46, 46, 47, 47, 48, 48, 54, 54, 55, 55,
56, 56, 58; 16:9, 15, 19
2Co 1:1, 6, 6, 6, 7, 12, 18, 21; 2:2, 2, 3, 6,
16; 3:5, 11, 11, 13, 14, 15, 15, 17, 17, 17;
4:3, 4, 13, 16, 17; 5:2, 5, 13, 13, 17; 6:2,
2, 11, 11; 7:4, 4, 14, 15; 8:10, 12, 15, 18,
19, 20, 23; 9:1, 8, 9, 12; 10:6, 7, 7, 10,
15, 15, 18; 11:3, 10, 14, 15, 21, 29, 29,
31; 12:1, 4, 9, 9, 13; 13:1, 3, 5, 7

Phm 1:6, 8, 12
Heb 1:8, 8; 2:6, 8, 11, 14, 18; 3:4, 4, 13, 15;
4:7, 10, 12, 12, 13, 13, 14; 5:1, 2, 4, 13,
13; 6:4, 7, 8, 8, 8, 10, 10, 20; 7:2, 5, 6, 7,
8, 12, 14, 15, 16, 18, 25, 26, 28; 8:1, 1, 3,
3, 6, 10, 13; 9:2, 3, 11, 15, 16, 17, 17, 20,
22, 24, 27; 10:3, 4, 7, 15, 16, 18, 18, 20,
23, 25, 31; 11:1, 6, 6, 6, 7, 10, 12, 16, 16,
27; 12:1, 2, 7, 13, 29; 13:4, 6, 9, 11, 15,
16, 17, 21, 23
Jas 1:6, 8, 9, 10, 11, 12, 12, 13, 14, 14, 15,
16, 17, 21, 23, 26, 27; 2:10, 17, 19, 20,
16, 17, 17, 18; 4:4, 4, 12, 12, 14, 14, 16,
17; 5:3, 4, 11, 13, 13, 14
1Pe 1:13, 16, 24, 25, 25; 2:3, 6, 7, 7, 15,
19, 20, 20; 3:4, 4, 12, 13, 13, 15, 17, 20,
22, 22; 4:5, 7, 12, 14, 14, 17; 5:2, 12, 13
2Pe 1:4, 9, 17, 20; 2:17, 19, 19, 20, 22, 22;
3:4, 8, 9, 9, 15
1Jn 1:3, 5, 5, 5, 7, 8, 9, 10; 2:2, 4, 4, 5, 7, 8,
18, 21, 22, 22, 22, 25, 27, 27, 29, 29; 3:2,
3, 4, 5, 7, 7, 8, 9, 9, 9, 10, 11, 15, 20, 23;
4:2, 2, 3, 3, 3, 3, 4, 4, 4, 6, 7, 7, 8, 10, 12,
15, 16, 17, 17, 18, 18, 20; 5:1, 1, 1, 3, 4,
4, 5, 5, 6, 6, 6, 9, 9, 11, 11, 14, 16, 16,
17, 17, 18, 18, 20, 20, 20
2Jn 1:6, 6, 7, 7, 11
3Jn 1:3, 11, 11, 11, 12
Jude 1:13, 24
Rev 1:3, 3, 4, 4, 5, 8, 8, 9; 2:7, 8, 13; 3:7, 7,
12; 4:8, 8; 5:2, 12, 13; 6:13, 14, 17; 7:17;
8:11; 9:11, 11, 12, 13, 19; 10:8; 11:2, 2,
8, 14, 18; 12:10, 10, 12, 14; 13:4, 4, 10,
15:1; 16:15, 17; 17:8, 8, 8, 9, 10, 10, 11,
11, 11, 14, 18; 18:2, 2, 2, 8, 10, 17, 18,
19; 19:7, 8, 10, 13; 20:2, 5, 6, 8, 12, 14;
21:1, 3, 6, 8, 16, 17, 23; 22:7, 10, 11, 11,
11, 11, 12, 17

IT (6132)

Ge 1:4, 6, 7, 9, 10, 10, 12, 15, 18, 21, 24,
24, 27, 29, 30, 31; 2:3, 3, 5, 5, 5, 10, 11,
13, 14, 15, 15, 17, 18; 3:3, 3, 6, 15, 17,
17, 18, 19; 4:3, 8, 12, 14; 6:1, 6, 6, 7, 17;
8:6, 13; 9:5, 13, 14, 16, 23; 10:9; 11:2, 9;
12:11, 13, 14; 13:10, 15, 17, 17, 17;
14:1; 16:2, 9, 11, 17; 16:2, 6, 10, 14;
17:11; 18:6, 7, 7, 8, 10, 11, 21, 28, 29,
30, 31, 32; 19:13, 17, 20, 20, 29, 34;
20:13, 15; 21:12, 14, 14, 22, 26; 22:1,
6, 14, 14, 20, 20; 23:8, 9, 9, 11, 11, 13,
13; 24:14, 15, 22, 30, 43, 52, 65; 25:11,
22; 26:8, 21, 22, 32, 33; 27:1, 4, 5, 10,
20, 20, 20, 25, 30, 31, 33, 40; 28:12,
12, 13, 16, 18, 18; 29:2, 7, 7, 10, 13,
19, 23, 25, 25, 26; 30:15, 25, 28, 30, 30,
33, 34, 35, 41; 31:2, 5, 10, 22, 32, 35,
37, 39, 44, 45, 47, 47, 48; 32:8, 18,
33:11, 15, 20; 34:7, 21, 25; 35:8, 12,
17, 18, 22, 22; 37:5, 9, 10, 14, 23, 24,
25, 26, 32, 32, 33, 33; 38:1, 9, 9, 13, 17,
18, 23, 24, 24, 27, 28, 29; 39:5, 7, 10, 11,
13, 15, 18, 19, 22, 22; 40:1, 8, 10, 10, 12,
14, 20; 41:1, 7, 8, 13, 13, 15, 16, 21,
24, 31, 32, 32, 42, 49; 42:6, 14, 27, 28,
35; 43:2, 11, 12, 12, 21, 21; 44:5, 9, 10,
10, 24, 31; 45:8, 12, 16, 28; 46:33; 47:18,
24, 26; 48:1, 14, 17, 17, 19, 19; 49:4, 7,
7, 15, 24; 50:9, 11, 20, 20
Ex 1:10, 16, 16, 21; 2:3, 3, 5, 6, 9, 9, 11, 18,
20, 23; 3:21; 4:3, 3, 3, 4, 4, 4, 6, 7, 7,
8, 9, 9, 24, 25; 5:11, 19, 22; 6:8, 8, 28;
7:9, 9, 10; 8:10, 16, 17, 26; 9:8, 9, 10, 10,
18, 24, 24, 28; 10:10, 13; 11:6, 6; 12:2, 4,
14, 22, 25, 26, 27, 29, 34, 39, 41, 41, 42,
46, 47, 48, 51; 13:2, 5, 9, 11, 11, 13, 14,
14, 15, 16; 14:2, 5, 12, 16, 20, 20, 20, 24,
27; 15:23; 16:5, 5, 10, 13, 15, 15, 15, 16,
18, 19, 20, 20, 21, 21, 22, 24, 24, 25, 26,
26, 27, 31, 31, 32, 33, 34; 17:6, 11, 12,
14, 15; 18:13, 18, 22, 22; 19:12, 13, 13,
13, 16, 18, 23; 20:8, 10, 11, 18, 25, 25,
25; 21:26, 29, 31, 33, 34, 35, 36; 22:1, 1,
4, 7, 9, 10, 10, 11, 11, 12, 13, 13, 14, 14,
14, 15, 15, 15, 26, 27, 30, 31; 23:4, 11, 14,
14, 15, 15, 15, 26, 27, 27, 30, 30, 31;
23:4, 11, 13, 15, 33; 24:6, 8, 10, 10, 16;
25:2, 9, 11, 11, 11, 12, 12, 12, 24, 25,
24, 31, 36; 27:2, 2, 4, 5, 7, 8, 8, 8, 21;
28:7, 7, 8, 15, 15, 16, 17, 28, 28, 38, 38,
43; 29:7, 12, 14, 16, 18, 18, 20, 21, 22,
25, 26, 26, 28, 28, 34, 34, 36, 36, 36,
37, 37; 30:1, 2, 3, 3, 4, 4, 4, 4, 6, 7, 8,
10, 10, 10, 16, 18, 21, 25, 25, 32, 32,
32, 32, 33, 33, 36, 36, 36, 36, 37;
31:13, 14, 14, 17; 32:4, 4, 5, 5, 8, 9, 13,
18, 19, 20, 20, 20, 20, 24, 24, 24, 30;
33:1, 7, 7, 7, 8, 9, 16, 22; 34:9, 10,
12, 20; 35:5, 24; 36:2, 3, 6, 7, 13, 18, 35;
38:37:1, 1, 1, 2, 2, 3, 3, 3, 11, 13, 21,
22, 24, 25, 25, 25, 26, 26, 26, 26, 27,
27, 27; 38:1, 2, 2, 4, 7, 8, 21, 30; 39:3, 3,
4, 4, 4, 5, 9, 10, 18, 19, 20, 21, 23, 30,
31, 31, 43, 43; 40:4, 9, 19, 11, 19, 19,
23, 29, 37, 38
Lev 1:3, 4, 6, 10, 11, 12, 13, 13, 15, 15,
16, 17, 17, 17; 2:1, 2, 2, 3, 4, 5, 6, 6,

7, 8, 8, 9, 9, 10, 15, 15, 16, 16; 3:1, 1, 1,
2, 4, 5, 5, 6, 7, 8, 9, 9, 10, 11, 11, 12, 13,
13, 15, 16, 17; 4:5, 8, 9, 10, 14, 17, 19,
20, 21, 24, 24, 25, 26, 30, 31, 31, 32, 33,
34, 35; 5:1, 1, 2, 2, 3, 3, 3, 4, 4, 5, 8, 9,
10, 11, 11, 12, 12, 12, 13, 16, 16, 17,
18, 18, 19; 6:3, 4, 5, 5, 5, 7, 9, 9, 12, 12,
12, 12, 13, 14, 15, 15, 16, 16, 17, 17,
18, 18, 20, 21, 21, 21, 21, 22, 23, 25, 25,
25, 26, 26, 26, 26, 27, 28, 28, 28, 29, 30; 7:1,
3, 4, 5, 6, 6, 7, 7, 9, 9, 10, 15, 16, 16, 17,
18, 18, 19, 6:3, 4, 5, 5, 5, 7, 9, 7, 8, 9,
12, 12, 13, 14, 15, 15, 16, 16, 17,
18, 18, 20, 21, 21, 21, 21, 22, 23, 25,
25, 26, 26, 26, 26, 27, 28, 28, 28, 29, 30;
7:1, 3, 4, 5, 6, 6, 7, 7, 9, 9, 10, 15, 16, 16,
17, 18, 18, 19, 25, 26, 26, 29, 30; 7:1,
3, 4, 5, 6, 6, 7, 7, 9, 9, 10, 15, 16, 16, 17,
18, 18, 19, 25, 28, 28; 19:5, 6, 6, 7, 8, 23, 23,
25; 20:14, 17, 21, 24, 24; 21:24; 22:7, 9,
9, 11, 14, 14, 20, 21, 23, 27, 27, 28, 28,
29, 30, 31, 32, 36, 41, 41, 41; 24:3, 3, 7,
8, 9, 9, 9, 18, 26; 25:5, 5, 10, 11,
11, 12, 12, 16, 21, 25, 25, 26, 27, 28, 28,
28, 29, 29, 29, 30, 30, 34, 50; 26:1,
16, 32, 34, 35, 35, 35, 35, 37; 27:4, 5, 6,
7, 7, 9, 10, 10, 10, 11, 12, 12, 12, 13,
14, 14, 14, 14, 15, 15, 15, 17, 18, 19, 19,
19, 20, 21, 24, 26, 26, 26, 27, 27, 27, 27,
27, 30, 33, 33, 33, 33
Nu 1:50, 50, 51, 51; 3:26; 4:5, 6, 9, 10, 10,
13, 15, 17, 25, 26, 27; 6:9, 18; 7:1, 1, 1,
5, 10, 84, 88; 8:24; 9:3, 3, 3, 11, 11, 12,
12, 12, 15, 16, 18, 20, 21, 22, 22;
10:11, 29, 32, 32, 35, 36; 11:1, 1, 8, 8, 8,
8, 8, 8, 9, 14, 17, 17, 18, 20, 20, 25, 25,
31, 31, 31, 33; 12:2; 13:18, 19, 20, 23,
27, 27, 30, 30, 32, 32; 14:3, 7, 8, 11, 13,
14, 23, 24, 35, 41; 15:11, 19, 20, 24, 25,
25, 26, 28, 34, 39, 39; 16:4, 7, 9, 13, 31,
42, 42; 17:5, 8; 18:10, 10, 10, 11, 13, 15,
19, 23, 26, 27, 29, 30, 30, 31, 31, 32, 32,
32; 19:6, 9, 9, 10, 12, 15, 18, 18, 20, 22;
20:5, 8, 19; 21:8, 8, 8, 9, 9, 9, 14, 17, 18,
28; 22:34, 41; 23:19, 19, 20, 22, 23, 27;
24:1, 8; 25:7, 13; 26:1; 27:11, 11, 13;
28:6, 8, 24; 29:1, 11; 30:7, 7, 8, 11, 13,
13; 31:23, 23, 23, 29, 29, 54; 32:39, 39,
42; 33:53, 55, 56; 34:5, 9, 12; 35:23, 25,
33, 33; 36:3
Dt 1:3, 17, 17, 21, 24, 25, 25, 36, 38, 39, 39;
2:16, 19, 24; 3:9, 11, 11, 18, 26, 27; 4:2,
5, 14, 26, 32, 32, 35, 38, 39, 40; 5:12, 14,
16, 23, 27, 27, 29, 31, 33; 6:1, 3, 3, 10,
18, 24, 25; 7:1, 12, 25, 26, 26, 26, 26;
8:9, 18, 18, 19; 9:6, 11, 13, 21, 21, 21,
21; 10:15; 11:8, 10, 10, 11, 13, 29,
29, 31; 12:1, 16, 24, 24, 25, 25, 28, 32,
32; 13:14, 15, 16, 16, 16; 14:8, 8, 10, 21,
21, 21, 24, 25, 28; 15:2, 2, 3, 4, 9, 16,
17, 18, 20, 21, 21, 22, 22, 23; 16:3, 7;
17:4, 4, 4, 14, 18, 19; 18:3, 19, 19, 22;
19:2, 13, 14; 20:2, 5, 5, 6, 6, 9, 10, 10,
11, 11, 11, 12, 12, 13, 19, 19, 20; 21:1, 1,
3, 7, 14, 16; 22:2, 2, 2, 7; 23:11, 13,
16, 20, 21, 21, 21, 22; 24:1, 1, 3, 13, 15,
15, 15, 19, 19, 20, 21, 21; 25:2, 6, 8, 9,
19, 19, 19; 26:1, 2, 4, 10, 12; 27:2, 4,
15; 28:1, 15, 21, 24, 38, 63, 63, 67, 67,
68; 29:8, 19, 22, 23, 27, 28; 30:1, 5, 11,
11, 12, 12, 12, 12, 13, 13, 13, 14, 16,
18; 31:6, 7, 8, 9, 13, 19, 19, 21, 21, 22,
24, 26, 26; 32:19, 27, 47, 47, 47; 34:4, 4
Jos 1:1, 7, 11, 15; 2:2, 5, 5, 14, 19, 21; 3:2,
3, 3, 4, 4, 13, 14; 4:1, 7, 11, 18, 24; 5:1,
8, 13; 6:5, 8, 11, 15, 16, 20, 20, 26;
7:9, 11, 14, 15, 19, 21, 22, 22; 8:2, 5, 7,
8, 14, 14, 18, 19, 24, 24, 25, 28, 29, 31;
9:1, 12, 12, 16, 24, 25; 10:1, 1, 2, 4, 5,
11, 14, 14, 17, 19, 24, 24, 27, 28, 30, 30,
30, 31, 31, 32, 32, 34, 34, 35, 35, 36, 37,
37, 38, 38, 39; 11:1, 20, 23; 12:6; 13:6;
14:7; 15:3, 4, 16, 17, 18; 16:6, 7; 17:9,
10, 10, 13, 18, 18, 18; 18:4, 5, 8, 9, 20;
19:14, 47, 47, 47; 21:11, 43; 22:12, 18,
22, 23, 24, 27, 28, 28, 34; 23:1, 10,
15; 24:4, 15, 17, 26, 27, 27, 29, 32
Jdg 1:1, 8, 15, 15, 17, 28; 2:4, 18, 19;
22; 3:16, 21, 27; 4:20, 21; 6:3, 5, 7, 11,
18, 19, 19, 24, 24, 25, 25, 27, 27, 27, 28,
30, 31, 37, 38, 39, 40; 7:4, 9, 9, 13, 13,
13, 15, 17; 8:27, 27, 33; 9:7, 25, 33, 42,
45, 47, 48, 48, 50, 51, 52, 52; 11:4, 5, 23,
31, 31, 35, 39; 12:5, 6; 13:16, 18, 19,
20, 20; 14:4, 11, 12, 12, 13, 13, 15, 15,
16, 16, 16, 17; 15:1, 15; 16:2, 2, 4, 9,
14, 16, 25, 29; 17:2, 3; 18:2, 9, 10, 12,
19, 28; 19:1, 5, 11, 26, 30, 30, 30;
20:9, 28; 21:4, 22
Ru 1:1, 13, 19; 2:6, 11, 17, 18, 22; 3:1, 4, 8,
12, 13, 14, 15, 15, 15; 4:4, 4, 4, 4, 4, 5,
6, 6, 7, 8, 16, 16, 17
1Sa 1:12, 20; 2:14, 16, 16, 19, 24, 30, 36;
3:2, 9, 11, 17, 18; 4:3, 3, 13, 18, 20; 5:1,

Idx

2, 2, 7, 9, 9, 9, 10, 11, 11; 6:2, 3, 3, 8, 8, 8, 9, 9, 9, 13, 15, 16, 21; 7:1, 2, 2, 6, 7, 9, 12, 12; 8:1; 9:20, 23, 24, 24, 24, 24, 26; 10:1, 1, 5, 7, 9, 11, 12, 25, 25; 11:2, 7, 9, 11, 11; 12:3, 6, 15, 17, 22; 13:3, 10, 22; 14:1, 6, 14, 15, 19, 27, 39; 15:11, 11, 12, 27, 28; 16:2, 6, 16, 23; 17:25, 27, 35, 39, 48, 49, 51, 54; 18:1, 4, 6, 16, 21, 11, 19, 23, 26, 30; 19:5, 13, 13, 19, 21; 20:2, 2, 4, 7, 9, 9, 12, 13, 13, 16, 27, 33, 35; 21:5, 6, 9, 9, 9; 22:1, 15, 17, 22; 23:6, 7, 13, 22, 23; 24:1, 1, 4, 5, 11, 16; 25:11, 20, 27, 30, 37, 38; 26:12, 12, 17, 22; 27:4; 28:1, 14, 17, 24, 24, 25; 29:4; 30:1, 1, 3, 25, 25; 31:4, 8, 9

2Sa 1:1, 2, 2, 18, 20, 20; 2:1, 23, 26, 26; 3:6, 18, 24, 26, 28, 29, 35, 36, 36, 37; 4:4, 12; 5:9, 17, 24; 6:3, 4, 6, 6, 10, 12, 13, 17, 17, 21; 7:1, 4, 15, 23, 29, 29, 29; 8:1; 10:1, 3, 3, 5, 7, 17; 11:1, 2, 14, 14, 16, 25; 12:3, 3, 4, 12, 15, 18, 21, 28, 28, 29, 29, 30; 13:1, 2, 5, 5, 8, 21, 30, 35, 36; 14:15, 15, 26, 26, 30, 32; 15:1, 2, 5, 7, 25, 32, 35, 35; 16:11, 12, 16; 17:9, 9, 13, 21, 27; 18:3, 10, 18, 29; 19:1, 6, 19, 25, 36; 20:8, 8, 15, 15, 20, 20, 22; 21:1, 10, 11, 18; 22:9, 48; 23:5, 12, 16, 16, 16, 17; 24:3, 12, 16, 16, 24

1Ki 1:11, 18, 21, 27, 41, 48, 51; 2:3, 15, 29, 37, 39, 41; 3:6, 15, 18, 19, 21, 21, 21, 26, 26, 26, 27; 5:7; 6:1, 7, 7, 7, 9, 14, 16, 17, 20, 21, 26, 38, 38; 7:3, 7, 23, 23, 24, 24, 24, 25, 26, 26, 37, 31; 8:10, 15, 17, 18, 18, 24, 24, 54; 9:1, 8, 10, 16, 16, 28; 10:6, 7, 18, 21; 11:4, 11, 12, 12, 15, 29, 30, 35, 38; 12:2, 2, 10, 20, 28; 13:3, 4, 4, 6, 9, 17, 20, 23, 24, 25, 26, 29, 31, 34, 34; 14:5, 6, 8, 10, 11, 25, 28; 15:13, 21, 29; 16:11, 18, 31, 31; 17:4, 7, 11, 12, 12, 13, 17; 18:1, 4, 6, 12, 13, 17, 23, 23, 23, 24, 25, 26, 27, 29, 33, 34, 34, 34, 34, 36, 36, 39, 44, 45; 19:4, 10, 13, 13, 14, 17; 20:1, 6, 6, 6, 11, 12, 13, 26, 29, 33, 40; 21:1, 2, 2, 2, 2, 3, 3, 6, 6, 15, 32, 33, 43, 43

2Ki 1:3, 6, 8, 16; 2:1, 3, 5, 8, 9, 10, 10, 11, 12, 20, 3:5, 14, 15, 20, 25, 25, 25; 4:6, 8, 8, 10, 11, 18, 23, 23, 25, 26, 26, 26, 26, 27, 40, 41, 44; 5:7, 8, 13, 16, 26; 6:5, 6, 6, 7, 7, 13, 26, 28, 25, 30; 7:2, 7, 8, 8, 11, 13, 18, 19, 20; 8:1, 3, 5, 7, 15, 15, 15; 9:3, 12, 13, 15, 15, 19, 19, 22, 22, 30; 10:7, 9, 15, 15, 19, 20, 25, 27; 11:6, 18; 12:5, 6, 7, 9, 9, 10, 11, 14, 15, 17, 17; 17:5, 7, 25; 18:1, 4, 4, 9, 9, 10, 16, 21, 21, 25, 25, 26; 19:1, 1, 4, 14, 14, 25, 25, 26, 26, 32, 32, 34, 34, 35, 37; 20:4, 7, 10, 11, 19; 21:12, 12, 13; 22:3, 5, 5, 8, 9, 10, 11; 23:6, 6, 15, 16, 16, 17, 24, 35; 24:2, 11, 20; 25:1, 1, 1, 17, 24, 25, 27

1Ch 4:10; 6:10, 55; 7:23; 9:32; 10:4, 8, 13; 11:7, 14, 18, 18, 18, 19, 19, 19; 12:15, 17, 22; 13:2, 2, 3, 6, 13; 14:8, 15; 15:1, 3, 12, 13, 26, 29; 16:1, 1, 19, 30; 17:1, 3, 11, 13, 24, 27, 27, 27; 18:1; 19:1, 8, 17; 20:1, 1, 2, 2, 2, 2, 3, 4, 27; 21:10, 15, 15, 17, 17, 22, 23, 23, 24, 30; 22:5, 7, 14; 23:26; 26:28; 27:24; 28:8, 10, 20; 29:12

2Ch 1:4, 4, 5, 6; 2:4, 16, 16; 3:4, 4, 8; 4:2, 3, 3, 3, 4, 5, 5, 16; 5:9, 11, 13; 6:7, 8, 8, 11, 13, 13, 15, 15; 7:20, 21, 22; 8:1, 3, 16; 9:5, 6, 17, 20; 10:2, 2, 10; 12:1, 2; 13:15; 14:11; 15:16, 16; 16:5; 18:5, 11, 31, 31, 32; 19:7; 20:1, 7, 25, 32; 21:17, 19; 22:8; 23:17, 18, 18; 24:4, 5, 8, 11, 11, 11, 12, 14, 22, 22; 25:3, 4, 8, 14, 16, 20; 26:2, 18, 18; 28:21; 29:10, 16, 16, 16, 22; 30:3, 5, 5, 18; 31:3, 21; 32:5, 12, 30; 33:14; 34:4, 10, 10, 11, 12, 16, 17, 18, 19, 19, 32; 36:22

Ezr 1:1; 2:68; 3:2, 4; 4:12, 13, 14, 19, 24; 5:8, 16, 16, 17, 17; 6:9; 12, 14, 18; 7:10, 20, 21, 23, 24, 26; 9:7, 11, 11, 12, 15; 10:3, 4, 9, 13

Ne 1:1, 4; 2:1, 1, 5, 5, 6, 7, 10, 10, 16, 19; 3:1, 1, 1, 13, 14, 15, 15; 4:1, 7, 8, 12, 15, 15, 16; 5:5, 9; 6:1, 3, 6, 6, 7, 9, 16; 7:1; 64; 8:5, 15; 9:8, 10, 23, 36, 37, 38, 38; 10:31, 34, 34, 36; 11:23; 13:3, 8, 19

Est 1:1, 17, 19, 19, 19, 20, 22; 2:8, 10, 22, 23, 23; 3:4; 8, 9, 9, 9, 9, 10, 11, 12; 4:4, 4, 5, 5, 8, 8; 5:1, 2, 3, 4, 6, 6, 8; 6:2, 9, 11, 7:2, 2, 3; 8:2, 5, 5, 8, 9, 10; 9:1, 12, 12, 13, 13, 14, 17, 18, 27, 32

Job 1:5, 5, 7, 19; 2:2; 3:3, 4, 4, 5, 5, 6, 6, 6, 8, 9, 9, 10, 21, 21; 4:5, 5, 16, 20; 5:5, 21, 27, 27, 27, 27; 6:3, 9, 17, 28, 29, 29; 7:16; 8:12, 12, 15, 15, 15, 18; 9:2, 7, 20, 22, 35; 10:3, 16; 11:8, 11, 14, 16; 12:8, 14; 13:1, 5, 9; 14:7, 7, 9, 21, 21; 15:18, 23, 32; 17:15; 18:2, 13, 14, 15, 15; 19:4; 20:12, 13, 13, 13, 14, 18, 19, 28, 30; 21:4, 19; 22:3, 3, 8, 19, 28, 30; 24:23, 25; 25:5; 26:3, 9; 27:6, 12, 14, 17, 17; 28:1, 5, 5, 5, 6, 6, 8, 8, 13, 14, 14, 15, 16, 17, 17, 19, 19, 19, 21, 27, 27, 27, 27; 29:11, 11, 14, 24; 30:18, 22; 31:11, 12, 26, 36, 36; 32:19; 33:14, 21, 27; 34:9, 10, 19, 28, 31, 33, 33, 35, 37, 43; 36:25, 25, 30, 32, 33; 37:3, 4, 12, 15; 38:5, 8, 8, 9, 10, 13, 13, 14, 18, 20, 21, 26, 29; 39:12, 24; 40:2, 24; 42:7

Ps 6:7; 7:2, 5, 12, 15; 10:11, 13, 14, 14; 17:12; 18:8, 32, 47; 19:6; 21:4; 22:2; 24:2, 2; 25:11; 30:9; 33:9, 9; 34:14; 35:9, 15, 21, 25; 37:5, 10, 34; 38:10; 39:4, 9; 40:3, 7, 14; 41:6; 48:5, 8, 13; 49:8; 50:3; 51:16; 52:9, 9; 54:6; 55:10, 10, 12, 12, 12, 13; 60:2, 2, 4, 12; 63:9; 65:9, 9, 9, 10; 68:9, 11, 14, 14, 16; 69:18, 22, 35, 36; 73:16, 28; 74:11; 75:3, 8; 78:28; 80:8, 9, 9, 10, 13, 13, 16, 16; 81:10; 84:6; 86:17; 87:5; 89:37, 39; 90:4, 6, 6, 10, 13, 17; 91:7; 92:1, 7; 93:1; 94:7, 15; 95:5, 10; 96:10; 99:3; 100:3; 101:3; 103:16, 16, 16; 104:5, 6, 20, 32; 105:12, 28; 106:9, 32; 107:42; 108:13; 109:17, 17, 18, 19, 23, 27; 112:10; 114:3; 118:8, 9, 23, 24; 119:20, 33, 34, 71, 90, 97, 106, 126, 130, 140, 175; 124:1, 2; 127:1, 2; 128:2; 129:6; 132:6, 6, 11, 13, 14; 133:1, 2; 135:3; 136:14; 137:7, 7; 139:4, 6, 6; 141:5, 5; 144:10; 147:1, 1

Pr 2:21, 22; 3:8, 14, 25, 27, 27, 27, 28; 4:5, 15, 15, 15, 23; 6:22, 22, 22, 22, 32; 7:23; 8:11, 33; 9:12; 10:22, 22, 22, 23, 24; 11:10, 12, 19; 14:1, 6; 15:23; 16:12, 14, 16, 19, 22, 26, 31; 17:8, 8, 14, 14, 16, 21; 18:5, 10, 13, 13, 21; 19:2, 11, 19, 23, 24; 20:3, 5, 35; 24:3, 12, 12, 12, 13, 14, 18, 18, 23, 27, 31, 32, 32; 25:2, 7, 7, 10, 27; 26:15, 15, 27; 28:14; 28:24; 29:4, 7, 11, 24; 30:15, 16, 17, 17, 21; 31:4, 4, 15, 16, 24

Ecc 1:6, 8, 9, 10, 10; 2:2, 2, 15, 15, 18, 21, 24; 3:10, 13, 14, 14, 14, 14; 4:8; 5:4, 5, 6, 18, 18; 6:1, 2, 2, 10, 10; 7:2, 2, 5, 11, 12, 18, 23, 24; 8:7, 8, 12, 13, 14, 14, 17, 17; 9:10, 12, 13, 14, 14, 14, 14, 15; 10:8; 11:1, 3, 7; 12:7, 7, 14, 14

SS 3:4, 7, 10; 5:2, 3; 6:13; 8:7, 7, 13

Isa 1:6, 7, 7, 13, 20, 21, 21, 31; 2:2, 2; 3:9, 10, 11, 24; 4:3; 5:2, 2, 2, 2, 2, 4, 4, 4, 5, 5, 6, 6, 6, 14, 18, 19, 19, 29, 29; 6:2, 7, 13; 7:1, 1, 1, 2, 6, 6, 7, 7, 8, 11, 13, 18, 20, 21, 21, 22, 23, 23, 25; 8:1, 10, 10, 20, 21, 21; 9:7, 7, 8, 18; 10:7, 12, 13, 15, 16, 15, 17, 17, 20, 26, 27; 11:10, 10, 11, 16, 16; 13:6, 9, 14, 14, 20, 20; 14:3, 9, 9, 23, 23, 24, 24, 24, 27, 27, 30; 15:5, 6, 12; 16:2, 5, 12, 12; 17:1, 4, 5, 5, 6, 10; 19:1, 16, 16, 16, 17, 20; 21:22; 20:1; 21:1, 3, 3, 17; 22:5, 7, 11, 14, 20, 25, 25; 23:1, 1, 9, 13, 13, 15, 17, 18; 24:1, 1, 2, 9, 13, 18, 20, 20, 21; 25:2, 8, 9; 26:5, 5, 5, 6, 15, 18, 19, 19, 21, 26:17, 27:3, 3, 3, 3, 8, 8, 11, 11, 19, 19, 20, 20, 28, 28, 28, 29, 2:5, 8, 5, 6, 10; 19:1, 16, 16, 16, 17, 20, 21, 22; 20:1; 21:1, 3, 3, 17; 22:5, 7, 11, 14, 20, 25, 25; 23:1; 28:1, 2, 3, 3, 8; 28:4, 4, 4, 15, 18, 19, 19; 29:1, 5, 5, 6, 7; 11:9, 9, 10, 11, 11, 13; 12:3, 3, 9; 13:2, 3, 4, 8, 9; 14:4, 6, 6, 7, 7, 7, 8, 8; 15:2; 16:9; 17:2, 5, 5, 9, 11; 18:24:1, 1, 2, 9, 13, 18, 20, 20, 21; 25:2, 8, 9; 26:5, 5, 5, 6, 15, 18, 19, 19, 21

Jer 1:3, 12; 2:19, 34; 3:5, 7, 9, 16, 16, 16, 17; 4:4, 9, 11, 18, 18, 23, 28, 28, 28; 5:1, 12, 13, 14, 15, 15, 19, 20, 20, 22, 22; 31; 6:10, 11, 19; 7:11, 12, 20, 23, 29, 30, 31, 32; 8:8, 16; 9:8, 12; 10:4, 4, 4, 5, 7, 18, 19, 23; 11:5, 5, 16, 16, 18, 18; 12:8, 8, 11, 11, 15, 16, 17, 19, 27; 14:5; 7; 15:2, 6, 7; 16:10, 14; 17:1, 9, 15, 21, 24, 27; 27, 18:4, 4, 7, 9, 10; 19:4, 5, 5, 15; 20:3, 4, 4, 10; 21:10, 10, 12, 14, 14, 22:14; 23:18, 18, 28, 32; 37:8, 8, 11, 14; 38:3; 43:3, 3, 2, 5, 6, 9, 9; 34:2, 2, 5; 35:11; 36:1, 3, 7, 9, 15, 15, 16, 21, 21, 23, 23, 23, 28, 32; 37:8, 8, 11, 14; 38:3; 15, 18, 20, 25; 39:1, 4; 40:3, 4, 4, 15; 41:1, 4, 4, 6, 7, 9, 9; 13; 42:4, 6, 6, 6, 7, 11, 21, 43:4, 10, 10, 20, 26; 47:6, 7, 7, 7; 48:1, 12, 14, 21, 22, 27, 33, 39; 50:13, 13, 15, 21, 34; 39; 51:11, 11, 33, 62, 62, 62, 63, 63; 52:3, 4, 4, 4, 21, 21, 22, 31

La 1:12, 13, 21; 2:6, 16; 3:22, 26, 27, 28, 37; 4:4, 8, 8, 11, 15; 5:18

Eze 1:1, 4, 14, 15, 17, 27, 27, 28; 2:10; 10; 3:3, 3, 16; 4:1, 1, 2, 2, 2, 2, 2, 3, 3, 3, 4, 4, 4, 7, 10, 12; 5:1, 2, 5, 13, 15, 15, 17; 7:6, 6, 10, 19, 20, 20, 21, 21, 22; 8:1, 17; 9:8; 10:1, 6, 7, 7, 11, 13; 11:3, 7, 7, 13; 12:3, 6, 6, 7, 7, 11, 12, 12, 13, 13, 25; 13:7, 10, 11, 11, 12, 12, 13, 14, 14, 15, 15; 14:13, 13, 13, 14, 15, 15, 16, 17, 18, 19, 19, 20, 20, 21, 21, 22, 23; 15:3, 4, 4, 4, 4, 5, 5, 5, 5; 16:14, 15, 16, 19, 19

23; 17:4, 4, 5, 5, 5, 6, 6, 7, 8, 8, 8, 8, 9, 9, 9, 9, 10, 10, 10, 10, 10, 14, 14, 14, 19, 21, 22, 22, 23, 23, 23, 24; 18:4, 20; 19:3, 3, 3; 20:1, 9, 14, 22, 28, 42, 47, 48, 48; 21:5, 7, 7, 7, 10, 10, 10, 10, 11, 11, 11, 12, 12, 13, 13, 14, 15, 15, 17, 19, 23, 27, 27, 27, 28, 30, 32; 22:3, 14, 14, 14, 14, 25, 27; 20, 20, 30; 23:32, 34, 34, 34, 39, 41; 24:3, 3, 4, 4, 5, 5, 6, 6, 6, 7, 7, 8, 8, 10, 11, 11, 11, 11, 11, 14, 14, 25, 26; 25:3, 3, 13, 13, 15; 26:1, 5, 5, 5, 14, 17; 28:10, 16, 17, 18, 19, 20; 30:3, 6, 9, 12, 20, 21, 21, 21, 25; 31:1; 32:1, 15, 17, 33:9, 13, 18, 19, 20; 33:18, 24; 35:2, 3, 7, 10, 15, 15; 36:5, 10, 17, 18, 19, 32, 34, 36, 36, 37; 37:14, 14, 16, 16, 26; 38:8, 10, 14, 16, 18; 39:5, 8, 8, 11, 11, 11, 13, 14, 14, 15, 15; 40:22, 25, 26, 26, 29, 29, 31, 33, 34, 35, 36, 37, 49; 41:15, 18, 19; 42:15, 20, 20; 43:3, 11, 17, 18, 20, 20, 20, 21, 22, 23, 26, 27; 44:1, 2, 2, 2, 3, 6, 7, 17, 24, 28, 31; 45:3, 4, 6, 9, 17, 19; 46:1, 1, 6, 9, 9, 9, 10, 10, 12, 13, 14, 16, 17, 17; 47:5, 9, 10, 10, 12, 13, 14, 16, 17, 18, 19, 20, 22, 22, 23; 48:8, 11, 14, 14, 18, 19, 21, 35

Da 1:1; 2:7, 11, 11, 40, 41, 44, 44, 45, 47; 3:1, 4, 14, 17, 18, 19; 4:2, 12, 12, 12, 14, 15, 17, 17, 21, 22, 23, 23, 25, 27, 31, 32; 5:21, 26; 6:1, 5, 8, 17; 7:4, 4, 5, 5, 5, 5, 6, 6, 7, 7, 7, 7, 7, 23, 23, 26; 8:2, 8, 10, 10, 12, 12, 18, 20, 27; 9:13, 14, 27; 11:12, 18, 27, 29, 35; 12:6, 7

Hos 1:5, 10, 10, 10; 2:7, 16, 21; 6:4; 7:4, 6, 9; 8:4, 5, 6, 6, 6, 6, 7, 7, 13, 14; 9:7; 10:5, 5, 5, 5, 6, 10, 12; 13:2

Joel 1:3, 5, 7, 7, 15; 2:1, 2, 11, 28, 32; 3:8, 18

Am 1:14; 2:2, 5, 11; 3:6; 4:7, 7, 7; 5:6, 6, 13, 15, 18, 20; 6:9; 7:1, 2, 3, 4, 13; 8:8, 8, 11, 12; 9:4, 5, 5, 6, 8, 11

Ob 1:15, 18

Jnh 1:2, 3, 5, 13, 14; 2:10; 3:2, 7, 10; 4:1, 3, 5, 6, 6, 7, 7, 8, 8, 10

Mic 1:5, 7, 9, 10; 2:1, 1, 4, 10, 10, 13; 3:1, 6; 4:1, 1, 1, 4, 8; 5:10; 6:9; 7:3, 10

Na 1:4; 3:1, 7, 8, 9, 15

Hab 1:5, 10; 2:2, 2, 3, 3, 3, 3, 3, 11, 13, 18, 19, 19, 19

Zep 1:8, 10, 12, 14; 2:3, 14; 3:16, 18

Hag 1:4, 6, 8, 9, 9, 9; 2:3, 3, 3, 6, 12, 13, 18

Zec 1:16, 21; 4:2, 3, 7, 9; 5:3, 3, 4, 4, 4, 4, 6, 8, 11, 11; 7:1, 13; 8:6, 6, 13, 20, 23; 9:2, 5, 5; 10:7; 11:9, 9, 10, 11, 11, 13; 12:3, 3, 9; 13:2, 3, 4, 8, 9; 14:4, 6, 6, 7, 7, 7, 8, 8, 10, 11, 13, 16, 17

Mal 1:8, 8, 8, 12, 13, 12; 2:2, 2, 3, 13; 3:10, 14, 14, 16; 4:1

Mt 1:22; 2:5, 9, 15, 23; 3:15, 15; 4:4, 6, 7, 10, 14; 5:13, 13, 15, 15, 21, 27, 29, 29, 29, 30, 30, 30, 30, 31, 34, 35, 35, 38, 43; 6:10; 7:2, 7, 7, 8, 14, 25, 25, 27, 28; 8:9, 10, 13, 19; 9:8, 18, 19, 20, 25, 26; 10:11, 10, 12, 14, 16, 22, 23, 24, 26; 12:2, 10, 11, 11, 11, 11, 13, 13, 15, 17, 24, 32, 32, 39, 41, 42, 44, 45; 13:11, 11, 19, 20, 27, 30, 32, 35, 40, 46, 48, 49, 53; 14:4, 9, 11, 12, 13, 15, 26, 27, 28; 15:5, 26, 26, 28; 16:2, 2, 3, 4, 7, 11, 11, 17, 18, 22, 25, 25, 27; 17:4, 6, 20; 18:6, 7, 8, 8, 9, 9, 17, 18, 23, 24, 25, 26, 30, 33; 19:5, 11, 12; 20:21, 15, 23, 23, 24, 26; 21:4, 13, 13, 19, 19, 20, 21, 25, 32, 33, 33, 33, 33, 34, 42, 44, 44; 22:5, 17, 39; 23:16, 18, 18, 20, 20, 21; 24:23, 24, 33; 25:28, 40, 40, 40, 45, 45; 26:1, 7, 8, 10, 12, 22, 24, 24, 25, 26, 26, 27, 29, 31, 39, 42, 54, 61, 62; 27:6, 6, 24, 29, 35, 40, 48, 48, 59, 60, 65; 28:1, 2

Mk 1:2, 9, 45; 2:1, 4, 9, 12, 15, 16, 17, 21, 23; 3:4, 5, 21; 4:4, 4, 5, 5, 5, 6, 6, 7, 11, 16, 19, 20, 22, 24, 30, 31, 31, 32, 32, 33, 37, 40; 5:14, 14, 16, 16, 43; 6:11, 15, 15, 16, 18, 28, 28, 29, 29, 49, 50, 56; 7:6, 11, 18, 19, 24, 27, 27, 36; 8:16, 17, 21, 26, 35, 35, 36; 9:5, 12, 13, 21, 22, 30, 33, 42, 43, 43, 45, 45, 47, 47, 50; 10:2, 14, 24, 25, 27, 40, 40, 41, 43, 47; 11:2, 13, 14, 14, 16, 17, 18, 20, 23; 12:1, 1, 11, 11, 11, 12, 13, 13, 15, 17, 24, 32, 32, 39, 41, 42, 43, 44, 45; 13:11, 11, 19, 20, 27, 28, 28, 29, 39, 49, 50, 56; 7:6, 11, 18, 19, 24, 27, 36; 8:16, 17, 21, 26, 35, 35, 36

Lk 1:3, 8, 23, 38, 41, 59; 2:1, 6, 15, 17, 18, 20, 23, 26, 43, 46, 49; 3:4, 21; 4:3, 4, 6, 8, 10, 12, 17, 20, 39, 42; 5:1, 8, 12, 17; 6:1, 4, 6, 9, 9, 12, 13, 38, 38, 48, 48, 49; 7:8, 11, 27, 39; 8:1, 5, 5, 6, 6, 7, 7, 10, 15, 16, 16, 16, 20, 24, 24, 29, 34, 36, 40; 9:7, 11, 18, 24, 24, 28, 33, 33, 36, 37, 39, 45, 45, 51, 57; 10:6, 6, 12, 14, 21, 38; 11:1, 9, 9, 10, 14, 14, 25, 27, 28, 29, 30, 33, 34, 51; 12:10, 10, 32, 49, 50, 54, 55, 56; 13:7, 7, 8, 8, 18, 19, 19, 19, 19, 21, 33; 14:1, 3, 18, 22, 28, 29, 34, 35, 35; 15:4, 5, 8, 9, 22, 23, 26; 16:2, 16, 17, 22; 17:1, 2, 6, 11, 14, 22, 26, 26, 28, 31; 18:15, 25, 25, 26, 30, 36; 19:1, 4, 7, 9, 13, 19; 20:1, 6, 6, 11, 46; 21:5, 13, 14, 21, 35; 22:16, 17, 19, 22, 23, 36, 38, 44, 64, 66; 23:3, 24, 26, 44, 53, 53, 53; 24:4, 4, 5, 5, 5, 5; 16:14, 15, 16, 19, 19,

10, 15, 21, 24, 29, 30, 30, 39, 43, 46, 51

Jn 1:5, 27, 32, 39; 2:5, 8, 9, 17, 19, 20; 3:8, 8, 8, 27; 4:6, 9, 10, 53; 5:10, 10, 13, 15; 6:17, 20, 31, 39, 42, 45, 46, 60, 61, 63, 65, 71; 7:7, 7, 10, 17, 22, 51; 8:9, 17, 44, 54, 56; 9:4, 14, 27, 32, 37; 10:10, 17, 18, 18, 18, 18, 22, 22, 34; 11:2, 22, 38, 38, 42, 50, 57; 12:14, 24, 24, 24, 25, 25, 28, 28, 29, 29; 13:19, 19, 24, 24, 25, 26, 26, 30; 14:2, 8, 14, 17, 21, 22, 27, 29, 29; 15:2, 2, 4, 7, 16, 18, 18; 16:7, 14, 13; 17:26; 18:10, 11, 14, 18, 25, 28, 31, 34; 19:2, 11, 14, 19, 20, 24, 24, 24, 29, 29, 30, 31, 35, 40; 20:1, 14, 27; 21:4, 6, 7, 7, 8, 12

Ac 1:7, 19, 20; 2:2, 3, 15, 17, 21, 24, 24; 3:10, 12, 17, 23; 4:3, 5, 10, 14, 16, 17, 19, 37, 37; 5:2, 2, 4, 4, 4, 7, 9, 38, 39, 39; 6:2, 15; 7:5, 5, 23, 31, 31, 42, 44, 53; 9:5, 6, 18, 32, 37, 42, 43; 10:4, 11, 28, 42; 11:4, 5, 5, 26, 30; 12:3, 9, 15, 15, 18, 22; 13:17, 33, 38, 41, 46, 46; 14:1, 6; 15:5, 5, 16, 28, 34; 16:16, 35; 17:14; 18:14, 15, 15; 19:1, 19, 39; 20:16, 35; 21:1, 3, 20, 22, 35; 22:6, 10, 17, 22, 25; 23:5, 12, 30, 31; 24:3, 21; 25:16, 27; 26:8, 14; 27:1, 8, 14, 25, 25, 28, 28, 35, 39, 39, 44; 28:8, 17, 19, 22, 28, 28

Ro 1:16, 17, 19; 2:24, 27; 3:4, 10, 19, 27, 30; 4:3, 10, 16, 16, 17, 22, 23, 23, 24; 5:10; 6:12; 7:11, 13, 16, 17, 17, 20, 20; 8:3, 7, 25, 33, 34, 36; 9:12, 13, 16, 20, 26, 26, 28, 32, 32, 33; 10:8, 15; 11:6, 6, 6, 7, 8, 26, 35; 12:8, 18, 19; 13:9, 11; 14:6, 6, 11, 14, 20, 21, 22; 15:3, 9, 21, 26, 27

1Co 1:11, 18, 19, 21, 31; 2:8, 9; 3:2, 13, 13, 13, 19; 4:2, 3, 7, 7, 9, 12; 5:1, 6:3, 15; 7:1, 5, 8, 9, 21, 21, 26, 29, 31; 8:7; 9:9, 10, 11, 15, 15, 25, 27; 10:7, 13, 16, 16, 28; 11:6, 13, 14, 15, 18, 24, 25; 12:6, 15, 16, 18, 26, 26; 13:3, 8; 14:7, 9, 10, 15, 21, 26, 27, 34, 35, 36; 15:11, 27, 32, 36, 37, 38, 38, 42, 42, 43, 43, 43, 43, 44, 44, 45; 16:4, 6, 15

2Co 1:6; 2:10, 10; 3:16; 4:3, 13; 5:10, 13, 13; 7:8, 11, 12; 8:11, 12, 15; 9:1, 5, 9; 11:15, 17, 17; 12:1, 4, 8, 13, 13, 16

Gal 1:12, 12, 13, 15; 2:6; 3:4, 5, 6, 10, 11, 13, 15, 15, 17, 18, 18, 19, 19; 4:15, 18, 22, 27, 29

Eph 2:8; 3:5; 4:9, 29; 5:3, 12, 25, 26, 27, 27, 29; 6:3

Php 1:6, 7, 20, 27, 29; 2:6, 13, 23, 25; 3:1, 4:4, 16, 17

Col 1:6, 6, 6, 9, 19; 2:14, 14, 15; 3:18, 23; 4:4, 16, 17

1Th 2:1, 13, 13; 3:1, 4; 4:10; 5:24

2Th 1:3, 6; 3:1

1Ti 1:8, 13; 4:4, 5; 5:16; 6:7

2Ti 2:11; 4:16

Tit 3:99;

Phm 1:14, 19, 19

Heb 2:10, 17; 3:13, 15, 17; 4:1, 2, 6, 6, 7; 6:4, 7, 7, 17, 18; 7:8, 11, 14, 15; 8:3; 9:5, 17, 23, 27; 10:4, 7, 31; 11:2, 4, 6, 18; 12:11, 13, 17, 20; 13:9, 17

Jas 1:2, 5, 11, 11, 15, 15; 2:14, 16, 17, 23; 3:3, 6, 8; 4:3, 14, 17, 17; 5:3, 7, 17, 17

1Pe 1:7, 11, 12, 16; 2:6, 13, 20, 20, 20; 3:3, 4, 11, 17; 4:4, 11, 12, 17

2Pe 1:13; 2:13, 21, 21, 22

1Jn 1:5; 2:18, 18, 21, 27; 3:1, 2; 4:3, 3; 5:6, 16

2Jn 1:6

Jude 1:3;

Rev 1:1, 11; 2:17; 3:8; 4:1; 5:6; 6:1, 11, 14; 7:2; 8:3, 5, 5, 8, 10, 10, 10; 9:4, 5, 6, 7, 9; 10:1, 9, 9, 9, 9, 10, 10, 10; 11:2, 2, 6; 12:4; 13:3, 7, 18; 14:3, 19; 15:2; 16:3, 17; 18:21; 19:6, 10, 15; 20:11, 13; 21:6, 16, 18, 21, 22, 23, 23, 24, 24, 25, 26, 27; 22:2, 3, 9

ME (4096)

Ge 3:12, 12, 13; 4:10, 14, 14, 25; 6:7, 13; 7:1; 9:12, 13, 15, 17; 12:12, 13, 18, 18, 19, 13; 13:8, 9; 14:21, 24; 15:2, 3, 9; 16:2, 5, 13, 13; 17:1, 2, 4, 7, 10, 11; 18:21, 27, 31; 19:8, 19, 19, 20; 20:5, 6, 9, 9, 11, 13, 13; 21:6, 6, 16, 23, 23, 23, 26, 30; 22:12; 23:4, 8, 8, 9, 9, 11, 13, 15, 15; 24:5, 7, 7, 7, 12, 17, 23, 27, 30, 37, 39, 40, 43, 44, 45, 48, 49, 54, 56, 56; 25:30, 31, 32, 33; 26:7, 27, 27, 27; 27:3, 4, 4, 7, 7, 9, 12, 12, 13, 13, 19, 19, 20, 25, 26, 31, 33, 34, 34, 36, 36, 38, 38, 46; 28:20, 20, 20, 20; 29:15, 15, 19, 21, 25, 25, 27, 32, 33, 34; 30:1, 6, 13, 14, 16, 18, 20, 20, 24, 25, 26, 26, 27, 28, 29; 31:7, 7, 7, 9, 11, 13, 26, 27, 28, 29, 31, 32, 35, 36, 40, 42, 42, 44, 48, 49, 50, 51, 52; 32:9, 11, 11, 16, 20, 20, 26, 29; 33:10, 11, 13, 14, 15, 15, 15; 34:4, 11, 11, 12, 12, 12, 30, 30, 30; 35:3, 3; 37:9, 14, 16; 38:16, 16, 17; 39:7, 8, 9, 12, 14, 14, 15, 17, 17, 18, 19; 40:8, 9, 14, 14, 14, 14, 15; 41:10, 10, 13, 14, 24, 51, 52; 42:20, 33, 34, 36, 36; 43:6, 8, 9, 16, 29; 44:21, 27, 28, 29, 34; 45:1, 4, 5, 5, 7, 8, 8, 9, 9, 10, 18; 46:30, 31; 47:29, 29, 30, 30, 31; 48:3, 3,

Idx

13:8, 18; 14:3, 16, 16, 16, 18, 18; 15:1;
16:13, 17, 17, 28; 17:2, 3, 3, 13; 18:24;
19:23, 24; 20:4, 5, 6, 23, 28
Ru 1:11, 11, 12, 13, 16, 16; 2:2, 8, 8, 13, 21,
21, 22; 3:1, 10, 11, 11, 16, 18; 4:4, 6, 10
1Sa 1:15, 15, 16, 26, 26, 27; 2:1, 1, 24, 28,
29, 29, 32, 35, 35, 35; 3:6, 16; 4:16; 9:5,
16, 16, 16, 17, 21; 10:2; 12:2, 2, 5; 14:29,
39, 40, 42; 15:11, 25, 30; 16:22; 18:17,
18, 18, 21; 19:2, 3, 3; 20:1, 1, 2, 2, 9, 12,
13, 13, 15, 29, 29, 42; 21:2, 8, 8, 15, 15;
22:3, 3, 8, 8, 8, 11, 12, 23; 23:10, 12, 17,
17; 24:6, 8, 10, 11, 11, 11, 15, 16, 21, 21,
21; 25:5, 11, 11, 11, 13, 24, 25, 25, 26,
26, 27, 27, 28, 28, 29, 30, 31, 31, 31, 39,
41; 26:17, 17, 17, 18, 19, 20, 21, 21, 23,
24, 25; 27:12; 28:9, 21, 21; 29:6, 8, 9;
30:13, 15, 23
2Sa 1:9, 10, 26; 2:22; 3:7, 12, 13, 13, 14, 18,
24, 28; 4:8, 9; 5:2; 7:5, 7, 8, 8, 10, 11,
13, 14, 15, 18; 9:7, 10, 11, 11; 11:11, 11,
11; 12:28; 13:4, 5, 5, 6, 6, 11, 12, 13, 20,
25, 26, 32, 33; 14:7, 7, 9, 9, 11, 12, 15,
16, 17, 17, 18, 19, 19, 20, 22, 24, 31;
15:7, 15, 21, 21; 16:3, 4, 9, 11, 11, 11;
18:5, 18, 22, 28, 31, 32, 33, 33, 33, 33,
33; 19:4, 4, 4, 12, 12, 13, 13, 19, 19,
20, 26, 26, 27, 27, 28, 28, 30, 35, 37, 37,
37; 20:9; 22:2, 2, 3, 3, 3, 3, 3, 3, 7, 7, 7,
7, 7, 18, 19, 19, 21, 21, 22, 25, 25, 29,
29, 30, 33, 33, 34, 34, 35, 37, 37, 39, 44,
47, 47; 23:2, 5, 5, 5; 24:3, 3, 17, 21,
22, 24
1Ki 1:2, 2, 13, 13, 17, 17, 18, 20, 20, 21, 21,
24, 24, 27, 27, 29, 30, 30, 31, 33, 35, 35,
36, 37, 37, 48; 2:15, 20, 24, 26, 26, 31,
32, 38, 44; 3:6, 7, 7, 14, 14, 14, 17, 20,
20, 21, 21, 22, 22, 23, 23, 26; 5:3, 4, 5, 5,
5, 6, 9, 9, 9; 6:12, 12, 12, 12, 13; 8:15,
16, 16, 16, 17, 18, 18, 19, 20, 24, 25, 25,
26, 28, 29, 59; 9:3, 4, 4, 6, 6, 7, 7, 13;
11:11, 11, 11, 13, 32, 33, 33, 33, 34, 34, 34,
36, 36, 38, 38, 38, 38, 38; 12:10, 10, 11,
11, 14, 14; 13:6, 30, 31; 14:7, 8, 8; 15:19;
16:2, 2; 17:1, 12, 18, 18, 20, 21; 18:7, 10,
12, 13; 19:4, 4, 10, 14, 20, 20; 20:4, 6, 7,
7, 7, 7, 9, 32, 34, 34; 21:2, 3, 4, 6; 22:4,
4, 49
2Ki 1:13, 14; 2:12, 12, 19; 3:7, 7; 4:1, 1, 16,
19, 19, 28, 29, 29; 5:3, 6, 13, 18, 18, 20,
22; 6:8, 12, 15, 21, 26, 28, 29; 8:5, 12;
9:7, 32; 10:6, 9, 15, 16; 13:14, 14; 14:9;
17:13, 13, 13; 18:23, 24, 27; 19:12, 23,
24, 28, 28, 34; 20:5, 6, 15, 19; 21:4, 7, 8,
15; 22:17; 23:27, 27
1Ch 4:10; 11:2, 2, 19; 16:22; 17:4, 6, 7, 7, 9,
10, 13, 13, 14, 25; 21:3, 3, 3, 17, 17, 23;
22:5, 7, 7, 7, 8, 8, 10, 10, 11, 14; 28:2, 2,
3, 4, 4, 4, 5, 5, 6, 6, 6, 7, 7, 9, 20; 29:1, 2,
2, 3, 3, 3, 14, 17, 19
2Ch 1:8, 9, 11; 2:3, 4, 7, 8, 13, 14, 15; 6:4,
5, 5, 5, 6, 6, 7, 8, 8, 9, 10, 15, 16, 16, 16,
19, 40; 7:13, 14, 14, 14, 16, 17, 17, 19,
19, 20, 20, 20; 8:11; 10:10, 10, 11, 11,
14, 14; 12:7, 8; 16:3; 18:3, 13; 25:16, 18;
29:11; 32:13, 14, 15; 33:4, 7; 34:25
Ezr 7:13, 28; 9:3, 3, 3, 3, 5, 5, 5, 5, 5, 6,
6, 10; 10:3
Ne 1:2, 6, 9, 9; 2:3, 3, 5, 8, 12, 12, 18; 4:16,
23, 23; 5:10, 10, 13, 14, 16, 17, 19; 6:9,
14, 19; 7:2, 5; 13:14, 14, 14, 19, 22,
29, 31
Est 4:16; 5:7, 7, 8, 8; 7:3, 3, 3, 3, 4; 8:6, 6
Job 1:5, 8; 2:1; 2:3; 3:10, 24, 24; 4:14, 15,
15; 5:8; 6:2, 2, 3, 4, 7, 7, 8, 11, 11, 12,
12, 13, 15, 21, 24, 29, 30, 30; 7:5, 5, 6, 7,
11, 11, 11, 13, 13, 13, 15, 15, 16, 19, 21;
9:14, 15, 16, 17, 18, 21, 21, 25, 25, 27,
28, 30; 10:1, 1, 1, 1, 6, 12, 15, 20; 11:4;
13:6, 6, 14, 14, 14, 16, 17, 17, 18, 19, 23,
23, 26, 27, 27, 27; 14:14, 14, 16, 16, 17;
16:4, 5, 5, 6, 7, 8, 8, 9, 12, 13, 13, 15, 15,
16, 17, 18, 18, 19, 19, 20; 17:1, 1, 7, 11,
11, 11, 13, 14, 14, 14, 15; 19:2, 5, 8,
8, 9, 9, 12, 13, 14, 14, 15, 16, 16, 17, 17,
19, 20, 20, 20, 20, 21, 22, 23, 25, 26, 26,
27; 20:2, 3, 7; 21:2, 4, 4, 6; 23:2, 2, 2, 4,
4, 7, 11, 12, 16, 17; 24:25; 27:2, 2, 3, 3,
4, 4, 5, 6, 6; 29:3, 4, 4, 5, 6, 7, 14, 18, 18,
19, 19, 20, 20, 20, 21, 22, 22, 24; 30:1,
10, 11, 12, 12, 13, 13, 16, 16, 17, 17, 17,
18, 18, 18, 22, 25, 27, 30, 30, 31, 31;
31:4, 4, 5, 7, 7, 8, 9, 10, 13, 13, 17, 18,
18, 20, 21, 21, 22, 24, 24, 25, 27, 27, 27,
30, 31, 32, 33, 33, 35, 36, 37, 38; 32:17,
19, 20, 22; 33:1, 1, 2, 2, 2, 3, 3, 3, 7,
11, 11; 34:2, 5, 6, 6, 10, 36; 35:2, 3, 10;
36:3, 3, 4; 37:1; 38:10; 40:4, 4, 8; 42:7, 7,
8, 8, 8
Ps 2:6, 6, 7; 3:2, 3, 4, 7; 4:1, 1, 2, 7; 5:1, 1,
2, 2, 2, 3, 3, 8; 6:2, 2, 3, 4, 6, 8, 8, 9, 9, 9;
7:1, 1, 2, 3, 3, 5, 5, 8, 10; 9:1, 4, 4, 13;
11:1, 1; 13:2, 2, 3, 5; 14:4; 16:1, 2, 2, 2,
3, 4, 5, 5, 7, 8, 9, 9, 9, 10; 17:1, 1, 2, 2,
5, 6, 9, 13; 18:1, 2, 2, 2, 2, 2, 2, 2, 6, 6,
6, 6, 17, 18, 18, 20, 20, 21, 24, 24, 28,
28, 28, 29, 32, 33, 33, 34, 36, 36, 38, 46;
46; 19:14, 14, 14, 14; 22:1, 1, 2, 9, 10,
10, 14, 14, 14, 15, 15, 15, 16, 17, 18,
18, 19, 20, 20, 22, 25, 25; 23:1, 3, 5, 6;
25:1, 2, 5, 7, 15, 17, 17, 18, 18, 20, 20;
26:2, 2, 9, 9, 12; 27:1, 1, 1, 2, 2, 3, 4, 7,
8, 8, 9, 9, 10; 28:1, 2, 6, 7, 7, 7, 7, 7,
7; 30:1, 2, 3, 6, 7, 9, 10, 11, 11, 11, 12;
31:1, 3, 3, 3, 4, 5, 7, 7, 8, 9, 9, 10, 10,

10, 11, 13, 14, 15, 22, 22; 32:3, 3, 4, 5, 5,
5, 7; 34:1, 2, 4; 35:1, 3, 4, 4, 7, 9, 10, 11,
12, 13, 13, 13, 14, 17, 17, 23, 23, 23, 23,
24, 27, 28; 36:1; 38:3, 3, 5, 5, 7, 7, 8,
9, 9, 10, 10, 11, 11, 11, 11, 12, 15, 22,
16, 17, 18, 21, 22; 39:1, 1, 1, 2, 2, 3, 3, 4,
5, 7, 8, 9, 10, 12, 12, 12; 40:1, 1, 2, 3, 5,
7, 8, 9, 9, 10, 10, 11, 11, 11, 12, 15, 16,
16, 17, 17, 17, 17; 41:4, 7, 9;
42:1, 2, 3, 3, 4, 5, 6, 6, 6, 8, 8, 9, 10, 11,
11; 43:1, 2, 4, 4, 5, 5, 5; 44:4, 6, 6, 15,
15; 45:1, 1; 49:3, 3, 4, 5, 15; 50:5, 7, 16,
16, 17; 51:1, 2, 3, 3, 5, 9, 14, 14, 15, 15;
53:4; 54:2, 2, 3, 4; 55:1, 1, 2, 4, 8, 13, 17,
18; 56:4, 5, 6, 6, 8, 8, 11, 13, 13; 57:1, 1,
4, 6, 6, 7, 7, 8; 59:1, 3, 3, 4, 9, 10, 10,
11, 16, 16, 16, 17, 17; 60:7, 8, 8; 61:1, 1,
2, 5, 8; 62:1, 1, 2, 2, 2, 5, 5, 6, 6, 6, 6, 7, 7,
7; 63:1, 1, 1, 3, 4, 5, 5, 6, 7, 8, 9; 64:1,
1, 1; 66:13, 14, 14, 16, 17, 17, 18, 19, 20;
68:22, 24, 24; 69:1, 3, 3, 3, 5, 5, 6, 10, 7,
8, 8, 10, 10, 11, 13, 18, 19, 19, 20, 20,
21, 21; 70:2, 2, 5, 5; 71:1, 3, 3, 3, 4, 5, 5,
5, 6, 6, 7, 8, 9, 10, 12, 12, 13, 13, 15, 17,
21, 22, 23, 23, 24, 24; 73:2, 2, 13, 13, 21,
21, 23, 26, 26, 26, 26, 28; 74:12; 77:1, 1,
2, 2, 2, 3, 6, 6, 10; 78:1, 1, 1; 81:8, 11,
11, 13, 13, 14; 83:13; 84:2, 2, 2, 3, 3, 8,
10; 86:2, 2, 4, 6, 6, 7, 11, 12, 13, 14;
87:7; 88:1, 2, 2, 3, 3, 9, 13, 14, 15; 89:1,
3, 3, 20, 21, 24, 24, 24, 26, 26, 26,
27, 28, 28, 30, 30, 31, 31, 33, 33, 34, 34,
35, 47, 50; 91:2, 2, 9, 14, 16; 92:10,
11, 11, 15; 94:17, 17, 18, 19, 19, 22, 22,
22; 95:9, 10, 11, 11; 101:2, 7, 7; 102:1, 1,
3, 3, 4, 4, 5, 5, 5, 9, 11, 23, 23, 24, 24;
103:1, 2, 22; 104:1, 1, 33, 33, 34, 35;
105:15; 108:1, 1, 8, 9, 9; 109:1, 4, 4, 5,
20, 22, 24, 24, 26, 30; 110:1, 1; 111:1;
116:1, 1, 4, 7, 8, 8, 11, 14, 16, 18; 118:6,
7, 7, 14, 14, 21, 28, 28; 119:5, 10, 13, 20,
24, 24, 25, 26, 28, 32, 34, 36, 39, 43, 48,
50, 50, 54, 54, 57, 58, 59, 69, 76, 77,
80, 81, 92, 97, 99, 99, 101, 103, 103,
105, 105, 108, 109, 109, 111, 111, 114, 114,
115, 116, 120, 129, 131, 133, 139, 143,
145, 149, 154, 157, 161, 167, 168, 169,
170, 171, 172, 174, 175; 120:1, 2, 6;
121:1, 2; 122:8; 129:1, 2, 3; 130:2, 2, 5,
6; 131:1, 2; 132:3, 3, 12, 12, 14; 137:5, 6,
6, 6; 138:1, 3; 139:2, 2, 3, 3, 4, 8, 13,
13, 14, 15, 16, 16, 23, 23; 140:4, 6, 6, 7,
7; 141:1, 2, 2, 3, 3, 4, 4, 5, 5, 6, 8, 8; 142:1,
1, 2, 2, 2, 2, 2; 145:1, 21; 146:1, 2
Pr 1:8, 10, 15, 23, 23, 24, 24, 25, 25, 30, 30;
2:1, 1, 1; 3:1, 1, 1, 11, 11, 21; 4:2, 3, 3, 4, 4,
5, 10, 10, 20, 20, 20; 5:1, 1, 1, 7, 12, 13,
20; 6:1, 3, 20; 7:1, 1, 1, 2, 2, 4, 6, 6, 14,
16, 17, 24; 8:4, 6, 7, 7, 7, 8, 10, 19, 19, 31,
32, 34, 34; 9:5; 19:27; 20:9, 9; 22:17;
23:15, 15, 16, 19, 26, 26; 24:13, 21;
27:11, 11; 30:9; 31:2, 2, 2
Ecc 1:13, 16, 17; 2:7, 9, 10, 10, 10, 10, 10,
11, 15, 15, 18, 19, 20; 3:18; 4:8; 7:15, 28;
8:9; 9:1; 12:12
SS 1:6, 7, 9, 12, 13, 13, 14, 15, 16; 2:2, 3,
6, 7, 8, 9, 10, 10, 10, 13, 13, 14, 16, 17;
3:1, 1, 2, 3, 4, 4, 5; 4:1, 7, 8, 9, 9, 9, 9,
10, 10, 11, 11, 12, 12, 16, 16; 5:1, 1, 1, 1, 1,
1, 1, 1, 1, 2, 2, 2, 2, 2, 2, 2, 2, 2, 3, 3, 4, 4,
5, 5, 5, 6, 6, 6, 7, 8, 10, 16, 16; 6:2, 3, 3,
4, 9, 9, 12; 7:9, 10, 11, 12, 13; 8:1, 1, 2,
2, 3, 4, 10, 12, 14
Isa 1:3, 12, 14, 25; 3:7, 12, 12, 15; 5:1, 1, 1,
3, 4, 5, 13; 6:7; 7:13; 8:4, 4, 16; 10:2, 6,
8, 10, 13, 13, 14, 14; 11:9; 12:2, 2, 2, 2;
13:3, 3, 3; 14:13, 25, 25; 15:5; 16:9, 11;
18:4, 4; 19:25, 25; 20:3; 21:3, 4, 4, 8, 8,
10, 10; 22:4, 20; 24:16, 16; 25:1; 26:9, 9,
19, 20; 27:5; 28:23, 23; 29:23; 30:1, 2;
32:9, 9, 13, 18; 33:1; 34:5, 5, 16; 36:8,
9, 12, 19, 20, 20; 37:12, 24, 25, 29, 29,
35; 38:10, 10, 12, 13, 15, 15, 16, 17, 17,
20; 39:4; 40:1, 27, 27, 27; 41:8, 8, 9,
10, 25; 42:1, 1, 1, 8, 8, 8, 14, 19, 19;
43:4, 6, 6, 7, 7, 10, 10, 10, 12, 13, 20, 21;
44:1, 2, 3, 8, 17, 21, 21, 21, 28, 28; 46:10,
11, 13, 13, 13; 47:6, 6, 6, 6, 7, 10; 48:3, 3,
5, 6, 6, 11, 12, 18; 49:1, 1, 2, 3, 4, 4, 4, 4,
5, 6, 6, 11, 14, 16, 16, 16, 17, 18; 50:1, 2, 2,
6, 6, 6, 7; 51:4, 4, 4, 5, 16, 16, 22; 52:6,
10, 10; 55:8, 8, 9, 11, 11; 56:1, 1, 4, 4,
5, 6, 7; 57:11, 13, 14, 21; 58:1, 2, 13;
59:21, 21, 21; 60:7, 10, 10, 13, 13, 21,
21; 61:10, 10; 62:1, 9; 63:3, 3, 4, 5, 5, 6,
8; 65:1, 3, 5, 8, 9, 9, 10, 11, 13, 13, 13,
14, 15, 19, 22, 25; 66:1, 1, 1, 2, 5, 18, 19,
19, 20
Jer 1:9, 9, 12, 16; 2:7, 11, 13, 19, 27, 31, 32;
3:4, 4, 13, 19; 4:1, 4, 11, 19, 19, 19, 19,
19, 19, 20, 20, 22, 31; 5:9, 14, 22, 26, 29,
31; 6:8, 12, 14, 19, 19, 26, 27; 7:10, 11,
12, 12, 12, 14, 15, 20, 23, 23, 25, 30, 30,
31; 8:7, 11, 18, 19, 21, 22; 9:1, 1, 2, 7, 9,
10, 10, 19, 19, 20, 20, 20, 20, 20, 20;
11:4, 4, 7, 10, 10, 15, 20; 12:7, 10, 10,
10, 14, 16, 14, 16, 16, 16, 20, 20, 20, 20;
14:14, 15, 17; 15:1, 1, 6, 7, 10, 10, 15, 18,
18, 19; 16:5, 11, 17, 18, 19, 19, 19, 21,
21; 17:3, 14, 17, 18; 18:2, 10, 10, 15, 20,
22; 19:5, 15; 20:9, 10, 10, 11, 12, 14, 15,
17, 17, 18; 21:10, 12; 22:18, 21, 24; 23:1,

2, 2, 3, 9, 11, 13, 22, 22, 22, 25, 27, 27,
27, 28, 28, 29, 30, 32, 39; 24:7; 25:8, 9,
13, 29; 26:4, 5; 27:5, 5, 6, 15; 29:9, 10,
19, 19, 21, 23, 32; 30:3, 10, 22; 31:1, 9,
14, 14, 18, 19, 19, 20, 20, 26, 32, 33, 33;
32:7, 8, 9, 31, 31, 34, 34, 35, 37, 38, 40, 41,
41; 33:5, 5, 20, 20, 21, 21, 21, 22, 24, 25,
26; 34:15, 15, 16, 18; 35:13, 15; 36:6;
37:20, 20; 38:9, 26; 39:16; 42:18, 18;
43:10; 44:4, 6, 10, 10, 11, 26, 26, 29;
45:3, 3; 46:27, 28; 49:25, 37, 38; 50:6;
51:20, 34, 35, 35, 45
La 1:9, 12, 13, 13, 14, 14, 14, 15, 15, 16, 16,
18, 18, 18, 19, 19, 20, 21, 22, 22, 22;
2:11, 11, 11, 21, 21, 22; 3:4, 4, 4, 7, 8, 9,
9, 11, 13, 14, 16, 17, 18, 18, 19, 20, 21,
24, 24, 48, 51, 53, 56, 56, 56, 58, 58, 59,
59; 4:3, 6, 10
Eze 1:28; 2:2, 7; 3:2, 3, 4, 10, 14, 17, 23, 24;
4:14, 14, 14; 5:6, 6, 6, 6, 7, 7, 11, 13, 13,
13; 6:12; 7:8, 14, 22, 22; 8:6; 9:6, 8; 10:2,
13, 19; 11:12, 12, 13, 20, 20; 12:7, 7, 13,
13, 28; 13:9, 10, 13, 13, 15, 18, 19, 19,
21, 23; 14:8, 8, 9, 9, 11, 11, 21; 15:7, 7;
16:8, 14, 17, 19, 21, 27, 42, 42, 60,
62; 17:19, 20, 20; 18:9, 9, 17, 17, 19,
25, 29; 20:8, 8, 9, 11, 11, 12, 13, 13, 13,
13, 14, 15, 16, 16, 16, 19, 19, 20, 21, 21,
21, 21, 21, 22, 24, 24, 24, 29, 29; 21:3, 4,
5, 10, 12, 14, 17, 31; 22:8, 20, 21, 22, 26,
26, 31; 23:18, 18, 25, 38, 38, 39; 24:13,
18, 21; 25:3, 14, 14, 14, 14, 17; 28:25;
29:3; 30:15, 24, 25; 32:3, 3, 10, 32; 33:7,
22, 22, 31; 34:6, 6, 8, 8, 8, 8, 8, 10, 10,
11, 12, 15, 17, 19, 22, 23, 24, 26, 30, 31;
31: 30:5, 5, 6, 6, 8, 12, 18, 20, 23, 23, 27,
27, 28; 37:12, 13, 14, 23, 24, 24, 24, 24;
25, 26, 27, 27, 28, 30; 38:14, 16, 16, 17, 18,
18, 19, 19, 20, 21; 39:7, 7, 7, 17, 19, 20,
21, 21, 21, 23, 24, 25, 29, 29; 43:3, 7, 7,
7, 8, 8, 8; 44:4, 7, 7, 7, 7, 7, 8, 8, 9, 11,
13, 15, 16, 16, 16, 23, 24, 24, 24, 24;
45:8, 8, 9; 46:18; 48:11
Da 1:10; 10; 2:3, 23; 3:14, 15; 4:4, 5, 5, 8, 9,
10, 13, 13, 18, 19, 24, 27, 30, 30, 36, 36,
36, 36, 36; 5:13; 6:22, 26; 7:2, 15, 15, 15,
28, 28, 28; 8:17, 18; 9:3, 4, 4, 18, 19, 20,
20, 20, 20, 20; 10:3, 8, 9, 9, 10, 10, 15,
16, 16, 16, 16, 16, 17, 17, 19; 12:8
Hos 1:9; 10; 2:2, 5, 5, 5, 5, 5, 5, 7, 9, 9, 9,
12, 12, 23, 23, 23; 4:6, 8, 12; 5:10, 15,
15; 6:5, 11; 7:2, 12; 8:1, 1, 2, 12; 9:8, 17;
10:10; 11:1, 7, 8; 12:8; 13:11
Joel 1:6, 7, 7, 13; 2:1, 25, 26, 27, 28, 29;
3:1, 2, 3, 5, 5, 5, 17
Am 2:7; 7:8, 15; 8:2; 9:3, 10, 12, 14
Ob 1:13, 16
Jnh 1:12; 2:2, 5, 6, 6, 7, 7; 4:2, 2, 3
Mic 1:9; 2:4, 7, 8, 9, 9; 3:3, 5; 6:3, 5, 7, 7, 7,
7, 16; 7:1, 7, 7, 9
Hab 1:12; 2:1; 3:16, 16, 16, 18, 18, 19, 19
Zep 2:8, 9, 9, 12; 3:8, 8, 8, 10, 10, 11
Hag 2:5, 23
Zec 1:6, 6, 6, 9, 16, 17; 2:11; 3:7, 7, 7, 7, 8;
4:4, 5, 6, 13; 5:4; 6:4, 8; 8:6, 7, 8; 11:4, 8,
10, 10, 12, 12; 12:5; 13:5, 6, 7, 7, 9, 9, 9;
14:5
Mal 1:6, 6, 11, 11, 11, 14; 2:2, 4, 5, 5, 9;
3:1, 17; 4:2, 4

Mt 2:6, 15; 3:17; 5:11; 7:21; 8:6, 8, 8, 9, 21;
9:18; 10:18, 22, 32, 33, 39; 11:10, 27, 29,
30, 30; 12:18, 18, 18, 18, 44, 48, 48, 49,
49, 50, 50; 13:30, 35; 15:13, 22; 16:17,
18, 25; 17:5; 18:5; 18:5, 10, 19, 20, 21, 35;
19:20, 29; 20:21, 23, 23, 23; 21:13,
28, 37; 22:4, 4, 4, 44, 44; 24:5, 9, 35, 36,
48; 25:27, 34, 40; 26:12, 12, 18, 18,
26, 28, 29, 38, 39, 42, 53; 27:35, 35, 46;
28:10
Mk 1:2, 11; 3:33, 33, 34, 34, 35, 35; 5:9, 23,
30; 6:23; 8:35, 38; 9:7, 17, 37, 39, 41;
10:20, 29, 40, 40, 51; 11:17; 12:6, 36, 36;
13:6, 9, 13, 31; 14:8, 14, 22, 24, 34;
15:34, 34; 16:17
Lk 1:18, 20, 25, 43, 44, 46, 47, 47; 2:49;
3:22; 6:47; 7:6, 7, 8, 27, 44, 44, 45, 46;
8:21, 21; 9:24, 26, 35, 38, 48, 59, 61;
10:22, 29, 40; 11:7, 24; 12:4, 13, 17, 18,
18, 18, 19, 45; 14:23, 24, 26, 27, 33;
15:6, 17, 18, 24, 29; 16:3, 5, 24, 27;
18:21, 41; 19:8, 23, 23, 46; 20:13, 42, 42;
21:8, 12, 17, 33; 22:11, 19, 20, 28, 29,
30, 30, 42; 23:46; 24:39, 39, 49
Jn 2:16; 3:29; 4:34, 49; 5:17, 24, 30, 31, 43,
47; 6:32, 51, 54, 54, 55, 55, 56, 56, 65;
7:6, 8, 16; 8:14, 16, 19, 19, 21, 28, 31,
31, 37, 38, 43, 43, 49, 51, 52, 54, 54, 56;
10:14, 15, 16, 17, 17, 18, 25, 26, 27, 27,
28, 29, 29, 30, 32, 37; 11:21, 32; 12:7,
26, 26, 27, 47, 48; 13:6, 8, 9, 9, 35, 37,
38; 14:2, 7, 12, 13, 14, 15, 20, 21, 21, 24,
26, 26, 36, 36, 37; 19:24, 24; 20:13, 17,
17, 17, 17, 21, 25, 27, 27, 27, 28, 28; 21:15,
16, 17
Ac 2:14, 17, 18, 18, 18, 25, 25, 26, 26, 26,
27, 34, 34; 7:34, 49, 49, 49, 50, 59; 9:15,
16; 10:30; 11:8; 13:22, 33; 15:7, 17, 19;
16:15; 20:24, 24, 25, 34; 22:1, 6;
24:14, 17; 25:26; 26:4, 4, 10; 28:19
Ro 1:8, 9, 9, 9; 2:16; 3:7; 7:4, 18, 23, 23, 23;
9:1, 2, 3, 3, 17, 17, 25, 25, 26; 10:1, 21;

11:3, 14, 27; 15:14, 24, 24, 24, 31; 16:3,
4, 5, 7, 7, 8, 9, 11, 21, 21, 25
1Co 1:4, 11; 2:4, 4; 4:14, 17, 17; 5:4; 7:25,
40; 8:13, 13; 9:1, 15, 17, 18, 18, 27;
10:14, 29; 11:24, 25, 33; 13:3, 3; 14:14,
18, 19, 19; 15:58; 16:6, 18, 24
2Co 1:16, 23; 2:3, 13, 13, 13; 6:13, 16, 18;
7:4, 4; 8:10, 23; 11:1, 26; 12:9, 19, 20
Gal 1:13, 14, 14, 15; 4:14, 14, 19, 20; 6:17
Eph 1:16; 3:4, 13, 14; 6:10, 19, 21
Php 1:3, 7, 7, 7, 8, 13, 14, 16, 19, 20, 20,
20, 22, 26; 2:2, 12, 12, 12, 25, 25; 3:1, 8;
4:1, 1, 1, 3, 14, 16, 19
Col 1:24; 2:4; 2:1; 4:7, 10, 11, 18
1Ti 1:2, 11
2Ti 1:2, 3, 3, 6, 16; 2:1, 8; 3:10; 4:6, 7, 16
Phm 1:4, 4, 10, 10, 20, 23, 24
Heb 1:5, 13; 2:12, 13; 3:9, 10, 11, 11; 4:3, 3,
5; 5:5; 8:9, 10; 10:16, 34, 38; 12:5; 13:6
Jas 1:2, 16, 19; 2:1, 3, 5, 14, 18, 18; 3:1, 10;
5:10, 12
1Pe 5:13;
2Pe 1:14, 15, 17
1Jn 2:1; 3:13, 18
3Jn 1:4;
Rev 1:20; 2:3, 13, 13, 13, 16, 20, 26, 27;
3:5, 8, 8, 10, 12, 12, 12, 12, 16, 16, 20,
21, 21; 10:10, 10; 11:3; 18:4; 21:7; 22:12

NOT (6596)

Ge 2:5, 5, 17, 18, 20, 25; 3:1, 3, 4, 11, 17;
4:5, 7, 7, 9, 12; 5:24; 6:3; 7:2, 8; 8:12, 21,
22; 9:4, 23; 11:7; 12:18; 13:6, 6, 9; 14:23,
23; 15:1, 4, 10, 13, 16; 16:10; 17:12, 14,
15; 18:3, 15, 21, 24, 25, 28, 29, 30, 30,
31, 32, 32; 19:7, 8, 17, 18, 20, 21, 31, 33,
35; 20:4, 5, 6, 7, 9, 12, 17; 21:10, 12, 16,
17, 23, 26; 22:12, 12, 16; 24:3, 5, 6, 8;
21, 27, 33, 37, 39, 41, 49, 56; 26:2, 22,
24, 29; 27:1, 2, 12, 21, 23, 36, 36; 28:1,
6, 8, 15, 19; 29:25, 26; 30:31, 33, 40, 42;
31:2, 5, 7, 15, 30, 34, 38, 38, 39, 52, 52; 32:10,
25, 26, 32; 34:7, 17, 19, 23; 35:5, 10, 17;
36:7; 37:4, 13, 21, 27, 29, 30; 38:9, 14,
16, 20, 23, 26; 40:8, 10, 23; 40:8, 23;
41:16, 21, 31, 36; 42:2, 4, 8, 13, 15, 20,
21, 22, 22, 22, 23, 32, 36, 36, 37, 38;
43:3, 5, 5, 5, 8, 9, 32; 44:4, 5, 15, 18,
26, 28, 30, 31, 32, 34; 45:1, 3, 5, 8, 9, 20,
26, 26; 46:3; 47:9, 18, 18, 19, 22, 22,
26, 29; 48:10, 11, 18; 49:4, 6, 6, 10;
50:19, 21
Ex 1:8, 17, 19; 2:3; 3:2, 3, 5, 19, 19, 21; 4:1,
8, 9, 10, 11, 14, 21; 5:2, 8, 9, 10, 11,
14, 19; 6:3, 9, 12; 7:4, 13, 16, 21, 24;
8:15, 18, 19, 21, 26, 26, 28, 29, 29, 31;
9:6, 7, 7, 11, 12, 17, 18, 19, 21, 30, 32,
32, 33; 10:7, 11, 15, 19, 20, 23, 26, 29,
27; 11:7, 9, 10; 12:9, 13, 23, 30, 30, 39,
39, 45, 46; 13:13, 17, 22; 14:12, 13, 20,
28; 15:23; 16:8, 15, 20, 24, 25; 17:7;
18:17, 18; 19:12, 13, 13, 15, 24; 20:4, 5,
7, 7, 10, 14, 15, 16, 17, 17, 19, 20, 26;
21:4, 6, 8, 9, 10, 14, 17, 18, 21, 23,
22:2, 2, 4, 6, 9, 18, 21, 25, 28, 29, 22,
23, 24, 25, 28; 23:22, 23, 24, 25, 28:
23, 32, 33:3, 11, 12, 15, 16, 20, 23;
34:10, 10, 25, 26, 29; 39:21, 23; 40:35,
37, 37
Lev 1:17; 2:12; 4:2, 13, 22, 27; 5:1, 7, 8, 11,
17, 18; 6:12, 17, 23; 7:15, 18, 19; 8:33,
35; 10:1, 6, 7, 9, 17, 18; 11:4, 4, 5, 6, 7,
8, 8, 10, 1, 13, 26, 41, 42, 43, 47; 12:8;
13:4, 4, 5, 6, 11, 13, 26, 41, 44, 55, 56;
15:11, 31; 16:2, 2, 13, 22; 17:4, 9, 16;
18:3, 3, 7, 8, 9, 10, 11, 12, 13, 14, 14,
15, 16, 17, 19, 20, 21, 22, 24, 26, 28,
30, 30; 19:4, 7, 9, 10, 11, 12, 13, 13, 14,
26, 27, 28, 29, 31, 33; 20:4, 19, 22, 23,
25; 21:4, 5, 6, 7, 10, 14, 17, 18, 21, 23;
22:2, 4, 6, 10, 12, 15, 15, 20, 20, 22,
23, 24, 25, 28; 23:22, 29; 25:5, 11, 14,
17, 20, 23, 28, 30, 34, 37, 39, 42, 43,
46, 53, 54; 26:11, 13, 14, 37, 39, 42, 43,
20, 21, 23, 26, 27, 31, 35, 44; 27:10, 11, 20,
20, 22, 27, 33, 33
Nu 1:47, 49; 2:33; 4:15, 18, 19, 20; 5:3, 14,
19, 28; 6:7; 9:6, 7, 13, 19, 22; 10:7, 30,
31; 11:11, 14, 15, 17, 19, 23, 25, 26;
12:2, 7, 8, 8, 11, 12, 14, 15; 13:20, 31;
14:3, 9, 9, 16, 22, 23, 24, 35, 40, 41, 42,
43, 44; 15:22, 34, 39; 16:12, 14, 14, 15,
15, 28, 29, 40, 40; 17:10; 18:3, 4, 17;
19:12, 12, 13, 13, 20, 20; 20:12, 12, 17,
12, 30, 34, 37, 37; 23:8, 8, 9, 13, 19, 19,
19, 19, 19, 21, 24, 26; 24:1, 12, 17, 17;
25:11; 26:11, 62, 64, 65; 27:3, 17; 29:7;
30:2, 5, 11, 12; 31:18, 23, 35, 49; 32:5, 9,
11, 18, 19, 23, 30; 33:55; 35:12, 23, 23,
27, 30, 33, 34; 36:7
Dt 1:9, 17, 17, 21, 26, 29, 32, 35, 37, 42, 42,
43, 45; 2:5, 5, 5, 9, 9, 9, 19, 19, 30, 36, 37;
3:2, 4, 4, 11, 22, 26, 27; 4:2, 21, 21, 22,
26, 31, 42; 5:3, 5, 8, 9, 11, 11, 14, 17, 32;
6:10, 11, 11, 11, 14, 16; 7:3, 7, 10, 14,
18, 21, 22, 25; 8:3, 3, 4, 9, 11, 11, 16, 20;

Idx

19, 22, 23; 13:10, 11, 25, 25, 27, 35, 39;
14:17, 18; 15:19, 38, 38; 16:7, 21; 17:4,
5, 6, 12, 24, 27, 29; 18:9, 9, 20; 19:2, 9,
26, 27, 30, 31, 32, 35; 20:10, 12, 16, 22,
27, 29, 31; 21:4, 12, 13, 14, 21, 34, 38;
22:9, 11, 18, 22; 23:5, 5, 9, 21; 24:4;
25:7, 11, 16, 24, 27; 26:19, 25, 26, 29,
32; 27:7, 10, 12, 14, 15, 21, 24, 34, 39;
28:4, 19, 24, 25, 26, 26

Ro 1:13, 16, 21, 28, 28, 32; 2:4, 8, 13, 14,
14, 21, 21, 22, 26, 27, 28, 29, 29; 3:3, 8,
10, 12, 17, 29; 4:2, 4, 5, 8, 10, 11, 12, 13,
16, 17, 19, 19, 20, 23; 5:3, 5, 11, 13, 14,
15, 16; 6:3, 6, 12, 14, 14, 15, 16; 7:1, 6,
7, 7, 7, 15, 16, 18, 19, 19, 20; 8:1, 3,
4, 7, 9, 9, 12, 15, 18, 20, 23, 24, 25, 26,
32, 32; 9:1, 6, 6, 8, 10, 11, 11, 16, 21, 24,
25, 25, 26, 30, 31, 32, 33; 10:2, 3, 6, 11,
14, 14, 16, 18, 18, 20, 20; 11:2, 2, 4, 7, 8,
8, 10, 18, 18, 20, 21, 21, 23, 25, 30, 31;
12:2, 3, 4, 11, 14, 16, 16, 19, 21; 13:1, 3,
4, 5, 9, 9, 9, 9, 13, 13, 13, 14; 14:1, 3,
3, 3, 3, 6, 6, 6, 6, 13, 15, 15, 16, 17, 20,
22, 23, 23; 15:1, 3, 18, 18, 20, 21, 21, 31;
16:4, 18

1Co 1:16, 17, 17, 20, 21, 26, 26, 26, 28; 2:1,
2, 4, 5, 6, 8, 9, 12, 13, 14; 3:1, 2, 2, 3, 4,
16; 4:3, 4, 6, 7, 7, 14, 15, 18, 19, 20; 5:1,
2, 6, 6, 8, 9, 10, 11, 11, 12; 6:1, 2, 3, 5, 5,
7, 7, 9, 9, 9, 12, 12, 13, 15, 16, 19, 19;
7:1, 4, 4, 5, 5, 6, 10, 10, 11, 12, 12, 12,
13, 15, 15, 16, 17, 18, 21, 23, 27, 28, 28,
30, 30, 30, 31, 35, 36, 38; 8:7, 8, 8, 10;
9:1, 1, 1, 1, 1, 3, 3, 4, 5, 7, 7, 9, 12, 12,
13, 16, 18, 21, 24, 26; 10:1, 5, 6, 13,
16, 16, 18, 20, 20, 23, 23, 27, 28, 29, 33;
11:6, 7, 8, 14, 17, 17, 20, 22, 22, 22, 29,
31, 32, 34; 12:1, 14, 15, 15, 15, 16, 16,
16; 13:1, 3, 4, 4, 4, 5, 5, 5, 6; 14:2, 11,
16, 17, 20, 21, 22, 22, 22, 23, 24, 33,
34, 39; 15:9, 10, 10, 13, 14, 15, 15, 16,
16, 17, 29, 32, 33, 34, 36, 37, 39, 46,
51, 58; 16:7, 12, 22

2Co 1:8, 9, 12, 18, 19, 23, 24; 2:1, 4, 5, 5,
11, 13, 17; 3:3, 3, 5, 6, 7, 8, 13, 13; 4:1,
2, 4, 5, 7, 8, 8, 9, 9, 16, 18, 18; 5:1, 3,
4, 7, 12, 12, 15, 19; 6:1, 3, 9, 12, 14, 17;
7:3, 7, 8, 9, 10, 12, 14; 8:5, 8, 10, 12, 12,
13, 19, 21; 9:4, 5, 7, 12; 10:2, 3, 4, 8,
9, 12, 12, 13, 14, 14, 15, 16, 18; 11:4, 4,
4, 5, 6, 11, 17, 29, 29, 31; 12:1, 4, 5, 6,
13, 14, 14, 14, 16, 16, 18, 20, 20, 21;
13:2, 3, 5, 6, 7, 10

Gal 1:1, 7, 10, 11, 16, 20; 2:5, 14, 14, 15,
16, 17, 20; 3:1, 1, 3:1, 10, 12, 16, 20; 4:8,
12, 14, 17, 18, 21, 27, 27, 30, 31; 5:1, 7,
8, 13, 15, 16, 18, 21, 26; 6:4, 7, 7, 9, 9

Eph 1:16, 21; 2:8, 9; 3:5, 13; 4:17, 20, 26,
26, 30; 5:3, 4, 7, 15, 17, 18, 27; 6:4, 6,
7, 12

Php 1:16, 22, 29; 2:4, 6, 12, 16, 21, 27, 30;
3:1, 9, 12, 13; 4:11, 17

Col 1:9, 23; 2:1, 8, 18, 19, 21, 21, 21, 23;
3:2, 9, 19, 21, 22, 23

1Th 1:5, 8, 8; 2:1, 3, 4, 8, 9, 13, 15, 17, 19;
4:5, 5, 7, 8, 9, 13, 15; 5:3, 4, 5, 6, 9,
19, 20

2Th 1:8, 8; 2:2, 3, 5, 10, 12; 3:2, 6, 7, 8, 9,
11, 12, 13, 14, 15

1Ti 1:9, 20; 2:7, 9, 12, 14; 3:3, 3, 3, 3, 5, 6,
8, 8, 8, 11; 4:14; 5:1, 8, 9, 13, 13, 16, 18,
19; 6:1, 2, 3, 17

2Ti 1:7, 8, 9, 12, 16; 2:5, 9, 13, 14, 15, 20,
24; 4:3, 8, 16

Tit 1:6, 7, 7, 7, 7, 11, 14; 2:3, 3, 5, 9, 10;
3:5, 14

Phm 1:14, 16, 19

Heb 1:12, 14; 2:5, 8, 8, 11, 16; 3:8, 10, 11,
15, 16, 17, 18, 18, 19; 4:2, 2, 6, 7, 8, 13,
15; 5:5, 12; 6:1, 10, 12; 7:6, 11, 16, 20,
21, 23, 27; 8:2, 4, 9, 9, 9, 11; 9:7, 8, 9,
11, 13, 14, 14; 10:1, 2, 4, 5, 8, 25, 35, 37, 39;
11:1, 3, 5, 5, 7, 8, 13, 16, 23, 27, 31, 31,
35, 38, 39, 40; 12:4, 5, 7, 8, 9, 18, 19, 20,
25, 25, 25, 26; 13:2, 6, 9, 9, 16, 17

Jas 1:5, 7, 16, 20, 22, 23, 25, 26; 2:1, 4, 5, 6,
7, 11, 11, 14, 16, 17, 21, 24, 25; 3:1, 2,
10, 14, 14, 15; 4:1, 2, 2, 3, 4, 11, 11,
14, 17; 5:6, 9, 12, 17, 17

1Pe 1:4, 8, 8, 12, 14, 18, 23; 2:6, 10, 10, 16,
18, 23, 23; 3:1, 3, 4, 6, 7, 9, 14, 21; 4:4,
12, 16, 17; 5:2, 2, 4

2Pe 1:12, 16, 21; 2:3, 3, 4, 5, 10, 11, 12, 21;
3:8, 9, 9

1Jn 1:6, 8, 10, 10; 2:1, 2, 4, 4, 11, 15, 15,
16, 19, 19, 21, 23, 27, 28; 3:1, 1, 2, 6,
6, 9, 10, 10, 10, 12, 13, 14, 18, 21; 4:1, 3,
3, 6, 6, 8, 8, 10, 18, 20, 20; 5:3, 6, 10, 10,
12, 12, 16, 16, 16, 17, 18, 18

2Jn 1:1, 5, 7, 8, 9, 9, 10, 10, 10, 12

3Jn 1:9, 10, 11, 11, 13

Jude 1:5, 6, 9, 10, 19

Rev 1:17; 2:2, 2, 3, 9, 11, 13, 21, 24, 24;
3:2, 3, 3, 4, 5, 8, 9, 17, 18; 4:8; 5:5; 6:6,
10; 7:1, 3; 8:12; 9:4, 4, 5, 6, 10, 20, 20;
10:4; 11:2, 6, 9; 12:8, 11; 13:8, 15; 14:4;
15:4; 16:9, 11, 18, 20; 17:8, 8, 8, 10, 11;
18:4, 4; 19:10; 20:4, 5, 15; 21:25; 22:9, 10

O (1086)

Ge 17:18; 24:12, 42; 27:34, 38; 32:9; 43:20;
44:18; 49:6, 18

Ex 4:10, 13; 15:6, 6, 11, 16, 17, 17; 32:4, 8;
34:9

Nu 10:36; 12:13; 16:22; 21:17, 29; 24:5, 5

Dt 3:24; 4:1; 5:1, 29; 6:3, 4; 9:1, 26; 20:3;
21:8; 26:10; 27:9; 32:1, 1, 6, 29, 43;
33:23, 29, 29

Jos 7:7, 8, 13

Jdg 3:19; 5:3, 3, 21, 31; 6:13, 15, 22; 13:8;
16:28, 28; 21:3

1Sa 1:11, 26; 4:9; 17:55; 20:12; 23:10, 11,
20; 26:17

2Sa 1:25; 7:18, 19, 19, 22, 25, 27, 28, 29;
14:4, 9, 22; 15:31, 34; 16:4; 18:33, 33;
19:4, 4, 26; 20:1; 22:29, 50; 23:17; 24:10

1Ki 1:13, 20, 24; 3:7, 17, 26; 8:26, 28, 53;
12:16, 28; 13:2; 17:18, 20, 21; 18:26, 37;
19:4; 20:4; 21:20; 22:28

2Ki 1:11, 13; 4:40; 6:12, 26; 8:5; 9:5, 5, 23;
13:14; 19:15, 19; 20:3

1Ch 16:13, 34, 35; 17:16, 17, 17, 19, 20,
25, 27; 21:17; 29:11, 11, 16, 18

2Ch 1:9; 6:14, 16, 17, 19, 41, 41, 42; 10:16;
13:12; 14:11, 11; 20:6, 12, 17, 20; 25:7

Ezr 9:6, 10, 15

Ne 1:5, 11; 4:4; 6:9; 13:14, 22, 29, 31

Est 7:3;

Job 6:8; 7:7, 20; 11:5; 13:5; 14:13; 16:18,
21; 19:21, 23, 23; 23:3; 29:2; 31:31, 35;
33:31; 34:2; 37:14

Ps 2:10; 3:3, 7, 7; 4:1, 2; 5:1, 3, 8, 10; 6:1, 2,
2, 3, 4, 4; 7:1, 3, 6, 9; 8:1, 9; 9:1, 2, 6,
13, 19, 20; 10:1, 12, 12; 12:7; 13:1, 3;
14:7; 16:1, 2; 17:1, 6, 7, 13, 14; 18:1, 15,
49; 19:14; 21:1; 22:2, 3, 19, 19; 24:6, 7,
9; 25:1, 2, 4, 6, 7, 11, 17, 20, 22; 26:1, 2,
6; 27:7, 9, 11; 28:1; 29:1; 30:1, 2, 3, 4, 8,
10; 31:1, 5, 9, 14, 17, 19, 23; 33:1, 1,
22; 34:3, 8, 9; 35:1, 22, 22, 24; 36:5, 6, 7,
9; 38:1, 15, 15, 21, 21, 22; 39:12, 13;
40:5, 8, 9, 11, 13, 13, 17; 41:10; 42:1, 5,
6, 11; 43:1, 1, 3, 4, 5; 44:1, 4, 23; 45:3, 6,
10; 47:1; 48:9, 10; 50:7, 7; 51:1, 10, 14,
15, 17; 52:1, 4; 53:6; 54:1, 2, 6; 55:1, 6,
23; 56:1, 2, 7, 12; 57:1, 5, 7, 9, 11;
58:1, 1, 6, 6; 59:1, 3, 5, 8, 11, 17; 60:1, 1,
10, 10; 61:1, 5, 7; 62:12; 63:1; 64:1; 65:1,
2, 5; 66:8, 10; 67:3, 4, 5; 68:7, 9, 10, 24,
28, 32, 35; 69:1, 5, 6, 6, 13, 13, 16, 29;
70:1, 1, 5; 71:1, 4, 5, 12, 12, 17, 18,
19, 19, 22, 22; 72:1; 73:20; 74:1, 10, 18,
19, 21, 22; 75:1; 76:6; 77:13, 16; 78:1;
79:1, 8, 9, 12; 80:1, 3, 4, 7, 14, 19; 81:8,
8, 13; 82:8; 83:1, 1, 13, 16; 84:1, 3, 8, 8;
9, 12; 85:4, 7; 86:1, 2, 3, 4, 4, 6, 8, 9, 11,
12, 14, 15, 16; 87:3; 88:1, 13; 89:5, 8, 15,
51; 90:13, 14; 92:1, 5, 9; 93:3, 5; 94:1, 1,
5, 12, 18; 95:1, 6; 96:1, 7, 9; 97:8; 98:1;
99:8; 101:1, 2; 102:1, 12, 24; 103:1, 2,
22; 104:1, 1, 24, 35; 105:1, 6; 106:1, 4, 4,
47; 107:1; 108:1, 3, 5, 11, 11; 109:1, 21,
26, 26; 113:1; 114:5; 115:1, 9, 10; 116:4,
7, 19; 117:1; 118:1, 25, 25, 29; 119:5, 8,
10, 12, 31, 33, 41, 52, 55, 57, 64, 65, 75,
89, 97, 107, 108, 137, 145, 149, 151,
156, 159, 169, 174; 120:2; 122:2; 123:1,
3; 125:4; 126:4; 130:1, 3; 132:8; 135:1, 9,
13, 13, 19, 19, 20; 136:1, 2, 3, 26; 137:5,
7, 8; 138:4, 8; 139:1, 4, 17, 19, 21, 23;
140:1, 4, 7, 9, 9; 141:3, 8; 142:5; 143:1,
7, 9, 11; 144:5, 9; 145:1, 10; 146:1, 10;
147:12, 12

Pr 4:10; 5:7; 6:9; 7:24; 8:4, 5, 32; 24:15;
30:13; 31:4

Ecc 10:16, 17; 11:9

SS 1:5, 7, 8, 9; 2:7, 14; 3:5, 11; 4:11, 16; 5:1,
1, 8, 9, 16; 6:1, 4, 13; 7:1, 6, 13; 8:1, 4, 12

Isa 1:2, 2; 2:5; 3:12; 5:3; 7:13; 8:8, 9; 10:5,
24, 30, 30; 12:1; 14:12, 31, 31; 16:9;
21:2, 2, 10, 13; 23:4, 10, 12; 24:17; 25:1;
26:8, 13, 15, 17; 27:12; 33:2; 37:16, 17,
17, 20; 38:3, 14, 16; 40:9, 9, 27, 27; 41:1;
43:1, 1, 22, 22; 44:1, 2, 21, 21, 23, 23;
45:15; 46:3, 8; 47:1, 1, 5; 48:1, 12, 18;
49:1, 3, 13, 13, 13; 51:4, 9, 17; 52:1, 1, 2,
2; 54:1, 11; 62:6; 63:16, 17; 64:1, 4, 8,
9, 12

Jer 2:4, 12, 28, 31; 3:14, 20; 4:1, 14, 19; 5:3,
15, 21; 6:1, 8, 18, 19, 23, 26; 7:29; 9:1, 2,
20; 10:1, 6, 7, 17, 23, 24; 11:5, 13, 20;
12:1, 3; 13:27; 14:7, 8, 9, 20, 22; 15:5,
15, 16; 16:19; 17:3, 13, 14; 18:6, 6, 19;
19:3; 20:7, 12; 21:12, 13; 22:2, 23, 29;
30:10, 10; 31:4, 7, 10, 21, 22, 23; 32:25;
34:4; 37:20; 42:19; 45:2; 46:11, 19, 27,
27, 28; 47:6; 48:2, 19, 28, 32, 43, 46;
49:3, 4, 8, 16, 30; 50:11, 24, 31, 42;
51:13, 25, 62

La 1:9, 11, 20; 2:13, 13, 18, 20; 3:55, 58, 59,
61, 64; 4:21, 22, 22; 5:1, 19, 21

Eze 3:25; 7:7; 8:15, 17; 10:13; 11:4, 5;
12:25; 13:4, 11; 16:35; 18:25, 29, 30, 31;
20:31, 39, 44; 23:22; 26:3; 27:3, 3, 8;
28:16, 22; 33:7, 8, 10, 11, 20; 34:9, 17;
35:3, 15; 36:8, 22, 32; 37:3, 4, 9, 12, 13;
38:3, 16; 39:1; 44:6; 45:9

Da 2:4, 23, 29, 31, 37; 3:4, 9, 10, 12, 14, 16,
17, 18, 24; 4:9, 18, 22, 24, 27, 31; 5:10,
18, 22; 6:7, 8, 12, 13, 15, 16, 20, 21, 22;
8:17; 9:4, 7, 8, 15, 16, 17, 18, 19, 19, 19,
19, 22; 10:11, 16, 19; 11:16; 12:4, 8

Hos 5:1, 1, 3, 8; 6:4, 4, 11; 8:5; 9:1, 14;
10:9; 13:9, 14, 14; 14:1

Joel 1:11, 11, 19; 2:21, 21; 3:4, 11

Am 2:11; 3:1; 4:5, 12, 12; 5:1, 25; 6:14; 7:2,
5, 12; 8:4, 14; 9:7

Ob 1:9;

Jnh 1:6, 14, 14; 2:6; 4:2, 3

Mic 1:2, 13, 15; 2:7, 12; 3:1; 4:8, 10, 13;
5:1; 6:2, 3, 5, 8; 7:8

Na 1:15; 3:18

Hab 1:2, 12, 12, 12; 3:2, 2

Zep 2:1, 5; 3:14, 14, 14

Hag 1:4; 2:4, 4, 23

Zec 1:9; 2:7, 10, 13; 3:2, 8; 4:7; 8:13;
9:9, 9, 13, 13; 11:1, 2, 7; 13:7

Mal 1:6; 2:1

Mt 3:7; 6:30; 8:26; 11:25; 12:34; 14:31;
15:22, 28; 16:3, 8; 17:17; 18:32; 20:30;
31; 23:37; 26:39, 42

Mk 9:19; 12:29

Lk 3:7; 5:8; 9:41; 10:21; 12:28; 13:34; 24:25

Jn 17:5, 25

Ac 1:1; 7:42; 13:10; 18:14; 25:26; 26:13, 19
Ro 2:1, 3; 7:24; 9:20; 11:33

1Co 7:16, 16; 15:55, 55

2Co 6:11;

Gal 3:1;

1Ti 6:11, 20

Heb 1:8; 10:7, 9

Jas 2:20;

Rev 4:11; 6:10; 11:17; 15:4; 16:5

OF (34750)

Ge 1:2, 2, 2, 6, 10, 14, 15, 17, 20, 24, 25,
26, 26, 27, 28, 28, 29, 29, 30, 30; 2:1, 4,
4, 5, 5, 6, 7, 7, 7, 9, 9, 9, 9, 9, 10, 11, 11,
12, 13, 13, 14, 15, 16, 16, 17, 17,
17, 19, 19, 19, 20, 20, 21, 23, 23, 23; 3:1,
1, 1, 2, 2, 3, 3, 3, 3, 6, 7, 8, 8, 8, 8, 11,
12, 14, 14, 17, 17, 17, 17, 17, 18, 19,
19, 20, 21, 22, 22, 22, 23, 24, 24, 24, 24;
4:2, 2, 3, 3, 3, 4, 4, 4, 10, 14, 16, 16, 16,
17, 17, 19, 19, 20, 20, 21, 23, 23, 25,
26; 5:1, 1, 1, 4, 8, 11, 14, 17, 20, 23, 27,
29, 29, 31; 6:1, 2, 2, 2, 4, 4, 4, 4, 5, 5, 5,
7, 7, 8, 9, 13, 14, 15, 15, 15, 18, 21, 21,
11, 11, 13, 13, 14, 15, 15, 16, 18, 21, 21,
21, 21, 22, 22, 23, 23; 8:2, 3, 4, 4, 5, 5,
6, 7, 8, 9, 10, 13, 13, 21, 21; 9:2, 2, 2, 2,
5, 5, 5, 5, 6, 10, 10, 10, 10, 11, 11,
12, 13, 15, 16, 17, 18, 18, 19, 19, 21;
22, 22, 23, 25, 26, 27, 29; 10:1, 1, 2, 3, 4,
5, 6, 7, 9, 10, 10, 14, 16, 16, 17, 18, 18,
19, 19, 20, 21, 22, 22, 23, 29; 11:1, 1, 2, 2,
5, 5, 5, 5, 6, 6, 10, 10, 10, 10, 10, 11,
12, 13, 15, 16, 17, 18, 18, 19, 19, 21, 21,
22, 22, 23, 25, 26, 27, 29; 10:1, 1, 2, 3, 4,
5, 6, 7, 9, 10, 10, 14, 16, 16, 17, 18, 18,
8, 11, 12, 13, 13, 14, 15, 16, 16, 22, 24,
25, 26, 28, 28, 28, 29, 29, 30, 31, 32,
34, 36, 37, 38, 38; 20:2, 2, 5, 5, 6, 11, 12,
12, 13, 16, 16, 18, 18, 18; 21:2, 3, 9, 10,
11, 12, 12, 13, 14, 14, 15, 16, 17, 17,
17, 17, 19, 21, 21, 21, 22, 25, 26, 27, 27,
28, 30, 31, 32, 32, 33; 22:2, 2, 2, 3, 6,
6, 8, 9, 11, 11, 13, 14, 14, 15, 15, 17, 17,
18, 21; 23:1, 1, 2, 3, 4, 4, 4, 5, 15, 17, 17,
18, 21; 23:1, 1, 2, 3, 4, 4, 4, 5, 15, 17, 17,
8, 9, 9, 9, 10, 10, 11, 12, 13, 16, 17, 17,
18, 21; 23:1, 1, 2, 3, 4, 4, 4, 5, 15, 17, 17,

38:2, 7, 12, 12, 19, 20, 21, 22, 27; 39:1,
1, 1, 1, 2, 5, 10, 11, 14, 19, 21, 21, 22,
22, 23; 40:1, 1, 1, 2, 2, 2, 3, 3, 4, 5, 5,
5, 7, 8, 12, 14, 14, 15, 15, 17, 17, 17, 20,
20; 41:1, 2, 3, 3, 5, 8, 10, 11, 12, 14, 15,
16, 17, 18, 19, 25, 26, 32, 36, 37, 38, 41,
42, 43, 44, 45, 45, 45, 45, 46, 46, 46, 48, 48,
48, 49, 50, 50, 50, 51, 52, 52, 53, 53, 54,
54, 55, 56, 56; 42:5, 5, 6, 7, 9, 9, 12, 13,
13, 15, 16, 16, 19, 19, 19, 21, 29, 30,
30, 32, 32, 33, 33, 33, 35, 35, 36; 43:2, 7,
7, 7, 9, 11, 12, 14, 16, 18, 19, 19, 21, 23,
27, 27, 29, 34; 44:1, 2, 4, 8, 8, 9, 16,
20, 20, 24, 31, 33; 45:2, 8, 8, 9, 10, 11,
12, 13, 13, 17, 18, 18, 18, 18, 19, 20, 25, 26, 27,
21, 21, 22, 22, 22, 23, 25, 25, 26, 27,
27; 46:1, 2, 3, 3, 5, 6, 8, 9, 10, 10, 11,
12, 12, 13, 14, 15, 15, 16, 17, 17, 18,
19, 20, 20, 20, 21, 22, 23, 24, 25, 26, 27,
27, 28, 31, 34; 47:1, 1, 1, 2, 4, 4, 6, 6,
6, 6, 9, 9, 9, 9, 9, 9, 9, 9, 11, 11, 13, 13,
13, 13, 14, 14, 14, 15, 16, 17, 21, 23, 28,
28, 30; 48:3, 4, 4, 5, 6, 7, 7, 10, 16, 16,
17, 19, 21, 22; 49:2, 3, 3, 3, 5, 8, 10,
11, 13, 13, 16, 16, 16, 20, 24, 24, 24, 28,
25, 25, 25, 26, 26, 26, 26, 27, 27, 28,
29, 30, 30, 30, 31, 31, 32, 32, 32;
Ex 1:1, 1, 5, 5, 7, 9, 9, 10, 12, 13, 14,
15, 15, 15, 16, 17, 18; 2:1, 1, 1, 3, 5,
6, 7, 10, 11, 13, 15, 15, 16, 19, 19, 23,
23, 23, 23, 25; 3:1, 1, 1, 1, 2, 2, 2, 2,
4, 4, 6, 6, 6, 7, 7, 8, 8, 9, 9, 9, 10,
10, 11, 13, 14, 15, 16, 16, 17, 17, 18, 18,
15, 16, 16, 16, 16, 16, 17, 17, 17, 18, 18,
18, 19, 21, 22, 22, 22; 4:5, 5, 5, 5, 7,
6, 6, 7, 9, 9, 11, 11, 13, 12, 12, 13, 13,
13, 13, 14, 14, 14, 14, 15, 15, 15, 15,
16, 16, 16, 16, 16, 17, 18, 19, 20,
20, 25, 26, 27, 28, 29, 29, 30, 31; 5:1, 3,
4, 5, 6, 8, 10, 11, 12, 14, 14, 15, 15,
18, 19, 19, 19, 21; 6:1, 3, 4, 4, 5, 5, 6,
6, 6, 7, 9, 9, 11, 11, 12, 13, 13, 13,
13, 13, 14, 14, 14, 14, 14, 15, 15, 16, 16, 16,
16, 16, 17, 17, 18, 18, 19, 20, 21, 21,
22, 23, 24, 24; 8:3, 5, 6, 6, 7, 12,
13, 13, 13, 16, 16, 17, 17, 17, 19, 21,
21, 21, 22, 24, 24, 24, 24, 24, 24, 24,
26, 26, 29, 31, 31; 9:1, 3, 4, 4, 4, 6, 6,
6, 6, 7, 7, 7, 7, 8, 9, 10, 11, 12, 13,
20, 20, 21, 22, 24, 24, 25, 25, 25, 27,
28, 28, 29, 30; 10:1, 2, 2, 3, 5,
5, 6, 6, 12, 12, 13, 14, 14, 15, 15, 15,
15, 15, 19, 20, 21, 22, 23; 11:2, 2, 2, 2,
3, 3, 3, 4, 4, 5, 5, 6, 7, 7, 9, 10;
12:1, 2, 3, 3, 3, 4, 5, 6, 6, 6, 7, 7, 9, 10,
10, 12, 12, 12, 13, 15, 16, 16, 16, 17, 17,
18, 18, 19, 21, 22, 22, 27, 27, 28,
29, 29, 29, 29, 30, 33, 33, 35, 35, 35, 35,
36; 17:1, 1, 1, 1, 3, 5, 5, 6, 6, 7, 7, 7,
9, 9, 12, 13, 14, 14, 15; 18:1, 1, 1, 3,
3, 4, 4, 4, 5, 7, 9, 9, 10, 10, 10, 10, 10,
12, 15, 16, 17, 21, 21, 21, 21, 24, 25,
25, 25, 25, 25; 19:1, 1, 1, 1, 2, 3, 3, 6,
6, 7, 8, 9, 11, 12, 13, 13, 16, 16, 16, 17,
17, 17, 17, 18, 18, 18, 19, 21, 22,
22, 23, 24, 24, 24, 25; 21:9, 10, 19, 26,
28, 30, 31, 32; 33:5, 14, 15, 17, 19, 21, 25,
23, 23, 25, 26, 27; 16:1, 1, 1, 1, 1, 1,
2, 2, 3, 3, 6, 6, 7, 9, 9, 10, 10, 12,
12, 14, 15, 15, 16, 16, 16, 17, 19, 19, 19,
27, 29, 29, 31, 31, 32, 32, 33, 33, 35, 35,
36; 17:1, 1, 1, 1, 3, 5, 5, 6, 6, 7, 7, 7,
9, 9, 12, 13, 14, 14, 15; 18:1, 1, 1, 3,
3, 4, 4, 4, 5, 7, 9, 9, 10, 10, 10, 10, 10,
12, 15, 16, 17, 21, 21, 21, 21, 24, 25,
25, 25, 25, 25; 19:1, 1, 1, 1, 2, 3, 3, 6,
6, 7, 8, 9, 11, 12, 13, 16, 16, 16, 17,
17, 17, 17, 18, 19, 19, 19, 19, 20, 22,
20, 22, 23, 24, 24, 24, 24, 25, 27,
28, 28, 29, 29, 30; 15:1, 3, 7, 8, 8, 14,
15, 15, 15, 16, 17, 19, 19, 19, 20, 22,
23, 23, 23, 26, 26, 27; 16:1, 1, 1, 1, 1,
2, 2, 3, 3, 6, 6, 7, 9, 9, 10, 10, 12,
12, 14, 15, 15, 16, 16, 16, 17, 19, 19, 19,

16, 16, 17, 18, 18, 19, 19, 20, 20, 20, 21, 21, 22, 22, 23, 23, 24, 24, 24, 24, 25, 25, 26, 26, 26, 26, 26, 26, 27, 27, 27, 27, 28, 29, 29, 30, 30, 30, 31, 32, 32, 32, 32, 33, 34, 36, 36, 39, 39; 18:1, 1, 1, 1, 1, 2, 3, 4, 5, 5, 7, 8, 9, 9, 9, 9, 9, 10, 10, 10, 10, 11, 11, 11, 12, 12, 13, 13, 13, 14, 14, 14, 14, 14, 14, 15, 15, 16, 16, 16, 16, 17, 17, 17, 18, 18, 19, 21, 21, 23, 24, 24, 24, 24, 26, 28, 28, 29, 30, 30, 31, 31, 31, 31, 32, 32, 32, 32, 33, 33, 33, 33, 33, 34, 34, 34, 34, 35, 35, 35, 37, 37, 37; 19:1, 2, 2, 3, 4, 4, 5, 6, 6, 6, 6, 8, 9, 9, 10, 10, 10, 11, 12, 12, 13, 13, 13, 13, 14, 14, 14, 15, 15, 15, 16, 17, 17, 18, 19, 19, 20, 20, 20, 21, 21, 22, 22, 23, 23, 23, 23, 24, 24, 25, 26, 26, 29, 29, 30, 30, 31, 31, 31, 31, 32, 35, 35, 36, 37, 37; 20:1, 4, 5, 5, 5, 6, 6, 6, 7, 8, 9, 11, 12, 12, 13, 13, 16, 18, 18, 18, 19, 20, 20, 20, 20; 21:2, 2, 2, 3, 3, 4, 4, 5, 5, 5, 6, 7, 7, 8, 9, 11, 12, 12, 12, 13, 13, 13, 14, 14, 15, 16, 17, 17, 17, 18, 18, 19, 20, 22, 22, 23, 24, 24, 24, 24, 25, 25, 25, 25, 26; 22:1, 1, 2, 3, 3, 3, 3, 4, 4, 5, 5, 5, 6, 7, 7, 8, 9, 9, 11, 12, 12, 12, 13, 13, 13, 14, 14, 14, 14, 15, 16, 16, 17, 18, 18, 18; 23:1, 1, 2, 2, 2, 2, 2, 2, 2, 2, 2, 3, 3, 4, 4, 4, 4, 4, 4, 4, 4, 5, 5, 5, 6, 6, 6, 7, 7, 8, 8, 8, 8, 8, 8, 9, 9, 10, 10, 10, 11, 11, 11, 12, 12, 12, 13, 13, 13, 13, 13, 13, 14, 15, 16, 16, 16, 17, 17, 17, 17, 18, 18, 19, 19, 19, 19, 19, 19, 20, 20, 21, 21, 21, 21, 21, 21, 22, 23, 23, 23, 23, 23, 23, 24, 24, 25, 25, 25, 26, 26, 27, 27, 27, 27, 27, 27, 27, 28, 28, 29, 30, 30;

1Ch 1:5, 6, 7, 8, 9, 9, 12, 17, 19, 23, 28, 29, 31, 32, 32, 33, 33, 34, 35, 36, 37, 38, 39, 40, 40, 41, 41, 42, 42, 43, 43, 43, 43, 44, 44, 45, 45, 46, 46, 46, 47, 48, 49, 50, 50, 50, 51, 54; 2:1, 3, 3, 3, 3, 4, 5, 6, 6, 7, 7, 8, 9, 10, 10, 16, 17, 18, 18, 21, 21, 22, 23, 23, 23, 24, 25, 25, 26, 27, 27, 28, 28, 29, 29, 30, 31, 31, 32, 33, 33, 42, 42, 42, 42, 42, 42, 43, 43, 44, 45, 45, 45, 46, 46, 46, 47, 47, 49, 49, 49, 50, 50, 50, 50, 51, 51, 52, 52, 53, 53, 54, 54, 54, 54, 55, 55, 55, 55; 3:1, 1, 1, 2, 2, 2, 3, 3, 5, 5, 9, 9, 15, 16, 17, 19, 19, 21, 21, 21, 21, 21, 22, 22, 23, 24; 4:1, 2, 2, 3, 3, 3, 4, 4, 4, 4, 5, 6, 7, 8, 8, 10, 11, 11, 12, 12, 13, 13, 14, 14, 15, 15, 16, 17, 17, 18, 18, 18, 18, 19, 19, 19, 20, 20, 21, 21, 21, 21, 21, 21, 22, 22, 24, 26, 26, 26, 26, 6:1, 2, 3, 3, 15, 16, 17, 17, 18, 18, 18, 19, 19, 19, 20, 20, 21, 21, 21, 21, 21, 22, 24, 26, 29, 31, 34, 35, 35, 35, 35, 36, 36, 36, 37, 37, 37, 37, 38, 38, 38, 38, 39, 39, 40, 40, 40, 41, 41, 42, 42, 43, 43, 44, 44, 44, 44, 45, 45, 45, 46, 46, 46, 47, 47, 47, 47, 47, 48, 48, 48, 49, 49, 49, 49, 50, 50, 54, 54, 54, 54, 55, 56, 56, 57, 57, 57, 60, 60, 61, 61, 61, 61, 61, 62, 62, 62, 62, 62, 62, 62, 63, 63, 63, 63, 63, 64, 65, 65, 65, 65, 65, 65, 66, 66, 66, 66, 66, 67, 67, 70, 70, 70, 70, 70, 71, 71, 71, 72, 72, 74, 74, 76, 76, 77, 77, 77, 77, 78, 78, 80, 80; 7:1, 2, 2, 2, 3, 3, 3, 4, 4, 5, 5, 6, 7, 7, 7, 7, 8, 8, 9, 9, 9, 9, 10, 10, 11, 11, 11, 12, 12, 13, 13, 14, 14, 15, 15, 16, 16, 17, 17, 17, 19, 20, 21, 29, 29, 29, 29, 30, 31, 31, 33, 33, 34, 35, 36, 38, 39, 40, 40, 40, 40; 8:3, 6, 6, 6, 6, 8, 9, 10, 11, 12, 13, 13, 13, 13, 14, 16, 17, 25, 27, 28, 29, 34, 35, 38, 39, 40, 40, 40, 40; 9:1, 1, 3, 3, 3, 3, 3, 4, 4, 4, 4, 4, 4, 5, 6, 7, 7, 7, 7, 7, 8, 8, 8, 8, 8, 9, 10, 11, 11, 11, 11, 11, 11, 12, 12, 12, 13, 13, 13, 14, 14, 14, 14, 14, 15, 15, 16, 16, 16, 16, 16, 16, 18, 19, 19, 19, 19, 19, 19, 20, 21, 21, 21, 21, 22, 23, 26, 26, 27, 28, 29, 30, 30, 30, 31, 31, 32, 32, 33, 33, 34, 35, 40, 40, 44; 10:1, 2, 3, 7, 9, 10, 10, 12, 12, 13, 13, 14; 11:3, 3, 4, 5, 5, 6, 7, 8, 9, 10, 10, 11, 11, 12, 12, 13, 13, 14, 15, 15, 15, 15, 17, 17, 18, 18, 18, 19, 19, 20, 20, 21, 22, 22, 22, 22, 22, 23, 23, 24, 24, 25, 25, 26, 26, 26, 30, 31, 31, 31, 32, 32, 34, 34, 35, 35, 37, 38, 38, 39, 39, 41, 42, 42, 43, 44, 45, 46; 12:1, 1, 1, 2, 2, 2, 3, 3, 7, 7, 8, 8, 8, 14, 14, 14, 14, 14, 15, 16, 16, 18, 18, 18, 19, 19, 19, 19, 20, 20, 21, 21, 22, 23, 23, 23, 24, 25, 25, 25, 26, 27, 28,

28, 29, 29, 29, 29, 29, 29, 30, 30, 30, 30, 31, 31, 32, 32, 32, 32, 33, 33, 33, 34, 35, 36, 37, 37, 37, 37, 37, 37, 38, 38, 40, 40; 13:1, 2, 2, 2, 3, 3, 4, 5, 5, 5, 6, 7, 7, 9, 10, 10, 12, 12, 13, 13, 14, 14, 14; 14:1, 1, 2, 4, 8, 9, 9, 10, 10, 12, 12, 14, 14, 15, 15, 16, 17, 17, 17; 15:1, 1, 2, 4, 8, 9, 10, 11, 11, 12, 13, 14, 14, 15, 15, 16, 16, 17, 17, 17, 17, 17, 18, 19, 21, 22, 22, 24, 27; 16:1, 2, 3, 3, 3, 4, 4, 6, 7, 9, 10, 12, 13, 14, 16, 17, 17, 17, 18, 19, 22, 27, 27, 28, 28, 29, 29, 29; 17:1, 1, 1, 3, 6, 6, 6, 7, 8, 9, 11, 17, 17, 17, 18, 21, 21, 24, 24, 24, 27; 18:1, 1, 3, 4, 5, 5, 5, 7, 7, 8, 9, 9, 9, 11, 12, 13, 16, 16, 16, 17; 19:1, 1, 2, 2, 2, 2, 3, 4, 4, 5, 6, 7, 7, 8, 9, 10, 10, 11, 11, 12, 13, 15, 16, 16, 17, 17; 20:1, 1, 3, 4, 5, 6, 7, 8; 21:2, 2, 3, 3, 5, 5, 7, 8, 10, 12, 12, 12, 12, 12, 15, 15, 15, 15, 16, 17, 17, 18, 18, 19, 20, 20, 22, 22, 23, 23, 24, 25, 26, 27, 28, 29; 22:1, 1, 2, 3, 3, 4, 5, 6, 7, 8, 9, 10, 11, 12, 12, 13, 14, 14, 16, 17, 17, 18, 18, 19, 21; 29:2, 2, 2, 2, 2, 2, 3, 3, 3, 4, 4, 4, 5, 5, 5, 6, 6, 7, 7, 7, 8, 8, 10, 12, 14, 14, 16, 17, 18, 18, 18, 18, 19, 20, 22, 22, 23, 23, 24, 25, 26, 28, 29, 29, 29, 29, 30;

2Ch 1:1, 2, 2, 2, 3, 3, 4, 4, 5, 5, 6, 9, 11, 12, 13, 16, 17, 17, 17; 2:1, 3, 4, 4, 6, 8, 10, 10, 10, 10, 10, 12, 13, 13, 14, 14, 14, 14, 14, 15, 15, 16, 17, 18, 18; 3:1, 1, 1, 2, 2, 3, 3, 4, 4, 4, 4, 6, 6, 8, 9, 9, 10, 11, 11, 11, 11, 12, 12, 13, 14, 15, 15, 16, 17; 4:1, 2, 2, 3, 3, 5, 5, 5, 5, 7, 7, 8, 8, 9, 9, 11, 12, 12, 13, 16, 16, 17, 18, 19, 20, 21, 22, 22, 22; 5:1, 1, 1, 2, 2, 2, 2, 2, 2, 3, 4, 5, 6, 7, 7, 7, 7, 7, 9, 9, 10, 10, 11, 12, 12, 13, 13, 13, 14, 14, 14, 14; 6:2, 3, 3, 4, 5, 5, 7, 7, 7, 9, 10, 11, 11, 12, 13, 16, 18, 19, 21, 21, 25, 27, 27, 28, 29, 30, 33, 33, 38, 41, 42, 42; 7:1, 1, 2, 2, 3, 3, 5, 6, 6, 7, 7, 8, 8, 9, 10, 11, 12, 18, 20, 22, 22; 8:1, 1, 2, 6, 6, 7, 7, 8, 8, 9, 9, 10, 11, 11, 11, 12, 13, 13, 13, 14, 14, 14, 15, 16, 16, 16, 16, 17, 18, 18, 18; 9:1, 1, 3, 3, 4, 4, 5, 5, 7, 7, 8, 8, 9, 10, 11, 11, 11, 11, 12, 13, 13, 14, 14, 14, 15, 16, 16, 16, 16, 17, 18, 18, 18; 9:1, 1, 1, 1, 3, 3, 4, 4, 4, 4, 5, 6, 6, 7, 8, 8, 8, 8, 8, 9, 11, 11, 11, 12, 13, 14, 14, 15, 16, 16, 16, 16, 17, 18, 18, 18, 18, 20; 10:1, 1, 1, 2, 3, 4, 6, 7, 7, 9, 10, 11; 11:1, 1, 3, 3, 5, 5, 6, 7, 8, 9, 10, 11, 12, 12, 12, 13, 14, 14, 16, 16, 16, 16, 17, 17, 17, 18, 18, 19, 20, 20, 21, 21, 21, 21, 22, 22, 23, 23, 23; 12:1, 2, 2, 3, 3, 4, 5, 6, 7, 9, 9, 9, 10, 10, 10, 10, 11, 13, 13, 13, 14, 15, 15, 16, 16, 16; 13:1, 2, 2, 3, 4, 4, 5, 6, 7, 8, 9, 9, 10, 10, 11, 11, 11, 11, 12, 13, 13, 14, 14, 15, 16, 16, 17, 17, 18, 18, 19, 19, 20, 20, 20, 20, 20, 20, 26, 28, 28, 28, 29, 29, 29, 31;

10:2, 2, 4, 13, 14, 15, 15, 16, 17, 17, 18, 19; 11:1, 1, 2, 2, 3, 3, 4, 4, 11, 11, 13, 16, 16, 16, 16, 16, 17, 17, 17, 18, 18, 18, 18, 20, 21, 21, 22, 22, 23; 12:1, 2, 2, 3, 5, 5, 6, 7, 7, 7, 8, 8, 9, 9, 9, 9, 10, 10, 10, 13:1, 2, 2, 3, 3, 3, 5, 5, 6, 6, 7, 7, 8, 8, 9, 9, 9, 9, 9, 9, 10, 11, 11, 11, 12, 12, 15, 15, 16, 17, 18, 18, 18, 20, 22, 22, 22; 14:1, 1, 3, 4, 5, 5, 8, 8, 9, 9, 10, 14, 15; 15:1, 1, 3, 5, 7, 8, 8, 9, 10, 14, 15, 15, 16, 17, 18; 16:1, 1, 1, 2, 2, 2, 3, 3, 3, 4, 4, 4, 5, 6, 7, 9, 10; 17:2, 2, 2, 2, 3, 3, 4, 4, 4, 5, 6, 6, 7, 7, 9, 9, 10, 11, 11, 11, 12, 13, 14, 16; 18:3, 4, 5, 5, 6, 7, 7, 7, 8, 10, 12, 14, 16, 17, 20, 23, 23, 24, 25;

29, 30, 31, 32, 32, 33, 34, 34, 34, 34, 34, 34, 35, 35, 37, 37; 21:1, 2, 2, 3, 3, 4, 4, 4, 6, 6, 6, 7, 8, 9, 10, 10, 11, 11, 12, 12, 12, 12, 12, 13, 13, 13, 13, 13, 13, 14, 14, 15, 15, 16, 17, 19, 19, 19, 19, 19, 20; 22:1, 1, 1, 1, 1, 1, 4, 5, 5, 5, 6, 7; 23:1, 1, 1, 1, 1, 1, 1, 1, 1, 2, 2, 3, 3, 3, 4, 4, 4, 4, 5, 5, 6, 6, 6, 7, 7; 25:1, 2, 4, 5, 6, 6, 6, 7, 7, 7, 9, 9; 26:1, 1, 3, 4, 5, 5, 6, 6, 8, 9, 11, 11, 11, 12, 12, 16, 16, 17, 18, 18, 19, 21, 21, 21, 22, 22, 22, 23; 27:1, 2, 3, 3, 3, 4, 5, 5, 5, 5, 5, 7, 7, 9; 28:1, 2, 2, 3, 3, 3, 5, 5, 6, 6, 6, 7, 7, 8, 8, 9, 9, 10, 11, 12, 12, 12, 13, 14, 15, 15, 16, 18, 18, 18, 18, 18, 19, 19, 20, 20, 21, 22, 23, 23, 23, 23, 24, 24, 24, 24, 25, 25, 26, 26, 26; 31:1, 1, 1, 2, 2, 3, 3, 4, 4, 5, 5, 5, 6, 6, 6, 6, 7, 10, 11, 12, 13, 13, 13, 14, 14, 14, 15, 15, 15, 17, 17, 17, 18, 18, 19, 19, 19, 19, 21; 32:1, 3, 4, 5, 6, 6, 6, 7, 8, 8, 9, 9, 10, 11, 11, 11, 13, 13, 13, 14, 14, 14, 14, 15, 15, 15, 17, 17, 17, 17, 17, 18, 19, 19, 19, 20, 21, 21, 21, 21, 22, 22, 23, 23, 26, 26, 26, 27, 28, 28, 29, 30, 30, 30, 30, 30, 31, 32, 32, 33, 33; 33:2, 2, 2, 3, 4, 5, 5, 6, 6, 6, 7, 7, 10, 8, 8, 9, 11, 11, 11, 13, 13, 14, 14, 14, 14, 15, 15, 15, 15, 16, 16, 18, 18, 18, 19, 19, 20, 25; 34:2, 2, 3, 3, 4, 4, 4, 6, 7, 8, 8, 8, 8, 9, 9, 9, 9, 10, 10, 10, 10, 11, 11, 12, 12, 12, 12, 13, 13, 13, 14, 15, 15, 17, 17, 17, 18, 19, 20, 21, 21, 22, 22, 22, 22, 22, 23, 24, 24, 25, 26, 26, 26, 27, 30, 31, 32; 35:1, 2, 3, 3, 4, 4, 4, 4, 5, 5, 5, 5, 6, 6, 7, 7, 8, 8, 9, 12, 12, 14, 14, 15, 16, 16, 16, 17, 18, 18, 18, 19, 19, 20, 21, 22, 22, 24, 24, 25, 26, 26, 27; 36:1, 1, 3, 3, 4, 5, 6, 7, 7, 8, 8, 9, 10, 10, 12, 12, 14, 15, 16, 16, 17, 17, 18, 18, 18, 18, 18, 19, 20, 21, 21, 22, 22, 22, 22, 22, 23, 23, 23;

Ezr 1:1, 1, 1, 1, 1, 1, 2, 2, 3, 3, 4, 4, 5, 5, 5, 5, 7, 7, 7, 8, 8, 8, 9, 9, 10, 10, 11, 11; 2:1, 2, 1, 1, 1, 2, 2, 2, 3, 4, 5, 6, 6, 7, 8, 9, 10, 11, 12, 13, 14, 14, 15, 16, 16, 17, 18, 19, 20, 21, 22, 23, 24, 25, 26, 27, 28, 29, 30, 31, 32, 33, 34, 35, 36, 36, 37, 38, 39, 40, 40, 41, 42, 42, 42, 42, 43, 43, 43, 44, 44, 45, 45, 49, 49, 50, 50, 50, 51, 51, 51, 52, 52, 53, 53, 54, 54, 55, 56, 56, 57, 58, 59, 60, 60, 61, 61, 61, 61, 63, 68, 68, 68, 69, 69, 69, 70; 3:1, 2, 2, 2, 2, 2, 2, 3, 3, 4, 4, 5, 5, 6, 6, 6, 6, 7, 7, 7, 8, 8, 8, 8, 8, 8, 8, 8, 9, 9, 10, 10, 10, 11, 11, 12, 12, 12, 13; 4:1, 1, 2, 2, 2, 3, 3, 4, 4, 4, 4, 5, 5, 5, 6, 6, 7, 7, 9, 10, 11, 12, 12, 13, 13, 13, 13, 14, 14, 15, 15, 17, 18, 19, 22, 23, 23, 24, 24; 5:1, 1, 1, 2, 2, 2, 2, 4, 5, 6, 6, 6, 7, 9, 10, 11, 11, 12, 13, 13, 14, 14, 14, 15, 16, 16, 16, 17; 6:1, 2, 3, 3, 4, 5, 5, 6, 7, 8, 8, 9, 10, 10, 11, 12, 13, 14, 14, 14, 14, 15, 16, 16, 16, 16, 17, 18, 18, 18, 18, 19, 20, 20, 20, 20, 20, 21, 22, 22, 22; 7:1, 1, 1, 1, 1, 2, 2, 3, 3, 4, 4, 5, 5, 5, 6, 6, 6, 7, 7, 7, 7, 7, 9, 10, 10, 10, 12, 14, 14, 15, 15, 15, 16, 16, 16, 17, 17, 18, 19, 19, 20, 21, 21, 21, 22, 22, 23, 23, 23;

29, 30, 31, 32, 32, 33, 33, 34, 34, 34, 34, 34, 35, 35, 37, 37; 21:1, 7, 8, 9, 10, 10, 11, 11, 12, 12, 12, 12, 12, 12, 12, 13, 13, 13, 14, 14, 15, 15, 16, 16, 17, 17, 19, 19, 19, 19, 20; 22:1, 1, 1, 1, 2, 3, 3, 4, 4, 5, 5, 5, 6, 6, 7, 7, 7, 7, 7, 8, 8, 8, 9, 9, 10, 10, 10, 11, 11, 11, 11, 11, 11, 12, 23:1, 1, 1, 4, 5, 5, 6, 6, 6, 7, 7, 8, 8, 9, 10, 11, 11, 11, 12, 12, 13, 13, 13, 13, 13, 13, 14, 14, 14, 15, 15, 15, 16, 16, 17, 17, 17, 18, 18, 18, 19, 19, 20, 20, 20, 21, 21, 21, 21, 21, 21, 22, 23, 23, 23, 23, 24, 24, 25, 25, 25, 27, 29, 29, 29, 31, 31, 32; 4:2, 2, 2, 4, 7, 8, 9, 10, 10, 14, 14, 15, 16, 16, 16, 17, 19, 20, 20, 21, 21, 23; 5:1, 3, 5, 5, 7, 7, 9, 9, 10, 11, 11, 11, 12, 12, 13, 13, 18, 18, 18; 6:1, 2, 7, 8, 10, 10, 10, 10, 10, 12, 14, 17, 17, 18, 18, 18; 7:2, 3, 3, 3, 5, 5, 6, 6, 6, 6, 7, 7, 8, 9, 10, 11, 12, 14, 14, 15, 17, 17, 18, 19, 19, 20, 21, 22, 22, 23, 23, 24, 25, 25, 26, 27, 27, 27, 28, 30, 30, 32, 32, 37, 38; 10:1, 9, 9, 9, 14, 28, 28, 28, 29, 29, 30, 31, 31, 31, 32, 32, 33, 33, 33, 34, 34, 34, 35, 35, 35, 35, 36, 36, 36, 36, 36, 36, 37, 37, 37, 37, 37, 37, 37, 37, 38, 38, 38, 39, 39, 39, 39, 39, 39; 11:1, 1, 1, 3, 3, 3, 4, 4, 4, 4, 4, 4, 4, 4, 4, 4, 5, 5, 5, 5, 5, 5, 6, 7, 7, 7, 7, 7, 7, 7, 7, 9, 9, 10, 10, 11, 11, 11, 11, 11, 11, 12, 12, 12, 12, 12, 13, 13, 13, 13, 14, 14, 14, 14, 15, 15, 15, 15, 16, 16, 16, 16, 17, 17, 17, 17, 17, 17, 20, 20, 20, 22, 22, 22, 22, 22, 22, 22, 22, 22, 24, 24, 24, 25, 25, 30, 30, 31, 35, 36; 12:1, 7, 7, 7, 12, 12, 12, 12, 12, 13, 13, 14, 14, 15, 15, 16, 16, 17, 17, 17, 18, 18, 19, 19, 20, 20, 21, 21, 22, 22, 22, 23, 23, 23, 23, 23, 24, 24, 24, 24, 25, 26, 26, 26, 26, 27, 27, 28, 28, 29, 29, 31, 31, 32, 32, 35, 35, 35, 35, 35, 36, 36, 37, 37, 37, 38, 38, 38, 38, 39, 39, 39, 39, 39; 13:1, 1, 2, 4, 4, 4, 5, 5, 5, 6, 6, 7, 7, 8, 9, 9, 10, 11, 12, 13, 13, 13, 14, 15, 16, 16, 16, 17, 19, 19, 20, 22, 23, 23, 24, 25, 26, 26, 28, 28, 28, 29, 29, 30;

Est 1:1, 2, 3, 3, 3, 4, 4, 5, 5, 6, 6, 8, 8, 10, 10, 14, 15, 16, 17, 18, 18, 18, 19, 21, 22; 2:1, 3, 3, 3, 3, 3, 5, 5, 6, 6, 8, 8, 8, 9, 9, 9, 11, 11, 12, 12, 12, 13, 14, 14, 15, 16, 17, 18, 20, 21, 21, 23, 23; 3:1, 5, 6, 6, 6, 7, 8, 9, 9, 9, 10, 12, 12, 12, 12, 13, 14; 4:1, 5, 6, 7, 7, 7, 8, 9, 11, 11; 5:1, 1, 2, 3, 4, 8, 9, 11, 11, 11, 11, 14, 14, 14; 6:1, 2, 2, 2, 4, 8, 9, 11, 11, 12; 7:2, 2, 7, 8, 8, 9, 11, 11, 12, 12; 8:1, 2, 3, 5, 6, 7, 9, 11, 11, 12, 12, 13, 15, 15, 15, 15, 15, 17, 17, 17; 9:1, 1, 2, 2, 3, 3, 3, 5, 10, 10, 10, 12, 15, 16, 17, 17, 18, 19, 19, 19, 20, 21, 21, 22, 24, 24, 26, 26, 26, 28, 28, 29, 29, 30, 30, 31, 31, 32, 32; 10:1, 2, 2, 2, 2, 2, 2, 3, 3, 3

Job 1:1, 3, 3, 3, 5, 5, 6, 10, 12, 15, 16, 17, 19, 21, 21; 2:1, 7, 9, 10, 10, 11; 3:5, 5, 6, 6, 9, 9, 10, 11, 14, 18, 25; 4:6, 9, 9, 10, 10, 10, 11, 13, 18, 19; 5:1, 5, 6, 6, 12, 13, 15, 17, 20, 21, 21, 22, 22, 23, 23, 25, 26; 6:3, 4, 4, 6, 10, 12, 12, 14, 15, 16, 17, 18, 19, 19, 22, 23, 26; 7:1, 2, 3, 4, 4, 5, 8, 11, 11, 20; 8:2, 6, 8, 8, 9, 10, 13, 17, 19, 19, 22; 9:2, 3, 6, 8, 9, 19, 19, 23, 24, 24, 28; 10:1, 1, 3, 4, 5, 7, 15, 18, 21, 21, 22, 22; 11:2, 6, 6, 20, 20; 12:4, 5, 6, 7, 8, 9, 10, 10, 12, 18, 20, 20, 21, 22, 24, 24, 24; 13:4, 4, 6, 12, 26, 27; 14:1, 1, 4, 5, 7, 9, 12, 14, 16, 18, 19, 19, 21; 15:5, 8, 11, 13, 14, 20, 22, 23, 26, 27, 30, 34, 34, 34; 16:5, 11, 16; 17:5, 6, 7, 11, 12, 16; 18:2, 4, 5, 7, 13, 13, 14, 28, 29, 29; 20:3, 3, 4, 5, 8, 11, 11, 14, 15, 16, 17, 20, 20, 21, 22, 23, 24, 25, 25, 28, 28, 29; 21:9, 12, 14, 16, 17, 20, 20, 21, 24, 25, 28, 28, 30, 30, 33; 22:4, 6, 9, 20; 23:12, 12, 15; 24:3, 4, 4, 6, 8, 8, 9, 12, 12, 13, 15, 17, 18, 18, 24, 24; 25:3, 4, 6; 26:9, 11, 14, 14, 14; 27:3, 8, 11, 13, 13, 13, 15, 21, 22, 23; 28:2, 2, 3, 3, 4, 5, 6, 6, 6, 12, 13, 16, 17, 17, 18, 18, 18, 19, 20, 21, 21, 24, 26, 28; 29:4, 4,

Idx

80; 2:2, 4, 4, 4, 4, 4, 9, 9, 10, 11, 13, 21, 21, 22, 22, 23, 24, 24, 24, 25, 27, 31, 32, 33, 34, 35, 36, 36, 36, 36, 36, 37, 38, 39, 40, 41, 42, 43, 46; 3:1, 1, 1, 1, 1, 1, 1, 1, 2, 2, 3, 3, 4, 4, 4, 4, 6, 7, 7, 8, 8, 9, 14, 15, 16, 23, 23, 23, 24, 24, 24, 24, 24, 25, 25, 25, 25, 25, 25, 25, 26, 26, 26, 27, 27, 27, 27, 27, 28, 28, 28, 28, 28, 29, 29, 29, 29, 30, 30, 30, 30, 31, 31, 31, 31, 31, 32, 32, 32, 32, 33, 33, 33, 33, 33, 34, 34, 34, 34, 35, 35, 35, 35, 35, 35, 36, 36, 36, 36, 36, 37, 37, 37, 37, 37, 38, 38, 38, 38; 4:1, 2, 3, 4, 4, 5, 5, 6, 9, 9, 14, 14, 15, 17, 18, 18, 19, 20, 22, 25, 25, 26, 26, 27, 27, 29, 29, 30, 30, 31, 31, 32, 32, 32, 32, 33, 33, 33, 33, 34, 34, 34, 34, 35, 35, 35, 35, 36, 36, 36, 36, 37, 38, 39, 40, 41, 42, 43, 43, 46; 5:1, 1, 2, 2, 3, 3, 6, 9, 10, 12, 12, 15, 15, 16, 17, 17, 17, 17, 17, 19, 24, 24, 27, 29, 29, 33, 33, 34, 36, 36; 6:1, 2, 4, 5, 5, 13, 15, 16, 17, 17, 17, 17, 17, 19, 20, 22, 26, 30, 30, 34, 35, 42, 44, 44, 45, 45, 45, 45, 45, 49; 7:1, 3, 3, 11, 12, 12, 12, 17, 18, 18, 19, 21, 21, 24, 34, 35, 36, 37, 38, 39, 42, 44; 8:1, 1, 2, 2, 3, 3, 4, 5, 10, 10, 11, 12, 13, 14, 21, 22, 23, 24, 25, 26, 27, 28, 29, 29, 32, 33, 35, 35, 36, 37, 37, 38, 41, 42, 43, 43, 44, 44, 46, 48, 49, 51; 9:2, 5, 7, 7, 8, 8, 8, 9, 11, 11, 11, 17, 19, 20, 22, 22, 26, 26, 26, 26, 27, 29, 31, 35, 36, 38, 43, 44, 44, 44, 45, 46, 47, 52, 55, 55, 56, 58, 58, 60, 62; 10:2, 6, 7, 9, 10, 11, 11, 11, 19, 21, 22, 30, 34, 35, 36; 11:1, 5, 6, 8, 11, 11, 15, 15, 16, 20, 20, 24, 26, 27, 28, 29, 30, 30, 31, 31, 31, 31, 32, 32, 34, 34, 34, 36, 36, 39, 39, 41, 42, 42, 44, 45, 46, 47, 48, 49, 50, 50, 50, 51, 51, 51, 52, 53, 54; 12:1, 1, 1, 1, 4, 6, 7, 7, 8, 8, 9, 10, 13, 15, 15, 16, 20, 25, 27, 28, 29, 30, 30, 31, 31, 39, 40, 42, 44, 48, 48, 48, 54, 56, 56, 57; 13:1, 7, 10, 11, 14, 15, 16, 18, 19, 19, 21, 25, 27, 28, 28, 29, 31, 33, 35; 14:1, 1, 5, 8, 8, 10, 14, 15, 15, 18, 19, 21, 21, 24, 24, 28, 32, 33; 15:4, 4, 8, 10, 10, 12, 12, 15, 17, 19, 26; 16:2, 2, 4, 4, 5, 7, 8, 9, 9, 15, 16, 17, 20, 24, 28; 17:2, 6, 7, 11, 15, 20, 20, 20, 21, 22, 22, 22, 24, 24, 25, 26, 26, 28, 29, 30; 18:3, 8, 12, 16, 16, 17, 24, 25, 29, 31, 34, 37, 38, 39; 19:3, 8, 9, 10, 11, 22, 29, 29, 31, 34, 37, 37, 37, 38, 39, 44, 46, 46, 47; 20:1, 4, 4, 6, 10, 10, 13, 15, 15, 17, 20, 20, 21, 21, 26, 27, 30, 32, 33, 34, 36, 36, 37, 37, 37, 38, 39, 42, 45, 46; 21:3, 4, 4, 4, 5, 9, 16, 17, 18, 21, 22, 24, 24, 24, 25, 26, 27, 30, 31, 34, 35, 36, 37; 22:1, 3, 3, 6, 7, 10, 11, 16, 18, 18, 18, 19, 21, 22, 23, 24, 25, 25, 30, 39, 44, 47, 48, 50, 50, 52, 53, 55, 58, 59, 59, 61, 66, 69, 69, 70, 71; 23:1, 3, 6, 8, 8, 17, 22, 23, 23, 26, 27, 27, 28, 35, 37, 38, 38, 39, 41, 45, 51, 51, 51, 51, 52; 24:1, 3, 7, 7, 10, 13, 14, 14, 17, 17, 18, 19, 22, 23, 24, 25, 31, 35, 35, 36, 42, 42, 44, 47, 48, 49, 49;

Jn 1:4, 7, 8, 12, 13, 13, 13, 13, 13, 14, 14, 14, 15, 15, 16, 18, 19, 22, 23, 23, 24, 29, 29, 30, 34, 35, 36, 40, 40, 42, 44, 44, 45, 45, 45, 46, 47, 49, 49, 51, 51; 2:1, 1, 3, 6, 6, 6, 8, 9, 9, 11, 11, 14, 15, 15, 16, 17, 21, 21, 21, 25; 3:1, 1, 3, 6, 6, 8, 10, 12, 13, 14, 18, 18, 22, 25, 29, 29, 31, 31, 34, 36; 4:5, 5, 7, 9, 9, 10, 13, 14, 14, 22, 30, 32, 34, 39, 39, 39, 41, 42, 42, 46, 47, 47, 52, 54; 5:1, 3, 3, 4, 6, 6, 6, 8, 9, 14, 14, 22, 25, 29, 29, 31, 31, 34, 36; 4:5, 5, 7, 9, 9, 11, 13, 14, 14, 22, 30, 32, 34, 39, 39, 39, 41, 42, 42, 46; 6:1, 1, 4, 7, 7, 8, 11, 13, 14, 18, 22, 25, 26, 27, 28, 29, 33, 35, 35, 38, 39, 40, 42, 45, 45, 45, 46, 48, 50, 52, 52, 58; 8:1, 12, 12, 13, 14, 17, 18, 19, 20, 22, 25, 29, 29, 33, 35, 38, 39, 44, 44, 44, 44, 46, 46, 47, 47, 52, 54, 59, 59; 9:3, 4, 5, 6, 6, 7, 11, 16, 16, 17, 18, 21, 22, 23, 31, 32, 33, 35, 40; 10:2, 5, 7, 14, 16, 18, 18, 20, 21, 21, 22, 25, 26, 28, 29, 32, 35, 36, 36, 37, 39, 41; 11:1, 1, 4, 4, 8, 9, 11, 13, 13, 13, 14, 19, 22, 27, 37, 39, 39, 40, 42, 45, 46, 47, 51, 52, 55; 12:2, 3, 3, 3, 4, 4, 7, 9, 11, 11, 13, 13, 15, 16, 17, 21, 21, 23, 26, 36, 37, 29, 29, 30, 31, 32, 42, 42, 43, 43, 49; 13:1, 1, 2, 18, 21, 30, 31, 34; 14:10, 21, 30; 15:4, 15, 16, 19, 19, 26, 26; 16:2, 4, 5, 8, 8, 9, 10, 11, 15, 17, 19, 21, 25, 33; 17:6, 7, 12, 12, 14, 14, 15, 16, 16, 24; 18:3, 5, 7, 9, 12, 15, 17, 18, 19, 19, 20, 22, 23, 25, 26, 26, 28, 32, 33, 34, 36, 36, 39; 19:2, 3, 5, 7, 14, 17, 19, 20, 21, 21, 25, 25, 29, 32, 34, 36, 38, 38, 38, 39, 40, 40, 42; 20:1, 2, 12, 19, 19, 24, 25, 25, 30, 31; 21:1, 2, 2, 2, 6, 6, 9, 10, 11, 12, 15, 16, 17, 24;

Ac 1:1, 3, 3, 3, 4, 4, 6, 8, 9, 11, 13, 13, 14, 15, 15, 16, 17, 18, 19, 20, 21, 22, 24, 24, 25; 2:1, 2, 3, 3, 5, 10, 10, 11, 13, 14, 15, 17, 17, 18, 19, 20, 21, 22, 22, 22, 23, 24, 24, 28, 28, 29, 30, 30, 31, 31, 33, 33, 36, 37, 38, 38, 38, 38, 42, 46; 3:1, 2, 2, 5, 6, 6, 10, 12, 13, 13, 13, 15, 16, 18, 19, 19, 21, 21, 22, 24, 25, 25; 4:1, 4, 4, 6, 8, 9, 10, 10, 16, 21, 24, 25, 26, 26, 32, 33, 33, 33,

11, 11, 13, 13, 15, 18, 19, 21, 22, 25, 26, 27, 27, 30, 31, 32, 32, 32, 32, 32, 33, 33, 34, 34, 34, 36, 36, 36; 5:2, 3, 3, 7, 9, 9, 12, 13, 14, 15, 15, 16, 17, 19, 20, 21, 21, 24, 24, 30, 31, 32, 34, 35, 36, 37, 37, 38, 39, 40, 41; 6:1, 1, 2, 2, 3, 3, 4, 5, 5, 7, 7, 7, 7, 8, 9, 9, 9, 9, 14, 15, 7:2, 3, 4, 4, 8, 10, 10, 10, 11, 16, 16, 16, 17, 22, 23, 24, 29, 30, 30, 31, 31, 32, 32, 32, 32, 33, 33, 36, 37, 37, 40, 40, 40, 41, 42, 42, 42, 43, 43, 44, 45, 45, 45, 46, 49, 52, 52, 53, 55, 55, 55, 56, 56, 58; 8:1, 3, 5, 7, 9, 10, 11, 12, 14, 16, 16, 16, 18, 20, 24, 26, 27, 27, 32, 32, 34, 34, 37, 39, 39; 9:1, 2, 2, 11, 11, 13, 15, 20, 24, 26, 27, 27, 32, 34, 34, 37, 39, 40, 41, 41, 43, 43, 44, 45, 45, 45, 46, 47, 47, 48, 49, 51; 9:2, 5, 6, 7, 8, 9, 11, 11, 11, 17, 19, 20, 22, 26, 26; 11:1, 2, 5, 6, 6, 8, 20, 22, 22, 23, 23, 24, 28, 30; 12:1, 1, 2, 2, 3, 3, 5, 6, 13, 16, 16, 17, 20, 21; 13:1, 1, 2, 3, 3, 4, 4, 10, 11, 12, 12; 14:7, 9, 10, 12, 14, 16, 17, 18, 20, 23, 23, 27, 27, 29, 29, 30, 31, 33; 16:1, 2, 2, 4, 5, 5, 14, 17, 18, 20; 11:1, 1, 1, 2, 4, 4, 5, 6, 6, 8, 8, 12, 12, 12, 12; 13:14, 14, 15, 15, 16, 17, 17, 17, 20, 20, 22, 24, 25, 25, 26, 29, 33, 33, 33, 34, 36; 12:1, 2, 2, 3, 3, 5, 6, 13, 16, 16, 17, 20, 21; 13:1, 1, 2, 3, 4, 4, 10, 11, 12, 14:7, 12, 14, 16, 17, 20, 20, 23, 24, 25, 25, 26, 26, 99

1Co 1:1, 1, 2, 2, 4, 6, 7, 8, 9, 10, 11, 11, 11, 18, 18, 19, 19, 20, 20, 21, 21, 24, 24, 25, 25, 27, 27, 28, 30; 2:1, 1, 1, 4, 4, 4, 5, 5, 6, 6, 7, 8, 8, 8, 9, 11, 11, 14, 15, 16, 16; 3:4, 4, 10, 13, 16, 16, 17, 17, 19, 20; 4:1, 1, 1, 1, 3, 5, 5, 5, 6, 8, 13, 13, 16, 17, 19, 20, 21; 5:4, 4, 5, 5, 8, 8, 10, 10; 6:1, 4, 9, 9, 10, 11, 11, 11, 12, 15, 15, 15, 19, 23, 25, 31, 33, 34, 34, 36, 40; 8:3, 4, 6, 6, 7, 9, 10; 9:2, 5, 7, 7, 7, 7, 9, 9, 10, 12, 12, 13, 14, 15, 15, 17, 18, 20; 10:4, 5, 7, 8, 9, 9, 10, 10, 11, 14, 16, 16, 16, 18, 18, 18, 21, 21, 21, 26, 29, 30, 31, 32, 33; 11:1, 1, 3, 3, 3, 7, 7, 8, 8, 14, 22, 23, 24, 25, 27, 27, 28, 28, 32; 12:3, 4, 5, 6, 7, 8, 9, 8, 9, 11, 12, 16, 21, 24, 24, 25, 26, 32, 33, 33,

15:3, 5, 5, 6, 6, 7, 7, 8, 8, 8, 9, 9, 10, 10, 12, 13, 15, 15, 19, 20, 21, 32, 34, 37, 37, 39, 39, 39, 39, 40, 40, 41, 41, 41, 42, 47, 49, 49, 50, 52, 56, 56, 58; 16:1, 2, 2, 10, 15, 15, 15, 17, 17, 19, 21, 23

2Co 1:1, 1, 1, 3, 3, 4, 4, 5, 6, 7, 7, 8, 8, 9, 11, 12, 12, 14, 16, 16, 19, 20, 20, 22, 24; 2:3, 3, 4, 4, 6, 9, 10, 11, 11, 12, 13, 14, 15, 16, 16, 17, 17, 17, 17; 3:1, 1, 2, 3, 3, 3, 5, 5, 5, 6, 6, 6, 7, 7, 7, 8, 9, 9, 10, 12, 13, 13, 14, 17, 18, 18; 4:2, 2, 2, 2, 2, 2, 4, 4, 4, 6, 6, 6, 6, 6, 7, 7, 7, 7, 8, 10, 11, 14, 14, 16, 16, 17, 5:1, 4, 5, 5, 9, 10, 11, 14, 18, 18, 19, 21; 6:1, 2, 2, 4, 7, 7, 7, 16, 16, 18; 7:1, 1, 4, 4, 6, 10, 10, 11, 12, 13, 14, 15; 8:1, 1, 1, 2, 2, 3, 4, 5, 8, 8, 8, 9, 11, 16, 17, 17, 19, 19, 21, 23, 23, 23, 24, 24; 9:2, 2, 2, 3, 4, 5, 5, 7, 10, 12, 12, 13, 13, 14; 10:1, 2, 4, 4, 5, 5, 7, 8, 8, 8, 13, 14, 15, 15, 16; 11:7, 8, 10, 10, 10, 10, 14, 15, 17, 20, 23, 23, 24, 26, 26, 28, 30, 31, 32; 12:1, 2, 3, 5, 5, 6, 6, 6, 7, 7, 9, 11, 12, 17, 17, 18, 21; 13:1, 3, 4, 4, 11, 11, 11, 14, 14, 14, 99

Gal 1:1, 2, 4, 6, 7, 10, 11, 12, 12, 13, 13, 14, 14, 19, 21, 22; 2:2, 4, 5, 6, 7, 7, 8, 9, 12, 14, 14, 15, 16, 16, 16, 16, 17, 20, 20, 21; 3:2, 2, 2, 5, 5, 7, 7, 9, 10, 10, 11, 11, 12, 13, 14, 14, 15, 16, 16, 17, 17, 18, 18, 19, 19, 20, 21, 22, 26, 27; 4:1, 2, 3, 4, 4, 5, 6, 7, 7, 9, 11, 13, 14, 15, 19, 20, 23, 23, 26, 28, 30, 30, 31, 31; 5:1, 4, 4, 5, 8, 11, 15, 16, 18, 19, 21, 21, 22, 26; 6:1, 2, 8, 8, 10, 10, 12, 14, 16, 18

Eph 1:1, 1, 3, 4, 5, 6, 6, 7, 7, 8, 10, 10, 11, 11, 11, 12, 13, 13, 14, 14, 14, 15, 16, 17, 17, 17, 18, 18, 18, 19, 19, 23; 2:2, 2, 2, 2, 3, 3, 3, 3, 7, 8, 8, 9, 12, 13, 14, 15, 15, 19, 19, 22; 3:1, 2, 2, 2, 4, 5, 6, 6, 7, 7, 8, 8, 9, 9, 10, 12, 14, 5, 16, 19, 19; 4:1, 1, 3, 3, 4, 6, 7, 7, 7, 9, 12, 12, 12, 12, 13, 13, 13, 13, 13, 14, 14, 16, 16, 16, 18, 18, 18, 23, 25, 29, 29, 30; 5:1, 4, 5, 5, 6, 6, 6, 8, 9, 11, 11, 12, 13, 14, 15, 15, 16, 16, 17, 17, 17, 19; 6:1, 2, 8, 8, 9, 11, 12, 12, 12, 13, 14, 14, 15, 15, 16, 16, 17, 18, 19, 21, 21, 22, 26; 6:1, 2, 8, 8, 11

Php 1:1, 3, 4, 6, 6, 7, 7, 8, 10, 11, 11, 12, 14, 15, 15, 16, 17, 17, 19, 19, 22, 25, 27, 27, 27, 28, 28, 28, 29; 2:1, 1, 2, 2, 3, 4, 6, 7, 7, 7, 8, 10, 10, 11, 13, 15, 15, 16, 16, 17, 19, 22, 26, 30, 30; 3:2, 2, 2, 5, 5, 5, 5, 8, 8, 8, 9, 13, 14, 15, 16, 16, 17, 17; 8:1, 3, 4, 4, 4, 5, 7, 8, 9, 10, 11, 11, 11, 12, 14, 18, 18; 4:2, 3, 7, 8, 9, 10, 11, 15, 18, 18, 22, 23

Col 1:1, 1, 3, 4, 4, 5, 5, 6, 6, 7, 7, 9, 10, 10, 12, 13, 13, 14, 15, 15, 16, 18, 20, 22, 23, 24, 24, 25, 25, 27, 27, 27; 2:2, 2, 2, 2, 2, 3, 5, 8, 8, 9, 10, 11, 11, 11, 12, 12, 13, 14, 14, 15, 16, 16, 17, 18, 18, 19, 20, 22, 23, 23, 23; 3:1, 6, 6, 8, 10, 12, 12, 12, 14, 15, 16, 17, 22, 24, 24, 25; 4:3, 3, 9, 11, 11, 12, 12, 16, 18

1Th 1:1, 2, 3, 3, 3, 3, 4, 5, 6, 6, 6, 8, 9, 9; 2:2, 3, 3, 4, 5, 6, 6, 6, 6, 8, 8, 9, 11, 12, 13, 13, 13, 13, 13, 14, 14, 14, 14, 19, 19, 19; 3:2, 2, 6, 6; 4:1, 3, 4, 5, 6, 9, 12, 15, 15, 16, 16; 5:1, 2, 5, 5, 5, 5, 8, 8, 8, 22, 23, 23, 28

2Th 1:1, 3, 3, 4, 4, 5, 5, 5, 8, 9, 9, 11, 11, 11, 12, 12; 2:1, 2, 3, 4, 7, 7, 8, 8, 9, 10, 10, 13, 13, 14; 3:1, 5, 6, 6, 8, 16, 17, 18

1Ti 1:1, 1, 5, 5, 5, 5, 7, 9, 9, 11, 14, 15, 15, 20; 2:1, 1, 3, 4, 7; 3:1, 2, 2, 3, 5, 5, 6, 7, 7, 8, 9, 10, 12, 13, 15, 15, 15, 16, 16; 4:1, 3, 4, 5, 6, 6, 6, 8, 10, 14; 5:8, 9, 10, 17, 18, 22, 25; 6:1, 1, 2, 3, 4, 5, 5, 5, 10, 10, 11, 12, 13, 14, 15, 20, 99

2Ti 1:1, 1, 3, 4, 6, 7, 7, 7, 7, 8, 8, 8, 8, 8, 10, 11, 13, 13, 15, 16, 16, 18; 2:2, 3, 4, 6, 8, 8, 9, 14, 15, 17, 18, 19, 19, 20, 20, 20, 22, 24, 25, 26, 26; 3:2, 3, 4, 4, 5, 6, 7, 8, 10, 11, 14, 14, 16, 16, 17; 4:2, 4, 5, 6, 7, 8, 10, 11, 14, 14, 15, 17, 99

Tit 1:1, 1, 1, 1, 2, 3, 6, 6, 7, 8, 8, 10, 12, 12, 14; 2:3, 5, 7, 8, 8, 10, 11, 13, 13, 14; 3:2, 4, 5, 5, 5, 7, 11, 99, 99, 99

Phm 1:1, 4, 5, 6, 6, 7, 9, 13, 14, 20, 25

Heb 1:2, 3, 3, 3, 3, 3, 4, 6, 7, 7, 8, 8, 9, 10, 14; 2:1, 2, 4, 6, 6, 7, 9, 9, 10, 11, 12, 14, 14, 14, 15, 16, 16, 17; 3:1, 1, 3, 5, 6, 8, 12, 13, 13, 14, 14, 16, 19; 4:1, 1, 3, 4, 6, 7, 9, 10, 11, 11, 12, 15, 16; 5:2, 4, 6, 7, 9, 10, 10, 11, 12, 12, 12, 13, 14; 6:1, 1, 1, 2, 2, 3, 3, 4, 4, 4, 5, 5, 5, 6, 7, 8, 10, 10, 17, 18, 19, 21, 22, 23, 24, 28; 8:1, 1, 1, 1, 2, 3, 5, 6, 8, 8, 9, 9, 10, 9:1, 3, 4, 4, 5, 6, 7, 8, 9, 9, 10, 11, 12, 13, 13, 15, 18, 21, 22, 23, 23, 24, 25, 26, 26, 27, 28; 10:1, 1, 2, 3, 4, 4, 7, 7, 10, 10, 16, 20, 29, 29, 29, 31, 33, 33, 34, 35, 36, 36, 36, 39; 11:1, 1, 3, 3, 4, 6, 7, 7, 7, 7, 9, 9, 11, 12, 13, 15, 18, 21, 22, 22, 23, 25, 26, 26, 27, 27, 28, 30, 31, 32, 33, 34, 35, 36, 36, 39, 39; 11:1, 2, 3, 12, 13, 14, 16, 17, 17, 19, 22, 23, 23, 24, 25, 26, 26, 27, 28, 29, 30, 31, 32, 32, 32, 33, 34, 34, 34, 36, 36, 38,

12:1, 2, 2, 3, 5, 5, 9, 9, 10, 11, 13, 15, 15, 15, 16, 17, 19, 19, 22, 22, 23, 23, 23, 24, 24, 24, 27, 27; 13:7, 7, 11, 15, 15, 20, 20, 20, 22, 24

Jas 1:1, 1, 3, 5, 5, 6, 7, 9, 10, 11, 11, 12, 13, 14, 17, 17, 18, 18, 18, 18, 20, 20, 21, 22, 23, 24, 25, 25; 2:1, 1, 1, 4, 5, 5, 9, 10, 11, 13, 15, 16, 23; 3:4, 6, 6, 6, 7, 7, 7, 7, 8, 9, 10, 13, 13, 17, 18; 4:1, 4, 4, 4, 10, 11, 11, 11, 11; 5:3, 4, 4, 4, 4, 4, 5, 7, 8, 10, 10, 11, 11, 11, 14, 14, 15, 16, 17, 19, 20, 20

1Pe 1:1, 2, 2, 2, 2, 3, 3, 5, 7, 7, 8, 9, 9, 19, 20, 22, 23, 23, 23, 24, 24, 25; 2:2, 4, 4, 7, 8, 8, 9, 9, 10, 12, 13, 14, 14, 15, 15, 16, 16, 25; 3:1, 3, 3, 3, 3, 4, 4, 4, 4, 7, 7, 8, 8, 12, 12, 13, 14, 15, 16, 16, 16, 17, 20, 20, 21, 21, 21, 22; 4:2, 2, 2, 3, 3, 3, 4, 4, 7, 8, 10, 10, 11, 11, 11, 11, 14, 14, 14, 14, 16, 17, 17, 17, 19, 19; 5:1, 1, 1, 2, 2, 4, 5, 6, 10, 12, 14

2Pe 1:1, 1, 2, 2, 3, 4, 8, 11, 12, 16, 16, 19, 20, 20, 21, 21; 2:2, 2, 2, 3, 3, 4, 5, 5, 6, 7, 9, 9, 10, 12, 13, 14, 15, 15, 15, 16, 17, 18, 18, 19, 19, 19, 20, 20, 21; 3:1, 2, 2, 2, 4, 4, 4, 5, 5, 5, 7, 7, 8, 10, 11, 12, 12, 14, 15, 16, 17, 18

1Jn 1:1, 1, 5, 7; 2:2, 5, 10, 14, 15, 16, 16, 16, 16, 16, 17, 18, 19, 19, 19, 21, 27, 29; 3:1, 1, 2, 4, 8, 8, 8, 9, 10, 10, 10, 12, 16, 17, 17, 19, 22, 23; 4:1, 2, 2, 3, 3, 4, 5, 5, 6, 6, 6, 6, 7, 7, 9, 13, 14, 15, 17; 5:1, 1, 2, 3, 4, 5, 9, 9, 9, 9, 10, 10, 12, 13, 13, 13, 15, 18, 19, 20

2Jn 1:3, 4, 9, 9, 11, 13

3Jn 1:3, 6, 7, 10, 11, 12, 12

Jude 1:1, 1, 3, 4, 4, 5, 6, 7, 8, 9, 10, 11, 11, 11, 12, 12, 13, 13, 14, 14, 15, 15, 16, 17, 17, 21, 21, 22, 23, 24

Rev 1:1, 2, 2, 2, 2, 2, 3, 5, 5, 5, 7, 7, 9, 9, 9, 10, 13, 14, 14, 15, 16, 18, 20, 20; 2:1, 1, 5, 5, 6, 7, 7, 7, 8, 9, 9, 10, 10, 10, 11, 12, 14, 14, 16, 17, 18, 18, 21, 22, 23, 24, 27, 27, 27; 3:1, 1, 5, 5, 7, 7, 9, 10, 10, 12, 12, 12, 12, 14, 14, 14, 16, 17, 18, 18; 4:1, 4, 5, 5, 5, 6, 6, 6, 8, 8; 5:1, 5, 5, 5, 5, 6, 6, 6, 7, 7, 8, 8, 8, 9, 9, 11, 11, 11; 6:1, 1, 1, 5, 6, 6, 6, 7, 8, 8, 9, 11, 11, 11; 7:1, 1, 2, 3, 4, 4, 4, 4, 5, 5, 5, 5, 5, 6, 6, 6, 6, 6, 7, 7, 7, 7, 7, 7, 7, 8, 17; 8:1, 3, 4, 4, 4, 5, 7, 8, 9, 10, 11, 11, 11, 12, 12; 9:1, 2, 2, 2, 3, 3, 4, 4, 5, 7, 7, 8, 8, 9, 9, 9, 9, 11, 13, 15, 16, 16, 16, 17, 17, 17, 17, 18, 20, 20, 20, 20, 21, 21, 21, 21; 10:1, 7, 7, 7, 8, 10; 11:1, 4, 5, 6, 7, 8, 9, 11, 13, 13, 13, 15, 15, 15, 18, 19, 19; 12:1, 4, 4, 5, 6, 10, 10, 10, 11, 12, 12, 14, 14, 15, 16, 16, 17, 17, 17; 13:1, 1, 1, 2, 2, 3, 8, 8, 11, 12, 13, 14, 14, 15, 17, 18, 18; 14:2, 2, 2, 5, 6, 7, 7, 8, 8, 10, 10, 10, 10, 10, 11, 11, 12, 12, 12, 14, 14, 15, 15, 17, 18, 18, 19, 19, 20, 20; 15:1, 2, 2, 2, 3, 3, 3, 3, 5, 5, 6, 7, 7, 7, 8, 8; 16:1, 1, 1, 2, 3, 4, 5, 6, 7, 9, 10, 10, 10, 11, 14, 14, 14, 17, 17; 17:1, 1, 2, 2, 3, 3, 3, 4, 4, 4, 4, 7, 7, 8, 8, 8, 11, 13, 13, 13, 15, 15, 16, 18, 19; 18:2, 2, 2, 3, 3, 3, 3, 3, 4, 4, 9, 9, 10, 10, 10, 10, 12, 13, 15, 15, 16, 16, 17, 17, 17, 18, 18, 18, 19, 19, 19, 21, 21, 21, 22, 23, 23, 23, 24, 24, 24; 19:1, 2, 5, 6, 6, 6, 7, 8, 9, 9, 10, 10, 10, 10, 12, 13, 13, 15, 15, 16, 17, 17, 18, 18, 18, 18, 18, 19, 20, 20, 21, 21, 21, 21; 17:1, 1, 2, 2, 3, 3, 3, 4, 5, 5, 6, 6, 7, 8, 8, 8, 9, 11, 11, 11; 20:1, 4, 4, 4, 5, 6, 6, 7, 8, 8, 9, 9, 10, 10, 10, 10, 12, 13, 13, 15, 15, 15; 21:2, 3, 3, 6, 6, 6, 9, 9, 10, 11, 12, 12, 12, 14, 14, 14, 16, 16, 17, 18, 18, 18, 19, 19, 19, 21, 21, 22, 22, 23, 23, 23, 24, 24, 24; 19:1, 2, 5, 6, 6, 6, 7, 26, 27; 22:1, 1, 1, 1, 1, 2, 2, 2, 2, 2, 2, 3, 3, 5, 5, 6, 9, 9, 9, 10, 10, 14, 16, 17, 18, 18, 18, 19, 19, 19, 19, 21

OUR (1165)

Ge 1:26, 26; 5:29, 29; 19:31, 32, 34; 23:6; 24:60; 29:26; 31:1, 1, 14, 15, 16, 16, 32; 33:12; 34:9, 14, 16, 17, 21, 31; 37:26, 27, 27, 27; 41:12; 42:13, 21, 32, 32; 43:4, 7, 7, 8, 18, 18, 21, 21, 21, 22, 22, 22, 28; 44:8, 25, 26, 26, 31; 46:34, 34; 47:3, 18, 18, 18, 18, 19, 19, 19, 25
Ex 1:10, 3:18; 5:3, 8, 21; 8:10, 26, 27; 10:9, 34:9; 9
Lev 25:20;
Nu 11:6, 6; 13:33; 14:3, 3; 20:3, 4, 15, 15, 16; 21:5; 27:3, 4, 4; 31:49, 50; 32:16, 16, 16, 26, 26, 32; 36:2, 3, 3, 4
Dt 1:6, 19, 20, 25, 28, 28, 41; 2:1, 8, 29, 33, 36, 37; 3:3, 3; 4:7; 5:2, 3, 24, 25, 27, 27; 6:4, 20, 22, 23, 24, 24, 25, 25; 21:7, 7, 20, 20; 26:3, 7, 7, 7, 7, 7, 15; 29:15, 18, 29, 29; 31:17; 32:3, 27, 31, 31
Jos 2:11, 13, 14, 14, 19, 20, 24, 5:13; 7:9; 9:11, 11, 11, 12, 13, 13, 13, 24; 17:4; 18:6; 21:2; 22:19, 24, 25, 27, 27, 27, 27, 28, 28, 29; 24:17, 17, 17, 18, 24
Jdg 6:13, 9:3; 10:10; 11:2, 6, 8, 24; 13:23;

16:23, 23, 23, 24, 24, 24, 24; 18:5; 19:19;
21:7, 18, 22
Ru 2:20; 3:2; 4:3
1Sa 2:2; 4:3; 5:7, 10, 11; 7:8; 8:20, 20; 9:6,
7, 8; 12:10, 19; 14:9, 10; 16:16; 17:9, 47;
20:29; 23:20; 25:14, 17; 30:23
2Sa 7:22; 10:12, 12; 12:18; 18:12; 19:9, 41,
43, 43; 22:32
1Ki 1:11, 43, 47; 8:21, 40, 53, 57, 57, 58,
58, 59, 61, 65; 12:4, 10; 20:31, 31
2Ki 7:9; 18:22; 19:19; 22:13
1Ch 12:17, 19; 13:2, 2, 3; 15:13; 16:14, 35;
17:20; 19:13, 13; 28:2, 8; 29:10, 13, 15,
15, 16, 18
2Ch 2:4, 5; 6:31; 10:4, 10; 13:10, 11, 12;
14:7, 11, 11; 19:7; 20:6, 7, 9, 12, 12;
28:13, 13, 13; 29:6, 6, 9, 9, 9, 9; 32:8, 8,
11; 34:21
Ezr 4:3; 5:12; 7:27; 8:17, 18, 21, 21, 21, 22,
23, 25, 30, 31, 33; 9:6, 6, 6, 7, 7, 7, 7, 8,
8, 8, 8, 9, 9, 9, 9, 10, 13, 13, 13, 15;
10:2, 3, 3, 14, 14, 14
Ne 4:4, 9, 9, 11, 15, 20, 23; 5:2, 2, 3, 4, 5, 5,
5, 5, 5, 5, 5, 5, 8, 8, 9, 9, 9; 6:1, 10, 16;
8:10; 9:9, 16, 32, 32, 32, 32, 32, 32, 34,
34, 34, 34, 36, 37, 37, 37, 38; 10:29, 30,
30, 32, 33, 34, 34, 34, 35, 36, 36, 36,
36, 36, 37, 37, 37, 37, 38, 39; 13:2, 4,
18, 27
Job 8:9; 17:16; 22:20; 28:22; 37:19
Ps 8:1, 9; 12:4, 4, 4; 17:11; 18:31; 20:5, 5, 7;
22:4; 33:20, 20, 20, 21; 35:21; 40:3; 44:1,
1, 5, 7, 9, 13, 18, 18, 20, 20, 24, 24, 25,
25, 26; 46:1, 7, 11; 47:3, 4, 6; 48:1, 8, 14,
14; 50:3; 59:11; 60:10, 12; 65:3, 5; 66:8,
9, 9, 11, 12; 67:6; 68:19, 20; 74:9; 77:13;
78:3, 5; 79:4, 9, 10, 12; 80:6, 6; 81:1,
3; 84:9; 85:4, 9, 12; 89:17, 18, 18; 90:1,
8, 8, 9, 9, 10, 12, 12, 14, 17, 17, 17;
92:13; 94:23; 95:1, 6, 7; 98:3; 99:5, 8, 9,
9; 103:10, 10, 12, 14; 105:7; 106:6, 7, 47;
108:11, 13; 113:5; 115:3; 116:5; 118:23;
122:2, 9; 123:2, 2, 4; 124:1, 2, 4, 5, 8;
126:2, 2, 4; 135:2, 5; 136:23, 24; 137:2;
141:7; 144:12, 12, 13, 13, 13, 14, 14;
147:1, 5, 7
Pr 1:13; 7:14
SS 1:16, 17, 17; 2:9, 12, 15; 7:13; 8:8
Isa 1:10; 3:6; 4:1, 1, 1; 20:6; 25:9; 26:8, 12,
13; 28:15; 33:2, 20, 22, 22, 22; 35:2;
36:7; 37:20; 38:20; 40:3, 8; 42:17; 47:4;
52:10; 53:1, 3, 4, 4, 5, 5, 5; 55:7; 58:3;
59:12, 12, 12, 13; 61:2, 6; 63:16, 16,
16, 17, 18; 64:6, 6, 7, 8, 8, 11, 11, 11, 11
Jer 3:22, 23, 24, 24, 25, 25, 25, 25, 25, 25;
5:19, 24; 6:24; 8:14; 9:18, 18, 19, 21, 21;
11:21; 12:4; 14:7, 7, 20, 20, 22; 16:10,
10, 10, 19; 17:12; 18:12; 20:10; 21:13;
23:6, 36; 26:16, 19; 31:6; 33:16; 35:6, 8,
8, 8, 8, 8, 10; 36:15; 37:3; 42:2, 6, 6, 20,
20; 43:2; 44:17, 17, 17, 17, 19, 19, 25; 46:16,
16; 50:28; 51:10, 10, 51
La 3:40; 4:1, 41, 44, 46; 4:17, 17, 17, 18, 18,
18, 18, 18, 19, 20; 5:1, 2, 3, 4, 4, 5, 7,
9, 9, 10, 15, 15, 16, 17, 17, 21
Eze 33:10, 10, 21; 37:11, 11, 11; 40:1
Da 1:13; 3:17; 9:6, 6, 6, 8, 8, 8, 9, 10, 12,
13, 13, 13, 14, 14, 15, 16, 16, 17, 18, 18, 18
Hos 7:5; 14:2, 3, 3
Joel 1:16; 16
Am 6:13;
Mic 2:4; 4:5, 11; 5:5, 5, 6, 6; 7:17, 19, 20
Zec 1:6, 6; 9:7
Mal 2:10;
Mt 3:9; 6:9, 11, 12, 12; 8:17, 17; 20:33;
21:42; 23:30; 25:8; 27:25
Mk 9:40; 11:10; 12:11, 29
Lk 1:55, 71, 72, 73, 74, 74, 75, 78, 79; 3:8; 7:5;
11:2, 3, 4; 13:26; 17:5, 10; 23:41; 24:20,
22, 32
Jn 3:11; 4:12, 20; 6:31; 7:51; 8:39, 53; 9:20;
11:11, 48; 12:38; 14:23; 19:7
Ac 2:8, 11, 39; 3:12, 13, 15; 5:30; 7:2, 11,
12, 15, 19, 19, 38, 39, 44, 45, 45; 13:17;
14:17; 15:10, 25, 26, 36; 16:20; 17:20,
28; 19:25, 27; 20:21; 21:5, 5, 6, 7, 15;
22:14; 24:6, 7; 26:5, 6, 7; 27:10, 19;
28:17, 25
Ro 1:3, 7; 3:5; 4:1, 12, 24, 25, 25; 5:1, 5, 11,
21; 6:6, 11, 23; 7:5, 25; 8:16, 23, 26, 39;
9:10; 10:16; 12:7; 13:11; 15:4, 6; 16:1, 9,
18, 20, 24
1Co 1:1, 2, 3, 7, 8, 9, 10; 2:7; 4:12; 5:4, 4, 7;
6:11; 9:1, 10, 10; 10:1, 6, 11; 12:23, 24;
15:3, 14, 31, 57; 16:12, 23
2Co 1:1, 2, 3, 4, 5, 7, 8, 11, 11, 12, 12, 18,
22; 3:2, 2, 5, 4; 4:3, 6, 10, 11, 14, 17; 5:1, 2,
12; 6:11, 11; 7:3, 4, 5, 12, 14; 8:9, 22, 23,
24; 9:3; 10:4, 8, 13, 14, 14, 15, 15, 16; 11:31
Gal 1:3, 4, 4; 2:4; 3:24; 6:14, 18
Eph 1:2, 3, 14, 17; 2:3, 3, 14; 3:11, 14; 5:20;
6:22, 24
Php 1:2; 3:20, 21; 4:20, 23
Col 1:1, 2, 3; 3:4
1Th 1:1, 2, 3, 3, 5; 2:1, 2, 3, 4, 8, 9, 19, 19,
20; 3:2, 2, 5, 7, 9, 9, 11, 11, 11, 13; 5:9,
23, 28
2Th 1:1, 2, 8, 10, 11, 12, 12; 2:1, 1, 14, 14,
16, 16; 3:6, 12, 14, 18
1Ti 1:1, 1, 2, 2, 12, 14; 2:3; 6:3, 14
2Ti 1:2, 8, 9, 10; 4:15
Tit 1:3, 4; 2:10, 13; 3:4, 6
Phm 1:1, 1, 2, 2, 3, 25
Heb 1:3; 3:1, 14; 4:14, 15; 7:14; 10:22, 22,
23; 12:2, 9, 10, 29; 13:15, 20, 23

Jas 2:1, 21; 3:6
1Pe 1:3; 2:24; 4:3
2Pe 1:1, 2, 8, 11, 14, 16; 3:15, 15, 18
1Jn 1:1, 1, 3, 9, 9; 2:2; 3:5, 16, 19, 20, 20,
21; 4:10, 17; 5:4
2Jn 1:12;
3Jn 1:12;
Jude 1:4, 4, 17, 21, 25
Rev 1:5; 5:10; 6:10; 7:3, 10, 12; 11:8, 15;
12:10, 10, 10; 19:1, 5; 22:21

OUT (2777)

Ge 2:9, 10, 19, 23; 3:19, 24; 4:14, 16; 8:10,
19; 9:10; 10:11, 14; 12:1, 4; 13:1; 14:8,
17; 15:4, 7, 14; 17:6; 19:5, 6, 8, 12, 14,
14, 24, 29, 30; 21:10, 17, 21; 22:11, 15;
23:4, 8; 24:11, 13, 15, 29, 44, 63; 25:25,
26; 26:8; 27:3, 30; 28:10, 16; 29:2; 30:16,
16; 31:13, 33; 32:25; 34:1, 6, 7, 24, 24,
26, 26; 35:9, 11; 37:14, 21, 22, 23, 28;
38:28, 28, 29, 30; 39:12, 15, 18; 40:14,
15, 17; 41:2, 3, 14, 18, 33, 45, 46; 43:2,
23, 31; 44:4, 8, 8, 16, 28; 45:1, 19, 24,
25; 46:26; 47:1, 10, 30; 48:12, 14, 22;
49:20; 50:24
Ex 1:5, 10, 10; 2:10, 11, 13, 19; 3:2, 4, 8, 8,
10, 11, 12, 17, 20; 4:6, 7, 9; 5:10; 6:1, 6,
6, 6, 7, 11, 13, 26, 27; 7:2, 4, 5, 15, 19;
8:6, 12, 13, 13, 16, 17, 29, 30; 9:15,
29, 33; 10:5, 6, 11, 12, 18, 21; 11:1, 4, 8,
8, 8, 10; 12:5, 15, 17, 21, 22, 33, 39, 39,
41, 42, 46, 51; 13:3, 3, 4, 4, 8, 9, 14, 16,
18; 14:8, 10, 11, 16, 21, 26, 30; 15:12,
20, 22; 16:1, 4, 6, 27, 29; 17:3, 6, 9, 9,
14; 18:1, 7, 9, 10, 10, 21, 25; 19:1, 3, 17;
20:2, 2; 21:2, 3, 3, 4, 5, 7, 11, 22; 22:6, 7,
23:13, 15, 16, 28, 29, 30, 31; 24:16;
25:32, 32, 32, 33, 35; 28:35; 29:23, 46;
32:1, 1, 4, 7, 8, 8, 11, 12, 19, 23, 24, 27,
32, 33; 33:1, 2, 7, 8, 11; 34:11, 18, 24,
34, 34; 37:7, 8, 9, 18, 18, 18, 19, 21
Lev 1:1, 15; 2:14; 4:12, 12, 18, 25, 30, 34;
5:9, 15, 18; 6:6, 12, 13; 7:14, 35; 8:26;
33; 9:9, 23, 24; 10:2, 4, 5, 7, 14; 11:45;
13:12, 20, 25, 56, 56, 56, 56; 14:3, 8, 38,
41, 43, 45, 53; 15:2, 16, 25; 16:17, 18;
17:3, 13; 18:24, 25, 28, 28; 19:36; 20:22,
23; 21:12; 22:33; 23:17, 43; 24:10, 23;
25:12, 28, 30, 31, 33, 38, 42, 51, 54, 55;
26:6, 13, 33, 45; 27:21
Nu 1:1; 3:9; 5:2, 3, 4, 23, 25; 6:19; 9:1;
10:12, 33, 34; 11:15, 20, 20, 24, 26; 12:4,
4, 12, 14, 15; 13:16, 17; 14:44; 15:41;
16:13, 14, 27, 35, 37, 46; 17:9; 18:29, 29;
20:5, 8, 10, 11, 16, 20; 21:5, 13, 23,
26, 28, 32, 32, 33; 22:5, 6, 11, 11, 23, 32,
36; 23:7, 22; 24:7, 8, 11, 17, 19; 26:4;
27:17, 17, 21; 28:26; 30:2, 6, 12; 31:5,
27, 28, 36; 32:11, 21, 23, 24; 33:1, 2, 2,
3, 12, 38, 52, 55; 34:5, 7, 8, 9, 10, 12;
35:25
Dt 1:22, 24, 27, 33, 44; 2:14, 23, 26, 32; 3:1,
8; 4:12, 15, 20, 20, 33, 34, 36, 36, 37, 37,
38, 45, 46; 5:4, 6, 15, 15, 22, 23, 24, 26;
6:12, 19, 21, 23; 7:1, 8, 8, 19, 19, 22; 8:3,
7, 9, 14, 15; 9:4, 4, 4, 12, 28, 29; 10:4, 14,
16, 17, 21, 26, 28, 28, 29, 29; 10:4; 11:2,
10, 23, 28; 12:3, 5, 27; 13:5, 5, 5, 10, 13;
15:11, 13, 14, 14, 14; 16:1, 3, 3, 6; 17:18;
18:5, 6, 12; 20:1, 1; 21:19; 22:21, 24;
23:4, 10, 23; 24:1, 2, 3, 5, 9, 11; 25:4, 6,
11, 17, 19; 26:4, 8, 13; 27:18; 28:6, 7, 19,
25, 38, 57; 29:7, 20, 21, 25, 28; 30:4;
31:2, 21; 32:13, 13, 39; 33:18, 27
Jos 1:8; 2:1, 2, 3, 5, 7, 10, 19; 3:10, 12, 12;
4:2, 2, 3, 3, 4, 8, 16, 17, 18, 19, 20; 5:4,
4, 5, 5, 6, 6; 6:1, 10, 22, 22, 23, 23, 25;
7:23, 23; 8:3, 5, 6, 14, 17, 18, 18, 19, 19,
22, 26; 9:12, 26; 10:22, 22, 23, 24; 11:4,
12, 14; 14:7, 11, 12; 15:3, 4, 4, 7, 9, 11,
11, 11, 63; 16:2, 3, 6, 7, 8, 8, 10; 17:12,
13, 18; 18:4, 12, 14, 15, 15, 19, 9, 12, 13,
17, 24, 27, 32, 34, 40, 47; 20:2, 8, 8, 8;
21:3, 4, 4, 4, 4, 5, 5, 5, 6, 6, 6, 6, 7, 7, 7,
9, 9, 16, 17, 20, 25, 27, 28, 30, 32,
34, 36, 38; 22:9, 31, 32; 23:5, 9, 13; 24:5,
6, 10, 12, 17, 18, 32
Jdg 1:16, 19, 19, 21, 24, 27, 28, 29, 30, 31,
32, 33; 2:1, 3, 12, 15, 16, 18, 21, 23;
3:10, 19, 20, 22, 22, 24; 4:6, 14, 18, 22;
5:4, 4, 14, 14, 14, 28; 6:8, 9, 9, 9, 19, 20,
21, 21, 30, 38; 7:23; 23, 23; 8:34; 9:4, 15,
17, 20, 20, 27, 29, 33, 35, 38, 39, 41, 42,
43; 10:12; 11:2, 3, 5, 7, 13, 24, 34, 36;
12:2; 13:5; 14:9, 12, 14, 14, 18; 15:17;
16:14, 20, 20, 21, 25; 17:7, 8; 18:2, 11,
11, 14, 17; 19:1, 16, 23, 24; 20:1, 1, 33,
33, 34, 38, 40, 42; 21:16, 17, 21, 21, 24
Ru 1:7, 13, 13, 21, 22; 2:6, 17, 22; 4:3
1Sa 3:3, 15, 16; 2:3, 5, 8, 10, 28; 3:3; 4:1, 3,
14; 8:8, 18, 20; 9:11, 14, 14, 16, 16, 26;
10:18, 18, 19, 19; 11:2, 3, 5, 7, 10; 12:6,
8, 10, 11; 13:10, 17, 23; 14:11, 48; 15:6;
16:16; 17:4, 4, 8, 23; 18:6, 16, 30, 35, 37,
37, 40, 46; 18:5, 6, 11, 13, 16; 19:3, 8,
10; 20:11, 11, 21, 35, 36, 41; 21:5; 23:13,
15, 23; 24:2, 7, 8, 14, 15, 21; 25:5, 5, 14,
29, 29, 37; 26:4, 19, 20, 24; 27:1; 28:1, 3,
9, 13, 17, 19; 29:6; 30:16, 16
2Sa 1:2, 3; 2:12, 13, 23; 3:18, 18, 25, 26;
4:4, 9; 5:2, 13, 24; 6:3, 4, 20; 7:6, 9, 12;

8:1; 9:5; 10:3, 8, 16; 11:8, 13, 17, 23;
12:7, 11; 13:9, 9, 9, 17, 18; 14:16, 16;
15:11, 24, 35; 16:5, 7, 7; 17:1, 21; 18:3,
4, 6; 19:9, 9, 9, 19; 20:7, 7, 8, 10, 12, 13,
16, 22; 21:10, 17; 22:1, 1, 7, 9, 9, 15, 17,
46; 23:4, 16, 16, 21, 29; 24:4, 7, 16, 20
1Ki 1:29; 2:27, 37, 42, 46; 3:7; 4:23, 33;
5:6, 13; 6:1, 8; 7:13, 47; 8:1, 8, 8, 9, 10,
16, 16, 19, 21, 41, 42, 44, 51, 53; 9:7, 7,
9, 12, 24; 10:28, 29, 29; 11:12, 18, 18,
29, 31, 32, 34, 35; 12:25, 28; 13:1, 3, 5;
14:15, 21, 24; 15:12, 17; 16:2, 7; 17:19, 23;
18:28, 44; 19:13; 20:16, 17, 17, 17, 18,
18, 19, 21, 24, 31, 39, 42; 21:10, 13, 26;
22:3, 32, 34, 35, 46
2Ki 2:23, 24; 3:6; 4:4, 5, 18, 21, 37, 39, 40,
40, 41; 5:2, 2, 11, 27; 6:7, 27, 27; 7:12,
12, 16, 20; 8:3; 9:2, 15, 19, 21, 21, 24,
30, 32; 10:3, 9, 25, 26, 28; 11:8, 9; 12:11,
12; 13:5, 25; 14:27; 16:3, 7, 7, 17:7,
8, 18, 20, 23, 23, 36, 36, 39; 18:18, 29,
31, 33, 34, 35, 35; 19:9, 19, 27, 31, 31,
35; 20:4, 6; 21:2, 7, 8, 15; 23:4, 6, 8, 16,
18, 27; 24:3, 7, 12, 13, 20; 25:7, 19,
21, 27
1Ch 5:18; 6:60, 61, 61, 62, 62, 62, 62, 63,
63, 63, 65, 65, 65, 66, 70, 71, 72, 74, 76,
77, 78, 80; 7:11; 9:28; 11:2, 18, 18, 23;
12:2, 17; 13:7; 14:8, 15, 17; 15:25, 29;
16:33; 17:21, 21; 18:1; 19:3, 6, 6, 6, 9,
10; 20:1, 2, 3; 21:16, 21; 26:14, 27; 27:1;
28:18
2Ch 1:10, 16, 17, 17; 2:2, 8, 14, 16; 4:18;
5:2, 9, 10, 11; 6:5, 9, 32, 34; 7:20, 20, 22;
8:11; 9:28, 28; 10:2; 11:13, 16; 12:3, 7,
13; 13:9; 14:5, 8, 8, 9, 10; 15:2, 5, 8, 8, 9,
9, 9, 17; 16:1, 2, 2, 7; 17:6; 18:20, 21, 21,
31, 33; 19:2, 3, 4; 20:4, 7, 10, 11, 17, 21;
21:15, 19; 22:7; 23:2, 7, 8, 11, 14; 24:5,
6, 6; 25:6, 10, 15; 26:11, 18, 20; 28:3,
9, 21, 21; 29:5, 7, 16, 16; 30:6, 25, 25;
31:1, 1; 32:11, 13, 14, 14, 15, 15, 15, 17,
17; 33:2, 8, 15, 15; 34:14, 21, 25, 33;
35:20, 24
Ezr 1:7; 2:1; 3:8; 5:14, 14; 6:4, 5, 21; 7:20,
28; 8:35; 9:5; 10:1
Ne 2:13; 3:25, 26, 27; 4:2, 5; 5:13, 13;
6:8; 7:6; 8:17; 9:7, 15, 18, 27; 12:27, 28,
29, 44; 13:8, 14
Est 2:9, 13, 23; 3:15; 4:1, 11; 5:2; 7:8, 8; 8:4,
14, 15; 9:4
Job 1:17, 21; 3:11, 24; 5:5, 6; 6:17; 8:10, 19;
9:6, 8, 10, 14; 10:7, 10, 18; 11:7, 7, 13;
12:15, 22, 22; 13:9; 14:4, 12, 18, 19;
15:13, 22, 25, 30; 16:13, 20; 18:4, 5, 6,
14, 18; 19:7; 20:15, 25, 25; 21:17; 22:16;
24:4, 12, 12, 24; 26:7; 27:21, 22, 23;
28:2, 2, 3, 4, 5, 10, 27; 29:6, 7, 16, 17,
19, 25; 30:16, 24; 31:7, 8, 12, 34; 32:11,
13; 33:6, 21; 35:9; 36:16, 26; 37:1, 2, 9,
9, 18, 22, 23; 38:1, 8, 13, 29; 39:3, 5;
40:6; 41:1, 19, 19, 20, 20, 21
Ps 3:4; 5:10; 8:2; 9:5; 10:5, 15, 16; 14:7;
15:5; 17:1; 18:6, 8, 14, 14, 16, 42, 45;
19:4, 5; 20:2; 21:8, 8; 22:7, 9, 14, 14;
25:15, 17, 22; 27:12; 31:4, 12; 34:6, 17,
19; 35:3; 37:14; 40:2, 2; 42:4; 43:3; 44:2,
2, 20, 21; 45:8; 50:2, 9, 9; 51:1, 9; 52:5,
5; 53:6; 54:7; 55:23; 58:6; 59:7; 60:6, 8,
10; 62:8; 64:6; 66:12; 68:6, 31, 31, 33,
35; 69:14, 14, 28; 71:4, 4, 6; 73:7, 10;
74:11; 75:8, 8; 77:17, 17; 78:15, 16, 20,
55, 65; 79:6; 80:8, 8, 11, 13; 81:5, 10, 16;
82:4, 5; 84:2; 85:5, 11; 88:9; 89:19, 34;
94:12; 97:10; 102:T; 104:2, 14, 35;
105:41; 107:3, 6, 13, 14, 19, 28; 108:7, 9;
109:10, 13, 14; 110:2; 111:2; 113:7, 7;
114:1; 118:26; 119:18, 43; 121:8; 124:7;
128:5; 130:1; 132:5; 134:3; 135:7, 21;
136:6, 11, 12; 142:2, 7; 143:11; 144:6, 7,
14; 147:18
Pr 1:23, 24; 2:6, 22; 3:10; 4:23; 5:15, 15;
6:9; 8:12; 9:1; 10:31; 11:8; 12:13; 13:9;
15:2, 28; 17:14, 23; 20:5, 20; 21:16;
22:10, 10; 24:20; 25:1, 2, 19; 26:20;
27:8; 30:17; 31:18, 20
Ecc 1:13; 3:11; 4:14; 7:24, 25, 27, 29; 8:3,
17, 17; 9:3, 9, 10
SS 3:6; 4:16; 8:11
Isa 2:3; 5:2, 25; 8:8; 9:12, 17, 21; 10:4; 11:1,
1, 16; 12:3, 6; 13:9, 13; 14:19, 26, 27, 29;
15:4, 5; 16:2, 4, 8, 10; 18:2, 7; 19:23;
21:11; 22:16, 16; 23:11; 24:18; 26:16, 17,
19, 21; 28:7, 7, 27; 29:4, 4, 4, 4, 19; 30:7,
7; 34:13, 25; 44:13, 13, 13, 22; 45:12, 23;
46:6, 7; 48:1, 3, 21, 21; 51:17, 22; 52:11,
11, 12; 53:2, 8, 12; 55:11, 12; 57:4, 14;
58:7, 10; 59:5, 21, 21, 21; 62:10, 12;
63:11; 65:2, 9, 9; 66:5, 11, 20
Jer 1:5, 10, 14; 2:6, 13; 3:18; 4:1, 16; 5:6, 6;
6:1, 1, 4, 7, 7, 11, 12; 7:15, 15, 18, 20,
22, 25; 8:1, 1; 9:8, 18, 19, 19; 10:3, 12,
13, 17, 18, 22, 25; 11:4, 7; 12:3, 8, 14,
14, 16; 14:16, 15:1, 6, 21, 21; 16:9, 13,
14, 16; 17:8, 16, 19, 22; 18:21, 23; 19:13;
20:3, 8, 18; 21:9, 12, 12; 22:3, 11, 14, 26,
28; 23:3, 7, 8, 16, 39; 24:5; 26:23; 27:10,
15; 30:7, 19; 31:32, 37; 32:4, 17, 21, 21,
37; 34:3, 13, 13, 36:6, 11, 21, 30;
37:4, 5, 21; 38:6, 10, 13, 18, 23,
23; 39:4, 4, 7, 14; 40:2; 44:7, 17, 17, 18,
19, 19, 25, 28; 46:20; 47:2; 48:15, 31, 44,

45; 49:5, 20; 50:3, 8, 8, 28, 45; 51:6, 15,
16, 25, 34, 44, 45, 55; 52:3, 7, 11, 25,
27, 31
La 1:10; 2:4, 8, 12, 19, 19; 3:7, 8, 38, 55;
4:1, 3, 11; 5:8
Eze 1:4, 4, 4, 5, 13; 3:25; 4:12; 5:2, 12; 6:14;
7:8; 9:8; 10:7, 19; 11:7, 9, 17, 19; 12:5,
12, 14; 13:2, 17, 21, 23; 14:9, 13, 19;
15:7; 16:5, 15, 27, 36; 19:14; 20:8, 9, 10,
13, 14, 21, 28, 33, 33, 34, 34, 34, 38,
38, 41, 41; 21:3, 4, 5, 19, 31; 22:15, 22,
31; 23:26, 34, 48; 24:6, 6, 12; 25:7, 7, 13,
16; 27:6, 33; 28:16; 29:4, 8; 30:13, 22,
25; 31:4, 11; 32:3, 7, 21; 33:21; 34:11,
12, 12, 12, 13, 25, 27; 35:3, 7, 11; 36:5,
20, 24, 26; 37:1, 12, 13, 23; 38:8, 8, 12,
15; 39:3, 3, 10, 10, 14, 27, 29; 42:11, 19;
43:6, 11, 23, 25; 44:3; 45:14, 15, 15, 15;
46:9, 18, 18, 20; 47:1, 2, 2, 8, 12;
48:19, 30
Da 2:34, 45; 3:15, 17; 5:2, 3, 13; 6:23, 23;
7:17, 24, 25; 8:4, 7, 9, 22; 9:15; 11:7, 41,
44, 44
Hos 1:11; 2:2, 10, 15, 17, 18; 4:2; 5:10; 7:5;
9:15; 10:11; 11:1, 11, 11; 12:8, 13; 13:3, 3
Joel 2:16, 28, 29; 3:7, 16
Am 3:4, 12, 12; 4:3, 11; 5:3, 6, 8; 6:4, 4, 10,
10; 7:11; 8:8; 9:3, 6, 7, 15
Ob 1:6, 8, 8
Jnh 1:4; 2:1, 2, 4, 10; 4:5
Mic 1:3; 2:9, 13; 4:6, 9, 10; 5:2, 10, 12, 13,
14; 6:4, 4; 7:2, 15, 17
Na 1:6, 11, 14; 2:2, 9
Hab 1:2; 2:11, 11; 3:4, 13, 14
Zep 1:4, 17; 2:4, 13; 3:11, 15, 19
Hag 2:5, 16, 16
Zec 1:21; 2:3, 13; 3:2; 4:1, 12; 5:9; 6:1, 12;
8:10, 23; 9:4, 7, 11; 10:4, 4, 4, 4, 10, 10;
11:6; 13:2, 2; 14:8
Mal 2:8, 12, 13; 3:10
Mt 2:6, 15; 3:5, 16; 4:4; 5:13, 26, 29; 7:4, 4,
5, 5, 5, 5, 22; 8:12, 16, 28, 29, 31, 32, 34,
34; 9:17, 32, 33, 34; 10:1, 8, 14; 11:7, 8,
9; 12:11, 14, 24, 26, 27, 28, 34, 35,
35, 43, 44; 13:1, 41, 52; 14:13, 26, 29,
35; 15:11, 17, 18, 19, 22; 17:5, 18, 19,
21; 18:9, 28; 20:1, 3, 5, 6, 30; 21:12, 16,
17, 33, 39, 41; 22:10; 23:24; 24:1, 17,
27, 25; 26:8, 30; 51, 55, 71, 75; 27:23,
32, 53, 60
Mk 1:5, 10, 23, 25, 26, 29, 34, 35, 39, 45;
3:5, 15, 21, 22, 23, 23; 4:3; 5:2, 2, 8, 10,
13, 14, 17, 30, 40; 6:1, 12, 13, 34, 34, 49,
54; 7:15, 19, 20, 21, 26, 29, 30; 8:23, 27;
9:7, 18, 24, 25, 26, 28, 38, 47; 10:26, 46,
47; 11:11, 15, 19; 12:1, 8; 13:1, 15;
14:26, 48, 68; 15:13, 14, 20, 21, 39, 46;
16:8, 9, 17
Lk 1:22, 42, 74; 2:1, 4; 4:14, 22, 29, 33, 35,
35, 36, 37, 38, 41, 41; 5:2, 3, 3, 4, 17, 36;
6:12, 17, 19, 22, 42, 42, 42, 45, 45;
7:12, 24, 25, 26; 8:2, 4, 5, 12, 27, 28, 29,
31, 33, 35, 35, 38, 46, 54; 9:5, 35, 38, 39,
40, 49; 10:10, 35; 11:14, 14, 15, 18, 19,
19, 20, 24, 24, 54; 12:54; 13:28, 31, 32,
33; 14:5, 7, 21, 23, 35; 15:28; 16:4;
17:24, 29; 19:22, 40, 45; 20:12, 15;
21:21, 37; 22:39, 52, 62; 23:18, 26;
24:31, 50
Jn 1:46; 2:8, 15, 15; 4:30, 47, 54; 6:37; 7:38,
41, 42, 52; 8:9, 59; 9:22, 34, 35; 10:3, 9,
28, 29, 39; 11:11, 31, 55; 12:17, 31, 34,
42; 13:1, 30, 31; 15:19; 16:2, 27; 17:6, 8,
15; 18:16, 29, 38; 19:6, 12, 15, 34; 20:2
Ac 1:9, 18, 21; 2:5, 17, 18; 3:19; 4:15; 5:6,
9, 16; 6:3, 4, 10, 12, 19, 21, 36, 40, 40,
45, 57, 58; 8:7, 9, 39; 9:1, 28; 10:45;
12:9, 10, 11, 17; 13:17, 42, 50; 14:14, 19;
15:14, 24; 16:13, 18, 18, 27, 27, 30, 37,
37, 39, 40, 40; 17:2, 5; 19:12, 16, 28, 33,
34; 21:5, 28, 30, 38; 24:7; 25:17, 26;
24:7; 27:19, 29, 30, 30, 38, 42; 28:3, 21,
23, 23
Ro 2:18; 3:12; 11:24, 26, 33; 13:11
1Co 5:7, 10; 9:9; 14:36; 15:8
2Co 1:8, 16; 2:4; 4:6; 6:17; 8:11; 12:2, 3
Gal 2:4; 4:15, 30
Eph 4:29;
Php 1:12; 2:12
Col 2:14, 14; 3:8
1Th 1:8;
2Th 2:7;
1Ti 1:5; 5:18; 6:7
2Ti 1:17; 2:22, 26; 3:11; 4:2, 17
Heb 3:16; 5:2; 7:5, 14; 8:9; 11:8, 8, 15, 34;
12:13
Jas 2:25; 3:10, 13
1Pe 2:9;
2Pe 2:9; 3:5
1Jn 2:19, 19; 4:1, 18
3Jn 1:10;
Jude 1:5, 13, 23
Rev 1:16; 2:5; 3:5, 5, 12, 12, 16; 4:5; 5:7, 9;
6:4, 14; 7:14; 8:4; 9:2, 3, 17, 18; 10:10;
11:2, 5, 7; 12:9, 9, 9, 15, 16; 13:1, 11;
14:10, 15, 17, 18, 20; 15:6; 16:1, 1, 2, 3,
4, 7, 8, 10, 12, 13, 13, 13, 17, 17, 21;
17:8; 18:4; 19:5, 15, 21; 20:7, 8, 9, 12;
21:2, 3, 10; 22:1, 19, 19

SHALL (9838)

Ge 1:29; 2:23, 24, 24, 24; 3:1, 3, 3, 4, 5, 5,
15, 16, 16, 18; 4:7, 12, 14, 14, 14, 15,

24; 5:29; 6:3, 3, 15, 17, 19, 20, 21; 8:22; 9:2, 3, 4, 6, 11, 11, 13, 14, 14, 15, 16, 25, 26, 27, 27, 27; 12:3, 12, 12, 12, 13; 13:16; 15:4, 4, 4, 5, 8, 8, 13, 13, 13, 14, 14, 16; 16:10, 12; 17:5, 5, 6, 10, 10, 11, 11, 12, 13, 14, 15, 16, 16, 17, 17, 19, 20, 21; 18:5, 10, 12, 13, 14, 17, 18, 18, 19, 25, 28, 29, 30, 31, 32; 19:2, 20; 20:7, 13; 21:10, 12; 22:14, 17, 18; 23:6, 9; 24:7, 14, 14, 14, 43, 55; 25:23, 23, 23, 32; 26:2, 4, 11, 22; 27:12, 12, 33, 37, 39, 40, 46; 28:14, 14, 21, 22; 29:15; 30:3, 15, 24, 30, 31, 32, 33, 33, 33; 31:8, 8; 32:4, 8, 19, 28; 34:10, 10, 11, 11, 12, 23, 30, 30; 35:10, 10, 11, 11; 37:10, 20, 30; 38:18; 40:13, 14, 19, 19, 19; 41:16, 27, 30, 30, 30, 31, 31, 36, 36, 40, 44; 42:15, 15, 16, 20, 20, 33, 34, 34, 38, 38; 43:3, 5, 16; 44:10, 10, 16, 16, 16, 17, 23, 29, 31, 31, 32, 34, 34; 45:6, 13, 13, 18; 46:4, 33, 33, 33, 34; 47:19, 23, 24, 24, 24; 48:5, 6, 6, 19, 19, 19, 19, 20, 20, 21; 49:1, 8, 8, 8, 9, 10, 10, 12, 13, 13, 13, 16, 17, 17, 19, 19, 20, 20, 25, 25, 26, 27, 27, 27; 50:17, 25

Ex 1:16, 16, 22, 22; 2:7; 3:12, 12, 13, 13, 13, 18, 18, 21, 21, 22, 22; 4:8, 9, 9, 15, 16, 16, 21; 5:7, 8, 8, 11, 18, 18, 19; 6:1, 1, 7, 12, 30; 7:1, 2, 4, 5, 9, 9, 17, 18, 18, 18; 8:3, 3, 4, 9, 11, 11, 21, 22, 23, 26, 26, 27, 28; 9:3, 4, 4, 5, 9, 9, 19, 19, 19, 28, 29, 29; 10:5, 5, 5, 6, 7, 8, 14, 26, 26; 11:1, 1, 5, 6, 7, 8, 8, 9; 12:2, 2, 3, 4, 5, 5, 6, 6, 7, 7, 8, 8, 10, 10, 11, 11, 13, 13, 14, 14, 14, 15, 15, 15, 15, 16, 16, 16, 17, 17, 18, 19, 19, 20, 20, 22, 22, 24, 25, 25, 26, 26, 27, 43, 44, 45, 45, 46, 46, 47, 48, 48, 48, 49; 13:3, 5, 6, 7, 7, 7, 9, 11, 11, 12, 14, 16, 19; 14:2, 4, 13, 14, 14, 14, 16, 17, 18; 15:9, 9, 14, 14, 15, 15, 15, 16, 16, 18, 24; 16:4, 5, 5, 6, 7, 8, 8, 12, 12, 22, 25, 26, 26; 17:4, 6; 18:19, 22, 22, 22, 22, 23; 19:5, 6, 12, 13, 13, 13, 13; 20:23, 23; 21:2, 2, 3, 3, 4, 4, 5, 6, 6, 6, 6, 7, 8, 8, 9, 10, 11, 12, 13, 15, 16, 17, 19, 19, 19, 20, 21, 22, 22, 23, 27, 28, 28, 29, 29, 30, 31, 32, 32, 32, 33, 33, 34, 34, 35, 35, 36, 36; 22:1, 1, 2, 3, 3, 4, 5, 5, 6, 7, 8, 9, 9, 9, 11, 11, 11, 12, 13, 14, 15, 16, 17, 19, 20, 22, 24, 24, 27, 27, 30, 31, 31, 31; 23:11, 15, 17, 18, 23, 25, 25, 26, 28, 33; 24:2, 2, 2; 25:2, 3, 9, 10, 10, 12, 15, 16, 17, 19, 20, 20, 20, 21, 23, 27, 31, 31, 32, 34, 35, 36, 36, 37, 39; 26:2, 2, 3, 6, 8, 8, 12, 13, 16, 16, 17, 20, 24, 24, 24, 24, 25, 28, 31, 32, 33, 37; 27:1, 1, 2, 7, 7, 8, 9, 10, 10, 11, 12, 13, 14, 14, 15, 16, 16, 17, 17, 18, 19, 21, 21; 28:4, 4, 5, 6, 7, 7, 8, 12, 16, 16, 16, 17, 17, 18, 20, 21, 21, 22, 24, 25, 26, 26; 29:9, 10, 15, 19, 21, 26, 28, 28, 29, 30; 30:2, 2, 2, 4, 7, 7, 8, 9, 9, 10, 10, 12, 13, 13, 14, 15, 15, 19, 20, 20, 20, 21, 21, 32; 31:11, 13, 14, 14, 14, 15, 16; 32:1, 13, 23, 30, 34; 33:14, 16, 16, 20, 22, 23; 34:3, 10, 13, 20, 23, 24, 25; 35:2, 2, 3, 3, 10; 40:9, 10, 15

Lev 1:2, 3, 4, 4, 5, 5, 6, 7, 8, 9, 9, 10, 11, 11, 13, 13, 13, 14, 15, 15, 16, 17, 17, 17; 2:1, 1, 2, 2, 2, 3, 4, 5, 7, 8, 9, 9, 10, 11, 11, 11, 11, 12, 12, 16; 3:1, 2, 2, 3, 6, 7, 8, 8, 9, 9, 10, 11, 11, 11, 12, 13, 13, 14, 15, 16, 17, 17; 4:2, 2, 4, 4, 5, 6, 7, 7, 8, 9, 10, 12, 12, 14, 15, 15, 16, 17, 18, 18, 19, 20, 20, 20, 21, 23, 24, 25, 25, 26, 26, 28, 29, 30, 30, 31, 31, 31, 32, 33, 34, 34, 35, 35, 35; 5:1, 2, 3, 4, 4, 5, 5, 6, 6, 7, 8, 8, 9, 9, 10, 10, 11, 11, 11, 12, 12, 13, 13, 13, 16, 16, 16, 17, 18, 18; 6:4, 4, 5, 5, 6, 7, 7, 9, 10, 10, 11, 12, 12, 12, 13, 13, 14, 15, 15, 16, 16, 16, 17, 18, 18, 18, 20, 21, 22, 22, 23, 23, 25, 25, 26, 26, 27, 27, 28, 28, 29, 30, 30; 7:2, 2, 3, 4, 5, 6, 6, 7, 8, 9, 9, 10, 12, 13, 13, 14, 15, 15, 16, 17, 18, 18, 19, 19, 20, 20, 21, 21, 23, 24, 25, 26, 27, 27, 29, 30, 30, 31, 31, 32, 33, 34, 34, 35; 9:6; 10:7, 9, 13, 14, 15, 15; 11:2, 3, 4, 8, 8, 9, 9, 10, 11, 11, 11, 12, 13, 13, 20, 23, 24, 24, 25, 26, 27, 28, 29, 31, 32, 32, 33, 33, 34, 34, 35, 35, 36, 37, 38, 39, 40, 40, 41, 42, 43, 43, 44, 44, 44, 45; 12:2, 2, 3, 4, 4, 4, 5, 5, 6, 7, 7, 8, 8; 13:2, 2, 3, 3, 3, 4, 4, 5, 5, 6, 6, 7, 8, 8, 10, 11, 11, 13, 13, 14, 15, 16, 17, 20, 21, 22, 23, 25, 26, 26, 27, 28, 28, 30, 31, 32, 33, 34, 34, 34, 35, 35, 35; 5:1, 2, 3, 4, 4, 5, 5, 6, 6, 7, 8, 8, 9, 9, 9, 10, 10, 11, 11, 12, 13, 13, 14, 15, 15, 16, 16, 16, 17, 18, 18; 6:4, 4, 5, 5, 6, 7, 7, 9, 10, 10, 11, 11, 12, 12, 13, 13, 13, 14, 15, 15, 15, 16, 16, 16, 17, 18, 18, 18, 20, 21, 22, 22, 22, 23, 25, 25, 26, 27, 27, 27; 7:2, 2, 3, 4, 5, 6, 6, 7, 8, 9, 9, 10, 11, 11, 12, 13, 14, 15, 15, 16, 16, 17, 17, 18, 18, 19, 19, 20, 21, 21, 23, 24, 24, 25, 26, 27, 27, 28, 28, 29, 30, 30; 9:6; 10:7, 9, 13, 14, 15, 15; 11:2, 3, 4, 8, 8, 9, 9, 10, 11, 11, 11, 12, 13, 13, 20, 23, 24, 24, 25, 26, 27, 28, 29, 31, 32, 32, 33, 33, 34, 34, 35, 35, 36, 37, 38, 39, 40, 40, 41, 42, 43, 43, 44, 44, 44; 12:2, 2, 3, 4, 4, 4, 5, 5, 6, 7, 7, 8, 8; 13:2, 2, 3, 3, 3, 4, 4, 5, 5, 6, 6, 7, 8, 8, 10, 11, 11, 13, 13, 14, 15, 16, 16, 17, 20, 21, 22, 23, 25, 26, 26, 27, 28, 28, 29, 30, 30, 31, 31, 32, 33, 33,

34; 17:4, 4, 6, 7, 7, 9, 12, 12, 13, 14, 14, 15, 15, 16; 18:3, 3, 4, 4, 5, 5, 6, 23, 26, 26, 29, 29, 30; 19:2, 3, 5, 6, 6, 7, 8, 8, 11, 12, 13, 15, 15, 19, 20, 20, 21, 22, 22, 23, 23, 23, 23, 24, 26, 26, 27, 28, 30, 33, 34, 35, 36, 37; 20:2, 2, 8, 9, 9, 10, 10, 11, 11, 12, 12, 13, 13, 14, 15, 15, 16, 16, 17, 17, 18, 18, 19, 20, 20, 20, 21, 24, 25, 25, 25, 26, 27, 27; 21:1, 4, 5, 5, 6, 6, 6, 7, 7, 8, 9, 10, 11, 13, 14, 14, 15, 18, 21, 21, 22, 22; 22:3, 4, 6, 6, 7, 7, 8, 9, 10, 10, 10, 11, 11, 13, 13, 14, 14, 15, 19, 20, 20, 21, 21, 22, 23, 24, 24, 25, 25, 27, 27, 27; 21:1, 4, 5, 5, 6, 6, 7, 7, 8, 9, 10, 11, 13, 14, 14, 15, 18, 21, 21, 22, 22; 23:2, 3, 3, 4, 7, 7, 8, 8, 10, 10, 11, 11, 12, 13, 14, 14, 15, 15, 16, 16, 17, 17, 18, 18, 19, 20, 20, 21, 21, 21, 24, 25, 25, 27, 27, 27, 28, 29, 29, 31, 31, 32, 32, 32, 34, 35, 35, 36, 36, 36, 37, 39, 39, 39, 40, 40, 41, 41, 42, 42; 24:3, 3, 4, 5, 8, 9, 9, 15, 16, 16, 17, 18, 19, 20, 21, 21, 21, 23; 25:2, 4, 6, 7, 8, 9, 10, 10, 10, 10, 11, 11, 12, 12, 13, 14, 15, 17, 18, 18, 19, 19, 20, 20, 21, 21, 21, 22, 23, 24, 25, 28, 28, 28, 30, 30, 31, 31, 33, 40, 40, 41, 41, 42, 44, 44, 45, 45, 46, 46, 50, 50, 51, 52, 52, 53, 54; 26:1, 1, 2, 4, 4, 5, 5, 6, 6, 6, 6, 7, 7, 8, 8, 8, 10, 11, 12, 15, 16, 16, 16, 17, 17, 17, 20, 20, 20, 22, 22, 22, 25, 28, 29, 29, 30, 31, 31, 33, 40, 40, 41, 41, 41, 42, 44, 44, 45, 45, 46, 46, 50, 50, 51, 52, 52, 53, 54; 26:1, 1, 2, 4, 4, 5, 5, 6, 6, 6, 6, 7, 7, 8, 8, 8, 10, 11, 12, 15, 16, 16, 16, 17, 17, 17, 20, 20, 20, 22, 22, 22, 23, 23, 24, 25, 28, 28, 28, 30, 31, 33, 40, 41, 41, 42, 44, 44, 45, 45, 46, 46, 50, 50, 51, 52, 52, 53, 54; 27:2, 2, 3, 3, 4, 5, 5, 6, 6, 7, 8, 9, 9, 10, 10, 10, 11, 12, 12, 13, 13, 13; 20:23, 23; 21:21, 22, 22, 23, 23, 24, 25, 26, 28, 28, 30, 31, 31, 33, 33, 34, 43; 27:2, 3, 4, 4, 5, 8, 9, 9, 15, 16, 16, 18, 19, 20, 21, 21, 23, 23, 26, 27, 29, 31, 32, 32, 33, 33, 33

Nu 1:3, 4, 5, 50, 50, 50, 51, 51, 51, 52, 53, 53; 2:2, 2, 3, 3, 5, 5, 7, 9, 10, 10, 12, 12, 14, 16, 17, 17, 18, 18, 20, 20, 22, 24, 25, 27, 27, 29, 31; 3:7, 8, 10, 10, 12, 13, 23, 24, 25, 29, 30, 31, 32, 35, 36, 38, 38, 45; 4:4, 5, 5, 6, 6, 6, 7, 7, 8, 8, 9, 10, 11, 11, 12, 12, 13, 14, 14, 15, 15, 19, 20, 25, 26, 27, 27, 28, 32; 5:3, 3, 6, 6, 7, 7, 8, 9, 10, 10, 15, 15, 15, 16, 17, 17, 18, 18, 19, 21, 21, 22, 23, 23, 24, 24, 25, 25, 26, 27, 27, 27, 28, 28, 30, 30, 31; 6:2, 3, 3, 3, 4, 4, 5, 5, 5, 6, 7, 7, 9, 9, 11, 11, 12, 12, 13, 14, 14, 16, 16, 17, 17, 18, 18, 19, 19, 20, 21, 21, 21, 23, 27; 7:11; 8:2, 10, 11, 12, 14, 15, 24, 25, 26, 26; 9:3, 3, 10, 10, 11, 11, 12, 13, 13, 14, 14, 14; 10:3, 3, 4, 5, 6, 6, 7, 7, 8, 8, 9, 9, 10, 32, 32, 32; 11:4, 17, 18, 18, 18, 19, 22, 22, 23; 12:8; 13:2; 14:13, 21, 23, 23, 24, 27, 29, 30, 31, 32, 33, 34, 34, 35, 35, 41, 43; 15:4, 9, 11, 12, 12, 13, 14, 15, 15, 16, 16, 19, 20, 20, 21, 24, 24, 25, 25, 26, 27, 28, 28, 30, 31, 35, 35, 38, 39, 39, 40, 40, 41; 16:7, 22, 28, 30, 38; 17:3, 5, 5, 13; 18:1, 1, 2, 3, 3, 4, 4, 5, 7, 7, 9, 9, 9, 9, 10, 10, 11, 12, 13, 13, 13, 14, 15, 15, 18, 23, 23, 24, 26, 27, 28, 28, 29, 30, 31, 32; 19:3, 4, 4, 5, 5, 6, 7, 7, 7, 7, 8, 8, 9, 9, 10, 10, 11, 11, 12, 12, 12, 13, 13, 14, 14, 16, 17, 18, 19, 19, 19, 20, 20, 20, 21, 21, 21, 22; 20:8; 21:2, 2, 4, 24, 26, 26; 21:8; 8; 22:4, 6, 8, 11, 20, 35, 38; 23:8, 8, 9, 9, 19, 23, 23, 24, 24; 24:7, 7, 7, 7, 8, 8, 8, 9, 14, 17, 17, 17, 17, 18, 18, 18, 19, 19, 20, 20, 20, 21, 21, 21; 26:53, 54, 55, 55, 56, 56, 65; 27:8, 9, 10, 11, 11, 11, 21, 21, 21, 28:2, 3, 7, 11, 14, 15, 17, 18, 19, 19, 24, 24, 25, 25, 26, 26, 27, 31; 29:1, 1, 2, 3, 7, 7, 8, 8, 9, 12, 13, 13, 14, 16, 16, 18, 19, 19, 21, 21, 22, 22, 24, 24, 24, 25, 25, 26, 27, 28, 28, 30, 30, 31, 33, 33, 34; 30:3, 3, 4, 4, 4, 4, 6, 7, 8, 8, 9; 7, 8, 9, 9;

Dt 1:17, 17, 22, 22, 28, 30, 35, 36, 38, 38, 39, 39; 2:4, 6, 6, 25, 25, 29; 3:18, 19, 20, 21, 22, 22, 28, 28; 4:2, 2, 6, 10, 22, 25, 25, 25, 26, 26, 26, 27, 27, 27, 28; 5:25, 27, 27, 32, 32, 33, 33; 6:6, 8, 10, 10, 14, 14, 17, 25; 7:1, 2, 5, 5, 5, 12, 12, 14, 16, 16, 19, 23, 23, 24, 24, 25; 8:1, 19, 19, 20; 9:3, 3; 11:8, 13, 13, 18, 19, 22, 23, 24, 24, 24, 24, 25, 25, 25, 29, 29, 31, 31, 32; 12:1, 2, 2, 3, 3, 4, 5, 5, 6, 7, 7, 8, 11, 11, 12, 14, 16, 16, 18, 20, 22, 26, 27, 29; 13:4, 4, 5, 8, 9, 9, 11, 11, 16, 16, 17, 14:1, 4, 6, 7, 8, 9, 9, 11, 12, 19, 23, 23, 29, 29; 15:2, 2, 3, 4, 4, 6, 10, 10, 11, 16, 17, 18, 20, 22; 16:2, 2, 3, 3, 4, 6, 10, 11, 16, 16, 17, 17; 17:6, 6, 6, 7, 8, 8, 10, 10, 11, 11, 12, 13, 15, 16, 16, 16, 17, 18; 17:6, 6, 7, 8, 8, 8, 10, 15, 16, 16, 16, 17, 18, 19, 19; 18:1, 1, 2, 3, 3, 6, 7, 8, 10, 15, 18, 18, 19, 19, 20, 20, 20, 21; 19:4, 5, 12, 13, 15, 15, 17, 17, 18, 19, 20, 20, 21, 21; 20:2, 3, 3, 4, 4, 4, 5, 5, 6, 8, 10, 11, 11; 21:2, 2, 3, 3, 4, 4, 5, 5, 6, 7, 8, 14, 20, 22; 22:5, 5, 5, 15, 16, 17, 18, 19, 19, 21, 21, 22, 24, 24, 25, 29, 29, 30; 23:1, 2, 2, 3, 3, 8, 10, 10, 11, 11, 13, 14, 16, 16, 17,

22; 24:5, 5, 5, 5, 6, 7, 8, 8, 11, 13, 15, 16, 16, 16, 19, 20, 20, 21; 25:1, 2, 2, 5, 5, 6, 6, 8, 9, 9, 9, 10, 12, 19; 26:1, 2, 3, 4; 27:2, 2, 4, 4, 12, 13, 14, 15, 16, 17, 18, 19, 20, 21, 22, 23, 24, 24, 25, 26; 28:1, 2, 4, 5, 7, 7, 8, 8, 9, 10, 10, 11, 12, 12, 13, 15, 15, 17, 18, 20, 21, 22, 22, 23, 23, 24, 24, 25, 26, 26, 28, 29, 30, 31, 31, 31, 32, 32, 33, 35, 36, 37, 38, 39, 40, 41, 42, 43, 43, 44, 44, 45, 45, 46, 48, 48, 49, 50, 51, 51, 52, 52, 53, 54, 54, 55, 55, 56, 57, 57, 57, 60, 62, 63, 63, 64, 65, 65, 66, 68, 68, 68; 29:19, 20, 20, 20, 21, 22, 22, 22, 24, 25, 30:1, 12, 13, 16, 18, 18; 31:3, 4, 5, 11, 17, 17, 17, 18, 20, 20, 20, 21, 21; 32:2, 2, 20, 22, 22, 24, 25, 35, 35, 36, 37, 42, 46, 47; 33:3, 10, 10, 12, 12, 12, 17, 19, 19, 22, 25, 27, 27, 28, 28, 28, 29

Jos 1:3, 4, 5, 8, 11, 14, 14, 15, 18; 2:5, 14, 19, 19, 19, 19, 19, 19; 3:3, 4, 8, 10, 13, 13, 13, 13; 4:3, 3, 7, 7, 21, 22; 6:3, 4, 4, 4, 5, 5, 5, 5, 10, 10, 10, 17, 17, 19, 26, 26; 7:8, 9, 9, 14, 14, 14, 14, 14, 14, 15, 15; 8:2, 4, 5, 7, 8, 8, 8; 9:7, 23; 10:8, 25; 14:9, 12; 15:4; 17:18, 18; 18:4, 4, 5, 5, 5, 6; 20:3, 4, 4, 4, 4, 4, 5, 6, 6, 6, 6; 22:22, 25, 28, 34; 23:5, 5, 10, 12, 13, 15, 15, 16, 16; 24:27, 27

Jdg 1:1, 2; 2:2, 2, 3, 3; 4:9, 9, 20; 5:11, 11, 14, 24; 6:15, 37; 7:4, 4, 4, 4, 11, 17; 8:23, 23; 9:33; 10:18; 11:9, 24, 31, 31; 13:5, 5, 5, 7, 8, 8, 12, 15, 22; 14:13, 16; 15:3, 18; 16:2, 7, 11, 17; 18:5, 10; 20:9, 18, 18, 23, 28, 28; 21:1, 5, 7, 11, 11, 16, 22

Ru 1:16; 2:2, 9; 3:1, 3, 4, 4, 13; 4:12, 15

1Sa 1:11, 28; 2:9, 9, 10, 10, 10, 25, 25, 30, 31, 32, 32, 33, 33, 33, 34, 34, 34, 35, 35, 36, 36, 36; 3:9, 11, 14; 4:8; 5:7, 8; 6:2, 2, 3, 3, 4, 4, 5, 5, 9, 20; 8:9, 11, 11, 17, 18, 18; 9:7, 13, 13, 17, 19; 10:2, 3, 5, 5, 27; 11:7, 9, 9, 10, 12, 13; 12:12, 14, 15, 17, 25, 25; 13:14; 14:10, 17, 39, 45, 45; 15:33; 16:16, 17:9, 25, 26, 47; 18:25; 19:6; 20:7, 10, 31, 32; 21:15; 23:2, 17, 17, 20, 23; 24:4, 12, 13, 20; 25:6, 11, 29, 29, 30, 30, 30, 31; 26:10, 10, 10; 27:1, 1, 1, 12; 28:8, 10, 11, 15, 19; 29:9; 30:8, 8, 23, 24, 24

2Sa 2:1, 1, 26, 26; 3:12, 39; 4:11; 5:8, 8, 19, 24; 6:9, 22; 7:10, 12, 13, 14, 16, 16; 14, 23, 23; 13:13; 14:7, 7, 10, 11, 17, 18; 15:8, 10, 14, 15, 21, 25, 35, 36; 16:3, 10, 20, 21, 21; 17:2, 3, 6, 10, 12, 12, 13; 19:21, 22, 37, 38, 38; 20:6, 18, 21; 21:3, 3, 4; 22:4, 44, 45, 45, 46, 46; 23:4, 6, 7, 7; 24:13, 13

1Ki 1:13, 13, 17, 17, 20, 21, 21, 21, 24, 24, 30, 30, 35, 35, 52, 52, 52; 2:4, 24, 32, 33, 33, 37, 37, 44, 45, 45; 3:5, 12, 13; 5:6, 9; 8:19, 19, 25, 29, 29, 30, 33, 38, 42, 42, 44, 47, 59; 9:3, 5, 6, 7, 8, 8, 8, 9; 11:2, 2, 3, 3, 22, 32; 12:10, 24, 26, 27, 27; 13:2, 2, 2, 3, 3, 32, 32; 14:3, 5, 15, 15, 16, 16; 16:4; 4; 17:1, 4, 14, 14; 18:12, 12, 12, 14, 31; 19:17, 17, 17; 20:6, 6, 6, 10, 14, 23, 25, 28, 36, 39, 40, 42; 21:19, 19, 23, 24, 24; 22:6, 6, 6, 12, 15, 15, 16, 20

2Ki 1:2; 2:9, 10, 10, 16, 21; 3:8, 17, 17, 17, 19, 19; 4:2, 10, 10, 13, 43, 43; 5:8, 10, 17, 27; 6:8, 15, 21, 21, 27; 7:1, 4, 4, 4, 12, 18; 8:1, 8, 9, 10, 10, 36, 37; 10:4, 10, 18, 19, 19, 24, 30; 11:5, 5, 6, 6, 7, 8; 12:5; 14:6, 6, 15:12; 16:13, 15, 15, 17:12, 15, 36, 36, 36, 37, 38, 38, 39, 39; 18:22, 29, 30, 19:6, 7, 7, 10, 10, 29, 29, 30, 31, 32, 33, 33; 20:8, 8, 9, 17, 17, 18, 18, 18; 21:12, 14; 22:17, 17, 18, 20; 23:27; 25:24

1Ch 11:6, 19; 12:17; 13:12; 14:10, 15; 16:30, 33; 17:9, 9, 9, 11, 13, 14, 27; 21:12; 22:9, 9, 10, 10; 23:26; 28:6, 21, 21

2Ch 1:7, 12; 2:8, 9, 14; 6:9, 9, 16, 21, 24, 29, 29, 29; 7:14, 15, 16, 18, 19, 21, 21, 22; 8:11; 10:10; 11:4; 12:7, 8; 13:12; 15:7; 18:5, 5, 11, 14, 14, 14, 15, 19; 19:9, 10, 10, 10, 11, 11; 20:16, 17, 20, 20; 23:3, 4, 4, 5, 6, 6, 7, 7; 25:4, 4, 4, 8, 9; 26:18; 28:13; 30:9, 9; 32:11, 12, 15, 17; 33:4; 34:25, 25, 26, 28; 35:3

Ezr 4:21; 6:8, 11, 12; 7:18, 20, 21, 24; 9:10; 10:38, 38, 39; 13:25, 27

Ne 2:6, 8; 4:3, 11, 12, 20; 5:8; 6:7, 9; 9:10; 10:38, 38, 39; 13:25, 27

Est 1:15, 17, 17, 17, 18, 18, 20, 20, 20; 4:11, 11, 14, 14; 5:3, 6, 6, 8; 6:6, 9, 11; 7:2, 2; 8:6; 9:12, 12

Job 1:21; 2:10, 10; 4:17, 17; 5:19, 19, 20, 23, 24, 25; 7:4, 7, 8, 9, 10, 10, 13, 13, 20, 21, 21; 8:2, 10, 13, 14, 14, 15, 15, 15, 15, 18, 19, 22; 9:14, 19, 20, 20, 31; 10:21; 11:3, 17, 19, 19, 20, 20, 31; 12:2, 7, 7, 8, 8; 13:11, 16, 16, 19, 19; 14:6, 12, 14, 22; 15:21, 22, 24, 29, 29, 29, 30, 30, 31, 32, 32, 33, 33, 34, 34; 16:3, 22, 22; 17:5, 8, 8, 9, 16, 16; 18:4, 5, 5, 6, 7, 7, 9, 9, 11, 11, 12, 12, 13, 13, 14, 14, 15, 16, 16, 16, 17, 17, 18, 19, 20; 19:25, 26, 27, 27; 20:7, 7, 8, 8, 8, 9, 9, 10, 10, 11, 15, 15, 16, 16, 16, 17, 18, 18, 18, 20, 20, 21, 21, 22, 23, 23, 24, 24, 26, 26, 28, 28; 21:19, 20, 20, 22, 26, 30, 31, 32, 33, 33;

22:21, 25, 27, 28, 28, 29, 30; 23:10; 24:15, 20, 20, 20, 20; 27:4, 6, 13, 14, 15, 15, 17, 17, 19, 19, 19, 22, 23, 23; 28:12, 15, 17, 18, 19; 29:18, 18; 31:14, 14; 33:3, 3, 7, 7, 25, 25, 26, 26, 28, 33; 34:11, 15, 15, 17, 20, 20, 24; 35:3; 36:4, 11, 12, 12; 37:19, 20, 20; 38:11, 15; 40:2, 4; 41:6, 6, 9; 42:8

Ps 1:3, 3, 3, 5, 6; 2:4, 4, 5, 8; 5:4, 5; 6:5; 7:7, 8, 16, 16; 9:3, 7, 8, 8, 17, 18, 18; 10:6, 6; 11:6, 6; 12:3; 13:2, 2, 5; 14:7, 7; 15:1, 1, 5; 16:4, 8, 9; 17:3, 15; 18:3, 43, 44, 44, 45; 19:13; 21:1, 7, 7, 8, 8, 9, 9; 22:25, 26, 26, 27, 27, 29, 30, 30, 31, 31; 31; 23:1, 6; 24:3, 3, 5, 7, 9; 25:12, 12, 13, 13, 15; 26:1; 27:1, 1, 3, 5, 5, 5, 6, 14; 28:5; 30:6, 9, 9; 31:24; 32:6, 6, 10, 10; 33:17, 21; 34:1, 2, 2, 10, 21, 21, 22; 35:9, 9, 10, 28; 36:8, 9, 12; 37:2, 4, 5, 6, 9, 9, 10, 10, 11, 11, 13, 15, 15, 17, 18, 19, 19, 20, 20, 20, 20, 22, 22, 24, 28, 29, 31, 34, 38, 38, 40, 40; 39:6; 40:3; 41:2, 5, 8; 42:2, 5, 8, 11; 43:5; 44:6, 21; 45:4, 11, 12, 14, 14, 15, 16, 17; 46:4, 5, 5; 47:3, 4; 49:3, 3, 5, 11, 14, 14, 14, 15, 17, 17, 19, 19; 50:3, 3, 3, 4, 6; 51:7, 7, 13, 14, 15, 19; 52:5, 5, 6, 6; 53:6, 6; 54:5; 55:16, 17, 19, 22, 22, 23; 56:7, 9; 57:3, 3; 58:9, 10, 10, 11; 59:10, 10; 60:12, 12; 61:7; 62:2, 3, 3, 6; 63:3, 5, 5, 9, 10, 10, 11, 11, 11; 64:5, 7, 7, 8, 8, 9, 9, 10, 10, 10; 65:1, 2, 4; 66:3, 4, 4, 4; 67:6, 6, 7, 7; 68:13, 21, 29, 31, 31; 69:31, 32, 32, 36, 36; 71:6, 15, 23, 24; 72:2, 3, 4, 4, 4, 5, 6, 7, 8, 9, 9, 9, 10, 11, 11, 12, 13, 13, 14, 14, 15, 15, 16, 16, 16, 17, 17, 17; 73:27; 74:10, 10; 75:2, 8, 10; 76:10, 12; 79:5; 80:3, 7, 19; 81:9, 9; 82:7; 85:11, 11, 12, 12, 13, 13; 86:9, 9; 87:5, 5, 6, 7; 88:10, 11, 12, 13; 89:2, 5, 12, 14, 15, 16, 16, 17, 21, 21, 22, 24, 24, 26, 28, 36, 37, 46, 48, 48; 91:1, 3, 4, 4, 7, 7, 10, 10, 11, 12, 15; 92:7, 9, 9, 10, 12, 12, 13, 14, 14; 94:3, 3, 4, 7, 9; 96:10, 10, 10, 12, 13; 98:9; 101:3, 4, 6, 6, 6, 7, 7; 102:15, 16, 16, 18, 18, 24, 26, 26, 27, 28, 28; 103:16; 104:12, 31, 31, 34; 107:42, 42, 43; 108:13, 13; 109:7, 31; 110:2, 3, 5, 6, 6, 6, 7, 7; 112:2, 2, 3, 6, 6, 7, 8, 9, 10, 10, 10; 115:14; 116:12; 118:7, 17, 20; 119:6, 7, 9, 27, 33, 34, 34, 42, 44, 88, 117, 144, 146, 165, 171, 172, 175; 120:3, 3; 121:4, 6, 7, 7, 8; 122:2, 6; 125:1, 3, 5, 5; 126:5, 6; 127:5, 5; 128:2, 3, 4, 5; 130:3, 8; 132:12, 12, 16, 18; 137:4, 8, 9; 138:4, 5, 7; 139:7, 7, 10, 10, 11, 11; 140:11, 13, 13; 141:5, 5, 5, 5, 6; 142:7; 143:2; 144:5; 145:4, 4, 6, 7, 7, 10, 10, 11, 21; 146:10; 148:6

Pr 1:5, 9, 13, 13, 28, 28, 28, 31, 32, 32, 33, 33; 2:11, 11, 21, 22; 3:2, 3:2, 6, 8, 10, 10, 22, 23, 24, 24, 26, 26, 35, 35; 4:6, 6, 8, 8, 15, 22, 22, 23, 23, 26; 6:11, 15, 15, 22, 22, 23; 7, 7, 35; 9:11, 11; 10:7, 8, 9, 10, 24, 24, 27, 28, 28, 29, 30, 30, 31; 11:3, 3, 5, 5, 6, 6, 7, 7, 9, 15, 18, 21, 21, 25, 25, 26, 26, 27, 28, 28, 29, 29, 31; 12:3, 3, 6, 7, 8, 8, 11, 13, 14, 14, 19, 21, 21, 24, 24; 13:2, 2, 3, 4, 9, 11, 11, 13, 13, 18, 18, 20; 14:3, 11, 11, 14, 14, 22, 26; 15:10, 27; 16:3, 5, 20, 21; 17:2, 2, 5, 11, 13; 18:20; 19:5, 8, 9, 9, 15, 16, 19, 21, 23, 23; 20:4, 17, 20, 20, 21, 22; 21:7, 13, 13, 15, 16, 16, 17, 17, 18, 28; 22:5, 8, 8, 9, 9, 10, 10, 11, 13, 14, 16, 18, 23; 23:11, 13, 13, 15, 16, 18, 21, 24, 24, 25; 24:3, 5, 6, 14, 14, 14, 22, 26; 15:10, 27; 16:3, 5, 20, 21; 17:2, 5, 11, 13; 18:20, 20; 19:5, 8, 9, 9, 15, 16, 19, 21, 23, 23; 20:4, 17, 20, 20, 21, 22; 21:7, 13, 13, 15, 16, 16, 17, 17, 18, 28; 22:5, 8, 8, 9, 9, 10, 10, 11, 13, 14, 16, 18, 23; 23:11, 13, 13, 15, 16, 18, 21, 24, 24, 25; 24:3, 3, 5, 6, 14, 14, 14, 16, 20, 20, 22, 24, 26, 26, 27, 27, 29; 25:4, 5, 8, 10, 13, 13, 14, 16, 18, 21, 21, 24, 24, 25, 26; 26:2, 26, 27; 27:14, 18, 18; 28:2, 8, 9, 10, 10, 13, 13, 14, 16, 17, 18, 18, 19, 19, 20, 20, 22, 23, 25, 26, 26, 27; 29:1, 14, 16, 17, 18, 21, 23, 23, 25; 30:17, 17; 31:11, 25, 30

Ecc 1:9, 9, 11, 11; 2:16, 18, 19, 19, 21; 3:14, 20; 6:4, 12; 7:18, 26, 26; 8:1, 5, 7, 7, 8, 10, 12, 13, 13, 15, 17, 17; 9:5; 10:8, 8, 9, 9, 14, 14, 20, 20; 11:2, 3, 4, 4, 4, 6, 8; 12:3, 3, 4, 4, 4, 5, 5, 5, 5, 7, 7, 14

SS 1:13; 5:3, 3; 7:8; 8:8, 8

Isa 1:18, 18, 19, 20, 27, 28, 28, 29, 29, 30, 31, 31, 31; 2:2, 2, 2, 2, 3, 3, 4, 4, 4, 4, 4, 11, 11, 11, 12, 12, 17, 17, 18, 19, 20; 3:4, 5, 5, 6, 7, 10, 10, 11, 11, 24, 24, 25, 26, 26; 4:1, 2, 2, 3, 3, 4, 4, 5, 6; 5:5, 5, 6, 6, 9, 10, 10, 14, 15, 15, 16, 16, 17, 17, 24, 24, 26, 27, 27, 27, 28, 29, 29, 29, 29, 30; 6:8, 13, 13, 13; 7:7, 7, 8, 9, 14, 14, 15, 16, 16, 17, 18, 18, 19, 19, 20, 20, 21, 22, 22, 23, 23, 23, 24, 25, 25; 8:4, 4, 7, 8, 8, 8, 9, 9, 10, 10, 13, 14, 15, 15, 15, 16, 17, 18, 18, 19, 19, 20, 20, 20, 21, 21, 22; 9:1, 5, 5, 6, 6, 7, 7, 7, 8, 11, 11, 12, 12, 13, 13, 13, 14, 14, 14, 15, 15, 15, 16, 16; 12:3, 4; 13:6, 7, 7, 8, 8, 8, 8, 9, 9, 10, 10, 13, 14, 14, 15, 15, 16, 16, 17, 17, 18, 18, 19, 20, 20,

SHALT (1616)

19; 4:7, 7, 12; 6:14, 14, 15, 16, 16, 16, 16, 18, 19, 21; 7:2; 12:2; 15:15, 15; 16:11, 11; 17:4, 9, 15, 19; 20:7, 7, 13; 21:23, 30; 24:3, 4, 7, 8, 37, 38, 40, 41, 41; 27:10, 40, 40, 40, 40, 40; 28:1, 6, 14, 22; 29:27; 30:31; 31:50, 50, 52; 32:18; 35:17; 37:8, 8; 40:13; 41:40; 43:9; 45:10, 10; 47:30; 49:4; 50:5

Ex 3:14, 15, 18; 4:9, 12, 15, 16, 17, 17, 22; 6:1; 7:2, 9, 15, 15, 16, 17; 9:15; 10:28; 12:46; 13:5, 6, 8, 10, 12, 13, 14; 15:17; 17:6; 18:20, 20, 21, 23, 23; 19:3, 6, 12, 24; 20:3, 4, 5, 7, 9, 10, 13, 14, 16, 17, 17, 22, 24, 24, 25, 26; 21:1, 14, 23; 22:18, 21, 25, 25, 26, 28, 29, 29, 30, 30; 23:1, 2, 2, 3, 4, 5, 6, 8, 9, 10, 11, 11, 12, 14, 14, 16, 18, 19, 19, 22, 24, 24, 27, 31, 32; 25:11, 11, 11, 12, 13, 14, 16, 17, 18, 18, 21, 21, 23, 24, 25, 25, 26, 28, 29, 29, 30, 31, 37; 26:1, 1, 4, 4, 5, 5, 6, 7, 7, 9, 9, 10, 11, 14, 15, 17, 18, 19, 22, 23, 26, 29, 29, 30, 31, 32, 33, 34, 35, 35, 36, 37, 37; 27:1, 2, 2, 3, 3, 4, 4, 5, 6, 8, 9, 20; 28:2, 3, 9, 11, 13, 15, 15, 15, 17, 22, 23, 23, 24, 25, 25, 26, 27, 27, 30, 31, 33, 36, 37, 39, 39, 40, 40, 40, 41, 41, 42; 29:1, 2, 3, 4, 4, 5, 6, 7, 8, 9, 9, 10, 11, 12, 13, 14, 15, 16, 16, 17, 18, 19, 20, 21, 22, 24, 24, 25, 26, 27, 31, 34, 35, 35, 36, 36, 37, 38, 39, 39, 41, 41; 30:1, 1, 3, 3, 4, 4, 5, 6, 6, 16, 18, 18, 18, 25, 26, 29, 30, 31, 37; 26:1, 4, 4, 5, 5, 6, 7, 7, 9, 9, 10, 11, 14, 18, 19, 22, 23, 29, 29, 30, 31, 32, 33, 34, 35, 35, 36, 37, 37; 27:1, 2, 2, 3, 3, 4, 4, 5, 6, 8, 9, 20; 28:2, 3, 9, 11, 13, 15, 15, 15, 17, 22, 23, 23, 24, 25, 25, 26, 27, 27, 30, 31, 33, 36, 37, 39, 39, 40, 40, 40, 41, 41, 42; 29:1, 2, 3, 4, 4, 5, 6, 7, 8, 9, 9, 10, 11, 12, 13, 14, 15, 16, 16, 17, 18, 19, 20, 21, 24, 24, 25, 26, 27, 31, 34, 35, 35, 36, 36, 37, 38, 39, 39, 41; 30:1, 1, 3, 3, 4, 4, 5, 6, 6, 16, 18, 18, 18, 20, 21, 21, 22, 24; 31:2, 11, 11, 12, 13, 13, 14, 16, 17, 18, 18, 21, 21, 23, 24, 24, 25, 25, 26, 28, 29, 29, 30, 30, 31, 37; 26:1, 4, 4, 5, 5, 6, 7, 7, 8, 9, 10, 11, 12, 13, 14, 15, 16, 16, 16, 17, 18, 19, 20, 21, 21, 22, 23, 23, 24, 25, 26, 27, 30, 31, 33, 33, 34, 34, 34, 41; 30:1, 3, 4, 4, 5, 6, 6, 16, 18, 18, 18, 20, 21, 21, 22, 24, 24, 25, 26, 27, 27, 28, 28, 29, 31, 32, 32, 34, 35, 35, 36, 37, 39, 39, 40, 40, 41, 41, 43, 44, 44, 48, 49, 53, 64, 65, 66, 66, 67, 67, 67, 67, 68; 30:1, 2, 2, 5, 8, 10, 17; 31:2, 3, 7, 11, 16, 23; 32:52, 52; 33:29; 34:4

Jos 1:6, 8, 8, 8; 2:18, 18; 3:8; 6:3; 8:2; 11:6; 17:17, 18, 18

Jdg 4:20; 6:14, 16, 23, 26; 7:5, 11; 9:33, 33; 11:2, 30; 13:3, 5, 7

Ru 2:21; 3:4, 4, 4

1Sa 2:16; 3:2; 3:9; 9:16; 10:2, 3, 3, 4, 5, 5, 6, 6, 8, 8, 8; 14:44; 16:3, 3, 16; 18:21; 19:11; 20:2, 8, 14, 15, 18, 19, 19, 31; 22:16, 23; 23:17; 24:20; 26:25, 25; 28:1, 2, 19; 30:8

2Sa 3:13; 5:2, 2, 6, 23, 24; 7:5, 8, 12; 9:7, 10; 10:11; 11:25; 12:13; 13:13; 15:33, 35, 35; 18:3, 20, 20, 20; 19:23, 38; 24:4, 17

1Ki 2:37, 37, 42; 5:6, 9, 9, 9; 8:19, 44; 11:37, 37; 12:10, 10; 13:17; 14:5; 17:4; 19:16, 16; 20:5, 13, 34, 39; 21:19, 19; 22:11, 22, 25, 25

2Ki 1:4, 4, 6, 6, 16, 16; 4:4, 4, 4, 16; 5:10; 6:22; 7:2, 2, 19, 19; 8:13; 9:7; 10:5; 13:17, 19; 19:11; 20:1, 5, 9, 18; 22:20

1Ch 11:2, 2, 5; 14:15, 15; 17:4, 7; 19:12; 21:22; 22:8, 13; 28:3

2Ch 2:16, 16; 6:9, 34; 7:17; 10:10, 10; 16:9; 18:10, 21, 21, 24, 24; 21:15; 34:28

Ezr 4:13, 15, 16; 7:20

Est 4:13; 6:13, 13

Job 5:21, 21, 22, 22, 23, 24, 24, 24, 25, 26; 7:21; 9:31; 11:15, 15, 15, 16, 17, 17, 18, 18, 18, 19; 14:15; 17:4; 22:23, 23, 24, 25, 26, 26, 27, 27, 28, 29; 35:14; 38:11

Ps 2:9, 9; 5:3, 6; 12:7, 7; 17:3; 21:9, 10, 12,

12; 31:20, 20; 32:7, 7, 8; 36:8; 37:3, 3, 10, 34; 50:15; 51:6, 19; 55:23; 59:8, 8; 65:3; 67:4; 71:20, 20, 21; 73:20, 24; 76:10; 82:8; 89:2; 91:4, 5, 8, 13, 13; 92:10; 102:12, 13, 26, 26; 119:32; 128:2, 2, 5, 6; 138:7; 142:7

Pr 2:5; 9; 3:4, 23, 24, 24; 4:12; 9:12, 12; 20:13; 22:24; 23:8, 14, 14, 34, 35; 24:6; 25:22; 27:27

Ecc 11:1; 12:1

Isa 1:26; 12:1; 14:4, 15, 20; 17:10, 10, 11, 11; 22:18; 23:12, 12; 25:5; 29:4, 4, 6; 30:19, 22, 22, 23; 33:1, 1, 1, 19; 37:11; 38:1; 39:7; 41:12, 12, 15, 15, 16, 16, 16; 43:2; 44:21, 26, 28; 47:1, 5, 11, 11, 11, 12; 49:18, 20, 21, 23; 51:22; 53:10; 54:3, 4, 4, 4, 4, 14, 14, 14, 17; 55:5; 58:9, 9, 11, 12, 12, 13, 14; 60:5, 16, 16, 16, 18; 62:2, 3, 4, 4, 12

Jer 1:7, 7; 2:36, 37, 37, 37; 3:19, 19; 4:1, 2, 30; 5:19; 7:27, 27, 28; 8:4; 13:12, 13; 14:17; 15:2, 19, 19; 16:2, 2, 8, 10, 11; 17:4; 18:22; 19:10, 11; 20:6, 6, 6; 21:8; 22:15, 22, 23; 23:33, 37; 25:27, 28; 26:4, 8; 28:13, 16; 29:24; 31:4, 4, 4, 5; 34:3, 3, 3, 4, 5, 14; 36:6, 29; 37:17; 38:17, 18, 23, 23, 24, 26; 39:17, 18; 40:16; 45:4; 46:11, 11; 48:2, 7; 49:12, 12; 51:26, 61, 61, 62, 63, 64

La 4:21, 21

Eze 2:4, 7; 3:18, 25, 26, 26, 27; 4:3, 4, 4, 5, 6, 7, 7, 8, 9, 9, 10, 10, 11, 11, 12, 12, 15; 5:2, 2, 2, 3; 8:6, 13, 15; 12:3, 4, 4, 6, 6; 16:41, 43, 61, 61, 62; 21:7, 32, 32; 22:2, 16, 16; 23:27, 32, 32, 33, 34, 34; 24:13, 16, 27, 27; 25:7; 26:14, 14, 21; 27:34, 36, 36; 28:8, 9, 10, 19, 19; 29:5, 5; 31:18, 18; 32:28, 28; 33:7, 8, 14; 35:4, 4, 12, 15; 36:12, 12, 14, 15, 15; 38:8, 8, 9, 10, 11, 14, 15, 16; 39:4, 5; 43:19, 20, 20, 21, 22, 23, 24, 25; 44:6; 45:3, 18, 20; 46:13, 13, 14

Da 4:26; 5:16, 16; 12:13

Hos 2:16, 16, 20; 3:3, 3, 3; 4:5, 6; 13:4

Am 7:17;

Ob 1:10;

Mic 1:14; 2:5; 4:10, 10, 10, 10, 13; 5:12, 13; 6:14, 14, 14, 15, 15, 15, 15

Na 3:11, 11, 11

Hab 2:7;

Zep 3:11, 11, 15

Zec 2:11; 3:7, 7; 4:7, 9; 13:3

Mt 1:21; 4:7, 10, 10; 5:21, 26, 27, 33, 33, 36, 43; 6:5; 7:5; 11:23; 12:37, 37; 16:19, 19; 17:27; 19:18, 18, 18, 18, 19, 21; 22:37, 39; 26:34, 75

Mk 6:23; 10:21; 12:30, 31; 14:30, 72

Lk 1:13, 14, 20, 31, 31, 76, 76; 4:8, 8, 12; 5:10; 6:42; 10:15, 27, 28; 12:59; 13:9; 14:10, 14, 14; 17:4, 8; 18:22; 22:34, 61; 23:43

Jn 1:33, 42, 50; 13:7, 8, 36; 21:18, 18

Ac 2:28; 13:11, 35; 16:31; 22:15; 23:5; 25:12, 22

Ro 2:3; 7:7; 10:9, 9, 9; 11:22; 12:20; 13:3, 9, 9, 9, 9, 9, 9

1Co 7:16, 16; 9:9; 14:16

Gal 5:14;

1Ti 4:6, 16; 5:18

Heb 1:12;

Jas 2:8;

3Jn 1:6;

Rev 2:10; 3:3, 3; 16:5; 18:14

SHE (981)

Ge 2:23, 23; 3:6, 12, 20; 4:1, 2, 17, 22, 25, 25; 8:9; 11:30; 12:14, 16, 18, 19; 15:9; 16:1, 4, 4, 4, 5, 5, 6, 8, 13, 13; 17:16; 18:15; 19:26, 33, 33, 35, 35, 38; 20:2, 3, 5, 5, 5, 12, 12, 16; 21:7, 9, 10, 14, 15, 16, 16, 16, 19; 22:20, 24; 24:14, 14, 16, 18, 18, 19, 19, 20, 24, 24, 25, 36, 44, 45, 46, 46, 47, 55, 58, 64, 64, 65, 65, 67; 25:2, 21, 22, 22, 26; 26:7, 7, 7, 9; 27:16, 17, 17, 42; 29:9, 12, 32, 32, 33, 33, 34, 35, 35, 35; 30:1, 3, 3, 4, 6, 8, 9, 9, 11, 13, 15, 17, 18, 20, 21, 21, 23, 24, 35; 31:35, 38; 32:14, 15; 34:1; 35:8, 16, 17, 18, 18; 36:12, 14; 38:3, 4, 4, 5, 5, 14, 14, 14, 15, 16, 16, 18, 19, 24, 24, 25, 25, 26, 28, 29; 39:7, 10, 12, 13, 14, 16, 17, 18; 45:23; 46:15, 18, 25

Ex 1:16; 2:2, 2, 3, 3, 3, 5, 5, 6, 6, 6, 7, 10, 10, 10, 22; 4:26; 6:20, 23, 25; 21:4, 7, 8, 11

Lev 12:2, 2, 4, 4, 5, 5, 5, 6, 7, 8, 8, 8; 15:19, 20, 20, 22, 23, 25, 25, 26, 26, 28, 28, 28, 29; 18:7, 9, 11, 12, 13, 14, 15, 19; 19:20, 20; 20:17, 18; 21:9, 9, 9; 22:12, 13; 26:43

Nu 5:13, 13, 14, 14, 27, 28; 12:10, 14; 15:27; 22:25, 27, 28, 33; 26:59; 30:4, 4, 5, 6, 6, 6, 7, 8, 8, 8, 10, 11

Dt 21:12, 13, 13, 14; 22:19, 21, 21, 24, 29; 24:1, 2, 2, 4; 25:6; 28:57, 57

Jos 2:6, 6, 8, 9, 15, 15, 16, 21, 21; 6:17, 17, 22, 23, 25, 25; 15:18, 18, 18

Jdg 1:14, 14, 14, 15; 4:4, 5, 6, 9, 18; 5:24, 25, 25, 26, 26, 26, 26, 29; 8:31; 11:34, 36, 37, 38, 39, 39; 13:9, 14; 14:3, 7, 17, 17; 15:2; 16:8, 9, 14, 15, 16, 18, 19; 19:9, 10; 19:3; 20:5

Ru 1:3, 6, 6, 6, 7, 7, 9, 15, 18, 18, 20; 2:2, 3, 7, 7, 7, 10, 13, 14, 14, 15, 16, 17,

17, 18, 18, 18, 18, 18, 19, 19, 23; 3:5, 6, 7, 9, 14, 14, 15, 15, 16, 16, 16, 17, 18; 4:13, 13

1Sa 1:7, 7, 7, 10, 11, 12, 13, 13, 18, 20, 20, 21, 22; 18:19, 21; 19:14; 25:3, 19, 19, 20, 20, 20, 23, 33, 36, 41, 42; 28:12, 14, 24, 25

2Sa 4:4; 6:16; 11:4, 4, 4, 26, 27; 12:24; 13:2, 8, 9, 10, 11, 12, 14, 16, 18; 14:4, 5, 11, 27; 20:17; 21:8, 8

1Ki 1:17, 22, 28; 2:13, 14, 16, 19, 20, 21; 3:19, 20, 26, 27; 10:1, 2, 2, 2, 6, 10, 13, 13; 14:5, 5, 6, 17; 15:13; 17:11, 12, 15, 15, 18; 21:8, 9, 11

2Ki 2:24; 4:2, 5, 5, 6, 7, 8, 9, 12, 13, 14, 15, 16, 21, 22, 23, 24, 25, 26, 27, 27, 28, 36, 37; 5:2, 3; 6:28, 29; 8:2, 3, 6, 6; 9:30, 31, 34; 11:1, 13, 14, 16, 16; 22:14, 15

1Ch 1:32; 2:21, 26, 29, 35, 49; 4:17; 7:14, 16, 23; 15:29

2Ch 9:1, 1, 1, 5, 9, 12, 12, 12; 15:16; 22:10, 11, 11; 23:12, 13, 15; 34:22, 23; 36:21, 21

Est 1:11, 15, 17, 19; 2:1, 7, 9, 10, 12, 13, 14, 14, 14, 15, 17, 20; 4:4, 4, 8; 5:2, 12, 14, 14, 15

Job 1:3; 39:16, 18, 18, 28, 29, 30; 42:12

Ps 45:14; 46:5; 68:12; 80:11; 84:3

Pr 1:20, 21, 21; 3:15, 18; 4:6, 6, 8, 8, 9, 9, 13; 7:11, 12, 13, 21, 21, 26; 8:2, 3; 9:1, 2, 2, 2, 3, 3, 4, 13, 14, 16; 12:4; 23:22, 25, 28; 30:20, 23; 31:12, 13, 14, 14, 15, 16, 16, 17, 18, 19, 20, 20, 21, 24, 24, 25, 26, 27, 30

SS 6:9, 9, 10; 8:5, 8, 9, 9

Isa 3:26; 8:3; 23:3, 17; 40:2; 49:15; 51:18, 18; 66:7, 7, 7, 8

Jer 3:1, 6, 7, 7, 9; 4:17; 6:6, 7; 11:15; 15:9, 9, 9; 33:16; 46:24; 50:9, 12, 14, 15, 15, 29, 29; 51:8, 9, 42, 53

La 1:1, 1, 1, 2, 2, 3, 4, 7, 8, 8, 9, 9, 9, 10, 11, 11, 17, 19, 21, 21, 21, 26; 8:2, 3; 9:1, 2, 2, 3, 3, 4, 13, 14, 16; 12:4

Eze 5:6; 16:46, 48, 49; 19:2, 2, 3, 5, 5, 5, 10, 11, 11, 12, 12, 13, 14; 23:5, 5, 7, 7, 8, 9, 10, 11, 11, 12, 13, 14, 14, 16, 16, 17, 18, 19, 19, 20, 43; 24:7, 7, 12; 26:2, 2, 2, 17; 32:20

Da 11:6, 6, 17

Hos 1:6, 8, 8; 2:2, 3, 5, 5, 6, 7, 7, 7, 8, 12, 13, 13, 13, 15, 15; 13:16

Am 5:2, 2

Mic 1:7, 13; 5:3; 7:10, 10

Na 2:7, 10; 3:10, 10

Zep 2:15; 3:2, 2, 2, 2

Zec 9:4;

Mal 2:14;

Mt 1:18, 21, 25; 8:15; 9:18, 21; 12:42; 14:7, 8, 11; 15:23, 25, 27; 20:21; 22:28; 26:10, 12, 12

Mk 1:31; 5:23, 23, 26, 27, 28, 29, 29, 42; 6:19, 24, 24, 25; 7:26, 28, 30, 30; 10:12; 12:23, 42, 44, 44; 14:3, 6, 8, 8, 9, 67; 16:10

Lk 1:29, 29, 36, 42, 45, 57, 57; 2:6, 7, 36, 37, 38; 4:39; 7:12, 37, 39, 44, 47, 47; 8:42, 47, 47, 47, 47, 47, 50, 52, 53, 55; 10:39, 40; 11:31; 13:13; 15:8, 8, 9, 9; 18:3, 5; 20:33; 21:4, 4

Jn 8:11; 11:20, 27, 28, 28, 29, 29, 31, 31, 32; 12:7; 16:21, 21, 21; 20:2, 11, 11, 13, 14, 14, 15, 16, 18

Ac 5:8, 10; 9:36, 37, 39, 40, 40, 40; 12:14, 14, 15; 16:14, 15, 15, 15, 18

Ro 7:2, 3, 3, 3, 3, 3; 16:2, 2

1Co 7:11, 12, 28, 34, 34, 34, 36, 39, 39, 40; 11:5

Gal 4:27;

Eph 5:33;

1Ti 2:15; 5:5, 6, 6, 10, 10, 10, 10, 10

Heb 11:11, 11, 31

Jas 2:25;

Rev 2:21; 6:13; 12:2, 5, 6, 14, 14; 14:8; 18:6, 6, 7, 7, 8, 19; 19:8

THAT (12914)

Ge 1:4, 10, 12, 18, 20, 20, 21, 21, 25, 25, 26, 28, 30, 31; 2:3, 4, 9, 11, 12, 13, 14, 17, 18, 19; 3:5, 6, 6, 6, 7, 11, 11, 13; 4:3, 8, 14, 14; 5:1, 5; 6:2, 2, 3, 4, 5, 6, 7, 17, 21, 22; 7:2, 4, 5, 8, 8, 10, 14, 19, 21, 22, 23; 8:1, 6, 11, 17, 17; 9:2, 3, 10, 10, 12, 14, 16, 16, 16, 17, 18; 10:11; 11:2, 7; 12:1, 3, 5, 5, 11, 11, 12, 13, 14, 14, 18, 18, 20; 13:1, 6, 10, 14, 16; 14:2, 5, 7, 10, 13, 14, 17; 15:4, 7, 8, 13, 13, 14, 17, 17; 16:2, 4, 5, 10, 13, 13, 17; 17:12, 12, 13, 13, 14, 14, 17, 17, 18, 23, 23; 18:5, 17, 18, 19, 19, 19, 24, 25, 25, 25; 19:5, 11, 11, 14, 21, 25, 28, 29, 29, 32, 33, 34, 34, 35; 20:6, 7, 7, 9, 9, 10, 13, 16; 21:3, 6, 6, 7, 8, 9, 17, 18, 20, 23; 22:3, 6, 8, 9, 11, 14, 14, 17, 20, 23:4, 6, 8, 9, 10, 11, 11, 15, 17, 17, 18, 20; 24:2, 2, 3, 6, 9, 14; 24:7, 12; 25:2, 2, 8, 9, 14, 21, 26, 28, 33, 35, 37, 40; 26:5, 15, 10, 11, 12, 12, 13, 13, 33; 27:5, 20; 28:1, 3, 3, 3, 4, 28, 28, 32, 35, 37, 38, 38, 41, 43; 29:1, 13, 13, 21, 22, 23, 27, 30, 30, 32, 38, 46, 46; 30:6, 6, 13, 14, 14, 14, 16, 20, 21, 29, 30, 38; 31:6, 6, 7, 11, 13, 13, 13, 14, 14, 14, 14, 16, 20; 32:1, 10, 10, 13, 18, 20, 25; 34:1, 3, 7, 7, 33; 30:1, 3, 9, 15, 16, 20, 22, 24; 19:8, 9, 12, 16, 16, 16; 20:4, 4, 4, 5, 6, 7, 10, 11, 12, 17, 20, 20, 20, 22, 26; 21:12, 12, 14, 15, 16, 17, 19, 22, 26, 28, 29, 35, 36; 22:2, 2, 6, 8, 25, 26, 27, 27; 23:5, 11, 12, 13, 22; 24:7, 12; 25:2, 2, 8, 9, 14, 21, 26, 28, 33, 35, 37, 40; 27:5, 20; 28:1, 3, 3, 3, 4, 28, 28, 32, 35, 38, 38, 41, 43; 29:1, 13, 13, 21, 22, 23, 27, 30, 30, 32, 38, 46, 46; 30:6, 6, 13, 14, 14, 16, 20, 21, 29, 30, 38; 31:6, 6, 7, 11, 13, 13, 13, 14, 14, 14, 16, 20; 32:1, 10, 10, 13, 18, 20, 25; 34:1, 3, 7, 7, 12; 35:1, 4, 8, 10, 22, 24, 25, 25, 34, 34, 35, 36:1, 4, 8, 18, 19; 37:8, 13; 38:15, 22, 24, 25, 26; 39:5, 7, 21, 21, 32, 42; 40:4, 9, 13, 15, 16, 17, 37

Lev 1:5, 8, 12, 17; 2:8, 10; 3:3, 3, 4, 5, 9, 9, 14, 14, 15, 17; 4:3, 5, 8, 8, 16; 6:3, 3, 3, 4, 4, 4, 5, 7, 18, 22, 26, 27; 7:3, 3, 4, 4, 7, 8, 9, 9, 14, 15, 16, 18, 19, 19, 20, 20, 21, 21, 24, 24, 25, 27, 29, 30, 33, 36, 38; 8:10, 16, 25, 26, 31, 32, 35; 9:1, 5, 6, 19; 10:3, 3, 10, 11, 12, 12, 20; 11:2, 3, 4, 4, 9, 9, 10, 10, 12, 12, 20, 21, 26, 27, 28, 29, 31, 34, 34, 36, 39, 39, 41, 42, 43, 43, 44, 45, 46, 46, 47, 47; 12:7; 13:4, 7, 8, 12, 13, 17, 24, 31, 31, 33, 37, 39, 41, 47, 50, 51, 52, 54, 55, 57; 14:4, 5, 6, 7, 8, 8, 9, 11, 12; 15:4, 6, 6, 6, 7, 7, 8, 8, 9, 11, 11, 16, 17, 17, 18, 19, 22, 28, 31, 31, 32, 33, 33; 16:2, 2, 13, 13, 15, 15, 16, 18, 26, 28, 28, 29, 30, 30; 17:3, 3, 4, 4, 5, 8, 8, 9, 10, 10, 10, 10, 11, 12, 13, 13, 15, 15, 15; 18:6, 26, 28, 28, 29, 30, 30; 19:8, 13, 20, 20, 25, 31, 34; 20:2, 2, 3, 3, 5, 5, 6, 9, 10, 10, 11, 14, 22, 24, 25, 25, 26, 27, 27; 21:2, 3, 7, 10, 17, 18, 21; 22:2, 3, 3, 4, 8, 11, 15, 21, 28, 29, 30, 30, 31, 33; 23:10, 14, 14, 15, 21, 28, 29, 30, 30; 24:7, 9, 11, 14, 16, 16, 17, 18, 21, 24:2; 25:5, 6, 7, 11, 11, 25, 27, 28, 28, 30, 30, 33, 35, 35, 39, 44, 45, 45, 47, 48; 49, 50, 51; 26:13, 15, 16, 17, 25, 36, 39, 44, 45, 45, 45; 27:8, 9, 15, 18, 19, 23, 28, 28

Nu 1:3, 5, 20, 21, 22, 22, 23, 24, 25, 26, 27, 28, 29, 30, 31, 32, 33, 34, 35, 36, 37, 38, 39, 40, 41, 42, 43, 44, 45, 45, 46, 50, 51, 53, 54; 2:4, 5, 6, 8, 9, 11, 16, 19, 21, 23, 24, 26, 27, 28, 30, 31, 32, 34; 3:1, 6, 10, 12, 13, 22, 26, 28, 30, 31, 34, 34, 37, 39, 43, 46, 49, 49, 51; 4:3, 15, 16, 19, 23, 25, 26, 30, 35, 36, 37, 39, 41, 42, 43, 44, 45, 46, 47, 48; 5:2, 2, 3, 6, 6, 17, 18, 19, 22, 24, 24, 27, 27, 27; 6:4, 6, 11, 11, 12, 20, 24, 26, 27, 27; 7:1, 2, 2, 5, 9, 10, 12, 88, 89; 8:11, 15, 17, 19, 20, 22, 24; 9:4, 5, 6, 6, 7, 13, 13, 14, 15, 17; 10:2, 5, 6, 9, 10, 11, 32, 35, 35; 11:1, 4, 11, 12, 13, 16, 16, 18, 18, 21, 26, 33, 33; 12:14, 14, 14; 13:2, 18, 19, 28, 31, 32, 32; 14:1, 2, 3, 6, 14, 14, 14, 14, 23, 29, 35, 37, 38, 42, 45; 15:4, 5, 14, 15, 16, 19, 23, 24, 24, 28, 29, 30, 30, 31, 32, 33, 38, 38, 39, 40; 16:7, 9, 11, 13, 14, 13, 13, 14, 21, 28, 30, 30, 31, 32, 33, 34, 35, 37, 39, 40, 40, 42, 45, 49, 49; 17:5, 8, 10;

11, 16; 12:1, 4, 4; 13:2, 3, 8, 14, 15, 15; 14:3, 4, 6, 16, 16, 16, 17, 17, 19, 19, 21, 25, 26, 26, 28, 29, 32; 15:7, 9; 16:2, 3, 12, 12, 13, 13, 14; 17:4, 4, 5, 7, 8, 9, 12, 14, 14; 18:2, 7; 19:3, 8, 8, 9, 9, 10, 13, 16, 17, 18, 19, 21, 23, 24; 20:1, 6; 21:3, 10, 14, 14; 22:1, 2, 3, 7, 8, 9, 11, 12, 16, 16, 16, 20, 20, 25, 25, 25; 23:1, 2, 13, 15, 15, 16, 16, 16, 17, 18; 24:6, 8, 9, 10, 18, 18, 21, 21, 21; 25:7, 9, 11; 26:1, 2, 5, 17, 19; 27:1, 1, 1, 2, 5, 6, 7, 7, 9, 11, 11, 12, 12, 13, 13; 28:1, 4, 5, 6, 6, 8, 9, 13, 14, 16, 19, 20, 20, 21; 29:4, 5, 7, 7, 7, 8, 11, 11, 12, 15, 16, 16, 18, 20, 21, 21, 24, 24; 30:1, 1, 1, 2, 5, 6, 8, 9, 9, 14, 14, 16, 18, 18, 18, 23, 23, 24, 26; 31:1, 2, 3, 3, 7; 32:3, 3, 9, 11, 20, 20; 33:1, 13, 13, 15, 15, 15, 15, 17, 18, 19, 20, 24; 34:1, 1; 35:4; 36:1, 5, 6, 11, 12, 12, 20, 20, 22; 37:1, 4, 6, 8, 16, 20, 20, 26, 26, 30, 31, 32, 34, 38; 38:3, 7, 7, 13, 18, 22; 39:1, 1, 2, 2, 4, 4, 6, 6, 7; 40:2, 2, 3, 9, 11, 20, 20, 20, 20, 22, 22, 23, 26, 26, 28, 29, 31; 41:3, 7, 7, 7, 11, 11, 12, 12, 20, 20, 22, 23, 23, 23, 24, 26, 26, 26, 26, 27, 28; 42:5, 5, 5, 5, 7, 8, 10, 10, 11, 16, 16, 17, 18, 19, 21, 23, 23; 43:1, 1, 7, 8, 8, 9, 10, 10, 12, 13, 25, 26; 44:2, 3, 7, 8, 9, 9, 10, 13, 18, 18, 20, 24, 24, 24, 24, 25, 25, 26, 26, 27, 28; 45:3, 3, 6, 6, 9, 9, 10, 15, 16, 18, 18, 19, 20, 20, 20, 21, 23, 24; 46:5, 10, 11, 12; 47:7, 8, 8, 13; 48:4, 8, 8, 8, 9, 16, 17, 18; 49:5, 6, 6, 7, 9, 9, 10, 15, 17, 19, 20, 23, 23, 25, 26, 26; 50:2, 4, 4, 6, 7, 8, 9, 10, 10, 10, 11, 11, 11; 51:1, 1, 2, 6, 7, 9, 10, 12, 12, 12, 13, 14, 14, 14, 15, 16, 18, 18, 22, 23, 23, 23; 52:5, 5, 6, 6, 6, 7, 7, 7, 7, 7, 11, 15, 15; 53:2; 54:1, 1, 9, 9, 10, 16, 16, 17, 17; 55:1, 1, 2, 2, 2, 5, 5, 10, 11, 11, 13; 56:2, 2, 2, 3, 4, 4, 5, 6, 6, 8, 11; 57:1, 11, 13, 15, 15, 19, 19; 58:2, 5, 6, 6, 7, 7, 7, 7, 12; 59:1, 1, 2, 5, 5, 15, 15, 16, 16, 20, 21; 60:8, 11, 11, 12, 14, 14, 15, 16, 21; 61:1, 2, 3, 3, 3, 9, 9, 11; 62:1, 6, 9, 9; 63:1, 1, 1, 2, 5, 7, 8, 11, 11, 12, 13; 64:1, 1, 1, 2, 4, 5, 5, 7, 7; 65:1, 1, 1, 2, 3, 3, 5; 66:1, 1, 11, 11, 12, 16, 16, 18, 20, 24; 66:1, 2, 3, 3, 3, 4, 5, 5, 5, 6, 10, 10, 11, 11, 13, 15, 27, 19, 23, 23, 24;

Jer 1:1, 7, 17; 2:2, 3, 5, 6, 6, 6, 8, 8, 11, 13, 17, 19, 19, 19, 24, 24, 28; 3:1, 6, 9, 13, 16, 17, 18; 4:4, 9, 9, 11, 14, 16, 31, 31, 31; 5:1, 1, 6, 7, 19, 22, 24, 26; 6:10, 11, 15, 15, 27; 7:1, 2, 7, 8, 18, 22, 23, 23, 25, 28; 8:1; 3, 10, 12, 13, 16, 16, 19, 19; 9:1, 1, 2, 2, 10, 12, 12, 12, 17, 17, 18, 24, 24, 25, 25, 26; 10:4, 11, 18, 23, 23, 25, 25; 11:1, 3, 4, 5, 7, 13, 14, 17, 19, 19, 19, 20, 20, 21, 21; 12:1, 4, 14, 15, 17; 13:4, 6, 11, 13, 20, 20, 23, 24, 26; 14:1, 8, 9, 15, 18, 18, 22; 15:4, 9, 10, 13, 15, 18; 16:3, 3, 3, 10, 12, 13, 14, 14, 15, 15, 21; 17:4, 5, 7, 8, 11, 13, 13, 16, 16, 18, 20, 23; 18:4, 8, 8, 10, 14, 16, 19, 20; 19:2, 6, 7, 8, 9, 11, 11, 15, 15; 20:1, 2, 3, 6, 12, 12, 12; 22:2, 2, 5, 10, 13, 13, 14, 21, 23, 25, 26, 30; 23:1, 2, 5, 7, 7, 8, 13, 13, 14, 21, 23, 25, 26, 30; 24:1, 2, 3, 5, 7, 8, 8, 10; 25:1, 1, 3, 7, 12, 13, 13, 15, 20, 24, 34, 34, 39; 24:1, 2, 3, 5, 7, 8, 8, 10; 25:1, 1, 3, 7, 12, 13, 13, 15, 20, 24, 31, 31, 33; 26:2, 3, 8, 8, 12, 13, 15, 20, 24; 27:5, 8, 8, 8, 10, 11, 13, 14, 15, 15, 16, 18, 19, 21, 22; 28:1, 3, 4, 5, 6, 7, 8, 9, 12, 14; 29:1, 2, 4, 6, 6, 8, 10, 11, 16, 16, 16, 16, 16, 26, 26, 31, 32; 30:1, 2, 3, 3, 8, 9, 10, 11, 17, 19, 19, 20, 21; 31:4, 6, 8, 10, 11, 17, 19, 24, 24, 27, 28, 30, 31, 32, 32, 33, 37, 38; 32:1, 7, 8, 8, 9, 11, 11, 12, 12, 14, 23, 24, 24, 29, 31, 31, 35, 39, 40, 40, 42; 33:2, 9, 9, 10, 11, 11, 13, 14, 14, 15, 20, 21, 22, 24, 26; 34:7, 8, 8, 9, 16, 16, 18, 20, 21; 35:7, 8, 10, 11, 14, 17, 18; 36:1, 2, 3, 3, 5, 6, 7, 8, 9, 13, 23, 23, 23, 24, 25, 27, 28, 31; 37:5, 7, 10, 11, 15, 18, 20, 21, 21; 38:1, 2, 2, 4, 5, 6, 7, 9, 14, 16, 16, 19, 21, 22, 25, 26, 27, 28; 39:4, 9, 9, 9, 14, 16, 17; 40:1, 1, 6, 7, 7, 10, 11, 11, 11, 11, 13, 14, 15; 41:1, 2, 3, 3, 5, 7, 7, 8, 9, 10, 10, 11, 11, 12, 13, 13, 14, 16, 16; 42:3, 3, 4, 6, 7, 10, 12, 16, 17, 17, 19, 20, 22; 43:1, 3, 5, 6, 10, 13; 44:1, 2, 3, 4, 8, 8, 8, 10, 12, 13, 14, 14, 15, 15, 16, 18, 20, 21, 23, 24, 24, 25, 26, 27, 28, 28, 29, 29, 30, 30, 30; 45:1, 4, 4; 46:7, 9, 9, 10, 13, 25, 26; 47:1, 2, 2, 4, 4; 48:9, 10, 10, 12, 12, 17, 18, 19, 19, 20, 28, 28, 35, 35, 36, 41, 44, 44, 45; 49:2, 2, 4, 5, 5, 8, 12, 13, 16, 16, 19, 19, 20, 22, 26, 31, 32, 34, 37, 39; 50:1, 4, 5, 7, 10, 12, 13, 14, 16, 20, 21, 28, 29, 29, 30, 31, 33, 34, 37, 44, 44, 44, 45, 45; 51:1, 1, 2, 3, 3, 4, 7, 12, 14, 14, 24, 46, 46, 47, 48, 50, 52, 60, 60, 62, 62, 63, 64; 52:2, 2, 3, 4, 14, 15, 15, 15, 17, 17, 19, 19, 20, 25, 25, 31, 32

La 1:1, 1, 6, 7, 8, 10, 10, 12, 16, 17, 21, 21, 21; 2:4, 13, 15, 15, 16, 17, 17, 19, 22, 22; 3:1, 6, 7, 22, 25, 25, 26, 27, 30, 37, 44, 57, 62; 4:5, 5, 6, 9, 9, 12, 13, 14, 17, 18, 18; 5:8, 16

Eze 1:1, 18, 23, 25, 26, 28, 28; 2:2, 2, 3, 5, 8, 8; 3:1, 2, 3, 10, 13, 15, 16, 21, 26, 27, 27; 4:4, 9, 12, 14, 17; 5:5, 6, 7, 7, 9, 13,

14, 14, 15; 6:6, 7, 8, 8, 9, 10, 10, 10, 12, 16, 12, 13, 14; 7:4, 7, 9, 9, 9, 13, 15, 15, 16, 27; 8:1; 3, 4, 6, 6, 9, 13, 17; 9:1, 4, 4, 8; 10:1, 6, 7, 7, 12, 15, 20, 20; 11:2, 5, 10, 12, 12, 13, 20, 24, 25; 12:4, 6, 10, 12, 14, 14, 15, 16, 16, 19, 19, 19, 20, 20, 22, 22, 25, 27, 27; 13:2, 2, 3, 6, 9, 9, 9, 11, 14, 14, 15, 15, 18, 18, 19, 19, 19, 20, 20, 21, 22, 23; 14:4, 4, 5, 7, 8, 8, 9, 10, 11, 15:7; 16:5, 15, 21, 24, 25, 27, 31, 31, 32, 33, 34, 37, 37, 37, 38, 44, 45, 46, 46, 47; 52, 52, 54, 54, 54, 57, 62, 63, 63; 17:7, 8, 8, 8, 9, 14, 14, 14, 15, 15, 16, 19, 19, 20, 21, 21, 24; 18:2, 4, 5, 8, 8, 10, 10, 11, 14, 15, 17, 17, 18, 19, 20, 21, 21, 22, 23, 23, 24, 24, 24, 24, 26, 27, 27, 28, 32; 19:5, 9, 11, 14; 20:1, 6, 9, 12, 12, 12, 14, 15, 20, 20, 22, 23, 26, 26, 26, 27, 32, 32, 38, 38, 42, 43, 44, 48; 21:4, 5, 5, 7, 10, 11, 14, 15, 19, 20, 23, 23, 24, 24, 24, 26, 26, 29, 29; 22:3, 4, 5, 5, 9, 10, 14, 16, 22, 24, 30, 30; 23:7, 13, 13, 14, 27, 37, 40, 43, 44, 45, 48, 49; 24:8, 8, 11, 11, 11, 19, 21, 24, 24, 26, 26, 27; 25:5, 7, 8, 10, 11, 12, 17; 26:1, 2, 2, 6, 17, 17, 18, 19, 20, 20, 20, 27; 27:3, 7, 7, 19, 22, 23, 24, 24, 24, 25, 26, 26, 28; 28:3, 8, 9, 9, 13, 14, 15, 17, 18, 19, 22, 23, 24, 24, 24, 25, 26, 26, 29:3, 6, 9, 12, 12, 15, 16, 18, 21, 21; 30:5, 6, 6, 7, 7, 8, 9, 12, 19, 20, 20, 25, 26; 31:1, 9, 9, 14, 14, 14, 16, 16, 17, 17, 17, 18; 32:1, 15, 15, 15, 17, 18, 20, 21, 24, 24, 25, 27, 28, 29, 29, 30, 30, 32; 33:5, 8, 11, 12, 12, 13, 13, 14, 15, 16, 16, 19, 21, 21, 24, 24, 27, 27, 28, 29, 30, 32, 33; 34:2, 3, 4, 4, 4, 10, 12, 12, 16, 16, 16, 16, 19, 21, 27, 29, 30; 35:4, 5, 7, 7, 8, 9, 12, 15; 36:3, 4, 4, 7, 11, 18, 23, 28, 30, 31, 33, 34, 35, 36, 36, 36, 38; 37:6, 9, 13, 14, 25, 28; 38:7, 8, 10, 11, 11, 12, 12, 14, 14, 16, 17, 17, 18, 19, 20, 20, 20, 20, 22, 23; 39:4, 6, 6, 7, 9, 10, 10, 10, 10, 11, 11, 12, 13, 14, 14, 16, 17, 17, 17, 18; 32:1, 15, 15, 15, 17, 18, 20, 21, 24, 25, 25, 27, 28, 29, 29, 30, 30, 32; 40:1, 4, 4, 4, 10, 10, 12, 20, 21, 24, 24, 35; 41:6, 11, 12, 42:1, 1, 1, 4, 5, 7, 9, 11, 11, 12, 14, 14, 15, 15, 17, 18, 20, 20, 21, 22, 23; 43:1, 3, 3, 8, 11, 11, 11, 19, 27, 44:3; 45:11, 13, 20, 20, 22; 46:1, 2, 4, 8, 9, 9, 12, 18, 19, 24; 47:2, 3, 5, 5, 9, 9, 10, 12, 19, 22, 23; 48:9, 11, 12, 15, 18, 19, 22, 35

Da 1:3, 5, 8, 8, 13, 16, 18, 20, 20; 2:8, 9, 10, 10, 11, 11, 13, 16, 16, 18, 18, 21, 25, 28, 29, 30, 30, 34, 34, 35, 40, 45, 45, 46, 47; 3:3, 3, 5, 5, 7, 7, 8, 10, 10, 11, 15, 15, 15, 18, 19, 20, 22, 28, 28, 29, 29; 4:1, 2, 6, 9, 9, 17, 17, 19, 20, 20, 25, 25, 26, 30, 32, 34, 34, 37; 5:2, 3, 5, 6, 13, 14, 14, 16, 16, 19, 21, 25, 29, 30; 6:2, 7, 8, 10, 12, 13, 13, 15, 15, 17, 22, 23, 25, 26, 27; 7:7, 14, 14, 16, 20, 20, 20, 20, 20, 21, 24, 24, 27; 8:1, 2, 4, 4, 6, 7, 13, 21, 22; 9:2, 4, 4, 7, 7, 7, 11, 12, 16, 17, 17, 18, 18, 21, 26, 27; 10:7, 7, 11, 12, 16, 19, 21; 11:3, 6, 6, 6, 16, 24, 26, 30, 31, 32, 33, 36, 36; 12:1, 1, 1, 1, 2, 3, 3, 5, 7, 7, 11, 11, 12

Hos 1:1, 5, 5, 10; 2:3, 5, 5, 6, 8, 12, 16, 18, 21, 23; 4:3, 4, 6, 14; 5:9, 10; 6:5, 8; 7:2, 7; 8:3, 4; 9:4, 10, 12; 10:5, 10, 11; 11:3, 4; 12:8, 9; 13:2, 3, 3, 8, 10; 14:7

Joel 1:1, 4, 4, 4; 2:5, 11, 16, 17, 25, 26, 27, 27, 28, 32; 3:1, 3, 6, 17, 18, 18, 21

Am 1:5, 8, 13; 2:7, 13, 15, 15, 15, 16, 16; 3:1, 12, 14, 14; 4:1, 2, 2, 3, 13; 5:3, 3, 8, 8, 9, 9, 10, 10, 13, 14, 15, 18; 6:1, 3, 4, 5, 6, 7, 7, 8, 9, 9, 10, 10; 7:2; 8:3, 4, 5, 5, 6, 6, 6, 8, 9, 9, 11, 13, 14; 9:1, 1, 1, 5, 5, 6, 6, 8, 11, 11, 12, 12, 13

Ob 1:3, 3, 7, 7, 8, 9, 11, 11, 12, 14, 14, 20

Jnh 1:2, 4, 5, 6, 6, 7, 8, 9, 9, 12; 2:8, 9, 9; 3:2, 2, 8, 9, 10, 10, 10; 4:2, 6, 7, 8, 8, 11, 11

Mic 1:1, 2, 4; 2:1, 4, 5, 6, 6, 7, 7, 8; 3:4, 5, 5, 5, 6, 6, 9; 4:1, 6, 6, 6, 7, 7, 11; 5:2, 3, 7, 10, 10; 6:5, 10, 14, 16; 7:3, 5, 10, 11, 11, 12, 13, 18

Na 1:5, 7, 11, 14, 15, 15; 2:1; 3:4, 7, 7, 8, 8, 19

Hab 1:3, 6, 6, 8, 13, 13, 14; 2:2, 2, 6, 6, 6, 7, 7, 8, 9, 9, 9, 12, 12, 13, 15, 15, 15, 15, 17, 18, 18, 19; 3:8, 16

Hag 1:2, 6, 9, 11; 2:3, 5, 13, 14, 18, 22, 23

Zec 1:8, 9, 10, 11, 13, 14, 15, 19; 2:3, 7, 8, 9, 11, 11; 3:2, 4, 7, 8, 9, 9, 10; 4:1, 1, 4, 5, 9, 14; 5:3, 3, 3, 3, 4, 5, 5, 6, 7, 10; 6:4, 7, 8, 15, 15; 7:1, 11, 13, 14; 8:9, 9, 9, 10, 13, 16, 17, 20, 23, 23, 23; 9:7, 8, 8, 12, 16; 11:1, 5, 9, 9, 9, 9, 9, 10, 11, 11, 11, 13, 14, 16, 16, 16, 17; 12:3, 4, 6, 7, 8, 8, 10, 11, 14; 13:1, 2, 2, 3, 3, 3, 4, 4, 4, 7, 8; 14:4, 6, 6, 7, 8, 8, 9, 13, 13, 15, 16, 16, 16, 17, 18, 18, 20, 21, 21

Mal 1:6, 7, 9, 10, 12, 13; 2:4, 4, 12, 12, 13, 15, 16, 16, 17; 3:3, 5, 5, 10, 10, 14, 14, 15, 15, 16, 16, 16, 17, 17, 18, 18; 4:1, 1, 1, 1, 1, 2, 3

Mt 1:6, 20, 22; 2:2, 6, 8, 12, 15, 16, 16, 17, 22, 23; 3:3, 9, 11; 4:3, 4, 12, 14, 17, 24,

24; 5:4, 14, 15, 16, 17, 20, 21, 22, 23, 27, 28, 29, 29, 30, 30, 32, 32, 33, 38, 39, 42, 42, 43, 44, 44, 45; 6:1, 2, 4, 5, 7, 16, 18, 23, 29, 32; 7:1, 3, 3, 6, 8, 8, 11, 12, 13, 14, 19, 21, 21, 22, 23, 25, 26, 27; 8:4, 8, 10, 10, 11, 15, 16, 17, 24, 27, 28, 28, 33, 34; 9:6, 6, 12, 12, 12, 13, 16, 26, 28, 30, 31, 38; 10:14, 15, 19, 20, 22, 25, 26, 26, 27, 34, 37, 37, 38, 39, 39, 40, 40, 40, 41, 41; 11:3, 8, 11, 11, 15, 24, 25, 28; 12:1, 2, 3, 5, 6, 10, 10, 16, 16, 19, 20, 22, 25, 26, 27, 34, 37, 37, 38, 39, 41, 44, 44, 46, 46, 47; 52, 53, 54; 14:1, 15, 20, 21, 33, 35, 35, 35, 36, 16:5, 4, 11, 11, 12, 17, 28, 30, 31, 37, 38; 16:1, 11, 11, 11, 12, 13, 14, 15, 18, 20, 20, 21, 21, 23, 23; 17:10, 12, 13, 18, 24, 27, 27; 18:6, 6, 7, 7, 10, 10, 11, 12, 13, 13, 14, 16, 19, 19, 25, 27, 28, 31, 32, 32, 34; 19:1, 4, 12, 13, 16, 17, 21, 22, 23, 28, 29, 30; 20:1, 7, 9, 10, 14, 21, 22, 22, 23, 23, 25, 30, 32, 33; 21:4, 9, 9, 9, 12, 12, 15, 16, 19, 21, 22, 24, 31, 34, 46; 22:3, 11, 12, 13, 17, 18, 19, 22, 22, 22, 26, 31, 35, 37, 39; 24:2, 4, 6, 13, 19, 19, 20, 24, 32, 33, 36, 38, 38, 43, 44, 46, 47, 48, 50; 25:3, 9, 10, 16, 17, 18, 20, 22, 24, 24, 25, 26, 26, 29, 32, 33, 36, 37, 39, 39, 41, 44, 44, 46, 48, 52, 53, 54, 55, 56, 57, 63, 63; 27:3, 4, 4, 4, 8, 9, 9, 14, 15, 16, 18, 19, 31, 31, 31; 21:3, 4, 7, 7, 12, 14, 14, 16, 16, 17, 20, 22, 23, 23, 23, 24, 25, 25

Mk 1:9, 14, 22, 27, 32, 32, 34, 36, 38, 45; 2:1, 2, 8, 10, 10, 12, 15, 16, 17, 17, 21, 23, 24, 25; 3:2, 9, 10, 12, 14, 14, 20, 24, 25, 29; 4:1, 8, 9, 10, 11, 12, 15, 22, 24, 25, 25, 25, 28, 31, 32, 37, 38, 40, 41; 5:4, 7, 10, 12, 14, 14, 15, 16, 16, 18, 23, 26, 29, 30, 30, 32, 36, 38, 40, 43, 43; 6:2, 5, 8, 10, 11, 11, 12, 14, 15, 15, 20, 21, 22, 25, 55, 55, 56; 7:2, 9, 11, 15, 15, 18, 20, 20, 26, 32, 34, 36, 38, 40, 43, 43; 8:1, 9, 11, 15, 18, 20, 20, 26, 28, 34, 36, 38, 40, 41; 9:1, 1, 7, 9, 10, 11, 12, 13, 18, 22, 22, 26, 30, 31, 32, 33; 9:1, 1, 7, 9, 10, 11, 12, 13, 18, 22, 22, 26, 30, 31, 32; 33, 37, 39, 40, 42, 42, 43, 45; 10:13, 13, 17, 18, 22, 23, 24, 29, 31, 35, 36, 37, 38, 38, 39, 39, 42, 47, 48, 51, 51; 11:3, 5, 9, 9, 9, 10, 15, 15, 16, 23, 24, 24, 25; 12:2, 12, 14, 15, 17, 19, 26, 28, 34, 34, 35, 41, 43, 44; 13:2, 11, 11, 13, 14, 14, 15, 16, 17, 17, 18, 20, 24, 25, 28, 29, 30, 32; 14:4, 9, 12, 12, 18, 21, 25, 28, 30, 35, 36, 42, 44, 44, 47, 58, 69, 70, 72; 15:5, 6, 7, 9, 10, 11, 12, 29, 29, 32, 32, 35, 39, 42; 16:1, 4, 7, 10, 11, 12, 16, 16, 17

Lk 1:4, 7, 8, 19, 20, 21, 22, 23, 28, 35, 41, 43, 45, 49, 50, 57, 59, 61, 65, 66, 71, 71, 74, 74, 79; 2:1, 1, 6, 6, 18, 20, 23, 24, 26, 35, 38, 38, 46, 47, 49, 49; 3:7, 8, 11, 11, 11, 13, 20, 21; 4:3, 4, 6, 18, 20, 26, 29, 40, 41, 42; 5:1, 3, 7, 7, 9, 17, 24, 24, 25, 29, 31, 31, 36; 6:1, 2, 4, 5, 6, 7, 12, 18, 21, 21, 23, 24, 25, 28, 28, 29, 30, 30, 31, 32, 38, 40, 41, 41, 42, 42, 45, 45, 48, 49, 49, 49; 7:3, 4, 6, 9, 10, 10, 11, 14, 15, 16, 16, 19, 20, 20, 21, 22, 28, 28, 29, 36, 37, 39, 43, 49, 49; 8:1, 8, 10, 12, 14, 15, 16, 16, 19, 20, 21, 21, 21, 22, 28, 28, 29, 33, 34, 34, 37, 38; 9:2, 3, 8, 11, 16, 17, 18, 20, 20, 24, 24, 27, 27, 33, 44; 28:1, 6, 8, 16, 19, 19, 20, 21, 22, 24, 25, 25, 26; 26:5, 8, 9, 19, 18, 20, 23, 23, 26, 27, 33, 43, 44; 28:1, 6, 8, 16, 19, 19, 20, 21, 22, 23, 25, 25, 26; 25:3, 4, 4, 16, 24, 25, 25, 26; 26:5, 8, 9, 19, 18, 20, 23, 23, 26, 27, 27, 33, 43, 44; 28:1, 6, 8, 16, 19, 19, 20, 21, 22, 23, 28, 30

Ro 1:7, 8, 9, 11, 12, 12, 13, 15, 16, 19, 20, 21, 22, 26, 27, 27, 32, 32; 2:1, 1, 2, 3, 3, 4, 8, 9, 10, 18, 19, 21, 22, 22, 23, 28, 29; 3:2, 4, 8, 8, 9, 11, 11, 12, 19, 19, 22, 24, 25, 26, 28; 4:1, 4, 5, 5, 9, 11, 11, 12, 13, 16, 16, 16, 18, 21, 23, 24; 5:3, 8, 12, 14, 14, 16, 20, 21; 6:1, 2, 3, 4, 6, 7, 9, 10, 12, 13, 16, 17, 17; 7:1, 1, 3, 3, 4, 4, 6, 6, 13, 13, 13, 14, 15, 15, 15, 16, 16, 17, 17, 18, 18, 19, 19, 20, 20, 20, 21, 24; 8:3, 4, 5, 5, 8, 9, 11, 11, 16, 16, 17, 17, 18, 18, 19, 20, 28, 29, 32, 33, 34, 34, 34, 37, 38; 9:2, 3, 8, 11, 11, 16, 16, 17, 17, 20, 20, 25, 26, 30, 32; 10:1, 6, 7, 9, 9, 11, 14, 14, 1; 11:2, 3, 5, 5, 13, 14, 17, 17, 18, 19, 22, 23, 23, 24, 28, 29, 32; 12:1, 2, 2, 3, 6, 7, 8, 8, 8, 9, 15, 15; 13:1, 2, 3, 4, 4, 8, 11, 11; 14:1, 2, 3, 3, 3, 4, 4, 6, 9, 14, 14, 18, 20, 22, 22, 23; 15:1, 3, 4, 6, 8, 9, 12, 19, 23, 24, 25, 26, 27, 27, 28, 30, 31, 31, 31, 32; 16:2, 2, 5, 11, 18, 19, 25

1Co 1:2, 2, 5, 7, 8, 10, 10, 11, 12, 14, 15, 18, 21, 21, 26, 28, 29, 31, 31; 2:5, 6, 6, 9, 12, 12, 16, 16; 3:7, 7, 7, 8, 8, 11, 16, 18, 20; 4:2, 3, 4, 6, 6, 6, 7, 8, 9, 19; 5:7, 5, 5, 7, 7, 12, 13, 22, 25, 26, 26, 29, 29, 30, 30, 30, 31, 31, 32, 32, 33, 33, 34, 34, 35, 35, 36, 37, 37, 38, 38, 40; 8:1, 2, 4, 4, 4, 5, 5, 7, 9; 9:3, 9, 10, 10, 10, 10, 13, 14, 15, 15, 18, 19, 20, 20, 20, 21, 24; 8:3, 4, 5, 5, 8, 9, 11, 11, 16, 16, 17, 17, 18, 20, 21, 21, 22, 23, 24, 24, 25, 26, 27; 10:1, 1, 4, 4, 6, 12, 13, 17, 19, 19, 20, 20, 25, 27, 28, 30, 33; 11:2, 3, 5, 5, 13, 14, 17, 17, 18, 19, 22, 23, 28, 29, 32, 34; 12:1, 2, 3, 3, 3, 11, 12, 24, 25, 25; 13:2, 10, 10; 14:1, 2, 3, 4, 4, 5, 5, 5, 5, 11, 11, 13, 13, 16, 19, 21, 22, 23, 23, 24, 23, 24, 25, 27, 30, 31, 37, 37, 46, 46, 48, 50, 54, 58; 16:2, 4, 6, 10, 11, 15, 15, 16, 16, 17, 18, 19

2Co 1:4, 7, 8, 8, 9, 10, 11, 12, 14, 15, 17, 17, 23, 24; 2:1, 2, 3, 4, 4, 5, 7, 8, 9, 15, 15; 3:5, 7, 10, 10, 11, 11, 12, 13, 13, 17; 4:3, 7, 10, 11, 14, 15; 5:1, 3, 4, 4, 5, 6, 9, 10, 10, 12, 14, 15, 15, 19, 21; 6:1, 3, 15; 7:3, 6, 6, 7, 8, 8, 9, 9, 9, 11, 12, 12, 16; 8:2, 4, 6, 6, 7, 8, 9, 9, 11, 12, 12, 13, 14, 14, 14, 15, 15, 19, 20; 9:2, 3, 4, 4, 5, 8, 10; 10:2, 2, 5, 7, 7, 9, 11, 12, 15, 15, 17, 18; 11:2, 3, 4, 7, 9, 12, 12, 16, 17, 18, 28, 28, 31; 12:4, 6, 6, 8, 9, 13, 19, 20, 21; 13:2, 5, 6, 6, 7, 7, 7, 7

Gal 1:4, 6, 6, 7, 8, 9, 11, 13, 16, 23; 2:2, 4, 4, 5, 7, 8, 9, 9, 10, 12, 13, 14, 16, 16, 19; 3:1, 5, 7, 8, 10, 11, 12, 13, 14, 14, 17, 17, 17, 22, 22, 24, 25; 4:1, 5, 5, 9, 15, 17, 21, 22, 27, 27, 29, 29; 5:2, 3, 3, 7, 8, 10, 10, 17, 17, 21, 24; 6:6, 6, 7, 8, 8, 13, 14

Eph 1:4, 10, 12, 13, 13, 13, 17, 18, 21, 21, 23; 2:2, 7, 8, 10, 11, 11, 12, 16, 17; 3:3, 6, 8, 10, 13, 16, 17, 17, 19, 20, 20, 20; 4:1, 9, 9, 10, 10, 10, 14, 16, 17, 18, 21, 22, 24, 28, 28, 29, 29; 5:5, 13, 14, 15, 26, 27, 27, 28, 33; 6:3, 5, 8, 9, 11, 13, 19, 19, 20, 21, 22, 22, 24

Php 1:6, 9, 10, 10, 10, 12, 13, 17, 19, 20, 20, 25, 26, 27, 27, 28; 2:2, 10, 11, 11, 15, 16, 16, 19, 22, 24, 25, 26, 26, 28, 28; 3:4, 8, 9, 10, 12, 12, 18, 21; 4:2, 10, 11, 14, 15, 17, 22

Col 1:9, 10, 16, 16, 18, 19, 21, 24, 28; 2:1, 2, 14; 3:9, 10, 24, 25; 4:1, 1, 3, 4, 5, 6, 8, 12, 13, 13, 16, 16, 17

1Th 1:7, 7, 8; 2:1, 2, 10, 12, 13, 16; 3:3, 3, 4, 6, 10, 10; 4:1, 3, 6, 6, 8, 9, 10, 11, 12, 12, 13, 14, 15; 5:1, 2, 4, 4, 7, 7, 14, 15, 15, 21, 24, 27

2Th 1:3, 4, 4, 5, 6, 8, 8, 10, 10, 11, 12; 2:2, 2, 3, 3, 4, 4, 4, 4, 5, 6, 8, 10, 10, 11, 12; 3:1, 2, 4, 6, 6, 9, 10, 11, 12, 14, 14

1Ti 1:3, 3, 8, 9, 10, 10, 12, 15, 16, 16, 20; 2:1, 2, 2, 8, 9; 3:4, 13, 15; 4:1, 8, 8, 10, 14, 15, 15, 16; 5:3, 4, 5, 6, 7, 14, 16, 16, 16, 17, 18, 20, 20, 21, 25; 6:1, 2, 5, 9, 14, 17, 17, 18, 18, 19, 20

2Ti 1:3, 4, 5, 5, 6, 12, 12, 14, 15, 18; 2:1, 2, 4, 4, 6, 8, 10, 14, 15, 18, 19, 19, 22, 23, 25, 26; 3:1, 3, 12, 15, 17; 4:8, 8, 13, 16, 17, 17

Tit 1:2, 5, 5, 9, 13, 14, 15, 16; 2:2, 3, 4, 5, 8, 8, 10, 11, 12, 13, 14; 3:4, 7, 8, 8, 10, 11, 11, 13, 14, 15, 15

Phm 1:6, 8, 12, 13, 14, 15, 18, 21, 22

Heb 2:3, 6, 6, 8, 8, 9, 11, 14, 14, 14, 17, 18, 18; 3:2, 4, 10, 16, 17, 18, 18, 19; 4:2, 6, 10, 11, 13, 14, 14, 16; 5:1, 2, 2, 4, 5, 7, 7, 9, 12, 13, 14; 6:7, 8, 9, 10, 11, 12, 18, 19; 7:2, 5, 5, 6, 8, 8, 11, 14, 15, 21, 25; 8:3, 4, 4, 5, 7, 9, 10, 13, 13; 9:4, 4, 8, 9, 9, 11, 15, 15, 23, 25, 28; 10:2, 4, 9, 14, 15, 16, 20, 23, 26, 28, 30, 33, 34, 36, 37, 39; 11:3, 3, 4, 5, 5, 6, 6, 6, 6, 13, 14, 16, 17, 18, 18, 19, 19, 28, 31, 35, 40; 12:1, 2, 3, 10, 13, 17, 18, 18, 19, 19, 20, 21, 24, 24, 25, 25, 25, 27, 27, 27; 13:3, 6, 9, 9, 12, 15, 17, 17, 17, 17, 19, 20, 20, 21, 23, 24

Jas 1:3, 4, 5, 6, 7, 7, 9, 10, 12, 18; 2:3, 5, 7, 11, 12, 13, 19, 20, 24; 3:1, 3, 6, 17, 18; 4:1, 3, 4, 5, 5, 9, 11, 12, 13, 14, 15, 15, 17; 5:1, 11, 16, 17, 20

1Pe 1:4, 7, 7, 10, 11, 12, 12, 18, 21, 21, 22; 2:2, 3, 6, 9, 12, 14, 14, 15, 18, 21, 23, 24; 3:1, 3, 4, 7, 9, 9, 10, 10, 12, 13, 13, 15, 15, 16, 16, 17, 18, 20; 4:1, 2, 4, 5, 6, 6, 11, 13, 17, 17, 19; 5:1, 4, 6, 9, 9, 10, 12, 13, 14

2Pe 1:1, 3, 3, 4, 4, 8, 9, 9, 14, 15, 19, 19, 20; 2:1, 4, 6, 8, 9, 10, 12; 3:1, 3, 4, 5, 6, 8, 9, 9, 10, 11, 14, 14, 15, 16

1Jn 1:1, 2, 3, 3, 4, 5, 6, 8, 10; 2:1, 3, 4, 5, 6, 9, 10, 11, 11, 13, 14, 15, 16, 16, 18, 19, 19, 21, 22, 22, 22, 23, 24, 24, 25, 26, 27, 28, 29, 29; 3:1, 2, 3, 5, 7, 8, 8, 10, 11, 11, 12, 14, 14, 15, 19, 22, 23, 23, 24, 24; 4:2, 2, 3, 3, 3, 4, 4, 4, 6, 7, 8, 9, 9, 10, 10, 10, 11, 12, 12, 13, 13, 13, 14, 14, 16, 16, 17, 18, 20, 21; 5:1, 1, 1, 2, 3, 4, 5, 5, 6, 6, 7, 8, 10, 10, 11, 12, 12, 13, 13, 13, 13, 14, 14, 15, 16, 16, 18, 18, 19, 20, 20, 20

2Jn 1:1, 4, 5, 6, 7, 7, 8, 8, 9, 11, 12

3Jn 1:2, 3, 4, 7, 8, 10, 11, 11, 11, 12

Jude 1:1, 3, 5, 5, 15, 18, 24

Rev 1:2, 3, 5, 9, 12, 18; 2:1, 6, 7, 7, 10, 11, 11, 14, 15, 17, 17, 17, 20, 22, 23, 25, 26, 29; 3:1, 1, 2, 5, 6, 7, 7, 7, 9, 10, 11, 11, 12, 13, 15, 17, 18, 18, 18, 18, 21, 22; 4:3, 9, 10, 10; 5:1, 7, 12, 13, 13, 14; 6:2, 4, 4, 4, 5, 8, 9, 10, 11, 11, 16; 7:1, 15; 8:3; 9:4, 5, 5, 17, 20; 10:6, 6, 6, 6; 11:1, 6, 7, 10, 10, 18, 18, 18; 12:6, 9, 12, 12, 13, 14, 15; 13:6, 8, 12, 13, 15, 15, 17, 17, 18; 14:3, 6, 7, 8, 12, 13, 15, 15, 16; 15:2, 4; 16:12, 14, 15; 17:1, 7, 8, 8, 8, 11, 14, 18; 18:4, 4, 10, 14, 16, 19, 19, 21, 24; 19:4, 5, 8, 10, 11, 12, 15, 17, 18, 18, 19, 20, 20, 20, 21; 20:3, 4, 4, 6, 6, 6, 10, 14, 15, 17, 27; 22:7, 11, 11, 11, 14, 14, 17, 17, 18, 18

THE (64039)

Ge 1:1, 1, 1, 2, 2, 2, 2, 2, 4, 4, 4, 5, 5, 5,

5, 5, 6, 6, 6, 6, 7, 7, 7, 7, 8, 8, 8, 9, 9, 9, 10, 10, 10, 11, 11, 11, 11, 12, 12, 13, 13, 13, 14, 14, 14, 14, 15, 15, 15, 16, 16, 16, 16, 16, 17, 17, 17, 18, 18, 18, 18, 19, 19, 20, 20, 20, 20, 21, 22, 22, 22, 23, 23, 23, 24, 24, 24, 24, 25, 25, 25, 26, 26, 26, 26, 26, 26, 27, 28, 28, 28, 28, 28, 29, 29, 29, 29, 29, 30, 30, 30, 31, 31, 31; 2:1, 1, 1, 2, 2, 3, 4, 4, 4, 4, 4, 4, 5, 5, 5, 5, 5, 5, 6, 6, 6, 7, 7, 7, 7, 8, 8, 9, 9, 9, 9, 9, 10, 11, 11, 12, 12, 13, 13, 13, 14, 14, 14, 14, 15, 15, 15, 16, 16, 16, 16, 16, 17, 17, 17, 18, 18, 19, 19, 19, 19, 20, 20, 20, 21, 21, 22, 22, 22, 22, 25; 3:1, 1, 1, 1, 1, 2, 2, 2, 2, 2, 3, 3, 3, 4, 4, 4, 6, 6, 7, 8, 8, 8, 8, 8, 8, 8, 9, 11, 11, 12, 12, 13, 13, 13, 14, 14, 14, 15, 16, 17, 17, 17, 17, 17, 18, 18, 18, 19, 19, 20, 21, 22, 22, 22, 23, 23, 23, 24, 24, 24; 4:1, 2, 3, 3, 3, 4, 4, 4, 6, 7, 8, 9, 10, 10, 11, 12, 12, 13, 14, 14, 14, 15, 15, 16, 16, 16, 16, 17, 17, 19, 19, 20, 20, 21, 22, 22, 26, 26; 5:1, 1, 1, 1, 2, 4, 5, 8, 11, 14, 17, 20, 23, 27, 29, 31; 6:1, 1, 2, 2, 3, 4, 4, 4, 5, 5, 5, 6, 7, 8, 9, 9, 11, 11, 11, 11, 11, 12, 12, 13, 13, 13, 14, 14, 14, 14, 15, 16, 17, 17, 17, 17, 18, 18, 19, 20, 20, 20, 21, 22, 22, 22; 7:1, 1, 1, 2, 2, 3, 3, 4, 4, 5, 5, 6, 6, 7, 8, 8, 9, 9, 9, 10, 10, 11, 11, 11, 12, 13, 13, 13, 14, 14, 14, 14, 16, 16, 16, 16, 16, 17, 17, 17, 18, 18, 18, 18, 19, 19, 20, 20, 21, 21, 21; 8:1, 1, 1, 1, 2, 2, 2, 3, 3, 3, 3, 4, 4, 4, 4, 5, 5, 5, 5, 5, 6, 6, 6, 7, 7, 8, 8, 9, 9, 9, 9, 10, 10, 11, 11, 11, 11, 13, 13, 13, 14, 14, 14, 14, 17, 17, 19, 20, 20, 21, 21, 21; 9:1, 2, 2, 2, 2, 3, 3, 4, 5, 5, 5, 6, 6, 6, 6, 6, 6, 7, 7, 8, 8, 8, 9, 10, 10, 11, 11, 11, 12, 12, 13, 13, 14, 14, 14, 14, 16, 16, 16, 16, 16, 17, 17, 17, 18, 18, 18, 18, 19, 19, 20, 20, 20, 21, 21; 10:2, 3, 3, 5, 7, 7, 7, 8, 8, 11, 12, 12, 16, 16, 16, 17, 17, 18, 18; 11:2, 3, 3, 3, 3, 3, 4, 4, 4, 5, 5, 6, 6, 7, 7, 7, 8, 8, 8, 8, 9, 9, 10, 11, 11, 11, 11, 11, 12, 12, 13, 13, 13, 14, 14, 14, 14; 12:1, 1, 2, 3, 5, 5, 5, 6, 6, 6, 6, 6, 7, 7, 8, 8, 9, 9, 10, 11, 11, 12, 13, 13, 15, 16, 16, 16, 17, 17, 17, 17, 18, 18, 18, 19, 19, 19, 20, 20, 20; 13:1, 2, 2, 3, 3, 5, 5, 7, 7, 7, 8, 8, 9, 10, 10, 11, 11, 12, 12, 13, 13, 14, 14, 15, 15, 16, 16, 16, 16, 17, 17, 17, 18; 14:1, 2, 2, 2, 3, 3, 3, 4, 4, 4, 4, 5, 5, 5, 5, 6, 6, 6, 7, 7, 7, 7, 8, 8, 8, 8, 9, 10, 10, 10, 11, 11, 11, 12, 12, 13, 13, 14, 14, 14, 14, 14, 16, 17, 17, 17, 18, 18; 15:1, 2, 3, 4, 4, 5, 5, 6, 7, 7, 7, 8, 8, 8, 10, 10, 11, 11, 11, 13, 13, 13, 14; 16:2, 3, 3, 5, 7, 7, 7, 7, 8, 8, 9, 10, 11, 12, 12, 13, 13, 14, 24; 15:1, 2, 3, 4, 4, 5, 6, 7, 7, 10, 10, 11, 12, 16, 16, 16, 16, 17, 18, 18, 18, 18, 19, 19, 20, 20, 20, 20, 21, 21; 16:2, 2, 3, 3, 5, 7, 7, 7, 7, 8, 8, 9, 11, 11, 11, 12, 13, 13, 14; 17:1, 1, 8, 8, 11, 11, 12, 12, 13, 13, 14; 17:1, 1, 8, 26, 27, 27, 27; 18:1, 1, 1, 1, 2, 2, 4, 6, 6, 7, 8, 8, 9, 10, 10, 11, 13, 14, 14, 14, 16, 16, 16, 18, 18, 19, 19, 20, 20, 21, 22, 22, 23, 23, 24, 24, 25, 25, 25, 26, 26, 27, 28, 28, 30, 31, 32, 33; 19:1, 1, 2, 4, 4, 4, 4, 4, 5, 5, 6, 6, 8, 8, 9, 10, 10, 11, 11, 11, 12, 12, 13, 13, 13, 14, 14, 15, 15, 15, 15, 16, 16, 16, 16, 17, 19, 21, 22, 23, 23, 24, 24, 25, 25, 25, 25, 27, 27, 28, 28, 29, 29, 29, 30, 31, 31, 32, 32, 32, 33, 37, 37, 37, 37, 38, 38, 38, 38; 20:1, 3, 6, 16, 16, 18; 21:1, 1, 2, 3, 8, 8, 9, 9, 10, 11, 12, 13, 13, 14, 14, 14, 15, 15, 15, 16, 16, 16, 16, 17, 17, 17, 17, 17, 18, 18, 19, 19, 19, 20, 20, 21, 22, 23, 23, 28, 32, 32, 32, 33, 33, 34; 22:2, 2, 3, 3, 3, 4, 5, 6, 6, 7, 7, 8, 9, 10, 10, 11, 11, 12, 12, 12, 12, 16, 17, 17, 17, 17, 17, 18, 21; 23:1, 1, 2, 2, 3, 5, 5, 7, 7, 8, 8, 9, 9, 10, 10, 10, 11, 11, 11, 11, 11, 12, 12, 13, 14, 14, 14, 16, 16, 17, 17, 20, 20, 21, 21, 22, 24, 24, 26, 26, 27, 27, 27, 28; 24:1, 1, 2, 4, 4, 5, 5, 6, 8, 9, 9, 9, 11, 11, 12, 12, 14, 16, 16, 16, 17, 17, 20, 21, 22, 23, 24, 25, 25, 26, 26, 27, 28, 28; 25:3, 4, 6, 6, 6, 7, 8, 8, 9, 9, 9, 10, 11, 11, 12, 12, 13, 13, 13, 14, 14, 14, 14, 16, 16, 17, 17, 17, 18, 18, 19, 20, 20, 20, 20, 21, 21, 22, 22, 23, 23, 23, 23, 25, 27, 27, 29, 32; 26:1, 1, 1, 2, 2, 3, 4, 4, 4, 7, 7, 7, 8, 10, 12, 13, 14, 14, 15, 15, 18, 18, 18, 18, 20, 20, 20, 20, 21, 21, 22, 22, 24, 24, 24, 25, 25, 26, 28, 29, 29, 31, 32, 32, 33, 33, 34, 34, 34; 27:2, 3, 5, 7, 9, 9, 15, 16, 16, 16, 18, 19, 20, 22, 22, 27, 27, 27, 28, 28, 28, 30, 34, 34, 39, 39, 40, 41, 41, 46, 46, 46, 46; 28:1, 2, 2, 4, 4, 5, 5, 6, 8, 9, 9, 11, 12, 12, 13, 13, 13, 14, 14, 14, 14, 14,

14, 16, 17, 17, 18, 18, 18, 19, 19, 19, 21, 22; 29:1, 1, 1, 2, 2, 2, 3, 3, 3, 3, 3, 3, 5, 6, 7, 7, 8, 8, 8, 8, 10, 10, 10, 10, 13, 14, 16, 16, 16, 20, 22, 22, 23, 25, 25, 26, 27, 31, 32, 33, 35; 30:2, 2, 13, 14, 14, 16, 16, 17, 19, 24, 27, 30, 32, 32, 32, 32, 33, 33, 35, 35, 35, 35, 35, 36, 37, 37, 37, 38, 38, 38, 38, 39, 39, 40, 40, 40, 40, 40, 41, 41, 41, 41, 41, 41, 42, 42, 42, 43; 31:1, 2, 3, 3, 4, 5, 8, 8, 8, 9, 10, 10, 10, 10, 11, 12, 12, 13, 13, 16, 18, 18, 19, 20, 21, 23, 24, 25, 25, 26, 27, 29, 33, 34, 34, 34, 35, 35, 38, 39, 40, 40, 40, 42, 42, 42, 46, 48, 49, 53, 53, 53, 53, 54, 54, 55; 32:1, 2, 3, 6, 7, 7, 7, 8, 12, 16, 17, 19, 19, 19, 20, 20, 21, 21, 22, 23, 24, 24, 25, 25, 26, 30, 30, 31, 32, 32, 32; 33:1, 1, 2, 3, 5, 5, 6, 8, 10, 13, 19; 34:1, 1, 1, 2, 2, 2, 3, 3, 5, 5, 6, 7, 7, 7, 8, 10, 12, 13, 13, 14, 15, 15, 17, 18, 18, 19, 19; 35:1, 2, 3, 4, 4, 4, 5, 5, 6, 7, 8, 12, 13, 14, 15, 15, 17, 19, 19, 20, 20, 21, 22, 23, 24, 25, 26, 27, 28, 29; 36:1, 2, 2, 2, 2, 2, 5, 5, 6, 6, 6, 6, 7, 9, 9, 9, 10, 10, 10, 10, 10, 11, 12, 13, 13, 14, 14, 15, 15, 15, 16, 16, 17, 17, 17, 17, 17, 18, 18, 18, 19, 20, 20, 20, 20, 21, 21, 21, 21, 21, 22, 22, 22, 23, 24, 24, 24, 24, 25, 25, 25, 26, 27, 28, 29, 29, 30, 30, 31, 31, 32, 32, 35, 37, 38, 38, 39, 39, 39, 40, 40, 40, 43, 43, 43, 43; 37:1, 1, 2, 2, 2, 2, 2, 2, 3, 5, 7, 8, 9, 9, 9, 10, 11, 13, 14, 14, 15, 15, 17, 22, 24, 27, 28, 28, 29, 29, 31, 31, 32, 33, 34, 36, 36; 38:7, 7, 9, 9, 9, 10, 10, 12, 12, 14, 17, 19, 20, 22, 24, 25, 25, 25, 26, 26, 27, 27, 28, 28, 29, 30, 30, 30, 30; 35:1, 2, 3, 4, 4, 4, 5, 5, 6, 7, 7, 8, 12, 12, 13, 14, 15, 15, 17, 17, 19, 20, 20, 21, 21, 22, 22, 23, 23, 23, 23; 40:1, 1, 1, 2, 2, 2, 3, 3, 3, 3, 4, 4, 5, 5, 5, 6, 7, 9, 10, 10, 11, 11, 12, 13, 15, 15, 16, 16, 17, 17, 17, 17, 17, 18, 18, 19, 20, 20, 20; 41:1, 1, 2, 3, 3, 3, 4, 4, 5, 6, 7, 7, 8, 9, 10, 10, 11, 12, 13, 14, 17, 18, 19, 20, 20, 20, 21, 21, 22, 23; 41:1, 1, 2, 3, 3, 4, 4, 8, 8, 11, 12, 14, 17, 17, 18, 19, 20, 20, 20, 20, 21, 21, 23, 24, 25, 26, 27, 27, 27, 28; 46:1, 2, 2, 3, 5, 6, 6, 8, 9, 10, 10, 11, 12, 14, 15, 15, 16, 17, 17, 19, 20, 20, 21, 27, 28, 31, 32, 34, 34; 47:1, 1, 4, 4, 4, 6, 6, 6, 6, 6, 9, 9, 9, 9, 11, 11, 13, 13, 13, 13, 13, 14, 14, 14, 15, 15, 15, 15, 17, 17, 18, 18, 19, 20, 20, 20, 20, 21, 21, 22, 22, 22, 23, 23, 24, 24, 24, 24, 25, 26, 26, 26, 26, 27, 27, 28, 28, 29, 31; 48:2, 3, 5, 6, 7, 7, 7, 7, 10, 12, 14, 14, 16, 16, 16, 16, 17, 18, 21, 22; 49:1, 3, 3, 3, 8, 9, 10, 10, 10, 11, 11, 13, 13, 13, 15, 16, 17, 17, 19, 22, 23, 24, 24, 24, 24, 25, 25, 25, 26, 26, 26, 26, 26, 26, 27, 27, 28, 29, 29, 30, 30, 30, 30, 32, 32, 32, 33, 33; 50:2, 2, 3, 3, 4, 4, 4, 5, 5, 5, 5, 5, 7, 7, 7, 8, 8, 8, 11, 11, 13, 13, 13, 15, 17, 17, 17, 19, 23, 23, 24, 25;

Ex 1:1, 5, 5, 7, 7, 9, 9, 10, 12, 12, 13, 14, 15, 15, 15, 15, 15, 16, 16, 17, 17, 17, 18, 18, 18, 18, 19, 19, 19, 19, 20, 20, 21; 2:1, 2, 3, 3, 3, 5, 5, 5, 5, 6, 6, 6, 6, 7, 8, 8, 9, 9, 10, 10, 12, 13, 13, 13, 13, 14, 14, 15, 15, 16, 16, 16, 17, 17, 19, 19, 20, 21, 23, 23, 23, 25; 3:1, 1, 1, 1, 1, 1, 2, 2, 2, 3, 3, 3, 4, 4, 5, 6, 6, 6, 7, 7, 8, 8, 8, 8, 8, 8, 9, 9, 9, 10, 12, 13, 13, 14, 15, 15, 15, 16, 16, 16, 17, 17, 17, 17, 17, 18, 18, 18, 19, 20, 21, 22; 4:1, 2, 3, 3, 4, 4, 4, 5, 6, 7, 7, 8, 8, 9, 9, 9, 10, 11, 11, 11, 11, 11, 13, 14, 14, 14, 16, 16, 16, 17, 17, 20, 20, 21, 22, 22, 24, 24, 25, 26, 27, 27, 28, 28, 28, 29, 30, 30, 30, 30, 31, 31; 5:1, 1, 8, 9, 10, 10, 10, 12, 13, 14, 14, 15, 6:1, 6, 13, 14, 14, 15, 16, 16, 16, 17, 18, 18, 19, 20, 21, 21, 22, 6:1, 2, 3, 4, 5, 5, 5, 6, 6, 6, 7, 7, 8, 8, 9, 10, 11, 12, 13, 13, 13, 15, 15, 16, 16, 17, 17, 18, 18, 19, 20, 20, 21, 22, 24,

28, 29, 29, 30; 7:1, 2, 3, 4, 4, 5, 5, 10, 11, 11, 11, 13, 14, 14, 15, 15, 15, 15, 16, 16, 16, 17, 17, 17, 17, 18, 18, 18, 18, 18, 19, 19, 19, 20, 20, 20, 20, 20, 20, 21, 21, 21, 21, 21, 21, 22, 22, 22, 24, 24, 24, 24, 25; 8:1, 1, 3, 3, 4, 5, 5, 5, 5, 6, 6, 7, 8, 9, 9, 10, 11, 11, 12, 12, 13, 13, 13, 13, 14, 15, 16, 16, 17, 17, 17, 17, 18, 18, 19, 19, 19, 20, 20, 20, 21, 21, 21, 21, 21, 21, 22, 22, 24, 24, 24, 24, 24, 25; 8:1, 1, 3, 3, 4, 5, 5, 5, 6, 6, 7, 9, 9, 9, 10; 12:1, 1, 3, 3, 5, 5, 6, 6, 6, 6, 6, 6, 7, 9, 9, 9, 10; 12:1, 1, 2, 2, 3, 3, 3, 3, 4, 4, 5, 5, 6, 6, 6, 6, 7, 7, 7, 7, 8, 8, 9, 9, 10; 12:1, 1, 6, 6, 7, 7, 7, 7, 8, 8, 9, 9, 9, 10, 11, 12, 12, 12, 13, 13, 13, 13, 14, 14, 15, 15, 16, 16, 16, 17, 17, 18, 18, 18, 19, 20, 21, 21, 22, 22, 22, 23, 23, 23, 23, 23, 25, 25, 26, 26, 27, 27, 27, 27, 27, 27, 27, 27, 28, 28, 29, 29, 30, 30, 30, 30, 30, 31, 31, 31, 31, 31; 15:1, 1, 1, 1, 1, 2, 3, 3, 4, 4, 5, 5, 7, 8, 8, 8, 8, 9, 9, 10, 11, 12, 13, 13, 13, 15, 16, 16, 17, 17, 17, 17, 18, 18, 19, 19, 19, 19, 19, 19, 19, 19, 20, 20, 21, 21, 22, 23, 23, 24, 25, 25, 25, 26, 26, 26, 27; 16:1, 1, 1, 1, 1, 1, 2, 2, 3, 3, 4, 5, 6, 7, 7, 7, 8, 8, 9, 9, 10, 10, 10, 10, 10, 10, 10, 10, 10, 11, 12, 13, 13, 14, 14, 14, 14, 15, 15, 15, 16, 16, 16, 19, 20, 21, 22, 23, 23, 24, 24, 25, 26, 26, 26, 26, 27, 16:1, 1, 1, 1, 1, 2, 2, 3, 3, 3, 3, 4, 5, 6, 7, 7, 8, 9, 9, 10, 10, 10, 11, 12, 13, 13, 14, 14, 15, 15, 16, 16, 16, 16, 16, 17, 17, 17, 17, 18, 19, 19, 19, 19, 20, 20, 20, 21, 22, 22, 22, 23, 23, 24, 24, 25; 20:2, 2, 2, 4, 4, 4, 4, 5, 5, 5, 5, 5, 7, 7, 7, 8, 10, 10, 10, 11, 11, 11, 11, 11, 18, 18, 18, 18, 18; 18, 20, 21, 21, 22, 22; 21:1, 2, 4, 5, 6, 6, 6, 9, 19, 22, 22, 23, 24, 24, 24, 28, 28, 29, 29, 30, 32, 32, 34, 34, 34, 34, 35, 35, 35, 36, 36; 22:3, 4, 5, 6, 6, 6, 6, 7, 7, 8, 8, 8, 9, 9, 9, 11, 12, 14, 15, 17, 20, 21, 24, 26, 28, 28, 29, 29, 30, 31; 23:1, 5, 6, 7, 7, 8, 8, 8, 9, 9, 10, 11, 11, 11, 12, 13, 14, 15, 15, 15, 16, 16, 16, 16, 16, 16, 16, 17, 17, 18, 18, 19, 19, 19, 20, 20, 23, 23, 23, 23, 25, 25, 26, 27, 28, 28, 29, 29, 30, 30, 31, 31, 31, 31, 31, 31, 31; 24:1, 1, 2, 2, 3, 3, 3, 3, 4, 4, 4, 4, 5, 5, 6, 6, 7, 7, 7, 8, 8, 8, 9, 10, 10, 11, 12, 12, 13, 14, 14, 16, 16, 16, 16, 17, 17, 17, 17, 18, 18; 25:1, 2, 3, 6, 7, 7, 9, 9, 9, 9, 10, 10, 10, 11, 11, 12, 12, 12, 12, 12, 13, 13, 13, 13, 14, 15, 16, 16,

(column 1, bottom left)

THE (64039)

Ge 1:1, 1, 2, 2, 2, 2, 2, 2, 4, 4, 4, 5, 5, 5,

Idx

22, 23, 23, 23, 24, 24, 26, 26, 26, 27, 27,
27, 27, 27, 27, 27, 27, 28, 28, 28, 29, 29, 29,
30, 30, 30, 32, 33, 33, 33, 33, 33, 33, 33,
33, 34, 34, 34, 34, 35, 35, 35, 35, 35, 35,
35, 35, 35, 36, 36, 36, 37; 27:1, 1, 2, 2, 2, 3,
4, 4, 5, 5, 5, 5, 5, 6, 7, 7, 7, 7, 7, 7, 8, 9, 9,
9, 9, 10, 10, 10, 11, 11, 11, 12, 12, 12,
13, 13, 13, 14, 14, 14, 15, 15, 16, 16, 17, 17, 18,
18, 18, 18, 19, 19, 19, 19, 19, 19, 20, 20,
20, 21, 21, 21, 21, 21, 21, 21; 28:1, 1, 1,
3, 4, 4, 6, 7, 7, 8, 8, 8, 8, 9, 9, 10, 10, 10,
11, 11, 11, 11, 11, 12, 12, 12, 12, 12, 14,
14, 14, 15, 15, 15, 16, 16, 17, 17, 17, 18, 19,
20, 21, 21, 21, 21, 21, 21, 21; 28:1, 1, 1,
23, 24, 24, 24, 24, 25, 25, 25, 25, 26,
26, 26, 26, 26, 27, 27, 27, 27, 27, 27, 28,
28, 28, 28, 28, 28, 28, 29, 29, 29, 29,
29, 30, 30, 30, 30, 30, 30, 31, 31, 31, 32,
32, 32, 32, 33, 33, 34, 34, 35, 35, 36, 36,
37, 37, 37, 38, 38, 38, 38, 39, 39, 39, 41,
42, 42, 43, 43, 43, 43; 29:1, 1, 3, 3, 3, 4,
4, 4, 5, 5, 5, 5, 5, 5, 5, 5, 6, 6, 7, 9,
10, 10, 10, 10, 11, 11, 11, 11, 11, 12, 12, 12,
12, 12, 12, 12, 12, 13, 13, 13, 13, 13, 13,
14, 14, 14, 14, 15, 15, 16, 16, 16, 17, 17, 18,
18, 18, 18, 19, 19, 19, 20, 20, 20, 20, 20,
20, 20, 20, 20, 21, 21, 21, 21, 22, 22, 22,
22, 22, 22, 22, 22, 22, 22, 22, 23, 23, 23, 24,
24, 24, 25, 25, 25, 26, 26, 26, 27, 27, 27,
27, 27, 27, 28, 28, 28, 28, 29, 29, 30, 30,
31, 31, 31, 32, 32, 32, 32, 32, 32, 32, 33,
34, 34, 34, 34, 34, 36, 37, 37, 38, 38, 39,
39, 39, 40, 40, 40, 40, 41, 41, 41, 41, 41,
42, 42, 42, 43, 43, 43, 43, 44, 44, 44, 45, 46,
46, 46; 30:2, 2, 2, 2, 2, 3, 3, 3, 4, 4, 4, 4,
5, 6, 6, 6, 6, 7, 8, 8, 10, 10, 10, 10, 10,
11, 12, 12, 12, 13, 13, 13, 13, 14, 14, 15, 15,
15, 16, 16, 16, 16, 16, 16, 17, 18, 18,
18, 20, 20, 20, 22, 24, 24, 24, 25, 25, 26,
26, 26, 26, 27, 27, 27, 28, 28, 30, 31, 32,
34, 35, 35, 36, 36, 36, 37, 37, 37; 31:1,
2, 2, 2, 3, 6, 6, 6, 7, 7, 7, 7, 7, 7, 7, 8, 9,
8, 9, 9, 10, 10, 10, 10, 11, 11, 12, 13,
13, 14, 15, 15, 15, 15, 16, 16, 16, 17, 17,
17, 18; 32:1, 1, 1, 1, 1, 2, 2, 3, 3, 4, 5, 6,
6, 7, 7, 8, 9, 11, 11, 11, 12, 12, 12, 12, 13,
14, 14, 15, 15, 15, 15, 15, 16, 16, 16,
16, 16, 17, 17, 17, 17, 18, 18, 19, 19, 19,
19, 19, 20, 20, 20, 20, 22, 22, 23, 23, 24,
25, 26, 26, 26, 26, 27, 27, 27, 28, 28, 29,
30, 30, 30, 31, 33, 34, 34, 34, 34, 35, 35;
33:1, 1, 1, 1, 2, 2, 2, 2, 2, 3, 3, 3, 4, 5, 5,
5, 6, 6, 7, 7, 7, 7, 7, 7, 7, 7, 8, 8, 8, 9,
9, 9, 9, 9, 10, 10, 10, 10, 10, 11, 11, 11, 11,
12, 16, 16, 16, 17, 19, 19, 19, 22; 34:1, 1,
1, 1, 2, 2, 2, 2, 3, 3, 4, 4, 4, 4, 4, 5, 5, 5, 5,
6, 6, 6, 7, 7, 7, 7, 7, 7, 8, 10, 10, 10,
10, 11, 11, 11, 11, 11, 11, 11, 11, 11, 11,
14, 15, 15, 18, 18, 18, 19, 20, 20, 20, 21, 21,
22, 22, 22, 23, 23, 23, 23, 24, 24, 25, 25,
25, 25, 25, 25, 26, 26, 26, 27, 28, 28, 28,
28, 28, 28, 29, 29, 29, 30, 30, 30, 31, 33,
34, 34, 35, 35, 35, 35; 36:1, 1, 1, 1, 2, 2,
3, 3, 3, 3, 4, 4, 4, 5, 5, 5, 6, 6, 6, 6, 6,
7, 7, 8, 8, 9, 9, 9, 9, 9, 10, 10, 10, 10, 10,
11, 11, 12, 12, 12, 12, 12, 13, 13, 14, 14,
15, 15, 15, 17, 17, 17, 17, 17, 17, 17, 18, 19,
20, 21, 21, 22, 22, 23, 23, 24, 25, 25, 25,
27, 27, 27, 28, 28, 29, 29, 29, 31, 31, 31,
32, 32, 32, 32, 33, 33, 33, 33, 34, 34,
34, 34, 38; 37:1, 1, 1, 1, 3, 3, 3, 5, 5, 5, 5,
5, 6, 6, 6, 6, 7, 7, 7, 7, 7, 8, 8, 8, 9, 9, 9,
10, 10, 10, 10, 12, 13, 13, 13, 13, 14, 14,
14, 14, 15, 15, 16, 16, 16, 17, 17, 17, 18,
18, 18, 18, 19, 19, 19, 19, 19, 20, 21, 21, 21,
22, 24, 24, 25, 26, 27, 27, 27, 28, 28, 28,
29, 29, 29, 29, 29, 29, 29, 29; 38:1, 1,
1, 1, 2, 2, 2, 2, 3, 3, 3, 3, 3, 3, 3, 4, 4,
4, 5, 5, 5, 6, 7, 7, 7, 7, 7, 8, 8, 8, 8, 8,
8, 9, 9, 10, 11, 11, 11, 12, 12, 13; 39:1, 1,
3, 3, 4, 5, 5, 5, 6, 6, 7, 7, 7, 7, 8, 8,
9, 9, 9, 10, 10, 11, 12, 13, 14, 14, 14, 14,
14, 15, 15, 16, 16, 16, 17, 17, 17, 17, 18,
18, 18, 18, 19, 19, 19, 19, 19, 19, 20, 20,
20, 20, 20, 20, 21, 21, 21, 21, 21, 21,
21, 22, 22, 23, 23, 23, 24, 24, 24, 24, 24, 25,
25, 25, 25, 26, 26, 26, 29, 30, 30, 30, 30,
31, 31, 32, 32, 32, 32, 32, 33, 33, 33, 33,
34, 34, 34, 35, 35, 35, 35, 36, 36, 36, 37,
37, 37, 37, 37, 38, 38, 38, 39, 39, 40,
40, 40, 40, 40, 40, 40, 40, 41, 41, 41,
41, 41, 41, 42, 42, 42, 43, 43; 40:1, 2, 2,
2, 2, 2, 3, 3, 3, 3, 4, 4, 4, 4, 4, 5, 5, 5, 5,
5, 5, 6, 6, 6, 6, 7, 7, 7, 7, 7, 8, 8, 8, 9,
9, 9, 10, 10, 10, 12, 12, 12, 13, 13, 13, 13,
15, 16, 17, 17, 17, 17, 17, 18, 18, 18, 19,
19, 19, 19, 20, 20, 20, 20, 20, 20, 21, 21,
21, 21, 21, 21, 22, 22, 22, 22, 22, 22, 22,
22, 23, 23, 23, 24, 24, 24, 24, 24, 25,

25, 25, 26, 26, 26, 26, 27, 28, 28, 28, 29,
29, 29, 29, 29, 29, 29, 29, 30, 30, 30, 30,
32, 32, 32, 32, 33, 33, 33, 33, 33, 33, 34,
34, 34, 34, 34, 35, 35, 35, 35, 35, 35, 36,
36, 36, 37, 37, 38, 38, 38, 38, 38;
Lev 1:1, 1, 1, 2, 2, 2, 2, 2, 3, 3, 3, 3, 4, 4,
5, 5, 5, 5, 5, 5, 5, 5, 6, 7, 7, 7, 7, 7, 8,
8, 8, 8, 8, 8, 9, 9, 9, 10, 10, 10, 10, 11,
11, 11, 11, 12, 12, 12, 12, 13, 13, 13, 13,
14, 14, 14, 14, 14, 15, 15, 15, 15, 16, 16,
16, 16, 17, 17, 17, 17, 17, 17, 17; 2:1, 2, 2, 2,
2, 2, 2, 2, 2, 3, 3, 3, 4, 4, 7, 8, 8, 8, 8,
9, 9, 9, 10, 10, 10, 11, 11, 12, 12, 12, 12,
13, 13, 14, 14, 14, 14, 16, 16, 16, 16, 16, 16;
3:1, 1, 2, 2, 2, 2, 2, 2, 2, 3, 3, 3, 3, 3, 3, 3,
4, 4, 4, 4, 4, 4, 5, 5, 5, 5, 6, 6, 7, 8, 8,
8, 8, 8, 9, 9, 9, 9, 9, 9, 9, 10, 10,
10, 10, 10, 10, 11, 11, 11, 11, 11, 12, 13,
13, 13, 13, 13, 14, 14, 14, 14, 15, 15, 16;
4:1, 2, 2, 2, 2, 3, 3, 3, 4, 4, 4, 4, 4, 4, 4, 4,
5, 5, 5, 6, 6, 6, 6, 6, 6, 7, 7, 7, 7, 7, 7,
7, 7, 7, 7, 7, 7, 7, 7, 7, 8, 8, 8, 8, 8, 8,
9, 9, 9, 9, 9, 10, 10, 10, 10, 10, 11, 11,
11, 11, 11, 12, 12, 12, 13, 13, 13, 13, 13, 13,
14, 14, 14, 14, 14, 14, 15, 15, 15, 15, 15,
15, 16, 16, 16, 16, 17, 17, 17, 18, 18, 18,
19, 20, 20, 20, 21, 21, 21, 21, 22, 22, 23,
24, 24, 24, 24, 24, 25, 25, 25, 25, 25,
25, 26, 26, 26, 26, 27, 27, 27, 27, 28, 28, 29,
29, 29, 29, 30, 30, 30, 30, 31, 31, 31, 31,
31, 32, 32, 32, 33, 33, 33, 33, 33, 35, 35;
5:1, 2, 3, 6, 6, 6, 6, 6, 6,
7, 7, 8, 8, 9, 9, 9, 9, 9, 9, 9, 10, 10, 10,
11, 11, 12, 12, 12, 12, 13, 13, 13, 14, 15,
15, 15, 15, 15, 15, 15, 16, 16, 16, 16, 16, 16;
16, 17, 17, 18, 18, 18, 19; 6:1, 2, 4, 4, 5,
5, 5, 6, 6, 6, 7, 7, 9, 9, 9, 9, 9, 9, 9,
10, 10, 10, 10, 10, 10, 11, 11, 12, 12, 12,
12, 12, 12, 13, 13, 14, 14, 14, 14, 14, 14,
16, 17, 17, 18, 18, 18, 19; 6:1, 2, 4, 4, 5,
5, 5, 6, 6, 6, 7, 7, 8, 9, 9, 9, 9, 9, 9, 9,
10, 10, 10, 10, 10, 10, 11, 11, 12, 12, 12,
15, 15, 15, 15, 15, 16, 16, 16, 16, 16,
16, 17, 17, 18, 18, 18, 19; 6:1, 2, 4, 4, 5,
5, 5, 6, 6, 6, 7, 7, 8, 9, 9, 9, 9, 9, 9, 9,
20, 20, 21, 21, 21, 22, 22, 24, 25, 25,
25, 25, 25, 26, 26, 26, 26, 27, 27, 27,
27, 28, 29, 29, 30, 30, 30, 30, 30, 30; 7:1, 1,
2, 2, 2, 2, 2, 3, 3, 3, 4, 4, 4, 4, 4, 4, 5,
5, 5, 6, 6, 7, 7, 7, 8, 8, 8, 9, 9, 9, 9,
11, 11, 11, 12, 13, 13, 14, 14, 14, 14, 14,
14, 15, 15, 15, 15, 16, 16, 16, 16, 17, 17,
17, 18, 18, 18, 18, 19, 19, 20, 20, 20, 20,
20, 21, 21, 21, 21, 21, 21, 23, 24, 24, 24,
25, 25, 25, 25, 25, 28, 29, 29, 29, 29, 29,
30, 30, 30, 30, 31, 31, 32, 32, 34,
33, 33, 34, 34, 34, 34, 34, 34, 35, 35,
35, 35, 35, 36; 9:1, 1, 2, 2, 3, 3, 3, 4, 4,
4, 4, 6, 6, 7, 7, 7, 8, 8, 9, 9, 10, 10, 10, 10,
10, 10, 11, 11, 11, 12, 12, 12, 13, 14, 14, 14,
15, 15, 15, 16, 17, 17, 17, 18, 18, 18, 19,
19, 19, 19, 21, 22, 22, 22, 22, 24, 24, 25,
25, 26, 26, 26, 27, 27, 28, 28, 29, 29, 29,
29, 30, 30, 30, 30, 31, 31, 31, 31, 32,
32, 32, 32, 33, 33, 33, 33, 34, 34, 35; 10:1, 1, 2, 2, 3,
4, 4, 4, 4, 5, 6, 6, 6, 6, 7, 7, 7, 7, 7, 7,
9, 9, 11, 11, 11, 11, 12, 12, 12, 13,
13, 13, 14, 14, 14, 14, 15, 15, 15, 15, 15,
16, 16, 16, 17, 17, 17, 17, 18, 18, 18, 18,
19, 19, 19; 11:1, 2, 2, 2, 2, 3, 3, 4, 4,
4, 4, 4, 5, 5, 5, 6, 7, 7, 7, 7, 8, 8, 8,
9, 9, 10, 10, 10, 12, 12, 12, 13, 13, 14, 14,
16, 16, 16, 16, 17, 17, 17, 17, 18, 18,
19, 19, 19, 19; 11:1, 2, 2, 2, 2, 3, 3, 4,
4, 4, 5, 5, 5, 6, 7, 7, 7, 7, 8, 8, 8,
13, 14, 14, 14, 14, 14, 15, 15, 15, 15, 16,
16, 17, 17, 17, 17, 18, 18, 18, 18, 19,
19, 19, 19, 21, 22, 22, 22, 22, 24, 24, 25,
25, 26, 26, 26, 27, 27, 28, 28, 29, 29, 29,
29, 30, 30, 30, 30, 31, 31, 31, 31, 32,
32, 32, 32, 33, 33, 33, 33, 34, 34; 14:1, 2,
2, 2, 2, 2, 3, 3, 3, 4, 4, 4, 4, 5, 5, 6,
6, 6, 6, 6, 6, 6, 7, 7, 7, 7, 7, 7, 8, 9,
9, 11, 11, 11, 11, 12, 12, 12, 13,
13, 13, 13, 13, 13, 14, 14, 14, 14, 14,

14, 14, 15, 15, 15, 16, 16, 16, 16, 17, 17,
17, 17, 17, 17, 17, 17, 18, 18, 18, 18, 18,
18, 18, 19, 19, 19, 20, 20, 20, 20, 20, 22,
24, 24, 25, 25, 25, 25, 25, 25, 25, 25, 26,
26, 26, 27, 27, 27, 28, 28, 28, 28, 28, 28,
28, 28, 28, 29, 29, 29, 29, 30, 30, 30,
30, 31, 31, 31, 31, 32, 32, 33, 34, 34,
34, 35, 35, 37, 37, 37, 38, 38, 38, 39,
39, 39, 39, 40, 40, 40, 40, 41, 41, 41, 41,
42, 42, 42, 43, 43, 43, 43, 43, 43, 44, 44,
45, 45, 45, 45, 45, 45, 46, 46, 46, 46,
48, 48, 48, 48, 48, 48, 49, 50, 50, 51, 51,
51, 51, 51, 51, 51, 51, 52, 52, 52, 52, 52,
52, 52, 52, 53, 53, 53, 53, 54, 55, 57;
15:1, 2, 4, 5, 6, 6, 7, 7, 8, 8, 9, 10, 10,
11, 11, 12, 12, 14, 14, 14, 14, 14, 14, 15,
15, 15, 15, 15, 16, 17, 17, 18, 18, 19, 21,
22, 23, 24, 25, 25, 25, 25, 26, 26, 26,
27, 29, 29, 29, 29, 30, 30, 30, 30, 30,
30, 31, 32, 33; 16:1, 1, 1, 1, 2, 2, 2, 2,
2, 2, 2, 3, 4, 4, 4, 5, 5, 6, 7, 7, 7, 7, 7,
8, 8, 8, 9, 9, 10, 10, 10, 10, 10, 11, 11,
11, 11, 12, 12, 12, 13, 13, 13, 13, 13, 13,
13, 14, 14, 14, 14, 15, 15, 15, 15, 15, 15,
15, 15, 16, 16, 16, 16, 16, 16, 16, 17, 17,
17, 18, 18, 18, 18, 18, 18, 18, 18, 18, 19,
19, 20, 20, 20, 20, 20, 21, 21, 21, 21, 21,
21, 21, 22, 22, 22, 23, 23, 23, 23, 23,
23, 24, 24, 24, 24, 25, 26, 26, 26, 26, 26, 27,
27, 27, 27, 28, 28, 29, 29, 30, 30, 31, 31,
32, 34, 34, 34, 34, 34, 34, 34, 35, 35, 35;
35:1, 1, 1, 2, 2, 2, 2, 3, 3, 3, 4, 4, 4,
4, 4, 6, 6, 7, 7, 7, 7, 7, 8, 9, 9, 10, 10, 10,
10, 11, 11, 11, 11, 11, 12, 12, 13, 14,
14, 14, 14, 15, 15, 15, 15, 15, 15, 15, 16,
16, 16, 16, 16, 17, 17, 17, 17, 17, 17,
18, 18, 19, 19, 20, 20, 20, 20, 21, 21, 21,
21, 21, 22, 22, 22, 22, 23, 23, 24, 24, 24,
24, 24, 24, 24, 25, 26, 27, 27, 28, 30, 32, 32, 33,
33, 33, 33, 34, 34, 35, 35, 35, 36, 36,
37, 37, 37, 37, 37, 37, 37, 37, 38,
38, 38, 38, 38, 38, 38, 38, 38, 39, 39,
39, 39, 39, 40, 40, 40, 40, 40, 41, 41, 41,
41, 41, 41, 41, 41, 41, 42, 42, 42, 43, 43, 44,
45, 45, 45, 45, 45, 45, 46, 46, 46, 46,
47, 47, 47, 47, 48, 48, 49, 50, 50, 50,
50, 50, 51, 51, 51, 51; 4:1, 2, 2, 2, 2, 3, 3,
3, 3, 4, 4, 4, 4, 6, 6, 6, 7, 7, 7, 7, 7,
7, 8, 8, 9, 9, 9, 10, 10, 10, 11, 11, 11, 12,
13, 14, 14, 14, 15, 15, 15, 15, 15, 15,
15, 15, 15, 15, 15, 15, 16, 16, 16, 16, 16, 16,
16, 16, 16, 16, 16, 16, 17, 17, 18, 18, 18,
18, 19, 20, 20, 20, 20, 21, 21, 21, 21, 21,
22, 23, 24, 24, 24, 24, 24; 10:1, 1, 2, 2, 3,
3, 3, 3, 4, 4, 4, 4, 5, 5, 5, 6, 6, 7, 7, 8, 10,
9, 9, 10, 10, 10, 10, 11, 11, 11, 11, 11,
13, 13, 13, 14, 14, 14, 15, 15, 15, 15, 15, 16,
16, 16, 16, 16, 16, 17, 17, 17, 17, 18, 18, 18,
19, 19, 19; 11:1, 2, 2, 2, 3, 3, 4, 4,
4, 4, 5, 5, 5, 6, 7, 8, 8, 13; 12:1, 2, 2, 2, 3, 3, 3,
3, 3, 3, 3, 4, 4, 4, 4, 4, 4, 5, 5, 5, 5,
5, 6, 6, 6, 6, 6, 6, 7, 7, 7, 7, 8, 8, 9,
9, 9, 11, 11, 11, 11, 12, 12, 12, 13;
13, 13, 13, 14, 14, 14, 14, 14, 14, 14,

14, 14, 15, 15, 15, 16, 16, 16, 16, 17, 17,
17, 17, 17, 17, 17, 17, 17, 18, 18, 18, 18,
18, 18, 19, 19, 20, 20, 20, 22, 22, 22, 22,
22, 23, 23, 23, 23, 23, 23, 24, 24, 24, 24,
24, 24, 25, 25, 25, 25, 25, 25, 25, 25, 26,
26, 26, 27, 27, 28, 28, 28, 28, 28, 28,
28, 28, 28, 29, 29, 29, 29, 30, 30, 30,
30, 30, 31, 31, 31, 31, 32, 33, 34, 34,
34, 35, 35, 36, 36, 36, 36, 36, 36, 36, 37,
37, 37, 37, 37, 38, 38, 38, 38, 39, 39, 39,
39, 39, 40, 40, 40, 40, 41, 41, 41,
42, 42, 43, 43, 43, 43, 43, 44, 44, 44, 45,
45, 46, 46, 46, 47, 47, 48, 49, 49, 49, 50,
50, 50, 51, 51, 51, 51, 51, 51, 51, 51,
52, 52, 53, 53, 53, 53, 54, 54, 54, 54, 55,
55, 55, 55, 55, 56, 56, 56, 56, 56, 56, 56,
57, 57, 57, 57, 58, 58, 58, 59, 59, 59;
14:1, 2, 2, 2, 3, 3, 3, 3, 3, 4, 4, 5, 5, 6,
6, 6, 6, 6, 6, 6, 6, 7, 8, 8, 9, 9, 10, 10,
11, 11, 11, 11, 11, 12, 12, 13, 13, 13, 13,
13, 13, 13, 13, 13, 14, 14, 14, 14, 14,

14, 14, 15, 15, 15, 16, 16, 16, 16, 17, 17,
17, 17, 17, 17, 18, 18, 18, 18, 18, 18,
18, 18, 19, 19, 20, 20, 20, 20, 22, 22, 22,
24, 24, 25, 25, 25, 25, 25, 25, 24, 24, 24,
24, 24, 24, 25, 25, 25, 25, 26, 26, 26, 26,
26, 26, 27, 27, 27, 28, 28, 29, 29, 29, 30,
30, 31, 31, 31, 31, 32, 32, 33, 33, 34, 34,
37, 37, 37, 37, 37, 37, 38, 38,
38, 38, 38; 8:1, 2, 2, 2, 3, 3, 3, 3, 4, 4, 4,
4, 4, 5, 5, 5, 7, 7, 7, 7, 7, 7, 8, 8, 8, 8,
9, 9, 9, 9, 10, 11, 11, 11, 11, 12, 13, 14,
14, 14, 14, 14, 15, 15, 15, 15, 15, 15, 15,
16, 16, 16, 16, 16, 16, 17, 17, 17, 17, 17, 17,
18, 18, 18, 19, 19, 20, 20, 20, 20, 20, 21,
21, 21, 21, 22, 22, 22, 22, 22, 23, 23, 24,
24, 24, 24, 25, 26, 27, 27, 27, 28, 30, 30, 32, 33;
23:1, 2, 2, 2, 3, 3, 3, 3, 4, 4, 5, 5, 5, 6,
6, 6, 6, 7, 8, 8, 8, 9, 10, 10, 10, 10, 10, 11,
11, 11, 11, 11, 11, 12, 12, 12, 12, 13, 13, 13,
13, 14, 14, 15, 15, 15, 16, 16, 16, 17, 17,
18, 18, 18, 18, 19, 19, 20, 20, 20, 20, 20,
20, 20, 21, 21, 22, 22, 22, 22, 23, 23, 24,
24, 24, 25, 25, 26, 27, 27, 28, 30, 32, 32, 33;
24:1, 2, 2, 2, 2, 3, 3, 3, 3, 3, 3, 4,
4, 4, 6, 6, 7, 7, 7, 9, 9, 10, 10, 10, 10,
10, 11, 11, 11, 11, 11, 12, 12, 12, 13, 14, 14,
15, 16, 16, 16, 16, 16, 16, 16, 22, 22, 23,
23, 23, 23; 25:1, 2, 2, 2, 2, 3, 4, 4, 4, 5, 5,
6, 6, 7, 7, 8, 8, 9, 9, 9, 9, 10, 10, 10, 11,
11, 11, 12, 12, 13, 13, 15, 15, 15, 16, 16,
16, 16, 16, 16, 18, 19, 20, 20, 21, 22,
22, 22, 23, 23, 24, 24, 26, 26, 27, 27, 27,
28, 28, 28, 30, 30, 30, 30, 31, 31, 31, 31,
31, 32, 32, 32, 32, 33, 33, 33, 33, 33,
33, 33, 34, 35, 35, 46, 47, 47, 47, 50, 50, 50,
50, 51, 51, 52, 52, 53, 54, 55, 55, 55;
26:1, 2, 4, 4, 4, 5, 5, 5, 6, 6, 6, 7, 8, 10,
10, 13, 13, 13, 16, 16, 19, 20, 20, 25, 25,
25, 25, 26, 26, 29, 29, 31, 32, 33, 34, 34,
36, 36, 38, 38, 39, 40, 41, 41, 42, 43, 43,
44, 44, 45, 45, 45, 45, 45, 46, 46, 46, 46;
27:1, 2, 2, 2, 3, 3, 3, 5, 5, 6, 6, 7, 8, 8,
9, 9, 10, 11, 11, 11, 12, 12, 14, 14, 14,
15, 15, 16, 16, 17, 18, 18, 18, 18, 18, 18,
19, 19, 19, 20, 20, 20, 21, 21, 21, 21, 22,
22, 23, 23, 23, 23, 23, 24, 24, 24, 24, 24,
25, 25, 25, 26, 26, 26, 26, 26, 27, 27, 27,
30, 30, 30, 30, 30, 30, 31, 32, 32, 32,
Nu 1:1, 1, 1, 1, 1, 1, 1, 2, 2, 2, 2, 4, 5,
5, 5, 5, 6, 7, 8, 9, 10, 10, 10, 10, 11, 12, 13,
14, 15, 16, 16, 16, 18, 18, 18, 18, 18, 18,
19, 19, 20, 20, 20, 20, 21, 22, 22, 22, 22,
23, 24, 24, 24, 24, 25, 25, 26, 26, 26, 27,
28, 28, 28, 29, 29, 30, 30, 30, 31, 32,
32, 32, 32, 32, 33, 33, 34, 34, 34, 35,
36, 36, 36, 37, 38, 38, 38, 39, 40, 40,
40, 40, 41, 42, 42, 42, 42, 43, 44, 44, 45,
45, 47, 47, 48, 49, 49, 49, 50, 50, 50, 50,
50, 50, 51, 51, 51, 51, 51, 51, 51, 51,
52, 52, 53, 53, 53, 53, 54, 54, 54, 54, 53,
53, 53, 53, 54, 54, 54; 2:1, 2, 2, 2, 3,
3, 3, 3, 3, 3, 5, 5, 5, 7, 7, 7, 9, 10, 10, 10,
10, 10, 10, 10, 11, 12, 12, 14, 14, 14, 14,
16, 16, 17, 17, 17, 17, 17, 18, 18, 18,
18, 18, 18, 20, 20, 20, 22, 22, 22, 22,
24, 24, 24, 24, 25, 25, 25, 25, 27, 27, 27,
27, 29, 29, 29, 31, 32, 32, 32, 32, 32,
33, 33, 33; 14:1, 1, 2, 2, 2, 3, 3, 5, 5, 5, 5, 6,
6, 6, 7, 7, 7, 8, 8, 9, 9, 9, 10, 10, 10, 10,
10, 10, 10, 11, 11, 12, 12, 13, 14, 15, 15, 16,
16, 16, 17, 18, 18, 18, 18, 18, 18, 19, 19,

12, 12, 13, 13, 13, 13, 13, 13, 14, 14, 15,
15, 15, 16, 16, 17, 18, 18, 19, 20, 20, 20, 20,
21, 21, 21, 21, 21, 21, 22, 22, 23, 23, 23,
24, 24, 24, 24, 24, 25, 25, 25, 25, 25, 25,
25, 25, 25, 25, 26, 26, 26, 26, 26, 26,
26, 26, 26, 27, 27, 27, 27, 27, 27, 27, 27,
27, 27, 28, 28, 28, 28, 29, 29, 29, 29, 30,
30, 30, 30, 30, 32, 32, 32, 32, 31, 31, 31, 31,
31, 31, 32, 32, 32, 32, 32, 32, 32, 32, 33,
33, 33, 33, 34, 34, 34, 35, 35, 35, 35, 35,
35, 36, 36, 36, 36, 36, 36, 36, 36, 37, 37,
38, 38, 38, 38, 38, 38, 38, 38, 38, 39, 39,
39, 39, 40, 40, 40, 40, 40, 40, 41, 41, 41,
41, 41, 41, 41, 42, 42, 42, 43, 43, 44,
45, 45, 45, 45, 45, 45, 46, 46, 46, 46,
47, 47, 47, 47, 48, 48, 49, 50, 50, 50,
50, 50, 51, 51, 51, 51; 4:1, 2, 2, 2, 2, 3, 3,
3, 3, 4, 4, 4, 4, 6, 6, 6, 7, 7, 7, 7, 7,
7, 8, 8, 9, 9, 9, 10, 10, 10, 11, 11, 11, 12,
13, 14, 14, 14, 15, 15, 15, 15, 15, 15,
15, 15, 15, 15, 15, 15, 16, 16, 16, 16, 16, 16,
16, 16, 16, 16, 16, 16, 17, 17, 18, 18, 18,
18, 19, 20, 20, 20, 20, 21, 21, 21, 21, 21,
22, 23, 24, 24, 24, 24, 24; 10:1, 1, 2, 2, 3,
3, 3, 3, 4, 4, 4, 4, 5, 5, 5, 6, 6, 7, 7, 8, 10,
9, 9, 10, 10, 10, 10, 11, 11, 11, 11, 11,
13, 13, 13, 14, 14, 14, 15, 15, 15, 15, 15, 16,
16, 16, 16, 16, 16, 17, 17, 17, 17, 18, 18, 18,
19, 19, 19; 11:1, 2, 2, 2, 3, 3, 4, 4,
4, 4, 5, 5, 5, 6, 7, 8, 8, 13; 12:1, 2, 2, 2, 3, 3, 3,
3, 3, 3, 3, 4, 4, 4, 4, 4, 4, 5, 5, 5, 5,
5, 6, 6, 6, 6, 6, 6, 7, 7, 7, 7, 8, 8, 9,
9, 9, 11, 11, 11, 11, 12, 12, 12, 13; 13:1, 2, 2, 3, 3, 3, 4, 4,
5, 5, 6, 6, 7, 7, 8, 8, 9, 9, 10, 10, 11,
11, 12, 12, 13, 13, 14, 14, 15, 15, 16, 16,
16, 16, 17, 17, 18, 19, 20, 20, 20, 20, 20,
20, 20, 21, 21, 21, 21, 22, 22, 22, 23, 23, 24,
24, 24, 25, 26, 26, 26, 26, 27, 27, 27,
27, 28, 28, 28, 29, 29, 29, 29, 29, 29, 29,
30, 30, 30, 31, 31, 31, 31, 31, 32, 32, 32,
33, 33; 14:1, 1, 2, 2, 2, 2, 3, 3, 3, 3, 5, 5,
6, 6, 7, 7, 7, 8, 9, 9, 9, 10, 10, 10, 10,
10, 10, 11, 11, 11, 11, 11, 12, 12, 12, 12,
15, 15, 16, 16; 13:1, 2, 2, 3, 3, 3, 4,
4, 5, 5, 6, 7, 7, 8, 8, 9, 9, 10, 10, 10, 11,
11, 12, 12, 13, 13, 14, 14, 15, 15, 16, 16, 16,
16, 16, 17, 17, 17, 18, 18, 18, 18, 18, 18,
19, 19, 19, 19, 19, 19, 20, 20, 20, 20, 20,
20, 21, 21, 21, 21, 21, 22, 22, 22, 23, 23, 23,
23, 23, 23, 23, 23; 10:1, 2, 2, 2, 2, 3, 3,
3, 3, 3, 3, 4, 4, 4, 5, 5, 5, 5, 5, 7, 7, 7, 8, 8, 9,
9, 10, 10, 10, 10, 10, 11, 11, 11, 11, 11,
11, 11, 12, 12, 12, 12, 13, 13, 14, 14,
14, 14, 15, 15, 15, 16, 16, 16, 17, 17, 18, 18, 18,
20, 21, 21, 21, 21, 22, 22, 22, 22, 22, 23, 23,
24, 24, 24, 25, 25, 25, 26, 26, 27, 27,
28, 28, 28, 29, 29, 29, 29, 29, 29, 30, 30,
31, 31, 31, 31, 31, 31, 31, 31, 32, 32, 32, 32,
33, 33, 33, 33, 33, 33, 33, 34, 34, 35;
12:1, 2, 2, 3, 3, 3, 3, 3, 4, 4, 5, 5, 5, 6, 6, 6,
6, 6, 8, 8, 9, 9, 9, 9, 9, 10, 10, 10, 10,
15, 15, 16, 16; 13:1, 2, 2, 3, 3, 3, 4,
4, 5, 5, 6, 7, 7, 8, 8, 9, 9, 10, 10, 10, 11,
11, 11, 12, 12, 13, 13, 14, 14, 15, 15, 16,
16, 16, 17, 17, 18, 19, 20, 20, 20, 20, 20,
20, 20, 21, 21, 21, 21, 22, 22, 22, 23, 23, 24,
24, 24, 25, 26, 26, 26, 26, 27, 27, 27,
28, 28, 28, 29, 29, 29, 29, 29, 29, 29,
30, 30, 30, 31, 31, 31, 31, 31, 32, 32, 32,
33, 33; 14:1, 2, 2, 2, 3, 3, 5, 5, 5, 5, 6,
6, 6, 7, 7, 7, 8, 8, 9, 9, 9, 10, 10, 10, 10,
10, 10, 10, 11, 11, 12, 12, 13, 14, 15, 15, 16,
16, 16, 17, 18, 18, 18, 18, 18, 18, 19, 19,

20, 21, 21, 21, 22, 23, 24, 25, 25, 25, 25, 25, 25, 26, 27, 27, 28, 30, 30, 30, 31, 33, 33, 34, 34, 34, 35, 36, 36, 36, 36, 37, 37, 37, 37, 38, 38, 38, 38, 39, 39, 40, 40, 40, 40, 41, 41, 41, 42, 43, 43, 43, 43, 43, 44, 44, 44, 44, 44, 45, 45; 15:1, 2, 2, 3, 3, 3, 3, 4, 4, 5, 5, 6, 7, 7, 8, 10, 12, 13, 13, 14, 15, 15, 15, 15, 16, 17, 18, 18, 19, 19, 19, 20, 20, 20, 21, 21, 22, 22, 23, 23, 23, 24, 24, 24, 24, 24, 25, 25, 25, 25, 26, 26, 26, 27, 27, 28, 29, 29, 29, 30, 30, 30, 31, 32, 32, 32, 33, 35, 35, 35, 35, 36, 36, 36, 37, 38, 38, 38, 39, 41, 41, 41; 16:1, 1, 1, 1, 1, 2, 2, 2, 3, 3, 3, 5, 7, 8, 8, 9, 9, 9, 9, 10, 11, 12, 13, 14, 15, 16, 17, 18, 18, 19, 19, 19, 19, 19, 19, 19, 19, 20, 22, 22, 22, 23, 24, 24, 25, 26, 26, 26, 27, 28, 28, 29, 29, 29, 30, 30, 30, 30, 31, 31, 32, 32, 32; 19:1, 2, 2, 2, 3, 3, 4, 4, 4, 5, 5, 6, 6, 6, 7, 7, 7, 7, 8, 9, 9, 10, 10, 10, 10, 11, 12, 12, 12, 13, 13, 13, 14, 14, 14, 16, 17, 17, 18, 18, 18, 19, 19, 19, 19, 19, 19, 19, 20, 20, 20, 20, 21, 21, 22, 22; 20:1, 1, 1, 1, 2, 3, 3, 4, 4, 6, 6, 6, 6, 6, 7, 8, 8, 8, 8, 9, 9, 10, 10, 10, 11, 11, 12, 12, 12, 13, 13, 13, 14, 14, 15, 16, 16, 17, 17, 17, 17, 17, 17, 18, 18, 18, 19, 22, 22, 23, 23, 23, 24, 24, 24, 27, 27, 27, 28, 28, 28, 29, 29; 21:1, 1, 1, 1, 2, 3, 3, 3, 3, 4, 4, 4, 4, 4, 5, 5, 6, 6, 6, 7, 7, 7, 7, 7, 8, 9, 10, 11, 11, 12, 13, 13, 13, 13, 13, 14, 14, 14, 14, 14, 15, 15, 15, 15, 16, 16, 16, 16, 18, 18, 18, 18, 20, 20, 21, 21, 22, 24, 24, 24, 24, 26, 28; 24:1, 2, 3, 3, 4, 4, 6, 6, 6, 6, 7, 8, 8, 11, 13, 13, 14, 15, 15, 16, 16, 16, 16, 17, 19, 20, 20, 21, 22, 24; 25:1, 1, 2, 2, 2, 3, 3, 4, 4, 4, 4, 6, 6, 6, 6, 6, 7, 7, 7, 7, 8, 8, 8, 8, 9, 10, 10, 11, 11, 11, 13, 14, 14, 14, 14, 15, 15, 16, 17, 18, 18, 18, 18, 18, 26:1, 1, 1, 1, 2, 2, 3, 3, 4, 4, 4, 4, 5, 5, 5, 5, 5, 6, 6, 6, 6, 7, 7, 8, 9, 9, 9, 10, 11, 12, 12, 12, 12, 12, 12, 12, 13, 13, 13, 13, 14, 14, 15, 15, 15, 15, 15, 16, 16, 16, 17, 17, 17, 17, 18, 19, 20, 20, 20, 20, 20, 20, 20, 21, 21, 21, 21, 22, 23, 23, 23, 23, 24, 24, 25, 25, 26, 26, 26, 27, 27, 27, 28, 29, 30, 31; 29:1, 1, 1, 2, 3, 4, 5, 6, 6, 6, 6, 7, 8, 8, 10, 11, 11, 11, 12, 12, 13, 13, 14, 14, 15, 16, 16, 17, 18, 18, 18, 18, 19, 19, 19, 20, 20, 21, 21, 22, 23, 23, 24, 24, 24, 24, 25, 25, 26, 26, 27, 27, 27, 27, 29, 30, 31; 29:1, 1, 2, 3, 4, 4, 5, 6, 6, 6, 6, 7, 8, 8, 10, 11; 30:1, 1, 1, 2, 3, 3, 4, 4, 5, 7, 8, 12, 13, 14, 16, 16, 16, 16; 31:1, 2, 2, 3, 3, 3, 4, 4, 4, 5, 6, 6, 6, 6, 6, 7, 7, 8, 8, 8, 9, 9, 11, 11, 12, 12, 12, 12, 12, 12, 12, 12, 12, 13, 13, 13, 14, 14,

14, 14, 15, 16, 16, 16, 16, 16, 16, 17, 18, 19, 19, 19, 21, 21, 21, 21, 21, 21, 22, 22, 22, 22, 22, 22, 23, 23, 23, 23, 24, 24, 25, 26, 26, 26, 26, 26, 27, 27, 27, 28, 28, 28, 28, 28, 29, 29, 30, 30, 30, 30, 31, 31, 32, 32, 32, 36, 36, 37, 37, 38, 38, 39, 39, 40, 40, 41, 41, 41, 42, 42, 43, 43, 47, 47, 47, 47, 47, 47, 48, 48, 48, 49, 49, 50, 50, 51, 51, 52, 52, 52, 52, 52, 53, 54, 54, 54, 54, 54, 54, 54; 32:1, 1, 1, 1, 2, 2, 2, 2, 4, 4, 6, 6, 7, 7, 7, 8, 9, 9, 9, 9, 10, 11, 11, 12, 12, 12, 13, 13, 13, 14, 14, 15, 17, 17, 17, 17, 18, 20, 21, 22, 22, 22, 23, 25, 25, 26, 27, 28, 28, 28, 28, 28, 29, 29, 29, 29, 29; 15:1, 2, 2, 4, 4, 4, 5, 5, 6, 7, 7, 9, 9, 11, 11, 12, 14, 15, 15, 17, 18, 19, 19, 19, 19, 20, 20, 20, 21, 22, 22, 22, 23; 16:1, 1, 1, 1, 2, 2, 2, 6, 6, 7, 7, 7, 8, 8, 8, 9, 9, 10, 10, 10, 11, 11, 11, 11, 11, 11, 11, 12, 13, 14, 14, 14, 14, 14, 15, 15, 16, 16, 16, 16, 16, 17, 17, 18, 18, 18, 18, 19, 19, 20; 18:1, 1, 1, 1, 2, 3, 3, 3, 3, 3, 4, 4, 5, 5, 6, 6, 7, 7, 7, 8, 9, 9, 10, 11, 11, 12, 12, 13, 14, 14, 15, 15, 16, 16, 16, 18, 18, 18, 19, 19, 19, 20, 20, 21, 21, 22; 19:1, 1, 2, 2, 3, 4, 4, 5, 5, 5, 6, 6, 7, 7, 8, 9, 9, 10, 12, 13, 14, 14, 15, 15, 15, 17; 20:1, 1, 2, 2, 4, 5, 5, 5, 5, 6, 6, 6, 6, 8, 9, 9, 9, 11, 13, 14, 14, 14, 15, 15, 15, 17; 21:1, 1, 1, 2, 3, 3, 3, 3, 4, 4, 4, 5, 5, 5, 6, 6, 6, 6, 8, 9, 9, 9, 10, 11, 11, 11, 11, 12, 12, 12, 13, 13, 13, 14, 14, 16, 16, 16, 16, 16, 16, 17, 17, 17, 17, 18, 19, 20, 20, 21; 22:4, 5, 6, 6, 6, 6, 6, 6, 6, 7, 7, 9, 9, 12, 15, 15, 15, 15, 15, 16, 16, 17, 17, 17, 18, 19, 19, 20, 20, 21; 23:1, 1, 2, 2, 2, 3, 3, 3, 3, 4, 4, 5, 5, 5, 8, 8, 9, 10, 11, 11, 12, 14, 14, 14, 15, 17, 18, 18, 18, 18, 18, 20, 21, 21, 23; 24:3, 3, 4, 4, 4, 6, 6, 7, 8, 8, 9, 11, 11, 12, 13, 13, 15, 15, 16, 16, 16, 17, 17, 18, 19, 19, 19, 20, 20, 20, 21, 21, 21, 22; 25:1, 1, 1, 2, 2, 4, 4, 5, 5, 6, 6, 7, 7, 7, 8, 9, 10, 11, 11, 11, 12, 12, 12, 12, 12, 13; 26:1, 1, 2, 2, 3, 3, 3, 3, 4, 4, 4, 5, 5, 6, 7, 7, 8, 8, 8, 9, 9, 10, 10, 10, 11, 11, 11, 11, 11, 12, 12, 13, 13, 13, 14, 15, 15, 16, 16, 17, 18, 19, 19, 19, 19, 20, 21, 21, 21, 22; 13:1, 2, 2, 2, 3, 3, 3, 3, 4, 4, 4, 4, 5, 5, 5, 5, 6, 6, 6, 6, 7, 8, 8, 8, 9, 9, 9, 9, 9, 10, 10, 10, 11, 11, 12, 12, 13, 13, 13, 13, 13, 14, 14, 15, 16, 16, 16, 16, 16, 16, 17, 19, 19, 21, 21, 21, 21, 22, 22, 22, 22, 23, 23, 23, 23, 24, 24, 25, 25, 26, 27, 27, 27, 27, 27, 28, 28, 28, 28, 30, 30, 30, 30, 32, 32, 33; 14:1, 1, 1, 1, 1, 1, 1, 1, 1, 2, 2, 2, 2, 3, 3, 3, 4, 4, 4, 4, 5, 5, 6, 6, 6, 6, 7, 7, 7, 7, 8, 8, 9, 10, 10, 11, 12, 12, 12, 12, 13, 14, 14, 14, 14, 15, 15, 15; 15:1, 1, 1, 1, 1, 1, 2, 2, 2, 3, 4, 5, 5, 6, 6, 7, 7, 7, 7, 7, 8, 8, 8, 8, 8, 8, 9, 9, 10, 10, 10, 10, 10, 11, 11, 11, 12, 12, 12, 15, 17, 17, 19, 19, 20, 20, 20, 21, 21, 21, 22, 22, 22, 22, 22, 22, 22, 23, 23, 23, 23, 23, 24, 24, 25, 25, 25, 26, 27, 27, 27, 27, 27, 28, 28, 28, 28, 30, 30, 30, 33; 14:1, 1, 1, 1, 1, 1, 1, 1, 6, 6, 6, 6, 6, 7, 7, 7, 7, 8, 8, 8, 8, 8, 9, 9, 9, 10, 10, 10, 10, 11, 11, 12, 12, 12, 12, 13, 14, 14, 14, 15, 15, 15; 15:1, 1, 1, 1, 1, 1, 1, 2, 2, 2, 3, 4, 5, 6, 6, 7, 7, 7, 7, 7, 7, 7, 8, 8, 8, 8, 8, 8, 8, 9, 10, 10, 11, 11, 11, 11, 11, 11, 12, 12, 12, 12, 12, 15, 17, 17, 19, 20, 20, 20, 20, 21, 21, 21, 28, 28; 19:1, 1, 1, 1, 1, 8, 8, 8, 8, 8, 9, 9, 9, 9, 9, 9, 9, 9, 10, 10,

10, 11, 11, 12, 12, 13, 14, 14, 14, 14, 16, 16, 17, 17, 22, 22, 22, 23, 23, 23, 24, 24, 24, 27, 27, 27, 27, 29, 29, 29, 29, 29, 29, 31, 31, 31, 32, 32, 32, 33, 34, 34, 34, 35, 39, 39, 39, 39, 39, 40, 40, 40, 40, 41, 46, 47, 47, 47, 47, 47, 47, 47, 48, 48, 48, 49, 49, 49, 50, 50, 50, 50, 51, 51, 51, 51, 51, 51, 51, 51, 51, 51; 20:1, 2, 2, 3, 3, 4, 4, 4, 4, 4, 5, 5, 6, 6, 6, 6, 6, 7, 7, 8, 8, 8, 8, 9, 9, 9, 9, 9, 9; 21:1, 1, 1, 1, 1, 1, 1, 1, 1, 1, 1, 2, 2, 2, 2, 3, 3, 3, 4, 4, 4, 4, 4, 4, 4, 4, 4, 4, 5, 5, 5, 5, 5, 5, 6, 6, 6, 6, 6, 6, 7, 7, 7, 8, 8, 8, 8, 9, 9, 9, 9, 9, 9, 9, 10, 10, 10, 10, 10, 11, 11, 11, 11, 12, 12, 12, 12, 13, 13, 13, 17, 19, 19, 19, 20, 20, 20, 20, 20, 20, 20, 21, 23, 25, 26, 26, 26, 27, 27, 27, 27, 28, 30, 32, 32, 33, 33, 34, 34, 34, 34, 36, 38, 38, 40, 40, 40, 40, 41, 41, 41, 41, 43, 43, 44, 44, 44, 45, 45; 22:1, 1, 1, 2, 2, 3, 3, 3, 4, 4, 4, 4, 4, 4, 5, 5, 5, 7, 7, 7, 8, 9, 9, 9, 9, 9, 9, 9, 9, 10, 10, 10, 10, 11, 11, 11, 11, 11, 11, 11, 12, 12, 12, 13, 13, 13, 13, 13, 13, 14, 14, 14, 15, 15, 15, 15, 16, 16, 16, 17, 17, 17, 18, 18, 18, 18, 18, 19, 20, 20, 20, 21, 21, 21, 21, 22, 22, 22, 23, 23, 25, 24, 25, 25, 25, 25, 27, 27, 27, 28, 28, 29, 29, 29, 29, 30, 30, 30, 30, 30, 30, 31, 31, 31, 31, 31, 31, 31, 31, 31, 32, 32, 32, 32, 32, 33, 33, 33, 33, 33, 34, 34, 34, 34; 23:1, 3, 3, 4, 4, 5, 6, 6, 6, 6, 7, 8, 9, 10, 11, 12, 13, 13, 14, 14, 14, 14, 14, 15, 15, 15, 16, 16, 16, 16, 16; 24:1, 1, 2, 2, 2, 2, 2, 2, 3, 3, 6, 6, 7, 7, 7, 7, 8, 8, 8, 9, 9, 11, 11, 11, 11, 11, 11, 11, 11, 13, 14, 14, 14, 14, 15, 15, 15, 15, 16, 16, 16, 17, 17, 17, 17, 17, 18, 18, 18, 18, 18, 19, 19, 20, 21, 21, 22, 22, 23, 23, 24, 24, 25, 25, 26, 26, 26, 26, 26, 27, 27, 27, 27, 28, 28, 29, 29, 29, 30, 30, 30, 30, 30, 31, 31, 31, 31, 31, 32, 32, 32, 32, 32, 33;

Jdg 1:1, 1, 1, 1, 2, 2, 3, 4, 4, 4, 5, 5, 8, 8, 8, 8, 9, 9, 9, 9, 9, 10, 11, 11, 13, 13, 15, 16, 16, 16, 16, 16, 16, 16, 16, 17, 17, 17, 18, 18, 18, 19, 19, 19, 19, 19, 19, 19, 21, 22, 22, 23, 23, 23, 24, 24, 24, 24, 25, 25, 25, 25, 25, 26, 26, 26, 26, 26, 27, 27, 27, 27, 27, 28, 29, 29, 30, 30, 31, 31, 32, 32, 32, 32, 33, 33, 33, 33, 34, 34, 34, 34, 35, 35, 35, 36, 36, 36; 2:1, 1, 2, 4, 4, 4, 4, 4, 5, 5, 6, 6, 6, 7, 7, 7, 7, 7, 8, 9, 9, 9, 10, 10, 11, 11, 11, 12, 12, 12, 12, 12, 12, 13, 14, 14, 14, 14, 15, 15, 15, 16, 16, 16, 17, 17, 18, 18, 18, 18, 18, 19, 20, 20, 21, 21, 22, 22, 23, 23; 3:1, 1, 1, 1, 1, 2, 3, 3, 3, 3, 3, 4, 4, 4, 5, 5, 7, 7, 7, 7, 8, 8, 8, 8, 9, 9, 9, 9, 10, 11, 11, 11, 12, 12, 14, 14, 15, 15, 15, 15, 16, 16, 16, 17, 17, 18, 18, 18, 19, 20, 21, 21, 22, 22, 23, 23; 3:1, 1, 1, 1, 2, 2, 2, 3, 3, 3, 3, 3, 4, 4, 4, 5, 5, 7, 7, 7, 7, 8, 8, 8, 8, 9, 9, 9, 9, 10, 11, 11, 11, 12, 12, 14, 14, 15, 15, 15, 15, 16, 16, 16, 17, 17, 18, 18, 18, 19, 20, 21, 21, 22, 22, 23, 24, 24, 24; 5:1, 2, 2, 2, 3, 3, 4, 4, 4, 4, 5, 5, 6, 6, 6, 6, 7, 7, 8, 9, 9, 9, 10, 11, 11, 11, 11, 11, 11, 11, 11, 11, 12, 12, 13, 13, 13, 14, 14, 15, 15, 15, 16, 16, 16, 16, 17, 17, 17, 17, 17, 17, 18, 18, 18, 18, 19, 19, 19, 19, 19, 19, 20, 20, 21, 21, 22, 22, 23, 23, 24, 24; 5:1, 2, 2, 2, 3, 3, 4, 4, 4, 4, 4, 5, 5, 6, 6, 6, 7, 7, 8, 9, 9, 9, 10, 11, 11, 11, 11, 11, 11, 11, 11, 12, 12, 12, 13, 13, 14, 15, 15, 16, 16, 16, 17, 18, 18, 18, 18, 19, 19, 19, 20, 20, 20, 21, 21, 21, 21, 21, 21, 21, 22, 22, 23, 23, 24, 24, 24; 5:1, 2, 2, 2, 3, 3, 4, 4, 4, 4, 4, 5, 5, 6, 6, 6, 6, 7, 7, 7, 8, 9, 9, 9, 10, 11, 11, 11, 11, 12, 13, 13, 14, 14, 15, 15, 15, 16, 16, 17, 18, 18, 18, 19, 19, 19, 19, 19, 19, 20, 20, 20, 20, 21, 21, 21, 21, 22, 22, 22, 23, 23, 24, 24, 24, 24; 6:1, 1, 1, 1, 2, 2, 2, 3, 3, 3, 3, 3, 4, 4, 5, 5, 6, 6, 6, 7, 7, 7, 7, 8, 8, 8, 9, 9, 9, 10, 10, 11, 11, 11, 12, 12, 13, 13, 13, 13, 13, 13, 13, 14, 14, 15, 15, 15, 16, 16, 16, 17, 17, 18, 18, 18, 19, 19, 19, 19, 19, 19, 20, 20, 20, 20, 21, 21, 21, 22, 22, 22, 22, 23, 23, 23, 24, 24, 25, 25, 25; 8:1, 1, 2, 2, 2, 3, 4, 4, 4, 5, 5, 6, 6, 6, 7, 7, 7, 8, 8, 9, 10, 10, 11, 11, 11, 11, 12, 12, 13, 14, 14, 14, 14, 15, 15, 16, 17, 18, 18, 20, 20, 20, 20, 23, 23, 24, 24, 24, 24; 9:1, 1, 1, 2, 2, 3, 3, 3, 4, 4, 4, 4, 4, 5, 5, 6, 6, 6, 6, 7, 8, 8, 9, 9, 10, 10, 11, 11, 12, 13, 14, 14, 15, 15, 15, 16, 17, 18, 18, 20, 20, 20, 23, 23, 24, 24, 24, 24, 25, 26, 26, 26, 27, 27, 28, 28, 28, 28, 30, 30, 30, 30, 31, 31, 32, 32, 32, 33, 33, 33, 34, 35, 35, 35, 35, 36, 36, 36, 36, 37, 37, 37, 38, 39, 40, 40, 40, 40, 42, 42, 42, 42, 42, 43, 43, 43, 44, 44, 44, 44, 44, 44, 45, 45, 45, 45, 45, 46, 46, 47, 47, 47, 48, 48, 48, 49, 49, 49, 49, 49, 49, 49, 49, 50, 51, 51, 51, 52, 52, 52, 54, 55, 56, 57, 57, 57, 57, 57, 10:1, 1, 4, 6, 6, 6, 6, 6, 6, 6, 6, 6, 6, 6, 7, 7, 7, 7, 8, 8, 8, 8, 8, 8, 8, 9, 9, 9, 11, 11, 11, 11, 12, 12, 14, 14, 15, 15, 16, 16, 17, 17, 18, 18, 18; 11:1, 2, 3, 4,

5, 5, 5, 6, 7, 8, 8, 8, 9, 9, 9, 10, 10, 11, 11, 11, 12, 12, 12, 13, 13, 13, 14, 14, 14, 15, 15, 15, 16, 16, 16, 16, 17, 17, 17, 17, 18, 18, 18, 18, 18, 18, 18, 19, 19, 19, 21, 21, 21, 21, 21, 22, 22, 22, 22, 23, 23, 24, 24, 25, 26, 26, 26, 27, 27, 27, 28, 28, 28, 29, 29, 29, 30, 30, 31, 31, 32, 32, 32, 33, 33, 33, 33, 35, 36, 36, 36, 37, 38, 39, 40, 40, 40; 12:1, 1, 2, 3, 3, 4, 4, 4, 4, 5, 5, 5, 5, 6, 6, 7, 7, 12, 12, 13, 15, 15, 15, 15; 13:1, 1, 1, 1, 1, 1, 2, 2, 3, 3, 3, 5, 5, 6, 6, 6, 7, 7, 7, 7, 8, 8, 9, 9, 9, 10, 10, 11, 11, 11, 12, 13, 13, 13, 14, 14, 15, 15, 15, 15; 14:1, 1, 3, 3, 4, 4, 4, 5, 5, 6, 6, 7, 7, 8, 8, 10, 10, 11, 11, 12, 12, 12, 13, 13, 13, 14, 14, 15, 15, 15, 15, 16, 16, 16, 17, 17, 17, 18, 18, 18, 18, 18, 19, 19, 19, 19, 19, 19, 20, 20, 20; 15:1, 1, 3, 3, 3, 4, 4, 5, 5, 6, 6, 6, 6, 7, 8, 8, 9, 9, 10, 10, 11, 11, 11, 11, 11, 12, 12, 12, 13, 13, 14, 14, 14, 14, 14, 15, 15, 16, 16, 16, 16, 17, 17, 18, 18, 18, 18, 19, 19, 20; 16:1, 2, 2, 2, 3, 3, 4, 4, 4, 4, 6, 6, 7, 7, 8, 8, 10, 10, 10, 11, 12, 13, 13, 13, 13, 14, 14, 14, 14, 15, 17, 8:2, 2, 4, 5, 6, 6, 7, 7, 8, 8, 9, 9, 9, 10, 10, 10, 11, 11, 11, 11, 11, 13, 14, 14, 15, 15, 17, 18, 19, 19, 20, 21, 21, 21, 22, 23, 23, 24, 24, 26, 26, 26, 26, 29, 29, 29, 29, 31; 31:1, 1, 1, 2, 3, 3, 7, 7, 7, 7, 7, 7, 8, 8, 8, 8, 9, 9, 9, 10, 10, 11, 11, 12, 12, 12, 12;

5, 5, 5, 6, 7, 8, 8, 8, 9, 9, 9, 10, 10, 11, 11, 11, 12, 12, 13, 13, 13, 14, 14, 15, 15, 15, 15, 16, 16, 16, 17, 17, 17, 17, 18, 18, 18, 18, 18, 18, 19, 21, 21, 21, 21, 21, 22, 22, 23, 24, 25, 26, 26, 27, 27, 27, 27; 14:1, 1, 2, 2, 3, 4, 4, 4, 4, 4, 4, 4, 4, 4, 5, 5, 5, 5, 6, 6, 6, 7, 7, 7, 8, 8, 8, 9, 9, 10, 10, 11, 11, 12, 12, 13, 13, 13, 14, 14, 14, 14, 15, 15, 16, 16, 16, 16, 17, 17, 18, 18, 18, 18, 19, 21, 21, 21, 21, 21, 22; 16:2, 2, 2, 2, 3, 3, 3, 3, 4, 5, 7, 8, 8, 10, 11, 12, 13, 13, 14, 14, 14, 14, 18, 18, 18, 18, 18, 18, 19, 20, 20; 16:2, 2, 2, 2, 2, 3, 3, 4, 5, 7, 8, 8, 9, 12, 13, 13, 14, 14, 14, 14, 18, 18, 18, 20, 20, 21, 22, 23, 23, 24, 24, 25, 25, 26, 26, 26, 26, 27, 27, 27, 27, 28, 28, 29, 29, 29, 30, 30, 30, 30, 30, 30, 31; 17:2, 2, 2, 3, 3, 3, 4, 4, 4, 5, 7, 8, 8, 9, 10, 10, 10, 11, 11, 11, 11, 12, 13, 13, 13, 13, 13, 13, 13, 13, 14, 14, 14, 14, 15, 15, 15, 17, 18, 18, 18, 18, 19, 20, 21, 21, 21, 21, 21, 22, 23, 23, 24, 24, 24, 25, 25, 25, 25, 26, 26, 26, 26, 26, 27, 27, 27, 27, 27, 28, 28; 20:1, 1, 1, 2, 2, 2, 2, 2, 3, 3, 4, 4, 4, 5, 6, 6, 6, 8, 10, 10, 10, 11, 12, 12, 12, 13, 13, 14, 14, 14, 15, 15, 15, 17, 18, 18, 18, 4:1, 1, 2, 2, 3, 3, 4, 4, 5, 5, 5, 5, 6, 7, 7, 9, 9, 10, 10, 10, 11, 12, 12, 13, 14, 16, 17, 17, 17, 18

22, 23, 23, 24, 24, 24, 25, 25, 25, 25, 26, 26, 26, 26, 27, 27, 27, 27; 10:1, 2, 2, 2, 2, 3, 5, 5, 5, 5, 6, 6, 10, 10, 11, 11, 11, 11, 11, 12, 12, 12, 13, 13, 14, 16, 16, 16, 17, 17, 17, 17, 18, 18, 18, 18, 18, 19, 21, 21, 21, 21, 21, 22, 22, 22, 23, 23, 23, 24, 24, 24, 24, 24, 24, 25, 25, 25, 25, 27; 11:1, 1, 1, 2, 2, 3, 3, 3, 4, 4, 4, 5, 7, 7, 7, 7, 7, 7, 7, 7, 8, 8; 12:2, 3, 5, 6, 6, 6, 6, 6, 7, 7, 8, 8, 9, 9, 9, 9, 9, 9, 10, 10, 10, 11, 11, 12, 12, 12, 13, 13, 14, 14, 14, 14, 14, 15, 15, 15, 15, 15, 15, 16, 17, 17, 17, 18, 18, 18, 18, 19, 19, 20, 20, 20, 22, 22, 23, 23, 23, 24; 13:2, 2, 3, 3, 3, 3, 4, 4, 5, 5, 5, 6, 6, 6, 7, 7, 7, 8, 8, 9, 9, 9, 10, 10, 11, 11, 12, 12, 13, 13, 13, 13, 14, 14, 14, 14, 14, 15, 15, 15, 15, 16, 16, 17, 17, 17, 18, 18, 18, 18, 19, 19, 20, 20, 20, 22, 22, 23, 23, 23, 24; 14:1, 1, 1, 1, 2, 2, 3, 3, 3, 4, 4, 4, 4, 4, 5, 5, 6, 6, 6, 6, 6, 6, 11, 11, 11, 12, 12, 12, 12, 13, 14, 14, 15, 15, 15, 15, 19, 19, 20, 20, 20, 20, 21, 21, 21, 22, 22, 23, 23, 24, 24, 24, 24, 25, 25, 26, 26, 27, 27, 27, 27, 28, 28, 28, 29, 29, 30, 30, 30, 30, 31, 31, 32, 32, 32, 32, 33, 33, 33, 34, 34, 34, 34, 34, 35, 35, 36, 36, 36, 37, 37, 37, 37, 37, 38, 38, 38, 39, 39, 39, 39, 40, 40, 40, 41, 41, 41, 41, 41, 42, 42, 42, 43, 43, 43, 43, 44, 44, 44, 44, 45, 45, 45, 45, 45, 46, 46, 46, 46, 47, 47, 47, 48, 48, 48, 49, 49, 49, 50, 50, 50, 51, 51, 51, 52, 52; 15:1, 1, 1, 1, 2, 2, 4, 5, 6, 6, 6, 6, 10, 11, 12; 16:1, 1, 1, 2, 2, 4, 5, 6, 7, 7, 7, 7, 7, 7, 14, 16, 18, 18, 19, 23; 17:1, 2, 2, 3, 3, 17:2, 2, 3, 3, 3, 4, 4, 5, 7, 8, 8, 9, 10, 11, 12, 12, 13, 13, 14, 14, 15, 15, 16, 16, 16, 17, 17, 18, 23, 23, 24, 25, 26, 26, 27, 27, 28, 28, 29, 29, 30, 30, 31, 32, 32, 33, 33, 33, 34, 34, 34, 35, 35, 35, 37; 14:1, 2, 3, 3, 4, 4, 4, 5, 6, 6, 7, 7, 7, 7, 8, 8, 9, 9, 10, 11, 13, 13, 23, 24, 25, 26, 27, 29, 29, 30, 31, 31, 32, 32, 32, 35, 36, 36, 37, 39; 14:1, 2, 3, 3, 4, 4, 4, 5, 5, 6, 6, 7, 7, 7, 8, 8, 9, 9, 10, 11, 11, 12, 13, 13, 13, 13, 14, 14, 15, 15, 15, 16, 16, 17, 17, 17, 18, 18, 18, 19, 19, 19, 19, 20, 21, 21, 21, 22, 22, 24, 24, 25, 25, 26, 26, 27, 27, 28, 29, 29, 29; 18:1, 2, 2, 2, 3, 3, 3, 4, 4, 5, 7; 20:3, 5, 5, 6, 6, 8, 9, 9, 10, 10, 10, 10, 11, 13, 15, 15, 16, 16, 20:3, 5, 5, 6, 8, 11, 11, 12, 13, 13, 14, 14, 14, 15, 15, 15, 15, 16, 16, 16, 17, 17, 18, 18, 18, 19, 19, 21, 21, 21, 22, 22, 23, 23, 23, 24, 24, 25, 25, 25, 25, 27, 27, 27, 27, 28, 28, 29, 30, 30, 30, 31, 31, 32, 32, 32, 34, 34, 34, 35, 35, 35, 37; 16:1, 1, 1, 2, 2, 2, 2, 2, 2, 2, 3, 3, 3, 4, 4, 5, 5, 5, 6, 6, 7, 7, 7, 7, 8, 8, 9, 9, 10, 10, 11, 11, 12, 13, 13, 14, 14, 15, 16, 22:1, 3, 4, 4, 5, 5, 5, 7, 7, 7, 8, 8, 8, 8, 9, 9, 9, 9, 10, 10, 11, 11, 11, 12, 13, 13, 14, 14, 14, 14, 15, 16, 16, 17, 17, 17, 17, 17, 18, 18, 18, 19, 19, 19, 19, 20, 20, 23:1, 3, 3, 3, 4, 4, 4, 4, 5, 6, 7, 7, 8, 8,

2Sa 1:1, 1, 1, 2, 2, 2, 3, 4, 4, 4, 6, 6, 10, 18, 18, 18, 18, 19, 19, 20, 20, 20, 20,

21, 21, 21, 22, 22, 22, 22, 22, 22, 22, 25, 25, 25, 26, 27, 27; 2:1, 1, 1, 1, 2, 3, 4, 4, 4, 5, 5, 6, 7, 8, 8, 8, 9, 9, 10, 11, 12, 12, 12, 13, 13, 13, 13, 14, 15, 15, 16, 16, 17, 17, 18, 18, 18; 3:1, 1, 1, 1, 2, 3, 3, 3, 3, 3, 3, 4, 4, 4, 4, 4, 4, 4, 4, 5, 5, 6, 6, 7, 8, 9, 9, 10, 10, 11, 11, 12, 12, 12, 13, 13, 14, 15, 15, 16, 16, 17, 17, 19, 19, 20, 21, 22, 22, 22, 22, 23, 24, 25, 26, 27, 27, 28, 28, 28, 29, 29, 30, 31, 31, 32, 32, 32, 33, 33, 34, 35, 35, 36, 36, 36, 36, 37, 37, 38, 38, 39, 39, 39; 4:1, 1, 2, 2, 2, 2, 2, 3, 3, 3, 4, 4, 4, 4, 4, 4, 5, 6, 7, 7, 7, 7, 8, 8, 9, 9, 10, 10, 11, 11, 11, 11, 12; 5:1, 1, 2, 2, 3, 3, 4, 4, 4, 5, 5, 6, 6, 6, 6, 7, 7, 8, 8, 8, 9, 9, 9, 10, 10, 10, 11, 11, 11, 11, 11, 11, 12, 13, 13, 13, 14, 14, 14, 15, 15, 15, 16, 16, 17, 17, 17, 17, 17, 18, 18, 19, 19, 19, 19, 19, 20, 20, 20, 20, 20, 21, 22, 22, 23, 23, 24, 24, 25, 25, 25; 6:1, 1, 1, 2, 2, 2, 2, 3, 3, 3, 4, 5, 6, 6, 7, 7, 8, 8, 9, 9, 10, 10, 10, 10, 11, 11, 11, 12, 12, 12, 12, 13, 13, 14, 14, 14, 15, 15, 16, 16, 16, 16, 17, 17, 18, 19, 19, 19, 20, 20, 20, 20, 21, 21, 22, 22, 23, 23; 7:1, 1, 1, 1, 2, 2, 2, 3, 4, 4, 4, 5, 5, 6, 7, 7, 7, 7, 8, 8, 8, 9, 9, 9, 9, 9, 9, 10, 10, 10, 11, 11, 12, 12, 12, 12, 13, 13, 13, 14, 14, 15, 15, 16, 16, 17, 18, 19, 19, 20, 21, 21, 21, 22, 22, 22, 22, 22, 23, 23, 23, 23, 24, 24, 24, 25, 25, 26, 27, 27, 28, 28, 29, 29, 30, 31, 31, 32, 32, 32, 33, 34, 34, 34, 34, 34, 35, 36, 36, 37, 38, 38, 39, 39, 39, 40, 40, 40, 41, 41, 41, 41, 42, 42, 42, 42, 43, 43, 43, 43, 43; 20:1, 2, 3, 3, 3, 3, 4, 4, 5, 5, 6, 7, 7, 7, 7, 7, 8, 8, 9, 10, 10, 10, 12, 12, 12, 12, 12, 14, 14, 15, 15, 16, 17, 17, 17, 18, 19, 19, 19, 20, 20, 21, 21, 21, 21, 22, 22, 22; 21:1, 1, 1, 1, 2, 2, 3, 3, 3, 3, 4, 5, 5, 5, 6, 6, 7, 7, 7, 7, 7, 8, 8, 8, 10, 10, 10, 11, 11, 12, 12, 12, 12, 12, 13, 13, 14, 14, 15, 15, 16, 16, 16, 16, 16, 17, 18, 19, 19, 19, 20, 20, 20, 20, 21, 21, 22; 21:1, 1, 1, 1, 2, 3, 3, 4, 4, 4, 4, 6, 7, 7, 7, 7, 8, 8, 8, 8, 8, 9, 9, 9, 9, 9, 9, 9, 10, 10, 10, 10, 10, 11, 11, 11, 11, 11, 11; 22:1, 3, 4, 4, 4, 5, 5, 5, 6, 6, 7, 7, 7, 7, 7, 8, 8, 8, 8, 9, 9, 9, 9, 9, 9, 11, 11, 11, 11, 11; 28:1, 3, 3, 4, 5, 5, 6, 6, 8, 8, 9, 9, 10, 10, 11, 12, 12, 13, 13, 14, 15, 16, 17, 17, 17, 18, 18, 18, 19, 19, 19, 19, 19, 19, 20, 20, 20, 20, 21, 22, 22, 23, 23, 24; 29:1, 1, 2, 2, 2, 3, 3, 3, 3, 4, 4, 4, 4, 4, 4, 5, 5, 6, 6, 6, 6, 6, 7, 7, 8, 8, 8, 9, 9, 10; 30:1, 1, 2, 2, 4, 5, 5, 6, 6, 6, 6, 7, 8, 9, 9, 10, 11, 14, 14, 14, 14, 15, 15, 16, 16, 16, 16, 16, 17, 17, 17, 18, 20, 20, 20, 21, 21, 22, 23, 24, 24, 26, 26, 26, 26, 27, 29, 29, 29, 29, 31; 31:1, 1, 1, 2, 3, 3, 7, 7, 7, 7, 7, 7, 8, 8, 8, 8, 9, 9, 9, 10, 10, 11, 11, 12, 12, 12, 12;

21, 21, 21, 22, 22, 22, 22, 22, 22, 22, 25, 25, 25, 26, 27, 27; 2:1, 1, 1, 1, 2, 3, 4, 4, 4, 5, 5, 6, 7, 8, 8, 8, 9, 10, 11, 11, 11, 12, 13, 13, 13, 13, 13, 14, 15, 15, 16, 17, 19, 19, 21, 22, 22, 22, 22, 22, 24, 24, 24, 25, 26, 27, 27, 28, 29, 29, 30, 31, 31, 32, 32, 32, 33, 34, 35, 35, 35; 36, 36, 36, 37, 37, 38, 39, 39; 4:1, 1, 2, 3, 3, 4, 4, 4, 4, 4, 5, 6, 6, 6, 7, 7, 7, 8, 8, 10, 10, 10, 11, 11, 12, 12, 12, 13, 14, 14, 14, 15, 15, 16, 16, 16, 17, 18, 18, 18, 18, 18, 18, 19, 20, 20, 20, 20, 20,

5, 5, 5, 6, 7, 8, 8, 8, 9, 9, 10, 10, 11, 11, 11, 12, 12, 13, 13, 13, 14, 14, 14, 15, 15, 15, 15, 16, 16, 16, 17, 17, 17, 17, 18, 18, 18, 18, 18, 18, 19, 21, 21, 21, 21, 21, 22, 22, 22, 22, 23, 23, 24, 24, 25, 26, 26, 26, 27, 27, 27, 28, 28, 28, 29, 29, 29, 30, 30, 31, 31, 32, 32, 32, 33, 33, 33, 33, 35, 36, 36, 36, 37, 38, 39, 40, 40, 40; 12:1, 1, 2, 3, 3, 4, 4, 4, 4, 5, 5, 5, 5, 6, 6, 7, 7, 12, 12, 13, 15, 15, 15, 15;

Ru 1:1, 1, 1, 1, 2, 2, 2, 2, 3, 4, 4, 4, 4, 6, 6, 6, 6, 7, 7, 7, 8, 8, 9, 9, 13, 13, 17, 19, 20, 21, 21, 21, 22, 22, 22; 2:1, 2, 2, 3, 3, 3, 3, 4, 4, 4, 4, 5, 5, 6, 6, 6, 6, 7, 7, 7, 7, 9, 9, 9, 10, 11, 11, 12, 12, 14, 14, 14, 14, 16, 17, 18, 19, 20, 20, 20, 20, 21, 23, 23; 3:2, 3, 3, 4, 6, 7, 7, 8, 8, 10, 10, 10, 11, 13, 13, 13, 13, 13, 13, 13, 14, 14, 15, 15, 16, 18, 18, 18; 4:1, 1, 2, 2, 3, 3, 4, 4, 4, 5, 5, 5, 5, 6, 7, 8, 9, 9, 10, 10, 10, 10, 10, 10, 11, 11, 11, 11, 11, 11, 11, 11, 11, 12, 13, 14, 14, 16, 17, 17, 17, 18

1Sa 1:1, 1, 1, 1, 2, 2, 2, 2, 3, 3, 3, 4, 5, 6, 7, 7, 8, 9, 11, 11, 11, 15, 16, 17, 18, 19, 19, 19, 20, 20, 20, 21, 21, 22, 22, 23, 23, 24, 24, 24, 25, 26, 26, 27, 27, 28, 28; 2:1, 1, 2, 3, 4, 4, 5, 6, 6, 6, 7, 7, 7, 8, 8, 8, 8, 8, 8, 8, 8, 8, 9, 9, 10, 10, 10, 10, 10, 10, 11, 11, 11, 12, 12, 13, 13, 13, 13, 13, 14, 14, 14, 14, 15, 15, 15, 16, 17, 17, 17, 17, 18, 19, 20, 20, 21, 21, 22, 22, 22, 22, 23, 23, 24, 24, 24, 24, 25, 25, 25, 25, 25, 26, 26, 26, 26, 26, 27, 27, 27, 28, 28, 28, 28, 28, 28, 29, 30, 30, 30, 30, 30, 31, 32, 32, 32, 33, 33, 33, 36; 3:1, 1, 1, 1, 3, 3, 3, 4, 6, 7, 7, 7, 7, 8, 10, 11, 11, 13, 14, 14, 15, 15, 15, 15, 15, 17, 17, 17, 18, 19, 19, 20, 21, 21, 21, 21; 4:1, 1, 1, 2, 2, 2, 3, 3, 3, 3, 3, 3, 4, 4, 4, 4, 4, 4, 5, 5, 5, 5, 6, 6, 6, 6, 6, 6, 6, 6, 7, 7, 8, 8, 8, 9, 10, 11, 11, 12, 13, 13, 13, 14, 14, 16, 16, 16, 17, 17, 17, 18, 18, 18, 19; 5:1, 1, 2, 2, 3, 3, 3, 4, 4, 4, 4, 4, 4, 4, 5, 5, 6, 6, 6, 7, 7, 7, 8, 8, 8, 8, 8, 8, 9, 9, 10, 10, 10, 11, 11, 11, 11, 11, 11, 11, 12; 6:1, 1, 1, 2, 2, 2, 3, 3, 4, 4, 4, 4, 5, 5, 6, 6, 6, 7, 7, 8, 8, 8, 8, 9, 9, 10, 10, 10, 11, 11, 11, 11, 11, 11; 28:1, 3, 3, 4, 5, 5, 6, 6, 8, 8, 9, 9, 10, 11, 12, 12, 13, 13, 14, 14, 15, 16, 17, 17, 17, 18, 18, 18, 19, 19, 19, 19, 19, 20, 20, 20, 20, 21, 22, 22, 23, 23, 24; 29:1, 1, 2, 2, 2, 3, 3, 3, 3, 4, 4, 4, 4, 4, 4, 5, 5, 6, 6, 6, 6, 6, 7, 7, 8, 8, 8, 9, 9, 10; 30:1, 1, 2, 2, 4, 5, 5, 6, 6, 6, 6, 7, 8, 9, 9, 10, 11, 14, 14, 14, 14, 15, 15, 16, 16, 16, 16, 16, 17, 17, 17, 18, 20, 20, 20, 21, 21, 22, 23, 24, 24, 26, 26, 26, 26, 27, 29, 29, 29, 29, 31; 31:1, 1, 1, 2, 3, 3, 7, 7, 7, 7, 7, 7, 8, 8, 8, 8, 9, 9, 9, 10, 10, 11, 11, 12, 12, 12, 12;

8, 8, 8, 8, 8, 9, 9, 9, 9, 9, 10, 10, 10, 10,
11, 11, 11, 11, 11, 11, 12, 12, 12, 12, 13, 13,
13, 13, 13, 13, 14, 14, 15, 15, 15, 15, 16, 16,
16, 16, 16, 16, 17, 17, 18, 18, 18, 19, 19, 20,
20, 20, 21, 21, 21, 22, 22, 23, 23, 24, 24,
24, 25, 25, 26, 26, 26, 27, 27, 27, 28, 28, 29,
29, 29, 30, 30, 31, 31, 32, 32, 33, 33, 33,
34, 34, 34, 34, 34, 35, 35, 36, 36, 37, 37,
37, 39; 24:1, 1, 2, 2, 2, 2, 2, 2, 2, 3, 3, 3,
3, 3, 3, 4, 4, 4, 4, 4, 4, 4, 4, 5, 5, 5, 5, 6,
7, 7, 7, 7, 7, 8, 8, 9, 9, 9, 9, 9, 10, 10,
10, 11, 11, 11, 11, 12, 14, 14, 14, 15, 15,
15, 15, 16, 16, 16, 16, 16, 16, 16, 16, 16,
17, 17, 17, 18, 18, 18, 19, 19, 20, 20, 20,
21, 21, 21, 21, 21, 22, 22, 23, 23, 23, 24,
24, 24, 24, 25, 25, 25;

1Ki 1:2, 2, 2, 3, 3, 4, 4, 4, 5, 7, 7, 8, 8, 8, 8,
9, 9, 9, 9, 10, 10, 11, 11, 12, 14, 15, 15,
15, 15, 15, 16, 16, 17, 18, 19, 19, 19, 19,
19, 20, 20, 20, 22, 22, 23, 23, 23, 23,
23, 25, 25, 25, 25, 26, 26, 27, 27, 28, 28,
28, 29, 29, 30, 31, 31, 32, 32, 32, 33, 33,
34, 34, 34, 34, 36, 36, 36, 37, 37, 37,
38, 38, 38, 38, 38, 39, 39, 39, 39, 40, 40,
40, 40, 41, 41, 41, 41, 42, 42, 44, 44, 44,
44, 44, 44, 44, 45, 45, 45, 45, 46, 46, 47,
47, 47, 47, 48, 48, 49, 50, 50, 51, 51, 51,
52, 53; 2:1, 2, 2, 3, 3, 3, 4, 4, 5, 5, 5, 5,
5, 5, 6, 7, 7, 8, 8, 8, 8, 9, 9, 11, 12, 13,
13, 15, 15, 17, 17, 18, 19, 19, 20, 21,
22, 22, 22, 22, 23, 24, 24, 25, 25, 26, 26,
26, 26, 27, 27, 27, 27, 28, 28, 28, 28, 29,
29, 29, 29, 30, 30, 30, 31, 31, 31, 32,
32, 32, 32, 32, 32, 33, 33, 33, 34, 34, 34,
35, 35, 35, 35, 36, 36, 37, 37, 38, 38, 38,
39, 39, 42, 42, 42, 42, 43, 43, 43, 44, 44,
44, 45, 45, 46, 46, 46, 46; 3:1, 1, 1, 1, 2,
2, 2, 3, 3, 4, 4, 5, 6, 8, 10, 10, 11, 13, 15,
15, 15, 16, 17, 17, 18, 18, 18, 18, 19, 21,
22, 22, 22, 22, 22, 22, 23, 23, 23, 23, 23,
23, 24, 24, 25, 25, 25, 25, 26, 26, 26, 26,
26, 27, 27, 27, 27, 27, 28, 28, 28; 4:2, 2, 2, 3,
3, 3, 4, 4, 4, 5, 5, 5, 5, 6, 6, 6, 7, 8, 9, 10,
10, 11, 11, 11, 12, 12, 13, 13, 13, 14, 14,
15, 16, 17, 18, 19, 19, 19, 19, 19, 19, 20,
20, 21, 21, 21, 21, 21, 22, 23, 23, 24, 24,
25, 28, 28, 28, 29, 29, 30, 30, 30, 30, 31,
31, 33, 33, 33, 34, 34; 5:1, 3, 3, 3, 3, 3, 4,
5, 5, 5, 6, 7, 7, 8, 8, 8, 9, 9, 12, 13, 14, 15, 16,
16, 16, 16, 17, 17, 17, 18; 6:1, 1, 1, 1,
1, 1, 1, 1, 2, 2, 2, 2, 2, 3, 3, 3, 3, 3, 3, 3,
3, 4, 5, 5, 5, 5, 5, 5, 6, 6, 6, 6, 6, 6, 6,
7, 7, 8, 8, 8, 8, 9, 9, 9, 9, 9, 10, 10, 11,
11, 13, 14, 15, 15, 15, 15, 15, 15, 15,
16, 16, 16, 16, 16, 16, 17, 17, 18, 18,
19, 19, 19, 19, 19, 20, 20, 20, 20, 21, 21,
21, 21, 22, 22, 22, 23, 23, 24, 24, 24, 24,
24, 24, 25, 25, 25, 26, 26, 26, 27, 27, 27,
27, 27, 27, 27, 27, 27, 27, 28, 28, 29,
29, 30, 30, 31, 31, 31, 31, 32, 32, 32, 33,
33, 33, 34, 34, 34, 34, 35, 36, 37, 37,
37, 37, 37, 38, 38, 38, 38, 38, 38; 7:2, 2,
2, 2, 2, 2, 3, 3, 5, 5, 6, 6, 6, 6, 6, 7, 7, 7, 7,
8, 8, 9, 9, 9, 9, 9, 10, 11, 12, 12, 12, 12,
12, 12, 14, 16, 16, 16, 16, 16, 16, 17, 17,
17, 17, 17, 18, 18, 18, 18, 19, 19, 19,
19, 20, 20, 20, 20, 20, 20, 21, 21, 21, 21,
21, 21, 21, 22, 22, 22, 23, 23, 24, 24,
24, 24, 24, 25, 25, 25, 25, 26, 26, 27, 27,
27, 28, 28, 28, 29, 29, 29, 30, 30, 30,
31, 31, 31, 31, 31, 31, 32, 32, 32, 32,
33, 33, 33, 34, 34, 34, 35, 35, 35, 35, 35,
35, 35, 36, 36, 36, 37, 38, 39, 39, 39,
39, 39, 39, 39, 40, 40, 40, 40, 40, 40, 40,
41, 41, 41, 41, 41, 41, 41, 41, 41, 41, 42,
42, 42, 42, 43, 43, 44, 44, 45, 45, 45, 45,
46, 46, 46, 47, 47, 47, 48, 48, 48, 48, 48,
48, 49, 49, 49, 49, 49, 49, 50, 50, 50, 50,
50, 50, 50, 50, 50, 50, 50, 50, 51, 51,
51, 51, 51, 51, 51, 51, 51; 8:1, 1, 1, 1,
4, 4, 4, 4, 4, 5, 5, 6, 6, 6, 6, 6, 6, 6, 6, 6,
7, 7, 7, 7, 7, 8, 8, 8, 8, 9, 9, 9, 9, 9,
10, 10, 10, 10, 10, 11, 11, 11, 11, 11, 11,
12, 12, 14, 14, 14, 15, 16, 16, 17, 17, 17,
18, 19, 19, 20, 20, 20, 20, 20, 21, 21, 21,
21, 21, 21, 22, 22, 22, 22, 23, 23, 24, 24,
24, 25, 25, 25, 25, 25, 26, 26, 27, 27, 27,
28, 28, 28, 29, 29, 29, 30, 30, 30,
31, 31, 31, 31, 31, 31, 32, 32, 32, 32, 32,
33, 33, 33, 34, 34, 34, 35, 35, 35, 35, 35,
35, 35, 36, 36, 36, 37, 38, 39, 39, 39,
39, 39, 39, 39, 40, 40, 40, 40, 40, 40, 40,
41, 41, 41, 41, 41, 41, 41, 41, 41, 41, 42,
42, 42, 42, 43, 43, 44, 44, 45, 45, 45, 45,
46, 46, 46, 47, 47, 47, 48, 48, 48, 48, 48,
48, 49, 49, 49, 49, 49, 49, 50, 50, 50, 50,
50, 50, 50, 50, 50, 50, 50, 50, 51, 51,
51, 51, 51, 51, 51, 51, 51; 8:1, 1, 1, 1,
4, 4, 4, 4, 4, 5, 5, 6, 6, 6, 6, 6, 6, 6, 6, 6,
7, 7, 7, 7, 7, 8, 8, 8, 8, 9, 9, 9, 9, 9,
10, 10, 10, 10, 10, 11, 11, 11, 11, 11, 11,
12, 12, 14, 14, 14, 15, 16, 16, 17, 17, 17,
18, 19, 19, 20, 20, 20, 20, 20, 21, 21, 21,
21, 21, 22, 22, 22, 22, 22, 25, 27, 28, 28,
28, 29, 29, 30, 31, 32, 32, 32, 32, 34, 34,
36, 37, 37, 38, 39, 39, 40, 40, 40, 43, 43, 44,
44, 44, 46, 46, 46, 47, 47, 48, 48, 48, 51,
51, 52, 52, 53, 53, 53, 54, 54, 54, 55, 56,
56, 57, 59, 59, 59, 59, 59, 59, 60, 60, 60, 61,
62, 62, 63, 63, 63, 63, 64, 64, 64, 64, 64,
64, 64, 64, 64, 64, 64, 64, 64, 64, 64, 65, 65,
65, 66, 66, 66, 66, 66; 9:1, 1, 1, 1, 1, 2, 2, 3,
5, 5, 7, 8, 9, 9, 9, 10, 10, 10, 10, 10, 11,
11, 12, 13, 14, 14, 15, 15, 15, 15, 16, 16,
17, 18, 18, 19, 19, 20, 20, 20, 21, 21, 22,
22, 23, 23, 23, 24, 24, 24, 24, 25, 25, 25,
26, 26, 27, 27, 27; 10:1, 1, 1, 1, 3, 4, 4, 5,
5, 5, 5, 5, 6, 7, 7, 7, 9, 9, 9, 10, 10, 11,
12, 12, 12, 12, 13, 14, 15, 15, 15, 19, 19,
15, 15, 17, 17, 17, 18, 18, 19, 19, 19, 19,
19, 20, 20, 20, 21, 22, 23, 25, 26, 26, 27,
22, 22, 23, 23, 24, 26, 27, 27, 27, 28,
28, 29, 29, 29; 11:1, 1, 2, 2, 2, 2, 4, 4, 5, 5,
5, 5, 6, 6, 6, 7, 7, 7, 7, 9, 9, 9, 10, 11, 11,
12, 13, 14, 14, 14, 15, 15, 15, 19, 19, 19,
19, 20, 20, 21, 21, 23, 23, 25, 25, 26, 26, 27,
27, 27, 27, 28, 28, 28, 29, 29, 29, 29, 29,
30, 31, 31, 31, 31, 32, 32, 33, 33, 33, 33,
33, 33, 34, 34, 35, 36, 39, 40, 41, 41, 41,
41, 42, 43; 12:2, 2, 3, 4, 5, 6, 8, 8, 8, 9,
10, 12, 12, 12, 12, 12, 13, 13, 14, 14, 15,
15, 15, 15, 15, 15, 16, 16, 16, 16, 17,

17, 18, 19, 20, 20, 20, 21, 21, 21, 21, 21,
22, 22, 23, 23, 23, 23, 24, 24, 24, 24, 24,
24, 26, 26, 27, 27, 27, 28, 28, 29, 29, 30,
30, 31, 31, 31, 32, 32, 32, 32, 32, 32,
32, 33, 33, 33, 33, 33, 33, 33; 13:1, 1, 1, 2, 2,
2, 2, 2, 2, 2, 2, 3, 3, 3, 3, 4, 4, 4, 4, 5, 5,
5, 5, 5, 5, 5, 6, 6, 6, 6, 6, 6, 7, 7, 7, 8,
9, 9, 9, 10, 11, 11, 11, 11, 11, 12, 13, 13, 14,
14, 17, 17, 17, 18, 18, 20, 20, 20, 20, 20,
21, 21, 21, 21, 21, 22, 22, 22, 22, 23, 23,
24, 24, 24, 24, 24, 24, 25, 25, 25, 26, 26,
26, 26, 26, 26, 26, 26, 26, 26, 27, 27, 28,
28, 28, 28, 28, 28, 29, 29, 29, 29, 29, 29, 29,
29, 31, 31, 32, 32, 32, 32, 32, 32, 32, 32,
33, 33, 33, 33, 33, 34, 34, 34, 34; 14:1, 1,
4, 5, 5, 6, 6, 7, 7, 8, 8, 10, 10, 10, 10, 11,
11, 11, 11, 11, 11, 12, 12, 13, 13, 13, 14,
14, 15, 15, 15, 15, 15, 16, 17, 17, 17, 18, 18,
18, 18, 19, 19, 19, 19, 19, 20, 20, 21, 21,
21, 22, 22, 24, 24, 24, 24, 24, 25, 26, 26,
26, 26, 26, 26, 27, 27, 27, 27, 27, 28, 28,
28, 28, 28, 29, 29, 29, 29, 31; 15:1, 1, 1,
2, 3, 3, 3, 4, 4, 5, 5, 5, 5, 5, 6, 7, 7, 7, 7, 7,
8, 9, 10, 11, 11, 12, 12, 12, 13, 14, 14, 14,
15, 15, 15, 15, 18, 18, 18, 18, 18, 18, 18,
18, 18, 18, 18, 20, 20, 20, 20, 20, 20, 23, 23,
23, 23, 24, 24, 24, 24, 24, 25, 25, 26, 27,
27, 29, 29, 29, 30, 30, 30, 31, 31, 31,
31, 31, 31, 33, 34, 34, 34, 34, 34; 16:1, 1,
1, 2, 2, 3, 3, 4, 4, 5, 5, 5, 5, 6, 7, 7, 8,
8, 10, 10, 12, 12, 12, 13, 14, 14, 14, 14,
15, 15, 15, 15, 16, 16, 16, 16, 17, 17, 17, 19,
19, 19, 19, 20, 20, 20, 21, 21, 21, 22,
22, 22, 22, 23, 23, 23, 23, 24, 25, 25, 25, 26,
26, 26, 27, 27, 28, 29, 29, 30, 30, 30, 31,
31, 31, 32, 33, 33, 34, 34, 35, 35, 35, 35,
35, 36, 36, 36, 36, 36, 36, 36, 36, 37, 37,
37, 38; 16:1, 1, 1, 2, 2, 3, 3, 3, 3, 3, 3, 3,
4, 4, 6, 6, 7, 7, 7, 7, 8, 8, 8, 8, 8, 9, 9, 9,
9, 10, 10, 10, 10, 11, 11, 12, 12, 12, 12,
12, 13, 13, 14, 14, 14, 14, 16, 16, 16, 17, 17, 17,
17, 17, 18, 18, 18, 18, 19, 19, 19, 19, 19,
20; 17:1, 1, 2, 2, 2, 4, 4, 4, 5, 5, 6, 6, 6, 6,
6, 7, 7, 7, 7, 7, 8, 8, 8, 8, 8, 9, 9, 9, 9, 11,
11, 11, 11, 12, 13, 13, 13, 13, 13, 14, 14,
15, 15, 16, 16, 16, 16, 17, 17, 17, 18, 18,
19, 19, 20, 20, 20, 21, 21, 21, 21, 22, 22, 23,
23, 24, 24, 24, 24, 25, 25, 25, 26, 26, 26,
26, 26, 26, 26, 26, 27, 27, 27, 27, 27, 27,
28, 28, 29, 29, 30, 30, 30, 30, 31, 31, 31,
32, 32, 32, 32, 33, 33, 33, 34, 34, 34, 34,
34, 34, 35, 36, 36, 37, 37, 37, 37, 38, 39,
39, 41; 18:1, 1, 2, 3, 4, 4, 4, 4, 4, 5, 5,
6, 6, 7, 7, 8, 8, 8, 8, 8, 9, 9, 10, 10, 14,
14, 15, 15, 15, 15, 15, 16, 16, 16, 16, 16,
16, 17, 17, 17, 17, 17, 18, 18, 18, 18, 18,
18, 19, 19, 20, 21, 22, 23, 24, 24, 25, 25,
25, 26, 26, 26, 26, 26, 26, 27, 27, 27, 27,
28, 28, 28, 29, 30, 30, 30, 30, 31, 31, 32,
32, 32, 32, 32, 33, 33, 33, 34, 34, 34,
39, 41; 18:1, 1, 2, 3, 4, 4, 4, 4, 4, 5, 5,
6, 6, 7, 7, 8, 8, 8, 8, 8, 9, 9, 10, 10, 14,
14, 15, 15, 15, 15, 15, 16, 16, 16, 16, 16,
16, 17, 17, 17, 17, 17, 18, 18, 18, 18, 18,
18, 19, 19, 20, 20, 20; 21:2, 2, 2, 2, 2, 3, 3, 4, 4, 4, 5,
5, 5, 5, 6, 6, 6, 7, 7, 7, 8, 8, 9, 9, 9, 10,
10, 11, 12, 13, 13, 13, 14, 14, 15, 16, 16,
17, 17, 17, 17, 17, 18, 19, 20, 20, 21,
21, 22, 22, 22, 23, 23, 24, 24, 24, 25,
25, 25, 25, 25, 26; 22:1, 2, 2, 2, 2, 2, 3, 3,
3, 3, 3, 3, 4, 4, 4, 4, 4, 4, 4, 4, 5, 5, 5, 5,

33, 33, 33; 7:1, 1, 1, 1, 2, 2, 2, 3, 3, 4, 4,
4, 4, 4, 5, 5, 5, 5, 5, 6, 6, 6, 6, 6, 6, 6, 6,
6, 7, 7, 7, 8, 8, 9, 9, 10, 10, 10, 10, 10, 11,
11, 12, 12, 12, 12, 12, 12, 12, 13, 13, 13, 13,
13, 13, 14, 14, 14, 14, 15, 15, 15, 15, 16, 16,
16, 16, 16, 17, 17, 17, 17, 17, 17, 17, 17,
18, 18, 18, 19, 19, 19, 20; 8:1, 1, 1, 2, 2,
2, 2, 2, 3, 3, 3, 3, 4, 4, 4, 4, 4, 5, 5, 5,
6, 6, 6, 6, 6, 6, 7, 7, 8, 8, 8, 10, 11, 11, 12,
12, 12, 13, 15, 16, 16, 16, 18, 18, 18, 18, 18,
18, 18, 19, 20, 21, 21, 21, 21, 22, 22, 22,
23, 23, 23, 23, 23, 24, 25, 25, 25, 26, 27,
27, 27, 27, 27, 27, 28, 28, 28, 29, 29,
29, 29; 9:1, 1, 1, 2, 2, 3, 3, 4, 4, 4, 4, 5, 5,
9, 9, 9, 9, 10, 10, 11, 12, 13, 13, 13, 14,
14, 15, 15, 15, 15, 15, 17, 17, 18, 18, 18,
18, 18, 19, 19, 19, 19, 19, 20, 20, 20, 21, 21,
21, 22, 22, 23, 23, 24, 25, 25, 25, 25, 25,
25; 10:1, 1,
3, 5, 5, 5, 5, 5, 6, 6, 6, 6, 6, 6, 6, 7, 7, 8, 8,
8, 8, 8, 9, 9, 10, 10, 10, 10, 10, 10, 11,
12, 12, 13, 13, 13, 13, 14, 14, 14, 15,
15, 16, 17, 17, 18, 19, 19, 19, 21, 21, 21,
22, 22, 23, 23, 23, 23, 24, 25, 25, 25,
25, 25, 25, 25, 25, 25, 25, 25, 25, 26, 27,
27, 29, 29, 29, 29, 30, 30, 30, 31, 31, 31,
32, 32, 33, 33, 33, 33, 33, 34, 34, 34, 34,
34, 36; 11:1, 1, 4, 4, 4, 4, 5, 5, 5, 6, 6, 6, 7,
7, 7, 7, 8, 8, 8, 8, 9, 9, 9, 9, 9, 10, 10,
10, 10, 11, 11, 11, 11, 11, 11, 11, 11, 12,
12, 12, 12, 13, 13, 13, 13, 13, 14, 14,
14, 14, 14, 14, 14, 15, 15, 15, 15, 15,
15, 15, 17, 17, 18, 18, 18, 18, 18, 18,
19, 19, 19, 19, 19, 19, 19, 19, 19, 19, 19,
19, 19, 19, 19, 19, 19, 19, 19, 20, 20, 20,
2, 3, 3, 3, 4, 4, 4, 4, 4, 4, 4, 4, 4, 4, 4, 4,
5, 5, 5, 6, 6, 6, 6, 7, 7, 7, 7, 7, 8, 8, 8, 8,
8, 8, 8, 9, 10, 10, 10, 10, 11, 11, 11, 11,
12, 12, 13, 13, 13, 13, 14, 14, 14, 14, 15,
15, 16, 17, 17, 18, 18, 18, 18, 18, 18, 18,
18, 18, 18, 18, 20, 20, 20, 20, 20, 20, 20;
15:1, 3, 3, 4, 4, 4, 5, 5, 5, 5, 5, 5, 5, 6, 6,
6, 6, 6, 7, 7, 8, 8, 9, 9, 9, 9, 9, 10, 10, 11, 11,
11, 11, 11, 11, 11, 12, 12, 12, 13, 13, 14, 14,
15, 15, 15, 15, 15, 16, 16, 17, 17, 17, 18, 18,
18, 18, 19, 19, 19, 19, 20, 20, 20, 21,
21, 21, 21, 21, 23, 23, 24, 24, 24, 24, 24,
25, 25, 25, 25, 26, 26, 26, 26, 27, 28,
28, 28, 29, 29, 29, 29, 29, 30, 30, 30, 30,
31, 31, 31, 32, 32, 32, 33, 33, 34, 34, 34,
35, 35, 35, 35, 35, 35, 37, 37, 37; 16:1, 1,
1, 2, 2, 2, 2, 3, 3, 3, 3, 3, 4, 4, 4, 4, 6, 6, 7,
7, 7, 8, 8, 8, 8, 9, 9, 9, 9, 9, 9, 10, 11, 11,
11, 11, 12, 12, 12, 13, 13, 13, 13, 13, 14,
14, 14, 14, 15, 15, 15, 16, 16, 16, 17, 17, 18,
18, 18, 18, 18, 18, 19, 19, 19, 19, 19, 19,
20; 17:1, 1, 2, 2, 2, 4, 4, 4, 5, 5, 6, 6, 6, 6,
6, 7, 7, 7, 7, 7, 8, 8, 8, 8, 8, 9, 9, 9, 11, 11,
11, 11, 12, 13, 13, 13, 13, 13, 14, 14,
15, 15, 16, 16, 16, 16, 17, 17, 17, 18, 18,
19, 19, 20, 20, 20, 21, 21, 21, 21, 22, 22, 23,
23, 24, 24, 24, 24, 25; 14:1, 1, 3, 4, 4, 4, 5, 5,
6, 6, 6, 6, 7, 7, 8, 8, 8, 9, 9, 9, 11, 12, 13,
13, 13, 13, 14, 14, 14, 14, 14, 14, 15,
15, 15, 15, 15, 16, 16, 17, 17, 18, 18, 18,
18, 19, 19, 19, 19, 19, 20, 20, 21, 21,
22, 23, 23, 24, 24, 24, 25, 25, 25, 25, 26, 27,
27, 27, 27, 28, 28, 28, 28, 29;

5, 5, 5, 5, 5, 5, 5, 5, 6, 7, 8, 8, 8, 8, 8, 8,
8, 9, 9, 9, 9, 9, 9, 9, 10, 10, 10, 10, 10,
10, 11, 11, 11, 11, 11, 12, 12, 12, 12, 12, 12, 12,
13, 13, 13, 13, 13, 13, 14, 14, 14, 14, 14, 14,
14, 14, 15, 15, 15, 16, 16, 16, 16, 17, 18,
18, 18, 19, 19, 19, 20, 20, 20; 23:1, 1, 2,
2, 2, 2, 2, 2, 2, 2, 2, 2, 2, 2, 2, 2, 2, 2, 2,
3, 3, 4, 4, 4, 4, 4, 4, 4, 4, 4, 4, 4, 4, 5,
5, 5, 5, 5, 5, 5, 5, 5, 6, 6, 6, 6, 6, 6, 6, 6,
6, 7, 7, 7, 7, 7, 7, 8, 8, 8, 8, 8, 8, 8, 8, 8,
8, 8, 9, 9, 9, 9, 10, 10, 10, 11, 11,
11, 11, 11, 11, 11, 11, 11, 11, 11, 11, 12, 12,
12, 12, 12, 12, 12, 12, 12, 12, 13, 13, 13,
13, 13, 13, 13, 13, 13, 13, 13, 13, 14, 14,
14, 15, 15, 15, 15, 15, 15, 16, 16, 16, 16,
16, 16, 16, 16, 17, 17, 17, 17, 17, 18, 18,
19, 19, 19, 19, 19, 19, 19, 20, 20, 20, 21, 21,
21, 21, 21, 22, 22, 22, 22, 23, 24, 24, 24,
24, 24, 24, 24, 24, 24, 27, 28, 28, 24, 24, 28,
25, 25, 25, 26, 26, 27, 28, 28, 28, 24, 28,
34, 34, 35, 35, 35, 35, 35, 35, 35, 35, 35,
36, 37, 37; 24:2, 2, 2, 2, 2, 2, 2, 2, 3, 3,
4, 4, 5, 5, 5, 5, 7, 7, 7, 7, 7, 7, 8, 9, 9, 10,
10, 11, 11, 12, 12, 12, 13, 13, 13, 13, 13,
13, 13, 13, 14, 14, 14, 14, 14, 15,
20; 25:1, 1, 1, 1, 2, 2, 3, 3, 3, 3, 3, 4, 4,
4, 4, 4, 4, 4, 4, 4, 5, 5, 5, 5, 5, 6, 6, 7, 7,
8, 8, 8, 8, 8, 9, 9, 9, 9, 10, 10, 10, 11, 12,
10, 11, 11, 11, 11, 11, 11, 11, 11, 11, 12,
12, 12, 12, 13, 13, 13, 13, 13, 13, 13, 14,
13, 14, 14, 14, 14, 15, 15, 15, 15, 16,
16, 16, 16, 17, 17, 17, 17, 17, 17, 17, 17,
17, 18, 18, 18, 18, 18, 19, 19, 19, 19, 19,
19, 19, 19, 19, 19, 19, 19, 19, 20, 20, 20,
22, 22, 22, 22, 23, 23, 23, 23, 23, 23, 23,
26, 26, 26, 26, 24, 27, 25, 27, 27, 27, 27,
28, 28, 29, 30;

1Ch 1:5, 6, 7, 8, 9, 9, 10, 12, 14, 14, 14, 15,
15, 15, 16, 16, 17, 19, 19, 19, 23, 27,
28, 29, 31, 32, 32, 33, 33, 34, 35, 36, 37,
38, 39, 40, 40, 41, 41, 42, 42, 43, 43, 43,
43, 43, 44, 45, 45, 46, 46, 46, 48, 49, 50,
50, 50, 51, 54; 2:1, 3, 3, 3, 3, 3, 4, 5, 6,
7, 7, 7, 8, 9, 10, 13, 14, 14, 15, 15,
16, 17, 17, 18, 21, 21, 22, 23, 23, 23, 23,
24, 25, 25, 26, 27, 27, 28, 28, 29, 29,
30, 31, 31, 31, 32, 32, 33, 42, 42, 42,
42, 42, 43, 43, 44, 45, 45, 47, 49, 49, 49,
50, 50, 50, 50, 51, 52, 52, 53, 53, 53,
53, 53, 53, 54, 54, 54, 54, 54, 55, 55,
55, 55, 55, 55, 55; 3:1, 1, 1, 1, 1, 2, 2, 2,
2, 3, 3, 3, 5, 9, 9, 9, 15, 15, 15, 15, 15,
16, 17, 19, 19, 21, 21, 21, 21, 22,
23, 24; 4:1, 2, 2, 2, 3, 3, 4, 4, 4, 4, 4, 5, 6,
7, 8, 8, 10, 11, 11, 12, 12, 13, 13, 14, 14,
15, 15, 15, 16, 17, 17, 18, 18, 18, 18, 18,
18, 19, 19, 19, 20, 20, 20, 21, 21, 21, 21,
21, 21, 21, 22, 22, 23, 24, 24, 26, 27, 27,
33, 34, 35, 35, 35, 37, 37, 37, 37, 37, 38,
39, 39, 39, 40, 41, 41, 42, 42, 43, 43; 5:1,
1, 1, 1, 1, 1, 1, 2, 2, 3, 3, 4, 6, 7, 7, 8, 8,
8, 9, 9, 9, 9, 9, 10, 10, 10, 10, 11, 11, 12,
13, 14, 14, 14, 14, 14, 14, 14, 14, 15, 15,
15, 16, 17, 17, 18, 18, 18, 19, 20, 20, 20,
22, 25, 26, 28, 28, 29, 31, 31, 33, 34, 34,
34, 35, 35, 35, 35, 35, 36, 37, 37, 38, 39,
37, 37, 38, 38, 38, 39, 39, 39, 40, 40, 40,
41, 41, 41, 42, 42, 42, 43, 43, 44, 44,
47, 47, 48, 48, 49, 49, 49, 49, 49, 49,
50, 54, 54, 54, 54, 55, 55, 56, 56, 56, 56,
57, 57, 57, 60, 61, 61, 61, 61, 62, 62, 62,
62, 62, 63, 63, 63, 63, 64, 64, 65, 65, 65,
65, 65, 65, 66, 66, 66, 66, 67, 70, 70, 70,
70, 71, 71, 71, 72, 74, 76, 77, 77, 77, 78,
78, 78, 78, 80; 7:1, 2, 2, 3, 3, 4, 5, 6, 6, 7, 7,
8, 8, 9, 9, 10, 10, 11, 11, 12, 12, 13, 13,
14, 14, 14, 15, 15, 15, 15, 16, 16, 17, 17,
17, 19, 20, 21, 21, 24, 24, 28, 28, 28, 29,
29, 29, 29, 30, 31, 31, 33, 33, 34, 35, 36,
38, 39, 40, 40, 40, 40, 40; 8:1, 1, 2, 2,
6, 6, 6, 6, 8, 10, 12, 22, 27, 29, 34, 35, 38, 39, 39,
18, 21, 25, 27, 28, 29, 34, 35, 38, 38, 39,
39, 40, 40; 9:1, 1, 2, 2, 2, 2, 2, 3, 3, 4,
4, 4, 4, 4, 5, 5, 6, 7, 7, 7, 7, 8, 8, 8, 8,
8, 9, 9, 10, 11, 11, 11, 11, 11, 11, 11, 12,
12, 12, 12, 12, 12, 12, 13, 13, 13, 13,
14, 14, 14, 14, 14, 15, 15, 15, 16, 16, 16,
16, 16, 16, 16, 17, 17, 18, 18, 19, 19, 19,
19, 19, 19, 19, 19, 19, 19, 19, 19, 19, 19,
20, 20, 20, 21, 21, 21, 22, 22, 23, 23, 23,
23, 23, 24, 24, 26, 26, 26, 27, 27, 27, 27,
28, 28, 28, 29, 29, 29, 30, 30, 31, 31, 31,
32, 32, 33, 33, 34, 34, 34, 34, 35, 35, 35,
36, 36, 37, 37, 38, 38, 39, 39, 39, 40,
40, 41, 41, 42, 42, 42, 43, 43, 44, 44, 44,

Idx

45, 45, 46, 46, 46, 47; 12:1, 1, 1, 2, 2, 3, 3, 3, 3, 3, 4, 4, 4, 4, 5, 6, 7, 8, 8, 8, 8, 8, 8, 8, 9, 9, 9, 10, 10, 11, 11, 12, 12, 13, 13, 14, 14, 14, 14, 15, 15, 15, 15, 16, 16, 17, 18, 18, 19, 19, 19, 19, 20, 21, 21, 22, 23, 23, 23, 23, 23, 23, 24, 24, 25, 25, 26, 27, 27, 29, 29, 29, 29, 30, 30, 31, 32, 32, 32, 35, 37, 37, 37, 37, 37, 38; 13:1, 2, 2, 2, 2, 3, 4, 4, 4, 5, 5, 6, 6, 6, 7, 7, 7, 9, 9, 9, 10, 10, 10, 11, 12, 13, 13, 13, 13, 14, 14, 14, 14; 14:2, 4, 8, 8, 9, 9, 10, 10, 11, 11, 13, 13, 14, 15, 15, 15, 15, 16, 16, 17, 17, 17; 15:1, 1, 2, 2, 2, 2, 3, 3, 4, 4, 5, 5, 6, 6, 7, 7, 8, 8, 9, 9, 10, 10, 11, 11, 12, 12, 12, 12, 12, 13, 13, 13, 14, 14, 14, 14, 15, 15, 15, 15, 16, 16, 16, 16, 17, 17, 17, 17, 17, 18, 18, 19, 21, 22, 23, 24, 24, 24, 25, 25, 25, 25, 25, 26, 26, 26, 26, 26, 27, 27, 27, 27, 27, 28, 28, 28, 28, 29, 29, 29, 29, 29; 16:1, 1, 1, 2, 2, 2, 2, 2, 4, 4, 4, 4, 5, 6, 6, 6, 7, 8, 8, 8, 10, 10, 10, 11, 12, 14, 14, 15, 16, 17, 18, 18, 23, 23, 24, 25, 26, 26, 26, 26, 28, 28, 28, 29, 29, 29, 29, 30, 30, 31, 31, 31, 31, 32, 32, 32, 33, 33, 33, 33, 34, 34, 35, 36, 36, 36, 37, 37, 37, 37, 38, 39, 39, 39, 39, 39, 40, 40, 40, 40, 40, 41, 41, 42, 43; 17:1, 1, 1, 3, 3, 4, 5, 6, 7, 7, 7, 8, 8, 8, 9, 9, 10, 10, 16, 16, 17, 18, 21, 23, 24, 24, 24, 27; 18:1, 1, 2, 3, 4, 5, 5, 6, 6, 7, 7, 8, 8, 8, 9, 11, 11, 11, 11, 11, 12, 12, 12, 13, 13, 15, 15, 15, 16, 16, 16, 17, 17, 17, 17; 19:1, 1, 2, 2, 2, 2, 3, 3, 3, 4, 5, 5, 5, 5, 6, 6, 7, 7, 8, 8, 9, 9, 9, 9, 9, 10, 10, 10, 11, 11, 11, 11, 12, 12, 13, 13, 14, 14, 14, 14, 15, 15, 15, 16, 16, 16, 16, 16, 17, 17, 17, 18, 18, 18, 18, 19, 19, 19, 19; 20:1, 1, 1, 1, 1, 1, 2, 2, 2, 3, 3, 4, 4, 4, 4, 5, 5, 5, 6, 7, 8, 8, 8; 21:2, 2, 2, 3, 3, 4, 5, 5, 6, 8, 9, 10, 11, 12, 12, 12, 12, 12, 12, 12, 12, 13, 13, 13, 14, 15, 15, 15, 16, 16, 16, 16, 16, 17, 17, 18, 18, 18, 18, 18, 18, 19, 19, 19, 20, 21, 21, 22, 22, 22, 22, 22, 23, 23, 23, 23, 24, 24, 24, 25, 26, 26, 26, 27, 27, 28, 28, 28, 28, 29, 29, 29, 29, 30, 30, 30; 22:1, 1, 1, 1, 2, 2, 2, 3, 3, 3, 4, 5, 5, 6, 7, 7, 7, 8, 8, 10, 11, 11, 12, 12, 12, 13, 13, 14, 14, 16, 16, 16, 16, 16, 17, 17, 18, 18, 18, 18, 19, 19, 19, 19, 19, 19, 19, 19; 23:2, 2, 2, 3, 3, 4, 4, 5, 5, 6, 7, 8, 8, 9, 9, 9, 10, 10, 11, 11, 12, 13, 13, 14, 14, 15, 16, 17, 17, 17, 18, 18, 19, 19, 19, 19, 19, 19, 20, 20, 21, 21, 21, 22, 23, 24, 24, 24, 24, 24, 24, 25, 26, 26, 26, 27, 27, 28, 28, 28, 28, 29, 29, 29, 29, 30, 31, 31, 31, 31, 31, 31, 32, 32, 32, 32, 32, 32, 32, 32, 32; 24:1, 1, 1, 2, 3, 3, 4, 4, 4, 4, 4, 4, 5, 5, 5, 5, 6, 6, 6, 6, 6, 6, 6, 6, 7, 7, 8, 8, 9, 9, 10, 10, 11, 11, 12, 12, 13, 13, 14, 14, 15, 15, 16, 16, 17, 17, 18, 18, 19, 19, 19, 19, 20, 20, 20, 20, 20, 21, 21, 22, 22, 23, 23, 23, 23, 24, 24, 24, 25, 25, 26, 26, 27, 29, 30, 30, 30, 30, 31, 31, 31, 31, 31, 31, 31, 32; 25:1, 1, 1, 1, 1, 1, 2, 2, 2, 2, 3, 3, 3, 3, 5, 5, 6, 6, 6, 6, 6, 6, 7, 7, 8, 8, 8, 8, 9, 9, 10, 10, 11, 11, 12, 13, 14, 15, 16, 17, 18, 19, 20, 21, 22, 23, 24, 25, 26, 27, 28, 29, 30, 30; 26:1, 1, 1, 1, 1, 1, 2, 2, 2, 2, 3, 3, 3, 4, 5, 5, 6, 7, 8, 8, 10, 10, 10, 10, 11, 11, 11, 12, 12, 12, 12, 12, 12, 12, 13, 13, 14, 14, 14, 16, 16, 16, 16, 16, 18, 19, 19, 19, 19, 20, 20, 20, 20, 20, 20, 21, 21, 21, 22, 22, 22, 22, 23, 23, 23, 23, 24, 24, 24, 24, 24, 25, 25, 25, 26, 26, 26, 26, 27, 27, 27, 27, 27, 27, 28, 28, 28, 28, 28, 29, 29, 29, 30, 30, 30, 30, 30, 31, 31, 31, 31, 32, 32, 32, 32, 32, 32, 32, 32, 32, 32; 27:1, 1, 1, 1, 1, 1, 2, 2, 2, 3, 3, 3, 3, 4, 4, 4, 4, 5, 5, 5, 6, 6, 7, 7, 8, 8, 8, 9, 9, 9, 9, 10, 10, 10, 10, 11, 11, 11, 12, 12, 12, 12, 13, 13, 13, 13, 14, 14, 14, 14, 15, 15, 15, 16, 16, 16, 16, 16, 16, 17, 17, 17, 17, 18, 18, 19, 19, 19, 19, 20, 20, 20, 20, 21, 21, 21, 22, 22, 22, 23, 23, 23, 23, 24, 24, 24, 24, 24, 25, 25, 25, 25, 25, 25, 26, 26, 26, 27, 27, 27, 27, 27, 28, 28, 28, 28, 28, 29, 29, 29, 29, 29, 30, 30, 30, 30, 31, 31, 31, 31, 31, 31, 32, 32, 32, 32; 28:1, 1, 1, 1, 1, 1, 1, 1, 1, 2, 2, 2, 2, 2, 2, 4, 4, 4, 4, 5, 5, 5, 5, 5, 8, 8, 8, 8, 9, 9, 9, 9, 10, 10, 11, 11, 11, 11, 11, 11, 11, 12, 12, 12, 12, 12, 12, 12, 13, 13, 13, 13, 13, 13, 13, 13, 13, 15, 15, 15, 15, 16, 17, 17, 18, 18, 18, 19, 19, 19, 20, 20, 20, 20, 21, 21, 21, 22, 22, 22, 22, 23, 23, 23, 23, 23, 24, 24, 25, 25, 25, 26, 26, 27, 27, 27, 27, 27, 27, 28, 28, 28, 28, 28, 29, 29, 29, 29, 29, 29, 29, 30, 30; 29:1, 1, 1, 1, 1, 1, 2, 2, 2, 2, 2, 3, 3, 3, 4, 4, 5, 5, 5, 5, 5, 6, 6, 6, 6, 7, 8, 8, 9, 9, 9, 10, 10, 11, 11, 11, 11, 11, 11, 11, 15, 17, 17, 18, 18, 18, 19, 19, 20, 20, 20, 20, 20, 20, 21, 21, 21, 21, 22, 22, 24, 24, 24, 25, 25, 26, 27, 29, 29, 29, 29, 29, 29, 29, 30, 30; 30:

2Ch 1:1, 1, 2, 2, 2, 2, 3, 3, 3, 3, 3, 3, 4, 4, 5, 5, 5, 5, 5, 5, 6, 6, 6, 7, 7, 9, 9, 11, 12, 12, 13, 13, 13, 14, 14, 15, 15, 15, 16, 16, 17, 17, 17; 2:1, 1, 2, 3, 4, 4, 4, 4, 4, 4, 4, 4, 5, 6, 7, 9, 10, 11, 11, 12, 12, 12, 14, 14, 14, 15, 15, 16, 17, 17, 17, 18, 18; 3:1, 1, 1, 1, 2, 2, 2, 3, 3, 3, 3, 4, 4, 4, 5, 6, 7, 7, 7, 8, 8, 8, 8, 9, 9, 9, 10, 11, 11, 11, 11, 11,

11, 11, 12, 12, 12, 12, 12, 12, 12, 13, 14, 15, 15, 15, 16, 16, 16, 16, 16, 17, 17, 17, 17, 17, 17; 4:1, 1, 2, 3, 3, 3, 4, 4, 4, 4, 5, 5, 5, 6, 6, 6, 6, 6, 6, 7, 7, 7, 7, 8, 8, 8, 8, 9, 9, 9, 9, 9, 10, 10, 10, 10, 11, 11, 11, 12, 12, 12, 12, 12, 12, 12, 12, 12, 12, 13, 13, 13, 13, 13, 14, 16, 16, 16, 16, 16, 16, 16, 16; 5:1, 1, 1, 1, 1, 1, 1, 1, 1, 1, 1, 2, 2, 2, 2, 2, 2, 2, 2, 2, 2, 2, 3, 3, 3, 3, 3, 3, 3, 3, 3, 3, 4, 4, 5, 5, 5, 5, 5, 6, 6, 7, 7, 7, 7, 8, 8, 8, 8, 9, 9, 10, 10, 10, 11, 11, 11, 12, 12, 12, 12; 6:1, 1, 3, 3, 3, 4, 5, 5, 5, 7, 7, 7, 8, 9, 9, 10, 10, 10, 10, 10, 10, 10, 11, 11, 11, 12, 12, 12, 13, 13, 13, 14, 14, 14, 14, 16, 18, 18, 19, 19, 19, 19, 20, 20, 20, 21, 21, 21, 21, 22, 22, 23, 24, 24, 25, 25, 25, 26, 27, 27, 28, 28, 30, 30, 31, 32, 33, 33, 33, 34, 34, 35, 37, 37, 38, 38, 38, 39, 40, 41, 42, 42; 7:1, 1, 1, 1, 4, 4, 4, 5, 5, 6, 6, 6, 6, 6, 6, 6, 6, 7, 7, 7, 7, 7, 7, 7, 7, 8, 9, 10, 10, 10, 11, 11, 12, 12, 13, 15, 18, 20, 21, 22, 22; 8:1, 1, 1, 2, 2, 4, 4, 5, 5, 6, 6, 6, 6, 7, 7, 7, 7, 7, 8, 9, 10, 10, 11, 11, 11, 11, 12, 12, 12, 13, 13, 13, 13, 14, 14, 14, 14, 14, 14, 15, 15, 15, 15, 16, 16, 16, 16, 17, 18, 18; 9:1, 1, 3, 3, 4, 4, 5, 5, 7, 7, 8, 9, 10, 10, 11, 11, 11, 11, 12, 12, 12, 13, 13, 14, 14, 14, 14, 15, 15, 15, 16, 16, 16, 16, 17, 17, 18, 18; 9:1, 1, 3, 3, 3, 4, 5, 5, 7, 7, 7, 8, 9, 10, 10, 11, 11, 11, 11, 12, 12, 12, 13, 13, 14, 14, 14, 14, 15, 15, 15, 16, 16, 16, 16, 17, 17, 18, 18, 18; 9:1, 1, 3, 3, 4, 4, 5, 5, 7, 7, 8, 9, 11, 11, 11, 12, 12, 13, 13, 14, 14, 15, 15, 16, 16, 17, 18, 18; 10:2, 2, 3, 4, 5, 5, 6, 6, 6, 7, 7, 7, 7, 8, 8, 8, 8, 9, 9, 10, 10, 10, 11, 11, 11, 12, 12, 13, 13, 14, 14, 14, 15, 15, 15, 15, 16, 16, 16, 16, 17, 17, 18, 19; 11:1, 1, 2, 2, 3, 3, 4, 4, 4, 11, 13, 13, 14, 14, 15, 15, 15, 16, 16, 17, 17, 17, 17, 18, 18, 18, 18, 19, 20, 20; 12:1, 1, 1, 1, 3, 3, 4, 5, 5, 5, 5, 6, 6, 6, 7, 7, 7, 7, 7, 8, 8, 9, 9, 9, 9, 9, 10, 10, 11, 11, 11, 12, 12, 12, 13, 13, 13, 13, 14, 15, 15, 16, 16; 13:1, 1, 2, 3, 3, 3, 3, 3, 4, 4, 4, 5, 5, 5, 6, 6, 7, 7, 7, 8, 8, 8, 8, 9, 9, 10, 10, 11, 11, 11, 11,

11, 11, 12, 12, 12, 12, 12, 12, 13, 14, 15, 15, 15, 16, 16, 16, 16, 16, 17, 17, 17, 17, 17; 4:1, 1, 2, 3, 3, 3, 4, 4, 4, 4, 5, 5, 5, 6, 6, 6, 6, 6, 6, 7, 7, 7, 7, 8, 8, 8, 8, 9, 9, 9, 9, 9, 10, 10, 10, 10, 11, 11, 11, 12, 12, 12, 12, 12, 12, 12, 12, 12, 12, 13, 13, 13, 13, 13, 14, 16, 16, 16, 16, 16, 16, 16, 16; 5:1, 1, 1, 1, 1, 1, 1, 1, 1, 1, 1, 2, 2, 2, 2, 2, 2, 2, 2, 2, 2, 2, 3, 3, 3, 3, 3, 3, 3, 3, 3, 3, 4, 4, 5, 5, 5, 5, 5, 6, 6, 7, 7, 7, 7, 8, 8, 8, 8, 9, 9, 10, 10, 10, 11, 11, 11, 12, 12, 12, 12; 6:1, 1, 3, 3, 3, 4, 5, 5, 5, 7, 7, 7, 8, 9, 9, 10, 10, 10, 10, 10, 10, 10, 11, 11, 11, 12, 12, 12, 13, 13, 13, 14, 14, 14, 14, 16, 18, 18, 19, 19, 19, 19, 20, 20, 20, 21, 21, 21, 21, 22, 22, 23, 24, 24, 25, 25, 25, 26, 27, 27, 28, 28, 30, 30, 31, 32, 33, 33, 33, 34, 34, 35, 37, 37, 38, 38, 38, 39, 40, 41, 42, 42; 7:1, 1, 1, 1, 4, 4, 4, 5, 5, 6, 6, 6, 6, 6, 6, 6, 6, 7, 7, 7, 7, 7, 7, 7, 7, 8, 9, 10, 10, 10, 11, 11, 12, 12, 13, 15, 18, 20, 21, 22, 22; 8:1, 1, 1, 2, 2, 4, 4, 5, 5, 6, 6, 6, 6, 7, 7, 7, 7, 7, 8, 9, 10, 10, 11, 11, 11, 11, 12, 12, 12, 13, 13, 13, 13, 14, 14, 14, 14, 14, 14, 15, 15, 15, 15, 16, 16, 16, 16, 17, 18, 18; 9:1, 1, 3, 3, 4, 4, 5, 5, 7, 7, 8, 9, 10, 10, 11, 11, 11, 11, 12, 12, 12, 13, 13, 14, 14, 14, 14, 15, 15, 15, 16, 16, 16, 16, 17, 17, 18, 18; 14:1, 1, 2, 2, 3, 3, 3, 3, 3, 4, 4, 5, 5, 6, 7, 7, 7, 9, 10, 11, 12, 12, 12, 13, 13, 14, 14, 14, 14, 15; 15:1, 1, 2, 2, 3, 4, 5, 5, 8, 8, 8, 8, 8, 8, 9, 10, 10, 10, 11, 11, 11, 12, 13, 14, 14, 15, 15, 16; 16:1, 1, 1, 1, 2, 2, 2, 2, 2, 4, 4, 6, 7, 7, 7, 7, 7, 8, 8, 8, 9, 9, 9, 9, 10, 10, 11, 11, 11, 12, 12, 12, 12, 14; 17:2, 2, 3, 3, 4, 5, 5, 6, 6, 7, 7, 9, 9, 9, 9, 10, 10, 11, 11, 13, 14, 15, 15, 16, 17, 18, 19; 10:1, 1, 1, 1, 2, 2, 2, 2, 4, 4, 6, 7, 7, 9, 9, 9, 10, 10, 10, 11, 11, 11, 12, 12, 13, 13, 14, 14, 15, 16; 13:1, 2, 2, 2, 3, 3, 3, 5, 5, 6, 6, 6, 6, 7, 7, 7, 7, 9, 9, 9, 9, 10, 10, 10, 10, 11, 11, 11, 11, 12, 12, 13, 13, 14, 14, 15, 15, 16; 15:1, 1, 1, 2, 3, 4, 4, 11, 13, 14; 16:1, 1, 1, 2, 2, 4, 6, 7, 7, 7, 7, 7, 8, 8, 8, 9, 9, 9, 9, 10, 10, 11, 11, 11, 12, 12, 12, 12, 14; 19:1, 2, 2, 2, 3, 3, 4, 4, 5, 5, 6, 6, 6, 7, 7, 8, 8, 8, 8, 9, 10, 10, 11, 11; 18:2, 3, 4, 4, 4, 5, 5, 6, 7, 7, 8, 8, 9, 9, 9, 9, 10, 10, 10, 11, 11, 11, 11, 12, 13, 14, 14, 14, 14, 15, 15, 15, 15, 16, 16, 17, 17, 18, 18, 18, 19, 20, 20, 20, 21, 21, 22, 22, 22, 23, 23, 23, 25, 25, 25, 26, 26, 27, 27, 28, 28, 29, 29, 29, 30, 30, 30, 30, 31, 31, 31, 31, 32, 32, 32, 33, 33, 34, 34, 34; 19:1, 2, 4, 4, 5, 6, 6, 6, 7, 7, 8, 8, 8, 8, 8, 9, 10, 11, 11, 11, 11, 11; 20:1, 1, 10, 13, 14, 14, 14, 14, 14, 14, 15, 15, 16, 16, 17, 17, 17, 18, 18, 19, 19, 19, 20, 21, 21, 21, 22, 22, 23, 23, 23, 23, 23, 24, 24, 24, 25, 25, 25, 26, 26, 26, 26, 26, 27, 27, 28, 28, 28, 29, 29, 30; 21:1, 2, 3, 3, 4, 4, 4, 5, 6, 6, 7, 7, 7, 8, 8, 9, 9, 10, 10, 10, 13, 13, 14, 15, 16, 16, 17, 17, 17, 18, 18, 19, 20, 20; 22:1, 1, 1, 1, 1, 2, 3, 4, 4, 4, 5, 5, 6, 7, 7, 7, 8, 8, 9, 9, 10, 10, 10, 11, 11, 11, 11, 12, 12, 12; 23:1, 1, 1, 1, 1, 1, 1, 2, 2, 2, 3, 3, 4, 4, 4, 4, 4, 5, 5, 5, 5, 6, 6, 6, 6, 7, 7, 7, 8, 8, 8, 8, 9, 9, 10, 10, 10, 10, 10, 11, 11, 11, 12, 12, 12, 13, 13, 13, 14, 14, 14, 14, 15, 15, 16, 16, 16, 17, 17, 18, 18, 18, 19, 20, 20, 20; 24:2, 2, 2, 2, 4, 4, 5, 5, 5, 5, 5, 5, 6, 6, 6, 6, 6, 6, 7, 7, 7, 7, 8, 8, 9, 9, 9, 10, 10, 11, 11, 11, 11, 11, 11, 12, 12, 12, 12, 12, 13, 13, 14, 14, 14, 14, 14, 14, 14, 14, 16, 16, 16, 17, 17, 17, 18, 18, 18, 19, 20, 20,

21, 21, 22, 23, 23, 23, 23, 23, 23, 23, 24, 24, 27, 27, 28; 26:1, 1, 2, 4, 4, 5, 5, 5, 9, 9, 10, 10, 10, 6, 6, 7, 7, 8, 8, 9, 9, 9, 10, 10, 10, 10, 11, 11, 11, 11, 11, 11, 11, 11, 11, 11, 11, 12, 12, 12, 12, 12, 12, 12, 12, 12, 13, 13, 14, 15, 15, 16, 16, 16, 16, 16, 17, 17, 18, 18, 19, 19, 19, 19, 19, 20, 20, 20, 20, 21, 21, 21, 22, 22, 22, 22, 22, 23, 23, 23; 27:1, 1, 2, 2, 3, 4, 4, 5, 5, 5, 5, 5, 5, 6, 7, 7, 7, 9, 9; 28:1, 1, 2, 3, 3, 3, 3, 4, 4, 4, 5, 5, 5, 6, 7, 7, 7, 8, 8, 9, 9, 9, 10, 10, 11, 12, 12, 13, 13, 13, 13, 14, 15, 15, 16, 16, 16, 17, 17, 17, 18, 18, 19, 20, 20, 21, 21, 22, 22, 23, 23, 23, 23, 24, 24, 24, 25, 25, 26, 26, 27, 27, 27, 27; 29:1, 1, 2, 3, 3, 4, 4, 4, 5, 5, 5, 6, 6, 6, 7, 7, 7, 8, 8, 8, 9, 10, 11, 11, 12, 12, 12, 12, 13, 15, 15, 15, 15, 16, 16, 16, 16, 16, 17, 18, 18, 19, 19, 20, 20, 21, 21, 22, 22, 22, 23, 23; 12:1, 1, 7, 7, 7, 8, 8, 8, 8, 8, 9, 9, 10, 10, 11, 11, 11, 11, 12, 12, 13, 13, 14, 14, 15, 15, 16; 13:1, 2, 3, 3, 3, 5, 5, 6, 6, 6, 6, 7, 7, 7, 7, 9, 9, 9, 9, 10, 10, 10, 10, 11, 11, 11, 11, 12, 12, 13, 13, 13, 14, 14, 15, 15, 16;

21, 21, 22, 23, 23, 23, 23, 23, 23, 24, 24, 24, 24, 24, 24, 25, 25, 26, 26, 26, 26, 27, 27, 28; 26:1, 1, 2, 4, 4, 5, 5, 5, 6, 6, 6, 6, 7, 7, 7, 8, 8, 8, 9, 9, 9, 10, 10, 10, 10, 11, 11, 11, 11, 11, 11, 11, 11, 11, 12, 12, 12, 12, 12, 12, 12, 12, 13, 13, 14, 15, 15, 15, 16, 16, 16, 16, 16, 16, 16, 17, 17, 18, 18, 18, 18, 18, 18, 19, 19, 19, 19, 19, 20, 20, 20, 20, 20, 20, 20, 21, 21, 21, 21, 21, 21, 22, 22, 22, 22, 23, 23, 23, 23, 24, 24, 25, 25, 25, 25, 25, 25, 25, 25, 26, 26, 26, 26, 27, 27, 27, 27, 27, 27, 27, 28, 28, 28, 28, 29, 30, 30, 30, 30, 30, 31, 31, 31, 31, 31, 31, 31, 32, 32, 32, 33, 34, 34, 34, 34, 34, 35, 35, 35, 35, 35, 35, 36, 36, 36; 30:1, 1, 1, 1, 2, 2, 2, 2, 3, 4, 4, 4, 4, 5, 5, 5, 5, 5, 6, 6, 7, 7, 7, 7, 7, 8, 8, 8, 9, 9, 9, 10, 10, 10, 12, 12, 12, 12, 12, 12, 12, 14, 15, 15, 15, 16, 16, 16, 16, 17, 17, 17, 17, 17, 17, 17, 17, 18, 18, 18, 19, 19, 19, 19, 19; 31:2, 2, 2, 3, 4, 4, 4, 4, 11, 13, 14, 14, 15, 15, 15, 15, 15, 16, 16, 17, 18, 18, 19, 19, 19, 19, 19; 32:1, 1, 1, 1, 3, 3, 4, 4, 4, 4, 5, 5, 5, 6, 6, 7, 7, 7, 8, 8, 8, 8, 8, 10, 11, 11, 11, 11, 11, 11, 11, 11, 11, 11, 12, 12, 13, 13, 14, 15, 16, 17, 17, 17, 18, 18, 18, 19, 19, 19, 19, 19, 19, 19, 19, 20, 20, 20, 21, 21, 21, 21, 21, 21, 22, 22, 22, 22, 23, 23, 23, 23, 24, 24, 24, 24, 24, 25, 25, 25, 26, 26, 26, 27, 27, 27, 27; 31:1, 1, 1, 1, 1, 1, 2, 2, 2, 2, 2, 2, 2, 2, 3, 3, 3, 3, 3, 3, 3, 3, 3, 3, 4, 4, 4, 4, 4, 4, 5, 5, 5, 5, 5, 5, 6, 6, 6, 7, 7, 7, 8, 8, 8, 8, 9, 9, 9, 10, 10, 10, 10, 10, 10, 11, 11, 11, 12, 12, 12, 12, 12, 12, 12, 13, 13, 14, 14, 14, 14, 14, 14, 14, 14, 15, 15, 15, 16, 16, 16, 17, 17, 17, 17, 17, 18, 18, 18, 18, 18, 18, 18, 18, 18, 19, 19, 22, 22, 22, 22, 23, 25, 25, 25, 25, 25; 34:2, 2, 3, 3, 3, 3, 3, 4, 4, 4, 4, 5, 5, 6, 7, 7, 7, 7, 7, 8, 8, 8, 8, 8, 8, 8, 8, 9, 9, 10, 10, 11, 11, 11, 11, 11, 12, 12, 12, 12, 13, 14, 14, 14, 14, 15, 15, 15, 16, 16, 16, 17, 18, 18, 18, 18, 18, 19, 19, 20, 20, 20, 20, 21, 21, 21, 21, 21, 21, 22, 22, 22, 22, 23, 23, 24, 24, 24, 24, 25, 26, 26, 27, 27; 35:1, 1, 1, 1, 2, 2, 2, 3, 3, 3, 3, 4, 4, 5, 5, 5, 5, 5, 6, 6, 7, 7, 7, 7, 7, 8, 8, 8, 8, 8, 8, 9, 9, 10, 10, 10, 11, 11, 11, 11, 12, 12, 12, 13, 13, 13, 13, 14, 14, 14, 14, 15, 15, 15, 16, 16, 16, 16, 16, 16, 16, 16, 17, 17, 18, 19, 20, 20, 21, 21, 21, 22, 22, 22, 22, 23, 23, 24, 24, 25, 25, 25, 26, 26, 26, 26, 27; 36:1, 1, 1, 3, 3, 4, 4, 5, 5, 7, 7, 7, 8, 8, 8, 8, 9, 9, 10, 10, 10, 10, 11, 11, 11, 11, 12, 12, 12, 13, 14, 14, 14, 14, 14, 14, 14, 14, 14, 15, 16, 16, 16, 17, 17, 17, 18, 18, 18, 18, 19, 19, 20, 20, 21, 21, 21, 22, 22, 22, 23, 23, 23, 23, 23;

Ezr 1:1, 1, 1, 1, 1, 2, 2, 3, 3, 3, 3, 4, 4, 4, 5, 5, 5, 5, 5, 7, 7, 7, 7, 7, 8, 8, 8, 9, 11; 2:1, 1, 1, 1, 2, 2, 2, 3, 4, 5, 6, 6, 7, 8, 9, 10, 11, 12, 13, 14, 15, 16, 17, 18, 19, 20, 21, 22, 23, 24, 25, 26, 26, 28, 29, 30, 31, 31, 32, 33, 34, 35, 36, 36, 36, 37, 38, 39, 40, 40, 40, 41, 41, 42, 42, 42, 42, 43, 43, 43, 43, 44, 44, 45, 45, 46, 46, 46, 47, 47, 47, 48, 48, 48, 49, 49, 49, 50, 50, 51, 51, 51, 52, 52, 53, 53, 53, 53, 54, 54, 55, 55, 55, 55, 56, 56, 56, 57, 57, 57, 57, 57, 58, 58, 60, 60, 60, 62, 62, 63, 63, 63, 63, 63, 63, 64, 65, 65, 66, 70, 70, 70, 70, 70, 71, 71, 71, 71, 72, 72, 73, 73, 73, 73, 73, 73, 73, 73; 8:1, 1, 1, 1, 1, 2, 2, 2, 2, 3, 3, 3, 3, 3, 3, 3, 3, 4, 4, 4, 5, 5, 5, 5, 6, 6, 6, 6, 7, 7, 7, 7, 8, 8, 8, 8, 9, 9, 9, 9, 9, 9, 9, 10, 10, 10, 11, 11, 11, 12, 13, 13, 13, 13, 13, 13, 13, 14, 14, 14, 14, 15, 16, 16, 16, 16, 16, 16, 17, 17, 17, 17, 17, 18, 18; 9:1, 1, 2, 2, 3, 3, 4, 4, 4, 5, 5, 6, 6, 6, 7, 7, 7, 8, 8, 8, 8, 8, 8, 9, 9, 10, 11, 11, 11, 11, 11, 12, 12, 12, 12, 13, 13, 13, 13, 13, 14, 14, 14, 14, 14, 15, 15, 16, 16, 16, 16, 16, 17, 17, 18; 9:1, 2, 3, 3, 3, 4, 4, 5, 5, 6, 6, 7, 7, 8, 8, 8, 8, 8, 8, 9, 9, 10, 10, 10, 10,

12, 13, 13, 13, 13, 13, 14, 14, 14, 15, 15, 15, 15, 15, 16, 16, 16, 16, 17, 17, 17, 17, 17, 17, 18, 20, 22, 22, 22, 22, 24, 24, 24, 24, 24; 5:1, 1, 1, 1, 1, 2, 2, 2, 3, 3, 3, 4, 4, 5, 5, 5, 5, 6, 6, 6, 6, 6, 7, 8, 8, 8, 8, 8, 9, 9, 10, 10, 10, 10, 10, 10, 10, 11, 11, 11, 11, 11, 12, 12, 12, 12, 12, 13, 13, 13, 13, 14, 14, 14, 14, 14, 14, 15, 15, 16, 16, 16, 16, 16, 17, 17, 17, 17, 17; 6:1, 1, 1, 1, 2, 2, 3, 3, 3, 3, 4, 4, 5, 5, 5, 6, 6, 7, 7, 7, 7, 8, 9, 9, 9, 10, 10, 12, 13, 13, 13, 14, 14, 14, 15, 15, 16, 16, 16, 16, 16, 16, 17, 17, 17, 18, 18, 19, 19, 19, 19, 19, 20, 20, 20, 20, 20, 20, 22, 22, 22, 22; 7:1, 1, 1, 2, 2, 2, 3, 3, 3, 4, 4, 5, 5, 5, 6, 6, 6, 7, 7, 7, 7, 8, 8, 8, 9, 9, 9, 10, 10, 11, 11, 11, 11, 12, 12, 12, 13, 13, 13, 14, 14, 14, 14, 14, 15, 15, 15, 16, 16, 16, 17, 17, 18, 18; 9:1, 1, 1, 1, 1, 2, 2, 3, 3, 3, 3, 3, 4, 5, 6, 6, 6, 7, 7, 7, 7, 8, 8, 8, 8, 9, 9, 9, 10, 10, 10, 11, 11, 11, 11, 11, 11, 11, 12, 12, 12, 13, 14, 14, 14, 14, 15, 19, 19, 19, 19, 19, 19, 21, 22, 22, 22, 22, 23, 23, 24, 24, 24, 24, 24, 24, 24, 24, 24, 25; 5:1, 1, 3, 4, 5, 7, 8, 8, 9, 9, 9, 11, 11, 11, 11, 12, 12, 13, 13, 14, 14, 14, 14, 14, 14, 15, 15, 15, 15, 16, 16, 16, 17, 17, 18, 18, 18; 6:1, 1, 1, 1, 1, 2, 2, 3, 4, 5, 6, 6, 7, 9, 10, 10, 10, 10, 10, 10, 10, 11, 11, 14, 14, 15, 15, 16, 17, 18, 18, 18, 7:1, 1, 1, 1, 1, 2, 2, 3, 3, 3, 3, 4, 4, 4, 5, 5, 5, 5, 6, 6, 6, 6, 7, 7, 7, 7, 8, 9, 10, 11, 11, 11, 12, 13, 13, 13, 14, 14, 14, 14, 15, 16, 17, 18, 18, 19, 20, 21, 21, 22, 23, 24, 25, 26, 27, 28, 29, 30, 31, 32, 33, 33, 34, 34, 35, 36, 37, 38, 39, 39, 40, 41, 42, 43, 43, 43, 43, 43, 44, 44, 44, 45, 45, 45, 45, 45, 46, 46, 46, 46, 46, 46, 47, 47, 47, 48, 48, 49, 49, 49, 50, 50, 50, 51, 51, 51, 51, 52, 52, 53, 53, 53, 53, 54, 54, 55, 56, 56, 57, 57, 57, 57, 58, 58, 58, 59, 59, 59, 59, 60, 60, 62, 62, 63, 63, 63, 63, 63, 64, 65, 65, 66, 70, 70, 70, 70, 71, 71, 71, 72, 72, 73, 73, 73, 73, 73, 73, 73; 8:1, 1, 1, 1, 2, 2, 2, 3, 4, 4, 5, 5, 5, 6, 6, 6, 7, 8, 8, 9, 10, 11, 11, 12, 12, 13, 14, 15, 16, 17, 18, 19, 20, 21, 22, 23, 24, 25, 26, 27, 28, 29, 30, 31, 32, 33, 33, 34, 34, 35, 36, 37, 38, 39, 39, 40, 41, 42, 43, 43, 43, 43, 44, 44, 45, 45, 45, 46, 46, 46, 47, 47, 47, 48, 48, 49, 49, 50, 50, 51, 51, 51, 52, 52, 53, 53, 53, 54, 54, 55, 55, 55, 55, 56, 56, 57, 57, 58, 58, 60, 61, 61, 61, 61, 61, 61, 61, 62, 63, 63, 64, 68, 68, 68, 68, 68, 69, 69, 70, 70, 70, 70, 70, 70; 3:1, 1, 1, 1, 2, 2, 2, 2, 2, 2, 2, 3, 3, 4, 4, 4, 4, 5, 5, 5, 5, 5, 5, 6, 6, 6, 6, 6, 6, 7, 7, 7, 7, 7, 8, 8, 8, 8, 9, 9, 9, 9, 10, 10, 10, 10, 10, 10, 10, 10, 11, 11, 11, 11, 11, 11, 12, 12, 12, 12, 12, 12, 12; 4:1, 1, 1,

12, 13, 13, 13, 13, 13, 14, 14, 14, 15, 15, 15, 15, 15, 16, 16, 16, 16, 16, 16, 17, 17, 17, 17, 17, 17, 18, 20, 20, 20, 20, 20, 20, 22, 22, 22, 24; 5:1, 1, 1, 1, 1, 2, 2, 2, 3, 3, 4, 4, 5, 5, 5, 6, 6, 6, 6, 6, 7, 8, 8, 8, 8, 8, 9, 9, 10, 10, 10, 10, 10, 11, 11, 11, 11, 11, 12, 12, 12, 12, 13, 13, 13, 13, 14, 14, 14, 14, 14, 14, 15, 15, 16, 16, 16, 16, 16, 17, 17, 17, 17, 17; 6:1, 1, 1, 1, 2, 2, 3, 3, 3, 3, 4, 4, 5, 5, 5, 6, 6, 7, 7, 7, 7, 8, 9, 9, 9, 10, 10, 12, 13, 13, 13, 14, 14, 14, 15, 15, 16, 16, 16, 16, 16, 16, 17, 17, 17, 18, 18, 19, 19, 19, 19, 19, 20, 20, 20, 20, 20, 20, 22, 22, 22, 22; 7:1, 1, 1, 2, 2, 2, 3, 3, 3, 4, 4, 5, 5, 5, 6, 6, 6, 7, 7, 7, 7, 8, 8, 8, 9, 9, 9, 10, 10, 11, 11, 11, 11, 12, 12, 12, 13, 13, 13, 14, 14, 14, 14, 14, 15, 15, 15, 16, 16, 16, 17, 17, 18, 18, 18; 8:1, 1, 1, 1, 1, 2, 2, 3, 4, 5, 6, 6, 7, 9, 10, 10, 10, 10, 10, 10, 10, 11, 11, 14, 14, 15, 15, 16, 17, 18, 18, 18,

12, 13, 13, 13, 13, 14, 14, 14, 15, 15, 15, 15, 15, 16, 16, 16, 16, 16, 17, 17, 17, 17, 17, 17, 18, 20, 22, 23, 24, 24, 24, 24; 5:1, 1, 1, 1, 1, 1, 2, 2, 2, 3, 3, 4, 4, 4, 5; 11:1, 1, 1, 1, 2, 2, 3, 3, 3, 3, 3, 4, 4, 5, 6, 7, 8, 9, 11, 11, 11, 12, 12, 12, 12, 13, 14, 15, 15, 16, 16, 17, 18, 19, 20, 21, 22, 23, 23; 11, 11, 11, 11, 11, 11, 12, 12, 12, 12, 12, 13, 14, 14, 14, 14, 15, 15, 15, 16, 16, 16, 17, 17, 17, 17, 17, 17, 18, 18, 18, 18, 18, 19, 20, 21, 22, 23, 23, 24, 24, 24, 25, 26, 27, 27, 28, 29, 30, 31, 32, 33, 33, 34, 34, 35, 36, 37, 38, 39, 39, 40, 41, 42, 43, 43, 43, 43, 43, 44, 44, 44, 45, 45, 45, 45, 45, 46, 46, 46, 46, 46, 46, 47, 47, 47, 48, 48, 49, 49, 49, 50, 50, 50, 51, 51, 51, 51, 52, 52, 53, 53, 53, 53, 54, 54, 54, 55, 56, 56, 57, 57, 57, 57, 58, 58, 58, 59, 59, 59, 59, 60, 60, 62, 62, 63, 63, 63, 63, 63, 64, 65, 65, 66, 70, 70, 70, 70, 71, 71, 71, 72, 72, 73, 73, 73, 73, 73, 73, 73; 8:1, 1, 1, 1, 2, 2, 2, 3, 4, 4, 5, 5, 5, 6, 6, 6, 7, 8, 8, 9, 10, 11, 11, 12, 12, 13, 14, 15, 16, 17, 18, 19, 20, 21, 22, 23, 24, 25, 26, 27, 28, 29, 30, 31, 32, 33, 33, 34, 34, 35, 36, 37, 38, 39, 39, 40, 41, 42, 43, 43, 43, 43, 44, 44, 45, 45, 45, 46, 46, 46, 47, 47, 47, 48, 48, 49, 49, 50, 50, 51, 51, 51, 52, 52, 53, 53, 53, 54, 54, 55, 55, 55, 55, 56, 56, 57, 57, 58, 58, 60, 61, 61, 61, 61, 61, 61, 61, 62, 63, 63, 64, 68, 68, 68, 68, 68, 69, 69, 70, 70, 70, 70, 70, 70; 3:1, 1, 1, 1, 2, 2, 2, 2, 2, 2, 2, 3, 3, 4, 4, 4, 4, 5, 5, 5, 5, 5, 5, 6, 6, 6, 6, 6, 6, 7, 7, 7, 7, 7, 8, 8, 8, 8, 9, 9, 9, 9, 10, 10, 10, 10, 10, 10, 10, 10, 11, 11, 11, 11, 11, 11, 12, 12, 12, 12, 12, 12, 12, 13, 13, 13, 13, 13, 13, 14, 14, 14, 14, 14, 14, 15, 15, 16, 16, 16, 16, 16, 16, 16, 16, 17, 17, 17, 17, 18; 9:1, 1, 1, 1, 2, 2, 3, 3, 3, 3, 3, 4, 4, 4, 5, 5, 5, 5, 6, 6, 6, 6, 7, 7, 7, 7, 8, 9, 10, 11, 11, 11, 12, 13, 13, 13, 14, 14, 14, 14, 15, 16, 17, 18, 18, 19, 20, 21, 21, 22, 23, 24, 25, 26, 27, 28, 29, 30, 31, 32, 33, 33, 34, 34, 35, 36, 37, 38, 39, 39, 40, 41, 42, 43, 43, 43, 43, 43, 44, 44, 44, 45, 45, 45, 45, 45, 46, 46, 46, 46, 46, 46, 47, 47, 47, 48, 48, 49, 49, 49, 50, 50, 50, 51, 51, 51, 51, 52, 52, 53, 53, 53, 53, 54, 54, 55, 56, 56, 57, 57, 57, 57, 58, 58, 58, 59, 59, 59, 59, 60, 60, 62, 62, 63, 63, 63, 63, 63, 64, 65, 65, 66, 70, 70, 70, 70, 71, 71, 71, 72, 72, 73, 73, 73, 73, 73, 73, 73;

12, 13, 13, 13, 13, 14, 14, 14, 15, 15, 15, 15, 15, 16, 16, 16, 16, 16, 17, 17, 17, 17, 17, 17, 18, 20, 22, 23, 24, 24; 5:1, 1, 1, 1, 1, 1, 2, 2, 2, 3, 3, 3, 4; 24; 5:1, 1, 1, 1, 1, 1, 2, 2, 2, 3, 3, 3, 4, 4, 5, 5, 5, 5, 6, 6, 6, 6, 6, 6, 7, 8, 8, 8, 8, 8, 8, 8; 10, 10, 10, 11, 11, 11, 11, 11, 12, 12, 12, 12, 13, 13, 13, 13, 13, 14, 14, 14, 14, 15, 15, 16, 16, 16, 17, 17, 17; 6:1, 1, 1, 1, 1, 2, 2, 3, 3, 4, 4, 5, 5, 5, 6, 6, 7, 7, 7, 8, 8, 9, 9, 10, 10, 11, 11, 12, 12, 13, 13, 14, 14, 14; 2, 2, 3, 3, 3, 4, 4, 5, 5, 5, 6, 6, 7, 7, 8, 8, 9, 9, 9, 9, 10, 10, 10, 11, 11, 11, 12, 13, 13, 14, 14, 14; 9, 9, 9, 10, 11, 11, 11, 11, 12, 12, 12, 12, 13, 13, 14, 14, 14, 14, 14, 14, 15, 15, 16, 17, 17, 18, 18; 9:1, 1, 2, 2, 3, 3, 4, 4, 5, 5, 5, 5, 6, 6, 7, 7, 8, 8, 8, 8, 8, 9, 9, 9, 10, 10, 11, 11, 11, 11, 11, 11, 12, 12, 13, 13, 14, 14, 14, 14, 15, 15, 15, 15, 15, 19, 19, 19, 19, 19, 21, 22, 22, 22, 22;

12, 13, 13, 13, 13, 13, 14, 14, 14, 15, 15, 15, 15, 15, 16, 16, 16, 16, 17, 17, 17, 17, 17; 6:1, 1, 1, 1, 2, 2, 3, 3, 3, 3, 4, 4, 5, 5, 5, 6, 6, 7, 7, 7, 7, 8, 9, 9, 9, 10, 10, 12, 13, 13, 13, 14, 14, 14, 15, 15, 16, 16, 16, 16, 16, 16, 17, 17, 17, 18, 18, 19, 19, 19, 19, 19, 20, 20, 20, 20, 20, 20, 22, 22, 22, 22; 24:5, 5, 5, 5, 5, 6, 7, 7, 7, 7, 7, 8, 9, 11; 2:1, 1, 1, 1, 1, 2, 2, 2, 3, 4, 5, 6, 6, 7, 8; 9, 10, 11, 12, 13, 14, 15, 16, 17, 18, 19, 20, 21, 21, 32, 33, 34, 35, 36, 36, 36, 37, 38, 39, 40, 40, 40, 41, 41, 42, 42, 42, 42, 42, 42, 42, 42, 43, 43, 43, 43, 44, 44, 45, 45, 46, 46, 46, 47, 47, 47, 48, 48, 48, 49, 49, 49, 50, 50, 51, 51, 51, 52, 52, 53, 53, 53, 53, 54, 54, 55, 55, 55, 55, 56, 56, 56, 57, 57, 57, 57, 57, 58, 58, 60, 60, 60, 62, 62, 63, 63, 63, 63, 63, 63, 64, 65, 65, 66, 70, 70, 70, 70, 70, 71, 71, 71, 71, 72, 72, 73, 73, 73, 73, 73, 73, 73, 73; 8:1, 1, 8; 9, 9, 9, 11, 11, 11, 11, 12, 12, 13, 13, 14, 14, 14, 14, 14, 14, 15, 15, 15, 15, 16, 16, 16, 17, 17, 18, 18, 18; 6:1, 1, 1, 1, 1, 2, 2, 3, 4, 5, 6, 6, 7, 9, 10, 10, 10, 10, 10, 10, 10, 11, 11, 14, 14, 15, 15, 16, 17, 18, 18, 18; 7:1, 1, 1, 1, 1, 2, 2, 3, 3, 3, 3, 4, 4, 4, 5, 5, 5, 5, 6, 6, 6, 6, 7, 7, 7, 7, 8, 9, 10, 11, 11, 11, 12, 13, 13, 13, 14, 14, 14, 14, 15, 16, 17, 18, 18, 19, 20, 21, 21, 22, 23, 24, 25, 26, 27, 28, 29, 30, 31, 32, 33, 33, 34, 34, 35, 36, 37, 38, 39, 39, 40, 41, 42, 43, 43, 43, 43, 43, 44, 44, 44, 45, 45, 45, 45, 45, 46, 46, 46, 46, 46, 46, 47, 47, 47, 48, 48, 49, 49, 49, 50, 50, 50, 51, 51, 51, 51, 52, 52, 53, 53, 53, 53, 54, 54, 55, 56, 56, 57, 57, 57, 57, 58, 58, 58, 59, 59, 59, 59, 60, 60, 62, 62, 63, 63, 63, 63, 63, 64, 65, 65, 66, 70, 70, 70, 70, 71, 71, 71, 72, 72, 73, 73, 73, 73, 73, 73, 73; 8:1, 1, 1, 1, 2, 2, 2, 3, 4, 4, 5, 5, 5, 6, 6, 6, 7, 8, 8, 9, 10, 11, 11, 12, 12, 13, 14, 15, 16, 17, 18, 19, 20, 21, 22, 23, 24, 25, 26, 27, 28, 29, 30, 31, 32, 33, 33, 34, 34, 35, 36, 37, 38, 39, 39, 40, 41, 42, 43, 43, 43, 43, 44, 44, 45, 45, 45, 46, 46, 46, 47, 47, 47, 48, 48, 49, 49, 50, 50, 51, 51, 51, 52, 52, 53, 53, 53, 54, 54, 55, 55, 55, 55, 56, 56, 57, 57, 58, 58, 60, 61, 61, 61, 61, 61, 61, 61, 62, 63, 63, 64, 68, 68, 68, 68, 68, 69, 69, 70, 70, 70, 70, 70, 70; 3:1, 1, 1, 1, 2, 2, 2, 2, 2, 2, 2, 3, 3, 4, 4, 4, 4, 5, 5, 5, 5, 5, 5, 6, 6, 6, 6, 6, 6, 7, 7, 7, 7, 7, 8, 8, 8, 8, 9, 9, 9, 9, 10, 10, 10, 10, 10, 10, 10, 10, 11, 11, 11, 11, 11, 11, 12, 12, 12, 12, 12, 12, 12; 4:1, 1, 1,

Ne 1:1, 1, 1, 1, 1, 2, 2, 3, 3, 3, 3, 3, 4, 5, 6, 6, 6, 6, 7, 7, 8, 8, 9, 9, 9, 11, 11, 11; 2:1, 1, 1, 1, 1, 2, 2, 3, 3, 3, 3, 4, 4, 5, 5, 5, 6, 6, 6, 6, 7, 7, 7, 7, 8, 8, 8, 8, 9, 9, 9, 9, 10, 10, 10, 12, 12, 12, 13, 13, 13, 13, 13, 14, 14, 14, 15, 15, 15, 15, 15, 16, 16, 16, 16, 16, 16, 17, 17, 17, 18, 18, 19, 19, 19, 19, 19, 20; 3:1, 1, 1, 1, 1, 1, 2, 2, 3, 3, 3, 3, 3, 3, 4, 4, 4, 4, 4, 5, 5, 5, 6, 6, 6, 6, 6, 7, 7, 7, 7, 7, 8, 8, 8, 8, 9, 9, 9, 10, 11, 11, 11, 11, 12, 12, 13, 13, 13, 13, 14, 14, 14, 14, 14, 14, 15, 15, 15, 15, 15, 15, 15, 16, 16, 16, 16, 16, 16, 16, 16, 17, 17, 17, 17, 18, 18, 18, 18, 19, 19, 19, 19, 19, 20, 20, 20, 20, 20, 20, 20, 21, 21, 21, 21, 22, 22, 22, 22, 23, 23, 24, 24, 24, 24, 24, 24, 24, 25, 25, 25, 25, 25, 25, 25, 25, 25, 26, 26, 26, 27, 27, 27, 27, 27, 28, 28, 28, 28, 29, 29, 29, 30, 30, 30, 30, 31, 31, 31, 31, 31, 31, 32; 4:1, 1, 2, 2, 2, 2, 3, 4, 5, 6, 6, 6, 6, 7, 7, 7, 7, 7, 8, 8, 8, 9, 9, 9, 9, 10, 10, 11, 12, 13, 13, 13, 13, 14, 14, 14, 14, 15, 16, 16, 16, 16, 16, 16, 16, 17, 17, 18, 18, 19, 19, 19, 19, 20, 21, 21, 21, 21, 21, 22, 22, 23, 23; 5:1, 1, 3, 4, 5, 7, 8, 8, 9, 9, 9, 11, 11, 11, 12, 13, 13, 13, 14, 14, 14, 14, 14, 14, 15, 15, 15, 16, 16, 17, 17, 18, 18, 18; 6:1, 1, 1, 1, 2, 2, 3, 4, 5, 6, 6, 7, 9, 10, 10, 10, 11, 11, 12, 12, 13, 14, 14, 15, 16, 17, 18, 19; 7:1, 1, 1, 2, 3, 3, 4, 5, 6, 6, 7, 9, 10, 11, 11, 11, 12, 12, 13, 14, 15, 16, 17, 18, 19, 20, 21, 22, 22, 22, 23, 24, 24, 24, 24, 24, 24, 27, 27, 28, 28, 28, 28, 28, 30, 30, 31, 32, 32, 33, 33, 34, 34, 35, 36, 37; 10:1, 1, 8, 9, 9, 9, 14, 14, 14, 29, 28, 28, 28, 28, 28, 28, 28, 28, 29, 29, 30, 30, 30, 31, 31, 31, 31, 31, 32, 32, 32, 33, 34, 34, 34, 34, 34, 34, 35, 35, 35, 35, 36, 36, 36, 36, 37, 37, 37, 37, 37, 37, 38, 38, 38, 38, 38, 38, 38, 38, 38, 38, 38, 38, 38, 39, 39, 39, 39; 11:1, 1, 1, 1, 1, 1, 1, 1, 1, 1, 2, 2, 2, 2, 3, 3, 3, 3, 3, 4, 4, 4, 4, 4, 4, 4, 4, 5, 5, 5, 5, 5, 6, 7, 7, 7, 7, 7, 7, 7, 7, 7, 9, 9,

9, 10, 10, 11, 11, 11, 11, 11, 11, 11, 12, 12, 12, 12, 12, 12, 12, 12, 12, 13, 13, 13, 13, 14, 14, 15, 15, 15, 15, 15, 16, 16, 16, 16, 16, 17, 17, 17, 17, 17, 17, 17, 17, 18, 18, 19, 19, 20, 20, 20, 21, 21, 22, 22, 22, 22, 22, 22, 22, 22, 22, 23, 24, 24, 24, 24, 24, 25, 25, 25, 25, 27, 28, 30, 30, 30, 31, 35, 36; 12:1, 1, 1, 7, 7, 7, 8, 8, 9, 12, 12, 12, 22, 22, 22, 22, 22, 23, 23, 23, 23, 23, 23, 23, 24, 24, 24, 24, 24, 25, 25, 25, 26, 26, 26, 26, 26, 26, 27, 27, 27, 27, 27, 28, 28, 28, 29, 29, 29, 30, 30, 30, 30, 30, 31, 31, 31, 31, 31, 32, 35, 35, 35, 35, 35, 35, 35, 36, 36, 36, 37, 37, 37, 37, 37, 37, 37, 38, 38, 38, 38, 38, 38, 39, 39, 39, 39, 39, 39, 39, 40, 40, 40, 40, 40, 41, 42, 43, 43, 43, 44, 44, 44, 44, 44, 44, 44, 44, 44, 44, 45, 45, 45, 45, 45, 45, 46, 46, 47, 47, 47, 47, 47, 47, 47, 47; 13:1, 1, 1, 1, 2, 2, 3, 3, 4, 4, 4, 4, 5, 5, 5, 5, 5, 5, 5, 5, 5, 5, 5, 6, 6, 7, 7, 7, 8, 8, 9, 9, 9, 9, 10, 10, 10, 10, 10, 11, 11, 11, 12, 12, 12, 13, 13, 13, 13, 13, 13, 14, 14, 15, 15, 15, 16, 16, 17, 17, 18, 19, 19, 19, 19, 19, 20, 21, 21, 22, 22, 22, 24, 24, 24, 28, 28, 28, 28, 29, 29, 29, 29, 30, 30, 30, 31, 31;

Est 1:1, 2, 2, 2, 3, 3, 3, 3, 4, 4, 4, 5, 5, 5, 5, 5, 6, 7, 7, 7, 8, 8, 8, 8, 9, 9, 9, 10, 10, 10, 10, 10, 11, 11, 11, 11, 11, 12, 12, 13, 13, 13, 13, 14, 14, 14, 14, 15, 15, 15, 15, 16, 16, 16, 16, 16, 16, 16, 16, 16, 17, 17, 17, 18, 18, 18, 19, 19, 19, 19, 19, 20, 20, 21, 21, 21, 21, 21, 22, 22, 22; 2:1, 2, 2, 3, 3, 3, 3, 3, 3, 3, 4, 4, 4, 4, 5, 5, 5, 6, 6, 7, 7, 8, 8, 8, 8, 9, 9, 9, 9, 9, 11, 11, 12, 12, 12, 12, 12, 13, 13, 13, 14, 14, 14, 14, 14, 14, 14, 14, 14, 15, 15, 15, 15, 15, 15, 15, 16, 16, 16, 17, 17, 17, 17, 18, 18, 18, 19, 19, 19, 19, 19, 20, 20, 21, 21, 21, 21, 21, 22, 22, 22, 22, 22, 23, 23, 23; 3:1, 1, 1, 2, 2, 2, 3, 3, 3, 6, 6, 6, 6, 7, 7, 7, 7, 7, 8, 8, 8, 8, 9, 9, 9, 9, 10, 10, 11, 11, 11, 12, 12, 12, 12, 12, 12, 12, 13, 13, 13, 13, 13, 13, 14, 14, 14, 15; 4:1, 1, 2, 2, 3, 3, 4, 5, 6, 6, 6, 7, 7, 7, 7, 8, 8, 8, 9, 11, 11, 11, 11, 11, 13, 14, 14, 16, 16; 5:1, 1, 1, 1, 1, 1, 1, 2, 2, 2, 2, 2, 3, 3, 3, 4, 4, 4, 4, 4, 5, 5, 5, 6, 6, 6, 7, 7, 8, 8; 6:1, 1, 1, 2, 2, 2, 2, 3, 3, 4, 4, 4, 4, 4, 4, 5, 5, 5, 6, 6, 6, 7, 7, 7, 8, 8, 8, 8, 9, 9, 9, 10, 10, 10, 10, 10, 11, 11, 11, 11, 12, 13, 13, 14; 7:1, 1, 2, 2, 2, 2, 3, 3, 4, 4, 5, 5, 6, 6, 6, 7, 7, 7, 7, 8, 8, 8, 8, 8, 8, 8, 9, 9, 9, 9, 9, 10, 10, 10, 10, 10, 10; 8:1, 1, 1, 1, 1, 2, 2, 3, 3, 3, 4, 4, 4, 5, 5, 5, 5, 5, 5, 6, 6, 6, 7, 7, 7, 7, 7, 8, 8, 8, 8, 8, 9, 9, 9, 9, 9, 9, 9, 9, 10, 10; 8:1, 1, 1, 1, 2, 2, 3, 3, 3, 4, 4, 4, 4, 5, 5, 5, 5, 5, 6, 6, 6, 7, 7, 7, 7, 7, 8, 8, 8, 8, 8, 9, 9, 9, 9, 9, 9, 10, 10; 9:1, 1, 1, 1, 1, 1, 1, 2, 2, 2, 2, 3, 3, 3, 3, 4, 4, 4, 5, 5, 5, 6, 6, 6, 6, 10, 10, 10, 10, 11, 11, 12, 12, 12, 12, 12, 12, 13, 13, 13, 14, 14, 14, 15, 15, 15, 16, 16, 16, 17, 17, 17, 17, 18, 18, 18, 18, 18, 19, 19, 19, 19, 19, 20, 20, 21, 21, 21, 21, 22, 22, 22, 23, 24, 24, 24, 24, 24, 25, 25, 25, 26, 26, 27, 28, 28, 29, 29, 29, 30, 30, 30, 30, 30, 31, 31, 31, 31, 31, 32, 32;

Job 1:1, 3, 3, 3, 5, 5, 5, 6, 6, 6, 7, 7, 7, 8, 8, 9, 9, 10, 10, 11, 12, 12, 12, 14, 14, 15, 15, 15, 16, 16, 16, 17, 17, 17, 17, 17, 17, 19, 19, 19, 19, 20, 21, 21, 21, 21; 2:1, 1, 1, 2, 2, 2, 3, 3, 4, 6, 6, 7, 7, 8, 10, 10, 10, 11, 11, 11, 13; 3:3, 3, 4, 4, 5, 5, 5, 6, 6, 6, 6, 8, 9, 9, 9, 9, 10, 11, 11, 11, 12, 12, 14, 14, 15, 17, 18, 18, 18, 18, 19, 19, 20, 22, 24, 25; 4:1, 3, 4, 6, 7, 8, 9, 9, 10, 10, 10, 10, 10, 11, 11, 13, 13, 15, 15, 16, 19; 5:1, 2, 3, 4, 4, 5, 5, 6, 6, 7, 10, 10, 12, 13, 13, 13, 14, 14, 15, 15, 15, 16, 16, 17, 17, 17, 17, 19, 21, 21, 22, 23, 23, 23, 25, 25; 6:2, 3, 4, 4, 4, 4, 4, 5, 5, 6, 7, 8, 10, 10, 12, 14, 14, 16, 16, 18, 19, 19, 23, 23, 26, 27; 7:1, 2, 2, 4, 4, 4, 8, 9, 9, 11, 11, 21, 21; 8:1, 2, 3, 5, 6, 8, 8, 11, 11, 13, 13, 16, 17, 17, 19, 19, 20, 20, 22, 22, 22, 23, 23, 23, 24, 24, 24, 24, 24, 26, 26, 30, 10:1, 3, 3, 3, 5, 9, 18, 19, 21, 21, 22; 11:1, 2, 6, 7, 9, 9, 9, 17, 17, 20, 20, 20, 20; 12:2, 4, 5, 6, 7, 7, 7, 8, 8, 8, 9, 9, 10, 11, 12, 15, 15, 16, 16, 17, 18, 19, 20, 20, 20, 20, 20, 21, 21, 22, 22, 23; 13:2, 3, 6, 19, 25, 26, 27, 27; 14:5, 7, 8, 8, 8, 9, 10, 11, 11, 12, 13, 14, 15, 18, 18, 19, 19, 19, 19, 19; 15:1, 2, 5, 7, 7, 8, 10, 11, 15, 19, 20, 21, 23, 24, 25, 26, 29, 29, 30, 30, 33, 33, 34, 34, 34; 16:5, 10, 11, 11, 11, 13, 15, 16, 18, 22; 17:1, 5, 6, 8, 8, 9, 11, 12, 12, 13, 13, 14, 16, 16, 16; 18:1, 4, 4, 5, 5, 6, 7, 9, 9, 9, 10, 10, 13, 13, 14, 17, 17, 18, 21, 21; 19:9, 19, 20, 21, 24, 25, 25, 28, 28, 29, 29, 29; 20:1, 3, 3, 5, 5, 5, 6, 6, 8, 9, 10, 11, 11, 14, 16, 16, 17, 17, 17, 18, 19, 20, 20, 20, 21, 21, 22, 22, 23, 24, 25, 27, 27, 28, 28, 29; 21:7, 9, 12, 12, 12, 13, 14, 15, 16, 16, 17, 17, 18, 18, 20, 20, 21, 21, 25, 26, 26, 27, 28, 28, 28, 29,

30, 30, 30, 32, 32, 33, 33; 22:1, 3, 6, 7, 7, 8, 8, 8, 9, 9, 12, 12, 12, 13, 14, 14, 17, 18, 18, 19, 19, 20, 20, 22, 23, 24, 24, 24, 25, 26, 28, 29, 30, 30, 30; 23:5, 7, 9, 9, 10, 12, 12, 14, 16, 17, 17; 24:1, 2, 3, 3, 3, 4, 4, 4, 4, 5, 5, 6, 6, 6, 7, 7, 8, 8, 9, 9, 9, 10, 10, 12, 12, 12, 13, 13, 13, 14, 14, 14, 14, 15, 15, 15, 15, 16, 16, 16, 16, 17, 17, 17, 17, 18, 18, 18, 18, 18, 19, 19, 20, 20, 21, 21, 22, 24, 24, 25:1, 5, 5, 6; 26:2, 3, 5, 5, 7, 7, 7, 8, 8, 9, 10, 10, 11, 12, 12, 13, 13, 14; 27:2, 3, 3, 7, 7, 8, 8, 10, 11, 11, 13, 13, 13, 14, 16, 16, 17, 17, 18, 19, 20, 21; 28:1, 2, 2, 3, 3, 4, 4, 4, 4, 5, 6, 6, 7, 8, 8, 9, 9, 10, 11, 11, 12, 13, 13, 14, 14, 15, 16, 16, 16, 17, 17, 17, 18, 19, 20, 21, 21, 21, 22, 23, 23, 24, 24, 24, 25, 25, 25, 26, 26, 26, 28, 28; 29:2, 4, 4, 5, 6, 7, 7, 7, 8, 8, 9, 10, 10, 11, 11, 12, 13, 13, 15, 15, 16, 16, 16, 17, 17, 17, 18, 19, 19, 23, 23, 24, 24, 25, 25; 30:1, 2, 3, 4, 6, 6, 6, 6, 7, 7, 8, 11, 12, 14, 15, 16, 17, 17, 18, 19, 22, 23, 24, 25, 25, 25; 31:2, 3, 7, 11, 13, 15, 15, 16, 16, 16, 17, 20, 21, 21, 22, 24, 26, 26, 28, 28, 29, 31, 32, 32, 34, 34, 35, 37, 38, 39, 39, 40; 32:2, 2, 2, 2, 5, 6, 6, 8, 8, 9, 18; 33:3, 4, 4, 4, 6, 8, 11, 15, 15, 16, 18, 19, 22, 22, 24, 25, 28, 28, 30, 30, 30; 34:3, 3, 8, 10, 11, 12, 13, 13, 16, 19, 19, 19, 20, 20, 21, 22, 25, 26, 28, 28, 28, 30, 30, 36; 35:5, 8, 9, 9, 9, 9, 10, 11, 11, 11, 12, 13; 36:6, 6, 6, 7, 7, 12, 13, 14, 15, 16, 17, 17, 19, 20, 26, 27, 27, 28, 29, 29, 29, 30, 30, 31, 32, 32, 33, 33, 33; 37:2, 2, 3, 3, 4, 4, 6, 6, 6, 6, 7, 8, 9, 9, 10, 10, 10, 11, 12, 12, 14, 15, 16, 16, 16, 17, 17, 18, 21, 21, 22; 38:1, 1, 4, 4, 5, 6, 6, 7, 8, 9, 12, 13, 13, 14, 14, 15, 15, 16, 16, 16, 16, 17, 17, 18, 18, 19, 19, 20, 20, 21, 22, 22, 23, 23, 24, 24, 25, 25, 26, 26, 27, 27; 39:1, 1, 1, 1, 2, 2, 5, 5, 5, 6, 6, 7, 7, 7, 7, 7, 8, 8, 9, 10, 10, 13, 13, 14, 14, 15, 15, 18, 19, 20, 21, 21, 22, 23, 23, 24, 24, 24, 25, 25, 25, 26, 26, 27, 27, 28, 28, 28, 29, 30; 40:1, 2, 3, 6, 6, 11, 12, 13, 16, 17, 19, 19, 20, 20, 20, 21, 21, 21, 22, 22; 41:6, 6, 8, 9, 9, 11, 13, 14, 18, 18, 23, 24, 25, 26, 26, 26, 28, 29, 30, 31, 31, 32, 34; 42:1, 5, 5, 7, 7, 7, 8, 9, 9, 10, 10, 11, 12, 12, 14, 14, 14, 14, 14, 15, 15;

Ps 1:1, 1, 1, 1, 1, 2, 2, 3, 4, 4, 4, 5, 5, 5, 6, 6, 6, 6, 6; 2:1, 1, 2, 2, 2, 4, 4, 7, 7, 8, 8, 8, 10, 11, 12; 3:3, 4, 5, 7, 7, 7, 8; 4:T, 3, 3, 5, 5, 6, 7; 5:T, 2, 3, 3, 5, 6, 6, 7, 10, 12; 6:T, 5, 6, 8, 8, 9, 9; 7:T, T, T, 5, 5, 5, 6, 6, 7, 7, 8, 8, 9, 9, 9, 9, 10, 11, 11, 13, 13, 15, 17, 17, 17; 8:T, 1, 1, 2, 2, 2, 3, 3, 3, 4, 5, 5, 6, 7, 7, 8, 8, 9, 9, 10, 11, 12, 12, 13, 14, 14, 15, 15, 16, 16, 16, 16, 17, 17, 17, 18, 18, 19, 20; 10:2, 2, 2, 3, 3, 3, 4, 4, 8, 8, 8, 8, 8, 9, 9, 10, 12, 13, 14, 14, 15, 15, 16, 16, 17, 18, 18, 18; 11:T, 1, 2, 2, 3, 3, 4, 4, 4, 5, 5, 6, 6, 7, 7; 12:T, 1, 1, 1, 2, 2, 3, 4, 5, 6, 6, 7, 7; 13:T, 3, 6; 14:T, 1, 2, 2, 4, 4, 5, 5, 6, 6, 6, 7, 7, 7, 7; 15:2, 4, 5; 16:2, 3, 3, 5, 5, 6, 7, 7, 8, 11; 17:1, 2, 2, 4, 4, 4, 8, 8, 8, 9, 11, 13, 14, 14; 18:T, T, T, T, T, T, T, T, 2, 2, 3, 4, 4, 4, 5, 5, 6, 7, 7, 9, 10, 10, 11, 13, 13, 15, 15, 15, 15, 18, 18, 20, 20, 21, 21, 22, 22, 25, 26, 26, 27, 27, 28, 28, 30, 30, 31, 35, 39, 40, 41, 42, 42, 42, 43, 43, 43, 43, 44, 45, 46, 46, 47, 48, 49; 19:T, 1, 1, 1, 4, 4, 4, 6, 6, 6, 6, 7, 7, 7, 8, 8, 8, 8, 8, 9, 9, 9, 10, 13, 14, 14; 20:T, 1, 1, 1, 2, 5, 5, 6, 6, 7, 9; 21:T, 1, 2, 3, 7, 7, 7, 7, 9, 9, 9, 10, 12; 22:T, 1, 2, 2, 3, 6, 7, 7, 8, 9, 10, 14, 15, 16, 16, 20, 20, 20, 21, 21, 21, 22, 22, 23, 23, 23, 24, 24, 25, 26, 26, 27, 27, 28, 29, 30; 23:1, 2, 3, 4, 4, 5, 6, 6, 6; 24:1, 1, 1, 2, 4, 4, 5, 5, 6, 6, 6, 6, 6, 6, 7, 7, 8, 8, 8, 9; 25:5, 5, 7, 8, 8, 9, 9, 9, 10, 10, 10, 12, 12, 13, 14, 14, 15, 17; 26:1, 5, 5, 7, 8, 8, 12, 12; 27:1, 1, 1, 2, 4, 4, 4, 4, 4, 4, 5, 6, 10, 12, 13, 13; 28:1, 2, 3, 4, 4, 5, 5, 6, 7, 8, 8; 29:1, 1, 2, 2, 2, 3, 3, 3, 3, 3, 3, 4, 4, 4, 4, 5, 5, 7, 7, 8, 8, 9, 9, 9, 10, 10, 10, 10, 11, 30:T, T, 3, 3, 4, 4, 5, 8, 9, 9; 31:T, 4, 6, 8, 8, 13, 15, 17, 17, 18, 18, 19, 20, 20, 20, 21, 22, 23, 23, 23, 23, 24; 32:2, 3, 4, 5, 5, 6, 8, 9, 11; 33:1, 1, 2, 2, 4, 4, 5, 5, 5, 5, 6, 6, 6, 6, 6, 6, 7, 7, 8, 8, 8, 9; 34:1, 2, 3, 4, 6, 7, 7, 8, 8, 9, 10, 11, 15, 16, 16, 18, 20, 27, 28; 35:3, 5, 5, 5, 5, 6, 6, 7, 7, 8, 8, 8, 8, 9, 10, 11, 11, 11, 12, 14, 14, 16, 17, 17, 17, 17, 18, 18, 18, 19, 19, 20, 20, 20, 20, 21, 21, 22, 23, 24, 25, 28, 28, 29, 30, 30, 31, 32, 32, 33, 34, 34, 34, 35, 37, 37, 38, 38, 38, 39, 39, 39, 39, 40, 40; 38:6, 8, 10, 12,

20; 39:T, 1, 3, 4, 8, 8, 10; 40:T, 1, 2, 3, 4, 4, 7, 7, 9, 10, 12, 12, 16, 17; 41:T, 1, 1, 2, 2, 2, 3, 3, 13; 42:T, T, 1, 1, 2, 4, 4, 4, 5, 6, 6, 7, 8, 8, 8, 8, 9, 9, 11; 43:1, 2, 2, 2, 4, 4, 5; 44:T, T, 1, 2, 2, 3, 3, 8, 10, 11, 14, 14, 14, 15, 15, 16, 16, 19, 19, 20, 21, 21, 22, 22, 25, 25; 45:T, T, 1, 1, 1, 2, 5, 5, 6, 7, 8, 9, 11, 12, 12, 12, 13, 14, 14, 15, 16, 17; 46:T, T, 2, 2, 2, 2, 3, 3, 4, 4, 4, 4, 4, 5, 6, 6, 6, 7, 7, 8, 8, 9, 9, 9, 9, 9; 47:T, T, 1, 2, 2, 3, 4, 5, 5, 7, 7, 8, 8, 9, 9, 9, 9, 9, 9; 48:T, 1, 1, 1, 2, 2, 2, 2, 2, 2, 4, 7, 8, 8, 9, 10, 10, 11, 12, 13; 49:T, T, 1, 3, 4, 5, 5, 6, 8, 10, 10, 12, 14, 14, 14, 14, 15, 15, 16, 19, 20; 50:1, 1, 1, 1, 1, 1, 2, 4, 4, 6, 10, 10, 11, 11, 11, 12, 12, 13, 13, 14, 15, 16, 23; 51:T, T, 1, 6, 6, 8, 12, 17, 18, 19; 52:T, T, 1, 1, 5, 6, 7, 7, 8, 8; 53:T, 1, 2, 4, 5, 6, 6; 54:T, T, 2, 4; 55:T, 3, 3, 3, 4, 7, 8, 9, 10, 10, 11, 14, 16, 18, 21, 22, 22, 23; 56:T, T, 7, 10, 13, 13; 57:T, T, 1, 3, 4, 5, 5, 6, 9, 9, 10, 10, 10, 11; 58:T, 2, 2, 3, 3, 4, 4, 5, 6, 8, 8, 9, 10, 10, 10, 10, 11; 59:T, 5, 2, 3, 5, 5, 6, 8, 10, 12, 12, 13, 14, 16, 16, 17; 60:T, T, 2, 2, 3, 4, 6, 7, 9, 11; 61:T, 2, 2, 2, 3, 4, 5, 6; 62:T, 7, 9; 63:T, 2, 6, 7, 9, 9, 10, 11, 11; 64:T, 1, 2, 2, 2, 2, 4, 6, 6, 9, 10, 10, 10; 65:T, 1, 4, 4, 5, 5, 5, 5, 6, 7, 7, 7, 7, 7, 8, 8, 9, 10, 10, 10, 11, 12, 12, 12, 13, 13; 66:T, 2, 3, 4, 5, 5, 6, 6, 7, 7, 8, 11, 15, 18, 19; 67:T, 3, 3, 4, 4, 4, 5, 6, 6, 7, 7; 68:T, 2, 2, 2, 3, 4, 5, 5, 6, 6, 7, 8, 8, 8, 8, 10, 11, 11, 11, 12, 13, 13, 14, 15, 15, 16, 16, 16, 17, 17, 18, 18, 19, 19, 19, 20, 20, 20, 21, 22, 22, 22, 23, 23, 23, 24, 24, 25, 25, 25, 26, 26, 27, 27, 27, 28, 28, 28, 29, 30, 30, 30, 31, 32, 33, 33, 33, 35; 69:T, 1, 2, 4, 9, 12, 12, 13, 13, 14, 14, 15, 15, 15, 16, 26, 28, 28, 30, 31, 32, 33, 34, 35, 36; 70:T; 71:4, 4, 4, 6, 8, 9, 15, 15, 16, 16, 20, 20, 22, 22, 24; 72:1, 1, 3, 3, 4, 4, 4, 4, 5, 6, 6, 6, 7, 7, 8, 8, 9, 9, 10, 10, 16, 17, 18, 18, 19, 19, 20, 20; 73:3, 3, 9, 9, 11, 12, 14, 17, 26, 28; 74:1, 2, 3, 13, 13, 13, 14, 14, 14, 14, 15, 15, 16, 16, 16, 16, 17, 17, 18, 18, 19, 19, 19, 20, 20, 20, 21, 21, 22, 23, 23; 75:T, 2, 3, 3, 4, 4, 4, 4, 6, 6, 6, 7, 8, 8, 8, 8, 8, 9; 76:T, 3, 3, 3, 3, 4, 4, 5, 6, 8, 9, 9, 10, 10, 10, 11, 11, 12, 12; 77:T, 2, 2, 5, 5, 5, 6, 7, 10, 10, 10, 11, 11, 11, 13, 14, 15, 15, 16, 16, 17, 17, 18, 18, 18, 18, 19, 19, 20; 78:1, 4, 4, 4, 6, 6, 7, 9, 9, 10, 12, 12, 12, 13, 13, 14, 14, 15, 15, 15, 16, 17, 17, 19, 20, 20, 20, 21, 23, 23, 24, 25, 26, 26, 26, 27, 27, 28, 31, 31, 31, 35, 40, 41, 42, 42, 43, 46, 46, 48, 49, 50, 51, 51, 52, 53, 54, 55, 55, 56, 60, 60, 61, 62, 63, 64, 65, 66, 67, 68, 68, 69, 70, 71, 72, 72; 79:1, 2, 2, 2, 2, 6, 6, 9, 10, 10, 10, 11, 11, 11; 80:T, 1, 4, 5, 8, 9, 10, 10, 10, 10, 11, 17; 81:T, 1, 2, 2, 3, 3, 4, 4, 5, 6, 6, 7, 10, 15, 16; 82:1, 1, 1, 2, 2, 3, 3, 4, 4, 4, 5, 6, 7, 8; 83:2, 4, 6, 6, 6, 6, 7, 7, 8, 9, 9, 12, 13, 13, 14, 14, 14, 18, 18; 84:T, T, 2, 2, 2, 3, 3, 5, 5, 6, 6, 6, 9, 10, 10, 11, 11, 12; 85:T, T, 1, 2, 3, 8, 11, 12, 13; 86:4, 6, 7, 8, 13, 14, 14, 16; 87:T, 1, 2, 2, 2, 5, 6, 6, 7, 7; 88:T, T, T, 3, 4, 5, 5, 5, 6, 6, 10, 10, 11, 12, 12, 13; 89:T, 1, 1, 2, 5, 5, 5, 6, 6, 6, 6, 6, 7, 7, 9, 9, 11, 11, 11, 11, 11, 12, 14, 15, 15, 16, 17, 18, 18, 19, 22, 25, 25, 26, 27, 27, 29, 32, 34, 36, 39, 41, 42, 43, 43, 44, 45, 48, 50, 50, 50, 50, 51, 52; 90:T, 2, 2, 2, 4, 5, 6, 6, 8, 10, 11, 15, 15, 17, 17, 17, 17; 91:1, 1, 1, 2, 3, 3, 3, 5, 6, 6, 6, 8, 9, 9, 11, 13; 92:T, 1, 2, 3, 3, 4, 7, 7, 7, 9, 10, 11, 12, 12, 13, 13, 13, 15; 93:1, 1, 1, 3, 3, 3, 4, 4, 4, 4, 4; 94:2, 2, 3, 3, 4, 4, 6, 6, 7, 7, 8, 9, 9, 10, 11, 12, 13, 13, 14, 15, 16, 16, 17, 19, 20, 21, 21, 21, 22, 22, 23; 95:1, 1, 3, 4, 4, 4, 4, 5, 6, 7, 8, 8, 8, 8; 96:1, 1, 1, 2, 3, 4, 5, 5, 5, 7, 7, 7, 8, 8, 9, 9, 9, 10, 10, 10, 11, 11, 11, 11, 12, 12, 12, 13, 13, 13, 15; 97:1, 1, 1, 2, 4, 4, 5, 5, 5, 5, 6, 6, 9, 10, 10, 10, 12; 98:1, 1, 2, 2, 3, 3, 3, 3, 9; 99:1, 1, 1, 1, 1, 2, 2, 4, 5, 6, 7, 7, 9, 9, 9; 100:1, 2, 3, 3, 5; 101:3, 6, 6, 8, 8, 8; 102:T, T, 2, 2, 5, 6, 6, 7, 8, 13, 13, 14, 15, 15, 15, 15, 16, 17, 17, 18, 18, 18, 19, 19, 20, 20, 21, 21, 22, 22, 23, 24, 25, 25, 25, 27, 28; 103:1, 2, 5, 6, 17, 19, 20, 20, 21, 22; 104:1, 2, 3, 3, 3, 5, 5, 6, 6, 6, 7, 8, 8, 9, 10, 10, 14, 15, 16, 16, 17, 17, 18, 18, 18, 19, 21, 22, 23, 26, 30, 31, 32, 32, 33, 35; 105:1, 1, 3, 3, 4, 5, 7, 8, 10, 10, 11, 16, 16, 19, 19, 20, 20, 23, 27, 30, 33, 34, 35, 35, 36, 36, 38, 39, 40, 40, 41, 41, 41, 44, 44, 44, 44, 45; 106:1, 1, 2, 4, 4, 5, 7, 7, 9, 9, 10, 11, 16, 20, 21, 22, 22, 23, 24, 25, 26, 27, 28,

29, 30, 32, 34, 34, 35, 38, 38, 38, 40, 40, 41, 41, 45, 47, 48, 48, 48; 107:1, 2, 2, 3, 3, 3, 3, 4, 9, 9, 9, 10, 11, 11, 11, 13, 14, 14, 15, 15, 16, 16, 18, 19, 21, 22, 23, 24, 24, 25, 25, 26, 26, 28, 29, 29, 31, 31, 32, 32, 32, 33, 34, 35, 36, 37, 40, 41, 42, 43, 43; 108:3, 3, 4, 5, 5, 7, 8, 10, 12; 109:T, 2, 2, 2, 2, 11, 11, 13, 14, 14, 14, 15, 15, 16, 16, 19, 20, 20, 21, 23, 23, 30, 31, 31; 110:1, 2, 2, 2, 3, 3, 3, 3, 4, 4, 5, 6, 6, 6, 7, 7; 111:1, 1, 1, 1, 1, 2, 2, 4, 6, 6, 6, 7, 10, 10, 10; 112:1, 1, 1, 2, 2, 4, 6, 7, 9, 10, 10, 10; 113:1, 1, 1, 1, 2, 2, 3, 3, 3, 3, 4, 4, 5, 6, 6, 7, 7, 7, 8, 9, 9; 114:1, 3, 4, 4, 7, 7, 7, 8, 8; 115:2, 3, 4, 9, 10, 11, 12, 12, 12, 13, 14, 15, 16, 16, 16, 16, 16, 17, 17, 18, 18; 116:1, 3, 3, 4, 4, 5, 6, 6, 7, 9, 9, 12, 13, 13, 13, 14, 15, 15, 15, 16, 17, 17, 17, 18, 18, 19, 19, 19, 19; 117:1, 2, 2, 2; 118:1, 3, 4, 5, 5, 6, 7, 8, 9, 10, 10, 11, 11, 12, 12, 13, 14, 15, 15, 15, 15, 15, 16, 16, 18, 19, 19, 19, 20, 20, 22, 22, 22, 23, 24, 24, 26, 26, 26, 26, 27, 27, 27, 29; 119:1, 1, 1, 1, 2, 13, 14, 19, 20, 21, 25, 27, 29, 30, 32, 33, 33, 35, 43, 49, 51, 53, 54, 55, 61, 61, 64, 69, 72, 78, 83, 84, 85, 88, 90, 95, 97, 100, 108, 110, 111, 112, 115, 119, 119, 122, 123, 130, 130, 134, 142, 144, 147, 147, 148, 155, 158, 160; 120:1, 4, 5; 121:1, 2, 5, 5, 6, 6, 7, 8; 122:1, 1, 4, 4, 4, 4, 4, 4, 5, 5, 6, 6, 9, 9; 123:1, 2, 2, 2, 2, 2, 4, 4, 4; 124:1, 2, 4, 4, 5, 6, 7, 7, 7, 8, 8; 125:1, 2, 3, 3, 3, 3, 5, 5; 126:1, 1, 2, 2, 3, 4, 4; 127:1, 1, 1, 1, 1, 2, 3, 3, 3, 4, 4, 5, 5, 5; 128:1, 2, 3, 4, 4, 4, 4, 6, 6, 7, 8, 8, 8, 8; 130:1, 2, 5, 6, 6, 6, 7, 7; 131:3; 132:2, 2, 3, 3, 3, 3, 3, 3; 134:1, 1, 1, 1, 2, 2, 3; 135:1, 1, 1, 1, 2, 2, 2, 3, 3, 4, 5, 6, 6, 7, 7, 7, 7, 8, 9, 11, 14, 14, 15, 15, 15, 19, 19, 20, 20, 20, 21; 136:1, 2, 3, 5, 6, 6, 9, 13, 14, 15, 16, 19, 20, 26; 137:1, 2, 3, 4, 6, 7, 7, 7, 9; 138:1, 3, 4, 4, 4, 5, 5, 5, 6, 6, 6, 7, 7, 8, 8; 139:T, 9, 9, 9, 9, 11, 11, 12, 12, 12, 12, 15, 15, 17, 18, 19, 24; 140:T, 1, 1, 4, 4, 4, 5, 5, 6, 6, 7, 7, 8, 8, 9, 9, 10, 11, 11, 12, 12, 12, 13, 13; 141:2, 2, 3, 5, 5, 7, 7, 8, 9, 9, 9, 10; 142:T, 1, 1, 3, 5, 5, 7; 143:3, 3, 5, 5, 7, 8, 8, 10; 144:1, 3, 5, 7, 10, 11, 12, 15; 145:3, 5, 6, 7, 8, 9, 11, 12, 12, 14, 15, 16, 17, 18, 19, 20, 20, 21, 21; 146:1, 2, 3, 5, 5, 6, 7, 7, 7, 7, 8, 8, 8, 8, 9, 9, 9, 9, 9, 10, 10; 147:1, 2, 2, 3, 4, 4, 6, 6, 6, 6, 7, 7, 8, 8, 9, 9, 10, 10, 10, 11, 12, 13, 14, 14, 16, 18, 20; 148:1, 1, 1, 1, 4, 5, 5, 7, 7, 11, 11, 13, 13, 13, 14, 14, 14, 14, 14; 149:1, 1, 2, 3, 3, 4, 4, 5, 6, 7, 7, 9, 9; 150:1, 1, 3, 3, 3, 4, 4, 5, 5, 6, 6;

Pr 1:1, 1, 2, 3, 4, 4, 6, 6, 6, 7, 7, 7, 8, 8, 11, 12, 12, 15, 17, 19, 19, 19, 20, 21, 21, 21, 21, 22, 29, 29, 31, 32, 32, 32; 2:5, 5, 5, 6, 7, 8, 8, 12, 12, 12, 13, 13, 14, 14, 16, 16, 17, 17, 18, 19, 20, 20, 21, 21, 21, 22, 22, 22; 3:3, 4, 5, 7, 9, 9, 11, 11, 12, 12, 13, 13, 14, 14, 14, 15, 19, 19, 19, 20, 20, 20, 25, 25, 25, 26, 26, 27, 28, 28, 28, 29, 29, 29, 31, 31, 34, 34, 35, 35; 4:1, 3, 5, 7, 10, 11, 14, 14, 17, 17, 17, 18, 18, 18, 19, 19, 21, 23, 26, 27, 27; 5:3, 6, 7, 8, 9, 11, 13, 14, 16, 18, 19, 20, 21, 21, 22, 22, 23; 6:2, 2, 3, 5, 5, 7, 8, 8, 9, 9, 9, 9, 10, 12, 12, 13, 16, 16, 20, 20, 22, 22, 23, 24, 27, 27, 27, 28, 29, 32, 34, 34, 35, 35, 35; 7:2, 3, 5, 5, 6, 7, 7, 8, 8, 9, 9, 9, 9, 10, 10, 20, 21, 22, 22, 23, 24, 27, 27; 8:2, 2, 2, 3, 3, 3, 4, 6, 8, 9, 9, 9, 9, 9, 10, 11, 13, 13, 13, 16, 16, 20, 20, 20, 22, 22, 23, 23, 25, 25, 26, 26, 29, 29, 30, 31, 31, 34, 34, 35; 9:3, 3, 5, 6, 6, 10, 10, 10, 10, 10, 11, 14, 14, 14, 18; 10:1, 1, 3, 3, 3, 3, 3, 4, 4, 6, 6, 6, 6, 7, 7, 7, 9, 10, 11, 11, 11, 13, 13, 14, 15, 15, 16, 16, 16, 16, 17, 19, 20, 20, 20, 21, 21, 22, 24, 24, 25, 25, 26, 26, 26, 27, 27, 27, 28, 28, 28, 29, 29, 29, 30, 30, 30, 31, 31, 31, 32, 32, 32; 11:1, 2, 3, 3, 4, 5, 5, 6, 6, 7, 8, 10, 10, 11, 11, 11, 11, 11, 13, 14, 14, 14, 17, 18, 20, 21, 21, 21, 23, 23, 23, 25, 26, 26, 28, 29, 29, 29, 30, 30, 31, 31, 31, 31; 12:2, 3, 3, 15, 5, 5, 6, 6, 6, 7, 7, 10, 10, 10, 12, 12, 13, 13, 13, 14, 14, 15, 18, 18, 19, 20, 20, 21, 21, 22, 23, 24, 24, 24, 25, 26, 26, 27, 27, 28, 28, 28, 29, 29, 30, 30, 30, 30, 31, 31, 31, 31; 12:2, 3, 3, 3, 3, 4, 5, 5, 5, 6, 6, 6, 7, 7, 7, 10, 10, 10, 12, 12, 13, 14, 14, 15, 18, 18, 18, 19, 20, 20, 21, 21, 22, 23, 23, 24, 24, 24, 25, 26, 26, 26, 27, 27, 28, 28, 28, 29, 30; 13:2, 2, 2, 4, 4, 4, 6, 6, 8, 8, 9, 9, 9, 9, 10, 12, 12, 13, 13, 14, 14, 14, 15, 16, 16, 17, 19, 19, 19, 22, 22, 22, 23, 23; 14:1, 2, 3, 3, 3, 4, 4, 4, 7, 7, 8, 8, 9, 10, 11, 11, 11, 11, 12, 12, 13, 14, 14, 15, 15, 16, 18, 19, 19, 19, 19, 20, 20, 20, 21, 23, 24, 24, 25, 26, 27, 27, 28, 28, 28, 30, 30, 30, 31, 31, 32, 33, 33, 35; 15:2, 2, 3, 3, 3, 4, 6, 6, 6, 7, 7, 10, 12, 13, 13, 14, 14, 15, 18, 18, 19, 20, 20, 21, 21, 22, 23, 24, 24, 24, 25, 26, 26, 27, 27, 28, 28, 29, 29, 29, 30, 30, 30, 31, 31, 31, 33, 33; 16:1, 1, 1, 1, 2, 2, 3, 4, 4, 5, 6, 6, 7, 9, 10, 11, 11, 11, 12, 13, 14, 15, 15, 15, 17,

17, 19, 19, 19, 20, 21, 21, 21, 22, 23, 23, 24, 24, 25, 25, 29, 31, 31, 32, 33, 33, 33, 33; 17:2, 2, 3, 3, 3, 3, 5, 6, 6, 8, 14, 15, 15, 15, 16, 18, 21, 21, 22, 23, 23, 24, 24, 24, 26; 18:3, 4, 4, 5, 5, 5, 7, 8, 8, 8, 10, 10, 10, 11, 12, 14, 15, 15, 15, 15, 18, 18, 19, 20, 20, 21, 21, 21, 22, 23, 23; 19:1, 2, 3, 3, 4, 6, 6, 6, 7, 7, 11, 12, 12, 12, 13, 13, 14, 14, 16, 17, 17, 21, 21, 22, 23, 23, 25, 27, 27, 28, 28, 29; 20:2, 2, 4, 4, 5, 7, 8, 10, 12, 12, 12, 14, 15, 21, 21, 22, 23, 24, 25, 26, 26, 27, 27, 27, 27, 27, 28, 29, 29, 29, 30, 30, 30; 21:1, 1, 1, 1, 2, 2, 3, 4, 4, 5, 5, 6, 7, 7, 8, 8, 9, 10, 10, 11, 11, 11, 12, 12, 12, 12, 13, 13, 14, 15, 15, 16, 16, 16, 18, 18, 18, 18, 19, 20, 20, 22, 22, 22, 25, 25, 26, 26, 27, 27, 28, 29, 30, 31, 31, 31; 22:2, 2, 2, 3, 3, 4, 4, 5, 5, 6, 7, 7, 7, 8, 9, 10, 10, 11, 11, 12, 12, 12, 12, 12, 13, 13, 14, 14, 15, 15, 16, 16, 17, 17, 19, 21, 21, 21, 22, 22, 22, 23, 23, 23, 28; 23:6, 8, 9, 9, 10, 10, 10, 12, 13, 13, 14, 17, 17, 17, 19, 21, 21, 23, 24, 24, 28, 30, 31, 31, 32, 34, 34, 34; 24:4, 7, 9, 9, 10, 12, 13, 14, 15, 15, 16, 18, 19, 20, 20, 20, 21, 21, 22, 23, 24, 24, 27, 29, 30, 30, 30, 30, 31, 31, 33; 25:1, 2, 2, 3, 3, 4, 4, 4, 5, 5, 6, 6, 6, 7, 7, 8, 13, 13, 13, 15, 22, 23, 24, 26; 26:2, 2, 2, 3, 3, 3, 6, 6, 7, 7, 7, 9, 9, 10, 10, 13, 13, 13, 14, 14, 15, 16, 17, 19, 20, 20, 22, 22, 22, 26; 27:3, 6, 6, 7, 7, 9, 9, 10, 22, 12, 14, 16, 16, 17, 18, 18, 19, 20, 21, 21, 23, 24, 25, 25, 25, 26, 26, 26, 27, 27; 28:1, 1, 2, 2, 3, 4, 4, 5, 6, 7, 8, 9, 10, 10, 11, 12, 12, 14, 15, 16, 17, 17, 23, 24, 24, 25, 27, 28, 28, 29; 29:2, 2, 2, 2, 4, 4, 4, 6, 7, 7, 7, 7, 10, 10, 10, 13, 13, 14, 14, 15, 16, 16, 18, 18, 21, 23, 25, 25, 26, 26, 27, 27, 27; 30:1, 1, 1, 1, 2, 3, 3, 4, 4, 4, 4, 9, 9, 14, 14, 14, 15, 16, 16, 16, 16, 17, 17, 17, 17, 19, 19, 19, 19, 19, 19, 20, 21, 24, 25, 25, 26, 26, 27, 28, 33, 33, 33; 31:1, 1, 2, 2, 5, 5, 7, 8, 8, 9, 9, 11, 12, 14, 16, 19, 19, 20, 20, 21, 23, 23, 24, 26, 27, 27, 30, 31, 31;

Ecc 1:1, 1, 1, 2, 3, 4, 5, 5, 6, 6, 6, 7, 7, 7, 7, 7, 8, 8, 9, 9, 12, 13, 14, 14; 2:3, 3, 3, 6, 8, 8, 8, 8, 11, 11, 11, 12, 12, 14, 14, 15, 16, 16, 16, 16, 16, 17, 17, 18, 18, 19, 19, 20, 20, 22, 22, 23, 24, 26; 3:1, 10, 10, 11, 11, 11, 11, 13, 13, 13, 16, 16, 16, 17, 17, 18, 18, 19, 19, 19, 20, 21, 21, 21, 21; 4:1, 1, 1, 2, 2, 3, 3, 5, 6, 7, 10, 15, 15, 15, 16; 5:1, 1, 3, 6, 6, 7, 7, 7, 8, 8, 8, 8, 9, 9, 9, 11, 12, 12, 12; 7:1, 1, 2, 2, 2, 3, 3, 3, 4, 4, 4, 4, 5, 5, 6, 6, 6, 7, 8, 8, 8, 8, 9, 10; 6:1, 3, 5, 5, 7, 7, 8, 8, 8, 9, 9, 9, 11, 12, 12; 7:1, 1, 2, 2, 2, 2, 3, 3, 3, 4, 4, 4, 4, 5, 5, 6, 6, 6, 7, 8, 8, 9, 10, 10, 11, 12, 13, 14, 14, 14, 14, 15, 19, 19, 25, 25, 26, 26, 27, 27; 8:1, 1, 1, 2, 2, 4, 5, 6, 8, 8, 8, 9, 10, 10, 10, 11, 11, 13, 14, 14, 14, 15, 15, 16, 16, 16, 17, 17, 17; 9:1, 1, 1, 2, 2, 2, 2, 2, 2, 3, 3, 3, 4, 5, 5, 5, 6, 9, 9, 9, 9, 9, 9, 10, 11, 11, 11, 11, 11, 11, 11, 12, 13, 15, 16, 17, 17; 10:1, 1, 3, 4, 4, 5, 5, 6, 7, 10, 10, 11, 12, 13, 13, 15, 15, 15, 16, 17, 18, 18, 18, 20, 20, 20, 20; 11:1, 2, 3, 3, 3, 3, 3, 3, 4, 4, 4, 5, 5, 5, 5, 6, 6, 6, 7, 7, 8, 9, 9, 9; 12:1, 1, 1, 2, 2, 2, 2, 3, 3, 3, 3, 4, 4, 4, 4, 5, 5, 5, 5, 6, 6, 7, 7, 8, 9, 9, 9, 10, 11, 11, 12, 13, 13

SS 1:1, 2, 3, 4, 4, 5, 5, 6, 6, 7, 8, 8, 8, 12, 12, 14, 17; 2:1, 1, 2, 2, 3, 3, 3, 4, 7, 7, 7, 8, 8, 8, 9, 9, 11, 11, 12, 12, 12, 12, 12, 13, 13, 13, 14, 14, 14, 15, 15, 15, 16, 17, 17, 17; 3:2, 2, 2, 3, 3, 4, 5, 5, 5, 6, 6, 7, 8, 8, 8, 9, 10, 10, 10, 10, 11, 11, 11, 11; 4:2, 4, 5, 6, 6, 6, 6, 8, 8, 8, 8, 10, 11, 11, 11, 14, 16; 5:2, 2, 2, 4, 4, 4, 5, 5, 7, 7, 7, 7, 10, 11, 14, 16; 6:2, 2, 3, 6, 9, 9, 9, 9, 10, 10, 11, 11, 11, 11, 12, 13; 7:1, 1, 1, 4, 4, 4, 5, 5, 5, 8, 8, 8, 8, 9, 9, 11, 11, 12, 12, 12, 12; 8:1, 2, 5, 5, 6, 6, 7, 7, 8, 11, 11, 12, 13, 13, 14

Isa 1:1, 1, 1, 2, 3, 3, 4, 4, 5, 5, 6, 6, 6, 8, 9, 10, 10, 10, 11, 11, 11, 11, 11, 13, 13, 13, 16, 17, 17, 17, 18, 19, 19, 20, 20, 20, 21, 23, 23, 23, 24, 24, 24, 24, 26, 26, 26, 28, 28, 28, 28, 29, 29, 31, 31; 2:1, 1, 2, 2, 2, 2, 2, 3, 3, 3, 3, 3, 3, 4, 4, 5, 5, 6, 6, 6, 6, 8, 9, 9, 10, 10, 10, 10, 11, 11, 11, 12, 12, 13, 13, 14, 14, 16, 17, 17, 17, 18, 19, 19, 19, 21, 21, 21; 3:1, 1, 1, 1, 1, 2, 2, 2, 2, 3, 3, 3, 3, 3, 5, 5, 5, 5, 6, 6, 6, 7, 7, 8, 11, 11, 12, 13, 14, 14, 14, 14, 14, 14, 15, 15, 16, 16, 16, 17, 17, 17, 18, 18, 19, 19, 20, 20, 20, 20, 20, 21, 21, 22, 22, 22, 23, 23, 23, 26; 4:2, 2, 2, 3, 4, 4, 4, 4, 4, 4, 5, 5, 5, 6, 6, 6; 5:2, 2, 2, 5, 5, 5, 6, 7, 7, 7, 7, 8, 8, 9, 10, 11, 12, 12, 12, 12, 12, 12, 15, 15, 15, 16, 17, 17, 17, 17, 19, 19, 23, 23, 24, 24, 24, 24, 24, 24, 25, 25, 25, 25, 26, 26, 26, 27, 27, 29, 30; 30, 30, 30, 30; 6:1, 1, 1, 2, 2, 3, 4, 4, 5, 5, 5, 6, 6, 8, 8, 10, 11, 11, 11, 12, 12, 12, 13, 13; 7:1, 1, 1, 1, 1, 1, 2, 2, 2, 2, 3, 3, 3, 5, 5, 5, 5, 5, 6, 6, 8, 9, 10, 11, 11, 11, 12, 14, 14, 14, 14, 14, 15, 15, 16, 17, 17, 18, 18, 19, 19, 20, 20, 20, 20, 20, 20, 21, 22, 22, 22, 23, 23, 24, 24, 24, 24, 24, 24, 25, 26; 4:2, 2, 2, 3, 4, 4, 4, 4, 4, 5, 5, 5, 6, 6; 5:2, 2, 2, 5, 5, 6, 7, 7, 7, 7, 8, 8, 9, 10, 11, 12, 12, 12, 12, 12, 15, 15, 15, 16, 17, 17, 17, 19, 19, 23, 23, 24, 24, 24, 24, 24, 24, 25, 25, 25, 25, 26, 26, 26, 27, 27, 29, 30, 30, 30, 30, 30; 6:1, 1, 1, 2, 2, 3, 4, 4, 5, 5, 5, 6, 6, 8, 8, 10, 11, 11, 11, 12, 12, 12, 13, 13; 7:1, 1, 1, 1, 1, 1, 2, 2, 2, 2, 3, 3, 3, 5, 5, 5, 5, 5, 6, 6, 8, 9, 10, 11, 11, 11, 12, 14, 14, 14, 14, 14, 15, 15, 16, 17, 17, 18, 18, 19, 19, 20, 20, 20, 20, 20, 20,

22, 22, 24, 25, 25, 25, 25; 8:1, 2, 2, 3, 3, 4, 4, 4, 4, 5, 6, 7, 7, 7, 7, 8, 8, 8, 10, 10, 11, 11, 13, 14, 14, 14, 16, 16, 17, 17, 17, 18, 18, 18, 19, 19, 20, 20, 22; 9:1, 1, 1, 1, 1, 1, 2, 2, 2, 2, 3, 3, 3, 3, 4, 4, 4, 5, 6, 6, 6, 6, 7, 7, 7, 7, 8, 8, 9, 9, 10, 10, 11, 11, 12, 12, 13, 13, 13, 14, 14, 15, 15, 15, 16, 17, 18, 18, 18, 18, 18, 18, 19, 19, 19, 20, 20, 20, 20; 10:2, 2, 2, 2, 3, 3, 4, 4, 5, 5, 6, 6, 6, 6, 6, 10, 12, 12, 12, 12, 12, 13, 13, 13, 14, 14, 14, 14, 14, 14, 15, 15, 15, 16, 16, 16, 17, 18, 19, 20, 20, 20, 20, 21, 21, 21, 22, 22, 22, 23, 23, 23, 23, 24, 24, 25, 26, 26, 26, 26, 26, 26, 27, 27, 29, 31, 32, 32, 33, 33, 34; 11:1, 2, 2, 2, 2, 2, 2, 2, 3, 3, 3, 3, 4, 4, 4, 4, 4, 5, 5, 6, 6, 6, 6, 6, 6, 6, 7, 7, 7, 8, 8, 8, 8, 9, 9, 9, 10, 11, 11, 11, 11, 11, 12, 12, 12, 13, 13, 14, 14, 14, 14, 14, 15, 15, 15, 16, 16; 12:2, 3, 4, 4, 5, 5, 6, 6; 13:1, 1, 2, 2, 2, 2, 2, 2, 4, 4, 4, 4, 4, 4, 4, 5, 5, 5, 5, 6, 6, 7, 8, 8, 9, 9, 9, 11, 11, 11, 11, 12, 13, 13, 13, 13, 14, 14, 15, 15, 16, 16, 17, 17, 17, 18, 18, 19, 19, 21, 21, 21, 22; 14:1, 1, 1, 2, 2, 2, 2, 3, 3, 3, 4, 4, 4, 5, 5, 5, 5, 6, 6, 7, 8, 8, 9, 9, 9, 9, 9, 11, 11, 11, 11, 12, 12, 12, 13, 13, 13, 13, 14, 14, 15, 15, 16, 16, 17, 17, 18, 18, 19, 19, 19, 20, 20, 21, 21, 21, 22, 22, 23, 23, 23, 23, 24, 24, 24, 24, 25, 25, 25, 26, 26, 26, 26, 27, 28, 29, 30, 31, 32, 32, 32; 15:1, 1, 1, 2, 3, 4, 4, 5, 5, 6, 6, 6, 6, 7, 8, 8, 8, 9, 9, 9, 9, 9; 16:1, 1, 1, 1, 1, 1, 2, 2, 2, 3, 3, 3, 3, 4, 4, 4, 4, 4, 5, 6, 7, 7, 8, 8, 8, 9, 9, 10, 10, 11, 11, 12, 12, 12, 13, 13, 14; 17:1, 2, 3, 3, 3, 3, 3, 4, 4, 5, 5, 5, 5, 6, 6, 6, 7, 7, 8, 8, 8, 9, 10, 10, 10, 11, 11, 11, 12, 12, 12; 18:1, 1, 2, 2, 2, 3, 3, 3, 4, 4, 5, 5, 5, 5, 5, 6, 6, 6, 6, 6, 7, 7, 7, 7, 7; 7, 8, 8, 8, 8, 8, 9, 9, 9, 9, 10, 10, 11, 11, 11, 11, 11, 11, 12, 12, 12, 13, 13, 13, 14, 14, 14, 14, 15, 15, 16, 16, 16, 16; 12:2, 3, 4, 4, 5, 5, 5, 5, 5, 6, 6, 6, 7, 7, 7, 8, 8, 8, 9, 9, 9, 9, 10, 10, 11, 11, 11, 13, 13, 14, 15, 16, 16, 16, 16, 17, 18, 18, 19, 19, 20, 20, 21, 22, 23, 23, 24, 24, 25, 25, 25; 20:1, 1, 2, 2, 2, 3, 3, 4, 4, 4, 4, 5, 5, 5, 5, 5, 8, 8, 9, 9, 9, 9, 10, 11, 11, 11, 11; 21:1, 2, 2, 2, 3, 3, 4, 4, 4, 4, 4, 5, 5, 6, 6, 7, 7, 7, 7, 7, 7, 7, 8, 8, 8, 9, 9, 9, 9, 10, 10, 11, 11, 11, 12, 12, 12, 12, 13, 13, 14, 15, 16, 17, 17, 17, 17, 17, 17, 18, 19, 19, 20, 20, 21, 21, 21; 27:1, 1, 1, 1, 3, 4, 6, 7, 7, 7, 7, 7, 7, 7, 8, 8, 8, 9, 9, 9, 9, 9, 10, 10, 10, 11, 11, 11, 11, 12, 12, 12, 12, 13, 13, 14, 14, 14; 22:1, 1, 1, 2, 2, 3, 3, 3, 3, 3, 3, 4, 4, 5, 6, 6, 6, 7, 8, 9, 9, 10, 11, 11, 11, 12, 14; 22:1, 1, 1, 2, 2, 2, 3, 3, 3, 3, 3, 4, 5, 6, 6, 6, 7, 8, 9, 9, 10, 11, 12, 12, 14; 23:1, 1, 2, 2, 2, 2, 3, 4, 5, 5, 5, 6, 7, 7, 7, 7, 8, 8, 8, 8, 9, 10, 10, 11, 11, 11, 12, 12, 12, 13, 13, 14, 14, 15, 15, 16, 16, 17, 17, 17, 18, 18, 18, 18, 19, 21, 21, 21, 23; 24:1, 1, 1, 1, 1, 2, 2, 2, 4, 4, 4, 4, 4, 5, 5, 6, 6, 6, 6, 7, 8, 10, 10, 11, 11, 11,

Jer 1:1, 1, 1, 1, 2, 2, 2, 2, 3, 3, 3, 3, 3, 3, 4, 4, 5, 5, 5, 7, 8, 9, 9, 10, 10, 11, 11, 12, 13, 13, 13, 13, 14, 14, 14, 14, 15, 15, 15, 15, 15, 15, 15, 15, 16, 18, 18, 18, 19; 2:1, 1, 2, 2, 2, 2, 3, 3, 3, 4, 4, 4, 4, 5, 6, 6, 6, 6, 7, 8, 8, 8, 9, 10, 12, 13, 15, 16, 16, 17, 17, 18, 18, 18, 18, 19, 19, 20, 21, 22, 23, 23, 24, 25, 26, 26, 27, 28, 28, 29, 31, 31, 33, 34, 34, 34, 37; 3:1, 1, 2, 2, 2, 2, 2, 3, 4, 5, 6, 6, 6, 8, 8, 9, 9, 10, 11, 11, 12, 12, 12, 13, 13, 13, 14, 16, 16, 16, 16, 17, 17, 17, 17, 17, 18, 18, 18, 18, 19, 20, 21, 21, 22, 23, 23, 23, 24, 25, 25; 4:1, 2, 2, 3, 3, 4, 4, 4, 5, 5, 5, 6, 6, 7, 7, 7, 8, 8, 9, 9, 9, 9, 9, 9, 10, 11, 11, 11, 16, 16, 17, 19, 19, 19, 20, 21, 21,

12, 12, 12, 13, 13, 13, 13, 14, 14, 14, 14, 14, 14, 15, 15, 16, 16, 16, 16, 17, 17, 18, 18, 19, 19, 20, 20, 20, 21, 21, 22, 22, 22, 22, 22, 23, 23, 24, 24, 24, 24, 24, 24, 24, 24, 24, 25, 25, 25, 27, 27, 27, 27, 27, 29, 30, 30, 30, 30, 31, 31, 32, 32, 33, 33, 34, 34, 36, 36, 36, 36, 36, 36, 38, 38, 38; 38:1, 1, 1, 2, 2, 4, 4, 4, 5, 5, 6, 6, 7, 7, 8, 8, 8, 9, 10, 10, 10, 11, 11, 11, 11, 11, 11, 15, 16, 17, 18, 18, 19, 19, 19, 19, 20, 20, 20, 20, 21, 21, 22, 22, 22, 22; 39:1, 2, 2, 2, 2, 2, 3, 3, 5, 5, 6, 6, 7, 7, 7, 7, 7, 8, 8, 8, 9, 10, 10, 11, 11, 11, 11, 11, 11, 15, 16, 17, 18, 18, 19, 19, 19, 20, 20, 20, 20, 21, 21, 22, 22, 22; 39:1, 2, 2, 2, 2, 2, 3, 3, 5, 5, 6, 6, 7, 7, 7, 7, 7, 7, 8, 9, 40:2, 3, 3, 3, 3, 4, 4, 5, 5, 5, 6, 6, 7, 7, 7, 7, 7, 8, 8, 9, 9, 9, 10, 11, 12, 12, 12, 12, 12, 12, 12, 12, 12, 14, 15, 15, 15, 15, 15, 16, 19, 21, 21, 21, 22, 22, 22, 23, 23, 23, 24, 24, 25, 26, 26, 27, 28, 28, 29, 30, 30, 31; 41:1, 2, 2, 2, 2, 3, 3, 4, 4, 4, 4, 4, 5, 5, 7, 7, 7, 7, 7, 8, 9, 9, 9, 10, 13, 14, 14, 15, 15, 15, 16, 16, 16, 17, 17, 18, 18, 18, 19, 19, 19, 19, 19, 19, 20, 20, 20, 21, 21, 22, 22, 23, 23, 25, 25, 25, 26, 27; 42:1, 2, 3, 4, 4, 5, 5, 5, 5, 6, 6, 6, 7, 7, 7, 7, 8, 9, 10, 10, 10, 10, 11, 11, 11, 11, 11, 11, 11, 11, 11, 12, 12, 13, 15, 15, 16, 17, 17, 19, 20, 21, 21, 22, 22, 22, 22; 43:1, 2, 2, 2, 2, 3, 3, 5, 5, 6, 6, 6, 6, 8, 8, 9, 9, 10, 10, 11, 11, 12, 12, 13; 44:2, 3, 4, 4, 5, 5, 5, 6, 6, 6, 6, 7, 7, 11, 12, 12, 12, 12, 12, 13, 13, 13, 14, 14, 14, 14, 14, 14, 16, 16, 17, 19, 19, 19, 23, 23, 24, 24, 24, 28, 28; 44:2, 3, 4, 4, 5, 5, 5, 6, 6, 6, 6, 7, 7, 11, 12, 12, 12, 12, 12, 13, 13, 13, 14, 14, 14, 14, 14, 14, 16, 16, 17, 19, 19, 19, 23, 23, 24, 24, 24, 28, 28; 45:1, 1, 1, 2, 2, 2, 3, 3, 3, 3, 5, 6, 6, 6, 6, 7, 7, 8, 8, 8, 9, 9, 9, 10, 11, 11, 11, 11, 12, 13, 14, 14, 14, 15, 17, 18, 18, 18, 18, 19, 19, 20, 20, 21, 22, 22, 23, 24, 25, 25; 46:1, 1, 1, 2, 3, 3, 3, 5, 6, 7, 9, 10, 10, 10, 11, 11; 47:1, 1, 1, 2, 2, 2, 2, 4, 4, 5, 5, 6, 7, 8, 9, 9, 9, 12, 13, 13, 13, 13, 14, 14, 14; 48:1, 1, 1, 1, 2, 2, 2, 3, 3, 5, 7, 7, 8, 10, 12, 12, 13, 13, 13, 14, 14, 16, 16, 16, 17, 17, 17, 18, 18, 19, 19, 20, 20, 20, 21, 21, 21, 21, 22; 49:1, 1, 2, 4, 5, 5, 5, 6, 6, 6, 6, 7, 7, 7, 7, 7, 8, 8, 8, 9, 9, 10, 10, 12, 12, 12, 13, 14, 15, 16, 18, 19, 20, 20, 22, 22, 23, 23, 23, 24, 24, 25, 25, 25, 26, 26; 50:1, 1, 2, 2, 3, 4, 4, 4, 4, 5, 6, 6, 7, 9, 9, 10, 10, 10, 11, 11; 51:1, 1, 1, 1, 3, 3, 3, 4, 5, 6, 6, 6, 6, 6, 7, 7, 8, 8, 9, 9, 9, 10, 10, 10, 10, 10, 11, 11, 12, 13, 13, 13, 13, 13, 13, 13, 14, 14, 15, 15, 15, 16, 16, 16, 17, 17, 17, 18, 18, 19, 19, 20, 20, 20, 22, 22, 22, 22, 23, 23, 23; 52:1, 1, 1, 2, 2, 3, 4, 4, 5, 5, 7, 7, 8, 8, 9, 10; 53:1, 1, 5, 6, 6, 7, 8, 8, 8, 9, 9, 10, 10, 11, 11, 12, 12, 12, 12, 12, 12; 54:1, 1, 1, 1, 2, 2, 3, 3, 3, 4, 4, 5, 5, 5, 5, 5, 6, 9, 9, 9, 10, 10, 10, 10, 10, 11, 11, 13, 13, 16, 16, 16, 17, 17, 17, 17; 55:1, 4, 4, 5, 5, 6, 7, 7, 7, 8, 9, 9, 10, 10, 10, 10, 10, 11, 11, 12, 12, 12, 13, 13, 13, 13, 13; 56:1, 2, 2, 3, 3, 3, 3, 4, 4, 4, 6, 6, 6, 6, 6, 6, 7, 8, 9, 9, 10, 11, 11, 11, 12; 57:1, 1, 1, 3, 3, 3, 3, 4, 5, 5, 5, 6, 6, 8, 8, 9, 10, 10, 13, 13, 14, 14, 14, 15, 15, 15, 15, 15, 16, 16, 16, 17, 17, 19, 19, 20, 20, 21; 58:1, 2, 2, 3, 4, 5, 6, 6, 6, 7, 7, 7, 8, 8, 8, 9, 9, 9, 9, 10, 10, 11, 12, 12, 12, 12, 12, 12, 12, 14, 14, 14, 14, 14, 14; 59:1, 5, 6, 8, 10, 10, 10, 13, 13, 14, 15, 17, 18, 19, 19, 19, 19, 19, 19, 20, 20, 21, 21, 21; 60:1, 1, 2, 2, 2, 2, 3, 3, 5, 5, 5, 5, 6, 6, 6, 6, 7, 7, 7, 8, 9, 9, 9, 9, 9, 10, 11, 11, 12, 12, 13, 13, 13, 13, 13, 14, 14, 14, 14, 14, 16, 16, 16, 16, 16, 16, 16, 19, 19, 20, 20; 61:1, 1, 1, 1, 1, 1, 1, 2, 2, 3, 3, 3, 3, 4, 4, 4, 4, 4, 5, 5, 6, 6, 7, 8, 10, 10, 10, 11, 11, 11, 11; 62:1, 1, 2, 2, 3, 3, 4, 4, 5, 5, 6, 7, 8, 8, 8, 9, 9, 10, 10, 10, 10, 11, 11, 11, 11, 12, 12, 12; 63:1, 2, 3, 3, 4, 4, 5, 6, 7, 7, 7, 7, 7, 7, 8, 8, 8, 9, 9, 9, 11, 11, 12, 12, 12, 13, 13, 13, 14, 14, 14, 14, 15, 15, 15, 17, 18; 64:1, 1, 2, 2, 2, 3, 4, 4, 4, 4, 4, 6, 8, 8; 65:2, 4, 4, 5, 7, 7, 7, 7, 8, 8, 8, 10, 10, 11, 11, 12, 13, 15, 15, 16, 16, 16, 16, 17, 19, 19, 20, 20, 21, 22, 22, 22, 23, 23, 23, 25, 25, 25, 25, 25, 25, 25; 66:1, 1, 1, 1, 1, 2, 5, 5, 5, 6, 6, 6, 8, 8, 9, 9, 9, 11, 12, 12, 14, 14, 14, 15, 16, 16, 16, 17, 17, 17, 17, 19, 19, 20, 20, 20, 20, 22;

21, 23, 23, 24, 24, 25, 25, 26, 26, 26, 26, 27, 27, 28, 28, 29, 29, 29, 29, 31, 31, 31; 5:1, 1, 1, 2, 3, 4, 4, 4, 5, 5, 5, 5, 5, 6, 6, 7, 7, 8, 9, 10, 11, 11, 11, 12, 14, 14, 15, 17, 18, 19, 19, 20, 22, 22, 22, 22, 22, 22, 24, 24, 24, 24, 24, 28, 28, 28, 28, 28, 29, 29, 30, 30, 31, 31, 31, 31; 6:1, 1, 1, 2, 3, 4, 4, 4, 6, 6, 6, 9, 9, 9, 9, 10, 10, 11, 11, 11, 11, 11, 11, 15, 16, 17, 18, 18, 19, 19, 19, 19, 22, 22, 22, 22, 22, 24; 11, 11, 11, 12, 12, 12, 13, 13, 13, 13, 14, 14, 15, 15, 16, 16, 16, 16, 17, 17, 19, 19, 20, 21, 21, 21, 22, 23, 23, 24, 25, 25; 25, 25, 26, 29, 29, 29, 29, 30; 7:1, 1, 2, 2, 2, 2, 2, 3, 3, 4, 4, 4, 4, 4, 4, 6, 7, 11, 12, 12, 13, 14, 15, 17, 17, 18, 18, 18, 18, 18, 19, 19, 20, 20, 20, 20, 20, 20, 20, 20, 21, 21, 22, 22, 23, 24, 24, 25, 25, 25, 28, 28, 29, 29, 30, 30, 30, 31, 31, 31, 32, 32, 32, 32, 32, 32, 32, 33, 33, 33, 33, 33, 33, 34, 34, 34, 34, 34; 8:1, 1, 1, 1, 1, 1, 1, 2, 2, 2, 2, 2, 2, 6, 7, 7, 7, 7, 7, 7, 8, 8, 8, 8, 9, 9, 9, 10, 10, 11, 11, 11, 12, 12, 13, 13, 13, 13, 13, 14, 14, 14, 16, 16, 16, 16, 16, 16, 16, 19, 19, 19, 20, 21, 22, 22; 9:1, 1, 2, 3, 3, 3, 5, 6, 6, 7, 7, 9, 10, 10, 10, 11, 11, 12, 12, 12, 12, 13, 14, 15, 15, 16, 16, 16, 17, 17, 18, 18, 19, 20, 20, 21, 21, 22, 22, 22; 9:1, 1, 2, 3, 3, 3, 5, 6, 6, 7, 7, 9, 10, 10, 10, 11, 11, 12, 12, 12, 12, 13, 14, 15, 15, 16, 16, 16, 17, 17, 18, 18, 19, 20, 20, 21, 21, 22, 22; 10:1, 1, 2, 2, 2, 2, 2, 3, 3, 3, 3, 3, 3, 3, 5, 7, 7, 7, 7, 8, 9, 9, 9, 9, 9, 10, 10, 10, 11, 11, 11, 11, 11, 11, 13, 14, 15, 15, 16, 16, 16, 17, 17, 18; 18, 18, 18, 18, 19, 21, 21, 21, 21, 21, 22, 22, 23, 23; 12:1, 1, 3, 3, 4, 4, 4, 4, 4, 5, 5, 6, 7, 7, 7, 8, 8, 8, 8, 9, 11, 12, 12, 12, 12, 12, 12, 12, 13, 13, 14, 15, 15, 16, 16, 16, 17, 17, 17, 17, 18, 18, 18, 20, 20, 20, 20, 20, 20, 21, 22, 22, 22, 23, 23; 12:1, 1, 3, 3, 4, 4, 4, 4, 4, 5, 5, 6, 7, 7, 7, 8, 8, 8, 8, 9, 11, 12, 12, 12, 12, 12, 13, 13, 14, 15, 15, 16, 16, 16, 17, 17, 17, 18, 18, 18, 18, 19, 19, 20, 20, 20, 20, 20, 20, 21, 22, 22, 22, 23, 23, 24, 24, 24, 24; 27:1, 1, 1, 1, 2, 3, 6, 7, 8, 8, 8, 8, 8, 8, 8, 8, 9, 11, 11, 11,

11, 12, 12, 13, 13, 13, 13, 13, 13, 14, 14, 14, 15, 15, 16, 16, 16, 16, 16, 17, 18, 18, 18, 18, 18, 18, 18, 18, 19, 19, 19, 19, 19, 19, 20, 20, 21, 21, 21, 21, 21, 21, 21, 21, 22, 22; 28:1, 1, 1, 1, 1, 1, 1, 1, 1, 1, 1, 1, 2, 2, 2, 2, 3, 3, 4, 4, 4, 4, 4, 4, 5, 5, 5, 5, 5, 5, 5, 6, 6, 6, 6, 6, 7, 7, 8, 9, 9, 9, 9, 9, 10, 10, 10, 11, 11, 11, 11, 11, 11, 11, 12, 12, 12, 12, 12, 12, 12, 13, 13, 14, 14, 14, 14, 14, 15, 15, 15, 15, 16, 16, 16, 16, 17, 17, 17; 29:1, 1, 1, 1, 1, 1, 1, 1, 2, 2, 2, 2, 2, 3, 3, 3, 4, 5, 7, 7, 7, 7, 8, 8, 8, 9, 10, 11, 11, 14, 14, 14, 14, 14, 14, 15, 15, 16, 16, 16, 17, 17, 17, 17, 17, 18, 18, 18, 18, 18, 18, 19, 19, 19, 20, 20, 20, 20, 21, 21, 21, 21, 21, 21, 21, 22, 22, 22, 22, 23, 24, 25, 25, 25, 25, 25, 25, 26, 26, 26, 26, 26, 28, 29, 29, 29, 30, 30, 31, 31, 31, 32, 32, 32, 32, 32; 30:1, 1, 2, 2, 3, 3, 3, 3, 4, 4, 5, 7, 8, 9, 10, 10, 11, 12, 14, 14, 14, 15, 17, 18, 18, 18, 18, 19, 19, 21, 21, 23, 23, 23, 23, 23, 24, 24, 24; 31:1, 1, 1, 1, 2, 2, 2, 2, 3, 4, 5, 5, 6, 6, 7, 7, 7, 7, 8, 8, 8, 8, 8, 9, 9, 10, 11, 11, 12, 12, 12, 12, 12, 12, 13, 13, 14, 14, 14, 15, 16, 16, 16, 16, 16, 16, 17, 18, 18, 19, 20, 21, 21, 22, 22, 23, 23, 23, 23, 23, 24, 25, 27, 27, 27, 27, 27, 28, 29, 29, 30, 31, 31, 31, 31, 32, 32, 32, 32, 32; 30:1, 1, 2, 2, 3, 3, 3, 3, 4, 4, 5, 7, 8, 9, 10, 11, 12, 14, 14, 15, 17, 18, 18, 18, 18, 19, 21, 21, 23, 23, 23, 23, 23, 24; 31:1, 1, 1, 1, 2, 2, 2, 2, 3, 4, 5, 5, 6, 6, 6, 7, 7, 7, 7, 8, 8, 8, 8, 8, 8, 9, 9, 10, 11, 11, 12, 12, 12, 12, 12, 12, 13, 13, 14, 14, 14, 15, 15, 16, 16, 16, 16, 17, 18, 18, 19, 20, 21, 21, 22, 22, 23, 23, 23, 23, 24, 25, 27, 27, 27, 27, 27, 28, 29, 29, 30, 30, 31, 31, 31, 32, 32, 32, 32, 32; 30:1, 1, 2, 2, 3, 3, 3, 3, 3, 4, 4, 5, 6, 7, 7, 8, 8, 8, 8, 8, 9, 9, 10, 10, 10, 11, 11, 11, 11, 12, 12, 12, 14, 14, 14, 15, 15, 16, 16, 16, 16, 19, 19, 20, 21, 24, 24, 24, 24, 24, 24, 24, 25, 25, 25, 26, 27, 28, 28, 28, 28, 29, 29, 30, 30, 30, 30, 30, 31, 32, 32, 32, 32, 32; 35:1, 1, 1, 11, 11, 11, 12, 12, 13, 13, 13, 14, 14, 15, 15, 16, 16, 16, 16, 17, 17, 17, 18, 18, 18, 18, 19, 19, 20, 21, 24, 24, 24, 24, 24, 24, 24, 25, 25, 25, 26, 27, 28, 28, 28, 29, 29, 30, 30, 30, 30, 30, 31, 32, 32, 32, 32; 35:1, 1, 2, 2, 3, 3, 3, 3, 3, 4, 4, 5, 5, 6, 6, 7, 7, 8, 8, 8, 9, 9, 10, 10, 10, 10, 10, 10, 10, 10, 10, 12, 12, 12, 12, 12, 13, 13, 13, 14, 14, 14, 14, 14, 15, 16, 18, 19, 20, 20, 20, 20, 20, 20, 21, 21, 21, 21, 21, 21, 21, 21, 22, 23, 23, 23, 23, 23, 24, 25, 25, 26, 26, 26, 26, 27, 27, 27, 27, 28, 28, 28, 29, 29, 30, 30, 30, 30, 30, 30, 31, 31, 31, 32, 32, 32, 32, 32; 37:1, 1, 1, 2, 2, 2, 2, 3, 3, 3, 3, 3, 4, 5, 6, 6, 7, 7, 7, 7, 8, 9, 9, 10, 10, 11, 11, 12, 12, 12, 13, 13, 13, 13, 13, 14, 14, 15, 15, 15, 15, 16, 16, 17, 17, 17, 17, 17, 17, 18, 18, 18, 19, 20, 20, 20, 20, 21, 21, 22, 22, 22, 22, 22; 43:1, 1, 1, 1, 2, 2, 2, 2, 3, 3, 3, 3, 4, 4, 4, 4, 4, 4, 4, 4, 5, 5, 5, 5, 5, 6, 6, 6, 6, 7, 7, 7, 7, 7, 7, 8, 8, 8, 8, 9, 9, 9, 9, 10, 11, 11, 12, 12, 13, 13, 13, 14, 14, 14, 15, 15, 15, 15, 16, 16, 17, 17; 44:1, 1, 1, 1, 2, 2, 2, 2, 4, 6, 6, 7, 7, 7, 7, 7, 7, 7, 8, 8, 9, 9, 10, 10, 10, 11, 11, 11, 12, 12, 12, 12, 13, 13, 13, 13, 13, 14, 14, 15, 15,

15, 15, 16, 16, 16, 17, 17, 17, 18, 18, 18, 19, 20, 20, 20, 20, 21, 21, 21, 21, 21, 21, 22, 22, 22, 23, 23, 23, 23, 24, 24, 24, 24, 25, 25, 25, 26, 26, 26, 26, 26, 26, 26, 26, 27, 27, 27, 27, 28, 28, 28, 28, 28, 29, 30, 30, 30, 30; 45:1, 1, 1, 1, 1, 1, 1, 1, 2, 2, 2, 3, 4, 4, 5; 46:1, 1, 1, 1, 2, 2, 2, 2, 3, 4, 4, 4, 5, 6, 6, 6, 7, 8, 8, 8, 8, 9, 9, 9, 9, 10, 10, 10, 10, 10, 11, 11, 11, 11, 12, 12, 12, 13, 13, 13, 13, 14, 15, 16, 16, 16, 17, 18, 18, 18, 18, 20, 21, 21, 21, 22, 23, 23, 23, 24, 24, 24, 24, 25, 25, 25, 25, 26, 26, 26, 26, 26, 27, 28; 47:1, 1, 1, 1, 2, 2, 2, 2, 2, 3, 3, 3, 3, 3, 4, 4, 4, 4, 4, 5, 6, 7, 7; 48:1, 1, 2, 5, 5, 5, 6, 6, 8, 8, 8, 8, 9, 9, 10, 10, 12, 12, 13, 14, 15, 15, 15, 15, 16, 17, 17, 18, 18, 19, 21, 24, 24, 25, 25, 26, 26, 28, 28, 28, 28, 29, 29, 30, 31, 32, 32, 32, 32, 32, 33, 33, 34, 34, 34, 35, 35, 35, 35, 35, 35, 36, 37, 37, 38, 38, 38, 39, 39, 39; 50:1, 1, 1, 1, 1, 2, 3, 4, 4, 4, 4, 5, 5, 6, 7, 7, 7, 7, 7, 8, 8, 8, 8, 9, 10, 11, 12, 12, 13, 13, 14, 14, 15, 15, 16, 16, 16, 16, 16, 16, 17, 21, 21, 21, 21, 21, 21, 22, 22, 23, 23, 23, 23, 24, 25, 25, 25, 25, 26, 27, 27, 28, 28, 28, 28, 30, 31, 32, 32, 32, 32, 32, 34, 34, 34, 34, 34, 35, 35, 35, 36, 36, 36, 37, 37, 38, 38, 39, 39, 39; 50:1, 1, 1, 1, 1, 2, 3, 4, 4, 4, 4, 5, 5, 6, 7, 7, 7, 7, 7, 7, 8, 8, 8, 8, 9, 10, 11, 12, 12, 13, 13, 13, 14, 14, 14, 15, 15, 15, 16, 16, 16, 16, 16, 17, 18, 18, 19, 19, 20, 20, 20, 21, 21, 22, 22, 22, 23, 23, 23, 23, 24, 25, 25, 25, 25, 26, 26, 27, 27, 28, 28, 28, 28, 30, 31, 31, 31, 31, 32, 32, 32, 32, 33, 33, 33, 33, 34, 35, 35, 35, 36, 39, 39, 39, 39, 39, 40, 41, 41, 42, 42, 42, 42, 43, 43, 44, 44, 44, 44, 45, 45, 45, 45, 45, 46, 46, 46, 46, 46, 46; 51:1, 1, 2, 3, 10, 10, 10, 11, 11, 11, 11, 11, 11, 11, 11, 11, 11, 12, 12, 12, 12, 13, 14, 15, 15, 15, 16, 16, 16, 16, 16, 16, 17, 18, 18, 18, 19, 19, 19, 19, 20, 21, 21, 22, 23, 23, 24, 24, 25, 25, 26, 27, 27, 27, 27, 27, 27, 27, 28, 28, 28, 28, 28, 29, 29, 30, 31, 32, 32, 32, 33, 33, 33, 33, 34, 34, 35, 35, 35, 36, 39, 39, 39, 39, 40, 41, 41, 41, 42, 42, 42, 42, 43, 43, 44, 44, 44, 44, 45, 45, 45, 45, 46, 46, 47, 47, 47, 47, 48, 48, 48, 48, 49, 49, 49, 50, 50, 50, 51, 51, 52, 52, 52, 53, 53, 54, 54, 55, 55, 56, 56, 57, 57, 58, 58, 58, 58, 58, 59, 59, 59, 59, 59, 59, 60, 63, 64, 64; 52:1, 2, 2, 3, 3, 4, 4, 4, 4, 5, 5, 6, 6, 6, 6, 6, 6, 7, 7, 7, 7, 7, 7, 9, 10, 10, 11, 11, 11, 12, 12, 12, 12, 12, 12, 13, 14, 14, 14, 15, 15, 16, 16, 16, 16, 16, 17, 17, 18, 18, 18, 20, 20, 20, 21, 21, 21, 22, 22, 22, 23, 23, 23, 24, 24, 24, 25, 25, 25, 25, 26, 26, 26, 27, 27, 28, 28, 29, 30, 30, 30, 30, 30, 30, 31, 31, 31, 31, 31, 32, 32, 33, 34, 34, 34;

La 1:1, 1, 1, 2, 3, 3, 4, 4, 5, 5, 5, 5, 6, 6, 7, 7, 7, 7, 7, 9, 10, 10, 11, 12, 12, 13, 14, 14, 15, 15, 15, 15, 15, 16, 16, 16, 17, 18, 19, 19, 20, 21; 2:1, 1, 1, 1, 1, 2, 2, 2, 2, 2, 2, 2, 3, 3, 4, 4, 4, 5, 5, 6, 6, 6, 6, 6, 7, 7, 7, 7, 7, 7, 8, 8, 8, 9, 9, 10, 11, 11, 11, 11, 11, 12, 12, 12, 13, 13, 15, 15, 15, 15, 15, 16, 16, 17, 17, 18, 18, 18, 18, 19, 19, 19, 19, 19, 20, 20, 20, 20, 20, 21, 21, 21, 21, 21; 3:1, 1, 3, 12, 13, 14, 18, 19, 19, 22, 24, 25, 25, 26, 27, 29, 31, 32, 33, 34, 34, 35, 35, 35, 36, 36, 38, 39, 40, 41, 45, 45, 45, 48, 48, 50, 51, 53, 55, 57, 58, 62, 62, 64, 66, 66; 4:1, 1, 1, 1, 1, 2, 2, 2, 2, 3, 3, 3, 3, 3, 4, 4, 4, 4, 5, 6, 6, 6, 6; 5:1, 1, 1, 2, 2, 6, 8, 9, 9, 9, 10, 10, 10, 11, 12, 12, 14, 15, 16, 16, 16, 16, 16, 16, 19, 19, 19, 20, 20, 20, 21, 21, 22; 5:6, 6, 6, 6, 9, 9, 9, 10, 11, 11, 12, 12, 12, 12, 13, 13, 13, 14, 14,

Eze 1:1, 1, 1, 1, 1, 1, 2, 2, 3, 3, 3, 3, 3, 3, 3, 4, 4, 4, 4, 4, 5, 5, 5, 7, 7, 7, 8, 10, 10, 10, 10, 10, 10, 12, 13, 13, 13, 13, 13, 13, 13, 14, 14, 16, 16, 16, 19, 19, 19, 20, 20, 20, 20, 21, 21, 21, 21, 21, 22, 22, 22, 22, 22, 23, 23, 23, 24, 24, 24, 24, 24, 24, 25, 26, 26, 26, 26, 26, 26, 26, 26, 27, 27, 27, 27, 27, 28, 28, 28, 28, 28, 28, 28, 28, 28; 2:2, 3, 4; 3:1, 4, 5, 7, 7, 11, 11, 11, 12, 12, 12, 13, 13, 13, 13, 13, 14, 14, 14, 14, 15, 15, 16, 16, 16, 17, 17, 18, 18, 19, 19, 21, 21, 22, 22, 22, 23, 23, 23, 23, 24, 24, 26, 27; 4:1, 2, 3, 3, 4, 4, 4, 4, 5, 5, 5, 5, 6, 6, 7, 8, 9, 9, 11, 13, 13, 13, 16; 5:1, 2, 2, 2, 2, 4, 4, 4, 4, 5, 5, 5, 6, 6, 7, 7, 7, 7, 8, 8, 9, 10, 10, 10, 10, 11, 11, 12, 12, 13, 14, 15, 15, 16, 16, 17; 6:1, 2, 3, 3, 3, 3, 3, 5, 5, 6, 7, 7, 8, 8, 8, 9, 10, 11, 11, 11, 12, 12, 13, 13, 14, 14, 14; 7:1, 2, 2, 3, 4, 4, 4, 5, 6, 6, 7, 8, 9, 10, 11, 11, 12, 12, 12, 13, 13, 14, 14, 14, 14, 15, 15, 15, 16, 17, 17, 18, 18, 18, 19, 19, 19, 20, 21; 8:1, 1, 2,

26, 26, 26, 27, 27, 27, 27, 27, 27; 8:1, 1, 1, 1, 1, 1, 1, 2, 2, 2, 2, 3, 3, 3, 3, 3, 3, 3, 3, 4, 4, 4, 4, 4, 5, 5, 5, 5, 5, 5, 5, 6, 6, 7, 7, 7, 8, 8, 9, 9, 10, 10, 10, 11, 11, 11, 11, 12, 12, 12, 12, 12, 12, 14, 14, 14, 14, 16, 16, 16, 16, 16, 16, 16, 16, 16, 17, 17, 17, 17; 9:1, 2, 2, 2, 2, 3, 3, 3, 3, 3, 3, 4, 4, 4, 4, 4, 4, 4, 4, 4, 4, 5, 5, 6, 6, 6, 6, 6, 7, 7, 7, 7, 7, 8, 8, 9, 9, 9, 9, 9, 9, 9, 9, 11, 11, 11; 10:1, 1, 1, 1, 1, 1, 1, 2, 2, 2, 2, 3, 3, 3, 3, 3, 3, 4, 4, 4, 4, 4, 4, 4, 4, 4, 5, 5, 5, 6, 6, 6, 6, 7, 7, 7, 7, 8, 8, 9, 9, 9, 9, 10, 11, 11, 11, 12, 12, 12, 12, 13, 13, 14, 14, 14, 14, 14, 14, 14, 14, 15, 15, 15, 16, 16, 16, 16, 16, 17, 18, 18, 18, 18, 18, 18, 19, 19, 19, 19, 19, 21, 22, 22; 11:1, 1, 1, 1, 1, 1, 1, 1, 1, 2, 3, 5, 5, 5, 5, 5, 5, 6, 7, 7, 7, 7, 7, 7, 8, 8, 9, 10, 10, 10, 11, 11, 11, 11, 12, 12, 12, 13, 13, 14, 14, 15, 15, 15, 16, 16, 16, 16, 17, 17, 18, 18, 18, 19, 19, 19, 19, 21, 22, 22, 23, 23, 23, 24, 24, 24, 24, 25, 25, 25; 12:1, 1, 2, 5, 6, 6, 6, 6, 6, 7, 7, 7, 8, 8, 9, 10, 10, 11, 11, 12, 12, 12, 13, 13, 14, 14, 15, 15, 16, 16, 16, 16, 17, 18, 19, 19, 19, 20, 20, 20, 21, 21, 22, 22; 11:1, 1, 1, 1, 1, 1, 1, 1, 1, 1, 2, 3, 5; 5, 5, 5, 5, 5, 6, 6, 7, 7, 7, 7, 8, 9, 10, 11, 11, 11, 12, 12, 13, 13, 14, 15, 16, 16, 16, 16, 17, 17, 17, 18, 19, 19, 19, 20, 20, 20, 20, 21, 22, 23; 13:1, 1, 2, 2, 3, 4, 4, 4, 4, 5, 6, 6, 7, 7, 7, 8, 8, 9, 9, 9, 9, 9, 12, 12, 12, 12, 13, 13, 14, 14, 15, 15, 15, 16, 16, 16, 16, 16, 17, 17, 18, 18, 18, 18, 19, 19, 20, 20, 20, 21, 22, 22, 23; 14:1, 2, 2, 3, 4, 4, 4, 4, 4, 4, 5, 6, 6, 7, 7, 7, 7, 8, 8, 9, 9, 9, 9, 10, 10, 11, 11, 11, 13, 13, 13, 14, 15, 15, 16, 16, 16, 17, 17, 17, 17, 18, 18, 19, 19, 20, 21, 21, 21, 22; 15:1, 1, 2, 2, 2, 2, 4, 4, 4, 5, 5, 5, 6, 6, 6; 16:1, 1, 3, 3, 4, 5, 5, 5, 7, 7, 8, 8, 14, 14, 15, 16, 16, 19, 21, 22, 23, 25, 26, 26, 27, 27, 27, 27, 28, 28, 28, 29, 30, 30, 31, 34, 34, 35, 36, 36, 36, 41, 41, 43, 43, 44, 44, 45, 45, 48, 49, 49, 49, 50, 53, 53, 56, 57, 57, 57, 58, 59, 59, 59, 59, 60, 63; 17:1, 1, 2, 3, 3, 3, 4, 5, 6, 7, 9, 9, 9, 9, 9, 10, 11, 11, 12, 12, 12, 12, 12, 13, 13, 13, 14, 15, 16, 16, 17, 18, 18, 19, 21, 21, 22, 22, 22, 23, 23, 23, 24, 24; 18:1, 1, 2, 2, 2, 3, 4, 4, 4, 4, 4, 6, 6, 7, 7, 7, 7, 9, 9, 10, 11, 12, 12, 12, 12, 12, 12, 13, 14, 15, 15, 16, 16, 17, 18, 19, 19, 20, 20, 20, 20, 21, 23, 24, 24, 24, 24, 25, 25, 25, 27, 29, 29, 29, 30, 32, 32; 19:1, 3, 4, 6, 6, 7, 7, 8, 9, 9, 9, 12, 12, 13, 14, 14, 14, 14; 20:1, 1, 1, 1, 1, 2, 2, 3, 3, 3, 4, 5, 5, 5, 5, 5, 6, 6, 7, 7, 7, 8, 8, 8, 9, 9, 10, 10, 12, 13, 13, 14, 15, 15, 15, 16, 16, 17, 18, 18, 19, 19, 20, 21, 22, 22, 23, 23, 23, 26, 26, 26, 26, 27, 27, 28, 28, 28, 28, 29, 30, 30, 31, 31, 32, 32, 32, 33, 34, 34, 35, 35, 36, 37, 37, 38, 38, 39, 40, 40, 40, 40, 41, 42, 42, 42, 42, 44, 44, 44, 45, 45, 46, 46, 46, 47, 47, 47, 48; 21:1, 1, 2, 2, 3, 3, 3, 4, 4, 4, 5, 6, 7, 7, 8, 8, 9, 10, 10, 11, 11, 11, 12, 13, 13, 13, 14, 14, 14, 14, 15, 15, 16, 16, 17, 18, 18, 19, 19, 19, 19, 19, 20, 20, 21, 21, 21, 21, 21, 21, 22, 23, 23, 24, 24, 26, 26, 26, 26, 27, 28, 28, 28, 29, 30, 30, 31, 31, 32, 32, 33, 34, 34, 35, 36, 37, 37, 38, 38, 38, 39, 40, 40, 40, 40, 41, 42, 42, 42, 42, 44, 44, 44, 44, 45, 45, 46, 46, 46, 46, 47, 47, 47, 48; 21:1, 1, 2, 2, 3, 3, 3, 4, 4, 4, 4, 5, 6, 7, 7, 8, 8, 9, 10, 10, 11, 11, 12, 14, 14, 14, 15, 15, 15, 17, 17, 19, 19, 20, 20, 20, 21, 21, 21, 21, 21, 21, 21, 21; 30:1, 1, 2,

2, 3, 3, 3, 3, 3, 4, 4, 5, 5, 5, 5, 6, 6, 6, 6, 6, 7, 7, 7, 7, 8, 9, 9, 10, 10, 10, 11, 11, 11, 12, 12, 12, 12, 12, 12, 12, 12, 12, 13, 13, 13, 13, 13, 13, 14, 14, 14, 14, 14, 14, 15, 15, 16, 16, 17, 19, 20, 20, 20, 21, 21, 22, 22, 22, 23, 23, 24, 24, 24, 24, 25, 25, 25, 25, 25, 25, 25, 25; 31:1, 1, 1, 1, 1, 1, 1, 1, 3, 3, 4, 4, 4, 4, 4, 5, 5, 5, 5, 6, 6, 6, 6, 7, 8, 8, 9, 9, 9, 10, 10, 11, 11, 11, 11, 12, 12, 12, 12, 12, 12, 13, 13, 13, 13, 13, 14, 14, 15, 15, 15, 15, 16, 16, 16, 17, 17, 18, 18, 18, 18, 18, 18, 18, 18, 18; 32:1, 1, 1, 1, 1, 1, 1, 1, 1, 2, 3, 3, 3, 4, 4, 4, 4, 4, 5, 6, 6, 6, 6, 6, 7, 7, 7, 8, 8, 9, 10, 11, 11, 11, 11, 12, 12, 12, 12, 12, 12, 12, 13, 13, 14, 12, 15, 15, 15, 17, 17, 17, 18, 19, 20, 20, 21, 21, 21, 22, 22, 22, 23, 23, 23, 24, 24, 24, 25, 25, 25, 26, 26, 27, 27, 27, 27, 28, 28, 29, 29, 30; 34:1, 1, 2, 2, 2, 2, 2, 3, 3, 3, 3, 4, 5, 5, 6, 6, 6, 7, 7, 8, 8, 9, 9, 10, 10, 10, 10, 11, 12, 12, 13, 13, 13, 13, 14, 14, 15, 16, 16, 17, 17, 17, 18, 18, 18, 18, 18, 20, 20, 21, 24, 24, 25, 25, 25, 25, 26, 26, 26, 27, 27, 27, 27, 27, 28, 29, 29, 30, 30, 30, 32; 35:1, 1, 1, 3, 4, 5, 5, 5, 5, 6, 6, 6, 7, 7, 7, 8, 8, 8, 9, 10, 11, 11, 11, 11, 11, 11, 12, 13, 13, 13, 14, 14, 14, 14, 15, 15, 15; 36:1, 1, 2, 2, 2, 3, 3, 3, 3, 4, 4, 4, 4, 5, 5, 5, 5, 6, 6, 6, 6, 6, 6, 7, 7, 7, 10, 10, 10, 11, 13, 14, 15, 19, 20, 20, 22, 23, 23, 23, 23, 23, 24, 26, 28, 29, 30, 30, 30, 30, 30, 32, 33, 33, 33, 34, 34, 35, 35, 36, 36, 36, 36, 37, 37, 38, 38, 38, 38; 37:1, 1, 1, 1, 1, 2, 2, 2, 3, 3, 4, 4, 4, 4, 4, 6, 6, 7, 7, 9, 9, 9, 10, 12, 12, 12, 13, 14, 14, 15, 15, 16, 16, 16, 17, 18, 19, 19, 19, 19, 20, 21, 22, 22, 22, 25, 26, 26, 26, 28, 28, 28, 28; 38:1, 1, 2, 2, 3, 3, 6, 6, 8, 8, 8, 8, 9, 9, 9, 10, 11, 11, 12, 12, 12, 13, 13, 14, 15, 16, 16, 16, 17, 17, 18, 18, 18, 19, 20, 20, 20, 20, 20, 21, 22, 22, 23; 39:1, 1, 2, 2, 2, 4, 4, 4, 4, 4, 5, 5, 6, 6, 7, 7, 7, 7, 8, 8, 9, 9, 9, 9, 9, 9, 10, 10, 11, 11, 11, 11, 11, 11, 12, 12, 13, 13, 13, 13, 14, 14, 14, 14, 14, 14, 15, 15, 15, 16, 16, 16, 17, 17, 17, 18, 18, 18, 23, 23, 25, 25, 25, 27, 27, 28, 29, 29; 40:1, 1, 1, 1, 1, 1, 1, 1, 1, 2, 2, 2, 3, 3, 4, 4, 4, 5, 5, 5, 5, 5, 5, 5, 6, 6, 6, 6, 7, 7, 7, 7, 8, 8, 9, 9, 9, 9, 10, 10, 10, 11, 11, 11, 11, 11, 11, 11, 11, 12, 12, 13, 13, 13, 14, 14, 14, 14, 14, 15, 15, 15, 15, 16, 16, 16, 16, 17, 17, 17, 18, 18, 18, 18, 19, 19, 19, 19, 19, 20, 20, 20, 20, 20, 20, 21, 21, 21, 21, 21, 21, 21, 21, 22, 22, 22, 23, 23, 23, 23, 24, 24, 24, 24, 25, 25, 25, 26, 26, 27, 27, 28, 28, 28, 29, 29, 29, 30, 31, 31, 31, 32, 32, 32, 33, 33, 33, 33, 34, 34, 34, 34, 35, 35, 36, 36, 36, 36, 36, 37, 37, 37, 38, 38, 39, 40, 40, 40, 40, 40, 40, 41, 41, 42, 42, 42, 42, 42, 43, 43, 43, 44, 44, 44, 44, 44, 44, 44, 44, 44, 44, 45, 45, 45, 45, 45, 46, 46, 46, 46, 46, 46, 46, 46, 46, 47, 47, 47, 47, 47, 48, 48, 48, 48, 48, 49, 49, 49, 49, 49; 41:1, 1, 1, 1, 1, 2, 2, 2, 2, 2, 2, 2, 2, 2, 3, 3, 3, 3, 3, 4, 4, 4, 5, 5, 5, 5, 6, 6, 6, 6, 6, 6, 7, 7, 7, 7, 7, 7, 7, 8, 8, 8, 9, 9, 9, 9, 9, 10, 10, 10, 11, 11, 11, 11, 11, 11, 11, 12, 12, 12, 12, 12, 12, 13, 13, 13, 13, 14, 14, 14, 14, 14, 14, 14, 14, 15, 15, 16, 16, 16, 16, 16, 16, 17, 17, 17, 17, 19, 19, 19, 19, 19, 19, 20, 20, 20, 20, 20, 22, 22, 22, 22, 23, 23, 23, 24, 24, 24, 24, 25, 25, 25, 25, 25, 26, 26, 26, 26, 26, 26; 42:1, 1, 1, 1, 1, 1, 1, 1, 2, 2, 2, 3, 3, 3, 4, 4, 5, 5, 5, 5, 6, 6, 6, 6, 6, 6, 6, 6, 6, 7, 7, 7, 8, 8, 8, 9, 9, 9, 10, 10, 10, 10, 10, 10, 10, 11, 11, 11, 11, 12, 12, 12, 12, 12, 12, 13, 13, 13, 13, 13, 13, 13, 13, 13, 14, 14, 14, 14, 14, 14, 15, 15, 16, 16, 16, 17, 17, 18, 18, 19, 19, 19, 20, 20, 20; 43:1, 1, 1, 2, 2, 2, 2, 3, 3, 3, 3, 4, 4, 4, 4, 5, 5, 5, 5, 6, 6, 6, 7, 7, 7, 7, 7, 7, 7, 7, 7, 8, 9, 9, 10, 10, 11, 11, 11, 11, 11, 12, 12, 12, 12, 12, 12, 13, 13, 13, 13, 13, 13, 14, 14, 14, 14, 14, 15, 15, 16, 16, 17, 17, 17, 17, 18, 18, 18, 19, 19, 19, 19, 21, 21, 21, 22, 22, 24, 24, 24, 25, 26, 27, 27, 27, 27; 44:1, 1, 1, 1, 2, 2, 2, 3, 3, 3, 3, 3, 4, 4, 4, 4, 4, 4, 4, 4, 4, 5, 5, 5, 5, 6, 6, 6, 7, 7, 8, 9, 10, 11, 11, 11, 11, 11, 11, 11, 11, 12, 12, 13, 13, 14, 14, 14, 14, 14, 14, 15, 16, 17, 17, 17, 17, 18, 18, 18, 19, 19, 19, 19, 21, 22, 22, 23, 23, 23, 23, 27, 27, 27, 27, 27, 29, 29, 29,

Idx

30, 30, 30, 30, 30, 30, 31; 45:1, 1, 1, 1,
1, 1, 2, 2, 3, 3, 3, 3, 4, 4, 4, 4, 4, 4, 5,
5, 5, 5, 5, 6, 6, 6, 6, 6, 6, 7, 7, 7, 7, 7, 7,
7, 7, 7, 7, 7, 7, 7, 7, 7, 7, 8, 8, 8, 9, 9,
11, 11, 11, 11, 11, 11, 11, 11, 12, 13, 13,
13, 14, 14, 14, 14, 14, 15, 15, 15, 16, 16, 16,
17, 17, 17, 17, 17, 17, 17, 17, 17, 17, 18,
18, 18, 18, 18, 19, 19, 19, 19, 19, 19, 19,
19, 19, 19, 19, 20, 20, 20, 21, 21, 21, 21,
22, 22, 22, 22, 23, 23, 23, 23, 25, 25, 25,
25, 25, 25, 25, 25, 25; 46:1, 1, 1, 1, 1, 1,
1, 1, 2, 2, 2, 2, 2, 2, 2, 2, 2, 3, 3, 3, 3,
3, 3, 4, 4, 4, 4, 5, 5, 5, 6, 6, 7, 8, 8, 8, 8,
9, 9, 9, 9, 9, 9, 9, 9, 9, 9, 9, 9, 9, 10,
10, 11, 11, 11, 11, 11, 12, 12, 12, 12, 12,
13, 13, 14, 14, 14, 14, 14, 15, 15, 15, 16,
16, 17, 17, 18, 18, 19, 19, 19, 19, 19, 19,
19, 20, 20, 20, 20, 20, 20, 21, 21, 21,
21, 22, 22, 23, 24, 24, 24, 24, 24; 47:1, 1,
1, 1, 1, 1, 1, 1, 1, 1, 1, 1, 2, 2, 2, 2, 2,
3, 3, 3, 3, 4, 4, 4, 4, 4, 5, 6, 6, 7, 7, 7,
7, 8, 8, 8, 8, 8, 9, 9, 10, 10, 10, 11, 11,
12, 12, 12, 12, 12, 12, 13, 13, 13, 13, 14,
15, 15, 15, 15, 15, 16, 16, 16, 17, 17, 17,
17, 17, 17, 18, 18, 18, 18, 18, 19, 19, 19,
19, 19, 20, 20, 20, 20, 21, 22, 22, 22, 22,
23, 23; 48:1, 1, 1, 1, 1, 1, 1, 2, 2, 2, 3,
3, 4, 4, 4, 5, 5, 5, 6, 6, 6, 7, 7, 7, 8, 8,
8, 8, 8, 8, 8, 9, 9, 9, 9, 10, 10, 10, 10, 10,
10, 10, 10, 11, 11, 11, 11, 12, 12, 12, 13,
13, 13, 13, 13, 14, 14, 14, 15, 15, 15, 15,
15, 15, 16, 16, 16, 16, 16, 17, 17, 17, 17,
17, 18, 18, 18, 18, 18, 18, 19, 19, 19, 19,
20, 20, 20, 20, 21, 21, 21, 21, 21, 21, 21,
21, 21, 21, 21, 21, 21, 21, 21, 21, 21, 21,
22, 22, 22, 22, 22, 22, 22, 22, 22, 23, 23,
23, 23, 24, 24, 24, 25, 25, 25, 26, 26, 26,
27, 27, 27, 28, 28, 28, 28, 28, 28, 29, 29,
29, 30, 30, 30, 31, 31, 31, 31, 32, 33, 34,
35, 35, 35;

Da 1:1, 1, 2, 2, 2, 2, 2, 2, 3, 3, 3, 3, 3, 4,
4, 4, 4, 5, 5, 5, 5, 6, 7, 7, 7, 8, 8, 8, 8,
8, 9, 9, 10, 10, 10, 10, 10, 10, 11, 11, 13, 13,
13, 13, 15, 15, 15, 15, 16, 16, 18, 18, 18,
18, 18, 19, 19, 20, 20, 21; 2:1, 1, 2, 2, 2,
2, 2, 2, 2, 3, 3, 4, 4, 4, 4, 5, 5, 5, 5, 6,
6, 6, 6, 7, 7, 7, 8, 8, 8, 9, 9, 9, 9, 10, 10,
10, 10, 11, 11, 11, 12, 12, 13, 13, 14, 14,
14, 15, 15, 15, 15, 15, 16, 16, 16, 17, 18, 18,
18, 19, 19, 20, 21, 21, 21, 22, 22, 23,
24, 24, 24, 24, 24, 24, 25, 25, 25, 25, 26,
26, 26, 27, 27, 27, 27, 27, 27, 27, 27, 27,
28, 28, 28, 30, 30, 30, 31, 34, 35, 35, 35,
35, 35, 35, 35, 35, 35, 35, 35, 36, 36, 36,
37, 38, 38, 38, 38, 38, 39, 40, 41, 41, 41,
41, 41, 42, 42, 42, 42, 43, 44, 44, 44, 45, 45,
45, 45, 45, 45, 45, 45, 45, 45, 46, 47,
48, 48, 48, 48, 49, 49, 49, 49, 49; 3:1, 1,
1, 1, 2, 2, 2, 2, 2, 2, 2, 2, 2, 2, 2, 2, 3,
3, 3, 3, 3, 3, 3, 3, 3, 3, 5, 5, 5, 6,
6, 7, 7, 7, 7, 7, 7, 7, 7, 8, 9, 10, 10, 10,
11, 12, 12, 12, 13, 14, 15, 15, 15, 15,
16, 17, 18, 19, 19, 20, 20, 21, 21, 22, 22,
22, 22, 23, 23, 24, 24, 24, 24, 25, 25, 25,
25, 25, 26, 26, 26, 26, 26, 27, 27, 27, 27,
28, 28, 29, 30, 30; 4:1, 1, 2, 2, 5, 5, 6, 6,
9, 9, 10, 10, 10, 10, 11, 11, 11, 11, 11, 11,
12, 12, 12, 12, 12, 12, 12, 13, 13, 13, 13,
15, 15, 15, 15, 15, 15, 15, 15, 15, 17, 17,
17, 17, 17, 17, 17, 17, 17, 18, 18, 18, 18,
19, 19, 19, 19, 19, 20, 20, 20, 20, 20, 21,
21, 21, 21, 22, 22, 22, 22, 23, 23, 23, 23,
23, 23, 23, 23, 24, 24, 24, 25, 25, 25,
25, 25, 26, 26, 26, 26, 27, 27, 27, 27,
28, 28, 29, 30, 30; 5:1, 1, 2, 2, 2, 3, 3, 3, 3,
5, 5, 5, 5, 5, 5, 5, 5, 5, 6, 7, 7, 7, 7, 7,
7, 7, 7, 8, 8, 8, 10, 10, 10, 10, 10, 11,
11, 11, 11, 11, 11, 11, 11, 12, 12, 12, 13,
13, 13, 13, 14, 14, 14, 15, 15, 15, 16, 16,
16, 16, 16, 16, 17, 17, 17, 18, 19, 21,
21, 21, 21, 21, 21, 21, 23, 23, 23, 23, 23, 23,
24, 25, 26, 26, 27, 28, 29, 29, 30, 30, 31, 31;
6:1, 1, 2, 2, 3, 3, 3, 4, 4, 5, 6, 7, 7, 7, 7, 7,
7, 7, 7, 8, 8, 8, 9, 9, 10, 12, 12, 12,
12, 12, 12, 13, 13, 13, 14, 14, 15, 16, 16, 16,
16, 16, 16, 16, 16, 17, 17, 17, 18, 19, 21,
21, 21, 21, 21, 22, 22, 22, 22, 22, 23,
23, 23, 23, 23, 24, 24, 24, 24, 24, 25, 25, 25,
25, 25, 26, 26, 26, 26, 27, 27, 27, 27,
27, 27, 27, 27, 27, 27, 27; 10:1, 1, 1, 1,
4, 4, 4, 4, 6, 6, 6, 7, 7, 7, 9, 9, 9, 9, 10,
10, 13, 13, 13, 14; 14, 14, 14, 15, 16, 16,
16, 17, 18, 20, 20, 21; 11:1, 1, 2, 2, 2, 4,

5, 5, 6, 6, 6, 6, 6, 6, 6, 7, 7, 7, 8, 8, 9, 9,
11, 11, 11, 11, 11, 12, 12, 13, 13, 13, 14, 14,
14, 14, 15, 15, 15, 15, 15, 16, 16, 17, 17, 18,
18, 19, 20, 20, 21, 21, 21, 22, 22, 22, 23,
24, 24, 24, 24, 25, 25, 25, 25, 26, 27, 27,
28, 28, 29, 29, 29, 30, 30, 30, 31, 31, 31,
32, 32, 33, 33, 33, 35, 35, 36, 36, 37, 37,
38, 39, 39, 40, 40, 40, 40, 40, 40, 40, 41,
41, 41, 42, 42, 43, 43, 43, 43, 44, 44, 45,
45, 45; 12:1, 1, 1, 2, 2, 3, 3, 3, 4, 4, 4, 4,
5, 5, 5, 5, 5, 6, 6, 6, 6, 7, 7, 7, 7, 7, 8,
9, 9, 9, 10, 10, 10, 11, 11, 11, 12, 13, 13,
13;

Hos 1:1, 1, 1, 1, 1, 2, 2, 2, 2, 2, 3, 4, 4,
4, 4, 4, 5, 5, 6, 7, 7, 10, 10, 10, 10, 10,
10, 10, 11, 11, 11, 11; 2:3, 4, 5, 9, 9, 10,
12, 12, 13, 13, 14, 15, 15, 15, 15, 16, 17,
18, 18, 18, 18, 18, 18, 18, 18, 20, 21,
21, 21, 22, 22, 22, 22, 23; 3:1, 1, 1, 1, 3,
4, 5, 5, 5, 5; 4:1, 1, 1, 1, 1, 1, 3, 3, 3, 3,
3, 4, 5, 5, 6, 8, 10, 11, 12, 13, 13, 13,
13, 14, 15, 15, 16, 16, 19; 5:1, 2, 4, 4, 4, 5, 6,
7, 8, 8, 9, 9, 10, 10, 10, 11, 13, 14; 6:1, 2,
3, 3, 3, 3, 4, 5, 5, 5, 6, 7, 9, 9, 10, 10,
11; 7:1, 1, 1, 1, 1, 3, 3, 4, 4, 5, 5, 6, 6, 8, 10,
10, 12, 12, 12, 16, 16, 16, 16; 8:1, 1, 1, 3, 3,
6, 6, 7, 7, 7, 7, 8, 10, 10, 10, 10, 11, 11,
11, 13, 13, 16, 17; 9:2, 2, 2, 3, 4, 4, 4, 4, 5, 6,
7, 7, 7, 7, 7, 8, 8, 8, 9, 10, 10, 10, 11, 11,
11, 13, 13, 16, 17; 10:1, 1, 1, 3, 4, 4, 5, 5,
5, 5, 5, 7, 7, 8, 8, 8, 8, 8, 9, 9, 9, 9, 10,
11, 12, 13, 13, 14, 14, 15; 11:4 5, 5, 6, 7,
9, 9, 9, 9, 10, 10, 10, 11, 11, 12, 12; 12:1,
1, 2, 3, 3, 4, 5, 7, 9, 9, 9, 9, 10, 10, 10,
11, 11, 12, 13; 13:2, 2, 2, 2, 3, 3, 3, 3,
3, 4, 4, 5, 5, 7, 8, 8, 12, 13, 13, 13, 14,
14, 15, 15, 15, 15, 16; 14:1, 2, 2, 3, 5,
5, 6, 7, 7, 7, 9, 9, 9, 9

Joel 1:1, 1, 1, 2, 2, 4, 4, 4, 4, 4, 5, 6, 6, 7,
11, 11, 11, 12, 12, 12, 12, 12, 12, 12, 12,
13, 13, 13, 13, 14, 14, 14, 14, 14, 15,
15, 15, 15, 16, 16, 17, 17, 17, 17, 18, 18,
18, 19, 19, 19, 19, 19, 20, 20, 20, 20,
20, 20; 2:1, 1, 1, 1, 1, 2, 2, 2, 2, 3, 3, 4, 4,
5, 5, 5, 5, 6, 7, 8, 9, 9, 9, 10, 10, 10,
10, 10, 11, 11, 11, 12, 13, 13, 14, 14, 14,
16, 16, 16, 16, 16, 16, 17, 17, 17, 17, 17,
17, 17, 18, 19, 20, 20, 20, 20, 21, 21, 22,
22, 22, 22, 22, 23, 23, 23, 23, 23, 24,
24, 25, 25, 25, 25, 26, 26, 27, 27, 29,
29, 30, 30, 31, 31, 31, 31, 32, 32, 32,
32; 3:1, 2, 2, 4, 6, 6, 6, 7, 8, 8, 8, 9,
9, 9, 10, 12, 12, 12, 13, 13, 13, 13, 14,
14, 14, 14, 15, 15, 15, 16, 16, 16, 16, 16,
16, 16, 17, 18, 18, 18, 18, 18, 19,
19, 21

Am 1:1, 1, 1, 1, 1, 2, 2, 2, 2, 3, 3, 4, 4, 5,
5, 5, 5, 5, 5, 6, 6, 6, 6, 7, 7, 8, 8, 8, 8, 8,
9, 9, 9, 9, 10, 10, 11, 11, 11, 12, 12, 13,
13, 13, 13, 14, 14, 14, 14, 14, 15; 2:1, 1,
1, 1, 2, 2, 2, 3, 3, 3, 3, 4, 4, 4, 4, 4, 5, 6,
6, 6, 6, 7, 7, 7, 7, 7, 7, 7, 8, 8, 9, 9, 9,
9, 10, 10, 10, 10, 11, 12, 12, 14, 14, 14,
14, 15, 15, 16, 16; 3:1, 1, 1, 2, 2, 4, 5, 5,
6, 6, 6, 6, 7, 7, 8, 8, 9, 9, 9, 9, 10, 11,
11, 11, 12, 12, 12, 12, 12, 13, 13, 13, 13,
14, 14, 14, 14, 14, 15, 15, 15, 15, 15, 15;
4:1, 1, 1, 2, 2, 3, 3, 3, 5, 5, 6, 7, 7, 8, 9,
9, 10, 10, 10, 10, 10, 11, 11, 13, 13, 13,
13, 13, 13, 13; 5:2, 3, 3, 3, 4, 4, 6, 6, 7, 8,
8, 8, 8, 8, 8, 8, 8, 9, 9, 9, 9, 10, 11, 12,
12, 12, 13, 14, 14, 15, 15, 15, 15, 16, 16,
16, 16, 16, 16, 17, 18, 18, 18, 18, 19, 19,
20, 20, 22, 23, 23, 25, 26, 26, 27, 27; 6:1,
1, 1, 2, 3, 3, 4, 4, 4, 4, 4, 4, 5, 5, 6, 7,
7, 8, 8, 8, 8, 10, 10, 10, 10, 10, 10, 11,
11, 11, 12, 12, 14, 14, 14, 14, 14; 7:1, 1,
1, 1, 1, 1, 2, 2, 3, 4, 4, 4, 6, 6, 6, 7, 8, 8,
8, 9, 9, 9, 9, 10, 10, 10, 10, 11, 12, 13,
13, 15, 15, 15, 16, 16, 16, 17, 17, 17; 8:1,
2, 2, 3, 3, 3, 4, 4, 4, 5, 5, 5, 5, 6, 6, 6,
6, 7, 7, 8, 8, 9, 9, 9, 10, 10, 11, 11, 11,
1, 1, 1, 1, 1, 1, 3, 3, 3, 4, 5, 5, 5, 6, 6,
6, 6, 6, 6, 6, 7, 7, 7, 7, 8, 8, 8, 8, 8, 8,
8, 9, 9, 9, 9, 10, 10, 10, 10, 11, 11, 12,
12, 13, 13, 13, 13, 13, 13, 13, 13, 14, 14, 14,
14, 15

Ob 1:1, 1, 1, 2, 3, 3, 3, 3, 4, 4, 5, 6, 7,
7, 7, 8, 8, 8, 9, 9, 11, 11, 11, 11, 12, 12,
12, 12, 12, 13, 13, 13, 13, 14, 14, 15, 15,
15, 16, 17, 18, 18, 18, 18, 19, 19, 19, 19,
19, 19, 19, 20, 20, 20, 20, 20, 20, 21,
21, 21

Jnh 1:1, 1, 1, 3, 3, 3, 3, 4, 4, 4, 4, 5, 5, 5,
5, 5, 5, 6, 7, 9, 9, 9, 9, 10, 10, 10, 10, 11,
11, 12, 12, 13, 13, 13, 14, 15, 15, 16, 16,
16, 17, 17, 17; 2:1, 1, 2, 2, 3, 3, 3, 3, 5, 5,
5, 5, 6, 6, 6, 7, 9, 9, 10, 10; 3:1, 1, 1, 1,
2, 3, 3, 4, 4, 5, 5, 5, 6, 7, 7, 8, 10; 4:2, 2, 4,
5, 5, 5, 5, 6, 6, 7, 7, 7, 8, 8, 8, 9, 10,
10, 10

Mic 1:1, 1, 1, 1, 2, 2, 3, 3, 3, 4, 4, 4, 5, 5,
5, 5, 5, 6, 6, 6, 6, 7, 7, 7, 7, 7, 7, 8, 8, 8,
9, 10, 10, 11, 12, 12, 12, 13, 13, 13, 13,
13, 13, 14, 14, 15, 16; 2:1, 1, 3, 4, 5, 5, 7,
7, 7, 8, 8, 9; 3:1, 2, 2, 3, 3, 4, 5, 6, 7, 7, 8,
8, 11, 11, 12; 3:1, 2, 2, 3, 3, 4, 5, 6, 7, 7,
6, 6, 7, 7, 8, 8, 9, 9, 11, 11, 11, 11, 11,
12, 12, 12, 12; 4:1, 1, 1, 1, 1, 1, 2, 2, 2,
2, 2, 2, 2, 2, 3, 3, 4, 4, 4, 4, 4, 4, 5, 5,
8, 10, 10, 10, 10, 12, 12, 12, 13, 13,
13; 5:1, 1, 2, 3, 3, 3, 4, 4, 4, 4, 4, 4, 5,
5, 6, 6, 6, 6, 7, 7, 7, 7, 8, 8, 8, 8,

8, 8, 10, 10, 11, 13, 13, 14, 15; 6:1, 1, 1, 1,
9, 9, 9, 10, 10, 10, 10, 11, 11, 12, 12, 12, 16,
14, 15, 16, 16, 16, 16, 16, 16; 7:1, 1, 1, 1, 2,
2, 3, 3, 3, 3, 4, 4, 4, 4, 5, 6, 6, 6, 6, 7, 7, 8,
9, 9, 9, 10, 10, 10, 10, 11, 11, 11, 12, 12, 13,
32, 32, 33, 33, 35, 35, 36, 36, 36, 37, 37,
38, 39, 39, 40, 40, 40, 40, 40, 41, 41, 41,
41, 41, 42, 42, 43, 43, 43, 43, 44, 44, 45,
45, 45; 12:1, 1, 1, 2, 2, 3, 3, 3, 4, 4, 4, 4,
13, 14, 14, 14, 14, 15, 15, 16, 17, 17, 17,
38, 39, 39, 40, 40, 40, 40, 40, 41, 41, 41,
41, 41, 42, 42, 42, 42, 43, 44, 44, 44, 45, 45,
13, 14, 14, 14, 15, 15, 15, 16, 17, 17, 17,
19, 20, 20, 20, 20, 20, 20, 21, 21,
21, 21

Na 1:1, 1, 1, 1, 2, 2, 2, 3, 3, 3, 3, 3, 4,
4, 4, 4, 4, 5, 5, 5, 6, 6, 7, 7, 8, 9, 9, 11, 12,
12, 14, 14, 14, 14, 15, 15, 15; 2:1, 1, 2, 2, 2,
2, 3, 3, 3, 3, 3, 4, 4, 4, 4, 5, 5, 6, 6, 6, 7,
9, 9, 9, 9, 10, 10, 10, 11, 11, 11, 11, 11,
11, 11, 12, 13, 13, 13, 13, 13; 3:1, 1, 2, 2,
8, 8, 10, 10, 11, 12, 12, 12, 13, 13, 13,
14, 14, 14, 15, 15, 15, 15, 15, 16, 16, 17,
17, 17, 17, 18, 18, 19, 19

Hab 1:1, 1, 4, 4, 4, 5, 6, 6, 6, 6, 8, 8, 9, 9,
2, 2, 3, 3, 4, 8, 8, 8, 8, 8, 9, 11, 11, 11,
16, 16, 17, 17, 17, 17, 17, 18, 18, 18, 18,
19, 19, 19, 20, 20; 3:1, 2, 2, 2, 2, 3, 3, 3,
4, 4, 5, 6, 6, 6, 6, 7, 7, 7, 8, 8, 8, 8, 9, 9,
9, 10, 10, 10, 10, 11, 11, 11, 12, 12, 12, 13,
13, 13, 13, 14, 14, 15, 15, 15, 16, 16,
16, 17, 17, 17, 17, 17, 17, 17, 17, 18, 18,
19

Zep 1:1, 1, 1, 1, 1, 1, 1, 2, 2, 3, 3, 3, 3,
3, 3, 4, 4, 4, 4, 4, 5, 5, 5, 6, 6, 6, 7, 7,
7, 7, 8, 8, 8, 9, 9, 9, 10, 10, 11, 11, 11,
11, 12, 12, 13, 14, 14, 14, 14, 14, 14, 16,
16, 16, 17, 17, 18, 18, 18, 18, 18; 2:2, 2,
2, 2, 2, 2, 3, 3, 3, 3, 4, 5, 5, 5, 5, 5,
5, 5, 6, 7, 7, 7, 7, 7, 7, 8, 8, 9, 9, 9, 9,
9, 9, 10, 10, 11, 11, 11, 11, 11, 13, 14,
14, 14, 14, 14, 14, 14, 14, 15; 3:1, 2,
2, 3, 3, 4, 4, 5, 5, 5, 6, 8, 8, 8, 8, 8, 8,
9, 9, 9, 10, 10, 11, 12, 12, 13, 13, 14, 14,
15, 15, 15, 17, 17, 18, 18, 20, 20, 20

Hag 1:1, 1, 1, 1, 1, 1, 1, 1, 1, 1, 2, 2, 2,
3, 3, 3, 5, 7, 8, 8, 9, 9, 10, 11, 11, 11, 11,
11, 11, 11, 11, 11, 12, 12, 12, 12, 12, 12,
12, 12, 12, 12, 12, 13, 13, 13, 13, 13, 14,
14, 14, 14, 14, 14, 14, 14, 14, 14, 14, 15,
15, 15, 15; 2:1, 1, 1, 1, 1, 2, 2, 2, 2, 2,
4, 4, 4, 4, 4, 5, 6, 6, 6, 6, 7, 7, 7, 8, 8,
9, 9, 9, 9, 10, 10, 10, 10, 10, 10, 11, 11,
12, 12, 12, 13, 14, 15, 15, 16, 16, 17, 17,
18, 18, 18, 18, 18, 19, 19, 19, 19, 19, 19,
20, 20, 20, 20, 21, 21, 21, 22, 22, 22, 22,
22, 22, 23, 23, 23, 23

Zec 1:1, 1, 1, 1, 1, 1, 2, 3, 3, 3, 4, 4, 4, 5,
6, 6, 7, 7, 7, 7, 7, 7, 7, 7, 8, 8, 9, 10,
10, 10, 10, 11, 11, 11, 11, 11, 12, 12, 12,
13, 13, 14, 14, 15, 15, 15, 16, 16, 17, 17, 19,
19, 20, 21, 21, 21, 21; 2:2, 2, 3, 4, 5, 5,
6, 6, 6, 6, 6, 6, 7, 8, 8, 8, 8, 9, 10, 10, 11,
11, 11, 12, 12, 13; 3:1, 1, 1, 1, 2, 2, 2, 3,
4, 5, 5, 6, 6, 7, 8, 8, 9, 9, 9, 9, 10, 10, 10;
4:1, 2, 2, 2, 3, 3, 3, 4, 5, 6, 6, 6, 7, 8, 8,
9, 9, 9, 10, 10, 10, 10, 10, 10, 11, 11, 11,
12, 12, 14, 14, 14; 5:2, 2, 3, 3, 3, 4, 4, 4,
4, 4, 4, 4, 5, 6, 7, 7, 8, 8, 8, 9, 9, 9, 9,
9, 10, 10, 11; 6:1, 2, 2, 3, 3, 4, 5, 5, 5, 5,
5, 6, 6, 6, 10, 11, 11, 11, 12, 12, 12, 12,
13, 13, 13, 14, 14, 14, 14, 15, 15, 15, 15,
15; 7:1, 1, 1, 1, 2, 2, 3, 3, 3, 3, 3, 3, 4,
5, 5, 5, 5, 7, 7, 7, 7, 7, 7, 8, 8, 9, 10,
10, 10, 10, 11, 11, 12, 12, 12, 13, 14, 14,
14, 14; 8:1, 1, 2, 3, 3, 3, 3, 4, 4, 5, 5, 5,
6, 6, 6, 6, 7, 7, 8, 9, 9, 9, 9, 9, 9, 9, 9,
10, 11, 11, 11, 12, 12, 12, 12, 13, 14,
14, 15, 15, 15, 16, 16, 16, 16, 16, 16, 17,
17; 10:1, 1, 1, 1, 1, 2, 2, 3, 3, 3, 3, 3, 4,
4, 5, 5, 5, 5, 6, 6, 6, 7, 9, 10, 10, 11,
2, 2, 3, 3, 3, 3, 4, 4, 5, 5, 5, 6, 6, 6, 6, 6,
7, 7, 7, 7, 9, 9, 10, 11, 11, 11, 11, 11, 13,
13, 13, 13, 13, 14, 15, 16, 16, 16, 16,
16, 17, 17, 17; 12:1, 1, 1, 1, 1, 1, 1, 2,
2, 3, 3, 4, 4, 4, 4, 5, 5, 6, 6, 6, 6, 6, 6, 6,
7, 7, 7, 7, 8, 8, 8, 8, 9, 10, 10, 10, 11,
12, 12, 12, 12, 13, 13, 13, 14; 13:1, 2, 2,
2, 2, 3, 3, 4, 4, 4, 4, 4, 4, 5, 6, 7, 7, 7, 7,
7, 8, 9, 9, 9; 14:1, 1, 1, 2, 2, 2
5, 5, 5, 5, 5, 5, 6, 7, 8, 8, 9, 9, 10,
10, 10, 10, 11, 11, 12, 12, 12, 13, 14,
14, 14, 17, 17, 18, 18, 18, 19, 20, 21,
22, 24, 24, 26, 27, 27, 29, 31, 31, 31, 31,
31, 31, 32, 32, 33, 35, 35, 36, 36, 36, 36,
37, 39, 39; 16:1, 2, 3, 3, 3, 3, 3, 4, 4,
5, 6, 6, 6, 9, 9, 9, 10, 11, 11, 11, 12, 12,
12, 12, 13, 13, 14, 14, 16, 16, 16, 18, 19,
19, 20, 21, 21, 23, 26, 27, 27, 28; 17:2,
2, 5, 6, 9, 9, 9, 9, 10, 12, 12, 13, 14, 15,
15, 18, 18, 19, 22, 22, 23, 25, 25, 25, 26,
27, 27; 18:1, 1, 1, 1, 2, 3, 4, 4, 6, 6, 7,
10, 11, 12, 12, 13, 14, 16, 16, 17, 20, 23,
26, 27, 27, 28, 28, 30, 34; 19:1, 3, 4, 8, 8,
10, 10, 12, 13, 14, 17, 20, 21, 22, 23, 24,
24, 28, 28, 28, 28, 30; 20:1, 2, 3, 3, 4,
5, 6, 6, 7, 8, 8, 8, 9, 9, 10, 11, 11, 12,
12, 16, 16, 17, 17, 18, 18, 19, 19, 20,
21, 21, 21, 22, 22, 23, 24, 24, 25, 25, 28,
30, 31, 31; 21:1, 2, 3, 4, 5, 5, 6, 7, 7, 8, 8,
8, 9, 9, 9, 10, 11, 11, 12, 12, 13, 14, 15,
17, 18, 18, 19, 19, 20, 20, 21, 21, 23, 23,
23, 23, 25, 26, 28, 30, 31, 31, 31, 31, 31,
32, 32, 32, 34, 34, 35, 35, 36, 38, 38,
38, 39, 40, 40, 41, 42, 42, 42, 42, 42,
42, 43, 43, 45, 46; 22:2, 3, 4, 6, 7, 8, 9,
10, 10, 11, 11, 13, 13, 15, 16, 16, 16, 19,
21, 21, 23, 23, 25, 26, 26, 26, 27, 28, 28,
29, 29, 30, 30, 31, 31, 32, 32, 32, 32, 32,
41, 42, 44; 23:1, 2, 2, 5, 6, 6, 6, 7, 9, 13,
14, 15, 16, 16, 16, 17, 17, 17, 18, 18, 19,
19, 19, 20, 21, 22, 22, 23, 23, 25, 25, 26,
26, 26, 29, 29, 29, 29, 30, 30, 30, 31, 31,
32, 33, 35, 35, 35, 35, 35, 37, 39, 39;
24:1, 1, 3, 3, 3, 3, 4, 6, 7, 9, 9, 11, 13, 13,
14, 14, 14, 15, 15, 15, 16, 17, 18, 20, 20,
21, 21, 22, 24, 26, 26, 27, 27, 27, 27, 27,
28, 28, 29, 29, 29, 29, 29, 30, 30, 30,
30, 30, 30, 31, 31, 32, 33, 36, 37, 40, 40,
30, 30, 31, 31, 32, 33, 36, 37, 40, 40,
38, 38, 38, 38, 39, 39, 39, 40, 40, 40, 41,
41, 41, 43, 43, 43, 44, 49, 50, 51; 25:1, 1,
4, 5, 8, 8, 9, 10, 13, 13, 14, 15, 15, 13, 13,
14, 16, 16, 18, 19, 21, 23, 24, 25, 27, 28,
30, 31, 31, 31, 32, 33, 33, 34, 34, 34,
34, 37, 40, 40, 41, 41, 45, 46; 26:2, 2, 2,
3, 3, 3, 3, 3, 5, 5, 6, 6, 9, 10, 11, 13,
14, 14, 17, 17, 17, 18, 18, 19, 19,
20, 20, 23, 23, 24, 24, 26, 26, 28, 28, 29,
30, 31, 31, 31, 34, 35, 36, 37, 40, 41, 41,
42, 44, 44, 44, 45, 45, 45, 46, 49, 50, 51,
51, 51, 51, 51, 51, 53, 53, 54, 54, 54, 54,
56, 56, 57, 58, 58, 59, 60, 60, 60, 60, 61,
62, 62, 62, 62, 64, 64, 64, 64, 64, 64, 66,
66; 28:1, 1, 1, 1, 1, 1, 2, 2, 2, 2, 4, 5, 5, 6,

6, 7, 8, 9, 11, 11, 11, 11, 12, 12, 14, 15, 15, 16, 19, 19, 19, 19, 20, 20;
Mk 1:1, 1, 1, 2, 3, 3, 3, 4, 4, 4, 5, 5, 7, 8, 10, 10, 10, 12, 12, 13, 13, 13, 14, 14, 15, 15, 15, 16, 16, 19, 19, 20, 20, 21, 21, 22, 24, 26, 27, 28, 29, 29, 31, 31, 32, 33, 33, 34, 35, 38, 42, 44, 45, 45; 2:1, 2, 2, 3, 4, 4, 4, 4, 4, 5, 5, 6, 9, 9, 10, 10, 10, 12, 13, 13, 14, 14, 16, 17, 17, 18, 18, 18, 18, 19, 19, 19, 19, 20, 20, 20, 21, 21, 21, 22, 22, 22, 23, 23, 23, 24, 24, 26, 26, 26, 26, 27, 27, 28, 28; 3:1, 2, 3, 3, 4, 5, 5, 5, 6, 6, 7, 9, 11, 17, 17, 17, 18, 18, 20, 22, 22, 22, 27, 28, 29, 32, 35, 35; 4:1, 1, 1, 1, 1, 4, 4, 4, 6, 7, 10, 10, 11, 11, 14, 14, 15, 15, 15, 16, 17, 18, 19, 19, 19, 19, 20, 26, 26, 27, 28, 28, 28, 28, 29, 29, 29, 30, 31, 31, 31, 32, 32, 32, 33, 35, 35, 35, 36, 36, 37, 37, 38, 38, 39, 39, 39, 41, 41; 5:1, 1, 1, 1, 2, 2, 3, 4, 4, 5, 5, 7, 8, 10, 11, 12, 12, 13, 13, 13, 13, 14, 14, 14, 14, 15, 15, 16, 16, 18, 18, 19, 21, 21, 22, 22, 23, 27, 29, 30, 31, 33, 33, 35, 35, 36, 36, 36, 37, 38, 38, 38, 38, 39, 40, 40, 40, 40, 41, 41, 42, 42; 6:2, 2, 3, 3, 6, 7, 11, 11, 14, 14, 15, 16, 22, 22, 22, 23, 24, 24, 25, 25, 25, 26, 27, 27, 28, 28, 30, 33, 35, 35, 36, 36, 39, 41, 41, 41, 43, 43, 44, 45, 45, 45, 47, 47, 47, 47, 48, 48, 48, 48, 49, 51, 51, 52, 52, 53, 53, 54, 56, 56, 56; 7:1, 1, 3, 3, 3, 3, 4, 4, 5, 5, 8, 8, 9, 10, 13, 14, 15, 15, 17, 17, 18, 19, 19, 20, 20, 21, 23, 24, 26, 26, 27, 27, 27, 28, 28, 28, 29, 30, 30, 31, 31, 31, 31, 31, 33, 35, 36, 36, 37, 37; 8:1, 2, 3, 4, 6, 6, 6, 6, 8, 10, 11, 13, 13, 14, 14, 15, 15, 15, 19, 19, 20, 20, 22, 22, 24, 24, 25, 25, 26, 27, 28, 28, 29, 31, 31, 31, 33, 34, 34, 35, 35, 35, 36, 38, 38, 38, 38; 9:1, 7, 9, 9, 9, 9, 10, 11, 12, 14, 15, 16, 17, 20, 20, 22, 22, 24, 24, 25, 25, 26, 27, 28, 31, 31, 31, 33, 33, 34, 34, 35, 35, 36, 42, 43, 44, 45, 46, 47, 48, 50; 10:1, 1, 1, 2, 5, 6, 6, 10, 10, 14, 15, 17, 19, 21, 23, 24, 24, 25, 25, 29, 30, 31, 32, 32, 33, 33, 33, 34, 34, 35, 37, 38, 39, 39, 41, 42, 44, 45, 46, 46, 47, 48, 50; 10:1, 1, 1, 2, 5, 7, 8, 8, 8, 9, 10, 10, 10, 10, 11, 11, 11, 12, 13, 15, 15, 15, 16, 17, 18, 18, 19, 19, 20, 20, 20, 21, 21, 23, 24, 27, 27, 30, 32; 12:1, 2, 2, 2, 2, 2, 4, 7, 7, 8, 9, 9, 9, 10, 10, 10, 10, 11, 12, 12, 13, 13, 14, 14, 17, 17, 18, 20, 21, 21, 22, 22, 23, 23, 24, 24, 25, 25, 26, 26, 26, 26, 27, 27, 27, 27, 28, 28, 29, 29, 29, 30, 30, 31, 32, 32, 32, 33, 33, 33, 34, 34, 35, 35, 36, 36, 37, 38, 38, 39, 39, 41, 41, 41, 43, 43, 43, 43, 44, 47, 48, 50; 13:1, 3, 4, 7, 8, 9, 10, 10, 12, 12, 12, 13, 13, 14, 14, 14, 15, 15, 15, 16, 18, 19, 19, 20, 20, 22, 22, 25, 25, 26, 26, 26, 26, 27, 27, 28, 29, 29, 29, 30, 30, 31, 31, 32, 32, 33, 33, 34, 34, 37, 38, 38, 39, 39, 41, 41, 41, 43; 13:1, 3, 3, 4, 7, 8, 9, 10, 12, 12, 13, 14, 14, 14, 14, 15, 15, 16, 18, 19, 19, 20, 20, 20, 22, 22, 24, 24, 25, 25, 26, 26, 26, 26, 28, 28, 29, 29, 29, 30, 30, 31, 32, 32, 32, 33, 33, 33, 34, 37, 38, 38, 38, 39, 39, 39, 41, 41, 41, 43; 13:1, 3, 3, 4, 7, 8, 9, 10, 12, 12, 12, 13, 14, 14, 14, 14, 16, 16, 17, 17, 20, 20, 20, 21, 21, 23, 24, 26, 26, 27, 27, 28, 29, 29, 29, 30, 30, 31, 32, 32, 33, 33, 33, 34, 37, 38, 38, 39, 39, 45, 46, 46, 46, 47; 16:1, 2, 2, 2, 2, 2, 3, 3, 3, 4, 5, 5, 6; 15:1, 1, 1, 1, 2, 2, 3, 7, 8, 8, 9, 10, 10, 12, 12, 12, 13, 14, 14, 14, 15, 16, 16, 16, 18, 19, 20, 21, 21, 22, 22, 23, 27, 29, 30, 31, 32, 33, 33, 33, 34, 37, 38, 39, 39, 41, 41, 43; 13:1, 3, 3, 4, 7, 8, 9, 10, 12; 16:1, 2, 2, 2, 2, 2, 2, 3, 3, 3, 4, 5, 5, 6;
Lk 1:2, 2, 3, 4, 5, 5, 5, 6, 6, 8, 8, 9, 9, 9, 10, 10, 10, 11, 11, 11, 13, 15, 15, 15, 16, 16, 17, 17, 17, 17, 17, 17, 17, 18, 19, 19, 20, 21, 21, 22, 23, 25, 25, 26, 26, 27, 27, 28, 28, 30, 30, 32, 32, 32, 32, 33, 34, 35, 35, 35, 36, 38, 38, 39, 40, 41, 41, 41, 42, 43, 44, 44, 45, 46, 46, 47, 48, 51, 52, 53, 53, 58, 59, 59, 59, 65, 66, 66, 67, 68, 69, 70, 70, 71, 72, 73, 74, 75, 76, 76, 76, 77, 78, 79, 79, 80, 80, 80; 2:1, 4, 4, 4, 6, 7, 8, 8, 9, 9, 9, 9, 10, 11, 11, 12, 13, 14, 14, 15, 15, 16, 16, 17, 18, 20, 20, 21, 21, 21, 22, 22, 23, 23, 23, 24, 24, 25, 25, 25, 26, 26, 26, 27, 27, 27, 27, 31, 32, 32, 34, 35, 36, 36, 37, 38, 38, 39, 39, 40, 40, 41, 41, 41, 42, 42, 43, 44, 44, 44, 46, 46, 46, 50; 3:1, 1, 1, 1, 2, 2, 2, 2, 3, 3, 3, 4, 4, 4, 4, 4, 4, 4, 5, 5, 6, 6, 7, 7, 9, 9, 9, 10, 14, 15, 15, 16, 16, 17, 17, 18, 19, 19, 21, 21, 22, 23, 23, 24, 24, 24, 24, 25, 25, 25, 26, 26, 26, 27, 27, 27, 27, 28, 28, 28, 29, 29, 30, 30, 30, 31, 31, 31, 31, 32, 32, 32, 32, 33, 33, 33, 34, 34, 34, 34, 34, 35, 35, 35, 36, 36, 36, 36, 37, 37, 37, 37, 37, 38, 38, 38, 38; 4:1, 1, 1, 2, 3, 3, 5, 5, 6, 6, 8, 9, 13, 13, 14, 14, 14, 16, 16, 17, 17, 17, 18, 18, 18, 18, 19, 19, 20, 20, 20, 20, 22, 25, 25, 25, 27, 27, 27, 27, 31, 32, 32, 34, 35, 36, 36, 38, 38, 38, 38; 4:1, 1, 1, 2, 2, 3, 3, 4, 4, 5, 5, 7, 7, 9, 9, 9, 10, 14, 15, 15, 16, 16, 17, 17, 18, 19, 19, 21, 21, 22, 23, 23, 23, 23; 3:1, 1, 2, 3, 4, 5, 5, 6, 8, 8, 13, 14, 14, 14, 16, 17, 17, 18, 18, 19, 19, 20, 20, 21, 21, 22, 22, 23, 24, 24, 24, 24, 24, 25, 25, 26, 26, 26, 26, 26, 27, 27, 27, 27, 27, 28, 28, 28, 28, 28, 29, 29, 29, 29, 30, 30, 30, 31, 31, 31, 31, 32, 32, 32, 32, 33, 33, 33, 34, 34, 34, 34, 34, 35, 35, 35, 35, 35, 36, 36, 36, 36, 37, 37, 37, 37, 37, 38, 38, 38, 38; 4:1, 1, 1, 2, 3, 3, 5, 5, 6, 6, 6, 7, 7, 8, 8, 8, 9, 9, 9, 10, 14, 15, 15, 16, 16, 17, 17, 19, 19, 19, 21, 21, 22, 23, 25, 25, 25, 25; 8:1, 1, 1, 3, 4, 5, 5, 6, 6, 7, 7, 7, 8, 8, 9, 11, 11, 11, 12, 12, 13, 14, 14, 15, 16, 16, 17, 18, 18, 18; 6:1, 1, 1, 1, 2, 2, 4, 4, 4, 5,

5, 6, 7, 7, 8, 8, 8, 9, 10, 10, 15, 16, 16, 17, 17, 17, 19, 20, 22, 23, 23, 26, 29, 29, 33, 35, 35, 35, 35, 38, 39, 39, 39, 40, 41, 41, 42, 42, 42, 42, 45, 45, 45, 45, 46, 48, 48, 48, 49, 49, 49; 7:1, 1, 3, 3, 6, 6, 9, 10, 10, 11, 12, 12, 12, 12, 12, 13, 14, 14, 17, 18, 19, 19, 22, 22, 22, 22, 22, 22, 24, 24, 24, 24, 28, 28, 29, 29, 29, 30, 30, 31, 31, 32, 33, 34, 36, 36, 37, 37, 38, 38, 39, 41, 41, 44, 44, 45, 47, 50; 8:1, 1, 1, 1, 3, 5, 5, 5, 7, 7, 10, 10, 11, 11, 11, 12, 12, 12, 13, 13, 15, 15, 16, 19, 21, 22, 22, 23, 24, 24, 24, 24, 25, 26, 26, 27, 27, 29, 29, 29, 29, 31, 32, 33, 33, 33, 33, 33, 34, 34, 35, 35, 35, 36, 37, 37, 37, 38, 38, 39, 40, 41, 41, 42, 44, 45, 47, 49, 49, 50, 51, 51, 51, 51, 54; 9:2, 2, 5, 6, 6, 7, 7, 8, 10, 10, 11, 11, 12, 12, 12, 12, 16, 16, 16, 16, 16, 18, 19, 19, 20, 22, 22, 24, 24, 25, 26, 26, 27, 27, 28, 29, 29, 29, 31, 32, 33, 35, 36, 37, 37, 38, 42, 42, 42, 43, 43, 44, 44, 47, 48, 51, 52, 56, 57, 58, 60, 60, 62, 62; 10:1, 2, 2, 2, 2, 4, 6, 7, 7, 9, 9, 10, 16, 21, 21, 22, 22, 35; 11:7, 13, 14, 14, 14, 15, 15, 20, 20, 24, 26, 26, 27, 27, 27, 28, 29, 29, 29, 30, 30, 31, 31, 31, 31, 31, 31, 32, 32, 33, 34, 34, 34, 35, 36, 36, 38, 39, 39, 42, 42, 43, 43, 44, 44, 47, 47, 48, 49, 50, 50, 50, 50, 51, 51, 51, 51, 52, 53, 12:1, 1, 3, 3, 4, 7, 8, 8, 9, 10, 10, 11, 12, 12, 13, 13, 15, 15, 16, 22, 23, 23, 24, 24, 26, 27, 28, 28, 28, 30, 31, 32, 33, 36, 37, 38, 38, 39, 39, 40, 42, 45, 46, 46, 48, 49, 53, 53, 53, 53, 53, 53, 53, 53, 53, 53, 54, 54, 56, 56, 56, 56, 58, 58, 58, 58, 58, 59; 13:1, 2, 4, 7, 7, 10, 10, 14, 14, 14, 14, 14, 14, 14, 15, 15, 15, 16, 17, 18, 18, 19, 19, 20, 21, 24, 25, 25, 25, 28, 28, 28, 29, 29, 29, 29, 31, 32, 33, 33, 34, 34, 35, 35, 35; 14:1, 1, 1, 2, 3, 5, 7, 8, 9, 9, 10, 10, 11, 11, 12, 13, 13, 15, 15, 15, 16, 21, 22, 23, 23, 28, 29, 30, 31, 31; 15:1, 2, 4, 4, 8, 9, 10, 10, 12, 12, 13, 16, 16, 21, 22, 22, 23, 25, 25, 26, 27, 30; 16:1, 3, 3, 4, 5, 8, 8, 8, 9, 10, 11, 11, 13, 13, 13, 14, 14, 16, 16, 16, 17, 21, 21, 21, 22, 22, 22, 24, 29, 30, 31, 31; 17:1, 2, 5, 5, 6, 6, 7, 9, 11, 14, 17, 20, 20, 20, 21, 22, 22, 22, 22, 24, 24, 24, 24, 26, 26, 26, 27, 27, 27, 28, 29, 30, 31, 31, 31, 34, 34, 35, 35, 36, 36, 36, 37; 18:6, 6, 8, 8, 10, 10, 10, 11, 12, 13, 14, 16, 17, 20, 22, 24, 25, 27, 29, 30, 31, 31, 31, 32, 33, 34, 35, 36, 39, 43; 19:2, 2, 3, 5, 8, 8, 8, 10, 11, 15, 15, 15, 16, 18, 23, 24, 29, 29, 30, 30, 30, 31, 33, 35, 35, 36, 36, 36, 37, 37; 20:1, 1, 1, 1, 1, 2, 3, 5, 8, 8, 8, 10, 11, 15, 15, 16, 16, 18, 23, 24, 24, 25, 26, 27, 27, 27, 28, 28, 29, 30, 30, 31, 35, 36, 36, 37, 37, 38, 39, 40, 41, 42, 45, 45, 46, 46, 46, 46, 46, 47; 21:1, 1, 4, 4, 5, 6, 6, 8, 9, 12, 20, 20, 21, 21, 21, 23, 23, 24, 24, 24, 24, 24, 25, 25, 25, 25, 25, 26, 26, 27, 27, 29, 31, 35, 35, 36, 37, 37, 37, 37, 38, 38, 38; 22:1, 1, 2, 2, 3, 3, 4, 6, 7, 7, 8, 10, 10, 11, 11, 11, 11, 13, 14, 14, 16, 17, 18, 18, 18, 20, 20, 21, 21, 22, 24, 25, 25, 26, 27, 29, 31, 35, 36, 36, 37, 37, 37, 37, 38, 38, 38, 22:1, 1, 2, 3, 3, 4, 6, 6, 7, 7, 8, 10, 10, 11, 11, 11, 11, 13, 14, 14, 16, 17, 18, 18, 18, 20, 21, 22, 23, 24, 24, 24, 24, 25, 25, 26, 27, 29, 29, 29, 29, 31, 32, 33; 24:1, 1, 1, 1, 1, 2, 2, 3, 3, 5, 5, 7, 7, 9, 9, 9, 10, 10, 12, 18, 18, 19, 19, 20, 21, 22, 24, 24, 25, 27, 27, 27, 29, 29, 32, 32, 33, 33, 33, 34, 44, 44, 44, 44, 45, 46, 46, 49, 49, 53;
Jn 1:1, 1, 1, 1, 2, 2, 4, 4, 5, 5, 7, 7, 9, 9, 10, 12, 13, 13, 13, 14, 14, 14, 14, 17, 18, 18, 18, 19, 19, 20, 23, 23, 23, 23, 24, 29, 29, 29, 29, 30, 30, 31, 33, 34, 35, 36, 37, 39, 40, 41, 41, 42, 43, 44, 45, 45, 48, 49, 49, 50, 51, 51; 2:1, 1, 2, 3, 5, 6, 6, 6, 7, 7, 9, 9, 9, 9, 9, 9, 10, 10, 13, 14, 14, 15, 15, 15, 15, 15, 18, 20, 21, 22, 22, 23, 23, 23; 3:1, 1, 2, 3, 4, 5, 5, 6, 8, 8, 8, 8, 13, 14, 14, 14, 16, 17, 17, 18, 19, 20, 20, 21, 22, 25, 26, 28, 29, 29, 29, 31, 31, 34, 34, 35, 35, 36, 36, 36; 4:1, 1, 5, 6, 6, 8, 9, 9, 10, 11, 11, 12, 14, 14, 15, 17, 18, 20, 21, 23, 25, 27, 28, 28, 29, 30, 31, 33, 34, 34, 35, 39, 39, 39, 40; 9:1, 1, 1, 2, 4, 5, 5, 6, 6, 9, 11, 12, 13, 13, 15, 15, 16, 16, 16, 16, 17, 18, 19, 19, 20, 21, 21, 21, 24, 25, 26, 27, 27, 27, 29, 29, 30, 30, 31, 31, 31, 31, 32, 34, 35, 38, 39, 39, 39, 40, 41; 10:1, 2, 3, 3, 6, 7, 9, 9, 9, 11, 11, 11, 12, 15, 16, 17, 17, 19, 19, 21, 21, 22, 22, 24, 30, 31, 32, 32, 36, 39; 9:1, 1, 3, 4, 4, 4, 4, 4, 4, 5, 5, 6, 7, 7, 8, 8, 8, 8, 9, 11, 11, 12, 12, 17, 17, 19, 21, 21, 22, 23, 24, 24, 25, 25, 26, 27, 27, 27; 6:1, 1, 4, 4, 10, 10, 10, 11, 11, 11, 11, 12, 12, 13, 14, 14, 14, 16, 16, 16, 17, 18, 19, 19, 21, 21, 21, 22, 22, 22, 23, 23, 23, 24, 25, 25, 26, 26, 27, 27, 27,

28, 29, 31, 32, 33, 33, 35, 37, 38, 39, 39, 40, 40, 40, 41, 41, 42, 44, 44, 45, 45, 46, 46, 49, 50, 51, 51, 51, 51, 52, 53, 53, 54, 57, 57, 59, 62, 63, 63, 63, 64, 67, 68, 69, 69, 71, 71; 7:1, 2, 3, 4, 7, 7, 10, 11, 12, 12, 13, 14, 14, 14, 15, 17, 18, 19, 19, 20, 22, 22, 23, 23, 24, 26, 26, 28, 31, 32, 32, 32, 35, 35, 35, 35, 36, 37, 37, 38, 39, 39, 40, 41, 42, 42, 43, 45, 45, 46, 47, 48, 48, 49; 8:1, 2, 2, 2, 3, 5, 6, 8, 9, 9, 9, 10, 12, 12, 13, 15, 16, 17, 18, 20, 20, 22, 25, 25, 26, 26, 28, 31, 32, 32, 32, 34, 35, 35, 35, 36, 39, 40, 41, 44, 44, 44, 45, 46, 48, 52, 52, 53, 57, 59; 9:3, 4, 4, 5, 5, 5, 6, 6, 6, 6, 7, 8, 11, 13, 14, 14, 15, 16, 16, 17, 18, 18, 22, 22, 24, 24, 30, 32, 32, 35, 40; 10:1, 1, 1, 2, 2, 2, 3, 3, 4, 5, 7, 7, 8, 9, 10, 11, 11, 12, 12, 12, 12, 12, 13, 14, 15, 15, 19, 21, 21, 22, 22, 23, 24, 24, 25, 31, 33, 35, 35, 36, 36, 37, 37, 38, 38, 40; 11:1, 2, 4, 4, 6, 8, 9, 9, 9, 10, 15, 17, 19, 20, 24, 24, 25, 25, 27, 27, 28, 31, 31, 31, 33, 33, 35, 36, 36, 36, 37, 38, 38, 39, 40, 41, 41, 41, 42, 45, 45, 46, 47, 48; 49, 50, 50, 52, 54, 54, 55, 55, 55, 56, 56, 57, 57; 12:1, 1, 2, 3, 3, 3, 5, 6, 6, 7, 8, 9, 9, 11, 12, 12, 12, 13, 13, 16, 17, 18, 19, 19, 20, 21, 23, 23, 24, 29, 31, 31, 32, 34, 34, 35, 35, 36, 36, 38, 38, 40, 42, 42, 43, 43, 46, 47, 47, 48; 49, 50, 50, 50, 50, 51, 51, 51, 51, 52, 53 12:1, 1, 2, 3, 3, 3, 4, 7, 8, 8, 9, 10, 10, 11, 12, 12, 13, 13, 15, 15, 15, 16, 18, 18, 21, 21, 22, 23, 23, 24, 26, 26, 27, 28, 28, 31, 31, 31, 32, 33, 33, 33, 34, 35, 35, 35, 35, 35, 38, 38, 41; 14:4, 5, 6, 6, 6, 9, 10, 10, 10, 10, 11, 11, 11, 12, 13, 13, 16, 17, 17, 19, 22, 24, 26, 26, 26, 27, 28, 30, 31, 31, 31, 31; 15:1, 1, 3, 4, 4, 5, 5, 5, 6, 9, 9, 15, 16, 18, 18, 19, 19, 19, 19, 20, 20, 24, 25, 26, 26, 26, 26, 27; 16:2, 2, 3, 4, 4, 7, 7, 8, 11, 13, 15, 16, 17, 17, 19, 20, 21, 21, 23, 25, 25, 26, 27, 28, 28, 28, 28, 32, 32, 33, 33; 17:1, 3, 4, 4, 5, 5, 6, 6, 9, 11, 11, 12, 12, 13, 14, 14, 15, 15, 16, 16, 18, 18, 19, 19, 21, 22, 24, 24, 25, 26; 18:1, 1, 2, 3, 6, 9, 10, 10, 11, 12, 12, 13, 14, 14, 15, 15, 15, 16, 16, 16, 17, 18, 19, 20, 20, 20, 22, 22, 23, 23, 33, 33, 35, 36, 37, 37, 38, 39, 40; 19:2, 3, 5, 5, 5, 6, 7, 7, 8, 9, 11, 12, 13, 13, 13, 14, 14, 14, 15, 15, 17, 17, 18, 19, 19, 20, 20, 20, 21, 21, 23, 23, 25, 25, 26, 26, 27, 28, 28, 28, 31, 32, 32, 32; 34, 34, 34, 34, 35, 35, 35, 35, 38, 38, 40, 40; 20:1, 1, 1, 1, 1, 1, 2, 2, 2, 3, 4, 5, 6, 6, 7, 7, 8, 9, 9, 10, 10, 11, 11, 11, 12, 12, 15, 18, 18, 19, 19, 19, 19, 20, 20, 22, 24, 25, 25, 25, 25, 26, 30, 31, 31; 21:1, 2, 4, 4, 6, 7, 7, 8, 8, 9, 11, 11, 12, 14, 14, 16, 17, 17, 20, 23, 24, 25, 25;
Ac 1:1, 2, 2, 2, 3, 3, 4, 4, 5, 6, 7, 7, 8, 8, 12, 13, 13, 14, 14, 15, 15, 15, 16, 16, 18, 18, 19, 19, 20, 21, 21, 22, 23, 24, 26, 26; 2:1, 2, 4, 4, 6, 9, 10, 11, 14, 15, 15, 16, 17, 19, 20, 20, 20, 21, 21, 22, 23, 24, 24, 28, 29, 30, 30, 31, 33, 33, 33, 34, 34, 36, 37, 37, 38, 38, 38, 38, 39, 41, 42, 43, 46, 47, 47, 47; 3:1, 1, 2, 2, 2, 3, 6, 7, 8, 9, 10, 11, 11, 11, 12, 13, 13, 13, 14, 14, 15, 16, 16, 16, 18, 19, 19, 21, 21, 21, 23, 24, 25, 25, 25, 25; 4:1, 1, 1, 1, 2, 2, 3, 4, 4, 5, 6, 6, 6, 7, 8, 8, 9, 9, 10, 10, 11, 11, 11, 13, 14, 15, 17, 18, 19, 20, 21, 22, 23, 24, 25, 25, 25, 26, 26, 27, 30, 31, 31, 32, 32, 33, 33, 33, 34, 34, 35, 36, 36, 37; 5:2, 2, 3, 3, 5, 6, 7, 8, 9, 9, 9, 10, 11, 12, 13, 14, 15, 16, 17, 17, 18, 18, 19, 19, 20, 20, 20, 21, 21, 21, 22, 24, 24, 24, 24, 25, 25, 25, 26, 26, 27, 29, 30, 31, 31, 31, 31, 32, 32, 32, 34, 36, 38, 38, 39, 40, 40, 40, 41, 41, 42; 6:1, 1, 1, 1, 1, 2, 2, 2, 3, 4, 4, 5, 6, 6, 7, 7, 7, 8, 9, 9, 10, 10, 11, 11, 11, 12, 13, 14, 15, 15, 16, 18, 19, 19, 20, 21, 22, 22, 23, 24, 24, 25, 25, 25, 26; 18:1, 1, 2, 3, 6, 9, 10, 10, 11, 12, 12, 12, 13, 14, 14, 15, 15, 15, 16, 16; 17:2, 2, 3, 4, 5, 6, 7, 7, 9, 11, 22, 23, 24, 24, 26, 26, 26, 27, 28, 28, 28, 31, 32, 33, 33, 33, 35, 36, 36, 37, 37, 38, 39, 39; 19:2, 3, 5, 5, 5, 6, 7, 7, 8, 9, 11, 12, 13, 13, 13, 14, 14, 14, 15, 15, 17, 17, 18, 19, 19, 20, 20, 20, 21, 21, 21, 21, 23, 23, 23, 24, 24, 25, 25, 25, 25; 20:1, 1, 1, 1, 2, 2, 3, 4, 5, 6, 6, 7, 7, 8, 9, 10, 11, 11, 12, 12, 14, 15, 18, 18, 19, 19, 19, 19, 20, 20, 22, 24, 25, 25, 25, 26, 30, 31; 21:1, 1, 2, 4, 4, 6, 6, 6, 6, 7, 7, 8, 8, 10, 11, 11, 12, 14, 14, 16, 17, 17, 20, 23, 24, 25, 25; 25;
Ac 1:1, 2, 2, 2, 3, 3, 4, 4, 5, 6, 7, 7, 8, 8, 12, 13, 13, 14, 14, 15, 15, 15, 16, 16, 18, 18, 19, 19, 20, 21, 21, 22, 24, 26, 26; 2:1, 2, 4, 4, 6, 9, 10, 11, 14, 15, 15, 16, 17, 19, 20, 20, 20, 21, 21, 22, 23, 24, 24, 28, 29, 30, 30, 31, 33, 33, 33, 34, 34, 36, 37, 37, 38, 38, 38, 38, 39, 41, 42, 43, 46, 47, 47, 47; 3:1, 1, 2, 2, 2, 3, 6, 7, 8, 9, 10, 11, 11, 11, 12, 13, 13, 13, 14, 14, 15, 16, 16, 16, 18, 19, 19, 21, 21, 21, 23, 24, 25, 25, 25, 25; 4:1, 1, 1, 1, 2, 2, 3, 4, 4, 5, 6, 6, 6, 7, 8, 8, 9, 9, 10, 10, 11, 11, 11, 13, 14, 15, 17, 18, 19, 20, 21, 22, 23, 24, 25, 25, 25, 26, 26, 27, 30, 31, 31; 5:2, 2, 3, 3, 3, 3, 3, 4, 4, 5, 5, 6, 7, 7, 7, 8, 8, 9, 9, 9, 10, 10, 10, 11, 11, 11, 12, 13, 13, 14, 14, 15, 15, 15, 15, 16, 16, 17, 17, 17, 18, 18, 22, 22, 23, 23, 23, 23, 23, 24, 25, 25, 27, 28, 28, 29, 31, 31;
Ro 1:1, 2, 3, 3, 4, 4, 4, 4, 5, 6, 7, 8, 9, 10, 17, 17, 18, 18, 20, 20, 20, 20, 23, 23, 24, 25, 25, 25, 26, 27, 27, 32; 2:1, 2, 3, 4, 4, 5, 5, 8, 9, 9, 10, 10, 12, 12, 13, 13, 13, 14, 14, 14, 14, 15, 15, 16, 16, 17, 18, 18, 20, 20, 20, 20, 23, 23, 24, 24, 25, 25, 26, 26, 27, 27, 28, 29, 29; 3:1, 2, 3, 5, 6, 7, 12, 13, 17, 19, 19, 19, 20, 20, 20, 20, 21, 21, 22, 23, 24, 25, 26, 27, 28, 28, 29, 29, 29, 30, 30, 31, 31, 31; 4:1, 3, 4, 5, 6, 6, 8, 9, 9, 11, 11, 12, 12, 13, 13, 13, 14, 14, 15, 15, 16, 16, 16, 16, 16, 17, 19, 20, 24; 5:2, 5, 5, 6, 10, 11, 12, 13, 13, 14, 14, 15, 15, 15, 15, 16, 16, 17, 18, 18, 19, 20, 20; 6:4, 4, 4, 5, 5, 6, 9, 12, 13, 14, 15, 17, 17, 18, 19, 20, 21, 23, 23; 7:1, 1, 2, 2, 2, 2, 4, 4, 4, 5, 5, 5, 6, 6, 7, 7, 7, 8, 8, 9, 9, 10, 11, 12, 12, 13, 14, 16, 19, 22, 23, 23, 24, 25, 25, 25; 8:1, 1, 2, 2, 2, 3, 3, 3, 4, 4, 5, 5, 7, 7, 8, 9, 9, 10, 11, 11, 12, 13, 13, 14, 14, 15, 16, 16, 16, 18, 18, 19, 20, 20, 20; 6:4, 4, 4, 5, 5, 6, 9, 12, 13, 14, 15, 17, 18, 18, 19, 19, 20, 21, 21, 21, 22, 23, 23, 23, 24, 25, 25, 25; 8:1, 1, 2, 4, 4,

28, 28, 28, 29, 29, 30, 30; 12:1, 1, 2, 2, 3, 3, 4, 5, 6, 6, 6, 6, 7, 7, 7, 7, 8, 9, 10, 10, 10, 10, 10, 11, 11, 11, 11, 11, 12, 12, 12, 13, 13, 14, 14, 14, 16, 17, 17, 17, 17, 17, 18, 18, 19, 20, 20, 22, 22, 23, 23, 23, 23, 24; 13:1, 1, 2, 2, 2, 4, 5, 5, 5, 6, 6, 6, 6, 7, 7, 7, 7, 8, 9, 10, 10, 10, 11, 11, 11, 11, 11, 12, 12, 13, 13, 14, 14, 14, 16, 17, 17, 17, 17, 17, 18, 18, 19, 20, 20, 21, 21, 21, 22, 22, 24; 14:1, 1, 1, 1, 2, 2, 3, 3, 4, 5, 5, 5, 6, 7, 9, 11, 11, 11, 11, 11, 12, 12, 12, 13, 13, 14, 14, 15, 15, 15, 17, 17, 17, 18, 18, 19, 20, 20, 21, 21, 21, 23, 23, 23, 23, 24; 13:1, 1, 2, 2, 2, 3, 3, 4, 5, 7, 7, 7, 8, 9, 10, 11, 11, 12, 12, 14, 14, 15, 15, 16, 16, 17, 17, 17, 18, 18, 19, 21, 22, 22, 22, 23, 23, 23, 25, 26, 26, 27, 27, 27, 27, 28; 15:1, 1, 2, 3, 3, 3, 3, 4, 4, 5, 5, 6, 7, 7, 7, 8, 10, 10, 11, 11, 12, 13, 14, 14, 14, 15, 15, 16, 16, 17, 17, 17, 18, 18, 19, 21, 22, 22, 22, 23, 23, 24, 26, 27, 28, 28, 30, 30, 31, 32, 33, 33, 35, 35, 36, 36, 38, 39, 39, 40, 40, 41; 16:1, 2, 3, 4, 4, 4, 5, 5, 6, 6, 7, 7, 7, 9, 9, 10, 10, 11, 12, 13, 13, 14, 15, 17, 17, 17, 17, 19, 20, 22, 23, 23, 23, 24, 24, 25, 25, 26, 26, 26, 26, 27, 27, 27, 28, 29, 29, 30, 30, 33, 33, 35, 35, 36, 36, 38, 39, 39, 40; 17:1, 2, 3, 4, 4, 5, 5, 5, 5, 5, 6, 6, 6, 7, 8, 8, 8, 9, 10, 10, 11, 11, 11, 12, 13, 14, 14, 16, 17, 17, 17, 17, 18, 18, 18, 21, 22, 23, 24, 25, 25, 25, 26, 26, 28, 29; 19:1, 2, 4, 4, 4, 4, 5, 6, 7, 8, 8, 8, 8, 9, 9, 9, 10, 10, 10, 11, 11, 11, 12, 13, 13, 13, 14, 14, 16, 17, 17, 17, 17, 18, 18; 18:3, 4, 5, 5, 5, 6, 6, 6, 7, 8, 8, 8, 8, 9, 9, 9, 10, 10, 10, 11, 11, 12, 13, 13, 13, 14, 14, 16, 17, 17, 17, 17, 17, 19, 20, 21, 21, 22, 22, 22, 23, 23, 23, 25, 25, 25, 25, 25, 26, 26, 27; 19:1, 2, 4, 4, 4, 5, 6, 7, 8, 8, 9, 9, 10, 10, 10, 11, 11, 12, 12, 13, 13, 13, 13, 14, 15, 16, 16, 17, 17, 17, 19; 20:1, 1, 3, 4, 6, 7, 7, 7, 8, 9, 11, 15, 15, 16, 16, 17, 17, 17, 18, 18, 19, 19, 19, 21, 21, 22, 22, 23, 23, 24, 24, 24, 25, 26, 27, 27, 28, 28, 28, 29, 31, 32, 35, 35, 35, 38, 38; 21:1, 3, 3, 4, 5, 5, 7, 8, 8, 8, 9, 11, 11, 11, 11, 13, 13, 14, 14, 16, 16, 17, 18, 18, 20, 20, 21, 21, 21, 22, 24, 25, 26, 26, 26, 27, 27, 28, 28, 28, 28, 29, 29, 30, 30, 30, 30, 31, 31, 32, 33; 34, 34, 34, 34, 35, 35, 35, 35, 35, 36, 36, 37, 37, 39, 40, 40, 40, 40; 22:2, 2, 3, 3, 3, 4, 5, 5, 5, 7, 9, 9, 10, 10, 11, 12, 12, 13, 14, 14, 14, 16, 16, 17, 20, 20, 21, 21, 22; 20; 23:1, 2, 2, 3, 3, 5, 5, 6, 6, 6, 6, 6, 6, 7, 7, 7, 8, 8, 9, 9, 10, 10, 11, 11, 12, 14, 15, 15, 16, 17, 17, 18, 19, 19, 19, 20, 22, 22, 23, 23, 24, 26, 27, 28, 30, 30, 31; 24:1, 1, 1, 5, 5, 5, 5, 6, 7, 9, 10, 10, 12, 13, 13, 15, 14, 14, 14, 14, 15, 15, 18, 20, 21, 21, 22, 24, 24, 26, 27; 25:1, 2, 2, 2, 3, 6, 6, 7, 8, 8, 9, 10, 10, 11, 13, 15, 15, 16, 16, 16, 16, 17, 17, 17, 18, 21, 22, 23, 23, 23, 23, 24, 24, 27; 26:1, 2, 2, 3, 4, 4, 5, 5, 6, 7, 8, 9, 10, 10, 12, 13, 13, 14, 14, 14, 14, 16, 17, 17, 18, 19, 20, 20, 20, 21, 22, 23, 23, 23, 25, 26, 27, 28, 29, 29, 30, 30, 30; 27:2, 3, 4, 5, 6, 7, 8, 9, 10, 11, 11, 12, 12, 13, 15, 15, 16, 17, 17, 18, 18, 19, 21, 22, 23, 27, 29, 29, 30, 30, 30, 31, 31, 31, 32, 32, 33, 34, 37, 38, 38, 38, 39, 39, 40, 40, 40, 40, 44; 28:1, 2, 2, 2, 3, 3, 4, 4, 4, 5, 7, 7, 7, 8, 9, 11, 13, 13, 15, 15, 16, 16, 16, 16, 17, 17, 17, 17, 17, 19, 20, 21, 21, 23, 23, 23, 24, 25, 25, 27, 28, 28, 29, 31, 31;
Ro 1:1, 2, 3, 3, 4, 4, 5, 6, 6, 16, 16, 16, 16, 17, 17, 18, 20, 20, 20, 20, 23, 23, 24, 25, 25, 26, 26, 27, 27, 32; 2:1, 2, 3, 4, 4, 5, 5, 6, 7, 8, 9, 9, 9, 11, 12, 13, 13, 13, 14, 14, 16, 16, 16, 17, 18, 18, 20, 20, 20, 20, 24; 5:2, 5, 5, 6, 10, 11, 12, 13, 13, 14, 14, 15, 15, 15, 15, 16, 16, 17, 18, 18, 19, 20, 20; 6:4, 4, 4, 5, 5, 6, 9, 12, 13, 14, 15, 17, 17, 18, 19, 19, 20, 21, 23, 23; 7:1, 1, 2, 2, 2, 2, 4, 4, 4, 4, 5, 5, 5, 5, 6, 7, 7, 7, 7, 8, 8, 9, 9, 10, 11, 12, 12, 13, 14, 16, 19, 22, 23, 23, 24, 25, 25, 25; 8:1, 1, 2, 2, 2, 3, 3, 3, 4, 4, 5, 5, 7, 7, 8, 9, 9, 10, 11, 11, 12, 13, 13; 10:3, 4, 4, 5, 5, 5, 6, 7, 8, 8, 9, 9, 10, 11, 12, 13, 13, 15, 15, 16, 17, 18, 18, 18; 11:1, 1, 2, 4, 4,

Idx

4, 5, 7, 7, 8, 8, 11, 12, 12, 12, 12, 12, 12, 13, 13, 15, 15, 15, 15, 16, 16, 16, 16, 17, 17, 17, 18, 18, 18, 19, 21, 22, 24, 24, 25, 25, 26, 28, 28, 28, 29, 33, 33, 33, 34, 34; 12:1, 2, 3, 3, 4, 6, 6, 11, 13, 16, 17, 19; 13:1, 1, 2, 2, 3, 3, 3, 4, 4, 4, 8, 10, 10, 11, 12, 12, 12, 12, 13, 14, 14, 14; 14:1, 6, 6, 6, 6, 6, 6, 8, 8, 9, 10, 11, 14, 17, 17, 19, 20; 15:1, 1, 3, 4, 5, 6, 7, 8, 8, 8, 9, 9, 11, 12, 12, 13, 13, 13, 15, 15, 16, 16, 16, 16, 16, 18, 19, 19, 19, 20, 25, 26, 27, 29, 29, 29, 30, 30, 30, 31, 32, 33; 16:1, 2, 4, 4, 5, 5, 7, 8, 11, 12, 12, 12, 13, 14, 15, 16, 17, 18, 18, 20, 20, 22, 23, 23, 23, 24, 25, 25, 25, 25, 26, 26, 26, 26, 26, 99, 99

1Co 1:1, 2, 2, 3, 4, 6, 7, 8, 8, 9, 10, 10, 10, 11, 13, 16, 17, 17, 18, 18, 18, 19, 19, 19, 19, 20, 20, 20, 20, 21, 21, 21, 22, 22, 23, 23, 24, 24, 25, 25, 26, 27, 27, 27, 27, 27, 27, 28, 31; 2:1, 4, 5, 5, 6, 6, 7, 7, 7, 8, 8, 9, 9, 10, 10, 11, 11, 11, 12, 12, 12, 13, 13, 14, 14, 14, 14, 16, 16, 16; 3:5, 6, 7, 10, 10, 13, 13, 16, 16, 17, 17, 19, 19, 20, 20, 20, 22; 4:1, 1, 4, 4, 5, 5, 5, 5, 5, 9, 9, 13, 13, 13, 15, 15, 15, 16, 17, 19, 19, 20, 21; 5:1, 4, 4, 5, 5, 5, 5, 6, 7, 8, 8, 8, 10, 10, 10; 6:1, 1, 2, 2, 2, 2, 2, 4, 6, 9, 9, 10, 10, 11, 11, 12, 12, 13, 13, 13, 13, 14, 14, 15, 15, 17, 18, 19, 19; 7:1, 3, 3, 3, 3, 4, 4, 4, 4, 5, 8, 10, 10, 10, 11, 12, 13, 14, 14, 14, 14, 15, 15, 17, 19, 19, 19, 19, 20, 20, 21; 8:1, 4, 4, 6, 7, 8, 8, 10, 10, 11, 12, 13; 9:1, 2, 2, 5, 7, 7, 7, 8, 9, 9, 12, 13, 13, 13, 13, 14, 14, 14, 16, 16, 17, 17, 18, 18, 18, 19, 20, 20, 20, 20, 20, 21, 21, 22, 23, 24, 25, 26; 10:1, 1, 2, 2, 3, 4, 4, 5, 7, 7, 10, 11, 13, 16, 16, 16, 16, 16, 16, 18, 18, 18, 19, 20, 20, 21, 21, 21, 21, 21, 22, 25, 26, 26, 26, 28, 28, 28, 29, 31, 32, 32, 32, 33; 11:2, 3, 3, 3, 3, 3, 6, 7, 7, 7, 7, 8, 8, 8, 9, 9, 9, 9, 11, 11, 11, 12, 12, 12, 12, 13, 14, 14, 16, 16, 17, 18, 20, 22, 23, 23, 23, 25, 25, 26, 27, 27, 27, 29, 32, 32, 34; 12:3, 3, 3, 4, 5, 6, 7, 7, 8, 8, 8, 9, 9, 9, 9, 10, 10, 11, 12, 12, 14, 15, 15, 15, 16, 16, 16, 16, 17, 17, 17, 18, 18, 19, 21, 21, 21, 21, 22, 23, 24, 25, 25, 26, 26, 27, 28, 30, 31; 13:1, 2, 3, 6, 13; 14:2, 4, 5, 7, 8, 9, 9, 10, 11, 11, 12, 12, 15, 15, 15, 15, 16, 16, 16, 17, 19, 21, 21, 23, 25, 27, 28, 29, 29, 30, 32, 32, 33, 33, 34, 34, 34, 35, 36, 37, 37, 37; 15:1, 3, 4, 4, 5, 6, 7, 9, 9, 9, 10, 10, 12, 12, 13, 14, 16, 16, 16, 17, 18, 18, 18, 19, 20, 20, 20, 20, 20, 21, 21, 22, 22, 23, 24, 24, 26, 28, 29, 29, 29, 32, 32, 34, 35, 39, 40, 40, 40, 41, 41, 41, 42, 42, 45, 45, 47, 47, 47, 48, 48, 49, 49, 49, 49, 50, 52, 52, 52, 54, 56, 56, 56, 57, 58, 58, 58; 16:1, 1, 1, 2, 2, 7, 7, 10, 10, 11, 12, 13, 15, 15, 15, 17, 19, 19, 19, 20, 21, 22, 23, 99, 99

2Co 1:1, 1, 1, 2, 3, 3, 3, 4, 5, 6, 6, 9, 9, 9, 11, 11, 12, 12, 12, 13, 14, 14, 17, 17, 19, 20, 20, 22; 2:2, 3, 4, 9, 10, 12, 14, 16, 16, 16, 16, 17; 3:3, 3, 3, 4, 6, 6, 6, 6, 7, 7, 7, 8, 9, 9, 10, 13, 13, 14, 14, 14, 15, 15, 16, 16, 17, 17, 17, 18, 18, 18; 4:2, 2, 2, 2, 4, 4, 4, 4, 5, 6, 6, 6, 7, 7, 10, 10, 10, 10, 11, 13, 14, 16, 16, 18; 5:1, 5, 5, 5, 6, 6, 8, 10, 11, 14, 16, 16, 18, 19, 19; 6:1, 2, 2, 2, 2, 4, 6, 7, 7, 7, 7, 13, 16, 16, 16, 17, 17, 18, 18, 18, 18; 7:1, 6, 6, 7, 7, 13, 16, 16, 16, 17, 18; 8:1, 5, 5, 5, 5, 6, 6, 6, 8, 10, 11, 11, 14, 16, 16, 18, 19, 19, 21; 6:1, 2, 2, 3, 4, 6, 7, 7, 7, 7, 13, 16, 16, 16, 17, 17, 18; 7:1, 1, 6, 7, 7, 7, 13, 16, 16, 18, 19, 19, 20, 20; 7:1, 1, 2, 4, 4, 4, 5, 5, 6, 8, 9, 11, 14, 16, 16, 18, 18, 19, 21; 6:1, 2, 2, 3, 4, 6, 7, 7, 7, 7, 13, 16, 16, 17, 18; 7:1, 1, 6, 7, 7, 7, 13, 16, 16, 18, 19, 19, 21, 21, 22, 23, 23, 24, 24; 9:1, 1, 2, 3, 5, 5, 9, 10, 10, 12, 12, 12, 13, 13, 14; 10:1, 2, 3, 3, 4, 4, 5, 5, 7, 8, 12, 13, 13, 14, 16, 16, 17, 18; 11:3, 3, 5, 7, 9, 10, 10, 13, 15, 16, 18, 18, 20, 20, 22, 22, 24, 25, 26, 26, 26, 28, 28, 30, 31, 32, 32, 32, 33; 12:1, 2, 2, 3, 3, 6, 6, 7, 7, 7, 7, 8, 9, 11, 12, 14, 14, 14, 14, 15, 15, 18, 18, 21; 13:1, 1, 2, 4, 4, 4, 4, 4, 5, 5, 8, 10, 10, 11, 13, 14, 14, 14, 14, 99, 99

Gal 1:1, 1, 2, 2, 3, 4, 6, 7, 10, 11, 12, 13, 13, 14, 16, 19, 19, 20, 21, 22, 23; 2:2, 5, 5, 7, 7, 7, 8, 8, 8, 9, 9, 9, 9, 10, 10, 11, 12, 12, 13, 14, 14, 14, 14, 14, 15, 16, 16, 16, 16, 16, 16, 16, 17, 17, 18, 18, 19, 20, 20, 20, 20, 21; 3:1, 2, 2, 2, 3, 3, 5, 5, 5, 5, 7, 8, 8, 10, 10, 10, 10, 11, 11, 11, 12, 13, 13, 14, 14, 14, 14, 15, 16, 17, 17, 17, 18, 18, 19, 19, 19, 21, 21, 22, 22, 23, 23, 24, 26, 29; 4:1, 2, 2, 3, 3, 4, 4, 4, 5, 5, 6, 6, 9, 13, 13, 13, 15, 16, 19, 19, 20, 21, 22, 23; 2:2, 5, 7, 8, 8, 9, 9, 9, 9, 10, 10, 11, 12, 13, 14, 16, 16, 17, 17, 17, 17, 18, 18, 18, 19, 19, 20, 20, 20, 20, 21, 21; 3:1, 2, 2, 2, 2, 3, 3, 5, 5, 5, 5, 7, 8, 8, 8, 8, 10, 10, 10, 10, 11, 11, 12, 13, 13, 14, 14, 15, 16, 17, 17, 17, 18, 99

Eph 1:1, 1, 2, 3, 3, 4, 4, 5, 5, 6, 6, 7, 7, 9, 9, 10, 10, 11, 11, 12, 13, 13, 14, 14, 14, 15, 15, 17, 17, 17, 18, 18, 18, 18, 19, 19, 20, 20, 20, 20, 23; 2:2, 2, 2, 2, 3, 3, 3, 3, 3, 7, 8, 11, 11, 11, 12, 12, 12, 13, 13, 14, 14, 14, 15, 16, 16, 16, 16, 16, 17, 18, 18, 19; 3:1, 2, 2, 2, 3, 3, 5, 5, 5, 5, 7, 8, 8, 8, 9, 9, 9, 10, 10, 11, 12, 14, 14, 16, 16, 17, 17, 18, 19, 20, 20, 20; 4:1, 1, 1, 3, 3, 3, 7, 7, 9, 9, 10, 12, 12, 21; 4:1, 1, 1, 3, 3, 3, 7, 7, 9, 9, 10, 12, 12,

12, 12, 12, 13, 13, 13, 13, 13, 13, 14, 15, 15, 16, 16, 16, 16, 16, 16, 17, 17, 18, 18, 18, 21, 22, 22, 22, 23, 23, 24, 26, 27, 28, 29, 29, 30, 30; 5:5, 6, 6, 8, 9, 9, 10, 11, 13, 14, 16, 16, 17, 17, 18, 19, 20, 20, 21, 22, 23, 23, 23, 23, 23, 24, 25, 26, 26, 29, 29, 32, 33; 6:1, 2, 3, 4, 4, 5, 6, 6, 6, 7, 8, 8, 9, 10, 11, 11, 11, 11, 12, 13, 13, 14, 15, 15, 16, 16, 17, 17, 17, 18, 19, 19, 21, 22, 23, 23, 23, 99

Php 1:1, 1, 1, 2, 5, 5, 6, 7, 7, 8, 10, 11, 11, 12, 13, 14, 14, 14, 14, 16, 17, 17, 19, 19, 22, 22, 24, 27, 27, 27, 29, 30; 2:1, 2, 4, 6, 7, 7, 8, 8, 9, 11, 11, 15, 15, 15, 16, 16, 17, 18, 19, 21, 22, 22, 24, 28, 28, 29, 30; 3:1, 1, 2, 3, 3, 3, 4, 4, 5, 5, 5, 5, 6, 6, 6, 8, 8, 8, 9, 9, 9, 10, 11, 11, 14, 14, 14, 16, 16, 16, 16, 20, 21; 4:1, 2, 2, 3, 3, 3, 4, 5, 5, 6, 6, 7, 8, 8, 8, 10, 11, 11, 14, 14, 14, 16, 16, 20, 20, 23, 99

Col 1:1, 2, 2, 3, 4, 4, 5, 5, 5, 6, 6, 6, 8, 9, 9, 10, 10, 12, 12, 12, 13, 13, 14, 15, 15, 15, 18, 18, 18, 18, 18, 18, 18, 19, 20, 22, 23, 23, 23, 24, 24, 25, 25, 26, 27, 27, 27, 27, 27; 2:1, 2, 2, 2, 3, 3, 5, 5, 6, 6, 7, 8, 8, 8, 9, 9, 10, 11, 11, 11, 11, 11, 12, 12, 12, 13, 14, 14, 16, 16, 17, 19, 19, 20, 20, 22, 23, 23, 23, 23; 3:1, 2, 5, 6, 6, 7, 9, 10, 10, 12, 14, 15, 15, 16, 16, 16, 17, 17, 18, 20, 22, 23, 24, 24, 24, 24, 25; 4:2, 3, 5, 7, 8, 11, 11, 12, 14, 15, 15, 16, 16, 16, 17, 17, 18, 18, 99

1Th 1:1, 1, 1, 1, 1, 3, 5, 6, 6, 6, 8, 8, 9, 10; 2:2, 4, 6, 8, 9, 13, 13, 13, 14, 14, 15, 16, 16, 16, 17, 19; 3:2, 5, 8, 9, 12, 13, 13; 4:1, 2, 3, 5, 6, 6, 10, 15, 15, 15, 15, 16, 16, 16, 16, 16, 17, 17, 17, 17, 17; 5:1, 1, 2, 2, 5, 5, 5, 5, 7, 7, 8, 8, 8, 12, 14, 14, 18, 19, 23, 23, 26, 27, 27, 28, 99, 99

2Th 1:1, 1, 1, 2, 3, 4, 5, 7, 8, 9, 9, 11, 11, 12, 12, 12; 2:1, 2, 3, 4, 7, 7, 8, 8, 8, 9, 10, 10, 12, 13, 13, 13, 14, 14, 14, 15; 3:1, 1, 3, 4, 4, 5, 5, 6, 6, 16, 16, 17, 17, 18, 99, 99

1Ti 1:1, 2, 5, 5, 7, 8, 9, 9, 9, 11, 11, 12, 14, 15, 17, 17, 18; 2:3, 4, 4, 5, 7, 7, 7, 11, 12, 14, 14; 3:1, 2, 5, 6, 6, 7, 7, 8, 9, 9, 10, 12, 12, 13, 13, 15, 15, 15, 15, 16, 16, 16, 16, 16; 4:1, 1, 1, 3, 5, 6, 6, 8, 10, 10, 12, 14, 14, 14, 14, 16; 5:1, 2, 2, 8, 9, 9, 10, 10, 11, 14, 14, 16, 17, 17, 18, 18, 18, 21, 21, 25; 6:1, 1, 2, 3, 3, 5, 10, 10, 12, 12, 13, 14, 15, 15, 16, 17, 19, 21, 99, 99

2Ti 1:1, 1, 2, 5, 6, 6, 7, 8, 8, 8, 9, 10, 10, 11, 12, 13, 14, 16, 16, 18, 18; 2:1, 2, 2, 4, 6, 6, 7, 8, 8, 9, 10, 10, 14, 14, 14, 15, 18, 18, 18, 19, 19, 19, 21, 22, 24, 24, 25, 25, 26, 26; 3:1, 5, 7, 7, 8, 8, 11, 14, 15, 17; 4:1, 1, 1, 2, 3, 4, 5, 6, 7, 8, 8, 11, 13, 13, 14, 14, 17, 17, 17, 17, 18, 19, 21, 22, 99, 99, 99, 99, 99

Tit 1:1, 1, 1, 2, 3, 4, 4, 5, 6, 7, 9, 9, 10, 12, 13, 14, 15; 2:1, 2, 3, 4, 5, 8, 10, 11, 13, 13; 3:4, 5, 5, 7, 9, 10, 13, 15, 99, 99

Phm 1:2, 3, 5, 6, 6, 7, 7, 9, 13, 13, 16, 16, 20, 20, 25

Heb 1:1, 1, 2, 3, 3, 3, 3, 4, 5, 6, 6, 6, 7, 8, 8, 9, 10, 10, 10, 10, 10, 12, 13; 2:1, 1, 2, 3, 3, 4, 5, 5, 6, 7, 7, 9, 9, 9, 10, 12, 12, 13, 14, 14, 14, 14, 16, 16, 17, 17; 3:1, 1, 1, 3, 3, 6, 6, 6, 6, 7, 8, 8, 12, 13, 14, 14, 15, 17; 4:2, 2, 3, 3, 3, 4, 4, 9, 11, 12, 12, 12, 12, 12, 14, 15, 16; 5:2, 2, 3, 6, 7, 8, 9, 9, 10, 12, 12, 12, 13; 6:1, 1, 1, 2, 2, 4, 4, 4, 5, 5, 6, 8, 9, 11, 14, 16, 18, 19, 19, 21; 6:1, 2, 2, 4, 4, 4, 5, 5, 6, 8, 8, 9, 11, 11, 11, 12, 12, 13, 15, 16, 16, 17, 18, 18, 19, 19, 19, 21, 25, 26, 27, 28, 28, 28, 28, 28; 8:1, 1, 1, 1, 1, 2, 2, 4, 5, 5, 5, 5, 8, 9, 10, 11, 13; 9:1, 2, 2, 2, 2, 3, 3, 4, 4, 4, 4, 5, 5, 6, 6, 7, 7, 8, 9, 10, 11, 11, 13; 9:1, 2, 2, 2, 2, 3, 3, 4, 4, 4, 4, 5, 5, 6, 6, 7, 7, 8, 9, 10, 11, 11, 13

Jas 1:1, 1, 3, 6, 6, 7, 9, 10, 10, 10, 11, 11, 11, 11, 11, 12, 12, 12, 17, 18, 20, 20, 21, 22, 23, 25, 25, 27, 27, 27; 2:1, 1, 3, 3, 5, 5, 6, 6, 7, 8, 8, 9, 10, 11, 12, 16, 19, 21, 23, 23, 25, 25, 26, 26; 3:1, 2, 2, 3, 4, 4, 5, 6, 6, 6, 6, 7, 8, 9, 9, 10, 11, 12, 14, 17, 18; 4:4, 4, 4, 4, 4, 5, 5, 6, 6, 10, 10, 11, 11, 11, 11, 14, 15; 5:3, 3, 4, 4, 4, 4, 4, 5, 6, 7, 7, 7, 7, 7, 7, 8, 9, 9, 10, 10,

11, 11, 11, 11, 12, 14, 14, 14, 14, 15, 15, 16, 17, 17, 18, 18, 19, 20, 20

1Pe 1:1, 2, 2, 2, 3, 3, 3, 5, 5, 7, 7, 9, 9, 10, 10, 11, 11, 11, 12, 12, 12, 12, 13, 13, 13, 14, 17, 19, 20, 20, 21, 22, 22, 22, 23, 24, 24, 24, 24, 25, 25, 25, 25; 2:2, 3, 6, 7, 7, 7, 7, 8, 9, 10, 11, 12, 13, 13, 14, 14, 15, 16, 17, 18, 18, 20, 20, 22, 24, 25; 3:1, 1, 1, 1, 3, 4, 4, 4, 4, 5, 5, 7, 7, 12, 12, 12, 15, 15, 16, 17, 17, 18, 18, 19, 21, 22; 4:1, 1, 1, 2, 2, 2, 2, 3, 3, 3, 4, 5, 5, 6, 6, 6, 7, 8, 10, 10, 11, 11, 11, 12, 13, 14, 14, 14, 15, 16, 17, 17, 18, 18, 19, 19; 5:1, 1, 1, 2, 2, 2, 3, 4, 4, 5, 5, 8, 9, 9, 9, 10, 12, 13

2Pe 1:1, 2, 3, 4, 4, 4, 8, 10, 11, 12, 16, 17, 18, 19, 19, 20, 20, 21, 21, 21; 2:1, 1, 2, 4, 5, 5, 5, 5, 5, 5, 6, 7, 7, 9, 9, 9, 9, 10, 10, 11, 12, 13, 13, 15, 15, 15, 16, 16, 16, 17, 18, 18, 19, 19, 20, 20, 20, 20, 20, 21, 21, 22, 22, 22, 22; 3:2, 2, 2, 2, 3, 4, 4, 4, 5, 5, 5, 6, 7, 7, 7, 7, 8, 9, 10, 10, 10, 10, 10, 10, 10, 10, 11, 12, 12, 12, 15, 15, 16, 16, 17, 18

1Jn 1:1, 1, 2, 3, 5, 6, 7, 7, 7, 8; 2:1, 1, 2, 2, 2, 4, 5, 7, 7, 7, 7, 8, 9, 10, 13, 13, 13, 14, 14, 14, 14, 15, 15, 15, 15, 15, 16, 16, 16, 16, 16, 16, 16, 17, 17, 17, 18, 18, 20, 21, 21, 22, 22, 22, 23, 23, 23, 23, 23, 24, 24, 24, 24, 25, 27, 27; 3:1, 1, 1, 2, 4, 4, 4, 8, 8, 8, 8, 8, 10, 10, 11, 11, 13, 14, 16, 16, 17, 19, 23; 4:1, 1, 2, 2, 3, 3, 4, 5, 5, 5, 6, 6, 9, 9, 10, 14, 14, 14, 14, 15, 16, 17; 5:1, 2, 3, 4, 4, 4, 5, 5, 6, 6, 7, 7, 7, 8, 8, 8, 8, 9, 9, 13, 14, 19, 20, 20

2Jn 1:1, 1, 1, 1, 2, 3, 3, 3, 4, 5, 6, 6, 7, 7, 9, 9, 9, 13

3Jn 1:1, 1, 1, 3, 3, 5, 6, 7, 8, 9, 9, 10, 10, 11, 11, 11, 12, 14

Jude 1:1, 1, 3, 3, 3, 4, 4, 5, 5, 5, 6, 6, 6, 7, 7, 8, 9, 9, 9, 11, 11, 11, 12, 13, 13, 14, 17, 17, 18, 19, 20, 21, 21, 23, 23, 23, 24, 25

Rev 1:1, 2, 2, 3, 3, 4, 4, 5, 5, 5, 5, 5, 7, 8, 8, 8, 8, 9, 9, 9, 9, 10, 10, 11, 11, 11, 12, 13, 13, 13, 15, 16, 16, 18, 18, 19, 19, 19, 20, 20, 20, 20, 20, 20, 20; 2:1, 1, 1, 1, 5, 6, 6, 7, 7, 7, 7, 8, 8, 8, 8, 9, 9, 10, 11, 11, 11, 11, 12, 12, 14, 14, 15, 15, 15, 16, 16, 16, 17, 17, 17, 17, 18, 18, 18, 19, 19, 23, 23, 24, 24, 26, 26, 26, 28, 29; 3:1, 1, 1, 2, 5, 5, 6, 6, 7, 7, 7, 9, 9, 10, 10, 10, 12, 12, 12, 12, 13, 14, 14, 14, 14; 6:1, 1, 1, 1, 1, 3, 3, 4, 5, 5, 6, 6, 6, 6, 7, 7, 8, 8, 8, 9, 10, 11, 11, 11, 11, 11, 11, 14, 15; 6:1, 1, 1, 1, 1, 3, 3, 4, 5, 5, 6, 6, 6, 6, 7, 7, 8, 8, 8, 9, 10, 11, 11, 11, 11, 11, 11, 14, 15; 7:1, 1, 1, 1, 1, 1, 2, 2, 2, 2, 3, 3, 3, 3, 4, 4, 4, 4, 5, 5, 6, 6, 6, 7, 7, 8, 9, 9, 9, 9, 9, 10; 8:1, 1, 1, 2, 3, 3, 3, 4, 4, 4, 5, 6, 7, 7, 7, 8, 8, 9, 9, 9, 9, 10, 10, 10, 11, 11, 11, 11, 11, 11, 11, 12, 12, 12, 12, 13, 13, 13, 13, 13; 9:1, 1, 1, 2, 2, 2, 2, 2, 2, 3, 3, 3, 3, 3, 4, 4, 4, 4, 4, 5, 5, 6, 6, 7, 7, 7, 7, 7, 8, 8, 8, 9, 9, 9, 10; 11:1, 1, 1, 2, 2, 2, 2, 4, 4, 4, 4, 6, 6, 7, 7, 8, 8, 8, 9, 9, 10, 10, 11, 13, 13, 13, 14, 15, 15, 15, 16, 18, 18; 18, 18, 18, 19, 19, 19; 12:1, 1, 4, 4, 4, 4, 6, 6, 7, 7, 9, 9, 9, 10, 10, 11, 11, 11, 12, 12, 12, 13, 13, 13, 14, 14, 14, 14, 15, 15, 15, 16, 16, 16, 16, 17, 17, 17, 17, 17; 13:1, 1, 1, 1, 2, 2, 2, 2, 3, 3, 3, 3, 4, 4, 4, 4, 5, 5, 6, 6, 7, 7, 7, 8, 8, 8, 8, 9, 9, 9, 10, 10, 10, 10, 10, 10, 10, 11, 11, 11, 12, 12, 12, 12, 13, 13, 13, 14, 14, 15, 15, 16, 16, 17, 17; 8:1, 3, 3, 3, 3, 4, 4, 4, 4, 5, 5, 5, 6, 7, 7, 7, 8, 9, 9, 9, 9, 9, 10, 11, 11, 12, 12, 13, 13, 14, 14, 15, 15, 15, 16, 16, 17, 18, 18; 14:1, 2, 2, 2, 3, 3, 3, 3, 3, 4, 4, 5, 5, 6, 6, 7, 7, 8, 8, 9, 9, 9, 9, 10, 10, 10, 10, 10, 10, 10, 11, 11, 12, 12, 12, 13, 13, 13, 14, 14, 14, 15, 15, 15, 15, 16, 16, 16, 17, 18, 18, 18, 18; 14:1, 2, 2, 2, 3, 3, 3, 3, 4, 4, 4, 5, 5, 6, 6, 6, 7, 7, 8, 8; 9, 9, 10, 10, 10, 10, 10, 10, 10, 10, 10, 11, 11, 12, 12, 13, 13, 13, 14, 14, 15, 15, 15, 15, 16, 16, 16, 17, 18; 18, 18, 18, 19, 19, 19, 19, 20, 20, 20, 20; 15:1, 1, 2, 2, 2, 2, 3, 3, 3, 3, 5, 5, 5, 6, 6, 6, 7, 7, 7, 8, 8, 8, 8, 8; 16:1, 1, 1, 1, 1, 2, 2, 2, 2, 2, 3, 3, 3, 3, 4, 4, 4, 5, 6, 7, 8, 9, 10, 10, 10, 11, 11, 12, 12, 13, 13, 14, 14, 14, 14, 14, 14, 16, 17, 17, 17, 18, 18, 18, 18, 19, 19, 19, 20; 17:1, 1, 1, 1, 1, 2, 2, 2, 2, 3, 3, 3, 3, 3, 4, 5, 5, 5, 5, 6, 6, 6, 6, 6, 6, 6, 9, 10, 11, 11, 11, 11, 12, 13, 14, 14, 14, 14, 16, 17, 17, 18, 18; 18:1, 2, 2, 3, 3, 3, 3, 3, 3, 4, 4, 4, 4, 5, 6, 7, 7, 8, 8, 9, 9, 9, 9, 10, 11, 11, 12, 12, 12, 13, 15, 15, 16, 16, 16, 17, 18, 18, 18, 19, 19, 20, 20, 20, 22, 22, 24, 99

THEIR (3931)

Ezr 1:6; 2:59, 59, 61, 62, 65, 65, 66, 66, 67, 67, 69, 70, 70; 3:8, 8, 9, 9, 10, 12; 4:5, 7, 9, 17, 23; 5:3, 5, 8, 10; 6:12, 13, 18, 18, 20, 22; 7:13, 16, 17, 17; 8:1, 19, 24, 26; 9:1, 2, 2, 11, 11, 12, 12, 12, 12; 10:16, 16, 19, 19, 19

Ne 2:18; 3:5, 5, 5, 18, 23; 4:3, 4, 4, 5, 5, 13, 13, 13, 15; 5:1, 1, 5, 6, 8, 11, 11, 11, 11, 14, 15; 6:6, 9, 14, 16; 7:61, 61, 63, 64, 67, 67, 68, 68, 69, 73, 73; 8:6, 6, 6, 7, 12, 15, 16; 9:2, 2, 3, 3, 4, 6, 9, 11, 15, 15, 16, 17, 17, 17, 20, 20, 21, 23, 23, 24, 24, 26, 27, 27, 27, 28, 29, 35, 35, 37; 10:10, 28, 28, 28, 29, 29, 30; 11:3, 9, 12, 14, 14, 19, 25, 30, 31; 12:7, 9, 24, 27, 42, 45; 13:11, 13, 13, 24, 25, 25, 25

Est 1:17, 17, 20, 22; 2:3, 12; 3:8, 12; 8:9, 9, 9, 11, 13; 9:2, 2, 5, 10, 15, 16, 16, 16, 16, 22, 27, 27, 27, 28, 31, 31, 31

Job 1:4, 4, 5, 5, 13, 18; 2:12, 12, 12; 3:8, 15; 4:21; 5:5, 12, 12, 13, 15; 6:17, 18; 8:4, 8, 10; 11:3, 20; 12:18; 14:12; 15:18, 35; 16:10; 17:2, 4; 19:12, 15; 20:10; 21:8, 8, 8, 8, 9, 10, 10, 11, 11, 13, 16, 16, 17, 29; 22:6, 18; 24:5, 5, 11, 11, 18, 23; 27:23; 29:9, 9, 10, 10, 10, 23, 25; 30:2, 4, 9, 9, 12; 31:16, 39; 33:16; 34:24, 25; 36:9, 9, 10, 11, 11, 14, 16; 36:3, 3, 4; 40:12, 13, 22; 42:15, 15

Ps 2:3, 3, 12; 4:7, 7; 5:9, 9, 9, 9, 10, 10, 11; 7:7; 9:5, 6, 10, 15; 10:17; 11:2, 2, 6; 16:4, 4, 4; 17:7, 10, 10, 11, 14, 14, 14; 18:45; 19:3, 4, 4; 21:10, 10, 12; 22:13; 26:10; 28:3, 3, 4, 4, 4, 4, 8; 33:15, 15, 19; 34:5, 15, 17; 35:6, 7, 16, 17, 21, 25; 36:7; 37:14, 15, 15, 15, 18, 39; 40:15; 44:1, 3, 3, 12; 49:6, 6, 8, 10, 11, 11, 11, 11, 11, 13, 13, 13, 13, 14, 14; 55:9, 15, 23; 56:5; 57:4; 58:4, 6, 6; 59:7, 7, 12, 12, 12; 62:4; 64:3, 3, 3, 8; 65:7; 68:27, 27; 69:22, 22, 23, 23, 25, 25, 27; 70:3; 72:14, 14; 73:4, 4, 7, 9, 9, 17, 20; 74:4, 8; 76:5, 5; 78:4, 5, 6, 7, 8, 8, 12, 18, 18, 28, 28, 29, 30, 30, 30, 33, 33, 33, 35, 35, 36, 36, 37, 38, 44, 44, 44, 46, 46, 47, 47, 48, 48, 50, 50, 51, 53, 55, 57, 58, 58, 63, 63, 64, 64; 79:3, 10, 12, 12; 81:12, 12, 14, 14, 15; 83:11, 11, 16; 85:2; 89:17, 32, 32; 90:10, 10; 91:12; 93:3, 3; 94:23, 23; 95:10; 98:8; 99:8; 102:17, 28; 104:11, 12, 17, 21, 21, 22, 27, 29, 29; 105:14, 24, 25, 29, 29, 30, 30, 31, 32, 33, 33, 33, 35, 35, 36, 36, 37; 106:11, 15, 15, 18, 20, 21, 25, 27, 29, 32, 35, 36, 37, 37, 38, 38, 39, 39, 42, 42, 43, 43, 44, 44; 107:5, 6, 6, 12, 13, 14, 17, 17, 18, 19, 19, 20, 26, 27, 28, 28, 30, 38; 109:10, 10, 11, 11; 119:70, 118; 123:2; 124:3, 6; 125:3, 4, 5; 129:3; 132:12; 135:12, 17; 136:10, 21; 140:2, 3, 3, 9; 141:4, 5, 6, 10; 144:8, 11, 12; 145:15, 19; 147:3, 4; 149:2, 5, 6, 6, 8, 8

Pr 1:6, 15, 16, 18, 18, 22, 31; 2:15; 4:16, 22; 8:21; 9:15; 10:15; 11:6, 20; 14:24; 17:6; 18:19; 20:29; 21:12; 22:23; 23:11, 11; 24:2, 2, 22; 25:27; 29:13, 16; 30:5, 11, 11, 12, 12, 13, 13, 14, 25, 26

Ecc 2:3; 3:11; 4:1, 9; 5:11, 13; 9:1, 3, 6, 6, 6; 10:8, 8; 12:1, 11, 12; 13:1, 14, 25, 26

Isa 2:4, 4, 7, 7, 7, 8, 8, 8; 3:4, 8, 8, 9, 9, 9, 12, 16, 17, 18, 18, 18, 18; 5:12, 13, 13, 14, 14, 14, 17, 21, 24, 24, 25, 27, 27, 28, 28, 28, 29; 6:10, 10, 10, 10, 10, 13; 8:12, 19, 21, 21; 9:17, 17; 10:2, 5, 13, 25, 29; 11:7, 14; 13:8, 10, 11, 11, 14, 16, 16, 16, 16, 16, 18, 20, 21, 22, 22; 14:1, 2, 2, 9, 21, 25; 15:2, 3, 3, 3, 4; 16:10, 10; 18:2, 7; 20:4, 5, 5; 21:14; 24:14; 25:11, 11; 26:11, 14, 21; 28:25; 29:13, 13, 13, 14, 14, 15, 15, 19; 30:6, 6, 6, 7, 26; 31:3, 4; 33:2, 7, 9, 23, 24; 34:2, 3, 3, 3, 4, 7, 7; 35:10; 36:12, 12, 20, 20; 37:18, 19, 27; 40:24, 26, 31; 41:1, 17, 29, 29; 42:11, 15; 43:9; 44:9, 9, 18, 18, 25; 45:12, 20; 46:1; 47:9; 49:9, 22, 22, 23, 23, 26, 26; 50:2, 3; 51:7, 11; 52:15; 53:11; 54:17; 55:12; 56:7, 7, 11; 57:2, 8; 58:1, 1, 2; 59:5, 6, 6, 6, 6, 7; 60:8, 8, 9, 9, 10, 11; 61:6, 7, 7, 8, 9, 9, 9, 9; 62:6; 63:3, 6, 8, 9, 10; 65:2, 4, 6, 7, 7, 22, 23; 66:3, 3, 3, 4, 4, 18, 18, 24, 24

Jer 1:8, 16, 16, 17; 2:11, 11, 26, 26, 26, 26, 27, 27, 27, 27; 3:17, 21, 21, 24, 24, 24, 24; 4:16; 5:3, 4, 5, 6, 6, 6, 16, 24, 27; 6:3, 10, 12, 12, 19, 23, 27; 7:18, 19, 24, 24, 26, 26, 26, 28, 28, 30, 31, 31; 8:1, 7, 10, 10, 12, 19; 9:3, 3, 5, 8, 14, 14, 16; 10:7, 9, 15, 21; 11:8, 8, 10, 10, 12, 14, 18, 22, 22, 23; 12:2, 2, 14; 13:10; 14:3, 3, 3, 3, 4; 16:10, 10, 10; 17:2, 7, 20:4, 5, 21:7, 7; 22:9; 23:3, 8, 10, 10, 11, 12, 12, 12, 22, 26, 27, 27, 31, 32; 24:5, 7, 7, 9, 10; 25:12, 14, 14, 36, 38; 26:3; 27:4, 8, 11, 11; 29:23; 30:3, 9, 9, 10, 20, 20, 21, 21; 31:12, 13, 13, 17, 23, 32, 33, 33, 34, 34; 32:18, 22, 30, 30, 32, 32, 32, 33, 34, 34, 35, 35, 38, 39, 40, 44; 33:8, 8, 12, 20, 26; 34:14, 16, 20, 20, 20, 21, 21, 21; 35:14; 36:3, 6, 3, 7; 37:7; 38:18, 19, 23; 40:7, 8, 9; 41:5, 5, 5, 8; 42:17; 43:1, 1; 44:3, 5, 5, 9, 10, 11, 15; 46:5, 10, 21, 21, 25, 25, 26, 27;

La 1:11, 14, 19, 19, 22; 2:10, 10, 12, 12, 12, 15, 15, 16, 18, 20; 3:14, 46, 60, 60, 61, 61, 62, 63, 63, 63, 64; 4:3, 7, 8, 8, 10, 10, 14, 20; 5:7, 8, 12, 14

Eze 1:5, 7, 7, 8, 8, 8, 8, 9, 10, 11, 11, 13, 16, 16, 16, 17, 18, 18, 20, 22, 23, 23, 24, 24, 25, 25, 26; 2:3, 6, 6, 6; 3:8, 8, 9; 4:4, 5, 12, 13, 17; 5:10, 16; 6:5, 9, 9, 9, 9, 13, 13, 13, 14; 7:11, 18, 19, 19, 19, 19, 19, 19, 20, 20, 24, 24, 27, 27; 8:16, 16, 17; 9:10; 10:10; 10:8, 10, 11, 12, 12, 12, 16, 16, 19, 21, 22; 11:19, 20, 21, 21, 21, 21, 21, 22; 12:3, 3, 4, 4, 5, 6, 7, 16, 19, 19; 13:2, 3, 17; 14:3, 3, 3, 5, 5, 10, 11, 11, 14, 14, 20, 20, 22, 22, 23, 23; 16:39, 40, 45, 45, 47, 47, 53, 55, 55; 19:4, 7, 7, 8, 8; 20:4, 8, 8, 8, 8, 8, 11, 11, 11, 13, 16, 16, 18, 18, 24, 24, 26, 28, 28, 28, 28, 30; 21:6, 14, 15, 15, 15, 23, 28, 29; 22:6, 10, 26, 31, 31; 23:3, 3, 3, 4, 7, 8, 15, 15, 15, 17, 20, 24, 30, 36, 37, 37, 37, 39, 39, 42, 42, 45, 47, 47; 24:25, 25, 25, 25, 25:4, 4; 26:10, 10, 16, 16, 16, 17; 27:9, 11, 29, 30, 30, 32, 32, 35; 28:7, 16, 16, 17, 17, 18, 19, 19, 23, 23, 25, 27; 30:4, 11, 23, 23, 23, 25, 25, 27; 38:16; 39:22, 23, 23, 24, 24, 26, 26, 26, 27, 28; 40:16, 22, 22, 22, 41, 44; 41:16; 42:4, 11, 11, 14; 43:7, 7, 7, 7, 8, 8, 8, 9, 10, 11; 44:10, 10, 12, 12, 13, 13, 18, 19, 19, 20, 20, 20, 22, 28, 28; 45:4, 8; 46:16, 18; 47:10, 10, 12; 48:29, 34

Da 1:15, 16; 2:30; 3:21, 21, 21, 21, 27, 28, 28, 29; 4:21; 6:24, 24, 24; 7:12, 12; 8:23; 9:7; 11:8, 8, 8, 32

Hos 1:7; 2:5, 17; 3:5, 5; 4:7, 8, 8, 9, 9, 12, 12, 12, 18, 19; 5:4, 4, 5, 6, 6, 7, 15, 15; 7:2, 2, 2, 3, 3, 6, 6, 6, 7, 10, 12, 14, 14, 15, 16, 16, 16; 8:4, 4, 13, 13; 9:4, 4, 4, 6, 6, 9, 9, 10, 11, 12, 15, 15, 16, 16; 10:2, 2, 2, 8, 10; 11:3, 4, 6, 6, 11; 12:11; 13:2, 2, 6, 8, 10, 16; 14:4;

Joel 1:3, 3, 17; 2:6, 7, 10, 17, 22; 3:6, 13, 15, 19, 21

Am 1:13, 15; 2:4, 4, 8; 3:10; 4:1; 5:12; 6:2, 4; 7:11; 8:7; 9:4, 15, 15

Ob 1:12, 13, 13, 13, 13, 13, 17

Jnh 1:2; 2:8; 3:8, 10, 10; 4:11, 11

Mic 2:1, 1, 9, 9, 12, 13; 3:2, 2, 2, 3, 4, 5, 5, 7; 4:3, 3, 13, 13; 6:12, 12, 16; 7:4, 13, 16, 16, 16, 16, 17, 19

Na 2:2, 5, 7; 3:3, 3, 17

Hab 1:7, 7, 8, 8, 8, 9, 15, 15, 16, 16, 16, 16, 17; 2:15; 3:11, 14

Zep 1:9, 12, 12, 13, 13, 17, 17, 18, 18; 2:7, 7, 8, 10, 14; 3:6, 6, 6, 7, 7, 13

Hag 1:12, 12, 14; 2:14, 22

Zec 1:21; 2:9; 5:6, 9; 7:2, 11, 12; 8:8, 12; 9:16; 10:2, 5, 6, 7, 7, 9; 11:3, 5, 6, 8, 16; 12:5, 5, 12, 12, 13, 13, 14; 14:12, 12, 12, 12, 12

Mal 4:6;

Mt 1:21; 2:11, 12; 3:6; 4:6, 20, 21, 21, 22, 23; 6:2, 5, 7, 14, 15, 16, 16; 7:6, 16, 20; 8:22, 33, 34; 9:2, 4, 29, 30, 35; 10:17, 21; 11:1, 5, 16; 12:9, 25; 13:15, 15, 15, 15, 15, 43, 54, 58; 14:14; 15:2, 8, 8, 8, 27; 17:6, 8, 25; 18:10, 31, 35; 19:12; 20:4, 8, 31, 34, 34; 21:7, 8, 41; 22:5, 7, 16, 18, 22; 23:3, 4, 4, 5, 5; 25:1, 3, 4, 4, 7; 26:43, 67; 27:39

Mk 1:5, 18, 19, 20, 23, 39; 2:5, 6; 3:4, 5; 4:12, 15; 5:17; 6:6, 8, 8, 26, 52; 7:3, 6, 6; 8:3; 9:34, 44, 46, 48; 10:42; 11:4, 7, 8; 12:12, 15, 44; 13:12; 14:40, 46, 56, 59, 65; 15:19, 29; 16:14

Lk 1:16, 20, 51, 52, 66, 77; 2:8, 39, 44; 3:15; 4:11, 15, 29; 5:2, 6, 7, 11, 15, 20, 30; 6:1, 8, 17, 22, 23, 26; 7:21; 8:3, 12; 9:47, 60; 11:17, 48; 12:36, 42; 13:1; 14:4; 16:4, 8; 17:13; 19:32, 35, 36, 40; 20:23, 26; 21:1, 4, 22; 22:66; 23:25, 48; 24:5, 11, 16, 31, 31, 44

Jn 3:19; 4:38; 8:9; 10:39; 11:19, 46; 12:40, 40, 40, 40; 13:12; 15:22, 25; 17:19, 20; 18:8; 19:3, 31; 20:10

Ac 1:9, 19, 26; 2:37, 45, 46; 4:5, 23, 24, 29; 5:18; 6:1, 6; 7:19, 34, 39, 41, 54, 57, 58, 60; 8:17, 36; 9:24; 10:9; 11:18; 12:17, 20, 20, 25; 13:3, 5, 18, 19, 22, 27, 33, 50, 51; 14:2, 3, 5, 11, 13, 14, 16; 15:3, 9, 13, 22; 26; 16:19, 22, 24, 33; 17:21, 26; 18:3; 19:18, 19; 21:21, 24; 22:22, 23, 30; 23:16, 28, 29; 25:19; 26:18; 27:13, 43; 28:6, 27, 27, 27, 27, 27, 27

Ro 1:21, 21, 24, 24, 26, 27, 28; 2:15, 15, 15; 3:3, 13, 13, 13, 15, 16, 16, 18; 8:10:3, 18; 11:9, 10, 10, 11, 12, 24, 27, 30; 13:7; 15:27, 27, 27; 16:4, 5, 18

1Co 3:19; 8:7, 12; 14:35; 16:19

2Co 3:14, 15; 5:19; 6:16; 8:2, 2, 3, 3, 5, 14, 14; 9:14; 11:15

Gal 2:13;

Eph 4:17, 18; 5:24, 28, 28

Php 2:21; 3:19, 19

Col 2:2;
1Th 2:15, 16; 5:13
2Th 3:12;
1Ti 3:11, 12, 12; 4:2; 5:4, 12; 6:1
2Ti 2:17; 3:2, 9; 4:3, 4, 16
Tit 1:12, 15; 2:4, 4, 5, 9; 3:13
Heb 2:10, 15; 3:10; 5:14; 7:5; 8:9, 10, 10, 12, 12, 12; 10:16, 16, 17; 11:16, 35; 12:10; 13:7
Jas 1:27; 3:3
1Pe 3:5, 12, 14; 4:14, 19
2Pe 2:2, 3, 8, 12, 13; 3:3, 16
3Jn 1:6;
Jude 1:6, 6, 13, 15, 15, 16, 16, 18
Rev 2:22; 3:4; 4:4, 10; 6:11, 11, 14; 7:3, 9, 11, 14, 17; 9:4, 5, 7, 7, 8, 9, 10, 10, 17, 18, 19, 19, 19, 19, 20, 21, 21, 21, 21; 10:3, 4; 11:5, 5, 6, 7, 8, 9, 9, 11, 12, 16, 16; 12:8, 11, 11; 13:16, 16; 14:1, 2, 5, 11, 13, 13; 15:6; 16:10, 11, 11, 11; 17:13, 17, 17; 18:11, 19; 19:19, 21; 20:4, 4, 12, 13; 21:3, 4, 8, 24; 22:4

THEM (6429)

Ge 1:14, 15, 17, 22, 26, 27, 28, 28; 2:1, 19, 19; 3:7, 21; 5:2, 2; 6:1, 2, 4, 7, 13, 13, 19, 20, 21; 7:13; 9:1, 19; 10:1; 11:3, 6, 8, 9, 29, 31; 12:3; 13:6; 14:8, 14, 15, 15, 24; 15:5, 10, 11, 13, 13; 18:2, 2, 8, 16, 16; 19:1, 1, 3, 3, 5, 5, 6, 8, 8, 9, 10, 12, 13, 17, 18; 20:14; 21:27, 27, 31; 22:6, 8; 23:8; 24:28, 53, 56, 60; 25:6, 26; 26:15, 15, 18, 18, 27, 30, 31; 27:9, 13, 14, 15; 28:11; 29:4, 5, 6, 7, 9, 9; 30:14, 35, 37, 40, 42; 31:5, 9, 32, 33, 34, 34, 34, 55; 32:2, 4, 16, 23, 23; 33:3, 13; 34:8, 14, 21, 21, 21, 23; 35:4, 5; 36:7; 37:6, 13, 17, 17, 18, 22; 38:26; 39:14; 40:3, 4, 4, 5, 9, 12, 14, 17, 18, 22, 22, 23, 24, 24, 24, 24, 25, 27, 28, 29, 36; 43:2, 11, 16, 23, 24, 27, 32, 34; 44:4, 4, 6, 6, 15; 45:1, 15, 21, 22, 24, 24, 26, 27, 47; 47:2, 6, 6, 6, 11, 17, 17, 20, 21, 22, 22, 24; 48:6, 9, 9, 10, 10, 10, 10, 12, 13, 16, 16, 20; 49:7, 28, 28, 28; 50:12, 14, 15;

Ex 1:7, 10, 10, 11, 11, 12, 14, 16, 17, 18, 19, 21; 2:17, 17, 25; 3:8, 8, 9, 13, 13, 16, 22; 4:20; 5:4, 5, 7, 8, 9, 13, 14, 21; 6:1, 1, 3, 4, 4, 13; 7:5, 6, 13, 22; 8:2, 14, 15, 19; 9:2, 2, 12, 17, 19; 10:2, 8, 10, 14, 14, 19, 27; 12:3, 16, 21, 33, 36, 38, 42; 13:17, 21, 21, 21; 14:3, 4, 7, 9, 9, 10, 13, 17, 19, 19, 20, 22, 23, 25, 28, 28, 29; 15:5, 7, 7, 9, 9, 10, 12, 13, 15, 16, 17; 16:4, 7, 7, 9, 10, 13, 15, 16, 17, 19, 20, 23; 17:2; 18:8, 8, 11, 16, 20, 20, 21, 22, 25; 19:10, 10, 21, 22, 24, 25; 20:5, 5, 5, 7; 21:1, 21:34; 22:11, 23, 23:23, 24, 24, 29, 30, 31, 32; 24:12, 14; 25:3, 8, 9, 11, 21, 22, 23, 23, 28; 26:1, 24, 37; 27:6; 28:9, 11, 14, 14, 25, 26, 27, 33, 40, 40, 41, 41, 41, 42; 29:1, 1, 2, 3, 4, 8, 9, 9, 13, 13, 17, 22, 24, 25, 25, 29, 30, 33, 35, 36; 30:18, 19, 19, 23, 30; 31:5; 32:2, 2, 3, 4, 8, 10, 12, 12, 13, 18, 18, 19, 20, 24, 24, 25, 33; 34:31, 31, 32, 33; 35:1, 1, 23, 26, 29; 33, 35, 36:8, 8, 14, 29, 36, 36; 37:4, 7, 15, 28; 38:6, 25; 39:7, 18, 19, 20, 43; 40:12, 14, 15

Lev 1:2, 12; 2:12; 3:4, 10, 15, 16; 4:2, 9, 10, 20, 20, 35; 5:8; 6:10, 17, 18; 7:4, 5, 7, 34, 35, 36, 36; 8:6, 10, 11, 13, 13, 13, 26, 27, 28, 28; 9:2, 7, 13, 14, 22; 10:1, 1, 2, 3, 4, 5, 11, 17; 11:1, 4, 4, 9, 22, 24, 25, 26, 28, 31, 32, 33, 42, 43, 45, 51; 15:2, 14, 15, 29, 31; 16:4, 7, 16, 21, 23, 28; 17:2, 5, 5, 7, 8, 16; 18:2, 5, 29; 19:2, 10, 31, 31, 37; 20:6, 8, 11, 11, 12, 12, 13, 13, 16, 22, 27, 27; 21:1, 23; 22:3, 9, 16, 16, 18, 22, 25, 25, 31; 23:2, 10, 20, 42; 24:6, 12; 25:2, 18, 31, 44, 45, 46, 46, 51; 26:3, 36, 39, 41, 41, 43, 43, 44, 44, 44; 27:2

Nu 1:3, 19, 21, 22, 23, 25, 27, 29, 31, 33, 35, 37, 39, 41, 43, 47, 49; 2:4, 13, 15, 19, 21, 23, 26, 28, 30; 3:6, 15, 16, 22, 22, 32, 34, 43, 47, 48, 49, 49, 51; 4:8, 12, 12, 12, 19, 19, 23, 26, 27, 29, 30, 36, 40, 44, 48; 5:3, 4, 12, 23; 6:2, 16, 19, 20, 23, 27; 7:1, 2, 3, 3, 5, 5, 6, 9, 13, 19, 25, 31, 37, 43, 49, 55, 61, 67, 73, 79; 8:6, 7, 7, 7, 7, 8, 9, 11, 13, 14, 15, 16; 9:8; 10:2, 2, 3, 3, 33, 34, 35; 11:1, 1, 3, 4, 12, 16, 16, 17, 24, 22, 22, 24, 24, 26, 26, 28, 29, 31, 32; 12:9; 13:2, 3, 17, 17, 26, 26; 14:2, 9, 9, 10, 11, 12, 12, 13, 14, 16, 16, 23, 28, 31, 40, 45, 45; 15:2, 18, 25, 26, 29, 38, 38, 39; 16:3, 3, 3, 3, 3, 19, 22, 24, 26, 26, 30, 31, 32, 33, 34, 38, 38, 45, 46, 49; 17:2, 4; 18:8, 11, 12, 12, 18, 20, 24, 26, 26, 30; 19:9, 10, 21; 20:6, 8, 10, 12, 13, 25, 26, 26, 28; 21:1, 3, 16, 30, 30, 33; 22:6, 6, 8, 11, 11, 12, 20; 23:11, 13, 13, 13, 13, 21, 22, 25, 25, 26, 27, 24:8, 10; 25:4, 8, 11, 17; 26:3, 7, 10, 25, 27, 34, 37, 43, 47, 50, 62, 62, 64, 65, 65; 27:3, 7, 7, 17, 17, 17; 28:2, 3, 31; 30:12, 12, 12, 14, 14, 15, 15; 31:3, 6, 6, 8, 13, 15, 27, 30, 30, 36, 47, 51; 32:7, 8,

Col 2:2 *(continued below right)*

Dt 1:3, 8, 8, 13, 15, 29, 39, 42; 2:5, 6, 6, 9, 11, 12, 12, 12, 12, 14, 15, 15, 19, 19, 20, 21, 21, 21, 22, 22, 23; 3:4, 6, 14, 20, 22; 28; 4:1, 3, 6, 7, 9, 10, 13, 14, 19, 19, 31; 37; 5:1, 1, 1, 9, 9, 9, 9, 22, 29, 29, 30, 31, 31, 31; 6:1, 7, 7, 8, 9; 7:2, 2, 2, 2, 2, 3, 5, 9, 10, 10, 11, 12, 15, 16, 17, 18, 20, 21, 22, 23, 23, 24, 25; 8:19; 9:3, 3, 3, 3, 4, 4, 5, 10, 12, 12, 14, 21, 24; 10:2, 4, 11, 15, 15; 11:4, 4, 6, 9, 16, 18, 19, 20, 21; 12:3, 18, 22, 22, 29, 30, 30; 13:2; 14:7, 7; 17:3, 5, 19; 18:2, 3, 12, 18, 18; 19:1, 9; 20:1, 3, 3, 17, 19, 19, 19, 19, 20; 21:5, 8, 10, 10, 18; 22:1, 1, 4, 4, 19, 22, 24, 24; 23:8; 24:8; 25:1, 5; 26:13, 13, 16; 27:2, 3, 4, 5, 26; 28:13, 14, 25, 25, 36, 31, 32, 39, 39, 41, 51, 57, 61; 29:1, 2, 7, 9, 17, 25, 25, 26, 26, 28; 30:1, 7, 17, 20; 31:2, 3, 4, 4, 5, 6, 7, 10, 16, 16, 17, 17, 17, 19, 20, 20, 21, 21, 23, 23, 24, 26, 28; 32:11, 11, 19, 20, 21, 21, 23, 23, 24, 26, 26, 28, 30, 30, 35, 38, 41, 46; 33:2, 2, 11, 11, 17, 27

Jos 1:2, 6, 14, 15; 2:4, 5, 5, 6, 6, 7, 7, 8, 15, 12; 5:1, 5, 6, 7, 7; 6:6, 8, 13, 23, 26; 7:2, 5, 5, 5, 11, 21, 21, 23, 23, 23, 24, 25, 25; 8:3, 4, 5, 6, 6, 9, 11, 12, 15, 16, 16, 22, 22, 24, 33, 33, 33, 35; 9:5, 8, 11, 11, 15, 15, 15, 16, 18, 18, 19, 19, 20, 20, 21, 21, 21, 21, 22, 22, 26, 26, 26, 26, 27; 10:1, 8, 8, 9, 10, 10, 10, 10, 11, 18, 19, 19, 19, 20, 20, 24, 25, 26, 26, 27, 27, 28, 39, 41; 11:4, 6, 6, 6, 7, 7, 8, 9, 11, 12, 12, 13, 13, 14, 17, 17, 20, 20, 21; 12:6; 13:6, 8, 8, 12, 14, 22, 22, 33; 14:1, 3, 12; 15:63; 17:4, 13, 15; 18:1, 4, 4, 7, 8, 10; 19:9, 9, 47, 49; 20:4, 4, 9; 21:2, 11, 21, 42, 44, 44; 22:2, 4, 6, 6, 7, 7, 8, 12, 16; 24:5, 7, 7, 8, 8, 11, 12, 13, 13, 25

Jdg 1:1, 4, 22, 25, 28, 29, 30, 32, 33, 34; 2:3, 3; 3:1, 2, 4, 8, 9, 13, 23, 25, 27, 28; 4:2; 5:14, 21, 30, 31; 6:1, 2, 3, 4, 9, 20, 35; 7:1, 4, 4, 6, 17, 24; 8:2, 4, 8, 10, 11, 12, 16, 19, 20, 23, 24, 33, 38, 43, 43, 43, 44, 49, 49, 51, 51, 57; 10:7, 14, 16; 11:9, 11, 21, 24, 25, 26, 32, 33, 35; 12:2, 3; 13:1; 14:9, 9, 12, 14, 18, 19, 19; 15:3, 3, 5, 7, 8, 11, 12; 16:3, 3, 9, 8, 12, 23, 25, 26; 17:4; 18:1, 1, 2, 4, 6, 7, 8, 9, 18, 21, 27, 31; 19:6, 8, 14, 15, 23, 23, 24, 24, 24, 25; 20:13, 20, 25, 28, 32, 34, 40, 41, 42, 42, 42, 43, 43, 45, 45, 45, 48; 21:6, 7, 7, 10, 12, 13, 14, 14, 15, 16, 17, 18, 22, 22, 22, 23, 23, 23

Ru 1:4, 5, 6, 9, 13, 13, 19, 20; 2:9, 16, 16

1Sa 2:8, 8, 8, 10, 16, 23, 25, 30, 34; 3:13; 5:6, 6, 6, 8; 6:6, 7, 10, 12, 15; 7:10, 11; 8:7, 8, 9, 9, 9, 11, 12, 14, 14, 16, 21, 22; 9:4, 4, 11, 11, 12, 14, 22, 24, 26; 10:5, 6, 10, 18; 11:2, 7, 7, 8, 11, 12; 12:5, 8, 9, 9; 13:16, 19; 14:8, 9, 9, 10, 11, 12; 15:3, 4, 6, 9, 15, 18; 16:5, 20; 17:3, 8, 23, 23, 31, 36, 39, 39, 40; 18:16, 27; 19:8, 20; 20:11, 21, 40; 21:13; 22:2, 4, 11; 23:5, 26; 24:7, 22; 25:7, 7, 14, 15, 16, 18, 20, 29, 43; 26:12, 12, 13; 27:5; 30:2, 8, 8, 17, 17, 19, 19, 21, 22, 27, 27, 28, 28, 29, 29, 29, 30, 30, 30, 31; 31:7, 12, 13

2Sa 1:10, 11, 18; 2:5, 7, 14; 3:22, 36; 4:7, 9, 12, 12; 5:3, 19, 20, 21, 23, 23; 6:22; 7:10, 10, 21; 8:1, 2, 2, 4, 7; 10:4, 5, 9, 10, 16, 19; 11:23; 12:11, 17, 31, 31; 13:9, 10, 11, 30; 14:6; 15:36, 36; 16:1; 17:9, 17, 18, 18, 20, 20, 22; 18:1, 4, 14, 31; 19:3, 28; 20:3, 3, 3, 8, 19; 21:2, 2, 2, 6, 6, 7, 9, 9, 10, 10, 12, 12, 13; 22:15, 15, 18, 23, 28, 31, 38, 38, 39, 39, 40, 41, 42, 43, 43, 43, 49; 23:6, 7, 18; 24:1, 12

1Ki 1:20, 33, 40; 2:5, 32; 5:3, 9, 9, 9, 9, 14, 18; 6:12, 15, 16, 32, 32, 35; 7:6, 6, 15, 25, 37, 46; 8:21, 34, 35, 36, 37, 44, 46, 46, 46, 47, 47, 48, 50, 50, 50, 50, 52, 53; 9:6, 7, 9, 9, 9, 13, 21; 10:17, 29; 11:2, 18, 24; 12:5, 7, 7, 7, 9, 10, 14, 16, 17, 28; 13:11, 12; 14:15, 23, 27, 28, 28; 15:18, 22; 18:4, 4, 6, 13, 23, 23, 26, 27, 28, 40, 40, 40, 40, 40; 19:2, 2, 21; 20:15, 18, 18, 19, 20, 20, 23, 25, 27, 27; 21:8, 8, 11, 11; 22:6, 10, 11, 13, 17

2Ki 1:2, 3, 5, 7, 12; 2:11, 12, 16, 18, 24, 24; 3:9, 10, 13, 21, 24; 4:3, 31, 33, 39, 39, 44; 5:12, 22, 23, 23, 24, 24; 6:4, 11, 16, 18, 19, 19, 19, 19, 21, 22, 22, 23, 23, 33; 7:10, 12, 15; 9:11, 17, 18, 19, 20; 10:1, 6, 6, 7, 7, 8, 14, 14, 14, 18, 22, 25, 25, 25, 26, 26, 26, 27, 28, 29, 32, 32, 33, 35, 35, 35; 18:11, 12, 12, 13, 18, 18, 22, 28, 29; 19:6, 11, 12, 18; 20:13, 13, 15; 21:3, 8, 8, 9, 14, 21, 24; 22:5, 5, 7, 9, 15; 23:4, 4, 5, 12,

12, 16, 19, 20; 24:2, 3, 16, 20; 25:13, 19, 20, 21, 21, 22, 24, 24
1Ch 2:6, 23, 53; 4:21, 41, 42; 5:11, 20, 20, 20, 25, 26, 26; 6:55, 67, 78; 7:3, 4, 9, 40; 8:6, 7, 8, 32; 9:20, 25, 27, 27, 28, 28, 29; 10:7, 12; 11:3, 14, 20; 12:15, 17, 17, 18, 18, 19, 29, 32, 34, 39, 40; 13:2; 14:8, 10, 10, 11, 14, 14, 14; 15:2, 12, 18; 16:10, 21, 41, 42; 17:9, 9; 18:1, 4, 7, 11; 19:4, 4, 5, 6, 10, 16, 17, 17; 20:3; 21:2, 6, 10; 23:6, 22, 31; 24:3, 6, 19; 25:7; 26:30, 31; 27:23, 26; 29:8
2Ch 2:2, 11, 17, 18; 3:10, 15, 16, 16; 4:4, 6, 6, 7, 8, 9, 17; 5:12, 12; 6:25, 25, 26, 27, 28, 34, 36, 36, 36, 38; 7:6, 19, 20, 20, 22, 22, 22, 22; 8:2, 8, 8, 18; 9:8, 8, 16; 10:5, 7, 7, 9, 10, 13, 14, 16, 17; 11:11, 12, 14, 16, 23; 12:5, 7, 7, 10, 11; 13:7, 9, 13, 13, 16, 17; 14:7, 9, 11, 13, 14, 14; 15:4, 6, 9, 15, 15; 16:8, 9; 17:8, 8, 9, 14; 18:5, 9, 9, 16, 31; 19:2, 4, 9, 10; 20:1, 10, 10, 12, 16, 16, 17, 23, 25, 25, 27, 27; 21:3; 22:8, 12; 23:3, 8, 14; 24:5, 13, 17, 19, 19, 20, 23; 25:5, 5, 5, 10, 12, 13, 14, 14, 14, 20; 26:9, 14; 27:5; 28:5, 5, 8, 9, 9, 12, 13, 15, 15, 15, 15, 23, 23; 29:3, 4, 5, 8, 21, 23, 24, 34; 30:7, 9, 9, 10, 10, 12, 14, 17, 18; 31:1, 6, 7, 11; 32:1, 6, 6, 18, 18, 22, 26; 33:3, 8, 11, 15, 22, 25; 34:4, 4, 4, 4, 12, 21, 23; 35:2, 11, 13, 15, 25; 36:7, 15, 17, 17, 20
Ezr 1:5, 6, 7, 8, 9, 11; 2:63, 65; 3:3, 7, 7; 4:2, 3, 4, 5, 20, 23; 5:1, 2, 2, 3, 4, 5, 9, 10, 12, 14, 15; 6:5, 9, 20, 21, 22, 22; 7:17, 24, 25, 25; 8:1, 13, 14, 15, 17, 17, 20, 22, 24, 25, 28, 29, 30, 33; 10:3, 6, 10, 14, 14, 15, 16, 44
Ne 1:2, 5, 9, 9, 9; 2:9, 10, 17, 18, 20, 20; 3:2, 4, 4, 4, 5, 7, 9, 10, 27, 29; 4:4, 8, 9, 9, 11, 11, 14, 16, 21, 23; 5:2, 5, 7, 7, 8, 10, 11, 11, 12, 12, 12, 15; 6:3, 4, 8, 17; 7:3, 3, 3, 5, 65; 8:8, 10, 10, 12, 16, 17; 9:1, 6, 10, 11, 12, 12, 13, 13, 14, 14, 15, 15, 15, 15, 17, 17, 18, 19, 19, 19, 19, 20, 21, 22, 22, 23, 24, 24, 24, 26, 26, 27, 27, 27, 27, 27, 28, 28, 28, 29, 29, 30, 30, 30, 31, 31, 34, 35, 35; 10:31; 11:23; 12:9, 24, 27, 29, 31, 32, 36, 37, 38, 38, 38, 40, 43, 44, 47; 13:2, 2, 10, 11, 11, 13, 15, 17, 21, 21, 25, 25, 25, 29, 30
Est 1:7; 2:3, 15; 3:4, 4, 8, 11, 13; 4:7, 8, 15; 5:8, 11; 8:11, 11, 17; 9:1, 1, 1, 2, 2, 3, 5, 21, 22, 22, 23, 24, 24, 24, 26, 27, 27, 28, 31
Job 1:4, 5, 5, 6, 14, 15, 15, 16, 17; 2:1; 3:8; 4:19, 21; 5:4; 6:19; 8:4; 9:5; 12:15, 23, 23, 24, 25; 14:21; 15:19; 17:4; 20:15, 15; 21:8, 9, 17, 26, 29; 22:17, 19, 20; 24:5; 12, 17, 17; 26:8; 29:22, 24; 30:5, 31; 32:8; 34:25, 26; 36:7, 9, 13, 31; 37:4, 12, 15, 21; 39:4, 14, 15, 15; 40:13; 41:16; 42:9, 15
Ps 2:4, 5, 5, 9, 9; 5:6, 10, 10, 10, 11, 11, 11; 6:10; 7:1; 9:6, 10, 12, 13, 20; 10:2, 5; 12:7, 7, 15:4; 17:7, 7; 18:14, 14, 17, 37, 38, 40, 41, 41, 42, 42; 19:4, 11, 11, 13; 21:9, 9, 9, 12, 12; 22:4, 18, 25; 24:6, 9; 25:3, 14, 14; 28:1, 4, 4, 4, 5, 5, 9, 9; 29:6; 31:6, 15, 17, 19, 19, 20, 20; 33:6, 18, 18, 19; 34:7, 7, 9, 19, 16, 17, 18, 19, 20, 22; 35:1, 1, 3, 4, 4, 4, 5, 5, 5, 9, 9, 26; 36:8, 10; 37:40, 40; 39:6; 40:5, 14, 14, 15; 41:10; 42:4; 43:3, 3; 44:2, 2, 3, 5, 7, 13; 48:6; 49:7, 14, 14; 50:21; 53:3, 5, 5; 54:3, 4, 5; 55:15, 15, 19, 23; 57:4; 58:7, 7, 8, 9; 59:1, 8, 11, 11, 11, 12, 13, 13, 14, 14, 15; 60:4; 62:10; 63:11; 64:5, 6, 7, 8; 65:3, 5, 9; 68:1, 2, 3, 3, 17, 18, 25; 69:6, 9, 11, 14, 22, 24, 24, 24, 27, 28; 70:2, 2, 3; 71:13, 13; 73:6, 6, 10, 18, 27; 74:8; 75:8, 8; 78:4, 5, 6, 11, 13, 14, 15, 24, 25, 27, 29, 31, 34, 38, 42, 45, 45, 45, 49, 49, 52, 53, 54, 55, 55, 66; 79:3, 4; 80:5, 5; 81:12, 16; 82:4; 83:4, 8, 9, 13, 15, 15, 17; 84:5, 7, 11; 85:8, 9; 86:5, 14; 87:4; 88:4, 8; 89:7, 9, 11, 12, 23; 90:5; 94:23, 23, 23; 97:10; 99:3, 6, 6, 7, 7, 8, 8; 101:3; 102:26, 26; 103:11, 13, 17, 18; 104:8, 12, 22, 27, 28; 105:3, 14, 17, 24, 27, 32, 37, 38, 38, 40, 44; 106:8, 9, 10, 10, 11, 15, 23, 26, 26, 27, 29, 34, 36, 41, 41, 41, 42, 43, 45, 46, 46; 107:5, 6, 7, 13, 14, 19, 20, 20, 22, 28, 30, 32, 34, 38, 40; 109:10, 15, 15, 20, 25, 28, 28, 29; 111:2, 6, 6; 115:8, 8, 8, 13; 118:4, 7, 7, 10, 11, 12, 19; 119:63, 63, 84, 93, 118, 129, 152, 165, 167; 125:4, 5; 126:1, 2; 127:5; 129:5, 6; 132:12; 135:18, 18, 18; 136:11; 139:16, 17, 18, 21, 22; 140:9, 10, 10; 143:7, 12; 144:6, 6; 145:15, 18, 19, 19, 20; 146:8; 147:4, 11, 18, 20; 148:5, 6, 13; 149:3, 3, 5, 9
Pr 1:12, 15, 32, 32; 2:7; 3:3, 3, 18, 21, 27; 4:21, 21, 22; 5:6, 13, 17; 6:21, 21; 7:3, 3; 8:8, 9, 17; 10:26; 11:3, 3, 6; 12:20, 26; 14:3, 22; 19:7; 20:10, 12, 26; 21:6, 7; 22:2, 5, 18, 21, 23, 26; 24:1, 11, 21, 22, 25, 25; 25:13; 27:3; 28:4, 13; 30:5, 7, 27; 31:29
Ecc 2:5, 10, 14; 3:12, 18, 19; 4:16; 5:11, 11; 7:11, 12, 18; 8:11, 12; 9:1, 5, 11, 12; 10:15; 11:8; 12:1
SS 3:4; 4:2; 5:3; 6:6

Isa 1:14, 23, 31; 2:9; 3:4, 9, 12; 4:2; 5:8, 11, 11, 18, 20, 21, 22, 25, 25, 26, 27, 30; 6:13; 7:19, 20; 8:7, 12, 15, 19, 20; 9:2, 10, 13, 16, 16; 10:1, 6, 10, 15, 19, 22; 11:6, 14, 14; 13:2, 3, 8, 15, 17; 14:1, 1, 2, 2, 2, 2, 18, 20, 22, 25; 16:4; 17:2, 13, 14, 14; 18:6, 6; 19:3, 4, 12, 21, 20, 22, 22; 23:1, 13, 18; 24:8, 9; 25:11; 26:5, 11, 14, 16; 27:4, 4, 6, 7, 11, 11, 11, 11, 11; 28:1, 6, 9, 13; 29:1, 15; 30:5, 6, 8, 22, 28; 31:1, 2, 4; 32:3; 33:4; 34:2, 2, 7, 16, 17, 17; 35:1, 4; 36:1, 4, 8; 37:6, 11, 12, 19; 38:21; 39:2, 2, 2, 4; 40:11, 22, 24, 24, 26, 29; 41:1, 1, 2, 3, 12, 12, 12, 15, 16, 16, 16, 17, 17, 22, 22, 22, 22, 27, 27, 28; 42:5, 5, 7, 9, 11, 12, 16, 16, 16, 16, 22; 43:9, 9, 9; 44:7, 7, 9, 11; 45:8, 16, 21, 21; 47:6, 6, 14; 48:3, 3, 5, 5, 7, 13, 14, 21, 21; 49:9, 10, 10, 10, 10, 18, 18, 26; 50:6, 9; 51:8, 8, 17, 23, 23; 52:4, 5, 5, 15; 54:2; 56:5, 5, 7, 7; 57:6, 8, 13, 13; 59:8, 12, 20, 21; 60:9, 14; 61:1, 3, 3, 7, 8, 9, 9; 62:12; 63:3, 3, 6, 7, 9, 9, 9, 9, 10, 11, 12, 12, 18; 65:1, 1, 8, 21, 21, 23; 66:4, 19, 19, 21
Jer 1:16, 17; 2:3, 13, 25, 28, 37; 3:2; 4:12; 5:3, 3, 5, 6, 6, 7, 13, 14, 19; 6:10, 13, 13, 15, 15, 18, 21, 30, 30; 7:16, 22, 22, 23, 25, 27, 27, 28, 31, 33; 8:2, 3, 4, 9, 10, 10, 12, 13, 13, 13, 19; 9:2, 7, 7, 9, 10, 13, 14, 14, 15, 16, 16, 16, 18; 10:2, 5, 5, 11, 14, 14, 18; 11:3, 4, 4, 5, 6, 7, 8, 8, 8, 10, 11, 11, 12, 14, 14, 20, 22, 25; 12:2, 3, 4, 6, 14, 14, 15, 15; 13:10, 10, 12, 13, 14, 14, 19, 20, 21; 14:10, 12, 12, 13, 14, 14, 14, 15, 16, 16, 16, 17, 17, 18; 15:1, 1, 2, 3, 4, 7, 7, 7; 16:4, 4, 5, 5, 5, 6, 6, 7; 17:11, 11, 18, 18, 18, 20; 18:8, 10, 15, 17, 17, 19, 20, 20, 22, 23, 23; 19:7, 7, 9, 9, 11, 11; 20:4, 4, 5, 5, 5, 12; 21:3, 4, 7, 7; 22:7, 9, 25, 25; 23:2, 2, 3, 4, 4, 7, 7; 22:7; 9, 25, 25; 23:2, 2, 3, 4, 4, 14, 17, 17, 19, 21, 22, 23, 28, 28; 24:1, 5, 6, 6, 6, 6, 6, 7, 8, 9, 9, 10; 25:4, 6, 6, 9, 9, 10, 14, 14, 16, 26, 27, 28, 30, 30, 31; 26:2, 3, 4, 5, 8, 9, 11, 16, 18, 18, 22, 22; 28:3, 13; 29:5, 5, 9, 17, 17, 18, 18, 18, 19, 19, 21, 22, 23, 28, 28, 31; 30:3, 9, 16, 19, 19, 19, 20, 21; 31:4, 5, 8, 8, 8, 9, 9, 13, 28, 28, 32, 32, 34, 34; 32:13, 14, 18, 22, 22, 23, 33, 33, 35, 37, 37, 37, 39, 39, 40, 40, 40, 41, 41, 41, 42, 42, 44; 33:5, 6, 6, 7, 8, 9, 11, 11, 13, 24, 24, 26; 34:8; 10, 11, 13, 14, 18, 18, 20, 22; 35:2, 2, 4, 5, 7, 7, 8, 10; 36:3, 6, 13, 14, 18, 18, 25, 25, 31, 32; 37:5, 10; 38:4, 11, 21, 27, 27, 30; 40:5; 46:5, 15, 21, 25, 26; 47:2; 48:39, 49:2, 11, 20, 20, 29, 32, 36, 37, 37, 37; 50:6, 6, 6, 7, 7, 20, 21, 27, 28, 33, 33, 33, 43, 44, 45, 45; 51:1, 1, 19, 39, 40; 52:3; 17, 25, 26, 26, 27, 27, 28, 33, 33, 33, 43, 44, 45, 45; 51:1, 1
La 1:13, 17, 22; 2:2, 21; 3:20, 25, 64, 65, 65, 66; 4:4, 15, 16, 16
Eze 1:18, 19, 20, 21; 2:4, 4, 5, 6, 7; 3:4, 6, 9, 11, 11, 11, 13, 15, 15, 17, 25, 25, 26, 27; 4:6, 9, 13; 5:2, 3, 4, 4, 4, 6, 13, 13, 16; 6:2, 10, 12, 14; 7:11, 11, 16, 16, 18, 19, 20, 22, 27; 8:11; 9:1, 2, 7; 10:12, 10, 11, 12, 14, 15, 15, 16, 19, 23, 28; 13:2, 6, 11, 15, 16, 18, 18, 21, 22, 24, 24, 25; 12:10, 12, 14, 15, 15, 16, 19, 23, 23, 28; 13:2, 6, 11, 15, 16, 18, 18, 20, 21, 23, 23; 16:2, 6, 6, 14, 16, 18; 17:5, 6; 19:5, 9, 9; 20:7, 8, 8, 9, 13, 13, 14, 16, 16, 16, 18, 19, 20, 22; 21:3; 22:6, 7, 11, 12, 25, 27, 29; 23:3, 3, 5, 7, 7, 8, 11, 13, 17, 18, 40, 44, 45, 48; 24:5, 19, 24; 26:2, 3, 4, 5; 27:3, 9, 12, 13, 14, 14, 14, 18, 25; 26, 28, 30, 31; 31:4, 6; 32:12, 13; 34:2, 4, 5, 5, 5, 10, 13, 14, 27, 28, 30, 31; 35:15; 36:6, 10, 12, 13, 17, 19, 20, 24, 27, 28, 30, 33, 33, 35, 36, 36, 38, 40, 41, 43, 44, 46, 50, 51, 51
Da 1:4, 5, 5, 12, 14, 14, 16, 17, 18, 19, 20, 20; 2:3, 21, 34, 35, 35, 38; 3:14, 20, 27; 4:7, 19; 5:3, 23; 6:2, 24, 24, 24; 7:8, 16, 21, 24; 8:9, 10; 9:4, 4, 7; 10:7; 11:7, 24, 30, 34, 34, 35, 35, 39; 12:2

Hos 1:6, 7, 7, 10, 10; 2:5, 7, 7, 12, 12, 13, 18, 18, 23; 4:9, 9, 12, 12, 16; 5:2, 4, 5, 6, 7, 10, 10; 6:5, 5, 8; 7:2, 7, 12, 12, 12, 13, 13; 8:4, 5, 10, 13; 9:2, 4, 6, 6, 12, 12, 12, 14, 14, 15, 15, 15, 17; 10:9, 10, 10; 11:2, 2, 3, 3, 4, 4, 4, 6, 7, 11; 13:2, 2, 7, 7, 8, 8, 14, 14, 14; 14:4, 7
Joel 2:3, 3, 3, 3, 3, 4, 10, 17, 17; 3:2, 2, 6, 7, 7, 8, 9
Am 1:6; 2:4, 9; 4:3, 9; 5:8, 11, 11, 22; 6:1, 7; 7:8; 8:2, 3; 9:1, 1, 1, 1, 1, 2, 2, 3, 3, 4, 4, 6, 14, 14, 15, 15
Ob 1:11, 18, 18
Jnh 1:3, 5, 9, 10, 12, 13; 3:5, 5, 7, 8, 10
Mic 2:1, 2, 2, 6, 6, 8, 12, 13, 13, 13; 3:2, 3, 3, 4, 4, 6; 4:4, 7, 12; 5:3; 6:11; 7:4, 13, 14
Na 1:7; 2:2, 10, 11; 3:18
Hab 1:10, 12, 12, 13, 14, 15, 15, 15, 16; 2:7, 17; 3:16
Zep 1:5, 5, 6, 13, 18, 18; 2:7, 9, 9, 11; 3:7, 8, 11, 13, 18, 19
Hag 2:22;
Zec 1:3, 21; 2:9; 3:5; 6:6, 10, 11, 13; 7:14, 14; 8:8; 9:8, 14, 15, 16; 10:1, 3, 5, 6, 6, 6, 6, 8, 8, 9, 9, 9, 10, 10, 10, 10, 12; 11:5, 5, 5, 6, 8, 12, 13, 13, 12:8; 13:9, 9, 9; 14:8, 13, 17, 21
Mal 1:4; 2:2, 5, 17; 3:3, 7, 16, 17; 4:1, 1

Mt 2:4, 7, 8, 9; 3:7; 4:8, 16, 19, 21, 24; 5:2, 19, 21, 27, 33, 44, 44, 44, 46; 6:1, 8, 26; 7:6, 11, 12, 16, 20, 23, 24, 26, 29; 8:4, 10, 15, 26, 30, 32, 33; 9:12, 15, 15, 15, 18, 24, 28, 30, 30; 10:1, 1, 5, 18, 21, 25, 26, 28, 29; 11:4, 5, 11, 25; 12:3, 4, 11, 13, 14, 15, 17, 19, 37; 13:3, 4, 7, 10, 14, 28, 28, 29, 30, 30, 31, 33, 34, 37, 39, 41, 42, 50, 51, 52, 54, 57; 14:6, 9, 14, 16, 16, 18, 25, 27; 15:3, 10, 14, 30, 30, 30, 32, 34, 36; 16:1, 2, 4, 6, 8, 11, 12, 14; 17:1, 3, 5, 17, 19, 22, 23, 24, 24, 24, 24, 24, 24, 24; 18:2, 8, 8, 12, 17, 19, 19, 24, 25, 25, 25, 31, 32, 34; 21:2, 2, 3, 7, 8, 8, 12, 12, 13, 14, 16, 17, 21, 24, 27, 31, 31, 36, 37, 42, 45; 22:1, 3, 4, 6, 6, 20, 22, 34, 34, 37, 24:2, 4, 10, 19, 22, 32, 34, 40, 41, 45; 26:10, 15, 19, 22, 30, 47; 31, 24:21, 22; 25:5, 6, 11; 26:10, 11, 11, 11, 11, 13, 18, 18, 20, 30; 27:9, 10, 21, 24, 33, 35, 42, 43; 28:3, 14, 17, 23, 27

Ro 1:19, 19, 24, 26, 28, 32, 32; 2:2, 3, 7, 8, 19; 3:2, 19, 22; 4:11, 11, 12; 5:14; 7:1; 8:1, 28, 28, 30, 30, 30; 9:25, 26; 10:2, 5, 15, 19, 20, 20; 11:8, 9, 11, 12, 12, 14, 14, 15, 15, 17, 17, 22, 23, 27, 32; 12:14, 15, 15; 15:3, 26, 27, 27, 28, 31; 16:10, 11, 14, 15, 17, 17
1Co 1:2, 11, 18, 21, 24; 2:6, 9, 10, 14; 4:19; 5:12, 12, 13; 6:4, 13, 15; 7:8, 9, 36; 8:9; 9:3, 20, 20, 21, 21; 10:4, 5, 7, 8, 9, 10, 11, 27; 11:2, 12; 12:18; 14:10, 20, 22, 22, 22, 34, 35; 15:20; 16:3, 18
2Co 1:4; 2:3, 13, 15, 15; 4:3, 4, 4; 5:12, 15; 6:16, 16, 17; 8:22, 24; 9:2, 13; 11:8, 12; 12:17; 13:2
Gal 1:17; 2:2, 2, 12, 14; 3:10, 12, 12, 22; 4:5, 8, 15, 17; 6:10, 16
Eph 2:10, 17; 4:18; 5:7, 11, 12; 6:4, 5, 9, 24
Php 1:28; 3:8, 17
Col 2:1, 15, 15; 3:7, 19; 4:5, 13, 13
1Th 2:16; 4:12, 13, 14, 15, 17; 5:3, 12, 13, 14
2Th 1:6, 8, 10; 2:10, 11; 3:12
1Ti 1:10, 16, 18; 3:7, 10; 4:3, 15, 16, 16; 5:4, 16, 16, 16, 20; 6:2, 2, 2, 17
2Ti 2:14, 14, 19, 22, 25; 3:11, 14; 4:8
Tit 1:13, 15; 2:9; 3:1, 13, 15
Heb 1:12, 14; 2:1, 3, 4, 11, 15, 18; 3:17, 18; 4:2, 2, 8; 5:2, 9, 14; 6:6, 7, 12, 16; 7:6, 8, 25, 25; 8:8, 9, 9, 10, 10; 9:10, 28; 10:14, 16, 16, 33, 39, 39; 11:6, 13, 13, 13, 16, 28, 31; 12:9, 11, 19; 13:3, 3, 3, 7, 9, 17, 24
Jas 1:12; 2:5, 16, 16, 25; 3:18; 5:3, 4, 11, 14
1Pe 1:11, 12; 2:7, 8, 14, 14; 3:7, 12; 4:4, 6, 17, 19
2Pe 1:1, 12; 2:1, 4, 4, 6, 6, 8, 10, 11, 18, 19, 20, 21, 21, 22; 3:5, 16
1Jn 2:26; 4:4, 5; 5:16
3Jn 1:9, 10, 10
Jude 1:1, 5, 7, 11, 15, 23
Rev 2:2, 2, 2, 9, 14, 15, 16, 22, 27; 3:9, 9, 10; 4:8; 5:8, 11, 13; 6:8, 9, 10, 11, 11; 7:4, 14, 15, 16, 17, 17; 8:2, 12; 9:3, 4, 5, 5, 6, 11, 16, 17, 17, 19; 10:4; 11:1, 5, 5, 6, 7, 7, 7, 10, 10, 11, 11, 11, 12, 12, 18; 12:4, 10, 12; 13:6, 7, 12, 14, 14; 14:6, 9, 13; 15:1, 2; 16:2, 6, 14, 16; 17:4; 18:14; 19:15, 18, 18, 20, 20; 20:4, 4, 4, 8, 9, 10, 11, 13; 21:3, 3, 14, 24; 22:5, 8, 9

Ge 2:4, 24, 25; 3:7, 7, 7, 8; 4:8; 5:2; 6:2, 2, 4, 19; 7:14, 15, 16, 23, 23; 8:17; 9:2, 23; 11:2, 2, 2, 3, 3, 3, 4, 6, 6, 6, 7, 8, 31, 31; 12:5, 5, 5, 5, 12, 12, 12, 20; 13:6, 6, 11; 14:4, 4, 7, 8, 10, 11, 12; 15:13, 14, 14, 16; 18:5, 8, 9, 19, 21; 19:2, 3, 3, 4, 4, 5, 8, 9, 9, 9, 11, 14, 16, 17, 33, 35; 20:11, 17; 21:30, 31, 32, 32; 22:6, 8, 9, 19; 24:19, 41, 54, 54, 57, 58, 59, 60, 61; 25:18; 26:18, 20, 21, 22, 28, 30, 31, 31, 32; 29:2, 3, 4, 5, 6, 8, 9, 20; 30:38, 38, 41; 31:23, 37, 43, 46, 46, 54; 32:18; 33:4, 6, 6, 7; 34:5, 7, 7, 14, 22, 23, 25, 26, 27, 28, 29, 30, 31; 35:4, 5, 5, 16; 36:7; 37:4, 5, 8, 16, 17, 18, 18, 19, 23, 24, 25, 25, 28, 28, 31, 32, 38; 38:21; 39:22; 40:4, 5, 6, 8, 15; 41:2, 14, 18, 21, 21, 21, 23; 42:7, 8, 10, 11, 21, 23, 26, 28, 29, 35, 35, 35; 43:2, 2, 7, 15, 18, 18, 19, 19, 24, 25, 25, 28, 28, 31, 32, 33, 34; 44:1, 3, 4, 7, 11, 13, 14; 45:3, 4, 24, 25, 27; 46:6, 6, 28, 32, 32; 47:1, 1, 3, 4, 14, 17, 18, 22, 25, 27; 48:5, 9; 49:6, 6, 26, 31, 31; 50:8, 10, 10, 11, 15, 16, 17, 17, 18, 26

Ex 1:10, 10, 11, 11, 12, 12, 14, 14, 19; 2:17; 3:13, 18; 4:1, 1, 5, 8, 8, 9, 18, 31, 31; 5:1, 3, 8, 8, 8, 9, 10, 16, 19,

Idx

Idx

Hos 1:11; 2:4, 8, 17, 21, 22, 23; 4:2, 4, 7, 7, 8, 8, 10, 10, 10, 12, 13, 14, 14, 14, 18, 19; 5:4, 4, 6, 6, 7, 7, 15, 15; 6:7, 7, 9; 7:1, 2, 2, 3, 4, 6, 6, 7, 10, 11, 11, 12, 13, 13, 13, 14, 14, 14, 14, 15, 16, 16; 8:1, 4, 4, 4, 4, 5, 7, 7, 8, 9, 9, 10, 10, 12, 13; 9:3, 3, 4, 4, 6, 9, 10, 10, 12, 16, 16, 17, 17; 10:1, 2, 3, 4, 8, 9, 10; 11:2, 2, 2, 3, 4, 5, 7, 10, 11; 12:1, 8, 11, 11; 13:2, 2, 3, 6, 6, 6, 16; 14:7, 7
Joel 1:18; 2:4, 5, 7, 7, 7, 8, 8, 9, 9, 9, 9, 17; 3:2, 3, 3, 8, 19
Am 1:3, 6, 9, 13, 13; 2:4, 6, 8, 8; 3:3, 10; 4:8; 5:10, 10, 12, 12, 12, 16, 16; 6:2, 6, 7, 9, 14; 7:2; 8:3, 12, 12, 14, 14; 9:2, 2, 3, 3, 4, 12, 14, 14, 14, 15
Ob 1:5, 5, 5, 7, 16, 16, 16, 16, 18, 19, 19, 19
Jnh 1:7, 7, 8, 11, 13, 14, 15; 2:8; 3:10
Mic 1:5, 7, 16; 2:1, 2, 2, 6, 6, 6, 12, 13; 3:3, 4, 4, 5, 7, 10, 11; 4:3, 3, 4, 4, 12, 12; 5:1, 4, 6, 15; 7:1, 2, 2, 3, 3, 16, 17, 17, 17
Na 1:10, 10, 10, 12, 12; 2:4, 4, 4, 5, 5, 8, 8; 3:3, 7, 10, 12, 12, 17, 17
Hab 1:7, 8, 9, 9, 10, 10, 10, 15, 15, 15, 16; 2:7; 3:10, 11, 14
Zep 1:11, 13, 13, 17, 17; 2:4, 7, 7, 8, 10, 10; 3:3, 4, 7, 9, 12, 13, 19
Hag 1:14; 2:14
Zec 1:4, 5, 5, 6, 6, 10, 11, 15; 2:9; 3:5, 8; 4:10, 10; 5:9, 9; 6:7, 7, 15; 7:2, 11, 11, 12, 12, 13, 13, 14, 14; 8:8, 8; 9:15, 15, 15, 16; 10:2, 2, 2, 5, 5, 6, 7, 8, 8, 9, 9, 12; 11:5, 6, 12; 12:2, 6, 10, 10, 10; 13:2, 4, 9, 9; 14:12, 13, 21
Mal 1:4, 4; 2:7; 3:3, 15, 15, 16, 17; 4:3
Mt 1:11, 12, 18, 23; 2:5, 9, 9, 9, 10, 10, 11, 11, 11, 11, 12, 14, 18, 20; 4:6, 18, 20, 22, 24; 5:4, 4, 5, 6, 6, 7, 8, 9, 10, 12, 16; 6:2, 2, 5, 5, 5, 7, 7, 16, 16, 16, 26, 26, 28, 28, 28; 7:6, 15; 8:16, 29, 32, 32, 33, 34, 34; 9:8, 11, 12, 12, 15, 17, 24, 28, 31, 31, 32, 32, 36; 10:17, 17, 19, 23, 25, 25, 36; 11:7, 8, 18, 19, 20, 21; 12:2, 3, 10, 10, 14, 16, 24, 27, 34, 34, 35, 36; 13:5, 5, 6, 6, 6, 13, 13, 15, 15, 16, 16, 41, 48, 51, 54, 56, 57; 14:5, 13, 15, 16, 16, 41, 48, 51, 54, 56, 57; 14:5, 13, 15, 16, 19, 20, 20, 21, 26, 34, 34, 34, 35, 36; 15:2, 2, 9, 12, 14, 18, 31, 31, 32, 32, 34, 37, 37, 38; 16:5, 7, 12, 14, 20, 28; 17:6, 8, 8, 9, 12, 12, 14, 20, 22, 23, 24; 18:19, 31; 19:5, 6, 7, 11, 25; 20:4, 7, 9, 9, 10, 10, 10, 11, 11, 18, 22, 24, 25, 29, 30, 31, 31, 33, 34; 21:1, 7, 15, 20, 25, 27, 31, 34, 36, 37, 39, 41, 45, 46, 46, 46; 22:3, 5, 8, 10, 15, 16, 19, 21, 22, 22, 28, 30, 33, 34, 42; 23:3, 3, 4, 4, 5, 5, 25; 24:9, 24, 26, 30, 31, 38; 25:3, 5, 10, 10, 44; 26:4, 5, 8, 15, 19, 21, 22, 26, 30, 30, 50, 52, 57, 60, 66, 67, 73; 27:2, 2, 4, 7, 9, 9, 13, 15, 16, 17, 18, 20, 21, 22, 23, 28, 29, 29, 29, 30, 31, 31, 34, 41, 45, 46, 46, 46; 28:3, 9, 10, 10, 11, 12, 12, 15, 15, 17, 17, 17
Mk 1:5, 16, 18, 20, 21, 22, 27, 27, 29, 29, 30, 32, 34, 36, 37, 37, 45; 2:3, 4, 4, 4, 4, 8, 15, 16, 17, 17, 18, 19, 19, 20, 23, 24, 25; 3:2, 2, 4, 6, 8, 8, 9, 10, 11, 12, 13, 14, 19, 20, 21, 21, 28, 30, 32; 4:10, 12, 12, 12, 15, 16, 16, 17, 18, 20, 33, 34, 36, 36, 38, 41, 45, 46, 46, 46; 5:1, 13, 14, 14, 14, 15, 15, 16, 17, 40, 42; 6:3, 8, 12, 13, 29, 30, 30, 31, 32, 34, 36, 37, 38, 41, 43, 44, 49, 49, 50, 52, 53, 54, 54, 55, 56, 56; 7:2, 2, 3, 4, 4, 4, 7, 15, 32, 36, 36; 8:2, 3, 5, 6, 7, 8, 9, 14, 16, 19, 20, 22, 28, 30; 9:1, 4, 6, 8, 8, 20, 30, 31, 32, 34, 34; 10:4, 8, 8, 13, 13, 23, 26, 32, 32, 32, 33, 34, 37, 39, 41, 42, 46, 49; 11:1, 4, 4, 6, 6, 7, 9, 9, 12, 15, 18, 18, 20, 20, 27, 31, 32, 33; 12:3, 4, 5, 6, 8, 12, 13, 14, 14, 16, 16, 17, 18, 23, 25, 25, 26, 43, 44; 13:9, 11, 26; 14:1, 2, 5, 11, 12, 16, 18, 19, 22, 23, 26, 31, 32, 40, 46, 50, 53, 64, 70; 15:4, 6, 13, 14, 16, 16, 17, 19, 20, 20, 21, 22, 23, 24, 24, 25, 27, 29, 32, 35; 16:1, 2, 3, 4, 4, 5, 5, 6, 8, 8, 8, 10, 11, 12, 3, 4, 4, 5, 13, 14, 14, 17, 17, 18, 18, 18, 20
Lk 1:2, 6, 7, 22, 58, 59, 59, 61, 62, 63, 66; 2:6, 9, 16, 17, 17, 18, 20, 22, 39, 42, 43, 43, 44, 44, 45, 45, 46, 48, 48, 50; 4:2, 11, 22, 28, 28, 29, 32, 36, 38, 40, 41; 5:6, 6, 7, 7, 7, 9, 11, 18, 19, 19, 19, 26, 26, 31, 31, 33, 35; 6:3, 7, 11, 11, 18, 18, 22, 39, 44; 7:4, 4, 10, 14, 16, 20, 25, 31, 32, 42, 49; 8:10, 10, 12, 12, 13, 13, 14, 14, 16, 22, 23, 23, 24, 24, 25, 25, 26, 31, 32, 34, 34, 35, 36, 37, 40, 45, 45, 53, 56, 56; 9:6, 9, 10, 10, 11, 12, 16, 22, 23, 24, 27, 27, 36, 48; 13:2, 4, 29, 34; 14:1, 4, 6, 7, 12, 14, 18; 15:24, 26, 26, 28, 28, 28, 28, 37; 18:9, 15, 15, 24, 26, 33, 34, 34, 37, 39, 43; 19:7, 7, 11, 11, 25, 30, 33, 35, 35, 36, 37, 42, 44, 48; 20:5, 6, 7, 7, 10, 11, 11, 12, 13, 19, 20, 20, 20, 21, 24, 26, 26, 27, 31, 35, 36, 36, 40, 41; 21:3, 7, 12, 16, 24, 27, 30; 22:2, 2, 5, 9, 13, 23, 23, 25, 28, 35, 38,

49, 49, 54, 55, 64, 64, 65, 70, 71; 23:2, 5, 12, 18, 21, 23, 26, 34, 34, 34, 56; 24:1, 1, 2, 3, 4, 5, 5, 8, 11, 14, 15, 16, 19, 22, 24, 28, 28, 29, 31, 32, 33, 35, 36, 37, 37, 41, 42, 45, 52
Jn 1:21, 22, 24, 25, 37, 38, 39; 2:3, 3, 7, 8, 12, 22, 23; 3:21, 23, 26; 4:24, 30, 35, 40, 45, 52; 5:12, 23, 25, 29, 29, 39, 39; 6:2, 9, 11, 12, 13, 14, 15, 19, 19, 19, 21, 21, 23, 24, 25, 28, 30, 34, 42, 45, 60, 63, 63, 64; 7:25, 26, 30, 39, 40, 45, 52; 8:3, 4, 6, 6, 7, 9, 19, 25, 27, 33, 39, 41, 59; 9:8, 10, 12, 13, 17, 18, 19, 22, 24, 26, 28, 34, 34, 35, 39, 39; 10:4, 5, 5, 6, 6, 10, 16, 19, 24, 26, 28, 41, 42, 53, 56, 56, 57; 12:2, 9, 9, 10, 11, 16, 18, 18, 37, 39, 40, 42, 42, 43; 15:6, 20, 20, 20, 20, 21, 21, 22, 24, 24, 25; 16:2, 3, 9, 18, 19, 17:3, 6, 7, 18, 18, 20, 21, 25, 28, 28, 30, 40; 19:2, 3, 6, 15, 16, 18, 23, 24, 24, 24, 29, 31, 33, 33, 37, 37, 40, 42; 20:2, 2, 4, 9, 13, 13, 13, 20, 23, 23, 29; 21:3, 3, 5, 6, 6, 8, 9, 9, 15, 25
Ac 1:4, 6, 6, 9, 10, 12, 13, 13, 23, 24, 26; 2:1, 2, 4, 7, 12, 18, 37, 37, 41, 42, 46; 3:2, 10, 10; 4:1, 2, 3, 7, 7, 13, 13, 13, 13, 14, 15, 15, 17, 18, 21, 21, 21, 23, 24, 24, 29, 31, 31, 31, 31, 32; 5:12, 15, 16, 16, 17, 21, 21, 21, 21, 21, 24, 26, 27, 27, 33, 33, 40, 40, 40, 40, 41, 41, 42; 6:5, 6, 6, 6, 10, 11, 12; 7:6, 7, 7, 19, 19, 25, 26, 27, 33, 41, 52, 54, 54, 54, 57, 59; 8:1, 4, 10, 11, 12, 12, 14, 15, 15, 16, 17, 17, 25, 25, 36, 38, 39; 10:9, 10, 22, 24, 39, 45, 46, 48; 11:2, 8, 18, 19, 20, 22, 23, 26, 30; 12:10, 10, 16, 16, 20, 20, 20, 21, 21, 22, 24, 25, 27, 33, 40, 40, 40, 40, 41, 41, 42; 6:5, 6, 6, 6, 10, 11, 12; 7:6, 7, 7, 19, 19, 25, 26, 27, 33, 41, 52, 54, 54, 54, 57, 59; 13:3, 3, 3, 4, 4, 5, 5, 6, 13, 14, 14, 17, 21, 27, 27, 28, 28, 29, 45, 46, 48; 11:2, 8, 18, 19, 20, 22, 23, 26, 30; 14:1, 3, 6, 7, 11, 12, 14, 16, 18, 21, 21, 23, 23, 24, 24, 29, 45, 60, 63, 63, 64; 15:2, 2, 3, 3, 4, 4, 4, 11, 13, 20, 23, 30, 30, 30, 31, 31, 33, 33, 36; 16:3, 4, 6, 7, 7, 8, 10, 13, 15, 19, 19, 20, 22, 23, 24, 27, 29, 32, 35, 35, 37, 38, 38, 40, 40; 17:5, 6, 8, 10, 14, 15, 18, 21, 23, 33, 34; 18:2, 5, 8, 11, 17, 18, 19, 21, 26, 27, 28; 19:2, 3, 6, 9, 12, 13, 14, 16, 17, 19, 19, 24, 24, 25, 28, 29, 30, 31, 32, 32, 33, 35; 20:5, 6, 7, 8, 11, 13, 15, 36, 37, 38, 38; 21:3, 4, 5, 6, 8, 12, 18, 26, 30, 30, 30, 31, 32, 33, 34, 35, 36, 36, 36, 45, 60, 63, 63, 64; 28:1, 2, 6, 6, 11, 14, 15, 15, 16, 17, 18

(Note: Long, dense reference columns continue. Full faithful transcription of every reference in these multi-column concordance entries is extensive.)

Ge 2:16, 17, 17, 17; 3:9, 11, 11, 11, 12, 13, 14, 14, 14, 14, 15, 15, 16, 17, 17, 17, 18, 19, 19, 19, 19; 4:6, 7, 7, 7, 7, 10, 11, 12, 12, 14; 6:14, 15, 16, 16, 16, 16, 18, 18, 19, 21, 21; 7:1, 2; 8:16; 10:19, 19, 30; 12:2, 11, 13, 18, 18, 19; 13:9, 9, 10, 14, 15; 14:23; 15:2, 3, 5, 15, 15; 16:8, 8, 11, 13; 17:1, 4, 8, 9, 15, 19; 18:5, 15, 23, 24, 28; 19:12, 12, 15, 17, 17, 19, 19, 21, 22, 34; 20:3, 3, 4, 6, 7, 7, 7, 7, 9, 9, 9, 10, 10, 13; 21:22, 23, 23, 23, 26, 29, 30; 22:2, 2, 12, 12, 12, 16, 18; 23:6, 6, 13; 24:3, 4, 5, 6, 6, 7, 8, 14, 14, 23, 31, 31, 37, 38, 40, 41, 41, 42, 44, 47, 58, 60, 60; 25:18; 26:9, 10, 10, 16, 29, 29; 27:10, 18, 19, 20, 21, 24, 32, 33, 36, 38, 40, 40, 40, 43, 45; 28:1, 3, 4, 13, 15, 22; 29:14, 15, 15, 25, 25, 27; 30:15, 15, 16, 26, 29, 29, 30, 30; 30:1, 2, 14, 23; 32:18; 32:9, 10, 11, 11; 33:8, 8, 10; 35:1, 17; 37:8, 8, 10, 15; 38:16, 16, 17, 17, 23, 29; 39:9, 17; 40:13, 13; 41:15, 39, 40, 40; 43:4, 5, 8, 9; 44:4, 18, 21, 23; 45:10, 10, 10, 10, 11, 11, 19; 46:30; 47:6, 8, 25, 30, 30; 48:6; 49:3, 4, 4, 4, 6, 6, 8, 9; 50:5
Ex 2:13, 14, 14; 3:5, 10, 12, 14, 15, 18, 18; 4:9, 9, 10, 12, 13, 15, 16, 17, 17, 21, 21, 22, 23, 25, 26; 5:15, 22, 22, 23; 6:1, 29; 7:2, 9, 15, 15, 16, 16, 17; 8:2, 10, 21, 22; 9:2, 14, 15, 17, 17, 19; 10:2, 3, 4, 7, 25, 28, 28, 29; 12:44, 46; 13:5, 6, 8, 10, 12, 13, 13, 13, 13, 14, 14:11, 11, 15, 16; 15:7, 7, 10, 12, 13, 13, 16, 17, 17, 17, 26; 17:3, 5, 6; 18:14, 14, 17, 18, 18, 19, 19, 20, 21, 23, 23; 19:3, 6, 12, 23, 23, 24; 20:3, 4, 5, 7, 9, 9, 10, 10, 10, 10, 14, 15, 16, 17, 17, 19, 22, 24, 25, 25, 25, 25, 26; 21:1, 2, 14, 23; 22:18, 21, 23, 25; 23:1, 2, 2, 3, 4, 5, 5, 6, 7, 8, 9, 10, 11, 11, 12, 12, 14, 15, 15, 15, 16, 18, 19, 19, 22, 24, 27, 30, 31, 31, 33; 24:1, 12; 25:11, 11, 12, 13, 14, 16, 17, 18, 18, 21, 21, 23, 23, 24, 25, 25, 26, 28, 29, 29, 30, 30, 31, 37, 40; 26:1, 1, 4, 4, 5, 5, 6, 7, 7, 9, 10, 11, 14, 15, 17, 18, 19, 22, 23, 24, 26, 27, 30, 31, 37; 27:1, 2, 2, 3, 3, 4, 4, 4, 5, 6, 7, 8, 9, 10, 14, 17, 18, 20; 28:1, 2, 3, 9, 11, 11, 12, 13, 14, 20, 21, 23, 24, 25, 26, 27, 28:1, 2, 3, 9, 11, 11, 12, 14, 14, 15, 19, 20; 25:7, 14, 17, 18; 26:5, 10, 17, 17, 17, 18, 18, 23; 27:1, 2, 16, 18, 18, 23, 25, 26, 29, 30, 36, 38, 38, 39, 39, 40, 40, 40, 41, 41, 42; 29:1, 2, 3, 4, 9, 11, 11, 12, 13, 13, 14, 15, 19, 20, 25; 25:7, 14, 17, 18; 26:5, 8, 8, 9, 10, 10, 11, 12, 13, 14, 16, 17, 20, 31, 31, 35, 36, 36, 38, 38, 39, 39, 39, 40, 40, 40, 41, 43, 44; 28:1, 1, 2, 4, 6, 6, 9, 10, 16, 17, 18, 21, 23, 25, 27, 27, 28

Idx

26, 27, 27, 27, 30, 30, 30, 31, 33, 34, 34, 35, 36, 38, 38, 39, 41; 7:17; 9:6; 10:4, 7, 10, 10, 10; 13:4; 14:11; 16:7, 8, 9, 9; 18:3, 3, 10, 12, 15, 21, 21, 24, 24, 27, 29, 33; 19:2, 3; 20:6, 6, 7, 9, 10, 11, 12, 15, 37; 21:12, 15; 24:6; 25:8, 15, 16, 16, 16, 19, 19, 19, 19, 19; 26:18; 34:26, 27, 27, 28; 35:21

Ezr 4:13, 15, 16; 7:14, 16, 17, 19, 20, 25; 9:11, 13, 14, 14, 15; 10:12

Ne 1:6, 7, 8, 10; 2:2, 4, 5, 6; 5:12; 6:6, 6, 6, 7, 8, 8, 14; 9:6, 6, 6, 6, 7, 8, 10, 10, 11, 11, 12, 13, 15, 17, 17, 19, 20, 21, 22, 23, 23, 24, 27, 27, 27, 27, 28, 28, 29, 30, 30, 31, 31, 33, 33, 34, 35, 35, 36, 37

Est 3:3; 4:13, 14, 14, 14; 5:3, 14, 14; 6:10, 10, 13, 13

Job 1:7, 8, 10, 10; 2:2, 3, 3, 9, 10; 4:2, 3, 3, 4, 5, 5; 5:1, 17, 21, 21, 22, 22, 23, 24, 24, 25, 26, 27; 7:12, 14, 17, 17, 18, 19, 20, 20, 21, 21; 8:2, 5, 6; 9:12, 28, 31; 10:2, 3, 3, 4, 4, 4, 6, 7, 8, 9, 10, 11, 12, 13, 14, 14, 15, 16, 16, 17, 18; 11:3, 4, 7, 7, 8, 8, 13, 15, 15, 16, 16, 17, 18, 18, 18, 19; 13:22, 22, 24, 25, 25, 26, 27, 27; 14:3, 5, 13, 13, 13, 15, 15, 16, 16, 17, 19, 19, 20, 20; 15:4, 5, 7, 7, 8, 8, 9, 9, 13; 16:3, 7, 8, 18; 17:4, 4, 14, 14; 20:4; 22:3, 3, 6, 7, 7, 9, 11, 13, 14, 15, 23, 23, 23, 24, 25, 26, 27, 27, 28, 29; 26:2, 2, 3, 3, 4; 30:20, 20, 21, 21, 22, 22, 23; 31:24; 33:5, 8, 12, 13, 32; 34:16, 17, 18, 32, 33, 33, 33; 35:2, 2, 3, 5, 6, 6, 6, 7, 7, 8, 14, 14, 14; 36:17, 21, 23, 24; 37:6, 15, 16, 18; 38:3, 4, 4, 5, 11, 12, 16, 16, 17, 18, 18, 20, 20, 21, 21, 22, 22; 31:24; 33:5, 8, 12, 13, 32; 39:1, 1, 2, 2, 10, 11, 11, 12, 13, 19, 19, 20; 40:7, 8, 8, 8, 9, 9; 41:1, 1, 2, 4, 5, 5, 7; 42:2, 4

Ps 2:7, 9, 9; 3:3, 7, 7; 4:1, 6, 7, 8; 5:3, 4, 5, 6, 10, 11, 12, 12; 6:3; 7:6, 7; 8:2, 2, 3, 4, 4, 5, 6, 6; 9:2, 4, 4, 5, 5, 6, 6, 10, 13; 10:1, 1, 13, 14, 14, 14, 15, 15, 17, 17, 17; 12:7, 7; 13:1, 1; 16:2, 2, 5, 10, 10, 11; 17:3, 3, 3, 6, 7, 7; 14; 18:25, 25, 26, 26, 27, 28, 35, 36, 39, 39, 40, 43, 43, 48, 48; 19:12; 21:2, 3, 3, 4, 5, 6, 6, 9, 10, 12, 13; 22:1, 1, 2, 3, 3, 4, 9, 9, 10, 15, 19, 21; 23:4, 5, 5; 25:5, 7, 17; 27:8, 9; 28:1; 30:1, 2, 3, 3, 7, 7, 9, 10, 11, 11; 31:2, 3, 4, 5, 7, 7, 8, 14, 19, 19, 20, 20, 22; 32:5, 6, 7, 7, 8; 35:17, 22; 36:6, 8; 37:1, 3, 3, 10, 34; 38:15; 39:5, 9, 11, 11; 40:5, 6, 6, 9, 11, 17; 41:2, 3, 10, 11, 12; 42:5, 5, 5, 9, 11, 11, 11; 43:2, 2, 5; 44:1, 2, 3, 4, 7, 9, 10, 11, 12, 13, 14, 19, 23, 24; 45:2, 7, 11, 16; 48:7; 49:16, 18; 50:15, 16, 16, 17, 18, 18, 19, 20, 21; 51:4, 4, 4, 4, 9; 53:5; 55:13, 23; 56:2, 8, 8, 13; 57:5, 11; 59:5, 8, 8, 16; 60:1, 1, 1, 2, 2, 3, 3, 4, 8, 10, 10; 61:3, 5, 7; 62:5, 12; 63:1, 7; 65:2, 3, 4, 5, 8, 9, 9, 9, 9, 10, 10, 10, 10, 11; 66:3, 10, 10, 11, 11, 12, 12; 67:4; 68:7, 7, 9, 9, 10, 18, 18, 28, 30, 35; 69:5, 19, 26, 26; 70:5; 71:3, 3, 3, 5, 5, 6, 7, 17, 20, 21, 22, 23; 73:18, 18, 20, 20, 23, 24, 27; 74:1, 2, 2, 2, 11, 13, 13, 14, 15, 15, 16, 17; 76:4, 7, 7, 7, 8, 10; 77:4, 14, 14, 15, 20; 79:5, 11; 80:1, 1, 4, 5, 6, 8, 8, 9, 12, 15; 17; 81:7, 8, 9; 82:8; 83:1, 18; 85:1, 1, 2, 2, 3, 3, 5, 5, 6; 86:2, 5, 7, 9, 10, 10, 13, 15, 17; 88:5, 6, 7, 8, 8, 10, 14, 14, 18; 89:2, 9, 9, 10, 10, 11, 12, 13, 17, 19, 26, 38, 38, 39, 39, 40, 40, 42, 42, 43, 44, 45, 45, 46, 47, 49; 90:1, 2, 2, 3, 5, 8, 15, 17, 17; 91:4, 5, 8, 9, 12, 13; 92:4, 8, 10; 93:2; 94:2, 12, 13; 97:9, 9; 99:4, 4, 8, 8, 8; 101:2; 102:10, 12, 13, 25, 26, 27, 28; 104:1, 1, 6, 8, 9, 20, 24, 24, 26, 27, 28, 28, 29, 29, 30, 30, 35; 106:4; 108:5, 11, 11; 109:6, 21, 21, 27, 28; 110:1, 2, 3, 4; 114:5, 5, 5, 7; 115:9; 116:8, 16; 118:13, 21, 28, 28; 119:4, 12, 18, 21, 25, 26, 28, 32, 37, 49, 57, 65, 68, 75, 82, 84, 86, 90, 93, 98, 102, 114, 117, 118, 119, 132, 132, 137, 138, 151, 152, 171; 120:3; 123:1; 128:2, 2, 5; 130:3; 4; 138:2; 137:8; 138:2, 3, 7, 7; 139:1, 2, 2, 3, 4, 5, 8, 8, 13, 19; 140:6, 7; 142:3, 5, 7; 143:10; 144:3, 3; 145:15, 16

Pr 1:10, 15; 3:6, 9, 12, 12; 5:9, 20; 3:4, 15, 23, 24, 24, 24, 28, 31; 4:8, 12, 12, 12; 5:2, 6, 6, 9, 11, 19, 20; 6:1, 1, 2, 2, 3, 6, 6, 9, 9, 22, 22, 22, 35; 7:4; 9:12, 12, 12, 12; 14:7; 19:19, 19, 20; 20:13, 13, 22; 22:18, 21, 24, 25, 26, 27, 29; 23:1, 2, 5, 6, 6, 8, 8, 14, 14, 17, 19, 31, 34, 35; 24:1, 6, 10, 11, 12, 13, 14, 19, 21, 24; 25:7, 8, 16, 16, 22; 26:4, 12; 27:1, 22, 23, 27; 29:20; 30:4, 6, 6, 10, 32, 32; 31:29

Ecc 5:1, 2, 4, 4, 5, 5, 6, 7, 8; 7:10, 10, 16, 17, 17, 18, 21, 22; 8:4; 9:9, 9, 10; 10:17; 11:1, 2, 5, 5, 6, 9; 12:1

SS 1:7, 7, 7, 8, 8, 9, 15, 15, 15, 16; 2:17; 4:1, 1, 1, 7, 9, 9, 16; 5:9, 9; 6:1, 4; 7:6; 8:1, 12, 13, 14

Isa 1:26; 2:6; 3:6, 6; 7:3, 16; 9:3, 4; 12:1, 1, 1, 6; 14:3, 4, 8, 10, 10, 12, 13, 15, 19, 20, 20, 29, 31; 16:4; 17:10, 10, 11, 11; 22:1, 2, 8, 10, 16, 16, 18; 23:2, 4, 12, 12, 14, 16, 16; 25:1, 1, 2, 4, 5; 26:3, 7, 12, 12, 14, 15, 15, 15, 15, 20; 27:8; 29:4, 6; 30:19, 22, 22, 23; 33:1, 1, 1, 1, 2, 19, 19, 19; 36:4, 5, 5, 5, 6, 7, 8, 9; 37:6, 10, 11, 11, 16, 16, 16, 20, 20, 21, 23, 23, 24, 26,

26, 29; 38:1, 12, 13, 16, 17, 17; 39:7, 8; 40:27, 28, 28; 41:8, 9, 9, 10, 12, 14, 15, 16, 16; 42:20; 43:1, 2, 2, 2, 4, 4, 22, 22, 23, 23, 24, 24, 24, 24, 26, 26; 44:2, 17, 21, 21, 21, 26, 28; 45:3, 4, 5, 9, 10, 10, 15; 47:1, 2, 5, 6, 6, 7, 7, 8, 10, 10, 10, 11, 11, 11, 12, 12, 13, 13, 15; 48:4, 5, 6, 6, 7, 7, 8, 8, 8, 17, 18; 49:3, 6, 6, 6, 9, 18, 20, 20, 21, 23; 51:9, 10, 12, 12, 16, 17, 21, 22, 23; 53:10; 54:1, 1, 3, 4, 4, 4, 4, 6, 11, 14, 14, 14, 17; 55:5, 5; 57:6, 6, 7, 7, 8, 8, 8, 8, 9, 10, 10, 10, 10, 11, 11, 11, 11, 12, 13, 14; 60:5, 15, 16, 16, 18; 62:2, 3, 4, 4, 8, 12; 63:2, 14, 16, 16, 16, 17, 19; 64:1, 1, 3, 3, 5, 5, 7, 8, 8, 12; 65:5

Jer 1:5, 7, 7, 11, 12, 13, 17, 17, 18, 18, 19, 20, 20, 21, 22, 23, 23, 23, 25, 27, 27, 28, 33, 33, 35, 35, 36, 36, 36, 37, 37; 3:1, 2, 2, 2, 3, 3, 4, 4, 5, 5, 6, 7, 19, 22; 4:1, 1, 1, 2, 10, 14, 19, 30, 30, 30, 30, 30, 30; 5:3, 3, 15, 17, 19; 6:8, 27; 7:16, 17, 27, 27, 28; 8:4; 10:6, 24; 11:3, 5, 5; 13:4, 12, 13, 21, 21, 22, 25, 27; 14:7, 8, 17, 17, 19, 19, 22, 22; 15:2, 5, 6, 6, 10, 14, 15, 15, 18, 21; 12:1, 2, 2, 3, 5, 5, 5; 13:4, 12, 13, 21, 21, 22, 25, 27; 14:7, 8, 17, 17, 19, 19, 22, 22; 16:2, 2, 8, 10, 11; 17:4, 4, 14, 16, 17; 18:22, 23:10; 19:10; 20:6, 6, 6, 6, 7, 7; 21:8; 22:2, 6, 15, 15, 21, 21, 22, 23, 23, 23, 37; 24:3; 25:27, 28, 30; 26:4, 8, 9; 27:13; 28:6, 7, 13, 13, 15, 16, 16; 29:24, 25, 26, 27; 30:10, 13, 13, 15; 31:4, 4, 5, 18, 18, 21, 22, 22; 32:3, 17, 18, 22, 24, 24, 25, 33:3, 24; 34:3, 3, 4, 5, 14; 36:6, 6, 6, 14, 17, 19, 29, 29; 37:13, 17, 20; 38:15, 15, 17, 17, 18, 18; 21, 23, 24, 25, 26; 39:17, 17, 18, 18; 40:14, 16, 16; 43:2; 44:16; 45:3, 4, 5, 5; 46:11, 11, 19, 27, 28; 47:5, 6, 6; 48:2, 7, 7, 18, 27, 27; 49:4, 12, 12, 12, 16, 16; 50:24, 24, 24, 24, 31; 51:13, 20, 26, 61, 62, 62, 63, 63, 64

La 1:10, 11, 21, 21, 22; 2:20, 21, 21, 22; 3:17, 42, 43, 43, 43, 44, 45, 56, 57, 57, 58, 58, 59, 59, 60, 61; 4:21; 5:19, 20, 21, 22, 22

Eze 2:4, 6, 6, 7, 8, 8; 3:1, 5, 6, 18, 18, 19, 19, 20, 21, 21, 25, 25, 26, 27; 4:1, 3, 3, 4, 4, 5, 6, 6, 7, 7, 8, 8, 9, 9, 9, 10, 10, 11, 11, 12, 12, 15, 5:1, 2, 2, 2, 3, 11; 7:2, 7; 8:6, 6, 12, 13, 15, 15, 17; 9:8, 11; 11:13; 12:2, 3, 3, 4, 4, 5, 6, 6, 6, 9, 9, 10; 13:2, 17, 17; 16:4, 4, 4, 5, 5, 6, 6, 7, 7, 7, 8, 13, 13, 13, 13, 15, 16, 17, 18, 19, 20, 20, 20, 21, 22, 22, 24, 25, 26, 28, 28, 29, 29, 30, 31, 31, 33, 34, 34, 36, 37, 37, 37, 41, 43, 43, 45, 45, 47, 47, 48, 48, 51, 52, 52, 52, 52, 52, 52, 54, 54, 54, 55, 58, 59, 61, 61, 62, 63, 63; 17:9; 19:1; 20:4, 4; 21:6, 7, 7, 14, 19, 19, 25, 28, 28, 30, 32, 32; 22:2, 2, 2, 2, 3, 4, 4, 4, 4, 8, 12, 12, 13, 16, 16, 24; 23:21, 27, 28, 30, 30, 31, 32, 32, 33, 34, 34, 35, 35, 36, 40, 41; 24:13, 13, 16, 19, 19, 25, 27, 27; 25:3, 6, 7; 26:14, 14, 17, 20, 21, 21; 27:2, 3, 7, 25, 33, 33, 34, 36; 28:2, 2, 2, 3, 4, 5, 6, 8, 9, 9, 10, 12, 13, 13, 14, 14, 14, 15, 15, 16, 17, 18, 19, 19; 29:5, 5, 7, 7; 31:2, 10, 18, 18, 18; 32:2, 2, 2, 6, 9, 19, 19, 28; 33:7, 7, 8, 8, 9, 9, 10, 12, 14, 27, 30, 32; 35:4, 4, 5, 6, 10, 11, 12, 15, 16, 16, 17; 37:3, 16, 18, 18, 20; 38:7, 7, 7, 8, 8, 9, 9, 10, 11, 13, 13, 14, 15, 16, 17; 39:1, 4, 4, 5, 17; 40:4, 4; 43:10, 19, 20, 20, 21, 22, 23, 24, 24; 44:6; 45:3, 18, 20; 46:13, 13, 14; 47:6

Da 1:13; 2:23, 23, 26, 30, 31, 34, 37, 38, 41, 41, 43, 45, 47; 3:10, 12, 12, 18; 4:18, 18, 20, 22, 25, 26, 32, 35; 5:13, 16, 16, 16, 18, 22, 22, 23, 23, 23, 27; 6:12, 13, 16, 20; 8:20, 26; 9:7, 23; 10:12, 19, 20; 12:4, 13, 13

Hos 2:16, 20, 23, 23; 3:3, 3, 3; 4:5, 6, 6, 6, 15; 5:3; 9:1, 1, 14; 10:9, 13; 12:6; 13:4, 9; 14:1

Am 5:23; 7:8, 12, 16, 16, 17; 8:2

Ob 1:2, 3, 4, 4, 5, 10, 11, 11, 12, 12, 13, 13, 14, 14, 15

Jnh 1:6, 8, 8, 10, 14; 2:2, 3, 6; 4:2, 4, 9, 10, 10

Mic 1:11, 13, 14; 2:5, 7; 4:8, 9, 10, 10, 10, 13; 5:2, 2, 12, 13; 6:1, 14, 14, 14, 14, 15, 15, 15; 7:19, 20, 20

Na 1:14; 3:8, 11, 11, 11, 16

Hab 1:2, 2, 3, 12, 12, 12, 13, 13; 2:7, 8, 10, 15, 16, 16; 3:8, 9, 12, 12, 13, 13, 14, 14, 15

Zep 3:7, 7, 11, 11, 11, 15, 16

Zec 1:3, 12, 12, 14; 2:2, 11; 3:7, 7, 7, 8; 4:2, 11, 13, 13, 15; 5:2; 6:10; 13:3, 3

Mal 1:2; 2:14

Mt 1:20, 21; 2:6, 13; 3:14; 4:3, 6, 6, 7, 9, 10, 10; 5:21, 22, 23, 25, 25, 26, 26, 27, 33, 36, 36, 42, 43; 6:2, 3, 3, 5, 6, 6, 6, 17, 17, 18; 7:3, 4, 5, 5; 8:2, 2, 3, 4, 8, 13, 19, 29, 29, 31; 9:27; 11:3, 23, 25; 12:37, 37; 13:10, 27, 28; 14:28, 31, 31, 33; 15:5, 12, 22, 28; 16:14, 16, 17, 18, 19, 19, 23; 17:4, 25, 27, 27, 27; 18:15, 28, 32, 33; 19:17, 17, 18, 18, 18, 19, 21, 21; 20:12, 13, 21, 30, 31; 21:16, 16, 21; 22:12, 16, 16, 16, 16, 17, 37, 39, 44; 23:26, 37; 25:20, 21, 21, 22, 23, 23, 24, 24, 24, 25, 26, 26, 27; 26:17, 25, 34,

39, 50, 53, 62, 63, 63, 64, 68, 69, 70, 73, 75; 27:4, 11, 11, 13, 19, 40, 40, 46

Mk 1:11, 24, 24, 24, 40, 40, 41, 44; 3:11; 4:38; 5:7, 7, 8, 31, 31, 35; 6:22, 23, 25; 7:11; 8:29, 33; 9:22, 23, 24, 25; 10:18, 19, 21, 21, 21, 35, 47, 48, 51; 11:21, 23, 23, 28; 12:14, 14, 30, 31, 32, 34, 36; 13:2; 14:12, 12, 30, 36, 37, 37, 60, 61, 67, 68, 70, 70, 72; 15:2, 2, 4, 29, 34

Lk 1:4, 6, 13, 14, 20, 20, 28, 28, 30, 31, 42, 76, 76; 2:29, 31, 48; 3:22; 4:3, 7, 8, 8, 9, 11, 12, 34, 34, 34, 41; 5:10, 12, 12, 13; 6:41, 42, 42, 42, 42; 7:6, 19, 20, 43, 44, 44, 45, 46; 8:28, 45; 9:54, 57, 60; 10:15, 21, 26, 27, 28, 36, 37, 40, 41; 11:27, 45; 12:19, 20, 20, 41, 58, 58, 58, 59, 59; 13:9, 12, 15, 26; 14:8, 8, 9, 10, 10, 12, 13, 14, 14, 22; 15:29, 30, 31; 16:2, 5, 7, 25, 25, 27; 17:4, 6, 6, 8; 18:19, 20, 22, 22, 22, 38, 39, 41; 19:17, 17, 17, 22, 24, 24, 24, 25, 26; 22:26, 28, 29, 29, 29, 30; 23:6, 10, 11, 11, 11, 12, 12, 13, 16, 16, 17, 19, 19, 25, 25, 26, 26, 31, 33; 28:1, 2, 4, 41; 29:12, 26; 32:4, 7, 8, 11, 11, 12, 12, 13, 32; 33:1, 5, 13, 13, 13, 13, 15, 16, 16, 16, 18; 34:9, 10, 16, 16, 19, 20, 24, 24, 24, 26, 26

Lev 2:5, 7, 13, 13, 13, 14, 14; 5:15, 18; 6:6; 9:7, 7; 10:9, 13, 13, 14, 14, 14, 15; 16:2; 18:7, 7, 7, 8, 8, 9, 9, 10, 10, 11, 11, 11, 12, 12, 13, 13, 14, 14, 15, 15, 16, 16, 20, 21, 21; 19:9, 9, 10, 10, 12, 13, 14, 15, 16, 16, 17, 17, 18, 18, 19, 19, 27, 29, 32; 20:19, 19; 21:8, 17; 23:22, 22; 25:3, 3, 4, 4, 5, 5, 6, 6, 6, 7, 7, 11, 14, 14, 15, 17, 25, 35, 36, 36, 37, 37, 39, 43, 44, 44, 47, 53; 27:2, 3, 3, 4, 5, 6, 6, 7, 8, 13, 15, 16, 17, 18, 19, 23, 25, 27

Nu 5:19, 20, 21, 21, 21, 22, 22, 22; 11:11, 11, 12, 15; 14:13, 14, 19, 20; 16:10, 11, 11, 11, 19, 19, 19, 20; 20:8, 14, 16, 17, 17, 19; 21:22, 22, 34; 22:32; 23:3, 15; 24:5, 5, 11, 12, 14, 21, 21, 27:13, 13; 31:2, 49; 32:4, 5, 5, 25, 27, 31

Dt 1:21, 21, 31; 2:7, 7, 7, 7, 24, 27, 30, 30; 3:2, 24, 24, 24, 24, 24; 4:3, 9, 9, 9, 9, 9, 10, 19, 21, 23, 24, 25, 29, 29, 29, 30, 31, 31, 37, 40, 40, 40; 5:6, 9, 11, 12, 13, 14, 14, 14, 14, 14, 14, 14, 14, 15, 15, 16, 16, 16, 16, 16, 20, 21, 21, 21, 21; 6:2, 2, 2, 2, 3, 5, 5, 5, 7, 9, 9, 10, 10, 12, 13, 13, 13, 13, 13, 13, 16, 18, 19, 19, 20, 21, 22, 23, 25; 8:2, 3, 4, 4, 5, 5, 6, 7, 10, 11, 13, 13, 13, 13, 14, 16, 16, 18, 19; 9:3, 13, 14, 5, 5, 5, 6, 6, 7, 12, 26, 26, 27, 29, 29, 29; 10:9, 11, 12, 12, 12, 12, 12, 12, 14, 15, 20, 20, 29; 11:1, 10, 10, 12, 12, 14, 14, 15, 15, 20, 29; 12:1, 7, 13, 14, 14, 15, 15, 15, 17, 17, 17, 17, 17, 17, 17, 18, 18, 18, 18, 18, 18, 18, 18, 20, 20, 20, 20, 21, 21, 21, 21, 21, 25, 26, 26, 27, 27, 27, 27, 28, 28, 29, 31; 13:5, 6, 6, 6, 6, 6, 6, 6, 10, 12, 12, 16, 17, 18, 18; 14:2, 21, 22, 23, 23, 23, 23, 23, 24, 24, 25, 26, 26, 26, 27, 28, 29, 29; 15:3, 4, 7, 7, 7, 7, 7, 7, 9, 9, 10, 10, 11, 11, 11, 11, 11, 11, 12, 14, 14, 14, 14, 17, 17, 18, 19, 19, 19, 19, 19, 20, 20, 21; 16:1, 1, 2, 3, 4, 5, 5, 6, 7, 7, 8, 10, 10, 11, 11, 11, 11, 11, 11, 11, 13, 13, 14, 14, 14, 14, 15, 15, 16, 16, 17, 18, 18, 20, 21, 21, 21; 17:1, 1, 2, 2, 8, 8, 10, 11, 13, 23, 23; 22:1, 1, 1, 2, 2, 3, 4, 5, 7, 8, 9, 9, 9, 12, 17; 23:5, 5, 6, 5, 6, 7, 13, 14, 14, 14, 16, 18, 18, 19, 20, 21, 21, 23, 23, 24, 24; 24:4, 9, 10, 13, 14, 14, 14, 14, 18, 19, 19, 19, 21; 25:3, 13, 15, 15, 16, 19, 19; 26:1, 2, 2, 3, 5, 10, 28:1, 1, 2, 4, 4, 4, 4, 5, 5, 7, 7, 7, 8, 8, 9, 11, 11, 12, 13, 15, 17, 17, 18, 18, 20, 21, 23, 23; 27:2, 3, 3, 5, 6, 6, 7, 13, 14, 14, 16, 17; 29:4, 5, 5, 6, 6, 10, 11, 11, 12, 13, 13, 15, 17, 17, 18, 18, 19, 19, 19, 19, 20, 20, 20; 31:3, 6, 11, 12, 12, 14, 16, 27, 27; 32:6, 7, 7, 50, 50; 33:3, 3, 8, 8, 8, 9, 10, 10, 18, 18, 25, 25, 25, 26, 27, 29, 29; 34:4;

Jos 1:5, 8, 8, 9, 17, 18, 18; 2:18, 18, 18, 18, 19; 5:15, 15; 7:9, 10, 10; 8:1, 18; 9:8, 9, 9, 24, 24; 10:6, 6; 14:9; 24:12, 12

Jdg 1:3; 5:12, 14; 6:14, 17, 25, 25, 26, 30; 7:10; 8:15, 22, 22; 9:38, 54; 11:10, 17, 24, 30, 36; 13:12, 16, 17, 17; 14:3, 13, 15, 15; 15:2, 18; 16:6, 15; 17:10; 18:19, 19, 25; 25, 25; 19:19, 19, 20

Ru 1:10, 15, 15, 16, 16; 2:11, 11, 11, 11, 12, 13, 13, 14; 3:3, 9, 12, 17; 4:12, 15, 15

1Sa 1:8, 14, 17, 18, 26; 2:1, 16, 27, 28, 29, 30, 30, 31, 34; 3:9, 10; 4:17; 8:5, 5; 9:20, 20; 10:2; 12:19, 19; 13:13, 13, 14; 14:7, 28; 15:15, 21, 24, 30, 33, 33, 33; 16:11, 16, 17, 17, 17, 17, 18, 22, 32, 34, 36, 44, 45, 58; 19:11; 20:1, 3, 3, 4, 6, 7, 8, 8, 8, 10, 15, 18, 20, 30, 30, 31, 42; 22:14, 14, 15, 16, 22, 23; 23:10, 11, 11, 20; 24:9, 11, 11, 16; 25:7, 8, 8, 8, 26, 28, 29, 29, 33, 35, 35; 26:15, 15, 17, 24, 27:5; 28:1, 2, 17, 19, 21, 21, 22; 29:6, 6, 6, 8, 10; 31:4

2Sa 1:16, 25, 25, 34, 34; 4:8; 5:1, 1; 6:21; 7:9, 12, 12, 12, 12, 16, 16, 19, 19, 20, 21, 21, 23, 23, 23, 24, 24, 25, 26, 26, 27, 27, 28, 28, 29, 29, 29; 9:2, 6, 7, 7, 8, 9, 10, 10, 10, 10, 10; 10:3; 11:8, 8, 10, 11, 11, 21, 24, 24, 25; 12:8, 8, 8, 9, 10, 11, 11, 11, 13, 13:5, 5, 7, 20, 20, 20, 24, 24, 35; 14:6, 11, 11, 15, 17, 19, 19, 20, 22, 22, 31; 15:2, 3, 8,

THY (4607)

Ge 3:10, 14, 14, 15, 15, 16, 16, 16, 17, 17, 17, 19; 4:6, 9, 10, 11, 11, 14; 6:18, 18, 18; 7:1; 8:16, 16, 16; 12:1, 1, 1, 2, 7, 13, 18, 19, 19; 13:8, 15, 16, 14:20; 15:1, 1, 5, 13, 15, 18; 16:5, 6, 6, 9, 10, 11; 17:5, 5, 7, 7, 8, 9, 10, 12, 13, 13, 15, 19; 18:3, 3, 9, 10; 19:12, 12, 15, 15, 17, 19, 19, 19; 20:6, 13, 16; 21:12, 12, 12, 13; 22:2, 12, 16, 17, 17, 18, 20; 23:6, 6, 11, 15; 24:2, 5, 7, 7, 14, 14, 14, 19, 23, 40, 43, 44, 46, 51, 60; 25:23, 23, 31; 26:3, 3, 4, 4, 4, 9, 10, 24, 24, 27:3, 3, 3, 3, 6, 6, 9, 10, 13, 19, 19, 20, 29, 29, 31, 32, 32, 35, 35, 37, 39, 40, 40, 40, 42, 44, 45; 28:2, 2, 4, 13, 13, 14, 14, 29:15, 18; 30:14, 15, 27, 28, 29, 31, 32, 33, 34; 31:3, 3, 8, 8, 13, 30, 31, 32, 37, 37, 38, 38, 38, 41, 41, 41; 32:4, 5, 6, 9, 9, 10, 12, 18, 20, 27, 28, 29; 33:5, 10, 10; 35:1, 10, 10, 10, 11, 12, 37:10, 10, 13, 14, 32; 38:8, 8, 11, 13, 18, 18, 18, 24; 39:19; 40:13, 19, 19; 41:40; 42:10, 11, 13; 43:28; 44:7, 8, 9, 16, 18, 18, 21, 23, 24, 27, 30, 31, 31, 32, 33; 45:9, 10, 10, 10, 11, 17; 46:3, 30, 34; 47:3, 4, 4, 5, 5, 6, 15, 29, 29; 48:1, 2, 4, 5, 6, 10, 11, 16, 18, 22; 49:4, 8, 8, 8, 18, 25, 26; 50:6, 16, 17, 17, 18

Ex 2:9, 13; 3:5, 5, 6, 18; 4:6, 7, 9, 10, 12, 15, 16, 19, 23, 23; 5:15, 16, 16, 23; 7:1, 1, 2, 9, 19; 8:2, 3, 3, 3, 3, 4, 4, 5, 9, 9, 9, 10, 11, 11, 16, 21, 21,

15, 17, 19, 19, 20, 22, 22, 31; 15:2, 3, 8,

22:2, 5, 5, 11, 13, 13, 14, 16, 16, 18, 20, 23, 26, 26, 26, 30, 32, 36, 37, 37, 37, 38, 40, 40, 41; 23:3, 3, 11, 12, 14, 17, 20, 23; 24:1, 1, 2, 10, 11, 11, 12, 13, 14, 25; 25:1, 2; 26:1, 2, 2, 18, 22, 25, 27, 37, 43, 47, 50, 53, 54, 54, 54, 54, 54, 55, 56, 59; 27:7, 8, 11, 14; 28:2, 7, 22, 30; 29:5, 9, 9, 14, 15, 18, 21, 24, 27, 30, 33, 37, 40; 30:2, 2, 13, 14; 31:4, 6, 6, 6, 13, 16, 21, 27, 28, 36, 50, 52; 32:2, 6, 6, 8, 14, 19, 20, 27, 29, 33, 33, 39; 33:2, 2, 14, 53, 54, 54, 54, 55, 56, 56; 34:4, 4, 4, 4, 8, 9, 10, 11, 12, 13, 13, 14, 14, 18, 29; 35:2, 3, 5, 6, 7, 8, 11, 16, 17, 18, 21, 24, 25, 30, 30, 30, 31, 32, 32; 36:2, 2, 2, 3, 3, 5, 6, 6, 7, 7, 9, 9

Dt 1:3, 5, 7, 7, 8, 8, 9, 14, 19, 27, 27, 28, 30, 33, 33, 33, 35, 36, 36, 38, 41, 41, 45; 2:4, 15, 16, 18, 22, 24, 25, 27, 31, 31, 32, 34; 3:1, 1, 3, 7, 12, 18, 24, 24, 24, 28; 4:1, 5, 9, 10, 13, 14, 14, 19, 20, 25, 25, 26, 26, 30, 34, 34, 36, 38, 38, 38; 5:4, 5, 12, 15, 23, 30, 31, 32, 32, 32; 6:1, 1, 2, 3, 10, 10, 10, 10, 19, 20, 23, 24, 24, 25; 7:1, 6, 9, 10, 10, 10, 10, 11, 12, 12, 13, 24, 25; 8:1, 2, 2, 2, 3, 6, 6, 6, 18; 9:1, 1, 1, 1, 4, 5, 6, 7, 8, 8, 9, 10, 11, 18, 18, 19, 20, 22, 23, 27, 27, 28, 28; 10:4, 6, 7, 8, 8, 8, 10, 11, 11, 12, 12, 12, 13, 15, 20; 11:4, 4, 8, 9, 9, 10, 11, 13, 16, 22, 22, 22, 22, 25, 28, 29, 29, 31, 31, 32; 12:1, 1, 5, 9, 9, 10, 11, 11, 13, 15, 19, 20, 21, 29, 30, 31, 31, 32; 13:2, 3, 5, 5, 5, 9, 9, 10, 12, 17, 18, 18, 18; 14:2, 23, 23, 24, 24; 15:4, 5, 5, 11, 11, 15, 18; 16:2, 6, 8, 9, 9, 9, 11, 17; 17:6, 6, 6, 7, 10, 10, 10, 11, 11, 11, 11, 12, 16, 16, 16, 16, 17, 17, 19, 19, 19, 20, 20, 20, 20; 18:5, 5, 8, 9, 10, 14, 16, 19, 20, 20, 22; 19:2, 3, 5, 5, 8, 9, 9, 9, 14, 16, 19; 20:1, 4, 4, 5, 9, 10, 18, 19, 19; 21:1, 5, 5, 10, 11, 12, 16, 22, 22; 22:2, 4, 6, 7, 14, 16, 21, 21, 22, 27; 23:2, 3, 4, 14, 14, 19, 20, 20, 20, 21, 22; 24:1, 3, 4, 4, 4, 6, 8, 8, 10, 11, 16, 16, 16, 16, 17, 18, 19, 22; 25:2, 2, 2, 2, 5, 5, 7, 7, 7, 8, 8, 11, 19; 26:2, 3, 5, 13, 13, 14, 14, 16, 17, 17, 17, 17, 18, 19; 27:12, 13, 18, 25, 26; 28:1, 1, 1, 7, 11, 12, 12, 13, 13, 14, 14, 14, 14, 15, 15, 20, 21, 25, 31, 31, 44, 44, 45, 50, 55, 56, 58, 63, 63, 63, 63, 63, 63; 29:1, 4, 4, 4, 8, 8, 13, 13, 13, 13, 18, 19, 19, 19, 21, 22, 27, 29; 30:1, 1, 2, 6, 10, 12, 16, 16, 16, 16, 18, 18, 19, 20, 20, 20, 20; 31:4, 4, 7, 7, 11, 12, 13, 13, 16, 21, 24, 28, 29, 29; 32:8, 8, 13, 16, 16, 17, 17, 17, 21, 21, 21, 21, 26, 30, 35, 40, 41, 43, 43, 45, 46, 46, 47; 33:7, 9, 17, 24; 34:1, 4, 5, 10, 11, 11, 11, 11

Jos 1:1, 2, 2, 5, 6, 7, 7, 7, 7, 8, 8, 11, 11, 11, 12, 12, 18; 2:1, 2, 2, 3, 3, 5, 6, 7, 16, 20, 23; 3:1, 2, 5, 7, 8, 13, 14, 14; 4:1, 6, 8, 10, 10, 11, 13, 18, 21, 23; 5:1, 6, 8, 13, 14; 6:5, 8, 15, 16, 17, 20, 25; 7:2, 3, 3, 6, 7, 7, 7, 13, 14, 14, 19; 8:1, 2, 3, 5, 8, 9, 10, 12, 14, 14, 16, 20, 20, 20, 23, 24, 34; 9:1, 2, 3, 6, 6, 10, 10, 10, 11, 11, 12, 15, 16, 20, 24, 24, 25; 10:1, 1, 1, 6, 6, 6, 10, 10, 11, 11, 12, 12, 13, 15, 18, 19, 20, 20, 21, 24, 25, 27, 28, 32, 32, 33, 35, 35, 37, 37, 38, 39, 39, 39, 39, 43; 11:1, 1, 1, 1, 2, 3, 3, 3, 5, 6, 11, 14, 17, 20, 23, 23; 12:3, 3, 7, 7; 13:1, 3, 4, 15, 24, 31; 14:1, 4, 7, 11, 11, 12; 15:1, 3, 3, 3, 3, 3, 6, 6, 6, 7, 8, 9, 9, 10, 10, 11, 11, 12, 12, 13, 13, 15, 16, 16, 17, 18, 18, 20; 16:1, 2, 2, 3, 3, 5, 6, 6, 6, 7, 7, 7; 17:1, 4, 4, 5, 7, 8, 13, 14, 15, 17, 17; 18:3, 3, 4, 4, 6, 8, 8, 9, 9, 10, 11, 12, 13, 13, 15, 16, 16, 16, 17, 17, 19, 20, 21, 28; 19:1, 1, 8, 8, 10, 11, 11, 12, 13, 13, 13, 15, 16, 16, 17, 17, 22, 23, 24, 26, 26, 27, 27, 27, 27, 29, 29, 29, 31, 32, 33, 34, 34, 34, 34, 39, 40, 47, 48, 49, 50; 20:2; 21:2, 2, 12, 13, 13, 21, 27, 32, 33, 38, 43, 44, 45; 22:5, 5, 5, 5, 5, 5, 9, 9, 10, 10, 12, 13, 13, 15, 15, 16, 18, 23, 23, 23, 24, 24, 26, 27, 27, 28, 28, 28, 29, 31, 31, 32, 33, 33; 23:1, 4, 6, 6, 6, 6, 7, 9, 12, 14, 15, 16; 24:1, 4, 9, 15, 16, 22, 29, 33

Jdg 1:1, 1, 7, 9, 12, 12, 13, 14, 14, 14, 23, 28, 28, 34, 34, 36; 2:1, 1, 4, 6, 12, 19, 19, 19, 22; 3:1, 2, 4, 4, 4, 6, 6, 9, 10, 18, 27, 28; 4:5, 7, 9, 10, 12, 17, 18, 18, 19, 24, 24; 5:3, 11, 16, 23, 23, 26, 26, 29, 30, 30; 6:5, 7, 11, 22, 25, 29, 31, 35; 7:2, 3, 5, 6, 6, 7, 10, 10, 11, 17, 20, 20, 22, 22, 25; 8:1, 3, 4, 8, 27, 33, 35, 35; 9:1, 3, 7, 8, 9, 10, 11, 13, 16, 21, 24, 24, 27, 28, 29, 29, 31, 31, 31, 36, 42, 48, 49, 50, 51, 51, 52, 53; 10:1, 9, 12, 18, 18; 11:3, 4, 6, 8, 9, 10, 12, 12, 16, 20, 24, 27, 31, 32, 33, 34, 34, 35, 36, 36, 39, 39, 40; 12:1, 1, 3, 6; 13:5, 7, 9, 11, 12, 17, 20, 20, 21, 21, 23, 25; 14:1, 2, 3, 3, 5, 5, 8, 8, 9, 10, 11, 15, 17, 17, 19, 19, 20; 15:1, 1, 1, 2, 4, 6, 10, 10, 10, 10, 11, 11, 12, 17; 16:1, 3, 4, 5, 6, 6, 6, 8, 10, 19, 19, 21, 22, 23, 23, 25; 17:3, 3, 4, 8, 8, 8, 9, 11, 13; 18:1, 2, 2, 2, 2, 7, 7, 8, 9, 9, 10, 14, 14, 15, 17, 19, 19, 19, 22, 23, 23, 25; 17:3, 3, 4, 8, 8, 9, 10, 14, 14, 15, 17, 19, 22, 22, 22; 21:2, 2, 9, 10, 16, 18, 21; 20:1, 3, 4, 4, 5, 8, 9, 10, 10, 10, 13, 13, 14, 14, 18, 18, 20, 20, 21, 23, 25, 28, 28, 31, 31, 31, 36, 39, 40, 40, 40, 47, 48, 48; 21:1, 1, 3, 3, 4, 5, 5, 5, 5, 7, 8, 8, 8, 8, 12,

13, 13, 13, 18, 19, 21, 21, 22, 22, 23, 24, 24, 24

Ru 1:1, 1, 7, 8, 12, 12, 16, 16, 17, 18, 19, 19, 19, 22; 2:2, 3, 8, 10, 12, 15, 18, 19, 19, 20, 20, 23; 3:2, 3, 6, 6, 7, 8, 11, 13, 13, 16, 16, 17; 4:1, 4, 4, 5, 6, 7, 7, 10, 10, 15, 17

1Sa 1:3, 3, 4, 4, 6, 7, 8, 8, 12, 19, 19, 20, 21, 25, 28, 28; 2:6, 8, 8, 10, 11, 11, 15, 15, 16, 19, 19, 19, 20, 24, 28, 28, 28, 28, 29, 33, 33, 35, 36, 36; 3:2, 2, 3, 6, 8, 11, 15, 17, 19, 20, 20, 21; 4:1, 1, 3, 4, 9, 12, 16, 18, 19; 5:3, 4, 4, 10, 10, 10, 10, 10, 19, 12; 6:2, 2, 3, 4, 4, 7, 9, 9, 10, 12, 12, 12, 13, 16, 18, 18, 20, 20, 20; 7:1, 2, 5, 6, 7, 8, 8, 10, 14, 16, 16, 16, 17; 8:1, 4, 5, 6, 8, 11, 12, 12, 12, 13, 13, 14, 14, 14, 17, 20, 21, 26, 26, 27, 27; 10:1, 2, 2, 3, 3, 3, 5, 5, 5, 5, 7, 7, 8, 8, 8, 9, 10, 11, 11, 11, 12, 13, 14, 14, 14, 17, 20, 21, 24, 25; 15:4, 4, 17, 17, 18, 21, 25, 26, 27, 27, 29, 29, 30, 33, 34; 16:1, 2, 2, 7, 8, 11, 11, 12, 13, 13, 15, 16, 21, 22, 22; 17:1, 4, 7, 9, 9, 9, 10, 10, 11, 11, 15, 16, 17, 18, 18, 18, 24; 18:1, 2, 6, 6, 8, 8, 9, 10, 11, 11, 12, 12, 13, 16, 16, 17, 19, 27, 29, 29, 31, 31, 33, 36, 37, 38, 40, 42, 42, 42, 43, 44, 45, 45, 45, 46; 19:2, 2, 3, 9, 10, 14, 15, 15, 16, 16, 17, 18, 19, 20; 20:2, 4, 6, 9, 10, 11, 12, 12, 13, 25, 25, 26, 28, 28, 30, 31, 32, 33, 33, 35, 37, 41, 42, 48, 48, 51, 52, 53

2Ki 1:3, 3, 3, 6, 6, 7, 9, 10, 16, 16, 17; 2:1, 2, 2, 3, 3, 4, 4, 5, 5, 6, 7, 9, 11, 15, 15, 15, 18, 20, 22, 25, 25; 3:1, 3, 5, 7, 7, 10, 12, 13, 13, 13, 15, 20, 21, 21, 23, 23, 24, 26, 27; 4:1, 1, 5, 6, 8, 8, 9, 10, 12, 13, 23, 13, 14, 14, 16, 17, 18, 18, 19, 10, 19, 20, 22, 23, 24, 26, 27, 27, 27, 29, 31, 35, 37, 38, 39, 40, 40, 44; 5:5, 6, 6, 7, 7, 7, 7, 8, 8, 10, 11, 13, 14, 15, 16, 17, 18, 18, 21, 22, 24, 26, 26, 26; 6:4, 7, 10, 18, 18, 19, 19, 20, 22, 23, 24, 28, 28, 30, 31, 32, 32; 7:1, 3, 5, 5, 6, 6, 6, 8, 9, 10, 11, 12, 12, 16, 16, 17, 18, 18, 20; 8:1, 3, 3, 5, 5, 5, 5, 5, 7, 9, 14, 14, 14, 15, 16, 17, 19, 19, 19, 21, 25, 26, 28, 29, 29; 9:1, 2, 4, 5, 5, 5, 7, 9, 14, 14, 15, 16, 17, 18, 18, 18, 19, 19, 22, 23, 25, 26, 27, 27, 28, 29, 30, 32, 33, 34, 37; 16:1, 2, 3, 3, 5, 5, 6, 7, 8, 9, 10, 10, 11, 12, 15, 16, 17, 18, 18; 11:4, 9, 9, 9, 10, 11, 13, 19, 21; 12:1, 4, 4, 5, 8, 8, 10, 11, 12, 12, 12, 12, 14, 15, 17, 17, 18, 20; 13:1, 2, 7, 10, 16, 21; 14:2, 3, 5, 6, 6, 6, 8, 9, 9, 9, 9, 9, 10, 11, 12, 13, 14, 19; 15:1, 2, 3, 9, 12, 13, 14, 16, 17, 18, 19, 20, 20, 23, 24, 27, 28, 32, 33, 34, 37; 16:1, 2, 3, 3, 5, 5, 6, 6, 7, 8, 9, 10, 10, 11, 12, 15, 17; 17:1, 4, 4, 5, 9, 11, 11, 13, 13, 14, 17, 17, 23, 26, 31, 35, 35, 36, 37; 18:1, 1, 2, 3, 4, 6, 8, 9, 14, 14, 16, 17, 17, 18, 18, 19, 22, 22, 23, 25, 26, 26, 27, 27, 27, 29, 31, 31, 32, 37; 19:1, 2, 3, 3, 4, 5, 6, 7, 7, 9, 10, 10, 16, 20, 23, 25, 25, 34, 35, 37; 20:1, 2, 4, 4, 10; 21:1, 6, 6, 6, 7, 7, 8, 8, 8, 9, 11, 14, 15, 16, 16; 22:1, 2, 2, 3, 3, 4, 4, 5, 5, 6, 8, 9, 11, 13, 15, 16, 16, 19, 19, 19, 19, 19, 20, 20, 20, 23, 25, 25, 25, 27, 30, 31, 32, 33, 33, 34, 37; 24:2, 2, 3, 3, 7, 8, 9, 12, 15, 15, 16, 17, 18, 19, 20; 25:1, 4, 6, 6, 7, 11, 12, 13, 20, 20, 23, 23, 24, 24, 24, 25, 26, 27, 27, 28

1Ch 1:10, 2:21, 23, 35, 35; 4:27, 39, 39, 42; 5:1, 18, 18, 18, 20, 26; 6:19, 32, 49, 49, 56, 57, 62, 64; 7:2, 11, 15, 21, 23, 40; 8:6; 9:1, 9, 22, 25, 25, 27, 29, 32; 10:4, 8, 8, 9, 11, 12, 13; 11:1, 3, 3, 4, 5, 10, 10, 13, 15, 15, 18, 18, 19, 21; 12:1, 1, 8, 15, 16, 17, 17, 17, 18, 19, 19, 19, 19, 20, 20, 22, 22, 23, 23, 23, 23, 23, 24, 31, 32, 32, 33, 36, 38, 38, 38; 13:2, 3, 5, 6, 6, 6, 6, 9, 10, 11, 12, 13, 13; 14:1, 1, 8, 11, 15, 15, 16; 15:2, 2, 2, 3, 3, 14, 15, 16, 16, 19, 21, 25, 26, 29, 29; 16:3, 4, 4, 4, 5, 7, 15, 17, 17, 20, 20, 21, 23, 25, 25, 33, 35, 37, 38, 40, 40, 41, 41, 43, 43; 17:1, 1, 3, 3, 4, 5, 7, 10, 11, 15, 16, 17, 19, 20, 22, 22; 18:1, 3, 5, 5, 11, 11, 11, 12, 12, 13; 19:2, 2, 4, 4, 6, 9, 11, 11, 12, 12, 14, 14, 14, 17, 17, 18, 18; 9:1, 1, 5, 8, 14, 14, 14, 17, 18, 9:1, 1, 5, 8

2Ch 1:2, 2, 2, 3, 4, 6, 8, 11, 13, 13; 2:1, 2, 2, 3, 3, 3, 4, 4, 4, 4, 6, 6, 7, 7, 8, 9, 9, 10, 11, 12, 14, 14, 14, 14, 16, 16, 16, 18, 18, 18; 3:1, 2, 4, 8, 8, 11, 11, 12, 12; 4:2, 6, 6, 7, 11, 12, 12, 13, 16; 5:2, 7, 11, 13, 13, 14; 6:1, 1, 3, 4, 11, 13, 13, 18, 23, 24, 25, 28, 34; 5:2, 5, 6, 6, 7, 8, 8, 9, 10, 11, 11, 14, 17, 18; 6:1, 1, 3, 4, 11, 13, 16, 16, 17, 18, 25, 25, 28, 28, 28, 28, 30; 31, 31, 32, 32, 32, 33, 36, 39, 39, 43, 43, 43, 44, 46, 52, 53, 54, 56, 58, 58, 61, 61, 64; 9:1, 1, 2, 3, 4, 5, 8, 10, 11, 12, 14,

15, 19, 21, 28, 28; 10:1, 2, 2, 6, 9, 9, 10, 13, 14, 16, 17, 24, 24, 27, 27; 11:2, 4, 11, 13, 15, 15, 17, 18, 24, 24, 27, 27; 12:1, 1, 1, 2, 5, 7, 9, 11, 12, 14, 14, 16, 16, 18, 18, 18; 11:1, 1, 1, 2, 3, 4, 13, 14, 16, 16, 16, 18, 18, 18, 18, 19, 21, 21, 21, 23, 23, 24, 24, 24, 26, 27, 27, 27, 28, 30; 13:1, 4, 4, 5, 10, 10, 17, 17, 17, 20, 22, 23, 23, 26, 27, 29, 29, 29, 31, 34, 34; 14:2, 2, 3, 4, 3, 4, 4, 4, 6, 8, 9, 9, 9, 9, 9, 9; 15:4, 4, 17, 17, 18, 21, 25, 25, 26, 27, 27, 29, 29, 30, 33, 34; 15:4, 4, 17, 17, 21, 25, 26, 27, 27, 29, 29, 31, 36, 40, 42, 42, 42, 43, 43, 43, 45, 45, 45, 46; 19:2, 2, 3, 9, 9, 10, 14, 15, 15, 16, 17, 20; 20:2, 4, 6, 9, 11, 12, 12, 13, 25, 26, 28, 28, 28, 30, 31, 33, 33; 21:1, 6, 6, 7, 7, 8, 8, 8, 9, 11, 14, 15, 16, 16; 22:1, 2, 2, 3, 3, 4, 5, 5, 6, 8, 9, 11, 13, 15, 16, 16, 19, 19, 19, 19, 19, 20, 20, 23, 25, 25, 27, 30, 31, 32, 33, 33; 24:1, 1, 1, 1, 2, 3, 5, 5, 6, 6, 6, 7, 10, 10, 11, 11, 11, 12, 13; 25:1, 5, 5, 6, 7, 10, 11, 17, 17, 17, 17, 17, 18, 18, 20, 23, 26, 26, 27, 27; 31:1, 1, 2, 2, 2, 3, 4, 7, 10, 10, 11, 14, 15, 15, 15, 15, 16, 17, 18, 19, 19, 21; 32:1, 2, 3, 5, 6, 6, 8, 8, 9, 11, 11, 13, 14, 15, 17, 18, 18, 20, 21, 23, 23, 24, 25, 30, 31, 31, 31; 33:1, 6, 6, 6, 7, 7, 8, 9, 9, 9, 9, 10, 10, 11, 11, 12, 12, 13, 14, 19, 19, 19, 19, 21; 12:1, 4, 4, 5, 8, 8, 10, 11, 12, 12, 12, 14, 15, 17, 17, 18, 20; 13:1, 2, 7, 10, 16, 21; 14:2, 3, 5, 6, 6, 6, 8, 9, 9, 9, 9, 10, 11, 12, 13, 14, 17, 17, 18, 19; 9:1, 1, 5, 8,

8, 8, 8, 11, 11, 12, 12, 13, 14, 15, 16, 18, 18, 21, 23, 26; 10:1, 1, 1, 2, 3, 6, 6, 7, 7, 9, 9, 11, 12, 12, 13, 16, 16, 16, 18, 18, 18; 11:1, 1, 1, 1, 2, 3, 4, 13, 14, 16, 16, 16, 18, 18, 18, 18; 12:1, 1, 1, 2, 3, 4, 13, 14, 16, 16, 16, 18, 18, 18; 13:1, 1, 1, 1, 2, 3, 4, 4, 4, 5, 7, 10; 13:15; 14:4, 4, 11, 15; 15:2, 5, 5, 9, 12; 13:16:1, 1, 2, 5, 7, 9, 9, 12, 12; 17:4, 5, 7, 7, 7, 7, 7, 14, 15; 18:2, 2, 2, 2, 3, 4, 5, 5, 11, 12, 12, 13, 14, 15, 16, 17, 23, 24, 25, 25, 28, 29, 29, 31, 31, 32, 33; 19:1, 1, 2, 2, 3, 4, 6, 8, 10; 20:1, 1, 3, 4, 4, 7, 11, 11, 11, 12, 16, 17, 17, 18, 19, 21, 22, 22, 23, 23, 24, 24, 25, 27, 27, 27, 28, 29, 30, 36, 36, 37, 37; 21:3, 4, 5, 6, 7, 7, 7, 11, 12, 13, 13, 19; 20:22:1, 2, 3, 4, 5, 6, 6, 7, 7, 8, 8, 9, 23:2, 7, 7, 8, 8, 8, 9, 10, 12, 13, 15, 17, 18; 24:1, 4, 4, 5, 5, 5, 6, 6, 9, 10, 11, 12, 12, 13, 14, 17, 19, 19, 22, 23, 23; 25:1, 3, 3, 5, 5, 5, 7, 7, 8, 8, 9, 9, 10, 10, 11, 13, 14, 14, 16, 16, 17, 18, 18, 18, 19, 18, 19, 18, 18, 21, 22, 23, 24, 24, 27, 26:2, 3, 4, 9, 11, 15, 15, 15, 15, 16, 18, 18, 21, 22, 23, 24, 24, 25, 25; 29:1, 2, 8, 8, 20; 27:1, 2, 8; 28:1, 5, 7, 8, 9, 10, 13, 13, 15, 15, 15, 16, 16, 23, 25, 25; 29:1, 2, 8, 8, 20; 30:1, 1, 1, 1, 2, 3, 5, 5, 5, 6, 6, 7, 10, 10, 11, 12, 12, 13, 16, 17, 19, 19, 20, 23, 24, 24, 27; 31:1, 1, 2, 2, 2, 2, 3, 4, 7, 10, 10, 11, 14, 15, 15, 15, 15, 16, 17, 18, 19, 19, 21; 32:1, 2, 3, 5, 6, 6, 8, 8, 9, 11, 11, 13, 14, 15, 17, 18, 18, 20, 21, 23, 23, 24, 25; 30, 31, 31; 33:1, 6, 6, 6, 7, 7, 8, 9, 9, 9, 9, 10, 10, 11, 12, 12, 13, 14, 19, 19, 21; 34:1, 2, 2, 3, 7, 8, 9, 9, 10, 10, 11, 11, 11, 12, 15, 16, 16, 17, 19, 21, 22, 22, 23, 25, 26, 28, 28, 31, 31, 31, 32, 32, 33, 33; 35:2, 4, 4, 5, 6, 7, 7, 8, 8, 10, 12, 12, 23, 24, 25, 26; 36:2, 4, 4, 5, 6, 6, 7, 9, 10, 11, 15, 18, 20, 20, 21, 21, 23

Ezr 1:2, 3, 5, 5; 2:68, 68; 3:1, 2, 4, 6, 7, 7, 7, 17, 21, 21, 22, 22, 23, 23; 5:2, 3, 3, 3, 5, 5, 8, 9, 9, 10; 4:2, 2, 3, 3, 5, 8, 12, 14, 17, 17, 21, 21, 22, 22, 23, 23; 5:2, 3, 3, 3, 5, 9, 9, 10, 10, 11, 13, 13, 17, 17, 17; 6:5, 8, 9, 12, 12, 12, 13, 14, 14, 17, 21, 22; 7:6, 8, 9, 9, 9, 10, 10, 11, 13, 14, 14, 15, 18, 18, 18, 20, 21, 22, 22, 22, 24, 26, 26, 26, 27, 28; 8:15, 15, 17, 21, 22, 22, 30, 30, 31, 32, 36; 9:1, 1, 6, 6, 7, 7, 7, 7, 8, 8, 8, 9, 9, 9, 9, 11, 11, 12; 10:3, 3, 3, 5, 5, 8, 10, 13, 16

Ne 1:1, 4, 9, 11, 11, 11; 2:1, 4, 6, 7, 8, 8, 8, 9, 10, 11, 12, 13, 14, 14, 14, 16, 16, 16, 16, 16, 19; 3:2, 5, 16, 19, 19, 21, 31; 4:1, 5, 6, 7, 7, 8, 8, 8, 10, 11, 12, 14, 14, 14, 19; 6:1, 2, 3, 6, 6, 7, 7, 7, 10, 10, 11, 14, 14, 16, 19, 19; 7:1, 3, 5, 6, 6, 63, 70, 71; 8:1, 1, 6, 7, 8, 12, 12, 12, 13, 13, 15; 9:8, 8, 8, 12, 15, 15, 16, 17, 17, 17, 17, 17, 19, 19, 19, 21, 24, 26, 26, 27, 28, 36; 10:29, 29, 29, 31, 32, 33, 34, 34, 35, 36, 36, 37, 38; 11:1, 1, 1, 2, 3, 17; 12:22, 24, 24, 24, 27, 27, 27, 44, 45; 13:3, 5, 5, 7, 10, 13, 13, 19, 19, 22, 22, 24, 26, 27, 27, 28

Est 1:1, 6, 7, 8, 8, 8, 9, 11, 11, 11, 12, 13, 15, 16, 16, 16, 17, 20, 20, 21, 22, 22, 22; 2:3, 8, 8, 8, 9, 9, 11, 12, 12, 12, 12, 13, 14, 15, 18, 18, 21, 22; 3:4, 4, 6, 6, 7, 7, 7, 8, 9, 9, 11, 11, 12, 12, 12, 13, 13, 13, 13, 14, 15; 4:4, 4, 5, 5, 5, 6, 7, 7, 8, 8, 8, 8, 8, 11, 11, 11, 11, 12, 13, 14, 14, 16, 17; 5:1, 2, 3, 5, 5, 6, 8, 8, 8, 12, 14, 14; 6:1, 2, 3, 4, 4, 6, 6, 6, 9, 7, 8, 9, 9, 9, 9, 10, 10, 11, 12, 12, 13, 14; 7:1, 2, 4, 4, 4, 5, 7, 7; 8:3, 5, 5, 6, 6, 7, 9, 9, 9, 9, 9, 9, 11, 11, 11, 11, 11, 13, 13; 9:1, 1, 1, 12, 13, 16, 19, 21, 21, 22, 22, 22, 23, 24, 24, 24, 27, 27, 29, 30, 31; 10:3

Job 1:4, 4, 5, 6, 7, 11, 15, 16, 17, 19; 2:1, 1, 2, 3, 5, 8, 11, 11, 11; 3:8, 20, 23; 4:2, 12, 14, 20; 5:1, 4, 11, 16, 24, 26; 6:7, 9, 14, 18, 24, 26; 7:1, 3, 3, 4, 9, 10, 20; 8:5, 8, 22; 9:14, 15, 18, 19, 26; 10:19, 21; 11:6; 12:3, 4, 5, 8, 22, 24, 25; 13:3, 3, 6, 12, 23, 25, 26; 14:15, 18, 21; 15:8, 20, 24, 28; 16:8, 11, 12; 17:5, 14, 14, 16; 18:11, 14; 19:3, 17, 20, 20; 20:2, 3, 6, 10, 18, 23; 21:4, 13, 30, 30, 31, 32; 22:3, 3, 7, 7, 14, 19, 23; 23:5; 26:4, 10; 28:3, 11, 24, 25, 28; 29:7, 10, 11, 12, 13, 13, 15, 15, 16; 30:1, 6, 10, 11, 21, 22, 23, 23, 24, 29, 29, 31; 31:3, 3, 5, 7, 11, 12, 16, 23, 24, 28, 30, 30, 32, 36; 32:1, 10, 11, 19; 22; 33:1, 6, 22, 23, 24, 25, 30, 30, 32, 32; 34:4, 11, 11, 16, 18, 18, 18, 19, 28, 31, 33; 35:2, 9; 36:2, 3, 6, 10, 27, 32; 37:6, 6, 6, 13, 15; 38:12, 14, 20, 20, 20, 26, 26, 27, 27, 34, 36, 40; 39:9, 11, 17, 21; 40:19; 41:10, 13, 16, 17, 31, 32, 32; 42:7, 8

Ps 4:T, 5:T, 1; 6:T, 6; 7:2, 6, 8, 8, 9, 17, 17; 8:T, 6; 9:T, 2, 6, 8, 11, 20; 10:9, 14, 17, 18; 11:T, 1, 1; 12:T; 13:T; 14:T, 2; 15:3, 4, 5; 16:2, 3, 3, 10; 17:11, 14; 18:T, 3, 20, 24, 24, 30, 34, 38, 41, 50, 50, 50, 50; 19:T, 4, 5, 10; 20:T, 4; 21:T, 1; 22:T, 7, 11, 15, 19, 29, 30; 23:2; 25:7; 27:2, 4, 4,

13; 28:1, 1, 3, 4, 4, 4; 29:6, 9; 30:1, 3, 7, 8, 9, 12, 12; 31:T, 2, 2, 11, 12, 14, 18; 32:10; 33:10, 11, 19, 19; 34:9, 16; 35:4, 4, 11, 12, 23, 24, 26; 36:T, 2, 3, 3, 10, 12; 37:5, 7, 8, 14, 14, 32, 34; 38:T, T, 17, 22; 39:T, T, 1, 4, 11; 40:T, 4, 5, 8, 12, 13, 13, 14, 14; 41:T, 6, 6, 13; 42:T, 4; 43:3; 44:T, 7, 9, 10, 13, 13, 20, 25; 45:T, 17; 46:T, 9; 47:T, 6; 48:1, 10, 13; 49:T, 4, 7, 10, 11, 18, 19; 50:4, 4, 8, 16, 16, 19, 22, 23; 51:T, T, 1, 6, 8; 52:T, T, 3; 53:T, 2, 5; 54:T, T, 2; 55:T, 1, 22; 56:T; 57:T; 58:T, 5, 7; 59:T, 4, 4, 5, 5; 60:T, T, 1, 2, 3, 4; 61:T, 2; 62:T, T, 4, 9, 12, 12; 63:2, 9; 64:T, 3, 8; 65:T, 4, 8; 66:T, 4, 8, 9, 12, 19; 67:T, 1; 68:T, 4, 16, 33; 69:T, 10, 11, 16, 20, 21, 23, 26; 70:T, T, 1, 1, 2; 71:1, 2, 3, 11, 13, 18, 18; 72:3, 8, 15; 73:1, 1, 10, 16, 24, 28, 28; 74:7, 14, 14; 75:T, 4, 9; 76:T, 7, 8, 9, 9, 11, 12; 77:T, 2, 6, 9; 78:1, 1, 4, 4, 5, 6, 6, 10, 13, 13, 16, 24, 25, 48, 48, 50, 50, 52, 54, 54, 55, 58, 58, 63, 66, 71, 72; 79:2, 3, 4, 4, 11, 11, 13; 80:T, 3, 5, 7, 9, 19; 81:T, 11; 82:3; 83:9, 9, 12, 17; 84:T, 7, 10; 85:T, 4, 5, 8, 8; 86:5, 6, 11; 87:4; 88:T, 10, 15; 89:1, 4, 7, 7, 8, 19, 29, 33, 39, 40, 41, 42, 43, 44, 44; 90:2, 3, 11, 12, 15; 91:11; 92:1, 1, 2, 15; 94:1, 1, 2; 95:1, 7; 96:2, 4, 4, 13; 98:9; 100:5; 101:3; 102:4, 5, 13, 18, 20, 20, 20, 21, 22; 103:8, 10, 17, 18, 18, 18; 104:9, 11, 14, 15, 15, 23, 26, 29, 33; 105:8, 10, 13, 13, 14, 22, 25, 25, 39; 106:8, 23, 26, 27, 27, 29, 45, 46, 47, 47, 48; 107:4, 7, 8, 12, 15, 21, 23, 26, 26, 27, 31, 36, 38, 40; 109:T, 12, 12, 16, 20, 26, 31; 111:4; 112:9; 113:16; 116:17; 118:8, 9, 9, 19; 119:4, 5, 9, 25, 27, 31, 35, 36, 38, 41, 42, 49, 58, 60, 62, 76, 91, 95, 103, 112, 121, 126, 128, 132, 135, 149, 154, 156, 159, 169, 170; 121:3; 122:4; 124:6; 125:4; 127:2, 2, 2; 130:2; 132:4, 4, 17; 133:1, 2; 135:7; 136:3, 4, 5, 6, 7, 8, 9, 10, 13, 14, 16, 17; 137:6, 7, 8; 139:T, 12; 140:T, 4, 11; 141:4, 4; 143:1, 3, 3, 8, 9, 10; 144:1, 4; 145:3, 4, 8, 9, 12, 12, 18; 146:4, 7; 147:1, 6, 8, 9, 9, 18; 149:7, 8, 9; 150:2

Pr 1:2, 2, 3, 4, 4, 4, 6, 16, 16; 2:2, 7, 12, 13, 14, 16; 3:2, 8, 8, 15, 18, 22, 27, 27, 28, 32; 4:1, 8, 9, 9, 16, 20, 22, 27, 27; 5:1, 5, 13; 6:4, 4, 6, 10, 18, 24, 26, 29, 30; 7:8, 15, 15, 21, 22, 23, 24, 25, 27, 27; 8:4, 7, 9, 9, 11, 11, 13, 21, 29; 9:4, 7, 9, 15, 16; 10:3, 16, 16, 23, 23, 26, 26, 26, 29; 11:1, 17, 18, 19, 19, 24, 29; 12:4, 6, 8, 20, 21, 22; 13:5, 14, 18, 19, 19, 19, 21, 22, 25; 14:8, 15, 22, 23, 27, 29, 34; 15:8, 18, 21, 24, 26, 28; 16:5, 7, 12, 12, 16, 16, 17, 19, 19, 19, 24, 30, 32; 17:4, 4, 15, 16, 16, 21, 23, 25, 25, 26, 26; 18:5, 5, 9, 18, 19; 19:6, 7, 10, 11, 23, 24, 27, 27; 20:2, 3, 10, 13, 17, 25, 25; 21:3, 3, 5, 5, 6, 9, 16, 16, 16, 19, 19, 20, 21, 25; 22:1, 7, 9, 16, 16, 16, 19, 19, 20, 21, 25, 27; 23:1, 2, 2, 4, 7, 12, 21, 30; 24:1, 8, 9, 11, 11, 12, 12, 13, 20, 21, 23, 23, 25, 29, 29, 29, 33; 25:2, 2, 8, 8, 9, 10, 13, 20, 21, 21, 24, 25, 27, 27; 26:4, 5, 8, 11, 15, 15, 17, 21, 21, 23, 24; 27:1, 4, 7, 14, 19, 19, 21, 23, 23, 24; 28:10, 17, 17, 20, 21, 22; 29:7, 12, 15, 19, 22, 23, 24, 25, 27; 30:14, 17, 23; 31:3, 4, 6, 8, 15, 15, 19, 20, 20, 25, 27

Ecc 1:5, 6, 11, 13, 13, 13, 16, 17, 17; 2:1, 3, 3, 6, 11, 12, 14, 14, 15, 16, 19, 20, 20, 21, 26, 26, 26, 26; 3:1, 1, 2, 2, 2, 2, 3, 3, 3, 3, 4, 4, 4, 4, 4, 5, 5, 5, 6, 6, 6, 6, 7, 7, 7, 7, 8, 8, 8, 10, 11, 15, 16, 17, 17; 4:10, 10, 14; 5:1, 1, 2, 4, 6, 6, 18, 19, 19; 6:2, 2, 6, 8; 7:2, 2, 2, 2, 2, 5, 5, 9, 11, 12, 14, 25, 25, 25, 27; 8:1, 2, 3, 6, 8, 8, 9, 11, 14, 14, 14, 14, 15, 15, 15, 16, 16, 17, 17, 17; 9:1, 2, 2, 2, 2, 2, 2, 3, 4, 4, 10, 11, 11, 11, 11, 11, 11; 10:1, 3, 10, 10, 15, 15, 16; 11:2, 2, 7; 12:5, 7, 10

SS 1:7, 9; 2:3, 4; 3:3; 4:6, 6; 5:2, 5, 5, 6; 6:2, 2, 2, 11, 11; 7:7, 8, 9, 12; 8:2, 11, 11, 13, 13, 14, 14

Isa 1:11, 12, 12, 14, 16, 17; 2:2, 3, 3, 19, 20, 20, 21, 21, 22; 3:4, 8, 10, 12, 12, 13, 15, 24; 4:1, 3; 5:1, 4, 5, 5, 8, 8, 22, 22, 26; 7:1, 1, 3, 7, 13, 15, 16, 18, 21, 22, 23; 8:2, 3, 4, 8, 10, 11, 12, 12, 14, 14, 19, 20, 20, 20, 21, 22; 9:3, 7, 7, 16; 10:2, 2, 3, 6, 6, 6, 7, 11, 12, 20, 26, 27, 28, 28, 30, 31; 11:10, 11, 11, 16; 13:5, 9, 10, 11, 14, 16, 18, 20, 22; 14:1, 2, 3, 3, 9, 17, 19, 19, 24, 25, 16, 19, 24; 15:1, 1, 2, 2, 2, 7; 16:1, 1, 4, 10, 12, 12, 12; 17:4, 7, 7, 8, 11, 12, 12; 18:1, 2, 2, 2; 19:3, 3, 3, 14, 18, 19, 21, 22, 23; 20:4, 6; 21:2, 11, 14, 16; 22:1, 4, 6, 7, 12, 12, 12, 13, 20, 21, 21, 23, 24; 23:1, 6, 7, 9, 9, 11, 12, 13, 15, 15, 17, 17, 18, 18; 24:2, 9, 16, 18, 18, 18; 25:2, 4, 4, 11, 12, 12; 26:5, 5, 8, 8, 10, 14, 21; 27:6, 7, 9, 12, 13; 28:1, 1, 2, 6, 6, 12, 12, 17, 19, 21; 29:1, 1, 1, 11, 12, 14, 15, 20, 20, 24; 30:1, 1, 2, 2, 2, 4, 6, 7, 7, 8, 10, 10, 11, 13, 13, 14, 14, 14, 21, 28, 28, 28, 29, 29, 30; 31:1, 1, 4, 9; 32:4, 5, 6, 6, 6, 6, 7; 33:1, 1, 1, 4; 34:1, 2, 5, 10, 12, 14, 17; 35:4, 10; 36:1, 2, 4, 6, 7, 7, 7, 8, 8, 10,

11, 12, 12, 12, 12, 14, 16, 16, 17, 22; 37:1, 3, 3, 4, 5, 7, 7, 9, 9, 10, 11, 17, 21, 22, 24, 24, 26, 26, 35, 38; 38:4, 5, 10, 12, 13, 16, 17, 18, 20, 20, 22; 39:1, 5, 6, 8; 40:2, 14, 16, 17, 18, 20, 22, 23, 25, 29; 29; 41:1, 2, 2, 2, 6, 22, 23, 27, 27; 42:1, 2, 5, 7, 7, 8, 8, 9, 10, 17, 23, 23, 24, 25; 43:6, 6, 14, 20, 20, 23, 24, 28, 28; 44:13, 15, 19, 19, 26, 26, 27, 28, 28; 45:1, 1, 1, 1, 9, 10, 11, 16, 18, 24; 46:1, 4, 4, 5, 11; 47:7, 8, 9, 11, 12, 14, 14, 14, 15; 48:3, 5, 5, 17, 18, 20, 21; 49:5, 5, 5, 6, 6, 6, 7, 7, 7, 8, 8, 8, 9, 9, 19, 20, 21, 22, 22, 23; 50:1, 2, 2, 4, 4, 4, 6, 6, 8; 51:1, 1, 4, 6, 8, 10, 13, 18, 23, 23; 52:4, 5, 8; 53:1, 6, 7, 10; 54:3, 4, 16; 55:1, 4, 4, 7, 10, 10, 13; 56:1, 1, 3, 6, 6, 6, 6, 9, 10, 10, 11, 12; 57:1, 1, 6, 7, 8, 9, 11, 15, 15, 18, 19, 19, 21; 58:2, 2, 4, 4, 4, 5, 5, 5, 6, 6, 6, 7, 7, 7, 10, 12, 14; 59:7, 7, 18, 18, 18, 18, 20; 60:3, 3, 4, 8, 8, 9, 9, 13; 61:1, 1, 1, 1, 1, 2, 2, 3, 3, 11, 11; 62:8, 11; 63:1, 5, 5, 6, 7, 7, 7, 10, 12, 14, 14, 17; 64:2, 2, 6, 7; 65:3, 3, 5, 10, 12, 12, 24; 66:2, 2, 5, 6, 8, 9, 10, 14, 17, 17, 18, 19, 19, 20, 23, 23, 23, 23

Jer 1:2, 7, 8, 10, 10, 10, 10, 10, 10, 12, 19; 2:1, 7, 18, 18, 18, 24, 27, 28, 33, 36; 3:1, 3, 5, 9, 12, 13, 14, 15, 16, 16, 17, 17, 18; 4:3, 4, 7, 9, 11, 11, 11, 11, 16, 22, 22; 5:1, 3, 3, 7, 19, 31; 6:1, 2, 6, 10, 13, 17, 19, 20, 20; 7:1, 2, 3, 6, 7, 7, 10, 12, 14, 14, 14, 16, 18, 18, 18, 19, 27, 30, 31, 34; 8:5, 6, 10, 10, 14, 14, 19; 9:3, 5, 5, 6, 8, 12, 15, 21, 21; 10:5, 7, 10, 13, 20, 20, 22, 23, 24; 11:1, 2, 4, 5, 8, 10, 10, 10, 11, 13, 13, 13, 13, 15, 17, 17, 19; 12:9, 11, 12, 13, 14, 15, 15, 15, 16, 16, 16; 13:2, 4, 6, 6, 6, 7, 10, 10, 10, 11, 11, 16, 18, 21, 23; 14:1, 3, 3, 8, 10, 10, 16, 16; 15:2, 2, 2, 2, 2, 3, 6, 8, 8, 9, 10, 10, 11, 14, 18, 20, 20; 16:5, 7, 7, 8, 8, 8, 9, 17, 17, 18, 19, 19, 20, 21, 21; 17:3, 4, 10, 11, 13, 15, 15, 16, 21, 24, 24, 24, 27, 27; 18:1, 2, 2, 3, 4, 4, 5, 7, 7, 8, 9, 11, 11, 15, 15, 16, 18, 19, 20, 21, 22, 23; 19:5, 7, 7, 9, 11, 12, 14, 14; 20:3, 4, 4, 5, 6, 6, 15, 17, 18; 21:2, 3, 9, 14; 22:1, 3, 8, 10, 17, 17, 20, 27, 27; 23:3, 13, 21, 22, 27, 27, 27, 28, 32, 35, 35, 37; 24:1, 6, 7, 9, 9, 10; 25:1, 2, 4, 5, 6, 6, 7, 7, 12, 14, 14, 15, 17, 17, 17, 20, 22, 22, 23, 25, 26, 26, 27; 39:4, 5, 5, 7, 7, 8, 8, 9, 11; 26:2, 2, 3, 4, 4, 4, 5, 5, 6, 8, 11, 11, 12, 15, 15, 16, 16, 17, 17, 17, 18, 19, 21, 22, 23, 23, 24, 24, 28, 28; 46:23:1, 1, 4, 5, 7, 13, 15, 23, 24, 27; 17:18, 22, 26, 27, 37, 45, 49, 53, 55, 57, 58, 59, 59, 61, 61, 63, 74, 74; 27:1, 1,

24:6, 6, 7, 8, 8, 9, 13, 14, 14, 14, 17, 19, 20, 26, 26, 27; 25:4, 7, 7, 14, 14, 15; 26:1, 3, 3, 5, 11, 13, 14, 15, 17, 17, 20; 27:5, 7, 9, 19, 30; 28:8, 17, 18, 21; 29:4, 5, 5, 6, 7, 14, 14, 14, 15, 15, 16, 16, 16, 16, 17, 18, 21; 30:9, 10, 11, 13, 20, 21, 21, 21, 21, 21, 22; 31:1, 2, 14, 14, 14, 15, 16, 16, 16, 18; 32:1, 4, 6, 12, 14, 17, 19, 20, 21, 21, 24, 27, 29, 30, 30; 33:2, 8, 9, 12, 13, 13, 21, 22, 27, 29, 30, 33; 34:2, 5, 8, 18, 18, 25, 26, 28; 35:11, 11, 12; 36:4, 4, 4, 4, 4, 4, 5, 6, 6, 6, 8, 8, 12, 15, 15, 19, 19, 20, 27, 28, 33, 37; 37:2, 5, 7, 9, 12, 17, 22; 38:9, 10, 11, 11, 12, 12, 12, 13, 13, 13, 13, 16, 18, 20; 39:2, 3, 4, 4, 11, 13, 14, 14, 17, 18, 20, 24, 24, 28; 40:4, 4, 13, 16, 24, 26, 27, 28, 28, 29, 31, 32, 33, 34, 35, 35, 36, 37, 39, 40, 46, 46, 48, 49; 41:1, 7, 7, 16, 17; 42:11, 11, 12, 14, 19, 20; 43:1, 3, 3, 3, 10, 14, 18, 18, 19, 19; 44:3, 6, 6, 7, 7, 11, 11, 12, 13, 13, 15, 15, 16, 16, 17, 17, 23, 24, 25, 25, 25; 45:4, 6, 7, 8, 13, 14, 15, 17, 17, 23, 24, 25, 25; 46:5, 5, 7, 9, 11, 11, 11, 11, 14, 17, 17, 17, 18, 20, 21; 47:3, 4, 4, 5, 6, 6, 9, 10, 10, 10, 10, 11, 12, 13, 14, 15, 19; 19, 21, 22, 22, 23; 48:1, 1, 1, 28

Da 1:2, 4, 7, 7, 7, 10, 10, 12; 2:2, 2, 3, 4, 5, 9, 12, 13, 14, 14, 16, 17, 21, 24, 26, 26, 28, 29, 29, 29, 30, 30, 35, 39, 43, 44, 45, 45; 3:2, 2, 4, 9, 13, 16, 16, 17, 17, 18, 18, 19, 19, 20, 20, 26, 27, 31, 31, 32, 32, 34, 37, 37; 5:1, 2, 7, 7, 8, 16, 17, 17, 17, 28; 6:1, 3, 4, 6, 7, 7, 8, 12, 14, 14, 18, 20, 20, 20; 7:4, 5, 6, 7, 12, 13, 13, 15, 16, 16, 23, 25; 8:2, 4, 6, 7, 7, 10, 11, 12, 13, 13, 15, 16, 23, 25; 9:2, 3, 4, 4, 6, 6, 7, 7, 8, 8, 8, 10, 16, 16, 17, 21, 22, 23, 24, 24, 24, 24, 24, 25, 25, 27; 10:6, 7, 12, 12, 13, 14, 20; 11:1, 1, 3, 4, 6, 6, 10, 14, 15, 16, 17, 18, 18, 19, 34, 35, 35, 35, 35, 36, 39, 44, 44, 45; 12:1, 2, 2, 3, 4, 4, 6, 6, 7, 12

Hos 1:2, 4, 5, 10; 2:1, 7, 9, 11, 13, 18, 21, 23; 3:1, 1, 2; 4:6, 10, 10, 12, 15; 6:3; 7:10, 10, 11, 11, 12, 15, 15; 5:2, 4, 5, 6, 12, 13, 13, 14, 14, 15; 6:3; 7:10, 10, 11, 11, 16; 8:1, 5, 9, 11, 11, 12, 13; 9:3, 4, 10, 12, 13; 10:1, 1, 6, 6, 8, 8, 11, 11, 12, 12; 11:1, 1, 3, 4, 4, 9; 12:2, 6, 7, 9, 14; 13:2, 6; 14:2, 3, 8

Joel 1:1, 19; 2:2, 9, 12, 13, 17, 23, 25, 28, 32; 3:4, 8, 8, 11, 12, 12, 18, 20

Am 1:6, 6, 9; 2:4, 7, 8, 10, 12; 3:10, 14; 4:1, 4, 7, 7, 9, 10, 12; 5:2, 3, 5, 5, 6, 10, 16, 18, 26, 27; 6:1, 1, 2, 2, 3, 5, 5, 9, 10, 13; 7:2, 4, 10, 10, 14; 8:4, 4, 9, 9, 12, 12; 9:2

Ob 1:3, 5, 5, 7, 9, 14, 21

Jnh 1:2, 3, 3, 3, 4, 5, 6, 7, 13, 13, 17; 2:5, 6; 3:3, 4, 5, 7; 4:2, 3, 3, 4, 6, 6, 8, 8, 8, 8, 8, 9, 9, 9

Mic 1:1, 7, 7, 9, 13, 14, 14; 2:1, 6, 6, 7; 3:1, 8; 4:1, 2, 2, 8, 10, 10; 5:2, 10; 6:8, 8, 8, 14; 7:1, 9, 11, 12, 12, 12, 15, 20, 20

Na 1:3; 2:5; 3:1, 7

Hab 1:3, 6, 8, 13, 17; 2:1, 6, 6, 9, 9, 10, 12, 15, 18, 19, 19; 3:9, 14, 14, 19, 19

Zep 1:8, 10, 12, 18; 2:15; 3:1, 1, 2, 4, 5, 8, 8, 8, 9, 9, 16, 16, 18, 19

Hag 1:1, 4, 6, 8, 9; 2:2, 2, 2, 5, 16, 16, 16, 17, 21

Zec 1:6, 6, 6, 10, 10, 11, 16, 21, 21, 21, 21; 2:2, 2, 3, 4, 9, 11; 3:1, 4, 7; 4:2, 4, 10; 5:3, 3, 10, 11; 6:7, 7, 7, 7, 14, 14, 14, 15; 7:1, 2, 3, 5, 9, 11, 13; 8:1, 10, 12, 13, 14, 14, 15, 16, 19, 20, 20, 21, 21, 22, 22, 23; 9:10, 10, 12, 12; 10:1, 6; 11:9, 13, 17; 12:9, 9, 13, 13:1, 1, 2, 3, 4, 4, 7; 14:2, 5, 6, 7, 8, 8, 9, 9, 16, 16, 18, 19; 16, 17, 18, 19

Mal 1:1; 2:2, 2, 2, 5, 8, 15, 16; 3:1, 5, 5, 10, 14, 16; 4:6, 6

Mt 1:11, 12, 17, 18, 19, 19, 20; 2:1, 2, 8, 12, 13, 13, 14, 14, 15; 4:1, 3, 16, 17, 17; 5:13, 13, 14, 15, 17, 22, 23, 28, 32, 39, 41, 42, 44, 45; 6:1, 5, 6, 6, 16, 18, 24, 30, 30; 7:2, 4, 5, 8, 11, 11, 12, 13, 13, 14, 14, 15, 16, 17, 17, 19, 20, 24, 24, 24, 27; 8:7, 9, 18:1, 3, 5, 7, 8, 10, 11, 12, 14, 21, 24, 24; 19:3, 7, 10, 12, 13, 14, 14, 16, 16, 17, 23, 34; 24:1, 6, 9, 17, 18, 19, 19, 21, 26, 27, 29, 34, 34, 43, 45; 25:1, 5, 9, 10, 10, 11, 15, 27, 45, 45; 26:1, 2, 8, 9, 16, 16, 21, 26, 27, 37, 45, 49, 53, 55, 55, 57, 58, 59, 59, 61, 61, 73, 74; 27:1, 1,

2, 3, 4, 4, 6, 7, 14, 15, 19, 24, 26, 31, 32, 33, 34, 46, 48, 49, 51, 58, 58, 60; 28:1, 1, 8, 9, 14, 20

Mk 1:7, 9, 17, 24, 24, 34, 40, 40, 44, 44, 45, 45, 45; 2:2, 9, 9, 9, 10, 10, 15, 17, 17, 18, 23, 23, 26; 3:4, 4, 4, 4, 7, 9, 11, 14, 15, 15, 15, 21; 4:1, 3, 4, 9, 11, 21, 23, 25, 33, 34, 34; 5:7, 14, 15, 16, 17, 17, 19, 20, 32, 37, 38, 39, 41, 41, 43; 6:2, 7, 18, 21, 27, 28, 28, 31, 34, 36, 37, 37, 39, 41, 41, 41, 45, 45, 46, 53, 55; 7:2, 4, 5, 11, 11, 12, 16, 27, 30, 32, 34, 37, 37; 8:1, 2, 3, 6, 6, 7, 11, 13, 14, 22, 22, 26, 31, 37, 38; 9:2, 5, 9, 15; 10:2, 4, 4, 7, 12, 13, 14, 17, 21, 24, 24, 28, 30, 32, 32, 33, 33, 33, 40, 40, 40, 41, 42, 42, 45, 45, 45, 46, 47, 49, 50; 11:1, 1, 2, 12, 13, 14, 14, 17, 17, 23, 33; 12:1, 1, 2, 12, 13, 14, 14, 17, 17, 23, 33, 33, 36, 38; 13:5, 9, 9, 12, 12, 14, 15, 16, 17, 17, 21, 22, 27, 29, 34, 34, 34; 14:1, 5, 8, 8, 10, 11, 14, 14, 20, 43, 44, 48, 53, 55, 55, 64, 65, 65, 65, 65, 69, 70, 71, 71, 72; 15:1, 8, 8, 15, 15, 18, 20, 21, 23, 36, 36, 38, 45; 16:8, 9, 15

Lk 1:1, 3, 3, 8, 9, 9, 16, 17, 17, 17, 19, 19, 20, 23, 23, 25, 27, 27, 38, 41, 43, 43, 49, 50, 55, 55, 55, 56, 59, 59, 62, 72, 72, 72, 73, 76, 77, 79, 79, 79; 2:1, 3, 5, 10, 14, 15, 15, 15, 21, 24, 24, 27, 29, 32, 38, 39, 39, 41, 42, 44, 45, 46; 3:7, 7, 7, 7, 8, 8, 8, 11, 12, 14, 16, 21, 23; 4:6, 9, 10, 16, 16, 18, 18, 18, 18, 18, 19, 20, 31, 34, 34, 41, 43; 5:1, 1, 7, 11, 12, 14, 14, 15, 15, 17, 17, 18, 18, 19, 20, 21, 31, 34, 34, 34, 43; 5:1, 1, 7, 11, 12, 14, 14, 15, 15, 17, 17, 18, 18, 19, 21, 23, 24, 34, 34, 47; 7:2, 4, 6, 7, 8, 8, 9, 9, 12, 17, 18, 19, 19, 24, 24, 25, 26, 32, 36, 38, 38; 22:5, 6, 15, 23, 23, 24, 26, 30, 32, 32, 32, 33; 14:1, 1, 3, 6, 7, 8, 9, 9, 12, 17, 17, 18, 19, 21, 23, 24, 28, 29, 29, 29, 30, 30, 31, 31, 33; 15:1, 2, 12, 12, 14, 15, 15, 17, 18, 19, 20, 21, 22, 24, 25, 29; 16:3, 4, 7, 9, 10, 16, 16, 19, 24, 28, 29, 30, 31, 31; 17:3, 4, 7, 10, 11, 11, 14, 14, 18, 22, 23, 31, 33; 18:1, 1, 1, 10, 13, 14, 16, 18, 25, 30, 31, 33, 35; 19:3, 4, 4, 5, 7, 8, 9, 10, 10, 12, 15, 15, 15, 19, 24, 28, 29, 29, 35, 37, 45, 46; 20:1, 9, 9, 10, 16, 19, 22, 35, 37, 37, 42, 42, 46; 21:7, 9, 12, 12, 13, 14, 16, 16, 21, 23, 24, 28, 29, 30, 36, 36, 38, 38; 22:5, 6, 15, 23, 31, 33, 39, 44, 45, 47, 52; 23:2, 2, 2, 4, 4, 5, 6, 7, 8, 8, 11, 15, 20, 20, 25, 30, 30, 30, 32, 32, 35, 37, 38, 38, 38, 40, 40, 43; 10:2, 2, 3, 5, 6, 8, 9, 11, 13, 13, 14, 15, 23; 24:4, 5, 9, 11, 12, 13, 17, 18, 20, 20, 21, 24, 24, 26, 26, 29, 30, 32, 32, 32, 33, 34, 46, 46, 50, 51, 52

Jn 1:7, 8, 12, 12, 12, 19, 22, 27, 31, 33, 38, 42, 47; 2:2, 4, 7, 12, 13; 3:2, 13, 17, 20, 21, 23, 26, 26, 33; 4:5, 5, 5, 7, 7, 8, 10, 10, 11, 15, 15, 20, 21, 28, 30, 32, 33, 34, 34, 35, 38, 52; 5:1, 7, 10, 16, 18, 26, 26, 27, 35, 36, 40, 45; 6:6, 11, 11, 15, 17, 24, 31, 35, 37, 38, 44, 52, 68; 7:1, 4, 4, 19, 22, 27, 31, 33, 38, 42, 44, 47, 56, 59; 9:11, 13; 10:3, 10, 10, 10, 18, 18, 24, 29, 31, 39; 11:7, 8, 15, 19, 19, 31, 38, 45, 46, 53, 53, 54, 55, 55, 56; 12:1, 5, 6, 10, 12, 12, 13, 20, 21, 21, 24, 26, 26, 29, 35; 14:2, 18, 21, 26, 27; 15:25; 16:5, 10, 12, 12, 12, 19, 22, 27, 31, 33; 17:1, 2, 4, 11, 13; 18:6, 13, 13, 14, 20, 31, 31, 36, 37; 19:4, 7, 10, 17, 20, 20, 21, 23, 27, 29, 33, 34, 35, 38, 39, 40; 20:2, 2, 5, 7, 10, 16, 18, 24, 26, 27; 21:1, 6, 9, 11, 14, 15, 16, 21, 22, 23

Ac 1:1, 3, 3, 6, 7, 16, 19, 22, 25; 2:4, 7, 12, 14, 17, 21, 25, 27, 28, 30, 30, 30, 37, 39, 45, 46, 47; 3:2, 3, 3, 9, 19, 23, 26; 4:5, 9, 10, 16, 16, 17, 18, 19, 23, 26; 5:2, 3, 3, 9, 11, 13, 14, 15, 17, 18, 20, 21, 21, 28, 28, 30, 34, 35, 35, 36, 36, 38, 39, 40, 41, 42; 6:4, 4, 7, 10, 13; 7:5, 5, 7, 13, 17, 18, 19, 21, 22, 23, 26, 27, 29, 30, 32, 34, 35, 37, 38, 38, 39; 8:2, 3, 5, 6, 7, 11, 24, 25, 26, 28, 29, 30, 32, 35, 36, 38, 39; 9:2, 2, 4, 5, 9, 10, 13, 15, 18, 20, 25, 25, 26, 28, 29, 29; 10:2, 2, 3, 5, 6, 8, 9, 11, 13, 13, 14, 15, 23; 11:2, 3, 5, 13, 17, 21, 24, 28, 29, 30; 12:1, 3, 4, 4, 4, 4, 10, 11, 12, 13, 17,

Idx

17, 19, 19, 20; 13:2, 4, 5, 7, 8, 10, 11, 13, 13, 14, 19, 22, 22, 23, 24, 25, 26, 31, 34, 34, 35, 42, 43, 43, 44, 46, 46, 47, 48; 14:1, 3, 5, 5, 9, 11, 16, 20, 21, 21, 22, 23, 24, 26, 26; 15:2, 4, 5, 5, 5, 6, 10, 10, 12, 14, 15, 19, 22, 22, 24, 25, 28, 28, 28, 29, 30, 34, 37, 38, 38; 16:1, 3, 4, 6, 7, 7, 8, 9, 10, 10, 11, 11, 12, 13, 15, 15, 16, 16, 18, 18, 20, 21, 21, 22, 23, 30, 32, 36, 36, 39; 17:1, 5, 5, 7, 14, 14, 15, 15, 16, 18, 20, 21, 21, 23, 25, 26, 29, 30; 18:1, 2, 5, 7, 9, 10, 12, 13, 13, 14, 15, 19, 20, 20, 24, 26, 27, 27; 19:1, 1, 13, 17, 21, 21, 27, 36, 36, 40; 20:1, 3, 3, 6, 7, 7, 13, 13, 14, 15, 16, 16, 17, 18, 20, 21, 21, 24, 26, 27, 28, 28, 30, 31, 32, 32, 32, 32, 34, 35, 35, 35; 21:1, 3, 4, 4, 7, 12, 12, 13, 13, 13, 13, 15, 17, 21, 21, 21, 23, 25, 26, 31, 33, 34, 37, 39; 22:2, 3, 5, 5, 5, 6, 9, 10, 12, 17, 24, 25, 30; 23:2, 3, 3, 3, 9, 10, 10, 10, 14, 15, 15, 15, 17, 18, 18, 18, 19, 20, 20, 22, 23, 23, 29, 29, 30, 30, 30, 31, 32, 32, 33, 33, 35; 24:2, 6, 6, 8, 10, 11, 11, 16, 17, 17, 19, 19, 23, 23, 23, 25, 27; 25:1, 3, 3, 6, 9, 9, 10, 10, 11, 13, 15, 16, 16, 16, 16, 16, 17, 19, 20, 21, 21, 22, 24, 25, 25, 26, 26, 27, 27, 27; 26:1, 3, 3, 7, 9, 9, 10, 10, 11, 12, 14, 14, 14, 14, 16, 18, 18, 18, 20, 20, 21, 21, 23, 23, 28, 29; 27:2, 3, 5, 12, 12, 12, 16, 21, 22, 26, 30, 31, 31, 33, 34, 35, 35, 35, 39, 40, 42, 43, 43, 44, 44; 28:4, 6, 8, 8, 13, 13, 14, 15, 16, 16, 16, 17, 19, 19, 20, 20, 22, 23, 23

Ro 1:1, 3, 4, 5, 7, 7, 10, 10, 11, 13, 14, 14, 14, 14, 15, 15, 16, 16, 16, 17, 22, 23, 23, 24, 24, 28, 28, 30; 2:2, 4, 6, 7, 10, 10, 10, 16; 3:15, 19, 25, 25, 26; 4:1, 2, 4, 5, 8, 9, 12, 13, 13, 16, 16, 16, 18; 6:2, 11, 16, 16, 16, 19, 19, 19, 22; 7:1, 2, 3, 3, 4, 4, 4, 5, 10, 10, 18, 18, 23; 8:1, 6, 6, 7, 12, 12, 15, 18, 20, 23, 23, 27, 28, 28, 29, 29, 31, 33, 38, 39; 9:3, 4, 11, 15, 20, 21, 22, 22, 26, 30, 31; 10:1, 2, 3, 4, 6, 7, 19; 11:2, 4, 4, 5, 11, 11, 13, 14, 23, 24, 25, 35, 36, 36; 12:2, 3, 3, 3, 3, 6, 6, 6, 9, 10, 13, 13, 16, 17; 13:2, 3, 3, 4, 4, 7, 7, 7, 8, 10, 11, 14; 14:1, 4, 4, 6, 6, 6, 7, 7, 9, 11, 11, 12, 13, 14, 14, 14, 18, 21, 21, 22; 15:1, 1, 2, 5, 5, 7, 8, 9, 12, 14, 15, 16, 17, 18, 20, 24, 24, 24, 25, 26, 27, 28, 30; 16:17, 25, 25, 25, 25, 26, 26, 27, 99

1Co 1:1, 2, 2, 17, 17, 18, 19, 21, 27, 27, 28, 28; 2:1, 2, 6, 12; 3:2, 5, 8, 10, 18, 22; 4:5, 6, 6, 6, 7, 8, 9, 9, 9, 14, 18, 19; 5:5, 9, 11, 11, 12, 12; 6:1, 2, 3, 4, 4, 5, 5, 6, 6, 7, 16; 7:1, 2, 5, 8, 9, 9, 11, 12, 12, 13, 15, 17, 25, 26, 27, 32, 39, 39; 8:2, 6, 8, 9, 9, 10, 10, 13, 13; 9:2, 3, 4, 4, 5, 6, 15, 16, 20, 21, 21, 21, 22, 22, 25, 27; 10:6, 7, 7, 13, 13, 13, 15, 19, 20, 20, 20, 22, 27, 27, 31, 32, 32; 11:2, 6, 7, 10, 15, 16, 20, 22, 22, 22, 29, 33; 12:3, 7, 7, 8, 8, 9, 9, 10, 10, 10, 10, 11, 13, 21, 22, 23, 24; 13:3, 3, 12; 14:3, 6, 8, 9, 12, 22, 22, 28, 28, 30, 32, 34, 34, 34, 38, 54, 57; 16:1, 3, 7, 12, 12, 15, 16, 99

2Co 1:2, 4, 8, 12, 13, 15, 16, 16, 16, 17, 23; 2:1, 3, 6, 7, 9, 10, 10, 12, 12, 14, 16, 16; 3:1, 1, 3, 4, 5, 7, 13, 16, 18; 4:2, 3, 6, 6, 15; 5:2, 8, 8, 10, 12, 12, 13, 18, 18, 19, 20, 21; 7:3, 3, 9, 10, 10, 11, 14, 14; 8:1, 3, 4, 5, 7, 8, 10, 10, 11, 12, 16, 19, 19, 24; 9:1, 1, 1, 2, 5, 8, 8, 9, 10, 11, 11; 10:2, 2, 4, 5, 6, 6, 7, 13, 13, 14, 15, 16, 16, 16; 11:1, 2, 2, 7, 8, 9, 9, 9, 15, 32; 12:1, 1, 2, 4, 6, 6, 7, 7, 11, 13, 13, 14, 14, 14, 14; 13:1, 2, 3, 7, 7, 10, 10, 10, 99

Gal 1:3, 4, 5, 10, 16, 17, 17, 18, 18; 2:1, 2, 3, 4, 5, 6, 6, 6, 6, 8, 9, 10, 11, 11, 14, 14, 17, 19; 3:5, 6, 10, 16, 16, 16, 18, 19, 22, 24, 24, 29; 4:5, 9, 9, 15, 18, 20, 20, 21, 24, 25; 5:3, 3, 13, 17; 6:3, 8, 8, 12, 12, 13, 16

Eph 1:1, 1, 2, 5, 5, 6, 7, 9, 11, 12, 16, 19, 19; 2:2, 2, 2, 7, 15, 17, 17, 18; 3:2, 7, 9, 10, 11, 16, 16, 18, 19, 20, 20; 4:3, 7, 14, 14, 16, 19, 22, 27, 28, 28, 29, 32; 5:2, 19, 19, 21, 24, 27, 28; 6:4, 5, 5, 7, 7, 11, 13, 16, 19, 20, 21, 23

Php 1:1, 7, 14, 16, 16, 19, 20, 21, 24, 23, 23, 24, 26, 28, 28, 29, 29, 30; 2:6, 11, 13, 13, 19, 23, 25, 25, 25, 30; 3:1, 1, 1, 7, 13, 21, 21; 4:11, 12, 12, 12, 12, 12, 18, 19, 99

Col 1:2, 3, 4, 9, 9, 11, 12, 20, 22, 23, 25, 25, 25, 26, 27, 29; 2:2, 14, 14, 17, 20, 22, 23; 3:9, 15, 16, 17, 21, 22, 23; 4:3, 4, 6, 10, 17, 17, 99

1Th 1:2, 7, 8, 8, 9, 9, 10, 10; 2:2, 4, 8, 15, 16, 16, 16, 16, 17; 3:1, 2, 2, 4, 5, 6, 6, 9, 12, 13; 4:1, 1, 4, 9, 11, 11, 11, 13, 17; 5:9, 9, 12, 13, 15, 16

2Th 1:3, 6, 6, 7, 10, 10, 12; 2:13, 13, 13, 14; 3:7, 8, 9, 9, 99

1Ti 1:3, 4, 7, 10, 11, 11, 15, 16, 16, 18, 20; 2:4, 4, 6, 12, 12, 12; 3:2, 2, 3, 5, 8, 13, 14, 15; 4:1, 3, 3, 3, 4, 8, 13, 13, 15; 5:4, 4, 11, 13, 13, 14, 14, 24; 6:3, 3, 3, 16, 17, 18, 20, 99

2Ti 1:1, 2, 4, 5, 8, 9, 9, 10, 12; 2:2, 2, 4, 8, 14, 14, 15, 15, 20, 20, 24, 25; 3:2, 7, 7, 15; 4:3, 6, 8, 9, 10, 11, 12, 14, 16, 18, 21

Tit 1:1, 3, 4, 7, 7, 9, 9, 14; 2:3, 4, 4, 4, 5, 5, 6, 8, 9, 9, 11; 3:1, 1, 1, 1, 1, 2, 2, 5, 7, 8, 12, 12, 12, 14, 99

Phm 1:2, 2, 3, 8, 11, 11, 11, 16, 19, 99

Heb 1:5, 5, 13, 14; 2:1, 1, 3, 4, 5, 10, 11, 15, 17, 17, 17, 18; 3:2, 5, 7, 13, 15, 18, 18; 4:1, 6, 7, 7, 9, 11, 12, 13, 16, 16, 18; 5:1, 3, 5, 5, 7, 11, 11, 12, 14, 14; 6:5, 6, 6, 6, 8, 10, 10, 11, 13, 14, 14, 18; 7:2, 5, 5, 13, 23, 25, 25, 25, 27; 8:3, 3, 4, 5, 5, 5, 9, 9, 10, 10, 11, 12, 13; 9:9, 11, 11, 13, 14, 14, 19, 19, 24, 26, 27, 28; 10:1, 2, 7, 9, 15, 19, 20, 24, 24, 31, 32, 39; 11:6, 6, 7, 8, 11, 15, 16, 19, 20, 24, 24, 31, 32, 39; 11:6, 6, 7, 8, 11, 15, 16, 19, 20, 24, 24, 31, 32, 39; 12:11, 19, 22, 23, 23, 23, 24, 24; 13:2, 8, 10, 14, 15, 15, 16, 16, 18, 19, 19, 21, 21, 99

Jas 1:1, 5, 12, 19, 19, 19, 21, 26, 27, 27; 2:3, 3, 5, 4, 9, 12, 12, 13, 13, 13, 15, 17, 17, 17; 5:1, 16, 17

1Pe 1:1, 2, 3, 4, 5, 12, 13, 13, 14, 17; 2:4, 5, 8, 13, 13, 15, 18, 18, 18, 23, 24; 3:1, 7, 15, 15, 18; 4:2, 2, 3, 4, 5, 6, 6, 6, 9, 10, 11, 12, 19, 19; 5:3, 5, 5, 11

2Pe 1:1, 3, 5, 5, 6, 6, 6, 7, 7, 10, 12, 13, 15, 17; 2:4, 4, 8, 9, 9, 10, 12, 13, 17, 21, 21, 22, 22; 3:2, 9, 10, 13, 15, 32

1Jn 1:9, 9; 2:6; 3:5, 16; 4:10, 11, 14, 16; 5:11, 14

2Jn 1:8, 12, 12, 12

3Jn 1:4, 5, 5, 8, 8, 9, 13, 14, 14

Jude 1:1, 3, 3, 4, 7, 13, 15, 15, 24, 24, 25

Rev 1:1, 1, 4, 4, 6, 8, 12, 13; 2:7, 7, 12, 14, 14, 14, 17, 17, 19, 20, 20, 20, 20, 21, 23, 26, 27; 3:2, 7, 9, 9, 10, 10, 18, 20, 21, 21; 4:3, 8, 9, 11; 5:2, 2, 3, 3, 4, 4, 4, 5, 5, 9, 9, 9, 12; 6:2, 4, 4, 8, 16; 7:2, 2, 2, 10, 14; 8:2, 6, 13, 13; 9:1, 5, 6, 9, 10, 14, 15; 10:4, 5, 7, 7; 11:6, 6, 6, 6, 9, 10, 12, 13, 17, 17, 18; 12:2, 4, 4, 4, 5, 5, 12, 14, 15, 17, 17, 18; 13:3, 3, 4, 5, 6, 7, 7, 12, 14, 15, 16, 16; 14:4, 6, 6, 7, 15, 15, 18; 15:8; 16:1, 6, 8, 9, 14, 14, 19; 17:17, 17; 18:6, 6, 17; 19:7, 8, 10, 17, 19; 20:8, 8, 8, 12, 13; 21:10, 15, 17, 23; 22:6, 8, 12, 14, 16

UNTO (9005)

Ge 1:9, 28; 2:19, 22, 24; 3:1, 2, 4, 6, 9, 9, 13, 14, 16, 17, 17, 19, 19, 21; 4:3, 4, 5, 6, 7, 9, 10, 12, 13, 15, 18, 19, 23, 23; 6:1, 4, 13, 20, 21; 7:1, 5, 9, 15; 8:9, 9, 12, 15, 20; 9:1, 8, 17, 24, 25; 10:1, 19, 19, 19, 21, 25, 30; 11:4, 31; 12:1, 1, 4, 6, 6, 7, 7, 7, 7, 8, 8, 11, 18; 13:3, 4, 8, 10, 14, 17, 18; 14:6, 14, 15, 17, 18, 21, 22; 15:1, 4, 5, 7, 9, 10, 13, 18, 18; 16:2, 2, 4, 5, 6, 9, 10, 11, 13; 17:1, 7, 8, 9, 15, 17, 18, 21, 23; 18:1, 6, 7, 7, 9, 10, 13, 14, 21, 27, 29, 30, 31, 33; 19:3, 5, 5, 5, 6, 8, 8, 12, 14, 14, 16, 18, 19, 20, 21, 31, 31, 34, 37, 38; 20:5, 6, 9, 9, 9, 30; 21:1, 3, 5, 9, 10, 12, 12, 14, 17, 22, 23, 23, 27, 29, 30; 22:1, 3, 5, 7, 11, 12, 15, 19, 20; 23:3, 5, 13, 14, 15, 16, 18, 20; 24:2, 3, 4, 4, 5, 5, 6, 7, 7, 7, 10, 12, 14, 20, 24, 24, 25, 29, 29, 30, 30, 36, 38, 38, 39, 40, 42, 45, 45, 47, 48, 50, 54, 56, 58, 60, 65; 25:5, 6, 6, 12, 17, 18, 23, 33; 26:1, 1, 2, 3, 3, 9, 9, 16, 24, 27, 29, 32, 33, 35; 27:1, 1, 6, 6, 13, 18, 19, 20, 21, 22, 26, 31, 31, 32, 34, 37, 37, 38, 38, 39, 42; 28:1, 4, 9, 19, 22; 29:4, 5, 6, 15, 20, 21, 21, 23, 24, 25, 30, 34; 30:1, 3, 4, 14, 15, 16, 17, 25, 25, 27, 29, 30, 40; 31:3, 3, 4, 5, 11, 12, 13, 14, 16, 24, 39; 32:6, 6, 9, 11, 13, 14, 14, 16, 14; 34:1, 3, 4, 6, 9, 9, 11, 11, 11, 12, 14, 14, 15, 16, 17, 20, 22, 23, 24, 24; 35:1, 1, 1, 2, 3, 4, 7, 9, 10, 11, 17, 20, 27, 27, 27, 29; 36:5, 37:2, 4, 6, 10, 13, 13, 18, 22, 23, 26, 29, 30, 35, 36; 38:2, 8, 8, 9, 12, 14, 16, 16, 16, 18; 39:8, 10, 14, 14, 14, 14, 17, 17, 19; 40:6, 8, 8, 12, 13, 14, 14, 16, 20, 21; 41:8, 9, 13, 14, 15, 17, 24, 25, 28, 32, 38, 38, 40, 41, 44, 50, 50, 55, 55, 56; 42:1, 7, 7, 7, 9, 10, 12, 14, 14, 16, 20, 22, 23, 25, 28, 28, 29, 29, 29, 31, 33, 34, 36, 37; 43:2, 3, 3, 5, 8, 9, 11, 13, 23, 29, 29, 32, 34; 44:4, 4, 6, 7, 8, 10, 15, 16, 17, 18, 20, 21, 22, 23, 24, 27, 32; 45:1, 3, 4, 9, 9, 10, 12, 17, 17, 17, 18, 24, 25, 27; 46:1, 2, 15, 18, 20, 20, 25, 28, 28, 29, 30, 31, 31, 31, 31, 34; 47:2, 3, 4, 5, 5, 8, 9, 9, 15, 17, 18, 18, 19, 23, 24, 26, 29, 31, 31; 48:2, 3, 4, 5, 7, 9, 9, 10, 11, 13, 15, 17, 18, 21; 49:1, 2, 6, 10, 11, 11, 13, 15, 26, 28, 29, 29, 33; 50:4, 12, 15, 16, 17, 17, 17, 19, 20, 21, 24, 24

Ex 1:9, 10, 18, 19, 19; 2:9, 10, 11, 20, 23, 25; 3:2, 4, 8, 8, 8, 9, 10, 11, 11, 12, 13, 13, 13, 13, 13, 14, 14, 14, 15, 15, 15, 16, 16, 17, 17, 18, 18; 4:1, 1, 2, 4, 6, 8, 10, 11, 15, 15, 16, 18, 18, 18, 19, 21, 22, 23, 30; 5:1, 3, 4, 4, 15, 16, 21, 22; 6:1, 2, 2, 3, 3, 3, 4, 4, 6, 9, 10, 11, 12, 13, 13, 13, 28, 29, 29, 29, 30; 7:1, 2, 4, 7, 8, 8, 9, 9, 13, 14, 16, 16, 19, 20, 20; 8:1, 1, 1, 5, 5, 8, 9, 9, 12, 13, 13, 22, 19, 20, 20; 9:1, 1, 8, 8, 12, 13, 13, 22, 27, 29, 29, 33; 10:1, 1, 3, 3, 4, 5, 6, 7, 7, 8,

8, 9, 10, 12, 21, 24, 25, 28; 11:1, 5, 8, 8, 9, 9; 12:1, 2, 3, 4, 14, 21, 21, 26, 29, 36, 42, 43, 49; 13:1, 2, 3, 5, 8, 9, 11, 12, 14; 14:1, 2, 10, 11, 13, 15, 15, 15, 22, 24, 26, 29; 15:1, 1, 11, 13, 20, 23, 23, 25, 28, 33, 35; 17:2, 4, 14, 14, 15, 15, 22, 24, 26, 29; 15:1, 1, 11, 13, 20, 23, 23, 25, 28, 33, 35; 17:2, 4, 14, 14, 15, 15, 22, 24, 26, 29; 18:5, 6, 10, 14, 15, 17, 22, 26; 19:3, 4, 7, 8, 8, 8, 9, 11, 12, 14, 17, 21, 24; 20:4, 5, 6, 11, 13, 13, 14, 16, 18, 18, 21, 22, 22, 22, 24; 20:4, 5, 6, 11, 13, 13, 14, 16, 18, 18, 21, 22, 22, 22, 24; 21:1, 5, 6, 6, 8, 8, 9, 11, 13, 29, 30, 34; 22:4, 4, 6, 9, 11, 13, 14; 13:1, 2, 17, 21, 22, 23, 26, 26, 26, 27, 32; 14:2, 3, 7, 11, 13, 16, 18, 19, 23, 26, 26, 28, 35, 39, 40, 44, 45; 15:1, 2, 2, 3, 17, 17, 17, 23, 33, 35, 36, 37, 37, 38, 38, 39; 23:1, 3, 4, 5, 6, 11, 13, 14, 17, 18, 18, 19, 21, 22, 24, 25, 33, 33, 35, 37, 38, 39, 40; 16:3, 5, 5, 5, 8, 9, 15, 16, 19, 19, 22, 22, 28, 29, 30, 33, 34, 35; 23:1, 3, 10, 12, 12, 13, 14, 15, 15, 16, 18, 18, 19; 15:7, 11, 11, 11, 11, 12, 12, 12, 13, 14, 19; 16:1, 5, 5, 7, 9, 10, 11, 12, 13, 13, 14, 15, 16, 17, 18, 23, 26, 28; 17:2, 3, 3, 4, 9, 9, 10, 10, 11; 18:1, 1, 2, 3, 4, 5, 6, 8, 8, 10, 12, 14, 15, 18, 19, 19, 21, 23, 23, 24, 25, 26, 27, 27, 29; 19:2, 3, 5, 6, 9, 11, 12, 13, 18, 21, 23, 23, 24, 24, 25, 28, 28, 30; 20:1, 14, 26, 32, 36, 42, 45, 45, 47; 21:1, 5, 12, 13, 22, 22, 22, 22, 23

Lev 1:1, 1, 2, 2, 9, 13, 15, 17; 2:1, 2, 8, 8, 8, 9, 11, 12, 14, 16; 3:3, 5, 6, 9, 11, 14; 4:1, 2, 3, 4, 12, 31, 35; 5:6, 7, 8, 12, 14, 15, 16, 18; 6:1, 2, 5, 6, 6, 8, 9, 11, 15, 17, 19, 20, 21, 24, 25; 7:5, 11, 14, 14, 18, 20, 21, 22, 23, 25, 28, 29, 29, 32, 34, 34, 35, 38; 8:1, 3, 4, 5, 7, 21, 28, 31; 9:2, 3, 4, 6, 7, 8, 9, 11, 12, 12, 15, 16, 21; 10:3, 4, 6, 10:3, 3, 4, 6, 6, 9, 10, 14, 14, 15, 22, 23, 24, 24, 25, 28, 29, 30, 30, 31, 34, 36, 41, 41, 43; 11:6, 8, 8, 9, 14, 17, 22, 23, 23; 12:1, 2, 3, 5, 6, 7, 7; 13:1, 3, 4, 5, 6, 9, 10, 11, 14, 15, 16, 17, 18, 46, 47, 63; 16:1, 2, 3, 5, 6, 8, 10; 17:7, 9, 14, 17; 18:3, 10, 18; 19:10, 12, 28, 33; 20:1, 2, 4, 4, 6, 10, 12, 13, 8, 27, 34, 43, 43, 44, 45; 22:2, 3, 4, 4, 4, 5, 6, 7, 17, 18, 19, 22, 23; 23:1, 2, 3, 4, 4, 5, 7, 8, 8, 9, 10, 11, 15, 19, 22, 23, 24, 27, 27, 27, 27, 28

Nu 1:1, 48, 50; 2:1, 1, 5; 3:5, 6, 9, 9, 11, 13, 14, 40, 44, 48, 51; 4:1, 1, 9, 17, 17, 19, 19, 21, 27, 30, 35, 39, 43, 47; 5:1, 4, 5, 6, 7, 7, 8, 8, 9, 11, 12, 15, 15, 19, 19, 19, 21, 22, 23, 23, 25; 7:4, 5, 6, 7, 8, 8, 9, 9, 11, 89, 89; 8:1, 2, 2, 4, 4, 4, 5, 7, 12, 13, 16, 16, 19, 20, 20, 22, 23, 24, 26; 9:1, 4, 7, 8, 8, 9, 10, 10, 12, 14, 21; 10:1, 4, 29, 29, 30, 32, 36; 11:2, 2, 11, 12, 12, 12, 13, 16, 16, 18, 20, 23, 23, 25, 25, 29, 30, 35; 12:4, 4, 4, 4, 6, 6, 11, 13, 14; 13:1, 2, 17, 21, 22, 23, 26, 26, 26, 27, 32; 14:2, 3, 7, 11, 13, 16, 18, 19, 23, 26, 26, 28, 35, 39, 40, 44, 45; 15:1, 2, 2, 3, 17, 17, 17, 23, 33, 35, 36, 37, 37, 38, 38, 39; 16:3, 5, 5, 5, 8, 9, 15, 16, 19, 19, 22, 22, 28, 29, 30, 33, 34, 35; 17:2, 3, 3, 4, 9, 9, 10, 10, 11; 18:1, 1, 2, 3, 4, 5, 6, 8, 8, 10, 12, 14, 15, 18, 19, 19, 21, 23, 23, 24, 25, 26, 27, 27, 29; 19:2, 3, 5, 6, 9, 11, 12, 13, 18, 21, 23, 23, 24, 24, 25, 28, 28, 30; 20:1, 14, 26, 32, 36, 42, 45, 45, 47; 21:1, 5, 12, 13, 22, 22, 22, 22, 23

Dt 1:1, 2, 3, 3, 6, 7, 7, 7, 8, 8, 9, 17, 20, 20, 21, 22, 24, 25, 29, 35, 39, 41, 42, 42, 43, 44, 45, 46; 2:1, 2, 4, 5, 9, 9, 12, 14, 17, 20, 23, 26, 27, 29, 31, 35, 36, 37, 37, 37, 37; 3:2, 2, 2, 6, 8, 10, 12, 13, 14, 16, 18, 20, 21, 26, 26; 4:1, 1, 2, 4, 7, 10, 11, 12, 12, 14, 19, 20, 21, 23, 30, 34, 41, 46; 5:1, 5, 9, 10, 11, 14, 15, 18, 21, 22, 23, 29:3, 3, 3, 4, 4, 6, 6, 8, 30; 3:15, 17, 24, 25, 26; 31:4

2Sa 1:3, 3, 4, 5, 14, 16, 26; 2:1, 1, 5, 5, 5, 6; 3:2, 7, 8, 12, 16, 21, 21, 24, 38; 4:8, 9; 5:1, 6, 6, 14, 19; 6:10, 12, 21, 23; 7:2, 4, 8, 9, 17, 20, 24, 27, 28;

9, 10, 12, 21, 24, 25, 28; 11:1, 5, 8, 8, 9, 9; 12:1, 2, 3, 4, 14, 21, 21, 26, 29, 36, 42, 43, 49; 13:1, 2, 3, 5, 8, 9, 11, 12, 14; 14:1, 2, 10, 11, 13, 15, 15, 15, 22, 24, 26, 29; 15:1, 1, 11, 13, 20, 23, 23, 25, 28, 33, 35; 17:2, 4, 14, 14, 15, 15, 22, 24, 26, 29; 18:5, 6, 10, 14, 15, 17, 22, 26; 19:3, 4, 7, 8, 8, 8, 9, 11, 12, 14, 17, 21, 24; 20:4, 5, 6, 11, 13, 13, 14, 16, 18, 18, 21, 22, 22, 22, 24; 21:1, 5, 6, 6, 8, 8, 9, 11, 13, 29, 30, 34; 22:4, 4, 6, 9, 11, 13, 14; 23:1, 2, 3, 4, 5, 7, 8, 8, 10, 12, 14, 16, 16, 16, 17, 19, 20, 20, 24, 24, 25, 26, 27, 27, 32, 32, 33; 24:1, 2, 3, 7, 9, 10, 13, 15; 25:1, 2, 2, 4, 5, 8, 8, 10, 10, 10, 10, 16, 27, 28, 39, 40, 41, 41, 47, 49, 50, 50, 51, 52, 52, 55; 26:1, 5, 5, 9, 14, 16, 18, 21, 21, 23, 24, 27, 27, 28, 28, 40, 41; 27:1, 2, 2, 3, 5, 6, 9, 9, 11, 13, 14, 15, 16, 18, 18, 19, 21, 22, 23, 23, 24, 28, 28, 30, 32

Jos 1:1, 2, 3, 3, 4, 4, 6, 6, 15, 17, 17, 18; 2:3, 4, 7, 8, 9, 10, 12, 12, 16, 17, 18, 21, 22, 24; 3:4, 5, 6, 7, 9, 15; 4:1, 5, 5, 7, 8, 8, 9, 10, 13, 13, 14, 14, 15; 6:2, 6, 7, 8, 16, 19, 22, 22, 25; 7:2, 3, 5, 9, 10, 19, 19, 22, 23, 23, 24, 26; 8:1, 2, 2, 5, 18, 24, 27, 29, 30, 31; 9:3, 6, 6, 7, 8, 8, 9, 11, 12, 15, 17, 18, 19, 19, 20, 21, 22, 25, 26, 25, 26, 27; 10:3, 3, 3, 3, 4, 6, 6, 8, 9, 14, 14, 15, 22, 23, 24, 24, 25, 28, 29, 30, 30, 31, 34, 36, 41, 41, 43; 11:6, 8, 8, 9, 14, 17, 22, 23, 23; 12:1, 2, 3, 5, 6, 7, 7; 13:1, 3, 4, 5, 6, 9, 10, 11, 14, 15, 16, 17, 18, 46, 47, 63; 16:1, 2, 3, 5, 6, 8, 10; 17:7, 9, 14, 17; 18:3, 10, 18; 19:10, 12, 28, 33; 20:1, 2, 4, 4, 6; 21:1, 1, 1, 2, 3, 8, 27, 34, 43, 43, 44, 45; 22:2, 3, 4, 4, 5, 6, 7, 8, 9, 10, 11, 15, 16, 19, 21, 23, 24, 27, 27, 27, 27, 28

Jdg 1:3, 14, 15, 20, 21, 24, 26, 33; 2:1, 1, 3, 4, 5, 6, 10, 12, 15, 17, 17, 19, 20, 26, 28; 4:3, 6, 7, 8, 11, 13, 14, 16, 18, 18, 19, 20, 21, 22; 5:3, 18; 6:4, 6, 7, 8, 8, 10, 11, 12, 12, 13, 15, 18, 19, 20, 23, 23, 24, 24, 25, 26, 27, 30, 31, 35, 35, 36, 39; 7:2, 4, 4, 4, 4, 5, 5, 7, 8, 9, 11, 13, 13, 14, 17, 19, 22, 24, 24; 8:1, 2, 5, 5, 6, 15, 22, 23, 24, 25, 27, 35; 9:1, 5, 7, 7, 7, 8, 9, 11, 12, 13, 14, 15, 16, 31, 36, 40, 48, 52, 52, 54, 54, 55, 56; 10:4, 10, 11, 14, 15, 15; 11:2, 6, 6, 7, 7, 8, 9, 10, 12, 12, 13, 13, 14, 15, 15, 16, 17, 17, 19, 19, 22, 22, 28, 29, 30, 32, 33, 34, 35, 36, 36, 37, 39; 12:1, 2, 3, 5, 9, 13; 13:3, 5, 6, 7, 8, 9, 10, 10, 11, 11, 12, 13, 13, 15, 16, 16, 18, 19, 22, 23; 14:3, 3, 10, 12, 12, 13, 14, 15, 15, 16, 16, 18, 18, 19; 15:7, 11, 11, 11, 11, 12, 12, 12, 13, 14, 15, 16, 16; 16:1, 5, 5, 7, 9, 10, 11, 12, 13, 13, 14, 15, 16, 17, 18, 23, 26, 28; 17:2, 3, 3, 4, 9, 9, 10, 10, 11; 18:1, 1, 2, 3, 4, 5, 6, 8, 8, 10, 12, 14, 15, 18, 19, 19, 23, 23, 24, 25, 26, 27, 27, 29; 19:2, 3, 5, 6, 9, 11, 12, 13, 18, 21, 23, 23, 24, 24, 25, 28, 28, 30; 20:1, 14, 26, 32, 36, 42, 45, 45, 47; 21:1, 5, 12, 13, 22, 22, 22, 22, 23

Ru 1:7, 8, 10, 10, 14, 15, 15, 18, 20; 2:2, 2, 19, 20, 20, 20, 21, 22, 23; 3:1, 3, 5, 5, 6, 13, 17; 4:1, 3, 8, 9, 9, 12, 13, 14, 15, 16

1Sa 1:3, 5, 10, 11, 11, 14, 21, 22, 23, 24, 26; 2:10, 11, 14, 16, 20, 22, 23, 25, 27, 27, 27, 28, 34; 3:1, 5, 7, 9, 14, 17; 4:3, 7, 8, 9, 16, 20; 5:1, 5, 8, 8; 6:5, 12, 14, 15, 17, 18, 18; 7:3, 3, 3, 5, 8, 9, 9, 14, 17; 8:4, 5, 6, 7, 7, 8, 8, 9, 9, 10, 22, 22, 22; 9:6, 10, 11, 16, 17, 19, 23, 23, 24; 10:2, 7, 8, 11, 14, 15, 16, 17, 18, 19; 11:1, 3, 3, 7, 9, 9, 9, 10, 10, 12; 12:1, 1, 1, 2, 6, 7, 8, 10, 12, 17, 18, 19, 19, 19, 20; 13:12, 15, 17; 14:1, 4, 6, 7, 8, 8, 9, 9, 10, 11, 11, 12, 17, 18, 19, 19, 23, 33, 34, 35, 35, 36, 36, 40, 40, 41, 45, 52; 15:1, 1, 6, 10, 11, 13, 15, 16, 16, 20, 21, 24, 26, 28, 32; 16:1, 3, 3, 5, 7, 10, 11, 11, 15, 17, 19, 20; 17:8, 8, 13, 17, 18, 23, 24, 34, 37, 39, 41, 43, 44, 46, 52, 52, 55; 18:1, 8, 18, 19; 19:4, 4, 6, 11, 17, 17, 20, 24, 5, 5, 12, 16, 18, 22, 29, 30, 30, 31, 32, 36, 40, 40; 21:1, 2, 2, 5, 8, 11, 14; 22:2, 3, 5, 7, 8, 13, 15, 17, 22; 23:2, 3, 17, 17, 27; 24:4, 4, 4, 6, 16, 19, 21, 22, 22, 27, 27, 31, 31, 34, 35, 40, 40; 26:1; 27:2, 5, 6, 6, 28:1, 7, 8, 8, 9, 11, 13, 14, 15, 18, 21, 21, 21, 22, 23; 29:3, 3, 4, 4, 4, 6, 6, 6, 8; 30:13, 15, 17, 24, 25, 26; 31:4

2Sa 1:3, 3, 4, 5, 14, 16, 26; 2:1, 1, 5, 5, 5, 6; 3:2, 7, 8, 12, 16, 21, 21, 24, 38; 4:8, 9; 5:1, 6, 6, 14, 19; 6:10, 12, 21, 23; 7:2, 4, 8, 9, 17, 20, 24, 27, 28;

17, 19, 25, 32, 37, 38; 17:2, 3, 5, 6, 10, 15, 15, 18, 19, 23, 29, 31, 34; 18:2, 6, 6, 14, 21, 26, 26; 19:2, 2, 3, 3, 3, 4, 12, 22, 24, 30, 31, 33; 20:1, 6, 7, 13, 20, 22, 24, 27, 28, 34, 38; 21:1, 1, 1, 2, 8, 11, 18, 20, 31, 32, 37, 37, 39, 40, 40; 22:1, 4, 5, 5, 6, 7, 7, 8, 10, 13, 13, 18, 20, 21, 21, 22, 25, 27; 23:3, 15, 17, 17, 18, 18, 18, 21, 23, 24, 26; 24:2, 4, 8, 10, 10, 14, 23; 26:6, 11, 11, 12, 13, 14, 21, 22, 26; 26:1, 6, 7, 11, 14, 16, 16, 17, 18, 19, 20, 22, 23, 28, 30; 32; 27:1, 3, 8, 10, 21, 40; 28:17, 19, 21, 25, 26, 28, 28, 30

Ro 1:1, 10, 11, 13, 16, 19, 26; 2:5, 8, 14; 3:2, 7, 22; 4:3, 6, 11; 5:5, 15, 16, 18, 21, 21; 6:10, 10, 11, 11, 13, 13, 13, 16, 16, 19, 19, 22; 7:4, 5, 10, 13, 16; 9:12, 17, 19, 21, 21, 23, 26, 29; 10:3, 10, 10, 12, 18, 20, 21; 11:4, 8, 9, 17, 27, 35; 12:1, 3, 19; 13:1; 14:6, 8, 8; 15:8, 9, 15, 19, 23, 25, 25, 27, 29, 32; 16:1, 4, 5, 19, 19

1Co 1:2, 3, 8, 9, 11, 18, 23, 23, 24, 30; 2:1, 7, 10, 14; 3:1, 1, 1, 1, 10; 4:9, 11, 13, 17, 21; 5:5, 9, 11; 6:12, 17; 7:1, 3, 3, 10, 27; 8:1, 4, 7, 7; 9:2, 11, 15, 16, 17, 18, 18, 20; 10:2, 11, 28, 28; 11:13, 14, 17, 23, 34; 12:2, 21, 31; 14:3, 2, 3, 6, 11, 11, 21, 26, 34, 36, 37; 15:1, 1, 2, 3, 6, 28, 28; 16:3, 5, 9, 11, 12, 16

2Co 1:1, 3, 15, 16, 20, 23; 2:3, 4, 4, 12, 14, 15, 16, 16; 3:15; 4:4, 11; 5:5, 11, 12, 15, 15, 19, 19, 19; 6:11, 13, 18; 7:12, 12; 8:2, 5, 17; 9:5, 12, 13, 13, 13, 15; 10:13, 14; 12:9, 17, 19, 20

Gal 1:2, 6, 8, 8, 9, 17, 20, 22; 2:2, 7, 7, 9, 9, 9, 14, 19; 3:8, 23, 24; 4:8, 13; 5:2, 4, 13; 6:6, 10, 10, 11, 14, 14, 99

Eph 1:5, 9, 14, 15, 17; 2:10, 16, 18, 21; 3:3, 5, 5, 7, 8, 10, 14, 20, 21; 4:7, 8, 13, 13, 16, 19, 29, 30; 5:10, 20, 22, 22, 24, 31; 6:5, 9, 13, 19, 22, 99

Php 1:2, 11, 12, 14, 22, 29; 2:8, 19, 27, 30; 3:10, 11, 13, 15, 21, 21; 4:5, 6, 16, 20

Col 1:2, 6, 8, 10, 11, 12, 20; 2:2; 3:18, 20, 23; 4:1, 3, 7, 8, 9, 10, 11, 11

1Th 1:1, 1, 5, 9; 2:1, 2, 8, 8, 9, 9, 12, 18; 3:6, 11; 4:7, 7, 8, 9, 15, 15; 5:1, 15, 23, 27, 99

2Th 1:1, 1, 2; 2:1; 3:9

1Ti 1:2, 6, 17, 18, 20; 2:4; 3:14, 14, 16; 4:7, 8, 16, 16; 6:16

2Ti 1:12, 14, 16, 16, 18, 18; 2:9, 15, 16, 21, 24; 3:9, 11, 15, 17; 4:4, 8, 9, 10, 10, 18, 99

Tit 1:3, 15, 15, 16; 2:9, 14; 3:2, 8, 12, 12, 13

Phm 1:1, 13, 16, 19, 21, 22

Heb 1:1, 2, 5, 8; 2:3, 5, 10, 12, 12, 17; 3:6, 14; 4:2, 2, 13, 16; 5:4, 5, 7, 9; 6:1, 6, 8, 11, 17; 7:3, 4, 19, 21, 25; 8:5; 9:20, 27, 28, 28; 10:24, 29, 30, 39; 11:4, 26; 12:2, 4, 5, 5, 9, 11, 18, 18, 22, 22; 13:6, 7, 13, 22

Jas 1:23; 2:2, 3, 16, 23; 4:6; 5:7

1Pe 1:2, 2, 3, 5, 7, 10, 12, 12, 12, 13, 22, 25; 2:4, 7, 7, 14, 14, 24, 25; 3:5, 7, 7, 12, 19, 22; 4:7, 12, 19; 5:5, 12

2Pe 1:2, 3, 3, 4, 11, 16, 19; 2:4, 6, 9, 21, 22; 3:1, 7, 12, 15, 15, 16

1Jn 1:2, 3, 4, 5; 2:1, 7, 8, 12, 13, 13, 14, 14, 21, 26; 3:14; 5:13, 16, 16, 17

2Jn 1:1, 5, 10, 12, 12

3Jn 1:1, 9, 13

Jude 1:2, 3, 3, 3, 6, 11, 21, 24

Rev 1:1, 1, 1, 4, 5, 6, 11, 11, 11, 11, 11, 14, 11, 11, 13, 15, 17; 2:1, 5, 7, 8, 10, 11, 14, 16, 17, 18, 18, 20, 23, 24, 24, 26, 29; 3:1, 6, 13, 14, 22; 4:3; 6; 5:5, 10, 13, 13; 6:2, 4, 8, 11, 11, 13; 7:10, 12, 13, 14, 17; 8:3; 9:1, 3, 7, 7, 10, 19; 10:4, 8, 9, 9, 11; 11:1, 2, 3, 12, 18; 12:5, 12, 13; 13:2, 4, 4, 5, 5, 7; 14:4, 6, 13, 14, 20; 15:7; 16:8, 14, 19; 17:1, 1, 7, 13, 15, 17; 18:5, 6, 9, 11, 9, 9, 9, 10, 17; 20:4; 21:5, 6, 6, 9, 11, 18; 22:6, 6, 9, 10, 16, 18, 18

UP (2381)

Ge 2:6, 21; 4:8; 7:11, 17, 17; 8:7, 13; 13:1, 10, 14; 14:22; 17:22; 18:2, 16; 19:1, 2, 14, 27, 28, 30; 20:18; 21:14, 16, 18, 32; 22:3, 3, 4, 13, 19; 23:3, 7; 24:16, 54, 63, 64; 25:8, 17, 34; 26:23, 31; 27:38; 28:12, 18, 18; 29:11; 31:10, 12, 17, 21, 35, 45, 55; 32:22; 35:1, 3, 13, 14, 29; 37:25, 28, 35; 38:8, 12, 13; 39:15, 16, 18; 40:13, 19, 20; 41:2, 3, 4, 5, 6, 18, 19, 20, 21, 23, 27, 34, 35, 44, 48, 48, 48; 43:2, 15, 29; 44:4, 17, 24, 30, 33; 45:9, 25; 46:4, 5, 29, 31; 47:14; 48:17; 49:4, 4, 9, 9, 33, 33; 50:5, 6, 7, 7, 9, 14, 23, 25

Ex 1:8, 10; 2:17, 23; 3:8, 17; 7:12, 20; 8:3, 4, 5, 6, 7, 20; 9:10, 13, 16, 32; 10:12, 14; 12:6, 30, 31, 34, 38; 13:18, 19; 14:10, 16; 15:7; 16:13, 14, 23, 24, 33, 34; 17:3, 10, 11, 12; 19:3, 12, 13, 20, 20, 23, 24, 24; 20:25, 26; 22:2; 24:1, 2, 4, 9, 12, 13, 13, 15, 18; 26:15, 30, 33; 29:27; 32:1, 1, 4, 6, 6, 8, 23, 30; 33:1, 1, 3, 5, 15; 34:2, 3, 4, 4, 24; 35:21, 26; 36:2, 20; 40:2, 8, 8, 17, 18, 18, 18, 21, 28, 33, 33, 36, 37, 37

Lev 6:10; 9:22; 11:45; 13:4, 5, 11, 21, 26,

31, 33, 37, 42, 50, 54; 14:38, 46; 19:16, 32; 22:30; 26:1, 1, 38

Nu 1:51; 6:26; 7:1; 9:15, 17, 21, 21, 22; 10:11, 21, 35; 11:32; 13:17, 17, 24, 30, 31, 31, 32, 32; 14:1, 13, 36, 37, 40, 40, 40, 42, 44; 15:19, 20; 16:2, 3, 12, 13, 14, 24, 25, 27, 30, 32, 34, 37, 45; 17:4, 7; 18:26; 19:9, 9; 20:4, 5, 11, 25, 27; 21:3, 5, 17, 33; 22:4, 4, 13, 14, 20, 21, 41; 23:7, 18, 18, 24, 24; 24:2, 3, 8, 9, 15, 20, 21, 23, 25; 25:4, 7; 26:10; 27:12; 31:52; 32:9, 11, 14; 33:38

Dt 1:21, 22, 24, 26, 28, 28, 41, 41, 42, 43; 2:13, 24; 3:1, 27, 27; 4:19; 5:5; 6:7; 8:14; 9:1, 9, 23; 10:1, 3; 11:6, 17, 18, 19; 14:25, 28; 16:22; 17:8, 20; 18:15, 18; 19:11, 15, 16; 20:1; 22:4, 14, 19; 23:14; 24:5; 25:7, 7, 9; 27:2, 4, 5; 28:7, 33, 43; 29:22; 30:12; 31:5, 16; 32:11, 17, 30, 34, 34, 36, 38, 40, 49, 50; 33:2; 34:1

Jos 2:6, 8, 10; 3:6, 6, 16; 4:5, 8, 9, 16, 17, 18, 18, 19, 23, 23; 5:1, 7, 13; 6:1, 5, 6, 12, 20, 26, 26; 7:2, 2, 3, 3, 4, 10, 13, 16, 16; 8:1, 3, 7, 10, 10, 11, 14, 20, 31; 9:4; 10:4, 5, 6, 9, 10, 12, 33, 36; 11:6, 17; 12:7; 14:8; 15:3, 3, 6, 6, 7, 7, 8, 8, 15; 16:1; 17:15; 18:1, 11, 12, 12, 17; 19:10, 11, 12, 47; 20:5; 22:12, 13; 24:17, 26, 32

Jdg 1:1, 2, 3, 4, 16, 22, 36; 2:1, 1, 4, 16, 18; 3:9, 15; 4:5, 10, 10, 12, 14; 6:3, 3, 5, 8, 13, 21, 35, 38; 7:1; 8:8, 11, 13, 20, 28; 9:7, 18, 32, 33, 34, 35, 43, 48, 51; 11:2, 13, 16, 31, 37; 12:3; 13:20; 14:2, 19; 15:5, 6, 9, 10, 10, 13; 16:3, 5, 8, 18, 18, 29, 31; 18:9, 12, 17, 30, 31; 19:5, 7, 9, 10, 17, 27, 28, 28, 30, 30; 20:3, 9, 18, 18, 19, 23, 23, 23, 26, 28, 30, 31, 33, 38, 40, 40; 21:2, 5, 8, 19

Ru 1:9, 14; 2:15, 18; 3:14; 4:1, 5, 10

1Sa 1:3, 5, 6, 7, 9, 19, 21, 22, 24; 2:6, 7, 8, 8, 14, 19, 35; 5:12; 6:9, 10, 13, 20, 21; 7:1, 7, 10; 8:8; 9:11, 13, 13, 14, 14, 19, 24, 26; 10:3, 18, 25; 11:1, 4; 12:6; 13:5, 15; 14:9, 10, 10, 12, 12, 13, 21, 46; 15:2, 6, 11, 12, 34; 16:12, 13; 17:20, 23, 25, 25; 19:15; 20:38; 21:12; 22:8; 23:11, 12, 19, 29; 24:7, 16, 22; 25:5, 13, 35; 26:19; 27:8; 28:8, 11, 11, 14, 15, 25; 29:9, 10, 10, 11, 11; 30:4

2Sa 2:1, 1, 1, 2, 3, 22, 27, 32; 3:10, 32; 4:4, 12; 5:8, 17, 19, 19, 22, 23; 6:2, 12, 15; 7:6, 12; 12:3, 3, 11, 17; 13:29, 34, 36; 14:14; 15:2, 20, 24, 30, 30, 30, 30; 17:16, 21; 18:9, 18, 24, 24, 28, 28, 31, 33; 19:34; 20:2, 3, 15, 19, 20, 21; 21:6, 8, 13; 22:9, 40, 49, 49; 23:1, 8, 18; 24:9, 11, 18, 19, 22

1Ki 1:3, 4, 6, 6, 7, 9, 13, 14, 16; 2:1, 11, 13, 35; 5:13, 14; 6:8; 7:21, 21, 21; 8:1, 3, 4, 4, 20, 35, 54; 9:16, 24; 10:5, 29; 11:14, 15, 23, 26, 27; 12:8, 10, 18, 24, 27, 28, 28; 13:4, 29; 14:10, 14, 15, 16, 25; 15:4; 16:17, 32, 34; 17:9, 19; 18:38, 41, 42, 42, 43, 44, 46; 20:1, 22, 26, 33; 21:16, 21, 25; 22:6, 12, 20, 29, 35, 38

2Ki 1:3, 4, 6, 6, 7, 9, 13, 14, 16; 2:1, 11, 13, 16, 23, 23, 23; 3:7, 8, 21, 22, 24; 4:21, 29, 34, 35, 36, 37; 6:7, 24; 7:5; 8:12; 9:1, 2, 8, 35, 36, 37; 6:7, 24; 7:5; 10:1, 5, 6, 15; 12:10, 10, 17, 17; 13:21; 14:10, 11, 26; 15:14, 16; 16:5, 7, 7, 7, 9; 17:3, 4, 5, 5, 7; 18:9, 13, 17, 17, 17, 25, 25; 19:4, 14, 23, 23, 24, 26, 28; 20:5, 8, 17, 21:3, 3; 22:4, 23, 23, 24, 26, 28; 24:1, 10; 25:4, 6, 27

1Ch 5:26; 11:6, 11, 20; 13:6, 6; 14:2, 8, 10, 10, 11, 14; 15:3, 12, 14, 16, 25, 28; 17:5, 11; 21:11, 16, 18, 18, 19, 27; 25:5; 26:16; 28:2

2Ch 1:4, 6, 17; 2:16; 3:17; 5:2, 4, 5, 5, 13; 6:10, 26; 7:13, 20; 8:11; 9:4; 10:8, 10, 18; 11:4; 12:2, 9; 13:4, 6; 16:1; 17:6; 18:2, 5, 11, 14, 19, 28, 34; 20:16, 19, 23; 21:4, 9, 16, 17; 24:7, 23; 25:14, 19, 21; 26:16, 19; 28:9, 12, 15; 29:20, 27, 30; 30:7, 27; 32:5, 5, 25; 33:3, 14, 19; 34:30; 35:20; 36:6, 15, 22, 23

Ezr 1:1, 3, 5, 5, 11, 11; 2:1, 59, 63, 68; 3:2; 4:2, 12, 12, 13, 18, 23; 5:2, 3, 9, 11; 6:1, 11; 7:6, 7, 9, 13, 28; 8:1; 9:5, 6, 6, 9; 10:6, 10

Ne 2:1, 15, 17, 18; 3:1, 1, 3, 6, 13, 14, 15, 19, 31, 32; 4:3, 7, 14; 5:2; 6:1, 10; 7:1, 5, 6, 61, 65; 8:5, 6; 9:3, 4, 5, 18; 10:38; 12:1, 31, 37, 37

Est 2:7, 20; 5:9; 7:7

Job 1:5, 7, 16; 2:2, 12, 12; 3:8, 10, 11; 4:15; 5:5, 5, 11, 18; 6:3, 4; 7:9; 8:11; 9:7; 10:15, 18; 11:10, 15, 20; 12:14, 15; 13:19; 14:10, 11, 17, 17; 15:30; 16:4, 8, 12; 17:8; 18:16; 19:8, 12, 20:6, 15, 27; 21:19; 22:22, 23, 24, 26, 29; 24:22; 26:8; 27:7, 16; 28:4, 5; 29:8; 30:4, 12, 20, 22, 28; 31:14, 18, 21, 29; 33:5; 34:7; 36:13; 37:7, 20; 38:3, 8, 10, 34; 39:4, 18, 27, 30; 40:7, 23, 23; 41:10, 15, 20; 42:8

Ps 3:1, 3; 4:6; 5:3; 7:6; 9:13; 10:12; 14:4; 15:3; 16:4; 17:5, 7; 18:8, 35, 39, 48, 48; 20:5; 21:9; 22:15; 24:4, 7, 7, 9, 9; 25:1; 27:2, 5, 6, 10, 12; 28:2, 5, 9; 30:1, 3; 31:8, 19; 33:7; 35:2, 11, 23, 25; 39:6; 40:2, 5, 12; 41:8, 9, 10; 44:5; 47:5; 53:4; 54:3; 56:1, 2; 57:3, 8; 59:1, 15; 63:4; 69:9, 15, 29; 71:6, 20; 74:3, 4, 5, 8, 15, 23; 75:3; 77:9; 78:21, 38, 48; 80:2; 81:3, 12; 83:2; 86:4; 87:6; 88:8, 15;

89:2, 4, 42; 90:5, 6; 91:12; 92:11; 93:3, 3; 94:2, 16, 16, 18; 97:3; 102:10, 16; 104:8; 105:35; 106:9, 17, 18, 26, 30; 107:25, 26; 109:23; 110:7; 113:7; 119:48, 117; 121:1; 122:4; 123:1; 124:2, 3; 127:2, 2; 129:6; 132:3; 134:2; 139:8, 21; 140:10; 141:2; 143:8; 144:12; 145:14; 147:2, 3, 6

Pr 1:12; 2:3, 7; 3:20; 7:1; 8:23, 30; 10:12, 14; 13:22; 15:1, 18; 16:27; 21:20; 22:6; 23:8; 24:16; 25:7; 26:9, 24; 28:25; 29:21, 22; 30:4, 13, 31, 32; 31:28

Ecc 2:26; 3:2, 3; 4:10, 10, 15; 10:4, 12; 12:4

SS 2:7, 10; 3:5; 4:2, 12; 5:5; 6:6; 7:8, 12, 13; 8:4, 5, 5

Isa 1:2, 6; 2:3, 4, 12, 13, 14; 3:13, 14; 5:5, 6, 11, 13, 24, 26; 6:1; 7:1, 6; 8:7, 7, 16; 9:11, 18, 18; 10:15, 15, 24, 26, 26, 28, 29, 30; 11:12, 16; 13:2, 14, 17; 14:4, 8, 9, 9, 22; 15:2, 5, 5, 5, 7; 18:3; 19:5, 6; 21:2; 22:1; 23:4, 4, 13, 18; 24:10, 14, 18, 22; 25:8; 26:11; 27:9; 28:4, 7, 21; 30:26; 32:9, 13; 33:3, 10, 12; 34:3, 10, 13; 35:9; 36:1, 10, 10; 37:4, 14, 23, 24, 25, 27, 29; 38:22; 39:6; 40:9, 9, 9, 15, 26, 31; 41:2, 25; 42:2, 11, 13, 15, 15; 43:6; 44:4, 11, 26, 27; 45:8, 13, 20; 47:13; 48:13; 49:6, 18, 19, 21, 22, 22, 23; 50:2, 9; 51:6, 8, 17, 18; 52:8; 53:2; 55:13, 13; 57:7, 8, 8, 14, 14, 14, 20; 58:1, 12; 59:19; 60:4, 7, 10; 61:1, 4; 62:10, 10, 10; 63:11; 64:7, 11

Jer 1:17; 2:6, 24; 3:2, 6; 4:3, 6, 7, 13, 29; 5:10, 17, 17, 17; 6:1, 4; 7:13, 16, 25, 29; 9:10, 10, 12, 18, 21; 10:17, 20, 25; 11:7, 13, 14; 12:17; 13:19, 20; 14:2, 6; 15:9; 16:14, 15; 18:7, 15, 21; 20:9; 21:2, 22; 22:20, 20, 22; 23:4, 7, 8, 10; 24:6; 25:32; 26:5, 10, 17; 27:22; 29:15, 19, 22; 30:9, 13; 31:6, 21, 28, 40; 32:2, 3, 33; 33:1, 15; 34:21; 35:11, 15; 36:5, 20; 37:10, 11; 38:10, 13, 13; 39:2, 5, 15; 42:10; 45:4; 46:4, 7, 8, 9, 9; 47:2, 6; 48:5, 9, 11; 49:5, 14, 19, 22, 28; 50:2, 3, 9, 21, 26, 32, 38, 41, 44; 51:1, 1, 3, 9, 11, 12, 12, 14, 27, 27, 34, 36, 42, 44, 53; 52:7, 9, 31

La 1:14, 14, 19; 2:2, 5, 5, 7, 10, 16, 17, 19, 22; 3:41, 62, 63; 4:5; 5:12

Eze 1:13, 19, 19, 20, 21, 21; 3:12, 14; 4:14; 7:11; 8:3, 5, 5, 11; 9:3; 10:4, 15, 16, 16, 17, 17, 19, 19; 11:1, 22, 23, 24, 24; 13:5, 5, 10; 14:3, 4, 7; 16:40; 17:9, 9, 14, 17, 24; 18:6, 12, 15; 19:1, 3, 6, 12, 12; 20:5, 6, 6, 15, 23, 28, 42; 21:15, 22; 22:30; 23:22, 27, 46, 47; 24:8; 26:3, 3, 8, 17, 19; 27:2, 30, 32; 28:2, 5, 12, 12, 14, 17; 29:4; 30:21; 31:4, 10, 10, 10, 14, 18, 39:2; 33:25; 34:4, 10, 18, 19, 24, 29; 36:3, 3, 7, 13; 37:6, 8, 10, 12, 13; 38:11, 16, 18; 39:2, 15; 40:6, 22, 26, 31, 34, 37, 40, 49; 41:16; 43:5, 24; 44:12; 47:14

Da 2:21, 44; 3:1, 2, 3, 5, 7, 12, 14, 18, 22, 24; 4:17, 34; 5:19, 20, 23; 6:23, 23; 7:3, 4, 5, 8, 8, 20; 8:3, 3, 8, 22, 22, 23, 25, 26, 27; 9:24; 10:5; 11:2, 2, 3, 4, 4, 6, 7, 10, 10, 12, 14, 15, 20, 21, 23, 25, 25; 12:1, 4, 7, 9, 11

Hos 1:11; 2:6, 15; 4:8, 15, 19; 6:1, 2; 8:4, 7, 8, 9; 9:6, 12, 16; 10:4, 8, 12; 11:8; 13:12, 15, 15, 16

Joel 1:6, 10, 12, 20; 2:9, 20, 20; 3:9, 9, 12

Am 1:6, 9, 13; 2:10, 11; 3:1, 5, 10; 4:10; 5:1, 2; 6:8, 10, 14; 7:1, 4; 8:4, 8, 10, 14; 9:2, 2, 5, 5, 6, 10, 11; 12:3; 13:2, 10

Ob 1:1, 6, 14, 21

Jnh 1:2, 3, 12, 15, 17; 2:6; 4:6, 10

Mic 2:4, 8, 13, 13; 3:10; 4:2, 3; 5:3, 9, 14; 6:4, 14; 7:3, 6

Na 1:4; 9; 7; 3:3, 15

Hab 1:3, 6, 9, 15; 2:4, 6, 7; 3:10, 16

Zep 2:4; 3:8

Hag 1:8, 14

Zec 1:18, 21, 21; 2:1, 13; 5:1, 5, 7, 9, 9; 6:1; 12; 9:3, 13, 16; 10:11, 12; 11:16, 17; 14:10, 13, 16, 17, 18, 18, 19

Mal 3:15; 17; 4:1, 2

Mt 3:9, 12, 16; 4:1, 5, 6, 8, 16; 5:1; 6:19, 20; 9:6, 16; 10:17, 19, 21, 21; 11:5; 12:42; 13:4, 5, 6, 7, 26, 28, 29, 29; 14:12, 19, 20, 23; 15:13, 29, 37; 16:9, 10, 24; 17:1, 8, 27, 27; 19:20; 20:12; 18; 22:7, 24; 23:13, 32; 24:9, 43; 26:52; 27:37, 50

Mk 1:10, 31, 35; 2:4, 9, 11, 12, 21; 3:13, 26; 4:4, 5, 6, 7, 8, 27, 32; 5:29; 6:29, 41, 43, 51; 7:34; 8:8, 19, 20, 24, 25, 34; 9:2, 27; 10:16, 21, 32, 33; 11:20; 12:19; 13:9, 11, 12, 16; 14:42, 60; 15:37, 39, 41; 16:18, 19

Lk 1:66, 69; 2:4, 28, 42; 3:8, 20; 4:5, 11, 16, 25, 29; 5:23, 24, 25, 25, 28; 6:8, 20; 7:15, 16; 8:6, 7, 8, 37; 9:16, 17, 23, 28, 51; 10:25, 34; 11:27, 31, 32; 12:19, 21; 13:11, 25; 14:10; 16:23; 17:6, 13; 18:10, 13, 21, 31; 19:4, 5, 20, 21, 22, 28; 20:28; 21:1, 12, 28, 28; 22:45; 23:5, 46; 24:33, 50, 51

Jn 2:7, 13, 17, 19, 20; 3:13, 14, 14; 4:14, 35; 5:1, 8, 9, 11, 12, 21; 6:3, 5, 12, 39, 40, 44, 54, 62; 7:8, 8, 10, 10, 14; 8:7, 10, 28, 59; 10:1, 31; 11:31, 41, 41, 55; 12:20, 32, 34; 12:17, 32; 13:4, 18, 22, 31; 17:1; 18:11; 19:30; 21:11

Ac 1:2, 9, 10, 11, 11, 13, 15, 22; 2:14, 14, 24, 30, 32; 3:1, 6, 7, 8, 13, 22, 26; 4:24, 26; 5:5, 6, 10, 17, 30, 34, 36, 37; 6:12; 7:20, 21, 37, 42, 43, 55; 8:31, 39; 9:40, 41; 10:4, 9, 16, 26, 26, 40; 11:2, 10, 28; 12:7, 7, 23; 13:1, 16, 22, 31, 33, 34,

43, 50; 14:2, 11, 20; 15:2, 5, 7, 16; 16:22; 17:13; 18:22; 20:9, 11, 32; 21:4, 12, 15, 15, 27; 22:3, 13, 22; 24:11, 12; 25:9, 18; 26:10, 30; 27:15, 17, 27, 40, 40

Ro 1:24, 26; 2:5; 4:24; 6:4; 8:11, 11, 32; 9:17; 10:7; 14:4; 15:16

1Co 4:6, 18, 19; 5:2; 6:14, 14; 8:1; 10:7; 13:4; 15:15, 15, 24, 35, 54

2Co 2:7; 4:14, 14; 5:4; 9:5; 12:2, 4, 14

Gal 1:17, 18; 2:1, 2; 3:23

Eph 2:6; 4:8, 10, 15; 6:4

Col 1:5, 24; 2:7, 18

1Th 2:16; 4:17

1Ti 2:8; 3:6, 16; 4:6; 5:10; 6:19

2Ti 1:6; 4:8

Heb 1:12; 5:7; 7:27, 27; 11:17, 17, 19; 12:12, 15

Jas 4:10; 5:15

1Pe 1:13, 21; 2:5, 5

2Pe 1:13; 3:1, 10

1Jn 3:17;

Jude 1:12, 20

Rev 4:1; 8:4, 7, 7; 10:4, 5, 9, 10; 11:12, 12; 12:5, 16; 13:1, 11; 14:11; 15:1; 16:12; 18:21; 19:3; 20:3, 9, 13, 13

UPON (2763)

Ge 1:2, 2, 11, 15, 17, 25, 26, 28, 29, 30; 2:5, 21; 3:14; 4:15, 26; 6:12, 12, 17; 7:3, 4, 6, 8, 10, 12, 14, 17, 18, 18, 19, 21, 21, 23, 24; 8:4, 17, 17, 19; 9:2, 2, 2, 2, 2, 16, 16, 17; 11:4, 8, 9; 12:8, 11; 15:11, 12, 12; 16:5; 17:17; 18:6, 19, 27, 31; 19:3, 9, 16, 16, 16, 23, 24, 24, 25; 22:2, 6, 9, 12, 17; 24:15, 16, 16, 18, 30, 47, 47, 61; 26:7, 10, 25; 27:12, 13, 15, 16, 16; 28:11, 18; 29:2, 3, 32; 30:3; 31:10, 12, 17, 34, 35, 46, 54; 32:31, 31, 32; 34:25, 27; 35:5, 20; 37:22, 27, 34; 38:28; 29, 30; 39:5, 7; 40:6, 17; 41:3, 5, 17, 42; 42:1, 21; 43:18, 30; 44:21; 45:14, 14, 15; 46:4; 47:31; 48:2, 14, 14, 17, 18; 50:1, 1, 23

Ex 1:16; 2:25; 3:6, 12, 22, 22; 4:9, 9, 20, 31; 5:3, 8, 9, 21; 7:4, 5, 17, 19, 19, 19, 19, 19; 8:3, 3, 4, 4, 5, 7, 14, 18, 18, 21, 21, 21; 9:3, 3, 3, 3, 3, 9, 10, 10, 11, 11, 14, 14, 14, 19, 19, 22, 22, 22, 23, 23, 33; 10:6, 12, 13, 14:1, 5, 12:13, 13, 23; 13:9, 16; 14:4, 4, 17, 17, 17, 17, 18, 18, 22, 22, 26, 26, 26, 29, 30, 31; 15:9, 16, 19, 26, 26; 16:14; 17:6; 18:8; 19:11, 16, 18, 20, 22, 24; 20:5, 12, 25; 21:14, 19, 22, 30; 22:3, 25; 24:11, 16; 25:11, 21, 22, 30; 26:4, 7, 32, 32, 34; 27:2, 4, 7; 28:8, 12, 12, 23, 26, 29, 30, 30, 33, 34, 35, 36, 37, 37, 38, 38, 41, 43, 43; 29:5, 6, 6, 7, 9, 12, 13, 13, 15, 16, 18, 19, 20, 20, 20, 20, 21, 21, 21, 21, 21, 22, 25, 38; 30:1, 4, 7, 8, 10, 10, 32, 33; 31:18; 32:16, 20, 21, 29, 29, 29, 34; 33:16, 21; 34:1, 7, 7, 28, 35; 35:3; 36:17, 17; 37:3, 3, 13, 16, 27; 39:5, 15, 19, 24, 25, 30, 31, 41, 42; 40:4, 10; 40:14, 17, 18; 50:1, 1, 23

Lev 1:4, 5, 7, 7, 8, 8, 11, 12, 13, 17, 17; 2:1, 2, 9, 15; 3:2, 2, 3, 5, 5, 8, 8, 9, 10, 11, 13, 13, 14, 15, 16; 4:4, 7, 8, 9, 10, 15, 18, 19, 24, 25, 26, 29, 30, 31, 33, 34, 35; 5:9, 11; 6:9, 10, 12, 12, 13, 15, 15, 27; 7:2, 5, 20, 31; 8:7, 7, 8, 9, 9, 11, 12, 13, 13, 14, 15, 15, 16, 18, 19, 21, 22, 23, 23, 23, 24, 24, 24, 25, 26, 27, 27, 28, 30, 30, 30, 30, 30, 30; 9:9, 10, 13, 14, 17, 18, 20, 24; 10:6, 7; 11:20, 21, 21, 27, 29, 32, 37, 38, 41, 42, 42, 42, 44, 46; 13:25, 27, 29, 30, 43, 45, 50; 14:7, 14, 14, 14, 17, 17, 17, 18, 20, 25, 25, 25, 28, 28, 28, 29, 41; 15:8, 9, 20, 20, 24, 26, 16:2, 2, 4, 8, 9, 13, 13, 14, 15, 18, 25; 17:6, 11; 18:25; 19:17; 19:28; 20:9, 11, 12, 13, 16, 27; 21:5; 10, 12; 22:3, 22; 23:37; 24:4, 6, 7, 14; 25:21; 26:21, 25, 30, 35, 36, 37

Nu 1:53; 4:7, 8, 10, 11, 14, 14, 25; 5:14, 14, 15, 25, 30, 30; 6:5, 7, 19, 25, 26, 27; 7:9, 89; 8:7, 10, 12, 24, 25; 9:15, 18, 19, 20, 22; 10:34; 11:9, 9, 17, 17, 25, 25, 26, 29, 31; 12:3, 10, 10; 13:23; 14:18, 36, 37; 15:31, 32, 38, 39; 16:3, 4, 7, 22, 33, 45; 17:2, 3; 18:5, 17; 19:2, 13, 13, 15, 18, 18, 18, 19, 20; 20:6, 26, 28; 21:8, 8, 9, 15, 22; 22:30; 23:4; 24:2; 27:18, 20, 23; 30:14; 31:27; 33:4; 35:22, 23

Dt 1:36; 2:25; 4:7, 10, 13, 26, 30, 32, 36, 39, 40; 5:9; 6:8, 9, 22, 22; 7:6, 7, 15, 15, 16, 22; 8:4; 11:12, 18, 20, 21, 25, 25, 29, 29; 12:1, 2, 16, 19, 24, 27, 27; 13:9, 17; 14:2; 15:23; 17:7, 18; 19:5, 10; 21:23; 22:6, 6, 8, 12, 14, 19; 23:13, 19, 19, 20, 20; 24:5, 6, 15, 20, 21; 28:8, 15, 20, 24, 45, 46, 48, 56, 60, 61; 29:5, 5, 20, 22, 27; 30:1, 3, 7, 18; 31:17; 32:2, 2, 23, 34, 35, 43; 33:10, 16, 16, 26, 28, 29; 34:9

Jos 1:3; 2:6, 8, 9, 15, 15, 19; 3:13, 16; 4:5; 7:6, 6, 10; 8:7, 20, 32; 9:4, 5, 5, 20; 10:11, 12, 13, 18, 24, 24, 26; 11:4, 7; 12:2; 13:9; 19:34; 20:8; 23:15, 15; 24:7

Jdg 3:10, 16, 22, 23; 4:16; 6:14, 20, 26, 28, 34, 37, 39, 39, 40; 7:5, 6, 25; 8:21; 9:5, 18, 24, 24, 33, 44, 49, 53, 57, 57; 11:29, 37, 38; 12:1; 13:19; 14:6, 17, 19; 15:12, 14, 14, 16; 16:3, 9, 12, 14, 17, 19, 20, 26,

WE (1844)

9:15; 10:1, 2, 5, 6, 7, 9, 10; 11:5; 12:2, 2, 17, 17, 17, 17, 19, 19; 15:11
2Co 1:8; 3:14; 5:1, 14; 7:5, 5, 5, 8, 9, 9, 13; 8:3; 11:17; 12:12, 13; 13:2
Gal 1:17, 22; 2:2, 6, 12, 12; 3:16, 23; 4:3, 3, 5; 5:12
Eph 1:13; 2:1, 3, 5, 12, 13, 17, 17; 5:8
Php 3:7, 12; 4:10, 18
Col 1:16, 16, 21
1Th 1:5, 7; 2:2, 2, 4, 7, 8, 8; 3:4, 7
2Th 3:10;
Tit 3:3;
Phm 1:14;
Heb 2:15; 3:5; 4:3; 5:8; 6:4, 4; 7:11, 21, 23, 23; 8:4; 9:6, 9, 15; 10:32, 33, 33; 11:3, 3, 13, 13, 23, 29, 30, 34, 35, 37, 37, 37, 37
Jas 5:3;
1Pe 1:18; 2:8, 10, 21, 24, 25; 3:20, 20
2Pe 1:16; 1:18; 2:1, 18; 3:2, 4, 5
1Jn 2:19, 19; 3:12
Jude 1:4, 17
Rev 1:14, 14; 4:1, 4, 5, 6, 8, 11; 6:1, 9, 11, 11, 14; 7:4, 4, 5, 5, 5, 5, 6, 6, 7, 7, 7, 8, 8, 8; 8:2, 5, 7, 8, 9, 9, 9, 10, 11; 9:2, 7, 7, 7, 8, 9, 10, 15, 15, 16, 17, 19, 20; 10:1; 11:13, 13, 15, 18, 19; 12:9, 14; 13:2, 3; 14:3, 3, 4, 4; 15:2, 8; 16:9, 18, 18, 20; 17:8; 18:14, 15, 19, 23, 23, 24; 19:6, 12, 12, 14, 20, 21, 21; 20:4, 5, 12, 12, 12, 13, 13, 13, 14; 21:1, 19, 21, 21; 22:2

WITH (6016)

Ge 3:6, 12; 4:8; 5:22, 24; 6:3, 9, 11, 13, 13, 14, 16, 18, 18, 19; 7:7, 13, 23; 8:1, 16, 17, 17, 18; 9:4, 8, 9, 9, 10, 10, 10, 11, 12; 11:31; 12:4, 13, 17; 13:1, 5; 14:2, 2, 5, 8, 9, 9, 9, 13, 17, 24; 15:14, 18; 16:6, 11; 17:3, 4, 12, 13, 19, 19, 21, 22, 23, 27, 27; 18:11, 16, 23, 25, 33; 19:1, 9, 9, 11, 30, 32, 33, 34, 34, 35, 36; 20:16, 16; 21:6, 10, 10, 19, 20, 22, 23, 23, 23; 22:3, 5; 23:4, 4, 4, 8, 16; 24:15, 32, 40, 45, 49, 54, 55, 58; 25:30; 26:3, 8, 10, 15, 20, 24, 28, 28; 27:15, 34, 35, 37, 44; 28:4, 15, 20; 29:6, 9, 9, 14, 19, 25, 27, 30; 30:8, 8, 15, 16, 16, 20, 20, 29, 33; 31:3, 5, 6, 21, 23, 25, 26, 27, 27, 27, 27, 32, 32, 36, 38, 42, 50; 32:4, 6, 7, 9, 10, 11, 15, 20, 24, 25, 28, 28; 33:1, 5, 7, 10, 11, 13, 13, 15; 34:2, 5, 6, 7, 8, 9, 10, 16, 20, 21, 22, 23, 26, 31, 31; 35:2, 3, 6, 13, 14, 15, 22; 37:2, 2, 2, 14, 14, 25; 38:14, 24, 25; 39:2, 3, 7, 8, 10, 12, 14, 14, 15, 18, 21, 23; 40:4, 7, 14; 41:6, 10, 12, 23, 27; 42:4, 6, 8, 8, 16, 16, 19, 26, 29, 30, 31, 33, 34; 45:1, 5, 15, 23, 23; 46:1, 4, 6, 7, 7, 15, 26; 47:12, 17, 29, 30; 48:1, 12, 21, 22, 22; 49:12, 12, 25, 29, 30; 50:7, 9, 10, 13, 14

Ex 1:1, 7, 10, 11, 13, 14, 14, 20; 2:3, 3, 21, 24, 24, 24; 3:2, 8, 12, 17, 20; 4:12, 15, 15; 5:3, 3, 3, 15; 6:1, 1, 4, 6, 6; 7:11, 17, 22; 8:2, 5, 7, 17, 18; 9:9, 10, 15, 24; 10:9, 9, 9, 9, 9, 10, 24, 26, 26; 12:8, 8, 9, 9, 9, 10, 11, 22, 38, 48; 13:5, 7, 7, 9, 13, 19, 19; 14:6, 8, 11; 15:8, 10, 19, 19, 20, 20; 16:3, 12, 28, 30, 31; 17:2, 2, 3, 5, 8, 9, 9, 10, 13, 16; 18:5, 6, 12, 18, 19, 22; 19:9, 17, 24; 20:19, 19, 22, 23; 21:3, 6, 8, 9, 14, 18, 20, 22, 29; 22:14, 15, 16, 19, 24, 30, 30, 30; 23:1, 5, 11, 11, 18, 32, 32; 24:2, 3, 8, 14; 25:2, 11, 13, 14, 20, 22, 22, 24, 28, 28, 33, 34, 39; 26:1, 1, 6, 29, 29, 31, 32, 36, 37; 27:2, 6, 8, 16, 17; 28:1, 3, 6, 11, 11, 15, 21, 21, 28, 41; 29:2, 2, 3, 4, 5, 9, 12, 14, 21, 21, 34, 40, 40, 43; 30:3, 5, 6, 10, 20, 28, 34, 36; 31:3, 6, 8, 9, 18, 18; 32:4, 11, 11; 33:3, 9, 12, 14, 15, 16, 22; 34:3, 5, 10, 12, 19, 20, 25, 27, 28, 29, 31, 32, 33, 34, 35; 35:12, 14, 16, 23, 24, 25, 31, 35; 36:8, 13, 34, 34, 35, 36, 38, 38; 37:2, 4, 9, 9, 11, 15, 26, 28; 38:2, 6, 7, 17, 23; 39:3, 6, 14, 21, 23, 37, 37; 40:3, 12, 14

Lev 1:12, 13, 16, 17; 2:2, 4, 4, 5, 7, 11, 13, 13, 16; 3:4, 10, 15; 4:9, 11, 11, 12, 20, 20, 25, 30, 34; 5:4, 4, 15, 16, 18; 6:6, 10, 16, 17, 21; 7:4, 10, 12, 12, 12, 12, 13, 17, 19, 24, 30; 8:2, 6, 7, 7, 7, 13, 15, 17, 30, 30, 31, 32; 9:4, 11, 13; 10:9, 14, 15, 15, 16; 11:43, 43, 44; 13:57, 14:10, 16, 21, 27, 31, 37, 52, 52, 52, 52, 52, 52; 15:3, 17, 18, 18, 24, 33; 16:3, 4, 4, 10, 14, 14, 15, 15, 19; 17:4, 13; 18:20, 22, 22, 23; 19:13, 19, 19, 20, 22, 26, 33, 34; 20:2, 5, 10, 10, 11, 12, 13, 13, 14, 15, 18, 20, 24, 27; 21:9; 22:6, 8, 11, 14; 23:13, 17, 18, 18, 20, 20, 24:23; 25:6, 23, 35, 35, 36, 40, 41, 43, 45, 46, 50, 50, 52, 53, 53, 54; 26:9, 39, 40, 42, 42, 42, 44

Nu 1:2, 4, 5; 2:2, 17, 31; 3:1; 4:5, 8, 11, 12, 32, 32; 5:7, 13, 13, 19, 19, 20, 21, 23; 6:15, 15, 17, 20; 7:13, 19, 25, 31, 37, 43, 49, 55, 61, 67, 73, 79, 87, 89; 8:8, 8, 26; 9:11; 10:3, 4, 8, 9, 10, 24; 11:15, 16, 17, 17, 18, 33; 12:8; 13:23, 27, 31; 14:8, 9, 10, 12, 21, 24, 27, 43; 15:4, 5, 6, 9, 9, 14, 15, 16, 24, 36; 16:2, 10, 13, 14, 18, 20, 20; 17:4, 13; 18:1, 1, 2, 2, 7, 11, 11, 19; 19:4, 6, 12, 12; 20:3, 11, 13, 18, 20, 20; 21:18, 24; 22:7, 8, 9, 12, 13,

14, 20, 21, 22, 27, 35, 35, 39, 40; 23:13, 17, 21; 24:8; 25:1, 14, 18; 26:3, 10; 27:21; 28:5, 9, 12, 12, 13, 20, 28; 29:3, 9, 14; 30:2, 8, 10; 31:6, 8, 10, 14, 14, 17, 18, 23, 35; 32:19, 29, 30, 33; 33:1, 3; 34:2, 12; 35:7, 16, 17, 18, 21, 23, 25

Dt 1:16, 37; 2:5, 7, 9, 19, 24, 26; 3:5, 13, 26, 27; 4:11, 11, 21, 23, 29, 29, 37, 40, 40; 5:2, 3, 3, 4, 14, 22, 23, 24, 29, 29, 33; 6:3, 3, 5, 5, 5, 18, 21; 7:2, 3, 5, 5, 8, 9, 23, 25; 8:3, 16; 9:8, 9, 10, 10, 15, 19, 20, 21, 26; 10:9, 12, 12, 14, 22; 11:2, 9, 10, 13, 13; 12:3, 12, 23, 25, 25, 28, 28; 13:3, 3, 10, 15, 15, 16; 14:27, 29; 15:3, 14, 16, 19; 16:3, 4, 10, 18; 17:5, 19; 18:1, 6, 11, 13; 19:5, 5, 13; 20:1, 4, 12, 13, 20; 21:3, 11; 22:2, 3, 3, 3, 6, 7, 10; 21, 22, 22, 23, 24, 25, 25, 28, 29; 23:4, 4, 11, 16, 23, 25; 24:5, 12; 25:3, 11; 26:5, 8, 8, 8, 8, 8, 9, 15, 16, 16; 27:1, 2, 3, 4, 14, 20, 21, 22, 28:22, 22, 22, 22, 22, 22, 22, 27, 27, 27, 27, 28, 30, 32, 35, 40, 47, 47, 67, 68; 29:1, 1, 10, 12, 12, 14, 15, 15, 15, 25; 30:2, 2, 6, 6, 10, 10; 31:6, 7, 8, 16, 16, 20, 23, 27; 32:10, 14, 14, 15, 16, 16, 16, 16, 21, 21, 21, 24, 24, 24, 24, 25, 34, 39, 42, 43, 43; 33:2, 3, 8, 8, 17, 20, 21, 23, 23, 24; 34:4

Jos 1:5, 5, 9, 17, 17; 2:6, 14, 19; 3:7, 7; 4:3; 5:6; 13; 6:4, 5, 5, 8, 9, 9, 10, 13, 13, 16, 17, 20, 20, 21, 24, 27; 7:12, 15, 15, 24, 25, 25, 25; 8:1, 5, 11, 24, 35; 9:2, 2, 2, 6, 7, 11, 11, 15, 15, 16; 10:1, 4, 4, 7, 10, 11, 11, 12, 14, 18, 19, 31; 13:8, 21; 14:4; 15:32, 36, 41, 44, 45, 46, 47, 47, 51, 54, 57, 59, 60, 62, 63; 16:9; 18:24, 28; 19:15, 16, 22, 30, 31, 38, 46, 47, 48; 21:2, 8, 11, 13, 13, 14, 14, 15, 16, 16, 16, 17, 17, 18, 18, 19, 21, 21, 22, 22, 23, 23, 24, 24, 24, 25, 26, 27, 27, 28, 28, 28, 29, 29, 30, 30, 31, 31, 32, 32, 32, 33, 34, 34, 35, 35, 36, 36, 37, 37, 38, 38, 38, 39, 41, 42; 22:5, 5, 8, 8, 8, 8, 8, 8, 8, 14, 15, 15, 18, 21, 24, 27, 27, 27, 30; 23:4, 12; 24:6, 8, 12, 12, 25

Jdg 1:3, 3, 3, 8, 16, 17, 18, 18, 19, 21, 22, 25; 2:1, 2, 18; 3:27, 31; 4:6, 7, 8, 8, 9, 9, 10, 10, 13, 15, 16; 5:15, 26; 6:5, 12, 13, 16, 17, 26, 39; 7:1, 2, 4, 4, 4, 5, 10, 11, 16, 18, 18, 19; 8:1, 1, 4, 7, 7, 15, 16, 16; 9:1, 1, 16, 19, 19, 23, 26, 32, 33, 34, 35, 38, 39, 44, 45, 48, 48, 52; 11:3, 6, 8, 11, 12, 33, 34, 34, 38, 39; 12:1, 1, 2, 4; 13:9, 19; 14:7, 11, 15, 18; 15:1, 5, 6, 8, 13, 14, 16, 16; 16:3, 7, 8, 9, 11, 13, 14, 14, 15, 16, 21, 29, 29, 30, 30; 17:2, 10, 11; 18:4, 7, 11, 16, 17, 17, 19, 23, 25, 27, 27, 28; 19:3, 4, 5, 10, 10, 20, 24, 29; 20:1, 37, 38, 40, 43, 48; 21:5, 10, 10, 12

Ru 1:6, 7, 8, 8, 8, 10, 11, 18, 20, 22; 2:4, 6, 19, 19, 22, 23; 3:1, 2

1Sa 1:24, 24; 2:4, 13, 13, 18, 19, 22, 26, 26, 29; 3:14, 19; 4:4, 5, 8, 12, 12, 19; 5:6, 7, 8, 9, 12; 6:11, 15, 19; 7:3, 10; 9:3, 5, 19, 24, 25; 10:5, 6, 7, 26; 11:1, 2, 7, 10; 12:2, 7, 20, 24; 13:2, 2, 4, 5, 15, 16, 22, 22, 22; 14:2, 7, 17, 18, 20, 21, 21, 21, 21, 27, 28, 32, 33, 34, 34, 43, 45; 15:6, 8, 25, 26, 30; 16:1, 2, 5, 16, 18, 19; 17:5, 9, 19, 20, 23, 25, 28, 32, 33, 34, 34, 36, 37, 38, 40, 41, 20:8, 9, 15, 16; 18:1, 6, 6, 6, 10, 11, 12, 14, 22, 28; 19:3, 8, 8, 9, 9, 16, 19, 23, 24:7, 8, 18; 21:1; 8; 22:2, 3, 4, 6, 8, 17, 19, 19, 23; 23:3, 5, 5, 6, 19, 23, 23; 24:7, 8, 18; 25:7, 15, 16, 25, 26, 29, 31, 33, 39, 42; 26:2, 6, 6, 8; 27:2, 2, 3, 3, 5; 28:1, 1, 8, 12, 14, 14, 19, 19; 29:2, 3, 4, 4, 6, 6, 8, 9, 10, 10; 30:1, 3, 4, 9, 14, 21, 22, 22, 23; 31:5

2Sa 1:2, 11, 17, 21, 24; 2:3, 3; 3:8, 12, 12, 13, 16, 17, 20, 20, 21, 22, 22, 23, 27, 31, 31; 5:3, 10; 6:2, 2, 12, 14, 14, 15, 15; 7:3, 7, 7, 9, 12, 14, 14, 22, 29; 8:2, 2, 2, 10, 10, 11; 10:13, 17, 19; 11:1, 4, 5, 9, 11, 13, 17; 12:3, 3, 9, 9, 11, 17, 24, 30; 13:11, 14, 18, 20, 24, 26, 26, 27, 28, 31; 14:2, 17, 19; 15:11, 12, 14, 14, 19, 19, 20, 20, 23, 24, 27, 30, 31, 32, 33, 35, 36; 16:1, 10, 14, 15, 17, 18, 21, 23; 17:2, 8, 10, 12, 16, 22, 24, 29; 18:1, 2, 2, 5, 14, 22, 28; 19:1, 7, 16, 17, 22, 25, 31, 33, 39, 42; 20:3, 6, 6, 8; 21:2, 2, 3, 3, 9, 21; 23:4, 8, 11, 18; 24:7, 8, 18; 25:7, 1, 15, 16, 25, 26, 29, 31, 33, 39, 42; 26:2, 6, 6, 8; 27:2, 2, 3, 3, 5; 28:1, 1, 8, 12, 14, 14, 19, 19; 29:2, 3, 4, 4, 6, 6, 8, 9, 10, 10; 30:1, 3, 4, 9, 14, 21, 22, 22, 23; 24:2

1Ki 1:1, 7, 7, 8, 14, 21, 22, 23, 31, 33, 34, 37, 37, 40, 40, 40, 41, 44, 49, 51; 2:4, 4, 8, 8, 8, 9, 10, 32, 43; 3:1, 6, 17, 18; 4:13; 5:6; 6:8, 9, 10, 12, 15, 15, 16, 18, 20, 21, 21, 22, 22, 28, 29, 30, 32, 36; 7:2, 3, 5, 7, 9, 12, 14, 18, 26, 31, 49; 8:5, 9, 15, 15, 21, 22, 22, 24, 25, 25, 26, 27, 28, 31, 42, 54, 55, 57, 57, 61, 62, 65; 9:11, 11, 16, 27; 10:1, 2, 2, 2, 18, 22, 26; 11:1, 4, 9, 16, 17, 18, 21, 22, 29, 38, 43; 12:6, 8, 8, 10, 11, 11, 14, 14, 18, 21; 13:7, 8, 15, 16, 16, 16, 18, 19; 14:3, 6, 8, 20, 22, 31; 15:3, 8, 14, 19, 20, 22, 24, 24, 30; 16:2, 6, 7, 13, 17, 18, 26, 28; 17:18; 18:4, 13, 28, 32, 33, 35, 45; 19:1, 10, 14, 19, 19, 21; 20:1, 20, 21, 34, 34, 38;

21:8, 8, 13; 22:4, 11, 13, 27, 27, 31, 31, 40, 44, 49, 50, 50

2Ki 1:8, 9, 11, 13, 14, 15, 15; 2:1, 16; 3:4, 7, 12, 13, 17, 19, 20, 26; 4:13, 26, 26, 26; 5:1, 3, 5, 9, 9, 23, 26; 6:1, 3, 4, 8, 15, 16, 16, 18, 18, 22, 22, 22, 32, 33; 7:2, 19; 8:2, 4, 9, 12, 12, 21, 24, 24, 28; 9:13, 15, 18, 19, 24, 28; 10:2, 2, 6, 13, 15, 16, 23, 25, 31, 35; 11:3, 4, 4, 8, 8, 9, 11, 14, 15, 20; 12:15, 21; 13:9, 12, 13, 13, 19, 23; 14:10, 15, 16, 16, 20, 22, 29, 29; 15:7, 7, 16, 19, 22, 25, 25, 38, 38; 16:15, 20, 20; 17:15, 18, 35, 36, 38; 18:7, 17, 26, 27, 28, 31; 37; 19:1, 2, 6, 23, 24, 32, 37; 20:3, 21; 21:6, 11, 11, 16; 22:7, 14, 17; 23:2, 3, 11, 14, 18, 24, 25, 25, 25, 26; 24:4, 6; 25:7, 9, 10, 11, 17, 24, 25, 25, 28

1Ch 2:23, 23; 4:9, 10, 23; 5:10, 18, 19, 19, 20; 6:32, 33, 57, 60, 61, 63; 7:1, 5, 10, 13, 14, 16, 16, 16, 17, 18, 20, 21; 8:12, 18, 24, 30, 31; 10:4, 10, 12; 11:2, 9, 10; 12:11, 14, 21; 13:10, 16, 20; 14:1, 10, 14, 18; 15:16; 16:7, 8, 19, 19; 17:1, 14; 18:1, 3, 20; 19:2, 7, 23; 20:1, 3, 17, 18, 19; 21:9, 19, 27; 20:8, 23; 23:1, 7, 11, 13, 14, 24; 24:1, 4, 21, 28, 31; 25:9, 16, 24; 26:17, 23, 24; 27:14, 22; 28:4, 20, 23; 29:3, 9, 24; 30:8, 16, 19, 22, 28; 31:13, 16, 17, 21, 26

Ecc 1:8, 8, 11, 16; 2:1, 3, 9; 4:6, 6, 8, 15; 5:2, 10, 10, 11, 17; 6:3, 4, 4, 10; 7:11; 8:12, 13, 15, 16; 9:7, 7, 9, 10; 11:5; 12:14

SS 1:2, 6, 10, 10, 11; 2:3, 5, 5, 13; 3:6, 6, 10, 11; 4:8, 8, 9, 9, 13, 13, 14, 14; 5:1, 1, 2, 2, 5, 5, 12, 14, 14; 6:1, 4, 10; 7:1, 2; 8:9

Isa 1:4, 6, 7, 13, 20, 22, 27, 27; 3:10, 11, 14, 16, 16, 17; 5:2, 13, 18, 18, 26; 6:2, 2, 2, 4, 6, 10, 10, 10; 7:2, 2, 4, 20, 24, 24, 25; 8:1, 10, 11; 9:5, 5, 7, 7, 10, 12; 10:22, 24, 33, 34; 11:4, 4, 4, 4, 6, 6, 15; 12:1, 3; 13:9; 14:1, 6, 19, 20, 21, 23, 30; 15:3, 5; 16:4, 9, 9, 14; 17:5, 10; 18:1, 5; 19:23, 24, 24; 20:4; 21:3, 7, 7, 9, 14; 22:2, 6, 12, 17, 21, 21; 23:17; 24:2, 2, 2, 2, 2, 2, 2, 2, 2, 2, 9, 12; 25:5, 11; 26:9, 9, 17, 18, 18, 27, 27, 27, 28, 28, 28; 29:3, 6, 6, 9, 9, 17, 21, 22, 30; 30:1, 24, 27, 28, 29:2, 6, 8, 9, 9, 17, 21, 22, 30; 2Ch 1:1, 3, 14; 2:3, 3, 7, 7, 8, 12, 13, 14, 14, 17; 3:4, 5, 5, 6, 7, 8, 10, 14; 4:13, 20; 5:10, 12, 12, 12, 13, 13; 6:4, 4, 11, 14, 15, 15, 15, 16, 18, 30, 38, 38, 41; 7:3, 6, 8, 18; 8:5, 18; 9:1, 1, 1, 17, 18, 21, 23, 31; 10:6, 8, 8, 10, 11, 11, 14, 14, 18; 12:1, 3, 3, 16; 13:3, 3, 8, 9, 11, 12, 12, 14, 17, 19, 19, 19, 14:1, 9, 11, 11, 11, 13; 15:2, 2, 6, 9, 9, 12, 12, 14, 14, 14, 15, 15; 16:3, 6, 8, 10, 10, 13, 14; 17:3, 14; 18:1, 2, 2, 3, 3, 9, 14, 16, 17, 17, 18, 18:1, 2, 3, 3; 20:1, 3, 17, 18, 19, 21, 25, 27, 28, 35, 36, 37; 21:1, 3, 4, 7, 9; 22:1, 5, 6, 7, 9; 23:1, 3, 7, 7, 8, 13, 13, 14, 18, 18, 21, 24:21, 24; 25:2, 7, 7, 7, 13, 14, 18, 21; 26:2, 19, 23; 27:5, 9; 28:5, 9, 10, 10, 15, 18, 18, 27; 29:8, 10, 18, 18, 24, 25, 25, 26, 26, 27, 27, 29, 30, 30, 30, 35; 30:6, 21, 21, 23, 25; 31:9, 21; 32:3, 7, 7, 7, 8, 9, 18, 21, 21, 23; 33:6, 6, 11, 21; 34:6, 25, 31, 35:12, 13, 21, 21, 21, 22; 36:10, 17, 19, 23

Ezr 1:3, 4, 4, 4, 5, 6, 6, 6, 6, 11; 2:2, 63, 63; 3:9, 9, 10, 10, 11, 12, 13; 4:2, 3; 5:2, 8; 6:4, 12, 16, 22; 7:13, 16, 17, 17, 18, 28; 8:1, 3, 4, 5, 6, 7, 8, 9, 10, 11, 12, 13, 14, 14; 10:3, 4, 12, 14, 16, 17

Ne 1:3; 2:3, 9, 12, 12, 13, 17; 3:1; 4:13, 17, 17, 17, 22; 5:7; 6:5; 7:7, 65; 8:2, 6, 6; 9:1, 1, 4, 6, 8, 13, 24, 24, 34; 10:32, 38; 11:25; 12:1, 24, 27, 27, 27, 27, 27, 35, 36, 40, 41, 42, 43; 13:2, 2, 9, 11, 17, 25

Est 1:6, 10, 11; 2:6, 6, 9, 12, 12, 13, 20; 3:1, 11, 12; 4:1, 1, 2, 13; 5:9, 12, 12, 14; 6:14; 7:1; 8:3, 8, 8, 10, 15, 15; 9:5, 29, 30

Job 1:4, 15, 17; 2:7, 10, 11, 13; 3:14, 15, 15; 4:2, 18; 5:14, 23, 23; 7:5, 14; 8:21, 21, 22; 9:2, 3, 14, 17, 18, 30, 35; 10:2, 11, 11, 13; 12:2, 5, 12, 13, 16, 18; 13:3, 17, 19; 14:3, 5; 15:2, 3, 10, 11, 11, 20, 27; 16:5, 8, 9, 10, 14, 16, 21; 17:2, 3, 9; 18:6; 19:2, 4, 6, 10, 20, 24, 20:11, 26, 21:8, 24, 25; 22:4, 16, 18, 21; 23:4, 6, 7, 14; 24:8, 14, 22, 25; 24:4, 16, 18, 21; 23:4, 6, 7, 14; 24:8, 14, 22, 25; 25:2; 4, 26:10, 12; 27:11, 13, 14; 28:14, 16, 16, 19, 22; 29:5, 6; 30:1, 21, 30; 31:1, 5, 13, 18, 20; 32:14; 33:19, 23, 29, 30; 34:8, 8, 9, 23, 30; 34:6, 7, 18, 32; 34:4, 36:4, 7, 18, 32; 34:3, 37:4, 18, 22, 24:10, 21; 35:2, 21:23, 10, 14, 21; 38:6, 23, 25; 37:9; 39:3, 7, 8; 40:4, 4, 5, 6; 41:1, 2, 2, 3, 3, 5, 7, 9, 14, 15, 16, 16, 16, 16, 17, 24, 28; 42:6, 8, 11, 17; 43:6, 12, 13; 44:8, 25, 25; 46:4, 10, 22, 22, 25, 28; 47:5; 48:7, 32, 33, 39; 49:2, 3, 20; 50:5, 39, 45; 51:5, 14, 14, 16, 20, 20, 21, 21, 22, 22, 23, 23, 28, 28, 32, 34, 40, 42, 58, 59; 52:13, 14, 22, 32

Ps 2:9, 11, 11; 3:4; 4:4; 5:4, 9, 12, 12; 6:6, 6; 7:4, 11, 14; 8:5; 9:1, 6; 10:14; 12:2, 2, 2; 4; 13:6; 15:3; 17:10, 14; 18:25, 25, 26, 26, 32, 39; 20:6; 21:3, 6; 22:13; 23:4, 5; 25:14, 19; 26:4, 4, 5, 7, 9, 9; 27:7; 28:3, 3, 7; 29:11; 30:11; 31:9, 10, 10; 32:7, 8, 9; 33:2, 2, 3; 34:3; 35:1, 1, 13, 16, 16, 19, 26; 36:8, 9; 37:12, 24; 38:7; 39:1, 1, 2, 3, 11, 12; 42:4, 4, 4, 4, 8, 10; 44:1, 2, 9; 45:3, 7, 12, 15; 46:3, 7, 11; 47:1, 5, 5, 7; 48:7; 50:5, 18, 18; 51:7, 12, 19, 19; 54:7; 4; 55:18, 20; 58:9; 59:7; 60:T, T, 5, 10; 62:4; 63:5, 5; 64:7; 65:4, 6, 9, 10, 11, 13, 13; 66:13, 15, 15, 17, 17; 68:6, 13, 13, 19, 25, 27, 30, 30; 69:10, 28, 30, 30; 71:8, 8, 13, 22, 22; 72:2, 2, 19; 73:7, 19, 23, 24; 74:6; 75:5; 77:1, 1, 6, 15; 78:8, 14, 14, 36, 36, 37, 47, 47, 58, 58, 62, 71; 80:5, 10, 16; 81:2, 16, 16; 83:5, 7, 8, 15, 15, 16; 85:5; 86:12; 87:4; 88:4, 7; 89:1, 3, 10, 20, 21, 24, 28, 32, 32, 38, 45; 90:5, 14; 91:4, 8, 15, 16; 92:3, 10; 93:1, 1; 94:20; 95:2, 2, 10; 96:13, 13; 98:5, 5, 6, 9; 100:2, 2, 4, 4; 101:2, 6; 102:9; 103:4, 5, 10; 104:1, 2, 2, 6, 6, 13, 28; 105:9, 18, 25, 37, 40, 43, 43; 106:4, 4, 5, 6, 29, 32, 33, 38, 39, 39, 43; 107:9,

Pr 1:11, 13, 15, 31; 2:1, 16; 3:5, 9, 9, 10, 30, 32; 4:7, 23; 5:10, 17, 18, 19, 20, 22; 6:1, 2, 2, 12, 13, 13, 22, 25, 32; 7:1, 5, 10, 13, 14, 16, 16, 16, 17, 18, 20, 21, 23; 8:12, 18, 24, 30, 31; 10:4, 18, 22; 11:2, 9, 10; 12:11, 14, 21; 13:10, 16, 20; 14:1, 10, 14, 18; 15:16; 16:7, 8, 19, 19; 17:1, 14; 18:1, 3, 20; 19:2, 7, 23; 20:8, 23; 23:1, 7, 11, 13, 14, 24; 24:1, 4, 21, 28, 31; 25:9, 16, 24; 26:17, 23, 24; 27:14, 22; 28:4, 20, 23; 29:3, 9, 24; 30:8, 16, 19, 22, 28; 31:13, 16, 17, 21, 26

Eze 1:15, 16, 16, 17; 5:2, 2, 11, 11, 12, 12; 6:9, 9, 11, 11; 7:15, 18, 27; 8:11, 16, 18; 9:1, 1, 2, 2, 3, 7, 11; 10:2, 2, 4, 6, 7; 11:6, 13; 12:7, 12, 18, 18, 18, 19, 19; 13:10, 11, 12, 13, 14, 15, 20, 22; 14:11; 16:8, 9, 9, 10, 10, 16; 17, 26, 28, 28, 36, 36, 37, 40, 40, 41, 59, 60, 62; 17:3, 7, 12, 13, 16, 17, 20, 21; 18:7, 16; 19:4, 11; 20:6, 7, 15, 18, 31, 33, 33, 33, 34, 34, 34, 35, 36, 36, 39, 39, 40, 41, 44; 21:6, 6, 21, 22, 24; 22:7, 11, 14, 28, 31; 23:6, 7, 7, 7, 8, 10, 14, 15, 16, 17, 17, 23, 24, 25, 29, 30, 33, 33, 37, 40, 42, 42, 43, 43, 47, 47; 24:4, 7, 12, 16, 26; 25:6, 6, 6, 10, 15; 26:7, 7, 7, 8, 9, 11, 16, 20, 20, 20; 27:7, 9, 11, 12, 14, 16, 21, 22, 22, 24, 31, 31, 33; 28:4, 7, 7, 7, 8, 10, 14, 15, 16, 17, 17, 18, 18, 18; 32:2, 3, 4, 4, 6, 7, 8, 18, 21, 24, 25, 25, 27, 27, 28, 29, 29, 30, 30, 30, 32, 32; 33:25, 31; 34:3, 4, 4, 16, 18, 19, 21, 21, 23, 25, 29; 35:8, 8, 13; 36:5, 5, 37, 38; 37:6, 19, 19, 23, 23, 26, 26, 27, 27; 38:4, 4, 5, 5, 6, 9, 13, 15, 22, 22, 22; 39:4, 9, 10, 14, 20, 20, 20; 40:3, 4, 4; 41:13, 15, 16, 18; 42:16, 16, 17, 18, 19;

YOU (2802)

HEBREW-ARAMAIC DICTIONARY-INDEX TO THE OLD TESTAMENT

FEATURES OF THE HEBREW-ARAMAIC TO ENGLISH DICTIONARY-INDEX

STRONG NUMBER	LEXICAL FORM AND TRANSLITERATION	PART OF SPEECH	G/K NUMBER
Matches the number at the end of context lines; one- to four-digit numbers in non-italic type are Hebrew and Aramaic (see the introduction, pages xii–xiv).	See the table below. Note that the lexical forms conform to modern resources and sometimes differ from Strong's original spelling.	The part of speech is abbreviated (see below and introduction, page xiv).	Cross reference to the G/K numbering system, widely used in up-to-date word study reference resources (see the introduction, page xiv).

122 אָדֹם *'ādōm,* a. GK: 137 [→ 131; cf. 119].

RELATED WORDS LIST
Hebrew and Aramaic words related by cognate are listed by Strong number (see the introduction, pages xiv–xv).

red, ruddy (skin):–

DEFINITION AND ETYMOLOGY
Words are defined, often with expanded explanations, and if a proper name, the possible definition (etymology) is given in italics (see the introduction, pages xiv–xv).

red [7], ruddy [1]

KJV WORD AND (FREQUENCY COUNT)
Following the symbol :– KJV words are listed according to their exact textual spelling and are organized according to frequency (see the introduction, page xiv).

displeased (+7451+871.1) [1],

MULTIPLE WORDS / MULTIPLE NUMBERS
More than one KJV word and/or more than one Strong number indicate multiple-word translations (see the introduction, pages xiii–xiv).

same[s] [1]

SUPERSCRIPT "S"
Indicates "substitution" translation (see the introduction, pages xiii–xv).

HEBREW-ARAMAIC SIMPLIFIED TRANSLITERATION AND PRONUNCIATION TABLE

Consonants

א	'	[no sound]	
ב, בּ	b	boy	
ג, גּ	g	girl	
ד, דּ	d	dog	
ה	h	hot	
ו	w	vote	
ז	z	zip	
ח	ḥ	Bach	
ט	ṭ	tip	

י	y	yes	
ךּ, כּ, כ	k	kit	
ל	l	let	
ם, מ	m	mother	
ן, נ	n	not	
ס	s	sip	
ע	'	[no sound]	
ף, פּ, פ	p	pet	
ץ, צ	ṣ	sits	
ק	q	torque	

ר	r	rot	
שׂ	ś	sip	
שׁ	š	ship	
ת, תּ	t	tip	

Vowels

ָ	â	father	
ָ	ā	father	
ַ	a	father	
ֲ	a	baton	

וּ	û	tune	
ֻ	u	sure	
ֵי	ê	they	
ֵ	ē	they	
	e	get	
if (vocal)	ᵉ	select	
ְ	ᵉ	select	
ִי	î	machine	
ִ	i	pin	
וֹ	ô	phone	

HEBREW-ARAMAIC DICTIONARY ABBREVIATIONS

&	and	intens.	intensive	vbl.	verbal
+	plus: in combination with	inter.	interrogative		
?	uncertain	interj.	interjection	**Hebrew Verbal Stems**	
[]	uncertain part of speech	l.	loanword		
→	see these related words	loc.	location	[H]	Hiphil
√	see this organizing word	m.	masculine	[Ho]	Hophal
1	first person	n.	noun	[Hotpaal]	Hotpaal
2	second person	neg.	negative	[Hotpael]	Hotpael
3	third person	num.	numeral	[Hsh]	Histaphel
a.	adjective	ord.	ordinal	[Ht]	Hitpael
abst.	abstract	p.	pronoun	[Htpal]	Hitpalpel
adv.	adverb	pl.	plural	[Htpalpal]	Hitpalpal
art.	article	poss.	possibly	[Htpo]	Hitpoel
c.	conjunction	pp.	preposition	[Htpoal]	Hitpoal
col.	collective	pr.	proper [noun]	[Htpol]	Hitpolel
com.	common gender	pref.	prefix	[Htpolal]	Hitpolal
demo.	demonstrative	prob.	probably	[N]	Niphal
den.	denominative	pt.	particle	[P]	Piel
du.	dual number	ptcp.	participle	[Pilal]	Pilal
emph.	emphatic	rel.	relative	[Pilel]	Pilel
excl.	exclamation	s.	singular	[Pilpal]	Pilpal
f.	feminine	subst.	substantive	[Pil]	Pilpel
fig.	figurative(ly)	suf.	suffix	[Po]	Poel
g.	gentilic	temp.	temporal	[Poal]	Poal
indecl.	indeclinable	tt.	technical term in Psalm title	[Poalal]	Poalal
indef.	indefinite	v.	verb	[Pol]	Polel
inf.	infinitive	var.	variant	[Polal]	Polal
				[Pu]	Pual

[Pualal]	Pualal
[Pul]	Pulal
[Pulpal]	Pulpal
[Q]	Qal
[Qp]	Qal passive

Aramaic Verbal Stems

[A]	Aphel
[H]	Haphel
[Ho]	Hophal
[Hp]	Haphel passive
[Hsh]	Hishtaphel
[Hth]	Hithaphal
[Htpa]	Hitpaal
[Htpe]	Hitpeel
[Htpol]	Hitpolel
[Htt]	Ettaphal
[Itpa]	Itpaal
[Itpe]	Itpeel
[Itpo]	Itpoal
[P]	Peal
[Pa]	Pael
[Pap]	Pael passive
[Peil]	Peil
[Po]	Poel
[Pol]	Polel
[Pp]	Peal passive (participle)

0.1 אָ *-ā'*, p.suf.3.f.s. GK: 2 [cf. 1886.3]. she, her:– *not translated* [1]

0.2 אָ *-ā'* (Aram.), art.suf. GK: 10002 [→ 1886.7]. the, a; indicates vocative: O; indicates emphatic state:– the [503], *usually untranslated* [258], O [24], a [13], that [5], continually (+8411+871.2) [2], the same [2], this [2], an [1], at what time (+1768+5732+871.2) [1], ever (+5705+5957) [1], ever (+5957) [1], for ever (+5957) [1], the same [1]

1 אָב *'āb*, n.m. GK: 3 [cf. 2 (also used with compound proper names)]. father, grandfather, forefather, ancestor; (pl.) ancestors (of both genders); by extension: originator, founder (of a city or profession); a title of respect referring to humans or god. The "house of a father" is a subdivision of a clan:– father [593], fathers [475], father's [118], fathers' [13], father's (+3807.1) [6], chief [2], families (+1004) [2], fatherless (+369) [1], forefathers (+7223) [1], patrimony [1], prince [1], principal [1]

2 אַב *'ab* (Aram.), n.m. GK: 10003 [cf. 1]. father, predecessor, ancestor (not necessarily male):– father [6], fathers [3]

3 אֵב *'ēb*, n.[m.]. GK: 4 [cf. 768; cf. 4]. new (plant) growth, shoot:– fruits [1], greenness [1]

4 אֵב *'ēb* (Aram.), n.m. GK: 10004 [cf. 3]. fruit:– fruit [3]

אֹב *'ōb*. See 178.

5 אֲבַגְתָא *'⁴bagtā'*, n.pr.m. GK: 5. Abagtha:– Abagtha [1]

6 אָבַד *'ābad*, v. GK: 6 [→ 8, 9, 10, 11, 12, 13; cf. 7]. [Q] perish, [P, H] destroy, demolish, annihilate; "to destroy the heart" means "to lose courage":– perish [65], destroy [39], destroyed [17], perished [17], lost [9], perisheth [6], destroyeth [4], surely perish (+6) [4], cause to perish [3], ready to perish [3], utterly destroy (+6) [2], utterly perish (+6) [2], broken [1], destroyest [1], destruction [1], failed (+4480) [1], faileth [1], have no (+4480) [1], lose [1], made to perish [1], not (+4480) [1], spendeth [1], take [1], undone [1], void [1]

7 אֲבַד *'bad* (Aram.), v. GK: 10005 [cf. 6]. [P] to perish; [H] to execute; [Ho] to be destroyed:– destroy [4], perish [2], destroyed [1]

8 אֹבֵד *'ōbēd*, n.[m.]. GK: 7 [→ 6]. ruin:– perish [2]

9 אֲבֵדָה *'bēdâ*, n.f. GK: 8 [→ 6]. lost item:– lost [3], that which was lost [1]

10 אֲבַדֹּה *'⁴baddōh*, n.f. GK: 9 [→ 11; cf. 6]. destruction; this can refer to the nether world of the dead, with a focus that this is the place of decay:– destruction [1]

11 אֲבַדּוֹן *'⁴baddôn*, n.f. GK: 10 & 11 [→ 10; cf. 6]. destruction; some translate as a proper noun, the Place of Destruction (the realm of the dead):– destruction [5]

12 אַבְדָן *'abdān*, n.[m.]. GK: 12 [→ 6]. destruction:– destruction [1]

13 אָבְדָן *'obdān*, n.[m.]. GK: 13 [→ 6]. destruction:– destruction [1]

14 אָבָה *'ābâ*, v. GK: 14 [→ 17, 15?, 34?; cf. 2968, 8373?]. [Q] to be willing, consent, yield; with the negative, to be unwilling, refuse:– would [39], will [6], consent [4], willing [4], rest content [1]

15 אֲבִי *'ābî*, interj. GK: 20 [→ 14?]. Oh, that!:– my desire [1]

16 אֵבֶה *'ēbeh*, n.[m.]. GK: 15. papyrus or reed (boat):– swift [1]

17 אֲבוֹי *'bôy*, interj. GK: 16 [→ 14]. sorrow (uneasiness); some parse as an interjection: woe!:– sorrow [1]

18 אֵבוּס *'ēbûs*, n.m. GK: 17 [→ 75]. manger:– crib [3]

19 אִבְחָה *'ibḥâ*, n.f. GK: 18 [cf. 2874]. slaughter:– point [1]

20 אֲבַטִּיחַ *'baṭṭîaḥ*, n.[m.]. GK: 19 [→ 982]. melon:– melons [1]

21 אֲבִי *'bî*, n.pr.m. GK: 23 [→ 29]. Abijah, Abiezrite, "*[my] father is Yahweh, Abi [my] father*":– Abi [1]

22 אֲבִיאֵל *'bî'ēl*, n.pr.m. GK: 24 [→ 410+1]. Abiel, "*[my] father is God [El]*":– Abiel [3]

23 אֲבִיאָסָף *'bî'āsāp*, n.pr.m. GK: 25 [→ 43]. Abiasaph, "*[my] father has gathered*":– Abiasaph [1]

24 אָבִיב *'ābîb*, n.m. GK: 26 [cf. 8512]. (month of) Abib, the first month of the Canaanite calendar equal to Nisan (March-April); head (of grain), already ripe but still soft:– Abib [6], green ears of corn [1], in the ear [1]

25 אֲבִי גִבְעוֹן *'bî gib'ôn*, n.pr.m. GK: 3 + 1500 [→ 1+1391]. father of Gibeon (1 + 1391):–

26 אֲבִיגַיִל *'bîgayil*, n.pr.f. GK: 28 [→ 1+1523?]. Abigail, "*[my] father rejoices* or *father [cause] of joy*":– Abigail [17]

27 אֲבִידָן *'bîdān*, n.pr.m. GK: 29 [→ 1+1777]. Abidan, "*[my] father is judge*":– Abidan [5]

28 אֲבִידָע *'bîdā'*, n.pr.m. GK: 30 [→ 1+3045]. Abida, "*[my] father knows*":– Abidah [1], Abida [1]

29 אֲבִיָּה *'biyyâ* or אֲבִיָּהוּ *'biyyāhû*, n.pr.m. & f. GK: 31 & 32 [→ 21]. Abijah, "*[my] father is Yahweh*":– Abijah [20], Abiah [4], Abia [1]

30 אֲבִיהוּא *'bîhû'*, n.pr.m. GK: 33 [→ 1+1931]. Abihu, "*he is [my] father*":– Abihu [12]

31 אֲבִיהוּד *'bîhûd*, n.pr.m. GK: 34 [→ 1+1935]. Abihud, "*[my] father has majesty*":– Abihud [1]

32 אֲבִיהַיִל *'bîhayil* or אֲבִיחַיִל *'bîhayil*, n.pr.m. GK: 35 & 38 [→ 1+2428]. Abihail, "*[my] father has strength/wealth* or *cause of strength/wealth*":– Abihail [6]

33 אֲבִי עֶזְרִי *'bî 'ezrî*, a.g. GK: 49 [→ 44]. Abiezrite, "*of Abiezer*":– Abi-ezrites [2], Abi-ezrite [1]

34 אֶבְיוֹן *'ebyôn*, a. GK: 36 [→ 14?]. poor, needy, often as a class of persons with physical needs, of low status and little political power, with an associative meaning of oppression and misery:– needy [35], poor [24], beggar [1], poor man [1]

35 אֲבִיּוֹנָה *'biyyônâ*, n.f. GK: 37. caper berry (that stimulates desire):– desire [1]

אֲבִיחַיִל *'bîhayil*. See 32.

36 אֲבִיטוּב *'bîṭûb*, n.pr.m. GK: 39 [→ 1+2896]. Abitub, "*[my] father is good*":– Abitub [1]

37 אֲבִיטָל *'bîṭāl*, n.pr.f. GK: 40 [→ 1+2919]. Abital, "*[my] father is [the] night dew*":– Abital [2]

38 אֲבִיּם *'biyyām*, n.pr.m. GK: 41 [→ 1+3220]. Abiyam, "*[my] father is Yam [the sea]*":– Abijam [5]

39 אֲבִימָאֵל *'bîmā'ēl*, n.pr.m. GK: 42 [→ 1+410]. Abimael, "*[my] father is God [El]*":– Abimael [1]

40 אֲבִימֶלֶךְ *'bîmelek*, n.pr.m. GK: 43 [→ 1+4428]. Abimelech, "*[my] father is king* or *[my] father is Molech*":– Abimelech [65], Abimelech's [2]

41 אֲבִינָדָב *'bînādāb*, n.pr.m. GK: 44 [→ 1+5068]. Abinadab, "*[my] father is generous* or *[my] father is Nadab*":– Abinadab [13]

42 אֲבִינֹעַם *'bînō'am*, n.pr.m. GK: 45 [→ 1+5278]. Abinoam, "*[my] father is graciousness*":– Abinoam [4]

אֲבִינֵר *'bînēr*. See 74.

43 אֲבִיאָסָף *'byāsāp*, n.pr.m. GK: 47 [→ 23]. Ebiasaph, "*[my] father has gathered*":– Ebiasaph [3]

44 אֲבִיעֶזֶר *'bî'ezer*, n.pr.m. GK: 48 [→ 33]. Abiezer, "*[my] father is help*":– Abi-ezer [7]

45 אֲבִי־עַלְבוֹן *'bî-'albôn*, n.pr.m. GK: 50 [→ 1]. Abi-Albon, "*[my] father is Albon*":– Abialbon [1]

46 אָבִיר *'ābîr*, a. GK: 51 [→ 47, 82, 83, 84]. mighty, powerful; (as a divine title) the Mighty One:– mighty one [3], mighty [3]

47 אַבִּיר *'abbîr*, a. GK: 52 [→ 46]. mighty, powerful; this can refer to strong animals, social leaders, and angelic beings:– bulls [4], mighty [4], stouthearted (+3820) [2], strong [2], valiant [2], angels' [1], chiefest [1], strong ones [1]

48 אֲבִירָם *'bîrām*, n.pr.m. GK: 53 [→ 1+7311; cf. 87]. Abiram, "*[my] father is exalted*":– Abiram [11]

49 אֲבִישַׁג *'bîšag*, n.pr.f. GK: 54 [→ 1+7683]. Abishag, "*[my] father strays*":– Abishag [5]

50 אֲבִישׁוּעַ *'bîšûa'*, n.pr.m. GK: 55 [→ 1+7770]. Abishua, "*[my] father is salvation*":– Abishua [5]

51 אֲבִישׁוּר *'bîšûr*, n.pr.m. GK: 56 [→ 1+7794]. Abishur, "*[my] father is a wall*":– Abishur [1]

52 אֲבִישַׁי *'bîšay* or אַבְשַׁי *'abšay*, n.pr.m. GK: 57 & 93 [→ 1+7862]. Abishai, "*[my] father is Jesse* or *father exists*":– Abishai [25]

53 אֲבִישָׁלוֹם *'bîšālôm* or אַבְשָׁלוֹם *'abšālôm*, n.pr.m. GK: 58 & 94 [→ 1+7965]. Abishalom, "*[my] father is peace*":– Absalom [104], Absalom's [5], Abishalom [2]

54 אֶבְיָתָר *'byātār*, n.pr.m. GK: 59 [→ 1+3498]. Abiathar, "*[my] father gives abundance* or *the father is preeminent*":– Abiathar [29], Abiathar's (+3807.1) [1]

55 אָבַךְ *'ābak*, v. GK: 60 [cf. 2015]. [Ht] to roll upward, to be borne along:– mount up [1]

56 אָבַל *'ābal*, v. GK: 61 & 62 [→ 57, 60]. [Q] to dry up, lie parched; to mourn, lament, grieve; [H] cause to mourn; mourning can be the emotion or attitude of sorrow, as well as the active observation of mourning rites and ceremonies; [Ht] to mourn, lament, grieve:– mourn [15], mourned [10], mourneth [8], caused a mourning [1], feign to be a mourner [1], lamented [1], lament [1], made to lament [1], mourning [1]

57 אָבֵל *'ābēl*, a. GK: 63 [→ 56]. mourning, grieving, weeping:– mourn [3], mourners [2], mourning [2], mourneth [1]

58 אָבֵל *'ābēl*, n.m. GK: 64 [→ 59, 62, 63, 64, 65, 66, 67, 180; cf. 2986]. meadow:– plain [1]

59 אָבֵל *'ābēl*, n.pr.loc. GK: 64 [→ 58]. Abel, "*meadow*":– Abel [4], Abel-beth-maachah [2]

60 אֵבֶל *'ēbel*, n.m. GK: 65 [→ 56]. ceremony of mourning, period of mourning; a mourning ceremony was a ritual for burial of the dead, with distinctive clothing, music, behaviors, and a set time period for the ritual, generally a longer period for more important people:– mourning [24]

61 אֲבָל *'bāl*, adv. GK: 66 [→ 1077]. but; however, surely, indeed:– but [4], verily [3], indeed [2], nevertheless [2]

62 אָבֵל בֵּית מַעֲכָה *'ābēl bêt ma'kâ*, n.pr.loc. GK: 68 [→ 58+1004+4601]. Abel Beth Maacah, "*meadow of the house of Maacah [oppression]*":–

63 אָבֵל הַשִּׁטִּים *'ābēl haššiṭṭîm*, n.pr.loc. GK: 69 [→ 58]. Abel Shittim, "*meadow of the acacia trees*":– Abel-shittim [1]

64 אָבֵל כְּרָמִים *'ābēl k⁴rāmîm*, n.pr.loc. GK: 70 [→ 58]. Abel Keramim, "*meadow of vineyards*":–

65 אָבֵל מְחוֹלָה *'ābēl m⁴ḥôlâ*, n.pr.loc. GK: 71 [→ 58+4246; cf. 4259?]. Abel Meholah, "*meadow of the round dance*":– Abel-meholah [3]

66 אָבֵל מַיִם *'ābēl mayim*, n.pr.loc. GK: 72 [→ 58+4325]. Abel Maim, "*meadow of waters*":– Abel-maim [1]

67 אָבֵל מִצְרַיִם *'ābēl miṣrayim*, n.pr.loc. GK: 73 [→ 58+4714]. Abel Mizraim, "*meadow of Egypt* or *mourning of Egypt*":– Abel-mizraim [1]

68 אֶבֶן *'eben*, n.f. GK: 74 [→ 72, 70?; cf. 69]. stone, rock, natural or shaped, sometimes of specific size for use in a balance scale; a "precious stone" is a gem or jewel; by extension: hailstone. Rock is a title of God, with a focus of strength and stability, a place of refuge:– stones [142], stone [105], divers weights (+68+2050.1) [6], weight [4], great hailstones (+417) [3], weights [3], stony [2], carbuncles (+688) [1], chalkstones (+1615) [1], hailstones (+1259) [1], hailstones (+1259+1886.1) [1], headstone (+7222) [1], masons (+2796+7023) [1], plummet (+913) [1], slingstones (+7050) [1]

69 אֶבֶן *'eben* (Aram.), n.f. GK: 10006 [cf. 68]. rock, stone, including hewn or unhewn stones, stone slabs and bricks:– stone [6], stones [2]

70 אָבְנָיִם *'obnayim*, n.[m.]. GK: 78 [→ 68?]. potter's wheel; delivery stool:– stools [1], wheels [1]

71 אֲבָנָה *'bānâ*, n.pr.loc. GK: 76 [cf. 549]. Abana:– Abana [1]

72 אֶבֶן הָעֵזֶר *'eben hā'ēzer*, n.pr.loc. GK: 75 [→ 68+5828]. Ebenezer, "*stone of help*":– Eben-ezer [3]

73 אַבְנֵט *'abnēṭ*, n.[m.]. GK: 77. (linen) sash, wrapped around the waist:– girdle [6], girdles [3]

74 אַבְנֵר *'abnēr* or אֲבִינֵר *'bînēr*, n.pr.m. GK: 46 & 79 [→ 1+5216]. Abner, "*[my] father is Ner [a lamp]*":– Abner [62], Abner's [1]

75 אָבַס *'ābas*, v. GK: 80 [→ 18, 3965]. [Qp] to be fattened:– fatted [1], stalled [1]

76 אֲבַעְבֻּעֹת *'ba'bu'ōt*, n.f.pl. GK: 81 [→ 5042]. festers, blisters:– blains [2]

77 אֶבֶץ *'ebeṣ*, n.pr.loc. GK: 82 [→ 78]. Ebez:– Abez [1]

78 אִבְצָן *'ibṣān*, n.pr.m. GK: 83 [→ 77]. Ibzan, "*swift*":– Ibzan [2]

79 אָבַק *'ābaq*, v.den. GK: 84 [cf. 3543?]. [N] to wrestle (with):– wrestled [2]

80 אָבָק *'ābāq*, n.m. GK: 85 [→ 81]. fine dust, powder:– dust [4], powder [1], small dust [1]

81 אֲבָקָה *'bāqâ*, n.f. GK: 86 [→ 80]. spice (scented powders):– powders [1]

82 אָבַר *'ābar*, v.den. GK: 87 [→ 83; cf. 46]. [H] to take flight, soar upward:– fly [1]

83 אָבָר *'ēber*, n.[m.]. GK: 88 [→ 82, 84; cf. 46]. feather, wing; other sources: the strong joint of the body to the wing, "pinion,"

with the associative meaning of strength that can bring freedom:– wings [2], longwinged (+750) [1]

84 אֶבְרָה *'ebrâ*, n.f. GK: 89 [→ 83; cf. 46]. feather, pinion, wing; in some contexts may have the associative meaning of protection:– feathers [2], wings [2]

85 אַבְרָהָם *'abrāhām*, n.pr.m. GK: 90 [cf. 87]. Abraham, "*father of many*":– Abraham [161], Abraham's [14]

86 אַבְרֵךְ *'abrēk*, l.excl. GK: 91. Make way!; others: Kneel down! or Watch out!:– bow the knee [1]

87 אַבְרָם *'abrām*, n.pr.m. GK: 92 [→ 1+7311; cf. 48, 85]. Abram, "*exalted father*":– Abram [54], Abram's [7]

אַבְשַׁי *'absay*. See 52.

אַבְשָׁלוֹם *'absālôm*. See 53.

88 אֵבֹת *'ōbōt*, n.pr.loc. GK: 95 [→ 2968?]. Oboth, "*fathers*":– Oboth [4]

89 אַגָא *'āgē'*, n.pr.m. GK: 96. Agee, "[poss.] *fugitive*":– Agee [1]

90 אֲגַג *'āgag*, n.pr.m. GK: 97 [→ 91?]. Agag, "[poss.] *violent*":– Agag [8]

91 אֲגָגִי *'āgāgî*, a.g. GK: 98 [→ 90?]. Agagite, "*of Agag*":– Agagite [5]

92 אֲגֻדָּה *'ăguddâ*, n.f. GK: 99. bunch, bundle; group, band; cord, bands; foundation, structure:– troop [2], bunch [1], burdens [1]

93 אֱגוֹז *'ĕgôz*, n.[m.]. GK: 100. nut tree:– nuts [1]

94 אָגוּר *'āgûr*, n.pr.m. GK: 101 [→ 103]. Agur, "*gatherer* [or poss.] *wage earner*":– Agur [1]

95 אֲגוֹרָה *'ăgôrâ*, n.f. GK: 102 [→ 107]. fee, payment, a piece of precious metal used as a medium of exchange (but not a minted coin):– piece [1]

96 אֶגֶל *'egel*, n.[m.]. GK: 103 [→ 97]. drop (of dew):– drops [1]

97 אֶגְלַיִם *'eglayim*, n.pr.loc. GK: 104 [→ 96]. Eglaim:– Eglaim [1]

98 אֲגַם *'ăgam*, n.[m.]. GK: 106 [→ 100]. swamp, pond, marsh (with reeds):– ponds [2], pools [2], pool [2], standing [2], reeds [1]

99 אָגֵם *'āgēm*, a. GK: 108 [cf. 5701]. sick, grieved:– ponds [1]

100 אַגְמוֹן *'agmôn*, n.[m.]. GK: 109 [→ 98]. reed; cord (made of reeds):– rush [2], bulrush [1], caldron [1], hook [1]

101 אַגָּן *'aggān*, n.[m.]. GK: 110. (large and deep) bowl, goblet:– basons [1], cups [1], goblet [1]

102 אֲגַף *'ăgap*, n.[m.]. GK: 111 [→ 1610]. troop, band:– bands [7]

103 אָגַר *'āgar*, v. GK: 112 [→ 94]. [Q] to gather (in):– gathereth [2], gather [1]

104 אִגְּרָא *'iggĕrā'* (Aram.), n.f. GK: 10007 [cf. 107]. letter:– letter [3]

105 אַגַרְטָל *'ăgarṭāl*, n.m. GK: 113. dish; in context made of precious metals:– chargers [2]

106 אֶגְרֹף *'egrōp*, n.[m.]. GK: 114 [→ 1640?]. fist (the hand clenched to strike):– fist [2]

107 אִגֶּרֶת *'iggeret*, n.f. GK: 115 [→ 95; cf. 104]. letter, document:– letters [6], letter [4]

108 אֵד *'ēd*, n.m. GK: 116. stream, fresh water that moves from a higher to lower place; in some contexts this may be an artesian spring:– mist [1], vapour [1]

109 אָדַב *'ādab*, v. GK: 117 [→ 110]. [H] to grieve:– grieve [1]

110 אַדְבְּאֵל *'adbĕ'ēl*, n.pr.m. GK: 118 [→ 109+410]. "*[the] grief of God [El]*":– Adbeel [2]

111 אֲדַד *'ădad*, n.pr.m. GK: 119 [→ 1908]. Hadad, "*sharp*":– Hadad [1]

112 אִדּוֹ *'iddô*, n.pr.m. GK: 120. Iddo, "[prob.] *Yahweh has adorned*":– Iddo [2]

אֱדוֹם *'ĕdôm*. See 123.

אֱדוֹמִי *'ĕdômî*. See 30.

113 אָדוֹן *'ādôn*, n.m. GK: 123 [→ 136, 137, 138, 138, 139, 140, 141]. lord, master, supervisor, one who has authority over another; husband; owner; the Lord, (with Yahweh [3068]) Sovereign. "Lord of lords" means the highest power or authority:– Lord/lord [216], master [77], master's [22], lord's [5], masters [5], lords [4], lord's (+3807.1) [3], masters' [1], owner [1], sir [1]

114 אַדּוֹן *'addôn*, n.pr.loc. GK: 124 [cf. 135]. Addon:– Addon [1]

115 אֲדוֹרַיִם *'ădôrayim*, n.pr.m. GK: 126 [→ 1752?]. Adoraim, "[poss.] *pair of knolls*":– Adoraim [1]

116 אֱדַיִן *'ĕdayin* (Aram.), adv. GK: 10008 [cf. 227]. then, thus, so then:– then (+871.2) [28], then [26], now (+1768) [1], that time [1], then (+4481+6925+871.2) [1]

117 אַדִּיר *'addîr*, a. GK: 129 [→ 142]. mighty, noble, majestic, splendid; (n.) any powerful or awesome person: noble, believer, elite soldier; (as a divine title) the Mighty One, with a focus on the power and splendor of God:– nobles [7], excellent [4], mighty [4], principal [3], gallant [1], glorious [1], goodly [1], lordly [1], mightier [1], mighty one [1], worthies [1]

118 אֲדַלְיָא *'ădalyā'*, n.pr.m. GK: 130. Adalia, "[poss.] *honorable*":– Adalia [1]

119 אָדֵם *'ādēm*, v. GK: 131 [→ 120, 121, 122, 123, 124, 125, 127, 130, 131, 132]. [Q] be ruddy; [Pu] be dyed red:– dyed red [5], red [3], made red [1], ruddy [1]

120 אָדָם *'ādām*, n.m. GK: 132 & 133 & 135 [→ 119]. man, human being; humankind, people, often in contrast to animals; "son of man" means a human being (Nu 23:9), but often assumes messianic significance (Ps 8):– man [388], men [106], Adam [20], man's [16], men's [10], persons (+5315) [3], persons [3], man (+1121) [2], man (+5315) [2], men (+1121) [2], person [2], another [1], husbandman (+376+5647) [1], hypocrite (+2611) [1], low (+1121) [1], men (+5315) [1], men of low degree (+1121) [1], sort [1]

121 אָדָם *'ādām*, n.pr.m. & loc. GK: 134 & 136 [→ 128; cf. 119]. Adam, "*[red] earth* or *[ruddy] skin color*":– Adam [2]

122 אָדֹם *'ādōm*, a. GK: 137 [→ 131; cf. 119]. red; ruddy (skin):– red [7], ruddy [1], sameS [1]

123 אֱדוֹם *'ĕdôm* or אֱדֹם *'ĕdōm*, n.pr.m. GK: 121 & 139 [→ 130, 5654; cf. 119]. Edom, referring to a person and his ancestral territory S.E. of the Dead Sea, "*red*":– Edom [87], Edomites [9], Idumea [4]

124 אֹדֶם *'ōdem*, n.[f.]. GK: 138 [→ 119]. ruby:– sardius [3]

125 אֲדַמְדָּם *'ădamdām*, a. GK: 140 [→ 119]. reddish, reddish-white:– reddish [4], somewhat reddish [2]

126 אַדְמָה *'admâ*, n.pr.loc. GK: 144. Admah, "*[red] earth*":– Admah [5]

127 אֲדָמָה *'ădāmâ*, n.f. GK: 141 & 143 [→ 119]. earth, the entire surface of the place where humans dwell, as well as smaller regions: land; with a focus on the elements of the earth: ground, soil, dust. A "man of the soil" is a farmer; "fruit of the soil" are crops:– land [122], earth [52], ground [43], lands [3], country [1], dust [1], husbandman (+376+1886.1) [1], husbandry [1]

128 אֲדָמָה *'ădāmâ*, n.pr.loc. GK: 142 [→ 121; cf. 119]. Adamah, "*[red] earth*":– Adamah [1]

אַדְמוֹנִי *'admônî*. See 132.

129 אֲדָמִי *'ădāmî*, n.pr.loc. GK: 146 [→ 119]. Adami [with Nekeb 5346], "*ground [of piercing]*":– Adami [1]

130 אֲדֹמִי *'ădōmî*, a.g. GK: 122 [→ 123; cf. 119; 726]. Edomite, "*of Edom*":– Edomite [7], Edomites [4]

131 אֲדֻמִּים *'ădummîm*, n.pr.loc. GK: 147 [→ 122; cf. 119]. Adummim, "*red [streaks]*":– Adummim [2]

132 אַדְמוֹנִי *'admônî*, a. GK: 145 [→ 119]. red; ruddy (skin):– ruddy [2], red [1]

133 אַדְמָתָא *'admātā'*, n.pr.m. GK: 148. Admatha, "*unrestrained*":– Admatha [1]

134 אֶדֶן *'eden*, n.m. GK: 149. base, footing, pedestal:– sockets [54], foundations [1], socket [1]

אָדוֹן *'ādôn*. See 113.

135 אַדָּן *'addān*, n.pr.loc. GK: 150 [cf. 114]. Addon:– Addan [1]

136 אֲדֹנָי *'ădōnāy*, n.[pr.]m. GK: 151 [→ 113]. the Lord, a title of the one true God, with a focus on his majesty and authority:– Lord/lord [430], God [1], Lord's [1]

137 אֲדֹנִי בֶזֶק *'ădōnî bezeq*, n.pr.m. GK: 152 [→ 113+966]. Adoni-Bezek, "*lord of Bezek*":– Adoni-bezek [3]

138 אֲדֹנִיָּה *'ădōniyyâ* or אֲדֹנִיָּהוּ *'ădōniyyāhû*, n.pr.m. GK: 125 & 153 & 154 [→ 2899]. Adonijah, "*[my] lord is Yahweh*":– Adonijah [26]

139 אֲדֹנִי־צֶדֶק *'ădōnî-ṣedeq*, n.pr.m. GK: 155 [→ 113+6664]. Adoni-Zedek, "*[my] lord is righteousness*":– Adoni-zedek [2]

140 אֲדֹנִיקָם *'ădōnîqām*, n.pr.m. GK: 156 [→ 113+6965]. Adonikam, "*[my] lord arises*":– Adonikam [3]

141 אֲדֹנִירָם *'ădōnîrām*, n.pr.m. GK: 157 [→ 151]. Adoniram, "*[my] lord is exalted*":– Adoniram [2]

142 אָדַר *'ādar*, v. GK: 158 [→ 117, 145, 143, 155]. [N] to prove oneself majestic, powerful; [H] to make glorious, powerful:– become glorious [1], glorious [1], make honourable [1]

143 אַדָּר *'addār*, n.pr.[m.]. GK: 160 [→ 142; cf. 144]. Adar, "[poss.] *dark, clouded*":– Adar [8]

144 אֲדָר *'ădār* (Aram.), n.pr.month. GK: 10009 [cf. 143]. Adar, "[poss.] *dark, clouded*":– Adar [1]

145 אֶדֶר *'eder*, n.[m.]. GK: 159 [→ 142]. splendor, handsomeness, of obvious quality:– goodly [1], robe [1]

146 אַדָּר *'addār*, n.pr.m. & loc. GK: 161 & 162 [→ 2692, 5853]. Addar, "*glorious*":– Adar [1], Addar [1]

147 אִדַּר *'iddar* (Aram.), n.m. GK: 10010. threshing floor:– threshingfloors [1]

148 אֲדַרְגָּזַר *'ădargāzar* (Aram.), n.m. GK: 10011. adviser, counselor, likely the king's "minister of information":– judges [2]

149 אַדְרַזְדָּא *'adrazdā'* (Aram.), adv. GK: 10012. with diligence, zealously:– diligently [1]

150 אֲדַרְכֹּנִים *'ădarkōnîm*, n.[m.pl.?]. GK: 163 [→ 1871]. darics, Persian gold coins:– drams [2]

151 אֲדוֹרָם *'ădôrām* or אֲדֹרָם *'ădōrām*, n.pr.m. GK: 127 & 164 [→ 141]. Adoram:– Adoram [2]

152 אַדְרַמֶּלֶךְ *'adrammelek*, n.pr.m. GK: 165 & 166. Adrammelech (pagan god and king), "*nobility of Molech [king]*":– Adrammelech [3]

153 אֶדְרָע *'edrā'* (Aram.), n.[f.]. GK: 10013 [→ 1872; cf. 248, 2220]. arm; fig., power, force:– force [1]

154 אֶדְרֶעִי *'edre'î*, n.pr.loc. GK: 167. Edrei, "*strong*":– Edrei [8]

155 אַדֶּרֶת *'adderet*, n.f. GK: 168 [→ 142]. cloak, royal robe, (hairy) garment:– mantle [5], garment [4], glory [1], goodly [1], robe [1]

156 אָדַשׁ *'ādaš*, v. GK: 169 [cf. 1758]. to thresh; see definitions at 1758:– threshing (+156) [2]

157 אָהַב *'āhab*, v. GK: 170 [→ 159, 158, 160]. [Q] to love, like, be a friend; [N] to be loved; [P] be a lover, an ally; love can refer to friendship, familial love, romantic love, or covenant loyalty:– love [75], loved [48], loveth [38], lovers [17], friends [8], lovest [7], beloved [5], friend [4], liketh [1], lovedst [1], lovely [1], loving [1]

158 אֹהַב *'ahab*, n.[m.]. GK: 172 [→ 157]. lover (negative); loving, charming (positive):– lovers [1], loving [1]

159 אֹהַב *'ōhab*, n.[m.]. GK: 171 [→ 157]. love; something loved:– loves [1]

160 אַהֲבָה *'ahăbâ*, n.f. GK: 173 & 174 [→ 157]. love; friendship, familial love, romantic love, or covenant loyalty:– love [33], loved [7]

161 אֹהַד *'ōhad*, n.pr.m. GK: 176. Ohad:– Ohad [2]

162 אֲהָהּ *'ăhāh*, interj. GK: 177. Ah!, Oh!, Alas!; an exclamation of emphasis, surprise, or sorrow:– ah [8], alas [7]

163 אַהֲוָא *'ahăwā'*, n.pr.loc. GK: 178. Ahava:– Ahava [3]

164 אֵהוּד *'ēhûd*, n.pr.m. GK: 179 [cf. 261?]. Ehud, "*united*":– Ehud [9]

165 אֲהִי *'ăhî*, adv. GK: 180. Where?:– be [2], where (+645) [1]

166 אָהַל *'āhal*, v. GK: 183 [→ 1984]. [H] to be bright:– shineth [1]

167 אָהַל *'āhal*, v.den. GK: 182 [→ 168]. [Q, P] to pitch a tent:– pitch tent [1], pitched tent [1], removed tent [1]

168 אֹהֶל *'ōhel*, n.m. GK: 185 [→ 167, 169, 170 (also used with compound proper names)]. tent, tent-dwelling; by extension: home, dwelling place, a permanent dwelling; family group. "The Tent of Meeting" was the worship tent built before the Temple:– tabernacle [187], tent [91], tents [50], tabernacles [11], dwelling place [2], covering [1], dwelling [1], home [1], places [1]

169 אֹהֶל *'ōhel*, n.pr.m. GK: 186 [→ 168]. Ohel, "*tent*":– Ohel [1]

170 אָהֳלָה *'oh°lâ*, n.pr.f. GK: 188 [→ 172, 173; cf. 168]. Oholah, "*she who has a tent*":– Aholah [5]

171 אָהֳלִיאָב *'oh°lî'āb*, n.pr.m. GK: 190 [→ 168+1]. Oholiab, "*tent of [my] father*":– Aholiab [5]

172 אָהֳלִיבָה *'oh°lîbâ*, n.pr.f. GK: 191 [→ 170+871.1+1886.3]. Oholibah, "*my tent is in her*":– Aholibah [6]

173 אָהֳלִיבָמָה *'oh°lîbāmâ*, n.pr.m. & f. GK: 192 [→ 168+1116?]. Oholibamah, "*[my] tent is a high place*":– Aholibamah [8]

174 אֲהָלוֹת *'°hālôt* or אֲהָלִים *'°hālîm*, n.[m.]. GK: 189 & 193. aloes; an aromatic wood from India:– aloes [3], trees of lign aloes [1]

175 אַהֲרֹן *'ah°rôn*, n.pr.m. GK: 195. Aaron:– Aaron [315], Aaron's [26], Aaron's (+3807.1) [4], Aaronites [2]

176 אוֹ *'ô*, c. GK: 196 [→ 194?]. or, or if, whether:– or [293], either [7], whether [7], and [2], nor [2], or if [2], also [1], at the least [1], if then (+227) [1], nor (+3808) [1], or else [1], otherwise [1], then [1]

177 אוּאֵל *'û'ēl*, n.pr.m. GK: 198 [→ 183?+410]. Uel, "*[poss.] will of God [El]*":– Uel [1]

178 אוֹב *'ôb*, n.m. GK: 199 & 200. wineskin, bag, a leather bag of goatskin turned inside out to hold fluids; medium, spiritist, one who communicates with and conjures ghosts or spirits:– familiar spirits [9], familiar spirit [7], bottles [1]

179 אוֹבִיל *'ôbîl*, n.pr.m. GK: 201 [→ 2986]. Obil, "*camel driver*":– Obil [1]

180 אוּבָל *'ubāl*, n.[m.]. GK: 67 [→ 58]. canal:– river [3]

181 אוּד *'ûd*, n.m. GK: 202 [→ 343]. burning stick:– brand [1], firebrands [1], firebrand [1]

182 אֹדוֹת *'ōdôt*, n.f. GK: 128. on account of, because of, for the reason that:– because of (+5921) [5], concerning (+5921) [2], causes [1], cause [1], sake [1]

183 אָוָה *'āwâ*, v. GK: 203 [→ 185, 1942, 3970, 8378 (also used with compound proper names)]. [P, Ht] to crave, desire, yearn for, long for:– desireth [7], desired [5], desire [3], longed [2], coveteth greedily (+8378) [1], covet [1], desirous [1], fell a lusting (+8378) [1], greatly desire [1], longeth [1], lusted exceedingly (+8378) [1], lusted [1], lusteth after [1]

184 אָוָה *'āwâ*, v. GK: 204 [→ 226?; cf. 8376, 8379, 8427]. [Ht] to run a line, measure:– point out [1]

185 אַוָּה *'awwâ*, n.f. GK: 205 [→ 1942; cf. 183]. wanting, craving; earnestness:– desire [3], lusteth after [3], pleasure [1]

186 אוּזַי *'ûzay*, n.pr.m. GK: 206. Uzai, "*Yahweh has given ear, listened*":– Uzai [1]

187 אוּזָל *'ûzāl*, n.pr.loc. [& m.]. GK: 207. Uzal, a person and a place:– Uzal [1]

188 אוֹי *'ôy*, interj. GK: 208 [→ 190]. Woe! Alas!:– woe [23], alas [1]

189 אֱוִי *'°wî*, n.pr.m. GK: 209. Evi, "*desire*":– Evi [2]

אֹיֵב *'ôyēb*. See 341.

190 אוֹיָה *'ôyâ*, interj. GK: 210 [→ 188]. Woe!, Alas!:– woe [1]

191 אֱוִיל *'°wîl*, a. GK: 211 [→ 196, 200; cf. 2973]. foolish; (n.) a fool:– fool [11], fools [7], foolish [5], fool's [2], foolish man [1]

192 אֱוִיל מְרֹדַךְ *'°wîl m°rōdak*, n.pr.m. GK: 213. Evil-Merodach, "*worshiper of Marduk[s];* [corrupted to read] *fool of blessing*":– Evil-merodach [2]

193 אוּל *'ûl*, n.[m.]. GK: 214 & 215 [→ 352; cf. 2974]. belly, sometimes referring to the whole body; leading man, noble; symbolic of strength:– strength [1]

194 אוּלַי *'ûlay*, adv. GK: 218 [→ 176?+3808?]. what if, perhaps, maybe; this is in an expression of hope, pleading, or fear:– peradventure [23], if so be [8], it may be that [7], it may be [5], if so be that [1], unless [1]

195 אוּלַי *'ûlay*, n.pr.loc. GK: 217. Ulai:– Ulai [2]

196 אֱוִלִי *'°wilî*, a. GK: 216 [→ 191]. foolish, without understanding:– foolish [1]

197 אוּלָם *'ûlām*, n.m. GK: 221 [→ 361]. portico; hall; colonnade:– porch [33], porches [1]

198 אוּלָם *'ûlām*, n.pr.m. GK: 220. Ulam, "*first, leader*":– Ulam [4]

199 אוּלָם *'ûlām*, adv. GK: 219. but, however, on the other hand, nevertheless:– but (+2050.1) [6], truly [4], but [2], in very

deed [2], surely [2], howbeit [1], wherefore (+2050.1) [1], would [1]

200 אִוֶּלֶת *'iwwelet*, n.f. GK: 222 [→ 191]. foolishness, folly; in some contexts this may refer to thoughtless speech:– folly [13], foolishness [10], foolishly [1], foolish [1]

201 אֹמָר *'ōmār*, n.pr.m. GK: 223 [→ 559]. Omar, "*speaker*":– Omar [3]

202 אוֹן *'ôn*, n.m. GK: 226 [→ 203, 207, 208, 209]. power, strength, vigor, manhood; wealth:– strength [7], might [2], force [1], goods [1], substance [1]

203 אוֹן *'ôn*, n.pr.m. GK: 227 [→ 208; cf. 202]. On, "*Sun [god] city*":– On [1]

204 אוֹן *'ôn*, n.pr.loc. GK: 228. On, "*Sun [god] city*":– On [3]

205 אָוֶן *'āwen*, n.m. GK: 224 & 230 [→ 578, 1007, 1126, 8383?]. evil, wickedness, iniquity; evildoer; an unfavorable circumstance: calamity, trouble, injustice; this can also refer to idols, with a focus that they are morally evil; mourning:– iniquity [47], vanity [6], wicked [6], affliction [3], mischief [3], Aven [2], unrighteous [2], wickedness [2], evil [1], false [1], idol [1], mourners [1], mourning [1], nought [1], sorrow [1], unjust [1], vain [1]

206 אָוֶן *'āwen*, n.pr.loc. GK: 225. Heliopolis; (Valley of) Aven, "*evil power, wickedness*":– Aven [1]

207 אוֹנוֹ *'ônô*, n.pr.loc. GK: 229 [→ 202]. Ono, "*strong*":– Ono [5]

208 אוֹנָם *'ônām*, n.pr.m. GK: 231 [→ 203; cf. 202]. Onam, "*intense, strong*":– Onam [4]

209 אוֹנָן *'ônān*, n.pr.m. GK: 232 [→ 202]. Onan, "*powerful, intense*":– Onan [8]

210 אוּפָז *'ûpāz*, n.pr.loc. GK: 233. Uphaz:– Uphaz [2]

211 אוֹפִיר *'ôpîr*, n.pr.m. & loc. GK: 234 & 235 [cf. 665]. Ophir:– Ophir [13]

212 אוֹפַן *'ôpan*, n.m. GK: 236 [cf. 655?]. wheel (of a vehicle):– wheels [24], wheel [11], fitly (+5921) [1]

אֹפִיר *'ōpir*. See 211.

213 אוּץ *'ûṣ*, v. GK: 237. [Q] to be in haste, be eager; to press (for an answer); to be small, narrow; [H] to urge, insist upon:– hasted [2], hastened [2], hasty [2], hasteth [1], labour [1], maketh haste [1], narrow [1]

214 אוֹצָר *'ôṣār*, n.m. GK: 238 [→ 686]. treasury, storehouse, storeroom, storage vault:– treasures [50], treasure [11], treasuries [7], treasury [3], cellars [2], storehouses [2], armoury [1], garners [1], storehouse (+1004) [1], store [1]

215 אוֹר *'ôr*, v. GK: 239 [→ 216, 217, 218, 219, 221, 224?, 3974, 3975? (also used with compound proper names)]. [Q] to shine, be bright; [H] to give light, make shine, brighten; [N] to be resplendent with light, shine on; the fig. extension "to make the face shine" is to establish favorable circumstance, peace and relief from trouble:– give light [8], cause to shine [5], enlightened [4], lighten [2], light [2], make to shine [2], maketh to shine [2], at break of day [1], enlightening [1], gave light [1], give light (+216) [1], giveth light [1], glorious [1], have light [1], kindle [1], lightened [1], lighteneth [1], make shine [1], set on fire [1], shew light [1], shewed light [1], shined [1], shineth more and more (+1980) [1], shineth [1], shine [1]

216 אוֹר *'ôr*, n.m. GK: 240 [→ 219; cf. 215]. light, contrasted with darkness; by extension: brightness; lightning; daylight, sunshine; the fig. extension "light of the face" is a positive, happy attitude, resulting from relief from trouble:– light [111], day [2], lights [2], bright [1], clear [1], give light (+215) [1], herbs [1], lightning [1], morning [1], sun [1]

217 אוֹר *'ûr*, n.m. GK: 241 [cf. 215]. light; east [the region of light], the direction of the sunrise:– fire [4], fires [1], light [1]

218 אוֹר *'ûr*, n.pr.m. & loc. GK: 243 & 244 [→ 215]. Ur, "*flame, light*":– Ur [5]

219 אוֹרָה *'ôrâ*, n.f. GK: 245 & 246 [→ 216; cf. 215]. light, morning light; happiness, serenity, cheerfulness; herb, mallow, a tasty, edible plant:– herbs [2], light [2]

220 אֻרָוָה *'°wērâ*, n.f. GK: 774 [→ 723]. (animal) stall, pen, stable; cf. 723:– cotes [1]

221 אוּרִי *'ûrî* or אֻרִי *'urî*, n.pr.m. GK: 247 & 788 [→ 215, 738]. Uri, "*Yahweh is [my] flame, light*":– Uri [8]

222 אוּרִיאֵל *'ûrî'ēl*, n.pr.m. GK: 248 [→ 215+410]. Uriel, "*God [El] is [my] flame, light*":– Uriel [4]

223 אוּרִיָּה *'ûriyyâ* or אוּרִיָּהוּ *'ûriyyāhû*, n.pr.m. GK: 249 & 250. Uriah, "*Yahweh is [my] flame, light*":– Uriah [26], Urijah [12], Uriah's [1]

224 אוּרִים *'ûrîm*, n.m.[pl.]. GK: 242 & 251 [→ 215? or 717? or 779?]. Urim, devices used by the high priest to make God's will known, possibly related to radiating or reflecting light:– Urim [7]

אוּרֶנָה *'ôrenâ*. See 728.

225 אוּת *'ût*, v. GK: 252. [N] to consent, agree:– consent [3], consented [1]

226 אוֹת *'ôt*, n.m. & f. GK: 253 [→ 184?; cf. 852]. sign, mark, symbol, a signal or event that communicates; a supernatural event or miracle as a sign from God:– sign [33], signs [27], token [10], tokens [4], miracles [2], ensigns [1], ensign [1], mark [1]

227 אָז *'āz*, adv. GK: 255 [→ 233; cf. 116]. then, at that time, meanwhile:– then [114], since (+4480) [6], that time [3], the beginning [3], old [2], time [2], also [1], at which time [1], even from (+4480) [1], for [1], hitherto (+4480) [1], if then (+176) [1], now [1], than (+4480) [1], then (+3588) [1], when once (+4480) [1], yet [1]

228 אֲזָה *'°zâ* (Aram.), v. GK: 10015. [P] to heat; [Pp] to be heated:– heat [2], hot [1]

229 אֶזְבַּי *'ezbāy*, n.pr.m. GK: 256 [→ 231?]. Ezbai:– Ezbai [1]

230 אַזְדָּא *'azdā'* (Aram.), a. GK: 10014. firm, assured:– gone [2]

231 אֵזוֹב *'ēzôb*, n.m. GK: 257 [→ 229?]. hyssop:– hyssop [10]

232 אֵזוֹר *'ēzôr*, n.m. GK: 258 [→ 247]. garments that are wrapped: belt, sash, loincloth:– girdle [13], girdles [1]

233 אֲזַי *'°zay*, adv. GK: 259 [→ 227]. (if not ...) then:– then [3]

234 אַזְכָּרָה *'azkārâ*, n.f. GK: 260 [→ 2142]. memorial offering, memorial portion; the portion of the meal burnt as a token of honor to the Lord:– memorial [7]

235 אָזַל *'āzal*, v. GK: 261 [cf. 236]. [Q] to go about, go away; disappear:– fail [1], gaddest about [1], going to and fro (+4480) [1], gone way [1], gone [1], spent [1]

236 אֲזַל *'°zal* (Aram.), v. GK: 10016 [cf. 235]. [P] to go, return:– went [5], go [1], went up [1]

237 אָזֵל *'āzēl*, n.pr.loc. GK: 262. Ezel:– Ezel [1]

238 אָזַן *'āzan*, v.den. GK: 263 [→ 241]. [H] to listen, pay attention, give ear:– give ear [29], hearken [5], gave ear [2], hear [2], giveth ear [1], hearkened [1], perceived by the ear [1]

239 אָזַן *'āzan*, v. GK: 264. [P] to ponder, give serious thought, an extension of weighing and testing on scales:– gave good heed [1]

240 אָזֵן *'āzēn*, n.[m.]. GK: 266 [cf. 241?]. equipment, tools, specifically a digging tool:– weapon [1]

241 אֹזֶן *'ozen*, n.f. GK: 265 [→ 238, 244, 245; cf. 240?]. ear: the organ for hearing; by extension: listening, and hence, responding, obeying. "To be in the ear" shows close proximity; "to reveal to the ear" means "to inform":– ears [100], ear [63], audience [7], hearing [5], shew (+1540) [4], advertise (+1540) [1], displeased (+7451+871.1) [1], hear (+8085) [1], revealed (+1540) [1], sheweth (+1540) [1], sheweth unto (+1540) [1], they[S] [1], told (+1540) [1]

242 אֹזֶן שְׁאֵרָה *'ozen še'°râ*, n.pr.loc. GK: 267 [cf. 7609]. Uzzen Sheerah, "[perhaps] *ear of Sheerah*":– Uzzen-sherah [1]

243 אַזְנוֹת תָּבוֹר *'aznôt tābôr*, n.pr.loc. GK: 268 [cf. 8396]. Aznoth Tabor, "[poss.] *peaks of Tabor*":– Aznoth-tabor [1]

244 אָזְנִי *'oznî*, n.pr.m. & a.g. GK: 269 & 270 [cf. 241]. Ozni, "*my ear, my hearing*"; Oznite, "*belonging to Ozni*":– Oznites [1], Ozni [1]

245 אֲזַנְיָה *'°zanyâ*, n.pr.m. GK: 271 [→ 241+3068]. Azaniah, "*Yahweh has listened*":– Azaniah [1]

246 אֲזִקִּים *'°ziqqîm*, n.[m.]. GK: 272 [cf. 2131]. chains, which in context refer to manacles or wrist cuffs:– chains [2]

247 אָזַר *'āzar*, v. GK: 273 [→ 232]. [Q] to gird up, belt on; [P] to gird someone; [N, Ht] to gird oneself; the action of wrapping a belt or sash around the waist; by extension "to take action" of various kinds: working, providing, going to battle:– girded [6], gird up [3], gird [2], girt [2], bindeth about [1], compass about [1], girdeth [1]

248 אֶזְרוֹעַ *'ezrôa'*, n.f. GK: 274 [cf. 2220; cf. 153]. arm, with the associative meaning of power and potency:– arm [2]

Heb

249 אֶזְרָח **'ezrāḥ**, n.m. GK: 275 [→ 2224]. native-born:– born [3], your own country [2], bay tree [1], born among [1], born in the country [1], homeborn [1], one born amongst [1], one of own country [1], that is born in land [1], that is born [1], that was born [1], your own nation [1]

250 אֶזְרָחִי **'ezrāḥî**, a.g. GK: 276 [→ 2226; cf. 2224]. Ezrahite, "of Ezrah":– Ezrahite [3]

251 אָח **'āḥ**, n.m. GK: 278 [→ 264, 269, 277; cf. 252 (also used with compound proper names)]. brother; by extension: family, kinsman, relative (of either gender); a term of endearment; anyone of the same race or large social group: countryman; associate. "Each to his brother" is usually translated "to each other" or "one to another.":– brethren [331], brother [244], brother's [24], anotherS [24], brethren's [1], brother's (+3807.1) [1], brotherly [1], kindred [1], like [1], otherS [1]

252 אָח **'āḥ** (Aram.), n.m. GK: 10017 [cf. 251]. brother:– brethren [1]

253 אָח **'āḥ**, interj. GK: 277. Alas!, Oh!:– ah [1], alas [1]

254 אָח **'āḥ**, n.f. GK: 279. firepot:– hearth [3]

255 אֹחַ **'ōaḥ**, n.[m.]. GK: 280. a howling animal: jackal, hyena, eagle owl:– doleful creatures [1]

256 אַחְאָב **'aḥ'āb** or אֶחָב **'eḥāb**, n.pr.m. GK: 281 & 282 [→ 251+1]. Ahab, "brother of father":– Ahab [91], Ahab's [2]

257 אַחְבָּן **'aḥbān**, n.pr.m. GK: 283. Ahban, "brother of intelligent one":– Ahban [1]

258 אָחַד **'āḥad**, v. GK: 284 [→ 2300]. prob. same as 2300: [Ht] to slash; to go one way or another:– go one way or other [1]

259 אֶחָד **'eḥād**, a.num. GK: 285 [→ 261; cf. 2297; 2300; cf. 2298]. one; a certain one; first:– one [681], a [60], first [37], another [35], other [31], any [15], once [11], certain [9], eleven (+6240) [9], each [8], every [7], some [7], an [5], together (+3509.1) [5], alone [4], eleventh (+6240) [4], every one [3], few [3], once (+6471) [3], somewhat [3], at once (+6471) [2], only [2], alike (+3509.1) [1], altogether (+871.1) [1], any (+3605) [1], apiece (+5982) [1], apiece [1], at once [1], daily (+3117+3807.1) [1], each man [1], each one [1], fro (+2008) [1], man [1], none (+369) [1], none (+3808) [1], once (+871.1) [1], one manner [1], one tenth deal (+6241) [1], one thing [1], the [1], threescore and one (+8346+2050.1) [1], toS (+2008) [1]

260 אָחוּ **'āḥû**, n.m.col. GK: 286. reeds:– meadow [2], flag [1]

261 אֵהוּד **'ēhûd**, n.pr.m. GK: 287 [→ 259; cf. 164?]. Ehud, "united":– Ehud [1]

262 אַחֲוָא **'aḥăwā'**, n.f. GK: 289 [→ 2331]. what is said, declaration:– declaration [1]

263 אַחֲוָיָה **'aḥăwāyâ** (Aram.), n.f. GK: 10018 [→ 2324]. declaring:– shewing [1]

264 אַחֲוָה **'aḥăwâ**, n.f. GK: 288 [→ 251]. brotherhood, community:– brotherhood [1]

265 אֲחוֹחַ **'ăḥôaḥ**, n.pr.m. GK: 291 [→ 266]. Ahoah, "brotherly":– Ahoah [1]

266 אֲחוֹחִי **'ăḥôḥî**, a.g. GK: 292 [→ 265]. Ahohite:– Ahohite [4], Ahohite (+1121) [1]

267 אֲחוּמַי **'ăḥûmay**, n.pr.m. GK: 293. Ahumai:– Ahumai [1]

268 אָחוֹר **'āḥôr**, subst. GK: 294 [→ 322; cf. 309]. back (of the body), rear, hindquarters; backward, from behind; west, as a compass point, because east (the direction of the sunrise) is the direction of orientation:– back [15], backward [10], behind [3], hinder parts [3], behind (+4480) [2], afterwards [1], back parts [1], backside [1], backs [1], backward (+3807.1) [1], hereafter [1], time to come [1], without [1]

269 אָחוֹת **'āḥôt**, n.f. GK: 295 [→ 251]. sister, by extension: half-sister, any female blood-relative; a term of endearment. "Each to her sister" is a marker of reciprocal reference: one to another:– sister [90], sisters [11], anotherS [6], sister's [5], otherS [1], together (+413+802) [1]

270 אָחַז **'āḥaz**, v. GK: 296 & 297 [→ 271, 272, 275, 276; (also used with compound proper names)]. [Q] grasp, seize, hold; to attach, cover, panel; [Op] to be fastened; [N] to be caught, acquire; [Ho] be attached; [P] to cover:– take hold [7], hold [6], took [6], taken [5], take [4], caught [3], fastened [3], held [3], taken hold upon [3], took hold [3], lay hold [2], portion [2], affrighted (+8178) [1], bar [1], caught hold [1], come upon [1], get possessions [1], had possession [1], handle [1], have possessions [1], hold on [1], holden [1], holdest [1], holdeth back [1], lay hold on [1], possessed [1], rested [1], surprised [1],

take possession [1], taketh hold on [1], taketh [1], took hold upon [1]

271 אָחָז **'āḥāz**, n.pr.m. GK: 298 [→ 274; cf. 270]. Ahaz, "he has grasped":– Ahaz [41]

272 אֲחֻזָּה **'ăḥuzzâ**, n.f. GK: 299 [→ 270]. property, possession:– possession [64], possessions [2]

273 אַחְזַי **'aḥzay**, n.pr.m. GK: 300 [→ 274]. Ahzai, "Yahweh has grasped":– Ahasai [1]

274 אֲחַזְיָה **'ăḥazyâ** or אֲחַזְיָהוּ **'ăḥazyāhû**, n.pr.m. GK: 301 & 302 [→ 271, 273, 276]. Ahaziah, "Yahweh has upheld":– Ahaziah [37]

275 אֲחֻזָּם **'ăḥuzzām**, n.pr.m. GK: 303 [→ 270]. Ahuzzam, "possessor":– Ahuzam [1]

276 אֲחֻזַּת **'ăḥuzzat**, n.pr.m. GK: 304 [→ 274; cf. 270]. Ahuzzath, "possession":– Ahuzzath [1]

277 אֲחִי **'ăḥî**, n.pr.m. GK: 306 [→ 251]. Ahi, "my brother, [poss.] Yahweh is [my] brother":– Ahi [2]

278 אֵחִי **'ēḥî**, n.pr.m. GK: 305 [→ 297]. Ehi, "my brother [is exalted]":– Ehi [1]

279 אֲחִיאָם **'ăḥî'ām**, n.pr.m. GK: 307 [→ 251+3963.1?]. Ahiam, "brother of mother":– Ahiam [2]

280 אֲחִידָה **'ăḥîdâ** (Aram.), n.f. GK: 10019 [cf. 2420]. riddle:– hard sentences [1]

281 אֲחִיָּה **'ăḥiyyâ** or אֲחִיָּהוּ **'ăḥiyyāhû**, n.pr.m. GK: 308 & 309 [→ 251+3068]. Ahijah, "[my] brother is Yahweh":– Ahijah [20], Ahiah [4]

282 אֲחִיהוּד **'ăḥîhûd**, n.pr.m. GK: 310 [→ 251+1935]. Ahihud, "[my] brother has majesty":– Ahihud [1]

283 אַחְיוֹ **'aḥyô**, n.pr.m. GK: 311 [→ 251+3068]. Ahio, "[my] brother is Yahweh":– Ahio [6]

284 אֲחִיחֻד **'ăḥîḥud**, n.pr.m. GK: 312 [→ 251+1935]. Ahihud, "[my] brother has majesty":– Ahihud [1]

285 אֲחִיטוּב **'ăḥîṭûb**, n.pr.m. GK: 313 [→ 251+2896]. Ahitub, "[my] brother is goodness":– Ahitub [15]

286 אֲחִילוּד **'ăḥîlûd**, n.pr.m. GK: 314 [→ 251+3205?]. Ahilud, "[my] brother is born":– Ahilud [5]

287 אֲחִימוֹת **'ăḥîmôt**, n.pr.m. GK: 315 [→ 251+4191]. Ahimoth, "[my] brother is my support [or poss.] [my] brother is Mot":– Ahimoth [1]

288 אֲחִימֶלֶךְ **'ăḥîmelek**, n.pr.m. GK: 316 [→ 251+4428]. Ahimelech, "[my] brother is king":– Ahimelech [16], Ahimelech's [1]

289 אֲחִימָן **'ăḥîman**, n.pr.m. GK: 317 [→ 251+?]. Ahiman, "[poss.] [my] brother is a gift":– Ahiman [4]

290 אֲחִימַעַץ **'ăḥîma'aṣ**, n.pr.m. GK: 318 [→ 251+4619]. Ahimaaz, "[my] brother is fury":– Ahimaaz [15]

291 אַחְיָן **'aḥyān**, n.pr.m. GK: 319 [→ 251+4993.1?]. Ahian, "little brother":– Ahian [1]

292 אֲחִינָדָב **'ăḥînādāb**, n.pr.m. GK: 320 [→ 251+5068]. Ahinadab, "[my] brother is willing":– Ahinadab [1]

293 אֲחִינֹעַם **'ăḥînō'am**, n.pr.f. GK: 321 [→ 251+5278]. Ahinoam, "[my] brother is pleasant":– Ahinoam [7]

294 אֲחִיסָמָךְ **'ăḥîsāmāk**, n.pr.m. GK: 322 [→ 251+5564]. Ahisamach, "[my] brother is a support":– Ahisamach [3]

295 אֲחִיעֶזֶר **'ăḥî'ezer**, n.pr.m. GK: 323 [→ 251+5828]. Ahiezer, "[my] brother is a help":– Ahiezer [6]

296 אֲחִיקָם **'ăḥîqām**, n.pr.m. GK: 324 [→ 251+6965]. Ahikam, "[my] brother stands":– Ahikam [20]

297 אֲחִירָם **'ăḥîrām**, n.pr.m. GK: 325 [→ 278, 298, 2361, 2438]. Ahiram, "[my] brother is exalted":– Ahiram [1]

298 אֲחִירָמִי **'ăḥîrāmî**, a.g. GK: 326 [→ 297]. Ahiramite, "of Ahiram":– Ahiramites [1]

299 אֲחִירַע **'ăḥîra'**, n.pr.m. GK: 327 [→ 251+7452 or 7453 or 7454]. Ahira, "[my] brother is my friend or my brother is evil":– Ahira [5]

300 אֲחִישָׁחַר **'ăḥîšāḥar**, n.pr.m. GK: 328 [→ 251+7835]. Ahishahar, "[my] brother was born at early dawn":– Ahishahar [1]

301 אֲחִישַׁר **'ăḥîšar**, n.pr.m. GK: 329. Ahishar, "[my] brother is upright or [my] brother has sung":– Ahishar [1]

302 אֲחִיתֹפֶל **'ăḥîtōpel**, n.pr.m. GK: 330 [→ 251+8603?]. Ahithophel, "[poss.] [my] brother is in the desert or [my] brother is foolishness":– Ahithophel [20]

303 אַחְלָב **'aḥlāb**, n.pr.loc. GK: 331. Ahlab, "fat, fruitful, healthy":– Ahlab [1]

304 אַחְלָי **'aḥlāy**, n.pr. GK: 333 [→ 251+410]. Ahlai, "Alas! I wish that!":– Ahlai [2]

305 אַחֲלַי **'aḥălay**, subst. GK: 332. Oh that!; If only!:– O that [1], would God [1]

306 אַחְלָמָה **'aḥlāmâ**, n.f. GK: 334. amethyst (exact identification uncertain):– amethyst [2]

307 אַחְמְתָא **'aḥm'tā** (Aram.), n.pr.loc. GK: 10020. Ecbatana, "[perhaps] place of gathering":– Achmetha [1]

308 אֲחַסְבַּי **'ăḥasbay**, n.pr.m. GK: 335 [→ 2620+871.1?+3068?]. Ahasbai, "I seek refuge in Yahweh":– Ahasbai [1]

309 אָחַר **'āḥar**, v. GK: 336 [→ 268, 310, 314, 319, 322, 4279, 4283; cf. 3186]. [Q] to remain, stay on; [P] to detain, delay, slow down; [H] to take longer (than a set time), come late:– tarry [3], defer [2], make tarrying [2], slack [2], continue [1], deferred [1], delay [1], hinder [1], late [1], stayed [1], tarried longer [1], tarry long [1]

310 אַחַר **'aḥar**, subst. & adv. & pp. GK: 339 & 343 [cf. 309; cf. 311]. (temporal) after, afterward, later, some time later; (spatial) back, behind, following:– after [477], behind [35], following [26], afterward [22], followed [+1980) [16], followed [16], afterward (+3651) [15], from (+4480) [12], behind (+4480) [11], follow (+1980) [9], afterwards [5], follow [5], after (+4480) [4], afterwards (+3651) [4], posterity [4], after that (+3651) [2], at [2], behind (+413) [2], followed (+1961) [2], followeth (+935) [2], following (+1980) [2], forasmuch [2], pursuing [2], since [2], when [2], after (+413) [1], after that (+3651+2050.1) [1], afterward (+3651+4480) [1], again [1], away from (+4480) [1], backside [1], back [1], behind (+5921) [1], beside [1], by [1], follow (+1961) [1], follow (+935) [1], followed (+3318) [1], followedst (+1980) [1], followeth [1], following (+3651) [1], following after [1], forasmuch as [1], hereafter [1], hinder and [1], outlived (+748+3117) [1], overlived (+748+3117) [1], pursue (+1980) [1], remnant [1], seeing that (+834) [1], thenceforth (+3651) [1], when (+4970) [1], when (+834) [1], with [1]

311 אַחַר **'aḥar** (Aram.), pp. GK: 10021 [→ 320, 318; cf. 310]. after, in the future:– hereafter (+1836) [2], after [1]

312 אַחֵר **'aḥēr**, a. GK: 337 [→ 313]. other, another, different; next, additional, more, extra:– other [96], another [55], others [9], next [2], another man's [1], following [1], other men [1], strange [1]

313 אַחֵר **'aḥēr**, n.pr.m. GK: 338 [→ 312]. Aher, "another, substitute":– Aher [1]

314 אַחֲרוֹן **'aḥărôn**, a.f. GK: 340 [→ 309]. (temporal) next, later, last, end; (spatial) at the back, behind, west, as a compass point, because east (the direction of the sunrise) is the direction of orientation:– last [19], latter [6], come [4], to come [3], after [2], come after [2], latter end [2], utmost [2], after (+871.1+1886.1) [1], afterward (+871.1+1886.1) [1], afterwards [1], afterward [1], following [1], hindermost [1], hinder [1], hindmost [1], last (+871.1+1886.1) [1], rereward [1], uttermost [1]

315 אַחְרַח **'aḥraḥ**, n.pr.m. GK: 341. Aharah, "brother of Rah":– Aharah [1]

316 אֲחַרְחֵל **'ăḥarḥēl**, n.pr.m. GK: 342. Aharhel, "brother of Rachel":– Aharhel [1]

317 אָחֳרִי **'oḥŏrî** (Aram.), a.f. GK: 10023 [→ 321]. other, another:– another [5], other [1]

318 אָחֳרֵן **'oḥŏrēn** (Aram.), adv. GK: 10024 [→ 311]. finally, at last:– last [1]

319 אַחֲרִית **'aḥărît**, n.f. GK: 344 [→ 309; cf. 320]. (spatial) the far side, the other side; (temporal) at the last, at the end, (in days) to come:– end [21], latter [11], latter end [8], last [6], last end [4], posterity [3], reward [2], hindermost [1], latter time [1], length [1], remnant [1], residue [1], uttermost parts [1]

320 אַחֲרִי **'aḥŏrî** (Aram.), n.f.constr. GK: 10022 [→ 311; cf. 319]. end (of days), (days) to come:– latter [1]

321 אָחֳרָן **'oḥŏrān** (Aram.), a.m. GK: 10025 [→ 317]. other, another, someone else:– other [3], another [2]

 אָחֳרֵן **'oḥŏrēn**. See 318.

322 אֲחֹרַנִּית **'ăḥōrannît**, adv. GK: 345 [→ 268; cf. 309]. backwardly, by turning around, in turning back:– backward [6], again [1]

323 אֲחַשְׁדַּרְפָּן *'ḥašdarpān*, n.m.pl. GK: 346 [cf. 324]. satraps, an administrative governor of a Persian province:– lieutenants [4]

324 אֲחַשְׁדַּרְפַּן *'ḥašdarpan* (Aram.), n.m. GK: 10026 [cf. 323]. satrap, a viceroy or governor having considerable power:– princes [9]

325 אֲחַשְׁוֵרוֹשׁ *'ḥašwêrôš* or אֲחַשְׁרֹשׁ *'ḥašērōš*, n.pr.m. GK: 347 & 348. Ahasuerus, Xerxes:– Ahasuerus [30], Ahasuerus' [1]

326 אֲחַשְׁתָּרִי *'ḥaštārî* or הָאֲחַשְׁתָּרִי *hā''ḥaštārî*, n.pr.m. or a.g. GK: 349 & 2028. Ahashtari; Haahashtari, "*the Ahashtarites*":– Haahashtari [1]

327 אֲחַשְׁתְּרָן *'ḥašt'rān*, a. GK: 350. royal, belonging to the king and used in the king's service:– camels [2]

328 אַט *'aṭ*, subst. & n.m. GK: 351 & 356. spirits of the dead; (adv.) gently, meekly, slowly:– softly (+3807.1) [2], charmers [1], gently (+3807.1) [1], secret [1], softly [1]

329 אָטָד *'āṭād* or אַטָד *'aṭād*, n.m. & n.pr.loc. GK: 353 & 354. thornbush; Atad, "*of the thorns [?]*":– bramble [3], Atad [2], thorns [1]

330 אֵטוּן *'êṭûn*, n.[m.] GK: 355. linen, possibly red in color:– fine linen [1]

331 אָטַם *'āṭam*, v. GK: 357. [Q] to stop up (one's ears); to hold (one's tongue); [Qp] to be narrow:– narrow [4], stoppeth [3], shutteth [1]

332 אָטַר *'āṭar*, v. GK: 358 [→ 333, 334]. [Q] to close:– shut [1]

333 אִטֵּר *'iṭṭēr*, n.pr.m. GK: 359 [→ 332]. Ater, "[poss.] *crippled one, left-handed one, or Etir*":– Ater [5]

334 אִטֵּר *'iṭṭēr*, a. GK: 360 [→ 332]. hindered on the right hand, (thus) left-handed; other sources: ambidextrous:– lefthanded (+3027+3225) [2]

335 אֵי *'ê*, adv.inter. GK: 361 [→ 346, 349, 351, 370, 375, 645?]. where?, which way?:– where [11], where (+2088) [10], whence (+2088+4480) [5], from whence (+2088+4480) [2], which (+2088) [2], by what (+2088) [1], how [1], of what (+2088+4480) [1], what (+2088) [1], what [1], whether (+2088) [1], which way (+2088) [1]

336 אִי *'î*, adv. GK: 364 [→ 348?, 350]. not:– island [1]

337 אִי *'î*, interj. GK: 365. Woe!:– woe [2]

338 אִי *'î*, n.m. GK: 363 [cf. 339?]. hyena, jackals; some understand this to be a spirit or demon:– wild beasts of the islands [2], wild beasts of the island [1]

339 אִי *'î*, n.m. & f. GK: 362 [cf. 338?]. island; coastland; distant shores:– isles [27], islands [5], isle [3], country [1]

340 אָיַב *'āyab*, v. GK: 366 [→ 341, 342, 347]. [Q] to be an enemy, be hostile towards:– enemy [1]

341 אֹיֵב *'ōyēb*, n.m. or v.ptcp. GK: 367 [→ 340]. enemy, foe:– enemies [199], enemy [77], enemies' [3], foes [2], enemy's [1]

342 אֵיבָה *'êbâ*, n.f. GK: 368 [→ 340]. hostility, enmity:– enmity [3], hatred [2]

343 אֵיד *'êd*, n.m. GK: 369 [→ 181]. disaster, calamity, destruction:– calamity [16], destruction [7], calamities [1]

344 אַיָּה *'ayyâ*, n.f. GK: 370 [→ 345]. black kite; falcon; vulture:– kite [2], vulture's [1]

345 אַיָּה *'ayyâ*, n.pr.m. GK: 371 [→ 344]. Aiah, "*black kite*":– Aiah [6]

346 אַיֵּה *'ayyēh*, adv.inter. GK: 372 [→ 335]. Where?:– where [45]

347 אִיּוֹב *'iyyôb*, n.pr.m. GK: 373 [→ 340]. Job, "*where is my father, [or perhaps] Where is my father, O God?*":– Job [57], Job's [1]

348 אִיזֶבֶל *'îzebel*, n.pr.f. GK: 374 [→ 336?+2073?]. Jezebel, "[poss.] *unhusbanded, unexalted*":– Jezebel [21], Jezebel's [1]

349 אֵיךְ *'êk* or אֵיכָה *'êkâ* or אֵיכָכָה *'êkākâ*, adv.inter. & excl. GK: 375 & 377 & 379 [→ 335; cf. 1963]. How? Why? How! Also!:– how [78], where [2], how can [1], what [1]

350 אִיכָבוֹד *'îkābôd* or אִי־כָבוֹד *'î-kābôd*, n.pr.m. GK: 376 [→ 336+3519]. Ichabod, "*where is the glory?*":– Ichabod's [1], Ichabod [1]

351 אֵיכֹה *'êkōh*, adv.inter. & excl. GK: 378 [→ 335]. Where?:– where [1]

 אֵיכָה *'êkâ* אֵיכָכָה *'êkākâ*. See 349.

352 אַיִל *'ayil*, n.m. GK: 380 & 381 & 382 & 383 & 442 & 443 & 444 [→ 193, 354, 356, 358, 359?, 362, 424, 425, 427, 436, 437, 438, 439, 879]. ram, a male sheep generally more aggressive and protective of the flock; by extension: leading man, ruler; oaks; or any large, mighty tree without reference to a specific species; projecting wall; jamb:– ram [90], rams [61], posts [17], rams' [5], post [4], mighty [3], trees [2], lintel [1], mighty men [1], oaks [1]

353 אֱיָל *'ĕyāl*, n.m. GK: 384 [→ 360; cf. 352]. strength:– strength [1]

354 אַיָּל *'ayyāl*, n.[m.] & f. GK: 385 [→ 355, 365, 357; cf. 352]. deer, young stag:– hart [9], harts [2]

355 אַיָּלָה *'ayyālâ*, n.f. GK: 387 [→ 354]. deer, doe:– hinds [4], hinds' [3], hind [1]

356 אֵילוֹן *'êlôn* or אֵילוֹן *'êlôn*, n.pr.m. & loc. GK: 390 & 391 & 472 [→ 436, 440; cf. 352]. Elon, "*species of a mighty tree*":– Elon [6]

357 אַיָּלוֹן *'ayyālôn*, n.pr.loc. GK: 389 [→ 354]. Aijalon, "*place of the deer*":– Aijalon [8], Ajalon [2]

358 אֵילוֹן בֵּית חָנָן *'êlôn bêt ḥānān*, n.pr.loc. GK: 392 [→ 352+1004+2605]. Elon Bethhanan, "*tree of Bethhanan*":– Elon-beth-hanan [1]

359 אֵילוֹת *'êlôt* or אֵילַת *'êlat*, n.pr.loc. GK: 393 & 397 [→ 352?]. Eloth, Elath, "*grove of large trees*":– Elath [5], Eloth [3]

360 אֱיָלוּת *'ĕyālût*, n.m. GK: 394 [→ 353; cf. 352]. Strength, Power, a title of the one true God, with a focus that he is potent to help:– strength [1]

361 אֵילָם *'êlām*, n.m. GK: 395 [→ 197]. portico, porch, hall:– arches [15]

362 אֵילִם *'êlim*, n.pr.loc. GK: 396 [→ 352; cf. 352]. Elim, "*big trees*":– Elim [6]

363 אִילָן *'îlān* (Aram.), n.m. GK: 10027 [cf. 436]. tree:– tree [6]

364 אֵיל פָּארָן *'êl pā'rān*, n.pr.loc. GK: 386 [→ 352+6290]. El Paran, "*tree of Paran*":– El-paran [1]

 אֵילֹן *'êlôn*. See 356.

365 אַיֶּלֶת *'ayyelet*, n.f. GK: 387 [→ 354]. deer, doe:– hind [2], Aijeleth [1]

 אַיִם *'ayim*. See 368.

366 אָיֹם *'āyōm*, a. GK: 398 [→ 367]. fearful; majestic, with an implication that this majesty instills awe that borders on fear:– terrible [3]

367 אֵימָה *'êmâ* or אֵמָה *'ēmâ*, n.f. GK: 399 & 568 [→ 366, 368; cf. 520; cf. 574]. terror, dread, fear:– fear [5], terror [4], terrors [1], terrible [1], dread [1], horror [1], idols [1]

368 אֵימִים *'êmîm*, n.pr.m.pl. GK: 400 [→ 367]. Emites, "*frightening beings*":– Emims [3]

369 אַיִן *'ayin*, subst.neg. GK: 401 [cf. 371]. there is no, not, none, without:– no [243], not [188], none [141], neither (+2050.1) [27], nothing [26], without [26], without (+4480) [18], no man [17], nor (+2050.1) [17], neither [13], nor any (+2050.1) [5], gone [4], never [4], nothing (+3972) [4], cannot [3], innumerable (+4557) [3], unsearchable (+2714) [3], without (+871.1) [3], neither any (+2050.1) [2], no (+3605) [2], no more [2], none (+376) [2], none (+4480) [2], nothing (+3605) [2], without (+5704) [2], abundance (+4557) [1], any [1], come to nought [1], else [1], except [1], faileth [1], fatherless (+1) [1], incurable (+4832) [1], infinite (+4557) [1], infinite (+7093) [1], infinite (+7097) [1], innumerable (+4557+5704) [1], more than (+3807.1) [1], neither (+637) [1], no (+1097) [1], no (+3605+3807.1) [1], no (+4480) [1], no where [1], none (+259) [1], none other [1], no any thing (+2050.1) [1], nothing else (+1115) [1], past (+5704) [1], there be no [1], there is none [1], there is not [1], well nigh (+3509.1) [1], without any (+4480) [1]

370 אַיִן *'ayin*, adv. GK: 402 [cf. 335]. where (from)?:– whence (+4480) [12], whence [4], where (+4480) [1]

371 אִין *'în*, subst.neg. GK: 403 [cf. 369]. there is not:– not [1]

372 אִיעֶזֶר *'î'ezer*, n.pr.m. GK: 404 [→ 373]. Iezer, "*my [father] is help*":– Jeezer [1]

373 אִיעֶזְרִי *'î'ezrî*, a.g. GK: 405 [→ 372]. Iezerite, "*of Iezer*":– Jeezerites [1]

374 אֵיפָה *'êpâ*, n.f. GK: 406. ephah (dry measure, about three-fifths of a bushel (22 liters); also a large basket of unspecified measure; "ephah and ephah" means "two differing measures," as a measure that is not standardized:– ephah [34], divers measures (+374+2050.1) [4], measure [2]

375 אֵיפֹה *'êpōh*, adv. GK: 407 [→ 335+6311]. where?:– where [9], what manner [1]

376 אִישׁ *'îš*, n.m. GK: 408 [→ 380, 792, 802 (also used with compound proper names)]. man, sometimes in contrast to woman, human, sometimes in contrast to animal (without gender distinction); by extension: husband, in contrast to wife; (p.) each, every, someone, a certain one, anyone, whoever. This word is often used in phrases meaning "one of a kind," so a "man of war" is a soldier; a "man of bow" is an archer, etc:– man [763], men [679], every man [163], every one [112], one [71], husband [66], man's [31], any [24], any man [17], certain [14], persons [10], every one (+376) [8], each man [7], another [6], every man's [6], he^S [6], none (+3808) [6], whatsoever man (+376) [6], each [5], whosoever (+834) [5], every man (+376) [4], footmen (+7273) [4], husbands [4], none (+408) [4], person [4], what man soever (+376) [4], whosoever [4], any man's [3], him^S [3], some [3], Benjamite (+3227) [2], Israel (+3478) [2], any man (+376) [2], an (+2], champion (+1143+1886.1) [2], each (+376) [2], either^S [2], every man's (+376+2050.1) [2], husband's [2], male [2], men's [2], none (+1115) [2], none (+369) [2], none (+376+3808) [2], one man [2], people [2], stranger (+2214) [2], stranger (+5237) [2], they^S [2], those^S [2], whosoever (+376) [2], whoso [2], Amalekite (+6003) [1], Benjamite (+1121+3227) [1], Egyptian (+4713) [1], Egyptian (+4713+1886.1) [1], Ishi [1], Israelite (+3478) [1], adulteress (+802) [1], adversary (+6862) [1], adversary (+7379) [1], all (+3605) [1], also [1], archers (+3384+7198+871.1+1886.1) [1], a [1], bear^S [1], bloodthirsty (+1818) [1], chapmen (+1886.1+8446) [1], consent [1], counseller (+6098) [1], counsellers (+6098) [1], destroyer (+4889) [1], divers [1], each one [1], eloquent (+1697) [1], every man's (+3807.1) [1], every [1], evil speaker (+3956) [1], familiar friend (+7965) [1], famous (+8034) [1], fellows [1], fellow [1], friends (+7965) [1], goodman [1], had war with (+1961+4421) [1], had wars with (+1961+4421) [1], high (+1121) [1], hunter (+6718) [1], husbandman (+120+5647) [1], husbandman (+127+1886.1) [1], in the flower of age [1], lender (+3867) [1], liar (+3577) [1], man carnally (+2233+7902) [1], mankind (+1320) [1], master (+1167) [1], men (+1121) [1], men of high degree (+1121) [1], merchantmen (+5503) [1], merchantmen (+8446) [1], none (+1097) [1], none (+3808+3807.1) [1], one man's [1], oppressor (+2555) [1], reprover (+3198) [1], servants (+3198) [1], shipmen (+591) [1], slothful (+6102) [1], steward (+834+5921) [1], stranger (+1616) [1], stranger (+2114) [1], strangers (+1616) [1], them^S [1], this^S [1], trade about cattle (+4735) [1], trade to feed cattle (+4735) [1], whatsoever (+834+3605) [1], whosoever (+3605) [1], workmen (+4399) [1], worthy [1], young men (+5288) [1]

377 אָשַׁשׁ *'āšaš* or אֹשׁ *'ôš*, v. GK: 899 → 809?; cf. 787]. [Htpol] to fix in one's mind:– shew yourselves men [1]

378 אִישׁ־בֹּשֶׁת *'îš-bōšet*, n.pr.m. GK: 410 [→ 376+1322]. Ish-Bosheth, "*man of shame*":– Ish-bosheth [11]

379 אִישְׁהוֹד *'îšhôd*, n.pr.m. GK: 412 [→ 376+1935]. Ishhod, "*man of grandeur*":– Ishod [1]

380 אִישׁוֹן *'îšôn*, n.[m.] GK: 413 & 854 [→ 376]. pupil, the black center of the eyeball, formally, "the little man (of the eye)," often translated as "the apple of the eye," an idiom of care and love:– apple [2], apple (+1323) [1], black [1], obscure [1]

 אִישׁ־חַי *'îš-ḥay*. See 381.

381 אִישׁ־חַיִל *'îš-ḥayil*, n.m. GK: 408 + 2657 [→ 376+2428]. valiant man (376 + 2428):–

382 אִישׁ־טוֹב *'îš-ṭôb*, n.pr.loc. GK: 411 [→ 376+2896]. Ish-Tob, "*man from Tob*":– Ish-tob [2]

 אִישׁ *'îš*. See 3448.

 אִיתוֹן *'îtôn*. See 2978.

383 אִיתַי *'îtay* (Aram.), pt. GK: 10029 [cf. 3426]. there is, there are; a manner of existence often called a "quasi-verb":– there is [5], be [3], have [2], art [1], have (+3807.2) [1], is [1], none (+1768+3809) [1], there are [1], will [1]

384 אִיתִיאֵל *'îtî'ēl*, n.pr.m. GK: 417 [cf. 863]. Ithiel, "*God [El] is with me*":– Ithiel [3]

385 אִיתָמָר *'îtāmār*, n.pr.m. GK: 418. Ithamar, "[poss.] *[is]land of palms; [father] of Tamar*":– Ithamar [21]

386 אֵיתָן *'êtān*, a. GK: 419 [→ 387, 388, 3496, 3497]. ever-flowing, of a stream that is always filled with water; by extension: never-failing, steady, established, eternal:– strong [5], mighty [4], strength [2], hard [1], rough [1]

387 אֵיתָן *'êtān*, n.prm. GK: 420 [→ 386]. Ethan, "*long lived, ever-flowing [streams]*":– Ethan [8]

388 אֵתָנִים *'êtānîm*, n.pr.[m.]. GK: 923 [→ 386]. Ethanim, "*ever-flowing [streams]*":– Ethanim [1]

389 אַךְ *'ak*, adv. GK: 421 [→ 403]. but, surely, only, however:– only [35], surely [34], but [33], yet [12], nevertheless [11], notwithstanding [6], verily [6], also [4], howbeit [4], even [3], truly [3], at least [1], certainly [1], howbeit yet (+3588) [1], in any wise [1], indeed only (+7535) [1], notwithstanding (+2050.1) [1], of a surety [1], save [1], wherefore (+3588) [1], yet but [1]

390 אַכַּד *'akkad*, n.pr.loc. GK: 422. Akkad:– Accad [1]

391 אַכְזָב *'akzāb*, a. GK: 423 [→ 3576]. deceptive, deceitful, referring to a stream or a person:– liar [1], lie [1]

392 אַכְזִיב *'akzîb*, n.pr.loc. GK: 424 [→ 3576?]. Aczib, "*deceit*":– Achzib [4]

393 אַכְזָר *'akzār*, a. GK: 425 [→ 394, 395]. deadly, ruthless, fierce, heartless:– cruel [3], fierce [1]

394 אַכְזָרִי *'akzārî*, a.g. GK: 426 [→ 393]. cruel, merciless:– cruel [7], cruel one [1]

395 אַכְזְרִיּוּת *'akz⁰riyyût*, n.f. GK: 427 [→ 393]. cruelty:– cruel [1]

396 אֲכִילָה *'⁰kîlâ*, n.f. GK: 428 [→ 398]. food:– meat [1]

397 אָכִישׁ *'ākîš*, n.pr.m. GK: 429. Achish, "*the king gives*":– Achish [21]

398 אָכַל *'ākal*, v. GK: 430 [→ 396, 400, 402, 3978, 3979, 3980, 4361; cf. 399]. [Q] to eat; [N] to be eaten; [Pu] be consumed, be destroyed; [H] to give to eat, feed; from the base meaning of eating food is the fig. extension of consuming and destroying something:– eat [471], eaten [74], devour [57], devoured [41], eateth [29], consumed [20], eat up [16], eating [13], consume [9], feed [8], devoureth [6], eaten at all (+398) [6], devouring [5], fed [5], meat [5], eaten up [4], eater [3], eatest [3], give to eat [3], ate [2], cause to eat [2], consumeth [2], consuming [2], eat in plenty (+398) [2], eaten freely (+398) [2], eateth up [2], freely eat (+398) [2], in no wise eat (+398+3808) [2], indeed eaten (+398) [2], quite devoured (+398) [2], burnt up [1], caused to eat [1], devourer [1], devourest up [1], dine [1], feedest [1], food [1], gave to eat [1], higher [1], moth-eaten (+6211) [1]

399 אֲכַל *'⁰kal* (Aram.), v. GK: 10030 [cf. 398]. [P] to eat (food); to destroy, devastate, devour (an object):– accused (+7170) [2], devoured [2], devour [2], eat [1]

400 אֹכֶל *'ōkel*, n.m. GK: 431 [→ 398]. food; a general word for food as anything edible:– meat [18], food [16], eating [4], victuals [3], prey [2], mealtime (+6256+1886.1) [1]

401 אֻכָל *'ukāl*, n.pr.m. GK: 432 [→ 3615]. Ucal, "[poss.] *I am consumed* or *I cease*":– Ucal [1]

402 אָכְלָה *'oklâ*, n.f. GK: 433 [→ 398]. what is consumed, food, fuel:– meat [8], fuel [3], devour [2], eat [2], consume [1], devoured [1], food [1]

403 אָכֵן *'ākēn*, adv. GK: 434 & 435 [→ 389+2005]. Surely! Truly!, an exclamation to emphasize the unexpected:– surely [9], but [3], truly [2], verily [2], certainly [1], nevertheless [1]

404 אָכַף *'ākap*, v. GK: 436 [→ 405]. [Q] to drive, press hard:– craveth [1]

405 אֶכֶף *'ekep*, n.m. GK: 437 [→ 404]. hand, with a focus that this part of the body that can exert pressure or press hard:– hand [1]

406 אִכָּר *'ikkār*, n.m. GK: 438. farmer, people who work in fields and vineyards:– husbandmen [3], husbandman [2], plowmen [2]

407 אַכְשָׁף *'akšāp*, n.pr.loc. GK: 439 [→ 3784]. Acshaph, "*fascination*":– Achshaph [3]

408 אַל *'al*, adv.neg. GK: 440 [cf. 409]. no, not:– not [558], neither (+2050.1) [61], no [42], nor (+2050.1) [24], nay [8], neither [6], none [6], none (+376) [4], nothing (+1697) [3], nothing [3], never (+5769+3807.1) [2], cannot [1], neither (+1571) [1], neither (+1571+2050.1) [1], neither yet (+2050.1) [1], no (+3972) [1], none (+3605+871.1) [1], nothing (+3605) [1], than [1], whither [1]

409 אַל *'al* (Aram.), neg.adv. GK: 10031 [cf. 408]. not:– not [3], nor (+2050.3) [1]

410 אֵל *'ēl*, n.m. GK: 445 & 446 [→ 430, 433 (also used with compound proper names)]. God, the Mighty One, as a title of majesty and power, often used in combination with other titles; also any false god, gods; any person who is strong and capable: mighty one; strength:– God/god [229], mighty [3], power [3], God's [2], gods [2], goodly [1], great [1], idols [1], mighty (+1121) [1], mighty one [1], might [1], power (+3027) [1], strong [1]

411 אֵל *'ēl*, pr.pl.m. & f. GK: 447 [→ 428; cf. 412]. these:– these [7], those [2]

412 אֵל *'ēl* (Aram.), p.demo.pl. GK: 10032 [→ 1836; cf. 411]. these:– these [1]

413 אֶל *'el*, pp. GK: 448 [→ 454, 454]. to, toward; in, into; with regard to:– unto [2855], to [1183], into [308], upon [169], against [148], in [87], for [57], at [51], toward [49], on [44], with [44], by [27], of [26], over [23], concerning [17], towards [16], before (+6440) [15], before [8], after [7], among [6], over against (+6440) [4], under (+8478) [4], straight forward (+5676+6440) [3], whithersoever (+834+3605) [3], within [3], according to [2], among (+996) [2], because of [2], before (+4136+6440) [2], behind (+310) [2], beside [2], hands together (+3709+3709) [2], over against (+4136+6440) [2], regard (+6437) [2], therein (+1886.3) [2], through [2], touching [2], under [2], whereupon (+1992.1) [2]*

414 אֵלָא *'ēlā'*, n.pr.m. GK: 452 [cf. 425]. Ela:– Elah [1]

415 אֵל אֱלֹהֵי יִשְׂרָאֵל *'ēl '⁰lōhê yiśrā'ēl*, n.pr.loc. GK: 449 [→ 410+430+3478]. El Elohe Israel, "*God, the God of Israel*":– El-Elohe-Israel [1]

416 אֵל בֵּית־אֵל *'ēl bêt-'ēl*, n.pr.loc. GK: 450 [→ 410+1004+410]. El Bethel, "*God [El] of Bethel*":– El-beth-el [1]

417 אֶלְגָּבִישׁ *'elgābîš*, n.[m.]. GK: 453 [cf. 1378]. hail(stone) or clump of ice:– great hailstones (+68) [3]

418 אַלְגּוּמִּים *'algûmmîm*, n.[m.].pl. GK: 454 [cf. 484]. algum (wood); a transliteration of the Hebrew, the exact identification of which is uncertain:– algum [2], algum trees [1]

419 אֶלְדָּד *'eldād*, n.pr.m. GK: 455 [→ 410+1730]. Eldad, "*beloved of God [El]*; [poss.] *Dadi is god*":– Eldad [2]

420 אֶלְדָּעָה *'eldā'â*, n.pr.m. GK: 456 [→ 410]. Eldaah, "*God [El] is [my] desire*":– Eldaah [2]

421 אָלָה *'ālâ*, v. GK: 458. [Q] to mourn, wail:– lament [1]

422 אָלָה *'ālâ*, v. GK: 457 [→ 423, 8381]. [Q] to utter a curse, swear an oath; [H] to bind under oath, take an oath:– swearing [2], adjured [1], cause to swear [1], cursedst [1], make swear [1]

423 אָלָה *'ālâ*, n.f. GK: 460 [→ 422]. curse, oath; sworn agreement; public charge:– oath [14], curse [9], curses [5], cursing [4], execration [2], swearing [2]

424 אֵלָה *'ēlâ*, n.f. GK: 461 [→ 425; cf. 363]. oak, terebinth, or any species of large tree:– oak [11], elms [1], teil tree [1]

425 אֵלָה *'ēlâ*, n.pr.m. & loc. GK: 462 & 463 [→ 352, 424; cf. 414]. Elah, "*a mighty tree*":– Elah [16]

426 אֱלָהּ *'⁰lāh* (Aram.), n.m. GK: 10033 [cf. 433]. God, in the singular usually the true God, but see Da 4:8; 6:7 for a pagan god; gods, in the plural:– God/god [81], gods [14]

427 אַלָּה *'allâ*, n.f. GK: 464 [→ 352]. oak, or any species of large tree:– oak [1]

428 אֵלֶּה *'ēlleh*, pr.pl.m. & f. GK: 465 [→ 411; cf. 429]. these:– these [647], those [39], them [10], this [10], some [6], such [4], they [4], one [3], other [3], such (+3509.1) [3], the same [2], whom [2], another [2], others [1], so [1], these things [1], the things [1], things [1], thus [1], which [1], who [1]

429 אֵלֶּה *'ēlleh* (Aram.), p.demo.pl. GK: 10034 [→ 1836; cf. 428]. these:– these [1]

אֵלֹהַּ *'lōah*. See 433.

430 אֱלֹהִים *'⁰lōhîm*, n.pl.m. & f. GK: 466 [→ 433; cf. 410]. God (plural of majesty: plural in form but singular in meaning, with a focus on great power); gods (true grammatical plural); any person characterized by greatness or power: mighty one, great one, judge:– God/god [2363], gods [216], God's [6], judges [4], goddess [2], mighty [2], God's [3807.1)] [1], angels [1], exceeding (+3807.1) [1], godly [1], great [1], judge [1], to God-ward (+4136+1886.1) [1], very great [1]

431 אֲלוּ *'⁰lû* (Aram.), interj. GK: 10035 [→ 718]. there!, behold!; a discourse marker of transition, emphasis, or attention:– behold [5]

432 אַלּוּ *'illû*, c. GK: 467 [→ 518+3863]. if:– if [1], though [1]

433 אֱלוֹהַּ *'⁰lôah*, n.m. GK: 468 [→ 430; cf. 410, 426]. God; god; idol:– God/god [56], God's [1]

434 אֱלוּל *'lûl*, n.m.?. GK: 470 [→ 457]. idols, images, gods:–

435 אֱלוּל *'⁰lûl*, n.pr. GK: 469. Elul:– Elul [1]

436 אֵלוֹן *'ēlôn*, n.[f.]. GK: 471 [→ 356; cf. 352; cf. 363]. great tree, large tree of an unspecified species:– plain [7], plains [2]

437 אַלּוֹן *'allôn*, n.m. GK: 473 [→ 438; cf. 352]. oak tree, large tree of an unspecified species:– oaks [5], oak [3]

438 אַלּוֹן *'allôn*, n.pr.loc. GK: 474 [→ 437; cf. 352]. Allon, "*oak*":– Allon [2]

439 אַלּוֹן בָּכוּת *'allôn bākût*, n.pr.loc. GK: 475 [→ 352+1058]. Allon Bacuth, "*oak of weeping*":– Allon-bachuth [1]

440 אֵלֹנִי *'ēlōnî*, a.g. GK: 533 [→ 356]. Elonite, "*of Elon*":– Elonites [1], Elon [1]

441 אַלּוּף *'allûp*, a. & n.m. GK: 476 & 477 [→ 502, 503]. close friend, partner, ally, companion; chief, leader:– duke [43], dukes [14], guide [4], governors [2], captains [1], chief friends [1], governor [1], oxen [1], ox [1], very friends [1]

442 אָלוּשׁ *'ālûš*, n.pr.loc. GK: 478. Alush:– Alush [2]

443 אֶלְזָבָד *'elzābād*, n.pr.m. GK: 479 [→ 410+2064]. Elzabad, "*God [El] has given*":– Elzabad [2]

444 אָלַח *'ālaḥ*, v. GK: 480. [N] to be, become (morally) corrupt, a fig. extension of milk turning sour, not found in the OT:– filthy [3]

445 אֶלְחָנָן *'elḥānān*, n.pr.m. GK: 481 [→ 410+2605]. Elhanan, "*God [El] is gracious*":– Elhanan [4]

אֵלִי *'ēlî*. See 1017.

446 אֱלִיאָב *'⁰lî'āb*, n.pr.m. GK: 482 [→ 410+1]. Eliab, "*God [El] is [my] father*":– Eliab [20], Eliab's [1]

447 אֱלִיאֵל *'⁰lî'ēl*, n.pr.m. GK: 483 [→ 410+2967.1+410]. Eliel, "*God [El] is [my] God*":– Eliel [10]

448 אֱלִיאָתָה *'⁰lî'ātâ* or אֱלִיָּתָה *'⁰liyyātâ*, n.pr.m. GK: 484 & 517 [→ 410+857]. Eliathah, "*God [El] comes*":– Eliathah [2]

449 אֱלִידָד *'⁰lîdād*, n.pr.m. GK: 485 [→ 410+1730]. Elidad, "*God [El] is [my] beloved*":– Elidad [1]

450 אֱלִידָע *'⁰lîdā'*, n.pr.m. GK: 486 [→ 410+3045]. Eliada, "*God [El] knows*":– Eliada [3], Eliadah [1]

451 אַלְיָה *'alyâ*, n.f. GK: 487. fat tail (of a sheep):– rump [5]

452 אֵלִיָּה *'ēliyyâ* or אֵלִיָּהוּ *'ēliyyāhû*, n.pr.m. GK: 488 & 489 [→ 410+3068]. Elijah, "*Yahweh is [my] God*":– Elijah [69], Eliah [2]

453 אֱלִיהוּ *'⁰lîhû* or אֱלִיהוּא *'⁰lîhû'*, n.pr.m. GK: 490 & 491 [→ 410+1931]. Elihu, "*Yahweh is [my] God*":– Elihu [11]

454 אֶלְיְהוֹעֵינַי *'elyhô'ênay* or אֶלְיוֹעֵינַי *'elyô'ênay*, n.pr.m. GK: 492 & 493 [→ 413+3068+5869]. Eliehoenai, Elioenai, "*my eyes [look] to Yahweh*":– Elioenai [8], Elihoenai [1]

455 אֶלְיַחְבָּא *'elyaḥbā'*, n.pr.m. GK: 494 [→ 410+2244]. Eliahba, "*God [El] hides*":– Eliahba [2]

456 אֱלִיחֹרֶף *'⁰lîḥōrep*, n.pr.m. GK: 495. Elihoreph:– Elihoreph [1]

457 אֱלִיל *'⁰lîl*, n.m. GK: 496 [→ 434]. idols, images, gods:– idols [16], idol [1], images [1], of no value [1], thing of nought [1]

458 אֱלִימֶלֶךְ *'⁰lîmelek*, n.pr.m. GK: 497 [→ 410+4428]. Elimelech, "*God [El] is [my] king*":– Elimelech [4], Elimelech's [2]

459 אִלֵּין *'illên* (Aram.), p.demo.pl. GK: 10036 [→ 1836]. these:– these [4]

460 אֶלְיָסָף *'elyāsāp*, n.pr.m. GK: 498 [→ 410+3254]. Eliasaph, "*God [El] has added*":– Eliasaph [6]

461 אֱלִיעֶזֶר *'⁰lî'ezer*, n.pr.m. GK: 499 [→ 410+5828]. Eliezer, "*God [El] is [my] help*":– Eliezer [14]

462 אֱלִיעֵינַי *'⁰lî'ênay*, n.pr.m. GK: 501 [→ 413+3068+5869]. Elienai, "*my eyes [look] to Yahweh*":– Elienai [1]

463 אֱלִיעָם *'⁰lî'ām*, n.pr.m. GK: 500 [→ 410+5971]. Eliam, "*God [El] is [my] kinsman*":– Eliam [2]

464 אֱלִיפַז *'⁰lîpaz*, n.pr.m. GK: 502 [→ 410+6337]. Eliphaz, "*God [El] is fine gold* or *God crushes*":– Eliphaz [15]

465 אֱלִיפָל *'⁰lîpāl*, n.pr.m. GK: 503 [→ 410+6419]. Eliphal, "*[my] God [El] sit in judgment*":– Eliphal [1]

466 אֱלִיפְלֵהוּ *'⁰lîp⁰lēhû*, n.pr.m. GK: 504 [→ 410+6381?]. Eliphelehu, "*God [El] distinguish him!*":– Elipheleh [2]

467 אֱלִיפֶלֶט 'ᵉlîpeleṭ or אֶלְפֶּלֶט 'elpeleṭ, n.pr.m. GK: 505 & 550 [→ 410+6404]. Eliphelet, Elpelet, "God [El] is [my] deliverance":– Eliphelet [6], Eliphalet [2], Elpalet [1]

468 אֱלִיצוּר 'ᵉlîṣûr, n.pr.m. GK: 506 [→ 410+6697]. Elizur, "God [El] is [my] Rock":– Elizur [5]

469 אֱלִיצָפָן 'ᵉlîṣāpān or אֶלְצָפָן 'elṣāpān, n.pr.m. GK: 507 & 553 [→ 410+6845]. Elizaphan, Elzaphan, "God [El] is [my] hiding place":– Elizaphan [4], Elzaphan [1]

470 אֱלִיקָא 'ᵉlîqā', n.pr.m. GK: 508 [→ 410+6965?]. Elika:– Elika [1]

471 אֶלְיָקִים 'elyāqîm, n.pr.m. GK: 509 [→ 410+6965]. Eliakim, "God [El] establishes":– Eliakim [12]

472 אֱלִישֶׁבַע 'ᵉlîšeba', n.pr.f. GK: 510 [→ 410; cf. 7652]. Elisheba, "God [El] is an oath; God [El] is my fill":– Elisheba [1]

473 אֱלִישָׁה 'ᵉlîšâ, n.pr.loc. GK: 511. Elishah, "God [El] saves":– Elishah [3]

474 אֱלִישׁוּעַ 'ᵉlîšûa', n.pr.m. GK: 512 [→ 410+7768]. Elishua, "God [El] is my salvation":– Elishua [2]

475 אֶלְיָשִׁיב 'elyāšîb, n.pr.m. GK: 513 [→ 410+7725]. Eliashib, "God [El] restores":– Eliashib [17]

476 אֱלִישָׁמָע 'ᵉlîšāmā', n.pr.m. GK: 514 [→ 410+8085]. Elishama, "God [El] has heard":– Elishama [17]

477 אֱלִישָׁע 'ᵉlîšā', n.pr.m. GK: 515 [→ 410+3467?]. Elisha, "God [El] is [my] salvation":– Elisha [58]

478 אֱלִישָׁפָט 'ᵉlîšāpāṭ, n.pr.m. GK: 516 [→ 410+8199]. Elishaphat, "God [El] is [my] judge":– Elishaphat [1]

אֱלִיָתָה 'ᵉlîātâ. See 448.

479 אִלֵּךְ 'illēk (Aram.), p.demo.pl. GK: 10037 [→ 1836]. these:– these [11], those [3]

480 אַלְלַי 'allay, interj. GK: 518. Woe!, What misery!, Alas!:– woe [2]

481 אָלַם 'ālam or אָלֵם 'ālam, v. GK: 519 & 520 [→ 483, 485, 492; cf. 481?]. [N] to be silenced, be speechless; [P] to bind:– dumb [6], became dumb [1], binding [1], put to silence [1]

482 אֵלֶם 'ēlem, n.[m.]. GK: 521 [cf. 481?]. silence [?]:– congregation [1]

אֵלָם 'ēlām. See 361.

אֵלֻם 'ēlum. See 485.

483 אִלֵּם 'illēm, a. GK: 522 [→ 481]. mute, unable to speak:– dumb [6]

484 אַלְמֻגִּים 'almuggîm, n.[m.]pl. GK: 523 [cf. 418]. almugwood; a transliteration of the Hebrew, the exact identification of which is uncertain:– almug [3]

485 אֲלֻמָּה 'ᵃlummâ, n.f. GK: 524 [→ 481]. sheaf:– sheaves [3], sheaf [2]

486 אַלְמוֹדָד 'almôdād, n.pr. GK: 525. Almodad, "God [El] is loved":– Almodad [2]

487 אַלַּמֶּלֶךְ 'allammelek, n.pr.loc. GK: 526 [→ 427?+4428]. Allammelech, "oak of the king or oak of Molech":– Alammelech [1]

488 אַלְמָן 'almān, a. & n.[f.]. GK: 527 & 528 [→ 490; cf. 759]. widowed (one forsaken); stronghold:– forsaken [1]

489 אַלְמֹן 'almōn, n.[m.]. GK: 529 [→ 490]. widowhood:– widowhood [1]

490 אַלְמָנָה 'almānâ, n.f. GK: 530 [→ 488, 489, 491]. widow:– widow [37], widows [12], widow's [3], desolate houses [1], desolate palaces [1], widow's (+802) [1]

491 אַלְמָנוּת 'almānût, n.f. GK: 531 [→ 490]. widowhood:– widowhood [3], widow's [1]

492 אַלְמֹנִי 'almōnî, a. GK: 532 [→ 481; cf. 6422, 6423]. a certain so-and-so, whoever, wherever, with a focus that this is not named or spoken out loud:– such a one (+6423) [1], such and such (+6423) [1], such [1]

אָלֵן 'illēn. See 459.

אֱלֹנִי 'ᵉlōnî. See 440.

493 אֶלְנַעַם 'elna'am, n.pr.m. GK: 534 [→ 410+5278]. Elnaam, "God [El] is pleasantness":– Elnaam [1]

494 אֶלְנָתָן 'elnātān, n.pr.m. GK: 535 [→ 410+5414]. Elnathan, "God [El] is given":– Elnathan [7]

495 אֶלָּסָר 'ellāsār, n.pr.loc. GK: 536. Ellasar:– Ellasar [2]

496 אֶלְעָד 'el'ād, n.pr.m. GK: 537 [→ 410+5749]. Elead, "God [El] has testified":– Elead [1]

497 אֶלְעָדָה 'el'ādâ, n.pr.m. GK: 538 [→ 410+5710]. Eleadah, "God [El] has adorned":– Eladah [1]

498 אֶלְעֻזַי 'el'ûzay, n.pr.m. GK: 539 [→ 410+5797?]. Eluzai, "God [El] is my strength":– Eleuzai [1]

499 אֶלְעָזָר 'el'āzār, n.pr.m. GK: 540 [→ 410+5826]. Eleazar, "God [El] is a help":– Eleazar [72]

500 אֶלְעָלֵא 'el'ālē' or אֶלְעָלֵה 'el'ālēh, n.pr.loc. GK: 541 & 542 [→ 410+5927]. Elealeh, "God [El] is high":– Elealeh [5]

501 אֶלְעָשָׂה 'el'āśâ, n.pr.m. GK: 543 [→ 410+6213]. Eleasah, "God [El] has fashioned":– Eleasah [4], Elasah [2]

502 אָלַף 'ālap, v. GK: 544 [→ 441]. [Q] to learn, become familiar with; [P] to teach, instruct:– learn [1], teacheth [1], teach [1], uttereth [1]

503 אָלַף 'ālap, v.den. GK: 545 [→ 441, 505; cf. 504]. [H] to increase by thousands, produce in abundance:– bring forth thousands [1]

504 אֶלֶף 'elep, n.m. GK: 546 [→ 441, 505; cf. 502]. cattle herd; oxen:– kine [4], oxen [3], family [1]

505 אֶלֶף 'elep, n.m. GK: 547 & 548 [→ 503; cf. 506]. thousand; by extension from "thousand," this refers to any large unit or group: (family) clan, (military) unit:– thousand [418], thousands [46], two thousand [29], eleven hundred (+3967+2050.1) [3], forty two thousand (+702+7239) [2], eighteen thousand (+7239+8083+2050.1) [1], four [1], threescore and one thousand (+7239+8337+2050.1) [1], twelve hundred (+3967+2050.1) [1]

506 אֲלַף 'ᵃlap (Aram.), n.m. GK: 10038 [cf. 505]. thousand; the phrase "thousands upon thousands" is an indefinitely large number:– thousand [3], thousands [1]

507 אֶלֶף 'elep, n.pr.loc. GK: 549. Eleph:– Eleph [1]

אַלּוּף 'allup. See 441.

אֶלְפֶּלֶט 'elpeleṭ. See 467.

508 אֶלְפַּעַל 'elpa'al, n.pr.m. GK: 551 [→ 410+6466]. Elpaal, "God [El] creates":– Elpaal [3]

509 אָלַץ 'ālaṣ, v. GK: 552. [P] to prod, urge, a fig. extension of pressing one object hard against another, not found in the OT:– urged [1]

אֶלְצָפָן 'elṣāpān. See 469.

510 אַלְקוּם 'alqûm, n.[m.]?. GK: 554. army:– no rising up [1]

511 אֶלְקָנָה 'elqānâ, n.pr.m. GK: 555 [→ 410+7069]. Elkanah, "God [El] has possessed":– Elkanah [21]

512 אֶלְקֹשִׁי 'elqōšî, a.g. GK: 556. Elkoshite, "of Elkosh":– Elkoshite [1]

513 אֶלְתּוֹלַד 'eltôlad, n.pr.loc. GK: 557 [cf. 8434]. Eltolad, "generation; kindred of God [El]; place where God [El] gives children":– Eltolad [2]

514 אֶלְתְּקֵא 'eltᵉqē' or אֶלְתְּקֵה 'eltᵉqēh, n.pr.loc. GK: 558 & 559. Eltekeh, "meeting place":– Eltekeh [2]

515 אֶלְתְּקֹן 'eltᵉqōn, n.pr.loc. GK: 560. Eltekon, "God [El] has arranged":– Eltekon [1]

516 אַל תַּשְׁחֵת 'al tašḥēt, adv.neg.+v. GK: 440 + 8845 [→ 408+7843]. Al-taschith (408 + 7843), "Do not destroy":– Al-taschith [4]

517 אֵם 'ēm, n.f. GK: 562. mother, grandmother, ancestress; by extension: a term of endearment; caregiver; fork (in a road):– mother [143], mother's [67], dam [5], mothers [3], mothers' [1], parting [1]

518 אִם 'im, c. & pt.inter. GK: 561 [→ 432]. if, whether, or; whenever, as often as:– if [587], but (+3588) [86], or [43], not [35], though [33], whether [28], surely (+3808) [23], when [20], save (+3588) [13], that [9], or (+2050.1) [8], nor (+2050.1) [7], except (+3588) [6], except (+3808) [5], no [5], surely not [4], surely [4], though (+3588) [4], neither [3], until (+5704) [3], until [834+5704] [3], and (+3588) [2], either [2], for (+3588) [2], none [2], nor [2], sith [2], surely (+3588) [2], than (+3588) [2], verily (+3808) [2], will (+3808) [2], yet (+3588) [2]*

519 אָמָה 'āmâ, n.f. GK: 563. slave woman; female servant, maidservant:– handmaid [22], maidservant [13], maid [5], bondwoman [4], maidservants [4], bondmaids [2], maids [2], handmaids [1], maidens [1], maidservant's [1], maidservants' [1]

אַמָּה 'ēmâ. See 367.

520 אַמָּה 'ammâ, n.f. GK: 564 & 567 [cf. 521]. cubit (measurement of length, from the elbow to end of fingers, about 18 to 22 inches [about half a meter]); an unspecified unit of time; pivot (of a door):– cubits [191], cubit [42], two cubits [9], measure [1], posts [1]

521 אַמָּה 'ammâ (Aram.), n.f. GK: 10039 [cf. 520]. cubit (measurement of distance from the elbow to the end of the fingers, about 18 to 22 inches):– cubits [4]

522 אַמָּה 'ammâ, n.pr.loc. GK: 565. Ammah, "cubit":– Ammah [1]

523 אֻמָּה 'ummâ, n.f. GK: 569 [cf. 524]. tribe, clan:– people [2], nations [1]

524 אֻמָּה 'ummâ (Aram.), n.f. GK: 10040 [cf. 523]. nation, people:– nations [7], nation [1]

525 אָמוֹן 'āmôn, n.m. GK: 570 [→ 542]. one brought up:– one brought up [1]

526 אָמוֹן 'āmôn, n.pr.m. GK: 571 [→ 532; cf. 527, 539]. Amon, "trustworthy":– Amon [17]

527 אָמוֹן 'āmôn, n.pr.[m.]. GK: 572 [→ 528; cf. 526, 539]. multitude, crowd; see also 1995:– multitude [2], populous [1]

528 אָמוֹן 'āmôn, n.pr.[m.]. GK: 572 [→ 527+4996; cf. 526, 539]. Amon (pagan god), "trustworthy":–

529 אֵמוּן 'ēmûn, n.[m.]. GK: 573 & 574 [→ 539]. faithful, trustworthy:– faithful [4], faith [1], truth [1]

530 אֱמוּנָה 'ᵉmûnâ, n.f. GK: 575 [→ 539]. faithfulness, steadiness, trustworthiness:– faithfulness [18], truth [13], faithfully (+871.1) [5], set office [5], faithful [3], faith [1], stability [1], steady [1], truly [1], verily [1]

531 אָמוֹץ 'āmôṣ, n.pr.[m.]. GK: 576 [→ 553]. Amoz, "strong":– Amoz [13]

532 אֲמִי 'ᵃmî, n.pr.[m.]. GK: 577 [→ 526; cf. 539]. Ami, "trustworthy, reliable, faithful":– Ami [1]

אֲמִינוֹן 'ᵃmînôn. See 550.

533 אַמִּיץ 'ammîṣ, a. GK: 579 [→ 553]. strong, mighty, brave:– strong [4], courageous (+3820) [1], mighty [1]

534 אָמִיר 'āmîr, n.m. GK: 580 [→ 559]. branch:– branch [1], uppermost bough [1]

535 אָמַל 'āmal, v. GK: 581 & 582 [→ 536, 537]. [Qp] to be weak-willed; to be hot, feverish; [Pul] to wither, languish, fade away:– languisheth [8], languish [5], languished [1], waxed feeble [1], weak [1]

536 אֻמְלַל 'umlal, a. GK: 583 [→ 535]. faint, fading away:– weak [1]

537 אֲמֵלָל 'ᵃmēlāl, a. GK: 584 [→ 535]. feeble, fading:– feeble [1]

538 אֲמָם 'ᵃmām, n.pr. GK: 585 [→ 4965]. Amam:– Amam [1]

539 אָמַן 'āman, v. GK: 586 & 587 [→ 526, 527, 529, 530, 532, 543, 544, 545, 548, 546, 547, 550, 551, 1968?; cf. 540, cf. 3330]. [Q] to nurse, nurture, care for; be a trustee, be a guardian; [Qp, N] to be nurtured, cared for; to be faithful, be trustworthy, be established; [H] to believe, trust, have confidence:– believed [21], believe [19], faithful [19], sure [11], established [6], believeth [4], brought up [3], verified [3], long continuance [2], nurse [2], stedfast [2], trust [2], assurance [1], bringers up [1], fail (+3808) [1], nursed [1], nursing fathers [1], nursing father [1], put trust [1], putteth trust [1], stablished [1], stand fast [1], surely [1], trusted [1], trusty [1]

540 אֲמַן 'ᵃman (Aram.), v. GK: 10041 [cf. 539]. [H] to trust in; [Hp] be trustworthy:– believed [1], faithful [1], sure [1]

541 אָמַן 'āman, v. GK: 3554 [→ 3225, 3231]. [H] to turn to the right; cf. 3231:– turn to the right hand [1]

542 אָמָּן 'ommān, n.m. GK: 588 [→ 525]. craftsman:– cunning workman [1]

543 אָמֵן 'āmēn, adv. GK: 589 [→ 539]. amen, surely; truth:– amen [27], truth [2], so be it [1]

544 אֹמֶן 'ōmen, n.[m.]. GK: 590 [→ 551, 552; cf. 539]. faithfulness:– truth [1]

545 אֹמְנָה 'omnâ, n.f. GK: 594 [→ 539]. bringing up, caring, tending, fostering:– brought up [1]

546 אָמְנָה 'omnâ, adv. GK: 593 [→ 539]. really, truly, indeed:– indeed [2]

547 אָמְנָה 'ōmᵉnâ, subst. GK: 595 [→ 539?]. doorpost:– pillars [1]

548 אֲמָנָה *'ᵃmānâ*, n.f. GK: 591 [→ 539]. binding agreement, trustworthy agreement:– certain portion [1], sure [1]

549 אֲמָנָה *'ᵃmānâ*, n.pr.loc. GK: 592 [cf. 71]. Amana, "*constant*":– Amana [1]

אֲמֻנָה *'ᵉmunâ*. See 530.

550 אֲמִינוֹן *'mînôn* or אַמְנוֹן *'amnôn*, n.pr.m. GK: 578 & 596 [cf. 539]. Amnon, "*trustworthy*":– Amnon [25], Amnon's [3]

551 אָמְנָם *'omnām*, adv. GK: 597 [→ 552; cf. 544, 539]. indeed, truly, assuredly:– of a truth [3], indeed [2], no doubt [1], surely [1], true [1], truly [1]

552 אֻמְנָם *'umnām*, adv. GK: 598 [→ 551; cf. 544, 539]. really, indeed; used in interrogative sentences:– indeed [3], in very deed [1], of a surety (+637) [1]

553 אָמֵץ *'āmēṣ*, v. GK: 599 [→ 531, 533, 554, 555, 556, 3981 (also used with compound proper names)]. [Q] to be strong, courageous; [P] to strengthen, support, establish; harden; [Ht] to persist, determine:– of good courage [9], strengthen [7], strengthened [3], courageous [2], made speed [2], madest strong [2], strengtheneth [2], stronger [2], strong [2], confirm [1], established [1], fortify [1], hardened [1], harden [1], increaseth [1], made obstinate [1], made strong [1], prevailed [1], stedfastly minded [1]

554 אָמֹץ *'āmōṣ*, a. GK: 600 [→ 553]. powerful, strong:– bay [2]

555 אֹמֶץ *'ōmeṣ*, n.[m.]. GK: 601 [→ 553]. strength:– stronger and stronger (+3254) [1]

אַמִּץ *'ammiṣ*. See 533.

556 אִמְצָה *'imṣâ*, n.f. GK: 602 [→ 553]. strength:– strength [1]

557 אַמְצִי *'amṣî*, n.pr.m. GK: 603 [→ 553; cf. 558?]. Amzi, "*[poss.] [Yahweh is] my strength*":– Amzi [2]

558 אֲמַצְיָה *'ᵃmaṣyâ* or אֲמַצְיָהוּ *'ᵃmaṣyāhû*, n.pr.m. GK: 604 & 605 [→ 557]. Amaziah, "*Yahweh is powerful*":– Amaziah [40]

559 אָמַר *'āmar*, v. GK: 606 & 607 [→ 201, 534, 561, 562, 565, 3982, 8560; cf. 560 (also used with compound proper names)]. [Q, H] to say, speak, think (say to oneself); [Qp, N] to be said; [Ht] to boast:– said [2776], saying [915], saith [581], say [560], spake [110], answered [91], speak [47], tell [29], commanded [25], saidst [19], sayest [18], spoken [15], told [14], answer [8], thought [8], speaketh [7], bade [6], bid [6], promised [5], called [4], call [3], commandeth [3], think [3], appointed [2], avouched [2], command [2], expressly say (+559) [2], intend [2], name [2], plainly say (+559) [2], purpose [2], reported [2], said indeed (+559) [2], say still (+559) [2], termed [2], verily thought (+559) [2], yet say (+559) [2], appoint [1], bidden [1], boast [1], certified [1], challengeth [1], charged [1], commandment [1], commune [1], consider [1], declared [1], demanded [1], desired [1], desireth [1], determined [1], gave a commandment [1], intendest [1], is [1], named [1], promisedst [1], published [1], requirest [1], spakest [1], suppose [1], talked [1], thinking [1], useˢ [1], uttereth [1]

560 אֲמַר *'mar* (Aram.), v. GK: 10042 [→ 3983; cf. 559]. [P] to say, tell; to command:– said [41], commanded [12], tell [5], told [4], saying [2], say [2], speak [2], declare [1], spake [1], spoken [1]

561 אֵמֶר *'ēmer*, n.m. GK: 609 & 610 & 611 [→ 559, 564; cf. 563]. word, saying; branched antlers; fawn, lamb:– words [43], sayings [2], speeches [2], answer [1], appointed unto [1]

562 אֹמֶר *'ōmer*, n.m. GK: 608 [→ 559]. saying, word:– speech [2], word [2], promise [1], thing [1]

563 אִמַּר *'immar* (Aram.), n.m. GK: 10043. male lamb:– lambs [3]

564 אִמֵּר *'immēr*, n.pr.m. & loc. GK: 612 & 613 [→ 561]. Immer, "*lamb*":– Immer [10]

565 אִמְרָה *'imrâ* or אֶמְרָה *'emrâ*, n.f. GK: 614 & 615 [→ 559]. word, saying, utterance:– word [26], speech [7], words [1], commandment [1]

566 אִמְרִי *'imrî*, n.pr.m. GK: 617 [→ 559+3068]. Imri, "*Yahweh spoke*":– Imri [2]

567 אֱמֹרִי *'ᵉmōrî*, a.g. GK: 616. Amorite, "*[poss.] hill dwellers; westerners*":– Amorites [73], Amorite [14]

568 אֲמַרְיָה *'ᵃmaryâ* or אֲמַרְיָהוּ *'ᵃmaryāhû*, n.pr.m. GK: 618 & 619. Amariah, "*Yahweh has said*":– Amariah [16]

569 אַמְרָפֶל *'amrāpel*, n.pr.m. GK: 620. Amraphel:– Amraphel [2]

570 אֶמֶשׁ *'emeš*, adv. GK: 621 [cf. 4871?]. last night; yesterday (evening):– yesternight [3], in former time [1], yesterday [1]

571 אֱמֶת *'ᵉmet*, n.f. GK: 622 [→ 573; cf. 539]. faithfulness, reliability, trustworthiness; truth, what conforms to reality in contrast to what is false; "the book of truth" is a reliable book, referring to heavenly scroll detailing future things:– truth [90], true [18], truly [4], right [3], truly (+871.1) [3], faithfully [2], assuredly (+871.1) [1], assured [1], establishment [1], faithful [1], sure [1], truth's [1], verity [1]

572 אַמְתַּחַת *'amtaḥat*, n.f. GK: 623 [→ 4969]. sack:– sacks [6], sack [5], sack's [3], sacks' [1]

573 אֲמִתַּי *'ᵃmittay*, n.pr.m. GK: 624 [→ 571; cf. 539]. Amittai, "*true*":– Amittai [2]

574 אֵימְתָן *'êmᵉtān* (Aram.), a. GK: 10028. frightening, terrible:– terrible [1]

575 אָן *'ān*, adv. GK: 625. how long?; where?:– whither (+1886.5) [16], how long (+5704+1886.5) [13], any whither (+575+1886.5+2050.1) [4], where (+1886.5) [3], whither (+575+1886.5+1886.5+2050) [2], how long (+5704) [1], whithersoever (+1886.5) [1], whither [1]

אֹן *'ōn*. See 204.

576 אֲנָה *'ᵃnâ* (Aram.), p.1.com.s. GK: 10044 [cf. 589]. I:– I [14], me [2]

577 אָנָּא *'onnā* or אָנָּה *'onnâ*, interj. GK: 626 & 629 [cf. 4994]. I ask you!, O! (preceding a request):– I beseech thee [5], beseech [2], oh [2], I pray thee [1], O [1], now [1], pray [1]

אֲנָה *'ᵃnâ*. See 576.

אָנָה *'ānâ*. See 575.

578 אָנָה *'ānâ*, v. GK: 627 [→ 205, 592, 3123, 8386; cf. 584, 596]. [Q] to mourn, lament, groan:– lament [1], mourn [1]

579 אָנָה *'ānâ*, v. GK: 628 [→ 8385]. [P] to make happen; [Pu] to befall, have happen to; [Ht] to pick a quarrel against:– befall (+413) [1], deliver [1], happen [1], seeketh a quarrel [1]

אָנָּה *'onnâ*. See 577.

580 אֲנוּ *'ᵃnû*, p.com.pl. GK: 630 [→ 587]. we:– we [1]

אֹנוֹ *'ōnô*. See 207.

581 אִנּוּן *'innûn* (Aram.), p.3.m.pl. GK: 10045 [→ 1932]. they; those:– are [1], them [1], these [1], which [1]

582 אֱנוֹשׁ *'ᵉnôš*, n.m. GK: 632 [→ 583; cf. 605; cf. 606]. man, humankind, mortal, with an emphasis on frailty; "a man of peace" is a "friend":– man [29], men [7], man's [3], anotherˢ [1], familiars (+7965) [1], mortal man [1]

583 אֱנוֹשׁ *'ᵉnôš*, n.pr.m. GK: 633 [→ 582; cf. 605]. Enosh, "*[mortal] man*":– Enos [6], Enoch [1]

584 אָנַח *'ānaḥ*, v. GK: 634 [→ 585; cf. 578, 596, 5117]. [N] to groan, moan:– sigh [7], groan [1], mourn [1], sighed [1], sighest [1], sigheth [1]

585 אֲנָחָה *'ᵃnāḥâ*, n.f. GK: 635 [→ 584]. groaning, sighing:– sighing [5], groaning [4], mourning [1], sighs [1]

586 אֲנַחְנָא *'ᵃnaḥnā'* (Aram.), p.1.com.pl. GK: 10047 [cf. 587]. we:– we [4]

587 אֲנַחְנוּ *'ᵃnaḥnû*, p.com.pl. GK: 636 [→ 580, 589, 595, 5168; cf. 586]. we:– we [111], us [3], we ourselves [3]

588 אֲנָחֲרַת *'ᵃnāḥᵃrat*, n.pr.loc. GK: 637. Anaharath:– Anaharath [1]

589 אֲנִי *'ᵃnî*, p.com.s. GK: 638 [→ 587; cf. 576]. I:– I [839], me [24], myself [2], I myself [1], mine [1], my [1], we [1], who [1]

590 אֳנִי *'ᵒnî*, n.m. GK: 639 [→ 591]. ships, fleet of ships:– navy [6], galley [1]

591 אֳנִיָּה *'ᵒniyyâ*, n.f. GK: 641 [→ 590]. ship, trading ship; (pl.) fleet of ships:– ships [26], ship [4], shipmen (+376) [1]

592 אֲנִיָּה *'ᵃniyyâ*, n.f. GK: 640 [→ 578]. lamentation, mourning:– lamentation [1], sorrow [1]

אַנִּין *'innîn*. See 581.

593 אֲנִיעָם *'ᵃnî'ām*, n.pr.m. GK: 642. Aniam, "*I am kinsman*":– Aniam [1]

594 אֲנָךְ *'ᵃnāk*, n.[m.]. GK: 643. plummet, weight for a plumb line:– plumbline [4]

595 אָנֹכִי *'ānōkî*, p.com.s. GK: 644 [→ 587]. I:– I [354], me [4], my [1]

596 אָנַן *'ānan*, v. GK: 645 [cf. 578 or 584]. [Htpol] to complain:– complained [1], complain [1]

597 אָנַס *'ānas*, v. GK: 646 [cf. 598]. [Q] to compel; "there is no compelling" means "to allow":– compel [1]

598 אֲנַס *'ᵃnas* (Aram.), v. GK: 10048 [cf. 597]. [P] to oppress, make difficult:– troubleth [1]

599 אָנַף *'ānap*, v. GK: 647 [→ 639, 649, 2739; cf. 600]. [Q] to be, become angry; [Ht] to feel angry:– angry [13], displeased [1]

600 אֲנַף *'ᵃnap* (Aram.), n.m. GK: 10049 [cf. 599]. face; "to fall on the face" is to assume a position of honor or reverence:– face [1], visage [1]

601 אֲנָפָה *'ᵃnāpâ*, n.f. GK: 649. heron, an unclean bird:– heron [2]

602 אָנַק *'ānaq*, v. GK: 650 [→ 603; cf. 5008, 5009]. [Q, N] to groan, lament, sigh:– cry [3], groan [1]

603 אֲנָקָה *'ᵃnāqâ*, n.f. GK: 651 [→ 602]. groaning, sighing:– sighing [2], crying out [1], groaning [1]

604 אֲנָקָה *'ᵃnāqâ*, n.f. GK: 652. gecko:– ferret [1]

605 אָנַשׁ *'ānaš*, v. GK: 631 & 653 [→ 605, 582, 583; cf. 5136]. [N] be ill, sickly; incurable, beyond cure; despairing:– incurable [5], desperately wicked [1], desperate [1], very sick [1], woeful [1]

606 אֱנָשׁ *'ᵉnāš* (Aram.), n.m. GK: 10050 [cf. 582]. man, human being; humankind, people, often in contrast to animals; "son of man" often means a human being, but in Da 7:13 assumes messianic significance:– men [12], man [8], man's [3], whosoever (+1768+1768+3606) [1], whosoever (+3606) [1]

אַנְתְּ *'ant*. See 859.

607 אַנְתְּ *'ant* or אַנְתָּה *'antâ* (Aram.), p.2.m.s. GK: 10051 & 10052 [cf. 859]. you, your:– thou [14], thee [1]

608 אַנְתּוּן *'antûn* (Aram.), p.2.m.pl. GK: 10053 [cf. 859]. you (all):– ye [1]

609 אָסָא *'āsā'*, n.pr.m. GK: 654. Asa, "*[poss.] healer; myrtle*":– Asa [57], Asa's [1]

610 אָסוּךְ *'āsûk*, n.[m.]. GK: 655 [→ 5480]. small (oil) jar, flask:– pot [1]

611 אָסוֹן *'āsôn*, n.m. GK: 656. serious injury, harm:– mischief [5]

612 אֵסוּר *'ēsûr*, n.m. GK: 657 [→ 631; cf. 613]. bindings, chains, fetters, shackles:– bands [2], prison (+1004+1886.1) [1]

613 אֱסוּר *'ᵉsûr* (Aram.), n.[m.]. GK: 10054 [→ 633; cf. 612]. bond, fetter; (pl.) imprisonment:– band [2], imprisonment [1]

614 אָסִיף *'āsîp*, n.[m.]. GK: 658 [→ 622]. (Feast of) Ingathering; harvest (from a threshing floor and winepress before the rainy season):– ingathering [1]

615 אָסִיר *'āsîr*, n.m. GK: 659 [→ 631]. prisoner, captive:– prisoners [8], bound [2], prisoner [2]

616 אַסִּיר *'assîr*, n.m.[col.]. GK: 660 [→ 617; cf. 631]. captive, prisoner:– prisoners [3]

617 אַסִּיר *'assîr*, n.pr.m. GK: 661 [→ 616; cf. 631]. Assir, "*prisoner*":– Assir [5]

618 אָסָם *'āsām*, n.m. GK: 662. barn, storehouse:– barns [1], storehouses [1]

619 אַסְנָה *'asnâ*, n.pr.m. GK: 663. Asnah, "*[poss.] thornbush; he who belongs to Nah*":– Asnah [1]

620 אָסְנַפַּר *'āsᵉnappar* (Aram.), n.pr.m. GK: 10055. Ashurbanipal, "*Ashur creates a son*":– Asnappar [1]

621 אָסְנַת *'āsᵉnat*, n.pr.f. GK: 664. Asenath, "*[belonging to] Neith*":– Asenath [1]

622 אָסַף *'āsap*, v. GK: 665 [→ 614, 623, 624, 625, 626, 627, 628]. [Q] to store, gather, harvest; [Qp] to be a victim; [N] to be gathered, assembled; [P] to be a rear guard, to bring in, gather; [Pu] to be gathered, collected; [Ht] to assemble; [H] to bring together:– gathered [49], gathered together [43], gather [25], assemble [9], taken away [7], gather together [6], assembled [5], rereward [5], gathereth [4], recover [4], withdraw [4], gather in [3], bring [2], gather up [2], gathered in [2], gathered up [2], generally gathered (+622) [2], surely assemble (+622) [2], took [2], assembled together [1], brought in [1], brought together [1], brought [1], consumed [1], destroy [1], fet [1], gathered together (+626) [1], gat [1], gotten [1], lose [1], put all together [1], put up [1], received in [1], receiveth [1], surely consume (+5486) [1], take away [1], take up [1], taken [1], takest away [1], take [1], utterly [1]

623 אָסָף 'āsāp, n.pr.m. GK: 666 [→ 622]. Asaph, "gatherer":– Asaph [45], Asaph's [1]

אָסִיף 'āsip. See 614.

624 אָסֻף 'āsōp, n.[m.]. GK: 667 [→ 622]. storehouse, storeroom:– Asuppim [2], thresholds [1]

625 אֹסֶף 'ōsep, n.m. GK: 668 [→ 622]. harvest (of fruit), gathering:– gathering [2], gathered [1]

626 אֲסֵפָה "ªsēpâ, n.f.vbl. GK: 669 [→ 622]. gathering (prisoners); imprisonment:– gathered together (+622) [1]

627 אֲסֻפָּה 'ªsuppâ, n.f. GK: 670 [→ 622]. collection (of sayings):– assemblies [1]

628 אֲסַפְסֻף "ªsapsup, n.[m.]. GK: 671 [→ 622]. rabble, collection (of grumblers):– mixt multitude [1]

629 אָסְפַּרְנָא 'osparnā' (Aram.), adv. GK: 10056. with diligence, surely, fully:– speedily [4], fast [1], forthwith [1], with speed [1]

630 אַסְפָּתָא 'aspātā', n.pr.m. GK: 672. Aspatha, "[poss.] given from a sacred horse":– Aspatha [1]

631 אָסַר 'āsar, v. GK: 673 [→ 612, 615, 616, 617, 632, 4147, 4149?, 4562?]. [Q] to bind, tie up; to obligate; [Qp] to be confined, be bound; [N] to be tied, be kept in prison; [Pu] to be captured, be taken prisoner:– bound [33], bind [11], bind fast (+631) [4], made ready [3], tied [3], prisoners [2], prison [2], bindeth [1], binding [1], girded [1], girdeth [1], harness [1], held [1], kept in prison [1], make ready [1], order [1], prepare [1], prison (+1004+1886.1) [1], put in bands [1], set in array [1], tie [1]

632 אֵסָר 'issār, n.m. GK: 674 [→ 631; cf. 633]. pledge, a binding obligation:– bond [7], bonds [3], binding [1]

633 אֱסָר "ªsār (Aram.), n.m. GK: 10057 [→ 613; cf. 632]. (enforced) decree, i.e., a legally binding edict, a fig. extension of a bond or fetter that inhibits or controls:– decree [7]

634 אֵסַר־חַדֹּן 'ēsar-ḥaddōn, n.pr.m. GK: 675. Esarhaddon, "Ashur has given a brother [for a lost son]":– Esar-haddon [3]

635 אֶסְתֵּר 'estēr, n.pr.f. GK: 676. Esther, "[Persian] star [poss.] Ishtar":– Esther [52], Esther's [3]

636 אָע 'ā' (Aram.), n.m. GK: 10058 [cf. 6086]. wood, timber:– timber [3], wood [2]

637 אַף 'ap, c. GK: 677 [cf. 638]. how much (better, worse; more, less); really, truly; too, also, even more:– also [53], yea [36], even [7], how much more (+3588) [7], how much less (+3588) [5], and [3], how much more (+518) [1], although (+3588) [1], and (+2050.1) [1], and when [1], but [1], furthermore [1], how much less (+3588+3808) [1], how much less [1], how much more then (+3588) [1], how much rather [1], moreover [1], much less (+3588) [1], much less for (+3588) [1], much more (+3588) [1], neither (+369) [1], of a surety (+552) [1], so [1], though (+3588) [1], with [1], yea (+3588) [1], yet [1]

638 אַף 'ap (Aram.), c. GK: 10059 [cf. 637]. even, also:– also [3], also (+2050.3) [1]

639 אַף 'ap, n.m. GK: 678 [→ 649; cf. 599; cf. 600]. nose (representing the face or some part of the face); "hot of nose" signifies anger; "long of nose" signifies patience; "high of nose" signifies arrogance:– anger [171], wrath [42], face [19], nostrils [13], nose [11], angry [4], longsuffering (+750) [4], faces [3], before (+3807.1) [1], before (+871.1) [1], countenance [1], forbearing [1], forehead [1], noses [1], provocation of anger [1], snout [1], worthy [1]

640 אָפַד 'āpad, v.den. GK: 679 [→ 642]. [Q] to fasten:– bound [1], gird [1]

אֵפֹד 'ēpōd. See 646.

641 אֵפֹד 'ēpōd, n.pr.m. GK: 681 [→ 646?; cf. 640]. Ephod, "ephod":– Ephod [1]

642 אֲפֻדָּה "ªpuddâ, n.f. GK: 682 [→ 640]. skillfully woven covering:– ephod [2], ornament [1]

643 אַפֶּדֶן 'appeden, n.[m.]. GK: 683. palace tent, royal tent:– palace [1]

644 אָפָה 'āpâ, v. GK: 684 & 685 [→ 3989; cf. 8601?]. [Q] to bake; [N] to be baked:– baker [8], bake [7], baken [3], baked [2], bakers [2], bakemeats (+3978+4639) [1], bakers' [1], baketh [1]

אֵפָה 'ēpâ. See 374.

645 אֵפוֹא 'ēpô', pt. GK: 686 [→ 335?+6311?]. then, so then:– now [10], where [3], here [1], where (+165) [1]

646 אֵפֹד 'ēpōd, n.m. GK: 680 [→ 641?; cf. 640]. ephod, a garment of a priest used for adornment and as an aid in priestly service:– ephod [49]

647 אַפִּיחַ "ªpîaḥ, n.pr.m. GK: 688. Aphiah:– Aphiah [1]

648 אָפִיל 'āpîl, a. GK: 689 [→ 652]. late-ripening, late in the season:– not grown up [1]

649 אַפַּיִם 'appayim, n.pr.m. GK: 691 [cf. 639, 599]. Appaim, "[pair of] nostrils":– Appaim [2]

650 אָפִיק 'āpîq, n.m. GK: 692 & 693 [→ 662]. stream, water channel; valley, ravine, the deepest part of a valley flowing with water; mighty, strong:– rivers [10], channels [3], brooks [1], mighty [1], scales (+4043) [1], streams [1], stream [1], strong pieces [1]

אוֹפִיר 'ôpîr. See 211.

651 אָפֵל 'āpēl, a. GK: 695 [→ 652]. dark, gloomy:– very dark [1]

652 אֹפֶל 'ōpel, n.m. GK: 694 [→ 648, 651, 653, 3990?, 3991?]. darkness, the absence of light, often with the associative meaning of gloom, despair; shadows:– darkness [7], obscurity [1], privily (+1119) [1]

653 אֲפֵלָה "ªpēlâ, n.f. GK: 696 [→ 652]. the dark, darkness, with the associative meaning of mental gloom and despair:– darkness [6], gloominess [2], dark [1], thick [1]

654 אֶפְלָל 'eplāl, n.pr.m. GK: 697 [→ 6419]. Ephlal, "judgment, arbitration":– Ephlal [2]

655 אֹפֶן 'ōpen, n.[m.]. GK: 698 [cf. 212?]. (right) time; aptly:– (right) time [1]

אוֹפָן 'ôpān. See 212.

656 אָפֵס 'āpēs, v. GK: 699 [→ 657, 658]. [Q] to come to an end, cease:– at an end [1], brought [1], clean gone [1], faileth [1], fail [1]

657 אֶפֶס 'epes, n.m. GK: 700 & 701 [→ 656; cf. 6446]. ends (of the earth); no, nothing; however, but, only, yet; an extremity of the body, which in context wades through shallow water: ankles, or possibly soles of the feet:– ends [13], none [4], no [4], nothing [2], none else [2], not [2], without (+871.1) [2], ankles [1], but [1], howbeit [1], nevertheless (+3588) [1], nor any (+2050.1) [1], not any [1], notwithstanding (+3588) [1], only [1], save [1], saving [1], thing of nought [1], uttermost parts [1], want [1], without cause (+871.1) [1]

658 אֶפֶס דַּמִּים 'epes dammîm, n.pr.loc. GK: 702 [→ 656]. Ephes Dammim, "border of Dammim [blood]":– Ephes-dammim [1]

659 אֶפַע 'epa', n. or a. GK: 703. worthless:– nought [1]

660 אֶפְעֶה 'ep'eh, n.[m.]. GK: 704 [→ 6463?]. snake, variously identified as an adder or viper:– viper [2], viper's [1]

661 אָפַף 'āpap, v. GK: 705. [Q] to surround, entangle, engulf:– compassed [3], compassed about [2]

662 אָפַק 'āpaq, v. GK: 706 [→ 650]. [Ht] to control oneself, restrain oneself; to feel compelled:– refrained [3], refrain [2], forced [1], restrained [1]

663 אֲפֵק "ªpēq, n.pr.loc. GK: 707 [→ 664]. Aphek, "stronghold":– Aphek [8], Aphik [1]

664 אֲפֵקָה "ªpēqâ, n.pr.loc. GK: 708 [→ 663]. Aphekah, "fortress":– Aphekah [1]

665 אֵפֶר 'ēper, n.[m.]. GK: 709 [→ 211]. ashes, dust:– ashes [22]

666 אֲפֵר "ªpēr, n.[m.]. GK: 710. headband:– ashes [2]

667 אֶפְרֹחַ 'eprōaḥ, n.m. GK: 711 [→ 6524]. young (of a bird), chick:– young ones [2], young [2]

668 אַפִּרְיוֹן 'appiryôn, n.[m.]. GK: 712. carriage; other sources: sedan chair, litter, or palanquin, a vehicle carried on poles by porters:– chariot [1]

669 אֶפְרַיִם 'eprayim, n.pr.m. GK: 713 [→ 6509?]. Ephraim, "doubly fruitful":– Ephraim [171], Ephraimites [5], Ephraim's [3], Ephraim's (+3807.1) [1]

670 פָּרְסָי "ªpār'sāy (Aram.), n.pr.pl.g. GK: 10060 [cf. 6539?]. Persian, from Persia:– Apharsites [1]

671 אֲפַרְסְכָי 'ªpars'kāy (Aram.), n.m.pl.[pr.g.?]. GK: 10061 & 10062. officials; transliterated in the KJV and ASV as the proper name "Apharsachites":– Apharsachites [1], Apharsathchites [1]

672 אֶפְרָת 'eprāt or אֶפְרָתָה 'eprātâ, n.pr.f. & loc. GK: 714 & 715 & 716 & 717 [→ 673, 3613]. Ephrath, Ephrathah, "fruitful land":– Ephratah [5], Ephrath [5]

673 אֶפְרָתִי 'eprātî, a.g. GK: 718 [→ 672]. Ephraimite, "of Ephraim":– Ephrathite [3], Ephraimite [1], Ephrathites [1]

674 אַפְּתֹם 'app'tōm (Aram.), n.m. GK: 10063. revenue, treasury:– revenue [1]

675 אֶצְבֹּן 'eṣbōn, n.pr.m. GK: 719. Ezbon:– Ezbon [2]

676 אֶצְבַּע 'eṣba', n.f. GK: 720 [cf. 677]. digit appendage of hand or foot: finger, toe; "four fingers" is a measurement of width (Jer 52:21):– finger [19], fingers [10], fingers and toes [1], toes [1]

677 אֶצְבַּע 'eṣba' (Aram.), n.f. GK: 10064 [cf. 676]. toe, finger:– toes [2], fingers [1]

678 אָצִיל 'āṣîl, n.[m.]. GK: 721 & 722 [→ 680, 682]. leader, with an implication of being noble and distinguished; far corner, the remote areas of the earth:– chief men [1], nobles [1]

679 אַצִּיל 'aṣṣîl, n.[f.]. GK: 723 [→ 680]. joint (of shoulder or wrist); "a cubit of the joint" (Eze 41:8) is an unknown length, translated as a "long cubit":– armholes (+3027) [2], great [1]

680 אָצַל 'āṣal, v.den. GK: 724 [→ 678, 679, 681, 683]. [Q] to turn aside; to take away; [N] to be smaller:– kept [1], reserved [1], straitened [1], take [1], took [1]

681 אֵצֶל 'ēṣel, subst.pp. GK: 725 [→ 680]. beside, near, at the side:– by [33], beside [11], with [3], at [2], from (+4480) [2], near [2], unto [2], besides [1], by (+4480) [1], hard by [1], near unto [1], toward [1], to [1]

682 אָצֵל 'āṣēl, n.pr.m. & loc. GK: 727 & 728 [→ 678]. Azel, "noble":– Azel [6], Azal [1]

683 אֲצַלְיָהוּ "ªṣalyāhû, n.pr.m. GK: 729 [→ 680+3068]. Azaliah, "Yahweh is keeping in reserve":– Azaliah [2]

684 אֹצֶם 'ōṣem, n.pr.m. GK: 730. Ozem:– Ozem [2]

685 אֶצְעָדָה 'eṣ'ādâ, n.f. GK: 731 [→ 6805]. armlet, armband; an ornamental chain worn on the wrist or the ankle:– bracelet [1], chains [1]

686 אָצַר 'āṣar, v. GK: 732 [→ 214, 687?]. [Q] to store up; [N] be stored; [H] to be in charge of a storeroom:– laid up in store [2], made treasurers [1], store up [1], treasured [1]

687 אֵצֶר 'ēṣer, n.pr.m. GK: 733 [→ 686?]. Ezer, "help":– Ezer [5]

688 אֶקְדָּח 'eqdāḥ, n.[m.]. GK: 734 [→ 6919]. sparkling jewel; some sources: beryl stone:– carbuncles (+68) [1]

689 אַקּוֹ 'aqqô, n.m. GK: 735 [→ 3243]. wild goat:– wild goat [1]

690 אֲרָא "ªrā', n.pr.m. GK: 736. Ara:– Ara [1]

691 אֶרְאֵל 'er'ēl, n.[m.]. GK: 737 [→ 739?]. brave man, hero:– valiant ones [1]

692 אַרְאֵלִי 'ar'ēlî, a.g. GK: 739 & 740 [→ 692; cf. 8634?]. Areli; Arelite, "of Areli":– Areli [2], Arelites [1]

693 אָרַב 'ārab, v. GK: 741 [→ 695, 696, 698?, 3993]. [Q] to lay in wait against, hide in ambush; [P] to ambush, waylay; [H] to set an ambush:– lie in wait [9], liers in wait [8], laid wait [5], ambush [4], lieth in wait [4], lay wait [3], lying in wait [2], ambushes [1], ambushments [1], lay in wait [1], lie in ambush [1], lie in wait against [1], liers in ambush [1]

694 אֲרָב "ªrāb, n.pr.loc. GK: 742 [cf. 701?]. Arab, "desert or steppe":– Arab [1]

695 אֶרֶב 'ereb, n.[m.]. GK: 743 [→ 693]. cover, hiding place, lair; hiding place (for an ambush):– dens [1], lie in wait [1]

696 אֹרֶב 'ōreb, n.[m.]. GK: 744 [→ 693]. trap, intrigue:– wait [1]

אַרְבֵּאל 'arbē'l. See 1009.

697 אַרְבֶּה 'arbeh, n.m. GK: 746 [→ 7235?]. locust, mature locust:– locusts [11], locust [9], grasshoppers [3], grasshopper [1]

698 אָרְבָּה 'orbâ, n.f. GK: 747 [→ 693?]. cleverness; other sources: nimble movements (of the hands), perhaps some concrete survival skill, such as swimming:– spoils [1]

699 אֲרֻבָּה "ªrubbâ, n.[f.]. GK: 748. floodgate; window; nest (nesting hole):– windows [8], chimney [1]

700 אֲרֻבּוֹת "ªrubbôt, n.pr.loc. GK: 749. Arubboth:– Aruboth [1]

701 אַרְבִּי 'arbî, a.g. GK: 750 [cf. 694?]. Arbite:– Arbite [1]

702 אַרְבַּע 'arba', n.m. & f. GK: 752 [→ 704, 705, 706, 7153, 7243, 7251, 7253?, 7255, 7256; cf. 703]. four, (pl.) forty; fourth, fortieth:– four [264], fourteenth (+6240) [23], fourteen (+6240) [19], fourth [5], forty two thousand (+505+7239) [2],

four apiece (+702) [2], threescore and fourteen (+7657+2050.1) [2], fourfold [1], thousand [1]

703 אַרְבַּע **'arba'** (Aram.), n.m. & f. GK: 10065 [→ 7244; cf. 702]. four:– four [8]

704 אַרְבַּע **'arba'**, n.pr.m. GK: 753 [→ 702]. Arba:– Arbah [2], Arba [1]

אַרְבָּעָה **'arbā'â**. See 702.

705 אַרְבָּעִים **'arbā'îm**, n.pl.indecl. GK: 754 [→ 702]. forty (pl. of "four"):– forty [131], fortieth [4], forty's [1]

706 אַרְבַּעְתַּיִם **'arba'tayim**, n.m. & f. GK: 752 [→ 702]. dual of 702: fourfold:–

707 אָרַג **'ārag**, v. GK: 755 [→ 708]. [Q] to weave, spin (a web):– weaver's [4], woven [3], weaver [2], weave [2], weavest [1], wove [1]

708 אֶרֶג **'ereg**, n.[m.]. GK: 756 [→ 707]. weaver's loom, weaver's shuttle:– beam [1], weaver's shuttle [1]

709 אַרְגֹּב **'argōb**, n.pr.m. & loc. GK: 758 & 759 [cf. 7263]. Argob, "mound":– Argob [5]

710 אַרְגְּוָן **'arg**e**wān**, n.[m.]. GK: 760 [cf. 713]. purple (yarn):– purple [1]

711 אַרְגְּוָן **'arg**e**wān** (Aram.), n.m. GK: 10066 [cf. 713]. purple (clothing), a sign of rulership:– scarlet [3]

712 אַרְגַּז **'argaz**, n.m. GK: 761 [→ 7264]. chest (containing objects); other sources: saddlebag:– coffer [3]

713 אַרְגָּמָן **'argāmān**, n.[m.]. GK: 763 [cf. 710; cf. 711]. purple (yarn):– purple [38]

714 אַרְד **'ard**, n.pr.m. GK: 764 [→ 715?, 716, 720?]. Ard, "hunchbacked":– Ard [2]

715 אַרְדּוֹן **'ardôn**, n.pr.m. GK: 765 [→ 714?]. Ardon, "hunchbacked":– Ardon [1]

716 אַרְדִּי **'ardî**, a.g. GK: 766 [→ 714]. Ardite, "of Ard":– Ardites [1]

717 אָרָה **'ārâ**, v. GK: 768 [→ 224?]. [Q] to gather, pick (fruit):– gathered [1], pluck [1]

718 אֲרוּ **'rû** (Aram.), interj. GK: 10067 [→ 431]. there!, behold!, i.e., a discourse marker of introduction, transition, or emphasis:– behold [4], lo [1]

719 אַרְוַד **'arwād**, n.pr.loc. GK: 770 [→ 721]. Arvad:– Arvad [2]

720 אֲרוֹד **'**a**rôd**, n.pr.m. GK: 769 [→ 714?]. Arod, see 722:– Arod [1]

721 אַרְוָדִי **'arwādî**, a.g. GK: 773 [→ 719]. Arvadite, "of Arvad":– Arvadite [2]

722 אֲרוֹדִי **'**a**rôdî**, n.pr.m. & a.g. GK: 771 & 772. Arodi, "hunchbacked"; Arodite, "of Arodi":– Arodites [1], Arodi [1]

723 אֻרְוָה **'urwâ** or אַרְיָה **'uryâ**, n.f. GK: 774 & 795 [→ 220]. (animal) stall, pen, stable, manger, crib:– stalls [3]

724 אֲרוּכָה **'**a**rûkâ**, n.f. GK: 776 [→ 748]. healing, health; repair:– health [4], made up (+5927) [1], perfected (+5927) [1]

725 אֲרוּמָה **'**a**rûmâ**, n.pr.loc. GK: 777 [cf. 7316]. Arumah, "lofty":– Arumah [1]

726 אֲרוֹמִי **'**a**rômî**, a.g. GK: 122 [cf. 130]. var. of 130: Edomite, "of Edom":– Syrians [1]

727 אֲרוֹן **'**a**rôn**, n.m. & f. GK: 778. ark, chest, box; coffin:– ark [195], chest [6], coffin [1]

728 אֲרַוְנָה **'**a**rawnâ** or אֲרַנְיָה **'**a**ranyâ**, n.pr.m. GK: 779 & 819. Araunah, Aranyah, "strong":– Araunah [9]

729 אָרוּז **'ārûz**, a. GK: 775 [→ 730?]. tight, solid:– made of cedar [1]

730 אֶרֶז **'erez**, n.m. GK: 780 [→ 729?, 731]. cedar; other sources: fir:– cedar [43], cedars [24], cedar trees [5], cedar tree [1]

731 אַרְזָה **'arzâ**, n.f.col. GK: 781 [→ 730]. beam of cedar; other sources: paneling (made of fir):– cedar work [1]

732 אָרַח **'āraḥ**, v. GK: 782 [→ 733?, 734, 736, 737?]. [Q] to go, travel; (ptcp.) traveler, wanderer; (ptcp.pl.) caravans:– wayfaring man [2], goeth [1], wayfaring men [1], wayfaring [1]

733 אָרַח **'āraḥ**, n.pr.m. GK: 783 [→ 732?]. Arah, "he wanders":– Arah [4]

734 אֹרַח **'ōraḥ**, n.m. GK: 784 [→ 732; cf. 735]. road, way, path, thoroughfare; by extension: way of life, manner of conduct; "the way of a woman" means "childbirth":– way [18], paths [16], path [9], ways [8], byways (+6106) [1], highways [1],

manner [1], race [1], ranks [1], traveller [1], troops [1], wayfaring man (+5674) [1]

735 אֹרַח **'raḥ** (Aram.), n.[m.?]. GK: 10068 [cf. 734]. road, way; fig., conduct or way of life (only used fig. in the Aramaic portion of the Bible):– ways [2]

736 אֹרְחָה **'ōrḥâ**, n.f. GK: 785 [→ 732]. caravan:– company [1], travelling companies [1]

737 אֲרֻחָה **'**a**ruḥâ**, n.f. GK: 786 [→ 732?]. allowance, provision; portion:– allowance [2], diet [2], dinner [1], victuals [1]

738 אֲרִי **'**a**rî**, n.m. GK: 787 & 793 [→ 221, 745; cf. 744]. (the African) lion, with the associative meanings of strength, fierceness, and sometimes nobility; sometimes fig. of people who are destructive:– lion [55], lions [17], lion's [4], lions' [2], young lion [1]

739 אֲרִאֵל **'**a**ri'ēl**, n.pr.m. GK: 738 [→ 691?]. best man, warrior, possibly "lionlike":– lion-like men [2]

740 אֲרִיאֵל **'**a**rî'ēl**, n.pr.m. & n.pr.f. GK: 790 & 791 [→ 741]. Ariel, "lioness of God [El]":– Ariel [6]

741 אֲרִיאֵל **'**a**rî'ēl**, n.m. GK: 789 [→ 739, 740; cf. 2025]. altar hearth:– altar [2]

742 אֲרִידַי **'**a**riday**, n.pr.m. GK: 767. Aridai, "[perhaps] delight of Hari":– Aridai [1]

743 אֲרִידָתָא **'**a**rîdātā'**, n.pr.m. GK: 792. Aridatha, "[perhaps] given by Hari":– Aridatha [1]

אַרְיֵה **'aryēh**. See 738.

744 אַרְיֵה **'aryēh** (Aram.), n.m. GK: 10069 [cf. 738]. lion, an animal with the associative meanings of being fierce and powerful, and so causing fear:– lions [8], lions' [1], lion [1]

745 אַרְיֵה **'aryēh**, n.pr.m. GK: 794 [→ 738]. Arieh, "lion":– Arieh [1]

אַרְיָה **'aryâ**. See 723.

746 אַרְיוֹךְ **'aryôk**, n.pr.m. GK: 796 & 10070. Arioch; note this name is Hebrew twice in Genesis and Aramaic five times in Daniel:– Arioch [7]

747 אֲרִיסַי **'**a**rîsay**, n.pr.m. GK: 798. Arisai:– Arisai [1]

748 אָרַךְ **'ārak**, v. GK: 799 [→ 724, 750, 752, 753; cf. 754]. [Q] to be, become long; [H] to lengthen, to have a long (life):– prolong [12], prolonged [5], long [3], drew out [1], lengthen [2], deferreth [1], defer [1], draw out [1], lengthened [1], made long [1], outlived (+310+3117) [1], overlived (+310+3117) [1], prolongeth [1], tarried long [1], tarried [1]

749 אֲרִיךְ **'**a**rîk** (Aram.), a.vbl. GK: 10071. proper, fitting:– meet [1]

750 אָרֵךְ **'ārēk**, a. GK: 800 [→ 748]. slow (to anger), patient, long-suffering:– slow [9], longsuffering (+639) [4], longwinged (+83) [1], patient [1]

751 אֶרֶךְ **'erek**, n.pr.loc. GK: 804 [cf. 756]. Erech:– Erech [1]

752 אָרֹךְ **'ārōk**, a. GK: 801 [→ 748]. length (spatial and temporal):– long [2], longer [1]

753 אֹרֶךְ **'ōrek**, n.[m.]. GK: 802 [→ 748]. length (spatial and temporal):– length [70], long [21], ever (+3117) [2], high [1], so long [1]

754 אַרְכָה **'arkâ** (Aram.), n.f. GK: 10073 [cf. 752]. continuing, prolongation, lengthening of time:– lengthening [1], prolonged [1]

755 אַרְכֻבָּה **'arkubbâ** (Aram.), n.f. GK: 10072 [cf. 1288]. knee; "knocking of the knees" indicates fear:– knees [1]

אַרְכָה **'arkâ**. See 724.

756 אַרְכְּוַי **'ark**e**wāy** (Aram.), n.pr.g. GK: 10074 [cf. 751]. Erech:– Archevites [1]

757 אַרְכִּי **'arkî**, a.g. GK: 805. Arkite:– Archite [5], Archi [1]

758 אֲרָם **'**a**rām**, n.pr.m. GK: 806 [→ 762, 761, 6307 (also used with compound proper names)]. Aram:– Syria [67], Syrians [56], Aram [7], Mesopotamia [1], Syria-damascus (+1834) [1], Syria-maachah [1]

759 אַרְמוֹן **'armôn**, n.m. GK: 810 [→ 764; cf. 488, 7411]. fortress, citadel, palace, stronghold, a military defensive building usually small of base but many floors high:– palaces [27], palace [4], castle [1]

760 אֲרַם צוֹבָה **'**a**ram ṣôbâ**, n.pr.loc. GK: 809 [→ 758+6678]. Aram Zobah:– Aram-zobah [1]

761 אֲרַמִּי **'**a**rammî**, a.g. GK: 812 [→ 758]. Aramean:– Syrian [7], Syrians [3], Aramitess [1]

762 אֲרָמִי **'**a**rāmî**, adv. GK: 811 [→ 758]. in Aramaic:– in the Syrian language [2], in the Syrian tongue [1], in Syriack [1]

763 אֲרַם נַהֲרַיִם **'**a**ram nah**a**rayim**, n.loc. GK: 808 [→ 758]. Aram Naharaim:– Mesopotamia [4], Aram-naharaim [1]

764 אַרְמֹנִי **'armōnî**, n.pr.m. GK: 813 [→ 759]. Armoni, "one born in the dwelling tower, the palace":– Armoni [1]

765 אֲרָן **'**a**rān**, n.pr.m. GK: 814. Aran, "wild goat":– Aran [2]

766 אֹרֶן **'ōren**, n.[m.]. GK: 815 [→ 767, 769?]. pine tree; other sources: laurel, sweet laurel, fir, cedar:– ash [1]

767 אֹרֶן **'ōren**, n.pr.m. GK: 816 [→ 766]. Oren, "fir or cedar; laurel":– Oren [1]

אֲרֹן **'**a**rōn**. See 727.

768 אַרְנֶבֶת **'arnebet**, n.f. GK: 817 [cf. 3]. rabbit; other sources: hare:– hare [2]

769 אַרְנוֹן **'arnôn**, n.pr.loc. GK: 818 [→ 766?]. Arnon:– Arnon [25]

אֲרַנְיָה **'**a**rnîah**. See 728.

770 אַרְנָן **'arnān**, n.pr.loc. GK: 820. Arnan:– Arnan [1]

771 אָרְנָן **'ornān**, n.pr.m. GK: 821. Araunah, "strong":– Ornan [12]

772 אֲרַע **'**a**ra'** (Aram.), n.[f.]. GK: 10075 [→ 773, 778; cf. 776]. earth, world, the dwelling place of all peoples; land, ground, the dwelling place of a specific people:– earth [20], inferior [1]

773 אַרְעִי **'ar'î** (Aram.), n.f.den. GK: 10076 [→ 772]. floor, bottom:– bottom [1]

774 אַרְפַּד **'arpād**, n.pr.loc. GK: 822. Arpad:– Arpad [4], Arphad [2]

775 אַרְפַּכְשַׁד **'arpakšad**, n.pr.m. GK: 823. Arphaxad:– Arphaxad [9]

776 אֶרֶץ **'ereṣ**, n.f. & m. GK: 824 [cf. 772, cf. 778]. world, earth, all inhabited lands; parts of the earth, land (in contrast to water), ground, soil; country, region, territory; "heaven and earth" means the totality of creation; "the ends of the earth" means "a very distant place":– land [1508], earth [712], ground [98], country [92], countries [48], lands [34], world [4], way [2], common [1], field [1], little way (+3530+1886.1) [1], nations [1], wilderness (+4057) [1]

777 אַרְצָא **'arṣā'**, n.pr.m. GK: 825. Arza, "[perhaps] gracious":– Arza [1]

778 אֲרַק **'**a**raq** (Aram.), n.[f.]. GK: 10077 [→ 772; cf. 776]. earth:– earth [1]

779 אָרַר **'ārar**, v. GK: 826 [→ 224?, 3994]. [Q] to curse, place a curse; [Qp] to be cursed, be under a curse; [N] to be cursed; [P] to bring a curse; [Ho] to bring a curse upon one:– cursed [44], curse [12], causeth the curse [5], curseth [2], bitterly [1], causeth curse [1], cursest [1]

780 אֲרָרַט **'**a**rāraṭ**, n.pr.m. GK: 827. Ararat:– Ararat [2], Armenia [2]

781 אָרַשׂ **'āraś**, v. GK: 829. [P] to betroth, pledge to marriage; [Pu] to be betrothed, be pledged to be married:– betrothed [6], betroth [4], espoused [1]

782 אֲרֶשֶׁת **'**a**rešet**, n.f. GK: 830 [→ 4180]. request, desire:– request [1]

783 אַרְתַּחְשַׁסְתְּא **'artaḥšast'** or אַרְתַּחְשַׁשְׂתְּ **'artaḥšaśt** or אַרְתַּחְשַׁשְׂתָּא **'artaḥšaśtā'**, n.pr.m. GK: 831 & 10078. Artaxerxes; note this name occurs nine times in Hebrew in Ezra and Nehemiah and six times in Aramaic in Ezra:– Artaxerxes [14], Artaxerxes' [1]

784 אֵשׁ **'ēš**, n.f. & m. GK: 836 [→ 800, 801; cf. 785]. fire, flame; lightning; same as 800:– fire [372], fiery [2], burning [1], fire (+3956) [1], flaming [1], hot [1]

785 אֶשָּׁא **'eššā'** (Aram.), n.[f.]. GK: 10080 [cf. 784, 801]. fire:– flame [1]

786 אֵשׁ **'iš**, subst. GK: 838 [→ 3426]. there is:– are there [1], can [1]

787 אֹשׁ **'ōš** (Aram.), n.m. GK: 10079 [cf. 8357]. foundation:– foundations [2], foundation [1]

788 אַשְׁבֵּל **'ašbēl**, n.pr.m. GK: 839 [→ 789; cf. 7640]. Ashbel, "[poss. a form of] man of Baal; having a long upper lip":– Ashbel [3]

789 אַשְׁבֵּלִי **'ašbēlî**, a.g. GK: 840 [→ 788; cf. 7640]. Ashbelite, "of Ashbel":– Ashbelites [1]

790 אֶשְׁבָּן *'ešbān*, n.pr.m. GK: 841. Eshban, "*man of understanding*":– Eshban [2]

791 אַשְׁבֵּעַ *'ašbēa'*, n.pr.loc. GK: 842 [→ 1004+791]. Ashbea:– Ashbea [1]

792 אֶשְׁבַּעַל *'ešba'al*, n.pr.m. GK: 843 [→ 376+1167]. Esh-Baal, "*man of Baal*":– Eshbaal [2]

793 אֶשֶׁד *'ešed*, n.[m.]. GK: 845 [→ 794]. foundation, bottom, lower part (slope):– stream [1]

794 אָשֵׁד *'āšēd*, n.f. GK: 844 [→ 793, 799]. slopes, mountain slopes:– springs [3]

795 אַשְׁדּוֹד *'ašdôd*, n.pr.loc. GK: 846 [→ 796, 797]. Ashdod, "[perhaps] *fortress*":– Ashdod [17]

796 אַשְׁדּוֹדִי *'ašdôdî*, a.g. GK: 847 [→ 795]. from Ashdod:– Ashdodites [1], Ashdothites [1], of Ashdod [1], them of Ashdod [1], they of Ashdod [1]

797 אַשְׁדּוֹדִית *'ašdôdît*, adv. GK: 848 [→ 795]. language of Ashdod:– in the speech of Ashdod [1]

798 אַשְׁדּוֹת הַפִּסְגָּה *'ašdôt happisgā*, n.pr.loc. GK: 849 [→ 794+1886.1+6449]. Ashdoth Pisgah:– Ashdoth-pisgah [3]

799 אֶשְׁדָּת *'ešdāt*, n.f. GK: 850 [→ 794]. mountain slope:– *not translated* [1]

800 אֵשׁ *'ēš*, n.f. & m. GK: 836 [→ 784]. fire, flame; lightning; same as 784:–

801 אִשֶּׁה *'iššeh*, n.m. GK: 852 [→ 784; cf. 785]. offering made by fire:– offering made by fire [35], offerings made by fire [15], sacrifice made by fire [9], sacrifices made by fire [3], offering by fire [2], offering made by fire (+7133) [1]

802 אִשָּׁה *'iššâ*, n.f. GK: 851 [→ 376; cf. 5389]. woman, in contrast to man; wife, in contrast to husband; "to take a woman" means "to marry":– wife [301], woman [211], wives [115], women [103], wife's [8], one [7], woman's [7], every one [3], each [2], female [2], married (+1961+3807.1) [2], marry (+1961+3807.1) [2], adulteress (+376) [1], every woman [1], every [1], married (+1167) [1], married (+3807.1) [1], none (+3808) [1], together (+269+413) [1], whore's (+2181) [1], widow's (+490) [1], wife (+3807.1) [1], womankind [1], women's [1]

803 אֲשׁוּיָה *'ašûyâ* or אָשְׁיָה *'ošyâ*, n.f. GK: 853 & 859. tower:– foundations [1]

804 אַשּׁוּר *'aššûr*, n.pr.g. & loc. GK: 855 [→ 839]. Asshur, Assyria:– Assyria [118], Assyrian [13], Asshur [8], Assyrians [6], Assyrians (+1121) [4], Assur [2]

805 אַשּׁוּרִי *'ašûrî*, a.g. & n.pr.g.pl. GK: 856. Ashuri; Asshurite, "*of Asshur*":– Ashurites [1], Asshurim [1]

806 אַשְׁחוּר *'ašḥûr*, n.pr.m. GK: 858. Ashhur:– Ashur [2]

807 אֲשִׁימָא *'ašîmā'*, n.pr.[m.]. GK: 860. Ashima:– Ashima [1]

אֲשֵׁירָה *'ašērâ*. See 842.

808 אָשִׁישׁ *'āšîš*, n.m. GK: 861. man:– foundations [1]

809 אֲשִׁישָׁה *'ašîšâ*, n.f. GK: 862 [→ 377?]. cake of raisins, made of dried, compressed grapes; used as food and as an offering:– flagons [2], flagon [2]

810 אֶשֶׁךְ *'ešek*, n.[m.]. GK: 863. testicle:– stones [1]

811 אֶשְׁכּוֹל *'eškôl*, n.m. GK: 864 [→ 812; cf. 7921]. cluster of grapes:– clusters [4], cluster [4], cluster of grapes [1]

812 אֶשְׁכּוֹל *'eškôl*, n.pr.m. & loc. GK: 865 & 866 [→ 811]. Eshcol, "*[grape] cluster*":– Eshcol [6]

813 אַשְׁכְּנַז *'ašk^enaz*, n.pr.m. GK: 867. Ashkenaz:– Ashchenaz [2], Ashkenaz [1]

814 אֶשְׁכָּר *'eškār*, n.[m.]. GK: 868. gifts; payment:– gifts [1], present [1]

815 אֶשֶׁל *'ešel*, n.m. GK: 869. tamarisk tree:– tree [2], grove [1]

816 אָשַׁם *'āšam*, v. GK: 870 [→ 817, 818, 819]. [Q] to be guilty; to be in a state of liable for a wrongdoing, with an implication of that one will suffer or be punished for the guilt; [N] to be suffering; [H] to declare guilty:– guilty [12], desolate [4], offend [4], certainly trespassed (+816) [2], greatly offended (+816) [1], made desolate [1], trespass [1], acknowledge offence [1], destroy [1], found faulty [1], found guilty [1], hath trespassed [1], hold guilty [1], offended [1]

817 אָשָׁם *'āšām*, n.m. GK: 871 [→ 816]. guilt offering, atoning sacrifice; guilt, penalty:– trespass offering [35], trespass [6], sin [2], guiltiness [1], offering for sin [1], trespasses [1]

818 אָשֵׁם *'āšēm*, a. GK: 872 [→ 816]. guilty, bearing guilt:– guilty [2], which is faulty [1]

819 אַשְׁמָה *'ašmâ*, n.f. GK: 873 [→ 816]. guilt, guiltiness:– trespass [9], sins [2], sin [2], cause of trespass [1], offended [1], trespass offering [1], trespassed [1], trespasses [1], trespassing [1]

אַשְׁמוּרָה *'ašmûrâ*. See 821.

820 אַשְׁמָן *'ašmān*, n.[m.]pl. GK: 875 [→ 8081?]. strong one:– desolate places [1]

821 אַשְׁמוּרָה *'ašmûrâ*, n.f. GK: 874 [→ 8104]. watch of the night (middle or last):– watch [4], watches [3]

822 אֶשְׁנָב *'ešnāb*, n.[m.]. GK: 876 [→ 5380]. lattice, a barred or grated window:– casement [1], lattice [1]

823 אַשְׁנָה *'ašnâ*, n.pr.loc. GK: 877. Ashnah:– Ashnah [2]

824 אֶשְׁעָן *'eš'ān*, n.pr.loc. GK: 878. Eshan, "*support*":– Eshean [1]

825 אַשָּׁף *'aššāp*, n.m. GK: 879 [cf. 826]. enchanter, conjurer, one of the profession of the secret arts, in communication with the dead:– astrologers [2]

826 אָשַׁף *'āšap* (Aram.), n.m. GK: 10081 [cf. 825]. enchanter, conjurer; astrologers [4], astrologer [2], astrologians [1]

827 אַשְׁפָּה *'ašpâ*, n.f. GK: 880. quiver (for arrows):– quiver [6]

828 אַשְׁפְּנַז *'ašp^enaz*, n.pr.m. GK: 881. Ashpenaz, "*guest*":– Ashpenaz [1]

829 אֶשְׁפָּר *'ešpār*, n.m. GK: 882 [→ 7782]. cake of dates:– good piece [2]

830 אַשְׁפֹּת *'ašpōt*, n.[m.]. GK: 883 [→ 8239]. ash heap; Dung (Gate):– dung [4], dunghill [2], dunghills [1]

831 אַשְׁקְלוֹן *'ašq^elôn*, n.pr.loc. GK: 884 [→ 832]. Ashkelon:– Ashkelon [9], Askelon [3]

832 אֶשְׁקְלוֹנִי *'ešq^elônî*, a.g. GK: 885 [→ 831]. Ashkelonite, "*of Ashkelon*":– Eshkalonites [1]

833 אָשַׁר *'āšar*, v. GK: 886 & 887 [→ 835, 836, 837, 838, 843]. [Q] to walk (straight); [P] to lead, guide; reprove; to call blessed, pronounce happy, speak well of; [Pu] to be guided; to be blessed; in some contexts, to give a blessing is to act kindly and impart benefits to the one being blessed; to be blessed implies the happy state that results:– call blessed [4], blessed [3], go [2], call happy [1], guide [1], happy [1], leaders [1], lead [1], led [1], relieve [1]

834 אֲשֶׁר *'^ašer*, pt.rel. GK: 889. (rel.) who, which, what; (c.) that, in order that, so that:– which [1819], that [1671], as (+3509.1) [382], whom [262], who [94], what [75], whose [69], where (+8033) [54], when (+3509.1) [47], wherewith [41], whither (+8033+1886.5) [38], because [36], whatsoever (+3605) [33], when [32], how [28], where [28], for [27], until (+5704) [27], whither (+8033) [27], because (+5921) [26], wherein [25], as [23], because (+3282) [19], whereof [19], according as (+3509.1) [16], wherein (+871.1) [15], such as [14], wherein (+871.1+1886.3) [14], whereby [12], whithersoever (+3605+871.1) [12], because (+8478) [11], like as (+3509.1) [11], wherewith (+871.1) [11], whereon (+5921) [10], till (+5704) [9], wherewith (+5921) [8], whosoever (+3605) [8], such [7], where (+8033+1886.5) [7], where (+871.1) [7], wherein (+8033) [7], as soon as (+3509.1) [6], forasmuch as (+3282) [5], how that [5], whatsoever [5], whither [5], whosoever (+376) [5], as when (+3509.1) [4], because (+1697+5921) [4], if [4], that (+4616+3807.1) [4], that when (+3509.1) [4], what soever (+3605) [4], wherein (+871.1+2050.2) [4], wherein (+871.1+3963.1) [4]*

835 אֶשֶׁר *'ešer*, n.[m.]. GK: 890 & 897 [→ 833, 837]. fortune, blessedness, happiness; (interj.) blessed!, happy!, a heightened state of happiness and joy, implying very favorable circumstances, often resulting from the kind acts of God:– blessed [27], happy [18]

836 אָשֵׁר *'āšēr*, n.pr.m. GK: 888 [→ 843; cf. 833]. Asher, "*Happy One!*":– Asher [43]

837 אֹשֶׁר *'ōšer*, n.[m.]. GK: 891 [→ 835; cf. 833]. fortune, blessedness, happiness:– happy [1]

838 אָשֻׁר *'āšur*, n.m. GK: 892 & 893 [→ 833]. steps, tracks:– steps [5], goings [2], going [1], step [1]

839 אַשּׁוּר *'aššur*, n.pr.g. & loc. GK: 894 [→ 804]. Asshur, Asshurite; cf. 804:– Ashurites [1]

אַשּׁוּר *'aššur*. See 804, 838.

840 אֲשַׂרְאֵל *'^aśar'ēl*, n.pr.m. GK: 832 [→ 841, 844, 845]. Asarel:– Asareel [1]

841 אֲשַׂרְאֵלָה *'^aśar'ēlâ*, n.pr.m. GK: 833 [→ 840; cf. 3480]. Asarelah:– Asarelah [1]

842 אֲשֵׁרָה *'^ašērâ*, n.pr.f. GK: 895 [cf. 6252?]. Asherah (pagan god), Asherah pole:– groves [24], grove [16]

843 אָשֵׁרִי *'āšērî*, a.g. GK: 896 [→ 836; cf. 833]. people of Asher:– Asherites [1]

844 אַשְׂרִיאֵל *'aśrî'ēl*, n.pr.m. GK: 835 [→ 840]. Asriel, "*God has filled with joy* or *[the object of] joy is God*":– Asriel [2], Ashriel [1]

845 אַשְׂרִיאֵלִי *'aśri'ēlî*, a.g. GK: 834 [→ 840]. Asrielite, "*of Asriel*":– Asrielites [1]

846 אֻשַּׁרְנָא *'uššarnā* (Aram.), n.m. GK: 10082. structure, a building or part of a building (various sources translate more specifically: "beams, roofing, paneling, scaffolding," etc.):– walls [1], wall [1]

847 אֶשְׁתָּאֹל *'eštā'ōl*, n.pr.loc. GK: 900 [→ 848; cf. 7592]. Eshtaol, "*[place of oracles,] inquiry*":– Eshtaol [7]

848 אֶשְׁתָּאֻלִי *'eštā'ulî*, a.g. GK: 901 [→ 847]. Eshtaolite, "*of Eshtaol*":– Eshtaulites [1]

849 אֶשְׁתַּדּוּר *'eštaddûr* (Aram.), n.m. GK: 10083 [→ 7712]. rebellion, sedition, revolt:– sedition [2]

850 אֶשְׁתּוֹן *'eštôn*, n.pr.m. GK: 902. Eshton, "[poss.] *hen-pecked [husband]* or *effeminate*":– Eshton [2]

851 אֶשְׁתְּמֹה *'ešt^emōh* or אֶשְׁתְּמֹעַ *'ešt^emōa'*, n.pr.m. & loc. GK: 903 & 904 [→ 8085]. Eshtemoa, Eshtemoh, "*[place where oracle is] heard*":– Eshtemoa [5], Eshtemoh [1]

אֵת *'at*. See 859.

852 אָת *'āt* (Aram.), n.m. GK: 10084 [cf. 226]. miraculous sign:– signs [3]

853 אֵת *'ēt*, pt. GK: 906 [cf. 3487]. usually not translated: marks the direct object:– *usually untranslated* [513], consecrated (+3027+4390) [5], consecrate (+3027+4390) [4], besought (+2470+6440) [3], aided (+2388+3027) [1]

854 אֵת *'ēt*, pp. GK: 907 [→ 856]. with, to, upon, beside, among, against:– with [606], from (+4480) [81], of (+4480) [71], against [27], to [20], before (+6440) [16], unto [14], by (+4480) [10], by [9], among [7], in [7], upon [7], for [3], of [3], amongst [2], and (+2050.1) [2], before [2], from [2], hath [2], also [1], at the hand of (+4480) [1], beside (+2050.1) [1], beside [1], delivered to keep (+6485+6487) [1], doing (+4480) [1], for (+2050.1) [1], had [1], have [1], knoweth [1], lie with at all (+7901+7901) [1], lien with (+7901) [1], lieth carnally with (+2233+7901+7902) [1], on side [1], on the behalf of (+4480) [1], out of (+4480) [1], own [1], requite (+6213) [1], than (+4480) [1], therewith (+2050.2) [1], towards [1], undo (+6213) [1], with (+4480) [1]

855 אֵת *'ēt*, n.[m.]. GK: 908. plowshare, mattock:– plowshares [3], coulters [1], coulter [1]

אַתָּה *'attâ*. See 859.

אָתָא *'ātā*. See 857.

856 אֶתְבַּעַל *'etba'al*, n.pr.m. GK: 909 [→ 854+1167]. Ethbaal, "*with [him is] Baal*":– Ethbaal [1]

857 אָתָה *'ātâ*, v. GK: 910 [→ 2978, 448; cf. 858]. [Q] to come; [H] to bring:– come [9], came [4], cometh [3], to come [2], brought (+7125) [1], come upon [1], coming [1]

858 אֲתָה *'^atâ* (Aram.), v. GK: 10085 [cf. 857]. [P] to come, go; [H] to bring; [Hp] to be brought:– brought [6], came [4], come [3], bring [2], brought out [1]

859 אַתָּה *'attâ*, p.m.s.; אַתְּ *'att* or אַתִּי *'attî*, p.f.s.; אַתֶּם *'attem*, p.m.pl.; אַתֵּן *'attēn*, p.f.pl. GK: 905 & 911 & 914 & 917 & 920 [cf. 607; cf. 608]. all forms of the second person pronoun: you, your, yourself; you (all), yours, yourselves:– thou [777], ye [251], you [29], thee [15], thyself [5], yourselves [4], yourselves [1], thou [1], thy [1]

860 אָתוֹן *'ātôn*, n.f. GK: 912. female donkey:– ass [16], asses [12], she asses [5], ass's [1]

861 אַתּוּן *'attûn* (Aram.), n.m. [& f.?]. GK: 10086. furnace:– furnace [10]

862 אַתּוּק *'attûq* or אַתִּיק *'attîq*, n.m. GK: 913 & 916. gallery, porch; other sources: street, passage:– galleries [3], gallery [2]

אַתִּי *'attî*. See 859.

863 אִיתַי *'îtay* or אִתַּי *'ittay*, n.pr.m. GK: 416 & 915 [cf. 384]. Ithai, Ittai, "[poss.] *with me*":– Ittai [8], Ithai [1]

864 אֵתָם *'ētām*, n.pr.loc. GK: 918. Etham, "[poss.] *fort*":– Etham [4]

אַתֶּן *'attem*. See 859.

865 אֶתְמוֹל **'etmôl**, subst.adv. GK: 919 [→ 8543]. yesterday; (adv.) before, formerly, lately, in the past:– before that time (+8032+3509.1) [1], beforetime (+4480+8032) [1], heretofore (+8032) [1], in time past (+1571+8032) [1], in times past (+8032) [1], late [1], old [1], yesterday (+3117) [1]

אַתֶּן **'atten**. See 859.

866 אֶתְנָה **'etnâ**, n.f. GK: 921 [→ 869]. payment (of a prostitute):– rewards [1]

אֶתְנָה **'attēnâ** or אַתֶּנָּה **'attēnnâ**. See 859.

867 אֶתְנִי **'etnî**, n.pr.m. GK: 922. Ethni, "gift or hire":– Ethni [1]

868 אֶתְנָן **'etnān**, n.pr.m. GK: 925 [→ 869]. Ethnan, "hire [of a prostitute]":– hire [7], reward [3], hires [1]

869 אֶתְנַן **'etnan**, n.m. GK: 924 [→ 866, 868, 8566; cf. 5414]. wages, payment (of a prostitute):– Ethnan [1]

870 אֲתַר **'ᵃtar** (Aram.), n.m. GK: 10087 & 10092 [→ 871.2; cf. 834]. site, place; after:– place [5], after [3]

871 אֲתָרִים **'ᵃtārîm**, n.pr.loc. GK: 926. Atharim, "[trad.] way of the spies":– spies [1]

871.1 בְ- **b⁽e⁾-**, pp.pref. GK: 928 [→ 1119, 1152, 1164, 1212; cf. 871.2]. in, on, among, over, through, against; when, whenever; a spatial, temporal, or logical marker to show relationship of objects, words, and phrases:– in [6850], with [1418], by [699], when [584], into [476], at [438], on [372], upon [340], against [335], among [299], of [274], for [248], through [152], to [151], among (+8432) [106], unto [104], therein [1886.3] [86], over [71], throughout [64], after [51], according to [43], by (+3027) [42], among (+7130) [41], before (+2962) [35], therein (+2050.2) [35], while [35], within [35], as [34], under [31], obey (+8085) [26], within (+7130) [25], every morning (+1242+871.1+1886.1+1886.1) [20], obeyed (+8085) [20], amongst [19], because of [19], in (+8432) [19], within (+8432) [18], without (+3808) [17], wherein (+834) [15], for sake (+5668) [14], wherein (+834+1886.3) [14], that [13], because [12], wherein (+4100) [12], whithersoever (+834+3605) [12], without (+2351+1886.1) [12], therewith (+1886.3) [11], wherewith (+834) [11], here (+2088) [10], that (+5668) [10], when (+3117) [10], wherein (+2050.2) [10], wherewith (+4100) [10], with (+3027) [10]*

871.2 בְ- **b⁽e⁾-** (Aram.), pp.pref. GK: 10089 [→ 870; cf. 871.1]. in, with, by:– in [103], then (+116) [28], at [18], with [15], by [6], into [4], over [4], aloud (+2429) [3], of [3], on [3], upon [3], concerning [2], continually (+0.2+8411) [2], without (+3809) [2], according to [1], at what time (+0.2+1768+5732) [1], for [1], more [1], then (+116+4481+6925) [1], therein (+1459+1886.9) [1], therein (+1886.9) [1], therein (+1952.1) [1], through [1], wherein (+1459) [1], wheresoever (+1768+3606) [1], whiles [1], within [1]

872 בֹּא **bi'â**, n.f. GK: 929 [→ 935]. entrance:– entry [1]

873 בִּאֵשׁ **bi'yš** (Aram.), a. GK: 10090 [→ 888]. wicked, evil, bad:– bad [1]

874 בָּאַר **bā'ar**, v. GK: 930. [P] to make plain, make clear, expound:– declare [1], make plain [1], plainly [1]

875 בְּאֵר **b⁽e⁾'ēr**, n.f. GK: 931 [→ 876, 877, 879, 883, 884, 878, 880, 881, 882, 885, 953, 1269, 1269 (also used with compound proper names)]. well, a shaft in the ground for extraction of water; pit, a depression in the earth with no focus on water:– well [23], well's [6], pit [3], wells [3], full of slimepits (+875+2564) [2]

876 בְּאֵר **b⁽e⁾'ēr**, n.pr.loc. GK: 932 [→ 875]. Beer, "cistern, well":– Beer [2]

877 בֹּאר **bō'r**, n.m. GK: 934 [→ 953; cf. 875]. pit, well, cistern; dungeon; a cistern is usually a shaft in the ground, hewn out of soft stone and plastered to hold water:–

878 בְּאֵרָא **b⁽e⁾'ērā'**, n.pr.loc. GK: 938 [→ 875]. Beera, "cistern, well":– Beera [1]

879 בְּאֵר אֵילִים **b⁽e⁾'ēr 'êlîm**, n.pr.loc. GK: 935 [→ 875+352; cf. 352]. Beer Elim, "cistern, well of Elim":– Beer-elim [1]

880 בְּאֵרָה **b⁽e⁾'ērâ**, n.pr.m. GK: 939 [→ 875]. Beerah, "cistern, well":– Beerah [1]

881 בְּאֵרוֹת **b⁽e⁾'ērôt**, n.pr.loc. GK: 940 [→ 886; cf. 875]. Beeroth, "cisterns, wells":– Beeroth [6]

882 בְּאֵרִי **b⁽e⁾'ērî**, n.pr.m. GK: 941 [→ 875]. Beeri, "[my] cistern, well":– Beeri [2]

883 בְּאֵר לַחַי רֹאִי **b⁽e⁾'ēr laḥay rō'î**, n.pr.loc. GK: 936 [→ 875+3807.1+2421]. Beer Lahai Roi, "well that belongs to the Living One seeing me":– well Lahai-roi [2], Beer-lahai-roi [1]

884 בְּאֵר שֶׁבַע **b⁽e⁾'ēr šeba'**, n.pr.loc. GK: 937 [→ 875+7651]. Beersheba, "seventh well":– Beer-sheba [34]

885 בְּאֵרֹת בְּנֵי-יַעֲקָן **b⁽e⁾'ērōt b⁽e⁾nê-ya⁽ᵃqān**, n.pr.loc. GK: 942 [→ 875+1121+3292]. Beeroth Bene-Jaakan, "wells of the sons of Jaakan":–

886 בְּאֵרֹתִי **b⁽e⁾'ērōtî**, a.g. GK: 943 [→ 881; cf. 1307]. Beerothite, "of Beeroth":– Beerothite [4], Beerothites [1]

887 בָּאַשׁ **bā'aš**, v. GK: 944 [→ 889, 891, 890; cf. 888]. [Q] to stink, smell; [N] to become a stench; [H] to make a stench, to cause a bad smell; [Ht] to make oneself a stench:– stank [3], stink [3], made utterly to abhor (+887) [2], abhorred [1], had in abomination [1], loathsome [1], made odious [1], made to be abhorred [1], make to stink [1], stinketh [1], stinking savour [1], stunk [1]

888 בְּאֵשׁ **b⁽e⁾'ēš** (Aram.), v. GK: 10091 [→ 873; cf. 887]. [P] to be distressed:– displeased [1]

889 בְּאֹשׁ **b⁽e⁾'ōš**, n.m. GK: 945 [→ 887]. stench, stink:– stink [1]

890 בָּאְשָׁה **bo'šâ**, n.f. GK: 947 [→ 887]. weeds, a plant of no value, variously identified:– cockle [1]

891 בְּאֻשׁ **b⁽e⁾'uš**, n.[m.]pl. GK: 946 [→ 887]. bad (putrid) fruit, rotten grapes:– wild grapes [2]

892 בָּבָה **bābâ**, n.f. GK: 949 [→ 893?]. apple (of the eye), eyeball, formally, "little child of the eye," a term of endearment:– apple [1]

893 בֵּבַי **bēbay**, n.pr.m. GK: 950 [→ 892?]. Bebai, "child":– Bebai [4]

894 בָּבֶל **bābel**, n.pr.loc. GK: 951 [cf. 3778; cf. 895]. Babel, Babylon, "gate of god[s]; [Ge 11:9] confused":– Babylon [249], Babylon's [8], Babylonians (+1121) [3], Babel [2]

895 בָּבֶל **bābel** (Aram.), n.pr.loc. GK: 10093 [→ 896; cf. 894]. Babylon, "gate of god(s)":– Babylon [25]

896 בָּבְלִי **bāb⁽e⁾lî** (Aram.), a.g. GK: 10094 [→ 895]. Babylonian, from Babylon:– Babylonians [1]

897 בַּג **bag**, var. GK: 952 [cf. 957, 6598?]. plunder, loot, despoiling:–

898 בָּגַד **bāgad**, v. GK: 953 [→ 899, 900, 901]. [Q] to be unfaithful, be faithless; to betray; act treacherously:– dealt treacherously [10], transgressors [8], deal treacherously [6], treacherous [3], deal very treacherously (+898) [2], dealt deceitfully [2], dealt very treacherously (+898) [2], transgressor [2], treacherous dealers [2], deal very treacherously (+899) [2], dealest treacherously [1], dealeth treacherously [1], dealt unfaithfully [1], dealt very treacherously (+899) [1], offend [1], transgressed [1], transgresseth [1], transgress [1], treacherous dealer [1], treacherously [1], unfaithful [1]

899 בֶּגֶד **beged**, n.m. GK: 954 & 955 [→ 898]. clothing, garment, cloak, robe; treachery:– clothes [73], garments [70], garment [37], raiment [12], cloth [9], apparel [4], robes [4], wardrobe [2], clothing [1], deal very treacherously (+898) [1], dealt very treacherously (+898) [1], lap [1], rags [1], vestures [1]

900 בֹּגְדוֹת **bōg⁽e⁾dôt**, n.pl.abst. GK: 956 [→ 898]. treachery:– treacherous [1]

901 בָּגוֹד **bāgôd**, a. GK: 957 [→ 898]. unfaithful, pertaining to being adulterous, with the implication that the actions were deceptive and treacherous:– treacherous [2]

902 בִּגְוַי **bigway**, n.pr.m. GK: 958. Bigvai, "fortunate":– Bigvai [6]

903 בִּגְתָא **bigtā'**, n.pr.m. GK: 960 [→ 904]. Bigtha, "gift of God":– Bigtha [1]

904 בִּגְתָן **bigtān** or בִּגְתָנָא **bigtānā'**, n.pr.m. GK: 961 & 962 [→ 903]. Bigthana, "gift of God":– Bigthana [1], Bigthan [1]

905 בַּד **bad**, n.m. GK: 963 & 964 [→ 909]. part, member, limb; pole, bar; (adv.) alone, apart, only; in addition to:– alone (+3807.1) [39], only (+3807.1) [39], staves [37], beside (+4480+3807.1) [30], besides (+4480+3807.1) [13], apart (+3807.1) [11], by themselves (+3807.1) [6], by themselves (+3807.1+3963.1) [4], beside (+3807.1) [3], branches [3], by himself (+2050.2+3807.1) [3], each a like (+905+871.1) [2], strength (+3807.1) [1], alone (+2050.2+3807.1) [1], bars [1], beside (+5921+3807.1) [1], besides (+3807.1) [1], by himself (+3807.1) [1], by themselves (+2006.1+3807.1) [1], by themselves (+3807.1+5089.1) [1], except (+3807.1) [1], myself (+2967.1) [1]

906 בַּד **bad**, n.[m.] GK: 965 [→ 909]. formally, a "(cut) piece (of a garment)," likely linen of the flax plant:– linen [23]

907 בַּד **bad**, n.m. GK: 966 & 967 [→ 908]. boasting, idle talk; false prophet, with a focus on empty, idle talk:– lies [3], liars [2], parts [1]

908 בָּדָא **bādā'**, v. GK: 968 [→ 907]. [Q] to choose; to make up, devise:– devised [1], feignest [1]

909 בָּדַד **bādad**, v. GK: 969 [→ 905, 906, 910]. [Q] to be alone, isolated:– alone [3]

910 בָּדָד **bādād**, n.m. GK: 970 [→ 909]. alone, by oneself, apart:– alone [6], alone (+3807.1) [1], desolate [1], only (+3807.1) [1], solitarily (+3807.1) [1], solitary [1]

911 בְּדַד **b⁽e⁾dad**, n.pr.m. GK: 971. Bedad, "solitary":– Bedad [2]

912 בְּדְיָה **bēd⁽e⁾yâ**, n.pr.m. GK: 973. Bedeiah, "servant of Yahweh":– Bedeiah [1]

913 בְּדִיל **b⁽e⁾dîl**, n.[m.]. GK: 974 & 975 [→ 914]. tin, an inexpensive metal that could be used as a medium of exchange; impurities, slag, the dross of the smelting process, used as a figure of moral and ceremonial impurities:– tin [5], plummet (+68) [1]

914 בָּדַל **bādal**, v. GK: 976 [→ 913, 915, 3995]. [N] separate oneself, be expelled; [H] to separate, sever completely, distinguish between:– separated [17], separate [7], divide [4], put difference [3], divide asunder [1], divided [2], severed [2], utterly separated (+914) [2], make a difference [1], make a separation [1], sever out [1]

915 בָּדָל **bādāl**, n.[m.]. GK: 977 [→ 914]. piece (of an ear):– piece [1]

916 בְּדֹלַח **b⁽e⁾dōlaḥ**, n.[m.]. GK: 978. aromatic resin; some sources: bdellium-gum (an aromatic, yellowish gum):– bdellium [2]

917 בְּדָן **b⁽e⁾dān**, n.pr.m. GK: 979 [→ 917]. Bedan, "son of judgment":– Bedan [2]

918 בָּדַק **bādaq**, v.den. GK: 980 [→ 919; cf. 1333]. [Q] to repair, mend:– repair [1]

919 בֶּדֶק **bedeq**, n.m. GK: 981 [→ 918]. breach (of a temple or a ship):– breaches [7], calkers (+2388) [2], breach [1]

920 בִּדְקַר **bidqar**, n.pr.m. GK: 982 [→ 1121?+1857?]. Bidkar, "son of Deker [piercing]":– Bidkar [1]

921 בְּדַר **b⁽e⁾dar** (Aram.), v. GK: 10095 [cf. 967, 6340]. [Pa] to scatter:– scatter [1]

922 בֹּהוּ **bōhû**, n.[m.]. GK: 983. emptiness, desolation, a void associated with chaos; "empty and void" is a state of total chaos:– void [1], emptiness [1]

923 בַּהַט **bahaṭ**, n.[m.]. GK: 985. porphyry (or some other precious stone):– red [1]

924 בְּהִילוּ **b⁽e⁾hîlû** (Aram.), n.f. GK: 10096 [→ 927; cf. 926]. hurry, haste; (as adv.) immediately:– haste [1]

925 בָּהִיר **bāhîr**, a. GK: 986 [→ 934]. bright, brilliant:– bright [1]

926 בָּהַל **bāhal**, v. GK: 987 [→ 928; cf. 1089; cf. 927, cf. 927]. [N] to be terrified, alarmed, dismayed, bewildered; [P] to make afraid, terrify; to make haste; [Pu] to be hastened, made to hurry; to cause terror; to cause to hurry:– troubled [13], vexed [3], afraid [2], amazed [2], hasty [2], troubleth [2], trouble [2], affrighted [1], dismayed [1], gotten hastily [1], hasted [1], hastened [1], hasteth [1], make afraid [1], make haste [1], rash [1], speedily [1], speedy [1], thrust out [1]

927 בְּהַל **b⁽e⁾hal** (Aram.), v. GK: 10097 & 10218 [→ 924; cf. 926]. [Pa] to frighten, terrify; [Htpe] to hurry, be at once; [Htpa] to be frightened:– troubled [6], haste [3], trouble [2]

928 בֶּהָלָה **behālâ**, n.f. GK: 988 [→ 926; cf. 924]. sudden terror; misfortune:– trouble [2], terrors [1], terror [1]

929 בְּהֵמָה **b⁽e⁾hēmâ**, n.f. GK: 989 [→ 930?]. beast, animal, livestock, herds, cattle:– beast [84], cattle [53], beasts [51], beasts (+929+2050.1) [2]

930 בְּהֵמֹות **b⁽e⁾hēmôt**, n.m. GK: 990 [→ 929?]. behemoth; sources variously identify as hippopotamus, crocodile, elephant; the plural form may indicate this is the ultimate creature, a composite description of the strongest attributes of the animal kingdom:– behemoth [1]

931 בֹּהֶן **bōhen**, n.[f.]. GK: 984 & 991 [→ 932?]. thumb, big toe:– great toe [6], thumb [6], thumbs (+3027) [2], great toes [1], thumbs [1]

932 בֹּהֶן *bōhan*, n.pr.m. GK: 992 [→ 931?]. Bohan, "*thumb, big toe*":– Bohan [2]

933 בֹּהַק *bōhaq*, n.m. GK: 993. harmless rash:– freckled spot [1]

934 בַּהֶרֶת *baheret*, n.f. GK: 994 [→ 925]. spot, bright spot (on the skin):– bright spot [9], bright spots [3]

935 בּוֹא *bô'*, v. GK: 995 [→ 872, 3996, 3997, 4126, 8393]. [Q] to come, go; [H] to bring, take; [Ho] to be brought:– come [627], came [621], brought [234], bring [222], go [88], cometh [83], enter [66], went [59], go in [58], went in [53], come in [39], entered [35], came in [31], brought in [25], bring in [23], comest [20], coming [14], goest [12], enter in [11], put [11], entering [10], carried [9], camest [8], come to pass [8], carry [7], entereth [7], get [7], goeth [7], gone [7], bringeth [6], certainly come (+935) [6], going down [6], bringing [5], cometh in [5], coming in [5], entering in [5], goeth in [5], stricken [5], attained [4], came to pass [4], down [4], go down [4], went down [4], go into [3], goeth down [3], apply [3], besieged (+4692+871.1+1886.1) [3], brought to pass [2], broughtest in [2], broughtest [2], come in (+935) [2], come upon [2], comest in [2], cometh surely to pass (+935) [2], doubtless come again (+935) [2], entered in [2], entrance [2], followeth (+310) [2], gat [2], gone in [2], indeed come (+935) [2], led [2], surely come (+935) [2], well stricken [2], abide (+871.1) [1], abideth (+871.1) [1], befell (+5921) [1], bring forth [1], bring to pass [1], bringest [1], bringing in [1], brought into [1], brought up [1], called for [1], came unto [1], came up [1], carried into [1], cause to come [1], cause to enter [1], cause to go down [1], caused to enter [1], cometh to pass [1], departed [1], eaten (+413+7130) [1], eaten up (+413+7130) [1], employ (+4480+6440) [1], enter into [1], entered into [1], entereth into [1], entereth in [1], fallen [1], fetch [1], follow (+310) [1], gave [1], get in [1], go in [1], goest in [1], going [1], gone down [1], granted [1], had (+413) [1], have [1], invade (+871.1) [1], invaded (+871.1) [1], laid [1], lifted [1], mentioned [1], pulled in [1], resort [1], run down [1], runneth [1], send [1], set [1], sold (+4242+871.1) [1], take [1], took in [1], way [1], went forward [1]

בּוּב *bûb*. See 892, 5014.

936 בּוּז *bûz*, v. GK: 996 [→ 937, 938?, 939, 940, 941]. [Q] to despise, scorn, deride:– despiseth [4], despise [4], despised [2], utterly contemned (+936) [2]

937 בּוּז *bûz*, n.m. GK: 997 [→ 936]. contempt:– contempt [7], despised [2], contemptuously [1], shamed [1]

938 בּוּז *bûz*, n.pr.m. GK: 998 [→ 936?]. Buz, "*contempt*":– Buz [3]

939 בּוּזָה *bûzâ*, n.f. GK: 999 [→ 936]. contempt:– despised [1]

940 בּוּזִי *bûzî*, a.g. GK: 1000 [→ 941; cf. 936]. Buzite, "*of Buz*":– Buzite [2]

941 בּוּזִי *bûzî*, n.pr.m. GK: 1001 [→ 940; cf. 936]. Buzi, "*contempt*":– Buzi [1]

942 בַּוַּי *bawway*, n.pr.m. GK: 1002 [cf. 1131]. Bavvai, cf. 1131:– Bavai [1]

943 בּוּךְ *bûk*, v. GK: 1003 [→ 3998]. [N] to wander around, mill about; to be bewildered:– perplexed [2], entangled [1]

944 בּוּל *bûl*, n.[m.]. GK: 1005 & 1006 [→ 8398?]. piece of wood, in context likely referring to a block of wood that has been crafted into an idol; produce, in context produce as a gift or tribute:– food [1], stock [1]

945 בּוּל *bûl*, n.pr. GK: 1004. Bul (month), the eighth month of the Canaanite calendar (modern October-November):– Bul [1]

בּוּם *bûm*. See 1116.

946 בּוּנָה *bûnâ*, n.pr.m. GK: 1007. Bunah:– Bunah [1]

בּוּנִי *bûnî*. See 1138.

947 בּוּס *bûs*, v. GK: 1008 [→ 4001, 8395]. [Q, P] to trample down; loathe; [Htpol] to kick about; [Ho] to be trodden down:– tread down [4], polluted [3], loatheth [1], tread under foot [1], tread under [1], trodden down [1], trodden under feet [1], trodden under foot [1]

948 בּוּץ *bûs*, n.[m.]. GK: 1009 [→ 949?, 1000]. fine linen; white linen:– fine linen [7], white linen [1]

949 בּוֹצֵץ *bôsēs*, n.pr.loc. GK: 1010 [→ 948? *or* 1206?]. Bozez, "*oozing place*":– Bozez [1]

950 בּוּקָה *bûqâ*, n.f. GK: 1011 [→ 4003, 5802?]. pillage, that which is made desolate and emptied:– empty [1]

951 בּוֹקֵר *bôqēr*, n.m.den. GK: 1012 [→ 1241; cf. 1239]. herdsman, usually a shepherd:– herdman [1]

952 בּוּר *bûr*, v. GK: 1013. [Q] to conclude:– declare [1]

953 בּוֹר *bôr*, n.m. GK: 1014 [→ 877; cf. 875, 3565, 6228]. pit, well, cistern; dungeon; a cistern is usually a shaft in the ground, hewn out of soft stone and plastered to hold water:– pit [41], dungeon [11], well [6], cistern [4], wells [3], cisterns [2], dungeon (+1004) [1], dungeon (+1004+1886.1) [1], fountain [1], pits [1]

954 בּוֹשׁ *bôš*, v. GK: 1017 & 1018 [→ 955, 1317, 1322, 4016]. [Q] to be put to shame, be ashamed, be disgraced; [Polal] to be delayed, be long; [Htpolal] to feel ashamed; [H] to bring shame, to cause disgrace, act shamefully:– ashamed [74], confounded [29], at all ashamed (+954) [4], put to shame [3], shamed [2], bringeth to shame [1], delayed [1], done shamefully [1], greatly ashamed (+1322) [1], long [1], maketh ashamed [1], put to confusion [1], shame [1]

955 בּוּשָׁה *bûšâ*, n.f. GK: 1019 [→ 954]. shame:– shame [4]

956 בִּית *bît* (Aram.), v.den. GK: 10102 [→ 1005]. [P] to spend the night:– passed the night [1]

957 בַּז *baz*, n.[m.]. GK: 1020 [→ 4122; cf. 962]. plunder, loot, despoiling:– prey [15], spoil [4], spoiled [2], take a prey (+962) [2], booty [1], take prey (+962) [1]

958 בָּזָא *bāzā'*, v. GK: 1021. [Q] to divide, likely referring to the washing out of rivers by force of the waters:– spoiled [2]

959 בָּזָה *bāzâ*, v. GK: 1022 [→ 960, 963, 964, 5240]. [Q] to despise, scorn, ridicule, show contempt for; [Qp] to be despised; [N] to be despised, be contemptible; [H] to cause to despise:– despised [26], despise [6], despiseth [4], contemptible [3], contemned [1], disdained [1], scorn [1], vile person [1]

960 בָּזֹה *bāzōh*, v.inf. GK: 1022 [→ 959]. inf. of 959: to despise, scorn, ridicule, show contempt for:– despiseth [1]

961 בִּזָּה *bizzâ*, n.f. GK: 1023 [→ 962]. plunder, booty, spoils:– spoil [6], prey [4]

962 בָּזַז *bāzaz*, v. GK: 1024 [→ 957, 961]. [Q] to plunder, loot, carry off spoils; [Qp, N, Pu] to be plundered:– spoiled [5], spoil [5], took for a prey [4], robbed [3], rob [3], take [3], prey [2], take a prey (+957) [2], take the spoil [2], utterly spoiled (+962) [2], caught [1], gathering [1], make a prey [1], prey upon [1], robbers [1], take away [1], take for a prey [1], take prey (+957) [1], taken spoil [1], took away [1], took spoil [1], took [1]

963 בִּזָּיוֹן *bizzāyôn*, n.[m.]. GK: 1025 [→ 964; cf. 959]. disrespect, contempt:– contempt [1]

964 בִּזְיוֹתְיָה *bizyôṯᵉyâ*, n.pr.loc. GK: 1026 [→ 963+3068]. Biziothiah, "*contempt of Yahweh*":– Bizjothjah [1]

965 בָּזָק *bāzāq*, n.[m.]. GK: 1027. flashes of lightning, lightning:– flash of lightning [1]

966 בֶּזֶק *bezeq*, n.pr.loc. GK: 1028 [→ 137]. Bezek, "*scattering, sowing*":– Bezek [1]

967 בָּזַר *bāzar*, v. GK: 1029 [cf. 6340; cf. 921]. [Q] to distribute; [P] to scatter:– scatter [2]

968 בִּזְתָא *bizzᵉṯā'*, n.pr.m. GK: 1030. Biztha, "[perhaps] *eunuch* or *bound*":– Biztha [1]

969 בָּחוֹן *bāḥôn*, n.[m.]. GK: 1031 [→ 974]. tester of metals, assayer:– tower [1]

970 בָּחוּר *bāḥûr*, n.m. GK: 1033 & 1037 [→ 979]. young man, able (fighting) man; bridegroom:– young men [35], young man [5], young [2], choice [1], chosen [1]

בְּחוּרֹת *bᵉḥûrôt*. See 979.

בַּחוּרִים *baḥûrîm*. See 980.

971 בַּחוּן *baḥûn*, n.[m.]. GK: 1032 & 1039 [→ 975]. siege tower, a moveable military engine used to attack a walled city:– towers [1]

972 בָּחִיר *bāḥîr*, n.m. GK: 1040 [→ 977]. chosen one, one preferred or selected by God with an implication of receiving special favor:– chosen [8], elect [4], choose [1]

973 בָּחַל *bāḥal*, v. GK: 1041 & 1042. [Q] to detest, disdain, feel an attitude of loathing; [Pu] to be gotten by greed:– abhorred [1]

974 בָּחַן *bāḥan*, v. GK: 1043 [→ 969, 976]. [Q] to test, try, probe, examine; [Qp, N, Pu] to be tested: to test and learn the genuineness of an object, fig. of assaying a metal to determine its purity or nature:– try [8], proved [6], tried [4], trieth [4], triest [3], examine [1], prove [1], tempt [1], trial [1]

975 בַּחַן *baḥan*, n.[m.]. GK: 1044 [→ 971]. watchtower:– towers [1]

976 בֹּחַן *bōḥan*, n.[m.]. GK: 1046 [→ 974]. tested (stone):– tried [1]

977 בָּחַר *bāḥar*, v. GK: 1034 & 1047 & 1048 [→ 972, 2984, 4004, 4005, 4006]. [Q] to choose, select, desire, prefer; to enter into a covenant; [Qp, N] to be chosen, choice, the best, preferred; [Pu] to be joined:– chosen [78], choose [50], chose [22], choice [6], choose out [3], chooseth [3], choosest [2], chose out [2], acceptable [1], appoint [1], excellent [1], rather [1], require [1]

בָּחוּר *bāḥur*. See 970.

978 בַּחֲרוּמִי *baḥᵃrûmî*, a.g. GK: 1049. Baharumite:– Baharumite [1]

979 בְּחוּרוֹת *bᵉḥûrôt* or בְּחוּרִים *bᵉḥûrîm*, n.f.&m.pl.abst. GK: 1035 & 1036 [→ 970]. youth, as a state of being:– youth [2], young men [1]

980 בַּחוּרִים *baḥûrîm*, n.pr.loc. GK: 1038 [cf. 1273]. Bahurim, "*young men*":– Bahurim [5]

981 בָּטָא *bāṭā'*, v. GK: 1051 [→ 4008]. [Q, P] to speak thoughtlessly, to speak rashly, recklessly:– pronounce [1], pronouncing [1], spake unadvisedly [1], speaketh [1]

982 בָּטַח *bāṭaḥ* or בָּטַה *bāṭah*, v. GK: 1053 & 1054 [→ 20, 983, 985, 987, 986, 4009]. [Q] to trust, rely on, put confidence in; to stumble, fall to the ground; [Qp] to be confident; [H] to lead to believe, make trust:– trust [46], trusted [18], trusteth [14], put trust [9], trustest [6], put confidence [4], secure [4], careless [3], trustedst [3], confident [2], make trust [2], putteth trust [2], bold [1], caused to trust [1], hoped [1], make hope [1], makest to trust [1], sure [1], trusting [1]

983 בֶּטַח *beṭaḥ*, n.[m.]. GK: 1055 [→ 982]. safety, security:– safely (+3807.1) [14], safety [8], carelessly (+3807.1) [3], safely [3], careless [2], safe [2], assurance [1], boldly [1], confidence [1], hope [1], in safety [1], securely (+3807.1) [1], securely [1], surely [1], without care [1]

984 בֶּטַח *beṭaḥ*, n.pr.loc. GK: 1056 [cf. 2880]. Betah, cf. 2875:– Betah [1]

985 בִּטְחָה *biṭḥâ*, n.f. GK: 1057 [→ 982]. trust, confidence:– confidence [1]

986 בִּטָּחוֹן *biṭṭāḥôn*, n.m. GK: 1059 [→ 982]. confidence, hope:– confidence [2], hope [1]

987 בַּטֻּחָה *baṭṭuḥâ*, n.f.pl. GK: 1058 [→ 982]. security, safety:– secure [1]

988 בָּטַל *bāṭal*, v. GK: 1060 [cf. 989]. [Q] to cease (activity):– cease [1]

989 בְּטַל *bᵉṭal* (Aram.), v. GK: 10098 [cf. 988]. [P] to come to a standstill; [Pa] to stop (another):– cause to cease [2], ceased [2], hindered [1], made to cease [1]

990 בֶּטֶן *beṭen*, n.f. GK: 1061. inmost part, viscera: abdomen, belly, stomach, womb; by extension: the inner person, the heart, the seat of emotion, thought, and desire:– womb [31], belly [30], body [8], as soon as born (+4480) [1], within (+871.1) [1], within [1]

991 בֶּטֶן *beṭen*, n.pr.loc. GK: 1062 [cf. 992?]. Beten, "*womb, bowels*":– Beten [1]

992 בָּטְנָה *boṭnâ*, n.[m.]pl. GK: 1063 [cf. 991?, 993?]. pistachio nut:– nuts [1]

993 בְּטֹנִים *bᵉṭōnîm*, n.pr.loc. GK: 1064 [cf. 992?]. Betonim, "*pistachio nuts*":– Betonim [1]

994 בִּי *bî*, pt.entreaty. GK: 1065. O!, please!:– O [11], alas [1]

995 בִּין *bîn*, v. GK: 1067 [→ 996, 998, 2985?, 8394]. [Q] to understand, discern, realize; be prudent; [N] to be discerning, be understanding; [Pol] to care for; to have skill, insight; to instruct, explain; [Htpolel/Htpolal] to look closely, consider with full attention, ponder:– understand [36], understanding [18], consider [17], understood [11], prudent [8], give understanding [5], hath understanding [5], understandeth [5], regard [4], make to understand [3], perceived [3], perceive [3], wise [3], caused to understand [2], consider diligently (+995) [2], considering [2], discern [2], discreet [2], giveth understanding [2], instructed [2], taught [2], understandest [2], attended [1], cause to understand [1], consider perfectly (+998) [1], considered (+413) [1], considereth [1], cunning [1], dealt wisely [1], diligently consider [1], directeth [1], discerned [1], eloquent [1], feel [1], had understanding [1], have understanding [1], having understanding [1], informed [1], instruct [1], intelligence [1], know [1], looketh well [1], make understand [1], mark [1], perceiveth [1], regardest [1], regardeth [1], skilful [1], skill [1], teacher [1], think [1], understand (+3045) [1], viewed [1]

996 בַּיִן *bayin*, subst. & pp. GK: 1068 [→ 1143; cf. 995; cf. 997]. between; separate from; whether … or:– between [194], among [28], betwixt [14], at even (+6153+1886.1) [6], at [6], from [4], in [4], whether [3], among

(+413) [2], with [2], among (+4480) [1], among (+5921) [1], among (+871.1) [1], amongst [1], asunder [1], midst [1], once in [1], out of (+4480) [1], part [5337] [1], spake unto [1], within [1]

997 בֵּין **bên** (Aram.), pp. GK: 10099 [cf. 996]. between, among:– among [1], between [1]

998 בִּינָה **bînâ**, n.f. GK: 1069 [→ 995; cf. 999]. understanding, insight, discernment, good sense, wisdom, usually referring to the wisdom that responds to the Lord and his instruction:– understanding [30], wisdom [2], come to understanding (+3045) [1], consider perfectly (+995) [1], had understanding (+3045) [1], knowledge [1], meaning [1], understand [1]

999 בִּינָה **bînâ** (Aram.), n.f. GK: 10100 [cf. 998]. discernment, insight:– understanding [1]

1000 בֵּיצָה **bêṣâ**, n.f. GK: 1070 [→ 948]. egg:– eggs [6]

1001 בִּירָה **bîrâ** (Aram.), n.f. GK: 10101 [cf. 1002]. citadel, fortress:– palace [1]

1002 בִּירָה **bîrâ**, n.f. GK: 1072 [cf. 1003; cf. 1001]. citadel, fort, palatial structure:– palace [16]

1003 בִּירָנִיָּה **bîrāniyyâ**, n.f. GK: 1073 [cf. 1002]. fortified place:– castles [2]

1004 בַּיִת **bayit**, n.m. GK: 1074 & 1428 [→ 1006, 1055; cf. 1005]. house, home; of royalty: palace; of deity: temple; a specific part of a house: room; place; by extension: household, family, clan, tribe; woven garment:– house [1766], houses [118], household [47], home [25], within (+4480) [14], temple [11], places [9], prison (+5470+1886.1) [8], households [7], place [7], inward (+1886.5) [5], prison (+3608+1886.1) [4], families (+1) [2], families [2], prison (+3608) [2], prison (+3628+1886.1) [2], within (+4480+1886.1) [2], contain [1], court [1], door [1], dungeon (+953) [1], dungeon (+953+1886.1) [1], family [1], hangings [1], homeborn (+3211) [1], inside [1], inward (+4480+1886.1) [1], palace [1], prison (+612+1886.1) [1], prison (+631+1886.1) [1], prison (+6486+1886.1) [1], steward (+834+5921) [1], storehouse (+214) [1], tablets (+5315) [1], ward (+4931) [1], web [1], winterhouse (+2779) [1], within (+1886.1+3807.1) [1], within (+1886.5) [1], within (+4480+3807.1) [1], within (+4480+3807.1) [1], within (+871.1+1886.1) [1], within [1], without (+413+4480) [1]

1005 בַּיִת **bayit** (Aram.), n.m. GK: 10103 [→ 956; cf. 1004]. a place of residence: house, home; residence of royalty: palace; residence of God or a god: temple:– house [42], houses [1]

1006 בַּיִת **bayit**, n.m. GK: 1074 [→ 1004]. same as 1004: Bayit, "house":– Bajith [1]

1007 בֵּית אָוֶן **bêt 'āwen**, n.pr.loc. GK: 1077 [→ 1004+205]. Beth Aven, "house of idolatry":– Beth-aven [7]

1008 בֵּית־אֵל **bêt-'ēl**, n.pr.loc. GK: 1078 [→ 1004+410]. Bethel, "temple [house] of God [El]":– Beth-el [66]

1009 בֵּית אַרְבֵּאל **bêt 'arbē'l**, n.pr.loc. GK: 1079 [→ 1004]. Beth Arbel, "house of Arbel":– Beth-arbel [1]

1010 בֵּית בַּעַל מְעוֹן **bêt ba'al mᵉ'ôn** or בֵּית מְעוֹן **bêt mᵉ'ôn**, n.pr.loc. GK: 1081 & 1110 [→ 1004+1186]. Beth Baal Meon, "house of Baal Meon"; Beth Meon, "house of habitation":– Beth-baal-meon [1], Beth-meon [1]

1011 בֵּית בִּרְאִי **bêt bir'î**, n.pr.loc. GK: 1082 [→ 1004]. Beth Biri, "house of Biri or den of a lioness":– Beth-birei [1]

1012 בֵּית בָּרָה **bêt bārâ**, n.pr.loc. GK: 1083 [→ 1004]. Beth Barah, "house of Barah [the river ford]":– Beth-barah [2]

1013 בֵּית־גָּדֵר **bêt-gādēr**, n.pr.loc. GK: 1084 [→ 1004+1445; cf. 1451]. Beth Gader, "house of Gader or site of a stone hedge":– Beth-gader [1]

1014 בֵּית גָּמוּל **bêt gāmûl**, n.pr.loc. GK: 1085 [→ 1004+1580]. Beth Gamul, "house of recompense":– Beth-gamul [1]

1015 בֵּית דִּבְלָתַיִם **bêt diblātayim**, n.pr.loc. GK: 1086 [→ 1004]. Beth Diblathaim, "house of Diblathaim":– Beth-diblathaim [1]

1016 בֵּית־דָּגוֹן **bêt-dāgôn**, n.pr.loc. GK: 1087 [→ 1004+1712]. Beth Dagon, "temple [house] of Dagon":– Beth-dagon [2]

1017 בֵּית הָאֱלִי **bêt hā'ēlî**, a.g. GK: 1088 [→ 1004+430; cf. 433]. the Bethelite, "of Bethel":– Bethelite [1]

1018 בֵּית הָאֵצֶל **bêt hā'ēṣel**, n.pr.loc. GK: 1089 [→ 1004+1886.1]. Beth Ezel, "house of Ezel or site nearby":– Beth-ezel [1]

1019 בֵּית הַגִּלְגָּל **bêt haggilgāl**, n.pr.loc. GK: 1090 [→ 1004+1886.1+1537]. Beth Gilgal:–

1020 בֵּית הַיְשִׁמוֹת **bêt hayšimôt**, n.pr.loc. GK: 1093 [→ 1004]. Beth Jeshimoth, "house of Jeshimoth or site of desolation":– Beth-jeshimoth [3], Beth-jesimoth [1]

1021 בֵּית הַכֶּרֶם **bêt-hakkerem**, n.pr.loc. GK: 1094 [→ 1004]. Beth Hakkerem, "house of Hakkerem or site of vineyard":– Beth-haccerem [2]

1022 בֵּית הַלַּחְמִי **bêt-hallaḥmî**, a.g. GK: 1095 [→ 1004]. the Bethlehemite, "of Bethlehem":– Beth-lehemite [4]

1023 בֵּית הַמֶּרְחָק **bêt hammerḥāq**, n.pr.loc. GK: 1092 [→ 1004+1886.1+7368]. Beth Hamerhaq:–

1024 בֵּית הַמַּרְכָּבוֹת **bêt-hammarkābôt** or מַרְכָּבוֹת **markābôt**, n.pr.loc. GK: 1096 & 1112 [→ 1004]. Beth Marcaboth, "site [house] of Marcaboth [chariots]":– Beth-marcaboth [2]

1025 בֵּית הָעֵמֶק **bêt hā'ēmeq**, n.pr.loc. GK: 1097 [→ 1004+1886.1+6010]. Beth Emek, "house of Emek or site of the valley":– Beth-emek [1]

1026 בֵּית הָעֲרָבָה **bêt hā'ᵃrābâ**, n.pr.loc. GK: 1098 [→ 1004]. Beth Arabah, "house of Arabah [desert, plain]":– Beth-arabah [3]

1027 בֵּית הָרָם **bêt hārām**, n.pr.loc. GK: 1099 [→ 1004]. Beth Haram:– Beth-aram [1]

1028 בֵּית הָרָן **bêt hārān**, n.pr.loc. GK: 1100 [→ 1004+2039]. Beth Haran, "house of the mountaineer":– Beth-haran [1]

1029 בֵּית הַשִּׁטָּה **bêt haššiṭṭâ**, n.pr.loc. GK: 1101 [→ 1004]. Beth Shittah, "house of Shittah [acacias]":– Beth-shittah [1]

1030 בֵּית־שִׁמְשִׁי **bêt-šimšî**, a.g. GK: 1128 [→ 1004]. of Beth Shemesh:– Beth-shemite [2]

1031 בֵּית חָגְלָה **bêt-ḥoglâ**, n.pr.loc. GK: 1102 [→ 1004+2295]. Beth Hoglah, "house of Hoglah or site of the partridge":– Beth-hoglah [2], Beth-hogla [1]

1032 בֵּית־חוֹרוֹן **bêt-ḥôrôn**, n.pr.loc. GK: 1103 [→ 1004]. Beth Horon, "house of Horon or site of ravine":– Beth-horon [14]

בֵּית חָנָן **bêt ḥānān**. See 358.

1033 בֵּית כָּר **bêt kār**, n.pr.loc. GK: 1105 [→ 1004]. Beth Car, "site [house] of a lamb":– Beth-car [1]

1034 בֵּית לְבָאוֹת **bêt lᵉbā'ôt**, n.pr.loc. GK: 1106 [→ 1004+3822]. Beth Lebaoth, "house of Lebaoth or den of the lioness":– Beth-lebaoth [1]

1035 בֵּית לֶחֶם **bêt leḥem**, n.pr.loc. GK: 1107 [→ 1004+3899]. Bethlehem, "house of bread; [poss.] temple [house] of Lakhmu":– Beth-lehem [31], Beth-lehem-judah (+3063) [10]

1036 בֵּית לְעַפְרָה **bêt lᵉ'aprâ**, n.pr.loc. GK: 1108 [→ 1004]. Beth Ophrah, "house of Ophrah or house of dust":– house of Aphrah [1]

1037 בֵּית מִלּוֹא **bêt millô'**, n.pr.loc. GK: 1109 [→ 1004+4390]. Beth Millo, "house of Millo or site of earth fill":–

1038 בֵּית מַעֲכָה **bêt ma'ᵃkâ**, n.pr.loc. GK: 1111 [→ 1004+4601]. Beth Maacah:– Beth-maachah [2]

1039 בֵּית נִמְרָה **bêt nimrâ**, n.pr.loc. GK: 1113 [→ 1004+5247]. Beth Nimrah, "house of Nimrah [spotted leopard]; house of a basin of clear, limpid water":– Beth-nimrah [2]

1040 בֵּית עֵדֶן **bêt 'eden**, n.pr.loc. GK: 1114 [→ 1004+5729]. Beth Eden, "house of Eden; garden place":–

1041 בֵּית־עַזְמָוֶת **bêt-'azmāwet**, n.pr.loc. GK: 1115 [→ 1004+5820]. Beth Azmaveth, "strong of death; house of Azmaveth [camel fodder]":– Beth-azmaveth [1]

1042 בֵּית־עֲנוֹת **bêt-'ᵃnôt**, n.pr.loc. GK: 1116 [→ 1004+6067]. Beth Anoth, "house of Anath [plural]":– Beth-anoth [1]

1043 בֵּית־עֲנָת **bêt-'ᵃnāt**, n.pr.loc. GK: 1117 [→ 1004+6067]. Beth Anath, "house of Anath":– Beth-anath [3]

1044 בֵּית־עֵקֶד **bêt-'ēqed**, n.pr.loc. GK: 1118 [→ 1004]. Beth Eked:– shearing [2]

1045 בֵּית עַשְׁתָּרוֹת **bêt 'aštārôt**, n.pr.loc.?. GK: 1119 [→ 1004+6252]. Beth Ashtaroth, "temple of the Ashtoreths":–

1046 בֵּית פֶּלֶט **bêt pelet**, n.pr.loc. GK: 1120 [→ 1004+6404]. Beth Pelet, "house of Pelet [escape]":– Beth-palet [1], Beth-phelet [1]

1047 בֵּית פְּעוֹר **bêt pᵉ'ôr**, n.pr.loc. GK: 1121 [→ 1004+6465]. Beth Peor, "house of Peor":– Beth-peor [4]

1048 בֵּית פַּצֵּץ **bêt paṣṣēṣ**, n.pr.loc. GK: 1122 [→ 1004]. Beth Pazzez:– Beth-pazzez [1]

1049 בֵּית־צוּר **bêt-ṣûr**, n.pr.loc. GK: 1123 [→ 1004+6697]. Beth Zur, "cliff house":– Beth-zur [4]

1050 בֵּית־רְחוֹב **bêt-rᵉḥôb**, n.pr.loc. GK: 1124 [→ 1004+7339]. Beth Rehob, "house of Rehob [main street, market]":– Beth-rehob [2]

1051 בֵּית רָפָא **bêt rāpā'**, n.pr.loc.?. GK: 1125 [→ 1004+7495]. Beth Rapha, "house of Rapha [healing]":– Beth-rapha [1]

1052 בֵּית־שְׁאָן **bêt-šᵉ'ān**, n.pr.loc. GK: 1126 [→ 1004]. Beth Shan, "site [house] of Shan [repose]":– Beth-shean [6], Beth-shan [3]

1053 בֵּית שֶׁמֶשׁ **bêt šemeš**, n.pr.loc. GK: 1127 [→ 1004+8121]. Beth Shemesh, "temple [house] of Shemesh":– Beth-shemesh [21]

1054 בֵּית־תַּפּוּחַ **bêt-tappûaḥ**, n.pr.loc. GK: 1130 [→ 1004+8598]. Beth Tappuah, "house of Tappuah [apricot; apple]":– Beth-tappuah [1]

1055 בִּיתָן **bîtān**, n.[m.]. GK: 1131 [→ 1004]. dwelling place, of royalty: palace, with a possible focus on the inner parts of the palace complex:– palace [3]

1056 בָּכָא **bākā'**, n.[m.]. GK: 1133 [→ 1058]. Baca, "balsam tree or weeping":– Baca [1]

1057 בָּכָא **bākā'**, n.[m.]. GK: 1132 [→ 1058]. balsam tree; some sources: baka-shrub:– mulberry trees [1]

1058 בָּכָה **bākâ**, v. GK: 1134 [→ 1057, 1056, 1059, 1065, 1068; cf. 1066]. [Q] to weep, wail, cry, sob, mourn; [P] to weep for, mourn for; this can refer to ritual mourning as well as personal sorrow:– wept [51], weep [26], weeping [8], bewail [3], weepeth [3], wept sore (+1065+1419) [3], mourned [2], weep at all (+1058) [2], weep more (+1058) [2], weep sore (+1058) [2], weepeth sore (+1058) [2], wept sore (+1058) [2], bewail (+5921) [1], bewailed [1], complain [1], made lamentation [1], tears [1], weepest [1], wept sore (+1059) [1], wept sore (+1065) [1]

1059 בֶּכֶה **bekeh**, n.[m.]. GK: 1135 [→ 1058]. weeping:– wept sore (+1058) [1]

1060 בְּכוֹר **bᵉkôr**, n.m. GK: 1147 [→ 1069]. firstborn, first male offspring (human or animal), the oldest son, with associative meanings of honor, status, prominence, and privileges of inheritance to the firstborn; by extension: one in a special relationship with God:– firstborn [102], firstling [9], eldest [3], eldest son [2], firstlings [1]

1061 בִּכּוּרִים **bikkûrîm**, n.m. GK: 1137 [→ 1069]. firstfruits, first ripened produce:– firstfruits [14], first ripe [2], firstripe figs [1], hasty fruit [1]

1062 בְּכוֹרָה **bᵉkôrâ**, n.f. GK: 1148 [→ 1069]. birthright, rights of the firstborn:– birthright [9], firstlings [5], firstborn [1]

1063 בִּכּוּרָה **bikkûrâ**, n.f. GK: 1136 [→ 1069, 1073]. same as 1073: early ripened fruit, usually ripening in June (late fruit ripens in August):– firstripe fruit [1], firstripe [1]

1064 בְּכוֹרַת **bᵉkôrat**, n.pr.m. GK: 1138 [→ 1069]. Becorath, "firstborn":– Bechorath [1]

1065 בְּכִי **bᵉkî**, n.m. GK: 1140 [→ 1058]. weeping:– weeping [20], wept sore (+1058+1419) [3], continual weeping (+1065) [2], weep [2], overflowing [1], weep aloud (+5414+6963+871.1) [1], wept sore (+1058) [1]

1066 בֹּכִים **bōkîm**, n.pr.loc. GK: 1141 [cf. 1058]. Bokim, "weepings":– Bochim [2]

1067 בְּכִירָה **bᵉkîrâ**, n.f. GK: 1142 [→ 1069]. first born (daughter):– firstborn [6]

1068 בְּכִית **bᵉkît**, n.f. GK: 1143 [→ 1058]. mourning, weeping:– mourning [1]

1069 בָּכַר **bākar**, v. GK: 1144 [→ 1061, 1063, 1064, 1067, 1070, 1071, 1060, 1062, 1072, 1074, 1076, 1075]. [P] bear early fruit; give the rights of the firstborn; [Pu] make a firstborn (dedication); [H] to bear one's first child:– bring forth new fruit [1], bringeth forth first child [1], firstling [1], make firstborn [1]

1070 בֶּכֶר **bēker**, n.f. GK: 1145 [→ 1071; cf. 1069]. young bull camel:– dromedaries [1]

1071 בֶּכֶר **beker**, n.pr.m. GK: 1146 [→ 1070, 1076, 1075; cf. 1069]. Beker, "young male camel":– Becher [5]

1072 בְּכְרָה **bikrâ**, n.f. GK: 1149 [→ 1069]. young cow-camel (having given birth to her first calf):– dromedary [1]

בְּכְרָה **bᵉkôrâ**. See 1062.

1073 בִּכּוּרָה **bikkûrâ**, n.f. GK: 1136 [→ 1063]. same as 1063: early ripened fruit, usually ripening in June (late fruit ripens in August):– first ripe [1]

1074 בֹּכְרוּ **bôkᵉrû**, n.pr.m. GK: 1150 [→ 1069]. Bokeru, "his first born":– Bocheru [2]

1075 בִּכְרִי **bikrî**, n.pr.m. or a.g. GK: 1152 [→ 1071; cf. 1069]. Bicri, "firstborn":– Bichri [8]

1076 בַּכְרִי **bakrî**, a.g. GK: 1151 [→ 1071; cf. 1069]. Bekerite, "of Beker":– Bachrites [1]

1077 בַּל **bal**, adv. GK: 1153 [→ 61, 1107; cf. 1086]. no, not, cannot, never:– not [52], nor (+2050.1) [3], no [3], cannot [2], neither (+2050.1) [2], lest [1], never (+5331+3807.1) [1], never (+5769+3807.1) [1], none [1], nothing (+4100) [1], nothing [1]

1078 בֵּל **bēl**, n.pr.m. GK: 1155 [→ 1112, 1085, 1095, 1114]. Bel, "Bel":– Bel [3]

1079 בַּל **bāl** (Aram.), n.[m.]. GK: 10104. heart, mind:– heart [1]

1080 בְּלָה **bᵉlâ** (Aram.), v. GK: 10106 [cf. 1086]. [Pa] to oppress, wear down:– wear out [1]

1081 בַּלְאֲדָן **balᵃdān**, n.pr.m. GK: 1156 [→ 4757]. Baladan:– Baladan [2]

1082 בָּלַג **bālag**, v. GK: 1158 [→ 1083, 1084]. [H] to flash (with a focus on suddenness); by extension: to smile, rejoice, gleam, have a cheerful attitude:– comfort [1], recover strength [1], strengtheneth [1], take comfort [1]

1083 בִּלְגָּה **bilgâ**, n.pr.m. GK: 1159 [→ 1082]. Bilgah, "gleam, smile":– Bilgah [3]

1084 בִּלְגַּי **bilgay**, n.pr.m. GK: 1160 [→ 1082]. Bilgai, "gleam, smile":– Bilgai [1]

1085 בִּלְדַּד **bildad**, n.pr.m. GK: 1161 [→ 1078?+1730]. Bildad, "Bel has loved":– Bildad [5]

1086 בָּלָה **bālâ**, v. GK: 1162 [→ 61, 1077, 1087, 1094, 1097, 1107, 1115, 8399; cf. 1080]. [Q] to wear out, waste away; [P] to enjoy, use to the full; to decay; to grow old; to oppress:– waxed old [4], wax old [3], waxen old [2], become old [1], consumeth [1], consume [1], long enjoy [1], made old [1], waste [1]

1087 בָּלֶה **bāleh**, a. GK: 1165 [→ 1086]. old, worn-out:– old [5]

1088 בָּלָה **bālâ**, n.pr.loc. GK: 1163 [cf. 1090]. Balah, "old, worn out":– Balah [1]

1089 בָּלַה **bālah**, v. GK: 1164 [→ 1090?, 1091?, 926.]. [P] to be troubled:–

1090 בִּלְהָה **bilhâ**, n.pr.f. & loc. GK: 1167 & 1168 [→ 1089?, 1172; cf. 1088]. Bilhah:– Bilhah [11]

1091 בַּלָּהָה **ballāhâ**, n.f. GK: 1166 [→ 1089]. sudden terror, horrible end; in some contexts a horrible end refers to death:– terrors [6], terror [3], trouble [1]

1092 בִּלְהָן **bilhān**, n.pr.m. GK: 1169. Bilhan, "foolish":– Bilhan [4]

1093 בְּלוֹ **bᵉlô** (Aram.), n.[m.]. GK: 10107. tribute, tax:– tribute [3]

1094 בְּלוֹי **bᵉlôy**, n.[m.]. GK: 1170 [→ 1086]. old, worn-out (things):– old [3]

1095 בֵּלְטְשַׁאצַּר **bēlᵉṭša'ṣṣar**, n.pr.m. GK: 1171 [→ 1078; cf. 1096]. Belteshazzar, "protect his life":– Belteshazzar [2]

1096 בֵּלְטְשַׁאצַּר **bēlᵉṭša'ṣṣar** (Aram.), n.pr.m. GK: 10108 [cf. 1113; cf. 1095]. Belteshazzar, "protect his life":– Belteshazzar [8]

1097 בְּלִי **bᵉlî**, subst. GK: 1172 [→ 1099, 1100; cf. 1086]. lacking, without; nothing:– not [10], without [9], no [5], without (+4480) [5], lack [3], none [3], none (+4480) [2], unwittingly (+1847+871.1) [2], without (+3807.1) [2], base men (+8034) [1], cannot [1], corruption [1], for want of (+4480) [1], ignorantly (+1847+871.1) [1], never (+5769+3807.1) [1], no (+369) [1], no (+4480) [1], no man [1], none (+376) [1], nothing (+3605) [1], nothing (+4100) [1], so long as endureth (+5704) [1], so that (+834+4480) [1], unawares (+1847+871.1) [1], want [1], without (+3509.1) [1], without (+871.1) [1]

1098 בְּלִיל **bᵉlîl**, n.m. GK: 1173. fodder, mash, fermented matter:– corn [1], fodder [1], provender [1]

1099 בְּלִימָה **bᵉlîmâ**, n.[m.]. GK: 1174 [→ 1097+4100]. nothing:–

1100 בְּלִיַּעַל **bᵉliyya'al**, n.[m.]. GK: 1175 [→ 1097+3276]. wicked one, vile one, evil one, worthless one, transliterated "Belial"; A "son of Belial" or "man of Belial" is a troublemaker and scoundrel:– Belial [16], wicked [5], ungodly men [2], ungodly [2], evil [1], naughty [1]

1101 בָּלַל **bālal**, v. GK: 1176 [→ 7642?, 8397, 8400; cf. 1104?]. [Q] to confuse; give fodder, feed; pour upon; [Qp] to mix (with); [Htpolal] to be thrown about, shaken back and forth:– mingled [37], confound [3], anointed [1], gave provender [1], mixed [1], tempered [1]

1102 בָּלַם **bālam**, v. GK: 1178. [Q] to be controlled, in check:– held in [1]

1103 בָּלַס **bālas**, v.den. GK: 1179. [Q] to nip (scratch open) unripe sycamore-fig fruit, so as to promote ripening and make more palatable:– gatherer [1]

1104 בָּלַע **bāla'**, v. GK: 1180 & 1181 & 1182 [→ 1105, 1106, 1108, 1109, 2991?; cf. 1101?]. [Q] to swallow up; [N] to be swallowed; be befuddled, confused; [P] to swallow up, gulp down, devour, consume; to communicate, spread abroad; confuse, turn away; [Pu] be swallowed up, be devoured; be communicated; to be led astray; [Ht] to be confused thoroughly:– swallowed up [17], swallow up [11], destroy [7], devoured [2], devoureth [2], swallow down [2], at wit's end (+2451+3605) [2], covered [1], destroyed [1], destroying [1], eateth up [1], spendeth up [1], swallowed down [1], swallowed [1]

1105 בֶּלַע **bela'**, n.[m.]. GK: 1183 & 1184 [→ 1104]. what is swallowed; harmful, with a likely focus on destruction, fig. of what is greedily swallowed up:– devouring [1], swallowed up [1]

1106 בֶּלַע **bela'**, n.pr.m. & loc. GK: 1185 & 1186 [→ 1104]. Bela, "swallower, devourer":– Bela [13], Belah [1]

1107 בִּלְעֲדֵי **bal'ᵃdê**, adv. GK: 1187 [→ 1077+5704]. apart from, except for, besides:– beside (+4480) [3], save (+4480) [3], without (+4480) [3], besides (+4480) [2], not [2], besides [1], else beside (+4480+5750) [1], save [1], without [1]

1108 בִּלְעִי **bal'î**, a.g. GK: 1188 [→ 1104]. Belaite, "of Bela":– Belaites [1]

1109 בִּלְעָם **bil'ām** or בִּלְעָם **bil'ām**, n.pr.m. & loc. GK: 1189 & 1190 [→ 1104]. Balaam, "[poss.] Baal [lord] of the people; [poss.] the clan brings forth; devourer, glutton"; Bileam, "[gift] brought to the people":– Balaam [57], Balaam's [3], Bileam [1]

1110 בָּלַק **bālaq**, v. GK: 1191 [→ 1111]. [Q] to devastate; [Pu] to be stripped, devastated:– maketh waste [1], waste [1]

1111 בָּלָק **bālāq**, n.pr.m. GK: 1192 [→ 1110]. Balak, "devastator":– Balak [42], Balak's [1]

1112 בֵּלְאשַׁצַּר **bēl'ša'ṣṣar**, n.pr.m. GK: 1157 [→ 1078; cf. 1113]. Belshazzar, "Bel protect the king":– Belshazzar [1]

1113 בֵּלְאשַׁצַּר **bēl'ša'ṣṣar** (Aram.), n.pr.m. GK: 10105 & 10109 [cf. 1112]. Belshazzar, "Bel protect the king":– Belshazzar [7]

1114 בִּלְשָׁן **bilšān**, n.pr.m. GK: 1193 [→ 1078]. Bilshan, "their Bel [lord]":– Bilshan [2]

1115 בִּלְתִּי **biltî**, subst. & adv. & pp. GK: 1194 [→ 1086]. no, not, without; except for; besides:– not [56], none [10], no [6], beside [3], nothing [3], save [3], without [3], except [2], from (+3807.1) [2], lest (+3807.1) [2], none (+376) [2], nor (+2050.1+3807.1) [2], not (+3807.1) [2], but (+518) [1], but [1], cannot [1], continual (+5627) [1], except (+518) [1], lest that (+3807.1) [1], neither (+2050.1) [1], neither [1], no (+3605) [1], no (+3807.1) [1], no more [1], nothing else (+369) [1], that no more (+3807.1) [1], that not (+3807.1) [1], unsatiable (+7654) [1], without (+3807.1) [1]

1116 בָּמָה **bāmâ**, n.f. GK: 1195 [→ 173?, 1117, 1120]. high place, worship shrine (an elevated place, often artificial, for the worship of a god); heights:– high places [83], high place [18], heights [1], waves [1]

1117 בָּמָה **bāmâ**, n.pr.loc. GK: 1196 [→ 1116]. Bamah, "high place":– Bamah [1]

1118 בִּמְהָל **bimhāl**, n.pr.m. GK: 1197 [→ 1121+4107]. Bimhal, "son of circumcision":– Bimhal [1]

1119 בְּמוֹ **bᵉmô**, pp. GK: 1198 [→ 871.1]. by, with, in:– in [2], with [2], for [1], into [1], privily (+652) [1], through [1]

1120 בָּמוֹת **bāmôt** or בָּמֹת בַּעַל **bāmōt ba'al**, n.pr.loc. GK: 1199 & 1200 [→ 1116+1167]. Bamoth, "high places [for cultic worship]", Bamoth Baal, "high places for Baal [worship]":– Bamoth [2], Bamoth-baal [1]

1121 בֵּן **bēn**, n.m. GK: 1201 [→ 1122, 1150; cf. 1129, 1248; cf. 1247 (also used with compound proper names)]. son, child (of either gender), descendant (in any generation), offspring (human or animal); by extension: a term of endearment; one of a class or kind or nation or family. A "son of man" is a "human being" (Nu 23:9), a term that often assumes messianic significance (Ps 8):– son [1906], children [1543], sons [1030], old [135], young [52], first year (+8141) [42], son's [21], sons' [21], men [17], Ammonites (+5983) [15], children's [15], child [10], first [9], strangers (+5236) [6], people (+5971) [5], sons' (+3807.1) [5], stranger (+5236) [5], Assyrians (+804) [4], valiant (+2428) [4], Babylonians (+894) [3], age [3], bullock (+1241) [3], Beno [2], calf (+1241) [2], calves (+6509) [2], fruitful bough (+6509) [2], hostages (+8594) [2], in a night (+3915) [2], lambs (+6629) [2], man (+120) [2], man [2], men (+120) [2], nephews (+1121) [2], ones [2], surely die (+4194) [2], whelps [2], young ones [2], Ahohite (+266) [1], Benjamite (+376+3227) [1], Benjamite [1], Egyptians (+4714) [1], Gileadites (+1569) [1], Grecians (+3125) [1], Hachmonite (+2453) [1], Levites (+3878) [1], Muth-labben (+4192+1886.1+3807.1) [1], afflicted (+6040) [1], appointed to death (+8546) [1], appointed to destruction (+2475) [1], appointed to die (+8546) [1], arrow (+7198) [1], arrows' [1], born [1], branch [1], breed [1], calves (+1241) [1], children (+3807.1) [1], children's (+3807.1) [1], colts [1], colt [1], common [1], corn [1], father's [1], foal [1], high's (+376) [1], kids (+5795) [1], low's (+120) [1], meet for the war (+2428) [1], men (+376) [1], men of high degree (+376) [1], men of low degree (+120) [1], mighty (+410) [1], one born [1], one [1], people [1], rebels (+4805) [1], robbers (+6530) [1], soldiers [1], sparks (+7565) [1], steward (+4943) [1], stranger's (+5236) [1], strong (+2428) [1], them's [1], valiantest (+2428) [1], very fruitful (+8081) [1], worthy to die (+4194) [1], worthy [1], youths [1]

1122 בֵּן **bēn**, n.pr.m. GK: 1202 [→ 1121]. Ben:– Ben [1]

1123 בֵּן **bēn** (Aram.), n.m. GK: 10110. a direct descendant, human or animal, male or of either gender: son, child; a distant descendant: grandson, grandchild, descendant; fig., one of a class or kind:– children [6], sons [3], captives (+1547) [1], young [1]

1124 בְּנָה **bᵉnâ** (Aram.), v. GK: 10111 [→ 1147; cf. 1129]. [P] to build, construct, rebuild; [Pp] to be built; [Htpe] to be constructed, be rebuilt:– builded [10], build [7], building [3], built [1], make [1]

1125 בֶּן־אֲבִינָדָב **ben-'ᵃbînādāb**, n.pr.m. GK: 1203 [→ 1121+1+5068]. Ben-Abinadab, "son of Abinadab":–

1126 בֶּן־אוֹנִי **ben-'ônî**, n.pr.m. GK: 1204 [→ 1121+205]. Ben-Oni, "son of my sorrow":– Ben-oni [1]

1127 בֶּן־גֶּבֶר **ben-geber**, n.pr.m. GK: 1205 [→ 1121+1397]. Ben-Geber, "son of strength":–

1128 בֶּן־דֶּקֶר **ben-deqer**, n.pr.[loc.?]. GK: 1206 [→ 1121+1856]. Ben-Deker, "son of Deker [pierces]":–

1129 בָּנָה **bānâ**, v. GK: 1215 [→ 1131, 1137, 1138, 1140, 1146, 4011, 8403; cf. 1121, 1323; cf. 1124 (also used with compound proper names)]. [Q] to make, build, rebuild, establish; [Qp, N] to be built, established:– built [152], build [132], builded [35], building [13], builders [10], build up [7], buildeth [7], buildest [3], built up [3], made [3], in building [2], repaired [2], surely built (+1129) [2], buildedst [1], have children [1], obtain children [1]

1130 בֶּן־הֲדַד **ben-hᵃdad**, n.pr.m. GK: 1207 [→ 1121+1908]. Ben-Hadad, "son of Hadad":– Ben-hadad [25]

1131 בִּנּוּי **binnûy**, n.pr.m. GK: 1218 [→ 1129; cf. 942]. Binnui, "son":– Binnui [7]

1132 בֶּן־זוֹחֵת **ben-zôḥēt**, n.pr.m. GK: 1209 [→ 1121+2105]. Ben-Zoheth, "son of Zoheth":– Ben-zoheth [1]

1133 בֶּן־חוּר **ben-ḥûr**, n.pr.m. GK: 1210 [→ 1121+2354]. Ben-Hur, "son of Hur":–

1134 בֶּן־חַיִל **ben-ḥayil**, n.pr.m. GK: 1211 [→ 1121+2428]. Ben-Hail, "son of strength":– Ben-hail [1]

1135 בֶּן־חָנָן **ben-ḥānān**, n.pr.m. GK: 1212 [→ 1121+2605]. Ben-Hanan, "son of grace":– Ben-hanan [1]

1136 בֶּן־חֶסֶד **ben-ḥesed**, n.pr.m. GK: 1213 [→ 1121+2617]. Ben-Hesed, "son of Hesed [loyal love]":–

1137 בָּנִי **bānî**, n.pr.m. GK: 1220 [→ 1129]. Bani, "descendant":– Bani [15]

1138 בֻּנִּי **bunnî**, n.pr.m. GK: 1221 [→ 1129]. Bunni:– Bunni [3]

1139 בְּנֵי־בְרַק **bᵉnê-bᵉraq**, n.pr.loc. GK: 1222 [→ 1121]. Bene Berak, "sons of Barak [lightning]":– Bene-berak [1]

1140 בִּנְיָה *binyâ*, n.f. GK: 1224 [→ 1129]. building, physical structure:– building [1]

1141 בְּנָיָה or בְּנָיָהוּ *bᵉnāyâ* or *bᵉnāyāhû*, n.pr.m. GK: 1225 & 1226 [→ 1129+3068]. Benaiah, "*Yahweh has built*":– Benaiah [42]

1142 בְּנֵי יַעֲקָן *bᵉnê yaʿqān*, n.pr.loc. GK: 1223. Bene Jaakan, "[poss.] *son of Jaakan*":– Bene-jaakan [2]

1143 בֵּנַיִם *bēnayim*, subst.[du.]. GK: 1227 [→ 996]. champion, single fighter:– champion (+376+1886.1) [2]

1144 בִּנְיָמִין or בֶּן־יָמִין *binyāmîn*, n.pr.m. GK: 1228 [→ 1145, 3227]. Benjamin, "*son of [the] right hand; southerner*":– Benjamin [158], Benjamin's [4], Benjamites [4]

1145 בֶּן־יְמִינִי or בְּנֵי־יְמִינִי *ben-yᵉmînî*, a.g. GK: 1229 [→ 1030]. Benjamite, of Benjamin, "*of Benjamin*":– Benjamite [5], Benjamites [3]

1146 בִּנְיָן *binyān*, n.m. GK: 1230 [→ 1129; cf. 1147]. building, structure; outer wall:– building [7]

1147 בִּנְיָן *binyān* (Aram.), n.[m.]. GK: 10112 [→ 1124; cf. 1146]. building:– building [1]

1148 בְּנִינוּ *bᵉnînû*, n.pr.m. GK: 1231 [→ 1121]. Beninu, "*our son*":– Beninu [1]

1149 בְּנַס *bᵉnas* (Aram.), v. GK: 10113. [P] to become angry:– angry [1]

1150 בִּנְעָא *binʿāʾ*, n.pr.m. GK: 1232 [→ 1121]. Binea:– Binea [2]

1151 בֶּן־עַמִּי *ben-ʿammî*, n.pr.m. GK: 1214 [→ 1121+5971+2967.1]. Ben-Ammi, "*son of my people*":– Ben-ammi [1]

1152 בְּסוֹדְיָה *bᵉsôdᵉyâ*, n.pr.m. GK: 1233 [→ 871.1+5475+3068; cf. 1153?]. Besodeiah, "*in secret council of Yahweh*":– Besodeiah [1]

1153 בֵּסַי *bēsay*, n.pr.m. GK: 1234 [cf. 1152?]. Besai, "*in secret council of Yahweh*":– Besai [2]

1154 בֶּסֶר *beser*, n.m. GK: 1235 [→ 1155]. unripe grapes, sour grapes:– unripe grape [1]

1155 בֹּסֶר *bōser*, n.m. GK: 1235 [→ 1154]. unripe grapes, sour grapes:– sour grape [3], sour grapes [1]

1156 בְּעָה *bᵉʿâ* (Aram.), v. GK: 10114 [→ 1159; cf. 1158]. [P] to ask for, request; when petitioning deity: pray for, plead for:– sought [3], ask [2], desired [2], asked [1], desire [1], maketh petition (+1159) [1], praying [1], requested [1]

1157 בְּעַד *bᵉʿad*, subst.pp. GK: 1237. behind; through, over; around; from; on behalf of, for (benefit of):– for [61], upon [9], about [7], through [7], at [4], within (+4480) [3], by means of [1], by [1], concerneth [1], in [1], out at [1], over [1], sealeth up (+2856) [1], to [1]

1158 בָּעָה or בָּעָא *bāʿâ* or *bāʿāʾ*, v. GK: 1239 & 1240 [cf. 1156]. [Q] to ask, inquire; to boil; [N] to be pillaged; other sources searched out, with an implication that what is found would be taken and so ransacked; to bulge, to be swollen:– inquire [2], causeth to boil [1], sought up [1], swelling out [1]

1159 בָּעוּ *bāʿû* (Aram.), n.f. GK: 10115 [→ 1156]. prayer, petition, request:– maketh petition (+1156) [1], petition [1]

1160 בְּעוֹר *bᵉʿôr*, n.pr.m. GK: 1242. Beor, "[perhaps] *a burning*":– Beor [10]

1161 בִּעֻתוּת *biʿût*, n.m.pl. GK: 1243 [→ 1204]. terror:– terrors [2]

1162 בֹּעַז *bōʿaz*, n.pr.m. GK: 1244 & 1245. Boaz, "[prob.] *in him is strength*":– Boaz [24]

1163 בָּעַט *bāʿaṭ*, v. GK: 1246. [Q] to kick (in scorn):– kicked [1], kick [1]

1164 בְּעִי *bᵉʿî*, n.[m.]. GK: 1247 [→ 871.1+5856]. ?:–

1165 בְּעִיר *bᵉʿîr*, n.m. GK: 1248 [→ 1197, 1198]. animals, livestock, cattle:– beasts [3], cattle [2], beast [1]

1166 בָּעַל *bāʿal*, v. GK: 1241 & 1249. [Q] to rule over; to marry, be a husband; [Qp, N] to be married, have a husband; (ptcp.) Beulah:– married [6], husband [3], Beulah [1], dominion [1], had dominion over [1], married wife [1], marrieth [1], marry [1], wife [1]

1167 בַּעַל *baʿal*, n.m. GK: 1251 [→ 1168, 1172, 1191, 4810; cf. 1166; cf. 1169 (also used with compound proper names)]. Baal (pagan god), "*master, owner, lord*"; husband, master, owner, citizen; used in many phrases to indicate mastery of an object: "lord of arrows" is a master archer; "lord of dreams" is an interpreter of dreams, etc.:– men [20], owner [10], husband [9], man [4], owners [4], having [2], him that hath [2], husbands [2], lords [2], master [2], adversary (+4941) [1], archers (+2671) [1], babbler (+3956+1886.1) [1], bird (+3671) [1], captain [1], chief man [1], confederate (+1285) [1], creditor (+3027+4874) [1], dreamer (+2472+1886.1) [1], furious (+2534) [1], had [1], him that is great [1], horsemen (+6571) [1], man's [1], married (+802) [1], master [376] [1], master's [1], masters [1], person [1], sworn (+7621) [1], that which hath [1], them that have [1], them to whom is due [1], theyˢ [1], those that are given to [1]

1168 בַּעַל *baʿal*, n.pr.m. GK: 1252 [→ 1167]. Baal, "*master, owner, lord*":– Baal [62], Baalim [18], Baal's [1]

1169 בְּעֵל *bᵉʿēl* (Aram.), n.m. GK: 10116 [cf. 1167]. master, lord; with 2941: "lord of the decree" is "commanding officer":– chancellor (+2942) [3]

1170 בַּעַל בְּרִית *baʿal bᵉrît*, n.pr. GK: 1253 [→ 1167+1285]. Baal-Berith, "*Baal [lord] of the covenant*":– Baal-berith [2]

1171 בַּעַל גָּד *baʿal gād*, n.pr.loc. GK: 1254 [→ 1167+1410]. Baal Gad, "*lord [Baal] of good luck*":– Baal-gad [3]

1172 בַּעֲלָה *baʿᵃlâ*, n.f. GK: 1266 [→ 1090, 1173?, 1175; cf. 1167]. mistress (of sorceries); (female) owner:– hath [2], mistress [2]

1173 בַּעֲלָה *baʿᵃlâ*, n.pr.loc. GK: 1267 [→ 1172?]. Baalah, "[fem. of Baal] *lady*":– Baalah [5]

1174 בַּעַל הָמוֹן *baʿal hāmôn*, n.pr.loc. GK: 1255 [→ 1167+1995]. Baal Hamon, "*lord [Baal] of Hamon* or *possessor of abundance*":– Baal-hamon [1]

1175 בְּעָלוֹת *bᵉʿālôt*, n.pr.loc. GK: 1268 [→ 1172]. Bealoth, "[fem. pl. of Baal] *lady*":– Aloth [1], Bealoth [1]

1176 בַּעַל זְבוּב *baʿal zᵉbûb*, n.pr. GK: 1256 [→ 1167+2070]. Baal-Zebub, "*Baal [lord] of the flies*":– Baal-zebub [4]

1177 בַּעַל חָנָן *baʿal ḥānān*, n.pr.m. GK: 1257 [→ 1167+2605]. Baal-Hanan, "*lord [Baal] is gracious*":– Baal-hanan [5]

1178 בַּעַל חָצוֹר *baʿal ḥāṣôr*, n.pr.loc. GK: 1258 [→ 1167+2691]. Baal Hazor, "*lord [Baal] of Hazor*":– Baal-hazor [1]

1179 בַּעַל חֶרְמוֹן *baʿal ḥermôn*, n.pr.loc. GK: 1259 [→ 1167+2768]. Baal Hermon, "*lord [Baal] of Hermon*":– Baal-hermon [2]

1180 בַּעֲלִי *baʿᵃlî*, n.m. GK: 1251 + 3276 [→ 1167+2967.1]. my husband; my Baal (1167 + 2967.1); translated as a proper name in the KJV: Baali:– Baali [1]

1181 בַּעֲלֵי בָמוֹת *baʿᵃlê bāmôt*, n.pr.loc. GK: 1251 + 1195 [→ 1167+1116]. lords of the high places (1167 + 1116):–

1182 בַּעַלְיָדָע *baʿalyādāʿ*, n.pr.m. GK: 1269 [→ 1167+3045]. Beeliada, "*the lord [Baal] knows*":– Beeliada [1]

1183 בְּעַלְיָה *bᵉʿalyâ*, n.pr.m. GK: 1270 [→ 1167+3045+3068]. Bealiah, "*Yahweh is Lord*":– Bealiah [1]

1184 בַּעֲלֵי יְהוּדָה *baʿᵃlê yᵉhûdâ*, n.pr.loc. GK: 1251 + 3373 [→ 1167+3063]. Baale of Judah (1167 + 3063):– Baale of Judah [1]

1185 בַּעֲלִיס *baʿᵃlîs*, n.pr.m. GK: 1271. Baalis, "[poss.] *son of delight* or *Baals*":– Baalis [1]

1186 בַּעַל מְעוֹן *baʿal mᵉʿôn*, n.pr.loc. GK: 1260 [→ 1167+4583?]. Baal Meon:– Baal-meon [3]

1187 בַּעַל פְּעוֹר *baʿal pᵉʿôr*, n.pr.m. GK: 1261 [→ 1167+6465]. Baal Peor, "*lord [Baal] of Peor*":– Baal-peor [6]

1188 בַּעַל־פְּרָצִים *baʿal-pᵉrāṣîm*, n.pr.loc. GK: 1262 [→ 1167+6556]. Baal Perazim, "*lord [Baal] of making a breech, breaking through*":– Baal-perazim [4]

1189 בַּעַל צְפֹן *baʿal ṣᵉpōn*, n.pr.loc. GK: 1263 [→ 1167+6828]. Baal Zephon, "*lord [Baal] of the north*":– Baal-zephon [3]

1190 בַּעַל שָׁלִשָׁה *baʿal šālišâ*, n.pr.loc. GK: 1264 [→ 1167+8031]. Baal Shalishah:– Baal-shalisha [1]

1191 בַּעֲלָת *baʿᵃlāt*, n.pr.loc. GK: 1272 [→ 1167]. Baalath, "*lady, goddess* [fem. of Baal]":– Baalath [3]

1192 בַּעֲלַת בְּאֵר *baʿᵃlat bᵉʾēr*, n.pr.loc. GK: 1273 [→ 1167+875]. Baalath Beer, "*lord [Baal] of the well*":– Baalath-beer [1]

1193 בַּעַל תָּמָר *baʿal tāmār*, n.pr.loc. GK: 1265 [→ 1167+8558]. Baal Tamar, "*lord [Baal] of the palm tree*":– Baal-tamar [1]

1194 בְּעֹן *bᵉʿōn*, n.pr.loc. GK: 1274. Beon:– Beon [1]

1195 בַּעֲנָא *baʿᵃnāʾ*, n.pr.m. GK: 1275 [→ 1196]. Baana, "*son of affliction*":– Baana [2], Baanah [1]

1196 בַּעֲנָה *baʿᵃnâ*, n.pr.m. GK: 1276 [→ 1195]. Baanah, "*son of affliction*":– Baanah [9]

1197 בָּעַר *bāʿar*, v. GK: 1277 & 1278 & 1279 [→ 1165, 1199, 1200, 8404]. [Q] to burn; to be senseless, to be brutal; [N] to be purged; to behave senselessly; [P] to light a fire, set a blaze; to purge, remove, get rid of; [Pu] to be burning; [Ht] to start a fire, consume with fire; [H] to graze:– burn [19], put away [13], kindled [9], brutish [7], burned [6], burning [6], burnt [6], burneth [4], kindle [4], take away [4], burnt up [2], eaten up [2], taken away [2], brought away [1], cause to be eaten [1], eaten [1], feed [1], heated [1], set on fire [1], set [1], taketh away [1], took out [1], wasted [1]

1198 בַּעַר *baʿar*, n.m. GK: 1280 [→ 1165]. senselessness, stupidity, ignorance, comparable to an animal:– brutish [3], brutish person [1], foolish [1]

1199 בַּעֲרָא *baʿᵃrāʾ*, n.pr.f. GK: 1281 [→ 1200; cf. 1197]. Baara, "*passionate [burning] one*":– Baara [1]

1200 בְּעֵרָה *bᵉʿērâ*, n.f. GK: 1282 [→ 1199; cf. 1197]. fire:– fire [1]

1201 בַּעְשָׁא *baʿšāʾ*, n.pr.m. GK: 1284. Baasha, "*boldness*":– Baasha [28]

1202 בַּעֲשֵׂיָה *baʿᵃśêyâ*, n.pr.m. GK: 1283. Baaseiah, "*the LORD is bold*":– Baaseiah [1]

1203 בְּעֶשְׁתְּרָה *bᵉʿeštᵉrâ*, n.pr.loc. GK: 1285 [cf. 6252?]. Be Eshtarah:– Beeshterah [1]

1204 בָּעַת *bāʿat*, v. GK: 1286 [→ 1205, 1161]. [N] to be afraid; [P] to torment, terrify, overwhelm:– make afraid [5], afraid [3], made afraid [1], terrify [1], terrifiest [1], troubled [1], troubleth [1]

1205 בְּעָתָה *bᵉʿātâ*, n.f. GK: 1287 [→ 1204]. terror:– trouble [2]

1206 בֹץ *bōṣ*, n.[m.]. GK: 1288 [→ 949?, 1207, 8405?]. mud, silt:– mire [1]

1207 בִּצָּה *biṣṣâ*, n.f. GK: 1289 [→ 1206]. marsh, swamp, waterlogged ground:– fens [1], mire [1], miry places [1]

1208 בָּצוּר *bāṣûr*, a. GK: 1290 [→ 1219]. fortified:–

1209 בֵּצַי *bēṣay*, n.pr.m. GK: 1291. Bezai:– Bezai [3]

1210 בָּצִיר *bāṣîr*, n.m. GK: 1292 & 1293 [→ 1219]. grape harvest; grapes; vineyard; dense, inaccessible (forest):– vintage [8]

1211 בָּצָל *bāṣāl*, n.m. GK: 1294 [→ 1213?]. onion:– onions [1]

1212 בְּצַלְאֵל *bᵉṣalʾēl*, n.pr.m. GK: 1295 [→ 871.1+6738+410]. Bezalel, "*in the shadow of God [El]*":– Bezaleel [9]

1213 בְּצָלוּת or בְּצָלִית *baṣlût* or *baṣlît*, n.pr.m. GK: 1296 & 1297 [→ 1211?]. Bazluth, Bazlith:– Bazlith [1], Bazluth [1]

1214 בָּצַע *bāṣaʿ*, v. GK: 1298 [→ 1215]. [Q] to cut off; to be greedy, make unjust gain; [P] to cut off; to finish; to make unjust gain:– cut off [2], greedy of gain (+1215) [2], coveteth [1], covetous [1], cut [1], finish [1], fulfilled [1], gained [1], get dishonest gain (+1215) [1], given to covetousness (+1215) [1], given [1], greedily gained [1], performed [1], wounded [1]

1215 בֶּצַע *beṣaʿ*, n.m. GK: 1299 [→ 1214]. ill-gotten gain, dishonest gain; cutting off:– covetousness [9], gain [5], profit [3], greedy of gain (+1214) [2], dishonest gain [1], get dishonest gain (+1214) [1], given to covetousness (+1214) [1], lucre [1]

1216 בָּצֵק *bāṣēq*, v. GK: 1301 [→ 1217, 1218]. [Q] to swell, become swollen:– swelled [1], swell [1]

1217 בָּצֵק *bāṣēq*, n.[m.]. GK: 1302 [→ 1216]. dough made of flour, not yet leavened:– dough [4], flour [1]

1218 בָּצְקַת *boṣqat*, n.pr.loc. GK: 1304 [→ 1216]. Bozkath, "*swollen* or *elevated spot*":– Boscath [1], Bozkath [1]

1219 בָּצַר *bāṣar*, v. GK: 1305 & 1306 & 1307 [→ 1208, 1210, 1221, 1223, 1224, 1225, 1226, 4013, 4014]. [Q] to harvest, gather grapes; to humble, break (the spirit); to be impossible, be thwarted; [P] to strengthen, fortify:– fenced [16], defenced [5], fortify [2], gather [2], grapegatherers [2], cut off [1], gathered [1], gatherest grapes [1], grapegatherer [1], mighty [1], restrained [1], strong [1], walled up [1], walled [1], withholden [1]

1220 בֶּצֶר *beṣer*, n.m. GK: 1309 [→ 1222]. same as 1222: gold ore:– defence [1], gold [1]

1221 בֶּצֶר *beṣer*, n.pr.m. & loc. GK: 1310 & 1311 [→ 1219]. Bezer, "*[metallic] ore* or *place of refuge*":– Bezer [5]

1222 בְּצָר *bᵉṣar*, n.[m.]. GK: 1309 [→ 1220]. same as 1220: gold ore:– gold [1]

1223 בָּצְרָה *boṣrâ*, n.f. GK: 1312 [→ 1219]. pen, sheep-fold:– Bozrah [1]

1224 בָּצְרָה *boṣrâ*, n.pr.loc. GK: 1313 [→ 1219]. Bozrah, "*enclosure (for sheep), fortress*":– Bozrah [8]

1225 בִּצָּרוֹן *biṣṣārôn*, n.[m.]. GK: 1315 [→ 1219]. fortress, stronghold:– strong hold [1]

1226 בַּצֹּרֶת *baṣṣārâ* or בַּצֹּרֶת *baṣṣōret*, n.f. GK: 1314 & 1316 [→ 1219]. drought; trouble:– dearth [1], drought [1]

1227 בַּקְבּוּק *baqbûq*, n.pr.m. GK: 1317 [→ 1228]. Bakbuk, "*gurgling (sound coming out of a bottle)*":– Bakbuk [2]

1228 בַּקְבֻּק *baqbuq*, n.[m.]. GK: 1318 [→ 1227, 1229, 1231, 1232]. jar; in some contexts a flask:– bottle [2], cruse [1]

1229 בַּקְבֻּקְיָה *baqbuqyâ*, n.pr.m. GK: 1319 [→ 1228+3068]. Bakbukiah, "*Yahweh pours out*":– Bakbukiah [3]

1230 בַּקְבַּקַּר *baqbaqqar*, n.pr.m. GK: 1320. Bakbakkar, "*investigator*":– Bakbakkar [1]

1231 בֻּקִּי *buqqî*, n.pr.m. GK: 1321 [→ 1228; cf. 1232]. Bukki, "*proved of Yahweh; mouth [gurgle sounds] of Yahweh*":– Bukki [5]

1232 בֻּקִּיָּהוּ *buqqiyyāhû*, n.pr.m. GK: 1322 [→ 1228+3068?; cf. 1231]. Bukkiah, "*proved of Yahweh*":– Bukkiah [2]

1233 בָּקִיעַ *bāqîaʿ*, n.[m.]. GK: 1323 [→ 1234]. breach (in a defense); bits, debris:– breaches [1], clefts [1]

1234 בָּקַע *bāqaʿ*, v. GK: 1324 [→ 1233, 1235, 1237]. [Q] to divide, split, tear open; [N] to be split, burst open; [P] to split open, burst forth; [Pu] to be cracked open, broken through, ripped open; [H] to break through, divide; [Ho] to be broken through; [Ht] to split apart:– rent [7], broken up [5], clave [5], cleave [3], ript up [3], brake [2], cleaveth [2], divided [2], divide [2], hatch [2], brake into [1], break forth [1], break out [1], break through [1], breaketh out [1], broken in pieces [1], clave asunder [1], cleft [1], cutteth out [1], dividing [1], made a breach [1], make a breach [1], ready to burst [1], rent asunder [1], rip up [1], tare [1], tear [1], win [1]

1235 בֶּקַע *beqaʿ*, n.[m.]. GK: 1325 [→ 1234]. beka (half-shekel, one-fifth of an ounce [five or six grams]):– bekah [1], half a shekel [1]

1236 בִּקְעָה *biqʿâ* (Aram.), n.f. GK: 10117 [cf. 1237]. plain, (broad) valley:– plain [1]

1237 בִּקְעָה *biqʿâ*, n.f. GK: 1326 [→ 1234; cf. 1236]. valley, plain:– valley [9], plain [7], valleys [4]

1238 בָּקַק *bāqaq*, v. GK: 1327 & 1328 [cf. 2999?]. [Q] to lay waste, ruin, destroy; to grow abundantly, spread out; [N] to be laid waste; [P] to devastate:– empty [2], utterly emptied (+1238) [2], emptied out [1], emptiers [1], fail [1], make void [1], maketh empty [1]

1239 בָּקַר *bāqar*, v. GK: 1329 [→ 1241, 1242, 1243, 1244; cf. 1240]. [P] to inspect, seek; look after; consider:– inquire [2], seek out [2], make inquiry [1], search [1], seek [1]

1240 בְּקַר *bᵉqar* (Aram.), v. GK: 10118 [cf. 1239]. [Pa] to make a search, inquire; [Htpa] to let a search be made:– search made [4], inquire [1]

1241 בָּקָר *bāqār*, n.m. GK: 1330 [→ 951; cf. 1239]. animal, cow, bull; cattle, oxen, herd:– oxen [75], herds [30], bullock (+6499) [28], herd [14], beeves [7], bullocks (+6499) [5], bullocks [4], bullock (+1121) [3], ox [3], calf (+1121) [2], heifer (+5697) [2], kine [2], bullock [1], bulls [1], calf (+5695) [1], calves (+1121) [1], cattle, cow's [1], great cattle [1], young cow (+5697) [1]

1242 בֹּקֶר *bōqer*, n.m. GK: 1332 [→ 1239]. morning:– morning [178], every morning (+1242+871.1+871.1+1886.1+1886.1) [20], morrow [4], day [3], every morning (+1242+1886.1+1886.1+3807.1+3807.1) [2], to morrow [2], days (+6153) [1], early (+1886.1+3807.1) [1], early (+871.1+1886.1) [1], to morrow (+871.1+1886.1) [1]

1243 בַּקָּרָה *baqqārâ*, n.f.vbl. GK: 1333 [→ 1239]. looking after, caring for:– seeketh out [1]

1244 בִּקֹּרֶת *biqqōret*, n.f. GK: 1334 [→ 1239]. due punishment (after investigation):– scourged [1]

1245 בָּקַשׁ *bāqaš*, v. GK: 1335 [→ 1246]. [P] to seek, search, look for, inquire about; [Pu] be sought, be investigated:– seek [103], sought [48], seeketh [19], require [10], seek after [7], seekest [7], sought for [6], make request [3], required [3], seek out [3], besought [2], asked [1], ask [1], begging [1], desire [1],

get [1], inquired of (+6440) [1], inquired [1], inquirest [1], inquisition was made [1], procureth [1], requested [1], requireth [1], sought after [1], sought out [1]

1246 בַּקָּשָׁה *baqqāšâ*, n.m. GK: 1336 [→ 1245]. request:– request [8]

1247 בַּר *bar* (Aram.), n.m. GK: 10120 [cf. 1248, 1121]. a direct descendant, human or animal, male or of either gender: son, child; a distant descendant: grandson, grandchild, descendant; fig., one of a class or kind:– son [7], old [1]

1248 בַּר *bar*, n.m. GK: 1337 [→ 1302; cf. 1121; cf. 1247]. son (exclusively male in the OT); the phrase translated "Kiss the Son" (Ps 2:12) is an act of homage to a king:– son [4]

1249 בַּר *bar*, a. GK: 1338 [→ 1305]. pure; empty; favorite; radiant, bright:– clean [3], pure [2], choice [1], clear [1]

1250 בַּר *bar*, n.m. GK: 1339 & 1340 [→ 1305; cf. 1257?; cf. 1251]. grain, wheat, that has been cleansed and threshed; wilds, in the open field:– corn [9], wheat [5]

1251 בַּר *bar* (Aram.), n.[m.]. GK: 10119 [cf. 1250]. open field, the wild, an area not populated by people, the place of undomesticated animals:– field [8]

1252 בֹּר *bōr*, n.m. GK: 1341 [→ 1305]. cleanness:– cleanness [4], pureness [1]

1253 בֹּר *bōr*, n.m. GK: 1342 [→ 1305]. soda, potash, lye, used in making soap:– make never so clean (+2141+871.1) [1], purely (+1886.1+3509.1) [1]

1254 בָּרָא *bārāʾ*, v. GK: 1343 & 1344 & 1345 [→ 1256, 1274, 1277, 1278; cf. 4806]. [Q] to create, Creator; [N] to be created; can refers to creating from nothing as well as to reforming existing materials, as in "create in me a pure heart" (Ps 51:10); [P] to cut, cut down, clear (a forest); [H] to fatten:– created [33], create [8], creator [3], choose [2], cut down [2], createth [1], dispatch [1], done [1], made [1], make fat [1], make [1]

1255 בְּרֹאדַךְ־בַּלְאֲדָן *bᵉrōʾdak-balʾᵃdān*, n.pr.m. GK: 1347 [→ 4757]. Berodach-Baladan; cf. 4757:– Berodach-baladan [1]

בְּרָאִי *birʾî*. See 1011.

1256 בְּרָאיָה *bᵉrāʾyâ*, n.pr.m. GK: 1349 [→ 1254+3068]. Beraiah, "*Yahweh has created*":– Beraiah [1]

1257 בַּרְבֻּר *barbur*, n.m.pl. GK: 1350 [cf. 1250?]. fowl, bird (of various species):– fowl [1]

1258 בָּרַד *bārad*, v.den. GK: 1351 [→ 1259]. [Q] to shower hail:– hail [1]

1259 בָּרָד *bārād*, n.m. GK: 1352 [→ 1258]. hail, hailstones:– hail [25], hailstones [2], hailstones (+68) [1], hailstones (+68+1886.1) [1]

1260 בֶּרֶד *bered*, n.pr.m. & loc. GK: 1354 & 1355. Bered, "[poss.] *freezing rain*":– Bered [2]

1261 בָּרֹד *bārōd*, a. GK: 1353. spotted, dappled:– grisled [4]

1262 בָּרָה *bārâ*, v. GK: 1346 & 1356 & 1357 [→ 1267, 1279, 1285]. [Q] to eat; [H] to give to eat, urge to eat:– eat [3], cause to eat [1], choose [1], give [1], meat [1]

1263 בָּרוּךְ *bārûk*, n.pr.m. GK: 1358 [→ 1288]. Baruch, "*be blessed*":– Baruch [26]

1264 בְּרֹמִים *bᵉrōmîm*, n.[m.]. GK: 1394. multicolored, a fabric of two-color webbing:– rich apparel [1]

1265 בְּרוֹשׁ *bᵉrôš*, n.m. GK: 1360 [cf. 1266]. pine tree; some sources: cypress or fir:– fir trees [8], fir [7], fir tree [5]

1266 בְּרוֹת *bᵉrôt*, n.m. GK: 1361 [cf. 1265]. fir tree; some sources: juniper or cypress:– fir [1]

1267 בָּרוּת *bārût*, n.f. GK: 1362 [→ 1262]. food:– meat [1]

1268 בֵּרוֹתָה *bērôtâ* or בֵּרֹתַי *bērōtay*, n.pr.loc. GK: 1363 & 1408. Berothah, Berothai, "*well*":– Berothah [1], Berothai [1]

1269 בִּרְזָוִת *birzāwit* or בִּרְזָיִת *birzāyit*, n.pr.f. GK: 1364 & 1365 [→ 875+2132]. Birzaith, Birzavith, "*well of olive oil*":– Birzavith [1]

1270 בַּרְזֶל *barzel*, n.m. GK: 1366 [→ 1271; cf. 6523]. iron, iron (implements):– iron [73], axe head [1], head [1], smith (+2796) [1]

1271 בַּרְזִלַּי *barzillay*, n.pr.m. GK: 1367 [→ 1270]. Barzillai, "*[made of] iron*":– Barzillai [12]

1272 בָּרַח *bāraḥ*, v. GK: 1368 & 1369 & 1370 [→ 1280, 1281, 4015]. [Q] to flee, run away, escape; [H] to drive out, make flee; [H] to injure; to make impassable:– fled [39], flee [10], flee away [3], would fain flee (+1272) [2], chased [1], chaseth

away [1], drove away [1], fleddest [1], fleeth [1], make flee [1], make haste [1], put to flight [1], ran away [1], reach [1], shoot [1]

בָּרִחַ *bāriaḥ*. See 1281.

1273 בַּרְחֻמִי *barḥumî*, a.g. GK: 1372 [cf. 980]. Barhumite:– Barhumite [1]

1274 בְּרִי *bᵉrî*, a. GK: 1374 [→ 1254, 1277; cf. 4806]. fat, choice, healthy:– fat [1]

1275 בֵּרִי *bērî*, n.pr.m. GK: 1373. Beri, "*wisdom*":– Beri [1]

1276 בֵּרִים *bērîm*, a.g. GK: 1379. Berite:– Berites [1]

1277 בָּרִיא *bārîʾ*, a. GK: 1374 [→ 1274]. fat, choice, healthy:– fat [5], fatfleshed (+1320) [2], rank [2], fatter [1], fed [1], firm [1], plenteous [1]

1278 בְּרִיאָה *bᵉrîʾâ*, n.f. GK: 1375 [→ 1254]. created thing, with a possible implication that it is something new:– new thing [1]

1279 בִּרְיָה *biryâ*, n.f. GK: 1376 [→ 1262]. food; in context it refers to food for sick people:– meat [3]

1280 בְּרִיחַ *bᵉrîaḥ*, n.m. GK: 1378 [→ 1272]. bar, gate bar, crossbar:– bars [36], bar [4], fugitives [1]

1281 בָּרִחַ *bāriaḥ*, a. GK: 1371 [→ 1272]. gliding; fugitive:– crooked [1], nobles [1], piercing [1]

1282 בָּרִיחַ *bārîaḥ*, n.pr.m. GK: 1377. Bariah, "[poss.] *board, bar; fugitive; descendant*":– Bariah [1]

1283 בְּרִיעָה *bᵉrîʿâ*, n.pr.m. GK: 1380 [→ 1284]. Beriah, "*prominent, excellent*":– Beriah [11]

1284 בְּרִיעִי *bᵉrîʿî*, a.g. GK: 1381 [→ 1283]. Beriite, "*of Beriah*":– Beriites [1]

1285 בְּרִית *bᵉrît*, n.f. GK: 1382 [→ 1286, 1170, 1262]. covenant, treaty, compact, agreement, an association between two parties with various responsibilities, benefits, and penalties; "to cut a covenant" is "make a covenant," a figure of the act of ceremonially cutting an animal into two parts, with an implication of serious consequences for not fulfilling the covenant:– covenant [264], league [15], in league [2], confederacy [1], confederate (+1167) [1], confederate [1]

1286 בְּרִית *bᵉrît*, n.pr.[loc.?]. GK: 451 [→ 410+1285]. Berith, "*covenant*":– Berith [1]

1287 בֹּרִית *bōrît*, n.f. GK: 1383 [→ 1305]. soap, made from soap plants or potash:– sope [2]

1288 בָּרַךְ *bārak*, v. GK: 1384 & 1385 [→ 1263, 1290, 1292, 1293, 1000; cf. 1289]. [Q] to kneel down; [P] to bless, pronounce blessings, give praise, give thanks, extol; [Qp, N, Pu] to be blessed, be praised; [Ht] to bless oneself, be blessed; this can mean to speak words invoking divine favor (bless), or speak of the excellence of someone (praise); [H] to make kneel:– blessed [173], bless [112], blesseth [8], salute [4], blessest [3], curse [3], abundantly bless (+1288) [2], altogether blessed (+1288) [2], bless at all (+1288) [2], bless indeed (+1288) [2], blessed altogether (+1288) [2], blessed still (+1288) [2], blessing [2], greatly bless (+1288) [2], congratulate [1], cursed [1], kneeled [1], kneel [1], made to kneel down [1], praised [1], praise [1], saluted [1], thanked [1]

1289 בְּרַךְ *bᵉrak* (Aram.), v. GK: 10121 & 10122 [→ 1291; cf. 1288]. [P] to kneel, an act of reverence to authority, often referring to God; [Pp] to be praised; [Pa] to praise; [Pap] to be praised, to give or receive words of excellence:– blessed [4], kneeled [1]

1290 בֶּרֶךְ *berek*, n.f. GK: 1386 [→ 1288, 1296; cf. 755, cf. 1291]. knee, the "buckling of the knees" means to falter, implying great fear or despair; "to bow the knee" means to be reverent or submissive:– knees [24], knee [1]

1291 בְּרַךְ *bᵉrak* (Aram.), n.[f.]. GK: 10123 [→ 1289; cf. 1290]. knee; "to kneel down on the knees" is to assume a position of reverence or worship:– knees [1]

1292 בָּרַכְאֵל *barakʾēl*, n.pr.m. GK: 1387 [→ 1288+410]. Barakel, "*God [El] blesses*":– Barachel [1]

1293 בְּרָכָה *bᵉrākâ*, n.f. GK: 1388 [→ 1294; cf. 1288]. blessing; gift:– blessing [50], blessings [11], blessed [3], present [3], Berachah [2], liberal [1]

1294 בְּרָכָה *bᵉrākâ*, n.pr.m. & loc. GK: 1389 & 1390 [→ 1293; cf. 1288]. Beracah, "*blessing*":– Berachah [1]

1295 בְּרֵכָה *bᵉrēkâ*, n.pr.m. GK: 1391. (man-made) pool, reservoir:– pool [15], pools [2], fishpools [1]

1296 בֶּרֶכְיָה *berekyâ* or בֶּרֶכְיָהוּ *berekyāhû*, n.pr.m. GK: 1392 & 1393 [→ 1290+3068]. Berekiah, "*Yahweh blesses*":– Berechiah [10], Berachiah [1]

1297 בְּרַם **bᵉram** (Aram.), adv.advers. GK: 10124. but, however, nevertheless:– but [2], yet [2], nevertheless [1]

1298 בֶּרַע **bera'**, n.pr.m. GK: 1396. Bera, "gift":– Bera [1]

1299 בָּרַק **bāraq**, v. GK: 1397. [→ 1300, 1301, 1303]. [Q] to flash lightning:– cast forth lightning (+1300) [1]

1300 בָּרָק **bārāq**, n.m. GK: 1398 [→ 1301, 1303; cf. 1299]. lightning bolt, flash of lightning:– lightnings [9], glittering [4], lightning [4], bright [1], cast forth lightning (+1299) [1], glistering sword [1], glitter [1]

1301 בָּרָק **bārāq**, n.pr.m. GK: 1399 [→ 1300; cf. 1299]. Barak, "lightning":– Barak [13]

1302 בַּרְקוֹס **barqôs**, n.pr.m. GK: 1401 [→ 1248]. Barkos, "son of Kos":– Barkos [2]

1303 בַּרְקָן **barqōn**, n.m.pl. GK: 1402 [→ 1300; cf. 1299]. brier, a thorny plant:– briers [2]

1304 בָּרֶקֶת **bāreqet** or בָּרְקַת **bārᵉqat**, n.f. GK: 1403 & 1404. beryl (a green stone, exact identification uncertain):– carbuncle [3]

1305 בָּרַר **bārar**, v. GK: 1359 & 1405 & 1406 [→ 1249, 1250, 1252, 1253, 1287]. [Q] to purge; [Qp] to be chosen, be choice; to be sharpened, polished, [N] to keep clean, be pure; [P] purify; [H] to cleanse; to sharpen; [Ht] to show oneself pure:– pure [3], choice [2], chosen [2], shew pure [2], cleanse [1], clean [1], clearly [1], make bright [1], manifest [1], polished [1], purge out [1], purge [1], purified [1]

1306 בִּרְשַׁע **birša'**, n.pr.m. GK: 1407. Birsha, "disagreeable in taste":– Birsha [1]

1307 בֵּרֹתִי **bērōtî**, a.g. GK: 1409 [cf. 886]. Berothite, "of Berothai [?]":– Berothite [1]

1308 בְּשׂוֹר **bᵉśôr**, n.pr.loc. GK: 1410. Besor:– Besor [3]

1309 בְּשׂוֹרָה **bᵉśôrâ**, n.f. GK: 1415 [→ 1319]. news, good news:– tidings [4], good tidings [1], reward for tidings [1]

1310 בָּשַׁל **bāšal**, v. GK: 1418 [→ 1311, 4018]. [Q] to ripen; boil; [P] to cook, boil, roast, bake; [Pu] to be cooked, be boiled; [H] ripen:– seethe [9], boil [4], sodden [4], boiled [2], baked [1], bake [1], brought forth ripe [1], ripe [1], roasted [1], roast [1], seething [1], sodden at all (+1311) [1], sod [1]

1311 בָּשֵׁל **bāšēl**, a. GK: 1419 [→ 1310]. cooked, boiled:– sodden at all (+1310) [1], sodden [1]

1312 בִּשְׁלָם **bišlām**, n.pr.m. GK: 1420. Bishlam, "son of Shalom [peace]":– Bishlam [1]

1313 בֶּשֶׂם **bāśām**, n.m. GK: 1411 [→ 1314, 1315, 3005]. same as 1314: spices, perfume, fragrance; this can refer to balsam oil or to perfume in general:– spice [1]

1314 בֹּשֶׂם **bōśem**, n.m. GK: 1411 [→ 1313]. same as 1313: spices, perfume, fragrance; this can refer to balsam oil or to perfume in general:– spices [22], spice [2], sweet odours [2], sweet [2], sweet smell [1]

1315 בָּשְׂמַת **bāśᵉmat**, n.pr.f. GK: 1412 [→ 1313]. Basemath, "fragrant":– Bashemath [6], Basmath [1]

1316 בָּשָׁן **bāšān**, n.pr.loc. GK: 1421 & 1422. Bashan, "fertile stoneless plain":– Bashan [59], Bashan-havoth-jair (+2334) [1]

1317 בָּשְׁנָה **bošnâ**, n.f. GK: 1423 [→ 954]. disgrace, shame:– shame [1]

1318 בָּשַׁס **bāšas**, v. GK: 1424. [Po] to trample:– treading [1]

1319 בָּשַׂר **bāśar**, v. GK: 1413 [→ 1309]. [P] to bring (good) news, proclaim (good) news; [Ht] to hear news:– bringeth good tidings [3], bear tidings [3], shew forth [3], bringest good tidings [2], publish [2], bringest tidings [1], bringeth tidings [1], brought good tidings [1], brought tidings [1], carry tidings [1], messenger [1], preach good tidings unto [1], preached [1], published [1], tidings [1]

1320 בָּשָׂר **bāśār**, n.m. GK: 1414 [cf. 1321]. flesh, the soft tissue mass of any animal; the whole body; particular parts of the body: meat, skin, genitals, etc.; by extension: humankind, living things:– flesh [256], body [2], fatfleshed (+1277) [2], kin [2], leanfleshed (+1851) [2], leanfleshed (+7534) [2], mankind (+376) [1], myself (+2967.1) [1], nakedness (+6172) [1], skin [1], thereofᵉ [1]

1321 בְּשַׂר **bᵉśar** (Aram.), n.m. GK: 10125 [cf. 1320]. flesh (human or creatures):– flesh [3]

בְּשׂוֹרָה **bᵉśōrâ**. See 1309.

1322 בֹּשֶׁת **bōšet**, n.f. GK: 1425 [→ 378; cf. 954]. shame, disgrace, humiliation:– shame [20], confusion [7], ashamed [1], greatly ashamed (+954) [1], shameful thing [1]

1323 בַּת **bat**, n.f. GK: 1426 [→ 1337, 1339, 1340; cf. 1129]. daughter, female child of any generation (granddaughter, etc.); by extension: any female, girl, woman; a term of endearment; fig., outlying village or settlement of a "mother" city):– daughter [280], daughters [245], towns [32], villages [12], owls (+3284) [6], daughter's [3], first [2], owl (+3284) [2], apple (+380) [1], apple [1], branches [1], company [1], first year (+8141) [1], old [1]

1324 בַּת **bat**, n.m. & f. GK: 1427 [cf. 1325]. bath (liquid measure, equal to an ephah, about six gallons [about 22 liters]; some sources: eight to nine gallons):– baths [7], bath [6]

1325 בַּת **bat** (Aram.), n.[m.]. GK: 10126 [cf. 1324]. bath (liquid measure):– baths [2]

1326 בָּתָה **bātâ**, n.f. GK: 1429 [→ 1327?]. wasteland:– waste [1]

1327 בַּתָּה **battâ**, n.f. GK: 1431 [→ 1326?]. steep ravine, face of a cliff:– desolate [1]

1328 בְּתוּאֵל **bᵉtû'êl**, n.pr.m. & loc. GK: 1432 & 1433 [→ 4962+410; cf. 1329?]. Bethuel, "man of God [El]":– Bethuel [10]

1329 בְּתוּל **bᵉtûl**, n.pr.loc. GK: 1434 [cf. 1328?]. Bethul:– Bethul [1]

1330 בְּתוּלָה **bᵉtûlâ**, n.f. GK: 1435 [→ 1331]. virgin, maiden; a marriageable woman who has never had sexual intercourse and still under the authority of her father; (unmarried) young woman:– virgin [24], virgins [14], maid [4], maidens [3], maids [3], maiden [1]

1331 בְּתוּלִים **bᵉtûlîm**, n.f. GK: 1436 [→ 1330]. virginity, proof of virginity, referring to a cloth with blood from a virgin's first sexual encounter:– virginity [8], maid [2]

1332 בִּתְיָה **bityâ**, n.pr.f. GK: 1437. Bithiah, "[poss.] worshiper of Yahweh or queen":– Bithiah [1]

1333 בָּתַק **bātaq**, v. GK: 1438 [cf. 918]. [P] to hack to pieces, slaughter:– thrust through [1]

1334 בָּתַר **bātar**, v. GK: 1439 [→ 1335, 1336, 1338]. [Q, P] to cut in pieces:– divided [2]

1335 בֶּתֶר **beter**, n.m. GK: 1440 [→ 1334]. piece:– parts [2], Bether [1], piece [1]

1336 בֶּתֶר **beter**, n.m. GK: 1441 [→ 1334]. ruggedness, referring to mountains with rugged ravines:–

1337 בַּת־רַבִּים **bat-rabbîm**, n.pr.loc. GK: 1442 [→ 1323+7235]. Bath Rabbim, "daughter of a multitude":– Bath-rabbim [1]

1338 בִּתְרוֹן **bitrôn**, n.[pr.loc.?]. GK: 1443 [→ 1334]. Bithron, "gully":– Bithron [1]

1339 בַּת־שֶׁבַע **bat-šeba'**, n.pr.f. GK: 1444 [→ 1323; cf. 7652]. Bathsheba, "seventh daughter or daughter of an oath":– Bath-sheba [11]

1340 בַּת־שׁוּעַ **bat-šûa'**, n.pr.f. GK: 1445 [→ 1323+7651?]. Bath-Shua:– Bath-shua [1]

1341 גֵּא **gē'**, a. GK: 1447 [→ 1342]. proud, arrogant:– proud [1]

1342 גָּאָה **gā'â**, v. GK: 1448 [→ 1341, 1344, 1343, 1346, 1347, 1348, 1349, 1466]. [Q] to grow tall, be high, to rise up; by extension: to be exalted:– triumphed gloriously (+1342) [4], grow up [1], increaseth [1], risen [1]

1343 גֵּאֶה **gē'eh**, a. GK: 1450 [→ 1342]. proud, arrogant:– proud [8]

1344 גֵּאָה **gē'â**, n.f. GK: 1449 [→ 1342]. pride, arrogance:– pride [1]

1345 גְּאוּאֵל **gᵉ'û'êl**, n.pr.m. GK: 1451 [→ 1341+410]. Geuel, "splendor of God [El]":– Geuel [1]

1346 גַּאֲוָה **ga'ᵃwâ**, n.f. GK: 1452 [→ 1342]. surging; majesty, glory, triumph; pride, arrogance, conceit:– pride [10], excellency [3], haughtiness [2], highness [1], proudly (+871.1) [1], proud [1], swelling [1]

1347 גָּאוֹן **gā'ôn**, n.m. GK: 1454 [→ 1342]. surging (waves), lush (high) thickets; majesty, splendor, glory; pride, arrogance:– pride [19], excellency [10], majesty [7], pomp [5], arrogancy [3], swelling [3], excellent [1], proud [1]

1348 גֵּאוּת **gē'ût**, n.f. GK: 1455 [→ 1342]. surging (sea), rising (smoke); majesty, glory, pride, arrogance:– majesty [2], pride [2], excellent things [1], lifting up [1], proudly (+871.1) [1], raging [1]

1349 גַּאֲיוֹן **ga'ᵃyôn**, n.[m.]. GK: 1456 [→ 1342]. arrogant, proud:– proud [1]

1350 גָּאַל **gā'al**, v. GK: 1453 & 1457 [→ 1353, 3008]. [Q] to redeem, deliver; (n.) avenger; kinsman-redeemer; [Qp] to be redeemed; [N] to be redeemed, redeem oneself; often this redemption is in the context of saving from danger or hostility, as a figure of purchasing a slave or indentured person. A "kinsman-redeemer" purchases a relative from slavery (actual or potential); a "kinsman-avenger" provides justice on behalf of a relative; both concepts are in the image of God as Redeemer:– redeemed [24], redeem [22], redeemer [18], kinsman [7], avenger [6], revenger [6], at all redeem (+1350) [4], do the part of a kinsman [2], in any wise redeem (+1350) [2], near kinsman [2], ransomed [2], deliver [1], do the kinsman's part [1], kinsfolks [1], next kinsmen [1], perform the part of a kinsman [1], purchase [1], redeemeth [1], revengers [1], stain [1]

1351 גָּאַל **gā'al**, v. GK: 1458 [→ 1352; cf. 1602]. [N] to be stained, defiled; [P] to defile; [Pu] to be unclean, defiled; [H/Aphel] to stain; [Ht] to defile oneself:– polluted [7], defile [2], defiled [1], stain [1]

1352 גֹּאַל **gō'al**, n.[m.]. GK: 1459 [→ 1351]. defilement:– defiled [1]

1353 גְּאֻלָּה **gᵉ'ullâ**, n.f. GK: 1460 [→ 1350]. redemption (of a person or object); right of redemption; blood relatives:– redemption [3], price of redemption [2], redeem (+1961) [2], redeemed (+1961) [2], kindred [1], redeem (+4672) [1], redeeming [1], redeem [1], right [1]

1354 גַּב **gab**, n.m. & f. GK: 1461 & 1462 [cf. 1355]. eyebrow; rim (of a wheel); mound, back; defense:– eminent place [3], bodies [2], rings [2], backs [1], back [1], bosses [1], eyebrows (+5869) [1], higher place [1], naves [1]

1355 גַּב **gab** (Aram.), n.[m.]. GK: 10128 [→ 1358?]. the back (body part):– back [1]

1356 גֵּב **gēb**, n.[m.]. GK: 1463 & 1464 [→ 1374; cf. 1358]. ditch; cistern; an architectural structure variously interpreted: beam, rafter, paneling:– full of ditches (+1356) [2], beams [1], pits [1]

1357 גֵּבָה **gēbâ**, n.[m.]. GK: 1466 [→ 1462]. swarm (of locust):– locusts [1]

1358 גֹּב **gōb** (Aram.), n.m. GK: 10129 [→ 1355?; cf. 1356]. den, pit (of lions), often an excavated hole:– den [10]

1359 גּוֹב **gôb**, n.pr.loc. GK: 1570 [→ 1461?]. Gob, "cistern":– Gob [2]

1360 גֶּבֶא **gebe'**, n.m. GK: 1465. cistern; marsh:– marishes [1], pit [1]

1361 גָּבַהּ **gābah**, v. GK: 1467 [→ 1362, 1364, 1363, 1365, 1405, 3011]. [Q] to be tall, tower high; to exalt; to be proud, haughty, arrogant; [H] to make high, grow tall; exalt; the attitude of pride or arrogance is a fig. extension the base meaning of being tall or high is "too high" cannot be understood:– lifted up [6], exalted [5], haughty [5], higher [4], exalt [3], high [2], exalteth [1], height [1], lift up [1], make high [1], mount up [1], on high [1], proud [1], raised up a great height [1], upward [1]

1362 גָּבֵהַּ **gābēah**, a. GK: 1468 [→ 1361]. high, towered; proud, haughty; the attitude of pride or arrogance is a fig. extension the base meaning of being tall or high:– high [2], proud [2]

1363 גֹּבַהּ **gōbah**, n.m. GK: 1470 [→ 1361]. tallness, height; splendor, majesty; pride, haughtiness, conceit; the attitude of pride or arrogance is a fig. extension the base meaning of being tall or high:– height [9], high [3], pride [2], excellency [1], haughty [1], loftiness [1]

1364 גָּבֹהַּ **gābōah**, a. GK: 1469 [→ 1361]. high, tall; proud, haughty; the attitude of pride or arrogance is a fig. extension the base meaning of being tall or high:– high [24], higher [5], exceeding proudly (+1364) [2], lofty [2], haughty [1], height [1], highest [1], proud [1]

1365 גַּבְהוּת **gabhût**, n.f. GK: 1471 [→ 1361]. arrogance:– loftiness [2], lofty [1]

1366 גְּבוּל **gᵉbûl**, n.m. GK: 1473 [→ 1367, 1379]. territory, boundary, border:– border [138], coast [46], coasts [23], borders [20], bound [4], landmark [4], space [2], bounds [1], limit [1], quarters [1]

1367 גְּבוּלָה **gᵉbûlâ**, n.f. GK: 1474 [→ 1366]. boundary stone, border marker:– coasts [5], bounds [2], borders [1], landmarks [1], place [1]

1368 גִּבּוֹר **gibbôr**, a. GK: 1475 [→ 1396; cf. 1401]. mighty one, mighty warrior, special guard:– mighty [133], strong [5], valiant [5], men [4], mighty ones [3], mighties [2], champion [1], chief [1], excel [1], giant [1], man [1], mightiest [1], strongest [1]

1369 גְּבוּרָה gᵉḇûrâ, n.f. GK: 1476 [→ 1396; cf. 1370]. power, strength, might, achievement:– might [27], strength [17], power [8], mighty acts [4], force [1], mastery [1], mighty (+5973) [1], mighty power [1], mighty [1]

1370 גְּבוּרָה gᵉḇûrâ (Aram.), n.f. GK: 10130 [→ 1400; cf. 1369]. power, might, strength:– might [2]

1371 גִּבֵּחַ gibbēaḥ, a. GK: 1477 [→ 1372]. bald forehead:– forehead bald [1]

1372 גַּבַּחַת gabbaḥat, n.f. GK: 1478 [→ 1371]. bald spot on the forehead; bare spot on cloth:– bald forehead [3], without [1]

1373 גַּבַּי gabbay, n.pr.m. GK: 1480. Gabbai, "collector":– Gabbai [1]

1374 גֵּבִים gēḇîm, n.pr.loc. GK: 1481 [→ 1356]. Gebim, "ditches":– Gebim [1]

1375 גָּבִיעַ gāḇîaʿ, n.m. GK: 1483 [→ 1392, 4021?]. cup, (drinking) bowl:– bowls [8], cup [5], pots [1]

1376 גְּבִיר gᵉḇîr, n.m. GK: 1484 [→ 1376; cf. 1396]. lord, master:– lord [2]

1377 גְּבִירָה gᵉḇîrâ, n.f. GK: 1485 [→ 1376; cf. 1396]. mistress (female lord); queen:– queen [6]

1378 גָּבִישׁ gāḇîš, n.m. GK: 1486 [cf. 417]. jasper:– pearls [1]

1379 גָּבַל gāḇal, v.den. GK: 1487 [→ 1366]. [Q] to set up a boundary; [H] to put limits around (a geographical area):– border [2], set bounds about [1], set bounds [1], set [1]

1380 גְּבַל gᵉḇal, n.pr.loc. GK: 1488 [→ 1382]. Gebal, "[poss.] border; hill":– Gebal [1]

1381 גְּבָל gᵉḇāl, n.pr.loc. GK: 1489. Gebal, "[poss.] border; hill":– Gebal [1]

גְּבֻלָה gᵉḇulâ. See 1367.

1382 גִּבְלִי giblî, a.g. GK: 1490 [→ 1380]. Gebalite, "of Gebal":– Giblites [1], stonesquarers [1]

1383 גַּבְלֻת gablut, n.f. GK: 1491 [→ 4020]. braided (gold chain):– at the ends [1], ends [1]

1384 גִּבֵּן gibbēn, a. GK: 1492 [→ 1386; cf. 1385]. hunchbacked:– crookbackt [1]

1385 גְּבִנָה gᵉḇinâ, n.f. GK: 1482 [cf. 1384]. cheese:– cheese [1]

1386 גַּבְנֹן gabnôn, n.[m.]. GK: 1493 [→ 1384]. ruggedness; a many-peaked mountain range with an appearance that suggests wonder and majesty:– high [2]

1387 גֶּבַע geba', n.pr.loc. GK: 1494 [→ 1389]. Geba, "hill":– Geba [13], Gibeah [4], Gaba [2]

1388 גִּבְעָא gib'ā', n.pr.loc. GK: 1495 [→ 1389?]. Gibea, "mound, hill":– Gibea [1]

1389 גִּבְעָה gib'â, n.f. GK: 1496 [→ 1387, 1388?, 1390, 1391, 1394, 1533]. hill, hill top, height:– hills [35], hill [30], little hills [4]

1390 גִּבְעָה gib'â, n.pr.loc. GK: 1497 [→ 1395; cf. 1389]. Gibeah, "mound, hill":– Gibeah [44], Gibeath [1]

1391 גִּבְעוֹן gib'ôn, n.pr.loc. GK: 1500 [→ 1393; cf. 1389]. Gibeon, "mound, hill":– Gibeon [37]

1392 גִּבְעֹל gib'ōl, n.[m.]. GK: 1499 [→ 1375]. bloom:– bolled [1]

1393 גִּבְעוֹנִי gib'ônî, a.g. GK: 1498 [→ 1391; cf. 1389]. Gibeonite, of Gibeon, "of Gibeon":– Gibeonites [6], Gibeonite [2]

1394 גִּבְעַת gib'at, n.pr.loc. GK: 1501 & 1502 [→ 1389]. same as 1390: Gibeath, "mound, hill":–

1395 גִּבְעָתִי gib'ātî, a.g. GK: 1503 [→ 1390]. Gibeathite, "of Gibeah":– Gibeathite [1]

1396 גָּבַר gāḇar, v. GK: 1504 [→ 1368, 1369, 1376, 1377, 1397, 1398, 1399, 1402, 1403, 1404]. [Q] to rise, flood; to be greater, stronger; to prevail, overwhelm; [P] to strengthen; [H] to cause to triumph, confirm (a covenant); [Ht] to show oneself as a victor:– prevailed [9], prevail [5], great [2], strengthen [2], confirm [1], exceeded [1], mighty [1], put to more [1], strengtheneth [1], stronger [1], valiant [1]

1397 גֶּבֶר geber, n.m. GK: 1505 [→ 1127, 1398, 1399, 1403; cf. 1396; cf. 1400]. (strong, young) man; in some contexts an indefinite pronoun: certain ones:– man [53], men [6], man's [2], mighty [2], every one [1], man child [1]

1398 גֶּבֶר geber, n.pr.m. GK: 1506 [→ 1397; cf. 1396]. Geber, "[strong young] man":– Geber [2]

1399 גְּבַר gᵉḇar, n.m. GK: 1505 [→ 1397]. (mighty) man; in some contexts an indefinite pronoun: certain ones:– man [1]

1400 גְּבַר gᵉḇar (Aram.), n.m. GK: 10131 [→ 1370, 1401; cf. 1397]. (mighty) man; in some contexts an indefinite pronoun: certain ones:– men [16], certain [2], man [2], most mighty men (+1401+2429) [1]

1401 גִּבָּר gibbar (Aram.), n.m. GK: 10132 [→ 1400; cf. 1368]. strong man, mighty one:– most mighty men (+1400+2429) [1]

1402 גִּבָּר gibbār, n.pr.m. GK: 1507 [→ 1396]. Gibbar, "[young vigorous] man, hero":– Gibbar [1]

גְּבֻרָה gᵉḇurâ. See 1369.

1403 גַּבְרִיאֵל gabrî'ēl, n.pr.m. GK: 1508 [→ 1397+410]. Gabriel, "[strong] man of God [El]":– Gabriel [2]

1404 גְּבֶרֶת gᵉḇeret, n.f. GK: 1509 [→ 1396]. queen:– mistress [7], lady [2]

1405 גִּבְּתוֹן gibbᵉtôn, n.pr.loc. GK: 1510 [→ 1361]. Gibbethon, "mound, hill":– Gibbethon [6]

1406 גָּג gāg, n.m. GK: 1511. roof, top:– roof [9], housetops [6], top [4], housetop [3], top of house [3], roof of house [2], roofs [2], tops of houses [1]

1407 גַּד gad, n.m. GK: 1512. coriander:– coriander [2]

1408 גַּד gad, n.[m.]. GK: 1513 [→ 1409, 1410, 1426, 1427]. same as 1409: good fortune; (as a pagan god) Fortune:–

1409 גַּד gad, n.[m.]. GK: 1513 [→ 1408]. same as 1408: good fortune; (as a pagan god) Fortune:– troop [2]

1410 גָּד gāḏ, n.pr.m. GK: 1514 [→ 1171, 1425, 1424; cf. 1408]. Gad, "fortune":– Gad [70]

1411 גְּדָבַר gᵉḏāḇar (Aram.), n.m. GK: 10133 [cf. 1490; cf. 1489]. treasurer:– treasurers [2]

1412 גֻּדְגֹּדָה gudgōḏâ, n.pr.loc. GK: 1516. Gudgodah, "cleft":– Gudgodah [2]

1413 גָּדַד gāḏaḏ, v. GK: 1517 & 1518 [→ 1416, 1417, 1418, 1464?; cf. 1414]. [Q] to band together; [Htpolal] to band together against; to cut oneself, slash oneself:– cut [5], assembled by troops [1], gather in troops [1], gather together [1]

1414 גְּדַד gᵉḏaḏ (Aram.), v. GK: 10134 [cf. 1413]. [P] to cut down:– hew down [2]

גְּדֻדָה gᵉḏuḏâ. See 1417.

1415 גָּדָה gāḏâ, n.f. GK: 1519 [→ 1428]. bank (of a river):– banks [4]

גַּדָּה gaddâ. See 2693.

1416 גְּדוּד gᵉḏûḏ, n.m. GK: 1522 [→ 1413]. band of raiders; band of rebels; bandits; troops, divisions:– bands [9], troop [7], band [5], army [4], company [3], troops [3], armies [1], companies [1]

1417 גְּדוּד gᵉḏûḏ, n.m. & f. GK: 1521 [→ 1413]. ridge (of a furrow):– cuttings [1]

1418 גְּדוּדָה gᵉḏûḏâ, n.m. & f. GK: 1523 [→ 1413]. slash, cut (of the skin):– furrows [1]

1419 גָּדוֹל gāḏôl, a. GK: 1524 & 2045 [cf. 1431]. great, large; much, more; this can refer to physical size, quantity, degree, and social status (great king, high priest):– great [412], high [22], greater [20], loud [19], greatest [9], elder [7], mighty [7], eldest [6], more [4], wept sore (+1058+1065) [3], aloud (+6963+871.1) [1], displeased exceedingly (+3415+7451) [1], elder (+4480) [1], exceeding glad (+8055+8057) [1], exceedingly afraid (+3372+3374) [1], exceedingly [1], far [1], feared exceedingly (+3372+3374) [1], great men [1], great multitude [1], greatness [1], grew great [1], grieved exceedingly (+7451+7489) [1], hated exceedingly (+3966+8130+8135) [1], long [1], loud (+6963+871.1) [1], nobles [1], proud [1], very (+3966) [1], very [1]

1420 גְּדוּלָה gᵉḏûllâ, n.f. GK: 1525 [→ 1431]. greatness, majesty, recognition, honor:– greatness [7], great things [3], dignity [1], majesty [1]

1421 גִּדּוּף giddûp or גִּדּוּפָה giddûpâ, n.m. GK: 1526 & 1528 [→ 1442]. taunt, scorn, insult, reviling:– revilings [2], reproaches [1]

1422 גְּדוּפָה gᵉḏûpâ, n.f. GK: 1527 [→ 1442]. taunt, scorn, reviling:– taunt [1]

גְּדוֹר gᵉḏôr. See 1446.

1423 גְּדִי gᵉḏî, n.m. GK: 1531 [→ 1429, 5872]. (male) young goat:– kid (+5795) [7], kid [6], kids [3]

1424 גַּדִּי gaddî, n.pr.m. GK: 1533 [→ 1410]. Gadi, "my fortune":– Gadi [2]

1425 גָּדִי gāḏî, a.g. GK: 1532 [→ 1410]. Gadite, of Gad, "of Gad":– Gadites [14], Gadite [1], Gad [1]

1426 גַּדִּי gaddî, n.pr.m. GK: 1534 [→ 1408]. Gaddi, "my fortune":– Gaddi [1]

1427 גַּדִּיאֵל gaddî'ēl, n.pr.m. GK: 1535 [→ 1408+410]. Gaddiel, "God [El] is my fortune; Gad is [my] God":– Gaddiel [1]

1428 גִּדְיָה gidyâ, n.f. GK: 1536 [→ 1415]. bank (of a river):–

1429 גְּדִיָּה gᵉḏiyyâ, n.f. GK: 1537 [→ 1423]. (female) young goat:– kids [1]

1430 גָּדִישׁ gāḏîš, n.m. GK: 1538 & 1539. shock of grain, sheaf of grain; tomb:– shock of corn [1], shocks [1], stacks of corn [1], tomb [1]

1431 גָּדַל gāḏal, v. GK: 1540 [→ 1419, 1420, 1432, 1433, 1435, 1434?, 1437, 4024, 4026 (also used with compound proper names)]. [Q] to grow up; be great, exalted; [P] to grow long, make great; to exalt, honor, glorify; [Pu] to be well-nurtured; [H] to make great, cause greatness; [Ht] to magnify oneself, show greatness:– magnified [17], great [16], magnify [15], grew [7], brought up [6], grown [5], grown up [4], greater [3], make great [3], waxed great [3], great things [2], grew up [2], made great [2], make greater [2], much set by [2], waxen great [2], advanced [1], became great [1], boasted [1], bring up [1], come to great estate [1], exceeded (+4480) [1], exceeded [1], excellent [1], great giveth [1], great things done [1], grow [1], increased [1], lift up [1], madest grow [1], magnifical [1], nourish up [1], nourished [1], nourishing [1], nourish [1], passed (+4480) [1], promoted [1], promote [1], proudly [1]

1432 גָּדֵל gāḏēl, a.vbl. or v.ptcp. GK: 1541 [→ 1431]. great, powerful:– great [2], grew [1]

1433 גֹּדֶל gōḏel, n.m. GK: 1542 [→ 1431]. greatness, majesty, strength; pride, arrogance:– greatness [11], stoutness [1], stout [1]

1434 גְּדִל gᵉḏil, n.[m.]pl. GK: 1544 [→ 1431?]. tassel, festoon:– fringes [1], wreaths [1]

1435 גִּדֵּל giddēl, n.pr.m. GK: 1543 [→ 1431]. Giddel, "big":– Giddel [4]

גָּדוֹל gāḏôl. See 1419.

גְּדֻלָה gᵉḏullâ. See 1420.

1436 גְּדַלְיָה gᵉḏalyâ or גְּדַלְיָהוּ gᵉḏalyāhû, n.pr.m. GK: 1545 & 1546 [→ 1431+3068]. Gedaliah, "great is Yahweh":– Gedaliah [32]

1437 גִּדַּלְתִּי giddaltî, n.pr.m. GK: 1547 [→ 1431]. Giddalti, "I pronounce [God as] Great; I reared up":– Giddalti [1]

1438 גָּדַע gāḏa', v. GK: 1548 [→ 1439, 1440, 1441]. [Q] to cut short, cut off, break; [P] to cut down, cut to pieces; [Qp, N, Pu] to be cut off, be cut down:– cut down [9], cut off [7], cut asunder [3], cut in sunder [2], hew down [1], hewn down [1]

1439 גִּדְעוֹן gid'ôn, n.pr.m. GK: 1549 [→ 1441; cf. 1438]. Gideon, "one who cuts, hacks":– Gideon [39]

1440 גִּדְעֹם gid'ōm, n.pr.loc. GK: 1550 [→ 1438]. Gidom, "cutting off, stop pursuit":– Gidom [1]

1441 גִּדְעֹנִי gid'ōnî, n.pr.m. GK: 1551 [→ 1439; cf. 1438]. Gideoni, "one who cuts, hacks":– Gideoni [5]

1442 גָּדַף gāḏap, v. GK: 1552 [→ 1421, 1422]. [P] to blaspheme, revile:– blasphemed [5], blasphemeth [1], reproacheth [1]

גִּדֻּף giddup, and גִּדֻּפָה giddupâ. See 1421.

1443 גָּדַר gāḏar, v. GK: 1553 [→ 1446, 1445, 1444, 1447, 1448, 1449, 1450, 1448, 1452, 1453]. [Q] to built a stone wall, heap up stones for a wall:– masons [2], close up [1], fenced up [1], hedged [1], inclosed [1], made up the hedge (+1447) [1], make a wall (+1447) [1], make up the hedge (+1447) [1], repairer [1]

1444 גֶּדֶר geḏer, n.m. GK: 1555 [→ 1443, 1447]. same as 1447: wall, fence, a wall made of loose stones from the field without mortar:– wall [2]

1445 גֶּדֶר geḏer, n.pr.loc. GK: 1554 [→ 1013; cf. 1013, 1443]. Geder, "wall [of stones]":– Geder [1]

1446 גְּדוֹר gᵉḏôr, n.pr.m. & loc. GK: 1529 & 1530 [→ 1443]. Gedor, "wall; pock-marked":– Gedor [7]

1447 גָּדֵר gāḏēr, n.pr.loc. GK: 1555 [→ 1444]. same as 1444: wall, fence, a wall made of loose stones from the field without mortar:– wall [5], fence [1], hedges [1], hedge [1], made up the

hedge (+1443) [1], make a wall (+1443) [1], make up the hedge (+1443) [1], walls [1]

1448 גְּדֵרָה *gᵉdērâ* or גְּדֵרֶה *gᵉderet*, n.f. GK: 1556 & 1560 [→ 1443, 1449, 1450, 1452, 1453; cf. 1443]. wall, pen (for sheep) made of stone walls:– hedges [4], folds [3], sheepcotes (+6629) [1], sheepfolds (+6629) [1], wall [1]

1449 גְּדֵרָה *gᵉdērâ*, n.pr.loc. GK: 1557 [→ 1448; cf. 1443]. Gederah, "*stone pen, sheep corral*":– Gederah [1]

1450 גְּדֵרוֹת *gᵉdērôt*, n.pr.loc. GK: 1558 [→ 1448; cf. 1443]. Gederoth, "*stone pens, sheep corrals*":– Gederoth [2]

1451 גְּדֵרִי *gᵉdērî*, a.g. GK: 1559 [cf. 1013]. Gederite, "*of Geder*":– Gederite [1]

1452 גְּדֵרָתִי *gᵉdērātî*, a.g. GK: 1561 [→ 1448; cf. 1443]. Gederathite, "*of Geder[ath]*":– Gederathite [1]

1453 גְּדֵרֹתָיִם *gᵉdērōtayim*, n.pr.loc. GK: 1562 [→ 1448; cf. 1443]. Gederothaim, "*two stone pens, two sheep corrals*":– Gederothaim [1]

1454 גֶּה *gēh*, var. GK: 1563. var. of 2088: this:– this [1]

1455 גָּהָה *gāhâ*, v. GK: 1564 [→ 1456, 4010]. [Q] to heal:– cure [1]

1456 גֵּהָה *gēhâ*, n.f. GK: 1565 [→ 1455]. healing, cure; that which promotes healing: medicine:– medicine [1]

1457 גָּהַר *gāhar*, v. GK: 1566. [Q] to bow down; stretch out in prostration:– stretched [2], cast down [1]

1458 גַּו *gaw*, n.[m.] GK: 1567 [→ 1460]. back (of the body); "to thrust behind the back" means "to reject:– back [2], backs [1]

1459 גַּו *gaw* (Aram.), n.m. GK: 10135 [cf. 1460]. middle, interior:– midst [10], the same (+1886.9) [1], therein (+871.2+1886.9) [1], wherein (+871.2) [1]

1460 גֵּו *gēw*, n.[m.] GK: 1568 & 1569 [→ 1458, 1465, 1471?, 1472; cf. 1459]. back (of the body); "to walk upon the back" is a sign of conquest and subjugation; "to send sin behind the back" is "to forgive"; among; fellow people, community:– back [5], among [1], body [1]

1461 גּוּב *gûb*, v. GK: 1572 [→ 1359?]. [Q] to dig:–

1462 גּוֹב *gôb* or גֹּבַי *gōbay*, n.m.[col] GK: 1571 & 1479 [→ 1357]. locust, locust swarm:– great grasshoppers (+1462) [2], grasshoppers [1]

1463 גּוֹג *gôg*, n.pr.m. GK: 1573 [→ 1996, 4031]. Gog, "*precious golden object*":– Gog [10]

1464 גּוּד *gûd*, v. GK: 1574 [→ 1413?]. [Q] to attack, invade:– overcome [2], invade with troops [1]

1465 גֵּוָה *gēwâ*, n.f. GK: 1576 [→ 1460]. back (of the body):– body [1]

1466 גֵּוָה *gēwâ*, n.f. GK: 1575 [→ 1342; cf. 1467]. pride, lifting up:– pride [2], lifting up [1]

1467 גֵּוָה *gēwâ* (Aram.), n.f. GK: 10136 [cf. 1466]. pride:– pride [1]

1468 גּוּז *gûz*, v. GK: 1577. [Q] to pass along, pass away:– brought [1], cut off [1]

1469 גּוֹזָל *gôzāl*, n.[m.] GK: 1578. young bird, hatchling:– young pigeon [1], young [1]

1470 גּוֹזָן *gôzān*, n.pr.loc. GK: 1579. Gozan:– Gozan [5]

1471 גּוֹי *gôy*, n.m. GK: 1580 & 1582. people, nation; regularly in the OT, any people in contrast to Israel: the Gentiles, pagan, heathen, uncultured:– nations [265], heathen [143], nation [107], Gentiles [30], people [11], every nation (+1471) [4], another [1]

1472 גְּוִיָּה *gᵉwiyyâ*, n.f. GK: 1581 [→ 1460]. dead body, corpse; carcass:– bodies [5], body [3], carcase [2], corpses [2], dead bodies [1]

1473 גּוֹלָה *gôlâ*, n.f. GK: 1583 [→ 1540; cf. 1547]. exile, captive, people deported to another place:– captivity [26], those carried away [3], carried away captives [2], carried away [2], removing [2], away [1], captives [1], captive [1], carried away captive [1], go into captivity [1], remove [1], them carried away [1]

1474 גּוֹלָן *gôlān*, n.pr.loc. GK: 1584. Golan:– Golan [4]

1475 גּוּמָץ *gûmmāṣ*, n.m. GK: 1585. pit:– pit [1]

1476 גּוּנִי *gûnî*, n.pr.m. GK: 1586 [→ 1477]. Guni, "*spotted sand grouse*":– Guni [4]

1477 גּוּנִי *gûnî*, a.g. GK: 1587 [→ 1476]. Gunite, "*of Guni*":– Gunites [1]

1478 גָּוַע *gāwa'*, v. GK: 1588. [Q] to perish, die, breath one's last:– die [7], gave up the ghost [4], died [3], give up the ghost [2], dead [1], dying [1], given up the ghost [1], giveth up the ghost [1], perished [1], perish [1], ready to die [1], yielded up the ghost [1]

1479 גּוּף *gûp*, v. GK: 1589. [H] to shut (a door):– shut [1]

1480 גּוּפָה *gûpâ*, n.f. GK: 1590 [→ 1610]. dead body, corpse:– bodies [1], body [1]

1481 גּוּר *gûr*, v. GK: 1591 & 1592 & 1593 [→ 1483?, 1616, 1628, 4032, 4033, 4034, 4036; cf. 1624, 1482?, 3025]. [Q] to live as an alien, dwell as a stranger, implying less social rights than a native; to be terrified, be afraid, fear, revere; to attack, stir up; [Htpol] to stay, gather together:– sojourn [31], sojourneth [15], dwell [11], sojourned [11], afraid [6], strangers [6], abide [2], fear [2], gather together [2], surely gather together (+1481) [2], assemble [1], dwelleth [1], feared [1], gathered together [1], gathered [1], inhabitant [1], remain [1], sojourners [1], sojourning [1], stand in awe [1]

1482 גּוּר *gûr*, n.m. GK: 1594 [→ 1484; cf. 1481?]. cub (young of lions, jackals):– whelps [3], whelp [3], young ones [1]

1483 גּוּר *gûr*, n.pr.loc. GK: 1595 [→ 1481?]. Gur:– Gur [1]

1484 גֹּר *gōr*, n.[m.] GK: 1596 [→ 1482]. cub (of lion):– whelps [2]

1485 גּוּר־בַּעַל *gûr-ba'al*, n.pr.loc. GK: 1597 [cf. 3017]. Gur Baal, "*sojourn of Baal*":– Gur-baal [1]

1486 גּוֹרָל *gôrāl*, n.m. GK: 1598. lot, device by which a decision was made, often a pebble, stick, or pottery shard either thrown or blindly pulled from a container; by extension: what is decided by lot, allotment (of land):– lot [61], lots [16]

1487 גּוּשׁ *gûš*, n.[m.] GK: 1599 & 1641. scab, something crusted:– clods [1]

1488 גֵּז *gēz*, n.[m.] GK: 1600 [→ 1494]. fleece, sheared wool; grass mowed:– fleece [2], mowings [1], mown grass [1]

1489 גִּזְבָּר *gizbār*, n.m. GK: 1601 [cf. 1411, cf. 1490]. treasurer:– treasurer [1]

1490 גִּזְבַּר *gizbar* (Aram.), n.m. GK: 10139 [cf. 1411; cf. 1489]. treasurer:– treasurers [1]

1491 גָּזָה *gāzâ*, v. GK: 1602 [→ 1496]. [Q] to bring forth, cut off (the umbilical cord):– took [1]

1492 גִּזָּה *gizzâ*, n.f. GK: 1603 [→ 1494]. wool fleece:– fleece [7]

1493 גִּזוֹנִי *gizônî*, a.g. GK: 1604. Gizonite, "*of Gizon*":– Gizonite [1]

1494 גָּזַז *gāzaz*, v. GK: 1605 [→ 1488, 1492, 1495]. [Q] to shear sheep; to shave one's head (in mourning):– shear [4], shearers [2], sheepshearers [1], cut down [1], cut off [1], poll [1], shaved [1], shearing [1], sheepshearers (+6629) [1]

1495 גָּזֵז *gāzēz*, n.pr.m. GK: 1606 [→ 1494]. Gazez, "[poss.] *sheep shearer*; [poss.] *one born at the time of shearing*":– Gazez [2]

1496 גָּזִית *gāzît*, n.f. GK: 1607 [→ 1491]. dressed stone, stone hewn or cut for masonry:– hewed stones [3], hewn stone [3], hewed stone [1], hewed [1], hewn stones [1], hewn [1], wrought [1]

1497 גָּזַל *gāzal*, v. GK: 1608 [→ 1499, 1498, 1500]. [Q] to rob, seize, snatch, take way; [Qp, N] to be robbed, be forcibly taken from:– spoiled [7], violently taken away [3], rob [2], away [1], caught [1], consume [1], exercised robbery (+1498) [1], pluck off [1], plucked [1], pluckt [1], pluck [1], robbed [1], robbeth [1], spoileth [1], take away from [1], take by force [1], take by violence [1], taken away [1], took violently away (+1500) [1], torn [1], violently take away [1]

1498 גָּזֵל *gāzēl*, n.[m.] GK: 1609 [→ 1500; cf. 1497]. stealing, robbery, implying violence:– robbery [2], exercised robbery (+1497) [1], thing taken away by violence [1]

1499 גֵּזֶל *gēzel*, n.[m.] GK: 1609 [→ 1497]. denial of rights:– violence [1], violent perverting [1]

גֹּזָל *gōzāl*. See 1469.

1500 גְּזֵלָה *gᵉzēlâ*, n.f. GK: 1611 [→ 1498; cf. 1497]. plunder, spoil, stolen things:– violence [3], robbed [1], spoil [1], took violently away (+1497) [1]

1501 גָּזָם *gāzām*, n.m. GK: 1612 [→ 1502, 3697]. locust swarm; some sources: caterpillar or a specific state in the development of a locust:– palmerworm [3]

1502 גַּזָּם *gazzām*, n.pr.m. GK: 1613 [→ 1501]. Gazzam, "*some kind of bird or insect*":– Gazzam [2]

1503 גֶּזַע *geza'*, n.m. GK: 1614. stump, root stock:– stock [2], stem [1]

1504 גָּזַר *gāzar*, v. GK: 1615 & 1616 [→ 1506, 1507?, 1508, 1509, 1511, 4037; cf. 1629; cf. 1505, cf. 1510]. [Q] to cut in two, divide, cut down; decide on; to disappear; to devour, eat, with a possible focus on carving or chewing up food; [N] to be cut off, be excluded:– cut off [6], divide [2], cut down [1], decreed [1], decree [1], divided [1], snatch [1]

1505 גְּזַר *gᵉzar* (Aram.), v. GK: 10140 [→ 1510; cf. 1504]. [P] to determine; (as noun) diviner, astrologer; note that a diviner determines the future through interpretations of omens, such as the movement of the stars (astrologer), or through interpreting the fissures in bodily organs of animals, such as livers; [Htpe] to cut out; [Itpe] to cut out:– soothsayers [4], cut out [2]

1506 גֶּזֶר *gezer*, n.[m.] GK: 1617 [→ 1504]. pieces (something divided and cut up):– parts [1], pieces [1]

1507 גֶּזֶר *gezer*, n.pr.loc. GK: 1618 [→ 1511; cf. 1504?]. Gezer, "[poss.] *pieces*":– Gezer [13], Gazer [2]

1508 גִּזְרָה *gizrâ*, n.f. GK: 1619 [→ 1504]. courtyard; appearance:– separate place [7], polishing [1]

1509 גְּזֵרָה *gᵉzērâ*, n.f. GK: 1620 [→ 1504; cf. 1510]. solitary place, unfertile land:– not inhabited [1]

1510 גְּזֵרָה *gᵉzērâ* (Aram.), n.f. GK: 10141 [→ 1505; cf. 1509]. decree, decision:– decree [2]

1511 גִּזְרִי *gizrî* or גִּרְזִי *girzî*, a.g. GK: 1621 & 1747 [→ 1507; cf. 1504]. Gizrite, Girzite:– Gezrites [1]

גִּיחוֹן *gîḥôn*. See 1521.

1512 גָּחוֹן *gāḥôn*, n.m. GK: 1623 [→ 1518]. belly (of reptile):– belly [2]

גֶּחֲזִי *gēḥᵃzî*. See 1522.

גַּחַל *gaḥol*. See 1513.

1513 גַּחַל *gaḥal* or גַּחֶלֶת *gaḥelet*, n.f. GK: 1624 & 1625. burning coals, hot embers:– coals [11], burning coals [3], coal [2], coals of fire [1], hot coals [1]

1514 גַּחַם *gaḥam*, n.pr.m. GK: 1626. Gaham, "*burning brightly*":– Gaham [1]

1515 גַּחַר *gaḥar*, n.pr.m. GK: 1627. Gahar, "*[born in the] year of little rain*":– Gahar [1]

גּוֹי *gôy*. See 1471.

1516 גַּיְא *gay'*, n.m. & f. GK: 1628 [→ 2798]. valley:– valley [52], valleys [8]

1517 גִּיד *gîd*, n.m. GK: 1630. sinew, tendon:– sinews [4], sinew [3]

1518 גִּיחַ *gîaḥ*, v. GK: 1622 & 1631 [→ 1520, 1521; cf. 1519]. [Q] to burst forth, surge, bring forth (a baby); [H] to charge; to thrash about:– brake forth [1], came forth [1], camest forth [1], draw up [1], labour to bring forth [1], took out [1]

1519 גּוּחַ *gûaḥ* (Aram.), v. GK: 10137 [cf. 1518]. [H] to churn up, stir up (the sea):– strove [1]

1520 גִּיחַ *gîaḥ*, n.pr.loc. GK: 1632 [→ 1518]. Giah, "*bubbling spring*":– Giah [1]

1521 גִּיחוֹן *gîḥôn*, n.pr.loc. GK: 1633 [→ 1518]. Gihon, "*to gush forth*":– Gihon [6]

1522 גֵּיחֲזִי *gêḥᵃzî*, n.pr.m. GK: 1634. Gehazi, "[poss.] *valley of vision*":– Gehazi [12]

1523 גִּיל *gîl*, v. GK: 1635 [→ 26?, 1524, 1525]. [Q] to rejoice, be glad, be joyful, the attitude and action of favorable circumstance, often expressed in shouts and song:– rejoice [23], glad [10], joyful [4], joy [2], rejoiced [2], delight [1], greatly rejoice (+1524) [1], rejoiceth [1]

1524 גִּיל *gîl*, n.[m.] GK: 1636 & 1637 [→ 1523]. gladness, delight, jubilance; age, stage in life:– joy [3], gladness [2], greatly rejoice (+1523) [1], rejoice exceedingly (+413+8056) [1], rejoice [1], rejoicing [1], sort [1]

1525 גִּילָה *gîlâ*, n.f. GK: 1638 [→ 1523]. rejoicing, delight:– joy [1], rejoicing [1]

גִּילֹה *gîlōh*. See 1542.

1526 גִּילֹנִי *gîlōnî*, a.g. GK: 1639 [→ 1542; cf. 1540]. Gilonite, "*of Gilon*":– Gilonite [2]

1527 גִּינַת *gînat*, n.pr.m. GK: 1640. Ginath, "*protector*":– Ginath [2]

1528 גִּיר *gîr* (Aram.), n.[m.] GK: 10142 [cf. 1615]. plaster:– plaister [1]

גֵּיר *gêr*. See 1616.

1529 גֵּישָׁן gêšān, n.pr.m. GK: 1642. Geshan:– Geshan [1]

1530 גַּל gal, n.m. GK: 1643 & 1644 [→ 1554, 1556]. waves, breaker waves, surging waves; fountain; heap, pile (of rocks, rubble):– waves [14], heap [12], heaps [6], Gallim [1], billows [1], spring [1]

1531 גֹּל gōl, n.f.? GK: 1646 [→ 1543]. same as 1543: bowl:– bowl [1]

גֹּלָא geʿlāʾ. See 1541.

1532 גַּלָּב gallāb, n.[m.]. GK: 1647. barber:– barber's [1]

1533 גִּלְבֹּעַ gilbōaʿ, n.pr.loc. GK: 1648 [→ 1389]. Gilboa, "bubbling":– Gilboa [8]

1534 גַּלְגַּל galgal, n.m. GK: 1649 & 1650 [cf. 1556; cf. 1535]. wheel; whirlwind; tumbleweed (a wheel-shaped plant):– wheels [6], wheel [3], heaven [1], rolling thing [1]

1535 גַּלְגַּל galgal (Aram.), n.m. GK: 10143 [→ 1560; cf. 1534, 1536]. wheel:– wheels [1]

1536 גִּלְגָּל gilgāl, n.[m.]. GK: 1651 [→ 1556; cf. 1535]. wheel:– wheel [1]

1537 גִּלְגָּל gilgāl, n.pr.loc. GK: 1652 [→ 1019; cf. 1556]. Gilgal, "circle of stones":– Gilgal [41]

1538 גֻּלְגֹּלֶת gulgōlet, n.f. GK: 1653 [→ 1556]. skull; individual, person:– polls [6], skull [2], every man [1], head [1], man [1], poll [1]

1539 גֶּלֶד gᵉled, n.m. GK: 1654. skin:– skin [1]

1540 גָּלָה gālâ, v. GK: 1655 [→ 1473, 1526, 1546, 1549, 1542; cf. 1541]. [Q] to tell, uncover, reveal; depart, leave, be exiled, banished; [Qp] to be opened, unseal; be made known; [N] to be revealed, be exposed; [P] to reveal, expose (nakedness) = sexual relations; [Pu] to be opened, exiled; [H] to depart, exile:– uncover [22], discovered [18], carried away [17], carried away captive [15], discover [10], revealed [10], uncovered [10], open [6], removed [4], shew (+241) [4], surely go into captivity (+1540) [4], departed [3], gone into captivity [3], opened [3], openeth [2], revealeth [2], carried captive [2], carry away [2], go captive [2], plainly appear (+1540) [2], published [2], remove [2], reveal [2], surely led away captive (+1540) [2], advertise (+241) [1], appeared [1], appeareth [1], bewray [1], brought [1], captives [1], captive [1], captivity [1], carry away captives [1], carry away into captivity [1], carry captive [1], carrying away captive [1], cause to go into captivity [1], caused to be carried away captives [1], caused to be carried away captive [1], caused to be carried away [1], caused to be led into captivity [1], depart [1], disclose [1], discovereth [1], exile [1], go into captivity [1], gone [1], led away captive [1], led captive [1], openly shewed [1], revealed (+241) [1], shamelessly uncovereth (+1540) [1], shewed [1], sheweth [1], sheweth unto (+241) [1], shew [1], told (+241) [1], told in [1], uncovereth [1], went into captivity [1]

1541 גְּלָה gᵉlâ (Aram.), v. GK: 10144 [cf. 1540]. [P] to reveal (mysteries); [Peil] to be revealed (i.e., mysteries); [H] to deport:– revealeth [3], revealed [2], brought over [1], carried away [1], revealer [1], reveal [1]

גֹּלָה gōlâ. See 1473.

1542 גִּלֹה gilōh, n.pr.loc. GK: 1656 [→ 1526; cf. 1540]. Giloh:– Giloh [2]

1543 גֻּלָּה gullâ, n.f. GK: 1657 & 1684 [→ 1531]. spring (of water); bowl-shaped capital (of a pillar):– springs [6], bowls [3], pommels [1], bowl [2]

1544 גִּלּוּלִים gillûlîm, n.m. GK: 1658 [→ 1556]. (pl.) idols:– idols [47], images [1]

1545 גְּלֹם gᵉlōm, n.[m.]. GK: 1659 [→ 1563?]. fabric:– clothes [1]

1546 גָּלוּת gālût, n.f. GK: 1661 [→ 1540; cf. 1547]. exile, captive:– captivity [10], captives [3], carried away captive [2]

1547 גָּלוּ gālû (Aram.), n.f. GK: 10145 [cf. 1546]. exile:– captivity [3], captives (+1123) [1]

1548 גָּלַב gālab, v. GK: 1662. [P] to shave off, cut off; [Pu] be shaved off; [Ht] to have oneself shaven, shave oneself:– shave [7], shaven [5], shave off [4], polled [1], caused to shave off [1], shaved off [1]

1549 גִּלָּיֹון gillāyôn, n.m. GK: 1663 [→ 1540]. scroll (some sources: wooden tablet with a wax cover); mirror:– glasses [1], roll [1]

1550 גָּלִיל gālîl, a. GK: 1664 [→ 1556]. turnable (door); rings; rods:– folding [2], rings [2]

1551 גָּלִיל gālîl, n.pr.loc. GK: 1665 [→ 1552, 1553; cf. 1556]. Galilee, "ring, circle, hence region":– Galilee [6]

1552 גְּלִילָה gᵉlîlâ, n.f. GK: 1666 [→ 1553; cf. 1551]. region, district:– borders [3], coasts [1], country [1]

1553 גְּלִילֹות gᵉlîlôt, n.pr.loc. GK: 1667 [→ 1552]. Geliloth, "region":– Geliloth [1]

1554 גַּלִּים gallîm, n.pr.loc. GK: 1668 [→ 1530; cf. 1556]. Gallim, "heaps":– Gallim [1]

1555 גָּלְיָת golyāt, n.pr.m. GK: 1669. Goliath, "exile":– Goliath [6]

1556 גָּלַל gālal, v. GK: 1670 & 1671 [→ 1530, 1561, 1534, 1536, 1537, 1538, 1544, 1550, 1551, 1552, 1553, 1554, 1557, 1559, 4039; cf. 4038?; cf. 1560]. [Q] to roll down, roll away; to commit, turn over; [N] to be rolled; [P] to roll; [Polal] to be rolled; [Htpol] to roll about, wallow; "to commit, trust" is a figure of rolling care or responsibility onto the Lord:– rolled [4], roll [3], commit [2], remove [1], roll down [1], rolled away [1], rolled together [1], rolleth [1], run down [1], seek occasion [1], trusted [1], wallowed [1]

1557 גָּלָל gālāl, n.[m.]. GK: 1672 [→ 1556]. dung, filth:– dung [1]

1558 גָּלָל gālāl, n.[m.]. GK: 1673. because of, on account of, for the sake of:– because of (+871.1) [4], sake [2], for (+871.1) [1], for sake (+871.1) [1], sakes [1], that for (+871.1) [1]

1559 גָּלָל gālāl, n.pr.m. GK: 1674 [→ 1562; cf. 1556]. Galal, "[poss.] tortoise; roll away":– Galal [3]

1560 גְּלָל gᵉlāl (Aram.), n.[m.]. GK: 10146 [→ 1535, 4040; cf. 1556]. (col.) stone blocks, formally, "stones of rolling" i.e., stones too large to carry:– great [2]

1561 גֵּל gēl, n.m. GK: 1645 [→ 1556]. dung, excrement, used for fuel in some contexts:– dung [4]

1562 גִּלֲלַי gilˊlay, n.pr.m. GK: 1675 [→ 1559]. Gilalai:– Gilalai [1]

1563 גָּלַם gālam, v. GK: 1676 [→ 1545?, 1564]. [Q] to roll up (clothing in a tight ball):– wrapt together [1]

1564 גֹּלֶם gōlem, n.[m.]. GK: 1677 [→ 1563]. unformed body, embryo:– substance yet being unperfect [1]

1565 גַּלְמוּד galmûd, a. GK: 1678. barren, haggard:– desolate [2], solitary [2]

1566 גָּלַע gālaʿ, v. GK: 1679. [Ht] to burst out (in quarrel); to defy:– intermeddleth [1], meddled with [1], meddling [1]

1567 גַּלְעֵד galʿēd, n.pr.loc. GK: 1681. Galeed; "heap of [stones that are a] witness":– Galeed [2]

1568 גִּלְעָד gilʿād, n.pr.loc. [& m.?]. GK: 1680 [→ 1569, 3003, 7433]. Gilead, "[perhaps] monument of stones":– Gilead [100], Gileadites [2], Gilead's [1], Ramoth-gilead [1]

1569 גִּלְעָדִי gilʿādî, a.g. GK: 1682 [→ 1568]. Gileadite, of Gilead:– "of Gilead":– Gileadite [9], Gileadites (+1121) [1], Gileadites [1]

1570 גָּלָשׁ gālāš, v. GK: 1683. [Q] to descend; some sources: to leap, frisk:– appear [2]

1571 גַּם gam, adv. GK: 1685 [cf. 4041]. also, surely, too; and, but, yet, even, moreover:– also [438], yea [55], even [49], and [45], both [30], yet [14], likewise [13], moreover [12], moreover (+2050.1) [10], nor [7], neither (+3808) [6], neither [6], also (+2050.1) [5], neither (+3808+2050.1) [5], likewise (+2050.1) [3], so [3], therefore [3], again [2], and (+2050.1) [2], and also [2], for [2], in like manner [2], in times past (+1571+8032+8543) [2], nay [2], nevertheless (+2050.1) [2], nor (+3808) [2], not [2], yea (+2050.1) [2], alike [1], and so much as [1], and yet [1], any [1], as soon as [1], as [1], both (+2050.1) [1], but (+2050.1) [1], but [1], either [1], except (+3588) [1], further [1], heretofore (+4480+4480+8032+8543) [1], howbeit (+2050.1) [1], in time past (+865+8032) [1], indeed [1], more yea [1], moreover as for [1], neither (+408) [1], neither (+408+2050.1) [1], neither yet (+3808+2050.1) [1], no not [1], nor (+3808+2050.1) [1], or [1], so much as [1], surely [1], then [1], therefore (+2050.1) [1], though [1], together with (+2050.1) [1], what [1], with [1], yet (+2050.1) [1]

1572 גָּמָא gāmāʾ, v. GK: 1686 [→ 1573?]. [P] to eat up, swallow up; [H] to give water (to sip):– drink [1], swalloweth [1]

1573 גֹּמֶא gōmeʾ, n.m. GK: 1687 [→ 1572?]. papyrus:– bulrushes [2], rushes [1], rush [1]

1574 גֹּמֶד gōmed, n.m. GK: 1688 [→ 1575?]. unit of measure: short cubit (the length from the elbow to the knuckles, about 12 to 18 inches):– cubit [1]

1575 גַּמָּדִים gammādîm, n.pr.g. GK: 1689 [→ 1574?]. men of Gammad, "[prob.] valiant men":– Gammadims [1]

1576 גְּמוּל gᵉmûl, n.m. GK: 1691 [→ 1580]. what is done; benefit; what is deserved, recompense:– recompence [10], reward [3], asˢ [1], benefits [1], benefit [1], desert [1], deserving [1], given [1]

1577 גָּמוּל gāmûl, n.pr.m. GK: 1690 [→ 1580]. Gamul, "weaned":– Gamul [1]

1578 גְּמוּלָה gᵉmûlâ, n.f. GK: 1692 [→ 1580]. what is done; retribution, recompense:– deeds [1], recompences [1], reward [1]

1579 גִּמְזֹו gimzô, n.pr.loc. GK: 1693. Gimzo, "place of sycamore trees":– Gimzo [1]

1580 גָּמַל gāmal, v. GK: 1694 [→ 1014, 1577, 1576, 1578, 1581?, 1582, 1583, 8408]. [Q] to do, produce, deal fully; to wean; to repay (what is deserved); [Qp, N] to be weaned:– weaned [9], rewarded [7], bestowed on [2], deal bountifully [2], dealt bountifully [2], did [2], recompense [2], weaned child [2], child weaned [1], doeth good [1], done [1], do [1], requite [1], reward [1], ripening [1], served [1], yielded [1]

1581 גָּמָל gāmāl, n.m. GK: 1695 [→ 1580?]. camel:– camels [45], camel [5], camels' [3], camel's [1]

1582 גְּמַלִּי gᵉmallî, n.pr.m. GK: 1696 [→ 1580]. Gemalli, "my reward":– Gemalli [1]

1583 גַּמְלִיאֵל gamlîʾēl, n.pr.m. GK: 1697 [→ 1580+410]. Gamaliel, "recompense of God [El]":– Gamaliel [5]

1584 גָּמַר gāmar, v. GK: 1698 [→ 1586, 1587; cf. 1585]. [Q] to bring to an end, fail; fulfill:– ceaseth [1], come to an end [1], fail [1], perfect [1], performeth [1]

1585 גְּמַר gᵉmar (Aram.), v. GK: 10147 [cf. 1584]. [Pp] to be finished; (as an introduction in a letter) Greetings:– perfect [1]

1586 גֹּמֶר gōmer, n.pr.m. & f. GK: 1699 & 1700 [→ 1584]. Gomer, "complete":– Gomer [6]

1587 גְּמַרְיָה gᵉmaryâ or גְּמַרְיָהוּ gᵉmaryāhû, n.pr.m. GK: 1701 & 1702 [→ 1584+3068]. Gemariah, "Yahweh has accomplished":– Gemariah [5]

1588 גַּן gan, n.m. GK: 1703 [→ 1593; cf. 1598]. garden:– garden [39], gardens [3]

1589 גָּנַב gānab, v. GK: 1704 [→ 1590, 1591, 1592?]. [Q] to steal, be a thief, kidnap; to deceive; [Qp, N, Pu] to be stolen, forcibly carried off; [Ht] to steal oneself away, sneak in:– stolen [11], steal [9], indeed stolen away (+1589) [2], stealeth [2], stealing [2], stolen (+1589) [2], stole [2], carrieth away [1], secretly brought [1], stale away unawares (+3820) [1], stale [1], steal away from [1], steal away [1], stealeth away [1], stealth [1], stolen away unawares (+3824) [1], stolen away [1]

1590 גַּנָּב gannāb, n.m. GK: 1705 [→ 1589]. thief; kidnapper:– thief [13], thieves [4]

1591 גְּנֵבָה gᵉnēbâ, n.f. GK: 1706 [→ 1589]. stolen possession:– theft [2]

1592 גְּנֻבַת gᵉnubat, n.pr.m. GK: 1707 [→ 1589?]. Genubath, "thief":– Genubath [2]

1593 גַּנָּה gannâ, n.f. GK: 1708 [→ 1594, 1588; cf. 1598]. same as 1594: garden, grove:– gardens [9], garden [3]

1594 גִּנָּה ginnâ, n.f. GK: 1708 [→ 1593]. same as 1593: garden, grove:– garden [4]

1595 גֶּנֶז genez, n.[m.]. GK: 1709 & 1710 [→ 1597; cf. 1596]. (royal) treasury; rug, carpet:– treasuries [2], chests [1]

1596 גְּנַז gᵉnaz (Aram.), n.m. GK: 10148 [cf. 1595]. place of treasure and archival documents:– treasure [2], treasures [1]

1597 גִּנְזַךְ ganzak, n.[m.]. GK: 1711 [→ 1595]. (temple) storeroom, where treasures are kept:– treasuries [1]

1598 גָּנַן gānan, v. GK: 1713 [→ 1588, 1593, 1594, 4043]. [Q] to defend, shield, protect:– defend [7], defending [1]

1599 גִּנְּתֹון ginnᵉtôn or גִּנְּתֹוי ginnᵉtôy, n.pr.m. GK: 1715 & 1714. Ginnethon, Ginnethoi:– Ginnethon [2], Ginnetho [1]

1600 גָּעָה gāʿâ, v. GK: 1716. [Q] to bellow, low (of cattle):– loweth [1], lowing [1]

1601 גֹּעָה gōʿâ, n.pr.loc. GK: 1717. Goah:– Goath [1]

1602 גָּעַל gāʿal, v. GK: 1718 [→ 1604, 1603; cf. 1351]. [Q] to abhor, despise, loathe; [N] to be defiled; [H] to cause defiling = fail to impregnate:– abhor [4], lothed [2], abhorred [1], faileth [1], lotheth [1], vilely cast away [1]

1603 גַּעַל gaʿal, n.pr.m. GK: 1720 [→ 1602]. Gaal, "loathing":– Gaal [9]

1604 גֹּעַל gōʿal, n.m. GK: 1719 [→ 1602]. despising, loathing:– lothing [1]

1605 נָעַר *gā'ar*, v. GK: 1721 [→ 1606, 4045]. [Q] to rebuke, reprimand; prevent (insects):– rebuke [7], rebuked [4], corrupt [1], rebuketh [1], reproved [1]

1606 גְּעָרָה *ge'ārâ*, n.f. GK: 1722 [→ 1605]. rebuke; threat:– rebuke [12], reproof [2], rebuking [1]

1607 גָּעַשׁ *gā'aš*, v. GK: 1723. [Q] to shake, tremble; [Pu] to be shaken; [Ht] to shake back and forth, stagger, surge, tremble back and forth:– moved [3], shook [3], shaken [1], toss [1], troubled [1]

1608 גַּעַשׁ *ga'aš*, n.pr.loc. GK: 1724. Gaash, "*rumble, quake*":– Gaash [4]

1609 גַּעְתָּם *ga'tām*, n.pr.m. GK: 1725. Gatam:– Gatam [3]

1610 גַּף *gap*, n.m. GK: 1726 & 1727 [→ 102, 1480]. height, elevation; body; by oneself:– himself (+2050.2) [3], highest places (+4791) [1]

1611 גַּף *gap* (Aram.), n.f. GK: 10149. wing:– wings [3]

1612 גֶּפֶן *gepen*, n.f. & m. GK: 1728. vine, grapevine:– vine [43], vines [9], plant of vine [1], tree [1], vine (+3196) [1]

1613 גֹּפֶר *gōper*, n.[m.]. GK: 1729. cypress (wood); exact identity of the wood is uncertain; "gopher wood" is simply a transliteration of the Hebrew:– gopher [1]

1614 גָּפְרִית *goprît*, n.f. GK: 1730. sulfur; older versions: brimstone:– brimstone [7]

1615 גִּר *gir*, n.[m.]. GK: 1732 [cf. 1528]. chalk:– chalkstones (+68) [1]

1616 גֵּר *gēr*, n.m. GK: 1731 [→ 1628; cf. 1481]. alien, stranger (in a foreign land):– stranger [69], strangers [18], alien [1], sojourner [1], stranger (+376) [1], stranger's [1], strangers (+376) [1]

גֵּר *gur*. See 1482.

1617 גֵּרָא *gērā'*, n.pr.m. GK: 1733. Gera, "[perhaps] *sojourner*":– Gera [9]

1618 גָּרָב *gārāb*, n.[m.]. GK: 1734 [→ 1619]. festering sore:– scurvy [2], scab [1]

1619 גָּרֵב *gārēb*, n.pr.m. & loc. GK: 1735 & 1736 [→ 1618]. Gareb, "*scabby*":– Gareb [3]

1620 גַּרְגַּר *gargar*, n.m. GK: 1737. ripe olives:– berries [1]

1621 גַּרְגְּרוֹת *garg'rôt*, n.f.pl. GK: 1738. neck, throat:– neck [4]

1622 גִּרְגָּשִׁי *girgāšî*, a.g. GK: 1739. Girgashite:– Girgashites [5], Girgashite [2]

1623 גָּרַד *gārad*, v. GK: 1740. [Ht] to scrape oneself (with a broken piece of pottery):– scrape [1]

1624 גָּרָה *gārâ*, v. GK: 1741 [→ 8409; cf. 1481]. [P] to stir up (a dispute); [Ht] to provoke (to war), engage (to battle):– meddle [4], contend [3], stirred up [3], stirreth up [3], striven [1]

1625 גֵּרָה *gērâ*, n.f. GK: 1742 [→ 1641]. cud:– cud [11]

1626 גֵּרָה *gērâ*, n.f. GK: 1743. gerah (measure, one-twentieth of a shekel, about half a gram):– gerahs [5]

גֹּרָה *gōrâ*. See 1484.

1627 גָּרוֹן *gārôn*, n.m. GK: 1744 [→ 1641]. throat, neck; by extension: mouth; an "outstretched neck" is a sign of arrogance and possibly of sexual misconduct:– throat [4], aloud (+871.1) [1], mouth [1], necks [1], neck [1]

1628 גֵּרוּת *gērût*, n.f.[pr.loc.] GK: 1745 [→ 1616]. habitation; place name: Geruth:– habitation [1]

1629 גָּרַז *gāraz*, v. GK: 1746 [→ 1631; cf. 1504]. [N] to be cut off, implying destruction:– cut off [1]

1630 גְּרִזִים *g'rizîm*, n.pr.loc. GK: 1748. Gerizim:– Gerizim [3], Gerizzim [1]

1631 גַּרְזֶן *garzen*, n.m. GK: 1749 [→ 1629]. ax, chisel:– axe [4]

1632 גָּרוֹל *gārôl*, a.var. GK: 1754. var. of 1419: large, great:–

גּוֹרָל *gōrāl*. See 1486.

1633 גָּרַם *gāram*, v.den. GK: 1750 & 1751 [→ 1634]. [Q] to leave, reserve; [P] to break, to break bones:– break [2], gnaw bones [1]

1634 גֶּרֶם *gerem*, n.[m.]. GK: 1752 [→ 1633, 1636?; cf. 1635]. bone, rawboned, bony; bareness:– bones [2], bone [1], strong [1], top [1]

1635 גְּרַם *g'ram* (Aram.), n.[m.]. GK: 10150 [cf. 1634]. bone:– bones [1]

1636 גַּרְמִי *garmî*, a.g. GK: 1753 [→ 1634?]. Garmite:– Garmite [1]

1637 גֹּרֶן *gōren*, n.m. GK: 1755. threshing floor:– threshingfloor [17], floor [10], void place [2], barnfloor [1], barn [1], cornfloor (+1715) [1], corn [1], floors [1], threshingfloors [1], threshingplace [1]

גָּרוֹן *gārōn*. See 1627.

1638 גָּרַס *gāras*, v. GK: 1756. [Q] to be crushed; [H] to break, crush:– breaketh [1], broken [1]

1639 גָּרַע *gāra'*, v. GK: 1757 & 1758 [→ 4052]. [Q] to take away, reduce, hinder; [Qp] to be cut off (of a beard); [N] to be reduced, be taken away, to disappear; [P] to draw up (drops of water):– diminish [6], taken [3], diminished [2], abated [1], clipt [1], done away [1], kept back [1], maketh small [1], minish [1], restrainest [1], restrain [1], taken away [1], withdraweth [1]

1640 גָּרַף *gārap*, v. GK: 1759 [→ 106, 4053]. [Q] to sweep away (of a river):– swept away [1]

1641 גָּרַר *gārar*, v. GK: 1760 [→ 1625, 1627, 4050; cf. 5064]. [Q] to chew; to drag away; [Polal] to be sawn; [Htpol] to drive, swirl:– catch [1], cheweth [1], continuing [1], destroy [1], sawed [1]

1642 גְּרָר *g'rār*, n.pr.loc. GK: 1761. Gerar, "*circle, region*":– Gerar [10]

1643 גֶּרֶשׂ *gereś*, n.[m.]. GK: 1762. (coarse) crushed grain, grits, groats:– beaten corn [1], beaten out [1]

1644 גָּרַשׁ *gāraš*, v. GK: 1763 & 1764 [→ 1645, 1646, 4054]. [Q] to cast up, toss up; to drive out; [Qp] to be divorced; [N] to be tossed, stirred up; to be banished; [P] to drive out, expel [Pu] to be banished:– drive out [11], cast out [8], thrust out [5], driven out [4], divorced [3], drave out [3], drove away [2], put away [2], surely thrust out (+1644) [2], cast up [1], driven forth [1], drive [1], driving out [1], drove out [1], expel [1], troubled [1]

1645 גֶּרֶשׁ *gereš*, n.[m.]. GK: 1765 [→ 1644]. yield, produce:– put forth [1]

1646 גְּרֻשָׁה *g'rušâ*, n.f. GK: 1766 [→ 1644]. dispossession:– exactions [1]

1647 גֵּרְשֹׁם *gēršōm*, n.pr.m. GK: 1768 [→ 1648]. Gershom, Gershon, "*temporary resident there*":– Gershom [14]

1648 גֵּרְשׁוֹן *gēršôn*, n.pr.m. GK: 1767 [→ 1647, 1649]. Gershon, "*temporary resident there*":– Gershon [17]

1649 גֵּרְשֻׁנִּי *gēršunnî*, a.g. GK: 1769 [→ 1648]. Gershonite, "*of Gershon*":– Gershonites [9], Gershonite [3], Gershon [1]

1650 גְּשׁוּר *g'šûr*, n.pr.m. GK: 1770 [→ 1651]. Geshur, "*bridge*":– Geshur [8], Geshurites [1]

1651 גְּשׁוּרִי *g'šûrî*, a.g. GK: 1771 [→ 1650]. Geshurite, people of Geshur, "*of Geshur*":– Geshurites [4], Geshuri [2]

1652 גָּשַׁם *gāšam*, v.den. GK: 1772 [→ 1653, 1654, 1656]. [H] to bring rain:– cause rain [1]

1653 גֶּשֶׁם *gešem*, n.m. GK: 1773 [→ 1654, 1656; cf. 1652]. rain, shower, downpour:– rain [29], shower [3], great rain [1], much rain [1], showers [1]

1654 גֶּשֶׁם *gešem* or גַּשְׁמוּ *gašmû*, n.pr.m. GK: 1774 & 1776 [cf. 1652, 1653]. Geshem, Gashmu, "*rain shower*":– Geshem [1], Gashmu [1]

1655 גְּשֵׁם *g'šēm* (Aram.), n.m. GK: 10151. body; the phrase "give up the body" is translated "to die":– body [3], bodies [2]

1656 גֹּשֶׁם *gōšem*, n.[m.]. GK: 1775 [→ 1653; cf. 1652]. shower, rain:– rained upon [1]

גַּשְׁמוּ *gašmû*. See 1654.

1657 גֹּשֶׁן *gōšen*, n.pr.loc. GK: 1777. Goshen, "*mound of earth*":– Goshen [15]

1658 גִּשְׁפָּא *gišpā'*, n.pr.m. GK: 1778. Gishpa, "*listener*":– Gispa [1]

1659 גָּשַׁשׁ *gāšaš*, v. GK: 1779. [P] to grope along, feel one's way (as if blind):– grope [2]

1660 גַּת *gat*, n.f. GK: 1780 [→ 1661, 1662, 1667, 1663, 1665]. winepress; also used as a hiding place:– winepress [2], press [1], wine presses [1], winefat [1]

1661 גַּת *gat*, n.pr.loc. GK: 1781 [→ 1663, 1665; cf. 1660]. Gath, "*winepress*":– Gath [33], Gath-hepher [1], Gittah-hepher [1]

1662 גַּת הַחֵפֶר *gat haḥēper* or גַּת חֵפֶר *gat ḥēper*, n.pr.loc. GK: 1783 [→ 1660+1886.1+2660]. Gath Hepher, "*winepress waterpit*":–

1663 גִּתִּי *gittî*, a.g. GK: 1785 [→ 1661; cf. 1660]. Gittite, "*of Gath*":– Gittite [8], Gittites [2]

1664 גִּתַּיִם *gittayim*, n.pr.loc. GK: 1786 [→ 1660]. Gittaim, "*two winepresses*":– Gittaim [2]

1665 גִּתִּית *gittît*, tt. GK: 1787 [→ 1661; cf. 1660]. gittith; unknown musical term, possibly the name of the tune, or the name of the instrument that played it, or even related in some way to ceremonies associated with the winepress:– Gittith [3]

1666 גֶּתֶר *geter*, n.pr.m. GK: 1788. Gether:– Gether [2]

1667 גַּת־רִמּוֹן *gat-rimmôn*, n.pr.loc. GK: 1784 [→ 1660+7416]. Gath Rimmon, "*winepress of pomegranate*":– Gath-rimmon [4]

1668 דָּא *dā'* (Aram.), p.demo.f. GK: 10154 [cf. 2090, 2097, 2088]. this, this one:– another [2], one [2], this [2]

1669 דָּאַב *dā'ab*, v. GK: 1790 [→ 1670, 1671]. [Q] to be dim (of eyes); to sorrow:– mourneth [1], sorrowful [1], sorrow [1]

1670 דְּאָבָה *d'ābâ*, n.f. GK: 1791 [→ 1669]. dismay, despair:– sorrow [1]

1671 דְּאָבוֹן *d'ābôn*, n.[m.]. GK: 1792 [→ 1669]. despair:– sorrow [1]

1672 דָּאַג *dā'ag*, v. GK: 1793 [→ 1673, 1674]. [Q] to worry, dread, be troubled, be afraid:– afraid [3], careful [1], sorroweth [1], sorry [1], take thought [1]

1673 דֹּאֵג *dō'ēg*, n.pr.m. GK: 1795 [→ 1672]. Doeg, "*anxious*":– Doeg [6]

1674 דְּאָגָה *d'āgâ*, n.f. GK: 1796 [→ 1672]. fear, anxiety, restlessness:– carefully [2], care [1], fear [1], heaviness [1], sorrow [1]

1675 דָּאָה *dā'â*, v. GK: 1797 [→ 1676; cf. 1772]. [Q] to swoop down, pounce; to soar:– fly [3], flieth [1]

1676 דָּאָה *dā'â*, n.f. GK: 1798 [→ 1675]. red kite (bird):– vulture [1]

1677 דֹּב *dōb*, n.m. GK: 1800 [→ 1680; cf. 1678]. bear (animal):– bear [10], bears [2]

1678 דֹּב *dōb* (Aram.), n.[m.]. GK: 10155 [cf. 1677]. bear:– bear [1]

1679 דֹּבֶא *dōbe'*, n.[m.]. GK: 1801. strength:– strength [1]

1680 דָּבַב *dābab*, v. GK: 1803 [→ 1677, 1681?, 1686?]. [Q] to flow over gently:– causing to speak [1]

1681 דִּבָּה *dibbâ*, n.f. GK: 1804 [→ 1680?]. bad report, slander, bad reputation, whisper:– slander [3], infamy [2], report [2], defaming [1], evil report [1]

1682 דְּבוֹרָה *d'bôrâ*, n.f. GK: 1805 [→ 1683; cf. 1696]. wild honey bee; (pl.) swarm of bees:– bees [3], bee [1]

1683 דְּבוֹרָה *d'bôrâ*, n.pr.f. GK: 1806 [→ 1682; cf. 1696]. Deborah, "*hornet, wasp, wild honey bee*":– Deborah [10]

1684 דְּבַח *d'baḥ* (Aram.), v. GK: 10156 [→ 1685, 4056; cf. 2076]. [P] to present a sacrifice as an act of worship:– offered [1]

1685 דְּבַח *d'baḥ* (Aram.), n.[m.]. GK: 10157 [→ 1684; cf. 2077]. sacrifice (i.e., animal):– sacrifices [1]

1686 דִּבְיוֹנִים *dibyônîm*, n.[m.]. GK: 1807 [→ 1680?+3123]. seed pods or doves' dung:– dove's dung [1]

1687 דְּבִיר *d'bîr*, n.m. GK: 1808 [→ 1688; cf. 1696?]. inner sanctuary, referring to the Most Holy Place:– oracle [16]

1688 דְּבִיר *d'bîr*, n.pr.m. & loc. GK: 1809 [→ 1687; cf. 1696]. Debir, "*back room [of a shrine temple for oracle pronouncement]*":– Debir [14]

1689 דִּבְלָה *diblâ*, n.pr.loc. GK: 1812. Diblah:– Diblath [1]

1690 דְּבֵלָה *d'bēlâ*, n.f. GK: 1811 [→ 1691?]. pressed fig cakes; poultice of figs:– cakes [2], lump [2], cake [1]

1691 דִּבְלַיִם *diblayim*, n.pr.m. GK: 1813 [→ 1690?]. Diblaim, "*lump of [two dried fig] cakes*":– Diblaim [1]

דִּבְלָתַיִם *diblātayim*. See 1015.

1692 דָּבַק *dābaq*, v. GK: 1815 [→ 1695, 1694; cf. 1693]. [Q] to be united, hold fast, keep, cling to; [H] to overtake, cause to cleave, press hard upon; [Pu] to be joined fast, be stuck together; [Ho] be made to cleave, stick to; from the base joining or fastening objects together comes the figure of close association of people:– cleave [13], clave [6], cleaveth [6], cleaved [3], followed

hard [3], overtook [3], keep [2], make cleave [2], abide fast [1], cause to stick [1], caused to cleave [1], cleave fast together [1], cleave to [1], follow close [1], followed hard after [1], followeth hard [1], joined together [1], joined [1], keep fast [1], kept fast [1], pursued hard [1], stick [1], stuck [1], take [1]

1693 דְּבַק **dᵉbaq** (Aram.), v. GK: 10158 [cf. 1692]. [P] to be united, having a very close association:– cleave [1]

1694 דֶּבֶק **debeq**, n.m. GK: 1817 [→ 1692]. welding; sections (of armor):– joints [2], sodering [1]

1695 דָּבֵק **dābēq**, a. GK: 1816 [→ 1692]. holding fast, sticking to:– cleave [1], joining [1], sticketh closer [1]

1696 דָּבַר **dābar**, v. GK: 1818 & 1819 [→ 1682, 1683, 1687?, 1688, 1697, 1698, 1699, 1699', 1700, 1702, 1703, 1705, 4057]. [Q. P, Ht] to say, speak, tell, command, promise; [P] to depart; to destroy; [H] to subdue:– [Qp, Pu] to be spoken (of); [N] to speak together; a general term for verbal communication, note the specific contextual translations in the KJV; [P] to depart; to destroy; [H] to subdue:– spake [318], speak [273], spoken [174], said [85], speaking [37], promised [29], talked [29], say [27], speaketh [22], told [15], communed [14], pronounced [13], speakest [11], talk [11], spakest [8], tell [7], saith [6], utter [5], commanded [4], commune [4], say on [4], gave [4], talking [3], bid [3], communing [2], promisedst [2], speak well (+1696) [2], talkest [2], taught [2], telleth [2], wont to speak (+1696) [2], answered [1], appointed [1], badest [1], bade [1], declared [1], declare [1], destroyed [1], give [1], named [1], pronounce [1], published [1], rehearsed [1], saidst [1], speak on [1], spokesman [1], subdueth [1], subdue [1], talketh [1], telling [1], thought [1], useth intreaties (+8469) [1], uttered [1], uttereth [1]

1697 דָּבָר **dābār**, n.m. GK: 1821 [→ 1696]. what is said, word (or any unit of speech such as a clause, or the whole of communication); matter (any event); thing (any object):– word [434], words [372], thing [178], acts [51], things [49], matter [47], chronicles (+3117) [33], nothing (+3808) [20], saying [20], commandment [15], manner [15], matters [15], business [8], said [8], book [7], speech [7], answer [6], cause [6], promise [5], chronicles (+3117+1886.1) [5], commandments [5], sayings [5], because (+834+5921) [4], portion [4], tidings [4], because of (+5921) [3], concerning (+5921) [3], deed [3], errand [3], message [3], nothing (+408) [3], rate [3], sentence [3], advice [2], affairs [2], answered (+7725) [2], any thing [2], causes [2], certain rate [2], deeds [2], it's [2], of [2], ought [2], questions [2], report [2], request [2], spoken [2], talk [2], answer (+7725) [1], answered [1], anyˢ [1], as the matter require [1], care [1], case [1], commune [1], communication [1], conferred (+1961) [1], counsel [1], dealings [1], decree [1], disease [1], due [1], duty required [1], duty [1], effect [1], eloquent (+376) [1], every thing [1], evil favouredness (+7451) [1], for (+5921) [1], for sake (+5921) [1], hurt [1], iniquities (+5771) [1], judgment (+4941) [1], language [1], lies (+3577) [1], lies (+8267) [1], lying (+8267) [1], no (+3808) [1], nothing (+3605+3808) [1], oracle [1], parts [1], provision [1], purpose [1], reason [1], sakes [1], sake [1], so (+2088+1886.1+1886.1+3509.1) [1], somewhat to say [1], some [1], song (+7892) [1], sort [1], spakest [1], such [1], tasks [1], task [1], that (+2088+1886.1+1886.1) [1], thing (+1886.1) [1], things concerning [1], thought [1], thus (+2088+1886.1+1886.1) [1], what (+4100+1886.1) [1], whatsoever (+4100) [1], what [1], wherewith [1], whit [1], word's [1], work required [1], works [1]

1698 דֶּבֶר **deber**, n.m. GK: 1822 & 1823 [→ 1696]. plague, pestilence, disease, a pandemic occurrence of sickness and death; some sources identify specific diseases in specific contexts; thorn:– pestilence [47], murrain [1], plagues [1]

1699 דֹּבֶר **dōber**, n.[m.] GK: 1824 [→ 1696]. pasture, in a remote place:– fold [1], manner [1]

1699' דִּבֵּר **dibbēr**, n.[m.] GK: 1825 [→ 1696]. word (of God):– word [2]

דְּבִר **dᵉbir**. See 1687, 1688.

1700 דִּבְרָה **dibrâ**, n.f. GK: 1826 [→ 1696; cf. 1701]. cause; order; therefore, because:– cause [1], end [1], estate [1], order [1], regard [1]

1701 דִּבְרָה **dibrâ** (Aram.), n.f. GK: 10159 [cf. 1700]. affair; matter:– intent [1], sakes [1]

דִּבְרָה **dᵉbōrâ** or דְּבֹרָה **dᵉbōrâ**. See 1682, 1683.

1702 דֹּבְרוֹת **dōbᵉrōt**, n.f.pl. GK: 1827 [→ 1696]. raft, a collection of logs towed behind a ship:– flotes [1]

1703 דַּבֶּרֶת **dabberet**, n.f. GK: 1830 [→ 1696]. instruction, word:– words [1]

1704 דִּבְרִי **dibrî**, n.pr.m. GK: 1828. Dibri, "[poss.] *speak*":– Dibri [1]

1705 דַּבְרַת **dabᵉrat**, n.pr.loc. GK: 1829 [→ 1696]. Daberath, "*pasture*":– Daberath [2], Dabareh [1]

1706 דְּבַשׁ **dᵉbaš**, n.m. GK: 1831 [→ 3031]. honey:– honey [52], honeycomb (+3295+1886.1) [1], honeycomb (+6688) [1]

1707 דַּבֶּשֶׁת **dabbešet**, n.f. GK: 1832 [→ 1708?]. hump (of a camel):– bunches [1]

1708 דַּבֶּשֶׁת **dabbešet**, n.pr.loc. GK: 1833 [→ 1707?]. Dabbesheth, "*hump*":– Dabbasheth [1]

1709 דָּג **dāg** or דָּאג **dā'g**, n.m. GK: 1834 & 1794 [→ 1711?, 1710, 1728, 1729, 1771; cf. 1770]. fish:– fish [11], fishes [8]

1710 דָּגָה **dāgâ**, n.f. GK: 1836 [→ 1709]. fish:– fish [14], fish's [1]

1711 דָּגָה **dāgâ**, v. GK: 1835 [→ 1709?]. [Q] to increase, multiply:– grow [1]

1712 דָּגוֹן **dāgôn**, n.pr.m. GK: 1837 [→ 1016, 1715]. Dagon (pagan god), "*[god of] grain; fish*":– Dagon [12], Dagon's [1]

1713 דָּגַל **dāgal**, v.den. GK: 1838 & 1839 [→ 1714]. [Q] to lift a banner; [Qp] to be outstanding, conspicuous; [N] be gathered around the banner(s), organized as troops:– banners [1], chiefest [1], set up banners [1], with banners [1]

1714 דֶּגֶל **degel**, n.m. GK: 1840 [→ 1713]. standard, banner:– standard [10], standards [3], banner [1]

1715 דָּגָן **dāgān**, n.m. GK: 1841 [→ 1712]. grain:– corn [37], wheat [2], cornfloor (+1637) [1]

1716 דָּגַר **dāgar**, v. GK: 1842. [Q] to care for; hatch eggs:– gather [1], sitteth [1]

1717 דַּד **dad**, n.m. GK: 1843. bosom, breast:– breasts [2], teats [2]

1718 דָּדָה **dādâ**, v. GK: 1844. [Ht] to walk, lead:– go softly [1], went with [1]

1719 דְּדָן **dᵉdān**, n.pr.loc. & g. GK: 1847 [→ 1720]. Dedan:– Dedan [11]

1720 דְּדָנִי **dᵉdānî**, a.g. GK: 1848 [→ 1719]. Dedanite, "*of Dedan*":– Dedanim [1]

1721 דֹּדָנִים **dōdānîm** or רֹדָן **rōdān**, n.pr.g.pl. GK: 1849 & 8102. Dodanim; Rhodes, Rodanim, "*people of Rhodes*":– Dodanim [2]

1722 דְּהַב **dᵉhab** (Aram.), n.m. GK: 10160 [cf. 2091]. gold:– gold [14], golden [9]

1723 דַּהֲוָא **dᵉhû'** (Aram.), pt. + pr. GK: 10161 & 10162 [→ 1768+1932]. that is (1768 + 1932):– Dehavites [1]

1724 דָּהַם **dāham**, v. GK: 1850. [N] to be taken by surprise, be astounded:– astonied [1]

1725 דָּהַר **dāhar**, v. GK: 1851 [→ 1726]. [Q] to gallop:– pransing [1]

1726 דַּהֲרָה **dahᵃrâ**, n.f. GK: 1852 [→ 1725]. galloping:– pransings [2]

דֹּאג **dō'ēg**. See 1673.

1727 דּוּב **dûb**, v. GK: 1853 [cf. 2100]. [H] to drain away, wear away; loss of life as a fig. extension of draining liquid out of a container:– cause sorrow [1]

דֹּב **dôb**. See 1677.

1728 דַּוָּג **dawwāg**, n.m. GK: 1854 [→ 1709]. fisherman:– fishers [1]

1729 דּוּגָה **dûgâ**, n.f. GK: 1855 [→ 1709]. fishing (hooks):– fishhooks (+5518) [1]

1730 דּוֹד **dōd**, n.m. GK: 1856 [→ 419, 449, 1085, 1732?, 1733, 1734?, 1737?]. uncle, cousin, relative; beloved one, lover; a term of endearment ranging from friendship and familial affection to romantic love:– beloved [32], uncle [10], love [7], uncle's [6], beloved's (+3807.1) [2], father's brothers' [1], father's brother [1], loves [1], well-beloved [1]

1731 דּוּד **dûd**, n.m. GK: 1857. basket; kettle, caldron, pot:– basket [2], baskets [1], caldrons [1], kettle [1], pots [1], pot [1]

1732 דָּוִד **dāwid**, n.pr.m. GK: 1858 [→ 1730?]. David, "*beloved one*":– David [1022], David's [50], David's (+3807.1) [3]

1733 דּוֹדָה **dôdâ**, n.f. GK: 1860 [→ 1730]. aunt (father's sister):– aunt [1], father's sister [1], uncle's wife [1]

1734 דּוֹדוֹ **dôdô** or דֹּדִי **dôdî**, n.pr.m. GK: 1861 & 1846 [→ 1730?]. Dodo, Dodai, "*beloved*":– Dodo [5]

1735 דֹּדָוָהוּ **dōdāwāhû**, n.pr.m. GK: 1845. Dodavahu, "*beloved of Yahweh*":– Dodavah [1]

1736 דּוּדָאִים **dûdā'îm** or דּוּדַי **dûday**, n.m. GK: 1859 & 1863. mandrake plant, thought to be a fertility aid or aphrodisiac:– mandrakes [6], baskets [1]

1737 דּוֹדַי **dôday**, n.pr.m. GK: 1862 [→ 1730?]. Dodai, "*beloved*":– Dodai [1]

1738 דָּוָה **dāwâ**, v. GK: 1864 [→ 1739, 1741, 1742, 1773?, 4064]. [Q] to have a monthly period, menstruate:– infirmity [1]

1739 דָּוֶה **dāweh**, a. GK: 1865 [→ 1738]. pertaining to the menstrual cycle; fainting:– faint [2], having sickness [1], menstruous cloth [1], sick [1]

1740 דּוּחַ **dûaḥ**, v. GK: 1866 [cf. 5080]. [H] to rinse, wash, cleanse:– washed [2], cast out [1], purged [1]

1741 דְּוַי **dᵉway**, n.[m.] GK: 1867 [→ 1738]. illness:– languishing [1], sorrowful [1]

1742 דַּוָּי **dawwāy**, a. GK: 1868 [→ 1738]. faint; afflicted:– faint [3]

דָּוִיד **dāwîd**. See 1732.

1743 דּוּךְ **dûk**, v. GK: 1870 [→ 4085; cf. 1790, 1792, 1794, 1854]. [Q] to crush (in a mortar):– beat [1]

1744 דּוּכִיפַת **dûkîpat**, n.f. GK: 1871. hoopoe:– lapwing [2]

1745 דּוּמָה **dûmâ**, n.f. GK: 1872 [→ 1826]. silence:– silence [2]

1746 דּוּמָה **dûmâ**, n.pr.loc. GK: 1873 & 1874. Dumah, "*silence*":– Dumah [4]

1747 דּוּמִיָּה **dûmiyyâ**, n.f. GK: 1875 [→ 1826; cf. 1820]. silence, stillness; rest:– waiteth [1], silence [1], silent [1]

1748 דּוּמָם **dûmām**, n.[m.] GK: 1876 [cf. 1826]. in silence, quietly; lifeless:– dumb [1], quietly wait [1], silent [1]

דּוּמֶשֶׂק **dûmešeq**. See 1833.

1749 דּוֹנַג **dônag**, n.m. GK: 1880. wax:– wax [4]

1750 דּוּץ **dûṣ**, v. GK: 1881. [Q] to leap:– turned into joy [1]

1751 דּוּק **dûq**, v. GK: 1882 [→ 1785]. [Q] to review:–

1752 דּוּר **dûr**, v. GK: 1883 & 1884 [→ 115, 1754, 1755, 4071; cf. 1756; cf. 1753]. [Q] to dwell; to pile logs (around, to burn):– burn [1], dwell [1]

1753 דּוּר **dûr** (Aram.), v. GK: 10163 [→ 1859, 4070, 8411; cf. 1752]. [P] to live, dwell:– dwell [3], dwelt [2], inhabitants [2]

1754 דּוּר **dûr**, n.[m.] GK: 1885 [→ 1752; cf. 8411]. all around, encircling; ball:– ball [1], round about (+1886.1+3509.1) [1]

1755 דּוֹר **dôr**, n.m. GK: 1886 & 1887 [→ 1752; cf. 1859]. generation, generation to come; descendant; house, dwelling:– generation [57], generations [50], all generations (+1755+2050.1) [26], many generations (+1755+2050.1) [12], all generations (+1755) [4], age [2], all generations (+1755+3605+2050.1) [2], evermore (+1755+2050.1) [2], every generation (+1755+2050.1) [2], every generation (+1755+3605+2050.1) [2], generations (+1755+2050.1) [2], never (+1755+3808+2050.1) [2], throughout all generations (+1755f) [2], anotherˢ [1], posterity [1]

1756 דֹּאר **dôr** or דֹּאר **dō'r**, n.pr.loc. GK: 1888 & 1799 [→ 2576, 5874; cf. 1752]. Dor:– Dor [7]

1757 דּוּרָא **dûrā'** (Aram.), n.pr.loc. GK: 10164. Dura:– Dura [1]

1758 דּוּשׁ **dûš**, v. GK: 1889 [→ 1786, 1788?, 4098; cf. 1759]. [Q] to tread, trample, thresh; [Qp, N, Ho] be trampled, be threshed:– thresh [3], threshed [2], threshing [2], trodden down [2], break [1], tear [1], tread out [1], treadeth out [1]

1759 דּוּשׁ **dûš** (Aram.), v. GK: 10165 [cf. 1758]. [P] to trample, tread down:– tread down [1]

1760 דָּחָה **dāḥâ** or דָּחַח **dāḥaḥ**, v. GK: 1890 & 1891 [→ 1762, 4072; cf. 5080; cf. 1761]. [Q] to push, push away; trip up; [Qp] to totter; [N] be brought down; to be pushed, pushed out; [Pu] to be thrown down:– outcasts [3], thrust sore (+1760) [2], cast down [1], chase [1], driven away [1], driven on [1], overthrow [1], tottering [1]

1761 דַּחֲוָה **daḥᵃwâ** (Aram.), n.f. GK: 10166. entertainment, variously interpreted as musical, dancing, sexual, culinary, etc:– instruments of musick [1]

1762 דְּחִי **dᵉḥî**, n.[m.] GK: 1892 [→ 1760]. stumbling; falling [2]

1763 דְּחַל **dᵉḥal** (Aram.), v. GK: 10167 [cf. 2119]. [P] to fear, reverence; [Pp] to be terrified, be awesome; [Pa] to make afraid:– dreadful [2], feared [1], fear [1], made afraid [1], terrible [1]

1764 דֹּחַן **dōḥan**, n.m. GK: 1893. (sorghum) millet:– millet [1]

1765 דָּחַף **dāḥap**, v. GK: 1894 [→ 4073]. [Qp] to be spurred on, be in haste; [N] to be eager, be rushed, hurry:– hasted [2], hastened [1], pressed on [1]

1766 דָּחַק **dāḥaq**, v. GK: 1895. [Q] to afflict, oppress:– thrust [1], vexed [1]

1767 דַּי **day**, subst. GK: 1896 [→ 1838, 4078]. enough, sufficient:– enough [6], from (+4480) [5], since (+4480) [3], sufficient [3], when (+4480) [3], in (+871.1) [2], very [2], ability [1], able (+3027+4672) [1], able (+3027+5381+3509.1) [1], able to bring (+3027+4672) [1], able [1], according to (+3509.1) [1], after (+4480) [1], among (+871.1) [1], as oft as (+4480) [1], much [1], so much as is sufficient [1], sufficient for [1], time [1]

1768 דִּי **dî** (Aram.), pt.rel. & c. GK: 10168 [cf. 2088, 2098]. who, that, of:– that [100], of [64], which [54], whom [13], forasmuch as (+3606+6903) [8], till (+5705) [8], for [5], because (+3606+6903) [4], when (+3509.4) [4], whereas [4], whomsoever (+4479) [4], whose, who who [3], because [2], until (+5705) [2], whatsoever (+1768+3606) [2], what [2], whoso (+4479) [2], whosoever (+3606) [2], whosoever (+606+1768+3606) [2], as (+3509.4) [1], as (+3606+6903) [1], at what time (+0.2+5732+871.2) [1], because (+4481) [1], but [1], none (+383+3809) [1], now (+116) [1], seeing [1], than [1], that which [1], therefore (+3606+6903) [1], those [1], though (+3606+6903) [1], what (+3964+3807.2) [1], whatsoever (+3606) [1], whatsoever (+4101) [1], wheresoever (+3606+871.2) [1], where [1]

1769 דִּיבוֹן **dîbôn**, n.pr.loc. GK: 1897 [→ 1769+1410; cf. 1775, 1776]. Dibon:– Dibon [9], Dibon-gad [2]

1770 דִּיג **dîg**, v.den. GK: 1899 [cf. 1709]. [Q] to catch fish:– fish [1]

1771 דַּיָּג **dayyāg**, n.m. GK: 1900 [→ 1709]. fisherman:– fishers [2]

1772 דַּיָּה **dayyâ**, n.f. GK: 1901 [cf. 1675]. falcon:– vultures [1], vulture [1]

1773 דְּיוֹ **dᵉyô**, n.m. GK: 1902 [→ 1738?]. ink, a writing substance made of soot or metal shavings mixed with oil or resin:– ink [1]

1774 דִּי זָהָב **dî zāhāb**, n.pr.loc. GK: 1903. Dizahab, "that which has gold":– Dizahab [1]

1775 דִּימוֹן **dîmôn**, n.pr.loc. GK: 1904 [cf. 1769]. Dimon:– Dimon [2]

1776 דִּימוֹנָה **dîmônâ**, n.pr.loc. GK: 1905 [cf. 1769]. Dimonah:– Dimonah [1]

1777 דִּין **dîn**, v. GK: 1906 [→ 1779, 1781, 1783, 1835, 4066, 4068, 4079, 4082, 4090; cf. 1778 (also used with compound proper names)]. [Q] to judge, punish; to plead, defend, vindicate, contend for; [N] to argue:– judge [14], judged [2], at strife [1], contend [1], execute [1], judgeth [1], minister judgment [1], plead the cause [1], plead [1], strive [1]

1778 דִּין **dîn** (Aram.), v. GK: 10169 [→ 1780, 1782, 1784, 4083; cf. 1777]. [P] to administer justice:– judge [1]

1779 דִּין **dîn**, n.[m.]. GK: 1907 [→ 1777; cf. 1780]. cause, legal case; judgment, justice:– judgment [9], cause [8], plea [2], strife [1]

1780 דִּין **dîn** (Aram.), n.m. GK: 10170 [→ 1778; cf. 1779]. judgment, court (place of judgment):– judgment [5]

1781 דַּיָּן **dayyān**, n.m. GK: 1908 [→ 1777; cf. 1782]. defender, judge:– judge [2]

1782 דַּיָּן **dayyān** (Aram.), n.m. GK: 10171 [→ 1778; cf. 1781]. judge:– judges [1]

1783 דִּינָה **dînâ**, n.pr.f. GK: 1909 [→ 1777]. Dinah, "female judge":– Dinah [7], Dinah's [1]

1784 דִּינָיֵא **dînāyē'** (Aram.), n.pr.g. GK: 10172 [→ 1778]. judge:– Dinaites [1]

דִּיפַת **dîpat**. See 7384.

1785 דָּיֵק **dāyēq**, n.m. GK: 1911 [→ 1751]. siege works:– forts [3], fort [3]

1786 דַּיִשׁ **dayiš**, n.m. GK: 1912 [→ 1758]. threshing (season):– threshing [1]

1787 דִּישֹׁן **dîšōn**, n.pr.m. GK: 1914 [→ 1788?]. Dishon, Dishan, "ibex[?]":– Dishon [6]

1788 דִּישׁוֹן **dîšôn**, n.m.[.]. GK: 1913 [→ 1787?, 1789?; cf. 1758?]. ibex:– pygarg [1]

1789 דִּישָׁן **dîšān**, n.pr.m. GK: 1915 [→ 1788?]. Dishan, "ibex[?]":– Dishan [5], Dishon [1]

1790 דַּךְ **dak**, a. GK: 1916 [→ 1795; cf. 1743, 1792, 1794, 1854]. oppressed:– oppressed [3], afflicted [1]

1791 דֵּךְ **dēk** (Aram.), p.demo.com. GK: 10173 [→ 1797]. this:– this [12], the same [1]

1792 דָּכָא **dākā'**, v. GK: 1917 [→ 1793; cf. 1743, 1790, 1794, 1854]. [N] to be contrite; [P] to crush; [Pu] to be crushed, be dejected, be humbled; [Ht] to lie crushed:– break in pieces [3], broken [2], crushed [2], beat to pieces [1], broken in pieces [1], bruised [1], bruise [1], contrite ones [1], crush [1], destroyed [1], destroy [1], humbled [1], oppress [1], smitten down [1]

1793 דַּכָּא **dakkā'**, a. & n.[m.]. GK: 1918 & 1919 [→ 1792]. crushed, contrite; dust:– contrite [2], destruction [1]

1794 דָּכָה **dākâ**, v. GK: 1920 [→ 1796; cf. 1743, 1790, 1792, 1854]. [Q, P] to crush; [N] to be crushed, contrite:– broken [2], contrite [1], croucheth [1], sore broken [1]

1795 דַּכָּה **dakkâ**, n.f. GK: 1921 [→ 1790]. crushing (of testicle):– stones [1]

1796 דְּכִי **dᵉkî**, n.[m.]. GK: 1922 [→ 1794]. pounding (waves):– waves [1]

1797 דִּכֵּן **dikkēn** (Aram.), p.demo.com. GK: 10174 [→ 1791]. that:– same [1], that [1], this [1]

1798 דְּכַר **dᵉkar** (Aram.), n.m. GK: 10175 [cf. 2145]. ram (male animal):– rams [3]

1799 דִּכְרוֹן **dikrôn** or דָּכְרָן **dokrān** (Aram.), n.[m.]. GK: 10176 & 10177 [cf. 2146]. memorandum, record:– records [2], record [1]

1800 דַּל **dal**, a. GK: 1924 [→ 1803; cf. 1809]. poor, needy, humble; weak, haggard, scrawny:– poor [43], needy [2], lean [1], weaker [1]

1801 דָּלַג **dālag**, v. GK: 1925. [Q, P] to scale, ascend, leap up over:– leaped over [2], leap [2], leaping [1]

1802 דָּלָה **dālâ**, v. GK: 1926 & 1927 [→ 1805, 1806, 1808]. [Q, P] to draw up, draw water (from a well); [Q] to hang limp, dangle:– drew water enough (+1802) [2], draw out [1], drew water [1], lifted up [1]

1803 דַּלָּה **dallâ**, n.f. GK: 1929 & 1930 [→ 1800, 1809]. poor, a class of people with little status, influence, and social value; threads remaining on the loom; flowing hair:– poor [5], hair [1], pining sickness [1], poorest sort [1]

1804 דָּלַח **dālaḥ**, v. GK: 1931. [Q] to churn, stir up:– trouble [2], troubledst [1]

1805 דְּלִי **dᵉlî**, n.[m.]. GK: 1932 [→ 1802]. (water) bucket, possibly made of leather:– buckets [1], bucket [1]

1806 דְּלָיָה **dᵉlāyâ** or דְּלָיָהוּ **dᵉlāyāhû**, n.pr.m. GK: 1933 & 1934 [→ 1802+3068]. Delaiah, "Yahweh draws up [like water in a bucket]":– Delaiah [6], Dalaiah [1]

1807 דְּלִילָה **dᵉlîlâ**, n.pr.f. GK: 1935 [→ 1809]. Delilah, "tease":– Delilah [6]

1808 דָּלִית **dālît**, n.f. GK: 1936 [→ 1802]. branch, bough:– branches [8]

1809 דָּלַל **dālal**, v. GK: 1937 & 1938 [→ 1800, 1803, 1807]. [Q] to be in need, be weak, fade; to dangle:– brought low [3], dried up [1], emptied [1], fail [1], impoverished [1], made thin [1], not equal [1]

1810 דִּלְעָן **dil'ān**, n.pr.loc. GK: 1939. Dilean, "cucumber; protrude":– Dilean [1]

1811 דָּלַף **dālap**, v. GK: 1940 & 1941 [→ 1812, 1813, 3044]. [Q] to leak; to pour out; to be weary, be sleepless:– droppeth through [1], melteth [1], poureth out [1]

1812 דֶּלֶף **delep**, n.m. GK: 1942 [→ 1811]. leaky roof:– continual dropping (+2956) [1], dropping [1]

1813 דַּלְפּוֹן **dalpôn**, n.pr.m. GK: 1943 [→ 1811]. Dalphon, "crafty; sleepless":– Dalphon [1]

1814 דָּלַק **dālaq**, v. GK: 1944 [→ 1816; cf. 1815]. [Q] to set on fire; to hunt, chase, pursue; [H] to inflame, kindle:– kindle [1], burning [1], chasing [1], hotly pursued [1], inflame [1], persecute [1], persecutors [1], pursued [1]

1815 דְּלַק **dᵉlaq** (Aram.), v. GK: 10178 [cf. 1814]. [P] to be ablaze, burn:– burning [1]

1816 דַּלֶּקֶת **dalleqet**, n.f. GK: 1945 [→ 1814]. inflammation:– inflammation [1]

1817 דֶּלֶת **delet**, n.f. [& m.?]. GK: 1923 & 1928 & 1946. door, gate; column, lid, leaf (of a door):– doors [48], door [21], gates [13], leaves [4], lid [1], two leaved gates [1]

1818 דָּם **dām**, n.m. GK: 1947. blood, lifeblood; by extension: bloodshed, death; blood-colored fluids: grape juice, wine; "to pour out blood" is "to kill" since life is in the blood:– blood [342], bloody [15], bloodguiltiness [1], bloodthirsty (+376) [1], person⁵ [1]

1819 דָּמָה **dāmâ**, v. GK: 1948 [→ 1823, 1824, 1825; cf. 1821]. [Q] to be like, liken, resemble; [N] to be like; [P] to think, plan, intend; to liken; [Ht] to consider oneself equal to:– like [14], liken [4], thought [4], likened [2], compared [1], devised [1], meaneth [1], think [1], thoughtest [1], used similitudes [1]

1820 דָּמָה **dāmâ**, v. GK: 1949 & 1950 [→ 1822?, 1824; cf. 1747, 1826]. [Q] to destroy; to cease; to be silent; [N] to perish, be ruined, be destroyed, be wiped out; to be silenced:– cut off [3], brought to silence [2], perish [2], utterly cut off (+1820) [2], ceaseth [1], cease [1], cut down [1], destroyed [1], destroy [1], undone [1]

1821 דְּמָה **dᵉmâ** (Aram.), v. GK: 10179 [cf. 1819]. [P] to look like, resemble:– like [2]

1822 דֻּמָה **dumâ**, n.f. GK: 1951 [→ 1820?]. one silenced:– destroyed [1]

1823 דְּמוּת **dᵉmût**, n.f. GK: 1952 [→ 1819]. likeness, figure, image, form:– likeness [19], similitude [2], fashion [1], like (+3509.1) [1], like as [1], manner [1]

1824 דְּמִי **dᵉmî** or דֳּמִי **dŏmî**, n.[m.]. GK: 1953 & 1954 [→ 1819, 1820]. silence, rest; prime (of life), a fig. extension of being at a midway point in a journey:– cutting off [1], keep silence [1], rest [1], silence [1]

1825 דִּמְיוֹן **dimyôn**, n.[m.]. GK: 1955 [→ 1819]. likeness:– like [1]

1826 דָּמַם **dāmam**, v. GK: 1957 & 1958 & 1959 [→ 1745, 1747, 1827; cf. 1748, 1820]. [Q] to perish; to be still, be silent, be quiet, rest; [N] to be laid waste, be silenced, be destroyed; [Po] to quiet; [H] to doom to perish:– silent [4], still [4], cut off [3], cut down [2], keep silence [2], kept silence [2], ceased [1], cease [1], forbear [1], held peace [1], keepeth silence [1], put to silence [1], quieted [1], rested [1], rest [1], stand still [1], stood still [1], tarry [1], wait [1]

1827 דְּמָמָה **dᵉmāmâ**, n.f. GK: 1960 [→ 1826]. hush, whisper:– calm [1], silence [1], still [1]

1828 דֹּמֶן **dōmen**, n.m. GK: 1961 [→ 4087]. refuse, dung:– dung [2]

1829 דִּמְנָה **dimnâ**, n.pr.loc. GK: 1962. Dimnah, "manure":– Dimnah [1]

1830 דָּמַע **dāma'**, v. GK: 1963 [→ 1831, 1832]. [Q] to weep:– weep sore (+1830) [2]

1831 דֶּמַע **dema'**, n.[m.]. GK: 1964 [→ 1830]. juice:– liquors [1]

1832 דִּמְעָה **dim'â**, n.f. GK: 1965 [→ 1830]. tears, weeping:– tears [23]

1833 דְּמֶשֶׁק **dᵉmeseq**, n.[m.?]. GK: 1967 [→ 1834?]. Damascus, damask [?]:– Damascus [1]

1834 דַּמֶּשֶׂק **dammeseq** or דּוּמֶּשֶׂק **dûmmeseq** or דַּרְמֶשֶׂק **darmeseq**, n.pr.loc. GK: 1877 & 1966 & 2008 [→ 1833?]. Damascus:– Damascus [44], Syria-damascus (+758) [1]

1835 דָּן **dān**, n.pr.m. & loc. GK: 1968 [→ 1842, 1839; cf. 1777. Dan, "judge":– Dan [71]

1836 דְּנָא **dᵉnâ** (Aram.), p.demo.com. GK: 10180 [→ 412, 429, 459, 479]. this, that:– this [38], therefore (+3606+6903) [3], these [3], hereafter (+311) [2], thus (+3509.4) [2], wherefore (+3606+6903) [2], aforetime (+4481+6928) [1], another [1], for this cause (+3606+6903) [1], one [1], such (+3509.4) [1], that (+3606+6903) [1], therefore (+5922) [1], which [1]

1837 דַּנָּה **dannâ**, n.pr.loc. GK: 1972 [→ 4091]. Dannah, "stronghold":– Dannah [1]

1838 דִּנְהָבָה **dinhābâ**, n.pr.loc. GK: 1973 [→ 1767+5107]. Dinhabah:– Dinhabah [2]

1839 דָּנִי **dānî**, a.g. GK: 1974 [→ 1835]. Danite, men of Dan, "of Dan":– Danites [4], Dan [1]

1840 דָּנִאֵל **dāni'ēl** or דָּנִיֵּאל **dāniyyē'l**, n.pr.m. GK: 1971 & 1975 [→ 1777+410; cf. 1841]. Danel, Daniel; this can refer to four different persons, the most prominent being the sage and prophet of the captivity, "*God is [my] judge*":– Daniel [29]

1841 דָּנִיֵּאל **dāniyyē'l** (Aram.), n.pr.m. GK: 10181 [cf. 1840]. Daniel, "*God (El) is my judge*":– Daniel [52]

1842 דָּן יַעַן **dān ya'an**, n.pr.loc. GK: 1970 [→ 1835]. Dan Jaan:– Dan-jaan [1]

1843 דֵּעַ **dēa'**, n.[m.]. GK: 1976 [→ 1844; cf. 3045]. what is known, knowledge:– opinion [3], knowledge [2]

1844 דֵּעָה **dē'â**, n.f. GK: 1978 [→ 1843; cf. 3045]. knowledge:– knowledge [6]

1845 דְּעוּאֵל **d'û'ēl**, n.pr.m. GK: 1979 [→ 3045+410]. Deuel, "*known of God [El]*":– Deuel [4]

1846 דָּעַךְ **dā'ak**, v. GK: 1980 [cf. 2193]. [Q] to snuff out, extinguish; [N] to vanish; [Pu] to die out:– put out [6], consumed [1], extinct [1], quenched [1]

1847 דַּעַת **da'at**, n.f. & m. GK: 1981 & 1982 & 1983 [→ 3045]. knowledge; understanding; learning; claim:– knowledge [80], know [4], unwittingly (+1097+871.1) [2], cunning [1], hath knowledge (+3045) [1], have knowledge (+3045) [1], ignorantly (+1097+871.1) [1], knew [1], knowest (+5921) [1], unawares (+1097+871.1) [1]

1848 דֳּפִי **d'pî**, n.[m.]. GK: 1984. blemish, stain; slander:– slanderest (+5414) [1]

1849 דָּפַק **dāpaq**, v. GK: 1985 [→ 1850]. [Q] to drive hard; to knock hard (= worry); [Ht] to pound (on a door):– beat [1], knocketh [1], overdrive [1]

1850 דָּפְקָה **dopqâ**, n.pr.loc. GK: 1986 [→ 1849]. Dophkah, "*drive [sheep]*":– Dophkah [2]

1851 דַּק **daq**, a. GK: 1987 [→ 1854]. gaunt, thin, dwarfed; finely ground (incense), fine (dust):– thin [5], small [4], leanfleshed (+1320) [2], beaten small [1], dwarf [1], very little thing [1]

1852 דֹּק **dōq**, n.[m.]. GK: 1988 [→ 1854]. canopy, thin veil:– curtain [1]

1853 דִּקְלָה **diqlâ**, n.pr.m.[loc.]. GK: 1989. Diklah, "*[place of] date palms*":– Diklah [2]

1854 דָּקַק **dāqaq**, v. GK: 1990 [→ 1851, 1852; cf. 1743, 1790, 1792, 1794; cf. 1855]. [Q] to finely crush or grind; [H] to grind to powder, break to pieces; [Ho] to be ground (to make bread):– powder [2], stampt small [2], beat in pieces [1], beat small [1], bruised [1], bruise [1], made dust [1], small [1], stamped [1], stamp [1], very small [1]

1855 דְּקַק **d'qaq** (Aram.), v. GK: 10182 [cf. 1854]. [P] to break to pieces; [H] to crush, smash, pulverize:– brake in pieces [5], break in pieces [3], breaketh in pieces [1], broken to pieces [1]

1856 דָּקַר **dāqar**, v. GK: 1991 [→ 1128, 1857, 4094]. [Q] to drive through, pierce, stab; [Op, N, Pu] to be pierced:– thrust through [8], pierced [1], stricken through [1], wounded [1]

1857 דֶּקֶר **deqer**, n.pr.m. GK: 1992 [→ 1856]. Deker:– Dekar [1]

1858 דַּר **dar**, n.[m.]. GK: 1993. mother-of-pearl:– white [1]

1859 דָּר **dār** (Aram.), n.[m.]. GK: 10183 [→ 1753; cf. 1755]. generation; the phrase "from generation to generation" indicates an unlimited span of time: "eternal, forever":– generation [4]

דֹּר **dōr**. See 1755.

1860 דְּרָאוֹן **dērā'ôn**, n.m. GK: 1994. loathing, contempt, aversion:– abhorring [1], contempt [1]

1861 דָּרְבָן **dorbān**, n.[m.]. GK: 1995 & 1996. (iron) goading stick:– goads [2]

1862 דַּרְדַּע **darda'**, n.pr.m. GK: 1997 [cf. 1873]. Darda:– Darda [1]

1863 דַּרְדַּר **dardar**, n.[m.]. GK: 1998. thistle:– thistles [1], thistle [1]

1864 דָּרוֹם **dārôm**, n.m. GK: 1999. south; south wind:– south [17]

1865 דְּרוֹר **d'rôr**, n.[m.]. GK: 2001 & 2002. freedom, liberty; an event required every fifty years to restore Israelite slaves to freedom and Israelite land to tribal allotments; oil of myrrh, stacte:– liberty [7], pure [1]

1866 דְּרוֹר **d'rôr**, n.f. GK: 2000. a kind of bird, perhaps swallow or dove:– swallow [2]

1867 דָּרְיָוֶשׁ **dār'yāweš**, n.pr.m. GK: 2003 [cf. 1868]. Darius, "*he who upholds the good*":– Darius [10]

1868 דָּרְיָוֶשׁ **dār'yāweš** (Aram.), n.pr.m. GK: 10184 [cf. 1867]. Darius, "*he who upholds the good*":– Darius [15]

1869 דָּרַךְ **dārak**, v. GK: 2005 [→ 1870, 4096]. [Q] to go out, set out, march on, walk upon, trample; to bend (a bow); [Op] to string (a bow), be bent (of a bow); [H] to shoot (a bow); to cause to tread, to enable to go; to lead, guide:– tread [12], bend [7], bent [7], trodden [6], treadeth [4], bendeth [2], lead [2], archers (+7198) [1], archer [1], come [1], drew [1], goeth [1], guide [1], leadeth [1], led forth [1], led [1], make go over [1], make to go [1], make to walk [1], shoot [1], thresh [1], tread out [1], tread upon [1], treaders [1], treader [1], treading [1], trodden down [1], trode down [1], trode [1], walk [1]

1870 דֶּרֶךְ **derek**, n.m. GK: 2006 [→ 1869]. way, path, route, road, journey; by extension: conduct, way of life; a pagan god (Am 8:14):– way [460], ways [164], toward [29], journey [23], manner [8], conversation [2], towards [2], along by (+4480) [1], away (+871.1) [1], by [1], custom [1], eastward (+6921+1886.1) [1], high way [1], in the way go (+5921+6310) [1], journeyed (+6213) [1], pass by (+5674) [1], passengers (+5674) [1], pathway (+5410) [1], through [1], transgression (+6588) [1], way side [1], wayfaring men (+1980) [1], wayside (+3027) [1], whithersoever (+834+871.1+1886.1) [1]

1871 דַּרְכְּמוֹנִים **dark'mônîm**, n.m.[pl.]. GK: 2007 [→ 150]. (pl.) drachmas (Persian: a unit of weight used as a money, the value of which is uncertain):– drams [4]

1872 דְּרָע **d'rā'** (Aram.), n.[f.]. GK: 10185 [→ 153; cf. 2220]. arm:– arms [1]

1873 דָּרַע **dāra'**, n.pr.m. GK: 2009 [cf. 1862]. Daraa:– Dara [1]

1874 דַּרְקוֹן **darqôn**, n.pr.m. GK: 2010. Darkon, "*[perhaps] rough or stern*":– Darkon [2]

1875 דָּרַשׁ **dāraš**, v. GK: 2011 [→ 4097]. [Q] to seek, inquire, consult; [Op] to ponder, be sought after; [N] to let oneself be inquired of, to allow a search to be made:– seek [54], inquire [29], sought [19], require [10], inquired [5], seeketh [5], inquired of [4], inquire of [3], search [3], diligently sought (+1875) [2], inquired of at all (+1875) [2], required [2], searcheth [2], seeking [2], sought after [2], sought out [2], surely require (+1875) [2], ask [1], cared [1], careth for [1], examine [1], inquired for [1], make inquisition [1], maketh inquisition [1], necromancer (+413+1886.1+4191) [1], questioned [1], regard [1], search for [1], searchest [1], seek after [1], seek out [1], seeketh after [1], sought for [1]

1876 דָּשָׁא **dāšā'**, v. GK: 2012 [→ 1877]. [Q] to become green (of pastures); [H] to produce, cause to shoot forth:– bring forth [1], spring [1]

1877 דֶּשֶׁא **deše'**, n.m. GK: 2013 [→ 1876; cf. 1883]. (new) green vegetation, (new) green grass:– grass [6], herb [4], tender grass [2], tender herb [2], green [1]

1878 דָּשֵׁן **dāšēn**, v. GK: 2014 [→ 1879, 1880]. [Q] to thrive, grow fat; [P] to anoint, give health; to remove the (fat) ashes; [Pu] to prosper, be satisfied, be soaked (with fat); [Hotpaal] to be covered with fat:– made fat [5], accept [1], anointest [1], maketh fat [1], receive ashes [1], take away ashes [1], waxen fat [1]

1879 דָּשֵׁן **dāšēn**, a. GK: 2015 [→ 1878]. rich (pertaining to food which is fresh and possibly juicy), fresh:– fat [3]

1880 דֶּשֶׁן **dešen**, n.m. GK: 2016 [→ 1878]. fat; ashes (the burned wood of the altar fire soaked with fat); by extension: abundance, riches, choice food; in the ancient Near East fatness was a positive, enviable state, though extreme obesity could be denounced or ridiculed:– ashes [8], fatness [7]

1881 דָּת **dāt**, n.f. GK: 2017 [cf. 1882]. command (either written or oral), prescription, custom, edict, law:– decree [9], law [6], laws [3], commandment [2], commissions [1], manner [1]

1882 דָּת **dāt** (Aram.), n.f. GK: 10186 [cf. 1881]. law, decree, usually a written, codified prescription by either human or deity; the "Law of God" can refer to the Torah, the first five books of the Hebrew Bible:– law [9], decree [3], laws [2]

1883 דֶּתֶא **dete'** (Aram.), n.[m.]. GK: 10187 [cf. 1877]. grass (of the open country):– tender grass [2]

1884 דְּתָבַר **d'tābar** (Aram.), n.m. GK: 10188 [cf. 1881]. judge:– counsellers [2]

1885 דָּתָן **dātān**, n.pr.m. GK: 2018. Dathan, "*strong*":– Dathan [10]

1886 דֹּתָן **dōtān**, n.pr.loc. GK: 2019. Dothan, "*two wells*":– Dothan [3]

1886.1 הַ- **ha-**, art.pref. GK: 2021 [cf. 0.2 (also used with compound proper names)]. the, a, who, this, that; often not translated:– the [18118], that [957], a [767], which [269], an [87], who [55], O [53], to day (+3117) [50], every morning (+1242+1242+871.1+871.1+1886.1) [20], he [17], for ever (+3117+3605) [15], it [12], without (+2351+871.1) [12], daily (+3117+3605) [11], those [10]*

1886.2 הֲ- **h'-**, inter.pt.pref. GK: 2022 [cf. 1886.6]. introduces a question; usually translated as a question mark:– *usually untranslated* [711], whether [23], if [5], as if [1], either [1], not [1], or [1]

1886.3 הָ- **-āh** or הַ- **-hā** or הַ- **-â** or הָא- **-hā'**, p.f.s.suf. GK: 2023 [→ 1886.4, 1930.2, 1958.1, 1992.1, 1993.1, 2006.1, 2009.1, 2050.2, 3963.1, 4123.1, 4993.1, 5089.1, 5105.2]. she, her; it, its:– her [1518], it [649], thereof [343], therein (+871.1) [86], his [81], she [44], their [24], the[s] [18], them [15], wherein (+834+871.1) [14], that [13], whose [13], therewith (+871.1) [11], thereon (+5921) [10], whereof [10]*

1886.4 הֹ- **-ōh**, p.m.s.suf. GK: 2024 [→ 1886.3]. he, his, him:– his [11], it [3], one [3], them [3], they [3], he [1], same [1], thereof [1]

1886.5 הָ- **-â**, adv.suf. GK: 2025. to, toward; a suffixed adverb or remnant of an archaic case ending:– to [269], into [97], toward [58], thither (+8033) [50], unto [49], upward (+4605) [45], on [41], whither (+834+8033) [38], upon [32], there (+8033) [31], westward (+3220) [21], northward (+6828) [20], above (+4480+4605+3807.1) [18], whither (+575) [16], eastward (+4217) [15], west (+3220) [15], east (+6921) [14], at [13], how long (+575+5704) [13], southward (+5045) [13], in [12], upward (+4605+3807.1) [12], eastward (+6924) [9], north (+6828) [9], towards (+2351) [8], southward (+8486) [8], where (+834+8033) [7], above (+4605+3807.1) [6], without (+2351) [6], east (+6924) [5], inward (+1004) [5], on high (+4605+3807.1) [5], therein (+8033) [5], above (+4605) [4], any whither (+575+575+1886.5+2050.1) [4], eastward (+6921) [4], out (+2351) [3], where (+575) [3], yearly (+3117+3117+4480) [3], exceedingly (+4605+3807.1) [2], exceedingly (+4605+5704+3807.1) [2], forward (+4605) [2], south (+5045) [2], south (+8486+1886.5) [2], still (+4605+3807.1) [2], upward (+4480+4605+3807.1) [2], very high (+4605+4605+1886.5) [2], whither (+575+575+1886.5+2050.1) [2], whither (+8033) [2], without (+2351+4480) [2], abroad (+413+2351+1886.1) [1], by [1], east (+4217+6924) [1], exceeding (+4605) [1], exceeding (+4605+3807.1) [1], for [1], hither (+2008) [1], in north (+6828) [1], north side (+6828) [1], northwards (+6828) [1], on high (+4480+4605+3807.1) [1], outward (+2351) [1], over (+4480+4605+3807.1) [1], over and above (+4480+4605+3807.1) [1], overturned (+2015+4605+3807.1) [1], south (+8486) [1], south [1], thitherward (+8033) [1], through [1], unto (+8033) [1], up (+4605+3807.1) [1], very (+4605+3807.1) [1], westward (+4628) [1], whereinto (+834+8033) [1], whereunto (+834+8033) [1], whithersoever (+575) [1], within (+1004) [1], within (+1004+4480) [1], without (+2351+1886.1) [1], without (+2435) [1]

1886.6 הֲ- **h'-** (Aram.), inter.pt. GK: 10190 [cf. 1886.2]. introduces a question, translated as a question mark rather than as a word:– *not translated* [6]

1886.7 הַ- **-â** (Aram.), art.suf. GK: 10191 [→ 0.2]. the, a:– the [32], The[s] [1], a [1], it [1], thereof [1], this [1]

1886.8 הֵ- **-ēh** (Aram.), p.s.m.3.m.s. GK: 10192 [→ 1958.2; cf. 1886.4]. he, his; it, its:– his [61], him [29], thereof [25], whose [11], it [4], the[s] [2], their [2], whom [2], he [1], his (+3807.2) [1], his own [1], same [1]

1886.9 הֵ- **-ah** (Aram.), p.s.m.3.f.s. GK: 10193 [cf. 1886.3]. she, her; it, its:– it [21], his [5], same [3], whom [2], whose [2], the same (+1459) [1], therein (+1459+871.2) [1], therein (+871.2) [1], thereof [1]

1887 הֵא **hē'**, interj. GK: 2026 [cf. 1888]. surely! see!, a discourse marker of emphasis:– behold [1], lo [1]

1888 הָא **hā'** or הֵא **hē'** (Aram.), demo.pt. GK: 10194 & 10195 [cf. 1887]. just as; look!, there!:– even [1], lo [1]

1889 הֶאָח **he'āḥ**, interj. GK: 2027. Ah!, Aha!:– aha [10], ah [1], ha, ha [1]

הָארָרִי **hā'rārî**. See 2043.

1890 הַבְהָב **habhab**, n.m. GK: 2037. gift:– offerings [1]

1891 הָבַל **hābal**, v.den. GK: 2038 [→ 1892]. [Q] to be worthless, meaningless; be proud, vain; [H] to fill with false hopes, cause to become vain:– vain [2], altogether vain (+1892) [1], become vain [1], make vain [1]

1892 הֶבֶל *hebel*, n.m. GK: 2039 [→ 1891; cf. 1893]. breath; by extension: something with no substance, meaninglessness, worthlessness, vanity, emptiness, futility; idol:– vanity [49], vanities [12], in vain [7], vain [4], altogether vain (+1891) [1]

1893 הֶבֶל *hebel*, n.pr.m. GK: 2040 [cf. 1892?]. Abel, "*morning mist*":– Abel [8]

1894 הׇבְנִים *hobnîm*, n.[m.]. GK: 2041. ebony:– ebeny [1]

1895 הָבַר *hābar*, v. GK: 2042. [Q] (ptcp.) astrologer, one who divides (classifies) the night sky for the purpose of telling the future:– astrologers (+8064) [1]

1896 הֵגֵא *hēgē'* or הֵגַי *hēgay*, n.pr.m. GK: 2043 & 2051. Hegai:– Hegai [3], Hege [1]

1897 הָגָה *hāgâ*, v. GK: 2047 [→ 1899, 1900, 1902]. [Q] to utter a sound, moan, meditate; [H] to mutter; from the base meaning of uttering a sound of any kind comes figure of meditation, the act of thoughtful deliberation with the implication of speaking to oneself:– meditate [6], mourn [3], speak [3], imagine [2], mourn sore (+1897) [2], studieth [2], muttered [1], mutter [1], roaring [1], speaketh [1], talk [1], uttering [1], utter [1]

1898 הָגָה *hāgâ*, v. GK: 2048 [cf. 3014]. [Q] to expel, remove:– take away [2], stayeth [1]

1899 הֶגֶה *hegeh*, n.m. GK: 2049 [→ 1897]. moaning, mourning, rumbling:– mourning [1], sound [1], tale [1]

1900 הָגוּת *hāgût*, n.f. GK: 2050 [→ 1897]. utterance, meditation, which can include thinking and planning:– meditation [1]

1901 הָגִיג *hāgîg*, n.m. GK: 2052. sighing, meditation:– meditation [1], musing [1]

1902 הִגָּיוֹן *higgāyôn*, n.m. GK: 2053 [→ 1897]. muttering (sounds spoken to no one in particular), meditation; Higgaion, melody:– Higgaion [1], device [1], meditation [1], solemn sound [1]

1903 הָגִין *hāgîn*, a. GK: 2054. corresponding:– directly [1]

1904 הָגָר *hāgār*, n.pr.f. GK: 2057 [→ 1905?]. Hagar, "*emigration, flight*":– Hagar [12]

1905 הַגְרִי *hagrî*, a.g. [& n.pr.m.?]. GK: 2058 [→ 1904?]. Hagrites, of Hagri, "*wanderer*":– Hagarites [3], Hagarenes [1], Hagerite [1], Haggeri [1]

1906 הֵד *hēd*, n.[m.]. GK: 2059 [→ 1959]. joyous shout:– sounding again [1]

1907 הַדָּבַר *haddābar* (Aram.), n.m. GK: 10196. royal adviser, official of the king:– counsellers [4]

1908 הֲדַד *h°dad*, n.pr.m. GK: 2060 [→ 111, 1130, 1909, 1910, 1913, 2582]. Hadad, "*thunderer*":– Hadad [12]

1909 הֲדַדְעֶזֶר *h°dad'ezer*, n.pr.m. GK: 2061 [→ 1908+5828]. Hadadezer, "*Hadad is a help*":– Hadadezer [9]

1910 הֲדַדרִמּוֹן *h°dad-rimmôn*, n.pr.m.[loc.?]. GK: 2062 [→ 1908+7417]. Hadad Rimmon:– Hadadrimmon [1]

1911 הָדָה *hādâ*, v. GK: 2063. [Q] to put, stretch out:– put [1]

1912 הֹדּוּ *hōddû*, n.pr.loc. GK: 2064. India:– India [2]

1913 הֲדוֹרָם *h°dôrām*, n.pr.m. GK: 2066 & 2067 [→ 1908+7311]. Hadoram, "*Hadad is exalted*":– Hadoram [4]

1914 הִדַּי *hidday*, n.pr.m. GK: 2068 [cf. 2355]. Hiddai:– Hiddai [1]

1915 הָדַךְ *hādak*, v. GK: 2070. [Q] to crush by treading upon:– tread down [1]

1916 הֲדֹם *h°dōm*, n.m. GK: 2071. footstool:– footstool (+7272) [5], footstool (+7272+3807.1) [1]

1917 הַדָּם *haddām* (Aram.), n.[m.]. GK: 10197. pieces, members (of an execution by dismemberment):– pieces [2]

1918 הֲדַס *h°das*, n.m. GK: 2072 [→ 1919]. myrtle tree:– myrtle trees [3], myrtle [2], myrtle tree [1]

1919 הֲדַסָּה *h°dassâ*, n.pr.f. GK: 2073 [→ 1918]. Hadassah, "*myrtle*; [poss.] bride or myrtle":– Hadassah [1]

1920 הָדַף *hādap*, v. GK: 2074. [Q] to shove, push, thrust, drive out:– thrust [3], cast out [2], drive [2], casteth away [1], driven [1], expel [1], thrust away [1]

1921 הָדַר *hādar*, v. GK: 2075 & 2065 [→ 1926, 1925, 1927; cf. 1922]. [Q] to show favoritism; show respect; [Qp] to be in splendor; [N] to be shown respect; [Ht] to exalt oneself:– honour [2], countenance [1], crooked places [1], glorious [1], honoured [1], put forth [1]

1922 הֲדַר *h°dar* (Aram.), v. GK: 10198 [→ 1923; cf. 1921]. [Pa] to glorify, honor, to speak words that elevate the status of another:– glorified [1], honoured [1], honour [1]

1923 הֲדַר *h°dar* (Aram.), n.[m.]. GK: 10199 [→ 1922; cf. 1926, 1925]. splendor, honor, majesty:– honour [2], majesty [1]

1924 הֲדַר *h°dar*, n.pr.m. GK: 2076 [→ 1928]. Hadar; cf. 1908:– Hadar [1]

1925 הֶדֶר *heder*, n.[m.]. GK: 2078 [→ 1921; cf. 1923]. splendor; "the royal splendor" may refer to the land of Israel, with the focus that this land is an valued ornament of the king:– glory [1]

1926 הָדָר *hādār*, n.m. GK: 2077 [→ 1921; cf. 1923]. majesty, splendor, glory, nobility; often related to the appearance of an object that is beautiful and instills awe:– glory [6], honour [5], beauty [3], comeliness [3], excellency [2], beauties [1], full of majesty [1], glorious [1], goodly [1]

1927 הֲדָרָה *h°dārâ*, n.f. GK: 2079 [→ 1921]. splendor, glory:– beauty [4], honour [1]

הֲדֹרָם *h°dōrām*. See 1913.

1928 הֲדַרְעֶזֶר *h°dar'ezer*, n.pr.m. GK: 2080 [→ 1924+5828]. Hadarezer:– Hadarezer [12]

1929 הָהּ *hāh*, interj. GK: 2081. Alas!:– woe [1]

1930 הוֹ *hô*, interj. GK: 2082 [→ 1945]. ah! (doubled for emphasis), with a strong implication of mourning or sorrow:– alas [2]

1930.1 הוּ *hû*, p.m.s. GK: 2083 [→ 1931]. he, she, it; that, which:– it [1]

1930.2 הוּ- *-hû*, p.m.s.suf. GK: 2084 [→ 1886.3]. he, his, him; it, its:– him [568], his [219], it [164], them [33], thereof [13], he [8], his own [4], that [3], their [3], they [3], which [3], whose [3], himself [2], the same [2], whom [2], her [1], himself (+4617) [1], man's [1], me [1], she [1], thereof (+4480) [1], there [1], whereof [1]

1931 הוּא *hû'*, p.m.s. or הִיא *hî'*, p.f.s. GK: 2085 & 2115 [→ 1930.1, 1992, 2007; cf. 1932 (also used with compound proper names)]. he, she, it; this, that:– he [623], that [432], it [245], she [103], this [63], which [63], the same [53], they [24], who [24], himself [16], same [14], him [13], the [6], her [2], such [2], their [2], the [2], those [2], his own [1], his [1], one [1], she herself [1], this same [1], thou [1], very [1], what (+834) [1], whom [1], whose [1]

1932 הוּא *hû'*, p.3.m.s. or הִיא *hî'* (Aram.), p.3.f.s. GK: 10200 & 10205 [→ 581; cf. 1931]. he, she, it:– *usually untranslated* [10], he [6], it [3], this [2], that [1]

1933 הָוָה *hāwâ*, v. GK: 2092 & 2093 [→ 1942, 1943, 1962; cf. 1961; cf. 1934]. [Q] to be, become; to get, have:– be [5], hath (+3807.1) [1]

1934 הֲוָה *h°wâ* (Aram.), v. GK: 10201 [cf. 1961, 1933]. [P] to be, become, happen:– *usually untranslated* [34], be [21], was [5], come to pass [3], became [2], been [1], have [1], might [1], offer [1], shall [1], so (+2050.3) [1]

1935 הוֹד *hôd*, n.m. GK: 2086 [→ 1936, 5989; cf. 3034 (also used with compound proper names)]. splendor, majesty, glory, strength:– glory [9], honour [6], majesty [4], beauty [1], comeliness [1], glorious [1], goodly [1], honourable [1]

1936 הוֹד *hôd*, n.pr.m. GK: 2087 [→ 1935]. Hod, "*grandeur*":– Hod [1]

1937 הוֹדְוָה *hôd°wâ*, n.pr.m. GK: 2088 [→ 1938, 1939]. Hodaviah, "*give thanks to Yahweh*":– Hodevah [1]

1938 הוֹדַוְיָה *hôdawyâ*, n.pr.m. GK: 2089 [→ 1939, 1937]. Hodaviah, "*give thanks to Yahweh*":– Hodaviah [3]

1939 הוֹדַוְיָהוּ *hôdawyāhû*, n.pr.m. GK: 2069 & 2090 [→ 1937, 1938]. Hodaviah, "*give thanks to Yahweh*":– Hodaiah [1]

1940 הוֹדִיָּה *hôdiyyâ*, n.pr.f. GK: 2091 [→ 1935+3068, 1941]. same as 1941: Hodiah, "*grandeur is Yahweh*":– Hodiah [1]

1941 הוֹדִיָּה *hôdiyyâ*, n.pr.m. GK: 2091 [→ 1940]. same as 1940: Hodiah, Hodijah, "*grandeur is Yahweh*":– Hodijah [5]

הָוָה *hāwâ*. See 1933.

הֲוָה *h°wâ*. See 1934.

1942 הַוָּה *hawwâ*, n.f. GK: 2094 & 2095 [→ 185, 1962; cf. 183; 1933]. (evil) desire, craving; destruction, ruin, corruption:– calamity [3], wickedness [3], calamities [1], iniquity [1], mischiefs [1], mischievous things [1],

mischievous [1], naughtiness [1], naughty [1], noisome [1], perverse things [1], substance [1]

1943 הֹוָה *hôwâ*, n.f. GK: 2096 [→ 1933]. calamity, disaster:– mischief [3]

1944 הוֹהָם *hôhām*, n.pr.m. GK: 2097. Hoham:– Hoham [1]

1945 הוֹי *hôy*, interj. GK: 2098 [→ 1930]. woe, ah!, oh!, alas!; (to invite) come!:– woe [36], ah [7], O [3], ho [3], alas [1]

1946 הוּךְ *hûk* (Aram.), v. GK: 10202 [→ 1981]. same as 1981: [P] to go, walk:– go [2], brought [1], came [1]

1947 הוֹלֵלוֹת *hôlēlôt*, n.f. GK: 2099 [→ 1984]. madness, delusion, folly:– madness [4]

1948 הוֹלֵלוּת *hôlēlût*, n.f. GK: 2100 [→ 1984]. madness, delusion, folly:– madness [1]

1949 הוּם *hûm*, v. GK: 2101 [→ 4103; cf. 1993, 2000, 5098]. [Q] to throw into confusion; [N] to be stirred up, be shook; [H] to be distraught; to throng:– rang again [2], destroy [1], make a noise [1], make great noise [1], moved [1]

1950 הוֹמָם *hômām*, n.pr.m. GK: 2102 [→ 1967]. Homam:– Homam [1]

1951 הוּן *hûn*, v. GK: 2103 [→ 1952]. [H] to think it easy:– ready [1]

1952 הוֹן *hôn*, n.m. GK: 2104 [→ 1951]. wealth, riches, possessions:– riches [10], substance [7], wealth [5], enough [2], nought (+3808) [1], rich [1]

1952.1 הוֹן- *-hôn* (Aram.), p.suf.3.m.pl. GK: 10203 [cf. 1992.1]. they, them, their:– their [21], them [16], the [3], their own [1], therein (+871.2) [1], these [1], whom [1], whose [1], your [1]

1953 הוֹשָׁמָע *hôšāmā'*, n.pr.m. GK: 2106 [→ 8085+3068]. Hoshama, "*Yahweh has heard*":– Hoshama [1]

1954 הוֹשֵׁעַ *hôšēa'*, n.pr.m. GK: 2107 [→ 3467+410 or 3068]. Hoshea; Joshua, "*salvation*":– Hoshea [11], Hosea [3], Oshea [2]

1955 הוֹשַׁעְיָה *hôša'yâ*, n.pr.m. GK: 2108 [→ 3467+3068]. Hoshaiah, "*Yahweh has saved*":– Hoshaiah [3]

1956 הוֹתִיר *hôtîr*, n.pr.m. GK: 2110 [→ 3498]. Hothir, "*one who remains*":– Hothir [2]

1957 הָזָה *hāzâ*, v. GK: 2111. [Q] to dream:– sleeping [1]

1958 הִי *hî*, n.[m.]. GK: 2113. woe!, an exclamation of sorrow:– woe [1]

הִיא *hî'*. See 1931, 1932.

1958.1 הִי- *-hî*, p.m.s.suf. GK: 2114 [→ 1886.3]. his, him:– his [1]

1958.2 הִי- *-hî* (Aram.), p.suf.3.m.s. GK: 10204 [→ 1886.8; cf. 1958.1]. he, his, him; it, its:– his [37], him [20], it [3], thereof [3], which [2], whose [2], himself [1], the [1], thereon (+5922) [1], ye [1]

1959 הֵידָד *hêdād*, n.m. GK: 2116 [→ 1906]. shout (of joy):– shouting [5], give a shout (+6030) [1], shout [1]

1960 הֻיֵּדֹת *huyy°dôt*, n.f.pl. GK: 2117 [→ 3034]. (pl.) songs of thanksgiving:– thanksgiving [1]

1961 הָיָה *hāyâ*, v. GK: 2118 & 181 [cf. 1933; cf. 1934]. [Q] to be, become, happen; [N] to be done, happen; the common verb of being, referring to state of being, change of state, existence, and the occurring of events, or even possession:– be [1277], was [525], came to pass [389], were [228], came [146], come to pass [125], is [75], had (+3807.1) [72], have (+3807.1) [72], been [71], become [64], became [59], are [56], have [26], am [20], had [18], wast [15], come [10], done [8], shall [8], became (+3807.1) [7], hath (+3807.1) [6], become (+3807.1) [4], being [4], did [4], fell [4], hath (+871.1) [4], went [4], art [3], continued [3], endure [3], fell on [3], follow [3], should [3], abode [2], be (+3807.1) [2], be altogether (+1961) [2], becamest [2], been (+1961) [2], came expressly (+1961) [2], continue [2], escape (+6413) [2], followed (+310) [2], go [2], had at all (+1961+3807.1) [2], hadst (+3807.1) [2], hast (+3807.1) [2], having [2], made [2], married (+802+3807.1) [2], marry (+802+3807.1) [2], pertained [2], quit [2], received (+3807.1) [2], redeem (+1353) [2], redeemed (+1353) [2], seemed (+5869+871.1) [2], shew (+3807.1) [2], surely become (+1961) [2], surely come to pass (+1961) [2], was altogether (+1961) [2], accomplished [1], after that (+4480+7093) [1], be at all (+1961) [1], brake [1], brought to pass [1], brought [1], came up [1], caused [1], cherish (+5532) [1], cherished (+5532) [1], come [1], cometh to pass [1], committed [1], conferred (+1697) [1], count (+3807.1) [1], coupled (+8535) [1], determined (+7760) [1], do [1], endured [1], enjoy (+3807.1) [1], escape (+6412) [1], fainted [1],

follow (+310) [1], give (+413) [1], gone [1], had (+5973) [1], had before (+4480) [1], had wars with (+376+4421) [1], had with (+376+4421) [1], happened [1], hast [1], hath [1], have (+871.1) [1], having (+3807.1) [1], held peace (+2790+3509.1) [1], help (+3444) [1], help (+8668) [1], keep (+4931) [1], keep [1], lasted [1], lay [1], let [1], lived (+2416) [1], liveth [1], make [1], marry [1], order (+4941) [1], pass [1], pertaineth [1], reach [1], rejoice (+8056) [1], remained [1], remain [1], required [1], seem (+5869+871.1) [1], shalt [1], since (+4480) [1], surely be (+1961) [1], take (+3807.1) [1], trembled (+2730) [1], use (+3807.1) [1], waited on (+6440+3807.1) [1], wear (+5921) [1], while (+871.1) [1], will [1], would [1]

1962 הַיָּה *hayyâ*, n.f. GK: 2119 [→ 1942; cf. 1933]. destruction:–

1963 הֵיךְ *hêk*, adv. GK: 2120 [cf. 349]. how?:– how [2]

1964 הֵיכָל *hêkāl*, n.m. GK: 2121 [cf. 1965]. a building of some kind: temple, sanctuary, palace; main hall:– temple [68], palace [7], palaces [3], temples [2]

1965 הֵיכַל *hêkal* (Aram.), n.m. GK: 10206 [cf. 1964]. residence of a deity: temple; residence of royalty: palace:– temple [8], palace [5]

1966 הֵילֵל *hêlēl*, n.m.[pr.?]. GK: 2122 [→ 1984]. from the base meaning "shining one," this refers to an object in the night sky, often translated "morning star," and possibly referring the planet Venus; fig. used as a title of the king of Babylon (Isa 14:12). The Latin "lucifer" also means "shining one," and has become a title of Satan due to a traditional equation of the king of Babylon with the devil:– Lucifer [1]

1967 הֵימָם *hêmām*, n.pr.m. GK: 2123 [→ 1950]. Homam:– Hemam [1]

1968 הֵימָן *hêmān*, n.pr.m. GK: 2124 [→ 3225? *or* 539?]. Homam:– Heman [17]

1969 הִין *hîn*, n.m. GK: 2125. hin (liquid measure of volume, one-sixth of a bath, about one gallon [four liters]):– hin [22]

1970 הָכַר *hākar*, v. GK: 2128 & 2686. [Q] to attack (vigorously) or to make oneself strange:– make strange [1]

1971 הַכָּרָה *hakkārâ*, n.f. GK: 2129 [→ 5234]. look (on a face) as a non-verbal communication, which in context may refer to personal bias:– shew [1]

הַל *hal*. See 1973.

1972 הָלָא *hālā'*, v.den. GK: 2133. [N] to be driven away, be removed:– cast far off [1]

1973 הָלְאָה *hāľ'â*, adv. GK: 2131 & 2134 [→ 1886.1+3807.1]. beyond; far (and wide), some distance away; out of the way!:– forward [5], beyond (+4480) [4], hitherto [2], back [1], beyond (+4480+2050.1) [1], henceforward [1], thenceforth [1], yonder [1]

1974 הִלּוּלִים *hillûlîm*, n.[m.]. GK: 2136 [→ 1984]. offering of praise; festival (related to a god):– merry [1], praise [1]

1975 הַלָּז *hallāz*, p.com.s. GK: 2137 [→ 1976]. this:– this [4], that [2], other [1]

1976 הַלָּזֶה *hallāzeh*, p.m. GK: 2138 [→ 1975, 1977; cf. 2098]. this:– this [2]

1977 הַלֵּזוּ *hallēzû*, p.f. GK: 2139 [→ 1976]. this:– this [1]

1978 הָלִיךְ *hālîk*, n.[m.]. GK: 2141 [→ 1980]. path, steps:– steps [1]

1979 הֲלִיכָה *hălîkâ*, n.f. GK: 2142 [→ 1980]. procession, way, walk; traveling merchants; affairs:– goings [2], ways [2], companies [1], walk [1]

1980 הָלַךְ *hālak*, v. GK: 2143 [→ 1978, 1979, 1982, 3212, 4108, 4109, 4447, 8418, 8437; cf. 1981]. [Q] to walk, go, travel; [N] to fade away; [P] to walk about, go about, [H] to drive back, get rid of; enable to walk; to lead; bring; [Ht] to move to and fro, wander, walk about; by extension: to walk as a lifestyle, a pattern of conduct:– go [417], went [348], walk [133], walked [97], come [78], departed [47], gone [35], walketh [34], goest [18], get [17], depart [16], followed (+310) [16], goeth [16], led [13], came [11], walking [11], going [10], follow (+310) [9], went away [9], brought [8], went on (+1980) [8], wentest [7], bring [4], walkest [4], camest [3], carry [3], departed (+4480) [3], going on [3], march [3], passeth away [3], walk to and fro [3], went along [3], went on [3], all along as went (+1980) [2], came apace (+1980) [2], came on (+1980) [2], carried [2], cause to go [2], cause to walk [2], come away [2], continually [2], conversant [2], departeth [2], flow [2], following (+310) [2], gat away [2], gat [2], go along [2], go away [2], go speedily (+1980) [2], go to [2], go up and down [2], goeth away [2], goeth forth (+1980) [2], leadeth away [2], lead [2], needs be gone (+1980) [2], quite gone (+1980) [2], ran [2], run [2], still went

on (+1980) [2], surely depart (+1980) [2], surely go (+1980) [2], travelleth [2], walked to and fro [2], walking up and down [2], waxed greater (+1980) [2], weak [2], went forth on a time (+1980) [2], went on continually (+1980) [2], went out [2], went up and down [2], wrought [2], along [1], at the point [1], away [1], bear [1], behaved [1], carry away [1], cause to run [1], caused to go [1], cometh out [1], cometh [1], coming [1], continually (+7725+2050.1) [1], depart (+4480) [1], eased (+4480) [1], enter [1], exercise [1], flowed [1], follow (+7272+871.1) [1], followedst (+310) [1], followed [1], get away [1], go forward [1], go in [1], go up [1], goeth about [1], goeth on still [1], gone away [1], gone up [1], grow [1], lead forth [1], leadeth [1], let down [1], made go [1], may [1], moveth [1], on [1], pass away [1], passeth [1], prospered [1], pursue (+310) [1], ran along [1], return again (+7725) [1], run continually [1], running [1], sent [1], shineth more and more (+215) [1], sounded long [1], spread abroad [1], spread [1], take away [1], takest [1], take [1], talebearer (+7400) [1], travellers (+5410) [1], vanisheth away [1], walk on [1], walk up and down [1], walked up and down [1], wandered [1], wandering [1], waxed greater [1], waxed stronger [1], waxed weaker [1], waxed [1], wayfaring men (+1870) [1], went abroad [1], went forward (+1980) [1], went way [1], whirleth about continually (+5437+5437) [1], wont to haunt [1]

1981 הֲלַךְ *hǎlak* (Aram.), v. GK: 10207 [→ 1983; cf. 1946; cf. 1980]. [P] to go; [Pa] to walk about; [H] to walk around:– walked [1], walking [1], walk [1]

1982 הֵלֶךְ *hēlek*, n.m. GK: 2144 [→ 1980]. oozing, flowing; visitor:– dropped [1], traveller [1]

1983 הֲלָךְ *hǎlāk* (Aram.), n.[m.]. GK: 10208 [→ 1981]. duty, toll, tax:– custom [3]

1984 הָלַל *hālal*, v. GK: 2145 & 2146 & 2147 & 2149 [→ 166, 1947, 1948, 1966, 1974, 1985, 4110, 8416 (also used with compound proper names)]. [Q] to be arrogant; [P] to praise; give thanks; cheer, extol; [Po] to make a fool of, to mock, rail against; [Pu] to be praised, be worthy of praise, be of renown; [Ht] to make one's boast in (the name of God); to act like a madman; act furiously; [H] to flash, radiate, shine; "Hallelujah" is a compound of the second person plural imperative and the personal name of God: hallelu-yah, praise Yah(weh):– praise [92], praised [19], glory [12], boast [5], mad [5], praising [4], boasteth [3], commended [2], foolish [2], maketh mad [2], rage [2], shined [2], boastest [1], celebrate [1], deal foolishly [1], feigned mad [1], fools [1], given to marriage [1], give [1], gloriest [1], glorieth [1], make boast [1], maketh fools [1], praises [1], praiseth [1], renowned [1], shine [1]

1985 הִלֵּל *hillēl*, n.pr.m. GK: 2148 [→ 1984]. Hillel, "*he has praises*":– Hillel [2]

1986 הָלַם *hālam*, v. GK: 2150 [→ 1989, 4112]. [Q] to strike, smash, beat, trample:– smote [2], beaten [1], beating down [1], break down [1], broken down [1], broken [1], overcome [1], smite [1]

1987 הֵלֶם *hēlem*, n.pr.m. GK: 2152. Helem, "*health*":– Helem [1]

1988 הֲלֹם *hǎlōm*, adv. GK: 2151. to here:– hither [6], here [2], hitherto (+5704) [2], thither [1]

1989 הַלְמוּת *halmût*, n.f. GK: 2153 [→ 1986]. hammer:– hammer [1]

1990 הָם *hām*, n.pr.loc. GK: 2154. Ham:– Ham [1]

1991 הָם *hām*, n.[m.]. GK: 2155 [cf. 1998]. wealth:– *not translated* [1]

1992 הֵם *hēm* or הֵמָּה *hēmmâ*, p.m.pl. GK: 2156 & 2160 [→ 1931; cf. 1994]. they, them:– they [368], those [52], these [26], them [20], who [7], themselves [5], same [4], that [3], their [3], which [3], it [2], whom (+834) [2], whom [2], the things [1], this [1], whereby (+834) [1], withal (+871.1) [1], ye [1]

1992.1 הֶם- *-hem* or הֵם- *-hēm*, p.m.pl.suf. GK: 2157 [cf. 1886.3]. they, them, their:– them [1496], their [1187], they [90], their (+3807.1) [38], themselves [26], their own [23]*

1992.2 הֹם- *-hōm* (Aram.), p.suf.3.m.pl. GK: 10209 [→ 2006.2; cf. 1992.1]. they, them, their:– them [7], their [4]

1993 הָמָה *hāmâ*, v. GK: 2159 [→ 1995, 1997?, 1998, 1999?; cf. 1949, 2000, 5098]. [Q] to make a noise, be tumultuous:– roar [6], disquieted [4], make a noise [4], sound [3], troubled [3], clamorous [1], concourse [1], cry aloud [1], in an uproar [1], loud [1], make a tumult [1], maketh a noise [1], mourning [1], moved [1], noise [1], raged [1], raging [1], roared [1], roareth [1], tumultuous [1]

1993.1 הֶמָה- *-hēmâ*, p.m.pl.suf. GK: 2161 [→ 1886.3]. they, them:– their [1]

1994 הִמּוֹ *himmô* (Aram.), p.3.pl. GK: 10210 [cf. 1992]. they, them:– them [8], those [1]

1995 הָמוֹן *hāmôn*, n.m. GK: 2162 & 2171 [→ 1174, 1996, 1997; cf. 1993]. commotion, tumult, confusion; many, populace, hoards, army:– multitude [59], noise [4], tumult [4], abundance [2], many [3], multitudes [3], Hamon-gog [2], company [1], great store [1], multiplied [1], riches [1], rumbling [1], sounding [1], store [1]

הַמֹּלֶכֶת *ham-mōleket*. See 4447.

1996 הֲמוֹן גּוֹג *hǎmôn gôg*, n.pr.loc. GK: 2163 [→ 1995+1463]. Hamon Gog, "*multitude of Gog*":–

1997 הֲמוֹנָה *hǎmônâ*, n.pr.loc. GK: 2164 [→ 1995?; cf. 1993]. Hamonah, "*multitude*":– Hamonah [1]

הֲמוּנֵךְ *hǎmûnēk*. See 2002.

1998 הֶמְיָה *hemyâ*, n.f. GK: 2166 [→ 1993; cf. 1991]. noise, sound, tone:– noise [1]

1999 הֲמֻלָּה *hǎmullâ*, n.f. GK: 2167 [→ 1993?]. tumult, sound, noise:– speech [1], tumult [1]

הַמֶּלֶךְ *ham-melek*. See 4429.

2000 הָמַם *hāmam*, v. GK: 2169 & 2170 [cf. 1949, 1993, 5098]. [Q] to throw into confusion; to rout; to drain:– discomfited [5], destroy [3], break [1], consume [1], crushed [1], troubled [1], vex [1]

הָמֹן *hāmōn*. See 1995.

2001 הָמָן *hāmān*, n.pr.m. GK: 2172. Haman:– Haman [50], Haman's [3], he[s] [1]

2002 המונכ *hmwnk* or הֲמְיָנַךְ *hamyānak* (Aram.), n.[m.]. GK: 10211 & 10212. chain, necklace:– chain [3]

2003 הֲמָסִים *hǎmāsîm*, n.[m.]. GK: 2173. twigs, brushwood:– melting [1]

2004 הֵן *hēn*, p.f.pl. GK: 2177 [→ 1886.3]. they, them, their:–

2005 הֵן *hēn*, adv.demo. *or* interj. GK: 2176 [→ 403, 2008, 2009, 5728; cf. 2006]. behold!, see!, surely!; if, yet, but, then:– behold [82], lo [11], if [5], though [1]

2006.1 הֶן- *-hēn* or הֶן- *-hen*, p.f.pl.suf. GK: 2177 [→ 1886.3]. they, them, their:– their [90], them [52], they [6], them (+871.1) [4], thereof [4], their (+3807.1) [2], their own [2], withal (+871.1) [2], by themselves (+905+3807.1) [1], it [1], thereby (+871.1) [1], these [1], those [1], wherein (+834+871.1) [1], wherein (+871.1) [1], withal (+834+871.1) [1]

2006.2 הֹן- *-hēn* (Aram.), p.suf.3.f.pl. GK: 10214 [→ 1992.2, 3861; cf. 1992.1]. they, them, their:– *usually untranslated* [6], the others [1], them [1]

2007 הֵנָּה *hēnnâ*, p.f.pl. GK: 2179 [→ 1931]. they, these, those:– they [13], these [7], them [4], those [3], such (+3509.1) [2], such things (+3509.1) [1], such [1], that [1], the [1], theirs [1], thence (+4480) [1], therein (+871.1+1886.1) [1], this [1], thither [1], wherein (+834+871.1) [1]

2008 הֵנָּה *hēnnâ*, adv. GK: 2178 [→ 5728; cf. 2005]. here, to here; on this side, on the opposite side:– hither [20], hitherto (+5704) [5], thither [3], here [2], hither (+5704) [2], thus far (+5704) [2], fro (+259) [1], hither (+1886.5) [1], hitherto (+5704+2050.1) [1], in hither [1], now [1], on this side [1], side [1], since (+5704) [1], that way [1], there [1], this side [1], this way [1], thitherward [1], to (+259) [1], yet (+5704) [1]

2009 הִנֵּה *hinnēh*, pt.demo. GK: 2180 [→ 2005]. look!, now!, here, there, a marker used to enliven a narrative, change a scene, emphasize an idea, or call attention to detail:– behold [928], lo [110], here [17], see [2], behold (+2088) [1], behold as soon as [1], behold here [1]

2009.1 הֲנָה- *-hǎnâ* or הֵנָּה- *-henâ*, p.f.pl.suf. GK: 2181 [→ 1886.3]. they, them, their:– them [2], their [1]

2010 הֲנָחָה *hǎnāhâ*, n.f. GK: 2182 [→ 3240]. holiday, an official day of rest and celebration:– release [1]

2011 הִנֹּם *hinnōm*, n.pr.m. & loc. GK: 2183. Hinnom:– Hinnom [13]

2012 הֵנַע *hēna'*, n.pr.loc. GK: 2184. Hena, "*Anath*":– Hena [3]

2013 הָסָה *hāsâ*, v.den. GK: 2187 & 2188. [H] to silence, cause to be still:– hold peace [2], keep silence [2], be silent [1], hold tongue [1], silence [1], stilled [1]

2014 הֲפֻגָה *hᵃpugâ*, n.f. GK: 2198 [→ 6313]. relief, stopping:– intermission [1]

2015 הָפַךְ *hāpak*, v. GK: 2200 [→ 2016, 2017, 2018, 2019, 4114, 4115, 8419; cf. 55]. [Q] to overthrow, overturn, turn around, change; [Qp] to be turned over; [N] to be changed, transformed, turned into; [Ho] to be overwhelmed; [Ht] to tumble around, flash back and forth, swirl; from the base meaning of turning an object over comes the fig. extension of "changing one's mind":– turned [48], turn [7], overthrow [5], overthrew [4], overthrown [4], overturneth [3], turneth [3], changed [2], become [1], came [1], change [1], converted [1], gave [1], make [1], overturned (+4605+1886.5+3807.1) [1], overturn [1], perverse [1], perverted [1], retired [1], tumbled [1], turned aside [1], turned back [1], turned every way [1], turned into [1], turned up [1], turning [1]

2016 הֶפֶךְ *hēpek*, n.m. GK: 2201 [→ 2015, 2017]. opposite, turning of things upside down, perversion:– contrary [2]

2017 הֹפֶךְ *hōpek*, n.m. GK: 2201 [→ 2016]. opposite, turning of things upside down, perversion:– turning upside down [1]

2018 הֲפֵכָה *hᵃpēkâ*, n.f. GK: 2202 [→ 2015]. catastrophe, demolition:– overthrow [1]

2019 הֲפַכְפַּךְ *hᵃpakpak*, a. GK: 2203 [→ 2015]. devious, crooked:– froward [1]

2020 הַצָּלָה *haṣṣālâ*, n.f. GK: 2208 [→ 5337]. deliverance:– deliverance [1]

2021 הֹצֶן *hōṣen*, n.[m.] GK: 2210. weapon (variously interpreted):– chariots [1]

2022 הַר *har*, n.m. GK: 2215 [→ 2023, 2042]. hill, mountain, range (of hills, mountains); referring to low hills as well as high mountains:– mount [224], mountains [156], mountain [105], hill [35], hills [23], hill country [1], hill's [1]

2023 הֹר *hōr*, n.pr.loc. GK: 2216 [→ 2022]. Hor, "[perhaps] *mountain*":– Hor [12]

2024 הָרָא *hārā'*, n.pr.loc. GK: 2217. Hara, "*hill, highland*":– Hara [1]

2025 הַרְאֵל *har'ēl*, n.[m.]. GK: 2219 [cf. 741]. altar hearth:– altar [1]

2026 הָרַג *hārag*, v. GK: 2222 [→ 2027, 2028]. [Q] to kill, put to death, murder, slaughter; [Qp, N, Pu] to be slain, be put to death, be slaughtered:– slew [57], slay [41], slain [31], kill [15], killed [3], slaying [3], kill out of hand (+2026) [2], killedst [2], slayeth [2], surely kill (+2026) [2], destroyed [1], killeth [1], killing [1], murderers [1], murderer [1], murder [1], put to death (+4194) [1], slaughter made (+2027) [1], slayer [1]

2027 הֶרֶג *hereg*, n.m. GK: 2223 [→ 2026]. slaughter, killing:– slaughter [3], slain [1], slaughter made (+2026) [1]

2028 הֲרֵגָה *hᵃrēgâ*, n.f. GK: 2224 [→ 2026]. slaughter:– slaughter [5]

2029 הָרָה *hārâ*, v. GK: 2225 [→ 2030, 2032]. [Q] to conceive, become pregnant, be with child; [Gp; Pu] to be conceived, born:– conceived [34], conceive [4], with child [2], bare [1], conceiving [1], progenitors [1]

2030 הָרֶה *hāreh* or הָרִיָּה *hāriyyâ*, a.f. GK: 2226 & 2230 [→ 2029]. pregnant, expecting (child):– with child [7], women with child [4], conceive [3], child [1], great [1]

2031 הַרְהֹר *harhōr* (Aram.), n.[m.]. GK: 10217. mental image (in a dream-like state):– thoughts [1]

2032 הֵרוֹן *hērôn* or הֵרָיוֹן *hērāyôn*, n.[m.]. GK: 2228 & 2231 [→ 2029]. childbearing, pregnancy:– conception [3]

2033 הֲרוֹרִי *hᵃrôrî*, a.g. GK: 2229. Harorite:– Harorite [1]

2034 הֲרִיסָה *hᵃrîsâ*, n.f. GK: 2232 [→ 2040]. ruin:– ruins [1]

2035 הֲרִיסוּת *hᵃrîsût*, n.f. GK: 2233 [→ 2040]. waste, ruin, destruction:– destruction [1]

2036 הֹרָם *hōrām*, n.pr.m. GK: 2235 [cf. 2037]. Horam, "*height*":– Horam [1]

2037 הָרוּם *hārûm*, n.pr.m. GK: 2227 [cf. 2036]. Harum, "*consecrated*":– Harum [1]

2038 הַרְמוֹן *harmôn*, n.pr.loc. GK: 2236. Harmon:– palace [1]

2039 הָרָן *hārān*, n.pr.m. GK: 2237 [→ 1028]. Haran, "*mountaineer* [perhaps *sanctuary*]":– Haran [7]

2040 הָרַס *hāras*, v. GK: 2238 [→ 2034, 2035]. [Q] to tear down, break down, destroy; [Qp] to be in ruins; [N] to be destroyed, in ruins; [P] to destroy:– thrown down [7], throw down [6], break down [4], broken down [4], destroyed [3], pull down [3], break through [2], overthrown [2], ruined [2], utterly overthrow (+2040) [2], beat down [1], breaketh down [1],

break [1], destroyers [1], destroy [1], overthroweth [1], overthrow [1], plucketh down [1]

2041 הֶרֶס *heres*, n.[m.]. GK: 2239 [→ 5892+2041]. destruction (= Heliopolis):– destruction [1]

2042 הָרָר *hārār*, n.m. GK: 2215 [→ 2022]. hill, mountain, range (of hills, mountains); referring to low hills as well as high mountains:– mountains [8], hills [2], mountain [2], mount [1]

2043 הֲרָרִי *hᵃrārî* or הָאֲרָרִי *hā'ᵃrārî*, a.g. GK: 2240 & 2034. Hararite:– Hararite [5]

2044 הָשֵׁם *hāšēm*, n.pr.m. GK: 2244. Hashem:– Hashem [1]

2045 הַשְׁמָעוּת *hašmā'ût*, n.f. GK: 2245 [→ 8085]. news, communication, information:– cause to hear [1]

2046 הִתּוּךְ *hittûk*, n.[m.]. GK: 2247 [→ 5413]. melting:– melted [1]

2047 הֲתָךְ *hᵃtāk*, n.pr.m. GK: 2251. Hathach, "*good*":– Hatach [4]

2048 הָתַל *hātal*, v. GK: 2252 & 9438 [→ 2049, 4123]. [P] to taunt, mock:– mocked [4], deceived [2], deal deceitfully [1], deceive [1], mocketh [1], mock [1]

2049 הֲתֻלִים *hᵃtulîm*, n.[m.]pl. GK: 2253 [→ 2048]. mockery:– mockers [1]

2050 הָתַת *hātat*, v. GK: 2109 & 2254. [Po] to overwhelm with reproaches:– imagine mischief [1]

2050.1 וְ‑ *wᵉ‑*, c.pref. GK: 2256 [cf. 2050.3]. a marker showing the relationship between words, clauses, sentences, and sections; generally, coordinating: and, also; contrasting: but, yet, however; showing a logical relationship: because, so then; emphasizing: even, indeed:– and [38504], but [1748], then [1316], that [991], so [597], also [592], therefore [524], neither (+3808) [415], and when [371], for [368], even [363], or [363], now [290], with [282], nor [254], now (+3808) [242], yet [186], yea [151], when [142], moreover [120], so that [110], thus [81], wherefore [77], which [66], neither (+408) [61], both [58], again [36], nevertheless [33], though [31], seeing [28], neither (+369) [27], howbeit [26], as [24], nor (+408) [24], neither [23], but when [19], nor (+369) [17], as for [16], if [16], lest (+3808) [14], all generations (+1755+1755) [13], now when [13], likewise [11], notwithstanding [11], as and [10], moreover (+1571) [10], whereas [10], while [10]*

2050.2 וֹ‑ ‑ô or וֹ‑ ‑w or וֹ‑ ‑û, p.m.s.suf. GK: 2257 [→ 1886.3]. he, him, his; it, its:– his [6106], him [2818], it [586], he [454], thereof [366], their [202], his own [152], them [138], his (+3807.1) [76], whose [72], himself [68], the$ [49], therein (+871.1) [35], thereon (+5921) [31], whom [27], her [23], the same [11], their own [11], wherein (+871.1) [10]*

2050.3 וְ‑ *wᵉ‑* (Aram.), c.pref. GK: 10221 [cf. 2050.1]. (connecting) and; (contrasting) or, but, however; (furthering) then, now:– and [612], but [20], or [10], that [10], nor (+3809) [7], even [6], also [5], then [5], so [4], which [4], neither (+3809) [3], nor [3], now [3], for [2], therefore [2], to [2], with [2], also (+638) [1], and that [1], as concerning [1], both [1], moreover [1], nor (+409) [1], nor (+5922) [1], so (+1934) [1], so that [1], therefore (+4481) [1], thus [1], upharsin (+6537) [1], yet [1]

2051 וְדָן *wᵉdān*, n.pr.loc.?. GK: 2258. Vedan; and Dan (2050.1 + 1835):–

2052 וָהֵב *wāhēb*, n.pr.loc.?. GK: 2259. Waheb:– what he did [1]

2053 וָו *wāw*, n.[m.]. GK: 2260. hook, peg:– hooks [13]

2054 וָזָר *wāzār*, a. GK: 2261. guilty:– strange [1]

2055 וַיְזָתָא *way'zātā'*, n.pr.m. GK: 2262. Vaizatha, "[poss.] *given of the best one*":– Vajezatha [1]

2056 וָלָד *wālād*, n.m. GK: 2263 [→ 3205]. child:– child [2]

2057 וַנְיָה *wanyâ*, n.pr.m. GK: 2264. Vaniah, "[poss.] *worthy of love*":– Vaniah [1]

2058 וָפְסִי *wopsî*, n.pr.m. GK: 2265. Vophsi:– Vophsi [1]

2059 וַשְׁנִי *wašnî*, n.pr.m.?. GK: 2266. Vashni:– Vashni [1]

2060 וַשְׁתִּי *waštî*, n.pr.f. GK: 2267. Vashti, "*one beautiful, desired*":– Vashti [10]

2061 זְאֵב *zᵉ'ēb*, n.m. GK: 2269 [→ 2062]. wolf:– wolf [4], wolves [3]

2062 זְאֵב *zᵉ'ēb*, n.pr.m. GK: 2270 [→ 2061]. Zeeb, "*wolf*":– Zeeb [6]

2063 זֹאת *zō't*, p.demo. & adv. GK: 2271 [→ 2088]. this, these:– this [15], herewith (+871.1) [2], it [2], she [2], so [2],

that [2], these [2], thus [2], hereby (+871.1) [1], herein (+871.1) [1], so much [1], such (+1886.1+3509.1) [1], such [1], the one [1], the other [1], the same [1], therefore (+871.1+2050.1) [1], thus (+871.1) [1]

2064 זָבַד *zābad*, v. GK: 2272 [→ 2065, 2066, 2067, 2071, 2072, 2080 (also used with compound proper names)]. [Q] to give (a gift), bestow:– endued [1]

2065 זֶבֶד *zēbed*, n.m. GK: 2273 [→ 2064]. gift:– dowry [1]

2066 זָבָד *zābād*, n.pr.m. GK: 2274 [→ 2064]. Zabad, "*he bestows*":– Zabad [8]

2067 זַבְדִּי *zabdî*, n.pr.m. GK: 2275 [→ 2064]. Zabdi, "*Yahweh bestows*":– Zabdi [6]

2068 זַבְדִּיאֵל *zabdî'ēl*, n.pr.m. GK: 2276 [→ 2064+410]. Zabdiel, "*God [El] bestows*":– Zabdiel [2]

2069 זְבַדְיָה *zᵉbadyâ* or זְבַדְיָהוּ *zᵉbadyāhû*, n.pr.m. GK: 2277 & 2278. Zebadiah, "*Yahweh bestows*":– Zebadiah [9]

2070 זְבוּב *zᵉbûb*, n.m. GK: 2279 [→ 1176]. fly (insect):– flies [1], fly [1]

2071 זָבוּד *zābûd*, n.pr.m. GK: 2280 [→ 2064]. Zabud, "*[he has] bestowed upon*":– Zabud [1]

2072 זַבּוּד *zabbûd*, n.pr.f. GK: 2281 [→ 2064; cf. 2080]. Zabbud, "*[he has] bestowed upon*":– Zabbud [1]

2073 זְבֻל *zᵉbul*, n.[m.]. GK: 2292 [→ 348?, 2074, 2082, 2083]. magnificent dwelling, princely mansion, lofty dwelling:– habitation [3], dwell in [1], dwelling [1]

2074 זְבוּלוּן *zᵉbûlûn*, n.pr.m. GK: 2282 [→ 2075; cf. 2073]. Zebulun, "*honor* Ge 30:20":– Zebulun [45]

2075 זְבוּלֹנִי *zᵉbûlōnî*, a.g. GK: 2283 [→ 2074; cf. 2073]. Zebulunite, "*of Zebulun*":– Zebulonite [2], Zebulunites [1]

2076 זָבַח *zābaḥ*, v. GK: 2284 [→ 2077, 2078, 4196; cf. 1684]. [Q, P] to offer a sacrifice; to slaughter, butcher:– sacrifice [44], sacrificed [29], offer [19], offered [17], sacrificeth [6], do sacrifice [3], kill [3], slew [3], killed [2], sacrificing [2], slain [2], offer a sacrifice (+2077) [1], offereth [1], offering [1], sacrificedst [1]

2077 זֶבַח *zebaḥ*, n.m. GK: 2285 [→ 2078; cf. 2076; cf. 1685]. sacrifice, offering:– sacrifice [101], sacrifices [53], offerings [6], offer a sacrifice (+2076) [1], offer [1]

2078 זֶבַח *zebaḥ*, n.pr.m. GK: 2286 [→ 2077; cf. 2076]. Zebah, "*sacrifice*":– Zebah [12]

2079 זַבַּי *zabbay*, n.pr.m. GK: 2287. Zabbai, "[perhaps] *God has given*":– Zabbai [2]

2080 זְבִידָה *zᵉbîdâ*, n.pr.f. GK: 2288 [→ 2064; cf. 2072]. Zebidah, "*given*":– Zebudah [1]

2081 זְבִינָא *zᵉbînā'*, n.pr.m. GK: 2289. Zebina, "*one bought, purchased*":– Zebina [1]

2082 זָבַל *zābal*, v. GK: 2290 [cf. 2073, 5445]. [Q] to honor, exalt; from the base meaning of lifting up or carrying an object, especially bringing presents, not found in the OT:– dwell with [1]

2083 זְבֻל *zᵉbul*, n.pr.m. GK: 2291 [→ 2073]. Zebul, "*elevation, height, lofty [temple]*":– Zebul [6]

זְבֻלוּן *zᵉbulûn*. See 2074.

2084 זְבַן *zᵉban* (Aram.), v. GK: 10223. [P] to try to gain (time), buy (time):– gain [1]

2085 זַג *zāg*, n.[m.]. GK: 2293 [cf. 2212]. skin, peel (of grape):– husk [1]

2086 זֵד *zēd*, a. GK: 2294 [→ 2087; cf. 2102]. arrogant, proud, haughty:– proud [12], presumptuous [1]

2087 זָדוֹן *zādôn*, n.m. GK: 2295 [→ 2086]. pride, arrogance, contempt, presumption:– pride [6], presumptuously (+871.1) [2], proud [2], most proud [1]

2088 זֶה *zeh*, p.demo. & adv. GK: 2296 [→ 2063, 2090, 2097, 2098; cf. 2098]. this, these, such:– this [1418], that [42], these [37], it [12], thus (+3509.1) [12], another [10], here (+871.1) [10], one [10], where (+335) [10], he [9], the [9], thus [9], hence (+4480) [7], the other [7], hence [6], such [5], whence (+335+4480) [5], one side [4], other side [4], same [4], such (+3509.1) [4], wherefore (+4100+3807.1) [4], hereby (+871.1) [3], that side [3]*

2089 זֶה *zeh*, n.m. & f. GK: 8445 [→ 7716]. lamb; var. for 7716:–

2090 זֹה *zōh*, p.demo. & adv. GK: 2297 [→ 2097; cf. 2088; cf. 1668]. this:– this [7], thus (+3509.1) [3], it [1], one [1], that [1]

2091 זָהָב **zāhāb**, n.m. GK: 2298 [→ 4314; cf. 6668; cf. 1722]. gold, nugget of gold, gold piece or coin:– gold [348], golden [40], fair weather [1]

2092 זָהַם **zāham**, v. GK: 2299 [→ 2093]. [P] to make repulsive, loathsome (to someone):– abhorreth [1]

2093 זַהַם **zaham**, n.pr.m. GK: 2300 [→ 2092]. Zaham, "*putrid, loathsome*":– Zaham [1]

2094 זָהַר **zāhar**, v. GK: 2302 [cf. 2114; cf. 2095]. [N] to be warned, take warning; [H] to give warning, dissuade; to shine:– warn [8], warned [4], admonished [2], taketh warning [2], give warning [1], given warning [1], givest warning [1], shine [1], teach [1], took warning [1]

2095 זְהִיר **zᵉhîr** (Aram.), v. GK: 10224 [cf. 2094]. careful, cautious:– take heed [1]

2096 זֹהַר **zōhar**, n.[m.]. GK: 2303. brightness, shining:– brightness [2]

2097 זוֹ **zô**, p.demo. GK: 2305 [→ 2090; cf. 2088]. this:– this [1]

2098 זוּ **zû**, p.demo. & rel. GK: 2306 [→ 2088; cf. 1976]. who, which, that:– this [4], that [3], wherein [2], which [2], that which [1], whom [1]

2099 זִיו **ziw**, n.pr. GK: 2304 [cf. 2122]. Ziv, "*bright [as colorful flowers]*":– Zif [2]

2100 זוּב **zûb**, v. GK: 2307 [→ 2101; cf. 1727]. [Q] to flow, gush out; discharge (of body fluids); "flowing with milk and honey" is a figure of sweet abundance:– floweth [12], issue [11], flowing [9], gushed out [3], running issue [3], hath an issue [2], hath [1], have an issue (+2101) [1], pine away [1], run [1]

2101 זוֹב **zôb**, n.m. GK: 2308 [→ 2100]. discharge (of body fluids):– issue [12], have an issue (+2100) [1]

2102 זִיד **zîd**, v. GK: 2326 [→ 2121, 5138; cf. 2086; cf. 2103]. [Q] to treat arrogantly, defy; [H] to cook; to act arrogantly, be contemptuous:– dealt proudly [4], presumptuously [2], come presumptuously [1], presume [1], proud [1], sod [1]

2103 זוּד **zûd** (Aram.), v. GK: 10225 [cf. 2102]. [H] to act proudly, act haughtily:– pride [1]

2104 זוּזִים **zûzîm**, n.pr.g. GK: 2309. Zuzite, "*strong nations; babblers*":– Zuzims [1]

2105 זוֹחֵת **zôḥēt**, n.pr.m. GK: 2311 [→ 1132]. Zoheth, "*proud*":– Zoheth [1]

2106 זָוִית **zāwît**, n.f. GK: 2312 [cf. 4200]. corner (of a palace, altar), pillar:– corner stones [1], corners [1]

2107 זוּל **zûl**, v. GK: 2313 [→ 2108]. [Q] to pour out, weigh out:– despise [1], lavish [1]

2108 זוּלָה **zûlâ**, n.[f.] pp.c. GK: 2314 [→ 2107]. but, only, except; apart from, besides:– save [6], besides [5], beside [2], but [2], only [1]

2109 זוּן **zûn**, v. GK: 2315 & 3469 [→ 4202; cf. 2110, cf. 4203]. [Q] to feed; [Pu] to be fed; to be lusty, be in the rut:– fed [1]

2110 זוּן **zûn** (Aram.), v. GK: 10226 [→ 4203; cf. 2109]. [Htpe] to be fed, live on:– fed [1]

2111 זוּעַ **zûa'**, v. GK: 2316 & 2398 [→ 2113; cf. 2189; cf. 2112]. [Q] to show fear, tremble; [Pil] to make tremble; terrify:– moved [1], tremble [1], vex [1]

2112 זוּעַ **zûa'** (Aram.), v. GK: 10227 [cf. 2111]. [P] to dread, fear, to have an attitude of terror or worship, a fig. extension of "to shake, tremble.":– trembled [1], tremble [1]

2113 זְוָעָה **zᵉwā‘â**, n.f. GK: 2317 [→ 2111]. abhorrence, terror, object of dread:– vexation [1]

2114 זוּר **zûr**, v. GK: 2319 & 2320 & 2424 [cf. 2094]. [Q, N, Ho] to go astray, turn aside, be estranged; [Q] to stink; by extension: to be offensive:– strangers [25], strange [20], stranger [18], estranged [4], another [2], another place [1], fanners [1], gone away [1], stranger (+376) [1], strangers' [1]

2115 זוּר **zûr**, v. GK: 2318 [→ 2116]. [Q] to squeeze, press upon, crush; [Qp] to be crushed:– closed [1], crush [1], thrust together [1]

2116 זוּרֶה **zûreh**, v.ptcp. GK: 2318 [→ 2115]. ptcp. of 2115:– that which is crushed:– crushed [1]

2117 זָזָא **zāzā'**, n.pr.m. GK: 2321. Zaza, "*form of a shortened nick name; term of endearment*":– Zaza [1]

2118 זָחַח **zāḥaḥ**, v. GK: 2310 & 2322. [N] to come loose, get out of place; to swing out:– loosed [2]

2119 זָחַל **zāḥal**, v. GK: 2323 & 2324 [→ 2120; cf. 1763]. [Q] to be afraid; to crawl, glide (of a snake):– afraid [1], serpents [1], worms [1]

2120 זֹחֶלֶת **zōḥelet**, n.pr.loc. GK: 2325 [→ 2119]. Zoheleth, "*crawling thing* or *fearsome thing*":– Zoheleth [1]

2121 זֵידוֹן **zêdôn**, a. GK: 2327 [→ 2102]. raging (water), implying it is out of control:– proud [1]

2122 זִיו **zîw** (Aram.), n.m. GK: 10228. radiant appearance: dazzling, splendor; terrified appearance: flushed, pale:– countenance [4], brightness [2]

2123 זִיז **zîz**, n.m. GK: 2328 & 2329. creatures; nipple (of a lactating breast):– abundance [1], wild beasts [1], wild beast [1]

2124 זִיזָא **zîzā'**, n.pr.m. GK: 2330 [→ 2125?]. Ziza, "*(childish abbreviation, like "mama," as a name of endearment]*":– Ziza [2]

2125 זִיזָה **zîzâ**, n.pr.m. GK: 2331 [→ 2124?]. Ziza, "*(childish abbreviation, like "mama," as a term of endearment]*":– Zizah [1]

2126 זִינָא **zînā'**, n.pr.m. GK: 2332 [cf. 2124]. Zina; cf. 2124:– Zina [1]

2127 זִיעַ **zîa'**, n.pr.m. GK: 2333. Zia, "*[poss.] trembler*":– Zia [1]

2128 זִיף **zîp**, n.pr.m. & loc. GK: 2334 & 2335 [→ 2130]. Ziph:– Ziph [10]

2129 זִיפָה **zîpâ**, n.pr.m. GK: 2336. Ziphah:– Ziphah [1]

2130 זִיפִי **zîpî**, a.g. GK: 2337 [→ 2128]. Ziphite, "*of Ziph*":– Ziphites [2], Ziphims [1]

2131 זִיקוֹת **zîqôt** or זֵק **zēq**, n.[m.]. GK: 2338 & 2414 & 2415 [cf. 246]. flaming torch, firebrand; chains, fetters:– chains [3], sparks [2], fetters [1], firebrands [1]

2132 זַיִת **zayit**, n.m. GK: 2339 [→ 1269, 1269, 2133, 2241?]. olive (tree, grove, oil, leaf):– olive [13], olive tree [8], olive trees [6], oliveyards [5], olives [4], Olivet [1], oliveyard [1]

2133 זֵיתָן **zêtān**, n.pr.m. GK: 2340 [→ 2132]. Zethan, "*olive tree* or *one who deals in olives*":– Zethan [1]

2134 זַךְ **zak**, a. GK: 2341 [→ 2141]. pure, clear; flawless, innocent, upright:– pure [9], clean [2]

2135 זָכָה **zākâ**, v. GK: 2342 [cf. 2141; cf. 2136]. [Q] to be pure; be justified, be acquitted; [P] to keep pure; [Ht] to make oneself clean, pure; usually referring to moral purity as a superior quality:– clean [2], cleansed [1], cleanse [1], clear [1], count pure [1], made clean [1], make clean [1]

2136 זָכוּ **zākû** (Aram.), n.f. GK: 10229 [cf. 2135]. innocence:– innocency [1]

2137 זְכוֹכִית **zᵉkôkît**, n.[f.]. GK: 2343 [→ 2141]. crystal, referring to a transparent ornament):– crystal [1]

2138 זָכוּר **zākûr**, n.m. GK: 2344 & 2345 [→ 2142]. male:– males [2], male [1], men children [1]

2139 זַכּוּר **zakkûr**, n.pr.m. GK: 2346 [→ 2142]. Zaccur, "*remembering*":– Zaccur [8], Zacchur [1]

2140 זַכַּי **zakkay**, n.pr.m. GK: 2347 [→ 2142+3068?]. Zaccai, "*Yahweh has remembered, [or perhaps] Yahweh remember*":– Zaccai [2]

2141 זָכַךְ **zākak**, v. GK: 2348 [→ 2134, 2137; cf. 2135]. [Q] to be pure, bright, clean:– clean [1], make never so clean (+1253+871.1) [1], purer [1], pure [1]

2142 זָכַר **zākar**, v. GK: 2349 & 2350 & 4654 [→ 234, 2138, 2139, 2143, 2144, 2145, 2146 (also used with compound proper names)]. [Q] to remember, commemorate, consider; [Qp] to remember; [N] to be remembered, be mentioned; to be born male; [H] to bring to remembrance, remind, mention, record:– remember [117], remembered [46], make mention [12], recorder [9], mindful [6], call to remembrance [3], mentioned [3], remembereth [3], bring to remembrance [2], earnestly remember (+2142) [2], mention [2], record [2], still in remembrance (+2142) [2], think [2], well remember (+2142) [2], bringeth to remembrance [1], bringing to remembrance [1], burneth [1], calling to remembrance [1], come to remembrance [1], in remembrance [1], keep in remembrance [1], made mention of [1], made mention [1], made to be remembered [1], make to be remembered [1], maketh mention [1], male [1], mention made [1], put in remembrance [1], recount [1], remembrest [1], remembering [1], think on [1]

2143 זֵכֶר **zēker** or זֶכֶר **zeker**, n.m. GK: 2352 & 2354 [→ 2142]. memory, memorial, remembrance (with an implication of honor, worship, and celebration); fame, renown:– remembrance [11], memorial [5], memory [5], remembered [1], sent [1]

2144 זֶכֶר **zeker**, n.pr.m. GK: 2353 [→ 2142]. Zeker, "*memorial*":– Zacher [1]

2145 זָכָר **zākār**, n.m. & a. GK: 2351 [→ 2142; cf. 1798]. male, man:– male [37], males [30], man [9], man child [2], mankind [2], him⁵ [1], men [1]

2146 זִכָּרוֹן **zikkārôn**, n.m. GK: 2355 [→ 2142; cf. 1799]. memorial, remembrance (with an implication of honor, worship, and celebration), commemoration, reminder:– memorial [17], remembrance [5], records [1], remembrances [1]

2147 זִכְרִי **zikrî**, n.pr.m. GK: 2356 [→ 2142?+3068?]. Zicri, "*Yahweh remembers*":– Zichri [12]

2148 זְכַרְיָה **zᵉkaryâ** or זְכַרְיָהוּ **zᵉkaryāhû**, n.pr.m. GK: 2357 & 2358 & 10230. Zechariah, "*Yahweh remembers*": note this name is Aramaic twice in Ezra:– Zechariah [39], Zachariah [4]

2149 זֻלּוּת **zullût**, n.f. GK: 2359 [→ 2151]. vileness:– vilest [1]

2150 זַלְזַל **zalzal**, n.[m.]. GK: 2360 [→ 2151; cf. 5550]. shoots, sprigs, tendrils:– sprigs [1]

2151 זָלַל **zālal**, v. GK: 2361 & 2362 [→ 2149, 2150]. [Q] to profligate, be a glutton, to gorge oneself; [N] to tremble (of mountains); [H] to despise, treat contemptibly:– glutton [2], vile [2], flow down [1], flowed down [1], riotous eaters [1], riotous [1]

2152 זַלְעָפָה **zal‘āpâ**, n.f. GK: 2363 [→ 2196]. raging (wind); indignation; fits of hunger:– horrible [1], horror [1], terrible [1]

2153 זִלְפָּה **zilpâ**, n.pr.f. GK: 2364. Zilpah, "*short nosed person*":– Zilpah [7]

2154 זִמָּה **zimmâ**, n.f. GK: 2365. lewdness, shamelessness, evil:– lewdness [14], wickedness [14], mischief [3], lewd [2], heinous crime [1], lewdly (+871.1) [1], purposes [1], thought [1], wicked devices [1], wicked mind [1]

2155 זִמָּה **zimmâ**, n.pr.m. GK: 2366. Zimmah, "*consider, plan*":– Zimmah [3]

2156 זְמוֹרָה **zᵉmôrâ**, n.[f.]. GK: 2367 [→ 2168; cf. 2231]. vine branch:– branch [3], slips [1], vine branches [1]

2157 זַמְזֻמִּים **zamzummîm**, n.pr.g. GK: 2368 [→ 2161?]. Zamzummite, "*babblers*":– Zamzummims [1]

2158 זָמִיר **zāmîr**, n.m. GK: 2369 [→ 2167]. song, music and song:– songs [3], psalmist [1], psalms [1], singing [1]

2159 זָמִיר **zāmîr**, n.[m.]. GK: 2370 [→ 2168]. pruning (of vines); vintage:– branch [1]

2160 זְמִירָה **zᵉmîrâ**, n.pr.m. GK: 2371 [→ 2172?; cf. 2167]. Zemirah, "*[poss.] song [with instrumental accompaniment]; [poss.] Yahweh has helped*":– Zemira [1]

2161 זָמַם **zāmam**, v. GK: 2372 [→ 2157?, 2162, 4209]. [Q] to determine, plan, plot, intend, resolve:– thought [4], devised [3], purposed [2], considereth [1], imagined [1], plotteth [1], thought evil [1]

2162 זָמָם **zāmām**, n.[m.]. GK: 2373 [→ 2161]. plan, plot:– wicked device [1]

2163 זָמַן **zāman**, v. GK: 2374 [→ 2165; cf. 2164]. [Pu] to be set, be designated, appointed:– appointed [3]

2164 זְמַן **zᵉman** (Aram.), v.den. GK: 10231 [→ 2166; cf. 2163]. [Htpe] to conspire, agree to; [H] to decide:– prepared [1]

2165 זְמָן **zᵉmān**, n.m. GK: 2375 [→ 2163; cf. 2166]. time, appointed time:– time [2], season [1], times [1]

2166 זְמַן **zᵉman** (Aram.), n.m. GK: 10232 [→ 2166; cf. 2165]. time, event, occurrence; a unit of time: indefinite period of time, set time, season:– time [6], times [3], seasons [1], season [1]

2167 זָמַר **zāmar**, v. GK: 2376 [→ 2158, 2160?, 2172, 2176, 4210; cf. 2170, cf. 2171]. [P] to sing, sing praises, to make music, to chant, sing, or play instruments to worship God and proclaim his excellence:– sing [38], give praise [2], sing psalms [2], praise [1], sing forth [1], sing praises [1]

2168 זָמַר **zāmar**, v. GK: 2377 [→ 2156, 2159, 4211, 4212]. [Q] to prune (vines); [N] to be pruned:– prune [2], pruned [1]

2169 זֶמֶר **zemer**, n.[m.]. GK: 2378 [cf. 2173?]. mountain sheep; some sources: gazelle:– chamois [1]

2170 זְמָר **zᵉmār** (Aram.), n.[m.]. GK: 10233 [→ 2171; cf. 2167]. music in general, or string music in particular:– musick [4]

זָמִיר **zāmir**. See 2158.

זְמֹר **zᵉmōr**. See 2156.

Heb

2171 זַמָּר *zammār* (Aram.), n.m. GK: 10234 [→ 2170; cf. 2167]. singer:– singers [1]

2172 זִמְרָה *zimrâ*, n.f. GK: 2379 [→ 2160?; cf. 2167]. singing, song, (instrumental) music:– melody [2], psalm [2]

2173 זִמְרָה *zimrâ*, n.f. GK: 2380 [→ 2174; cf. 2169?]. best product, having a high value:– best fruits [1]

זְמִרָה *zᵉmirâ*. See 2158.

זְמֹרָה *zᵉmōrâ*. See 2156.

2174 זִמְרִי *zimrî*, n.pr.m. & loc. GK: 2381 & 2382 [→ 2173]. Zimri, "*wild goats, sheep*; [poss.] *awe of Yahweh*":– Zimri [15]

2175 זִמְרָן *zimrān*, n.pr.m. GK: 2383. Zimran, "*wild goats, sheep*":– Zimran [2]

2176 זִמְרָת *zimrāt*, n.f. GK: 2384 [→ 2167?]. song or strength:– song [3]

2177 זַן *zan*, n.[m.]. GK: 2385 [cf. 2178]. kind, sort:– all manner of store (+413+2177+4480) [2], divers kinds [1]

2178 זַן *zan* (Aram.), n.[m.]. GK: 10235 [cf. 2177]. kind, sort:– kinds [4]

2179 זָנַב *zānab*, v.den. GK: 2386 [→ 2180]. [P] to cut off from the rear position, attack from the rear, as a fig. extension of the base meaning "to cut off a tail":– smite the hindmost [1], smote the hindmost [1]

2180 זָנָב *zānāb*, n.m. GK: 2387 [→ 2179]. tail; stump:– tail [9], tails [2]

2181 זָנָה *zānâ*, v. GK: 2388 & 2389 [→ 2185, 2183, 2184, 8457]. [Q] to be, become a prostitute; to be sexually immoral, be promiscuous, commit adultery; to feel a dislike for; [Pu] to be solicited for prostitution; [H] to make a prostitute, to turn to prostitution:– harlot [18], go a whoring [8], played the harlot [8], commit whoredom [6], went a whoring [5], gone a whoring [4], whore [4], whorish [3], committed great whoredom (+2181) [2], committed whoredom continually (+2181) [2], committed whoredoms [2], harlot's [2], harlots [2], play the harlot [2], played the whore [2], playedst the harlot [2], playing the harlot [2], whores [2], cause to be a whore [1], caused to commit fornication [1], commit fornication [1], commit whoredoms (+8457) [1], commit whoredoms [1], committed fornication [1], committest whoredom [1], fall to whoredom [1], harlots' [1], made to go a whoring [1], make go a whoring [1], play the whore [1], playeth the harlot [1], playing the whore [1], whore's (+802) [1], whoredoms [1], whoredom [1]

2182 זָנוֹחַ *zānôaḥ*, n.pr.m. & loc. GK: 2391 & 2392 [→ 2186]. Zanoah, "*rejected*":– Zanoah [5]

2183 זְנוּנִים *zᵉnûnîm*, n.[m.]. GK: 2393 [→ 2181]. wanton lust, prostitution, adultery; by extension: idolatry, as unfaithfulness to God:– whoredoms [11], whoredom [1]

2184 זְנוּת *zᵉnût*, n.f.abst. GK: 2394 [→ 2181]. prostitution, sexual immorality, unfaithfulness; by extension: idolatry, as unfaithfulness to God:– whoredom [7], whoredoms [2]

2185 זֹנָה *zōnâ*, n.f. *or* v. GK: 2390 [→ 2181]. prostitute, harlot; translated as "armor" in the KJV:– armour [1].

2186 זָנַח *zānaḥ*, v. GK: 2395 & 2396 [→ 2182]. [Q] to reject, cast out; [H] to declare rejected; to remove; to stink:– cast off [16], cast away [1], castest off [1], removed far off [1], turn far away [1]

2187 זָנַק *zānaq*, v. GK: 2397. [P] to spring out:– leap [1]

2188 זֵעָה *zēʿâ*, n.f. GK: 2399 [→ 3154]. sweat; the "sweat of the brow" refers to do heavy manual labor:– sweat [1]

2189 זַעֲוָה *zaʿᵃwâ*, n.f. GK: 2400 [→ 2190; cf. 2111]. thing of horror, terror:– removed [6], trouble [1]

2190 זַעֲוָן *zaʿᵃwān*, n.pr.m. GK: 2401 [→ 2189+4993.1?]. Zaavan, "[poss.] *trembling, terror*":– Zaavan [1], Zavan [1]

2191 זְעֵיר *zᵉʿêr*, n.[m.]. GK: 2402 [→ 4213; cf. 6819; cf. 2192]. little; a little longer:– little [5]

2192 זְעֵיר *zᵉʿêr* (Aram.), a. GK: 10236 [cf. 2191]. little, small; fig., insignificant, light in status:– little [1]

2193 זָעַךְ *zāʿak*, v. GK: 2403 [cf. 1846]. [N] to be extinguished:– extinct [1]

2194 זָעַם *zāʿam*, v. GK: 2404 [→ 2195]. [Q] to express wrath, show fury, denounce; [Qp] to be under wrath, be accursed; [N] to be scolded, be cursed:– indignation [4], angry [2], defy [2], abhorred [1], abhor [1], abominable [1], defied [1]

2195 זַעַם *zaʿam*, n.m. GK: 2405 [→ 2194]. wrath, anger, indignation, insolence:– indignation [20], anger [1], rage [1]

2196 זָעַף *zāʿap*, v. GK: 2406 & 2407 [→ 2152, 2197, 2198]. [Q] to rage against, become angry; to look dejected, look pitiful:– wroth [2], fretteth [1], sad [1], worse liking [1]

2197 זַעַף *zaʿap*, n.m. GK: 2408 [→ 2196]. rage, wrath:– indignation [2], rage [2], raging [1], wrath [1]

2198 זָעֵף *zāʿēp*, a. GK: 2409 [→ 2196]. angry, raging:– displeased [2]

2199 זָעַק *zāʿaq*, v. GK: 2410 [→ 2201; cf. 6817; cf. 2200]. [Q] to cry out, call to, weep aloud, howl; [N] to be called, be summoned; be assembled; [H] to summon, cause to gather together, issue a proclamation:– cried [26], cry [20], cried out [5], cry out [5], called [3], assemble [2], criest [2], gathered together [2], gathered [2], assembled [1], caused to be proclaimed [1], comest with a company [1], crieth out [1], crying [1], make to cry [1]

2200 זְעִק *zᵉʿiq* (Aram.), v. GK: 10237 [cf. 3815, cf. 6817]. [P] to call out, shout:– cried [1]

2201 זַעֲקָה *zaʿᵃqâ*, n.f. GK: 2411 [→ 2199]. outcry, shout, lament, wail:– cry [17], crying [1]

2202 זִפְרוֹן *ziprôn*, n.pr.loc. GK: 2412. Ziphron:– Ziphron [1]

2203 זֶפֶת *zepet*, n.f. GK: 2413. pitch (resin):– pitch [3]

זִק *ziq* or זֵק *zēq*. See 2131.

2204 זָקֵן *zāqēn*, v. GK: 2416 [→ 2206]. [Q] to be old; [H] to grow old; this can refer to maturity in contrast to youth or to advanced age:– old [22], waxed old [2], aged man [1], old man [1], wax old [1]

2205 זָקֵן *zāqēn*, a. GK: 2418 [→ 2206]. elder, old, aged, veteran; (n.) elder, leader, dignitary; "elder" can refer to a formal position as a community leader and arbiter:– elders [114], old [21], old men [9], ancient [9], old man [9], ancient [5], aged [3], ancient men [1], elder (+3117+3807.1) [1], eldest [1], old men's [1], old women [1], senators [1]

2206 זָקָן *zāqān*, n.m. GK: 2417 [→ 2204, 2205, 2207, 2209, 2208]. beard, whiskers (a sign of maturity or age); chin:– beard [15], beards [4]

2207 זֹקֶן *zōqen*, n.[m.]. GK: 2419 [→ 2206]. old age:– age [1]

2208 זְקֻנִים *zᵉqunîm*, n.pl.[m.]. GK: 2421 [→ 2206]. old age:– old age [4]

2209 זִקְנָה *ziqnâ*, n.f. GK: 2420 [→ 2206]. old age, growing old:– old age [3], old [3]

2210 זָקַף *zāqap*, v. GK: 2422 [cf. 2211]. [Q] to lift up:– raiseth up [1], raiseth [1]

2211 זְקַף *zᵉqap* (Aram.), v. GK: 10238 [cf. 2210]. [Pp] to be lifted up:– set up [1]

2212 זָקַק *zāqaq*, v. GK: 2423 [cf. 2085]. [Q] to refine, distill; [P] to refine; [Pu] to be refined, be purified:– refined [2], fine [1], pour down [1], purge [1], purified [1], well refined [1]

2213 זֵר *zēr*, n.m. GK: 2425 [→ 2237]. molding:– crown [10]

2214 זָרָא *zārā*, n.[f.]. GK: 2426. loathsome thing:– stranger (+376) [2], loathsome [1], strangers [1]

2215 זָרַב *zārab*, v. GK: 2427. [Pu] to become dry:– wax warm [1]

2216 זְרֻבָּבֶל *zᵉrubbābel*, n.pr.m. GK: 2428 [→ 2232+894; cf. 2217]. Zerubbabel, "*offspring [seed] of Babylon; scion* i.e., *one grafted into the [plant of] Babylon*":– Zerubbabel [21]

2217 זְרֻבָּבֶל *zᵉrubbābel* (Aram.), n.pr.m. GK: 10239 [cf. 2216]. Zerubbabel, "*seed of Babylon* or *one grafted into Babylon*":– Zerubbabel [1]

2218 זֶרֶד *zered*, n.pr.loc. GK: 2429. Zered, "*[valley of some kind of] plant*":– Zered [3], Zared [1]

2219 זָרָה *zārâ*, v. GK: 2430 & 2431 [→ 2239, 4214, 4215]. [Q, P] to scatter, spread out; winnow; to measure off, discern; [N, Pu] to be scattered, spread out:– scatter [12], disperse [7], scattered [6], fan [4], scattereth [2], spread [2], cast away [1], compassest [1], dispersed [1], strawed [1], winnowed [1], winnoweth [1]

2220 זְרוֹעַ *zᵉrôaʿ*, n.f. GK: 2432 [cf. 248; cf. 153, cf. 1872]. arm, forearm, shoulder; power, strength, force:– arm [59], arms [24], power [3], shoulder [2], holpen [1], mighty [1], strength [1]

2221 זֵרוּעַ *zērûaʿ*, n.[m.]. GK: 2433 [→ 2232]. (plants from) seeds:– sowing [1], things that are sown [1]

2222 זַרְזִיף *zarzîp*, n.[m.]. GK: 2434 & 2449. dripping:– water [1]

זְרוֹעַ *zᵉrôʿâ*. See 2220.

2223 זַרְזִיר *zarzîr*, a. GK: 2435 [→ 2237?]. a strutting animal, variously interpreted: rooster, horse, greyhound:– greyhound (+4975) [1]

2224 זָרַח *zāraḥ*, v. GK: 2436 [→ 249, 250, 2225, 2226, 2227, 4217 (also used with compound proper names)]. [Q] to rise, dawn (of the sun); by extension: to appear bright red (as with a skin disorder):– ariseth [4], arise [3], risen [3], riseth [2], rose up [2], arose [1], rise [1], rose [1], shone [1], up [1]

2225 זֶרַח *zeraḥ*, n.[m.]. GK: 2437 [→ 2226, 2227; cf. 2224]. dawning (of light):– rising [1]

2226 זֶרַח *zeraḥ*, n.pr.m. GK: 2438 [→ 250; cf. 2224, 2225]. Zerah, "*dawning, shining* or *flashing [red or scarlet] light*":– Zerah [20], Zarah [1]

2227 זַרְחִי *zarḥî*, a.g. GK: 2439 [→ 2226; cf. 2224, 2225]. Zerahite, "*of Zerah*":– Zarhites [6]

2228 זְרַחְיָה *zᵉraḥyâ*, n.pr.m. GK: 2440 [→ 2224+3068]. Zerahiah, "*Yahweh shines brightly [red or scarlet]; Yahweh has risen [like the sun]*":– Zerahiah [5]

2229 זָרַם *zāram*, v. GK: 2441 & 2442 [→ 2230]. [Q] to sweep away, put an end to; [Po] to pour down:– carriest away as with a flood [1], poured out [1]

2230 זֶרֶם *zerem*, n.m. GK: 2443 [→ 2229]. rain, rainstorm, thunderstorm, torrent rains:– storm [3], tempest [3], flood [1], overflowing [1], showers [1]

2231 זִרְמָה *zirmâ*, n.f. GK: 2444 [cf. 2156]. male genitals or emission:– issue [2]

2232 זָרַע *zāraʿ*, v. GK: 2445 [→ 2221, 2233, 2235, 4218; cf. 2234 (also used with compound proper names)]. [Q] to sow seed, plant seed; [Qp] to be sown upon; [Pu] to be sown; [N] to be sown, be planted, to have children, have descendants; [H] to yield seed, to become pregnant; from the base meaning of scattering seed onto the ground comes the fig. extension "to have children":– sow [26], sown [14], yielding [3], sowed [2], sower [2], soweth [2], bearing [1], conceive seed (+2233) [1], conceived seed [1], set [1], sow seeds [1], sow with seed [1], sowedst [1]

2233 זֶרַע *zeraʿ*, n.m. GK: 2446 [→ 2232; cf. 2234]. seed, semen, that which propagates a species; by extension: that which is propagated, child, offspring, descendant, line, race:– seed [218], child [2], conceive seed (+2232) [1], fruitful [1], lie carnally (+5414+7903+3807.1) [1], lieth carnally with (+854+7901+7902) [1], man carnally (+376+7902) [1], seed (+7902) [1], seed's [1], seedtime [1], sowing time [1]

2234 זְרַע *zᵉraʿ* (Aram.), n.[m.]. GK: 10240 [cf. 2233]. seed, "seed" of a person is translated "descendant":– seed [1]

זְרֹעַ *zᵉrōaʿ*. See 2220.

2235 זֵרֹעִים *zērōʿîm* or זֵרְעֹנִים *zērᵉʿōnîm*, n.[m.]. GK: 2447 & 2448 [cf. 2232]. vegetables:– pulse [2]

זְרֹעָה *zᵉrōʿâ*. See 2220.

2236 זָרַק *zāraq*, v. GK: 2450 & 2451 [→ 4219]. [Q] to sprinkle, to scatter, to toss (in the air); to creep in; [Pu] to be sprinkled:– sprinkled [16], sprinkle [14], scatter [2], here and there [1], sprinkleth [1], strowed [1]

2237 זָרַר *zārar*, v. GK: 2452 & 2453 [→ 2213, 2223?]. [Qp] to be pressed out; [Po] to sneeze:– neesed [1]

2238 זֶרֶשׁ *zereš*, n.pr.f. GK: 2454. Zeresh, "[poss.] *Kirsha; gold; mop-headed*":– Zeresh [4]

2239 זֶרֶת *zeret*, n.f. GK: 2455 [→ 2219]. handbreadth, span (of an open hand, a measure of about nine inches [23 cm]):– span [7]

2240 זַתּוּא *zattû*, n.pr.m. GK: 2456. Zattu, "[poss.] *olive tree*":– Zattu [3], Zatthu [1]

2241 זֵתָם *zētām*, n.pr.m. GK: 2457 [→ 2132?]. Zetham, "[poss.] *olive tree*":– Zetham [1]

2242 זֵתַר *zētar*, n.pr.m. GK: 2458. Zethar, "[poss.] *conqueror; slayer*":– Zethar [1]

2243 חֹב *ḥōb*, n.[m.]. GK: 2460 [→ 2245; cf. 2244]. heart:– bosom [1]

2244 חָבָא *ḥābā*, v. GK: 2461 [→ 455, 4224; cf. 2243, 2246?, 2247, 3160?]. [N] to be hidden, to hide oneself; [Pu] to keep oneself in hiding; [H] to hide (another); [Ho] to be hidden; [Ht] to keep oneself hidden:– hid [24], hide [7], held peace (+6963) [1], hideth [1], secretly [1]

2245 חָבַב *ḥābab*, v. GK: 2462 [→ 2243, 2246?, 3160?]. [Q] to love:– loved [1]

2246 חֹבָב ḥōbāb, n.pr.m. GK: 2463 [→ 2245?; cf. 2244?]. Hobab, "*beloved*; [poss.] *deceit*":– Hobab [2]

2247 חָבָה ḥābâ, v. GK: 2464 [→ 2252, 2253; cf. 2244]. [Q] to conceal oneself:– hide [4]

2248 חֲבוּלָה ḥᵃbûlâ (Aram.), n.f. GK: 10242 [→ 2255]. wrong, crime:– hurt [1]

2249 חָבוֹר ḥābôr, n.pr.loc. GK: 2466. Habor:– Habor [3]

2250 חַבּוּרָה ḥabbûrâ, n.f. GK: 2467 [→ 2266]. bruise, welt, wound, injury:– stripe [2], blueness [1], bruises [1], hurt [1], stripes [1], wounds [1]

2251 חָבַט ḥābaṭ, v. GK: 2468. [Q] to thresh, beat out; [N] to be beaten:– beat off [1], beat out [1], beaten out [1], beatest [1], threshed [1]

2252 חֲבַיָּה ḥᵃbayyâ, n.pr.m. GK: 2469 [→ 2247+3068]. Hobaiah, "*Yahweh has hidden*":– Habaiah [2]

2253 חֶבְיוֹן ḥebyôn, n.[m.]. GK: 2470 [→ 2247]. hiding, covering:– hiding [1]

2254 חָבַל ḥābal, v. GK: 2471 & 2472 & 2473 [→ 2256, 2258; cf. 2255]. [Q] to require a pledge, demand a security; to act wickedly, to offend; [P] to destroy, ruin, work havoc; to conceive, be pregnant, be in labor; [Pu] to be broken:– destroy [5], take a pledge [3], at all take to pledge (+2254) [2], bands [2], brought forth [2], dealt very corruptly (+2254) [2], destroyed [2], take to pledge [2], corrupt [1], laid to pledge [1], offend [1], spoil [1], take for a pledge [1], taken a pledge [1], taketh to pledge [1], travaileth [1], withholden the pledge (+2258) [1]

2255 חֲבַל ḥᵃbal (Aram.), v. GK: 10243 [→ 2248, 2257; cf. 2254]. [Pa] to destroy, hurt; [Htpa] to be destroyed:– destroyed [3], destroy [2], hurt [1]

2256 חֶבֶל ḥebel or חֵבֶל ḥēbel, n.m. GK: 2474 & 2475 & 2476 & 2477 & 2482 [→ 2254, cf. 2259, 2260]. rope, cord, line, rigging; share, portion, region, district; procession, group, union; destruction, ruin; labor pains, anguish of birth pangs:– cords [12], sorrows [10], line [5], coast [4], cord [4], lot [3], region [3], ropes [3], company [2], lines [2], pangs [2], portions [2], portion [2], bands [1], country [1], destruction [1], pain [1], snare [1], tacklings [1]

2257 חֲבַל ḥᵃbal (Aram.), n.m. GK: 10244 [→ 2255]. physical harm, wound, hurt; fig.: damage resulting from the lowering of status:– hurt [2], damage [1]

2258 חֲבֹל ḥᵃbōl or חֲבֹלָה ḥᵃbōlâ, n.[m.]. GK: 2478 & 2481 [→ 2254]. pledge for a loan:– pledge [3], withholden the pledge (+2254) [1]

2259 חֹבֵל ḥōbēl, n.m. GK: 2480 [cf. 2256]. seaman, sailor:– pilots [4], shipmaster (+7227+1886.1) [1]

2260 חִבֵּל ḥibbēl, n.[m.]. GK: 2479 [→ 2256]. (ship's) rigging, mast:– mast [1]

2261 חֲבַצֶּלֶת ḥᵃbaṣṣelet, n.f. GK: 2483. rose; crocus:– rose [2]

2262 חֲבַצִּנְיָה ḥᵃbaṣṣinyâ, n.pr.m. GK: 2484. Habazziniah, "[poss.] *exuberant in Yahweh*":– Habaziniah [1]

2263 חָבַק ḥābaq, v. GK: 2485 [→ 2264]. [Q] to hold in one's arms, embrace; to fold one's hands; [P] to embrace, hug:– embrace [8], embraced [3], embracing [1], foldeth together [1]

2264 חִבֻּק ḥibbuq, n.[m.]. GK: 2486 [→ 2263]. folding (of idle hands):– folding [1]

2265 חֲבַקּוּק ḥᵃbaqqûq, n.pr.m. GK: 2487. Habakkuk, "*garden plant*":– Habakkuk [2]

2266 חָבַר ḥābar, v. GK: 2248 & 2488 & 2489 [→ 2250, 2267, 2268, 2270, 2271, 2272, 2274, 5683, 2275, 2276, 2277, 2278, 2279, 4226, 4225]. [Q] to join, unite, be attached, to be touching; to cast spells, to enchant; [Qp] to be joined; [P] to fasten, join; [Pu] to be fastened, be closely compacted; [Ht] to make an alliance, become allies; [H] to make fine speeches:– joined [6], coupled [5], couple together [3], coupled together [2], couple [2], joined together [2], charmer (+2267) [1], charming (+2267) [1], compact [1], fellowship [1], heap up [1], join together [1], joined to [1], join [1], league [1]

2267 חֶבֶר ḥeber, n.[m.]. GK: 2490 [→ 2266]. sharing; band, group; magic spell:– enchantments [2], wide [2], charmer (+2266) [1], charming (+2266) [1], company [1]

2268 חֶבֶר ḥeber, n.pr.m. GK: 2491 [→ 2277; cf. 2266]. Heber, "*associate*":– Heber [10], Heber's [1]

2269 חֲבַר ḥᵃbar (Aram.), n.m. GK: 10245 [→ 2273; cf. 2270]. friend, companion:– fellows [2], companions [1]

2270 חָבֵר ḥābēr, a. & n.m. GK: 2492 [→ 2266; cf. 2269, cf. 2273]. companion, associate, partner, friend:– companions [5], fellows [3], companion [2], fellow [1], knit together [1]

2271 חַבָּר ḥabbār, n.m. GK: 2493 [→ 2266]. (fellow) trader, one of a community of traders:– companions [1]

2272 חֲבַרְבֻּרֹת ḥᵃbarburōt, n.f. GK: 2494 [→ 2266]. spots (of a leopard):– spots [1]

2273 חֲבְרָא ḥabrâ (Aram.), n.f. GK: 10246 [→ 2269; cf. 2270]. companion (horn):– fellows [1]

2274 חֶבְרָה ḥebrâ, n.f. GK: 2495 [→ 2266]. company, association:– company [1]

2275 חֶבְרוֹן ḥebrôn, n.pr.m. & loc. GK: 2496 & 2497 [→ 2276; cf. 2266, 5683?]. Hebron, "*association*":– Hebron [71]

2276 חֶבְרוֹנִי ḥebrônî, a.g. GK: 2498 [→ 2275; cf. 2266, 5683]. Hebronite, "*of Hebron*":– Hebronites [6]

2277 חֶבְרִי ḥebrî, a.g. GK: 2499 [→ 2268; cf. 2266]. Heberite, "*of Heber*":– Heberites [1]

2278 חֲבֶרֶת ḥᵃberet, n.f. GK: 2500 [→ 2266]. partner, (marriage) companion:– companion [1]

2279 חֹבֶרֶת ḥōberet, n.f. GK: 2501 [→ 2266]. set (of curtains):– coupleth [2], coupling [2]

2280 חָבַשׁ ḥābaš, v. GK: 2502 [cf. 2805]. [Q] to tie, bind, saddle; [Qp] to be saddled; to be twisted, wrapped around; [P] to bind up; [Pu] to be bound, bandaged:– saddled [10], bind up [3], bindeth up [3], bind [3], bound up [3], saddle [3], put [2], bindeth [1], bound [1], girded about [1], govern [1], healer [1], wrapt about [1]

2281 חֲבִתִּים ḥᵃbittîm, n.[m.]pl. GK: 2503 [→ 4227]. offering bread (flat cakes, baked in a pan):– pans [1]

2282 חַג ḥag, n.m. GK: 2504 [→ 2287]. religious feast, festival; festal procession:– feast [50], feasts [3], keep a feast (+2287) [2], sacrifice [2], solemn feasts [2], sacrifices [1], solemn feast [1], solemnity [1]

2283 חָגָא ḥoggā', n.[f.]. GK: 2505. terror; some sources: confusion:– terror [1]

2284 חָגָב ḥāgāb, n.m. GK: 2506 [→ 2285, 2286]. grasshopper, locust (in some cultures distinguished from a grasshopper and used as a food source):– grasshoppers [2], grasshopper [2], locusts [1]

2285 חָגָב ḥāgāb, n.pr.m. GK: 2507 [→ 2286; cf. 2284]. Hagab, "*locust*":– Hagab [1]

2286 חֲגָבָא ḥᵃgābā' or חֲגָבָה ḥᵃgābâ, n.pr.m. GK: 2508 & 2509 [→ 2285; cf. 2284]. Hagaba, Hagabah, "*locust*":– Hagabah [1], Hagaba [1]

2287 חָגַג ḥāgag, v. GK: 2510 [→ 2282, 2291, 2292, 2293, 2294; cf. 2328]. [Q] to hold a festival, celebrate a festival; this can refer to a religious celebration or a revel:– keep [6], keep a feast (+2282) [2], celebrate [1], dancing [1], hold a feast [1], keep a feast [1], keep a solemn feast [1], keep feast [1], kept holyday [1], reel to and fro [1]

2288 חָגוּ ḥāgû, n.m.pl. GK: 2511. clefts (of a rock) that can be used as a hiding place or retreat from danger:– clefts [3]

2289 חָגוֹר ḥāgôr, a. GK: 2513 [→ 2296]. belted (around the waist):– girdle [2], girded with [1], girdles [1]

2290 חֲגוֹר ḥᵃgôr or חֲגוֹרָה ḥᵃgôrâ, n.m. & f. GK: 2512 & 2514 [→ 2296]. covering; belt, sash:– girdle [3], aprons [1], gird [1], put on armour (+2296) [1]

2291 חַגִּי ḥaggî, n.pr.m. & a.g. GK: 2515 [→ 2287]. Haggi, "*festal; born on the feast day*":– Haggi [2], Haggites [1]

2292 חַגַּי ḥaggay, n.pr.m. GK: 2516 & 10247 [→ 2287]. Haggai, "*festal; born on the feast day*": note this name is Aramaic twice in Ezra:– Haggai [11]

2293 חַגִּיָּה ḥaggiyyâ, n.pr.m. GK: 2517 [→ 2287+3068]. Haggiah, "*feast of Yahweh*":– Haggiah [1]

2294 חַגִּית ḥaggît, n.pr.f. GK: 2518 [→ 2287]. Haggith, "*festal; born on the feast day*":– Haggith [5]

2295 חָגְלָה ḥoglâ, n.pr.f. GK: 2519 [→ 1031; cf. 2728]. Hoglah, "*partridge*":– Hoglah [4]

2296 חָגַר ḥāgar, v. GK: 2520 [→ 2289, 2290, 4228]. [Q] to tie, strap, fasten; to tuck (lower robe) into one's belt, gird; [Qp] to be tucked in, girded:– girded [13], gird with [7], gird [5], appointed [3], girded on [3], gird up [2], girded with [2], afraid [1], gird on [1], girdeth on [1], girdeth [1], girding with [1], on every side [1], put on armour (+2290) [1], restrain [1]

2297 חַד ḥad, a. GK: 2522 [cf. 259]. one, each:– one [1]

2298 חַד ḥad (Aram.), a. & subst. GK: 10248 [cf. 259]. one, first, a; time, occurrence:– one [5], a [4], first [4], together (+3509.4) [1]

2299 חַד ḥad, a. GK: 2521 [→ 2300]. sharp (sword):– sharp [4]

2300 חָדַד ḥādad or חָדָה ḥādâ, v. GK: 2523 & 2527 [→ 258, 2299, 2303, 2307; cf. 2302]. [Q] to be fierce, sharp; to sharpen; [H] to sharpen; [Ho] to be sharpened; [Ht] to slash:– sharpened [3], sharpeneth [2], fierce [1]

2301 חֲדַד ḥᵃdad, n.pr.m. GK: 2524. Hadad, "*sharp, fierce*":– Hadad [1]

2302 חָדָה ḥādâ, v. GK: 2525 & 2526 [→ 2304, 3164, 3165; cf. 2300]. [Q] to be delighted; [N] to be seen; to be joined; [P] to make glad:– joined [1], made [1], rejoiced [1]

2303 חַדּוּד ḥaddûd, a. GK: 2529 [→ 2300]. jagged, pointed:– sharp [1]

2304 חֶדְוָה ḥedwâ, n.f. GK: 2530 [→ 2302; cf. 2305]. joy:– gladness [1], joy [1]

2305 חֶדְוָה ḥedwâ (Aram.), n.f. GK: 10250 [cf. 2304]. joy:– joy [1]

2306 חֲדֵה ḥᵃdēh (Aram.), n.m. GK: 10249 [cf. 2373]. chest, breast:– breast [1]

2307 חָדִיד ḥādîd, n.pr.loc. GK: 2531 [→ 2300]. Hadid, "*sharp*":– Hadid [3]

2308 חָדַל ḥādal, v. GK: 2532 & 2533 [→ 2310, 2311?]. [Q] to stop, cease, refrain, fail; to become fat, have success:– forbear [17], cease [12], ceased [6], left off [4], forbare [3], leave [3], left [2], alone (+4480) [1], alone [1], ceaseth [1], ceasing [1], endeth [1], failed [1], forbeareth [1], forborn [1], forsake [1], off [1], rest [1], unoccupied [1], wanteth [1]

2309 חֶדֶל ḥedel, n.[m.]. GK: 2535. world (of the living); some sources: the Underworld, the realm of the dead:– world [1]

2310 חָדֵל ḥādēl, a. GK: 2534 [→ 2308]. refused, rejected, fleeting:– forbeareth [1], frail [1], rejected [1]

2311 חֶדְלַי ḥedlay, n.pr.m. GK: 2536 [→ 2220 or 2308]. Hadlai, "*resting; fat, stout*":– Hadlai [1]

2312 חֵדֶק ḥēdeq, n.[m.]. GK: 2537. brier, thorn:– brier [1], thorns [1]

2313 חִדֶּקֶל ḥiddeqel, n.pr.loc. GK: 2538. Hiddekel = Tigris, "*arrow*":– Hiddekel [2]

2314 חָדַר ḥādar, v. GK: 2539 [→ 2315]. [Q] to close in on every side, surround:– entereth into privy chambers [1]

2315 חֶדֶר ḥeder, n.m. GK: 2540 [→ 2314, 2316]. room, chamber, bedroom; shrine; "the chambers of the belly" means "the most inner parts"; "the chambers of death" means "Sheol":– chamber [10], inner chamber (+2315+871.1) [8], chambers [7], bedchamber (+4904) [4], bedchamber (+4296) [2], innermost parts [2], inward parts [2], parlours [1], south [1], within (+4480) [1]

2316 חֲדַר ḥᵃdar, n.pr.m. GK: 2540 [→ 2315]. Hadar:– Hadar [1]

2317 חַדְרָךְ ḥadrāk, n.pr.loc. GK: 2541. Hadrach:– Hadrach [1]

2318 חָדַשׁ ḥādaš, v. GK: 2542 [→ 2319, 2320, 2321, 2322]. [Q] to renew, restore, repair, reaffirm; [Ht] to renew oneself:– renew [3], repair [3], renewed [2], renewest [2]

2319 חָדָשׁ ḥādāš, a. GK: 2543 [→ 2318; cf. 2323]. new, recent, fresh:– new [52], fresh [1]

2320 חֹדֶשׁ ḥōdeš, n.m. [& f.?]. GK: 2544 [→ 2321; cf. 2318]. month; new moon, new moon festival:– month [216], months [37], new moon [20], new moons [9], every month (+2320+871.1) [2], another^s [1], monthly [1]

2321 חֹדֶשׁ ḥōdeš, n.pr.f. GK: 2545 [→ 2320; cf. 2318]. Hodesh, "*new moon*":– Hodesh [1]

2322 חֲדָשָׁה ḥᵃdāšâ, n.pr.loc. GK: 2546 [→ 2318]. Hadashah, "*new*":– Hadashah [1]

2323 חֲדַת ḥᵃdat (Aram.), a. GK: 10251 [cf. 2319]. new:– new [1]

2324 חֲוָה ḥᵃwâ (Aram.), v. GK: 10252 [→ 263; cf. 2331]. [Pa] to reveal, tell, show; [H, A] tell, explain, make known, interpret:– shew [14]

2325 חוּב ḥûb, v. GK: 2549 [→ 2326]. [P] to forfeit (one's head):– make endanger [1]

2326 חוב **ḥôb**, n.[m.]. GK: 2550 [→ 2325]. loan, debt:– debtor [1]

2327 חובה **ḥôbâ**, n.pr.loc. GK: 2551. Hobah:– Hobah [1]

2328 חוג **ḥûg**, v. GK: 2552 [→ 2329, 4230; cf. 2287]. [Q] to encircle:– compassed with (+5921+6440) [1]

2329 חוג **ḥûg**, n.[m.]. GK: 2553 [→ 2328]. circle, horizon:– circle [1], circuit [1], compass [1]

2330 חוד **ḥûd**, v.den. GK: 2554 [→ 2420; cf. 258]. [Q] to tell a riddle, set forth an allegory:– put forth [3], put forth a riddle (+2420) [1]

2331 חוה **ḥāwâ**, v. GK: 2555 [→ 262; cf. 263, cf. 2324]. [P] to tell, explain, show, display:– shew [5], sheweth [1]

2332 חוה **ḥawwâ**, n.pr.f. GK: 2558 [cf. 2421]. Eve, "life":– Eve [2]

2333 חוה **ḥawwâ**, n.f. GK: 2557. settlement, camp; an unwalled village, a tent camp of nomadic peoples, more or less permanent:– towns [3], small towns [1]

2334 חות יאיר **ḥawwôt yāʾîr**, n.pr.m. & n.f. GK: 2596 [cf. 2971]. Havvoth Jair, "villages of Jair":– Havoth-jair [2], Bashan-havoth-jair (+1316) [1]

2335 חוזי **ḥôzāy**, n.m. GK: 2559 [→ 2374; cf. 2372]. Hozai:–

2336 חוח **ḥôaḥ**, n.m. GK: 2560 [cf. 2397]. thicket, thistle, thornbush, bramble, briers; hook:– thistle [4], thorns [3], thorn [2], brambles [1], thistles [1]

2337 חוח **ḥôaḥ**, n.m. GK: 2561. hollows, cleft in rock; thicket:– thickets [1]

2338 חוט **ḥûṭ** (Aram.), v. GK: 10253. [H] to repair:– joined [1]

2339 חוט **ḥûṭ**, n.m. GK: 2562 [cf. 2338]. line, cord, ribbon, thread:– thread [4], cord [1], fillet [1], line [1]

2340 חוי **ḥiwwî**, a.g. GK: 2563. Hivite:– Hivites [16], Hivite [9]

2341 חוילה **ḥᵃwîlâ**, n.pr.loc. GK: 2564 [→ 2344]. Havilah, "stretch of sand":– Havilah [7]

2342 חול or חיל **ḥûl** or **ḥîl**, v. GK: 2565 & 2655 & 2656 [→ 2427, 2428, 2479, 4234, 4235, 4246, 4257?; cf. 2426]. [Q] to swirl, turn, fall, dance; to writhe, tremble, be in labor, give birth; to endure, prosper; [Pol] to wait; to dance (the round dance); to give birth; be in deep anguish; to twist; [Polal] to be brought forth, be given birth; [Htpalpal] be in distress; [Htpol] to be in torment; to wait patiently; to swirl down; in some contexts this refers to a whirlwind; [H] to shake; [Ho] to be born:– formed [5], in pain [4], brought forth [3], fear [2], grieved [2], grievous [2], have great pain (+2342) [2], shaketh [2], stayed [2], travailed [2], trembled [2], tremble [2], wounded [2], abide [1], afraid [1], bare [1], calve [1], danced [1], dance [1], driveth away [1], fall grievously [1], fall with pain [1], in anguish [1], look for [1], made to bring forth [1], made [1], maketh to calve [1], much pained [1], pained [1], rest [1], shapen [1], sore pained [1], sorely pained [1], sorrowful [1], sorrow [1], tarried [1], travail with child [1], travaileth with pain [1], travail [1], trust [1], wait patiently [1], waited carefully [1]

2343 חול **ḥûl**, n.pr.m. GK: 2566. Hul:– Hul [2]

2344 חול **ḥôl**, n.m. GK: 2567 & 2568 [→ 2341]. sand, grains of sand, with the associative meanings that the sands are vast and innumerable; palm tree or phoenix bird:– sand [23]

2345 חום **ḥûm**, a. GK: 2569 [→ 2552]. dark-colored; some shade of gray:– brown [4]

2346 חומה **ḥômâ**, n.f. GK: 2570 [→ 3181]. wall, with various associative meanings: protection, safety, or impenetrability:– wall [92], walls [35], two walls [4], walled [2]

2347 חוס **ḥûs**, v. GK: 2571. [Q] to show pity, mercy, have compassion, spare:– spare [12], pity [5], spare (+5921) [2], spared [1], had pity [1], pitied [1], regard (+5869) [1]

2348 חוף **ḥôp**, n.[m.]. GK: 2572 [→ 2653]. coast, seashore, haven (for ships):– haven [2], shore [2], coasts [1], coast [1], side [1]

2349 חופם **ḥûpām**, n.pr.m. GK: 2573 [→ 2350]. Hupham:– Hupham [1]

2350 חופמי **ḥûpāmî**, a.g. GK: 2574 [→ 2349]. Huphamite, "of Hupham":– Huphamites [1]

2351 חוץ **ḥûṣ**, n.[m.]. GK: 2575 [→ 2435; cf. 2434]. out, outside; street, market area; countryside, fields, outdoors:– without (+4480) [43], streets [35], without (+871.1+1886.1) [12], out (+4480) [9], street [9], abroad (+1886.5) [8], abroad [6], out [6], without (+1886.5) [6], out (+1886.5) [3], without [3], abroad (+4480) [2], fields [2], forth [2], outside [2], without (+1886.1+3807.1) [2], without

(+4480+1886.5) [2], abroad (+1886.1+3807.1) [1], abroad (+413+1886.1+1886.5) [1], abroad (+4480+1886.1) [1], abroad (+871.1+1886.1) [1], highways [1], more [1], outward (+1886.5) [1], utter [1], without (+1886.1+1886.5) [1], without (+413+1886.1) [1], without (+4480+1886.1) [1]

חק **ḥōq**. See 2436.

חקק **ḥûqōq**. See 2712.

2352 חר **ḥur**, n.[m.]. GK: 2987 [→ 2356]. hole, pit:– holes [1], hole [1]

2353 חור **ḥûr**, n.[m.]. GK: 2580 [→ 2357]. white garments, white linen:– white [2]

2354 חור **ḥûr**, n.pr.m. GK: 2581 [→ 1133, 5991?]. Hur, "[perhaps] child":– Hur [16]

2355 חורי **ḥôray**, n.m. GK: 2583 [→ 2357]. fine linen; networks [1]

2356 חר **ḥōr**, n.[m.]. GK: 2986 [→ 2352, 2735]. hole (in various forms):– holes [3], hole [3], caves [1]

2357 חור **ḥāwar**, v. GK: 2578 [→ 2353, 2355, 2751; cf. 2358]. [Q] to grow pale:– wax pale [1]

2358 חור **ḥiwwār** (Aram.), a. GK: 10254. white, a color of purity and lack of defilement:– white [1]

חורון **ḥôrōn**. See 1032.

חורי **ḥōrî**. See 2753.

2359 חורי **ḥûrî**, n.pr.m. GK: 2585 [→ 2357]. Huri, "linen weaver":– Huri [1]

2360 חורי **ḥûray**, n.pr.m. GK: 2584 [→ 2357]. Hurai:– Hurai [1]

2361 חורם **ḥûrām**, n.pr.m. GK: 2586 & 2587 [→ 297?+1]. Huram, Hiram, "[my] brother is elevated":– Huram [12]

2362 חורן **ḥawrān**, n.pr.loc. GK: 2588. Hauran, "black":– Hauran [2]

2363 חוש **ḥûš**, v. GK: 2590 & 2591 [→ 2439, 2440, 4122]. same as 2439: [Q] to go quickly, hasten, rush upon; to be greatly disturbed; to find enjoyment; [Qp] to be ready; [H] to make hurry, hasten; to be dismayed:– make haste [9], hasten [4], hasted [2], haste [2], hasteth [1], made haste [1], ready [1]

2364 חושה **ḥûšâ**, n.pr.m. GK: 2592 [→ 2843]. Hushah, "[perhaps] haste":– Hushah [1]

2365 חושי **ḥûšay**, n.pr.m. GK: 2593 [cf. 7862?]. Hushai:– Hushai [14]

2366 חושים **ḥûšîm** חשים **ḥušim** or חשם **ḥušim**, n.pr.f. & m. GK: 2594 & 3123. Hushim, Hushite:– Hushim [4]

2367 חושם **ḥûšām**, n.pr.m. GK: 2595 [cf. 2828]. Husham:– Husham [4]

2368 חותם **ḥôtām**, n.m. GK: 2597 [→ 2369; cf. 2856]. seal, signet ring:– signet [8], seal [5], signets [1]

2369 חותם **ḥôtām**, n.m. GK: 2598 [→ 2368; cf. 2856]. Hotham, "signet ring, seal":– Hotham [1], Hothan [1]

2370 חזה **ḥᵃzâ** (Aram.), v. GK: 10255 [→ 2376, 2379; cf. 2372]. [P] to see, look, watch, realize; [Pp] to be usual, be customary:– saw [9], sawest [7], beheld [6], see [4], seen [3], had⁵ [1], wont [1]

2371 חזאל **ḥᵃzāʾēl** or חזהאל **ḥᵃzāhʾēl**, n.pr.m. GK: 2599 & 2604 [→ 2372+410]. Hazael, "God [El] sees":– Hazael [23]

2372 חזה **ḥāzâ**, v. GK: 2600 [→ 2335, 2374, 2377, 2380, 2378, 2384, 4236, 4237, 4238; cf. 2370 (also used with compound proper names)]. [Q] to see, look, observe, gaze; by extension: to choose (one thing over another); to have visions, to prophesy:– see [15], seen [9], saw [8], behold [7], look [3], seeth [3], prophesy [2], seest [2], provide [1], sawest [1]

2373 חזה **ḥāzeh**, n.m. GK: 2601 [cf. 2306]. breast (portion of sacrifice):– breast [11], breasts [2]

2374 חזה **ḥōzeh**, n.m. GK: 2602 & 2603 [→ 2335, 3626; cf. 2372]. seer, one who receives a communication from God, with a possible focus that the message has a visual component; agreement:– seer [11], seers [5], see [2], agreement [1], prophets [1], seeing [1], stargazers (+3556+871.1+1886.1) [1]

חזהאל **ḥᵃzāhʾēl**. See 2371.

2375 חזו **ḥᵃzô**, n.pr.m. GK: 2605. Hazo:– Hazo [1]

2376 חזו **ḥᵃzû** (Aram.), n.m. GK: 10256 [→ 2370]. vision, appearance:– visions [9], vision [2], look [1]

2377 חזון **ḥāzôn**, n.m. GK: 2606 [→ 2372]. vision, revelation, a message from God, with a possible focus on the visual aspects of the message:– vision [32], visions [3]

2378 חזות **ḥᵃzôt**, n.[f.]. GK: 2608 [→ 2372]. visions:– visions [1]

2379 חזות **ḥᵃzôt** (Aram.), n.f. GK: 10257 [→ 2370]. visible sight:– sight [2]

2380 חזות **ḥāzût**, n.f. GK: 2607 [→ 2372]. vision; prominent appearance:– vision [2], agreement [1], notable ones [1], notable [1]

2381 חזיאל **ḥᵃzîʾēl**, n.pr.m. GK: 2609 [→ 2372+410]. Haziel, "vision of God [El]":– Haziel [1]

2382 חזיה **ḥᵃzāyâ**, n.pr.m. GK: 2610 [→ 2372+3068]. Hazaiah, "Yahweh sees":– Hazaiah [1]

2383 חזיון **ḥezyôn**, n.pr.m. GK: 2611. Hezion, "vision; one with floppy ears":– Hezion [1]

2384 חזיון **ḥizzāyôn**, n.m. GK: 2612 [→ 2372]. vision, dream, revelation:– vision [6], visions [3]

2385 חזיז **ḥᵃzîz**, n.[m.]. GK: 2613. storm cloud, dark and producing lightning and thunder:– lightning [2], bright clouds [1]

2386 חזיר **ḥᵃzîr**, n.m. GK: 2614 [→ 2387, 3170]. pig, boar:– swine's [4], swine [2], boar [1]

2387 חזיר **ḥēzîr**, n.pr.m. GK: 2615 [→ 2386]. Hezir, "boar":– Hezir [2]

2388 חזק **ḥāzaq**, v. GK: 2616 [→ 2389, 2390, 2391, 2392, 2393, 2394 (also used with compound proper names)]. [Q] to be strong, hard, harsh, severe; [P] to harden (one's heart); to give strength, repair, encourage; [H] to grasp, seize, hold; to make repairs; [Ht] to establish oneself firmly; to encourage, to rally strength; from the base meaning of physical hardness come by extension: physical and internal strength of character; (negative) hardness of the heart, failure to respond to a person or message:– repaired [39], strong [38], strengthened [28], strengthen [14], hardened [9], prevailed [8], repair [8], take hold [7], of good courage [6], caught [5], encouraged [5], held [5], hold [5], make strong [5], encourage [4], harden [4], laid hold [4], stronger [4], took hold [4], took [4], caught hold [3], hold fast [3], made strong [3], sore [3], taketh [3], calkers (+919) [2], confirm [2], courageous [2], fortified [2], lay hold [2], mend [2], prevail [2], taken hold [2], taken [2], withstand (+6440+3807.1) [2], aided (+853+3027) [1], became mighty [1], behave valiantly [1], clave [1], confirmed [1], constant [1], constrained [1], continued [1], courageously [1], established [1], fastened [1], fasten [1], force [1], fortify [1], give strength [1], good courage [1], held fast [1], help (+3027+871.1) [1], help [1], holden [1], holdeth fast [1], holdeth [1], lay hold on [1], layeth hold [1], leaneth [1], made harder [1], maintain [1], obtain [1], play the men [1], received [1], recovered [1], relieve [1], retained (+871.1) [1], retained [1], retaineth [1], retain [1], seized [1], shew strong [1], stout [1], stronger than [1], sure [1], take fast hold [1], taken hold on [1], taketh hold [1], took courage [1], urgent [1], waxed mighty [1], waxen strong [1]

2389 חזק **ḥāzāq**, a. GK: 2617 [→ 2388]. mighty, powerful, strong, hard, severe; from the base meaning of physical hardness come by extension: physical and internal strength of character; (negative) hardness of the heart, failure to respond to a person or message:– strong [26], mighty [20], sore [3], stronger [2], harder [1], hottest [1], impudent (+4696) [1], loud [1], stiff [1]

2390 חזק **ḥāzēq**, a.vbl. GK: 2618 [→ 2388]. strong, loud:– stronger [1], waxed louder and louder (+3966) [1]

2391 חזק **ḥēzeq**, n.[m.]. GK: 2619 [→ 2388]. strength:– strength [1]

2392 חזק **ḥōzeq**, n.m. GK: 2620 [→ 2388]. might, strength, power:– strength [5]

2393 חזקה **ḥezqâ**, n.f. GK: 2621 [→ 2388]. strength, power:– strong [2], mightily (+871.1) [1], strengthened [1], strength [1]

2394 חזקה **ḥozqâ**, n.f. GK: 2622 [→ 2388]. force, harshness, urgency:– force [2], mightily (+871.1) [1], repair [1], sharply (+871.1) [1]

2395 חזקי **ḥizqî**, n.pr.m. GK: 2623 [→ 2388+3068]. Hizki, "Yahweh is [my] strength or my strength":– Hezeki [1]

2396 חזקיה **ḥizqiyyâ** or חזקיהו **ḥizqiyyāhû**, n.pr.m. GK: 2624 & 2625 [→ 2388+3068]. Hezekiah, "Yahweh is [my] strength":– Hezekiah [85], Hizkiah [1], Hizkijah [1]

2397 חח **ḥāḥ**, n.m. GK: 2626 [cf. 2336]. hook; brooch:– chains [2], hooks [2], hook [2], bracelets [1]

חחי **ḥāḥî**. See 2397.

2398 חטא **ḥāṭāʾ**, v. GK: 2627 [→ 2399, 2400, 2401, 2402, 2403]. [Q] to sin, do wrong, miss the way; [P] to purify, cleanse, to offer a sin offering; [H] to bring a sin upon, cause to commit a

sin; [Ht] to purify oneself; "to sin," to willfully act contrary to the will and law of God, is a figure of missing or moving from a standard or mark:– sinned [101], sin [38], made to sin [20], sinneth [13], sinner [8], cleanse [7], purify [7], committed [5], cause to sin [4], made sin [4], offended [4], purified [3], bear the blame [2], done [2], make sin [2], sinning [2], bare loss [1], cleansing [1], fault [1], grievously sinned (+2399) [1], harm done [1], make reconciliation [1], make an offender [1], miss [1], offered for sin [1], offereth for sin [1], purge [1], purifieth [1], sin committed (+2403) [1], sinful [1], sinnest [1], trespass [1]

2399 חֵטְא *ḥēṭ',* n.m. GK: 2628 [→ 2398; cf. 2408]. sin, action contrary to the will and law of God, with a strong implication that guilt follows, error:– sin [21], sins [7], committed a sin [1], faults [1], grievously sinned (+2398) [1], offences [1], punishment of sins [1]

2400 חַטָּא *ḥaṭṭā',* a. & n.m. GK: 2629 [→ 2398]. sinful, guilty; (n.) sinner, wicked one:– sinners [16], offenders [1], sinful [1]

2401 חֲטָאָה *ḥᵃṭā'â,* n.f. GK: 2630 & 2631 [→ 2398]. sin, guilt, condemnation; sin offering:– sin [7], sin offering [1]

2402 חַטָּאָה *ḥaṭṭā'â,* n.f. GK: 2632 [→ 2398]. sin, wickedness, fault:–

2403 חַטָּאת *ḥaṭṭā't,* n.f. GK: 2633 [→ 2398; cf. 2409]. sin, wrong, iniquity; sin offering, purification offering:– sin offering [115], sin [100], sins [70], punishment [2], purification for sin [2], punishment of sin [1], purifying [1], sin committed (+2398) [1], sin offerings [1], sinful [1], sinner [1], sins committed [1]

2404 חָטַב *ḥāṭab,* v. GK: 2634. [Q] to cut, chop (wood); (n.) woodcutter, woodsman; [Pu] to carve:– hewers [5], cut down [1], hewer [1], hew [1], polished [1]

2405 חֲטֻבוֹת *ḥᵃṭubôt,* n.f.pl. GK: 2635. colored, embroidered (fabric):– carved [1]

2406 חִטָּה *ḥiṭṭâ,* n.f. GK: 2636 [→ 2590; cf. 2591]. wheat:– wheat [29], wheaten [1]

2407 חַטּוּשׁ *ḥaṭṭûš,* n.pr.m. GK: 2637. Hattush:– Hattush [5]

2408 חֲטָי *ḥᵃṭāy* (Aram.), n.[m.]. GK: 10259 [→ 2409; cf. 2399]. sin:– sins [1]

2409 חַטָּיָא *ḥaṭṭāyā'* (Aram.), n.f. GK: 10260 [→ 2408; cf. 2403]. sin offering:– sin offering [1]

2410 חֲטִיטָא *ḥᵃṭîṭā',* n.pr.m. GK: 2638. Hatita:– Hatita [2]

2411 חַטִּיל *ḥaṭṭîl,* n.pr.m. GK: 2639. Hattil, *"talkative":–* Hattil [2]

2412 חֲטִיפָא *ḥᵃṭîp̄ā',* n.pr.m. GK: 2640 [→ 2414]. Hatipha, *"taken captive":–* Hatipha [2]

2413 חָטַם *ḥāṭam,* v. GK: 2641 [→ 2748]. [Q] to hold back, restrain:– refrain [1]

2414 חָטַף *ḥāṭap̄,* v. GK: 2642 [→ 2412]. [Q] to seize, carry off (by force):– catch [3]

2415 חֹטֶר *ḥōṭer,* n.m. GK: 2643. rod, switch; shoot, twig:– rod [2]

2416 חַי *ḥay,* n.m. & a. GK: 2644 & 2645 & 2646 & 2651 & 2652 & 2653 [→ 2421; cf. 2417; cf. 2423]. life, state of living (in contrast to death), lifetime; "as I live" is a formula for an oath, implying death should follow if what is sworn is not true; family, kin; band, army; animal, beast, livestock, living creature; living, alive, with an implication that life has movement and vigor; "living meat" is "raw meat"; "living water" is "fresh, running water":– life [143], living [80], liveth [67], live [46], beasts [41], beast [34], alive [30], living creatures [9], running [7], living creature [6], raw [5], lived [4], living thing [4], quick [3], congregation [2], lives [2], troop [2], alive (+871.1+1886.1) [1], appetite [1], company [1], life (+5315) [1], lifetime [1], lived (+1961) [1], lively [1], livest [1], maintenance [1], maketh merry (+8055) [1], multitude [1], old (+3117+8141) [1], quick raw (+4241) [1], springing [1], whole age (+3117+8141) [1], wild beasts [1]

2417 חַי *ḥay* (Aram.), a. GK: 10261 [→ 2418; cf. 2416]. living, alive:– living [4], life [1], lives [1], liveth [1]

2418 חֲיָה *ḥᵃyâ* (Aram.), v. GK: 10262 [→ 2417, 2423; cf. 2421]. [P] to live; [H] to spare, let live:– live [5], kept alive [1]

2419 חִיאֵל *ḥî'ēl,* n.pr.m. GK: 2647 [→ 251+410]. Hiel, *"God [El] lives here":–* Hiel [1]

חִיב *ḥāyab.* See 2325.

2420 חִידָה *ḥîdâ,* n.f. GK: 2648 [→ 2330; cf. 280]. riddle, hard question, allegory; hidden things, intrigue; scorn (the asking of a riddle as a game could imply scorn and ridicule toward the person asked):– riddle [8], dark sayings [2], hard questions [2],

dark saying [1], dark sentences [1], dark speeches [1], proverb [1], put forth a riddle (+2330) [1]

2421 חָיָה *ḥāyâ,* v. GK: 2649 [→ 2416, 2422, 2424, 2425, 4241; cf. 2332; cf. 2418 (also used with compound proper names)]. same as 2425: [Q] to live; recover, revive; [P] to keep alive, preserve life; [H] to keep alive, save a life, spare a life, restore a life:– live [113], lived [44], surely live (+2421) [18], quicken [12], save alive [10], God save [8], keep alive [8], revive [8], saved alive [8], recover [4], restored to life [4], revived [4], certainly recover (+2421) [2], kept alive [2], liveth [2], make alive [2], preserve alive [2], preserve [2], quickened [2], recovered [2], save life [2], surely recover (+2421) [2], given life [1], giveth life [1], left alive [1], make to live [1], maketh alive [1], nourished up [1], nourish [1], preservest [1], preserveth life [1], promising life [1], repaired [1], save lives [1], saved lives [1], save [1], saving [1], suffer to live [1], whole [1]

2422 חָיֶה *ḥāyeh,* a. GK: 2650 [→ 2421]. vigorous:– lively [1]

2423 חֵיוָא *ḥêwâ* (Aram.), n.f. GK: 10263 [→ 2418; cf. 2416]. beast, animal; this can refer to physical creatures of earth as well as to fig. creatures of visions and parables:– beasts [13], beast [6], beast's [1]

2424 חַיּוּת *ḥayyût,* n.f.abst. GK: 2654 [→ 2421]. lifetime:– living [1]

2425 חָיַי *ḥāyay,* v. GK: 2649 [→ 2421]. same as 2421: [Q] to live; recover, revive; [P] to keep alive, preserve life; [H] to keep alive, save a life, spare a life, restore a life:–

2426 חֵל *ḥēl,* n.m. GK: 2658 [→ 2430; cf. 2342]. ramparts, outer fortification, defense walls:– host [2], rampart [2], army [1], bulwarks [1], trench [1], walls [1], wall [1]

חיל *ḥîl.* See 2342.

2427 חִיל *ḥîl* or חִילָה *ḥîlâ,* n.m. GK: 2659 & 2660 [→ 2342]. pain, anguish, any kind of physical trauma, as a fig. extension of the labor pains of birth:– pain [3], pangs [2], sorrow [2]

2428 חַיִל *ḥayil,* n.m. GK: 2657 [→ 32, 1134; cf. 2342; cf. 2429]. strength, capability, skill, valor, wealth; army, troop, warrior:– army [51], valour [37], host [28], valiant [16], forces [14], strength [12], riches [11], wealth [10], power [9], substance [8], might [6], valiantly [5], armies [4], strong [4], valiant (+1121) [4], able [3], virtuous [3], goods [2], activity [1], army (+6635) [1], band of men [1], band [1], company [1], hosts [1], meet for the war (+1121) [1], mighty [1], strong (+1121) [1], train [1], valiantest (+1121) [1], very able [1], virtuously [1], war [1], worthily [1], worthy [1]

2429 חַיִל *ḥayil* (Aram.), n.m. GK: 10264 [cf. 2428]. strength, power; an army:– aloud (+871.2) [3], army [2], most mighty men (+1400+1401) [1], power [1]

2430 חֵילָה *ḥêlâ,* n.f. GK: 2658 [→ 2426]. ramparts, outer fortification, defense walls:– bulwarks [1]

2431 חֵילָם *ḥêlām* or חֵלָאם *ḥēlā'm,* n.pr.loc. GK: 2663 & 2691. Helam, *"health":–* Helam [2]

2432 חִילֵן *ḥîlēn,* n.pr.loc. GK: 2664. Hilen:– Hilen [1]

2433 חִין *ḥîn,* n.[m.]. GK: 2665 [→ 2603]. gracefulness:– comely [1]

2434 חַיִץ *ḥayiṣ,* n.[m.]. GK: 2666 [cf. 2351]. flimsy wall, inner wall:– wall [1]

2435 חִיצוֹן *ḥîṣôn,* a. GK: 2667 [→ 2351]. outer, outside, exterior:– utter [13], outward [7], without [3], without (+1886.5) [1], without (+871.1+1886.1) [1]

2436 חֵיק *ḥêq* or חֹק *ḥōq,* n.[m.]. GK: 2668 & 2576 [→ 2710]. lap, bosom, the area to which one holds and cradles a loved one; by extension: the inner person, heart, seat of affection; fold of a cloak, gutter:– bosom [32], bottom [3], lap [1], midst [1], within (+871.1) [1]

2437 חִירָא *ḥîrā',* n.pr.m. GK: 2669. Hirah:– Hirah [2]

2438 חִירוֹם *ḥîrôm* or חִירָם *ḥîrām,* n.pr.m. GK: 2670 & 2671 [→ 297?]. Hiram, *"[my] brother is elevated":–* Hiram [22], Hiram's [1]

2439 חִישׁ *ḥîš,* v. GK: 2590 [→ 2363]. same as 2363: [Q] to go quickly, hasten, rush upon; [Qp] to be ready; [H] to make hurry, hasten:–

2440 חִישׁ *ḥîš,* adv. GK: 2673 [→ 2363]. quickly, in haste:– soon [1]

2441 חֵךְ *ḥēk,* n.m. GK: 2674. (area of the) mouth: lips, tongue (taste), roof of mouth:– mouth [9], roof of mouth [5], taste [4]

2442 חָכָה *ḥākâ,* v. GK: 2675. [Q] to wait; [P] to lie in wait (ambush); hope for, long for:– wait [5], waiteth [3], tarry [2], waited [2], long for [1], wait for [1]

2443 חַכָּה *ḥakkâ,* n.f. GK: 2676. fishhook:– angle [2], hook [1]

2444 חֲכִילָה *ḥᵃkîlâ,* n.pr.loc. GK: 2677 [→ 2447]. Hakilah:– Hachilah [3]

2445 חַכִּים *ḥakkîm* (Aram.), n.m. GK: 10265 [→ 2452; cf. 2450]. wise man (usually pertaining to a social class):– wise [14]

2446 חֲכַלְיָה *ḥᵃkalyâ,* n.pr.m. GK: 2678 [→ 2447+3068]. Hacaliah, *"dark":–* Hachaliah [2]

2447 חַכְלִילִי *ḥaklîlî,* a. GK: 2679 [→ 2444, 2446, 2448]. darker, some sources: sparkling:– red [1]

2448 חַכְלִלוּת *ḥaklilût,* n.f. GK: 2680 [→ 2447]. bloodshot (eyes); some sources: sparkling:– redness [1]

2449 חָכַם *ḥākam,* v. GK: 2681 [→ 2450, 2451, 2454, 2453?; cf. 2445]. [Q] to be wise, be skillful, gain wisdom; [P] to make wiser, to teach wisdom; [Pu] to be skillful; [H] to make wise; [Ht] to deal shrewdly; to show oneself wise; to be wise implies understanding and acting in a manner that is effective and usually moral:– wise [15], wiser [2], deal wisely [1], exceeding wise (+2450) [1], made wiser [1], made wise [1], make wise [1], maketh wiser [1], making wise [1], shewed wise [1], teach wisdom [1], wisely [1]

2450 חָכָם *ḥākām,* a. GK: 2682 [→ 2449; cf. 2445]. wise, skilled, shrewd, craftsman; (n.) wise person, sage, one who interprets divination or prophecy, one who has fear of the Lord and understanding that leads to effective (moral) action:– wise [120], cunning [10], unwise (+3808) [2], wise men [2], wiser [2], exceeding wise (+2449) [1], subtil [1]

2451 חָכְמָה *ḥokmâ,* n.f. GK: 2683 [→ 2449; cf. 2452]. wisdom, skill, learning; this can refer to skill in life, trade, war, or spiritual things:– wisdom [144], wit's end (+1104+3605) [1], skilful [1], wisdom (+2050.2) [1], wisely (+4480) [1], wisely (+871.1) [1]

2452 חָכְמָה *ḥokmâ* (Aram.), n.f. GK: 10266 [→ 2445; cf. 2451]. wisdom:– wisdom [8]

2453 חַכְמוֹנִי *ḥakmônî,* n.pr.m.[g.?]. GK: 2685 [→ 2449?]. Hacmoni; Hacmonite, *"wise":–* Hachmonite (+1121) [1], Hachmoni [1]

2454 חָכְמוֹת *ḥokmôt,* n.f.pl.abst. GK: 2684 [→ 2449]. wisdom; the plural form may imply in its essential or supreme condition:– wisdom [4]

חֵל *ḥēl.* See 2426.

2455 חֹל *ḥōl,* n.[m.]. GK: 2687 [→ 2490]. common use, not holy, ordinary:– profane [4], common [2], unholy [1]

2456 חָלָא *ḥālā',* v. GK: 2688 [→ 2457, 2458, 8463; cf. 2470]. [Q] to be ill:– diseased [1]

2457 חֶלְאָה *ḥel'â,* n.f. GK: 2689 [→ 2458; cf. 2456]. deposit, encrustation, rust:– scum [5]

2458 חֶלְאָה *ḥel'â,* n.pr.f. GK: 2690 [→ 2457; cf. 2456]. Helah, *"necklace; rust":–* Helah [2]

2459 חֵלֶב *ḥēleb,* n.m. GK: 2693. fat, fat portions; by extension: finest, best part; callous (heart that is dull and unresponsive):– fat [79], best [5], fatness [4], finest [2], grease [1], marrow [1]

2460 חֵלֶב *ḥēleb,* n.pr.m. GK: 2694 [cf. 2466]. Heleb, cf. 2466:– Heleb [1]

2461 חָלָב *ḥālāb,* n.m. GK: 2692 [→ 2464]. milk:– milk [42], cheeses (+2757) [1], sucking [1]

2462 חֶלְבָּה *ḥelbâ,* n.pr.loc. GK: 2695. Helbah, *"fertile region":–* Helbah [1]

2463 חֶלְבּוֹן *ḥelbôn,* n.pr.loc. GK: 2696. Helbon, *"fertile":–* Helbon [1]

2464 חֶלְבְּנָה *ḥelbᵉnâ,* n.f. GK: 2697 [→ 2461]. galbanum (aromatic gum resin used to make incense):– galbanum [1]

2465 חֶלֶד *ḥeled,* n.[m.]. GK: 2698 [→ 2466, 2469]. life, duration of life; this world:– age [2], world [2], short time [1]

2466 חֵלֶד *ḥēled,* n.pr.m. GK: 2699 [→ 2465]. Heled, *"mole":–* Heled [1]

2467 חֹלֶד *ḥōled,* n.[m.]. GK: 2700 [→ 2468]. weasel; some sources: rat or mole:– weasel [1]

2468 חֻלְדָּה *ḥuldâ,* n.pr.m. GK: 2701 [→ 2467]. Huldah, *"weasel":–* Huldah [2]

2469 חֶלְדָּי *ḥelday*, n.pr.m. GK: 2702 [→ 2465]. Heldai, "*mole*":– Heldai [2]

2470 חָלָה *ḥālâ*, v. GK: 2703 & 2704 [→ 2483, 4245, 4248?, 4249?, 4250?, 4251, 4257?; cf. 2456]. [Q] to be ill, be weak, be faint, become diseased, be wounded; [N] to be made sick, be incurable; [P] to afflict; to entreat, implore, seek favor, intercede; [Pu] to become weak; [H] to make ill, to cause to suffer; [Ho] to be wounded; [Ht] to pretend to be ill, to feel sick:– sick [24], fell sick [4], grievous [4], besought (+853+6440) [3], diseased [3], pray [3], weak [3], wounded [3], besought (+6440) [2], grieved [2], intreat [2], made sick [2], make sick [2], sore [2], become weak [1], beseech (+6440) [1], fallen sick [1], grief [1], in travail [1], infirmity [1], intreat favour (+6440) [1], intreated [1], laid [1], made prayer [1], made supplication [1], make suit [1], maketh sick [1], put to grief [1], put to pain [1], sorry [1]

2471 חַלָּה *ḥallâ*, n.f. GK: 2705 [→ 2490]. (ring-shaped) bread cakes:– cakes [7], cake [7]

2472 חֲלוֹם *ḥᵃlôm*, n.m. GK: 2706 [→ 2492; cf. 2493]. dream, dreamer; this can refer to a supernatural revelation by God by words and images:– dream [44], dreams [19], dreamer (+1167+1886.1) [1], dreamers [1]

2473 חֹלוֹן *ḥōlôn*, n.pr.loc. GK: 2708. Holon, "[perhaps] *sandy*":– Holon [3]

2474 חַלּוֹן *ḥallôn*, n.m. & f. GK: 2707 & 2709 [→ 2490]. window, narrow openings, parapet openings:– windows [18], window [13]

2475 חֲלוֹף *ḥᵃlôp*, n.m. GK: 2710 [→ 2498]. destitute, vanishing:– appointed to destruction (+1121) [1]

2476 חֲלוּשָׁה *ḥᵃlûšâ*, n.f. GK: 2711 [→ 2522]. defeat:– overcome [1]

2477 חֲלַח *ḥᵃlaḥ*, n.pr.loc. GK: 2712. Halah:– Halah [3]

2478 חַלְחוּל *ḥalḥûl*, n.pr.loc. GK: 2713. Halhul:– Halhul [1]

2479 חַלְחָלָה *ḥalḥālâ*, n.f. GK: 2714 [→ 2342]. anguish, pain, trembling:– great pain [2], much pain [1], pain [1]

2480 חָלַט *ḥālaṭ*, v. GK: 2715. [Q] to accept a statement:– catch [1]

2481 חֲלִי *ḥᵃlî*, n.m. GK: 2717 [→ 2484]. ornament, jewel:– jewels [1], ornament [1]

2482 חֲלִי *ḥᵃlî*, n.pr.loc. GK: 2718. Hali, "*adornment*":– Hali [1]

2483 חֳלִי *ḥᵒlî*, n.m. GK: 2716 [→ 2470]. illness, sickness, affliction; wound, injury:– sickness [11], disease [7], grief [3], griefs [1], sicknesses [1], sick [1]

2484 חֶלְיָה *ḥelyâ*, n.f. GK: 2719 [→ 2481]. jewelry, ornament:– jewels [1]

2485 חָלִיל *ḥālîl*, n.m. GK: 2720 [→ 2490, 5155?]. flute:– pipes [3], pipe [1]

2486 חָלִיל *ḥālîl*, subst. GK: 2721 [→ 2490]. far be it!, never!:– God forbid [8], far be it [4], be it far [3], forbid [3], that be far [2], forbid it [1]

2487 חֲלִיפָה *ḥᵃlîpâ*, n.f. GK: 2722 [→ 2498]. set, sequence, shift; renewal, relief:– changes [7], change [4], courses [1]

2488 חֲלִיצָה *ḥᵃlîṣâ*, n.f. GK: 2723 [→ 2502]. belongings, equipment:– armour [1], spoil [1]

2489 חֵלְכָה *ḥēlkâ*, a. GK: 2724. victim:– poor [3]

2490 חָלַל *ḥālal*, v. GK: 2725 & 2726 & 2727 [→ 2455, 2471, 2474, 2485, 2486, 2491, 4247, 5155?, 8462]. [Q] to be wounded; to play the flute; [N] to defile oneself, be profaned, be desecrated; [P] to pierce, wound; to defile, profane, desecrate; to enjoy; to play the flute; [Pu] to be killed; to be defiled; [Poll] to pierce, wound; [Polal] to be wounded; [H] to begin, to proceed, launch; [Ho] to be begun:– began [33], profane [17], profaned [15], polluted [13], begin [12], pollute [8], begun [7], defiled [5], break [3], wounded [3], defile [2], polluting [2], profaning [2], beginnest [1], broken [1], cast as profane [1], defiledest [1], defileth [1], eat as common things [1], eaten [1], eat [1], first [1], gather the grapes [1], piped [1], players on instruments [1], profaneth [1], prostitute [1], slain [1], slayeth [1], sorrow [1], stain [1], take inheritance [1]

2491 חָלָל *ḥālāl*, n.m. & a. GK: 2728 & 2729 [→ 2490]. dead, slain, casualty; defiled, profane (moral or ceremonial failure):– slain [73], wounded [9], slew [4], profane [3], kill [2], deadly wounded [1], that is slain [1], that were slain [1]

 חֲלִלָה *ḥᵃlilâ*. See 2486.

2492 חָלַם *ḥālam*, v. GK: 2730 & 2731 [→ 2472]. [Q] to grow strong; to dream; [H] to restore to health; to encourage one to

have dreams:– dreamed [19], dreamer [3], dreameth [2], dream [2], cause to be dreamed [1], in good liking [1], recover [1]

2493 חֵלֶם *ḥēlem* (Aram.), n.m. GK: 10267 [cf. 2472]. dream:– dream [21], dreams [1]

2494 חֵלֶם *ḥēlem*, n.pr.m. GK: 2732 [cf. 2469]. Helem, cf. 2469:– Helem [1]

2495 חַלָּמוּת *ḥallāmût*, n.f. GK: 2733. egg or mallow:– egg [1]

2496 חַלָּמִישׁ *ḥallāmîš*, n.m. GK: 2734. flinty rock, hard rock:– flint [3], flinty [1], rock [1]

2497 חֵלֹן *ḥēlōn*, n.pr.m. GK: 2735. Helon, "*strength, power*":– Helon [5]

2498 חָלַף *ḥālap*, v. GK: 2736 [→ 2475, 2487, 2500, 4252?, 4253; cf. 2499]. [Q] to go by, pass on, sweep by; to be new; to pierce, cut through; [P] to change; [H] to change, exchange, replace, renew:– changed [6], change [4], groweth up [2], renew [2], abolish [1], alter [1], cut off [1], go on [1], over [1], pass through [1], passed away [1], passed [1], passeth on [1], pass [1], renewed [1], sprout [1], stricken through [1], strike through [1]

2499 חֲלַף *ḥᵃlap* (Aram.), v. GK: 10268 [cf. 2498]. [P] to pass by, pass over:– pass [4]

2500 חֵלֶף *ḥēlep*, n.[m.]. GK: 2739 [→ 2498]. in return for:– for [2]

2501 חֵלֶף *ḥēlep*, n.pr.loc. GK: 2738. Heleph, "[poss.] *sharp, cutting*":– Heleph [1]

2502 חָלַץ *ḥālaṣ*, v. GK: 2740 & 2741 [→ 2488, 2503, 4254]. [Q] to take off; [Qp] to be taken off; to be armed (for battle); [N] to be delivered, be rescued; to arm oneself; [P] to rescue, deliver; to tear out, rob; [H] to strengthen:– armed [11], delivered [9], deliver [5], delivereth [2], go armed [2], ready armed [2], armed soldiers [1], army [1], arm [1], draw out [1], loosed [1], loose [1], make fat [1], prepared [1], put off [1], ready prepared for [1], take away [1], taken away [1], withdrawn [1]

2503 חֶלֶץ *ḥeleṣ*, n.[m.]. GK: 2742 [→ 2502]. Helez, "*vigor; he has saved*":– Helez [5]

2504 חֲלָצִים *ḥᵃlāṣîm*, n.[f.]. GK: 2743 [cf. 2783]. waist, stomach, the area between the lowest ribs and the hip-bones; by extension: body, flesh; the inner person, heart:– loins [9], reins [1]

2505 חָלַק *ḥālaq*, v. GK: 2744 & 2745 & 2746 [→ 2506, 2509, 2510, 2511, 2512, 2513, 2514, 2515, 2517, 2518, 2519, 2520, 4256]. [Q] to be smooth, slippery; deceitful; to divide, apportion, assign; [N] to be divided, be dispersed, be distributed; [P] to divide, allot, apportion; to destroy; [Pu] to be divided; [Ht] to divide among themselves; [H] to speak deceit, flatter, be seductive; to get one's share:– divided [21], divide [18], flattereth [5], dealt [2], distributed [2], parted [2], part [2], distributeth [1], distribute [1], dividing [1], flatter [1], given [1], have part [1], imparted [1], partner [1], received [1], separate [1], smoother [1], smootheth [1], took away a portion [1]

2506 חֵלֶק *ḥēleq*, n.m. GK: 2749 & 2750 [→ 2505, 2513, 2520; cf. 2505; cf. 2508 (also used with compound proper names)]. smoothness; share, portion, allotment, plot of ground:– portion [36], part [18], parts [4], portions [4], flattering [1], flattery (+3807.1) [1], inheritance [1], partaker [1]

2507 חֵלֶק *ḥēleq*, n.pr.m. GK: 2751 [→ 2516; cf. 2518?]. Helek, "*portion, lot*":– Helek [2]

2508 חֲלָק *ḥᵃlāq* (Aram.), n.[m.]. GK: 10269 [→ 4255; cf. 2506]. portion, lot in life:– portion [3]

2509 חָלָק *ḥālāq*, a. GK: 2747 [→ 2505, 2511]. smooth, slippery, pleasant, flattering:– flattering [2], smoother [1], smooth [1]

2510 חָלָק *ḥālāq*, n.pr.loc. GK: 2748 [→ 2505]. Halak:– Halak [2]

2511 חַלָּק *ḥallāq*, a. GK: 2747 [→ 2509]. smooth, slippery, pleasant, flattering:– smooth [1]

2512 חַלֻּק *ḥalluq*, a. GK: 2752 [→ 2505]. smooth (stones):– smooth [1]

2513 חֶלְקָה *ḥelqâ*, n.f. GK: 2753 & 2754 [→ 2505, 2506]. smoothness; plot, field, tract:– portion [6], parcel [5], field [3], piece [3], flattering [2], piece of land [2], plat [2], smooth [2], flattery [1], ground [1], part [1], slippery [1]

2514 חֲלַקָּה *ḥᵃlaqqâ*, n.f. GK: 2756 [→ 2505]. smoothness, flattery:– flatteries [1]

2515 חֲלֻקָּה *ḥᵃluqqâ*, n.f. GK: 2755 [→ 2505]. part, portion, division:– division [1]

2516 חֶלְקִי *ḥelqî*, a.g. GK: 2757 [→ 2507]. Helekite, "*of Helek*":– Helekites [1]

2517 חֶלְקַי *ḥelqay*, n.pr.m. GK: 2758 [→ 2506+3068?]. Helkai, "*Yahweh is [my] portion*":– Helkai [1]

2518 חִלְקִיָּה or חִלְקִיָּהוּ *ḥilqiyyâ* or *ḥilqiyyāhû*, n.pr.m. GK: 2759 & 2760 [cf. 2507?]. Hilkiah, "*Yahweh is [my] portion*":– Hilkiah [33], Hilkiah's [1]

2519 חֲלַקְלַק *ḥᵃlaqlaq*, n.f.abst. GK: 2761 [→ 2505]. slippery, slick and hard to walk on; by extension: slippery words, intrigue, insincere:– flatteries [2], slippery [2]

2520 חֶלְקַת *ḥelqat*, n.pr.loc. GK: 2762 [→ 2521; cf. 2505, 2506]. Helkath, "*portion*":– Helkath [2]

2521 חֶלְקַת הַצֻּרִים *ḥelqat haṣṣurîm*, n.pr.loc. GK: 2763 [→ 2520]. Helkath Hazzurim, "[poss.] *portion [field] of rock or swords; portion [field] of snare*":– Helkath-hazzurim [1]

2522 חָלַשׁ *ḥālaš*, v. GK: 2764 & 2765 [→ 2476, 2523]. [Q] to be laid low; to overcome, defeat:– discomfited [1], wasteth away [1], weaken [1]

2523 חַלָּשׁ *ḥallāš*, a. GK: 2766 [→ 2522]. weak, weakling:– weak [1]

2524 חָם *ḥām*, n.m. GK: 2767 [→ 2537, 2545]. father-in-law:– father in law [4]

2525 חָם *ḥām*, a. GK: 2768 [→ 2552]. hot, sweltering:– hot [1], warm [1]

2526 חָם *ḥām*, n.pr.m. & loc. GK: 2769 [→ 2536, 2537]. Ham:– Ham [16]

2527 חֹם *ḥōm*, n.m. GK: 2770 [→ 2552]. heat:– heat [9], hot [4], warm [1]

2528 חֱמָא *ḥᵉmâ* (Aram.), n.f. GK: 10270 [cf. 2534]. fury, rage; "to be in fury and rage" refers to anger of highest degree:– fury [1]

 חֵמָא *ḥēmā'*. See 2534.

2529 חֶמְאָה *ḥem'â*, n.f. GK: 2772 [cf. 4260]. curds, curdled milk; butter, cream:– butter [10]

2530 חָמַד *ḥāmad*, v. GK: 2773 & 2776 [→ 2531, 2532, 2533, 4261, 4262]. [Q] to covet, lust, desire; delight in; [Qp] (n.) what is coveted: treasure, wealth; [N] to be pleasing, be desirable; [P] to delight; this can refer to proper delight and fondness, as well as to improper lust and desire:– desired [5], desire [4], covet [3], desireth [2], beauty [1], coveted [1], delectable [1], delight in [1], lust after [1], pleasant [1], with great delight [1]

2531 חֶמֶד *ḥemed*, n.[m.]. GK: 2774 [→ 2530]. fruitfulness, lushness; pleasantness; handsomeness:– desirable [3], pleasant [2]

2532 חֶמְדָּה *ḥemdâ*, n.f. GK: 2775 [→ 2530]. desirable, pleasant, fine, valuable (things):– pleasant [11], precious [4], desire [3], greatly beloved [3], goodly [2], desired [1], pleasant things [1]

2533 חֶמְדָּן *ḥemdān*, n.pr.m. GK: 2777 [→ 2530; cf. 2566]. Hemdan, "*desirable*":– Hemdan [1]

2534 חֵמָה *ḥēmâ* or חֵמָא *ḥēmā'*, n.f. GK: 2779 & 2771 [→ 3179; cf. 2528]. anger, wrath, fury, rage, from the base meaning of heat (as in "hot-headed"); by extension: venom (poison that causes a burning sensation):– fury [67], wrath [34], poison [6], furious [4], hot displeasure [3], rage [2], anger [1], bottles [1], furious (+1167) [1], furiously (+871.1) [1], heat [1], indignation [1], wrathful [1], wroth [1]

2535 חַמָּה *ḥammâ*, n.f. GK: 2780 [→ 2552]. heat (of the sun):– sun [5], heat [1]

2536 חַמּוּאֵל *ḥammû'ēl*, n.pr.m. GK: 2781 [→ 2526+410; cf. 2537]. Hammuel, "*God [El] of Ham*":– Hamuel [1]

2537 חֲמוּטַל or חֲמִיטַל *ḥᵃmûṭal* or *ḥᵃmîṭal*, n.pr.f. GK: 2782 & 2795 [→ 2524+2919; 2526]. Hamutal, Hamital, "*my husband's father is like dew*":– Hamutal [3]

2538 חָמוּל *ḥāmûl*, n.pr.m. GK: 2783 [→ 2539; cf. 2550]. Hamul, "*pitied*":– Hamul [3]

2539 חָמוּלִי *ḥāmûlî*, a.g. GK: 2784 [→ 2538; cf. 2550]. Hamulite, "*of Hamul*":– Hamulites [1]

2540 חַמּוֹן *ḥammôn*, n.pr.loc. GK: 2785 [→ 2552]. Hammon, "*hot springs*":– Hammon [2]

2541 חָמוֹץ *ḥāmôṣ*, n.[m.]. GK: 2787 [→ 2556]. oppressor; oppressed:– oppressed [1]

2542 חַמּוּק *ḥammûq*, n.[m.]. GK: 2788 [→ 2559]. gracefulness, curve:– joints [1]

2543 חֲמוֹר *ḥᵃmôr*, n.m. GK: 2789 [→ 2544; cf. 2565, 2560]. donkey:– ass [55], asses [39], ass's [1], he asses [1]

2544 חֲמוֹר, n.prm. GK: 2791 [→ 2543; cf. 2560]. Hamor, "*male donkey*":– Hamor [12], Hamor's [1]

2545 חֲמוֹת, n.f. GK: 2792 [→ 2524]. mother-in-law:– mother in law [11]

2546 חֹמֶט, n.[m.]. GK: 2793. skink (lizard):– snail [1]

2547 חֻמְטָה, n.prloc. GK: 2794. Humtah, "*[unclean] reptile*":– Humtah [1]

2548 חָמִיץ, a. GK: 2796 [→ 2556]. sour mash, sorrel-fodder:– clean [1]

2549 חֲמִישִׁי, a.num.ord. GK: 2797 [→ 2568]. fifth:– fifth [45]

2550 חָמַל, v. GK: 2798 & 2800 [→ 2538, 2539, 2551, 2602, 4263]. [Q] to spare, take pity on, have mercy on:– spare [13], have pity [8], pitied [4], pity [4], spared [4], had compassion [3], had pity [2], have compassion [2], spareth [1]

2551 חֶמְלָה, n.f. GK: 2799 [→ 2550]. mercy:– merciful [1], pity [1]

2552 חָמַם, v. GK: 2801 [→ 2345, 2525, 2527, 2535, 2540, 2553, 2575, 2578, 2577; cf. 3179]. [Q] to be hot, be warm; by extension: to be aroused; be in a rage; [N] to burn with lust; [P] to let warm; [Ht] to warm oneself:– warm [3], hot [2], warmeth [2], get heat [1], have heat [1], inflaming [1], warmed [1], waxed hot [1], waxed warm [1]

2553 חַמָּן, n.m. GK: 2802 [→ 2552]. incense altar:– images [7], idols [1]

2554 חָמַס, v. GK: 2803 & 2804 [→ 2555, 8464?]. [Q] to do violence, harm, to lay waste; to be stripped off; to think up, devise; [N] to be mistreated:– do violence [1], done violence [1], made bare [1], shake off [1], violated [1], violently taken away [1], wrongeth [1], wrongfully imagine [1]

2555 חָמָס, n.m. GK: 2805 [→ 2554]. violence, destruction, malice, ruthlessness, fierceness:– violence [39], violent [6], cruelty [4], wrong [3], false [2], cruel hatred (+8135) [1], damage [1], injustice [1], oppressor (+376) [1], unrighteous [1], violent dealing [1]

2556 חָמֵץ, v. GK: 2806 & 2807 & 2808 [→ 2541, 2548, 2557, 2558]. [Q] to have yeast added, be leavened; to be cruel, oppress; [Qp] to be stained crimson; [Ht] to be grieved, embittered:– leavened [4], cruel [1], dyed [1], grieved [1], that which is leavened [1]

2557 חָמֵץ, n.m. GK: 2809 [→ 2556]. something leavened, made with yeast:– leavened bread [5], leaven [5], leavened [1]

2558 חֹמֶץ, n.m. GK: 2810 [→ 2556]. vinegar, wine vinegar:– vinegar [6]

2559 חָמַק, v. GK: 2811 [→ 2542]. [Q] to leave, turn away; [Ht] to wander, turn here and there:– go about [1], withdrawn [1]

2560 חָמַר, v. GK: 2812 & 2813 & 2814 [→ 2543, 2565, 2544, 2561, 2563, 2564, 3180]. [Q] to foam; to coat, cover, to apply pitch as a sealant; [Poalal] to be reddened, glow:– troubled [3], daubed [1], foul [1], red [1]

2561 חֶמֶר, n.[m.]. GK: 2815 [→ 2560; cf. 2562]. (foaming, fermenting) wine:– pure [1], red wine [1]

2562 חֲמַר (Aram.), n.m. GK: 10271 [cf. 2561]. wine:– wine [6]

חֲמֹר ḥᵃmōr. See 2543.

2563 חֹמֶר, n.[m.]. GK: 2816 & 2817 & 2818 [→ 2560]. churning, storming (sea waters); clay, mortar, mud; "defenses of clay" are weak arguments; homer (dry measure of volume, roughly the amount a donkey could carry, variously reckoned from six to eleven bushels [220 to 394 liters]):– clay [11], homer [10], morter [4], mire [2], upon heaps (+2563) [2], heap [1], homers [1]

2564 חֵמָר, n.[m.]. GK: 2819 [→ 2560]. tar (used in waterproofing or mortar):– slime [2], full of slimepits (+875+875) [1]

2565 חֲמֹרָה, n.f. GK: 2790 [→ 2560; cf. 2543]. heap:– heaps [2]

2566 חַמְרָן, n.prm. GK: 2820 [cf. 2533]. Hamran, cf. 2533:– Amram [1]

2567 חָמַשׁ, v.den. GK: 2821 [→ 2571; cf. 2568]. [Qp] to be organized for war; [P] to take a fifth:– take up the fifth [1]

2568 חָמֵשׁ, n.m. & f. GK: 2822 [→ 2549, 2567, 2569, 2571, 2572]. five, (pl.) fifty:– five [299], fifteenth (+6240) [17], fifteen (+6240) [16], fifth [6], five apiece (+2568) [2], threescore

and fifteen (+7657+2050.1) [2], fifteen (+6235+2050.1) [1], threescore and fifteen (+7657+2050.1+2050.1) [1]

2569 חֹמֶשׁ, n.[m.]. GK: 2823 [→ 2568]. fifth:– fifth [1]

2570 חֹמֶשׁ, n.m. GK: 2824. stomach, belly:– fifth [4]

2571 חָמֻשׁ, v.ptcp. GK: 2821 & 2826 [→ 2567; cf. 2568]. organized for war, armed:– armed [3], harnessed [1]

חֲמִשָּׁה ḥᵃmiššâ. See 2568.

חֲמִשִּׁי ḥᵃmiššî. See 2549.

2572 חֲמִשִּׁים, n.pl. GK: 2825 [→ 2568]. fifty (pl. of "five"):– fifty [149], fifties [6], fiftieth [4], by fifty (+2572) [2], fifty every where (+2572+871.1+1886.1) [2]

2573 חֵמֶת, n.[m.]. GK: 2827. skin (for water or wine):– bottle [4]

2574 חֲמָת, n.prloc. GK: 2828 & 4217 [→ 2578, 2577]. Hamath, "*fortress*":– Hamath [34], Hemath [1], Hamath-zobah [1]

חֲמֹת ḥᵃmōt. See 2545.

2575 חַמַּת, n.prm. & loc. GK: 2830 & 2829 [→ 2576; cf. 2552]. Hammath, "*hot springs*":– Hammath [1], Hemath [1]

2576 חַמֹּת דֹּאר, n.prloc. GK: 2831 [→ 2575+1756]. Hammoth Dor, "*hot spring of Dor*":– Hammoth-dor [1]

2577 חֲמָתִי, a.g. GK: 2833 [→ 2574; cf. 2552]. Hamathite, "*of Hamath*":– Hamathite [2]

2578 חֲמָת צוֹבָה, n.prloc. GK: 2832 [→ 2574+6678]. Hamath Zobah:– Hamath Zobah [1]

2579 חֲמָת רַבָּה, n.prloc. GK: 2828 + 8051 [→ 2574+7237]. Hamath Rabbah:–

2580 חֵן, n.m. GK: 2834 [→ 2582, 2584, 2600; cf. 2603 (also used with compound proper names)]. favor, grace; charm; grace is the moral quality of kindness, displaying a favorable disposition; "to find grace in someone's eyes" means to be in a state of favor:– grace [38], favour [26], gracious [2], pleasant [1], precious [1], wellfavoured (+2896) [1]

2581 חֵן, n.prm. GK: 2835 [→ 2603]. Hen, "*gracious*":– Hen [1]

2582 חֵנָדָד, n.prm. GK: 2836 [→ 2580+1908]. Henadad, "*favor of Hadad*":– Henadad [4]

2583 חָנָה, v. GK: 2837 [→ 2588, 4264, 4266, 8466]. [Q] to set up camp, pitch camp, encamp:– pitched [67], encamped [33], encamp [10], pitch [9], abode in tents [3], camp [3], dwelt [3], encampeth [2], lie [2], pitch tents [2], pitched tent [2], rested in tents [2], abide [1], camped [1], encamp about [1], encamping [1], groweth to an end [1], pitched tents [1]

2584 חַנָּה, n.prf. GK: 2839 [→ 2580; cf. 2603]. Hannah, "*favor*":– Hannah [13]

2585 חֲנוֹךְ, n.prm. & loc. GK: 2840 & 2841 [→ 2599; cf. 2593, 2596]. Enoch; Hanoch, "*initiated; follower*":– Enoch [9], Hanoch [5], Henoch [2]

2586 חָנוּן, n.prm. GK: 2842 [→ 2603]. Hanun, "*favored*":– Hanun [11]

2587 חַנּוּן, a. GK: 2843 [→ 2603]. gracious, compassionate:– gracious [13]

2588 חָנוּת, n.f. GK: 2844 [→ 2583]. vaulted cell:– cabins [1]

2589 חֲנֹּת, v. GK: 2838. verbal forms of 2603: gracious, intreated:– gracious [1], intreated [1]

2590 חָנַט, v. GK: 2845 & 2846 & 2847 [→ 2406]. [Q] to embalm; to ripen:– embalmed [3], embalm [1], putteth forth [1]

2591 חִנְטָא (Aram.), n.f. GK: 10272 [cf. 2406]. wheat:– wheat [2]

2592 חַנִּיאֵל, n.prm. GK: 2848 [→ 2603+410]. Hanniel, "*favored of God [El]*":– Haniel [1], Hanniel [1]

2593 חָנִיךְ, a. GK: 2849 [→ 2596; cf. 2585]. trained (and trusted person):– trained [1]

2594 חֲנִינָה, n.f. GK: 2850 [→ 2603]. favor, kindness:– favour [1]

2595 חֲנִית, n.f. GK: 2851. spear:– spear [34], javelin [6], spears [6], spear's [1]

2596 חָנַךְ, v. GK: 2852 [→ 2585, 2593, 2598, 2599]. [Q] to dedicate, to devote an object to deity; to train (morally and religiously):– dedicated [3], dedicate [1], train up [1]

2597 חֲנֻכָּה (Aram.), n.f. GK: 10273 [cf. 2598]. (ceremonial religious) dedication:– dedication [4]

2598 חֲנֻכָּה, n.f. GK: 2853 [→ 2596; cf. 2597]. dedication, offering for dedication:– dedication [6], dedicating [2]

2599 חֲנֹכִי, a.g. GK: 2854 [→ 2585; cf. 2596]. Hanochite, "*of Hanoch*":– Hanochites [1]

2600 חִנָּם, subst.adv. GK: 2855 [→ 2580; cf. 2603]. without cause, for no reason, for nothing:– without cause [10], for nought [6], without a cause [5], causeless [1], cost nothing [1], for nothing [1], freely [1], free [1], in vain [1], innocent [1], vain [1], without cost [1], without wages [1]

2601 חֲנַמְאֵל, n.prm. GK: 2856 [→ 2580+410]. Hanamel, "*God [El] is gracious*":– Hanameel [4]

2602 חֲנָמָל, n.[m.]. GK: 2857 [→ 2550]. sleet:– frost [1]

2603 חָנַן, v. GK: 2858 & 2859 [→ 2433, 2580, 2581, 2584, 2586, 2587, 2594, 2600, 2605, 8465?, 8467, 8468, 8469, 8470?; cf. 2604 (also used with compound proper names)]. [Q] to be gracious, to have mercy, to take pity, be kind; to be loathsome; [Pol] to move to pity, be kind, be charming; [Ho] to be shown compassion, mercy; [Ht] to plead for grace, beg for mercy; this word implies acts of kindness, not simply feelings of pity:– gracious [12], have mercy [12], merciful [12], make supplication [7], besought [3], favour [3], made supplication [3], hath mercy [2], have pity [2], shew favour [2], very gracious (+2603) [2], besought (+413) [1], dealt graciously [1], fair [1], favour shewed [1], favourable [1], favoured [1], findeth favour [1], grant graciously [1], hath pity [1], intreated [1], pity [1], pray [1], shew mercy [1], sheweth favour [1], sheweth mercy [1], supplication made (+8467) [1]

2604 חֲנַן (Aram.), v. GK: 10274 [cf. 2603]. [P] to be kind, show mercy; [Htpa] to ask, implore:– making supplication [1], shewing mercy [1]

2605 חָנָן, n.prm. GK: 2860 [→ 2603 (also used with compound proper names)]. Hanan, "*gracious*":– Hanan [12]

2606 חֲנַנְאֵל, n.prm. GK: 2861 [→ 2603+410]. Hananel, "*God [El] is gracious*":– Hananeel [4]

2607 חֲנָנִי, n.prm. GK: 2862 [→ 2603+3068]. Hanani, "*gracious*":– Hanani [11]

2608 חֲנַנְיָה or חֲנַנְיָהוּ, n.prm. GK: 2863 & 2864 & 10275 [→ 2603+3068]. Hananiah, "*Yahweh is gracious*": note this name is Aramaic once in Daniel:– Hananiah [29]

2609 חָנֵס, n.prloc. GK: 2865. Hanes:– Hanes [1]

2610 חָנֵף, v. GK: 2866 [→ 2611, 2612, 2613]. [Q] to be desecrated, be defiled; [H] to corrupt, defile, pollute:– defiled [3], greatly polluted (+2610) [2], polluted [2], corrupt [1], defileth [1], pollute [1], profane [1]

2611 חָנֵף, a. GK: 2867 & 2868 [→ 2610]. godless, ungodly; limping:– hypocrite [6], hypocrites [3], hypocritical [2], hypocrite (+120) [1], hypocrite's [1]

2612 חֹנֶף, n.[m.]. GK: 2869 [→ 2610]. ungodliness, godlessness:– hypocrisy [1]

2613 חֲנֻפָּה, n.f. GK: 2870 [→ 2610]. ungodliness, godlessness:– profaneness [1]

2614 חָנַק, v. GK: 2871 [→ 4267]. [N] to hang oneself; [P] to strangle:– hanged [1], strangled [1]

2615 חַנָּתֹן, n.prloc. GK: 2872. Hannathon:– Hannathon [1]

2616 חָסַד, v. GK: 2873 & 2874 [→ 1136, 2617, 2618, 2623, 2624]. [P] to put to shame, reproach, with the strong implication of an insult; [Ht] to conduct oneself as faithful:– shew merciful [2], put to shame [1]

2617 חֶסֶד, n.m. GK: 2875 & 2876 [→ 1136, cf. 2616, 2618, 2619?, 2623]. unfailing love, loyal love, devotion, kindness, often based on a prior relationship, especially a covenant relationship; disgrace:– mercy [137], kindness [38], lovingkindness [26], goodness [12], mercies [9], kindly [5], lovingkindnesses [4], favour [3], merciful [3], mercy's [3], merciful kindness [2], good deeds [1], goodliness [1], pity [1], reproach [1], wicked thing [1]

2618 חֶסֶד, n.prm. GK: 2877 [→ 2617; cf. 2616]. Hesed:– Hesed [1]

2619 חֲסַדְיָה *ḥ*ᵃ*sadyâ*, n.pr.m. GK: 2878 [→ 2617+3068]. Hasadiah, "*Yahweh is faithful*":– Hasadiah [1]

2620 חָסָה *ḥāsâ*, v. GK: 2879 [→ 308, 2622, 4268 (also used with compound proper names)]. [Q] to take refuge in, to trust in:– trust [19], put trust [12], trusteth [2], hope [1], make refuge [1], putteth trust [1], trusted [1]

2621 חֹסָה *ḥōsâ*, n.pr.m. & loc. GK: 2880 & 2881. Hosah, "*refuge*":– Hosah [5]

2622 חָסוּת *ḥāsût*, n.f. GK: 2882 [→ 2620]. refuge:– trust [1]

2623 חָסִיד *ḥāsîd*, a.m. GK: 2883 [→ 2624; cf. 2616, 2617]. godly, saints, the people of God with a focus on their faithfulness; this can refer to a prominent individual, with messianic significance (Ps 16:10):– saints [19], godly [3], holy [3], merciful [3], holy one [2], good [1], ungodly (+3808) [1]

2624 חֲסִידָה *ḥ*ᵃ*sîdâ*, n.f. GK: 2884 [→ 2623; cf. 2616]. stork; some sources: heron:– stork [5], ostrich [1]

2625 חָסִיל *ḥāsîl*, n.m. GK: 2885 [→ 2628]. grasshoppers, locusts at a particular stage of development:– caterpillar [5], caterpillars [1]

2626 חָסִין *ḥ*ᵃ*sîn*, a. GK: 2886 [→ 2634]. mighty, strong:– strong [1]

2627 חַסִּיר *ḥassîr* (Aram.), a. GK: 10276 [cf. 2638]. wanting, lacking in quality or quantity, deficient:– wanting [1]

2628 חָסַל *ḥāsal*, v. GK: 2887 [→ 2625]. [Q, H] to devour, consume:– consume [1]

2629 חָסַם *ḥāsam*, v. GK: 2888 [→ 4269]. [Q] to muzzle (an animal); to block (the way):– muzzle [1], stop [1]

2630 חָסַן *ḥāsan*, v.den. GK: 2889 [→ 2633; cf. 2631]. [N] to be stored up:– laid up [1]

2631 חֲסַן *ḥ*ᵃ*san* (Aram.), v. GK: 10277 [→ 2632; cf. 2630]. [H] to take possession of, occupy:– possessed [1], possess [1]

2632 חֱסֵן *ḥ*ᵉ*sēn* (Aram.), n.m. GK: 10278 [→ 2631; cf. 2633]. power, might, force:– power [2]

2633 חֹסֶן *ḥōsen*, n.m. GK: 2890 [→ 2630; cf. 2632]. stored treasure, riches, wealth:– strength [2], treasure [2], riches [1]

2634 חָסֹן *ḥāsōn*, a. GK: 2891 [→ 2626]. mighty, strong:– strong [2]

2635 חֲסַף *ḥ*ᵃ*sap* (Aram.), n.[m.]. GK: 10279. (formed, molded) clay, baked clay:– clay [9]

2636 חָסַף *ḥāspas*, v. GK: 2892. [Pualal] to flake; some sources: to be scale-like, pertaining to the shape of an object; to crisp, crackle, pertaining to the brittleness of an object:– round thing [1]

2637 חָסֵר *ḥāsēr*, v. GK: 2893 [→ 2638, 2639, 2640, 2642, 4270]. [Q] to lack; to have nothing; to go down, recede; [P] to make lower; to deprive; [H] to cause to lack, withhold:– want [4], lack [3], fail [2], lacked [2], wanteth [2], abated [1], bereave [1], cause to fail [1], decreased [1], had lack [1], have need [1], made lower [1], wanted [1]

2638 חָסֵר *ḥāsēr*, a. GK: 2894 [→ 2637]. lacking; wanting:– void [6], wanteth [4], lacketh [3], destitute [1], faileth [1], fail [1], lacked [1], need [1], want [1]

2639 חֶסֶר *ḥeser*, n.m. GK: 2895 [→ 2637]. poverty, lack:– poverty [1], want [1]

2640 חֹסֶר *ḥōser*, n.[m.]. GK: 2896 [→ 2637]. poverty, lack:– want [3]

2641 חַסְרָה *ḥasrâ*, n.pr.m. GK: 2897 [cf. 2745]. Hasrah:– Hasrah [1]

2642 חֶסְרוֹן *ḥesrôn*, n.m. GK: 2898 [→ 2637]. what is lacking:– that which is wanting [1]

2643 חַף *ḥap*, a. GK: 2899 [→ 2653]. clean, pure:– innocent [1]

2644 חָפָא *ḥāpā'*, v. GK: 2901. [P] to do secretly:– secretly [1]

2645 חָפָה *ḥāpâ*, v. GK: 2902 [→ 2646, 2647; cf. 2653]. [Q] to cover; [Qp] to be covered; [N] to be sheathed, be covered; [P] to panel, overlay, cover:– covered [7], overlaid [4], cieled [1]

2646 חֻפָּה *ḥuppâ*, n.f. GK: 2903 [→ 2647; cf. 2645]. canopy, shelter; chamber, pavilion (of marriage ceremony):– chamber [1], closet [1], defence [1]

2647 חֻפָּה *ḥuppâ*, n.pr.m. GK: 2904 [→ 2646; cf. 2645]. Huppah, "*canopy*, hence *protection*":– Huppah [1]

2648 חָפַז *ḥāpaz*, v. GK: 2905 [→ 2649]. [Q] to hurry away (in alarm or terror):– haste [3], hasted away [2], made haste [2], hasteth [1], tremble [1]

2649 חִפָּזוֹן *ḥippāzôn*, n.[m.]. GK: 2906 [→ 2648]. haste:– haste [3]

2650 חֻפִּים *ḥuppîm*, n.pr.m. & a.g. GK: 2907. Huppim; Huppite, "*coast people*":– Huppim [3]

2651 חֹפֶן *ḥōpen*, n.[m.]. GK: 2908. hollow of the hand, handful (sometimes as a measure of volume):– hands [2], both hands [1], fists [1], handfuls (+4393) [1], hand [1]

2652 חָפְנִי *ḥopnî*, n.pr.m. GK: 2909. Hophni, "*tadpole*":– Hophni [5]

2653 חָפַף *ḥāpap*, v. GK: 2910 [→ 2348, 2643; cf. 2645]. [Q] to shield, shelter:– cover [1]

2654 חָפֵץ *ḥāpēṣ*, v. GK: 2911 & 2912 [→ 2655, 2656, 2657]. [Q] to desire, delight in, be pleased with, have pleasure in; to sway; some sources: to hang:– delight [15], delighteth [12], delighted [10], pleased [7], desire [6], please [5], will [3], any pleasure at all (+2654) [2], desirest [2], like [2], pleasure [2], delight in [1], desired [1], favourest [1], favoureth [1], moveth [1], pleaseth [1], take delight in [1], well pleased [1], would [1]

2655 חָפֵץ *ḥāpēṣ*, a.vbl. GK: 2913 [→ 2654]. desire, delight, pleasure:– desire [2], pleasure [2], delight [1], desireth [1], favour [1], please [1], willing [1], wish [1], would [1]

2656 חֵפֶץ *ḥēpeṣ*, n.m. GK: 2914 [→ 2654]. desire, delight, pleasure:– pleasure [16], desire [9], delight [3], purpose [3], desired [2], acceptable [1], delightsome [1], desireth [1], matter [1], pleasant [1], willingly (+871.1) [1]

2657 חֶפְצִי־בָהּ *ḥepṣî-bāh*, n.pr.f. GK: 2915 [→ 2654+871.1+1886.3]. Hephzibah, "*my pleasure is in her*":– Hephzi-bah [1]

2658 חָפַר *ḥāpar*, v. GK: 2916 [→ 1662, 2660, 2663, 2661, 6512]. [Q] to dig, scoop, to paw, to make a hole of any depth in soil; by extension: to spy out, search for, look about, seek out:– digged [13], dig [3], search out [3], diggeth [1], paweth [1], seeketh [1]

2659 חָפֵר *ḥāpar*, v. GK: 2917. [Q] to feel dismay, be disgraced, be humiliated, be in confusion; [H] to bring disgrace, be ashamed, be humiliated:– confounded [6], ashamed [4], brought to confusion [2], bringeth reproach [1], brought unto shame [1], cometh to shame [1], put to shame [1], shame [1]

2660 חֵפֶר *ḥēper*, n.pr.m. & loc. GK: 2918 & 2919 [→ 1662, 2662; cf. 2658]. Hepher, "[perhaps] *help*":– Hepher [9]

2661 חֲפַרְפָּרָה *ḥ*ᵃ*parpārâ*, n.f. GK: 2923 [→ 2658, 6512]. rodent (an object of worship):– moles (+6512) [1]

2662 חֶפְרִי *ḥeprî*, a.g. GK: 2920 [→ 2660]. Hepherite, "*of Hepher*":– Hepherites [1]

2663 חֲפָרַיִם *ḥ*ᵃ*pārayim*, n.pr.loc. GK: 2921 [→ 2658]. Hapharaim, "*place of two trenches*":– Hapharaim [1]

חֲפַרְפֵּרָה *ḥ*ᵃ*parpērâ*. See 2661.

2664 חָפַשׂ *ḥāpaś*, v. GK: 2924 [→ 2665]. [Q] to search for, examine, plot; [N] to be ransacked; [P] to search, look around, track down, hunt down; [Pu] to go into hiding, to devise; [Ht] to disguise oneself, become like:– disguised [5], search [5], disguise [2], search out [2], searched [2], changed [1], diligent [1], hidden [1], made diligent search [1], searched out [1], searchest for [1], searching [1]

2665 חֵפֶשׂ *ḥēpeś*, n.m. GK: 2925 [→ 2664]. plan, plot:– search [1]

2666 חָפַשׁ *ḥāpaš*, v. GK: 2926 [→ 2670]. [Pu] to be freed:– free [1]

2667 חֹפֶשׁ *ḥōpeš*, n.[m.]. GK: 2927. material (for saddle blanket):– precious [1]

2668 חֻפְשָׁה *ḥupšâ*, n.f. GK: 2928 [→ 2670]. freedom:– freedom [1]

2669 חָפְשׁוּת *ḥopšût* or חָפְשִׁית *ḥopšît*, n.f. GK: 2929 & 2931 [→ 2670]. separation, exemption (from duties):– several [2]

2670 חָפְשִׁי *ḥopšî*, a. GK: 2930 [→ 2666, 2668, 2669]. free; set apart, exempt:– free [16], liberty [1]

2671 חֵץ *ḥēṣ*, n.m. GK: 2932 [→ 2678]. arrow; archer:– arrows [37], arrow [11], archers (+1167) [1], dart [1], shaft [1], wound [1]

חֻץ *ḥuṣ*. See 2351.

2672 חָצַב *ḥāṣēb*, v. GK: 2933 & 2934 & 2935 [→ 4274]. [Q] to dig; hew out, cut out; to strike (with lightning); [Qp, N, Pu] to be dug, be engraved, be cut out; [H] to cut in pieces:– hewers [4], digged [3], masons [3], hewed out [2], hew [2], cut [1], diggedst [1], dig [1], divideth [1], graven [1], hewed [1], heweth out [1], heweth [1], hewn out [1], hewn [1], made [1]

2673 חָצָה *ḥāṣâ*, v. GK: 2936 [→ 2676, 2677, 2677, 3183, 3185, 4275, 4276; cf. 2686, 2687]. [Q] to divide; set apart; to rise up to; [N] to be divided, be parceled out:– divided [8], divide [2], divide into two parts [1], live out half [1], midst [1], parted [1], part [1]

2674 חָצוֹר *ḥāṣôr*, n.pr.loc. GK: 2937 & 2938 [→ 2691, 5877]. Hazor, "*enclosure*":– Hazor [18]

2675 חָצוֹר חֲדַתָּה *ḥāṣôr ḥ*ᵃ*dattâ*, n.pr.loc. GK: 2939 [→ 2691]. Hazor Hadattah, "*new Hazor*":– Hazor Hadattah [1]

2676 חָצוֹת *ḥ*ᵃ*ṣôt*, n.f. GK: 2940 [→ 2673]. middle (of the night), mid(night):– at midnight (+3915) [2], midnight (+3915+1886.1) [1]

2677 חֲצִי *ḥ*ᵃ*ṣî*, n.m. GK: 2942 & 2944 [→ 2673, 2679, 2680]. half, halfway, middle, midst:– half [107], midst [8], midnight (+3915+1886.1) [4], part [3], middle [1], one half [1], two parts [1]

2678 חֵצִי *ḥēṣî*, n.m. GK: 2943 [→ 2671]. arrow:– arrow [4]

2679 חֲצִי הַמְּנֻחוֹת *ḥ*ᵃ*ṣî hamm*ᵉ*nuḥôt*, n.m.+a.g. GK: 2942 [→ 2677]. half of the Manahethites:– Manahethites [1]

2680 חֲצִי הַמְּנַחְתִּי *ḥ*ᵃ*ṣî hamm*ᵉ*naḥtî*, n.m.+a.g. GK: 2942 [→ 2677]. half of the Manahethites:– Manahethites [1]

2681 חָצִיר *ḥāṣîr*, n.[m.]. GK: 2948. home, abode, haunt:– court [1]

2682 חָצִיר *ḥāṣîr*, n.m. GK: 2945 & 2946 & 2947 [→ 2690, 2689, 2695, 2696]. (green) grass; hay; leeks; reed:– grass [17], hay [2], herb [1], leeks [1]

2683 חֵצֶן *ḥēṣen*, n.m. GK: 2949 [→ 2684, 2785?]. bosom (of a garment):– bosom [1]

2684 חֹצֶן *ḥōṣen*, n.m. GK: 2950 [→ 2683]. arms, folds of a robe:– arms [1], lap [1]

2685 חֲצַף *ḥ*ᵃ*sap* (Aram.), v. GK: 10280. [H] to show harshness:– hasty [1], urgent [1]

2686 חָצַץ *ḥāṣaṣ*, v. GK: 2951 & 2952 [cf. 2673]. [Q] to be in order, in ranks; [P] to divide, share; to sing; some sources: to distribute water; [Pu] to come to an end:– archers [1], by bands [1], cut off in the midst [1]

2687 חָצָץ *ḥāṣāṣ*, n.[m.]. GK: 2953 [cf. 2673]. gravel:– arrows [1], gravel stones [1], gravel [1]

2688 חַצְצוֹן תָּמָר *ḥaṣ*ᵉ*ṣôn tāmār*, n.pr.loc. GK: 2954 [cf. 8558]. Hazazon Tamar, "*Hazazon of the palm trees*":– Hazazon-tamar [1], Hazezon-tamar [1]

2689 חֲצֹצְרָה *ḥ*ᵃ*ṣōṣ*ᵉ*râ*, n.f. GK: 2956 [→ 2690; cf. 2682]. trumpet, a metal instrument used for signaling and music:– trumpets [26], trumpeters [2], trumpet [1]

2690 חַצֹּצֵר *ḥaṣṣar* or חָצַר *ḥāṣar*, v.den. GK: 2955 & 2957 [→ 2689; cf. 2682]. [P] to sound a trumpet, play a trumpet:– sounded [2], blow [1], sounded trumpets [1], sounding [1], trumpeters [1]

2691 חָצֵר *ḥāṣēr*, n.m. GK: 2958 [→ 1178, 2674, 2675, 2691, 2692, 2693, 2694, 2701, 2702, 2703, 2704, 2705, 2699, 2700; cf. 2691]. courtyard, court of a house, enclosed areas; village, a permanent settlement but without walls:– court [116], villages [47], courts [24], Hazar-hatticon [1], towns [1]

2692 חֲצַר־אַדָּר *ḥ*ᵃ*ṣar-'addār*, n.pr.loc. GK: 2960 [→ 146+2691]. Hazar Addar, "*settlement of Addar*":– Hazar-addar [1]

2693 חֲצַר גַּדָּה *ḥ*ᵃ*ṣar gaddâ*, n.pr.loc. GK: 2961 [→ 2691]. Hazar Gaddah, "*settlement of Gad*":– Hazar-gaddah [1]

2694 חֲצֵר הַתִּיכוֹן *ḥāṣēr hattîkôn*, n.pr.loc. GK: 2962 [→ 2691]. Hazer Hatticon, "*place of Hatticon*":–

2695 חֶצְרוֹ *ḥeṣrô* or חֶצְרַי *ḥeṣray*, n.pr.m. GK: 2968 & 2974 [→ 2682]. Hezro, Hezrai:– Hezrai [1], Hezro [1]

2696 חֶצְרוֹן *ḥeṣrôn*, n.pr.m. & loc. GK: 2969 & 2970 [→ 2697, 7152; cf. 2682]. Hezron, "*enclosure*":– Hezron [17], Hezron's [1]

2697 חֶצְרוֹנִי *ḥeṣrônî*, a.g. GK: 2971 [→ 2696; cf. 2682]. Hezronite, "*of Hezron*":– Hezronites [2]

2698 חֲצֵרוֹת *ḥ*ᵃ*ṣērôt*, n.pr.loc. GK: 2972. Hazeroth, "*settlements*":– Hazeroth [6]

2699 חֲצֵרִים *ḥ*ᵃ*ṣērîm*, n.pr.loc. GK: 2973 [→ 2691]. Hazerim:– Hazerim [1]

2700 חֲצַרְמָוֶת *ḥ*ᵃ*ṣarmāwet*, n.pr.m. GK: 2975 [→ 2691+4194]. Hazarmaveth, "*village of Maveth*":– Hazarmaveth [2]

2701 חֲצַר סוּסָה **ḥ°ṣar sûsâ**, n.pr.loc. GK: 2963 [→ 2691+5484]. Hazar Susah, *"settlement of Susah [horse]"*:– Hazar-susah [1]

2702 חֲצַר סוּסִים **ḥ°ṣar sûsîm**, n.pr.loc. GK: 2964 [→ 2691]. Hazar Susim, *"settlement of Susah [horse]"*:– Hazar-susim [1]

2703 חֲצַר עֵינוֹן **ḥ°ṣar 'ênôn**, n.pr.loc. GK: 2965 [→ 2691]. Hazar Enan, *"settlement of Enan"*:– Hazar-enan [1]

2704 חֲצַר עֵינָן **ḥ°ṣar 'ênân**, n.pr.loc. GK: 2966 [→ 2691+5881]. Hazar Enan, *"settlement of Enan"*:– Hazar-enan [3]

2705 חֲצַר שׁוּעָל **ḥ°ṣar šû'āl**, n.pr.loc. GK: 2967 [→ 2691+7776]. Hazar Shual, *"settlement of Shual [jackal]"*:– Hazar-shual [4]

חֵק **ḥēq**. See 2436.

2706 חֹק **ḥōq**, n.m. GK: 2976 [→ 2708, 2711; cf. 2710]. decree, statute, prescription, a clear communication of what someone should do; allotment, share, portion, prescribed amount of something:– statutes [74], statute [13], decree [7], ordinance [6], due [4], law [4], ordinances [3], portion [3], bounds [2], custom [2], commandments [1], convenient [1], decreed [1], measure [1], necessary [1], ordinary [1], set time [1], task [1], thing that is appointed [1]

2707 חָקָה **ḥāqâ**, v. GK: 2977 [cf. 2710]. [Pu] to be carved, be portrayed; [Ht] mark for oneself; from the base meaning of carving or engraving is by extension of the act of writing; the communication itself, regulation:– pourtrayed [2], carved work [1], settest a print [1]

2708 חֻקָּה **ḥuqqâ**, n.f. GK: 2978 [→ 2706; cf. 2710]. decree, ordinance, regulation, statute:– statutes [57], statute [20], ordinance [12], ordinances [10], customs [2], appointed [1], manners [1], rites [1]

2709 חֲקוּפָא **ḥ°qûpā'**, n.pr.m. GK: 2979. Hakupha, *"crooked"*:– Hakupha [2]

2710 חָקַק **ḥāqaq**, v. GK: 2980 [→ 2436, 2706, 2708; cf. 2707]. [Q] to mark out, inscribe, chisel, engrave; [Qp] to be portrayed; [Po] to command, be a leader, ruler; staff (of a commander); [Pu] to be decreed; [Ho] to be written:– lawgiver [6], decree [2], governors [2], appointed [1], graven [1], graveth [1], law [1], note [1], pourtrayed [1], pourtray [1], printed [1], set [1]

2711 חֵקֶק **ḥēqeq**, n.m. GK: 2981 [→ 2706]. decree, statute, prescription:– decrees [1], thoughts [1]

2712 חֻקֹּק **ḥuqqōq** or חוּקֹק **ḥûqōq**, n.pr.loc. GK: 2982 & 2577. Hukkok, Hukok:– Hukkok [1], Hukok [1]

2713 חָקַר **ḥāqar**, v. GK: 2983 [→ 2714, 4278]. [Q] to explore, search out, probe; [N] to be determined, be searched; [P] to search out:– search [7], searched out [4], search out [3], searched [3], found out [2], searcheth out [2], make search [1], searcheth [1], seek [1], sought out [1], sounded [1], try [1]

2714 חֵקֶר **ḥēqer**, n.m. GK: 2984 [→ 2713]. searching, finding out, often negatively stated: what cannot be search thoroughly or found out:– search [3], unsearchable (+369) [3], searching [2], finding out [1], number [1], searched out [1], searchings [1]

2715 חֹר **ḥōr**, n.m. GK: 2985. noble, free person:– nobles [13]

חֻר **ḥur**. See 2352.

2716 חֲרָאִים **ḥ°rā'îm**, n.[m.]. GK: 2989 [→ 4280; cf. 2755]. filth, excrement:–

2717 חָרֵב **ḥārēb**, v. GK: 2990 & 2991 & 2993 [→ 2719, 2720, 2721, 2722?, 2723, 2724, 2725; cf. 2718]. [Q] to be dried up, be parched; to be desolate, lay in ruins; [N] to be ruined, be desolate; to be slaughtered; [Pu] to be dried up; [H] to lay waste, devastate, cause to dry up; [Ho] to lie in ruins:– laid waste [8], dried up [6], desolate [3], dried [3], dry up [2], dry [2], made waste [2], surely slain (+2717) [2], utterly wasted (+2717) [2], wasted [2], decayeth [1], destroyed [1], destroyer [1], drieth up [1], lie waste [1], make waste [1], slay [1], waste [1]

2718 חֲרֵב **ḥ°rab** (Aram.), v. GK: 10281 [cf. 2717]. [Ho] to be destroyed, be devastated:– destroyed [1]

2719 חֶרֶב **ḥereb**, n.f. GK: 2995 [→ 2717]. sword; dagger; knife; cutting tool; by extension: battle, war; used fig. of God's judgment:– sword [385], swords [17], dagger [3], knives [3], knife [2], axes [1], mattocks [1], tool [1]

2720 חָרֵב **ḥārēb**, a. GK: 2992 [→ 2717]. dry, desolate, wasted, in ruins:– waste [6], desolate [2], dry [2]

2721 חֹרֶב **ḥōreb** or חֹרֶב **ḥōreb**, n.m. GK: 2996 & 2997 [→ 2717]. heat, dryness, drought, fever; waste, rubble, object of horror, desolation:– heat [4], drought [3], dry [3], waste [2], desolation (+2723) [1], utterly waste (+2723) [1]

2722 חֹרֵב **ḥōrēb**, n.pr.loc. GK: 2998 [→ 2717?]. Horeb, *"dry, desolate"*:– Horeb [17]

2723 חָרְבָּה **ḥorbâ**, n.f. GK: 2999 [→ 2717]. ruins, desolate place:– wastes [7], waste [7], desolation [5], desolate places [4], waste places [4], desolations [3], deserts [2], desolate [2], laid waste [2], decayed places [1], desert [1], destructions [1], places desolate [1], utterly waste (+2721) [1], wasted [1]

2724 חֲרָבָה **ḥārābâ**, n.f. GK: 3000 [→ 2717]. dry land, dry ground:– dry [8]

2725 חֲרָבוֹן **ḥ°rābôn**, n.m. GK: 3001 [→ 2717]. dry heat, implying a drought:– drought [1]

2726 חַרְבוֹנָא **ḥarbônā'** or חַרְבוֹנָה **ḥarbônâ**, n.pr.m. GK: 3002 & 3003. Harbona, *"donkey driver"*:– Harbonah [1], Harbona [1]

2727 חָרַג **ḥārag**, v. GK: 3004. [Q] to come out trembling:– afraid [1]

2728 חַרְגֹּל **ḥargōl**, n.[m.]. GK: 3005 [cf. 2295]. cricket; some sources: locust, grasshopper:– beetle [1]

2729 חָרַד **ḥārad**, v. GK: 3006 [→ 2730, 2731, 2732?, 2733?]. [Q] to tremble, quake, shudder, be startled; [H] to make afraid, frighten, make tremble:– make afraid [10], afraid [8], tremble [6], trembled [4], fray away [2], made afraid [2], careful [1], discomfited [1], fray [1], quaked [1], trembled (+2731) [1], trembleth [1], trembling [1]

2730 חָרֵד **ḥārēd**, a.vbl. GK: 3007 [→ 2729]. trembling, fearful:– tremble [3], afraid [1], trembled (+1961) [1], trembled [1], trembleth [1]

2731 חֲרָדָה **ḥ°rādâ**, n.f. GK: 3010 [→ 2729]. panic, fear, terror, horror:– trembling [4], fear [2], care [1], quaking [1], trembled (+2729) [1]

2732 חֲרָדָה **ḥ°rādâ**, n.pr.loc. GK: 3011 [→ 2729?]. Haradah, *"place of fear"*:– Haradah [2]

2733 חֲרֹדִי **ḥ°rōdî**, a.loc. GK: 3012 & 3009 [→ 2729?]. Harodite:– Harodite [2]

2734 חָרָה **ḥārâ**, v. GK: 3013 [→ 2740, 2750, 8474; cf. 2787]. [Q] to be angry, be aroused; to burn with anger; [N] to rage; [H] to be jealous; [Tiphel] to compete, contend with; [Ht] to fret:– kindled [44], wroth [12], angry [8], hot [5], fret [4], wax hot [4], displeased [3], incensed [2], very wroth (+2734) [2], burn [1], displease (+5869+871.1) [1], earnestly [1], grieved [1], very angry [1], waxed hot [1]

2735 חֹר הַגִּדְגָּד **ḥōr haggidgād**, n.pr.loc. GK: 2988 [→ 2356]. Hor Haggidgad, *"cavern of the Gidgad"*:– Hor-hagidgad [2]

2736 חַרְהֲיָה **ḥarh°yâ**, n.pr.m. GK: 3015 & 3029. Harhaiah:– Harhaiah [1]

2737 חֲרוּזִים **ḥ°rûzîm**, n.[m.]pl. GK: 3016. string of jewels; some sources: string of beads or shells:– chains [1]

2738 חָרוּל **ḥārûl**, n.[m.]. GK: 3017. weeds, undergrowth, variously identified:– nettles [3]

חֹרוֹן **ḥōrôn**. See 1032, 2772.

2739 חֲרוּמַף **ḥ°rûmap**, n.pr.m. GK: 3018 [→ 2763+639]. Harumaph, *"disfigured nose"*:– Harumaph [1]

2740 חָרוֹן **ḥārôn**, n.m. GK: 3019 [→ 2734]. fierce (anger), burning (anger), wrath:– fierce [23], fierceness [9], wrath [5], fierce wrath [1], fury [1], sore displeasure [1], wrathful [1]

2741 חֲרוּפִי **ḥ°rûpî** or חֲרִיפִי **ḥ°rîpî**, a.g. GK: 3020 & 3042 [→ 2756; cf. 2778]. Haruphite, Hariphite:– Haruphite [1]

2742 חָרוּץ **ḥārûṣ**, n.m. & a. GK: 3021 & 3022 & 3023 & 3025 & 3026 [→ 2782]. gold; trench, ditch, moat, a military defense; threshing sledge, sharp instrument for harvest; decision; diligent, industrious:– diligent [5], gold [4], decision [2], fine gold [2], threshing [2], sharp pointed [1], sharp [1], wall [1]

2743 חָרוּץ **ḥārûṣ**, n.pr.m. GK: 3027 [→ 2782?]. Haruz, *"[perhaps] gold or eager"*:– Haruz [1]

2744 חַרְחוּר **ḥarḥûr**, n.pr.m. GK: 3028 [→ 2746; cf. 2787]. Harhur, *"[poss.] fever; [poss.] raven; one born during mother's fever"*:– Harhur [1]

2745 חַרְחַס **ḥarḥas**, n.pr.m. GK: 3030 [cf. 2641]. Harhas:– Harhas [1]

2746 חַרְחֻר **ḥarḥur**, n.m. GK: 3031 [→ 2744; cf. 2787]. scorching heat; some souces: fever:– extreme burning [1]

2747 חֶרֶט **ḥereṭ**, n.[m.]. GK: 3032. pen; fashioning tool, stylus:– graving tool [1], pen [1]

חָרִט **ḥārîṭ**. See 2754.

2748 חַרְטֹם **ḥarṭōm**, n.m. GK: 3033 [→ 2413; cf. 2749]. magician:– magicians [11]

2749 חַרְטֹם **ḥarṭōm** (Aram.), n.m. GK: 10282 [cf. 2748]. magician:– magicians [4], magician [1]

2750 חֳרִי **ḥ°rî**, n.m. GK: 3034 [→ 2734]. hot, burning, fierce (anger):– fierce [3], great [2], heat [1]

חֳרִי **ḥ°rî**. See 2716.

2751 חֹרִי **ḥōrî**, n.[m.]. GK: 3035 [→ 2357]. (white) bread or cake:– white [1]

2752 חֹרִי **ḥōrî**, n.pr.m. GK: 3036. Hori, *"cave-dweller"*:– Horites [3], Horims [2], Horite [1]

2753 חֹרִי **ḥōrî**, a.g. GK: 3037. Horite, *"of Hor[i]"*:– Hori [4]

2754 חָרִיט **ḥārîṭ**, n.m. GK: 3038. bag, purse:– bags [1], crisping pins [1]

2755 חִרְיוֹנִים **ḥiryyônîm**, n.[m.]. GK: 3039 [cf. 2716+3123]. dove's dung [?], see 2716:–

2756 חָרִיף **ḥārîp**, n.pr.m. GK: 3040 [→ 2741; cf. 2778]. Hariph, *"one born at harvest time"*:– Hariph [2]

2757 חָרִיץ **ḥārîṣ**, n.m. GK: 3043 & 3044 [→ 2782]. portion, slice; pick, hoe, an iron tool:– harrows [2], cheeses (+2461) [1]

2758 חָרִישׁ **ḥārîš**, n.m. GK: 3045 [→ 2790]. plowing, time of plowing:– earing time [1], earing [1], ground [1]

2759 חֲרִישִׁי **ḥ°rîšî**, a. GK: 3046 [→ 2790?]. scorching:– vehement [1]

2760 חָרַךְ **ḥārak**, v. GK: 3047. [Q] to roast; some sources: to capture:– roasteth [1]

2761 חֲרַךְ **ḥ°rak** (Aram.), v. GK: 10283. [Htpa] to be singed (i.e., hair burnt):– singed [1]

2762 חֲרַכִּים **ḥ°rakkîm**, n.[m.]pl. GK: 3048. lattice, a window covered by crossed strips of wood:– lattice [1]

חָרֻל **ḥārul**. See 2738.

2763 חָרַם **ḥāram**, v. GK: 3049 & 3050 [→ 1179, 2739, 2764, 2766?, 2767, 2768, 2769]. [Qp] to be disfigured, mutilated, any split portion of the face, possibly a cleft palate; [H] to completely destroy, devote to destruction, exterminate, annihilate [Ho] to be destroyed, be devoted to destruction; this can refer to anything which is under the ban from common use, some things are set apart for use by priests, other things are destroyed utterly as devoted to the LORD:– utterly destroyed [19], utterly destroy [9], destroyed utterly [4], utterly destroy (+2763) [4], destroy utterly [3], destroying utterly [3], utterly destroying [1], consecrate [1], devoted [1], devote [1], flat nose [1], forfeited [1], make accursed [1], utterly make away [1], utterly to slay [1]

2764 חֵרֶם **ḥērem**, n.m. GK: 3051 & 3052 [→ 2763]. devoted, set apart for destruction; this can refer to anything which is under the ban from common use, some things are set apart for use by priests, other things are destroyed utterly as devoted to the LORD; net, fishnet, trap:– accursed thing [9], net [5], curse [4], nets [4], accursed [3], cursed thing [3], devoted [3], devoted thing [2], appointed to utter destruction [1], dedicate thing [1], thing accursed [1], things utterly destroyed [1], utter destruction [1]

2765 חֹרֵם **ḥ°rēm**, n.pr.loc. GK: 3054. Horem, *"consecrated"*:– Horem [1]

2766 חָרִם **ḥārim**, n.pr.m. GK: 3053 [→ 2763?]. Harim, *"consecrated [to Yahweh]"*:– Harim [11]

2767 חָרְמָה **ḥormâ**, n.pr.loc. GK: 3055 [→ 2763]. Hormah, *"consecration"*:– Hormah [9]

2768 חֶרְמוֹן **ḥermôn**, n.pr.loc. GK: 3056 [→ 1179, 2769; cf. 2763]. Hermon, *"consecrated place"*:– Hermon [13]

2769 חֶרְמוֹנִים **ḥermônîm**, n.pr.loc. GK: 3057 [→ 2768; cf. 2763]. heights of Hermon:– Hermonites [1]

2770 חֶרְמֵשׁ **ḥermēš**, n.[m.]. GK: 3058. sickle (for harvest of grain):– sickle [2]

2771 חָרָן **ḥārān**, n.pr.m. & loc. GK: 3059 & 3060. Haran, *"mountaineer perhaps sanctuary"*:– Haran [12]

חָרֹן **ḥārōn**. See 2740.

2772 חֹרֹנִי **ḥōrōnî**, a.g. GK: 3061. Horonite:– Horonite [3]

2773 חוֹרֹנַיִם **ḥōrōnayim**, n.pr.loc. GK: 2589. Horonaim, *"twin hollows, twin caves"*:– Horonaim [4]

2774 חַרְנֶפֶר **ḥarneper**, n.pr.m. or loc. GK: 3062. Harnepher, *"Horus is merciful"*:– Harnepher [1]

Heb

2775 חֶרֶס ḥeres or חַרְסָה ḥarᵉsâ, n.m. GK: 3063 & 3064 & 3066 [→ 2776, 8556]. sun; itch, any eruptive skin rash:– sun [3], itch [1]

2776 חֶרֶס ḥeres, n.pr.loc. GK: 3065 [→ 2775, 8556]. Heres, "sun":– Heres [1]

2777 חַרְסוּת ḥarsût or חַרְסִית ḥarsît, n.f.col. GK: 3067 & 3068 [→ 2789]. potsherd:– east [1]

2778 חָרַף ḥārap, v. GK: 3069 & 3070 & 3071 & 3072 [→ 2756, 2741, 2779, 2780, 2781; cf. 2741?]. [Q] to treat with contempt, insult, reproach, taunt; to (spend the time of) winter; [N] to be promised to a man, engaged; [P] to defy, ridicule, taunt, mock, insult; to disillusion, confuse:– reproached [12], reproach [10], defied [5], reproacheth [5], defy [3], betrothed [1], blasphemed [1], jeoparded [1], rail [1], upbraid [1], winter [1]

2779 חֹרֶף ḥōrep, n.m. GK: 3074 [→ 2778]. winter (the early time of the harvest cycle); prime (the early time of one's youth):– winter [4], cold [1], winterhouse (+1004) [1], youth [1]

2780 חָרֵף ḥārēp, n.pr.m. GK: 3073 [→ 2778]. Hareph, "autumn or sharp; scornful":– Hareph [1]

2781 חֶרְפָּה ḥerpâ, n.f. GK: 3075 [→ 2778]. disgrace, contempt, scorn, insult:– reproach [65], shame [3], rebuke [2], reproaches [1], reproacheth [1], reproachfully (+871.1) [1]

2782 חָרַץ ḥāraṣ, v. GK: 3024 & 3076 & 3077 [→ 2742, 2743?, 2757]. [Q] to pronounce, determine; to pay attention, act quickly; [Qp, N] to be determined, be decreed; to be maimed, mutilated, pertaining to what has been cut:– determined [6], bestir [1], decided [1], decreed [1], maimed [1], moved [1], move [1]

2783 חֲרַץ ḥᵃraṣ (Aram.), n.[m.]. GK: 10284 [cf. 2504]. hips, hip joints:– loins [1]

חָרֻץ ḥārûṣ. See 2742.

2784 חַרְצֹב ḥarṣōb, n.[f.]. GK: 3078. struggle; chains:– bands [2]

חָרִץ ḥāriṣ. See 2757.

2785 חַרְצָן ḥarṣān, n.m.pl. GK: 3079 [→ 2683?]. seeds (of grapes); some sources: unripe fruit:– kernels [1]

2786 חָרַק ḥāraq, v. GK: 3080. [Q] to gnash, grind (teeth):– gnasheth [2], gnash [2], gnashed [1]

2787 חָרַר ḥārar, v. GK: 3081 & 3082 [→ 2744, 2746, 2788; cf. 2734]. [Q] to burn (heated metal) glow; [N] be parched, burned, charred; to be hoarse; [Pil] to kindle, cause to burn, glow; by extension: to have a fever:– burnt [5], burned [2], angry [1], burn [1], dried [1], kindle [1]

2788 חֲרֵרִים ḥᵃrērîm, n.[m.]. GK: 3083 [→ 2787]. parched place, a hot, lifeless desert place:– parched places [1]

2789 חֶרֶשׂ ḥereś, n.[m.]. GK: 3084 [→ 2777, 7025]. clay pot, earthenware; potsherd; fragment of pottery:– earthen [8], potsherd [4], earth [1], potsherds [1], sheards [1], sheard [1], stones [1]

2790 חָרֵשׁ ḥārēš, v. GK: 3086 & 3087 [→ 2758, 2759?, 2791, 2792?, 2794, 2795, 2796, 2797?, 2798, 2799, 4281, 4282]. [Q] to plow; engrave; plan, plot; to be silent, be quiet; [Qp] to be inscribed; [N] to be plowed; [H] to be quiet, say nothing, be silent; [Ht] to make no moves, keep silent; [H] to plot against:– hold peace [11], held peace [8], plow [6], plowed [5], altogether hold peace (+2790) [4], devise [3], keep silence [3], altogether holdest peace (+2790) [2], deviseth [2], hold tongue [2], holdeth peace [2], kept silence [2], plowing [2], plowman [2], cease [1], conceal [1], deaf [1], ear [1], graven [1], held peace (+1961+3509.1) [1], held tongue [1], holdest tongue [1], imagine [1], left off speaking [1], make hold peace [1], plowers [1], quiet [1], rest [1], secretly practised [1], silent [1], speak not a word [1], still [1], worker [1]

2791 חֶרֶשׁ ḥereš, n.[m.] (used as adv.). GK: 3089 [→ 2790]. secretly, silently:– artificer [1], craftsmen [1], secretly [1]

2792 חֶרֶשׁ ḥereš, n.pr.m. GK: 3090 [→ 2790?]. Heresh, "deaf, silent":– Heresh [1]

2793 חֹרֶשׁ ḥōreš, n.m.[loc.] GK: 3091 & 3092 [→ 2796?; cf. 2800]. wooded place, forest, thicket; as place name: Horesh, "woodsman or craftsman":– wood [4], bough [1], forests [1], shrowd [1]

2794 חָרָשׁ ḥārāš, v.ptcp. GK: 3086 [→ 2790]. ptcp. of 2790: one who plows; engraves; plans:– artificer [1]

2795 חֵרֵשׁ ḥērēš, a. GK: 3094 [→ 2790]. deaf (person):– deaf [9]

2796 חָרָשׁ ḥārāš, n.m. GK: 3088 & 3093 [→ 2790, 2793?]. skilled craftsman: blacksmith, carpenter, gemcutter, idol-maker, etc.; the ironic phrase "craftsman of destruction" means people who are very good at destroying things (Eze 21:31); magic, sorcery:– carpenters [6], workman [5], craftsmen [4], carpenters (+6086) [3], engraver [3], artificers [2], smith [2], carpenter (+6086) [1], carpenter [1], craftsman [1], makers [1], masons (+68+7023) [1], masons (+7023) [1], skilful [1], smith (+1270) [1], workers [1], workmen [1], wrought [1]

2797 חַרְשָׁא ḥaršā', n.pr.m. GK: 3095 [→ 8521; cf. 2790?]. Harsha, "deaf":– Harsha [2]

2798 חֲרָשִׁים ḥᵃrāšîm, n.pr.loc. GK: 3096 & 1629 [→ 1516; cf. 2790]. Harashim; Ge Harashim, "valley of the craftsmen":– Charashim [1]

2799 חֲרֹשֶׁת ḥᵃrōšet, n.f. GK: 3098 [→ 2790]. cutting (stone), working (wood):– carving [2], cutting [2]

2800 חֲרֹשֶׁת ḥᵃrōšet, n.pr.loc. GK: 3099 [→ 1471; cf. 2793]. Harosheth:– Harosheth [3]

2801 חָרַת ḥārat, v. GK: 3100. [Qp] to be engraved:– graven [1]

2802 חֶרֶת ḥeret, n.pr.loc. GK: 3101. Hereth:– Hareth [1]

2803 חָשַׁב ḥāšab, v. GK: 3108 & 3110 [→ 2807, 2808, 2809, 2810, 2811, 2815, 4284; cf. 2804]. [Q] to plan, plot, purpose, consider; to credit, account, impute; [N] to be thought, considered, regarded; to be reckoned, accounted; [P] to determine, plan, plot; to compute, account; [Ht] to consider oneself:– counted [18], devise [12], cunning [9], thought [9], imagine [6], think [6], accounted [5], devised [5], deviseth [4], esteemed [4], purposed [4], reckoned [4], count [3], reckon [3], counteth [2], cunning workman [2], imagined [2], imputed [2], purpose [2], conceived [1], considered [1], esteemeth [1], esteem [1], find out [1], forecast against [1], forecast [1], holdest [1], imagineth [1], imputeth [1], impute [1], invent [1], like [1], makest account [1], meant [1], reckoning made [1], regardeth [1], regard [1], thinkest [1], thinketh [1], those that devise cunning work (+4284) [1], thought on [1]

2804 חֲשַׁב ḥᵃšab (Aram.), v. GK: 10285 [cf. 2803]. [Pp] to be regarded, be respected:– reputed [1]

2805 חֵשֶׁב ḥēšeb, n.m. GK: 3109 [cf. 2280]. waistband:– curious girdle [8]

2806 חֲשַׁבַּדָּנָה ḥašbaddānâ, n.pr.m. GK: 3111 [cf. 2811]. Hashbaddanah, "[prob.] Yahweh has considered me":– Hashbadana [1]

2807 חֲשֻׁבָה ḥᵃšubâ, n.pr.m. GK: 3112 [→ 2803]. Hashubah, "consideration":– Hashubah [1]

2808 חֶשְׁבּוֹן ḥešbôn, n.m. GK: 3113 [→ 2803]. scheme, plan:– account [1], device [1], reason [1]

2809 חֶשְׁבּוֹן ḥešbôn, n.pr.loc. GK: 3114 [→ 2803]. Heshbon, "reckoning":– Heshbon [38]

2810 חִשָּׁבוֹן ḥiššābôn, n.m. GK: 3115 [→ 2803]. catapult machine (for hurling against ramparts); scheme:– engines [1], inventions [1]

2811 חֲשַׁבְיָה ḥᵃšabyâ or חֲשַׁבְיָהוּ ḥᵃšabyāhû, n.pr.m. GK: 3116 & 3117 [→ 2803+3068; cf. 2806]. Hashabiah, "Yahweh has reckoned":– Hashabiah [15]

2812 חֲשַׁבְנָה ḥᵃšabnâ, n.pr.m. GK: 3118. Hashabnah, "[prob.] Yahweh has considered me":– Hashabnah [1]

2813 חֲשַׁבְנְיָה ḥᵃšabnᵉyâ, n.pr.m. GK: 3119. Hashabneiah, "[prob.] Yahweh has considered me":– Hashabniah [2]

2814 חָשָׁה ḥāšâ, v. GK: 3120. [Q] to be silent, be hushed; [H] to keep silent; to do nothing, hesitate:– hold peace [5], still [3], held peace [2], hold my peace [1], holden peace [1], keep silence [1], silence [1], silent [1], stilled [1]

2815 חַשּׁוּב ḥaššûb, n.pr.m. GK: 3121 [→ 2803]. Hashub, "considerate":– Hashub [4], Hasshub [1]

2816 חֲשׁוֹךְ ḥᵃšôk (Aram.), n.[m.]. GK: 10286 [cf. 2822]. darkness:– darkness [1]

2817 חֲשׁוּפָא ḥᵃšûpā', n.pr.m. GK: 3102. Hasupha:– Hashupha [1], Hasupha [1]

חָשׁוּק ḥāšûq. See 2838.

2818 חֲשַׁח ḥᵃšaḥ, v. or חַשְׁחָה ḥašḥâ (Aram.), n.f. GK: 10287 & 10288 [→ 2819]. [P] to be in need; (n.) need:– careful [1], have need of [1]

2819 חַשְׁחוּ ḥašḥû (Aram.), n.f.col. GK: 10289 [→ 2818]. what is needed:– needful [1]

חֲשֵׁכָה ḥᵃšêk'h. See 2825.

חֻשִׁים ḥušîm. See 2366.

2820 חָשַׂךְ ḥāśak, v. GK: 3104. [Q] to keep back, to withhold, halt, spare; [N] to be spared, be relieved:– spareth [3], spare [3], withheld [3], reserved [2], spared [2], asswaged [1], forbear [1], held back [1], hindereth [1], keep back [1], keepeth back [1], kept back [1], kept [1], punished [1], refrained [1], refraineth [1], refrain [1], withholdeth [1]

2821 חָשַׁךְ ḥāšak, v. GK: 3124 [→ 2822, 2823, 2824, 2825, 4285]. [Q] to grow dark, be dim, be black; [H] to darken, make dark; often darkness has the associative meanings of gloom, despair, terror, ignorance, or hard to understand:– darkened [7], dark [3], blacker [1], cause darkness [1], darkeneth [1], darken [1], dim [1], hideth [1], made dark [1], maketh dark [1]

2822 חֹשֶׁךְ ḥōšek, n.m. GK: 3125 [→ 2821; cf. 2816]. darkness, dark; blackness, gloom; often darkness has the associative meanings of gloom, despair, terror, ignorance, or hard to understand:– darkness [70], dark [7], obscurity [2], night [1]

2823 חָשֹׁךְ ḥāšōk, a. GK: 3126 [→ 2821]. obscure, dark, unknown:– mean [1]

2824 חֶשְׁכָה ḥeškâ, n.f.a. GK: 3128 [→ 2821, 2825]. same as 2825: darkness:– dark [1]

2825 חֲשֵׁכָה ḥᵃšēkâ, n.f.a. GK: 3128 [→ 2824]. same as 2824: darkness:– darkness [5]

2826 חָשַׁל ḥāšal, v. GK: 3129. [N] to lag (behind), be worn out:– feeble [1]

2827 חֲשַׁל ḥᵃšal (Aram.), v. GK: 10290. [P] to smash, pulverize:– subdueth [1]

2828 חָשֻׁם ḥāšum, n.pr.m. GK: 3130 [→ 2829, 2832; cf. 2367. Hashum, "broad-nosed":– Hashum [5]

חֻשָׁם ḥušām. See 2367.

חֻשִׁם ḥušim. See 2366.

2829 חֶשְׁמוֹן ḥešmôn, n.pr.loc. GK: 3132 [→ 2828]. Heshmon:– Heshmon [1]

2830 חַשְׁמַל ḥašmal, n.[m.]. GK: 3133. glowing metal; some sources: electrum:– amber [3]

2831 חַשְׁמַן ḥašman, n.m. GK: 3134. envoy:– princes [1]

2832 חַשְׁמֹנָה ḥašmōnâ, n.pr.loc. GK: 3135 [→ 2828]. Hashmonah:– Hashmonah [2]

2833 חֹשֶׁן ḥōšen, n.m. GK: 3136. breastpiece:– breastplate [25]

2834 חָשַׂף ḥāśap, v. GK: 3103 & 3106 & 3107 [→ 2835, 4286]. [Q] to strip bare, lay bare; to scoop out, draw out; [Qp] to be bared; [P] to bring to premature birth:– made bare [2], uncovered [2], bare [1], discovereth [1], discover [1], draw out [1], made clean [1], make bare [1], take [1]

2835 חָשִׂף ḥāśip, n.m. GK: 3105 [→ 2834]. small flock:– little flocks [1]

2836 חָשַׁק ḥāšaq, v. GK: 3137 & 3138 [→ 2837, 2838, 2839]. [Q] to set one's affection, desire, love, be attached to; [P] to make bands, make joints for binding; [Pu] to have bands:– filleted [3], desired (+2837) [2], set love [2], had delight [1], hast a desire [1], in love [1], longeth [1]

2837 חֵשֶׁק ḥēšeq, n.m. GK: 3139 [→ 2836]. thing desired, thing longed for:– desired (+2836) [2], desire [1], pleasure [1]

2838 חָשׁוּק ḥāšûq, n.[m.]. GK: 3122 [→ 2836]. band, binding:– fillets [8]

2839 חִשֻּׁק ḥiššuq, n.[m.]. GK: 3140 [→ 2836]. spokes (of a wheel):– felloes [1]

2840 חִשֻּׁר ḥiššur, n.[m.]. GK: 3141 [→ 2841]. hub (of a wheel):– spokes [1]

2841 חַשְׁרָה ḥašrâ, n.f. GK: 3142 [→ 2840]. collection, mass:– dark [1]

חֲשֻׁפָא ḥᵃšupā'. See 2817.

2842 חֲשַׁשׁ ḥᵃšaš, n.m. GK: 3143. chaff, dry grass:– chaff [2]

2843 חֻשָׁתִי ḥušātî, a.g. GK: 3144 [→ 2364]. Hushathite:– Hushathite [5]

2844 חַת ḥat, n.m. & a. GK: 3145 & 3146 [→ 2865]. fear, dread, terror; terrified, broken:– broken [1], dismayed [1], dread [1], fear [1]

2845 חֵת ḥēt, n.pr.m. GK: 3147 [→ 2850]. Hittite, "descendants of Heth":– Heth [14]

2846 חָתָה ḥātâ, v. GK: 3149 [→ 4289]. [Q] to get, snatch, take away:– take [2], heap [1], take away [1]

2847 חִתָּה ḥittâ, n.f. GK: 3150 [→ 2865]. terror:– terror [1]

2848 חִתּוּל *ḥittûl*, n.[m.]. GK: 3151 [→ 2853]. splint, bandage:– roller [1]

2849 חֲתַת *ḥathat*, n.[m.]. GK: 3152 [→ 2865]. horror, terror, danger:– fears [1]

2850 חִתִּי *ḥittî*, a.g. GK: 3153 [→ 2845]. Hittite, "*descendants of Heth*":– Hittite [26], Hittites [22]

2851 חִתִּית *ḥittît*, n.f. GK: 3154 [→ 2865]. terror:– terror [8]

2852 חָתַךְ *ḥātak*, v. GK: 3155. [N] to be decreed:– determined [1]

2853 חָתַל *ḥātal*, v. GK: 3156 [→ 2848, 2854]. [Pu, Ho] to be wrapped in strips of cloth:– swaddled at all (+2853) [2]

2854 חֲתֻלָּה *ḥᵉtullâ*, n.f. GK: 3157 [→ 2853]. band (of cloth) for wrapping:– swaddling band [1]

2855 חֶתְלוֹן *ḥetlôn*, n.pr.loc. GK: 3158. Hethlon:– Hethlon [2]

2856 חָתַם *ḥātam*, v. GK: 3159 [→ 2368, 2369, 2858; cf. 2857]. [Q] to seal (with a signet ring); to seal up; by extension: to be a model; [Op] to be sealed, be enclosed; [N] to be sealed; [P] to seal in; [H] to block, obstruct:– sealed [12], seal [5], sealed up [2], marked [1], seal up [1], sealest up [1], sealeth up (+1157) [1], sealeth up [1], sealeth [1], stopped [1]

2857 חֲתַם *ḥᵃtam* (Aram.), v. GK: 10291 [cf. 2856]. [P] to seal (with a signet ring):– sealed [1]

חֹתָם *ḥōtām*. See 2368.

2858 חֹתֶמֶת *ḥōtemet*, n.f. GK: 3160 [→ 2856]. signet ring seal:– signet [1]

2859 חָתַן *ḥātan*, v.den. GK: 3161 & 3162 & 3165 [→ 2860]. [Q, Ht] to intermarry; to become or have a son-in-law:– father in law [21], son in law [5], make marriages [3], join in affinity [1], joined affinity [1], made affinity [1], mother in law [1]

2860 חָתָן *ḥātān*, n.m. GK: 3163 [→ 2859, 2861]. son-in-law; bridegroom:– bridegroom [8], son in law [8], husband [2], sons in law [2]

2861 חֲתֻנָּה *ḥᵃtunnâ*, n.f. GK: 3164 [→ 2860]. wedding, marriage:– espousals [1]

2862 חָתַף *ḥātap*, v. GK: 3166 [→ 2863]. [Q] to snatch away:– taketh away [1]

2863 חֶתֶף *ḥetep*, n.[m.]. GK: 3167 [→ 2862]. bandit, robber; prey [1]

2864 חָתַר *ḥātar*, v. GK: 3168 [→ 4290]. [Q] to dig, break into; row (in rough seas):– dig [5], digged [2], rowed hard [1]

2865 חָתַת *ḥātat*, v. GK: 3169 [→ 2844, 2847, 2849, 2851, 2866, 2867?, 4287?, 4288]. [Q] to be shattered, dismayed, terrified; [N] to be discouraged, terrified; [P] to frighten; break; [H]·to shatter, terrify:– dismayed [26], afraid [5], broken in pieces [5], broken [3], broken down [2], abolished [1], affrighted [1], amazed [1], beaten down [1], broken to pieces [1], cause to be dismayed [1], chapt [1], confound [1], discouraged [1], go down [1], made afraid [1], scarest [1], terrify [1]

2866 חַתַּת *ḥᵃtat*, n.[m.]. GK: 3170 [→ 2866; cf. 2865]. something dreadful, horrible:– casting down [1]

2867 חֲתַת *ḥᵃtat*, n.pr.m. GK: 3171 [→ 2866?; cf. 2865?]. Hathath, "[poss.] *terror;* [poss.] *weakness*":– Hathath [1]

2868 טְאֵב *ṭᵉʾēb* (Aram.), v. GK: 10293 [→ 2869; cf. 3191; cf. 2895, 3190]. [P] to be good = to have joy:– glad [1]

2869 טָב *ṭāb* (Aram.), a. GK: 10294 [→ 2868; cf. 2896]. good, pleasing, pure:– fine [1], good [1]

2870 טָבְאַל *ṭāḇᵉʾal* or טָבְאֵל *ṭāḇᵉʾēl*, n.pr.m. GK: 3174 & 3175 [→ 2896+410]. Tabeal, Tabeel, "*God [El] is good*":– Tabeal [1], Tabeel [1]

2871 טְבוּלִים *ṭᵉḇûlîm*, n.m. GK: 3178. turban:– exceeding in dyed attire (+5628) [1]

2872 טַבּוּר *ṭabbûr*, n.[m.]. GK: 3179. center (of the land), as a fig. extension of the navel of the body, not found in the OT:– middle [1], midst [1]

2873 טָבַח *ṭāḇaḥ*, v. GK: 3180 [→ 2874, 2876, 2879, 2878, 4293]. [Q] to slaughter, butcher; [Qp] to be slaughtered:– killed [1], slaughter [3], slay [2], kill [1], slain [1], sore slaughter (+2874) [1]

2874 טֶבַח *ṭeḇaḥ*, n.m. GK: 3181 [→ 2875; cf. 19, 2873]. slaughtering:– slaughter [9], beasts [1], sore slaughter (+2873) [1]

2875 טֶבַח *ṭeḇaḥ*, n.pr.m. & loc. GK: 3182 & 3183 [→ 2874; cf. 2880]. Tebah, "[poss.] *one born at the time or place of slaughtering*":– Tebah [1]

2876 טַבָּח *ṭabbāḥ*, n.m. GK: 3184 [→ 2879; cf. 2873; cf. 2877]. cook, butcher; by extension: executioner; guard, imperial guard:– guard [29], cook [2], guard's [1]

2877 טַבָּח *ṭabbāḥ* (Aram.), n.m. GK: 10295 [cf. 2876]. (royal) body-guard, executioner; an elite unit guarding a king, execution only one of its functions:– guard [1]

2878 טִבְחָה *ṭibḥâ*, n.f. GK: 3186 [→ 2873]. slaughtered meat, butchered meat:– slaughter [2], flesh [1]

2879 טִבְחָה *ṭibḥâ*, n.f. GK: 3185 [→ 2876; cf. 2873]. (female) cook (of meat):– cooks [1]

2880 טִבְחַת *ṭibḥat*, n.pr.loc. GK: 3187 [cf. 984, 2875]. Tebah, "[poss.] *one born at the time or place of slaughtering*":– Tibhath [1]

2881 טָבַל *ṭāḇal*, v. GK: 3188. [Q] to dip, plunge; bathe, soak; [N] to be dipped:– dip [9], dipped [3], dipt [3], plunge [1]

2882 טַבַלְיָהוּ *ṭᵃḇalyāhû*, n.pr.m. GK: 3189 [→ 2919+3807.1?+3068?]. Tabaliah, "*Yahweh has dipped*":– Tebaliah [1]

2883 טָבַע *ṭāḇaʿ*, v. GK: 3190 [→ 2884, 2885]. [Q] to sink down, to fall into; [Pu] to be drowned; [Ho] to be sunk, be settled into:– sunk [4], sink [2], drowned [1], fastened [1], settled [1], sunk down [1]

2884 טַבָּעֹת *ṭabbāʿôt*, n.pr.m. GK: 3191 [→ 2885; cf. 2883]. Tabbaoth, "*[ornamental or signet] ring*":– Tabbaoth [2]

2885 טַבַּעַת *ṭabbaʿat*, n.f. GK: 3192 [→ 2884; cf. 2883]. ring; signet ring:– rings [40], ring [9]

2886 טַבְרִמּוֹן *ṭabrimmōn*, n.pr.m. GK: 3193 [→ 2896+7417]. Tabrimmon, "*Rimmon is good*":– Tabrimon [1]

2887 טֵבֵת *ṭēḇēt*, n.pr. GK: 3194. Tebeth:– Tebeth [1]

2888 טַבַּת *ṭabbat*, n.pr.loc. GK: 3195. Tabbath, "[poss.] *good*":– Tabbath [1]

2889 טָהוֹר *ṭāhôr*, a. GK: 3196 [→ 2891, 2890]. clean, pure, flawless, free from impurity; moral or ceremonial purity as a fig. extension of an object being free from defect or filth:– clean [51], pure [40], fair [2], pureness [1], purer [1]

2890 טְהוֹר *ṭᵉhôr*, n.[m.]. GK: 3196 [→ 2889]. same as 2889: cleanness, purity, flawlessness:–

2891 טָהֵר *ṭāhēr*, v. GK: 3197 [→ 2889, 2890, 2892, 2893]. [Q] to be (ceremonially) clean, purified; [P] to pronounce clean, cleanse, make ceremonially clean, to purify; [Ht] to cleanse oneself, purify oneself; this can mean moral or ceremonial purity:– clean [26], cleansed [23], cleanse [16], pronounce clean [10], purged [4], purified [3], purify [3], made clean [2], pure [2], cleanseth [1], make clean [1], maketh clean [1], purge [1], purifier [1]

2892 טֹהַר *ṭōhar*, n.[m.]. GK: 3198 & 3199 [→ 2891]. purity; cleanness; clearness, brightness, splendor:– purifying [2], cleanness [1], glory [1]

2893 טָהֳרָה *ṭāhŏrâ*, n.f. GK: 3200 [→ 2891]. cleansing, purification; pronouncement of (ceremonial) cleansing:– cleansing [7], purifying [3], purification [2], cleansed [1]

2894 טָאטֵא *ṭāʾṭēʾ*, v. GK: 3173 [→ 4292; cf. 2916]. [Pil] to sweep away:– sweep [1]

2895 טוֹב *ṭôb*, v. GK: 3201 [→ 2896, 2897, 2898; cf. 3190; cf. 2868, cf. 3191]. [Q] to be good, well, pleasing; [H] to do well, do good, prosper; this can refer to quality as well as to moral goodness:– well [8], good [5], please [4], do good [3], didst well [2], please (+5921) [2], better [1], cheer [1], do better [1], doest good [1], done well [1], do [1], goodly [1], made goodly [1]

2896 טוֹב *ṭôb*, a. & n.m. GK: 3202 & 3203 [→ 2895, 2897; cf. 2869 (also used with compound proper names)]. good, pleasing, desirable; goodness; this can refer to quality as well as to moral goodness:– good [361], better [72], well [20], goodness [16], goodly [8], merry [7], best [6], fair [6], prosperity [6], precious [4], wealth [3], any thing better (+2896) [2], fair (+4758) [2], fairer [2], fine [2], glad [2], goodliest [2], goods [2], kindly [2], pleasant [2], pleased (+5869+871.1) [2], pleaseth (+5869+871.1) [2], please [2], pleasure [2], beautiful (+4758) [1], beautiful [1], bountiful [1], cheerful [1], ease [1], favour (+5869+871.1) [1], fine (+6668) [1], good deeds [1], goodlier [1], goodly (+8389) [1], graciously [1], in favour [1], joyful [1], kindness [1], kind [1], liketh (+5869+871.1) [1], liketh best (+871.1+1886.1) [1], loving [1], most [1], pleaseth (+6440+3807.1) [1], pleasing [1], ready [1], sweet [1], think best (+5869+871.1) [1], welfare [1], wellfavoured (+2580) [1]

2897 טוֹב *ṭôb*, n.pr. GK: 3204 [→ 2896; cf. 2895]. Tob, "*good*":– Tob [2]

2898 טוּב *ṭûb*, n.m. GK: 3206 [→ 2895]. good, best; goodness, prosperity; this can refer to quality as well as to moral goodness:– goodness [13], good [9], goods [3], fair [1], gladness [1], goeth well [1], good things [1], good thing [1], goodness' [1], joy [1]

2899 טוֹב אֲדֹנִיָּה *ṭôb ʾᵃḏōniyyâ*, n.prm. GK: 3207 [→ 2897+138]. Tob-Adonijah, "*good is [my] Lord Yahweh*":– Tob-adonijah [1]

2900 טוֹבִיָּה *ṭôḇiyyâ* or טוֹבִיָּהוּ *ṭôḇiyyāhû*, n.pr.m. GK: 3209 & 3210 [→ 2896+3068]. Tobiah; Tobijah, "*Yahweh is good*":– Tobiah [15], Tobijah [3]

2901 טָוָה *ṭāwâ*, v. GK: 3211 [→ 4299]. [Q] to spin (yarn):– spin [1], spun [1]

2902 טוּחַ *ṭûaḥ* or טָחַח *ṭāḥaḥ*, v. GK: 3212 & 3220 [→ 2915]. [Q] to cover with whitewash; overlay with plaster; [N] to be plastered, be coated:– daubed [6], plaistered [3], daub [1], overlay [1], plaister [1], shut [1]

2903 טוֹטָפֹת *ṭôṭāpōt*, n.f.pl. GK: 3213 [→ 5197]. symbol, sign (later, phylactery, a small box of Scripture verses worn as a sign of obedience to the covenant):– frontlets [3]

2904 טוּל *ṭûl*, v. GK: 3214 [→ 2925]. [P] to hurl; [H] to thrown, hurl; [Ho] to be overpowered, be fallen, be hurled:– cast forth [4], cast [4], cast out [2], carry away [1], cast down [1], sent out [1], utterly cast down [1]

2905 טוּר *ṭûr*, n.m. GK: 3215 [→ 2918]. row, course:– row [14], rows [12]

2906 טוּר *ṭûr* (Aram.), n.m. GK: 10296 [cf. 6697]. mountain:– mountain [2]

2907 טוּשׂ *ṭûś*, v. GK: 3216. [Q] to swoop down; some sources: to flutter:– hasteth [1]

2908 טְוָת *ṭᵉwāt* (Aram.), adv. GK: 10297. without eating, in hunger, in fasting:– fasting [1]

2909 טָחָה *ṭāḥâ*, v. GK: 3217. [Pil] to shoot (an arrow the distance of a bowshot; the distance of a bowshot is still in sight, though it is out of hearing range):– bowshot (+7198) [1]

2910 טֻחוֹת *ṭuḥôt*, n.f.pl. GK: 3219. inner parts; heart, with a possible focus that this is a mysterious and unknowable part of a person:– inward parts [2]

2911 טְחוֹן *ṭᵉḥôn*, n.[m.]. GK: 3218 [→ 2912]. hand-mill, grinding-mill:– grind [1]

2912 טָחַן *ṭāḥan*, v. GK: 3221 & 3223 [→ 2911, 2913]. [Q] to grind to flour, crush to powder:– grind [4], ground [2], grinders [1], ground very small (+3190) [1]

2913 טַחֲנָה *ṭaḥᵃnâ*, n.f. GK: 3222 [→ 2912]. grinding-mill:– grinding [1]

2914 טְחֹרִים *ṭᵉḥōrîm*, n.m. GK: 3224. tumor, hemorrhoids:– emerods [7]

2915 טִיחַ *ṭîaḥ*, n.[m.]. GK: 3225 [→ 2902]. coating (of whitewash); some sources: coating of clay:– daubing [1]

2916 טִיט *ṭîṭ*, n.m. GK: 3226 [→ 2894, 4292; cf. 2917]. mud, dirt, mire, clay:– mire [8], clay [3], dirt [2]

2917 טִין *ṭîn* (Aram.), n.[m.]. GK: 10298 [cf. 2916]. (wet) clay:– miry [2]

2918 טִירָה *ṭîrâ*, n.f. GK: 3227 [→ 2905; cf. 3195?]. camp (protected by stone walls); tower, battlement:– castles [2], goodly castles [1], habitation [1], palaces [1], palace [1], rows [1]

2919 טַל *ṭal*, n.m. GK: 3228 [→ 37, 2537, 2882; cf. 2920]. dew, night mist:– dew [31]

2920 טַל *ṭal* (Aram.), n.[m.]. GK: 10299 [cf. 2919]. dew:– dew [5]

2921 טָלָא *ṭālāʾ*, v. GK: 3229. [Qp] to be spotted; be variegated; [Pu] to be patched:– spotted [6], clouted [1], divers colours [1]

2922 טְלָא *ṭᵉlāʾ*, n.m. GK: 3231 [→ 2923, 2924]. same as 2924: lamb:– lambs [1]

2923 טְלָאִים *ṭᵉlāʾîm*, n.pr.loc. GK: 3230 [→ 2922]. Telaim, "*lambs*":– Telaim [1]

2924 טָלֶה *ṭāleh*, n.m. GK: 3231 [→ 2922]. same as 2922: lamb:– lamb [2]

2925 טַלְטֵלָה *ṭalṭēlâ*, n.f. GK: 3232 [→ 2904]. hurling, throwing:– captivity [1]

2926 טָלַל *ṭālal*, v. GK: 3233 [cf. 6751]. [P] to cover with a roof:– covered [1]

2927 צֵלַל *ṣᵉlal* (Aram.), v. GK: 10300 [cf. 6751]. [H] to find shelter:– shadow [1]

2928 טֶלֶם *ṭelem*, n.prm. & loc. GK: 3234 & 3235 [cf. 2929]. Telem, "brightness":– Telem [2]

2929 טַלְמוֹן *ṭalmôn*, n.prm. GK: 3236 [cf. 2928]. Talmon, "[perhaps] brightness":– Talmon [5]

2930 טָמֵא *ṭāmē'*, v. GK: 3237 & 3239 [→ 2931, 2932, 2933]. [Q] to be unclean, defiled; [N] to be made unclean, become defiled, impure; [P] to make unclean, defile, desecrate; [Pu] to become defiled; [Ht] to make oneself unclean, defiled; [Hotpaal] to be defiled; this can mean to be ceremonially impure or to be immoral in action:– unclean [61], defiled [45], defile [24], polluted [12], pronounce unclean [10], pollute [2], pronounce utterly unclean (+2930) [2], defile yourselves [1], defileth [1], made unclean [1], make unclean [1], take uncleanness [1]

2931 טָמֵא *ṭāmē'*, a. GK: 3238 [→ 2930]. unclean, defiled, impure; this can mean to be ceremonial impurity or active immorality:– unclean [80], defiled [5], infamous (+8034+1886.1) [1], polluted [1], pollution [1]

2932 טֻמְאָה *ṭum'â*, n.f. GK: 3240 [→ 2930]. uncleanness, impurity, filthiness; this can mean ceremonial impurity or a physical impurity on the body or in an object:– uncleanness [25], filthiness [7], unclean [3], uncleannesses [1]

2933 טָמָה *ṭāmâ*, v. GK: 3241 [→ 2930?]. [N] to be considered stupid; some sources: to be regarded as unclean:– make unclean [1], reputed vile [1]

2934 טָמַן *ṭāman*, v. GK: 3243 [→ 4301]. [Q] to hide; bury; [Op] to be hidden; [N] to hide oneself; [H] to keep hidden:– hid [17], hide [5], hideth [2], hidden [1], hiding [1], laid privily [1], laid [1], laying privily [1], privily laid [1], secret [1]

2935 טֶנֶא *ṭene'*, n.m. GK: 3244. basket:– basket [4]

2936 טָנַף *ṭānap*, v. GK: 3245. [P] to soil, make dirty:– defile [1]

2937 טָעָה *ṭā'â*, v. GK: 3246 [cf. 8582]. [H] to lead astray:– seduced [1]

2938 טָעַם *ṭā'am*, v. GK: 3247 [→ 2940, 4303; cf. 2939]. [Q] to taste; to see, discover by experience:– taste [5], did but taste (+2938) [2], tasted [2], perceiveth [1], tasteth [1]

2939 טְעֵם *ṭᵉ'ēm* (Aram.), v. GK: 10301 [→ 2941; cf. 2938]. [Pa] to eat:– make to eat [2], fed [1]

2940 טַעַם *ṭa'am*, n.m. GK: 3248 [→ 2938; cf. 2941]. taste; discretion; discernment; decree, judgment; "to turn from discernment" means "to pretend to be insane" (1Sa 21:13):– taste [5], behaviour [2], advice [1], decree [1], discretion [1], judgment [1], reason [1], understanding [1]

2941 טְעֵם *ṭa'am* (Aram.), n.m. GK: 10302 [→ 2939, 2942; cf. 2940]. same as 2942: order, decree, command:– commandment [1], commanded [1], matter [1]

2942 טְעֵם *ṭᵉ'ēm* (Aram.), n.m. GK: 10302 [→ 2941]. same as 2941: order, decree, command; tact, good sense; report, advice; with 2562 "under the command of wine" means "to be intoxicated"; with 1169, "lord of the decree" is translated "commanding officer":– decree [13], chancellor (+1169) [3], commanded (+7761) [3], commandment [2], accounts [1], regarded (+7761) [1], tasted [1], wisdom [1]

2943 טָעַן *ṭā'an*, v. GK: 3250. [Q] to load:– lade [1]

2944 טָעַן *ṭā'an*, v. GK: 3249. [Pu] to be pierced:– thrust through [1]

2945 טַף *ṭap*, n.m. GK: 3251 & 3252 [→ 2952]. (little) children, women and children, those (as a class) not able or barely able to march; drops:– little ones [29], children [9], little children [3], families [1]

2946 טָפַח *ṭāpaḥ*, v.den. GK: 3253 & 3254 [→ 2947, 2948, 2949, 4304]. [P] to spread out; to care for; some sources: to bear healthy children:– spanned [1], swaddled [1]

2947 טֵפַח *ṭepaḥ* or טֹפַח *ṭōpâ*, n.[m.]. GK: 3255 & 3257 & 3258 [→ 2946, 2948]. span, handbreadth (the width of the hand at the base of the four fingers, about three inches (8 cm)); a figure of a short unit of time, a few years:– handbreadth [3], coping [1]

2948 טֹפַח *ṭōpaḥ*, n.m. GK: 3256 [→ 2947; cf. 2946]. handbreadth, span of the hand:– hand breadth [2], handbreadth [1], hand broad [1]

2949 טִפֻּחִים *ṭippuḥîm*, n.[m.]pl.abst. GK: 3259 [→ 2946]. caring for (children):– span long [1]

2950 טָפַל *ṭāpal*, v. GK: 3260 [cf. 8602]. to smear, cover:– forged [1], forgers [1], sewest up [1]

2951 טִפְסָר *ṭipsār*, n.[m.]. GK: 3261. official, clerk:– captains [1], captain [1]

2952 טָפַף *ṭāpap*, v. GK: 3262 [→ 2945]. [Q] to take little steps, trip along:– mincing [1]

2953 טְפַר *ṭᵉpar* (Aram.), n.m. GK: 10303 [cf. 6856]. finger and toe nails (of a human); claws (of an animal):– nails [2]

2954 טָפַשׁ *ṭāpaš*, v. GK: 3263. [Q] to be unfeeling, insensible:– fat [1]

2955 טָפַת *ṭāpat*, n.pr.f. GK: 3264. Taphath, "[poss.] little child":– Taphath [1]

2956 טָרַד *ṭārad*, v. GK: 3265 [→ 4308; cf. 2957]. [Q] to constantly drip:– continual dropping (+1812) [1], continual [1]

2957 טְרַד *ṭᵉrad* (Aram.), v. GK: 10304 [cf. 2956]. [P] to drive away (as noun) one driven away; [Peil] to be driven away:– driven [2], drive [2]

2958 טְרוֹם *ṭᵉrôm*, adv.temp. GK: 3266 [→ 2961, 2962]. before:–

2959 טָרַח *ṭāraḥ*, v. GK: 3267 [→ 2960]. [H] to load down, burden with:– wearieth [1]

2960 טֹרַח *ṭōraḥ*, n.m. GK: 3268 [→ 2959]. burden, problem, load:– cumbrance [1], trouble [1]

2961 טָרִי *ṭārî*, a. GK: 3269 [→ 2958]. fresh (bone); open, moist (sore):– new [1], putrifying [1]

2962 טֶרֶם *ṭerem*, adv.temp. & c. GK: 3270 [→ 2958]. a marker of time: before; negative: not, not yet:– before (+871.1) [35], before [11], not yet [3], before (+3808+871.1) [2], ere [2], but ere (+871.1) [1], ere (+871.1) [1], neither yet (+2050.1) [1]

2963 טָרַף *ṭārap*, v. GK: 3271 [→ 2964, 2965, 2966]. [Q] to tear, mangle; [Qp, N, Pu] to be torn (to pieces); [H] to provide (to enjoy):– torn in pieces (+2963) [4], ravening [3], teareth [3], tear [3], catch [2], tear in pieces [2], without doubt rent in pieces (+2963) [2], feed [1], prey [1], ravin [1], teareth in pieces [1], torn in pieces [1], torn [1]

2964 טֶרֶף *ṭerep*, n.m. GK: 3272 [→ 2963]. prey (food for wild animals):– prey [18], meat [3], leaves [1], spoil [1]

2965 טָרָף *ṭārāp*, a. GK: 3273 [→ 2963]. fresh-picked (leaf or vegetation):– pluckt off [1]

2966 טְרֵפָה *ṭᵉrēpâ*, n.f. GK: 3274 [→ 2963]. animal torn by wild beasts:– torn [4], that which was torn [2], ravin [1], that which is torn [1], torn in pieces [1]

2967 טַרְפְּלָי *ṭarpᵉlāy* (Aram.), n.pr.g. GK: 10305. from Tripolis (Tarpel):– Tarpelites [1]

2967.1 י- *-î*, p.s.com.suf. GK: 3276 [→ 447, 5105.1, 5204.1]. I, me, my:– my [3551], me [1946], mine [494], I [241], my (+3807.1) [64], mine (+3807.1) [50], mine own [30], myself [21], our [7], us [7], me (+5315) [5], mine own (+3807.1) [3], the⁵ [3], Ammi (+5971) [1], for my sake [1], me (+6440) [1], mine (+5978) [1], mine (+8478) [1], my (+871.1) [1], myself (+1320) [1], myself (+3820) [1], myself (+5315) [1], myself (+905) [1], we [1]

2967.2 י- *-î* (Aram.), p.suf.1.com.s. GK: 10307 [→ 5204.2; cf. 2967.1]. I, me, my:– my [32], me [22], I [10], mine [5]

2968 יָאַב *yā'ab*, v. GK: 3277 [→ 88?, 3053?; cf. 14?, 8373?]. [Q] to long for:– longed [1]

2969 יָאָה *yā'â*, v. GK: 3278. [Q] to be fitting, be proper:– appertain [1]

יְאוֹר *yᵉ'ôr*. See 2975.

2970 יַאֲזַנְיָה *ya'ᵃzanyâ* or יַאֲזַנְיָהוּ *ya'ᵃzanyāhû*, n.pr.m. GK: 3279 & 3280. Jaazaniah, "Yahweh listens":– Jaazaniah [4]

2971 יָאִיר *yā'îr*, n.pr.m. GK: 3281 [→ 2334, 2972]. Jair, "he gives light":– Jair [9]

2972 יָאִרִי *yā'irî*, a.g. GK: 3285 [→ 2971]. Jairite, "of Jair":– Jairite [1]

2973 יָאַל *yā'al*, v. GK: 3282 [cf. 191]. [N] to become foolish, act foolishly:– done foolishly [1], dote [1], foolish [1], fools [1]

2974 יָאַל *yā'al*, v. GK: 3283 [cf. 193, 4136]. [H] to begin; to determine; be intent upon; to agree to; to be content, be pleased; to be bold:– content [7], please [3], would [3], taken upon [2], assayed [1], began [1], pleased [1], willingly [1]

2975 יְאֹר *yᵉ'ōr*, n.m. GK: 3284. river, stream, the Nile river; likely the Tigris river in Daniel:– river [35], rivers [15], flood [6], brooks [5], river's [3], streams [1]

2976 יָאַשׁ *yā'aš*, v. GK: 3286. [N] to be despairing of, be without hope, give up; [P] to let despair:– no hope [3], cause to despair [1], despair [1], desperate [1]

2977 יֹאשִׁיָּה *yō'šiyyâ* or יֹאשִׁיָּהוּ *yō'šiyyāhû*, n.pr.m. GK: 3287 & 3288 [cf. 3068]. Josiah, "let or may Yahweh give":– Josiah [53]

2978 יִאתוֹן *yi'tôn* or אִיתוֹן *'îtôn*, n.m. GK: 3289 & 415 [→ 857]. entrance:– entrance [1]

2979 יְאָתְרַי *yᵉ'ātᵉray*, n.pr.m. GK: 3290. Jeatherai:– Jeaterai [1]

2980 יָבַב *yābab*, v. GK: 3291 [→ 3103]. [P] to cry out, lament:– cried [1]

2981 יְבוּל *yᵉbûl*, n.m. GK: 3292 [→ 2986]. crops, produce, harvest:– increase [10], fruit [3]

2982 יְבוּס *yᵉbûs*, n.pr.loc. GK: 3293 [→ 2983]. Jebus:– Jebus [4]

2983 יְבוּסִי *yᵉbûsî*, a.g. GK: 3294 [→ 2982]. Jebusite, "of Jebus":– Jebusites [25], Jebusite [14], Jebusi [2]

2984 יִבְחָר *yibḥar*, n.pr.m. GK: 3295 [→ 977]. Ibhar, "he chooses":– Ibhar [3]

2985 יָבִין *yābîn*, n.pr.m. GK: 3296 [→ 995]. Jabin, "perceptive":– Jabin [7], Jabin's [1]

יָבֵשׁ *yābēš*. See 3003.

2986 יָבַל *yābal*, v. GK: 3297 [→ 58, 179, 2981, 2988, 2989, 3105; cf. 2987]. [H] to bring, take (a gift); [Ho] to be brought, be led, be carried off:– brought [6], bring [5], carried [3], brought forth [1], carry [1], lead [1], led forth [1]

2987 יְבַל *yᵉbal* (Aram.), v. GK: 10308 [cf. 2986]. [H] to bring, take:– brought [2], carry [1]

יוֹבֵל *yôbēl*. See 3104.

2988 יָבָל *yābāl*, n.[m.]. GK: 3298 [→ 2986]. stream, watercourse:– courses [1], streams [1]

2989 יָבָל *yābāl*, n.pr.m. GK: 3299 [→ 2986]. Jabal:– Jabal [1]

יוֹבֵל *yôbēl*. See 3104.

2990 יַבֶּלֶת *yabbelet*, a. GK: 3301 [→ 3104]. wart; some sources: running sore:– having a wen [1]

2991 יִבְלְעָם *yibᵉl'ām*, n.pr.loc. GK: 3300 [→ 1104?]. Ibleam:– Ibleam [3]

2992 יָבַם *yābam*, v.den. GK: 3302 [→ 2993]. [P] to fulfill the procreational duty of the brother-in-law:– marry [1], perform the duty of a husband's brother [1], perform the duty of husband's brother [1]

2993 יָבָם *yābām*, n.m. GK: 3303 [→ 2992, 2994]. husband's brother:– husband's brother [2]

2994 יְבָמָה *yᵉbāmâ*, n.f. GK: 3304 [→ 2993]. brother's widow; sister-in-law, husband's brother's widow:– brother's wife [3], sister in law [2]

2995 יַבְנְאֵל *yabnᵉ'ēl*, n.pr.loc. GK: 3305 [→ 1129+410; cf. 2996]. Jabneel, "God [El] will build":– Jabneel [2]

2996 יַבְנֵה *yabnēh*, n.pr.loc. GK: 3306 [cf. 2995]. Jabneh:– Jabneh [1]

2997 יִבְנְיָה *yibnᵉyâ*, n.pr.m. GK: 3307 [→ 1129+3068]. Ibneiah, "Yahweh built":– Ibneiah [1]

2998 יִבְנִיָּה *yibniyyâ*, n.pr.m. GK: 3308 [→ 1129+3068]. Ibnijah, "Yahweh built":– Ibnijah [1]

2999 יַבֹּק *yabbōq*, n.pr.loc. GK: 3309 [→ 1238? or 79?]. Jabbok, "flowing or wrestling":– Jabbok [7]

3000 יְבֶרֶכְיָהוּ *yᵉberekyāhû*, n.pr.m. GK: 3310 [→ 1288+3068]. Jeberekiah, "Yahweh blesses":– Jeberechiah [1]

3001 יָבֵשׁ *yābēš*, v. GK: 3312 [→ 3002, 3003, 3004, 3006]. [Q] to dry up, be dry, be withered, be shriveled up; [P] to make wither, dry up; [H] to make wither, dry up:– dried up [18], withered [9], wither [7], dry up [6], withereth [5], dry [3], clean dried up (+3001) [2], dried [2], utterly wither (+3001) [2], withered away [2], ashamed [1], confounded [1], driedst up [1], drieth up [1], drieth [1], make dry [1], maketh dry [1]

3002 יָבֵשׁ *yābēš*, a.vbl. or v.ptcp. GK: 3313 [→ 3001]. dry, withered, by extension: a paralyzed person (whose limbs have a shriveled appearance):– dry [7], dried away [1], dried [1]

3003 יָבֵשׁ *yābēš*, n.pr.m. & loc. GK: 3314 & 3315 & 3316 [→ 3001+1568]. Jabesh, "dry":– Jabesh-gilead [12], Jabesh [12]

3004 יַבָּשָׁה *yabbāšâ*, n.f. GK: 3317 [→ 3001; cf. 3007]. dry ground, dry land (in contrast to bodies of water):– dry [13], land [1]

3005 יִבְשָׂם *yibśām*, n.pr.m. GK: 3311 [→ 1313]. Ibsam, "*fragrance*":– Jibsam [1]

3006 יַבֶּשֶׁת *yabbešet*, n.f. GK: 3318 [→ 3001]. dry ground, dry land:– dry [2]

3007 יַבֶּשָׁה *yabbᵉšâ* (Aram.), n.f. GK: 10309 [cf. 3004]. earth; dry land (in contrast to the sea):– earth [1]

3008 יִגְאָל *yigʾāl*, n.pr.m. GK: 3319 [→ 1350]. Igal, "*he redeems*":– Igal [2], Igeal [1]

3009 יָגַב *yāgab*, v. GK: 3320 [→ 3010]. [Q] to work a field, do farm work:– husbandmen [2]

3010 יָגֵב *yāgēb*, n.m. GK: 3321 [→ 3009]. field:– fields [1]

3011 יָגְבְּהָה *yogbᵉhâ*, n.pr.loc. GK: 3322 [→ 1361]. Jogbehah, "*height*":– Jogbehah [2]

3012 יִגְדַּלְיָהוּ *yigdalyāhû*, n.pr.m. GK: 3323 [→ 1431+3068]. Igdaliah, "*Yahweh is great*":– Igdaliah [1]

3013 יָגָה *yāgâ*, v. GK: 3324 [→ 3015, 8424; cf. 3014]. [N] to be grieved; [P] to bring grief; [H] to torment, bring grief:– afflicted [3], afflict [1], cause grief [1], grieve [1], sorrowful [1], vex [1]

3014 יָגָה *yāgâ*, v. GK: 3325 [cf. 1898, 3013]. [H] to remove:– removed [1]

3015 יָגוֹן *yāgôn*, n.[m.]. GK: 3326 [→ 3013]. sorrow, anguish, grief:– sorrow [12], grief [2]

3016 יָגוֹר *yāgôr*, a.vbl. GK: 3328 [→ 3025]. fearing, filled with fear:– afraid [1], fearest [1]

3017 יָגוּר *yāgûr*, n.pr.loc. GK: 3327 [cf. 1485]. Jagur:– Jagur [1]

3018 יְגִיעַ *yᵉgîaʿ*, n.m. GK: 3330 [→ 3021]. labor, heavy work; the result of labor: produce, gain:– labour [12], labours [3], work [1]

3019 יָגִיעַ *yāgîaʿ*, a. GK: 3329 [→ 3021]. weary, exhausted:– weary (+3581) [1]

3020 יָגְלִי *yoglî*, n.pr.m. GK: 3332. Jogli, "[perhaps] *may God reveal*":– Jogli [1]

3021 יָגַע *yāgaʿ*, v. GK: 3333 [→ 3019, 3018, 3024, 3022, 3023]. [Q] to labor, toil, be weary; [P] to make weary; [H] to make weary:– labour [7], weary [7], wearied [5], laboured [4], fainted [1], make to labour [1], wearieth [1]

3022 יְגַע *yᵉgaʿ*, n.[m.]. GK: 3334 [→ 3021]. what is toiled for, the produce of labor:– that which laboured for [1]

3023 יָגֵעַ *yāgēaʿ*, a. GK: 3335 [→ 3021]. worn out, weary, wearisome:– weary [2], full of labour [1]

3024 יְגִעָה *yᵉgiʿâ*, n.f. GK: 3331 [→ 3021]. weariness:– weariness [1]

3025 יָגֹר *yāgōr*, v. GK: 3336 [→ 3016; cf. 1481]. [Q] to fear, dread:– afraid [4], fear [1]

3026 יְגַר שָׂהֲדוּתָא *yᵉgar śāhᵃdûtāʾ*, n.[m.]. & n.m. GK: 3337. Jegar Sahadutha, the Aramaic name of a stone monument, "*witness heap*":– Jegar-sahadutha [1]

3027 יָד *yād*, n.f. & m. GK: 3338 [cf. 3028]. hand, by extension: arm, finger; fig. of control, power, strength, direction, care:– hand [1087], hands [271], by (+871.1) [42], next unto (+5921) [13], power [11], with (+871.1) [10], place [8], tenons [5], consecrate (+4390) [5], consecrated (+853+4390) [5], custody [4], means [4], next to (+5921) [4], parts [4], side [4], stays [4], beside (+5921) [3], large (+7342) [3], next (+5921) [3], able to get (+5381) [2], armholes (+679) [2], as able [2], axletrees [2], because of (+871.1) [2], by (+5921) [2], consecrated (+4390) [2], dominion [2], force [2], from (+4480) [2], ledges [2], lefthanded (+334+3225) [2], ministry [2], near (+5921) [2], of (+4480) [2], order [2], paw [2], service [2], take [2], thumbs [2], times [2], to (+871.1) [2], wide (+7342) [2], ability (+5381) [1], able (+1767+4672) [1], able (+1767+5381+3509.1) [1], able (+4979) [1], able to bring (+1767+4672) [1], able to bring (+5381) [1], about (+3807.1) [1], aided (+853+2388) [1], as ordained by (+5921) [1], at (+3807.1) [1], beside (+3807.1) [1], borders [1], border [1], bounty [1], broad (+7342) [1], brokenhanded (+7667) [1], by side [1], by [1], can get (+5381) [1], charge [1], coasts [1], creditor (+1167+4874) [1], dominion (+4475) [1], drew with full strength (+4390+871.1) [1], exaction of debt (+4853) [1], fallen in decay (+4131) [1], fellowship (+8667) [1], for (+871.1) [1], get (+5381) [1], give (+5414+871.1) [1], hand

is able to get (+5381) [1], handed [1], handstaves (+4731) [1], handywork (+4639) [1], he (+2050.2) [1], help (+2388+871.1) [1], in (+871.1) [1], labour [1], large enough (+7342) [1], near (+413) [1], occasion serve (+4672) [1], occupied (+5503) [1], of (+871.1) [1], ordained by (+5921) [1], ordinance [1], own [1], places [1], power (+410) [1], power (+871.1) [1], presumptuously (+7311+871.1) [1], sore [1], stroke [1], sware (+5375) [1], swear (+5375) [1], sworn (+3678+5921) [1], sworn [1], thee (+3509.2) [1], themselves [1], thou (+3509.2) [1], through (+871.1) [1], throwing [1], under (+871.1) [1], wait on [1], wax rich (+5381) [1], way side (+4570) [1], wayside (+1870) [1], where [1], work [1], yield (+5414) [1]

3028 יַד *yad* (Aram.), n.f. GK: 10311 [cf. 3027]. hand (of a human), paw (of an animal); fig., power, control, action:– hand [12], hands [4], power [1]

3029 יְדָא *yᵉdāʾ* (Aram.), v. GK: 10312 [cf. 3034]. [H] to give thanks, confess praise:– gave thanks [1], thank [1]

3030 יִדְאֲלָה *yidʾᵃlâ*, n.pr.loc. GK: 3339. Idalah:– Idalah [1]

3031 יִדְבָּשׁ *yidbāš*, n.pr.m. GK: 3340 [→ 1706]. Idbash, "*honey*":– Idbash [1]

3032 יָדַד *yādad*, v. GK: 3341 [cf. 3034]. [Q] to cast (lots for decision making):– cast [3]

3033 יְדִדוּת *yᵉdidût*, n.f. GK: 3342 [→ 3039]. loved one, beloved:– dearly beloved [1]

3034 יָדָה *yādâ*, v. GK: 3343 & 3344 [→ 1935, 1937, 1938, 1939, 1960, 8426; cf. 3032; cf. 3029]. [Q] to shoot (a bow); [P] to throw (down); [H] to express praise, give thanks, extol, make a public confession, make an admission; to praise is to speak of the excellence of someone or something; to give thanks has a focus on the gratitude of the speaker:– praise [52], give thanks [31], confess [11], thank [4], confessed [3], thanksgiving [2], cast out [1], cast [1], confesseth [1], confessing [1], giving thanks [1], made confession [1], making confession [1], praised [1], shoot [1], thankful [1], thanking [1]

3035 יִדּוֹ *yiddô* or יַדַּי *yadday*, n.pr.m. GK: 3345 & 3346 & 3350 [→ 3039?]. Iddo, Jaddai, "[prob.] *Yahweh has adorned*":– Iddo [1], Jadau [1]

3036 יָדוֹן *yādôn*, n.pr.m. GK: 3347. Jadon, "*frail one* or *Yahweh rules*":– Jadon [1]

3037 יַדּוּעַ *yaddûaʿ*, n.pr.m. GK: 3348 [→ 3045]. Jaddua, "*one known*":– Jaddua [3]

3038 יְדוּתוּן *yᵉdûtûn* or יְדִיתוּן *yᵉdîtûn*, n.pr.m. GK: 3349 & 3357. Jeduthun:– Jeduthun [17]

3039 יָדִיד *yādîd*, a. GK: 3351 & 3353 [→ 3033, 3035?, 3040, 3041]. lovely, beloved, love song (referring to a wedding song):– beloved [5], well-beloved [2], amiable [1], loves [1]

3040 יְדִידָה *yᵉdîdâ*, n.pr.f. GK: 3352 [→ 3039]. Jedidah, "*beloved; lovely, beloved*":– Jedidah [1]

3041 יְדִידְיָה *yᵉdîdᵉyāh*, n.pr.m. GK: 3354 [→ 3039+3068]. Jedidiah, "*beloved of Yahweh*":– Jedidiah [1]

3042 יְדָיָה *yᵉdāyâ*, n.pr.m. GK: 3355. Jedaiah, "*Yahweh has favored* or *Yahweh knows*":– Jedaiah [2]

3043 יְדִיעֲאֵל *yᵉdî ʿᵃʾēl*, n.pr.m. GK: 3356 [→ 3045+410]. Jediael, "*known of God [El]*":– Jediael [6]

3044 יִדְלָף *yidlāp*, n.pr.m. GK: 3358 [→ 1811]. Jidlaph, "*he weeps*":– Jidlaph [1]

3045 יָדַע *yādaʿ*, v. GK: 3359 [→ 1843, 1844, 1847, 3037, 3049, 4093, 4129, 4130; cf. 3046 (also used with compound proper names)]. [Q] to know, recognize, understand; to have sexual relations; [Qp] to be respected; [N] to be known, make oneself known; [P] to cause to know; [Pu] to be well known; [H] to show, teach, make known; [Ho] to be made aware; [Ht] to make oneself known; this can range in meaning from the mere acquisition and understanding of information to intimacy in relationship, including sexual relations:– know [404], knew [83], known [80], knowest [66], knoweth [58], make known [14], shew [12], perceived [11], knowledge [10], made known [8], tell [8], wist [7], acquaintance [6], certainly know (+3045) [6], perceive [6], wot [6], acknowledge [5], cause to know [5], knewest [5], make know [5], shewed [5], teach [5], consider [4], cunning [4], know certainly (+3045) [4], know for certain (+3045) [4], sure [4], understood [4], declared [3], declare [3], ignorant (+3808) [3], learned (+5612) [3], make to know [3], mark [3], skill [3], taught [3], understand [3], aware [2], certainly knoweth (+3045) [2], come to knowledge [2], considereth [2], could [2], diligent to know [2], discern [2], endued [2], feel [2], knew certainly (+3045) [2], know assuredly (+3045) [2], know for a certain (+3045) [2], know for a certainty (+3045) [2], know of a surety (+3045) [2], knowing [2], skilful [2], takest

knowledge [2], wit [2], acknowledged [1], acquainted with [1], advise [1], answer [1], appointed [1], can skill [1], cannot (+3808) [1], cause to discern [1], caused to know [1], come to understanding (+998) [1], comprehend [1], discerneth [1], discovered [1], familiar friends [1], famous [1], felt [1], given knowledge [1], had knowledge [1], had respect unto [1], had understanding (+998) [1], hast [1], hath knowledge [1], hath [1], have knowledge (+1847) [1], have knowledge [1], have [1], having knowledge [1], instructed [1], kinsfolks [1], know well [1], madest known [1], make to be known [1], making known [1], perceivest [1], privy [1], prognosticators [1], regardeth [1], take knowledge [1], unawares (+3808) [1], understand (+995) [1], will [1], wotteth [1]

3046 יְדַע *yᵉdaʿ* (Aram.), v. GK: 10313 [→ 4486; cf. 3045]. [P] to know, understand, acknowledge; [Pp] to be known; [H] to make known, tell, inform:– know [13], make known [12], known [5], knowledge [5], certify [3], knew [2], maketh known [2], certified [1], knewest [1], knoweth [1], made know [1], teach [1]

3047 יָדָע *yādāʿ*, n.pr.m. GK: 3360. Jada, "*shrewd one; [God] has cared*":– Jada [2]

3048 יְדַעְיָה *yᵉdaʿyâ*, n.pr.m. GK: 3361 [→ 3045+3068]. Jedaiah, "*Yahweh has favored* or *Yahweh knows*":– Jedaiah [11]

3049 יִדְּעֹנִי *yiddᵉʿōnî*, n.m. GK: 3362 [→ 3045]. spiritist, soothsayer:– wizards [9], wizard [2]

3050 יָהּ *yāh*, n.pr.m. GK: 3363 [→ 3068]. LORD (Yahweh):– the LORD* [45], LORD* [3], Jah [1]

3051 יָהַב *yāhab*, v. GK: 2035 & 3364 [cf. 3052]. [Q] to give; (interj.) come!, give!, put!, ascribe!:– give [24], go to [4], bring [2], ascribe [1], come on [1], set [1], take [1]

3052 יְהַב *yᵉhab* (Aram.), v. GK: 10314 [cf. 5415; cf. 3051]. [P] to give; [Pp] to be given; [Htpe] to be given as payment; be entrusted:– given [16], gave [4], give [2], delivered [1], giveth [1], laid [1], paid [1], were [1], yielded [1]

3053 יְהָב *yᵉhāb*, n.[m.]. GK: 3365 [→ 2968?]. care, burden:– burden [1]

3054 יָהַד *yāhad*, v.den. GK: 3366 [→ 3064; cf. 3063]. [Ht] to become a Jew, this can mean to join the Jewish faith or simply to act like a Jew:– became Jews [1]

3055 יְהֻד *yᵉhūd*, n.pr.loc. GK: 3372. Jehud, "*declare*":– Jehud [1]

3056 יֶהְדַּי *yahdāy*, n.pr.m. GK: 3367. Jahdai, "*Yahweh lead*":– Jahdai [1]

3057 יְהֻדִיָּה *yᵉhudiyyâ*, a.g. GK: 3368 [→ 3063]. Jewish, Judean:– Jehudijah [1]

3058 יֵהוּא *yēhûʾ*, n.pr.m. GK: 3369 [→ 3068+1931]. Jehu, "*Yahweh is he*":– Jehu [58]

3059 יְהוֹאָחָז *yᵉhôʾāḥāz*, n.pr.m. GK: 3370 [→ 3068+270]. Jehoahaz, "*Yahweh holds*":– Jehoahaz [20]

3060 יְהוֹאָשׁ *yᵉhôʾāš*, n.pr.m. GK: 3371 [→ 3068+376]. Joash; Jehoash, "*Yahweh bestows; man of Yahweh*":– Jehoash [17]

3061 יְהוּד *yᵉhûd* (Aram.), n.pr.loc. GK: 10315 [→ 3062; cf. 3063]. Judah, "*praised*":– Judah [5], Jewry [1], Judea [1]

3062 יְהוּדָי *yᵉhûdāy* (Aram.), n.g. GK: 10316 [→ 3061; cf. 3064]. Jew:– Jews [10]

3063 יְהוּדָה *yᵉhûdâ*, n.pr.m. & loc. GK: 3373 [→ 3054, 3057, 3064, 3065, 3066, 3067; cf. 3061]. Judah, of Judah, Judean, "*praised*":– Judah [804], Beth-lehem-judah (+1035) [10], Judah's [4]

3064 יְהוּדִי *yᵉhûdî*, a.g. GK: 3374 [→ 3054, 3065, 3067; cf. 3063; cf. 3062]. (person) of Judah, Judean, Jew, Jewish, "*of Judah*":– Jews [63], Jew [10], Jews' [2], Judah [1]

3065 יְהוּדִי *yᵉhûdî*, n.pr.m. GK: 3375 [→ 3064; cf. 3063]. Jehudi, Yaudi, "*of Judah*":– Jehudi [4]

3066 יְהוּדִית *yᵉhûdît*, a.g.f. (used as adv.). GK: 3376 [→ 3063]. in Hebrew (language), in the language of Judah:– in the Jews' language [5], in the Jews' speech [1]

3067 יְהוּדִית *yᵉhûdît*, n.pr.f. GK: 3377 [→ 3064; cf. 3063]. Judith, "*Jewess* or *Judahite*":– Judith [1]

3068 יהוה *yhwh* or יֱהוִה *yehwih*, n.pr.m. GK: 3378 [→ 3050, 3069 (also used with compound proper names)]. LORD (Yahweh), the proper name of the one true God; knowledge and use of the name implies personal or covenant relationship; the name pictures God as the one who exists and/or causes existence:– the LORD* [6044], LORD* [364], GOD* [309], the LORD'S* [79], the LORD'S* (+3807.1) [28], Jehovah [4], LORD'S* [1], heˢ [1]

3069 יְהוִה *yehwih*, n.pr.m. GK: 3378 [→ 3068]. same as 3068: LORD (Yahweh), with vowels points used in combination with 136:–

3070 יְהוָה יִרְאֶה *yhwh yir'eh*, n.pr.loc. GK: 3378 + 8011 [→ 3068+7200]. Yahweh yireh, "The LORD (Yahweh) will see" (3068 + 7200):– Jehovah-jireh [1]

3071 יְהוָה נִסִּי *yhwh nissî*, n.pr.loc. GK: 3378 + 5812 + 3276 [→ 3068+5251+2967.1]. "LORD (Yahweh) is my banner" (3068 + 5251 + 2967.1):– Jehovah-nissi [1]

3072 יְהוָה צִדְקֵנוּ *yhwh ṣidqēnû*, n.pr.m. GK: 3378 + 7406 + 5646 [→ 3068+6664+5105.1]. "LORD (Yahweh) is our righteousness" (3068 + 6664 + 5105.1):–

3073 יְהוָה שָׁלוֹם *yhwh šālôm*, n.pr.loc. GK: 3378 + 8934 [→ 3068+7965]. "LORD (Yahweh) is peace" (3068 + 7965):– Jehovah-shalom [1]

3074 יְהוָה שָׁמָּה *yhwh šammâ*, n.pr.loc. GK: 3378 + 9004 + 2025 [→ 3068+8033+1886.5]. "LORD (Yahweh) is there" (3068 + 8033 + 1886.5):–

3075 יְהוֹזָבָד *yᵉhôzābād*, n.pr.m. GK: 3379 [→ 3068+2064]. Jehozabad, "*Yahweh endows*":– Jehozabad [4]

3076 יְהוֹחָנָן *yᵉhôḥānān*, n.pr.m. GK: 3380 [→ 3068+2603]. Jehohanan, "*Yahweh has been gracious*":– Jehohanan [6], Johanan [3]

3077 יְהוֹיָדָע *yᵉhôyādā'*, n.pr.m. GK: 3381 [→ 3068+3045]. Jehoiada, "*Yahweh has known*":– Jehoiada [51]

3078 יְהוֹיָכִין *yᵉhôyākîn*, n.pr.m. GK: 3382 [→ 3204, 3659]. Jehoiachin, "*Yahweh supports*":– Jehoiachin [10]

3079 יְהוֹיָקִים *yᵉhôyāqîm*, n.pr.m. GK: 3383 [→ 3068+6965]. Jehoiakim, "*Yahweh lifts up, establishes*":– Jehoiakim [37]

3080 יְהוֹיָרִיב *yᵉhôyārîb*, n.pr.m. GK: 3384 [→ 3068+7378]. Jehoiarib, "*Yahweh argues [for me]*":– Jehoiarib [2]

3081 יְהוּכַל *yᵉhûkal*, n.pr.m. GK: 3385 [→ 3068+3201; cf. 3116]. Jehucal, "*Yahweh is capable*":– Jehucal [1]

3082 יְהוֹנָדָב *yᵉhônādāb*, n.pr.m. GK: 3386 [→ 3068+5068]. Jonadab; Jehonadab, "*Yahweh is generous, noble*":– Jonadab [5], Jehonadab [3]

3083 יְהוֹנָתָן *yᵉhônātān*, n.pr.m. GK: 3387 [→ 3068+5414]. Jonathan; Jehonathan, "*gift of Yahweh*":– Jonathan [76], Jehonathan [3], Jonathan's [3]

3084 יְהוֹסֵף *yᵉhôsēp*, n.pr.m. GK: 3388 [cf. 3254]. Joseph, "*he will add*":– Joseph [1]

3085 יְהוֹעַדָּה *yᵉhô'addâ*, n.pr.m. GK: 3389. Jehoaddah:– Jehoadah [1]

3086 יְהוֹעַדִּין or יְהוֹעַדָּן *yᵉhô'addîn* or *yᵉhô'addān*, n.pr.f. GK: 3390 & 3391. Jehoaddin, Jehoaddan, "[prob.] *Yahweh is delight*":– Jehoaddan [2]

3087 יְהוֹצָדָק *yᵉhôṣādāq*, n.pr.m. GK: 3392 [→ 3068+6663; cf. 3136]. Jehozadak, "*Yahweh is just*":– Josedech [6], Jehozadak [2]

3088 יְהוֹרָם *yᵉhôrām*, n.pr.m. GK: 3393 [→ 3068+7311]. Joram; Jehoram, "*Yahweh exalts*":– Jehoram [23], Joram [6]

3089 יְהוֹשֶׁבַע *yᵉhôšeba'*, n.pr.f. GK: 3394 [→ 3068; cf. 7652]. Jehosheba, "*Yahweh is an oath; Yahweh gives plenty, satisfies*":– Jehosheba [2]

3090 יְהוֹשַׁבְעַת *yᵉhôšab'at*, n.pr.f. GK: 3395 [→ 3068; cf. 7652]. Jehosheba, "*Yahweh is an oath; Yahweh gives plenty, satisfies*":– Jehoshabeath [2]

3091 יְהוֹשֻׁעַ *yᵉhôšua'*, n.pr.m. GK: 3397 [→ 3068+7768]. Joshua, "*Yahweh saves*":– Joshua [216], Jeshua [2]

3092 יְהוֹשָׁפָט *yᵉhôšāpāṭ*, n.pr.m. & loc. GK: 3398 & 3399 [→ 3068+8199]. Jehoshaphat, "*Yahweh has judged*":– Jehoshaphat [84]

3093 יָהִיר *yāhîr*, a. GK: 3400. arrogant, haughty:– haughty [1], proud [1]

3094 יְהַלֶּלְאֵל *yᵉhallel'ēl*, n.pr.[m.]. GK: 3401 [→ 3094+410]. Jehallelel, "*he shall praise God [El]; God [El] shines forth*":– Jehalelel [1], Jehaleleel [1]

3095 יַהֲלֹם *yahᵉlōm*, n.[m.]. GK: 3402. emerald (precious stone, exact identification uncertain):– diamond [3]

3096 יַהַץ *yahaṣ* or יַהְצָה *yahṣâ*, n.pr.loc. GK: 3403 & 3404. Jahaz, Jahzah, "[perhaps] *a trodden* or *open place*":– Jahaz [5], Jahazah [3], Jahzah [1]

3097 יוֹאָב *yô'āb*, n.pr.m. GK: 3405 [→ 5854]. Joab, "*Yahweh is father*":– Joab [138], Joab's [8]

3098 יוֹאָח *yô'āḥ*, n.pr.m. GK: 3406 [→ 3068+251]. Joah, "*Yahweh is brother*":– Joah [11]

3099 יוֹאָחָז *yô'āḥāz*, n.pr.m. GK: 3407 [→ 3068+270]. Jehoahaz; Joahaz, "*Yahweh grips, holds*":– Jehoahaz [3], Joahaz [1]

3100 יוֹאֵל *yô'ēl*, n.pr.m. GK: 3408 [→ 3068+410]. Joel, "*Yahweh is God [El]*":– Joel [19]

3101 יוֹאָשׁ *yô'āš*, n.pr.m. GK: 3409 [→ 3068+376]. Joash; Jehoash:– Joash [47]

3102 יוֹב *yôb*, n.pr.m. GK: 3410. Job:– Job [1]

3103 יוֹבָב *yôbāb*, n.pr.m. GK: 3411 & 3412 [→ 2980]. Jobab, "*howl*":– Jobab [9]

3104 יוֹבֵל *yôbēl*, n.m. GK: 3413 [→ 2990]. ram's horn; (blowing of ram's horn) jubilee, (Year of) Jubilee:– jubile [21], rams' horns [4], ram's [1], trumpet [1]

3105 יוּבַל *yûbal*, n.[m.]. GK: 3414 [→ 2986]. stream, watercourse:– river [1]

3106 יוּבָל *yûbāl*, n.pr.m. GK: 3415. Jubal:– Jubal [1]

3107 יוֹזָבָד *yôzābād*, n.pr.m. GK: 3416 [→ 3068+2064]. Jozabad, "*Yahweh bestowed*":– Jozabad [9], Josabad [1]

3108 יוֹזָכָר *yôzākār*, n.pr.m. GK: 3417. Jozakar:– Jozachar [1]

3109 יוֹחָא *yôḥā'*, n.pr.m. GK: 3418. Joha:– Joha [2]

3110 יוֹחָנָן *yôḥānān*, n.pr.m. GK: 3419 [→ 3068+2603]. Johanan, "*Yahweh is gracious*":– Johanan [24]

יוּטָה *yûṭâ*. See 3194.

3111 יוֹיָדָע *yôyādā'*, n.pr.m. GK: 3421 [→ 3068+3045]. Joiada, "*Yahweh knows*":– Joiada [4], Jehoiada [1]

3112 יוֹיָכִין *yôyākîn*, n.pr.m. GK: 3422 [→ 3068+3559]. Jehoiachin, "*Yahweh supports*":– Jehoiachin's [1]

3113 יוֹיָקִים *yôyāqîm*, n.pr.m. GK: 3423 [→ 3068+6965]. Joiakim, "*Yahweh lifts up*":– Joiakim [1]

3114 יוֹיָרִיב *yôyārîb*, n.pr.m. GK: 3424 [→ 3068+7378]. Joiarib, "*Yahweh contends, pleads [your case]*":– Joiarib [5]

3115 יוֹכֶבֶד *yôkebed*, n.pr.f. GK: 3425 [→ 3068+3513]. Jochebed, "*Yahweh is glorious*":– Jochebed [2]

3116 יוּכַל *yûkal*, n.pr.m. GK: 3426 [cf. 3081]. Jehucal, "*Yahweh is capable*":– Jucal [1]

3117 יוֹם *yôm*, n.m. GK: 3427 & 3428 [→ 3119; cf. 3118]. day (24 hours), daytime (in contrast to night); by extension: an indefinite period of time, an era with a certain characteristic, such as "the day of the LORD" and the prophetic "on that day"; storm, wind; breath:– day [1217], days [666], time [54], to day (+1886.1) [50], chronicles [1697] [30], for ever (+3605+1886.1) [15], days' [13], daily (+3117) [12], every day (+3117+871.1) [12], daily (+3605+1886.1) [11], daily (+3117+871.1) [10], when (+871.1) [10], continually (+3605+1886.1) [9], while [6], yearly (+3117+4480+1886.5) [6], year [6], age [6], as long as (+3605) [5], chronicles (+1697+1886.1) [5], daily (1886.1+3807.1) [5], day's [5], two full years (+8141) [5], years [5], alway (+3605+1886.1) [4], two days [4], always (+3605+1886.1) [3], ever (+3605+1886.1) [3], life [3], season [3], space [3], times [3], whole [3], yearly [3], as long as (+834+3605+1886.1) [2], at all times (+3117+871.1) [2], at other times (+3117+871.1) [2], daily (+3117+2050.1) [2], daily [2], day by day (+1886.1+3807.1) [2], each day (+3117) [2], ever (+753) [2], every day (+3117+3605+2050.1) [2], every day's (+3117+871.1) [2], every sabbath (+3117+7676+7676+871.1+871.1+1886.1+1886.1) [2], every year's (+3117+3807.1) [2], for every day (+3117+871.1) [2], full month (+3391) [2], full year [2], in process of time (+3117+4480+3807.1) [2], live [2], now (+1886.1) [2], now [2], perpetually (+3605+1886.1) [2], time (+4557) [2], upon day (+3117+871.1) [2], afternoon (+5186+1886.1) [1], ago [1], always (+3605) [1], any time [1], as long as (+3605+1886.1) [1], as long as (+871.1) [1], birthday (+3205) [1], continually (+3605) [1], continuance [1], daily (+259+3807.1) [1], daily (+3605+871.1) [1], day (+1886.1) [1], each$ [1], elder (+2205+3807.1) [1], elder [1], everlasting (+5769) [1], evermore (+3605+1886.1) [1], for evermore (+3605+1886.1) [1], full weeks (+7620) [1], how long (+4100+8141+3509.1) [1], in process of time (+4480) [1], in process of time (+7235+1886.1) [1], in trouble (+7186) [1], livest$ [1], midday (+4276+1886.1) [1], now a days (+1886.1) [1], old (+2416+8141) [1], old [1], outlived (+310+748) [1], overlived (+310+748) [1], presently (+1886.1+3509.1) [1], presently (+871.1+1886.1) [1], process of time (+7227+1886.1+1886.1) [1], prolong life

(+3117+3254+5921) [1], remaineth [1], sabbath (+7676) [1], since (+4480) [1], since (+4480+1886.1+3807.1) [1], so long as (+3605+1886.1) [1], so long as (+4480) [1], then (+1886.1) [1], to morrow (+4279) [1], two$ [1], weather [1], when [1], while (+1886.1+3509.1) [1], while (+4480) [1], whole age (+2416+8141) [1], whole weeks (+7620) [1], within a while after (+4480) [1], yesterday (+865) [1], young (+6810+3807.1) [1], younger (+6810) [1]

3118 יוֹם *yôm* (Aram.), n.m. GK: 10317 [cf. 3117]. a period of time which is indefinite in scope: it can range widely in meaning from "daytime" (in contrast to night); "day," a period of time approximately 24 hours; to longer periods (seasons or years). The title "Ancient of Days" is a title of God as old (eternal), emphasizing wisdom and power:– days [9], day [5], time [2]

3119 יוֹמָם *yômām*, subst. & adv. GK: 3429 [→ 3117]. day; in the daytime, by day:– day [24], by day [17], in daytime [4], daytime [3], daily [2], by day time [1]

3120 יָוָן *yāwān*, n.pr.g. GK: 3430 [→ 3125]. Javan; Greeks; Greece:– Javan [7], Grecia [3], Greece [1]

3121 יָוֵן *yāwēn*, n.[m.]. GK: 3431. mire, mud, sediment:– mire [1], miry [1]

3122 יוֹנָדָב *yônādāb*, n.pr.m. GK: 3432 [→ 3068+5068]. Jonadab, "*Yahweh is generous, noble*":– Jonadab [7]

3123 יוֹנָה *yônâ*, n.f. GK: 3433 [→ 1686, 3124; cf. 578, 2755]. dove; pigeon:– dove [14], pigeons [9], doves [5], doves' [2], pigeon [1]

3124 יוֹנָה *yônâ*, n.pr.m. GK: 3434 [→ 3123]. Jonah, "*dove*":– Jonah [19]

3125 יְוָנִי *yᵉwānî*, a.g. GK: 3436 [→ 3120]. Javanite = Greek:– Grecians (+1121) [1]

3126 יוֹנֵק *yônēq*, n.m. GK: 3437 [→ 3243]. infant, one nursing; tender shoot:– tender plant [1]

3127 יוֹנֶקֶת *yôneqet*, n.f. GK: 3438 [→ 3243]. new shoot, young shoot (of a plant):– branches [3], branch [1], tender branch [1], young twigs [1]

3128 יוֹנַת אֵלֶם רְחֹקִים *yônat 'ēlem rᵉḥōqîm*, tt. GK: 3439 [→ 3123+352+7368]. Dove of the Distant Oaks:– Jonath-elem-rechokim [1]

3129 יוֹנָתָן *yônātān*, n.pr.m. GK: 3440 [→ 3068+5414]. Jonathan, "*gift of Yahweh*":– Jonathan [42]

3130 יוֹסֵף *yôsēp*, n.pr.m. GK: 3441 [→ 3254]. Joseph, "*he will add*":– Joseph [193], Joseph's [20]

3131 יוֹסִפְיָה *yôsipyâ*, n.pr.m. GK: 3442 [→ 3254+3068]. Josiphiah, "*Yahweh will add*":– Josiphiah [1]

3132 יוֹעֵאלָה *yô'ē'lâ*, n.pr.m. GK: 3443. Joelah, "*let him help*":– Joelah [1]

3133 יוֹעֵד *yô'ēd*, n.pr.m. GK: 3444 [→ 3068+5707]. Joed, "*Yahweh is witness*":– Joed [1]

3134 יוֹעֶזֶר *yô'ezer*, n.pr.m. GK: 3445 [→ 3068+5828]. Joezer, "*Yahweh is help*":– Joezer [1]

3135 יוֹעָשׁ *yô'āš*, n.pr.m. GK: 3447 [→ 3068+5789]. Joash, "*Yahweh has bestowed*":– Joash [2]

3136 יוֹצָדָק *yôṣādāq*, n.pr.m. GK: 3449 & 10318 [→ 3068+6663, 3087]. Jozadak, "*Yahweh is righteous*": note this name is Aramaic once in Ezra:– Jozadak [5]

3137 יוֹקִים *yôqîm*, n.pr.m. GK: 3451 [→ 3068?+6965]. Jokim, "*Yahweh lifts up*":– Jokim [1]

3138 יוֹרֶה *yôreh*, n.[m.]. GK: 3453 [→ 7301]. autumn (i.e., the time of the early rains, from the end of October to the beginning of December):– first rain [1], former [1]

3139 יוֹרָה *yôrâ*, n.pr.m. GK: 3454. Jorah, "*one born during harvest*":– Jorah [1]

3140 יוֹרַי *yôray*, n.pr.m. GK: 3455. Jorai, "[poss.] *Yahweh sees; whom Yahweh teaches*":– Jorai [1]

3141 יוֹרָם *yôrām*, n.pr.m. GK: 3456 [→ 3068+7311]. Joram; Jehoram, "*Yahweh is exalted*":– Joram [20]

3142 יוּשַׁב חֶסֶד *yûšab ḥesed*, n.pr.m. GK: 3457. Jushab-Hesed, "*loyal love will be returned*":– Jushabhesed [1]

3143 יוֹשִׁבְיָה *yôšibyâ*, n.pr.m. GK: 3458 [→ 3427+3068]. Joshibiah, "*Yahweh places*":– Josibiah [1]

3144 יוֹשָׁה *yôšâ*, n.pr.m. GK: 3459. Joshah, "*gift of Yahweh*":– Joshah [1]

3145 יוֹשַׁוְיָה *yôšawyâ*, n.pr.m. GK: 3460 [→ 3427+3068]. Joshaviah, "*Yahweh places*":– Joshaviah [1]

3146 יוֹשָׁפָט *yôšāpāṭ*, n.pr.m. GK: 3461 [→ 3068+8199]. Joshaphat, "*Yahweh judges*":– Jehoshaphat [1], Joshaphat [1]

3147 יוֹתָם *yôtām*, n.pr.m. GK: 3462 [→ 3068+8535]. Jotham, "*Yahweh will complete*":– Jotham [24]

3148 יוֹתֵר *yôtēr*, n.m. or v.ptcp. GK: 3463 [→ 3498]. the rest; gain, advantage, profit; more than:– more [2], better [1], further [1], more than [1], moreover [1], over [1], profit [1]

3149 יְזוּאֵל *y^ezû'ēl* or יְזִיאֵל *y^ezî'ēl*, n.pr.m. GK: 3464 & 3465 [cf. 3150?, 3151?]. Jeziel, Jezuel, "*may God sprinkle [in atonement]; God unites*":– Jeziel [1]

3150 יִזִּיָּה *yizziyyâ*, n.pr.m. GK: 3466 [cf. 3149?]. Izziah, "*may Yahweh sprinkle [in atonement]; Yahweh unites*":– Jeziah [1]

3151 יָזִיז *yāzîz*, n.pr.m. GK: 3467 [cf. 3149?]. Jaziz:– Jaziz [1]

3152 יְזְלִיאָה *yizlî'â*, n.pr.m. GK: 3468. Izliah, "*long living, eternal; Yahweh delivers*":– Jezliah [1]

3153 יְזַנְיָה *y^ezanyâ* or יְזַנְיָהוּ *y^ezanyāhû*, n.pr.m. GK: 3470 & 3471. Jezaniah, Jaazaniah, "*Yahweh listens*":– Jezaniah [2]

3154 זֵעַ *yeza'*, n.[m.]. GK: 3472 [→ 2188]. perspiration, sweat:– sweat [1]

3155 יִזְרָח *yizrāḥ*, a.g. GK: 3473. Izrahite:– Izrahite [1]

3156 יִזְרַחְיָה *yizraḥyâ*, n.pr.m. GK: 3474 [→ 2224+3068]. Izrahiah; Jezrahiah, "*Yahweh shines or will arise*":– Izrahiah [2], Jezrahiah [1]

3157 יִזְרְעֵאל *yizr^e'e'l*, n.pr.m. & loc. GK: 3475 & 3476 [→ 3158, 3159]. Jezreel, "*God [El] will sow*":– Jezreel [36]

3158 יִזְרְעֵאלִי *yizr^e'ē'lî*, a.g. GK: 3477 [→ 3157, 3159]. Jezreelite, of Jezreel, "*of Jezreel*":– Jezreelite [8]

3159 יִזְרְעֵאלִית *yizr^e'ē'lît*, a.g. GK: 3477 [→ 3158]. f. of 3158: Jezreelite, of Jezreel, "*of Jezreel*":– Jezreelitess [5]

3160 יְחֻבָּה *y^eḥubbâ*, n.pr.m. GK: 3478 & 2465 [→ 2245?; cf. 2244?]. Jehubbah, "*God has hidden [someone from danger]*":– Jehubbah [1]

3161 יָחַד *yāḥad*, v. GK: 3479 [→ 3162, 3173]. [Q] to join, be united; [P] to unite:– joined with [1], united [1], unite [1]

3162 יַחַד *yaḥad*, n.[m.] or יַחְדָּו *yaḥdāw*, adv. GK: 3480 & 3481 [→ 3161]. together, along with, in close proximity or concord either in space or time; by extension: close association in relationships, unity:– together [118], alike [5], altogether [5], at once [2], likewise [2], withal [2], at all [1], both [1], coupled together (+8535) [1], even as [1], knit (+3807.1) [1], only [1], together in unity [1]

3163 יַחְדּוֹ *yaḥdô*, n.pr.m. GK: 3482. Jahdo, "*[God] gives joy*":– Jahdo [1]

3164 יַחְדִּיאֵל *yaḥdî'ēl*, n.pr.m. GK: 3484 [→ 2302+410]. Jahdiel, "*God [El] gives joy*":– Jahdiel [1]

3165 יֶחְדְּיָהוּ *yeḥd^eyāhû*, n.pr.m. GK: 3485 [→ 2302+3068]. Jehdeiah, "*Yahweh rejoices [in his works]*":– Jehdeiah [2]

יְחַוְאֵל *y^eḥaw'ēl*. See 3171.

3166 יַחֲזִיאֵל *yaḥ^azî'ēl*, n.pr.m. GK: 3487 [→ 2372+410]. Jahaziel, "*God [El] will see*":– Jahaziel [6]

3167 יַחְזְיָה *yaḥz^eyâ*, n.pr.m. GK: 3488 [→ 2372+3068]. Jahzeiah, "*Yahweh sees*":– Jahaziah [1]

3168 יְחֶזְקֵאל *y^eḥezqē'l*, n.pr.m. GK: 3489 [→ 2388+410]. Ezekiel; Jehezkel, "*God [El] gives strength*":– Ezekiel [2], Jehezekel [1]

3169 יְחִזְקִיָּה *y^eḥizqiyyâ* or יְחִזְקִיָּהוּ *y^eḥizqiyyāhû*, n.pr.m. GK: 3490 & 3491 [→ 2388+3068]. Hezekiah, "*Yahweh is [my] strength*"; Jehizkiah, "*Yahweh gives strength*":– Hezekiah [43], Jehizkiah [1]

3170 יַחְזֵרָה *yaḥzērâ*, n.pr.m. GK: 3492 [→ 2386]. "[poss.] *prudent*":– Jahzerah [1]

3171 יְחוּאֵל *y^eḥû'ēl* or יְחִיאֵל *y^eḥî'ēl*, n.pr.m. GK: 3486 & 3493 [→ 3172]. Jehuel, Jehiel, "*God [El] lives*":– Jehiel [14]

3172 יְחִיאֵלִי *y^eḥî'ēlî*, n.pr.m. GK: 3494 [→ 3171]. Jehieli, "*of Jehiel*":– Jehieli [2]

3173 יָחִיד *yāḥîd*, a. & subst. GK: 3495 [→ 3161]. only son, only child (special and unique to the parents); precious life; alone, solitary:– only [7], darling [2], child [1], desolate [1], solitary [1]

3174 יְחִיָּה *y^eḥiyyâ*, n.pr.m. GK: 3496 [→ 2421+3068]. Jehiah, "*Yahweh lives*":– Jehiah [1]

3175 יָחִיל *yāḥîl*, a.vbl. GK: 3497 [→ 3176]. waiting:– hope [1]

3176 יָחַל *yāḥal*, v. GK: 3498 [→ 3175, 3177, 3178, 8431]. [N] to wait; [P] to wait for, put hope in, expect; [H] to wait, put hope in:– hope [17], waited [6], wait [5], hoped [3], tarry [2], trust [2], caused to hope [1], made to hope [1], stayed [1], tarried [1], waiteth [1]

3177 יַחְלְאֵל *yaḥl^e'ēl*, n.pr.m. GK: 3499 [→ 3178]. Jahleel, "*wait for God [El]; [poss.] may God [El] show himself friendly*":– Jahleel [2]

3178 יַחְלְאֵלִי *yaḥl^e'ēlî*, a.g. GK: 3500 [→ 3177]. Jahleelite, "*of Jahleel*":– Jahleelites [1]

3179 יָחַם *yāḥam*, v. GK: 3501 [→ 2534; cf. 2552]. [Q] to be in (breeding) heat, be in the rut; [P] to be in (breeding) heat, to mate, to conceive:– conceive [4], conceived [2], hot [2], gat heat [1], warm [1]

3180 יַחְמוּר *yaḥmûr*, n.[m.]. GK: 3502 [→ 2560]. roebuck, the roe deer:– fallow deer [1], fallowdeer [1]

3181 יַחְמַי *yaḥmay*, n.pr.m. GK: 3503 [→ 2346]. Jahmai, "*protect*":– Jahmai [1]

3182 יָחֵף *yāḥēp*, a. GK: 3504. barefoot:– barefoot [4], unshod [1]

3183 יַחְצְאֵל *yaḥṣ^e'ēl*, n.pr.m. GK: 3505 [→ 3184]. Jahzeel, "*God [El] apportions*":– Jahzeel [2]

3184 יַחְצְאֵלִי *yaḥṣ^e'ēlî*, a.g. GK: 3506 [→ 3183]. Jahzeelite, "*of Jahzeel*":– Jahzeelites [1]

3185 יַחְצִיאֵל *yaḥṣî'ēl*, n.pr.m. GK: 3507 [→ 2673+410]. Jahziel:– Jahziel [1]

3186 יָחַר *yāḥar*, v. GK: 3508 [cf. 309]. var. of 309: to wait, hesitate:–

3187 יָחַשׂ *yāḥas*, v. GK: 3509 [→ 3188]. [Ht] to enroll oneself in a genealogical record, be in a family register:– genealogy [5], reckoned by genealogies [5], reckoned by genealogy [5], genealogy reckoned [2], genealogies [1], number after genealogy [1], throughout genealogy [1]

3188 יַחַשׂ *yaḥas*, n.[m.]. GK: 3510 [→ 3187]. (book of) genealogy:– genealogy [1]

3189 יַחַת *yaḥat*, n.pr.m. GK: 3511. Jahath, "*snatch up*":– Jahath [8]

3190 יָטַב *yāṭab*, v. GK: 3512 [→ 3192, 3193, 4105, 4315; cf. 2895; cf. 2868, cf. 3191]. [Q] to be good, go well; to be glad, pleased; [H] to do good, right; to make successful, cause to prosper; "to be good in the eyes" indicates pleasure in and acceptance of a person or situation:– well [20], do good [14], pleased (+5869+871.1) [8], go well [4], merry [4], amend [3], do well [3], accepted [2], dealt well [2], diligently [2], doeth good [2], good [2], pleased well (+5869+871.1) [2], surely do good (+3190) [2], throughly amend (+3190) [2], benefit [1], best [1], better [1], comely [1], content (+5869+871.1) [1], deal well [1], diligent [1], doest well [1], done good [1], do [1], dresseth [1], earnestly (+3807.1) [1], entreated well [1], found favour [1], give [1], glad [1], ground very small (+2912) [1], made better [1], make better [1], make good [1], make sweet [1], maketh cheerful [1], making merry [1], please (+413) [1], pleased (+6440+3807.1) [1], pleased [1], pleaseth (+5869+871.1) [1], please [1], shewed more [1], skilfully [1], throughly [1], tired [1], trimmest [1], useth aright [1], very [1]

3191 יְטַב *y^eṭab* (Aram.), v. GK: 10320 [cf. 2868; cf. 3190]. [P] to seem best, be pleasing:– seem good [1]

3192 יָטְבָה *yoṭbâ*, n.pr.loc. GK: 3513 [→ 3190]. Jotbah, "*good, pleasant*":– Jotbah [1]

3193 יָטְבָתָה *yoṭbātâ*, n.pr.loc. GK: 3514 [→ 3190]. Jotbathah, "*good, pleasant*":– Jotbathah [2], Jotbath [1]

3194 יֻטָּה *yûṭṭâ*, n.pr.loc. GK: 3420. Juttah, "*extended, inclined*":– Juttah [2]

3195 יְטוּר *y^eṭûr*, n.pr.m. & g. GK: 3515 [cf. 2918?]. Jetur:– Jetur [3]

3196 יַיִן *yayin*, n.m. GK: 3516. wine, an alcoholic beverage made of naturally fermented fruit juice (usually grapes), usually diluted with water for general consumption:– wine [137], banqueting [1], vine (+1612) [1], vine [1], winebibbers (+5433) [1]

3197 יַד *yak*, var. GK: 3517. var. of 3027: hand, side:–

יָכוֹל *yākôl*. See 3201.

יְכָנְיָה *y^ekon^eyâ*. See 3204.

3198 יָכַח *yākaḥ*, v. GK: 3519 [→ 8433]. [N] to reason together (in a legal case); to be vindicated; [H] to rebuke, discipline, punish; decide, argue, defend, judge; [Ho] to be chastened; [Ht] to lodge a charge against:– reprove [15],

rebuke [7], reproved [4], plead [3], rebuketh [3], reproveth [3], correcteth [2], in any wise rebuke (+3198) [2], reason [2], surely reprove (+3198) [2], appointed out [1], appointed [1], arguing [1], chastened [1], chasten [1], convinced [1], correction [1], correct [1], daysman [1], dispute [1], judge [1], maintain [1], reason together [1], rebuked [1], reprover [1], reprover (+376) [1]

יְכִילְיָה *y^ekîl^eyâ*. See 3203.

3199 יָכִין *yākîn*, n.pr.m. GK: 3520 & 3521 [→ 3200, 3559]. Jakin, "*he establishes*":– Jachin [8]

3200 יָכִינִי *yākînî*, a.g. GK: 3522 [→ 3199; cf. 3559]. Jakinite, "*of Jakin*":– Jachinites [1]

3201 יָכֹל *yākōl*, v. GK: 3523 [→ 3203; cf. 3202 (also used with compound proper names)]. [Q] to be able, capable; overcome, prevail, have victory:– could [45], able [41], cannot (+3808) [36], prevail [12], may [11], can [10], prevailed [8], canst [5], mayest [5], any power at all (+3201) [2], any ways able (+3201) [2], endure [2], might [2], still prevail (+3201) [2], well able to overcome (+3201) [2], attain [1], can do [1], cannot away with (+3808) [1], canst do [1], could endure [1], couldest [1], prevailed against [1], suffer [1]

3202 יְכֹל *y^ekōl* (Aram.), v. GK: 10321 [cf. 3201]. [P] to be able:– able [4], canst [2], can [2], cannot (+3809) [1], couldest [1], could [1], prevailed [1]

3203 יְכָלְיָה *y^ekolyâ* or יְכָלְיָהוּ *y^ekolyāhû*, n.pr.f. GK: 3524 & 3525 [→ 3201+3068]. Jecoliah, "*Yahweh is able*":– Jecholiah [1], Jecoliah [1]

3204 יְכוֹנְיָה *y^ekôn^eyâ* or יְכָנְיָה *y^ekon^eyâ* or יְכָנְיָהוּ *y^ekonyāhû*, n.pr.m. GK: 3518 & 3526 & 3527 [→ 3078]. Jeconiah, "*Yahweh supports*":– Jeconiah [7]

3205 יָלַד *yālad*, v. GK: 3528 & 4256 [→ 2056, 3206, 3207, 3208, 3209, 3211, 4138, 4140, 8434?, 8435]. [Q] to give birth to, have a child, become the father of; [Qp, N, Pu, Ho] to be born, be a descendant; [P] to assist in childbirth, be a midwife; [H] to become the father of, cause to come to birth:– begat [179], bare [111], born [78], bear [17], bring forth [12], beget [10], brought forth [10], in travail [9], begotten [7], midwives [7], delivered [5], bearing [3], begetteth [3], borne [3], travailed [3], travaileth [3], beareth [2], begettest [2], birth [2], brought up [2], cause to bring forth [2], child [2], labour [2], midwife [2], bearest [1], birthday (+3117) [1], bring forth children [1], bring forth young [1], calved [1], children [1], come [1], declared pedigrees [1], delivered of a child [1], delivery [1], do the office of a midwife [1], gendered [1], hatcheth [1], maketh bring forth [1], son [1], travail with child [1], travaileth with child [1], travailing woman [1], travailing [1], travail [1]

3206 יֶלֶד *yeled*, n.m. GK: 3529 [→ 3205]. male child, young boy; this can refer to a wide range of ages, from infant to young adult:– child [38], children [30], young men [6], sons [3], young ones [3], child's [2], men children [2], boys [1], boy [1], fruit [1], young man [1]

3207 יַלְדָּה *yaldâ*, n.f. GK: 3530 [→ 3205]. female child, young girl; this can refer to a wide range of ages, from infant to young adult:– damsel [1], girls [1], girl [1]

3208 יַלְדוּת *yaldût*, n.f. GK: 3531 [→ 3205]. youth, childhood:– youth [2], childhood [1]

3209 יִלּוֹד *yillôd*, a. GK: 3533 [→ 3205]. born (children):– born [5]

3210 יָלוֹן *yālôn*, n.pr.m. GK: 3534. Jalon:– Jalon [1]

3211 יָלִיד *yālîd*, a. GK: 3535 [→ 3205]. born (child, slave child); (pl.) descendants, children:– children [4], born [2], sons [2], that is born [1], he that is born [1], homeborn [1] (+1004) [1], that were born [1]

3212 יָלַךְ *yālak*, v. 2143 [→ 1980]. all forms of this assumed root are aligned with 1980:–

3213 יָלַל *yālal*, v. GK: 3536 [→ 3214, 3215]. [H] to wail, howl:– howl [27], howled [1], howlings [1], make to howl [1]

3214 יְלֵל *y^elēl*, n.[m.]. GK: 3537 [→ 3213]. howling, wailing-cry:– howling [1]

3215 יְלָלָה *y^elālâ*, n.f. GK: 3538 [→ 3213]. wailing, lamentation, howling:– howling [5]

3216 לָעַע *lā'a'* or יָלַע *yāla'*, v. GK: 4363 [→ 3930; cf. 5966]. [Q] to sip, lap, slurp:– devoureth [1]

3217 יַלֶּפֶת *yallepet*, n.f. GK: 3539. running sore; some sources: scab, ringworm:– scabbed [2]

3218 יֶלֶק **yeleq**, n.m. GK: 3540. locust, grasshopper; young locust, possibly some stage in the development of the locust:– cankerworm [6], caterpillars [3]

3219 יַלְקוּט **yalqûṭ**, n.[m.]. GK: 3541 [→ 3950]. pouch:– scrip [1]

3220 יָם **yām**, n.m. GK: 3542 [cf. 39; cf. 3221]. sea; seashore; the west (the direction of the Mediterranean Sea relative to the Near East); by extension: a large container for holding water; the recurring image of the sea as a terrifying danger and opponent of the LORD has its source in the Sea (Yamm) as a hostile Canaanite god:– sea [297], west [33], seas [24], westward (+1886.5) [21], west [+1886.5] [15], west side [3], seafaring [1], south [1], western [1]

3221 יָם **yam** (Aram.), n.m. GK: 10322 [cf. 3220]. a body of water usually referring to ocean, sea, or lake; fig., the nether regions of mystery, chaos, and monsters:– sea [2]

3222 יַמִּם **yēmim**, n.[m.]. GK: 3553 [→ 3224?]. hot springs; traditionally: mules; others: adders:– mules [1]

3223 יְמוּאֵל **yᵉmû'ēl**, n.pr.m. GK: 3543 [cf. 5241]. Jemuel:– Jemuel [1]

3224 יְמִימָה **yᵉmîmâ**, n.pr.f. GK: 3544 [→ 3222?]. Jemimah, "dove":– Jemima [1]

3225 יָמִין **yāmîn**, n.f. GK: 3545 [→ 541, 1144, 1145, 1968?, 3226, 3228, 3233, 8486, 8488]. (direction) right; south, southward (south is right when facing east, the direction of orientation in the ancient Near East); the right is considered culturally to be stronger and of greater prestige than the left; to be seated on the right side of a ruler is a greater position than on the left side:– right hand [106], right [22], right side [6], south [3], lefthanded (+334+3027) [2]

3226 יָמִין **yāmîn**, n.pr.m. GK: 3546 [→ 3228; cf. 3225]. Jamin, "[poss.] right hand; south, an indication of [good] fortune":– Jamin [6]

3227 יְמִינִי **yᵉmînî**, a.g. GK: 3549 [→ 1144]. Benjamite, "of Benjamin":– Benjamite (+376) [2], Benjamite (+376+1121) [1]

3228 יְמִינִי **yāmînî**, a.g. GK: 3547 [→ 3226; cf. 3225]. Jaminite, "of Jamin":– Benjamites [1], Jaminites [1]

3229 יִמְלָא **yimlā'** or יִמְלָה **yimlâ**, n.pr.m. GK: 3550 & 3551 [→ 4390]. Imla, Imlah, "fullness":– Imlah [2], Imla [2]

3230 יַמְלֵךְ **yamlēk**, n.pr.m. GK: 3552 [→ 4427?]. "he will reign":– Jamlech [1]

3231 יָמַן **yāman**, v.den. GK: 3554 [→ 541, 3225]. [H] to go the right; (ptcp.) right-handed:– go to the right [1], on the right hand [1], turn to the right hand [1], use the right hand [1]

3232 יִמְנָה **yimnâ**, n.pr.m. GK: 3555 [→ 4487]. Imnah; Imnite, "good fortune":– Imnah [2], Jimnah [1], Jimna [1], Jimnites [1]

3233 יְמָנִי **yᵉmānî**, a. GK: 3556 & 3548 [→ 3225]. (direction) right:– right [32], right hand [1]

3234 יִמְנָע **yimnā'**, n.pr.m. GK: 3557 [→ 4513]. Imna, "[poss.] he is withheld; luck, fortune":– Imna [1]

3235 יָמַר **yāmar**, v. GK: 3558. [H] to change, exchange:– boast [1], changed [1]

3236 יִמְרָה **yimrâ**, n.pr.m. GK: 3559 [→ 4784]. Imrah, "he rebels":– Imrah [1]

3237 יָמַשׁ **yāmaš**, v. GK: 3560 [cf. 4184, 4959]. [H] to touch:–

3238 יָנָה **yānâ**, v. GK: 3561 & 3435. [Q] to oppress, to crush; [H] to mistreat, take advantage of, oppress:– oppress [5], oppressed [3], oppressing [3], vexed [2], vex [2], destroy [1], do wrong [1], oppressor [1]

3239 יָנוֹחַ **yānôaḥ** or יָנוֹחָה **yānôḥâ**, n.pr.loc. GK: 3562 & 3563 [→ 3240]. Janoah, Janohah, "resting place":– Janohah [2], Janoah [1]

יָנוּם **yānum**. See 3241.

3240 יָנַח **yānaḥ**, v. GK: 5663 [→ 2010, 3239, 4494, 4495, 4496, 4506, 5117, 5118, 5119?, 5183, 5184, 5207]. same as 5117: [Q] to settle, rest, wait; [H] to put, keep, settle, rest; to leave, allow; [Ho] to be placed, find rest:– leave [13], left [11], set [6], lay up [5], lay [5], put [5], let alone [4], laid [3], suffer [3], placed [2], set down [2], suffered [2], bestowed [1], cast down [1], laid down [1], leave off [1], pacifieth [1], place [1], remain still [1], withdraw [1], withhold [1]

3241 יָנוּם **yānûm** or יָנִם **yānîm**, n.pr.loc. GK: 3564 & 3565 [→ 5123?]. Janum, Janim:– Janum [1]

3242 יְנִיקָה **yᵉnîqâ**, n.f. GK: 3566 [→ 3243]. shoot (of a plant):– young twigs [1]

3243 יָנַק **yānaq**, v. GK: 3567 & 4787 [→ 689, 3126, 3127, 3242; cf. 5134]. [Q] to suck, be nursing; [H] to give nourishment, nurse:– nurse [7], suck [7], sucking child [3], sucklings [3], suckling [3], give suck [2], gave suck [1], given suck [1], made to suck [1], milch [1], nursing mothers [1], sucked [1], those that suck [1]

3244 יַנְשׁוּף **yanšûp**, n.[m.]. GK: 3568 [→ 5398]. great owl (an unclean bird, variously identified):– great owl [2], owl [1]

3245 יָסַד **yāsad**, v. GK: 3569 & 3570 [→ 3246, 3247, 3248, 4143, 4144, 4145, 4146, 4328, 4527; cf. 5475]. [Q] to lay a foundation, establish, ordain; [N] to be founded; to associate, conspire (together); [P] to lay a foundation, establish; [Pu, Ho] to be founded, have a foundation laid:– founded [8], foundation laid [7], laid foundation [5], established [2], foundation [2], laid foundations [2], lay foundations [2], lay foundation [2], appointed [1], instructed [1], laid [1], lay for a foundation [1], lay the foundation [1], layeth foundation [1], ordained [1], ordain [1], set [1], sure foundation (+4143) [1], take counsel [1], took counsel [1]

3246 יְסוּד **yᵉsud**, n.[m.]. GK: 3571 [→ 3245]. foundation, beginning:– began [1]

3247 יְסוֹד **yᵉsôd**, n.f. & m. GK: 3572 [→ 3245]. foundation; base (of an altar); foot (base of the body); by extension: what is firm or enduring:– bottom [9], foundation [7], foundations [3], repairing [1]

3248 יְסוּדָה **yᵉsûdâ**, n.f. GK: 3573 [→ 3245]. foundation:– foundation [1]

3249 יָסוּר **yāsûr**, var. GK: 6073 [→ 5627, 5493; cf. 5494, 5495]. one who departs:–

3250 יִסּוֹר **yissôr**, n.m. GK: 3574 [→ 3256]. corrector, fault-finder, reprover:– instruct [1]

3251 יָסַךְ **yāsak**, v. GK: 3575 [cf. 5258, 5480]. same as 5480: [Q] to anoint, to use oils or perfumes or lotions:– poured [1]

3252 יִסְכָּה **yiskâ**, n.pr.f. GK: 3576. Iscah:– Iscah [1]

3253 יִסְמַכְיָהוּ **yismakyāhû**, n.pr.m. GK: 3577 [→ 5564+3068]. Ismakiah, "Yahweh sustains":– Ismachiah [1]

3254 יָסַף **yāsap**, v. GK: 3578 [→ 23, 43, 460, 3130, 3131; cf. 3084, cf. 3255]. [Q] to add to, to do once more, to do again; [N] to be added to, to gain more, to be joined; [H] to increase, to cause to add to, to continue on, to add to, to happen again:– again [40], more [39], add [22], more (+5750) [10], any more [7], henceforth [6], again (+5750) [5], increaseth [5], yet again (+5750) [5], increased [4], increase [4], put [4], added [3], addeth [3], further [3], any more (+5750) [2], continued (+5375) [2], do more [2], exceed [2], make so many moe [2], more and more [2], yet the more (+5750) [2], added more [1], any more at all [1], bring more [1], bring [1], came again [1], came more [1], can more (+5750) [1], caused again [1], cease [1], do again (+5750) [1], done [1], exceedest [1], exceedeth [1], gave [1], gotten more [1], increase (+5921) [1], increase more and more [1], increased more [1], join [1], longer [1], maketh [1], more (+5750+3807.1) [1], more also (+3541) [1], more also [1], more and more (+3605+5921) [1], moreover given [1], proceed further [1], proceeded [1], proceed [1], prolong life (+3117+3117+5921) [1], prolongeth [1], put more [1], set again [1], stronger and stronger (+555) [1], yet more (+5750) [1], yield [1]

3255 יְסַף **yᵉsap** (Aram.), v. GK: 10323 [cf. 3254]. [Ho] to be added:– added [1]

3256 יָסַר **yāsar**, v. GK: 3579 & 3580 & 3581 [→ 3250, 4148, 4561]. [Q] to correct, discipline; [N] to accept correction, be warned, be disciplined; [P] to punish, correct, discipline; to instruct, train; to strengthen; [H] to catch; [Nitpael] to let oneself take warning:– chastised [6], chastise [6], correct [6], instructed [5], chasten [3], instruct [3], chastened sore (+3256) [2], chasteneth [2], taught [2], bound [1], chastened [1], chastenest [1], chastiseth [1], corrected [1], punish [1], reformed [1], reproveth [1]

3257 יָע **yā'**, n.[m.]. GK: 3582 [→ 3261]. shovel (for altar fires):– shovels [9]

3258 יַעְבֵּץ **ya'bēṣ**, n.pr.m. & loc. GK: 3583 & 3584. Jabez, "to grieve":– Jabez [4]

3259 יָעַד **yā'ad**, v. GK: 3585 [→ 4150, 4151, 4152, 5129; cf. 5712]. [Q] to select, appoint, set out; [N] to meet with, assemble, band together, join forces; [H] to summon, challenge; [Ho] to be set, be ordered:– meet [7], appointed [3], assembled [3], gathered together [3], appoint the time [2], betrothed [2], set [2], agreed [1], assemble [1], gather [1], made an appointment [1], meet together [1], met together [1], set a time [1]

3260 יֶעְדּוֹ **ye'dô** or יַעְדִּי **ye'dî**, n.pr.m. GK: 3587 & 3588 [→ 5710 or 5716]. Iddo, Iddi, "[prob.] Yahweh has adorned":– Iddo [1]

יְעְדּוֹ **yᵉ'dô**. See 3260.

3261 יָעָה **yā'â**, v. GK: 3589 [→ 3257, 3262?, 3273?]. [Q] to sweep away:– sweep away [1]

3262 יְעוּאֵל **yᵉ'û'ēl**, n.pr.m. GK: 3590 [→ 3273]. Jeuel, "God [El] has preserved":– Jeuel [1]

3263 יְעוּץ **yᵉ'ûṣ**, n.pr.m. GK: 3591 [→ 3268]. Jeuz, "he comes to help; [poss.] encouraged":– Jeuz [1]

3264 יָעוֹר **ya'ôr**, n.m. GK: 3623 [→ 3293, 3295]. same as 3293: forest, woods, thicket:–

3265 יָעוּר **yā'ûr** or יָעִיר **yā'îr**, n.pr.m. GK: 3592 & 3600 [→ 5782]. Jaur, Jair, "he gives light":– Jair [1]

3266 יְעוּשׁ **yᵉ'ûš**, n.pr.m. GK: 3593 [→ 5789; cf. 3274]. Jeush, "[perhaps] may God aid":– Jeush [8], Jehush [1]

3267 יָעַז **yā'az**, v. GK: 3594 [cf. 5810]. [N] to be arrogant, be insolent:– fierce [1]

3268 יַעֲזִיאֵל **ya'ăzî'ēl**, n.pr.m. GK: 3595. Jaaziel, "God [El] strengthens":– Jaaziel [1]

3269 יַעֲזִיָּהוּ **ya'ăziyyāhû**, n.pr.m. GK: 3596. Jaaziah, "may Yahweh nourish":– Jaaziah [2]

3270 יַעֲזֵיר **ya'ăzêr**, n.pr.loc. GK: 3597 [→ 5826]. Jazer, "he helps":– Jazer [11], Jaazer [2]

3271 יָעַט **yā'aṭ**, v. GK: 3598 [cf. 5844]. [Q] to array, cover:– covered with [1]

3272 יְעַט **yᵉ'aṭ** (Aram.), v. GK: 10324 & 10325 [→ 5843; cf. 3289]. [Itpa] to take counsel together, implying mutual agreement and choices:– counsellers [2], consulted together [1]

3273 יְעִיאֵל **yᵉ'î'ēl**, n.pr.m. GK: 3599 [→ 3262]. Jeiel, "God [El] has preserved; [poss.] God [El] sweeps up":– Jeiel [11], Jehiel [2]

יָעִיר **yā'îr**. See 3265.

3274 יְעִישׁ **yᵉ'îš**, n.pr.m. GK: 3601 [→ 5789; cf. 3266]. Jeish:–

3275 יַעְכָּן **ya'kān**, n.pr.m. GK: 3602. Jacan:– Jachan [1]

3276 יָעַל **yā'al**, v. GK: 3603 [→ 1100]. [H] to have value, have use, have value, have benefit:– profit [17], profit at all (+3276) [2], do good [1], profitable [1], profiteth [1], set forward [1]

3277 יָעֵל **yā'ēl**, n.[m.]. GK: 3604 [→ 3278, 3279, 3280]. mountain goat, wild goat:– wild goats [3]

3278 יָעֵל **yā'ēl**, n.pr.f. GK: 3605 [→ 3277]. Jael, "mountain goat":– Jael [6]

3279 יַעֲלָא **ya'ălā'** or יַעֲלָה **ya'ălâ**, n.pr.m. GK: 3606 & 3608 [→ 3280; cf. 3277]. Jaala, Jaalah:– Jaalah [1], Jaala [1]

3280 יַעֲלָה **ya'ălâ**, n.f. GK: 3607 [→ 3279; cf. 3277]. (female) mountain goat, ibex; deer:– roe [1]

3281 יַעְלָם **ya'lām**, n.pr.m. GK: 3609 [→ 5934]. Jalam:– Jaalam [4]

3282 יַעַן **ya'an**, subst.pp.c. GK: 3610 [→ 6031]. for, because, since:– because [56], because [+834] [19], forasmuch as (+834) [5], because (+3588) [3], because (+3282+871.1) [2], because (+871.1) [2], because of [2], because that [2], as [1], forasmuch as (+3588) [1], forsomuch as (+3588) [1], seeing then [1], that (+834) [1], therefore [1], whereas (+834) [1]

3283 יָעֵן **yā'ēn**, n.[m.]. GK: 3612 [cf. 3284]. (male) ostrich:– ostriches [1]

3284 יַעֲנָה **ya'ănâ**, n.f. GK: 3613 [cf. 3283]. owl; horned owl:– owls (+1323) [6], owl (+1323) [2]

3285 יַעֲנַי **ya'nay**, n.pr.m. GK: 3614 [→ 6030?]. Janai, "he will answer":– Jaanai [1]

3286 יָעֵף **yā'ēp**, v. GK: 3615 [→ 3287, 3288; cf. 5774, 5889]. [Q] to grow tired, be faint, exhaust oneself:– weary [4], faint [3], caused to fly [1], fainteth [1]

3287 יָעֵף **yā'ēp**, a.g. GK: 3617 [→ 3286]. weary, exhausted, fatigued:– faint [1], weary [1]

3288 יְעָף **yᵉ'āp**, n.[m.]. GK: 3618 & 3616. flight; some source: tiredness, weariness:– swiftly (+871.1) [1]

3289 יָעַץ **yā'aṣ**, v. GK: 3619 & 3446 [→ 4156, 6098; cf. 5779; cf. 3272]. [Q] to give advise, give counsel; to purpose, plan, plot, determine; [Qp] to be determined; [N] to seek advise, consult; to confer, to plot (together); [Ht] to consult together, conspire against:– counsellers [12], counseller [10], consulted [7],

purposed [5], took counsel [5], counselled [4], counsel [3], take counsel [3], taken counsel [3], counsel gave (+6098) [2], counsel given (+6098) [2], counsel give [2], determined [2], deviseth [2], give counsel (+6098) [2], give counsel [2], taken [2], took counsel with [2], advertise [1], advise [1], advise [1], consulted with [1], consult [1], given counsel [1], guide [1], taken counsel (+6098) [1], took advice [1], well advised [1]

3290 יׇעֲקֹב *ya*ʿ*qōb*, n.pr.m. & g. GK: 3620 [cf. 6119?, 6120?]. Jacob, "*follower, replacer, one who follows at the heel*":– Jacob [332], Jacob's [16], Jacob's (+3807.1) [1]

3291 יׇעֲקֹבׇה *ya*ʿ*qōbâ*, n.pr.m. GK: 3621. Jaakobah, "*may [deity] protect*":– Jaakobah [1]

3292 יׇעְקׇן *ya*ʿ*qān*, n.pr.loc. GK: 3622 [→ 885; cf. 6130?]. Jaakan:– Jaakan [1], Jakan [1]

3293 יׇעַר *ya'ar*, n.m. & pr. GK: 3623 & 3624 & 3625 [→ 3264, 3295]. forest, woods, thicket; (cultivated) tree groves; honeycomb; as n.pr. Jaar:– forest [37], wood [18], forests [1], honeycomb [1], woods [1]

3294 יׇעְרׇה *ya'râ* or יׇעְדׇה *ya'dâ*, n.pr.m. GK: 3628 & 3586 [→ 5710?]. Jarah, Jadah, "*honeycomb*":– Jarah [2]

3295 יׇעְרׇה *ya'râ*, n.f. GK: 3626 & 3627 [→ 3264, 3293]. forest; honeycomb:– forests [1], honeycomb (+1706+1886.1) [1]

3296 יׇעֲרֵי אֹרְגִים *ya*ʿ*rê 'ōr^egīm*, n.pr.m. GK: 3629. Jaare-Oregim:– Jaare-oregim [1]

3297 יׇעֲרִים *ya*ʿ*ārīm*, n.pr.loc. GK: 3630 [→ 7157]. Jearim, "*timberlands*":– Jearim [1]

3298 יׇעֲרֶשְׁיׇה *ya*ʿ*rešyâ*, n.pr.m. GK: 3631 [→ 3068]. Jaareshiah, "*Yahweh plants*":– Jaresiah [1]

3299 יׇעֲשׂוּ *ya*ʿ*śû* or יׇעֲשָׂי *ya*ʿ*śāy*, n.pr.m. GK: 3632 & 3633 [→ 6213]. Jaasu, Jaasai:– Jaasau [1]

3300 יׇעֲשִׂיאֵל *ya*ʿ*śî'ēl*, n.pr.m. GK: 3634 [→ 6213+410]. Jaasiel, "*God [El] does*":– Jaasiel [1], Jasiel [1]

3301 יִפְדְיׇה *yipd^eyâ*, n.pr.m. GK: 3635. Iphdeiah, "*Yahweh redeems*":– Iphedeiah [1]

3302 יׇפׇה *yāpâ*, v. GK: 3636 [→ 3303, 3304, 3305?, 3308]. [Q] to be beautiful, delightful; [P] to adorn, make beautiful; [Ht] to adorn oneself:– fair [3], beautiful [2], deck [1], fairer [1], make fair [1]

3303 יׇפֶה *yāpeh*, a. GK: 3637 [→ 3302]. beautiful, fair, lovely, handsome:– fair [20], beautiful [5], well [5], fairest [3], beautiful (+8389) [2], fair one [2], beauty [1], comely [1], fair (+8389) [1], goodly (+8389) [1], pleasant [1]

3304 יְפֵה־פִיׇה *y^epêpiyyâ* or יְפֵה־פִיׇה *y^epēh-piyyâ*, a.f. GK: 3645 & 3638 [→ 3302]. beautiful, pretty:– very fair [1]

3305 יׇפוֹ *yāpô*, n.pr.loc. GK: 3639 [→ 3302?]. Joppa, "*beautiful*":– Joppa [3], Japho [1]

3306 יׇפַח *yāpaḥ*, v. GK: 3640 [→ 3307; cf. 6315]. [Ht] to gasp for breath:– bewaileth [1]

3307 יׇפֵחַ *yāpēaḥ*, a. GK: 3641 [→ 3306]. breathing out, with a strong implication that this breath results in an action or communication:– breathe out [1]

3308 יְפִי *y^epî*, n.m. GK: 3642 [→ 3302]. beauty:– beauty [19]

3309 יׇפִיעַ *yāpîa*ʿ, n.pr.m. & loc. GK: 3644 [→ 3313]. Japhia, "*[perhaps] may the deity shine*":– Japhia [5]

3310 יׇפְלֵט *yaplēṭ*, n.pr.m. GK: 3646 [→ 3311; cf. 6403]. Japhlet, "*he delivers;* [poss.] *he escapes*":– Japhlet [3]

3311 יׇפְלֵטִי *yaplēṭî*, a.g. GK: 3647 [→ 3310; cf. 6403]. Japhletite, "*of Japhlet*":– Japhleti [1]

3312 יְפֻנֶּה *y^epunneh*, n.pr.m. GK: 3648 [→ 6437]. Jephunneh, "*[perhaps] may he [God] turn or turned*":– Jephunneh [16]

3313 יׇפַע *yāpa*ʿ, v. GK: 3649 [→ 3309, 3314]. [H] to shine forth, flash; smile:– shine [2], caused to shine [1], light [1], shew [1], shine forth [1], shined forth [1], shined [1]

3314 יִפְעׇה *yip'â*, n.f. GK: 3650 [→ 3313]. shining splendor:– brightness [2]

3315 יֶפֶת *yepet*, n.pr.m. GK: 3651 [→ 6601]. Japheth, "*enlarge*":– Japheth [11]

3316 יִפְתׇּח *yiptāḥ*, n.pr.m. & loc. GK: 3652 & 3653 [→ 6605]. Jephthah, Iphtah, "*Yahweh opens, frees*":– Jephthah [29], Jiphtah [1]

3317 יִפְתַּח־אֵל *yiptāḥ-'ēl*, n.pr.loc. GK: 3654 [→ 6605+410]. Iphtah El, "*God [El] opens*":– Jiphthah-el [2]

3318 יׇצׇא *yāṣā'*, v. GK: 3655 & 3448 [→ 3329, 4161, 4162, 4163, 6631, 6792, 8444]. [Q] to go out, come out; [H] to bring out, lead forth; produce; [Ho] to be brought out; emptied; by extension: to grow (of plants), to have offspring:– went out [162], go forth [92], go out [82], brought forth [70], came out [63], went forth [54], brought out [51], come out [48], bring forth [39], came forth [35], come forth [35], bring out [32], gone out [18], goeth out [13], bringeth forth [12], goeth forth [12], gone forth [12], cometh forth [10], departed [10], going out [10], carry forth [9], came [8], carry out [7], proceed [7], bringeth out [6], cometh out [6], proceedeth [6], goest out [5], broughtest out [4], camest forth [4], get out [4], goeth [4], issued out [4], broughtest forth [3], cometh [3], depart [3], going forth [3], go [3], lieth out [3], utter [3], assuredly go forth (+3318) [2], at any time come (+3318) [2], bring up [2], bring [2], brought up [2], brought [2], camest out [2], carried out [2], coming out [2], failed [2], go on [2], goest forth [2], got [2], have forth [2], issue [2], laid out [2], leddest out [2], proceeded [2], put away [2], scarce gone out (+3318) [2], surely come out (+3318) [2], surely go forth (+3318) [2], uttereth [2], westest forth [2], after (+3509.1+6259) [1], appeared [1], bear out [1], begotten [1], be [1], break out [1], bringing forth [1], bringing out [1], bringing up [1], brought forth out of [1], brought forth out [1], brought of [1], camest [1], carried forth [1], carry forth out [1], carry [1], cause to go out [1], caused to go forth [1], come abroad [1], departing [1], departure [1], do^s [1], draw forth [1], drawn forth [1], drew forth [1], end [1], escaped [1], escape [1], exacted [1], fall out [1], falleth [1], fell out [1], fell [1], fet forth [1], fetch [1], followed (+310) [1], get away [1], get forth [1], get hence [1], go away [1], go way forth [1], goeth on [1], grow [1], have out [1], in departing [1], issue out [1], lead out [1], out [1], pluck out [1], plucked out [1], proceed out [1], pull out [1], risen [1], shooteth forth [1], spread [1], spring out [1], springeth out [1], stand out [1], take forth [1], took out [1], to [1], uttered [1], westest out [1], went [1]

3319 שֵׁיצִיא *šêṣî'* or יְצׇא *y^eṣā'* (Aram.), v. GK: 10707. [Sh] to complete, finish:– finished [1]

3320 יׇצַב *yāṣab*, v. GK: 3656 [cf. 5324; cf. 3321]. [Ht] to stand one's ground, confront; to stand before, present oneself, commit oneself:– stand [16], stood [7], present [5], set [5], presented [4], stand still [2], stand up [2], able to withstand (+5973) [1], remaining [1], resorted [1], setteth [1], stand fast [1], stand forth [1], standing [1]

3321 יְצַב *y^eṣab* (Aram.), v. GK: 10326 [→ 3330; cf. 3320]. [Pa] to make certain, to know the truth:– know the truth [1]

3322 יׇצַג *yāṣag*, v. GK: 3657 [cf. 3332]. [H] to set, place, present; touch; [Ho] to be left behind:– set [8], made [2], put [2], establish [1], leave [1], presented [1], stayed [1]

3323 יִצְהׇר *yiṣhār*, n.[m.]. GK: 3658 [→ 3324, 3325; cf. 6671]. olive oil:– oil [22], anointed [1]

3324 יִצְהׇר *yiṣhār*, n.pr.m. GK: 3659 [→ 3323; cf. 6671]. Izhar, "*the shining one*":– Izhar [8], Izehar [1]

3325 יִצְהׇרִי *yiṣhārî*, a.g. GK: 3660 [→ 3323; cf. 6671]. Izharite, "*of Izhar*":– Izharites [2], Izeharites [1]

3326 יׇצוּעַ *yāṣûa*ʿ or יׇצִיעַ *yāṣîa*ʿ, n.m. GK: 3661 & 3662 & 3666 [→ 3331]. bed, couch; structure, room, often referring to an annex, wing, or level of a building:– bed [3], chambers [2], bed (+6210) [1], chamber [1], couch [1]

3327 יִצְחׇק *yiṣḥāq*, n.pr.m. GK: 3663 [→ 6711; cf. 3446]. Isaac, "*he laugh, he will laugh* or *mock; [God] laughs*":– Isaac [104], Isaac's [4]

3328 יִצְחׇר *yiṣhār*, n.pr.m. GK: 3664 [cf. 6714]. Jizhar:– Jezoar [1]

3329 יׇצִיא *yāṣî'*, a. GK: 3665 [→ 3318]. coming forth:– came forth [1]

3330 יַצִּיב *yaṣṣîb* (Aram.), a. GK: 10327 [→ 3321]. certain, true, reliable:– true [2], certainty [1], certain [1], truth [1]

יׇצִיעַ *yāṣîa*ʿ. See 3326.

3331 יׇצַע *yāṣa*ʿ, v. GK: 3667 [→ 3326, 4702]. [H] to spread out bedding; [Ho] to be spread out:– spread [2], lay [1], make bed [1]

3332 יׇצַק *yāṣaq*, v. GK: 3668 [→ 3333, 4164, 4166, 4690?, 6694?; cf. 3322]. [Q] to pour out, cast out; [Qp] to be cast out, be poured out, be smelted; [H] to pour out, spread out; [Ho] to be poured out, be washed away; be anointed:– cast [11], pour [11], poured [9], molten [6], poured out [4], firm [2], pour out [2], cleaveth fast [1], groweth [1], hard [1], laid out [1], overflown [1], ran out [1], set down [1], steadfast [1]

3333 יְצֻקׇה *y^eṣuqâ*, n.f. GK: 3669 [→ 3332]. casting (of metal), with a focus that this is one piece:– cast [1]

3334 יׇצַר *yāṣar*, v. GK: 7674 [→ 4712, 6862, 6869, 6872, 6887; cf. 6696]. same as 6887: [Q] to bind up, wrap up, tie up; to hamper, oppress, be in distress; [Qp] be bound, be confined; [Pu] to be mended; [H] to bring trouble, distress, oppress:– distressed [4], straitened [2], in straits [1], narrow [1], vexed [1]

3335 יׇצַר *yāṣar*, v. GK: 3670 & 3450 [→ 3336, 3337, 3338, 3339, 3340]. [Q] to form, fashion, shape, create; (of God) the Maker, the Creator; [N] to be formed; [Pu] to be formed; [Ho] to be forged, be formed; usually from existing material; God as Creator or Maker, has its focus his planning and forming the creation as a skilled craftsman:– formed [23], potter [8], potter's [7], maker [4], fashioneth [3], fashioned [2], former [2], formeth [2], made [2], earthen [1], form [1], framed [1], frameth [1], frame [1], make [1], potters' [1], potters [1], purposed [1]

3336 יֵצֶר *yēṣer*, n.m. GK: 3671 [→ 3337; cf. 3335]. something formed, creation; inclination, disposition, motivation:– imagination [4], frame [1], imaginations [1], mind [1], thing framed [1], work [1]

3337 יֵצֶר *yēṣer*, n.pr.m. GK: 3672 [→ 3339, 3340; cf. 3335, 3336]. Jezer, "*formed, fashioned*":– Jezer [3]

3338 יְצֻרִים *y^eṣurîm*, n.m.pl. GK: 3674 [→ 3335]. frame, body, limbs, that which gives visible form to a person:– members [1]

3339 יִצְרִי *yiṣrî*, a.g. & n.pr.m. GK: 3673 [→ 3337; cf. 3335]. same as 3340: Izri; Jezerite, "*Yahweh designs*":– Izri [1]

3340 יִצְרִי *yiṣrî*, a.g. & n.pr.m. GK: 3673 [→ 3337]. same as 3339: Izri; Jezerite, "*Yahweh designs*":– Jezerites [1]

3341 יׇצַת *yāṣat*, v. GK: 3675 [cf. 6702]. [Q] to set ablaze; [N] to burn, be burned; [H] to kindle, set on fire:– kindle [8], burnt [7], set [6], kindled [4], burnt up [2], desolate [1], set on [1]

3342 יֶקֶב *yeqeb*, n.m. GK: 3676 [cf. 5344]. winepress; (wine or oil) vat:– winepress [7], fats [2], presses [2], winepresses [2], pressfat [1], wine presses [1], wine [1]

3343 יְקַבְצְאֵל *y^eqabṣ^e'ēl*, n.pr.loc. GK: 3677 [→ 6908+410]. Jekabzeel, "*God [El] gathers*":– Jekabzeel [1]

3344 יׇקַד *yāqad*, v. GK: 3678 & 3683 [→ 3350, 4168, 4169; cf. 3345, cf. 3346]. [Q] to burn; to kindle a fire; [Qp or n.m.] hearth (of a fireplace); [Ho] to be burning, be kindled:– burning [3], burn [3], burneth [1], hearth [1], kindle [1]

3345 יְקַד *y^eqad* (Aram.), v. GK: 10328 [→ 3346; cf. 3344]. [P] to burn:– burning [8]

3346 יְקֵדׇה *y^eqēdâ* (Aram.), n.f. GK: 10329 [→ 3345]. blazing, burning:– burning [1]

3347 יׇקְדְעׇם *yoqd^e'ām*, n.pr.loc. GK: 3680. Jokdeam:– Jokdeam [1]

3348 יׇקֶה *yāqeh*, n.pr.m. GK: 3681. Jakeh, "*prudent*":– Jakeh [1]

3349 יְקׇהׇה *y^eqāhâ*, n.f. GK: 3682. obedience:– gathering [1], obey [1]

3350 יְקוֹד *y^eqôd*, n.[m.]. GK: 3679 [→ 3344]. blazing, burning:– burning [2]

3351 יְקוּם *y^eqûm*, n.[m.]. GK: 3685 [→ 6965]. living thing, living creature:– living substance [2], substance [1]

3352 יׇקוֹשׁ *yāqôš*, n.[m.]. GK: 3686 [→ 3369]. fowler, bait-layer:– fowler [1]

3353 יׇקוּשׁ *yāqûš*, n.[m.]. GK: 3687 [→ 3369]. fowler, one who snares birds:– fowler [2], snares [1]

3354 יְקוּתִיאֵל *y^eqûtî'ēl*, n.pr.m. GK: 3688. Jekuthiel, "*God [El] will nourish*":– Jekuthiel [1]

3355 יׇקְטׇן *yoqṭān*, n.pr.m. GK: 3690 [→ 3364]. Joktan, "*smaller*":– Joktan [6]

3356 יׇקִים *yāqîm*, n.pr.m. GK: 3691 [→ 6965]. Jakim, "*he will establish*":– Jakim [2]

3357 יׇקִּיר *yaqqîr*, a. GK: 3692 [→ 3365; cf. 3358]. dear, precious:– dear [1]

3358 יׇקִּיר *yaqqîr* (Aram.), a. GK: 10330 [→ 3367; cf. 3366]. honorable; difficult, with an implication that such difficulty makes something unlikely or improbable:– noble [1], rare [1]

3359 יְקַמְיׇה *y^eqamyâ*, n.pr.m. GK: 3693 [→ 6965+3068]. Jekamiah, "*Yahweh will establish*":– Jekamiah [2], Jecamiah [1]

3360 יְקַמְעׇם *y^eqam'ām*, n.pr.m. GK: 3694 [→ 6965+5971]. Jekameam, "*[my] kinsman establishes*":– Jekameam [1]

3361 יׇקְמְעׇם *yoqm^e'ām*, n.pr.loc. GK: 3695 [→ 3362?]. Jokmeam, "*let the people arise*":– Jokmeam [1], Jokneam [1]

3362 יָקְנְעָם *yoqn^e'ām*, n.pr.loc. GK: 3696 [→ 3361?]. Jokneam:– Jokneam [3].

3363 יָקַע *yāqa'*, v. GK: 3697 [cf. 5361]. [Q] to turn (away), wrench; [H] to kill and expose; [Ho] to be killed and exposed:– alienated [2], hang up [2], hanged [2], depart [1], out of joint [1]

3364 יָקַץ *yāqaṣ*, v. GK: 3699 [→ 3355; cf. 6972]. [Q] to wake up, awake:– awoke [6], awaked [4], awake [1]

יָקַף *yāqap*. See 5362.

3365 יָקַר *yāqar*, v. GK: 3700 [→ 3357, 3368, 3366]. [Q] to be precious, be costly; become well known; [H] to make scarce:– precious [7], make precious [1], prised [1], set by [1], withdraw [1]

3366 יְקָר *y^eqār*, n.m. GK: 3702 [→ 3365; cf. 3367]. honor, splendor, riches, valuable things:– honour [12], precious things [2], precious thing [1], precious [1], price [1]

3367 יְקָר *y^eqār* (Aram.), n.m. GK: 10331 [→ 3358; cf. 3366]. glory, honor, majesty:– glory [5], honour [2]

3368 יָקָר *yāqār*, a. GK: 3701 [→ 3365]. precious, valuable, quality, pertaining to items that are rare, beloved, or splendid:– precious [25], costly [4], excellent [2], brightness [1], clear [1], fat [1], honourable [1], reputation [1]

3369 יָקַשׁ *yāqaš*, v. GK: 3704 [→ 3352, 3353, 3370, 4170; cf. 5367, 6983]. [Q] to lay a bird snare, set a trap; [N, Pu] to be ensnared, be trapped:– snared [5], fowlers [1], laid a snare [1], laid [1]

3370 יָקְשָׁן *yoqšān*, n.pr.m. GK: 3705 [→ 3369]. Jokshan:– Jokshan [4]

3371 יָקְתְאֵל *yoqt^e'ēl*, n.pr.loc. GK: 3706 [→ 410]. Joktheel:– Joktheel [2]

יָרָא *yārā'*. See 3384.

3372 יָרֵא *yārē'*, v. GK: 3707 [→ 3373, 3374, 4172]. [Q] to be afraid, be frightened; to revere, respect; [N] to be awesome, be dreadful, be feared; [P] to frighten, terrify, intimidate; in some contexts fear relates to terror and fright, in other contexts fear relates to honor, respect and awe, as in "the fear of the LORD":– fear [146], afraid [75], feared [36], terrible [28], dreadful [5], feareth [2], fearful [2], made afraid [2], put in fear [2], reverence [2], affright [1], dread [1], durst not [1], exceedingly afraid (+1419+3374) [1], feared exceedingly (+1419+3374) [1], fearest [1], fearfully [1], fearing [1], had in reverence [1], reverend [1], terrible acts [1], terrible things [1], terribleness [1]

3373 יָרֵא *yārē'*, a.vbl. GK: 3710 [→ 3372]. fear; worship:– fear [35], feareth [11], feared [9], afraid [3], fearful [2], one that feareth [2], one that feared [1]

3374 יִרְאָה *yir'â*, n.f. GK: 3711 [→ 3372]. fear, reverence, piety:– fear [41], dreadful [1], exceedingly afraid (+1419+3372) [1], feared exceedingly (+1419+3372) [1], fearfulness [1]

3375 יִרְאוֹן *yir'ôn*, n.pr.loc. GK: 3712. Iron:– Iron [1]

3376 יִרְאִיָּיה *yir'iyyāyh*, n.pr.m. GK: 3713 [→ 7200+3068]. Irijah, "Yahweh sees":– Irijah [2]

3377 יָרֵב *yārēb*, n.m. GK: 3714 [→ 7231]. great (king):– Jareb [2]

3378 יְרֻבַּעַל *y^erubba'al*, n.pr.m. GK: 3715 [→ 7231+1167]. Jerub-Baal, "Baal contends":– Jerubbaal [14]

3379 יָרָבְעָם *yārob'ām*, n.pr.m. GK: 3716 [→ 7231+5971]. Jeroboam, "the people increase":– Jeroboam [102], Jeroboam's [2]

3380 יְרֻבֶּשֶׁת *y^erubbešet*, n.pr.m. GK: 3717 [→ 7231+954]. Jerub-Besheth, "Shame [Baal] contends":– Jerubbesheth [1]

3381 יָרַד *yārad*, v. GK: 3718 [→ 3383, 4174]. [Q] to come down, go down, descend; [H] to bring down, lower; [Ho] to be brought down, be taken down:– go down [73], went down [63], come down [53], came down [41], bring down [26], brought down [17], gone down [14], descended [12], get down [9], descend [6], goeth down [5], let down [5], run down [5], took down [4], camest down [3], cast down [3], take down [3], bringeth down [2], came indeed down (+3381) [2], carry down [2], cause to come down [2], coming down [2], down [2], fell [2], runneth down [2], abundantly [1], casteth down [1], caused to run down [1], cometh down [1], descending [1], goeth down [1], hang down [1], let fall down [1], lighted down [1], lighted [1], put down [1], put off [1], ran down [1], sank [1], subdued [1], taken down [1], went down [1]

3382 יֶרֶד *yered*, n.pr.m. GK: 3719. Jared; Jered, "rose; servant":– Jared [5], Jered [2]

3383 יַרְדֵּן *yardēn*, n.pr.loc. GK: 3720 [→ 3381]. Jordan, "descending":– Jordan [182]

3384 יָרָה *yārâ*, v. GK: 3721 & 3722 & 3723 & 3452 [→ 3385, 3406, 3412, 4175, 4176, 8451, 8452]. [Q] to throw, cast; shoot; [N] to be shot through; [H] to shoot (an arrow), to hurl; to water upon, rain, shower; to teach, instruct, give guidance, in a formal or informal setting, with an implied authority for the teacher and the content of what is taught; [Ho] to be refreshed:– teach [33], shoot [11], shot [6], taught [5], cast [4], archers [3], teachers [3], teacheth [3], shot through (+3384) [2], archers (+376+7198+871.1+1886.1) [2], casteth [1], direct [1], former rain [1], inform [1], instructed [1], laid [1], rain [1], shewed [1], teacher [1], teaching [1], watered [1]

3385 יְרוּאֵל *y^erû'ēl*, n.pr.loc. GK: 3725 [→ 3384+410]. Jeruel, "God [El] is a foundation":– Jeruel [1]

3386 יָרוֹחַ *yārôaḥ*, n.pr.m. GK: 3726 [→ 3391]. Jaroah, "soft, delicate":– Jaroah [1]

3387 יָרוֹק *yārôq*, n.[m.]. GK: 3728 [→ 3418]. green plant:– green thing [1]

3388 יְרוּשָׁא *y^erûšā'* or יְרוּשָׁה *y^erûšâ*, n.pr.f. GK: 3729 & 3730 [→ 3423]. Jerusha, "possession":– Jerushah [1], Jerusha [1]

3389 יְרוּשָׁלַם *y^erûšālaim*, n.pr.loc. GK: 3731 [cf. 3390]. Jerusalem, "foundation of Shalem [peace]":– Jerusalem [640], Jerusalem's [3]

3390 יְרוּשְׁלֵם *y^erûš^elem* (Aram.), n.pr.loc. GK: 10332 [cf. 3389]. Jerusalem, "foundation of Shalem (peace)":– Jerusalem [26]

3391 יֶרַח *yerah*, n.m. GK: 3732 [→ 3386, 3392, 3394, 3405; cf. 732; cf. 3393]. moon; (lunar) month:– months [5], month [4], full month (+3117) [1], moon [2]

3392 יֶרַח *yerah*, n.pr.m. GK: 3733 [→ 3391]. Jerah, "moon [god?]":– Jerah [2]

3393 יְרַח *y^erah* (Aram.), n.m. GK: 10333 [cf. 3391]. month:– months [1], month [1]

3394 יָרֵחַ *yārēaḥ*, n.m. GK: 3734 [→ 3391]. moon:– moon [26]

יְרֵחוֹ *y^erēḥô*. See 3405.

3395 יְרֹחָם *y^erōḥām*, n.pr.m. GK: 3736 [→ 7355]. Jeroham, "he will be compassionate":– Jeroham [10]

3396 יְרַחְמְאֵל *y^eraḥm^e'ēl*, n.pr.m. GK: 3737 [→ 7355+410]. Jerahmeel, "God [El] will have compassion":– Jerahmeel [8]

3397 יְרַחְמְאֵלִי *y^eraḥm^e'ēlî*, a.g. GK: 3738 [→ 7355+410]. Jerahmeelite, "of Jerahmeel":– Jerahmeelites [2]

3398 יַרְחָע *yarḥā'*, n.pr.m. GK: 3739. Jarha:– Jarha [2]

3399 יָרַט *yāraṭ*, v. GK: 3740. [Q] to throw (into someone's custody); to be reckless, a fig. extension of going down a steep ravine:– perverse [1], turned over [1]

3400 יְרִיאֵל *y^erî'ēl*, n.pr.m. GK: 3741 [cf. 3404]. Jeriel, "founded of God [El]; God [El] will see":– Jeriel [1]

3401 יָרִיב *yārîb*, n.[m.]. GK: 3742 [→ 7378]. contender, accuser, adversary, opponent:– contend with [1], contendeth with [1], strive with [1]

3402 יָרִיב *yārîb*, n.pr.m. GK: 3743. Jarib, "Yahweh contends":– Jarib [3]

3403 יְרִיבַי *y^erîbay*, n.pr.m. GK: 3744 [→ 7380?]. Jeribai, "Yahweh pleads":– Jeribai [1]

3404 יְרִיָּה *y^eriyyâ* or יְרִיָּהוּ *y^eriyyāhû*, n.pr.m. GK: 3745 & 3746 [cf. 3400]. Jeriah, "Yahweh founds":– Jeriah [2], Jerijah [1]

3405 יְרִחוֹ *y^eriḥô* or יְרֵחוֹה *y^erēḥôh*, n.pr.loc. GK: 3735 & 3747 [→ 3391]. Jericho, "moon city":– Jericho [57]

3406 יְרִימוֹת *y^erîmôt* or יְרֵמוֹת *y^erāmôt* or יְרֵמוֹת *y^erēmôt*, n.pr.m. GK: 3748 & 3755 & 3756 [→ 3384+4191?]. Jeramoth; Jerimoth, "swollen or obese":– Jerimoth [8], Jeremoth [5]

3407 יְרִיעָה *y^erî'â*, n.f. GK: 3749 [→ 3415]. tent curtain; tent, shelter, dwelling:– curtains [31], curtain [23]

3408 יְרִיעוֹת *y^erî'ôt*, n.pr.m. GK: 3750 [→ 3415]. Jerioth, "tents":– Jerioth [1]

3409 יָרֵךְ *yārēk*, n.f. GK: 3751 [→ 3411; cf. 3410]. the area and components of the torso: thigh, hip, breast, leg, side; by extension: side, base, of any object:– thigh [19], side [7], shaft [3], loins [2], thighs [2], body [1]

3410 יַרְכָה *yarkâ* (Aram.), n.f. GK: 10334 [cf. 3409]. (upper) thigh; some sources translate as "loin" (the lower back, as the soft area between the lower ribs and the hip joints):– thighs [1]

3411 יְרֵכָה *y^erēkâ*, n.[f.]. GK: 3752 [→ 3409]. far end, ends (of the earth); remote area: heights, depths:– sides [15], two sides [4], coasts [3], parts [2], side [2], border [1], quarters [1]

3412 יַרְמוּת *yarmût*, n.pr.loc. GK: 3754 [→ 3384+4191?]. Jarmuth, "height":– Jarmuth [7]

יְרֵמוֹת *y^erēmôt*. See 3406.

3413 יְרֵמַי *y^erēmay*, n.pr.m. GK: 3757 [cf. 3414?]. Jeremai, "[poss.] fat":– Jeremai [1]

3414 יִרְמְיָה *yirm^eyâ* or יִרְמְיָהוּ *yirm^eyāhû*, n.pr.m. GK: 3758 & 3759 [cf. 3413?]. Jeremiah, "Yahweh loosens [the womb]; Yahweh lifts up; [poss.] Yahweh shoots, establishes":– Jeremiah [146], Jeremiah's [1]

3415 יָרַע *yāra'*, v. GK: 3760 [→ 3407, 3408]. [Q] to tremble, be faint-hearted:– displeased (+5869+871.1) [6], grieved [3], grievous [3], evil [2], displease (+7489+871.1) [1], displeased (+7489+871.1) [1], displeased exceedingly (+1419+7451) [1], do harm [1], go ill [1], ill [1], sad [1]

3416 יִרְפְּאֵל *yirp^e'ēl*, n.pr.loc. GK: 3761 [→ 7495+410]. Irpeel, "God [El] heals":– Irpeel [1]

3417 יָרַק *yāraq*, v. GK: 3762 [cf. 7556]. [Q] to spit (in the face as an act of contempt):– but spit (+3417) [2], spit [1]

3418 יֶרֶק *yereq*, n.m. GK: 3764 [→ 3387, 3419, 3420, 3422]. green (of plants, foliage, shoots, grass):– green [3], green thing [1], grass [1]

3419 יָרָק *yārāq*, n.[m.]. GK: 3763 [→ 3418]. vegetables, vegetable greens:– herbs [3], green [2]

יַרְקוֹן *yarqôn*. See 4313.

3420 יֵרָקוֹן *yērāqôn*, n.m. GK: 3766 [→ 3418]. paleness (of face); mildew (of grain):– mildew [5], paleness [1]

3421 יָרְקְעָם *yorq^e'ām*, n.pr.m. GK: 3767 [→ 7554]. Jorkeam:– Jorkoam [1]

3422 יְרַקְרַק *y^eraqraq*, a. GK: 3768 [→ 3418]. yellowish-green, pale-green (mildew); shining-yellowish (gold):– greenish [2], yellow [1]

3423 יָרַשׁ *yāraš*, v. GK: 3769 [→ 3388, 3424, 3425, 4180, 4181, 7558, 7568, 8492; cf. 7326]. [Q] to be an heir, gain an inheritance, have as a possession; [N] to become destitute, to be poor; [P] to take possession of; [H] to drive away, push out, destroy; to cause to inherit; many of these meanings have a common element of gaining (by right or violence) or losing possession (by force or circumstance):– possess [93], drive out [26], inherit [19], possessed [19], cast out [11], heir [9], utterly drive out (+3423) [4], come to poverty [3], succeeded [3], dispossessed [2], dispossess [2], drave out [2], driven out [2], enjoy [2], expelled [2], inherited [2], succeedest [2], take possession [2], without fail drive out (+3423) [2], consume [1], destroy [1], disinherit [1], drive [1], driving out [1], drove out [1], drove [1], given to inherit [1], giveth to possess [1], got in possession [1], have in possession [1], heirs [1], inheritor [1], leave an inheritance [1], magistrate (+6114) [1], makest to possess [1], maketh poor [1], poor [1], possessest [1], possesseth [1], seize upon [1], take in possession [1], take that have [1], taken possession [1]

3424 יְרֵשָׁה *y^erēšâ*, n.f. GK: 3771 [→ 3423]. possession conquered:– possession [2]

3425 יְרֻשָּׁה *y^erussâ*, n.f. GK: 3772 [→ 3423]. possession, inheritance:– possession [11], inheritance [2], heritage [1]

3426 יֵשׁ *yēš*, subst. GK: 3780 [→ 786, 3449?; cf. 8454; cf. 383]. there is, it exists:– there is [35], there [16], is there [13], be [12], is [9], have (+3807.1) [8], there were [6], have [4], had (+3807.1) [3], are [2], hast [2], hath (+3807.1) [2], it is [2], it was [2], there [2], wilt [2], are there [1], do [1], had [1], hast (+3807.1) [1], hath (+871.1) [1], hath [1], have (+5973) [1], is able [1], it be [1], substance [1], there was [1], were [1], will [1], wouldest [1]

3427 יָשַׁב *yāšab*, v. GK: 3782 [→ 4186, 7675, 7871?, 8453; cf. 3488 (also used with compound proper names)]. [Q] to live, inhabit, dwell, stay; [N] to be settled, be inhabited; [Ho] to set up; to cause to settle, make dwell, to cause to sit; by extension: to marry, with a focus that the spouses live together:– inhabitants [190], dwell [184], dwelt [182], sat [72], sit [54], abode [33], inhabitant [31], abide [29], inhabited [28], sitteth [24], sat down [22], dwelleth [19], dwell in [16], dwelling [15], sitting [14], set [13], dwellest [12], tarry [12], remain [11], remained [10], inhabit [8], dwelled [6], sittest [6], tarried [6], placed [5], sit down [5], taken [5], abideth [4], dwelt in [4], continued [3], abiding [2], continue [2], dwellest in [2], endure [2], habitation [2], made to dwell [2], make to dwell [2], satest [2], sit still [2], situate [2], abide in [1], abodest [1], bring to place [1], cause to dwell in [1], cause to dwell [1], caused to

dwell [1], downsitting [1], dwelleth in [1], dwelling in [1], dwelt amongst [1], dwelt at [1], dwelt with [1], ease [1], establish [1], haunt [1], inhabitest [1], inhabiteth [1], lurking [1], made dwell [1], made to abide [1], make to be inhabited [1], makest dwell [1], maketh to dwell [1], maketh to keep [1], married [1], marrying [1], not fail to sit (+3427) [1], place [1], remainest [1], remaineth [1], setteth [1], settle [1], sit in [1], sit up [1], sitteth still [1], sitting down [1], still [1], tarrieth [1], tarry abroad [1]

3428 יְשֵׁבְאָב *yeŝeb'āb*, n.pr.m. GK: 3784 [→ 7725+1]. Jeshebeab, "*father lives*":– Jeshebeab [1]

3429 יֹשֵׁב בַּשֶּׁבֶת *yōŝēb baŝŝebet*, n.pr.m. GK: 3783. Josheb-Basshebeth, "*one sitting in the seat*":–

3430 יִשְׁבּוֹ בְּנֹב *yiŝbô b°nōb* or יֹשְׁבִי בְּנֹב *yiŝbî b°nōb*, n.pr.m. GK: 3785 & 3787. Ishbo-Benob, Ishbi-Benob:– Ishbi-benob [1]

3431 יִשְׁבָּח *yiŝbāḥ*, n.pr.m. GK: 3786 [→ 7623]. Ishbah, "*he boasts, congratulates*":– Ishbah [1]

3432 יָשׁוּבִי *yāŝûbî*, a.g. GK: 3795 [→ 3437; cf. 7725]. Jashubite, "*of Jashub*":– Jashubites [1]

3433 יָשֻׁבִי לֶחֶם *yāŝubî leḥem*, n.pr.m. GK: 3788 [→ 3899]. Jashubi Lehem, "*[they] returned to Lehem*":– Jashubi-lehem [1]

3434 יָשָׁבְעָם *yāŝob'ām*, n.pr.m. GK: 3790. Jashobeam, "*the people return*":– Jashobeam [3]

3435 יִשְׁבָּק *yiŝbāq*, n.pr.m. GK: 3791 [→ 7733]. Ishbak:– Ishbak [1]

3436 יָשָׁבְקָשָׁה *yoŝb°qāŝâ*, n.pr.m. GK: 3792. Joshbekashah, "*one sitting in request [prayer?]*":– Joshbekashah [2]

3437 יָשׁוּב *yāŝûb* or יָשִׁיב *yāŝîb*, n.pr.m. GK: 3793 & 3806 [→ 3432; cf. 7725]. Jashub, Jashib, "*he returns*":– Jashub [3]

3438 יִשְׁוָה *yiŝwâ*, n.pr.m. GK: 3796 [→ 7737]. Ishvah, "*he will level*":– Ishuah [1], Ishuai [1]

3439 יְשׁוֹחָיָה *y°ŝôḥāyâ*, n.pr.m. GK: 3797 [→ 3068+8817?]. Jeshohaiah, "*[poss.] Yahweh humbles*":– Jeshohaiah [1]

3440 יִשְׁוִי *yiŝwî*, n.pr.m. GK: 3798 [→ 7737]. Ishvi:– Ishui [2], Isuah [1], Jesui [1]

3441 יִשְׁוִי *yiŝwî*, a.g. GK: 3799 [→ 7737]. Ishvite, "*of Ishvi*":– Jesuites [1]

3442 יֵשׁוּעַ *yēŝûa'*, n.pr.m. & loc. GK: 3800 & 3801 [cf. 3467; cf. 3443]. Jeshua, "*Yahweh saves*":– Jeshua [29]

3443 יֵשׁוּעַ *yēŝûa'* (Aram.), n.pr.m. GK: 10336 [cf. 3442]. Jeshua, "*Yahweh saves*":– Jeshua [1]

3444 יְשׁוּעָה *y°ŝû'â*, n.f. GK: 3802 [→ 3467]. salvation, deliverance, help, rescue from a dangerous circumstance or harmful state by a savior; divine salvation usually has its focus on rescue from earthly enemies, occasionally referring to salvation from guilt, sin, and punishment:– salvation [65], deliverance [2], health [2], help [2], deliverances [1], help (+1961) [1], helping [1], save [1], saving health [1], saving [1], welfare [1]

3445 יֵשַׁח *yeŝaḥ*, n.[m.]. GK: 3803. emptiness; some sources: filth, dung:– casting down [1]

3446 יִשְׁחָק *yiŝḥāq*, n.pr.m. GK: 3773 [→ 7832; cf. 3327]. Isaac, "*he laughs, he will laugh or mock, [God] laughs*":– Isaac [4]

3447 יָשַׁט *yāŝaṭ*, v. GK: 3804. [H] to extend; hold out:– held out [2], hold out [1]

3448 יִשַׁי *yiŝay*, n.pr.m. GK: 3805. Jesse:– Jesse [42]

יָשִׁיב *yāŝîb*. See 3437.

3449 יִשִּׁיָּה *yiŝŝiyyâ* or יִשִּׁיָּהוּ *yiŝŝiyyāhû*, n.pr.m. GK: 3807 & 3808 [→ 3426?+3068]. Isshiah, Ishijah, "*Yahweh forgets*":– Isshiah [3], Jesiah [2], Ishiah [1], Ishijah [1]

3450 יְשִׂימְאֵל *y°ŝîmi'ēl*, n.pr.m. GK: 3774 [→ 7760+410]. Jesimiel, "*God [El] will establish*":– Jesimiel [1]

3451 יְשִׂימָה *y°ŝîmâ* or יְשִׂימוֹת *yaŝŝîmâwet*, n.f. GK: 3809 & 3812 [→ 3456]. desolation, devastation:–

3452 יְשִׁימוֹן *y°ŝîmôn*, n.m. GK: 3810 [→ 3456]. Jeshimon; wasteland:– Jeshimon [6], desert [4], wilderness [2], solitary [1]

יְשִׁימוֹת *y°ŝîmôt*. See 1020, 3451.

3453 יָשִׁישׁ *yāŝîŝ*, a. GK: 3813 [→ 3454?; cf. 3486]. old, aged:– aged [1], ancient [1], very aged men [1], very old [1]

3454 יְשִׁישַׁי *y°ŝîŝay*, n.pr.m. GK: 3814 [→ 3453?]. Jeshishai, "*aged*":– Jeshishai [1]

3455 יָשַׂם *yāŝam*, v. GK: 3775 [cf. 7760]. prob. same as 7760: to place, set:– put [1]

3456 יָשַׁם *yāŝam*, v. GK: 3815 [→ 3451, 3452; cf. 8074]. [Q] to be desolate:– desolate [4]

3457 יִשְׁמָא *yiŝmā'*, n.pr.m. GK: 3816 [→ 3458]. Ishma, "*desolate; God [El] he heard*":– Ishma [1]

3458 יִשְׁמָעֵאל *yiŝmā'ē'l*, n.pr.m. GK: 3817 [→ 3457, 3459]. Ishmael, "*God [El] he heard*":– Ishmael [47], Ishmael's [1]

3459 יִשְׁמְעֵאלִי *yiŝm°'ē'lî*, a.g. GK: 3818 [→ 3458]. Ishmaelite, "*of Ishmael*":– Ishmeelites [4], Ishmaelites [2], Ishmaelite [1], Ishmeelite [1]

3460 יִשְׁמַעְיָה *yiŝma'yâ* or יִשְׁמַעְיָהוּ *yiŝma'yāhû*, n.pr.m. GK: 3819 & 3820 [→ 3461?]. Ishmaiah, "*Yahweh heard*":– Ishmaiah [1], Ismaiah [1]

3461 יִשְׁמְרַי *yiŝm°ray*, n.pr.m. GK: 3821 [→ 3460?]. Ishmerai, "*Yahweh guards*":– Ishmerai [1]

3462 יָשֵׁן *yāŝēn*, v. GK: 3822 & 3823 [→ 3463, 3464?, 3465, 8142]. [Q] to sleep, fall asleep; [N] to live a long time, be old, chronic; [P] to put to sleep:– sleep [9], slept [5], made sleep [1], old store (+3465) [1], old [1], remained long [1], sleepest [1]

3463 יָשֵׁן *yāŝēn*, a. GK: 3825 [→ 3462]. sleeping, pertaining to sleep:– sleep [5], asleep [2], sleepeth [2], sleeping [1], slept [1]

3464 יָשֵׁן *yāŝēn*, n.pr.m. GK: 3826 [→ 3462?]. Jashen, "*[poss.] asleep*":– Jashen [1]

3465 יָשָׁן *yāŝān*, a. GK: 3824 [→ 3466?; cf. 3462]. old; pertaining to last year:– old [7], old store (+3462) [1]

3466 יְשָׁנָה *y°ŝānâ*, n.pr.loc. GK: 3827 [→ 3465?]. Jeshanah, "*old*":– Jeshanah [1]

3467 יָשַׁע *yāŝa'*, v. GK: 3828 & 3830 & 4635 [→ 3444, 3468, 4190, 4338, 4337, 8668 (also used with compound proper names)]. [N] to be rescued, be delivered, be saved; [H] to save, rescue, deliver; divine salvation has its focus on rescue from earthly enemies, occasionally referring to salvation from guilt, sin, and punishment:– save [103], saved [35], saviour [13], help [10], delivered [8], saveth [7], preserved [4], deliver [3], savest [3], avenging [2], brought salvation [2], deliverer [2], helped [2], save at all (+3467) [2], saviours [2], avenged [1], defend [1], gotten victory [1], having salvation [1], preservest [1], rescue [1], safe [1]

3468 יֶשַׁע *yēŝa'*, n.m. GK: 3829 [→ 3442; cf. 3467 (also used with compound proper names)]. salvation, deliverance, protection, often implying a victory is at hand; (of God) Savior, a title of God that focuses on rescue from earthly enemies, occasionally referring to salvation from guilt, sin, and punishment:– salvation [32], safety [3], saving [1]

3469 יִשְׁעִי *yiŝ'î*, n.pr.m. GK: 3831 [→ 3467?+3068?]. Ishi, "*God has saved*":– Ishi [5]

3470 יְשַׁעְיָה *y°ŝa'yâ* or יְשַׁעְיָהוּ *y°ŝa'yāhû*, n.pr.m. GK: 3832 & 3833 [→ 3467+3068]. Jeshaiah, "*Yahweh will save*":– Isaiah [31], Jeshaiah [5], Jesaiah [2], Esai [1]

3471 יַשְׁפֵה *yāŝ°pēh*, n.[m.]. GK: 3835. jasper (exact identification uncertain):– jasper [3]

3472 יִשְׁפָּה *yiŝpâ*, n.pr.m. GK: 3834 [→ 8192]. Ishpah, "*[poss.] barren way, empty path*":– Ispah [1]

3473 יִשְׁפָּן *yiŝpān*, n.pr.m. GK: 3836 [→ 8192?]. Ishpan, "*[poss.] may God judge*":– Ishpan [1]

3474 יָשַׁר *yāŝar*, v. GK: 3837 [→ 3475, 3476, 3477, 3483, 3484, 4334, 4339, 8289, 8290]. [Q] to do good, do right, be straight; [P] to make straight, make smooth; [Pu] to be evenly hammered; [H] to make straight, gaze straight; from the base meaning of straightening out a crooked object comes the fig. extension of doing an act that is not perverse, but right or just:– direct [3], make straight [3], pleased (+5869+871.1) [3], pleased well (+5869+871.1) [3], brought straight [1], directeth [1], esteem to be right [1], fitted [1], go right [1], good [1], look straight [1], meet [1], please (+5869+871.1) [1], pleaseth well (+5869) [1], right [1], took straight [1], uprightly [1], upright [1]

3475 יֵשֶׁר *yēŝer*, n.pr.m. GK: 3840 [→ 3474]. Jesher, "*[perhaps] the deity shows himself just*":– Jesher [1]

3476 יֹשֶׁר *yōŝer*, n.m. GK: 3841 [→ 3474]. uprightness, straightness, honesty, integrity:– uprightness [9], right [2], equity [1], meet [1], upright [1]

3477 יָשָׁר *yāŝar*, a. & n.pr.m. GK: 3838 & 3839 [→ 3474]. straight (not crooked or twisted); by extension, something morally straight: right, upright, innocent; (n.) upright person; as n.pr. Jashar:– right [53], upright [41], righteous [9], straight [3], Jasher [2], convenient for (+413+1886.1) [1], convenient [1], equity [1], just [1], meetest [1], meet [1], most upright [1], pleased well (+5869+871.1) [1], upright ones [1], uprightly [1], uprightness [1]

3478 יִשְׂרָאֵל *yiŝrā'ēl*, n.pr.m. & g. GK: 3776 [→ 415, 3481, 3482; cf. 8280; cf. 3479]. Israel, "*he struggles with God [El]*":– Israel [2476], Israelites [16], Israel's [10], Israel (+376) [2], Israelite (+376) [1]

3479 יִשְׂרָאֵל *yiŝrā'ēl* (Aram.), n.prg. GK: 10335 [cf. 3478]. Israel, "*he struggles with God [El]*":– Israel [8]

3480 יְשַׂרְאֵלָה *y°ŝar'ēlâ*, n.pr.m. GK: 3777 [cf. 841]. Jesarelah:– Jesharelah [1]

3481 יִשְׂרְאֵלִי *yiŝr°'ēlî*, a.g. GK: 3778 [→ 3478, 3482]. Israelite, "*of Israel*":– Israelite [1], Israel [1]

3482 יִשְׂרְאֵלִית *yiŝr°'ēlît*, a.g. GK: 3778 [→ 3481]. f. of 3481: Israelite, "*of Israel*":– Israelitish [3]

3483 יִשְׂרָה *yiŝrâ*, n.f. GK: 3842 [→ 3474]. uprightness:– uprightness [1]

3484 יְשֻׁרוּן *y°ŝurûn*, n.pr.m. GK: 3843 [→ 3474]. Jeshurun, "*upright*":– Jeshurun [4]

3485 יִשָּׂשכָר *yiŝŝāŝkār*, n.pr.m. GK: 3779 [→ 376+7939]. Issachar, "*there is reward [Ge. 30:18]; may [God] show mercy; hired hand*":– Issachar [43]

3486 יָשֵׁשׁ *yāŝēŝ*, a. GK: 3844 [→ 3453]. aged, decrepit:– him that stooped for age [1]

3487 יָת *yāt* (Aram.), pt. GK: 10337 [cf. 853]. not translated, indicates the direct object:–

3488 יְתֵב *y°tib* (Aram.), v. GK: 10338 [cf. 3427]. [P] to live in, dwell; to sit, be seated; [H] to cause to settle, cause to dwell in:– set [2], sit [2], dwell [1]

3489 יָתֵד *yātēd*, n.f. GK: 3845. tent peg, stake, pin (of a loom); tool for digging:– pins [10], nail [8], pin [3], stakes [2], paddle [1]

3490 יָתוֹם *yātôm*, n.[m.]. GK: 3846. fatherless, orphan:– fatherless [38], fatherless children [2], fatherless child [1], orphans [1]

3491 יְתוּר *y°tûr*, var. GK: 3847 [cf. 8446]. range, extent; poss. a form of 8446:– range [1]

3492 יַתִּיר *yattîr*, n.pr.loc. GK: 3848 [→ 3498]. Jattir, "*[poss.] preeminence*":– Jattir [4]

3493 יַתִּיר *yattîr* (Aram.), a. GK: 10339 [cf. 3471]. exceptional, outstanding; (as adv.) so, very, exceedingly:– excellent [5], exceeding [2], exceedingly [1]

3494 יִתְלָה *yitlâ*, n.pr.loc. GK: 3849 [→ 8518]. Ithlah, "*hanging, lofty place*":– Jethlah [1]

3495 יִתְמָה *yitmâ*, n.pr.m. GK: 3850. Ithmah, "*fatherless; purity*":– Ithmah [1]

3496 יַתְנִאֵל *yatni'ēl*, n.pr.m. GK: 3853 [→ 386+410]. Jathniel, "*God [El] hires; God [El] is forever*":– Jathniel [1]

3497 יִתְנָן *yitnān*, n.pr.loc. GK: 3854 [→ 386]. Ithnan:– Ithnan [1]

3498 יָתַר *yātar*, v. GK: 3855 [→ 1956, 3148, 3492?, 3499, 3500, 3501, 3502, 3503, 3504, 3506, 3508, 4195, 4340; cf. 3493 (also used with compound proper names)]. [N] to remain, be left over, the rest; [H] to have left over, spare, preserve:– left [46], remain [12], rest [12], leave [6], remained [5], remainder [4], remaineth [4], remnant [3], residue [3], make plenteous [2], reserved [2], come to remain [1], excel [1], had reserved [1], leave a remnant [1], left behind [1], preserve [1], remaining [1], too much [1]

3499 יֶתֶר *yeter*, n.m. GK: 3856 & 3857 [→ 3323, 4340; cf. 3498]. remainder, remnant, the rest, what is left over; thong, cord, bowstring:– rest [63], remnant [14], residue [8], excellency [3], left [3], withs [3], abundant [1], cord [1], exceeding [1], excellent [1], leave [1], plentifully [1], string [1]

3500 יֶתֶר *yeter*, n.pr.m. GK: 3858 [→ 3505; cf. 3498, 3499]. Jether; Jethro:– Jether [8], Jethro [1]

3501 יִתְרָא *yitrā'*, n.pr.m. GK: 3859 [→ 3498]. Jether, "*abundance*":– Ithra [1]

3502 יִתְרָה *yitrâ*, n.f. GK: 3860 [→ 3498]. wealth, abundance:– abundance [1], riches [1]

3503 יִתְרוֹ *yitrô*, n.pr.m. GK: 3861 [→ 3498]. Jethro, "*remainder*":– Jethro [9]

3504 יִתְרוֹן *yitrôn*, n.[m.]. GK: 3862 [→ 3498]. profit, gain, increase:– profit [5], excelleth [2], better [1], excellency [1], profitable [1]

3505 יִתְרִי *yitrî*, a.g. GK: 3863 [→ 3500; cf. 3498]. Ithrite:– Ithrite [4], Ithrites [1]

3506 יִתְרָן *yitrān*, n.pr.m. GK: 3864 [→ 3498]. Ithran, "*what is over, profit; excellent*":– Ithran [3]

3507 יִתְרְעָם *yitr⁰'ām*, n.pr.m. GK: 3865 [→ 3499+5971]. Ithream, "*remainder of the people*":– Ithream [2]

3508 יֹתֶרֶת *yōteret*, n.f. GK: 3866 [→ 3498]. covering, lobe (of certain animal livers):– caul [11]

3509 יְתֵת *y⁰tēt*, n.pr.m. GK: 3867. Jetheth:– Jetheth [2]

3509.1 כְּ- *k⁰-*, subst.pref. GK: 3869 [→ 3644; cf. 3509.4]. marker of comparison: as, like; marker of similarity or correspondence: according to; marker of time: when, as soon as, about:– as [1044], as (+834) [382], according to [367], like [361], when [164], after [75], about [47], when (+834) [47], according unto [29], like unto [23], as it were [20], according as (+834) [16], as soon as [13], so [13], thus (+2088) [12], like as (+834) [11]*

3509.2 ךָ- *-kā* or ךָ- *-āk*, כָה- *-kēh*, p.m.s.suf. GK: 3870 [→ 3509.3, 3641.1, 3654.1]. you, your:– thy [3403], thee [2501], thine [639], thou [282], thyself [46], thine own [45], you [34], thine (+3807.1) [29], thy (+3807.1) [24], your [8], ye [3], thine own (+3807.1) [2], his [1], of thy [1], theˢ [1], thee (+3027) [1], thee (+3807.1) [1], thee-ward [1], thine own self [1], thou (+3027) [1], thyself (+3807.1) [1], whose [1]

3509.3 ךְ- *-k* or כִי- *-kî*, p.f.s.suf. GK: 3871 [→ 3509.2]. you, your:– thy [619], thee [458], thine [101], thou [63], thine own [9], thy (+3807.1) [7], thine (+3807.1) [3], thyself [3], thyself (+5315) [1], whom [1]

3509.4 כְּ- *k⁰-* (Aram.), pp.pref. GK: 10341 [cf. 3509.1]. as, like, according to:– like [10], as [9], according to [5], when (+1768) [4], after [2], how (+4101) [2], thus (+1836) [2], about [1], after sort [1], as (+1768) [1], for [1], such (+1836) [1], together (+2298) [1], when [1]

3509.5 ךְ- *-k* (Aram.), p.suf.2.m.s. GK: 10342 [cf. 3509.2]. you, your:– thee [44], thy [44], thine [7], thou [3], thyself [1]

3510 כָּאַב *kā'ab*, v. GK: 3872 [→ 3511, 4341]. [Q] to feel pain, ache; [H] to bring pain:– sorrowful [2], grieving [1], have pain [1], made sad [1], maketh sore [1], mar [1], sore [1]

3511 כְּאֵב *k⁰'ēb*, n.m. GK: 3873 [→ 3510]. pain, anguish, suffering:– sorrow [3], grief [2], pain [1]

3512 כָּאָה *kā'â*, v. GK: 3874 [cf. 3543]. [N] to be brokenhearted, lose heart; [H] to dishearten, cause to lose heart:– broken [1], grieved [1], made sad [1]

3513 כָּבֵד *kābēd*, v. GK: 3877 [→ 3514, 3515, 3516, 3517, 3519, 3520, 3520]. [Q] to be heavy; to be wealthy, honored, glorified; to be failing, dull; [N] to be glorified, honored, renowned; [P] to honor, glorify, reward; [Pu] to be honored; [H] to make heavy, make hard; [Ht] to make numerous; honor oneself. If the base meaning is "to be weighty or heavy," then by extension, negatively: hard, dull, stubborn, difficult in circumstance; positively: substantial, honored, glorious, wealthy:– honourable [15], honour [15], heavy [9], glorify [7], glorified [6], hardened [6], honoured [5], made heavy [5], glorious [4], honoureth [4], chargeable [2], heavier [2], make many [2], promote unto great honour (+3513) [2], come unto honour (+3513) [2], went sore [2], abounding [2], boast [1], bring to honour [1], come to honour [1], dim [1], do honour [1], get honour [1], glorifieth [1], glory [1], gotten honour [1], grievous [1], had in honour [1], harden [1], heavily laid [1], honourest [1], ladeth with [1], made glorious [1], make glorious [1], make heavy [1], more grievously afflict [1], more laid [1], nobles [1], prevailed [1], promote to honour [1], rich [1], sore [1], stopped [1]

3514 כֹּבֶד *kōbed*, n.[m.]. GK: 3880 [→ 3513]. heaviness; heavy mass (density, piles):– heavy [2], great number [1], grievousness [1]

3515 כָּבֵד *kābēd*, a. GK: 3878 [→ 3513]. heavy, severe, difficult, an extended degree or amount, positive or negative:– heavy [9], great [8], grievous [8], sore [4], hard [2], much [2], slow [2], hardened [1], heavier [1], laden [1], thick [1]

3516 כָּבֵד *kābēd*, n.m. GK: 3879 [→ 3513]. liver; heart:– liver [14]

כָּבֹד *kābôd*. See 3519.

3517 כְּבֵדֻת *k⁰bēdut*, n.f. GK: 3881 [→ 3513]. difficulty, awkwardness:– heavily (+871.1) [1]

3518 כָּבָה *kābâ*, v. GK: 3882. [Q] to be quenched, snuffed out; [P] to quench, put out, snuff out:– quenched [9], quench [8], put out [3], goeth out [2], go out [1], went out [1]

3519 כָּבוֹד *kābôd*, n.m. GK: 3883 [→ 350; cf. 3513]. glory, honor, splendor, wealth; while related words can be positive or negative in context, this word is almost exclusively positive in the OT; "the Glory" a title for God focuses on his splendor and high status; "my glory" means "myself" (Ge 49:8):– glory [156], honour [32], glorious [10], gloriously [1], honourable [1]

3520 כְּבוּדָּה *k⁰búddâ*, n.f. GK: 3884 & 3885 [→ 3513]. possession, valuable property; glorious, elegant:– carriage [1], glorious [1], stately [1]

3521 כָּבוּל *kābûl*, n.pr.loc. GK: 3886 [→ 3525]. Cabul, "*good for nothing*":– Cabul [2]

3522 כַּבּוֹן *kabbôn*, n.pr.loc. GK: 3887. Cabbon:– Cabbon [1]

3523 כָּבִיר *kābîr*, n.[m.]. GK: 3889 [→ 3527]. something braided; in context referring to goat's hair:– pillow [2]

3524 כַּבִּיר *kabbîr*, a. GK: 3888 [→ 3527]. great, mighty (of God and humans), with a focus on potency or ability:– mighty [5], much [2], feeble (+3808) [1], most [1], strong [1]

3525 כֶּבֶל *kebel*, n.[m.]. GK: 3890 [→ 3521]. shackles, fetters:– fetters [2]

3526 כָּבַס *kābas*, v. GK: 3891 [cf. 3533]. [Q] (ptcp.) washer, fuller; [P] to wash, launder; [Pu] to be washed; [Hotpael] to be washed off:– wash [39], washed [7], fuller's [3], fullers' [1], washing [1]

3527 כָּבַר *kābar*, v. GK: 3892 [→ 3524, 3523, 3528, 3529, 3531, 3530, 4342, 4346]. [H] to multiply; provide in abundance:– multiplieth [1]

3528 כְּבָר *k⁰bār*, adv. GK: 3893 [→ 3527]. already, before:– already [5], now [4]

3529 כְּבָר *k⁰bār*, n.pr.loc. GK: 3894 [→ 3527]. Kebar:– Chebar [8]

3530 כִּבְרָה *kibrâ*, n.f. GK: 3896 [→ 3527]. (a certain) distance; some sources: as far as a horse can run; as far as one can see; about seven miles:– little [2], little way (+776+1886.1) [1]

3531 כְּבָרָה *k⁰bārâ*, n.f. GK: 3895 [→ 3527]. sieve:– sieve [1]

3532 כֶּבֶשׂ *kebeś*, n.m. GK: 3897 [→ 3535; cf. 3775]. ram-lamb, young ram sheep:– lambs [59], lamb [41], he lamb [3], sheep [2], he lambs [1], lamb (+7716) [1]

3533 כָּבַשׁ *kābaš*, v. GK: 3899 [→ 3534, 3536; cf. 3526, 3728]. [Q] to subdue, overcome, enslave; [N] be subdued, be subject, be brought under control; [P] to subdue; [H] subdue, subjugate:– subdued [5], subdue [3], brought into subjection [2], bring into bondage [1], brought unto bondage [1], force [1], keep under [1]

3534 כֶּבֶשׁ *kebeš*, n.[m.]. GK: 3900 [→ 3533]. footstool:– footstool [1]

3535 כִּבְשָׂה *kibśâ*, n.f. GK: 3898 [→ 3532]. ewe-lamb, young female sheep:– ewe lambs [3], ewe lamb [3], lamb [2]

3536 כִּבְשָׁן *kibšān*, n.m. GK: 3901 [→ 3533]. furnace, likely in context referring to a kiln or forge for making glass, pottery, smelting, etc:– furnace [4]

3537 כַּד *kad*, n.f. GK: 3902. jar, pitcher (of the size that could by carried on the shoulder):– pitcher [10], pitchers [4], barrel [3], barrels [1]

3538 כְּדַב *k⁰dab* (Aram.), a. GK: 10343 [cf. 3577]. misleading, false:– lying [1]

3539 כַּדְכֹּד *kadkōd*, n.[m.]. GK: 3905. ruby (exact identification unknown):– agates [1], agate [1]

3540 כְּדָרְלָעֹמֶר *k⁰dorlā'ōmer* or כְּדָרְלָעֹמֶר *k⁰dor-lā'ōmer*, n.pr.m. GK: 3906. Kedorlaomer, "*servant of [the deity] Lagamar*":– Chedorlaomer [5]

3541 כֹּה *kōh*, adv.demo. GK: 3907 [→ 3602; cf. 3542]. this is what, thus:– thus [520], so [23], also [7], here [4], hitherto (+5704) [2], in the mean while (+3541+5704+5704+2050.1) [2], this [2], and (+2050.1) [1], and [1], more also (+3254) [1], much [1], on the other side [1], on this side [1], on this wise [1], such [1], that manner [1], that way [1], this manner [1], this way [1], yonder (+5704) [1], yonder [1]

3542 כָּה *kâ* (Aram.), adv. GK: 10345 [cf. 3541]. here, up to this point:– hitherto (+5705) [1]

3543 כָּהָה *kāhâ*, v. GK: 3908 & 3909 [→ 3544, 3545; cf. 3512]. [Q] to grow dim, be weak; [P] to fade, become faint; to rebuke, set (someone) right, with an implication that future bad behavior is curtailed:– dim [3], utterly darkened (+3543) [1], fail [1], faint [1], restrained [1]

3544 כֵּהֶה *kēheh*, a. GK: 3910 [→ 3543]. dull; weak; smoldering; despairing:– somewhat dark [5], darkish [1], dim [1], heaviness [1], smoking [1]

3545 כֵּהָא *kēhâ*, n.f. GK: 3911 [→ 3543]. healing, relief:– healing [1]

3546 כְּהַל *k⁰hal* (Aram.), v. GK: 10346 [cf. 3202]. [P] to be able:– able [2], could [2]

3547 כָּהַן *kāhan*, v.den. GK: 3912 [→ 3548]. [P] to serve as a priest:– minister in the priest's office [15], executed the priest's office [2], ministered in the priest's office [2], decketh with [1], do the office of a priest [1], executing the priest's office [1], priest [1]

3548 כֹּהֵן *kōhēn*, n.m. GK: 3913 [→ 3547, 3550; cf. 3549]. priest, who not only had religious duties, but also examined persons and things for medical diagnosis, policed the unruly, and taught the word of God:– priest [421], priests [298], priest's [14], priests' [8], hisˢ own (+1886.1) [2], priest's (+3807.1) [2], chief rulers [1], chief ruler [1], priests' (+3807.1) [1], princes [1], principal officer [1]

3549 כָּהֵן *kāhēn* (Aram.), n.m. GK: 10347 [cf. 3548]. priest:– priests [6], priest [2]

3550 כְּהֻנָּה *k⁰hunnâ*, n.f. GK: 3914 [→ 3548]. priesthood, priestly office:– priesthood [9], priest's office [4], priests' offices [1]

3551 כַּוָּה *kawwâ* (Aram.), n.f. GK: 10348. window:– windows [1]

3552 כּוּב *kûb*, n.pr.g. GK: 3915. Kub:– Chub [1]

3553 כּוֹבַע *kôba'*, n.m. GK: 3916 [cf. 6959]. helmet:– helmet [4], helmets [2]

3554 כָּוָה *kāwâ*, v. GK: 3917 [→ 3555, 3587, 4348]. [N] to be burned, be scorched:– burnt [2]

כּוֹחַ *kôaḥ*. See 3581.

3555 כְּוִיָּה *k⁰wiyyâ*, n.f. GK: 3918 [→ 3458]. burn spot, scar (of a burn):– burning [2]

3556 כּוֹכָב *kôkāb*, n.m. GK: 3919. star, planet, a luminary in the night sky; by extension: human power (such as a king), heavenly power (that serve God); stargazer, one who studies the movements of the stars to predict the future:– stars [34], star [2], stargazers (+2374+871.1+1886.1) [1]

3557 כּוּל *kûl*, v. GK: 3920 [cf. 3634?]. [Q] to hold, seize; [Pil] to hold; to provide, supply, sustain; [H] to hold; to bear, endure:– sustain [4], contain [3], fed [3], feed [3], abide [2], contained [2], nourish [2], receive [2], able to abide [1], bear [1], comprehended [1], containeth [1], forbearing [1], guide [1], held [1], holding in [1], hold [1], made provision [1], nourished [1], nourisher [1], present [1], provided of sustenance [1], provided victuals [1], provided victual [1]

3558 כּוּמָז *kûmāz*, n.[m.]. GK: 3921. ornament, necklace:– tablets [2]

3559 כּוּן *kûn*, v. GK: 3922 & 5788 [→ 3078, 3112, 3199, 3562, 3651, 3663, 4349, 4350, 4368, 4369, 5225, 8498, 8499; cf. 3653]. [N] to be established, be steadfast, be firm, be prepared; [Pol] to establish, set in place, make secure; [Polal] to be made firm, be prepared; [H] to establish, make preparations, provide; [Ho] to be made ready, be established, be attached:– prepared [53], established [42], prepare [28], establish [12], ready [9], fixed [4], made ready [4], make ready [4], right [4], stablished [4], stablish [4], prepareth [3], set [3], certain [2], confirmed [2], fashioned [2], firm [2], order [2], provideth [2], provide [2], certainty [1], confirm [1], could frame [1], directed [1], directeth [1], direct [1], faithfulness [1], fashion [1], fastened [1], fitted [1], made provision [1], make preparation [1], meet [1], ordained [1], ordered [1], perfect [1], preparation [1], preparest [1], provided for [1], set aright [1], set forth [1], set in order [1], setteth fast [1], stable [1], stablisheth [1], standeth [1], stood [1], tarry [1], very deed [1]

3560 כּוּן *kûn*, n.pr.loc. GK: 3923. Cun, "*chosen*":– Chun [1]

3561 כַּוָּן *kawwān*, n.[m.]. GK: 3924. cake of bread (presented as an offering):– cakes [2]

3561.1 כוֹן *-kôn* (Aram.), p.suf.2.m.pl. GK: 10349 [→ 3641.2; cf. 3641.1]. you, your:– you [6], ye [2], your [2]

3562 כּוֹנַנְיָהוּ *kônanyāhû*, n.pr.m. GK: 3925 [→ 3559+3068]. Conaniah:– Cononiah [2], Conaniah [1]

3563 כּוֹס *kôs*, n.f. GK: 3926 & 3927. cup; little owl:– cup [30], little owl [2], cups [1], owl [1]

3564 כּוּר *kûr*, n.[m.]. GK: 3929 [cf. 3600]. (little) furnace (for smelting metals); by extension: the testing and purification process:– furnace [9]

כּוֹר *kôr*. See 3733.

3565 כּוֹר עָשָׁן *kôr 'āšān*, n.pr.loc. GK: 3930 [cf. 953]. Kor Ashan:– Chor-ashan [1]

3566 כּוֹרֶשׁ, n.pr.m. GK: 3931 [cf. 3567]. Cyrus:- Cyrus [15]

3567 כּוֹרֶשׁ (Aram.), n.pr.m. GK: 10350 [cf. 3566]. Cyrus:- Cyrus [8]

3568 כּוּשׁ *kûs*, n.pr.m. & loc. GK: 3932 & 3933 [→ 3569, 3570, 3571]. Cush:- Ethiopia [19], Cush [8], Ethiopians [3]

3569 כּוּשִׁי *kûsî*, a.g. GK: 3934 [→ 3568]. Cushite, "*of Cush*":- Cushi [10], Ethiopians [9], Ethiopian [8]

3570 כּוּשִׁי *kûsî*, n.pr.m. GK: 3935 [→ 3568]. Cushi:-

3571 כּוּשִׁית *kûsît*, a.g. GK: 3934 [→ 3569]. f. of 3569: Cushite, "*of Cush*":-

3572 כּוּשָׁן *kûsān*, n.pr.loc. GK: 3936. Cushan:- Cushan [1]

3573 כּוּשַׁן רִשְׁעָתַיִם *kûsan ris'ãtayim*, n.pr.m. GK: 3937. Cushan-Rishathaim, "*man of Cush, doubly guilty*":- Chushan-rishathaim [4]

3574 כּוּשָׁרָה *kôsãrâ*, n.f. GK: 3938 [cf. 7891]. singing or prosperity, fortune:- chains [1]

3575 כּוּת *kût* or כּוּתָה *kûtâ*, n.pr.loc. GK: 3939 & 3940. Cuthah:- Cuthah [1], Cuth [1]

3576 כָּזַב *kãzab*, v. GK: 3941 [→ 391, 392?, 3577, 3578, 3580]. [Q] to lie; [N] to be proven a liar, be false; [P] to lie, deceive, prove false; to fail; [H] to prove someone a liar:- lie [8], lied [2], fail [1], found a liar [1], in vain [1], liars [1], lying [1], make a liar [1]

3577 כָּזָב *kãzãb*, n.m. GK: 3942 [→ 3576; cf. 3538]. lie, falsehood; by extension: delusion; false god (worshiped by a deluded person):- lies [21], leasing [2], lie [2], lying [2], deceitful [1], false [1], liar (+376) [1], lies (+1697) [1]

3578 כּוֹזֵבָא *kôzēbã'*, n.pr.loc. GK: 3943 [→ 3576]. Cozeba, "*liar*":- Chozeba [1]

3579 כָּזְבִּי *kozbî*, n.pr.f. GK: 3944. Cozbi, "*deceitful; luxuriant*":- Cozbi [2]

3580 כְּזִיב *kᵉzîb*, n.pr.loc. GK: 3945 [→ 3576]. Kezib, "*deceit*":- Chezib [1]

3581 כֹּחַ *kôah*, n.m. GK: 3946 & 3947. strength, power, might, ability; often physical strength and the vigor of good health, sometimes simply ability to accomplish an action; monitor lizard; some sources: any kind of lizard:- strength [57], power [47], might [7], force [3], ability [2], able [2], able (+6113) [1], chameleon [1], fruits [1], in strength [1], powerful [1], substance [1], wealth [1], weary (+3019) [1]

3582 כָּחַד *kãhad*, v. GK: 3948. [N] to be hidden; be destroyed, perish; [P] to hide, conceal, keep from; [H] to hide; to destroy, annihilate, get rid of:- cut off [10], hide [10], hid [6], concealed [2], conceal [2], cut down [1], desolate [1]

3583 כָּחַל *kãhal*, v. GK: 3949. [Q] to paint (eyes):- paintedst [1]

3584 כָּחַשׁ *kãhas*, v. GK: 3950 [→ 3585, 3586]. [Q] to be thin; [N] to cringe, feign obedience; [P] to lie, deceive; fail; to cringe, feign obedience; [Ht] to cringe, feign obedience:- deny [3], submit [3], denied [2], fail [2], lying [2], belied [1], deceive [1], dissembled [1], faileth [1], found liars [1], lied [1], lieth [1], lie [1], submitted [1]

3585 כַּחַשׁ *kahas*, n.m. GK: 3951 [→ 3584]. lie, deception; gauntness, thinness, leanness:- lies [4], leanness [1], lying [1]

3586 כֶּחָשׁ *kehãs*, a. GK: 3952 [→ 3584]. deceitful, untruthful:- lying [1]

3587 כִּי *kî*, n.[m.]. GK: 3953 [→ 3554]. branding:- burning [1]

3588 כִּי *kî*, c. GK: 3954. a marker that shows the relationship between clauses, sentences, or sections; logical: for, that, because; contrast: but, except; introducing a statement, often untranslated:- for [2322], that [696], because [442], when [237], but [173], if [168], but (+518) [86], surely [44], though [37], save (+518) [13], seeing [12], how [11], yet [10], although [9], yea [9], therefore [8], how much more (+637) [7], even [6], except (+518) [6], how much less (+637) [5], how that [5], because (+5921) [4], for (+5921) [4], nevertheless [4], so that [4], though (+518) [4], until (+5704) [4], whereas [4], assuredly [3], because (+3282) [3], else [3], in that [3], so [3], while [3], and (+518) [2], as [2], because (+3651+5921) [2], because (+6118) [2], because that [2], for (+518) [2], for if [2], forasmuch as [2], if not [2], or (+2050.1) [2], surely (+518) [2], than (+518) [2], to be [2], truly [2], whether [2], yet (+518) [2], also [1], although (+637) [1], and when [1], and [1], because (+8478) [1], because of [1], but (+518+3808) [1], but for (+518) [1], but that (+518) [1], but that [1], certainly [1], doubtless [1], either [1], even so [1], except (+1571) [1], except (+3884) [1], except (+518+3808) [1], except [1], for (+2088) [1], for (+4480) [1], for

(+5973) [1], for surely (+518) [1], for that (+8478) [1], for then [1], for though (+518) [1], forasmuch as (+3282) [1], forasmuch as (+3651+5921) [1], forasmuch [1], forsomuch as (+3282) [1], how much less (+637+3808) [1], how much more then (+637) [1], howbeit yet (+389) [1], howbeit [1], inasmuch as [1], moreover [1], most [1], much less (+637) [1], much less for (+637) [1], much more (+637) [1], neither (+3808) [1], nevertheless (+518) [1], nevertheless (+657) [1], notwithstanding (+657) [1], now (+6258) [1], now [1], of a truth (+518) [1], rightly [1], save only (+518) [1], saving (+518) [1], seeing that [1], shall (+518) [1], since [1], than that [1], that (+518) [1], that when [1], then (+227) [1], then [1], thereof [1], though (+5973) [1], though (+637) [1], thus [1], till (+5704) [1], too [1], to [1], unless (+3884) [1], unless (+518) [1], until (+518) [1], wherefore (+389) [1], which [1], whom [1], whose [1], yea (+637) [1]

3589 כִּיד *kîd*, n.[m.]. GK: 3957. destruction:- destruction [1]

3590 כִּידוֹד *kîdôd*, n.m. GK: 3958. spark:- sparks [1]

3591 כִּידוֹן *kîdôn*, n.[m.]. GK: 3959 [→ 3592?]. javelin, lance, spear:- spear [5], shield [2], lance [1], target [1]

3592 כִּידֹן *kîdõn*, n.pr.loc. GK: 3961 [→ 3591?]. Kidon:- Chidon [1]

3593 כִּידוֹר *kîdôr*, n.[m.]. GK: 3960. attack, battle:- battle [1]

3594 כִּיּוּן *kiyyûn*, n.m. GK: 3962. pedestal:- Chiun [1]

3595 כִּיּוֹר *kiyyôr*, n.m. GK: 3963. basin, pan, firepot:- laver [15], lavers [5], hearth [1], pan [1], scaffold [1]

3596 כִּילַי *kîlay*, n.m. GK: 3964 [→ 5230?]. scoundrel:- churl [2]

3597 כֵּילַפּוֹת *kêlappôt*, n.[f.]. GK: 3965 [→ 3619?]. an iron-tipped tool: ax, crowbar, pickax, etc:- hammers [1]

3598 כִּימָה *kîmâ*, n.f. GK: 3966. Pleiades (a constellation):- Pleiades [2], seven stars [1]

3599 כִּיס *kîs*, n.m. GK: 3967. bag, purse:- bag [4], purse [1]

3600 כִּיר *kîr*, n.[m.]. GK: 3968 [cf. 3564]. cooking pot, stove, a small portable cooking hearth, the form of the word suggesting it is large enough for a pair of pots:- ranges for pots [1]

כִּיּוֹר *kîor*. See 3595.

3601 כִּישׁוֹר *kîsôr*, n.[m.]. GK: 3969. distaff, spindle, whorl, the small disk at the bottom of a distaff to promote turning:- spindle [1]

3602 כָּכָה *kãkâ*, adv. GK: 3970 [→ 3541]. this is what, this is how, thus:- thus [17], so [8], after this manner [3], even so [3], after that manner [1], even thus [1], in such a case [1], this [1]

3603 כִּכָּר *kikkâr*, n.f. GK: 3971 [→ 3769; cf. 3604]. plain (geographical area); loaf of bread; cover (of lead); talent (unit of weight or value, about 75 pounds [34 kg]):- talents [35], plain [12], talent [10], two talents [3], loaf [2], loaves [2], piece [2], morsel [1], plain country [1]

3604 כַּכַּר *kakkar* (Aram.), n.[f.]. GK: 10352 [cf. 3603]. talent (unit of weight or value, probably about 75 lbs [34 k]):- talents [1]

3605 כֹּל *kôl*, n.m. GK: 3972 [→ 3626; cf. 3634; cf. 3606, cf. 3635]. all, everyone, everything, totality of a mass or collective; every, any, a particular of a totality:- all [4291], every [362], any [169], whole [130], every one [95], no (+3808) [43], whosoever [34], whatsoever (+834) [33], whatsoever [23], for ever (+3117+1886.1) [15], none (+3808) [13], whithersoever (+834+871.1) [12], daily (+3117+1886.1) [11], continually (+3117+1886.1) [9], wholly [9], whosoever (+834) [8], any thing [7], as long as (+3117) [5], altogether [4], alway (+3117+1886.1) [4], every man [4], every province (+4082+4082+2050.1) [4], every thing [4], nothing (+3808) [4], what soever (+834) [4], all things [3], always (+3117+1886.1) [3], always (+6256+871.1) [3], as many as [3], ever (+3117+1886.1) [3], nothing (+3808+1886.1) [3], what [3], whatsoever (+871.1) [3], whithersoever (+413+834) [3], whomsoever (+834) [3], as long as (+834+3117+1886.1) [2], every city (+5892+5892+2050.1) [2], no (+369) [2], nothing (+369) [2], perpetually (+3117+1886.1) [2], that [2], throughout (+871.1) [2], whatsoever (+3807.1) [2], whatsoever (+834+3509.1) [2], whoso [2], all (+376) [1], all generations (+1755+1755+2050.1) [1], all manner [1], all over [1], always (+3117) [1], always (+871.1) [1], any (+259) [1], any manner [1], any thing (+3972) [1], as (+834+3509.1) [1], as long as (+3117+1886.1) [1], as long as [1], as many as (+834) [1], as much as (+3509.1) [1], as much as (+834) [1], at wit's end (+1104+2451) [1], continually (+3117) [1], daily (+3117+871.1) [1], enough [1], everlasting (+5769) [1], evermore (+3117+1886.1) [1], every

day (+3117+3117+2050.1) [1], every generation (+1755+1755+2050.1) [1], every man's [1], every where [1], every year (+8141+8141+2050.1) [1], for evermore (+3117+1886.1) [1], generally [1], howsoever (+834) [1], many [1], more and more (+3254+5921) [1], no (+1115) [1], no (+369+3807.1) [1], none (+408+871.1) [1], nor (+2050.1) [1], nothing (+1097) [1], nothing (+1697+3808) [1], nothing (+408) [1], open [1], ought else (+3972) [1], ought [1], so long as (+3117+1886.1) [1], so long as (+871.1) [1], soever [1], theˢ [1], throughout all [1], utterly [1], whatsoever (+3509.1) [1], whatsoever (+3627+1886.1) [1], whensoever (+871.1) [1], wheresoever (+3807.1) [1], wheresoever (+413) [1], wheresoever (+834+871.1) [1], wheresoever any (+834+8033) [1], while (+5750) [1], whithersoever (+834+8033) [1], whithersoever (+834+4033) [1], whosoever (+376) [1], whosoever (+376+834) [1], withal [1], yearly (+8141+8141+871.1+2050.1) [1]

3606 כֹּל *kôl* (Aram.), n.m. GK: 10353 [→ 3635; cf. 3605]. all, totality, completion of an event; a part of a totality: any, every:- all [51], any [8], forasmuch as (+1768+6903) [8], whole [6], because (+1768+6903) [4], every [4], no (+3809) [3], therefore (+1836+6903) [3], wherefore (+1836+6903) [2], whosoever (+1768) [2], as (+1768+6903) [1], for this cause (+1836+6903) [1], manner [1], noˢ [1], none (+3809) [1], that (+1836+6903) [1], therefore (+1768+6903) [1], though (+1768+6903) [1], whatsoever (+1768) [1], whatsoever (+1768+1768) [1], wheresoever (+1768+871.2) [1], whosoever (+606) [1], whosoever (+606+1768+1768) [1]

3607 כָּלָא *kãlã'*, v. GK: 3973 & 3974 [→ 3608, 3628, 4356; cf. 3615, 3627]. [Q] to stop, withhold, contain; [Qp] to be confined; [N] to be restrained; [P] to finish:- shut up [4], stayed [3], refrained [2], restrained [2], withhold [2], finish [1], forbid [1], keep back [1], kept [1], retain [1]

3608 כֶּלֶא *kele'*, n.[m.]. GK: 3975 [→ 3607; cf. 3628]. prison, (house of) imprisonment:- prison (+1004+1886.1) [4], prison [4], prison (+1004) [2]

3609 כִּלְאָב *kil'ãb*, n.pr.m. GK: 3976. Kileab:- Chileab [1]

3610 כִּלְאַיִם *kil'ayim*, n.[m.]. GK: 3977. (things of) two kinds:- diverse kind [1], divers [1], mingled of linen and woollen (+8162) [1], mingled [1]

3611 כֶּלֶב *keleb*, n.m. GK: 3978 [→ 3612; cf. 3619]. dog; by extension of a person of low status: a dead dog; an immoral person: male prostitute:- dogs [16], dog [14], dog's [2]

3612 כָּלֵב *kãlēb*, n.pr.m. GK: 3979 [→ 3613, 3614, 3619, 3621; cf. 3611]. Caleb, "*dog; snappish, warding off*":- Caleb [31], Caleb's [4]

3613 כָּלֵב אֶפְרָתָה *kãlēb 'eprãtâ*, n.pr.loc. GK: 3980 [→ 3612+672]. Caleb Ephrathah:- Caleb-ephratah [1]

3614 כָּלִבִּי *kãlibbî*, a.g. GK: 3981 & 3982 [→ 3612]. Calebite, "*of Caleb*":- of the house of Caleb [1]

3615 כָּלָה *kãlâ*, v. GK: 3983 [→ 401, 3616, 3617, 3631, 3630, 4357, 8502, 8503; cf. 3607, 3627, 3634, 5239]. [Q] to finish, fulfill, complete; to fail, cease, perish; [P] to finish, complete, fulfill; to destroy, end, wipe out; [Pu] to be completed, be concluded:- made an end [41], consumed [36], consume [22], finished [19], fail [12], done [9], accomplished [7], ended [7], accomplish [5], determined [4], faileth [4], spend [4], spent [4], end [2], fainteth [2], fulfilled [2], left [2], make an end [2], bringeth to pass [1], caused to fail [1], ceaseth [1], cease [1], consumed away [1], destroy utterly [1], destroyeth [1], expired [1], failed [1], finish [1], fulfil [1], fully [1], left off [1], longed [1], make clean riddance [1], pluck [1], quite take away [1], utterly destroyed [1], wasted [1], waste [1], wholly reap (+3807.1+7114) [1]

3616 כָּלֶה *kãleh*, a. GK: 3985 [→ 3615]. failing with desire, longing:- fail [1]

3617 כָּלָה *kãlâ*, n.f. GK: 3986 [→ 3615]. destruction, complete destruction:- full end [8], altogether [3], consumption [2], utter end [2], consumed [1], consume [1], consummation [1], determined [1], end [1], riddance [1], utterly consume [1]

3618 כַּלָּה *kallâ*, n.f. GK: 3987 [→ 3623]. (before marriage) bride; daughter-in-law:- daughter in law [14], bride [9], spouse [6], daughters in law [3], spouses [2]

כְּלוּא *kᵉlû'*. See 3628.

3619 כְּלוּב *kᵉlûb*, n.m. GK: 3990 [→ 3597?, 3611, 3612, 3619, 3620?]. (fruit) basket; (bird) cage:- basket [2], cage [1]

3620 כְּלוּב *kᵉlûb*, n.pr.m. GK: 3991 [→ 3619?]. Kelub, "*basket*":- Chelub [2]

3621 כְּלוּבַי **k^elûbāy**, n.pr.m. GK: 3992 [→ 3612]. Caleb, "*dog; snappish warding off*":– Chelubai [1]

3622 כְּלוּהִי **k^eluhî** or כְּלוּהוּ **k^elûhû**, n.pr.m. GK: 3988 & 3993. Keluhi:– Chelluh [1]

3623 כְּלוּלֹה **k^elûlōt**, n.f. GK: 3994 [→ 3618]. time of betrothal, state of betrothal:– espousals [1]

3624 כֶּלַח **kelaḥ**, n.m. GK: 3995. full vigor:– full age [1], old age [1]

3625 כֶּלַח **kelaḥ**, n.pr.loc. GK: 3996. Calah, "*strength, vigor*":– Calah [2]

3626 כָּל־חֹזֶה **kol-ḥōzeh**, n.pr.m. GK: 3997 [→ 3605+2374]. Col-Hozeh, "*every seer*":– Col-hozeh [2]

3627 כְּלִי **k^elî**, n.m. GK: 3998 [cf. 3607?; 3615?]. article, utensil, thing; a general term that can be used of any object:– vessels [132], instruments [37], vessel [34], jewels [20], armourbearer [+5375] [18], weapons [17], stuff [14], thing [11], weapons [10], furniture [7], weapon [4], bag [2], carriage [2], instrument [2], artillery [1], carriages [1], furnish (+6213) [1], jewel [1], one another^S [1], pot [1], psaltery (+5035) [1], sacks [1], that is made [1], that which pertaineth [1], things made [1], tool [1], wares [1], whatsoever (+3605+1886.1) [1]

3628 כְּלוּא **k^elû**' or כְּלִיא **k^elî**', n.[m.]. GK: 3989 & 3999 [→ 3607; cf. 3608]. imprisonment:– prison (+1004+1886.1) [2]

3629 כִּלְיָה **kilyâ**, n.f. GK: 4000. kidney; by extension: inmost being: heart, mind, spirit, the seat of thought and emotion of the inner person; kernel (of wheat):– kidneys [18], reins [13]

3630 כִּלְיוֹן **kilyôn**, n.pr.m. GK: 4002 [→ 3615]. Kilion, "*annihilation*":– Chilion [2], Chilion's [1]

3631 כִּלָּיוֹן **killāyôn**, n.m. GK: 4001 [→ 3615]. destruction, annihilation; weariness, failure (of the eyes):– consumption [1], failing [1]

3632 כָּלִיל **kālîl**, a. & subst. GK: 4003 [→ 3634]. entire, whole, perfect; whole burnt offering:– wholly [4], perfect [3], all [2], whole [2], every whit [1], flame [1], perfection [1], utterly [1]

3633 כַּלְכֹּל **kalkōl**, n.pr.m. GK: 4004 [→ 3634?]. Calcol:– Calcol [1], Chalcol [1]

3634 כָּלַל **kālal**, v. GK: 4005 [→ 3605, 3626, 3632, 3633?, 3636, 4358, 4360, 4359; cf. 3557?; 3615; cf. 3606, cf. 3635]. [Q] to bring to perfection, make complete:– made perfect [1], perfected [1]

3635 כְּלַל **k^elal** (Aram.), v. GK: 10354 [→ 3606; cf. 3634]. [Sh] to finish, restore; [Hsh] to be finished:– set up [4], make up [2], finished [1]

3636 כְּלָל **k^elāl**, n.pr.m. GK: 4006 [→ 3634]. Kelal, "*perfection, completeness*":– Chelal [1]

3637 כָּלַם **kālam**, v. GK: 4007 [→ 3639, 3640]. [N] to be disgraced, be humiliated, be put to shame; [H] to disgrace, humble, bring to shame; [Ho] to be mistreated, be despairing:– ashamed [11], confounded [11], put to shame [5], blush [3], hurt [2], done shame [1], make ashamed [1], put to confusion [1], reproached [1], reproach [1], shameth [1]

3638 כִּלְמָד **kilmad**, n.pr.loc. GK: 4008. Kilmad:– Chilmad [1]

3639 כְּלִמָּה **k^elimmâ**, n.f. GK: 4009 [→ 3637]. disgrace, shame, scorn:– shame [20], confusion [6], dishonour [3], reproach [1]

3640 כְּלִמּוּת **k^elimmût**, n.f. GK: 4010 [→ 3637]. shame, disgrace, insult:– shame [1]

3641 כָּלְנֶה **kalnēh** or כַּלְנוֹ **kalnô**, n.pr.loc. GK: 4011 & 4012. Calneh, Calno, "*all of them*":– Calneh [2], Calno [1]

3641.1 כֶּם- **-kem**, p.m.pl.suf. GK: 4013 [→ 3509.2]. you, your:– you [1209], your [1175], ye [145], your (+3807.1) [44], your own [22], yourselves [22], yourselves (+5315) [6], yours (+3807.1) [4], thee [2], thou [1], thy [1], your (+4480) [1], yours [1]

3641.2 כֹם- **-kōm** (Aram.), p.suf.2.m.pl. GK: 10355 [→ 3641.2; cf. 3641.1]. you, your:– you [3], your [2]

3642 כָּמַהּ **kāmah**, v. GK: 4014 [→ 3643]. [Q] to long for, yearn for:– longeth [1]

3643 כִּמְהָם **kimhām** or כִּמְוהָם **kimwhām**, n.pr.m. GK: 4016 & 4018 [cf. 3642]. Kimham, Kimuham:– Chimham [4]

3644 כְּמוֹ **k^emô**, adv. & c. GK: 4017 [→ 3509.1+4100]. like, as; for, with, when:– as [60], like [41], like unto [17], according to [2], as it were [2], as well as [2], like to [2], such as [2], and [1], both [1], even [1], in comparison of [1], like as [1], so [1], the like [1], thus [1], when [1], worth [1]

3645 כְּמוֹשׁ **k^emôš** or כְּמִישׁ **k^emîš**, n.pr. GK: 4019 & 4020. Chemosh, Chemish (pagan god):– Chemosh [8]

3646 כַּמֹּן **kammōn**, n.m. GK: 4021. cummin (a small, flavorful seed of the carrot family):– cummin [3]

3647 כָּמַס **kāmas**, v. GK: 4022 [→ 4363]. [Qp] to be kept in reserve:– laid up in store [1]

3648 כָּמַר **kāmar**, v. GK: 4023 [→ 3649]. [N] to become hot; become aroused, be excited (with compassion):– black [1], kindled [1], yerned [1], yern [1]

3649 כֹּמֶר **kōmer**, n.m. GK: 4024 [→ 3648]. priest, in the OT always one who serves a foreign god, with a possible focus on manic rituals and altered states of awareness:– Chemarims [1], idolatrous priests [1], priests [1]

3650 כִּמְרִיר **kamrîr**, n.m. GK: 4025. blackness, deep gloom:– blackness [1]

3651 כֵּן **kēn**, a. & adv. GK: 4026 & 4027 [cf. 3559; cf. 3652]. honest; right, correct, orderly; (adv.) marker to show sequence of logic: so, thus, therefore; marker to show sequence of events: so, then:– so [283], therefore (+3807.1) [176], therefore (+5921) [125], wherefore (+5921) [22], thus [20], wherefore (+3807.1) [18], this [17], afterward (+310) [15], that [12], likewise [11], such [7], true [5], afterwards (+310) [4], right [4], as [3], because (+5921) [3], in like manner [3], like [3], well [3], after that (+310) [2], because (+3588+5921) [2], even so [2], surely (+3807.1) [2], according [1], after that (+310+2050.1) [1], afterward (+310+4480) [1], also [1], aright [1], as (+834+3509.1) [1], as yet (+5704) [1], certainly [1], even as (+834+3509.1) [1], following (+310) [1], for which cause (+3807.1) [1], for which cause (+5921) [1], forasmuch (+3807.1) [1], forasmuch as (+3588+5921) [1], howbeit (+2050.1) [1], if so (+518) [1], state [1], straightway [1], that (+5921) [1], the more [1], thenceforth (+310) [1], therefore [1], which thing [1]

3652 כֵּן **kēn** (Aram.), adv. GK: 10357 [cf. 3651]. this is what, thus:– thus [8]

3653 כֵּן **kēn**, n.m. GK: 4029 & 4030 [→ 3662, 3663; cf. 3559]. position; place; stand (of a basin):– foot [8], estate [4], base [2], office [1], place [1], well [1]

3654 כֵּן **kēn**, n.[m.]. GK: 4031 & 4038. gnats, flies:– lice [6], in manner [1]

3654.1 -כֶן- **-ken** or כֶנָה- **-kenâ**, p.f.pl.suf. GK: 4032 [→ 3509.2]. you, your:– your [16], you [2], ye [1]

3655 כָּנָה **kānâ**, v. GK: 4033. [P] to bestow a title or name of honor; to flatter by giving a name of honor:– give flattering titles [2], surnamed [1], surname [1]

3656 כַּנֶּה **kanneh**, n.pr.loc. GK: 4034. Canneh:– Canneh [1]

3657 כַּנָּה **kannâ**, n.f. GK: 4035. root:– vineyard [1]

3658 כִּנּוֹר **kinnôr**, n.m. GK: 4036. a stringed instrument: harp, lyre, lute, zither:– harp [25], harps [17]

3659 כָּנְיָהוּ **konyāhû**, n.pr.m. GK: 4037 [→ 3078]. Jehoiachin:– Coniah [3]

3660 כְּנֵמָא **k^enēmā**' (Aram.), adv. GK: 10358. as follows, thus:– thus [2], after this manner [1], in this sort [1], so [1]

3661 כָּנַן **kānan**, var. GK: *. to plant a vineyard:–

3662 כְּנָנִי **k^enānî**, n.pr.m. GK: 4039 [→ 3663]. Kenani, "*Yahweh strengthens*":– Chenani [1]

3663 כְּנַנְיָה **k^enanyâ** or כְּנַנְיָהוּ **k^enanyâhû** or כְּנַנְיָהוּ **kānanyāhû**, n.pr.m. GK: 4040 & 4041 & 4042 [→ 3068+3559, 3662]. Kenaniah, Conaniah, "*Yahweh strengthens*":– Chenaniah [3]

3664 כָּנַס **kānas**, v. GK: 4043 [→ 4370; cf. 3673]. [Q, P] to assemble, gather, store up; [Ht] to wrap around:– gather together [3], gathered [2], gathereth together [2], gather [2], heap up [1], wrap [1]

3665 כָּנַע **kāna**', v. GK: 4044 [→ 3666]. [N] to be humbled, be subdued, be subjected; [H] to subdue, humble, subject:– humbled [13], subdued [9], bring down [2], humbleth [2], humble [2], bring low [1], brought down [1], brought into subjection [1], brought low [1], brought under [1], humbledst [1], subduedst [1], subdue [1]

3666 כִּנְעָה **kin'â**, n.f. GK: 4045 [→ 3665]. bundle of belongings:– wares [1]

3667 כְּנַעַן **k^ena'an**, n.pr.m. & loc. GK: 4046 & 4047 [→ 3668?, 3669]. Canaan; Canaanite, "*land of purple, hence merchant, trader*":– Canaan [89], merchant [3], traffickers [1], traffick [1]

3668 כְּנַעֲנָה **k^ena'a^anâ**, n.pr.m. GK: 4049 [→ 3667?]. Kenaanah, "*toward Canaan*":– Chenaanah [5]

3669 כְּנַעֲנִי **k^ena'a^anî**, a.g. & n.m. GK: 4048 & 4050 & 4051 [→ 3667]. Canaanite, of Canaan, in Canaan, "*of Canaan*"; merchant, trader:– Canaanite [55], Canaanites [12], Canaanitess [1], Canaanitish woman [1], Canaanitish [1], Canaan [1], merchants [1], merchant [1]

3670 כָּנַף **kānap**, v.den. GK: 4052 [→ 3671]. [N] to hide oneself, be hidden:– removed into a corner [1]

3671 כָּנָף **kānāp**, n.f. GK: 4053 [→ 3670]. extreme part: wing (of creatures that fly); corner, hem (of garment); ends (of the earth):– wings [60], wing [13], skirt [12], borders [2], corners [2], ends [2], feathered [2], one another (+413+3671) [2], skirts [2], sort [2], winged [2], bird (+1167) [1], flying [1], other^S [1], overspreading [1], quarters [1], two wings [1], uttermost part [1]

3672 כִּנְּרוֹת **kinrôt** or כִּנֶּרֶת **kinneret** or כִּנְרוֹת **kin^erôt**, n.pr.loc. GK: 4054 & 4055. Kinnereth, Kinneroth, "*zithers, lyres*":– Chinnereth [3], Cinneroth [3], Cinnereth [1]

3673 כְּנַשׁ **k^enaš** (Aram.), v. GK: 10359 [→ 3664]. [P] to assemble (persons); [Htpa] to be assembled:– gathered together [2], gather together [1]

3674 כְּנָת **k^enāt**, n.f. GK: 4056 [cf. 3675]. associate, companion:– companions [1]

3675 כְּנָת **k^enāt** (Aram.), n.m. GK: 10360 [cf. 3674]. associate, colleague:– companions [7]

3676 כֵּס **k's**, var. GK: 4058 [→ 3678+3050; cf. 3764]. poss. short form of 3678: seat, throne:–

3677 כֵּסֶא **kese**', n.[m.]. GK: 4057 & 4060 [→ 3678]. full moon:– appointed [1], time appointed [1]

3678 כִּסֵּא **kissē**' or כִּסֵּה **kissēh**, n.m. GK: 4058 & 4061 [→ 3676]. seat, chair; in a public and civic setting: place of authority, seat of honor; of royalty or deity: throne:– throne [123], seat [7], thrones [4], stool [1], sworn (+3027+5921) [1]

3679 כַּשְׂדָּי **kasdāy** (Aram.), n.pr.g. GK: 10361 [cf. 3779]. Chaldean:– Chaldean [1]

3680 כָּסָה **kāsâ**, v. GK: 4059 [→ 3681, 3682, 4372, 4374]. [Qp] to be covered; [N] to be covered; [P] to cover, conceal; to decorate; to overwhelm; [Pu] to be covered, be shrouded; [Ht] to cover oneself, put on clothing:– covered [61], cover [50], covereth [21], concealeth [2], conceal [2], coveredst [2], covering [2], hide [2], hid [2], overwhelmed [1], clad [1], closed [1], clothed [1], coverest [1], flee to hide [1], hideth [1]

כֵּסֶה **keseh**. See 3677.

כִּסֵּה **kissēh**. See 3678.

3681 כָּסוּי **kāsûy**, n.[m.]. GK: 4062 [→ 3680]. covering:– covering [2]

3682 כְּסוּת **k^esût**, n.f. GK: 4064 [→ 3680]. covering, cloak, clothing:– covering [6], raiment [1], vesture [1]

3683 כָּסַח **kāsaḥ**, v. GK: 4065. [Qp] to be cut down (of brush):– cut down [1], cut up [1]

3684 כְּסִיל **k^esîl**, n.m. GK: 4067 [→ 3685; cf. 3688]. foolish, stupid, insolent; (n.) fool, insolent person:– fool [34], fools [22], foolish [4], fools [4], fool's [1]

3685 כְּסִיל **k^esîl**, n.m. GK: 4068 [→ 3684; cf. 3688]. Orion (and its adjoining constellations):– Orion [3], constellations [1]

3686 כְּסִיל **k^esîl**, n.pr.loc. GK: 4069. Kesil:– Chesil [1]

3687 כְּסִילוּת **k^esîlût**, n.f. GK: 4070 [→ 3688]. folly, stupidity, insolence, with a possible implication of rebellion:– foolish [1]

3688 כָּסַל **kāsal**, v. GK: 4071 [→ 3694, 3684, 3685, 3687, 3689, 3690, 3693, 3692]. [Q] to be foolish, be stupid:– foolish [1]

3689 כֶּסֶל **kesel**, n.m. GK: 4072 & 4073 [→ 3688, 3696?]. waist, back; (pl.) loins; trust, confidence; stupidity:– flanks [6], hope [3], folly [2], confidence [1], loins [1]

3690 כִּסְלָה **kislâ**, n.f. GK: 4074 [→ 3688]. confidence; folly:– confidence [1], folly [1]

3691 כִּסְלֵו **kislēw**, n.pr.[m.]. GK: 4075. Kislev:– Chisleu [2]

3692 כִּסְלוֹן **kislôn**, n.pr.m. GK: 4077 [→ 3688]. Kislon, "*slow; strength*":– Chislon [1]

3693 כִּסְלֹן **k^esālôn**, n.pr.loc. GK: 4076 [→ 3688]. Kesalon:– Chesalon [1]

3694 כְּסֻלּוֹת **k^esullôt**, n.pr.loc. GK: 4063 [→ 3688]. Kesulloth, "*loins* or *flanks [of Mt. Tabor]*":– Chesulloth [1]

3695 כַּסְלֻחִים **kasluḥîm**, n.pr.g. GK: 4078. Casluhite:– Casluhim [2]

3696 כִּסְלֹת תָּבֹר **kislōt tābōr**, n.pr.loc. GK: 4079 [→ 3689?+8396]. Kisloth Tabor:– Chislothtabor [1]

3697 כָּסַם **kāsam**, v. GK: 4080 [→ 3698; cf. 1501, 3765]. [Q] to trip, clip (hair):– only poll (+3697) [2]

3698 כֻּסֶּמֶת **kussemet**, n.f. GK: 4081 [→ 3697]. spelt, emmer wheat:– rye [2], fitches [1]

3699 כָּסַס **kāsas**, v. GK: 4082 [→ 4371, 4373]. [Q] to determine, reckon, compute:– make count [1]

3700 כָּסַף **kāsap**, v. GK: 4083 [→ 3701]. [Q] to long for; be hungry; [N] to long for, yearn for; to be ashamed:– sore longedst (+3700) [2], desired [1], greedy [1], have desire [1], longeth [1]

3701 כֶּסֶף **kesep**, n.m. GK: 4084 [→ 3700; cf. 3702]. silver, silver piece = money:– silver [287], money [112], price [3], silverlings [1]

3702 כְּסַף **keʸsap** (Aram.), n.m. GK: 10362 [cf. 3701]. silver:– silver [12], money [1]

3703 כָּסִפְיָא **kāsipyāʾ**, n.pr.loc. GK: 4085. Casiphia:– Casiphia [2]

3704 כֶּסֶת **keset**, n.f. GK: 4086. magic charm band:– pillows [2]

3705 כְּעַן **keʸʿan** (Aram.), adv. GK: 10363 [→ 3706]. now, furthermore, to the present:– now [13]

3706 כְּעֶנֶת **keʸʿenet** or כְּעֶת **keʸʿet** (Aram.), adv. GK: 10364 & 10365 [→ 3705]. (and) now, a marker to connect what follows; the phrase "Peace and now" is a formal greeting in a letter:– at such a time [1], such a time [1]

3707 כָּעַס **kāʿas**, v. GK: 4087 [→ 3708; cf. 3708]. [Q] to be angry, be vexed, be incensed; [P] to anger, provoke; [H] to provoke to anger:– provoke to anger [24], provoked to anger [14], provoking to anger [3], angry [2], provoked [2], grieved [1], provoke unto wrath [1], provoked sore (+3708) [1], provoketh to anger [1], provoke [1], sorrow [1], took indignation [1], vex [1], wroth [1]

3708 כַּעַס **kaʿas** or כַּעַשׂ **kaʿaś**, n.m. GK: 4088 & 4089 [→ 3707, 3708]. general uneasiness and anxiety, inwardly focused: anguish, grief; focused toward an object: anger, resentment:– grief [7], wrath [4], provocation [3], sorrow [3], anger [2], angry [1], indignation [1], provocations [1], provoked sore (+3707) [1], provoking [1], spite [1]

כְּעֶת **keʸʿet**. See 3706.

3709 כַּף **kap**, n.f. GK: 4090 [→ 3721]. hand (of a person), palm of the hand, sole of the foot, paw (of an animal); by extension: power, strength; something hollowed: socket, (shallow) dish; a measure of quantity: handful:– hands [69], hand [55], sole [12], spoons [12], spoon [12], soles [7], hands together (+413+3709) [4], hollow [4], palms [3], handful (+4393) [2], palm of hand [2], apiece (+1886.1) [1], branches [1], clouds [1], foot (+7272) [1], handled (+8610+871.1+1886.1) [1], handles [1], middle [1], palms of hands [1], paws [1], power [1], took a handful (+4390) [1]

3710 כֵּף **kēp**, n.[m.]. GK: 4091. rock:– rocks [2]

3711 כָּפָה **kāpâ**, v. GK: 4092. [Q] to soothe, avert (anger):– pacifieth [1]

3712 כִּפָּה **kippâ**, n.f. GK: 4093 [→ 3721]. palm branch, palm frond:– branch [3]

3713 כְּפוֹר **keʸpôr**, n.m. GK: 4094 & 4095 [→ 3722]. bowl, dish (made of gold or silver); frost:– basons [4], every bason (+3713+2050.1) [4], hoar frost [1], hoarfrost [1], hoary frost [1]

3714 כָּפִיס **kāpîs**, n.m. GK: 4096. beam (of woodwork); some sources: rafter:– beam [1]

3715 כְּפִיר **keʸpîr**, n.m. GK: 4097 & 4099 [→ 3722, 3723]. young lion; village:– young lions [12], young lion [12], lion [4], lions [2], villages [1], young [1]

3716 כְּפִירָה **keʸpîrâ**, n.pr.loc. GK: 4098 [→ 3723]. Kephirah, "village":– Chephirah [4]

3717 כָּפַל **kāpal**, v. GK: 4100 [→ 3718, 4375]. [Q] to fold double; [Qp] to be folded double; [N] to be doubled:– doubled [3], double [2]

3718 כֶּפֶל **kepel**, n.[m.]. GK: 4101 [→ 3717]. double; two sides:– double [3]

3719 כָּפַן **kāpan**, v. GK: 4102 [→ 3720]. [Q] to hunger, send out roots in hunger:– bend [1]

3720 כָּפָן **kāpān**, n.[m.]. GK: 4103 [→ 3719]. hunger, famine:– famine [2]

3721 כָּפַף **kāpap**, v. GK: 4104 [→ 3709, 3712]. [Q] to bow down in distress; [Qp] be bowed down; [N] bow down (before):– bowed down [3], bow down [1], bow [1]

3722 כָּפַר **kāpar**, v. GK: 4105 & 4106 [→ 3713, 3715, 3724, 3725, 3727]. [Q] to coat, cover (with pitch); [Nitpael] to be atoned (for); [P] to make atonement; make amends, pardon, release, appease, forgive; [Pu] to be atoned for, be annulled; [Ht] to allow for atonement; atonement may be a figure of covering over and therefore forgetting (forgiving) sin:– make an atonement [58], make atonement [6], made an atonement [5], purged [5], make reconciliation [4], atonement made [2], merciful [2], purge away [2], purge [2], reconcile [2], appease (+6440) [1], cleansed [1], disannulled [1], forgave [1], forgiven [1], forgive [1], maketh an atonement [1], maketh atonement [1], pacified [1], pacify [1], pardon [1], pitch [1], put off [1], reconciling [1]

3723 כָּפָר **kāpār**, n.m. GK: 4107 [→ 3716, 3715, 3724, 3726]. (unwalled) village:– villages [2]

3724 כֹּפֶר **kōper**, n.m. GK: 4108 & 4109 & 4110 & 4111 [→ 3722, 3723]. pitch (used to cover and seal the ark of Noah); (unwalled) village; henna, henna blossom; ransom, compensation, payment; bribe:– ransom [8], bribe [2], camphire [2], satisfaction [2], pitch [1], sum of money [1], villages [1]

3725 כִּפֻּרִים **kippurîm**, n.pl.abst. GK: 4113 [→ 3722]. atonement; atonement may be a figure of covering over and therefore forgetting (forgiving) sin; "day of Atonement" is an annual day of rest and with ceremonies accomplishing full atonement for the nation of Israel:– atonement [7], atonements [1]

3726 כְּפַר הָעַמֹּנִי **keʸpar hāʿammōnî**, n.pr.loc. GK: 4112 [→ 3723]. Kephar Ammoni, "village of Ammonites":– Chephar-haammonai [1]

3727 כַּפֹּרֶת **kappōret**, n. GK: 4114 [→ 3722]. atonement cover (traditionally: mercy seat); the golden cover on the ark of the covenant, the place where atonement is made:– mercy seat [26], mercy seatward [1]

3728 כָּפַשׁ **kāpaš**, v. GK: 4115 [cf. 3533]. [H] to trample down:– covered [1]

3729 כְּפַת **keʸpat** (Aram.), v. GK: 10366. [Peil] to be bound; [Pa] to tie up; [Pap] to be tied:– bound [3], bind [1]

3730 כַּפְתּוֹר **kaptôr**, n.m. GK: 4117. bud; top of a pillar or column:– knop [10], knops [6], lintel of the door [1], upper lintels [1]

3731 כַּפְתּוֹר **kaptôr**, n.pr.loc. GK: 4116 [→ 3732]. Caphtor:– Caphtor [3]

3732 כַּפְתֹּרִי **kaptōrî**, a.g. GK: 4118 [→ 3731]. Caphtorite, "of Caphtor":– Caphthorim [1], Caphtorims [1], Caphtorim [1]

3733 כַּר **kar**, n.m. GK: 4119 & 4120 & 4121 [→ 3769]. (young) ram; battering ram; meadow, pastureland; saddle, saddle-bag:– lambs [9], pastures [2], rams [2], captains [1], furniture [1], lamb [1]

3734 כֹּר **kōr**, n.[m.]. GK: 4123 & 10367. cor (measure of dry or liquid volume, about 60 gallons [220 liters]): note this word is Aramaic once in Ezra:– measures [8], cor [1]

3735 כְּרָא **keʸrāʾ** (Aram.), v. GK: 10369. [Itpe] to be troubled, distressed:– grieved [1]

3736 כִּרְבֵּל **kirbēl**, v.den. GK: 4124 [cf. 3737]. [Pu] to be clothed, be wrapped:– clothed [1]

3737 כַּרְבְּלָה **karbeʸlâ** (Aram.), n.f. GK: 10368. headdress of some kind: turban, cap; the etymology suggests something wrapped around the head:– hats [1]

3738 כָּרָה **kārâ**, v. GK: 4125 & 4127 & 4128 [→ 3740, 3741, 4351, 4379]. [Q] to dig; to hew (stone); to hollow out; to prepare a feast; to tie together:– digged [8], dig [2], made [2], diggeth up [1], diggeth [1], opened [1], pierced [1]

3739 כָּרָה **kārâ**, v. GK: 4126. [Q] to barter; purchase:– bought [1], buy [1], make a banquet [1], prepared [1]

3740 כֵּרָה **kērâ**, n.f. GK: 4130 [→ 3738]. feast, banquet; provision:– provision [1]

3741 כָּרָה **kārâ**, n.f. GK: 4129 [→ 3738]. cistern, well:– cottages [1]

3742 כְּרוּב **keʸrûb**, n.m. GK: 4131. cherub, (pl.) cherubim, a class of supernatural beings that serve in the presence of God; used as ornamental figures on the atonement cover of the ark of the covenant and in the temple as well as on the walls and doors of the temple:– cherubims [63], cherub [27], cherubims' [1]

3743 כְּרוּב **keʸrûb**, n.pr.loc. GK: 4132. Kerub:– Cherub [2]

3744 כָּרוֹז **kārôz** (Aram.), n.m. GK: 10370 [→ 3745]. herald, proclaimer:– herald [1]

3745 כְּרַז **keʸraz** (Aram.), v.den. GK: 10371 [→ 3744]. [H] to proclaim:– made a proclamation [1]

3746 כָּרִי **kārî**, a.g. GK: 4133. Carite:– captains [2]

3747 כְּרִית **keʸrît**, n.pr.loc. GK: 4134 [→ 3772]. Kerith, "cut off, perish":– Cherith [2]

3748 כְּרִיתוּת **keʸrîtût**, n.f. GK: 4135 [→ 3772]. divorce:– divorcement [3], divorce [1]

3749 כַּרְכֹּב **karkōb**, n.[m.]. GK: 4136. ledge, rim, edge:– compass [1]

3750 כַּרְכֹּם **karkōm**, n.[m.]. GK: 4137. saffron (plant):– saffron [1]

3751 כַּרְכְּמִישׁ **karkeʸmîš**, n.pr.loc. GK: 4138. Carchemish:– Carchemish [3]

3752 כַּרְכַּס **karkas**, n.pr.m. GK: 4139. Carcas, "[perhaps] vulture":– Carcas [1]

3753 כִּרְכָּרָה **kirkārâ**, n.f. GK: 4140 [→ 3769]. (fast running) female camel:– swift beasts [1]

3754 כֶּרֶם **kerem**, n.m. GK: 4142 [→ 3755, 3756?, 3757?, 3759]. vineyard:– vineyards [45], vineyard [44], vines [3], vintage [1]

3755 כֹּרֵם **kōrēm**, n.[m.] or v.ptcp. GK: 4144 [→ 3754]. worker in the vineyard, vine growers, vinedressers:– vinedressers [5]

3756 כַּרְמִי **karmî**, n.pr.m. GK: 4145 [→ 3757; cf. 3754?]. Carmi, "[poss.] [fruitful] vine, vineyard owner":– Carmi [8]

3757 כַּרְמִי **karmî**, a.g. GK: 4146 [→ 3756; cf. 3754?]. Carmite, "of Carmi":– Carmites [1]

3758 כַּרְמִיל **karmîl**, n.[m.]. GK: 4147. crimson (yarn):– crimson [3]

3759 כַּרְמֶל **karmel**, n.m. GK: 4149 & 4152 [→ 3760, 3761, 3762; cf. 3754]. fertile land, fruitful land; this can refer to an orchard or plantation; new grain, newly ripe grain:– fruitful field [6], plentiful field [2], corn of full ears [1], fruitful place [1], full ears of corn [1], green ears [1], plentiful [1]

3760 כַּרְמֶל **karmel**, n.pr.loc. GK: 4150 & 4151 [→ 3759, 3761]. Carmel, "orchard planted with vine and fruit trees":– Carmel [26]

3761 כַּרְמְלִי **karmeʸlî**, a.g. GK: 4153 [→ 3760, 3762; cf. 3759]. Carmelite, of Carmel, "of Carmel":– Carmelite [5], Carmelitess [2]

3762 כַּרְמְלִית **karmeʸlît**, a.g. GK: 4153 [→ 3761]. f. of 3761: Carmelite, of Carmel, "of Carmel":–

3763 כְּרָן **keʸrān**, n.pr.m. GK: 4154. Keran:– Cheran [2]

3764 כָּרְסֵא **korseʾ** (Aram.), n.m. GK: 10372 [cf. 3676]. seat, chair; of power and position: throne; "to come down from the throne" means to be deposed and so lose power:– throne [2], thrones [1]

3765 כִּרְסֵם **kirsēm**, v. GK: 4155 [cf. 3697]. [P] to ravage, eat away:– waste [1]

3766 כָּרַע **kāraʿ**, v. GK: 4156 [→ 3767]. [Q] to kneel down, crouch, often with the associative meaning of respect and honor or of readiness for action; [H] to make bow down, make kneel (an act of oppression), make miserable:– bowed [10], bow down [5], bow [4], boweth down [2], brought very low (+3766) [2], fell [2], subdued [2], bowed down [1], brought down [1], cast down [1], couched [1], feeble [1], kneeling [1], smote down [1], stooped down [1], sunk down [1]

3767 כֶּרַע **keraʿ**, n.[f.]. GK: 4157 [→ 3766]. leg bone (the shank bone, between the knee and ankle):– legs [9]

3768 כַּרְפַּס **karpas**, n.m. GK: 4158. (fine) linen:– green [1]

3769 כָּרַר **kārar**, v. GK: 4159 [→ 3564?, 3603, 3733, 3753]. [Pil] to dance:– danced [1], dancing [1]

3770 כָּרֵשׂ **kārēś**, n.[m.]. GK: 4160. stomach, belly:– belly [1]

כֹּרֶשׁ **kōreš**. See 3567.

3771 כַּרְשְׁנָא **karšeʸnāʾ**, n.pr.m. GK: 4161. Carshena, "[poss.] black":– Carshena [1]

3772 כָּרַת **kārat**, v. GK: 4162 [→ 3747?, 3748, 3773]. [Q] to cut off, cut down; to make (a covenant, agreement); [Qp] to be cut off, broken off; [N] to be cut off, be destroyed; [Pu] to be cut off; [H] to cut off, get rid of, destroy, kill; [Ho] to be cut off; "to cut a covenant" is "make a covenant," a figure of the act of ceremonially cutting an animal into two parts, with an

implication of serious consequences for not fulfilling the covenant:- cut off [146], made [52], make [30], cut down [21], cut [6], fail [5], want [3], covenanted [2], destroyed [2], destroy [2], hew [2], utterly cut off (+3772) [2], are [1], chewed [1], cut out [1], cutteth [1], fail (+3807.1) [1], feller [1], freed [1], hew down [1], heweth down [1], leese [1], madest [1], make a covenant [1], maketh [1], making [1], perish [1]

3773 כְּרֻתוֹת **kᵉrutôt**, n.[f.pl.] GK: 4164 [→ 3772]. beams (trimmed and cut):- beams [3]

3774 כְּרֵתִי **kᵉrētî**, a.g. GK: 4165 [cf. 6432?]. Kerethite:- Cherethites [1], Cherethims [1]

3775 כֶּשֶׂב **keśeb**, n.[m.]. GK: 4166 [→ 3776; cf. 3532]. ram-lamb, young sheep:- sheep [8], lamb [3], lambs [1], sheep (+7716) [1]

3776 כִּשְׂבָּה **kiśbâ**, n.f. GK: 4167 [→ 3775]. ewe-lamb, young sheep:- lamb [1]

3777 כֶּשֶׂד **keśed**, n.pr.m. GK: 4168 [→ 3778]. Kesed, "*Chaldean, Babylonian*":- Chesed [1]

3778 כַּשְׂדִּים **kaśdîm**, n.pr.g. GK: 4169 [→ 3777; cf. 894; cf. 3679, cf. 3779]. Chaldean, Babylonian, astrologers:- Chaldeans [59], Chaldees [13], Chaldea [7], Chaldeans' [1], Chaldees' [1]

3779 כַּשְׂדָּי **kaśdāy** (Aram.), n.pr.g. GK: 10373 [cf. 3679; cf. 3778]. Chaldean; Babylonian; (as a common noun) astrologer:- Chaldeans [6], Chaldean [1]

3780 כָּשָׂה **kāśâ**, v. GK: 4170. [Q] to become sleek, heavy, stubborn, headstrong:- covered [1]

3781 כַּשִּׁיל **kaššîl**, n.[m.]. GK: 4172 [→ 3782]. axe:- axes [1]

3782 כָּשַׁל **kāšal**, v. GK: 4173 [→ 3781, 3783, 4383, 4384]. [Q] to stumble, falter, fail; [N] be caused to stumble, be brought down; [H] to cause to stumble, overthrow, bring to ruin; [Ho] to be overthrown:- fall [17], stumble [13], feeble [4], cast down [3], stumbled [3], cause to fall [2], caused to stumble [2], fallen [2], overthrown [2], utterly fall (+3782) [2], decayed [1], faileth [1], falling [1], fell down [1], fell [1], made to fall [1], make fall [1], make to fall [1], ruined [1], ruin [1], stumbleth [1], weak [1]

3783 כִּשָּׁלוֹן **kiššālôn**, n.[m.]. GK: 4174 [→ 3782]. falling down, stumbling:- fall [1]

3784 כָּשַׁף **kāšap**, v.den. GK: 4175 [→ 407, 3785, 3786]. [P] to engage in witchcraft, be a sorcerer:- sorcerers [3], witch [2], used witchcraft [1]

3785 כֶּשֶׁף **kešep**, n.m. GK: 4176 [→ 3784]. witchcraft, sorcery, often with the associative meanings of rebellion and seduction into false religion:- witchcrafts [4], sorceries [1]

3786 כַּשָּׁף **kaššāp**, n.m. GK: 4177 [→ 3784]. sorcerer:- sorcerers [1]

3787 כָּשֵׁר **kāšēr**, v. GK: 4178 [→ 3788]. [Q] to be right, successful; [H] to bring success:- direct [1], prosper [1], seem right [1]

3788 כִּשְׁרוֹן **kišrôn**, n.[m.]. GK: 4179 [→ 3787]. skill, achievement; benefit:- equity [1], good [1], right [1]

3789 כָּתַב **kātab**, v. GK: 4180 [→ 3791, 3793, 4385; cf. 3790]. [Q] to write, engrave (on stone tablets); [Qp] to be written, be inscribed; [N] to be written down, be listed, be recorded; [P] to issue a written statement; writing can refer to ink on leather or papyrus, stylus on wax or clay, or carving in stone:- written [137], write [35], wrote [34], describe [4], described [2], subscribed [2], subscribe [2], writest [2], prescribed [1], recorded [1], were written [1], writeth [1], writing [1]

3790 כְּתַב **kᵉtab** (Aram.), v. GK: 10374 [→ 3792; cf. 3789.] [P] to write; [Pp, Peil] to be written:- wrote [5], written [2], write [1]

3791 כְּתָב **kᵉtāb**, n.m. GK: 4181 [→ 3789; cf. 3792]. written communication in various forms: script, text, record, book (as a scroll or tablet):- writing [14], register [2], scripture [1]

3792 כְּתָב **kᵉtāb** (Aram.), n.m. GK: 10375 [→ 3790; cf. 3791]. writing, inscription, decree:- writing [10], prescribing [1], written [1]

3793 כְּתֹבֶת **kᵉtōbet**, n.f. GK: 4182 [→ 3789]. tattoo mark:- any [1]

3794 כִּתִּיִּים **kittiyyîm**, a. & n.g. GK: 4183. Kittim, Cyprus; western coastlands:- Chittim [6], Kittim [2]

3795 כָּתִית **kātît**, a. GK: 4184 [→ 3807]. beaten or pressed olives; in some contexts this refers to virgin olive oil:- beaten [4], pure [1]

3796 כֹּתֶל **kōtel**, n.[m.]. GK: 4185 [cf. 3797]. wall (of a house):- wall [1]

3797 כְּתַל **kᵉtal** (Aram.), n.[m.]. GK: 10376. wall:- walls [1], wall [1]

3798 כִּתְלִישׁ **kitlîš**, n.pr.loc. GK: 4186. Kitlish:- Kithlish [1]

3799 כָּתַם **kātam**, v. GK: 4187. [N] be stained, be defiled:- marked [1]

3800 כֶּתֶם **ketem**, n.m. GK: 4188 [cf. 4387?]. gold, pure gold:- fine gold [4], gold [3], golden wedge [1], most [1]

3801 כֻּתֹּנֶת **kuttōnet**, n.f. GK: 4189. garment, robe, tunic:- coat [16], coats [7], garments [3], garment [2], robe [1]

3802 כָּתֵף **kātēp**, n.f. GK: 4190. shoulder, the part an animal or human that carries a load; by extension: shoulder piece; slope (of a hill), side, wall (of a building):- side [30], shoulders [13], shoulder [9], shoulderpieces [4], sides [4], undersetters [4], corner [2], arm [1]

3803 כָּתַר **kātar**, v. GK: 4192 & 4193 & 4194 [→ 3804, 3805]. [P] to bear with, have patience with; to surround, encircle; [H] to gather about; hem in; to crown, wear as a headdress:- compass about [2], beset round [1], crowned [1], inclosed round about [1], suffer [1]

3804 כֶּתֶר **keter**, n.m. GK: 4195 [→ 3803]. crown (probably not jeweled), royal headdress, crest, high turban:- crown [3]

3805 כֹּתֶרֶת **kōteret**, n.f. GK: 4196 [→ 3803]. capital (of a pillar or column):- chapiters [12], chapiter [12]

3806 כָּתַשׁ **kātaš**, v. GK: 4197 [→ 4388]. [Q] to grind, pound (in a mortar):- bray [1]

3807 כָּתַת **kātat**, v. GK: 4198 [→ 3795, 3796]. [Q] to crush, beat; [Qp] to be crushed, be shattered; [P] to beat, crush, break to pieces; [Pu] to be crushed; [H] to beat down; [Ho] to be battered to pieces:- beat [3], destroyed [3], beat down [1], beaten down [1], beaten to pieces [1], beaten [1], brake in pieces [1], broken in pieces [1], crushed [1], discomfited [1], smite [1], smitten [1], stamped [1]

3807.1 לְ **lᵉ-**, pp.pref. GK: 4200 [→ 1973, 2882?, 3815, 4192, 3926, 3927, 3942; cf. 3807.2]. to; toward; in, through; before, at, with; temporally: before, until, when; logically: so that, in order to; agency: by means of:- to [4509], unto [2352], for [2001], of [1133], before (+6440) [958], in [462], that [358], with [227], therefore (+3651) [176], that (+4616) [167], by [163], into [131], against [122], had [122], after [116], at [116], have [110], according to [102], why (+4100) [92], on [81], upon [81], his (+2050.2) [76], had (+1961) [72], have (+1961) [72], wherefore (+4100) [70], hath [64], my (+2967.1) [64], before [59], throughout [56], mine (+2967.1) [50], for sake (+4616) [45], your (+3641.1) [44], alone (+905) [39], only (+905) [39], their (+1992.1) [38], among [37], as [37], concerning [31], beside (+905+4480) [30], toward [30], thine (+3509.2) [29], the LORD'S* (+3068) [28], from [27], over [27], hast [26], thy (+3509.2) [24], to (+4616) [19], above (+4480+4605+1886.5) [18], before [5048] [18], wherefore (+3651) [18], before (+4480+6440) [17], over against (+5980) [15], safely (+983) [14], and [13], besides (+905+4480) [13], our (+5105.1) [13], because of (+4616) [12], from (+4480) [12], upward (+4605+1886.5) [12], according to (+6310) [11], apart (+905) [11], when [10]*

3807.2 לְ **lᵉ-** (Aram.), pp.pref. GK: 10378 [cf. 3807.1]. to, for, toward, into; belonging to, with regard to:- to [101], unto [54], for [21], into [16], of [10], had [6], at [5], against [4], that [4], before (+6903) [3], by [2], in [2], why (+4101) [2], according to (+6903) [1], according to [1], against (+6655) [1], hast [1], have (+383) [1], his (+1886.8) [1], never (+3809+5957) [1], on [1], over [1], upon [1], what (+1768+3964) [1]

3808 לֹא **lō'** or לֹה **lōh**, adv. GK: 4202 & 4257 [→ 194?, 3810, 3818, 3819; cf. 3809 (also used with compound proper names)]. no, not:- not [3448], no [490], neither (+2050.1) [415], nor (+2050.1) [242], none [71], neither [58], cannot [57], no (+3605) [43], cannot (+3201) [36], surely (+518) [23], nothing [21], nothing (+1697) [20], nay [18], never [17], without (+871.1) [17], lest (+2050.1) [14], nor [14], none (+3605) [13], never (+5769+3807.1) [9], without [9], neither (+1571) [6], none (+376) [6], except (+518) [5], neither (+1571+2050.1) [5], nothing (+3972) [5], ere [4], nothing (+3605) [4], ignorant (+3045) [3], neither any (+2050.1) [3], nothing (+3605+1886.1) [3], without (+871.1) [3], before (+2962+871.1) [2], before (+871.1) [2], by no means [2], never (+5331+3807.1) [2], no more [2], nor (+1571) [2], nought [2], unequal (+8505) [2], unwise (+2450) [2], verily (+518) [2], will (+518) [2], afore [1], but (+518) [1], but [1], but (+518+3588) [1], but [1], cannot (+3045) [1], cannot (+518) [1], cannot away with

(+3201) [1], else (+518) [1], except (+518+3588) [1], fail (+539) [1], feeble (+3524) [1], feeble (+6099) [1], forbidden [1], how much less (+637+3588) [1], in no wise eat (+398+398) [1], lest (+4616+3807.1) [1], lest (+834) [1], measured (+4058) [1], neither (+2050.2) [1], neither (+3588) [1], neither yet (+1571+2050.1) [1], never (+1755+1755+2050.1) [1], never (+4480+5769) [1], never (+5331+5704) [1], never (+5704+5769) [1], never (+8548) [1], never again (+5750) [1], nevertheless (+2050.1) [1], no (+1697) [1], no (+3972) [1], none (+2050.2) [1], none (+259) [1], none (+376+376) [1], none (+376+3807.1) [1], none (+4480) [1], none (+802) [1], none (+834) [1], none (+1571+2050.1) [1], nor (+176) [1], not (+518) [1], not (+5704) [1], not even [1], nothing (+1697+3605) [1], notwithstanding (+2050.1) [1], nought (+1952) [1], nought (+3972) [1], of a truth (+518) [1], or ever (+834+5704) [1], or ever [1], otherwise than (+871.1+3509.1) [1], out of (+2050.1) [1], out of (+871.1) [1], unaccustomed (+3925) [1], unawares (+3045) [1], ungodly (+2623) [1], unless (+518) [1], unrighteousness (+6664) [1], want of [1], wanting [1], whether (+518) [1], without (+2050.1) [1], without any (+2050.1) [1], wrong (+4941) [1], wrongfully (+4941+871.1) [1], yet neither (+2050.1) [1]

3809 לָא **lā'** (Aram.), adv.neg. GK: 10379 & 10384 [cf. 3808.] no, not, never:- not [49], nor (+2050.3) [7], no [7], neither (+2050.3) [3], no (+3606) [3], nor [2], without (+871.2) [1], without [2], cannot (+3202) [1], ever [1], never (+5957+3807.2) [1], none (+3606) [1], none (+383+1768) [1], none [1], nothing [1]

 לֻא **lu'**. See 3863.

3810 לֹא דְבָר **lō' dᵉbār** or לֹא דְבָר **lō' dᵉ bār** or לֹו דְבָר **lô dᵉbār**, n.pr.loc. GK: 4203 & 4274 [→ 3808+1696]. Lo Debar, "*no pasture*":- Lodebar [3]

3811 לָאָה **lā'â**, v. GK: 4206 [→ 8513; cf. 3856]. [Q] to be weary; [N] to wear oneself out, be weary; [H] to wear someone out, try one's patience, frustrate:- weary [9], wearied [5], faintest [1], grieved [1], grieveth [1], lothe [1], made weary [1]

3812 לֵאָה **lē'â**, n.pr.f. GK: 4207. Leah, "[poss.] *wild-cow; wild cow, gazelle; cow*":- Leah [29], Leah's [5]

 לְאֹם **lᵉ'owm**. See 3816.

3813 לָאַט **lā'aṭ**, v. GK: 4209 [cf. 3874]. [Q] to cover:- covered [1]

3814 לָאט **lā'ṭ**, n.[m.]. GK: 4319 [→ 3874, 3909]. same as 3909: quietly, privately, secretly, a fig. extension of the base meaning "no physical sound"; (pl.) secret arts, with a focus on mysterious and hidden elements of this magic:- softly (+871.1+1886.1) [1]

3815 לָאֵל **lā'ēl**, n.pr.m. GK: 4210 [→ 3807.1+410]. Lael, "*[belonging] to God [El]*":- Lael [1]

3816 לְאֹם **lᵉ'ōm**, n.m. GK: 4211. people, nation:- people [24], nations [9], folk [1], nation [1]

3817 לְאֻמִּים **lᵉ'ummîm**, n.pr.g. GK: 4212. Leummite:- Leummim [1]

3818 לֹא עַמִּי **lō' 'ammî**, n.pr.m. GK: 4204 [→ 3808]. Lo-Ammi, "*not my people*":- Lo-ammi [1]

3819 לֹא רֻחָמָה **lō' ruḥāmâ**, n.pr.f. GK: 4205 [→ 3808]. Lo-Ruhamah, "*no compassion*":- Lo-ruhamah [2]

3820 לֵב **lēb**, n.m. GK: 4213 [→ 3823, 3824, 3834; cf. 3821]. heart; by extension: the inner person, self, the seat of thought and emotion: conscience, courage, mind, understanding:- heart [483], hearts [20], midst [12], mind [12], understanding [10], hearted [9], wisdom [6], comfortably (+5921) [4], double heart (+3820+2050.1) [4], care (+7760) [2], considered [2], friendly (+5921) [2], heart's [2], mark well (+7760) [2], regard (+7896) [2], stouthearted (+47) [2], well (+7760) [2], bethink (+413+7725) [1], broken-hearted (+7665) [1], consent [1], consider (+7760) [1], considered (+7896) [1], courageous (+533) [1], hardhearted (+7186) [1], kindly (+5921) [1], kindly [1], merryhearted (+8056) [1], minded (+5973) [1], myself (+2967.1) [1], regard (+7760) [1], regarded (+7760) [1], stale away unawares (+1589) [1], take heed (+5414) [1], very heart (+7023) [1], willingly (+4480) [1]

3821 לֵב **lēb** (Aram.), n.[m.]. GK: 10380 [→ 3825; cf. 3820]. heart, mind:- heart [1]

3822 לְבָאוֹת **lᵉbā'ôt**, n.pr.loc. GK: 4219 [→ 1034; cf. 3833]. Lebaoth, "*lionesses*":- Lebaoth [1]

3823 לָבַב **lābab**, v.den. GK: 4220 & 4221 [→ 3826, 3834; cf. 3820]. [N] to be made wise, be made intelligent; [P] to steal one's heart (from a lover's glance); to make special bread or

pastry (heart-shaped?):– ravished heart [2], made cakes [1], make cakes (+3834) [1], wise [1]

3824 לֵבָב **lēbâb**, n.m. & f. GK: 4222 [→ 3820; cf. 3825]. heart; by extension: the inner person, self, the seat of thought and emotion: conscience, courage, mind, understanding:– heart [208], hearts [35], consider (+7760) [5], mind [4], understanding [3], bethink (+413+7725) [1], breasts [1], comfortably (+5921) [1], courage [1], fainthearted (+7390+1886.1) [1], fainthearted (+7401) [1], hearted [1], midst [1], stolen away unawares (+1589) [1]

3825 לְבַב **lǝbab** (Aram.), n.m. GK: 10381 [→ 3821; cf. 3824]. heart (a physical organ); fig., the inner person that thinks, feels, and chooses: mind, heart, will; "one's heart" can mean "oneself":– heart [7]

לִבְבָה **lǝbibâ**. See 3834.

3826 לִבָּה **libbâ**, n.[f.]. GK: 4226 [→ 3823]. rage:– hearts [6], heart [2]

3827 לַבָּה **labbâ**, n.f. GK: 4225 [cf. 3852]. flame:– flame [1]

3828 לְבוֹנָה **lǝbônâ** or לְבֹנָה **lǝbōnâ**, n.f. GK: 4227 & 4247 [→ 3829, 3836]. frankincense:– frankincense [15], incense [6]

3829 לְבוֹנָה **lǝbônâ**, n.pr.loc. GK: 4228 [→ 3828]. Lebonah, "*frankincense*":– Lebonah [1]

3830 לְבוּשׁ **lǝbûš**, n.m. GK: 4229 & 4230 [→ 3847; cf. 3831]. clothing, garment, robe:– clothing [9], apparel [8], garment [7], garments [2], vesture [2], clothed [1], put on [1], raiment [1], vestments [1]

3831 לְבוּשׁ **lǝbûš** (Aram.), n.m. GK: 10382 [→ 3848; cf. 3830]. clothing, garment:– garments [1], garment [1]

3832 לָבַט **lābaṭ**, v. GK: 4231. [N] to come to ruin, be trampled:– fall [3]

לִבִּי **lubbî**. See 3864.

3833 לָבִיא **lābî'** or לְבִיא **lǝbiyyâ'** or לְבָאָה **lib'â** or לֶבָא **lebe'**, n.m. & f. GK: 4216 & 4218 & 4233 & 4234 [→ 1034, 3822]. lion, lioness:– lion [4], great lion [3], old lion [2], lionesses [1], lioness [1], lions [1], stout lion's [1], young⁵ [1]

3834 לְבִבָה **lǝbibâ**, n.f. GK: 4223 [→ 3823; cf. 3820]. special bread (heart-shaped?):– cakes [2], make cakes (+3823) [1]

3835 לָבַן **lāban**, v. GK: 4235 & 4236 [→ 3828, 3829, 3836, 3837, 3838, 3839, 3840, 3841?, 3842, 3844]. [Q] to make bricks; [H] to make white, be whitened; [Ht] to show oneself spotless, purified:– made white [2], make brick (+3843) [1], make white [1], making brick [1], whiter [1], white [1]

3836 לָבָן **lābān**, a. GK: 4237 [→ 3828, 3837, 3842; cf. 3835]. white:– white [29]

3837 לָבָן **lābān**, n.pr.m. & loc. GK: 4238 & 4239 [→ 3836]. Laban, "*white*":– Laban [51], Laban's [4]

לִבֵּן **labbēn**. See 4192.

3838 לְבָנָה **lǝbānâ** or לְבָנָה **lǝbānāh'**, n.pr.loc. GK: 4245 & 4241 [→ 3842]. Lebanah; Lebana, "*white*":– Lebanah [1], Lebana [1]

3839 לִבְנֶה **libneh**, n.[m.]. GK: 4242 [→ 3835]. poplar tree; some sources: storax tree:– poplars [1], poplar [1]

3840 לְבֵנָה **lǝbēnâ**, n.f. GK: 4246 [→ 3835, 3843, 4404]. same as 3843: brick; tablet:– paved [1]

3841 לְבָנָה **libnâ**, n.pr.loc. GK: 4243 [→ 3835?]. Libnah, "*white*":– Libnah [18]

3842 לְבָנָה **lǝbānâ**, n.f. GK: 4244 [→ 3838; cf. 3836]. bright (full) moon:– moon [3]

3843 לְבֵנָה **lǝbēnâ**, n.f. GK: 4246 [→ 3840]. same as 3840: brick; tablet:– bricks [4], brick [3], make brick (+3835) [2], altars of brick [1], tile [1]

לְבֹנָה **lǝbōnâ**. See 3828.

3844 לְבָנוֹן **lǝbānôn**, n.pr.loc. GK: 4248 [→ 3835]. Lebanon, "*white, snow*":– Lebanon [71]

3845 לִבְנִי **libnî**, n.pr.m. GK: 4249 [→ 3846]. Libni, "*[descendant of] Libni* or *white*":– Libni [5]

3846 לִבְנִי **libnî**, a.g. GK: 4250 [→ 3845]. Libnite, "*of Libni*":– Libnites [1]

3847 לָבַשׁ **lābaš**, v. GK: 4252 [→ 3830, 4403, 8516; cf. 3848]. [Q] to put on clothing, dress, clothe; [Qp] to be dressed; [Pu] to be dressed; [H] to dress another, clothe someone:– put on [30], clothed with [20], clothed [15], clothe with [8], put upon [8], clothed in [4], clothe [4], wear [4], armed [3], arrayed [3], came upon [3], array [2], put [2],

apparelled [1], apparel [1], arrayed in [1], clothest with [1], put on clothing (+8516) [1]

3848 לְבַשׁ **lǝbaš** (Aram.), v. GK: 10383 [→ 3831; cf. 3847]. [P] to be clothed; [H] to clothe (another):– clothed with [3]

לְבֻשׁ **lǝbuš**. See 3830.

3849 לֹג **lōg**, n.m. GK: 4253. log (liquid measure, about a third of a quart or liter):– log [5]

3850 לֹד **lōd**, n.pr.loc. GK: 4254. Lod:– Lod [4]

לִדְבִר **lidbir**. See 3810.

3851 לַהַב **lahab**, n.m. GK: 4258 [→ 3852, 7957]. flame of fire; by extension: flash (of a blade), blade of a sword:– flame [6], blade [2], flames [2], bright [1], glittering [1]

3852 לֶהָבָה **lehābâ**, n.f. GK: 4259 [→ 3851; cf. 3827]. flame, blaze, flash; (iron) point (of a blade):– flame [12], flaming [5], flames [1], head [1]

3853 לְהָבִים **lǝhābîm**, n.pr.g. GK: 4260. Lehabite:– Lehabim [2]

3854 לַהַג **lahag**, n.m. GK: 4261. study, devotion to books:– study [1]

3855 לַהַד **lāhad**, n.pr.m. GK: 4262. Lahad, "*[perhaps] slow, indolent*":– Lahad [1]

3856 לָהַהּ **lāhah**, v. GK: 3532 & 4263 & 4264 & 4271 [cf. 3811]. [Q] to languish, faint; [Ht] to behave like a madman:– fainted [1], mad [1]

3857 לָהַט **lāhaṭ**, v. GK: 4265 & 4266 [→ 3858; cf. 3938]. [Q] to burn, flame; to devour; (n.) ravenous beast; [P] to set afire, set ablaze, consume:– set on fire [3], burn up [1], burneth up [1], burneth [1], burnt up [1], burnt [1], flaming [1], kindleth [1], setteth on fire [1]

3858 לַהַט **lahaṭ**, n.[m.]. GK: 4267 & 4268 [→ 3857; cf. 3874]. flame, referring to the supernatural blade of a sword; secret arts, sorceries:– enchantments [1], flaming [1]

3859 לָהַם **lāham**, v. GK: 4269. [Ht] to let oneself swallow greedily; (ptcp.) choice morsels:– wounds [2]

3860 לָהֵן **lāhēn**, c. GK: 4270 [cf. 3861]. therefore:–

3861 לָהֵן **lāhēn** (Aram.), c. GK: 10385 & 10386 [→ 3809; cf. 3860]. so then, therefore; except, but, unless:– except [3], but [2], save [2], therefore [2], wherefore [1]

3862 לַהֲקָה **lahăqâ**, n.f. GK: 4272. group, community:– company [1]

לֹא **lō'**. See 3808.

3863 לוּ **lû**, c. GK: 4273 [→ 432, 3884]. if! if only!; O that!:– if [6], O that [5], would God [2], I pray thee [1], I would [1], if haply [1], neither [1], oh that [1], peradventure [1], though (+2050.1) [1], would God that [1], would to God (+2050.1) [1], would [1]

3864 לוּב **lûb**, n.g.pl. GK: 4275 [→]. Libya, Libyan:– Lubims [2], Libyans [1], Lubim [1]

3865 לוּד **lûd**, n.pr.m. & g. GK: 4276 [→ 3866]. same as 3866: Lud, Ludite; Lydia, Lydians:– Lud [4], Ludim [2], Lydians [1], Lydia [1]

3866 לוּדִים **lûdîm**, n.pr.m. & g. GK: 4276 [→ 3865]. same as 3865: Lud, Ludite; Lydia, Lydians:–

3867 לָוָה **lāwâ**, v. GK: 4277 & 4278 [→ 3878, 3881, 3880, 3882; cf. 3924]. [Q] to accompany; to borrow; [N] to be joined, be attached, be bound to; [H] to lend:– joined [8], lend [4], lendeth [3], borrower [2], join [2], abide with [1], borrowed [1], borroweth [1], borrow [1], cleave [1], lender (+376) [1], lender [1]

3868 לוּז **lûz**, v. GK: 4279 [→ 3891]. [Q] to depart (from one's sight); [N] to be devious, be perverse, be deceitful; [H] to depart (from one's sight):– depart [2], froward [2], perverseness [1], perverse [1]

3869 לוּז **lûz**, n.[m.]. GK: 4280 [→ 3870]. almond tree (branch):– hazel [1]

3870 לוּז **lûz**, n.pr.loc. GK: 4281 [cf. 3869]. Luz, "*almond tree*":– Luz [8]

3871 לוּחַ **lûaḥ**, n.m. GK: 4283 [→ 3872; cf. 3892]. tablets (of stone); board, panel (of wood); plate (metal):– tables [34], boards [4], table [4], plates [1]

3872 לוּחִית **lûḥît** or לֻחֹת **luḥōt**, n.pr.loc. GK: 4284 & 4304 [→ 3871; cf. 3892]. Luhith, Luhoth:– Luhith [2]

3873 לוֹחֵשׁ **lôḥēš** or הַלּוֹחֵשׁ **hallôḥēš**, n.pr.m. GK: 4285 & 2135 [→ 1886.1+3907]. Lohesh or Hallohesh, "*the whisperer*":– Hallohesh [2]

3874 לוּט **lûṭ**, v. GK: 4286 [→ 3875, 3814, 3909, 3910; cf. 3813, 3858]. [Q] to cover, enfold; [Qp] to be wrapped up; [H] to cover, wrap up:– cast [1], wrapped [1], wrapt [1]

3875 לוֹט **lôṭ**, n.m. GK: 4287 [→ 3874]. shroud, covering:– covering [1]

3876 לוֹט **lôṭ**, n.pr.m. GK: 4288 [→ 3877]. Lot:– Lot [32], Lot's [1]

3877 לוֹטָן **lôṭān**, n.pr.m. GK: 4289 [→ 3876]. Lotan, "*of Lot*":– Lotan [5], Lotan's [2]

3878 לֵוִי **lēwî**, n.pr.m. GK: 4290 [→ 3867; cf. 3879]. Levi; Levite, "*of Levi*":– Levi [64], Levites (+1121) [1]

3879 לֵוָי **lēwāy** (Aram.), n.g. GK: 10387 [cf. 3878, 3881]. Levite, "*of Levi*":– Levites [4]

3880 לִוְיָה **liwyâ**, n.f. GK: 4292 [→ 3867]. garland, wreath:– ornament [2]

3881 לֵוִי **lēwî**, a.g. GK: 4291 [→ 3867; cf. 3879]. Levite, of Levi, "*of Levi*":– Levites [259], Levite [26]

3882 לִוְיָתָן **liwyātān**, n.m. GK: 4293 [→ 3867]. Leviathan, sea-monster; this refers both to a serpent-like sea creature and to a mythological monster of chaos opposed to the true God:– leviathan [5], mourning [1]

3883 לוּל **lûl**, n.[m.]. GK: 4294. stairway; some sources: trap door:– winding stairs [1]

3884 לוּלֵא **lûlē'**, c. GK: 4295 [→ 3863]. if not, unless:– except [3], if not [3], unless [3], were it not that [2], except (+3588) [1], not [1], unless (+3588) [1]

3885 לוּן **lûn** or לִין **lîn**, v. GK: 4296 & 4328 [→ 4411, 4412, 8519; cf. 3915, 3917]. [Q] to spend the night, stay the night; [N] to grumble against, blame; [H] to grumble against, blame; to hold back overnight, leave overnight; [Htpolal] to stay for the night; by extension: to stay, dwell an indeterminate amount of time:– lodge [18], murmured [7], murmur [6], abideth [3], abide [3], remain [3], tarried all night [3], tarry all night [3], abide all night [2], lie all night [2], lodge in [2], remain all night [2], remaineth [2], tarry [2], all night [1], cause to lodge [1], continue [1], dwell [1], endure [1], grudge [1], lay all night [1], left [1], lodge all night [1], lodgest [1], lodging [1], made to murmur [1], tarry for a night [1], tarry night [1]

3886 לוּעַ **lûa'**, v. GK: 4362. [Q] to talk impetuously, to dedicate (something) rashly; a fig. extension of drinking in a hurried, careless manner:– swallow down [1], swallowed up [1]

3887 לוּץ **lûṣ** or לִיץ **lîṣ**, v. GK: 4329 & 4370 [→ 3944, 3945, 4426]. [Q] to mock, scorn, talk big; [H] to mock; [Htpolal] to show oneself a mocker:– scorner [11], scorners [3], interpreter [2], scorneth [2], ambassadors [1], had in derision [1], make a mock at [1], mockers [1], mocker [1], scornest [1], scornful [1], scorn [1], teachers [1]

3888 לוּשׁ **lûš**, v. GK: 4297. [Q] to knead (bread dough):– kneaded [3], knead [2]

3889 לוּשׁ **lûš**, n.pr.loc. GK: 4298 [→ 3918]. Lawish; var. of 3919:–

3890 לְוָת **lǝwāt** (Aram.), pp. GK: 10388 [cf. 3807.2]. near, beside:– from (+4481) [1]

לֻחֹת **luḥōt**. See 3872.

לָז **lāz** and לָזֶה **lāzeh**. See 1975 and 1976.

3891 לָזוּת **lāzût**, n.f. GK: 4299 [→ 3868]. crookedness, perversity, referring to a kind of speech:– perverse [1]

3892 לַח **laḥ**, a. GK: 4300 [→ 3871, 3872, 3893]. fresh, fresh-cut, still moist:– green [5], moist [1]

3893 לֵחַ **lēaḥ**, n.m. GK: 4301 [→ 3892]. strength:– natural force [1]

לֻחַ **luaḥ**. See 3871.

3894 לָחוּם **lāḥûm**, n.[m.]. GK: 4302 & 4303 [→ 3898]. entrails; blow, wound; act of eating:– eating [1], flesh [1]

3895 לְחִי **lǝḥî**, n.m. GK: 4305 [→ 3896?, 7437?]. jaw, jawbone; by extension: cheek, jowl:– cheek [5], cheeks [4], jaws [4], jawbone [3], jaw [3], cheek bone [1], two cheeks [1]

3896 לֶחִי **leḥî**, n.pr.loc. GK: 4306 [→ 3895?]. Lehi, "*jawbone*":– Lehi [3]

3897 לָחַךְ **lāḥak**, v. GK: 4308. [Q] to lick up; [P] to lick up, subdue:– lick up [2], lick [2], licked up [1], licketh up [1]

3898 לָחַם **lāḥam**, v. GK: 4309 & 4310 [→ 3894, 3899, 3901, 4421]. [Q] to fight against, attack; to eat, dine; [Qp] to be consumed; [N] to fight against, attack:– fight [85], fought [57], warred [7], eat [5], made war [4], fighteth [3], ever fight

(+3898) [2], fighting [2], make war [2], overcome [2], warring [2], devoured [1], fought against [1], maketh war [1], making war [1], prevail [1], war [1]

3899 לֶחֶם *leḥem*, n.m. & f. GK: 4312 [→ 1035, 3433, 3898; cf. 3900]. bread, bread loaf; any kind of food; time or act of eating, meal; "bread of the Presence" is a regular offering to the LORD presented on a designated table in the tabernacle and temple:– bread [238], food [21], meat [18], loaves [5], shewbread (+6440) [3], shewbread (+6440+1886.1) [3], shewbread (+4635+1886.1) [2], victuals [2], eat [1], feast [1], fruit [1], provision [1], shewbread (+4635) [1], shewbread [1]

3900 לְחֵם *l̄ḥem* (Aram.), n.m. GK: 10389 [cf. 3899]. bread; banquet meal:– feast [1]

3901 לֶחֶם *lāḥem*, n.[m.]. GK: 4311 [→ 3898]. war; other sources vary:– war [1]

 לָחֶם *lāḥum*. See 3894.

3902 לַחְמִי *laḥmî*, n.pr.m. GK: 4313. Lahmi:– Lahmi [1]

3903 לַחְמָס *laḥmās*, n.pr.loc. GK: 4314. Lahmas:– Lahmam [1]

3904 לְחֵנָה *l̄ḥēnâ* (Aram.), n.f. GK: 10390. concubine, a class of spouse generally of lower status than a wife (the exact marriage relationship of a concubine varied in different cultures), usually for status and pleasure of the husband, also translated "mistress, consort":– concubines [3]

3905 לָחַץ *lāḥaṣ*, v. GK: 4315 [→ 3906; cf. 5169]. [Q] to oppress, crush, confine; [N] to be pressed close:– oppressed [7], oppress [5], afflict [1], crusht [1], forced [1], hold fast [1], oppresseth [1], oppressors [1], thrust [1]

3906 לַחַץ *laḥaṣ*, n.m. GK: 4316 [→ 3905]. oppression, affliction; short ration (of bread or water):– oppression [7], affliction [5]

3907 לָחַשׁ *lāḥaš*, v. GK: 4317 [→ 3873, 3908; cf. 5172]. [P] to charm, enchant (i.e., whisper); [Ht] to whisper together:– charmers [1], whispered [1], whisper [1]

3908 לַחַשׁ *laḥaš*, n.[m.]. GK: 4318 [→ 3907]. charming, whispering; charm, enchanter:– charmed [1], earrings [1], enchantment [1], orator [1], prayer [1]

3909 לָט *lāṭ*, n.[m.]. GK: 4319 [→ 3814]. quietly, privately, secretly, a fig. extension of the base meaning "no physical sound"; (pl.) secret arts, with a focus on mysterious and hidden elements of this magic:– enchantments [3], privily (+871.1+1886.1) [1], secretly (+871.1+1886.1) [1], softly (+871.1+1886.1) [1]

3910 לֹט *lōṭ*, n.[m.]. GK: 4320 [→ 3874]. myrrh (a resinous, fragrant and slightly bitter to the taste); some sources: mastic bark (a resinous gum of the rockrose plant):– myrrh [2]

3911 לְטָאָה *l̄ṭā'â*, n.f. GK: 4321. wall lizard; some sources: gecko:– lizard [1]

3912 לְטוּשִׁם *l̄ṭûšîm*, n.pr.g. GK: 4322 [→ 3913]. Letushite, "*sharpened*":– Letushim [1]

3913 לָטַשׁ *lāṭaš*, v. GK: 4323 [→ 3912]. [Q] to sharpen; to forge, hammer; to pierce (with the eyes); [Pu] to be sharpened:– instructor [1], sharpeneth [1], sharpen [1], sharp [1], whet [1]

3914 לֹיָה *lōyâ*, n.f. GK: 4324 [cf. 3924]. wreath, garland; some translate as a technical architectural term: border, rim:– additions [2], addition [1]

3915 לַיִל *layil* or לַיְלָה *laylâ*, n.m. GK: 4325 & 4326 [→ 3917; cf. 3885; cf. 3916]. night; sometimes with the implication that it is the time of illicit, illegal, or immoral activity:– night [199], nights [15], midnight (+2677+1886.1) [4], to night (+1886.1) [4], at midnight (+2676) [2], in a night (+1121) [2], night season [2], in night [1], midnight (+2676+1886.1) [1], midnight (+8432+1886.1) [1], night seasons [1], to night [1]

3916 לֵילֵי *lêlê* (Aram.), n.[m.]. GK: 10391 [cf. 3915]. night:– night [5]

3917 לִילִית *lîlît*, n.f. GK: 4327 [→ 3915; cf. 3885]. night creature; Lilith, a female demon of the night:– shrich owl [1]

3918 לַיִשׁ *layiš*, n.m. GK: 4330 [→ 3889, 3919]. lion:– old lion [1], lion [1]

3919 לַיִשׁ *layiš* or לַיְשָׁה *lay'šâ*, n.pr.m. & loc. GK: 4331 & 4332 & 4333 [→ 3918; cf. 3959]. Laish, Laishah, "*lion*":– Laish [7]

3920 לָכַד *lākad*, v. GK: 4334 [→ 3921, 4434]. [Q] to capture, seize, take as a possession; [N] to be taken captive, be seized, be taken:– taken [44], took [43], take [19], taketh [5], caught [3], catch [2], taken at all (+3920) [2], frozen [1], holden [1], stick together [1]

3921 לֶכֶד *leked*, n.[m.]. GK: 4335 [→ 3920]. snaring, capturing:– taken [1]

3922 לְכָה *lēkâ*, n.pr.loc. GK: 4336. Lecah, "*to you*":– Lecah [1]

3923 לָכִישׁ *lākîš*, n.pr.loc. GK: 4337. Lachish:– Lachish [24]

3924 לֻלָאֹת *lulā'ōt*, n.f. GK: 4339 [cf. 3867, 3914]. (pl.) loops:– loops [13]

3925 לָמַד *lāmad*, v. GK: 4340 [→ 3928, 4451, 8527]. [Q] to learn, train for; [Qp] to be trained; [P] to teach, instruct, cause to learn; [Pu] to be trained; with implication that the learning will be put to use:– teach [32], taught [17], learn [16], learned [5], teacheth [5], diligently learn (+3925) [2], instructed [2], expert [1], instruct [1], skilful [1], teachers [1], teachest [1], teaching [1], unaccustomed (+3808) [1]

 לִמֻּד *limmud*. See 3928.

3926 לְמוֹ *l̄mô*, pp. GK: 4344 [→ 3807.1]. for, in, over:– at [1], for [1], to [1], upon [1]

3927 לְמוּאֵל *l̄mû'ēl*, n.pr.m. GK: 4345 [→ 3807.1+410]. Lemuel, "*[belonging] to God [El]*":– Lemuel [1]

3928 לִמֻּד *limmud*, a. GK: 4341 [→ 3925]. accustomed to; (n.) a disciple, one who is taught, a follower:– learned [2], accustomed to [1], disciples [1], taught [1], used to [1]

3929 לֶמֶךְ *lemek*, n.pr.m. GK: 4347. Lamech:– Lamech [11]

3930 לֹעַ *lōa'*, n.[m.]. GK: 4350 [→ 3216]. throat:– throat [1]

3931 לָעַב *lā'ab*, v. GK: 4351. [H] to mock, make sport of (someone), make a game of (someone):– mocked [1]

3932 לָעַג *lā'ag*, v. GK: 4352 [→ 3933, 3934; cf. 5926]. [Q] to mock, scoff, ridicule; [N] to stammer, speak as a foreigner; [H] to mock, ridicule:– laughed to scorn [3], mocketh [3], laugh to scorn [2], laugh [2], mocked [2], mock [2], derision [1], have in derision [1], mockest [1], stammering [1]

3933 לַעַג *la'ag*, n.[m.]. GK: 4353 [→ 3932]. scorn, ridicule, derision:– derision [3], scorning [2], scorn [2]

3934 לָעֵג *lā'ēg*, a. GK: 4354 [→ 3932]. people of stammering lips or foreign language:– mockers [1], stammering [1]

3935 לַעְדָּה *la'dâ*, n.pr.m. GK: 4355 [→ 3936]. Laadah, "[perhaps] *having a fat throat or neck*":– Laadah [1]

3936 לַעְדָּן *la'dān*, n.pr.m. GK: 4356 [→ 3935]. Ladan:– Laadan [7]

3937 לָעַז *lā'az*, v. GK: 4357. [Q] to speak a foreign tongue, speak an unintelligible language:– strange language [1]

3938 לָעַט *lā'aṭ*, v. GK: 4358 [cf. 3857]. [H] to let (someone) gulp down:– feed [1]

3939 לַעֲנָה *la'nâ*, n.f. GK: 4360. gall (bitter to the taste, possibly poisonous); by extension: bitterness as a concept:– wormwood [7], hemlock [1]

3940 לַפִּיד *lappîd*, n.m. GK: 4365 [→ 3941?]. torch, firebrand; by extension: lightning:– lamps [4], lamp [3], brands [1], burning lamps [1], firebrands [1], firebrand [1], lightnings [1], torches [1], torch [1]

3941 לַפִּידוֹת *lappîdôt*, n.pr.m. GK: 4366 [→ 3940?]. Lappidoth, "*flames*":– Lapidoth [1]

3942 לִפְנֵי *lipnê*, pp.+n.m. GK: 4367 [→ 3807.1+6437]. before, in front of, in the presence of (3807.1 + 6440):–

3943 לָפַת *lāpat*, v. GK: 4369. [Q] to reach toward; [N] be turned aside; in some contexts there is an implication of touching or grasping the object reached toward:– took hold [1], turned aside [1], turned [1]

3944 לָצוֹן *lāṣôn*, n.[m.]. GK: 4371 [→ 3887]. mockery, scoffing, hostile speech of fools:– scornful [2], scorning [1]

3945 לָצַץ *lāṣaṣ*, n.[m.] or v.ptcp. GK: 4372 [→ 3887]. mocker, scoffer, with an implication that this class of person is foolish and rebellious:– scorners [1]

3946 לַקּוּם *laqqûm*, n.pr.loc. GK: 4373. Lakkum:– Lakum [1]

3947 לָקַח *lāqaḥ*, v. GK: 4374 [→ 3948, 3949, 4455, 4457, 4727, 4728]. [Q] to take, receive; [Qp] to be led away; [N] to be captured, taken away; [Pu] to be taken away, brought; [Ht] to flash back and forth; by extension: to gain possession, exercise authority; "to take a woman" means "to marry a wife":– took [347], take [343], taken [72], receiveth [35], received [22], fetch [19], bring [17], take away [16], took away [12], taketh [10], brought [9], taken away [9], fetched [5], fet [5], get [5], married [4], receiveth [4], carried away [3], buy [2], carry away [2], fetcht [2], have [2], accept [1], buyeth [1], drawn unto [1], getteth [1], infolding [1], mingled [1], placed [1], put [1],

3948 לֶקַח *leqaḥ*, n.m. GK: 4375 [→ 3947]. teaching, instruction, learning:– doctrine [4], learning [4], fair speech [1]

3949 לִקְחִי *liqḥî*, n.pr.m. GK: 4376 [→ 3947]. Likhi, "*take, marry*":– Likhi [1]

3950 לָקַט *lāqaṭ*, v. GK: 4377 [→ 3219, 3951]. [Q] to gather; [P] to gather, pick up, glean; [Pu] to be gathered up; [Ht] to gather oneself about; this act of gathering is general, and can refer to the second or final gleanings of the field or orchard:– gather [13], gathered [9], glean [7], gleaned [5], gathered up [2], gathereth [1]

3951 לֶקֶט *leqeṭ*, n.[m.]. GK: 4378 [→ 3950]. gleanings (of a harvest):– gleanings [1], gleaning [1]

3952 לָקַק *lāqaq*, v. GK: 4379. [Q, P] to lap up, lick up:– lapped [2], lappeth [2], licked up [1], licked [1], lick [1]

3953 לָקַשׁ *lāqaš*, v.den. GK: 4380 [→ 3954, 4456]. [P] to glean:– gather [1]

3954 לֶקֶשׁ *leqeš*, n.[m.]. GK: 4381 [→ 3953]. second crop, late grass at spring time:– latter growth [2]

3955 לְשָׁד *lāšād*, n.m. GK: 4382. moist (food), strength:– fresh [1], moisture [1]

3956 לָשׁוֹן *lāšôn*, n.m. GK: 4383 [→ 3960; cf. 3961]. tongue; by extension: language, speech, noise (of an animal); something tongue-shaped: wedge (of precious metal), bay, gulf, flame of fire:– tongue [89], language [9], tongues [9], bay [3], wedge [2], babbler (+1167+1886.1) [1], evil speaker (+376) [1], fire (+784) [1], languages [1], talkers [1]

3957 לִשְׁכָּה *liškâ*, n.f. GK: 4384 [cf. 5393]. room, chamber; hall; storeroom:– chambers [31], chamber [15], parlour [1]

3958 לֶשֶׁם *lešem*, n.[m.]. GK: 4385. jacinth (exact identification is uncertain):– ligure [2]

3959 לֶשֶׁם *lešem*, n.pr.loc. GK: 4386 [cf. 3919]. Leshem, "*lion*":– Leshem [2]

3960 לָשַׁן *lāšan*, v.den. GK: 4387 [→ 3956]. [Po] to slander; [H] to slander:– accuse [1], slandereth [1]

3961 לִשָּׁן *liššān* (Aram.), n.m. GK: 10392 [cf. 3956]. language, tongue:– languages [6], language [1]

3962 לֶשַׁע *leša'*, n.pr.loc. GK: 4388. Lasha:– Lasha [1]

3963 לֶתֶךְ *letek*, n.[m.]. GK: 4390. lethek (a dry measure, half a cor, about 6 bushels [220 liters]):– half homer [1]

 מַ *ma-*, or מָ *mā-*. See 4100.

3963.1 ־ָם *-ām* or ־ָם *-m*, p.m.pl.suf. GK: 4392 [→ 279?, 1886.3]. they, them, their:– them [1859], their [1501], they [263], their own [46], it [16], whose [15], whom [14], these [11], those [11], themselves [10], thereof [9], the^s [6], theirs [4], which [6], you [6], by themselves (+905+3807.1) [4], therein (+871.1) [4], wherein (+834+871.1) [4], themselves (+5315) [3], whom (+834) [3], his [2], thereby (+871.1) [2], ye [2], man's^s [1], others [1], the^s people [1], their he [1], they (+5315) [1], wherein (+871.1) [1], wherein [1], whereof (+834) [1], whereof [1], wherewith (+834+871.1) [1], wherewith (+871.1) [1]

3964 מָא *mā'* (Aram.), p.inter. & indef. GK: 10394 [→ 4101; cf. 4100]. what?:– what (+1768+3807.2) [1]

3965 מַאֲבוּס *ma'ăbûs*, n.[m.]. GK: 4393 [→ 75]. granary:– storehouses [1]

3966 מְאֹד *m̄'ōd*, n.m. (used as adv.). GK: 4394. a marker of great degree or quantity: very, greatly, exceedingly, much:– very [129], greatly [47], sore [20], great [12], exceeding [10], exceeding (+3966+871.1) [8], much [7], very (+5704) [7], exceedingly (+3966) [6], exceedingly (+3966) [6], diligently [4], exceedingly (+3966+871.1) [4], exceedingly [4], good [3], far [2], greatly (+5704) [2], mightily [2], might [2], utterly (+5704) [2], very sore (+5704) [2], ask never so much (+7235) [1], diligent [1], especially [1], exceeding (+5704) [1], exceeding (+7235) [1], exceedingly (+7235) [1], far off [1], fast [1], hated exceedingly (+1419+8130+8135) [1], mighty [1], quickly [1], right well [1], so much [1], sore (+5704) [1], so [1], very (+1419) [1], very (+5704+3807.1) [1], very great [1], very much (+5704) [1], waxed louder and louder (+2390) [1], well [1]

3967 מֵאָה *mē'â*, n.f. GK: 4395 [→ 3968?; cf. 3969]. hundred:– hundred [465], two hundred [76], hundreds [27], eleven hundred (+505+2050.1) [3], hundredth [3], one hundred [3], hundredfold (+6471) [1], hundredfold (+8180) [1], sixscore (+6242+2050.1) [1], twelve hundred (+505+2050.1) [1]

3968 מֵאָה *mē'â*, n.pr.loc. GK: 4396 [→ 3967?; cf. 3969]. (the Tower of) the Hundred:– Meah [2]

3969 מְאָה *m^e'â* (Aram.), n.f. GK: 10395 [cf. 3967, 3968]. hundred; (dual) two hundred:– hundred [7], two hundred [1]

3970 מַאֲוַיִּים *ma'awiyyîm*, n.[m.pl.]. GK: 4397 [→ 183]. desires:– desires [1]

מוֹאָל *mô'l*. See 4136.

3971 מְאוּם *m^e'ûm* or מוּם *mûm*, n.m. GK: 4398 & 4583 [→ 3972]. defect, blemish, flaw, injury; by extension: shame, defilement:– blemish [15], spot [3], blot [2], blemishes [1]

3972 מְאוּמָה *m^e'ûmâ*, p.indef. GK: 4399 [→ 3971]. something, anything; (with negation) nothing:– any thing [13], nothing (+3808) [5], nothing (+369) [4], ought [4], any thing (+3605) [1], no (+3808) [1], no (+408) [1], nought (+3808) [1], ought else (+3605) [1], somewhat [1]

3973 מָאֹס *mā'ôs*, n.[m.]. GK: 4400 [→ 3988]. refuse, trash:– refuse [1]

3974 מָאֹר *mā'ôr*, n.m. GK: 4401 [→ 215]. light source, luminary, light-bearer:– light [15], lights [3], bright [1]

3975 מְאוּרָה *m^e'ûrâ*, n.f. GK: 4402 [→ 215?]. nest hole (of a viper):– den [1]

3976 מֹאזְנַיִם *mō'znayim*, n.m.[du.] GK: 4404 [cf. 3977]. set of scales, (two) balance pans for weight measurement, with an emphasis on honesty and standardized measurements; by extension: righteous evaluation of motives and actions:– balances [8], balance [7]

3977 מֹאזְנֵא *mō'znē* (Aram.), n.m.emph. GK: 10396 [cf. 3976]. scale, balance, with a focus that the device is an objective implement for judging truth:– balances [1]

מֵאִיָּה *mē'yâ*. See 3967.

3978 מַאֲכָל *ma'akāl*, n.m. & f. GK: 4407 [→ 398]. food, supplies, something to eat:– meat [22], food [5], bakemeats (+644+4639) [1], fruit [1], victual [1]

3979 מַאֲכֶלֶת *ma'akelet*, n.f. GK: 4408 [→ 398]. (butcher) knife, sometimes with a ceremonial or sacrificial focus:– knife [3], knives [1]

3980 מַאֲכֹלֶת *ma'akōlet*, n.f. GK: 4409 [→ 398]. fuel (for a fire); a fig. extension of food that is consumed:– fuel [2]

3981 מַאֲמָץ *ma'amāṣ*, n.[m.]. GK: 4410 [→ 553]. effort, exertion:– strength [1]

3982 מַאֲמָר *ma'amār*, n.m. GK: 4411 [→ 559; cf. 3983]. command, decree, instruction:– commandment [2], decree [1]

3983 מֵאמַר *mē'mar* (Aram.), n.[m.]. GK: 10397 [→ 560; cf. 3982]. declaration, request:– appointment [1], word [1]

3984 מָאן *mā'n* (Aram.), n.m. GK: 10398. article, container, goblet:– vessels [7]

3985 מָאֵן *mā'an*, v. GK: 4412 [→ 3986, 3987]. [P] to refuse, reject:– refused [24], refuse [9], refuseth [5], utterly refuse (+3985) [2], refusedst [1]

3986 מָאֵן *mā'ēn*, a.v. GK: 4413 [→ 3985]. refusing:– refuse [4]

3987 מֵאֵן *mē'ēn*, a. GK: 4414 [→ 3985]. refusing:– refuse [1]

3988 מָאַס *mā'as*, v. GK: 4415 & 4416 [→ 3973, cf. 4529, 4549]. [Q] to reject, despise, spurn, disdain; [N] to be rejected, become vile; to be festering, be dissolving; be vanishing:– rejected [16], despised [12], despise [9], cast away [7], refused [5], utterly rejected (+3988) [4], cast off [3], despiseth [3], refuse [3], abhorred [2], abhorreth [1], abhor [1], become loathsome [1], contemneth [1], contemn [1], disdained [1], loathe [1], melt away [1], refuseth [1], reject [1], reprobate [1], vile [1]

3989 מַאֲפֶה *ma'apeh*, n.[m.]. GK: 4418 [→ 644]. something baked:– baken [1]

3990 מַאֲפֵל *ma'apēl*, n.[m.]. GK: 4419 [→ 652?]. darkness:– darkness [1]

3991 מַאְפֵלְיָה *ma'pēlyâ*, n.f. GK: 4420 [→ 652?]. great darkness:– darkness [1]

3992 מָאַר *mā'ar*, v. GK: 4421. [H] to be destructive; to be painful:– fretting [3], pricking [1]

מָאֹר *mā'ôr*. See 3974.

3993 מַאֲרָב *ma'arāb*, n.m. GK: 4422 [→ 693]. ambush; troops in an ambush:– ambushment [2], lie in ambush [1], lurking places [1], lying in wait [1]

3994 מְאֵרָה *m^e'ērâ*, n.f. GK: 4423 [→ 779]. curse:– curse [4], cursing [1]

מְאֹרָה *m^e'ōrâ*. See 3974.

3995 מִבְדָּלוֹת *mibdālôt*, n.f. GK: 4426 [→ 914]. set aside, selected, singled out:– separate [1]

3996 מָבוֹא *mābô'*, n.m. GK: 4427 [→ 3997, 4126; cf. 935]. entrance, entryway, gateway; "the place where the sun goes (sets)" is the direction west:– entry [5], going down [5], entrance [3], entering in [2], came [1], cometh [1], coming in [1], enter into [1], entering [1], goeth down [1], the west (+8121+1886.1) [1], westward (+8121+1886.1) [1]

3997 מְבוֹאָה *m^ebô'â*, n.m. GK: 4427 [→ 3996]. same as 3996: entrance, entryway, gateway:– entry [1]

3998 מְבוּכָה *m^ebûkâ*, n.f. GK: 4428 [→ 943]. confusion, confused terror:– perplexity [2]

3999 מַבּוּל *mabbûl*, n.m. GK: 4429 [→ 5035]. flood (waters):– flood [13]

4000 מְבוֹנִים *m^ebônîm*, v.ptcp. GK: 4430. ptcp. of 995: knowing, taught:–

4001 מְבוּסָה *m^ebûsâ*, n.f. GK: 4431 [→ 947]. trampling down, implying subjugation:– treading down [1], trodden down [1], trodden under foot [1]

4002 מַבּוּעַ *mabbûa'*, n.[m.]. GK: 4432 [→ 5042]. (a bubbling) spring (of water):– springs [2], fountain [1]

4003 מְבוּקָה *m^ebûqâ*, n.f. GK: 4433 [→ 950]. plundering, devastation, desertion:– void [1]

4004 מִבְחוֹר *mibbôr*, n.[m.]. GK: 4435 [→ 977]. choicest (trees); major (towns):– choice [2]

4005 מִבְחָר *mibḥār*, n.[m.] & f. GK: 4436 [→ 4006; cf. 977]. choicest, best, elite, finest (persons or things):– choice [7], chosen [4], choicest [1]

4006 מִבְחָר *mibḥār*, n.pr.m. GK: 4437 [→ 4005; cf. 977]. Mibhar, "*choice*":– Mibhar [1]

4007 מַבָּט *mabbāṭ*, n.m. GK: 4438 [→ 5027]. hope, trust in, relying on:– expectation [3]

4008 מִבְטָא *mibṭā'*, n.[m.]. GK: 4439 [→ 981]. rash promise, rashness:– that which uttered [1], uttered ought out [1]

4009 מִבְטָח *mibṭāḥ*, n.[m.]. GK: 4440 [→ 982]. security, trust, confidence:– confidence [8], trust [4], confidences [1], hope [1], sure [1]

4010 מַבְלִיגִית *mablîgît*, n.f. GK: 4443 [→ 1455]. comfort, smile, cheerfulness:– comfort [1]

4011 מִבְנֶה *mibneh*, n.m. GK: 4445 [→ 1129]. building, structure:– frame [1]

4012 מְבֻנַּי *m^ebunnay*, n.pr.m. GK: 4446. Mebunnai, "*well built*":– Mebunnai [1]

4013 מִבְצָר *mibṣār*, n.m. GK: 4448 & 4450 [→ 4014; cf. 1219]. fortress, fortification, stronghold; ore:– fenced [11], strong holds [10], defenced [4], fortress [4], fortresses [2], strong hold [2], strong [2], holds [1], most fenced [1]

4014 מִבְצָר *mibṣār*, n.pr.m. GK: 4449 [→ 4013; cf. 1219]. Mibzar, "*bastion*":– Mibzar [2]

מִבְצָרָה *mibṣārâ*. See 4013.

4015 מִבְרָח *mibrāḥ*, n.m. GK: 4451 [→ 1272]. fleeing, refugee:– fugitives [1]

4016 מְבוּשִׁים *m^ebûšîm*, n.[m.]. GK: 4434 [→ 954]. private parts, (male) genitals, with a possible focus on shame if exposed:– secrets [1]

4017 מִבְשָׂם *mibśām*, n.pr.m. GK: 4452. Mibsam, "*sweet odor*":– Mibsam [3]

4018 מְבַשְּׁלוֹת *m^ebaššᵉlôt*, n.f.pl. GK: 4453 [→ 1310]. places for fire, cooking-places:– boiling places [1]

מָג *māg*. See 7248, 7249.

4019 מַגְבִּישׁ *magbîš*, n.pr.m. GK: 4455. Magbish, "[perhaps] *thick*":– Magbish [1]

4020 מִגְבָּלוֹת *migbālôt*, n.f.pl. GK: 4456 [→ 1383]. (braided) chains, (twisted) cords:– ends [1]

4021 מִגְבָּעָה *migbā'â*, n.f.pl. GK: 4457 [→ 1375?]. headband:– bonnets [4]

4022 מֶגֶד *meged*, n.m. GK: 4458 [→ 4023, 4025, 4030]. choice things, best gifts:– precious things [4], pleasant [3], precious [1]

4023 מְגִדּוֹ *m^egiddô* or מְגִדּוֹן *m^egiddôn*, n.pr.loc. GK: 4459 & 4461 [cf. 4022]. Megiddo, "*place of troops*":– Megiddo [11], Megiddon [1]

4024 מִגְדּוֹל *migdôl* or מִגְדֹּל *migdōl*, n.m. & n.pr.loc. GK: 4460 & 4465 [→ 1431, 4026]. Migdol, "*tower*"; great:– Migdol [4], tower [3]

4025 מַגְדִּיאֵל *magdî'ēl*, n.pr.m. GK: 4462 [→ 4022+410]. Magdiel, "*choice gift of God [El]*":– Magdiel [2]

4026 מִגְדָּל *migdāl*, n.m. GK: 4463 [→ 4024, 4027, 4028, 4029; cf. 1431]. tower, watchtower, usually a tall, narrow building used for defense; high platform (made of wood and used for public speaking to crowds); an elevated area such as a garden with mounds, terraces:– tower [34], towers [13], castles [1], flowers [1], pulpit [1]

מִגְדֹּל *migdōl*. See 4024.

מִגְדָּלָה *migdālâ*. See 4026.

4027 מִגְדַּל־אֵל *migdal-'ēl*, n.pr.loc. GK: 4466 [→ 4026+410; cf. 1431]. Migdal El, "*tower of God [El]*":– Migdal-el [1]

4028 מִגְדַּל־גָּד *migdal-gad*, n.pr.loc. GK: 4467 [→ 4026+1410; cf. 1431]. Migdal Gad, "*tower of Gad*":– Migdal-gad [1]

4029 מִגְדַּל־עֵדֶר *migdal-'ēder*, n.pr.loc. GK: 4468 [→ 4026+5740]. Migdal Eder, "*tower of Eder [flock]*":–

4030 מִגְדָּנוֹת *migdānôt*, n.f.[pl.]. GK: 4469 [→ 4022]. costly gifts, articles of value:– precious things [3], presents [1]

4031 מָגוֹג *māgôg*, n.pr.loc. GK: 4470 [→ 1463]. Magog, "[perhaps] *land of Gog*":– Magog [4]

4032 מָגוֹר *māgôr*, n.m. GK: 4471 [→ 4034; cf. 1481]. terror, horror:– fear [6], terrors [1], terror [1]

4033 מָגוֹר *māgôr*, n.[m.]. GK: 4472 & 4473 [→ 1481, 4035, 4460]. to live as an alien, stay as a stranger; place to live, place to lodge; grain pit, storage chamber = heart, mind:– pilgrimage [4], stranger [3], dwellings [2], sojourn [1], strangers [1]

4034 מְגוֹרָה *m^egôrâ*, n.f. GK: 4475 [→ 4032; cf. 1481]. dread, fear:– fear [1]

4035 מְגוּרָה *m^egûrâ*, n.f. GK: 4476 [→ 4033]. barn, grain-pit, storage chamber:– fears [2], barn [1]

4036 מָגוֹר מִסָּבִיב *māgôr missābîb*, n.pr.m. GK: 4474 [→ 1481]. Magor-Missabib, "*terror on every side*":– Magor-missabib [1]

4037 מַגְזֵרָה *magzērâ*, n.f. GK: 4477 [→ 1504]. ax:– axes [1]

4038 מַגָּל *maggāl*, n.[m.]. GK: 4478 [cf. 1556?]. sickle:– sickle [2]

4039 מְגִלָּה *m^egillâ*, n.f. GK: 4479 [→ 1556; cf. 4040]. scroll (a rolled up document made of leather or papyrus):– roll [20], volume [1]

4040 מְגִלָּה *m^egillâ* (Aram.), n.f. GK: 10399 [→ 1560; cf. 4039]. scroll:– roll [1]

4041 מְגַמָּה *m^egammâ*, n.f. GK: 4480 [cf. 1571]. horde:– sup up [1]

4042 מָגַן *māgan*, v. GK: 4481 [→ 4043]. [P] to hand over, deliver to, present with:– deliver [2], delivered [1]

4043 מָגֵן *māgēn*, n.m. GK: 4482 & 4483 & 4484 [→ 1598, 4042, 4044]. (small) shield used for defense, usually of oiled leather; by extension, ruler, a leader who protects; fig. of the impregnable scales of leviathan; insolent; gift, present (gifts made in return):– shield [33], shields [15], buckler [6], bucklers [3], armed [2], defence [2], rulers [1], scales (+650) [1]

4044 מְגִנָּה *m^eginnâ*, n.f. GK: 4485 [→ 4043]. veil, covering:– sorrow [1]

4045 מִגְעֶרֶת *mig'eret*, n.f. GK: 4486 [→ 1605]. rebuke, reproach:– rebuke [1]

4046 מַגֵּפָה *maggēpâ*, n.f. GK: 4487 [→ 5062]. plague; blow, strike, slaughter:– plague [20], slaughter [3], plagued [1], plagues [1], stroke [1]

4047 מַגְפִּיעָשׁ *magpî'āš*, n.pr.m. GK: 4488. Magpiash, "*moth killer*":– Magpiash [1]

4048 מָגַר *māgar*, v. GK: 4489 [cf. 4049]. [Qp] to be thrown; [P] to cast, throw down:– cast down [1], terrors [1]

4049 מְגַר *m^egar* (Aram.), v. GK: 10400 [cf. 4048]. [Pa] to overthrow:– destroy [1]

4050 מְגֵרָה *m^egērâ*, n.f. GK: 4490 [→ 1641]. saw (stone-cutting tool):– saws [3], axes [1]

4051 מִגְרוֹן *migrôn*, n.pr.loc. GK: 4491. Migron, "*precipice*":– Migron [2]

4052 מִגְרָעוֹת *migrā'ôt*, n.f. GK: 4492 [→ 1639]. offset ledge, recess, rebatement (of a wall):– narrowed rests [1]

4053 מֶגְרָפָה *megrāpâ*, n.f. GK: 4493 [→ 1640]. clods (of earth) or a digging instrument: hoe, spade, shovel:– clods [1]

4054 מִגְרָשׁ *migrāš* or מִגְרְשׁוֹת *migrᵉšôt*, n.m. GK: 4494 & 4495 [→ 1644]. pastureland, untilled open land (belonging to a town):– suburbs [114], cast out [1]

4055 מַד *mad*, n.m. GK: 4496 [→ 4058; cf. 4063]. clothing, garment; measure, decree:– garment [3], armour [2], clothes [1], garments [1], judgment [1], measures [1], measure [1], raiment [1]

4056 מִדְבַּח *madbaḥ* (Aram.), n.[m.]. GK: 10401 [→ 1684; cf. 4196]. altar:– altar [1]

4057 מִדְבָּר *midbār*, n.m. GK: 4497 & 4498 [→ 1696]. desert, wasteland, barren wilderness, desolate land that supports little life; open country, suitable for grazing; mouth, instrument of speech:– wilderness [255], desert [13], south [1], speech [1], wilderness (+776) [1]

4058 מָדַד *mādad*, v. GK: 4499 [→ 4055, 4059, 4060, 4461]. [Q] to measure a distance; consider a plan; [N] to be measured; [P] to measure off; [Htpol] to stretch oneself out:– measured [39], measure [7], mete out [2], measured (+3808) [1], mete [1], stretched [1]

4059 מָדַד *middad*, v. GK: 4499 [→ 4058]. same as 4058: [P] to measure off:– gone [1]

4060 מִדָּה *middâ*, n.f. GK: 4500 & 4501 [→ 4058; cf. 5414; cf. 4061]. measurement, size, length; section (of a wall), length of life; tax:– measure [15], measures [12], measuring [10], piece [7], size [3], stature [3], garments [1], great stature [1], meteyard [1], tribute [1], wide [1]

4061 מִדָּה *middâ* or מִנְדָה *mindâ* (Aram.), n.f. GK: 10402 & 10429 [cf. 4060]. tax, revenue, tribute:– toll [3], tribute [1]

4062 מַדְהֵבָה *madhēbâ*, n.f. GK: 4502 [cf. 7292]. fury; others: golden:– golden city [1]

4063 מָדוּ *mādû* or מַדְוֶה *madweh*, n.m. GK: 4503 [cf. 4055]. garment:– garments [2]

4064 מַדְוֶה *madweh*, n.m. GK: 4504 [→ 1738]. disease, sickness:– diseases [2]

4065 מַדּוּחִים *maddûḥîm*, n.[m.]. GK: 4505 [→ 5080]. misleading, able to deceive:– causes of banishment [1]

4066 מָדוֹן *mādôn*, n.m. GK: 4506 [→ 4067; cf. 1777]. dissension, quarrel, strife, contention:– strife [7], contentions [4], contention [3], contentious [3], brawling [2], discord [2], strifes [1]

4067 מִדְיָן *midyān* or מָדוֹן *mādôn*, n.m. GK: 4517 [→ 4066, 4079, 4080, 4084, 4090, 4092; cf. 1777]. quarrel, strife, contention:– stature [1]

4068 מָדוֹן *mādôn*, n.pr.loc. GK: 4507 [→ 1777]. Madon, "contention":– Madon [2]

4069 מַדּוּעַ *maddûaʿ*, adv. GK: 4508. Why?, What is the meaning?:– why [43], wherefore [28], how [1]

4070 מָדוֹר *mᵉdôr* or מְדָר *mᵉdār* (Aram.), n.[m.]. GK: 10403 & 10407 [→ 1753]. living, dwelling:– dwelling [4]

4071 מְדוּרָה *mᵉdûrâ*, n.f. GK: 4509 [→ 1752]. (circular) pile of wood, fire pit:– pile for fire [1], pile [1]

4072 מִדְחֶה *midḥeh*, n.m. GK: 4510 [→ 1760]. ruin, downfall:– ruin [1]

4073 מַדְחֵפָה *madḥēpâ*, n.f. GK: 4511 [→ 1765]. blow, thrust; (pl.) blow after blow:– overthrow [1]

4074 מָדַי *māday*, n.pr.g & loc. GK: 4512 [→ 4075; cf. 4076]. Madai; Media, Medes:– Medes [8], Media [6], Madai [2]

4075 מָדִי *mādî*, a.g. GK: 4513 [→ 4074]. Mede:– Mede [1]

4076 מָדַי *māday* (Aram.), n.pr.g. GK: 10404 [cf. 4074, 4077]. same as 4077: Mede; Media:– Medes [5], Median [1]

4077 מָדַי *māday* (Aram.), n.pr.g. GK: 10404 [→ 4076]. same as 4076: Mede; Media:–

4078 מַדַּי *madday*, n.[m.]. GK: 1896 [→ 1767]. prob. same as 1767: sufficiently:– sufficiently (+3807.1) [1]

4079 מִדְיָן *midyān*, n.m. GK: 4506 [→ 4067; cf. 1777]. same as 4066: dissension, quarrel, strife, contention:–

4080 מִדְיָן *midyān*, n.pr.m. GK: 4518 [→ 4084; cf. 1777, 4067]. Midian, Midianite:– Midian [39], Midianites [20]

4081 מִדִּין *middîn*, n.pr.loc. GK: 4516. Middin:– Middin [1]

4082 מְדִינָה *mᵉdînâ*, n.f. GK: 4519 [→ 1777; cf. 4083]. province, district, region:– provinces [27], every province (+4082+2050.1) [10], every province (+3605+4082+2050.1) [8], province [8]

4083 מְדִינָה *mᵉdînâ* (Aram.), n.f. GK: 10406 [→ 1778; cf. 4082]. province, district:– province [8], provinces [3]

4084 מִדְיָנִי *midyānî*, a.g. GK: 4520 [→ 4080, 4092; cf. 1777, 4067]. Midianite, "of Midian":– Midianites [3], Midianitish [2], Medanites [1], Midianite [1], Midianitish woman [1]

4085 מְדֹכָה *mᵉdōkâ*, n.f. GK: 4521 [→ 1743]. mortar:– mortar [1]

4086 מַדְמֵן *madmēn*, n.pr.loc. GK: 4522 [→ 4088, 4089]. Madmen, "[sounds like] be silenced":– Madmen [1]

4087 מַדְמֵנָה *madmēnâ*, n.f. GK: 4523 [→ 1828]. manure-pile, dung-heap:– dunghill [1]

4088 מַדְמֵנָה *madmēnâ*, n.pr.loc. GK: 4524 [→ 4086]. Madmenah, "dunghill":– Madmenah [1]

4089 מַדְמַנָּה *madmannâ*, n.pr.m. & loc. GK: 4525 & 4526 [→ 4086]. Madmannah, "dung place":– Madmannah [2]

4090 מְדָן *mᵉdān*, n.m. GK: 4506 [→ 4067; cf. 1777]. same as 4066: dissension, quarrel, strife, contention:–

4091 מְדָן *mᵉdān*, n.pr.m. GK: 4527 [→ 1837]. Medan, "dissension":– Medan [2]

4092 מִדָנִי *mᵉdānî*, a.g. GK: 4520 [→ 4084]. same as 4084: Midianite, "of Midian":–

4093 מַדָּע *maddāʿ*, n.m. GK: 4529 [→ 3045; cf. 4486]. knowledge:– knowledge [4], science [1], thought [1]

מוֹדָע *môdāʿ*. See 4129.

מַדָּע *madûaʿ*. See 4069.

4094 מַדְקָרָה *madqērâ*, n.f. GK: 4532 [→ 1856]. piercing (of a sword):– piercings [1]

מְדֹר *mᵉdôr*. See 4070.

4095 מַדְרֵגָה *madrēgâ*, n.f. GK: 4533. cliff, (steep) mountainside (with footholds and hiding places):– stairs [1], steep places [1]

מְדֻרָה *mᵉdurâ*. See 4071.

4096 מִדְרָךְ *midrāk*, n.[m.]. GK: 4534 [→ 1869]. foot-width, footprint:– breadth [1]

4097 מִדְרָשׁ *midrāš*, n.[m.]. GK: 4535 [→ 1875]. annotation, study, writing, exposition:– story [2]

4098 מְדֻשָׁה *mᵉdušâ*, n.f. GK: 4536 [→ 1758]. that which is crushed (by trampling on a threshing floor):– threshing [1]

4099 הַמְּדָתָא *hammᵉdātā'* or מְדָתָא *mᵉdātā'*, n.pr.m. GK: 2158. Hammedatha, "given by the moon [god]":– Hammedatha [5]

4100 מָה *mâ*, p.inter. & indef. GK: 4537 [→ 1099, 3644, 4972; cf. 4478; cf. 3964, cf. 4101]. why?, what? how?; O!, who, whoever, whatever:– what [404], why (+3807.1) [92], wherefore (+3807.1) [70], how [51], why [28], wherein (+871.1) [12], wherefore (+5921) [10], wherewith (+871.1) [10], that [6], wherefore [6], how long (+5704) [4], wherefore (+2088+3807.1) [4], why (+5921) [3], how great [2], how long (+3509.1) [2], how many (+3509.1) [2], how many (+5704+3509.1) [2], how much [2], how oft (+3509.1) [2], howsoever [2], what (+3509.1) [2], what (+3807.1) [2], wherein [2], which [2], because (+3807.1) [1], how (+3509.1) [1], how long (+3117+8141+3509.1) [1], nor (+2050.1) [1], nothing (+1077) [1], nothing (+1097) [1], not [1], so many (+3509.1) [1], thing [1], to what end (+3807.1) [1], until (+5704) [1], what (+1697+1886.1) [1], what (+2088) [1], what aileth (+3807.1) [1], what good (+3807.1) [1], what profit (+3807.1) [1], whatsoever (+1697) [1], whatsoever [1], whereby (+871.1) [1], wherefore (+8478) [1], wherein (+871.1+1886.1) [1], whereon (+5921) [1], whereto (+3807.1) [1], whereupon (+5921) [1], wherewithal (+871.1) [1], whether [1], why (+2088+3807.1) [1], why (+871.1) [1], why then (+2088+3807.1) [1]

4101 מָה *mâ* (Aram.), p.inter. & indef. GK: 10408 [→ 2987; cf. 4479; cf. 4100]. why?, what?; what:– what [6], how (+3509.4) [2], why (+3807.2) [2], that which [1], whatsoever (+1768) [1], why (+5922) [1]

4102 מָהַהּ *māhah*, v. GK: 4538. [Htpal] to wait, delay, linger, hesitate:– tarry [3], lingered [2], tarried [2], delayed [1], stay [1]

4103 מְהוּמָה *mᵉhûmâ*, n.f. GK: 4539 [→ 1949]. turmoil, confusion, panic, discomfiture:– destruction [3], trouble [3], discomfiture [1], tumults [1], tumult [1], vexations [1], vexation [1], vexed [1]

4104 מְהוּמָן *mᵉhûmān*, n.pr.m. GK: 4540. Mehuman:– Mehuman [1]

4105 מְהֵיטַבְאֵל *mᵉhêṭab'ēl*, n.pr.m. & f. GK: 4541 [→ 3190+410]. Mehetabel, "God [El] does good":– Mehetabel [2], Mehetabeel [1]

4106 מָהִיר *māhîr*, a. GK: 4542 [→ 4116]. skilled, well versed, experienced; speedy, prompt:– ready [2], diligent [1], hasting [1]

4107 מָהַל *māhal*, v. GK: 4543 [→ 1118; cf. 4135]. [Qp] to be diluted, changed to an adulterated state; referring to dilution by water:– mixt [1]

4108 מַהְלֵךְ *mahlēk*, n.m. GK: 4544 [→ 1980, 4109]. same as 4109: passageway; journey:– places to walk [1]

4109 מַהֲלָךְ *mah²lāk*, n.m. GK: 4544 [→ 4108]. same as 4108: passageway; journey:– journey [3], walk [1]

4110 מַהֲלָל *mah²lāl*, n.[m.]. GK: 4545 [→ 4111; cf. 1984]. praise, good reputation:– praise [1]

4111 מַהֲלַלְאֵל *mah²lal'ēl*, n.pr.m. GK: 4546 [→ 4110+410]. Mahalalel, "praise of God [El]":– Mahalaleel [7]

4112 מַהֲלֻמוֹת *mah²lumôt*, n.f.pl. GK: 4547 [→ 1986]. (pl.) beating, thrashing, repeated blows to the body:– stripes [1], strokes [1]

4113 מַהֲמֹרוֹת *mah²mōrôt*, n.f.[pl.]. GK: 4549. miry pits, pits filled with rain water:– deep pits [1]

4114 מַהְפֵּכָה *mahpēkâ*, n.f. GK: 4550 [→ 2015]. overthrow, destruction, demolishing:– overthrew [3], overthrow [2], overthrown [1]

4115 מַהְפֶּכֶת *mahpeket*, n.f. GK: 4551 [→ 2015]. stocks (confining a prisoner, suggesting in a crooked posture or distortion):– prison [2], stocks [2]

4116 מָהַר *māhar*, v. GK: 4554 [→ 4106, 4117, 4118, 4120, 4122]. [N] to be swept away; to be impetuous, rash, disturbed; [P] to be quick, hasten, hurry, do at once:– hasted [14], make haste [8], haste [5], made haste [5], soon [3], swift [3], hastened [2], hasten [2], hasteth [2], hastily [2], in haste [2], make speed [2], carried headlong [1], cause to make haste [1], fearful [1], fetch quickly [1], hasteneth [1], make ready quickly [1], quickly [1], rash [1], shortly [1], speedily [1], straightway [1], suddenly [1]

4117 מָהַר *māhar*, v.den. GK: 4555 & 4556 [→ 4116, 4119]. [Q] to pay the purchase price for a bride:– surely endow (+4117) [2]

4118 מַהֵר *maher*, adv. GK: 4557 [→ 4116]. swiftly:– quickly [8], speedily [4], hastily [2], at once [1], hasteth [1], suddenly [1]

מָהִיר *māhir*. See 4106.

4119 מֹהַר *mōhar*, n.m. GK: 4558 [→ 4117, 4121]. bride-price, compensation to the father of the bride:– dowry [3]

4120 מְהֵרָה *mᵉhērâ*, n.f. GK: 4559 [→ 4116]. haste, quickness, speed; (adv.) quickly, swiftly, soon, at once:– quickly [8], speedily [4], hastily [1], make speed [1], pass quickly [1], quickly (+871.1) [1], shortly [1], soon [1], speed [1], very swiftly (+5704) [1]

4121 מַהְרַי *mah²ray*, n.pr.m. GK: 4560 [→ 4119]. Maharai, "impetuous":– Maharai [3]

4122 מַהֵר שָׁלָל חָשׁ בַּז *maher šālāl ḥāš baz*, n.pr.m. GK: 4561 [→ 4116+7998+2363+957]. Maher-Shalal-Hash-Baz, "quick to the plunder, swift to the spoil":– Maher-shalal-hash-baz [2]

4123 מַהֲתַלָּה *mah²tallâ*, n.f. GK: 4562 [→ 2048]. illusion, deception:– deceits [1]

4123.1 מוֹ *-mô* or מוּ *-mû*, p.suf. GK: 4564 [→ 1886.3]. he, him; they, them:– them [58], their [22], their (+3807.1) [6], themselves [6], they [5], he [2], him [2], his (+3807.1) [2], their own [2], whom [2], himself [1], his [1], that [1], thereto (+3807.1) [1], those [1], wherein (+5921) [1], which (+3807.1) [1]

4124 מוֹאָב *mô'āb*, n.pr.m. & loc. GK: 4565 & 4566 [→ 4125, 6355]. Moab, Moabite:– Moab [166], Moabites [15]

4125 מוֹאָבִי *mô'ābî*, a.g. GK: 4567 [→ 4124]. Moabite, from Moab, "of Moab":– Moabitess [6], Moabites [4], Moabite [3], Moabitish [1], of Moab [1], women of Moab [1]

מוֹאֵל *mô'l*. See 4136.

4126 מוֹבָא *môbā'*, n.[m.]. GK: 4569 [→ 3996; cf. 935]. coming in; entrance (way):– coming in [1], comings in [1]

4127 מוּג *mûg*, v. GK: 4570. [Q] to melt, waste away; [N] to melt away (in fear), be disheartened; to collapse; [Pol] to soften; to toss about; [Htpol] to melt away, flow from; from the base meaning the melting of a substance is the fig. extension of the

inner person melting is fear:– dissolved [3], faint [3], melt [3], melted [2], consumed [1], dissolvest [1], fainthearted [1], makest soft [1], melt away [1], melted away [1]

4128 מוד **môd**, v. GK: 4571. [Pol] to shake, convulse, set into motion:– measured [1]

4129 מֹדָע **môdāʿ**, n.m. GK: 4530 [→ 4130; cf. 3045]. (distant) relative, kinsman:– kinsman [1], kinswoman [1]

4130 מֹדַעַת **môdaʿat**, n.f. GK: 4531 [→ 4129; cf. 3045]. (distant) kinsman:– kindred [1]

4131 מוט **môṭ**, v. GK: 4572 [→ 4132, 4133]. [Q] to slip, fall, totter, stagger; [N] to be shaken, be caused to move, be toppled; [H] to bring down, to cause to fall; [Htpol] to be thoroughly shaken, be continually shaken:– moved [19], removed [5], moved exceedingly (+4131) [2], slippeth [2], carried [1], cast [1], fallen in decay (+3027) [1], falling down [1], fall [1], out of course [1], ready [1], shaketh [1], slide [1], slip [1]

4132 מוט **môṭ**, n.[m.]. GK: 4573 [→ 4131]. carrying frame; pole; yoke bar:– bar [2], moved [2], staff [1], yoke [1]

4133 מוֹטָה **môṭâ**, n.f. GK: 4574 [→ 4131]. yoke bar, pole, bar; by extension: oppression of subjected people:– yokes [4], yoke [4], bands [2], heavy [1], staves [1]

4134 מוּך **mûk**, v. GK: 4575 [cf. 4355]. [Q] to become poor:– waxen poor [3], poorer [1], wax poor [1]

4135 מוּל **mûl**, v. GK: 4576 & 4577 [→ 4139; cf. 4107, 5243]. [Q] to circumcise; [Qp] to be circumcised; [N] to be circumcised, undergo circumcision, circumcise oneself; "to circumcise the heart" means to commit to covenant obedience from within, not only formally; [H] to cut off, ward off:– circumcised [23], circumcise [5], destroy [1], must needs be circumcised (+4135) [2], circumcising [1], cut down [1], cut in pieces [1]

4136 מוּל or מוֹאל **mûl** or **môʾl**, subst. & pp. GK: 4578 & 4568 [cf. 2974]. before, opposite, in front of:– over against [10], against [5], forefront (+6440) [3], over against (+4480) [3], before (+413+6440) [2], over against (+413+6440) [2], against (+413) [1], before (+413) [1], before [1], forepart (+6440) [1], from (+4480) [1], off (+4480) [1], over against (+413) [1], to God-ward (+430+1886.1) [1], towards (+413) [1], towards (+4480) [1], upon (+413) [1]

4137 מוֹלָדָה **môlādâ**, n.pr.loc. GK: 4579. Moladah, "*generation*":– Moladah [4]

4138 מוֹלֶדֶת **môledet**, n.f. GK: 4580 [→ 3205]. family, relatives, children; (land of) birth, native (land):– kindred [11], nativity [6], born [2], begotten [1], issue [1], native [1]

4139 מוּלָה **mûlâ**, n.f. GK: 4581 [→ 4135]. circumcision:– circumcision [1]

4140 מוֹלִיד **môlîd**, n.pr.m. GK: 4582 [→ 3205]. Molid, "*descendant*":– Molid [1]

מוּם **muwm**. See 3971.

מוֹמֻכָן **mômukān**. See 4462.

4141 מוּסָב **mûsāb**, v.ptcp. GK: 6015 [→ 4142, 4524, 5252, 5437, 5438, 5439]. ptcp. of 5437: turning, winding:–

4142 מוּסַבָּה **mûsabbâ**, v.ptcp. GK: 6015 [→ 4141]. ptcp. of 5437: turning, winding:–

4143 מוּסָד **mûsād**, n.m. GK: 4586 [→ 4145; cf. 3245]. foundation, laying the foundation stone:– foundation [1], sure foundation (+3245) [1]

4144 מוֹסָד **môsād**, n.m. GK: 4587 [→ 4146; cf. 3245]. foundation:– foundations [3]

4145 מוּסָדָה **mûsādâ**, n.f. GK: 4588 [→ 4143, 4328; cf. 3245]. foundation:– grounded [1]

4146 מוֹסָדָה **môsādâ**, n.m. GK: 4589 [→ 4144; cf. 3245]. foundation:– foundations [10]

4147 מוֹסֵר **môsēr** or מוֹסֵרָה **môsērâ**, n.m. GK: 4591 & 4593 [→ 4149; cf. 631]. bonds, shackles, straps, chains, fetters:– bands [6], bonds [5]

4148 מוּסָר **mûsār**, n.m. GK: 4592 [→ 4561; cf. 3256]. discipline, instruction, correction; wisdom and teaching that imply correcting errant behavior:– instruction [30], correction [8], chastening [3], chastisement [3], bond [1], chasteneth [1], check [1], discipline [1], doctrine [1], rebuker [1]

4149 מוֹסֵרָה **môsērâ** or מֹסְרוֹת **môsērôt**, n.pr.loc. GK: 4594 & 5035 [→ 631?]. Moserah, Moseroth, "*bond, prison [?]*":– Moseroth [1], Mosera [1]

4150 מוֹעֵד **môʿēd**, n.m. GK: 4595 [→ 3259]. (Tent of) Meeting; appointed time, designated time, season:– congregation [149], time appointed [9], solemn feasts [8],

feasts [6], set time [6], season [5], set feasts [5], appointed season [4], appointed [3], seasons [3], solemnities [3], time [3], solemn feast [2], solemn [2], appointed feasts [2], appointed sign [1], appointed times [1], appointed time [1], assemblies [1], assembly [1], congregations [1], due season [1], feast [1], places of assembly [1], solemn assembly [1], solemn days [1], solemnity [1], synagogues [1], times [1]

4151 מוֹעָד **môʿād**, n.[m.] GK: 4596 [→ 3259]. ranks, appointed place of a soldier:– appointed times [1]

4152 מוּעָדָה **mûʿādâ**, n.f. GK: 4597 [→ 3259]. designation, appointment:– appointed [1]

4153 מוֹעַדְיָה **môʿadyâ**, n.pr.m. GK: 4598 [→ 4154+3068; cf. 4572]. Moadiah, "[perhaps] *Yahweh assembles* or *Yahweh promises*":– Moadiah [1]

4154 מוּעֶדֶת **mûʿedet**, v.ptcp. GK: 5048 [→ 4153, 4571, 4572, 4573, 5976]. ptcp. of 4571: dislocated:– out of joint [1]

4155 מוּעָף **mûʿāp**, n.[m.]. GK: 4599 [→ 4588, 6079; cf. 5890]. gloom, darkness; fig. of the emotional state of sadness and despondency:– dimness [1], foundations [1]

4156 מוֹעֵצָה **môʿēṣâ**, n.f. GK: 4600 [→ 3289]. plan, scheme, device, intrigue:– counsels [6], devices [1]

4157 מוּעָקָה **mûʿāqâ**, n.f. GK: 4601 [→ 5781?]. burden, misery, hardship:– affliction [1]

4158 מוֹפַעַת **môpaʿat** or מֵיפַעַת **mêpaʿat**, n.pr.loc. GK: 4602 & 4789. Mophaath, Mephaath, "*splendor*":– Mephaath [4]

4159 מוֹפֵת **môpēt**, n.m. GK: 4603. wonder, sign, miracle, portent; symbol:– wonders [19], sign [8], wonder [6], miracles [1], miracle [1], wondered at [1]

4160 מֵץ **mēṣ** or מוּץ **mûṣ**, n.m. GK: 5160 [→ 4330]. oppressor:– extortioner [1]

4161 מוֹצָא **môṣāʾ**, n.m. GK: 4604 [→ 3318]. act of going out, springing out, exiting, moving on; by extension, (n.) what goes out: spring (of water), mine shaft, sunrise, east:– going forth [4], goings out [4], brought out [2], spring [2], watersprings (+4325) [2], bud [1], east [1], go forth [1], going out [1], outgoings [1], proceeded out [1], springs [1], that proceedeth out [1], that which came out [1], that which is gone out [1], thing that is gone out [1], vein [1], watercourse (+4325) [1]

4162 מֹצָא **môṣāʾ**, n.pr.m. GK: 4605 [→ 3318]. Moza, "*sunrise*":– Moza [5]

4163 מוֹצָאָה **môṣāʾâ**, n.f. GK: 4606 [→ 3318]. origin, coming out; latrine:– goings forth [1]

4164 מוּצָק **mûṣāq**, n.[m.]. GK: 4607 [→ 4166; cf. 3332]. casting (of metal):– straitened [1], straitness [1], vexation [1]

4165 מוּצָק **mûṣāq**, n.[m.]. GK: 4608 [→ 6693]. restriction, constraint; distress, hardship:– casting [1], hardness [1]

4166 מוּצָקָה **mûṣāqâ**, n.f. GK: 4609 [→ 4164; cf. 3332]. casting (into one piece); channel, spout or lip (of a lamp):– cast [1], pipes [1]

4167 מוּק **mûq**, v. GK: 4610. [H] to scoff:– corrupt [1]

4168 מוֹקֵד **môqēd**, n.[m.]. GK: 4611 [→ 4169; cf. 3344]. hearth, (place of) glowing embers, burning embers:– burnings [1], hearth [1]

4169 מוֹקְדָה **môqdâ**, n.f. GK: 4612 [→ 4168; cf. 3344]. hearth, place of burning:– burning [1]

4170 מוֹקֵשׁ **môqēš**, n.m. GK: 4613 [→ 3369]. snare, trap, that which captures prey; by extension: ensnarement, entrapment (of a person):– snare [14], snares [6], grins [2], ensnared [1], gin [1], snared [1], traps [1], trap [1]

4171 מוּר **mûr**, v. GK: 4614 & 4615 [→ 8545]. [N] to be changed; to shake, quake; [H] to exchange, substitute, change:– changed [4], change [3], at all change (+4171) [2], change at all (+4171) [2], changeth [1], exchange [1], removed [1]

4172 מוֹרָא **môrāʾ** or מוֹרָה **môrâ**, n.m. GK: 4616 & 4624 [→ 3372]. fear, terror, respect, reverence; awesome deed:– fear [6], terror [3], dread [1], feared [1], terribleness [1], terrors [1]

4173 מוֹרַג **môrag**, n.m. GK: 4617. threshing sledge:– threshing instruments [2], threshing instrument [1]

4174 מוֹרָד **môrād**, n.m. GK: 4618 [→ 3381]. slope, road going down; something hammered down:– going down [3], made thin [1], steep place [1]

4175 מוֹרֶה **môreh**, n.[m.] or v.ptcp. GK: 4619 & 4620 & 4621 [→ 3384]. archer; autumn rains; teacher:– former rain [2], archers (+7198+871.1+1886.1) [1], rain [1], shooters [1]

4176 מוֹרֶה **môreh**, n.pr.[loc.?]. GK: 4622 [→ 3384]. Moreh:– Moreh [3]

4177 מוֹרָה **môrâ**, n.m. GK: 4623 [→ 6168]. razor:– rasor [3]

4178 מוֹרָט **môrāṭ**, v.ptcp. GK: 5307 [→ 4803; cf. 4804, cf. 4873]. ptcp. of 4803: polished, rubbed; skinned:– peeled [2]

4179 מוֹרִיָּה **môriyyâ**, n.pr.loc. GK: 5317. Moriah:– Moriah [2]

4180 מוֹרָשׁ **môrāš**, n.[m.]. GK: 4625 & 4626 [→ 782, 4181; cf. 3423]. possession, inheritance; desire:– possessions [1], possession [1], thoughts [1]

4181 מוֹרָשָׁה **môrāšâ**, n.f. GK: 4627 [→ 4180; cf. 3423]. possession:– possession [6], inheritance [2], heritage [1]

4182 מוֹרֶשֶׁת גַּת **môrešet gat**, n.pr.loc. GK: 4628 [→ 4183]. Moresheth Gath, "*possession of Gath*":– Moresheth-gath [1]

4183 מוֹרַשְׁתִּי **môraštî**, a.g. GK: 4629 [→ 4182]. of Moresheth:– Morasthite [2]

4184 מוּשׁ **mûš**, v. GK: 4630 [cf. 3237, 4959]. [Q] to touch, feel; [H] be able to feel, touch:– feel [1], handle [1]

4185 מוּשׁ **mûš**, v. GK: 4631. [Q] to depart, leave, move away, vanish; [H] to remove:– depart [8], remove [4], departed [2], removed [2], cease [1], departeth [1], gone back from [1], took away [1]

4186 מוֹשָׁב **môšāb**, n.m. GK: 4632 [→ 3427]. dwelling, settlement, place to live, place:– dwellings [8], habitations [8], seat [7], dwelling [4], habitation [4], dwelling places [3], dwelt [2], sitting [2], assembly [1], dwell in [1], dwelling place [1], inhabited places [1], situation [1], sojourning [1]

4187 מוּשִׁי **mûšî**, n.pr.m. GK: 4633 [→ 4188]. Mushi:– Mushi [8]

4188 מוּשִׁי **mûšî**, a.g. GK: 4634 [→ 4187]. Mushite, "*of Mushi*":– Mushites [2]

4189 מֹשְׁכוֹת **môškôt**, n.f. GK: 5436 [→ 4900]. cords, chains, fetters:– bands [1]

4190 מוֹשָׁעָה **môšāʿâ**, n.f. GK: 4636 [→ 3467]. act of salvation, act of helping:– salvation [1]

4191 מוּת **mût**, v. GK: 4637 [→ 4194, 4463, 8546 (also used with compound proper names)]. [Q] to die, be killed, be dead; [Pol] to kill, slay, put to death; [H] to kill, make die, put to death, assassinate; [Ho] to be put to death, be murdered:– die [232], died [153], dead [134], surely put to death (+4191) [56], put to death [44], slew [40], surely die (+4191) [40], slay [38], kill [23], slain [18], dieth [16], death [10], killed [6], in wise slay (+4191) [4], die (+4191) [2], killeth [2], must needs die (+4191) [2], surely be put to death (+4191) [2], surely kill (+4191) [2], cause to die [1], crying [1], dead man [1], destroyers [1], destroy [1], diest [1], necromancer (+7843+1875+1886.1) [1], slayeth [1], slaying [1]

4192 מוּת לַבֵּן **mût labbēn**, tt. GK: 4240 [→ 3807.1+1886.1+1121]. t.t. in Ps 9, poss. "death of the son" (4637 + 3807.1 + 1886.1 + 1121):– Muth-labben (+1121+1886.1+3807.1) [1]

4193 מוֹת **môt** (Aram.), n.[m.]. GK: 10409 [cf. 4194]. death:– death [1]

4194 מָוֶת **māwet**, n.m. GK: 4638 [→ 2700; cf. 4191; cf. 4193]. death, dying:– death [126], dead [8], died [8], die [6], dieth [5], surely die (+1121) [2], deadly [2], deaths [1], put to death (+2026) [1], slay [1], worthy to die (+1121) [1]

מוּת לַבֵּן **mût lab-bēn**. See 4192.

4195 מוֹתָר **môtār**, n.m. GK: 4639 [→ 3498]. profit, advantage:– hath preeminence [1], plenteousness [1], profit [1]

4196 מִזְבֵּחַ **mizbēaḥ**, n.m. GK: 4640 [→ 2076; cf. 4056]. altar:– altar [349], altars [52]

4197 מֶזֶג **mezeg**, n.m. GK: 4641. blended wine, mixed wine (likely spiced):– liquor [1]

4198 מָזֶה **māzeh**, a. GK: 4642. empty (from hunger), implying an unhealthy loss of weight and breakdown in health:– burnt [1]

4199 מִזָּה **mizzâ**, n.pr.m. GK: 4645. Mizzah, "*terror*":– Mizzah [3]

4200 מָזוּ **māzû**, n.m. GK: 4646 [cf. 2106]. barn, granary:– garners [1]

4201 מְזוּזָה **mᵉzûzâ**, n.f. GK: 4647. doorframe, doorpost, doorjamb; by extension: posts [10], side posts [4], post [3], door posts [1], door post [1]

4202 מָזוֹן **mazôn**, n.m. GK: 4648 [→ 2109]. provisions, food:– meat [1], victual [1]

4203 מָזוֹן **mazôn** (Aram.), n.[m.]. GK: 10410 [→ 2110; cf. 2109]. food:– meat [2]

Heb

4204 מָזוֹר **māzôr**, n.m. GK: 4650. trap, ambush:– wound [1]

4205 מָזוֹר **māzôr**, n.[m.] GK: 4649. sore, boil, ulcer:– wound [2], bound up [1]

מְזוּזָה **mᵉzuzā**. See 4201.

4206 מֵזַח מֵזִיחַ **mēzaḥ** or מֵזִיחַ **māzîaḥ**, n.m. GK: 4651 & 4652 & 4653 [→ 4231]. belt, leather girdle worn next to the skin; harbor; an area in which wind and wave are restricted as a fig. extension of a girdle or belt that restrains:– strength [2], girdle [1]

4207 מַזְלֵג **mazlēg** or מִזְלָגָה **mizlāgâ**, n.m. & f. GK: 4656 & 4657 & 4658. (three-tined) meat fork:– fleshhooks [5], fleshhook [2]

4208 מַזָּל **mazzāl**, n.[f.]pl. GK: 4655 [cf. 4216]. constellation (possibly of the zodiac signs):– planets [1]

4209 מְזִמָּה **mᵉzimmâ**, n.f. GK: 4659 [→ 2161]. discretion; scheme, plan, purpose, intent:– discretion [4], wicked devices [3], devices [2], thoughts [2], device [1], intents [1], lewdness [1], mischievous device [1], mischievous [1], thought [1], wickedly (+3807.1) [1], witty inventions [1]

4210 מִזְמוֹר **mizmôr**, n.[m.] GK: 4660 [→ 2167]. psalm, melody:– psalm [57]

4211 מַזְמֵרָה **mazmērâ**, n.f. GK: 4661 [→ 2168]. pruning hook, pruning knife, vine-knife:– pruninghooks [3], pruning hooks [1]

4212 מְזַמֶּרֶת **mᵉzammeret**, n.f. GK: 4662 [→ 2168]. wick trimmer (scissors, possibly also used as a snuffer):– snuffers [5]

4213 מִזְעָר **miz'ār**, n.[m.]. GK: 4663 [→ 2191]. small matter, few:– very little while (+4592) [2], few [1], small [1]

מָזֹר **māzōr**. See 4205.

4214 מִזְרֶה **mizreh**, n.[m.]. GK: 4665 [→ 2219]. winnowing fork, shovel:– fan [1]

4215 מְזָרִים **mᵉzārîm**, n.m. or v.ptcp. GK: 4668 [→ 2219]. driving (north) winds:– north [1]

4216 מַזָּרוֹת **mazzārôt**, n.[f.]pl. GK: 4666 [cf. 4208]. constellations, variously specified:– Mazzaroth [1]

4217 מִזְרָח **mizrāḥ**, n.[m.]. GK: 4667 [→ 2224]. direction of the sunrise, east, eastern; the east was the direction of orientation in the ancient Near East:– east [32], eastward (+1886.5) [15], rising [7], sunrising (+8121) [6], eastward [3], the sunrising (+8121+1886.5) [2], east (+6924+1886.5) [1], east side (+8121) [1], east side [1], eastward (+1886.1+3807.1) [1], eastward (+8121+1886.1) [1], rising of the sun [1], sunrising (+8121) [1], sunrising [1], the east side (+8121+1886.1) [1]

4218 מִזְרָע **mizrā'**, n.[m.]. GK: 4669 [→ 2232]. seeded field, land sown:– sown [1]

4219 מִזְרָק **mizrāq**, n.m. GK: 4670 [→ 2236]. sacred bowl used for sprinkling (the altar):– bowl [13], basons [11], bowls [8]

4220 מֵחַ **mēaḥ**, n.[m.]. GK: 4671 [→ 4221; cf. 4229]. fat sheep; (representing) the rich:– fat ones [1], fatlings [1]

4221 מֹחַ **mōaḥ**, n.m. GK: 4672 [→ 4220; cf. 4229]. marrow (of the bones):– marrow [1]

4222 מָחָא **māḥā'**, v. GK: 4673 [→ 4232; cf. 4223]. [Q] to clap (hands in joy):– clap [2], clapped [1]

4223 מְחָא **mᵉḥā'** (Aram.), v. GK: 10411 [cf. 4272]. [P] to strike; [Pa] to hold back, prevent; [Htpe] to be impaled:– smote [2], hanged [1], stay [1]

4224 מַחֲבֵא **maḥᵃbē'** or מַחֲבֹא **maḥᵃbō'**, n.[m.]. GK: 4675 & 4676 [→ 2244]. shelter, hiding place (from wind):– hiding place [1], lurking places [1]

4225 מַחְבֶּרֶת **maḥberet**, n.f. GK: 4678 [→ 2266]. place of joining, seam, set (of curtains):– coupling [8]

4226 מְחַבְּרוֹת **mᵉḥabbᵉrôt**, n.f. GK: 4677 [→ 2266]. fittings, braces (of iron), joists, truss (of timber):– couplings [1], joinings [1]

4227 מַחֲבַת **maḥᵃbat**, n.f. GK: 4679 [→ 2281]. (metal) griddle or baking pan:– pan [5]

4228 מַחֲגֹרֶת **maḥᵃgōret**, n.f. GK: 4680 [→ 2296]. girding (of sackcloth wrapped around the body):– girding [1], king [1]

4229 מָחָה **māḥâ**, v. GK: 4681 & 4682 & 4683 [→ 4239, 8547?; cf. 4220, 4221, 4222; cf. 4223]. [Q] to wash off, wipe out, blot out, destroy; to continue along, stretch along; [N] to be blotted out, be wiped out, be exterminated; [Pu] (choice food-dishes) to be filled with marrow; [H] to cause to blot out:– blot out [9], blotted out [5], destroyed [3], destroy [2], put out [2], utterly put out (+4229) [2], wipeth [2], abolished [1], blotteth

out [1], blot [1], destroyeth [1], full of marrow [1], reach [1], wipe away [1], wipe out [1], wiped away [1], wipe [1], wiping [1]

4230 מְחוּגָה **mᵉḥûgâ**, n.f. GK: 4684 [→ 2328]. compass (for making circles):– compass [1]

4231 מָחוֹז **māḥôz**, n.[m.]. GK: 4685 [→ 4206]. haven, harbor, which might include a population center like a repair yard and city:– haven [1]

4232 מְחוּיָאֵל **mᵉḥûyā'ēl** or מְחִיָּיאֵל **mᵉḥiyyāy'ēl**, n.pr.m. GK: 4686 & 4696 [→ 4222+410]. Mehujael, Mehijael:– Mehujael [2]

4233 מַחֲוִים **maḥᵃwîm**, a.g. GK: 4687. Mahavite:– Mahavite [1]

4234 מָחוֹל **māḥôl**, n.m. GK: 4688 [→ 4235, 4246; cf. 2342]. circle-dancing, round-dancing:– dance [4], dances [1], dancing [1]

4235 מָחוֹל **māḥôl**, n.pr.m. GK: 4689 [→ 4234; cf. 2342]. Mahol, "place of round dancing":– Mahol [1]

מְחֹלָה **mᵉḥōlâ**. See 65, 4246.

4236 מַחֲזֶה **maḥᵃzeh**, n.[m.]. GK: 4690 [→ 2372]. vision:– vision [4]

4237 מֶחֱזָה **meḥᵉzâ**, n.f. GK: 4691 [→ 2372]. light, place of seeing, in some contexts referring to a window:– light [4]

4238 מַחֲזִיאוֹת **maḥᵃzî'ôt**, n.pr.m. GK: 4692 [→ 2372]. Mahazioth, "visions":– Mahazioth [2]

4239 מְחִי **mᵉḥî**, n.[m.]. GK: 4693 [→ 4229]. blow (of a battering ram):– engines [1]

4240 מְחִידָא **mᵉḥîdā'**, n.pr.m. GK: 4694. Mehida, "[poss.] bought as slave":– Mehida [2]

4241 מִחְיָה **miḥyâ**, n.f. GK: 4695 [→ 2421]. saving of a life; raw flesh; food, sustenance; relief, recovering:– reviving [2], preserve life (+2416) [1], quick raw [1], quick [1], recover [1], sustenance [1], victuals [1]

מְחִיָּיאֵל **mᵉḥiyyāy'ēl**. See 4232.

4242 מְחִיר **mᵉḥîr**, n.m. GK: 4697 [→ 4243]. price, cost, money:– price [11], gain [1], hire [1], sold (+871.1+935) [1], worth [1]

4243 מְחִיר **mᵉḥîr**, n.pr.m. GK: 4698 [→ 4242]. Mehir, "hired hand":– Mehir [1]

4244 מַחְלָה **maḥlâ**, n.pr.f. [& m.?]. GK: 4702. Mahlah, "[perhaps] weak one":– Mahlah [4], Mahalah [1]

4245 מַחֲלֶה **maḥᵃleh** or מַחֲלָה **maḥᵃlâ**, n.m. & f. GK: 4700 & 4701 [cf. 2470]. sickness, disease:– sickness [3], diseases [1], disease [1], infirmity [1]

4246 מְחֹלָה **mᵉḥōlâ**, n.f. GK: 4703 [→ 4234; cf. 65, 2342]. circle-dance, round-dance:– dances [5], dancing [2], company [1]

4247 מְחִלָּה **mᵉḥillâ**, n.f. GK: 4704 [→ 2490]. hole:– caves [1]

4248 מַחְלוֹן **maḥlôn**, n.pr.m. GK: 4705 [→ 2470?]. Mahlon:– Mahlon [3], Mahlon's [1]

4249 מַחְלִי **maḥlî**, n.pr.m. GK: 4706 [→ 2470?]. Mahli, "[perhaps] shrewd, cunning":– Mahli [11], Mahali [1]

4250 מַחְלִי **maḥlî**, a.g. GK: 4707 [→ 2470?]. Mahlite, "of Mahli":– Mahlites [2]

4251 מַחֲלֻיִים **maḥᵃluyîm**, n.m. GK: 4708 [→ 2470]. sickness (caused by wounding):– diseases [1]

4252 מַחֲלָף **maḥᵃlāp**, n.[m.]. GK: 4709 [→ 2498?]. utensil, perhaps a pan:– knives [1]

4253 מַחְלָפָה **maḥlāpâ**, n.f. GK: 4710 [→ 2498]. braids (of hair):– locks [2]

4254 מַחֲלָצוֹת **maḥᵃlāṣôt**, n.f.[pl.]. GK: 4711 [→ 2502]. fine robes, fine, white, festival garments:– change of raiment [1], changeable suits of apparel [1]

4255 מַחְלְקָה **maḥlᵉqâ** (Aram.), n.f. GK: 10412 [→ 2508; cf. 4256]. group, division (of priests):– courses [1]

4256 מַחֲלֹקֶת **maḥᵃlōqet**, n.f. GK: 4713 [→ 2505; cf. 4255]. portion, share (of land); division, group (of people):– course [18], courses [14], divisions [8], companies by course [1], portions [1]

4257 מַחֲלַת **maḥᵃlat**, n.f. GK: 4714 [→ 2342? or 2470?]. mahalath (t.t. in the Psalms):– Mahalath [2]

4258 מַחֲלַת **maḥᵃlat**, n.pr.f. GK: 4715. Mahalath, "suffering of affliction NIV; sickness or suffering poem JB":– Mahalath [2]

4259 מְחֹלָתִי **mᵉḥōlātî**, a.g. GK: 4716 [cf. 65?]. Meholathite, of Meholah, "of Meholah":– Meholathite [2]

4260 מַחְמָאֹת **maḥmā'ōt**, n.f.pl. GK: 4717 [cf. 2529]. butter; some sources: curds, yogurt:– butter [1]

4261 מַחְמָד **maḥmād**, n.m. GK: 4718 [→ 2530]. thing of value, something of delight, treasure; "the delight of the eyes" is someone or something especially cherished:– pleasant things [4], desire [3], pleasant [3], beloved [1], goodly [1], lovely [1]

4262 מַחְמֹד **maḥmōd**, n.[m.]. GK: 4719 [→ 2530]. treasure, something precious:– pleasant things [1]

4263 מַחְמָל **maḥmāl**, n.[m.]. GK: 4720 [→ 2550?]. yearning:– pitieth [1]

4264 מַחֲנֶה **maḥᵃneh**, n.m. & f. GK: 4722 [→ 4266; cf. 2583]. camp, group (military or civilian):– camp [129], host [57], camps [7], company [5], tents [5], hosts [4], armies [3], battle [1], companies [1], drove [1], two armies [1]

4265 מַחֲנֵה־דָן **maḥᵃnēh-dān**, n.pr.loc. GK: 4723. Mahaneh Dan, "camp of Dan":– Mahaneh-dan [1]

4266 מַחֲנַיִם **maḥᵃnayim**, n.pr.loc. GK: 4724 [→ 4264; cf. 2583]. Mahanaim, "double camp":– Mahanaim [13]

4267 מַחֲנַק **maḥᵃnaq**, n.[m.]. GK: 4725 [→ 2614]. strangling, suffocation:– strangling [1]

4268 מַחְסֶה **maḥseh**, n.m. GK: 4726 [→ 4271; cf. 2620]. refuge, shelter:– refuge [13], hope [2], place of refuge [2], shelter [2], trust [1]

4269 מַחְסוֹם **maḥsôm**, n.m. GK: 4727 [→ 2629]. muzzle, a covering for the mouth to keep silence:– bridle [1]

4270 מַחְסוֹר **maḥsôr**, n.[m.]. GK: 4728 [→ 2637]. need, lack of, scarcity, hence poverty:– want [7], lack [1], need [1], penury [1], poor [1], poverty [1], wants [1]

4271 מַחְסֵיָה **maḥsēyâ**, n.pr.m. GK: 4729 [→ 4268+3068]. Mahseiah:– Maaseiah [2]

4272 מָחַץ **māḥaṣ**, v. GK: 4730 [→ 4273; cf. 4223]. [Q] to beat to pieces, crush, shatter:– wound [3], smite [2], wounded [2], dipped [1], pierce through [1], pierced [1], smiteth through [1], strike through [1], woundedst [1], woundeth [1]

4273 מַחַץ **maḥaṣ**, n.[m.]. GK: 4731 [→ 4272]. wound (from a blow):– stroke [1]

4274 מַחְצֵב **maḥṣēb**, n.[m.]. GK: 4732 [→ 2672]. dressed (stone), hewn (stone):– hewn [2], hewed [1]

4275 מֶחֱצָה **meḥᵉṣâ**, n.f. GK: 4733 [→ 2673]. half:– half [2]

4276 מַחֲצִית **maḥᵃṣît**, n.f. GK: 4734 [→ 2673]. half; noon, middle of the day:– half [14], half so much [1], midday (+3117+1886.1) [1]

4277 מָחַק **māḥaq**, v. GK: 4735. [Q] to crush, smash, pierce:– smote off [1]

4278 מֶחְקָר **meḥqār**, n.[m.]. GK: 4736 [→ 2713]. (unexplored) depths (of the earth):– deep places [1]

4279 מָחָר **māḥār**, n.m. (used as adv.). GK: 4737 [→ 4283; cf. 309]. tomorrow, the next day, in the future:– to morrow [43], in time to come [7], to come [1], to morrow (+3117) [1]

4280 מַחֲרָאָה **maḥᵃrā'â**, n.f. GK: 4738 [→ 2716]. latrine:– draught house [1]

4281 מַחֲרֵשָׁה **maḥᵃrēšâ**, n.f. GK: 4739 [→ 2790, 4282]. same as 4282: plowshare:– mattocks [1], mattock [1]

4282 מַחֲרֶשֶׁת **maḥᵃrešet**, n.f. GK: 4739 [→ 4281]. same as 4281: plowshare:– share [1]

4283 מׇחֳרָת **moḥᵒrāt**, n.f. GK: 4740 [→ 4279; cf. 309]. the next day, the day after:– morrow [26], morrow after [3], next day [2], next [1]

4284 מַחֲשָׁבָה **maḥᵃšābâ**, n.f. GK: 4742 [→ 2803]. thought, plan, scheme, plot, design:– thoughts [27], devices [8], device [4], imaginations [3], purposes [3], purpose [3], cunning works [2], cunning [1], curious works [1], devised [1], invented [1], means [1], those that devise cunning work (+2803) [1], thought [1]

4285 מַחְשָׁךְ **maḥšāk**, n.m. GK: 4743 [→ 2821]. place of darkness, hiding place:– darkness [4], dark places [2], dark [1]

4286 מַחְשֹׂף **maḥśōp**, n.m. GK: 4741 [→ 2834]. exposing, laying bare (of wood):– made appear [1]

4287 מַחַת **maḥat**, n.pr.m. GK: 4744 [→ 2865?]. Mahath, "[perhaps] tough":– Mahath [3]

4288 מְחִתָּה **mᵉḥittâ**, n.f. GK: 4745 [→ 2865]. ruin, undoing; terror, horror:– destruction [7], terror [2], dismaying [1], ruin [1]

4289 מַחְתָּה *maḥtâ*, n.f. GK: 4746 [→ 2846]. censer, firepan, tray:– censers [8], censer [7], firepans [4], snuffdishes [3]

4290 מַחְתֶּרֶת *maḥteret*, n.m. GK: 4747 [→ 2864]. (the act of) breaking into (a house) and so trespassing:– breaking up [1], secret search [1]

4291 מְטָא *mᵉṭā'* (Aram.), v. GK: 10413. [P] to reach out, extend towards:– came [4], reached [2], come [1], reacheth [1]

4292 מַטְאֲטֵא *maṭ'ᵃṭē'*, n.[m.]. GK: 4748 [→ 2894; cf. 2916]. broom:– besom [1]

4293 מַטְבֵּחַ *maṭbēaḥ*, n.[m.]. GK: 4749 [→ 2873]. place of slaughter, slaughter yard:– slaughter [1]

4294 מַטֶּה *maṭṭeh*, n.m. [& f.?]. GK: 4751 [→ 5186]. staff, rod, club, a stick used to assist in walking, discipline, and guidance, often highly individualized and used for identification; of royalty: scepter; by extension: tribe, as a major unit of national group or clan (fig. identified with or under authority of a leader's staff):– tribe [163], rod [42], tribes [20], staff [15], rods [8], staves [1]

4295 מַטָּה *maṭṭâ*, adv. GK: 4752 [→ 5186]. below, beneath, lower, bottom:– downward (+3807.1) [5], beneath (+4480+3807.1) [4], beneath [2], underneath (+4480+3807.1) [2], very low (+4295) [2], beneath (+3807.1) [1], down (+3807.1) [1], less [1], under [1]

4296 מִטָּה *miṭṭâ*, n.f. GK: 4753 [→ 5186]. bed, couch, a piece of furniture on which one reclines for rest or sleep; by extension: bier, to carry the dead; carriage or palanquin (a vehicle carried on poles by porters):– bed [23], bedchamber (+2315) [2], beds [2], bed's [1], bier [1]

4297 מֻטֶּה *muṭṭeh*, n.[m.]. GK: 4754 [→ 5186]. injustice, warping (of justice), crookedness (of law):– perverseness [1]

4298 מֻטָּה *muṭṭâ*, n.f. GK: 4755 [→ 5186]. outspreading (of wings):– stretching out [1]

4299 מַטְוֶה *maṭweh*, n.[m.]. GK: 4757 [→ 2901]. that which is spun, yarn:– spun [1]

4300 מָטִיל *māṭîl*, n.m. GK: 4758. (iron) rod:– bars [1]

4301 מַטְמוֹן *maṭmôn*, n.m. GK: 4759 [→ 2934]. (hidden) treasure, (hidden) riches:– hid treasures [2], hidden riches [1], treasures [1], treasure [1]

4302 מַטָּע *maṭṭā'*, n.m. GK: 4760 [→ 5193]. (the act or place of) planting:– planting [2], plantation [1], plantings [1], plants [1], plant [1]

4303 מַטְעָם *maṭ'ām*, n.m. GK: 4761 [→ 2938]. tasty food, delicacy:– savoury meat [6], dainties [1], dainty meats [1]

4304 מִטְפַּחַת *miṭpaḥat*, n.f. GK: 4762 [→ 2946]. cloak, shawl:– vail [1], wimples [1]

4305 מָטַר *māṭar*, v.den. GK: 4763 [→ 4306]. [N] to be rained upon; [H] to send rain down on; [Ho] to be rained upon; rain has a generally positive associations of growth and refreshment, though excessive or ill-timed rain is potentially destructive to crops and even life-threatening:– rained [5], rain [5], cause to rain [3], caused to rain [3], rained down [1]

4306 מָטָר *māṭār*, n.m. GK: 4764 [→ 4305, 4309]. rain, rain shower:– rain [35], great [1], showers [1], small [1]

4307 מַטָּרָא *maṭṭārâ*, n.f. GK: 4766 [→ 5201]. (the court of the) guard, i.e., place of confinement; (the Gate of the) Guard (a place); target:– prison [13], mark [3]

4308 מַטְרֵד *maṭrēd*, n.pr.f. GK: 4765 [→ 2956]. Matred, "[perhaps] *spear*":– Matred [2]

4309 מַטְרִי *maṭrî*, a.g. GK: 4767 [→ 4306]. Matri:– Matri [1]

4310 מִי *mî*, p.inter. GK: 4769 [→ 4316?, 4317, 4318, 4319, 4320, 4322, 4321, 4332]. who?, what?, which?; anyone, whoever:– who [284], whom [47], what [25], O that (+5414) [17], whose [11], whose (+3807.1) [7], which [6], oh that [3], whosoever [3], whoso [3], any [2], he [2], would God (+5414) [2], would to God (+5414) [2], him [1], none [1], that [1], what (+2088) [1], who else [1], whosoever (+834) [1], would God that (+5414) [1], would [1]

4311 מֵידְבָא *mêdᵉbā'*, n.pr.loc. GK: 4772. Medeba:– Medeba [5]

4312 מֵידָד *mêdād*, n.pr.m. GK: 4773. Medad, "*beloved*":– Medad [2]

4313 מֵי הַיַּרְקוֹן *mê hayyarqôn*, n.pr.loc. GK: 4770 [→ 4325]. Me Jarkon, "*waters of Jarkon [greenish?]*":– Me-jarkon [1]

4314 מֵי זָהָב *mê zāhāb*, n.pr.m. GK: 4771 [→ 4325+2091]. Me-Zahab, "*waters of gold*":– Mezahab [2]

4315 מֵיטָב *mêṭāb*, n.[m.]. GK: 4774 [→ 3190]. best (part of something):– best [6]

4316 מִיכָא *mîkā'*, n.pr.m. GK: 4775 [→ 4317?, 4318; cf. 4310?]. Mica, "*Who is like Yahweh?*":– Micha [4], Micah [1]

4317 מִיכָאֵל *mîkā'ēl*, n.pr.m. GK: 4776 [→ 4316?]. Michael, "*Who is like God [El]?*":– Michael [13]

4318 מִיכָה *mîkâ*, n.pr.m. GK: 4777 [→ 4316]. Micah; Mica; Micaiah, "*Who is like Yahweh?*":– Micah [24], Michah [4], Micah's [3], Micaiah [1]

4319 מִיכָהוּ *mîkāhû*, n.pr.m. GK: 4778 [→ 4310+3509.1+1930.2]. Micahu, cf. 4322:–

4320 מִיכָיָה *mîkāyâ*, n.pr.m. GK: 4779 [→ 4322, 4321]. Micaiah, "*Who is like Yahweh?*":– Michaiah [3]

4321 מִיכָיְהוּ *mîkāyᵉhû*, n.pr.m. GK: 4781 [→ 4320]. Micaiah, "*Who is like Yahweh?*":– Micaiah [17], Micah [2], Michaiah [2]

4322 מִיכָיָהוּ *mîkāyāhû*, n.pr.m. & f. GK: 4780 [→ 4320]. Micaiah, "*Who is like Yahweh?*":– Michaiah [2]

4323 מִיכָל *mîkāl*, n.[m.]. GK: 4782 [→ 4324]. brook, stream; some sources: pool, reservoir:– brook [1]

4324 מִיכַל *mîkal*, n.pr.f. GK: 4783 [→ 4323]. Michal, "*Who is like God [El]?*":– Michal [18]

4325 מַיִם *mayim*, n.m. GK: 4784 [→ 66, 4313, 4314, 4956]. water; in nature: ocean, lake, flood, river; from the body: tears, urine:– water [306], waters [267], piss (+7272) [2], watersprings (+4161) [2], washing [1], watercourse (+4161) [1], waterflood (+7641) [1], watering [1]

4326 מִיָּמִין *miyyāmîn*, n.pr.m. GK: 4785 [→ 4509]. Mijamin, "*from the right hand*":– Miamin [2], Mijamin [2]

4327 מִין *mîn*, n.[m.]. GK: 4786 [→ 8544]. kind: genus or species:– kind [30], kinds [1]

4328 מְיֻסָּדָה *mᵉyussādâ*, v.ptcp. GK: 4588 [→ 4145]. ptcp. of 3245: foundation:–

4329 מוּסָךְ *mûsāk* or מֵיסָךְ *mêsāk*, n.m. GK: 4590 & 4788 [→ 5526]. canopy:– covert [1]

 מֵיפַעַת *mêpa'at*. See 4158.

4330 מִיץ *mîṣ*, n.m. GK: 4790 [→ 4160]. pressing, squeezing:– churning [1], forcing [1], wringing [1]

4331 מֵישָׁא *mêšā'*, n.pr.m. GK: 4791. Mesha:– Mesha [1]

4332 מִישָׁאֵל *mîšā'ēl*, n.pr.m. GK: 4792 [→ 4310+7945+410; cf. 4333]. Mishael, "*Who belongs to God [El]?*":– Mishael [7]

4333 מִישָׁאֵל *mîšā'ēl* (Aram.), n.pr.m. GK: 10414 [cf. 4332]. Mishael, "*who belongs to God [El]*":– Mishael [1]

4334 מִישׁוֹר *mîšôr*, n.m. GK: 4793 [→ 3474]. (geographical) plateau, plain, level ground; (of ruling and right living) uprightness, justice, straightness:– plain [10], equity [2], even place [1], made straight [1], plains [1], righteously [1], right [1], straight [1], uprightness [1]

4335 מֵישַׁךְ *mêšak*, n.pr.m. GK: 4794 [cf. 4336]. Meshach, "*[perhaps] I have become weak*":– Meshach [1]

4336 מֵישַׁךְ *mêšak* (Aram.), n.pr.m. GK: 10415 [cf. 4335]. Meshach, "*[perhaps] I have become weak*":– Meshach [14]

4337 מֵישַׁע *mêšā'*, n.pr.m. GK: 4796 [→ 3467]. Mesha:– Mesha [1]

4338 מֵישַׁע *mêšā'*, n.pr.m. GK: 4795 [→ 3467]. Mesha:– Mesha [1]

4339 מֵישָׁרִים *mêšārîm*, n.m. GK: 4797 [→ 3474]. uprightness, fairness, equity, justice; moral uprightness and justice are fig. extensions of an object that is straight rather than crooked:– equity [4], uprightly [3], uprightness [3], right things [2], agreement [1], aright (+871.1) [1], righteously (+871.1) [1], sweetly (+3807.1) [1], things that are equal [1], things that are right [1], upright [1]

4340 מֵיתָר *mêtār*, n.m. GK: 4798 [→ 3499]. rope, cord; bow-string:– cords [8], laid up [2], strings [1]

4341 מַכְאֹב *mak'ōb*, n.m. GK: 4799 [→ 3510]. pain, grief, sorrow, suffering:– sorrow [7], sorrows [5], grief [2], pain [2]

4342 מַכְבִּיר *makbîr*, v.ptcp. GK: 3892 [→ 3527]. ptcp. of 3527: abundance:– abundance [1]

4343 מַכְבֵּנָה *makbēnâ*, n.pr.loc. GK: 4800 [cf. 4344]. Macbenah, "*bond*":– Machbenah [1]

4344 מַכְבַּנַּי *makbannay*, n.pr.m. GK: 4801 [cf. 4343]. Macbannai, "*clad with a cloak*":– Machbanai [1]

4345 מַכְבָּר *makbār*, n.[m.]. GK: 4803 [→ 4346]. grating, lattice-work:– grate [6]

4346 מַכְבֵּר *makbēr*, n.[m.]. GK: 4802 [→ 4345]. thick cloth, with a focus that it is twisted, braided, or woven:– thick cloth [1]

4347 מַכָּה *makkâ*, n.f. GK: 4804 [→ 5221]. wound, injury, physical damage to the body; by extension: plague, affliction, calamity, disaster:– slaughter [13], plagues [9], wound [8], wounds [6], plague [5], stripes [2], stroke [2], beaten [1], blow [1], slaughter made (+5221) [1], smote [1], sores [1], wounded [1]

4348 מִכְוָה *mikwâ*, n.f. GK: 4805 [→ 3554]. burn (on the skin), scar; in context this is not an intentional mark or tattoo:– burning [4], burneth [1]

4349 מָכוֹן *mākôn*, n.m. GK: 4806 [→ 3559]. (established) place, site; foundation (of earth or throne):– place [11], dwelling place [2], habitation [2], foundations [1], settled place [1]

4350 מְכוֹנָה *mᵉkônâ*, n.f. GK: 4807 [→ 3559, 4369]. movable stand; (established) place, foundation:– bases [16], base [8], every (+1886.1) [1]

4351 מְכוּרָה *mᵉkûrâ*, n.f. GK: 4808 [→ 3738]. ancestry, origin, parentage:– birth [1], habitation [1], nativity [1]

4352 מָכִי *mākî*, n.pr.m. GK: 4809. Maki, "[perhaps] *reduced or bought*":– Machi [1]

4353 מָכִיר *mākîr*, n.pr.m. GK: 4810 [→ 4354]. Makir, Makirite, "*bought*":– Machir [22]

4354 מָכִירִי *mākîrî*, a.g. GK: 4811 [→ 4353]. Makirite, "*of Makir*":– Machirites [1]

4355 מָכַךְ *mākak*, v. GK: 4812 [cf. 4134]. [Q] to sink, go down, waste away; [N] to sag, be sunk down; [Ho] to be brought low:– brought low [2], decayeth [1]

4356 מִכְלָא *miklā'*, n.[m.]. GK: 4813 [→ 3607]. pen, fold (for sheep or goats):– folds [1], fold [1], sheepfolds (+6629) [1]

4357 מִכְלוֹת *miklôt*, n.[f.]. GK: 4816 [→ 3615]. solid (gold), purest (gold):– perfect [1]

4358 מִכְלוֹל *miklôl*, n.m. GK: 4814 [→ 3634]. fullness, completeness, perfection:– all sorts [1], most gorgeously [1]

4359 מִכְלָל *miklāl*, n.m. GK: 4817 [→ 3634]. perfection:– perfection [1]

4360 מִכְלוּל *maklûl*, n.m. GK: 4815 [→ 3634]. beautiful garment, finery, with a focus the excellence of the item:– all sorts of things [1]

4361 מַכֹּלֶת *makkōlet*, n.f. GK: 4818 [→ 398]. food:– food [1]

4362 מִכְמָן *mikmān*, n.[m.]. GK: 4819. (hidden) treasure:– treasures [1]

4363 מִכְמָס *mikmās* or מִכְמָשׁ *mikmāš*, n.pr.loc. GK: 4820 & 4825 [cf. 3647]. Micmas, Micmash, "[perhaps] *hidden place*":– Michmash [9], Michmas [2]

4364 מִכְמָר *mikmār* or מַכְמֹר *makmōr*, n.[m.]. GK: 4821 & 4822 [cf. 4365]. net, snare (for capture of game):– nets [1], net [1]

4365 מִכְמֶרֶת *mikmeret* or מִכְמֹרֶת *mikmōret*, n.f. GK: 4823 & 4824 [cf. 4364]. net, snare; fishing net, dragnet (for fish):– drag [2], nets [1]

 מִכְמָשׁ *mikmāš*. See 4363.

4366 מִכְמְתָת *mikmᵉtāt*, n.pr.loc. GK: 4826. Micmethath:– Michmethath [1]

4367 מַכְנַדְבַי *maknadbay*, n.pr.m. GK: 4827. Macnadebai, "[poss.] *possession of Nebo*":– Machnadebai [1]

 מְכֹנָה *mᵉkōnâ*. See 4350.

4368 מְכֹנָה *mᵉkōnâ*, n.pr.loc. GK: 4828 [→ 3559]. Meconah, "*foundation*":– Mekonah [1]

4369 מְכֻנָה *mᵉkunâ*, n.f. GK: 4807 [→ 4350]. same as 4350: movable stand; (established) place, foundation:–

4370 מִכְנָס *miknās*, n.m. GK: 4829 [→ 3664]. undergarment, some kind of shorts or trousers:– breeches [5]

4371 מֶכֶס *mekes*, n.m. GK: 4830 [→ 3699]. tribute, cultic dues or taxes:– tribute [6]

4372 מִכְסֶה *mikseh*, n.m. GK: 4832 [→ 3680]. covering:– covering [16]

4373 מִכְסָה *miksâ*, n.f. GK: 4831 [→ 3699]. number (of persons); amount, valuation (of a thing):– number [1], worth [1]

4374 מְכַסֶּה *mᵉkasseh*, n.m. GK: 4833 [→ 3680]. covering (of a body or building); layer of fat (on the kidneys):– clothing [1], covered [1], covereth [1], cover [1]

4375 מַכְפֵּלָה *makpēlâ*, n.pr.loc. GK: 4834 [→ 3717]. Machpelah, "*double [cave]*":– Machpelah [6]

4376 מָכַר *mākar*, v. GK: 4835 [→ 4377, 4378?, 4465, 4466]. [Q] to sell; [N] to be sold; [Ht] to sell oneself:– sold [44], sell [22], selleth [5], seller [3], sell at all (+4376) [2], sell ought (+4465) [1], sellers [1], sellest [1], sold (+4466) [1]

4377 מֶכֶר *meker*, n.m. GK: 4836 [→ 4376]. worth, value; merchandise:– pay (+5414) [1], price [1], ware [1]

4378 מַכָּר *makkār*, n.m. GK: 4837 [→ 4376?]. treasurer:– acquaintance [1]

4379 מִכְרֶה *mikreh*, n.m. GK: 4838 [→ 3738]. (salt) pit:– saltpits (+4417) [1]

4380 מְכֵרָה *mᵉkērâ*, n.[f.]. GK: 4839. sword, weapon:– habitations [1]

מְכֹרָה *mᵉkōrâ*. See 4351.

4381 מִכְרִי *mikrî*, n.pr.m. GK: 4840. Micri:– Michri [1]

4382 מְכֵרָתִי *mᵉkērātî*, a.g. GK: 4841. Mekerathite:– Mecherathite [1]

4383 מִכְשׁוֹל *mikšôl*, n.m. GK: 4842 [→ 3782]. stumbling block, obstacle; (occasion of) stumbling, downfall:– stumblingblock [7], offence [2], caused to fall [1], offend [1], ruins [1], ruin [1], stumblingblocks [1]

4384 מַכְשֵׁלָה *makšēlâ*, n.f. GK: 4843 [→ 3782]. heap of ruins, heap of rubble:– ruin [1], stumblingblocks [1]

4385 מִכְתָּב *miktāb*, n.m. GK: 4844 [→ 3789]. writing, inscription, letter:– writing [9]

4386 מְכִתָּה *mᵉkittâ*, n.f. GK: 4845 [→ 3807]. pieces, crushed fragments:– bursting [1]

4387 מִכְתָּם *miktām*, n.[m.]. GK: 4846 [→ 3800?]. miktam (t.t. in the Psalms, of uncertain meaning):– Michtam [6]

4388 מַכְתֵּשׁ *maktēš*, n.m. GK: 4847 [→ 3806, 4389]. hollow place; mortar; market district (at a hollow place in the city?):– hollow place [1], mortar [1]

4389 מַכְתֵּשׁ *maktēš*, n.pr.m. GK: 4847 [→ 4388]. same as 4388 as n.pr.: Maktesh:– Maktesh [1]

מֻל *mul*. See 4136.

4390 מָלֵא *mālē’* or מָלָא *mālâ*, v. GK: 4848 & 4862 [→ 3229, 4392, 4393, 4394, 4395, 4396, 4402, 4407; cf. 4391 (also used with compound proper names)]. [Q] to fill up, be full; [Qp] to be ordained, fulfilled; [N] to be filled, become filled up; [P] to fill up, satisfy; ordain, consecrate; [Pu] to be set; [Ht] to unite together; "to fill the hand" means to ordain or consecrate for service to God:– filled [72], full [46], fill [32], fulfilled [20], fulfil [8], accomplished [6], wholly [6], consecrate (+3027) [5], consecrated (+853+3027) [5], replenished [5], set [5], consecrate (+853+3027) [2], expired [1], consecrated (+3027) [2], filleth [2], replenish [2], accomplish [1], at an end [1], become full [1], confirm [1], consecrate [1], drew with full strength (+3027+871.1) [1], durst presume [1], fenced [1], filledst [1], fillest [1], fully set [1], fully [1], fulness [1], furnish unto [1], gather together [1], gathered [1], gather [1], gave in full tale [1], overfloweth (+5921) [1], overflown (+5921) [1], satisfied [1], satisfy [1], space [1], took a handful (+3709) [1], went fully [1]

4391 מְלָא *mᵉlā’* (Aram.), v. GK: 10416 [cf. 4390]. [P] to fill; [Htpe] to be filled:– filled [1], full [1]

4392 מָלֵא *mālē’*, a. GK: 4849 [→ 4390]. filled, full; "full of days" means "very old":– full [58], filled [2], all [1], fill [1], fully [1], multitude [1], with child [1], worth [1]

4393 מְלֹא *mᵉlō’*, n.m. GK: 4850 [→ 4390]. what fills, what makes something full; fullness, everything:– full [12], fulness [8], all that is therein [6], fill [2], handful (+3709) [2], multitude [2], take handful (+7061+7062) [2], all along (+6967) [1], all that is in [1], all that therein is [1], handfuls (+2651) [1]

מִלֹּא *millō’*. See 4407.

4394 מִלֻּאִים *millu’îm*, n.m. GK: 4854 [→ 4390]. ordination, consecration (of a priest); mounting, setting (of gem stones):– consecration [6], consecrations [5], set [4]

4395 מְלֵאָה *mᵉlē’â*, n.f. GK: 4852 [→ 4390]. full yield (of crops):– fruit [1], fulness [1], ripe fruits [1]

4396 מִלֻּאָה *millu’â*, n.f. GK: 4853 [→ 4390]. mounting (of jewels), setting (of jewels):– inclosings [2], settings [1]

4397 מַלְאָךְ *mal’āk*, n.m. GK: 4855 [→ 4399, 4400, 4401?; cf. 4398]. messenger, a human representative; angel, a supernatural representative of God, sometimes delivering messages, sometimes protecting God's people; the "angel of the LORD" sometimes shares divine characteristics and is sometimes thought to be a manifestation of God himself, or of the preincarnate Christ:– angel [101], messengers [74], messenger [24], angels [10], ambassadors [4]

4398 מַלְאַךְ *mal’ak* (Aram.), n.m. GK: 10417 [cf. 4397]. messenger; angel, a class of being that serves God, often to communicate with or rescue his faithful on earth:– angel [2]

4399 מְלָאכָה *mᵉlā’kâ*, n.f. GK: 4856 [→ 4397]. work, deed, duty, craft, service; thing, something:– work [126], business [12], workmanship [5], workmen (+6213+1886.1) [4], workmen (+6213) [3], works [3], goods [2], cattle [1], industrious (+6213) [1], labour [1], made [1], occupation [1], occupied (+6213) [1], officers (+6213+1886.1) [1], stuff [1], thing [1], use [1], workmen (+376) [1]

4400 מַלְאָכוּת *mal’ākût*, n.f. GK: 4857 [→ 4397]. message (from a commissioned messenger):– message [1]

4401 מַלְאָכִי *mal’ākî*, n.pr.m. GK: 4858 [→ 4397?]. Malachi, "my messenger or messenger of Yahweh":– Malachi [1]

4402 מִלֵּאת *millē’t*, n.f. GK: 4859 [→ 4390]. setting, mounting, the solid base in which a gem is set:– fitly [1]

4403 מַלְבּוּשׁ *malbûš*, n.m. GK: 4860 [→ 3847]. clothing, robe, attire, garment:– apparel [4], raiment [3], vestments [1]

4404 מַלְבֵּן *malbēn*, n.[m.]. GK: 4861 [→ 3840]. brickwork, brick pavement; (the act of) brickmaking:– brickkiln [3]

4405 מִלָּה *millâ*, n.f. GK: 4863 [→ 4448; cf. 4406]. word, what is said; the act of speaking, speech:– words [21], speech [4], speaking [2], speeches [2], word [2], answer (+7725) [1], any thing to say [1], byword [1], matter [1], speak [1], talking [1], what to say [1]

4406 מִלָּה *millâ* (Aram.), n.f. GK: 10418 [→ 4449; cf. 4405]. word, command; matter, thing, affair; a general term like the English "thing":– thing [9], words [5], matter [4], things [2], word [2], commandment [1], matters [1]

מְלֹו *mᵉlô* or מְלֹוא *mᵉlô’*. See 4393.

4407 מִלֹּוא *millô’* or מִלֹּא *millō’*, n.pr.loc. GK: 4864 & 4851 [cf. 4390]. Millo, "supporting terrace":– Millo [10]

4408 מַלּוּחַ *mallûaḥ*, n.[m.]. GK: 4865 [→ 4417]. salt herb (collected by the destitute and banished):– mallows [1]

4409 מַלּוּךְ *mallûk* or מְלִיכוּ *mᵉlîkû* or מַלּוּכִי *mallûkî* or מְלִיכוּ *mᵉlîkû*, n.pr.m. GK: 4866 & 4868 & 4883 [→ 4428; cf. 4427]. Malluch, Melichu, "counselor; king":– Malluch [6], Melicu [1]

4410 מְלוּכָה *mᵉlûkâ*, n.f. GK: 4867 [→ 4427]. kingship, rulership, royalty:– kingdom [18], royal [4], king's [2]

4411 מָלֹון *mālôn*, n.m. GK: 4869 [→ 3885]. place of overnight lodging, place where one spends the night:– inn [3], lodging place [2], lodgings [1], place where lodged [1], taken up lodging [1]

4412 מְלוּנָה *mᵉlûnâ*, n.f. GK: 4870 [→ 3885]. hut, structure (of a watchman in the field):– cottage [1], lodge [1]

4413 מַלֹּותִי *mallôtî*, n.pr.m. GK: 4871 [→ 4448]. Mallothi, "my expression":– Mallothi [2]

4414 מָלַח *mālaḥ*, v.den. GK: 4872 & 4873 [→ 4417, 4418]. [Q] to season with salt; [N] to vanish, be dispersed; [Pu] to be salted; [Ho] to be rubbed with salt:– salted at all (+4414) [2], season [1], tempered together [1], vanish away [1]

4415 מְלַח *mᵉlaḥ* (Aram.), v.den. GK: 10419 [→ 4416; cf. 4414]. [P] to eat salt (i.e., be under obligation to); "to eat the salt of the palace" is to be under the solemn obligation to the king's interests:– have maintenance (+4416) [1]

4416 מְלַח *mᵉlaḥ* (Aram.), n.m. GK: 10420 [→ 4415; cf. 4417]. salt, a condiment for food; also used in ceremonies:– salt [2], have maintenance (+4415) [1]

4417 מֶלַח *melaḥ*, n.m. GK: 4875 [→ 4408, 4414, 4419, 4420, 5898, 8528; cf. 4415, cf. 4416]. salt, a staple of the ancient world; positively: for flavoring, as a nutrient, as a food preservative; as a medicine; for curing animal skins; negatively: used on fields to prevent or inhibit productive plant growth:– salt [28], saltpits (+4379) [1]

4418 מֶלַח *melaḥ*, n.[m.]. GK: 4874 [→ 4414]. worn-out clothes, rags:– rotten rags [2]

4419 מַלָּח *mallāḥ*, n.m. GK: 4876 [→ 4417]. sailor, mariner:– mariners [4]

4420 מְלֵחָה *mᵉlēḥâ*, n.f. GK: 4877 [→ 4417]. salt flat, salt waste-lands, barren country:– barrenness [1], barren [1], salt [1]

4421 מִלְחָמָה *milḥāmâ*, n.f. GK: 4878 [→ 3898]. fighting, battle (a particular engagement), war (as an ongoing event):– war [150], battle [144], wars [8], battles [6], fight [5], warriors

4422 מָלַט *mālaṭ*, v. GK: 4880 & 4881 [→ 4423?, 4424; cf. 6403]. [N] to deliver oneself, escape, flee; [P] to save, deliver, rescue; [H] to rescue; to deliver (a child); [Ht] to shoot out (of sparks); to escape; to be bald:– escaped [25], escape [21], delivered [16], deliver [16], save [4], escapeth [3], speedily escape (+4422) [2], surely deliver (+4422) [2], get away [1], lay [1], leap out [1], let alone [1], preserve [1], saved [1]

4423 מֶלֶט *meleṭ*, n.[m.]. GK: 4879 [→ 4422?]. clay flooring:– clay [1]

4424 מְלַטְיָה *mᵉlaṭyâ*, n.pr.m. GK: 4882 [→ 4422+3068]. Melatiah, "Yahweh sets free":– Melatiah [1]

4425 מְלִילָה *mᵉlîlâ*, n.f. GK: 4884. (rubbed) kernels (of grain):– ears [1]

4426 מְלִיצָה *mᵉlîṣâ*, n.[f.]. GK: 4886 [→ 3887]. allusive saying, parable; ridicule:– interpretation [1], taunting [1]

4427 מָלַךְ *mālak*, v.den. GK: 4887 & 4888 [→ 3230?, 4410, 4428, 4467, 4468; cf. 4431]. [Q] to reign as king; [N] to ponder, consider carefully within oneself; [H] to make one a king, have a coronation; [Ho] to be made a king:– reigned [159], reign [115], made king [30], reigneth [11], made king [10], king [4], made a king (+4428) [3], indeed reign (+4427) [2], surely be king (+4427) [2], consulted [1], made queen [1], made to reign [1], made [1], make a king (+4428) [1], queen [1], reigned over (+4428) [1], reigning [1], rule [1], set a king (+4428) [1], set up kings [1], set up to be king (+4428) [1]

4428 מֶלֶךְ *melek*, n.m. GK: 4889 [→ 4409, 4429, 4432, 4436, 4435, 4438, 4445, 4446; cf. 4427; cf. 4430 (also used with compound proper names)]. king, royal ruler, human and divine; "the great king" is the more prominent of the leaders in a convenant agreement and is used of God (Ps 48:2); the "king of kings" is the supreme sovereign and is not used of God in the OT:– king [1966], kings [282], king's [254], king's (+871.1) [4], kings' [3], made a king (+4427) [3], king's (+3807.1) [2], royal [2], make a king (+4427) [2], reigned over (+4427) [1], set a king (+4427) [1], set up to be king (+4427) [1]

4429 מֶלֶךְ *melek*, n.pr.m. GK: 4890 [→ 4428; cf. 4427]. Melech, "king":– Hammelech [2], Melech [2], Moloch [1]

4430 מֶלֶךְ *melek* (Aram.), n.m. GK: 10421 [→ 4433, 4437; cf. 4428]. king, royal ruler:– king [147], king's [17], kings [15], royal [1]

4431 מְלַךְ *mᵉlak* (Aram.), n.m. GK: 10422 [cf. 4427]. advice, counsel:– counsel [1]

4432 מֹלֶךְ *mōlek*, n.pr.[m.]. GK: 4891 [→ 4428]. Molech (pagan god), "(shameful) king":– Molech [8]

4433 מַלְכָּא *malkâ* (Aram.), n.f. GK: 10423 [→ 4430; cf. 4436]. queen, the wife of a king, with very high status but not likely equal status to the king; queen mother, mother or grandmother of a king:– queen [2]

4434 מַלְכֹּדֶת *malkōdet*, n.f. GK: 4892 [→ 3920]. trap, snare:– trap [1]

4435 מִלְכָּה *milkâ*, n.pr.f. GK: 4894 [→ 4428; cf. 4427]. Milcah, "queen":– Milcah [11]

4436 מַלְכָּה *malkâ*, n.f. GK: 4893 [→ 4428; cf. 4427; cf. 4433]. queen (outside Israel), a female ruler of a kingdom; wife of a king, royalty but without much actual governmental power:– queen [33], queens [2]

4437 מַלְכוּ *malkû* (Aram.), n.f. GK: 10424 [→ 4430; cf. 4438]. kingdom, dominion, reign:– kingdom [47], reign [4], realm [3], kingdoms [2], kingly [1]

4438 מַלְכוּת *malkût*, n.f. GK: 4895 [→ 4428; cf. 4427; cf. 4437]. kingdom, empire, realm; reign, royal power, position as a king:– kingdom [49], reign [21], royal [13], realm [4], kingdoms [2], empire [1], royal estate [1]

4439 מַלְכִּיאֵל *malkî’ēl*, n.pr.m. GK: 4896 [→ 4440]. Malkiel, "God [El] is [my] king":– Malchiel [3]

4440 מַלְכִּיאֵלִי *malkî’ēlî*, a.g. GK: 4897 [→ 4439]. Malkielite, "of Malkiel":– Malchielites [1]

4441 מַלְכִּיָּה *malkiyyâ* or מַלְכִּיָּהוּ *malkiyyāhû*, n.pr.m. GK: 4898 & 4899 [→ 4428+3068]. Malkijah, "Yahweh is [my] king":– Malchiah [9], Malchijah [6], Melchiah [1]

4442 מַלְכִּי־צֶדֶק *malkî-ṣedeq*, n.pr.m. GK: 4900 [→ 4428+6664]. Melchizedek, "[my] king is Zedek [just]":– Melchizedek [2]

4443 מַלְכִּירָם *malkîrām*, n.pr.m. GK: 4901 [→ 4428+7311]. Malkiram, "[my] king is exalted":– Malchiram [1]

4444 מַלְכִּי־שׁוּעַ malkî-šûa', n.pr.m. GK: 4902 [→ 4428+7768]. Malki-Shua, "*[my] king saves*":– Malchishua [4], Melchishua [1]

4445 מַלְכָּם malkām or מִלְכֹּם milkōm, n.pr.m. GK: 4903 & 4904 [→ 4428+3963.1]. Malcam, Milcom, Molech, "*their king*" or *[servant of] Malk*":– Milcom [3], Malcham [2]

4446 מְלֶכֶת m^eleket, n.f. GK: 4906 [→ 4428]. Queen (of Heaven):– queen [5]

4447 מֹלֶכֶת mōleket or הַמֹּלֶכֶת hammōleket, n.pr.f. GK: 4907 & 2168 [→ 1980]. Moleketh, Hammoleketh, "*the queen*":– Hammoleketh [1]

4448 מָלַל mālal, v. GK: 4910 & 4911 [→ 4405, 4413; cf. 4449]. [Q] to signal by rubbing or scraping; [P] to say, speak, proclaim:– utter [2], said [1], speaketh [1], speak [1]

4449 מְלַל m^elal (Aram.), v. GK: 10425 [→ 4406; cf. 4448]. [Pa] to speak:– spake [2], said [1], speaking [1], speak [1]

4450 מִלְלַי mil'lay, n.pr.m. GK: 4912. Milalai:– Milalai [1]

4451 מַלְמָד malmād, n.m. GK: 4913 [→ 3925]. oxgoad, cattle prod, a (metal-tipped) poker used to guide animals, which could also be used as a weapon:– goad [1]

4452 מָלַץ mālaṣ, v. GK: 4914. [N] to be smooth, pleasant, palatable, sweet:– sweet [1]

4453 מֶלְצַר melṣar, n.m. GK: 4915 [→ 5341]. guard, guardian, official:– Melzar [1]

4454 מָלַק mālaq, v. GK: 4916. [Q] to wring off, pinch off (the head of a bird):– wring off [2]

4455 מַלְקוֹחַ malqôaḥ or מַלְקוֹחַיִם malqôḥayim, n.m. GK: 4917 & 4918 [→ 3947]. spoils of war, plunder, war-booty; (du.) roof of the mouth, palate:– prey [6], booty [1], jaws [1]

4456 מַלְקוֹשׁ malqôš, n.m. GK: 4919 [→ 3953]. spring rains, latter rains of March-April:– latter rain [6], latter [2]

4457 מֶלְקָחַיִם melqāḥayim, n.m.|du. GK: 4920 [→ 3947]. (pair of) wick trimmers; (pair of) tongs:– tongs [5], snuffers [1]

4458 מֶלְתָּחָה meltāḥâ, n.f. GK: 4921. wardrobe:– vestry [1]

4459 מַלְתָּעוֹת maltā'ôt, n.f.pl. GK: 4922 [→ 4973]. fangs, teeth; some sources: jawbone:– great teeth [1]

4460 מַמְּגוּרָה mamm^egûrâ, n.f.pl. GK: 4923 [→ 4033]. granary, grain-pit:– barns [1]

4461 מֵמַד mēmād, n.[m.]. GK: 4924 [→ 4058]. dimensions, measurement:– measures [1]

4462 מְמוּכָן m^emûkān or מוּמְכָן m^ewmukān, n.pr.m. GK: 4925 & 4584. Memucan, Mumecan:– Memucan [3]

4463 מָמוֹת māmôt, n.[m.]. GK: 4926 [→ 4191]. death:– deaths [2]

4464 מַמְזֵר mamzēr, n.m. GK: 4927. one born of a forbidden marriage; foreigner; this can have the associative meaning of being an unprivileged or despised class:– bastard [2]

4465 מִמְכָּר mimkār, n.m. GK: 4928 [→ 4376]. what is sold, goods, merchandise:– sale [2], sold [2], sell ought (+4376) [1], that was sold [1], that which cometh of sale [1], that which is sold [1], that which sold [1], ware [1]

4466 מִמְכֶּרֶת mimkeret, n.f. GK: 4929 [→ 4376]. selling, sale:– sold (+4376) [1]

4467 מַמְלָכָה mamlākâ, n.f. GK: 4930 [→ 4427]. kingdom, royal dominion, reign:– kingdom [62], kingdoms [48], royal [4], reign [2], king's [1]

4468 מַמְלָכוּת mamlākût, n.f. GK: 4931 [→ 4427]. kingdom, realm, royal dominion:– kingdom [8], reign [1]

4469 מִמְסָךְ mimsāk, n.m. GK: 4932 [→ 4537]. bowl of mixed wine, with a focus on the wine:– drink offering [1], mixt wine [1]

4470 מֶמֶר memer, n.[m.]. GK: 4933 [→ 4843]. bitterness, annoyance:– bitterness [1]

4471 מַמְרֵא mamrē', n.pr.m. & loc. GK: 4934 & 4935 [→ 4806?]. Mamre, "*strength*":– Mamre [10]

4472 מַמְרֹרִים mamm^erōrîm, n.m.[pl.]. GK: 4936 [→ 4843]. misery, bitterness:– bitterness [1]

4473 מִמְשַׁח mimšaḥ, n.[m.]. GK: 4937 [→ 4886]. anointing:– anointed [1]

4474 מִמְשָׁל mimšāl, n.[m.]. GK: 4938 [→ 4910]. leader, ruler; power, dominion, sovereign authority:– dominion [2], ruled [1]

4475 מֶמְשָׁלָה memšālâ, n.f. GK: 4939 [→ 4910]. dominion, power to govern, authority to rule:– dominion [10], rule [4], dominion (+3027) [1], government [1], power [1]

4476 מִמְשָׁק mimšāq, n.[m.]. GK: 4940 [→ 4943]. place, ground (overgrown with weeds):– breeding [1]

4477 מַמְתַקִּים mamtaqqîm, n.m.[pl.]. GK: 4941 [→ 4985]. sweetness, sweet things:– most sweet [1], sweet [1]

4478 מָן mān, n.m. GK: 4942 [cf. 4100]. manna, a food given by God to the generation of the Exodus: "the grain of heaven":– manna [14]

4479 מַן man (Aram.), p.inter. & indef. GK: 10426 [cf. 4101]. who? what?; anyone, whoever:– whomsoever (+1768) [4], who [3], whoso (+1768) [2], what [1]

4480 מִן min or מִנִּי minnî, pp. GK: 4946 & 4974 [→ 4648; cf. 4481]. marker of a source or extension from a source: from, out of, of; temporary: since, after; logically: because of; of degree: more than:– from [2335], out of [1397], out of [970], than [227], on [204], from (+5921) [152], at [116], for [103], from (+854) [81], more than [73], of (+854) [71], by [62], with [57], because of (+6440) [54], before (+6440) [50], from (+5973) [46], without (+2351) [43], above [38], in [38], thence (+8033) [34], because of [32], from (+6440) [31], too [31], beside (+905+3807.1) [30], by reason of [25], among [24], because [24], since [23], of (+6440) [20], round about (+5439) [20], above (+4605) [19], not [19], out of (+5921) [19], above (+4605+1886.5+3807.1) [18], afar off (+7350) [18], without (+369) [18], after [17], before (+6440+3807.1) [17], both [17], thereof (+5105.2) [16], on every side (+5439) [15], from among [14], within (+1004) [14], beneath (+8478) [13], besides (+905+3807.1) [13], of (+5973) [13], under (+8478) [13], above (+5921) [12], because (+6440) [12], for (+6440) [12], from (+310) [12], from (+3807.1) [12], through [12], whence (+370) [12], against [11], before [11], behind (+310) [11], that [11], upon (+5921) [11], by (+854) [10]*

4481 מִן min (Aram.), pp. GK: 10427 [cf. 4480]. from, to, out of, more than:– from [31], of [27], out of [11], part [6], before (+6925) [4], of (+6925) [3], with [3], according to [2], after [2], for [2], aforetime (+1836+6928) [1], ago (+6928) [1], because (+1768) [1], because [1], by [1], concerning (+6655) [1], from (+3890) [1], from (+6925) [1], more than [1], of a truth (+7187) [1], over (+5924) [1], partly (+7118) [1], partly [1], since [1], than [1], then (+116+6925+871.2) [1], therefore (+2050.3) [1], to [1], upon [1], when [1]

4482 מֵן mēn, n.[m.]. GK: 4944 & 4945 [→ 4487]. share, portion; (music of) stringed instruments:– in [1], stringed instruments [1], whereby [1]

4483 מְנָא m^enâ (Aram.), v. GK: 10431 [→ 4484, 4510; cf. 4487]. [P] to number; [Pa] to appoint, set (over):– set [3], numbered [1], ordained [1]

4484 מְנֵא m^enē' (Aram.), n.[m.]. GK: 10428 [→ 4483; cf. 4487]. mene (unit of weight, about 1.25 lbs. [0.6 kg]):– mene [3]

4485 מַנְגִּינָה mangînâ, n.f. GK: 4947 [→ 5059]. mocking song:– musick [1]

מִנְדָּה mindâ. See 4061.

4486 מַנְדַּע manda' (Aram.), n.[m.]. GK: 10430 [→ 3046; cf. 4093]. knowledge, understanding; in some contexts, sanity:– knowledge [2], reason [1], understanding [1]

מְנָה m^enâ. See 4483.

4487 מָנָה mānâ, v. GK: 4948 [→ 3232, 4482, 4488, 4490, 4489, 4507, 4521, 8553?, 8554, 8556?; cf. 4483]. [Q] to count, number, take a census; [N] to be counted, be numbered; [P] to assign, appoint, provide; [Pu] to be assigned, be appointed:– numbered [7], number [7], appointed [4], prepared [4], telleth [2], count [1], prepare [1], set [1], told [1]

4488 מָנֶה māneh, n.m. GK: 4949 [→ 4487; cf. 4484]. mina (unit of weight, about 1.25 pounds [0.6 kg]):– pound [4], maneh [1]

4489 מֹנֶה mōneh, n.[m.]. GK: 4951 [→ 4487]. time, occurrence:– times [2]

4490 מָנָה mānâ, n.f. GK: 4950 [→ 4487]. share, portion, piece:– portions [6], portion [4], part [3], such things as belonged [1]

4491 מִנְהָג minhāg, n.m. GK: 4952 [→ 5090]. driving (of a chariot):– driving [2]

4492 מִנְהָרָה minhārâ, n.f. GK: 4953. shelter, hole, cave (in mountain clefts):– dens [1]

4493 מָנוֹד mānôd, n.[m.]. GK: 4954 [→ 5110]. shaking of the head (in scorn or derision):– shaking [1]

4494 מָנוֹחַ mānôaḥ, n.m. GK: 4955 [→ 4495, 4496; cf. 3240]. resting place; the home of a person or the lair of an animal, with the focus that this is a place of rest, satisfaction, and contentment:– rest [6], place of rest [1]

4495 מָנוֹחַ mānôaḥ, n.pr.m. GK: 4956 [→ 4494; cf. 3240]. Manoah, "*rest*":– Manoah [18]

4496 מְנוּחָה m^enûḥâ, n.f. GK: 4957 [→ 4494; cf. 3240]. resting place:– rest [15], comfortable [1], quiet [1], resting places [1], resting place [1], still [1], with ease [1]

4497 מָנוֹן mānôn, n.m. GK: 4959. grief:– son [1]

4498 מָנוֹס mānôs, n.m. GK: 4960 [→ 4499; cf. 5127]. place to flee, place of escape, refuge:– refuge [4], escape [1], fled apace (+5127) [1], flight [1], way to flee [1]

4499 מְנוּסָה m^enûsâ, n.f. GK: 4961 [→ 4498; cf. 5127]. flight, fleeing:– fleeing [1], flight [1]

4500 מָנוֹר mānôr, n.m. GK: 4962. (weaver's) rod, beam (of weavers):– beam [4]

4501 מְנוֹרָה m^enôrâ, n.f. GK: 4963 [→ 5216]. lampstand (holding an oil lamp; not a candlestick, holding a wax candle):– candlestick [32], candlesticks [6], every candlestick (+4501+2050.1) [4]

4502 מִנְזָר minn^ezār, n.m.pl. GK: 4964 [cf. 5144]. guard, watchman, with a possible implication of status and rank:– crowned [1]

4503 מִנְחָה minḥâ, n.f. GK: 4966 [cf. 4504]. grain offering; animal offering or sacrifice; gift, tribute, present:– meat offering [122], offering [29], present [22], meat offerings [10], gifts [6], presents [6], oblation [5], sacrifice [5], offerings [4], gift [1], oblations [1]

4504 מִנְחָה minḥâ (Aram.), n.f. GK: 10432 [cf. 4503]. offering, gift; grain offering:– meat offerings [1], oblation [1]

מְנוּחָה m^enuḥâ. See 4496.

מְנֻחוֹת m^enuḥôt. See 2679.

4505 מְנַחֵם m^enaḥēm, n.pr.m. GK: 4968 [→ 5162]. Menahem, "*comforter*":– Menahem [8]

4506 מָנַחַת mānaḥat, n.pr.m. & loc. GK: 4969 & 4970 [→ 3240]. Manahath, "*resting place*":– Manahath [3]

מְנַחְתִּי m^enaḥtî. See 2680.

4507 מְנִי m^enî, n.pr. GK: 4972 [→ 4487]. Destiny (pagan god):– number [1]

מִנִּי minnî. See 4480, 4482.

4508 מִנִּי minnî, n.pr.loc. GK: 4973. Minni:– Minni [1]

מְנָיוֹת m^enāyôt. See 4521.

4509 מִנְיָמִן minyāmin, n.pr.m. GK: 4975 [→ 4326]. Miniamin, "*from the right, good, fortune*":– Miniamin [3]

4510 מִנְיָן minyān (Aram.), n.[m.]. GK: 10433 [→ 4483]. number:– number [1]

4511 מִנִּית minnît, n.pr.loc. GK: 4976. Minnith:– Minnith [2]

4512 מִנְלֶה minleh, n.[m.]. GK: 4978 [cf. 5186]. possession, acquisition:– perfection [1]

מְנֻסָה m^enusâ. See 4499.

4513 מָנַע māna', v. GK: 4979 [→ 3234]. [Q] to keep from, withhold, deny, refuse; [N] to be kept from, be withheld, be denied:– withholden [8], withhold [5], withheld [3], kept back [2], refrain [2], denied [1], deny [1], hinder [1], keep back [1], keep still [1], keepeth back [1], restrained [1], withheldest [1], withholdeth [1]

4514 מַנְעוּל man'ûl, n.[m.]. GK: 4980 [→ 5274]. bolt, lock (of a door):– locks [5], lock [1]

4515 מִנְעָל min'āl, n.m. GK: 4981 [→ 5274]. bolt (on a gate):– shoes [1]

4516 מַנְעַמִּים man'ammîm, n.m.[pl]. GK: 4982 [→ 5276]. (edible) delicacies:– dainties [1]

4517 מְנַעַנְעִים m^ena'an'îm, n.m.pl. GK: 4983 [→ 5128]. sistrum, rattle, percussion instrument not precisely identified:– cornets [1]

4518 מְנַקִּית m^enaqqît, n.f. GK: 4984 [→ 5352]. bowl (used for drink offering):– bowls [3], cups [1]

מְנֹרָה m^enôrâ. See 4501.

4519 מְנַשֶּׁה **mᵉnaššeh**, n.pr.m. GK: 4985 [→ 4520; cf. 5382]. Manasseh, "one that makes to forget":– Manasseh [141], Manasseh's [3], Manasseh's (+3807.1) [1], Manassites [1]

4520 מְנַשִּׁי **mᵉnaššî**, a.g. GK: 4986 [→ 4519; cf. 5382]. Manassite, of Manasseh, "of Manasseh":– Manasseh [2], Manassites [2]

4521 מְנָת **mᵉnāt**, n.f. GK: 4987 [→ 4487]. portion, lot, assigned share:– portion [4], portions [3]

4522 מַס **mas**, n.m. GK: 4989. forced labor, slave labor:– tribute [12], levy [4], tributaries [4], discomfited [1], taskmasters (+8269) [1], tributary [1]

4523 מָס **mās**, a. GK: 4988 [→ 4549]. despairing (man):– afflicted [1]

4524 מֵסַב **mēsab** or מְסִבָּה **mᵉsibbâ**, n.[m.]. GK: 4990 & 4991 [cf. 4141]. surrounding; round table, circle of feasters; (adv.) around, round about:– round about [2], compass about [1], places round about [1], table [1]

מְסִבָּה **musabbâ**. See 4142.

4525 מַסְגֵּר **masgēr**, n.[m.]. GK: 4993 & 4994 [cf. 5462]. prison, dungeon; artisan, craftsman; some sources: metalworker, locksmith:– smiths [4], prison [3]

4526 מִסְגֶּרֶת **misgeret**, n.f. GK: 4995 [→ 5462]. side panels (of a building); rim (of a table and base); stronghold; den:– borders [8], border [6], close places [2], holes [1]

4527 מַסַּד **massad**, n.[m.]. GK: 4996 [→ 3245]. foundation:– foundation [1]

מוֹסָדָה **mōsādâ**. See 4146.

4528 מִסְדְּרוֹן **misdᵉrôn**, n.[m.]. GK: 4997 [→ 5468?]. porch, vestibule:– porch [1]

4529 מָסָה **māsâ**, v. GK: 4998 [cf. 3988, 4549]. [H] to melt, dissolve; to consume; to drench (with tears):– made melt [1], makest to consume away [1], melteth [1], water [1]

4530 מִסָּה **missâ**, n.f. GK: 5002. proportion, measure:– tribute [1]

4531 מַסָּה **massâ**, n.f. GK: 4999 & 5000 [→ 4532, 4549; cf. 5254]. trial, test, temptation; despair:– temptations [3], temptation [1], trial [1]

4532 מַסָּה **massâ**, n.pr.loc. GK: 5001 [→ 4531?; cf. 5254?]. Massah, "test, try":– Massah [4]

4533 מַסְוֶה **masweh**, n.[m.]. GK: 5003 [→ 5497]. veil, covering:– vail [3]

4534 מְסוּכָה **mᵉsûkâ**, n.f. GK: 5004 [→ 4881]. thorn hedge:– thorn hedge [1]

4535 מַסָּח **massāḥ**, n.m. or adv. GK: 5005 [cf. 5255?]. in turn, taking turns:– not broken down [1]

4536 מִסְחָר **misḥār**, n.m. GK: 5006 [cf. 5503]. revenue:– traffick [1]

4537 מָסַךְ **māsak**, v. GK: 5007 [→ 4469, 4538]. [Q] to mingle, mix (substances into drinks):– mingled [4], mingle [1]

4538 מֶסֶךְ **mesek**, n.[m.]. GK: 5008 [→ 4537]. mixture (of spices):– mixture [1]

4539 מָסָךְ **māsāk**, n.[m.]. GK: 5009 [→ 5526]. curtain, covering; by extension: shield, defense:– hanging [17], covering [7], curtain [1]

4540 מְסֻכָה **mᵉsukâ**, n.f. GK: 5010 [→ 5526]. (woven) covering:– covering [1]

4541 מַסֵּכָה **massēkâ**, n.f. GK: 5011 & 5012 & 5013 [→ 5258, 5259]. image, idol (of cast metal); (woven) blanket, (interwoven) covering; alliance:– molten image [10], molten images [8], molten [7], covering [2], vail [1]

4542 מִסְכֵּן **miskēn**, a. GK: 5014 [→ 4544; cf. 5533]. poor, needy (one):– poor [4]

4543 מִסְכְּנוֹת **miskᵉnôt**, n.f.pl. GK: 5016 [→ 5532]. storage places, warehouses:– store [5], storehouses [1], treasure [1]

4544 מִסְכֵּנֻת **miskēnut**, n.f. GK: 5017 [→ 4542; cf. 5533]. scarcity, poverty:– scarceness [1]

4545 מַסֶּכֶת **masseket**, n.f. GK: 5018 [→ 5259]. warp-threads (the lengthwise threads of a loom):– web [2]

4546 מְסִלָּה **mᵉsillâ**, n.f. GK: 5019 [→ 5549]. main road; (raised) highway, ramp, stairs; by extension: lifestyle, conduct in life:– highway [14], highways [5], causeway [2], courses [1], high way [1], paths [1], path [1], terraces [1], ways [1]

4547 מַסְלוּל **maslûl**, n.m. GK: 5020 [→ 5549]. highway:– highway [1]

4548 מַסְמֵר **masmēr**, n.m. GK: 5021 [→ 5568]. nail:– nails [4]

4549 מָסַס **māsas**, v. GK: 5022 [→ 4523, 4531, 8557; cf. 3988, 4529, 4885]. [Q] to waste away, dissolve; [N] to be melted, dissolved; [H] to cause to melt:– melted [6], melt [4], melteth [2], utterly melt (+4549) [2], discouraged [1], fainteth [1], faint [1], loosed [1], melt away [1], molten [1], refuse [1]

4550 מַסַּע **massa'**, n.m.]. GK: 5023 [→ 5265]. journey, travels from place to place:– journeys [9], journeyings [1], journeying [1], journey [1]

4551 מַסָּע **massā'**, n.[m.]. GK: 5024 & 5025 [→ 5265]. quarry; a weapon probably thrown like a spear or javelin; dart:– brought [1], dart [1]

4552 מִסְעָד **mis'ād**, n.[m.]. GK: 5026 [→ 5582]. supports (for a building):– pillars [1]

4553 מִסְפֵּד **mispēd**, n.m. GK: 5027 [→ 5594]. wailing, howling, weeping, mourning:– mourning [6], wailing [6], lamentation [3], mourneth [1]

4554 מִסְפּוֹא **mispô'**, n.m. GK: 5028. fodder, animal feed:– provender [5]

4555 מִסְפָּחָה **mispāḥâ**, n.f. GK: 5029 [→ 5596]. veil, (head) covering:– kerchiefs [2]

4556 מִסְפַּחַת **mispaḥat**, n.f. GK: 5030 [→ 5597]. (uninfectious) breaking out of skin, rash or scab; referring to something relatively harmless:– scab [3]

4557 מִסְפָּר **mispār**, n.m. GK: 5031 [→ 4558?, 4559?; cf. 5612]. number, quantity; listing, inventory, census:– number [109], few [5], all [3], innumerable (+369) [3], sum [2], time (+3117) [2], abundance (+369) [1], account [1], few (+4962) [1], infinite (+369) [1], innumerable (+369+5704) [1], numbered [1], numbers [1], tale [1], telling [1]

4558 מִסְפָּר **mispār**, n.pr.m. GK: 5032 [→ 4559; cf. 4557?, 5612]. Mispar, "number":– Mizpar [1]

מֹסְרוֹת **môsᵉrôt**. See 4149.

4559 מִסְפֶּרֶת **misperet**, n.pr.m. GK: 5033 [→ 4558; cf. 4557?]. Mispereth:– Mispereth [1]

4560 מָסַר **māsar**, v. GK: 5034 [→ 4562?]. [Q] to supply, deliver; [N] to be supplied:– commit [1], delivered [1]

4561 מוֹסָר **môsār**, n.m. GK: 5036 [→ 4148; cf. 3256]. same as 4148: instruction:– instruction [1]

4562 מָסֹרֶת **māsōret**, n.f. GK: 5037 [→ 631? or 4560?]. bond, obligation, duty:– bond [1]

4563 מִסְתּוֹר **mistôr**, n.[m.]. GK: 5039 [→ 5641]. hiding place, shelter (from the elements):– covert [1]

4564 מַסְתֵּר **mastēr**, n.[m.]. GK: 5040 [→ 5641]. (the act of) hiding:– hid [1]

4565 מִסְתָּר **mistār**, n.[m.]. GK: 5041 [→ 5641]. hiding place, covered place (from which to ambush):– secret places [7], secretly (+871.1+1886.1) [2], secret [1]

מְעָא **mᵉ'ā'**. See 4577.

4566 מַעְבָּד **ma'bād**, n.[m.]. GK: 5042 [→ 5647; cf. 4567]. deed, action:– works [1]

4567 מַעְבָּד **ma'bād** (Aram.), n.[m.]. GK: 10434 [→ 5648; cf. 4566]. what one does, work:– works [1]

4568 מַעֲבֶה **ma'ăbeh**, n.[m.]. GK: 5043 [→ 5666]. mold, foundry:– clay [1]

4569 מַעֲבָר **ma'ăbār** or מַעְבָּרָה **ma'bārâ**, n.[m.]. GK: 5044 & 5045 [→ 5674]. stroke (of a rod); (geographical) pass; ford (of a river):– passages [4], fords [3], passage [2], ford [1], pass [1]

4570 מַעְגָּל **ma'gāl**, n.m. GK: 5046 & 5047 [→ 5696]. (rutted) path (of a cart or wagon); (circled) camp, encampment:– paths [6], path [3], trench [2], goings [2], way side (+3027) [1], ways [1]

4571 מָעַד **mā'ad**, v. GK: 5048 [→ 4154]. [Q] to slip, waver, wobble; [Pu] to become lame; [H] cause to wobble, to bend, wrench (one's back):– slip [3], slide [2], make to shake [1]

מוֹעֵד **mô'ēd**. See 4150.

4572 מַעֲדַי **ma'ăday**, n.pr.m. GK: 5049 [→ 4573; cf. 4153]. Maadai, "ornaments":– Maadai [1]

4573 מַעַדְיָה **ma'adyâ**, n.pr.m. GK: 5050 [→ 4572]. Moadiah, "[perhaps] Yahweh assembles or Yahweh promises":– Maadiah [1]

4574 מַעֲדַנִּים **ma'ădannîm**, n.[m.pl.]. GK: 5052 [→ 5727]. delicacy; delight:– dainties [1], delicately (+3807.1) [1], delicately [1], delight [1]

4575 מַעֲדַנּוֹת **ma'ădannôt**, n.[f.pl.]. GK: 5051 [→ 5727; cf. 6029]. beautiful; some sources: bands, cords used for binding; (adv.) confidently:– sweet influences [1]

4576 מַעְדֵּר **ma'dēr**, n.[m.]. GK: 5053 [→ 5737]. hoe (to cultivate ground):– mattock [1]

4577 מְעֵה **mᵉ'ēh** (Aram.), n.[m.]pl. GK: 10435 [cf. 4578]. belly:– belly [1]

4578 מֵעֶה **mē'eh**, n.m. GK: 5055 [cf. 4577]. viscera: stomach, heart, bowels, womb; (body as a whole); by extension: of the inner person, the seat of emotions: anguish, tenderness:– bowels [27], belly [3], heart [1], womb [1]

4579 מָעָה **mā'â**, n.f. GK: 5054. grain (of sand):– gravel [1]

4580 מָעוֹג **mā'ôg**, n.[m.]. GK: 5056 [→ 5746]. provision, supply; some sources: flat bread:– cake [1], feasts [1]

4581 מָעוֹז **mā'ôz**, n.[m.]. GK: 5057 [cf. 5810]. refuge, stronghold, fortress, place of protection; (used with "head") helmet:– strength [24], fortress [3], strong [2], forces [1], fort [1], most strong [1], rock [1], strengthen [1], strong holds [1], strong hold [1]

4582 מָעוֹךְ **mā'ôk**, n.pr.m. GK: 5059 [cf. 4601]. Maoch, "poor one":– Maoch [1]

4583 מָעוֹן **mā'ôn**, n.[m.]. GK: 5060 & 5061 [→ 1010, 1186, 4584, 4585]. dwelling place; help:– habitation [9], dwelling place [3], dwelling [3], den [2], habitations [1], place [1]

4584 מָעוֹן **mā'ôn**, n.pr.m. & g. & loc. GK: 5062 & 5063 [→ 4583]. Maon; Maonite, "dwelling":– Maon [7], Maonites [1]

4585 מְעוֹנָה **mᵉ'ônâ**, n.f. GK: 5104 [→ 4583]. hiding place, refuge; dwelling place, (animal) den:– dens [4], den [1], dwelling place [1], habitations [1], places [1], refuge [1]

4586 מְעוּנִים **mᵉ'ûnîm**, n.pr.g. GK: 5064 [→ 4583]. Meunim, Meunite, "people of Maon":– Mehunims [1], Mehunim [1], Meunim [1]

4587 מְעוֹנֹתַי **mᵉ'ônôtay**, n.pr.m. GK: 5065. Meonothai, "my dwellings":– Meonothai [1]

4588 מָעוּף **mā'ûp**, n.[m.]. GK: 5066 [→ 4155]. gloom, darkness:– dimness [1]

4589 מָעוֹר **mā'ôr**, n.[m.]. GK: 5067 [→ 5783]. exposed genitals, nakedness:– nakedness [1]

מָעֹז **mā'ōz**. See 4581.

מָעֻז **mā'uz**. See 4581.

4590 מַעַזְיָה **ma'azyâ** or מַעַזְיָהוּ **ma'azyāhû**, n.pr.m. GK: 5068 & 5069. Maaziah, "Yahweh is a refuge":– Maaziah [2]

4591 מָעַט **mā'aṭ**, v. GK: 5070 [→ 4592]. [Q] to dwindle, decrease, become few; [P] to become few; [H] to let reduce, make diminish, make collect little:– diminished [3], few [3], give less [3], diminish [2], little [2], bring to nothing [1], fewness [1], gathered least [1], gathered little [1], give few [1], less [1], make few in number [1], minished [1], suffereth to decrease [1]

4592 מְעַט **mᵉ'aṭ**, subst. GK: 5071 [→ 4591]. little (of size), few (of quantity), short (of time):– little [47], few [22], almost (+3509.1) [4], little while [4], small thing [4], by little and little (+4592) [2], small matter [2], small [2], soon (+3509.1) [2], very little while (+4213) [2], almost (+5750) [1], few (+4962) [1], fewer [1], fewest [1], lightly (+3509.1) [1], little worth (+3509.1) [1], some (+3509.1) [1], very little (+6985) [1], very small (+3509.1) [1], very [1]

4593 מָעֹט **mā'ōṭ**, v.ptcp. GK: 6487 [→ 5844]. ptcp. of 5844: grasped, wrapped up:– wrapt up [1]

4594 מַעֲטֶה **ma'ăṭeh**, n.[m.]. GK: 5073 [→ 5844]. garment, mantle, wrap:– garment [1]

4595 מַעֲטָפֶת **ma'ăṭepet**, n.f. GK: 5074 [→ 5848]. cape, outer garment:– mantles [1]

4596 מְעִי **mᵉ'î**, n.[m.]. GK: 5075 [→ 5856]. heap (of ruins):– heap [1]

4597 מָעַי **mā'ay**, n.pr.m. GK: 5076. Maai, "to be compassionate":– Maai [1]

4598 מְעִיל **mᵉ'îl**, n.m. GK: 5077. robe, cloak:– robe [17], mantle [7], robes [2], cloke [1], coat [1]

מֵעִים **mē'îm**. See 4578.

מְעִין **mᵉ'în** (Aram.). See 4577.

4599 מַעְיָן **ma'yān**, n.m. GK: 5078 [→ 5869]. spring, fountain, well; by extension: source of life (satisfaction,

blessing):– fountain [9], fountains [7], wells [3], springs [2], well [2]

מְעִינִי *mᵉ'înî*. See 4586.

4600 מָעַךְ *mā'ak*, v. GK: 5080. [Qp] be pressed (into the ground), be crushed, be bruised; [Pu] be fondled:– bruised [1], pressed [1], stuck [1]

4601 מַעֲכָה *ma'ăkâ* or מַעֲכָת *ma'ăkāt*, n.pr.m. & f. & g. GK: 5081 & 5082 & 5083 → 4602; cf. 4582 (also used with compound proper names)]. Maacah, "[perhaps *dull, stupid*":– Maachah [18], Maacah [3], Maachathites [1]

4602 מַעֲכָתִי *ma'ăkātî*, a.g. GK: 5084 [→ 4601]. Maacathite, of Maacah, "*of Maacah*":– Maachathite [4], Maachathites [3], Maachathi [1]

4603 מָעַל *mā'al*, v. GK: 5085 [→ 4604]. [Q] to act unfaithfully, break faith, commit a violation:– trespassed [11], transgressed [5], commit a trespass (+4604) [4], committed a trespass (+4604) [3], transgress [2], committed trespass (+4604) [1], committed [1], do a trespass (+4604) [1], done trespass (+4604) [1], transgressed much (+4604) [1], transgressed sore (+4604) [1], transgresseth [1], transgression committed (+4604) [1], trespassing grievously (+4604) [1], trespass [1]

4604 מַעַל *ma'al*, n.m. GK: 5086 [→ 4603]. unfaithfulness:– trespass [8], transgression [5], commit a trespass (+4603) [4], committed a trespass (+4603) [3], committed trespass (+4603) [1], do a trespass (+4603) [1], done trespass (+4603) [1], falsehood [1], transgressed much (+4603) [1], transgressed sore (+4603) [1], transgression committed (+4603) [1], trespasses [1], trespassing grievously (+4603) [1]

4605 מַעַל *ma'al*, subst.adv. & pp. GK: 5087 [→ 5927]. above, beyond; this refer to spatial position, to degree, and to time (afterward):– upward (+1886.5) [45], above (+4480) [19], above (+4480+1886.5+3807.1) [18], upward (+1886.5+3807.1) [12], above (+1886.5+3807.1) [6], on high (+1886.5+3807.1) [5], above (+1886.5) [4], above [4], upon (+4480) [4], exceedingly (+1886.5+3807.1) [2], exceedingly (+5704+1886.5+3807.1) [2], forward (+1886.5) [2], still (+1886.5+3807.1) [2], upward (+4480+1886.5+3807.1) [2], very high (+4605+1886.5+1886.5) [2], above (+4480+3807.1) [1], exceeding (+1886.5) [1], exceeding (+1886.5+3807.1) [1], from above (+4480) [1], on high (+4480+1886.5+3807.1) [1], over (+1886.5+3807.1) [1], over (+4480+1886.5+3807.1) [1], over and above (+4480+1886.5 +3807.1) [1], overturned (+2015+1886.5+3807.1) [1], up (+1886.5+3807.1) [1], very (+1886.5+3807.1) [1]

מֵעַל *mē'al*. See 5921.

4606 מֵעָל *me'āl* (Aram.), n.[m.]. GK: 10436 [→ 5954]. going in, (+ 8122) sunset:– going down [1]

4607 מֹעָל *mō'al*, n.[m.]. GK: 5089 [→ 5927]. lifting (of hands):– lifting up [1]

4608 מַעֲלֶה *ma'ăleh*, n.m. GK: 5090 [→ 5927]. and ascent: hill, mount, (geographical) pass; stairs:– going up [9], ascent [2], chiefest [1], cliff [1], goeth up [1], hill [1], mounting up [1], stairs [1], up [1]

4609 מַעֲלָה *ma'ălâ*, n.f. GK: 5091 & 5092 [→ 5927]. ascent: steps, stairway, paces; what goes through (or rises into) one's mind:– degrees [24], steps [11], stairs [5], dial [2], go up [1], high degree [1], stories [1], things that come into [1]

4610 מַעֲלֵה עַקְרַבִּים *ma'ălēh 'aqrabbîm*, n.pr.loc. GK: 5091 + 6832 [→ 4609+6137]. Maaleh-akkrabim, the ascent of Akrabbim (or the Scorpions):– Maaleh-acrabbim [1]

4611 מַעֲלָל *ma'ălāl*, n.m. GK: 5095 [→ 5953]. deeds, actions, practices, what is done:– doings [35], works [3], inventions [2], endeavours [1]

4612 מַעֲמָד *ma'ămād*, n.[m.]. GK: 5096 [→ 5975]. attendance, serving; position of attendant:– attendance [2], office [1], place [1], state [1]

4613 מָעֳמָד *mo'ŏmād*, n.[m.]. GK: 5097 [→ 5975]. foothold, firm ground:– standing [1]

4614 מַעֲמָסָה *ma'ămāsâ*, n.f. GK: 5098 [→ 6006]. heavy stone, hard-to-lift rock:– burdensome [1]

4615 מַעֲמַקִּים *ma'ămaqqîm*, n.m.pl. GK: 5099 [→ 6009]. depths (of waters or seas):– depths [3], deep [2]

4616 מַעַן *ma'an*, subst.pp.c. GK: 5100 [→ 6031]. for the sake of, on account of, because; therefore, so that:– that (+3807.1) [167], for sake (+3807.1) [45], to (+3807.1) [19], because of (+3807.1) [12], for sakes (+3807.1) [5], for (+3807.1) [4], that (+834+3807.1) [4], to the end (+3807.1) [4], to the end that (+3807.1) [4], for that (+3807.1) [2], to the

intent that (+3807.1) [2], lest (+3808+3807.1) [1], therefore (+3807.1) [1], to [1]

4617 מַעֲנֶה *ma'neh*, n.m. GK: 5101 & 5102 [→ 6030, 6031]. reply, answer, response; purpose:– answer [7], himself (+1930.2) [1]

4618 מַעֲנָה *ma'ănâ*, n.f. GK: 5103 [cf. 6031]. furrow, plow path:– acre [1], furrows [1]

מַעֲנָה *mᵉ'ônâ*. See 4585.

4619 מַעַץ *ma'aṣ*, n.pr.m. GK: 5106 [→ 290]. Maaz, "[perhaps] *angry* or *wrath*":– Maaz [1]

4620 מַעֲצֵבָה *ma'ăṣēbâ*, n.f. GK: 5107 [→ 6087]. place of torment, place of pain:– sorrow [1]

4621 מַעֲצָד *ma'ăṣād*, n.[m.]. GK: 5108. chiseling tool (for wood carving); some sources: ax, adze:– axe [1], tongs [1]

4622 מַעֲצוֹר *ma'ṣôr*, n.[m.] GK: 5109 [→ 6113]. hindrance:– restraint [1]

4623 מַעֲצָר *ma'ṣār*, n.[m.]. GK: 5110 [→ 6113]. self-control:– rule [1]

4624 מַעֲקֶה *ma'qeh*, n.[m.]. GK: 5111. parapet, a short wall around the upper level of a house:– battlement [1]

4625 מַעֲקַשִּׁים *ma'ăqaššîm*, n.[m.]. GK: 5112 [→ 6140]. rough places, uneven terrain, rugged country:– crooked things [1]

4626 מַעַר *ma'ar*, n.[m.]. GK: 5113 [→ 4629]. nakedness; available space:– nakedness [1], proportion [1]

4627 מַעֲרָב *ma'ărāb*, n.[m.]. GK: 5114 [→ 6148]. wares, goods (for trade, exchange, or barter):– merchandise [5], market [4]

4628 מַעֲרָב *ma'ărāb*, n.[m.]. GK: 5115 [→ 6150]. west (the place of the sunset):– west [10], westward [2], westward (+1886.1+3807.1) [1], westward (+1886.5) [1]

4629 מַעֲרֶה *ma'reh*, n.[m.]. GK: 5116 [→ 4626]. approaches, vicinity:– meadows [1]

4630 מַעֲרָה *ma'ărâ*, n.f. GK: 5120 [→ 4634, 6186]. var. of 4634: things arranged in a row: battle line, row of army ranks:–

4631 מְעָרָה *mᵉ'ārâ*, n.f. GK: 5117. cave:– cave [32], caves [3], cave's [1], dens [1], den [1], holes [1]

4632 מְעָרָה *mᵉ'ārâ*, n.f. GK: 5118 [→ 4638; cf. 6168]. wasteland, bare field:– Mearah [1]

4633 מַעֲרָךְ *ma'ărāk*, n.[m.]. GK: 5119 [→ 6186]. plan, consideration, arrangement:– preparations [1]

4634 מַעֲרָכָה *ma'ărākâ*, n.f. GK: 5120 [→ 4630]. things arranged in a row: battle line, row of army ranks; row, layer (of things); by extension: proper arrangement of something fitting and suitable:– army [8], armies [7], fight [1], ordered place [1], rank [1], rows [1], set in order [1]

4635 מַעֲרֶכֶת *ma'reket*, n.f. GK: 5121 [→ 6186]. (consecrated) bread set in rows:– shewbread [3], row [2], shewbread (+3899+1886.1) [2], in order [1], shewbread (+3899) [1]

4636 מַעֲרֹם *ma'rōm*, n.m. GK: 5122 [→ 6168]. nakedness, naked person:– naked [1]

4637 מַעֲרָצָה *ma'ărāṣâ*, n.f. GK: 5124 [→ 6206]. terrifying power:– terror [1]

4638 מַעֲרָת *ma'ărāt*, n.pr.loc. GK: 5125 [→ 4632?; cf. 6168]. Maarath, "*barren*":– Maarath [1]

4639 מַעֲשֶׂה *ma'śeh*, n.m. GK: 5126 [→ 4640, 4641; cf. 6213]. work, labor, deed; something made, something done:– work [116], works [73], acts [4], needlework (+7551) [4], art [3], doings [3], labours [3], deeds [2], network (+7568) [2], occupation [2], operation [2], wares of making [2], bakemeats (+644+3978) [1], business [1], deed [1], doing [1], do [1], handywork (+3027) [1], labour [1], possessions [1], purpose [1], things made [1], things offered [1], things that were made [1], well set hair (+4748) [1], working [1], workmanship [1], wrought with needlework (+7551) [1]

4640 מַעֲשַׂי *ma'śay*, n.pr.m. GK: 5127 [→ 4639+3068]. Maasai, "*work of Yahweh*":– Maasiai [1]

4641 מַעֲשֵׂיָה *ma'śēyâ* or מַעֲשֵׂיָהוּ *ma'śēyāhû*, n.pr.m. GK: 5128 & 5129 [→ 4639+3068; cf. 6213]. Maaseiah, "*Yahweh is a refuge*":– Maaseiah [23]

4642 מַעֲשַׁקּוֹת *ma'ăšaqqôt*, n.f. GK: 5131 [→ 6229]. (col.pl) extortion:– oppressions [1], oppressor [1]

4643 מַעֲשֵׂר *ma'śēr*, n.[m.]. GK: 5130 [→ 6237]. tithe, setting aside a tenth:– tithes [16], tithe [11], tenth part [2], tenth [2], tithing [1]

4644 מֹף *mōp*, n.pr.loc. GK: 5132 [cf. 5297]. Moph = Memphis:– Memphis [1]

מְפִבֹשֶׁת *mᵉpibōšet*. See 4648.

4645 מִפְגָּע *mipga'*, n.[m.] GK: 5133 [→ 6293]. target:– mark [1]

4646 מַפָּח *mappāḥ*, n.[m.]. GK: 5134 [→ 5301]. (a dying) gasp, exhaling (of soul), with an implication of despair and affliction:– giving up of the ghost (+5315) [1]

4647 מַפֻּחַ *mappuaḥ*, n.[m.]. GK: 5135 [→ 5301]. bellows:– bellows [1]

4648 מְפִיבֹשֶׁת *mᵉpibōšet* or מְפִי־בֹשֶׁת *mᵉpî-bōšet*, n.pr.m. GK: 5136 [→ 4480+6310+1322]. Mephibosheth, "*from the mouth of Shame* [a derogatory name for Baal]":– Mephibosheth [15]

4649 מֻפִּים *muppîm*, n.pr.m. GK: 5137. Muppim:– Muppim [1]

4650 מֵפִיץ *mēpîṣ*, n.m. GK: 5138 [→ 6327]. war club:– maul [1]

4651 מַפָּל *mappāl*, n.m. GK: 5139 [→ 4654; cf. 5307]. sweepings, waste, refuse (of wheat); (fleshy) folds (of the leviathan):– flakes [1], refuse [1]

4652 מִפְלָאוֹת *miplā'ôt*, n.f.[pl.]. GK: 5140 [→ 6381]. wonders, marvelous works:– wondrous works [1]

4653 מִפְלַגָּה *miplaggâ*, n.f. GK: 5141 [→ 6385]. division (of family groups), subgroup of a clan:– divisions [1]

4654 מַפָּלָה *mappālâ* or מַפֵּלָה *mappēlâ*, n.f. GK: 5142 & 5143 [→ 4651; cf. 5307]. ruin, heap of rubble:– ruin [2], ruinous [1]

4655 מִפְלָט *miplāṭ*, n.[m.]. GK: 5144 [→ 6403]. place of shelter, refuge, escape:– escape [1]

4656 מִפְלֶצֶת *mipleṣet*, n.f. GK: 5145 [→ 6426]. repulsive image, disgraceful (idol):– idol [4]

4657 מִפְלָשׂ *miplāś*, n.[m.]. GK: 5146. floating, hovering (clouds):– balancings [1]

4658 מַפֶּלֶת *mappelet*, n.f. GK: 5147 [→ 5307]. downfall, collapse; (something downfallen) a shipwreck; carcass:– fall [5], ruin [2], carcase [1]

4659 מִפְעָל *mip'āl* or מִפְעָלָה *mip'ālâ*, n.m. & f. GK: 5148 & 5149 [→ 6466]. deed, work:– works [3]

4660 מַפָּץ *mappāṣ*, n.m. GK: 5150 [→ 5310]. shattering, wrecking (weapon), implying death will follow its effective use:– slaughter [1]

4661 מַפֵּץ *mappēṣ*, n.m. GK: 5151 [→ 5310]. war club:– battle axe [1]

4662 מִפְקָד *mipqād*, n.m. & pr.loc. GK: 5152 [→ 4663, 6485]. appointment (by a king); number, counting (of the people); Inspection (Gate):– number [2], Miphkad [1], appointed place [1], commandment [1]

4663 מִפְקָד *mipqād*, n.pr.loc. GK: 5152 [→ 4662]. same as 4662: Miphkad, "Inspection (Gate)":–

4664 מִפְרָץ *miprāṣ*, n.[m.]. GK: 5153 [→ 6555]. cove, inlet, landing-place:– breaches [1]

4665 מַפְרֶקֶת *mapreqet*, n.f. GK: 5154 [→ 6561]. neck:– neck [1]

4666 מִפְרָשׂ *miprāś*, n.[m.]. GK: 5155 [→ 6566]. spreading (used of clouds and canvas sail):– spreadings [1], which spreadest forth [1]

4667 מִפְשָׂעָה *mipśā'â*, n.f. GK: 5156 [cf. 6585]. buttocks, posterior area:– buttocks [1]

מוֹפֵת *mōpēt*. See 4159.

4668 מַפְתֵּחַ *maptēaḥ*, n.m. GK: 5158 [→ 6605]. key:– key [2], opening [1]

4669 מִפְתָּח *miptāḥ*, n.m. GK: 5157 [→ 6605]. opening (of lips):– opening [1]

4670 מִפְתָּן *miptān*, n.[m.]. GK: 5159 [cf. 6596]. threshold:– threshold [8]

4671 מֹץ *mōṣ*, n.m. GK: 5161. chaff:– chaff [8]

4672 מָצָא *māṣā'*, v. GK: 5162. [Q] to find, find out, discover, uncover; [N] to be found out; be caught; [H] to hand over, present; to bring upon, cause to encounter; "to find favor in the eyes" means to "be please":– found [261], find [82], present [17], find out [16], findeth [12], come upon [5], found out [5], befallen [3], met [3], presented [3], certainly found (+4672) [2], findest [2], finding [2], get [2], gotten [2], here [2], hit [2], left [2],

meet [2], suffice [2], able (+1767+3027) [1], able to bring (+1767+3027) [1], befall [1], befell [1], came to hand [1], came to [1], catch [1], cause to find [1], causeth to come [1], come on [1], come unto [1], cometh [1], delivered [1], deliver [1], enough [1], find occasion [1], foundest [1], gat hold upon [1], hath (+3807.1) [1], lighted on [1], lighteth upon [1], occasion serve (+3027) [1], ready [1], received [1], redeem (+1353) [1], sped [1], sufficed [1], taken hold on [1]

מָצָא *mōṣā'*. See 4161.

4673 מַצָּב *maṣṣāb*, n.m. GK: 5163 [→ 4675; cf. 5324]. standing place; office; outpost, garrison:– garrison [7], stood [2], station [1]

4674 מֻצָּב *muṣṣāb*, n.[m.] GK: 5164 [→ 5324]. pillar, tower:– mount [1]

4675 מַצָּבָה *maṣṣābâ* or מִצָּבָה *miṣṣābâ*, n.f. GK: 5165 & 5166 [→ 4673, 5324]. guard, watch, outpost, garrison of soldiers on the perimeter of a guarded area:– army [1], garrison [1]

4676 מַצֵּבָה *maṣṣēbâ*, n.f. GK: 5167 [→ 4678; cf. 5324]. sacred (upright) stone, stone pillar:– images [13], pillar [9], image [4], pillars [2], garrisons [1], standing images [1], standing image [1]

4677 מְצֹבָיָה *mᵉṣōbāyâ*, a.g. GK: 5168. Mezobaite:– Mesobaite [1]

4678 מַצֶּבֶת *maṣṣebet*, n.f. GK: 5169 & 5170 [→ 4676, 5324]. (tree) stump; sacred (upright) stone, stone pillar:– pillar [5], substance [2]

4679 מְצָד *mᵉṣād*, n.f. GK: 5171 [→ 6679; cf. 4686]. stronghold, fortress (with difficult access):– strong holds [5], hold [1], castle [1], forts [1], holds [1], munitions [1]

מְצָדָה *mᵉṣudâ*. See 4686.

4680 מָצָה *māṣâ*, v. GK: 5172 [cf. 4711]. [Q] to squeeze out; to drain dry; [N] to be drained out:– wrung out [4], suck out [1], wring out [1], wringed [1]

4681 מֹצָה *mōṣâ*, n.pr.loc. GK: 5173. Mozah:– Mozah [1]

4682 מַצָּה *maṣṣâ*, n.f. GK: 5174 [cf. 4711?]. unleavened bread, bread made without yeast; bread quickly made, without waiting for the dough to rise:– unleavened bread [34], unleavened [18], without leaven [1]

4683 מַצָּה *maṣṣâ*, n.f. GK: 5175 [→ 5327]. quarrel, strife:– contention [1], debate [1], strife [1]

4684 מְצָהֲלוֹת *mishālôt*, n.f.[pl.]. GK: 5177 [→ 6670]. neighing:– neighings [1], neighing [1]

4685 מָצוֹד *māṣôd* or מְצוֹדָה *mᵉṣôdâ*, n.m. & f. GK: 5178 & 5179 & 5182 & 5183 [→ 6679]. fortress, prison (a place difficult to access); plunder; stronghold; (hunting) snare, net:– net [2], bulwarks [1], holds [1], munition [1], snares [1]

4686 מְצוּדָה *mᵉṣûdâ*, n.f. GK: 5180 & 5181 [→ 6679; cf. 4679]. stronghold, fortress, prison (a place difficult to access); (hunting) snare, net; prey:– fortress [6], hold [6], net [2], snare [2], castle [1], defence [1], fort [1], hunted [1], strong hold [1], strong place [1]

4687 מִצְוָה *miṣwâ*, n.f. GK: 5184 [→ 6680]. command, order, prescription, instruction:– commandments [130], commandment [43], precepts [3], commanded [2], law [1], ordinances [1], precept [1]

4688 מְצוֹלָה *mᵉṣôlâ* or מְצֻלָה *mᵉṣulâ*, n.f. GK: 5185 & 5198 [→ 4699, 6683]. depths, the deep:– deep [5], deeps [3], depths [2], bottom [1]

4689 מָצוֹק *māṣôq*, n.[m.]. GK: 5186 [→ 4691; cf. 6693]. distress, suffering, stress, hardship:– straitness [4], anguish [1], distress [1]

4690 מָצוּק *māṣûq*, n.m. GK: 5187 [→ 3332?]. foundation, pillar, support:– pillars [1], situate [1]

4691 מְצוּקָה *mᵉṣûqâ*, n.f. GK: 5188 [→ 4689; cf. 6693]. distress, anguish, stress, affliction:– distresses [5], anguish [1], distress [1]

4692 מָצוֹר *māṣôr*, n.[m.]. GK: 5189 & 5190 [→ 4694; cf. 6696]. stronghold, fortification, defense; siege; siege works, ramparts:– siege [13], besieged (+935+871.1+1886.1) [3], besieged (+871.1+1886.1) [2], strong [2], bulwarks [1], defence [1], fenced [1], strong hold [1], tower [1]

4693 מָצוֹר *māṣôr*, n.pr.loc. GK: 5191 [→ 4714]. Egypt:– besieged [2], defence [1], fortified [1], fortress [1]

4694 מְצוּרָה *mᵉṣûrâ* or מְצֻרָה *maṣṣārâ*, n.f. GK: 5193 & 5211 [→ 4692, 5341; cf. 6696]. fortification, defense, fortress; guard, watch:– fenced [5], forts [1], munition [1], strong holds [1]

4695 מַצּוּת *maṣṣût*, n.f. GK: 5194 [→ 5327]. enemy, person of strife:– contended with [1]

4696 מֵצַח *mēṣaḥ*, n.m. GK: 5195 [→ 4697; cf. 6705?]. forehead:– forehead [9], foreheads [2], brow [1], impudent (+2389) [1]

4697 מִצְחָה *miṣḥâ*, n.f. GK: 5196 [→ 4696; cf. 6705?]. greaves (armor for the front or back of leg from ankle to knee):– greaves [1]

מְצֹלָה *mᵉṣōlâ*. See 4688.

מְצֻלָה *mᵉṣulâ*. See 4688.

4698 מְצִלָּה *mᵉṣillâ*, n.f. GK: 5197 [→ 6750]. (small) bell (on a horse):– bells [1]

4699 מְצֻלָה *mᵉṣullâ*, n.f. GK: 5185 [→ 4688]. same as 4688: depths, the deep:– bottom [1]

4700 מְצִלְתַּיִם *mᵉṣiltayim*, n.f.du. GK: 5199 [→ 6750]. (pair of) cymbals:– cymbals [13]

4701 מִצְנֶפֶת *miṣnepet*, n.f. GK: 5200 [→ 6801]. turban, headband:– mitre [11], diadem [1]

4702 מַצָּע *maṣṣā'*, n.m. GK: 5201 [→ 3331]. bed, couch:– bed [1]

4703 מִצְעָד *miṣ'ād*, n.[m.]. GK: 5202 [→ 6805]. step; (position of submission in a) train:– steps [2], goings [1]

4704 מִצְעִירָה *miṣ'ᵉîrâ*, a.g. GK: 5203 [→ 4705, 6819]. form of 4705: small, little, lowly:– little [1]

4705 מִצְעָר *miṣ'ār*, n.m. GK: 5203 [→ 4704]. small quantity, few:– little one [2], small [2], little while [1]

4706 מִצְעָר *miṣ'ār*, n.pr.loc. GK: 5204 [→ 6819]. Mizar, "small":– Mizar [1]

4707 מִצְפֶּה *miṣpeh*, n.m. GK: 5205 [→ 4708, 4709; cf. 6822]. watchtower (used for military defense and surveillance), any place that overlooks:– watch tower [1], watchtower [1]

4708 מִצְפֶּה *miṣpeh*, n.pr.loc. GK: 5206 [→ 4707; cf. 6822]. Mizpah, "lookout point":– Mizpah [9], Mizpah [5]

4709 מִצְפָּה *miṣpâ*, n.pr.loc. GK: 5207 [→ 4707; cf. 6822]. Mizpah, "lookout point":– Mizpah [18], Mizpeh [14]

4710 מַצְפֻּן *maṣpôn*, n.[m.]. GK: 5208 [→ 6845]. hidden treasure, hiding place:– hid things [1]

4711 מָצַץ *māṣaṣ*, v. GK: 5209 [cf. 4680?]. [Q] to drink deeply, quaff:– milk out [1]

מֻצָּקָה *muṣāqâ*. See 4166.

4712 מֵצַר *mēṣar*, n.[m.]. GK: 5210 [→ 3334]. anguish, distress, hardship:– distress [1], pains [1], straits [1]

מָצֻק *māṣuq*. See 4690.

מְצֻקָה *mᵉṣuqâ*. See 4691.

מְצֻרָה *mᵉṣurâ*. See 4694.

4713 מִצְרִי *miṣrî*, a.g. GK: 5212 [→ 4714]. Egyptian:– Egyptian [16], Egyptians [5], Egyptian's [4], Egyptian (+376) [1], Egyptian (+376+1886.1) [1], Egypt [1], of Egypt [1]

4714 מִצְרַיִם *miṣrayim*, n.pr.loc. & g. GK: 5213 [→ 67, 4693, 4713]. Mizraim; Egypt, Egyptian:– Egypt [585], Egyptians [90], Mizraim [44], Egyptian [2], Egyptians (+1121) [1]

4715 מִצְרֵף *maṣrēp*, n.[m.]. GK: 5214 [→ 6884]. crucible, melting pot for metal:– fining pot [1]

4716 מַק *maq*, n.m. GK: 5215 [→ 4743]. stench, smell of decay:– rottenness [1], stink [1]

4717 מַקֶּבֶת *maqqebet*, n.f. GK: 5216 [→ 5344]. hammer:– hammers [2], hammer [2]

4718 מַקֶּבֶת *maqqebet*, n.f. GK: 5217 [→ 5344]. quarry:– hole [1]

4719 מַקֵּדָה *maqqēdâ*, n.pr.loc. GK: 5218 [→ 5348]. Makkedah, "locality of shepherds":– Makkedah [9]

4720 מִקְדָּשׁ *miqdāš*, n.m. GK: 5219 [→ 6942]. holy place, sanctuary, shrine:– sanctuary [64], sanctuaries [5], holy places [2], chapel [1], hallowed [1], holy place [1]

4721 מַקְהֵל *maqhēl*, n.[m.]. GK: 5220 [→ 6951]. assembly, congregation:– congregations [2]

4722 מַקְהֵלוֹת *maqhēlôt*, n.pr.loc. GK: 5221 [→ 6951]. Makheloth, "assemblies":– Makheloth [2]

4723 מִקְוֶה *miqweh*, n.[m.]. GK: 5223 & 5224 [→ 6960]. hope; collection (of water), reservoir; other sources: linen yarn:–

hope [4], linen yarn [4], abiding [1], gathering together [1], plenty [1], pools [1]

4724 מִקְוָה *miqwâ*, n.f. GK: 5225 [→ 6960]. reservoir:– ditch [1]

4725 מָקוֹם *māqôm*, n.m. GK: 5226 [→ 6965]. place, site:– place [370], places [20], home [3], room [3], whithersoever (+834) [2], country [1], open [1], space [1]

4726 מָקוֹר *māqôr*, n.m. GK: 5227 [→ 6979]. fountain, spring, source (of a flow), often with an implication of abundance or freshness:– fountain [11], spring [2], wellspring [2], issue [1], springs [1], well [1]

4727 מִקָּח *miqqāḥ*, n.[m.]. GK: 5228 [→ 3947]. taking, accepting (a bribe):– taking [1]

4728 מַקָּחוֹת *maqqāḥôt*, n.f. GK: 5229 [→ 3947]. (pl.) merchandise, wares:– ware [1]

4729 מִקְטָר *miqṭār*, n.m. GK: 5230 [→ 6999]. burning:– burn [1]

מְקַטְּרָה *mᵉqaṭṭᵉrâ*. See 6999.

4730 מִקְטֶרֶת *miqṭeret*, n.f. GK: 5233 [→ 6999]. censer, incense burner:– censer [3]

4731 מַקֵּל *maqqēl*, n.m. & f. GK: 5234. branch, stick; staff, a stick used to assist in walking, discipline, and guidance; war club:– staff [7], rods [6], rod [2], staves [2], handstaves (+3027) [1]

4732 מִקְלוֹת *miqlôt*, n.pr.m. GK: 5235. Mikloth, "rods":– Mikloth [4]

4733 מִקְלָט *miqlāṭ*, n.[m.]. GK: 5236 [→ 7038]. refuge, place of protection:– refuge [20]

4734 מִקְלַעַת *miqla'at*, n.f. GK: 5237 [→ 7049]. carving, engraving (on wood):– carved figures (+6603) [1], carved [1], carvings [1], gravings [1]

מָקוֹם *māqôm*. See 4725.

מְקוֹמָה *mᵉqômâ*. See 4725.

4735 מִקְנֶה *miqneh*, n.m. GK: 5238 [→ 4737; cf. 7069]. livestock, (animals from) herds and flocks:– cattle [61], flocks [3], possession [3], possessions [2], substance [2], flocks (+6629) [1], herds [1], purchase [1], trade about cattle (+376) [1], trade to feed cattle (+376) [1]

4736 מִקְנָה *miqnâ*, n.f. GK: 5239 [→ 7069]. something bought, purchased, acquisition:– bought [5], purchase [5], price [2], possession [1], that is bought [1], that were bought [1]

4737 מִקְנֵיָהוּ *miqnēyāhû*, n.pr.m. GK: 5240 [→ 4735+3068; cf. 7069]. Mikneiah, "Yahweh acquires":– Mikneiah [2]

4738 מִקְסָם *miqsām*, n.[m.]. GK: 5241 [→ 7080]. divination:– divination [2]

4739 מָקַץ *māqaṣ*, n.pr.loc. GK: 5242. Makaz:– Makaz [1]

4740 מִקְצוֹעַ *miqṣôa'*, n.m. GK: 5243 [→ 4742]. corner (of a base); angle of a wall:– corners [5], turning [5], every corner (+4740) [2]

4741 מַקְצֻעָה *maqṣu'â*, n.[f.]. GK: 5244 [→ 7106]. (wood) chisel:– planes [1]

4742 מְקֻצְעָה *mᵉquṣ'â*, v.ptcp. GK: 7910 [→ 4740, 7106]. ptcp. of 7106: made with corners:– corners [2]

4743 מָקַק *māqaq*, v. GK: 5245 [→ 4716]. [N] to rot, waste away, fester; dissolve; [H] to cause to rot:– consume away [4], pine away [4], corrupt [1], dissolved [1]

מָקֹר *māqōr*. See 4726.

4744 מִקְרָא *miqrā'*, n.m. GK: 5246 [→ 7121]. assembly, calling the community together, usually for a religious ceremony:– convocation [16], convocations [3], assemblies [2], calling [1], reading [1]

4745 מִקְרֶה *miqreh*, n.m. GK: 5247 [→ 7136]. happening by chance; fate, destiny:– befalleth [3], event [3], chance [1], happeneth [1], hap [1], something befallen [1]

4746 מְקָרֶה *mᵉqāreh*, n.[m.]. GK: 5248 [→ 6982]. rafters, roof beams:– building [1]

4747 מְקֵרָה *mᵉqērâ*, n.f. GK: 5249 [→ 6979]. coolness; cool room, summer home:– summer [2]

מֹקֵשׁ *mōqēš*. See 4170.

4748 מִקְשֶׁה *miqšeh*, n.m. GK: 5250 [→ 4749]. well-dressed hair:– well set hair (+4639) [1]

4749 מִקְשָׁה *miqšâ*, n.f. GK: 5251 [→ 4748]. hammered work; some sources: embossed metal work:– beaten work [6], beaten out of one piece [1], beaten [1], upright [1], whole piece [1]

4750 מִקְשָׁה *miqšā*, n.f. GK: 5252 [→ 7180]. melon field, cucumber field:– garden of cucumbers [1]

4751 מַר or מָרָה *mar* or *mārā*, a. & subst. GK: 5253 & 5287 [cf. 4843]. bitter; bitterness, ranging from being merely disagreeable to the taste to being poisonous; by extension: anxiety, despair:– bitter [21], bitterness [9], bitterly [3], angry (+5315) [1], chafed [1], discontented (+5315) [1], great bitterness (+4843) [1], heavy [1]

4752 מַר *mar*, n.[m.]. GK: 5254. drop (in a bucket):– drop [1]

4753 מֹר *mōr*, n.m. GK: 5255 [→ 4843]. myrrh:– myrrh [12]

4754 מָרָא *mārā*, v. GK: 5256 & 5257 [cf. 4784]. [Q] to flap, spread the feathers as it runs; this can also refer to the feet kicking up dirt; [Ho] to be obstinate:– filthy [1], lifteth up [1]

4755 מָרָא *mārā'*, n.pr.f. GK: 5259 [→ 4843]. Mara, "*bitter*":– Mara [1]

4756 מָרֵא *mārē'* (Aram.), n.m. GK: 10437. lord; (of God) the Lord; "Lord of kings" is one who is an authority over any and all other authorities:– Lord/lord [4]

מֹרֵא *mōrē'*. See 4172.

4757 מְרֹדַךְ־בַּלְאֲדָן *mᵉrōdak-bal'ᵃdān*, n.pr.m. GK: 5282 [→ 4781+1081; cf. 1255]. Merodach-Baladan, "*Marduk has given a son*":– Merodach-baladan [1]

4758 מַרְאֶה *mar'eh*, n.m. GK: 5260 [→ 7200]. what is seen with the eye, appearance; by extension: vision, supernatural revelation with a focus on visual communication, but can include verbal content:– appearance [33], vision [11], sight [10], countenance [9], favoured [8], in sight [8], look upon [4], appearances [2], countenances [2], fair (+2896) [2], apparently [1], appeareth [1], beautiful (+2896) [1], beauty [1], form [1], goodly [1], look on [1], look to [1], looketh (+5869) [1], pattern [1], saw [1], seem [1], see [1], visage [1]

4759 מַרְאָה *mar'â*, n.f. GK: 5261 & 5262 [→ 7200]. vision; mirror:– vision [6], visions [5], looking-glasses [1]

4760 מֻרְאָה *mur'â*, n.f. GK: 5263 [cf. 4784]. crop (of a bird):– crop [1]

מֵרָאוֹן *mᵉr'ôn*. See 8112.

4761 מְרַאֲשׁוֹת *mᵉra'ᵃšōt*, n.[f.]pl.den. GK: 5265 [→ 4762, 4763]. same as 4763: head rest, place near the head, headship:– principalities [1]

4762 מָרֵשָׁה *mārēšâ*, n.pr.m. & loc. GK: 5358 & 5359 [→ 4761, 4763]. Mareshah, "[perhaps] *head place*":– Mareshah [8]

4763 מְרַאֲשֹׁת *mᵉra'ᵃšōt*, n.[f.]pl.den. GK: 5265 [→ 4761]. same as 4761: head rest, place near the head:– bolster [6], pillows [2], head [1]

4764 מֵרָב *mērab*, n.pr.f. GK: 5266 [→ 7231]. Merab, "*abundant*":– Merab [3]

4765 מַרְבַד *marbad*, n.[m.]. GK: 5267 [→ 7234]. covering:– coverings of tapestry [2]

4766 מַרְבֶּה *marbeh*, n.[m.]. GK: 5269 [→ 7235]. abundance, increase:– great [1], increase [1]

4767 מִרְבָּה *mirbâ*, n.f. GK: 5268 [→ 7235]. so much:– much [1]

4768 מַרְבִית *marbît*, n.f. GK: 5270 [→ 7235]. great number; most, majority; profit:– increase [2], greatest part [1], greatness [1], multitude [1]

4769 מַרְבֵּץ *marbēṣ*, n.[m.]. GK: 5271 [→ 7257]. lair, resting place, place to lie down:– couching place [1], place to lie down in [1]

4770 מַרְבֵּק *marbēq*, n.[m.]. GK: 5272. fattening (of a calf):– stall [2], fatted [1], fat [1]

מֹרַג *mōrag*. See 4173.

4771 מַרְגּוֹעַ *margôa'*, n.[m.]. GK: 5273 [→ 7280]. resting place:– rest [1]

4772 מַרְגְּלוֹת *margᵉlôt*, n.[f.]pl.den. GK: 5274 [→ 7272]. (place of) the feet:– feet [5]

4773 מַרְגֵּמָה *margēmâ*, n.f. GK: 5275 [→ 7275]. sling:– sling [1]

4774 מַרְגֵּעָה *margē'â*, n.f. GK: 5276 [→ 7280]. place of repose, resting-place:– refreshing [1]

4775 מָרַד *mārad*, v. GK: 5277 [→ 4777, 4778?, 4780]. [Q] to rebel, revolt:– rebelled [12], rebel [8], rebellest [2], rebel against [1], rebellious [1], rebels [1]

4776 מְרַד *mᵉrad* (Aram.), n.[m.]. GK: 10438 [→ 4779; cf. 4777]. rebellion:– rebellion [1]

4777 מֶרֶד *mered*, n.[m.]. GK: 5278 [→ 4778; cf. 4775; cf. 4776]. rebellion:– rebellion [1]

4778 מֶרֶד *mered*, n.pr.m. GK: 5279 [→ 4777?; cf. 4775]. Mered, "*rebel*":– Mered [2]

4779 מָרָד *mārād* (Aram.), a. GK: 10439 [→ 4776]. rebellious:– rebellious [2]

4780 מַרְדוּת *mardût*, n.f. GK: 5280 [→ 4775]. rebellion, revolt:– rebellious [1]

4781 מְרֹדָךְ *mᵉrōdāk*, n.pr. GK: 5281 [→ 4757, 4782]. Marduk, Merodak (pagan god):– Merodach [1]

4782 מָרְדֳּכַי *mordᵉkay*, n.pr.m. GK: 5283 [→ 4781]. Mordecai, "*Marduk*":– Mordecai [58], Mordecai's [2]

4783 מֻרְדָּף *murdāp*, n.f. & m. GK: 5284 [→ 7291]. aggression:– persecuted [1]

4784 מָרָה *mārâ*, v. GK: 5286 [→ 3236, 4805, 4812?, 4850; cf. 4754, 4760]. [Q] to rebel, defy, become disobedient; some: to be bitter; [H] to act as a rebel, defy by one's action:– rebelled [14], rebellious [9], provoked [4], rebel [4], disobedient [2], grievously rebelled (+4784) [2], provoke [2], bitter [1], changed [1], disobeyed [1], provocation [1], provoking [1], rebelled against [1], rebels [1]

4785 מָרָה *mārâ*, n.pr.f. GK: 5288 [→ 4796; cf. 4843]. Marah, "*bitter*":– Marah [5]

מֹרֶה *mōreh*. See 4175.

4786 מֹרָה *mōrâ*, n.f. GK: 5289 [→ 4843]. bitterness, grief:– grief [1]

4787 מָרָּה *morrâ*, n.f. GK: 5285 [→ 4843]. bitterness:– bitterness [1]

4788 מָרוּד *mārûd*, n.[m.]. GK: 5291 [→ 7300]. wandering, wanderer; homeless, with a focus on poverty:– cast out [1], miseries [1], misery [1]

4789 מֵרוֹז *mērôz*, n.pr.loc. GK: 5292. Meroz:– Meroz [1]

4790 מָרוֹחַ *mārôaḥ*, n.[m.]. GK: 5293 [→ 4799]. damaged (by pounding or grinding):– broken [1]

4791 מָרוֹם *mārôm*, n.m. GK: 5294 [→ 7311]. heights, (place) on high, being in an elevated position; by extension: pride, haughtiness, arrogance, an improperly high opinion of oneself; exaltation, high in honor and status:– high [16], on high [11], height [9], above [4], high places [4], dignity [1], far above [1], haughty [1], heights [1], high ones [1], highest places (+1610) [1], loftily (+4480) [1], on high (+871.1+1886.1) [1], upward [1], very high (+5704) [1]

4792 מֵרוֹם *mērôm*, n.pr.loc. GK: 5295 [→ 7311]. Merom, "*high place*":– Merom [2]

4793 מֵרוֹץ *mērôṣ*, n.[m.]. GK: 5296 [→ 7323]. foot race, running:– race [1]

4794 מְרוּצָה *mᵉrûṣâ*, n.f. GK: 5297 [→ 7323]. manner or mode of running; course of a race:– course [2], running [2]

4795 מְרוּקִים *mᵉrûqîm*, n.[m.]. GK: 5299 [→ 4838]. beauty treatments (including massage and ointments):– purifications [1]

מְרוֹר *mᵉrôr*. See 4844.

מְרוֹרָה *mᵉrôrâ*. See 4846.

4796 מָרוֹת *mārôt*, n.pr.loc. GK: 5300 [→ 4785; cf. 4843]. Maroth, "*bitterness*":– Maroth [1]

4797 מַרְזֵחַ *marzēaḥ*, n.m. GK: 5301 [→ 4798]. same as 4798: funeral meal; cultic feast:– banquet [1]

4798 מַרְזֵחַ *marzēaḥ*, n.m. GK: 5301 [→ 4797]. same as 4797: funeral meal; cultic feast:– mourning [1]

4799 מָרַח *māraḥ*, v. GK: 5302 [→ 4790]. [Q] to apply by spreading on or rubbing in:– lay for a plaister [1]

4800 מֶרְחָב *merḥāb*, n.[m.]. GK: 5303 [→ 4800+3050; cf. 7337]. spaciousness, wideness, with the associative meaning that such a wide area is comfortable, and possibly safe and free:– large place [4], breadth [1], large room [1]

4801 מֶרְחָק *merḥāq*, n.m. GK: 5305 [→ 7368]. distance, far away:– far [11], afar off (+4480) [2], afar [1], far countries [1], far off (+4480) [1], far off [1], very far off [1]

4802 מַרְחֶשֶׁת *marḥešet*, n.f. GK: 5306 [→ 7370]. cooking pan (with a lid):– fryingpan [2]

4803 מָרַט *māraṭ*, v. GK: 5307 [→ 4178]. [Q] to pull out (hair); [Qp] to be polished, rubbed; [N] to lose one's hair, become bald; [Pu] to be polished, burnished, smooth (skinned):–

4804 מְרַט *mᵉraṭ* (Aram.), v. GK: 10440 [cf. 4178]. [Peil] to be torn off, plucked out:– pluckt [1]

4805 מְרִי *mᵉrî*, n.m. GK: 5308 [→ 4784]. rebellion; some: bitter:– rebellious [17], rebellion [4], bitter [1], rebels (+1121) [1]

4806 מְרִיא *mᵉrî'*, n.[m.]. GK: 5309 [→ 1254, 1274, 1277, 4471?, 4813?]. fattened animal (choice for consumption):– fat cattle [3], fatlings [2], fat beasts [1], fatling [1], fed beasts [1]

4807 מְרִיב בַּעַל *mᵉrîb ba'al*, n.pr.m. GK: 5311 [→ 1167; cf. 4810]. Merib-Baal, "*Baal contends*":– Merib-baal [3]

4808 מְרִיבָה *mᵉrîbâ*, n.f. GK: 5312 [→ 4809; cf. 7378]. quarreling, strife; rebellion, with a focus on the feelings of enmity:– strife [5], provocation [1]

4809 מְרִיבָה *mᵉrîbâ*, n.pr.loc. GK: 5313 [→ 4808; cf. 7378]. Meribah:– Meribah [6], Meribah-Kadesh [1]

4810 מְרִי־בַעַל *mᵉrî-ba'al*, n.pr.m. GK: 5314 [→ 1167; cf. 4807]. Merib-Baal, "*Baal contends*":– Merib-baal [1]

4811 מְרָיָה *mᵉrāyâ*, n.pr.m. GK: 5316. Meraiah, "*loved by Yahweh*":– Meraiah [1]

מֹרִיָּה *mōrîâ*. See 4179.

4812 מְרָיוֹת *mᵉrāyôt*, n.pr.m. GK: 5318 [→ 4784?]. Meraioth, "*rebellious*":– Meraioth [7]

4813 מִרְיָם *miryām*, n.pr.f. & m. GK: 5319 [→ 4806?]. Miriam, "[variously] bitterness; plump one; wished-for child; one who loves or is loved":– Miriam [15]

4814 מְרִירוּת *mᵉrîrût*, n.f. GK: 5320 [→ 4843]. bitterness:– bitterness [1]

4815 מְרִירִי *mᵉrîrî*, a. GK: 5321 [→ 4843]. bitter, in context referring to something deadly:– bitter [1]

4816 מֹרֶךְ *mōrek*, n.[m.]. GK: 5322 [→ 7401]. fearfulness, despondency:– faintness [1]

4817 מֶרְכָּב *merkāb*, n.m. GK: 5323 [→ 7392]. seat, saddle, chariot:– chariots [1], covering [1], saddle [1]

4818 מֶרְכָּבָה *merkābâ*, n.f. GK: 5324 [→ 7392]. chariot:– chariot [23], chariots [21]

4819 מַרְכֹּלֶת *markōlet*, n.f. GK: 5326 [→ 7402]. marketplace, place of merchandising:– merchandise [1]

4820 מִרְמָה *mirmâ*, n.f. GK: 5327 [→ 4821; cf. 7411]. deceit, deception, dishonesty, treachery:– deceit [19], deceitful [8], false [2], guile [2], craft [1], deceitfully (+3807.1) [1], deceitfully (+871.1) [1], deceitfully [1], deceits [1], feigned [1], subtilty [1], treachery [1]

4821 מִרְמָה *mirmâ*, n.pr.m. GK: 5328 [→ 4820?; cf. 7411?]. Mirmah, "*deceit*":– Mirma [1]

4822 מְרֵמוֹת *mᵉrēmôt*, n.pr.m. GK: 5329. Meremoth, "*elevations*":– Meremoth [6]

4823 מִרְמָס *mirmās*, n.[m.]. GK: 5330 [→ 7429]. trampling down, running over:– trodden down [3], that which trodden [1], tread down (+7760) [1], treading [1], trodden under foot [1]

4824 מֵרֹנֹתִי *mērōnōtî*, a.g. GK: 5331 [→]. Meronothite, of Meronoth, "*of Meronoth*":– Meronothite [2]

4825 מֶרֶס *meres*, n.pr.m. GK: 5332. Meres, "*worthy*":– Meres [1]

4826 מַרְסְנָא *marsᵉnā'*, n.pr.m. GK: 5333. Marsena:– Marsena [1]

4827 מֵרַע *mēra'*, n.m. or v.ptcp. GK: 5334 [→ 7489]. evil, atrocity:– do mischief [1]

4828 מֵרֵעַ *mērēa'*, n.[m.] or v.ptcp. GK: 5335 [→ 7462]. close friend, companion, personal adviser:– companion [3], friends [3], companions [1]

4829 מִרְעֶה *mir'eh*, n.m. GK: 5337 [→ 7462]. pasture, grazing place:– pasture [11], feeding place [1], pastures [1]

4830 מִרְעִית *mar'ît*, n.f. GK: 5338 [→ 7462]. pasture, place of grazing:– pasture [8], flocks [1], pastures [1]

4831 מַרְעֲלָה *mar'ᵃlâ*, n.pr.loc. GK: 5339 [→ 7477]. Maralah:– Maralah [1]

4832 מַרְפֵּא *marpē'*, n.m. GK: 5340 & 5341 [→ 7503; cf. 7495]. healing, remedy; calmness, composure:– health [5], healing [3], remedy [3], cure [1], incurable (+369) [1], sound [1], wholesome [1], yielding [1]

4833 מִרְפָּשׂ *mirpāś*, n.[m.]. GK: 5343 [→ 7511]. what is muddy, fouled (by trampling):– that which fouled [1]

Heb

4834 מָרַץ *māraṣ*, v. GK: 5344. [N] to be painful, hurtful; [H] to provoke, irritate:– emboldeneth [1], forcible [1], grievous [1], sore [1]

4835 מְרוּצָה *mᵉrûṣâ*, n.f. GK: 5298 [→ 7533]. extortion:– violence [1]

4836 מַרְצֵעַ *marṣēa'*, n.[m.]. GK: 5345 [→ 7527]. awl (piercing tool):– aul [2]

4837 מַרְצֶפֶת *marṣepet*, n.f. GK: 5346 [→ 7528]. (stone) base, stone-layer:– pavement [1]

4838 מָרַק *māraq*, v. GK: 5347 [→ 4795, 4839, 8562]. [Q] to polish; [Qp] to be polished; [Pu] to be thoroughly scoured; [H] to cleanse:– bright [1], furbish [1], scoured [1]

4839 מָרָק *mārāq*, n.m. GK: 5348 [→ 4838]. broth (juice stewed out of meat):– broth [3]

4840 מֶרְקָח *merqāḥ*, n.[m.]. GK: 5349 [→ 7543]. aromatic herb, scented spice, perfume:– sweet [1]

4841 מֶרְקָחָה *merqāḥâ*, n.f. GK: 5350 [→ 7543]. ointment jar, spice-pot:– pot of ointment [1], well [1]

4842 מִרְקַחַת *mirqaḥat*, n.f. GK: 5351 [→ 7543]. mixture of fragrant spices, blend of perfumes:– apothecaries' [1], compound [1], ointment [1]

4843 מָרַר *mārar*, v. GK: 5352 [→ 4470, 4472, 4751, 4753, 4755, 4787, 4785, 4786, 4796, 4814, 4815, 4844, 4845, 4846, 8563]. [Q] to be bitter; suffer anguish; [P] to make bitter, weep bitterly; [H] to make bitter; to grieve bitterly; [Htpal] to enrage oneself, be furious; from the base meaning "to taste bitter" come extensions of bitter feelings: anger, fury, anguish, rebellion:– in bitterness [2], moved with choler [2], vexed [2], bitterly [1], bitterness [1], bitter [1], dealt bitterly [1], great bitterness (+4751) [1], grieved [1], grieveth [1], made bitter [1], provoke [1], sorely grieved [1]

4844 מְרֹר *mārōr*, n.m. GK: 5353 [→ 4843]. bitter things:– bitter [2], bitterness [1]

4845 מְרֵרָה *mᵉrērâ*, n.f. GK: 5354 [→ 4843]. gall (bitter fluid from the gall bladder):– gall [1]

4846 מְרֹרָה *mᵉrōrâ*, n.f. GK: 5355 [→ 4843]. gall bladder; venom, poison (of snakes):– bitter [2], gall [2]

4847 מְרָרִי *mᵉrārî*, n.[m.]. GK: 5356 [→ 4848]. Merari; Merarite, "*bitter*":– Merari [39]

4848 מְרָרִי *mᵉrārî*, a.g. GK: 5357 [→ 4847]. Merarite, "*of Merari*":– Merarites [1]

מָרֵשָׁה *mārēšâ*. See 4762.

4849 מִרְשַׁעַת *mirša'at*, n.f. GK: 5360 [→ 7561]. wickedness, of a person (that) wicked woman:– wicked woman [1]

4850 מְרָתַיִם *mᵉrātayim*, n.pr.f. GK: 5361 [→ 4784]. Merathaim, "*double rebellion*":– Merathaim [1]

4851 מַשׁ *maš*, n.pr.m. GK: 5390. prob. same as 4902: Mash, Meshech:– Mash [1]

4852 מֵשָׁא *mēšā'*, n.pr.loc. GK: 5392 [→ 4854?]. Mesha:– Mesha [1]

4853 מַשָּׂא *maśśā'*, n.m. GK: 5362 & 5363 [→ 4984]. burden, load, what is lifted and carried; by extension: oppression; singing (lifting the voice); oracle, prophetic utterance, pronouncement, with the focus on the content of the message:– burden [52], burdens [5], song [3], prophecy [2], carry away [1], exaction of debt (+3027) [1], set [1], tribute [1]

4854 מַשָּׂא *maśśā'*, n.pr.g. & loc. GK: 5364 [→ 4852?]. Massa, "*burden, oracle*":– Massa [2]

4855 מַשָּׁא *maššā'*, n.m. GK: 5391 [→ 5378]. debt; exacting of usury:– usury [2]

4856 מַשֹּׁא *maššō'*, n.m. GK: 5365 [→ 4984]. partiality:– respect [1]

4857 מַשְׁאָב *maš'āb*, n.[m.]. GK: 5393 [→ 7579]. watering channel, place to draw water:– places of drawing [1]

מֹשָׁאָה *mᵉšō'â*. See 4875.

4858 מַשָּׂאָה *maśśā'â*, n.f. GK: 5366 [→ 4984]. uplifted (clouds of smoke):– burden [1]

4859 מַשָּׁאָה *maššā'â*, n.f. GK: 5394 [→ 5378]. (secured) loan:– debts [1], lend (+5383) [1]

מַשֻּׁאָה *maššu'â*. See 4876.

4860 מַשָּׁאוֹן *maššā'ôn*, n.[m.]. GK: 5396 [→ 5377]. deception:– deceit [1]

4861 מִשְׁאָל *miš'āl*, n.pr.loc. GK: 5398 [cf. 4913]. Mishal:– Mishal [1], Misheal [1]

4862 מִשְׁאָלָה *miš'ālâ*, n.f. GK: 5399 [→ 7592]. desire:– desires [1], petitions [1]

4863 מִשְׁאֶרֶת *miš'eret*, n.f. GK: 5400 [→ 7603]. kneading trough:– kneadingtroughs [2], store [2]

4864 מַשְׂאֵת *maś'ēt*, n.f. GK: 5368 [→ 4984]. what is lifted up: portion (of food), tax, tribute, gift, burden:– burdens [2], collection [2], flame [2], mess [2], burden [1], gifts [1], lifting up [1], messes [1], oblations [1], reward [1], sign of fire [1]

מוֹשָׁב *môšāb*. See 4186.

מְשֻׁבָה *mᵉšubâ*. See 4878.

4865 מִשְׁבְּצוֹת *mišbᵉṣôt*, n.f.pl. GK: 5401 [→ 7660]. filigree settings (ornamental work with fine gold wire usually for setting jewels):– ouches [8], wrought [1]

4866 מַשְׁבֵּר *mašbēr*, n.[m.]. GK: 5402 [→ 7665]. opening of the womb, the point where birth first occurs:– birth [2], breaking forth [1]

4867 מִשְׁבָּר *mišbār*, n.[m.]. GK: 5403 [→ 7665]. breakers, waves:– waves [4], billows [1]

4868 מִשְׁבָּת *mišbāt*, n.[m.]. GK: 5404 [→ 7673]. destruction, cessation, finish:– sabbaths [1]

4869 מִשְׂגָּב *miśgāb*, n.m. & loc. GK: 5369 [→ 7682]. fortress, refuge, stronghold; Misgab:– defence [6], refuge [5], high tower [3], Misgab [1], high fort [1], place of defence [1]

4870 מִשְׁגֶּה *mišgeh*, n.m. GK: 5405 [→ 7686]. inadvertent mistake, oversight:– oversight [1]

4871 מָשָׁה *māšâ*, v. GK: 5406 [→ 4872; cf. 570?]. [Q] to draw out; [H] to cause to draw out:– drew out [2], drew [1]

4872 מֹשֶׁה *mōšeh*, n.pr.m. GK: 5407 [→ 4871]. Moses, "*drawn out* [Ex 2:10]; Egyptian for *child*":– Moses [750], Moses' [15], Moses (+3807.1) [1]

4873 מֹשֶׁה *mōšeh* (Aram.), n.pr.m. GK: 10441 [cf. 4872]. Moses, "*drawn out* [Ex 2:10]; [Egyptian for] *child*":– Moses [1]

4874 מַשֶּׁה *maššeh*, n.m. GK: 5408 [→ 5378]. credit, loan; "the lord of the loan" is a "creditor":– creditor (+1167+3027) [1]

4875 מְשׁוֹאָה *mᵉšô'â*, n.f. GK: 5409. wasteland, desolate land:– waste [2], desolation [1]

4876 מַשּׁוּאָה *maššû'â* or מַשֻּׁאוֹת *maššu'ôt*, n.m. & f.[pl.]. GK: 5410 & 5397 [→ 5377]. ruin, rubble, desolation; deception:– desolations [1], destruction [1]

4877 מְשׁוֹבָב *mᵉšôbāb*, n.pr.m. GK: 5411 [→ 7725]. Meshobab:– Meshobab [1]

4878 מְשׁוּבָה *mᵉšûbâ*, n.f. GK: 5412 [→ 7725]. waywardness, backsliding, faithlessness, apostasy:– backsliding [7], backslidings [4], turning away [1]

4879 מְשׁוּגָה *mᵉšûgâ*, n.f. GK: 5413 [cf. 7683, 7686]. error:– error [1]

4880 מָשׁוֹט *māšôṭ* or מִשּׁוֹט *miššôṭ*, n.[m.]. GK: 5414 & 5415 [→ 7751]. oar:– oars [1], oar [1]

4881 מְשׂוּכָה *mᵉśûkkâ* or מְשֻׂכָה *mᵉśukâ*, n.f. GK: 5372 & 5379 [→ 4534]. (thorn) hedge (which impedes movement):– hedge [2]

4882 מְשׁוּסָה *mᵉšiwssâ*, var. GK: 5416 [cf. 4933]. plunder, loot, booty; cf. 4934:–

4883 מַשּׂוֹר *maśśôr*, n.[m.]. GK: 5373. saw (cutting tool):– saw [1]

4884 מְשׂוּרָה *mᵉśûrâ*, n.f. GK: 5374. (liquid) measure of quantity, measure of capacity:– measure [4]

4885 מָשׂוֹשׂ *māśôś*, n.m. GK: 5375 & 5376 [→ 7797; cf. 4549]. joy, delight, celebration; wasting away, rotting away:– joy [12], mirth [1], rejoiceth [1], rejoice [1]

4886 מָשַׁח *māšaḥ*, v. GK: 5417 [→ 4473, 4888, 4899; cf. 4887]. [Q] to anoint; [Qp] to be spread, be anointed; [N] to be anointed; usually referring to pouring or smearing sacred oil on a person in a ceremony of dedication, possibly symbolizing divine empowering to accomplish the task or office:– anointed [42], anoint [25], anointedst [1], painted [1]

4887 מְשַׁח *mᵉšaḥ* (Aram.), n.[m.]. GK: 10442 & 10443 [cf. 4888]. olive oil, used for food, lamp oil, and ceremonies; measure:– oil [2]

4888 מִשְׁחָה *mišḥâ* or מׇשְׁחָה *mošḥâ* or מׇשְׁחָה *mišḥâ*, n.f. GK: 5418 & 5419 & 5420 & 5421 [→ 4886]. portion; anointing (oil), usually referring to pouring or smearing sacred oil on a person in a ceremony of dedication, possibly symbolizing divine empowering to accomplish the task or office:– anointing [24], anoint [1], ointment [1]

4889 מַשְׁחִית *mašḥît*, n.[m.]. GK: 5422 [→ 7843]. destroyer, one who destroys; destruction, corruption; bird trap:– destroy [4], corruption [2], destruction [2], destroyer (+376) [1], destroying [1], trap [1], utterly (+3807.1) [1]

4890 מִשְׂחָק *miśḥāq*, n.[m.]. GK: 5377 [→ 7832]. (scoffing) laughter:– scorn [1]

4891 מִשְׁחָר *mišḥār*, n.[m.]. GK: 5423 [→ 7835]. dawn, early morning light:– morning [1]

4892 מַשְׁחֵת *mašḥēt*, n.[m.]. GK: 5424 [→ 7843]. destruction, annihilation:– destroying [1]

4893 מִשְׁחָת *mišḥāt* or מׇשְׁחָת *mošḥāt*, n.[m.]. GK: 5425 & 5426 [→ 7843]. deformity, defect, corruption, disfigurement, implying ugliness and repulsion:– corruption [1], marred [1]

4894 מִשְׁטוֹחַ *mišṭôaḥ*, n.[m.]. GK: 5427 [→ 7849]. place for spreading out nets, drying yard for nets:– place to spread forth [1], spread upon [1], spreading [1]

4895 מַשְׂטֵמָה *maśṭēmâ*, n.f. GK: 5378 [→ 7852]. hostility, animosity, enmity:– hatred [2]

4896 מִשְׁטָר *mišṭār*, n.[m.]. GK: 5428 [→ 7860]. dominion, rule; some sources: heavenly writing (the starry sky as God's communication):– dominion [1]

4897 מֶשִׁי *mešî*, n.[m.]. GK: 5429. costly fabric for garments; possibly referring to silk:– silk [2]

מֻשִׁי *mušî*. See 4187.

4898 מְשֵׁיזַבְאֵל *mᵉšêzab'ēl*, n.pr.m. GK: 5430 [cf. 7804]. Meshezabel, "*God [El] delivers*":– Meshezabeel [3]

4899 מָשִׁיחַ *māšîaḥ*, n.m. GK: 5431 [→ 4886]. anointed (one), usually refers to pouring or smearing sacred oil on a person in a ceremony of dedication, possibly symbolizing divine empowering to accomplish the task or office; the Anointed One, the Messiah, God's ultimate chosen one, identified in the NT in Jesus:– anointed [37], Messiah [2]

4900 מָשַׁךְ *māšak*, v. GK: 5432 [→ 4901, 4189]. [Q] to draw up, drag; to extend, spread out; [N] to be prolonged, delayed; [Pu] to be deferred; to be tall:– draw [7], drew [4], draw out [3], prolonged [3], draweth [2], drawn [2], scattered [2], continue [1], deferred [1], draw away [1], draw along [1], drew up [1], extend unto [1], forbear (+5921) [1], give [1], handle [1], make a long blast [1], soundeth long [1], soweth [1], stretched out [1]

4901 מֶשֶׁךְ *mešek*, n.[m.]. GK: 5433 [→ 4900]. (leather) bag, pouch (= price):– precious [1], price [1]

4902 מֶשֶׁךְ *mešek*, n.pr.g. GK: 5434. Meshech:– Meshech [8], Mesech [1]

4903 מִשְׁכַּב *miškab* (Aram.), n.[m.]. GK: 10444 [cf. 4904]. bed, formally "a place for lying," which can refer to simple mats and even outer cloaks, as well as to pieces of furniture:– bed [6]

4904 מִשְׁכָּב *miškāb*, n.m. GK: 5435 [→ 7901; cf. 4903]. bed, couch, used as a place for sleep, meditation, convalescence, marital relations, and worship:– bed [28], beds [5], bedchamber (+2315) [4], lying with [4], couch [1], lay on a bed (+7901) [1], lien [1], lieth with [1]

מִשְׁכָּה *mᵉsukâ*. See 4881.

4905 מַשְׂכִּיל *maśkîl*, n.m. GK: 5380 [→ 7919]. maskil (t.t. in the Psalms, perhaps "wisdom song"):– Maschil [13]

מַשְׂכִּים *maśkîm*. See 7925.

4906 מַשְׂכִּית *maśkît*, n.f. GK: 5381 [→ 7919]. carved image, sculpture, figurine; what is imagined, imagination:– pictures [2], conceit [1], imagery [1], image [1], wish [1]

4907 מִשְׁכַּן *miškan* (Aram.), n.[m.]. GK: 10445 [→ 7932; cf. 4908]. dwelling, abode:– habitation [1]

4908 מִשְׁכָּן *miškān*, n.m. GK: 5438 [→ 7931; cf. 4907]. dwelling place, habitat, tent, tabernacle, the tent used as the central place of worship before the temple:– tabernacle [114], dwellings [6], tabernacles [5], dwelling places [3], habitation [3], dwelling place [2], habitations [2], dwelling [1], tents [1], where dwelleth [1]

4909 מַשְׂכֹּרֶת *maśkōret*, n.f. GK: 5382 [→ 7936]. wage:– wages [3], reward [1]

4910 מָשַׁל *māšal*, v. GK: 5440 [→ 4474, 4475, 4915]. [Q] to rule, govern, control; [H] make one a ruler, (n.) dominion:– rule [15], ruler [14], ruleth [7], ruled [5], reign [4], rulers [4], governor [3], have dominion [3], reigned [3], have power [2], have rule [2], indeed have dominion (+4910) [2], rule over [2], rulest [1], ruling [2], bare rule [1], barest rule [1], bear rule [1], beareth rule [1], cause to rule over [1], dominion [1], governors [1], had dominion [1], madest to have dominion [1], reignest [1], ruler's [1]

4911 מָשַׁל *māšal*, v. GK: 5439 [→ 4912, 4915, 4914]. [Q] to quote (a proverb or saying), to make up a proverb; [N] to liken, be like; [P] to tell a proverb; [H] to liken, compare to; [Ht] to show oneself like:– become like [3], like [2], use proverb (+4912) [2], compare [1], like unto [1], speak a parable (+4912) [1], speak in proverbs [1], speak [1], use as a proverb [1], use proverb [1], useth proverbs [1], utter [1]

4912 מָשָׁל *māšāl*, n.m. GK: 5442 [→ 4911]. wisdom sayings of various types: proverb, a short, pithy saying, easy to remember; parable, a brief story with a symbolic meaning; oracle, a discourse type of prophecy; taunt, ridicule, a stylized form for mocking an enemy:– parable [16], proverb [12], proverbs [5], use proverb (+4911) [2], byword [1], like unto [1], parables [1], speak a parable (+4911) [1]

4913 מָשָׁל *māšāl*, n.pr.loc. GK: 5443 [cf. 4861]. Mashal:– Mashal [1]

4914 מְשֹׁל *mᵉšōl*, n.[m.]. GK: 5446 [→ 4911]. byword:– byword [1]

4915 מֹשֶׁל *mōšel*, n.[m.]. GK: 5444 & 5445 [→ 4910, 4911]. likeness, similarity; power, dominion:– dominion [2], like [1]

מִשְׁלֹשׁ *mišlôš*. See 7969.

4916 מִשְׁלוֹחַ *mišlôaḥ* or מִשְׁלָח *mišlāḥ*, n.[m.]. GK: 5447 & 5448 [→ 7971]. giving, sending (presents); laying on (hands):– puttest unto [2], sending [2], settest unto [1], lay upon [1], put unto [1], sending forth [1], settest [1]

4917 מִשְׁלַחַת *mišlaḥat*, n.f. GK: 5449 [→ 7971]. discharge (from military); band, company (of angels):– discharge [1], sending [1]

4918 מְשֻׁלָּם *mᵉšullām*, n.pr.m. GK: 5450 [→ 4920; cf. 7999]. Meshullam, "*restitution*":– Meshullam [25]

4919 מְשִׁלֵּמוֹת *mᵉšillēmôt*, n.pr.m. GK: 5451 [→ 4921; cf. 7999]. Meshillemoth, "*restitution*":– Meshillemoth [2]

4920 מְשֶׁלֶמְיָה *mᵉšelemyâ* or מְשֶׁלֶמְיָהוּ *mᵉšelemyāhû*, n.pr.m. GK: 5452 & 5453 [→ 4918+3068]. Meshelemiah, "*Yahweh repays*":– Meshelemiah [4]

4921 מְשִׁלֵּמִית *mᵉšillēmît*, n.pr.m. GK: 5454 [→ 4919; cf. 7999]. Meshillemith, "*restitution*":– Meshillemith [1]

4922 מְשֻׁלֶּמֶת *mᵉšullemet*, n.pr.f. GK: 5455 [→ 7999]. Meshullemeth, "*restitution*":– Meshullemeth [1]

4923 מְשַׁמָּה *mᵉšammâ*, n.f. GK: 5457 [→ 8074]. object of horror, desolate waste, dried up place:– desolate [3], most desolate (+8077+2050.1) [3], astonishment [1]

4924 מִשְׁמָן *mišmān*, n.m. GK: 5458 & 5460 [→ 8081]. fatness; by extension: sturdiness, stoutness; richness, fertility, abundance, prosperity; choice food, festive food, rich with oil or fat (rare and valued in the ancient Near East):– fatness [3], fat ones [1], fattest places [1], fattest [1], fat [1]

4925 מִשְׁמַנָּה *mišmannâ*, n.pr.m. GK: 5459 [→ 8081]. Mishmannah, "*fatness*":– Mishmannah [1]

4926 מִשְׁמָע *mišmā'*, n.[m.]. GK: 5461 [→ 4927; cf. 8085]. what one hears, rumor, hearsay:– hearing [1]

4927 מִשְׁמָע *mišmā'*, n.pr.m. GK: 5462 [→ 4926; cf. 8085]. Mishma, "*rumor*":– Mishma [4]

4928 מִשְׁמַעַת *mišma'at*, n.f. GK: 5463 [→ 8085]. bodyguard; subject, one obligated to allegiance:– guard [2], bidding [1], obey [1]

4929 מִשְׁמָר *mišmār*, n.[m.]. GK: 5464 [→ 8104]. guard or guarding, custody, imprisonment:– ward [12], watch [4], guard [3], diligence [1], offices [1], prison [1]

4930 מַשְׂמֵרָה *maśmērâ*, n.m. GK: 5383 [cf. 5568]. nail (on the end of a goad):– nails [1]

4931 מִשְׁמֶרֶת *mišmeret*, n.f. GK: 5466 [→ 8104]. responsibility, duty, service; requirement, obligation; guard, watch, what is cared for:– charge [45], kept [6], ward [5], watch [5], charges [4], ordinance [3], wards [3], watches [2], charge of [1], in safeguard [1], keep (+1961) [1], offices [1], ward (+1004) [1]

4932 מִשְׁנֶה *mišneh*, n.[m.]. GK: 5467 [→ 8138]. second, next (in a series); twice, double:– second [9], double [8], next [6], college [2], copy [2], twice [2], fatlings [1], next to [1], second degree [1], second order [1], second sort [1], twice as much [1]

4933 מְשִׁסָּה *mᵉšissâ*, n.f. GK: 5468 [→ 7601; cf. 4882]. plunder, loot, booty:– spoil [4], booties [1], booty [1]

4934 מִשְׁעוֹל *miš'ôl*, n.m. GK: 5469 [→ 8168]. narrow path:– path [1]

4935 מִשְׁעִי *miš'î*, n.f. GK: 5470. cleansing, implying cleansing by washing and rubbing:– supple [1]

4936 מִשְׁעָם *miš'ām*, n.pr.m. GK: 5471. Misham:– Misham [1]

4937 מִשְׁעָן *miš'ān*, n.m. & f. GK: 5472 & 5473 [→ 8172]. support, supplies:– stay [5]

4938 מִשְׁעֵנָה *maš'ēnâ* or מִשְׁעֶנֶת *miš'enet*, n.f. GK: 5474 & 5475 [→ 8172]. staff, stick; support, supply:– staff [11], staves [1]

4939 מִשְׂפָּח *miśpāḥ*, n.[m.]. GK: 5384 [cf. 5596]. bloodshed, with a focus on violence:– oppression [1]

4940 מִשְׁפָּחָה *mišpāḥâ*, n.f. GK: 5476 [→ 8198]. clan, family, people:– families [169], family [117], kindred [6], every family (+4940) [4], kindreds [3], every family (+4940+2050.1) [2], kinds [2]

4941 מִשְׁפָּט *mišpāṭ*, n.m. GK: 5477 [→ 5880; cf. 8199]. justice, judgment; law, regulation, prescription, specification:– judgment [188], judgments [108], manner [34], right [18], cause [12], that which is lawful [7], ordinances [6], ordinance [5], worthy [4], after the manner [2], discretion [2], fashion [2], law [2], manners [2], measure [2], order [2], sentence [2], adversary (+1167) [1], as required [1], ceremonies [1], charge [1], crimes [1], custom [1], deserts [1], determination [1], disposing [1], due order [1], due [1], execute the judgment (+8199) [1], fashions [1], form [1], judged [1], judgment (+1697) [1], justice [1], justly [1], just [1], order (+1961) [1], order commanded to do [1], usest to do [1], wrong (+3808) [1], wrongfully (+3808+871.1) [1]

4942 מִשְׁפְּתַיִם *mišpᵉtayim*, n.[m.]du. GK: 5478 [→ 8239]. (dual) campfires or two saddlebags:– sheepfolds [1], two burdens [1]

4943 מֶשֶׁק *mešeq*, n.[m.]. GK: 5479 [→ 4476]. inheritance, possession:– steward (+1121) [1]

4944 מַשָּׁק *maššāq*, n.[m.]. GK: 5480 [→ 8264]. onslaught, assault; formally "rushing," this is the sudden, aggressive movement of a swarm:– running to and fro [1]

4945 מַשְׁקֶה *mašqeh*, n.m. GK: 5482 & 5483 [→ 8248]. cupbearer; drink (liquid); drinking vessel; irrigation:– drinking [2], drink [2], butlership [1], fat pastures [1], well watered [1]

4946 מִשְׁקוֹל *mišqôl*, n.[m.]. GK: 5484 [→ 8254]. weight:– weight [1]

4947 מַשְׁקוֹף *mašqôp*, n.m. GK: 5485 [→ 8259]. top (upper crosspiece of a door), lintel:– lintel [2], upper door post [1]

4948 מִשְׁקָל *mišqāl*, n.m. GK: 5486 [→ 8254]. weight:– weight [46], weigh [2], full weight [1]

4949 מִשְׁקֶלֶת *mišqelet*, n.f. GK: 5487 [→ 8254?]. plumb line, leveling instrument:– plummet [2]

4950 מִשְׁקָע *mišqā'*, n.[m.]. GK: 5488 [→ 8257]. clear (settled) water:– deep [1]

4951 מִשְׂרָה *miśrâ*, n.f. GK: 5385 [→ 7786]. dominion, rule:– government [2]

4952 מִשְׁרָה *mišrâ*, n.f. GK: 5489 [→ 8281]. (grape) juice:– liquor [1]

4953 מַשְׁרוֹקִי *mašrôqî* (Aram.), n.f. GK: 10446. flute, musical pipe, a cylinder-shaped instrument producing a high shrill sound, made of wood, reed, or bone:– flute [4]

4954 מִשְׁרָעִי *miśrā'î*, a.g. GK: 5490. Mishraite:– Mishraites [1]

4955 מִשְׂרָפוֹת *miśrāpôt*, n.[f.pl.]. GK: 5386 [→ 8313]. (complete) burning, funeral fire:– burnings [2]

4956 מִשְׂרְפוֹת מַיִם *miśrᵉpôt mayim*, n.pr.loc. GK: 5387 [→ 8313+4325]. Misrephoth Maim, "*waters of Misrephoth /lime burning/*":– Misrephoth-maim [2]

4957 מַשְׂרֵקָה *maśrēqâ*, n.pr.loc. GK: 5388 [→ 8320]. Masrekah, "*[perhaps] vineyard*":– Masrekah [2]

4958 מַשְׂרֵת *maśrēt*, n.m. GK: 5389 [→ 7603]. cooking pan:– pan [1]

4959 מָשַׁשׁ *māšaš*, v. GK: 5491 [cf. 3237, 4184]. [Q] to touch, feel; [P] to grope, search thoroughly; [H] to let one feel:– grope [3], felt [2], searched [2], feel [1], gropeth [1]

4960 מִשְׁתֶּה *mišteh*, n.m. GK: 5492 [→ 8354; cf. 4961]. feast, banquet, dinner, with an focus on drinking:– feast [21], banquet [10], feasting [7], drink [3], drank [2], feasts [2], feasted (+6213) [1]

4961 מִשְׁתֵּא *mištē'* (Aram.), n.m. GK: 10447 [→ 8355; cf. 4960]. banquet (hall); feast (hall), a place of merriment and celebration, often associated with drinking bouts:– banquet [1]

4962 מֹת *mōt*, n.m. GK: 5493 [→ 1328, 4968]. men; few (people):– men [14], few [2], few (+4557) [1], few (+4592) [1], friends [1], number [1], persons [1], small [1]

4963 מַתְבֵּן *matbēn*, n.[m.]. GK: 5495 [→ 8401]. heap of straw:– straw [1]

4964 מֶתֶג *meteg*, n.m. GK: 5496 [→ 4965]. bridle or bit:– bridle [3], Metheg-ammah [1], bit [1]

4965 מֶתֶג הָאַמָּה *meteg hā'ammâ*, n.pr.loc. GK: 5497 [→ 4964+1886.1+538]. Metheg Ammah:– Metheg Ammah [1]

4966 מָתוֹק *mātôq*, a. GK: 5498 [→ 4985]. sweet, sweetness; by extension: pleasant, delightful:– sweet [8], sweeter [2], sweetness [2]

4967 מְתוּשָׁאֵל *mᵉtûšā'ēl*, n.pr.m. GK: 5499 [→ 4191+7945+410]. Methushael, "*[perhaps] man of God*":– Methusael [2]

4968 מְתוּשֶׁלַח *mᵉtûšelaḥ*, n.pr.m. GK: 5500 [→ 4962+7971?]. Methuselah, "*man of the javelin*":– Methuselah [6]

4969 מָתַח *mātaḥ*, v. GK: 5501 [→ 572]. [Q] to spread out:– spreadeth out [1]

4970 מָתַי *mātay*, adv.inter. GK: 5503. How long?; When?:– how long (+5704) [28], when [12], for how long (+5704) [1], when (+310) [1], when (+3807.1) [1]

מְתִים *mᵉtîm*. See 4962.

4971 מַתְכֹּנֶת *matkōnet*, n.f. GK: 5504 [→ 8505]. measure, formula:– composition [2], measure [1], state [1], tale [1]

4972 מַתְלָאָה *mattᵉlā'â*, p.indef.+n.f. GK: 5505 [→ 4100+8513]. what a burden! (4100 + 8513):– weariness [1]

4973 מְתַלְּעוֹת *mᵉtall'ôt*, n.f.pl. GK: 5506 [→ 4459]. jaw; teeth:– cheek-teeth [1], jaw teeth [1], jaws [1]

4974 מְתֹם *mᵉtōm*, n.[m.]. GK: 5507 [→ 8552]. health, soundness:– soundness [3], men [1]

מֶתֶן *meten*. See 4981.

4975 מָתְנַיִם *motnayim*, n.m.du. GK: 5516 [→ 4981?]. (dual) waist, lower back (lumbar region), loins; "girding the loins" involves tucking the skirt of a tunic or robe into the belt, thus preparing for action: running, working, fighting, etc:– loins [42], side [4], greyhound (+2223) [1]

4976 מַתָּן *mattān*, n.m.col. GK: 5508 [→ 4977, 4982, 4983; cf. 5414; cf. 4978]. gift, present:– gift [4], giveth gifts [1]

4977 מַתָּן *mattān*, n.pr.m. GK: 5509 [→ 4976; cf. 5414]. Mattan, "*gift*":– Mattan [3]

4978 מַתְּנָא *mattᵉnā* (Aram.), n.f. GK: 10448 [→ 5415; cf. 4976]. gift:– gifts [3]

4979 מַתָּנָה *mattānâ*, n.f. GK: 5510 [→ 4980; cf. 5414]. gift, something given, such as an offering to deity or a bribe:– gifts [11], gift [5], able (+3027) [1]

4980 מַתָּנָה *mattānâ*, n.pr.loc. GK: 5511 [→ 4979; cf. 5414]. Mattanah, "*gift*":– Mattanah [2]

4981 מִתְנִי *mitnî*, a.g. GK: 5512 [→ 4975?]. Mithnite:– Mithnite [1]

4982 מַתְּנַי *mattᵉnay*, n.pr.m. GK: 5513 [→ 4976+3068]. Mattenai, "*gift*":– Mattenai [3]

4983 מַתַּנְיָה *mattanyâ* or מַתַּנְיָהוּ *mattanyāhû*, n.pr.m. GK: 5514 & 5515 [→ 4976+3068]. Mattaniah, "*gift of Yahweh*":– Mattaniah [16]

מָתְנַיִם *motnayim*. See 4975.

4984 מִתְנַשֵּׂא *mitnaśśē'*, v.ptcp. GK: 5951 [→ 4853, 4853, 4856, 4858, 4864, 5375, 5379, 5385, 5387, 7613, 7721, 7863?, 7865?; cf. 5376]. ptcp. of 5375: lifted up, exalted:–

4985 מָתַק *mātaq*, v. GK: 5517 [→ 4477, 4966, 4986, 4987, 4988, 4989?]. same as 4988: [Q] to be, become sweet; [H] to taste sweet, enjoy sweetness:– sweet [3], made sweet [1], took sweet [1]

4986 מָתֵק *mātēq*, n.m. GK: 5518 [→ 4985]. sweetness; by extension: pleasantness:– sweetness [2]

4987 מֹתֶק *mōteq*, n.[m.]. GK: 5519 [→ 4985]. sweetness:– sweetness [1]

4988 מָתָק *mātāq*, v. GK: 5517 [→ 4985]. same as 4985: [Q] to be, become sweet:– feed sweetly on [1]

4989 מִתְקָה *mitqâ*, n.pr.loc. GK: 5520 [→ 4985?]. Mithcah, "*sweetness*":– Mithcah [2]

4990 מִתְרְדָת *mitrᵉdāt*, n.pr.m. GK: 5521. Mithredath, "*gift to Mithra*":– Mithredath [2]

4991 מַתָּת *mattat*, n.f. GK: 5522 [→ 4993; cf. 5414]. gift, something given:– gift [3], give [2], reward [1]

4992 מַתַּתָּה *mattattâ*, n.pr.m. GK: 5523 [→ 5414]. Mattattah, "*gift*":– Mattathah [1]

4993 מַתִּתְיָה *mattityâ* or מַתִּתְיָהוּ *mattityāhû*, n.pr.m. GK: 5524 & 5525 [→ 4991+3068]. Mattithiah, "*gift of Yahweh*":– Mattithiah [8]

4993.1 ן־ *-ān* or ן־ *-n*, p.f.pl.suf. GK: 5527 [→ 1886.3, 2190]. they, them, their:– their [14], them [11], they [8], thereof [1]

4994 נָא *nā'*, pt. GK: 5528 [→ 577]. often not translated, marks entreaty or exhortation: please!, I beg you!, now!:– now [167], I pray thee [150], I pray you [34], I beseech thee [22], we pray thee [10], we beseech thee [6], oh [5], go to [3], I pray [2], let [2], O [1]

4995 נָא *nā'*, a. GK: 5529. raw (meat):– raw [1]

4996 נֹא *nō'*, n.pr.loc. GK: 5530 [→ 527+4996]. No = Thebes:– no [5]

4996.1 נָא־ *-nā'* (Aram.), p.suf.1.com.pl. GK: 10450 [cf. 5105.1]. we, our:– us [7], our [2], we [1]

4997 נֹאד *nō'd*, n.m. GK: 5532. skin vessel (skinned in one piece, the appendages tied or sewn, the neck the funnel, used to hold liquid):– bottle [4], bottles [2]

נְאֹדְרִי *ne'dārî*. See 142.

4998 נָאָה *nā'â*, v. GK: 5533 [→ 5000; cf. 5115]. [Pilel] to be beautiful, adorn:– beautiful [1], becometh [1], comely [1]

4999 נָוֶה *nāwâ*, n.f. GK: 5661 [→ 5380]. pasture, pastureland; (generally) abode, dwelling, camp, place:– habitations [5], pastures [5], houses [1], pleasant places [1]

5000 נָאוֶה *nā'weh*, a. GK: 5534 [→ 4998]. lovely, fitting, suited:– comely [6], seemly [2], becometh [1]

5001 נָאַם *nā'am*, v.den. GK: 5535 [→ 5002]. [Q] to declare as a prophet:– say [1]

5002 נְאֻם *ne'um*, n.m. GK: 5536 [→ 5001]. declaration, oracle, utterance; often a marker introducing or punctuating prophetic discourse:– saith [366], said [9], spake [1]

5003 נָאַף *nā'ap*, v. GK: 5537 [→ 5005, 5004; cf. 5130]. [Q, P] to commit adultery; [ptcp.] adulterer, adulteress; by extension: to be unfaithful to God (by having illicit relations with other gods):– commit adultery [6], committed adultery [6], adulterers [5], committeth adultery [4], adulterer [3], adulteresses [2], adulteress [2], adulterous [1], break wedlock [1], committing adultery [1]

5004 נָאִפִים *ni'upîm*, n.[m.]. GK: 5539 [→ 5003]. adultery:– adulteries [2]

5005 נַאֲפוּפִים *na'ăpûpîm*, n.[m.pl.]. GK: 5538 [→ 5003]. (marks of) unfaithfulness, adultery; such marks might refer to jewelry or adornments which signal that a woman is available for illicit sex:– adulteries [1]

5006 נָאַץ *nā'aṣ*, v. GK: 5540 [→ 5007]. [Q] to spurn, despise, reject; [P] to treat with contempt, revile, despise; [Htpo] be blasphemed, be reviled:– despised [6], abhorred [5], blasphemed [2], given great occasion to blaspheme (+5006) [2], provoked [2], provoke [2], abhorreth [1], abhor [1], blaspheme [1], contemned [1], contemn [1], despiseth [1], despise [1], provoked unto anger [1]

5007 נְאָצָה *ne'āṣâ* or נֶאָצָה *ne'āṣâ*, n.f. GK: 5541 & 5542 [→ 5006]. disgrace, shame; contemptible things, blasphemies:– blasphemy [2], provocations [2], blasphemies [1]

5008 נָאַק *nā'aq*, v. GK: 5543 [→ 5009; cf. 602]. [Q] to groan:– groan [2]

5009 נְאָקָה *ne'āqâ*, n.f. GK: 5544 [→ 5008; cf. 602]. groaning:– groanings [2], groaning [2]

5010 נָאַר *nā'ar*, v. GK: 5545. [P] to renounce, abandon:– abhorred [1], made void [1]

5011 נֹב *nōb*, n.pr.loc. GK: 5546. Nob:– Nob [6]

5012 נָבָא *nābā'*, v.den. GK: 5547 [→ 5030; cf. 5013]. to prophesy, speak as a prophet; prophecy has its focus on encouraging or restoring covenant faithfulness, the telling of future events encourages obedience or warns against disobedience:– prophesy [68], prophesied [40], prophesieth [3], maketh a prophet [2], prophesying [2]

5013 נְבָא *nebā'* (Aram.), v. GK: 10451 [→ 5017, 5029; cf. 5012]. [Htpa] to prophesy, act as a prophet:– prophesied [1]

5014 נָבַב *nābab*, v. GK: 5554 & 5548. [Q] to hollow out; by extension to be foolish:– hollow [3], vain [1]

5015 נְבוֹ *nebô*, n.pr.m. & loc. GK: 5549 & 5550 & 5551 [→ (used with compound proper names)]. Nebo (pagan god), Nebo (loc.), "*height* or *Mount of Nabu [Nebo]*":– Nebo [13]

5016 נְבוּאָה *nebû'â*, n.f. GK: 5553 [→ 5030; cf. 5017]. prophecy, the word of the prophet; prophecy has its focus on encouraging or restoring covenant faithfulness, the telling of future events encourages obedience or warns against disobedience:– prophecy [3]

5017 נְבוּאָה *nebû'â* (Aram.), n.f. GK: 10452 [→ 5013; cf. 5016]. prophesying, preaching:– prophesying [1]

5018 נְבוּזַרְאֲדָן *nebûzar'ădān* or נְבוּזַר־אֲדָן *nebûzar-'ădān*, n.pr.m. GK: 5555 [→ 5015+2232]. Nebuzaradan, "*Nebo [Nabu] has given seed [offspring]*":– Nebuzar-adan [15]

5019 נְבוּכַדְנֶאצַּר *nebûkadne'ṣṣar* or נְבוּכַדְנֶצּוֹר *nebûkadneṣṣôr* or נְבוּכַדְרֶאצַּר *nebûkadre'ṣṣar* or נְבוּכַדְרֶאצּוֹר *nebûkadre'ṣṣar* or נְבֻכַדְרֶאצֹּר *nebukadre'ṣṣôr*, n.pr.m. GK: 5556 & 5557 [→ 5015; cf. 5020]. Nebuchadnezzar, Nebuchadrezzar, "*Nebo protect my boundary stone; Nebo protect my son!*":– Nebuchadrezzar [31], Nebuchadnezzar [29]

5020 נְבוּכַדְנֶצַּר *nebûkadneṣṣar* (Aram.), n.pr.m. GK: 10453 [cf. 5019]. Nebuchadnezzar, "*Nebo protect my boundary stone or Nebo protect my son!*":– Nebuchadnezzar [31]

5021 נְבוּשַׁזְבָּן *nebûšazbān* or נְבוּשַׁז־בָּן *nebûšaz-bān*, n.pr.m. GK: 5558 [→ 5015]. Nebushazban, "*Nebo [Nabu] save me!*":– Nebushazban [1]

5022 נָבוֹת *nābôt*, n.pr.m. GK: 5559. Naboth, "*sprout*":– Naboth [22]

5023 נְבִזְבָּה *nebizbâ* (Aram.), n.f. GK: 10454. present, gift; this can be a gift given as a recompense for a proper service, a reward:– rewards [2]

5024 נָבַח *nābaḥ*, v. GK: 5560 [→ 5025?]. [Q] to bark:– bark [1]

5025 נֹבַח *nōbaḥ*, n.pr.m. & loc. GK: 5561 & 5562 [→ 5024?]. Nobah, "*barking*":– Nobah [3]

5026 נִבְחַז *nibḥaz*, n.pr.[m.]. GK: 5563. Nibhaz (pagan god):– Nibhaz [1]

5027 נָבַט *nābaṭ*, v. GK: 5564 [→ 4007, 5028]. [P] to look at; [H] to look at, gaze at, consider:– look [21], looked [11], behold [9], consider [5], regard [4], see [4], looketh [3], have respect [2], look down [2], beheld (+413) [1], beheld [1], beholdest [1], cause to behold [1], look upon [1], looked about [1], lookest [1], respect [1]

5028 נְבָט *nebāṭ*, n.pr.m. GK: 5565 [→ 5027]. Nebat, "*look to, regard [approvingly]*":– Nebat [25]

5029 נְבִיא *nebî'* (Aram.), n.m. GK: 10455 [→ 5013; cf. 5030]. prophet, one who speaks for God in inspired utterance, often including the application of the message:– prophets [2], prophet [2]

5030 נָבִיא *nābî'*, n.m. GK: 5566 [→ 5012, 5016, 5031; cf. 5029]. prophet (true or false):– prophet [165], prophets [147], prophecy [1], prophesy [1], prophet's [1]

5031 נְבִיאָה *nebî'â*, n.f. GK: 5567 [→ 5030]. prophetess (true or false):– prophetess [6]

5032 נְבָיוֹת *nebāyôt*, n.pr.g. GK: 5568. Nebaioth:– Nebajoth [5]

5033 נֵבֶךְ *nēbek*, n.[m.]. GK: 5569. source springs (of the sea):– springs [1]

5034 נָבֵל *nābēl*, v. GK: 5570 & 5571 [→ 5036, 5037, 5038, 5039, 5040?]. [Q] to wither, shrivel, fade, decay; to play the fool, act disdainfully; [P] to treat with contempt, dishonor, reject:– fadeth [3], fade [3], fade away [2], fadeth away [2], fading [2], surely wear away (+5034) [2], wither [2], cometh to nought [1], disgrace [1], dishonoureth [1], done foolishly [1], fall down [1], falleth off [1], falling [1], lightly esteemed [1], make vile [1]

5035 נֵבֶל *nēbel*, n.m. GK: 5574 & 5575 [→ 3999]. (wine) skin; water jar, jug, pot (of clay); lyre, harp (stringed instrument):– psalteries [14], psaltery [8], bottle [5], bottles [3], viols [2], viol [2], flagons [1], pitchers [1], psaltery (+3627) [1], vessel [1]

5036 נָבָל *nābāl*, a. GK: 5572 [→ 5037; cf. 5034]. foolish, lacking understanding, (n.) fool; often pertaining to insolence, pride, and disobedience to God:– foolish [7], fool [7], fools [2], vile person [2]

5037 נָבָל *nābāl*, n.pr.m. GK: 5573 [→ 5036; cf. 5034]. Nabal, "*fool*":– Nabal [18], Nabal's [4]

5038 נְבֵלָה *nebēlâ*, n.f. GK: 5577 [→ 5034]. dead body, carcass:– carcase [28], carcases [7], dead body [3], dead bodies [2], dieth of itself [2], beast that dieth of itself [1], body [1], dead carcase [1], that is dead of itself [1], that which died of itself [1], that which dieth of itself [1]

5039 נְבָלָה *nebālâ*, n.f. GK: 5576 [→ 5034]. (very) wicked thing, disgraceful thing; vileness, something a fool would do:– folly [10], villany [2], vile [1]

5040 נַבְלוּת *nablût*, n.f. GK: 5578 [→ 5034?]. (female) genitals:– lewdness [1]

5041 נְבַלָּט *neballāṭ*, n.pr.loc. GK: 5579. Neballat:– Neballat [1]

5042 נָבַע *nāba'*, v. GK: 5580 [→ 76, 4002]. [H] to gush forth, bubble out, spew forth:– utter [3], poureth out [2], abundantly utter [1], belch out [1], cause to send forth [1], flowing [1], pour out [1], uttereth [1]

5043 נֶבְרְשָׁה *nebreśâ* (Aram.), n.f.emph. GK: 10456. lampstand:– candlestick [1]

5044 נִבְשָׁן *nibšān*, n.pr.loc. GK: 5581. Nibshan:– Nibshan [1]

5045 נֶגֶב *negeb*, n.[pr.m.]. GK: 5582 [→ 7418]. south, the Negev:– south [88], southward (+1886.5) [13], south side [5], south (+1886.5) [2], south (+4480) [1], southward (+4480) [1], southward (+871.1+1886.1) [1], southward [1]

5046 נָגַד *nāgad*, v. GK: 5583 [→ 5048, 5057; cf. 5047]. [H] to tell, report, inform; [Ho] to be told, have reported to:– told [150], tell [66], declare [45], shew [34], shewed [18], declared [13], sheweth [5], surely tell (+5046) [4], declareth [3], utter [3], certainly declare (+5046) [2], certainly told (+5046) [2], fully been shewed (+5046) [2], messenger [2], report [2], shew forth [2], telleth [2], told plainly (+5046) [2], uttered [2], another [1], bewrayeth [1], certify [1], declaring [1], denounce [1], expounded [1], expound [1], profess [1], rehearsed [1], sheweth forth [1], speaketh [1]

5047 נְגַד *negad* (Aram.), v. GK: 10457 [→ 5049; cf. 5046]. [P] to flow:– issued [1]

5048 נֶגֶד *neged*, subst. & adv. & pp. GK: 5584 [→ 5046; cf. 5049]. before, in front of, opposite of, beyond:– before [59], before (+3807.1) [18], over against [16], against [6], in (+3807.1) [4], in the presence [4], over against (+3807.1) [4], presence [4], before (+4480) [3], from (+4480) [3], over against (+4480) [3], against (+4480) [2], meet for (+3509.1) [2], straight before [2], view (+4480) [2], about [1], afar off (+4480) [1], against (+3807.1) [1], aloof from (+4480) [1], before (+6440) [1], far (+4480) [1], far off (+4480) [1], in presence [1], in the sight [1], in [1], of (+4480) [1], on the other side (+4480) [1], other side [1], over (+3807.1) [1], over [1], right against [1], sight [1], withstand (+5975) [1], withstood (+5975+3807.1) [1]

5049 נֶגֶד *neged* (Aram.), pp. GK: 10458 [→ 5047; cf. 5048]. toward, before, facing:– toward [1]

5050 נָגַהּ *nāgah*, v. GK: 5585 [→ 5051, 5052, 5054]. [Q] to shine; [H] to cause to shine, give light:– shine [2], cause to shine [1], enlighten [1], lighten [1], shined [1]

5051 נֹגַהּ *nōgah*, n.f. GK: 5586 [→ 5052; cf. 5050; cf. 5053]. brightness, radiance, splendor, brilliance:– brightness [11], shining [5], bright [1], clear shining [1], light [1]

5052 נֹגַהּ *nōgah*, n.pr.m. GK: 5587 [→ 5051; cf. 5050]. Nogah, "*joy, splendor*":– Nogah [2]

5053 נְגַהּ *negah* (Aram.), n.[f.]. GK: 10459 [cf. 5051]. brightness (i.e., first light of dawn):– morning [1]

5054 נְגֹהָה *negōhâ*, n.f. GK: 5588 [→ 5050]. brightness, luster:– brightness [1]

5055 נָגַח *nāgaḥ*, v. GK: 5590 [→ 5056]. [Q] to gore (a bull into a person); [P] to gore, push back, butt; to engage in pushing back, butting, thrusting:– push [5], gored [1], push down [1], pushing [1], pusht [1]

5056 נַגָּח *naggāḥ*, a. GK: 5591 [→ 5055]. (the act of) goring (a bull into a person):– used to push [1], wont to push with his horn [1]

5057 נָגִיד *nāgîd*, n.m. GK: 5592 [→ 5046]. leader, ruler, official, officer:– ruler [18], prince [8], captain [5], leader [3], captains [1], chief governor [1], chief ruler [1], excellent things [1], governor [1], leaders [1], nobles [1], princes [1], rulers [1]

5058 נְגִינָה *negînâ*, n.f. GK: 5593 [→ 5059]. stringed instrument; song that mocks, taunts:– Neginoth [6], song [4], Neginah [1], musick [1], songs [1], stringed instruments [1]

5059 נָגַן *nāgan*, v. GK: 5594 [→ 4485, 5058]. [Q] to play a stringed instrument, (n.) musician; [P] to play a stringed instrument:– played [4], play [3], minstrel [2], melody [1], play on an instrument [1], players on instruments [1], player [1], playing [1], sing the stringed instruments [1]

5060 נָגַע *naga'*, v. GK: 5595 [→ 5061]. [Q] to touch; to strike; [Qp] to be plagued, be stricken; [N] to let oneself be driven back (in a battle); [P] to inflict, afflict; [Pu] to be plagued; [H] to extend, reach out, cause to touch; ranging in meaning from simple contact to violence:– toucheth [37], touch [31], touched [24], come [10], came [6], reacheth [4], reach [4], plagued [3], reaching [3], smote [3], bring [2], happeneth [2], beaten [1], bring down [1], bringeth [1], brought down [1], cast [1], come close [1], come nigh [1], cometh [1], draw near [1], draw nigh [1], draweth near [1], draweth nigh [1], drew near [1], getteth up [1], join [1], laid [1], near [1], reached [1], smitten [1], stricken [1], strike [1]

5061 נֶגַע *nega'*, n.m. GK: 5596 [→ 5060]. plague, blow (of various kinds); mildew, infection, sores, scourge, disaster:– plague [64], sore [5], stroke [4], stripes [2], plagues [1], stricken [1], wound [1]

5062 נָגַף *nāgap*, v. GK: 5597 [→ 4046, 5063]. [Q] to strike, afflict (with a plague); [N] to be defeated:– smitten [12], smite [9], smote [6], put to the worse [5], hurt [2], plagued [2], slain [2], smitten down (+5062) [1], smitten down [2], stumble [2], beaten [1], dash [1], plague [1], strake [1], struck [1]

5063 נֶגֶף *negep*, n.m. GK: 5598 [→ 5062]. plague; stumbling (caused by a stone):– plague [6], stumbling [1]

5064 נָגַר *nāgar*, v. GK: 5599 [cf. 1641]. [N] to be spilled, flow; [H] to pour out, hand over, deliver over; [Ho] to be poured down (a slope):– fall [1], flow away [1], pour down [1], pour out [1], poured [1], poureth out [1], ran [1], shed [1], spilt [1], trickleth down [1]

5065 נָגַשׂ *nāgaś*, v. GK: 5601 [cf. 5066]. [Q] to oppress, exploit, (n.) a slave driver; [N] to be oppressed, be hard pressed:– oppressor [5], taskmasters [5], exact [3], distressed [2], oppressed [2], oppressors [2], driver [1], exacted [1], exactors [1], taxes [1]

5066 נָגַשׁ *nāgaš*, v. GK: 5602 [cf. 5065]. [Q] to come near, approach; [N] to come near, approach; [H] to bring forth, present; [Ho] to be brought, be presented; [Ht] to draw near, assemble:– came near [17], come near [16], came [9], brought [8], come nigh [7], bring hither [6], come [6], drew near [6], draw near [5], approach [4], bring [4], offer [4], brought near [3], drew nigh [3], went near [3], bring forth [2], bring near [2], offered [2], overtake [2], approached nigh [1], brought forth [1], brought thither [1], came nigh [1], cause to come near [1], give place [1], go near [1], go [1], make to approach [1], near [1], offereth [1], presented [1], put [1], stand [1], went hard [1], went nigh [1]

5067 נֵד *nēd*, n.m. GK: 5603. heap, wall, barrier, dam:– heap [6]

5068 נָדַב *nādab*, v. GK: 5605 [→ 5070, 5071, 5081, 5082; cf. 5069 (also used with compound proper names)]. [Q] to be willing; to prompt, incite; [Ht] to willingly offer oneself, volunteer, give a freewill offering:– willingly offered [6], offered willingly [4], made willing [2], offer willingly [2], giveth willingly [1], offered freely [1], willing [1]

5069 נְדַב *nᵉdab* (Aram.), v. GK: 10461 [cf. 5068]. [Htpa] to be willing, to give freely; (as noun) a freewill offering:– freely offered [1], freewill offering [1], minded of own freewill [1], offering willingly [1]

5070 נָדָב *nādāb*, n.pr.m. GK: 5606 [→ 5072; cf. 5068]. Nadab, *"volunteer, free will offering"*:– Nadab [20]

5071 נְדָבָה *nᵉdābâ*, n.f. GK: 5607 [→ 5068]. free, voluntary; freewill offering:– freewill offering [8], freewill offerings [7], free offerings [2], freely (+871.1) [1], freely [1], plentiful [1], voluntarily [1], voluntary offering [1], voluntary [1], willing offering (+3807.1) [1], willing [1]

5072 נְדַבְיָה *nᵉdabyâ*, n.pr.m. GK: 5608 [→ 5070]. Nedabiah, *"Yahweh volunteers"*:– Nedabiah [1]

5073 נִדְבָּךְ *nidbāk* (Aram.), n.m. GK: 10462. course (of timber or stone in building):– rows [1], row [1]

5074 נָדַד *nādad*, v. GK: 5610 [→ 5076; cf. 5077, 5110; cf. 5075]. [Q] to flee, be a fugitive; to wander, stray; [Pol] to flee away; [H] to banish, put to flight; [Ho] to be banished, be cast aside:– fled [3], wandereth [4], flee apace (+5074) [2], flee away [2], chased away [1], chased [1], could not [1], departed [1], flee [1], moved [1], removed [1], thrust away [1], wanderers [1], wandereth abroad [1], wandering [1], wander [1]

5075 נְדַד *nᵉdad* (Aram.), v. GK: 10463 [cf. 5111; cf. 5074]. [P] to flee (i.e., sleep flees = insomnia):– went [1]

5076 נָדֻדִים *nᵉdudîm*, n.m.pl. GK: 5611 [→ 5074]. tossing and turning, restlessness (in bed in the night):– tossings to and fro [1]

5077 נָדָא *nādā'* or נָדָה *nādâ*, v. GK: 5604 & 5612 [→ 5079, 5206; cf. 5074, 5110]. [P] to exclude; to put off thoughts, suppose to be far off; [H] detach, remove from:– cast out [1], put far away [1]

5078 נֵדֶה *nēdeh*, n.m. GK: 5613. gift, reward; likely referring to a fee for service:– gifts [1]

5079 נִדָּה *niddâ*, n.f. GK: 5614 [→ 5206; cf. 5077]. period of menstruation; (water used in) cleansing, "unclean" water; (act of) impurity, corruption, defilement:– separation [14], filthiness [2], flowers [2], menstruous [2], put apart [2], far [1], removed woman [1], removed [1], that was set apart [1], unclean thing [1], uncleanness [1], unclean [1]

5080 נָדַח *nādaḥ*, v. GK: 5615 & 5616 [→ 4065; cf. 1740, 1760]. [Q] to wield (an ax); (to have hand) be put (to the ax); [N] to be scattered, be exiled, be outcast; [Pu] be thrust into; [H] to cause to scatter, banish, drive out; to bring; [Ho] to be driven, be hunted:– driven [15], driven away [4], driven out [4], outcasts [4], cast out [3], drive [3], banished [2], drive out [2], bring [1], cast down [1], chased [1], compelled [1], drave [1], drawn away [1], expelled [1], fetcheth a stroke [1], forced [1], forcing [1], go astray [1], outcast [1], thrust away [1], thrust [1], withdrawn [1]

5081 נָדִיב *nādîb*, a. (used as noun). GK: 5618 [→ 5082; cf. 5068]. willing, generous; prince, noble, ruler, official:– princes [10], nobles [4], prince [4], willing [3], free [2], liberal [2], prince's [1]

5082 נְדִיבָה *nᵉdîbâ*, n.f. GK: 5619 [→ 5081; cf. 5068]. something noble; dignity, nobility:– liberal [2], soul [1]

5083 נָדָן *nādān*, n.m. GK: 5621 [cf. 5414]. gift, wages of illicit sexual favors:– gifts [1]

5084 נָדָן *nādān*, n.m. GK: 5620 [cf. 5085]. sheath (of a sword):– sheath [1]

5085 נִדְנֶה *nidneh* (Aram.), n.m. GK: 10464. sheath (of the spirit = the body):– body [1]

5086 נָדַף *nādap*, v. GK: 5622. [Q] to blow away, scatter; [N] to be windblown, be fleeting:– driven away [2], drive away [1], driven to and fro [1], driven [1], driveth away [1], shaken [1], thrusteth down [1], tossed to and fro [1]

5087 נָדַר *nādar*, v. GK: 5623 [→ 5088; cf. 5144, 5145]. [Q] to make a vow:– vowed [16], vow [10], vowest [2], made [1], vowedst [1], voweth [1]

5088 נֶדֶר *nēder*, n.m. GK: 5624 [→ 5087]. vow:– vows [30], vow [28], make a singular vow (+6381) [1], vowed [1]

5089 נֹהַ *nōah*, n.[m.]. GK: 5625. value, distinction:– wailing [1]

5089.1 נָה *-nâ*, p.f.s.suf. GK: 5626 [→ 1886.3]. her; it, its:– it [121], her [27], the same [11], them [9], she [5], thereof (+4480) [3], they [3], thence [2], therefrom (+4480) [2], thereof [2], by themselves (+905+3807.1) [1], their [1], therein [1], thereon [1], these things [1], this [1]

5090 נָהַג *nāhag*, v. GK: 5627 & 5628 [→ 4491, cf. 5101]. [Q] to drive, lead, guide; [Qp] to be led; [P] to drive, lead forth, guide; to moan, sob, lament:– lead [7], drave [4], carried away [3], brought [2], lead away [2], led forth [2], led [2], acquainting [1], brought away [1], brought in [1], drive away [1], driveth [1], drive [1], guided [1], guide [1], leadest [1]

5091 נָהָה *nāhâ*, v. GK: 5629 & 5630 [→ 5092, 5093, 5204]. [Q] to mourn, wail; [N] to be taunted (with a mournful song); to keep close, stay loyal:– lamented [1], lament [1], wail [1]

5092 נְהִי *nᵉhî*, n.[m.]. GK: 5631 [→ 5204; cf. 5091]. wailing, mourning, often related to mournful songs: lamentation:– wailing [4], lamentation [2]

5093 נִהְיָה *nihyâ*, n.f. GK: 5632 [→ 5091]. wailing, lamentation, mourning:– doleful lamentation [1]

5094 נְהִיר *nᵉhîr* or נְהִירוּ *nahîrû* (Aram.), n.m. GK: 10466 & 10467 [cf. 5105]. light; insight, illumination (of the mind):– light [3]

5095 נָהַל *nāhal*, v. GK: 5633 [→ 5096, 5097]. [P] guide, bring along, lead; [Ht] to move along:– guide [3], guided [2], carried [1], fed [1], gently lead [1], lead on [1], leadeth [1]

5096 נַהֲלָל *nahᵃlāl* or נַהֲלֹל *nahᵃlōl*, n.pr.loc. GK: 5634 & 5636 [→ 5095, 5097]. Nahalal, Nahalol, *"watering place"*:– Nahalal [1], Nahallal [1], Nahalol [1]

5097 נַהֲלֹל *nahᵃlōl*, n.m. GK: 5635 [→ 5096; cf. 5095]. watering hole:– bushes [1]

5098 נָהַם *nāham*, v. GK: 5637 [→ 5099, 5100; cf. 1949, 1993, 2000]. [Q] to growl, roar; to groan:– mourn [2], roar [2], roaring [1]

5099 נַהַם *naham*, n.[m.]. GK: 5638 [→ 5098]. roaring, growling:– roaring [2]

5100 נְהָמָה *nᵉhāmâ*, n.f. GK: 5639 [→ 5098]. roaring, growling; anguish, groaning:– disquietness [1], roaring [1]

5101 נָהַק *nāhaq*, v. GK: 5640 [cf. 5090]. [Q] to bray (of a donkey):– brayed [1], bray [1]

5102 נָהַר *nāhar*, v. GK: 5641 & 5642 [→ 5104, 5105; cf. 5216]. [Q] to stream (like a river flow); to be radiant (with joy), beam (with joy):– flow [5], lightened [1]

5103 נְהַר *nᵉhar* (Aram.), n.m. GK: 10468 [cf. 5104]. river, stream:– river [14], stream [1]

5104 נָהָר *nāhār*, n.m. GK: 5643 [→ 763, 5102; cf. 5103]. river, stream, canal; the River, which can refer to the Euphrates, Tigris, or Nile:– river [67], rivers [31], floods [10], flood [8], streams [2], river side [1]

5105 נְהָרָה *nᵉhārâ*, n.f. GK: 5644 [→ 5102; cf. 5094]. (beaming) light:– light [1]

5105.1 נוּ *-nû*, p.com.pl.suf. GK: 5646 [→ 2967.1]. us, our:– us [775], our [749], we [67], our (+3807.1) [13], our own [8], ours (+3807.1) [5], ourselves [4], it [1], ours [1], thereof (+4480) [1], us-ward (+413) [1], we (+5315) [1]

5105.2 נוּ *-nû* or נוֹ *-nô*, p.m.s.suf. GK: 5647 [→ 1886.3]. him, his; it, its:– him [217], it [120], them [36], he [34], thereof (+4480) [16], thereof [12], the same [4], they [4], his [2], themselves, thereat (+4480) [2], every one of them [1], him (+5315) [1], himself [1], theˢ [1], their [1], thence [1], thereby [1], therefrom (+4480) [1], thereout (+4480) [1], therewith [1], which [1], whom (+834) [1], whom [1], whosoever (+834) [1]

5106 נוּא *nû'*, v. GK: 5648 [→ 8569]. [Q] to hinder; [H] to forbid, thwart, discourage:– disallowed [1], disallow [2], break [1], discouraged [1], discourage [1], maketh of none effect [1]

5107 נוּב *nûb*, v. GK: 5649 [→ 1838, 5108, 8570]. [Q] to bring forth, bear fruit, increase; [Pol] to make thrive:– bring forth fruit [1], bringeth forth [1], increase [1], make cheerful [1]

5108 נוֹב *nôb* or נִיב *nîb*, n.[m.]. GK: 5650 & 5762 [→ 5107]. fruit; "fruit of the lips" is praise:– fruit [2]

5109 נוֹבַי *nôbay* or נֵיבַי *nêbāy*, n.pr.m. GK: 5651 & 5763. Nebai, Nobai, *"thrive"*:– Nebai [1]

5110 נוּד *nûd*, v. GK: 5653 [→ 4493, 5112, 5113, 5205; cf. 5074, 5077; cf. 5111]. [Q] to sway, wander, be aimless, become homeless; to mourn, express sympathy (by shaking the head:– bemoan [5], remove [4], vagabond [2], bemoaned [1], bemoaning [1], flee [1], get [1], make move [1], mourn [1], removed [1], shaken [1], skippedst for joy [1], sorry [1], take pity [1], wag [1], wandering [1]

5111 נוּד *nûd* (Aram.), v. GK: 10469 [cf. 5075; cf. 5110]. [P] to flee:– get away [1]

5112 נוֹד *nôd*, n.[m.]. GK: 5654 [→ 5110]. lament; some sources: wandering, homelessness:– wanderings [1]

5113 נוֹד *nôd*, n.pr.loc. GK: 5655 [→ 5110]. Nod, *"wandering"*:– Nod [1]

5114 נוֹדָב *nôdāb*, n.pr.g. GK: 5656. Nodab:– Nodab [1]

5115 נָוָה *nāwâ*, v. GK: 5657 & 5658 [→ 5116; cf. 4998]. [Q] to be at rest, reach one's aim; [H] to praise:– keepeth at home [1], prepare a habitation [1]

5116 נָוֶה *nāweh*, n.m. GK: 5659 & 5660 [→ 5115, 4999; cf. 4998]. dwelling, abiding; pasture, pastureland, with a possible hue that this is a place of rest and peace; (generally) abode, dwelling, house:– habitation [21], fold [3], dwelling [2], sheepcote [2], comely [1], dwelling place [1], dwellings [1], folds [1], habitations [1], pleasant place [1], stable [1], tarried [1]

5117 נוּחַ *nûaḥ*, v. GK: 5663 & 5664 [→ 3240; cf. 584]. [Q] to settle, rest, wait; to lament, wail; [H] to give, place, put, set, settle, rest; to leave, allow; [Ho] to be placed, find rest:– rest [15], given rest [12], rested [7], cause to rest [4], give rest [4], at rest [3], caused to rest [3], gave rest [3], resteth [2], ceased [1], confederate [1], giveth rest [1], lay [1], let down [1], make to rest [1], quieted [1], quiet [1], remain [1], set down [1], set [1]

5118 נוֹחַ *nôaḥ*, n.f. GK: 5665 [→ 5119; cf. 3240]. resting place:– rested [2], resting place [1], rest [1]

5119 נוֹחָה *nôḥâ*, n.pr.m. GK: 5666 [→ 5118?; cf. 3240]. Nohah, *"rest"*:– Nohah [1]

5120 נוּט *nûṭ*, v. GK: 5667. [Q] to shake, quake:– moved [1]

5121 נָווֹת *nāwôt* or נָוִית *nāwît*, n.pr.loc. GK: 5662 & 5668 & 5766. Navoth, Navith, Naioth, *"dwellings"*:– Naioth [6]

5122 נְוָלוּ *n*ᵉ*wālû* (Aram.), n.f. GK: 10470. pile of rubble, garbage-heap:– dunghill [3]

5123 נוּם *nûm*, v. GK: 5670 [→ 3241?, 5124, 8572]. [Q] to sleep, slumber, implying detachment from activities and others; by extension: to be dead:– slumber [5], slept [1]

5124 נוּמָה *nûmâ*, n.f. GK: 5671 [→ 5123]. drowsiness:– drowsiness [1]

5125 נוּן *nûn*, v. GK: 5672 [cf. 5126?]. [N] to propagate, increase:– continued [1]

5126 נוּן *nûn*, n.pr.m. & f. GK: 5673 [cf. 5125?]. Nun, "*fish* hence *fertile, productive*":– Nun [29], Non [1]

5127 נוּס *nûs*, v. GK: 5674 [→ 4498, 4499, 5211]. [Q] to flee away, escape; [Pol] to drive along; [H] to put to flight, get to safety:– fled [80], flee [52], flee away [8], fleeth [5], fled away [3], flee away (+5127) [2], abated [1], displayed [1], fled apace (+4498) [1], fleddest [1], fleeing [1], hide [1], lift up a standard [1], made flee [1], put to flight [1], ran away [1]

5128 נוּעַ *nûa'*, v. GK: 5675 [→ 4517]. [Q] to shake, sway, swagger, wander; [N] to be shaken; [H] to make wander, to set trembling, shake, toss:– moved [5], promoted [3], shaken [3], wandered [3], continually vagabonds (+5128) [2], fugitive [2], reel to and fro (+5128) [2], shake [2], stagger [2], wag [2], wander [2], gone away [1], made wander [1], make [1], moveable [1], move [1], removed [1], scatter [1], set [1], shaked [1], sift [1], sift [1], wander up and down [1]

5129 נוֹעַדְיָה *nô'adyâ*, n.pr.m. & f. GK: 5676 [→ 3259+3068]. Noadiah, "*meet with Yahweh*":– Noadiah [2]

5130 נוּף *nûp*, v. GK: 5677 & 5678 [→ 5299, 5317, 8573; cf. 5003]. [Q] to sprinkle with myrrh (a bed); [Pol] to wave (the fist) threateningly; [H] to wave, present (an offering) by waving; to shake, wield, sweep; to cause (rain) to fall; [Ho] to be waved:– wave [11], shake [5], waved [5], lift up [4], offer [3], offered [2], shaketh [2], move [1], perfumed [1], send [1], sift [1], strike [1]

5131 נוֹף *nôp*, n.[m.]. GK: 5679 [→ 5299, 5316]. loftiness, elevation, height:– situation [1]

5132 נוּץ *nûṣ*, v. GK: 5680. [Q] to leave, go away:– fled away [1]

5133 נֹצָה *nôṣâ* or נוֹצָה *nôṣâ*, n.f. GK: 5901 & 5902 & 5681. contents (of a bird's crop); plumage, feathers; falcon or other bird:– feathers [4]

5134 נוּק *nûq*, v. GK: 5682 [cf. 3243]. [H] to suckle, nurse:– nursed [1]

5135 נוּר *nûr* (Aram.), n.f. & m. GK: 10471 [cf. 5216]. fire; used for heat, purification, and as a form of execution:– fiery [10], fire [7]

5136 נוּשׁ *nûš*, v. GK: 5683 [cf. 605]. [Q] to be sick:– full of heaviness [1]

5137 נָזָה *nāzâ*, v. GK: 5684 & 5685. [Q] to spatter; [H] to sprinkle; to leap, spring:– sprinkle [17], sprinkled [6], sprinkleth [1]

5138 נָזִיד *nāzîd*, n.[m.]. GK: 5686 [→ 2102]. stew, thick boiled food:– pottage [6]

5139 נָזִיר *nāzîr*, n.m. GK: 5687 [→ 5144]. Nazirite, with the designated meaning of separation; a class of people dedicated to God; untended vine, dedicated to God in the sabbatical year of rest:– Nazarite [9], Nazarites [3], vine undressed [2], separate from [1], separated from [1]

5140 נָזַל *nāzal*, v. GK: 5688 & 5689. [Q] to flow down, pour down, stream down; [H] to make flow:– floods [3], streams [2], caused to flow [1], distil [1], drop [1], flow out [1], flowing [1], flow [1], gush out [1], melted [1], pour down [1], pour [1], running waters [1]

5141 נֶזֶם *nezem*, n.m. GK: 5690. ring (in the nose or ear of male or female):– earrings [9], earring [5], jewel [2], jewels [1]

5142 נְזַק *n*ᵉ*zaq* (Aram.), v. GK: 10472 [cf. 5143]. [P] to suffer loss; [H] to cause to suffer, be a detriment, be troublesome:– damage [1], endamage [1], hurtful [1], hurt [1]

5143 נֶזֶק *nēzeq*, n.[m.]. GK: 5691 [cf. 5142]. burden, trouble:– damage [1]

5144 נָזַר *nāzar*, v. GK: 5692 & 5693 [→ 5139, 5145; cf. 4502, 5087]. [N] to separate oneself, consecrate oneself; [H] to keep separate; to abstain, separate as a Nazirite:– separate [4], separateth [3], consecrate [1], separated [1], separating [1]

5145 נֶזֶר *nēzer*, n.m. GK: 5694 [→ 5144; cf. 5087]. separation, dedication (to God); diadem, crown (as a sign of consecration); Nazirite, a class of people dedicated to God:– crown [11], separation [11], consecration [2], hair [1]

5146 נֹחַ *nōaḥ*, n.pr.m. GK: 5695 [→ 5162]. Noah, "*rest, comfort*":– Noah [44], Noah's [2]

5147 נַחְבִּי *naḥbî*, n.pr.m. GK: 5696. Nahbi, "[perhaps] *hidden* or *timid*":– Nahbi [1]

5148 נָחָה *nāḥâ*, v. GK: 5697. [Q, H] to lead, guide:– lead [16], guide [4], led [4], bringeth [2], brought [2], guided [2], leddest [2], bestowed [1], govern [1], leadeth [1], led forth [1], led on [1], put [1], straiteneth [1]

5149 נְחוּם *n*ᵉ*ḥûm*, n.pr.m. GK: 5700 [cf. 7348]. Nehum, "*comfort*":– Nehum [1]

5150 נִחֻמִים *niḥumîm*, n.m.[pl.]. GK: 5719 [→ 5162]. comfort, compassion:– comfortable [1], comforts [1], repentings [1]

5151 נַחוּם *naḥûm*, n.pr.m. GK: 5699 [→ 5162]. Nahum, "*comfort*":– Nahum [1]

5152 נָחוֹר *nāḥôr*, n.pr.m. GK: 5701. Nahor, "*the mound of Nahuru*":– Nahor [15], Nahor's [2], Nachor [1]

5153 נָחוּשׁ *nāḥûš*, a. GK: 5702 [→ 5178]. (made) of bronze:– brass [1]

5154 נְחוּשָׁה *n*ᵉ*ḥûšâ*, n.f. GK: 5703 [→ 5178; cf. 5174]. copper, bronze:– brass [7], steel [3]

5155 נְחִילוֹת *n*ᵉ*ḥîlôt*, n.f. GK: 5704 [→ 2485?; cf. 2490?]. flutes (a t.t. in Ps 5):– Nehiloth [1]

5156 נָחִיר *nāḥîr*, n.[m.]. GK: 5705 [→ 5170, 5170]. (dual) nostrils:– nostrils [1]

5157 נָחַל *nāḥal*, v.den. GK: 5706 [→ 5159]. [Q] to take as an appearance, take possession; [P] to assign an inheritance, allot; [H] to cause to inherit, give an inheritance; [Ho] to be allotted; [Ht] to obtain an inheritance for oneself; to distribute an inheritance:– inherit [16], cause to inherit [5], inherited [3], possess [3], giveth to inherit [2], have inheritance (+5159) [2], cause to possess [1], caused to inherit [1], distribute for inheritance [1], distributed for inheritance [1], divide an inheritance among [1], divide by inheritance [1], divide for an inheritance [1], divide inheritance unto [1], divided for an inheritance [1], divided inheritance [1], divide [1], dividing for inheritance [1], give inheritance [1], given for an inheritance [1], had [1], have inheritance [1], inheritance [1], inheriteth [1], leave for an inheritance [1], leaveth an inheritance [1], made to possess [1], make inherit [1], maketh to inherit [1], possession [1], take as inheritance [1], take for inheritance [1], taken as an heritage [1], took inheritance [1]

5158 נַחַל *naḥal* or נַחְלָה *naḥ*ᵃ*lâ*, n.m. & loc. GK: 5707 & 5711 [→ 5160]. river, stream, brook, torrent; ravine, gorge, valley; wadi (of Egypt):– river [46], brook [37], valley [18], brooks [9], rivers [8], stream [7], valleys [5], streams [4], flood [3], floods [2]

5159 נַחֲלָה *naḥ*ᵃ*lâ*, n.f. GK: 5709 [→ 5157]. inheritance, property:– inheritance [188], heritage [26], have inheritance (+5157) [2], inherit [2], river [2], have inheritance (+5307) [1], heritages [1], inheritances [1], possession [1]

5160 נַחֲלִיאֵל *naḥ*ᵃ*lî'ēl*, n.pr.loc. GK: 5712 [→ 5158+410]. Nahaliel, "*wadi of God [El]*":– Nahaliel [2]

5161 נֶחֶלָמִי *neḥ*ᵉ*lāmî*, a.g. GK: 5713. Nehelamite:– Nehelamite [3]

5162 נָחַם *nāḥam*, v. GK: 5714 [→ 4505, 5146, 5151, 5149, 5163, 5164, 5165, 5166, 5150, 5167, 8575, 8576]. [N] to relent, repent, change one's mind; be grieved; [P] to comfort, console, express sympathy; [Pu] to be comforted, be consoled; [Ht] to console oneself; to change one's mind; avenge oneself:– comfort [32], comforted [20], repent [19], repented [17], comforters [5], comforter [4], comforteth [3], repenteth [3], comfortedst [1], ease [1], receive comfort [1], repentest [1], repenting [1]

5163 נַחַם *naḥam*, n.pr.m. GK: 5715 [→ 5162]. Naham, "*repent, console*":– Naham [1]

5164 נֹחַם *nōḥam*, n.m. GK: 5716 [→ 5162]. compassion, pity:– repentance [1]

5165 נֶחָמָה *neḥāmâ*, n.f. GK: 5717 [→ 5162]. comfort, consolation:– comfort [2]

5166 נְחֶמְיָה *n*ᵉ*ḥemyâ*, n.pr.m. GK: 5718 [→ 5162+3068]. Nehemiah, "*Yahweh has comforted*":– Nehemiah [8]

5167 נַחֲמָנִי *naḥ*ᵃ*mānî*, n.pr.m. GK: 5720 [→ 5162]. Nahamani, "*Yahweh has consoled*":– Nahamani [1]

5168 נַחְנוּ *naḥnû*, p.com.pl. GK: 5721 [→ 587]. we:– we [6]

5169 נָחַץ *nāḥaṣ*, v. GK: 5722 [cf. 3905]. [Qp] to be urgent:– haste [1]

5170 נַחַר *naḥar* or נַחֲרָה *naḥ*ᵃ*râ*, n.m. & f. GK: 5724 & 5725 [→ 5156]. snorting (of a horse):– nostrils [1], snorting [1]

5171 נַחְרַי *naḥray*, n.pr.m. GK: 5726. Naharai:– Naharai [2]

5172 נָחַשׁ *nāḥaš*, v.den. GK: 5727 [→ 5173; cf. 3907]. [P] to practice divination, interpret omens and signs:– certainly divine (+5172) [2], indeed divineth (+5172) [2], used enchantments [1], diligently observe [1], enchanter [1], enchantments [1], learned by experience [1], use enchantment [1]

5173 נַחַשׁ *naḥaš*, n.[m.]. GK: 5728 [→ 5172]. sorcery, magic curse, spell:– enchantments [1], enchantment [1]

5174 נְחָשׁ *n*ᵉ*ḥāš* (Aram.), n.m. GK: 10473 [cf. 5154, 5178]. bronze material; "brass" is a copper alloy dating from Roman times:– brass [9]

5175 נָחָשׁ *nāḥāš*, n.m. GK: 5729 [→ 5176, 5177]. snake, serpent; by extension: a mythological creature of chaos opposed to God:– serpent [25], serpents [4], serpent's [2]

5176 נָחָשׁ *nāḥāš*, n.pr.m. GK: 5731 [→ 5175]. Nahash, "*viper*" or "*copper*":– Nahash [9]

נְחֻשָׁה *n*ᵉ*ḥušâ*. See 5154.

5177 נַחְשׁוֹן *naḥšôn*, n.pr.m. GK: 5732 [→ 5175]. Nahshon, "*small viper*":– Nahshon [9], Naashon [1]

5178 נְחֹשֶׁת *n*ᵉ*ḥōšet*, n.m. GK: 5733 & 5734 [→ 5153, 5154; cf. 5180; cf. 5174]. copper, bronze; this can refer to bronze as a medium of exchange; menstruation:– brass [101], brasen [28], fetters [2], chains [2], fetters of brass [2], chain [1], copper [1], filthiness [1], steel [1]

5179 נְחֻשְׁתָּא *n*ᵉ*ḥuštā'*, n.pr.f. GK: 5735. Nehushta, "*[strong as* or *color of] bronze*":– Nehushta [1]

5180 נְחֻשְׁתָּן *n*ᵉ*ḥuštān*, n.pr. GK: 5736 [cf. 5178]. Nehushtan, "*bronze viper*":– Nehushtan [1]

5181 נָחַת *nāḥat*, v. GK: 5737 [→ 5183, 5185; cf. 8478; cf. 5182]. [Q] to descend, go down; [N] to be pierced, penetrate; [P] to bend (a bow); to level off; [H] to bring down:– broken [2], cause to come down [1], come down [1], entereth [1], presseth sore (+5921) [1], settlest [1], stick fast [1]

5182 נְחַת *n*ᵉ*ḥat* (Aram.), v. GK: 10474 [cf. 5181]. [P] to come down; [H, A] to deposit, store; [Ho] to be deposited:– came down [1], carry [1], coming down [1], deposed [1], laid up [1], place [1]

5183 נַחַת *naḥat*, n.f. & m. GK: 5738 & 5739 [→ 5181, 5184; cf. 3240]. coming down, descending; rest, peace, tranquillity:– rest [4], lighting down [1], quietness [1], quiet [1], that which be set on [1]

5184 נַחַת *naḥat*, n.pr.m. GK: 5740 [→ 5183; cf. 3240]. Nahath, "*descent*; [poss.] *rest*":– Nahath [5]

5185 נָחֵת *nāḥēt*, a. GK: 5741 [→ 5181]. going down, descending:– come down [1]

5186 נָטָה *nāṭâ*, v. GK: 5742 [→ 4294, 4295, 4296, 4297, 4298]. [Q] to spread out, stretch out; [Qp] to be outstretched, be spread out, be extended; [N] to be spread out, be stretched out; [H] to turn aside, pervert, lead astray; [Ho] to be outspread:– stretched out [37], stretch out [25], incline [15], inclined [13], stretched forth [9], turn aside [9], turned [9], pitched [8], turn [7], bowed [5], spread [5], stretch forth [5], bow down [4], stretcheth out [4], declined [3], decline [3], outstretched [3], turned aside [3], turned away [3], wrest [3], bow [2], carried aside [2], declineth [2], extended [2], pervert [2], stretcheth forth [2], afternoon (+3117+1886.1) [1], apply [1], bowing down [1], bowing [1], caused to yield [1], deliver [1], extend [1], go down [1], goeth down [1], intended [1], laid [1], lay down [1], let down [1], offer [1], overthrow [1], perverted [1], perverteth [1], prolong [1], put away [1], shewed [1], spread forth [1], spreadeth out [1], stretchedst out [1], stretched [1], stretchest out [1], stretch [1], took aside [1], turn away [1], turned in [1], turneth aside [1], turneth [1]

5187 נָטִיל *nāṭîl*, a. GK: 5744 [→ 5190]. weighing (of precious metals); by extension, trading: buying, selling, and bartering:– bear [1]

5188 נְטִפָה *n*ᵉ*ṭipâ*, n.[f.]. GK: 5755 [→ 5197]. pendant, a drop-shaped ornament:– chains [1], collars [1]

5189 נְטִישׁוֹת *n*ᵉ*ṭîšôt*, n.f. GK: 5746 [→ 5203]. spreading branches, tendrils:– battlements [1], branches [1], plants [1]

5190 נָטַל *nāṭal*, v. GK: 5747 [→ 5187, 5192; cf. 5191]. [Q] to lay upon; to weigh; [P] to lift:– bare [1], borne [1], offer [1], taketh up [1]

5191 נְטַל *n*ᵉ*ṭal* (Aram.), v. GK: 10475 [cf. 5190]. [P] to raise up, lift up; [Peil] to be lifted up:– lift up [1], lifted up [1]

5192 נֵטֶל *nēṭel*, n.[m.]. GK: 5748 [→ 5190]. burden, load:– weighty [1]

5193 נָטַע *nāṭa'*, v. GK: 5749 [→ 4302, 5195, 5194, 5196]. [Q] to plant (seed or stock); by extension: to place, set, set up (any object on any surface):– plant [31], planted [21], plantedst [2], planteth [2], fastened [1], planters [1]

5194 נֶטַע *neṭa'*, n.[m.]. GK: 5750 [→ 5193]. garden, plants; young plant:– plant [3], plants [1]

5195 נְטִיעַ *nāṭîa'*, n.[m.]. GK: 5745 [→ 5193]. shoot (of a young plant):– plants [1]

5196 נְטָעִים *nᵉṭā'îm*, n.pr.loc. GK: 5751 [→ 5193]. Netaim:– plants [1]

5197 נָטַף *nāṭap*, v. GK: 5752 [→ 2903, 5188, 5198, 5199, 5200]. [Q] to pour down; gently fall, drip; [H] to (drip words) preach, prophesy:– drop [6], dropped [5], prophesy [4], drop down [1], dropping [1], prophet [1]

5198 נָטָף *nāṭāp*, n.[m.]. GK: 5753 & 5754 [→ 5197]. gum resin, drops of stacte (the resin of a shrub); drop (of water):– drops [1], stacte [1]

5199 נְטֹפָה *nᵉṭōpâ*, n.pr.loc. GK: 5756 [→ 5200; cf. 5197]. Netophah, "*trickle, drip*":– Netophah [2]

5200 נְטֹפָתִי *nᵉṭōpātî*, a.g. GK: 5743 [→ 5199; cf. 5197]. Netophathite, "*of Netophah*":– Netophathite [8], Netophathites [2], Netophathi [1]

5201 נָטַר *nāṭar*, v. GK: 5757 [→ 4307; cf. 5341]. [Q] to care for, tend; to be angry, harbor a grudge:– keep [3], bear any grudge against [1], keepers [1], keeper [1], kept [1], reserveth [1], reserve [1]

5202 נְטַר *nᵉṭar* (Aram.), v. GK: 10476 [cf. 5341]. [P] to keep (in one's mind or heart):– kept [1]

5203 נָטַשׁ *nāṭaš*, v. GK: 5759 [→ 5189]. [Q] to abandon, forsake, reject; [Qp] to be scattered; [N] to spread out; to be deserted; [Pu] to be abandoned:– forsake [7], left [7], forsaken [6], leave [5], spread [3], forsook [2], cast off [1], drawn [1], fall [1], joined [1], leave off [1], lie still [1], loosed [1], spread abroad [1], stretched out [1], suffered [1]

5204 נִי *nî*, n.[m.]. GK: 5760 [→ 5092; cf. 5091]. wailing:– wailing [1]

5204.1 נִי- *-nî*, p.com.s.suf. GK: 5761 [→ 2967.1]. I, me, my:– me [1072], I [217], my [7], us [3], myself [2], it [1], let me [1], mine (+4480) [1], mine [1], send me [1]

5204.2 נִי- *-nî* (Aram.), p.suf.1.com.s. GK: 10477 [→ 2967.2; cf. 5204.1]. I, me, my:– me [18]

5205 נִיד *nîd*, n.m. GK: 5764 [→ 5110]. comfort:– moving [1]

5206 נִידָה *nîdâ*, n.f. GK: 5765 [→ 5079; cf. 5077]. uncleanness, impurity:– removed [1]

5207 נִיחֹחַ *nîḥōaḥ*, n.[m.]. GK: 5767 [→ 3240; cf. 5208]. pleasing, soothing, appeasing:– sweet [42], sweet odours [1]

5208 נִיחֹחַ *nîḥōaḥ* (Aram.), n.[m.]. GK: 10478 [cf. 5207]. incense, pleasing scent:– sweet odours [1], sweet savours [1]

5209 נִין *nîn*, n.[m.]. GK: 5769. offspring, children, posterity:– son [3]

5210 נִינְוֵה *nînᵉwēh*, n.pr.loc. GK: 5770. Nineveh:– Nineveh [17]

5211 נִיס *nîs*, n.m. or v. GK: 5771 [→ 5127]. flight, fleeing:–

5212 נִיסָן *nîsān*, n.pr. GK: 5772. Nisan:– Nisan [2]

5213 נִיצֹץ *nîṣôṣ*, n.[m.]. GK: 5773 [→ 5340]. spark:– spark [1]

5214 נִיר *nîr*, v. GK: 5774 [→ 5215]. [Q] to break up, bring into cultivation:– break up [2]

5215 נִיר *nîr*, n.[m.]. GK: 5776 [→ 5214]. unplowed ground, likely referring to ground not plowed for the current season:– fallow ground [1], plowing [1], tillage [1]

5216 נִיר *nîr* or נֵר *nēr*, n.m. GK: 5775 & 5944 [→ 74, 4501, 5369, 5374; cf. 5102; cf. 5135]. lamp (fueled by olive oil); by extension: life (as a burning lamp); light (showing the way of truth):– lamps [26], lamp [9], candle [8], light [4], candles [1]

5217 נָכָא *nākā'*, v. GK: 5777 [→ 5218, 5219?; cf. 5221]. [N] to be driven out (by whipping or scourging):– viler [1]

5218 נָכָא *nākā'* or נָכֵא *nākē'*, a. GK: 5778 & 5779 [→ 5217]. crushed, beaten, broken; grieving (as one unmercifully beaten):– broken [2], stricken [1], wounded [1]

5219 נְכֹאת *nᵉkō't*, n.f. GK: 5780 [→ 5217?]. spices, resin:– spicery [1], spices [1]

5220 נֶכֶד *neked*, n.m. GK: 5781. descendant, progeny:– nephew [2], son's son [1]

5221 נָכָה *nākâ*, v. GK: 5782 [→ 4347, 5223, 5222; cf. 5217]. [N] to be struck; [Pu] to be destroyed; [H] to kill, slaughter, destroy, defeat; [Ho] to be beat, be struck, be wounded, be killed:– smote [193], smite [95], slew [57], smitten [42], slain [21], killeth [11], smiteth [11], slay [8], slaughter [5], smiting [5], beaten [4], beat [4], kill [4], slay (+5315) [4], given [3], killed [3], stricken [3], wounded [3], indeed smitten (+5221) [2], killeth (+5315) [2], slaying [2], surely smite (+5221) [2], beatest [1], cast forth [1], clapt [1], murderers [1], punish [1], slaughter made (+4347) [1], slayer [1], slewest [1], smiters [1], smitest [1], smotest [1], strike [1], stripes give [1], stripes [1], strooke [1]

5222 נֵכֶה *nēkeh*, a. GK: 5784 [→ 5221]. attacker:– abjects [1]

5223 נָכֶה *nākeh*, a. GK: 5783 [→ 5221]. lame, crippled; contrite:– lame [2], contrite [1]

5224 נְכֹה *nᵉkōh* or נְכֹו *nᵉkô*, n.pr.m. GK: 5785 & 5786. Neco:– Necho [3]

5225 נָכֹון *nākôn*, n.pr.m. GK: 5789 [→ 3559]. Nacon, "*established*":– Nachon's [1]

5226 נֵכַח *nēkaḥ*, subst. (used as pp. & adv.). GK: 5790 [→ 5227, 5228]. same as 5227: opposite, before, in front of:– before (+3807.1) [1], over against [1]

5227 נֹכַח *nōkaḥ*, subst. (used as pp. & adv.). GK: 5790 [→ 5226]. same as 5226: opposite, before, in front of:– before [7], over against [7], against [4], before (+3807.1) [1], directly (+413) [1], for (+3807.1) [1], right before (+6440) [1], right on (+3807.1) [1]

5228 נָכֹחַ *nākōaḥ*, a. & subst. GK: 5791 [→ 5226, 5229]. same as 5229: proper, right, honest, what is straight:– right [2], plain [1], uprightness [1]

5229 נְכֹחָה *nᵉkōḥâ*, a. & subst. GK: 5791 [→ 5228]. same as 5228: proper, right, honest, what is straight:– right [2], equity [1], uprightness [1]

5230 נָכַל *nākal*, v. GK: 5792 [→ 3596?, 5231]. [Q, P] to cheat, treat cunningly; [Ht] to conspire, plot:– beguiled [1], conspired against [1], deal subtilly [1], deceiver [1]

5231 נֵכֶל *nēkel*, n.[m.]. GK: 5793 [→ 5230]. deception, cunning:– wiles [1]

5232 נְכַס *nᵉkas* (Aram.), n.[m.]. GK: 10479 [cf. 5233]. treasury; fine:– goods [2]

5233 נְכָסִים *nᵉkāsîm*, n.m.[pl.]. GK: 5794 [cf. 5232]. riches, wealth, possessions:– wealth [4], riches [1]

5234 נָכַר *nākar*, v. GK: 5795 & 5796 [→ 1971, 5235, 5236, 5237]. [N] to disguise oneself, be not recognized; [P] to regard, consider; to favor; to misunderstand; to treat as foreign; [H] to recognize, acknowledge; [Ht] to pretend to be a stranger; to make known:– knew [8], know [8], acknowledge [6], discern [4], respect [4], discerned [2], known [2], take knowledge [2], acknowledged [1], behave strangely [1], could [1], delivered [1], dissembleth [1], estranged [1], feign to be another [1], feignest to be another [1], knoweth [1], made strange [1], perceived [1], regardeth [1], took notice [1]

5235 נֵכֶר *nēker*, n.[m.]. GK: 5798 [→ 5234]. misfortune, disaster:– strange punishment [1], stranger [1]

5236 נֵכָר *nēkār*, n.[m.]. GK: 5797 [→ 5234]. (one from a foreign land) foreigner, alien, stranger:– strange [17], strangers (+1121) [6], stranger (+1121) [5], strangers [3], stranger [3], alien [1], stranger's (+1121) [1]

5237 נָכְרִי *nokrî*, a. GK: 5799 [→ 5234]. foreign, alien; (n.) foreigner:– strange [20], stranger [14], alien [3], stranger (+376) [2], strangers [2], aliens [1], foreigners [1], foreigner [1], outlandish [1]

5238 נְכֹת *nᵉkōt*, n.[f.]. GK: 5800. treasure, storage:– precious things [2]

5239 נָלָה *nālâ*, v. GK: 5801 [cf. 3615]. [H] to stop:– make an end [1]

5240 נִמְבְזֶה *nᵉmibzeh*, v.ptcp. GK: 1022 [→ 959]. ptcp. of 959: despised, contemptible:– vile [1]

5241 נְמוּאֵל *nᵉmû'ēl*, n.pr.m. GK: 5803 [→ 5242; cf. 3223, 5272?]. Nemuel:– Nemuel [3]

5242 נְמוּאֵלִי *nᵉmû'ēlî*, a.g. GK: 5804 [→ 5241]. Nemuelite, "*of Nemuel*":– Nemuelites [1]

5243 נָמַל *nāmal* or מָלַל *mālal*, v. GK: 4909 [cf. 4135]. [Q] to circumcise; to wither away; [N] to be cut off; [Pol] to wither;

5244 נְמָלָה *nᵉmālâ*, n.f. GK: 5805. ant:– ants [1], ant [1]

5245 נְמַר *nᵉmar* (Aram.), n.[m.]. GK: 10480 [cf. 5246]. leopard, panther:– leopard [1]

5246 נָמֵר *nāmēr*, n.m. GK: 5807 [cf. 5245]. leopard:– leopard [4], leopards [2]

נִמְרֹד *nimrōd*. See 5248.

5247 נִמְרָה *nimrâ*, n.pr.loc. GK: 5809 [→ 1039, 5249]. Nimrah, "*spotted leopard; basin of limpid [clear] water*":– Nimrah [1]

5248 נִמְרֹד *nimrōd*, n.pr.m. GK: 5808. Nimrod, "[perhaps] *to rebel* or *the Arrow, the mighty hero*":– Nimrod [4]

5249 נִמְרִים *nimrîm*, n.pr.loc. GK: 5810 [→ 5247]. Nimrim, "*limpid [clear] waters; wholesome waters*; [poss.] *waters of leopards*":– Nimrim [2]

5250 נִמְשִׁי *nimšî*, n.pr.m. GK: 5811. Nimshi:– Nimshi [5]

5251 נֵס *nēs*, n.[m.]. GK: 5812 [→ 5264; cf. 5263, 5264]. banner, standard, signal pole:– standard [7], ensign [6], banner [2], pole [2], sail [2], sign [1]

5252 נְסִבָּה *nᵉsibbâ*, n.f. GK: 5813 [→ 4141]. turn of events:– cause [1]

5253 נָסַג *nāsag* or סוּג *sûg*, v. GK: 6047 [→ 5472, 7734; cf. 5473, 5509, 5873]. prob. same as 5472: [Q] to turn away, be faithless, be disloyal; [N] to be turned back, be disloyal, be faithless; [H] to move, displace; [Ho] to be driven back:– remove [4], departing away [1], removeth [1], take hold [1], take [1], turned away [1]

נְסָה *nᵉsâ*. See 5375.

5254 נָסָה *nāsâ*, v. GK: 5814 [→ 4531, 4532?]. [P] to test (usually to prove character or faithfulness), to attempt; to test God implies a lack of confidence in his revealed character, thus is wicked:– prove [14], tempted [8], proved [5], tempt [4], adventure [1], assayed [1], assay [1], proveth [1], try [1]

5255 נָסַח *nāsaḥ*, v. GK: 5815 [cf. 4535?; cf. 5256]. [Q] to tear down; [N] to be uprooted, be torn down:– destroy [1], plucked [1], pluck [1], rooted [1]

5256 נְסַח *nᵉsaḥ* (Aram.), v. GK: 10481 [cf. 5255]. [Htpe] to be pulled out:– pulled down [1]

5257 נָסִיךְ *nāsîk*, n.m. GK: 5816 & 5817 [cf. 5258]. drink offering; metal image, idol; prince, leader:– princes [3], drink offerings [1], dukes [1], principal [1]

5258 נָסַךְ *nāsak*, v. GK: 5818 & 5820 [→ 4541, 5257, 5262; cf. 3251, 5480; cf. 5260]. [Q] to pour out; to install, set; [N] to be poured out; to be appointed; [P] to pour out; [H] to pour out; [Ho] to be poured out; usually of pouring out a drink offering to deity:– poured out [7], pour out [5], cover [3], offer [2], poured [2], cause to be poured [1], melteth [1], molten [1], pour [1], set up [1], set [1]

5259 נָסַךְ *nāsak*, v. GK: 5819 [→ 4541, 4545; cf. 5526, 7753]. [Qp] to be woven:– spread [1]

5260 נְסַךְ *nᵉsak* (Aram.), v. GK: 10482 [→ 5261; cf. 5258]. [Pa] to present (an offering):– offer [1]

5261 נְסַךְ *nᵉsak* (Aram.), n.[m.]. GK: 10483 [→ 5260; cf. 5262]. drink offering, libation:– drink offerings [1]

5262 נֶסֶךְ *nesek*, n.m. GK: 5821 & 5822 [→ 5258; cf. 5261]. drink offering; metal image, idol:– drink offerings [30], drink offering [29], molten image [3], cover withal [1], molten images [1]

נִסְמָן *nismān*. See 5567.

5263 נָסַס *nāsas*, v. GK: 5823 [cf. 5251, 5264]. [Q] to falter:– standard-bearer [1]

5264 נָסַס *nāsas*, v. GK: 5824 [→ 5251; cf. 5251, 5263]. [Htpol] to unfurl; to sparkle:– lifted up as an ensign [1]

5265 נָסַע *nāsa'*, v. GK: 5825 [→ 4550, 4551]. [Q] to set out, move on, leave, travel on; [N] to be pulled up; [H] to lead, bring out; to pull out:– departed [30], journeyed [28], removed [26], set forward [13], went [8], took journey [7], take journey [5], go forward [3], brought [2], set forth [2], setteth forward [2], went away [2], brought out [1], caused to blow [1], get [1], go away [1], go forth [1], go [1], journeying [1], made to go forth [1], marched [1], on way [1], removeth [1], remove [1], set aside [1], still (+2050.1) [1], took [1], went forth [1], went onward [1], went out [1]

5266 נָסַק *nāsaq* or סָלַק *sālaq*, v. GK: 5826. [Q] to go up:– ascend up [1]

5267 נְסַק *neˢaq* or סְלַק *seˢlaq* (Aram.), v. GK: 10513 [→ 5559]. prob. same as 5559: [P] to come up, go up; [H] to lift up; [Ho] to be lifted up:– take up [1], taken up [1], took up [1]

5268 נִסְרֹךְ *nisrōk*, n.pr.[m.]. GK: 5827. Nisroch (pagan god):– Nisroch [2]

5269 נֵעָה *nēˢâ*, n.pr.loc. GK: 5828. Neah:– Neah [1]

5270 נֹעָה *nōˢâ*, n.pr.f. GK: 5829. Noah, "*rest, comfort*":– Noah [1]

5271 נְעוּרִים *neˢûrîm* or נְעוּרֹת *neˢûrôt*, n.m. & f.pl. GK: 5830 & 5831 [→ 5286, 5288]. youth, childhood:– youth [46], childhood [1]

5272 נְעִיאֵל *neˢîˢēl*, n.pr.loc. GK: 5832 [cf. 5241?]. Neiel:– Neiel [1]

5273 נָעִים *nāˢîm*, a. GK: 5833 & 5834 [→ 5276]. pleasant, charming; singing, sweetly sounding, musical:– pleasant [9], pleasures [2], sweet [2]

5274 נָעַל *nāˢal*, v. GK: 5835 & 5836 [→ 4514, 4515, 5275]. [Q] to lock up, bolt; to put on a sandal; [Qp] to be locked up, be sealed; [H] to provide with sandals:– locked [2], shod [2], bolted [1], bolt [1], inclosed [1], shut up [1]

5275 נַעַל *naˢal*, n.f. GK: 5837 [→ 5274]. sandal (normal footware); not to wear sandals could have the associative meaning of being in poverty, misery, or disgrace:– shoes [11], shoe [9], dryshod [1], shoelatchet (+8288) [1]

5276 נָעֵם *nāˢēm*, v. GK: 5838 [→ 42, 293, 493, 4516, 5273, 5277, 5278, 5279, 5281, 5280, 5283, 5282]. [Q] to be pleasant, be dear, be favored:– pleasant [5], delight [1], in beauty [1], sweet [1]

5277 נַעַם *naˢam*, n.pr.m. GK: 5839 [→ 5276]. Naam, "*pleasant*":– Naam [1]

5278 נֹעַם *nōˢam*, n.m. GK: 5840 [→ 42, 293, 493; cf. 5276]. pleasantness, favor:– beauty [4], pleasant [2], pleasantness [1]

5279 נַעֲמָה *naˢᵃmâ*, n.pr.f. & loc. GK: 5841 & 5842 [→ 5276]. Naamah, "*pleasant*":– Naamah [5]

5280 נַעֲמִי *naˢᵃmî*, a.g. GK: 5844 [→ 5281; cf. 5276]. Naamite, "*of Naaman*":– Naamites [1]

5281 נָעֳמִי *noˢᵒmî*, n.pr.f. GK: 5843 [→ 5276]. Naomi, "*my joy*":– Naomi [20], Naomi's [1]

5282 נַעֲמָנִים *naˢᵃmānîm*, n.[m.]. GK: 5846 [→ 5276]. finest (of Adonis [?]):– pleasant [1]

5283 נַעֲמָן *naˢᵃmān*, n.pr.m. GK: 5845 [→ 5280; cf. 5276]. Naaman, "*pleasantness*":– Naaman [15], Naaman's [1]

5284 נַעֲמָתִי *naˢᵃmātî*, a.g. GK: 5847. Naamathite:– Naamathite [1]

5285 נַעֲצוּץ *naˢᵃṣûṣ*, n.[m.]. GK: 5848. thornbush:– thorns [1], thorn [1]

5286 נָעַר *nāˢar*, v. GK: 5849 [→ 5271, 5289?, 5288?]. [Q] to growl:– yell [1]

5287 נָעַר *nāˢar*, v. GK: 5850 [→ 5296]. [Q] to shake off; to refuse; [Qp] be shaken out; [N] to shake oneself free, be shaken off; [P] to shake off, sweep away; [Ht] to shake oneself free:– overthrew [2], shake [2], shake off [1], shake out [1], shaken out [1], shaken [1], shaketh [1], shook [1], tossed up and down [1]

5288 נַעַר *naˢar*, n.m. GK: 5853 [→ 5271, 5290, 5291, 5292, 5294?; cf. 5286?]. young man, boy, child, ranging in age from infancy to young adulthood; by extension: servant, attendant, steward, with a possible focus on lower social status:– child [44], young men [39], young man [37], lad [32], servant [32], servants [22], young [14], children [7], youth [5], babe [1], boys [1], lads [1], men [1], young men (+376) [1], youths [1]

5289 נַעַר *naˢar*, n.[m.]. GK: 5852 [→ 5286?]. scattering, shaking; (n.) scattered ones:– young one [1]

5290 נֹעַר *nōˢar*, n.m. GK: 5854 [→ 5288]. youth:– youth [2], child's [1], child [1]

נָעוּר *nāˢur*. See 5271.

5291 נַעֲרָה *naˢᵃrâ*, n.f. GK: 5855 [→ 5292; cf. 5288]. young woman, girl, ranging in age from infancy to young adulthood; by extension: servant, maid, with a possible focus on lower social status:– damsel [24], maidens [12], damsel's [8], maid [4], young [4], maiden [3], damsels [2], every maid's (+5291+2050.1) [2], maids [2], young maidens [1], young woman [1]

5292 נַעֲרָה *naˢᵃrâ*, n.pr.f. & loc. GK: 5856 & 5857 [→ 5291; cf. 5288, 5293?, 5295]. Naarah, "*[young] woman*":– Naarah [3], Naarath [1]

נְעֻרָה *neˢurâ*. See 5271.

5293 נַעֲרַי *naˢᵃray*, n.pr.m. GK: 5858 [cf. 5292?]. Naarai, "*young man of Yahweh*":– Naarai [1]

5294 נְעַרְיָה *neˢaryâ*, n.pr.m. GK: 5859 [→ 5288?+3068]. Neariah, "*[young] man of Yahweh*":– Neariah [3]

5295 נַעֲרָן *naˢᵃrān*, n.pr.loc. GK: 5860 [cf. 5292]. Naaran:– Naaran [1]

5296 נְעֹרֶת *neˢōret*, n.f. GK: 5861 [→ 5287]. tinder (broken fibers shaken off flax):– tow [2]

נַעֲרָתָה *naˢᵃrātâ*. See 5292.

5297 נֹף *nōp*, n.pr.loc. GK: 5862 [cf. 4644]. Noph = Memphis:– Noph [7]

5298 נֶפֶג *nepeg*, n.pr.m. GK: 5863. Nepheg, "*sprout, shoot*":– Nepheg [4]

5299 נָפָה *nāpâ*, n.f. GK: 5864 & 5865 [→ 5130, 5131; cf. 5316]. height, yoke; sieve (winnowing device):– borders [1], coast [1], region [1], sieve [1]

5300 נְפוּשְׂסִים *neˢpûšsîm* or נְפוּסִים *neˢpûsîm* or נְפִישְׂסִים *neˢpîšˢsîm*, n.pr.g.?. GK: 5867 & 5866 & 5875 [→ 5304]. Nephushsim, Nephussim, Nephishsim:– Nephishesim [1], Nephusim [1]

5301 נָפַח *nāpaḥ*, v. GK: 5870 [→ 4646, 4647, 8598; cf. 6315]. [Q] to blow upon, breathe upon; [Qp, Pu] to be blown upon; [H] to sniff out; to cause to breathe out:– blow [3], seething [2], bloweth [1], blown [1], breathed [1], breathe [1], caused to lose [1], given up the ghost (+5315) [1], snuffed [1]

5302 נֹפַח *nōpaḥ*, n.pr.loc. GK: 5871. Nophah:– Nophah [1]

5303 נְפִלִים *neˢpîlîm*, n.m.pl. GK: 5872 [→ 5307]. Nephilim:– giants [3]

5304 נְפִיסִים *neˢpîsîm*, n.pr.g.?. GK: 5873 [→ 5300]. Nephissim:–

5305 נָפִישׁ *nāpîš*, n.pr.m. GK: 5874 [→ 5314]. Naphish, "*refreshed*":– Naphish [2], Nephish [1]

5306 נֹפֶךְ *nōpek*, n.[m.]. GK: 5876. turquoise (green semi-precious stone):– emerald [3], emeralds [1]

5307 נָפַל *nāpal*, v. GK: 5877 [→ 4651, 4654, 4658, 5303, 5309; cf. 5308]. [Q] to fall, fail; [Pilal?] to fall; [H] to cause to fall, to cast down, drop; (used of casting lots) to allocate; [Ht] to fall prostrate (to worship); to fall upon (to attack); by extension: to happen (of circumstance falling on a person):– fall [136], fell [98], fallen [52], fell down [20], cast [16], falleth [9], cast down [7], cause to fall [7], fall down [5], divide [4], failed [4], fallen down [3], falling [3], fell away [3], overthrown [3], present [3], rot [3], accepted [2], caused to fall [2], divided [2], fail [2], inferior [2], lay along [2], lighted [2], lost [2], overthrow [2], surely fall (+5307) [2], cast in [1], cast out [1], castedst down [1], casteth into [1], casting down [1], cause to lie down [1], ceased [1], died [1], fall away [1], fallest away [1], fell out [1], felled [1], fellest [1], felling [1], fugitives [1], have inheritance (+5159) [1], judged [1], keepeth [1], lay down [1], lay [1], liest [1], lighted down [1], lying [1], make fall [1], manˢ [1], overwhelm (+5921) [1], perish [1], presented [1], presenting [1], slew [1], smite out [1], throw down [1]

5308 נְפַל *neˢpal* (Aram.), v. GK: 10484 [cf. 5307]. [P] to fall:– fall down [3], fell [3], falleth down [2], fell down [2], have occasion [1]

5309 נֶפֶל *nepel*, n.m. GK: 5878 [→ 5307]. stillborn child, miscarriage:– untimely birth [3]

נְפִל *neˢpil*. See 5303.

5310 נָפַץ *nāpaṣ*, v. GK: 5879 & 5880 [→ 4660, 4661, 5311; cf. 6327]. [Q] to shatter; to scatter; [P] to shatter; (of log raft) to separate; [Pu] to be crushed:– break in pieces [9], scattered [2], beaten in sunder [1], brake [1], break [1], broken [1], cause to be discharged [1], dash in pieces [1], dasheth [1], dash [1], dispersed [1], overspread [1], scatter [1]

5311 נֶפֶץ *nepeṣ*, n.[m.]. GK: 5881 [→ 5310]. bursting, pelting (of rain):– scattering [1]

5312 נְפַק *neˢpaq* (Aram.), v. GK: 10485 [→ 5313]. [P] to go out, come out; [H] to take out, remove:– came forth [3], taken out [2], come forth [1], gone forth [1], take [1], took forth [1], took [1], went forth [1]

5313 נִפְקָא *nipqâ* (Aram.), n.f. GK: 10486 [→ 5312]. expense, cost:– expences [2]

5314 נָפַשׁ *nāpaš*, v.den. GK: 5882 [→ 5305, 5315]. [N] to be refreshed, refresh oneself:– refreshed [3]

5315 נֶפֶשׁ *nepeš*, n.f. GK: 5883 [→ 5314]. breath; by extension: life, life force, soul, an immaterial part of a person, the seat of emotion and desire; a creature or person as a whole: self, body, even corpse:– soul [416], life [100], souls [58], lives [18], persons [13], person [13], heart [12], mind [11], creature [9], himself (+2050.2) [8], yourselves (+3641.1) [6], dead [5], dead body [4], minds [4], slay (+5221) [4], will [4], desire [3], me (+2967.1) [3], persons (+120) [3], pleasure [3], themselves (+3963.1) [3], any [2], beast [2], body [2], hearts [2], herself (+1886.3) [2], him (+2050.2) [2], killeth (+5221) [2], lust [2], man (+120) [2], thing [2], angry (+4751) [1], appetite [1], breath [1], deadly (+871.1) [1], desire (+5375) [1], discontented (+4751) [1], fish [1], given to appetite (+4606) [1], given up the ghost (+5301) [1], giving up the ghost (+4646) [1], greedy (+5794) [1], have a desire (+5375) [1], he (+2050.2) [1], heart's [1], hearty [1], her (+1886.3) [1], he [1], him (+5105.2) [1], himˢ (+2050.2) [1], his own (+2050.2) [1], life (+2416) [1], men (+120) [1], mortally [1], moving creature [1], myself (+2967.1) [1], one [1], soul's [1], tablets (+1004) [1], they (+3963.1) [1], thyself (+3509.3) [1], we (+5105.1) [1]

5316 נֶפֶת *nepet* or נָפֹת *nāpōt*, n.f. or loc. GK: 5884 & 5868 [→ 5131; cf. 5299]. hill; or Nephet, Naphoth, "*heights*":– countries [1]

5317 נֹפֶת *nōpet*, n.m. GK: 5885 [→ 5130]. honey of the honeycomb:– honeycomb [1], honeycomb (+6688) [1]

5318 נֶפְתּוֹחַ *neptôaḥ*, n.pr.loc. GK: 5886. Nephtoah, "*opening*":– Nephtoah [2]

5319 נַפְתּוּלִים *naptûlîm*, n.[m.pl.]. GK: 5887 [→ 6617]. struggles, wrestlings:– wrestlings [1]

5320 נַפְתֻּחִים *naptuḥîm*, n.pr.loc. & a.g. GK: 5888. Naphtuhite:– Naphtuhim [1]

5321 נַפְתָּלִי *naptālî*, n.pr.m. GK: 5889 [→ 6617?]. Naphtali, "*wrestling*":– Naphtali [50], Kedesh-naphtali (+6943) [1]

5322 נֵץ *nēṣ*, n.m. GK: 5890 & 5891 [→ 5323, 5340]. blossom; hawk or falcon (bird of prey):– hawk [3], blossoms [1]

5323 נְצָא *neˢṣāˢ*, v. GK: 5892 [→ 5322]. [Q] to fly:– flee [1]

5324 נָצַב *nāṣab*, v. GK: 5893 & 5894 [→ 4673, 4674, 4675, 4676, 4678, 5325, 5333, 5334; cf. 3320]. [N] to stand oneself before; (n.) officer, official; to be wretched, exhausted; [H] to station, set up, establish; [Ho] to be set up; to be decreed:– stood [17], set [11], stand [8], set up [7], officers [6], standing [4], standeth [3], stood upright [2], Huzzab [1], appointed [1], at best state [1], deputy [1], erected [1], establish [1], laid [1], made to stand [1], pillar [1], present [1], reared up [1], settest [1], settled [1], sharpen [1], stablish [1], standeth still [1], stoodest [1]

נְצִיב *neˢṣib*. See 5333.

5325 נִצָּב *niṣṣāb*, n.m. GK: 5896 [→ 5324]. handle, hilt (of sword, dagger or knife):– haft [1]

5326 נִצְבָּה *niṣbâ* (Aram.), n.f. GK: 10487. hardness, firmness, a quality of strength of a metal:– strength [1]

5327 נָצָה *nāṣâ*, v. GK: 5897 & 5898 [→ 4683, 4695]. [Q] to lie in ruins; [N] to fight (quarreling that can come to blows and struggles); to be laid waste, be desolate; [H] to rebel, engage in a struggle:– strove together [3], strove [3], ruinous [2], strive [2], laid waste [1]

נֹצָה *nōṣâ*. See 5133.

5328 נִצָּה *niṣṣâ*, n.f. GK: 5900 [→ 5340]. blossom:– flower [2]

נְצוּרָה *neˢṣûrâ*. See 5341.

5329 נָצַח *nāṣaḥ*, v. GK: 5904 [→ 5331, 5335; cf. 5330]. [N] to be enduring, lasting; [P] to direct, supervise; (n.) director (of music, t.t. in the Psalms), supervisor:– chief Musician [55], set forward [4], overseers [2], chief singer [1], excel [1], oversee (+5921) [1], perpetual [1]

5330 נְצַח *neˢṣaḥ* (Aram.), v. GK: 10488 [cf. 5329]. [Htpa] to distinguish oneself:– preferred [1]

5331 נֵצַח *nēṣaḥ*, n.m. GK: 5905 [→ 5329]. glory, majesty, splendor; forever, unending, everlasting, always; "the Glory of Israel" as a title of God probably emphasizes both glory and eternity:– ever [20], always (+3807.1) [2], end [2], ever (+3807.1) [2], for ever [2], never (+3808+3807.1) [2], perpetual [2], strength [2], victory [2], alway (+3807.1) [1], constantly (+3807.1) [1], for evermore [1], never (+1077+3807.1) [1], never (+3808+5704) [1], perpetual (+3807.1) [1], surely never (+518+3807.1) [1]

5332 נֵצַח *nēṣaḥ*, n.m. GK: 5906. juice (= blood):– blood [1], strength [1]

5333 נְצִיב *neˢṣîb*, n.m. GK: 5907 [→ 5334; cf. 5324]. garrison, outpost; pillar:– garrisons [5], garrison [4], officer [1], pillar [1]

5334 נְצִיב n°ṣîb, n.pr.loc. GK: 5908 [→ 5333; cf. 5324]. Nezib, "*pillar, garrison*":– Nezib [1]

5335 נְצִיחַ n°ṣîaḥ, n.pr.m. GK: 5909 [→ 5329]. Neziah, "*director [of worship]*":– Neziah [2]

5336 נָצִיר nāṣîr, a. GK: 5910 [→ 5341]. preserved:–

5337 נָצַל nāṣal, v. GK: 5911 [→ 2020; cf. 5338]. [N] to be saved, be delivered, be spared; [P] to plunder, take away, tear away; [H] to deliver, save, rescue; [Ho] to be snatched; [Ht] to strip off oneself:– deliver [112], delivered [56], delivereth [7], delivered at all (+5337) [4], surely deliver (+5337) [4], rid [3], pluckt [2], recovered [2], recover [2], without fail recover (+5337) [2], defended [1], deliverer [1], deliverest [1], escape (+5869) [1], escaped [1], part (+996) [1], preserved [1], rescued [1], rescue [1], saved [1], spoiled [1], spoil [1], stript off [1], stript [1], taken away [1], taken out [1], taken [1], taketh [1], take [1]

5338 נְצַל n°ṣal (Aram.), v. GK: 10489 [cf. 5337]. [H] to save, rescue, deliver:– deliver [2], rescueth [1]

5339 נִצָּנִים niṣṣānîm, n.[m.]. GK: 5912 [→ 5340]. blossoms:– flowers [1]

5340 נָצַץ nāṣaṣ, v. GK: 5913 & 5914 [→ 5213, 5322, 5328, 5339]. [Q] to gleam, sparkle; [H] to bloom, blossom:– bud forth [1], budded [1], flourish [1], sparkled [1]

5341 נָצַר nāṣar, v. GK: 5915 [→ 4453, 4694, 5336; cf. 5201; cf. 5202]. [Q] to guard, watch, protect, keep, preserve; [Qp] to be kept secret, be hidden:– keep [26], preserve [11], keepeth [7], kept [4], watchmen [3], besieged [2], hidden [1], keeper [1], keeping [1], monuments [1], observe [1], preserved [1], preserver [1], preserveth [1], subtil [1], watchers [1]

5342 נֵצֶר nēṣer, n.m. GK: 5916. branch, shoot (of a plant):– branch [4]

5343 נְקֵא n°qē' (Aram.), a. GK: 10490 [cf. 5355]. pure, clean; this purity can be symbolized by the color white, as of lamb's wool:– pure [1]

5344 נָקַב nāqab, v. GK: 5918 & 5919 [→ 4717, 4718, 5345, 5346, 5347; cf. 3342, 6895]. [Q] to bore (a hole), pierce; to designate, bestow; to blaspheme; [Qp] to have a hole; to be notable; [N] to be designated, be registered:– expressed [6], curse [4], blasphemeth [2], curse at all (+5344) [2], pierce [2], appoint [1], blasphemed [1], bore through [1], bored [1], cursed [1], holes [1], named [1], name [1], pierceth [1], strike through [1]

5345 נֶקֶב neqeb, n.[m.]. GK: 5920 [→ 5344]. mounting (used in gold jewelry):– pipes [1]

5346 נֶקֶב neqeb, n.pr.loc. GK: 5921 [→ 5344]. Nekeb:– Nekeb [1]

5347 נְקֵבָה n°qēbâ, n.f. GK: 5922 [→ 5344]. female, woman:– female [18], woman [2], maid child [1], women [1]

5348 נָקֹד nāqōd, a. GK: 5923 [→ 4719, 5351, 5350]. speckled, spotted:– speckled [9]

5349 נֹקֵד nōqēd, n.m. GK: 5924. shepherd, one who raises sheep:– herdmen [1], sheepmaster [1]

5350 נִקֻּדִים niqqudîm, n.[m.]. GK: 5926 [→ 5348]. (small) cakes; crumbling (food supplies):– mouldy [2], cracknels [1]

5351 נְקֻדָּה n°quddâ, n.f. GK: 5925 [→ 5348]. point, drops (of silver on a gold earring):– studs [1]

5352 נָקָה nāqâ, v. GK: 5927 [→ 4518, 5355, 5356]. [Q] to go unpunished; [N] be innocent, be released, go unpunished; [P] to leave unpunished, consider innocent, pardon:– unpunished [6], innocent [4], hold guiltless [3], altogether go unpunished (+5352) [2], at all acquit (+5352) [2], cleanse [2], clear (+5352) [2], clearing (+5352) [2], clear [2], cut off [2], free [2], guiltless [2], leave altogether unpunished (+5352) [2], leave wholly unpunished (+5352) [2], utterly unpunished (+5352) [2], acquit [1], blameless [1], cleansed [1], desolate [1], go unpunished [1], hold innocent [1], quit [1]

5353 נְקוֹדָא n°qôdā', n.pr.m. GK: 5928. Nekoda:– Nekoda [4]

5354 נָקַט nāqaṭ or קוּט qûṭ, v. GK: 7752 [→ 6900, 6962, cf. 6973, 8262]. prob. same as 6962: [Q] to feel anger, loathing; [N] to feel loathing; [Htpolal] to loathe, abhor:– weary [1]

5355 נָקִי nāqî or נָקִיא nāqî', a. GK: 5929 & 5930 [→ 5352; cf. 5343]. innocent, free of blame, not guilty:– innocent [29], guiltless [4], blameless [3], innocents [2], quit [1], clean [1], clear [1], exempted [1], free [1]

5356 נִקָּיוֹן niqqāyôn, n.[m.]. GK: 5931 [→ 5352]. cleanness, purity; by extension: moral or ceremonial innocence, purity, cleanness; "cleanness of teeth" is a sign of lack of food in famine:– innocency [4], cleanness [1]

5357 נָקִיק nāqîq, n.m. GK: 5932. crevice, cleft, crack:– holes [2], hole [1]

5358 נָקַם nāqam, v. GK: 5933 [→ 5359, 5360]. [Q] to seek vengeance, avenge; [N] to be avenged, avenge oneself; [P] to avenge; [Ho or Qp] to be avenged; [Ht] to take one's own vengeance:– avenged [8], avenge [7], avenger [2], revengeth [2], surely punished (+5358) [2], take vengeance [2], avenge (+5360) [1], avenge the quarrel (+5359) [1], avenged (+5359) [1], punished [1], revenged [1], revenge [1], take vengeance (+5359) [1], take vengeance (+5360) [1], taken vengeance (+5359) [1], taking vengeance (+5359) [1], tookest vengeance [1], vengeance taken [1]

5359 נָקָם nāqām, n.m. GK: 5934 [→ 5360; cf. 5358]. vengeance, revenge:– vengeance [12], avenge the quarrel (+5358) [1], avenged (+5358) [1], take vengeance (+5358) [1], taken vengeance (+5358) [1], taking vengeance (+5358) [1]

5360 נְקָמָה n°qāmâ, n.f. GK: 5935 [→ 5359; cf. 5358]. vengeance, revenge:– vengeance [18], avengeth (+5414) [2], revenge [2], avenge (+5358) [1], avenge (+5414) [1], avenged (+5414) [1], revenging [1], take vengeance (+5358) [1]

5361 נָקַע nāqa', v. GK: 5936 [cf. 3363]. [Q] to turn away in disgust:– alienated [3]

5362 נָקַף nāqap, v. GK: 5937 & 5938 [→ 5363, 5364; cf. 8622]. [Q] to go through a yearly cycle; [P] to cut down; to be destroyed; [H] to surround, encircle, engulf:– compassed about [2], compassed [2], compassing [2], compass [2], go round about [2], compass about [1], cut down [1], destroy [1], going about [1], gone about [1], gone round about [1], inclosed [1], kill [1], round [1]

5363 נֹקֶף nōqep, n.[m.]. GK: 5939 [→ 5362]. beating (fruit off olive tree in harvest):– shaking [2]

5364 נִקְפָּה niqpâ, n.f. GK: 5940 [→ 5362]. rope (around waist):– rent [1]

5365 נָקַר nāqar, v. GK: 5941 [→ 5366]. [Q] to gouge out, peck out (an eye); [P] to gouge out; to pierce; [Pu] to be hewn out (of quarry rock):– put out [2], digged [1], pick out [1], pierced [1], thrust out [1]

5366 נְקָרָה n°qārâ, n.f. GK: 5942 [→ 5365]. cleft; cavern:– clifts [1], clift [1]

5367 נָקַשׁ nāqaš, v. GK: 5943 [cf. 3369, 6983; cf. 5368]. [N] to be ensnared; [P] to lay out snares; [Ht] to lay out traps, set a trap:– snared [2], catch [1], lay snares [1], layest a snare [1]

5368 נְקַשׁ n°qaš (Aram.), v. GK: 10491 [cf. 5367]. [P] to knock (together):– smote [1]

נֵר nēr, נִיר nîr. See 5215, 5216.

5369 נֵר nēr, n.pr.m. GK: 5945 [→ 5216]. Ner, "*lamp*":– Ner [16]

5370 נֵרְגַל nēr°gal, n.pr. GK: 5946 [→ 5371]. Nergal (pagan god):– Nergal [1]

5371 נֵרְגַל שַׁר־אֶצֶר nērgal śar-'eṣer, n.pr.m. GK: 5947 [→ 5370+8272]. Nergal-Sharezer, "*Nergal protect the prince!*":– Nergal-sharezer [3]

5372 נִרְגָּן nirgān, v.ptcp. GK: 8087 [→ 7279]. ptcp. of 7279: grumbling, gossiping:– talebearer [3], whisperer [1]

5373 נֵרְדְּ nērd, n.m. GK: 5948. nard (aromatic ointment):– spikenard [3]

נֵרָה nērâ. See 5216.

5374 נֵרִיָּה nēriyyâ or נֵרִיָּהוּ nēriyyāhû, n.pr.m. GK: 5949 & 5950 [→ 4490]. Neriah, "*lamp of Yahweh*":– Neriah [10]

5375 נָשָׂא nāśā', v. GK: 5951 [→ 4984]. [Q] to bear, carry, lift up; forgive; [Qp] to be forgiven, honored, carried; [N] to be carried off, lifted up; [P] to elevate, carry along; [H] to cause to carry, to bring; [Ht] to exalt oneself, lift up oneself; from the base meaning of rise in elevation come fig. extensions "to exalt, honor," as the lifting up of a person in status, and "to forgive," as the removal of guilt and its penalties; "to lift up the eyes" means "to look up":– lift up [121], bear [96], lifted up [37], bare [33], take [30], took up [22], take up [20], armourbearer (+3627) [18], took [18], carry [14], borne [13], carried [13], brought [11], bearing [10], bring [8], forgive [8], take away [8], beareth [7], exalted [7], set up [7], accept [6], taken [5], took away [5], carry away [4], forgiven [4], honourable (+6440) [4], laid [4], obtained [4], suffer [4], bringing [3], carrying [3], pardon [3], receive [3], spare [3], stirred up [3], taken away [3], accept (+6440) [2], accepted (+6440) [2], advanced [2], bring forth [2], burnt [2], carried away [2], continued (+3254) [2], exalt [2], forgavest [2], forgiving [2], high [2], laden [2], lifteth up [2], must needs be borne (+5375) [2], regard [2], respect [2], set [2], taketh [2], utterly take away (+5375) [2], wear [2], able to

bear [1], accepted [1], accepteth [1], arise [1], bare up [1], barest [1], bear up [1], been [1], brought forth [1], carrieth away [1], cast [1], contain [1], desire (+5315) [1], ease [1], exalted above [1], extolled [1], fetch [1], fet [1], furnished [1], furthered [1], gift [1], given [1], hadst [1], have a desire (+5315) [1], helped [1], help [1], hold up [1], laded [1], liftest up [1], lifting up [1], lofty [1], magnified [1], married (+3807.1) [1], offer [1], pardoneth [1], pluck up [1], raise up [1], raise [1], regard (+6440) [1], regard persons (+4480+6440) [1], regardeth [1], respected [1], setteth [1], suffer to bear [1], suffered [1], sware (+3027) [1], swear (+3027) [1], swear [1], taken up [1], takest [1], taketh up [1], wearing [1], went on journey (+7272) [1], yield [1]

5376 נְשָׂא n°śā' (Aram.), v. GK: 10492 [cf. 4984]. [P] to take away, carry away; [Htpa] to revolt, rise up:– carried away [1], made insurrection [1], take [1]

5377 נָשָׁא nāšā', v. GK: 5958 [→ 4860, 4876]. [N] to be deceived; [H] to deceive:– deceive [7], deceived [4], greatly deceived (+5377) [2], beguiled [1], seize [1], utterly forget (+5382) [1]

5378 נָשָׁא nāšā', v. GK: 5957 [→ 4855, 4859, 4874, 5383, 5386; cf. 5392]. [Q] to give a loan, be a creditor; [H] to make a loan; to subject one to tribute:– exact [2], debt [1], taker of usury [1]

נָשָׂא nāsi'. See 5387.

נְשֻׂאָה n°su'â. See 5385.

5379 נִשֵּׂאת niśśē't, v.ptcp. GK: 5951 [→ 4984]. ptcp. of 5375: something lifted up, taken; gift:–

5380 נָשַׁב nāšab, v. GK: 5959 [→ 822; cf. 5395, 5398]. [Q] to blow; [H] to cause to blow; to drive away:– bloweth [1], causeth to blow [1], drove away [1]

5381 נָשַׂג nāśag, v. GK: 5952. [H] to overtake, catch up, attain; to reach, to be able to afford:– overtake [13], overtook [7], take hold [3], able to get (+3027) [2], obtain [2], reach unto [2], surely overtake (+5381) [2], ability (+3027) [1], able (+1767+3027+3509.1) [1], able (+3027) [1], able to bring (+3027) [1], attain unto [1], attained unto [1], can get (+3027) [1], get (+3027) [1], get [1], hand is able to get (+3027) [1], layeth [1], overtaken [1], overtaketh [1], put [1], remove [1], take hold on [1], taken hold upon [1], take [1], wax rich (+3027) [1]

5382 נָשָׁה nāšâ, v. GK: 5960 [→ 4519, 4520, 5388; cf. 7876]. [Q] to forget; [N] to be forgotten; [P] to make forget; [H] to make one forget; to allow one to forget:– deprived [1], exacteth [1], forgat [1], forgotten [1], made forget [1], utterly forget (+5377) [1]

5383 נָשָׁה nāšâ, v. GK: 5957 [→ 5378]. same as 5378: [Q] to give a loan, be a creditor; [H] to make a loan; to subject one to tribute:– exact [2], lent on usury [2], creditors [1], creditor [1], extortioner [1], giver of usury [1], lend (+4859) [1], lendeth [1], lend [1], usurer [1]

5384 נָשֶׁה nāšeh, n.[m.]. GK: 5962. tendon (attached to the hip), perhaps the sciatic nerve:– shrank [2]

5385 נְשׂוּאָה n°śû'â, n.f. GK: 5953 [→ 4984]. burden, load (of images that are carried about):– carriages [1]

5386 נְשִׁי n°šî, n.[m.]. GK: 5963 [→ 5378]. debt:– debt [1]

5387 נָשִׂיא nāśî', n.m. GK: 5954 & 5955 [→ 4984]. leader, ruler, chief, prince; cloud, rising mist, damp fog:– prince [55], princes [40], captain [12], chief [9], rulers [3], ruler [3], vapours [3], chief over [1], clouds [1], governor [1], prince's (+3807.1) [1], prince's [1]

5388 נְשִׁיָּה n°šiyyâ, n.f. GK: 5964 [→ 5382]. oblivion, place forgotten (by the LORD):– forgetfulness [1]

נָשִׁים nāšîm. See 802.

5389 נְשִׁין n°šîn (Aram.), n.f.pl. GK: 10493 [cf. 802]. wives, women:– wives [1]

5390 נְשִׁיקָה n°šîqâ, n.f. GK: 5965 [→ 5401]. kiss:– kisses [2]

5391 נָשַׁךְ nāšak, v. GK: 5966 & 5967 [→ 5392]. [Q] to bite; earn interest; to claim interest against; [Qp] to be bitten; [P] to bite; [H] to charge interest:– bite [6], lend upon usury [3], biteth [2], bitten [2], bit [2], lent upon usury [1]

5392 נֶשֶׁךְ nešek, n.[m.]. GK: 5968 [→ 5391; cf. 5378]. interest, usury:– usury [12]

5393 נִשְׁכָּה niškâ, n.f. GK: 5969 [cf. 3957]. room (for various uses: living, storage, etc.):– chamber [2], chambers [1]

5394 נָשַׁל nāšal, v. GK: 5970. [Q] to take off, come off; to drive out:– cast out [1], cast [1], drave [1], loose [1], put off [1], put out [1], slippeth [1]

5395 נָשַׁם *nāšam*, v. GK: 5971 [→ 5397, 8580; cf. 5380, 5398]. [Q] to gasp, pant:– destroy [1]

5396 נִשְׁמָא *nišmâ* (Aram.), n.f. GK: 10494 [cf. 5397]. breath, air that enters and exhales the lungs; fig., that which is animate and conscious: life:– breath [1]

5397 נְשָׁמָה *nᵉšāmâ*, n.f. GK: 5972 [→ 5395; cf. 5396]. breath, blast of breath; by extension: life, life force, spirit:– breath [11], blast [2], breathed [2], breathe [2], spirit [2], breath (+7307) [1], breatheth [1], inspiration [1], souls [1]

5398 נָשַׁף *nāšap*, v. GK: 5973 [→ 3244, 5399; cf. 5380, 5395]. [Q] to blow:– blow [2]

5399 נֶשֶׁף *nešep*, n.m. GK: 5974 [→ 5398]. dusk, dawn (of morning); twilight (of evening):– twilight [6], night [3], dark [1], dawning of the day [1], dawning of the morning [1]

5400 נָשַׂק *nāśaq*, v. GK: 5956. [N] to be kindled; [H] to kindle a fire, burn:– burn [1], kindled [1], kindleth [1]

5401 נָשַׁק *nāšaq*, v. GK: 5975 & 5976 [→ 5390, 5402]. [Q] to be equipped, arm oneself; to kiss; [P] to kiss (repeatedly or intensely); a kiss can show familial or romantic affection, as well as homage and submission; [H] to brush against, touch up against:– kissed [21], kiss [9], armed [3], ruled [1], touched [1]

5402 נֶשֶׁק *nešeq*, n.[m.]. GK: 5977 [→ 5401]. weapon; armory; armour [3], weapons [2], armed men [1], armoury [1], battle [1], harness [1], weapon [1]

5403 נְשַׁר *nᵉšar* (Aram.), n.m. GK: 10495 [cf. 5404]. eagle, vulture:– eagle's [1], eagles' [1]

5404 נֶשֶׁר *nešer*, n.m. GK: 5979 [cf. 5403]. eagle; vulture:– eagle [19], eagles [5], eagle's [1], eagles' [1]

5405 נָשַׁת *nāšat*, v. GK: 5980. [Q] to be dry, be parched; [N] to be dried up:– failed [1], faileth [1], fail [1]

נְתִיבָה *nᵉtîbâ*. See 5410.

5406 נִשְׁתְּוָן *ništᵉwān*, n.[m.]. GK: 5981 [cf. 5407]. letter, writing:– letter [2]

5407 נִשְׁתְּוָן *ništᵉwān* (Aram.), n.m. GK: 10496 [cf. 5406]. official letter, decree:– letter [3]

נָתוּן *nātûn*. See 5411.

5408 נָתַח *nātaḥ*, v. GK: 5983 [→ 5409]. [P] to cut into pieces:– cut [4], cut in pieces [3], divided [1], hewed in pieces [1]

5409 נֵתַח *nētaḥ*, n.m. GK: 5984 [→ 5408]. piece (of butchered things or persons):– pieces [9], piece [3], parts [1]

5410 נָתִיב *nātîb* or נְתִיבָה *nᵉtîbâ*, n.m. & f. GK: 5985 & 5986. path, way, road; by extension: behavior, lifestyle:– paths [14], path [8], way [2], pathway (+1870) [1], travellers (+1980) [1]

5411 נָתִין *nātîn*, n.m. GK: 5987 [cf. 5414; cf. 5412]. temple servant:– Nethinims [17]

5412 נְתִין *nᵉtîn* (Aram.), n.m.pl. GK: 10497 [→ 5415; cf. 5411]. temple servant:– Nethinims [1]

5413 נָתַךְ *nātak*, v. GK: 5988 [→ 2046]. [Q] to pour out; [N] to be poured out, be melted; [H] to pour out (liquid or money); to melt; [Ho] to be melted:– poured out [7], poured forth [3], poured [3], melted [2], melt [2], dropped [1], gathered together [1], gathered [1], molten [1]

5414 נָתַן *nātan*, v. GK: 5989 [→ 866, 869, 868, 4976, 4977, 4979, 4980, 4991, 4992, 5411, 5416; cf. 4060, 5083; cf. 5415 (also used with compound proper names)]. [Q] to give, put; [Qp] to be given, dedicated; [N] to be given; [Ho or Qp] to be given; note the many contextual translations in the KJV:– give [471], gave [252], given [246], put [185], set [99], delivered [94], giveth [71], deliver [72], make [66], made [45], lay [22], gavest [21], O that (+4310) [17], yield [13], grant [12], laid [11], suffer [11], bring [10], granted [9], recompense [9], appointed [7], caused [5], givest [5], suffered [5], give up [6], send [6], cast [5], cause [5], committed [5], giving [5], shew [5], uttered [5], let [4], sent [4], surely give (+5414) [4], traded [4], utter [4], wholly given (+5414) [4], appoint [3], brought [3], fasten [3], occupied [3], place [3], putteth [3], set up [3], uttereth [3], add [2], applied [2], ascribed [2], ascribe [2], assigned [2], avengeth (+5360) [2], bestowed [2], bestow [2], bringeth [2], deliver up [2], delivered up [2], doubtless deliver (+5414) [2], fastened [2], given forth [2], hang up [2], indeed deliver (+5414) [2], laid up [2], maketh [2], offer [2], ordained [2], pay [2], surely given (+5414) [2], willingly give (+5414) [2], without fail deliver (+5414) [2], would God (+4310) [2], would to God (+4310) [2], God [1], appoint out [1], are delivered [1], avenge (+5360) [1], avenged (+5360) [1], be [1], bring forth [1], bringeth forth [1], causeth [1], charged [1], charge [1], cometh [1], commit [1], considered [1], count [1], cried [1], crieth out (+6963+871.1) [1], cry (+6963) [1], deliver over [1],

deliveredst [1], delivereth [1], direct [1], distribute [1], done [1], frame [1], gave up [1], gift [1], give [1], give forth [1], give leave [1], give out [1], give over [1], given over [1], given up [1], gotten [1], hang [1], hath [1], having the oversight (+871.1) [1], layeth up [1], leave [1], left [1], lend [1], let (+3807.1) [1], let out [1], lie (+7903) [1], lie carnally (+2233+7903+3807.1) [1], lie with (+7903) [1], lift up [1], liftest up [1], made sit [1], paid (+4377) [1], perform [1], placed [1], planted [1], plant [1], pour [1], presented [1], print [1], pulled [1], put forth [1], put in [1], put on [1], put out [1], puttest [1], putteth out [1], putting [1], recompensed [1], recompensing [1], render [1], requite [1], restored [1], send out [1], sendeth forth [1], sendeth [1], sent out [1], set forth [1], setting [1], shewedst [1], shewed [1], shoot forth [1], shoot up [1], shot up [1], sing (+6963) [1], slanderest (+1848) [1], strike [1], submitted [1], suffereth [1], surely delivered (+5414) [1], take heed (+3820) [1], taken up [1], thrust [1], tied [1], took [1], turned [1], turn [1], wept aloud (+1065+6963+871.1) [1], withdrew (+5637) [1], would God that (+4310) [1], yelled (+6963) [1], yield (+3027) [1], yieldeth [1]

5415 נְתַן *nᵉtan* (Aram.), v. GK: 10498 [→ 4978, 5412; cf. 3052; cf. 5414]. [P] to give, provide, supply:– giveth [3], bestow [2], give [1], pay [1]

5416 נָתָן *nātān*, n.pr.m. GK: 5990 [→ 5414]. Nathan, "*gift*":– Nathan [42]

5417 נְתַנְאֵל *nᵉtan'ēl*, n.pr.m. GK: 5991 [→ 5321+410]. Nethanel, "*God [El] has given*":– Nethaneel [14]

5418 נְתַנְיָה *nᵉtanyâ* or נְתַנְיָהוּ *nᵉtanyāhû*, n.pr.m. GK: 5992 & 5993 [→ 5414+3068]. Nethaniah, "*Yahweh has given*":– Nethaniah [20]

5419 נְתַן־מֶלֶךְ *nᵉtan-melek*, n.pr.m. GK: 5994 [→ 5414+4428]. Nathan-Melech, "*gift of king* or *gift of Melek, Molech, Malk*":– Nathan-melech [1]

5420 נָתָס *nātas*, v. GK: 5995 [cf. 5421, 5422, 5428]. [Q] to break up, tear up:– mar [1]

5421 נָתַע *nāta'*, v. GK: 5996 [cf. 5420, 5422, 5428]. [N] to be broken down, be knocked out (of teeth):– broken [1]

5422 נָתַץ *nātaṣ*, v. GK: 5997 [cf. 5420, 5421, 5428]. [Q] to break down, tear down, demolish; [Qp] to be broken down; [N] to be shattered, lay in ruins; [P] to tear down, break down, shatter, destroy; [Pu] to be demolished; [Ho] to be broken up:– brake down [12], break down [5], broken down [5], destroy [4], beat down [3], cast down [3], thrown down [3], pull down [2], break out [1], destroyed [1], overthrow [1], threw down [1], throw down [1]

5423 נָתַק *nātaq*, v. GK: 5998 [→ 5424]. [Q] to draw away, pull off; [Qp] to be torn; [N] to be lured away, be shattered, be torn, be broken; [P] to break, tear; [H] to lure away, drag off; [Ho] to be drawn away:– broken [6], burst [3], brake [2], drawn away [2], brake in sunder [1], break asunder [1], break [1], broken off [1], burst in sunder [1], drawn [1], draw [1], lift up [1], pluck off [1], plucked away [1], pluck [1], pull out [1], pull up [1], rooted out [1]

5424 נֶתֶק *neteq*, n.m. GK: 5999 [→ 5423]. diseased area of skin: itch; some sources: ringworm, eczema:– scall [13], dry scall [1]

5425 נָתַר *nātar*, v. GK: 6000 & 6001 & 6002. [Q] to leap up; [P] to hop up; [H] to make leap up, jump up; to let loose, set free, release, untie; withdraw:– drove asunder [1], leap [1], loosed [1], looseth [1], loose [1], maketh [1], moved [1], undo [1]

5426 נְתַר *nᵉtar* (Aram.), v. GK: 10499. [H/A] to strip off, shake off:– shake off [1]

5427 נֶתֶר *neter*, n.[m.]. GK: 6003. natron (a sodium carbonate for washing):– nitre [2]

5428 נָתַשׁ *nātaš*, v. GK: 6004 [cf. 5420, 5421, 5422]. [Q] to uproot; [N] to be uprooted; [Ho] to be uprooted:– pluck up [6], plucked up [2], utterly pluck up (+5428) [2], destroyed [1], forsaken [1], pluck out [1], pluck up by the roots [1], plucked out [1], pluckt up [1], pluck [1], pulled up [1], root out [1], root up [1], rooted out [1]

5429 סְאָה *sᵉ'â*, n.f. GK: 6006. seah (dry measure, one-third of an ephah, about seven quarts or liters):– two measures [4], measure [3], measures [2]

5430 סְאוֹן *sᵉ'ôn*, n.m. GK: 6007 [→ 5431]. boot:– battle [1]

5431 סָאַן *sā'an*, v.den. GK: 6008 [→ 5430]. [Q] to tramp along in boots:– warrior [1]

5432 סַאסְּאָה *sa'ss'â*, n.f. GK: 6009. warfare, chasing away:– measure [1]

5433 סָבָא *sābā'*, v. or סְבָא *sābā'*, n.m. GK: 6010 [→ 5435]. [Q] to be a drunkard, drink too much; [Qp] to be drunk; others: bind-weed, shrub; others: Sabean, cf. 5434:– drunkard [1], drunken [1], fill [1], winebibbers (+3196) [1]

5434 סְבָא *sᵉbā'*, n.pr.m. GK: 6013 [→ 5436]. Seba:– Seba [4]

5435 סֹבֶא *sōbe'*, n.m. GK: 6011 [→ 5433]. wine, drink, implying drunkenness:– drink [1], drunkards [1], wine [1]

5436 סְבָאִי *sᵉbā'î*, n.pl.g. GK: 6014 [→ 5434]. Sabean:– Sabeans [2]

5437 סָבַב *sābab*, v. GK: 6015 [→ 4141]. [Q] to go around, surround, encircle, engulf; [N] to change direction; to be surrounded; [P] to change; [Pol] to surround, shield, go about; [H] to turn about, circle around; [Ho] to be set, mounted, surrounded; to be changed:– turned [21], compassed [15], compassed about [10], turn [10], compass [9], compass about [7], turned about [6], go about [5], carried about [3], compasseth [3], led about [3], beset round about [2], changed [2], compassed in [2], driven [2], fetch a compass [2], go round about [2], inclosed [2], remove [2], returned [2], turn away [2], turned away [2], whirleth about continually (+1980+5437) [2], winding about [2], about on every side [1], applied [1], avoided [1], beset about [1], besieged [1], bring about [1], bring again [1], brought about [1], came round about [1], cast about [1], caused about [1], circuit [1], closed round about [1], compass round about (+5439) [1], compass round about [1], compassed round [1], compasseth about [1], environ round [1], fetch about [1], fetched a compass [1], fetcht a compass [1], gone about [1], make about [1], occasioned [1], on every side [1], removed [1], round about compassing (+5439) [1], set [1], sit down [1], stood round about [1], turn aside [1], turn back [1], turned aside [1], turned back [1], turneth about [1], turneth [1], turning [1], walk about [1]

5438 סִבָּה *sibbâ*, n.f. GK: 6016 [→ 4141]. turning, arrangement (of events):– cause [1]

5439 סָבִיב *sābîb*, subst. (used as pp. & adv.) GK: 6017 [→ 4141]. all around, on all sides, surrounding, encircling:– round about [204], round about (+5439) [52], about [24], round about (+4480) [20], on every side (+4480) [15], on every side [7], every side [3], on every side (+5439) [2], about (+4480) [1], all about [1], circuits [1], compass round about (+5437) [1], compass [1], in compass [1], places round about [1], round about compassing (+5437) [1]

5440 סָבַךְ *sābak*, v. GK: 6018 [→ 5442, 5441; cf. 7730]. [Qp, Pu] to be entangled, entwined:– folden together [1], wrapped [1]

5441 סְבֹךְ *sᵉbōk*, n.[m.]. GK: 6020 [→ 5440]. thicket, underbrush (where animals can live or hide):– thicket [1]

5442 סְבַךְ *sᵉbak*, n.m. GK: 6019 [→ 5440]. thicket, underbrush:– thickets [2], thicket [1], thick [1]

5443 שַׂבְּכָא *śabbᵉkā'* or סַבְּכָא *sabbᵉkā'* (Aram.), n.[f.]. GK: 10676 & 10501 [cf. 7638]. lyre (triangular instrument with four strings):– sackbut [4]

5444 סִבְּכַי *sibbᵉkay*, n.pr.m. GK: 6021. Sibbecai:– Sibbecai [2], Sibbechai [1]

5445 סָבַל *sābal*, v. GK: 6022 [→ 5447, 5448, 5449, 5450; cf. 2082; cf. 5446]. [Q] to bear, carry, sustain; [Pu] to be (heavy) laden; [Ht] to drag oneself along:– carry [3], bear [2], borne [1], burden [1], carried [1], strong to labour [1]

5446 סְבַל *sᵉbal* (Aram.), v. GK: 10502 [cf. 5445]. [Po] to be laid:– strongly laid [1]

5447 סֵבֶל *sēbel*, n.[m.]. GK: 6023 [→ 5445]. burden; forced labor:– burdens [1], burden [1], charge [1]

5448 סֹבֶל *sōbel*, n.m. GK: 6024 [→ 5445]. burden:– burden [2]

5449 סַבָּל *sabbāl*, n.[m.]. GK: 6025 [→ 5445]. carrier, burden-bearer:– bearers of burdens [3], burdens [2]

5450 סְבָלוֹת *siblôt*, n.f. GK: 6026 [→ 5445]. forced labor, burden-bearer:– burdens [6]

5451 סִבֹּלֶת *sibbōlet*, n.f. GK: 6027 [cf. 7641]. Sibboleth, "*ear of grain* or *torrent of water*":– sibboleth [1]

5452 סְבַר *sᵉbar* (Aram.), v. GK: 10503 [cf. 7663]. [P] to try, strive, seek:– think [1]

5453 סַבְרַיִם *sibrayim*, n.pr.loc. GK: 6028. Sibraim:– Sibraim [1]

5454 סַבְתָּא *sabtā'* or סַבְתָּה *sabtâ*, n.pr.g. GK: 6029 & 6030. Sabta, Sabtah:– Sabtah [1], Sabta [1]

5455 סַבְתְּכָא *sabtᵉkā'*, n.pr.g. GK: 6031. Sabteca:– Sabtecha [2]

5456 סָגַד *sāgad*, v. GK: 6032 [cf. 5457]. [Q] to bow down (in worship):– fall down [2], falleth down [2]

5457 סְגִד *sᵉgid* (Aram.), v. GK: 10504 [cf. 5456]. [P] to worship, pay honor:– worship [8], worshipped [2], worshippeth [2]

5458 סְגוֹר *sᵉgôr*, n.[m.]. GK: 6033 [→ 5462]. enclosure, closing (of the heart):– caul [1], gold [1]

5459 סְגֻלָּה *sᵉgullâ*, n.f. GK: 6035. treasured possession, personal property:– peculiar treasure [3], peculiar [2], jewels [1], proper good [1], special [1]

5460 סְגַן *sᵉgan* (Aram.), n.m. GK: 10505 [cf. 5461]. prefect, governor:– governors [5]

5461 סֶגֶן *segen*, n.m. GK: 6036 [cf. 5532; cf. 5460]. official, officer, commander:– rulers [16], princes [1]

5462 סָגַר *sāgar*, v. GK: 6037 & 6034 [→ 4525, 4526, 5458, 5474; cf. 5534; cf. 5463]. [Q] to shut, close; [Qp] to be shut; [N] to be confined, to be shut up, be imprisoned; [P] to deliver; [Pu] to be shut up, be barred, be closed; [H] to surrender, give over, deliver up; to put in isolation:– shut [30], shut up [23], pure [8], deliver up [5], deliver [5], delivered up [3], delivered [3], gave over [2], straitly shut up (+5462+2050.1) [2], closed up [1], closed [1], gave up [1], given up [1], inclosed [1], repaired [1], shut in [1], shutteth up [1], shutting [1], stop [1]

5463 סְגַר *sᵉgar* (Aram.), v. GK: 10506 [cf. 5462]. [P] to shut, close up:– shut [1]

5464 סַגְרִיר *sagrîr*, n.[m.]. GK: 6039. heavy rain, downpour of rain:– very rainy [1]

5465 סַד *sad*, n.[m.]. GK: 6040 [cf. 7702]. shackles:– stocks [2]

5466 סָדִין *sādîn*, n.[m.]. GK: 6041. linen garment:– fine linen [2], sheets [2]

5467 סְדֹם *sᵉdōm*, n.pr.loc. GK: 6042. Sodom:– Sodom [39]

5468 סֵדֶר *sēder*, n.[m.]. GK: 6043 [→ 4528?; cf. 7713]. order, arrangement; "the land of disorder" refers to the Underworld, the region of darkness and chaos:– order [1]

5469 סַהַר *sahar*, n.[m.]. GK: 6044 [→ 5470]. roundness; referring to the shape of a bowl:– round [1]

5470 סֹהַר *sōhar*, n.[m.]. GK: 6045 [→ 5469]. prison:– prison (+1004+1886.1) [8]

5471 סוֹא *sô'*, n.pr.m. GK: 6046. So:– So [1]

5472 סוּג *sûg*, v. GK: 6047 [→ 5253]. [Q] to turn away, depart; [N] to be turned back, be disloyal, be faithless; [H] to move, displace; [Ho] to be driven back:– turned [6], turned away [3], backslider [1], driven [1], gone back [1], go [1], turned back [1]

5473 סוּג *sûg*, v. GK: 6048 [cf. 5253; 7735?]. [Qp] to be encircled, be bordered (by lilies):– set about [1]

סוּג *sûg*. See 5509.

5474 סוּגַר *sûgar*, n.[m.]. GK: 6050 [→ 5462]. cage; some sources: neck-stock (of iron or wood):– ward [1]

5475 סוֹד *sôd*, n.[m.]. GK: 6051 [→ 1152; cf. 3245]. confidential talk, conspiracy; council, confidant:– secret [7], assembly [5], counsel [5], secrets [2], inward [1], secret counsel [1]

5476 סוֹדִי *sôdî*, n.pr.m. GK: 6052. Sodi, "*Yahweh confides*":– Sodi [1]

5477 סוּחַ *sûaḥ*, n.pr.m. GK: 6053. Suah, "[poss.] *offal, dung, viscera*":– Suah [1]

5478 סוּחָה *sûḥâ*, n.f. GK: 6054 [→ 5501]. refuse, garbage, offal:– torn [1]

סוּת *sût*. See 7750.

5479 סוֹטַי *sôṭay*, n.pr.m. GK: 6055. Sotai:– Sotai [2]

5480 סוּךְ *sûk*, v. GK: 6057 [→ 610; cf. 3251, 5258]. [Q] to anoint, to use oils or perfumes or lotions; [H] to put on lotions; [Ho] to be poured on; this can refer to the application of oils, perfumes, lotions, or resins to the body:– anoint [4], anointed [3], anoint at all (+5480) [1]

סוֹלְלָה *sôlᵉlâ*. See 5550.

5481 סוּמְפֹּנְיָה *sûmpōnᵉyā'* or סוּפֹּנְיָא *sûppōnᵉyā'* or סִפֹּנְיָא *sippōnᵉyā'* (Aram.), n.f. GK: 10507 & 10510 & 10512. musical instrument; sources vary widely: a wind instrument: pipe, bagpipe, double flute; a stringed instrument: dulcimer; a percussion instrument: drum, cymbal:– dulcimer [3]

5482 סְוֵנֵה *sᵉwēnêh*, n.pr.loc. GK: 6059. Syene = Aswan:– Syene [2]

5483 סוּס *sûs*, n.m. GK: 6061 & 6062 [→ 5484, 5485]. (male) horse, stallion; swallow, swift:– horses [97], horse [35], crane [2], horseback [2], on horseback (+7392) [2], horsehoofs (+6119) [1], horses' [1]

5484 סוּסָה *sûsâ*, n.f. GK: 6063 [→ 2701; cf. 5483]. (female) horse, mare:– company of horses [1]

5485 סוּסִי *sûsî*, n.f. GK: 6064 [→ 5483]. Susi, "*[my] horse*":– Susi [1]

5486 סוּף *sûp*, v. GK: 6066 [→ 5490, 5492; cf. 5487]. [Q] to come to an end; demolish; die; [H] to sweep away:– consume [3], consumed [2], have an end [1], perish [1], surely consume (+622) [1]

5487 סוּף *sûp* (Aram.), v. GK: 10508 [→ 5491; cf. 5486]. [P] to be fulfilled; [H] to bring to an end:– consume [1], fulfilled [1]

5488 סוּף *sûp*, n.m. GK: 6068 [→ 5489, 5492]. reed; Reed Sea (traditionally, Red Sea):– Red [24], flags [3], weeds [1]

5489 סוּף *sûp*, n.pr.loc. GK: 6069 [→ 5488]. Suph, "*reeds, bushes*":– Red [1]

5490 סוֹף *sôp*, n.m. GK: 6067 [→ 5486; cf. 5491]. end, conclusion, destiny; rear guard:– end [3], conclusion [1], hinder part [1]

5491 סוֹף *sôp* (Aram.), n.[m.]. GK: 10509 [→ 5487; cf. 5490]. end (of space, time, or circumstance):– end [5]

5492 סוּפָה *sûpâ*, n.f. & loc. GK: 6070 & 6071 [→ 5486, 5488]. storm wind, whirlwind, tempest, gale; Suphah, "*reeds, bushes*"; poss. Red (Reed) Sea:– whirlwind [10], storm [3], Red sea [1], tempest [1], whirlwinds [1]

5493 סוּר *sûr* or שׁוּר *śûr*, v. GK: 6073 & 8462 [→ 3249, 7795?]. [Q] to turn away, depart, leave; to saw; [Qp] to be rejected; [Pol] to drag from, turn aside; [H] to remove, get rid of, take off; [Ho] to be removed, be abolished; by extension: to forsake, reject:– depart [41], take away [41], departed [31], removed [20], taken away [18], put away [14], remove [14], turn aside [14], turned aside [14], took away [10], turn in [7], took off [4], turn away [4], turned in [4], turned [4], departeth [3], taken [3], took [3], turn [3], depart away [2], departing [2], escheweth [2], go aside [2], put off [2], take off [2], taketh away [2], take [2], beheaded (+7218) [1], brought [1], call back [1], declined [1], decline [1], eschewed [1], get out [1], go away [1], goeth [1], gone aside [1], gone away [1], go [1], grievous [1], laid by [1], lay away [1], left undone [1], past [1], pluck away [1], put away (+4480) [1], put down [1], put [1], rebel [1], removeth away [1], removing to and fro [1], revolted [1], sour [1], turned away [1], turned back [1], turneth away [1], went [1], withdraw [1], without [1]

5494 סוּר *sûr*, a.vbl. GK: 6074 [cf. 3249]. corrupt:– degenerate [1]

5495 סוּר *sûr*, n.pr.loc. GK: 6075 [cf. 3249]. Sur:– Sur [1]

5496 סוּת *sût*, v. GK: 6077. [H] to incite, entice, urge, mislead:– moved [4], persuade [3], stirred up [2], entice [1], movedst [1], persuaded [1], persuadeth [1], provoked [1], removed [1], set on [1], setteth on [1], take away [1]

5497 סוּת *sût*, n.[m.]. GK: 6078 [→ 4533]. robe, garment:– clothes [1]

5498 סָחַב *sāḥab*, v. GK: 6079 [→ 5499]. [Q] to drag down:– draw out [2], drawn [1], draw [1], tear [1]

5499 סְחָבָה *sᵉḥābâ*, n.f. GK: 6080 [→ 5498]. rag:– cast clouts [2]

5500 סָחָה *sāḥâ*, v. GK: 6081 [cf. 5501]. [P] to scrape away:– scrape [1]

5501 סְחִי *sᵉḥî*, n.[m.]. GK: 6082 [→ 5478; cf. 5500]. scum, refuse:– offscouring [1]

סָחִישׁ *sāḥîš*. See 7823.

5502 סָחַף *sāḥap*, v. GK: 6085. [Q] to wash away (of rain); [N] to be washed away, be laid low:– sweeping [1], swept away [1]

5503 סָחַר *sāḥar*, v. GK: 6086 [→ 5504, 5505, 5506; cf. 4536]. [Q] to be a trader, a merchant; [Pealal] to pound, throb (of the heart):– merchants [9], merchant [4], trade [2], go about [1], merchant's [1], merchantmen (+376) [1], occupied (+3027) [1], panteth [1], traffick [1]

5504 סַחַר *saḥar*, n.m. GK: 6087 [→ 5503]. same as 5505: merchandise, profit (from merchandising in the marketplace):– merchandise [4]

5505 סַחַר *saḥar*, n.m. GK: 6087 [→ 5503]. same as 5504: merchandise, profit (from merchandising in the marketplace):– merchandise [2], mart [1]

5506 סְחֹרָה *sᵉḥōrâ*, n.f. GK: 6088 [→ 5503]. customer:– merchandise [1]

5507 סֹחֵרָה *sōḥērâ*, n.f. GK: 6089. rampart, wall:– buckler [1]

5508 סֹחֶרֶת *sōḥeret*, n.f. GK: 6090. costly stone (not specifically defined):– black [1]

סֵט *sēṭ*. See 7750.

5509 סוּג *sûg* or סִיג *sîg*, n.[m.]. GK: 6049 & 6092 [cf. 5253, 7873]. dross (usually of silver):– dross [8]

5510 סִיוָן *sîwān*, n.pr. GK: 6094. Sivan:– Sivan [1]

5511 סִיחוֹן *sîḥôn*, n.pr.m. GK: 6095. Sihon:– Sihon [37]

5512 סִין *sîn*, n.pr.loc. GK: 6096 & 6097. Sin = Pelusium; Sin (a desert area between Sinai and Elim, having nothing to do with sinfulness), "*[desert] of clay* [or poss.] *[desert] of Sin*":– Sin [6]

5513 סִינִי *sînî*, a.g. GK: 6098. Sinite:– Sinite [2]

5514 סִינַי *sînay*, n.pr.loc. GK: 6099. Sinai, "*Sin; glare [from white chalk]*":– Sinai [35]

5515 סִינִים *sînîm*, a.g.pl. GK: 6100. Sinim, Chinese [?]:– Sinim [1]

5516 סִיסְרָא *sîsᵉrā'*, n.pr.m. GK: 6102. Sisera:– Sisera [21]

5517 סִיעָא *sî'ā'* or סִיעֲהָא *sî'ᵃhā'*, n.pr.m. GK: 6103 & 6104. Sia, Siaha, "*assembly*":– Siaha [1], Sia [1]

סִיפֹּנְיָא *sîpōnᵉyā'*. See 5481.

5518 סִיר *sîr* or סִירָה *sîrâ*, n.m. & f. GK: 6105 & 6106 [cf. 5626]. pot, pan, caldron, washbasin; thorn, thornbush; fishhook, barb:– pot [12], pots [9], thorns [4], caldron [3], caldrons [2], washpot (+7366) [2], fishhooks (+1729) [1], pans [1]

5519 סָךְ *sāk*, n.[m.]. GK: 6107 [→ 5526]. multitude, throng:– multitude [1]

5520 סֹךְ *sōk*, n.[m.]. GK: 6108 [→ 5521, 5523; cf. 7900]. covering, dwelling (of human or lion):– covert [1], den [1], pavilion [1]

5521 סֻכָּה *sukkâ*, n.f. GK: 6109 [→ 5523; cf. 5520]. tabernacle, shrine; booth, shelter, dwelling, tent:– booths [9], tabernacles [9], pavilions [3], tabernacle [3], booth [2], pavilion [2], cottage [1], covert [1], tents [1]

5522 סִכּוּת *sikkût*, n.pr.?. GK: 6110. Sikkut (pagan god?):– tabernacle [1]

5523 סֻכּוֹת *sukkôt*, n.pr.loc. GK: 6111 [→ 5521; cf. 5520]. Succoth, "*booths*":– Succoth [18]

5524 סֻכּוֹת בְּנוֹת *sukkôt bᵉnôt*, n.pr. GK: 6112. Succoth Benoth (pagan god):– Succoth-benoth [1]

5525 סֻכִּיִּים *sukkiyyîm*, n.pr.m.pl. GK: 6113. Sukkite:– Sukkiims [1]

5526 סָכַךְ *sākak*, v. GK: 6114 & 6115 [→ 4329, 4539, 4540, 5519, 5527; cf. 5259, 7753]. [Q] to cover, conceal, overshadow, shield; to knit together; [Pol] to knit together; [H] to cover, shield; to relieve oneself:– covered [8], cover [5], covereth [2], covering [2], defence [1], defendest (+5921) [1], hedged in [1], join together [1], set [1], shut up [1]

5527 סְכָכָה *sᵉkākâ*, n.pr.loc. GK: 6117 [→ 5526]. Secacah, "*thicket, cover*":– Secacah [1]

5528 סָכַל *sākal*, v. GK: 6118 [→ 5530, 5529, 5531]. [N] to do a foolish thing; [P] to turn into foolishness; [H] to act like a fool:– done foolishly [5], maketh foolish [1], played the fool [1], turn into foolishness [1]

5529 סֶכֶל *sekel*, n.m. GK: 6120 [→ 5528]. foolishness, fool:– folly [1]

5530 סָכָל *sākāl*, n.m. GK: 6119 [→ 5528]. foolish (one), senseless, stupid:– fool [4], foolish [2], sottish [1]

5531 סִכְלוּת *siklût* or שִׂכְלוּת *śiklût*, n.f. GK: 6121 & 8508 [→ 5528]. folly:– folly [5], foolishness [2]

5532 סָכַן *sākan*, v. GK: 6122 & 6125 [→ 4543; cf. 5461]. [Q] to be of use, benefit, profit; [H] to be in the habit; be familiar with; to get along well with:– ever wont (+5532) [2], profitable [2], acquainted [1], acquaint [1], advantage [1], cherish (+1961) [1], cherished (+1961) [1], profiteth [1], treasurer [1], unprofitable (+3808) [1]

5533 סָכַן *sākan*, v. GK: 6123 & 6124 [cf. 4542, 4544]. [N] to be endangered; [Pu] to be poor:– endangered [1], so impoverished [1]

5534 סָכַר *sākar*, v. GK: 6126 & 6127 [cf. 5462]. [N] to be closed; be silent; [P] to hand over, deliver:– stopped [2], give over [1]

5535 סָכַת *sākat*, v. GK: 6129. [H] to be silent, be still:– take heed [1]

סֻכּוֹת *sukkōt*. See 5523.

5536 סַל *sal*, n.m. GK: 6130. basket:– basket [13], baskets [2]

5537 סָלָא *sālā'*, v. GK: 6131 [→ 5543, 5544?; cf. 5541]. [Pu] to be weighed (in correlation to gold):– comparable [1]

5538 סִלָּא *sillā'*, n.pr.loc. GK: 6133. Silla, "embankment":– Silla [1]

5539 סָלַד *sālad*, v. GK: 6134 [→ 5540?]. [P] to skip (for joy):– harden [1]

5540 סֶלֶד *seled*, n.pr.m. GK: 6135 [→ 5539?]. Seled, "jump for joy":– Seled [2]

5541 סָלָה *sālā*, v. GK: 6136 & 6137 [cf. 5537]. [Q] to reject, toss aside; [P] to reject; [Pu] to be bought, be paid for:– valued [2], trodden down [1], trodden under foot [1]

5542 סֶלָה *selā*, n.[f.] GK: 6138 [cf. 5549?]. selah (t.t. in the Psalms):– Selah [74]

5543 סַלּוּא *sallu'* or סַלּוּ *sallû* or סָלוּא *sālū'* or סַלַּי *sallay*, n.pr.m. GK: 6132 & 6139 & 6140 & 6144 [→ 5537]. Sallu, Salu, Sallai, "[poss.] he restores":– Sallu [3], Sallai [2], Salu [1]

5544 סִלּוֹן *sillôn*, n.m. GK: 6141 [→ 5537?]. thorn, brier:– brier [1], thorns [1]

5545 סָלַח *sālaḥ*, v. GK: 6142 [→ 5546, 5547]. [Q] to forgive, release, pardon; [N] to be forgiven:– forgive [18], forgiven [13], pardon [11], pardoned [2], forgiveth [1], spare [1]

5546 סַלָּח *sallāḥ*, a. GK: 6143 [→ 5545]. forgiving:– ready to forgive [1]

סַלַּי *sallay*. See 5543.

5547 סְלִיחָה *sᵉlîḥâ*, n.f. GK: 6145 [→ 5545]. forgiveness, pardon:– forgivenesses [1], forgiveness [1], ready to pardon [1]

5548 סַלְכָּה *salkâ*, n.pr.loc. GK: 6146. Salecah:– Salcah [2], Salchah [2]

5549 סָלַל *sālal*, v. GK: 6147 & 6148 [→ 4546, 4547, 5550, 5551, 5552; cf. 5542?]. [Q] to build up, heap up (a highway), extol; to pile up; [Pil] to esteem, cherish; [Htpol] to behave haughtily, insolently:– cast up [6], raise up [2], exaltest [1], exalt [1], extol [1], made plain [1]

5550 סֹלְלָה *sōlᵉlâ*, n.f. GK: 6149 [→ 5549; cf. 2150]. siege ramp, siege mound:– mount [5], bank [3], mounts [3]

5551 סֻלָּם *sullām*, n.m. GK: 6150 [→ 5549]. stairway; some sources: ladder:– ladder [1]

5552 סַלְסִלָּה *salsillâ*, n.[f.]. GK: 6151 [→ 5549]. branch, shoot; some sources: basket:– baskets [1]

5553 סֶלַע *sela'*, n.m. GK: 6152 [→ 5554, 5555, 5638?]. rock, stone; rock formation: cliff, crag; by extension: stronghold, fortress; God as a "Rock" focuses on stability, faithfulness, and protection:– rock [47], rocks [9], ragged rocks [1], stones [1], stony [1], strong hold [1]

5554 סֶלַע *sela'*, n.pr.loc. GK: 6153 [→ 5553]. Sela, "rock crags, cliffs":– Selah [1], Sela [1]

5555 סֶלַע הַמַּחְלְקוֹת *sela' hammaḥlᵉqôt*, n.pr.loc. GK: 6154 [→ 5553]. Sela Hammahlekoth:– Sela-hammahlekoth [1]

5556 סָלְעָם *sol'ām*, n.m. GK: 6155 [→ 5553?]. edible locust or katydid:– bald locust [1]

5557 סָלַף *sālap*, v. GK: 6156 [→ 5558]. [P] to twist; to overthrow; to frustrate:– overthroweth [4], perverteth [2], pervert [1]

5558 סֶלֶף *selep*, n.m. GK: 6157 [→ 5557]. duplicity, perversity, deceit:– perverseness [2]

5559 סְלִק *sᵉlaq* (Aram.), v. GK: 10513 [→ 5267]. [P] to come up, go up; [H] to lift up; [Ho] to be lifted up:– came up [4], came [1]

5560 סֹלֶת *sōlet*, n.f. GK: 6159. fine flour (likely wheat flour):– fine flour [35], flour [17], fine [1]

5561 סַם *sam*, n.m. GK: 6160. fragrant perfume:– sweet [13], sweet spices [3]

5562 סַמְגַּר־נְבוֹ *samgar-nᵉbô*, n.pr.m. GK: 6162 [→ 5015]. Samgar-Nebo:– Samgar-nebo [1]

5563 סְמָדַר *sᵉmādar*, n.m. GK: 6163. blossom (of a vine):– tender grape [2], tender grapes [1]

5564 סָמַךְ *sāmak*, v. GK: 6164 [→ 294, 3253, 5565]. [Q] to sustain, uphold; to lay (one's hand upon); [Qp] to be braced, be steadfast; [N] to lean upon, rely upon, gain confidence; [P] to

strengthen, refresh:– lay [12], laid [6], put [5], uphold [5], sustained [3], upholdeth [3], lean [2], stay [2], borne up [1], established [1], holden up [1], leaned [1], lieth hard [1], rested [1], set [1], stand fast [1], stayed [1], upheld [1]

5565 סְמַכְיָהוּ *sᵉmakyāhû*, n.pr.m. GK: 6165 [→ 5564]. Semakiah, "Yahweh sustains, consecrates":– Semachiah [1]

5566 סֶמֶל *semel*, n.m. GK: 6166. image, idol:– idol [2], image [2], figure [1]

5567 סָמַן *sāman*, v. GK: 6168. [N] to be appointed, apportioned:– appointed [1]

5568 סָמַר *sāmar*, v. GK: 6169 [→ 4548, 5569; cf. 4930]. [Q] to tremble, shudder (i.e., to have goose bumps, gooseflesh); [P] to bristle, stand on end (of hair):– stood up [1], trembleth [1]

5569 סָמָר *sāmār*, a. GK: 6170 [→ 5568]. bristling (locust):– rough [1]

5570 סְנָאָה *sᵉnā'â* or הַסְּנָאָה *hassᵉnā'â*, n.pr.m. GK: 6171 & 2189 [→ 1886.1, 8130, cf. 5574]. Hassenaah, Senaah, "the hated one":– Senaah [2], Hassenaah [1]

סְנוּאָה *sᵉnu'â*. See 5574.

5571 סַנְבַלַּט *sanballaṭ*, n.pr.m. GK: 6172. Sanballat, "Sin has given life":– Sanballat [10]

5572 סְנֶה *sᵉneh*, n.m. GK: 6174. bush, thorny shrub:– bush [6]

5573 סֶנֶּה *senneh*, n.pr.loc. GK: 6175. Seneh, "thorny; [poss.] [cliff shaped like] a tooth":– Seneh [1]

סַנָּה *sannâ*. See 7158.

5574 סְנוּאָה *sᵉnû'â* or הַסְּנוּאָה *hassᵉnu'â*, n.pr.m. GK: 6176 & 2190 [→ 1886.1+8130; cf. 5570]. Senuah, Hassenuah, "the hated one":– Hasenuah [1], Senuah [1]

5575 סַנְוֵרִים *sanwērîm*, n.[m.pl.]. GK: 6177. blindness:– blindness [3]

5576 סַנְחֵרִיב *sanḥērîb*, n.pr.m. GK: 6178. Sennacherib, "Sin has increased the brothers; Sin replace the [lost] brothers!":– Sennacherib [13]

5577 סַנְסִנָּה *sansinnâ*, n.[m.]pl. GK: 6180. fruit cluster (of date tree):– boughs [1]

5578 סַנְסַנָּה *sansannâ*, n.pr.loc. GK: 6179. Sansannah, "palm branch":– Sansannah [1]

5579 סְנַפִּיר *sᵉnappîr*, n.[m.]. GK: 6181. fin:– fins [5]

5580 סָס *sās*, n.m. GK: 6182. (garment) moth; some sources: worm:– worm [1]

סוּס *sus*. See 5483.

5581 סִסְמַי *sismay*, n.pr.m. GK: 6183. Sismai, "[poss.] belonging to Sisam":– Sisamai [2]

5582 סָעַד *sā'ad*, v. GK: 6184 [→ 4552; cf. 5583]. [Q] to sustain, support, refresh:– comfort [3], strengthen [2], held up [1], hold up [1], holden [1], refresh [1], stablish [1], strengtheneth [1], upholden [1]

5583 סְעַד *sᵉ'ad* (Aram.), v. GK: 10514 [cf. 5582]. [Pa] to help, support:– helping [1]

5584 סָעָה *sā'â*, v. GK: 6185. [Q] to slander, defame, speak with malice:– storm [1]

5585 סָעִיף *sā'îp*, n.[m.]. GK: 6186 & 6187 [→ 5586, 5587, 5588, 5589, 5634]. cleft, crag; bough, branch:– branches [2], top [2], clifts [1], tops [1]

5586 סָעַף *sā'ap*, v.den. GK: 6188 [→ 5585]. [P] to lop off, trim down:– lop [1]

5587 סְעִפִּים *sᵉ'ippîm* or שְׂעַפִּים *śᵉ'ippîm*, n.f. GK: 6191 & 8546 [→ 5588, 8312; cf. 5585]. disquieted thoughts, troubled thoughts; division, divided opinion, a fig. extension of hobbling on crutches made of boughs:– thoughts [2], opinions [1]

5588 סֵעֵף *sē'ēp*, a. GK: 6189 [→ 5587; cf. 5585]. double-minded, divided in heart:– thoughts [1]

5589 סְעַפָּה *sᵉ'appâ*, n.f. GK: 6190 [→ 5585]. bough:– boughs [2]

5590 סָעַר *sā'ar*, v. GK: 6192 [→ 5591; cf. 8175]. [Q] to grow stormier, rougher; [N] to be enraged; [P] to scatter in a wind; [Po] to scatter, swirl; [Pu] to be lashed by storms:– tempestuous [2], came out as a whirlwind [1], driven with a whirlwind [1], scattered with a whirlwind [1], sore troubled [1], tossed with tempest [1]

5591 סַעַר *sa'ar* or סְעָרָה *sᵉ'ārâ*, n.m. GK: 6193 & 6194 [cf. 5590]. windstorm, tempest, gale:– whirlwind [11], tempest [6], stormy [4], storm [1], whirlwind (+7307) [1], whirlwinds [1]

5592 סַף *sap*, n.m. GK: 6195 & 6196 & 6197 [→ 5605]. threshold, door frame, entrance, doorway; doorkeeper; basin, bowl; wool, hide, skin:– door [10], threshold [6], basons [2], bason [2], bowls [2], doors [2], gates [2], posts [2], thresholds [2], cup [1], door posts [1]

5593 סַף *sap*, n.pr.m. GK: 6198 [cf. 5598]. Saph, "basin, threshold":– Saph [1]

5594 סָפַד *sāpad*, v. GK: 6199 [→ 4553, 5636?]. [Q] to beat the breast, mourn, lament, weep; [N] to be mourned:– lament [9], mourn [9], mourned [6], lamented [4], mourners [1], wail [1]

5595 סָפָה *sāpâ*, v. GK: 6200. [Q] to sweep away; take away; bring disaster; [N] to be swept away; be destroyed:– consumed [5], add [3], destroy [3], destroyed [2], perish [2], augment [1], consume [1], heap [1], joined [1], put [1]

5596 סָפַח *sāpaḥ* or שָׂפַח *śāpaḥ*, v. GK: 6202 & 6203 & 8558 [→ 4555, 5599; cf. 4939, 8198]. [Q] to associate, attach to; [N] to be attached, be united; [P] to pour out; to bring sores, make scabby; [Pu] be joined together; [Ht] to feel oneself attached to:– abiding [1], cleave [1], gathered together [1], puttest [1], put [1], smite with a scab [1]

5597 סַפַּחַת *sappaḥat*, n.f. GK: 6204 [→ 4556]. rash, skin eruption:– scab [2]

5598 סִפַּי *sippay*, n.pr.m. GK: 6205 [cf. 5593]. Sippai:– Sippai [1]

5599 סָפִיחַ *sāpîaḥ*, n.[m.]. GK: 6206 & 6207 [→ 5596]. what grows on its own, after-growth in a fallow year; torrent, downpour:– such as groweth of itself [1], such things as grow of themselves [1], that which groweth of it own accord [1], that which groweth of itself [1], things which grow [1]

5600 סְפִינָה *sᵉpînâ*, n.f. GK: 6208 [→ 5603]. ship (with a covering or deck):– ship [1]

5601 סַפִּיר *sappîr*, n.[m.]. GK: 6209. sapphire; some sources: lapis lazuli:– sapphire [7], sapphires [3], sapphire stone [1]

5602 סֵפֶל *sēpel*, n.[m.]. GK: 6210. bowl (for water or curdled milk):– bowl [1], dish [1]

5603 סָפַן *sāpan*, v. GK: 6211 [→ 5600, 5604; cf. 8226]. [Q] to cover; [Qp] to be roofed, be paneled, be roofed:– covered [3], cieled [2], seated [1]

5604 סִפֻּן *sippun*, n.[m.]. GK: 6212 [→ 5603]. ceiling:– cieling [1]

5605 סָפַף *sāpap*, v.den. GK: 6214 [→ 5592]. [Htpol] to stand at the threshold:– doorkeeper [1]

5606 סָפַק *sāpaq* or שָׂפַק *śāpaq*, v. GK: 6215 & 6216 & 8562 & 8563 [→ 5607]. [Q] to clap hands (in derision); beat one's breast; to punish, slap; to wallow, splash; to be enough; [H] to clasp hands:– clap [2], clappeth [1], please [1], smite [1], smote together [1], smote [1], striketh [1], suffice [1], wallow [1]

5607 סֵפֶק *sepeq* or שֶׂפֶק *śepeq*, n.[m.]. GK: 6217 & 8565 [→ 5606]. riches, abundance, plenty, sufficiency:– stroke [1], sufficiency [1]

5608 סָפַר *sāpar*, v. GK: 6218 & 6221 [→ 5612; cf. 5613]. [Q] to count, number, take a census; [N] to be counted, be recorded; by extension: [P] to tell, proclaim, recount (an event or principle); [Pu] to be told:– scribe [42], told [26], declare [20], tell [12], numbered [11], number [10], scribes [6], shew forth [5], count [4], declared [4], counted [2], scribe's [2], speak [2], writer's [2], writer [2], accounted [1], commune [1], numberest [1], numbering [1], penknife (+8593+1886.1) [1], reckon [1], shewing [1], talk [1], tellest [1], telling [1], told out [1]

5609 סְפַר *sᵉpar* (Aram.), n.m. GK: 10515 [→ 5613; cf. 5612]. record, archive, book (though not a book in the sense of a codex with bound pages); the phrase "book of Moses" means the first five books of the Bible:– book [3], books [1], rolls [1]

5610 סְפָר *sᵉpār*, n.[m.]. GK: 6222 [→ 5612]. census:– numbering [1]

5611 סְפָר *sᵉpār*, n.pr.loc. GK: 6223 [cf. 8234]. Sephar:– Sephar [1]

5612 סֵפֶר *sēper* or סִפְרָה *siprâ*, n.m. GK: 6219 & 6225 [→ 4557, 4558?, 4559, 5608, 5610, 5615, 5618, 7158; cf. 5609]. book (as a scroll or tablet), scroll, letter, certificate, deed, dispatch:– book [136], letters [16], letter [13], evidence [6], bill [4], learned (+3045) [3], books [2], evidences [2], learning [2], register [1], scrole [1]

5613 סָפַר *sāpar* (Aram.), n.m. GK: 10516 [→ 5609; cf. 5608]. teacher of the Law; secretary (an official); scribe:– scribe [6]

5614 סְפָרַד *s°parad*, n.pr.loc. GK: 6224. Sepharad:– Sepharad [1]

סִפְרָה *siprâ*. See 5612.

5615 סְפֹרוֹת *s°pōrôt*, n.f. GK: 6228 [→ 5612]. measure, number; some sources: art of writing:– numbers [1]

5616 סְפַרְוִים *s°parwîm*, a.g. GK: 6227 [→ 5617]. Sepharvite, "of Sepharvaim":– Sepharvites [1]

5617 סְפַרְוַיִם *s°parwayim*, n.pr.loc. GK: 6226 [→ 5616]. Sepharvaim:– Sepharvaim [6]

5618 סֹפֶרֶת *sōperet* or סוֹפֶרֶת *sôperet*, n.[pr.]m. GK: 6230 & 6072 [→ 5612]. (office of) scribes; as n.pr. Sophereth, "scribe":– Sophereth [2]

5619 סָקַל *sāqal*, v. GK: 6232. [Q] to stone (as an execution); [N] to be stoned; [P] to throw stones (out or away), pelt with stones; [Pu] to be stoned:– stone [7], stoned [6], surely stoned (+5619) [4], cast [1], gathered out stones [1], gather [1], stoning [1], threw [1]

5620 סַר *sar*, a. GK: 6234 [→ 5637]. sullen, dejected, discouraged:– heavy [2], so sad [1]

5621 סָרָב *sārāb*, n.m. GK: 6235. briers:– briers [1]

5622 סַרְבָּל *sarbāl* (Aram.), n.[m.]. GK: 10517. robe, garment; variously translated as "hose, trousers, tunic, mantle, coat, cloak":– coats [2]

5623 סַרְגוֹן *sargôn*, n.pr.m. GK: 6236. Sargon, "firm, faithful king; the king is legitimate":– Sargon [1]

5624 סֶרֶד *sered*, n.pr.m. GK: 6237 [→ 5625]. Sered:– Sered [2]

5625 סַרְדִּי *sardî*, a.g. GK: 6238 [→ 5624]. Seredite, "of Sered":– Sardites [1]

5626 סִרָה *sirâ*, n.pr.[loc.]. GK: 6241 [→ 953+5626; cf. 5518]. Sirah:– Sirah [1]

5627 סָרָא *sārâ*, n.f. GK: 6239 & 6240 [→ 3249, 5637]. ceasing, stopping; rebellion, revolt:– rebellion [2], revolt [2], continual (+1115) [1], revolted [1], turn away [1], wrong [1]

5628 סָרַח *sāraḥ*, v. GK: 6243 & 6244 & 6242 [→ 5629; cf. 8294]. [Q] to hang down, overhang, spread over; [Qp] to be overhanged; [N] to be spoiled, become stinking:– hang [2], exceeding in dyed attire (+2871) [1], spreading [1], stretched [1], stretch [1], vanished [1]

5629 סֶרַח *seraḥ*, n.m. GK: 6245 [→ 5628]. overhang, what projects over:– remnant [1]

5630 סִרְיוֹן *siryôn*, n.[m.]. GK: 6246 [cf. 8302, 8303]. (scale) armor, coat of mail:– brigandines [1], brigandine [1]

5631 סָרִיס *sārîs*, n.m. GK: 6247 [→ 7249]. court official, palace officer, eunuch:– eunuchs [15], chamberlains [9], officers [7], officer [5], chamberlain [4], eunuch [2]

5632 סָרַךְ *sārak* (Aram.), n.m. GK: 10518. administrator:– presidents [5]

5633 סֶרֶן *seren*, n.[m.]. GK: 6248 & 6249. axle; ruler, prince:– lords [21], plates [1]

5634 סַרְעַפָּה *sar'appâ*, n.f. GK: 6250 [→ 5585]. bough:– boughs [1]

5635 סָרַף *sārap*, v. GK: 6251 [cf. 8313]. [P] to burn:– burneth [1]

5636 סִרְפָּד *sirpād*, n.[m.]. GK: 6252 [→ 5594?]. briers, stinging nettles:– brier [1]

5637 סָרַר *sārar*, v. GK: 6253 [→ 5620, 5627]. [Q] to be stubborn, be obstinate, be rebellious:– rebellious [6], stubborn [4], revolters [2], away [1], backsliding [1], revolting [1], slideth back [1], withdrew (+5414) [1]

5638 סְתָו *s°tāw*, n.m. GK: 6255. winter, rainy season:– winter [1]

5639 סְתוּר *s°tûr*, n.pr.m. GK: 6256 [→ 5641]. Sethur, "concealed [by deity]":– Sethur [1]

5640 סָתַם *sātam* or שָׂתַם *śātam*, v. GK: 6258 & 8608. [Q] to stop up, block off, seal; [Qp] to be closed up, (by extension) to be in a secret place; [N] to be closed; [P] to stop up:– stopped [5], shut up [2], stop [2], closed up [1], hidden [1], secret [1], shutteth out [1], stopt [1]

5641 סָתַר *sātar*, v. GK: 6259 [→ 4563, 4564, 4565, 5639, 5643; cf. 5642]. [Q] to be hidden, be concealed, have a refuge; [P] to hide; [Pu] to be hidden; [H] to hide, conceal; [Ht] to hide oneself, keep oneself hidden:– hide [32], hid [29], hidest [5], hideth [5], secret [3], kept close [2], surely hide (+5641) [2], absent [1], conceal [1], keep secret [1]

5642 סְתַר *s°tar* (Aram.), v. GK: 10519 & 10520 [cf. 5641, cf. 8368]. [P] to destroy, demolish; [Pap] to be hidden; (as noun) hidden things:– destroyed [1], secret [1]

5643 סֵתֶר *sēter* or סִתְרָה *sitrâ*, n.[m.]. GK: 6260 & 6261 [cf. 5641]. hiding place, secret place, shelter; covering, veil; (adv.) secretly, in secret:– secretly (+871.1+1886.1) [9], secret [9], covert [5], secret place [4], hiding place [3], backbiting [1], covering [1], disguiseth (+7760) [1], privily [1], protection [1], secret places [1]

5644 סִתְרִי *sitrî*, n.pr.m. GK: 6262. Sithri, "[poss.] Yahweh is my hiding place":– Zithri [1]

5645 עָב *'āb*, n.m. GK: 6265 & 6266 [→ 5743]. clouds; thicket:– clouds [15], cloud [7], thick clouds [5], thick cloud [2], clay [1], thickets [1], thick [1]

5646 עָב *'āb*, n.m. GK: 6264. overhang, overhanging roof:– thick beam [1], thick planks [1], thick [1]

5647 עָבַד *'ābad*, v. GK: 6268 [→ 4566, 5650, 5652, 5653, 5656, 5657, 5659, 5744 (also used with compound proper names); cf. 5648]. [Q] to work, serve, labor, do; to worship, minister, work in ministry; [N] to be plowed, be cultivated; [Pu] to be worked; [H] to reduce to servitude, enslave, cause to serve; [Ho] to be caused to serve, worship (a god):– serve [153], served [61], do [14], worshippers [5], servants [4], till [4], do service [3], made to serve [3], serveth [3], work [3], caused to serve [2], dress [2], labour [2], serving [2], tilled [2], tilleth [2], beenS [1], bondmen [1], bondservice [1], bring to pass [1], cause to serve [1], compel to serve (+5656) [1], do work [1], done [1], eared [1], ear [1], execute [1], husbandman (+120+376) [1], keep in bondage [1], keep [1], labouring [1], made serve [1], servant [1], servedst [1], set a work [1], tiller [1], tillest [1], useth service [1], wrought [1]

5648 עֲבַד *'°bad* (Aram.), v. GK: 10522 [→ 4567, 5649, 5673; cf. 5647]. [P] to do, make; [Htpe] to be done, be made, be turned into; a general word of activity and occurrence; the context determines the best translation, "do, make, obey, happen," etc:– made [7], do [5], done [4], cut [2], did [2], doest [1], doeth [1], executed [1], goeth on [1], kept [1], moved [1], worketh [1], wrought [1]

5649 עֲבַד *'°bēd* (Aram.), n.m. GK: 10523 [→ 5648; cf. 5650]. servant:– servants [6], servant [1]

5650 עֶבֶד *'ebed*, n.m. GK: 6269 [→ 5647, 5651, 5658, 5660, 5661; cf. 5649 (also used with compound proper names)]. servant, slave, attendant; indentured servants and owned slaves had varying levels of status and responsibilities; according to the OT Law, a Hebrew slave could be sold to a Hebrew master for only six years, but there was no time limit for Gentile slaves:– servants [370], servant [362], bondmen [15], manservant [12], bondage [10], menservants [9], servant's [8], bondman [6], servants' [4], bondservant [1], manservant's [1], manservants [1]

5651 עֶבֶד *'ebed*, n.pr.m. GK: 6270 [→ 5650]. Ebed, "servant":– Ebed [6]

5652 עֲבָד *'°bād*, n.m. GK: 6271 [→ 5647]. what is done, deed, act:– works [1]

5653 עַבְדָּא *'abdā'* (Aram.), n.pr.m. GK: 6272 [→ 5647]. Abda, "servant of Yahweh":– Abda [2]

5654 עֹבֵד-אֱדֹם *'ōbēd-'°dôm*, n.pr.m. GK: 6273 [→ 5647+123]. Obed-Edom, "servant [worshiper] of Edom":– Obed-edom [20]

5655 עַבְדְּאֵל *'abd°'ēl*, n.pr.m. GK: 6274 [→ 5650+410; cf. 5661]. Abdeel, "servant of God [El]":– Abdeel [1]

5656 עֲבֹדָה *'°bōdâ*, n.f. GK: 6275 [→ 5647; cf. 5673]. work, service, labor, task, duty, job; special work and service to God: service, ministry; forced labor: slavery:– service [94], servile [12], work [10], bondage [8], act [2], all manner of service (+5656+2050.1) [2], any manner of service (+5656+2050.1) [2], every kind of service (+5656+2050.1) [2], servitude [2], tillage [2], compel to serve (+5647) [1], effect [1], labour [1], ministering [1], ministry [1], office [1], serveth [1], use [1], wrought [1]

5657 עֲבֻדָּה *'°buddâ*, n.f. GK: 6276 [→ 5647]. servant, slave:– household [1], servants [1]

5658 עַבְדּוֹן *'abdôn*, n.pr.m. & loc. GK: 6277 & 6278 [cf. 5650]. Abdon, "servant":– Abdon [8]

5659 עַבְדֻּת *'abdut*, n.f. GK: 6285 [→ 5647]. slavery, servitude:– bondage [3]

5660 עַבְדִּי *'abdî*, n.pr.m. GK: 6279 [→ 5661?]. Abdi, "servant of Yahweh or my servant":– Abdi [3]

5661 עַבְדִּיאֵל *'abdî'ēl*, n.pr.m. GK: 6280 [→ 5655, 5660?; cf. 5655]. Abdiel, "servant of God [El]":– Abdiel [1]

5662 עֹבַדְיָה *'ōbadyâ* or עֹבַדְיָהוּ *'ōbadyāhû*, n.pr.m. GK: 6281 & 6282 [→ 5647+3068]. Obadiah, "servant [worshiper] of Yahweh":– Obadiah [20]

5663 עֶבֶד-מֶלֶךְ *'ebed-melek*, n.pr.m. GK: 6283 [→ 5650+4428]. Ebed-Melech, "servant of Melek [king] or Malk":– Ebed-melech [6]

5664 עֲבֵד נְגוֹ *'°bēd n°gô*, n.pr.m. GK: 6284 [→ 5650+5015; cf. 5665]. Abednego, "servant of Nego or Nebo":– Abed-nego [1]

5665 עֲבֵד נְגוֹ *'°bēd n°gô* (Aram.), n.pr.m. GK: 10524 [→ 5649; cf. 5664]. Abednego, "servant of Nego or Nebo":– Abed-nego [14]

5666 עָבָה *'ābâ*, v. GK: 6286 [→ 4568, 5672]. [Q] to be thick:– thicker [2], grown thick [1]

5667 עֲבוֹט *'°bôṭ*, n.[m.]. GK: 6287 [→ 5670, 5671]. pledge, (garment) security (for a loan):– pledge [4]

5668 עָבוּר *'°bûr*, pp. & c. GK: 6288. marker of cause or reason: for, because; marker of purpose or intent: on account of; in order to; a marker of result: then; benefit: for:– for sake (+871.1) [14], that (+871.1) [10], for (+871.1) [7], because of (+871.1) [5], to (+871.1) [3], because (+871.1) [2], for sakes (+871.1) [2], and (+871.1) [1], for cause (+871.1) [1], for to (+871.1+3807.1) [1]

5669 עָבוּר *'°bûr*, n.[m.]. GK: 6289 [→ 5674]. produce, yield:– old corn [1]

5670 עָבַט *'ābaṭ*, v.den. GK: 6292 & 6293 [→ 5667]. [Q] to borrow, i.e., take or receive a pledge; [P] to swerve, change (a course), implying a lack of purpose; [H] to lend on a pledge:– surely lend (+5670) [2], borrow [1], break [1], fetch [1], lend [1]

5671 עַבְטִיט *'abṭîṭ*, n.[m.]intens. GK: 6294 [→ 5667]. heavy pledges, excessive mortgage for a debt; there may be an implication of undue force being used to keep the pledge:– thick clay [1]

5672 עֳבִי *'°bî*, n.[m.]. GK: 6295 [→ 5666]. thickness, density, mold:– thickness [2], thick [2]

5673 עֲבִידָה *'°bîdâ* (Aram.), n.f. GK: 10525 [→ 5648; cf. 5656]. work, service, administration:– work [3], affairs [2], service [1]

5674 עָבַר *'ābar*, v. GK: 6296 & 6297 [→ 4569, 5669, 5676, 5677, 5678, 5679, 5682]. [Q] to pass over, cross over, travel through; [N] to be crossed; [P] to extend; to breed; [H] to make pass through, let pass, send over; by extensions: to forgive, as the passing over of guilt; [Ht] to be very angry, show oneself angry:– pass [46], passed over [43], pass over [40], passed [34], go over [29], passed by [17], went over [17], pass through [14], passeth [14], transgressed [12], went [11], gone over [10], passed on [10], come over [9], go [9], past [9], pass on [8], passed along [7], cause to pass [6], go through [6], gone [6], pass away [6], caused to pass [5], come [5], pass by [5], passeth by [5], wroth [5], goeth [4], passed through [4], passengers [4], passeth away [4], passing [4], put away [4], transgress [4], went on [4], caused to pass through [3], made pass [3], made to pass [3], make to pass [3], went through [3], at all brought over (+5674) [2], brought over [2], brought [2], carry over [2], cause to pass through [2], fail [2], go beyond [2], go by [2], go on [2], made a proclamation (+6963) [2], make go [2], overpast [2], passest over [2], passest [2], sent over [2], speedily pass over (+5674) [2], sweet smelling [2], take away [2], turn away [2], alienate [1], altered [1], beyond [1], bring over [1], brought through [1], came along [1], came by [1], came over [1], came [1], carried over [1], cause to sound [1], caused to be proclaimed (+6963) [1], charged (+5921) [1], cometh [1], coming on [1], conduct over [1], conducted [1], convey over [1], current [1], delivered [1], do away [1], enter [1], escape [1], gendereth [1], get over [1], go in [1], goeth forth [1], goeth over [1], going over [1], going [1], have away [1], have more than [1], laid [1], made a partition [1], made proclamation (+6963) [1], made to pass by [1], made to pass through [1], make pass [1], make proclamation (+6963) [1], make sound [1], make to transgress [1], maketh to pass through [1], meddleth [1], overcome [1], overpass [1], overran [1], overrunning [1], over [1], pass away from [1], pass by (+1870) [1], passage [1], passed away [1], passed beyond [1], passedst over [1], passengers (+1870) [1], passest on [1], passeth along [1], passeth on along [1], passeth out [1], passeth over [1], passeth through [1], passing by [1], passing through [1], perishing [1], perish [1], proclaim (+6963) [1], proveketh to anger [1], rageth [1], raiser [1], removed [1], set apart [1], shave (+8593) [1], taken [1], took away [1], took [1], transgressest [1], transgressing [1], transgressors [1], translate [1], wayfaring man (+734) [1], went away [1], went forth [1], went throughout (+871.1) [1]

5675 עֲבַר **ᵃbar** (Aram.), n.m. GK: 10526 [cf. 5676]. the opposite bank (of a river); Trans(-Euphrates) or "beyond the River)" is to the east of Israel:– beyond [7], side [7]

5676 עֵבֶר **ēber**, n.m. GK: 6298 [→ 5674; cf. 5675]. what is on the other side, what is beyond, across; i.e., east or west; Trans-Euphrates:– side [56], beyond (+871.1) [8], beyond [7], beyond (+4480) [6], sides [4], straight forward (+413+6440) [3], against (+6440) [1], by (+3807.1) [1], from (+4480) [1], over [1], passages [1], passage [1], quarter [1]

5677 עֵבֶר **ēber**, n.pr.m. GK: 6299 [→ 5674]. Eber, "[regions] beyond [the river]":– Eber [13], Heber [2]

5678 עֶבְרָה **ebrâ**, n.f. GK: 6301 [→ 5674]. wrath, anger, fury, rage; insolence:– wrath [31], rage [2], anger [1]

5679 עֲבָרָה **ᵃbārâ**, n.f. GK: 6302 [→ 5682; cf. 5674]. ford, crossing:– ferry boat [1]

5680 עִבְרִי **ibrî**, a. & n.g. GK: 6303 [→ 5681]. Hebrew:– Hebrews [17], Hebrew [11], Hebrew women [2], Hebrew man [1], Hebrew woman [1], Hebrewess [1], Hebrews' [1]

5681 עִבְרִי **ibrî**, n.pr.m. GK: 6304 [→ 5680]. Ibri, "Hebrew":– Ibri [1]

5682 עֲבָרִים **ᵃbārîm**, n.pr.loc. GK: 6305 [→ 5679; cf. 5674]. Abarim, "geographical regions beyond":– Abarim [4]

5683 עֶבְרֹן **ebrōn**, n.pr.loc. GK: 6306 [→ 2266; cf. 5658]. Ebron, Hebron, "association":– Hebron [1]

5684 עֶבְרֹנָה **ᵃbrōnâ**, n.pr.loc. GK: 6307. Abronah:– Ebronah [2]

5685 עָבַשׁ **ābaš**, v. GK: 6308. [Q] to shrivel, wither, dry up:– rotten [1]

5686 עָבַת **ābat**, v. GK: 6309 [→ 5687, 5688]. [P] to conspire, twist:– wrap up [1]

5687 עָבֹת **ᵃbōt**, a. GK: 6290 [→ 5686]. leafy, dense, interwoven foliage:– thick [4]

5688 עֲבֹת **ᵃbōt**, n.m. GK: 6310 & 6291 [→ 5686]. rope, cord, chains, ties; fetters, harness; thick foliage:– wreathen [8], cords [5], bands [3], thick boughs [3], ropes [2], band [1], rope [1], thick branches [1]

5689 עָגַב **āgab**, v. GK: 6311 [→ 5691, 5689; cf. 5748]. [Q] to lust, have sensual desire for:– doted [6], lovers [1]

5690 עֲגָבִים **ᵃgābîm**, n.[m.]. GK: 6313 [→ 5689]. devotion, love:– much love [1], very lovely [1]

5691 עֲגָבָה **ᵃgābâ**, n.f. GK: 6312 [→ 5689]. lust, sensual desire:– inordinate love [1]

5692 עֻגָה **ugâ**, n.f. GK: 6314 [→ 5746]. (round, flat) bread cakes:– cakes [4], cake [3]

עָגוֹל **āgôl**. See 5696.

5693 עָגוּר **āgûr**, n.[m.]. GK: 6315. (short footed) thrush (a bird):– swallow [2]

5694 עָגִיל **āgîl**, n.[m.]. GK: 6316 [→ 5696]. earring:– earrings [2]

5695 עֵגֶל **egel**, n.m. GK: 6319 [→ 5696]. bull-calf; calf-shaped idol:– calf [20], calves [11], bullocks [1], bullock [1], calf (+1241) [1], calf's [1]

5696 עָגֹל **āgōl**, a. GK: 6318 [→ 4570, 5694, 5696, 5695, 5697, 5698, 5699, 5700]. circular, round:– round [6]

5697 עֶגְלָה **eglâ**, n.f. GK: 6320 [→ 5698; cf. 5696]. heifer-calf, young cow:– heifer [9], heifer (+1241) [2], calves [1], heifer's [1], young cow (+1241) [1]

5698 עֶגְלָה **eglâ**, n.pr.f. GK: 6321 [→ 5697]. Eglah, "heifer":– Eglah [2]

5699 עֲגָלָה **ᵃgālâ**, n.f. GK: 6322 [→ 5696]. cart:– cart [15], wagons [8], chariot [1], wagon [1]

5700 עֶגְלוֹן **eglôn**, n.pr.m. & loc. GK: 6323 & 6324 [→ 5696]. Eglon, "circle; young bull":– Eglon [13]

5701 עָגַם **āgam**, v. GK: 6327 [cf. 99]. [Q] to grieve for, have pity on:– grieved [1]

5702 עָגַן **āgan**, v. GK: 6328. [N] to keep withdrawn (from marital relations):– stay [1]

5703 עַד **ad**, n.m. GK: 6329. a unit of time, referring to the past: old, ancient; without limit: forever, eternal, for ever and ever; continual, always:– ever [39], everlasting [2], for ever [2], eternity [1], ever (+5769) [1], evermore [1], for ever (+5769+2050.1) [1], old [1], perpetually (+3807.1) [1], world without end (+5704+5769) [1]

5704 עַד **ad**, pp. GK: 6330 [→ 1107, 5728; cf. 5710?; cf. 5705]. until, up to, as far as:– unto [376], until [249], to [167], for [75], till [68], how long (+4970) [28], until (+834) [27], and [13], how long (+575+1886.5) [13], till (+834) [9], into [8], and (+2050.1) [7], both (+4480) [7], very (+3966) [7], by [5], even [5], hitherto (+2008) [5], or [5], how long (+4100) [4], toward [4], until (+3588) [4], until (+7945) [4], while [4]*

5705 עַד **ad** (Aram.), pp. & c. GK: 10527 [→ 5709?; cf. 5704]. up to, until:– till (+1768) [8], to [5], for [4], unto [4], till [3], until [3], until (+1768) [2], at [1], ever (+0.2+5957) [1], hitherto (+3542) [1], on [1], or [1], within [1]

5706 עַד **ad**, n.[m.]. GK: 6331 [→ 5710]. prey, plunder:– prey [3]

5707 עֵד **ēd**, n.m. GK: 6332 [→ 3133; cf. 5749]. witness, testimony; an object that serves as a memorial or a person giving of legal evidence:– witness [45], witnesses [21], take witnesses (+5749) [2], took witnesses (+5749) [1]

5708 עִדָּה **iddâ**, n.f. GK: 6340. menstruation:– filthy [1]

עֹד **ōd**. See 5750.

5709 עֲדָא **dâ** (Aram.), v. GK: 10528 [→ 5705?; cf. 5710]. [P] to be taken, be repealed; [H] to take away:– altereth [2], departed [1], pass away [1], passed [1], removeth [1], take away [1], taken away [1], took [1]

עֹדֵד **ōdēd**. See 5752.

5710 עָדָה **ādâ**, v. GK: 6334 & 6335 [→ 497, 3260?, 3294?, 5704?, 5711, 5706, 5716; cf. 5709]. [Q] to adorn oneself, put on jewelry; to prowl; [H] to take away, remove:– decked [3], adorned [3], adorneth with [1], deckedst with ornaments (+5716) [1], deckest with [1], deck [1], passed [1], taketh away [1]

5711 עָדָה **ādâ**, n.pr.f. GK: 6336 [→ 5716; cf. 5710]. Adah, "adornment":– Adah [8]

5712 עֵדָה **ēdâ**, n.f. GK: 6337 [cf. 3259]. community, assembly, with a possible focus on the unity of the congregation; this can refer to good or evil groups; human or animal groups:– congregation [124], company [13], assembly [8], assemblies [1], multitude [1], people [1], swarm [1]

5713 עֵדָה **ēdâ**, n.f. GK: 6338 [→ 5749]. witness:– testimonies [21], witness [4], testimony [1]

5714 עִדֹּא **iddō'** or עִדּוֹ **iddô**, n.pr.m. GK: 6333 & 6341 & 6342 & 10529. Iddo, "[prob.] Yahweh has adorned": note this name is Aramaic twice in Ezra:– Iddo [10]

5715 עֵדוּת **ēdût**, n.f. GK: 6343 [→ 5749]. testimony, statute, stipulation, regulation; this can also mean "the Testimony" as a formal written copy of the precepts and stipulations of a covenant:– testimony [40], testimonies [15], witness [4], Shoshannim-Eduth (+7799) [1]

5716 עֲדִי **ᵃdî**, n.[m.]. GK: 6344 [→ 3260, 5711, 5717, 5718; cf. 5710 (also used with compound proper names)]. ornament, beautiful jewelry:– ornaments [7], excellent ornaments (+5716) [2], mouth [2], ornament [2], deckedst with ornaments (+5710) [1]

5717 עֲדִיאֵל **ᵃdî'ēl**, n.pr.m. GK: 6346 [→ 5716+410]. Adiel, "adornment of God [El]":– Adiel [3]

5718 עֲדָיָה **ᵃdāyâ** or עֲדָיָהוּ **ᵃdāyāhû**, n.pr.m. GK: 6347 & 6348 [→ 5716+3068]. Adaiah, "adornment of Yahweh":– Adaiah [9]

5719 עָדִין **ādîn**, a. GK: 6349 [→ 5727]. voluptuous, wantonness:– given to pleasures [1]

5720 עָדִין **ādîn**, n.pr.m. GK: 6350 [→ 5727]. Adin, "voluptuous, luxurious":– Adin [4]

5721 עֲדִינָא **ᵃdînā'**, n.pr.m. GK: 6351 [→ 5727]. Adina, "adorned":– Adina [1]

5722 עֲדִינוֹ **ᵃdînô**, n.pr.m. GK: 6352. Adino:– Adino [1]

5723 עֲדִיתַיִם **ᵃdîtayim**, n.pr.loc. GK: 6353. Adithaim, "double [row] of adornments":– Adithaim [1]

5724 עַדְלַי **adlay**, n.pr.m. GK: 6354. Adlai, "be just":– Adlai [1]

5725 עֲדֻלָּם **ᵃdullām**, n.pr.loc. GK: 6355 [→ 5726]. Adullam, "retreat or refuge; [poss.] [they are] just":– Adullam [8]

5726 עֲדֻלָּמִי **ᵃdullāmî**, a.g. GK: 6356 [→ 5725]. Adullamite, of Adullam, "of Adullam":– Adullamite [3]

5727 עָדַן **ādan**, v.den. GK: 6357 [→ 4575, 4574, 5719, 5720, 5721, 5730; cf. 5734?]. [Ht] to revel in the good life, luxuriate:– delighted [1]

5728 עֲדֶן **den** or עֲדֶנָּה **denâ**, adv. GK: 6362 & 6364 [→ 5704+2008]. yet, still:– yet [2]

5729 עֵדֶן **eden**, n.pr.loc. GK: 6361 [→ 1040]. Eden, "paradise, delight, [poss.] flat land":– Eden [4]

5730 עֵדֶן **ēden** or עֶדְנָה **ednâ**, n.[m.]. GK: 6358 & 6366 [→ 5727, 5731, 5734; cf. 5733]. delight, delicacy; finery; (sexual) pleasure:– delicates [1], delights [1], pleasures [1], pleasure [1]

5731 עֵדֶן **ēden**, n.pr.m. & loc. GK: 6359 & 6360 [→ 5730]. Eden, "paradise, delight, [poss.] flat land":– Eden [16]

5732 עִדָּן **iddān** (Aram.), n.m. GK: 10530. time (general or specific period); "time, times, and half a time" likely means three-and-one-half periods of time:– times [6], time [6], at what time (+0.2+1768+871.2) [1]

5733 עַדְנָא **adnā'**, n.pr.m. GK: 6363 [cf. 5730, 5734]. Adna, "delight":– Adna [2]

5734 עַדְנָה **adnâ**, n.pr.m. GK: 6365 & 6367 [→ 5730; cf. 5727?, 5733]. Adnah, "delight":– Adnah [2]

5735 עַדְעָדָה **ad'ādâ**, n.pr.loc. GK: 6368. Adadah:– Adadah [1]

5736 עָדַף **ādap**, v. GK: 6369. [Q] (ptcp.) what is left over, what is additional; [H] to have a surplus:– remaineth [3], had over [1], more [1], odd number [1], over and above (+5921) [1], overplus [1], remaineth over [1]

5737 עָדַר **ādar**, v. GK: 6370 & 6371 & 6372 [→ 4576, 5739; cf. 5826]. [Q] to help, serve; referring to a fighting unit that acts as a group; [N] to be cultivated, be weeded; to be missing; be lacking; [P] to let be lacking:– faileth [3], digged [2], lacked [2], fail [1], keep rank [1], keep [1], lacking [1]

5738 עֵדֶר **eder**, n.pr.m. GK: 6376 [→ 5740]. Eder, "flock":– Ader [1]

5739 עֵדֶר **ēder**, n.m. GK: 6373 [→ 5737]. flock, herd:– flocks [16], flock [16], drove [2], every drove (+5739) [2], herds [2], droves [1]

5740 עֵדֶר **ēder**, n.pr.m. & loc. GK: 6374 & 6375 [→ 4029, 5738, 5741]. Eder, "flock":– Eder [3], Edar [1]

5741 עַדְרִיאֵל **adrî'ēl**, n.pr.m. GK: 6377 [→ 5740+410]. Adriel, "[my] help is God [El]":– Adriel [2]

5742 עֲדָשִׁים **ᵃdāšîm**, n.f. GK: 6378. lentils:– lentiles [4]

עַוָּא **awwā'**. See 5755.

5743 עוּב **ûb**, v.den. GK: 6380 [→ 5645]. [H] to cover with a cloud:– covered with a cloud [1]

5744 עוֹבֵד **ôbēd**, n.pr.m. GK: 6381 [→ 5647]. Obed, "servant [worshiper]":– Obed [10]

5745 עוֹבָל **ôbāl**, n.pr.g. GK: 6382 [cf. 5858]. Obal:– Obal [1]

5746 עוּג **ûg**, v.den. GK: 6383 [→ 4580, 5692]. [Q] to bake a (round, flat) cake of bread:– bake [1]

5747 עוֹג **ôg**, n.pr.m. GK: 6384. Og:– Og [22]

5748 עוּגָב **ûgāb**, n.m. GK: 6385 [cf. 5689]. flute:– organ [3], organs [1]

5749 עוּד **ûd**, v.den. GK: 6386 & 6387 [→ 496, 5707, 5713, 5715, 5750, 5752, 8584]. [Q] to bear witness; [P] to surround (with ropes); [Pil] to sustain, relieve; [H] to admonish, warn, charge, declare; to testify, to call on a witness; [Ho] to be warned; [Htpol] to hold each other up; from the base meaning of binding (with ropes) come the fig. extensions of "to warn, charge, testify" (bind with words) and "to help, sustain" (bind oneself to another in aid and comfort):– testified [7], testify [6], call to record [2], earnestly protested (+5749) [2], protest solemnly (+5749) [2], solemnly protest (+5749) [2], take witnesses (+5707) [2], testifiedst [2], admonished [1], bear witness against [1], call to witness [1], chargedst [1], charge [1], gave witness to [1], give warning [1], lifteth up [1], protesting [1], relieveth [1], robbed [1], stand upright [1], take to witness [1], took to record [1], took witnesses (+5707) [1], witnessed against [1], witness [1]

5750 עֹד **ōd**, subst. (used as adv.). GK: 6388 [→ 5749; cf. 5751]. longer, again, still, more:– yet [125], more [114], any more [72], again [44], still [21], while yet [12], else [10], more (+3254) [10], besides [6], again (+3254) [5], as yet [5], moreover [5], within (+871.1) [5], yet again (+3254) [5], moe [3], any longer [2], any more [2], any more at all (+5750) [2], further [2], henceforth [2], longer [2], while have being (+871.1) [2], whiles [2], while [2], yet the more (+3254) [2], after [1], again (+2050.1) [1], all life long (+4480) [1], almost (+4592) [1], any more at all (+3254) [1], any [1], beside [1], but [1], can more (+3254) [1], do again

(+3254) [1], else beside (+1107+4480) [1], ever since (+4480) [1], furthermore [1], good while [1], more (+3254+3807.1) [1], moreover (+2050.1) [1], mo [1], never again (+3808) [1], once [1], since [1], while (+3605) [1], while (+871.1) [1], whilst yet [1], within the space of (+871.1) [1], yet (+3807.1) [1], yet again [1], yet more (+3254) [1]

5751 עוֹד *'ôd* (Aram.), adv. GK: 10531 [cf. 5750]. still, yet:– while [1]

5752 עוֹדֵד *'ôdēd*, n.pr.m. GK: 6389 [→ 5749]. Oded, "*restorer*":– Oded [3]

5753 עָוָה *'āwâ*, v. GK: 6390 [→ 5754, 5771, 5773, 5856]. [Q] to do wrong; [N] to be perverse, be warped; [P] to ruin, make crooked; [H] to do wrong, pervert; from the base meaning of twisting an object comes the fig. extension of twisting morality: to be perverse, to do wrong:– commit iniquity [2], committed iniquity [2], perverse [2], perverted [2], bowed down [1], did perversely [1], done amiss [1], done perversely [1], done wickedly [1], done wrong [1], made crooked [1], troubled [1], turneth [1]

5754 עַוָּה *'awwâ*, n.f. GK: 6392 [→ 5857; cf. 5753]. ruin, wreckage, rubble:– overturn [3]

5755 עַוָּא *'awwā'* or עַוָּה *'awwâ* or עִוָּה *'iwwâ*, n.pr.loc. GK: 6379 & 6393 & 6394 [→ 5757, 5761]. Avva, Avvah, Ivvah:– Ivah [3], Ava [1]

עָוֹן *'āwôn*. See 5771.

5756 עוּז *'ûz*, v. GK: 6395 [→ 5797; cf. 5810]. [Q] to take refuge; [H] to bring to refuge, give shelter:– gather to flee [2], gather [1], retire [1]

5757 עַוִּים *'awwîm*, a.g. GK: 6398 [→ 5755]. Avvite:–

5758 עֲוָיָא *'wāyâ* (Aram.), n.f. GK: 10532. wickedness, iniquity:– iniquities [1]

5759 עֲוִיל *'wîl*, n.m. GK: 6396 [→ 5763]. little boys:– little ones [1], young children [1]

5760 עֲוִיל *'wîl*, n.m. GK: 6397 [→ 5765]. evil one, unjust one:– ungodly [1]

5761 עַוִּים *'awwîm*, n.pr.loc. GK: 6399 [→ 5755]. Avvim:– Avites [2], Avims [1], Avim [1]

5762 עֲוִית *'wît* or עַיּוֹת *'yôt*, n.pr.loc. GK: 6400 & 6511. Avith, Aioth:– Avith [2]

5763 עוּל *'ûl*, v. GK: 6402 [→ 5759, 5764, 5768]. [Q] to nurse, suckle:– milch [2], great with young [1], with young [1], young [1]

5764 עוּל *'ûl*, n.m. GK: 6403 [→ 5763]. nursing infant, baby:– infant [1], sucking child [1]

5765 עָוַל *'āwal*, v.den. GK: 6401 [→ 5760, 5766, 5767]. [P] to do evil, act wrong:– deal unjustly [1], unrighteous [1]

עוֹל *'ôl*. See 5923.

5766 עֶוֶל *'āwel* or עַוְלָה *'awlâ* or עֹלָה *'ôlâ*, n.m. GK: 6404 & 6406 & 6593 [→ 5765]. wrong, evil, sin, injustice, what is morally perverted, warped, and twisted, an extension of the base meaning of a physically twisted, crooked object (not found in the OT):– iniquity [35], wickedness [7], unrighteousness [3], unjust [2], iniquities [1], perverseness [1], unjustly [1], unrighteously [1], wickedly [1], wicked [1]

5767 עַוָּל *'awwāl*, n.m. GK: 6405 [→ 5765]. wicked one, evil one, unjust one:– wicked [3], unjust [1], unrighteous [1]

עוֹלָה *'ôlâ*. See 5930.

5768 עוֹלֵל *'ôlēl* or עוֹלָל *'ôlāl*, n.m. GK: 6407 & 6408 [→ 5763]. child, little one:– children [10], young children [3], babes [2], infants [2], child [1], infant [1], little ones [1]

5769 עוֹלָם *'ôlām*, n.m. GK: 6409 [cf. 5865; cf. 5957]. everlasting, forever, eternity; from of old, ancient, lasting, for a duration:– ever [210], everlasting [59], for ever [47], perpetual [21], old [17], evermore [15], never (+3808+3807.1) [9], ever (+3807.1) [5], ancient [4], of old [4], everlasting (+3807.1) [3], alway (+3807.1) [2], always (+3807.1) [2], any more (+5704) [2], ever (+5704) [2], ever throughout [2], for ever (+3807.1) [2], long [2], never (+408+3807.1) [2], old time [2], world [2], always [1], ancient (+4480) [1], ancient times [1], any time [1], continuance [1], eternal [1], ever (+4480+1886.1) [1], ever (+5703) [1], ever of old (+4480) [1], everlasting (+3117) [1], everlasting (+3605) [1], for ever (+5703+2050.1) [1], lasting [1], long time [1], never (+1077+3807.1) [1], never (+1097+3807.1) [1], never (+3808+4480) [1], never (+3808+5704) [1], of old time [1], of old time (+4480) [1], perpetual (+5704) [1], since the beginning of the world (+5703+5704) [1], world without end (+5703+5704) [1]

5770 עָיַן *'āyan*, v.den. GK: 6523 [→ 5869]. [Q] to keep an eye on, look at (with suspicion or jealousy):– eyed [1]

5771 עָוֹן *'āwôn*, n.m. GK: 6411 [→ 5753; cf. 5758]. sin, wickedness, iniquity, often with a focus on the guilt or liability incurred, and the punishment to follow:– iniquity [167], iniquities [48], punishment of iniquity [5], punishment [4], fault [2], affliction [1], iniquities (+1697) [1], mischief [1], punishments [1], sin [1]

5772 עֹנָה *'ônâ*, n.f. GK: 6703 [→ 6031?]. marital rights (of intercourse):– duty of marriage [1], furrows [1]

5773 עִּעִּים *'iw'îm*, n.pl.abst. GK: 6413 [→ 5753]. (col. pl.) dizziness, staggering, frenzy:– perverse [1]

5774 עוּף *'ûp*, v. GK: 6414 & 6545 & 6758 [→ 5775, 5888, 5889; cf. 3286]. [Q] to fly; to be faint, be exhausted; [Pol] to dart about (of a flying bird or a snake); to brandish; [H] to let (eyes) glance; [Ht] to fly away:– fly [8], flying [6], fly away [5], faint [2], flieth [2], brandish [1], flew [1], flieth away [1], set [1], shine forth [1], waxed faint [1], weary [1]

5775 עוֹף *'ôp*, n.m. GK: 6416 [→ 5774; cf. 5776]. bird, winged creatures, flying creatures:– fowls [36], fowl [23], birds [6], bird [3], flying [2], flieth [1]

5776 עוֹף *'ôp* (Aram.), n.[m.]. GK: 10533 [cf. 5775]. bird; a "bird of heaven" is any wild bird:– fowls [1], fowl [1]

5777 עֹפֶרֶת *'ōperet*, n.m. GK: 6769. lead (a mineral):– lead [9]

5778 עֵיפַי *'êpay* or עוֹפַי *'ôpay*, n.pr.m. GK: 6550 & 6417. Ephai, Ophai, "*my bird*":– Ephai [1]

5779 עוּץ *'ûṣ*, v. GK: 6418 [cf. 3289]. [Q] to consider, devise, plan:– take advice [1], take counsel together (+6098) [1]

5780 עוּץ *'ûṣ*, n.pr.m. & loc. GK: 6419 & 6420. Uz:– Uz [7], Huz [1]

5781 עוּק *'ûq*, v. GK: 6421 [→ 4157?, 6125]. [Q] to crush, totter; [H] to crush, cause to totter:– pressed [2]

5782 עוּר *'ûr*, v. GK: 6424 [→ 3265, 5892, 5895, 6147, 6179, 6180]. [Q] to awake; [N] to be aroused, stirred up, wakened; [Pol] to awaken, arouse, raise up; [Pil] to raise, keep up; [H] to stir up, rouse, waken; [Htpol] to rouse oneself:– awake [24], stir up [12], raised up [9], stirred up [5], raise up [4], stirreth up [4], lift up [3], raised [3], raise [2], wakened [2], wakeneth [2], arise [1], awake up [1], awakest [1], dare stir up [1], lifting up [1], master [1], raising [1], wake up [1], waked [1], waketh [1]

5783 עוּר *'ûr*, v. GK: 6423 [→ 4589, 5785?; cf. 6168]. [N] to be uncovered, be laid bare:– made quite naked (+6181) [1]

5784 עוּר *'ûr* (Aram.), n.[m.]. GK: 10534. chaff, the husk particles of threshed grain, used fig. to indicate something worthless:– chaff [1]

5785 עוֹר *'ôr*, n.m. GK: 6425 [→ 5783?]. skin, hide, leather:– skin [73], skins [23], hide [2], leather [1]

5786 עָוַר *'āwar*, v. GK: 6422 [→ 5787, 5788?]. [P] to make blind:– put out [3], blindeth [1], blind [1]

5787 עִוֵּר *'iwwēr*, a. GK: 6426 [→ 5786]. blind:– blind [26]

עוֹרֵב *'ôrēb*. See 6159.

5788 עִוָּרוֹן *'iwwārôn* or עַוֶּרֶת *'awweret*, n.[m.]. GK: 6427 & 6428 [→ 5786]. blindness, blinding:– blindness [2], blind [1]

5789 עוּשׁ *'ûš*, v. GK: 6429 [→ 3135, 3266, 3274; cf. 5790]. [Q] to be quick or to help:– assemble [1]

5790 עוּת *'ût*, v. GK: 6431 [→ 5793; cf. 5789]. [Q] to sustain, help:– speak in season [1]

5791 עָוַת *'āwat*, v. GK: 6430 [→ 5792]. [P] to make crooked, pervert; [Pu] to be twisted, be made crooked; [Ht] to stoop down, bend over; from the base meaning of twisting an object comes the fig. extension of twisting morality: to pervert:– pervert [3], bow [1], dealt perversely with [1], falsifying [1], made crooked [1], overthrown [1], subvert [1], turneth upside down [1]

5792 עַוָּתָה *'awwātâ*, n.f. GK: 6432 [→ 5791]. wrong:– wrong [1]

5793 עוּתַי *'ûtay*, n.pr.m. GK: 6433 [→ 5790]. Uthai, "[poss.] *superiority of Yahweh*; [poss.] *[my] restoration*":– Uthai [2]

5794 עַז *'az*, a. GK: 6434 & 6435 [→ 5810, 5815?]. strong, mighty, powerful, fierce:– strong [12], fierce [4], mighty [3], greedy (+5315) [1], power [1], roughly [1], stronger [1]

5795 עֵז *'ēz*, n.m. GK: 6436 [→ 5810?; cf. 5796]. goat; goat hair:– goats [40], goats' [10], kid (+1423) [7], goat [5], she goats [3], he goat (+6842) [2], she goat [2], goat (+7716) [1], he goats (+6842) [1], kids (+1121) [1], kids [1], kid [1]

5796 עֵז *'ēz* (Aram.), n.[f.]. GK: 10535. goat (male and female):– he goats (+6841) [1]

5797 עֹז *'ōz*, n.m. GK: 6437 [→ 5813, 5818; cf. 5756, 5810]. strength, power, might; stronghold, fortification; strong-willed, stubborn:– strength [60], strong [17], power [11], might [2], boldness [1], loud [1], mighty [1]

5798 עֻזָּא *'uzzā'* or עֻזָּה *'uzzâ*, n.pr.m. GK: 6438 & 6446 [→ 6560]. Uzza, Uzzah, "*strong, fierce one*":– Uzza [10], Uzzah [1]

5799 עֲזָאזֵל *'zā'zēl*, n.[m. or pr.]. GK: 6439. scapegoat, a goat sent into the wilderness of the Day of Atonement, symbolically carrying away the sin of the community; some see this word as the name of the desert spirit (Azazel) to whom the goat is sent:– scapegoat [4]

5800 עָזַב *'āzab*, v. GK: 6440 & 6441 [→ 5801, 5805, 5806]. [Q] to leave, abandon, reject, desert; to restore, help; [Qp] be left, be abandoned, be freed; [N] be abandoned, be forsaken, be neglected; [Pu] be deserted, be abandoned:– forsaken [60], forsake [46], left [41], leave [28], forsook [5], forsaketh [5], faileth [2], forsookest [2], leave off [2], leaveth [2], left off [2], surely help (+5800) [2], committeth [1], fortified [1], fortify [1], help [1], left destitute [1], leftest [1], refuseth [1]

5801 עִזָּבוֹנִים *'izbônîm*, n.[m.]. GK: 6442 [→ 5800]. merchandise, goods:– fairs [6], wares [1]

5802 עַזְבּוּק *'azbûq*, n.pr.m. GK: 6443 [→ 950?]. Azbuk:– Azbuk [1]

5803 עַזְגָּד *'azgād*, n.pr.m. GK: 6444. Azgad, "*strong is Gad*":– Azgad [4]

5804 עַזָּה *'azzâ*, n.pr.loc. GK: 6445 [→ 5841]. Gaza, "*strong*":– Gaza [18], Azzah [3]

5805 עֲזוּבָה *'zûbâ*, n.f. GK: 6447 [→ 5800]. forsaking, desolation:– forsaking [1]

5806 עֲזוּבָה *'zûbâ*, n.pr.f. GK: 6448 [→ 5800]. Azubah, "*adornment*":– Azubah [4]

5807 עֱזוּז *'zûz*, n.[m.]. GK: 6449 [→ 5810]. power, strength:– strength [2], might [1]

5808 עִזּוּז *'izzûz*, a. GK: 6450 [→ 5810]. strong, powerful:– power [1], strong [1]

5809 עַזּוּר *'azzur*, n.pr.m. GK: 6473. Azzur, "*help*":– Azur [2], Azzur [1]

5810 עָזַז *'āzaz*, v. GK: 6451 [→ 4581, 5794, 5795?, 5807, 5808, 5811, 5812, 5815, 5819, 5821; cf. 3267, 5756, 5797]. [Q] to be strong, overpower; [H] to put on a bold face, be brazen:– strengthened [3], prevailed [2], strengthen [2], hardeneth [1], impudent [1], prevail [1], strengtheneth [1], strong [1]

5811 עָזָז *'āzāz*, n.pr.m. GK: 6452 [→ 5810]. Azaz, "*strong*":– Azaz [1]

5812 עֲזַזְיָהוּ *'zazyāhû*, n.pr.m. GK: 6453 [→ 5810+3068]. Azaziah, "*Yahweh is strong*":– Azaziah [3]

5813 עֻזִּי *'uzzî*, n.pr.m. GK: 6454 [→ 5797]. Uzzi, "*Yahweh is [my] strength*":– Uzzi [11]

5814 עֻזִּיָּא *'uzziyyā'*, n.pr.m. GK: 6455 [cf. 5818]. Uzzia, "*[my] strength* or *Yahweh is [my] strength*":– Uzzia [1]

5815 עֲזִיאֵל *'zî'ēl*, n.pr.m. GK: 6456 [→ 5794?+410?]. Aziel, "*God is my strength*":– Aziel [1]

5816 עֻזִּיאֵל *'uzzî'ēl*, n.pr.m. GK: 6457 [→ 5817]. Uzziel, "*God [El] is [my] strength*":– Uzziel [16]

5817 עֲזִיאֵלִי *'ozzî'ēlî*, a.g. GK: 6458 [→ 5816]. Uzzielite, "*of Uzziel*":– Uzzielites [2]

5818 עֻזִּיָּה *'uzziyyâ* or עֻזִּיָּהוּ *'uzziyyāhû*, n.pr.m. GK: 6459 & 6460 [→ 5797+3068; cf. 5814]. Uzziah, "*Yahweh is [my] strength*":– Uzziah [27]

5819 עֲזִיזָא *'zîzā'*, n.pr.m. GK: 6461 [→ 5810]. Aziza, "*powerful*":– Aziza [1]

5820 עַזְמָוֶת *'azmāwet*, n.pr.m. & loc. GK: 6462 & 6463 [→ 1041]. Azmaveth, "*strong one of death; camel fodder, plant of the plumose family*":– Azmaveth [8]

5821 עַזָּן *'azzān*, n.pr.m. GK: 6464 [→ 5810]. Azzan, "*strong*":– Azzan [1]

5822 עָזְנִיָּה *'ozniyyâ*, n.f. GK: 6465. black vulture:– ospray [2]

5823 עָזַק *'āzaq*, v. GK: 6466. [P] to dig:– fenced [1]

5824 עִזְקָא *'izqâ* (Aram.), n.f. GK: 10536. signet-ring, used to validate official business:– signet [2]

5825 עֲזֻקָה ^ᵃzēqâ, n.pr.loc. GK: 6467. Azekah, "[poss.] *hoe [the ground]*":– Azekah [7]

5826 עָזַר 'āzar, v. GK: 6468 [→ 499, 3270, 5828, 5829, 5830, 5832, 5835, 5836, 5838; cf. 5737]. [Q] to help, support; [Op] to be helped; [N] to be helped:– help [44], helped [17], helper [7], helpers [4], holpen [3], helpeth [2], succour [2], helped forward [1], succoured [1]

5827 עֵזֶר 'ezer, n.pr.m. GK: 6472 [→ 5828]. Ezer, "*help*":– Ezer [1]

5828 עֵזֶר 'ēzer, n.m. GK: 6469 [→ 5829, 5827, 5833, 5834; cf. 5826 (also used with compound proper names)]. help, helper:– help [21]

5829 עֵזֶר 'ēzer, n.pr.m. GK: 6470 [→ 5828; cf. 5826]. Ezer, "*help*":– Ezer [4]

עָזּוּר 'azzur. See 5809.

5830 עֶזְרָא 'ezrā', n.pr.m. GK: 6474 [→ 5826; cf. 5831]. Ezra, "*help*":– Ezra [22]

5831 עֶזְרָא 'ezrā' (Aram.), n.pr.m. GK: 10537 [cf. 5830]. Ezra, "*help*":– Ezra [3]

5832 עֲזַרְאֵל 'zar'ēl, n.pr.m. GK: 6475 [→ 5826+410]. Azarel, "*God [El] has helped*":– Azareel [5], Azarael [1]

5833 עֶזְרָה 'ezrâ, n.f. GK: 6476 [→ 5834; cf. 5828]. help, aid, support; helper, ally:– help [24], helped [1], helpers [1]

5834 עֶזְרָה 'ezrâ, n.pr.m. GK: 6477 [→ 5833]. Ezrah:– Ezra [1]

5835 עֲזָרָה 'zārâ, n.f. GK: 6478 [→ 5826]. court, enclosure; ledge, barrier:– settle [6], court [3]

5836 עֶזְרִי 'ezrî, n.pr.m. GK: 6479 [→ 5826+3068? or 2967.1?]. Ezri, "*my help*":– Ezri [1]

5837 עֲזְרִיאֵל 'zri'ēl, n.pr.m. GK: 6480 [→ 5828+410]. Azriel, "*God [El] is [my] help*":– Azriel [3]

5838 עֲזַרְיָה 'zaryâ or עֲזַרְיָהוּ 'zaryāhû, n.pr.m. GK: 6481 & 6482 [→ 5826+3068; cf. 5839]. Azariah, "*Yahweh has helped*":– Azariah [48]

5839 עֲזַרְיָה 'zaryâ (Aram.), n.pr.m. GK: 10538 [cf. 5838]. Azariah, "*Yahweh has helped*":– Azariah [1]

5840 עֲזְרִיקָם 'azrîqām, n.pr.m. GK: 6483 [→ 5828+6965]. Azrikam, "*[my] help arises*":– Azrikam [6]

5841 עֲזָּתִי 'azzātî, a.g. GK: 6484 [→ 5804]. Gazite, "*of Gaza*":– Gazathites [1], Gazites [1]

5842 עֵט 'ēt, n.m. GK: 6485. (iron) engraving tool, stylus; (reed) pen:– pen [4]

5843 עֵטָא 'ēṭâ (Aram.), n.f. GK: 10539 [→ 3272; cf. 6098]. counsel, wisdom:– counsel [1]

5844 עָטָה 'āṭâ, v. GK: 6486 & 6487 [→ 4593, 4594; cf. 3271]. [Q] to cover, wrap oneself; to grasp; [Pu] to be grasped; [H] cover, wrap another (thing):– cover [4], covered with [2], surely cover (+5844) [2], array with [1], clad with [1], covered [1], coverest [1], covereth [1], filleth [1], put a covering [1], putteth on [1], turneth aside [1]

5845 עֲטִין 'ṭîn, n.[m.]. GK: 6489. body, part of body; or pail, bucket:– breasts [1]

5846 עֲטִישָׁה 'ṭîšâ, n.f. GK: 6490. snorting, sneezing:– neesings [1]

5847 עֲטַלֵּף 'ṭallēp, n.[m.]. GK: 6491 [→ 5848+3807.1]. bat (animal):– bat [2], bats [1]

5848 עָטַף 'āṭap, v. GK: 6488 & 6493 & 6494 [→ 4595, 5847]. [Q] to clothe, mantle; to turn aside; to grow faint; [N] to be faint; [H] to be feeble; [Ht] to ebb away, grow faint:– overwhelmed [5], fainted [2], covered over [1], covereth [1], fail [1], faint [1], feebler [1], feeble [1], hideth [1], swooned [1], swoon [1]

5849 עָטַר 'āṭar, v. GK: 6496 & 6497 [→ 5850, 5851, 5852, 5853, 5854, 5855]. [Q] to surround, close in upon; [P] to crown, place a wreath (on the head); [H] to bestow a crown:– crowned [2], compassed round about [1], compass [1], crownest [1], crowneth [1], crowning [1]

5850 עֲטָרָה 'ṭārâ, n.f. GK: 6498 [→ 5849]. crown, wreath, placed on the head as a symbol of celebration or status; can be made of plants or precious metals:– crown [20], crowns [3]

5851 עֲטָרָה 'ṭārâ, n.pr.f. GK: 6499 [→ 5849]. Atarah, "*circlet, wreath*":– Atarah [1]

5852 עֲטָרוֹת 'ṭārôt, n.pr.loc. GK: 6500 [→ 5853, 5854; cf. 5849]. Ataroth, "*circlets, wreaths*":– Ataroth [5]

5853 עֲטָרוֹת אַדָּר 'ṭārôt 'addār, n.pr.loc. GK: 6501 [→ 5852+146]. Ataroth Addar, "*wreaths of majesty*":– Ataroth-adar [1], Ataroth-addar [1]

5854 עֲטָרוֹת בֵּית יוֹאָב 'ṭārôt bêt yô'āb, n.pr.loc. GK: 6502 [→ 5852+1004+3097]. Atroth Beth Joab, "*circlets, folds of the house of Joab*":–

5855 עֲטָרוֹת שׁוֹפָן 'ṭārôt šôpān, n.pr.loc. GK: 6503 [→ 5849]. Atroth Shophan, "*circlets, folds of Shophan*":– Atroth Shophan [1]

5856 עִי 'î, n.[m.]. GK: 6505 [→ 1164, 4596, 5859, 5863, 5864; cf. 5753]. heap of rubble; (of a person) a broken man:– heaps [3], grave [1], heap [1]

5857 עַי 'ay or עַיָּה 'ayyat or עַיָּא 'ayyâ, n.pr.loc. GK: 6504 & 6509 & 6569 [cf. 5754]. Ai, Aiath, Ayyah; Aija, "*ruin, the heap*":– Ai [36], Hai [2], Aiath [1], Aija [1]

5858 עֵיבָל 'êbāl, n.pr.m. & g. & loc. GK: 6506 & 6507 & 6508 [cf. 5745]. Ebal:– Ebal [8]

עַיָּה 'ayâ. See 5857.

5859 עִיּוֹן 'iyyôn, n.pr.loc. GK: 6510 [→ 5856]. Ijon, "*place of heaps [of stone]*":– Ijon [3]

5860 עִיט 'îṭ, v. GK: 6512 & 6513 [→ 5861, 5862?]. [Q] to hurl insults; to pounce upon (with shrieks and screams):– flew [1], fly [1], railed [1]

5861 עַיִט 'ayiṭ, n.m. GK: 6514 [→ 5862?; cf. 5860]. (coll) birds of prey, carrion birds:– fowls [3], birds [1], bird [1], fowl [1], ravenous bird [1], ravenous [1]

5862 עֵיטָם 'êṭām, n.pr.loc. GK: 6515 [→ 5861?+3963.1?]. Etam, "*[poss.] place of birds of prey*":– Etam [5]

5863 עִיֵּי הָעֲבָרִים 'iyyê hā'bārîm, n.pr.loc. GK: 6516 [→ 5856]. Iye Abarim, "*heaps of Abarim [regions beyond]*":– Ije-abarim [2]

5864 עִיִּים 'iyyîm, n.pr.loc. GK: 6517 [→ 5856]. Iyim; Iim, "*heaps, ruins*":– Iim [2]

5865 עֵילוֹם 'êlôm, n.m. GK: 6518 [cf. 5769]. forever:– ever [1]

5866 עִילַי 'îlay, n.pr.m. GK: 6519. Ilai:– Ilai [1]

5867 עֵילָם 'êlām, n.pr.m. & g. & loc. GK: 6520 & 6521 [cf. 5962]. Elam, "*highland*":– Elam [28]

5868 עֲיָם 'yām, n.[m.]. GK: 6522. scorching (of wind):– mighty [1]

5869 עַיִן 'ayin, n.f. & m. GK: 6524 [→ 4599, 5770, 5871, 5879, 5881; cf. 5870 (also used with compound proper names)]. eye; by extension: sight; spring, fountain; to be "evil of eye" is to be displeased; to be "good of eye" is to be pleased; to be "good in one's eyes" is to be pleasing "right in one's eyes" means acceptable to one's personal standards:– eyes [420], sight [216], eye [77], colour [12], face [10], well [10], seemeth unto (+871.1) [9], pleased (+3190+871.1) [8], presence [8], fountain [7], before (+3807.1) [6], displeased (+3415+871.1) [6], seem unto (+871.1) [6], seemeth (+871.1) [6], conceit [6], fountains [4], looks [3], look [3], pleased (+3474+871.1) [3], pleased well (+3474+871.1) [3], seemed to (+871.1) [3], thought (+871.1) [3], before (+871.1) [2], displease (+7489+871.1) [2], look well (+7760) [2], pleased (+2896+871.1) [2], pleased well (+3190+871.1) [2], pleaseth (+2896+871.1) [2], seemed (+1961+871.1) [2], seemeth to (+871.1) [2], thinkest (+871.1) [2], content (+3190+871.1) [1], countenance [1], displease (+2734+871.1) [1], displease (+6213+7451+871.1) [1], displeased (+7489+871.1) [1], escape (+5337) [1], eye sight [1], eye's [1], eyebrows (+1354) [1], eyed [1], eyesight [1], favour (+2896+871.1) [1], for (+871.1) [1], humble person (+7807) [1], liketh (+2896+871.1) [1], looketh (+4758) [1], open place (+6607) [1], openly (+871.1+1886.1) [1], outward appearance [1], please (+3474+871.1) [1], please not (+7451+871.1) [1], pleased not (+7451+871.1) [1], pleased well (+3477+871.1) [1], pleaseth (+3190+871.1) [1], pleaseth well (+3474) [1], regard (+2347) [1], resemblance [1], seem (+1961+871.1) [1], seem (+871.1) [1], seem unto (+3807.1) [1], seemed unto (+871.1) [1], think (+871.1) [1], think best (+2896+871.1) [1], thinking (+871.1) [1], wells [1], with (+871.1) [1], without knowledge (+4480) [1]

5870 עַיִן 'ayin (Aram.), n.f. GK: 10540 [cf. 5869]. eye:– eyes [4], eye [1]

5871 עַיִן 'ayin, n.pr.loc. GK: 6526 [→ 5869]. Ain, "*eye/ball*" or *spring of water*":– Ain [5]

5872 עֵין גֶּדִי 'ên gedî, n.pr.loc. GK: 6527 [→ 5869+1423]. En Gedi, "*spring of young goat*":– En-gedi [6]

5873 עֵין גַּנִּים 'ên gannîm, n.pr.loc. GK: 6528 [→ 5869]. En Gannim, "*spring of gardens*":– En-gannim [3]

5874 עֵין־דֹּאר 'ên-dō'r or עֵין־דּוֹר 'ên-dôr, n.pr.loc. GK: 6529 [→ 5869+1756]. Endor, "*spring of Dor*":– En-dor [3]

5875 עֵין הַקּוֹרֵא 'ên haqqôrē', n.pr.loc. GK: 6530 [→ 5869]. En Hakkore, "*spring of the partridge or caller*":– En-hakkore [1]

עֵינוֹן 'ênôn. See 2703.

5876 עֵין חַדָּה 'ên ḥaddâ, n.pr.loc. GK: 6532 [→ 5869]. En Haddah, "*spring of gladness*":– En-haddah [1]

5877 עֵין חָצוֹר 'ên ḥāṣôr, n.pr.loc. GK: 6533 [→ 5869+2674]. En Hazor, "*spring of Hazor*":– En-hazor [1]

5878 עֵין חֲרֹד 'ên ḥ'rōd, n.pr.loc. GK: 6534 [→ 5869]. En Harod, "*spring of Harod*":– Harod [1]

5879 עֵינַיִם 'ênayim or עֵינָם 'ênām, n.pr.loc. GK: 6542 & 6543 [→ 5869+3963.1]. Enam, Enaim, "*two springs*":– Enam [1]

5880 עֵין מִשְׁפָּט 'ên mišpāṭ, n.pr.loc. GK: 6535 [→ 5869+4941]. En Mishpat, "*spring of judgment*":– En-mishpat [1]

5881 עֵינָן 'ênān, n.pr.m. GK: 6544 [→ 2704]. Enan, "*spring*":– Enan [5]

5882 עֵין עֶגְלַיִם 'ên 'eglayim, n.pr.loc. GK: 6536 [→ 5869]. En Eglaim, "*spring of two calves*":– En-eglaim [1]

5883 עֵין רֹגֵל 'ên rōgēl, n.pr.loc. GK: 6537 [→ 5869]. En Rogel, "*spring of the fuller or wanderer or spy*":– En-rogel [4]

5884 עֵין רִמּוֹן 'ên rimmôn, n.pr.loc. GK: 6538 [→ 5869+7417]. En Rimmon, "*spring of Rimmon*":– En-rimmon [1]

5885 עֵין שֶׁמֶשׁ 'ên šemeš, n.pr.loc. GK: 6539 [→ 5869+8121]. En Shemesh, "*spring of Shemesh*":– En-shemesh [2]

5886 עֵין תַּנִּים 'ên tannîm, n.pr.loc. GK: 6524 + 9478 [→ 5869+8565]. En Tannim, "*Well of the Jackal*" (5869 + 8565):–

5887 עֵין תַּפּוּחַ 'ên tappûaḥ, n.pr.loc. GK: 6540 [→ 5869+8599]. En Tappuah, "*spring of apple*":– En-tappuah [1]

5888 עִיף 'îp, v. GK: 6545 [→ 5774]. [Q] to be faint, be exhausted:– wearied [1]

5889 עָיֵף 'āyēp, a. GK: 6546 [→ 5774; cf. 3286]. weary, faint; famished, parched:– weary [8], faint [6], thirsty [3]

5890 עֵיפָה 'êpâ, n.f. GK: 6547 [→ 5891; cf. 4155]. darkness:– darkness [2]

5891 עֵיפָה 'êpâ, n.pr.m. & f. & g. GK: 6548 & 6549 [cf. 5890]. Ephah, "*darkness*":– Ephah [5]

5892 עִיר 'îr, n.f. GK: 6551 & 6552 [→ 5542, 6144? (also found with compound proper names)]. city, town, village, a general term for a population center; anguish, terror, wrath:– city [650], cities [421], several city (+5892+2050.1) [6], every city (+3605+5892+2050.1) [4], any city (+5892+2050.1) [4], town [4], towns [3], cities every one (+5892) [2]

5893 עִיר 'îr, n.pr.m. GK: 6553 [→ 5895]. Ir, "*[poss.] stallion donkey*":– Ir [1]

5894 עִיר 'îr (Aram.), n.m. GK: 10541 [cf. 5782]. messenger (of God), watcher, one who is a sentinel to guard and protect:– watcher [2], watchers [1]

5895 עַיִר 'ayir, n.m. GK: 6554 & 6555 [→ 5782, 5893, 5896, 5901, 5902]. (male) donkey:– ass colts [2], colt [2], young asses [2], foals [1], foal [1]

5896 עִירָא 'îrā', n.pr.m. GK: 6562 [→ 5895]. Ira, "*[poss.] stallion donkey*":– Ira [6]

5897 עִירָד 'îrād, n.pr.m. GK: 6563 [→ 6171]. Irad:– Irad [2]

5898 עִיר הַמֶּלַח 'îr hammelaḥ, n.pr.loc. GK: 6558 [→ 5892+1886.1+4417]. Ir Hammelak, "*the city of salt*":–

5899 עִיר הַתְּמָרִים 'îr hatt'mārîm, n.pr.loc. GK: 6559 [→ 5892+1886.1+8558]. Ir Hattemarim, "*the city of palms*":–

5900 עִירוּ 'îrû, n.pr.m. GK: 6564. Iru:– Iru [1]

5901 עִירִי 'îrî, n.pr.m. GK: 6565 [→ 5895]. Iri, "*[perhaps] donkey's colt*":– Iri [1]

5902 עִירָם 'îrām, n.pr.m. GK: 6566 [→ 5895+3963.1]. Iram:– Iram [2]

5903 עֵירֹם 'êrōm, a. (used as noun). GK: 6567 [→ 6168]. naked; nakedness:– naked [9], nakedness [1]

5904 עִיר נָחָשׁ 'îr nāḥāš, n.pr.loc. GK: 6560 [→ 5892]. Ir Nahash, "*city of Nahash*":– Irnahash [1]

5905 עִיר שֶׁמֶשׁ *ʿîr šemeš*, n.pr.loc. GK: 6561 [→ 5892+8121].
Ir Shemesh, "*city of Shemesh*":– Ir-shemesh [1]

5906 עַיִשׁ or עָשׁ *ʿayiš* or *ʿāš*, n.f. GK: 6568 & 6933 [→ 6211].
constellation: the Bear or the Lion, or some other constellation:–
Arcturus [2]

עֵיָה *ʿayāt*. See 5857.

5907 עַכְבּוֹר *ʿakbôr*, n.pr.m. GK: 6570 [→ 5909]. Acbor,
"*mouse* or *jerboa*":– Achbor [7]

5908 עַכָּבִישׁ *ʿakkābîš*, n.m. GK: 6571. spider:– spider's [2]

5909 עַכְבָּר *ʿakbār*, n.m. GK: 6572 [→ 5907]. (jumping) rat,
jerboa:– mice [4], mouse [2]

5910 עַכּוֹ *ʿakkô*, n.pr.loc. GK: 6573. Acco:– Accho [1]

5911 עָכוֹר *ʿākôr*, n.pr.loc. GK: 6574 [→ 5916]. Achor,
"*trouble*":– Achor [5]

5912 עָכָן *ʿākān*, n.pr.m. GK: 6575. Achan, "*troubler*":–
Achan [6]

5913 עָכַס *ʿākas*, v.den. GK: 6576 [→ 5914, 5915]. [P] to
jingle, rattle (of ankle ornaments):– making a tinkling [1]

5914 עֶכֶס *ʿekes*, n.[m.]. GK: 6577 [→ 5913]. bangle, ankle
ornament:– stocks [1], tinkling ornaments [1]

5915 עַכְסָה *ʿaksâ*, n.pr.f. GK: 6578 [→ 5913]. Acsah,
"*decorative anklet*":– Achsah [5]

5916 עָכַר *ʿākar*, v. GK: 6579 [→ 5911, 5917, 5918]. [Q] to
bring trouble, make trouble; [N] to be troubled, be anguished:–
troubled [4], troubleth [4], trouble [4], stirred [1], troubler [1]

5917 עָכָר *ʿākār*, n.pr.m. GK: 6580 [→ 5916]. Achar,
"*trouble*":– Achar [1]

5918 עָכְרָן *ʿokrān*, n.pr.m. GK: 6581 [→ 5916]. Ocran,
"*trouble*":– Ocran [5]

5919 עַכְשׁוּב *ʿakšûb*, n.m. GK: 6582. (horned) viper; other
sources: asp:– adder's [1]

5920 עַל *ʿal*, subst. GK: 6583 [→ 5927; cf. 5921; cf. 5943].
(the) Most High:– above [2], most high [2], above (+4480) [1],
on high [1]

5921 עַל *ʿal*, pp. & c. GK: 6584 [→ 4480+5921; cf. 5920;
cf. 5922]. marker of relationship: spatial: on, upon, over, against,
toward; logical: because of, according to; temporal: on, when,
during:– upon [1572], against [538], over [413], in [318],
for [305], on [292], by [215], to [167], from (+4480) [152],
unto [150], therefore (+3651) [125], with [106], at [87],
concerning [79], off [63], above [56], of [55], into [47], before
(+6440) [43], according to [32], thereon (+2050.2) [31], because
(+834) [26], because of [26], because [25], upon (+6440) [23],
wherefore (+3651) [22], after [20], out of (+4480) [19],
toward [15], next unto (+3027) [13], about [12], above
(+4480) [12], beside [12], before [11], upon (+4480) [11],
thereon (+1886.3) [10], wherefore (+4100) [10], whereon
(+834) [10]*

5922 עַל *ʿal* (Aram.), pp. GK: 10542 [→ 5924, 5928, 5943,
5952, 5946; cf. 5921]. upon, over, against, toward,
concerning:– upon [19], unto [16], over [13], in [10], against [7],
to [7], concerning [6], for [6] of [5], about [3], above [1], from [1],
more [1], nor (+2050.3) [1], on [1], therefore (+1836) [1],
thereon (+1958.2) [1], why (+4101) [1], with [1]

5923 עֹל *ʿōl*, n.m. GK: 6585 [→ 5953]. yoke, placed on draft
animals; by extension: a figure of oppression or of proper
training:– yoke [40]

5924 עֵלָּא *ʿellāʾ* (Aram.), adv. GK: 10543 [→ 5922; cf. 5921].
over, above:– over (+4481) [1]

5925 עֻלָּא *ʿullāʾ*, n.pr.m. GK: 6587 [→ 5927]. Ulla:– Ulla [1]

5926 עִלֵּג *ʿillēg*, a. GK: 6589 [cf. 3932]. speaking
inarticulately; (pl.n.) stammerers:– stammerers [1]

5927 עָלָה *ʿālâ*, v. GK: 6590 [→ 500, 4605, 4607, 4608,
4609, 5920, 5925, 5929, 5930, 5935, 5941, 5940,
5942, 5933, 5944, 5945, 8585]. [Q] to go up, ascend, rise; [N]
to be lifted up, withdraw, be exalted; [H] to take up, set up, offer
a sacrifice; [Ho] to be offered up, be carried away, be recorded;
[Ht] to raise oneself up; from the base meaning of rise in
elevation comes the fig. extension "to exalt, honor," as the
lifting up of a person in status:– went up [156], go up [123],
come up [81], came up [77], brought up [58], offered [35], bring
up [32], offer [29], gone up [21], get up [18], come [11], goeth
up [10], taken up [9], offering [8], brought [7], gat up [7],
ascended [6], came [6], cause to come up [6], cheweth [6],
cometh up [6], offer up [5], rise up [5], ascended up [4],
ascend [4], carry up [4], going up [4], go [4], mount up [4], take
up [4], went [4], bringeth up [3], bring [3], carried up [3], causeth

to ascend [3], chew [3], climb up [3], cometh [3], increased [3],
made to come up [3], offereth [3], took up [3], arose [2],
ascending [2], cast up [2], cause to burn [2], depart [2],
exalted [2], fell [2], go up at once (+5927) [2], lifteth up [2],
lighted [2], light [2], offered up [2], put [2], raised [2], setteth
up [2], spring [2], surely bring up (+5927) [2], wentest up [2],
arise up [1], ariseth [1], arise [1], ascend up [1], breaketh [1],
breaking [1], broken up [1], broughtest up [1], broughtest [1],
burnt [1], cause come up [1], caused to come up [1], causeth to
come up [1], climbed up [1], climb [1], cometh in [1], cut off [1],
dawning [1], departed [1], excellest [1], fetch up [1], fetched
up [1], fetcht up [1], getteth up [1], goest up [1], goeth [1], gone
away [1], grow up [1], groweth [1], grown over [1], grow [1],
increaseth [1], laid [1], leaped [1], leap [1], lift up [1], lightest [1],
lighteth [1], made to go up [1], made up (+724) [1], make rise
up [1], make to pay [1], mentioned [1], offering up [1], perfected
(+724) [1], prefer [1], put on [1], raised up [1], recovered [1],
restore [1], riseth up [1], rising [1], rose up [1], rose [1],
scaleth [1], set up [1], set [1], shooting up [1], shot forth [1],
spring up [1], stir up [1], take away [1], upon levy [1], vapour [1],
went away [1], wrought [1]

5928 עֲלָוָה *ʿălāwâ* (Aram.), n.f. GK: 10545 [→ 5922;
cf. 5930]. burnt offering:– burnt offerings [1]

5929 עָלֶה *ʿāleh*, n.m. GK: 6591 [→ 5927]. leaves, foliage:–
leaf [11], branches [4], branch [1], leaves [1]

5930 עֹלָה *ʿōlâ*, n.f. GK: 6592 [→ 5927; cf. 5928]. burnt
offering, wholly dedicated to God:– burnt offering [183], burnt
offerings [82], burnt sacrifice [17], burnt sacrifices [4], ascent [1],
go up [1]

5931 עִלָּה *ʿillâ* (Aram.), n.f. GK: 10544 [cf. 5953]. grounds,
basis, pretext (for charges):– occasion [3]

5932 עַלְוָה *ʿalwâ*, n.f. GK: 6594. evil, wickedness:– iniquity [1]

5933 עַלְוָה *ʿalwâ* or עַלְיָה *ʿalyâ*, n.pr.m. GK: 6595 & 6607
[→ 5927]. Alvah, Aliah:– Aliah [1], Alvah [1]

5934 עֲלוּמִים *ʿălûmîm*, n.pl.abst. GK: 6596 [→ 3281, 5958,
5959, 5961]. (abst.pl.) youthfulness, (the vigor of) youth:–
youth [4]

5935 עַלְוָן *ʿalwān* or עַלְיָן *ʿalyān*, n.pr.m. GK: 6597 & 6615
[→ 5927]. Alvan, Alian, "[poss.] *ascending one* or *tall*":–
Alian [1], Alvan [1]

5936 עֲלוּקָה *ʿălûqâ*, n.f. GK: 6598. leech:– horseleach [1]

5937 עָלַז *ʿālaz*, v. GK: 6600 [→ 5938, 5947; cf. 5965]. [Q] to
rejoice, be jubilant:– rejoice [8], joyful [2], rejoiced [2],
triumph [2], greatly rejoiceth [1], rejoicest [1]

5938 עָלֵז *ʿālēz*, a. (used as n.). GK: 6601 [→ 5937]. reveling,
exultant; (n.) reveler:– rejoiceth [1]

5939 עֲלָטָה *ʿălāṭâ*, n.f. GK: 6602. darkness, dusk:– twilight [3],
dark [1]

5940 עֱלִי *ʿĕlî*, n.[m.]. GK: 6605 [→ 5927]. pestle (of a
mortar):– pestle [1]

5941 עֵלִי *ʿēlî*, n.pr.m. GK: 6603 [→ 3068 *or* 410+5927]. Eli,
"*Yahweh is exalted; God [El] is exalted*":– Eli [32], Eli's [1]

5942 עִלִּי *ʿillî*, a. GK: 6606 [→ 5927; cf. 5952]. upper:–
upper [2]

5943 עִלַּי *ʿillāy* (Aram.), a. GK: 10546 [→ 5922]. highest,
superior; the Most High, a title of God indicating his supreme
status and power:– most high [9], high [1]

עֶלְיָה *ʿelyâ*. See 5933.

5944 עֲלִיָּה *ʿăliyyâ*, n.f. GK: 6608 [→ 5927; cf. 5952]. upper
room, upper parts:– chambers [4], chamber [4], parlour [4], going
up [2], upper chambers [2], upper chamber [2], ascent [1], loft [1]

5945 עֶלְיוֹן *ʿelyôn*, a. GK: 6609 & 6610 [→ 5927; cf. 5943,
cf. 5946]. upper, also used in place names; (the) Most High, a
title of God with a focus on supremacy in status and power:–
most high [27], high [9], upper [8], higher [4], highest [3], on
high [1], uppermost [1]

5946 עֶלְיוֹן *ʿelyôn* (Aram.), a. GK: 10548 [→ 5922; cf. 5945].
highest, superior; (as a title) the Most High:– most high [4]

5947 עַלִּיז *ʿallîz*, a. GK: 6611 [→ 5937]. rejoicing, exulting;
reveling, wild:– joyous [3], rejoice [3], rejoicing [1]

5948 עֲלִיל *ʿălîl*, n.[m.]. GK: 6612 [→ 5953]. furnace:–
furnace [1]

5949 עֲלִילָה *ʿălîlâ*, n.f. GK: 6613 [→ 5953]. what is done,
deed, action:– doings [13], works [3], deeds [2], occasions [2],
actions [1], acts [1], doing [1], inventions [1]

5950 עֲלִילִיָּה *ʿălîliyyâ*, n.f. GK: 6614. deed:– work [1]

5951 עֲלִיצֻת *ʿălîṣut*, n.f. GK: 6617 [→ 5970; cf. 5965].
rejoicing, exaltation, including verbal expressions of joy and
praise; from a negative perspective: haughtiness, presumption,
gloating:– rejoicing [1]

5952 עִלִּי *ʿillî* (Aram.), n.f. GK: 10547 [→ 5922; cf. 5942].
upstairs room, a storage or guest room on the flat roof of a
house:– chamber [1]

5953 עָלַל *ʿālal*, v. GK: 6618 & 6619 & 6620 & 6621
[→ 4611, 5923, 5948, 5949, 5955, 8586; cf. 5954]. [Po] to act
or play the child; (n.) youths; to deal with; to glean, go over a
second time; to thrust (in); [Poal] to be dealt with (in a way that
causes suffering); [Ht] to deal harshly, abuse, mistreat; [Htpo] to
take part in (wickedness):– done [3], abuse [2], glean [2],
throughly glean (+5953) [2], abused [1], affecteth [1],
children [1], defiled [1], do [1], gleaned [1], mocked [1], mock [1],
practise [1], wrought wonderfully [1], wrought [1]

5954 עֲלַל *ʿălal* (Aram.), v. GK: 10549 [→ 4606; cf. 5953]. [P]
to go in; [H] to take in, bring before; [Ho] to be brought in,
introduced before:– bring in [3], brought in [3], came in [3], went
in [2], brought [1], came [1], went [1]

עֹלָל *ʿōlāl*. See 5768.

עֹלָה *ʿōlâ*. See 5949.

5955 עֹלֵלוֹת *ʿōlēlôt*, n.f.pl.intens. GK: 6622 [→ 5953].
gleanings:– gleaning grapes [3], gleaning of grapes [1],
grapegleanings [1], grapes [1]

5956 עָלַם *ʿālam*, v. GK: 6623 [→ 8587]. [Qp] to be in secret;
[N] to be concealed, be hidden, be unaware; [H] to hide, shut off,
conceal; [Ht] to hide oneself from, ignore:– hid [11], hide [7], any
ways hide (+5956) [2], hideth [2], secret [2], blind [1],
dissemblers [1], hidden [1], hidest [1]

5957 עָלַם *ʿālam* (Aram.), n.[m.]. GK: 10550 [cf. 5769].
forever, eternal, everlasting; ancient, a long time ago:– ever [10],
everlasting [4], old [2], ever (+0.2) [1], ever (+0.2+5705) [1], for
ever (+0.2) [1], never (+3809+3807.2) [1]

5958 עֶלֶם *ʿelem*, n.m. GK: 6624 [→ 5934]. boy, young man:–
stripling [1], young man [1]

עוֹלָם *ʿôlām*. See 5769.

5959 עַלְמָה *ʿalmâ*, n.f. GK: 6625 [→ 5934; cf. 5961]. girl,
young woman, (in certain contexts) virgin:– maid [2], virgins [2],
virgin [2], damsels [1]

5960 עַלְמוֹן *ʿalmôn*, n.pr.loc. GK: 6626 [→ 5963]. Almon:–
Almon [1]

5961 עֲלָמוֹת *ʿălāmôt*, n.f. GK: 6628 [→ 5934; cf. 5959].
alamoth (t.t. in the Psalms):– Alamoth [2]

עַלְמוּת *ʿalmût*. See 4192.

5962 עֵלָמַי *ʿēlāmay* (Aram.), n.g.pl. GK: 10551 [cf. 5867].
Elamite:– Elamites [1]

5963 עַלְמוֹן דִּבְלָתָיְמָה *ʿalmôn diblātāyim*, n.pr.loc. GK: 6627
[→ 5960]. Almon Diblathaim, "*way of the double fig cakes*":–
Almon-diblathaim [2]

5964 עָלֶמֶת *ʿālemet*, n.pr.m. & loc. GK: 6630 & 6631.
Alemeth, "*concealment*":– Alemeth [3], Alameth [1]

5965 עָלַס *ʿālas*, v. GK: 6632 [cf. 5937, 5951, 5970]. [Q] to
enjoy; [N] to appear glad; [Ht] to enjoy one another:–
peacocks [1], rejoice [1], solace [1]

5966 עָלַע *ʿālaʿ*, v. GK: 6633 [cf. 3216]. [Palpal] to drink, feast
on:– suck up [1]

5967 עֲלַע *ʿălaʿ* (Aram.), n.f. GK: 10552 [cf. 6763]. rib:– ribs [1]

5968 עָלַף *ʿālap*, v. GK: 6634. [Pu] to faint; to be withered; be
decorated, covered; [Ht] to disguise oneself; to grow faint:–
fainted [2], faint [1], overlaid [1], wrapped [1]

5969 עֻלְפֶּה *ʿulpeh*, var. GK: 6635. form of 5968: faint:–
fainted [1]

5970 עָלַץ *ʿālaṣ*, v. GK: 6636 [→ 5951; cf. 5965]. [Q] to
rejoice, be jubilant:– rejoice [4], rejoiceth [2], joyful [1],
triumph [1]

5971 עַם *ʿam*, n.[m.]. GK: 6638 & 6639 [cf. 5972 (also used
with compound proper names)]. people, nation, countrymen;
army, troop; father's relatives, one's people:– people [1829],
nations [15], every people (+5971+2050.1) [8], people
(+1121) [5], each people (+5971+2050.1) [2], folk [2],
nation [2], people's [2], Ammi (+2967.1) [1], men [1]

5972 עַם *ʿam* (Aram.), n.m. GK: 10553 [cf. 5971]. people,
nation:– people [15]

5973 עַם **'im**, pp. GK: 6640 [→ 6005; cf. 6004; cf. 5974]. marker of association or proximity: to, toward; with, among:– with [778], from (+4480) [46], against [36], unto [32], by [22], in [18], of (+4480) [13], among [11], to [11], and [7], for [5], of [5], before [4], by (+4480) [4], as [3], beside [3], at [2], towards [2], able to withstand (+3320) [1], accompanying [1], according to mind (+4480) [1], as long as [1], before (+4480) [1], besides [1], between [1], by reason of [1], for (+3588) [1], given of (+4480) [1], had (+1961) [1], had [1], have (+3426) [1], have [1], help [1], in the behalf of [1], lest (+2050.1) [1], lieth with (+7901) [1], like [1], mighty [1369] [1], minded (+3820) [1], more than [1], near [1], on side [1], shew (+6213) [1], though (+3588) [1], to (+4480) [1], together with [1], toward [1], unto (+4480) [1], upon [1], withal [1]

5974 עַם **'im** (Aram.), pp. GK: 10554 [cf. 5973]. with, along with, to, for; a marker showing association in various meanings:– with [14], from [2], to [2], by [1], like [1], toward [1], unto [1]

5975 עָמַד **'āmad**, v. GK: 6641 [→ 4612, 4613, 5977, 5978, 5979, 5982]. [Q] to stand, stand up, stand still; [H] to cause to stand, present; to appoint, assign; [Ho] to be presented, be caused to stand:– stood [175], stand [123], set [31], standeth [13], stand up [12], set up [11], stood still [11], appointed [10], standing [10], stay [8], stayed [7], present [6], stand still [6], continue [4], endureth [4], remained [4], standest [4], stood up [4], waited [4], endure [3], establish [3], made [3], remain [3], abideth [2], abide [2], appoint [2], at a stay [2], confirmed [2], left [2], set forth [2], setteth [2], standing up [2], stayed up [2], stoodest [2], withstand [2], able to stand [1], abode [1], arise [1], arose [1], caused to stand [1], ceased [1], continued [1], continueth [1], dwell [1], employed [1], enduring [1], established [1], made to serve [1], made to stand [1], ordained [1], over (+5921) [1], placed [1], presented [1], raised up [1], raiseth [1], remaineth [1], repair [1], served (+6440+3807.1) [1], serve [1], settled [1], settle [1], stablished [1], stablisheth [1], stand by [1], standeth (+3807.1) [1], stood fast [1], tarried [1], tarry [1], waited on [1], withstand (+5048) [1], withstand (+6440+3807.1) [1], withstood (+5048+3807.1) [1], withstood (+5921) [1]

5976 עָמַד **'āmad** for מָעַד **mā'ad**, v. GK: 5048 [→ 4154]. var. of 4571: [H] cause to wobble, to bend:– madest to be at a stand [1]

5977 עֹמֶד **'ōmed**, n.[m.]. GK: 6642 [→ 5975]. standing-place (a position, station, or post):– place [6], upright (+5921) [2], stood [1], where stood [1]

5978 עִמָּד **'immād**, pp. GK: 6643 [→ 5975]. with:– with [25], unto [7], against [1], by [1], from (+4480) [1], in [1], mine (+2967.1) [1], of (+4480) [1], take [1], upon [1], within [1]

עַמֻּד **'ammud**. See 5982.

5979 עֶמְדָה **'emdâ**, n.f. GK: 6644 [→ 5975]. place to stand, protection:– standing [1]

5980 עֻמָּה **'ummâ**, n.f. (used as pp.). GK: 6645 [→ 6004]. close by; alongside; adjoining:– over against (+3807.1) [15], against (+3807.1) [6], against [1], besides (+3807.1) [2], answerable (+3807.1) [1], at (+3807.1) [1], hard by (+3807.1) [1], points [1]

5981 עֻמָּה **'ummâ**, n.pr.loc. GK: 6646. Ummah:– Ummah [1]

5982 עַמּוּד **'ammûd**, n.m. GK: 6647 [→ 5975]. pillar, post, column; used fig. of the pillar-shaped cloud of God's presence:– pillars [80], pillar [29], apieceˢ (+259) [1], themˢ [1]

5983 עַמּוֹן **'ammôn**, n.pr.[loc.]. GK: 6648 [→ 5984; cf. 5971]. Ammonite; Ammon, "my people [Ge 19:38]":– Ammon [90], Ammonites (+1121) [15], Ammonites [1]

5984 עַמּוֹנִי **'ammônî**, a.g. GK: 6649 [→ 5983, 5985]. Ammonite, from Ammon, "of Ammon":– Ammonite [9], Ammonites [7], Ammonitess [4], of Ammon [1]

5985 עַמּוֹנִית **'ammônît**, a.g. GK: 6649 [→ 5984]. f. of 5984: Ammonite, from Ammon, "of Ammon":–

5986 עָמוֹס **'āmôs**, n.pr.m. GK: 6650 [→ 6006?]. Amos, "burden bearer":– Amos [7]

5987 עָמוֹק **'āmôq**, n.pr.m. GK: 6651 [→ 6009]. Amok, "capable":– Amok [2]

5988 עַמִּיאֵל **'ammî'ēl**, n.pr.m. GK: 6653 [→ 5971+410]. Ammiel, "God [El] is my kinsman":– Ammiel [6]

5989 עַמִּיהוּד **'ammîhûd**, n.pr.m. GK: 6654 [→ 5971+1935]. Ammihud, "[my] people have majesty":– Ammihud [10]

5990 עַמִּיזָבָד **'ammîzābād**, n.pr.m. GK: 6655 [→ 5971+2064]. Ammizabad, "[my] people have given a gift":– Ammizabad [1]

5991 עַמִּיחוּר **'ammîḥûr**, n.pr.m. GK: 6656 [→ 5971+2354?]. Amihur, cf. 5989:–

5992 עַמִּינָדָב **'ammînādāb**, n.pr.m. GK: 6657 [→ 5971+5068]. Amminadab, "[my] people are generous":– Amminadab [12]

5993 עַמִּי נָדִיב **'ammî Nādîb**, n.pr.m. GK: 6652 + 5618 [→ 5971+5081]. Amminadib, "[my] people are generous":– Ammi-nadib [1]

5994 עַמִּיק **'ammîq** (Aram.), a. GK: 10555 [cf. 6013]. deep; (as noun) the deep things, which are normally impenetrable and so secret and hidden, with the implication that such things are mysterious, profound, and valuable:– deep [1]

5995 עָמִיר **'āmîr**, n.[m.]. GK: 6658 [→ 6014]. (newly) cut grain:– sheaves [2], handful [1], sheaf [1]

5996 עַמִּישַׁדָּי **'ammîšadday**, n.pr.m. GK: 6659 [→ 5971+7706]. Ammishaddai, "Shaddai is [my] kinsman":– Ammishaddai [5]

5997 עָמִית **'āmît**, n.m. GK: 6660 [→ 6004]. neighbor, countryman, associate (one in close, united relation):– neighbour [7], anotherˢ [2], neighbour's [2], fellow [1]

5998 עָמַל **'āmal**, v. GK: 6661 [→ 5999, 6000, 6001]. [Q] to labor, toil, pour forth effort:– laboured [5], labour [2], taketh [2], laboureth [1], took [1]

5999 עָמָל **'āmāl**, n.m. & f. GK: 6662 [→ 5998]. trouble, work, labor, toil:– labour [25], mischief [9], misery [3], travail [3], trouble [3], sorrow [2], grievance [1], grievousness [1], iniquity [1], miserable [1], painful [1], pain [1], perverseness [1], toil [1], wearisome [1], wickedness [1]

6000 עָמָל **'āmāl**, n.pr.m. GK: 6663 [→ 5999; cf. 5998]. Amal, "laborer, troubler":– Amal [1]

6001 עָמֵל **'āmēl**, n.m. GK: 6664 & 6665 [→ 5998]. misery; workman, laborer:– laboureth [2], in misery [1], laboured [1], labour [1], taken [1], takest [1], wicked [1], workmen's [1]

6002 עֲמָלֵק **'amālēq**, n.pr.m. GK: 6667 [→ 6003]. Amalek; Amalekite:– Amalek [24], Amalekites [15]

6003 עֲמָלֵקִי **'amālēqî**, a.g. GK: 6668 [→ 6002]. Amalekite, "of Amalek":– Amalekites [9], Amalekite [2], Amalekite (+376) [1]

6004 עָמַם **'āmam**, v. GK: 6669 & 6670 [→ 5973, 5980, 5997]. [Q] to be rival to, be equal to; to grow dark; [Ho] to lose luster, grow dark:– hide [2], become dim [1]

6005 עִמָּנוּ אֵל **'immānû 'ēl**, n.pr.m. GK: 6672 [→ 5973+5105.1+410]. Immanuel, "God with us":– Immanuel [2]

6006 עָמַס **'āmas**, v. GK: 6673 [→ 4614, 5986?, 6007]. [Q] to load a burden, carry a burden; [Qp] to be burdensome, be upheld; [H] to lay a burden upon:– laded [2], borne [1], burden [1], heavy loaden [1], lade [1], lading (+5921) [1], loadeth [1], put [1]

6007 עֲמַסְיָה **'amasyâ**, n.pr.m. GK: 6674 [→ 6006+3068]. Amasiah, "Yahweh carries a load":– Amasiah [1]

6008 עַמְעָד **'am'ād**, n.pr.loc. GK: 6675. Amad:– Amad [1]

6009 עָמַק **'āmaq**, v. GK: 6676 [→ 1025, 4615, 5987, 6010, 6013, 6011, 6012, 7104]. [Q] to be profound; [H] to make deep (in various senses):– deep [3], deeply [2], depth [1], made deep [1], profound to make [1], seek deep [1]

6010 עֵמֶק **'ēmeq**, n.m. GK: 6677 [→ 1025; cf. 6009]. valley; (low-lying) plain:– valley [54], valleys [9], vale [4], dale [2]

6011 עֹמֶק **'ōmeq**, n.[m.]. GK: 6679 [→ 6009]. depth:– depth [1]

6012 עָמֵק **'āmēq**, a. GK: 6680 [→ 6009]. obscure, unintelligible, by extension of what is physically deep (not found in the OT):– strange [2], deeper [1], depths [1]

6013 עָמֹק **'āmōq**, a. GK: 6678 [→ 6009; cf. 5994]. deep; profound:– deeper [8], deep [7], exceeding deep (+6013) [2]

6014 עָמַר **'āmar**, v.den. GK: 6682 & 6683 [→ 5995, 6016, 6017, 6019, 6020, 6192, 6191; cf. 6192]. [P] to bind sheaves (of newly cut grain); [Ht] to treat brutally, deal tyrannically with:– bindeth sheaves [1], make merchandise [1], maketh merchandise [1]

6015 עֲמַר **'amar** (Aram.), n.m. GK: 10556 [cf. 6785]. wool:– wool [1]

6016 עֹמֶר **'ōmer**, n.m. GK: 6684 & 6685 [→ 6014]. sheaf of grain; omer (dry measure, one-tenth of an ephah, about two quarts or liters):– sheaf [6], omer [5], sheaves [2], omers [1]

6017 עֲמֹרָה **'ōmorâ**, n.pr.loc. GK: 6686 [→ 6014]. Gomorrah, "to overwhelm with water":– Gomorrah [19]

6018 עָמְרִי **'omrî**, n.pr.m. GK: 6687 [→ 6020]. Omri, "thrive, live long":– Omri [18]

6019 עַמְרָם **'amrām**, n.pr.m. GK: 6688 [→ 6020]. Amram, "exalted people":– Amram [13], Amram's [1]

6020 עַמְרָמִי **'amrāmî**, a.g. GK: 6689 [→ 6019]. Amramite, "of Amram":– Amramites [2]

עָמַשׁ **'āmaś**. See 6006.

6021 עֲמָשָׂא **'amāśā'**, n.pr.m. GK: 6690 [→ 6022]. Amasa, "[my] people are from Jesse":– Amasa [16]

6022 עֲמָשַׂי **'amāśay**, n.pr.m. GK: 6691 [→ 6021]. Amasai, "[my] people are from Jesse":– Amasai [5]

6023 עֲמָשְׂסַי **'amaśśay**, n.pr.m. GK: 6692. Amashai:– Amashai [1]

6024 עֲנָב **'anāb**, n.pr.loc. GK: 6693 [→ 6025]. Anab, "grape":– Anab [2]

6025 עֵנָב **'ēnāb**, n.m. GK: 6694 [→ 6024]. cluster of grapes:– grapes [17], grape [1], wine [1]

6026 עָנַג **'ānag**, v. GK: 6695 [→ 6027, 6028, 8588]. [Pu] to be delicate; [Ht] to delight oneself, enjoy, to mock:– delight [5], delicateness [1], delicate [1], delighted [1], have delight [1], sport [1]

6027 עֹנֶג **'ōneg**, n.[m.]. GK: 6696 [→ 6026]. delight, luxury, enjoyment:– delight [1], pleasant [1]

6028 עָנֹג **'ānōg**, a. GK: 6697 [→ 6026]. sensitive, delicate:– delicate [3]

6029 עָנַד **'ānad**, v. GK: 6698 [cf. 4575]. [Q] to bind around, bind upon:– bind [1], tie [1]

6030 עָנָה **'ānâ**, v. GK: 6699 & 6702 & 4361 [→ 3285?, 4617, 6031?, 6035?; cf. 6032]. [Q] to answer, reply, respond; to sing; [N] to be answered; usually verbal, the response can involve action; [P] to sing to or sing about; (inf.) leannoth (t.t. in Ps 88):– answered [175], answer [54], hear [29], heard [11], testify [8], answereth [5], sing [5], speak [5], spake [3], testified [3], answeredst [1], answerest [1], bear [1], cry [1], gave answer [2], witness [2], beareth witness [1], beareth [1], brought low [1], give a shout (+1959) [1], give an answer [1], given answer [1], giveth account [1], giveth answer [1], heardest [1], hearest [1], lift up [1], make answer [1], said [1], sang [1], scholar [1], shout [1], sung [1], testifieth [1], utter [1]

6031 עָנָה **'ānâ**, v. GK: 6700 & 6701 [→ 3282, 4616, 4617, 4618, 5772? 6030?, 6035, 6037, 6038, 6039, 6040, 6041, 6045, 6256, 6258, 6261, 6262, 8589]. [Q] to be afflicted; to stoop down; to be concerned about, to be worried about; [N] to be afflicted, humbled, oppressed; [P] to afflict, oppress, subdue, humble, mistreat; [Pu] to be afflicted, deny oneself; [H] to afflict another, oppress; to keep occupied, keep oneself busy; [Ht] to humble oneself; humbling by force implies dishonor:– afflict [28], afflicted [21], humbled [7], forced [4], humble [4], afflict in any wise (+6031) [2], exercised [2], Leannoth [1], abase [1], afflictest [1], afflictions [1], answereth [1], chasten [1], dealt hardly with [1], defiled [1], force [1], gentleness [1], hurt [1], ravished [1], sing [1], submit [1], troubled [1], weakened [1]

6032 עֲנָה **'ānâ** (Aram.), v. GK: 10558 [cf. 6030]. [P] to answer, reply; usually a reaction to a direct question, but can be a more general response:– answered [16], spake [14]

6033 עֲנֵה **'ānēh** (Aram.), a. GK: 10559 [cf. 6041, 6035]. oppressed, needy, poor, implying that such persons are miserable in their life situation:– poor [1]

6034 עֲנָה **'ānâ**, n.pr.m. GK: 6704 [→ 6067]. Anah:– Anah [12]

6035 עָנָו **'ānāw** or עָנִי **'ānayw**, n.m. GK: 6705 & 6718 [cf. 6031; cf. 6033]. humble, afflicted, poor, oppressed:– meek [13], humble [5], lowly [2], poor [1] ·

6036 עָנוּב **'ānûb**, n.pr.m. GK: 6707. Anub, "fruitful":– Anub [1]

6037 עַנְוָה **'anwâ**, n.f. GK: 6709 [→ 6031]. humility:– gentleness [1], meekness [1]

6038 עֲנָוָה **'ānāwâ**, n.f. GK: 6708 [→ 6031]. humility:– humility [3], meekness [1]

6039 עֱנוּת **'ĕnût**, n.f. GK: 6713 [→ 6031]. suffering, affliction:– affliction [1]

6040 עֳנִי **'ŏnî**, n.m. GK: 6715 [→ 6031]. affliction, suffering, misery:– affliction [32], trouble [3], afflicted (+1121) [1]

6041 עָנִי **'ānî**, a. GK: 6714 [→ 6031; cf. 6033]. needy, poor, afflicted, oppressed, often referring to a class of persons of low status and lacking resources:– poor [59], afflicted [15], lowly [1]

6042 עֻנִּי **'unnî**, n.pr.m. GK: 6716. Unni, "*Yahweh has answered*":– Unni [3]

6043 עֲנָיָה **'ănāyâ**, n.pr.m. GK: 6717 [→ 6030+3068]. Anaiah, "*Yahweh responds*":– Anaiah [2]

עָנָיו **'ănāyw** See 6035.

6044 עָנִים **'ānîm**, n.pr.loc. GK: 6719. Anim, "*springs*":– Anim [1]

6045 עִנְיָן **'inyān**, n.m. GK: 6721 [→ 6031]. task, work, labor; misfortune, cares, troubles:– travail [6], business [2]

6046 עָנֵם **'ānēm**, n.pr.loc. GK: 6722. Anem, "*springs*":– Anem [1]

6047 עֲנָמִים **'ănāmîm**, n.pr.g. GK: 6723. Anamite:– Anamim [2]

6048 עֲנַמֶּלֶךְ **'anammelek**, n.pr.[m.]. GK: 6724 [→ 6067+4428]. Anammelech (pagan god), "*Anath is king*":– Anammelech [1]

6049 עָנַן **'ānan**, v.den. GK: 6725 & 6726 [→ 6031, 6051, 6052, 6053, 6054, 6055]. [P] to bring clouds; [Po] to practice sorcery, practice divination, cast spells:– observed times [2], soothsayers [2], Meonenim [1], bring a cloud (+6051) [1], enchanters [1], observe times [1], observer of times [1], observers of times [1], sorceress [1]

6050 עֲנַן **'ănan** (Aram.), n.[m.]. GK: 10560 [cf. 6051]. cloud:– clouds [1]

6051 עָנָן **'ānān**, n.m. GK: 6727 [→ 6053; cf. 6049; cf. 6050]. cloud, of moisture or smoke, natural or supernatural:– cloud [74], clouds [6], cloudy [6], bring a cloud (+6049) [1]

6052 עָנָן **'ānān**, n.pr.m. GK: 6728 [→ 6051; cf. 6049]. Anan, "*cloud*":– Anan [1]

6053 עֲנָנָה **'ănānâ**, n.f. GK: 6729 [→ 6051]. cloud, likely referring to a dense rain cloud:– cloud [1]

6054 עֲנָנִי **'ănānî**, n.pr.m. GK: 6730 [→ 6049+3068]. Anani, "*Yahweh is a covering*":– Anani [1]

6055 עֲנַנְיָה **'ănan^eyâ**, n.pr.m. & loc. GK: 6731 & 6732 [→ 6049+3068]. Ananiah, "*Yahweh is a covering*":– Ananiah [2]

6056 עֲנַף **'ănap** (Aram.), n.[m.]. GK: 10561 [cf. 6057]. branch, bough:– branches [3], boughs [1]

6057 עָנָף **'ānāp**, n.[m.]. GK: 6733 [→ 6058; cf. 6056]. branches:– boughs [3], branches [3], branch [1]

6058 עָנֵף **'ānēp**, a. GK: 6734 [→ 6057]. full of branches:– full of branches [1]

6059 עָנַק **'ānaq**, v.den. GK: 6735 [→ 6060]. [Q] to put on (as a necklace); [H] to supply, a fig. extension of putting an adornment around the neck:– furnish liberally (+6059) [2], compasseth about as a chain [1]

6060 עֲנָק **'ănāq**, n.m. GK: 6736 [→ 6059]. necklace chain:– chains [2], chain [1]

6061 עֲנוֹק **'ănôq**, n.pr.[m. or loc.]. GK: 6710 [→ 6062]. Anak, "*neck*":– Anak [9]

6062 עֲנָק **'ănāq**, n.[m.] & g. GK: 6737 [→ 6061]. Anak, "*neck*", Anakites:– Anakims [9]

6063 עָנֵר **'ānēr**, n.pr.m. & loc. GK: 6738 & 6739. Aner:– Aner [3]

6064 עָנַשׁ **'ānaš**, v.den. GK: 6740 & 6711 [→ 6066; cf. 6065]. [Q] to levy a fine (as a punishment or recompense); [N] to be fined, be punished:– punished [3], condemned [2], surely punished (+6064) [2], amerce [1], punish [1]

6065 עֲנַשׁ **'ănaš** (Aram.), n.[m.]. GK: 10562 [cf. 6066]. confiscation; some sources translate as "fine," a monetary penalty without the necessary confiscation of property:– confiscation [1]

6066 עֹנֶשׁ **'ōneš**, n.[m.]. GK: 6741 [→ 6064]. levy, penalty, fine:– punishment [1], tribute [1]

עֶנֶת **'enet** See 3706.

6067 עֲנָת **'ānāt**, n.pr.m. GK: 6742 [→ 1042, 1043, 6034, 6048, 6068, 6069]. Anath, "*Semitic goddess*":– Anath [2]

6068 עֲנָתוֹת **'ănātôt**, n.pr.f. & loc. GK: 6743 & 6744 [→ 6067]. Anathoth, "*plural of Anath*":– Anathoth [15]

6069 עַנְּתֹתִי **'ann^etōtî**, a.g. GK: 6745 [→ 6067]. from Anathoth, "*of Anathoth*":– Antothite [2], Anathoth [1], Anethothite [1], Anathothite [1]

6070 עֲנְתֹתִיָּה **'antōtiyyâ**, n.pr.m. GK: 6746. Anthothijah:– Antothijah [1]

6071 עָסִיס **'āsîs**, n.m. GK: 6747 [→ 6072]. new wine (relatively sweet); nectar:– new wine [2], sweet wine [2], juice [1]

6072 עָסַס **'āsas**, v. GK: 6748 [→ 6071]. [Q] to trample down:– tread down [1]

6073 עֳפִי **'ŏpî**, n.[m.]. GK: 6751 [cf. 6074]. branch:– branches [1]

6074 עֳפִי **'ŏpî** (Aram.), n.m. GK: 10564 [cf. 6073]. leaves, foliage:– leaves [3]

6075 עָפַל **'āpal**, v. GK: 6752 & 6753 [→ 6076, 6077]. [Pu] to be puffed up, be swelled; [H] to have presumption, to have the audacity to:– lifted up [1], presumed [1]

6076 עֹפֶל **'ōpel**, n.m. GK: 6754 [→ 6075]. tumor, hemorrhoid, abscess:– emerods [1], forts [1], tower [1]

6077 עֹפֶל **'ōpel**, n.[m.]. GK: 6755 [→ 6076]. hill; (as a proper name) the hill of Ophel:– Ophel [5], strong hold [1]

6078 עָפְנִי **'opnî**, n.pr.loc. GK: 6756. Ophni:– Ophni [1]

6079 עַפְעַף **'ap'appayim**, n.m. GK: 6757 [→ 4155]. flashing rays (of dawn); glances or flitting of eyes or eyelids:– eyelids [9], dawning [1]

6080 עָפַר **'āpar**, v.den. GK: 6759 [→ 6083]. [P] to shower (with dust or dirt):– cast [1]

6081 עֵפֶר **'ēper**, n.pr.m. GK: 6761 [→ 6085]. Epher, "*[small] gazelle*":– Epher [4]

6082 עֹפֶר **'ōper**, n.m. GK: 6762 [→ 6084; cf. 6083]. fawn (of a deer or gazelle):– young [5]

6083 עָפָר **'āpār**, n.m. GK: 6760 [→ 6080; cf. 6082]. dust, earth, soil in any form; used as a figure of something that cannot be counted:– dust [92], earth [8], powder [3], ashes [2], morter [2], rubbish [2], ground [1]

עֶפְרָה **'aprâ**. See 1036.

6084 עָפְרָה **'oprâ**, n.pr.m. & loc. GK: 6763 & 6764 [cf. 6082]. Ophrah, "*young gazelle*":– Ophrah [8]

6085 עֶפְרוֹן **'eprôn**, n.pr.m. & loc. GK: 6766 & 6767 [cf. 6081]. Ephron, "*gazelle*":– Ephron [13], Ephrain [1]

עֹפֶרֶת **'ōperet**. See 5777.

6086 עֵץ **'ēṣ**, n.m. GK: 6770 [→ 6097; cf. 636]. tree; by extension, the product of the tree: wood, any wooden object:– wood [107], tree [84], trees [78], timber [23], stick [9], gallows [8], sticks [5], staff [4], carpenters (+2796) [3], stocks [2], stock [2], branches [1], carpenter (+2796) [1], helve [1], planks [1], stalks [1]

6087 עָצַב **'āṣab**, v. GK: 6771 & 6772 [→ 4620, 6089, 6090, 6091, 6092, 6093, 6094; cf. 6088]. [Q] to interfere with; [Qp] to be distressed; [N] to be grieved, be distressed; [P] to grieve; to shape; [H] to grieve; to make an image (of the Queen of Heaven); [Ht] to be filled with grief, be filled with pain:– grieved [8], grieve [2], displeased [1], hurt [1], made [1], sorry [1], vexed [1], worship.[1], wrest [1]

6088 עֲצִיב **'ṣîb** (Aram.), v. GK: 10565. anguished, sorrowful:– lamentable [1]

6089 עֶצֶב **'eṣeb**, n.m. GK: 6775 & 6776 [→ 6087]. pot, vessel; pain, toil, hard work:– sorrow [2], grievous [1], idol [1], labours [1], labour [1], sorrows [1]

6090 עֹצֶב **'ōṣeb**, n.m. GK: 6777 & 6778 [→ 6087]. idol; pain, toil:– sorrow [2], idol [1], wicked [1]

6091 עָצָב **'āṣāb**, n.[m.]. GK: 6773 [→ 6087]. idol, image, a crafted object believed to represent or even possess a spirit or god:– idols [16], images [1]

6092 עָצָב **'aṣṣāb**, n.[m.]. GK: 6774 [→ 6087]. (hard) worker, toiler:– labours [1]

6093 עִצָּבוֹן **'iṣṣābôn**, n.[m.]. GK: 6779 [→ 6087]. pain, hardship, distress:– sorrow [2], toil [1]

6094 עַצֶּבֶת **'aṣṣebet**, n.f. GK: 6780 [→ 6087]. pain, sorrow, grief:– sorrows [2], sorrow [2], wounds [1]

6095 עָצָה **'āṣâ**, v. GK: 6781. [Q] to wink (the eye), as a non-verbal communication of what is evil, malicious, or lurid:– shutteth [1]

6096 עָצֶה **'āṣeh**, n.[m.]. GK: 6782. backbone, tailbone:– back bone [1]

6097 עֵצָה **'ēṣâ**, n.f.col. GK: 6785 [→ 6086]. (coll.) wood; this can refer to wooden idols:– trees [1]

6098 עֵצָה **'ēṣâ**, n.f. GK: 6783 [→ 3289; cf. 5843]. advice, counsel, plan, purpose, scheme:– counsel [72], counsel gave (+3289) [2], counsel given (+3289) [2], counsels [2], give counsel (+3289) [2], purpose [2], advice [1], advisement [1], counseller (+376) [1], counsellers (+376) [1], take counsel together (+5779) [1], taken counsel (+3289) [1]

6099 עָצוּם **'āṣûm**, a. GK: 6786 [→ 6110; cf. 6105]. strong, mighty, powerful:– strong [13], mighty [8], mightier [7], feeble (+3808) [1], great [1], much [1]

6100 עֶצְיוֹן גֶּבֶר **'eṣyôn geber**, n.pr.loc. GK: 6787. Ezion Geber, "*giant, the giant backbone*":– Ezion-geber [4], Ezion-gaber [3]

6101 עָצַל **'āṣal**, v. GK: 6788 [→ 6102, 6103, 6104]. [N] to hesitate, be sluggish, be slow:– slothful [1]

6102 עָצֵל **'āṣēl**, a. GK: 6789 [→ 6101]. sluggish, slow, lazy; (n.) sluggard, one with no discipline or motivation, a moral failure:– slothful [7], sluggard [6], slothful (+376) [1]

6103 עַצְלָה **'aṣlâ**, n.f. GK: 6790 & 6792 [→ 6101]. laziness, slowness, sluggishness:– much slothfulness [1], slothfulness [1]

6104 עַצְלוּת **'aṣlût**, n.f. GK: 6791 [→ 6101]. idleness, sluggishness, laziness:– idleness [1]

6105 עָצַם **'āṣam**, v. GK: 6793 & 6794 [→ 6099, 6106, 6107, 6108, 6108, 6109, 6111, 8592]. [Q] to close (the eyes); to be vast, powerful, numerous; [P] to tightly shut (the eyes); to crush bones; [H] to make numerous, make powerful, make vast:– increased [4], strong [4], mighty [2], moe [2], waxed mighty [2], broken bones [1], closed [1], great [1], made stronger [1], mightier [1], shutteth [1]

6106 עֶצֶם **'eṣem**, n.f. GK: 6795 [→ 6107; cf. 6105]. bone; by extension: the whole body, any part of the body, limb; strength of the body, vigor; (adv.) that very (day); "one's bone and flesh" is a close relative:– bones [89], bone [15], selfsame [11], same [5], body [2], very [2], life [1], strength [1]

6107 עֶצֶם **'eṣem**, n.pr.loc. GK: 6796 [→ 6106; cf. 6105]. Ezem, "*bone [strength]*":– Azem [2], Ezem [1]

6108 עֹצֶם **'ōṣem**, n.[m.]. GK: 6797 & 6798 [→ 6105]. might, strength; framework (of bones of the human body):– might [1], strong [1], substance [1]

עָצֻם **'āṣum**. See 6099.

6109 עָצְמָה **'oṣmâ**, n.f. GK: 6800 [→ 6105]. power, potency, might:– strength [2], abundance [1]

6110 עֲצֻמוֹת **'ṣumôt**, n.f.[pl.]. GK: 6802 [→ 6099]. defensive arguments, strong words:– strong [1]

6111 עַצְמוֹן **'aṣmôn**, n.pr.loc. GK: 6801 [→ 6106; cf. 6105]. Azmon, "*strongly [built body]*":– Azmon [3]

6112 עֶצְנִי **'eṣnî**, n.pr. or a.g.?. GK: 6804. Eznite:– Eznite [1]

6113 עָצַר **'āṣar**, v. GK: 6806 [→ 4622, 4623, 6114, 6115, 6116]. [Q] to refrain, hold back, restrain; [Qp] to be enslaved, be constrained; [N] to be stopped, be detained:– shut up [15], stayed [7], detain [2], fast closed up (+6113) [2], retained [2], able (+3581) [1], able [1], be [1], detained [1], keep still [1], kept close [1], kept [1], prevail [1], recover [1], refrained [1], reign [1], restrained [1], retain [1], shut [1], slack [1], stop [1], withholdeth [1], withhold [1]

6114 עֶצֶר **'eṣer**, n.[m.]. GK: 6807 [→ 6113]. restraint, oppression:– magistrate (+3423) [1]

6115 עֹצֶר **'ōṣer**, n.[m.]. GK: 6808 [→ 6113]. oppression; barrenness:– barren [1], oppression [1], prison [1]

6116 עֲצָרָה **'ṣārâ**, n.f. GK: 6809 [→ 6113]. assembly, usually on a festive day:– solemn assembly [8], assembly [1], solemn assemblies [1], solemn meeting [1]

6117 עָקַב **'āqab**, v. GK: 6810 [→ 6120; cf. 6119, 6120, 6906]. [Q] to deceive; to grasp at the heel; [P] to hold the heel, to hold back:– utterly supplant (+6117) [2], stay [1], supplanted [1], took by the heel [1]

6118 עֵקֶב **'ēqeb**, n.[m.]. (used as adv. & c.). GK: 6813 [→ 6119]. (c.) because; (n.) a reward; unto the end:– because [3], reward [3], because (+3588) [2], because (+834) [2], end [2], by [1], for [1], if [1]

6119 עָקֵב **'āqēb**, n.m. GK: 6811 [→ 6118, 6121; cf. 3290, 6117, 6120, 6906]. heel, hoof; footstep, footprint; by extension: rear guard of a military formation; a euphemism for private parts:– heel [4], footsteps [2], heels [2], horsehoofs (+5483) [1], liers in wait [1], steps [1], last [1]

6120 עָקֵב **'āqēb**, a.vbl. GK: 6812 [→ 6117, 6121, 6122; cf. 3290, 6117, 6119, 6906]. deceiver:– heels [1]

6121 עָקֹב **'āqōb**, a. [& n.] GK: 6814 & 6815 [→ 6119, 6120]. deceitful; rough, bumpy; footprint:– crooked [1], deceitful [1], polluted [1]

6122 עָקְבָּה **'oqbâ**, n.f. GK: 6817 [→ 6120]. deceptiveness, cunning, craftiness:– subtilty [1]

6123 עָקַד **'āqad**, v. GK: 6818 [→ 6124]. [Q] to bind (feet):– bound [1]

עֶקֶד **'ēqed**. See 1044.

6124 עָקֹד **'āqōd**, a. GK: 6819 [→ 6123]. streaked, striped:– ringstraked [7]

6125 עָקָה **'āqâ**, n.f. GK: 6821 [→ 5781]. pressure; oppressive look, stare, or actions:– oppression [1]

6126 עַקּוּב **'aqqûb**, n.pr.m. GK: 6822. Akkub, "guard":– Akkub [8]

6127 עָקַל **'āqal**, v. GK: 6823 [→ 6128, 6129]. [Pu] to be perverted, be distorted, be crooked:– wrong [1]

6128 עֲקַלְקַל **'ăqalqāl**, a.intens. GK: 6824 [→ 6127]. crooked, winding:– byways (+734) [1], crooked ways [1]

6129 עֲקַלָּתוֹן **'ăqallātôn**, a. GK: 6825 [→ 6127]. coiling (serpent):– crooked [1]

6130 עָקָן **'āqān**, n.pr.m. GK: 6826 [→ 3292?]. Akan:– Akan [1]

6131 עָקַר **'āqar**, v.den. GK: 6827 & 6828 [→ 6135, 6133, 6134; cf. 6132, cf. 6136]. [Q] to root up; [N] to be uprooted; [P] to hamstring (to cut the tendon and render helpless or useless):– houghed [3], digged down [1], hough [1], pluck up [1], rooted up [1]

6132 עֲקַר **'ăqar** (Aram.), v.den. GK: 10566 [→ 6136; cf. 6131]. [Itpe] to be uprooted, plucked out:– pluckt up by roots [1]

6133 עֵקֶר **'ēqer**, n.m. GK: 6830 [→ 6131]. offspring, as the fig. extension of a plant that grows up from a root:– stock [1]

6134 עֵקֶר **'ēqer**, n.pr.m. GK: 6831 [→ 6131?]. Eker, "[poss.] offspring":– Eker [1]

6135 עָקָר **'āqār**, a. GK: 6829 [→ 6131]. barren, sterile, without children:– barren [10], female barren [1], male⁵ [1]

6136 עִקַּר **'iqqar** (Aram.), n.[m.]. GK: 10567 [→ 6132]. stump, root:– stump [3]

6137 עַקְרָב **'aqrāb**, n.m. GK: 6832 [→ 7128]. scorpion:– scorpions [6], Akrabbim [2]

6138 עֶקְרוֹן **'eqrôn**, n.pr.loc. GK: 6833 [→ 6139]. Ekron, "[perhaps] barren place or fertile place":– Ekron [22]

6139 עֶקְרוֹנִי **'eqrônî**, a.g. GK: 6834 [→ 6138]. Ekronite, of Ekron, "of Ekron":– Ekronites [2]

6140 עָקַשׁ **'āqaš**, v. GK: 6835 [→ 4625, 6141, 6142, 6143]. [N] to be perverse, be crooked; [P] to take crooked paths; to distort; [H] to pronounce guilty:– made crooked [1], perverse [1], perverteth [1], pervert [1], prove perverse [1]

6141 עִקֵּשׁ **'iqqēš**, a. GK: 6836 [→ 6142; cf. 6140]. perverse, crooked, warped:– froward [6], perverse [4], crooked [1]

6142 עִקֵּשׁ **'iqqēš**, n.pr.m. GK: 6837 [→ 6141; cf. 6140]. Ikkesh, "crooked, perverted":– Ikkesh [3]

6143 עִקְּשׁוּת **'iqqᵉšût**, n.f. GK: 6838 [→ 6140]. perversion, corruption, crookedness:– froward [2]

עָר **'ār**. See 5892.

6144 עָר **'ār**, n.pr.loc. GK: 6840 [→ 5892?]. Ar, "[poss.] city":– Ar [6]

6145 עָר **'ār**, n.m. GK: 6839 [→ 6209?]. enemy, adversary:– enemies [1], enemy [1]

6146 עָר **'ār** (Aram.), n.m. GK: 10568 [cf. 6862]. adversary, foe:– enemies [1]

6147 עֵר **'ēr**, n.pr.m. GK: 6841 [→ 5782; cf. 5894]. Er, "watchful, watcher":– Er [10]

6148 עָרַב **'ārab**, v. GK: 6842 & 6843 [→ 4627, 6154, 6157, 6161, 6162, 8594; cf. 6150; cf. 6151]. [Q] to put up a security, make a guarantee, give a pledge; [Ht] to make a bargain, make a wager; to mingle, join in with, share with:– surety [4], give pledges [2], meddle [2], mingled [2], surety for [1], became surety [1], becometh surety (+6161) [1], engaged [1], intermeddle [1], mortgaged [1], occupiers [1], occupy [1], put in a surety [1], sureties [1], undertake [1]

6149 עָרַב **'ārab**, v. GK: 6844 [→ 6156]. [Q] to be pleasing, be pleasant, be acceptable:– sweet [5], pleasant [1], pleasing [1], taken pleasure [1]

6150 עָרַב **'ārab**, v.den. GK: 6845 [→ 4628, 6153; cf. 6148]. [Q] to become evening; (opposite of joy) turn to gloom; [H] to do something in the evening:– evening [2], darkened [1]

6151 עֲרַב **'ărab** (Aram.), v. GK: 10569 [cf. 6148]. [Pap] to be mixed; [Htpa] (ptcp.) mixture:– mixed [2], mingle [1], mixt [1]

6152 עֲרָב **'ărāb**, n.pr.loc. & g. GK: 6851 [→ 6160]. Arabia, Arab:– Arabia [5]

6153 עֶרֶב **'ereb**, n.[m.]. GK: 6847 [→ 6150]. evening, twilight, dusk, the fading of the day; twilight can extend into the dark of the night:– even [67], evening [47], at even (+996+1886.1) [6], every evening (+6153+871.1+1886.1+1886.1) [4], night [4], mingled people [3], eveningtide (+6256) [2], Arabia [1], days (+1242) [1], eventide (+6256+1886.1) [1], eventide (+6437) [1], eventide [1], people [1]

6154 עֵרֶב **'ēreb**, n.m. GK: 6849 & 6850 [→ 6148]. foreign people; knitted or woven material:– woof [9], mixed multitude [1], mixed [1]

6155 עֲרָבָה **'ărābâ**, n.[f.]. GK: 6857 [→ 6164]. poplar tree:– willows [5]

6156 עָרֵב **'ārēb**, a. GK: 6853 [→ 6149]. pleasant, sweet (voice):– sweet [2]

6157 עָרֹב **'ārōb**, n.m. GK: 6856 [→ 6148]. swarms of flies:– swarms [5], divers sorts [2], swarm [2]

6158 עֹרֵב **'ōrēb**, n.m. GK: 6854 [→ 6159]. raven:– raven [6], ravens [4]

6159 עֹרֵב **'ōrēb**, n.pr.m. GK: 6855 [→ 6158]. Oreb, "raven":– Oreb [7]

6160 עֲרָבָה **'ărābâ**, n.f. GK: 6858 [→ 6152, 6163]. plains (a geographical region of desert, wilderness or wasteland); (pr.n.) Arabah:– plain [22], plains [20], desert [8], wilderness [5], Arabah [2], champaign [1], deserts [1], evenings [1], heavens [1]

6161 עֲרֻבָּה **'ărubbâ**, n.f. GK: 6859 [→ 6148]. security, pledge; assurance:– becometh surety (+6148) [1], pledge [1]

6162 עֵרָבוֹן **'ērābôn**, n.[m.]. GK: 6860 [→ 6148]. pledge, security:– pledge [3]

6163 עַרְבִי **'arbî** or עַרְבִי **'ārbî**, a.g. GK: 6861 & 6862 [→ 6160]. Arab, of Arabia; may also refer to bedouin in general:– Arabians [5], Arabian [4]

6164 עַרְבָתִי **'arbātî**, a.g. GK: 6863 [→ 6155]. Arbathite, "of Arabah":– Arbathite [2]

6165 עָרַג **'ārag**, v. GK: 6864 [→ 6170?]. [Q] to pant for, long for (as a thirsty animal):– panteth [2], cry [1]

6166 עֲרָד **'ărād**, n.pr.m. & loc. GK: 6865 & 6866 [→ 6171]. Arad, "wild donkey":– Arad [5]

6167 עֲרָד **'ărād** (Aram.), n.m. GK: 10570 [cf. 6171]. wild donkey:– wild asses [1]

6168 עָרָה **'ārâ**, v. GK: 6867 [→ 4177, 4632, 4636, 5903, 6172, 6174, 6181, 6196, 8593; cf. 6209, 5783]. [N] to be poured; [P] to lay bare, empty, expose, strip; [H] to make exposed; to cause to pour out; to dishonor; [Ht] to show oneself naked:– emptied [2], rase [2], discovered [1], discovering [1], discover [1], leave destitute [1], make naked [1], poured out [1], poured [1], spreading [1], uncovered [1], uncovereth [1], uncover [1]

6169 עָרָה **'ārâ**, n.f. GK: 6868. plants, bulrushes:– paper reeds [1]

6170 עֲרוּגָה **'ărûgâ**, n.f. GK: 6870 [→ 6165?]. garden bed, garden plot:– furrows [2], beds [1], bed [1]

6171 עָרוֹד **'ārôd**, n.[m.]. GK: 6871 [→ 5897, 6166; cf. 6167]. wild donkey:– wild ass [1]

6172 עֶרְוָה **'erwâ**, n.f. GK: 6872 [→ 6168; cf. 6173]. nakedness (indecent or shameful in certain situations); "to expose the nakedness" is to have sexual relations:– nakedness [50], nakedness (+1320) [1], shame [1], uncleanness [1], unclean [1]

6173 עֶרְוָה **'arwâ** (Aram.), n.f. GK: 10571 [cf. 6172]. nakedness, fig., dishonor, lowering of one's status in a community resulting in disgrace or shame:– dishonour [1]

6174 עָרוֹם **'ārôm**, a. GK: 6873 [→ 6168]. naked, stripped:– naked [16]

6175 עָרוּם **'ārûm**, a. GK: 6874 [→ 6191]. wise and understanding; with a positive connotation: prudent, clever; with a negative connotation: crafty:– prudent [8], crafty [3], subtil [2]

6176 עֲרוֹעֵר **'ărô'ēr**, n.[m.]. GK: 6875 [→ 6177; cf. 6209]. (juniper) bush:– heath [1]

6177 עֲרוֹעֵר **'ărô'ēr** or עֲרֹעֵר **'ărō'ēr**, n.pr.loc. GK: 6876 & 6898 [→ 6200; cf. 6176, 6209]. Aroer, "juniper":– Aroer [16]

6178 עָרוּץ **'ārûṣ**, a. GK: 6877 [→ 6206]. dry or dreadful:– clifts [1]

6179 עֵרִי **'ērî**, n.pr.m. GK: 6878 [→ 6180; cf. 5782]. Eri, "watcher":– Eri [2]

6180 עֵרִי **'ērî**, a.g. GK: 6879 [→ 6179; cf. 5782]. Erite, "of Eri":– Erites [1]

6181 עֶרְיָה **'eryâ**, n.f. GK: 6880 [→ 6168]. bareness, nakedness, the state of being uncovered:– bare [4], made quite naked (+5783) [1], naked [1]

6182 עֲרִיסָה **'ărîsâ**, n.f. GK: 6881. ground meal (dough in the first phase of bread making):– dough [4]

6183 עֲרִיפִים **'ărîpîm**, n.[m.pl.]. GK: 6882 [→ 6201]. cloud:– heavens [1]

6184 עָרִיץ **'ārîṣ**, a. GK: 6883 [→ 6206]. ruthless, cruel, fierce:– terrible [8], terrible ones [3], oppressors [2], great power [1], mighty [1], oppressor [1], strong [1], terrible one to nought [1], terrible one [1], violent [1]

6185 עֲרִירִי **'ărîrî**, a. GK: 6884 [→ 6209]. childless, very undesireable and even shameful in the ancient Near East:– childless [4]

6186 עָרַךְ **'ārak**, v.[den.]. GK: 6885 [→ 6187, 4633, 4630, 4634, 4635]. [Q] to arrange in rows; put in order, take up (battle) positions; [Qp] to be arranged, be put in order, be put in formation; [H] to set a value:– put in array [14], set in array [12], order [6], set in order [5], lay in order [4], expert [3], value [3], equal [2], estimate [2], laid in order [2], ordained [2], ordered [2], prepared [2], prepare [2], compared [1], compare [1], directed [1], direct [1], esteem [1], furnished [1], furnish [1], handle [1], joined [1], preparest [1], put in order [1], reckoned up in order [1], set in order (+6187) [1], taxed [1]

6187 עֵרֶךְ **'ērek**, n.m. GK: 6886 [→ 6186]. proper estimated value:– estimation [23], equal (+3509.1) [1], estimations [1], price [1], proportion [1], set at [1], set in order (+6186) [1], set in order [1], suit [1], taxation [1], valuest [1]

6188 עָרַל **'āral**, v.den. GK: 6887 [→ 6190]. [Q] to regard as forbidden, leave unharvested:– count as uncircumcised (+6190) [1], foreskin uncovered [1]

6189 עָרֵל **'ārēl**, a. GK: 6888 [→ 6190]. uncircumcised (i.e., having a foreskin of the penis):– uncircumcised [34], uncircumcised person [1]

6190 עָרְלָה **'orlâ**, n.f. GK: 6889 [→ 1394, 6188, 6189]. foreskin (of the penis):– foreskin [8], foreskins [5], uncircumcised [1], count as uncircumcised (+6188) [1]

6191 עָרַם **'āram**, v. GK: 6891 [→ 6175, 6193, 6195]. [Q] to be crafty, show prudence; [H] to initiate cunning plans:– dealeth very subtilly (+6191) [2], beware [1], prudent [1], taken crafty [1]

6192 עָרַם **'āram**, v. GK: 6890 [→ 6194; cf. 6014]. [N] to be piled up, be dammed up:– gathered together [1]

6193 עֹרֶם **'ōrem**, n.[m.]. GK: 6892 [→ 6191]. craftiness:– craftiness [1]

עֵרֹם **'ērōm**. See 5903.

עָרֹם **'ārōm**. See 6174.

6194 עֲרֵמָה **'ărēmâ**, n.f. GK: 6894 [→ 6192]. heap, mound (of grain):– heaps [5], heap [3], by heaps (+6194) [2], sheaves [1]

6195 עָרְמָה **'ormâ**, n.f. GK: 6893 [→ 6191]. prudence, cunning:– guile [1], prudence [1], subtilty [1], wilily (+871.1) [1], wisdom [1]

עֲרֵמָה **'arēmâ**. See 6194.

6196 עַרְמוֹן **'ermôn**, n.[m.]. GK: 6895 [→ 6168]. plane tree:– chesnut trees [1], chesnut tree [1]

6197 עֵרָן **'ērān**, n.pr.m. GK: 6896 [→ 6198]. Eran, "watcher, watchful":– Eran [1]

6198 עֵרָנִי **'ērānî**, a.g. GK: 6897 [→ 6197]. Eranite, "of Eran":– Eranites [1]

עֲרֹעֵר **'ărō'ēr**. See 6177.

6199 עַרְעָר **'ar'ār**, a. GK: 6899 [cf. 6209]. destitute, naked, stripped; (juniper) bush:– destitute [1], heath [1]

עֲרֹעֵר **'ărō'ēr**. See 6177.

6200 עֲרֹעֵרִי **'ărō'ērî**, a.g. GK: 6901 [→ 6177; cf. 6209]. Aroerite, "of Aroer":– Aroerite [1]

6201 עָרַף ʿārap, v. GK: 6903 [→ 6183, 6205?; cf. 7491]. [Q] to trickle, drip:– drop down [1], drop [1]

6202 עָרַף ʿārap, v.den. GK: 6904. [Q] to break; [Qp] be broken:– break neck [2], beheaded [1], break down [1], cut off neck [1], strike off neck [1]

6203 עֹרֶף ʿōrep, n.m. GK: 6902 [→ 6204]. neck; to be "stiff of neck" is to be obstinate, stubborn, implying rebellion:– neck [11], necks [6], stiffnecked (+7186) [6], back [4], backs [3], stiffnecked (+7185) [2], turn backs [1]

6204 עָרְפָּה ʿorpâ, n.pr.f. GK: 6905 [→ 6203]. Orpah, "neck, the girl with the full mane[?]":– Orpah [2]

6205 עֲרָפֶל ʿᵃrāpel, n.m. GK: 6906 [→ 6201?]. dark or thick clouds; deep gloom:– thick darkness [8], darkness [3], dark [2], gross darkness [2]

6206 עָרַץ ʿāraṣ, v. GK: 6907 [→ 4637, 6178, 6184]. [Q] to shake, to shake in terror; to be feared; [N] to dread, stand in awe:– afraid [3], dread [3], fear [2], shake terribly [2], affrighted [1], break [1], feared [1], oppress [1], prevail [1], terrified [1]

6207 עָרַק ʿāraq, v. GK: 6908. [Q] to gnaw:– flying [1], sinews [1]

6208 עַרְקִי ʿarqî, a.g. GK: 6909. Arkite:– Arkite [2]

6209 עָרַר ʿārar, v. GK: 6910 [→ 6145?, 6176, 6177, 6185, 6199, 6200; cf. 6168]. [Q] to strip off; [Po] to strip; [Pil] to level, demolish; [Htpal] to be laid utterly bare:– utterly broken (+6209) [2], make bare [1], raised up [1]

6210 עֶרֶשׂ ʿereś, n.f. GK: 6911. bed, couch:– bed [4], bedstead [2], couch [2], bed (+3326) [1], couches [1]

6211 עָשׁ ʿāš, n.m. GK: 6931 & 6933 [→ 5906, 6244]. moth, which consumes some natural fabrics; Bear or Lion (a constellation):– moth [6], moth-eaten (+398) [1]

6211' עֲשַׂב ʿᵃsab (Aram.), n.[m.]. GK: 10572 [cf. 6212]. grass, (green) plants:– grass [5]

6212 עֵשֶׂב ʿēseb, n.m. GK: 6912 [cf. 6211']. green plant, vegetation, grass:– grass [16], herb [12], herbs [5]

6213 עָשָׂה ʿāsâ, v. GK: 6913 & 6914 [→ 501, 3299, 3300, 4639, 4640, 4641, 6214, 6221, 6222]. [Q] to do, make; [Qp] to be done; [N] to be done, be made; [P] to caress, squeeze; [Pu] to be made; a generic of action, seen in the many contextual translations of the KJV:– do [607], made [393], done [339], did [319], make [232], wrought [52], doeth [42], offer [41], keep [30], committed [27], execute [24], deal [23], maketh [23], prepare [22], work [22], shew [19], doest [18], kept [18], dealt [17], shewed [17], commit [16], executed [15], doing [14], maker [13], prepared [13], didst [12], perform [12], gotten [9], dealeth [7], dress [7], bring forth [6], maintain [6], offered [6], worketh [6], yield [6], dressed [5], executeth [5], performed [5], bear [4], brought forth [4], certainly make (+6213) [4], committeth [4], makest [4], workmen (+4399+1886.1) [4], bring to pass [3], doer [3], observe [3], ordained [3], practise [3], set [3], workmen (+4399) [3], yielding [3], accomplish [2], appointed [2], bruised [2], certainly do (+6213) [2], deal with [2], do great things (+6213) [2], do indeed (+6213) [2], doers [2], doth [2], fulfil [2], gat [2], get [2], holden [2], labour [2], made ready [2], meet [2], offering [2], procured [2], procure [2], sacrifice [2], sheweth [2], shewing [2], surely deal (+6213) [2], surely perform (+6213) [2], surely shew (+6213) [2], throughly execute (+6213) [2], used [2], warriors (+4421) [2], advanced [1], apt [1], at [1], become [1], bestow [1], bringeth to pass [1], bruising [1], busy [1], caused to be made [1], cause [1], charge [1], come to pass [1], committing [1], dealest [1], dealt with [1], deckedst [1], displease (+5869+7451+871.1) [1], effect [1], executedst [1], executest [1], executing [1], exercise [1], fashioned [1], feasted (+4960) [1], fighting (+4421) [1], fitteth [1], followed [1], fulfilled [1], fulfilling [1], furnish (+3627) [1], gathered [1], getteth [1], given [1], give [1], go about [1], govern [1], granted [1], held [1], hinder (+8442) [1], industrious (+4399) [1], journeyed (+1870) [1], laboured [1], madest [1], maintained [1], making [1], observed [1], occupied (+4399) [1], occupied [1], officers (+4399+1886.1) [1], pare [1], practised [1], preparest [1], preparing [1], provided [1], provide [1], put in execution [1], put [1], ready dressed [1], require (+854) [1], sacrificed [1], served [1], shew (+5973) [1], shewest [1], sinneth through ignorance (+7684+871.1) [1], spendeth [1], surely [1], taken [1], take [1], trimmed [1], undo (+854) [1], used to do [1], vex (+7451) [1], workers [1], working [1], workmen [1], wroughtest [1]

6214 עֲשָׂהאֵל ʿᵃsāh'el or עֲשָׂה-אֵל ʿᵃsāh-'el, n.pr.m. GK: 6915 [→ 6213+410]. Asahel, "God [El] has made":– Asahel [18]

6215 עֵשָׂו ʿēsāw, n.pr.m. GK: 6916. Esau, "hairy":– Esau [85], Esau's [12]

6216 עָשׁוֹק ʿāšôq, n.[m.]. GK: 6934 [→ 6231]. oppressor:– oppressor [1]

6217 עֲשׁוּקִים ʿᵃšûqîm, n.pl.abst. GK: 6935 [→ 6231]. oppression:– oppressions [2], oppressed [1]

6218 עָשׂוֹר ʿāśôr, n.[m.]. GK: 6917 [→ 6237]. (group of) ten:– tenth [12], instrument of ten strings [3], ten [1]

6219 עָשׁוֹת ʿāšôt, a. GK: 6936 [→ 6245]. wrought, fashioned (iron):– bright [1]

6220 עַשְׁוָת ʿašwāt, n.pr.m. GK: 6937. Ashvath, "[poss.] wrought iron":– Ashvath [1]

6221 עֲשִׂיאֵל ʿᵃsî'ēl, n.pr.m. GK: 6918 [→ 6213+410]. Asiel, "God [El] has made":– Asiel [1]

6222 עֲשָׂיָה ʿᵃsāyâ, n.pr.m. GK: 6919 [→ 6213+3068]. Asaiah, "Yahweh has made":– Asaiah [6], Asahiah [2]

6223 עָשִׁיר ʿāšîr, a. (used as n.). GK: 6938 [→ 6238]. rich, wealthy; (n.) the rich, rich person:– rich [23]

6224 עֲשִׂירִי ʿᵃsîrî, a.num.ord. GK: 6920 [→ 6237]. tenth:– tenth [29]

6225 עָשַׁן ʿāšan, v.den. GK: 6939 [→ 6227, 6226]. [Q] to envelope in smoke, smolder:– smoke [5], angry [1]

6226 עָשֵׁן ʿāšēn, a. GK: 6942 [→ 6225]. smoking, smoldering:– smoking [2]

6227 עָשָׁן ʿāšān, n.m. GK: 6940 [→ 953+6228; cf. 6225]. smoke (billowing, ascending, blowing):– smoke [24], smoking [1]

6228 עָשָׁן ʿāšān, n.pr.loc. GK: 6941 [cf. 953]. Ashan, "smoke":– Ashan [4]

6229 עָשַׂק ʿāsaq, v. GK: 6921 [→ 4642]. [Ht] to dispute, quarrel:– strove [1]

6230 עֵשֶׂק ʿēseq, n.pr.loc. GK: 6922. Esek, "dispute":– Esek [1]

6231 עָשַׁק ʿāšaq, v. GK: 6943 [→ 6216, 6217, 6232, 6233, 6234]. [Q] to oppress, mistreat; to defraud, extort; [Qp] to be oppressed, be tormented; [Pu] to be crushed:– oppressed [10], oppress [9], oppresseth [3], defrauded [2], do wrong [2], oppressors [2], oppressor [2], cruelly oppressed (+6233) [1], deceitfully gotten (+6233) [1], deceived [1], defraud [1], doeth violence [1], drinketh up [1], used oppression (+6233) [1]

עָשֻׁק ʿāšuq. See 6217.

6232 עֵשֶׁק ʿēšeq, n.pr.m. GK: 6944 [→ 6231]. Eshek, "oppressor":– Eshek [1]

6233 עֹשֶׁק ʿōšeq, n.m. GK: 6945 [→ 6231]. oppression, tyranny; extortion:– oppression [11], cruelly oppressed (+6231) [1], deceitfully gotten (+6231) [1], extortion [1], used oppression (+6231) [1]

6234 עָשְׁקָה ʿošqâ, n.f. GK: 6946 [→ 6233; cf. 6231]. trouble, oppression:– oppressed [1]

6235 עֶשֶׂר ʿeser or עֲשָׂרָה ʿᵃsārâ, n.m. & f. GK: 6924 & 6927 [→ 6237; cf. 6236]. ten:– ten [168], tens [3], fifteen (+2568+2050.1) [1], seventeen (+7651+2050.1) [1], ten's [1]

6236 עֲשַׂר ʿᵃsar (Aram.), n.m. & f. GK: 10573 [→ 6243; cf. 6235]. ten:– ten [4], twelve (+8648) [2]

6237 עָשַׂר ʿāsar, v.den. GK: 6923 [→ 4643, 6218, 6224, 6235, 6240, 6241, 6242, 6240]. [Q] to take a tenth; [P] to give a tenth, set aside a tenth; [H] to give or receive a tenth:– surely give the tenth (+6237) [2], take the tenth [2], truly tithe (+6237) [2], take tithes [1], tithes [1], tithing [1]

6238 עָשַׁר ʿāšar, v.den. GK: 6947 [→ 6223, 6239]. [Q] to be, become rich; [H] to make rich, bring wealth:– rich [5], maketh rich [4], enrich [2], made rich [2], become rich [1], enrichest [1], richer (+6239) [1], waxen rich [1]

6239 עֹשֶׁר ʿōšer, n.m. GK: 6948 [→ 6238]. wealth, riches:– riches [36], richer (+6238) [1]

6240 עָשָׂר ʿāsār, n. or a.num. GK: 6925 & 6926 & 6930 [→ 6237]. ten (always used in combined numbers):– twelve (+8147) [109], fourteenth (+702) [23], twelfth (+8147) [22], sixteen (+8337) [21], fourteen (+702) [19], eighteen (+8083) [18], fifteenth (+2568) [17], fifteen (+2568) [16], eleventh (+6249) [13], thirteen (+7969) [13], eighteenth (+8083) [11], thirteenth (+7969) [11], eleven (+259) [9], seventeen (+7651) [8], eleven (+6249) [6], seventeenth (+7651) [6], eleventh (+259) [4], nineteenth (+8672) [4], nineteen (+8672) [3], sixteenth (+8337) [3], sixscore (+8147) [1]

עָשֹׂר ʿāsōr. See 6218.

6241 עִשָּׂרוֹן ʿiśśārôn, n.m. GK: 6928 [→ 6237]. tenth part:– tenth deals [18], several tenth deal (+6241) [10], tenth deal [3], one tenth deal (+259) [1], three tenth deals (+7969) [1]

6242 עֶשְׂרִים ʿesrîm, n.pl.indecl. GK: 6929 [→ 6237; cf. 6243]. twenty (pl. of "ten"):– twenty [277], twentieth [36], sixscore (+3967+2050.1) [1], twenty's [1]

6243 עֶשְׂרִין ʿesrîn (Aram.), n.pl.indecl. GK: 10574 [→ 6236; cf. 6242]. twenty; note that this is the grammatical plural of "ten":– twenty [1]

6244 עָשֵׁשׁ ʿāšaš, v. GK: 6949 [→ 6211]. [Q] to grow weak:– consumed [3]

6245 עָשַׁת ʿāšat, v. GK: 6950 & 6951 [→ 6219, 6247, 6248, 6250; cf. 6246]. [Q] to grow sleek (i.e., smooth or shiny); [Ht] to take notice:– shine [1], think [1]

6246 עֲשִׁת ʿᵃšit (Aram.), v. GK: 10575 [cf. 6245]. [P] to plan, intend:– thought [1]

6247 עֶשֶׁת ʿešet, n.[m.]. GK: 6952 [→ 6245]. polished piece, slab, plate:– bright [1]

6248 עַשְׁתּוּת ʿaštût, n.f. GK: 6953 [→ 6245]. thought:– thought [1]

6249 עַשְׁתֵּי ʿaštê, n. or a.num. GK: 6954. eleven, eleventh:– eleventh (+6240) [13], eleven (+6240) [6]

6250 עֶשְׁתֹּנֶת ʿeštōnet, n.f. GK: 6955 [→ 6245]. plan, thought:– thoughts [1]

6251 עַשְׁתְּרֹת ʿašteret, n.f. GK: 6957. lamb or ewe:– flocks [4]

6252 עַשְׁתָּרֹת ʿaštārōt, n.pr.loc. GK: 6958 [→ 1045, 6253, 6255, 6254; cf. 842, 1203?]. Ashtaroth:– Ashtaroth [10], Astaroth [1]

6253 עַשְׁתֹּרֶת ʿaštōret, n.pr.f. GK: 6956 [→ 6252]. Ashtoreth (pagan god):– Ashtoreth [3], Ashtaroth [1]

6254 עַשְׁתְּרָתִי ʿašᵉrātî, a.g. GK: 6960 [→ 6252]. Ashterathite:– Ashterathite [1]

6255 עַשְׁתְּרֹת קַרְנַיִם ʿašᵉrōt qarnayim, n.pr.loc. GK: 6959 [→ 6252+7161]. Ashteroth Karnaim, "Ashteroth of the pair of horns [twin peaks?]":– Ashteroth Karnaim [1]

6256 עֵת ʿēt, n.f. GK: 6961 [→ 6031]. time (in general); a unit of time (of various lengths), season:– time [233], times [24], season [8], due season [5], when (+871.1) [5], always (+3605+871.1) [3], eveningtide (+6153) [2], seasons [2], after (+3318+3509.1) [1], after (+3807.1) [1], certain [1], continually (+3605+871.1) [1], due season (+2050.2) [1], eventide (+6153+1886.1) [1], long [1], mealtime (+400+1886.1) [1], noontide (+6672) [1], when (+871.1) [1], when (+3807.1) [1], when [1]

6257 עָתַד ʿātad, v. GK: 6963 [® 6259, 6260?, 6264]. [P] to make ready; [Ht] to be destined:– make fit [1], ready to become [1]

עַתּוּד ʿattud. See 6260.

6258 עַתָּה ʿattâ, adv. GK: 6964 [→ 6031]. now:– now [407], therefore [8], henceforth [6], this time forth [3], this time [2], I pray thee [1], as yet (+5704) [1], even now (+2088) [1], now (+3588) [1], straightway [1], whereas [1], yet (+5704) [1]

6259 עָתוּד ʿātûd, a. GK: 6965 [→ 6257]. supply, treasure:– treasures [1]

6260 עַתּוּד ʿattûd, a. GK: 6966 [→ 6257?]. male goat; (of humans) a leader:– he goats [15], goats [11], rams [2], chief ones [1]

6261 עִתִּי ʿittî, a. GK: 6967 [→ 6031]. available:– fit [1]

6262 עַתַּי ʿattay, n.pr.m. GK: 6968 [→ 6031]. Attai, "timely, [or perhaps] an abbreviation of Athaiah":– Attai [4]

6263 עֲתִיד ʿᵃtîd (Aram.), a. GK: 10577 [cf. 6264]. ready:– ready [1]

6264 עָתִיד ʿātîd, a. GK: 6969 [→ 6257; cf. 6263]. ready, prepared:– ready [4], things that shall come [1]

6265 עֲתָיָה ʿᵃtāyâ, n.pr.m. GK: 6970. Athaiah, "[poss.] [the] superiority of Yahweh":– Athaiah [1]

6266 עָתִיק ʿātîq, a. GK: 6971 [→ 6275]. fine, choice, select:– durable [1]

6267 עַתִּיק ʿattîq, a. GK: 6972 [→ 6275]. taken, removed (from place or time):– ancient [1], drawn [1]

6268 עַתִּיק ʿattîq (Aram.), a. GK: 10578. old, ancient; (as a title) the Ancient (of Days), a title of veneration and honor emphasizing wisdom and power:– ancient [3]

6269 עָתָךְ ʿātāk, n.pr.loc. GK: 6973. Athach:– Athach [1]

Heb

6270 עַתְלָי **ʿatlāy**, n.pr.m. & f. GK: 6974 [→ 6271]. Athlai, "[poss.] Yahweh is exalted; oldest of Yahweh":– Athlai [1]

6271 עֲתַלְיָה **talyâ** or עֲתַלְיָהוּ **talyāhû**, n.pr.m. & f. GK: 6975 & 6976 [→ 5830, 6270]. Athaliah, "[poss.] Yahweh is exalted; oldest of Yahweh":– Athaliah [17]

6272 עָתַם **ʿātam**, v. GK: 6977. [N] to be destroyed; in context, to be scorched:– darkened [1]

6273 עָתְנִי **ʿotnî**, n.pr.m. GK: 6978 [→ 6274]. Othni:– Othni [1]

6274 עָתְנִיאֵל **ʿotnîʾēl**, n.pr.m. GK: 6979 [→ 6273+410]. Othniel:– Othniel [7]

6275 עָתֵק **ʿātaq**, v. GK: 6980 [→ 6266, 6267, 6277, 6276; cf. 6268]. [Q] to move; to grow old, grow weak; [H] to move on; to fail; to copy:– removed [4], become old [1], copied out [1], left off (+4480) [1], removeth [1], waxeth old [1]

6276 עָתֵק **ʿātēq**, a. GK: 6982 [→ 6275]. enduring (wealth):– durable [1]

6277 עָתָק **ʿātāq**, a. GK: 6981 [→ 6275]. arrogant, insolent, outstretched:– arrogancy [1], grievous things [1], hard [1], stiff [1]

6278 עֵת קָצִין **ʿēt qāṣîn**, n.pr.loc. GK: 6962 [cf. 7101]. Eth Kazin:– Ittah-kazin [1]

6279 עָתַר **ʿātar**, v. GK: 6983 [→ 6281?, 6282; cf. 6280?]. [Q] to pray; [N] to respond to prayer, be moved by an entreaty; [H] to pray, make entreaty:– intreated [12], intreat [6], make prayer [1], pray [1]

6280 עָתַר **ʿātar**, v. GK: 6984 [→ 6283; cf. 6279?]. [N] to be multiplied; [H] to multiply:– deceitful [1], multiplied [1]

6281 עֶתֶר **ʿeter**, n.pr.loc. GK: 6987 [→ 6279?]. Ether, "[perhaps] perfume":– Ether [2]

6282 עָתָר **ʿātār**, n.[m.]. GK: 6985 & 6986 [→ 6279]. worshiper; fragrance, perfume:– suppliants [1], thick [1]

6283 עֲתֶרֶת **ʿteret**, n.f. GK: 6988 [→ 6280]. abundance:– abundance [1]

אֹא **pōʾ**. See 6311.

6284 פָּאָה **pāʾâ**, v. GK: 6990 & 6991 [→ 6285]. [H] to split into pieces, scatter:– scatter into corners [1]

6285 פֵּאָה **pēʾâ**, n.f. GK: 6991 [→ 6284]. side, edge, boundary; forehead or crown of the head; piece, part:– side [63], corners [11], corner [5], quarter [3], end [1], part [1], quarter (+3807.1) [1], sides [1]

6286 פָּאַר **pāʾar**, v. GK: 6995 [→ 6287?, 8597]. [P] to honor, adorn, endow with splendor; to knock down olives a second time; [Ht] to glorify oneself, display one's splendor; (negatively) to boast:– glorified [6], beautify [3], boast [1], glorify [1], glory [1], go over the boughs [1], vaunt [1]

6287 פְּאֵר **pʾēr**, n.m. GK: 6996 [→ 6286?]. turban, headdress:– bonnets [2], beauty [1], goodly [1], ornaments [1], tire of head [1], tires [1]

6288 פֹּארָה **pōʾrâ** or פֻּארָה **puʾrâ**, n.f. GK: 6997 & 6998. branch, leafy bough:– branches [4], boughs [1], bough [1], sprigs [1]

6289 פָּארוּר **pāʾrûr**, n.[m.]. GK: 6999 [→ 6517]. growing pale, turning pale; some sources: to burn, glow:– blackness [2]

6290 פָּארָן **pāʾrān**, n.pr.loc. GK: 7000 [→ 364; cf. 6501?]. Paran, "plain":– Paran [11]

6291 פַּג **pag**, n.f. GK: 7001. early fruit, in context, unripe fig buds:– green figs [1]

6292 פִּגּוּל **piggûl**, n.m. GK: 7002. (ceremonially) unclean meat, kept too long after a sacrifice:– abominable [3], abomination [1]

6293 פָּגַע **pāgaʿ**, n.m. GK: 7003 [→ 4645, 6294, 6295]. to strike, touch; intercede for, plead with; [H] to make intercession, intervene; strike; cause to encounter:– fall [6], meet [5], reacheth [5], fell [4], met [3], fall upon [2], intreat [2], made intercession [2], make intercession [2], meeteth [2], reached [2], came [1], cause to entreat [1], cometh betwixt [1], fell upon [1], intercessor [1], laid [1], lighted [1], meetest [1], met together [1], pray [1], run [1]

6294 פֶּגַע **pegaʿ**, n.m. GK: 7004 [→ 6293]. chance, occurrence:– chance [1], occurrent [1]

6295 פַּגְעִיאֵל **pagʿîʾēl**, n.pr.m. GK: 7005 [→ 6293+410]. Pagiel:– Pagiel [5]

6296 פָּגַר **pāgar**, v. GK: 7006 [→ 6297]. [P] to be exhausted:– faint [2]

6297 פֶּגֶר **peger**, n.m. GK: 7007 [→ 6296]. dead body, corpse; carcass; by extension: lifeless idol, with a focus that it is unclean and impotent:– carcases [12], dead bodies [6], corpses [2], carcase [1], dead carcases [1]

6298 פָּגַשׁ **pāgaš**, v. GK: 7008. [Q] to meet; to attack; [N] to have in common, to meet together; [P] to come upon, encounter:– met [6], meet [4], meet together [2], meeteth [1], met together [1]

6299 פָּדָה **pādâ**, v. GK: 7009 [→ 6302, 6303, 6304, 6306 (also used with compound proper names)]. [Q] to redeem, ransom, deliver, rescue, buy; [Qp] to be redeemed, be ransomed; [N] to be ransomed, be redeemed; [H] to let be ransomed; [Ho] to be brought to ransomed; this can mean to purchase a devoted animal from sacrifice or to purchase a person from slavery to freedom or new ownership; by extension: divine salvation from oppression, death, or sin:– redeemed [22], redeem [21], deliver [3], at all redeemed (+6299) [2], by any means redeem (+6299) [2], delivered [2], surely redeem (+6299) [2], ransomed [1], ransom [1], redeemedst [1], redeemeth [1], rescued [1]

6300 פְּדַהְאֵל **pʾdahʾēl**, n.pr.m. GK: 7010 [→ 6299+410]. Pedahel, "God [El] ransoms":– Pedahel [1]

6301 פְּדָהצוּר **pʾdāhṣûr** or פְּדָה־צוּר **pʾdāh-ṣûr**, n.pr.m. GK: 7011 [→ 6299+6697]. Pedahzur, "the Rock ransoms":– Pedahzur [5]

6302 פְּדוּיִם **pʾdûyim**, n.[m.]pl.abst. GK: 7012 [→ 6299]. redemption, ransom, paid to purchase firstborn Israelites from dedication to God:– redeemed [2], them that were redeemed [1], those that are redeemed [1]

6303 פָּדוֹן **pādôn**, n.pr.m. GK: 7013 [→ 6299]. Padon, "ransom":– Padon [2]

6304 פְּדוּת **pʾdût** or פְּלֻת **pʾlut**, n.f. GK: 7014 & 7151 [→ 6299, 6395]. redemption, ransom, always of divine action; distinction:– redemption [2], division [1], redeem [1]

6305 פְּדָיָה **pʾdāyâ** or פְּדָיָהוּ **pʾdāyāhû**, n.pr.m. GK: 7015 & 7016 [→ 6299+3068]. Pedaiah, "Yahweh ransoms":– Pedaiah [8]

6306 פִּדְיוֹם **pidyôm** or פִּדְיוֹן **pidyôn**, n.m. GK: 7017 & 7018 [→ 6299]. redemption, ransom; redemption money, ransom payment:– redemption [2], ransom [1]

6307 פַּדָּן **paddān** אֲרָם **ʾarām** or פַּדַּן **paddan** אֲרָם **ʾrām**, n.pr.loc. GK: 7019 & 7020 [→ 758]. Paddan, "plain"; Paddan Aram, "plain of Aram":– Padan-aram [10], Padan [1]

6308 פָּדַע **pādaʿ**, v. GK: 7021. [Q] to spare, deliver:– deliver [1]

6309 פֶּדֶר **peder**, n.[m.]. GK: 7022. suet (the hard fat about kidney's and loins of animals):– fat [3]

פְּדֻת **pʾdut**. See 6304.

6310 פֶּה **peh**, n.m. GK: 7023 [→ 6366, 6374; cf. 6433]. mouth (human or animal); by extension: speech, command, testimony; any opening; edge (of a sword):– mouth [329], commandment [37], edge [35], word [15], mouths [12], according to (+3807.1) [11], according to (+3509.1) [6], hole [6], according to (+5921) [4], another[5] [3], according unto (+3509.1) [2], appointment [2], one end [2], portion [2], tenor [2], according as (+834+3509.1) [2], according to (+834+5921) [1], according unto (+3807.1) [1], accord [1], after (+3807.1) [1], collar [1], command [1], eat (+871.1) [1], edges [1], end [1], entry [1], file (+6477) [1], in (+3807.1) [1], in the way go (+1870+5921) [1], mind [1], out of (+4480) [1], parts [1], saith (+871.1) [1], sayings [1], skirts [1], so that (+3509.1) [1], sound [1], speech [1], spoken [1], talk [1], to (+3807.1) [1], told (+7760+871.1) [1], twoedged [1], when (+3807.1) [1], wish [1], with assent [1]

6311 פֹּה **pōh**, adv.loc. GK: 7024 [→ 375, 645?]. here:– here [44], that side [13], this side [12], one side [5], other side [5], hither [2], hitherto (+5704) [1]

פֹּא **pōʾ**. See 375.

6312 פּוּאָה **pûʾâ** or פֻּאָה **puʾâ** or פֻּוָּה **puwwâ**, n.pr.m. GK: 7025 & 7026 & 7030 [→ 6324]. Puah, Puvah, "[perhaps] girl":– Puah [2], Phuvah [1], Pua [1]

6313 פּוּג **pûg**, v. GK: 7028 [→ 2014, 6314]. [Q] to grow numb, be feeble; [N] to be benumbed, be feeble:– ceased [1], fainted [1], feeble [1], slacked [1]

6314 פּוּגָה **pûgâ**, n.f. GK: 7029 [→ 6313]. relief, relaxation:– rest [1]

6315 פּוּחַ **pûaḥ**, v. GK: 7031 & 7032 [→ 6368; cf. 3306, 5301]. [Q] to blow, become dawn (of the day); to breathe out; [H] to blow (of wind); to breathe out, sneer, malign:– speaketh [5], blow [2], break [2], puffeth [2], bring into a snare [1], speak [1], utter [1]

6316 פּוּט **pûṭ**, n.pr.g. GK: 7033. Put:– Libya [2], Phut [2], Put [2], Libyans [1]

6317 פּוּטִיאֵל **pûṭîʾēl**, n.pr.m. GK: 7034 [→ 410]. Putiel, "he whom God [El] gives":– Putiel [1]

6318 פּוֹטִיפַר **pôṭîpar**, n.pr.m. GK: 7035 [cf. 6319]. Potiphar, "he whom Ra gives":– Potiphar [2]

6319 פּוֹטִי פֶרַע **pôṭî peraʿ**, n.pr.m. GK: 7036. Potiphera, "he whom Ra gives":– Poti-pherah [3]

6320 פּוּךְ **pûk**, n.[m.]. GK: 7037. turquoise (stone); (eye) paint, possibly derived from turquoise:– fair colours [1], glistering [1], painting [1]

6321 פּוֹל **pôl**, n.[m.]col. GK: 7038. beans:– beans [2]

6322 פּוּל **pûl**, n.pr.m. GK: 7040 [→ 6467; cf. 6466]. Pul:– Pul [4]

6323 פּוּן **pûn**, v. GK: 7041. [Q] to be in despair:– distracted [1]

6324 פֻּוָּא **puʾî** or פּוּנִי **pûnî**, a.g. GK: 7027 & 7043 [→ 6312]. Puite, Punite, "of Puah":– Punites [1]

6325 פּוּנֹן **pûnōn**, n.pr.loc. GK: 7044 [cf. 6373]. Punon:– Punon [2]

6326 פּוּעָה **pûʿâ**, n.pr.f. GK: 7045. Puah, "[perhaps] girl":– Puah [1]

6327 פּוּץ **pûṣ** or פָּצַץ **pāṣaṣ**, v. GK: 7046 & 7047 & 7207 [→ 1048, 4650, 6483, 8600; cf. 5310]. [Q] to be scattered; flow, overflow; [Qp] to be scattered; [N] to be scattered; [H] to cause to scatter; [Pol] to break to pieces, shatter; [Pil] to crush, smash; [Htpol] to be crumbled, be shattered:– scattered [31], scatter [16], scattered abroad [3], cast abroad [2], dispersed [2], scatter abroad [2], scattereth [2], spread abroad [2], breakth in pieces [1], dasheth in pieces [1], disperse [1], drive [1], retired [1], scattereth abroad [1], shaken to pieces [1]

6328 פּוּק **pûq**, v. GK: 7048 [→ 6330; cf. 6329, 6375]. [Q] to stumble, totter; [H] to totter:– move [1], stumble [1]

6329 פּוּק **pûq**, v. GK: 7049 [cf. 6328]. [H] to bring out, furnish, promote:– obtaineth [2], affording [1], draw out [1], further [1], getteth [1], obtain [1]

6330 פּוּקָה **pûqâ**, n.f. GK: 7050 [→ 6328]. staggering, stumbling:– grief [1]

6331 פּוּר **pûr**, v. GK: 7051 [cf. 6565]. [H] to destroy:– bringeth to nought [1], broken [1], utterly take [1]

6332 פּוּר **pûr**, n.m. GK: 7052. pur (the lot), pebbles, sticks, or pottery shards that were thrown to make decisions; (pl.) Purim, a Jewish festival celebrating God's control over the casting of lots:– Purim [5], Pur [3]

6333 פּוּרָה **pûrâ**, n.f. GK: 7053. trough of the winepress; measure (equal to the filling of the winepress):– press [1], winepress [1]

פּוּרִים **pûrîm**. See 6332.

6334 פּוֹרָתָא **pôrātāʾ**, n.pr.m. GK: 7054. Poratha:– Poratha [1]

6335 פּוּשׁ **pûš**, v. GK: 7055 & 7056. [Q] to leap, frolic, gallop; this may refer to the playful pawing action of a young animal; [N] to be scattered:– grow up [1], grown fat [1], scattered [1], spread [1]

6336 פּוּתִי **pûtî**, a.g. GK: 7057. Puthite:– Puhites [1]

6337 פָּז **paz**, n.m. GK: 7058 [→ 464, 6338]. pure gold:– fine gold [8], pure gold [1]

6338 פָּזַז **pāzaz**, v. GK: 7059 [→ 6337]. [Ho] to be set with pure gold:– best [1]

6339 פָּזַז **pāzaz**, v. GK: 7060. [Q] to be limber; [P] to leap:– leaping [1], made strong [1]

6340 פָּזַר **pāzar**, v. GK: 7061 [cf. 967]. [Qp] to be scattered; [P] to scatter; [N] to be scattered; [Pu] to be dispersed:– scattered [6], scattereth [2], dispersed [1], scattered abroad [1]

6341 פַּח **paḥ**, n.m. GK: 7062 & 7063 [→ 6351]. thin sheets (of hammered metal); snare, bird trap:– snare [18], snares [5], gin [1], grin [1], plates [1], thin plates [1]

6342 פָּחַד **pāḥad**, v. GK: 7064 [→ 6343, 6345]. [Q] to tremble, be afraid; [P] to live in terror, fear; [H] to make shake, make tremble:– afraid [9], fear [8], feared [2], in great fear (+6343) [2], feareth [1], greatly feared (+6343) [1], made to shake [1], standeth in awe [1]

6343 פַּחַד *paḥad*, n.m. GK: 7065 [→ 6342; cf. 6765]. fear, terror, dread:– fear [40], dread [3], in great fear (+6342) [2], terror [2], dreadful [1], greatly feared (+6342) [1]

6344 פַּחַד *paḥad*, n.[m.]. GK: 7066. thigh:– stones [1]

6345 פַּחְדָּה *paḥdâ*, n.f. GK: 7067 [→ 6342]. awe, dread:– fear [1]

6346 פֶּחָה *peḥâ*, n.m. GK: 7068 [→ 6355?; cf. 6347]. governor, officer:– governor [10], captains [7], governors [7], captain [2], deputies [2]

6347 פֶּחָה *peḥâ* (Aram.), n.m. GK: 10580 [cf. 6346]. governor:– governor [6], captains [4]

6348 פָּחַז *pāḥaz*, v. GK: 7069 [→ 6349, 6350]. [Q] to be arrogant, be insolent:– light [2]

6349 פַּחַז *paḥaz*, n.[m.]. GK: 7070 [→ 6348]. turbulence, recklessness:– unstable [1]

6350 פַּחֲזוּת *paḥ⁰zût*, n.f. GK: 7071 [→ 6348]. insolence, arrogance, with an implication of recklessness:– lightness [1]

6351 פָּחַח *pāḥaḥ*, v.den. GK: 7072 [→ 6341]. [H] to trap; [Ho] to be entrapped:– snared [1]

6352 פֶּחָם *peḥām*, n.[m.]. GK: 7073. coal, charcoal:– coals [3]

6353 פֶּחָר *peḥār* (Aram.), n.m. GK: 10581. potter; sources translate "clay":– potter's [1]

6354 פַּחַת *paḥat*, n.m. GK: 7074 [→ 6356]. pit, cave:– pit [8], hole's [1], snare [1]

6355 פַּחַת מוֹאָב *paḥat mô'āb*, n.pr.m. GK: 7075 [→ 6346?+4124]. Pahath-Moab, "*supervisor of Moab*":– Pahath-moab [6]

6356 פְּחֶתֶת *p⁰ḥetet*, n.m. GK: 7076 [→ 6354]. mildew (that eats away at a garment):– fret [1]

6357 פִּטְדָה *piṭdâ*, n.f. [*or* m.?]. GK: 7077. topaz; some sources: chrysolite:– topaz [4]

6358 פָּטַר *pāṭar*, v.ptcp. GK: 7080 [→ 6359, 6362, 6363]. ptcp. of 6362: open:– open [4]

6359 פְּטִירִים *p⁰ṭîrîm*, var. GK: 7078 [→ 6358]. open, unoccupied:–

6360 פַּטִּישׁ *paṭṭîš*, n.m. GK: 7079. (sledge-)hammer:– hammer [3]

6361 פַּטִּישׁ *paṭṭîš* (Aram.), n.[m.]. GK: 10582. trousers, leggings; some sources identify as other parts of clothing: coat, tunic, shirt, trousers, hose, hat, etc:– hosen [1]

6362 פָּטַר *pāṭar*, v. GK: 7080 [→ 6358]. [Q] to elude, escape, release; [Qp] to be opened; [H] to open wide the mouth (as an insult):– dismissed [1], free [1], letteth out [1], shoot out [1], slipt away [1]

6363 פֶּטֶר *peṭer*, n.m. or פִּטְרָה *piṭrâ*, n.f. GK: 7081 & 7082 [cf. 6358]. first offspring, firstborn:– openeth [5], firstling [4], that openeth [2], open [1]

6364 פִּי־בֶסֶת *pî-beset*, n.pr.loc. GK: 7083. Bubastis (Piy-Beset), "*house of the cat goddess Basht*":– Phi-beseth [1]

6365 פִּיד *pîd*, n.[m.]. GK: 7085. misfortune, distress, calamity:– destruction [2], ruin [1]

6366 פִּיָה *pîyâ*, n.m. GK: 7023 [→ 6310]. f. of 6310: mouth; by extension: edge (of a sword):–

6367 פִּי הַחִירוֹת *pî haḥîrôt*, n.pr.loc. GK: 7084. Pi Hahiroth, "*temple [house] of Hathor*":– Pi-hahiroth [4]

6368 פִּיחַ *pîaḥ*, n.[m.]. GK: 7086 [→ 6315]. soot (from a furnace):– ashes [2]

6369 פִּיכֹל *pîkōl*, n.pr.m. GK: 7087. Phicol:– Phichol [3]

6370 פִּילֶגֶשׁ *pîlegeš*, n.f. GK: 7108. concubine, a female consort generally with lower status and fewer rights than a wife, with the function of giving social status or pleasure to the husband; once this refers to a woman's male consorts (Eze 23:20):– concubine [22], concubines [14], paramours [1]

6371 פִּימָה *pîmâ*, n.f. GK: 7089. fat, referring to an abundant life:– collops of fat [1]

6372 פִּינְחָס *pîn⁰ḥās*, n.pr.m. GK: 7090 [cf. 8471]. Phinehas, "*the black man*":– Phinehas [24], Phinehas' [1]

6373 פִּינֹן *pînōn*, n.pr.m. GK: 7091 [cf. 6325]. Pinon, "*darkness* [name related to famous copper mines]":– Pinon [2]

6374 פִּיפִיּוֹת *pîpiyyôt*, n.[f.pl.?]. GK: 7092 [→ 6310]. double-edged, with many teeth:– teeth [1], twoedged [1]

6375 פִּק *piq*, n.[m.]. GK: 7211 [cf. 6328]. giving way, shaking (of knees):– smite together [1]

6376 פִּישׁוֹן *pîšôn*, n.pr.loc. GK: 7093. Pishon:– Pison [1]

6377 פִּיתוֹן *pîtôn*, n.pr.m. GK: 7094. Pithon:– Pithon [2]

6378 פַּךְ *pak*, n.[m.]. GK: 7095 [→ 6379]. flask, (small) jug-box [2], vial [1]

6379 פָּכָה *pākâ*, v. GK: 7096 [→ 6378]. [P] to trickle:– ran out [1]

6380 פֹּכֶרֶת הַצְּבָיִים *pōkeret haṣṣ⁰bāyîm*, n.pr.m. GK: 7097. Pokereth-Hazzebaim, "*pitfall of gazelles, i.e., gazelle hunter*":– Pochereth Zebaim [1], Pochereth of Zebaim [1]

6381 פָּלָא *pālā'*, v.den. GK: 7098 [→ 466?, 4652, 6381, 6382, 6383, 6384, 6411, 6396; cf. 6395]. [N] to be wonderful, be marvelous, be amazing; to be hard, be amazing; [P] to fulfill; [H] to show a wonder, to cause to astound; [Ht] to show oneself marvelous:– wondrous works [10], wonders [9], marvellous [7], wonderful works [7], hard [5], wonderful [5], marvellous works [4], wondrous [4], marvellously [2], performing [2], accomplish [1], do a marvellous work [1], hidden [1], high [1], make a singular vow (+5088) [1], make wonderful [1], marvellous work [1], marvels [1], miracles [1], separate [1], shewed marvellous [1], shewest marvellous [1], wonderfully made [1], wonderfully [1], wondrously (+3807.1) [1], wondrously [1]

6382 פֶּלֶא *pele'*, n.m. GK: 7099 [→ 6381]. wonder, miracle, astounding thing:– wonders [7], wonderful [2], marvellous things [1], wonderful things [1], wonderfully [1], wonder [1]

6383 פִּלְאִי *pil'î*, a. GK: 7100 [→ 6381]. wonderful, beyond understanding:– secret [1], wonderful [1]

6384 פַּלֻּאִי *pallu'î*, a.g. GK: 7101 [→ 6396; cf. 6381]. Palluite, "*wonderful*":– Palluites [1]

פְּלָאיָה *p⁰lā'yâ*. See 6411.

פִּלְאֶסֶר *pil'eser*. See 8407.

6385 פָּלַג *pālag*, v. GK: 7103 [→ 4653, 6388, 6390, 6391; cf. 6418; cf. 6386, 6387]. [N] to be divided; [P] to cut open, divide:– divided [3], divide [1]

6386 פְּלַג *p⁰lag* (Aram.), v. GK: 10583 [→ 6387, 6392; cf. 6385]. [Pp] to be divided:– divided [1]

6387 פְּלַג *p⁰lag* (Aram.), n.[m.]. GK: 10584 [→ 6386; cf. 6388]. half:– dividing [1]

6388 פֶּלֶג *peleg*, n.m. GK: 7104 [→ 6385]. stream, artificial irrigation canal:– rivers [8], river [1], streams [1]

6389 פֶּלֶג *peleg*, n.pr.m. GK: 7105. Peleg, "*water canal*":– Peleg [7]

6390 פְּלַגָּה *p⁰laggâ*, n.f. GK: 7106 [→ 6385]. district, division; stream:– divisions [2], rivers [1]

6391 פְּלֻגָּה *p⁰luggâ*, n.f. GK: 7107 [→ 6385; cf. 6392]. division (of a clan or family):– divisions [1]

6392 פְּלֻגָּה *p⁰luggâ* (Aram.), n.f. GK: 10585 [→ 6386; cf. 6391]. division (of priests):– divisions [1]

פִּלֶגֶשׁ *pilegeš*. See 6370.

6393 פְּלָדֹת *p⁰lādōt*, n.f. GK: 7110. (polished) metal:– torches [1]

6394 פִּלְדָּשׁ *pildāš*, n.pr.m. GK: 7109. Pildash, "*steely; spider*":– Pildash [1]

6395 פָּלָה *pālâ*, v. GK: 7111 [→ 6397, 6411, 6423, 6304; cf. 6381]. [N] to be distinguished; [H] to deal differently, make a distinction:– sever [2], marvellous [1], put a difference [1], separated [1], set apart [1], shew marvellous [1]

6396 פַּלּוּא *pallû'*, n.pr.m. GK: 7112 [→ 6384; cf. 6381]. Pallu, "*wonderful*":– Pallu [4], Phallu [1]

6397 פַּלֹּנִי *p⁰lônî*, a.g. GK: 7113 [→ 6395]. Pelonite:– Pelonite [3]

6398 פָּלַח *pālaḥ*, v. GK: 7114 [→ 6400, 6401; cf. 6399]. [Q] to plow; [P] to cut up, pierce; to bring forth (from the womb):– bring forth [1], cleaveth asunder [1], cutteth [1], shred [1], strike through [1]

6399 פְּלַח *p⁰laḥ* (Aram.), v. GK: 10586 [→ 6402; cf. 6398?]. [P] to serve, worship, work for (deity or deities):– serve [7], servest [2], ministers [1]

6400 פֶּלַח *pelaḥ*, n.f. GK: 7115 [→ 6398]. millstone; half (of a pomegranate); slice (of a cake):– piece [6]

6401 פִּלְחָא *pilḥā'*, n.pr.m. GK: 7116 [→ 6398]. Pilha, "*millstone; plowman; harelip*":– Pileha [1]

6402 פָּלְחָן *polḥān* (Aram.), n.m. GK: 10587 [→ 6399]. worship, service, work (for deity):– service [1]

6403 פָּלַט *pālaṭ*, v. GK: 7117 [→ 3310, 3311, 4655, 6404, 6405, 6408, 6409, 6410, 6412, 6413; cf. 4422]. [Q] to escape; [P] to rescue, deliver; [H] to bring to safety:– deliver [11], deliverer [5], delivered [3], calveth [1], carry away safe [1], cause to escape [1], deliverest [1], delivereth [1], escape [1]

6404 פֶּלֶט *pelet*, n.pr.m. GK: 7118 [→ 6407; cf. 6403 (also used with compound proper names)]. Pelet, "*rescue*":– Pelet [2]

פָּלֵט *pālēt*. See 6412.

6405 פַּלֵּט *pallēt*, n.[m.]. GK: 7119 [→ 6403]. deliverance:– escape [3], deliverance [1], escaped [1]

פְּלֵטָה *p⁰lēṭâ*. See 6413.

6406 פַּלְטִי *palṭî*, n.pr.m. GK: 7120 [→ 6409]. Palti; Paltiel, "*God [El] is [my] deliverance*":– Palti [1], Phalti [1]

6407 פַּלְטִי *palṭî*, a.g. GK: 7121 [→ 6404]. Paltite:– Paltite [1]

6408 פִּלְטַי *pilṭay*, n.pr.m. GK: 7122 [→ 6403]. Piltai, "*Yahweh rescues*":– Piltai [1]

6409 פַּלְטִיאֵל *palṭî'ēl*, n.pr.m. GK: 7123 [→ 6406]. Paltiel, "*God [El] is [my] deliverance*":– Paltiel [1], Phaltiel [1]

6410 פְּלַטְיָה *p⁰laṭyâ* or פְּלַטְיָהוּ *p⁰laṭyāhû*, n.pr.m. GK: 7124 & 7125 [→ 6403+3068]. Pelatiah, "*Yahweh rescues*":– Pelatiah [5]

פָּלִיא *pālî'*. See 6383.

6411 פְּלָאיָה *p⁰lā'yâ* or פְּלָיָה *p⁰lāyâ*, n.pr.m. GK: 7102 & 7126 [→ 6381+3068 or 6395+3068]. Pelaiah, "*Yahweh is spectacular*":– Pelaiah [3]

6412 פָּלִיט *pālîṭ* or פָּלֵט *pālēṭ*, n.m. GK: 7127 & 7128 [→ 6403]. fugitive, one who escapes:– escape [9], escaped [6], escapeth [2], escape (+1961) [1], fugitives [1], one that escaped [1], that escaped [1]

6413 פְּלֵיטָה *p⁰lêṭâ*, n.f. GK: 7129 [→ 6403]. fugitive, one who escapes, survivors, remnant:– deliverance [5], escaped [4], escape [4], escape (+1961) [2], that is escaped [2], they that escape [2], escaping [1], him that escapeth [1], remnant to escape [1], remnant [1], such as are escaped [1], that are escaped [1], them that are escaped [1], them that be escaped [1], which is escaped [1]

6414 פָּלִיל *pālîl*, n.m. GK: 7130 [→ 6419]. judge:– judges [3]

6415 פְּלִילָה *p⁰lîlâ*, n.f. GK: 7131 [→ 6419]. decision:– judgment [1]

6416 פְּלִילִי *p⁰lîlî*, a. GK: 7132 [→ 6419]. for a judge, calling for judgment:– judge [1]

6417 פְּלִילִיָה *p⁰lîliyyâ*, n.f. GK: 7133 [→ 6419]. rendering of a decision, the calling for a judgment:– judgment [1]

6418 פֶּלֶךְ *pelek*, n.[m.]. GK: 7134 & 7135 [cf. 6385]. spindle-whorl, which could be used as a crutch; district:– part [8], distaff [1], staff [1]

6419 פָּלַל *pālal*, v. GK: 7136 & 7137 [→ 654, 6414, 6415, 6416, 6417, 6420, 6421, 8605 (also used with compound proper names)]. [P] to mediate, intervene; to expect; to furnish justification; [Ht] to pray:– pray [35], prayed [30], praying [5], prayeth [4], executed judgment [1], intreat [1], judged [1], judge [1], made prayer [1], make supplication [1], make [1], prayer made [1], prayer make (+8605) [1], thought [1]

6420 פָּלָל *pālāl*, n.pr.m. GK: 7138 [→ 6419]. Palal, "*he has judged*":– Palal [1]

6421 פְּלַלְיָה *p⁰lalyâ*, n.pr.m. GK: 7139 [→ 6419+3068]. Pelaliah, "*Yahweh intercedes in arbitration*":– Pelaliah [1]

6422 פַּלְמֹנִי *palmōnî*, p. GK: 7140 [cf. 492, 6423]. certain one:– certain [1]

פִּלְנְאֶסֶר *piln⁰'eser*. See 8407.

6423 פְּלֹנִי *p⁰lōnî*, p. GK: 7141 [→ 6395; cf. 492, 6422]. certain one:– such a one (+492) [1], such and such (+492) [1], such [1]

פִּלְנֶסֶר *pilneser*. See 8407.

6424 פָּלַס *pālas*, v.den. GK: 7142 & 7143 [→ 6425]. [P] to make level, make smooth, prepare; to examine, observe:– ponder [2], weigh [2], made [1], pondereth [1]

6425 פֶּלֶס *peles*, n.[m.]. GK: 7144 [→ 6424]. balance, scale:– scales [1], weight [1]

פְּלֶסֶר *p⁰leser*. See 8407.

6426 פָּלַץ *pālaṣ*, v. GK: 7145 [→ 4656, 6427, 8606]. [Ht] to tremble, shake:– tremble [1]

6427 פַלָּצוּת *pallāṣût*, n.f. GK: 7146 [→ 6426]. trembling, shuddering, shaking:– horror [2], fearfulness [1], trembling [1]

6428 פָלַשׁ *pālaš*, v. GK: 7147. [Ht] to roll oneself (in the dust or ash):– wallow [3], roll [1]

6429 פְלֶשֶׁת *pelešet*, n.pr.loc. GK: 7148 [→ 6430]. Philistia; Philistine:– Palestina [3], Philistia [3], Palestine [1], Philistines [1]

6430 פְלִשְׁתִּי *pelištî*, a.g. GK: 7149 [→ 6429]. Philistine:– Philistines [245], Philistine [33], Philistims [5], Philistines' [4], Philistim [1]

6431 פֶלֶת *pelet*, n.pr.m. GK: 7150. Peleth, "[perhaps] *swift* or *swiftness*":– Peleth [2]

6432 פְלֵתִי *pelêtî*, a.g. GK: 7152 [cf. 3774?]. Pelethite:– Pelethites [7]

6433 פֻם *pum* (Aram.), n.m. GK: 10588. mouth:– mouth [5], mouths [1]

6434 פֵן *pēn*, n.m. GK: 7157 [→ 6437, 6438]. same as 6438: corner (of a structure), cornerstone (as a crucial element); stronghold; by extension: leader:– corner [2]

6435 פֶן *pen*, c. GK: 7153 [→ 6437?]. lest, not:– lest [114], not [7], lest peradventure [5], that not [4], none [1], peradventure [1], that [1]

6436 פַנַּג *pannag*, n.[m.]. GK: 7154. food, confection:– Pannag [1]

6437 פָנָה *pānâ*, v. GK: 7155 [→ 3312, 3942, 6435?, 6440, 6434, 6438, 6439, 6441, 6442]. [Q] to turn (in various senses); [P] to prepare; to turn away; [H] to turn; [Ho] to be caused to turn:– turned [33], turn [16], looked [14], looking [9], look [9], looketh [8], prepare [4], look back [3], respect [3], turneth [3], have respect [2], regard (+413) [2], beholdeth [1], cast out [1], cometh on [1], corner [1], dawning [1], empty [1], eventide (+6153) [1], goeth away [1], lieth [1], look toward [1], looked back [1], looked toward [1], mark (+413) [1], passed away [1], preparedst [1], prepared [1], regardeth (+413) [1], regard [1], respecteth (+413) [1], return [1], right [1], turn away [1], turn back [1], turned aside [1], turned back [1], turned faces [1], turnest [1], turneth away [1], when appeared (+3807.1) [1]

פָנֶה *pāneh*. See 6440.

6438 פִנָּה *pinnâ*, n.f. GK: 7157 [→ 6434]. same as 6434: corner (of a structure), cornerstone (as a crucial element); stronghold; by extension: leader:– corner [16], corners [6], chief [2], towers [2], bulwarks [1], stay [1]

6439 פְנוּאֵל *penû'ēl* or פְנִיאֵל *penî'ēl*, n.pr.m. & loc. GK: 7158 & 7159 & 7160 & 7161 [→ 6437]. Penuel, Peniel, "*face of God [El]*":– Penuel [8], Peniel [1]

פָנִי *pānî*. See 6443.

6440 פָנֶה *pāneh*, n.m. & f. GK: 7156 [→ 6753, 6441; cf. 6437]. face; by extension: appearance, presence; (pp.) before, in front of, in the presence of; to "show one's face" is a sign of favor; to "turn" or "hide one's face" is a sign of rejection:– before (+3807.1) [958], face [328], presence [70], before [67], faces [63], because of (+4480) [54], before (+5921) [43], sight [33], from (+4480) [31], countenance [30], upon (+5921) [23], of (+4480) [20], before (+4480+3807.1) [17], before (+854) [16], before (+413) [15], open [13], because (+4480) [12], for (+4480) [12], persons [10], person [10], by reason of (+4480) [9], fear [7], before (+871.1) [6], prospect [6], toward (+5921) [6], with (+3807.1) [6], against (+3807.1) [5], over against (+5921) [5], sight (+3807.1) [5], forefront [4], from (+4480+3807.1) [4], honourable (+5375) [4], in (+5921) [4], over against (+413) [4], presence (+3807.1) [3], according to (+5921) [3], anger [3], at (+4480) [3], because [3], beforetime (+3807.1) [3], besought (+853+2470) [3], favour [3], for (+3807.1) [3], forefront (+4136) [3], forepart [3], meet [3], of (+4480+3807.1) [3], say nay (+7725) [3], shewbread (+3899) [3], shewbread (+3899+1886.1) [3], straight forward (+413+5676) [3], unto (+3807.1) [3], accept (+5375) [2], accepted (+5375) [2], afore (+3807.1) [2], aforetime (+3807.1) [2], before (+413+4136) [2], besought (+2470) [2], from (+3807.1) [2], from off (+4480+5921) [2], looketh [2], looks [2], of old (+3807.1) [2], over against (+413+4136) [2], seemeth unto (+3807.1) [2], unto [2], withstand (+2388+3807.1) [2], against (+413) [1], against (+5676) [1], appease (+3722) [1], as (+5921) [1], as long as (+3807.1) [1], at (+3807.1) [1], attend upon [1], because (+834+4480) [1], before (+5048) [1], before face [1], beforetime [1], beforetime (+4480+3807.1) [1], beseech (+2470) [1], by (+4480) [1], compassed with (+2328+5921) [1], disappoint (+6923) [1], edge [1], employ (+935+4480) [1], endure (+3807.1) [1], evident [1], first (+3807.1) [1], for

(+4480+3807.1) [1], for fear of (+4480) [1], forefront (+3807.1) [1], forepart (+4136) [1], form [1], forward (+3807.1) [1], front [1], heaviness [1], himself (+2050.2) [1], impudent (+7186) [1], in former time (+3807.1) [1], in front (+5921) [1], in old time (+3807.1) [1], in presence (+7200) [1], in sight (+3807.1) [1], in the presence [1], in the sight (+3807.1) [1], in time past [1], in times past (+3807.1) [1], inquired of (+1245) [1], intreat favour (+2470) [1], looked [1], look [1], me (+2967.1) [1], more than (+3807.1) [1], mouth [1], out of (+4480+5921) [1], over against [1], partial [1], pleased [1], pleaseth (+3190+3807.1) [1], purposed [1], regard (+3807.1) [1], regard persons (+4480+5375) [1], right before (+5227) [1], right forth (+3807.1) [1], send good speed (+7136+3807.1) [1], served (+5975+3807.1) [1], set [1], shewbread [1], state [1], themselves (+1992.1) [1], through (+4480) [1], throughout (+5921) [1], till (+3807.1) [1], towards (+4480) [1], towards (+4480) [1], toward [1], to [1], upside down (+5921) [1], upside down [1], waited on (+1961+3807.1) [1], whom (+834+4480) [1], with (+4480) [1], within (+4480+3807.1) [1], within [1], withstand (+5975+3807.1) [1]

6441 פְנִימָה *penîmâ*, adv. *or* pp. GK: 7163 [→ 6442; cf. 6440, 6437]. inner, inside, within:– within (+4480) [3], within [3], inward (+3807.1) [2], within (+3807.1) [2], inner part [1], in [1], within (+413) [1]

6442 פְנִימִי *penîmî*, a. GK: 7164 [→ 6441]. inner:– inner [30], inward (+413+1886.1) [1], within (+871.1+1886.1) [1]

6443 פְנִינִים *penînîm*, n.[f.]pl. GK: 7165 [→ 6444]. rubies or corals:– rubies [6]

6444 פְנִנָּה *peninnâ*, n.pr.f. GK: 7166 [→ 6443]. Peninnah, "[poss.] *pearls, coral branches; woman with rich hair*":– Peninnah [3]

6445 פָנַק *pānaq*, v. GK: 7167. [P] to pamper:– delicately bringeth up [1]

6446 פַס *pas*, n.[m.]. GK: 7168 [→ 6450; cf. 657; cf. 6447]. ornamentation, many-colored or long-sleeved garment:– of many colours [3], divers colours [2]

6447 פַס *pas* (Aram.), n.m. GK: 10589 [cf. 6446]. (palm of) hand; this may also refer to the entire hand:– part [2]

6448 פָסַג *pāsag*, v. GK: 7170. [P] to look over or to walk among:– consider [1]

6449 פִסְגָה *pisgâ*, n.pr.loc. GK: 7171 [→ 798]. Pisgah:– Pisgah [5]

6450 פַס דַּמִּים *pas dammîm*, n.pr.loc. GK: 7169 [→ 6446]. Pas Dammim, "*place of blood*":– Pas-dammim [1]

6451 פִסָּה *pissâ*, n.f. GK: 7172. abundance, plenty:– handful [1]

6452 פָסַח *pāsaḥ*, v. GK: 7173 & 7174 [→ 6453, 6454, 6455, 8607]. [Q] to pass over; to be limp; [N] to become crippled; to worship in a limping dance:– pass over [2], became lame [1], halt [1], leapt [1], passed over [1], passing over [1]

6453 פֶסַח *pesaḥ*, n.m. GK: 7175 [→ 6452]. Passover; this can refer to the festival, the meal, or the lamb sacrificed at the festival:– passover [48], passovers [1]

6454 פָסֵחַ *pāsēaḥ*, n.pr.m. GK: 7176 [→ 6452]. Paseah, "*hobbling one*":– Paseah [3], Phaseah [1]

6455 פִסֵּחַ *pissēaḥ*, a. GK: 7177 [→ 6452]. lame, crippled:– lame [14]

6456 פָסִיל *pāsîl*, n.m. GK: 7178 [→ 6458]. idol, carved image:– graven images [18], carved images [3], quarries [2]

6457 פָסַךְ *pāsak*, n.pr.m. GK: 7179. Pasach, "*to divide*":– Pasach [1]

6458 פָסַל *pāsal*, v. GK: 7180 [→ 6456, 6459]. [Q] to chisel out, carve (stone or wood):– hew [3], hewed [2], graven [1]

6459 פֶסֶל *pesel*, n.m. GK: 7181 [→ 6458]. idol, usually an image carved of wood or stone:– graven image [26], carved image [2], graven images [2], graven [1]

6460 פְסַנְתֵּרִין *pesantērîn* (Aram.), n.[m.]. GK: 10590. harp (triangular stringed instrument):– psaltery [4]

6461 פָסַס *pāsas*, v. GK: 7182. [Q] to vanish:– fail [1]

6462 פִסְפָה *pispâ*, n.pr.m. GK: 7183. Pispah:– Pispah [1]

6463 פָעָה *pā'â*, v. GK: 7184 [→ 660?]. [Q] to cry out, groan (in childbirth):– cry [1]

6464 פָעוּ *pā'û* or פָעִי *pā'î*, n.pr.loc. GK: 7185 & 7187. Pau, Pai, "*groaning, bleating*":– Pai [1], Pau [1]

6465 פְעוֹר *pe'ôr*, n.pr.loc. GK: 7186 [→ 1047, 1187; cf. 6473?]. Peor, "*opening*":– Peor [4], Peor's [1]

פָעִי *pā'î*. See 6464.

6466 פָעַל *pā'al*, v. GK: 7188 [→ 508, 4659, 6322, 6467, 6468, 6469]. [Q] to do, make:– workers [19], work [7], wrought [7], do [5], worketh [4], done [3], made [3], commit [1], didst [1], doers [1], doest [1], maker [1], maketh [1], ordaineth [1], working [1]

6467 פֹעַל *pō'al*, n.m. GK: 7189 [→ 6322; cf. 6466]. work, deed, labor:– work [27], deeds [2], done acts [2], works [2], act [2], do [1], getting [1], maker [1], reward of work [1]

6468 פְעֻלָה *pe'ullâ*, n.f. GK: 7190 [→ 6469; cf. 6466]. work, deed, recompense:– work [8], labour [2], works [2], reward [1], wages [1]

6469 פְעֻלְתַי *pe'ulltay*, n.pr.m. GK: 7191 [→ 6468; cf. 6466]. Peullethai, "*worker, wage earner*":– Peulthai [1]

6470 פָעַם *pā'am*, v. GK: 7192 [→ 6471, 6472]. [Q] to push, impel; [N] to be troubled; [Ht] to be troubled:– troubled [4], move at times [1]

6471 פַעַם *pa'am*, n.f. GK: 7193 [→ 6472; cf. 6470]. step, foot; time, occurrence:– times [38], at other times (+6471+871.1) [12], time [12], once [8], feet [6], now [5], twice [5], steps [4], thrice (+7969) [4], corners [3], once (+259) [3], at once (+259) [2], now (+1886.1) [2], ranks [2], second time [2], anvil [1], footsteps [1], goings [1], hundredfold (+3967) [1], oftentimes (+7227) [1], oftentimes (+7969) [1], once (+871.1+1886.1) [1], order [1], two times [1], wheels [1]

6472 פַעֲמֹן *pa'amōn*, n.[m.]. GK: 7194 [→ 6471; cf. 6470]. bell (on a robe):– bell [4], bells [3]

6473 פָעַר *pā'ar*, v. GK: 7196 [cf. 6465?, 6474?]. [Q] to open wide (mouth):– opened [2], gaped [1], opened wide [1]

6474 פַעֲרַי *pa'aray*, n.pr.m. GK: 7197 [cf. 6473?]. Paarai, "*devotee of Peor*":– Paarai [1]

6475 פָצָה *pāṣâ*, v. GK: 7198. [Q] to open (mouth); to deliver, set free:– opened [7], open [3], rid [2], delivereth [1], gaped [1], uttered [1]

6476 פָצַח *pāṣaḥ*, v. GK: 7200. [Q] to break forth, burst forth; [P] to break (in pieces):– break forth [6], break [1], make a loud noise [1]

6477 פְצִירָה *peṣîrâ*, n.f. GK: 7201. sharpening (of plowshare):– file (+6310) [1]

6478 פָצַל *pāṣal*, v. GK: 7202 [→ 6479]. [P] to peel (bark off boughs):– pilled [2]

6479 פְצָלוֹת *peṣālôt*, n.f.pl. GK: 7203 [→ 6478]. stripes (made by peeling bark):– strakes [1]

6480 פָצַם *pāṣam*, v. GK: 7204. [Q] to tear open:– broken [1]

6481 פָצַע *pāṣa'*, v. GK: 7205 [→ 6482]. [Q] to bruise, wound; [Qp] to be emasculated (by crushing):– wounded [3]

6482 פֶצַע *peṣa'*, n.m. GK: 7206 [→ 6481]. wound, bruise:– wounds [4], wound [3], wounding [1]

פַצֵּץ *paṣṣēṣ*. See 1048.

6483 פִצֵּץ *piṣṣēṣ* or הַפִּצֵּץ *happiṣṣēṣ*, n.pr.m. GK: 7209 & 2204 [→ 1886.1+6327]. Pizzez, Happizzez, "*one who breaks*":– Aphses [1]

6484 פָצַר *pāṣar*, v. GK: 7210 [cf. 6555]. [Q] to insist on, bring pressure, persuade; [H] to be arrogant:– urged [4], pressed [2], stubbornness [1]

6485 פָקַד *pāqad*, v. GK: 7212 & 7217 [→ 4662, 6486, 6487, 6488, 6489, 6490, 6496]. [Q] to pay attention, care for; to count, number; to punish; [Qp] to be counted, listed; [N] to be missing, empty; [P] to muster; [Pu] to be robbed; to be recorded; [H] to appoint, give a charge; [Ho] to be appointed; [Ht] be mustered, counted; [Hotpaal] to be counted:– numbered [103], visit [31], punish [27], visited [17], number [14], appoint [10], set [6], surely visit (+6485) [6], made governor [5], appointed [4], committed [4], officers [4], punished [4], visiting [4], charged [3], counted [3], empty [3], missed [3], at all miss (+6485) [2], by any means missing (+6485) [2], commit [2], do judgment [2], lacking [2], laid up [2], made overseer [2], made ruler [2], numberest [2], overseers [2], oversight [2], surely visited (+6485) [2], visitest [2], wanting [2], avenge [1], bestowed [1], calledst to remembrance [1], chargest [1], delivered to keep (+854+6487) [1], deprived [1], enjoined [1], given a charge [1], go see [1], had oversight [1], have oversight [1], hurt [1], lacked [1], lacketh [1], look [1], made rulers [1], make [1], missing [1], mustereth [1], reckon [1], remember [1], set over [1], sum [1], visiteth [1], want [1]

6485 פִּקֻּד. See 6490.

6486 פְּקֻדָּה *pᵉquddâ*, n.f. GK: 7213 [→ 6485]. positive appointment, charge, visitation; negative: punishment:– visitation [13], office [3], officers [2], offices [2], oversight [2], account [1], charge [1], custody [1], numbers [1], orderings [1], prison (+1004+1886.1) [1], reckoning [1], that have charge over [1], that laid up [1]

6487 פִּקָּדוֹן *piqqādôn*, n.m. GK: 7214 [→ 6485]. something entrusted, something in reserve:– delivered to keep (+854+6485) [1], store [1], that which was delivered to keep [1]

6488 פִּקְדֻת *pᵉqidut*, n.f. GK: 7215 [→ 6485]. (captain of the) guard:– ward [1]

6489 פְּקוֹד *pᵉqôd*, n.pr.loc. GK: 7216 [→ 6485]. Pekod, "*visitation*":– Pekod [2]

6490 פִּקּוּדִים *piqqûdîm*, n.m.[pl.]. GK: 7218 [→ 6485]. precepts, directions, orders:– precepts [21], commandments [2], statutes [1]

6491 פָּקַח *pāqaḥ*, v. GK: 7219 [→ 6492?, 6493, 6494, 6495]. [Q] to open; [Qp] to be opened; [N] to be opened:– open [10], opened [7], openeth [2], opening [1]

6492 פֶּקַח *peqaḥ*, n.pr.m. GK: 7220 [→ 6491?]. Pekah, "*he has opened*":– Pekah [11]

6493 פִּקֵּחַ *piqqēaḥ*, a. GK: 7221 [→ 6491]. (normal) sighted:– seeing [1], wise [1]

6494 פְּקַחְיָה *pᵉqaḥyâ*, n.pr.m. GK: 7222 [→ 6491+3068]. Pekahiah, "*Yahweh opens*":– Pekahiah [3]

6495 פְּקַח־קוֹחַ *pᵉqaḥ-qôaḥ*, n.[m.]. GK: 7223 [→ 6491]. opening (of eyesight); some sources: opening a prison house to release prisoners:– opening of the prison [1]

6496 פָּקִיד *pāqîd*, n.m. GK: 7224 [→ 6485]. chief officer, supervisor, commissioner:– overseer [4], officers [3], officer [2], charge [1], governor [1], overseers [1], set [1]

6497 פְּקָעִים *pᵉqāʿîm*, n.m.pl. GK: 7225 [→ 6498]. gourds:– knops [3]

6498 פַּקֻּעֹת *paqquʿōt*, n.[f.]pl. GK: 7226 [→ 6497]. gourds:– gourds [1]

6499 פַּר *par*, n.m. GK: 7228 [→ 6510]. bull:– bullock [60], bullocks [31], bullock (+1241) [28], bullocks (+1241) [5], bullock's [3], bulls [2], oxen [2], calves [1], young [1]

6500 פָּרָא *pārā'*, v. GK: 7229 [cf. 6509]. [H] to thrive in fruitfulness:– fruitful [1]

6501 פֶּרֶא *pere'* or פֶּרֶה *pereh*, n.m. or f. GK: 7230 & 7241 [→ 6290?, 6502]. wild donkey; some sources: zebra, onager:– wild asses [4], wild ass [4], wild ass's [1], wild [1]

פֹּרָאֽה *pōrā'h*. See 6288.

6502 פִּרְאָם *pir'ām*, n.pr.m. GK: 7231 [→ 6501]. Piram, "[poss.] *wild donkey; indomitable*; [poss.] *zebra*":– Piram [1]

6503 פַּרְבָּר *parbār* or פַּרְוָר *parwār*, n.[m.]. GK: 7232 & 7247. court (of the temple):– Parbar [2], suburbs [1]

6504 פָּרַד *pārad*, v. GK: 7233 [→ 6505, 6506, 6507]. [Qp] to be separated out; [N] to be separated, be parted; [P] to consort with; [Pu] to be scattered; [H] to set apart, divide, separate; [Ht] to be scattered, be parted:– separated [8], divided [3], parted [2], separateth [2], separate [2], dispersed [1], out of joint [1], parteth [1], part [1], scattered abroad [1], scattered [1], severed [1], stretched [1], sundered [1]

6505 פֶּרֶד *pered*, n.m. GK: 7234 [→ 6506; cf. 6504]. mule:– mules [8], mule [6], mules' [1]

6506 פִּרְדָּה *pirdâ*, n.f. GK: 7235 [→ 6505]. (female) mule:– mule [3]

6507 פְּרֻדוֹת *pᵉrudōt*, n.f.[pl.]. GK: 7237 [→ 6504]. grain (of seed); some sources: dried fig:– seed [1]

6508 פַּרְדֵּס *pardēs*, n.[m.]. GK: 7236. park, forest, orchard:– forest [1], orchards [1], orchard [1]

6509 פָּרָה *pārâ*, v. GK: 7238 [→ 669?, 6513, 6529; cf. 6500]. [Q] to be fruitful, flourish; [H] to make fruitful:– fruitful [13], make fruitful [5], increased [3], fruitful bough (+1121) [2], beareth [1], bring forth [1], bring fruit [1], caused to be fruitful [1], grew [1], grow [1]

6510 פָּרָה *pārâ*, n.f. GK: 7239 [→ 6499]. cow, heifer:– kine [18], heifer [6], cow [2]

6511 פָּרָה *pārâ*, n.pr.loc. GK: 7240. Parah, "*cow*":– Parah [1]

פֶּרֶה *pereh*. See 6501.

6512 פֵּרוֹת *pērôt* or חַפַרְפָּרָה *ḥᵃparpārâ*, n.f. GK: 7249 & 2923 [→ 2658, 2661]. rodent (an object of worship):– moles (+2661) [1]

6513 פֻּרָה *purâ*, n.pr.m. GK: 7242 [→ 6509]. Purah, "*branch; imposing*":– Phurah [2]

6514 פְּרוּדָא *pᵉrûdā'* or פְּרִידָא *pᵉrîdā'*, n.pr.m. GK: 7243 & 7263. Peruda, Perida, "*single, unique*":– Perida [1], Peruda [1]

פְּרוֹזִי *pᵉrôzî*. See 6521.

6515 פָּרוּחַ *pārûaḥ*, n.pr.m. GK: 7245 [→ 6524]. Paruah, "*blooming; cheerful*":– Paruah [1]

6516 פַּרְוַיִם *parwayim*, n.pr.loc. GK: 7246. Parvaim:– Parvaim [1]

6517 פָּרוּר *pārûr*, n.[m.]. GK: 7248 [→ 6289]. cooking pot:– pot [2], pans [1]

פַּרְוָר *parwār*. See 6503.

6518 פָּרָז *pārāz*, n.[m.]. GK: 7250. warrior:– villages [1]

6519 פְּרָזוֹת *pᵉrāzôt*, n.f.[pl.]. GK: 7252 [→ 6520, 6521, 6522?]. rural, open country:– towns without walls [1], unwalled villages [1], unwalled [1]

6520 פְּרָזוֹן *pᵉrāzôn*, n.[m.]. GK: 7251 [→ 6519]. dwellers in the open country; warriors:– villages [2]

6521 פְּרָזִי *pᵉrāzî*, n.[m.]. GK: 7253 [cf. 6519]. rural, open country:– country [1], unwalled [1], villages [1]

6522 פְּרִזִּי *pᵉrizzî*, a.g. GK: 7254 [→ 6519]. Perizzite:– Perizzites [18], Perizzite [5]

6523 פַּרְזֶל *parzel* (Aram.), n.m. GK: 10591 [cf. 1270]. iron:– iron [20]

6524 פָּרַח *pāraḥ*, v. GK: 7255 & 7256 & 7257 [→ 667, 6515, 6525, 6526?]. [Q] to sprout, blossom; break out, flourish; to fly; (n.) a bird; [H] to make flourish, bring to bud:– flourish [7], blossom [3], budded [3], blossom abundantly (+6524) [2], break out abroad (+6524) [2], breaking forth [2], broken out [2], bud [2], grow [2], make fly [2], break out [1], flourished [1], groweth [1], made to flourish [1], make to flourish [1], spreading [1], springeth up [1], spring [1], sprung up [1]

6525 פֶּרַח *peraḥ*, n.m. GK: 7258 [→ 6524]. blossom, bud; floral work:– flowers [9], flower [5], blossom [1], buds [1], bud [1]

6526 פִּרְחָח *pirḥaḥ*, n.m.col. GK: 7259 [→ 6524?]. offspring, brood, tribe, with a focus on energetic behavior:– youth [1]

6527 פָּרַט *pāraṭ*, v. GK: 7260 [→ 6528?]. [Q] to strum, improvise (on a musical instrument):– chant [1]

6528 פֶּרֶט *pereṭ*, n.[m.]col. GK: 7261 [→ 6527?]. fallen grapes:– grape [1]

6529 פְּרִי *pᵉrî*, n.m. GK: 7262 [→ 6509]. fruit, produce, crops; by extension: offspring of any creature; result of any action; "fruit of the lips" is speech, praise; "fruit of the hand" is something earned:– fruit [107], fruits [7], fruitful [2], boughs [1], firstfruits (+7225) [1], reward [1]

פְּרִידָא *pᵉrîdā'*. See 6514.

פֻּרִים *purîm*. See 6332.

6530 פָּרִיץ *pārîṣ*, n.m. GK: 7264 & 7265 [→ 6555]. ferocious (animal); robber; violent one:– robbers [2], destroyer [1], ravenous [1], robbers (+1121) [1], robber [1]

6531 פֶּרֶךְ *perek*, n.m. GK: 7266. ruthlessness, brutality, violence:– rigour [5], cruelty [1]

6532 פָּרֹכֶת *pārōket*, n.f. GK: 7267. curtain:– vail [25]

6533 פָּרַם *pāram*, v. GK: 7268. [Q] to tear; [Qp] to be torn:– rend [2], rent [1]

6534 פַּרְמַשְׁתָּא *parmašᵉtā'*, n.pr.m. GK: 7269. Parmashta, "*very first*":– Parmashta [1]

6535 פַּרְנַךְ *parnak*, n.pr.m. GK: 7270. Parnach:– Parnach [1]

6536 פָּרַס *pāras*, v. GK: 7271 [→ 6538?, 6541, 6537?]. [Q] to offer food, share food; [H] to have a divided hoof:– divideth [5], divide [4], parteth [2], deal [1], hoofs [1], tear [1]

6537 פְּרַס *pᵉras*, v. and פְּרֵס *pᵉrēs* (Aram.), n.[m.]. GK: 10592 [cf. 6536]. [Peil] to be divided; parsin, peres (unit of measure and weight):– divided [1], peres [1], upharsin (+2050.3) [1]

6538 פֶּרֶס *peres*, n.[m.]. GK: 7272 [→ 6536?]. vulture:– ossifrage [1]

6539 פָּרַס *pāras*, n.pr.loc. GK: 7273 [→ 6542; cf. 6540, cf. 6543]. Persia; Persian:– Persia [27], Persians [4]

6540 פָּרַס *pāras* (Aram.), n.pr.loc. & g. GK: 10594 [→ 6543; cf. 6539]. Persia, Persian:– Persians [4], Persia [2]

6541 פַּרְסָה *parsâ*, n.f. GK: 7274 [→ 6536]. hoof:– hoof [12], hoofs [5], claws [2], clovenfooted (+8156+8157) [2]

6542 פַּרְסִי *pārᵉsî*, a.g. GK: 7275 [→ 6539; cf. 6543]. Persian:– Persian [1]

6543 פַּרְסָי *parsāy* (Aram.), a.g. GK: 10595 [→ 6540; cf. 6542]. Persian:– Persian [1]

6544 פָּרַע *pāra'*, v.den. GK: 7276 & 7277 [→ 6546]. [Q] to take the lead; to be out of control, be unkempt; to ignore, avoid; [Qp] to be unkempt, be running wild; [N] be unrestrained; [H] to let neglect; to promote wickedness:– uncover [3], made naked [2], refuseth [2], avenging (+6546) [1], avoid [1], bare [1], go back [1], let [1], naked [1], perish [1], refuse [1], set at nought [1]

6545 פֶּרַע *pera'*, n.[m.]. GK: 7279 [cf. 6546?]. long hair of head:– locks [2]

6546 פֶּרַע *pera'*, n.[m.]. GK: 7278 [→ 6544; cf. 6545?]. leader, prince:– avenging (+6544) [1], revenges [1]

6547 פַּרְעֹה *par'ōh*, n.m. GK: 7281 [→ 6548, 6549]. Pharaoh:– Pharaoh [222], Pharaoh's [43], Pharaoh's (+3807.1) [3]

6548 פַּרְעֹה חָפְרַע *par'ōh ḥopra'*, n.pr.m. GK: 7281 + 2922 [→ 6547]. Pharaoh Hophra:– Pharaoh-hophra [1]

6549 פַּרְעֹה נְכֹה *par'ōh nᵉkōh*, n.pr.m. GK: 7281 + 5785 [→ 6547]. Pharaoh Neco:– Pharaoh-nechoh [4], Pharaoh-necho [1]

6550 פַּרְעֹשׁ *par'ōš*, n.m. GK: 7282 [→ 6551]. flea:– flea [1]

6551 פַּרְעֹשׁ *par'ōš*, n.pr.m. GK: 7283 [→ 6550]. Parosh, "*flea*":– Parosh [5], Pharosh [1]

6552 פִּרְעָתוֹן *pir'ātôn*, n.pr.loc. GK: 7284 [→ 6553]. Pirathon:– Pirathon [1]

6553 פִּרְעָתוֹנִי *pir'ātônî*, a.g. GK: 7285 [→ 6552]. Pirathonite, from Pirathon, "*of Pirathon*":– Pirathonite [5]

6554 פַּרְפַּר *parpar*, n.pr.loc. GK: 7286. Pharpar:– Pharpar [1]

6555 פָּרַץ *pāraṣ*, v. GK: 7287 [→ 1188, 4664, 6530, 6556, 6557, 6560, 6558, 6559; cf. 6484]. [Q] to break out, burst forth; [Qp] to be broken through; [N] to spread abroad; [Pu] to be broken down; [Ht] to break oneself away:– broken down [5], increased [4], brake down [3], break down [3], break forth [3], breaketh [2], broken forth [2], broken up [2], broken [2], made a breach (+6556) [2], pressed [2], abroad every where [1], brake in [1], breaches [1], break away [1], break out [1], breaker [1], breaketh out [1], broken in upon [1], burst out [1], came abroad [1], compelled [1], dispersed [1], grew [1], increase [1], made a breach [1], open [1], scattered [1], spread abroad [1], urged [1]

6556 פֶּרֶץ *pereṣ*, n.m. GK: 7288 [→ 1188, 7428; cf. 6555]. breech, break, gap caused by something breaking through; by extension: outburst of anger:– breach [9], breaches [3], breaking in [2], made a breach (+6555) [2], breaking forth [1], gaps [1], gap [1]

6557 פֶּרֶץ *pereṣ*, n.pr.m. GK: 7289 [→ 6558; cf. 6555]. Perez, "*breaking out*":– Pharez [12], Perez [3]

6558 פַּרְצִי *parṣî*, a.g. GK: 7291 [→ 6557; cf. 6555]. Perezite:– Pharzites [1]

6559 פְּרָצִים *pᵉrāṣîm*, n.pr.loc. GK: 7292 [→ 6556; cf. 6555]. Perazim, "*breaking out*":– Perazim [1]

6560 פֶּרֶץ עֻזָּא *pereṣ 'uzzā'* or פֶּרֶץ עֻזָּה *pereṣ 'uzzâ*, n.pr.loc. GK: 7290 [→ 6556+5798]. Perez Uzzah, "*breaking out of Uzzah*":– Perez-uzzah [1], Perez-uzza [1]

6561 פָּרַק *pāraq*, v. GK: 7293 [→ 4665, 6563, 6564; cf. 6562]. [Q] to rip to pieces; to free (by tearing away); [P] to take off, tear off; [Ht] to take off from oneself, tear off from oneself:– break off [2], brake off [1], break [1], broken [1], deliver [1], redeemed [1], rending in pieces [1], rent [1], tear in pieces [1]

6562 פְּרַק *pᵉraq* (Aram.), v. GK: 10596 [cf. 6561]. [P] to break off, tear away; to loosen, abolish; to renounce:– break off [1]

6563 פֶּרֶק *pereq*, n.[m.]. GK: 7294 [→ 6561]. crossroad; plunder:– crossway [1], robbery [1]

6564 פָּרָק *pārāq*, n.[m.]. GK: 7295 [→ 6561]. fragment:–

6565 פָּרַר *pārar*, v. GK: 7296 & 7297 [cf. 6331]. [Q] to split asunder; [Pil] to shatter; [Pol] to split open; [Htpol] to split asunder; [H] to break, violate, nullify; [Ho] to be broken, revoked, thwarted:– break [13], broken [8], any ways make void

(+6565) [2], brake [2], breaking [2], clean dissolved (+6565) [2], defeat [2], disannul [2], made void [2], utterly made void (+6565) [2], broken asunder [1], brought to nought [1], castest off [1], cause to cease [1], come to nought [1], disappointed [1], disappointeth [1], divide [1], fail [1], frustrateth [1], frustrate [1], make void [1], none effect [1]

6566 פָּרַשׂ *paras*, v. GK: 7298 [→ 4666; cf. 6576]. [Q] to spread out, scatter; [Qp] to be spread out; [N] to be scattered; [P] to scatter, spread out:– spread [29], spread forth [10], spread out [6], spread abroad [4], spreadeth [3], scattered [2], spreadeth forth [2], stretch forth [2], breaketh [1], chop in pieces [1], layeth open [1], spreadeth abroad [1], stretch out [1], stretched forth [1], stretched out [1], stretcheth out [1], stretch [1]

6567 פָּרַשׁ *paras*, v. GK: 7300 & 7301 [→ 6571, 6575; cf. 6569; cf. 6568]. [Q] to make clear; [N] to be given; [Pu] to be made clear; [H] to secrete poison:– declared [1], distinctly [1], scattered [1], shewed [1], stingeth [1]

6568 פְּרַשׁ *peras* (Aram.), v. GK: 10597 [cf. 6566]. [Pap] to be translated, be made clear, with an implication that each and every element of the letter be read and made clear:– plainly [1]

6569 פֶּרֶשׁ *pereš*, n.[m.]. GK: 7302 [→ 6570; cf. 6567]. offal, dung or intestinal contents of a butchered animal:– dung [7]

6570 פֶּרֶשׁ *pereš*, n.pr.m. GK: 7303 [→ 6569]. Peresh, "*offal eviscerated; dung; contents of stomach [not intestine]*":– Peresh [1]

6571 פָּרָשׁ *paraš*, n.m. GK: 7304 & 7305 [→ 6567]. horse; horseman:– horsemen [55], horseman [1], horsemen (+1167) [1]

6572 פַּרְשֶׁגֶן *paršegen* or פַּתְשֶׁגֶן *patšegen*, n.m. GK: 7306 & 7358 [cf. 6573]. copy (of a text):– copy [4]

6573 פַּרְשֶׁגֶן *paršegen* (Aram.), n.m. GK: 10598 [cf. 6572]. copy (of a document):– copy [3]

6574 פַּרְשְׁדֹן *parš⁽e⁾don*, n.[m.]. GK: 7307. back (of a person), back door [?]:– dirt [1]

6575 פָּרָשָׁה *paraša*, n.f. GK: 7308 [→ 6567]. exact amount, exact statement:– declaration [1], sum [1]

6576 פַּרְשֵׁז *parséz*, a.vbl. *or* v. GK: 7299 [cf. 6566]. spreading:– spreadeth [1]

6577 פַּרְשַׁנְדָּתָא *paršandāta'*, n.pr.m. GK: 7309. Parshandatha:– Parshandatha [1]

6578 פְּרָת *p⁽e⁾rāt*, n.pr.loc. GK: 7310. Euphrates (mighty river of Mesopotamia); Perath (small river or valley in the book of Jeremiah):– Euphrates [19]

פֹּרָת *pôrāt*. See 6509.

6579 פַּרְתְּמִים *part⁽e⁾mîm*, n.m.pl. GK: 7312. nobles, princes:– most noble [1], nobles [1], princes [1]

6580 פַּשׁ *paš*, n.[m.]. GK: 7317. wickedness or weakness, foolishness:– extremity [1]

6581 פָּשָׂה *pasá*, v. GK: 7313. [Q] to spread:– spread [13], spread much abroad (+6581) [6], spread much (+6581) [2], spreadeth [1]

6582 פָּשַׁח *pašah*, v. GK: 7318. [P] to mangle:– pulled in pieces [1]

6583 פַּשְׁחוּר *pašhûr*, n.pr.m. GK: 7319. Pashhur, "[perhaps] *be quiet* and *round about*":– Pashur [14]

6584 פָּשַׁט *pašat*, v. GK: 7320. [Q] to take off, strip; to make a sudden dash, raid; [P] to strip; [H] to take off, strip off; [Ht] to strip oneself:– put off [6], strip [6], invaded [4], flay [3], stripped [3], fell [2], spoileth [2], stript [2], flayed [1], made a road [1], made an invasion [1], pull [1], ran [1], rushed forward [1], rushed [1], set [1], spoil [1], spread abroad [1], spread [1], strip out of [1], stripped off [1], stript off [1], stript out of [1]

6585 פָּשַׂע *pasa'*, v. GK: 7314 [→ 6587; cf. 4667]. [Q] to march, step forth:– go [1]

6586 פָּשַׁע *paša'*, v. GK: 7321 [→ 6588]. [Q] to rebel, revolt (against human or divine authority):– transgressed [13], transgressors [8], rebelled [6], revolted [5], transgress [3], offended [1], revolt [1], transgressing [1], transgression [1], transgressor [1], trespassed [1]

6587 פֶּשַׂע *pesa'*, n.[m.]. GK: 7315 [→ 6585]. step:– step [1]

6588 פֶּשַׁע *peša'*, n.m. GK: 7322 [→ 6586]. rebellion, revolt, sin, transgression (against human or divine authority):– transgressions [46], transgression [37], trespass [1], sins [1], rebellion [1], sin [1, +1870 [1]

6589 פָּשַׂק *pasaq*, v. GK: 7316. [Q] to open wide (the lips in talking or smirking); [P] to spread the feet or legs (in immorality):– opened [1], openeth wide [1]

6590 פְּשַׁר *p⁽e⁾šar* (Aram.), v. GK: 10599 [→ 6591; cf. 6592, 6622]. [P] to give an interpretation; [Pa] to interpret; (as noun) an interpreter:– interpreting [1], make interpretations (+6591) [1]

6591 פְּשַׁר *p⁽e⁾šar* (Aram.), n.m. GK: 10600 [→ 6590; cf. 6592]. interpretation, explanation, what something means:– interpretation [30], make interpretations (+6590) [1]

6592 פֵּשֶׁר *pešer*, n.[m.]. GK: 7323 [cf. 6590, cf. 6591]. explanation, interpretation:– interpretation [1]

6593 פֵּשֶׁת *pešet*, n.[m.]. GK: 7324 [→ 6594]. flax, linen (made of flax):– linen [9], flax [7]

6594 פִּשְׁתָּה *pištá*, n.f. GK: 7325 [→ 6593]. flax, wick (made of flax):– flax [3], tow [1]

6595 פַּת *pat* or פָּתוֹת *p⁽e⁾tôt*, n.f. GK: 7326 & 7336 [→ 6598, 6626]. little piece, morsel (of food):– morsel [8], pieces [2], piece [2], meat [1], morsels [1], part in pieces (+6626) [1]

6596 פֹּת *pôt*, n.[f.]. GK: 7327 [cf. 4670]. scalp, forehead; socket (for doors):– hinges [1], secret parts [1]

פִּתְאָ *pit⁽e⁾'ā*. See 6612.

6597 פִּתְאֹם *pit'ōm*, subst. (used as adv.). GK: 7328 [→ 6621]. suddenly, unexpectedly, all at once, in an instant:– suddenly [20], sudden [2], straightway [1], suddenly (+871.1) [1], very suddenly (+6621+871.1) [1]

6598 פַּת־בַּג *pat-bag*, n.[m.]. GK: 7329 [→ 6595+897?]. (fine) food, choice provisions:– portion of meat [5], meat [1]

6599 פִּתְגָם *pitgām*, n.m. GK: 7330 [cf. 6600]. edict, decree; sentence (for a crime):– decree [1], sentence [1]

6600 פִּתְגָם *pitgām* (Aram.), n.m. GK: 10601 [cf. 6599]. word: report, reply, edict, decision, decree:– answer [2], matter [2], letter [1], word [1]

6601 פָּתָה *pātá*, v.den. GK: 7331 & 7332 [→ 3315, 6612, 6615; cf. 6613]. [Q] to be simple, easily deceived, enticed; [P] to seduce, entice, deceive, allure; [N] to be enticed, deceived; [Pu] to be deceived, enticed, persuaded; [H] to provide ample space, make spacious:– entice [7], deceived [6], persuade [3], deceive [2], enticed [2], allure [1], enlarge [1], enticeth [1], flattereth [1], flatter [1], persuaded [1], silly one [1], silly [1]

6602 פְּתוּאֵל *p⁽e⁾tû'ēl*, n.pr.m. GK: 7333 [→ 6612+410]. Pethuel, "*God's opening*":– Pethuel [1]

6603 פִּתּוּחַ *pittûah*, n.m. GK: 7334 [→ 6605]. engraving, inscription:– engravings [5], graving [2], carved figures (+4734) [1], carved work [1], grave (+3807.1+6605) [1], graven [1]

6604 פְּתוֹר *p⁽e⁾tôr*, n.pr.loc. GK: 7335. Pethor:– Pethor [2]

6605 פָּתַח *pātah*, v. GK: 7337 & 7338 [→ 3316, 3317, 4669, 4668, 6603, 6607, 6608, 6609, 6610, 6611; cf. 6606]. [Q] to open; [Qp] to be opened; [N] to be opened; [P] to loosen, release, take off; to engrave, carve; [Pu] to be engraved; [Ht] to free oneself:– opened [51], open [47], loose [6], loosed [5], open wide (+6605) [4], openeth [4], grave [3], engrave [2], graved [2], openest [2], appear [1], break forth [1], drawn out [1], drawn [1], go free [1], grave (+3807.1+6603) [1], graven [1], loose from [1], looseth [1], opening [1], put off [1], putteth off [1], set forth [1], set wide [1], spread out [1], ungirded [1], unstopped [1], vent [1]

6606 פְּתַח *p⁽e⁾tah* (Aram.), v. GK: 10602 [cf. 6605]. [Pp, Peil] to be opened:– opened [1], open [1]

6607 פֶּתַח *petah*, n.m. GK: 7339 [→ 6605]. entrance, opening; of a building or city: door, gate:– door [116], entering [17], doors [11], entry [7], gate [4], gates [3], entrance [2], entrances [1], entries [1], open place (+5869) [1], openings [1]

6608 פֵּתַח *pētah*, n.m. GK: 7340 [→ 6605]. revelation, disclosure, an extension opening a door or gate:– entrance [1]

פָּתוּחַ *pātuah*. See 6603.

6609 פְּתִחָה *p⁽e⁾tihá*, n.[f.]. GK: 7347 [→ 6605]. drawn sword:– drawn swords [1]

6610 פִּתָּחוֹן *pittāhôn*, n.[m.]. GK: 7341 [→ 6605]. opening (of mouth for communication):– opening [1], open [1]

6611 פְּתַחְיָה *p⁽e⁾tahyá*, n.pr.m. GK: 7342 [→ 6605+3068]. Pethahiah, "*Yahweh opens*":– Pethahiah [4]

6612 פְּתִי *peti*, n.f. & a. GK: 7343 & 7344 [→ 6601, 6602]. simple, naive, someone easily deceived or persuaded; simple ways, simplemindedness:– simple [15], simple ones [1], foolish [1], simplicity [1]

6613 פְּתִי *p⁽e⁾tāy* (Aram.), n.[m.]. GK: 10603. width, breadth:– breadth [1]

6614 פְּתִיגִיל *p⁽e⁾tîgîl*, n.[m.]. GK: 7345. fine clothing:– stomacher [1]

6615 פְּתַיּוּת *p⁽e⁾tayyût*, n.f. GK: 7346 [→ 6601]. undisciplined, deceptive:– simple [1]

6616 פָּתִיל *pātîl*, n.m. GK: 7348 [→ 6617]. cord, strands, string:– lace [4], bracelets [2], bound [1], line [1], ribband [1], thread [1], wires [1]

6617 פָּתַל *pātal*, v. GK: 7349 [→ 5319, 5321?, 6616, 6618]. [N] to have a struggle; to be wily, be crooked; [Ht] to show oneself shrewd:– froward [2], shew froward [1], shew unsavoury [1], wrestled [1]

6618 פְּתַלְתֹּל *p⁽e⁾taltōl*, a. GK: 7350 [→ 6617]. crooked, perverse:– crooked [1]

6619 פִּתֹם *pitōm*, n.pr.loc. GK: 7351. Pithom, "*temple [house] of Atum*":– Pithom [1]

6620 פֶּתֶן *peten*, n.m. GK: 7352. cobra, serpent; some sources: viper:– asps [3], adder [2], asp [1]

6621 פֶּתַע *peta'*, subst. (used as adv.). GK: 7353 [→ 6597]. instant; (adv.) suddenly, in an instant:– suddenly [3], instant [2], suddenly (+871.1) [1], very suddenly (+6597+871.1) [1]

6622 פָּתַר *pātar*, v. GK: 7354 [→ 6623; cf. 6590, cf. 6591]. [Q] to interpret, give the meaning (of a dream):– interpret [4], interpreted [3], interpretation [1], interpreter [1]

6623 פִּתָּרוֹן *pittārôn*, n.m. GK: 7355 [→ 6622]. interpretation, meaning:– interpretation [4], interpretations [1]

6624 פַּתְרוֹס *patrôs*, n.pr.loc. GK: 7356 [→ 6625]. Upper Egypt (Patros):– Pathros [5]

6625 פַּתְרֻסִים *patrusîm*, a.g.pl. GK: 7357 [→ 6624]. Pathrusite:– Pathrusim [2]

פַּתְשֶׁגֶן *patšegen*. See 6572.

6626 פָּתַת *pātat*, v. GK: 7359 [→ 6595]. [Q] to crumble:– part in pieces (+6595) [1]

6627 צֵאָה *sē'á*, n.f. GK: 7362. excrement, dung:– cometh from [1], cometh out [1]

צֹאָה *sô'á*. See 6675.

צְאוֹן *s⁽e⁾'ôn*. See 6629.

6628 צֶאֱלִים *se'⁽e⁾lîm*, n.m.pl. GK: 7365. lotus plant:– shady trees [2]

6629 צֹאן *sô'n*, n.col.f. *or* m. GK: 7366 [→ 6792; cf. 3318]. flock, sheep, goats (in contrast to larger mammals: cattle, donkeys, camels, etc.):– sheep [111], flock [84], flocks [53], cattle [14], lambs (+1121) [2], shepherds (+7462) [2], flocks (+4735) [1], lamb [1], sheepcotes (+1448) [1], sheepfolds (+1448) [1], sheepfolds (+4356) [1], sheepshearers (+1494) [1], shepherd (+7462) [1], small⁵ [1]

6630 צַעֲנָן *sa'⁽a⁾nān*, n.pr.loc. GK: 7367 [cf. 6799?]. Zaanan:– Zaanan [1]

6631 צֶאֱצָאִים *se'⁽e⁾sā'îm*, n.m.[pl.]. GK: 7368 [→ 3318]. offspring, descendant:– offspring [9], that come forth [1], that which cometh out [1]

6632 צָב *sāb*, n.[m.]. GK: 7369 & 7370 [→ 6637, 6638?]. (covered) wagon; some sources: litter without wheels; lizard (of unspecified species):– covered [1], litters [1], tortoise [1]

6633 צָבָא *sābā'*, v. GK: 7371 [→ 6635]. [Q] to fight, do battle; to serve in (temple) corps:– fight [3], assembled [2], mustered [2], warred [2], assembling [1], fought [1], perform service (+6635) [1], wait (+6635) [1]

6634 צְבָא *s⁽e⁾bā* (Aram.), v. GK: 10605 [→ 6640]. [P] to wish, desire, want, long for:– will [5], would [5]

6635 צָבָא *sābā'*, n.m. & f. GK: 7372 [→ 6633]. army, host, divisions (of an army); as a title of God: of Hosts (the heavenly armies), the Almighty, with a focus on great power to conquer or rule, a fig. extension of the leader of an earthly army:– hosts [293], host [101], war [41], armies [22], army [7], battle [5], service [4], appointed time [2], warfare [2], army (+2428) [1], battle (+4421) [1], company [1], perform service (+6633) [1], soldiers [1], time appointed [1], wait (+6633) [1], waiting upon [1]

6636 צְבֹאִים *s⁽e⁾bō'îm* or צְבֹיִים *s⁽e⁾bōyîm*, n.pr.loc. GK: 7375 & 7387 [cf. 6643]. Zeboiim, "*gazelles*":– Zeboim [3], Zeboiim [2]

6637 צֹבֵבָה *sōbēbá*, n.pr.m. GK: 7376 [→ 6632]. Zobebah:– Zobebah [1]

6638 צָבָה *sābá*, v. GK: 7377 [→ 6632?, 6639]. [Q] to swell; [H] to cause to swell:– fight [1], make to swell [1], swell [1]

6639 צָבֶה *ṣābeh*, a. GK: 7379 [→ 6638]. swollen:– swell [1]

צֹבָא *ṣōbâ*. See 6678.

6640 צְבוּ *ṣᵉbû* (Aram.), n.f. GK: 10606 [→ 6634]. situation, matter, affair, thing:– purpose [1]

6641 צָבֻעַ *ṣābûaʿ*, a. GK: 7380 [→ 6641, 6648; 6649, 6650]. speckled, variegated, pertaining to the pattern on a winged creature:– speckled [1]

6642 צָבַט *ṣābaṭ*, v. GK: 7381 [cf. 6653]. [Q] to offer (food to another person):– reached [1]

6643 צְבִי *ṣᵉbî*, n.m. GK: 7373 & 7374 & 7382 & 7383 [→ 6644, 6645, 6646; cf. 6636, 6719; cf. 6634]. ornament, beautiful (thing), glory; gazelle:– glory [8], roe [6], glorious [5], roebuck [4], roes [3], beauty [2], beautiful [1], goodly [1], pleasant [1], roebucks [1]

6644 צִבְיָא *ṣibyā'*, n.pr.m. GK: 7384 [→ 6643]. Zibia, "*gazelle*":– Zibia [1]

6645 צִבְיָה *ṣibyâ*, n.pr.f. GK: 7385 [→ 6643]. Zibiah, "*gazelle*":– Zibiah [2]

6646 צְבִיָּה *ṣᵉbiyyâ*, n.f. GK: 7386 [→ 6643]. (female) gazelle:– roes [2]

צְבִיִּים *ṣᵉbîîm*. See 6636.

צְבָיִם *ṣᵉbāyim*. See 6380.

6647 צְבַע *ṣᵉbaʿ* (Aram.), v. GK: 10607. [Pa] to drench, make wet; [Htpa] to be drenched, made wet:– wet [5]

6648 צֶבַע *ṣebaʿ*, n.[m.]. GK: 7389 [→ 6641; cf. 6647]. colorful (dyed) garment:– divers colours [3]

6649 צִבְעוֹן *ṣibʿôn*, n.pr.m. GK: 7390 [cf. 6641, 6650]. Zibeon, "*hyena*":– Zibeon [8]

6650 צְבֹעִים *ṣᵉbōʿîm*, n.pr.loc. GK: 7391 [cf. 6641, 6649]. Zeboim, "*hyenas*":– Zeboim [2]

6651 צָבַר *ṣābar*, v. GK: 7392 [→ 6652]. [Q] to store up, heap up, pile up:– gathered together [1], gathered [1], heap up [1], heaped up [1], heapeth up [1], heap [1], lay up [1]

6652 צִבֻּר *ṣibbur*, n.m. GK: 7393 [→ 6651]. pile, heap:– heaps [1]

6653 צֶבֶת *ṣebet*, n.[m.]pl. GK: 7395 [cf. 6642]. bundle (of grain with the stalk):– handfuls [1]

6654 צַד *ṣad*, n.m. GK: 7396 [→ 6657; cf. 6655]. side (of something):– side [20], sides [9], beside (+4480) [3], anotherˢ [1]

6655 צַד *ṣad* (Aram.), n.[m.]. GK: 10608 [cf. 6654]. side:– against (+3807.2) [1], concerning (+4481) [1]

6656 צְדָא *ṣᵉdā'* (Aram.), n.[m.]. GK: 10609. purpose, (with 1886.6) is it true?:– true [1]

6657 צְדָד *ṣᵉdād*, n.pr.loc. GK: 7398 [→ 6654]. Zedad, "*side*":– Zedad [2]

6658 צָדָה *ṣādâ*, v. GK: 7399 & 7400 [→ 6660]. [Q] to lie in wait, hunt down a person; [N] to be destroyed, be laid waste:– destroyed [1], huntest [1], lie in wait [1]

צֵדָה *ṣēdâ*. See 6720.

6659 צָדוֹק *ṣādôq*, n.pr.m. GK: 7401 [→ 6663]. Zadok, "*righteous one*":– Zadok [52], Zadok's (+3807.1) [1]

6660 צְדִיָּה *ṣᵉdiyyâ*, n.f. GK: 7402 [→ 6658; cf. 6656]. ambush, lying-in-wait (with malicious intent):– laying of wait [2]

6661 צִדִּים *ṣiddîm*, n.pr.loc. GK: 7403. Ziddim, "*place on the sides or flanks [of the hill]*":– Ziddim [1]

6662 צַדִּיק *ṣaddîq*, a. GK: 7404 [→ 6663]. righteous, upright, just, innocent; in accordance with a proper (God's) standard, and so implying innocence:– righteous [163], just [42], lawful [1]

צִדֹנִי *ṣidōnî*. See 6722.

6663 צָדַק *ṣādaq*, v.den. GK: 7405 [→ 3087, 3136, 6659, 6662, 6664, 6666, 6667]. [Q] to be righteous, be innocent, be vindicated; in accordance with a proper (God's) standard, and so implying innocence:– justified [12], righteous [10], justify [7], just [3], justifieth [2], justifying [2], cleansed [1], clear [1], do justice [1], justice [1], turn to righteousness [1]

6664 צֶדֶק *ṣedeq*, n.m. GK: 7406 [→ 139, 4442, 6667; cf. 6663]. righteousness, justice, rightness, acting according to a proper (God's) standard, doing what is right, being in the right:– righteousness [78], justice [10], just [10], righteous [8], righteously [3], right [3], altogether (+6664) [2], even [1], righteous cause [1], righteousness' [1], unrighteousness (+3808) [1]

6665 צִדְקָה *ṣidqâ* (Aram.), n.f. GK: 10610 [cf. 6666]. what is right:– righteousness [1]

6666 צְדָקָה *ṣᵉdāqâ*, n.f. GK: 7407 [→ 6663; cf. 6665]. righteousness, acting according to a proper (God's) standard, doing what is right, being in the right:– righteousness [124], justice [15], right [9], righteous acts [3], righteousnesses [3], moderately (+3807.1) [1], righteously [1], righteousness' [1]

6667 צִדְקִיָּה *ṣidqiyyâ* or צִדְקִיָּהוּ *ṣidqiyyāhû*, n.pr.m. GK: 7408 & 7409 [→ 6664+3068]. Zedekiah, "*Yahweh is [my] righteousness*":– Zedekiah [61], Zedekiah's [1], Zidkijah [1]

6668 צָהַב *ṣāhab*, v. GK: 7410 [→ 6669, 6678; cf. 2091]. [Ho] to be polished, gleaming copper color:– fine (+2896) [1]

6669 צָהֹב *ṣāhōb*, a. GK: 7411 [→ 6668]. yellow, blond; some sources: gleaming red:– yellow [3]

6670 צָהַל *ṣāhal*, v. GK: 7412 & 7413 [→ 4684, cf. 6671]. [Q] to shout out, celebrate; to neigh (of a horse); [H] to make shine:– cry aloud [2], bellow [1], cry out [1], lift up [1], make to shine [1], neighed [1], rejoiced [1], shout [1]

6671 צָהַר *ṣāhar*, v.den. GK: 7414 [→ 3323, 3324, 3325, 6672; cf. 6670]. [H] to press olives; some sources: to spend the noontime:– make oil [1]

6672 צֹהַר *ṣōhar*, n.f. and צָהֳרַיִם *ṣoḥᵒrayim*, n.[m.]. GK: 7415 [→ 6671]. roof, covering (for the ark of Noah); noon, noonday, midday:– noon [11], noonday [8], midday [1], noon day [1], noondays [1], noontide (+6256) [1], window [1]

6673 צַו *ṣaw*, n.[m.]. GK: 7417 [→ 7723? or 6680?]. worthless thing, an idol or utterance (perhaps a nonsense syllable, a mocking sound):– precept [8], commandment [1]

6674 צוֹא *ṣô'î*, a. GK: 7364. filthy, befouled (with excrement):– filthy [2]

6675 צוֹא *ṣô'â*, n.f. GK: 7363. filth, excrement, dung; by extension: moral filth:– dung [2], filthiness [2], filth [1]

6676 צַוָּאר *ṣawwa'r* (Aram.), n.m. GK: 10611 [cf. 6677]. neck:– neck [3]

6677 צַוָּאר *ṣawwā'r* or צַוְּרֹנִים *ṣawwᵉrōnîm*, n.m. GK: 7418 & 7454 [cf. 6676]. (back of) neck; necklace:– neck [32], necks [10]

6678 צוֹבָא *ṣôbā'* or צוֹבָה *ṣôbâ*, n.pr.loc. GK: 7419 & 7420 [→ 760, 2578; cf. 6668]. Zobah:– Zobah [10], Zoba [2]

6679 צוּד *ṣûd* or צִיד *ṣîd*, v. GK: 7421 & 7472 [→ 4679, 4685, 4686, 6718, 6719, 6720]. [Q] to hunt, stalk; [Pil] to ensnare; by extension to stalk people for capture or oppression; [Ht] to pack provisions for oneself:– hunt [10], chased sore (+6679) [1], hunt for [1], huntest [1], hunteth [1], taken [1], take [1], took provision [1]

6680 צָוָה *ṣāwâ*, v. GK: 7422 [→ 4687, 6673?]. [P] to command, order, instruct, give direction; [Pu] to be commanded, be directed, be ordered:– commanded [333], command [84], charged [23], commandeth [6], appointed [4], commandedst [4], gave a charge [4], bade [3], gave charge [3], give a charge [3], give charge [3], charge [2], commandest [2], gave commandment [2], given a commandment [2], set in order [2], appoint [1], commander [1], commanding [1], forbad [1], forbidden [1], gave a commandment [1], gave in commandment [1], give in commandment [1], given a charge [1], given commandment [1], given in commandment [1], put in order [1], sent a messenger [1], sent with commandment [1]

6681 צָוַח *ṣāwaḥ*, v. GK: 7423 [→ 6682]. [Q] to shout, cry aloud:– shout [1]

6682 צְוָחָה *ṣᵉwāḥâ*, n.f. GK: 7424 [→ 6681]. cry of distress, wail:– cry [2], complaining [1], crying [1]

6683 צוּלָה *ṣûlâ*, n.f. GK: 7425 [→ 4688, 4699; cf. 6749]. the watery deep, the ocean abyss:– deep [1]

6684 צוּם *ṣûm*, v. GK: 7426 [→ 6685]. [Q] to fast, to voluntarily abstain from food as dedication to deity, as a sign of mourning, or possibly as a medical treatment:– fasted [11], fast [7], at all fast (+6684) [2], fasted (+6685) [1]

6685 צוֹם *ṣôm*, n.m. GK: 7427 [→ 6684]. fast, time of fasting, act of fasting:– fast [16], fasting [8], fasted (+6684) [1], fastings [1]

6686 צוּעָר *ṣûʿār*, n.pr.m. GK: 7428 [→ 6819]. Zuar, "*little one*":– Zuar [5]

6687 צוּף *ṣûp*, v. GK: 7429 [→ 6688, 6689, 6824?]. [Q] to flow; [H] to make float; to overwhelm (with water):– flowed [1], made to overflow [1], swim [1]

6688 צוּף *ṣûp*, n.m. GK: 7430 [→ 6687]. honeycomb (dripping with honey):– honeycomb (+1706) [1], honeycomb (+5317) [1]

6689 צוּף *ṣûp* or צוֹפַי *ṣôpay* or צוֹפִי *ṣôpî* or צִיף *ṣîp*, n.pr.m. & g. & loc. GK: 7431 & 7433 & 7434 & 7487 [→ 6687, 6688]. Zuph; Zuphite; Zophai; Ziph, "*[dripping, full] honeycomb*":– Zuph [3], Zophai [1], Ziph [1]

6690 צוֹפַח *ṣôpaḥ*, n.pr.m. GK: 7432 [→ 6838]. Zophah, "*bellied jug*":– Zophah [2]

צוֹפַי *ṣôpay*. See 6689.

6691 צוֹפַר *ṣôpar*, n.pr.m. GK: 7436 [→ 6833?]. Zophar, "[poss.] *peep, twitter [as a bird]*":– Zophar [4]

6692 צוּץ *ṣûṣ*, v. GK: 7437 & 7438 [→ 6731, 6733, 6734]. [Q] to bud, blossom; [H] to put forth blossoms; to cause to flourish; to peer at, look at:– flourish [3], flourisheth [2], bloomed [1], blossomed [1], blossom [1], shewing [1]

6693 צוּק *ṣûq*, v. GK: 7439 [→ 4165, 4689, 4691, 6695, 6695; cf. 6845]. [H] to oppress, compel, nag, inflict:– distress [5], oppressor [2], constraineth [1], lay sore upon [1], pressed [1], straiten [1]

6694 צוּק *ṣûq*, v. GK: 7440 [→ 3332?]. [Q] to pour out:– poured out [2], molten [1]

6695 צוֹק *ṣôq* or צוּקָה *ṣûqâ*, n.m. & f. GK: 7441 & 7442 [→ 6693]. trouble, distress, oppression:– anguish [3], troublous [1]

6696 צוּר *ṣûr*, v. GK: 7443 & 7444 & 7445 [→ 4692, 4694, 4699, 6736?; cf. 6737, 3334]. [Q] to siege, besiege, enclose; to oppose, harass; to fashion, shape:– besieged [14], besiege [6], distress [2], lay siege [2], adversary [1], assault [1], beset [1], besiege (+5921) [1], bind up [1], bind [1], bound [1], cast [1], distressed [1], fashioned [1], fortify [1], inclose [1], laid siege [1], put up [1]

6697 צוּר *ṣûr*, n.m. GK: 7446 & 7447 [→ 468, 1049, 6301, 6698, 6700, 6701, 6864; cf. 2906]. rock; pebble, flint; stone mass, rocky crag; a title of God, with a focus of stability, and possibly as a place of security and safety:– rock [57], rocks [7], strength [5], sharp [2], God [1], edge [1], mighty God [1], mighty one [1], stones [1], strong [1]

6698 צוּר *ṣûr*, n.pr.m. GK: 7448 [→ 6697]. Zur, "*rock*":– Zur [5]

צֹר *ṣōr*. See 6865.

צַוָּר *ṣawwār*. See 6677.

6699 צוּרָה *ṣûrâ*, n.f. GK: 7451 [→ 6696]. design, form:– forms [2], form [2], beauty [1]

צַוָּרֹן *ṣawwārōn*. See 6677.

6700 צוּרִיאֵל *ṣûrî'ēl*, n.pr.m. GK: 7452 [→ 6697+410]. Zuriel, "*God [El] is [my] rock*":– Zuriel [1]

6701 צוּרִישַׁדַּי *ṣûrîšadday* or צוּרִי־שַׁדָּי *ṣûrî-šadday*, n.pr.m. GK: 7453 [→ 6697+7706]. Zurishaddai, "*Shaddai is [my] rock*":– Zurishaddai [5]

6702 צוּת *ṣût*, v. GK: 7455 [cf. 3341]. [H] to set on fire:– burn [1]

6703 צַח *ṣaḥ*, a. GK: 7456 [→ 6705]. radiant, shimmering, scorching, clear:– clear [1], dry [1], plainly [1], white [1]

צִחֶא *ṣiḥâ'*. See 6727.

6704 צִחֶה *ṣiḥeh*, a. GK: 7457 [cf. 6705]. parched:– dried up [1]

6705 צָחַח *ṣāḥaḥ*, v. GK: 7458 [→ 4696?, 4697?, 6703, 6706, 6707, 6710; cf. 6704, 6708]. [Q] to be white:– whiter [1]

6706 צָחִיחַ *ṣāḥîaḥ*, n.[m.]. GK: 7460 [→ 6705; cf. 6708]. bare (rock or place in a wall):– top [4], higher places [1]

6707 צְחִיחָה *ṣᵉḥîḥâ*, n.f. GK: 7461 [→ 6705]. bare, (sun-)scorched land:– dry [1]

6708 צְחִיחִי *ṣᵉḥîḥî*, n.[m.]. GK: 7459 [cf. 6705, 6706]. bare (rock or place in a wall):–

6709 צַחֲנָה *ṣaḥᵃnâ*, n.f. GK: 7462. putrid smell, stench:– ill savour [1]

6710 צְחִצָחוֹת *ṣaḥṣāḥôt*, n.[f.pl.]. GK: 7463 [→ 6705]. bare, (sun-)scorched land:– drought [1]

6711 צָחַק *ṣāḥaq*, v. GK: 7464 [→ 3327, 6712; cf. 7832]. [Q] to laugh; [P] to mock, make sport, caress; this can mean to laugh with delight or in scorn:– laughed [3], laugh [3], mock [2], made sport [1], mocked [1], mocking [1], play [1], sporting with [1]

6712 צְחֹק *ṣᵉḥōq*, n.[m.]. GK: 7465 [→ 6711]. laughter, scorn:– laughed to scorn [1], laugh [1]

6713 צָחַר *ṣāḥar*, n. & pr.m. GK: 7466 [→ 6715]. white; as n.pr. Zahar, "*yellowish red, tawny*":– white [1]

6714 צֹחַר ṣōḥar, n.pr.m. GK: 7468 [→ 6715; cf. 3328]. Zohar, "*yellowish red, tawny*":– Zohar [4]

6715 צָחֹר ṣāḥōr, a. GK: 7467 [→ 6713, 6714]. white, yellowish red, tawny:– white [1]

6716 צִי ṣî, n.m. GK: 7469. ship:– ships [3], ship [1]

6717 צִיבָא ṣîbā', n.pr.m. GK: 7471. Ziba, "*gazelle*":– Ziba [16]

6718 צַיִד ṣayid, n.m. GK: 7473 & 7474 [→ 6679]. food supply, provision; (hunting) game; hunter:– venison [8], hunter [2], provision [2], victuals [2], catcheth [1], food [1], hunter (+376) [1], hunting [1], took in hunting [1]

6719 צַיָּד ṣayyād, n.m. GK: 7475 [→ 6679]. hunter:– hunters [1]

6720 צֵידָה ṣêdâ, n.f. GK: 7476 [→ 6679]. food, provisions, supplies:– victuals [4], provision [2], victual [2], meat [1]

6721 צִידוֹן ṣîdôn, n.pr.loc. GK: 7477 [→ 6722]. Sidon, "*fishery*":– Zidon [20], Sidon [2]

6722 צִידֹנִי ṣîdōnî, a.g. GK: 7479 [→ 6721]. Sidonian, people of Sidon:– Zidonians [10], Sidonians [5], Zidon [1]

6723 צִיָּה ṣiyyâ, n.f. GK: 7480 [→ 6728, 6724]. desert, parched land, dry land, waterless region:– dry [9], drought [2], wilderness [2], barren [1], dry land [1], solitary place [1]

6724 צָיוֹן ṣāyôn, n.[m.]. GK: 7481 [→ 6723]. desert, waterless country:– dry place [2]

6725 צִיּוּן ṣiyyûn, n.m. GK: 7483. sign, stone marker:– sign [1], title [1], waymarks [1]

6726 צִיּוֹן ṣiyyôn, n.pr.loc. GK: 7482. Zion, "*citadel*":– Zion [153], Zion's [1]

6727 צִיחָא ṣîḥā', n.pr.m. GK: 7484. Ziha:– Ziha [3]

6728 צִי ṣî, n.m. GK: 7470 [→ 6723]. desert creature, referring to known animals or presumed spirits or demons; tribe of the desert:– wild beasts of the desert [3], inhabiting the wilderness [1], that dwell in the wilderness [1], them that dwell in the wilderness [1]

6729 צִינֹק ṣînōq, n.[m.]. GK: 7485. neck-iron, iron collar:– stocks [1]

6730 צִיעֹר ṣî'ōr, n.pr.loc. GK: 7486 [→ 6819]. Zior, "*small, insignificant*":– Zior [1]

צִיף ṣîp. See 6689.

6731 צִיץ ṣîṣ, n.m. GK: 7488 & 7490 [→ 6692, 6733, 6734]. flower, blossom; (ornamental) plate; salt:– flower [6], flowers [4], plate [3], blossoms [1], wings [1]

6732 צִיץ ṣîṣ, n.pr.loc. GK: 7489. Ziz, "*[poss.] ascent where the flowers grow*":– Ziz [1]

6733 צִיצָה ṣîṣâ, n.f. GK: 7491 [→ 6731; cf. 6692]. flower:– flower [1]

6734 צִיצִת ṣîṣit, n.f. GK: 7492 [→ 6731; cf. 6692]. tassel of threads; tuft of hair:– fringe [2], fringes [1], lock [1]

צִיקְלַג ṣîqᵉlag. See 6860.

6735 צִיר ṣîr, n.[m.]. GK: 7494 & 7495. hinge, (door-)pivot; pains, pangs, anguish; envoy, messenger:– ambassador [3], pangs [3], ambassadors [1], hinges [1], messengers [1], messenger [1], pains [1], sorrows [1]

6736 צִיר ṣîr, n.m. GK: 7497 [→ 6696?]. idol:– idols [1]

6737 צִיר ṣîr, v.den. GK: 7493 [cf. 6696]. [Ht] to act as a delegation:– made as if ambassadors [1]

6738 צֵל ṣēl, n.m. GK: 7498 [→ 1212, 6741, 6752, 6757, 6765; cf. 6751]. shadow, shade, protection:– shadow [45], defence [3], shade [1]

6739 צְלָא ṣᵉlâ (Aram.), v. GK: 10612. [Pa] to pray:– prayed [1], pray [1]

6740 צָלָה ṣālâ, v. GK: 7499 [→ 6748]. [Q] to roast (meat):– roasted [1], roasteth [1], roast [1]

6741 צִלָּה ṣillâ, n.pr.f. GK: 7500 [→ 6738; cf. 4980]. Zillah, "*[God is my] shadow, i.e., protection*":– Zillah [3]

6742 צְלוּל ṣᵉlûl or צָלִיל ṣālîl, n.m. GK: 7501 & 7508. cake, round loaf:– cake [1]

6743 צָלַח ṣālaḥ, v. GK: 7502 & 7503 [cf. 6744]. [Q] to be powerful, come forcefully; to rush; to prosper, prevail, succeed, avail; [H] to make a success, grant prosperity, make victorious:– prosper [33], prospered [6], came [5], made to prosper [3], came mightily [2], make prosperous [2], prosperous [2], break out [1], cause to prosper [1], come [1], good [1], made prosperous [1],

meet [1], profitable [1], prospereth [1], prosperously effected [1], prosperously [1], send prosperity [1], went over [1]

6744 צְלַח ṣᵉlaḥ (Aram.), v. GK: 10613 [cf. 6743]. [H] to cause to prosper; to promote; to make progress:– prospered [2], promoted [1], prospereth [1]

6745 צַלַּחַת ṣallaḥat, n.[f.]. GK: 7505 [→ 6746, 6747]. dish, pan:– pans [1]

6746 צְלֹחִית ṣᵉlōḥît, n.f. GK: 7504 [→ 6745]. (shallow) bowl; some sources: pan, cruse, dish:– cruse [1]

6747 צֵלַחַת ṣēlaḥat, n.[f.]. GK: 7506 [→ 6745]. pot for cooking:– bosom [2], dish [1]

6748 צָלִי ṣālî, a. GK: 7507 [→ 6740]. roasted (meat):– roast [3]

6749 צָלַל ṣālal, v. GK: 7510 [cf. 6683]. [Q] to sink down:– sank [1]

6750 צָלַל ṣālal, v. GK: 7509 [→ 4698, 4700, 6767]. [Q] to tingle; to quiver:– tingle [3], quivered [1]

6751 צָלַל ṣālal, v. GK: 7511 [→ 1212, 6738, 6741, 6752, 6753, 6757, 6765; cf. 2926; cf. 2927]. [Q] to grow dark; [H] to give shade:– dark [1], shadowing [1]

6752 צֵלֶל ṣēlel, n.m. GK: 7498 [→ 6738]. same as 6738:– shadow, shade, protection:– shadows [3], shadow [1]

6753 צַלְלְפּוֹנִי haṣṣᵉlelpônî, n.pr.f. GK: 2209 [→ 1886.1+6751+6440+2967.1]. Hazzelelponi:– Hazelelponi [1]

6754 צֶלֶם ṣelem, n.m. GK: 7512 & 7513 [→ 6756?; cf. 6755]. image (usually referring to an object of worship), idol; phantom, fantasy, shadowy thing:– images [10], image [6], in a vain shew [1]

6755 צֶלֶם ṣᵉlēm (Aram.), n.m. GK: 10614 [cf. 6754]. sculptured image, statue; this can refer to a statue, not necessarily worshiped, or to an idol, which is:– image [15], form [1], image's [1]

6756 צַלְמוֹן ṣalmôn, n.pr.m. & loc. GK: 7514 & 7515 [→ 6754?]. Zalmon, "*in his image, copy*" or "*black hill*":– Zalmon [2], Salmon [1]

6757 צַלְמָוֶת ṣalmāwet, n.[m.]. GK: 7516 [→ 6738+4191]. shadow, darkness, gloom, blackness:– shadow of death [18]

6758 צַלְמֹנָה ṣalmōnâ, n.pr.loc. GK: 7517. Zalmonah, "*dark, gloomy, shaded place*":– Zalmonah [2]

6759 צַלְמֻנָּע ṣalmunnā', n.pr.m. GK: 7518. Zalmunna, "*protection refused*":– Zalmunna [12]

6760 צָלַע ṣāla', v. GK: 7519 [→ 6761]. [Q] to be lame, limp:– halted [2], halteth [2]

6761 צֶלַע ṣela', n.[m.]. GK: 7520 [→ 6760]. stumbling, falling, slipping:– adversity [1], halt [1]

6762 צֵלָע ṣēlā', n.pr.loc. GK: 7522 [→ 6763]. Zela, Zelah, "*side, slope*":– Zelah [2]

6763 צֵלָע ṣēlā', n.f. & m. GK: 7521 [→ 6762; cf. 5967]. side:– side [15], side chambers [7], sides [4], boards [2], corners [2], side chamber [2], anotherˢ [1], beams [1], chambers [1], chamber [1], halting [1], leaves [1], oneˢ [1], planks [1], ribs [1], rib [1]

6764 צָלָף ṣālāp, n.pr.m. GK: 7523. Zalaph, "*low, prickly shrub [caper plant]*":– Zalaph [1]

6765 צְלָפְחָד ṣᵉlopḥād, n.pr.m. GK: 7524 [→ 6738+6343]. Zelophehad, "*shadow of dread, terror i.e., protection from terror or dread*":– Zelophehad [11]

6766 צֶלְצַח ṣelṣaḥ, n.pr.loc. GK: 7525. Zelzah:– Zelzah [1]

6767 צְלָצַל ṣᵉlāṣal or צִלְצָל ṣilṣāl, n.m. GK: 7526 & 7527 & 7528 & 7529 [→ 6750]. (swarm of) locust; some sources: cricket; whirring, buzzing; (fishing) spear; cymbals:– cymbals [3], locust [1], shadowing [1], spears [1]

6768 צֶלֶק ṣeleq, n.pr.m. GK: 7530. Zelek, "*cry aloud*":– Zelek [2]

6769 צִלְּתַי ṣillᵉtay, n.pr.m. GK: 7531. Zillethai, "*shadow of Yahweh*":– Zilthai [2]

צֹם ṣōm. See 6685.

6770 צָמֵא ṣāmē', v. GK: 7532 [→ 6772, 6771, 6773, 6774]. [Q] to thirst, be thirsty:– athirst [2], thirsted [2], thirsteth [2], thirsty [2], suffer thirst [1], thirst [1]

6771 צָמֵא ṣāmē', a. GK: 7534 [→ 6770]. thirsty, used of humans and animals; used fig. of parched ground:– thirsty [7], thirsteth [1], thirst [1]

6772 צָמָא ṣāmā', n.[m.]. GK: 7533 [→ 6770]. thirst (of humans and animals); used fig. of parched ground:– thirst [16], thirsty [1]

6773 צִמְאָה ṣim'â, n.f. GK: 7535 [→ 6770]. thirst:– thirst [1]

6774 צִמָּאוֹן ṣimmā'ôn, n.[m.]. GK: 7536 [→ 6770]. thirsty ground:– drought [1], dry ground [1], thirsty land [1]

6775 צָמַד ṣāmad, v. GK: 7537 [→ 6776, 6781]. [N] to be joined together; [Pu] to be strapped on; [H] to harness, attach to:– joined [2], fastened [1], frameth [1], joined unto [1]

6776 צֶמֶד ṣemed, n.m. GK: 7538 [→ 6775]. yoke, team of two, pair; this can refer to a measurement of land, as the acreage a team of animals can plow:– yoke [6], couple [4], two [2], acres [1], together [1], yoke of oxen [1]

6777 צַמָּה ṣammâ, n.f. GK: 7539. veil:– locks [4]

6778 צִמּוּקִים ṣimmûqîm, n.m.[pl.]. GK: 7540 [→ 6784]. raisin cakes:– bunches of raisins [2], clusters of raisins [2]

6779 צָמַח ṣāmaḥ, v. GK: 7541 [→ 6780]. [Q] to sprout up, spring up; [P] to grow; [H] to cause to grow, bring to fruition:– grown [3], spring forth [3], cause to spring forth [2], grew [2], grow [2], spring up [2], beareth [1], bring forth [1], bringeth forth [1], bud [1], cause to bud forth [1], cause to grow up [1], causeth to grow [1], causeth to spring forth [1], grow up [1], groweth [1], grown up [1], made to grow [1], make to bud [1], make to grow [1], maketh to grow [1], sprang up [1], spring out [1], spring [1], sprung up [1]

6780 צֶמַח ṣemaḥ, n.m. GK: 7542 [→ 6779]. growth (which sprouts); (as a messianic title) the Branch:– branch [5], bud [3], grew [1], springing [1], spring [1], that which grew [1]

6781 צָמִיד ṣāmîd, n.m. GK: 7543 & 7544 [→ 6775]. bracelet; lid, cover:– bracelets [6], covering [1]

6782 צַמִּים ṣammîm, n.m. GK: 7545. snare:– robber [2]

6783 צְמִתֻת ṣᵉmitut, n.f. GK: 7552 [→ 6789]. permanence, finality:– ever [2]

6784 צָמַק ṣāmaq, v. GK: 7546 [→ 6778]. [Q] to be dry, shriveled (of breasts):– dry [1]

6785 צֶמֶר ṣemer, n.m. GK: 7547 [→ 6787, 6788; cf. 6015]. wool:– wool [11], woollen [5]

6786 צְמָרִי ṣᵉmārî, a.g. GK: 7548. Zemarite:– Zemarite [2]

6787 צְמָרַיִם ṣᵉmārayim, n.pr.loc. GK: 7549 [→ 6785]. Zemaraim, "*[poss.] double peak*":– Zemaraim [2]

6788 צַמֶּרֶת ṣammeret, n.f. GK: 7550 [→ 6785]. top (of a tree):– top [3], highest branch [2]

6789 צָמַת ṣāmat, v. GK: 7551 [→ 6783]. [Q] to silence; [N] to be silenced; [Pil] to destroy; [P] to wear out; [H] to put to silence, destroy:– cut off [8], destroy [4], consumed [1], destroyed [1], vanish [1]

צְמִתֻת ṣᵉmitut. See 6783.

6790 צִן ṣin, n.pr.loc. GK: 7554. Zin:– Zin [10]

6791 צֵן ṣēn, n.[m.]. GK: 7553 [→ 6793, 6796]. thorn; hook:– thorns [2]

6792 צֹנֵא ṣōnā' or צֹנֶה ṣōneh, [n.m.]. GK: 7555 & 7556 [→ 6629; cf. 3318]. flocks (of sheep and goats):– sheep [2]

6793 צִנָּה ṣinnâ, n.f. GK: 7557 & 7558 & 7559 [→ 6791]. coolness; (large) shield; hook:– shield [9], buckler [3], targets [3], bucklers [2], target [2], cold [1], hooks [1], shields [1]

6794 צִנּוֹר ṣinnôr, n.m. GK: 7562 [→ 6804]. water shaft; waterfall:– gutter [1], waterspouts [1]

6795 צָנַח ṣānaḥ, v. GK: 7563. [Q] to get down; to go down:– fastened [1], lighted off (+4480+5921) [1], lighted [1]

6796 צְנִינִים ṣᵉnînîm, n.[m.pl.]. GK: 7564 [→ 6791]. thorns:– thorns [2]

6797 צָנוּף ṣānûp or צָנִיף ṣānîp or צְנִיפָה ṣᵉnîpâ, n.m. GK: 7561 & 7565 & 7566 [→ 6801]. turban, an ornamental head wrap:– diadem [2], mitre [2], hoods [1]

6798 צָנַם ṣānam, v. GK: 7567 & 7568. [Q] to dry up, harden, wither:– withered [1]

6799 צְנָן ṣᵉnān, n.pr.loc. GK: 7569 [cf. 6630?]. Zenan, "*place of flocks*":– Zenan [1]

צָנִן ṣānin. See 6796.

6800 צָנַע ṣāna', v. GK: 7570 & 7560 [→ 5204]. [H] to show a humble (walk with God), as an extension of acting in a cautious manner:– humbly [1], lowly [1]

6801 צָנַף *ṣānap*, v. GK: 7571 [→ 4701, 6797, 6802]. [Q] to wrap around, wind around:– surely violently turn and toss (+6801+6802) [2], attired [1]

6802 צְנֵפָה *ṣᵉnēpâ*, n.f. GK: 7572 [→ 6801]. winding, wrapping:– surely violently turn and toss (+6801+6801) [1]

6803 צִנְצֶנֶת *ṣinṣenet*, n.f. GK: 7573. vessel, receptacle, likely referring to a jar:– pot [1]

6804 צַנְתָּרוֹת *ṣantārôt*, n.m.pl. GK: 7574 [→ 6794]. pipes:– pipes [1]

6805 צָעַד *ṣāʿad*, v. GK: 7575 [→ 685, 4703, 6806, 6807]. [Q] to step, march; [H] to make march:– bring [1], gone paces (+6806) [1], go [1], march through [1], marchedst [1], march [1], run [1], went [1]

6806 צַעַד *ṣaʿad*, n.m. GK: 7576 [→ 6805]. step, stride:– steps [11], goings [1], gone paces (+6805) [1], go [1]

6807 צְעָדָה *ṣᵉʿādâ*, n.f. GK: 7577 & 7578 [→ 6805]. marching; ankle chains:– going [2], ornaments of the legs [1]

6808 צָעָה *ṣāʿâ*, v. GK: 7579. [Q] to lay down, stoop, incline; [P] to tip, pour out:– captive exile [1], cause to wander [1], travelling [1], wanderers [1], wanderest [1]

צָעוֹר *ṣāʿôr*. See 6810.

6809 צָעִיף *ṣāʿîp*, n.[m.]. GK: 7581. veil:– vail [3]

6810 צָעִיר *ṣāʿîr*, a. GK: 7582 [→ 6819; cf. 6812]. younger, small, little, lowly:– younger [7], least [4], youngest [3], little ones [2], little [2], small one [1], small [1], young (+3117+3807.1) [1], younger (+3117) [1]

6811 צָעִיר *ṣāʿîr*, n.pr.loc. GK: 7583. Zair, "*small, insignificant, hence narrow pass*":– Zair [1]

6812 צְעִירָה *ṣᵉʿîrâ*, n.f. GK: 7584 [cf. 6810]. youth, youngest (offspring):– youth [1]

6813 צָעַן *ṣāʿan*, v. GK: 7585. [Q] to pack up, move (a tent):– taken down [1]

6814 צֹעַן *ṣōʿan*, n.pr.loc. GK: 7586. Zoan:– Zoan [7]

6815 צַעֲנַנִּים *ṣaʿᵃnannîm*, n.pr.loc. GK: 7588. Zaanannim:– Zaanaim [1], Zaanannim [1]

6816 צַעֲצֻעִים *ṣaʿᵃṣuʿîm*, n.[m.]pl. GK: 7589. sculptured work (by metal casting):– image [1]

6817 צָעַק *ṣāʿaq*, v. GK: 7590 [→ 6818; cf. 2199; cf. 2200]. [Q] to cry; [N] to be called out, be summoned; [P] to keep crying; [H] to call together, summon:– cried [27], cry [13], gathered together [3], called together [2], cried out [2], crieth [2], cry at all (+6817) [2], criest [1], cry out [1], gathered themselves together [1], gathered [1]

6818 צְעָקָה *ṣᵉʿāqâ*, n.f. GK: 7591 [→ 6817]. cry of distress, outcry, wailing:– cry [19], crying [2]

6819 צָעַר *ṣāʿar*, v. GK: 7592 [→ 4704, 4705, 4706, 6686, 6730, 6810, 6820; cf. 2191]. [Q] to be trivial, insignificant, little:– brought low [1], little ones [1], small [1]

6820 צֹעַר *ṣōʿar*, n.pr.loc. GK: 7593. Zoar, "*small, insignificant*":– Zoar [10]

6821 צָפַד *ṣāpad*, v. GK: 7594. [Q] to shrivel:– cleaveth [1]

6822 צָפָה *ṣāpâ*, v. GK: 7595 [→ 4707, 4708, 4709, 6828, 6829, 6830, 6836, 6837?]. [Q] to keep watch, be a lookout; [Qp] to be spied out; [P] to watch, lookout:– watchman [14], watchmen [5], watch [4], beholding [1], behold [1], espy [1], kept watch [1], look up [1], looketh well [1], looketh [1], look [1], waited [1], watched [1], watcheth [1], watching [1], watchman's [1]

6823 צָפָה *ṣāpâ*, v. GK: 7596 [→ 6826, 6844, 6858, 6857?]. [Q] to arrange; [P] to overlay, cover, adorn; [Pu] to be overlaid, be coated:– overlaid [28], overlay [12], covered [5], garnished [1]

6824 צָפָה *ṣāpâ*, n.f. GK: 7597 [→ 6687?]. out-flow, discharge:– swimmest [1]

6825 צְפוֹ *ṣᵉpô* or צְפִי *ṣᵉpî*, n.pr.m. GK: 7598 & 7609. Zepho, Zephi, "*poss. gaze*":– Zepho [2], Zephi [1]

6826 צִפּוּי *ṣippûy*, n.[m.]. GK: 7599 [→ 6823]. overlaying, (metal) plating:– covering [3], overlaying [1]

6827 צְפוֹן *ṣᵉpôn*, n.pr.m. GK: 7602 [→ 6831; cf. 6837]. Zephon, "[poss.] *gaze*; [poss.] *look out [tower], watch*":– Zephon [1]

6828 צָפוֹן *ṣāpôn*, n.f. GK: 7600 [→ 1189, 6829, 6830; cf. 6822]. north, northern:– north [105], northward (+1886.5) [20], north side [10], north (+1886.5) [9], northward (+4480) [2], in north (+1886.5) [1], north side (+1886.5) [1],

north side (+4480) [1], north wind [1], northern (+4480) [1], northwards (+1886.5) [1], northward [1]

6829 צָפוֹן *ṣāpôn*, n.pr.loc. GK: 7601 [→ 6828; cf. 6822]. Zaphon, "[poss.] *North* or [proper name of a god], *Zephon*":– Zaphon [1]

6830 צְפוֹנִי *ṣᵉpônî*, a. GK: 7603 [→ 6828; cf. 6822]. northern; (n.) northerner:– northern [1]

6831 צְפוֹנִי *ṣᵉpônî* or צִפְיוֹנִי *ṣipyônî*, a.g. GK: 7604 & 7612 [→ 6827, 6837]. Zephonite, "*of Zephon*":– Zephonites [1]

6832 צָפוּעַ *ṣāpûaʿ* or צְפִיעַ *ṣᵉpîaʿ*, n.[m.]. GK: 7605 & 7616. manure, dung:– dung [1]

6833 צִפּוֹר *ṣippôr*, n.f. & m. GK: 7606 [→ 6691?, 6834, 6855]. bird (individual and collective):– bird [21], birds [10], fowl [5], sparrow [2], bird's [1], fowls [1]

6834 צִפּוֹר *ṣippôr*, n.pr.m. GK: 7607 [→ 6833; cf. 6853]. Zippor, "*bird, swallow*":– Zippor [7]

6835 צַפַּחַת *ṣappaḥat*, n.f. GK: 7608 [→ 6838]. jug, jar (for liquid), a portable convex or spherical shape, with a lid or plug for transport:– cruse [7]

6836 צְפִיָּה *ṣᵉpiyyâ*, n.f. GK: 7610 [→ 6822]. watchtower, lookout:– watching [1]

6837 צִפְיוֹן *ṣipyôn*, n.pr.m. GK: 7611 [→ 6831; cf. 6822?, 6827]. Ziphion, cf. 6829:– Ziphion [1]

6838 צַפִּיחִת *ṣappîḥit*, n.f. GK: 7613 [→ 6690, 6835]. wafer, flat-cake:– wafers [1]

6839 צֹפִים *ṣōpîm*, n.pr.[loc.?]. GK: 7614. Zophim:– Zophim [1]

6840 צָפִין *ṣāpîn*, n.[m.]. GK: 7615 [→ 6845]. hidden thing:–

6841 צְפִיר *ṣᵉpîr* (Aram.), n.m. GK: 10615 [cf. 6842]. male goat:– he goats (+5796) [1]

6842 צָפִיר *ṣāpîr*, n.[m.]. GK: 7618 [cf. 6841]. (male) goat:– goat [3], he goat (+5795) [2], he goats (+5795) [1], he goats [1]

6843 צְפִירָה *ṣᵉpîrâ*, n.f. GK: 7619. crown, wreath; doom:– morning [2], diadem [1]

6844 צָפִית *ṣāpît*, n.f. GK: 7620 [→ 6823]. rug, carpet:– watchtower [1]

6845 צָפַן *ṣāpan*, v. GK: 7621 & 7636 [→ 4710, 6840; cf. 6693 (also used with compound proper names)]. [Q] to hide, conceal, store up; [Qp] to be treasured, be cherished; [N] to be stored up, be concealed; [H] to hide:– hid [8], hide [5], laid up [3], hidden [2], hideth [2], lay up [2], layeth up [1], lurk privily [2], esteemed [1], hidden ones [1], keep secretly [1], privily set [1], secret places [1], secret [1]

צָפֹן *ṣāpōn*. See 6828.

6846 צְפַנְיָה *ṣᵉpanyâ* or צְפַנְיָהוּ *ṣᵉpanyāhû*, n.pr.m. GK: 7622 & 7623 [→ 6845+3068]. Zephaniah, "*Yahweh has hidden [to shelter]* or *Yahweh has hidden [as a treasure]*":– Zephaniah [10]

6847 צָפְנַת פַּעְנֵחַ *ṣāpᵉnat paʿnēaḥ*, n.pr.m. GK: 7624. Zaphenath-Paneah, "*the [pagan] god speaks and he [the newborn] lives*":– Zaphnath-paaneah [1]

6848 צֶפַע *ṣepaʿ* or צִפְעֹנִי *ṣipʿōnî*, n.m. GK: 7625 & 7626. viper, serpent:– cockatrice' [2], adder [1], cockatrices [1], cockatrice [1]

6849 צְפִעָה *ṣᵉpiʿâ*, n.f. GK: 7617. offshoots, leaf:– issue [1]

צִפְעֹנִי *ṣipʿōnî*. See 6848.

6850 צָפַף *ṣāpap*, v. GK: 7627 [→ 6851]. [Pil] to chirp; to whisper:– chatter [1], peeped [1], peep [1], whisper [1]

6851 צַפְצָפָה *ṣapṣāpâ*, n.f. GK: 7628 [→ 6850]. willow:– willow tree [1]

6852 צָפַר *ṣāpar*, v. GK: 7629. [Q] to leave, depart:– depart early [1]

6853 צְפַר *ṣᵉpar* (Aram.), n.f. GK: 10616 [cf. 6834]. bird:– fowls [3], birds' [1]

צִפֹּר *ṣippōr*. See 6833.

6854 צְפַרְדֵּעַ *ṣᵉpardēaʿ*, n.f. GK: 7630. frogs:– frogs [13]

6855 צִפֹּרָה *ṣippōrâ*, n.pr.f. GK: 7631 [→ 6833]. Zipporah, "*bird, swallow*":– Zipporah [3]

6856 צִפֹּרֶן *ṣippōren*, n.[m.]. GK: 7632 [cf. 2953]. nail (of finger or toe); (flint or hard stone) point (of a stylus):– nails [1], point [1]

6857 צְפַת *ṣᵉpat*, n.pr.loc. GK: 7634 [→ 6823?]. Zephath, "*watcher*":– Zephath [1]

6858 צֶפֶת *ṣepet*, n.f. GK: 7633 [→ 6823]. capital (of a pillar):– chapiter [1]

6859 צְפָתָה *ṣᵉpātâ*, n.pr.loc. GK: 7635. Zephathah, "*watchtower*":– Zephathah [1]

צָץ *ṣiṣ*. See 6732.

6860 צִקְלַג *ṣiqlag*, n.pr.loc. GK: 7637. Ziklag:– Ziklag [15]

6861 צִקָּלוֹן *ṣiqqālôn* or בְּצִקְלֹן *biṣqālōn*, n.[m.]. GK: 7638 & 1303. head of grain; garment, bag:– husk [1]

6862 צַר *ṣar*, a. & n.m. GK: 7639 & 7640 & 7641 [→ 3334, 6864, 6887; cf. 6146]. (n.) trouble, distress, anguish; (a.) narrow; enemy, foe, adversary, opponent; flint, known for its hardness:– enemies [26], adversaries [21], trouble [17], enemy [10], adversary [5], distress [4], affliction [3], strait [3], enemy's [2], foes [2], narrow [2], adversary (+376) [1], adversity [1], afflicted [1], anguish [1], close [1], distresses [1], small [1], sorrow [1], tribulation [1]

6863 צֵר *ṣēr*, n.pr.loc. GK: 7643. Zer:– Zer [1]

6864 צֹר *ṣōr*, n.[m.]. GK: 7644 [→ 6697, 6862, 6865, 6872, 6876]. flint knife:– flint [1], sharp stone [1]

6865 צֹר *ṣōr* or צוֹר *ṣôr*, n.pr.loc. GK: 7645 & 7450 [→ 6876; cf. 6864]. Tyre, "*rocky place*":– Tyrus [22], Tyre [20]

צֻר *ṣur*. See 6697.

6866 צָרַב *ṣārab*, v. GK: 7646 [→ 6867]. [N] to be scorched:– burnt [1]

6867 צָרָב *ṣārāb* or צָרֶבֶת *ṣārebet*, a. & n.f. GK: 7647 & 7648 [→ 6866]. scorching; scar:– burning [2], inflammation [1]

6868 צְרֵדָה *ṣᵉrēdâ*, n.pr.loc. GK: 7649. Zeredah:– Zeredathah [1], Zereda [1]

6869 צָרָה *ṣārâ*, n.f. GK: 7650 & 7651 [→ 6862, 6887; cf. 3334]. trouble, distress, calamity, anguish; rival-wife:– trouble [34], troubles [10], distress [8], affliction [7], anguish [5], adversity [4], tribulation [2], adversary [1], adversities [1], tribulations [1]

6870 צְרוּיָה *ṣᵉrûyâ*, n.pr.f. GK: 7653. Zeruiah, "*perfumed resin*":– Zeruiah [26]

6871 צְרוּעָה *ṣᵉrûʿâ*, n.pr.loc. GK: 7654 [→ 6879]. Zeruah, "*one with skin disease*":– Zeruah [1]

6872 צְרוֹר *ṣᵉrôr*, n.m. & pr. GK: 7655 & 7656 & 7657 [cf. 3334, 6864]. pouch, purse, sachet, bag; pebble; as n.pr. Zeror, "*money bag, pouch,* [or poss.] *pebbles*":– bag [3], bundle [3], Zeror [1], bindeth [1], bundles [1], least grain [1], small stone [1]

6873 צָרַח *ṣāraḥ*, v. GK: 7658. [Q] to shout, cry out; [H] to raise the battle cry:– cry [1], roar [1]

6874 צְרִי *ṣᵉrî*, n.pr.m. GK: 7662 [→ 6875]. Zeri, "*balsam*":– Zeri [1]

6875 צְרִי *ṣᵉrî*, n.[m.]. GK: 7661 [→ 6874]. balm, mastic (resin), usually obtained from processing from the bark of a tree:– balm [6]

6876 צֹרִי *ṣōrî*, a.g. GK: 7660 [→ 6865]. Tyrian, of Tyre:– Tyre [2], of Tyre [2], men of Tyre [1]

6877 צְרִיחַ *ṣᵉrîaḥ*, n.[m.]. GK: 7663. pit, (underground) stronghold, likely referring to a man-made pit:– hold [3], high places [1]

6878 צֹרֶךְ *ṣōrek*, n.[m.]. GK: 7664. need:– need [1]

6879 צָרַע *ṣāraʿ*, v.den. GK: 7665 [→ 6871, 6879?, 6883]. [Qp, Pu] to become, afflicted with an infectious skin disease:– leper [13], leprous [6], lepers [1]

6880 צִרְעָה *ṣirʿâ*, n.f.col. GK: 7667 [→ 6879?]. hornets or discouragement:– hornet [2], hornets [1]

6881 צָרְעָה *ṣārᵉʿâ*, n.pr.loc. GK: 7666 [→ 6882]. Zorah:– Zorah [8], Zareah [1], Zoreah [1]

6882 צָרְעִי *ṣārᵉʿî* or צָרְעָתִי *ṣārᵉʿātî*, a.g. GK: 7668 & 7670 [→ 6881]. Zorite; Zorathite, "*of Zorah*":– Zareathites [1], Zorathites [1], Zorites [1]

6883 צָרַעַת *ṣāraʿat*, n.f. GK: 7669 [→ 6879]. infectious skin disease; (of clothing) mildew:– leprosy [35]

6884 צָרַף *ṣārap*, v. GK: 7671 [→ 4715, 6885]. [Q] to smelt, refine (metals); (n.) gold- or silver-)smith:– tried [8], founder [5], goldsmith [3], try [3], goldsmiths [2], pure [2], refined [2], casteth [1], finer [1], melteth [1], melt [1], purge away [1], refiner's [1], refiner [1], refine [1]

6885 צֹרְפִי *ṣōrᵉpî*, n.[m.]col. GK: 7672 [→ 6884]. (member of the) goldsmiths:– goldsmith's [1]

6886 צָרְפַת *ṣār^epat*, n.pr.loc. GK: 7673. Zarephath, "[poss.] *smelting place; place of pigmenting, staining*":– Zarephath [3]

6887 צָרַר *ṣārar*, v. GK: 7674 & 7675 & 7677 [→ 3334, 6862, 6869]. [Q] to be a rival-wife; to be an enemy, adversary; to bind up, wrap up, tie up; to hamper, oppress, be in distress; [Qp] to be bound, be confined; [Pu] to be mended; [H] to bring trouble, distress, oppress:– enemies [9], enemy [5], vex [5], besiege [4], bound up [4], adversaries [3], distress [3], afflicted [2], afflict [2], bound [2], distressed [2], in a strait [2], in pangs [2], affliction [1], bind up [1], bindeth up [1], bring distress [1], in distress [1], in trouble [1], narrower [1], oppresseth [1], shut up [1], strait [1], trouble [1], vexed [1]

6888 צְרֵרָה *ṣ^erērâ*, n.p.loc. GK: 7678. Zererah:– Zererath [1]

6889 צֶרֶת *ṣeret*, n.pr.m. GK: 7679 [→ 6890]. Zereth, "*splendor*":– Zereth [1]

6890 צֶרֶת הַשַּׁחַר *ṣeret haššaḥar*, n.pr.loc. GK: 7680 [→ 6889]. Zereth Shahar, "*glory of dawn*":– Zareth-shahar [1]

6891 צָרְתָן *ṣār^etān*, n.pr.loc. GK: 7681. Zarethan:– Zaretan [1], Zartanah [1], Zarthan [1]

6892 קֵא *qē'* or קִיא *qî'*, n.m. GK: 7683 & 7795 [→ 6958]. vomit:– vomit [4]

6893 קָאַת *qā'at*, n.[f.]. GK: 7684. desert owl:– pelican [3], cormorant [2]

6894 קַב *qab*, n.[m.]. GK: 7685 [→ 6898]. cab (dry measure, one-eighteenth of an ephah, about one quart or liter):– kab [1]

6895 קָבַב *qābab*, v. GK: 7686 [cf. 5344]. [Q] to curse:– curse [6], cursed [1]

6896 קֵבָה *qēbâ*, n.f. GK: 7687 [→ 6897]. same as 6897: maw (4th stomach of cud-chewing animals); (of humans) belly, stomach area:– maw [1]

6897 קֹבָה *qōbâ*, n.f. GK: 7687 [→ 6896]. same as 6896: maw (4th stomach of cud-chewing animals); (of humans) belly, stomach area:– belly [1]

6898 קֻבָּה *qubbâ*, n.f. GK: 7688 [→ 6894]. woman's section (of a tent):– tent [1]

6899 קִבּוּץ *qibbûṣ*, n.m. GK: 7689 [→ 6908]. collection (of idols):– companies [1]

6900 קְבוּרָה *q^ebûrâ*, n.f. GK: 7690 [→ 5354, 6912, 6962]. tomb, grave, burial:– sepulchre [5], burial [4], grave [4], buryingplace [1]

6901 קָבַל *qābal*, v. GK: 7691 [→ 6904; cf. 6902]. [P] to receive, take; [H] to match, correspond:– received [3], receive [3], took [3], choose [1], held [1], take hold [1], undertook [1]

6902 קְבַל *q^ebal* (Aram.), v.den. GK: 10618 [→ 6903; cf. 6901]. [Pa] to receive; to take over:– receive [1], take [1], took [1]

6903 קֳבֵל *q^obēl* (Aram.), subst. & pp. & c. GK: 10619 [→ 6902]. before, in front of; since, because of:– forasmuch as (+1768+3606) [8], because (+1768+3606) [4], before (+3807.2) [3], therefore (+1836+3606) [3], wherefore (+1836+3606) [2], according to (+3807.2) [1], against [1], as (+1768+3606) [1], for this cause (+1836+3606) [1], means [1], reason [1], that (+1836+3606) [1], therefore (+1768+3606) [1], though (+1768+3606) [1]

6904 קֹבֶל *q^obōl*, n.[m.]. GK: 7692 [→ 6901, 6905]. prob. same as 6905: (something) in front of, battering ram:– war [1]

6905 קְבָל *q^ebōl*, n.[m.]. GK: 7692 [→ 6904]. prob. same as 6904: (something) in front of, battering ram:– before [1]

6906 קָבַע *qāba'*, v. GK: 7693 [cf. 6117, 6120]. [Q] to rob, plunder:– robbed [3], rob [1], spoiled [1], spoil [1]

6907 קֻבַּעַת *qubba'at*, n.f. GK: 7694. cup, goblet:– dregs [2]

6908 קָבַץ *qābaṣ*, v. GK: 7695 [→ 6899, 6910, 6911 (also used with compound proper names)]. [Q] to collect, gather, assemble; [Qp] to be assembled; [N] to be gathered, be assembled, be joined; [P] to gather, assemble; [Pu] to be gathered; [Ht] to gather (themselves) together:– gather [43], gathered together [33], gathered [22], gather together [10], assemble [5], gathereth [4], gather up [2], surely gather (+6908) [2], assembled [1], brought together [1], gathered up [1], heapeth [1], resort [1], taketh up [1]

6909 קַבְצְאֵל *qabṣ^e'ēl*, n.pr.loc. GK: 7696 [→ 6908+410]. Kabzeel, "*God [El] collects*":– Kabzeel [3]

6910 קְבֻצָה *q^ebuṣâ*, n.f. GK: 7697 [→ 6908]. gathering:– gather [1]

6911 קִבְצַיִם *qibṣayim*, n.pr.loc. GK: 7698 [→ 6908]. Kibzaim:– Kibzaim [1]

6912 קָבַר *qābar*, v. GK: 7699 [→ 6900, 6913, 6914]. [Q] to store up, pile up, heap up:– buried [96], bury [32], burying [2], in any wise bury (+6912) [2], buriers [1]

6913 קֶבֶר *qeber*, n.m. GK: 7700 [→ 6914]. burial site, tomb, grave:– grave [19], graves [16], sepulchre [14], sepulchres [12], buryingplace [6]

6914 קִבְרוֹת הַתַּאֲוָה *qibrôt hatta'^awâ*, n.pr.loc. GK: 7701 [→ 6913]. Kibroth Hattaavah, "*graves of lust, greed*":– Kibroth-hattaavah [5]

6915 קָדַד *qādad*, v. GK: 7702 [→ 6936?]. [Q] to bow low, bow down:– bowed down head [3], bowed heads [3], bowed down heads [2], bowed head [2], bowed [2], stooped [2], bowed the head [1]

6916 קִדָּה *qiddâ*, n.f. GK: 7703. cassia (a spice):– cassia [2]

6917 קְדוּמִים *q^edûmîm*, n.[m.pl.]. GK: 7704 [→ 6923]. age-old, ancient:– ancient [1]

6918 קָדוֹשׁ *qādôš*, a. GK: 7705 [→ 6942; cf. 6922]. holy, sacred, consecrated, set apart as dedicated to God; by extension: pure, innocent, free from impurity; (n.) holy people of God, saints; as a title of God, "the Holy One" focuses on God as unique, wholly other:– holy [63], holy one [41], saints [9], saint [3]

6919 קָדַח *qādaḥ*, v. GK: 7706 [→ 688, 6920]. [Q] to kindle, light (a fire):– kindled [3], burneth [1], kindle [1]

6920 קַדַּחַת *qaddaḥat*, n.f. GK: 7707 [→ 6919]. fever, inflammation:– burning ague [1], fever [1]

6921 קָדִים *qādîm*, n.m. GK: 7708 [→ 6923]. east, eastern, the direction of orientation in the ancient Near East (facing the sunrise); east is also the direction of the great desert, thus an east or desert wind is particularly hot:– east [36], east (+1886.5) [14], east wind [10], eastward (+1886.5) [4], eastward [3], east side [1], eastward (+1870+1886.1) [1]

6922 קַדִּישׁ *qaddîš* (Aram.), a. GK: 10620 [cf. 6918]. holy, ceremonial or moral purity; (as noun) holy one, saint, which can refer to human beings or angels:– saints [6], holy [4], holy one [2], holy ones [1]

6923 קָדַם *qādam*, v.den. GK: 7709 [→ 6917, 6921, 6924, 6927, 6926, 6929, 6930, 6932, 6934, 6931, 6935; cf. 6925, cf. 6933]. [P] to be in front of, meet, confront:– prevented [8], prevent [6], come before [5], met [5], before [1], disappoint (+6440) [1], go before [1], preventest [1], went before [1]

6924 קֶדֶם *qedem* or קֵדְמָה *qēd^emâ*, n.[m.]. GK: 7710 & 7711 & 7714 [→ 6923]. (as a direction) east, eastern; the direction of orientation in the ancient Near East (facing the sunrise); (used of time) ancient, eternal, long ago, possibly relating to east as the direction of origin (as the sunrise):– east [27], eastward (+1886.5) [9], old [9], of old [8], ancient [6], east (+1886.5) [5], east side [5], before [2], aforetime [1], ancient times [1], ancient time [1], before (+4480) [1], east (+4217+1886.5) [1], east country [1], east end [1], east parts [1], east part [1], eastward (+4480) [1], eastward [1], eternal [1], everlasting [1], forward [1], or ever was (+4480) [1], past [1]

6925 קֳדָם *q^odām* (Aram.), pp. GK: 10621 [→ 6928, 6933; cf. 6924]. before, in the presence of:– before [29], before (+4481) [4], of (+4481) [3], from (+4481) [1], in the presence [1], then (+116+4481+871.2) [1], thought [1]

קָדִם *qādim*. See 6921.

6926 קִדְמָה *qidmâ*, n.f. GK: 7713 [→ 6923]. east:– east [2], eastward [1], toward east [1]

6927 קַדְמָה *qadmâ*, n.f. GK: 7712 [→ 6923; cf. 6928]. past, antiquity; ancient (city):– former estate [3], afore [1], antiquity [1], old estates [1]

6928 קַדְמָה *qadmâ* (Aram.), n.f. GK: 10622 [→ 6925; cf. 6927]. before times; (as adv.) formerly:– aforetime (+1836+4481) [1], ago (+4481) [1]

קֵדְמָה *qēd^emâ*. See 6924.

6929 קֵדְמָה *qēd^emâ*, n.pr.m. GK: 7715 [→ 6923]. Kedemah, "*east*":– Kedemah [2]

6930 קַדְמוֹן *qadmôn*, a. GK: 7716 [→ 6931, 6935; cf. 6923]. eastern:– east [1]

6931 קַדְמֹנִי *qadmōnî*, a. GK: 7719 [→ 6930; cf. 6923]. (of a direction) eastern; (of time) old, former, past:– east [4], former [2], ancients [1], of old [1], old [1], they that went before [1]

6932 קְדֵמוֹת *q^edēmôt*, n.pr.loc. GK: 7717 [→ 6923]. Kedemoth, "*east*":– Kedemoth [4]

6933 קַדְמָי *qadmāy* (Aram.), a. GK: 10623 [→ 6925; cf. 6924]. first; earlier, former:– first [3]

6934 קַדְמִיאֵל *qadmî'ēl*, n.pr.m. GK: 7718 [→ 6923+410]. Kadmiel, "*[stand] before God [El]*":– Kadmiel [8]

קַדְמֹנִי *qadmōnî*. See 6931.

6935 קַדְמֹנִי *qadmōnî*, a.g. GK: 7720 [→ 6930; cf. 6923]. Kadmonite:– Kadmonites [1]

6936 קָדְקֹד *qodqōd*, n.[m.]. GK: 7721 [→ 6915?]. top or crown of the head:– crown of the head [4], crown of head [2], crown [1], pate [1], scalp [1], top of head [1], top of the head [1]

6937 קָדַר *qādar*, v. GK: 7722 [→ 6938, 6939, 6940, 6941]. [Q] to grow dark, be black; to mourn, wail, grieve; [H] to make dark, bring gloom; [Ht] to grow dark:– black [4], mourning [4], dark [2], make dark [2], blackish [1], caused to mourn [1], darkened [1], heavily [1], mourn [1]

6938 קֵדָר *qēdār*, n.pr.g. GK: 7723 [→ 6937]. Kedar, "*mighty*":– Kedar [12]

6939 קִדְרוֹן *qidrôn*, n.pr.loc. GK: 7724 [→ 6937]. Kidron:– Kidron [11]

6940 קַדְרוּת *qadrût*, n.f. GK: 7725 [→ 6937]. darkness, blackness:– blackness [1]

6941 קְדֹרַנִּית *q^edōrannît*, adv. GK: 7726 [→ 6937]. in mourner's attire, in an unkempt manner:– mournfully [1]

6942 קָדַשׁ *qādaš*, v.den. GK: 7727 [→ 4720, 6918, 6943, 6944, 6945, 6946, 6947, 6948]. [Q] to be holy, sacred, consecrated; [N] to show oneself holy, be consecrated; [P] to consecrate, make holy; [Pu] to be dedicated, consecrated; [Ht] to consecrate oneself; [H] to set apart, consecrate, dedicate, regard as holy; to set apart as dedicated to God; by extension: pure, innocent, free from impurity:– sanctify [64], sanctified [45], hallow [15], hallowed [10], prepare [7], dedicated [5], holy [5], dedicate [4], consecrated [3], consecrate [2], wholly dedicated (+6942) [2], appointed [1], bid [1], defiled [1], holier [1], holy kept [1], holy places [1], keep holy [1], proclaim [1], purified [1], sanctified ones [1]

6943 קֶדֶשׁ *qedeš*, n.pr.loc. GK: 7730 [→ 6942]. Kedesh, "*sacred place*":– Kedesh [11], Kedesh-naphtali (+5321) [1]

6944 קֹדֶשׁ *qōdeš*, n.m. GK: 7731 [→ 6942]. holy or sacred thing, holy or sacred place, sanctuary; holiness, set apart as dedicated to God; the "holy of holies" is the most holy place, set apart exclusively for the Presence of God, with very limited high priestly access:– holy [256], most holy (+6944) [88], sanctuary [68], holiness [30], hallowed [9], dedicated [7], dedicate [5], consecrated [2], thing most holy (+6944) [2], holy dwelling [1], saints [1]

6945 קָדֵשׁ *qādēš*, n.m. GK: 7728 [→ 6942, 6948]. (male or female) shrine prostitute:– sodomites [4], unclean [1], whore [1]

6946 קָדֵשׁ *qādēš*, n.pr.loc. GK: 7729 [→ 4809+6946; cf. 6942]. Kadesh, "*sacred place*":– Kadesh [17]

קָדוֹשׁ *qādôš*. See 6918.

6947 קָדֵשׁ בַּרְנֵעַ *qādēš barnēa'*, n.pr.loc. GK: 7732 [→ 6942]. Kadesh Barnea, "*sacred place of Barnea*":– Kadesh-barnea [10]

6948 קְדֵשָׁה *q^edēšâ*, n.m. GK: 7728 [→ 6945]. f. of 6945: female shrine prostitute:– harlot [3], harlots [1], sodomite [1]

6949 קָהָה *qāhâ*, v. GK: 7733. [Q] to be dull, blunt (of teeth); [P] to be dull:– set on edge [3], blunt [1]

6950 קָהַל *qāhal*, v.den. GK: 7735 [→ 6951]. [N] to be gathered, be assembled; [H] to summon, call together, cause to assemble:– gathered together [15], assembled [8], gather together [7], gathered [5], assembled together [3], gather [1]

6951 קָהָל *qāhāl*, n.m. GK: 7736 [→ 4721, 4722, 6950, 6951, 6952, 6953, 6954, 7035; cf. 6963]. assembly, community, often of Israel assembled for religious ceremony:– congregation [86], assembly [17], company [16], multitude [3], companies [1]

6952 קְהִלָּה *q^ehillâ*, n.f. GK: 7737 [→ 6951]. assembly, meeting:– assembly [1], congregation [1]

6953 קֹהֶלֶת *qōhelet*, n.m. GK: 7738 [→ 6951]. (as a title or name) the Teacher, one who calls together and instructs the assembly:– preacher [7]

6954 קְהֵלָתָה *q^ehēlātâ*, n.pr.loc. GK: 7739 [→ 6951]. Kehelathah, "*assembly*":– Kehelathah [2]

6955 קְהָת *q^ehāt*, n.pr.m. GK: 7740 [→ 6956]. Kohath, Kohathite:– Kohath [32]

6956 קְהָתִי qᵉhātî, a.g. GK: 7741 [→ 6955]. Kohathite, "*of Kohath*":– Kohathites [15]

6957 קַו qāw, n.m. GK: 7742 & 7744 [→ 6960?, 6978; cf. 6961]. measuring line, ruler; qav (a mocking sound, like blah-blah):– line [20], rule [1]

6958 קִא qî', v. GK: 7794 [→ 6892, 7006]. same as 7006: [Q] to vomit; [H] to vomit out, spit out:– spue out [2], vomit up [2], spued out [1], vomited out [1], vomiteth out [1], vomit [1]

6959 קוֹבַע qôba', n.[m.]. GK: 7746 [cf. 3553]. helmet:– helmet [2]

6960 קָוָה qāwâ, v. GK: 7747 & 7748 [→ 4723, 4724, 6957?, 8615, 8616]. [Q] to hope in; [N] to be gathered; [P] to hope for, wait for, look for:– wait [13], looked [8], waited [6], look [4], wait for [4], wait on [4], wait upon [2], waited patiently for (+6960) [2], gathered together [1], gathered [1], looked for [1], looketh [1], tarrieth [1], waited for [1]

6961 קָוֶה qāweh, n.m. GK: 7749 [cf. 6957]. measuring line, ruler:–

קֹוחַ qôaḥ. See 6495.

6962 קוּט qût, v. GK: 7752 & 7753 [→ 5354, 6900, 6990]. [Q] to feel anger, loathing; to be fragile; [N] to feel loathing; [Htpolal] to loathe, abhor:– grieved [3], lothe [3]

6963 קוֹל qôl or קֹל qōl, n.m. GK: 7754 & 7825 & 7826 [→ 6964?, 7043; cf. 6951; cf. 7032]. sound, voice, noise; lightness, (i.e., frivolity or light-heartedness):– voice [381], noise [49], sound [39], thunder [7], thunders [3], made a proclamation (+5674) [2], thunderings [2], voices [2], aloud (+1419+871.1) [1], bleating [1], caused to be proclaimed (+5674) [1], crackling [1], crieth out (+5414+871) [1], cry (+5414) [1], cry [1], fame [1], held peace (+2244) [1], lightness [1], loud (+1419+871.1) [1], lowing [1], made proclamation (+5674) [1], make proclamation (+5674) [1], proclaim (+5674) [1], proclamation [1], shouted aloud (+7311+8643+871.1+3807.1) [1], sing (+5414) [1], speaketh [1], wept aloud (+1065+5414+871.1) [1], yelled (+5414) [1]

6964 קוֹלָיָה qôlāyâ, n.pr.m. GK: 7755 [→ 6963?]. Kolaiah, "*Yahweh's voice*":– Kolaiah [2]

6965 קוּם qûm, v. GK: 7756 [→ 3351, 3356, 4725, 6967, 6968, 7009, 7012, 7054, 8617, 8618; cf. 6966 (also used with compound proper names)]. [Q] to get up, arise, stand, establish; [P] to establish, confirm, restore; [Pol] to raise up; [H] to set up, establish, restore; [Ho] to be set up, be raised up; [Htpol] to raise up against:– arise [103], arose [101], rose up [62], rise up [45], rise [28], raise up [26], stand [25], set up [23], establish [17], stood up [15], perform [13], performed [11], risen up [11], up [10], raised up [9], reared up [9], rose [8], established [7], riseth up [6], risen [5], confirm [4], raise [4], set [4], stand up '[4], arose up [3], confirmeth [3], continue [3], riseth [3], stablish [3], stirred up [3], ariseth [2], confirmed [2], lift up [2], made sure [2], newly set (+6965) [2], raiseth up [2], rear up [2], risest up [2], rose up against [2], stablished [2], surely accomplish (+6965) [2], surely lift up again (+6965) [2], surely stand (+6965) [2], abide [1], arise up [1], arising [1], assured [1], clearer [1], decreed [1], dim [1], endure [1], enemies [1], enjoined (+5921) [1], establisheth [1], get up [1], help up [1], hold [1], made to stand [1], make arise up [1], make good [1], maketh [1], ordained [1], performeth [1], pitch [1], raised [1], rear [1], remain [1], rise again [1], rise up again [1], rising up [1], rising [1], rouse up [1], stir up [1], strengthen [1], succeed [1], upholden [1], uprising [1]

6966 קוּם qûm (Aram.), v. GK: 10624 [→ 7010?, 7011; cf. 6965]. [P] to stand, rise up; [Pa] to issue (a decree); [H, A] to set up, establish; [Ho] to be set up, be established; from the base meaning of "standing up" (in contrast to sitting or lying) comes fig. extension of causing something to be or come into existence, implying a lively, active state:– set up [10], arise [4], stood [4], set [3], establish [2], rose up [2], setteth up [2], appointeth [1], arose [1], establisheth [1], made stand [1], made [1], raised up [1], rise [1], stand [1]

6967 קוֹמָה qômâ, n.f. GK: 7757 [→ 6965]. height:– height [30], stature [7], high [5], tall [2], all along (+4393) [1]

6968 קוֹמְמִיּוּת qômᵉmiyyût, n.f. GK: 7758 [→ 6965]. (adv.) with head held high:– upright [1]

6969 קוּן qîn, v.den. GK: 7801 [→ 7015]. [Pol] to chant a lament, sing a dirge:– lament [4], lamented [1], mourning [1]

6970 קוֹעַ qôa', n.pr.g. GK: 7760 [cf. 7772]. Koa:– Koa [1]

6971 קוֹף qôp, n.[m.]. GK: 7761. ape:– apes [1]

6972 קִיץ qîṣ or קוּץ qûṣ, v. GK: 7810 [→ 7019; cf. 3364]. [Q] to pass the summer; [H] to rouse, awaken:– summer [1]

6973 קוּץ qûṣ, v. GK: 7762 [→ 6975?; cf. 5354, 8262]. [Q] to detest, be disgusted, loathe:– abhorred [1], distressed [1], weary [1], abhorrest [1], distressed [1], grieved [1], loatheth [1], vex [1]

6974 קוּץ qûṣ, v. GK: 7763. [H] to rouse, awaken; to tear apart:– awake [10], awaked [4], awaketh [3], wake [2], arise [1], awakest [1], watcheth [1]

6975 קוֹץ qôṣ, n.m. GK: 7764 & 7765 [→ 6976?; cf. 6973?, 7093]. thorns, thornbush; shreds of a wick:– thorns [10], thorn [2]

6976 הַקּוֹץ haqqôṣ or קוֹץ qôṣ, n.prm. GK: 2212 & 7766 [→ 1886.1+6975?]. Hakkoz, Koz, "*the thorn*":– Koz [4], Coz [1], Hakkoz [1]

6977 קְווּצּוֹת qᵉwuṣṣôt, n.f.pl. GK: 7767. locks of hair:– locks [2]

6978 קַו־קַו qaw-qaw, n.m. GK: 7743 & 7744 [→ 6957]. strange speech; qav-qav (a mocking sound, like blah-blah):– meted out (+6978) [1]

6979 קוּר qûr or קָרַר qārar, v. GK: 7769 & 7981 & 7982 [→ 4726, 4747, 7119, 7120, 7135]. [Q] to dig (a well or water hole); [Pil] to tear down:– casteth out [2], digged [2], breaking down [1], destroy [1]

6980 קוּר qûr, n.m. GK: 7770. thread (of a spider cobweb):– webs [1], web [1]

6981 קֹרֵא qōrē', n.pr.m. GK: 7927 [→ 7124; cf. 7121]. Kore, "*proclaimer*":– Kore [3]

6982 קוֹרָה qôrâ, n.f. GK: 7771 [→ 4746]. beam, pole, roof beams, tree:– beams [2], beam [2], roof [1]

6983 קוּשׁ qûš, v. GK: 7772 [cf. 3369, 5367]. [Q] to set a snare:– lay a snare [1]

6984 קוּשָׁיָהוּ qûšāyāhû, n.pr.m. GK: 7773 [cf. 7029]. Kushaiah:– Kushaiah [1]

6985 קָט qāṭ, pt. GK: 7775. little; soon:– very little (+4592) [1]

6986 קֶטֶב qeṭeb, n.m. GK: 7776 [→ 6987]. same as 6987: plague, destruction:– destruction [2], destroying [1]

6987 קֹטֶב qōṭeb, n.m. GK: 7776 [→ 6986]. same as 6986: plague, destruction:– destruction [1]

6988 קְטוֹרָה qᵉṭôrâ, n.m. GK: 7777 [→ 6999]. smoke (of sacrifice):– incense [1]

6989 קְטוּרָה qᵉṭûrâ, n.pr.f. GK: 7778 [→ 6999]. Keturah, "*incense, scented one*":– Keturah [4]

6990 קוּט qûṭ or קָטַט qāṭaṭ, v. GK: 7752 & 7753 [→ 6962]. [Q] to be fragile; cut off; cf. 6962:– cut off [1]

6991 קָטַל qāṭal, v. GK: 7779 [→ 6993; cf. 6992]. [Q] to slay, kill:– slay [2], killeth [1]

6992 קְטַל qᵉṭal (Aram.), v. GK: 10625 [cf. 6991]. [P] to put to death, kill; [Peil] to be slain; [Htpe] to be put to death; [Pa] to kill; [Htpa] to be put to death:– slain [4], slew [2], slay [1]

6993 קֶטֶל qeṭel, n.[m.]. GK: 7780 [→ 6991]. slaughter:– slaughter [1]

6994 קָטֹן qāṭōn, v. GK: 7781 [→ 6995, 6996, 6997]. [Q] to be unworthy, not enough, trifling; [H] to make a (measure) small:– small thing [2], making small [1], not worthy [1]

6995 קֹטֶן qōṭen, n.m. GK: 7782 [→ 6994]. little finger; possibly a euphemism for penis:– little [2]

6996 קָטָן qāṭān or קָטֹן qāṭōn, a. GK: 7783 & 7785 [→ 6994, 6997]. small (in size); few (in quantity); by extension, of status: lesser, insignificant; of age: young(est):– small [33], little [19], youngest [15], younger [14], least [10], less [3], lesser [2], little one [2], small quantity [1], smallest [1], young [1]

6997 קָטָן qāṭān or הַקָּטָן haqqāṭān, n.pr.m. GK: 7784 & 2214 [→ 1886.1+6996; cf. 6994]. Katan, Hakkatan, "*the small one*":– Hakkatan [1]

6998 קָטַף qāṭap, v. GK: 7786. [Q] to pick off (grain), break off (twigs); [N] to be picked off:– crop off [1], cropt off [1], cut down [1], cut up [1], pluck [1]

6999 קָטַר qāṭar, v.den. GK: 7787 [→ 4729, 4730, 6988, 6989, 7002, 7003, 7004, 7008]. [P] to burn an offering (of incense smoke); [Pu] to be perfumed; [H] to make a burned smoking offering; [Ho] to be burned as an offering:– burn [34], burnt incense [25], burn incense [23], burnt [13], burned incense [3], burneth incense [2], not fail to burn (+6999) [2], offer [2], altars for incense [1], burn sacrifice [1], burned [1], burning incense [1], burnt incense (+7004) [1], incense [1], kindle [1], offer incense [1], offered incense [1], offered [1], offering incense [1], perfumed [1]

7000 קָטַר qāṭar, v. GK: 7788. [Qp] to be enclosed:– joined [1]

7001 קְטַר qᵉṭar (Aram.), n.m. GK: 10626. joint (of the hip); difficult problem, "to solve a difficult problem" means to explain an enigma, as a fig. extension of untying a tight, hard-to-undo knot:– doubts [2], joints [1]

7002 קִטֵּר qiṭṭēr, n.f. GK: 7789 [→ 6999]. incense, often as or accompanying an offering to God:– incense [1]

7003 קִטְרוֹן qiṭrôn, n.pr.loc. GK: 7790 [→ 6999]. Kitron, "*incense, [sacrificial] smoke*":– Kitron [1]

7004 קְטֹרֶת qᵉṭōret, n.f. GK: 7792 [→ 6999]. incense, smoke offering, its pleasant fragrance symbolic of God's acceptance:– incense [56], perfume [3], burnt incense [1]

7005 קַטָּת qaṭṭāt, n.pr.loc. GK: 7793. Kattath:– Kattath [1]

7006 קִא qî' or קָיָה qāyâ, v. GK: 7794 & 7796 [→ 6958]. [Q] to vomit; [H] to vomit out, spit out:– spue [1]

7007 קַיִט qayiṭ (Aram.), n.[m.]. GK: 10627 [cf. 7019]. summer:– summer [1]

7008 קִיטוֹר qîṭôr, n.m. GK: 7798 [→ 6999]. smoke:– smoke [3], vapour [1]

7009 קִים qîm, n.m. GK: 7799 [→ 6965]. foe, adversary:– substance [1]

7010 קְיָם qᵉyām (Aram.), n.[m.]. GK: 10628 [→ 6966?]. edict, statute, decree:– statute [2]

7011 קַיָּם qayyām (Aram.), a. GK: 10629 [→ 6966]. enduring:– stedfast [1], sure [1]

7012 קִימָה qîmâ, n.f. GK: 7800 [→ 6965]. standing up; rising up [1]

קִימוֹשׁ qîmôš. See 7057.

7013 קַיִן qayin, n.[m.]. GK: 7802. spearhead, spear:– spear [1]

7014 קַיִן qayin, n.pr.m. & g. & loc. GK: 7803 & 7804 & 7805 [→ 7017, 7018, 8423; cf. 7069]. Cain, "*metal worker; brought forth, acquired* [Ge 4:1]"; Kenite, "*metal workers*" Kain, "*place of metal workers [?]*":– Cain [17], Kenites [1], Kenite [1]

7015 קִינָה qînâ, n.f. GK: 7806 [→ 6969]. lament, mourning song, dirge:– lamentation [15], lamentations [3]

7016 קִינָה qînâ, n.pr.loc. GK: 7807. Kinah, "*lament, dirge*":– Kinah [1]

7017 קֵינִי qênî, a.g. GK: 7808 [→ 7014]. Kenite:– Kenites [7], Kenite [5]

7018 קֵינָן qênān, n.pr.m. GK: 7809 [→ 7014]. Kenan:– Cainan [5], Kenan [1]

7019 קַיִץ qayiṣ, n.m. GK: 7811 [→ 6972; cf. 7007]. summer; by extension, summer fruit, ripe fruit:– summer [11], summer fruits [6], summer fruit [1]

7020 קִיצוֹן qîṣôn, a. GK: 7812 [→ 7093]. end, outermost:– uttermost [3], outmost [1]

7021 קִיקָיוֹן qîqāyôn, n.m. GK: 7813. caster-oil vine; some sources: cucumber plant:– gourd [5]

7022 קִיקָלוֹן qîqālôn, n.[m.]. GK: 7814 [→ 7043]. disgrace:– shameful spuing [1]

7023 קִיר qîr, n.m. GK: 7815 [→ 7024; cf. 7176 (also used with compound proper names)]. wall (of a building or city); by extension, any surface of a construction: side, ceiling, surface; one who "urinates on a wall" is male:– wall [50], walls [16], sides [2], side [2], masons (+2796) [1], masons (+68+2796) [1], town [1], very heart (+3820) [1]

7024 קִיר qîr, n.pr.loc. GK: 7816 & 7817 [→ 7023]. Kir, "*walled enclosure*":– Kir [5]

7025 קִיר־חֶרֶשׂ qîr-ḥeres or קִיר חֲרֶשֶׂת qîr ḥᵃreset, n.pr.loc. GK: 7818 & 7819 [→ 7023+2789]. Kir Heres, Kir Hareseth, "*walled [city] of pottery fragments*":– Kir-heres [1], Kir-haraseth [1], Kir-hareseth [1], Kir-haresh [1]

7026 קֵרוֹס qêrôs, n.pr.m. GK: 7820. Keros:– Keros [2]

7027 קִישׁ qîš, n.pr.m. GK: 7821. Kish, "*bow, power*":– Kish [21]

7028 קִישׁוֹן qîšôn, n.pr.loc. GK: 7822. Kishon, "*cunning*":– Kishon [5], Kison [1]

7029 קִישִׁי qîšî, n.pr.m. GK: 7823 [cf. 6984]. Kishi, "*[poss.] gift; snarer*":– Kishi [1]

7030 קִיתְרֹס qîtᵉrōs or קַתְרֹס qatrôs (Aram.), n.[m.]. GK: 10630 & 10644. a stringed instrument, translated variously as "zither, lute, lyre," etc.:– harp [4]

7031 קַל qal, a. GK: 7824 [→ 7043]. fleet-footed, swift, speedy:– swift [9], swiftly [2], light [1], swifter [1]

7032 קָל qāl (Aram.), n.m. GK: 10631 [cf. 6963]. sound, voice:– sound [4], voice [1]

קֹל qōl. See 6963.

7033 קָלָא qālâ, v. GK: 7828 [→ 7039]. [Q] to burn; [Qp] to be roasted; [N] to have a burning sensation:– dried [1], loathsome [1], parched [1], roasted [1]

7034 קָלָה qālâ, v. GK: 7829 [→ 7036; cf. 7043]. [N] to lightly esteemed, to be a nobody, be degraded; [H] to dishonor, treat with contempt:– base [1], contemned [1], despised [1], lightly esteemed [1], setteth light [1], vile [1]

7035 קָלַה qālah, v.den. GK: 7827 [→ 6951]. var. of 6950: [N] to be gathered:–

7036 קָלוֹן qālôn, n.m. GK: 7830 [→ 7034]. shame, disgrace, dishonor:– shame [13], confusion [1], dishonour [1], ignominy [1], reproach [1]

7037 קַלַּחַת qallaḥat, n.f. GK: 7831. caldron, (cooking) pot:– caldron [2]

7038 קָלַט qālaṭ, v. GK: 7832 [→ 4733, 7042]. [Qp] to be stunted:– lacking in parts [1]

7039 קָלִי qālî, n.m. GK: 7833 [→ 7033]. roasted grain, parched grain:– parched [6]

7040 קַלַּי qallāy, n.pr.m. GK: 7834. Kallai, "swift":– Kallai [1]

7041 קֵלָיָה qēlāyâ, n.pr.m. GK: 7835. Kelaiah, "[perhaps] Yahweh has dishonored":– Kelaiah [1]

7042 קְלִיטָא qᵉlîṭā', n.pr.m. GK: 7836 [→ 7038]. Kelita:– Kelita [3]

7043 קָלַל qālal, v. GK: 7837 [→ 7022, 7031, 6963, 7044, 7045, 7052; cf. 7034]. [Q] to recede, grow smaller; to be vile, to disdain, despise; to be swift; [N] to be trivial, insignificant; to be swift; [P] to curse, blaspheme, revile; [Pu] to be accursed; [H] to lighten; to humble; to treat with contempt; [Htpal] to be shaken:– cursed [17], curse [17], curseth [6], swifter [5], light thing [4], make lighter [3], vile [3], abated [2], despised [2], ease somewhat [2], lighten [2], light [2], slightly (+5921) [2], accursed [1], bring into contempt [1], despise [1], easier (+4480) [1], easy [1], lightly afflicted [1], lightly esteemed [1], made bright [1], made vile [1], make somewhat lighter [1], moved lightly [1], revile [1], set light [1], swift [1], whet [1]

7044 קָלָל qālāl, a. GK: 7838 [→ 7043]. burnished, polished:– burnished [1], polished [1]

7045 קְלָלָה qᵉlālâ, n.f. GK: 7839 [→ 7043]. curse, condemnation:– curse [24], cursing [4], curses [1], accursed [1], cursings [1]

7046 קָלַס qālas, v. GK: 7840 [→ 7047, 7048]. [P] to scorn; [Ht] to make fun of:– mocked [1], mock [1], scoff [1], scornest [1]

7047 קֶלֶס qeles, n.[m.]. GK: 7841 [→ 7046]. derision, reproach:– derision [3]

7048 קַלָּסָה qallāsâ, n.f. GK: 7842 [→ 7046]. laughingstock, object of derision:– mocking [1]

7049 קָלַע qāla', v. GK: 7843 & 7844 [→ 4734, 7050]. [Q] to hurl a stone (from a sling); to carve; [P] to hurl a stone (from a sling):– carved [2], sling out [2], slang [1], sling [1]

7050 קֶלַע qela', n.[m.]. GK: 7845 & 7846 [→ 7049, 7051]. sling (a weapon); curtains:– hangings [15], sling [4], leaves [1], slingstones (+68) [1], slings [1]

7051 קַלָּע qallā', n.m. GK: 7847 [→ 7050]. slinger (one who uses a sling):– slingers [1]

7052 קְלֹקֵל qᵉlōqēl, a. GK: 7848 [→ 7043]. miserable (food), starvation (rations):– light [1]

7053 קִלְּשֹׁון qillᵉšôn, n.[m.]. GK: 7849. (sharp pointed, three-pronged) fork:– forks (+7969) [1]

7054 קָמָה qāmâ, n.f. GK: 7850 [→ 6965]. standing grain:– standing corn [5], corn [2], grown up [2], stalk [1]

7055 קְמוּאֵל qᵉmû'ēl, n.pr.m. GK: 7851 [→ 6965+410]. Kemuel, "God's [El's] mound":– Kemuel [3]

7056 קָמוֹן qāmôn, n.pr.loc. GK: 7852. Kamon:– Camon [1]

7057 קִמּוֹשׂ qimmôś, n.m. GK: 7853 [→ 7063]. thorns, nettles, briers (weeds of all kinds):– nettles [2]

7058 קֶמַח qemaḥ, n.[m.]. GK: 7854. flour:– meal [10], flour [4]

7059 קָמַט qāmaṭ, v. GK: 7855. [Q] to seize; [Pu] to be seized:– cut down [1], filled with wrinkles [1]

7060 קָמַל qāmal, v. GK: 7857. [Q] to wither:– hewn down [1], wither [1]

7061 קָמַץ qāmaṣ, v. GK: 7858 [→ 7062]. [Q] to take a handful:– take handful (+4393+7062) [2], take a handful [1]

7062 קֹמֶץ qōmeṣ, n.[m.]. GK: 7859 [→ 7061]. handful; (pl.) abundance:– take handful (+4393+7061) [2], handfuls [1], handful [1]

7063 קִמָּשׂוֹן qimmāśôn, n.m. GK: 7853 [→ 7057]. same as 7057: thorns, nettles, briers (weeds of all kinds):– thorns [1]

7064 קֵן qēn, n.m. GK: 7860 [→ 7077]. nest:– nest [12], rooms [1]

7065 קָנָא qānā', v.den. GK: 7861 [→ 7067, 7068, 7072]. [P] (of negative attitude) to be jealous, be envious, (of positive attitude) to be zealous:– jealous [8], envied [5], envious [4], very jealous (+7065) [4], envy [3], moved to jealousy [2], provoked to jealousy [2], enviest [1], move to jealousy [1], zealous (+7068) [1], zealous [1], zeal [1]

7066 קְנָא qᵉnā' (Aram.), v. GK: 10632 [cf. 7069]. [P] to buy:– buy [1]

7067 קַנָּא qannā', a. GK: 7862 [→ 7072; cf. 7065]. jealous; an adjective or title used exclusively of God, focusing on his desire for exclusive relationships:– jealous [6]

7068 קִנְאָה qin'â, n.f. GK: 7863 [→ 7065]. jealousy, envy, zeal:– jealousy [24], zeal [9], envy [7], envied [1], jealousies [1], zealous (+7065) [1]

7069 קָנָה qānâ, v. GK: 7864 & 7865 [→ 511, 4735, 4736, 4737, 7075; cf. 7014, cf. 7066]. [Q] to buy, acquire, get; to create, bring forth; (as a title of God) Creator; [N] to be bought:– bought [21], buy [21], get [9], purchased [5], buyer [3], getteth [3], got [3], possessed [3], buyest [2], possessor [2], surely buy (+7069) [2], verily buy (+7069) [2], attain [1], buy (+7075) [1], gotten [1], owner [1], possessors [1], provoketh to jealousy [1], recover [1], redeemed [1], taught [1]

7070 קָנֶה qāneh, n.m. GK: 7866 [→ 7071]. branch, rod; (calamus) reed, stalk, shaft, cane; by extension: a measure of length, variously reckoned:– reed [22], branches [19], reeds [6], branch [5], calamus [3], stalk [2], balance [1], bone [1], cane [1], spearmen [1], sweet cane [1]

7071 קָנָה qānâ, n.pr.loc. GK: 7867 [→ 7070]. Kanah, "reed":– Kanah [3]

7072 קַנּוֹ qannô', a. GK: 7868 [→ 7067; cf. 7065]. jealous:– jealous [2]

7073 קְנַז qᵉnaz, n.pr.m. GK: 7869 [→ 7074]. Kenaz, "hunting":– Kenaz [11]

7074 קְנִזִּי qᵉnizzî, a.g. GK: 7870 [→ 7073]. Kenizzite:– Kenezite [3], Kenizzites [1]

7075 קִנְיָן qinyān, n.[m.]. GK: 7871 [→ 7069]. goods, property, possessions:– substance [4], getting [2], goods [2], buy (+7069) [1], riches [1]

7076 קִנָּמוֹן qinnāmôn, n.m. GK: 7872. cinnamon (a spice from the far east):– cinnamon [3]

7077 קָנַן qānan, v.den. GK: 7873 [→ 7064]. [P] to make a nest; [Pu] to be nestled, nested:– make nests [1], make nests [1], make nest [1], makest nest [1], maketh nest [1]

7078 קֶנֶץ qeneṣ, n.[m.]. GK: 7874 [→ 7093]. end, an extension of a snare or net that captures or restrains (not found in the OT):– end [1]

7079 קְנָת qᵉnāt, n.pr.loc. GK: 7875. Kenath, "possession":– Kenath [2]

7080 קָסַם qāsam, v.den. GK: 7876 [→ 4738, 7081]. [Q] to practice divination, be a soothsayer, seek an omen:– diviners [7], divine [6], divination [1], divineth [1], prudent [1], soothsayer [1], use divination (+7081) [1], used divination (+7081) [1], useth divination (+7081) [1]

7081 קֶסֶם qesem, n.[m.]. GK: 7877 [→ 7080]. divination: pagan practice of determining the future by examining the position of stars, communication with the dead or with spirits, examining animal organs, or casting lots:– divination [4], divinations [1], divine sentence [1], rewards of divination [1], use divination (+7080) [1], used divination (+7080) [1], useth divination (+7080) [1], witchcraft [1]

7082 קָסַס qāsas, v. GK: 7878 [cf. 7193]. [Pol] to strip off:– cut off [1]

7083 קֶסֶת qeset, n.[f.]. GK: 7879. writing kit, writing-case:– inkhorn [3]

7084 קְעִילָה qᵉ'îlâ, n.pr.loc. GK: 7881. Keilah:– Keilah [18]

7085 קַעֲקַע qa'ăqa', n.[m.]. GK: 7882. tattoo:– marks [1]

7086 קְעָרָה qᵉ'ārâ, n.f. GK: 7883 [→ 8258]. plate, dish:– charger [13], dishes [3], chargers [1]

קוֹף qôp. See 6971.

7087 קָפָא qāpā', v. GK: 7884. [Q, N] to congeal, thicken; [H] to curdle:– congealed [1], cruddled [1], dark [1], settled [1]

7088 קָפַד qāpad, v. GK: 7886 [→ 7090, 7089; cf. 7091]. [P] to roll up:– cut off [1]

7089 קְפָדָה qᵉpādâ, n.[f.]. GK: 7888 [→ 7088]. terror, anguish:– destruction [1]

7090 קִפֹּד qippōd, n.[m.]. GK: 7887 [→ 7088]. screech owl; some sources: hedgehog:– bittern [3]

7091 קִפּוֹז qippôz, n.m. GK: 7889 [cf. 7088, 7092]. owl; some sources: tree snake:– great owl [1]

7092 קָפַץ qāpaṣ, v. GK: 7890 [cf. 7091]. [Q] to draw together, shut; [N] to be gathered up; [P] to bound, leap:– shut [2], shut up [1], skipping [1], stoppeth [1], stop [1], taken out of the way [1]

7093 קֵץ qēṣ, n.m. GK: 7891 [→ 7020; cf. 7078, 7112]. end, limit, boundary:– end [51], after (+4480) [6], after [2], after (+3807.1) [1], after that [1] (1961+4480) [1], borders [1], border [1], have an end (+369) [1], infinite (+369) [1], process [1], utmost border [1]

קוֹץ qōṣ. See 6975.

7094 קָצַב qāṣab, v. GK: 7892 [→ 7095]. [Q] to cut off; [Qp] to be shorn, be cut off:– cut down [1], even shorn [1]

7095 קֶצֶב qeṣeb, n.m. GK: 7893 [→ 7094]. shape, foundation:– size [2], bottoms [1]

7096 קָצָה qāṣâ, v. GK: 7894 [→ 7097, 7098, 7099, 7117; cf. 7112]. [P] to cut off, reduce; [H] to scrape off:– cut short [1], cutteth off [1], cutting off [1], scrape off [1], scraped [1]

7097 קָצֶה qāṣeh or קֵצֶה qēṣeh, n.[m.]. GK: 7895 & 7897 [→ 7096]. end, boundary, limit, outskirts, edge:– end [50], edge [6], ends [6], uttermost part [6], outside [3], border [2], otherˢ [2], utmost part [2], after (+4480) [1], borders [1], brim [1], brink [1], coasts [1], every quarter [1], frontiers [1], infinite (+369) [1], otherˢ (+8064) [1], outmost coast (+4480) [1], outmost parts [1], quarter [1], shore [1], side [1], some of (+4480) [1], utmost [1], uttermost (+4480) [1], uttermost part (+4480) [1], uttermost parts [1], uttermost [1]

7098 קָצָה qāṣâ, n.f. & m.[pl.]. GK: 7896 [→ 7096]. end, fringe, edge:– ends [18], end [4], lowest [3], edges [2], selvedge [2], uttermost part [2], coasts [1], corners [1], parts [1], quarters [1]

7099 קָצוּ qāṣû, n.[m.]. GK: 7898 [→ 7096]. ends, borders (of the earth):– ends [4], uttermost parts [1]

7100 קֶצַח qeṣaḥ, n.m. GK: 7902. caraway, cummin:– fitches [3]

7101 קָצִין qāṣîn, n.m. GK: 7903 [→ 6278]. commander, ruler, leader:– captain [2], princes [2], prince [2], rulers [2], ruler [1], captains [1], guide [1]

7102 קְצִיעָה qᵉṣî'â, n.f. GK: 7904 [→ 7103; cf. 7106]. cassia:– cassia [1]

7103 קְצִיעָה qᵉṣî'â, n.pr.f. GK: 7905 [→ 7102; cf. 7106]. Keziah, "cassia [cinnamon]":– Kezia [1]

7104 קְצִיץ qᵉṣîṣ, n.pr.loc. GK: 7906 & 6681 [→ 6009; cf. 7093]. Keziz:– Keziz [1]

7105 קָצִיר qāṣîr, n.m. GK: 7907 & 7908 [→ 7114]. harvest, time of reaping; branch, bough, twig, shoot:– harvest [46], boughs [3], branch [2], cuttest down harvest (+7114) [1], harvest time [1], harvestman [1]

7106 קָצַע qāṣa', v. GK: 7909 & 7910 [→ 4741, 4742, 7102, 7103]. [H] to scrape off; [Pu, Ho] to be made with corners:– cause to be scraped [1], corners [1]

7107 קָצַף qāṣap, v. GK: 7911 [→ 7110; cf. 7108]. [Q] to be angry; [H] to provoke to anger; [Ht] to be enraged:– wroth [22], provoked to wrath [3], angry [2], sore displeased (+7110) [2], angered [1], displeased [1], fret [1], provokedst to wrath [1], wrath [1]

7108 קְצַף qᵉṣap (Aram.), v. GK: 10633 [→ 7109; cf. 7107]. [P] to become furious:– furious [1]

7109 קְצַף qᵉṣap (Aram.), n.[m.]. GK: 10634 [→ 7108; cf. 7110]. wrath, fury:– wrath [1]

7110 קֶצֶף *qeṣep*, n.m. GK: 7912 & 7913 [→ 7107, 7111; cf. 7109]. wrath, anger, fury; twig (snapped off):– wrath [23], indignation [3], sore displeased (+7107) [2], foam [1]

7111 קְצָפָה *qᵉṣāpâ*, n.f. GK: 7914 [→ 7110]. stump, splintering:– barked [1]

7112 קָצַץ *qāṣaṣ*, v. GK: 7915 & 7899 [cf. 7093, 7096]. [Q] to cut off, cut off, take away; [P] to be cut off, maimed:– cut off [6], in the utmost [2], cut in pieces [2], cut asunder [1], cutteth in sunder [1], cut [1]

7113 קְצַץ *qᵉṣaṣ* (Aram.), v. GK: 10635 [cf. 7112]. [Pa] to trim off, cut off:– cut off [1]

7114 קָצַר *qāṣar*, v. GK: 7917 & 7918 & 7900 [→ 7105, 7115, 7116]. [Q] to reap, harvest, gather; to be short; (by extension) to be impatient, angry; [P] to cut short; [H] to shorten, cut short:– reap [18], reapers [7], shortened [4], shortened at all (+7114) [2], shorter [2], cuttest down harvest (+7105) [1], discouraged [1], grieved [1], harvestman [1], lothed [1], mower [1], reaper [1], reapest [1], reapeth [1], reaping [1], straitened [1], troubled [1], vexed [1], waxed short [1], wholly reap (3615+3807.1+7114) [1]

7115 קֹצֶר *qōṣer*, n.[m.]. GK: 7919 [→ 7114]. discouragement, despondency, an extension of shortness or lack (of spirit):– anguish [1]

7116 קָצֵר *qāṣēr*, a. GK: 7920 [→ 7114]. shortened: quick-tempered, impatient:– small [2], few [1], hasty [1], soon [1]

7117 קְצָת *qᵉṣāt*, n.f. GK: 7921 [→ 7096; cf. 7118]. end, extremity:– end [3], part (+4480) [1], some (+4480) [1]

7118 קְצָת *qᵉṣāt* (Aram.), n.f. GK: 10636 [cf. 7117]. part; the end:– end [2], partly (+4481) [1]

7119 קַר *qar*, a. GK: 7922 [→ 6979]. cool, cold (water); cool-headed, even-tempered (of one's spirit):– cold [2]

קִר *qir*. See 7023.

7120 קֹר *qōr*, n.[m.]. GK: 7923 [→ 6979]. cold:– cold [1]

7121 קָרָא *qārā'*, v. GK: 7924 [→ 4744, 7124, 6981, 7148, 7150; cf. 7123]. [Q] to call, summon, announce, proclaim; [Qp] to be invited as a guest, be appointed; [N] to be called, be summoned; [Pu] to be called: "to call on the name of the LORD" means to proclaim or praise the excellence of Yahweh, to worship Yahweh, or to summon Yahweh by name for help:– called [366], call [115], cried [51], cry [35], read [35], proclaim [20], call upon [14], calleth [13], proclaimed [11], called upon [10], named [9], crieth [4], guests [4], called for [3], calledst [3], calling [3], cried unto [3], gave [3], invited [3], renowned [3], bidden [2], criest [2], cry unto [2], named (+8034) [2], preach [2], proclaiming [2], reading [2], bewrayeth [1], call for [1], call on [1], called forth [1], crying [1], famous (+8034) [1], famous [1], made proclamation [1], mentioned (+871.1) [1], proclaim (+871.1) [1], proclaimed (+871.1) [1], proclaimeth [1], pronounced [1], publish [1], readeth [1], said [1]

7122 קָרָא *qārā'*, v. GK: 7925 [→ 7125; cf. 7136]. [Q] to meet, encounter, happen; [N] to have met, have happened, [H] to cause to happen:– befall [4], met [2], befallen [1], came upon [1], caused to come upon [1], chance to be [1], come unto [1], come upon [1], falleth out [1], happened by chance (+7136) [1], happened to be [1], happened unto [1]

7123 קְרָא *qᵉrā'* (Aram.), v. GK: 10637 [cf. 7121]. [P] to call, proclaim, read out loud; [Pp, Peil] to be read out loud; [Htpe] to be called, be summoned:– read [7], cried [3], called [1]

7124 קֹרֵא *qōrē'*, n.m. GK: 7926 [→ 6981; cf. 7121]. partridge:– partridge [2]

7125 קִרְאָה *qir'â*, v.inf. GK: 7925 [→ 7122]. inf. of 7122: meeting, encounter, happening:– meet [69], against [39], met [4], brought (+857) [1], come against [1], come [1], coming [1], help [1], in the way (+3807.1) [1], meet with [1], meeting [1], seek [1]

7126 קָרַב *qārab*, v. GK: 7928 [→ 6137, 7131, 7128, 7132, 7133, 7138; cf. 7127]. [Q] to come near, approach; [N] to present oneself, be brought near; [P] to bring near, approach; [H] to bring near, offer, present:– offer [79], bring [32], brought [24], come near [20], offered [16], came near [11], approach [9], offereth [9], came [6], come nigh [5], at hand [4], bring near [4], come [4], draw nigh [4], drew near [4], drew nigh [4], draw near [3], came nigh [2], cause to come near [2], cause to draw near [2], caused to come near [2], comest nigh [2], draweth near [2], go near [2], presented [2], went [2], approached [1], brought forth [1], brought near [1], came together [1], camest [1], cause to be brought [1], caused to draw near [1], causest to approach [1], draweth near the time [1], drewest near [1], goeth [1], go [1], joined [1], lay [1], lay [1], went near [1]

7127 קְרֵב *qᵉrēb* (Aram.), v. GK: 10638 [→ 7129; cf. 7126]. [P] to come near, approach; [Pa] to offer (a sacrifice); [H] to bring near, offer (a sacrifice):– came near [4], brought near [1], came [1], offered [1], offer [1], sacrifices [1]

7128 קְרָב *qᵉrāb*, n.[m.]. GK: 7930 [→ 6137; cf. 7126; cf. 7129]. war, battle:– battle [5], war [4]

7129 קְרָב *qᵉrāb* (Aram.), n.[m.]. GK: 10639 [→ 7127; cf. 7128]. war:– war [1]

7130 קֶרֶב *qereb*, n.[m.]. GK: 7931. inner parts; by extension: heart or mind as the seat of thought and emotion; interior, midst; (pp.) among, in the midst of:– midst [73], among (+871.1) [41], among [26], within (+871.1) [25], inwards [19], in (+871.1) [8], amongst (+871.1) [7], through (+871.1) [5], inward [3], out of (+4480) [3], amongst [2], into (+5921) [2], inward parts [2], before (+871.1) [1], bowels [1], charge [1], eaten (+413+935) [1], eaten up (+413+935) [1], heart [1], inwardly (+871.1) [1], purtenance [1], therein (+871.1) [1], therein (+871.1+1886.3) [1], within [1]

7131 קָרֵב *qārēb*, a.v. GK: 7929 [→ 7126]. approaching, coming near:– cometh nigh [4], come near [2], cometh near (+7131) [2], drew near [2], approach [1], came [1]

קָרֹב *qārōb*. See 7138.

7132 קִרְבָה *qirbâ*, n.f. GK: 7932 [→ 7126]. nearness, approach:– approaching to [1], draw near [1]

7133 קָרְבָּן *qorbān* or קֻרְבָּן *qurbān*, n.m. GK: 7933 & 7934 [→ 7126]. gift, offering, sacrifice; contribution, supply (of wood):– offering [65], oblation [11], oblations [1], offered [1], offering made by fire (+801) [1], offerings [1], sacrifice [1]

7134 קַרְדֹּם *qardōm*, n.[m.]. GK: 7935. ax; some sources: adze:– axes [3], axe [2]

7135 קָרָה *qārâ*, n.f. GK: 7938 [→ 6979]. cold:– cold [5]

7136 קָרָה *qārâ*, v. GK: 7936 [→ 4745, 7137, 7147; cf. 7122]. [Q] to happen, meet, encounter; [N] to meet with, have happen; [P] to make beams, build beams; [H] to give success, to select oneself:– met [4], happeneth [3], befall [2], happen [2], laid beams [2], appoint [1], befallen [1], befell [1], brought [1], come to pass [1], come [1], floor [1], happened [1], happened by chance (+7122) [1], layeth beams [1], light on [1], make beams [1], meet [1], send good speed (+6440+3807.1) [1]

7137 קָרֶה *qāreh*, n.[m.]. GK: 7937 [→ 7136]. emission (at night):– chanceth [1]

קֹרָא *qōrâ*. See 6982.

7138 קָרֹב *qārōb*, a. GK: 7940 [→ 7126]. near, close:– near [33], nigh [12], next [5], at hand [4], neighbours [3], approach [2], near of kin [2], neighbour [2], allied [1], come nigh [1], hand [1], kinsfolk [1], kinsmen [1], kin [1], near (+871.1) [1], near unto [1], nearer [1], newly (+4480) [1], nigh at hand [1], ready [1], short (+4480) [1], shortly (+4480) [1], short [1]

7139 קָרַח *qāraḥ*, v. GK: 7942 [→ 7142, 7143, 7141, 7144, 7145, 7146]. [Q] to shave, make bald; [N] to shave oneself, make oneself bald; [H] to shave another, make bald; [Ho] to be rubbed bare, be make bald:– make bald [2], make utterly bald (+7139) [2], made bald [1], make baldness (+7144) [1]

7140 קֶרַח *qeraḥ*, n.m. GK: 7943. ice, frost, hail:– frost [3], ice [3], crystal [1]

7141 קֹרַח *qōraḥ*, n.pr.m. GK: 7946 [→ 7145; cf. 7139]. Korah, "shaven, bald":– Korah [37]

7142 קֵרֵחַ *qērēaḥ*, a. GK: 7944 [→ 7139]. bald, bald-headed:– bald head [2], bald [1]

7143 קָרֵחַ *qārēaḥ*, n.pr.m. GK: 7945 [→ 7139]. Kareah, "bald head":– Kareah [13], Careah [1]

7144 קָרְחָה *qorḥâ*, n.f. GK: 7947 [→ 7139]. baldness, shaving the head:– baldness [8], bald [1], make baldness (+7139) [1]

7145 קָרְחִי *qorḥî*, a.g. GK: 7948 [→ 7141; cf. 7139]. Korahite, "of Korah":– Korhites [4], Korahites [2], Korahite [1], Kore [1]

7146 קָרַחַת *qāraḥat*, n.f. GK: 7949 [→ 7139]. bald spot (not the forehead area); bare spot (of articles):– bald head [3], bare within [1]

7147 קְרִי *qᵉrî*, n.[m.]. GK: 7950 [→ 7136]. hostile encounter, hostility:– contrary [7]

7148 קָרִיא *qārî'*, a. GK: 7951 [→ 7121]. summoned, called:– famous [2]

7149 קִרְיָה *qiryâ* (Aram.), n.f. GK: 10640 [cf. 7151]. city, town:– city [8], cities [1]

7150 קְרִיאָה *qᵉrî'â*, n.f. GK: 7952 [→ 7121]. message, appeal:– preaching [1]

7151 קִרְיָה *qiryâ* or קִרְיַת *qiryat*, n.f. [& pr.] GK: 7953 & 7956 [→ 7176; cf. 7149]. city, town; as n.pr. Kiriath:– city [32]

7152 קְרִיּוֹת *qᵉriyyôt*, n.pr.loc. GK: 7954 [→ 7176]. Kerioth, "town":– Kerioth [4]

7153 קִרְיַת אַרְבַּע *qiryat 'arba'* or קִרְיַת הָאַרְבַּע *qiryat hā'arba'*, n.pr.loc. GK: 7957 & 7959 [→ 7176+702]. Kiriath Arba, "city of four":– Kirjath-arba [9]

7154 קִרְיַת־בַּעַל *qiryat-ba'al*, n.pr.loc. GK: 7958 [→ 7176+1167]. Kiriath Baal:– Kirjath-baal [2]

7155 קִרְיַת חֻצוֹת *qiryat ḥuṣôt*, n.pr.loc. GK: 7960 [→ 7176]. Kiriath Huzoth, "city of Huzoth [outside spaces]":– Kirjath-huzoth [1]

7156 קִרְיָתַיִם *qiryātayim*, n.pr.loc. GK: 7964 [→ 7176]. Kiriathaim, "two cities":– Kiriathaim [3], Kirjathaim [3]

7157 קִרְיַת יְעָרִים *qiryat yᵉ'ārîm*, n.pr.loc. GK: 7961 [→ 7176+3297]. Kiriath Jearim, "city of timberlands":– Kirjath-jearim [18], Kirjath-arim [1], Kirjath [1]

7158 קִרְיַת־סַנָּה *qiryat-sannâ* or קִרְיַת־סֵפֶר *qiryat-sēper*, n.pr.loc. GK: 7962 & 7963 [→ 7176+5612]. Kiriath Sannah, "city of Sannah"; Kiriath Sepher, "city of a scribe or book":– Kirjath-sepher [4], Kirjath-sannah [1]

7159 קָרַם *qāram*, v. GK: 7965. [Q] to cover with, spread; [N] to be spread over:– cover with [1], covered [1]

7160 קָרַן *qāran*, v.den. GK: 7966 [→ 7161]. [Q] to be radiant; [H] to be with horns:– shone [1], horns [1]

7161 קֶרֶן *qeren*, n.f. or קְרָנַיִם *qᵉrānayim*, n.pr.loc. GK: 7967 & 7969 → 6255, 7160, 7163; cf. 7162]. horn, (pair) of horns; something made of horns: wind instrument, container; horn often symbolizes strength and status, as in "horn of salvation"; as n.pr. Karnaim, "horns":– horns [43], horn [28], two horns [4], hill [1]

7162 קֶרֶן *qeren* (Aram.), n.f. GK: 10641 [cf. 7161]. horn (of an animal), also referring to a musical instrument:– horns [5], horn [5], cornet [4]

7163 קֶרֶן הַפּוּךְ *qeren happûk*, n.pr.f. GK: 7968 [→ 7161]. Keren-Happuch, "horn of [cosmetic] eye shadow; i.e., cosmetic case":– Keren-happuch [1]

7164 קָרַס *qāras*, v. GK: 7970 [→ 7165, 7166]. [Q] to stoop low, bend down:– stoopeth [1], stoop [1]

7165 קֶרֶס *qeres*, n.[m.]. GK: 7971 [→ 7164]. clasp, hook (of curtains):– taches [10]

קֶרֹס *qērōs*. See 7026.

7166 קַרְסֹל *qarsōl*, n.[f.]. GK: 7972 [→ 7164]. (dual) ankles:– feet [2]

7167 קָרַע *qāra'*, v. GK: 7973 [→ 7168]. [Q] to tear, rend, rip; [Qp] to be torn; [N] to be torn to pieces, be split apart:– rent [46], rend [5], tear [3], surely rend (+7167) [2], cutteth out [1], cut [1], rend away [1], rent away [1], rent in pieces (+7168) [1], rentest [1], tare [1]

7168 קְרָעִים *qᵉrā'îm*, n.m.[pl.]. GK: 7974 [→ 7167]. torn pieces (of a garment), rags:– pieces [2], rags [1], rent in pieces (+7167) [1]

7169 קָרַץ *qāraṣ*, v. GK: 7975 [→ 7171; cf. 7170]. [Q] to maliciously wink, purse (the lips); [Pu] to be shaped:– winketh [2], formed [1], moving [1], wink [1]

7170 קְרַץ *qᵉraṣ* (Aram.), n.[m.]. GK: 10642. piece, "to eat pieces" is slander, denouncement:– accused (+399) [2]

7171 קֶרֶץ *qereṣ*, n.m. GK: 7976 [→ 7169]. gadfly; some sources: mosquito:– destruction [1]

7172 קַרְקַע *qarqa'*, n.[m.]. GK: 7977 [→ 7173, 7174]. floor:– floor [6], bottom [1], otherˢ [1]

7173 קַרְקַע *qarqa'*, n.pr.loc. GK: 7978 [→ 7172]. Karka, "floor, ground":– Karkaa [1]

7174 קַרְקֹר *qarqōr*, n.pr.loc. GK: 7980 [→ 7172]. Karkor:– Karkor [1]

7175 קֶרֶשׁ *qereš*, n.m. GK: 7983. frame:– boards [33], board [17], benches [1]

7176 קֶרֶת *qeret*, n.f. GK: 7984 [→ 7151, 7152, 7156, 7177, 7178; cf. 7023 (also used with compound proper names)]. city, town:– city [5]

7177 קַרְתָּה *qartâ*, n.pr.loc. GK: 7985 [→ 7176]. Kartah, "city":– Kartah [1]

7178 קַרְתָּן *qartān*, n.pr.loc. GK: 7986 [→ 7176]. Kartan:– Kartan [1]

7179 קַשׁ *qaš*, n.m. GK: 7990 [→ 7197]. stubble, chaff, straw:– stubble [15], gather stubble (+7197) [1]

7180 קִשֻּׁאָה *qiššu'â*, n.f. GK: 7991 [→ 4750]. cucumber:– cucumbers [1]

7181 קָשַׁב *qāšab*, v. GK: 7992 [→ 7182, 7183]. [Q] to listen; [H] to pay attention, give heed, listen:– hearken [21], attend [7], hearkened [5], give heed [2], attend to [1], attend unto [1], attended [1], cause to be heard [1], cause to hear [1], giveth heed [1], hearkened diligently (+7182) [1], incline [1], mark well [1], marked [1], regarded [1]

7182 קֶשֶׁב *qešeb*, n.m. GK: 7993 [→ 7181]. paying attention, responding:– hearing [1], hearkened diligently (+7181) [1], heed [1], regarded [1]

7183 קַשָּׁב or קַשֻּׁב *qaššāb* or *qaššub*, a. GK: 7994 & 7995 [→ 7181]. attentive:– attentive [3], attent [2]

7184 קַשְׂוָה *qaśwâ*, n.f. GK: 7987. pitcher, jar:– covers [3], cups [1]

7185 קָשָׁה *qāšâ*, v. GK: 7996 [→ 7186, 7190]. [Q] to be hard, harsh, cruel; [N] to be distressed; [P] to have great difficulty (in labor); [H] to make stiff, harden, be difficult:– hardened [8], hard [4], hardeneth [1], harden [2], made grievous [2], stiffnecked (+6203) [2], cruel [1], fiercer [1], hard thing [1], hardly bestead [1], hardly [1], made stiff [1], sore [1], stiffened [1]

7186 קָשֶׁה *qāšeh*, a. GK: 7997 [→ 7185]. hard, harsh, difficult, fierce; stubborn, stiff(-necked), obstinate:– hard [6], stiffnecked (+6203) [6], roughly [3], cruel [3], grievous [3], sore [2], churlish [1], hardhearted (+3820) [1], heavy [1], impudent (+6440) [1], in trouble (+3117) [1], obstinate [1], prevailed [1], rough [1], sorrowful [1], stiff [1], stubborn [1]

7187 קְשֹׁט *qᵉšōt* (Aram.), n.[m.]. GK: 10643 [cf. 7189]. truth; (as adv.) surely, truly, rightly:– of a truth (+4481) [1], truth [1]

7188 קָשַׁח *qāšaḥ*, v. GK: 7998. [H] to harden:– hardened against [1], hardened [1]

7189 קֹשְׁט or קֹשֶׁט *qōšṭ* or *qōšeṭ*, n.m. GK: 7999 & 8000 [cf. 7198; cf. 7187]. truth; bow (weapon):– certainty [1], truth [1]

קֹשֹׁט *qōšōṭ*. See 7187.

7190 קְשִׁי *qᵉšî*, n.[m.]. GK: 8001 [→ 7185]. stubbornness:– stubbornness [1]

7191 קִשְׁיוֹן *qišyôn*, n.pr.loc. GK: 8002. Kishion:– Kishion [1], Kishon [1]

7192 קְשִׂיטָה *qᵉśîṭâ*, n.f. GK: 7988. piece of silver (unknown unit of weight or value):– piece of money [1], pieces of money [1], pieces of silver [1]

7193 קַשְׂקֶשֶׂת *qaśqeśet*, n.f. GK: 7989 [cf. 7082]. scales (as on skin of marine creatures); scale armor:– scales [7], mail [1]

7194 קָשַׁר *qāšar*, v. GK: 8003 [→ 7195, 7196]. [Q] to tie, bind; to plot, conspire; [Qp] to be bound up; be strong; [N] to be joined with; [P] to bind; [Pu] to be strong; [Ht] to conspire together:– conspired [18], bind [11], made a conspiracy (+7195) [4], bound [3], stronger [2], bound up [1], conspiracy made (+7195) [1], conspirators [1], joined together [1], knit [1], wrought [1]

7195 קֶשֶׁר *qešer*, n.m. GK: 8004 [→ 7194]. conspiracy, treason:– treason [5], conspiracy [4], made a conspiracy (+7194) [4], confederacy [1], conspiracy made (+7194) [1]

→**7196** קִשֻּׁרִים *qiššurîm*, n.[m.]pl. GK: 8005 [→ 7194]. sashes, wedding ornaments:– attire [1], headbands [1]

7197 קָשַׁשׁ *qāšaš*, v.den. GK: 8006 & 8007 [→ 7179]. [Q] to gather together; [Pol] to gather; [Htpol] to gather together:– gathering [3], gather together [2], gather stubble (+7179) [1], gathered [1], gather [1]

7198 קֶשֶׁת *qešet*, n.f. [& m.?]. GK: 8008 [→ 7199; cf. 7189]. bow (weapon); by extension, something bow shaped: rainbow:– bow [55], bows [13], archers [2], archers (+1869) [1], archers (+376+3384+871.1+1886.1) [1], archers (+4175+871.1+1886.1) [1], arrow (+1121) [1], bowmen (+7411) [1], bowshot (+2909) [1]

7199 קַשָּׁת *qaššāt*, n.m. GK: 8009 [→ 7198]. archer:– archer (+7235) [1]

7200 רָאָה *rā'â*, v. GK: 8011 [→ 7204, 4758, 4759, 7201?, 7202, 7203, 7207, 7209, 7210, 7212 (also used with compound proper names)]. [Q] to see, look, view; to realize, know, consider; [Qp] to be selected; [N] to become visible, appear, show oneself; [Pu] to be seen; [H] to cause to see, show; [Ho] to be shown; [Ht] to look at each other, meet with; a

general word for visual perception; note the many contextual translations in the KJV:– see [349], saw [305], seen [161], behold [57], looked [53], look [50], appeared [39], shewed [37], seest [27], seeth [27], shew [27], appear [24], beheld [23], consider [15], seeing [11], seer [10], sawest [6], spied [5], considered [4], looketh [4], perceived [4], appeareth [3], enjoy [3], lo [3], respect [3], sheweth [3], beholdest [3], considereth [2], foreseeth [2], indeed look (+7200) [2], look out [2], looked on [2], looked upon [2], provided [2], provide [2], regarded [2], saw certainly (+7200) [2], see indeed (+7200) [2], surely seen (+7200) [2], take heed [2], advise [1], approveth [1], beholding [1], caused to see [1], discern [1], espied [1], gaze [1], had experience [1], hath respect [1], in presence (+6440) [1], joyfully [1], make enjoy [1], mark [1], meet [1], near [1], perceive [1], presented [1], regardeth [1], regard [1], respecteth [1], seemeth [1], seer's [1], shewedst [1], sight [1], spy [1], stare [1], thinketh [1], view [1], visions [1]

7201 רָאָה *rā'â*, n.f. GK: 8012 [→ 7200?]. red kite:– glede [1]

7202 רָאֶה *rā'eh*, a. GK: 8013 [→ 7200]. seeing:–

7203 רֹאֶה *rō'eh*, n.[m.]. GK: 8014 & 8015 [→ 7200]. seer; vision:– seers [1], vision [1]

7204 הָרֹאֶה or רֹאֶה *hārō'eh* or *rō'eh*, n.pr.m. GK: 2218 [→ 7200]. Haroeh, "*the seer*":– Haroeh [1]

7205 רְאוּבֵן *rᵉ'ûbēn*, n.pr.m. GK: 8017 [→ 7206]. Reuben, "*see, a son! [Ge 29:32]; substitute a son*":– Reuben [72]

7206 רְאוּבֵנִי *rᵉ'ûbēnî*, a.g. GK: 8018 [→ 7205]. Reubenite, of Reuben, "*of Reuben*":– Reubenites [16], Reubenite [1], Reuben [1]

7207 רַאֲוָה *ra'ᵃwâ*, n.f. GK: 8019 [→ 7200]. spectacle, sight:– beholding [1]

7208 רְאוּמָה *rᵉ'ûmâ*, n.pr.f. GK: 8020 [→ 7355? *or* 7214?]. Reumah:– Reumah [1]

7209 רְאִי *rᵉ'î*, n.m. GK: 8023 [→ 7200]. mirror:– looking glass [1]

7210 רֳאִי *rᵒ'î*, n.[m.]. GK: 8024 [→ 7200; cf. 7299]. appearance, spectacle:– seen [2], gazing-stock [1], look to [1], seest [1], seeth [1]

7211 רְאָיָה *rᵉ'āyâ*, n.pr.m. GK: 8025 [→ 7200+3068]. Reaiah, "*Yahweh has seen*":– Reaiah [3], Reaia [1]

7212 רְאִית *rᵉ'ît*, n.f. GK: 8026 [→ 7200]. look, sight:–

7213 רָאַם *rā'am*, v. GK: 8027 [→ 7216; cf. 7311]. [Q] to rise up high:– lifted up [1]

7214 רְאֵם *rᵉ'ēm*, n.m. GK: 8028 [→ 7208?]. wild oxen:– unicorn [6], unicorns [3]

7215 רָאמָה *rā'mâ*, n.[f.pl.]. GK: 8029. coral:– coral [2]

7216 רָאמוֹת *rā'môt*, n.pr.loc. GK: 8030 [→ 7213; cf. 7311]. Ramoth, "*height*":– Ramoth [4]

7217 רֵאשׁ *rē'š* (Aram.), n.m. GK: 10646 [cf. 7218]. head (for functions of sight and thought as a crucial part of the body); fig., leader; or the very first part of an event, the beginning:– head [11], chief [1], heads [1], sum [1]

7218 רֹאשׁ *rō'š*, n.m. GK: 8031 [→ 7220, 7221, 7222, 7223, 7224, 7225, 7226; cf. 7217]. head (of the body); by extension: top (of an object); high in status or authority: leader, chief; source or origin: first, beginning; "to lift up the head" can mean to take a census, to behead, or to restore to a position:– head [263], chief [95], heads [85], top [67], beginning [12], sum [9], tops [8], companies [7], captains [6], first [6], company [5], principal [5], captain [4], chapiters [4], high [3], bands [2], beginnings [2], ends [2], rulers [2], beheaded (+5493) [1], chief place [1], chief things [1], chiefest [1], every [1], excellent [1], forefront [1], height [1], highest part [1], lead [1], of [1]

7219 רֹאשׁ *rō'š*, n.m. GK: 8032. poison; gall; bitterness:– gall [9], hemlock [1], poison [1], venom [1]

7220 רֹאשׁ *rō'š*, n.pr.m. & g. & loc. GK: 8033 & 8396 [→ 7218]. Rosh, "*head, leader*":– Rosh [1]

רֵאשׁ *rē'š*. See 7389.

7221 רִאשָׁה *ri'šâ*, n.f. GK: 8035 [→ 7218]. beginning, before:– beginnings [1]

7222 רֹאשָׁה *rō'šâ*, n.f. GK: 8036 [→ 7218]. uppermost, cap(stone):– headstone (+68) [1]

7223 רִאשׁוֹן *ri'šôn*, a. GK: 8037 [→ 7224; cf. 7218]. (of position) first, foremost; (of time) former, beginning, earlier:– first [128], former [32], beginning [4], old [3], foremost [3], before (+871.1+1886.1) [2], old time [2], aforetime (+871.1+1886.1) [1], ancestors [1], beforetime

(+871.1+1886.1) [1], before [1], eldest [1], first (+871.1+1886.1) [1], forefathers (+1) [1], past [1]

7224 רִאשֹׁנִי *ri'šōnî*, a. GK: 8038 [→ 7223; cf. 7218]. first:– first [1]

7225 רֵאשִׁית *rē'šît*, n.f. GK: 8040 [→ 7218]. what is first; beginning:– beginning [18], firstfruits [10], first [10], chief [8], chiefest [1], first time [1], firstfruits (+6529) [1], firstfruit [1], principal thing [1]

7226 רַאֲשֹׁת *ra'ᵃšōt*, n.m. GK: 8031 [→ 7218]. pl. of 7218: place of the head:–

7227 רַב *rab*, a. & n. GK: 8041 & 8042 [→ 7237, 7248, 7249, 7262; cf. 7231; cf. 7229, cf. 7261]. many, much; great, abundant, numerous; commander, chief officer, high official:– many [191], great [117], much [33], captain [24], long [10], moe [8], enough [7], multitude [6], mighty [5], greater [4], more [4], greatly [3], manifold [3], plenteous [3], suffice [3], too much [3], abundantly [2], abundant [2], exceedingly [2], increased [2], long enough [2], many a time [2], princes [2], aboundeth [1], abound [1], common [1], elder [1], full [1], great men [1], great multitude [1], great one [1], great store [1], in abundance [1], in multitude [1], master [1], multiply [1], officers [1], oftentimes (+6471) [1], populous [1], process of time (+3117+1886.1+1886.1) [1], shipmaster (+2259+1886.1) [1], sufficient [1], too many [1]

7228 רַב *rab*, n.m. GK: 8043 [→ 7232]. archer:– archers [2]

7229 רַב *rab* (Aram.), a. GK: 10647 [→ 7236, 7260; cf. 7227]. great, large, many, chief; this can refer to a large object (great, large), a large amount of objects (many, much), or high status (chief):– great [9], master [2], captain [1], chief [1], lord [1], very great [1]

רִב *rib*. See 7378.

7230 רֹב *rōb*, n.m. GK: 8044 [→ 7231]. greatness, abundance; multitude:– multitude [69], abundance [32], greatness [9], great [7], much [7], abundantly (+3807.1) [3], many [3], abundance (+3807.1) [2], long [2], plenty [2], abundantly [1], all [1], common [1], excellent [1], great number (+3807.1) [1], great things [1], greatly (+3807.1) [1], huge (+3807.1) [1], in abundance (+3807.1) [1], increased [1], most [1], much (+3807.1) [1], number [1], plentifully (+3807.1) [1], plenty (+3807.1) [1], very [1]

7231 רָבַב *rābab*, v. GK: 8045 [→ 3377, 3378, 3379, 3380, 4764, 7227, 7230, 7233, 7237, 7239, 7241, 7245; cf. 7235]. [Q] to abound, increase, be great; [Pu] to increase by tens of thousands:– many [6], increased [3], multiplied [3], manifold [1], moe [1], more [1], multiply [1], ten thousands [1]

7232 רָבַב *rābab*, v. GK: 8046 [→ 7228; cf. 7235]. [Q] to shoot (an arrow):– shot out [1], shot [1]

7233 רְבָבָה *rᵉbābâ*, n.f. GK: 8047 [→ 7231]. ten thousand, myriad; (virtually) countless number:– ten thousands [8], ten thousand [2], many [1], millions [1], multiply [1]

7234 רָבַד *rābad*, v. GK: 8048 [→ 4765, 7242]. [Q] to cover:– deckt [1]

7235 רָבָה *rābâ*, v. GK: 8049 & 8050 & 2221 [→ 697?, 1337, 4767, 4766, 4768, 8635, 8636; cf. 7231, 7232; cf. 7236]. [Q] to increase in number, multiply, grow large; to shoot; (ptcp.) archer; [P] to rear (offspring); to gain; make numerous; [H] to cause to increase, make numerous, enlarge:– multiply [38], multiplied [29], much [24], increase [19], many [19], increased [15], great [6], increaseth [5], more [5], give more [3], long [3], made many [3], greatly multiply (+7235) [3], made great [2], make many [2], much more [2], multiplieth [2], multiply exceedingly (+7235) [2], over much [2], very [2], abundance [1], abundantly [1], any more [1], archer (+7199) [1], ask never so much (+3966) [1], brought in abundance [1], brought up [1], continued [1], enlarge [1], exceeding (+3966) [1], exceedingly (+3966) [1], excelled [1], full [1], gathered much [1], give many [1], givest many [1], great store [1], greater [1], grow up [1], had many [1], heap [1], in authority [1], in process of time (+3117+1886.1) [1], increasest [1], make to multiply [1], many a time [1], more and more [1], much greater [1], multipliedst [1], multiplying [1], nourished [1], number [1], plenteous [1], plenty [1], so much as (+4480) [1], sore [1], store [1], take much [1], throughly [1], use many [1]

7236 רְבָה *rᵉbâ* (Aram.), v. GK: 10648 [→ 7229, 7240?, 7238, 7260, 7261; cf. 7235]. [P] to become large, be great; [Pa] to place in a high position, make great:– grown [3], grew [2], made great [1]

7237 רַבָּה *rabbâ*, n.pr.loc. GK: 8051 [→ 7227; cf. 7231]. Rabbah, "*chief, capital [city]*":– Rabbah [13], Rabbath [2]

7238 רְבוּ *rᵉbû* (Aram.), n.f. GK: 10650 [→ 7236]. greatness, high position:– majesty [3], greatness [2]

7239 רִבּוֹא *ribbô'*, n.f. GK: 8052 [→ 7231; cf. 7240]. ten thousand; myriad, (virtually) countless number:– thousand [3], forty two thousand (+505+702) [2], eighteen thousand (+505+8083+2050.1) [1], ten thousands [1], ten thousand [1], threescore and one thousand (+505+8337+2050.1) [1], twenty thousand [1]

7240 רִבּוֹ *ribbô* (Aram.), n.f. GK: 10649 [→ 7236?; cf. 7239]. ten thousand, myriad, (virtually) countless number:– ten thousand [2]

7241 רְבִיבִים *rᵉbîbîm*, n.m. GK: 8053 [→ 7231]. rain shower, abundant rain, gentle rain:– showers [6]

7242 רָבִיד *rābîd*, n.[m.]. GK: 8054 [→ 7234]. necklace, ornamental chain:– chain [2]

7243 רְבִיעִי *rᵉbî'î*, a.num.ord. GK: 8055 [→ 702; cf. 7244]. fourth:– fourth [55], foursquare [1]

7244 רְבִיעַי *rᵉbî'ay* (Aram.), a.num.ord. GK: 10651 [→ 703; cf. 7243]. fourth:– fourth [6]

7245 רַבִּית *rabbît*, n.pr.loc. GK: 8056 [→ 7231]. Rabbith, "*great*":– Rabbith [1]

7246 רָבַך *rābak*, v. GK: 8057. [Ho] to be kneaded, mixed (of dough):– fried [2], baken [1]

7247 רִבְלָה *riblâ*, n.pr.loc. GK: 8058. Riblah:– Riblah [11]

7248 רַב מָג *rab māg*, n.m. GK: 8059 [→ 7227]. high official:– Rab-mag [2]

7249 רַב־סָרִיס *rab-sārîs*, n.m. GK: 8060 [→ 7227+5631]. chief officer:– Rab-saris [3]

7250 רָבַע *rāba'*, v.den. GK: 8061 [→ 7252; cf. 7257]. [Q] to lie down with, have sexual relations with; [H] to mate, cross-breed:– lie down [1], gender with [1]

7251 רָבַע *rāba'*, v.den. GK: 8062 [→ 702]. [Qp, P] to be squared, have four corners:– foursquare [8], square [3], squared [1]

7252 רֶבַע *reba'*, v.inf. GK: 8061 [→ 7250]. inf. of 7250: to lie down:– lying down [1]

7253 רֶבַע *reba'*, n.m. GK: 8063 [→ 7254?; cf. 702?]. fourth-part, quarter; side (of a square thing):– sides [3], fourth part [2], squares [2]

7254 רֶבַע *reba'*, n.pr.m. GK: 8064 [→ 7253?; cf. 702?]. Reba:– Reba [2]

7255 רֹבַע *rōba'*, n.[m.]. GK: 8065 [→ 702]. fourth-part, quarter:– fourth part [1]

7256 רִבֵּעַ *ribbêa'*, a. GK: 8067 [→ 702]. fourth; (n.) the fourth generation:– fourth [4]

רְבִיעִי *rᵉbî'î*. See 7243.

7257 רָבַץ *rābaṣ*, v. GK: 8069 [→ 4769, 7258; cf. 7250]. [Q] to lie down; [H] to make lie down; to cause to rest:– lie down [9], lieth [3], lie [3], lay down [2], lying [2], cause to lie down [1], causing to lie down [1], couched [1], couching down [1], fell down [1], lay [1], make fold [1], makest to rest [1], maketh to lie down [1], sitting [1]

7258 רֵבֶץ *rēbeṣ*, n.[m.]. GK: 8070 [→ 7257]. resting place:– resting place [2], place to lie down in [1], where lay [1]

7259 רִבְקָה *ribqâ*, n.pr.f. GK: 8071. Rebekah, "[poss.] *choice calf*":– Rebekah [28], Rebekah's [2]

7260 רַבְרַב *rabrab* (Aram.), a. GK: 10647 [→ 7229]. same as 7229: great, large, many, chief; this can refer to a large object (great, large), a large amount of objects (many, much), or high status (chief):– great [7], stout [1]

7261 רַבְרְבָנִין *rabrᵉbānîn* (Aram.), n.m.pl. GK: 10652 [→ 7236]. nobles, lords:– lords [6], princes [2]

7262 רַב־שָׁקֵה *rab-šāqēh*, n.m. GK: 8072 [→ 7227+8248]. Assyrian officer: (field) commander, cupbearer:– Rab-shakeh [16]

7263 רֶגֶב *regeb*, n.m. GK: 8073 [→ 709]. clod of dirt:– clods [2]

7264 רָגַז *rāgaz*, v. GK: 8074 [→ 712, 7267, 7268, 7269; cf. 7265]. [Q] to quake, shake, tremble; to be angry, be in anguish; [H] to cause to shake, make tremble, cause a disturbance; [Ht] to enrage oneself (against):– tremble [8], rage [4], moved [4], trembled [3], troubled [3], disquieted [2], move [2], afraid [1], disquiet [1], fall out [1], fretted [1], made to tremble [1], much moved [1], provoke [1], quaked [1], quake [1], shaketh [1], shake [1], shook [1], stand in awe [1], wroth [1]

7265 רְגַז *rᵉgaz* (Aram.), v. GK: 10653 [→ 7266; cf. 7264]. [H] to anger, enrage:– provoked unto wrath [1]

7266 רְגַז *rᵉgaz* (Aram.), n.m. GK: 10654 [→ 7265; cf. 7267]. rage:– rage [1]

7267 רֹגֶז *rōgez*, n.m. GK: 8075 [→ 7264; cf. 7266]. turmoil, excitement, tumult:– trouble [2], fear [1], noise [1], rage [1], troubling [1], wrath [1]

7268 רַגָּז *raggāz*, a. GK: 8076 [→ 7264]. anxious, trembling:– trembling [1]

7269 רָגְזָה *rogzâ*, n.f. GK: 8077 [→ 7264]. shuddering, agitation:– trembling [1]

7270 רָגַל *rāgal*, v.den. GK: 8078 [→ 7272, 8637]. [Q] to slander; [P] to spy, explore:– spies [10], spy out [7], backbiteth [1], espy out [1], searched out [1], slandered [1], spied out [1], spy [1], taught to go [1], viewed [1], view [1]

7271 רְגַל *rᵉgal* (Aram.), n.[f.]. GK: 10655 [cf. 7272]. foot:– feet [7]

7272 רֶגֶל *regel*, n.f. GK: 8079 [→ 4772, 7270, 7273, 8637; cf. 7271]. foot; by extension, body parts associated with the foot: sole, legs, big toe, ankle; a euphemism for the genitals; footing or base of an object; footstep, as a measure of length:– feet [152], foot [63], footstool (+1916) [5], times [4], after (+871.1) [3], follow (+871.1) [3], great toes [2], piss (+4325) [2], able to endure (+3807.1) [1], after (+3807.1) [1], brokenfooted (+7667) [1], coming [1], follow (+1980+871.1) [1], followed (+871.1) [1], foot (+3709) [1], footstool (+1916+3807.1) [1], goeth [1], haunt [1], legs [1], possession [1], went on journey (+5375) [1]

7273 רַגְלִי *raglî*, a. GK: 8081 [→ 7272]. (persons) on foot (i.e., not riding):– footmen [7], footmen (+376) [4], on foot [1]

7274 רְגָלִים *rōg·lîm*, n.pr.loc. GK: 8082. Rogelim, "*[place of] treaders, fullers [one who cleans clothes by kneading with no soap]*":– Rogelim [2]

7275 רָגַם *rāgam*, v. GK: 8083 [→ 4773, 7277]. [Q] to execute by hurling stones:– stone [9], stoned [5], certainly stone (+7275) [1]

7276 רֶגֶם *regem*, n.pr.m. GK: 8084 [→ 7278; cf. 8638]. Regem, "*friend*":– Regem [1]

7277 רִגְמָה *rigmâ*, n.f. GK: 8086 [→ 7275]. great throng, crowd, a bustling, noisy group:– council [1]

7278 רֶגֶם מֶלֶך *regem melek*, n.pr.m. GK: 8085 [→ 7276+4428]. Regem-Melech, "*friend of the king; [poss.] chief of troops of the king*":– Regemmelech [1]

7279 רָגַן *rāgan*, v. GK: 8087 [→ 5372]. [Q] to complain; [N] to be grumbling, be gossiping:– murmured [3]

7280 רָגַע *rāga'*, v. GK: 8088 & 8089 & 8090 [→ 4771, 4774, 7281, 7282]. [Q] to stir up, churn up; to harden, crust over; [N] to cease; [H] to find repose, bring rest; to do something in an instant:– divideth [2], rest [2], suddenly [2], broken [1], cause to rest [1], divided [1], find ease [1], give rest [1], make to rest [1], moment [1]

7281 רֶגַע *rega'*, n.m. GK: 8092 [→ 7280]. moment, instant; peace, tranquillity:– moment [13], in a moment [3], instant [2], every moment (+3807.1) [1], in a moment (+3509.1) [1], space [1], suddenly [1]

7282 רָגֵעַ *rāgēa'*, a. GK: 8091 [→ 7280]. quiet, resting:– quiet [1]

7283 רָגַשׁ *rāgaš*, v. GK: 8093 [→ 7285; cf. 7284]. [Q] to be restless, be in tumult, likely referring to a rebellious conspiracy:– rage [1]

7284 רְגַשׁ *rᵉgaš* (Aram.), v. GK: 10656 [cf. 7283]. [H] to go in as a group (causing an uproar), implying that those in the group are bumping into one another:– assembled [3]

7285 רֶגֶשׁ *regeš* or רִגְשָׁה *rigšâ*, n.[m.]. GK: 8094 & 8095 [→ 7283]. crowd, throng:– company [1], insurrection [1]

7286 רָדַד *rādad*, v. GK: 8096 [→ 7289]. [Q] to subdue, beat down; [H] to hammer out flat:– spent [1], spread [1], subdueth [1], subdue [1]

7287 רָדָה *rādâ*, v. GK: 8097 & 8098 [→ 7288]. [Q] to rule over; to scoop out, scrape out; [H] to cause to dominate:– dominion [5], rule [5], ruled [3], bare rule [2], have dominion [2], made have dominion over [2], bear rule [1], made rule over [1], prevaileth [1], reign [1], rule over [1], ruler [1], taken [1], took [1]

7288 רַדַּי *radday*, n.pr.m. GK: 8099 [→ 7287]. Raddai, "[poss.] *beating down; Yahweh rules*":– Raddai [1]

7289 רָדִיד *rᵉdîd*, n.[m.]. GK: 8100 [→ 7286]. cloak, shawl, something wrapped around:– vails [1], vail [1]

7290 רָדַם *rādam*, v. GK: 8101 [→ 8639]. [N] to be in a heavy sleep:– fast asleep [2], in a deep sleep [2], cast into a dead sleep [1], sleeper [1], sleepeth [1]

7291 רָדַף *rādap*, v. GK: 8103 [→ 4783]. [Q] to pursue, chase, persecute; [N] to be pursued, be hounded; [P] to pursue, chase; [Pu] to be chased; [H] to chase:– pursued [35], pursue [28], persecute [15], chased [8], follow [8], persecutors [7], pursueth [7], chase [5], followeth after [5], persecuted [5], pursuers [5], pursuing [4], follow after [3], followed [2], followeth [1], hunt [1], past [1], persecution [1], pursuer [1], put to flight [1]

7292 רָהַב *rāhab*, v. GK: 8104 [→ 7293, 7294, 7296, 7295; cf. 4062]. [Q] to rise up against; press one's plea; [H] to overwhelm; make bold:– behave proudly [1], make sure [1], overcome [1], strengthenedst [1]

7293 רַהַב *rahab*, n.m. GK: 8105 [→ 7292]. same as 7294: pride, strength:– proud [2], strength [1]

7294 רַהַב *rahab*, n.pr. GK: 8105 [→ 7292]. same as 7293: Rahab, a sea monster of chaos that opposes God; used of the land of Egypt, with a focus on affliction or arrogance:– Rahab [3]

7295 רָהָב *rāhāb*, a. GK: 8107 [→ 7292]. proud, defiant:– proud [1]

7296 רֹהָב *rōhab*, n.[m.]. GK: 8106 [→ 7292]. pride or hurry:– strength [1]

7297 רָהָה *rāhâ* or יָרַה *yārah*, v. GK: 8109 & 3724. [Q] to fear:– afraid [1]

7298 רַהַט *rahaṭ*, n.[m.]. GK: 8110 & 8111 [→ 7351]. tress, rafter; watering trough:– gutters [2], galleries [1], troughs [1]

7299 רֵו *rēw* (Aram.), n.m. GK: 10657. appearance:– form [2]

רוּב *rûb*. See 7378.

7300 רוּד *rûd*, v. GK: 8113 [→ 4788]. [Q] to roam; [H] to grow restless, cause restlessness:– dominion [1], lords [1], mourn [1], ruleth [1]

7301 רָוָה *rāwâ*, v. GK: 8115 [→ 3138, 7302, 7310, 7377]. [Q] to drink to satisfaction, quench the thirst; [P] to drench, refresh, satisfy; [H] to lavish upon, cause to refresh; from the base meaning of quenching thirst come the fig. extensions of refreshment, satisfaction, and fulfillment:– watereth [2], abundantly satisfied [1], bathed [1], filled [1], made drunken [1], made drunk [1], satiated [1], satiate [1], satisfy [1], soaked [1], take fill [1], waterest abundantly [1], water [1]

7302 רָוֶה *rāweh*, a. GK: 8116 [→ 7301]. well-watered, drenched:– watered [2], drunkenness [1]

7303 רָהְגָּה *rohgâ* or רוֹהֲגָה *rôhᵉgâ*, n.pr.m. GK: 8108 & 8117. Rohagah, Rohgah:– Rohgah [1]

7304 רָוַח *rāwaḥ*, v. GK: 8118 [→ 7305, 7307, 7309, 7306, 7381]. [Q] to feel relief; [Pu] to be spacious:– refreshed [2], large [1]

7305 רֶוַח *rewaḥ*, n.m. GK: 8119 [→ 7304]. relief; space:– enlargement [1], space [1]

7306 רִיחַ *rîaḥ* or רוּחַ *rûaḥ*, v. GK: 8193 [→ 7381; cf. 7304]. [H] to smell (an aroma or odor):– smell [5], smelled [2], accept [1], make of quick understanding [1], smelleth [1], toucheth [1]

7307 רוּחַ *rûaḥ*, n.f. GK: 8120 [→ 7304; cf. 7308]. breath, wind; by extension: spirit, mind, heart, as the immaterial part of a person that can respond to God, the seat of life; spirit being, especially the Spirit of God:– spirit [227], wind [81], breath [27], winds [11], mind [5], side [5], spirits [5], blast [4], vain [4], air [1], anger [1], breath (+5397) [1], cool [1], courage [1], quarters [1], sides [1], spiritual [1], tempest [1], whirlwind (+5591) [1], windy [1]

7308 רוּחַ *rûaḥ* (Aram.), n.f. GK: 10658 [cf. 7382; cf. 7307]. wind, breath, spirit; from the base meaning of "wind" (or "breath") come the meaning of "spirit" as an immaterial supernatural being, and as the immaterial part of the inner person, with a possible focus on the reasoning and thinking faculty: "mind" or "heart":– spirit [8], mind [1], winds [1], wind [1]

7309 רְוָחָה *rᵉwāḥâ*, n.f. GK: 8121 [→ 7304]. relief, respite:– breathing [1], respite [1]

7310 רְוָיָה *rᵉwāyâ*, n.f. GK: 8122 [→ 7301]. place of abundance, overflowing:– runneth over [1], wealthy [1]

7311 רוּם *rûm* or רָמַם *rāmam*, v. GK: 8123 & 8249 & 8225 [→ 4791, 4792, 7213, 7312, 7315, 7316, 7317, 7318, 7319, 7410, 7415, 7427, 8641, 8642, 7413, 7426; cf. 7313 (also used with compound proper names)]. [Q] to be high, raise up; to be proud, haughty; to be full of maggots, be wormy; [Pol] to

Heb

exalt, lift high; [Polal] to be exalted, be lifted up; [H] to cause to lift up, present (an offering); to raise up against, rebel; [Ho] to be presented, be taken away; to exalt oneself; from the base meaning of being high in spatial position come the fig. extensions of being high in status: exalted, and high in attitude: proud, arrogant:– exalted [27], lift up [25], high [22], exalt [17], offer [11], lifted up [8], set up [6], take up [5], gave [4], exalteth [3], lifteth up [3], lofty [3], offer up [3], take off [3], take [3], tall [3], extol [2], heaved [2], held up [2], higher [2], liftest up [2], promotion [2], took up [2], bred [1], bring up [1], brought up [1], extolled [1], give [1], haughty [1], heaved up [1], heave [1], high ones [1], levy [1], lifted up on high [1], lifter up [1], lifteth [1], lifting up [1], loud [1], make on high [1], mount up [1], offered up [1], offered [1], presumptuously (+3027+871.1) [1], promote [1], proud [1], set up on high [1], setteth up [1], shouted aloud (+6963+8643+871.1+3807.1) [1], take away [1], taken away [1], taken off [1], taller [1], went up [1]

7312 רוּם **rûm**, n.[m.]. GK: 8124 [→ 7311; cf. 7314]. height; haughtiness, pride:– haughtiness [3], high [2], height [1]

7313 רוּם **rûm** (Aram.), v. GK: 10659 [→ 7314; cf. 7311]. [P] to become arrogant; [Pol] to exalt, praise; [H] to promote, cause to rise (in rank); [Htpol] to rise up (against); all of these meanings are from the base meaning of "high":– lifted up [2], extol [1], set up [1]

7314 רוּם **rûm** (Aram.), n.m. GK: 10660 [→ 7313; cf. 7312?]. height; the top:– height [5]

7315 רֹם **rôm**, adv. GK: 8125 [→ 7311]. on high:– on high [1]

7316 רוּמָה **rûmâ**, n.pr.loc. GK: 8126 [→ 7311; cf. 725]. Rumah, "*height*":– Rumah [1]

7317 רֹמָה **rômâ**, adv. GK: 8127 [→ 7311]. proudly, haughtily:– haughtily [1]

7318 רוֹמָם **rômām**, n.[m.]. GK: 8128 [→ 7311]. praise, exaltation:–

7319 רוֹמֵמֻת **rômēmut**, n.f. GK: 8129 [→ 7311, 7427]. rising up, lifting up:– high [1]

7320 רֹמַמְתִּי עֶזֶר **rōmamtî 'ezer**, n.pr.m. GK: 8251 [→ 7311+5828]. Romamti-Ezer, "*he is my] highest help*":– Romamti-ezer [2]

7321 רוּע **rûa'**, v. GK: 8131 [→ 7452, 8643]. [H] to raise a battle cry; sound a trumpet blast; shout in triumph or exaltation:– shouted [10], shout [10], make a joyful noise [7], triumph [3], cried [2], sound an alarm [2], blow an alarm [1], cry alarm [1], cry aloud [1], cry out aloud (+7452) [1], cry out [1], cry [1], gave a shout [1], shout for joy [1], shouted for joy [1], shouting [1], smart (+7451) [1]

7322 רָפַף **rāpap** or רוּף **rûp**, v. GK: 8344. [Poal] to quake, shake:– tremble [1]

7323 רוּץ **rûṣ**, v. GK: 8132 [→ 4793, 4794; cf. 7519?]. [Q] to run, hurry, be a messenger; [Pol] to dart about, run to and fro; [H] to chase; to bring quickly:– run [34], ran [28], guard [14], posts [6], running [6], runneth [4], make run [2], post [2], anotherˢ [1], brake down [1], brought hastily [1], divided speedily [1], footmen [1], runnest [1], stretch out [1]

7324 רִיק **rîq** or רוּק **rûq**, v. GK: 8197 [→ 7385, 7386, 7387]. [H] to pour forth, empty out; to draw (a sword):– draw out [5], empty [4], draw [3], emptied [2], armed [1], cast out [1], make empty [1], pour out [1], poured forth [1]

7325 רִיר **rîr** or רוּר **rûr**, v. GK: 8201 [→ 7388]. [Q] to flow:– run [1]

7326 רוּשׁ **rûš**, v. GK: 8133 [→ 7389; cf. 3423]. [Q] to be poor, be in poverty, be oppressed; [Htpol] to pretend to be poor:– poor [21], lack [1], maketh poor [1], needy [1]

 רוֹשׁ **rôš**. See 7219.

7327 רוּת **rût**, n.pr.f. GK: 8134 [→ 7462?]. Ruth, "*friendship; refreshed [as with water]*; [poss.] *comrade, companion*":– Ruth [12]

7328 רָז **rāz** (Aram.), n.m. GK: 10661. mystery, secret:– secret [6], secrets [3]

7329 רָזָה **rāzâ**, v. GK: 8135 [→ 7330, 7332, 7334]. [Q] to destroy; [N] to waste away:– famish [1], wax lean [1]

7330 רָזֶה **rāzeh**, a. GK: 8136 [→ 7329]. lean, barren:– lean [2]

7331 רְזוֹן **r'zôn**, n.pr.m. GK: 8139 [→ 7336]. Rezon, "*prince; high official*":– Rezon [1]

7332 רָזוֹן **rāzôn**, n.[m.]. GK: 8137 [→ 7329]. wasting disease; short, scrimped (ephah):– leanness [2], scant [1]

7333 רָזוֹן **rāzôn**, n.[m.]. GK: 8138 [→ 7336]. prince, dignitary:– prince [1]

7334 רָזִי **rāzî**, n.[m.]. GK: 8140 [→ 7329]. wasting away, leanness:– leanness [2]

7335 רָזַם **rāzam**, v. GK: 8141. [Q] to wink, flash the eyes:– wink [1]

7336 רָזַן **rāzan**, v. GK: 8142 [→ 7333, 7331]. [Q] to be a ruler; (ptcp.) a prince, ruler:– princes [5], rulers [1]

7337 רָחַב **rāḥab**, v. GK: 8143 [→ 4800, 7338, 7341, 7342, 7343, 7339, 7345, 7346]. [Q] to be wide; to swell (with joy); to boast; [N] to be roomy, be broad; [H] to enlarge, broaden, make wide:– enlarged [8], enlarge [7], enlargeth [2], large [2], enlarging [1], made room [1], make wide [1], maketh room [1], open wide [1], opened wide [1]

7338 רַחַב **raḥab**, n.[m.]. GK: 8144 [→ 7337]. spacious place, vast expanse:– breadth [1], broad place [1]

7339 רְחֹב **r'ḥōb**, n.f. GK: 8148 [→ 1050, 7340, 7344; cf. 7337]. public square, open street:– street [21], streets [19], broad ways [2], broad places [1]

7340 רְחֹב **r'ḥōb**, n.p.rm. & loc. GK: 8149 & 8150 [→ 7339]. Rehob, "*broad, wide [place, market]*":– Rehob [10]

7341 רֹחַב **rōḥab**, n.[m.]. GK: 8145 [→ 7337]. breadth, width:– breadth [74], broad [22], thickness [2], largeness [1], thick [1], wideness [1]

7342 רָחָב **rāḥāb**, a. GK: 8146 [→ 7343?; cf. 7337]. spacious, broad, roomy:– broad [4], large [4], large (+3027) [3], proud [3], wide (+3027) [2], broad (+3027) [1], broader [1], large enough (+3027) [1], liberty [1], wide [1]

7343 רָחָב **rāḥāb**, n.pr.f. GK: 8147 [→ 7342?; cf. 7337]. Rahab, "*spacious, broad*":– Rahab [5]

7344 רְחֹבוֹת **r'ḥōbôt**, n.pr.loc. GK: 8151 [→ 7339]. Rehoboth, "*broad, wide [places, markets]*":– Rehoboth [4]

7345 רְחַבְיָה **r'ḥabyâ** or רְחַבְיָהוּ **r'ḥabyāhû**, n.pr.m. GK: 8152 & 8153 [→ 7337+3068]. Rehabiah, "*Yahweh has enlarged*":– Rehabiah [5]

7346 רְחַבְעָם **r'ḥab'ām**, n.pr.m. GK: 8154 [→ 7337+5971]. Rehoboam, "*[my] people will enlarge, expand*":– Rehoboam [50]

 רְחֹבֹת **r'ḥōbōt**. See 7344.

7347 רֵחַיִם **rēḥayim**, n.[m.]. GK: 8160. handmill; pair of mill stones:– millstones [2], mills [1], mill [1], nether [1]

 רְחוֹב **r'ḥôb**. See 7339, 7340.

7348 רְחוּם **r'ḥûm**, n.pr.m. GK: 8156 & 10662 [→ 7355; cf. 5149, 7359]. Rehum, "*[he] is compassionate*": note this name is Aramaic four times in Ezra.– Rehum [8]

7349 רַחוּם **raḥûm**, a. GK: 8157 [→ 7355]. compassionate, merciful:– merciful [8], full of compassion [5]

7350 רָחוֹק **rāḥôq**, a. (used as noun). GK: 8158 [→ 7368; cf. 7352]. far, distant; (n.) distance, afar:– far [31], afar off (+4480) [18], far off [13], afar off [4], afar [3], great while to come (+4480) [2], long ago (+4480+3807.1) [2], old [2], afar off (+4480+5704+3807.1) [1], afar off (+5704+3807.1) [1], afar off (+871.1) [1], even afar off (+4480) [1], far abroad (+4480+5704+3807.1) [1], far off (+4480) [1], long (+4480) [1], long ago (+4480) [1], space [1]

7351 רָהִיט **rāhîṭ**, n.m.col. GK: 8112 [→ 7298]. rafters:– rafters [1]

7352 רַחִיק **raḥîq** (Aram.), a. GK: 10663 [cf. 7350]. far away:– far [1]

7353 רָחֵל **rāḥēl**, n.f. GK: 8161 [→ 7354]. ewe-sheep:– ewes [2], sheep [1]

7354 רָחֵל **rāḥēl**, n.pr.f. GK: 8162 [→ 7353]. Rachel, "*ewe*":– Rachel [41], Rachel's [5], Rahel [1]

7355 רָחַם **rāḥam**, v.den. GK: 8163 [→ 3395, 3396, 3397, 7208?, 7348, 7349, 7362; cf. 7358]. [Q] to love; [P] to have compassion on, show mercy, take pity on; [Pu] to find compassion, be loved; feelings of compassion are usually accompanied by acts of compassion:– have mercy [22], have compassion [7], shew mercy [3], hath mercy [2], pitieth [2], surely have mercy (+7355) [2], Ruhamah [1], findeth mercy [1], had compassion [1], had mercy [1], have pity [1], love [1], merciful [1], mercy [1], obtained mercy [1]

7356 רַחֲמִים **raḥ'mîm**, n.m.pl.abst. GK: 8171 [→ 7358; cf. 7359]. compassion, mercy, pity:– mercies [14], tender mercies [11], mercy [4], womb [4], bowels [2], compassions [2], compassion [2], damsel [1], mercies' [1], pitied [1], pity [1], tender love [1]

7357 רַחַם **raḥam**, n.pr.m. GK: 8165 [→ 7360]. Raham, "*compassion*":– Raham [1]

7358 רֶחֶם **reḥem**, n.m. GK: 8167 [→ 7361, 7356; cf. 7355]. womb; by extension: mother, any female, birth; an "open womb" is able to conceive; a "closed womb" cannot conceive:– womb [20], matrix [5], wombs [1]

7359 רַחֲמִין **raḥ'mîn** (Aram.), n.[m.]pl.intens. GK: 10664 [cf. 7348; cf. 7356]. mercy, compassion:– mercies [1]

7360 רָחָם **rāḥām** or רָחָמָה **rāḥāmâ**, n.[m.]. GK: 8164 & 8168 [→ 7357]. carrion-vulture; some sources: osprey:– gier eagle [1]

7361 רַחְמָה **raḥ'mâ**, n.f. GK: 8169 [→ 7358]. womb; slang for woman:– twoˢ [1]

7362 רַחֲמָנִי **raḥ'mānî**, a. GK: 8172 [→ 7355]. compassionate:– pitiful [1]

7363 רָחַף **rāḥap**, v. GK: 8173. [Q] to tremble, shake; [P] to hover:– fluttereth [1], moved [1], shake [1]

7364 רָחַץ **rāḥaṣ**, v. GK: 8175 [→ 7366, 7367]. [Q] to wash, bathe; [Pu] to be cleansed; [Ht] to wash oneself:– wash [36], bathe [18], washed [16], washed away [1], washing [1]

7365 רְחַץ **r'ḥaṣ** (Aram.), v. GK: 10665. [Htpe] to put one's trust in, rely on:– trusted [1]

7366 רַחַץ **raḥaṣ**, n.[m.]. GK: 8176 [→ 7364]. washing:– washpot (+5518) [2]

7367 רַחְצָה **raḥṣâ**, n.f. GK: 8177 [→ 7364]. washing:– washing [2]

7368 רָחַק **rāḥaq**, v. GK: 8178 [→ 1023, 3128, 4801, 7350, 7369]. [Q] to be far off; to avoid, stand aloof; [P] to send far away, extend; [H] to remove far away, drive far off, go very far:– far [19], far off [4], remove far [4], put away far [3], put far [3], far removed [2], go far [2], removed far [2], very far away (+7368) [2], afar off [1], cast far off [1], drive far [1], far away [1], flee far [1], go far off [1], gone away far [1], gone far [1], good way off [1], good way [1], keep far [1], put far away [1], refrain [1], remove far off [1], removed far away [1], withdraw far [1]

7369 רָחֵק **rāḥēq**, a.vbl. GK: 8179 [→ 7368]. one who is far away:– far from [1]

 רָחֹק **rāḥōq**. See 7350.

7370 רָחַשׁ **rāḥaš**, v. GK: 8180 [→ 4802]. [Q] to be stirred up (one's heart):– inditing [1]

7371 רַחַת **raḥat**, n.f. GK: 8181. winnowing fork, shovel:– shovel [1]

7372 רָטַב **rāṭab**, v. GK: 8182 [→ 7373]. [Q] to be drenched, be wet:– wet [1]

7373 רָטֹב **rāṭōb**, a. GK: 8183 [→ 7372]. well-watered (plant):– green [1]

7374 רֶטֶט **reṭeṭ**, n.[m.]. GK: 8185 [cf. 7578]. panic:– fear [1]

7375 רֻטֲפַשׁ **ruṭ'paš**, v. GK: 8186. [Qp] to be renewed:– fresher [1]

7376 רָטַשׁ **rāṭaš**, v. GK: 8187. [P] to dash to pieces; [Pu] to be dashed to pieces:– dashed in pieces [3], dash to pieces [1], dashed to pieces [1], dash [1]

7377 רִי **rî**, n.[m.]. GK: 8188 [→ 7301]. moisture:– watering [1]

7378 רִיב **rîb**, v. GK: 8189 [→ 3080, 3114, 3401, 4807, 4808, 4809, 7379]. [Q] to quarrel, contend, plead for:– plead [22], strive [7], contend [6], chide [4], contended [3], strove [3], chode [2], ever strive (+7378) [2], pleaded [2], throughly plead (+7378) [2], adversaries [1], complain [1], contend with [1], contendest [1], contendeth [1], debate with [1], debate [1], laid wait [1], plead for [1], pleadeth the cause [1], rebuked [1], strive together [1], striveth [1]

7379 רִיב **rîb**, n.m. GK: 8190 & 8191 [→ 7378]. contention, grievance, strife, legal dispute:– cause [23], strife [14], controversy [9], contention [2], strivings [2], adversary (+376) [1], causes [1], chiding [1], contended [1], controversies [1], multitude [1], pleadings [1], strive with [1], suit [1]

7380 רִיבַי **rîbay**, n.pr.m. GK: 8192 [→ 3403?]. Ribai, "*opponent*":– Ribai [2]

7381 רֵיחַ **rîaḥ**, n.m. GK: 8194 [→ 7306; cf. 7304; cf. 7382]. aroma; pleasing and acceptable: fragrance; unpleasing and unacceptable: stench; both connotations are used of sacrifices as accepted or rejected by God:– savour [45], smell [11], sent [2]

7382 רֵיחַ **rîaḥ** (Aram.), n.f. GK: 10666 [cf. 7308; cf. 7381]. (singed, scorched) smell:– smell [1]

 רֵים **rêm**. See 7214.

 רֵיעַ **rêa'**. See 7453.

7383 רִיפוֹת **rîpôt**, n.[f.]. GK: 8195. grain:– ground corn [1], wheat [1]

7384 רִיפַת or דִּיפַת **rîpat** or **dîpat**, n.pr.g. GK: 8196 & 1910. Riphath, Diphath:– Riphath [2]

7385 רִיק **rîq**, n.[m.]. GK: 8198 [→ 7324]. emptiness, nothingness, vanity:– vain [8], vanity [2], empty [1], no purpose [1]

7386 רֵיק **rêq**, a. GK: 8199 [→ 7324]. empty; idle, worthless:– vain [7], empty [6], emptied [1]

7387 רֵיקָם **rêqām**, adv. GK: 8200 [→ 7324]. empty-handed, without cause or satisfaction:– empty [12], without cause [2], in vain [1], void [1]

7388 רִיר **rîr**, n.m. GK: 8202 [→ 7325]. saliva; white (of an egg); some sources: a kind of plant juice:– spittle [1], white [1]

7389 רֵישׁ **rêš**, n.m. GK: 8203 [→ 7326]. poverty:– poverty [7]

7390 רַךְ **rak**, a. GK: 8205 [→ 7401]. gentle, tender, weak, soft:– tender [10], soft [3], fainthearted (+3824+1886.1) [1], tender one [1], weak [1]

7391 רֹךְ **rōk**, n.[m.]. GK: 8204 [→ 7401]. gentleness, tenderness, softness:– tenderness [1]

7392 רָכַב **rākab**, v. GK: 8206 [→ 4817, 4818, 7393, 7395, 7394, 7396, 7398]. [Q] to ride or mount an riding animal:– rode [15], riding [10], ride [8], rider [7], rideth [7], riders [5], carried [3], caused to ride [3], put [3], cause to ride [2], made ride [2], on horseback (+5483) [2], ride on [2], set [2], bring [1], brought on horseback [1], causest to ride [1], gat up [1], made to ride [1], make to ride [1], ridden [1]

7393 רֶכֶב **rekeb**, n.m. GK: 8207 [→ 7392]. chariot; large upper mill stone:– chariots [86], chariot [29], millstone [2], upper millstone [1], wagons [1]

7394 רֵכָב **rēkāb**, n.pr.m. GK: 8209 & 8211 [cf. 7392]. Recab, "[prob.] rider or horseman [from to ride, mount]":– Rechab [13]

7395 רַכָּב **rakkāb**, n.m. GK: 8208 [→ 7392]. chariot driver, horseman:– chariot man [1], driver of chariot [1], horseman [1]

7396 רִכְבָּה **rikbâ**, n.f. GK: 8210 [→ 7392]. act of riding:– chariots [1]

7397 רֵכָה **rēkâ**, n.pr.loc. GK: 8212. Recah:– Rechabites [4], Rechah [1]

7398 רְכוּב **rᵉkûb**, n.[m.]. GK: 8213 [→ 7392]. chariot:– chariot [1]

7399 רְכוּשׁ **rᵉkûš**, n.m. GK: 8214 [→ 7408]. possessions, property, goods, equipment:– goods [12], substance [11], riches [5]

7400 רָכִיל **rākîl**, n.[m.]. GK: 8215 [→ 7402?]. slanderer, gossip:– slanders [2], talebearer [2], carry tales [1], talebearer (+1980) [1]

7401 רָכַךְ **rākak**, v. GK: 8216 [→ 4816, 7391, 7390]. [Q] to be soft, faint-hearted; [Pu] to be soothed; [H] to make faint:– faint [2], tender [2], fainthearted (+3824) [1], maketh soft [1], mollified [1], softer [1]

7402 רָכַל **rākal**, v. GK: 8217 [→ 4819, 7400?, 7403?, 7404]. [Q] to do trade, act as a merchant; (n.) trader, merchant:– merchants [14], merchant [3]

7403 רָכָל **rākāl**, n.pr.loc. GK: 8218 [→ 7402?]. Racal, "trade":– Rachal [1]

7404 רְכֻלָּה **rᵉkullâ**, n.f. GK: 8219 [→ 7402]. trading of merchandise:– merchandise [2], traffick [2]

7405 רָכַס **rākas**, v. GK: 8220 [→ 7406, 7407?; cf. 7409]. [Q] to tie, bind:– bind [2]

7406 רֶכֶס **rekes**, n.[m.]. GK: 8221 [→ 7405]. rugged place:– rough places [1]

7407 רֹכֶס **rōkes**, n.[m.]. GK: 8222 [→ 7405?]. intrigue, plot, conspiracy:– pride [1]

7408 רָכַשׁ **rākaš**, v. GK: 8223 [→ 7399]. [Q] to tie, bind:– gotten [4], gathered [1], got [1]

7409 רֶכֶשׁ **rekeš**, n.m.col. GK: 8224 [cf. 7405]. team of horses; fast horses (for couriers):– mules [2], dromedaries [1], swift beast [1]

רְכֻשׁ **rᵉkuš**. See 7399.

רֵם **rēm**. See 7214.

7410 רָם **rām**, n.pr.m. GK: 8226 [→ 7311]. Ram, "high, exalted":– Ram [7]

רֻם **rum**. See 7311.

7411 רָמָה **rāmâ**, v. GK: 8227 & 8228 [→ 759, 3414, 4820, 4821, 7419, 7423, 8649; cf. 7503?; cf. 7412]. [Q] to hurl (horse and rider); to shoot (arrows); [P] to deceive, betray:– deceived [4], beguiled [2], thrown [2], betray [1], bowmen (+7198) [1], carrying [1], deceiveth [1]

7412 רְמָא **rᵉmâ** (Aram.), v. GK: 10667 [cf. 7411]. [P] to throw; to impose; [Peil] to be thrown, be set in place; [Htpe] to be thrown:– cast [11], impose [1]

7413 רָמָה **rāmâ**, n.f. GK: 8229 [→ 7414, 7433, 7418, 7432, 7434, 7437, 7435; cf. 7311]. lofty shrine; height:– high place [3], high places [1]

7414 רָמָה **rāmâ** or רָמָתַיִם **rāmātayim**, n.pr.loc. GK: 8230 & 8259 [→ 7413]. Ramah, Ramoth, "elevated spot, height"; Ramathaim, "two heights":– Ramah [36], Ramath [1]

7415 רִמָּה **rimmâ**, n.f. GK: 8231 [→ 7311]. worm, maggot:– worm [5], worms [2]

7416 רִמּוֹן **rimmôn**, n.m. GK: 8232 [→ 1667, 7417, 7428]. pomegranate: the tree, its fruit, or decorative objects shaped like the fruit:– pomegranates [22], pomegranate [8], pomegranate tree [1]

7417 רִמּוֹן **rimmôn** or רִמּוֹנוֹ **rimmônô**, n.pr.m. & loc. GK: 8233 & 8234 & 8235 & 8237 [→ 1910, 2886, 5884]. Rimmon, "pomegranate or pagan god Rimmon"; for Remmon-methoar, see also 1886.1 and 8388:– Rimmon [14], Remmon-methoar (+8388+1886.1) [1], Remmon [1]

רָמוֹת **rāmôt**. See 7418, 7433.

7418 רָמוֹת־נֶגֶב **rāmôt-negeb**, n.pr.loc. GK: 8241 [→ 7418+5045]. Ramoth Negev, "heights of Negev [the south]":– Ramoth [1]

7419 רָמוּת **rāmût**, n.f. GK: 8239 [→ 7411]. remains, refuse, rubbish:– height [1]

7420 רֹמַח **rōmaḥ**, n.[m.]. GK: 8242. spear:– spears [9], spear [3], buckler [1], javelin [1], lancets [1]

7421 רַמִּי **rammî**, n.pr.m. GK: 8246. Ramite or Aramean:– Syrians [1]

7422 רַמְיָה **ramyâ**, n.pr.m. GK: 8243 [→ 7311?+3068?]. Ramiah, "Yahweh is exalted":– Ramiah [1]

7423 רְמִיָּה **rᵉmiyyâ**, n.f. GK: 8244 & 8245 [→ 7411]. laziness, laxness, slackness; deceit:– deceitful [4], deceitfully [3], deceit [2], slothful [1], false [1], guile [1], idle [1], slack [1]

7424 רַמְכָה **rammākâ**, n.[f.]. GK: 8247. fast mare:– dromedaries [1]

7425 רְמַלְיָהוּ **rᵉmalyāhû**, n.pr.m. GK: 8248 [→ 3068]. Remaliah, "Yahweh has adorned":– Remaliah [11], Remaliah's [1]

7426 רָמַם **rāmam**, v. GK: 8250 [cf. 7311]. [Q] to be exalted; [N] to rise upward; to get away:– exalted [3], get up [1], lift up [1], lifted up [1], mounted up [1]

7427 רוֹמֵמֻת **rômēmut**, n.f. GK: 8129 [→ 7319]. same as 7319: rising up, lifting up:– lifting up [1]

רִמֹּן **rimmōn**. See 7416.

7428 רִמּוֹן פֶּרֶץ **rimmôn pereṣ**, n.pr.loc. GK: 8236 [→ 7416+6556]. Rimmon Perez, "pomegranate pass [breach]":– Rimmon-parez [1]

7429 רָמַס **rāmas**, v. GK: 8252 [→ 4823]. [Q] to trample, tread upon; [N] to be trampled:– tread down [4], tread [2], trode down [2], trode upon [2], oppressors [1], stamped upon [1], stamped [1], trample under feet [1], trample [1], treadeth down [1], treadeth [1], trodden [1], trode under foot [1]

7430 רָמַשׂ **rāmaś**, v. GK: 8253 [→ 7431]. [Q] to move along (ground or in the water):– creepeth [9], moveth [5], creep [2], moved [1]

7431 רֶמֶשׂ **remeś**, n.m. GK: 8254 [→ 7430]. creatures that move along (ground or sea):– creeping things [7], creeping thing [7], moving thing [1], thing that creepeth [1], things creeping [1]

7432 רֶמֶת **remet**, n.pr.loc. GK: 8255 [→ 7413]. Remeth, "heights":– Remeth [1]

7433 רָמוֹת גִּלְעָד **rāmôt gil'ād**, n.pr.loc. GK: 8240 [→ 7413+1568]. Ramoth Gilead, "heights in Gilead":– Ramoth-gilead [18], Ramoth [3]

7434 רָמַת הַמִּצְפֶּה **rāmat hammiṣpeh**, n.pr.loc. GK: 8256 [→ 7413]. Ramath Mizpah, "height [hill] of Mizpah [watch tower]":– Ramath-mizpeh [1]

7435 רָמָתִי **rāmātî**, a.g. GK: 8258 [→ 7413]. Ramathite, "of Ramah":– Ramathite [1]

7436 רָמָתַיִם צוֹפִים **rāmātayim ṣôpîm**, n.pr.loc. GK: 8259 + 7435 [→ 7413+6822]. Ramathaim Zophim:– Ramathaim-zophim [1]

7437 רָמַת לֶחִי **rāmat lᵉḥî**, n.pr.loc. GK: 8257 [→ 7413+3895?]. Ramath Lehi, "height [hill] of Lehi":– Ramath-lehi [1]

רָן **rān**. See 1028.

7438 רֹן **rōn**, n.[m.]. GK: 8260 [→ 7442]. (joyful) song:– songs [1]

7439 רָנָה **rānâ**, v. GK: 8261 [→ 7440, 7441; cf. 7442]. [Q] to rattle:– rattleth [1]

7440 רִנָּה **rinnâ**, n.f. GK: 8262 [→ 7441; cf. 7439, 7442]. shout of joy, song of joy; cry of pleading:– cry [12], singing [9], joy [3], rejoicing [3], gladness [1], proclamation [1], shouting [1], sing [1], songs [1], triumph [1]

7441 רִנָּה **rinnâ**, n.pr.m. GK: 8263 [→ 7440; cf. 7439]. Rinnah, "ringing cry [of joy] to Yahweh":– Rinnah [1]

7442 רָנַן **rānan**, v. GK: 8264 [→ 7438, 7444, 7445, 7443; cf. 7439, 7440]. [Q] to shout for joy, sing for joy; to cry, plead; [P] to sing for joy; [Polal] to sing for joy; [H] to make sing, call for songs of joy:– sing [17], rejoice [9], shout for joy [4], sing aloud [4], crieth [2], caused to sing for joy [1], crieth out [1], cry out [1], greatly rejoice [1], into joy sing [1], joyful [1], makest to rejoice [1], sang [1], shout aloud for joy (+7444) [1], shouted [1], shouteth [1], shout [1], sing for joy [1], sing out [1], singing [1], triumph [1]

7443 רְנָנִים **rᵉnānîm**, n.[m.]pl. GK: 8266 [→ 7442]. female ostrich:– goodly [1]

7444 רַנֵּן **rannēn**, v.inf. GK: 8264 [→ 7442]. inf. of 7442: to shout for joy, sing for joy:– shout aloud for joy (+7442) [1], singing [1]

7445 רְנָנָה **rᵉnānâ**, n.f. GK: 8265 [→ 7442]. shout of joy, joyful song:– joyful voice [1], joyful [1], singing [1], triumphing [1]

7446 רִסָּה **rissâ**, n.pr.loc. GK: 8267 [→ 7450?]. Rissah, "dew":– Rissah [2]

7447 רָסִיס **rāsîs**, n.[m.]. GK: 8268 & 8269 [→ 7450]. broken piece (of rubble); drop (of moisture):– breaches [1], drops [1]

7448 רֶסֶן **resen**, n.m. GK: 8270. bridle:– bridle [4]

7449 רֶסֶן **resen**, n.pr.loc. GK: 8271. Resen:– Resen [1]

7450 רָסַס **rāsas**, v. GK: 8272 [→ 7446?, 7447]. [Q] to moisten, sprinkle:– temper [1]

7451 רַע **ra'**, a. & n. GK: 8273 & 8274 & 8288 [cf. 7489]. bad, disagreeable, inferior in quality; by extension: evil, wicked in ethical quality; what is disagreeable to God is ethically evil; God's actions of judgment are disagreeable to the wicked (Eze 14:21), but are not ethically evil:– evil [436], wickedness [58], wicked [25], hurt [20], mischief [19], bad [13], sore [9], trouble [9], evils [8], ill [6], affliction [5], harm [5], adversity [3], naught [3], grievous [2], ill favoured [2], mischiefs [2], noisome [2], sad [2], adversities [1], afflictions [1], calamities [1], displease (+5869+6213+871.1) [1], displeased (+241+871.1) [1], displeased exceedingly (+1419+3415) [1], displeasure [1], distress [1], doest evil [1], evil favouredness (+1697) [1], evil men [1], great wickedness (+7465) [1], grief [1], grieved exceedingly (+1419+7489) [1], heavy [1], hurtful [1], mischievous [1], misery [1], naughty [1], please not (+5869+871.1) [1], pleased not (+5869+871.1) [1], sadly [1], smart (+7321) [1], sorrow [1], troubles [1], vex (+6213) [1], wicked ones [1], wickedly (+871.1) [1], wickedly [1], worse [1], worst [1], wretchedness [1], wrong [1]

7452 רֵעַ **rēa'**, n.m.vbl. GK: 8275 [→ 7321]. shouting, roar:– cry out [1], noise [1], shouted [1]

7453 רֵעַ **rēa'**, n.m. GK: 8276 [→ 7462]. neighbor; friend, companion, associate:– neighbour [73], friend [28], neighbour's [26], another's [21], friends [14], fellow [8], companion [3], neighbours [2], other's [2], another's (+7794) [1], another's [1], brother [1], companions' [1], companions [1], fellow's [1], fellows [1], husband [1], lovers [1], neighbour's (+3807.1) [1], neighbours' [1]

7454 רֵעַ **rēa'**, n.[m.]. GK: 8277. thought, intention:– thoughts [1], thought [1]

7455 רֹעַ **rōa'**, n.[m.]. GK: 8278 [→ 7489]. bad, disagreeable, inferior in quality; by extension: evil, wicked in ethical quality:– evil [11], wickedness [3], badness [1], bad [1], naughtiness [1], sadness [1], sorrow [1]

7456 רָעֵב **rā'ēb**, v. GK: 8279 [→ 7458, 7457, 7459]. [Q] to be hungry, be famished, be starving:– hungry [3], hunger [2],

suffer hunger [2], famished [1], suffer to famish [1], suffered to hunger [1]

7457 רָעֵב *rā'ēb*, a. GK: 8281 [→ 7456]. hungry:– hungry [22], hunger-bitten [1]

7458 רָעָב *rā'āb*, n.m. GK: 8280 [→ 7456]. hunger, famine, starvation:– famine [87], hunger [8], dearth [5], famished [1]

7459 רְעָבוֹן *r'ābôn*, n.[m.]. GK: 8282 [→ 7456]. hunger, famine, starvation:– famine [3]

7460 רָעַד *rā'ad*, v. GK: 8283 [→ 7461]. [Q, H] to tremble:– trembling [2], trembleth [1]

7461 רַעַד *ra'ad* or רְעָדָה *r'ādâ*, n.m. & f. GK: 8284 & 8285 [→ 7460]. trembling:– trembling [4], fearfulness [1], fear [1]

7462 רָעָה *rā'â*, v. GK: 8286 & 8287 & 8289 [→ 4828, 4829, 4830, 7327?, 7453, 7463, 7464, 7466, 7467, 7468, 7469, 7471, 7472, 7473, 7474]. [Q] to be a companion, be a friend; to be a shepherd, to care for flocks, graze; by extension: to rule, with a focus on care and concern; [P] to be an attendant of the groom (of a wedding); [H] feed [55], shepherds [31], shepherd [27], fed [11], herdmen [7], pastors [7], feedeth on [3], feeding [3], kept [3], companion [2], feedeth [2], shepherds (+6629) [2], broken [1], devour [1], eat up [1], eaten up [1], eat [1], evil entreateth [1], feedest [1], friend [1], keeper [1], keepeth company with [1], keepeth [1], keeping [1], make friendship [1], pastor [1], shepherd (+6629) [1], shepherd's [1], shepherds' [1], shew friendly [1], wander [1], waste [1]

7463 רֵעֶה *rē'eh*, n.m. GK: 8291 [→ 7462]. friend, personal advisor:– friend [3]

7464 רֵעָה *rē'â*, n.f. GK: 8292 [→ 7462]. companion, friend:– companions [2], fellows [1]

7465 רֹעָה *rō'â*, v.ptcp. GK: 8318 [→ 7489; cf. 7492, 7533]. ptcp. of 7489: broken:– broken [1], great wickedness (+7451) [1]

7466 רְעוּ *r'û*, n.pr.m. GK: 8293 [→ 7462; cf. 7472]. Reu, "*friend [of God]*":– Reu [4], Rehu [1]

7467 רְעוּאֵל *r'û'ēl*, n.pr.m. GK: 8294 [→ 7462+410]. Reuel, "*friend of God [El]*":– Reuel [10], Raguel [1]

7468 רְעוּת *r'ût*, n.f. GK: 8295 [→ 7462]. (female) neighbor; fellow (female):– another [2], mate [2], neighbour [2]

7469 רְעוּת *r'ût*, n.f. GK: 8296 [cf. 7470]. chasing after:– vexation [7]

7470 רְעוּ *r'û* (Aram.), n.f. GK: 10668 [→ 7476; cf. 7469]. will, decision:– pleasure [1], will [1]

7471 רְעִי *r'î*, n.[m.]. GK: 8297 [→ 7462]. pastured (cattle):– pastures [1]

7472 רֵעִי *rē'î*, n.pr.m. GK: 8298 [→ 7462; cf. 7466]. Rei, "*friendly* or *[my] friend*":– Rei [1]

7473 רֹעִי *rō'î*, v.ptcp. GK: 8286 [→ 7462]. ptcp. of 7462: shepherd:– shepherd's [1], shepherd [1]

7474 רַעְיָה *ra'yâ*, n.f. GK: 8299 [→ 7462]. darling, beloved, formally, companion, friend, a woman who is the object of a man's love and affection:– love [9]

7475 רַעְיוֹן *ra'yôn*, n.[m.]. GK: 8301 [→ 7462]. chasing after, striving for:– vexation [3]

7476 רַעְיוֹן *ra'yôn* (Aram.), n.m. GK: 10669 [→ 7470; cf. 7475]. thought (in one's mind):– thoughts [5], cogitations [1]

7477 רָעַל *rā'al*, v. GK: 8302 [→ 4831, 7478, 7479, 8653]. [Ho] to be made to quiver:– terribly shaken [1]

7478 רַעַל *ra'al*, n.[m.]. GK: 8303 [→ 7477]. reeling:– trembling [1]

7479 רְעָלָה *r'ālâ*, n.[f.]. GK: 8304 [→ 7477]. veil:– mufflers [1]

7480 רְעֵלָיָה *r'ēlāyâ*, n.pr.m. GK: 8305 [cf. 7485]. Reelaiah:– Reelaiah [1]

7481 רָעַם *rā'am*, v.den. GK: 8306 & 8307 [→ 7482, 7485]. [Q] to be confused, distorted; to storm, thunder; [H] to irritate, agitate; to make thunder, make storm:– roar [3], thundered [3], thundereth [3], thunder [2], make fret [1], troubled [1]

7482 רַעַם *ra'am*, n.[m.]. GK: 8308 [→ 7481]. thunder; thunderous shout:– thunder [6]

7483 רַעְמָה *ra'mâ*, n.f. GK: 8310. mane (of a horse):– thunder [1]

7484 רַעְמָה *ra'mâ* or רַעְמָא *ra'mā'*, n.pr.m. & loc. GK: 8311 & 8309. Raamah:– Raamah [5]

7485 רַעְמְיָה *ra'myâ*, n.pr.m. GK: 8313 [→ 7481+3068; cf. 7480]. Raamiah, "*Yahweh has thundered*":– Raamiah [1]

7486 רַעְמְסֵס *ra'm'sēs*, n.pr.loc. GK: 8314. Rameses, a town in Egypt and a region in the Nile Delta, "*Ra created him*":– Rameses [4], Raamses [1]

7487 רַעֲנַן *ra'anan* (Aram.), a. GK: 10670 [cf. 7488?]. prosperous, flourishing:– flourishing [1]

7488 רַעֲנָן *rā'an*, v. or רַעֲנַן *ra'anān*, a. GK: 8316 [cf. 7487]. [Palel] to flourish; (n.) spreading (tree), verdant, luxuriant:– green [18], flourishing [1], fresh [1]

7489 רָעַע *rā'a'*, v.den. GK: 8317 & 8318 [→ 4827, 7451, 7455, 7465]. [Q] to be distressed, be displeased; (by extension) to be bad, be evil; to break, shatter; [N] to suffer harm; [H] to do wickedness; bring trouble, mistreat; this refers to what is displeasing from a personal perspective; what is displeasing to God is ethically evil; [Htpol] to come to ruin:– evildoers [10], do evil [9], hurt [6], evil [4], wicked [4], afflicted [3], do harm [3], done evil [3], worse [3], afflict [2], break [2], displease (+5869+871.1) [2], done evil indeed (+7489) [2], done wickedly [2], evil entreated [2], still do wickedly (+7489) [2], utterly broken down (+7489) [2], associate [1], behaved ill [1], break in pieces [1], bring evil [1], broken [1], brought evil [1], deal worse [1], dealt ill [1], destroyed [1], did worse [1], displease (+3415+871.1) [1], displeased (+3415+871.1) [1], displeased (+5869+871.1) [1], do hurt [1], do wickedly [1], done mischief [1], evil doers [1], evildoer [1], grieved exceedingly (+1419+7451) [1], hurting [1], ill [1], punish [1], vexed [1], wicked doer [1], wickedly [1]

7490 רְעַע *r'a'* (Aram.), v. GK: 10671 [cf. 7533]. [P] to break, crush; [Pa] to break to pieces, shatter:– breaketh [1], bruise [1]

7491 רָעַף *rā'ap*, v. GK: 8319 [cf. 6201]. [Q] to drop, fall, overflow; [H] to cause to rain:– drop down [2], drop [2], distil [1]

7492 רָעַץ *rā'aṣ*, v. GK: 8320 [cf. 7465, 7533]. [Q] to shatter:– dashed in pieces [1], vexed [1]

7493 רָעַשׁ *rā'aš*, v. GK: 8321 [→ 7494]. [Q] to shake, quake, tremble; [N] to be made to quake; [H] to cause to shake, make to tremble:– shake [13], trembled [5], tremble [3], moved [2], shook [2], made to shake [1], made to tremble [1], make afraid [1], quake [1], remove [1]

7494 רַעַשׁ *ra'aš*, n.m. GK: 8323 [→ 7493]. commotion, rattling, earthquake; this can mean a quaking motion and the sounds from a quaking motion; by extension: any clamor, discord, or frenzy:– earthquake [6], rushing [3], shaking [3], commotion [1], confused noise [1], fierceness [1], quaking [1], rattling [1]

7495 רָפָא *rāpā'*, v. GK: 8324 [→ 4832, 7498, 7500, 7505, 7499, 8644 (also used with compound proper names)]. [Q] to heal; [N] to be healed, be cured; [P] to heal, repair; [Ht] to recover:– healed [31], heal [21], healeth [4], physicians [4], cause to be thoroughly healed (+7495) [2], cure [1], made whole [1], make whole [1], physician [1], repaired [1]

7496 רְפָאִים *r'pā'îm*, n.m. GK: 8327 [cf. 7503?]. dead, the spirits of the departed:– dead [7], deceased [1]

7497 רְפָאִים *r'pā'îm*, n.pr.g. GK: 8328 & 8329 [cf. 7503?]. Rephaite, "*mighty*"; Rephaim, "*sunken, powerless ones [giants]*; [poss.] *shades, ghosts of the dead ones [giants]*":– giants [10], giant [7], Rephaim [6], Rephaims [2]

7498 רָפָא *rāpā'* or רָפָה *rāpâ*, n.pr.m. GK: 8325 & 8334 [→ 7495; cf. 7501]. Rapha, Raphah, "*[poss.] one healed*":– Rapha [2]

7499 רְפֻאָה *r'pû'â*, n.f. GK: 8337 [→ 7495]. healing:– medicines [2], healed [1]

7500 רִפְאוּת *rip'ût*, n.f. GK: 8326 [→ 7495]. health, healing:– health [1]

7501 רְפָאֵל *r'pā'ēl*, n.pr.m. GK: 8330 [→ 7495+410; cf. 7498]. Rephael, "*God [El] heals*":– Rephael [1]

7502 רָפַד *rāpad*, v. GK: 8331 [→ 7507, 7508]. [Q] to spread (mud, so as to leave a trail); [P] to spread out; to refresh:– comfort [1], made [1], spreadeth [1]

7503 רָפָה *rāpâ*, v. GK: 8332 [→ 4832, 7504, 7510; cf. 7411?, 7496?, 7497?]. [Q] to hang limp, sink down, be feeble; [N] to be lazy; [P] to lower; discourage; [H] to leave alone, abandon, withdraw; [Ht] so show oneself slack:– fail [4], let alone [4], feeble [4], idle [3], let go [3], slack [3], stay [3], faint [3], forsake [2], let down [2], waxed feeble [2], weakened [2], weakeneth [2], abated [1], cease [1], consumeth [1], draweth [1], give respite [1], go [1], leave [1], slothful [1], still [1], wax feeble [1], weak [1]

7504 רָפֶה *rāpeh*, a. GK: 8333 [→ 7503]. weak, feeble:– weak [4]

רָפָא, רָפָה *rāpâ, rāpâ*. See 7497, 7498.

7505 ripâ. See 7383.

7505 רָפוּא *rāpû'*, n.pr.m. GK: 8336 [→ 7495]. Raphu, "*healed*":– Raphu [1]

7506 רֶפַח *repaḥ*, n.pr.m. GK: 8338. Rephah, "*[poss.] rich; easy [life]*":– Rephah [1]

7507 רְפִידָה *r'pîdâ*, n.f. GK: 8339 [→ 7502]. base (of a royal carriage); some sources: seat cover:– bottom [1]

7508 רְפִידִים *r'pîdîm*, n.pr.loc. GK: 8340 [→ 7502]. Rephidim, "*[poss.] supports, rests; resting place*":– Rephidim [5]

7509 רְפָיָה *r'pāyâ*, n.pr.m. GK: 8341 [cf. 7498?]. Rephaiah, "*Yahweh heals*":– Rephaiah [5]

7510 רִפָּיוֹן *rippāyôn*, n.[m.]. GK: 8342 [→ 7503]. hanging limp, possibly referring to despair:– feebleness [1]

7511 רָפַס *rāpas* or רָפַשׂ *rāpaś*, v. GK: 8346 [→ 4833, 7515; cf. 7512]. same as 7515: [Q] to muddy (a stream by trampling through); [N] to be muddied; [Ht] to be humbled, humble oneself:– humble [1], submit [1]

7512 רְפַס *r'pas* (Aram.), v. GK: 10672 [cf. 7511]. [P] to trample down:– stamped [2]

7513 רַפְסֹדוֹת *rapsōdôt*, n.[f.pl.]. GK: 8343. (log) rafts:– flotes [1]

7514 רָפַק *rāpaq*, v. GK: 8345. [Ht] to lean oneself (upon):– leaning [1]

7515 רָפַשׂ *rāpaś*, v. GK: 8346 [→ 7511]. same as 7511: [Q] to muddy (a stream by trampling through); [N] to be muddied; [Ht] to be humbled, humble oneself:– fouledst [1], foul [1], troubled [1]

7516 רֶפֶשׁ *repeš*, n.[m.]. GK: 8347. mire (of the sea):– mire [1]

7517 רֶפֶת *repet*, n.[m.]. GK: 8348. stall, enclosure for cattle:– stalls [1]

7518 רַץ *raṣ*, n.[m.]. GK: 8349. bar (of silver):– pieces [1]

7519 רָצָא *rāṣā'*, v. GK: 8351 & 8352 [→ 7521; cf. 7323?]. [Q] to take pleasure in, accept; to run forth:– ran [1]

7520 רָצַד *rāṣad*, v. GK: 8353. [P] to gaze in hostility:– leap [1]

7521 רָצָה *rāṣâ*, v. GK: 8354 & 8355 [→ 7519, 7522, 7525?, 7526?, 8656]. [Q] to be pleased, delight in, accept; to pay for (sin); [Qp] to be favored, be esteemed; [N] to be accepted; to be paid for; [P] to make amends; [H] to enjoy; [Ht] to regain favor:– accept [13], accepted [7], enjoy [3], favourable [3], please [3], taketh pleasure [3], accepteth [2], delighteth [2], pleased with [2], pleased [2], take pleasure [2], acceptable [1], accomplish [1], approve [1], consentedst [1], delight in [1], delightest in [1], delight [1], enjoyed [1], hadst a favour [1], hast pleasure [1], liked [1], pardoned [1], reconcile [1], set affection [1]

7522 רָצוֹן *rāṣôn*, n.[m.]. GK: 8356 [→ 7521]. pleasure, acceptance, favor, will:– favour [15], will [9], acceptable [7], delight [5], accepted [4], pleasure [4], desire [3], good will [2], would [2], acceptable (+3807.1) [1], acceptance [1], good pleasure [1], selfwill [1], voluntary will [1]

7523 רָצַח *rāṣaḥ*, v. GK: 8357 [→ 7524]. [Q] to murder, kill; [N] to be murdered, killed; [P] to murder, kill:– slayer [17], murderer [13], kill [4], murder [3], slain [3], manslayer [2], killed [1], killing [1], murderers [1], put to death [1], slayeth [1]

7524 רֶצַח *reṣaḥ*, n.[m.]. GK: 8358 [→ 7523]. slaughter, murder, agony of death:– slaughter [1], sword [1]

7525 רִצְיָא *riṣyā'*, n.pr.m. GK: 8359 [cf. 7521?]. Rizia, "*[poss.] pleasant one*":– Rezia [1]

7526 רְצִין *r'ṣîn*, n.pr.m. GK: 8360 [→ 7521?]. Rezin:– Rezin [1]

7527 רָצַע *rāṣa'*, v. GK: 8361 [→ 4836]. [Q] to pierce (ear):– bore through [1]

7528 רָצַף *rāṣap*, v. GK: 8362 [→ 4837, 7531]. [Qp] to be inlaid, be fitted:– paved [1]

7529 רֶצֶף *reṣep*, n.f. GK: 8363 [→ 7530, 7531, 7532]. hot coals, live coals:– baken on the coals [1]

7530 רֶצֶף *reṣep*, n.pr.loc. GK: 8364 [→ 7529]. Rezeph, "*heated stones, live coals*":– Rezeph [2]

7531 רִצְפָה *riṣpâ*, n.f. GK: 8365 & 8367 [→ 7528, 7529]. live coal, hot coal; (stone) pavement:– pavement [7], live coal [1]

7532 רִצְפָה *riṣpâ*, n.pr.f. GK: 8366 [→ 7529]. Rizpah, "*heated stones, live coals*":– Rizpah [4]

7533 רָצַץ *rāṣaṣ*, v. GK: 8368 [→ 4835; cf. 7465, 7492, cf. 7490]. [Q] break, smash, oppress; [Qp] to be smashed, broken, splintered, oppressed; [N] to be broken, splintered; [P] to

oppress, crush; [H] to crush to pieces; [Htpol] to jostle each other:– oppressed [6], broken [4], bruised [2], all to brake [1], brakest in pieces [1], break [1], crushed [1], crush [1], discouraged [1], struggled together [1]

7534 רַק **raq**, a. GK: 8369 [→ 7535, 7541, 7542, 7550, 7557]. lean, thin, lank:– leanfleshed (+1320) [1], lean [1], thin [1]

7535 רַק **raq**, adv. GK: 8370 [→ 7534]. only, but, however, except:– only [60], but [20], howbeit [5], nevertheless [5], surely [3], notwithstanding [2], save [2], yet [2], at the least [1], except [1], howsoever [1], in any wise [1], indeed only (+389) [1], nothing but [1], save only [1], save that [1], so that (+518) [1], so [1]

7536 רֹק **rōq**, n.[m.]. GK: 8371 [→ 7556]. spit, saliva; "to swallow one's spit" means a very brief time:– spitting [1], spittle [1], spit [1]

7537 רָקַב **rāqab**, v. GK: 8372 [→ 7538, 7539]. [Q] to rot, become worm-eaten:– rot [2]

7538 רָקָב **rāqāb**, n.[m.]. GK: 8373 [→ 7537]. rottenness, decay:– rottenness [4], rotten thing [1]

7539 רִקָּבוֹן **riqqābôn**, n.[m.]. GK: 8375 [→ 7537]. rottenness:– rotten [1]

7540 רָקַד **rāqad**, v. GK: 8376. [Q] to skip, dance; [P] to leap about, dance; [H] to make skip:– dance [3], skipped [2], dancing [1], jumping [1], leap [1], maketh to skip [1]

7541 רַקָּה **raqqâ**, n.f. GK: 8377 [→ 7534]. temple (of the head):– temples [5]

7542 רַקּוֹן **raqqôn**, n.pr.loc. GK: 8378 [→ 7534]. Rakkon, "narrow place":– Rakkon [1]

7543 רָקַח **rāqaḥ**, v. GK: 8379 [→ 4840, 4841, 4842, 7544, 7545, 7546, 7547, 7548]. [Q] to make perfume, mix spices; [Pu] to be blended (of perfume); [H] to mix spices:– apothecary [4], compoundeth [1], made [1], prepared [1], spice [1]

7544 רֶקַח **reqaḥ**, n.[m.]. GK: 8380 [→ 7545; cf. 7543]. (powdered) spice:– spiced [1]

7545 רֹקַח **rōqaḥ**, n.[m.]. GK: 8381 [→ 7544; cf. 7543]. fragrant blend, spice-blend:– confection [1], ointment [1]

7546 רַקָּח **raqqāḥ**, n.m. GK: 8382 [→ 7543]. perfume-maker, ointment-mixer:– apothecaries [1]

7547 רִקֻּחַ **riqquaḥ**, n.[m.]. GK: 8383 [→ 7543]. perfume, ointment:– perfumes [1]

7548 רַקָּחָה **raqqāḥâ**, n.f. GK: 8384 [→ 7543]. perfume-maker, ointment-mixer:– confectionaries [1]

7549 רָקִיעַ **rāqîa'**, n.m. GK: 8385 [→ 7554]. expanse (of the sky or heaven); the space above the earth that holds visible objects: clouds, planets, stars:– firmament [17]

7550 רָקִיק **rāqîq**, n.m. GK: 8386 [→ 7534]. wafer, (thin, flat) cake:– wafers [4], wafer [3], cakes [1]

7551 רָקַם **rāqam**, v. GK: 8387 [→ 7552?, 7553]. [Q] to embroider, weave colored thread; [Pu] to be woven together:– needlework (+4639) [4], embroiderer [2], curiously wrought [1], needlework [1], wrought with needlework (+4639) [1]

7552 רֶקֶם **reqem** or רָקֶם **rāqem**, n.pr.m. & loc. GK: 8388 & 8389 & 8390 [→ 7551?]. Rakem, Rekem, "friendship":– Rekem [5], Rakem [1]

7553 רִקְמָה **riqmâ**, n.f. GK: 8391 [→ 7551]. embroidered work; varied colored things:– broidered work [5], broidered [2], divers colours [2], needlework [2], raiment of needlework [1]

7554 רָקַע **rāqa'**, v. GK: 8392 [→ 3421, 7549, 7555]. [Q] to spread out; stamp upon, trample; [P] to hammer out thin, overlay (with precious metal); [Pu] to be hammered, be beaten thin; [H] to cause to spread out, make into plated metal:– beat [1], made broad [1], spread abroad [1], spread forth [1], spread into plates [1], spread out [1], spreadeth abroad [1], spreadeth over [1], stamped [1], stamp [1], stretched out [1]

7555 רִקֻּעַ **riqqua'**, n.[m.]. GK: 8393 [→ 7554]. sheet, something beaten thin:– broad [1]

7556 רָקַק **rāqaq**, v. GK: 8394 [→ 7536; cf. 3417]. [Q] to spit saliva:– spit [1]

7557 רַקַּת **raqqat**, n.pr.loc. GK: 8395 [→ 7534]. Rakkath, "narrow place":– Rakkath [1]

7558 רִשְׁיוֹן **rišyôn**, n.[m.]. GK: 8397 [→ 3423]. authorization, permission:– grant [1]

7559 רָשַׁם **rāšam**, v. GK: 8398 [cf. 7560]. [Qp] to be written, be inscribed:– noted [1]

7560 רְשַׁם **rᵉšam** (Aram.), v. GK: 10673 [cf. 7559]. [P] to put in writing, publish; [Peil] to be written, be published:– signed [4], written [2], sign [1]

7561 רָשַׁע **rāša'**, v.den. GK: 8399 [→ 4849, 7562, 7563, 7564]. [Q] to do evil, act wickedly; to be guilty; [H] to declare guilty, condemn, inflict punishment; to do wrong:– condemn [11], do wickedly [4], done wickedly [4], wicked [4], condemneth [2], wickedly departed [2], committed wickedness [1], condemned [1], condemning [1], dealt wickedly [1], make trouble [1], very wickedly [1], vexed [1]

7562 רֶשַׁע **reša'**, n.m. GK: 8400 [→ 7561]. evil, wickedness, wrongdoing:– wickedness [25], wicked [4], iniquity [1]

7563 רָשָׁע **rāšā'**, a. GK: 8401 [→ 7561]. wicked, evil, guilty:– wicked [252], ungodly [8], condemned [1], guilty [1], him that did wrong [1]

7564 רִשְׁעָה **riš'â**, n.f. GK: 8402 [→ 7561]. wickedness:– wickedness [13], fault [1], wickedly [1]

7565 רֶשֶׁף **rešep**, n.m. GK: 8404 [→ 7566]. flame:– coals [2], arrows [1], burning coals [1], burning heat [1], hot thunderbolts [1], sparks (+1121) [1]

7566 רֶשֶׁף **rešep**, n.pr.m. GK: 8405 [→ 7565]. Resheph, "flame, flash of fire":– Resheph [1]

7567 רָשַׁשׁ **rāšaš**, v. GK: 8406 [→ 8658?, 8659?]. [Pol] to destroy, shatter; [Pu] to be crushed, shattered:– impoverished [1], impoverish [1]

7568 רֶשֶׁת **rešet**, n.f. GK: 8407 [→ 3423]. net, snare, trap (for catching game); network (net-like metal grating):– net [20], network (+4639) [2]

7569 רַתּוֹק **rattôq**, n.[m.]. GK: 8408 [→ 7576]. chain:– chain [1]

7570 רָתַח **rātaḥ**, v. GK: 8409 [→ 7571]. [P] to bring to a boil; [Pu] to be caused to churn; [H] to make to churn:– boiled [1], make boil well (+7571) [1], maketh to boil [1]

7571 רֶתַח **retaḥ**, n.[m.]. GK: 8410 [→ 7570]. boiling:– make boil well (+7570) [1]

7572 רַתִּיקָה **rattîqâ**, n.[f.]. GK: 8411 [→ 7576]. chain:– chains [1]

7573 רָתַם **rātam**, v. GK: 8412 [→ 7574, 7575?]. [Q] to tie up, harness (horse team):– bind [1]

7574 רֹתֶם **rōtem**, n.m. GK: 8413 [→ 7575; cf. 7573?]. broom tree:– juniper tree [2], juniper [2]

7575 רִתְמָה **ritmâ**, n.pr.loc. GK: 8414 [→ 7574; cf. 7573?]. Rithmah, "[place of] broom plants":– Rithmah [2]

7576 רָתַק **rātaq**, v. GK: 8415 [→ 7569, 7572, 7577]. [Pu] to be bound with chains:– bound [1], loosed [1]

7577 רְתֻקוֹת **rᵉtuqôt**, n.[f.pl.]. GK: 8416 [→ 7576]. chains:– chains [1]

7578 רְתֵת **rᵉtēt**, n.[m.]. GK: 8417 [cf. 7374]. trembling, fright:– trembling [1]

7578.1 -שֶׁ **ša-**, pt.rel.pref. GK: 8611 [→ 4332, 4967, 7706]. who, that, because; see under 7945:–

7579 שָׁאַב **šā'ab**, v. GK: 8612 [→ 4857]. [Q] to draw and carry water:– draw [9], drew [5], drawers [3], drawer [1], drawn [1]

7580 שָׁאַג **šā'ag**, v. GK: 8613 [→ 7581]. [Q] to roar:– roar [10], roared [4], roaring [3], mightily roar (+7580) [2], roareth [1]

7581 שְׁאָגָה **šᵉ'āgâ**, n.f. GK: 8614 [→ 7580]. roar, groan:– roaring [6], roarings [1]

7582 שָׁאָה **šā'â**, v. GK: 8615 & 8616 [→ 7585, 7588, 7591, 7612, 7866?, 7898?, 8663]. [Q] to lie wasted; [N] to be ruined; to roar; [H] to turn into desolation:– lay waste [2], desolate [1], make a rushing [1], rush [1], wasted [1]

7583 שָׁאָה **šā'â**, v. GK: 8617 [cf. 8159]. [Ht] to watch closely, gaze at:– wondering [1]

7584 שַׁאֲוָה **ša'ᵃwâ**, n.f. GK: 8618. devastating storm:–

7585 שְׁאוֹל **šᵉ'ôl**, n.f. & m. GK: 8619 [→ 7582; cf. 8040]. grave; by extension, realm of death, deepest depths, transliterated "Sheol":– hell [31], grave [30], pit [3], grave's [1]

7586 שָׁאוּל **šā'ûl**, n.pr.m. GK: 8620 [→ 7587; cf. 7592]. Saul, Shaul, "asked, [poss.] dedicated to God":– Saul [368], Saul's [28], Shaul [7], Saul's (+3807.1) [3]

7587 שָׁאוּלִי **šā'ûlî**, a.g. GK: 8621 [→ 7586]. Shaulite, "of Shaul":– Shaulites [1]

7588 שָׁאוֹן **šā'ôn**, n.m. GK: 8623 [→ 7582]. roar, uproar, tumult, loud noise; waste, desolation:– noise [8], rushing [3], tumult [3], tumultuous [2], horrible [1], pomp [1]

7589 שְׁאָט **šᵉ'āṭ**, n.[m.]. GK: 8624. malice:– despiteful [2], despite [1]

7590 שׁוּט **šûṭ** or שָׁאט **šā'ṭ**, v. GK: 8764. [Q] to malign, act malicious:– despise [2], despised [1]

7591 שְׁאִיָּה **šᵉ'iyyâ**, n.f. GK: 8625 [→ 7582]. desolation, ruin:– destruction [1]

7592 שָׁאַל **šā'al**, v. GK: 8626 [→ 847, 848, 4862, 7586, 7587, 7956, 7957, 7961; cf. 7593 (also used with compound proper names)]. [Q] to ask, inquire, request; [Qp] to be given over; [N] to ask permission; [P] to ask intently, beg; [H] to give what is asked for:– asked [46], ask [38], inquire [15], inquire [7], asketh [4], borrow [4], desired [4], earnestly asked (+7592) [4], lent [4], required [4], asking [3], demand [3], requested [3], require [3], saluted (+7965+3807.1) [3], asked straitly (+7592) [2], beg [2], borrowed [2], desire [2], salute (+7965+3807.1) [2], surely ask (+7592) [2], ask on [1], ask petition (+7596) [1], askest [1], consulted [1], consulter [1], demanded [1], desire a request (+7596) [1], desiredst [1], desireth [1], greet (+7965+3807.1) [1], laid to charge [1], obtained [1], pray [1], wished [1], wishing [1]

7593 שְׁאֵל **šᵉ'ēl** (Aram.), v. GK: 10689 [→ 7595; cf. 7592]. [P] to ask, question:– asked [3], demanded [1], requireth [1], require [1]

7594 שְׁאָל **šᵉ'āl**, n.pr.m. GK: 8627 [→ 7592]. Sheal, "May God grant!, asking":– Sheal [1]

שְׁאֹל **šᵉ'ōl**. See 7585.

7595 שְׁאֵלָה **šᵉ'ēlâ** (Aram.), n.f. GK: 10690 [→ 7593; cf. 7596]. verdict, decision:– demand [1]

7596 שְׁאֵלָה **šᵉ'ēlâ**, n.f. GK: 8629 [→ 7956; cf. 7592; cf. 7595]. petition, request:– petition [9], request [2], ask petition (+7592) [1], desire a request (+7592) [1], loan [1]

7597 שְׁאַלְתִּיאֵל **šᵉ'altî'ēl** or שַׁלְתִּיאֵל **šalti'ēl**, n.pr.m. GK: 8630 & 9003 [→ 7592+410]. Shealtiel, "I have asked [him] of God [El]; [poss.] God [El] is a shield, God [El] is a victor":– Shealtiel [8], Salathiel [1]

7598 שְׁאַלְתִּיאֵל **šᵉ'altî'ēl** (Aram.), n.pr.m. GK: 10691 [cf. 7597]. Shealtiel:– Shealtiel [1]

7599 שָׁאַן **šā'an**, v. GK: 8631 [→ 7600, 7946]. [Palpal] to be at ease, be at rest, be secure:– at ease [2], quiet [2], rest [1]

7600 שַׁאֲנָן **ša'ᵃnān**, a. GK: 8633 [→ 7599]. at ease, complacent, secure; insolent, proud:– at ease [6], quiet [2], tumult [2]

7601 שָׁסַס **šāsas** or שָׁאס **šā'as**, v. GK: 9116 [→ 4933, 8155; cf. 8154]. same as 8155: [Q] to plunder, ransack; [N] to be looted, be ransacked:– spoil [1]

7602 שָׁאַף **šā'ap**, v. GK: 8634 & 8635 [cf. 7779]. [Q] to pant after, long for, pursue; to trample, crush:– swallow up [4], desire [1], devour [1], earnestly desireth [1], hasteth [1], panted [1], pant [1], snuffed up [1], snuffeth up [1], swallowed up [1], swalloweth up [1]

7603 שְׂאֹר **šᵉ'ōr**, n.m. GK: 8419 [→ 4958, 4863]. yeast, leaven:– leaven [4], leavened bread [1]

7604 שָׁאַר **šā'ar**, v. GK: 8636 [→ 7605, 7610, 7609, 7611; cf. 7606]. [Q] to remain; [N] to be left, remain; [H] to leave, spare:– left [64], remained [23], remain [15], leave [12], remaineth [8], remnant [4], let [3], rest [2], left behind [1], reserve [1]

7605 שְׁאָר **šᵉ'ār**, n.m. GK: 8637 [→ 7604; cf. 7606]. remainder, remnant, the rest:– remnant [11], rest [10], residue [4], other [1]

7606 שְׁאָר **šᵉ'ār** (Aram.), n.m. GK: 10692 [cf. 7605]. the rest, remainder:– rest [9], residue [2], more [1]

7607 שְׁאֵר **šᵉ'ēr**, n.m. GK: 8638 [→ 7608]. flesh, meat; by extension the body as a whole; blood relative, as one's "flesh and blood":– flesh [7], near kinswoman [2], body [1], food [1], kinsman [1], kin [1], near kin [1], near [1], that is nigh unto [1]

7608 שַׁאֲרָה **ša'ᵃrâ**, var. GK: 8640 [→ 7607+1886.3]. blood relative, as one's "flesh and blood":– near kinswomen [1]

7609 שֶׁאֱרָה **še'ᵉrâ**, n.pr.f. GK: 8641 [→ 7604; cf. 242]. Sheerah, "blood relationship or female relative; remainder":– Sherah [1]

7610 שְׁאָר יָשׁוּב **šᵉ'ār yāšûb**, n.pr.m. GK: 8639 [→ 7604+3427]. Shear-Jashub, "remnant will return":– Shear-jashub [1]

7611 שְׁאֵרִית **šᵉʾērît**, n.f. GK: 8642 [→ 7604]. remnant, remainder, the rest:– remnant [44], residue [13], rest [3], remainder [2], escaped [1], left [1], posterity [1], remain [1]

7612 שְׁאֵת **šᵉʾēt**, n.f. GK: 8643 [→ 7582]. ruin, desolation:– desolation [1]

7613 שְׂאֵת **šᵉʾēt**, n.f. GK: 8420 & 8421 [→ 4984, 7863?, 7865?; cf. 4984]. swelling; splendor, honor, loftiness, acceptance:– rising [7], dignity [2], excellency [2], accepted [1], highness [1], raiseth up [1]

7614 שְׁבָא **šᵉbāʾ**, n.pr.m. & loc. GK: 8644 [→ 7615]. Sheba, "seven or oath":– Sheba [22], Sabeans [1]

7615 שְׁבָאִים **šᵉbāʾîm**, a.g. GK: 8645 [→ 7614]. Sabeans:– Sabeans [1]

7616 שְׁבָבִים **šᵉbābîm**, n.m.[pl]. GK: 8646 [→ 7632]. broken pieces, splinters:– broken in pieces [1]

7617 שָׁבָה **šābâ**, v. GK: 8647 [→ 7619, 7622, 7628, 7633, 7870]. [Q] to take captive; [Qp, N] to be taken captive:– carried away captive [7], carried captives [5], carry away captives (+7617) [4], captives [3], carried away [3], taken captives [3], taken captive [3], carried captive [2], carry away captive [2], lead captive [2], took captives [2], brought away captive [1], carried away captives (+7633) [1], carry away captives [1], driven away [1], led away captive [1], led captive [1], take captives [1], taken captive (+7628) [1], took away [1], took captive [1], took prisoners (+7628) [1]

7618 שְׁבוֹ **šᵉbô**, n.[f.]. GK: 8648. agate (exact identification is uncertain):– agate [2]

7619 שׁוּבָאֵל **šûbāʾēl** or שְׁבוּאֵל **šᵉbûʾēl**, n.pr.m. GK: 8742 & 8649 [→ 7617?+410]. Shubael, Shebuel, "[poss.] captive of God [El] or God [El] restores":– Shebuel [3], Shubael [3]

7620 שָׁבוּעַ **šābûaʿ**, n.m. GK: 8651 [→ 7650]. week (a time period of seven); Feast of Weeks, a festival celebrating the first produce of the harvest; a unit of time used in the book of Daniel, possibly a "week" of seven years:– weeks [12], week [4], full weeks (+3117) [1], seven [1], two weeks [1], whole weeks (+3117) [1]

7621 שְׁבוּעָה **šᵉbûʿâ**, n.f. GK: 8652 [→ 7650]. sworn oath:– oath [25], oaths [2], charge with an oath (+7650+871.1) [1], curse [1], sworn (+1167) [1]

7622 שְׁבוּת **šᵉbût** or שְׁבִית **šᵉbît**, n.f. GK: 8654 & 8669 [→ 7617]. captivity, exile, fortunes:– captivity [31], captives [1]

7623 שָׁבַח **šābaḥ**, v. GK: 8655 & 8656 [→ 3431; cf. 7624]. [P] to glorify, commend, extol; to keep still; [H] to cause stillness; [Ht] to glory in:– praise [4], commended [1], glory [1], keepeth [1], praised [1], stillest [1], stilleth [1], triumph [1]

7624 שְׁבַח **šᵉbaḥ** (Aram.), v. GK: 10693 [cf. 7623]. [Pa] to praise, honor:– praised [3], praise [2]

7625 שְׁבַט **šᵉbaṭ** (Aram.), n.m. GK: 10694 [cf. 7626]. tribe, a subgroup of a nation:– tribes [1]

7626 שֵׁבֶט **šēbeṭ**, n.m. GK: 8657 [→ 8275; cf. 7625]. rod, staff, a stick used to assist in walking, discipline, and guidance, often highly individualized and used for identification; of royalty: scepter; by extension: tribe, as a major unit of national group or clan (fig. identified with or under authority of a leader's staff), people, clan, family:– tribes [84], tribe [57], rod [34], sceptre [9], staff [2], correction [1], darts [1], pen [1], sceptres [1]

7627 שְׁבָט **šᵉbāṭ**, n.pr.m. GK: 8658. Shebat, "[month of] destroying [rain]":– Sebat [1]

7628 שְׁבִי **šᵉbî**, n.m. GK: 8660 [→ 7617]. captivity, exile; captive, prisoner:– captivity [35], captives [6], captive [3], prisoners [1], taken away [1], taken captive (+7617) [1], taken [1], took prisoners (+7617) [1]

7629 שֹׁבִי **šōbî**, n.pr.m. GK: 8661. Shobi, "[poss.] captive or Yahweh returns":– Shobi [1]

7630 שֹׁבַי **šōbay**, n.pr.m. GK: 8662. Shobai, "[poss.] captive or Yahweh returns":– Shobai [2]

7631 שְׁבִיב **šᵉbîb** (Aram.), n.m. GK: 10695 [cf. 7632]. flame:– flame [2]

7632 שָׁבִיב **šābîb**, n.m. GK: 8663 [→ 7616; cf. 7631]. flame; some sources: spark:– spark [1]

7633 שִׁבְיָה **šibyâ** or שְׁבִיָּה **šᵉbiyyâ**, n.f. GK: 8664 & 8665 [→ 7617]. captive, prisoner; captivity:– captives [7], captivity [1], carried away captives [1]

7634 שָׁבְיָה **šobyâ** or שָׁכְיָה **šāḵᵉyâ**, n.pr.m. GK: 8499 [→ 3068]. Shobia, "exile"; Sakia, "[poss.] one who looks to Yahweh":– Shachia [1]

7635 שְׁבִיל **šᵉbîl**, n.[m.]. GK: 8666 [→ 7640]. way, path:– paths [1], path [1]

7636 שָׁבִיס **šābîs**, n.[m.]. GK: 8667. headband:– cauls [1]

7637 שְׁבִיעִי **šᵉbîʿî**, a.num.ord. GK: 8668 [→ 7651]. seventh:– seventh [98]

שְׁבִית **šᵉbît**. See 7622.

7638 שָׂבָךְ **śābāḵ**, n.[m.]. GK: 8422 [→ 7639, 7730; cf. 5443]. same as 7639: network, lattice, interwoven mesh:–

שַׂבְּכָא **śabbᵉḵāʾ**. See 5443.

7639 שְׂבָכָה **śᵉbāḵâ**, n.f. GK: 8422 [→ 7638]. same as 7638: network, lattice, interwoven mesh:– network [5], networks [2], wreathen work [2], wreaths [2], checker [1], lattice [1], nets [1], snare [1], wreath [1]

7640 שֹׁבֶל **šōbel**, n.[m.]. GK: 8670 [→ 788, 789, 7635, 7641]. skirt, hem of skirt:– leg [1]

7641 שִׁבֹּלֶת **šibbōlet**, n.f. GK: 8672 & 8673 [→ 7640; cf. 5451]. head of grain; flood, torrent, flow:– ears [11], ears of corn [3], branches [1], channel [1], floods [1], shibboleth [1], waterflood (+4325) [1]

7642 שַׁבְּלוּל **šabbᵉlûl**, n.m. GK: 8671 [→ 1101?]. slug, snail; some sources: miscarriage:– snail [1]

שִׁבֹּלֶת **šibbōlet**. See 7641.

7643 שְׁבָם **šᵉbām** or שִׂבְמָה **śibmâ**, n.pr.loc. GK: 8423 & 8424. Sebam, Sibmah, "sweet smell":– Sibmah [4], Shebam [1], Shibmah [1]

7644 שֶׁבְנָא **šebnāʾ** or שֶׁבְנָה **šebnâ**, n.pr.m. GK: 8674 & 8675 [→ 7645?]. Shebna, "[Yahweh] return now":– Shebna [9]

7645 שְׁבַנְיָה **šᵉbanyâ** or שְׁבַנְיָהוּ **šᵉbanyāhû**, n.pr.m. GK: 8676 & 8677 [→ 7644?]. Shebaniah:– Shebaniah [7]

7646 שָׂבַע **śābaʿ**, v. GK: 8425 [→ 7647, 7648, 7649, 7654, 7653]. [Q] to be satisfied, have enough, be satiated; the filling and even overfilling of appetites and desires:– satisfied [38], filled [21], full [14], satisfy [7], filleth [2], have enough [2], satisfieth [2], filled full [1], filledst [1], fill [1], had enough [1], had plenty [1], have plenty [1], satiate [1], satisfiest [1], sufficed [1], weary [1]

7647 שָׂבָע **śābāʿ**, n.m. GK: 8426 [→ 7646]. abundance, overflowing:– plenty [4], plenteous [2], abundance [1], plenteousness [1]

7648 שֹׂבַע **śōbaʿ**, n.[m.]. GK: 8427 [→ 7646]. one's fill to contentment, all one wants:– full [3], fill [2], fulness [1], satisfying [1], sufficed [1]

7649 שָׂבֵעַ **śābēaʿ**, a. GK: 8428 [→ 7646]. full, abounding:– full [8], satisfied [2]

7650 שָׁבַע **šābaʿ**, v. GK: 8678 [→ 884, 7620, 7621, 7637, 7651, 7657, 7658, 7659]. [N] to swear an oath, make a sworn promise; [H] to make one swear an oath, give a charge:– sware [70], sworn [41], swear [32], sweareth [7], made swear [6], charge [5], swarest [5], took an oath [4], adjure [2], made to swear [2], straitly charged with an oath (+7650) [2], straitly sworn (+7650) [2], adjured [1], cause to swear [1], charge by an oath [1], charge with an oath (+7621+871.1) [1], charged with the oath [1], fed to the full [1], make swear [1], make to swear [1], swearers [1]

7651 שֶׁבַע **šebaʿ**, n.m. & f. GK: 8679 [→ 884, 1340?, 7637, 7658; cf. 7650; cf. 7655]. seven; (pl.) seventy:– seven [360], seventh [12], seventeen (+6240) [8], seventeenth (+6240) [6], by sevens (+7651) [4], sevenfold [3], seventy (+6235+2050.1) [1], seventy [1], threescore and seventeen (+7657+2050.1) [1], threescore and ten [1]

7652 שֶׁבַע **šebaʿ**, n.pr.m. & loc. GK: 8680 & 8681 [cf. 472, 1339, 3089, 3090, 7656]. Sheba, "seven or oath":– Sheba [10]

שָׁבֻעַ **šābuaʿ**. See 7620.

7653 שִׂבְעָה **śibʿâ**, n.f. GK: 8430 [→ 7646]. abundance, plenty:– fulness [1]

7654 שָׂבְעָה **śobʿâ**, n.f. GK: 8429 [→ 7646]. abundance, satisfaction, enough:– enough [2], full [1], satisfieth [1], sufficiently (+3807.1) [1], unsatiable (+1115) [1]

שִׁבְעָה **šibʿâ**. See 7651.

7655 שְׁבַע **šᵉbaʿ** (Aram.), n.m. & f. GK: 10696 [cf. 7651]. seven; the phrase "seven times" (Da 3:19) likely means to be as hot as possible:– seven [6]

7656 שִׁבְעָה **šibʿâ**, n.pr.loc. GK: 8683 [cf. 7652]. Shibah:– Shebah [1]

שִׁבְעָה **šᵉbuʿâ**. See 7620.

שְׁבִיעִי **šᵉbîʿî**. See 7637.

7657 שִׁבְעִים **šibʿîm**, n.pl. GK: 8684 [→ 7650]. seventy (pl. of "seven"):– seventy [57], threescore and ten [21], threescore and fifteen (+2568+2050.1) [2], threescore and fourteen (+702+2050.1) [2], threescore and twelve (+8147+2050.1) [2], seven [1], threescore and fifteen (+2568+2050.1+2050.1) [1], threescore and seventeen (+7651+2050.1) [1], threescore and sixteen (+8337+2050.1) [1], threescore and thirteen (+7969+1886.1+2050.1) [1], threescore and thirteen (+7969+2050.1) [1]

7658 שִׁבְעָנָה **šibʿānâ**, n.m. GK: 8685 [→ 7651; cf. 7650]. seven:– seven [1]

7659 שִׁבְעָתַיִם **šibʿātayim**, n.f.du. GK: 8686 [→ 7650]. seven-fold, seven times:– sevenfold [5], seven times [1]

7660 שָׁבַץ **šābaṣ**, v. GK: 8687 [→ 4865, 7661, 8665]. [P] to weave; [Pu] to be woven (of fine metal), (n.) a filigree setting:– embroider [1], set [1]

7661 שָׁבָץ **šābāṣ**, n.m. GK: 8688 [→ 7660]. seizure, cramp, referring to death throes:– anguish [1]

7662 שְׁבַק **šᵉbaq** (Aram.), v. GK: 10697. [P] to leave, have remain; [Htpe] to be left:– leave [3], alone [1], left [1]

7663 שָׂבַר **śābar**, v. GK: 8431 & 8432 [→ 7664; cf. 5452]. [Q] to examine; [P] to wait for, hope for:– hoped [2], viewed [2], wait [2], hope [1], tarry [1]

7664 שֵׂבֶר **śēber**, n.m. GK: 8433 [→ 7663]. hope:– hope [2]

7665 שָׁבַר **šābar**, v. GK: 8689 & 8653 [→ 4866, 4867, 7667, 7669, 7670, 7671; cf. 8406]. [Q] to break, destroy, crush; [Qp] to be broken; [N] to be destroyed, be smashed, be broken; [P] to break, smash, shatter; [H] to bring to break through (of birth); [Ho] to be crushed:– broken [63], break [30], brake [15], destroyed [7], breaketh [5], brake in pieces [4], brakest [4], hurt [3], destroy [2], quite break down (+7665) [2], torn [2], brake down [1], brake up [1], break down [1], break in pieces [1], breakest [1], bring to the birth [1], broken down [1], broken off [1], broken-hearted (+3820) [1], crush [1], quench [1]

7666 שָׁבַר **šābar**, v.den. GK: 8690 [→ 7668]. [Q] to buy grain or food; [H] to sell, allow to buy grain:– buy [14], sell [3], sold [2], bought [1], selleth [1]

7667 שֶׁבֶר **šeber** or שֵׁבֶר **šēber**, n.m. GK: 8691 & 8694 [→ 7671; cf. 7665]. destruction, brokenness, injury; "destruction of spirit" is discouragement, and so lacking motivation and being faint-hearted; interpretation (of a dream):– destruction [21], breach [6], hurt [4], affliction [2], breaking [2], bruise [2], breaches [1], breakings [1], brokenfooted (+7272) [1], brokenhanded (+3027) [1], crashing [1], interpretation [1], vexation [1]

7668 שֶׁבֶר **šeber**, n.[m.]. GK: 8692 [→ 7666]. grain:– corn [8], victuals [1]

7669 שֶׁבֶר **šeber**, n.pr.m. GK: 8693 [→ 7667 or 7668]. Sheber, "[poss.] lion; [poss.] breaking or crushing or roughly broken grain":– Sheber [1]

7670 שִׁבָּרוֹן **šibbārôn**, n.[m.]. GK: 8695 [→ 7665]. destruction, brokenness:– breaking [1], destruction [1]

7671 שְׁבָרִים **šᵉbārîm**, n.m.[pl]. GK: 8696 [→ 7667]. stone quarry:– Shebarim [1]

7672 שְׁבַשׁ **šᵉbaš** (Aram.), v. GK: 10698. [Htpa] to be baffled, be perplexed:– astonied [1]

7673 שָׁבַת **šābat**, v. GK: 8697 [→ 4868, 7674, 7676, 7677, 7678]. [Q] to rest, observe the Sabbath; [N] to come to an end, disappear; [H] to put to an end, stop:– cause to cease [17], cease [6], ceased [6], rest [6], make to cease [5], causeth [4], rested [4], made to cease [3], caused to fail [1], causeth to cease [1], celebrate sabbath (+7676) [1], keep a sabbath (+7676) [1], kept sabbath [1], left without [1], make cease [1], make rest [1], make to fail [1], maketh to cease [1], put away [1], put down [1], puttest away [1], rid [1], still [1], suffer to be lacking [1], took away [1]

7674 שֶׁבֶת **šebet**, n.f. GK: 8700 [→ 7673]. cessation, doing-nothing:– cease [1], loss of time [1], sit still [1]

7675 שֶׁבֶת **šebet**, n.f. GK: 8699 [→ 3427]. place of sitting or settling, site, seat:– seat [3], habitation [1], place [1]

7676 שַׁבָּת **šabbāt**, n.f. & m. GK: 8701 [→ 7677, 7678; cf. 7673]. Sabbath, the seventh day of the week in the Hebrew calendar (modern Saturday) with a focus on this day as a day of rest and worship; by extension: sabbath, any day or year or period of rest:– sabbath [67], sabbaths [34], every sabbath (+3117+3117+7676+871.1+871.1+1886.1+1886.1) [2], every sabbath (+7676) [2], every sabbath (+7676+871.1) [2],

another⁵ [1], celebrate sabbath (+7673) [1], keep a sabbath (+7673) [1], sabbath (+3117) [1]

7677 שַׁבָּתוֹן *šabbātôn*, n.m. GK: 8702 [→ 7676]. (day of) rest:– rest [8], sabbath [3]

7678 שַׁבְּתַי *šabbᵉtay*, n.pr.m. GK: 8703 [→ 7676]. Shabbethai, "*one born at Sabbath*":– Shabbethai [3]

7679 שָׂגָא *śāgā'*, v. GK: 8434 [→ 7689; cf. 7685; cf. 7680]. [H] to make great, extol:– increaseth [1], magnify [1]

7680 שְׂגָא *śᵉgā'* (Aram.), v. GK: 10677 [→ 7690; cf. 7679, 7685]. [P] to grow great:– multiplied [2], grow [1]

7681 שָׁגֶה *šāgeh*, n.pr.m. GK: 8707 [→ 7686?]. Shagee, "*wanderer, meanderer [like grazing sheep]*":– Shage [1]

7682 שָׂגַב *śāgab*, v. GK: 8435 [→ 4869, 7687]. [Q] to be too strong for; [N] to be lofty, be exalted; [P] to lift high; to protect; [Pu] to be kept safe; [H] to act exalted:– exalted [5], high [3], defend [2], safe [2], exalteth [1], excellent [1], lofty [1], set on high [1], set up on high [1], set up [1], setteth on high [1], strong [1]

7683 שָׁגַג *šāgag*, v. GK: 8704 [→ 49; cf. 4879, 7686]. [Q] to err unintentionally, go astray:– deceived [1], erred [1], sinneth ignorantly [1], went astray [1]

7684 שְׁגָגָה *šᵉgāgâ*, n.f. GK: 8705 [cf. 7686]. unintentional wrong, accidental error:– ignorance [11], error [2], unawares (+871.1) [2], unawares [2], sinneth through ignorance (+6213+871.1) [1], unwittingly (+871.1) [1]

7685 שָׂגָא *śāgā'*, v. GK: 8436 [cf. 7679]. [Q] to be prosperous, thrive, grow; [H] to increase (in wealth):– grow [1], increase [2]

7686 שָׁגָה *šāgâ*, v. GK: 8706 [→ 4870; cf. 4879, 7683, 7684, 7681?, 7691]. [Q] to sin unintentionally, go astray, wander:– erred [6], err [4], ravisht [2], causeth to go astray [1], deceived [1], deceiver [1], erreth [1], go astray [1], maketh to wander [1], sin through ignorance [1], wandered [1], wander [1]

7687 שְׂגוּב *śᵉgûb* or שְׂגִיב *śᵉgîb*, n.pr.m. GK: 8437 & 8439 [→ 7682]. Segub, Sebig, "*exalted*":– Segub [3]

7688 שָׂגַח *śāgaḥ*, v. GK: 8708. [H] to gaze, stare:– looketh [2], narrowly look [1]

7689 שַׂגִּיא *śaggî'*, a. GK: 8438 [→ 7679; cf. 7690]. exalted:– excellent [1], great [1]

7690 שַׂגִּיא *śaggî'* (Aram.), a. GK: 10678 [→ 7680; cf. 7689]. great, large, abundant:– much [4], great [3], many [2], exceeding [1], greatly [1], sore [1], very [1]

7691 שְׂגִיאָה *śᵉgî'â*, n.f. GK: 8709 [cf. 7686]. error, mistake:– errors [1]

7692 שִׁגָּיוֹן *šiggāyôn*, tt. or n.m. GK: 8710. shiggaion, shigionoth:– Shiggaion [1], Shigionoth [1]

7693 שָׁגַל *šāgal*, v. GK: 8711 [→ 7694]. [Q] to ravish, sexually violate; [Qp, N, Pu] to be ravished, be raped:– lien [1]

7694 שֵׁגָל *šēgal*, n.f. GK: 8712 [→ 7693; cf. 7695]. queen, royal bride:– queen [2]

7695 שֵׁגָל *šēgal* (Aram.), n.f. GK: 10699 [cf. 7694?]. wife, concubine:– wives [3]

7696 שָׂגַע *śāga'*, v. GK: 8713 [→ 7697]. [Pu] to be mad, act like a maniac; [Ht] to carry on like a madman:– mad [5], mad men [1], play the mad man [1]

7697 שִׁגָּעוֹן *šiggā'ôn*, n.m. GK: 8714 [→ 7696]. madness:– madness [2], furiously (+871.1) [1]

7698 שֶׁגֶר *šeger*, n.f. GK: 8715. calf, offspring (of cattle):– increase [4], cometh [1]

7699 שַׁד *šad* or שֹׁד *šōd*, n.m. GK: 8716 & 8718 [→ 7705]. (female) breast:– breasts [19], breast [3], paps [1], teats [1]

7700 שֵׁד *šēd*, n.[m.]. GK: 8717. demon, evil spirit:– devils [2]

7701 שֹׁד *šōd*, n.m. GK: 8719 [→ 7703]. destruction, ruin, violence:– destruction [7], spoil [4], spoiled [3], spoiling [3], desolation [1], robbery [1], wasting [1], oppression [1], spoiler [1]

7702 שָׂדַד *śādad*, v. GK: 8440 [→ 7708; cf. 5465, 7713]. [P] to till, harrow, break up the ground:– break clods [1], break clods [1], harrow [1]

7703 שָׁדַד *šādad*, v. GK: 8720 [→ 7701, 7736]. [Q] to destroy, devastate; [Qp] to be destroyed; [H] to be ruined; [P, Pol] to ravage, destroy; [Pu] to be destroyed, be ruined; [Ho] to be ruined:– spoiled [19], spoiler [8], spoil [8], laid waste [4], spoilers [3], robbers [2], utterly spoiled (+7703) [2], wasted [2], dead [1], destroyed [1], destroyer [1], destroy [1], oppress [1], spoilest [1], spoileth [1], wasteth [1]

7704 שָׂדֶה *śādeh* or שָׂדַי *śāday*, n.m. GK: 8441 & 8442. area of land, usually cultivated; field, open country, countryside:– field [245], fields [47], country [17], land [7], wild [7], ground [4], lands [4], soil [1], wild (+871.1+1886.1) [1]

7705 שִׁדָּה *šiddâ*, n.f. GK: 8721 [→ 7699]. lady, concubine; (pl.) harem:– musical instruments of all sorts (+7705) [2]

7706 שַׁדַּי *šadday*, n.[pr.m.]. GK: 8724 [→ 6701, 7707? (also used with compound proper names)]. Almighty:– Almighty [48]

7707 שְׁדֵיאוּר *šᵉdê'ûr*, n.pr.m. GK: 8725 [→ 7706?+301]. Shedeur, "*Shaddai is light* or *Shaddai is fire*":– Shedeur [5]

7708 שִׂדִּים *śiddîm*, n.pr.loc. GK: 8443 [→ 7702]. Siddim:– Siddim [3]

7709 שְׁדֵמָה *šᵉdēmâ*, n.f. GK: 8727. (cultivated) field; terrace:– fields [5]

7710 שָׁדַף *šādap*, v. GK: 8728 [→ 7711; cf. 7805]. [Qp] to be scorched:– blasted [3]

7711 שְׁדֵפָה *šᵉdēpâ* or שִׁדָּפוֹן *šiddāpôn*, n.f. & m. GK: 8729 & 8730 [→ 7710]. scorching; blight:– blasting [5], blasted [2]

7712 שְׁדַר *šᵉdar* (Aram.), v. GK: 10700 [→ 849]. [Htpa] to make every effort, strive:– laboured [1]

7713 שְׂדֵרָה *śᵉdērâ*, n.f. GK: 8444 [cf. 5468, 7702]. ranks, rows; planks (architectural term):– ranges [3], boards [1]

7714 שַׁדְרַךְ *šadrak*, n.pr.m. GK: 8731 [cf. 7715]. Shadrach, "*servant of Aku*":– Shadrach [1]

7715 שַׁדְרַךְ *šadrak* (Aram.), n.pr.m. GK: 10701 [cf. 7714]. Shadrach, "*servant of the (pagan moon god) Aku*":– Shadrach [14]

7716 שֶׂה *śeh*, n.m. & f. GK: 8445 [→ 2089]. sheep, lamb:– sheep [17], lamb [8], cattle [8], ewe [1], goat (+5795) [1], lamb (+3532) [1], lesser cattle [1], sheep (+3775) [1], small cattle [1]

7717 שָׂהֵד *śāhēd*, n.[m.]. GK: 8446. witness:– record [1]

7718 שֹׁהַם *šōham*, n.m. GK: 8732 [→ 7719]. onyx (exact identification is uncertain):– onyx [11]

7719 שֹׁהַם *šōham*, n.pr.m. GK: 8733 [→ 7718]. Shoham, "*carnelian [precious stone]*":– Shoham [1]

7720 שַׂהֲרֹנִים *śah°rōnîm*, n.m. GK: 8448. ornamental crescent (or moon shaped) necklace:– ornaments [2], round tires like the moon [1]

שָׂו *śaw*. See 7723.

7721 שׂוֹא *śô'*, v.inf. GK: 5951 [→ 4984]. inf. of 5375: to lift up, arise:–

7722 שׁוֹא *šô'* or שׁוֹאָה *šô'â*, n.f. GK: 8738 & 8739. trouble, ruin, disaster, desolation; ravage:– desolation [5], desolate [2], destruction [2], destroy [1], destructions [1], storm [1], wasteness [1]

7723 שָׁוְא *šāw'*, n.[m.]. GK: 8736 [→ 6673?]. worthlessness, vanity, falseness:– vanity [22], vain [17], false [5], in vain [3], in vain (+1886.1+3807.1) [2], lying [2], falsely [1], lies [1]

7724 שְׁוָא *šᵉwā'*, n.pr.m. GK: 8737 [→ 7737; cf. 7864]. Sheva, "*vanity, emptiness; one who will emulate*":– Sheva [1]

7725 שׁוּב *šûb*, v. GK: 8740 [→ 3437, 3432, 4877, 4878, 7726, 7727, 7728, 7729, 8666; cf. 8421 (also used with compound proper names)]. [Q] to turn back, turn to, return; [Qp] to return; [Pol] to restore, bring back; [Polal] to be recovered; [H] to restore, recover, bring back; [Ho] to be returned, be brought back; from the base meaning of turning back comes the fig. extension of restoration of relationship, as when one returns in repentance to God:– return [223], returned [147], turn [71], bring again [54], turn away [36], turn again [32], turned [32], again [30], come again [30], brought again [25], restore [25], render [16], came again [15], restored [13], turned away [13], brought back [12], cause to return [12], turned back [12], answer [11], go again [11], turned again [10], turn back [9], turneth [9], bring back [6], bring [6], returneth [6], turneth away [6], recompensed [5], recovered [5], certainly return (+7725) [4], put again [4], went back [4], carry back [3], caused to return [3], cometh again [3], go back [3], recompense [3], relieve [3], rendered [3], repent [3], restored again [3], reverse [3], say nay (+6440) [3], answered (+1697) [2], answered [2], bring again indeed (+7725) [2], bringeth back [2], bringing back [2], brought [2], carried again [2], certainly requite (+7725) [2], deliver again [2], drew back [2], give again [2], gone back [2], hinder [2], in any case bring again (+7725) [2], in any case deliver again (+7725) [2], in any wise go back (+7725) [2], in any wise return (+7725) [2], may [2], must needs bring again (+7725) [2], restore again (+7725) [2], restorer [2], return at all (+7725) [2], reward [2], surely bring back again (+7725) [2], turnest [2], went again [2], withdrawn [2], answer (+1697) [1],

answer (+4405) [1], answereth [1], at all turn (+7725) [1], averse [1], back again [1], bethink (+413+3820) [1], bethink (+413+3824) [1], bring home [1], bringeth [1], call [1], came back [1], camest back [1], carry again [1], cause to answer [1], cause to turn [1], causing to return [1], cease [1], considereth [1], consider [1], continually (+1980+2050.1) [1], converted [1], converting [1], converts [1], convert [1], deliver [1], deny (+6440) [1], drawn [1], fetch again [1], fro [1], gave [1], get again [1], get back again [1], giveth [1], give [1], go home [1], let [1], make return [1], makest to turn [1], more [1], out [1], past [1], pay [1], perverted [1], pull in again [1], put up again [1], put [1], recall [1], recover [1], refresheth [1], rendered again [1], reported [1], requited [1], requite [1], requiting [1], rescue [1], restoreth [1], retire [1], return again (+1980) [1], return again [1], returned back [1], rewardeth [1], sent back [1], set again [1], slidden back [1], still [1], take back [1], taken off [1], take [1], turn back again [1], turn from [1], turneth back [1], turning away [1], turning [1], withdrawest [1], withdraw [1], withdrew [1]

שׁוּבָאֵל *šûbā'ēl*. See 7619.

7726 שׁוֹבָב *šôbāb*, a. GK: 8743 [→ 7725]. faithless, rebellious, apostate:– backsliding [2], frowardly [1]

7727 שׁוֹבָב *šôbāb*, n.pr.m. GK: 8744 [→ 7725]. Shobab, "*one who turns back, repents*":– Shobab [4]

7728 שׁוֹבֵב *šôbēb*, a. GK: 8745 [→ 7725]. unfaithful, traitorous, apostate:– backsliding [2]

7729 שׁוּבָה *šûbâ*, n.f. GK: 8746 [→ 7725]. returning, i.e., repentance:– returning [1]

7730 שׂוֹבֶךְ *śôbek*, n.[m.]. GK: 8449 [→ 7638; cf. 5440]. tangle of branches:– thick boughs [1]

7731 שׁוֹבָךְ *šôbak*, n.pr.m. GK: 8747 [cf. 7780]. Shobach:– Shobach [2]

7732 שׁוֹבָל *šôbāl*, n.pr.m. GK: 8748. Shobal, "*basket*":– Shobal [9]

7733 שׁוֹבֵק *šôbēq*, n.pr.m. GK: 8749 [→ 3435]. Shobek, "*victor*":– Shobek [1]

7734 סוּג *sûg* or שׂוּג *śûg*, v. GK: 6047 [→ 5253]. same as 5472: [N] to be turned back, be disloyal:– turned [1]

7735 שׂוּג *śûg*, v. GK: 8451 [cf. 5473?]. [Pil] to cause growth, raise:– make to grow [1]

7736 שׁוּד *šûd* or שָׁדַד *šādad*, v. GK: 8720 [→ 7703]. same as 7703: [Q] to destroy, devastate:– wasteth [1]

שׁוֹד *šôd*. See 7699, 7701.

7737 שָׁוָה *šāwâ*, v. GK: 8750 & 8751 [→ 3438, 3440, 3441, 7724, 7740, 7741, 7862; cf. 7739]. [Q] to be like, be equal; to be appropriate, be deserved; [N] to be like; [P] to make smooth; to set, place, bestow; [H] to liken; to count as equal:– laid [3], compared [2], equal [2], maketh [2], alike [1], availeth [1], behaved [1], bringeth forth [1], countervail [1], like [1], made plain [1], make equal [1], profited [1], profit [1], reckoned [1], set [1]

7738 שָׁוָה *šāwâ*, var. GK: *. to destroy:–

7739 שְׁוָה *šᵉwâ* (Aram.), v. GK: 10702 [cf. 7737]. [Peil] to be made like; [Pa] to make like; [Htpa] to be made into:– made [2]

7740 שָׁוֵה *šāwēh*, n.pr.loc. GK: 8753 [cf. 7737]. Shaveh, "*level [valley]*":– Shaveh [1]

7741 שָׁוֵה קִרְיָתַיִם *šāwēh qiryātayim*, n.pr.loc. GK: 8754 [→ 7737+7176]. Shaveh Kiriathaim:– Shaveh Kiriathaim [1]

7742 שׂוּחַ *śûaḥ*, v. GK: 8452. [Q] to meditate:– meditate [1]

7743 שׁוּחַ *šûaḥ*, v. GK: 8755 [→ 7745, 7746?, 7845; cf. 7812, 7817]. [Q] sink down:– bowed down [1], humbled [1], inclineth [1]

7744 שׁוּחַ *šûaḥ*, n.pr.m. GK: 8756 [→ 7747]. Shuah, "*depression, lowland [an Aramean land on the Euphrates River]*":– Shuah [2]

7745 שׁוּחָה *šûḥâ*, n.f. GK: 8757 [→ 7746?; cf. 7743, 7882]. pit, rift:– pit [3], ditch [1], pits [1]

7746 שׁוּחָה *šûḥâ*, n.pr.[m.?]. GK: 8758 [→ 7745?; cf. 7743?]. Shuhah, "*pit, depression*":– Shuah [1]

7747 שׁוּחִי *šûḥî*, a.g. GK: 8760 [→ 7744]. Shuhite:– Shuhite [5]

7748 שׁוּחָם *šûḥām*, n.pr.m. GK: 8761 [→ 7749]. Shuham:– Shuham [1]

7749 שׁוּחָמִי *šûḥāmî*, a.g. GK: 8762 [→ 7748]. Shuhamite, "*of Shuham*":– Shuhamites [2]

7750 שׂוּט *śûṭ*, v. GK: 8454 [→ 7846?; cf. 7847]. [Q] to turn aside (to false gods):– turn aside [2]

7751 שׁוּט **šûṭ**, v.den. GK: 8763 [→ 4880, 7752, 7850, 7885]. [Q] to roam, go about; to oar (a boat); [Pol] to wander, go here and there; [Htpol] to rush here and there:– run to and fro [6], going to and fro [2], gone [1], go [1], mariners [1], rowers [1], went about [1]

7752 שׁוֹט **šôṭ**, n.m. GK: 8765 & 8867 [→ 7850; cf. 7751]. whip, lash, scourge:– scourge [5], whips [4], whip [2]

7753 שׂוּךְ **šûk**, v. GK: 8455 [→ 7754, 7755; cf. 5259, 5526]. [Q] to block with thorn hedges:– fenced [1], hedge up [1], made a hedge [1]

7754 שׂוֹךְ **šôk** or שׂוֹכָה **šôkâ**, n.f. GK: 8456 & 8457 [→ 7753]. branch or brushwood:– bough [2]

7755 שׂוֹכֹה **šôkōh** or שׂוֹכוֹ **šôkô**, n.pr.loc. GK: 8458 & 8459 [→ 7753]. Soco, Socoh, "[poss.] thorny place":– Shochoh [2], Socoh [2], Shocho [1], Shoco [1], Sochoh [1], Socho [1]

7756 שׂוּכָתִי **šûkātî**, a.g. GK: 8460. Sucathite:– Suchathites [1]

7757 שׁוּל **šûl**, n.m. GK: 8767 [cf. 7887]. hem (of a robe); skirt:– hem [5], skirts [4], hems [1], train [1]

7758 שׁוֹלָל **šôlāl** or שֵׁילָל **šêlāl**, a. GK: 8768 & 8871 [→ 7997]. barefoot, stripped:– spoiled [2], stript [1]

7759 שׁוּלַמִּית **šûlammît**, a.g.[f.]. GK: 8769. Shulammite:– Shulamite [2]

7760 שִׂים **šîm** or שׂוּם **šûm**, v. GK: 8492 [→ 3450, 8667; cf. 3455, 7761]. [Q] to place, put, establish, appoint; [Qp] to be placed, set upon; [H] to cause to place, put; [Ho] to be set:– put [142], set [114], make [64], made [48], laid [35], lay [23], appoint [11], set up [10], appointed [8], maketh [8], consider (+3824) [5], give [5], putteth [5], brought [4], gave [4], layeth [4], makest [3], put in [3], care (+3820) [2], considered (+3820) [2], disposed [2], in any wise set (+7760) [2], lay up [2], look well (+5869) [2], mark well (+3820) [2], ordained [2], painted (+7760+871.1+1886.1) [2], placed [2], put on [2], put to [2], puttest [2], set on [2], take [2], turneth [2], wholly set (+7760) [2], bring [1], called [1], cast [1], caused to be set [1], change [1], charged [1], commit [1], consider (+3807.1) [1], consider (+3820) [1], consider [1], convey [1], determined (+1961) [1], disguiseth (+5643) [1], doeth [1], done [1], gavest [1], get [1], given [1], had [1], heap up [1], holdeth [1], impute [1], laid up [1], laidst [1], lay down [1], layest [1], leave [1], made out [1], named (+8034) [1], ordain [1], ordereth [1], place [1], preserve [1], purposed [1], putting [1], regard (+3820) [1], regarded (+3820) [1], regarding [1], rehearse [1], rewarded [1], settest [1], setteth [1], shed [1], shewed [1], shew [1], stedfastly [1], told (+6310+871.1) [1], took [1], tread down (+4823) [1], turned [1], turn [1], will^S [1], wrought [1]

7761 שִׂים **šîm** (Aram.), v. GK: 10682 [cf. 7760]. [P] to place (an order); value (a decree); [Peil] to be placed, be issued; [Htpe] to be put, be laid (to rubble):– made [10], make [5], commanded (+2942) [3], laid [2], given [1], give [1], named (+8036) [1], regarded (+2942) [1], regardeth [1], set [1]

7762 שׁוּמִים **šûmîm**, n.[m.]. GK: 8770. garlic:– garlick [1]

7763 שֹׁמֵר **šōmēr**, n.pr.m. GK: 9071 [→ 8116]. Shomer, "guardian, watchman":– Shomer [2]

7764 שׁוּנִי **šûnî**, n.pr.m. GK: 8771 [→ 7765]. Shuni:– Shuni [2]

7765 שׁוּנִי **šûnî**, a.g. GK: 8772 [→ 7764]. Shunite, "of Shuni":– Shunites [1]

7766 שׁוּנֵם **šûnēm**, n.pr.loc. GK: 8773 [→ 7767]. Shunem:– Shunem [3]

7767 שׁוּנַמִּי **šûnammî**, a.g. GK: 8774 [→ 7766]. Shunammite, "of Shunem":– Shunammite [8]

7768 שָׁוַע **šāwaʿ**, v. GK: 8775 [→ 7769, 7771, 7773, 7775 (also used with compound proper names)]. [P] to cry for help, plead:– cried [10], cry [6], crieth out [1], crieth [1], cry aloud [1], cry out [1], shout [1]

7769 שׁוּעַ **šûaʿ**, n.[m.]. GK: 8780 & 8782 [→ 7768, 7770; cf. 7771]. cry for help; wealth:– cry [1], riches [1]

7770 שׁוּעַ **šûaʿ**, n.pr.m. GK: 8781 [→ 7769; cf. 7771]. Shua, "prosperity":– Shuah [2], Shua [1]

7771 שׁוֹעַ **šôaʿ**, a. & n.m. GK: 8777 & 8779 [→ 50, 7768, 7770, 7769]. crying out; highly respected, noble; (n.) the rich:– bountiful [1], crying [1], rich [1]

7772 שׁוֹעַ **šôaʿ**, n.pr.g. GK: 8778 [cf. 6970]. Shoa, "rich":– Shoa [1]

7773 שֶׁוַע **šewaʿ**, n.[m.]. GK: 8776 [→ 7768]. cry for help:– cry [1]

7774 שׁוּעָא **šûʿāʾ**, n.pr.f. GK: 8783. Shua, "prosperity":– Shua [1]

7775 שַׁוְעָה **šawʿâ**, n.f. GK: 8784 [→ 7768]. cry for help:– cry [11]

7776 שׁוּעָל **šûʿāl**, n.m. GK: 8785 [→ 2705, 7777]. fox; jackal:– foxes [6], fox [1]

7777 שׁוּעָל **šûʿāl**, n.pr.m. & loc. GK: 8786 & 8787 [→ 7776]. Shual, "fox or jackal":– Shual [2]

7778 שׁוֹעֵר **šôʿēr**, n.m. GK: 8788 [→ 8179; cf. 8652]. gatekeeper, doorkeeper:– porters [31], porter [4], doorkeepers [2]

7779 שׁוּף **šûp**, v. GK: 8789 & 8790 [cf. 7602]. [Q] to strike; to crush; some sources: bruise, a wound that is not fatal:– bruise [2], breaketh [1], cover [1]

7780 שׁוֹפָךְ **šôpak**, n.pr.m. GK: 8791 [cf. 7731]. Shophach:– Shophach [2]

7781 שׁוּפָמִי **šûpāmî**, a.g. GK: 8793 [→ 8197]. Shuphamite, "of Shupham":– Shuphamites [1]

שׁוֹפָן **šôpān**. See 5855.

7782 שׁוֹפָר **šôpār**, n.m. GK: 8795 [→ 829; cf. 8231]. trumpet, ram's horn:– trumpet [48], trumpets [20], cornet [3], cornets [1]

7783 שׁוּק **šûq**, v. GK: 8796 [→ 7785, 7784; cf. 8264?]. [H] to prove narrow, overflow; [Polel] to water abundantly:– overflow [2], waterest [1]

7784 שׁוּק **šûq**, n.m. GK: 8798 [→ 7783]. street:– streets [3], street [1]

7785 שׁוֹק **šôq**, n.[f.]. GK: 8797 [→ 7783; cf. 8243]. (lower) thigh; leg:– shoulder [13], legs [4], hip [3], thigh [1]

7786 שׂוּר **šûr**, v.den. GK: 8606 [→ 4951, 8269, 8323]. same as 8323: [Q] to rule, govern; [H] to choose a prince:– had power [1], made princes [1], reigned [1]

7787 שׂוּר **šûr**, v. GK: *. [Q] to saw:– cut [1]

7788 שׁוּר **šûr**, v. GK: 8801. [Q] to travel, descend:– sing [1], wentest [1]

7789 שׁוּר **šûr**, v. GK: 8800 [→ 7790, 7791, 7793?, 7791, 8284]. [Q] to see, look, view:– behold [5], see [4], lay wait [1], looketh [1], look [1], observed [1], observe [1], perceiveth [1], regard [1]

7790 שׁוּר **šûr**, n.[m.]. GK: 8803 [→ 7791, 7793; cf. 7789; cf. 7792]. enemy:– enemies [1]

7791 שׁוּר **šûr** or שׁוּרָה **šûrâ**, n.m. & f. GK: 8803 & 8805 [→ 7790, 8284; cf. 7789]. wall, supporting wall (of a terrace):– wall [3], walls [1]

7792 שׁוּר **šûr** (Aram.), n.m. GK: 10703 [cf. 7790]. wall:– walls [3]

7793 שׁוּר **šûr**, n.pr.loc. GK: 8804 [→ 7790; cf. 7789?]. Shur, "wall":– Shur [6]

7794 שׁוֹר **šôr**, n.m. GK: 8802 [→ 51, 8670; cf. 8450]. bull, ox:– ox [54], bullock [11], oxen [8], cow [2], another's^S (+7453) [1], bullocks [1], bull [1], wall [1]

7795 שׁוֹרָה **šôrâ**, n.[f.]. GK: 8463 [→ 5493?; cf. 8184?]. place, row or a type of grain:– principal [1]

שׂוֹרֵק **šôrēq**. See 8321.

7796 שׂוֹרֵק **šôrēq**, n.pr.loc. GK: 8604 [→ 8320]. Sorek, "blood red grapes":– Sorek [1]

7797 שׂוּשׂ **šûś**, v. GK: 8464 [→ 4885, 8342]. [Q] to rejoice, be pleased, be delighted:– rejoice [12], glad [4], rejoiced [3], rejoiceth [3], greatly rejoice (+7797) [2], exceedingly rejoice (+8057+871.1) [1], joy [1], make mirth [1]

7798 שׁוֹשָׁא **šawšāʾ**, n.pr.m. GK: 8807. Shavsha:– Shavsha [1]

7799 שׁוּשַׁן **šûšan**, n.m. GK: 8808. lily plant; some sources: lotus plant:– lilies [8], lily [5], Shoshannim [2], Shoshannim-Eduth (+5715) [1]

7800 שׁוּשַׁן **šûšan**, n.pr.loc. GK: 8809 [cf. 7801]. Susa:– Shushan [21]

7801 שׁוּשַׁנְכָי **šûšankāy** (Aram.), n.pr.g. & loc. GK: 10704 [cf. 7800]. of Susa:– Susanchites [1]

7802 שׁוּשַׁן עֵדוּת **šûšan ʿēdût**, t.t. GK: 8808 + 6343 [→ 7799+5715]. Shushan Eduth, "Lily of the covenant":– Shushan-eduth [1]

שׁוּשַׁק **šûšaq**. See 7895.

7803 שׁוּתָלַח **šûtelaḥ**, n.pr.m. GK: 8811 [→ 8364]. Shuthelah:– Shuthelah [4]

7804 שֵׁיזִב **šêzib** (Aram.), v. GK: 10706. [Sh] to rescue, save:– deliver [6], delivered [2], delivereth [1]

7805 שָׁזַף **šāzap**, v. GK: 8812 [cf. 7710]. [Q] to see; to be darkened:– looked [1], saw [1], seen [1]

7806 שָׁזַר **šāzar**, v. GK: 8813. [Ho] to be finely twisted:– twined [21]

7807 שַׁח **šaḥ**, a. GK: 8814 [→ 7817]. downward, bent, low:– humble person (+5869) [1]

7808 שֵׂחַ **śēaḥ**, n.[m.]. GK: 8465 [→ 7878]. thoughts:– thought [1]

7809 שָׁחַד **šāḥad**, v. GK: 8815 [→ 7810]. [Q] to give a gift; pay a bribe; pay a ransom:– give a reward [1], hirest [1]

7810 שֹׁחַד **šōḥad**, n.m. GK: 8816 [→ 7809]. bribe, gift-reward [7], gift [6], gifts [4], bribes [3], present [2], bribery [1]

7811 שָׂחָה **śāḥâ**, v. GK: 8466 [→ 7813]. [Q] to swim; [H] to make swim, flood:– make to swim [1], swimmeth [1], swim [1]

7812 שָׁחָה **šāḥâ**, v. GK: 8817 [cf. 7743, 7817]. [Q] to bow down; [H] to weigh down, cause to bow:– worship [54], worshipped [39], bowed [31], bow down [14], bowed down [4], made obeisance [4], bow [3], obeisance [3], reverence [3], worshippeth [3], worshipping [3], did obeisance [2], fall down [2], crouch [1], did reverence [1], fell down [1], fell flat [1], humbly beseech [1], maketh stoop [1], reverenced [1]

7813 שָׂחוּ **śāḥû**, n.[m.]. GK: 8467 [→ 7811]. water deep enough to swim in:– swim [1]

7814 שְׂחוֹק **śᵉḥôq**, n.[m.]. GK: 8468 [→ 7832]. laughter, which can communicate joy or ridicule; object of ridicule:– laughter [6], derision [5], laughed to scorn [1], laughing [1], one mocked [1], sport [1]

7815 שְׁחוֹר **šᵉḥôr**, n.[m.]. GK: 8818 [→ 7835]. soot:– coal [1]

שִׁיחוֹר **šîḥôr**. See 7883.

שָׁחוֹר **šāḥôr**. See 7838.

7816 שְׁחוּת **šᵉḥût**, n.f. GK: 8819 [→ 7825]. trap, pit:– pit [1]

7817 שָׁחַח **šāḥaḥ** or שִׁיחַ **śîaḥ**, v. GK: 8820 & 8863 [→ 7807; cf. 7743, 7812]. [Q] to bow down, bend low; [N] to be brought low; [H] to humble, bring low:– bowed down [4], cast down [4], bow [2], brought low [2], bending [1], boweth down [1], bring down [1], bringeth down [1], brought down [1], couch [1], humbleth [1], low [1], stoop [1]

7818 שָׂחַט **śāḥaṭ**, v. GK: 8469. [Q] to squeeze out (juice from grapes):– pressed [1]

7819 שָׁחַט **šāḥaṭ**, v. GK: 8821 & 8823 [→ 7821]. [Q] to slaughter, kill; [Qp, N] to be killed, be slaughtered:– kill [23], slew [21], killed [15], slay [9], slain [4], killeth [3], killing [1], offer [1], shot out [1], slaughter [1], slaying [1]

7820 שָׁחַט **šāḥaṭ**, v. GK: 8822. [Qp] to be hammered, beaten; some sources: to be alloyed, blended, referring to the mixing of metals:– beaten [5]

7821 שְׁחִיטָה **šᵉḥîṭâ**, n.f. GK: 8824 [→ 7819]. killing, slaughter:– killing [1]

7822 שְׁחִין **šᵉḥîn**, n.m. GK: 8825. boils, skin sores:– boil [9], boils [2], botch [2]

7823 שָׁחִיס **šāḥîs** or סָחִישׁ **sāḥîš**, n.[m.]. GK: 8826 & 6084. growth, what springs up on its own (in the second year):– that which springeth of the same [2]

7824 שָׁחִיף **šāḥîp**, a. GK: 8470. covered, paneled:– cieled [1]

7825 שְׁחִית **šᵉḥît**, n.f. GK: 8827 [→ 7816]. pit, trap, grave:– destructions [1], pits [1]

7826 שַׁחַל **šaḥal**, n.m. GK: 8828 [→ 7827]. lion:– lion [4], fierce lion [3]

7827 שְׁחֵלֶת **šᵉḥēlet**, n.f. GK: 8829 [→ 7826]. onycha (a fragrant spice):– onycha [1]

7828 שַׁחַף **šaḥap**, n.[m.]. GK: 8830. gull or possibly bat:– cuckow [2]

7829 שַׁחֶפֶת **šaḥepet**, n.f. GK: 8831. wasting disease, consumption:– consumption [2]

7830 שַׁחַץ **šaḥaṣ**, n.[m.]. GK: 8832 [→ 7831]. pride, dignity:– lion's [1], pride [1]

7831 שַׁחֲצוּמָה **šaḥᵃṣûmâ** or שַׁחֲצִימָה **šaḥᵃṣîmâ**, n.pr.loc. GK: 8833 & 8834 [→ 7830]. Shahazimah, Shahazumah, "elevated place":– Shahazimah [1]

7832 שָׂחַק **śāḥaq**, v. GK: 8471 [→ 3446, 4890, 7814; cf. 6711]. [Q] to laugh, be amused; to laugh at, mock, scoff; [P] to celebrate, rejoice, frolic; [H] to scorn; this can communicate

joy or ridicule:– laugh [8], play [5], played [3], make merry [2], playing [2], rejoicing [2], scorneth [2], deride [1], derision [1], in sport [1], laughed to scorn [1], laughed [1], laugheth [1], made sport [1], make sport [1], mockers [1], mocketh [1], mock [1], rejoice [1]

7833 שָׁחַק *šāḥaq*, v. GK: 8835 [→ 7834]. [Q] to grind, wear away:– beat small [2], beat [1], wear [1]

7834 שַׁחַק *šaḥaq*, n.m. GK: 8836 [→ 7833]. clouds, skies:– clouds [11], skies [5], heaven [1], sky [1], small dust [1]

 שְׂחֹק *s*ᵉḥōq*. See 7814.

7835 שָׁחַר *šāḥar*, v. GK: 8837 [→ 300, 4891, 7815, 7838, 7225, 7839, 7840, 7842]. [Q] to become black:– black [1]

7836 שָׁחַר *šāḥar*, v.den. GK: 8838 [→ 7841; cf. 7837?]. [Q] to seek, look; [P] to earnestly seek, search for:– seek early [4], betimes [1], diligently seeketh [1], diligently seek [1], early seek [1], inquired early after [1], rising betimes [1], seek betimes [1], seek in the morning [1]

7837 שַׁחַר *šaḥar*, n.m. GK: 8840 [→ 7223, 7842; cf. 7836?]. dawn, daybreak:– morning [12], day [5], early [2], Shahar [1], day began [1], dayspring [1], light [1], riseth [1]

 שָׁחֹר *šiḥōr*. See 7883.

7838 שָׁחֹר *šāḥōr*, a. GK: 8839 [→ 7835]. black, dark:– black [6]

7839 שַׁחֲרוּת *šaḥᵃrût*, n.f. GK: 8841 [→ 7835]. vigor, prime of youth, an extension of dark hair color (or perhaps of the dawn):– youth [1]

7840 שְׁחַרְחֹר *s*ᵉḥarḥōr*, a. GK: 8842 [→ 7835]. dark, swarthy (complexion):– black [1]

7841 שְׁחַרְיָה *s*ᵉḥaryâ*, n.pr.m. GK: 8843 [→ 7836]. Shehariah, "*he seeks Yahweh*":– Shehariah [1]

7842 שַׁחֲרַיִם *šaḥᵃrayim*, n.pr.m. GK: 8844 [→ 7837; cf. 7835]. Shaharaim, "*one born at early [reddish] dawn*":– Shaharaim [1]

7843 שָׁחַת *šāḥat*, v. GK: 8845 [→ 4889, 4892, 4893; cf. 7844]. [N] to be corrupt, be ruined, be marred; [P] to corrupt, destroy, ruin; [H] to destroy, corrupt, bring to ruin:– destroy [68], destroyed [22], corrupted [11], corrupt [10], destroying [5], mar [4], marred [3], corrupters [2], destroyer [2], destroyeth [2], spoilers [2], utterly corrupt (+7843) [2], waster [2], battered [1], cast off [1], corrupting [1], corruptly [1], destroyers [1], destroyest [1], destruction [1], lose [1], perish [1], spilled [1], wasted [1]

7844 שְׁחַת *s*ᵉḥat* (Aram.), v. GK: 10705 [cf. 7843]. [Pp] to be corrupt, wicked; (as noun) corruption:– fault [2], corrupt [1]

7845 שַׁחַת *šaḥat*, n.f. GK: 8846 [→ 7743]. pit, dungeon; corruption, decay:– pit [14], corruption [4], destruction [2], ditch [1], grave [1]

7846 שֵׂט *šēṭ*, n.[m.]. GK: 8473 [→ 7750?]. rebel:– revolters [1]

7847 שָׂטָה *šāṭâ*, v. GK: 8474 [cf. 7750]. [Q] to go astray:– gone aside [2], decline [1], go aside [1], goeth aside [1], turn [1]

7848 שִׁטָּה *šiṭṭâ*, n.f. GK: 8847 [→ 7851]. acacia wood:– shittim [27], shittah tree [1]

7849 שָׂטַח *šāṭaḥ*, v. GK: 8848 [→ 4894]. [Q] to spread out, enlarge, scatter; [P] to spread out:– spread all abroad (+7849) [2], spread [2], enlargeth [1], stretched out [1]

7850 שֹׁטֵט *šōṭēṭ*, n.[m.]. GK: 8849 [→ 7752; cf. 7751]. whip, scourge:– scourges [1]

7851 שִׁטִּים *šiṭṭîm*, n.pr.loc. GK: 8850 [→ 7848]. Shittim, "*acacia trees*":– Shittim [5]

7852 שָׂטַם *šāṭam*, v. GK: 8475 [→ 4895; cf. 7853]. [Q] to hold a grudge, hold hostility toward:– hated [2], hate [2], hateth [1], opposest [1]

7853 שָׂטַן *šāṭan*, v.den. GK: 8476 [→ 7854, 7855, 7856; cf. 7852]. [Q] to accuse, slander:– adversaries [5], resist [1]

7854 שָׂטָן *šāṭān*, n.m.[pr.]. GK: 8477 [→ 7853]. (human) adversary, accuser, one who opposes, slanderer; (as a proper name) Satan, the spirit being who is an opponent of God and slanderer of his creation:– Satan [19], adversary [6], adversaries [1], withstand [1]

7855 שִׂטְנָה *šiṭnâ*, n.f. GK: 8478 [→ 7856; cf. 7853]. accusation:– accusation [1]

7856 שִׂטְנָה *šiṭnâ*, n.pr.loc. GK: 8479 [→ 7855]. Sitnah, "*hostility*":– Sitnah [1]

7857 שָׁטַף *šāṭap*, v. GK: 8851 [→ 7858, 8241]. [Q] to overflow, flood, wash away; [N] to be rinsed, be swept away;

[Pu] to be rinsed:– overflow [10], overflowing [8], rinsed [3], drown [1], flowing [1], overflowed [1], overflown [1], overwhelmed [1], ran [1], rusheth [1], throughly washed away [1], washed [1], washest away [1]

7858 שֶׁטֶף *šeṭep*, n.m. GK: 8852 [→ 7857; cf. 8241]. flood, torrents (of rain):– flood [3], floods [1], outrageous [1], overflowing of waters [1]

7859 שְׂטַר *s*ᵉṭar* (Aram.), n.m. GK: 10680. side:– side [1]

7860 שֹׁטֵר *šōṭēr*, n.m. GK: 8853 [→ 4896, 7861]. [Q] to keep a record; (n.) official, officer, foreman:– officers [23], overseer [1], ruler [1]

7861 שִׁטְרַי *šiṭray* or שֻׁרְטֵי *širṭay*, n.pr.m. GK: 8855 & 9231 [→ 7860]. Shitrai, Shirtai, "*scribe, officer*":– Shitrai [1]

7862 שַׁי *šay*, n.m. GK: 8856 [→ 52, 7737; cf. 2365?]. gift:– presents [2], present [1]

7863 שִׂיא *s*î'*, n.m. GK: 8480 [→ 7865; cf. 4984; 7613?]. height:– excellency [1]

7864 שֵׁיָא *s*ᵉyā'*, n.pr.m. GK: 8857 [cf. 7724]. Sheya, cf. 7724:–

7865 שִׂיאֹן *s*î'ôn*, n.pr.loc. GK: 8481 [→ 7863; cf. 4984; 7613]. Siyon:– Sion [1]

7866 שִׂיאָן *s*î'ôn*, n.pr.loc. GK: 8858 [→ 7582?]. Shion:– Shion [1]

7867 שִׂיב *s*îb*, v. GK: 8482 [→ 7869, 7872; cf. 7868]. [Q] to be gray(-haired); hence, old:– grayheaded [1]

7868 שִׂיב *s*îb* (Aram.), v. GK: 10681 [cf. 7867]. [P] to be gray-haired, (ptcp.) elder, a community leader with considerable political, social, and judicial authority, as a fig. extension of being gray-haired, implying wisdom and honor:– elders [5]

7869 שֵׂיב *s*êb*, n.[m.]. GK: 8483 [→ 7867]. gray-headedness, old age:– age [1]

7870 שִׁיבָה *šîbâ*, n.f. GK: 8860 [→ 7617; cf. 7622]. captives:– captivity [1]

7871 שִׁיבָה *šîbâ*, n.f. GK: 8859 [→ 3427?]. stay:– lay [1]

7872 שֵׂיבָה *s*êbâ*, n.f. GK: 8484 [→ 7867]. gray-haired (person), old age:– old age [6], gray hairs [5], hoar head [2], hoary head [2], gray head [1], grayheaded [1], hoar hairs [1], hoary [1]

7873 שִׂיג *s*îg*, n.[m.]. GK: 8485 [cf. 5253, 5509]. busyness; perhaps: bowel movement:– pursuing [1]

7874 שִׂיד *s*îd*, v.den. GK: 8486 [→ 7875]. [Q] to coat with (a whitewash) plaster:– plaister [2]

7875 שִׂיד *s*îd*, n.[m.]. GK: 8487 [→ 7874]. lime, plaster (used as a whitewash):– lime [2], plaister [2]

7876 שָׁיָה *šāyâ*, v. GK: 8861 [cf. 5382]. [Q] to desert, forget:– unmindful [1]

7877 שִׁיזָא *šîzā'*, n.pr.m. GK: 8862. Shiza:– Shiza [1]

7878 שִׂיח *s*îaḥ*, v.den. GK: 8488 [→ 7808, 7879, 7881]. [Q] to meditate, muse on, consider, think on:– meditate [5], talk [5], speak [4], commune [1], complained [1], complain [1], declare [1], muse [1], pray [1]

7879 שִׂיח *s*îaḥ*, n.m. GK: 8490 [→ 7878]. complaint, lament:– complaint [9], babbling [1], communication [1], meditation [1], prayer [1], talking [1]

7880 שִׂיח *s*îaḥ*, n.[m.]. GK: 8489 [→ 7878]. bush, shrub:– bushes [2], plant [1], shrubs [1]

7881 שִׂיחָה *s*îḥâ*, n.f. GK: 8491 [→ 7878]. meditation:– meditation [2], prayer [1]

7882 שִׂיחָה *s*îḥâ*, n.f. GK: 8864 [cf. 7745]. pit, pitfall:– pits [1], pit [1]

7883 שִׁיחוֹר *šîḥôr*, n.pr.loc. GK: 8865 [→ 7884]. Shihor, "[poss.] *black water*, [Egyptian] *Canal of Horus*":– Sihor [3], Shihor [1]

7884 שִׁיחוֹר לִבְנָת *šîḥôr libnāt*, n.pr.loc. GK: 8866 [→ 7883]. Shihor Libnath:– Shihor-libnath [1]

7885 שַׁיִט *šayiṭ*, n.m. GK: 8868 [→ 7751]. oar:– oars [1]

7886 שִׁילֹה *šilōh*, n.pr.loc.?. GK: 8869 [→ 7887]. Shiloh:– Shiloh [1]

7887 שִׁילוֹ *šîlô* or שִׁלוֹ *šilô* or שִׁלֹה *šilōh*, n.pr.loc. GK: 8870 & 8926 & 8931 [→ 7886, 7888; cf. 7757, 8387]. Shiloh:– Shiloh [32]

7888 שִׁילוֹנִי *šîlônî*, a.g. GK: 8872 [→ 7887, 8023]. Shilonite, of Shiloh, "*of Shiloh*":– Shilonite [5], Shilonites [1]

 שִׁילָל *šêlāl*. See 7758.

7889 שִׁימוֹן *šîmôn*, n.pr.m. GK: 8873. Shimon:– Shimon [1]

7890 שַׁיִן *šayin*, n.[m.]. GK: 8875 [→ 8366]. urine:–

7891 שִׁיר *šîr*, v. GK: 8876 [→ 7892; cf. 3574]. [Q] to sing; [P ptcp.] singer, musician:– singers [36], sing [32], singing [9], sang [6], behold [1], singer [1], singeth [1], sung [1]

7892 שִׁיר *šîr*, n.m. & f. GK: 8877 & 8878 [→ 7891]. song, music:– song [62], songs [12], musick [7], singing [4], musical [2], singers [1], sing [1], song (+1697) [1]

 שִׁישׁ *šîs*. See 7797.

7893 שַׁיִשׁ *šayiš*, n.[m.]. GK: 8880 [→ 8336]. alabaster:– marble [1]

7894 שִׁישָׁא *šîšā'*, n.pr.m. GK: 8881. Shisha:– Shisha [1]

7895 שׁוּשַׁק *šûšaq* or שִׁישַׁק *šîšaq*, n.pr.m. GK: 8810 & 8882. Shushak, Shishak:– Shishak [7]

7896 שִׁית *šît*, v. GK: 8883 [→ 7897, 8351, 8352; cf. 8371]. [Q] to place, put, set; [Ho] to be demanded:– set [21], make [12], put [11], laid [8], lay [5], made [5], appoint [2], regard (+3820) [2], alone (+4480) [1], apply [1], appointed [1], bring [1], considered (+3820) [1], lay up [1], layeth up [1], look [1], make turn [1], makest [1], mark [1], set in array [1], settest [1], shew [1], stayed [1], take [1]

7897 שִׁית *šît*, n.m. GK: 8884 [→ 7896]. garment:– attire [1], garment [1]

7898 שַׁיִת *šayit*, n.[m.]. GK: 8885 [→ 7582?]. thorns, thorn-bushes:– thorns [7]

7899 שֵׂךְ *sēk*, n.[m.]. GK: 8493. barb, splinter, thorn:– pricks [1]

7900 שֹׂךְ *sōk*, n.[m.]. GK: 8494 [cf. 5520]. dwelling place:– tabernacle [1]

7901 שָׁכַב *šākab*, v. GK: 8886 [→ 4904, 7902, 7903]. [Q] to lie down, rest; sleep with; (as a euphemism of sexual intercourse) to lie with, sleep with; [H] to make lie down; [Ho] to be laid down:– lie [41], slept [37], lay [32], lie down [15], lieth [15], lay down [11], sleep [10], laid down [9], laid [8], liest down [3], lieth down [3], lie with at all (+854+7901) [2], lien [2], lying [2], ravished [2], take rest [2], casting down [1], lain [1], lay down to sleep [1], lay on a bed (+4904) [1], lie together [1], lie with [1], lien with (+854) [1], liest [1], lieth carnally with (+854+2233+7902) [1], lieth with (+5973) [1], lodged [1], lying down [1], make to lie down [1], overlaid (+5921) [1], sleepest [1], stay [1], taketh rest [1]

7902 שְׁכָבָה *šikbâ*, n.f. GK: 8887 [→ 7901]. emission, discharge:– copulation [3], lay [2], lieth carnally with (+854+2233+7901) [1], man carnally (+376+2233) [1], seed (+2233) [1]

7903 שְׁכֹבֶת *s*ᵉkōbet*, n.f. GK: 8888 [→ 7901]. sexual relations, sexual intercourse:– lain [1], lie (+5414) [1], lie carnally (+2233+5414+3807.1) [1], lie with (+5414) [1]

7904 שָׁכָה *šākâ*, v. GK: 8889. [H] to be well-fed; lusting:– morning [1]

7905 שֻׁכָּה *šukkâ*, n.f. GK: 8496. harpoon:– barbed irons [1]

7906 שֶׁכוּ *šekû*, n.pr.loc. GK: 8497. Secu, "*lookout point*":– Sechu [1]

7907 שֶׂכְוִי *sekwî*, n.[m.]. GK: 8498. mind; some sources: mist:– heart [1]

7908 שְׁכוֹל *s*ᵉkôl*, n.[m.]. GK: 8890 [→ 7921]. forlornness, loss of children:– loss of children [2], spoiling [1]

7909 שַׁכּוּל *šakkûl* or שְׁכוּלָה *s*ᵉkûlâ*, a. GK: 8891 & 8892 [→ 7921]. bereaved (of children):– barren [2], bereaved of children [1], bereaved of whelps [1], robbed of whelps [1], robbed [1]

7910 שִׁכּוֹר *šikkôr*, a. GK: 8893 [→ 7937]. drunk, drunkenness; (n.) a drunkard:– drunken [6], drunkards [3], drunkard [2], drunk [2]

7911 שָׁכַח *šākaḥ*, v. GK: 8894 [→ 7913; cf. 7912]. [Q] to forget; [N] to be forgotten; [P] to make forget; [H] to make forget; [Ht] to be forgotten:– forget [46], forgotten [39], forgat [7], forgetteth [3], do at all forget (+7911) [2], forgettest [2], cause to forget [1], caused to be forgotten [1], forgot [1]

7912 שְׁכַח *s*ᵉkaḥ* (Aram.), v. GK: 10708 [cf. 7911]. [H] to find; [Htpe] to be found:– found [12], find [6]

7913 שָׁכֵחַ *šākēaḥ*, a. GK: 8895 [→ 7911]. forgetting:– forget [1]

7914 שְׂכִיָּה *s*ᵉkiyyâ*, n.f. GK: 8500. marine vessel, ship:– pictures [1]

Heb

7915 שַׂכִּין *śakkîn*, n.[m.]. GK: 8501. knife:– knife [1]

7916 שָׂכִיר *śākîr*, a. GK: 8502 [→ 7917, 7936]. hired worker, servant under contract:– hired servant [8], hireling [6], him that is hired [1], hired men [1], hired [1]

7917 שְׂכִירָה *śᵉkîrâ*, a. GK: 8502 [→ 7916]. f. of 7916: hired worker, servant under contract:– hired [1]

7918 שָׁכַךְ *śākak*, v. GK: 8896. [Q] to recede, reside; [H] to get rid of:– appeased [1], asswaged [1], make to cease [1], pacified [1], setteth [1]

7919 שָׂכַל *śākal*, v. GK: 8505 & 8506 [→ 4905, 7922; cf. 7920]. [Q] to have success; [P] to cross (the hands and arms in an extended motion); [H] to have insight, wisdom, understanding; to prosper, successful; the potent capacity to understand and so exercise skill in life, a state caused by proper training and teaching, enhanced by careful observation:– wise [11], understand [8], prosper [6], behaved wisely [4], understanding [4], instruct [2], prudent [2], understood [2], wisdom [2], behave wisely [1], considereth [1], consider [1], deal prudently [1], expert [1], give skill [1], guiding wittingly [1], handleth wisely [1], have good success [1], have understanding [1], instructed [1], made understand [1], make wise [1], prospered [1], prospereth [1], skilful [1], skill [1], taught knowledge (+7922) [1], teacheth [1], understandeth [1], wisely considereth [1], wisely consider [1]

7920 שְׂכַל *śᵉkal* (Aram.), v. GK: 10683 [→ 7924; cf. 7919]. [Htpa] to think about, consider:– considered [1]

7921 שָׂכַל *śākal*, v. GK: 8897 [→ 811, 7908, 7909, 7923]. [Q] to be bereaved (of children); [P] to make childless, bring bereavement, suffer miscarriage; [H] to miscarry:– bereave [3], barren [2], bereaved of children [2], bereaved [1], cast young [2], bereave of children [1], bereave of men [1], bereaveth [1], cast fruit before the time [1], casteth her calf [1], childless [1], deprived [1], destroy [1], lost children [1], made childless [1], miscarrying [1], rob of children [1], spoil [1]

7922 שֶׂכֶל *śekel*, n.m. GK: 8507 [→ 7919; cf. 7924]. understanding, wisdom, discretion:– understanding [7], wisdom [3], discretion [1], policy [1], prudence [1], sense [1], taught knowledge (+7919) [1], wise [1]

שַׂכֻּל *śakkul*. See 7909.

שִׂכְלוּת *siklût*. See 5531.

7923 שִׁכֻּלִים *śikkulîm*, n.[m.]pl.abst. GK: 8898 [→ 7921]. (state of) bereavement (of children):– lost [1]

7924 שָׂכְלְתָנוּ *śokᵉltānû* (Aram.), n.f. GK: 10684 [→ 7920]. intelligence, understanding, insight:– understanding [3]

7925 שָׁכַם *śākam*, v.den. GK: 8899 [→ 7926]. [H] to do early in the morning; to do again and again:– rose up early [18], rose early [9], arose early [8], rising early [6], rising up early [6], rise up early [5], early [4], be up early [1], early rose up [1], gat up early [1], get up early [1], get up early [1], morning [1], rise early [1], rising up betimes [1], rose up betimes [1]

7926 שְׁכֶם *śᵉkem*, n.m. GK: 8900 [→ 7925, 7927, 7928, 7929, 7930]. shoulder (upper part of the back); by extension: ridge of land:– shoulder [12], shoulders [5], back [2], consent [2], portion [1]

7927 שְׁכֶם *śᵉkem*, n.pr.m. & loc. GK: 8901 & 8902 [→ 7926]. Shechem, "*shoulders [and upper part of the back]; [poss.] shoulder [saddle of a hill]*":– Shechem [49], Sichem [1]

7928 שֶׁכֶם *śekem*, n.pr.m. GK: 8903 [→ 7930; cf. 7926]. Shechem, "*shoulders [and upper part of the back]*":– Shechem [13], Shechem's [2]

7929 שִׁכְמָה *śikmâ*, n.m. GK: 8900 [→ 7926]. f. of 7926: shoulder (upper part of the back); by extension: ridge of land:– shoulder blade [1]

7930 שִׁכְמִי *śikmî*, a.g. GK: 8904 [→ 7928]. Shechemite, "*of Shechem*":– Shechemites [1]

7931 שָׁכַן *śākan*, v. GK: 8905 [→ 4908, 7933, 7934, 7935; cf. 7932]. [Q] to dwell, abide, live among, stay; [P] to make to dwell, make a home; [H] to cause to dwell, settle in, set up a dwelling:– dwell [61], dwelleth [8], dwelt [8], abode [6], place [5], cause to dwell [3], dwell in [3], dwellest [3], dwelt in [3], habitation [2], inhabit [2], placed [2], remain [2], set [2], abide [1], abiding [1], at rest [1], cause to remain [1], continue [1], dwellers [1], dwelleth [1], dwelling [1], inhabitants [1], inhabited [1], inhabiteth [1], lay [1], made to dwell [1], make dwell [1], remaineth [1], remaining [1], rested [1], rest [1], set up [1]

7932 שְׁכַן *śᵉkan* (Aram.), v. GK: 10709 [→ 4907; cf. 7931]. [P] to dwell; [Pa] to cause to dwell:– caused to dwell [1], habitation [1]

7933 שֶׁכֶן *śeken*, v.inf. GK: 8905 [→ 7931]. inf. of 7931: to dwell, abide:–

7934 שָׁכֵן *śākēn*, a. GK: 8907 [→ 7931]. neighbor; inhabitant:– neighbours [11], neighbour [6], inhabitants [1], inhabitant [1], nigh [1]

7935 שְׁכַנְיָה *śᵉkanyâ* or שְׁכַנְיָהוּ *śᵉkanyāhû*, n.pr.m. GK: 8908 & 8909 [→ 7931+3068]. Shecaniah, "*Yahweh has taken up his abode*":– Shechaniah [8], Shecaniah [2]

7936 שָׂכַר *śākar* or סָכַר *śākar*, v. GK: 8509 & 6128 [→ 3485, 4909, 7916, 7917, 7938, 7939, 7940]. [Q] to hire; [Qp] to be hired; [N] to hire oneself; [Ht] to earn wages for oneself:– hired [12], earneth wages [2], hire [2], rewardeth [2], surely hired (+7936) [2], hired out [1]

7937 שָׁכַר *śākar*, v. GK: 8910 & 8912 [→ 7941, 7941, 7943]. [Q] to become drunk, drink to one's fill; [P] to make drunk; [H] to make drunk; [Ht] to behave drunken:– drunken [8], make drunk [3], make drunken [2], drink abundantly [1], filled with drink [1], made drunken [1], made drunk [1], makest drunken [1], merry [1]

7938 שֶׂכֶר *śeker*, n.[m.]. GK: 8512 [→ 7936]. wage, reward:– reward [1], sluces [1]

7939 שָׂכָר *śākār*, n.m. GK: 8510 [→ 7940; cf. 7936 (also used with compound proper names)]. wage, reward:– hire [9], reward [7], wages [6], price [2], rewarded [2], fare [1], worth [1]

7940 שָׂכָר *śākār*, n.pr.m. GK: 8511 [→ 7939; cf. 7936]. Sacar, "*reward [given by God]*", [poss.] *hired hand*":– Sacar [2]

7941 שֵׁכָר *śēkār*, n.[m.]. GK: 8911 [→ 7937]. fermented drink, beer:– strong drink [21], drunkards (+8354) [1], strong wine [1]

שִׁכּוֹר *śikkôr*. See 7910.

7942 שִׁכְּרוֹן *śikkᵉrôn*, n.pr.loc. GK: 8914. Shikkeron, "[poss.] *drunkenness; hog bean plant*":– Shicron [1]

7943 שִׁכָּרוֹן *śikkārôn*, n.[m.]. GK: 8913 [→ 7937]. drunkenness:– drunkenness [2], drunken [1]

7944 שַׁל *śal*, n.[m.]. GK: 8915. irreverent act:– error [1]

7945 שֶׁל *śel*, pt. GK: 8611 [→ 4332, 4967, 7706]. what, which, usually as prefix 7578.1:– that [54], which [20], whom [7], who [6], when [5], because [4], for [4], until (+5704) [4], wherein [3], whereof [3], till (+5704) [2], wherewith [2], as (+3509.1) [1], as [1], because (+871.1) [1], but (+5704) [1], by (+5921) [1], for cause (+871.1) [1], for sake (+871.1) [1], from whence [1], increase [1], it [1], of (+4480+3807.1) [1], when (+3509.1) [1], where [1], while (+5704) [1], whither (+8033) [1], whose (+2050.2) [1], whose [1]

7946 שַׁלְאֲנָן *śal'ᵃnan*, a. GK: 8916 [→ 7599]. secure:– at ease [1]

7947 שָׁלַב *śālab*, v. GK: 8917 [→ 7948]. [Pu] to be joined, set parallel, dovetailed:– equally distant [1], set in order [1]

7948 שָׁלָב *śālāb*, n.[m.]pl. GK: 8918 [→ 7947]. upright, crossbar:– ledges [3]

7949 שָׁלַג *śālag*, v.den. GK: 8919 [→ 7950]. [H] to snow:– snow [1]

7950 שֶׁלֶג *śeleg*, n.m. GK: 8920 & 8921 [→ 7949; cf. 8517]. snow; soap (processed from the soapwort plant):– snow [19], snowy [1]

7951 שָׁלָה *śālâ*, v. GK: 8922 [→ 7961, 7959, 7962, 7968, 7987, 7988; cf. 7952]. [Q] to be at ease, have peace; [N] to give oneself to rest; [H] to raise hopes:– prosper [3], happy [1], in safety [1]

7952 שָׁלָה *śālâ*, v. GK: 8923 [→ 7953, cf. 7951]. [Q] to take away, extract; to deceive:– deceive [1], negligent [1]

7953 שָׁלָה *śālâ*, v. GK: 8923 [→ 7952]. prob. same as 7952: [Q] to take away, extract:– taketh away [1]

7954 שְׁלֵה *śᵉlēh* (Aram.), a. GK: 10710 [→ 7960, 7963; cf. 7961]. contented, at ease:– rest [1]

שִׁלֹה *śilōh*. See 7887.

7955 שָׁלָה *śillâ* (Aram.), n.f. GK: 10685 [cf. 5541]. insolence, rebellion:–

שֵׁלָה *śēlâ*. See 7596.

7956 שֵׁלָה *śēlâ*, n.f. & n.pr.m. GK: 8924 & 8925 [→ 8024; cf. 7592]. petition; n.pr. Shelah, "*missile [a weapon], sprout*":– Shelah [3]

7957 שַׁלְהֶבֶת *śalhebet*, n.f. GK: 8927 [→ 3851]. flame:– flame [2], most vehement flame [1]

שָׁלָו *śālaw*. See 7951.

7958 שְׁלָו *śᵉlāw*, n.f. GK: 8513. quail:– quails [4]

7959 שָׁלוּ *śālû*, n.[m.]. GK: 8930 [→ 7951; cf. 7960]. secure feeling, ease:– prosperity [1]

שִׁלֹו *śilô*. See 7887.

7960 שָׁלוּ *śālû* (Aram.), n.f. GK: 10712 [→ 7954; cf. 7959]. negligence:– fail [2], any thing amiss [1], error [1]

7961 שָׁלֵו *śālēw*, a. GK: 8929 [→ 7951; cf. 7954]. quiet, at ease, carefree:– at ease [2], peaceable [1], prosperity [1], prosper [1], quietness [1], quiet [1], wealthy [1]

7962 שַׁלְוָה *śalwâ*, n.f. GK: 8932 [→ 7951; cf. 7963]. security, ease:– prosperity [3], abundance [1], peaceably (+871.1) [1], peaceably [1], peace [1], quietness [1]

7963 שְׁלֵוָה *śᵉlēwâ* (Aram.), n.f. GK: 10713 [→ 7954; cf. 7962]. prosperity:– tranquillity [1]

7964 שִׁלּוּחִים *śillûḥîm*, n.[m.]pl. GK: 8933 [→ 7971]. parting gifts; sending away:– presents [1], present [1], sent [1]

7965 שָׁלוֹם *śālôm*, n.m. GK: 8934 [→ 53, 8010, 8015, 8019; cf. 7999; cf. 8001]. peace, safety, prosperity, well-being; intactness, wholeness; peace can have a focus of security, safety which can bring feelings of satisfaction, well-being, and contentment:– peace [174], well [13], peaceably [7], welfare [5], prosperity [4], safe [3], saluted (+7592+3807.1) [3], how did (+3807.1) [2], peaceable [2], perfect peace (+7965) [2], salute (+7592+3807.1) [2], all is well [1], did [1], familiar friend (+376) [1], familiars (+582) [1], fare [1], favour [1], friends (+376) [1], greet (+7592+3807.1) [1], how doest (+3807.1) [1], how prospered (+3807.1) [1], in good health [1], in health [1], peaceably (+3807.1) [1], peaceably (+871.1) [1], prosperous [1], rest [1], safely [1], salute [1], wholly [1]

7966 שִׁלּוּם *śillûm*, n.[m.]. GK: 8936 [→ 7999]. retribution, reckoning; bribe, gift:– recompences [1], recompence [1], reward [1]

7967 שַׁלּוּם *śallûm*, n.pr.m. GK: 8935 [→ 7999]. Shallum, "*peace, well-being, prosperity*":– Shallum [27]

שְׁלֹמִית *śᵉlōmît*. See 8019.

7968 שַׁלּוּן *śallûn*, n.pr.m. GK: 8937 [→ 7951]. Shallun, "*recompense*":– Shallun [1]

7969 שָׁלֹשׁ *śālōš*, n.m. & f. GK: 8993 [→ 7991, 7992, 8027, 8028, 8030, 8032, 8029, 7970; cf. 8531]. three; (pl.) thirty:– three [389], thirteen (+6240) [13], thirteenth (+6240) [11], third [9], thrice (+6471) [4], forks (+7053) [1], oftentimes (+6471) [1], three tenth deals (+6241) [1], threescore and thirteen (+7657+1886.1+2050.1) [1], threescore and thirteen (+7657+2050.1) [1]

7970 שְׁלֹשִׁים *śᵉlōšîm*, n.indecl. GK: 9001 [→ 7969]. thirty (pl. of "three"):– thirty [163], thirtieth [9], captains [1]

שָׁלֻת *śālût*. See 7960.

7971 שָׁלַח *śālaḥ*, v. GK: 8938 [→ 4916, 4917, 7964, 7973, 7975, 7974, 7976, 7977; cf. 7972]. [Q] to send out; [Qp] to be sent away; [N] to be sent; [P] to send away, let go, release; [Pu] to be sent away, thrust out; [H] to send out; "to let go" from a marriage relationship is to divorce:– sent [405], send [140], let go [69], sent away [36], put forth [24], send away [10], put [9], sent forth [9], sending [8], sent out [8], cast out [7], lay [7], stretch forth [7], cast [6], laid [6], put away [6], sendeth [5], set [5], put out [4], go [3], send forth [3], sentest [3], shot forth [3], soweth [3], stretch out [3], depart [2], earnestly send (+7971) [2], in any wise let go (+7971) [2], let depart [2], let down [2], let go in any wise (+7971) [2], let loose [2], put in [2], putteth forth [2], sendest away [2], sendest [2], sendeth out [2], stretched forth [2], stretched out [2], appoint [1], away [1], bring on way [1], brought [1], cast away [1], conduct [1], forsaken [1], gave up [1], givest [1], layeth [1], left [1], let go away [1], letting go [1], loose [1], push away [1], putting away [1], putting forth [1], reacheth forth [1], send out [1], sendest forth [1], sendest out [1], sendeth forth [1], sending away [1], sent for [1], sentest forth [1], shoot out [1], shooteth forth [1], shot [1], spreadeth out [1], suffer to grow long [1]

7972 שְׁלַח *śᵉlaḥ* (Aram.), v. GK: 10714 [cf. 7971]. [P] to send out; [Pp, Peil] to be sent:– sent [12], put [1], send [1]

7973 שֶׁלַח *śelaḥ* or שְׁלָחִים *śᵉlāḥîm*, n.[m.]. GK: 8939 & 8945 [→ 7971]. weapon, sword, javelin; shoots, sprouts of a plant (in a closed, private garden):– sword [3], weapon [2], darts [1], plants [1], put off [1]

7974 שֶׁלַח *śelaḥ*, n.pr.m. GK: 8941 [→ 7973?; cf. 7971]. Shelah, "*missile [a weapon], sprout*":– Salah [6], Shelah [3]

7975 שֶׁלַח *šelaḥ* or שִׁלוֹחַ *šilôaḥ*, n.pr.loc. GK: 8940 & 8942 [→ 7971]. Siloam, Shiloah, "sent":– Shiloah [1], Siloah [1]

7975 שֶׁלַח *šilluaḥ*. See 7964.

7976 שְׁלֻחוֹת *šᵉluḥôt*, n.f. GK: 8943 [→ 7971]. shoot (of a vine):– branches [1]

7977 שִׁלְחִי *šilḥî*, n.pr.m. GK: 8944 [→ 7971]. Shilhi, "[poss.] [my] javelin [thrower?]":– Shilhi [2]

7978 שִׁלְחִים *šilḥîm*, n.pr.loc. GK: 8946. Shilhim:– Shilhim [1]

7979 שֻׁלְחָן *šulḥān*, n.m. GK: 8947. table:– table [55], tables [14], every table (+7979+2050.1) [2]

7980 שָׁלַט *šālaṭ*, v. GK: 8948 [→ 7983, 7986, 7989; cf. 7981]. [Q] to control, lord over; [H] to let rule, enable:– bare rule [1], given power [1], giveth power [1], have dominion [1], have power [1], have rule [1], ruleth [1], rule [1]

7981 שְׁלֵט *šᵉlēṭ* (Aram.), v. GK: 10715 [→ 7984, 7985, 7990; cf. 7980]. [P] to rule over, overpower; [H] to make rule over:– made ruler [2], ruler [2], bear rule [1], mastery [1], power [1]

7982 שֶׁלֶט *šeleṭ*, n.m. GK: 8949. small (round) shield:– shields [7]

7983 שִׁלְטוֹן *šilṭôn*, n.[m.]. GK: 8950 [→ 7980; cf. 7985]. supremacy:– power [2]

7984 שִׁלְטָן *šilṭān* (Aram.), n.m. GK: 10716 [→ 7981; cf. 7983]. high official:– rulers [2]

7985 שָׁלְטָן *šolṭān* (Aram.), n.m. GK: 10717 [→ 7981; cf. 7983?]. dominion, power, authority:– dominion [13], dominions [1]

7986 שַׁלֶּטֶת *šalleṭet*, a. GK: 8951 [→ 7980]. brazen, domineering:– imperious [1]

7987 שְׁלִי *šᵉlî*, n.[m.]. GK: 8952 [→ 7951]. privateness, uninterruptedness:– quietly (+871.1+1886.1) [1]

7988 שִׁלְיָה *šilyâ*, n.f. GK: 8953 [→ 7951]. afterbirth:– young one [1]

7988 שְׁלָיו *šᵉlāyw*. See 7958.

7988 שָׁלֵו *šalêw*. See 7961.

7989 שַׁלִּיט *šallîṭ*, a. GK: 8954 [→ 7980; cf. 7990]. ruler, governor:– governor [1], mighty [1], power [1], ruler [1]

7990 שַׁלִּיט *šallîṭ* (Aram.), a. GK: 10718 [→ 7981; cf. 7989]. mighty, powerful, sovereign, ruling:– ruleth [3], ruled [2], ruler [2], captain [1], lawful [1], rule [1]

7991 שָׁלִישׁ *šālîš* or שָׁלֹשׁ *šālîšî*, n.[m.]. GK: 8955 & 8956 & 8998 [→ 7969]. [the] Three, a rank of officer; bowlful, basketful (a unit of measure, probably of one-third of something); (three-stringed?) lute:– captains [8], lord [3], captain [2], measure [1], excellent things [1], great lords [1], instruments of musick [1], princes [1]

7992 שְׁלִישִׁי *šᵉlîšî*, a.num.ord. GK: 8958 [→ 7969; cf. 8523, cf. 8532]. third:– third [97], third part [3], third time [3], three years old [2], third rank [1], three [1]

7993 שָׁלַךְ *šālak*, v. GK: 8959 [→ 7994?, 7995]. [H] to throw, hurl, scatter; [Ho] to be thrown, be cast:– cast [77], cast out [13], cast away [11], cast down [11], cast forth [3], cast off [2], adventured [1], cast in [1], castest [1], casteth forth [1], hurl [1], pluckt [1], threwest [1], thrown [1]

7994 שָׁלָךְ *šālāk*, n.[m.]. GK: 8960 [→ 7993?]. cormorant:– cormorant [2]

7995 שַׁלֶּכֶת *šalleket*, n.f. GK: 8961 [→ 7993]. cutting down:– cast [1]

7996 שַׁלֶּכֶת *šalleket*, n.pr.loc. GK: 8962 [→ 7993]. Shallecheth, "[poss.] [gate of] sending forth":– Shallecheth [1]

7997 שָׁלַל *šālal*, v. GK: 8963 & 8964 [→ 7758, 7998]. [Q] to pull out; to plunder, loot; [Htpol] to be plundered:– spoiled [4], spoil [3], let fall of purpose (+7997) [2], take a spoil (+7998) [2], take [2], make a spoil [1], maketh prey [1], take spoil (+7998) [1]

7998 שָׁלָל *šālāl*, n.m. GK: 8965 [→ 4122; cf. 7997]. plunder, spoil, loot:– spoil [58], prey [10], take a spoil (+7997) [2], spoils won [1], spoils [1], take spoil (+7997) [1]

7999 שָׁלֵם *šālēm*, v. GK: 8966 [→ 4918, 4919, 4921, 4922, 7965, 7967, 7966, 8002, 8003, 8004, 8005, 8006, 8011, 8010, 8013, 8015, 8016, 8019, 8020, 8021 (also used with compound proper names)]. [Q] to be finished, be completed; be at peace; [Qp] to repay, make restitution, fulfill (a vow); [Pu] to be repaid, be fulfilled; [H] to make peace; cause to fulfill; [Ho] to be brought into peace:– pay [17], recompense [8], restore [8], render [7], made peace [6], make good [5], repay [5], perform [4], reward [4], at peace [3], finished [3], rewarded [3],

rewardeth [3], ended [2], make an end [2], make full restitution (+7999) [2], make restitution [2], performeth [2], recompensed [2], requite [2], surely make good (+7999) [2], surely make restitution [2], surely pay (+7999) [2], surely requite (+7999) [2], give again [1], make amends [1], make peace [1], make prosperous [1], maketh to be at peace [1], pay again [1], payed [1], payeth again [1], peaceable [1], perfect [1], performed [1], prospered [1], recompensest [1], renderest [1], rendereth [1], repayed [1], repayeth [1], requited [1]

8000 שְׁלִם *šᵉlim* (Aram.), v. GK: 10719 [→ 8001; cf. 7999]. [P] to be finished; [H] to (deliver) completely, bring to an end:– finished [2], deliver [1]

8001 שְׁלָם *šᵉlām* (Aram.), n.m. GK: 10720 [→ 8000; cf. 7965]. (as salutation) cordial greetings!; prosperity, well-being, good health:– peace [4]

8002 שֶׁלֶם *šelem*, n.[m.]. GK: 8968 [→ 7999]. fellowship (offering):– peace offerings [77], peace [6], peace offering [4]

8003 שָׁלֵם *šālēm*, a. GK: 8969 [→ 7999; cf. 8000]. safe, complete, whole:– perfect [16], whole [4], full [2], just [1], made ready [1], peaceable [1], perfected [1], quiet [1]

8004 שָׁלֵם *šālēm*, n.pr.loc. GK: 8970 [→ 7999]. Salem, "peace":– Salem [2], Shalem [1]

8004 שָׁלוֹם *šālôm*. See 7965.

8005 שִׁלֵּם *šillēm*, n.pr.loc. GK: 8972 [→ 7999]. recompense:– recompence [1]

8006 שִׁלֵּם *šillēm*, n.pr.m. GK: 8973 [→ 8016; cf. 7999]. Shillem, "recompense; [poss.] whole, healthy, complete":– Shillem [2]

8006 שִׁלֻּם *šillum*. See 7966.

8006 שַׁלּוּם *šallum*. See 7967.

8007 שַׁלְמָא *šalmā'*, n.pr.m. GK: 8514 [→ 8009, 8012]. Salma, "little spark":– Salma [4]

8008 שַׂלְמָה *salmâ*, n.f. GK: 8515 [cf. 8071]. clothing, garment, cloak, robe:– raiment [5], garments [4], garment [4], clothes [3]

8009 שַׂלְמָה *salmâ*, n.pr.m. GK: 8516 [→ 8007]. Salmah:– Salmon [1]

8010 שְׁלֹמֹה *šᵉlōmōh*, n.pr.m. GK: 8976 [→ 7965; cf. 7999]. Solomon, "peace, well-being":– Solomon [271], Solomon's [18], Solomon's (+3807.1) [4]

8011 שִׁלֻּמָה *šillumâ*, n.f. GK: 8974 [→ 7999]. punishment, retribution:– reward [1]

8012 שַׂלְמוֹן *salmôn*, n.pr.m. GK: 8517 [→ 8007]. Salmon, "little spark":– Salmon [1]

8013 שְׁלֹמוֹת *šᵉlōmôt*, n.pr.m. GK: 8977 [→ 7999]. Shelomoth, "at peace":– Shelomoth [2]

8014 שַׁלְמַי *šalmay*, n.pr.m. GK: 8518 [cf. 8073]. Salmai, cf. 8073:– Shalmai [1]

8015 שְׁלֹמִי *šᵉlōmî*, n.pr.m. GK: 8979 [→ 8019; cf. 7965]. Shelomi, "at peace":– Shelomi [1]

8016 שִׁלֵּמִי *šillēmî*, a.g. GK: 8980 [→ 8006]. Shillemite, "of Shillem":– Shillemites [1]

8017 שְׁלֻמִיאֵל *šᵉlumî'ēl*, n.pr.m. GK: 8981 [→ 7999+410]. Shelumiel, "God [El] is [my] peace":– Shelumiel [5]

8018 שֶׁלֶמְיָה *šelemyâ* or שֶׁלֶמְיָהוּ *šelemyāhû*, n.pr.m. GK: 8982 & 8983 [→ 7999+3068]. Shelemiah, "Yahweh pays back [poss.] he restores peace offering of Yahweh":– Shelemiah [10]

8019 שְׁלֹמִית *šᵉlōmît*, n.pr.m. & f. GK: 8984 & 8985 [→ 8015; cf. 7999]. Shelomith, "at peace":– Shelomith [9]

8020 שַׁלְמָן *šalman*, n.pr.m. GK: 8986 [→ 7999]. Shalman, "[abbreviation of] Shalmaneser":– Shalman [1]

8021 שַׁלְמֹנִים *šalmōnîm*, n.[m.pl.]. GK: 8988 [→ 7999]. gifts:– rewards [1]

8022 שַׁלְמַנְאֶסֶר *šalman'eser*, n.pr.m. GK: 8987. Shalmaneser, "Shulman is chief or Sulmanu is leader":– Shalmaneser [2]

8023 שִׁלֹנִי *šilōnî*, a.g. GK: 8872 [→ 7888]. same as 7888: Shilonite, of Shiloh, "of Shiloh":– Shiloni [1]

8024 שֵׁלָנִי *šēlānî*, a.g. GK: 8989 [→ 7956]. Shelanite, of Shelah, "of Shelah":– Shelanites [1]

8025 שָׁלַף *šālap*, v. GK: 8990. [Q] to draw out (a sword); remove (a sandal); [Qp] to be drawn (sword):– drew [13], drawn [5], draw [4], drew off [1], groweth up [1], plucked off [1]

8026 שֶׁלֶף *šelep*, n.pr.m. GK: 8991. Sheleph, "one plucked out, drawn out":– Sheleph [2]

8027 שָׁלַשׁ *šālaš*, v.den. GK: 8992 [→ 7969]. [P] to do a third time, on the third day; [Pu] to be three years old, in three parts:– three years old [3], did the third time [1], divide into three parts [1], do the third time [1], stayed three days [1], threefold [1], three [1]

8028 שֶׁלֶשׁ *šeleš*, n.pr.m. GK: 8994 [→ 7969]. Shelesh, "triplet; [poss.] obedient or gentle":– Shelesh [1]

8028 שָׁלֹשׁ *šālōš*. See 7969.

8029 שִׁלֵּשִׁים *šillēšîm*, a. GK: 9000 [→ 7969]. third (generation):– third [5]

8030 שִׁלְשָׁה *šilšâ*, n.pr.m. GK: 8996 [→ 7969]. Shilshah, "[poss.] obedient or gentle; third [part, child?], triplet":– Shilshah [1]

8031 שָׁלִשָׁה *šālišâ*, n.pr.loc. GK: 8995 [→ 1190]. Shalisha, "third part":– Shalisha [1]

8031 שְׁלֹשָׁה *šᵉlōšâ*. See 7969.

8032 שִׁלְשׁוֹם *šilšôm*, adv. GK: 8997 [→ 7969]. formally, three days ago; used with 8543: "yesterday and three days ago," as an adverb of time:– formerly, previously:– heretofore (+8543) [4], in time past (+4480+8543) [4], before (+8543) [3], before that time (+865+3509.1) [1], beforetime (+4480+8543) [1], beforetime (+8543) [1], beforetime (+865+4480) [1], heretofore (+1571+4480+4480+8543) [1], heretofore (+4480+8543) [1], heretofore (+865) [1], in time past (+8543) [1], in time past (+865+1571) [1], in times past (+1571+1571+8543) [1], in times past (+4480+8543) [1], in times past (+865) [1], these three days (+8543) [1]

8032 שְׁלֹשִׁים *šᵉlōšîm*. See 7970.

8032 שַׁלְתִּיאֵל *šaltî'ēl*. See 7597.

8033 שָׁם *šām*, adv. GK: 9004 [cf. 8536]. there, where:– there [424], thence [66], where (+834) [54], thither (+1886.5) [50], whither (+834+1886.5) [38], thence (+4480) [34], there (+1886.5) [31], whither (+834) [27], where [22], thither [20], where (+834+1886.5) [7], wherein (+834) [7], therein (+1886.5) [5], therein [5], thereof (+4480) [4], on [3], whence [3], here [2], whence (+834) [2], whence (+834+4480) [2], whereunto (+834) [2], whither (+1886.5) [2], whither [2], in it [1], place where [1], the same place [1], thereout (+4480) [1], thitherward (+1886.5) [1], unto (+1886.5) [1], where (+834+871.1) [1], whereinto (+834+1886.5) [1], wherein [1], wheresoever any (+834+3605) [1], whereunto (+834+1886.5) [1], which⁵ [1], whither (+7945) [1], whithersoever (+834+3605) [1], whithersoever (+834+5921) [1], whom (+834) [1], whom⁵ [1]

8034 שֵׁם *šēm*, n.m. GK: 9005 [→ 8035?, 8050, 8061, 8062; cf. 8036]. name, a proper designation of a person, place, or thing; by extension: renown, fame; "to call on the name of the LORD" means to proclaim or praise the excellence of the LORD, to worship Yahweh, or to summon Yahweh by name for help:– name [738], names [81], name's [19], renown [7], fame [4], named [3], famous [2], named (+7121) [2], other names (+8034) [2], base men (+1097) [1], famous [376) [1], famous (+7121) [1], infamous (+2931+1886.1) [1], named (+7760) [1], report [1]

8035 שֵׁם *šēm*, n.pr.m. GK: 9006 [→ 8034?]. Shem, "name, fame":– Shem [17]

8036 שֻׁם *šum* (Aram.), n.m. GK: 10721 [cf. 8034]. name, what someone is called:– name [8], names [3], named (+7761) [1]

8037 שַׁמָּא *šammā'*, n.pr.m. GK: 9007 [cf. 8048]. Shamma; Shammah, "astonishment":– Shamma [1]

8038 שְׁמְאֵבֶר *šem'ēber*, n.pr.m. GK: 9008. Shemeber:– Shemeber [1]

8039 שִׁמְאָה *šim'â*, n.pr.m. GK: 9009 [cf. 8043]. Shimeah, "he has heard or he is obedient":– Shimeah [1]

8040 שְׂמֹאל *śᵉmō'l*, n.[m.]. GK: 8520 [→ 8041, 8042; cf. 7585]. left (opposite of right); north:– left [36], left hand [17], left side [1]

8041 שָׂמַאל *śāma'l*, v.den. GK: 8521 [→ 8040]. [H] to go to the left; be left-handed:– left [2], go to the left [1], on the left [1], turn to the left [1]

8042 שְׂמָאלִי *śᵉmā'lî*, a. GK: 8522 [→ 8040]. on the left; northern:– left [9]

8043 שִׁמְאָם *šim'ām*, n.pr.m. GK: 9010 [cf. 8039]. Shimeam:– Shimeam [1]

8044 שַׁמְגַּר **šamgar**, n.pr.m. GK: 9011. Shamgar, "*Shimke gave [a son]*":– Shamgar [2]

8045 שָׁמַד **šamad**, v. GK: 9012 [cf. 8046]. [N] to be destroyed; [H] to destroy, demolish, annihilate:– destroyed [42], destroy [39], destroyed (+8045) [2], utterly destroy (+8045) [2], bring to nought [1], destruction [1], overthrown [1], perished [1], quite pluck down [1]

8046 שְׁמַד **šᵉmad** (Aram.), v. GK: 10722 [cf. 8045]. [H] to completely destroy, exterminate:– consume [1]

שָׁמֵא **šameh**. See 8064.

8047 שַׁמָּה **šammâ**, n.f. GK: 9014 [→ 8074]. thing of horror; desolation, devastation, what is laid waste:– astonishment [13], desolation [11], desolate [10], waste [3], desolations [1], wonderful [1]

8048 שַׁמָּה **šammâ**, n.pr.m. GK: 9015 [→ 8049, 8054, 8060?; cf. 8037, 8085? or 8121?]. Shammah, "*waste*":– Shammah [8]

8049 שְׁמָהוּת **šamhût**, n.pr.m. GK: 9016 [→ 8054; cf. 8048]. Shamhuth, "*[poss.] one born at a time of a horrible event*":– Shamhuth [1]

8050 שְׁמוּאֵל **šᵉmû'ēl**, n.pr.m. GK: 9017 [→ 8034+410]. Samuel; Shemuel, "*his name is God [El]; heard of God; the unnamed god is El*":– Samuel [137], Shemuel [3]

שְׁמֹנֶה **šᵉmôneh**. See 8083.

שְׁמֹנָה **šᵉmônâ**. See 8083.

שְׁמֹנִים **šᵉmônîm**. See 8084.

8051 שַׁמּוּעַ **šammûa'**, n.pr.m. GK: 9018 [→ 8085+3068?]. Shammua, "*[poss.] [Yahweh] hears; rumor*":– Shammua [5]

8052 שְׁמוּעָה **šᵉmû'â**, n.f. GK: 9019 [→ 8085]. message, rumor, report:– rumour [9], tidings [8], report [4], fame [2], bruit [1], doctrine [1], mentioned [1], news [1]

8053 שָׁמוּר **šamûr**, n.pr.m. GK: 9020 [cf. 8069]. Shamur, cf. 8069:–

8054 שַׁמּוֹת **šammôt**, n.pr.m. GK: 9021 [→ 8049; cf. 8048]. Shammoth, "*desolation*":– Shammoth [1]

8055 שָׂמַח **šamaḥ**, v. GK: 8523 [→ 8056, 8057]. [Q] to rejoice, be glad, delight in:– rejoice [65], glad [33], rejoiced [19], make glad [4], maketh glad [4], rejoiceth [4], joy [3], made to rejoice [3], made glad [2], making very glad (+8055) [2], caused to rejoice [1], cheer up [1], cheereth [1], exceeding glad (+1419+8057) [1], hath joy [1], have joy [1], made joyful [1], made rejoice [1], make joyful [1], make rejoice [1], maketh merry (+2416) [1], merry [1], rejoicing [1]

8056 שָׂמֵחַ **šamēaḥ**, a.vbl. GK: 8524 [→ 8055]. rejoicing, gladness, delight:– glad [4], rejoiced [4], rejoice [4], joyful [3], merry [2], making merry [1], merrily [1], merryhearted (+3820) [1], rejoice (+1961) [1], rejoice exceedingly (+413+1524) [1], rejoicing [1]

8057 שִׂמְחָה **šimḥâ**, n.f. GK: 8525 [→ 8055]. joy, gladness, pleasure, delight:– joy [43], gladness [32], mirth [8], rejoice [2], rejoicing [2], exceedingly glad (+1419+8055) [1], exceedingly rejoice (+7797+871.1) [1], exceeding [1], glad [1], joyfulness [1], pleasure [1], rejoiced [1]

8058 שָׁמַט **šamaṭ**, v. GK: 9023 [→ 8059]. [Q] to drop down, stumble; to lie unplowed; [N] to be thrown down; [H] to cancel a debt:– release [2], discontinue [1], overthrown [1], rest [1], shook [1], stumbled [1], threw down [1], throw down [1]

8059 שְׁמִטָּה **šᵉmiṭṭâ**, n.f. GK: 9024 [→ 8058]. canceling of debt:– release [5]

8060 שַׁמַּי **šammay**, n.pr.m. GK: 9025 [→ 8085? or 8048?]. Shammai, "*Yahweh has heard*":– Shammai [6]

8061 שְׁמִידָע **šᵉmîda'**, n.pr.m. GK: 9026 [→ 8062]. Shemida, "*[poss.] the name knows; [poss.] Eshmun has known*":– Shemida [3]

8062 שְׁמִידָעִי **šᵉmîda'î**, a.g. GK: 9027 [→ 8061; cf. 8034]. Shemidaite, "*of Shemida*":– Shemidaites [1]

8063 שְׂמִיכָה **šᵉmîkâ**, n.f. GK: 8526. covering:– mantle [1]

8064 שָׁמַיִם **šamayim**, n.m. GK: 9028 [cf. 8065]. region above the earth: the heavens: place of the stars, sky, air; heaven: the invisible realm of God:– heaven [289], heavens [109], air [21], astrologers (+1895) [1], other (+7097) [1]

8065 שְׁמַיִן **šᵉmayin** (Aram.), n.m.pl. GK: 10723 [cf. 8064]. the heavens (of this world), sky, air; heaven (the realm of God); "heaven" is also a euphemism for "God"; the phrase "heaven and earth" combine into one meaning "the universe," the totality of all that exists:– heaven [35], heavens [3]

8066 שְׁמִינִי **šᵉmînî**, a.num.ord. GK: 9029 [→ 8083]. eighth:– eighth [27], eight [1]

8067 שְׁמִינִית **šᵉmînît**, tt. GK: 9030 [→ 8083]. sheminith:– Sheminith [3]

8068 שָׁמִיר **šamîr**, n.m. GK: 9031 & 9032 [→ 8104; cf. 8069?]. briers; hardest stone; (other contexts) flint or emery:– briers [8], adamant stone [1], adamant [1], diamond [1]

8069 שָׁמִיר **šamîr**, n.pr.m. & loc. GK: 9033 & 9034 [cf. 8053, 8068?]. Shamir, "*[poss.] thorny or emery [flint]*":– Shamir [4]

8070 שְׁמִירָמוֹת **šᵉmîramôt** or שְׁמִרִימוֹת **šᵉmiramôt**, n.pr.m. GK: 9035 & 9082. Shemiramoth, Shemiramoth, "*heights, heavens; [poss. prn. of pagan goddess]*":– Shemiramoth [4]

8071 שִׂמְלָה **šimlâ**, n.f. GK: 8529 [→ 8072; cf. 8008]. clothing, garment, cloak:– raiment [11], clothes [6], garment [4], apparel [2], clothing [2], cloth [2], garments [2]

8072 שַׂמְלָה **šamlâ**, n.pr.m. GK: 8528 [→ 8071, 8073]. Samlah:– Samlah [4]

8073 שַׂמְלַי **šamlay** or שַׁלְמַי **šalmay** or שַׂמְלַי **šamlay**, n.pr.m. GK: 8530 & 8978 & 9036 [→ 8072; cf. 8014]. Samlai, Shalmai, Shamlai, "*[perhaps] Yahweh is well-being*":– Shalmai [1]

8074 שָׁמֵם **šamēm**, v. GK: 9037 [→ 4923, 8047, 8076, 8077, 8078; cf. 3456; cf. 8075]. [Q] to be desolate, be appalled; [N] to become desolate, be appalled; [Pol] to cause desolation, be appalled; [H] to bring to devastation, cause to be appalled; [Ho] to lie desolate; [Htpol] to destroy oneself, be appalled:– desolate [31], astonished [14], astonied [6], make desolate [5], desolations [4], made desolate [4], lieth desolate [3], destroy [2], laid desolate [2], laid waste [2], maketh desolate [2], wondered [2], astonishment [1], bring into desolation [1], bring unto desolation [1], desolate places [1], desolation [1], destitute [1], destroyed [1], lay desolate [1], lie waste [1], make amazed [1], make waste [1], make [1], making desolate [1], waste [1]

8075 שְׁמַם **šᵉmam** (Aram.), v. GK: 10724 [cf. 8074]. [Itpo] to be greatly perplexed, implying one is in a state of severe distress, a fig. extension of destroying an object:– astonied [1]

8076 שָׁמֵם **šamēm**, a. GK: 9038 [→ 8074]. desolate, deserted:– desolate [2]

8077 שְׁמָמָה **šᵉmāmâ** or שִׁמָּמָה **šimmâ**, n.f. GK: 9039 & 9040 [→ 8074]. desolation, ruin, wasteland:– desolate [36], desolation [12], most desolate (+4923+2050.1) [3], desolations [2], most desolate (+8077+2050.1) [2], utterly [1], waste [1]

8078 שִׁמָּמוֹן **šimmāmôn**, n.[m.]. GK: 9041 [→ 8074]. despair, which may border on feelings of horror and shuddering:– astonishment [1]

8079 שְׁמָמִית **šᵉmāmît**, n.f. GK: 8532. lizard; some sources: gecko:– spider [1]

8080 שָׁמֵן **šamēn**, v. GK: 9042 [→ 8081]. [Q] to grow fat; [H] to show as well-fed; by extension: to be calloused, unresponsive of heart:– waxed fat [2], became fat [1], make fat [1], waxen fat [1]

8081 שֶׁמֶן **šemen**, n.m. GK: 9043 [→ 820?, 4924, 4925, 4924, 8080, 8082]. olive, the tree and its products: olive berry, olive oil, olive wood; olive oil was a staple of diet in biblical times, and was also used as a medicine, lamp fuel, and in religious offerings and ritual:– oil [165], ointment [11], olive [4], ointments [3], fat things [2], fat [2], oiled [1], anointing [1], fatness [1], pine [1], very fruitful (+1121) [1]

8082 שָׁמֵן **šamēn**, a. GK: 9045 [→ 8081]. rich, fertile:– fat [8], lusty [1], plenteous [1]

8083 שְׁמֹנֶה **šᵉmôneh**, n.m. & f. GK: 9046 [→ 8066, 8067, 8084]. eight; (pl.) eighty:– eight [74], eighteen (+6240) [18], eighteenth (+6240) [11], eighth [5], eighteen thousand (+505+7239+2050.1) [1]

8084 שְׁמֹנִים **šᵉmônîm**, n.pl.indecl. GK: 9047 [→ 8083]. eighty (pl. of "eight"):– fourscore [34], eighty [3], eightieth [1]

8085 שָׁמַע **šama'**, v. GK: 9048 [→ 851, 2045, 3458, 3460, 3461, 4926, 4927, 4928, 8052, 8060, 8087, 8088, 8089, 8090, 8093, 8094, 8095, 8096, 8097, 8099, 8100, 8101; cf. 1002]. [Q] to hear, listen, obey; [N] to be heard; [P] to summon, call together; [H] to proclaim, summon, make hear; from the base meaning of hearing come the extensions of understanding and obedience:– heard [362], hear [150], hearkened [73], heareth [26], obey (+871.1) [26], obeyed (+871.1) [20], obeyed [14], publish [12], heardest [11], obey [11], obedient [8], hearest [6], hearing [6], understand [6], cause to be heard [5], cause to hear [4], diligently hearken (+8085) [4], hear diligently (+8085) [4], heareth (+8085) [4], hearken diligently

(+8085) [5], publisheth [4], shewed [4], make to be heard [3], call together [2], carefully hearken (+8085) [2], certainly heard (+8085) [2], diligently obey (+8085) [2], discern [2], hear indeed (+8085) [2], hearkeneth [2], indeed obey (+8085) [2], made to hear [2], obey indeed (+8085+871.1) [2], obeyedst (+871.1) [2], obeyeth (+871.1) [2], reported [2], shew [2], surely hear (+8085) [2], surely heard (+8085) [2], tell [2], told [2], called together [1], caused to be heard [1], caused to hear [1], consented [1], considered [1], content [1], declared [1], declareth [1], declare [1], gathered together [1], gave ear [1], hear (+241) [1], hear attentively (+8085) [1], diligently [1], hearken unto [1], hearkenedst [1], hearkening [1], listen [1], made a sound [1], made proclamation [1], make a sound [1], make hear [1], make noise [1], make to hear [1], making a noise [1], obeyeth [1], obeying (+871.1) [1], obeying [1], perceived [1], perceive [1], proclaimed [1], published [1], regardeth [1], sang loud [1], shew forth [1], sounding [1], sound [1], understandest [1], understanding [1], understood [1], witness [1]

8086 שְׁמַע **šᵉma'** (Aram.), v. GK: 10725 [cf. 8085]. [P] to hear; [Htpa] to obey:– heard [4], hear [4], obey [1]

8087 שֶׁמַע **šema'**, n.pr.m. GK: 9050. Shema, "*he hears*":– Shema [5]

8088 שֵׁמַע **šēma'**, n.[m.]. GK: 9051 [→ 8085]. what is heard, report, news, rumor:– fame [5], report [5], tidings [2], bruit [1], heard [1], hearing [1], hear [1], loud [1], speech [1]

8089 שֹׁמַע **šōma'**, n.m. GK: 9053 [→ 8085]. report; reputation:– fame [4]

8090 שֶׁמַע **šema'**, n.pr.loc. GK: 9054 [→ 8085]. Shema, "*he hears*":– Shema [1]

8091 שָׁמָע **šāmā'**, n.pr.m. GK: 9052 [→ 8085+3068?]. Shama, "*one obedient [to Yahweh]*":– Shama [1]

8092 שִׁמְעָא **šim'ā'**, n.pr.m. GK: 9055 [→ 8085+3068?]. Shimea; Shammua, "*he has heard or obedient one*":– Shimea [5], Shimma [1]

8093 שִׁמְעָה **šim'â**, n.pr.m. GK: 9056 [→ 8101]. Shimeah, "*he has heard or he is obedient*":– Shimeah [2]

8094 שִׁמְעָה **šᵉmā'â**, n.pr.m. GK: 9057 [→ 8085]. Shemaah, "*[poss.] Yahweh hears*":– Shemaah [1]

8095 שִׁמְעוֹן **šim'ôn**, n.pr.m. GK: 9058 [→ 8099; cf. 8085]. Simeon, Simeonite, "*he has heard or obedient one*":– Simeon [43], Shimeon [1]

8096 שִׁמְעִי **šim'î**, n.pr.m. GK: 9059 [→ 8097]. Shimei, "*Yahweh has heard or famous*":– Shimei [41], Shimhi [1], Shimi [1]

8097 שִׁמְעִי **šim'î**, a.g. GK: 9060 [→ 8096]. Shimeites, of Shimei, "*of Shimei*":– Shimei [1], Shimites [1]

8098 שְׁמַעְיָה **šᵉma'yâ** or שְׁמַעְיָהוּ **šᵉma'yāhû**, n.pr.m. GK: 9061 & 9062 [→ 8085+3068]. Shemaiah, "*Yahweh hears*":– Shemaiah [41]

8099 שִׁמְעֹנִי **šim'ōnî**, a.g. GK: 9063 [→ 8095]. Simeonite, of Simeon, "*of Simeon*":– Simeonites [3], Simeon [1]

8100 שִׁמְעָת **šim'āt**, n.pr.f. GK: 9064 [→ 8085]. Shimeath, "*guardian, watcher*":– Shimeath [2]

8101 שִׁמְעָתִי **šim'ātî**, a.g. GK: 9065 [→ 8093]. Shimeathite, "*of Shimeath*":– Shimeathites [1]

8102 שֶׁמֶץ **šemeṣ**, n.[m.]. GK: 9066 [→ 8103?]. whisper:– little [2]

8103 שִׁמְצָה **šimṣâ**, v. GK: 9067 [→ 8102?]. laughingstock, derision:– shame [1]

8104 שָׁמַר **šamar**, v. GK: 9068 [→ 821, 4929, 4931, 8068, 8105, 8106?, 8108, 8109, 8110, 8111, 8113, 8107, 8118, 8119 (also used with compound proper names)]. [Q] to keep, watch, observe, guard; [Qp] to be set aside, be secured; [N] to be careful, beware; [P] to cling to; [Ht] to keep oneself; to observe for oneself:– keep [183], kept [70], observe [41], take heed [31], keepeth [19], keepers [15], keeper [13], beware [9], preserve [9], keeping [7], preserved [6], preserveth [6], watch [5], diligently keep (+8104) [4], mark [4], watchman [4], watchmen [4], keepest [3], observed [3], regardeth [3], marked [2], regard [2], took heed [2], wait [2], circumspect [1], lay wait [1], lookest narrowly [1], markest [1], marketh [1], observest [1], observeth [1], reserveth [1], saved [1], save [1], spies [1], sure [1], takest heed [1], taking heed [1], wait on [1], waited [1], waiteth on [1], waiteth [1], waiting [1], watched [1], watcht [1]

8105 שֶׁמֶר **šemer**, n.m. GK: 9069 [→ 8106? cf. 8104]. dregs (of wine); aged wine:– lees [2], wines on the lees [2], dregs [1]

8106 שֶׁמֶר *šemer*, n.pr.m. GK: 9070 [→ 8105?]. Shemer, "[poss.] *watch*; [poss.] *sediment of wine from which clear wine is made*":– Shamer [2], Shemer [2], Shamed [1]

8107 שִׁמֻּרִים *šimmurîm*, n.[m.pl.]. GK: 9081 [→ 8104]. vigil, night-watch:– much observed [1], observed [1]

שֹׁמֵר *šōmēr*. See 7763.

8108 שָׁמְרָה *šomrâ*, n.f. GK: 9072 [→ 8104]. guard, watch:– watch [1]

8109 שְׁמֻרָה *š°murâ*, n.f. GK: 9073 [→ 8104]. eyelid (that covers and protects the eye):– waking [1]

8110 שִׁמְרוֹן *šimrôn*, n.pr.m. & loc. GK: 9074 & 9075 [→ 8104, 8117]. Shimron, "*guardian, watchman*":– Shimron [5]

8111 שֹׁמְרוֹן *šōm°rôn*, n.pr.m. GK: 9076 [→ 8118; cf. 8104; cf. 8115]. Samaria, the capital city of northern kingdom of Israel; by extension, the northern kingdom itself, "*belonging to the clan of Shemer [1Ki 16:24]*":– Samaria [109]

8112 שִׁמְרוֹן מְראֹון *šimrôn m°r'ôn*, n.pr.loc. GK: 9077. Shimron Meron:– Shimron-meron [1]

8113 שִׁמְרִי *šimrî*, n.pr.m. GK: 9078 [→ 8104]. Shimri, "*Yahweh guards, preserves*":– Shimri [3], Simri [1]

8114 שְׁמַרְיָה *š°maryâ* or שְׁמַרְיָהוּ *š°maryāhû*, n.pr.m. GK: 9079 & 9080 [→ 8104+3068]. Shemariah, "*Yahweh guards, preserves*":– Shemariah [3], Shamariah [1]

שְׁמָרִימוֹת *š°mārîmôt*. See 8070.

8115 שָׁמְרַיִן *šām°rayin* (Aram.), n.pr.loc. GK: 10726 [cf. 8111]. Samaria, "*belonging to the clan of Shemer*":– Samaria [2]

8116 שִׁמְרִית *šimrît*, n.pr.f. GK: 9083 [→ 7763]. "*guardianess, watch woman*":– Shimrith [1]

8117 שִׁמְרֹנִי *šimrōnî*, a.g. GK: 9084 [→ 8110]. Shimronite, "*of Shimron*":– Shimronites [1]

8118 שֹׁמְרֹנִי *šōm°rōnî*, a.g. GK: 9085 [→ 8111]. of Samaria, "*of Samaria*":– Samaritans [1]

8119 שִׁמְרָת *šimrāt*, n.pr.m. GK: 9086 [→ 8104]. Shimrath, "*guardian, watchman*":– Shimrath [1]

8120 שְׁמַשׁ *š°maš* (Aram.), v. GK: 10727 [→ 8122?]. [Pa] to attend to, serve:– ministered [1]

8121 שֶׁמֶשׁ *šemeš*, n.f. & m. GK: 9087 [→ 1053, 1030, 5885, 5905, 8048, 8123; cf. 8122]. sun:– sun [119], sunrising (+4217) [6], the sunrising (+4217+1886.1) [2], east side (+4217) [1], eastward (+4217+1886.1) [1], sunrising (+4217+1886.1) [1], the east side (+4217+1886.1) [1], the west (+3996+1886.1) [1], westward (+3996+1886.1) [1], windows [1]

8122 שְׁמַשׁ *š°maš* (Aram.), n.[m.]. GK: 10728 [→ 8120?, 8122; cf. 8121]. sun:– sun [1]

8123 שִׁמְשׁוֹן *šimšôn*, n.pr.m. GK: 9088 [→ 8121]. Samson, "*little one of Shemesh* or *strong*":– Samson [35], Samson's [3]

שִׁמְשִׁי *šimšî*. See 1030.

8124 שִׁמְשַׁי *šimšay* (Aram.), n.pr.m. GK: 10729 [→ 8122]. Shimshai, "*one given to (pagan sun god) Shemesh*":– Shimshai [4]

8125 שַׁמְשְׁרַי *šamš°ray*, n.pr.m. GK: 9091. Shamsherai, "*may Shemesh guard*":– Shamsherai [1]

8126 שֻׁמָתִי *šumātî*, a.g. GK: 9092. Shumathite:– Shumathites [1]

8127 שֵׁן *šēn*, n.f. & m. GK: 9094 [→ 8143; cf. 8150; cf. 8128]. tooth (human or animal); by extension, anything tooth shaped: rocky crag; "*cleanness of teeth*" is a sign of lack of food in famine:– teeth [31], ivory [10], tooth [9], sharp [2], crag [1], forefront [1], tooth's [1]

8128 שֵׁן *šēn* (Aram.), n.[f.]. GK: 10730 [cf. 8127]. tooth; in the dual number it is a set of teeth, the upper and lower rows of teeth in a mouth:– teeth [3]

8129 שֵׁן *šēn*, n.pr.loc. GK: 9095 [→ 8150]. Shen, "*tooth, crag [of rock]*":– Shen [1]

8130 שָׂנֵא *śānē'*, v. GK: 8533 [→ 5570, 5574, 8135, 8146; cf. 8131]. [Q] to hate, be an enemy; [Qp] to be unloved; [N] to be hated, be shunned; [P] to be an adversary, be a foe; "*hate*" can be active, as an adversary, or passive, as someone unloved or shunned:– hate [68], hated [40], hateth [20], hatest [5], enemies [3], enemy [2], utterly hated (+8130) [2], foes [1], hated exceedingly (+1419+3966+8135) [1], hateful [1], haters [1], hating [1], odious [1]

8131 שְׂנָא *śnā'* (Aram.), v. GK: 10686 [cf. 8130]. [P] to hate; (as noun) an enemy:– hate [1]

8132 שְׁנָא *šānā'*, v. GK: 9096 [→ 8125?]. prob. same as 8138: [Q] to become dull; to change; [P] to change, alter; [Pu] to be changed:– changed [3]

8133 שְׁנָה *š°nâ* (Aram.), v. GK: 10731 [→ 8140; cf. 8138]. [P] to be changed, be different; [Pa] to change; defy; [Pap] to be different; [H] to change, alter; [Itpa] to be changed, be turned into:– changed [12], diverse [5], alter [2], changeth [1], change [1]

שְׁנָא *šēnā'*. See 8142.

8134 שִׁנְאָב *šin'āb*, n.pr.m. GK: 9098. Shinab, "*Sin is his father*":– Shinab [1]

8135 שִׂנְאָה *śin'â*, n.f. GK: 8534 [→ 8130]. hatred, malice:– hatred [12], hated [2], cruel hatred (+2555) [1], hated exceedingly (+1419+3966+8130) [1], hatefully (+871.1) [1]

8136 שִׁנְאָן *šin'ān*, n.[m.]. GK: 9099 [→ 8125?]. high in rank or number:– angels [1]

8137 שֶׁנְאַצַּר *šen'aṣṣar*, n.pr.m. GK: 9100. Shenazzar, "*may Sin protect*":– Shenazar [1]

8138 שָׁנָה *šānâ*, v. GK: 9101 [→ 4932, 8132?, 8136?, 8141, 8144?, 8145, 8147; cf. 8150; cf. 8133]. [Q] to repeat, do again; [N] to be repeated; [P] to change, alter; to pretend; [Pu] to be changed; [Ht] to disguise oneself:– changed [3], again [2], change [2], diverse [2], alter [1], changest [1], did the second time [1], disguise [1], do again [1], do the second time [1], doubled [1], given to change [1], pervert [1], preferred [1], repeateth [1], returneth [1], second time [1]

8139 שְׁנָה *š°nâ* (Aram.), n.f. GK: 10733 [cf. 8142]. sleep:– sleep [1]

8140 שְׁנָה *š°nâ* (Aram.), n.f. GK: 10732 [→ 8133; cf. 8141]. year:– year [6], years [1]

8141 שָׁנָה *šānâ*, n.f. GK: 9102 [→ 8138; cf. 8140]. year:– years [446], year [288], first year (+1121) [42], two years [6], two full years (+3117) [5], every year (+3605+8141+2050.1) [2], year by year (+8141) [2], year by year (+8141+871.1) [2], yearly (+3605+8141+871.1+2050.1) [2], yearly (+8141+871.1) [2], years old [2], years' [2], first year (+1323) [1], how long (+3117+4100+3509.1) [1], long [1], old (+2416+3117) [1], two year [1], whole age (+2416+3117) [1], year's [1], yearly [1]

8142 שֵׁנָא *šēnā'* or שֵׁנָה *šēnâ*, n.f. GK: 9097 & 9104 [→ 3462, 8153; cf. 8139]. sleep, with a focus of rest and inactivity, sometimes laziness; by extension: death:– sleep [23]

8143 שֶׁנְהַבִּים *šenhabbîm*, n.m.[pl.]. GK: 9105 [→ 8127]. ivory:– ivory [2]

8144 שָׁנִי *šānî*, n.[m.]. GK: 9106 [→ 8138?]. scarlet, crimson (thread):– scarlet (+8438) [31], scarlet [6], scarlet (+8438+1886.1) [2], scarlet thread [2], crimson [1]

8145 שֵׁנִי *šēnî*, a.num.ord. GK: 9108 [→ 8147; cf. 8138; cf. 8578, cf. 8579]. second:– second [84], other [37], second time [16], again [7], another [7], more [3], either [1], second rank [1]

8146 שָׂנִא *śānî'*, a. GK: 8535 [→ 8130]. not loved, disdained:– hated [1]

8147 שְׁנַיִם *š°nayim*, n.m. & f. GK: 9109 [→ 8145; cf. 8138; cf. 8648]. two:– two [528], twelve (+6240) [109], both [75], twelfth (+6240) [22], second [10], twain [6], double [5], twice [4], threescore and twelve (+7657+2050.1) [2], twenty [2], both twain [1], couple [1], sixscore (+6240) [1], twice (+871.1) [1]

8148 שְׁנִינָה *š°nînâ*, n.f. GK: 9110 [→ 8150]. object of ridicule:– byword [3], taunt [1]

8149 שְׂנִיר *š°nîr*, n.pr.loc. GK: 8536. Senir:– Senir [2], Shenir [2]

8150 שָׁנַן *šānan*, v. GK: 9111 & 9112 [→ 8127, 8129, 8143, 8148; cf. 8138]. [Q] to sharpen; [Qp] to be sharpened; [P] to impress, repeat; [Htpol] to be embittered:– sharp [4], whet [2], pricked [1], sharpened [1], teach diligently [1]

8151 שָׁנַס *šānas*, v. GK: 9113. [P] to tuck up the cloak (into the belt):– girded up [1]

8152 שִׁנְעָר *šin'ār*, n.pr.loc. GK: 9114. Shinar; Babylonia:– Shinar [7], Babylonish [1]

8153 שְׁנָת *š°nāt*, n. GK: 9104 [→ 8142]. same as 8142: sleep:– sleep [1]

8154 שָׁסָא *šāsâ*, v. GK: 9115 [cf. 7601]. [Q] to raid, loot, plunder; [Qp] to be looted:– spoiled [3], spoil [3], spoilers [2], destroyers [1], robbed [1], rob [1]

8155 שָׁסַס *šāsas*, v. GK: 9116 [→ 7601]. same as 7601: [Q] to plunder, ransack; [N] to be looted, be ransacked:– spoiled [3], rifled [1], spoil [1]

8156 שָׁסַע *šāsa'*, v. GK: 9117 [→ 8157]. [Q] to divide; [Qp] be divided; [P] to tear apart:– clovenfooted (+6541+8157) [2], rent [2], cleaveth [1], cleave [1], clovenfooted (+8157) [1], cloven [1], stayed [1]

8157 שֶׁסַע *šesa'*, n.[m.]. GK: 9118 [→ 8156]. cleft (split hoof):– clovenfooted (+6541+8156) [2], cleft [1], clovenfooted (+8156) [1]

8158 שָׁסַף *šāsap*, v. GK: 9119. [P] to hack to pieces (for execution):– hewed in pieces [1]

8159 שָׁעָה *šā'â*, v. GK: 9120 [cf. 7583]. [Q] to look with favor, have regard for, pay attention to:– look [3], dismayed [2], respect [2], depart [1], dim [1], have respect [1], look away [1], looked [1], regard [1], spare [1], turn [1]

8160 שָׁעָה *šā'â* (Aram.), n.f. GK: 10734. moment, short time; (as adv.) immediately, suddenly, for a time:– hour [5]

שְׂעוֹר *s°'ôr*. See 8184.

שְׂעוֹרָה *s°'ôrâ*. See 8184.

8161 שַׁעֲטָה *š°'āṭâ*, n.f. GK: 9121. galloping, pounding (hooves):– stamping [1]

8162 שַׁעַטְנֵז *ša'aṭnēz*, n.m. GK: 9122. woven cloth; likely referring to a wide mesh:– garment of divers sorts [1], mingled of linen and woollen (+3610) [1]

8163 שָׂעִיר *śā'îr*, a. & n.m. GK: 8537 & 8538 & 8539 [→ 8166; cf. 8175]. hairy, shaggy; male goat; goat idol:– kid [26], goat [21], devils [2], goats [2], hairy [2], kids [2], he goats [1], rough [1], satyrs [1], satyr [1]

8164 שָׂעִיר *śā'îr*, n.[m.]. GK: 8540. rain shower:– small rain [1]

8165 שֵׂעִיר *śē'îr*, n.pr.m. & loc. GK: 8541 & 8542 & 8543 [→ 8167; cf. 8175]. Seir, "*hairy, shaggy, covered with trees*; [poss.] *the place of the goats* or *the place of Esau [Ge 25:25 BDB]*; *small forest, rich forest*":– Seir [39]

8166 שְׂעִרָה *s°'irâ*, n.f. GK: 8544 [→ 8163]. female goat:– kid [2]

8167 שְׂעִירָה *s°'îrâ*, n.pr.loc. GK: 8545 [→ 8165]. Seirah, "*place of the goats*; [poss.] *woody hills; shaggy forest*":– Seirath [1]

8168 שֹׁעַל *šō'al*, n.[m.]. GK: 9123 [→ 4934, 8171?]. hollow of the hand; handful, a measure of volume:– handfuls [2], hollow of hand [1]

שֻׁעָל *šu'āl*. See 7776.

8169 שַׁעַלְבִּים *ša'albîm* or שַׁעֲלַבִּין *ša'°labbîn*, n.pr.loc. GK: 9124 & 9125. Shaalbim, Shaalabbin, "*site of foxes*":– Shaalbim [2], Shaalabbin [1]

8170 שַׁעַלְבֹנִי *ša'albōnî*, a.g. GK: 9126. Shaalbonite:– Shaalbonite [2]

8171 שַׁעֲלִים *ša'°lîm*, n.pr.loc. GK: 9127 [→ 8168?]. Shaalim, "*[poss.] land of hollow depth*":– Shalim [1]

8172 שָׁעַן *šā'an*, v. GK: 9128 [→ 4937, 4938]. [N] to lean oneself upon, rely on:– stay [5], leaned [4], lean [4], relied [3], rest [2], leaneth [1], lieth [1], rely [1], resteth [1]

8173 שָׁעַע *šā'a'*, v. GK: 9129 & 9130 [→ 8191]. [Q] be blinded; [Pil] to take joy in, delight in; [Pulpal] to be dandled; [H] to make close the eyes; [Htpal] to blind oneself; a fig. extension of smearing over or pasting objects together; to delight oneself in:– delight [4], cry out [1], cry [1], dandled [1], play [1], shut [1]

שָׁעִיף *šā'ip*. See 5587.

8174 שַׁעַף *ša'ap*, n.pr.m. GK: 9131. Shaaph:– Shaaph [2]

8175 שָׂעַר *śā'ar*, v.den. GK: 8547 & 8548 & 8549 [→ 8163, 8165, 8166, 8167, 8178, 8181, 8183, 8184, 8185; cf. 5590]. [Q] to shudder, bristle with horror; to sweep away (by the wind); to know about, be acquainted with; [N] to be in a storm; [P] to sweep away (by a wind); [Ht] to storm against:– afraid [1], as a storm hurleth [1], come like a whirlwind [1], feared [1], horribly afraid [1], sore afraid (+8178) [1], take away as with a whirlwind [1], tempestuous [1]

8176 שָׁעַר *šā'ar*, v. GK: 9132 [→ 8180]. [Q] to think, estimate, calculate:– thinketh [1]

8177 שְׂעַר *s°'ar* (Aram.), n.m. GK: 10687 [cf. 8181]. hair (of the head or body):– hair [2], hairs [1]

8178 שַׂעַר *śa'ar*, n.[m.]. GK: 8550 & 8551 [→ 8175]. horror, shudder, an extension of the bristling of hair (in excitement or

fear); wind storm, gale:– affrighted (+270) [1], horribly [1], sore afraid (+8175) [1], storm [1]

8179 שַׁעַר *ša'ar*, n.m. GK: 9133 [→ 7778, 8182, 8189; cf. 8651]. gate, gateway; often referring to the entrance to a city, a key point of the city's defense and a place for public hearings and decisions:– gate [249], gates [112], every gate (+8179+2050.1) [6], cities [2], city [1], doors [1], door [1], porters [1], port [1]

8180 שַׁעַר *ša'ar*, n.[m.]. GK: 9134 [→ 8176]. measure (of grain):– hundredfold (+3967) [1]

שָׂעִיר *sā'ir*. See 8163.

8181 שֵׂעָר *śē'ār*, n.m. GK: 8552 [→ 8175; cf. 8177]. hair:– hair [23], hairy [3], hairs [1], rough [1]

שֹׂעֵר *śō'ēr*. See 7778.

8182 שֹׂעָר *śō'ār*, a. GK: 9135 [→ 8179]. burst open, i.e., poor quality (figs):– vile [1]

8183 שְׂעָרָה *ś'ārâ*, n.f. GK: 8554 [→ 8175]. storm, gale:– storm [1], tempest [1]

8184 שְׂעֹרָה *ś'ōrâ*, n.f. GK: 8555 [→ 8175; cf. 7795?]. barley:– barley [34]

8185 שַׂעֲרָה *śa"râ*, n.f. GK: 8553 [→ 8175]. hair:– hair [5], hairs [2]

8186 שַׂעֲרוּר *śa"rûr* or שַׂעֲרוּרִי *śa"rûrî*, n.f. GK: 9136 & 9137. something horrible, shocking thing:– horrible thing [4]

8187 שְׂעַרְיָה *ś'aryâ*, n.pr.m. GK: 9138 [→ 3068]. Sheariah, "[poss.] *Yahweh breaks*":– Sheariah [2]

8188 שְׂעֹרִים *ś'ōrîm*, n.pr.m. GK: 8556. Seorim, "*one born at the time of the barley [harvest]*":– Seorim [1]

8189 שַׁעֲרַיִם *ša"rayim*, n.pr.loc. GK: 9139 [→ 8179]. Shaaraim, "*double gates*":– Shaaraim [1], Sharaim [1]

שַׂעֲרִירִיָה *śa"rîrîâ* and שַׂעֲרֻרָת *śa"rurit*. See 8186.

8190 שַׁעַשְׁגַּז *ša'ašgaz*, n.pr.m. GK: 9140. Shaashgaz:– Shaashgaz [1]

8191 שַׁעֲשֻׁעִים *ša"šū'îm*, n.[m.]pl.intens. GK: 9141 [→ 8173]. delight:– delight [4], delights [3], pleasant [1]

8192 שָׂפָה *śāpâ*, v. GK: 9142 [→ 3472, 3473?, 8194?, 8195?, 8205]. [N, Pu] to be swept bare:– high [1], stick out [1]

8193 שָׂפָה *śāpâ*, n.f. & m. GK: 8557 [→ 8222]. lips (of the mouth); by extension: speech, language; edge of an object, rim, border; the "lip of the sea" is the seashore:– lips [110], bank [10], brim [8], edge [8], language [7], shore [6], speech [6], brink [5], border [3], side [3], lip [2], prating [2], vain [1], band [1], binding [1], full of talk [1], other [1]

8194 שְׁפוֹת *š'pôt*, n.f. GK: 9147 [→ 8192?]. milk product: cream, curds, cheese, etc:– cheese [1]

8195 שְׁפוֹ *š'pô* or שְׁפִי *š'pî*, n.pr.m. GK: 9143 & 9156 [→ 8192?, 8205?]. Shepho, Shephi, "[poss.] *barren way, empty path*":– Shephi [1], Shepho [1]

8196 שְׁפוֹט *š'pôṭ*, n.m. GK: 9144 [→ 8199]. judgment, punishment:– judgment [2]

8197 שְׁפוּפָם *š'pûpām* or שְׁפוּפָן *š'pûpān* or שׁוּפָם *šûpām*, n.pr.m. GK: 9145 & 9146 & 8792 [→ 7781, 8207?]. Shephuphan, Shephupham, Shupham, "[perhaps] *serpent*":– Shephuphan [1], Shupham [1]

8198 שִׁפְחָה *šiphâ*, n.f. GK: 9148 [→ 4940; cf. 5596]. maidservant, female slave:– handmaid [22], maid [12], handmaids [7], maidservants [5], bondwomen [3], maidservant [3], womenservants [3], handmaidens [2], maiden [2], bondmaid [1], maidens [1], servant [1], wench [1]

8199 שָׁפַט *šāpaṭ*, v. GK: 9149 [→ 4941, 8195, 8196, 8201, 8202, 8204; cf. 8200 (also used with compound proper names)]. [Q] to judge, decide; lead, defend, vindicate; [N] to execute judgment, be brought to trial; to argue a matter; [Po] (ptcp.) judge:– judge [102], judges [37], judged [28], plead [7], judgeth [5], judging [4], avenged [2], judgest [2], needs be a judge (+8199) [2], plead with [2], condemn [1], contendeth [1], defend [1], deliver [1], execute the judgment (+4941) [1], executing judgment [1], pleaded [1], pleadeth [1], reason [1], ruled [1]

8200 שְׁפַט *š'paṭ* (Aram.), v. GK: 10735 [cf. 8199]. [P] to judge; (as noun) judge:– magistrates [1]

8201 שֶׁפֶט *šepeṭ*, n.m. GK: 9150 [→ 8199]. judgment, punishment:– judgments [14], judgment [2]

8202 שָׁפָט *šāpāṭ*, n.pr.m. GK: 9151 [→ 8199]. Shaphat, "*he judges*":– Shaphat [8]

8203 שְׁפַטְיָה *š'paṭyâ* or שְׁפַטְיָהוּ *š'paṭyāhû*, n.pr.m. GK: 9152 & 9153 [→ 8199+3068]. Shephatiah, "*Yahweh has judged*":– Shephatiah [12], Shephathiah [1]

8204 שִׁפְטָן *šipṭān*, n.pr.m. GK: 9154 [→ 8199]. Shiphtan, "*he has judged*":– Shiphtan [1]

8205 שְׁפִי *š'pî*, n.m. GK: 9155 [→ 8195; cf. 8192]. barren height:– high places [8], high place [1]

8206 שֻׁפִּים *šuppîm*, n.pr.m. & a.g. GK: 9157 & 9158 [→ 8221]. Shuppim; Shuppites:– Shuppim [3]

8207 שְׁפִיפֹן *š'pîpōn*, n.[m.]. GK: 9159 [→ 8197?]. viper:– adder [1]

8208 שָׁפִיר *šāpîr*, n.pr.loc. GK: 9160 [→ 8231]. "*lovely*":– Saphir [1]

8209 שַׁפִּיר *šappîr* (Aram.), a. GK: 10736 [→ 8232]. beautiful, fair, lovely:– fair [2]

8210 שָׁפַךְ *šāpak*, v. GK: 9161 [→ 8211, 8212]. [Q] to pour out, shed, spill; [Qp, N, Pu] to be outpoured, be shed; [Ht] be scattered, ebb away; "to shed blood" means to kill:– shed [34], pour out [23], poured out [19], pour [10], cast [6], poured [6], poureth out [4], cast up [2], poureth [2], sheddeth [2], casting up [1], gushed out [1], pouredst out [1], pouring out [1], shed out [1], shedder [1], slipt [1]

8211 שֶׁפֶךְ *šepek*, n.[m.]. GK: 9162 [→ 8210]. dump (for throwing out ash refuse):– poured out [2]

8212 שׇׁפְכָה *šopkâ*, n.f. GK: 9163 [→ 8210]. male organ (fluid duct):– privy member [1]

8213 שָׁפֵל *šāpēl*, v. GK: 9164 [→ 8216, 8217, 8218, 8219, 8220; cf. 8214, cf. 8215]. [Q] to be humble, be brought low; [H] to humble, bring low:– humbled [4], bring down [3], abase [2], brought down [2], humbleth [2], lay low [2], layeth low [2], made low [2], bring low [1], bringeth low [1], brought low [1], cast down [1], casteth down [1], debase [1], humble [1], low [1], put lower [1], putteth down [1]

8214 שְׁפַל *š'pal* (Aram.), v. GK: 10737 [→ 8215; cf. 8213]. [H] to humble, subdue, bring low:– abase [1], humbled [1], put down [1], subdue [1]

8215 שְׁפַל *š'pal* (Aram.), a. GK: 10738 [→ 8214; cf. 8217]. low; (as superlative) lowliest:– basest [1]

8216 שֵׁפֶל *šepel*, n.[m.]. GK: 9165 [→ 8213]. low estate, humble condition:– low estate [1], low place [1]

8217 שָׁפָל *šāpāl*, a. GK: 9166 [→ 8213]. low, deep:– low [5], base [4], humble [4], lower [4], basest [1], lowly [1]

8218 שִׁפְלָה *šiplâ*, n.f. GK: 9168 [→ 8213]. state of lowliness, condition of humiliation:– low place [1]

8219 שְׁפֵלָה *š'pēlâ*, n.f. GK: 9169 [→ 8213]. (western) foothills, Shephelah, a major buffer area between the (Philistine) coastal plain and the highlands of Judah:– valley [6], vale [5], plain [3], low country [2], low plains [2], valleys [2]

8220 שִׁפְלוּת *šiplût*, n.f. GK: 9170 [→ 8213]. idleness, inactivity, an extension of lowering the hands to a position of rest:– idleness [1]

8221 שְׁפָם *š'pām*, n.pr.loc. GK: 9172 [→ 8225?]. Shepham, "*nakedness*":– Shepham [2]

8222 שָׂפָם *śāpām*, n.[m.]. GK: 8559 [→ 8193]. (the area of the) mustache; lower part of the face:– lips [3], beard [1], upper lip [1]

8223 שָׂפָם *śāpām*, n.pr.m. GK: 9171. Shapham:– Shapham [1]

8224 שִׂפְמוֹת *śipmôt*, n.pr.loc. GK: 8560. Siphmoth:– Siphmoth [1]

8225 שִׁפְמִי *šipmî*, a.g. GK: 9175 [→ 8221?]. Shiphmite:– Shiphmite [1]

8226 שָׂפַן *śāpan*, v. GK: 8561 [cf. 5603]. [Qp] to be hidden:– treasures [1]

8227 שָׁפָן *šāpān*, n.m. & n.pr.m. GK: 9176 & 9177. coney; n.pr. Shaphan, "*rock badger*":– Shaphan [30], conies [2], coney [1], cony [1]

8228 שֶׁפַע *šepa'*, n.[m.]. GK: 9179. abundance:– abundance [1]

8229 שִׁפְעָה *šip'â*, n.f. GK: 9180. (of water) flood; mass (of humans or animals):– abundance [3], company [2], multitude [1]

8230 שִׁפְעִי *šip'î*, n.pr.m. GK: 9181. Shiphi, "*flowing abundance*":– Shiphi [1]

שָׂפַק *śāpaq*. See 5606.

8231 שָׁפַר *šāpar*, v. GK: 9182 [→ 8208, 8233, 8235, 8236, 8237; cf. 7782, cf. 8232]. [Q] to be delightful, pleasing:– goodly [1]

8232 שְׁפַר *š'par* (Aram.), v. GK: 10739 [→ 8209, 8238?; cf. 8231]. [P] to be pleased, have pleasure:– acceptable [1], good [1], pleased [1]

8233 שֶׁפֶר *šeper*, n.[m.]. GK: 9183 [→ 8231]. beauty, loveliness:– goodly [1]

8234 שֶׁפֶר *šeper*, n.pr.loc. GK: 9184 [cf. 5611]. Shepher:– Shepher [2]

שׁוֹפָר *šôpār*. See 7782.

8235 שִׁפְרָה *šiprâ*, n.f. GK: 9185 [→ 8231]. fairness, clearness (of skies):– garnished [1]

8236 שִׁפְרָה *šiprâ*, n.pr.f. GK: 9186 [→ 8231]. Shiphrah, "*beautiful, fair*":– Shiphrah [1]

8237 שַׁפְרוּר *šaprûr* or שַׁפְרִיר *šaprîr*, n.[m.]. GK: 9187 & 9188 [→ 8231]. royal canopy, pavilion:– royal pavilion [1]

8238 שְׁפַרְפַּר *š'parpār* (Aram.), n.[m.]. GK: 10740 [→ 8232?]. dawn:– very early [1]

8239 שָׁפַת *šāpat*, v.den. GK: 9189 [→ 830, 4942, 8240]. [Q] to place, put:– set on [3], brought [1], ordain [1]

8240 שְׁפַתַּיִם *š'pattayim*, n.[m.]du. GK: 9190 & 9191 [→ 8239]. double-pronged hooks; area of inactivity: (place of the) fireplaces; some sources: saddlebags or sheepfolds:– hooks [1], pots [1]

8241 שֶׁצֶף *šeṣep*, n.m. GK: 9192 [cf. 7857, 7858]. surging, flooding (of anger):– little [1]

8242 שַׂק *śaq*, n.m. GK: 8566. sackcloth; sack:– sackcloth [41], sack [4], sacks [2], sackclothes [1]

8243 שָׁק *šāq* (Aram.), n.[m.]. GK: 10741 [cf. 7785]. lower leg, shank:– legs [1]

8244 שָׂקַד *śāqad*, v. GK: 8567. [N] to be bound:– bound [1]

8245 שָׁקַד *šāqad*, v. GK: 9193 [→ 8246, 8247]. [Q] to be awake, watch, stand guard:– watch [6], watched [2], hasten [1], remain [1], waketh [1], watching [1]

8246 מְשֻׁקָּד *m'šuqqād*, n.m. GK: 5481 [cf. 8245]. shape of almond flowers:– made like almonds [3], made like unto almonds [2], made after the fashion of almonds [1]

8247 שָׁקֵד *šāqēd*, n.m. GK: 9196 [cf. 8245]. almond tree, almond nuts:– almond tree [2], almonds [2]

8248 שָׁקָה *šāqâ*, v. GK: 9197 [→ 4945, 8249, 8250, 8268; cf. 8354]. [N] to be given a drink; [Pu] to be moistened; [H] to give a drink to:– water [9], butler [8], give drink [7], give a drink to [6], watered [6], gave drink [5], made drink [5], cause to drink [4], make drink [4], made to drink [3], cupbearers [2], drink [2], gave to drink [2], given to drink [2], butlers [1], cupbearer [1], givest to drink [1], giveth drink [1], giving drink [1], moistened [1], wateredst [1], watereth [1]

8249 שִׁקּוּו *šiqquw*, n.[m.]. GK: 9198 [→ 8248]. drink; nourishing drink:– drink [1]

8250 שִׁקּוּי *šiqqûy*, n.[m.]. GK: 9198 [→ 8248]. same as 8249; drink; nourishing drink:– drink [1], marrow [1]

8251 שִׁקּוּץ *šiqqûṣ*, n.m. GK: 9199 [→ 8262]. detestable thing, vileness, abomination:– abominations [13], abomination [7], detestable things [5], abominable filth [1], abominable idols [1], detestable [1]

8252 שָׁקַט *šāqaṭ*, v. GK: 9200 [→ 8253; cf. 8367]. [Q] to be at rest, be at peace; [H] to keep silent, remain quiet, remain calm:– quiet [14], rest [5], had rest [4], at rest [2], in rest [2], quietness [2], still [2], appeaseth [1], give rest [1], giveth quietness [1], idleness [1], in quietness [1], in quiet [1], quieteth [1], rested [1], settled [1], take rest [1]

8253 שֶׁקֶט *šeqeṭ*, n.[m.]. GK: 9201 [→ 8252]. quietness:– quietness [1]

8254 שָׁקַל *šāqal*, v. GK: 9202 [→ 4946, 4948, 4949?, 8255; cf. 8625]. [Q] to weigh out, make payment; [N] to be weighed:– weighed [11], pay [4], throughly weighed (+8254) [2], weigh [2], receiver [1], receive [1], spend [1]

8255 שֶׁקֶל *šeqel*, n.m. GK: 9203 [→ 8254; cf. 8625]. shekel (a unit of weight and value, about two-fifths of an ounce [11.5 grams]):– shekels [46], shekel [42]

8256 שִׁקְמָה *šiqmâ*, n.f. GK: 9204. sycamore-fig tree:– sycamore trees [5], sycamore fruit [1], sycomores [1]

8257 שָׁקַע šaqaʿ, v. GK: 9205 [→ 4950]. [Q] to sink down; [N] to sink; [H] to make sink down, make settle:– drowned [2], lettest down [1], make deep [1], quenched [1], sink [1]

8258 שְׁקַעֲרוּרָה šᵉqaʿᵃrûrâ, n.f. GK: 9206 [→ 7086]. depression, hollow:– hollow strakes [1]

8259 שָׁקַף šaqap, v. GK: 9207 [→ 4947, 8260?, 8261]. [N] to look down on, overlook; [H] to look down on:– looked [6], looked out [4], look down [3], looked down [3], looketh [3], appeareth [1], looketh forth [1], looking [1]

8260 שֶׁקֶף šaqep, n.[m.]. GK: 9208 [→ 8259?]. frame work (of a door):– windows [1]

8261 שְׁקֻפִּים šᵉqupîm, n.m. GK: 9209 [→ 8259]. clerestory window (a high place window):– lights [1], windows [1]

8262 שָׁקַץ šaqaṣ, v. GK: 9210 [→ 8251, 8263; cf. 5354, 6973]. [P] to detest, abhor, defile:– abomination [2], make abominable [2], utterly detest (+8262) [2], abhorred [1]

8263 שֶׁקֶץ šeqeṣ, n.m. GK: 9211 [→ 8262]. detestable thing:– abomination [9], abominable [2]

שִׁקֻּץ šiqquṣ. See 8251.

8264 שָׁקַק šaqaq, v. GK: 9212 [→ 4944; cf. 7783?]. [Q] to rush forth, charge forth; [Htpal] to rush back and forth:– appetite [1], justle against [1], longing [1], ranging [1], run to and fro [1], run [1]

8265 שָׂקַר šaqar, v. GK: 8568. [P] to flirt, ogle (with the eyes):– wanton [1]

8266 שָׁקַר šaqar, v.den. GK: 9213 [→ 8267]. [Q] to deal falsely with; [P] to deceive, lie, betray:– lie [3], deal falsely [1], dealt falsely [1], suffer to fail [1]

8267 שֶׁקֶר šeqer, n.m. GK: 9214 [→ 8266]. lie, falseness, deception; vanity:– lying [21], false [20], lies [18], falsehood [13], lie [10], falsely [7], falsely (+1886.1+3807.1) [4], wrongfully [4], vain [3], deceitful [2], deceit [1], falsely (+5921) [1], falsely (+871.1+1886.1) [1], feignedly (+871.1) [1], in vain (+1886.1+3807.1) [1], in vain [1], liar [1], lies (+1697) [1], lying (+1697) [1], vain thing [1], without a cause [1]

8268 שֹׁקֶת šōqet, n.f. GK: 9216 [→ 8248]. watering-trough:– troughs [1], trough [1]

8269 שַׂר śar, n.m. GK: 8569 [→ 5371, 8282, 8310; cf. 7786]. ruler of various spheres (military, religious, governmental); commander, official, prince, chief, leader; "Prince of Peace" is a title of the child who would rule on David's throne, referring to the Messiah:– princes [189], captains [80], captain [48], chief [33], rulers [23], prince [19], ruler [10], governor [4], chief captain [3], keeper [1], governors [1], principal [2], general [1], lords [1], master [1], stewards [1], taskmasters (+4522) [1]

8270 שֹׁר śōr, n.[m.]. GK: 9219 [→ 8307, 8326]. navel; umbilical cord:– navel [2]

8271 שְׁרָא šᵉrâ (Aram.), v. GK: 10742 [cf. 8281]. [P] to loosen, solve (a problem); [Pp] to be loosened; to dwell; [Pa] to begin; [Htpal] to be loose and shaking (of legs giving way):– began [1], dissolve [1], dissolving [1], dwelleth [1], loosed [1], loose [1]

8272 שַׂרְאֶצֶר śarʾeṣer, שַׂר־אֶצֶר śar-ʾeṣer, n.pr.m. GK: 8570 [→ 5371]. Sharezer, "[god] protect the king!":– Sharezer [2], Sherezer [1]

8273 שָׁרָב šārāb, n.m. GK: 9220 [→ 8274?]. parching heat; burning hot sand:– heat [1], parched ground [1]

8274 שֵׁרֵבְיָא šērēbyâ, n.pr.m. GK: 9221 [→ 8273?+3068]. Sherebiah, "[poss.] Yahweh has sent burning heat":– Sherebiah [8]

8275 שַׁרְבִיט šarbîṭ, n.m. GK: 9222 [→ 7626]. scepter, staff:– sceptre [4]

8276 שָׂרַג śārag, v. GK: 8571 [→ 8299]. [Pu] to be close-knit, be intertwined; [Ht] to be woven together:– wrapt together [1], wreathed [1]

8277 שָׂרַד śārad, v. GK: 8572 [→ 8300]. [Q] to run away, escape:– remained [1]

8278 שְׂרָד śᵉrād, n.[m.]. GK: 8573 [→ 8279?]. woven material (with some kind of braiding woven in it):– service [4]

8279 שֶׂרֶד śered, n.[m.]. GK: 8574 [→ 8278?]. marker (for wood chiseling):– line [1]

8280 שָׂרָה śārâ, v. GK: 8575 [→ 415, 3478, 3481, 3482, 8304]. [Q] to struggle, contend:– as a prince hast power [1], had power [1]

8281 שָׁרָה šārâ, v. GK: 9223 [→ 4952, 8302; cf. 8271]. [Q] to unleash; to deliver, set free:– remnant [1]

8282 שָׂרָה śārâ, n.f. GK: 8576 [→ 8269, 8283; cf. 7786]. woman of nobility, lady of royal birth, queen:– ladies [2], princesses [1], princess [1], queens [1]

8283 שָׂרָה śārâ, n.pr.f. GK: 8577 [→ 8282; cf. 8297]. Sarah, "princess":– Sarah [36], Sarah's [2]

8284 שָׂרָה śārâ, n.[m.]. GK: 9224 [→ 7791; cf. 7789]. vineyard:– walls [1]

8285 שֵׂרָה śērâ or שֹׂר śēr, n.[f.]. GK: 9225 & 9217. bracelet:– bracelets [1]

8286 שְׂרוּג śᵉrûg, n.pr.m. GK: 8578. Serug, "descendant i.e., younger branch":– Serug [5]

8287 שָׁרוּחֶן šārûḥen, n.pr.loc. GK: 9226. Sharuhen:– Sharuhen [1]

8288 שְׂרוֹךְ śᵉrôk, n.[m.]. GK: 8579 [→ 8308]. thong (of a sandal):– latchet [1], shoelatchet (+5275) [1]

8289 שָׁרוֹן šārôn or לַשָּׁרוֹן laššārôn, n.pr.loc. GK: 9227 & 4389 [→ 8290; cf. 3474]. Sharon, "plain, level country"; Lasharon, "[belonging to] Sharon":– Sharon [6], Lasharon [1]

8290 שָׁרוֹנִי šārônî, a.g. GK: 9228 [→ 8289; cf. 3474]. Sharonite, "of Sharon":– Sharonite [1]

8291 שָׂרוּק śārûq, n.[m.]. GK: 8602 [→ 8320]. choice vines:– principal plants [1]

8292 שְׂרוּקָה śᵉrûqâ or שְׁרִקָה šᵉriqâ, n.[f.]. GK: 9229 & 9241 [→ 8319; cf. 8322]. whistling; scorn; some sources: flute playing:– bleatings [1], hissing [1]

8293 שֵׁרוּת šērût, var. GK: 9230 [cf. 8281]. freedom:–

8294 שֶׂרַח śeraḥ, n.pr.f. GK: 8580 [cf. 5628]. Serah, "one who explains, opens, extends; abundance":– Serah [2], Sarah [1]

8295 שָׂרַט śāraṭ, v. GK: 8581 [→ 8296]. [Q] to make a cut, incise the skin; [N] to make oneself incised, cut oneself:– cut in pieces (+8295) [2], make any cuttings (+8296) [1]

8296 שֶׂרֶט śereṭ or שָׂרֶטֶת śāreṭet, n.[m.]. GK: 8582 & 8583 [→ 8295]. cut, incision; this may refer to a tattoo:– cuttings [1], make any cuttings (+8295) [1]

8297 שָׂרַי śāray, n.pr.f. GK: 8584 [cf. 8283]. Sarai, "princess":– Sarai [16], Sarai's [1]

8298 שָׂרַי śāray, n.pr.m. GK: 9232. Sharai:– Sharai [1]

8299 שָׂרִיג śārîg, n.[m.]. GK: 8585 [→ 8276]. branch, tendril (of grape vines and fig trees):– branches [3]

8300 שָׂרִיד śārîd, n.[m.]. GK: 8586 [→ 8277]. survivor; those left:– remaining [9], remain [8], left [3], remaineth [3], remnant [2], alive [1], remained [1], rest [1]

8301 שָׂרִיד śārîd, n.pr.loc. GK: 8587. Sarid, "survivor":– Sarid [2]

8302 שִׁרְיָה širyâ or שִׁרְיוֹן širyôn, n.f. GK: 9233 & 9234 [→ 8281; cf. 5630]. coat of scale armor; a weapon that is thrown: javelin, lance, light spear; some sources: arrowhead:– coat [3], habergeons [2], harness [2], breastplate [1], habergeon [1]

8303 שִׁרְיוֹן širyôn, n.pr.loc. GK: 8590 [cf. 5630]. Sirion, "coat of mail":– Sirion [2]

8304 שְׂרָיָה śᵉrāyâ or שְׂרָיָהוּ śᵉrāyāhû, n.pr.m. GK: 8588 & 8589 [→ 8280+3068]. Seraiah, "Yahweh persists; Yahweh is prince; Yahweh contends":– Seraiah [20]

8305 שָׂרִיק śārîq, a. GK: 8591. combed (flax, as a first step for making linen):– fine [1]

8306 שָׁרִיר šārîr, n.[m.]. GK: 9235 [→ 8307]. muscle:– navel [1]

8307 שְׁרִרוּת šᵉrirût, n.f. GK: 9244 [→ 8270, 8306, 8325, 8326]. stubbornness:– imagination [9], lust [1]

8308 שָׂרַךְ śārak, v. GK: 8592 [→ 8288]. [P] to run here and there (aimlessly):– traversing [1]

8309 שְׂרֵמוֹת śᵉrēmôt, var. GK: 9236. var. of 7709: field:–

8310 שַׂר־סְכִים śar-sᵉkîm, n.pr.m. GK: 8593 [→ 8269]. Sarsekim:– Sarsechim [1]

8311 שָׂרַע śāraʿ, v. GK: 8594. [Qp] to be deformed; [Ht] to stretch oneself:– hath any thing superfluous [1], stretch [1], superfluous [1]

8312 שַׂרְעַפִּים śarʿappîm, n.[m.]pl. GK: 8595 [→ 5587]. anxiety, anxious thoughts:– thoughts [2]

8313 שָׂרַף śārap, v. GK: 8596 [→ 4955, 4956, 8314, 8315, 8316; cf. 5635]. [Q] to burn, set a fire; [Qp, N, Pu] to be burned up:– burnt [64], burn [38], burneth [4], burned [3], utterly burnt (+8313) [2], burn thoroughly (+8316+3807.1) [1], burn up [1],
burnt up [1], cause to be burnt [1], kindled [1], made a burning (+8316) [1]

8314 שָׂרָף śārāp, n.m. GK: 8597 [→ 8315; cf. 8313]. venomous snake; seraph (six-winged being):– fiery [3], fiery serpent [2], seraphims [2]

8315 שָׂרָף śārāp, n.pr.m. GK: 8598 [→ 8314; cf. 8313]. Saraph, "burning one, serpent":– Saraph [1]

8316 שְׂרֵפָה śᵉrēpâ, n.f. GK: 8599 [→ 8313]. burning:– burning [8], burnt [2], burn thoroughly (+8313+3807.1) [1], burnt up [1], made a burning (+8313) [1]

8317 שָׁרַץ šāraṣ, v. GK: 9237 [→ 8318]. [Q] to teem, swarm, move about:– creepeth [4], bring forth abundantly [2], creep [2], breed abundantly [1], bring forth abundantly (+8318) [1], brought forth abundantly [1], brought forth in abundance [1], increased abundantly [1], moveth [1]

8318 שֶׁרֶץ šereṣ, n.m. GK: 9238 [→ 8317]. creatures that teem, swarm, move about:– creeping thing [7], creeping things [4], creep [2], bring forth abundantly (+8317) [1], move [1]

8319 שָׁרַק šāraq, v. GK: 9239 [→ 8322, 8292]. [Q] to whistle, hiss, scoff:– hiss [12]

8320 שָׂרֹק śārōq, a. GK: 8601 [→ 4957, 7796, 8291, 8321]. brown, dark red (color of grapes):– speckled [1]

8321 שֹׂרֵק śōrēq or שְׂרֵקָה śᵉrēqâ, n.m. & f. GK: 8603 & 8605 [→ 8320]. choice vines:– choicest vine [1], noble vine [1]

8322 שְׁרֵקָה šᵉrēqâ, n.f. GK: 9240 [→ 8319; cf. 8292]. object of scorn, thing of derision, something held in contempt; an extension of the act of whistling or shrieking in derision:– hissing [7], choice vine [1]

8323 שָׂרַר śārar, v.den. GK: 8606 [→ 7786]. [Q] to rule, govern; [H] to choose a prince; [Ht] to act out as a ruler:– make altogether a prince (+8323) [2], rule [2], bear rule [1]

8324 שׂוֹרֵר śôrēr, n.m. GK: 8806. enemy, adversary:– enemies [5]

8325 שָׁרָר šārār, n.pr.m. GK: 9243 [→ 8307]. Sharar, "firm":– Sharar [1]

8326 שֹׁרֶר šōrer, n.m. GK: 9219 [→ 8270]. same as 8270: navel; umbilical cord:– navel [1]

8327 שָׁרַשׁ šāraš, v.den. GK: 9245 [→ 8328]. [P] to uproot; [Poel/Poal] to take root; [Pu] to be uprooted; [H] to take root:– root out [2], cause to take deep root (+8328) [1], cause to take root [1], rooted out [1], take root [1], taken root [1], taking root [1]

8328 שֹׁרֶשׁ šōreš, n.m. GK: 9247 [→ 8327, 8329; cf. 8330]. root of a plant; by extension: base or bottom of any object; source of a family line; "the Root of Jesse" is a messianic title, emphasizing Davidic origin:– root [16], roots [13], bottom [1], cause to take deep root (+8327) [1], heels [1], take root [1]

8329 שֶׁרֶשׁ šereš, n.pr.m. GK: 9246 [→ 8328]. Sheresh, "root, rootstock, sucker [of a plant]":– Sheresh [1]

8330 שְׁרֹשׁ šᵉrōš (Aram.), n.m. GK: 10743 [→ 8332; cf. 8328]. root:– roots [3]

8331 שַׁרְשָׁה šaršâ, n.f. GK: 9248 [→ 8333]. chain:– chains [1]

8332 שְׁרֹשׁוּ šᵉrōšû or שְׁרֹשִׁי šᵉrōšî (Aram.), n.f. GK: 10744 & 10745 [→ 8330]. banishment, uprooting (from community):– banishment [1]

8333 שַׁרְשְׁרָה šaršᵉrâ, n.f. GK: 9249 [→ 8331]. chain:– chains [6], chain [1]

8334 שָׁרַת šārat, v. GK: 9250 [→ 8335]. [P] to minister, serve, attend:– minister [48], ministered [15], ministers [15], servant [4], served [4], serve [4], service [2], do service [1], ministering [1], servants [1], servitor [1], waited on [1]

8335 שָׁרֵת šārēt, n.m. GK: 9251 [→ 8334]. cultic service:– minister [1], ministry [1]

8336 שֵׁשׁ šēš, n.m. GK: 9253 & 9254 [→ 7893]. fine linen, byssus (processed from the flax plant); alabaster:– fine linen [37], marble [2], blue marble [1], silk [1]

8337 שֵׁשׁ šēš, n.m. GK: 9252 [→ 8345, 8346; cf. 8353]. six; (pl.) sixty:– six [187], sixteen (+6240) [21], sixteenth (+6240) [3], sixth [2], threescore and one thousand (+505+7239+2050.1) [1], threescore and sixteen (+7657+2050.1) [1]

8338 שָׁשָׂא šāśāʾ, v.intens. GK: 9255. [P] to lead along:– leave the sixth part [1]

8339 שֵׁשְׁבַּצַּר šēšbaṣṣar, n.pr.m. GK: 9256 [cf. 8339]. Sheshbazzar, "may Sin protect [the father]":– Sheshbazzar [2]

8340 שֵׁשְׁבַּצַּר **šēšbaṣṣar** (Aram.), n.pr.m. GK: 10746 [cf. 8339]. Sheshbazzar, "*may (the pagan moon god) Sin protect (the father)*":– Sheshbazzar [2]

שָׁסָא **šāsâ**. See 8154.

8341 שָׁשָׂה **šāśâ**, v.den. GK: 9257. [P] to give a sixth part:– give the sixth part [1]

8342 שָׂשׂוֹן **śāśôn**, n.m. GK: 8607 [→ 7797]. joy, gladness:– joy [15], gladness [3], mirth [3], rejoicing [1]

8343 שָׁשַׁי **šāšay**, n.pr.m. GK: 9258. Shashai, "*noble*":– Shashai [1]

8344 שֵׁשַׁי **šēšay**, n.pr.m. GK: 9259. Sheshai, "[poss.] *sixth /child/*":– Sheshai [3]

8345 שִׁשִּׁי **šiššî**, a.num.ord. GK: 9261 [→ 8337]. sixth:– sixth [28]

8346 שִׁשִּׁים **šiššîm**, n.indecl. GK: 9262 [→ 8337; cf. 8361]. sixty (pl. of "six"):– threescore [46], sixty [12], threescore and one (+259+2050.1) [1]

8347 שֵׁשַׁךְ **šēšak**, n.pr.loc. GK: 9263. Sheshach, "[cryptogram for] *Babel*":– Sheshach [2]

8348 שֵׁשָׁן **šēšān**, n.pr.m. GK: 9264. Sheshan:– Sheshan [5]

שׁוֹשָׁן **šôšān**. See 7799.

8349 שָׁשַׁק **šāšaq**, n.pr.m. GK: 9265. Shashak:– Shashak [2]

8350 שָׁשֵׁר **šāšēr**, n.[m.]. GK: 9266. red color (from lead, iron rust, or insects):– vermilion [2]

8351 שֵׁת **šēt**, n.pr.m. GK: 9269 [→ 7896, 8352]. same as 8352: Seth, Sheth, "*determined, granted, Ge 4:25; restitution*":–

8352 שֵׁת **šēt**, n.pr.m. GK: 9269 [→ 8351]. same as 8353: Seth, Sheth, "*determined, granted, Ge 4:25; restitution*":– Seth [7], Sheth [2]

8353 שֵׁת **šēt** (Aram.), n.m. & f. GK: 10747 [→ 8361; cf. 8337]. six:– sixth [1], six [1]

8354 שָׁתָה **šātâ**, v. GK: 9272 [→ 4960, 8358, 8360; cf. 8248; cf. 8355]. [Q] to drink; by extension: to be drunk; [N] to be drunken:– drink [160], drunk [17], drinking [12], drank [8], drunken [6], drunken [3], assuredly drunken (+8354) [2], certainly drink (+8354) [1], drinketh up [2], surely drink (+8354) [2], banquet [1], drinkers [1], drunkards (+7941) [1]

8355 שְׁתָה **šᵉtâ** (Aram.), v. GK: 10748 [→ 4961; cf. 8354]. [P] to drink; this can refer to common consumption of liquid, or it can refer to drinking in worship to pagan gods and in insult to the true God (by drinking with his vessels):– drank [3], drink [1], drunk [1]

8356 שֵׁתָה **šētâ**, n.m. GK: 9271 [→ 8354?, 8359]. worker in weaving:– foundations [1], purposes [1]

8357 שֵׁת **šēt**, n.[m.]. GK: 9268. foundation; buttocks:– buttocks [2]

8358 שְׁתִי **šᵉtî**, n.[m.]. GK: 9275 [→ 8354]. drunkenness, drinking:– drunkenness [1]

8359 שְׁתִי **šᵉtî**, n.m. GK: 9274 [→ 8356]. woven material, made on a loom; some sources: warp, the vertical threads on a loom:– warp [9]

8360 שְׁתִיָּה **šᵉtiyyâ**, n.f. GK: 9276 [→ 8354]. (manner of) drinking:– drinking [1]

שְׁתַיִם **šᵉttayim**. See 8147.

8361 שִׁתִּין **šittîn** (Aram.), n.indecl. GK: 10749 [→ 8353; cf. 8346]. sixty:– threescore [4]

8362 שָׁתַל **šātal**, v. GK: 9278 [→ 8363]. [Q] to plant; [Qp] to be planted:– planted [8], plant [2]

8363 שָׁתִיל **šātîl**, n.[m.]. GK: 9277 [→ 8362]. slip, cutting (of a plant):– plants [1]

8364 שֻׁתַלְחִי **šutalḥî**, a.g. GK: 9279 [→ 7803]. Shuthelahite, "*of Shuthelah*":– Shuthalhites [1]

שָׁתַם **śātam**. See 5640.

8365 שָׁתַם **šātam**, v. GK: 9280 & 9281. [Qp] to be opened:– open [2]

8366 שָׁתַן **šātan** or שִׁין **šîn**, v. GK: 9282 & 8874 [→ 7890]. [H, Hiphtil] to urinate (against a wall), i.e., a male:– pisseth [6]

8367 שָׁתַק **šātaq**, v. GK: 9284 [cf. 8252]. [Q] to become calm, die down:– calm [1], ceaseth [1], quiet [1]

8368 שָׁתַר **šātar**, v. GK: 8609 [cf. 5642]. [N] to be broken out (with tumors):– secret parts [1]

8369 שֵׁתָר **šētār**, n.pr.m. GK: 9285. Shethar:– Shethar [1]

8370 שְׁתַר בּוֹזְנַי **šᵉtar bôzᵉnay** (Aram.), n.pr.m. GK: 10750. Shethar-Bozenai:– Shethar-boznai [4]

8371 שָׁתַת **šātat**, v. GK: 7896. [Q] to be destined, appoint, lay claim:– laid [1], set [1]

8372 תָּא **tā'**, n.m. GK: 9288. alcove for guards, guardroom:– little chambers [9], chamber [2], little chamber [2]

8373 תָּאַב **tā'ab**, v. GK: 9289 [→ 8375; cf. 14? or 2968?]. [Q] to long for, desire:– longed [2]

8374 תָּאַב **tā'ab**, v. GK: 9290 [cf. 8581]. [P] to abhor, loathe:– abhor [1]

8375 תַּאֲבָה **ta'ăbâ**, n.f. GK: 9291 [→ 8373]. longing, desiring:– longing [1]

8376 תָּאָה **tā'â**, v. GK: 9292 [cf. 184, 8427]. [P] to draw a line, mark out (territory):– point out [2]

8377 תְּאוֹ **tᵉ'ô**, n.m. GK: 9293. antelope; some sources: wild ox or sheep:– wild bull [1], wild ox [1]

8378 תַּאֲוָה **ta'ăwâ**, n.f. GK: 9294 [→ 183]. longing, desire, craving:– desire [14], coveteth greedily (+183) [1], dainty [1], fell a lusting (+183) [1], lusted exceedingly (+183) [1], lust [1], pleasant [1]

8379 תַּאֲוָה **ta'ăwâ**, n.f. GK: 9295 [→ 8427]. boundary:– utmost bound [1]

8380 תּוֹאֲמִים **tô'ămîm** or תְּאוֹמִים **tᵉ'ômîm**, n.m. GK: 9339 & 9296 [→ 8382]. twins, (something) double:– twins [4]

8381 תַּאֲלָה **ta'ălâ**, n.f. GK: 9297 [→ 422]. curse:– curse [1]

8382 תָּאַם **tā'am**, v.den. GK: 9298 [→ 8380]. [H] to have twins:– beareth twins [2], coupled together [1], coupled [1]

תָּאֹם **tā'ōm**. See 8380.

8383 תְּאֻנִים **tᵉ'unîm**, n.[m.]. GK: 9303 [→ 205?]. efforts, toil:– lies [1]

8384 תְּאֵנָה **tᵉ'ēnâ**, n.f. GK: 9300. fig; fig tree:– fig tree [17], figs [15], fig trees [6], fig [1]

8385 תַּאֲנָה **ta'ănâ** or תֹּאֲנָה **tô'ănâ**, n.f. GK: 9299 & 9301 [→ 579]. occasion, opportunity; (time of) heat, rut:– occasion [2]

8386 תַּאֲנִיָּה **ta'ăniyyâ**, n.f. GK: 9302 [→ 578]. mourning:– heaviness [1], mourning [1]

8387 תַּאֲנַת שִׁלֹה **ta'ănat šilōh**, n.pr.loc. GK: 9304 [cf. 7887]. Taanath Shiloh, "[poss.] *approach to Shiloh*":– Taanath-shiloh [1]

8388 תָּאַר **tā'ar**, v. GK: 9305 & 9306 [→ 8389; cf. 8446?]. [Q] to turn toward; [P] to mark out a form, make an outline; [Pu] to be turned toward:– drawn [5], marketh out [2], Remmon-methoar (+7417+1886.1) [1]

8389 תֹּאַר **tō'ar**, n.m. GK: 9307 [→ 8388]. form, shape; beauty, fine-looking person:– form [3], beautiful (+3303) [2], favoured [2], comely [1], countenance [1], fair (+3303) [1], goodly (+2896) [1], goodly (+3303) [1], goodly [1], resembled (+3509.1) [1], visage [1]

8390 תַּאֲרֵעַ **ta'rēa'**, n.pr.m. GK: 9308 [cf. 8475]. Tarea:– Tarea [1]

8391 תְּאַשּׁוּר **tᵉ'aššûr**, n.f. GK: 9309. cypress tree, cypress wood:– box tree [1], box [1]

8392 תֵּבָה **tēbâ**, n.f. GK: 9310. box-shaped thing: chest, ark, basket:– ark [28]

8393 תְּבוּאָה **tᵉbû'â**, n.f. GK: 9311 [→ 935]. harvest, crops, produce:– increase [22], fruit [7], fruits [6], revenues [3], revenue [2], gain [1], yieldeth increase [1]

8394 תְּבוּנָה **tᵉbûnâ**, n.f. GK: 9312 [cf. 995]. understanding, insight; ability, skill, wisdom:– understanding [38], discretion [1], reasons [1], skilfulness [1], wisdom [1]

8395 תְּבוּסָה **tᵉbûsâ**, n.f. GK: 9313 [→ 947]. downfall, ruin:– destruction [1]

8396 תָּבוֹר **tābôr**, n.pr.loc. GK: 9314 [→ 3696; cf. 243]. Tabor:– Tabor [10]

8397 תֶּבֶל **tebel**, n.[m.]. GK: 9316 [→ 1101]. perversion, abominable confusion:– confusion [1]

8398 תֵּבֵל **tēbēl**, n.f. & m. GK: 9315 [→ 944?]. world, earth:– world [35], habitable part [1]

תֻּבַל **tubal**. See 8422.

8399 תַּבְלִית **tablît**, n.f. GK: 9318 [→ 1086]. destruction:– destruction [1]

8400 תְּבַלֻּל **tᵉballul**, n.[m.]. GK: 9319 [→ 1101]. defect (obscuring vision); likely referring to a cataract:– blemish [1]

8401 תֶּבֶן **teben**, n.m. GK: 9320 [→ 4963]. straw:– straw [15], chaff [1], stubble [1]

8402 תִּבְנִי **tibnî**, n.pr.m. GK: 9321. Tibni:– Tibni [3]

8403 תַּבְנִית **tabnît**, n.f. GK: 9322 [→ 1129]. image, form, shape:– pattern [9], likeness [5], form [3], similitude [2], figure [1]

8404 תַּבְעֵרָה **tab'ērâ**, n.pr.loc. GK: 9323 [→ 1197]. Taberah, "*burning*":– Taberah [2]

8405 תֵּבֵץ **tēbēṣ**, n.pr.loc. GK: 9324 [→ 1206?]. Thebez:– Thebez [3]

8406 תְּבַר **tᵉbar** (Aram.), v. GK: 10752 [cf. 7665]. [Pp] to be brittle, not to have flexibility, implying such an object is fragile and easy to break:– broken [1]

8407 תִּגְלַת פִּלְאֶסֶר **tiglat pil'eser** or תִּגְלַת פִּלְנֶאֶסֶר **tiglat pilnᵉ'eser** or תִּלְּגַת פִּלְאֶסֶר **tillᵉgat pil'eser** or תִּלְּגַת פִּלְנֶסֶר **tillᵉgat pilneser**, n.pr.m. GK: 9325 & 9433. Tiglath-Pileser, Tiglath-Pilneser, "*my trust is in the son of [the temple] Esharra*":– Tiglath-pileser [3], Tilgath-pilneser [3]

8408 תַּגְמוּל **tagmûl**, n.m. GK: 9326 [→ 1580]. benefit, gracious act:– benefits [1]

8409 תִּגְרָה **tigrâ**, n.f. GK: 9327 [→ 1624]. agitation, blow:– blow [1]

תֹּגַרְמָה **tōgarmâ**. See 8425.

8410 תִּדְהָר **tidhār**, n.[m.]. GK: 9329. fir tree; some sources: elm or ash tree:– pine tree [1], pine [1]

8411 תְּדִיר **tᵉdîr** (Aram.), n.f. GK: 10753 [→ 1753]. duration, encircling; (as adv.) continually:– continually (+0.2+871.2) [2]

8412 תַּדְמֹר **tadmōr**, n.pr.loc. GK: 9330. Tadmor, "*palm tree*":– Tadmor [2]

8413 תִּדְעָל **tid'āl**, n.pr.m. GK: 9331. Tidal:– Tidal [2]

8414 תֹּהוּ **tōhû**, n.m. GK: 9332. formless, waste, empty; (of speech) useless, confused, vain:– vanity [4], confusion [3], in vain [2], vain [2], wilderness [2], without form [2], empty place [1], nothing [1], nought [1], thing of nought [1], waste [1]

8415 תְּהוֹם **tᵉhôm**, n.f. & m. GK: 9333. the deep, depths, with the associative meanings of darkness and secrecy, controlled or inhabited by mysterious powers; "the depths of the earth" is the abode of the dead:– deep [19], depths [10], depth [5], deep places [1], deeps [1]

8416 תְּהִלָּה **tᵉhillâ**, n.f. GK: 9335 [→ 1984]. praise, renown, glory; praise is proclaiming the excellence of a person or object:– praise [52], praises [5]

8417 תָּהֳלָה **toholâ**, n.f. GK: 9334. error:– folly [1]

8418 תַּהֲלֻכָה **tahᵃlukâ**, n.f. GK: 9336 [→ 1980]. procession:– went [1]

תְּהֹם **tᵉhōm**. See 8415.

8419 תַּהְפֻּכוֹת **tahpukôt**, n.f. GK: 9337 [→ 2015]. perversity, confusing things:– frowardness [3], froward [3], froward things [2], perverse things [1], very froward [1]

8420 תָּו **tāw**, n.m. GK: 9338 [→ 8427]. mark (on the forehead); signing (a document):– desire [1], mark [1], set a mark (+8427) [1]

8421 תּוּב **tûb** (Aram.), v. GK: 10754 [cf. 7725]. [P] to return, restore; [H] to give back, return, answer:– returned [4], answered [1], answer [1], restored [1], returned answer [1]

8422 תֻּבַל **tubal**, n.pr.loc. GK: 9317. Tubal:– Tubal [8]

8423 תּוּבַל קַיִן **tûbal qayin**, n.pr.m. GK: 9340 [→ 7014]. Tubal-Cain:– Tubal-cain [2]

תּוֹבֵנָה **tôbunâ**. See 8394.

8424 תּוּגָה **tûgâ**, n.f. GK: 9342 [→ 3013]. grief, sorrow:– heaviness [3], sorrow [1]

8425 תֹּגַרְמָה **tōgarmâ**, n.pr.loc. GK: 9328. Togarmah:– Togarmah [4]

8426 תּוֹדָה **tôdâ**, n.f. GK: 9343 [→ 3034]. thank offering; thanksgiving, confession of thankfulness; song of thanksgiving; thanks is the speaking of the excellence of a person or object, with a focus on the personal gratitude of the speaker:– thanksgiving [16], praise [3], thank offerings [3], thanks [3], confession [2], praises [1], sacrifice of praise [1], sacrifice of thanksgiving [1], thanksgivings [1]

8427 תָּוָה **tāwâ**, v.den. GK: 9344 [→ 8379, 8420; cf. 184, 8376]. [P] to put a mark, place a sign:– scrabled [1], set a mark (+8420) [1]

8428 תָּוָה *tāwâ*, v. GK: 9345. [H] to vex, bring pain:– limited [1]

8429 תְּוַה *t^ewah* (Aram.), v. GK: 10755 [cf. 8539]. [P] to be amazed, be alarmed, an attitude or emotion that shows either fear or awe:– astonied [1]

8430 תּוֹחַ *tôaḥ*, n.pr.m. GK: 9346 [cf. 8459]. Toah:– Toah [1]

8431 תּוֹחֶלֶת *tôḥelet*, n.f. GK: 9347 [→ 3176]. hope, expectation:– hope [6]

תּוּךְ *tôk*. See 8496.

8432 תָּוֶךְ *tāwek*, subst. GK: 9348 [→ 8484]. middle, midst, center, among, within:– midst [204], among (+871.1) [106], among [28], in (+871.1) [19], within (+871.1) [18], amongst (+871.1) [7], middle [6], midst (+871.1) [4], between (+871.1) [3], therein (+871.1+1886.3) [3], amongst [2], out of (+4480) [2], through (+871.1) [2], half [1], in (+413) [1], into (+413) [1], into (+871.1) [1], midnight (+3915+1886.1) [1], of (+871.1) [1], to (+413) [1], unto (+413) [1], wherein (+834+871.1) [1], whereinto (+413) [1], with (+871.1) [1], within (+413) [1], within [1]

8433 תּוֹכֵחָה *tôkēḥâ* or תּוֹכַחַת *tôkaḥat*, n.f. GK: 9349 & 9350 [→ 3198]. rebuke, punishment, correction:– reproof [12], rebuke [4], rebukes [3], reproofs [2], reproved [2], arguments [1], chastened [1], correction [1], punishments [1], reasoning [1]

תּוּכִי *tûkkî*. See 8500.

8434 תּוֹלָד *tôlād*, n.pr.loc. GK: 9351 [→ 3205?; cf. 513]. Tolad, "*birth, generation [?]*":– Tolad [1]

8435 תּוֹלֵדוֹת *tôlēdôt*, n.f.pl. GK: 9352 [→ 3205]. account, record, genealogy, family line:– generations [38], birth [1]

8436 תּוֹלֹן *tôlôn* or תִּילֹן *tîlôn*, n.pr.m. GK: 9353 & 9400. Tilon, Tolon:– Tilon [1]

8437 תּוֹלָל *tôlāl*, n.m. GK: 9354 [→ 1980]. tormentor, oppressor:– wasted [1]

8438 תּוֹלָע *tôlā'* or תּוֹלֵעָה *tôlē'â*, n.[m.]. GK: 9355 & 9357 [→ 8439, 8440, 8529]. (deep) red, purple; scarlet yarn, scarlet yarn; worm, maggot:– scarlet (+8144) [31], worm [5], worms [3], scarlet (+8144+1886.1) [2], crimson [2], scarlet [1]

8439 תּוֹלָע *tôlā'*, n.pr.m. GK: 9356 [→ 8440; cf. 8438]. Tola:– Tola [6]

8440 תּוֹלָעִי *tôlā'î*, a.g. GK: 9358 [→ 8439; cf. 8438]. Tolaite, "*of Tola*":– Tolaites [1]

8441 תּוֹעֵבָה *tô'ēbâ*, n.f. GK: 9359 [→ 8581?]. detestable thing, loathsome thing, abomination:– abominations [61], abomination [52], abominable [3], abominable things [1]

8442 תּוֹעָה *tô'â*, n.f. GK: 9360 [→ 8582]. trouble, error:– error [1], hinder (+6213) [1]

8443 תּוֹעָפֹת *tô'āpôt*, n.f. GK: 9361. best, choice; strength; some sources: horns:– strength [2], plenty [1]

8444 תּוֹצָאוֹת *tôṣā'ôt*, n.f. GK: 9362 [→ 3318]. end, limit, starting point:– goings out [11], outgoings [7], issues [2], borders [1], going forth [1], goings forth [1]

8445 תּוֹקַהַת *towq^ehat*, n.pr.m. GK: 9363. Tokehath, Tavkehath:–

8446 תּוּר *tûr*, v. GK: 9365 [cf. 3491, 8388?]. [Q] to explore, investigate, search out; [H] to send out to spy:– search [6], searched [4], search out [3], spy out [2], chapmen (+376+1886.1) [1], espied [1], excellent [1], merchantmen (+376) [1], searching [1], seek [1], sent to descry [1], sought [1]

8447 תּוֹר *tôr*, n.m. GK: 9366 [→ 8448]. same as 8448: turning; earring:– turn [2], borders [1], rows [1]

8448 תּוֹר *tôr*, n.m. GK: 9366 [→ 8447]. same as 8447: turning; earring:– estate [1]

8449 תּוֹר *tôr*, n.f. & m. GK: 9367. dove:– turtle-doves [6], turtle-dove [3], turtles [3], turtle [2]

8450 תּוֹר *tôr* (Aram.), n.m. GK: 10756 [cf. 7794]. young bull or castrated bull, steer, ox, easier to handle for plowing, pulling, and threshing:– oxen [3], bullocks [3]

8451 תּוֹרָה *tôrâ*, n.f. GK: 9368 [→ 3384, 8452]. law, regulation, teaching, instruction; often referring to the five books of Moses in whole and in part:– law [206], laws [13]

8452 תּוֹרָה *tôrâ*, n.f. GK: 9368 [→ 8451]. same as 8451: manner, direction:– manner [1]

8453 תּוֹשָׁב *tôšāb*, n.m. GK: 9369 [→ 3427]. temporary resident, stranger, alien:– sojourner [7], sojourners [2], stranger [2], foreigner [1], inhabitants [1], strangers [1]

8454 תּוּשִׁיָּה *tûšiyyâ*, n.f. GK: 9370 [cf. 3426]. success, victory; sound judgment, wisdom:– wisdom [4], sound wisdom [3], enterprise [1], substance [1], that which is [1], thing as it is [1], working [1]

8455 תּוֹתָח *tôtāḥ*, n.m. GK: 9371. (stout) club:– Darts [1]

8456 תָּזַז *tāzaz*, v. GK: 9372. [H] to cut down:– cut down [1]

8457 תַּזְנוּת *taznût*, n.f.abst. GK: 9373 [→ 2181]. promiscuity, prostitution, act of lust:– whoredoms [14], whoredom [3], commit whoredoms (+2181) [1], fornications [1], fornication [1]

8458 תַּחְבֻּלוֹת *taḥbulôt*, n.f. GK: 9374. guidance, advice, giving direction:– counsels [2], counsel [1], good advice [1], wise counsels [1], wise counsel [1]

8459 תֹּחוּ *tōḥû*, n.pr.m. GK: 9375 [cf. 8430]. Tohu:– Tohu [1]

8460 תְּחוֹת *t^eḥôt* (Aram.), pp. GK: 10757 [→ 8479; cf. 8478]. under:– under [4]

8461 תַּחְכְּמֹנִי *taḥk^emōnî*, a.g. GK: 9376. Tahkemonite:– Tachmonite [1]

8462 תְּחִלָּה *t^eḥillâ*, n.f. GK: 9378 [→ 2490]. beginning, at first:– beginning [14], first [3], first (+871.1+1886.1) [2], first time [2], begin [1]

8463 תַּחֲלֻאִים *taḥ^alu'îm*, n.pl.m. GK: 9377 [→ 2456]. diseases:– diseases [2], grievous [1], sicknesses [1], them that are sick [1]

8464 תַּחְמָס *taḥmās*, n.[m.]. GK: 9379 [→ 2554?]. screech owl:– night hawk [2]

8465 תַּחַן *taḥan*, n.pr.m. GK: 9380 [→ 8470; cf. 2603?]. Tahan, "[poss.] *grace, favor*":– Tahan [2]

8466 תַּחֲנָה *taḥ^anâ*, n.f. GK: 9381 [→ 2583]. encampment:– camp [1]

8467 תְּחִנָּה *t^eḥinnâ*, n.f. GK: 9382 [→ 8468; cf. 2603]. plea, petition, request, supplication:– supplication [21], favour [1], grace [1], supplication made (+2603) [1], supplications [1]

8468 תְּחִנָּה *t^eḥinnâ*, n.pr.m. GK: 9383 [→ 8467; cf. 2603]. Tehinnah, "*supplication for favor*":– Tehinnah [1]

8469 תַּחֲנוּן *taḥ^anûn*, n.[m.]pl.abst. GK: 9384 [→ 2603]. plea for mercy, petition, supplication:– supplications [17], useth intreaties (+1696) [1]

8470 תַּחֲנִי *taḥ^anî*, a.g. GK: 9385 [→ 8465; cf. 2603?]. Tahanite, "*of Tahan*":– Tahanites [1]

8471 תַּחְפַּנְחֵס *taḥpanḥēs*, n.pr.loc. GK: 9387 [cf. 6372]. Tahpanhes, "*fortress of Penhase [the black man]*":– Tahpanhes [5], Tahapanes [1], Tehaphnehes [1]

8472 תַּחְפְּנֵס *taḥp^enês*, n.pr.f. GK: 9388. Tahpenes, "*wife of the king*":– Tahpenes [3]

8473 תַּחְרָא *taḥrā'*, n.[m.]. GK: 9389. collar, edge around an opening in a garment:– habergeon [2]

8474 תַּחֲרָה *taḥ^arâ*, v. GK: 3013 [→ 2734]. form of 2734: to be angry; to compete, contend with:– closest [1], contend [1]

8475 תַּחְרֵעַ *taḥrēa'*, n.pr.m. GK: 9390 [cf. 8390]. Tahrea, "[poss.] *clever one*":– Tahrea [1]

8476 תַּחַשׁ *taḥaš*, n.m. GK: 9391 [→ 8477]. (leather of) a sea cow:– badgers' [13], badgers' skins [1]

8477 תַּחַשׁ *taḥaš*, n.pr.m. GK: 9392 [→ 8476]. Tahash, "*species of dolphin*":– Thahash [1]

8478 תַּחַת *taḥat*, n.[m.] & adv. & pp. GK: 9393 [→ 8480, 8481, 8482; cf. 5181]. under, in place of, succeeding (on a sequence):– under [220], in stead [89], for [59], instead of [32], beneath (+4480) [13], under (+4480) [13], because (+834) [11], in place [11], in room [5], in the room of [5], beneath [4], under (+413) [4], in [3], place [3], flat [2], for sake [2], in rooms [2], in the stead of [2], instead of [2], as [1], because (+3588) [1], because [1], for that (+3588) [1], in a place [1], in places [1], in steads [1], in the place of [1], in the place where [1], in the place [1], in the same place [1], mine (+2967.1) [1], on behalf [1], room [1], underneath (+4480) [1], unto [1], where (+1886.3) [1], whereas (+834) [1], whereas [1], wherefore (+4100) [1], with [1]

8479 תְּחֹת *t^eḥōt* (Aram.), pp. GK: 10757 [→ 8460]. same as 8460: under:– under [1]

8480 תַּחַת *taḥat*, n.pr.m. & loc. GK: 9394 & 9395 [→ 8478]. Tahath, "*compensation*":– Tahath [6]

תַּחַת *t^eḥōt*. See 8460.

8481 תַּחְתּוֹן *taḥtôn*, a. GK: 9396 [→ 8478]. lower:– lower [5], nether [5], lowest [5], nethermost [1]

8482 תַּחְתִּי *taḥtî*, a. & subst. GK: 9397 [→ 8478]. lower; (n.) depths, below, sometimes referring to the underworld, the realm of the dead:– nether parts [5], lowest [3], nether [3], lower parts [2], lower [2], in low parts [1], lowest parts [1], low [1], nether part [1]

8483 תַּחְתִּים חָדְשִׁי *taḥtîm ḥodšî*, n.pr.loc. GK: 9398. Tahtim Hodshi:– Tahtim-hodshi [1]

8484 תִּיכוֹן *tîkôn*, a. GK: 9399 [→ 8432]. middle, center:– middle [8], middlemost [2], midst [1]

8485 תֵּימָא *têmā'*, n.pr.loc. [& m.?]. GK: 9401. Tema, "*on the right [not left] side, hence south country*":– Tema [5]

8486 תֵּימָן *têmān*, n.f. GK: 9402 [→ 8487; cf. 3225]. south, southward, south wind:– south [10], southward (+1886.5) [8], south side [2], south (+1886.5) [1], south (+1886.5+1886.5) [1], south wind [1]

8487 תֵּימָן *têmān*, n.pr.loc. GK: 9403 [→ 8489; cf. 3225, 8486]. Teman, "*on the right [not left] side, hence south country*":– Teman [11]

8488 תֵּימְנִי *têm^enî*, n.pr.m. GK: 9405 [→ 3225]. Temeni, "*one from the right [not left], hence southerner*":– Temeni [1]

8489 תֵּימָנִי *têmānî*, a.g. GK: 9404 [→ 8487]. Temanite, "*of Teman*":– Temanite [6], Temanites [1], Temani [1]

8490 תִּימָרָה *tîmārâ*, n.f. GK: 9406 [→ 8560?, 8564; cf. 8558]. column (of smoke):– pillars [2]

8491 תִּיצִי *tîṣî*, a.g. GK: 9407. Tizite:– Tizite [1]

8492 תִּירוֹשׁ *tîrôš*, n.m. GK: 9408 [→ 3423]. new wine:– wine [26], new wine [11], sweet wine [1]

8493 תִּירְיָא *tîr^eyā'*, n.pr.m. GK: 9409. Tiria:– Tiria [1]

8494 תִּירָס *tîrās*, n.pr.m. [& m.?]. GK: 9410. Tiras:– Tiras [2]

תִּירֹשׁ *tîrôš*. See 8492.

8495 תַּיִשׁ *tayiš*, n.m. GK: 9411. male goat:– he goats [3], he goat [1]

8496 תֹּךְ *tōk*, n.m. GK: 9412 [→ 8501]. oppression, threat:– deceit [2], fraud [1]

8497 תָּכָה *tākâ*, v. GK: 9413. [Pu] to bow down:– sat down [1]

8498 תְּכוּנָה *t^ekûnâ*, n.f. GK: 9414 [→ 3559, 8499]. same as 8499: dwelling; arrangement, supply:– fashion [1], store [1]

8499 תְּכוּנָה *t^ekûnâ*, n.f. GK: 9414 [→ 8498]. same as 8498: dwelling; arrangement, supply:– seat [1]

8500 תֻּכִּיִּים *tukkiyyîm*, n.m.[pl.]. GK: 9415. baboons; some sources: monkeys, peacocks, poultry:– peacocks [2]

8501 תֹּכָכִים *tōkākîm*, n.m.pl. GK: 9412 [→ 8496]. pl. of 8496: oppression, threat:– deceitful [1]

8502 תִּכְלָה *tiklâ*, n.f. GK: 9416 [→ 3615]. perfection:– perfection [1]

8503 תַּכְלִית *taklît*, n.f. GK: 9417 [→ 3615]. end, limit, boundary:– perfection [2], come to an end [1], end [1], perfect [1]

8504 תְּכֵלֶת *t^ekēlet*, n.f. GK: 9418. blue material:– blue [49]

8505 תָּכַן *tākan*, v. GK: 9419 [→ 4971, 8506, 8508; cf. 8626; cf. 8627]. [Q] to weigh, estimate; [N] to be just, be weighted; [P] to hold firm, mark off, understand; [Pu] to be determined:– equal [7], ponderethe [2], unequal (+3808) [2], weigheth [2], bear up [1], directed [1], meted out [1], told [1], weighed [1]

8506 תֹּכֶן *tōken*, n.m. GK: 9420 [→ 8505]. full quota, fixed measure; size, measurement:– measure [1], tale [1]

8507 תֹּכֶן *tōken*, n.pr.loc. GK: 9421. Token, "*measure*":– Tochen [1]

8508 תָּכְנִית *toknît*, n.f. GK: 9422 [→ 8505]. (perfect) example, design:– pattern [1], sum [1]

8509 תַּכְרִיךְ *takrîk*, n.m. GK: 9423. robe, mantle:– garment [1]

8510 תֵּל *tēl*, n.[m.]. GK: 9424 [→ 8512, 8521, 8528, 8524, 8534?]. mound, heap, ruin:– heap [4], strength [1]

8511 תָּלָא *tālā'*, v. GK: 9428 [cf. 8518]. [Q] to hang; [Qp] to be suspended, be determined:– bent [1], hang in doubt [1], hanged [1]

8512 תֵּל אָבִיב *tēl 'ābîb*, n.pr.loc. GK: 9425 [→ 8510+24]. Tel Abib, "*mound of barley; mound of storm tide; mound of flood*":– Tel-abib [1]

8513 תִּלְאָה *t^elā'â*, n.f. GK: 9430 [→ 4972; cf. 3811]. hardship, burden:– travail [3], trouble [1]

Heb

Heb

8514 תַּלְאֻבוֹת **tal'ubôt**, n.f. GK: 9429. burning heat:– great drought [1]

8515 תְּלַאשָּׁר **t'la'ššar** or תְּלַשָּׁר **t'laššar**, n.pr.loc. GK: 9431 & 9445. Telassar, Tel Assar, "*ruined city, mound of Assar*":– Telassar [1], Thelasar [1]

8516 תִּלְבֹּשֶׁת **tilbōšet**, n.f. GK: 9432 [→ 3847]. clothing, what is worn:– put on clothing (+3847) [1]

8517 תְּלַג **t'lag** (Aram.), n.[m.]. GK: 10758 [cf. 7950]. snow:– snow [1]

 תִּלְגַת **tilgat**. See 8407.

 תֹּלְדָה **tōl'dâ**. See 8435.

8518 תָּלָה **tālâ**, v. GK: 9434 [→ 3494, 8522; cf. 8511]. [Q, P] to hang, suspend; [Qp, N] to be hung:– hanged [16], hang [7], hanged up [2], hangeth [1], hanging [1]

8519 תְּלֻנּוֹת **t'lunnôt**, n.f. GK: 9442 [→ 3885]. grumbling, complaint:– murmurings [8]

8520 תֶּלַח **telah**, n.pr.m. GK: 9436. Telah, "*fissure, split, fracture*":– Telah [1]

8521 תֵּל חַרְשָׁא **tēl ḥarša'**, n.pr.loc. GK: 9426 [→ 8510+2793 or 2796]. Tel Harsha, "*mound of the forest or craftsman*":– Tel-haresha [1], Tel-harsa [1]

8522 תְּלִי **t'lî**, n.[m.]. GK: 9437 [→ 8518]. quiver (case to hold arrows that hangs or dangles):– quiver [1]

8523 תְּלִיתָי **t'lîtāy** (Aram.), a. GK: 10759 [→ 8531; cf. 7992]. third:– third [2]

8524 תָּלוּל **tālûl**, a. GK: 9435 [→ 8510]. lofty, towering:– eminent [1]

8525 תֶּלֶם **telem**, n.m. GK: 9439 [→ 8526]. furrow, plowed line:– furrows [3], furrow [1], ridges [1]

8526 תַּלְמַי **talmay**, n.pr.m. GK: 9440 [→ 8525]. Talmai, "[poss.] *[my] furrow maker*":– Talmai [6]

8527 תַּלְמִיד **talmîd**, n.[m.]. GK: 9441 [→ 3925]. student, pupil:– scholar [1]

8528 תֵּל מֶלַח **tēl melaḥ**, n.pr.loc. GK: 9427 [→ 8510+4417]. Tel Melah, "*mound of salt*":– Tel-melah [2]

 תְּלֻנָּה **t'lunnâ**. See 8519.

8529 תָּלַע **tāla'**, v.den. GK: 9443 [→ 8438]. [Pu] to be clad in scarlet material:– in scarlet [1]

 תֹּלַעַת **tōla'at**. See 8438.

8530 תַּלְפִּיּוֹת **talpiyyôt**, n.f.pl. GK: 9444. elegance or courses of stones:– armoury [1]

 תְּלַשָּׁר **t'laššar**. See 8515.

8531 תְּלָת **t'lāt** (Aram.), n.m. GK: 10760 [→ 8523, 8532, 8533; cf. 7969]. three:– third [2]

8532 תַּלְתָּא **taltā'** (Aram.), a.aden. GK: 10761 [→ 8531; 7992]. third highest; this can refer to ruling over a third of the kingdom, or ruling as third in command, or ruling in a triumvirate; some sources translate less specifically as a high official of indeterminate rank:– three [10], third [1]

 תַּלְתִּי **taltiy**. See 8523.

8533 תְּלָתִין **t'lātîn** (Aram.), n.indecl. GK: 10762 [→ 8531; cf. 7970]. thirty:– thirty [2]

8534 תַּלְתָּל **taltāl**, n.f.?. GK: 9446 [→ 8510?]. wavy:– bushy [1]

8535 תָּם **tām**, a. GK: 9447 [→ 3147; cf. 8552]. blameless, flawless, perfect:– perfect [9], undefiled [2], coupled (+1961) [1], coupled together (+3162) [1], plain [1], upright [1]

8536 תָּם **tammâ** (Aram.), adv. GK: 10764 [cf. 8033]. there:– there [2], thence [1], where [1]

8537 תֹּם **tōm**, n.[m.]. GK: 9448 [→ 8550; cf. 8552]. blamelessness, integrity, innocence:– integrity [11], uprightness [2], upright [1], venture [1], full [1], perfection [1], perfect [1], simplicity [1], uprightly (+871.1) [1], uprightly [1]

 תֵּמָא **tēmā'**. See 8485.

8538 תֻּמָּה **tummâ**, n.f. GK: 9450 [→ 8552]. integrity, blamelessness:– integrity [5]

8539 תָּמַהּ **tāmah**, v. GK: 9449 [→ 8541; cf. 8429, cf. 8540]. [Q] to be astonished, be astounded, be stunned; [Htpal] to be stunned in oneself:– wonder [3], marvelled [2], amazed [1], astonished [1], marvellously [1], marvel [1]

8540 תְּמַהּ **t'mah** (Aram.), n.m. GK: 10763. wonder, miracle:– wonders [3]

8541 תִּמָּהוֹן **timmāhôn**, n.[m.]. GK: 9451 [→ 8539]. confusion, panic:– astonishment [2]

8542 תַּמּוּז **tammûz**, n.pr.[m.]. GK: 9452. Tammuz (pagan god):– Tammuz [1]

8543 תְּמוֹל **t'môl**, subst.adv. GK: 9453 [→ 865]. yesterday; (generally) before, in the past:– heretofore (+8032) [4], in time past (+4480+8032) [4], yesterday [4], before (+8032) [3], beforetime (+4480+8032) [1], beforetime (+8032) [1], heretofore (+1571+4480+4480+8032) [1], heretofore (+4480+8032) [1], in time past (+8032) [1], in times past (+1571+1571+8032) [1], in times past (+4480+8032) [1], these three days (+8032) [1]

8544 תְּמוּנָה **t'mûnâ**, n.f. GK: 9454 [→ 4327]. form, image, likeness:– likeness [5], similitude [4], image [1]

8545 תְּמוּרָה **t'mûrâ**, n.f. GK: 9455 [→ 4171]. substitution, transfer, exchange:– exchange [2], change [1], changing [1], recompence [1], restitution [1]

8546 תְּמוּתָה **t'mûtâ**, n.f. GK: 9456 [→ 4191]. death:– appointed to death (+1121) [1], appointed to die (+1121) [1]

8547 תֶּמַח **temah**, n.pr.m. GK: 9457 [→ 4229?]. Temah:– Tamah [1], Thamah [1]

8548 תָּמִיד **tāmîd**, n.m. (used as adv.). GK: 9458. (adv.) continually, constantly, regularly, daily:– continually [53], continual [26], daily [7], always [6], alway [4], ever [3], perpetual [2], continual employment [1], evermore [1], never (+3808) [1]

8549 תָּמִים **tāmîm**, a. GK: 9459 [→ 8552]. without defect, blameless, perfect:– without blemish [44], perfect [18], upright [8], without spot [6], whole [4], uprightly [3], sincerely (+871.1) [2], complete [1], full [1], sincerity [1], sound [1], undefiled [1], uprightly (+871.1) [1]

8550 תֻּמִּים **tummîm**, n.m.[pl.]. GK: 9460 [→ 8537; cf. 8552]. Thummim, formally "Perfections," devices used by the high priest to make God's will known, possibly related to the casting of lots:– Thummim [5]

8551 תָּמַךְ **tāmak**, v. GK: 9461. [Q] to take hold of, grasp, hold secure; [N] to be seized:– uphold [3], holdeth [2], retaineth [2], retain [2], held up [1], hold up [1], holden [1], holding [1], hold [1], maintainest [1], stayed up [1], stay [1], take hold on [1], take hold [1], upholdest [1], upholdeth [1]

 תָּמֹל **t'môl**. See 8543.

8552 תָּמַם **tāmam**, v. GK: 9462 [→ 3147, 4974, 8535, 8537, 8538, 8549, 8550]. [Q] to complete, finish, perfect; [H] to end, stop, complete; [Ht] to show oneself blameless:– consumed [23], ended [5], finished [4], clean [3], spent [3], consume [2], done [2], end [2], failed [2], shew upright [2], wasted [2], accomplished [1], accomplish [1], all gone [1], all [1], cease [1], come to end [1], come to the full [1], make an end [1], makest perfect [1], perfect [1], sum [1], upright [1], utterly [1], whole [1]

 תֵּמָן **tēmān**, **tēmān**. See 8486, 8487.

8553 תִּמְנָה **timnâ**, n.pr.loc. GK: 9463 [→ 8554; cf. 4487?]. Timnah, "*lot, portion*":– Timnah [8], Timnath [3], Thimnathah [1]

 תִּמְנָה **t'munâ**. See 8544.

8554 תִּמְנִי **timni**, a.g.GK: 9464 [→ 8553; cf. 4487?]. Timnite, "*of Timnah*":– Timnite [1]

8555 תִּמְנָע **timna'**, n.pr.m. & f. GK: 9465. Timna, "*lot, portion*":– Timna [4], Timnah [2]

8556 תִּמְנַת־חֶרֶס **timnat-ḥeres** or תִּמְנָת־סֶרַח **timnat-serah**, n.pr.loc. GK: 9466 & 9467 [→ 4487?+2776]. Timnath Heres, Timnath Serah, "*place of the sun [worship]*":– Timnath-serah [2], Timnath-heres [1]

8557 תֶּמֶס **temes**, n.m. GK: 9468 [→ 4549]. melting away:– melteth [1]

8558 תָּמָר **tāmār**, n.m. GK: 9469 [→ 1193, 2688, 5899, 8559, 8560, 8561; cf. 8490]. palm tree:– palm trees [7], palm tree [4], palm [1]

8559 תָּמָר **tāmār**, n.pr.f. & loc. GK: 9470 & 9471 [→ 8558]. Tamar, "*date palm*":– Tamar [24]

8560 תֹּמֶר **tōmer**, n.m. & loc. GK: 9472 & 9473 [→ 559, 8490?, 8558]. the Palm (of Deborah), "*date palm*"; scarecrow:– palm tree [2]

8561 תִּמֹרָה **timōrâ**, n.f. GK: 9474 [→ 8558]. palm tree:– palm trees [16], palm tree [3]

 תַּמֹּר **tammōr**. See 8412.

 תִּמְרָה **timārâ**. See 8490.

8562 תַּמְרוּק **tamrûq**, n.[m.]. GK: 9475 [→ 4838]. beauty treatment (including massages and cleansing rituals), cosmetics:– things for purification [2], cleanseth away [1], things for the purifying [1]

8563 תַּמְרוּרִים **tamrûrîm**, n.m. GK: 9476 [→ 4843]. bitterness:– bitter [2], most bitterly [1]

 תַּמְרֻק **tamruq** and תַּמְרִיק **tamrîq**. See 8562.

8564 תַּמְרוּרִים **tamrûrîm**, n.m. GK: 9477 [→ 8490]. guidepost:– high heaps [1]

8565 תַּן **tan**, n.[m. & f.]. GK: 9478 [→ 8568, 8577]. jackal:–

8566 תָּנָה **tānâ**, v. GK: 9479 [→ 869]. [Q, H] to sell oneself as a prostitute:– hired [1]

8567 תָּנָה **tānâ**, v. GK: 9480. [P] to commemorate, recount:– lament [1], rehearse [1]

8568 תַּנָּה **tannâ**, n.[m. & f.]. GK: 9478 [→ 8565]. same as 8565: jackal:–

8569 תְּנוּאָה **t'nû'â**, n.f. GK: 9481 [→ 5106]. fault, opposition, what one has against another:– breach of promise [1], occasions [1]

8570 תְּנוּבָה **t'nûbâ**, n.f. GK: 9482 [→ 5107]. crop, produce:– fruit [2], increase [2], fruits [1]

8571 תְּנוּךְ **t'nûk**, n.[m.]. GK: 9483. lobe (of the ear):– tip [8]

8572 תְּנוּמָה **t'nûmâ**, n.f. GK: 9484 [→ 5123]. slumber, sleep:– slumber [4], slumberings [1]

8573 תְּנוּפָה **t'nûpâ**, n.f. GK: 9485 [→ 5130]. wave offering, what it waved:– wave offering [13], offering [7], wave [6], shaking [2], wave offerings [1], waved [1]

8574 תַּנּוּר **tannûr**, n.m. GK: 9486. oven, furnace, firepot (a portable oven for cooking bread):– oven [10], furnaces [2], furnace [2], ovens [1]

8575 תַּנְחוּמוֹת **tanḥûmôt** or תַּנְחוּמִים **tanḥûmîm**, n.pl.m. & f. GK: 9487 & 9488 [→ 5162]. consolation, comfort:– consolations [3], comforts [1], consolation [1]

8576 תַּנְחֻמֶת **tanḥumet**, n.pr.m. GK: 9489 [→ 5162]. Tanhumeth, "*comfort*":– Tanhumeth [2]

8577 תַּנִּין **tannîn**, n.m. GK: 9490 [→ 8565]. serpent, snake; monster of the deep; (pr.n.) Jackal (Well); can refer to large sea creatures as well as to mythological monsters of chaos opposed to God:– dragons [16], dragon [6], serpent [2], whale [2], sea monsters [1], serpents [1], whales [1]

8578 תִּנְיָן **tinyān** (Aram.), a. GK: 10765 [→ 8648]. second:– second [1]

8579 תִּנְיָנוּת **tinyānût** (Aram.), adv. GK: 10766 [→ 8648]. once more, in the second time:– again [1]

8580 תִּנְשֶׁמֶת **tinšemet**, n.f. GK: 9491 & 9492 [→ 5395]. white owl; chameleon:– swan [2], mole [1]

8581 תָּעַב **tā'ab**, v.den. GK: 9493 [→ 8441?; cf. 8374]. [N] to be repulsive, be vile, be rejected; [P] to detest, abhor, loathe, despise; [H] to behave in a vile manner:– abhor [8], abominable [4], abhorred [2], abhorreth [2], done abominable [2], utterly abhor (+8581) [2], abominably [1], made to be abhorred [1]

 תֹּעֵבָה **tō'ēbâ**. See 8441.

8582 תָּעָה **tā'â**, v. GK: 9494 [→ 8442; cf. 2937]. [Q] to wander, go astray; [N] to deceive oneself; to stagger around (as a drunk); [H] to lead astray, make wander, mislead:– went astray [6], caused to err [4], cause to err [3], err [3], go astray [3], wandered [3], causeth to wander [2], erred [2], gone astray [2], made to err [2], out of the way [2], seduced [2], wander [2], caused to go astray [1], caused to wander [1], causing to err [1], deceived [1], dissembled [1], erreth [1], going astray [1], make err [1], maketh to stagger [1], panted [1], seduceth [1], staggereth [1], wandereth [1], wandering [1]

8583 תֹּעוּ **tō'û** or תֹּעִי **tō'î**, n.pr.m. GK: 9495 & 9497. Toi, Tou:– Toi [3], Tou [2]

8584 תְּעוּדָה **t'ûdâ**, n.f. GK: 9496 [→ 5749]. testimony; method of legalizing transactions (sandal transaction):– testimony [3]

8585 תְּעָלָה **t'ālâ**, n.f. GK: 9498 & 9499 [→ 5927]. trench, channel, aqueduct; healing:– conduit [4], trench [3], cured [1], healing [1], little rivers [1], watercourse [1]

8586 תַּעֲלוּלִים **ta'ălûlîm**, n.m.pl.abst. GK: 9500 [→ 5953]. wantonness; harsh treatment, referring to impulsive people:– babes [1], delusions [1]

8587 תַּעֲלֻמָה **ta'ălumâ**, n.f. GK: 9502 [→ 5956]. secret; hidden thing:– secrets [2], thing that is hid [1]

8588 תַּעֲנוּג **ta'ănûg**, n.m. GK: 9503 [→ 6026]. delight, pleasure; living in luxury:– delights [2], delicate [1], delight [1], pleasant [1]

8589 תַּעֲנִית *ta*a*nît*, n.f. GK: 9504 [→ 6031]. self-abasement, mortification:– heaviness [1]

8590 תַּעֲנָךְ *ta*a*nak*, n.pr.loc. GK: 9505. Taanach:– Taanach [6], Tanach [1]

8591 תָּעַע *tā*a*', v. GK: 9506 [→ 8595]. [Pil] to mock; [Htpal] to scoff at:– deceiver [1], misused [1]

8592 תַּעֲצֻמוֹת *ta*a*sumôt*, n.f.[pl.]. GK: 9508 [→ 6105]. strength, might:– power [1]

8593 תַּעַר *ta*ar*, n.m. GK: 9509 [→ 6168]. razor, knife, scabbard:– sheath [6], rasor [4], penknife (+5608+1886.1) [1], scabbard [1], shave (+5674) [1]

8594 תַּעֲרוּבוֹת *ta*a*rûbôt*, n.f.[pl.]. GK: 9510 [→ 6148]. hostage, formally "son of a pledge":– hostages (+1121) [2]

8595 תַּעְתֻּעִים *ta*tu*'îm*, n.[m.]pl.abst. GK: 9511 [→ 8591]. mockery:– errors [1]

8596 תֹּף *tōp*, n.m. GK: 9512 & 9513 [→ 8608]. tambourine, timbrel; setting, jewelry; some sources uncertain in meaning:– tabrets [5], timbrel [5], timbrels [4], tabret [3]

8597 תִּפְאֶרֶת *tip*eret*, n.f. GK: 9514 [→ 6286]. glory, splendor, honor:– glory [22], beauty [10], beautiful [6], honour [4], fair [3], glorious [2], bravery [1], comely (+3807.1) [1], excellent [1]

8598 תַּפּוּחַ *tappûaḥ*, n.[m.]. GK: 9515 [→ 1054, 8599; cf. 5301]. apple, apple tree:– apple tree [3], apples [3]

8599 תַּפּוּחַ *tappûaḥ*, n.pr.m. & loc. GK: 9516 & 9517 [→ 5887, 8598; cf. 5301]. Tappuah, "*apple*":– Tappuah [6]

8600 תְּפוֹצָה *t*e*pûṣâ*, n.f.pl. GK: 9518 [→ 6327]. shattering, dispersing:– dispersions [1]

8601 תֻּפִינִים *tupînîm*, n.[m.]pl. GK: 9519 [cf. 644?]. broken into pieces:– baken [1]

8602 תָּפֵל *tāpēl*, n.[m.]. GK: 9521 & 9522 [→ 8604, cf. 2950]. tasteless (food); worthless (prophetic visions); whitewash:– untempered [5], foolish things [1], that which is unsavoury [1]

8603 תֹּפֶל *tōpel*, n.pr.loc. GK: 9523 [→ 302?]. Tophel, "*cement*":– Tophel [1]

8604 תִּפְלָה *tiplâ*, n.f. GK: 9524 [→ 8602]. repulsiveness, wrongdoing:– folly [2], foolishly [1]

8605 תְּפִלָּה *t*e*pillâ*, n.f. GK: 9525 [→ 6419]. prayer, plea, petition:– prayer [74], prayers [2], prayer make (+6419) [1]

8606 תִּפְלֶצֶת *tipleṣet*, n.f. GK: 9526 [→ 6426]. terror, horror, a state of great fear even to the point of shuddering:– terribleness [1]

8607 תִּפְסַח *tipsaḥ*, n.pr.loc. GK: 9527 [→ 6452]. Tiphsah:– Tiphsah [2]

8608 תָּפַף *tāpap*, v.den. GK: 9528 [→ 8596]. [Q] to tap (play) a tambourine; [Pol] to beat (the breast):– playing timbrels [1], tabring [1]

8609 תָּפַר *tāpar*, v. GK: 9529. [Q] to sew, mend; [P] to sew (together):– sew [2], sewed together [1], sewed [1]

8610 תָּפַשׂ *tāpaś*, v. GK: 9530. [Q] to take hold of, seize, capture; [Qp] to be covered; [N] to be seized, be caught, be captured; [P] to catch (a lizard):– took [17], taken [11], take [9], handle [5], caught [3], handleth [2], lay hold on [2], surely taken (+8610) [2], surprised [2], catch [1], handled (+3709+871.1+1886.1) [1], handling [1], holdest [1], hold [1], laid over [1], lay hold [1], stopped [1], take hold [1], taketh hold [1], taking [1], took hold [1]

8611 תֹּפֶת *tōpet*, n.f. GK: 9531. spitting:– tabret [1]

8612 תֹּפֶת *tōpet*, n.pr.loc. GK: 9532. Topheth:– Tophet [8], Topheth [1]

8613 תָּפְתֶּה *topteh*, n.pr.loc. GK: 9533. Topheth:– Tophet [1]

8614 תִּפְתָּי *tiptāy* (Aram.), n.m.pl. GK: 10767. magistrate, a general or legal authority such as a chief of police:– sheriffs [2]

תֹּצָאָה *tōṣā*'â*. See 8444.

8615 תִּקְוָה *tiqwâ*, n.f. GK: 9535 & 9536 [→ 6960, 8616]. hope, expectation; cord:– hope [23], expectation [7], line [2], expected [1], thing long for [1]

8616 תִּקְוָה *tiqwâ*, n.pr.m. GK: 9537 [→ 8615; cf. 6960]. Tikvah, "*hope*":– Tikvah [2], Tikvath [1]

8617 תְּקוּמָה *t*e*qûmâ*, n.f. GK: 9538 [→ 6965]. ability to stand:– power to stand [1]

8618 תְּקוֹמֵם *t*e*qômēm*, v.ptcp. GK: 9539 [→ 6965]. ptcp. of 6965: to rise up against:– rise up [1]

8619 תָּקוֹעַ *tāqôa*', n.[m.]. GK: 9540 [→ 8628]. trumpet, for battle signals:– trumpet [1]

8620 תְּקוֹעַ *t*e*qôa*', n.pr.loc. GK: 9541 [→ 8621; cf. 8628]. Tekoa:– Tekoa [6], Tekoah [1]

8621 תְּקוֹעִי *t*e*qô*'î*, a.g. GK: 9542 [→ 8620]. Tekoite, of Tekoa, "*of Tekoa*":– Tekoite [3], Tekoah [2], Tekoites [2]

8622 תְּקוּפָה *t*e*qûpâ*, n.f. GK: 9543 [cf. 5362]. turning, course:– end [2], circuit [1], come about (+3807.1) [1]

8623 תַּקִּיף *taqqîp*, a. GK: 9544 [→ 8630; cf. 8624]. strong, mighty:– mightier [1]

8624 תַּקִּיף *taqqîp* (Aram.), a. GK: 10768 [→ 8631; cf. 8623]. strong, powerful, mighty:– strong [3], mighty [2]

8625 תְּקַל *t*e*qal*, v. or תְּקֵל *t*e*qēl* (Aram.), n.[m.]. GK: 10769 & 10770 [cf. 8254, cf. 8255]. [Peil] to be weighed; (n.) tekel, (i.e., shekel of weight):– tekel [2], weighed [1]

8626 תָּקַן *tāqan*, v. GK: 9545 [cf. 8505; cf. 8627]. [Q] to be straight; [P] to straighten, set in order:– made straight [1], make straight [1], set in order [1]

8627 תְּקַן *t*e*qan* (Aram.), v. GK: 10771 [cf. 8626, 8505]. [Ho] to be restored, to be reestablished:– established [1]

8628 תָּקַע *tāqa*', v. GK: 9546 & 9364 [→ 8619, 8620, 8621, 8629]. [Q] to sound (a trumpet); to pitch, camp; to strike, clap; [Qp] to be driven; [N] to be sounded (a trumpet); to put up a security:– blow [22], blew [18], fastened [4], blown [3], blowing [2], clap [2], pitched [2], sounded [2], strike [2], thrust [2], blow up [1], bloweth [1], cast [1], fasten [1], pitch [1], smote [1], stricken [1], striketh [1], suretiship [1]

8629 תֵּקַע *tēqa*', n.[m.]. GK: 9547 [→ 8628]. sounding, blast (of a trumpet):– sound [1]

תְּקֹעִי *t*e*qō*'î*. See 8621.

8630 תָּקַף *tāqap*, v. GK: 9548 [→ 8623, 8633; cf. 8631]. [Q] to overpower, overwhelm:– prevail against [2], prevailest against [1]

8631 תְּקִף *t*e*qip* (Aram.), v. GK: 10772 [→ 8624, 8632; cf. 8630]. [P] to become strong, become hard; [Pa] to enforce, make hard:– strong [3], hardened [1], make firm [1]

8632 תְּקֹף *t*e*qōp* or תְּקָף *t*e*qāp* (Aram.), n.[m.]. GK: 10773 & 10774 [→ 8631; cf. 8633]. might, strength:– might [1], strength [1]

8633 תֹּקֶף *tōqep*, n.m. GK: 9549 [→ 8630; cf. 8632]. power, strength, authority:– authority [1], power [1], strength [1]

תְּקֻפָה *t*e*qupâ*. See 8622.

תֹּר *tōr*. See 8447, 8449.

8634 תַּרְאֵלָה *tar*'ēlâ*, n.pr.loc. GK: 9550 [→ 692?]. Taralah:– Taralah [1]

8635 תַּרְבּוּת *tarbût*, n.f. GK: 9551 [→ 7235]. a group of the same kind, brood:– increase [1]

8636 תַּרְבִּית *tarbît*, n.f. GK: 9552 [→ 7235]. excessive interest, exorbitant interest:– increase [5], unjust gain [1]

8637 רָגַל *rāgal* or תִּרְגַּל *tirgal*, v.den. GK: 8078 [→ 7270]. same as 7270: [Tiphil] to teach to walk:–

8638 תִּרְגֵּם *tirgēm*, v. GK: 9553 [→ 7276]. [Pu] to be interpreted, be translated:– interpreted [1]

תֹּרָה *tōrâ*. See 8451.

8639 תַּרְדֵּמָה *tardēmâ*, n.f. GK: 9554 [→ 7290]. deep (supernatural) sleep, often a state of divine revelation and activity:– deep sleep [7]

8640 תִּרְהָקָה *tirhāqâ*, n.pr.m. GK: 9555. Tirhakah:– Tirhakah [2]

8641 תְּרוּמָה *t*e*rûmâ*, n.f. GK: 9556 [→ 7311]. offering, special gift, contribution:– heave offering [21], offering [19], oblation [17], offerings [8], heave [4], heave offerings [3], oblations [2], gifts [1], offered [1]

8642 תְּרוּמִיָּה *t*e*rûmiyyâ*, n.f.den. GK: 9557 [→ 7311]. special gift, tribute:– oblation [1]

8643 תְּרוּעָה *t*e*rû*'â*, n.f. GK: 9558 [→ 7321]. trumpet blast, battle cry:– shout [10], shouting [8], alarm [6], joy [2], blowing of trumpets [1], blowing trumpets [1], blow [1], high sounding [1], joyful sound [1], jubile [1], loud noise [1], rejoicing [1], shouted aloud (+6963+7311+871.1+3807.1) [1], sounding [1]

8644 תְּרוּפָה *t*e*rûpâ*, n.f. GK: 9559 [→ 7495]. healing:– medicine [1]

8645 תִּרְזָה *tirzâ*, n.f. GK: 9560. cypress tree:– cypress [1]

8646 תֶּרַח *teraḥ* or תָּרַח *tāraḥ*, n.pr.m. & loc. GK: 9561 & 9562. Terah, Tarah:– Terah [11], Tarah [2]

8647 תִּרְחֲנָה *tirḥ*a*nâ*, n.pr.[f.?]. GK: 9563. Tirhanah:– Tirhanah [1]

8648 תְּרֵין *t*e*rên* or תַּרְתֵּין *tartên* (Aram.), n.m. & f. GK: 10775 & 10778 [→ 8578, 8579; cf. 8147]. two:– twelve (+6236) [2], second [1], two [1]

8649 תַּרְמוּת *tarmût* or תַּרְמִית *tarmît*, n.f. GK: 9566 & 9567 [cf. 7411]. deceitfulness, delusion:– deceit [4], deceitful [1], privily (+871.1) [1]

תְּרוּמָה *t*e*rûmâ*. See 8641.

8650 תֹּרֶן *tōren*, n.m. GK: 9568. (sailing) mast; flagstaff (on top of hill):– beacon [1], masts [1], mast [1]

8651 תְּרַע *t*e*ra*' (Aram.), n.m. GK: 10776 [→ 8652; cf. 8179]. gate, door; opening (of a furnace); (royal) court, the entourage of a king:– gate [1], mouth [1]

8652 תָּרָע *tārā*' (Aram.), n.m. GK: 10777 [→ 8651; cf. 7778]. gatekeeper, doorkeeper:– porters [1]

8653 תַּרְעֵלָה *tar*'ēlâ*, n.f. GK: 9570 [→ 7477]. staggering, reeling:– trembling [2], astonishment [1]

8654 תִּרְעָתִים *tir*'ātîm*, n.pr.m.pl. GK: 9571. Tirathite:– Tirathites [1]

8655 תְּרָפִים *t*e*rāpîm*, n.m.pl. GK: 9572. household god, idol:– teraphim [6], images [5], image [2], idolatry [1], idols [1]

8656 תִּרְצָה *tirṣâ*, n.pr.f. & loc. GK: 9573 & 9574 [→ 7521]. Tirzah, "*pleasant one* or *compensation*":– Tirzah [18]

8657 תֶּרֶשׁ *tereš*, n.pr.m. GK: 9575. Teresh, "[perhaps] *desire*":– Teresh [2]

8658 תַּרְשִׁישׁ *taršîš*, n.m. GK: 9577 [→ 7567?]. chrysolite:– beryl [7]

8659 תַּרְשִׁישׁ *taršîš*, n.pr.m. & loc. GK: 9576 & 9578 [→ 7567?]. Tarshish, "[poss.] *yellow jasper*; [poss.] *greedy one*; *foundry, refinery*"; ships of Tarshish = trading ships:– Tarshish [24], Tharshish [4]

8660 תִּרְשָׁתָא *tiršātā*' , n.m. GK: 9579. governor:– Tirshatha [5]

תַּרְתֵּין *tartên*. See 8648.

8661 תַּרְתָּן *tartān*, n.m. GK: 9580 [cf. 8648]. supreme commander, second in command:– Tartan [2]

8662 תַּרְתָּק *tartāq*, n.pr.[m.]. GK: 9581. Tartak (pagan god):– Tartak [1]

8663 תְּשֻׁאָה *t*e*šu*'â*, n.f. GK: 9583 & 9589 [→ 7582]. shouting, commotion, thundering, storm:– crying [1], noise [1], shoutings [1], stirs [1]

תֹּשָׁב *tōšāb*. See 8453.

8664 תִּשְׁבִּי *tišbî*, a.g. or תִּשְׁבֵּי *tišbê*, n.pr.loc. GK: 9585. Tishbe; Tishbite, "*of Tishbe*":– Tishbite [6]

8665 תַּשְׁבֵּץ *tašbēṣ*, n.[m.]. GK: 9587 [→ 7660]. woven or checkered fabric:– broidered [1]

8666 תְּשׁוּבָה *t*e*šûbâ*, n.f. GK: 9588 [→ 7725]. spring [time of year]; answer:– expired [3], return [3], answers [2]

8667 תְּשׂוּמָה *t*e*śûmâ*, n.f. GK: 9582 [→ 7760]. pledge, security:– fellowship (+3027) [1]

8668 תְּשׁוּעָה *t*e*šû*'â*, n.f. GK: 9591 [→ 3467]. deliverance, salvation, victory; divine salvation has its focus on rescue from earthly enemies, occasionally referring to salvation from guilt, sin, and punishment:– salvation [17], deliverance [5], help [4], safety [4], victory [3], help (+1961) [1]

8669 תְּשׁוּקָה *t*e*šûqâ*, n.f. GK: 9592 [→ 7794]. desire, longing:– desire [3]

8670 תְּשׁוּרָה *t*e*šûrâ*, n.f. GK: 9593 [→ 7794]. gift, present:– present [1]

תַּשְׁחֵת *tašḥēt*. See 516.

תֻּשִׁיָּה *tušîâ*. See 8454.

8671 תְּשִׁיעִי *t*e*šî*'î*, a.num.ord. GK: 9595 [→ 8672]. ninth:– ninth [18]

תְּשֻׁעָה *t*e*šu*'â*. See 8668.

8672 תֵּשַׁע *tēša*', n.m. & f. GK: 9596 [→ 8671, 8673]. nine, (pl.) ninety:– nine [45], ninth [6], nineteenth (+6240) [4], nineteen (+6240) [3]

8673 תִּשְׁעִים *tiš*'îm*, n.indecl. GK: 9597 [→ 8672]. ninety (pl. of "nine"):– ninety [20]

8674 תַּתְּנַי *tatt*e*nay* (Aram.), n.pr.[m.]. GK: 10779. Tattenai:– Tatnai [4]

GREEK DICTIONARY-INDEX TO THE NEW TESTAMENT

FEATURES OF THE GREEK TO ENGLISH DICTIONARY-INDEX

STRONG NUMBER	LEXICAL FORM AND TRANSLITERATION	PART OF SPEECH	G/K NUMBER
Matches the number at the end of context lines; Greek Strong numbers are in *italics* (see the introduction, pages xii, xiv).	See the table below. Note that the lexical forms conform to modern resources and sometimes differ from Strong's original spelling.	The part of speech is abbreviated (see below and introduction, page xiv).	Cross reference to the G/K numbering system, widely used in up-to-date word study reference resources (see the introduction, pages xiv).

223 ʼΑλέξανδρος, *Alexandros,* n.pr. GK: *235* [→ *221, 222*].

RELATED WORDS LIST
Greek words related by common elements are listed by Strong number (see the introduction, page xiv, xv).

Alexander, *"defender of men"*:–

DEFINITION AND ETYMOLOGY
Words are defined, often with expanded explanations, and if a proper name, the possible definition (etymology) is given in italics (see the introduction, page xiv, xv).

Alexander [6],

KJV WORD AND (FREQUENCY COUNT)
Following the symbol :– KJV words are listed according to their exact textual spelling and are organized according to frequency (see the introduction, page xiv).

one another (+*1520*+*3588*) [2]

MULTIPLE WORDS / MULTIPLE NUMBERS
More than one KJV word and/or more than one Strong number indicate multiple-word translations (see the introduction, pages xii–xiv).

one another[S] [2]

SUPERSCRIPT "S"
Indicates "substitution" translation (see the introduction, pages xiii, xiv).

GREEK TRANSLITERATION AND PRONUNCIATION TABLE

Α, α	*A, a*	father	Κ, κ	*K, k*	kit	Τ, τ	*T, t*	tip	γγ	*ng*	thi*ng*
Β, β	*B, b*	boy	Λ, λ	*L, l*	let	Υ, υ	*Y, y*	put	γκ	*nk*	thi*nk*
Γ, γ	*G, g*	girl	Μ, μ	*M, m*	mother	Φ, φ	*Ph, ph*	phone	γξ	*nx*	thi*nks*
Δ, δ	*D, d*	dog	Ν, ν	*N, n*	not	Χ, χ	*Ch, ch*	Bach	γχ	*nch*	thi*nk*
Ε, ε	*E, e*	get	Ξ, ξ	*X, x*	fox	Ψ, ψ	*Ps, ps*	lips			
Ζ, ζ	*Z, z*	adze	Ο, ο	*O, o*	hot	Ω, ω	*Ō, ō*	phone	αυ	*au*	kraut
Η, η	*Ē, ē*	they	Π, π	*P, p*	pot				ευ	*eu*	you
Θ, θ	*Th, th*	they	Ρ, ρ	*R, r*	rot	ʼΡ, ῥ	*Rh, rh*	myrrh	ου	*ou*	through
Ι, ι	*I, i*	pin, machine	Σ, σ, ς	*S, s, s*	sip	ʽ	*H, h*	hot	υι	*ui*	we

GREEK DICTIONARY ABBREVIATIONS

&	and	comp.	comparative	inter.	interrogative	pl.	plural
?	uncertain	cond.	conditional	interj.	interjection	poss.	possessive
+	plus: in combination with	contr.	contraction	intr.	intransitive	pp.	preposition
[]	uncertain part of speech	demo.	demonstrative	l.	loanword	pp.*	improper preposition
→	see these related words	disj.	disjunctive	letter	letter of the alphabet	pr.	proper [noun]
√	see this organizing word	emph.	emphatic	mid.	middle	pt.	particle
a.	adjective	excl.	exclamation	n.	noun	recip.	reciprocal
act.	active	fig.	figurative(ly)	neg.	negative	reflex.	reflexive
adv.	adverb	g.	gentilic	neu.	neuter	rel.	relative
adver.	adversative	imper.	impersonal	num.	numeral	super.	superlative
aff.	affirmative	indef.	indefinite	p.	pronoun	temp.	temporal
art.	article	infer.	inferential	pass.	passive	trans.	transitional
c.	conjunction	inten.	intensive	pers.	personal	v.	verb

1 α, *a*, letter. GK: *1 & 270* [→ *1*; *1.1:* *4, 22, 35, 36, 46, 50, 51, 52, 56, 57, 62, 77, 82, 83, 84, 87, 88, 89, 90, 91, 92, 93, 94, 95, 96, 97, 101, 102, 106, 110, 112, 113, 114, 115, 120, 121, 167, 168, 169, 170, 171, 172, 175, 176, 177, 178, 179, 180, 181, 182, 183, 185, 186, 192, 193, 194, 208, 209, 210, 215, 216, 225, 226, 227, 228, 230, 249, 253, 255, 261, 262, 263, 267, 269, 272, 273, 274, 275, 276, 277, 278, 279, 280, 282, 283, 298, 299, 335, 338, 358, 361, 368, 369, 370, 371, 379, 382, 410, 411, 412, 413, 415, 418, 419, 421, 422, 423, 428, 434, 448, 449, 453, 454, 458, 459, 460, 462, 504, 505, 506, 512, 517, 521, 531, 532, 540, 543, 544, 545, 551, 552, 562, 563, 564, 569, 570, 571, 639, 640, 676, 677, 678, 679, 691, 692, 729, 731, 732, 761, 762, 763, 764, 765, 766, 767, 769, 770, 771, 772, 776, 777, 781, 784, 786, 790, 793, 794, 795, 799, 800, 801, 802, 803, 804, 805, 806, 807, 808, 809, 810, 811, 812, 813, 814, 815, 818, 819, 820, 821, 823, 824, 852, 853, 854, 855, 857, 858, 861, 862, 865, 866, 870, 877, 878, 880, 884, 886, 888, 889, 890, 893, 895, 1280, 1820, 2673;* **1.2:** *12, 816;* **1.3:** *79, 271?, 1811, 1872, 2628, 3877, 4870, 5359, 5360, 5361, 5569*]. 1) letter of the Greek alphabet, Alpha, "*First* or *Beginning*"; 2) inseparable prefix: *1.1* alpha privative (as non- or un- in English), *1.2* prefix of intensity, *1.3* prefix of similarity, collectivity or association; also used as the numeral "1" in the superscriptions of some Greek manuscripts:– Alpha [4]

2 Ἀαρών, *Aarōn*, n.pr. GK: *2*. Aaron (referring to both the person and his priesthood):– Aaron [4], Aaron's [1]

3 Ἀβαδδών, *Abaddōn*, n.pr. GK: *3*. Abaddon, "*destruction*":– Abaddon [1]

4 ἀβαρής, *abarēs*, a. GK: *4* [→ *1.1+922*]. not burdensome:– from being burdensome [1]

5 ἀββᾶ, *abba*, l.[n.]. GK: *5*. Aramaic for "father":– Abba [3]

6 Ἅβελ, *Habel*, n.pr. GK: *6*. Abel, "*morning mist*":– Abel [4]

7 Ἀβιά, *Abia*, n.pr. GK: *7*. Abijah, "*[my] father is Yahweh*":– Abia [3]

8 Ἀβιαθάρ, *Abiathar*, n.pr. GK: *8*. Abiathar, "*[my] father gives abundance* or *the father is preeminent*":– Abiathar [1]

9 Ἀβιληνή, *Abilēnē*, n.pr. GK: *9*. Abilene, a territory on the south end of the Ante-Lebanon mountain range, "[prob.] *meadow*":– Abilene [1]

10 Ἀβιούδ, *Abioud*, n.pr. GK: *10*. Abiud, "*[my] father has majesty*":– Abiud [2]

11 Ἀβραάμ, *Abraam*, n.pr. GK: *11*. Abraham, "*father of many*":– Abraham [68], Abraham's [5]

12 ἄβυσσος, *abyssos*, n. GK: *12* [→ *1.2+1037*]. Abyss, the deep place, the underworld, the abode of the dead and demons, "*unfathomable depth*":– bottomless [7], deep [2]

13 Ἅγαβος, *Hagabos*, n.pr. GK: *13*. Agabus:– Agabus [2]

14 ἀγαθοεργέω, *agathoergeō*, v. GK: *14* [→ *18+2041*]. to do good:– do good [1]

15 ἀγαθοποιέω, *agathopoieō*, v. GK: *16* [→ *18+4160*]. to do good, to do right:– do good [5], do well [2], well doing [2], did good [1], doeth good [1]

16 ἀγαθοποιΐα, *agathopoiia*, n. GK: *17* [→ *18+4160*]. doing good:– well doing [1]

17 ἀγαθοποιός, *agathopoios*, a. GK: *18* [→ *18+4160*]. one who does good, right:– do well [1]

18 ἀγαθός, *agathos*, a. GK: *19* [→ *14, 15, 16, 17, 19, 865, 5358*]. good; good as a positive quality (vs. bad), good as a moral quality (vs. evil):– good [98], goods [2], benefit [1], well [1]

19 ἀγαθωσύνη, *agathōsynē*, n. GK: *20* [→ *18*]. goodness:– goodness [4]

20 ἀγαλλίασις, *agalliasis*, n. GK: *21* [→ *21*]. delight, great joy:– gladness [3], exceeding joy [1], joy [1]

21 ἀγαλλιάω, *agalliaō*, v. GK: *22* [→ *20*]. to be filled with delight, with great joy:– rejoiced [4], rejoice [3], exceeding glad [1], exceeding joy [1], glad [1], greatly rejoice [1]

22 ἄγαμος, *agamos*, n. GK: *23* [→ *1.1+1062*]. unmarried (man or woman):– unmarried [4]

23 ἀγανακτέω, *aganakteō*, v. GK: *24* [→ *24*]. to be indignant:– had indignation [2], much displeased [2], indignation [1], moved with indignation [1], sore displeased [1]

24 ἀγανάκτησις, *aganaktēsis*, n. GK: *25* [→ *23*]. indignation:– indignation [1]

25 ἀγαπάω, *agapaō*, v. GK: *26* [→ *26, 27*]. to love; in the NT usually the active love of God for his Son and his people, and the active love his people are to have for God, each other, and even enemies:– love [73], loved [39], loveth [20], beloved [7], lovest [2], lovedst [1]

26 ἀγάπη, *agapē*, n. GK: *27* [→ *25*]. love, in the NT usually the active love of God for his Son and his people, and the active love his people are to have for God, each other, and even enemies; love feast, the common meal shared by Christians in connection with church meetings:– love [85], charity [27], charitably (+2596) [1], dear [1], feasts of charity [1], love's [1]

27 ἀγαπητός, *agapētos*, a. GK: *28* [→ *25*]. dearly loved one; the object of special affection and of special relationship, as with Jesus the beloved of the Father:– beloved [47], dearly beloved [9], dear [4], wellbeloved [3]

28 Ἀγάρ, *Hagar*, n.pr. GK: *29*. Hagar:– Agar [2]

29 ἀγγαρεύω, *angareuō*, v. GK: *30*. to force, compel, press into service in military or civil matters:– compel to go [1], compelled [1], compel [1]

30 ἀγγεῖον, *angeion*, n. GK: *31*. jar, flask, a container for liquid, basket:– vessels [2]

31 ἀγγελία, *angelia*, n. GK: *32* [→ *32*]. message:– message [1]

32 ἄγγελος, *angelos*, n. GK: *34* [→ *31, 518, 312, 743, 1229, 1804, 1860, 1861, 1862, 2097, 2098, 2099, 2465, 2604, 2605, 3852, 3853, 4279, 4283, 4293; cf. 71*]. angel, messenger; this can refer to a human messenger, such as John the Baptist, or messengers sent by John the Baptist or Jesus, or to the supernatural class of being that serves God: the angel:– angel [96], angels [80], messenger [4], messengers [3], angel's [2]

33 ἄγε, *age*, v.imper. of *71*. GK: *72* [→ *71*]. look, pay attention, listen:–

34 ἀγέλη, *agelē*, n. GK: *36* [→ *71*]. herd (of pigs):– herd [8]

35 ἀγενεαλόγητος, *agenealogētos*, a. GK: *37* [→ *1.1+1096+3004*]. without genealogy:– without descent [1]

36 ἀγενής, *agenēs*, a. GK: *38* [→ *1.1+1096*]. lowly, insignificant, implying low social standing:– base [1]

37 ἁγιάζω, *hagiazō*, v. GK: *39* [→ *40*]. to sanctify, set apart, make holy; this can mean active dedication and service to God or the act of regarding or honoring as holy:– sanctified [16], sanctify [6], sanctifieth [4], hallowed [2], holy [1]

38 ἁγιασμός, *hagiasmos*, n. GK: *40* [→ *40*]. holiness:– holiness [5], sanctification [5]

39 ἅγιον, *hagion*, a.neut. of *40*. GK: *41* [→ *40*]. holy (moral quality), holy place = sanctuary:–

40 ἅγιος, *hagios*, a. GK: *41* [→ *37, 38, 39, 41, 42; cf. 53*]. holy (moral quality), consecrated ([ceremonially] acceptable to God); holy person/people = saint(s), holy place = sanctuary:– holy [163], saints [60], holy one [4], sanctuary [4], holiest of all (+40) [2], holiest [2], holy thing [1], most holy [1], saints' [1], saint [1]

41 ἁγιότης, *hagiotēs*, n. GK: *42* [→ *40*]. holiness, a characteristic of God, shared by his people, requiring a lifestyle acceptable to God:– holiness [1]

42 ἁγιωσύνη, *hagiōsynē*, n. GK: *43* [→ *40*]. holiness, a characteristic of God, shared by his people, requiring a lifestyle acceptable to God:– holiness [3]

43 ἀγκάλη, *ankalē*, n. GK: *44* [→ *1723*]. arm:– arms [1]

44 ἄγκιστρον, *ankistron*, n. GK: *45* [→ *45*]. fish-hook, fish line with a hook on it:– hook [1]

45 ἄγκυρα, *ankyra*, n. GK: *46* [→ *44*]. anchor; used fig. of security:– anchors [3], anchor [1]

46 ἄγναφος, *agnaphos*, a. GK: *47* [→ *1.1+1102*]. unshrunk, new cloth that has not been laundered:– new [2]

47 ἁγνεία, *hagneia*, n. GK: *48* [→ *53*]. purity, in the sense of moral purity and proper sexual conduct:– purity [2]

48 ἁγνίζω, *hagnizō*, v. GK: *49* [→ *53*]. to purify, ceremonially cleanse:– purify [3], purified [2], purifieth [1], purifying [1]

49 ἁγνισμός, *hagnismos*, n. GK: *50* [→ *53*]. purification:– purification [1]

50 ἀγνοέω, *agnoeō*, v. GK: *51* [→ *1.1+1097*]. to be ignorant, not know, not understand:– ignorant [10], ignorantly [2], know not [2], understood not [2], unknown [2], have ignorant [1], knew not [1], not knowing [1], understand not [1]

51 ἀγνόημα, *agnoēma*, n. GK: *52* [→ *1.1+1097*]. sin committed in ignorance:– errors [1]

52 ἄγνοια, *agnoia*, n. GK: *53* [→ *1.1+1097*]. ignorance:– ignorance [4]

53 ἁγνός, *hagnos*, a. GK: *54* [→ *47, 48, 49, 54, 55; cf. 40*]. pure (in some contexts morally pure), innocent:– pure [4], chaste [3], clear [1]

54 ἁγνότης, *hagnotēs*, n. GK: *55* [→ *53*]. purity:– pureness [1]

55 ἁγνῶς, *hagnōs*, adv. GK: *56* [→ *53*]. sincerely, purely:– sincerely [1]

56 ἀγνωσία, *agnōsia*, n. GK: *57* [→ *1.1+1097*]. ignorance, with a focus on talk or action that opposes God:– ignorance [1], not knowledge [1]

57 ἄγνωστος, *agnōstos*, a. GK: *58* [→ *1.1+1097*]. unknown:– unknown [1]

58 ἀγορά, *agora*, n. GK: *59* [→ *59*]. marketplace (as a center of social and commercial life):– markets [4], marketplace [3], market [2], marketplaces [1], streets [1]

59 ἀγοράζω, *agorazō*, v. GK: *60* [→ *58, 60, 238, 1215, 1805; cf. 71*]. to buy, purchase; this refers to buying and acquiring possessions, as in a market place, and to setting a slave free through purchase, often to God's purchase (redemption) of sinners:– bought [13], buy [13], redeemed [3], buyeth [2]

60 ἀγοραῖος, *agoraios*, a. GK: *61* [→ *59*]. marketplace, place where the courts meet:– baser sort [1], law [1]

61 ἄγρα, *agra*, n. GK: *62* [→ *64, 69, 70, 2221*]. catch (of fish), a net full:– draught [2]

62 ἀγράμματος, *agrammatos*, a. GK: *63* [→ *1.1+1125*]. unschooled, probably in the sense of not having a formal rabbinic education:– unlearned [1]

63 ἀγραυλέω, *agrauleō*, v. GK: *64* [→ *68+833*]. to live outdoors, spend a night in the elements:– in country abiding [1]

64 ἀγρεύω, *agreuō*, v. GK: *65* [→ *61*]. to catch:– catch [1]

65 ἀγριέλαιος, *agrielaios*, n. GK: *66* [→ *68+1636*]. wild olive tree:– olive tree which is wild [1], wild olive tree [1]

66 ἄγριος, *agrios*, a. GK: *67* [→ *68*]. wild; undomesticated as well as uncontrolled:– wild [2], raging [1]

67 Ἀγρίππας, *Agrippas*, n.pr. GK: *68* [→ *68+2462*]. Agrippa, "*wild horse*":– Agrippa [12]

68 ἀγρός, *agros*, n. GK: *69* [→ *63, 65, 66, 67*]. field, countryside, both tilled and untilled ground:– field [21], country [8], lands [3], farm [1], fields [1], land [1], piece of ground [1]

69 ἀγρυπνέω, *agrypneō*, v. GK: *70* [→ *61+5258*]. to keep awake, keep alert:– watch [3], watching [1]

70 ἀγρυπνία, *agrypnia*, n. GK: *71* [→ *61+5258*]. sleeplessness, wakefulness:– watchings [2]

71 ἄγω, *agō*, v. GK: *72* [→ *33, 34, 72, 321, 411, 520, 747, 1236, 1334, 1396, 1521, 1555, 1806, 1834, 1863, 1877, 1898, 1996, 2023, 2024, 2230, 2231, 2232, 2233, 2519, 2609, 2723, 3329, 3594, 3595, 3807, 3831, 3855, 3919, 3920, 3931, 4013, 4254, 4285, 4316, 4317, 4318, 4755, 4812, 4863, 4864, 4879, 5217, 5468, 5490, 5497, 5524; cf. 32, 59, 514, 2723*]. to bring, lead; as a command: look, pay attention, listen:– brought [32], bring [13], led [10], go [8], bring out [1], bringing [1], carried [1], going [1], is [1], kept [1], leadeth [1], lead [1], led away [1], open [1]

72 ἀγωγή, *agōgē*, n. GK: *73* [→ *71*]. way of life, personal conduct:– manner of life [1]

73 ἀγών, *agōn*, n. GK: *74* [→ *74, 75, 464, 1864, 2610, 4865*]. struggle, fight, often an athletic contest:– conflict [2], fight [2], contention [1], race [1]

74 ἀγωνία, *agōnia*, n. GK: *75* [→ *73*]. anguish, anxiety:– agony [1]

75 ἀγωνίζομαι, *agōnizomai*, v. GK: *76* [→ *73*]. to fight, struggle, often an athletic contest:– fight [2], fought [1], labouring fervently [1], striveth for the mastery [1], strive [1], striving [1]

76 Ἀδάμ, *Adam*, n.pr. GK: *77*. Adam, "*[red] earth* or *[ruddy] skin color*":– Adam [8], Adam's [1]

77 ἀδάπανος, *adapanos*, a. GK: *78* [→ *1.1+1160*]. free of charge, without payment:– without charge [1]

78 Ἀδδί, *Addi*, n.pr. GK: *79*. Addi, "[poss.] *my witness* or *adorned*":– Addi [1]

79 ἀδελφή, *adelphē*, n. GK: *80* [→ *80; cf. 1.3*]. sister, fellow countrywoman; by extension a female believer, a sister in the family of faith:– sister [15], sisters [8], sister's [1]

80 ἀδελφός, *adelphos*, n. GK: *81* [→ *1.3, 79, 81, 5359, 5360, 5361, 5569*]. brother, fellow countryman, neighbor (often inclusive in gender); by extension a fellow believer in the family of faith; in the plural "brothers" regularly refers to men and women:– brethren [226], brother [113], brother's [7]

81 ἀδελφότης, *adelphotēs*, n. GK: *82* [→ *80*]. brotherhood, fellowship of believers (men and women):– brethren [1], brotherhood [1]

82 ἄδηλος, *adēlos*, a. GK: *83* [→ *1.1+1212*]. not clear:– appear not [1], uncertain [1]

83 ἀδηλότης, *adēlotēs*, n. GK: *84* [→ *1.1+1212*]. uncertainty:– uncertain [1]

84 ἀδήλως, *adēlōs*, adv. GK: *85* [→ *1.1+1212*]. aimlessly, uncertainly:– uncertainly [1]

85 ἀδημονέω, *adēmoneō*, v. GK: *86 & 194*. to be troubled, distressed:– very heavy [2], full of heaviness [1]

86 ᾅδης, *hadēs*, n. GK: *87*. Hades, the grave, the place of the dead, "*the underworld*":– hell [10], grave [1]

87 ἀδιάκριτος, *adiakritos*, a. GK: *88* [→ *1.1+1223+2919*]. impartial, free from prejudice:– without partiality [1]

88 ἀδιάλειπτος, *adialeiptos*, a. GK: *89* [→ *1.1+1223+3007*]. constant, unceasing:– continual [1], without ceasing [1]

89 ἀδιαλείπτως, *adialeiptōs*, adv. GK: *90* [→ *1.1+1223+3007*]. constantly, unceasingly:– without ceasing [4]

90 ἀδιαφθορία, *adiaphthoria*, n. GK: *91* [→ *1.1+1223+5351*]. sincerity, integrity:– uncorruptness [1]

91 ἀδικέω, *adikeō*, v. GK: *92* [→ *1.1+1349*]. to do wrong, mistreat:– hurt [10], wrong [3], done wrong [2], unjust [2], wronged [2], did wrong [1], doeth wrong [1], injured [1], offender [1], suffer wrong [1], suffered wrong [1], take wrong [1], wrong done [1]

92 ἀδίκημα, *adikēma*, n. GK: *93* [→ *1.1+1349*]. crime, unrighteous or unjust act:– evil doing [1], iniquities [1], wrong [1]

93 ἀδικία, *adikia*, n. GK: *94* [→ *1.1+1349*]. wickedness, evil, wrongdoing:– unrighteousness [16], iniquity [6], unjust [2], wrong [1]

94 ἄδικος, *adikos*, a. GK: *96* [→ *1.1+1349*]. unjust, unrighteous, used of things and persons; as a noun: unbeliever, wicked person:– unjust [8], unrighteous [4]

95 ἀδίκως, *adikōs*, adv. GK: *97* [→ *1.1+1349*]. unjustly:– wrongfully [1]

96 ἀδόκιμος, *adokimos*, a. GK: *99* [→ *1.1+1209*]. failing the test, rejected:– reprobates [3], reprobate [3], castaway [1], rejected [1]

97 ἄδολος, *adolos*, a. GK: *100* [→ *1.1+1388*]. pure, uncontaminated or tainted:– sincere [1]

98 Ἀδραμυττηνός, *Adramyttēnos*, a.pr.g. GK: *101*. of Adramyttium:– Adramyttium [1]

99 Ἀδρίας, *Adrias*, n.pr. GK: *102*. Adriatic Sea:– Adria [1]

100 ἁδρότης, *hadrotēs*, n. GK: *103*. liberal gift, liberality:– abundance [1]

101 ἀδυνατέω, *adynateō*, v. GK: *104* [→ *1.1+1410*]. to be impossible:– unpossible [2]

102 ἀδύνατος, *adynatos*, a. GK: *105* [→ *1.1+1410*]. impossible, powerless:– impossible [4], unpossible [2], could not do [1], impotent [1], not possible [1], weak [1]

103 ᾄδω, *adō*, v. GK: *106* [→ *5603*]. to sing:– singing [2], sung [2], sing [1]

104 ἀεί, *aei*, adv. GK: *107* [→ *126*]. always:– alway [4], always [3], ever [1]

105 ἀετός, *aetos*, n. GK: *108*. eagle (a noble, powerful bird), vulture (a carrion bird):– eagles [2], eagle [2]

106 ἄζυμος, *azymos*, a. GK: *109* [→ *1.1+2219*]. unleavened, (the Feast of) Unleavened Bread, made without yeast; fig. of purity:– unleavened bread [8], unleavened [1]

107 Ἀζώρ, *Azōr*, n.pr. GK: *110*. Azor:– Azor [2]

108 Ἄζωτος, *Azōtos*, n.pr. GK: *111*. Azotus, another name for Ashdod:– Azotus [1]

109 ἀήρ, *aēr*, n. GK: *113* [→ *822; cf. 143, 833*]. air, sky:– air [7]

ἀθά, *atha*. See *3134*.

110 ἀθανασία, *athanasia*, n. GK: *114* [→ *1.1+2348*]. immortality:– immortality [3]

111 ἀθέμιτος, *athemitos*, a. GK: *116*. unlawful, detestable:– abominable [1], unlawful [1]

112 ἄθεος, *atheos*, a. GK: *117* [→ *1.1+2316*]. without God, excluded from the heritage of Israel:– without God [1]

113 ἄθεσμος, *athesmos*, a. GK: *118* [→ *1.1+5087*]. lawless, unprincipled:– wicked [2]

114 ἀθετέω, *atheteō*, v. GK: *119* [→ *1.1+5087*]. to reject, set aside:– despiseth [6], reject [2], bring to nothing [1], cast off [1], despised [1], despise [1], disannulleth [1], frustrate [1], rejected [1], rejecteth [1]

115 ἀθέτησις, *athetēsis*, n. GK: *120* [→ *1.1+5087*]. setting aside, doing away with:– disannulling [1], put away [1]

116 Ἀθῆναι, *Athēnai*, n.pr.c. GK: *121* [→ *117*]. Athens:– Athens [6]

117 Ἀθηναῖος, *Athēnaios*, a.pr.g. GK: *122* [→ *116*]. Athenian, resident of Athens:– Athenians [1], of Athens [1]

118 ἀθλέω, *athleō*, v. GK: *123* [→ *119, 4866*]. to compete in a contest:– strive for masteries [1], strive [1]

119 ἄθλησις, *athlēsis*, n. GK: *124* [→ *118*]. contest, struggle:– fight [1]

120 ἀθυμέω, *athymeō*, v. GK: *126* [→ *1.1+2372*]. to be discouraged, lose heart:– discouraged [1]

121 ἄθῳος, *athōos*, a. GK: *127* [→ *1.1+5087*]. innocent:– innocent [1]

122 αἴγειος, *aigeios*, a. GK: *128*. of a goat:– goatskins (+*1192*) [1]

123 αἰγιαλός, *aigialos*, n. GK: *129* [→ *217*]. shore, beach:– shore [6]

124 Αἰγύπτιος, *Aigyptios*, a.pr.g. GK: *130* [→ *125*]. Egyptian, person of Egypt:– Egyptian [3], Egyptians [2]

125 Αἴγυπτος, *Aigyptos*, n.pr. GK: *131* [→ *124*]. Egypt:– Egypt [24]

126 ἀΐδιος, *aidios*, a. GK: *132* [→ *104*]. eternal (referring to God's power, chains of punishment):– eternal [1], everlasting [1]

127 αἰδώς, *aidōs*, n. GK: *133 & 1290* [→ *335, 1167, 1168, 1169, 1171, 1175, 1174*]. decency, modesty:– reverence [1], shamefastness [1]

128 Αἰθίοψ, *Aithiops*, n.pr.g. GK: *134*. Ethiopian, person of Ethiopia:– Ethiopians [1], Ethiopia [1]

129 αἷμα, *haima*, n. GK: *135* [→ *130, 131*]. blood; extended meanings: killing, death, sacrifice:– blood [99]

130 αἱματεκχυσία, *haimatekchysia*, n. GK: *136* [→ *129+1632*]. shedding, pouring out of blood:– shedding of blood [1]

131 αἱμορροέω, *haimorroeō*, v. GK: *137* [→ *129+4482*]. to be subject to bleeding, to experience loss of blood:– diseased with an issue of blood [1]

132 Αἰνέας, *Aineas*, n.pr. GK: *138* [→ *136*]. Aeneas, "[poss.] *praise*":– Aeneas [2]

133 αἴνεσις, *ainesis*, n. GK: *139* [→ *136*]. praise, speaking of the excellence of someone or something:– praise [1]

134 αἰνέω, *aineō*, v. GK: *140* [→ *136*]. to praise; in the NT, speaking of the excellence of God:– praising [6], praise [3]

135 αἴνιγμα, *ainigma*, n. GK: *141*. poor reflection, indistinct image:– darkly (+*1722*) [1]

136 αἶνος, *ainos*, n. GK: *142* [→ *132, 133, 134, 1866, 1867, 1868, 3867*]. praise:– praise [2]

137 Αἰνών, *Ainōn*, n.pr. GK: *143*. Aenon, "*spring*":– Aenon [1]

138 αἱρέομαι, *haireomai*, v. GK: *145* [→ *139, 140, 141, 336, 337, 830, 851, 1243, 1244, 1807, 2506, 2507, 4014, 4255*]. to choose:– choose [1], choosing [1], chosen [1]

139 αἵρεσις, *hairesis*, n. GK: *146* [→ *138*]. sect (religious party), faction, heresy:– sect [5], heresies [3], heresy [1]

140 αἱρετίζω, *hairetizō*, v. GK: *147* [→ *138*]. to choose (for the purpose of showing special favor):– chosen [1]

141 αἱρετικός, *hairetikos*, a. GK: *148* [→ *138*]. divisive, heretick [1]

142 αἴρω, *airō*, v. GK: *149* [→ *522, 1808, 1869, 3332, 4868, 5097, 5098, 5229*]. to take up, take away:– take up [14], take [14], took up [13], taken away [9], take away [7], taketh away [6], away with [5], taketh [5], taken [4], taken up [3], took [3], bear up [2], bear [2], lifted up [2], removed [2], took away [2], borne [1], carry [1], lift up [1], lift [1], loosing [1], make to doubt (+*3588+5590*) [1], put away [1], takest up [1], taking up [1]

143 αἰσθάνομαι, *aisthanomai*, v. GK: *150* [→ *144, 145; cf. 109*]. to grasp, understand, to have the capacity to perceive something clearly:– perceived [1]

144 αἴσθησις, *aisthēsis*, n. GK: *151* [→ *143*]. insight:– judgment [1]

145 αἰσθητήριον, *aisthētērion*, n. GK: *152* [→ *143*]. sense, faculty:– senses [1]

146 αἰσχροκερδής, *aischrokerdēs*, a. GK: *153* [→ *150+2771*]. pursuing dishonest gain:– greedy of filthy lucre [1], given to filthy lucre [1]

147 αἰσχροκερδῶς, *aischrokerdōs*, adv. GK: *154* [→ *150+2771*]. in greediness for money:– for filthy lucre [1]

148 αἰσχρολογία, *aischrologia*, n. GK: *155* [→ *150+3004*]. filthy language, vulgar speech:– filthy communication [1]

149 αἰσχρόν, *aischron*, a.neut. of *150*. GK: *156* [→ *150*]. disgraceful, shameful:– shame [3]

150 αἰσχρός, *aischros*, a. GK: *156* [→ *146, 147, 148, 149, 151, 152, 153, 422, 1870, 2617*]. disgraceful, shameful:– filthy [1]

151 αἰσχρότης, *aischrotēs*, n. GK: *157* [→ *150*]. obscenity:– filthiness [1]

152 αἰσχύνη, *aischynē*, n. GK: *158* [→ *150*]. shamefulness:– shame [5], dishonesty [1]

153 αἰσχύνομαι, *aischynomai*, v. GK: *159* [→ *150*]. to be ashamed:– ashamed [5]

154 αἰτέω, *aiteō*, v. GK: *160* [→ *155, 523, 1809, 1871, 3868, 4319*]. to ask, ask for (of other humans or God), demand:– ask [38], desired [10], asketh [5], desire [5], asked [3], begged [2], desiring [2], asked for [1], askest [1], called for [1], craved [1], require [1], requiring [1]

155 αἴτημα, *aitēma*, n. GK: *161* [→ *154*]. request:– petitions [1], requests [1], required [1]

156 αἰτία, *aitia*, n. GK: *162* [→ *157, 158, 159, 338, 4256*]. (legal) charge; reason, cause:– cause [9], accusation [3], fault [3], wherefore (+*1223+3739*) [3], case [1], crimes [1]

157 αἰτίαμα, *aitiama*, n. GK: *163 & 166* [→ *156*]. charge, complaint:– complaints [1]

158 αἴτιον, *aition*, a.neut. of *159*. GK: *165* [→ *156*]. basis, reason or cause (for legal charges), source:– cause [2], fault [2]

159 αἴτιος, *aitios*, a. GK: *165* [→ *156*]. basis, reason or cause (for legal charges), source:– author [1]

160 αἰφνίδιος, *aiphnidios*, a. GK: *167* [→ *869?, 1810, 1819*]. sudden, unexpected:– sudden [1], unawares [1]

161 αἰχμαλωσία, *aichmalōsia*, n. GK: *168* [→ *164*]. captivity:– captivity [3]

162 αἰχμαλωτεύω, *aichmalōteuō*, v. GK: *169* [→ *164*]. to take captive:– lead captive [1], led captive [1]

163 αἰχμαλωτίζω, *aichmalōtizō*, v. GK: *170* [→ *164*]. to take captive, take prisoner:– bringing into captivity [2], led away captive [1]

164 αἰχμάλωτος, *aichmalōtos*, a. GK: *171* [→ *161, 162, 163, 4869; cf. 259*]. prisoner:– captives [1]

165 αἰών, *aiōn*, n. GK: *172* [→ *166*]. eternity, age (time period); "this age" can mean the universe or even the current world system, the "god of this age" refers to the devil:– ever [68], world [35], never (+*1519+3361+3588+3756*) [5], ages [2], eternal [2], ever (+*1519+3588*) [2], evermore (+*165*) [2], evermore [2], world without end (+*165+3588+3588*) [2], worlds [2], beginning of the world [1], course [1], ever (+*1519+3588+3956*) [1], ever (+*2250*) [1], never (+*1487+1519+3588+3756*) [1], never (+*1519+3588+3756*) [1]

166 αἰώνιος, *aiōnios*, a. GK: *173* [→ *165*]. eternal, long ago:– eternal [42], everlasting [25], world began (+*5550*) [2], for ever [1], since world began (+*5550*) [1]

167 ἀκαθαρσία, **akatharsia**, n. GK: *174* [→ *1.1+2513*]. impurity, a state of moral filthiness, especially in relation to sexual sin:– uncleanness [10]

168 ἀκαθάρτης, **akathartēs**, n. GK: *175* [→ *1.1+2513*]. uncleanness:– filthiness [1]

169 ἀκάθαρτος, **akathartos**, a. GK: *176* [→ *1.1+2513*]. unclean, evil:– unclean [28], foul [2]

170 ἀκαιρέομαι, **akaireomai**, v. GK: *177* [→ *1.1+2540*]. to have no opportunity, have no time:– lacked opportunity [1]

171 ἀκαίρως, **akairōs**, adv. GK: *178* [→ *1.1+2540*]. out of season, lack of a favorable opportunity:– out of season [1]

172 ἄκακος, **akakos**, a. GK: *179* [→ *1.1+2556*]. blameless, innocent, unsuspecting:– harmless [1], simple [1]

173 ἄκανθα, **akantha**, n. GK: *180* [→ *206*]. thorn, thornbush:– thorns [14]

174 ἀκάνθινος, **akanthinos**, a. GK: *181* [→ *206*]. of thorns, thorny:– of thorns [2]

175 ἄκαρπος, **akarpos**, a. GK: *182* [→ *1.1+2590*]. unfruitful, unproductive, something generally useless:– unfruitful [6], without fruit [1]

176 ἀκατάγνωστος, **akatagnōstos**, a. GK: *183* [→ *1.1+2596+1097*]. not condemned, what cannot be criticized:– cannot be condemned [1]

177 ἀκατακάλυπτος, **akatakalyptos**, a. GK: *184* [→ *1.1+2596+2572*]. uncovered:– uncovered [2]

178 ἀκατάκριτος, **akatakritos**, a. GK: *185* [→ *1.1+2596+2919*]. uncondemned, without a proper trial:– uncondemned [2]

179 ἀκατάλυτος, **akatalytos**, a. GK: *186* [→ *1.1+2596+3089*]. indestructible, unstoppable:– endless [1]

180 ἀκατάπαυστος, **akatapaustos**, a. GK: *187 & 188* [→ *1.1+2596+3973*]. never stopping:– cannot cease from [1]

181 ἀκαταστασία, **akatastasia**, n. GK: *189* [→ *1.1+2596+2476*]. disorder, rebellion, riot:– confusion [2], tumults [2], commotions [1]

182 ἀκατάστατος, **akatastatos**, a. GK: *190* [→ *1.1+2596+2476*]. unstable, restless:– unstable [1]

183 ἀκατάσχετος, **akataschetos**, a. GK: *191* [→ *1.1+2596+2192*]. uncontrollable:– unruly [1]

184 Ἀκελδαμάχ, **Hakeldamach**, n.pr. GK: *192*. Akeldama (traditionally located south of the valley of Hinnom), "*field of blood*":– Aceldama [1]

185 ἀκέραιος, **akeraios**, a. GK: *193* [→ *1.1+2767*]. innocent, pure, not mixed with evil:– harmless [2], simple [1]

186 ἀκλινής, **aklinēs**, a. GK: *195* [→ *1.1+2827*]. unswerving, without wavering:– without wavering [1]

187 ἀκμάζω, **akmazō**, v. GK: *196* [→ *206*]. to be or become ripe:– fully ripe [1]

188 ἀκμήν, **akmēn**, adv. GK: *197* [→ *206*]. still, even yet:– yet [1]

189 ἀκοή, **akoē**, n. GK: *198* [→ *191*]. (act of) hearing, what is heard:– hearing [10], ears [4], fame [3], report [2], rumours [2], audience [1], heard [1], preached [1]

190 ἀκολουθέω, **akoloutheō**, v. GK: *199* [→ *1.3, 1811, 1872, 2628, 3877, 4870*]. to follow; accompany; fig., to follow or be a disciple of a leader's teaching:– followed [53], follow [30], followeth [5], following [3], reached [1]

191 ἀκούω, **akouō**, v. GK: *201* [→ *189, 1251, 1522, 1873, 3876, 3878, 4257, 5218, 5219, 5255*]. to hear, pay attention, understand, obey:– heard [239], hear [141], heareth [23], hearing [13], hearken [6], hearest [4], gave audience [2], hearers [2], came [1], come to ears (+*1909*) [1], give audience [1], in audience [1], noised [1], reported [1], understandeth [1]

192 ἀκρασία, **akrasia**, n. GK: *202* [→ *1.1+2904*]. lack of self-control:– excess [1], incontinency [1]

193 ἀκρατής, **akratēs**, a. GK: *203* [→ *1.1+2904*]. without self-control:– incontinent [1]

194 ἄκρατος, **akratos**, a. GK: *204* [→ *1.1+2767*]. undiluted (of wine not watered down):– without mixture [1]

195 ἀκρίβεια, **akribeia**, n. GK: *205* [→ *198*]. thoroughness, strictness:– perfect manner [1]

196 ἀκριβέστατος, **akribestatos**, a.super. GK: *206* [→ *198*]. strictest:– most straitest [1]

197 ἀκριβέστερον, **akribesteron**, a.compar. GK: *206* [→ *198*]. more strict:– more perfectly [3], more perfect [1]

198 ἀκριβόω, **akriboō**, v. GK: *208* [→ *195, 196, 197, 199*]. to find out exactly:– diligently inquired [1], inquired diligently [1]

199 ἀκριβῶς, **akribōs**, adv. GK: *209* [→ *198*]. accurately, carefully, well:– diligently [2], circumspectly [1], perfectly [1], perfect [1]

200 ἀκρίς, **akris**, n. GK: *210*. locust (in some cultures distinguished from a grasshopper and used as a food source):– locusts [4]

201 ἀκροατήριον, **akroatērion**, n. GK: *211* [→ *202*]. audience room (of the procurator), in which hearings were held and justice was privately dispensed:– place of hearing [1]

202 ἀκροατής, **akroatēs**, n. GK: *212* [→ *201, 1874*]. hearer:– hearers [2], hearer [2]

203 ἀκροβυστία, **akrobystia**, n. GK: *213* [→ *206*]. uncircumcision, foreskin; fig., not of the Mosaic covenant, a Gentile:– uncircumcision [16], not circumcised [1], uncircumcised (+*1722*) [1], uncircumcised (+*2192*) [1], uncircumcised [1]

204 ἀκρογωνιαῖος, **akrogōniaios**, a. GK: *214* [→ *206+1137*]. cornerstone, an essential stone in the construction of a building:– chief corner [2]

205 ἀκροθίνιον, **akrothinion**, n. GK: *215* [→ *206*]. plunder, booty, fine spoils:– spoils [1]

206 ἄκρον, **akron**, n. GK: *216* [→ *173, 174, 187, 188, 203, 204, 205, 891, 5230*]. end, top:– uttermost part [2], end [1], other^S [1], tip [1], top [1]

207 Ἀκύλας, **Akylas**, n.pr. GK: *217*. Aquila, "*eagle*":– Aquila [6]

208 ἀκυρόω, **akyroō**, v. GK: *218* [→ *1.1+2964*]. to nullify, make void:– disannul [1], made of none effect [1], making of none effect [1]

209 ἀκωλύτως, **akōlytōs**, adv. GK: *219* [→ *1.1+2967*]. without hinderance:– no forbidding [1]

210 ἄκων, **akōn**, a. GK: *220* [→ *1.1+1635*]. not voluntary, unwilling:– against will [1]

211 ἀλάβαστρος, **alabastros**, n. GK: *222 & 223*. alabaster jar; a long-necked flask, the top of which was broken off to empty its contents:– alabaster box [3], box [1]

212 ἀλαζονεία, **alazoneia**, n. GK: *224* [→ *213, 214*]. boasting, pretension, arrogance:– boastings [1], pride [1]

213 ἀλαζών, **alazōn**, n. GK: *225* [→ *212*]. boaster, braggart:– boasters [2]

214 ἀλαλάζω, **alalazō**, v. GK: *226* [→ *212*]. to clang, wail:– tinkling [1], wailed [1]

215 ἀλάλητος, **alalētos**, a. GK: *227* [→ *1.1+2980*]. inexpressible, unspeakable:– cannot be uttered [1]

216 ἄλαλος, **alalos**, a. GK: *228* [→ *1.1+2980*]. mute, unable to speak:– dumb [3]

217 ἅλας, **halas**, n. GK: *221 & 229* [→ *123, 231, 232, 233, 251, 252, 358, 1724, 3882; cf. 2281*]. salt; the impure salt of the ancient could become tasteless in adverse conditions, and its residue useless:– salt [8]

218 ἀλείφω, **aleiphō**, v. GK: *230* [→ *1813*]. to pour on, anoint (usually with olive oil):– anointed [5], anoint [3], anointing [1]

219 ἀλεκτοροφωνία, **alektorophōnia**, n. GK: *231* [→ *220+5456*]. crowing of a rooster; the third Roman watch of the night (about midnight to 3:00 a.m.):– cockcrowing [1]

220 ἀλέκτωρ, **alektōr**, n. GK: *232* [→ *219*]. rooster:– cock [12]

221 Ἀλεξανδρεύς, **Alexandreus**, n.pr.g. GK: *233* [→ *223*]. Alexandrian, person of Alexandria:– Alexandrians [1], at Alexandria [1]

222 Ἀλεξανδρῖνος, **Alexandrinos**, a.pr.g. GK: *234* [→ *223*]. Alexandrian, of Alexandria:– Alexandria [2]

223 Ἀλέξανδρος, **Alexandros**, n.pr. GK: *235* [→ *221, 222*]. Alexander, "*defender of men*":– Alexander [6]

224 ἄλευρον, **aleuron**, n. GK: *236* [→ *229*]. flour:– meal [2]

225 ἀλήθεια, **alētheia**, n. GK: *237* [→ *1.1+2990*]. truth, truthfulness; corresponding to reality:– truth [103], of a truth (+*1909*) [3], true [1], truly (+*1909*) [1], truth's [1], verity [1]

226 ἀληθεύω, **alētheuō**, v. GK: *238* [→ *1.1+2990*]. to be truthful, tell the truth:– speaking the truth [1], tell the truth [1]

227 ἀληθής, **alēthēs**, a. GK: *239* [→ *1.1+2990*]. true, genuine, reliable, trustworthy, valid:– true [23], truly [1], truth [1]

228 ἀληθινός, **alēthinos**, a. GK: *240* [→ *1.1+2990*]. true, genuine:– true [27]

229 ἀλήθω, **alēthō**, v. GK: *241* [→ *224*]. to grind grain (with a handmill operated by two women):– grinding [2]

230 ἀληθῶς, **alēthōs**, adv. GK: *242* [→ *1.1+2990*]. truly, surely:– indeed [6], of a truth [6], surely [3], truly [2], in truth [1], of a surety [1], verily [1], very [1]

231 ἁλιεύς, **halieus**, n. GK: *243* [→ *217*]. fisherman (by occupation):– fishers [4], fishermen [1]

232 ἁλιεύω, **halieuō**, v. GK: *244* [→ *217*]. to catch fish, either by net or by line:– fishing [1]

233 ἁλίζω, **halizō**, v. GK: *245* [→ *217*]. to salt, make salty:– salted [3]

234 ἀλίσγημα, **alisgēma**, n. GK: *246*. pollution, ritually defiled:– pollutions [1]

235 ἀλλά, **alla**, pt.adver. GK: *247* [→ *243*]. but, instead, yet, except:– but [573], yea [15], yet [11], nevertheless [10], howbeit [8], nay [4], therefore [3], and [2], save [2], also (+*2532*) [1], and (+*1065*) [1], howbeit (+*3303*) [1], moreover (+*2532*) [1], not so much as (+*3761*) [1], notwithstanding [1], no [1], than (+*2228*) [1], yet doubtless (+*1065*) [1]

236 ἀλλάσσω, **allassō**, v. GK: *248* [→ *465, 525, 604, 1259, 2643, 2644, 3337, 3883; cf. 243*]. to change, exchange:– changed [4], change [2]

237 ἀλλαχόθεν, **allachothen**, adv.pl. GK: *249* [→ *243*]. from another way:– some other way [1]

238 ἀλληγορέω, **allēgoreō**, v. GK: *251* [→ *243+59*]. to take figuratively, speak allegorically, to employ an analogy or likeness in communication:– allegory [1]

239 ἀλληλουϊά, **hallēlouia**, l.[v.+n.pr.]. GK: *252*. hallelujah; from Hebrew hallelu-yah, praise Yah(weh):– alleluia [4]

240 ἀλλήλων, **allēlōn**, p.recip. GK: *253* [→ *243*]. one another, each other:– one another [74], themselves [12], yourselves [3], each other [2], one another's [2], one the other [2], mutual [1], one to the other [1], together (+*3326*) [1], together (+*4314*) [1], yourselves together [1]

241 ἀλλογενής, **allogenēs**, a. GK: *254* [→ *243+1096*]. foreign:– stranger [1]

242 ἅλλομαι, **hallomai**, v. GK: *256* [→ *1814, 2177; cf. 4531*]. to jump up, well up, quick movement of both humans and water:– leaped [1], leaping [1], springing up [1]

243 ἄλλος, **allos**, a.&n. GK: *257* [→ *235, 237, 238, 240, 241, 244, 245, 246, 247, 526; cf. 236*]. another, other:– another [61], other [52], others [29], some [10], one [4], another (+*5100*) [1], moe [1], otherwise [1], some (+*3303*) [1]

244 ἀλλοτριεπίσκοπος, **allotriepiskopos**, n. GK: *258* [→ *243+1909+4648*]. meddler, busybody; formally rendered "one who oversees what belongs to another" (in an unwarranted manner):– busybody in other men's matters [1]

245 ἀλλότριος, **allotrios**, a. GK: *259* [→ *243*]. belonging to another:– another [4], strangers [3], other [2], strange [2], aliens [1], others [1], stranger [1]

246 ἀλλόφυλος, **allophylos**, a. GK: *260* [→ *243+5443*]. Gentile, foreigner:– one of another nation [1]

247 ἄλλως, **allōs**, adv. GK: *261* [→ *243*]. differently:– otherwise [1]

248 ἀλοάω, **aloaō**, v. GK: *262* [→ *257, 3389, 3964*]. to tread, thresh, to separate grain kernels from the husks by beating or treading on:– treadeth out the corn [2], thresheth [1]

249 ἄλογος, **alogos**, a. GK: *263* [→ *1.1+3004*]. unreasonable, without reason, brutish and living by instinct:– brute [2], unreasonable [1]

250 ἀλόη, **aloē**, n. GK: *264*. aloes:– aloes [1]

251 ἅλς, **hals**, n. GK: *265* [→ *217*]. salt:– salt [1]

252 ἁλυκός, **halykos**, a. GK: *266* [→ *217*]. salt spring, salty:– salt [1]

253 ἄλυπος, **alypos**, a. GK: *267* [→ *1.1+3077*]. free from anxiety; in the comparative, less anxiety:– less sorrowful [1]

254 ἅλυσις, **halysis**, n. GK: *268*. chain (the state of imprisonment):– chains [7], chain [3], bonds [1]

255 ἀλυσιτελής, *alysitelēs*, a. GK: *269* [→ *1.1+3089+5056*]. unadvantageous, without special benefit:– unprofitable [1]

256 Ἀλφαῖος, *Halphaios*, n.pr. GK: *271*. Alphaeus:– Alpheus [5]

257 ἅλων, *halōn*, n. GK: *272* [→ *248*]. threshing floor:– floor [2]

258 ἀλώπηξ, *alōpēx*, n. GK: *273*. fox; this can refer to a wicked person with the probable implication of being cunning or treacherous:– foxes [2], fox [1]

259 ἅλωσις, *halōsis*, n. GK: *274* [→ *355, 2654, 4321; cf. 164*]. capture, catch:– taken [1]

260 ἅμα, *hama*, adv.&pp.*. GK: *275* [→ *537, 716; cf. 573*]. together, at the same time:– together [3], withal [3], also (+*2532*) [1], and [1], early in the morning (+*4404*) [1], with [1]

261 ἀμαθής, *amathēs*, a. GK: *276* [→ *1.1+3129*]. ignorant, without a formal education:– unlearned [1]

262 ἀμαράντινος, *amarantinos*, a. GK: *277* [→ *1.1+3133*]. unfading, without loss of pristine character:– fadeth not away [1]

263 ἀμάραντος, *amarantos*, a. GK: *278* [→ *1.1+3133*]. never fading:– fadeth not away [1]

264 ἁμαρτάνω, *hamartanō*, v. GK: *279* [→ *265, 266, 268, 361, 4258*]. to sin, do wrong; usually to do any act contrary to the will and law of God:– sin [16], sinned [15], sinneth [7], trespass [3], faults [1], offended [1]

265 ἁμάρτημα, *hamartēma*, n. GK: *280* [→ *264*]. sin, wrongdoing; usually any act contrary to the will and law of God:– sins [3], sin [1]

266 ἁμαρτία, *hamartia*, n. GK: *281* [→ *264*]. sin, wrongdoing; usually any act contrary to the will and law of God:– sin [94], sins [78], offence [1], sinful [1]

267 ἀμάρτυρος, *amartyros*, a. GK: *282* [→ *1.1+3144*]. without testimony, without witness:– without witness [1]

268 ἁμαρτωλός, *hamartōlos*, a. GK: *283* [→ *264*]. (a.) sinful, as an absolute moral failure; (n.) sinner, one who violates God's will or law; in some contexts, one who does not keep orthodox traditions and behaviors:– sinners [31], sinner [12], sinful [4]

269 ἄμαχος, *amachos*, a. GK: *285* [→ *1.1+3163*]. peaceable, not quarrelsome, without conflict:– no brawlers [1], not a brawler [1]

270 ἀμάω, *amaō*, v. GK: *286*. to mow, cut down:– reaped [1]

271 ἀμέθυστος, *amethystos*, n. GK: *287* [→ *1.3?+3184*]. amethyst, usually purple or violet in color:– amethyst [1]

272 ἀμελέω, *ameleō*, v. GK: *288* [→ *1.1+3199*]. to neglect, ignore:– neglect [2], made light of [1], negligent [1], regarded not [1]

273 ἄμεμπτος, *amemptos*, a. GK: *289* [→ *1.1+3201*]. blameless, faultless:– blameless [3], faultless [1], unblameable [1]

274 ἀμέμπτως, *amemptōs*, adv. GK: *290* [→ *1.1+3201*]. blamelessly:– blameless [1], unblameably [1]

275 ἀμέριμνος, *amerimnos*, a. GK: *291* [→ *1.1+3308*]. free from concern, free from care:– secure (+*4160*) [1], without carefulness [1]

276 ἀμετάθετος, *ametathetos*, a. GK: *292* [→ *1.1+3326+5087*]. unchangeable, unchanging:– immutability [1], immutable [1]

277 ἀμετακίνητος, *ametakinētos*, a. GK: *293* [→ *1.1+3326+2795*]. not moveable, immovable:– unmoveable [1]

278 ἀμεταμέλητος, *ametamelētos*, a. GK: *294* [→ *1.1+3326+3199*]. without regret, so, not revocable:– not repented of [1], without repentance [1]

279 ἀμετανόητος, *ametanoētos*, a. GK: *295* [→ *1.1+3326+3563*]. unrepentant:– impenitent [1]

280 ἄμετρος, *ametros*, a. GK: *296* [→ *1.1+3358*]. beyond limits, immeasurable:– without measure [2]

281 ἀμήν, *amēn*, l.[adv.]. GK: *297*. amen, the truth; a formula of solemn expression of certainty. In the Gospel of John it is doubled in the sayings of Jesus for emphasis:– verily [101], amen [51]

282 ἀμήτωρ, *amētōr*, a. GK: *298* [→ *1.1+3384*]. without a mother:– without mother [1]

283 ἀμίαντος, *amiantos*, a. GK: *299* [→ *1.1+3392*]. pure:– undefiled [4]

284 Ἀμιναδάβ, *Aminadab*, n.pr. GK: *300*. Amminadab, "*my people are generous*":– Aminadab [3]

285 ἄμμος, *ammos*, n. GK: *302*. sand, often used as a figure of things that cannot be counted:– sand [5]

286 ἀμνός, *amnos*, n. GK: *303*. lamb:– lamb [4]

287 ἀμοιβή, *amoibē*, n. GK: *304*. repayment, recompense:– requite (+*591*) [1]

288 ἄμπελος, *ampelos*, n. GK: *306* [→ *289, 290*]. vine, grapevine:– vine [9]

289 ἀμπελουργός, *ampelourgos*, n. GK: *307* [→ *288+2041*]. one who takes care of a vineyard:– dresser of vineyard [1]

290 ἀμπελών, *ampelōn*, n. GK: *308* [→ *288*]. vineyard:– vineyard [23]

291 Ἀμπλίας, *Amplias*, n.pr. GK: *309*. Amplias:– Amplias [1]

292 ἀμύνομαι, *amynomai*, v. GK: *310*. to defend, help, come to the aid of:– defended [1]

293 ἀμφίβληστρον, *amphiblēstron*, n. GK: *312* [→ *906*]. casting net, fishing net (not a dragnet):– net [2]

294 ἀμφιέννυμι, *amphiennymi*, v. GK: *313 & 314* [cf. *2439*]. to dress, clothe:– clothed [2], clothe [2]

295 Ἀμφίπολις, *Amphipolis*, n.pr. GK: *315* [→ *4172*]. Amphipolis, "*a city surrounded* or *a city conspicuous*":– Amphipolis [1]

296 ἄμφοδον, *amphodon*, n. GK: *316* [→ *3598*]. street, usually within a city:– place where two ways met [1]

297 ἀμφότερος, *amphoteros*, a. GK: *317*. both, all:– both [14]

298 ἀμώμητος, *amōmētos*, a. GK: *318* [→ *1.1+3201*]. blameless, unblemished:– blameless [1], without rebuke [1]

299 ἄμωμος, *amōmos*, a. GK: *320* [→ *1.1+3201*]. unblemished, blameless:– without blemish [2], faultless [1], unblameable [1], without blame [1], without fault [1], without spot [1]

300 Ἀμών, *Amōn*, n.pr. GK: *321*. Amon, "*trustworthy*":– Amon [2]

301 Ἀμώς, *Amōs*, n.pr. GK: *322*. Amos, "*burden bearer*":– Amos [1]

302 ἄν, *an*, pt. GK: *323* [→ *1437, 1875, 2579, 3752*]. not easily translated: indicates potential or condition:– whosoever (+*3739*) [32], till (+*2193*) [16], would have [15], would [8], should [7], whatsoever (+*3739*) [7], whatsoever (+*3745*) [6], until (+*2193*) [5], had [4], should have [4], whithersoever (+*3699*) [4], whomsoever (+*3739*) [4], as many as (+*3745*) [3], might [3], soever [3], that (+*3704*) [3], what (+*5101*) [3], whatsoever (+*3739+5100*) [3], whom (+*3739*) [3], whoso (+*3739*) [3], whosoever (+*3739+3956*) [3], whosoever (+*3748*) [3], as (+*5613*) [2], whatsoever (+*302+3739+5100*) [2], when (+*2259*) [2], wheresoever (+*3699*) [2], whosoever (+*3745*) [2], as (+*2530*) [1], as (+*3739+5100*) [1], as oft as (+*3740*) [1], as often as (+*3740*) [1], except (+*1509*) [1], he that (+*3739*) [1], how (+*1063+4459*) [1], howbeit whereinsoever (+*1161+1722+3739*) [1], if [1], may [1], might have [1], once (+*575+3739*) [1], so soon as (+*5613*) [1], soever (+*3739*) [1], that (+*3739*) [1], till (+*891+3739*) [1], whatsoever (+*3748*) [1], when (+*3704*) [1], when (+*5613*) [1], whereunto (+*5101*) [1], wherewith soever (+*3745*) [1], which (+*3748*) [1], which (+*5101*) [1], who (+*5101*) [1], would (+*2172*) [1], wouldest have [1]

303 ἀνά, *ana*, pp. GK: *324* [→ *306, 308, 309, 310, 311, 508, 312, 313, 314, 319, 320, 321, 322, 323, 324, 325, 326, 327, 328, 329, 330, 331, 333, 336, 337, 339, 340, 341, 342, 343, 344, 345, 346, 347, 348, 349, 350, 351, 352, 353, 354, 355, 356, 357, 359, 360, 362, 363, 364, 365, 366, 372, 373, 374, 376, 375, 377, 378, 380, 381, 383, 384, 385, 386, 387, 388, 389, 390, 391, 392, 394, 396, 397, 398, 399, 400, 401, 402, 403, 404, 414, 420, 424, 425, 429, 430, 433, 447, 450, 456, 461, 463, 466, 1815, 1817, 1877, 1878, 1879, 1880, 1881, 1882, 2654, 4320, 4321, 4322, 4323, 4872, 4873, 4874, 4875, cf. 395, 426, 455, 507*]. each, in turn, among:– by [3], apiece [2], every man [2], among (+*3319*) [1], between (+*3319*) [1], by course (+*3313*) [1], in [1], several (+*1520*) [1], through [1]

304 ἀναβαθμός, *anabathmos*, n. GK: *325* [→ *305*]. step; (pl.) a flight of steps:– stairs [2]

305 ἀναβαίνω, *anabainō*, v. GK: *326* [→ *304, 307, 531, 576, 898, 939, 949, 950, 951, 952, 953, 968, 1041, 1224,* 1226, 1545, 1684, 1687, 1688, 1910, 1913, 2597, 2600, 2601, 3327, 3845, 3847, 3848, 4260, 4262, 4263, 4264, 4320, 4782, 4819, 4822, 4872, 5233]. to go up, rise:– went up [23], go up [9], come up [7], ascended up [5], ascended [4], ascend [3], ascending [2], coming up [2], entered [2], going up [2], gone up [2], arise [1], arose [1], ascend up [1], ascendeth up [1], ascending up [1], came unto [1], came up [1], came [1], climbed up [1], climbeth up [1], cometh up [1], goeth up [1], grew up [1], groweth up [1], rise up [1], rose up [1], sprang up [1], sprung up [1], went upon [1]

306 ἀναβάλλω, *anaballō*, v. GK: *327* [→ *303+906*]. to adjourn a proceeding (a legal term):– deferred [1]

307 ἀναβιβάζω, *anabibazō*, v. GK: *328* [→ *305*]. to pull up, bring up:– drew [1]

308 ἀναβλέπω, *anablepō*, v. GK: *329* [→ *303+991*]. to look up, receive sight:– received sight [8], receive sight [7], looked up [5], looking up [3], look up [1], looked [1], see [1]

309 ἀνάβλεψις, *anablepsis*, n. GK: *330* [→ *303+991*]. recovery of sight:– recovering of sight [1]

310 ἀναβοάω, *anaboaō*, v. GK: *331* [→ *303+995*]. to cry out:– cried out [1], cried [1], crying aloud [1]

311 ἀναβολή, *anabolē*, n. GK: *332* [→ *303+906*]. delay, postponement:– delay (+*4160*) [1]

312 ἀναγγέλλω, *anangellō*, v. GK: *334* [→ *303+32*]. to tell, report, announce:– shew [4], told [4], declare [2], shewed [2], tell [2], declared [1], rehearsed [1], reported [1], spoken [1]

313 ἀναγεννάω, *anagennaō*, v. GK: *335* [→ *303+1096*]. to give new birth, cause to be born again; used in the sense of spiritual rebirth, similar to being born again/from above:– begotten again [1], born again [1]

314 ἀναγινώσκω, *anaginōskō*, v. GK: *336* [→ *303+1097*]. to read, read aloud:– read [28], readeth [3], readest [2]

315 ἀναγκάζω, *anankazō*, v. GK: *337* [→ *318*]. to compel, force:– compelled [3], constrained [3], compellest [1], compel [1], constrain [1]

316 ἀναγκαῖος, *anankaios*, a. GK: *338* [→ *318*]. necessary, indispensable:– necessary [5], more needful [1], near [1], necessity [1]

317 ἀναγκαστῶς, *anankastōs*, adv. GK: *339* [→ *318*]. a must, by compulsion:– by constraint [1]

318 ἀνάγκη, *anankē*, n. GK: *340* [→ *315, 316, 317, 1876*]. necessity; distress, hardship:– necessity [7], distress [3], must needs [2], necessities [2], necessary [1], needeth (+*2250*) [1], needful (+*2192*) [1], needs [1]

319 ἀναγνωρίζω, *anagnōrizō*, v. GK: *341* [→ *303+1097*]. to tell, make known again:– made known [1]

320 ἀνάγνωσις, *anagnōsis*, n. GK: *342* [→ *303+1097*]. reading, public reading:– reading [3]

321 ἀνάγω, *anagō*, v. GK: *343* [→ *303+71*]. to lead up, bring up; (mid.) to put out to sea:– brought [3], launched [3], departed [2], loosed [2], sailed [2], bring forth [1], bring up again [1], brought again [1], depart [1], launched forth [1], led up [1], led [1], loosing [1], offered [1], sail [1], set forth [1], taking up [1]

322 ἀναδείκνυμι, *anadeiknymi*, v. GK: *344* [→ *303+1166*]. to show, appoint:– appointed [1], shew [1]

323 ἀνάδειξις, *anadeixis*, n. GK: *345* [→ *303+1166*]. public appearance:– shewing [1]

324 ἀναδέχομαι, *anadechomai*, v. GK: *346* [→ *303+1209*]. to receive, welcome:– received [2]

325 ἀναδίδωμι, *anadidōmi*, v. GK: *347* [→ *303+1325*]. to deliver, hand over:– delivered [1]

326 ἀναζάω, *anazaō*, v. GK: *348* [→ *303+2198*]. to become alive again:– alive again [2], revived [2], lived again [1]

327 ἀναζητέω, *anazēteō*, v. GK: *349* [→ *303+2212*]. to look for, search for:– seek [1], sought [1]

328 ἀναζώννυμι, *anazōnnymi*, v. GK: *350* [→ *303+2224*]. to gird (the loins), bind (to prepare for action); used fig. of "girding the loins of the mind" (1Pe 1:13) to prepare mentally for action:– gird up [1]

329 ἀναζωπυρέω, *anazōpyreō*, v. GK: *351* [→ *303+2198+4442*]. to fan a flame, rekindle:– stir up [1]

330 ἀναθάλλω, *anathallō*, v. GK: *352* [→ *303+2337*]. to renew, cause to grow or bloom again:– flourished again [1]

331 ἀνάθεμα, **anathema**, n. GK: *353* [→ *332, 334, 2652, 2653*]. curse, oath; one cursed:– accursed [4], anathema [1], bound under a great curse (+*332*) [1]

332 ἀναθεματίζω, **anathematizō**, v. GK: *354* [→ *331*]. to bind with an oath:– bound under a curse [1], bound under a great curse (+*331*) [1], bound with an oath [1], curse [1]

333 ἀναθεωρέω, **anatheōreō**, v. GK: *355* [→ *303*+*2334*]. to look carefully at:– beheld [1], considering [1]

334 ἀνάθημα, **anathēma**, n. GK: *356* [→ *331*]. gifts dedicated to God, devoted exclusively to the service of deity:– gifts [1]

335 ἀναίδεια, **anaideia**, n. GK: *357* [→ *1.1*+*127*]. boldness:– importunity [1]

336 ἀναίρεσις, **anairesis**, n. GK: *358* [→ *303*+*138*]. death:– death [2]

337 ἀναιρέω, **anaireō**, v. GK: *359* [→ *303*+*138*]. to kill, put to death; (mid.) take for oneself:– kill [6], killed [4], slain [3], slew [3], put to death [2], slay [2], didst [1], taketh away [1], took up [1]

338 ἀναίτιος, **anaitios**, a. GK: *360* [→ *1.1*+*156*]. innocent:– blameless [1], guiltless [1]

339 ἀνακαθίζω, **anakathizō**, v. GK: *361* [→ *303*+*2523*]. to sit up (from a reclining or lying position):– sat up [2]

340 ἀνακαινίζω, **anakainizō**, v. GK: *362* [→ *303*+*2537*]. to bring back, restore:– renew [1]

341 ἀνακαινόω, **anakainoō**, v. GK: *363* [→ *303*+*2537*]. to renew:– renewed [2]

342 ἀνακαίνωσις, **anakainōsis**, n. GK: *364* [→ *303*+*2537*]. renewal:– renewing [2]

343 ἀνακαλύπτω, **anakalyptō**, v. GK: *365* [→ *303*+*2572*]. to unveil, uncover:– open [1], untaken away (+*3361*) [1]

344 ἀνακάμπτω, **anakamptō**, v. GK: *366* [→ *303*+*2578*]. to return, come back:– return [2], returned [1], turn again [1]

345 ἀνάκειμαι, **anakeimai**, v. GK: *367* [→ *303*+*2749*]. to recline for a meal, dine (reclining was the normal posture at meals):– sat at meat [4], guests [2], sitteth at meat [2], leaning [1], lying [1], sat down [1], sat [1], set down [1], table [1]

346 ἀνακεφαλαιόω, **anakephalaioō**, v. GK: *368* [→ *303*+*2776*]. to bring together under one head, summarize:– briefly comprehended [1], gather together in one [1]

347 ἀνακλίνω, **anaklinō**, v. GK: *369* [→ *303*+*2827*]. to cause to lie down, recline (to eat):– sit down [3], laid [1], made sit down [1], make sit down to meat [1], make sit down [1], sat down to meat [1]

348 ἀνακόπτω, **anakoptō**, v. GK: *370* [→ *303*+*2875*]. to hinder, restrain:– hinder [1]

349 ἀνακράζω, **anakrazō**, v. GK: *371* [→ *303*+*2896*]. to cry out:– cried out [5]

350 ἀνακρίνω, **anakrinō**, v. GK: *373* [→ *303*+*2919*]. to examine, judge (in both a general and a legal sense):– examined [4], judged [3], asking question [2], judgeth [2], discerned [1], examine [1], examining [1], judge [1], searched [1]

351 ἀνάκρισις, **anakrisis**, n. GK: *374* [→ *303*+*2919*]. investigation:– examination [1]

352 ἀνακύπτω, **anakyptō**, v. GK: *376* [→ *303*+*2955*]. to straighten up, stand erect:– lift up [3], look up [1]

353 ἀναλαμβάνω, **analambanō**, v. GK: *377* [→ *303*+*2983*]. to take up, lift up, bring up:– received up [3], taken up [3], take in [1], take unto [1], take [1], taking [1], took in [1], took up [1], took [1]

354 ἀνάλημψις, **analēmpsis**, n. GK: *378* [→ *303*+*2983*]. taking up, ascension:– received up [1]

355 ἀναλίσκω, **analiskō**, v. GK: *379* & *384* [→ *303*+*259*]. to destroy, consume (with a possible implication of being used up):– consume [2], consumed [1]

356 ἀναλογία, **analogia**, n. GK: *381* [→ *303*+*3004*]. proportion, right relationship:– proportion [1]

357 ἀναλογίζομαι, **analogizomai**, v. GK: *382* [→ *303*+*3004*]. to consider, think carefully:– consider [1]

358 ἄναλος, **analos**, a. GK: *383* [→ *1.1*+*217*]. not salty:– lost saltness [1]

359 ἀνάλυσις, **analysis**, n. GK: *385* [→ *303*+*3089*]. departure (death):– departure [1]

360 ἀναλύω, **analyō**, v. GK: *386* [→ *303*+*3089*]. to depart (die), return:– depart [1], return [1]

361 ἀναμάρτητος, **anamartētos**, a. GK: *387* [→ *1.1*+*264*]. without sin:– without sin [1]

362 ἀναμένω, **anamenō**, v. GK: *388* [→ *303*+*3306*]. to wait for, expect:– wait for [1]

363 ἀναμιμνῄσκω, **anamimnēskō**, v. GK: *389* [→ *303*+*3421*]. to remember, remind:– bring into remembrance [1], call to remembrance [1], called to mind [1], calling to remembrance [1], put in remembrance [1], remembereth [1]

364 ἀνάμνησις, **anamnēsis**, n. GK: *390* [→ *303*+*3421*]. reminder, remembrance:– remembrance [4]

365 ἀνανεόομαι, **ananeoomai**, v. GK: *391* [→ *303*+*3501*]. to be made new, renewed:– renewed [1]

366 ἀνανήφω, **ananēphō**, v. GK: *392* [→ *303*+*3525*]. to come to one's senses:– recover [1]

367 Ἀνανίας, **Hananias**, n.pr. GK: *393*. Ananias, "*Yahweh is gracious*":– Ananias [11]

368 ἀναντίρρητος, **anantirrētos**, a. GK: *394* [→ *1.1*+*473*+*4487*]. undeniable, indisputable:– cannot be spoken against [1]

369 ἀναντιρρήτως, **anantirrētōs**, adv. GK: *395* [→ *1.1*+*473*+*4487*]. without raising any objection, indisputable:– without gainsaying [1]

370 ἀνάξιος, **anaxios**, a. GK: *396* [→ *1.1*+*514*]. not competent, unworthy:– unworthy [1]

371 ἀναξίως, **anaxiōs**, adv. GK: *397* [→ *1.1*+*514*]. in an unworthy manner, possibly in a careless manner:– unworthily [2]

372 ἀνάπαυσις, **anapausis**, n. GK: *398* [→ *303*+*3973*]. rest, resting place:– rest [4], rest (+*2192*) [1]

373 ἀναπαύω, **anapauō**, v. GK: *399* [→ *303*+*3973*]. to rest, be refreshed; (act.) to give rest:– refreshed [3], rest [3], take rest [2], give rest [1], refresh [1], resteth [1], take ease [1]

374 ἀναπείθω, **anapeithō**, v. GK: *400* [→ *303*+*3982*]. to persuade, with an implication of inciting resistance:– persuadeth [1]

375 ἀναπέμπω, **anapempō**, v. GK: *402* [→ *303*+*3992*]. to send:– sent again [2], sent [2]

376 ἀνάπειρος, **anapeiros**, a. GK: *401* [→ *303*]. crippled:– maimed [2]

377 ἀναπίπτω, **anapiptō**, v. GK: *404* [→ *303*+*4098*]. recline, sit down, lie down (usually referring to the normal posture at meals):– sit down [4], sat down [3], leaned [1], sat down to meat [1], set down [1], sit down to meat [1]

378 ἀναπληρόω, **anaplēroō**, v. GK: *405* [→ *303*+*4137*]. to fulfill, make complete:– fill up [1], fulfilled [1], fulfil [1], occupieth [1], supplied [1], supply [1]

379 ἀναπολόγητος, **anapologētos**, a. GK: *406* [→ *1.1*+*575*+*3004*]. without excuse:– inexcusable [1], without excuse [1]

380 ἀναπτύσσω, **anaptyssō**, v. GK: *408* [→ *303*+*4428*]. to unroll (a scroll):– opened [1]

381 ἀνάπτω, **anaptō**, v. GK: *409* [→ *303*+*681*]. to set on fire:– kindled [2], kindleth [1]

382 ἀναρίθμητος, **anarithmētos**, a. GK: *410* [→ *1.1*+*706*]. countless:– innumerable [1]

383 ἀνασείω, **anaseiō**, v. GK: *411* [→ *303*+*4579*]. to stir up, incite:– moved [1], stirreth up [1]

384 ἀνασκευάζω, **anaskeuazō**, v. GK: *412* [→ *303*+*4632*]. to trouble, upset:– subverting [1]

385 ἀνασπάω, **anaspaō**, v. GK: *413* [→ *303*+*4685*]. to pull up, draw out:– drawn up [1], pull out [1]

386 ἀνάστασις, **anastasis**, n. GK: *414* [→ *303*+*2476*]. resurrection, rising to life; from the base meaning of the act of rising from a prone or sitting position to a standing position. In the NT it means returning to life after death, usually referring to the raising to life of Jesus Christ:– resurrection [39], raised to life again (+*1537*) [1], rise [1], rising again [1]

387 ἀναστατόω, **anastatoō**, v. GK: *415* [→ *303*+*2476*]. to cause trouble, start a revolt:– madest an uproar [1], trouble [1], turned upside down [1]

388 ἀνασταυρόω, **anastauroō**, v. GK: *416* [→ *303*+*4716*]. to crucify again:– crucify afresh [1]

389 ἀναστενάζω, **anastenazō**, v. GK: *417* [→ *303*+*4728*]. to sigh deeply:– sighed deeply [1]

390 ἀναστρέφω, **anastrephō**, v. GK: *418* [→ *303*+*4762*]. to conduct oneself, live (in a certain way); to return:– had conversation [2], live [2], abode [1], behave [1], overthrew [1], pass [1], returned [1], return [1], used [1]

391 ἀναστροφή, **anastrophē**, n. GK: *419* [→ *303*+*4762*]. way of life, behavior:– conversation [13]

392 ἀνατάσσομαι, **anatassomai**, v. GK: *421* [→ *303*+*5021*]. to draw up (an account), compile:– set forth in order [1]

393 ἀνατέλλω, **anatellō**, v. GK: *422* [→ *395*]. to rise, dawn:– up [2], arise [1], maketh to rise [1], rise out [1], risen [1], rising [1], sprang [1], sprung up [1]

394 ἀνατίθημι, **anatithēmi**, v. GK: *423* [→ *303*+*5087*]. to set before, declare before:– communicated [1], declared [1]

395 ἀνατολή, **anatolē**, n. GK: *424* [→ *393, 1816, cf. 303*]. east, rising of the sun; note that the east is the compass direction of orientation in the ancient Near East, just as the north is in the modern western world:– east [7], east (+*2246*) [2], dayspring [1]

396 ἀνατρέπω, **anatrepō**, v. GK: *426* [→ *303*+*5157*]. to overturn, destroy:– overthrow [1], subvert [1]

397 ἀνατρέφω, **anatrephō**, v. GK: *427* [→ *303*+*5142*]. to bring up, care for:– brought up [1], nourished up [1], nourished [1]

398 ἀναφαίνω, **anaphainō**, v. GK: *428* [→ *303*+*5316*]. to appear:– appear [1], discovered [1]

399 ἀναφέρω, **anapherō**, v. GK: *429* [→ *303*+*5342*]. to lead up, offer (a sacrifice), bear (sin):– offer up [2], bare [1], bear [1], bringeth up [1], carried up [1], leadeth up [1], offered up [1], offered [1], offer [1]

400 ἀναφωνέω, **anaphōneō**, v. GK: *430* [→ *303*+*5456*]. to exclaim, cry out loudly:– spake out [1]

401 ἀνάχυσις, **anachysis**, n. GK: *431* [→ *1632; cf. 303*]. flood, wide stream:– excess [1]

402 ἀναχωρέω, **anachōreō**, v. GK: *432* [→ *303*+*5562*]. to withdraw, leave:– departed [8], withdrew [2], give place [1], gone aside [1], turned aside [1], went aside [1]

403 ἀνάψυξις, **anapsyxis**, n. GK: *433* [→ *303*+*5594*]. refreshment, relaxation, relief:– refreshing [1]

404 ἀναψύχω, **anapsychō**, v. GK: *434* [→ *303*+*5594*]. to refresh, revive:– refreshed [1]

405 ἀνδραποδιστής, **andrapodistēs**, n. GK: *435* [→ *435*+*4228*]. slave trader, kidnapper:– menstealers [1]

406 Ἀνδρέας, **Andreas**, n.pr. GK: *436* [→ *435*]. Andrew, "*manly*":– Andrew [13]

407 ἀνδρίζομαι, **andrizomai**, v. GK: *437* [→ *435*]. to act courageously:– quit like men [1]

408 Ἀνδρόνικος, **Andronikos**, n.pr. GK: *438* [→ *435*+*3529*]. Andronicus, "*victor over men*":– Andronicus [1]

409 ἀνδροφόνος, **androphonos**, n. GK: *439* [→ *435*+*5408*]. murderer:– manslayers [1]

410 ἀνέγκλητος, **anenklētos**, a. GK: *441* [→ *1.1*+*1722*+*2564*]. blameless, free from accusation:– blameless [4], unreproveable [1]

411 ἀνεκδιήγητος, **anekdiēgētos**, a. GK: *442* [→ *1.1*+*1537*+*1223*+*71*]. indescribable, with the associative meanings of marvelous and wonderful:– unspeakable [1]

412 ἀνεκλάλητος, **aneklalētos**, a. GK: *443* [→ *1.1*+*1537*+*2980*]. inexpressible:– unspeakable [1]

413 ἀνέκλειπτος, **anekleiptos**, a. GK: *444* [→ *1.1*+*1537*+*3007*]. not exhaustible, unfailing:– faileth not [1]

414 ἀνεκτός, **anektos**, a. GK: *445* [→ *303*+*2192*]. bearable, tolerable; used only in the comparative: more bearable:– more tolerable [6]

415 ἀνελεήμων, **aneleēmōn**, a. GK: *446* [→ *1.1*+*1656*]. ruthless, merciless:– unmerciful [1]

416 ἀνεμίζω, **anemizō**, v. GK: *448* [→ *417*]. to be moved by the wind:– driven with the wind [1]

417 ἄνεμος, **anemos**, n. GK: *449* [→ *416*]. wind, gale:– wind [20], winds [1]

418 ἀνένδεκτος, **anendektos**, a. GK: *450* [→ *1.1*+*1722*+*1209*]. impossible:– impossible [1]

419 ἀνεξεραύνητος, **anexeraunētos**, a. GK: *451*
[→ *1.1+1537+2045*]. unsearchable, inscrutable:–
unsearchable [1]

420 ἀνεξίκακος, **anexikakos**, a. GK: *452*
[→ *303+2192+2556*]. not resentful, patient:– patient [1]

421 ἀνεξιχνίαστος, **anexichniastos**, a. GK: *453*
[→ *1.1+1537+2487*]. unsearchable, incomprehensible:– past
finding out [1], unsearchable [1]

422 ἀνεπαίσχυντος, **anepaischyntos**, a. GK: *454*
[→ *1.1+1909+150*]. unashamed:– needeth not to be
ashamed [1]

423 ἀνεπίλημπτος, **anepilēmptos**, a. GK: *455*
[→ *1.1+1909+2983*]. above reproach, not open to blame:–
blameless [2], unrebukeable [1]

424 ἀνέρχομαι, **anerchomai**, v. GK: *456* [→ *303+2064*]. to
go up:– went up [3]

425 ἄνεσις, **anesis**, n. GK: *457* [→ *863; cf. 303*]. rest,
relaxation, relief:– rest [3], eased [1], liberty [1]

426 ἀνετάζω, **anetazō**, v. GK: *458* [→ *1833; cf. 303*]. to
question, examine, interrogate:– examined [2]

427 ἄνευ, **aneu**, pp.*. GK: *459*. without, apart from:–
without [3]

428 ἀνεύθετος, **aneuthetos**, a. GK: *460*
[→ *1.1+2095+5087*]. unsuitable, poor:– commodious [1]

429 ἀνευρίσκω, **aneuriskō**, v. GK: *461* [→ *303+2147*]. to
find:– finding [1], found [1]

430 ἀνέχομαι, **anechomai**, v. GK: *462* [→ *303+2192*]. to
put up with, endure:– suffer [7], bear with [4], endure [2],
forbearing [2]

431 ἀνεψιός, **anepsios**, n. GK: *463*. cousin:– sister's son [1]

432 ἄνηθον, **anēthon**, n. GK: *464*. dill, a plant used for
seasoning:– anise [1]

433 ἀνήκω, **anēkō**, v. GK: *465* [→ *303+2240*]. to be fitting,
proper; to do one's duty:– convenient [2], fit [1]

434 ἀνήμερος, **anēmeros**, a. GK: *466* [→ *1.1*]. brutal,
savage:– fierce [1]

435 ἀνήρ, **anēr**, n. GK: *467* [→ *405, 406, 407, 408, 409,
3527, 5220, 5362*]. man, male, husband; usually an adult
male, but in some contexts the emphasis is on maturity rather
than gender (1Co 13:11; Eph 4:13; Jas 3:2):– men [79],
man [75], husband [38], husbands [12], sirs [6], fellows [1],
man's [1], murderer (+*5406*) [1]

436 ἀνθίστημι, **anthistēmi**, v. GK: *468* [→ *473+2476*]. to
resist, oppose, rebel, withstand:– resist [7], withstood [4],
resisted [1], resisteth [1], withstand [1]

437 ἀνθομολογέομαι, **anthomologeomai**, v. GK: *469*
[→ *473+3670*]. to give thanks, praise:– gave thanks unto [1]

438 ἄνθος, **anthos**, n. GK: *470*. flower, blossom:– flower [4]

439 ἀνθρακιά, **anthrakia**, n. GK: *471* [→ *440*]. charcoal
fire:– fire of coals [2]

440 ἄνθραξ, **anthrax**, n. GK: *472* [→ *439*]. coal, charcoal:–
coals [1]

441 ἀνθρωπάρεσκος, **anthrōpareskos**, a. GK: *473*
[→ *444+700*]. one who wins favor, who pleases people:–
menpleasers [2]

442 ἀνθρώπινος, **anthrōpinos**, a. GK: *474* [→ *444*]. human,
common to mankind:– man's [3], after the manner of men [1],
common to man [1], of mankind [1], of man [1]

443 ἀνθρωποκτόνος, **anthrōpoktonos**, n. GK: *475*
[→ *444+615*]. murderer:– murderer [3]

444 ἄνθρωπος, **anthrōpos**, n. GK: *476* [→ *441, 442, 443,
5363, 5364*]. human being, person; humankind, people; man,
husband; used of human beings in contrast to animals or deity;
in some contexts it is used of male/husband in contrast to
female/wife. "The Son of Man" is an OT phrase usually
meaning "human being," that in the NT is used almost
exclusively as a messianic title (see Da 7:13), emphasizing Jesus'
humanity. "The outer person" is the corporeal body in contrast
to "the inner (or hidden) person" of the spirit:– man [346],
men [190], man's [10], men's [5], certain [2], Romans
(+*4514*) [1], enemy (+*2190*) [1], householder (+*3617*) [1], men
(+*3686*) [1], nobleman (+*2104*) [1]

445 ἀνθυπατεύω, **anthypateuō**, v. GK: *477* [→ *446*]. to be
proconsul:– deputy [1]

446 ἀνθύπατος, **anthypatos**, n. GK: *478* [→ *445; cf. 473*].
proconsul:– deputy [3], deputies [1]

447 ἀνίημι, **aniēmi**, v. GK: *479* [→ *863; cf. 303*]. loosen,
untie; leave, abandon:– loosed [2], forbearing [1], leave [1]

448 ἀνίλεως, **anileōs**, a. GK: *447 & 480* [→ *1.1+1656*].
merciless:– without mercy [1]

449 ἄνιπτος, **aniptos**, a. GK: *481* [→ *1.1+3538*].
unwashed:– unwashen [3]

450 ἀνίστημι, **anistēmi**, v. GK: *482* [→ *303+2476*]. to get
up, stand up, come back to life:– arose [14], rise [13],
rose up [13], raise up [8], rise again [8], stood up [7], rose [5],
raised up [4], risen again [4], rise up [2], risen [2], arise up [1],
ariseth [1], lift up [1], raised up again [1], raised [1], rising up [1],
rising [1], rose again [1], stand up [1], stand [1]

451 Ἅννα, **Hanna**, n.pr. GK: *483*. Anna, "*grace*":– Anna [1]

452 Ἅννας, **Hannas**, n.pr. GK: *484*. Annas, "*grace*":–
Annas [4]

453 ἀνόητος, **anoētos**, a. GK: *485 & 493* [→ *1.1+3563*].
foolish, senseless:– foolish [4], fools [1], unwise [1]

454 ἄνοια, **anoia**, n. GK: *486* [→ *1.1+3563*]. folly,
senselessness; fury:– folly [1], madness [1]

455 ἀνοίγω, **anoigō**, v. GK: *487 & 1986* [→ *457, 1272, 455;
cf. 303*]. to open:– opened [53], open [21], openeth [3]

456 ἀνοικοδομέω, **anoikodomeō**, v. GK: *488*
[→ *303+3624+1430*]. to rebuild:– build again [2]

457 ἄνοιξις, **anoixis**, n. GK: *489* [→ *455*]. (the act of)
opening:– open [1]

458 ἀνομία, **anomia**, n. GK: *490* [→ *1.1+3551*].
wickedness, lawlessness, lawless deed:– iniquity [9],
iniquities [3], transgresseth law (+*4160*) [1], transgression of
law [1], unrighteousness [1]

459 ἄνομος, **anomos**, a. GK: *491* [→ *1.1+3551*]. without
law, transgressing law (by not regarding it); as a noun this can
mean a Gentile (without God's covenant law); Paul uses the
definite article to speak of "the lawless one" (1Th. 2:8), often
considered a title of the antichrist:– without law [4],
transgressors [2], wicked [2], lawless [1], unlawful [1]

460 ἀνόμως, **anomōs**, adv. GK: *492* [→ *1.1+3551*]. apart
from law, without law:– without law [2]

461 ἀνορθόω, **anorthoō**, v. GK: *494* [→ *303+3717*]. to
restore, rebuild, strengthen:– lift up [1], made straight [1], set
up [1]

462 ἀνόσιος, **anosios**, a. GK: *495* [→ *1.1+3741*]. unholy,
wicked:– unholy [2]

463 ἀνοχή, **anochē**, n. GK: *496* [→ *303+2192*]. tolerance,
forbearance, clemency:– forbearance [2]

464 ἀνταγωνίζομαι, **antagōnizomai**, v. GK: *497*
[→ *473+73*]. to struggle against:– striving [1]

465 ἀντάλλαγμα, **antallagma**, n. GK: *498* [→ *473+236*].
something given in exchange:– in exchange for [2]

466 ἀνταναπληρόω, **antanaplēroō**, v. GK: *499*
[→ *473+303+4137*]. to fill up, complete:– fill up [1]

467 ἀνταποδίδωμι, **antapodidōmi**, v. GK: *500*
[→ *473+575+1325*]. to repay, return:– recompense [3],
recompensed [2], render again [1], repay [1]

468 ἀνταπόδομα, **antapodoma**, n. GK: *501*
[→ *473+575+1325*]. repayment, retribution:– recompence [2]

469 ἀνταπόδοσις, **antapodosis**, n. GK: *502*
[→ *473+575+1325*]. reward, repayment:– reward [1]

470 ἀνταποκρίνομαι, **antapokrinomai**, v. GK: *503*
[→ *473+575+2919*]. to talk back, answer (with implication of
contradicting someone):– answer again [1], repliest against [1]

471 ἀντέπω, **antepō**, v. GK: *515* [→ *473+3004*]. to speak
against, talk back, contradict:– gainsay [1], say against [1]

472 ἀντέχω, **antechō**, v. GK: *504* [→ *473+2192*]. to be
devoted, hold firmly to; pay attention to:– hold to [2], holding
fast [1], support [1]

473 ἀντί, **anti**, pp. GK: *505* [→ *368, 369, 436, 437, 464,
465, 466, 467, 468, 469, 470, 471, 472, 474, 475, 476, 477,
478, 479, 480, 481, 482, 483, 484, 485, 486, 487, 488, 489,
492, 493, 494, 495, 496, 497, 498, 499, 500, 503, 528, 529,
1725, 2658, 4876, 4877, 4878, 5221, 5222; cf. 446, 1725*]. in
exchange for (often as a sign of benefaction), in place of (often as
a sign of contrast), instead of (often as a sign of an exchange of a
relationship), one after another (often as a sign of purpose or

result). Note that this preposition used in absolute does not
mean to be "against" or "in opposition to" something:– for [14],
because (+*3739*) [4], for cause [1], for that (+*3588*) [1], in the
room of [1], therefore (+*3739*) [1]

474 ἀντιβάλλω, **antiballō**, v. GK: *506* [→ *473+906*]. to
discuss, exchange (words):– have [1]

475 ἀντιδιατίθημι, **antidiatithēmi**, v. GK: *507*
[→ *473+1223+5087*]. to oppose:– oppose themselves [1]

476 ἀντίδικος, **antidikos**, n. GK: *508* [→ *473+1349*].
enemy, opponent (in battle or in court):– adversary [5]

477 ἀντίθεσις, **antithesis**, n. GK: *509* [→ *473+5087*].
opposition, objection:– oppositions [1]

478 ἀντικαθίστημι, **antikathistēmi**, v. GK: *510*
[→ *473+2596+2476*]. to resist, oppose, contest against:–
resisted [1]

479 ἀντικαλέω, **antikaleō**, v. GK: *511* [→ *473+2564*]. to
invite in reciprocation:– bid again [1]

480 ἀντίκειμαι, **antikeimai**, v. GK: *512* [→ *473+2749*]. to
be an opponent, in conflict:– adversaries [4], contrary [2],
adversary [1], opposeth [1]

481 ἄντικρυς, **antikrys**, adv. GK: *513* [→ *473*]. opposite of,
in proximity to:– over against [1]

482 ἀντιλαμβάνω, **antilambanō**, v. GK: *514*
[→ *473+2983*]. to help, come to the aid of, benefit:–
holpen [1], partakers [1], support [1]

483 ἀντιλέγω, **antilegō**, v. GK: *515* [→ *473+3004*]. to
speak against, talk back, contradict:– spake against [2], spoken
against [2], answering again [1], contradicting [1], deny [1],
gainsayers [1], gainsaying [1], speaketh against [1]

484 ἀντίλημψις, **antilēmpsis**, n. GK: *516* [→ *473+2983*].
help, ability to aid:– helps [1]

485 ἀντιλογία, **antilogia**, n. GK: *517* [→ *473+3004*].
argument, opposition, rebellion:– contradiction [2],
gainsaying [1], strife [1]

486 ἀντιλοιδορέω, **antiloidoreō**, v. GK: *518*
[→ *473+3060*]. to retaliate:– reviled again [1]

487 ἀντίλυτρον, **antilytron**, n. GK: *519* [→ *473+3089*].
ransom; the purchase price to bring liberation from oppression;
it is the means to redemption. This refers to Jesus (in person and
work) as the price of salvation:– ransom [1]

488 ἀντιμετρέω, **antimetreō**, v. GK: *520* [→ *473+3358*].
to measure in return:– measured again [2]

489 ἀντιμισθία, **antimisthia**, n. GK: *521* [→ *473+3408*].
an exchange; penalty:– recompence [2]

490 Ἀντιόχεια, **Antiocheia**, n.pr. GK: *522* [→ *491*].
Antioch:– Antioch [18]

491 Ἀντιοχεύς, **Antiocheus**, n.pr.g. GK: *523* [→ *490*].
from Antioch:– Antioch [1]

492 ἀντιπαρέρχομαι, **antiparerchomai**, v. GK: *524*
[→ *473+3844+2064*]. to pass by on the opposite side:– passed
by on the other side [2]

493 Ἀντιπᾶς, **Antipas**, n.pr. GK: *525* [→ *473+3962*].
Antipas:– Antipas [1]

494 Ἀντιπατρίς, **Antipatris**, n.pr. GK: *526*
[→ *473+3962*]. Antipatris:– Antipatris [1]

495 ἀντιπέρα, **antipera**, adv. GK: *527* [→ *473+4008*].
across from, opposite of:– over against [1]

496 ἀντιπίπτω, **antipiptō**, v. GK: *528* [→ *473+4098*]. to
resist, oppose:– resist [1]

497 ἀντιστρατεύομαι, **antistrateuomai**, v. GK: *529*
[→ *473+4756*]. to wage war against:– warring against [1]

498 ἀντιτάσσω, **antitassō**, v. GK: *530* [→ *473+5021*]. to
oppose, rebel, resist:– resisteth [3], opposed [1], resist [1]

499 ἀντίτυπος, **antitypos**, a. GK: *531* [→ *473+5180*].
copy, representation:– figures [1], like figure [1]

500 ἀντίχριστος, **antichristos**, n. GK: *532* [→ *473+5547*].
antichrist:– antichrist [4], antichrists [1]

501 ἀντλέω, **antleō**, v. GK: *533* [→ *502*]. to draw (water):–
draw [2], draw out [1], drew [1]

502 ἄντλημα, **antlēma**, n. GK: *534* [→ *501*]. container to
draw water with:– draw with [1]

503 ἀντοφθαλμέω, **antophthalmeō**, v. GK: *535*
[→ *473+3788*]. to head into, face (the wind):– bear up into [1]

504 ἄνυδρος, **anydros**, a. GK: *536* [→ *1.1+5204*]. arid, without water:– dry [2], without water [2]

505 ἀνυπόκριτος, **anypokritos**, a. GK: *537* [→ *1.1+5259+2919*]. sincere, genuine, without hypocrisy; of good character, lacking pretense and prideful show:– unfeigned [4], without dissimulation [1], without hypocrisy [1]

506 ἀνυπότακτος, **anypotaktos**, a. GK: *538* [→ *1.1+5259+5021*]. rebellious, disobedient; not made subject to, independent:– unruly [2], disobedient [1], not put under [1]

507 ἄνω, **anō**, adv.pl. GK: *539* [→ *509, 510, 511, 1274, 1883, 5231; cf. 303*]. above, upward, heavenward, top:– above [5], up [2], high [1], the brim [1]

508 ἀνάγαιον, **anagaion**, n. GK: *333* [→ *303+1093*]. upper room:– upper room [2]

509 ἄνωθεν, **anōthen**, adv.pl. GK: *540* [→ *507*]. from above; from the beginning; again, anew:– from above [5], again [3], top [3], from beginning [1], from the very first [1]

510 ἀνωτερικός, **anōterikos**, a. GK: *541* [→ *507*]. interior, upper (regions):– upper [1]

511 ἀνώτερος, **anōteros**, a. GK: *542* [→ *507*]. higher, better in social standing; earlier, previously, first:– above [1], higher [1]

512 ἀνωφελής, **anōphelēs**, a. GK: *543* [→ *1.1+5623*]. unprofitable, useless:– unprofitableness [1], unprofitable [1]

513 ἀξίνη, **axinē**, n. GK: *544* [→ *2608*]. ax:– axe [2]

514 ἄξιος, **axios**, a. GK: *545* [→ *370, 371, 515, 516, 2661; cf. 71*]. worthy, deserving, in keeping with, corresponding to:– worthy [35], meet for [2], meet [2], due reward [1], unworthy (+*3756*) [1]

515 ἀξιόω, **axioō**, v. GK: *546* [→ *514*]. to consider worthy, consider wise or fitting:– counted worthy [2], thought [2], count worthy [1], desire [1], thought good [1]

516 ἀξίως, **axiōs**, adv. GK: *547* [→ *514*]. in a worthy manner, suitably:– worthy [3], becometh [2], after a sort [1]

517 ἀόρατος, **aoratos**, a. GK: *548* [→ *1.1+3708*]. invisible, not seen:– invisible [5]

518 ἀπαγγέλλω, **apangellō**, v. GK: *33 & 550* [→ *575+32*]. to tell, report, proclaim, announce, bring news, be a messenger:– told [19], shewed [6], tell [6], shew [4], declare [2], bring word again [1], bring word [1], declared [1], reported [1], report [1], shew again [1], told how [1]

519 ἀπάγχω, **apanchō**, v. GK: *551*. to hang (oneself):– hanged [1]

520 ἀπάγω, **apagō**, v. GK: *552* [→ *575+71*]. to lead away, bring before (an official):– led away [8], lead away [2], leadeth [2], bring [1], carried away [1], put to death [1], took away [1]

521 ἀπαίδευτος, **apaideutos**, a. GK: *553* [→ *1.1+3816*]. stupid, uneducated:– unlearned [1]

522 ἀπαίρω, **apairō**, v. GK: *554* [→ *575+142*]. to take away:– taken away [2], taken from [1]

523 ἀπαιτέω, **apaiteō**, v. GK: *555* [→ *575+154*]. to demand back:– ask again [1], required [1]

524 ἀπαλγέω, **apalgeō**, v. GK: *556*. to lose all sensitivity, become callous:– past feeling [1]

525 ἀπαλλάσσω, **apallassō**, v. GK: *557* [→ *575+236*]. (act.) to set free, release; (pass.) to be reconciled, come to a settlement (in court); to be cured:– delivered [1], deliver [1], departed [1]

526 ἀπαλλοτριόω, **apallotrioō**, v. GK: *558* [→ *575+243*]. to be excluded, separated, alienated:– alienated [2], aliens [1]

527 ἀπαλός, **hapalos**, a. GK: *559*. tender (referring to sprouts):– tender [2]

528 ἀπαντάω, **apantaō**, v. GK: *560* [→ *575+473*]. to meet, encounter:– met [5], meet [2]

529 ἀπάντησις, **apantēsis**, n. GK: *561* [→ *575+473*]. (the act of) meeting, encountering:– meet [4]

530 ἅπαξ, **hapax**, adv. GK: *562* [→ *2178*]. once, once more, once for all; the Greek idiom "once and yet twice" means to do something repeatedly, "again and again" (Php 4:16):– once [15]

531 ἀπαράβατος, **aparabatos**, a. GK: *563* [→ *1.1+3844+305*]. permanent, unchangeable:– unchangeable [1]

532 ἀπαρασκεύαστος, **aparaskeuastos**, a. GK: *564* [→ *1.1+3844+4632*]. unprepared, unready:– unprepared [1]

533 ἀπαρνέομαι, **aparneomai**, v. GK: *565* [→ *575+720*]. to disown, deny, repudiate:– deny [11], denied [2]

534 ἀπάρτι, **aparti**, adv. [pp.+adv.]. GK: *567* [→ *575+737*]. from now on, again:– henceforth [1]

535 ἀπαρτισμός, **apartismos**, n. GK: *568* [→ *575+737*]. completion, finishing:– finish [1]

536 ἀπαρχή, **aparchē**, n. GK: *569* [→ *575+757*]. firstfruits, the first of any crop or livestock offered to God before the rest could be used:– firstfruits [7], firstfruit [1]

537 ἅπας, **hapas**, a. GK: *570* [→ *260+3956*]. all, every, whole:– all [39], whole [3], every one [1], every [1]

538 ἀπατάω, **apataō**, v. GK: *572* [→ *539*]. to deceive, cheat, trick:– deceived [2], deceiveth [1], deceive [1]

539 ἀπάτη, **apatē**, n. GK: *573* [→ *538, 1818, 5422, 5423*]. deception, deceitfulness:– deceitfulness [3], deceitful [1], deceit [1], deceivableness [1], deceivings [1]

540 ἀπάτωρ, **apatōr**, a. GK: *574* [→ *1.1+3962*]. fatherless:– without father [1]

541 ἀπαύγασμα, **apaugasma**, n. GK: *575* [→ *575+827*]. radiance, brilliance:– brightness [1]

542 ἀπείδω, **apeidō**, v. GK: *927* [→ *575+3708*]. to fix one's eyes; look away:– see [1]

543 ἀπείθεια, **apeitheia**, n. GK: *577* [→ *1.1+3982*]. disobedience:– unbelief [4], disobedience [3]

544 ἀπειθέω, **apeitheō**, v. GK: *578* [→ *1.1+3982*]. to disobey, be disobedient:– believed not [4], disobedient [4], not believed [2], obey not [2], believeth not [1], not believe [1], obey [1], unbelieving [1]

545 ἀπειθής, **apeithēs**, a. GK: *579* [→ *1.1+3982*]. disobedient:– disobedient [6]

546 ἀπειλέω, **apeileō**, v. GK: *580* [→ *547*]. to threaten, warn:– straitly threaten [1], threatened [1]

547 ἀπειλή, **apeilē**, n. GK: *581* [→ *546, 4324*]. threat:– threatenings [2], threatening [1]

548 ἄπειμι¹, **apeimi¹**, v. GK: *582* [→ *575+1510*]. to be absent:– absent [7]

549 ἄπειμι², **apeimi²**, v. GK: *583* [→ *575*]. to go away:– went [1]

550 ἀπεῖπον, **apeipon**, v. GK: *584* [→ *575+3004*]. to renounce, disown:– renounced [1]

551 ἀπείραστος, **apeirastos**, a. GK: *585* [→ *1.1+3984*]. incapable of being tempted, without temptation:– cannot be tempted (+*1510*) [1]

552 ἄπειρος, **apeiros**, a. GK: *586* [→ *1.1+3984*]. not acquainted with:– unskilful [1]

553 ἀπεκδέχομαι, **apekdechomai**, v. GK: *587* [→ *575+1537+1209*]. wait eagerly for:– look for [2], wait for [2], waiting for [2], waiteth for [1]

554 ἀπεκδύομαι, **apekdyomai**, v. GK: *588* [→ *575+1537+1416*]. to take off, disarm:– put off [1], spoiled [1]

555 ἀπέκδυσις, **apekdysis**, n. GK: *589* [→ *575+1537+1416*]. removal, putting off:– putting off [1]

556 ἀπελαύνω, **apelaunō**, v. GK: *590* [→ *575+1643*]. to eject from (court), drive away:– drave [1]

557 ἀπελεγμός, **apelegmos**, n. GK: *591* [→ *575+1651*]. disrepute, discredit:– nought [1]

558 ἀπελεύθερος, **apeleutheros**, n. GK: *592* [→ *575+1658*]. freedman, one no longer a slave:– freeman [1]

559 Ἀπελλῆς, **Apellēs**, n.pr. GK: *593*. Apelles:– Apelles [1]

560 ἀπελπίζω, **apelpizō**, v. GK: *594* [→ *575+1680*]. to expect nothing in return:– hoping for again [1]

561 ἀπέναντι, **apenanti**, pp.*. GK: *595* [→ *575+1725*]. opposite, in front of, against (opposition to):– before [2], over against [2], contrary [1], in the presence [1]

ἀπέπω, **apepō**. See *550*.

562 ἀπέραντος, **aperantos**, a. GK: *596* [→ *1.1+4008*]. endless, unlimited:– endless [1]

563 ἀπερισπάστως, **aperispastōs**, adv. GK: *597* [→ *1.1+4012+4685*]. undivided, without distraction:– without distraction [1]

564 ἀπερίτμητος, **aperitmētos**, a. GK: *598* [→ *1.1+4012+5114*]. uncircumcised (with a possible implication of being stubborn and obstinate):– uncircumcised [1]

565 ἀπέρχομαι, **aperchomai**, v. GK: *599* [→ *575+2064*]. to go away, withdraw:– went [45], departed [23], go [17], went away [7], go away [4], come [3], depart [3], gone away [3], goest [2], past [2], came [1], depart out [1], go after [1], go aside [1], go out [1], goeth way [1], going [1], gone [1], passed away [1], went back (+*1519+3588+3694*) [1], went way [1]

566 ἀπέχει, **apechei**, v.3.s. of *568*. GK: *600* [→ *575+2192*]. to receive (in full), have enough:–

567 ἀπέχομαι, **apechomai**, v.mid. of *568*. GK: *600* [→ *575+2192*]. to abstain, avoid:–

568 ἀπέχω, **apechō**, v. GK: *600* [→ *575+2192*]. to receive (in full); to be distant; (mid.) to abstain, avoid:– have [4], abstain from [3], abstain [3], from [3], enough [1], is from [1], off [1], received [1], receive [1]

569 ἀπιστέω, **apisteō**, v. GK: *601* [→ *1.1+4103*]. to disbelieve, be faithless, unfaithful. In some contexts unbelief has no implication of faithlessness or hardheartedness (Lk 24:11); in other contexts unbelief is a moral failure, not acting like a true follower (2Ti 2:13):– believed not [4], believe not [1], believeth not [1], not believe [1]

570 ἀπιστία, **apistia**, n. GK: *602* [→ *1.1+4103*]. unbelief, lack of faith (often with the implication of stubbornly refusing to believe or act in accord with God's will or law):– unbelief [12]

571 ἄπιστος, **apistos**, a. GK: *603* [→ *1.1+4103*]. unbelieving, lacking in trust, doubting; as a noun: an unbeliever or outsider, one who does not believe the Gospel:– unbelieving [5], believe not [4], faithless [4], unbelievers [4], believeth not [3], infidel [2], incredible [1]

572 ἁπλότης, **haplotēs**, n. GK: *605* [→ *573*]. Formally "the quality of singleness," translated "generosity," the state of giving things in a manner that shows liberality; "sincerity," the moral quality of honesty expressing singleness of purpose or motivation:– simplicity [3], singleness [2], bountifulness [1], liberality [1], liberal [1]

573 ἁπλοῦς, **haplous**, a. GK: *606* [→ *572, 574; cf. 260*]. good in the sense of healthy, formally, "singleness." Some think "a good eye" means to be generous and liberal in giving.:– single [2]

574 ἁπλῶς, **haplōs**, adv. GK: *607* [→ *573*]. generously, without reserve:– liberally [1]

575 ἀπό, **apo**, pp. GK: *608* [→ *379, 467, 468, 469, 470, 518, 520, 522, 523, 525, 526, 528, 529, 533, 534, 535, 536, 541, 542, 548, 549, 550, 553, 554, 555, 556, 557, 558, 560, 561, 565, 566, 567, 568, 576, 577, 578, 579, 580, 581, 582, 583, 584, 585, 586, 587, 588, 589, 590, 591, 592, 593, 594, 595, 596, 597, 598, 599, 600, 601, 602, 603, 604, 605, 606, 607, 608, 609, 610, 611, 612, 613, 614, 616, 617, 618, 619, 620, 621, 622, 623, 626, 627, 628, 629, 630, 631, 632, 633, 634, 635, 636, 637, 638, 641, 642, 643, 644, 645, 646, 647, 648, 649, 650, 653, 654, 655, 656, 657, 658, 659, 660, 661, 662, 663, 664, 665, 666, 667, 668, 669, 670, 671, 672, 673, 674, 684, 851, 856, 864, 867, 868, 871, 872, 873, 874, 879, 3405, 3406, 4217, 4879, 4880, 4881; cf. 683, 863*]. from, away from; by means of; out of; against:– from [386], of [149], out of [25], for [10], at [9], by [9], off [6], afar off (+*3113*) [5], on [5], since [5], in [4], since (+*3739*) [4], with [4], from among [3], a year ago (+*4070*) [2], before [2], henceforth (+*737*) [2], hereafter (+*737*) [2], since began [2], a good while ago (+*744+2250*) [1], ago [1], away from [1], away [1], because of [1], forsake (+*646*) [1], from beginning [1], henceforth (+*3568+3588*) [1], hereafter (+*3568+3588*) [1], in that [1], now (+*737*) [1], once (+*302+3739*) [1], out [1], since the time (+*3739*) [1], somewhat (+*3313*) [1], some [1], space of [1], that (+*3739*) [1], upon [1]

576 ἀποβαίνω, **apobainō**, v. GK: *609* [→ *575+305*]. to leave, get out; to result in, turn to, lead to:– come [1], gone out [1], turn to [1], turn [1]

577 ἀποβάλλω, **apoballō**, v. GK: *610* [→ *575+906*]. to throw away:– cast away [1], casting away [1]

578 ἀποβλέπω, **apoblepō**, v. GK: *611* [→ *575+991*]. to look ahead, pay attention:– respect [1]

579 ἀπόβλητος, **apoblētos**, a. GK: *612* [→ *575+906*]. rejected (as unclean):– refused [1]

580 ἀποβολή, **apobolē**, n. GK: *613* [→ *575+906*]. rejection; loss:– casting away [1], loss [1]

581 ἀπογίνομαι, **apoginomai**, v. GK: *614* [→ *575+1096*]. to die:– dead [1]

582 ἀπογραφή, *apographē*, n. GK: *615* [→ *575+1125*]. census, registration:– taxing [2]

583 ἀπογράφω, *apographō*, v. GK: *616* [→ *575+1125*]. to take a census, register, record:– taxed [3], written [1]

584 ἀποδείκνυμι, *apodeiknymi*, v. GK: *617* [→ *575+1166*]. to display, exhibit, proclaim; prove, accredit, attest:– approved [1], prove [1], set forth [1], shewing [1]

585 ἀπόδειξις, *apodeixis*, n. GK: *618* [→ *575+1166*]. demonstration, proof:– demonstration [1]

586 ἀποδεκατόω, *apodekatoō*, v. GK: *619 & 620* [→ *575+1176*]. to give a tenth, tithe; collect a tithe:– give tithes [1], pay tithe of [1], take tithes [1], tithe [1]

587 ἀπόδεκτος, *apodektos*, a. GK: *621* [→ *575+1209*]. pleasing, pleasant:– acceptable [2]

588 ἀποδέχομαι, *apodechomai*, v. GK: *622* [→ *575+1209*]. to welcome, accept, receive; acknowledge, acclaim:– received [3], accept [1], gladly received [1], receive [1]

589 ἀποδημέω, *apodēmeō*, v. GK: *623* [→ *575+1218*]. to go away on a journey:– went into a far country [3], took journey [2], travelling into a far country [1]

590 ἀπόδημος, *apodēmos*, a. GK: *624* [→ *575+1218*]. going away on a journey:– taking a far journey [1]

591 ἀποδίδωμι, *apodidōmi*, v. GK: *625* [→ *575+1325*]. give, give away; pay, pay back:– give [8], render [8], pay [7], reward [6], sold [3], paid [2], delivered again [1], delivered [1], gave again [1], gave [1], payment made [1], perform [1], recompense [1], rendering [1], repay [1], requite (+*287*) [1], restore [1], rewarded [1], yielded [1], yieldeth [1]

592 ἀποδιορίζω, *apodiorizō*, v. GK: *626* [→ *575+1223+3724*]. to divide, separate, cause a division:– separate [1]

593 ἀποδοκιμάζω, *apodokimazō*, v. GK: *627* [→ *575+1209*]. to reject:– rejected [7], disallowed [2]

594 ἀποδοχή, *apodochē*, n. GK: *628* [→ *575+1209*]. acceptance, approval:– acceptation [2]

595 ἀπόθεσις, *apothesis*, n. GK: *629* [→ *575+5087*]. removal, putting aside, getting rid of; this can be a euphemism for death (2Pe 1:14):– put off [1], putting away [1]

596 ἀποθήκη, *apothēkē*, n. GK: *630* [→ *575+2344*]. barn, storehouse:– barns [2], barn [2], garner [2]

597 ἀποθησαυρίζω, *apothēsaurizō*, v. GK: *631* [→ *575+2344*]. to store up treasure:– laying up in store [1]

598 ἀποθλίβω, *apothlibō*, v. GK: *632* [→ *575+2346*]. to press against, crowd up to:– press [1]

599 ἀποθνήσκω, *apothnēskō*, v. GK: *633* [→ *575+2348*]. to die (in a literal or fig. sense); to be about to die, be mortal:– die [41], died [32], dead [29], dying [4], dieth [2], death [1], perished [1], slain (+*5408*) [1]

600 ἀποκαθίστημι, *apokathistēmi*, v. GK: *634 & 635* [→ *575+2596+2476*]. to (completely) restore, reestablish, cure:– restored [5], restore again [1], restoreth [1], restore [1]

601 ἀποκαλύπτω, *apokalyptō*, v. GK: *636* [→ *575+2572*]. to reveal, disclose:– revealed [22], reveal [4]

602 ἀποκάλυψις, *apokalypsis*, n. GK: *637* [→ *575+2572*]. revelation, what is revealed, disclosure, to make information known with an implication that the information can be understood. This refers in the NT to God making information known, especially to his close associates:– revelation [10], revealed [2], revelations [2], appearing [1], coming [1], lighten [1], manifestation [1]

603 ἀποκαραδοκία, *apokaradokia*, n. GK: *638 & 2839* [→ *575+2898+1380*]. eager expectation:– earnest expectation [2]

604 ἀποκαταλλάσσω, *apokatallassō*, v. GK: *639* [→ *575+2596+236*]. to reconcile, reunite:– reconcile [2], reconciled [1]

605 ἀποκατάστασις, *apokatastasis*, n. GK: *640* [→ *575+2596+2476*]. restoration:– restitution [1]

606 ἀπόκειμαι, *apokeimai*, v. GK: *641* [→ *575+2749*]. to be stored up, destined:– laid up [3], appointed [1]

607 ἀποκεφαλίζω, *apokephalizō*, v. GK: *642* [→ *575+2776*]. to behead:– beheaded [4]

608 ἀποκλείω, *apokleiō*, v. GK: *643* [→ *575+2808*]. to close:– shut to [1]

609 ἀποκόπτω, *apokoptō*, v. GK: *644* [→ *575+2875*]. to cut off; emasculate:– cut off [6]

610 ἀπόκριμα, *apokrima*, n. GK: *645* [→ *575+2919*]. sentence, verdict:– sentence [1]

611 ἀποκρίνομαι, *apokrinomai*, v. GK: *646* [→ *575+2919*]. to answer, reply; sometimes used in the NT in the Hebraic sense of continuing a discourse:– answered [201], answering [29], answer [12], answerest [4], answereth [4]

612 ἀπόκρισις, *apokrisis*, n. GK: *647* [→ *575+2919*]. answer:– answer [3], answers [1]

613 ἀποκρύπτω, *apokryptō*, v. GK: *648* [→ *575+2928*]. to hide, conceal:– hid [3], hid from [2], hidden [1]

614 ἀπόκρυφος, *apokryphos*, a. GK: *649* [→ *575+2928*]. concealed, hidden, secret:– hid [2], kept secret [1]

615 ἀποκτείνω, *apokteinō*, v. GK: *650 & 651* [→ *443*]. to kill (either natural life or spiritual life):– kill [28], killed [21], slain [7], put to death [6], slew [4], killeth [3], slay [3], killest [2], killing [1]

616 ἀποκυέω, *apokyeō*, v. GK: *652* [→ *575+2949*]. to give birth to, bring into being:– begat [1], bringeth forth [1]

617 ἀποκυλίω, *apokyliō*, v. GK: *375 & 653* [→ *575+2947*]. to roll away, roll back:– rolled away [2], roll away [1], rolled back [1]

618 ἀπολαμβάνω, *apolambanō*, v. GK: *655* [→ *575+2983*]. to receive, be repaid:– receive [7], receive again [1], receivedst [1], received [1], receiving [1], took [1]

619 ἀπόλαυσις, *apolausis*, n. GK: *656* [→ *575*]. enjoyment, pleasure:– enjoy [1], pleasures [1]

620 ἀπολείπω, *apoleipō*, v. GK: *657* [→ *575+3007*]. to leave behind:– left [3], remaineth [3]

621 ἀπολείχω, *apoleichō*, v. GK: *658 & 2143 & 3314 & 4336* [→ *575*]. lick, lick off:– licked [1]

622 ἀπόλλυμι, *apollymi*, v. GK: *660* [→ *575+3639*]. to destroy (an inanimate object), to kill (by taking a life), cause to lose (especially a life); to die or perish. Violence and strife is often the associative meaning related to this word:– perish [25], destroy [19], lose [17], lost [13], destroyed [7], perished [5], perisheth [3], die [1], loseth [1], marred [1]

623 Ἀπολλύων, *Apollyōn*, n.pr. GK: *661* [→ *575+3639*]. Apollyon, "*destroyer*":– Apollyon [1]

624 Ἀπολλωνία, *Apollōnia*, n.pr. GK: *662* [→ *625*]. Apollonia:– Apollonia [1]

625 Ἀπολλῶς, *Apollōs*, n.pr. GK: *663* [→ *624*]. Apollos:– Apollos [10]

626 ἀπολογέομαι, *apologeomai*, v. GK: *664* [→ *575+3004*]. to defend oneself, speak in one's own behalf:– answer [3], answer for [1], answered for himself [1], answered for [1], excuse ourselves [1], excusing [1], made defence [1], spake for [1]

627 ἀπολογία, *apologia*, n. GK: *665* [→ *575+3004*]. defense; answer or reply (of reason or accounting):– answer [3], defence [1], answer for [1], clearing [1]

628 ἀπολούω, *apolouō*, v. GK: *666* [→ *575+3068*]. to wash away:– wash away [1], washed [1]

629 ἀπολύτρωσις, *apolytrōsis*, n. GK: *667* [→ *575+3089*]. redemption, ransom, release:– redemption [9], deliverance [1]

630 ἀπολύω, *apolyō*, v. GK: *668* [→ *575+3089*]. to release (forgive, grant clemency); divorce, send away:– let go [13], put away [13], release [13], sent away [7], send away [6], released [4], dismissed [2], loosed [2], set at liberty [2], departed [1], depart [1], divorced [1], forgiven [1], forgive [1], let depart [1], putteth away [1]

631 ἀπομάσσω, *apomassō*, v. GK: *669* [→ *575+3146*]. to wipe off (this refers to an action of protest):– wipe off against [1]

632 ἀπονέμω, *aponemō*, v. GK: *671* [→ *575+3551*]. to treat with, show, pay (respect):– giving [1]

633 ἀπονίπτω, *aponiptō*, v. GK: *672* [→ *575+3538*]. to wash off:– washed [1]

634 ἀποπίπτω, *apopiptō*, v. GK: *674* [→ *575+4098*]. to fall away, drop off:– fell [1]

635 ἀποπλανάω, *apoplanaō*, v. GK: *675* [→ *575+4106*]. to deceive, mislead; (pass.) to wander:– erred [1], seduce [1]

636 ἀποπλέω, *apopleō*, v. GK: *676* [→ *575+4126*]. to sail away from:– sailed [3], sail [1]

637 ἀποπλύνω, *apoplynō*, v. GK: *677* [→ *575+4150*]. to wash off, wash out:– washing [1]

638 ἀποπνίγω, *apopnigō*, v. GK: *678* [→ *575+4155*]. to choke, smother; (pass.) to be drowned, choked (with water):– choked [3]

639 ἀπορέω, *aporeō*, v. GK: *679* [→ *1.1+4198*]. to be puzzled, at a loss, in wonder:– doubted [1], doubting [1], perplexed [1], stand in doubt [1]

640 ἀπορία, *aporia*, n. GK: *680* [→ *1.1+4198*]. perplexity, consternation:– perplexity [1]

641 ἀπορίπτω, *aporiptō*, v. GK: *681* [→ *575+4496*]. to jump into, throw oneself into:– cast [1]

642 ἀπορφανίζω, *aporphanizō*, v. GK: *682* [→ *575+3737*]. to make an orphan of:– taken [1]

643 ἀποσκευάζω, *aposkeuazō*, v. GK: *683 & 2171* [→ *575+4632*]. to pack up, get ready, make preparations:– took up carriages [1]

644 ἀποσκίασμα, *aposkiasma*, n. GK: *684* [→ *575+4639*]. shadow:– shadow [1]

645 ἀποσπάω, *apospaō*, v. GK: *685* [→ *575+4685*]. to draw out, draw away, attract; (pass.) to withdraw:– draw away [1], drew [1], gotten from [1], withdrawn [1]

646 ἀποστασία, *apostasia*, n. GK: *686* [→ *575+2476*]. turning away, rebellion, abandonment, apostasy:– falling away [1], forsake (+*575*) [1]

647 ἀποστάσιον, *apostasion*, n. GK: *687* [→ *575+2476*]. divorce:– divorcement [2], writing of divorcement [1]

648 ἀποστεγάζω, *apostegazō*, v. GK: *689* [→ *575+4722*]. to make an opening in a roof, remove a roof:– uncovered [1]

649 ἀποστέλλω, *apostellō*, v. GK: *690* [→ *651, 652, 1821, 4882, 5570*]. to send, send out, send away (especially used of the official sending out of the disciples):– sent [92], send [17], sent forth [8], send forth [5], sent away [3], sendeth forth [2], sent out [2], putteth in [1], send away [1], sendeth [1], set [1]

650 ἀποστερέω, *apostereō*, v. GK: *691 & 935* [→ *575*]. to defraud, cheat, steal; deprive, deny, withhold, keep back:– defraud [3], defrauded [1], destitute [1], kept back by fraud [1]

651 ἀποστολή, *apostolē*, n. GK: *692* [→ *649*]. apostleship, ministry / office of an apostle:– apostleship [4]

652 ἀπόστολος, *apostolos*, n. GK: *693* [→ *649*]. apostle, representative, messenger, envoy; often used in a technical sense for the divinely appointed founders of the church:– apostles [54], apostle [19], apostles' [5], he that is sent [1], messengers [1], messenger [1]

653 ἀποστοματίζω, *apostomatizō*, v. GK: *694* [→ *575+4750*]. to besiege with questions, interrogate closely:– provoke to speak [1]

654 ἀποστρέφω, *apostrephō*, v. GK: *695* [→ *575+4762*]. to turn away from, rebel, mislead; to desert, reject; to return, put back:– turn away [3], brought again [1], perverteth [1], put up again [1], turn away from [1], turn from [1], turned away from [1], turning away [1]

655 ἀποστυγέω, *apostygeō*, v. GK: *696* [→ *575+4767*]. to hate, abhor, loathe:– Abhor [1]

656 ἀποσυνάγωγος, *aposynagōgos*, a. GK: *697* [→ *575+4864*]. put out of the synagogue, excommunicated:– put out of the synagogue [2], out of the synagogues [1]

657 ἀποτάσσω, *apotassō*, v. GK: *698* [→ *575+5021*]. to say good-by, leave; give up, renounce, forsake:– bade farewell [1], bid farewell [1], forsaketh [1], sent away [1], taking leave of [1], took leave [1]

658 ἀποτελέω, *apoteleō*, v. GK: *699* [→ *575+5056*]. to bring to completion; (pass.) to be full-grown, mature, completed:– finished [1]

659 ἀποτίθημι, *apotithēmi*, v. GK: *700* [→ *575+5087*]. to put aside, get rid of:– put off [2], cast off [1], laid down [1], lay apart [1], lay aside [1], laying aside [1], putting away [1]

660 ἀποτινάσσω, *apotinassō*, v. GK: *701* [→ *1614; cf. 575*]. to shake off, stomp off:– shake off [1], shook off [1]

661 ἀποτίνω, *apotinō*, v. GK: *702* [→ *575+5099*]. to pay back, make restitution:– repay [1]

662 ἀποτολμάω, *apotolmaō*, v. GK: *703* [→ *575+5111*]. to bring forth boldly:– very bold [1]

663 ἀποτομία, *apotomia*, n. GK: *704* [→ *575+5114*]. sternness, severity:– severity [2]

664 ἀποτόμως, *apotomōs*, adv. GK: *705* [→ *575+5114*]. harshly, sharply, severely, rigorously:- sharply [1], sharpness [1]

665 ἀποτρέπω, *apotrepō*, v. GK: *706* [→ *575+5157*]. to have nothing to do with, turn away from completely, avoid:- from turn away [1]

666 ἀπουσία, *apousia*, n. GK: *707* [→ *575+1510*]. absence:- absence [1]

667 ἀποφέρω, *apopherō*, v. GK: *708* [→ *575+5342*]. to carry away, lead away:- carried away [3], bring [1], carried [1]

668 ἀποφεύγω, *apopheugō*, v. GK: *709* [→ *575+5343*]. to escape (from):- escaped [2], escaped from [1]

669 ἀποφθέγγομαι, *apophthengomai*, v. GK: *710* [→ *575+5350*]. to say, speak out, address, declare, in some contexts with the inference of urgency or boldness:- said [1], speak forth [1], utterance [1]

670 ἀποφορτίζομαι, *apophortizomai*, v. GK: *711* [→ *575+5342*]. to unload:- unlade [1]

671 ἀπόχρησις, *apochrēsis*, n. GK: *712* [→ *575+5530*]. using up, consumption:- using [1]

672 ἀποχωρέω, *apochōreō*, v. GK: *713* [→ *575+5562*]. to go away from, leave:- departeth [1], departing [1], depart [1]

673 ἀποχωρίζω, *apochōrizō*, v. GK: *714* [→ *575+5565*]. to part company, be separated; to recede, be split:- departed asunder [1], departed [1]

674 ἀποψύχω, *apopsychō*, v. GK: *715* [→ *575+5594*]. faint (some translate "to die"):- hearts failing [1]

675 Ἄππιος, *Appios*, n.pr. GK: *716*. Appius:- Appii [1]

676 ἄπροσιτος, *aprositos*, a. GK: *717* [→ *1.1+4314*]. unapproachable:- which no can approach unto [1]

677 ἀπρόσκοπος, *aproskopos*, a. GK: *718* [→ *1.1+4314+2875*]. blameless, clear; not causing one to stumble, not giving offense:- none offence [1], void of offence [1], without offence [1]

678 ἀπροσωπολήμπτως, *aprosōpolēmptōs*, adv. GK: *719* [→ *1.1+4383+2983*]. impartially, without prejudice:- without respect of persons [1]

679 ἄπταιστος, *aptaistos*, a. GK: *720* [→ *1.1+4417*]. without falling, without stumbling:- falling [1]

680 ἅπτομαι, *haptomai*, v.mid. of 681. GK: *721* [→ *381, 681, 860, 2510, 681*]. to touch, hold, handle; "to touch a woman" means "to get married":-

681 ἅπτω, *haptō*, v. GK: *721 & 4312* [→ *680*]. to touch, hold, handle; (act.) to start a fire; "to touch a woman" means "to get married":- touched [21], touch [13], lighted [2], toucheth [2], kindled [1], light [1]

682 Ἀπφία, *Apphia*, n.pr. GK: *722*. Apphia:- Apphia [1]

683 ἀπωθέω, *apōtheō*, v. GK: *723* [→ *1856; cf. 575*]. to reject, repudiate, push aside:- cast away [2], put away [1], put from [1], thrust away [1], thrust from [1]

684 ἀπώλεια, *apōleia*, n. GK: *724* [→ *575+3639*]. destruction, ruin, waste:- perdition [8], destruction [5], waste [2], damnable [1], damnation [1], die [1], perish (+*1510+1519*) [1], pernicious ways [1]

685 ἀρά, *ara*, n. GK: *725* [→ *1944, 2671, 2672*]. curse:- cursing [1]

686 ἄρα, *ara*, pt.infer. GK: *726*. then, so, therefore, consequently:- then [14], therefore (+*3767*) [7], so [4], therefore [4], so then [2], else (+*1893*) [1], haply (+*1065*) [1], haply [1], if so be that (+*1512*) [1], no doubt [1], now [1], perhaps [1], then (+*1065*) [1], truly [1], wherefore (+*1065*) [1], wherefore [1]

687 ἆρα, *ara*, pt.inter. GK: *727*. difficult to translate directly: introduces direct questions, showing anxiety or impatience:- what (+*5101*) [2], therefore [1], what man (+*5101*) [1]

688 Ἀραβία, *Arabia*, n.pr. GK: *728* [→ *690*]. Arabia, "*desert* or *steppe*":- Arabia [2]

 ἄραγε, *arage*. See **686** and **1065**.

689 Ἀράμ, *Aram*, n.pr. GK: *730*. Aram, Ram, "*high, exalted*":- Aram [3]

690 Ἄραψ, *Araps*, n.pr.g. GK: *732* [→ *688*]. Arab, "*desert dweller*":- Arabians [1]

691 ἀργέω, *argeō*, v. GK: *733* [→ *1.1+2041*]. to be idle, grow weary:- lingereth [1]

692 ἀργός, *argos*, a. GK: *734* [→ *1.1+2041*]. idle, lazy, useless, ineffective; careless:- idle [6], barren [1], slow [1]

693 ἀργύρεος, *argyreos*, a. GK: *735* [→ *696*]. (made of) silver:- silver [2], of silver [1]

694 ἀργύριον, *argyrion*, n. GK: *736* [→ *696*]. silver (always referring to money):- money [11], silver [9]

695 ἀργυροκόπος, *argyrokopos*, n. GK: *737* [→ *696+2875*]. silversmith:- silversmith [1]

696 ἄργυρος, *argyros*, n. GK: *738* [→ *693, 694, 695, 866, 5365, 5366*]. silver:- silver [5]

697 Ἄρειος πάγος, *Areios pagos*, n.pr. GK: *740 & 4076* [→ *698*]. meeting of the Areopagus; Mars' Hill, "*hill of the Greek god Ares*":- Areopagus [1], Mars' hill [1]

698 Ἀρεοπαγίτης, *Areopagitēs*, n.pr.g. GK: *741* [→ *697*]. member of the Areopagus:- Areopagite [1]

699 ἀρεσκεία, *areskeia*, n. GK: *742* [→ *700*]. pleasing, striving to please:- pleasing [1]

700 ἀρέσκω, *areskō*, v. GK: *743* [→ *441, 699, 701, 2100, 2101, 2102*]. to please, accommodate:- please [11], pleased [5], pleasing [1]

701 ἀρεστός, *arestos*, a. GK: *744* [→ *700*]. pleasing, desirable, right:- pleased (+*1510*) [1], please [1], pleasing [1], reason [1]

702 Ἀρέτας, *Haretas*, n.pr. GK: *745*. Aretas, "*virtuous*":- Aretas [1]

703 ἀρετή, *aretē*, n. GK: *746*. (moral) goodness, excellence, virtue:- virtue [4], praises [1]

704 ἀρήν, *arēn*, n. GK: *748* [→ *721*]. lamb:- lambs [1]

705 ἀριθμέω, *arithmeō*, v. GK: *749* [→ *706*]. to count:- numbered [2], number [1]

706 ἀριθμός, *arithmos*, n. GK: *750* [→ *382, 705, 2674*]. number:- number [18]

707 Ἀριμαθαία, *Harimathaia*, n.pr. GK: *751*. Arimathea:- Arimathea [4]

708 Ἀρίσταρχος, *Aristarchos*, n.pr. GK: *752* [→ *757*]. Aristarchus, "*best ruler*":- Aristarchus [5]

709 ἀριστάω, *aristaō*, v. GK: *753* [→ *712*]. to eat (breakfast):- dine [2], dined [1]

710 ἀριστερός, *aristeros*, a. GK: *754*. left side, left hand; the left is considered culturally to be weaker than the right; a weapon in the left hand is a defensive weapon; to be seated on the left side of a ruler is a lesser position than on the right side:- left [2], left hand [1]

711 Ἀριστόβουλος, *Aristoboulos*, n.pr. GK: *755* [→ *1014*]. Aristobulus, "*best advisor*":- Aristobulus' [1]

712 ἄριστον, *ariston*, n. GK: *756* [→ *709*]. meal, feast:- dinner [3]

713 ἀρκετός, *arketos*, a. GK: *757* [→ *714*]. enough, sufficient:- enough [1], suffice [1], sufficient [1]

714 ἀρκέω, *arkeō*, v. GK: *758* [→ *713, 841, 842, 1884*]. (mid./pass.) to be content, satisfied; (act.) to be sufficient:- content [4], sufficient [2], enough [1], sufficeth [1]

715 ἄρκος, *arkos*, n. GK: *759 & 760*. bear:- bear [1]

716 ἅρμα, *harma*, n. GK: *761* [→ *260*]. chariot, carriage (for traveling or military uses):- chariot [3], chariots [1]

717 Ἁρμαγεδών, *Harmagedōn*, n.pr. GK: *762 & 3403*. Armageddon, "*Mount Megiddo*":- Armageddon [1]

718 ἁρμόζω, *harmozō*, v. GK: *764* [→ *719, 4883*]. to promise for marriage, betroth:- espoused [1]

719 ἁρμός, *harmos*, n. GK: *765* [→ *718*]. joint (where bones connect):- joints [1]

720 ἀρνέομαι, *arneomai*, v. GK: *766* [→ *533*]. to deny, disown, renounce, repudiate:- denied [14], deny [7], denieth [4], denying [4], refused [2]

721 ἀρνίον, *arnion*, n. GK: *768* [→ *704*]. lamb, sheep; the Lamb (a title of Christ):- lamb [27], lamb's [2], lambs [1]

722 ἀροτριάω, *arotriaō*, v. GK: *769* [→ *723*]. to plow, furrow:- ploweth [1], plowing [1], plow [1]

723 ἄροτρον, *arotron*, n. GK: *770* [→ *722*]. plow, furrow-maker:- plough [1]

724 ἁρπαγή, *harpagē*, n. GK: *771* [→ *726*]. greediness, confiscation, robbery, plunder:- extortion [1], ravening [1], spoiling [1]

725 ἁρπαγμός, *harpagmos*, n. GK: *772* [→ *726*]. something to hold onto:- robbery [1]

726 ἁρπάζω, *harpazō*, v. GK: *773* [→ *724, 725, 727, 1283, 4884*]. to catch, steal, carry off:- caught up [4], take by force [3], pluck [2], catcheth away [1], catcheth [1], caught away [1], pulling [1]

727 ἅρπαξ, *harpax*, a. GK: *774* [→ *726*]. swindling, robbing, implying violence in the process; (destructively) ferocious, ravenous; as a noun, a (violent) robber or swindler:- extortioners [3], extortioner [1], ravening [1]

728 ἀρραβών, *arrabōn*, n. GK: *775*. deposit which guarantees, downpayment, pledge:- earnest [3]

729 ἄραφος, *araphos*, a. GK: *731* [→ *1.1+4476*]. seamless:- without seam [1]

730 ἄρρην, *arrēn*, n. GK: *776 & 781* [→ *733*]. male:- male [4], men [3], man [2]

731 ἄρρητος, *arrētos*, a. GK: *777* [→ *1.1+4487*]. inexpressible, not to be spoken (in context, things or words too sacred to tell):- unspeakable [1]

732 ἄρρωστος, *arrōstos*, a. GK: *778 & 779* [→ *1.1+4517*]. sick, ill:- sick [4], sickly [1]

733 ἀρσενοκοίτης, *arsenokoitēs*, n. GK: *780* [→ *730+2749*]. one engaging in homosexual acts (likely referring to the active male partner), sexual deviant:- abusers with mankind [1], them that defile with mankind [1]

734 Ἀρτεμᾶς, *Artemas*, n.pr. GK: *782* [→ *735+1325*]. Artemas, "*[given by] Artemis*":- Artemas [1]

735 Ἄρτεμις, *Artemis*, n.pr. GK: *783* [→ *734*]. Artemis:- Diana [5]

736 ἀρτέμων, *artemōn*, n. GK: *784*. foresail, sail:- mainsail [1]

737 ἄρτι, *arti*, adv. GK: *785* [→ *534, 535, 738, 739, 1822, 2675, 2676, 2677, 4294*]. now, at once, immediately:- now [22], henceforth (+*575*) [2], hereafter (+*575*) [2], hitherto (+*2193*) [2], even now [1], henceforth [1], now (+*575*) [1], presently [1], present [1], this day [1], this hour [1], this present [1]

738 ἀρτιγέννητος, *artigennētos*, a. GK: *786* [→ *737+1096*]. newborn:- newborn [1]

739 ἄρτιος, *artios*, a. GK: *787* [→ *737*]. thorough, complete, capable, proficient, able to meet all demands:- perfect [1]

740 ἄρτος, *artos*, n. GK: *788*. (loaf of) bread, food:- bread [72], loaves [22], shewbread (+*3588+4286*) [3], loaf [1], shewbread (+*4286*) [1]

741 ἀρτύω, *artyō*, v. GK: *789*. to make salty, season:- seasoned [2], season [1]

742 Ἀρφαξάδ, *Arphaxad*, n.pr. GK: *790*. Arphaxad:- Arphaxad [1]

743 ἀρχάγγελος, *archangelos*, n. GK: *791* [→ *757+32*]. archangel:- archangel [2]

744 ἀρχαῖος, *archaios*, a. GK: *792* [→ *757*]. ancient, of old:- old [8], of old time [3], a good while ago (+*575+2250*) [1]

745 Ἀρχέλαος, *Archelaos*, n.pr. GK: *793* [→ *757+2992*]. Archelaus, "*ruler of people*":- Archelaus [1]

746 ἀρχή, *archē*, n. GK: *794* [→ *757*]. beginning, origin, first; ruler, power, authority; position of authority, domain:- beginning [39], principalities [6], first [3], corners [2], principality [2], beginnings [1], first estate [1], magistrates [1], power [1], principles [1], rule [1]

747 ἀρχηγός, *archēgos*, n. GK: *795* [→ *757+71*]. author, originator, founder; leader, ruler:- prince [2], author [1], captain [1]

748 ἀρχιερατικός, *archieratikos*, a. GK: *796* [→ *757+2413*]. of the high priest:- high priest [1]

749 ἀρχιερεύς, *archiereus*, n. GK: *797* [→ *757+2413*]. chief priest, high priest:- chief priests [63], high priest [51], high priest's [4], high priests [3], chief of the priests [1], priests [1]

750 ἀρχιποίμην, *archipoimēn*, n. GK: *799* [→ *757+4166*]. chief shepherd:- chief shepherd [1]

751 Ἄρχιππος, *Archippos*, n.pr. GK: *800* [→ *757+2462*]. Archippus, "*master of the horse*":- Archippus [2]

752 ἀρχισυνάγωγος, *archisynagōgos*, n. GK: *801* [→ *757+4864*]. leader of the synagogue, an official whose duty it was to care for the physical needs for the worship service:-

Grk

ruler of the synagogue [5], ruler of the synagogue's [2], rulers of the synagogue [2]

753 ἀρχιτέκτων, *architektōn*, n. GK: *802* [→ *757+5078*]. expert builder:– masterbuilder [1]

754 ἀρχιτελώνης, *architelōnēs*, n. GK: *803* [→ *757+5057*]. chief tax collector:– chief among publicans [1]

755 ἀρχιτρίκλινος, *architriklinos*, n. GK: *804* [→ *757+5140+2827*]. master of the banquet, head waiter:– governor of the feast [2], ruler of the feast [1]

756 ἄρχομαι, *archomai*, v.mid. of *757*. GK: *806* [→ *757*]. to begin:– began [64], begin [11], beginning [7], begun [1], from the beginning [1]

757 ἄρχω, *archō*, v. GK: *806* [→ *536, 708, 743, 744, 745, 746, 747, 748, 749, 750, 751, 752, 753, 754, 755, 756, 758, 775, 1481, 1543, 1728, 1885, 3966, 3980, 4173, 4278, 4391, 4759, 5075, 5076, 5223, 5224, 5225, 5506*]. (act.) to rule; (mid.) to begin:– reign over [1], rule over [1]

758 ἄρχων, *archōn*, n. GK: *807* [→ *757*]. ruler, leader, official:– rulers [14], prince [8], ruler [8], princes [3], chief [2], magistrate [1], ruler's [1]

759 ἄρωμα, *arōma*, n. GK: *808*. spices, salves, scented oils, perfumes:– spices [4]

760 Ἀσά, *Asa*, n.pr. GK: *809 & 811*. Asa, "[poss.] *healer; myrtle*":– Asa [2]

761 ἀσάλευτος, *asaleutos*, a. GK: *810* [→ *1.1+4531*]. unshakable, immovable, fixed:– cannot be moved [1], unmoveable [1]

762 ἄσβεστος, *asbestos*, a. GK: *812* [→ *1.1+4570*]. unquenchable, inextinguishable:– never be quenched [2], unquenchable [2]

763 ἀσέβεια, *asebeia*, n. GK: *813* [→ *1.1+4576*]. ungodliness, godlessness, impiety (in thought and act):– ungodliness [4], ungodly [2]

764 ἀσεβέω, *asebeō*, v. GK: *814* [→ *1.1+4576*]. to do ungodly acts, act impiously:– those that live ungodly [1], ungodly committed [1]

765 ἀσεβής, *asebēs*, a. GK: *815* [→ *1.1+4576*]. ungodly, wicked, impious:– ungodly [9]

766 ἀσέλγεια, *aselgeia*, n. GK: *816* [→ *1.1*]. debauchery, sensuality, lewdness:– lasciviousness [6], wantonness [2], filthy [1]

767 ἄσημος, *asēmos*, a. GK: *817* [→ *1.1+4592*]. ordinary, obscure, insignificant:– mean [1]

768 Ἀσήρ, *Asēr*, n.pr. GK: *818*. Asher, "*happy one*":– Aser [2]

769 ἀσθένεια, *astheneia*, n. GK: *819* [→ *1.1+4599*]. weakness, illness, infirmity:– infirmities [10], infirmity [7], weakness [5], diseases [1], sickness [1]

770 ἀσθενέω, *astheneō*, v. GK: *820* [→ *1.1+4599*]. to be weak, ill:– sick [17], weak [16], impotent [2], diseased [1]

771 ἀσθένημα, *asthenēma*, n. GK: *821* [→ *1.1+4599*]. failing, weakness:– infirmities [1]

772 ἀσθενής, *asthenēs*, a. GK: *822* [→ *1.1+4599*]. weak, ill (of physical weakness or illness, also of moral or spiritual weakness):– weak [13], sick [6], weakness [2], impotent [1], more feeble [1], weaker [1], without strength [1]

773 Ἀσία, *Asia*, n.pr. GK: *823* [→ *774, 775*]. Asia:– Asia [19]

774 Ἀσιανός, *Asianos*, n.pr.g. GK: *824* [→ *773*]. one from the Roman province of Asia:– of Asia [1]

775 Ἀσιάρχης, *Asiarchēs*, n.pr. GK: *825* [→ *773+757*]. official of the province of Asia, Asiarch, a wealthy and influential man, probably connected with the Imperial cult:– chief of Asia [1]

776 ἀσιτία, *asitia*, n. GK: *826* [→ *1.1+4621*]. going without food:– abstinence [1]

777 ἄσιτος, *asitos*, a. GK: *827* [→ *1.1+4621*]. going without food:– fasting [1]

778 ἀσκέω, *askeō*, v. GK: *828*. to strive, do one's best:– exercise [1]

779 ἀσκός, *askos*, n. GK: *829*. wineskin, leather bag holding wine:– bottles [12]

780 ἀσμένως, *asmenōs*, adv. GK: *830* [→ *2237*]. warmly, gladly:– gladly [2]

781 ἄσοφος, *asophos*, a. GK: *831* [→ *1.1+4680*]. unwise, foolish:– fools [1]

782 ἀσπάζομαι, *aspazomai*, v. GK: *571 & 832* [→ *783*]. to give greetings (hello or good-bye):– salute [32], greet [14], saluted [5], saluteth [5], embraced [2], greeteth [1], taken leave [1]

783 ἀσπασμός, *aspasmos*, n. GK: *833* [→ *782*]. greeting:– salutation [6], greetings [3], salutations [1]

784 ἄσπιλος, *aspilos*, a. GK: *834* [→ *1.1+4696*]. without spot, defect or blemish:– without spot [3], unspotted [1]

785 ἀσπίς, *aspis*, n. GK: *835*. viper, asp, cobra:– asps [1]

786 ἄσπονδος, *aspondos*, a. GK: *836* [→ *1.1+4689*]. unforgiving, not reconcilable:– implacable [1], trucebreakers [1]

787 ἀσσάριον, *assarion*, n. GK: *837*. assarion (coin worth one-sixteenth of a day's wage):– farthings [1], farthing [1]

788 ἆσσον, *asson*, adv. GK: *839*. nearer:– close by [1]

789 Ἆσσος, *Assos*, n.pr. GK: *840*. Assos:– Assos [2]

790 ἀστατέω, *astateō*, v. GK: *841* [→ *1.1+2476*]. to be homeless, a vagabond:– have no certain dwelling place [1]

791 ἀστεῖος, *asteios*, a. GK: *842*. not ordinary, beautiful, pleasing:– exceeding fair (+*2316+3588*) [1], proper [1]

792 ἀστήρ, *astēr*, n. GK: *843* [→ *798*]. star:– stars [13], star [11]

793 ἀστήρικτος, *astēriktos*, a. GK: *844* [→ *1.1+4741*]. unstable, weak:– unstable [2]

794 ἄστοργος, *astorgos*, a. GK: *845* [→ *1.1*]. without love, heartless:– without natural affection [2]

795 ἀστοχέω, *astocheō*, v. GK: *846* [→ *1.1*]. to wander away, miss the mark; to turn to, deviate from:– erred [2], swerved [1]

796 ἀστραπή, *astrapē*, n. GK: *847* [→ *797, 1823, 4015*]. lightning; light, ray of light:– lightnings [4], lightning [4], bright shining [1]

797 ἀστράπτω, *astraptō*, v. GK: *848* [→ *796*]. to flash, gleam like lightning:– lighteneth [1], shining [1]

798 ἄστρον, *astron*, n. GK: *849* [→ *792*]. star, constellation:– stars [3], star [1]

799 Ἀσύγκριτος, *Asynkritos*, n.pr.v. GK: *850* [→ *1.1+4862+2919*]. Asyncritus, "*incomparable*":– Asyncritus [1]

800 ἀσύμφωνος, *asymphōnos*, a. GK: *851* [→ *1.1+4862+5456*]. disagreeable, not harmonious:– agreed not (+*1510*) [1]

801 ἀσύνετος, *asynetos*, a. GK: *852* [→ *863*]. senseless, dull, without understanding, foolish:– without understanding [3], foolish [2]

802 ἀσύνθετος, *asynthetos*, a. GK: *853* [→ *1.1+4862+5087*]. faithless, untrustworthy:– covenantbreakers [1]

803 ἀσφάλεια, *asphaleia*, n. GK: *854* [→ *755; cf. 1.1*]. security, safety; certainty, truth:– safety [2], certainty [1]

804 ἀσφαλής, *asphalēs*, a. GK: *855* [→ *754, 757; cf. 1.1*]. safe, firm, certain; definite; the truth:– certainty [2], certain [1], safe [1], sure [1]

805 ἀσφαλίζω, *asphalizō*, v. GK: *856* [→ *755; cf. 1.1*]. to make secure; fasten:– made sure [2], made fast [1], make sure [1]

806 ἀσφαλῶς, *asphalōs*, adv. GK: *857* [→ *755; cf. 1.1*]. carefully, securely; under guard; assuredly, beyond a doubt:– safely [2], assuredly [1]

807 ἀσχημονέω, *aschēmoneō*, v. GK: *858* [→ *1.1+4976*]. to act improperly, dishonorably, indecently, rudely:– behave unseemly [1], behaveth uncomely [1]

808 ἀσχημοσύνη, *aschēmosynē*, n. GK: *859* [→ *1.1+4976*]. indecent act, shame:– shame [1], unseemly [1]

809 ἀσχήμων, *aschēmōn*, a. GK: *860* [→ *1.1+4976*]. unpresentable, shameful, indecent:– uncomely [1]

810 ἀσωτία, *asōtia*, n. GK: *861* [→ *1.1+4982*]. debauchery, dissipation, wildness:– riot [2], excess [1]

811 ἀσώτως, *asōtōs*, adv. GK: *862* [→ *1.1+4982*]. wildly, in debauchery, in dissipation:– riotous [1]

812 ἀτακτέω, *atakteō*, v. GK: *863* [→ *1.1+5021*]. to be idle, lazy:– behaved disorderly [1]

813 ἄτακτος, *ataktos*, a. GK: *864* [→ *1.1+5021*]. idle, lazy:– unruly [1]

814 ἀτάκτως, *ataktōs*, adv. GK: *865* [→ *1.1+5021*]. idly, irresponsibly:– disorderly [2]

815 ἄτεκνος, *ateknos*, a. GK: *866* [→ *1.1+5088*]. childless, without children:– without children [2], childless [1]

816 ἀτενίζω, *atenizō*, v. GK: *867* [→ *1614; cf. 1.2*]. to look intently, gaze, stare:– looked stedfastly [2], earnestly beholding [1], earnestly looked [1], fastened eyes [1], fastening eyes [1], look earnestly [1], looked [1], looking stedfastly [1], set eyes [1], stedfastly beholding [1], stedfastly behold [1], stedfastly look [1]

817 ἄτερ, *ater*, pp.*. GK: *868*. without, apart from:– in the absence of [1], without [1]

818 ἀτιμάζω, *atimazō*, v. GK: *869 & 870* [→ *1.1+5092*]. to dishonor, disgrace, treat shamefully, insult:– dishonour [2], despised [1], dishonourest [1], entreated shamefully [1], suffer shame [1]

819 ἀτιμία, *atimia*, n. GK: *871* [→ *1.1+5092*]. dishonor, disgrace, shame; common use:– dishonour [4], reproach [1], shame [1], vile [1]

820 ἄτιμος, *atimos*, a. GK: *872* [→ *1.1+5092*]. without honor, dishonored, despised:– without honour [2], despised [1], less honourable [1]

821 ἀτιμόω, *atimoō*, v. GK: *873* [→ *1.1+5092*]. to disgrace:– shamefully handled [1]

822 ἀτμίς, *atmis*, n. GK: *874* [→ *109*]. mist, vapor; billows (of smoke):– vapour [2]

823 ἄτομος, *atomos*, a. GK: *875* [→ *1.1+5114*]. in a flash, in a moment, an indivisible unit of time:– moment [1]

824 ἄτοπος, *atopos*, a. GK: *876* [→ *1.1+5117*]. wrong, wicked; unusual, surprising:– amiss [1], harm [1], unreasonable [1]

825 Ἀττάλεια, *Attaleia*, n.pr. GK: *877*. Attalia:– Attalia [1]

826 αὐγάζω, *augazō*, v. GK: *878 & 2964* [→ *827*]. to see; shine (forth):– shine [1]

827 αὐγή, *augē*, n. GK: *879* [→ *541, 826, 1306, 5081*]. daylight, dawn:– break of day [1]

828 Αὔγουστος, *Augoustos*, n.pr. GK: *880*. Augustus, "*reverant, holy*":– Augustus [1]

829 αὐθάδης, *authadēs*, a. GK: *881* [→ *846+2237*]. overbearing, arrogant, stubborn, self-willed:– selfwilled [2]

830 αὐθαίρετος, *authairetos*, a. GK: *882* [→ *846+138*]. on one's own initiative, of one's own accord:– of own accord [1], willing of themselves [1]

831 αὐθεντέω, *authenteō*, v. GK: *883* [→ *846*]. to have authority over:– usurp authority over [1]

832 αὐλέω, *auleō*, v. GK: *884* [→ *836*]. to play the flute:– piped [3]

833 αὐλή, *aulē*, n. GK: *885* [→ *63, 1886, 4259; cf. 109, 835*]. palace, house; courtyard, sheepfold:– palace [7], hall [2], court [1], fold [1], sheepfold (+*3588+4263*) [1]

834 αὐλητής, *aulētēs*, n. GK: *886* [→ *836*]. flute player:– minstrels [1], pipers [1]

835 αὐλίζομαι, *aulizomai*, v. GK: *887* [cf. *833*]. to spend the night, find lodging:– abode [1], lodged [1]

836 αὐλός, *aulos*, n. GK: *888* [→ *832, 834*]. flute:– pipe [1]

837 αὐξάνω, *auxanō*, v. GK: *889 & 891* [→ *838, 4885, 5232*]. to cause to grow; (intr.) to grow, increase:– grew [6], grow [5], increased [3], increase [2], gave increase [1], giveth increase [1], groweth [1], grown [1], increaseth [1], increasing [1]

838 αὔξησις, *auxēsis*, n. GK: *890* [→ *837*]. growth, increase:– increase [2]

839 αὔριον, *aurion*, adv. GK: *892* [→ *1887*]. tomorrow, the next day:– to morrow [9], morrow [4], next day [1], on morrow [1]

840 αὐστηρός, *austeros*, a. GK: *893* [→ *850*]. hard, severe, strict, exacting:– austere [2]

841 αὐτάρκεια, *autarkeia*, n. GK: *894* [→ *846+714*]. contentment, having all of one's needs, sufficiency:– contentment [1], sufficiency [1]

842 αὐτάρκης, *autarkēs*, a. GK: *895* [→ *846+714*]. content; (possibly) self-sufficient:– content [1]

843 αὐτοκατάκριτος, *autokatakritos*, a. GK: *896* [→ *846+2596+2919*]. self-condemned:– condemned of himself [1]

844 αὐτόματος, *automatos*, a. GK: *897* [→ *846*]. by itself, automatic:– of herself [1], of own accord [1]

845 αὐτόπτης, *autoptēs*, n. GK: *898* [→ *846*+*3708*]. eyewitness:– eyewitnesses [1]

846 αὐτός, *autos*, p.inten. GK: *899* [→ *829, 830, 831, 841, 842, 843, 844, 845, 847, 848, 849, 1438, 1683, 1763, 1824, 1888, 3910, 4572, 5024, 5367, 5615*]. he, she, it, they; also used as inten.p., himself, herself, itself, themselves; the same one; also an adv. of place: here, there, where:– him [1942], them [1145], his [1093], their [313], he [265], her [242], it [183], usually untranslated [166], they [134], same [77], himself [51], his own [30], thereof [29], therein (+*1722*) [16], their own [12], yourselves [12], myself [10], themselves [10], the same [9], she [8], itself [7], that [7], those [7], together (+*1909*+*3588*) [7], ourselves [6], this [5], therein (+*1519*) [4], there [4], very [4], ye [4], own [3], selfsame [3], theirs [3], thereof (+*1537*) [3], thereon (+*1722*) [3], thyself [3], whose [3], he himself [2], into one place (+*1909*+*3588*) [2], likeminded (+*3588*+*5426*) [2], thee [2], there (+*1722*) [2], thereby (+*1223*) [2], thereon (+*1883*) [2], thereon [2], therewith (+*1722*) [2], we [2], which [2], whom [2], who [2], I myself [1], I [1], JesusS [1], and [1], even all one as if (+*1520*+*2532*+*3588*) [1], her own [1], here [1], herself [1], his own self [1], in one place (+*1909*+*3588*) [1], in the like manner (+*2596*+*3588*) [1], man's [1], myself (+*1473*) [1], nothing (+*1537*+*3361*) [1], one [1], own selves [1], so (+*2596*+*3588*) [1], the houseS [1], the otherS [1], the said [1], the same (+*3778*) [1], the very [1], their own company [1], thereat (+*1223*) [1], thereby (+*1722*) [1], thereinto (+*1519*) [1], therein [1], thereon (+*1909*) [1], thereunto (+*1519*+*3778*) [1], these [1], they themselves [1], the [1], things [1], together (+*2596*+*3588*) [1], we ourselves [1]

847 αὐτοῦ, *autou*, p.gen. of *846*. GK: *899* [→ *846*]. as an adv. of place: here, there, where:–

848 αὑτοῦ, *autou*, p.gen. of *846*. GK: *899* [→ *846*]. of him, her, it, them:–

849 αὐτόχειρ, *autocheir*, a. or n. GK: *901* [→ *846*+*5495*]. with one's own hand:– with own hands [1]

850 αὐχμηρός, *auchmēros*, a. GK: *903* [→ *840*]. dark:– dark [1]

851 ἀφαιρέω, *aphaireō*, v. GK: *904* [→ *575*+*138*]. to take away from, remove; to cut (off):– take away [5], cut off [2], smote off [1], taken away [1], taketh away [1]

852 ἀφανής, *aphanēs*, a. GK: *905* [→ *1.1*+*5316*]. hidden, invisible:– not manifest [1]

853 ἀφανίζω, *aphanizō*, v. GK: *906* [→ *1.1*+*5316*]. to destroy, disfigure; to perish, vanish, disappear:– corrupt [2], disfigure [1], perish [1], vanisheth away [1]

854 ἀφανισμός, *aphanismos*, n. GK: *907* [→ *1.1*+*5316*]. disappearance, destruction:– vanish away [1]

855 ἄφαντος, *aphantos*, a. GK: *908* [→ *1.1*+*5316*]. disappearing, invisible:– vanished out of sight (+*1096*) [1]

856 ἀφεδρών, *aphedrōn*, n. GK: *909* [→ *575*+*1476*]. latrine:– draught [2]

857 ἀφειδία, *apheidia*, n. GK: *910* [→ *1.1*+*5339*]. harsh treatment, unsparing:– neglecting [1]

858 ἀφελότης, *aphelotēs*, n. GK: *911* [→ *1.1*]. sincerity, simplicity:– singleness [1]

859 ἄφεσις, *aphesis*, n. GK: *912* [→ *863*]. forgiveness, pardon, release, cancellation of a debt:– remission [9], forgiveness [6], deliverance [1], liberty [1]

860 ἀφή, *haphē*, n. GK: *913* [→ *681*]. ligament, joint:– joints [1], joint [1]

861 ἀφθαρσία, *aphtharsia*, n. GK: *914* [→ *1.1*+*5351*]. imperishableness, immortality:– incorruption [4], immortality [2], sincerity [2]

862 ἄφθαρτος, *aphthartos*, a. GK: *915* [→ *1.1*+*5351*]. imperishable, immortal, lasting forever:– incorruptible [4], immortal [1], not corruptible [1], uncorruptible [1]

863 ἀφίημι, *aphiēmi*, v. GK: *918 & 1889* [→ *425, 447, 801, 859, 1455, 3929, 3935, 4907, 4908, 4920; cf. 575*]. to forgive, pardon, remit, cancel; to leave, abandon; to allow, permit, tolerate:– left [36], forgive [23], forgiven [21], leave [9], let [8], suffer [8], let alone [6], suffered [6], forsook [4], leaving [3], forgave [2], forsaken [2], leave undone [2], leaveth [2], put away [2], sent away [2], cried [1], forgiveth [1], laying aside [1], let be [1], let go [1], let have [1], omitted [1], remitted [1], remit [1], yielded up [1]

864 ἀφικνέομαι, *aphikneomai*, v. GK: *919* [→ *575*+*2425*]. to reach:– come abroad [1]

865 ἀφιλάγαθος, *aphilagathos*, a. GK: *920* [→ *1.1*+*5384*+*18*]. not loving good:– despisers of good [1]

866 ἀφιλάργυρος, *aphilargyros*, a. GK: *921* [→ *1.1*+*5384*+*696*]. not loving money, not greedy:– not covetous [1], without covetousness [1]

867 ἄφιξις, *aphixis*, n. GK: *922* [→ *575*+*2425*]. leaving, departure:– departing [1]

868 ἀφίστημι, *aphistēmi*, v. GK: *923* [→ *575*+*2476*]. to leave, withdraw, abandon; to revolt, mislead:– departed [6], depart [4], depart from [1], departing [1], drew away [1], fall away [1], refrain [1], withdraw [1]

869 ἄφνω, *aphnō*, adv. GK: *924* [→ *160?*]. suddenly:– suddenly [3]

870 ἀφόβως, *aphobōs*, adv. GK: *925* [→ *1.1*+*5401*]. fearlessly, without the slightest qualm, boldly:– without fear [4]

871 ἀφομοιόω, *aphomoioō*, v. GK: *926* [→ *575*+*3664*]. (pass.) to be like, similar:– made like unto [1]

872 ἀφοράω, *aphoraō*, v. GK: *927* [→ *575*+*3708*]. to fix one's eyes; look away:– looking [1]

873 ἀφορίζω, *aphorizō*, v. GK: *928* [→ *575*+*3724*]. to separate, set apart, exclude:– separated [4], separate [4], divideth [1], sever [1]

874 ἀφορμή, *aphormē*, n. GK: *929* [→ *575*+*3730*]. opportunity, opening, pretext:– occasion [7]

875 ἀφρίζω, *aphrizō*, v. GK: *930* [→ *876*]. to foam at the mouth:– foameth [1], foaming [1]

876 ἀφρός, *aphros*, n. GK: *931* [→ *875, 1890*]. foam, froth:– foameth (+*3326*) [1]

877 ἀφροσύνη, *aphrosynē*, n. GK: *932* [→ *1.1*+*5424*]. foolishness, lack of sense:– foolishly (+*1722*) [2], folly [1], foolishness [1]

878 ἄφρων, *aphrōn*, a. GK: *933* [→ *1.1*+*5424*]. foolish, ignorant:– fool [6], foolish [2], fools [2], unwise [1]

879 ἀφυπνόω, *aphypnoō*, v. GK: *934* [→ *575*+*5258*]. to fall asleep:– fell asleep [1]

880 ἄφωνος, *aphōnos*, a. GK: *936* [→ *1.1*+*5456*]. silent, mute, without speech; without meaning:– dumb [3], without signification [1]

881 Ἀχάζ, *Achaz*, n.pr. GK: *937 & 941*. Ahaz, "*he has grasped*":– Achaz [2]

882 Ἀχαΐα, *Achaia*, n.pr. GK: *938* [→ *883*]. Achaia:– Achaia [11]

883 Ἀχαϊκός, *Achaikos*, n.pr. GK: *939* [→ *882*]. Achaicus, "*belonging to Achaia*":– Achaicus [2]

884 ἀχάριστος, *acharistos*, a. GK: *940* [→ *1.1*+*5463*]. ungrateful:– unthankful [2]

885 Ἀχίμ, *Achim*, n.pr. GK: *943*. Akim, "*Yahweh is my brother*":– Achim [2]

886 ἀχειροποίητος, *acheiropoiētos*, a. GK: *942* [→ *1.1*+*5495*+*4160*]. not made by human hands, implying not of human origin:– made without hands [2], not made with hand [1]

887 ἀχλύς, *achlys*, n. GK: *944*. mistiness, dimness of sight:– mist [1]

888 ἀχρεῖος, *achreios*, a. GK: *945* [→ *1.1*+*5530*]. worthless, useless, unworthy:– unprofitable [2]

889 ἀχρειόω, *achreioō*, v. GK: *946* [→ *1.1*+*5530*]. (pass.) to become worthless, depraved:– unprofitable [1]

890 ἄχρηστος, *achrēstos*, a. GK: *947* [→ *1.1*+*5530*]. useless, worthless:– unprofitable [1]

891 ἄχρι, *achri*, pp.*&c. GK: *948* [→ *206*]. until, up to, as far as, as long as:– until [12], unto [12], till [12], till [4], until (+*3739*) [4], as far as [2], for [2], while (+*3739*) [2], even to [1], even unto [1], hitherto (+*1204*+*3588*) [1], into [1], in [1], till (+*302*+*3739*) [1], to [1]

892 ἄχυρον, *achyron*, n. GK: *949*. chaff:– chaff [1]

893 ἀψευδής, *apseudēs*, a. GK: *950* [→ *1.1*+*5574*]. not a liar, free from deceit, trustworthy:– cannot lie [1]

894 ἄψινθος, *apsinthos*, n. GK: *951 & 952*. (m.) Wormwood, referring to a bitter herb (absinthe); (f.) bitterness:– wormwood [2]

895 ἄψυχος, *apsychos*, a. GK: *953* [→ *1.1*+*5594*]. lifeless, inanimate:– without life [1]

896 Βάαλ, *Baal*, n.pr. GK: *955*. Baal, "*master, owner, lord*":– Baal [1]

897 Βαβυλών, *Babylōn*, n.pr. GK: *956*. Babylon, "*gate of god[s]*":– Babylon [12]

898 βαθμός, *bathmos*, n. GK: *957* [→ *305*]. standing, rank:– degree [1]

899 βάθος, *bathos*, n. GK: *958* [→ *901*]. depth, deep thing; extreme:– depth [4], deep (+*2596*) [1], deep things [1], deepness [1], deep [1], depths [1]

900 βαθύνω, *bathynō*, v. GK: *959* [→ *901*]. to go down deep, dig deep:– deep [1]

901 βαθύς, *bathys*, a. GK: *960* [→ *899, 900*]. deep; (as a time of day) early:– deep [2], very early in the morning (+*3722*) [1]

902 βάϊον, *baion*, n. GK: *961*. (palm) branch:– branches [1]

903 Βαλαάμ, *Balaam*, n.pr. GK: *962*. Balaam, "[poss.] *Baal [lord] of the people* or *the clan brings forth*":– Balaam [3]

904 Βαλάκ, *Balak*, n.pr. GK: *963*. Balak, "*devastator*":– Balac [1]

905 βαλλάντιον, *ballantion*, n. GK: *964*. purse, money-bag:– purse [3], bags [1]

906 βάλλω, *ballō*, v. GK: *311 & 965* [→ *293, 306, 311, 474, 577, 579, 580, 956, 992, 1000, 1001, 1002, 1225, 1228, 1544, 1546, 1685, 1911, 1915, 2598, 2602, 3036, 3328, 3846, 3850, 3925, 4016, 4018, 4261, 4820, 5146, 5234, 5235, 5236, 5260*]. to throw, pour; to put, set:– cast [81], put [11], casting [6], laid [3], send [3], thrust [3], casteth [2], putteth [2], threw [2], thrust in [2], arose [1], cast in [1], dung (+*2874*) [1], lieth [1], lying [1], poured [1], poureth [1], put up [1], strike with the palms of hands (+*4475*) [1], thrown [1]

907 βαπτίζω, *baptizō*, v. GK: *966* [→ *911*]. to baptize, wash; the baptizer:– baptized [61], baptize [9], baptizing [4], baptizeth [1], Baptist [1], baptizest [1], washed [1], wash [1]

908 βάπτισμα, *baptisma*, n. GK: *967* [→ *911*]. baptism:– baptism [22]

909 βαπτισμός, *baptismos*, n. GK: *968* [→ *911*]. baptism, ceremonial washing:– washing [2], baptisms [1], washings [1]

910 βαπτιστής, *baptistēs*, n. GK: *969* [→ *911*]. Baptist, a surname of John:– Baptist [13], Baptist's [1]

911 βάπτω, *baptō*, v. GK: *970* [→ *907, 908, 909, 910, 1686*]. to dip (in):– dipped [1], dipt [1], dip [1]

912 Βαραββᾶς, *Barabbas*, n.pr. GK: *972*. Barabbas, "*son of a father poss. son of a rabbi*":– Barabbas [11]

913 Βαράκ, *Barak*, n.pr. GK: *973*. Barak, "*lightning*":– Barak [1]

914 Βαραχίας, *Barachias*, n.pr. GK: *974*. Berekiah, "*Yahweh blesses*":– Barachias [1]

915 βάρβαρος, *barbaros*, a. GK: *975*. non-Greek, foreign, "barbarian"; someone who speaks an unintelligible language:– barbarian [3], barbarians [2], barbarous people [1]

916 βαρέω, *bareō*, v. GK: *976* [→ *922*]. (pass.) to be burdened, under pressure:– heavy [3], burdened [1], charged [1], pressed [1]

917 βαρέως, *bareōs*, adv. GK: *977* [→ *922*]. with difficulty:– dull [2]

918 Βαρθολομαῖος, *Bartholomaios*, n.pr. GK: *978*. Bartholomew, "*son of Talmai*":– Bartholomew [4]

919 Βαριησοῦς, *Bariēsous*, n.pr. GK: *979*. Bar-Jesus, "*son of Jesus [Joshua]*":– Barjesus [1]

920 Βαριωνᾶς, *Bariōnas*, n.pr. GK: *980 & 981*. son of Jonah, Bar-Jona, "*son of Jonah* or *John*":– Barjona [1]

921 Βαρνάβας, *Barnabas*, n.pr. GK: *982*. Barnabas, "*son of comfort*":– Barnabas [29]

922 βάρος, *baros*, n. GK: *983* [→ *4, 916, 917, 925, 926, 927, 1912, 2599*]. burden, weight; this can refer either to difficulty or importance:– burden [3], burdensome (+*1722*) [1], burdens [1], weight [1]

923 Βαρσαββᾶς, *Barsabbas*, n.pr. GK: *984*. Barsabbas, "*son of the Sabbath* or *son of Saba*":– Barsabas [2]

924 Βαρτιμαῖος, *Bartimaios*, n.pr. GK: *985*. Bartimaeus, "*son of Timai* or *son of uncleanness*":– Bartimeus [1]

925 βαρύνω, *barynō*, v. GK: *986 & 2852* [→ *922*]. to burden, grieve:– overcharged [1]

Grk

926 βαρύς, *barys*, a. GK: *987* [→ *922*]. burdensome, heavy, important; savage, fierce:– grievous [3], heavy [1], weightier [1], weighty [1]

927 βαρύτιμος, *barytimos*, a. GK: *988* [→ *922+5092*]. very expensive:– very precious [1]

928 βασανίζω, *basanizō*, v. GK: *989* [→ *931*]. to torture, torment; (pass.) to be tortured, tormented, in pain:– tormented [5], torment [3], pained [1], toiling [1], tossed [1], vexed [1]

929 βασανισμός, *basanismos*, n. GK: *990* [→ *931*]. torment, torture, agony:– torment [6]

930 βασανιστής, *basanistēs*, n. GK: *991* [→ *931*]. torturer:– tormentors [1]

931 βάσανος, *basanos*, n. GK: *992* [→ *928, 929, 930*]. torment, severe pain, torture:– torments [2], torment [1]

932 βασιλεία, *basileia*, n. GK: *993* [→ *935*]. kingdom, kingship, royal rule:– kingdom [157], kingdoms [4], reigneth (+*2192*) [1]

933 βασίλειον, *basileion*, a.neut. of *934*. GK: *994* [→ *935*]. as a noun, a residence of royalty: palace:– kings' courts [1]

934 βασίλειος, *basileios*, a. GK: *994* [→ *935*]. royal, kingly; as a noun, a residence of royalty: palace:– royal [1]

935 βασιλεύς, *basileus*, n. GK: *995* [→ *932, 933, 934, 936, 937, 938, 4821*]. king:– king [86], kings [29], king's [2], kings' [1]

936 βασιλεύω, *basileuō*, v. GK: *996* [→ *935*]. to reign as a king, become king:– reign [13], reigned [5], kings [1], reigned as kings [1], reigneth [1]

937 βασιλικός, *basilikos*, a. GK: *997 & 998* [→ *935*]. royal, noble, kingly; as a noun, royal official (possibly of the Herodian family):– nobleman [2], royal [2], king's [1]

938 βασίλισσα, *basilissa*, n. GK: *999* [→ *935*]. queen:– queen [4]

939 βάσις, *basis*, n. GK: *1000* [→ *305*]. foot:– feet [1]

940 βασκαίνω, *baskainō*, v. GK: *1001*. to bewitch:– bewitched [1]

941 βαστάζω, *bastazō*, v. GK: *1002* [→ *1419*]. to carry, bear up, carry off; to tolerate, help, support:– bear [11], bare [4], borne [4], bearing [3], bearest [1], carried [1], carrieth [1], carry [1], took up [1]

942 βάτος¹, *batos*¹, n. GK: *1003*. bush, brier, thornbush:– bush [4], bramble bush [1]

943 βάτος², *batos*², n. GK: *1004*. bath (a unit of liquid measure, between eight and nine gallons):– measures [1]

944 βάτραχος, *batrachos*, n. GK: *1005*. frog:– frogs [1]

945 βατταλογέω, *battalogeō*, v. GK: *1006* [→ *3004*]. to babble, prattle:– use vain repetitions [1]

946 βδέλυγμα, *bdelygma*, n. GK: *1007* [→ *947, 948*]. abomination, something detestable:– abomination [4], abominations [2]

947 βδελυκτός, *bdelyktos*, a. GK: *1008* [→ *946*]. detestable, abominable:– abominable [1]

948 βδελύσσομαι, *bdelyssomai*, v. GK: *1009* [→ *946*]. (mid.) to abhor, detest; (pass.) to be vile, abhorrent:– abhorrest [1], abominable [1]

949 βέβαιος, *bebaios*, a. GK: *1010* [→ *305*]. firm, sure, certain, binding:– stedfast [4], sure [2], firm [1], force [1], more sure [1]

950 βεβαιόω, *bebaioō*, v. GK: *1011* [→ *305*]. to confirm; keep strong:– confirmed [2], confirm [2], confirming [1], established [1], stablished [1], stablisheth [1]

951 βεβαίωσις, *bebaiōsis*, n. GK: *1012* [→ *305*]. confirmation:– confirmation [2]

952 βέβηλος, *bebēlos*, a. GK: *1013* [→ *305*]. godless, irreligious, profane, worldly:– profane [5]

953 βεβηλόω, *bebēloō*, v. GK: *1014* [→ *305*]. to desecrate, profane:– profane [2]

954 Βεελζεβούλ, *Beelzeboul*, n.pr. GK: *1015*. Beelzebub, "*lord [baal] of the flies*":– Beelzebub [7]

955 Βελίαλ, *Belial*, n.pr. GK: *1016*. Belial, "*wicked, without use*":– Belial [1]

956 βέλος, *belos*, n. GK: *1018* [→ *906*]. arrow:– darts [1]

957 βελτίων, *beltiōn*, a. GK: *1019*. having a detailed knowledge, translated "better, very well":– very well [1]

958 Βενιαμίν, *Beniamin*, n.pr. GK: *1020 & 1021*. Benjamin, "*son of the right hand* or *Southerner*":– Benjamin [4]

959 Βερνίκη, *Bernikē*, n.pr. GK: *1022* [→ *5342+3529*]. Bernice, "*victorious*":– Bernice [3]

960 Βέροια, *Beroia*, n.pr. GK: *1023* [→ *961*]. Berea:– Berea [2]

961 Βεροιαῖος, *Beroiaios*, a.prg. GK: *1024* [→ *960*]. Berean, person of Berea:– Berea [1]

962 Βηθαβαρά, *Bēthabara*, n.pr. GK: *1028 & 1030*. Bethabara:– Bethabara [1]

963 Βηθανία, *Bēthania*, n.pr. GK: *1029*. Bethany, "*House of Ananiah* [or *the poor* or *unripe figs*]":– Bethany [11]

964 Βηθεσδά, *Bēthesda*, n.pr. GK: *1031 & 1032*. Bethesda, "*site [house] of mercy*":– Bethesda [1]

965 Βηθλέεμ, *Bēthleem*, n.pr. GK: *1033*. Bethlehem, "*house of bread poss. temple of Lakhmu*":– Bethlehem [8]

966 Βηθσαϊδά, *Bēthsaida*, n.pr. GK: *1034 & 1035*. Bethsaida, "*site [house] of fishing*":– Bethsaida [7]

967 Βηθφαγή, *Bēthphagē*, n.pr. GK: *1036*. Bethphage, "*house of unripe figs*":– Bethphage [3]

968 βῆμα, *bēma*, n. GK: *1037* [→ *305*]. judicial court, judge's seat; this can refer to human or divine judgment:– judgment seat [10], set on [1], throne [1]

969 βήρυλλος, *bēryllos*, n. GK: *1039*. beryl, a semi-precious stone of sea-green color:– beryl [1]

970 βία, *bia*, n. GK: *1040* [→ *971, 972, 973, 3849*]. force, violence, pounding (of surf):– violence [4]

971 βιάζω, *biazō*, v. GK: *1041* [→ *970*]. (mid.) to force one's way:– presseth [1], suffereth violence [1]

972 βίαιος, *biaios*, a. GK: *1042* [→ *970*]. violent, strong:– mighty [1]

973 βιαστής, *biastēs*, n. GK: *1043* [→ *970*]. forceful one:– violent [1]

974 βιβλαρίδιον, *biblaridion*, n. GK: *1044 & 1045* [→ *976*]. little scroll:– little book [4]

975 βιβλίον, *biblion*, n. GK: *1046* [→ *976*]. scroll, book, certificate:– book [25], books [4], bill [1], scrole [1], writing [1]

976 βίβλος, *biblos*, n. GK: *1047* [→ *974, 975*]. book, scroll:– book [12], books [1]

977 βιβρώσκω, *bibrōskō*, v. GK: *1048* [→ *1033, 1034, 1035, 4598, 4662*]. to eat:– eaten [1]

978 Βιθυνία, *Bithynia*, n.pr. GK: *1049*. Bithynia:– Bithynia [2]

979 βίος, *bios*, n. GK: *1050* [→ *980, 981, 982, 3969*]. (everyday) life; what one lives on, property, possessions:– life [5], living [5], good [1]

980 βιόω, *bioō*, v. GK: *1051* [→ *979*]. to live:– live [1]

981 βίωσις, *biōsis*, n. GK: *1052* [→ *979*]. the way one lives:– manner of life [1]

982 βιωτικός, *biōtikos*, a. GK: *1053* [→ *979*]. (lesser things) of this life:– of life [1], pertaining to life [1], that pertain to life [1]

983 βλαβερός, *blaberos*, a. GK: *1054* [→ *984*]. harmful:– hurtful [1]

984 βλάπτω, *blaptō*, v. GK: *1055* [→ *983*]. to hurt, injure:– hurt [2]

985 βλαστάνω, *blastanō*, v. GK: *1056 & 1057* [→ *986*]. to sprout, bud:– brought forth [1], budded [1], spring [1], sprung up [1]

986 Βλάστος, *Blastos*, n.pr. GK: *1058* [→ *985*]. Blastus, "*sprout [of a vine or branch]*":– Blastus [1]

987 βλασφημέω, *blasphēmeō*, v. GK: *1059* [→ *988, 989; cf. 5346*]. to blaspheme, insult, slander, curse:– blasphemed [7], blaspheme [6], speak evil [5], evil spoken of [4], blasphemeth [2], blasphemers [1], blasphemest [1], blaspheming [1], blasphemously [1], defamed [1], railed on [1], railed [1], reviled [1], slanderously reported [1], speaking evil [1], spoken blasphemy [1]

988 βλασφημία, *blasphēmia*, n. GK: *1060* [→ *987*]. blasphemy, slander, malicious talk:– blasphemy [11], blasphemies [5], evil speaking [1], railings [1], railing [1]

989 βλάσφημος, *blasphēmos*, a. GK: *1061* [→ *987*]. blasphemous, slanderous, abusive, evil, hurtful (speech); as a noun, a reviler, blasphemer:– blasphemous [2], blasphemers [1], blasphemer [1], railing [1]

990 βλέμμα, *blemma*, n. GK: *1062* [→ *991*]. act of seeing:– seeing [1]

991 βλέπω, *blepō*, v. GK: *1063* [→ *308, 309, 578, 990, 1227, 1689, 1914, 4017, 4265*]. to see, look at; to watch out, beware, pay attention:– see [48], take heed [14], seeth [11], saw [9], seen [9], seeing [8], beware [7], seest [5], look [4], beholdest [3], behold [3], beheld [2], beholding [2], sight [2], lieth [1], look on [1], looked [1], looketh on [1], looking [1], perceive [1], regardest (+*1519*) [1], regardest [1]

992 βλητέος, *blēteos*, a. GK: *1064* [→ *906*]. must be put:– must be put [1], put [1]

993 Βοανηργές, *Boanērges*, i.[pr.n.]. GK: *1065*. Boanerges, "*sons of thunder*":– Boanerges [1]

994 βοάω, *boaō*, v. GK: *1066* [→ *995*]. to call, cry out, shout:– crying [6], cried [3], cry [2]

995 βοή, *boē*, n. GK: *1068* [→ *310, 994, 996, 997, 998, 1916*]. cry, shout:– cries [1]

996 βοήθεια, *boētheia*, n. GK: *1069* [→ *995*]. help; support (to hold something together with ropes or cables):– helps [1], help [1]

997 βοηθέω, *boētheō*, v. GK: *1070* [→ *995*]. to help, come to the aid of:– help [5], helped [1], succoured [1], succour [1]

998 βοηθός, *boēthos*, a. GK: *1071* [→ *995*]. helpful (one):– helper [1]

999 βόθυνος, *bothynos*, n. GK: *1072 & 1073*. pit, cistern:– ditch [2], pit [1]

1000 βολή, *bolē*, n. GK: *1074* [→ *906*]. throwing:– cast [1]

1001 βολίζω, *bolizō*, v. GK: *1075* [→ *906*]. to take a sounding (a nautical technical term):– sounded [2]

1002 βολίς, *bolis*, n. GK: *1076* [→ *906*]. missile, arrow, javelin:– dart [1]

1003 Βοόζ, *Booz*, n.pr. GK: *1067 & 1077 & 1078*. Boaz, "*[perhaps] in him is strength*":– Booz [3]

1004 βόρβορος, *borboros*, n. GK: *1079*. mud, filth, slime:– mire [1]

1005 βορρᾶς, *borras*, n. GK: *1080*. the north:– north [2]

1006 βόσκω, *boskō*, v. GK: *1081* [→ *1008*]. to feed, tend; (pass.) to eat, graze:– feeding [3], feed [3], fed [1], kept [1]

1007 Βοσόρ, *Bosor*, n.pr. GK: *1026 & 1027 & 1082*. Bosor:– Bosor [1]

1008 βοτάνη, *botanē*, n. GK: *1083* [→ *1006*]. crop (from any kind of plant or vegetation):– herbs [1]

1009 βότρυς, *botrys*, n. GK: *1084*. grape cluster, bunch of grapes:– clusters [1]

1010 βουλευτής, *bouleutēs*, n. GK: *1085* [→ *1014*]. member of a council (an advisory or legislative body):– counseller [2]

1011 βουλεύω, *bouleuō*, v. GK: *1086* [→ *1014*]. to make plans, consider, decide, plot:– minded [2], purpose [2], consulted [1], consulteth [1], determined [1], took counsel [1]

1012 βουλή, *boulē*, n. GK: *1087* [→ *1014*]. plan, purpose, will, decision:– counsel [9], advised (+*5087*) [1], counsels [1], will [1]

1013 βούλημα, *boulēma*, n. GK: *1088* [→ *1014*]. plan, will, choice:– purpose [1], will [1]

1014 βούλομαι, *boulomai*, v. GK: *1089* [→ *711, 1010, 1011, 1012, 1013, 1917, 2103, 3851, 4823, 4824, 4825*]. to wish, will, desire; to choose, determine, plan:– will [11], would [10], willing [5], minded [2], disposed [1], intending [1], intend [1], listeth (+*2116*) [1], of own will [1], would have [1]

1015 βουνός, *bounos*, n. GK: *1090*. hill:– hills [1], hill [1]

1016 βοῦς, *bous*, n. GK: *1091*. ox, cattle:– oxen [4], ox [4]

1017 βραβεῖον, *brabeion*, n. GK: *1092* [→ *1018*]. prize (from a contest or foot race):– prize [2]

1018 βραβεύω, *brabeuō*, v. GK: *1093* [→ *1017, 2603*]. to rule:– rule [1]

1019 βραδύνω, *bradynō*, v. GK: *1094* [→ *1021*]. to delay, hesitate:– slack [1], tarry long [1]

1020 βραδυπλοέω, **bradyploeō**, v. GK: *1095* [→ *1021+4126*]. to sail slowly:– sailed slowly [1]

1021 βραδύς, **bradys**, a. GK: *1096* [→ *1019, 1020, 1022*]. slow:– slow [3]

1022 βραδύτης, **bradytēs**, n. GK: *1097* [→ *1021*]. slowness:– slackness [1]

1023 βραχίων, **brachiōn**, n. GK: *1098* [→ *1024*]. arm; a figure of power and authority:– arm [3]

1024 βραχύς, **brachys**, a. GK: *1099* [→ *1023*]. little, short:– little [4], few [1], little space [1], little while [1]

1025 βρέφος, **brephos**, n. GK: *1100*. baby, infant:– babe [4], babes [1], child [1], infants [1], young children [1]

1026 βρέχω, **brechō**, v. GK: *1101* [→ *1028*]. to rain down (water or sulfur); to make wet:– rained [2], rain [+*5205*] [1], rain [1], sendeth rain [1], washed [1], wash [1]

1027 βροντή, **brontē**, n. GK: *1103*. thunder:– thunderings [4], thunders [4], thunder [3], thundered (+*1096*) [1]

1028 βροχή, **brochē**, n. GK: *1104* [→ *1026*]. rain:– rain [2]

1029 βρόχος, **brochos**, n. GK: *1105*. restriction, restraint (from the base meaning of a snare or noose, not found in the NT):– snare [1]

1030 βρυγμός, **brygmos**, n. GK: *1106* [→ *1031*]. gnashing, grinding:– gnashing [7]

1031 βρύχω, **brychō**, v. GK: *1107* [→ *1030*]. to gnash, grind:– gnashed [1]

1032 βρύω, **bryō**, v. GK: *1108*. to flow, pour forth:– send forth [1]

1033 βρῶμα, **brōma**, n. GK: *1109* [→ *977*]. food, what is eaten:– meat [10], meats [6], victuals [1]

1034 βρώσιμος, **brōsimos**, a. GK: *1110* [→ *977*]. eatable:– meat [1]

1035 βρῶσις, **brōsis**, n. GK: *1111* [→ *977*]. consumable, food, rust, corrosion:– meat [6], rust [2], eating [1], food [1], morsel of meat [1]

1036 βυθίζω, **bythizō**, v. GK: *1112* [→ *1037*]. (act.) to plunge; (pass.) to sink:– drown [1], sink [1]

1037 βυθός, **bythos**, n. GK: *1113* [→ *12, 1036*]. open sea, the deep:– deep [1]

1038 βυρσεύς, **byrseus**, n. GK: *1114*. tanner:– tanner [3]

1039 βύσσινος, **byssinos**, a. GK: *1115 & 3327* [→ *1040*]. made of fine linen, a product of the flax plant:– fine linen [4]

1040 βύσσος, **byssos**, n. GK: *1116* [→ *1039*]. fine linen:– fine linen [2]

1041 βωμός, **bōmos**, n. GK: *1117* [→ *305*]. altar:– altar [1]

1042 Γαββαθᾶ, **Gabbatha**, n.pr. GK: *1119*. Gabbatha, "[poss.] *height, ridge*":– Gabbatha [1]

1043 Γαβριήλ, **Gabriēl**, n.pr. GK: *1120*. Gabriel, "*[strong] man of God [El]*":– Gabriel [2]

1044 γάγγραινα, **gangraina**, n. GK: *1121*. gangrene:– canker [1]

1045 Γάδ, **Gad**, n.pr. GK: *1122*. Gad, "*fortune*":– Gad [1]

1046 Γαδαρηνός, **Gadarēnos**, a.pr.g. GK: *1123*. Gadarene, "*from Gadara*":– Gadarenes [3]

1047 γάζα², **gaza²**, n. GK: *1125* [→ *1049*]. treasury:– treasure [1]

1048 Γάζα¹, **Gaza¹**, n.pr. GK: *1124*. Gaza, "*strong*":– Gaza [1]

1049 γαζοφυλάκιον, **gazophylakion**, n. GK: *1126* [→ *1047+5442*]. treasury, place where offerings are put:– treasury [5]

1050 Γάϊος, **Gaios**, n.pr. GK: *1127* [→ *1093*]. Gaius:– Gaius [5]

1051 γάλα, **gala**, n. GK: *1128*. milk:– milk [5]

1052 Γαλάτης, **Galatēs**, n.pr.g. GK: *1129* [→ *1053*]. Galatian, "*from Galatia*":– Galatians [2]

1053 Γαλατία, **Galatia**, n.pr. GK: *1130* [→ *1052, 1054*]. Galatia:– Galatia [4]

1054 Γαλατικός, **Galatikos**, a.pr.g. GK: *1131* [→ *1053*]. Galatian:– of Galatia [1]

1055 γαλήνη, **galēnē**, n. GK: *1132*. calm:– calm [3]

1056 Γαλιλαία, **Galilaia**, n.pr. GK: *1133* [→ *1057*]. Galilee, "*ring, circle, hence region*":– Galilee [63]

1057 Γαλιλαῖος, **Galilaios**, a.pr.g. GK: *1134* [→ *1056*]. Galilean, "*from Galilee*":– Galileans [5], Galilean [3], of Galilee [3]

1058 Γαλλίων, **Galliōn**, n.pr. GK: *1136*. Gallio:– Gallio [3]

1059 Γαμαλιήλ, **Gamaliēl**, n.pr. GK: *1137*. Gamaliel, "*recompense of God [El]*":– Gamaliel [2]

1060 γαμέω, **gameō**, v. GK: *1138* [→ *1062*]. to marry:– marry [16], married [9], marrieth [3], marrying [1]

1061 γαμίσκω, **gamiskō**, v. GK: *1139 & 1140* [→ *1062*]. to give in marriage, marry; (pass.) to be given in marriage:– given in marriage [1]

1062 γάμος, **gamos**, n. GK: *1141* [→ *22, 1060, 1061, 1547, 1548, 1918*]. wedding banquet (a festive time in the community):– marriage [9], wedding [7]

1063 γάρ, **gar**, c. GK: *1142* [→ *5105*]. shows inference or continuation: for, because, indeed, but:– for [1026], and [4], because [4], why [4], but [2], verily [2], yet (+*2532*) [2], as [1], even [1], how (+*302+4459*) [1], indeed [1], no doubt [1], seeing [1], that [1], then [1], therefore [1], when (+*5613*) [1], yet [1]

1064 γαστήρ, **gastēr**, n. GK: *1143*. belly, womb, gluttony:– with child (+*1722+2192*) [5], child [2], bellies [1], womb [1]

1065 γέ, **ge**, pt.emph. GK: *1145* [→ *2534, 2544, 3304, 3386*]. emphatic particle: indeed, surely:– yet [2], and (+*235*) [1], at least (+*2532*) [1], did [1], haply (+*686*) [1], then (+*686*) [1], wherefore (+*686*) [1], yet doubtless (+*235*) [1]

1066 Γεδεών, **Gedeōn**, n.pr. GK: *1146*. Gideon, "*one who cuts, hacks*":– Gedeon [1]

1067 γέεννα, **geenna**, n. GK: *1147*. Gehenna, hell, "*Valley of Hinnom*":– hell [12]

1068 Γεθσημανῆ, **Gethsēmanē**, n.pr. GK: *1148 & 1149*. Gethsemane, "*olive oil press*":– Gethsemane [2]

1069 γείτων, **geitōn**, n. GK: *1150*. neighbor:– neighbours [4]

1070 γελάω, **gelaō**, v. GK: *1151* [→ *1071, 2606*]. to laugh:– laugh [2]

1071 γέλως, **gelōs**, n. GK: *1152* [→ *1070*]. laughter:– laughter [1]

1072 γεμίζω, **gemizō**, v. GK: *1153* [→ *1073*]. to fill:– filled [7], fill [1], full [1]

1073 γέμω, **gemō**, v. GK: *1154* [→ *1072, 1117*]. to be full:– full [9], full of [2]

1074 γενεά, **genea**, n. GK: *1155* [→ *1096*]. generation, one's own kind or race, descendant; fig., age, period of time (as in "to all generations"):– generation [31], generations [6], ages [2], nation [1], times [1], time [1]

1075 γενεαλογέω, **genealogeō**, v. GK: *1156* [→ *1096+3004*]. to trace genealogical descent:– descent counted [1]

1076 γενεαλογία, **genealogia**, n. GK: *1157* [→ *1096+3004*]. genealogy, lineage:– genealogies [2]

1077 γενέσια, **genesia**, n. GK: *1158 & 1159 & 1160* [→ *1096*]. birthday (a day that was celebrated):– birthday [2]

1078 γένεσις, **genesis**, n. GK: *1161* [→ *1096*]. birth; genealogy, descent; (course of one's) life:– generation [1], natural [1], nature [1]

1079 γενετή, **genetē**, n. GK: *1162* [→ *1096*]. birth:– birth [1]

1080 γεννάω, **gennaō**, v. GK: *1164* [→ *1096*]. to become the father of; to bear, give birth to; (pass.) to be conceived, born:– begat [42], born [39], begotten [7], bare [1], bear [1], brought forth [1], conceived [1], delivered [1], gendereth [1], gender [1], made [1], sprang [1]

1081 γέννημα, **gennēma**, n. GK: *1163 & 1165* [→ *1096*]. fruit, product, yield, harvest; offspring, brood:– generation [4], fruit [3], fruits [2]

1082 Γεννησαρέτ, **Gennēsaret**, n.pr. GK: *1166*. Gennesaret:– Gennesaret [2], Genesaret [1]

1083 γέννησις, **gennēsis**, n. GK: *1167* [→ *1096*]. birth:– birth [2]

1084 γεννητός, **gennētos**, a. GK: *1168* [→ *1096*]. pertaining to birth; "those born among women" means "all humankind":– born [2]

1085 γένος, **genos**, n. GK: *1169* [→ *1096*]. family, offspring; nation, people, native (of a region); classification or kind:– kindred [3], kind [3], offspring [3], born [2], kinds [2], nation [2], stock [2], countrymen [1], diversities [1], generation [1], of the country of [1]

1086 Γεργεσηνός, **Gergesēnos**, a.pr.g. GK: *1170 & 1171*. Gergesene, "*from Gergesa*":– Gergesenes [1]

1087 γερουσία, **gerousia**, n. GK: *1172* [→ *1088*]. assembly of the elders:– senate [1]

1088 γέρων, **gerōn**, n. GK: *1173* [→ *1087; cf. 1094*]. old person:– old [1]

1089 γεύομαι, **geuomai**, v. GK: *1174*. to taste, eat, partake of (implying enjoyment of the experience):– taste [7], tasted [5], eaten [2], eat [1]

1090 γεωργέω, **geōrgeō**, v. GK: *1175* [→ *1093+2041*]. to farm, cultivate:– dressed [1]

1091 γεώργιον, **geōrgion**, n. GK: *1176* [→ *1093+2041*]. (farmer's) field:– husbandry [1]

1092 γεωργός, **geōrgos**, n. GK: *1177* [→ *1093+2041*]. farmer, tenant farmer, share-cropper:– husbandmen [16], husbandman [1]

1093 γῆ, **gē**, n. GK: *1178* [→ *508, 1050, 1090, 1091, 1092, 1919*]. earth, world, country, region; land, ground, soil:– earth [188], land [42], ground [18], country [2], earthly (+*1537+3588*) [1], world [1]

1094 γῆρας, **gēras**, n. GK: *1179* [→ *1095; cf. 1088*]. old age:– old age [1]

1095 γηράσκω, **gēraskō**, v. GK: *1180* [→ *1094*]. to grow old, age:– old [1], waxeth old [1]

1096 γίνομαι, **ginomai**, v. GK: *1181* [→ *35, 36, 241, 313, 581, 738, 1074, 1075, 1076, 1077, 1078, 1079, 1080, 1081, 1083, 1084, 1085, 1103, 1104, 1118, 1230, 1549, 1920, 2104, 2225, 3439, 3824, 3854, 4266, 4269, 4772, 4773, 4836, 5041, 5042*]. to be, become, happen; to come into existence, be born. It is used in certain contexts to introduce a new section or paragraph in a narrative in Hebrew narrative style: and then, and it came to pass:– was [103], be [84], made [67], came to pass [65], done [63], come [27], were [26], become [21], came [21], is [20], became [17], God forbid (+*3361*) [15], come to pass [15], been [14], arose [11], are [5], have [5], become (+*1519*) [4], becometh [4], being [4], fulfilled [3], had [3], made (+*1519*) [3], married [3], ariseth [2], doing [2], grow [2], past [2], preferred before (+*1715*) [2], seemed [2], wrought [2], assembled [1], as [1], at even (+*3798*) [1], awaking out of sleep (+*1853*) [1], became (+*1519*) [1], befell [1], behaved [1], brought to pass [1], brought [1], came pass [1], camest [1], come by (+*4031*) [1], cometh to pass [1], cometh [1], continued [1], did [1], drawing [1], ended [1], falling headlong (+*4248*) [1], fell [1], finished [1], followed [1], found [1], give [1], happened [1], in [1], laid wait for (+*1917*) [1], obey (+*5255*) [1], ordained [1], partakest (+*4791*) [1], performed [1], preferred [1], published [1], purposed (+*1100*) [1], ran together (+*4890*) [1], require [1], shewed [1], sounded [1], spent [1], taken [1], there [1], thundered (+*1027*) [1], trembled (+*1719*) [1], trembled (+*1790*) [1], turned [1], vanished out of sight (+*855*) [1], was noised abroad (+*3588+5456*) [1], waxed (+*1519*) [1], waxed [1], wept (+*2805*) [1], were (+*1510*) [1]

1097 γινώσκω, **ginōskō**, v. GK: *1182* [→ *50, 51, 52, 56, 57, 176, 314, 319, 320, 1106, 1107, 1108, 1109, 1110, 1231, 1232, 1233, 1921, 1922, 2589, 2607, 4267, 4268, 4774*]. to know, come to know, recognize, understand; to have sexual relations:– know [94], known [45], knew [30], knoweth [16], perceived [7], knowest [5], knowing [5], understood [4], understand [3], perceive [2], sure [2], allow [1], canst speak [1], can [1], felt [1], knewest [1], knowledge [1], resolved [1], understandest [1], ware of [1], ware [1]

1098 γλεῦκος, **gleukos**, n. GK: *1183* [→ *1099*]. (sweet) wine:– new wine [1]

1099 γλυκύς, **glykys**, a. GK: *1184* [→ *1098*]. sweet, fresh (water):– sweet [3], fresh [1]

1100 γλῶσσα, **glōssa**, n. GK: *1185* [→ *1101, 2084*]. tongue; language; sometimes refers to the supernatural gift of tongues:– tongues [26], tongue [24]

1101 γλωσσόκομον, **glōssokomon**, n. GK: *1186* [→ *1100+2889*]. container for money:– bag [2]

1102 γναφεύς, **gnapheus**, n. GK: *1187* [→ *46; cf. 2833*]. bleacher, fuller, one who cleans and sizes woolen cloth:– fuller [1]

Grk

1103 γνήσιος, **gnēsios**, a. GK: *1188* [→ *1096*]. true, loyal, sincere, genuine:– own [2], sincerity [1], true [1]

1104 γνησίως, **gnēsiōs**, adv. GK: *1189* [→ *1096*]. genuinely, sincerely:– naturally [1]

1105 γνόφος, **gnophos**, n. GK: *1190*. darkness:– blackness [1]

1106 γνώμη, **gnōmē**, n. GK: *1191* [→ *1097*]. purpose, resolve; judgment; consent:– judgment [3], mind [2], advice [1], agree (+*1520*+*4160*) [1], purposed (+*1096*) [1], will [1]

1107 γνωρίζω, **gnōrizō**, v. GK: *1192* [→ *1097*]. to make known, tell, reveal:– made known [9], make known [6], declare [2], certify [1], declared [1], give to understand [1], known [1], wit [1], wot [1]

1108 γνῶσις, **gnōsis**, n. GK: *1194* [→ *1097*]. knowledge, understanding:– knowledge [28], science [1]

1109 γνώστης, **gnōstēs**, n. GK: *1195* [→ *1097*]. one well acquainted with, expert in:– expert [1]

1110 γνωστός, **gnōstos**, a. GK: *1196* [→ *1097*]. known:– known [11], acquaintance [2], know (+*1510*) [1], notable [1]

1111 γογγύζω, **gongyzō**, v. GK: *1197* [→ *1112, 1113, 1234*]. to grumble, complain, mutter:– murmured [6], murmur [2]

1112 γογγυσμός, **gongysmos**, n. GK: *1198* [→ *1111*]. complaint, grumbling; whispering, private talk:– murmuring [2], grudging [1], murmurings [1]

1113 γογγυστής, **gongystēs**, n. GK: *1199* [→ *1111*]. grumbler, complainer:– murmurers [1]

1114 γόης, **goēs**, n. GK: *1200*. imposter:– seducers [1]

1115 Γολγοθᾶ, **Golgotha**, n.pr. GK: *1201*. Golgotha, "*skull*":– Golgotha [3]

1116 Γόμορρα, **Gomorra**, n.pr. GK: *1202*. Gomorrah, "*to overwhelm with water*":– Gomorrha [5]

1117 γόμος, **gomos**, n. GK: *1203* [→ *1073*]. cargo, freight:– merchandise [2], burden [1]

1118 γονεύς, **goneus**, n. GK: *1204* [→ *1096*]. (pl.) parents:– parents [19]

1119 γόνυ, **gony**, n. GK: *1205* [→ *1120*]. knee; "to bend the knee" means "to kneel (in submission or worship)":– kneeled down (+*3588*+*5087*) [5], knees [4], knee [3]

1120 γονυπετέω, **gonypeteō**, v. GK: *1206* [→ *1119*+*4098*]. to kneel (before in submission or worship):– kneeling down [2], bowed the knee [1], kneeled [1]

1121 γράμμα, **gramma**, n. GK: *1207* [→ *1125*]. letter (of the alphabet); document, Scriptures, written code; education:– letter [6], letters [2], bill [2], learning [1], scriptures [1], writings [1], written (+*1722*) [1]

1122 γραμματεύς, **grammateus**, n. GK: *1208* [→ *1125*]. teacher or expert in the law, scholar, scribe, city clerk:– scribes [62], scribe [4], townclerk [1]

1123 γραπτός, **graptos**, a. GK: *1209* [→ *1125*]. written:– written [1]

1124 γραφή, **graphē**, n. GK: *1210* [→ *1125*]. (s.) a passage of Scripture; (pl.) the collective whole of the Scriptures; holy, authoritative collection of writings:– scripture [31], scriptures [20]

1125 γράφω, **graphō**, v. GK: *1211* & *2863* [→ *62, 582, 583, 1121, 1122, 1123, 1124, 1449, 1923, 1924, 4270, 5261, 5498*]. to write:– written [135], write [50], wrote [21], describeth [1], writing [1]

1126 γραώδης, **graōdēs**, a. GK: *1212* [→ *1491*]. old wives' tale:– old wives' [1]

1127 γρηγορέω, **grēgoreō**, v. GK: *1213* [→ *1453*]. to keep watch, be on guard:– watch [16], watched [2], vigilant [1], wake [1], watcheth [1], watchful [1], watching [1]

1128 γυμνάζω, **gymnazō**, v. GK: *1214* [→ *1131*]. to train, exercise:– exercised [3], exercise [1]

1129 γυμνασία, **gymnasia**, n. GK: *1215* [→ *1131*]. training, exercise:– exercise [1]

1130 γυμνητεύω, **gymnēteuō**, v. GK: *1216* & *1217* [→ *1131*]. to be in ragged clothing, poorly dressed:– naked [1]

1131 γυμνός, **gymnos**, a. GK: *1218* [→ *1128, 1129, 1130, 1132*]. naked, without clothing; needing (more or better) clothing:– naked [14], bare [1]

1132 γυμνότης, **gymnotēs**, n. GK: *1219* [→ *1131*]. nakedness, insufficiently clothed:– nakedness [3]

1133 γυναικάριον, **gynaikarion**, n. GK: *1220* [→ *1135*]. weak-willed woman, "little woman":– silly women [1]

1134 γυναικεῖος, **gynaikeios**, a. GK: *1221* [→ *1135*]. feminine, weaker:– wife [1]

1135 γυνή, **gynē**, n. GK: *1222* [→ *1133, 1134*]. woman; wife:– woman [96], wife [80], women [33], wives [12]

1136 Γώγ, **Gōg**, n.pr. GK: *1223*. Gog:– Gog [1]

1137 γωνία, **gōnia**, n. GK: *1224* [→ *204, 5068*]. corner; cornerstone, capstone, keystone:– corner [6], corners [2], quarters [1]

1138 Δαβίδ, **Dabid**, n.pr. GK: *1226* & *1253*. David, "*beloved one*":– David [58], David's [1]

1139 δαιμονίζομαι, **daimonizomai**, v. GK: *1227* [→ *1140*]. to be demon-possessed:– possessed with devils [4], possessed with the devil [3], possessed of the devils [2], hath a devil [1], one possessed with a devil [1], possessed with a devil [1], vexed with a devil [1]

1140 δαιμόνιον, **daimonion**, n. GK: *1228* [→ *1139, 1141, 1142, 1175, 1174*]. demon, (pagan) god:– devils [41], devil [18], gods [1]

1141 δαιμονιώδης, **daimoniōdēs**, a. GK: *1229* [→ *1140*+*1491*]. of the devil, demonic:– devilish [1]

1142 δαίμων, **daimōn**, n. GK: *1230* [→ *1140*]. demon, evil spirit:– devils [4], devil [1]

1143 δάκνω, **daknō**, v. GK: *1231*. to bite:– bite [1]

1144 δάκρυον, **dakryon**, n. GK: *1232* [→ *1145*]. teardrop:– tears [11]

1145 δακρύω, **dakryō**, v. GK: *1233* [→ *1144*]. to weep, shed tears:– wept [1]

1146 δακτύλιος, **daktylios**, n. GK: *1234* [→ *1147*]. (finger) ring:– ring [1]

1147 δάκτυλος, **daktylos**, n. GK: *1235* [→ *1146, 5554; cf. 1166*]. finger:– finger [5], fingers [3]

1148 Δαλμανουθά, **Dalmanoutha**, n.pr. GK: *1236*. Dalmanutha:– Dalmanutha [1]

1149 Δαλματία, **Dalmatia**, n.pr. GK: *1237*. Dalmatia, "*deceitful*":– Dalmatia [1]

1150 δαμάζω, **damazō**, v. GK: *1238* [→ *1151*]. to tame, subdue, control:– tamed [2], tame [2]

1151 δάμαλις, **damalis**, n. GK: *1239* [→ *1150*]. heifer, young cow:– heifer [1]

1152 Δάμαρις, **Damaris**, n.pr. GK: *1240*. Damaris:– Damaris [1]

1153 Δαμασκηνός, **Damaskēnos**, a.pr.g. GK: *1241* [→ *1154*]. Damascene, "*from Damascus*":– Damascenes [1]

1154 Δαμασκός, **Damaskos**, n.pr. GK: *1242* [→ *1153*]. Damascus:– Damascus [15]

1155 δανείζω, **daneizō**, v. GK: *1244* & *1247* [→ *1156*]. to lend, (mid.) to borrow:– lend [3], borrow [1]

1156 δάνειον, **daneion**, n. GK: *1245* & *1249* [→ *1155, 1157*]. debt, loan:– debt [1]

1157 δανειστής, **daneistēs**, n. GK: *1246* & *1250* [→ *1156*]. moneylender, creditor:– creditor [1]

1158 Δανιήλ, **Daniēl**, n.pr. GK: *1248*. Daniel, "*God [El] is my judge*":– Daniel [2]

1159 δαπανάω, **dapanaō**, v. GK: *1251* [→ *1160*]. to spend; to pay expenses:– spent [2], charges [1], consume [1], spend [1]

1160 δαπάνη, **dapanē**, n. GK: *1252* [→ *77, 1159, 1550, 4325*]. cost, expense:– cost [1]

1161 δέ, **de**, pt.&c. GK: *1254* [→ *1847, 1848, 3365, 3366, 3367, 3368, 3369, 3760, 3761, 3762, 3763, 3764*]. but, and, then, rather:– and [1214], but [935], now [168], then [132], when [40], yet [20], for [19], so [15], howbeit [12], nevertheless [12], also [10], yea [10], moreover [9], notwithstanding [8], therefore [4], while [4], even [3], and yet [2], neither (+*3756*) [2], or [2], they (+*3588*) [2], though [2], wherefore [2], and forasmuch as [1], and part (+*3588*) [1], and partly (+*3778*) [1], and to [1], as for [1], as [1], but and [1], but though (+*1487*+*2532*) [1], but though [1], furthermore [1], howbeit whereinsoever (+*302*+*1722*+*3739*) [1], moreover (+*2089*) [1], moreover (+*3062*+*3739*) [1], neither any

(+*3762*) [1], now about (+*2235*) [1], other (+*3588*) [1], so then [1], when (+*5613*) [1], who (+*3588*) [1]

1162 δέησις, **deēsis**, n. GK: *1255* [→ *1189*]. prayer, request, petition:– prayer [7], prayers [5], supplication [4], supplications [2], request [1]

1163 δεῖ, **dei**, v.imper. GK: *1256* [→ *1210*]. it is a must, it is necessary (one should, ought):– must [58], ought [25], must needs [5], ought to [3], meet [2], oughtest [2], should [2], behoved [1], must needs (+*3843*) [1], needful [1], need [1], ought to have [1], oughtest to have [1], should have [1], shouldest have [1]

1164 δεῖγμα, **deigma**, n. GK: *1257* [→ *1165, 1730, 3856, 5262; cf. 1166*]. example:– example [1]

1165 δειγματίζω, **deigmatizō**, v. GK: *1258* [→ *1164*]. to expose to public disgrace; to make a spectacle of:– made a shew [1]

1166 δεικνύω, **deiknyō**, v. GK: *1259* & *1260* [→ *322, 323, 584, 585, 1731, 1732, 1925, 5263; cf. 1147, 1164*]. to show, point out, make known:– shew [20], shewed [8], sheweth [2], shewest [1]

1167 δειλία, **deilia**, n. GK: *1261* [→ *127*]. timidity, cowardice:– fear [1]

1168 δειλιάω, **deiliaō**, v. GK: *1262* [→ *127*]. to be afraid, cowardly, timid:– afraid [1]

1169 δειλός, **deilos**, a. GK: *1264* [→ *127*]. afraid, cowardly, timid:– fearful [3]

1170 δεῖνα, **deina**, n. GK: *1265*. a certain one, a person or thing one cannot or does not wish to name:– such a man [1]

1171 δεινῶς, **deinōs**, adv. GK: *1267* [→ *127*]. terribly, fiercely:– grievously [1], vehemently [1]

1172 δειπνέω, **deipneō**, v. GK: *1268* [→ *1173*]. to eat supper, dine:– sup [2], supped [1], supper [1]

1173 δεῖπνον, **deipnon**, n. GK: *1270* & *1271* [→ *1172*]. banquet, supper, evening meal:– supper [13], feasts [3]

1174 δεισιδαίμων, **deisidaimōn**, a. GK: *1273* [→ *127*+*1140*]. (compar.) very religious:– too superstitious [1]

1175 δεισιδαιμονία, **deisidaimonia**, n. GK: *1272* [→ *127*+*1140*]. religion:– superstition [1]

1176 δέκα, **deka**, n.num. GK: *1274* [→ *586, 586, 1177, 1178, 1179, 1180, 1181, 1182, 1183, 1427, 1428, 1429, 1733, 1734, 4003, 5065*]. ten:– ten [24], eighteen (+*2532*+*3638*) [3]

1177 δεκαδύο, **dekadyo**, n.num. GK: *1275* [→ *1176*+*1417*]. twelve:– twelve [1]

1178 δεκαπέντε, **dekapente**, n.num. GK: *1278* [→ *1176*+*4002*]. fifteen:– fifteen [3]

1179 Δεκάπολις, **Dekapolis**, n.pr. GK: *1279* [→ *1176*+*4172*]. Decapolis, "*[league of] ten cities*":– Decapolis [3]

1180 δεκατέσσαρες, **dekatessares**, n.num. GK: *1280* [→ *1176*+*5064*]. fourteen:– fourteen [5]

1181 δεκάτη, **dekatē**, a.num.f. of *1182*. GK: *1281* [→ *1176*]. tenth in a series of things or events; as a noun, the tenth part, ten percent of something, tithe:– tenth [2], tithes [2]

1182 δέκατος, **dekatos**, a.num. GK: *1281* [→ *1176*]. tenth in a series of things or events; as a noun, the tenth part, ten percent of something, tithe:– tenth [3]

1183 δεκατόω, **dekatoō**, v. GK: *1282* [→ *1176*]. to collect a tenth; (pass.) to pay a tenth:– payed tithes [1], received tithes [1]

1184 δεκτός, **dektos**, a. GK: *1283* [→ *1209*]. acceptable, favorable:– accepted [3], acceptable [2]

1185 δελεάζω, **deleazō**, v. GK: *1284* [→ *1388*]. to entice, seduce, lure:– allure [1], beguiling [1], enticed [1]

1186 δένδρον, **dendron**, n. GK: *1285*. tree:– tree [17], trees [9]

1187 δεξιολάβος, **dexiolabos**, n. GK: *1286* & *1287* [→ *1188*+*2983*]. spearman; other sources: bowman, slinger, bodyguard:– spearmen [1]

1188 δεξιός, **dexios**, a. GK: *1288* [→ *1187*]. the right hand or side in contrast to the left; the right is considered culturally to be stronger and of greater prestige than the left; to be seated on the right side of a ruler is a greater position than on the left side; to "give the right hand of fellowship" in Galatians is a sign of friendship, trust, and covenant:– right hand [38], right [12], right side [2], right hands [1]

1189 δέομαι, *deomai*, v. GK: *1289* [→ *1162, 1729, 4326*]. to pray; ask, beg, plead:– pray [7], beseech [6], besought [3], prayed [2], praying [2], making request [1], prayed to [1]

δέον, *deon*. See **1163**.

1190 Δερβαῖος, *Derbaios*, a.pr.g. GK: *1291* [→ *1191*]. from Derbe, "*from Derbe*":– of Derbe [1]

1191 Δέρβη, *Derbē*, n.pr. GK: *1292* [→ *1190*]. Derbe:– Derbe [3]

1192 δέρμα, *derma*, n. GK: *1293* [→ *1194*]. skin, leather:– goatskins (+*122*) [1]

1193 δερμάτινος, *dermatinos*, a. GK: *1294* [→ *1194*]. made of leather:– leathern [1], skin [1]

1194 δέρω, *derō*, v. GK: *1296* [→ *1192, 1193*]. to beat up, strike, flog, slap:– beaten [5], beat [5], beateth [1], beating [1], smitest [1], smite [1], smote [1]

1195 δεσμεύω, *desmeuō*, v. GK: *1297* [→ *1210*]. to tie up, bind; to arrest:– binding [1], bind [1]

1196 δεσμέω, *desmeō*, v. GK: *1298* [→ *1210*]. to tie, bind:– bound [1]

1197 δέσμη, *desmē*, n. GK: *1299* [→ *1210*]. bundle:– bundles [1]

1198 δέσμιος, *desmios*, n. GK: *1300* [→ *1210*]. prisoner, one under arrest:– prisoner [11], prisoners [3], bonds [1], in bonds [1]

1199 δεσμός, *desmos*, n. GK: *1301* [→ *1210*]. chain, fetter, imprisonment:– bonds [14], bands [3], bond [1], chains [1], string [1]

1200 δεσμοφύλαξ, *desmophylax*, n. GK: *1302* [→ *1210+5442*]. jailer, warden:– keeper of the prison [2], jailor [1]

1201 δεσμωτήριον, *desmōtērion*, n. GK: *1303* [→ *1210*]. prison, jail:– prison [4]

1202 δεσμώτης, *desmōtēs*, n. GK: *1304* [→ *1210*]. prisoner:– prisoners [2]

1203 δεσπότης, *despotēs*, n. GK: *1305* [→ *3616, 3617; cf. 1210*]. master; Sovereign Lord:– Lord/lord [5], masters [4], master's [1]

1204 δεῦρο, *deuro*, adv.pl. GK: *1306* [→ *1205*]. come, come here:– come [6], hither [2], hitherto (+*891+3588*) [1]

1205 δεῦτε, *deute*, adv. GK: *1307* [→ *1204*]. come, come here (pl. of *1204*):– come [12], follow (+*3694*) [1]

1206 δευτεραῖος, *deuteraios*, a. GK: *1308* [→ *1417*]. on the following day, on the second day:– next day [1]

1207 δευτερόπρωτος, *deuteroprōtos*, a. GK: *1310* [→ *1417+4413*]. lit: "second-first":– second after the first [1]

1208 δεύτερος, *deuteros*, a. GK: *1309 & 1311* [→ *1417*]. second; (adv.) for the second time, secondly:– second [36], second time (+*1537*) [4], again (+*1537*) [2], second time [2], afterward [1], again [1], secondarily [1]

1209 δέχομαι, *dechomai*, v. GK: *1312* [→ *96, 324, 418, 553, 587, 588, 593, 594, 1184, 1237, 1240, 1381, 1382, 1383, 1384, 1403, 1523, 1551, 1561, 1735, 1920, 2144, 3580, 3829, 3830, 3858, 4327, 5264*]. to welcome, receive, accept:– receive [24], received [16], receiveth [11], take [3], accepted [2], took [2]

1210 δέω, *deō*, v. GK: *1313* [→ *1163, 1195, 1196, 1197, 1198, 1199, 1200, 1201, 1202, 1238, 3611, 4019, 4886, 4887, 5265, 5266; cf. 1203*]. to tie, bind, imprison:– bound [28], bind [9], tied [4], in bonds [1], knit [1], wound [1]

1211 δή, *dē*, pt.emph. GK: *1314* [→ *1221, 1222, 1894, 1895*]. indeed, therefore; can show urgency or certainty:– also [1], doubtless [1], now [1], therefore [1]

1212 δῆλος, *dēlos*, a. GK: *1316* [→ *82, 83, 84, 1213, 1552, 2612, 4271*]. clear, plain, evident:– bewrayeth (+*4160*) [1], certain [1], evident [1], manifest [1]

1213 δηλόω, *dēloō*, v. GK: *1317* [→ *1212*]. to make clear, bring to light, show, point:– declared [2], declare [1], shewed [1], signifieth [1], signifying [1], signify [1]

1214 Δημᾶς, *Dēmas*, n.pr. GK: *1318* [→ *1218 or 1216*]. Demas, "*common folks*":– Demas [3]

1215 δημηγορέω, *dēmēgoreō*, v. GK: *1319* [→ *1218+59*]. to deliver a public address:– made an oration [1]

1216 Δημήτριος, *Dēmētrios*, n.pr. GK: *1320* [→ *1214?*]. Demetrius, "*of Demeter*":– Demetrius [3]

1217 δημιουργός, *dēmiourgos*, n. GK: *1321* [→ *1218+2041*]. builder, craftsman, maker:– maker [1]

1218 δῆμος, *dēmos*, n. GK: *1322* [→ *589, 590, 1214?, 1215, 1217, 1219, 1553, 1736, 1927, 3530, 3927, 4898*]. people, crowd:– people [4]

1219 δημόσιος, *dēmosios*, a. GK: *1323* [→ *1218*]. public, publicly:– publickly [2], common [1], openly [1]

1220 δηνάριον, *dēnarion*, n. GK: *1324*. denarius [about a day's wage]:– penny [9], pence [5], pennyworth [2]

1221 δήποτε, *dēpote*, adv. GK: *1325* [→ *1211+4226*]. whatever:–

1222 δήπου, *dēpou*, adv. GK: *1327* [→ *1211+4226*]. surely, of course:– verily [1]

1223 διά, *dia*, pp. GK: *1328* [→ *87, 88, 89, 90, 411, 475, 592, 1224, 1225, 1226, 1227, 1228, 1229, 1230, 1231, 1232, 1233, 1234, 1235, 1236, 1237, 1238, 1239, 1240, 1241, 1242, 1243, 1244, 1245, 1246, 1251, 1252, 1253, 1254, 1255, 1256, 1257, 1258, 1259, 1260, 1261, 1262, 1263, 1264, 1265, 1266, 1267, 1268, 1269, 1270, 1271, 1272, 1273, 1274, 1275, 1276, 1277, 1278, 1279, 1280, 1281, 1282, 1283, 1284, 1285, 1286, 1287, 1288, 1289, 1290, 1291, 1292, 1293, 1294, 1295, 1296, 1297, 1298, 1299, 1300, 1301, 1302, 1303, 1304, 1305, 1306, 1307, 1308, 1309, 1310, 1311, 1312, 1313, 1314, 1315, 1316, 1326, 1327, 1328, 1329, 1330, 1331, 1334, 1335, 1336, 1338, 1339, 1340, 1352, 1353, 1355, 1357, 1358, 1360, 1368, 1555, 1928, 1930, 3859*]. (gen.) through, by means of; (acc.) because of, for the sake of, therefore:– by [247], through [86], for [58], therefore (+*3778*) [43], for sake [35], because of [24], because (+*3588*) [21], with [17], for this cause (+*3778*) [14], for sakes [12], because [9], in [8], wherefore (+*3778*) [7], after [3], always (+*3956*) [3], by reason of [3], of [3], throughout [3], whereby (+*3739*) [3], wherefore (+*156+3739*) [3], at [2], thereby (+*846*) [2], thereby [2], wherefore (+*3739*) [2], among [1], avoid [1], because by reason of [1], because that (+*3588*) [1], briefly (+*3641*) [1], by (+*3588*) [1], by (+*5495*) [1], by occasion [1], by reason hereof (+*3778*) [1], by reason of (+*3588*) [1], by the means of [1], continually (+*3956*) [1], for (+*3588*) [1], from [1], glorious (+*1391*) [1], out of [1], that (+*3588*) [1], threat (+*846*) [1], therefore [1], though [1], throughout (+*3650*) [1], to [1], wherein (+*3739*) [1], within [1]

Δία, *Dia*. See **2203**.

1224 διαβαίνω, *diabainō*, v. GK: *1329* [→ *1223+305*]. to pass through, come over, cross:– come over [1], passed through [1], pass [1]

1225 διαβάλλω, *diaballō*, v. GK: *1330* [→ *1223+906*]. (pass.) to have accusations brought upon someone:– accused [1]

1226 διαβεβαιόομαι, *diabebaioomai*, v. GK: *1331* [→ *1223+305*]. to confidently affirm, stress, insist on:– affirm constantly [1], affirm [1]

1227 διαβλέπω, *diablepō*, v. GK: *1332* [→ *1223+991*]. to see clearly; to open eyes wide:– see clearly [2]

1228 διάβολος, *diabolos*, a. [used as n.]. GK: *1333* [→ *1223+906*]. devilish, malicious, slanderous; as a noun, the devil, Satan, or a wicked person who is like the devil:– devil [35], false accusers [2], slanderers [1]

1229 διαγγέλλω, *diangellō*, v. GK: *1334* [→ *1223+32*]. to proclaim (throughout); to give notice:– declared [1], preach [1], signify [1]

1230 διαγίνομαι, *diaginomai*, v. GK: *1335* [→ *1223+1096*]. to pass, elapse (of time):– after [1], past [1], spent [1]

1231 διαγινώσκω, *diaginōskō*, v. GK: *1336* [→ *1223+1097*]. to determine, decide:– inquire [1], know the uttermost [1]

1232 διαγνωρίζω, *diagnōrizō*, v. GK: *1337* [→ *1223+1097*]. to give an exact report:– made known abroad [1]

1233 διάγνωσις, *diagnōsis*, n. GK: *1338* [→ *1223+1097*]. decision:– hearing [1]

1234 διαγογγύζω, *diagongyzō*, v. GK: *1339* [→ *1223+1111*]. to mutter, grumble, complain:– murmured [2]

1235 διαγρηγορέω, *diagrēgoreō*, v. GK: *1340* [→ *1223+1453*]. to become fully awake:– awake [1]

1236 διάγω, *diagō*, v. GK: *1341* [→ *1223+71*]. to live, conduct one's life:– lead [1], living [1]

1237 διαδέχομαι, *diadechomai*, v. GK: *1342* [→ *1223+1209*]. to receive (in turn):– came after [1]

1238 διάδημα, *diadēma*, n. GK: *1343* [→ *1223+1210*]. crown, diadem:– crowns [3]

1239 διαδίδωμι, *diadidōmi*, v. GK: *1344* [→ *1223+1325*]. to distribute, divide up:– distributed [1], distribute [1], distribution [1], divideth [1], give [1]

1240 διάδοχος, *diadochos*, n. GK: *1345* [→ *1223+1209*]. successor:– came into room (+*2983*) [1]

1241 διαζώννυμι, *diazōnnymi*, v. GK: *1346* [→ *1223+2224*]. to wrap around, tie around, put on:– girded [2], girt [1]

1242 διαθήκη, *diathēkē*, n. GK: *1347* [→ *1223+5087*]. covenant, a solemn agreement between two parties; will, testament, a legal document by which property is transferred to heirs, usually upon death (Heb 9:16):– covenant [17], testament [13], covenants [3]

1243 διαίρεσις, *diairesis*, n. GK: *1348* [→ *1223+138*]. difference, variety:– diversities [2], differences [1]

1244 διαιρέω, *diaireō*, v. GK: *1349* [→ *1223+138*]. to divide, distribute, apportion:– divided [1], dividing [1]

1245 διακαθαρίζω, *diakatharizō*, v. GK: *1350 & 1351* [→ *1223+2513*]. to clear out, clean out (with a possible implication that the cleaning is thorough):– throughly purge [2]

1246 διακατελέγχομαι, *diakatelenchomai*, v. GK: *1352* [→ *1223+2596+1651*]. to refute (thoroughly):– convinced [1]

1247 διακονέω, *diakoneō*, v. GK: *1354* [→ *1249*]. to serve, wait on, help, attend to; this often refers to spiritual and practical ministry in the Church. "To wait upon tables" (Ac 6:2) may mean to literally help in serving food, though some believe it refers (also) to the handling of finances:– ministered [14], minister [8], serve [7], administered [2], serveth [2], ministering [1], served [1], use the office of deacon [1], used the office of deacon [1]

1248 διακονία, *diakonia*, n. GK: *1355* [→ *1249*]. ministry, service, this can refer to helps and service of various kinds which can range in meaning from "spiritual" biblical teaching (Ac 6:4) to the "practical" giving of provisions, supplies, support, and finances to those in need (2Co 9:12):– ministry [16], ministration [6], ministering [3], service [3], administrations [1], administration [1], minister [1], office [1], relief (+*1519*) [1], serving [1]

1249 διάκονος, *diakonos*, n. GK: *1356* [→ *1247, 1248*]. servant, minister, a person who renders service and help to others, in some contexts with an implication of lower status; also transliterated as "deacon," a trusted officer of helps and service in the local church:– minister [14], ministers [6], servant [5], deacons [3], servants [3]

1250 διακόσιοι, *diakosioi*, a.num. GK: *1357* [→ *1417*]. two hundred:– two hundred [8]

1251 διακούω, *diakouō*, v. GK: *1358* [→ *1223+191*]. to give a (legal) hearing:– hear [1]

1252 διακρίνω, *diakrinō*, v. GK: *1359* [→ *1223+2919*]. to make a distinction, judge a dispute; (mid./pass.) to doubt, hesitate, waver:– judge [3], doubting [2], doubt [2], contended [1], contending [1], discerning [1], discern [1], doubteth [1], maketh to differ [1], making a difference [1], partial [1], put difference [1], staggered [1], wavereth [1], wavering [1]

1253 διάκρισις, *diakrisis*, n. GK: *1360* [→ *1223+2919*]. distinguishing, differentiation; passing judgment:– discerning [1], discern [1], disputations [1]

1254 διακωλύω, *diakōlyō*, v. GK: *1361* [→ *1223+2967*]. to deter, prevent:– forbad [1]

1255 διαλαλέω, *dialaleō*, v. GK: *1362* [→ *1223+2980*]. to talk about, discuss:– communed [1], noised abroad [1]

1256 διαλέγομαι, *dialegomai*, v. GK: *1363* [→ *1223+3004*]. to reason, discuss, discourse; to argue, dispute:– reasoned [4], disputed [3], disputing [3], preached [1], preaching [1], speaketh [1]

1257 διαλείπω, *dialeipō*, v. GK: *1364* [→ *1223+3007*]. to stop, cease:– ceased [1]

1258 διάλεκτος, *dialektos*, n. GK: *1365* [→ *1223+3004*]. language, dialect, a communication code whether written or oral; in the NT this always refers to known languages commonly spoken in the ancient world:– tongue [5], language [1]

1259 διαλλάσσομαι, *diallassomai*, v. GK: *1367* [→ *1223+236*]. to become reconciled:– reconciled [1]

1260 διαλογίζομαι, *dialogizomai*, v. GK: *1368* [→ *1223+3004*]. to think, wonder about; to talk, discuss, argue:– reasoned [5], reason [5], cast in mind [1], consider [1], disputed [1], mused [1], reasoning [1], thought [1]

1261 διαλογισμός, *dialogismos*, n. GK: *1369* [→ *1223+3004*]. thought, doubt; argument, dispute:– thoughts [8], disputings [1], doubtful [1], doubting [1], imaginations [1], reasoning [1], thought [1]

1262 διαλύω, *dialyō*, v. GK: *1370* [→ *1223+3089*]. to disperse, break up:– scattered [1]

1263 διαμαρτύρομαι, *diamartyromai*, v. GK: *1371* [→ *1223+3144*]. to (solemnly) warn or charge; to (solemnly) testify about:– testified [6], testify [4], charge [2], charging [1], testifying [1], witnesseth [1]

1264 διαμάχομαι, *diamachomai*, v. GK: *1372* [→ *1223+3163*]. to argue vigorously, contend sharply:– strove [1]

1265 διαμένω, *diamenō*, v. GK: *1373* [→ *1223+3306*]. to remain (constantly):– continue [2], continued [1], remained [1], remainest [1]

1266 διαμερίζω, *diamerizō*, v. GK: *1374* [→ *1223+3313*]. to divide, distribute:– parted [5], divided [4], cloven [1], divide [1], parted among [1]

1267 διαμερισμός, *diamerismos*, n. GK: *1375* [→ *1223+3313*]. division:– division [1]

1268 διανέμω, *dianemō*, v. GK: *1376* [→ *1223+3551*]. (pass.) to be spread:– spread [1]

1269 διανεύω, *dianeuō*, v. GK: *1377* [→ *1223+3506*]. to make signs, nod, beckon:– beckoned [1]

1270 διανόημα, *dianoēma*, n. GK: *1378* [→ *1223+3563*]. thought:– thoughts [1]

1271 διάνοια, *dianoia*, n. GK: *1379* [→ *1223+3563*]. mind, thinking, understanding; this is a part of the inner person that thinks and processes information into understanding, including the making of choices, the seat of which is the heart:– mind [7], understanding [3], minds [2], imagination [1]

1272 διανοίγω, *dianoigō*, v. GK: *1380* [→ *455*; cf. *1223*]. to open; (pass.) to be opened; to explain:– opened [6], openeth [1], opening [1]

1273 διανυκτερεύω, *dianyktereuō*, v. GK: *1381* [→ *1223+3571*]. to spend the (entire) night:– all night [1]

1274 διανύω, *dianyō*, v. GK: *1382* [→ *1223+507*]. to continue:– finished [1]

1275 διαπαντός, *diapantos*, adv. GK: *1383* [→ *1223+3956*]. always, continually, constantly:– always [3], alway [2], continually [1]

1276 διαπεράω, *diaperaō*, v. GK: *1385* [→ *1223+4008*]. to cross over:– passed over [3], gone over [1], pass [1], sailing over [1]

1277 διαπλέω, *diapleō*, v. GK: *1386* [→ *1223+4126*]. to sail across, sail through:– sailed over [1]

1278 διαπονέομαι, *diaponeomai*, v. GK: *1387* [→ *1223+4192*]. to be greatly disturbed, troubled, annoyed:– grieved [2]

1279 διαπορεύομαι, *diaporeuomai*, v. GK: *1388* [→ *1223+4198*]. to go through, travel through:– went through [2], in journey [1], pass by [1], went [1]

1280 διαπορέω, *diaporeō*, v. GK: *1389* [→ *1223+1.1+4198*]. to be perplexed, puzzled, in wonder:– doubted [2], perplexed [2], doubt [1]

1281 διαπραγματεύομαι, *diapragmateuomai*, v. GK: *1390* [→ *1223+4238*]. to gain, earn:– gained by trading [1]

1282 διαπρίω, *diapriō*, v. GK: *1391* [→ *1223+4249*]. (pass.) to be furious:– cut [2]

1283 διαρπάζω, *diarpazō*, v. GK: *1395* [→ *1223+726*]. to rob, carry off (many possessions):– spoil [4]

1284 διαρήσσω, *diarēssō*, v. GK: *1392 & 1393 & 1396* [→ *1223+4486*]. to tear (clothes), break (chains):– rent [3], brake [2]

1285 διασαφέω, *diasapheō*, v. GK: *1397* [→ *1223*]. to tell, explain (in detail):– told [1]

1286 διασείω, *diaseiō*, v. GK: *1398* [→ *1223+4579*]. to extort money, as a fig. extension of a violent shaking motion:– violence [1]

1287 διασκορπίζω, *diaskorpizō*, v. GK: *1399* [→ *1223+4650*]. to scatter:– scattered abroad [2], scattered [2], strawed [2], wasted [2], dispersed [1]

1288 διασπάω, *diaspaō*, v. GK: *1400* [→ *1223+4685*]. (pass.) to be torn to pieces:– plucked asunder [1], pulled in pieces [1]

1289 διασπείρω, *diaspeirō*, v. GK: *1401* [→ *1223+4687*]. (pass.) to be scattered:– scattered abroad [3]

1290 διασπορά, *diaspora*, n. GK: *1401* [→ *1223+4687*]. scattering, dispersion, Diaspora:– dispersed among [1], scattered abroad (+*1722+3588*) [1], scattered throughout [1]

1291 διαστέλλω, *diastellō*, v. GK: *1403* [→ *1223+4724*]. (mid.) to give orders, command, authorize; (pass.) what was commanded:– charged [6], commanded [1], gave commandment [1]

1292 διάστημα, *diastēma*, n. GK: *1404* [→ *1223+2476*]. later time, interval:– space after [1]

1293 διαστολή, *diastolē*, n. GK: *1405* [→ *1223+4724*]. difference, distinction:– difference [2], distinction [1]

1294 διαστρέφω, *diastrephō*, v. GK: *1406* [→ *1223+4762*]. (act.) to subvert, pervert, make turn away; (pass.) to be perverted, depraved, turned from the truth:– perverse [4], perverting [1], pervert [1], turn [1]

1295 διασῴζω, *diasōzō*, v. GK: *1407* [→ *1223+4982*]. save, spare, bring safely through a dangerous or distressing situation, with a focus that the rescue is complete or full; to heal, with a focus that the injured or sick person goes from the danger of ill health to the safety of a completely restored or healthy life:– escaped [2], bring safe [1], escaped safe [1], heal [1], made perfectly whole [1], saved [1], save [1]

1296 διαταγή, *diatagē*, n. GK: *1408* [→ *1223+5021*]. putting into effect, institution:– disposition [1], ordinance [1]

1297 διάταγμα, *diatagma*, n. GK: *1409* [→ *1223+5021*]. edict, command:– commandment [1]

1298 διαταράσσω, *diatarassō*, v. GK: *1410* [→ *1223+5015*]. (pass.) to be greatly troubled, perplexed, confused:– troubled [1]

1299 διατάσσω, *diatassō*, v. GK: *1411* [→ *1223+5021*]. (act./mid.) to command, order, direct; (pass.) to be required, ordered, put into effect:– commanded [6], appointed [4], ordained [2], commanding [1], given order [1], ordain [1], set in order [1]

1300 διατελέω, *diateleō*, v. GK: *1412* [→ *1223+5056*]. to continue, remain:– continued [1]

1301 διατηρέω, *diatēreō*, v. GK: *1413* [→ *1223+5083*]. to keep, treasure:– keep [1], kept [1]

1302 διατί, *diati*, pt.inter. GK: *1414* [→ *1223+5101*]. why?:– why [23], wherefore [4]

1303 διατίθεμαι, *diatithemai*, v. GK: *1415* [→ *1223+5087*]. to make a covenant or a will; to confer, assign; to decree, ordain:– make [2], testator [2], appointed [1], appoint [1], made [1]

1304 διατρίβω, *diatribō*, v. GK: *1417* [→ *1223+5147*]. to stay, remain, spend some time:– abode [4], continued [2], tarried [2], abiding [1], been [1]

1305 διατροφή, *diatrophē*, n. GK: *1418* [→ *1223+5142*]. food, sustenance:– food [1]

1306 διαυγάζω, *diaugazō*, v. GK: *1419* [→ *1223+827*]. to dawn, shine through:– dawn [1]

1307 διαφανής, *diaphanēs*, a. GK: *1420 & 1421* [→ *1223+5316*]. transparent:– transparent [1]

1308 διαφέρω, *diapherō*, v. GK: *1422* [→ *1223+5342*]. (tr.) to carry, spread out; (intr.) to differ; to be more valuable than:– better than [3], differeth from [2], more value than [2], carry [1], driven up and down [1], excellent [1], maketh matter [1], more excellent [1], published [1]

1309 διαφεύγω, *diapheugō*, v. GK: *1423* [→ *1223+5343*]. to escape, flee:– escape [1]

1310 διαφημίζω, *diaphēmizō*, v. GK: *1424 & 5775* [→ *1223+5346*]. to spread news about, circulate:– blaze abroad [1], commonly reported [1], spread abroad fame [1]

1311 διαφθείρω, *diaphtheirō*, v. GK: *1425* [→ *1223+5351*]. to destroy, corrupt:– destroy [2], corrupteth [1], corrupt [1], destroyed [1], perish [1]

1312 διαφθορά, *diaphthora*, n. GK: *1426* [→ *1223+5351*]. decay:– corruption [6]

1313 διάφορος, *diaphoros*, a. GK: *1427* [→ *1223+5342*]. different; superior, outstanding, excellent:– more excellent [2], differing [1], divers [1]

1314 διαφυλάσσω, *diaphylassō*, v. GK: *1428* [→ *1223+5442*]. to guard carefully:– keep [1]

1315 διαχειρίζω, *diacheirizō*, v. GK: *1429* [→ *1223+5495*]. (mid.) to kill, murder, formally, "to lay violent hands on":– kill [1], slew [1]

1316 διαχωρίζω, *diachōrizō*, v. GK: *1431* [→ *1223+5565*]. (pass.) to be separated:– departed [1]

1317 διδακτικός, *didaktikos*, a. GK: *1434* [→ *1321*]. able to teach, skillful at instructing:– apt to teach [2]

1318 διδακτός, *didaktos*, a. GK: *1435* [→ *1321*]. taught, instructed:– teacheth [2], taught [1]

1319 διδασκαλία, *didaskalia*, n. GK: *1436* [→ *1321*]. teaching, doctrine:– doctrine [15], doctrines [4], learning [1], teaching [1]

1320 διδάσκαλος, *didaskalos*, n. GK: *1437* [→ *1321*]. teacher, instructor, one who provides instruction, implying authority over the students or followers:– master [46], teachers [6], teacher [4], doctors [1], masters [1]

1321 διδάσκω, *didaskō*, v. GK: *1438* [→ *1317, 1318, 1319, 1320, 1322, 2085, 2312, 2567, 3547, 5572*]. to teach, instruct, to provide information in a manner intended to produce understanding, either in a formal or informal setting:– taught [40], teach [26], teaching [21], teachest [7], teacheth [3]

1322 διδαχή, *didachē*, n. GK: *1439* [→ *1321*]. (the activity or content of) teaching, instruction:– doctrine [28], doctrines [1], taught [1]

1323 δίδραχμον, *didrachmon*, n. GK: *1440* [→ *1417+1405*]. two-drachma (temple tax):– tribute money [1], tribute [1]

1324 Δίδυμος, *Didymos*, n.pr. GK: *1441* [→ *1417*]. Didymus, "twin":– Didymus [3]

1325 δίδωμι, *didōmi*, v. GK: *1442 & 1443* [→ *325, 467, 468, 469, 591, 734, 1239, 1390, 1394, 1395, 1431, 1432, 1433, 1434, 1554, 1560, 1929, 2130, 3330, 3405, 3406, 3860, 3862, 3970, 4272, 4273; cf. 1435*]. to give; that this can have many different specific meanings and referents depending on the context, as noted in the list of NIV translations:– give [141], given [123], gave [73], giveth [13], gavest [11], grant [7], put [5], giving [4], granted [3], shew [3], bestowed [2], delivered [2], had power [2], make [2], offer [2], suffer [2], adventure [1], brought forth [1], committed [1], deliver (+*4991*) [1], delivered up [1], gave forth [1], gave up [1], hinder (+*1464*) [1], minister [1], receive [1], set [1], shewed [1], smote with hands (+*4475*) [1], stroke with the palm of hand (+*4475*) [1], taking [1], utter [1], yielded [1], yield [1]

1326 διεγείρω, *diegeirō*, v. GK: *1444* [→ *1223+1453*]. to get up, arouse, stimulate:– arose [2], stir up [2], awake [1], awoke [1], raised [1]

1327 διέξοδος, *diexodos*, n. GK: *1447* [→ *1223+1537+3598*]. (street) corner:– highways (+*3588+3598*) [1]

1328 διερμηνευτής, *diermēneutēs*, n. GK: *1449 & 2256* [→ *1223+2059*]. interpreter, translator:– interpreter [1]

1329 διερμηνεύω, *diermēneuō*, v. GK: *1450* [→ *1223+2059*]. to interpret, translate, explain:– interpret [4], expounded [1], interpretation [1]

1330 διέρχομαι, *dierchomai*, v. GK: *1451* [→ *1223+2064*]. to go through, travel throughout:– passed through [5], go through [3], passed [3], pass [3], go [2], pass through [2], passing through [2], walketh through [2], went through [2], come [1], departed [1], go over [1], going [1], gone over [1], gone throughout [1], gone through [1], gone [1], pass over [1], passed by [1], passed into [1], passed throughout [1], past [1], pierce through [1], travelled [1], went about [1], went abroad [1], went every where [1], went over [1]

1331 διερωτάω, *dierōtaō*, v. GK: *1452* [→ *1223+2065*]. to find out, ask:– made inquiry [1]

1332 διετής, *dietēs*, a. GK: *1453* [→ *1417+2094*]. two years old:– two years old [1]

1333 διετία, *dietia*, n. GK: *1454* [→ *1417+2094*]. two years:– two years [2]

1334 διηγέομαι, *diēgeomai*, v. GK: *1455* [→ *1223+71*]. to tell, report, describe:– declared [2], tell [2], told [2], declare [1], shew [1]

1335 διήγησις, *diēgēsis*, n. GK: *1456* [→ *1223+71*]. account, narrative:– declaration [1]

1336 διηνεκής, *diēnekēs*, a. GK: *1457* [→ *1223+5342*]. forever, endless, for all time:– continually (+*1519+3588*) [2], for ever (+*1519+3588*) [2]

1337 διθάλασσος, *dithalassos*, a. GK: *1458* [→ *1417+2281*]. sandbar, sandbank (surrounded on both sides by sea):– where two seas met [1]

1338 διϊκνέομαι, *diikneomai*, v. GK: *1459* [→ *1223+2425*]. to penetrate, pierce:– piercing [1]

1339 διΐστημι, *diistēmi*, v. GK: *1460* [→ *1223+2476*]. to leave, pass:– gone further [1], parted [1], space after [1]

1340 διϊσχυρίζομαι, *diischyrizomai*, v. GK: *1462* [→ *1223+2479*]. to assert, insist, maintain firmly:– confidently affirmed [1], constantly affirmed [1]

1341 δικαιοκρισία, *dikaiokrisia*, n. GK: *1464* [→ *1349+2919*]. righteous judgment:– righteous judgment [1]

1342 δίκαιος, *dikaios*, a. GK: *1465* [→ *1349*]. right, righteous, upright; in the NT this refers to God's proper standards and actions, expressed in the covenants; as a noun it refers to a person in accord with God's standards, in proper relationship with God:– righteous [41], just [31], right [5], just one [2], meet [2]

1343 δικαιοσύνη, *dikaiosynē*, n. GK: *1466* [→ *1349*]. righteousness, what is right, justice, the act of doing what is in agreement with God's standards, the state of being in proper relationship with God:– righteousness [90], righteousness' [2]

1344 δικαιόω, *dikaioō*, v. GK: *1467* [→ *1349*]. to justify, vindicate, declare righteous, to put someone in a proper relationship with another, usually referring to God's relationship to humankind, implying a proper legal or moral relationship:– justified [31], justify [4], justifieth [2], freed [1], justifier [1], righteous [1]

1345 δικαίωμα, *dikaiōma*, n. GK: *1468* [→ *1349*]. regulation, requirement, commandment; act of righteousness:– righteousness [4], ordinances [3], judgments [1], judgment [1], justification [1]

1346 δικαίως, *dikaiōs*, adv. GK: *1469* [→ *1349*]. justly, uprightly, righteously:– justly [2], righteously [2], righteousness [1]

1347 δικαίωσις, *dikaiōsis*, n. GK: *1470* [→ *1349*]. justification:– justification [2]

1348 δικαστής, *dikastēs*, n. GK: *1471* [→ *1349*]. judge:– judge [3]

1349 δίκη, *dikē*, n. GK: *1472 & 2869* [→ *91, 92, 93, 94, 95, 476, 1341, 1342, 1343, 1344, 1345, 1346, 1347, 1348, 1556, 1557, 1558, 1738, 2613, 2993, 2994, 5267*]. punishment, with a focus that the penalty is justly deserved and right; this can also refer to a pagan Greek goddess, "Justice" (Ac 28:4), who would seek out the guilty and punish the wrongdoer:– vengeance [2], judgment [1], punished (+*5099*) [1]

1350 δίκτυον, *diktyon*, n. GK: *1473*. (fish) net:– nets [6], net [6]

1351 δίλογος, *dilogos*, a. GK: *1474* [→ *1417+3004*]. insincere, double-tongued:– doubletongued [1]

1352 διό, *dio*, c.infer. GK: *1475* [→ *1223+3739*]. therefore, that is why, for this reason:– wherefore [39], therefore [9], for which cause [2], therefore (+*2532*) [1], wherefore (+*2532*) [1], wherefore seeing that [1]

1353 διοδεύω, *diodeuō*, v. GK: *1476* [→ *1223+3598*]. to go through, travel through:– passed through [1], went throughout [1]

1354 Διονύσιος, *Dionysios*, n.pr. GK: *1477*. Dionysius, "*belonging to Dionysus*":– Dionysius [1]

1355 διόπερ, *dioper*, c.infer. GK: *1478* [→ *1223+3739+4007*]. therefore, for this reason:– wherefore [3]

1356 διοπετής, *diopetēs*, a. GK: *1479* [→ *2203+4098*]. (the image) fallen from heaven (given by the pagan god Zeus):– fell down from Jupiter [1]

1357 διόρθωσις, *diorthōsis*, n. GK: *1481* [→ *1223+3717*]. a new order:– reformation [1]

1358 διορύσσω, *dioryssō*, v. GK: *1482* [→ *1223+3736*]. to break in:– break through [2], broken through [1], broken up [1]

Διός, *Dios*. See **2203**.

1359 Διόσκουροι, *Dioskouroi*, n.pr. GK: *1483* [→ *2203+2751*]. the twin gods Castor and Pollux, the Dioscuri, "*sons of Zeus*":– Castor and Pollux [1]

1360 διότι, *dioti*, c. GK: *1484* [→ *1223+3739+5101*]. therefore, because:– because [11], for [8], because that [2], therefore [1]

1361 Διοτρέφης, *Diotrephēs*, n.pr. GK: *1485* [→ *2203+5142*]. Diotrephes, "*nurtured by Zeus*":– Diotrephes [1]

1362 διπλοῦς, *diplous*, a. GK: *1486 & 1487* [→ *1417*]. double, twice as much:– double [3], twofold more than [1]

1363 διπλόω, *diploō*, v. GK: *1488* [→ *1417*]. to double, pay back double:– double [1]

1364 δίς, *dis*, adv. GK: *1489* [→ *1417*]. twice, again:– twice [4], again [2]

Δίς, *Dis*. See **2203**.

1365 διστάζω, *distazō*, v. GK: *1491* [→ *1417*]. to doubt:– doubted [1], doubt [1]

1366 δίστομος, *distomos*, a. GK: *1492* [→ *1417+4750*]. double-edged:– twoedged [2], with two edges [1]

1367 δισχίλιοι, *dischilioi*, a.num. GK: *1493* [→ *1417+5507*]. two thousand:– two thousand [1]

1368 διϋλίζω, *diylizō*, v. GK: *1494* [→ *1223+5208*]. to strain out, filter out:– strain out [1]

1369 διχάζω, *dichazō*, v. GK: *1495* [→ *1417*]. to turn (one against another), cause a separation:– set at variance [1]

1370 διχοστασία, *dichostasia*, n. GK: *1496* [→ *1417+2476*]. division, dissension:– divisions [2], seditions [1]

1371 διχοτομέω, *dichotomeō*, v. GK: *1497* [→ *1417+5114*]. to cut to pieces, likely a figure for severe punishment rather than execution:– cut asunder [1], cut in sunder [1]

1372 διψάω, *dipsaō*, v. GK: *1498* [→ *1373*]. to be thirsty:– thirst [10], athirst [3], thirsty [3]

1373 δίψος, *dipsos*, n. GK: *1499* [→ *1372*]. thirst:– thirst [1]

1374 δίψυχος, *dipsychos*, a. GK: *1500* [→ *1417+5594*]. double-minded:– double minded [2]

1375 διωγμός, *diōgmos*, n. GK: *1501* [→ *1377*]. persecution:– persecutions [5], persecution [5]

1376 διώκτης, *diōktēs*, n. GK: *1502* [→ *1377*]. persecutor:– persecutor [1]

1377 διώκω, *diōkō*, v. GK: *1503* [→ *1375, 1376, 1559, 2614*]. to pursue, persecute, to systematically oppress and harass a person or group, as an extended meaning of pursuing a person on foot in a chase; also from the image of the chase comes the meaning of striving and pressing on to a goal with intensity: to press on:– persecuted [13], persecute [8], follow [7], persecutest [6], suffer persecution [3], followed [2], ensue [1], follow after [1], given to [1], persecuting [1], press [1]

1378 δόγμα, *dogma*, n. GK: *1504* [→ *1380*]. decree, regulation:– decrees [2], ordinances [2], decree [1]

1379 δογματίζω, *dogmatizō*, v. GK: *1505* [→ *1380*]. (pass.) to submit to a rule, regulation:– subject to ordinances [1]

1380 δοκέω, *dokeō*, v. GK: *1506* [→ *603, 1378, 1379, 2106, 2107, 4328, 4329, 4909; cf. 1391*]. to think, consider, regard, an action of the mind and heart for processing information into understanding and choices, sometimes with a focus on appearances. Often in the impersonal form translated, "it seems" (Ac 17:18):– think [22], seemeth [5], seem [5], thought [5], thinkest [4], seemed good [3], seemed [3], suppose [3], accounted [2], pleased [2], supposed [2], supposing [2], thinketh [2], of reputation [1], pleasure [1], trow [1]

1381 δοκιμάζω, *dokimazō*, v. GK: *1507* [→ *1209*]. to test, try, examine; interpret:– prove [6], proved [3], approve [2], try [2], allowed [1], alloweth [1], approvest [1], discern (+*1492*) [1], discern [1], examine [1], like [1], proving [1], tried [1], trieth [1]

1382 δοκιμή, *dokimē*, n. GK: *1509* [→ *1209*]. character, test, proof:– proof [3], experience [2], experiment [1], trial [1]

1383 δοκίμιον, *dokimion*, n. GK: *1510* [→ *1209*]. testing, proved genuineness:– trial [1], trying [1]

1384 δόκιμος, *dokimos*, a. GK: *1511* [→ *1209*]. approved by testing, genuine:– approved [6], tried [1]

1385 δοκός, *dokos*, n. GK: *1512*. plank, beam of wood:– beam [6]

δόκω, *dokō*. See **1380**.

1386 δόλιος, *dolios*, a. GK: *1513* [→ *1388*]. deceitful, dishonest, tricky:– deceitful [1]

1387 δολιόω, *dolioō*, v. GK: *1514* [→ *1388*]. to practice deceit, deceive:– used deceit [1]

1388 δόλος, *dolos*, n. GK: *1515* [→ *97, 1185, 1386, 1387, 1389*]. deceit, slyness, trickery, as a fig. extension of the base meaning (not used in the NT) of trapping an animal by baiting or by cunning:– guile [7], deceit [3], subtilty [2], craft [1]

1389 δολόω, *doloō*, v. GK: *1516* [→ *1388*]. to distort, falsify:– handling deceitfully [1]

1390 δόμα, *doma*, n. GK: *1517* [→ *1325*]. gift:– gifts [3], gift [1]

1391 δόξα, *doxa*, n. GK: *1518* [→ *1392, 1740, 1741, 2754, 2755, 3861, 4888; cf. 1380*]. This word has a wide range of meanings in the NT, corresponding closely to the Hebrew 3883: glory, splendor, brilliance, from the base meaning of the awesome light that radiates from God's presence and is associated with his acts of power; honor, praise, speaking of words of excellence and assigning highest status to God:– glory [145], glorious [6], honour [6], praise [4], glorious (+*1722*) [3], dignities [2], glorious (+*1223*) [1], worship [1]

1392 δοξάζω, *doxazō*, v. GK: *1519* [→ *1391*]. to glorify, give praise, honor:– glorified [34], glorify [17], glorifying [3], full of glory [1], had glory [1], have glory [1], honoured [1], honoureth [1], honour [1], made glorious [1], magnify [1]

1393 Δορκάς, *Dorkas*, n.pr. GK: *1520*. Dorcas, "*gazelle*":– Dorcas [2]

1394 δόσις, *dosis*, n. GK: *1521* [→ *1325*]. gift, act of giving:– gift [1], giving [1]

1395 δότης, *dotēs*, n. GK: *1522* [→ *1325*]. giver:– giver [1]

1396 δουλαγωγέω, *doulagōgeō*, v. GK: *1524* [→ *1401+71*]. to enslave, bring to subjection:– bring into subjection [1]

1397 δουλεία, *douleia*, n. GK: *1525* [→ *1401*]. slavery, bondage:– bondage [5]

1398 δουλεύω, *douleuō*, v. GK: *1526* [→ *1401*]. to serve (as a slave):– serve [13], in bondage [4], serving [3], did service [1], do service [1], doing service [1], served [1], serveth [1]

1399 δούλη, *doulē*, n. GK: *1527* [→ *1401*]. female servant, female slave:– handmaidens [1], handmaiden [1], handmaid [1]

1400 δοῦλον, *doulon*, a.neut. of *1401*. GK: *1529* [→ *1401*]. slavish, servile, completely controlled, as a fig. extension of a slavery system in the ancient world, see *1401*:–

1401 δοῦλος, *doulos*, n. GK: *1528* [→ *1396, 1397, 1398, 1399, 1400, 1402, 2615, 3787, 4889*]. servant, slave; in the NT a person owned as a possession for various lengths of times (Hebrew slaves no more than seven years, Gentile slaves without time limit), of lower social status than free persons or masters; slaves could earn or purchase their freedom:– servant [66], servants [53], bond [6], bondman [1], servant's [1]

1402 δουλόω, *douloō*, v. GK: *1530* [→ *1401*]. to enslave, to cause one to become a slave; (pass.) to become enslaved; see also *1401*:– servants [2], bring into bondage [1], brought in bondage [1], given [1], in bondage [1], made servant [1], under bondage [1]

1403 δοχή, *dochē*, n. GK: *1531* [→ *1209*]. banquet:– feast [2]

1404 δράκων, *drakōn*, n. GK: *1532*. dragon:– dragon [13]

1405 δράσσομαι, *drassomai*, v. GK: *1533* [→ *1323, 1406*]. to catch, seize:– taketh [1]

1406 δραχμή, *drachmē*, n. GK: *1534* [→ *1405*]. silver coin, drachma:– piece [2], silver [1]

δρέμω, *dremō*. See **5143**.

1407 δρέπανον, *drepanon*, n. GK: *1535*. sickle:– sickle [8]

1408 δρόμος, *dromos*, n. GK: *1536* [→ *5143*]. race, course; career:– course [3]

1409 Δρούσιλλα, *Drousilla*, n.pr. GK: *1537*. Drusilla:– Drusilla [1]

δῦμι, *dumi*. See **1416**.

1410 δύναμαι, *dynamai*, v. GK: *1538* [→ *101, 102, 1411, 1412, 1413, 1414, 1415, 1743, 2616*]. to be able, have ability, to have the power to accomplish an action; humans have variously limited abilities, God is unlimited:– can [63], cannot

Grk

(+*3756*) [45], able [41], could [29], canst [9], may [8], mayest [4], might [3], cannot (+*3361*) [2], might have [2], been [1], can do [1], possible [1], power [1]

1411 δύναμις, *dynamis*, n. GK: *1539* [→ *1410*]. power, ability; miracle; ruler, an extended meaning of a person or supernatural being who has administrative power:– power [71], mighty works [10], miracles [7], strength [7], powers [6], might [4], virtue [3], mighty [2], ability [1], abundance [1], meaning [1], mightily [1], mighty deeds [1], mighty work [1], miracle [1], violence [1], wonderful works [1], workers of miracles [1]

1412 δυναμόω, *dynamoō*, v. GK: *1540* [→ *1410*]. (pass.) to be strengthened:– strengthened [1]

1413 δυνάστης, *dynastēs*, n. GK: *1541* [→ *1410*]. ruler, sovereign, (court) official:– mighty [1], of great authority [1], potentate [1]

1414 δυνατέω, *dynateō*, v. GK: *1542* [→ *1410*]. to be able, powerful, strong:– mighty [1]

1415 δυνατός, *dynatos*, a. GK: *1543* [→ *1410*]. possible (based on power); powerful, able, the Mighty One:– possible [13], able [10], mighty [7], strong [3], could [1], power [1]

1416 δύνω, *dynō*, v. GK: *1544* [→ *554*, *555*, *1424*, *1562*, *1737*, *1742*, *1744*, *1745*, *1746*, *1902*, *1903*, *1931*, *3921*]. to set (of the sun):– setting [1], set [1]

1417 δύο, *dyo*, n.num. GK: *1545* [→ *1177*, *1206*, *1207*, *1208*, *1250*, *1323*, *1324*, *1332*, *1333*, *1337*, *1351*, *1362*, *1363*, *1364*, *1365*, *1366*, *1367*, *1369*, *1370*, *1371*, *1374*, *1427*, *1428*, *1429*]. two:– two [123], twain [10], both [2], two hundred thousand thousand (+*3461*) [1]

1418 δυσ-, *dus-*, inseparable prefix. GK: * [→ *1419*, *1420*, *1421*, *1422*, *1423*, *1425*, *1426*]. prefix conveying the idea of difficulty, opposition, injuriousness:–

1419 δυσβάστακτος, *dysbastaktos*, a. GK: *1546* [→ *1418*+*941*]. hard to carry:– grievous to be borne [2]

1420 δυσεντερία, *dysenteria*, n. GK: *1547* & *1548* [→ *1418*; cf. *1722*]. dysentery:– bloody flixe [1]

1421 δυσερμήνευτος, *dysermēneutos*, a. GK: *1549* [→ *1418*+*2059*]. hard to explain:– hard [1]

1422 δύσκολος, *dyskolos*, a. GK: *1551* [→ *1418*, *1423*; cf. *2967*]. hard, difficult:– hard [1]

1423 δυσκόλως, *dyskolōs*, adv. GK: *1552* [→ *1418*, *1422*]. hard, with difficulty:– hardly [3]

1424 δυσμή, *dysmē*, n. GK: *1553* [→ *1416*]. west (setting of the sun):– west [5]

1425 δυσνόητος, *dysnoētos*, a. GK: *1554* [→ *1418*+*3563*]. hard to understand:– hard to be understood [1]

1426 δυσφημία, *dysphēmia*, n. GK: *1556* [→ *1418*+*5346*]. bad report, slander:– evil report [1]

δύω, *duō*. See **1416**.

1427 δώδεκα, *dōdeka*, n.num. GK: *1557* [→ *1417*+*1176*]. twelve:– twelve [72]

1428 δωδέκατος, *dōdekatos*, a. GK: *1558* [→ *1417*+*1176*]. twelfth:– twelfth [1]

1429 δωδεκάφυλον, *dōdekaphylon*, n. GK: *1559* [→ *1417*+*1176*+*5443*]. twelve tribes:– twelve tribes [1]

1430 δῶμα, *dōma*, n. GK: *1560* [→ *456*, *1739*, *2026*, *3618*, *3619*, *3620*, *4925*]. roof, housetop:– housetop [4], housetops [2], house [1]

1431 δωρεά, *dōrea*, n. GK: *1561* [→ *1325*]. gift:– gift [11]

1432 δωρεάν, *dōrean*, adv. GK: *1562* [→ *1325*]. freely, free of charge, without payment:– freely [6], for nought [1], in vain [1], without a cause [1]

1433 δωρέομαι, *dōreomai*, v. GK: *1563* [→ *1325*]. to give, confer, bestow:– given [2], gave [1]

1434 δώρημα, *dōrēma*, n. GK: *1564* [→ *1325*]. gift:– gift [2]

1435 δῶρον, *dōron*, n. GK: *1565* [→ *2333*; cf. *1325*]. gift, offering:– gift [10], gifts [8], offerings [1]

1436 ἔα, *ea*, pt.excl. GK: *1568*. ha!, aha!:– let alone [2]

1437 ἐάν, *ean*, c. GK: *1569* [→ *1487*+*302*]. if (usually used in general conditions or conditions that imply some doubt):– if [214], whosoever (+*3739*) [19], whatsoever (+*3739*) [15], though [12], whomsoever (+*3739*) [4], if (+*4007*) [3], whatsoever (+*3699*) [3], that (+*3739*) [2], whatsoever (+*3745*) [2], when [2], whether (+*5037*) [2], whom (+*3739*) [2], according to that (+*2526*) [1], and whether (+*5037*) [1], as many

as (+*3745*) [1], as often as (+*3740*) [1], but (+*3361*) [1], except (+*3361*) [1], in what place soever (+*3699*) [1], or (+*5037*) [1], though (+*2532*) [1], what (+*3739*) [1], whatsoever (+*3739*+*5100*) [1], whatsoever (+*3748*+*3956*+*5100*) [1], whensoever (+*5613*) [1], whithersoever (+*3699*) [1], whithersoever (+*3757*) [1], whomsoever (+*5100*) [1], whoso (+*3739*) [1]

ἐὰν μή, *ean mē*. See **3361** and **3362**.

1438 ἑαυτοῦ, *heautou*, p.reflex. GK: *1571* [→ *846*]. himself, herself, itself, themselves; (pl., in some contexts) reciprocal relationship, to one another:– himself [111], themselves [57], yourselves [36], ourselves [20], his [19], their [15], itself [9], his own [8], their own [7], them [7], one another [6], herself [5], you [5], her [4], your own selves [4], your own [4], him [3], her own [2], they [2], alone (+*2596*) [1], he himself [1], he [1], our own [1], she [1], their own home [1], their own selves [1], thine own [1], thyself [1], ye [1], your [1]

1439 ἐάω, *eaō*, v. GK: *1572* [→ *4330*]. to let, allow, permit:– suffered [5], suffer [2], committed [1], left [1], let alone [1], let [1], sufferest [1], suffereth [1]

1440 ἑβδομήκοντα, *hebdomēkonta*, n.num. GK: *1573* [→ *2033*]. seventy:– seventy [2], threescore and fifteen (+*4002*) [1], threescore sixteen (+*1803*) [1], threescore ten [1]

1441 ἑβδομηκοντάκις, *hebdomēkontakis*, adv. GK: *1574* [→ *2033*]. seventy times:– seventy times [1]

1442 ἕβδομος, *hebdomos*, a. GK: *1575* [→ *2033*]. seventh:– seventh [9]

1443 Ἔβερ, *Eber*, n.pr. GK: *1576*. Eber, "[regions] beyond [the river]" or source of the word "Hebrew"":– Heber [1]

1444 Ἑβραϊκός, *Hebraikos*, a.pr. GK: *1577* [→ *1445*]. Hebrew:– Hebrew [1]

1445 Ἑβραῖος, *Hebraios*, n.pr.g. GK: *1578* [→ *1444*, *1446*, *1447*]. a Hebrew; a Hebraic Jew:– Hebrews [4], Hebrew [1]

1446 Ἑβραΐς, *Hebrais*, n.pr. GK: *1579* [→ *1445*]. Aramaic, Hebrew dialect:– in Hebrew [3]

1447 Ἑβραϊστί, *Hebraisti*, adv.pr. GK: *1580* [→ *1445*]. in Aramaic, in the Hebrew dialect:– in the Hebrew tongue [3], in the Hebrew [2], in Hebrew [1]

1448 ἐγγίζω, *engizō*, v. GK: *1581* [→ *1451*]. come near, draw near:– at hand [9], come nigh [6], drew nigh [6], drew near [4], come near [3], draw nigh [3], draweth nigh [3], came near [2], came nigh [2], nigh [2], approacheth [1], approaching [1], draweth near [1]

1449 ἐγγράφω, *engraphō*, v. GK: *1582* [→ *1722*+*1125*]. to write in, write on, record:– written [2]

1450 ἔγγυος, *engyos*, a. GK: *1583*. (n.) guarantee, guarantor:– surety [1]

1451 ἐγγύς, *engys*, adv. GK: *1584* [→ *1448*, *1452*, *4331*]. near, close:– nigh [12], at hand [6], nigh at hand [4], near [3], nigh to [2], from [1], near to [1], ready [1]

1452 ἐγγύτερον, *engyteron*, adv.comp. GK: *1585* [→ *1451*]. nearer, closer:– nearer [1]

1453 ἐγείρω, *egeirō*, v. GK: *1586* [→ *1127*, *1235*, *1326*, *1454*, *1825*, *1892*, *4891*]. to arise, to stand from a prone or sleeping position. From this base meaning are several fig. extended meanings: to wake from sleep; to restore from a dead or damaged state: to heal, raise to life; to cause something to exist: raise up (give birth to) a child:– raised [29], risen [20], raised up [16], rise [16], arise [13], arose [12], raise up [6], rise up [6], rose [4], awake [2], lift up [2], raise [2], risen up [2], ariseth [1], awoke [1], lift out [1], lifted up [1], raiseth up [1], raiseth [1], rear up [1], riseth [1], stand [1], took up [1]

1454 ἔγερσις, *egersis*, n. GK: *1587* [→ *1453*]. resurrection:– resurrection [1]

1455 ἐγκάθετος, *enkathetos*, a. GK: *1588* [→ *863*]. (n.) spy:– spies [1]

1456 ἐγκαίνια, *enkainia*, n. GK: *1589* [→ *1722*+*2537*]. Feast of Dedication (Hanukkah):– dedication [1]

1457 ἐγκαινίζω, *enkainizō*, v. GK: *1590* [→ *1722*+*2537*]. (pass.) to be put into effect, inaugurate; (act.) to open:– consecrated [1], dedicated [1]

1458 ἐγκαλέω, *enkaleō*, v. GK: *1592* [→ *1722*+*2564*]. to bring charges, accuse; (pass.) to be charged with, have an accusation brought to:– accused [4], called in question [1], implead [1], lay to the charge [1]

1459 ἐγκαταλείπω, *enkataleipō*, v. GK: *1593* [→ *1722*+*2596*+*3007*]. to forsake, leave, abandon:– forsaken [4], forsake [1], forsaking [1], forsook [1], leave [1], left [1]

1460 ἐγκατοικέω, *enkatoikeō*, v. GK: *1594* [→ *1722*+*2596*+*3624*]. to live among:– dwelling [1]

1461 ἐγκεντρίζω, *enkentrizō*, v. GK: *1596* [→ *1722*+*2759*]. to graft into:– graffed in [3], graff in [1], graffed into [1], graffed [1]

1462 ἔγκλημα, *enklēma*, n. GK: *1598* [→ *1722*+*2564*]. charge, accusation:– crime laid [1], laid to charge [1]

1463 ἐγκομβόομαι, *enkomboomai*, v. GK: *1599* [→ *1722*]. to clothe (oneself) with, put on:– clothed with [1]

1464 ἐγκοπή, *enkopē*, n. GK: *1600* & *1715* [→ *1722*+*2875*]. hinderance, restraint:– hinder (+*1325*) [1]

1465 ἐγκόπτω, *enkoptō*, v. GK: *1601* [→ *1722*+*2875*]. to hinder, stop, impede progress:– hindered from [1], hindered [1], tedious [1]

1466 ἐγκράτεια, *enkrateia*, n. GK: *1602* [→ *1722*+*2904*]. self-control:– temperance [4]

1467 ἐγκρατεύομαι, *enkrateuomai*, v. GK: *1603* [→ *1722*+*2904*]. to have control (of oneself):– contain [1], temperate [1]

1468 ἐγκρατής, *enkratēs*, a. GK: *1604* [→ *1722*+*2904*]. disciplined, self-controlled:– temperate [1]

1469 ἐγκρίνω, *enkrinō*, v. GK: *1605* [→ *1722*+*2919*]. to classify:– make of the number [1]

1470 ἐγκρύπτω, *enkryptō*, v. GK: *1606* [→ *1722*+*2928*]. to mix, put into:– hid [2]

1471 ἔγκυος, *enkyos*, a. GK: *1607* [→ *1722*+*2949*]. pregnant:– great with child [1]

1472 ἐγχρίω, *enchriō*, v. GK: *1608* [→ *1722*+*5548*]. to put on, rub on, anoint:– anoint [1]

1473 ἐγώ, *egō*, p.pers. GK: *1609* [→ *1683*, *1691*, *1698*, *1699*, *1700*, *2248*, *2249*, *2251*, *2254*, *2257*, *2504*, *3165*, *3365*, *3427*, *3450*]. I, me, my; we, us, our; often added for emphasis: myself, ourselves:– me [798], my [527], I [425], us [396], our [312], we [173], mine [24], mine own [4], ours [4], usward [2], myself (+*846*) [1], myself [1], ourselves [1], what have I to do (+*5101*) [1]

1474 ἐδαφίζω, *edaphizō*, v. GK: *1610* [→ *1475*]. to dash to the ground, raze:– lay even with the ground [1]

1475 ἔδαφος, *edaphos*, n. GK: *1611* [→ *1474*]. ground:– ground [1]

1476 ἑδραῖος, *hedraios*, a. GK: *1612* [→ *856*, *1477*, *1747*, *1748*, *1749*, *2145*, *2516*, *4332*, *4892*; cf. *2516*]. firm, steadfast:– stedfast [2], settled [1]

1477 ἑδραίωμα, *hedraiōma*, n. GK: *1613* [→ *1476*]. foundation:– ground [1]

1478 Ἐζεκίας, *Hezekias*, n.pr. GK: *1614*. Hezekiah, "God [El] strengthens":– Ezekias [2]

1479 ἐθελοθρησκία, *ethelothrēskia*, n. GK: *1615* [→ *2309*+*2357*]. self-imposed religion:– will worship [1]

ἐθέλω, *ethelō*. See **2309**.

1480 ἐθίζω, *ethizō*, v. GK: *1616* [→ *1485*]. (pass.) to be accustomed, required:– custom [1]

1481 ἐθνάρχης, *ethnarchēs*, n. GK: *1617* [→ *1484*+*757*]. governor:– governor [1]

1482 ἐθνικός, *ethnikos*, a. GK: *1618* [→ *1484*]. pagan, Gentile:– heathen [2]

1483 ἐθνικῶς, *ethnikōs*, adv. GK: *1619* [→ *1484*]. like a Gentile, like a pagan:– after the manner of Gentiles [1]

1484 ἔθνος, *ethnos*, n. GK: *1620* [→ *1481*, *1482*, *1483*]. Gentile, pagan; (foreign) nation, a people:– Gentiles [93], nations [37], nation [27], heathen [5], people [2]

1485 ἔθος, *ethos*, n. GK: *1621* [→ *1480*, *1486*, *1486*, *2239*, *2550*, *4914*]. custom, practice, habit:– customs [5], manner [4], custom [2], as wont (+*2596*+*3588*) [1]

1486 ἔθω, *ethō*, v. GK: *1622* & *1665* [→ *1485*]. to be accustomed; to have a custom:– wont [2], custom [1], manner [1]

1487 εἰ, *ei*, pt.cond. GK: *1623* [→ *1437*, *3375*, *1512*, *1513*, *1535*, *2579*, *5616*, *5619*]. if, since:– if [270], whether [21], that [6], although (+*2532*) [1], but (+*1622*+*3361*) [1], but (+*3361*) [1], but though (+*1161*+*2532*) [1], except (+*1622*+*3361*) [1], forasmuch [1], had [1], if (+*3305*) [1], it may

be (+*5177*) [1], it may chance (+*5177*) [1], never (+*165*+*1519*+*3588*+*3756*) [1], not [1], no [1], since [1], though (+*2532*) [1], unless (+*1622*+*3361*) [1], what if [1]

1488 εἶ, **ei**, v.2.s of *1510*. GK: *1639* [→ *1510*]. you are, thou art; see *1510*:–

1489 εἴγε, **eige**, pt.emph. GK: *1623* + *1145* [→ *1487*+*1065*]. if indeed, seeing that, unless; (with neg.) otherwise:– if [4], if so be that [1]

1490 εἰ δὲ μή (γε), **ei de mē (ge)**, pt.emph. GK: *1623* + *1254* + *3590* (+ *1145*) [→ *1487*+*1161*+*3361*+*1065*]. but if not, or else, otherwise:– else [4], or else [4], if not [2], if otherwise [2], and if not [1], otherwise [1]

1491 εἶδος, **eidos**, n. GK: *1626* [→ *1126*, *1141*, *2396*, *2397*, *2400*, *3708*, *4075*, *5237*; cf. *1497*]. form, appearance, sight:– shape [2], appearance [1], fashion [1], sight [1]

1492 εἶδα, **eidō**; or οἶδα, **oida**, v. GK: *3857* [→ *4893?*, *4941?*; cf. *2467*]. to know, to possess information; recognize, realize, to come to know; to understand, to be able to use knowledge:– saw [188], know [176], see [78], knowing [38], seen [34], knew [28], knoweth [22], knowest [15], beheld [10], tell [9], seeing [8], sawest [7], known [6], looked [6], wist [6], behold [4], knewest [3], perceive [3], perceiving [3], sure [3], wot [3], can [2], know how [2], aware [1], consider [1], discern (+*1381*) [1], knowledge [1], looked on [1], understandeth [1], understand [1]

1493 εἰδωλεῖον, **eidōleion**, n. GK: *1627* [→ *1497*]. temple of an idol:– idol's temple [1]

1494 εἰδωλόθυτος, **eidōlothytos**, a. GK: *1628* [→ *1497*+*2380*]. (food) sacrificed to idols:– things offered to idols [2], things sacrificed unto idols [2], meats offered to idols [1], offered in sacrifice to idols [1], offered in sacrifice unto idols [1], thing offered unto an idol [1], things offered in sacrifice unto idols [1], things offered unto idols [1]

1495 εἰδωλολατρία, **eidōlolatria**, n. GK: *1630* [→ *1497*+*2999*]. idolatry, the reverence and worship of idols:– idolatry [3], idolatries [1]

1496 εἰδωλολάτρης, **eidōlolatrēs**, n. GK: *1629* [→ *1497*+*2999*]. idolater, one who worships idols and so practices idolatry:– idolaters [5], idolater [2]

1497 εἴδωλον, **eidōlon**, n. GK: *1631* [→ *1493*, *1494*, *1496*, *1495*, *2712*; cf. *1491*]. idol, an object that is worshiped, formed by casting or carving (with the possible implication that a god or demon is intrinsic to the idol):– idols [7], idol [4]

1498 εἴην, **eiēn**, v.subj. or opt. of *1510*. GK: *1639* [→ *1510*]. it may (could, might, should, would) be; see *1510*:–

1499 εἰ καί, **ei kai**, conj. GK: *1623* + *2779* [→ *1487*+*2532*]. even if, although:– though [11], and if [1], if also [1], if that [1], though but [1]

1500 εἰκῆ, **eikē**, adv. GK: *1632*. in vain, for nothing, to no purpose:– in vain [5], vainly [1], without a cause [1]

1501 εἴκοσι, **eikosi**, n.num. GK: *1633*. twenty:– twenty [12]

1502 εἴκω, **eikō**, v. GK: *1634* [→ *5226*]. to give in, yield:– gave place [1]

1503 ἔοικα, **eoika**, v. GK: *2036* [→ *1504*, *1932*, *1933*]. to be like, resemble:– like [2]

1504 εἰκών, **eikōn**, n. GK: *1635* [→ *1503*]. image, likeness, portrait:– image [23]

1505 εἰλικρίνεια, **eilikrineia**, n. GK: *1636* [→ *1506*]. sincerity, the positive moral quality of purity (especially in motives), a fig. extension of an unadulterated or unmixed substance:– sincerity [3]

1506 εἰλικρινής, **eilikrinēs**, a. GK: *1637* [→ *1505*]. pure, wholesome:– pure [1], sincere [1]

1507 εἱλίσσω, **heilissō**, v. GK: *1813* [→ *1667*]. to roll up, roll together:– rolled together [1]

1508 εἰ μή, **ei mē**, conj. GK: *1623* + *3590* [→ *1487*+*3361*]. if not, except, but:– but [52], save [17], except [7], saving [2], more than [1], save only [1], till (+*3752*) [1]

1509 εἰ μή τι, **ei mē ti**, conj. GK: *1623* + *3590* + *5516* [→ *1508*+*5100*]. unless indeed, except, unless perhaps:– except [2], except (+*302*) [1]

1510 εἰμί, **eimi**, v. GK: *1639* [→ *548*, *666*, *1488*, *1498*, *1511*, *1526*, *1751*, *1762*, *1832*, *1849*, *1967*, *2070*, *2071*, *2075*, *2076*, *2077*, *2252*, *2258*, *2277*, *2468*, *3689*, *3776*, *3918*, *3952*, *4041*, *4840*, *4895*, *5123*, *5600*, *5607*; cf. *1849*]. to be, exist, be present; all forms of this verb are indexed under *1510*:– is [829], be [366], was [349], are [345], were [155],

am [139], art [85], being [37], been [24], have [23], had [16], be (+*1519*) [9], wast [6], come to pass [4], come [3], shall [3], meaneth [2], meant [2], mean [2], agree together (+*2470*) [1], agreed not (+*800*) [1], agreed together (+*2470*) [1], agree [1], belonged [1], belongeth [1], belong [1], cannot (+*3756*) [1], cannot be tempted (+*551*) [1], cometh [1], consisteth [1], continued [1], did [1], down [1], dureth [1], endure [1], exceedingly fear (+*1630*) [1], followed (+*3326*) [1], follow [1], for [1], give [1], hast [1], have being [1], having [1], held [1], know (+*1110*) [1], let [1], live long (+*3118*) [1], love husbands (+*5362*) [1], make [1], may [1], meaneth (+*2309*) [1], must [1], oweth [1], pass the flower of age (+*5230*) [1], perish (+*684*+*1519*) [1], please well (+*2101*) [1], pleased (+*701*) [1], profiteth (+*5624*) [1], remaineth (+*3062*+*3588*) [1], should [1], sojourn (+*3941*) [1], so [1], stand [1], used to [1], were (+*1096*) [1], were (+*4218*) [1], wert [1], while (+*1722*+*3588*) [1], wholly given to idolatry (+*2712*) [1], will [1], wrestle (+*3823*) [1]

1511 εἶναι, **einai**, v.infin. of *1510*. GK: *1639* [→ *1510*]. to be, exist, be present; see *1510*:–

εἵνεκεν, **heineken**. See *1752*.

1512 εἴπερ, **eiper**, pt.cond. GK: *1642* [→ *1487*+*4007*]. if indeed, if in fact, since:– if so that [2], if so be that (+*686*) [1], if so [1], seeing [1], though (+*2532*) [1]

1513 εἴπως, **eipōs**, pt. GK: *1643* [→ *1487*+*4226*]. if perhaps, if somehow:– if by any means [4]

1514 εἰρηνεύω, **eirēneuō**, v. GK: *1644* [→ *1515*]. to live in peace, be at peace:– have peace [1], live in peace [1], live peaceably [1], peace [1]

1515 εἰρήνη, **eirēnē**, n. GK: *1645* [→ *1514*, *1516*, *1517*, *1518*]. peace, harmony, tranquility; safety, welfare, health; often with an emphasis on lack of strife or reconciliation in a relation, as when one has "peace with God." Often used as a verbal and written greeting. This word generally follows the meanings and usage of the Hebrew word *7965*:– peace [89], quietness [1], rest [1], set at one (+*1519*+*4900*) [1]

1516 εἰρηνικός, **eirēnikos**, a. GK: *1646* [→ *1515*]. peace-loving, peaceable, peaceful, with a focus of having freedom from emotional worry and frustration:– peaceable [2]

1517 εἰρηνοποιέω, **eirēnopoieō**, v. GK: *1647* [→ *1515*+*4160*]. to make peace, to cause reconciliation between two parties, as in Christ causing the believer's peace with God:– made peace [1]

1518 εἰρηνοποιός, **eirēnopoios**, a. GK: *1648* [→ *1515*+*4160*]. peacemaker, one who restores peace and reconciliation between persons and even nations:– peacemakers [1]

εἴρω, **eirō**. See *1515*, *4483*, *5346*.

1519 εἰς, **eis**, pp. GK: *1650* [→ *1521*, *1522*, *1523*, *1524*, *1525*, *1528*, *1529*, *1530*, *1531*, *1532*, *1533*, *1898*, *2072*, *2080*, *2081*, *2082*, *3919*, *3920*, *3921*, *3922*, *3923*, *4897*]. to, toward, into; for. Spatially: movement toward or into an area (extending to a goal); logically: a marker of purpose or result; of time: extending to or up to a certain time:– into [543], to [316], unto [206], for [141], in [140], on [59], against [27], that (+*3588*) [27], to (+*3588*) [24], upon [24], at [21], among [18], towards [15], toward [14], be (+*1510*) [9], that [6], whereunto (+*3739*) [6], concerning [5], never (+*165*+*3361*+*3588*+*3756*) [5], throughout [5], become (+*1096*) [4], of [4], therein (+*846*) [4], to the end (+*3588*) [4], back (+*3588*+*3694*) [3], made (+*1096*) [3], therefore (+*3778*) [3], wherein (+*3739*) [3], abroad (+*5318*) [2], before [2], by [2], continually (+*1336*+*3588*) [2], for ever (+*1336*+*3588*) [2], for purpose [2], for this cause (+*3778*) [2], so that (+*3588*) [2], thereunto (+*3778*) [2], to this end (+*3778*) [2], why (+*5101*) [2], abundantly (+*4050*) [1], afar off (+*3112*) [1], after that (+*3195*+*3588*) [1], again (+*3588*+*3694*) [1], as concerning (+*3056*) [1], backward (+*3588*+*3694*) [1], became (+*1096*) [1], before (+*4383*) [1], by continual (+*5056*) [1], despised (+*3049*+*3762*) [1], ever (+*165*+*3588*+*3956*) [1], far more exceeding (+*2596*+*5236*+*5236*) [1], for to (+*3588*) [1], forth (+*3319*+*3588*) [1], from [1], grew (+*2064*) [1], hereunto (+*3778*) [1], home (+*2398*+*3588*) [1], in among [1], in no wise (+*3361*+*3588*+*3838*) [1], insomuch that (+*3588*) [1], lest (+*3361*+*3588*) [1], made ready to hand (+*2092*) [1], make mad (+*3130*+*4062*) [1], make war against (+*4171*+*4820*) [1], never (+*165*+*1487*+*3588*+*3756*) [1], never (+*165*+*3588*+*3756*) [1], peculiar (+*4047*) [1], perish (+*684*+*1510*) [1], regardest (+*991*) [1], relief (+*1248*) [1], set at one (+*1515*+*4900*) [1], thereinto (+*846*) [1], thereunto (+*846*+*3778*) [1], throughout (+*3837*) [1], till [1], to end [1], to make [1], to the intent (+*3588*) [1], took shipping (+*1684*+*3588*+*4143*) [1], until [1],

waxed (+*1096*) [1], went back (+*565*+*3588*+*3694*) [1], wherefore (+*3739*) [1], wherefore (+*5101*) [1], whereinto (+*3739*) [1], whereto (+*3739*) [1], wherewith [1], while standeth [1], whither (+*3739*) [1], with [1]

1520 εἷς, **heis**, n.num. GK: *1651* [→ *1733*, *1734*, *1775*, *1847*, *1848*, *3367*, *3391*, *3762*]. one, single:– one [289], a [13], first [8], some [6], the other[s] [6], certain [5], any [2], an [2], man [2], one (+*5100*) [2], one another (+*1520*+*3588*) [2], agree (+*1106*+*4160*) [2], another [1], each (+*1538*) [1], even all one as if (+*846*+*2532*+*3588*) [1], every (+*1538*+*2596*) [1], every (+*1538*) [1], no not one (+*2193*+*3756*) [1], one by one (+*2596*) [1], only [1], other[s] [1], particularly (+*1538*+*2596*) [1], several (+*303*) [1], whether (+*3739*) [1]

1521 εἰσάγω, **eisagō**, v. GK: *1652* [→ *1519*+*71*]. to bring in, take in:– brought into [4], brought in [3], bring in [1], bringeth in [1], led into [1]

1522 εἰσακούω, **eisakouō**, v. GK: *1653* [→ *1519*+*191*]. (pass.) to be heard, listened to:– heard [4], hear [1]

1523 εἰσδέχομαι, **eisdechomai**, v. GK: *1654* [→ *1519*+*1209*]. to receive, welcome:– receive [1]

1524 εἴσειμι, **eiseimi**, v. GK: *1655* [→ *1519*]. to go in, enter:– entered [1], go in [1], went in [1], went [1]

1525 εἰσέρχομαι, **eiserchomai**, v. GK: *1656* [→ *1519*+*2064*]. to go in, enter:– enter [55], entered [48], went into [14], went in [11], come in [8], came in [7], enter in [7], go in [7], come into [6], entered in [5], coming in [3], entereth [3], entering [3], came into [2], come [2], go into [2], arose [1], came to [1], camest in [1], come in [1], come unto [1], cometh into [1], enter in through [1], entereth in [1], entering in [1], goeth into [1], gone [1], go [1], in [1], wentest in [1], went [1]

1526 εἰσί, **eisi**, v.3.pl. of *1510*. GK: *1639* [→ *1510*]. they are; see *1510*:–

1527 εἷς καθ᾽ εἷς, **heis kath᾽ heis**, idiom. GK: *1651* + *2848* [→ *1520*+*2596*+*1520*]. one by one:– one by one [2], each [1]

1528 εἰσκαλέομαι, **eiskaleomai**, v. GK: *1657* [→ *1519*+*2564*]. to invite into:– called in [1]

1529 εἴσοδος, **eisodos**, n. GK: *1658* [→ *1519*+*3598*]. entering, entrance; reception, welcome:– coming [1], entering in [1], enter [1], entrance in [1], entrance [1]

1530 εἰσπηδάω, **eispēdaō**, v. GK: *1659* [→ *1519*]. to rush in:– ran in [1], sprang in [1]

1531 εἰσπορεύομαι, **eisporeuomai**, v. GK: *1660* [→ *1519*+*4198*]. to go in, enter:– entered [3], entereth [3], entereth in [2], entering [2], came in [1], come in [1], coming in [1], enter in [1], entering into [1], entering in [1], went into [1]

1532 εἰστρέχω, **eistrechō**, v. GK: *1661* [→ *1519*+*5143*]. to run in:– ran in [1]

1533 εἰσφέρω, **eispherō**, v. GK: *1662* [→ *1519*+*5342*]. to bring in, bring led in:– bring in [2], brought [2], bringest [1], lead into [1], lead [1]

1534 εἶτα, **eita**, adv. GK: *1663* [→ *1899*, *3347*]. then, after that, next:– then [11], after that [3], afterward [1], furthermore (+*3303*+*3588*) [1]

1535 εἴτε, **eite**, pt. GK: *1664* [→ *1487*+*5037*]. if, whether...or:– or [33], whether [28], or whether [3], if [1]

1536 εἴ τις, **ei tis**, pt.cond.+p. GK: *1623* + *5516* [→ *1487*+*5100*]. if any, whoever, whatever:– if any [45], if a man [6], that [2], whosoever [2], if ought [1], that which [1], whether any [1]

1537 ἐκ, **ek**, pp. GK: *1666* [→ *411*, *412*, *413*, *419*, *421*, *553*, *554*, *555*, *1327*, *1544*, *1545*, *1546*, *1547*, *1548*, *1549*, *1550*, *1551*, *1552*, *1553*, *1554*, *1555*, *1556*, *1557*, *1558*, *1559*, *1560*, *1561*, *1562*, *1567*, *1568*, *1569*, *1570*, *1571*, *1572*, *1573*, *1574*, *1575*, *1576*, *1577*, *1578*, *1579*, *1580*, *1581*, *1582*, *1583*, *1584*, *1585*, *1586*, *1587*, *1588*, *1589*, *1590*, *1591*, *1592*, *1593*, *1594*, *1597*, *1598*, *1599*, *1600*, *1601*, *1602*, *1603*, *1604*, *1605*, *1606*, *1607*, *1608*, *1609*, *1611*, *1612*, *1613*, *1615*, *1620*, *1622*, *1624*, *1625*, *1626*, *1627*, *1628*, *1629*, *1630*, *1631*, *1633*, *1634*, *1804*, *1805*, *1806*, *1807*, *1808*, *1809*, *1810*, *1811*, *1813*, *1814*, *1815*, *1816*, *1817*, *455*, *1818*, *1819*, *1820*, *1821*, *1822*, *1823*, *1824*, *1825*, *1826*, *1827*, *1828*, *1829*, *1830*, *1831*, *1832*, *1833*, *1834*, *1837*, *1839*, *1840*, *1841*, *1842*, *1843*, *1844*, *1845*, *1846*, *1847*, *1848*, *1849*, *1851*, *1852*, *1853*, *1854*, *1855*, *1856*, *1857*, *2078*, *2079*, *3924*, *4898*, *4899*, *5240*; cf. *1614*, *1632*]. of, out of; from, away from. Spatially: extension from a space to a goal outer in reference, separation; logically: the means or source of an activity, disassociation or separation:– of [441], from [185], out of [112], by [55], on [34], with [26],

in [7], among [5], over [4], second time (+*1208*) [4], at [3], by reason of [3], from among [3], thereof (+*846*) [3], through [3], again (+*1208*) [2], because of [2], for [2], out [2], abundantly (+*4053*) [1], as much as lieth in [1], between [1], betwixt [1], beyond [1], by the means of [1], earthly (+*1093+3588*) [1], exceedingly (+*4053+5228*) [1], from thenceforth (+*3778*) [1], grudgingly (+*3077*) [1], heartily (+*5590*) [1], heavenly (+*3772*) [1], hereby (+*3778*) [1], highly (+*4053*) [1], nothing (+*846+3361*) [1], of company [1], off [1], over against (+*1727*) [1], raised to life again (+*386*) [1], since began [1], third time (+*5154*) [1], to [1], unto [1], vehemently (+*4053*) [1], whereof (+*3739*) [1], whereof [1], your (+*4771*) [1]

1538 ἕκαστος, *hekastos*, a. GK: *1667* [→ *1539*]. each, every:– every man [34], every one [19], every [18], every man's [3], any man [1], both [1], daily (+*2250+2596*) [1], each (+*1520*) [1], each one [1], every (+*1520+2596*) [1], every (+*1520*) [1], every woman [1], particularly (+*1520+2596*) [1]

1539 ἑκάστοτε, *hekastote*, adv. GK: *1668* [→ *1538+3739+5037*]. always, at any time:– always [1]

1540 ἑκατόν, *hekaton*, n.num. GK: *1669* [→ *1541, 1542, 1543*]. hundred:– hundred [14], hundredfold [2], hundreds [1]

1541 ἑκατονταετής, *hekatontaetēs*, a. GK: *1670* [→ *1540+2094*]. a hundred years old:– hundred year old [1]

1542 ἑκατονταπλασίων, *hekatontaplasiōn*, a. GK: *1671* [→ *1540*]. a hundred times:– hundredfold [3]

1543 ἑκατοντάρχης, *hekatontarchēs*, n. GK: *1672 & 1673* [→ *1540+757*]. centurion, officer:– centurion [17], centurions [3], centurion's [1]

1544 ἐκβάλλω, *ekballō*, v. GK: *1675* [→ *1537+906*]. to take out, remove; to drive out, expel; bring out, send out:– cast out [46], bringeth forth [3], casteth out [3], casting out [3], cast [3], pull out [3], send forth [3], thrust out [3], put forth [2], cast forth [1], casteth [1], driveth [1], drove out [1], expelled [1], leave [1], plucked out [1], put out [1], putteth forth [1], put [1], sent away [1], sent out [1], took out [1]

1545 ἔκβασις, *ekbasis*, n. GK: *1676* [→ *1537+305*]. way out; outcome, end, result:– end [1], way to escape [1]

1546 ἐκβολή, *ekbolē*, n. GK: *1678* [→ *1537+906*]. throwing out (a ship's cargo), jettisoning:– lightened the ship (+*4160*) [1]

1547 ἐκγαμίζω, *ekgamizō*, v. GK: *1679* [→ *1537+1062*]. to marry, give in marriage:– given in marriage [2], giveth in marriage [2], giving in marriage [1]

1548 ἐκγαμίσκω, *ekgamiskō*, v. GK: *1680* [→ *1537+1062*]. to give in marriage:– given in marriage [2]

1549 ἔκγονος, *ekgonos*, a. GK: *1681* [→ *1537+1096*]. (n.) grandchild:– nephews [1]

1550 ἐκδαπανάω, *ekdapanaō*, v. GK: *1682* [→ *1537+1160*]. (pass.) to be completely expended, exhausted:– spent [1]

1551 ἐκδέχομαι, *ekdechomai*, v. GK: *1683* [→ *1537+1209*]. to wait for, expect, look forward to:– expecting [1], look for [1], looked for [1], tarry for [1], waited for [1], waited [1], waiteth for [1], waiting for [1]

1552 ἔκδηλος, *ekdēlos*, a. GK: *1684* [→ *1537+1212*]. clear, very evident, plain:– manifest [1]

1553 ἐκδημέω, *ekdēmeō*, v. GK: *1685* [→ *1537+1218*]. to be away, absent:– absent [3]

1554 ἐκδίδωμι, *ekdidōmi*, v. GK: *1686* [→ *1537+1325*]. (mid.) to rent, lease:– let out [3], let forth [1]

1555 ἐκδιηγέομαι, *ekdiēgeomai*, v. GK: *1687* [→ *1537+1223+71*]. to tell:– declare [1], declaring [1]

1556 ἐκδικέω, *ekdikeō*, v. GK: *1688* [→ *1537+1349*]. to avenge, take revenge; to grant justice, get justice:– avenge [4], avenged [1], revenge [1]

1557 ἐκδίκησις, *ekdikēsis*, n. GK: *1689* [→ *1537+1349*]. justice; vengeance; punishment:– vengeance [4], avenge (+*3588+4160*) [1], avenged (+*4160*) [1], avenge [1], punishment [1], revenge [1]

1558 ἔκδικος, *ekdikos*, a. GK: *1690* [→ *1537+1349*]. punishing, avenging:– avenger [1], revenger [1]

1559 ἐκδιώκω, *ekdiōkō*, v. GK: *1691* [→ *1537+1377*]. to drive out, persecute (severely):– persecuted [1], persecute [1]

1560 ἔκδοτος, *ekdotos*, a. GK: *1692* [→ *1537+1325*]. handed over, given up, delivered up:– delivered [1]

1561 ἐκδοχή, *ekdochē*, n. GK: *1693* [→ *1537+1209*]. expectation:– looking for [1]

1562 ἐκδύω, *ekdyō*, v. GK: *1694* [→ *1537+1416*]. to strip off clothing, unclothe:– stripped of raiment [1], stripped [1], took off from [1], took off [1], unclothed [1]

1563 ἐκεῖ, *ekei*, adv. GK: *1695* [→ *1564, 1565, 1566, 1900, 2546, 2547, 2548, 5238*]. there, in a place where:– there [86], thither [7], thitherward [1], to yonder place [1], yonder [1]

1564 ἐκεῖθεν, *ekeithen*, adv. GK: *1696* [→ *1563*]. from there, from that place:– thence [16], from thence [7], from that place [1], there [1]

1565 ἐκεῖνος, *ekeinos*, p.demo. GK: *1697* [→ *1563*]. that, those; he, she, it:– that [105], he [40], those [40], they [15], the same [12], them [8], his [7], same [6], him [5], she [4], their [2], it [1], same (+*4012*) [1], selfsame [1], the other[S] [1], the same (+*2596*) [1], theirs [1], this [1]

1566 ἐκεῖσε, *ekeise*, adv. GK: *1698* [→ *1563*]. there, a place where:– there [2]

1567 ἐκζητέω, *ekzēteō*, v. GK: *1699* [→ *1537+2212*]. to seek out, seek earnestly; (pass.) to be held responsible:– required [2], after [1], diligently seek [1], inquired [1], seek after [1], sought carefully [1]

1568 ἐκθαμβέω, *ekthambeō*, v. GK: *1701* [→ *1537+2285*]. (pass.) to be overwhelmed with wonder, distressed, alarmed:– affrighted [2], greatly amazed [1], sore amazed [1]

1569 ἔκθαμβος, *ekthambos*, a. GK: *1702* [→ *1537+2285*]. (utterly) astonished:– greatly wondering [1]

1570 ἔκθετος, *ekthetos*, a. GK: *1704* [→ *1537+5087*]. thrown out, exposed (to elements), abandoned:– cast out (+*4160*) [1]

1571 ἐκκαθαίρω, *ekkathairō*, v. GK: *1705* [→ *1537+2513*]. to cleanse, clean out, get rid of:– purge out [1], purge [1]

1572 ἐκκαίω, *ekkaiō*, v. GK: *1706* [→ *1537+2545*]. (pass.) to be inflamed, have a strong desire:– burned [1]

1573 ἐκκακέω, *ekkakeō*, v. GK: *1591 & 1707* [→ *1537+2556*]. to give up, become discouraged, lose heart:– faint [4], weary [2]

1574 ἐκκεντέω, *ekkenteō*, v. GK: *1708* [→ *1537+2759*]. to pierce:– pierced [1]

1575 ἐκκλάω, *ekklaō*, v. GK: *1709* [→ *1537+2806*]. (pass.) to be broken off:– broken off [3]

1576 ἐκκλείω, *ekkleiō*, v. GK: *1710* [→ *1537+2808*]. to alienate, shut out, exclude:– excluded [1], exclude [1]

1577 ἐκκλησία, *ekklēsia*, n. GK: *1711* [→ *1537+2564*]. church, congregation, assembly; a group of people gathered together. It can refer to the OT assembly of believers (Ac 7:38), or a riotous mob (Ac 19:32), but usually to a Christian assembly, a church: as a totality (Eph 3:10), or in a specific locale (Col. 4:15). In the NT a church is never a building or meeting place:– church [78], churches [36], assembly [3], in every church (+*2596*) [1]

1578 ἐκκλίνω, *ekklinō*, v. GK: *1712* [→ *1537+2827*]. to turn away, turn aside:– avoid [1], eschew [1], gone out of the way [1]

1579 ἐκκολυμβάω, *ekkolymbaō*, v. GK: *1713* [→ *1537+2860*]. to swim away:– swim out [1]

1580 ἐκκομίζω, *ekkomizō*, v. GK: *1714* [→ *1537+2889*]. to carry out:– carried out [1]

1581 ἐκκόπτω, *ekkoptō*, v. GK: *1716* [→ *1537+2875*]. to cut off, cut down:– cut off [3], hewn down [3], cut down [2], cut off from [1], cut out [1], hindered [1]

1582 ἐκκρεμάννυμι, *ekkremannymi*, v. GK: *1717* [→ *1537+2910*]. (mid.) to hang upon (words), to consider something seriously:– very attentive [1]

1583 ἐκλαλέω, *eklaleō*, v. GK: *1718* [→ *1537+2980*]. to tell:– tell [1]

1584 ἐκλάμπω, *eklampō*, v. GK: *1719* [→ *1537+2989*]. to shine:– shine forth [1]

1585 ἐκλανθάνομαι, *eklanthanomai*, v. GK: *1720* [→ *1537+2990*]. to forget:– forgotten [1]

1586 ἐκλέγομαι, *eklegomai*, v. GK: *1721* [→ *1537+3004*]. to chose, pick, select:– chosen [16], chose [3], chose out [1], made choice [1]

1587 ἐκλείπω, *ekleipō*, v. GK: *1722* [→ *1537+3007*]. to fail, end, stop:– fail [3]

1588 ἐκλεκτός, *eklektos*, a. GK: *1723* [→ *1537+3004*]. elect, chosen, the Chosen One:– elect [13], chosen [7], elect's [2], elects' [1]

1589 ἐκλογή, *eklogē*, n. GK: *1724* [→ *1537+3004*]. election, choice, selection:– election [6], chosen [1]

1590 ἐκλύω, *eklyō*, v. GK: *1725* [→ *1537+3089*]. (pass.) to lose heart; give up; collapse in weariness:– faint [5], fainted [1]

1591 ἐκμάσσω, *ekmassō*, v. GK: *1726* [→ *1537+3146*]. to wipe off, dry off:– wiped [3], wipe [2]

1592 ἐκμυκτηρίζω, *ekmyktērizō*, v. GK: *1727* [→ *1537+3456*]. to sneer at, ridicule:– derided [2]

1593 ἐκνεύω, *ekneuō*, v. GK: *1728* [→ *1537+3506*]. to slip away, withdraw:– conveyed away [1]

1594 ἐκνήφω, *eknēphō*, v. GK: *1729* [→ *1537+3525*]. to come to one's sense, become sober:– awake [1]

1595 ἑκούσιος, *hekousios*, a. GK: *1730* [→ *1635*]. spontaneous, willing:– willingly (+*2596*) [1]

1596 ἑκουσίως, *hekousiōs*, adv. GK: *1731* [→ *1635*]. willingly; deliberately, intentionally:– wilfully [1], willingly [1]

1597 ἔκπαλαι, *ekpalai*, adv. GK: *1732* [→ *1537+3819*]. for a long time, long ago:– of a long time [1], of old [1]

1598 ἐκπειράζω, *ekpeirazō*, v. GK: *1733* [→ *1537+3984*]. to test, put to a test, try, tempt:– tempt [3], tempted [1]

1599 ἐκπέμπω, *ekpempō*, v. GK: *1734* [→ *1537+3992*]. to send away, send out:– sent away [1], sent forth [1]

ἐκπερισσού, *ekperissou*. See **1537** and **4053**.

1600 ἐκπετάννυμι, *ekpetannymi*, v. GK: *1736* [→ *1537+4072*]. to hold out, spread out:– stretched forth [1]

1601 ἐκπίπτω, *ekpiptō*, v. GK: *1738* [→ *1537+4098*]. to fall off; to fail; to run aground, be dashed to pieces:– fall [2], cast [1], faileth [1], fall from [1], fall off [1], fallen from [1], falleth away [1], falleth [1], fell off [1], taken none effect [1]

1602 ἐκπλέω, *ekpleō*, v. GK: *1739* [→ *1537+4126*]. to sail (from):– sailed away [1], sailed thence [1], sailed [1]

1603 ἐκπληρόω, *ekplēroō*, v. GK: *1740* [→ *1537+4137*]. to (utterly) fulfill:– fulfilled [1]

1604 ἐκπλήρωσις, *ekplērōsis*, n. GK: *1741* [→ *1537+4137*]. end, completion:– accomplishment [1]

1605 ἐκπλήσσω, *ekplēssō*, v. GK: *1742* [→ *1537+4141*]. (pass.) to be amazed, astonished:– astonished [10], amazed [3]

1606 ἐκπνέω, *ekpneō*, v. GK: *1743* [→ *1537+4154*]. to breathe one's last breath, die:– gave up the ghost [3]

1607 ἐκπορεύομαι, *ekporeuomai*, v. GK: *1744* [→ *1537+4198*]. to go out, come out, leave:– went out [6], cometh out [2], depart [2], goeth out [2], proceeded [2], proceedeth [2], proceed [2], came forth [1], come forth [1], come out [1], come [1], departed [1], go forth [1], going out [1], gone forth [1], issued out [1], issued [1], out goeth [1], proceed out [1], proceeded out [1], proceedeth out [1], proceeding out [1], went [1]

1608 ἐκπορνεύω, *ekporneuō*, v. GK: *1745* [→ *1537+4204*]. to engage in sexual immorality:– giving over to fornication [1]

1609 ἐκπτύω, *ekptyō*, v. GK: *1746* [→ *1537+4429*]. to scorn, spit out:– rejected [1]

1610 ἐκριζόω, *ekrizoō*, v. GK: *1748* [→ *1537+4491*]. to uproot:– plucked up by the roots [1], plucked up by the root [1], root up [1], rooted up [1]

1611 ἔκστασις, *ekstasis*, n. GK: *1749* [→ *1537+2476*]. amazement, astonishment, bewilderment; a trance:– trance [3], amazed (+*2983*) [1], amazed [1], amazement [1], astonishment [1]

1612 ἐκστρέφω, *ekstrephō*, v. GK: *1750* [→ *1537+4762*]. (pass.) to be warped, perverted:– subverted [1]

1613 ἐκταράσσω, *ektarassō*, v. GK: *1752* [→ *1537+5015*]. to throw into an uproar, into confusion:– exceedingly trouble [1]

1614 ἐκτείνω, *ekteinō*, v. GK: *1753* [→ *660, 816, 1616, 1617, 1618, 1619, 1621, 1901, 2159, 3905, 4385, 4401, 5239, 5500*; cf. *1537*]. to stretch out, reach out; point, motion:– stretched forth [5], stretch forth [4], put forth [3], stretched out [2], cast [1], stretching forth [1]

1615 ἐκτελέω, *ekteleō*, v. GK: *1754* [→ *1537+5056*]. to finish, bring to a conclusion:– finish [1]

1616 ἐκτένεια, *ekteneia*, n. GK: *1755* [→ *1614*]. earnestness:– instantly (+*1722*) [1]

1617 ἐκτενέστερον, *ektenesteron*, adv.compar. of *1618*. GK: *1757* [→ *1614*]. more deeply, more earnestly:– more earnestly [1]

1618 ἐκτενής, *ektenēs*, a. GK: *1756* [→ *1614*]. deep, earnest:– fervent [1], without ceasing [1]

1619 ἐκτενῶς, *ektenōs*, adv. GK: *1757* [→ *1614*]. deeply, earnestly:– fervently [1]

1620 ἐκτίθημι, *ektithēmi*, v. GK: *1758* [→ *1537*+*5087*]. (mid.) to explain; (pass.) to be placed out in the elements, exposed, abandoned:– expounded [3], cast out [1]

1621 ἐκτινάσσω, *ektinassō*, v. GK: *1759* [→ *1614*]. to shake off, shake out:– shake off [2], shook off [1], shook [1]

1622 ἐκτός, *ektos*, adv. GK: *1760* [→ *1537*]. outside, beyond, except:– out of [2], but (+*1487*+*3361*) [1], except (+*1487*+*3361*) [1], excepted [1], other than [1], outside [1], unless (+*1487*+*3361*) [1], without [1]

1623 ἕκτος, *hektos*, a. GK: *1761* [→ *1803*]. sixth, noon (the sixth hour):– sixth [14]

1624 ἐκτρέπω, *ektrepō*, v. GK: *1762* [→ *1537*+*5157*]. to turn away, wander away from; be disabled:– turned aside [2], avoiding [1], turned out of the way [1], turned [1]

1625 ἐκτρέφω, *ektrephō*, v. GK: *1763* [→ *1537*+*5142*]. to feed, nourish; to bring up, rear (children):– bring up [1], nourisheth [1]

1626 ἔκτρωμα, *ektrōma*, n. GK: *1765* [→ *1537*+*5134*]. abnormal or untimely birth:– born out of due time [1]

1627 ἐκφέρω, *ekpherō*, v. GK: *1766* [→ *1537*+*5342*]. to bring out, carry out; to produce:– carry out [2], beareth [1], bring forth [1], brought forth [1], carried out [1], carrying forth [1]

1628 ἐκφεύγω, *ekpheugō*, v. GK: *1767* [→ *1537*+*5343*]. to escape:– escape [4], escaped [1], fled out [1], fled [1]

1629 ἐκφοβέω, *ekphobeō*, v. GK: *1768* [→ *1537*+*5401*]. to frighten, terrify:– terrify [1]

1630 ἔκφοβος, *ekphobos*, a. GK: *1769* [→ *1537*+*5401*]. frightened, terrified:– exceedingly fear (+*1510*) [1], sore afraid [1]

1631 ἐκφύω, *ekphyō*, v. GK: *1770* [→ *1537*+*5453*]. to come out, put forth:– putteth forth [2]

1632 ἐκχέω, *ekcheō*, v. GK: *1772* & *1773* [→ *130*, *401*, *2022*, *2708*, *4378*, *4797*, *4799*, *5240*, *5517*, *5522*; cf. *1537*]. to pour out, shed, scatter; (pass.) to be poured out, shed; to rush (for profit):– poured out [9], shed [9], pour out [3], spilled [2], gushed out [1], ran greedily after [1], runneth out [1], shed abroad [1], shed forth [1]

1633 ἐκχωρέω, *ekchōreō*, v. GK: *1774* [→ *1537*+*5562*]. to go out, go away:– depart out [1]

1634 ἐκψύχω, *ekpsychō*, v. GK: *1775* [→ *1537*+*5594*]. to die, expire:– gave up the ghost [2], yielded up the ghost [1]

1635 ἑκών, *hekōn*, a. GK: *1776* [→ *210*, *1595*, *1596*]. voluntarily, by one's own choice:– willingly [2]

1636 ἐλαία, *elaia*, n. GK: *1777* [→ *65*, *1637*, *1638*, *2565*]. olive, olive tree; in the proper name "the Mount of Olives," a ridge on the east side of the Kidron Valley, overlooking Jerusalem and the Temple mount:– olives [11], olive tree [2], olive berries [1], olive trees [1]

1637 ἔλαιον, *elaion*, n. GK: *1778* [→ *1636*]. olive oil:– oil [11]

1638 ἐλαιών, *elaiōn*, n. GK: *1779* [→ *1636*]. Mount of Olives, olive grove:– Olivet [1]

1639 Ἐλαμίτης, *Elamitēs*, n.pr.g. GK: *1780*. Elamite, "*highland*":– Elamites [1]

1640 ἐλάσσων, *elassōn*, a. [also used as adv.]. GK: *1781* & *1784* [→ *1641*, *1642*, *1646*, *1647*]. lesser, cheaper, younger:– less [1], under [1], worse [1], younger [1]

1641 ἐλαττονέω, *elattoneō*, v. GK: *1782* [→ *1640*]. to have too little:– had lack [1]

1642 ἐλαττόω, *elattoō*, v. GK: *1783* [→ *1640*]. to make lower than; (pass.) to be made lower than, become lesser, diminish:– decrease [1], made lower [1], madest lower [1]

1643 ἐλαύνω, *elaunō*, v. GK: *1785* [→ *556*, *4900*]. to row (with oars); (pass.) to be driven:– driven [2], carried [1], rowed [1], rowing [1]

1644 ἐλαφρία, *elaphria*, n. GK: *1786* [→ *1645*]. lightness, levity:– lightness [1]

1645 ἐλαφρός, *elaphros*, a. GK: *1787* [→ *1644*]. light, not burdensome:– light [2]

1646 ἐλάχιστος, *elachistos*, a. GK: *1788* [→ *1640*]. least, very small, trivial:– least [9], very small [2], smallest matters [1], very little [1]

1647 ἐλαχιστότερος, *elachistoteros*, a.compar. of *1646*. GK: *1788* [→ *1640*]. far less, smallest:– least [1]

1648 Ἐλεάζαρ, *Eleazar*, n.pr. GK: *1789*. Eleazar, "*God [El] is a help*":– Eleazar [2]

1649 ἔλεγξις, *elenxis*, n. GK: *1792* [→ *1651*]. rebuke, reproof:– rebuked [1]

1650 ἔλεγχος, *elenchos*, n. GK: *1791* & *1793* [→ *1651*]. certainty, proof; rebuke, reproof:– evidence [1], reproof [1]

1651 ἐλέγχω, *elenchō*, v. GK: *1794* [→ *557*, *1246*, *1649*, *1650*, *1827*]. to expose; to rebuke, refute, show fault; to convince, convict:– rebuke [4], reproved [3], reprove [3], convinced [2], convicted [1], convinceth [1], convince [1], rebuked [1], tell fault [1]

1652 ἐλεεινός, *eleeinos*, a. GK: *1795* [→ *1656*]. pitiful:– miserable [1], most miserable [1]

1653 ἐλεέω, *eleeō*, v. GK: *1790* & *1796* [→ *1656*]. to have mercy on, pity; to show mercy to, show pity to another who is in serious need, usually with a focus on an act of kindness that will help meet the need:– have mercy [14], obtained mercy [6], had compassion [2], obtain mercy [2], sheweth mercy [2], had mercy [1], had pity [1], hath mercy [1], have compassion [1], received mercy [1]

1654 ἐλεημοσύνη, *eleēmosynē*, n. GK: *1797* [→ *1656*]. gift to the poor, alms, charitable gift; any act of generosity to someone in serious need, often referring to giving gifts of substance or money:– alms [13], almsdeeds [1]

1655 ἐλεήμων, *eleēmōn*, a. GK: *1798* [→ *1656*]. merciful, including feelings of pity, with a focus of showing compassion to those in serious need:– merciful [2]

1656 ἔλεος, *eleos*, n. GK: *1799* [→ *415*, *448*, *1652*, *1653*, *1654*, *1655*]. mercy, pity; the moral quality of feeling compassion and especially of showing kindness toward someone in need. This can refer to a human kindness and to God's kindness to humankind:– mercy [27], tender mercy (+*4698*) [1]

1657 ἐλευθερία, *eleutheria*, n. GK: *1800* [→ *1658*]. freedom, liberty, not enslaved:– liberty [11]

1658 ἐλεύθερος, *eleutheros*, a. GK: *1801* [→ *558*, *1657*, *1659*]. free, released, liberated from various kinds of ownership, confinement, and distress: prison confinement, political domination and oppression, physical sickness, release from the marriage contract in death, and God's release of the sinner from sin. A free person is often contrasted to a slave:– free [19], freewoman [1], liberty [1]

1659 ἐλευθερόω, *eleutheroō*, v. GK: *1802* [→ *1658*]. to set free, liberate, cause someone to receive liberty or freedom:– made free [4], make free [2], delivered [1]

ἐλεύθω, *eleuthō*. See *2064*.

1660 ἔλευσις, *eleusis*, n. GK: *1803* [→ *2064*]. coming, advent:– coming [1]

1661 ἐλεφάντινος, *elephantinos*, a. GK: *1804*. made of ivory (derivative of the Greek word for "elephant," not found in the NT):– ivory [1]

1662 Ἐλιακείμ, *Eliakeim*, n.pr. GK: *1805* & *1806*. Eliakim, "*God [El] establishes*":– Eliakim [3]

1663 Ἐλιέζερ, *Eliezer*, n.pr. GK: *1808*. Eliezer, "*God [El] is [my] help*":– Eliezer [1]

1664 Ἐλιούδ, *Elioud*, n.pr. GK: *1809*. Eliud, "*God [El] is [my] grandeur*":– Eliud [2]

1665 Ἐλισάβετ, *Elisabet*, n.pr. GK: *1810*. Elizabeth, "*God [El] is [my] oath*":– Elisabeth [8], Elisabeth's [1]

1666 Ἐλισσαῖος, *Elissaios*, n.pr. GK: *1811* & *1812*. Elisha, "*God [El] is [my] salvation*":– Eliseus [1]

1667 ἑλίσσω, *helissō*, v. GK: *1813* [→ *1507*]. to roll up, fold up [1]

1668 ἕλκος, *helkos*, n. GK: *1814* [→ *1669*]. sore, abscess:– sores [2], sore [1]

1669 ἑλκόω, *helkoō*, v. GK: *1815* [→ *1668*]. (pass.) to be covered with sores:– full of sores [1]

1670 ἑλκύω, *helkyō*, v. GK: *1816* [→ *1828*]. to drag, draw, pull in:– draw [4], drew [3], drew out [1]

1671 Ἑλλάς, *Hellas*, n.pr. GK: *1817* [→ *1672*]. Greece:– Greece [1]

1672 Ἕλλην, *Hellēn*, n.pr. GK: *1818* [→ *1671*, *1673*, *1674*, *1675*, *1676*]. Greek; Gentile, a class of person distinguished from the Jewish race and nation (not necessarily Greek):– Greeks [13], Greek [7], Gentiles [5], Gentile [2]

1673 Ἑλληνικός, *Hellēnikos*, a.pr. GK: *1819* [→ *1672*]. Greek (language):– Greek [2]

1674 Ἑλληνίς, *Hellēnis*, n.pr. GK: *1820* [→ *1672*]. Greek, Gentile, a class of person distinguished from the Jewish race and nation (not necessarily Greek):– Greeks [1], Greek [1]

1675 Ἑλληνιστής, *Hellēnistēs*, n.pr.g. GK: *1821* [→ *1672*]. Grecian Jew, Hellenist:– Grecians [3]

1676 Ἑλληνιστί, *Hellēnisti*, adv.pr. GK: *1822* [→ *1672*]. in Greek (language):– Greek [2]

1677 ἐλλογέω, *ellogeō*, v. GK: *1823* & *1824* [→ *1722*+*3004*]. to charge (to one's account):– imputed [1], put on account [1]

ἕλλομαι, *hellomai*. See *138*.

1678 Ἐλμωδάμ, *Elmōdam*, n.pr. GK: *1825* & *1826*. Elmodam:– Elmodam [1]

1679 ἐλπίζω, *elpizō*, v. GK: *1827* [→ *1680*]. to hope, hope for, put hope in, expect, an attitude of confidently looking forward to what is good and beneficial:– trust [15], hope [5], hoped [3], hope for [2], trusted [2], hoped for [1], hopeth [1], hoping [1], trusteth [1]

1680 ἐλπίς, *elpis*, n. GK: *1828* [→ *560*, *1679*, *4276*]. hope, expectation:– hope [53], hope's [1]

1681 Ἐλύμας, *Elymas*, n.pr. GK: *1829*. Elymas, "[poss.] *wise one* hence *magician*":– Elymas [1]

1682 ἐλωΐ, *elōi*, l.[n.+p.]. GK: *1830* [cf. *2241*]. Eloi [Aramaic: my God]:– eloi [1]

1683 ἐμαυτοῦ, *emautou*, p.reflex. GK: *1831* [→ *1473*+*846*]. myself, my own, of my own accord:– myself [30], me [4], mine own self [2], mine own [1]

1684 ἐμβαίνω, *embainō*, v. GK: *1832* [→ *1537*+*305*]. to get into, step into, embark:– entered [7], went [3], come [2], get [2], entering [1], stepped in [1], took shipping (+*1519*+*3588*+*4143*) [1], took [1]

1685 ἐμβάλλω, *emballō*, v. GK: *1833* [→ *1722*+*906*]. to throw into:– cast [1]

1686 ἐμβάπτω, *embaptō*, v. GK: *1834* & *1835* [→ *1722*+*911*]. to dip into:– dippeth [2], dipped [1]

1687 ἐμβατεύω, *embateuō*, v. GK: *1836* [→ *1722*+*305*]. to go into great detail about:– intruding into [1]

1688 ἐμβιβάζω, *embibazō*, v. GK: *1837* [→ *1722*+*305*]. to put on board (a vessel):– put [1]

1689 ἐμβλέπω, *emblepō*, v. GK: *1838* [→ *1722*+*991*]. to look (closely, directly) at, gaze at:– beheld [3], looked upon [2], looking upon [2], beholding [1], behold [1], gazing up [1], saw [1], see [1]

1690 ἐμβριμάομαι, *embrimaomai*, v. GK: *1839* [→ *1722*]. to warn sternly, rebuke harshly; to be deeply moved:– straitly charged [2], groaned [1], groaning [1], murmured against [1]

1691 ἐμέ, *eme*, p.pers.acc. of *1473*. GK: *1609* [→ *1473*]. me; see *1473*:–

1692 ἐμέω, *emeō*, v. GK: *1840*. to spit out:– spue [1]

1693 ἐμμαίνομαι, *emmainomai*, v. GK: *1841* [→ *1722*+*3105*]. to be enraged:– mad against [1]

1694 Ἐμμανουήλ, *Emmanouēl*, n.pr. GK: *1842*. Immanuel, "*God with us*":– Emmanuel [1]

1695 Ἐμμαοῦς, *Emmaous*, n.pr. GK: *1843*. Emmaus, "*hot springs*":– Emmaus [1]

1696 ἐμμένω, *emmenō*, v. GK: *1844* [→ *1722*+*3306*]. to remain in, stay in; remain faithful, continue in:– continue in [1], continued [1], continueth [1]

1697 Ἐμμώρ, *Hemmōr*, n.pr. GK: *1846*. Hamor, "*male donkey*":– Emmor [1]

1698 ἐμοί, *emoi*, p.pers.dat. of *1473*. GK: *1609* [→ *1473*]. in me; to me; my; see *1473*:–

1699 ἐμός, *emos*, a.poss. GK: *1847* [→ *1473*]. my, mine:– my [49], mine [12], mine own [11], me [4], I have [1]

1700 ἐμοῦ, *emou*, p.pers.gen. of *1473*. GK: *1609* [→ *1473*]. my, mine; see *1473*:–

1701 ἐμπαιγμός, *empaigmos*, n. GK: *1849* [→ *1722*+*3815*]. jeering, scoffing, mocking:– mockings [1]

1702 ἐμπαίζω, **empaizō**, v. GK: *1850* [→ *1722+3815*]. to mock, ridicule:– mocked [8], mock [3], mocking [2]

1703 ἐμπαίκτης, **empaiktēs**, n. GK: *1851* [→ *1722+3815*]. scoffer, mocker:– mockers [1], scoffers [1]

1704 ἐμπεριπατέω, **emperipateō**, v. GK: *1853* [→ *1722+4012+3961*]. to walk among:– walk in [1]

1705 ἐμπίπλημι, **empiplēmi**, v. GK: *1854 & 1855 & 1857 & 1858* [→ *1722+4130*]. (act.) to provide, fill, satisfy; (pass.) to be filled to satisfaction; to enjoy one's company:– filled [3], filling with [1], full [1]

1706 ἐμπίπτω, **empiptō**, v. GK: *1860* [→ *1722+4098*]. to fall into:– fall [5], fallen [1], fell [1]

1707 ἐμπλέκω, **emplekō**, v. GK: *1861* [→ *1722+4120*]. (mid./pass.) to be involved in, become entangled:– entangled [1], entangleth with [1]

ἐμπλήθω, **emplēthō**. See **1705**.

1708 ἐμπλοκή, **emplokē**, n. GK: *1862 & 4451* [→ *1722+4120*]. braiding (possibly associated with high fashion):– plaiting [1]

1709 ἐμπνέω, **empneō**, v. GK: *1863* [→ *1722+4154*]. to breath:– breathing out [1]

1710 ἐμπορεύομαι, **emporeuomai**, v. GK: *1864* [→ *1722+4198*]. to carry on business; exploit:– buy and sell [1], make merchandise [1]

1711 ἐμπορία, **emporia**, n. GK: *1865* [→ *1722+4198*]. business, trade:– merchandise [1]

1712 ἐμπόριον, **emporion**, n. GK: *1866* [→ *1722+4198*]. market, marketplace:– merchandise [1]

1713 ἔμπορος, **emporos**, n. GK: *1867* [→ *1722+4198*]. merchant:– merchants [4], merchant [1]

1714 ἐμπρήθω, **emprēthō**, v. GK: *1856 & 1859 & 1868* [→ *1722+4092*]. to burn, set on fire:– burnt up [1]

1715 ἔμπροσθεν, **emprosthen**, adv.&pp.*. GK: *1869* [→ *1722+4314*]. before, in front of, in the presence of:– before [38], in sight [2], preferred before (+*1096*) [2], against [1], at [1], in the presence [1], in the sight [1], of [1], went forth [1]

1716 ἐμπτύω, **emptyō**, v. GK: *1870* [→ *1722+4429*]. to spit on, spit at:– spit upon [2], spit [2], spit on [1], spitted on [1]

1717 ἐμφανής, **emphanēs**, a. GK: *1871* [→ *1722+5316*]. seen, revealed, visible:– manifest [1], openly [1]

1718 ἐμφανίζω, **emphanizō**, v. GK: *1872* [→ *1722+5316*]. to show; report; to present (legal) charges; petition; (pass.) to appear:– informed [3], manifest [2], appeared [1], appear [1], declare plainly [1], shewed [1], signify [1]

1719 ἔμφοβος, **emphobos**, a. GK: *1873* [→ *1722+5401*]. afraid, terrified:– afraid [3], affrighted [2], trembled (+*1096*) [1]

1720 ἐμφυσάω, **emphysaō**, v. GK: *1874* [→ *1722+5453*]. to breathe on:– breathed on [1]

1721 ἔμφυτος, **emphytos**, a. GK: *1875* [→ *1722+5453*]. implanted:– engrafted [1]

1722 ἐν, **en**, pp. GK: *1877* [→ *410, 418, 1449, 1455, 1456, 1457, 1458, 1459, 1460, 1461, 1462, 1463, 1464, 1465, 1466, 1467, 1468, 1469, 1470, 1471, 1472, 1677, 1684, 1685, 1686, 1687, 1688, 1689, 1690, 1693, 1696, 1701, 1702, 1703, 1704, 1705, 1714, 1706, 1707, 1708, 1709, 1710, 1711, 1712, 1713, 1714, 1715, 1716, 1717, 1718, 1719, 1720, 1721, 1723, 1724, 1725, 1728, 1729, 1730, 1731, 1732, 1735, 1736, 1737, 1738, 1739, 1740, 1741, 1742, 1743, 1744, 1745, 1746, 1747, 1748, 1749, 1750, 1751, 1753, 1754, 1755, 1756, 1757, 1758, 1759, 1760, 1761, 1762, 1764, 1765, 1770, 1771, 1772, 1773, 1774, 1776, 1777, 1779, 1780, 1782, 1783, 1784, 1786, 1787, 1788, 1789, 1790, 1791, 1792, 1793, 1794, 1795, 1796, 1797, 1798, 1799, 1801, 1902, 1903, 2714, 3925, 3926, 4278, 5241; cf. 1420, 1785*]. Spatially: in, inside, at, among, with; logically: by means of, with, because of; of time: during, while:– in [1877], with [145], by [141], at [110], among [104], on [46], through [38], wherein (+*3739*) [23], to [18], therein (+*846*) [16], as (+*3588*) [15], of [15], within [13], into [12], when (+*3588*) [12], unto [9], amongst [8], hereby (+*3778*) [8], as [7], herein (+*3778*) [7], for [6], whereby (+*3739*) [6], among (+*3319*) [5], throughout [5], while (+*3588*) [5], with child (+*1064+2192*) [5], shortly (+*5034*) [4], upon [4], when [4], where (+*3739*) [4], glorious (+*1391*) [3], in (+*3588*) [3], openly (+*5318*) [3], thereon (+*846*) [3], towards [3], wherewith (+*5101*) [3], while (+*3739*) [3], almost (+*3641*) [2], always (+*2540+3956*) [2], because of [2], foolishly (+*877*) [2], quickly (+*5034*) [2], there (+*846*) [2], therein (+*3778*) [2], therewith

(+*846*) [2], under [2], when (+*3739*) [2], whereas (+*3739*) [2], wherewithal (+*3739*) [2], wherewith (+*3739*) [2], about [1], accused (+*2724*) [1], after (+*1836+3588*) [1], afterward (+*2517+3588*) [1], after [1], against [1], age (+*2250+4260*) [1], all (+*3650*) [1], altogether (+*4183*) [1], at (+*3588*) [1], because [1], before (+*3319+3588*) [1], before [1], being [1], between [1], boldly (+*3954*) [1], burdensome (+*922*) [1], by (+*3588*) [1], by way of [1], darkly (+*135*) [1], first (+*4413*) [1], for sake [1], gorgeously (+*1741*) [1], howbeit whereinsoever (+*302+1161+3739*) [1], in that (+*3588*) [1], in the mean time (+*3739*) [1], instantly (+*1616*) [1], inwardly (+*2927+3588*) [1], known openly (+*3954*) [1], namely (+*3588*) [1], openly (+*3954*) [1], outward (+*3588+5318*) [1], outwardly (+*3588+5318*) [1], over [1], plainly (+*3954*) [1], scattered abroad (+*1290+3588*) [1], speedily (+*5034*) [1], that (+*3588*) [1], that (+*3739*) [1], that [1], thereby (+*846*) [1], thereby [1], therein [1], throughly (+*3956*) [1], uncircumcised (+*203*) [1], wherein (+*3739+3778*) [1], wherein [1], while (+*1510+3588*) [1], whilst (+*3588*) [1], wholly to [1], written (+*1121*) [1]

1723 ἐναγκαλίζομαι, **enankalizomai**, v. GK: *1878* [→ *1722+43*]. to take in one's arms:– taken in arms [1], took up in arms [1]

1724 ἐνάλιος, **enalios**, a. GK: *1879* [→ *1722+217*]. creatures pertaining to the sea:– in the sea [1]

1725 ἔναντι, **enanti**, adv. [used as pp.*]. GK: *1882* [→ *561, 1726, 1727, 2713, 5121, 5227*]. before (spatial); fig., in the eyes of:– before [1]

1726 ἐναντίον, **enantion**, adv. [used as pp.*]. GK: *1883* [→ *1725*]. before (spatial); fig., in the sight of:– before [4], in the sight [1]

1727 ἐναντίος, **enantios**, a. GK: *1885* [→ *1725*]. against, opposite, in hostility:– contrary [6], against [1], over against (+*1537*) [1]

1728 ἐνάρχομαι, **enarchomai**, v. GK: *1887* [→ *1722+757*]. to begin:– begun [2]

1729 ἐνδεής, **endeēs**, a. GK: *1890* [→ *1722+1189*]. needy, poor, impoverished:– lacked [1]

1730 ἔνδειγμα, **endeigma**, n. GK: *1891* [→ *1722+1164*]. evidence, plain indication:– manifest token [1]

1731 ἐνδείκνυμι, **endeiknymi**, v. GK: *1892* [→ *1722+1166*]. to show, display:– shew [6], shewing [2], did [1], shew forth [1], shewed [1]

1732 ἔνδειξις, **endeixis**, n. GK: *1893* [→ *1722+1166*]. demonstration, proof, sign:– declare [2], evident token [1], proof [1]

1733 ἕνδεκα, **hendeka**, n.num. GK: *1894* [→ *1520+1176*]. eleven:– eleven [6]

1734 ἑνδέκατος, **hendekatos**, a. GK: *1895* [→ *1520+1176*]. eleventh:– eleventh [3]

1735 ἐνδέχομαι, **endechomai**, v.imper. GK: *1896* [→ *1722+1209*]. it is possible:– cannot (+*3756*) [1]

1736 ἐνδημέω, **endēmeō**, v. GK: *1897* [→ *1722+1218*]. to be at home:– present [2], at home [1]

1737 ἐνδιδύσκω, **endidyskō**, v. GK: *1898* [→ *1722+1416*]. to put on, dress (another); (mid.) dress oneself:– clothed in [1], ware [1]

1738 ἔνδικος, **endikos**, a. GK: *1899* [→ *1722+1349*]. just, deserved:– just recompence [1], just [1]

1739 ἐνδόμησις, **endomēsis**, n. GK: *1900 & 1908* [→ *1722+1430*]. what something is made of, construction, material:– building [1]

1740 ἐνδοξάζομαι, **endoxazomai**, v. GK: *1901* [→ *1722+1391*]. to be glorified, honored:– glorified [2]

1741 ἔνδοξος, **endoxos**, a. GK: *1902* [→ *1722+1391*]. honored, having high status and so thought to be wonderful, a fig. extension of the feature of an object being radiant or expensive:– glorious [2], gorgeously (+*1722*) [1], honourable [1]

1742 ἔνδυμα, **endyma**, n. GK: *1903* [→ *1722+1416*]. clothing, garment:– raiment [5], garment [2], clothing [1]

1743 ἐνδυναμόω, **endynamoō**, v. GK: *1904* [→ *1722+1410*]. to give strength, strengthen; (mid./pass.) to be strong, strengthened:– strong [3], enabled [1], increased in strength [1], made strong [1], strengthened [1], strengtheneth [1]

1744 ἐνδύνω, **endynō**, v. GK: *1905* [→ *1722+1416*]. to worm one's way, creep in:– creep [1]

1745 ἔνδυσις, **endysis**, n. GK: *1906* [→ *1722+1416*]. putting on:– putting on [1]

1746 ἐνδύω, **endyō**, v. GK: *1907* [→ *1722+1416*]. to clothe, dress; (mid.) clothe oneself:– put on [17], clothed in [2], clothed with [2], arrayed in [1], clothed with a garment [1], clothed [1], endued with [1], had on [1], having on [1], putting on [1]

ἐνέγκω, **enegkō**. See **5342**.

1747 ἐνέδρα, **enedra**, n. GK: *1909* [→ *1722+1476*]. plot, ambush:– laying wait (+*4160*) [1], lying in wait [1]

1748 ἐνεδρεύω, **enedreuō**, v. GK: *1910* [→ *1722+1476*]. to wait in ambush, lie in wait for:– laying wait for [1], lie in wait for [1]

1749 ἔνεδρον, **enedron**, n. GK: *1911* [→ *1722+1476*]. plot, ambush:–

1750 ἐνειλέω, **eneileō**, v. GK: *1912* [→ *1722*]. to wrap in:– wrapped in [1]

1751 ἔνειμι, **eneimi**, v. GK: *1913* [→ *1722+1510*]. to be inside; contents:– have [1]

1752 ἕνεκα, **heneka**; or ἕνεκεν, **heneken**; or εἵνεκεν, **heineken**, pp.*. GK: *1914 & 1915 & 1641*. for the sake of; for this reason, because:– for sake [14], for cause [2], for this cause (+*3778*) [2], because (+*3739*) [1], because that [1], by reason of [1], for causes [1], for [1], that [1], wherefore (+*5101*) [1]

1753 ἐνέργεια, **energeia**, n. GK: *1918* [→ *1722+2041*]. working, power, energy:– working [4], effectual working [2], operation [1], strong [1]

1754 ἐνεργέω, **energeō**, v. GK: *1919* [→ *1722+2041*]. to be at work in; to produce:– worketh [10], work [2], do [1], effectual fervent [1], effectually worketh [1], effectual [1], mighty in [1], shew forth in [1], shew forth [1], wrought effectually in [1], wrought [1]

1755 ἐνέργημα, **energēma**, n. GK: *1920* [→ *1722+2041*]. working, activity:– operations [1], working [1]

1756 ἐνεργής, **energēs**, a. GK: *1921* [→ *1722+2041*]. active, effective:– effectual [2], powerful [1]

1757 ἐνευλογέω, **eneulogeō**, v. GK: *1922* [→ *1722+2095+3004*]. (pass.) to be blessed:– blessed [2]

1758 ἐνέχω, **enechō**, v. GK: *1923* [→ *1722+2192*]. to oppose, be hostile toward, bear a grudge against; (pass.) to be burdened:– entangled [1], had a quarrel against [1], urge [1]

1759 ἐνθάδε, **enthade**, adv. GK: *1924* [→ *1722*]. here, in this place, to this place:– hither [4], here [3], there [1]

1760 ἐνθυμέομαι, **enthymeomai**, v. GK: *1445 & 1926* [→ *1722+2372*]. to consider, reflect on:– think [1], thought on [1], thought [1]

1761 ἐνθύμησις, **enthymēsis**, n. GK: *1927* [→ *1722+2372*]. thought, reflection; design, idea:– thoughts [3], device [1]

1762 ἔνι, **eni**, v. GK: *1928* [→ *1722+1510*]. there is:– is [5]

1763 ἐνιαυτός, **eniautos**, n. GK: *1929* [→ *846*]. year:– year [11], years [2], year by year (+*2596*) [1]

1764 ἐνίστημι, **enistēmi**, v. GK: *1931* [→ *1722+2476*]. to be present, (ptcp.) the present:– present [5], at hand [1], come [1]

1765 ἐνισχύω, **enischyō**, v. GK: *1932* [→ *1722+2479*]. to strengthen (another); to regain (one's own) strength:– strengthened [1], strengthening [1]

1766 ἔνατος, **enatos**, a. GK: *1888* [→ *1767*]. ninth (ninth hour = three p.m.):– ninth [10]

1767 ἐννέα, **ennea**, n.num. GK: *1933* [→ *1766, 1768*]. nine:– nine [5]

1768 ἐνενήκοντα, **enenēkonta**, n.num. GK: *1916* [→ *1767*]. ninety:– ninety [4]

1769 ἐννεός, **enneos**, a. GK: *1917 & 1934*. speechless:– speechless [1]

1770 ἐννεύω, **enneuō**, v. GK: *1935* [→ *1722+3506*]. to make a sign, nod:– made signs [1]

1771 ἔννοια, **ennoia**, n. GK: *1936* [→ *1722+3563*]. attitude, thought:– intents [1], mind [1]

1772 ἔννομος, **ennomos**, a. GK: *1937* [→ *1722+3551*]. under law, subject to the law; legal (assembly):– lawful [1], under law [1]

1773 ἔννυχος, **ennychos**, a. [used as adv.]. GK: *1939* [→ *1722+3571*]. while it is still dark, at night:– before day [1]

1774 ἐνοικέω, **enoikeō**, v. GK: *1940* [→ *1722+3624*]. to live in, live with:– dwelleth [2], dwell [2], dwelt [1]

1775 ἑνότης, **henotēs**, n. GK: *1942* [→ *1520*]. unity:– unity [2]

1776 ἐνοχλέω, **enochleō**, v. GK: *1943* [→ *1722+3793*]. (act.) to cause trouble; (pass.) to be troubled:– trouble [1]

1777 ἔνοχος, **enochos**, a. GK: *1944* [→ *1722+2192*]. subject to; guilty, liable for:– guilty [4], in danger [4], danger [1], subject [1]

1778 ἔνταλμα, **entalma**, n. GK: *1945* [→ *1785*]. rule, commandment, precept:– commandments [3]

1779 ἐνταφιάζω, **entaphiazō**, v. GK: *1946* [→ *1722+5028*]. to prepare (a corpse) for burial, bury:– burial [1], bury [1]

1780 ἐνταφιασμός, **entaphiasmos**, n. GK: *1947* [→ *1722+5028*]. preparation for burial, burial:– burying [2]

1781 ἐντέλλω, **entellō**, v. GK: *1948* [→ *1785*]. (mid.) to command, give orders, give instructions:– commanded [6], command [4], gave commandment [2], give charge [2], charged [1], enjoined [1], given commandments [1]

1782 ἐντεῦθεν, **enteuthen**, adv. GK: *1925 & 1949* [→ *1722*]. from here, from this place:– hence [6], from hence [3], of either side (+*1782+2532*) [2], on either side one (+*1782+2532*) [2]

1783 ἔντευξις, **enteuxis**, n. GK: *1950* [→ *1722+5177*]. prayer, intercession:– intercessions [1], prayer [1]

1784 ἔντιμος, **entimos**, a. GK: *1952* [→ *1722+5092*]. highly valued, honored, precious:– precious [2], dear [1], more honourable than [1], reputation [1]

1785 ἐντολή, **entolē**, n. GK: *1953* [→ *1778, 1781; cf. 1722*]. command, commandment, regulation, an order that has authority:– commandment [42], commandments [27], precept [2]

1786 ἐντόπιος, **entopios**, a. GK: *1954* [→ *1722+5117*]. resident, local:– place [1]

1787 ἐντός, **entos**, adv. GK: *1955* [→ *1722*]. inside, within:– within [2]

1788 ἐντρέπω, **entrepō**, v. GK: *1956* [→ *1722+5157*]. to cause shame; (pass.) to be ashamed; (mid.) to care about, respect:– reverence [3], ashamed [2], gave reverence [1], regarded [1], regard [1], shame [1]

1789 ἐντρέφω, **entrephō**, v. GK: *1957* [→ *1722+5142*]. (pass.) to be brought up, reared, trained:– nourished up [1]

1790 ἔντρομος, **entromos**, a. GK: *1958* [→ *1722+5141*]. trembling:– quake [1], trembled (+*1096*) [1], trembling [1]

1791 ἐντροπή, **entropē**, n. GK: *1959* [→ *1722+5157*]. shame, humiliation:– shame [2]

1792 ἐντρυφάω, **entryphaō**, v. GK: *1960* [→ *1722+5172*]. to revel, carouse:– sporting [1]

1793 ἐντυγχάνω, **entynchanō**, v. GK: *1961* [→ *1722+5177*]. to intercede, appeal, petition:– maketh intercession [3], dealt with [1], make intercession [1]

1794 ἐντυλίσσω, **entylissō**, v. GK: *1962* [→ *1722*]. to wrap up (a body); (pass.) to be folded:– wrapped [2], wrapped together [1]

1795 ἐντυπόω, **entypoō**, v. GK: *1963* [→ *1722+5180*]. (pass.) to be engraved, carved:– engraven [1]

1796 ἐνυβρίζω, **enybrizō**, v. GK: *1964* [→ *1722+5196*]. to insult:– done despite unto [1]

1797 ἐνυπνιάζομαι, **enypniazomai**, v. GK: *1965* [→ *1722+5258*]. to (have supernatural) dreams or visions:– dreamers [1], dream [1]

1798 ἐνύπνιον, **enypnion**, n. GK: *1966* [→ *1722+5258*]. dream:– dreams [1]

1799 ἐνώπιον, **enōpion**, pp.*. GK: *1967* [→ *1722+3708*]. before, in the presence of; in behalf of, by authority of:– before [62], in the sight [16], in the presence [6], in sight [5], in presence [2], before face [1], here before [1], presence [1], to [1]

1800 Ἐνώς, **Enōs**, n.pr. GK: *1968*. Enosh, "*[mortal] man*":– Enos [1]

1801 ἐνωτίζομαι, **enōtizomai**, v. GK: *1969* [→ *1722+3775*]. to listen carefully, pay attention to:– hearken [1]

1802 Ἐνώχ, **Henōch**, n.pr. GK: *1970*. Enoch, "*initiated; follower*":– Enoch [3]

ἐξ, *ex*. See *1537*.

1803 ἕξ, **hex**, n.num. GK: *1971* [→ *1623, 1812, 1835*]. six:– six [11], threescore sixteen (+*1440*) [1]

1804 ἐξαγγέλλω, **exangellō**, v. GK: *1972* [→ *1537+32*]. to declare, proclaim:– shew forth [1]

1805 ἐξαγοράζω, **exagorazō**, v. GK: *1973* [→ *1537+59*]. (act.) to redeem, as a fig. extension of the act of purchasing something in the marketplace; (mid.) to make the most (of the time):– redeeming [2], redeemed [1], redeem [1]

1806 ἐξάγω, **exagō**, v. GK: *1974* [→ *1537+71*]. to lead out, bring out, escort:– brought out [5], led out [3], brought forth [1], fetch out [1], lead out [1], leadeth out [1], leddest out [1]

1807 ἐξαιρέω, **exaireō**, v. GK: *1975* [→ *1537+138*]. (act.) to gouge, take out, tear out; (mid.) to rescue, set free:– delivered [2], deliver [2], pluck out [2], delivering [1], rescued [1]

1808 ἐξαίρω, **exairō**, v. GK: *1976* [→ *1537+142*]. to expel, remove, drive away:– put away [1], taken away [1]

1809 ἐξαιτέω, **exaiteō**, v. GK: *1977* [→ *1537+154*]. (mid.) to ask for:– desired [1]

1810 ἐξαίφνης, **exaiphnēs**, adv. GK: *1978 & 2005* [→ *1537+160*]. suddenly, unexpectedly:– suddenly [5]

1811 ἐξακολουθέω, **exakoloutheō**, v. GK: *1979* [→ *1537+190; cf. 1.3*]. to follow, obey:– followed [1], following [1], follow [1]

1812 ἑξακόσιοι, **hexakosioi**, a.num. GK: *1980* [→ *1803*]. six hundred:– six hundred [1]

1813 ἐξαλείφω, **exaleiphō**, v. GK: *1981* [→ *1537+218*]. to wipe away, blot out, cancel:– wipe away [2], blot out [1], blotted out [1], blotting out [1]

1814 ἐξάλλομαι, **exallomai**, v. GK: *1982* [→ *1537+242*]. to jump up:– leaping up [1]

1815 ἐξανάστασις, **exanastasis**, n. GK: *1983* [→ *1537+303+2476*]. resurrection:– resurrection [1]

1816 ἐξανατέλλω, **exanatellō**, v. GK: *1984* [→ *395; cf. 1537*]. to spring up:– sprang up [1], sprung up [1]

1817 ἐξανίστημι, **exanistēmi**, v. GK: *1985* [→ *1537+303+2476*]. to raise up (seed) = have children; (intr.) to stand up:– raise up [2], rose up [1]

1818 ἐξαπατάω, **exapataō**, v. GK: *1987* [→ *1537+539*]. to deceive, cheat:– deceive [3], beguiled [1], deceived [1]

1819 ἐξάπινα, **exapina**, adv. GK: *1988* [→ *1537+160*]. suddenly:– suddenly [1]

1820 ἐξαπορέω, **exaporeō**, v. GK: *1989* [→ *1537+1.1+4198*]. (mid.) to despair; (pass.) to be in despair:– despaired [1], in despair [1]

1821 ἐξαποστέλλω, **exapostellō**, v. GK: *1990* [→ *1537+649*]. to send out, send away:– sent away [4], sent forth [4], send [1], sent out [1], sent [1]

1822 ἐξαρτίζω, **exartizō**, v. GK: *1992* [→ *1537+737*]. to finish, complete; (pass.) to be equipped, furnished:– accomplished [1], throughly furnished [1]

1823 ἐξαστράπτω, **exastraptō**, v. GK: *1993* [→ *1537+796*]. to flash like lightning:– glistering [1]

1824 ἐξαυτῆς, **exautēs**, adv. GK: *1994* [→ *1537+846*]. immediately, at once, right now:– immediately [2], by and by [1], immediately already [1], presently [1], straightway [1]

1825 ἐξεγείρω, **exegeirō**, v. GK: *1995* [→ *1537+1453*]. to raise, awaken (from the dead):– raise up [1], raised up [1]

1826 ἔξειμι, **exeimi**, v. GK: *1996* [→ *1537*]. to leave, go out, go away:– departed [1], depart [1], get [1], gone out [1]

1827 ἐξελέγχω, **exelenchō**, v. GK: *1998* [→ *1537+1651*]. to convict:– convince [1]

1828 ἐξέλκω, **exelkō**, v. GK: *1999* [→ *1537+1670*]. (pass.) to be dragged away:– drawn away [1]

1829 ἐξέραμα, **exerama**, n. GK: *2000* [→ *1537*]. vomit, what is disgorged:– vomit [1]

1830 ἐξεραυνάω, **exeraunaō**, v. GK: *2001* [→ *1537+2045*]. to search intently, inquire carefully:– searched diligently [1]

1831 ἐξέρχομαι, **exerchomai**, v. GK: *2002* [→ *1537+2064*]. to go out, leave:– went out [59], came out [30], departed [22], went forth [19], come out [18], gone out [10], go out [9], depart [6], came forth [5], went [5], come forth [4], go forth [4], get out [3], came [2], come [2], go [2], out [2], spread abroad [2], went abroad [2], came out of [1],

camest forth [1], cometh out [1], coming out [1], depart out [1], departing [1], escaped [1], go thence [1], gone [1], out come [1], proceeded forth [1], proceedeth [1], proceed [1], went away [1], went from [1]

1832 ἔξεστι, **exesti**, v.imper. GK: *1997 & 2003* [→ *1537+1510*]. it is legal, it is proper, it is permitted:– lawful [28], lawful for [1], let [1], mayest [1], may [1]

1833 ἐξετάζω, **exetazō**, v. GK: *2004* [→ *426; cf. 1537*]. to make a search; to ask, inquire, question:– ask [1], inquire [1], search [1]

1834 ἐξηγέομαι, **exēgeomai**, v. GK: *2007* [→ *1537+71*]. to tell, make known, describe, report:– declared [4], declaring [1], told [1]

1835 ἑξήκοντα, **hexēkonta**, n.num. GK: *2008* [→ *1803*]. sixty:– threescore [4], sixty [3], sixtyfold [1]

1836 ἑξῆς, **hexēs**, adv. GK: *2009* [→ *2192*]. next, afterward:– next [2], after (+*1722+3588*) [1], following [1], on morrow [1]

1837 ἐξηχέω, **exēcheō**, v. GK: *2010* [→ *1537+2279*]. (pass.) to ring out, be caused to sound out:– sounded out [1]

1838 ἕξις, **hexis**, n. GK: *2011* [→ *2192*]. constant use, practice:– use [1]

1839 ἐξίστημι, **existēmi**, v. GK: *2012 & 2013 & 2014* [→ *1537+2476*]. to amaze, astound; confuse; (intr.) to be amazed, out of one's senses:– amazed [6], astonished [5], bewitched [2], beside himself [1], besides ourselves [1], made astonished [1], wondered [1]

1840 ἐξισχύω, **exischyō**, v. GK: *2015* [→ *1537+2479*]. to have power, be strong enough:– able [1]

1841 ἔξοδος, **exodos**, n. GK: *2016* [→ *1537+3598*]. exodus, departure:– decease [2], departing [1]

1842 ἐξολεθρεύω, **exolethreuō**, v. GK: *2017* [→ *1537+3639*]. (pass.) to be completely cut off from:– destroyed [1]

1843 ἐξομολογέω, **exomologeō**, v. GK: *2018* [→ *1537+3670*]. (act.) to consent; (mid.) to openly confess, admit, praise:– confess [5], confessing [2], thank [2], confessed [1], promised [1]

ἐξόν, *exon*. See *1832*.

1844 ἐξορκίζω, **exorkizō**, v. GK: *2019* [→ *1537+3727*]. to charge under oath, adjure:– adjure [1]

1845 ἐξορκιστής, **exorkistēs**, n. GK: *2020* [→ *1537+3727*]. one driving out evil spirits, exorcist:– exorcists [1]

1846 ἐξορύσσω, **exoryssō**, v. GK: *2021* [→ *1537+3736*]. to dig through, tear out:– broken up [1], plucked out [1]

1847 ἐξουδενόω, **exoudenoō**, v. GK: *2022 & 2023* [→ *1537+3756+1161+1520*]. (pass.) to be rejected, treated with contempt:– set at nought [1]

1848 ἐξουθενέω, **exoutheneō**, v. GK: *2024 & 2025* [→ *1537+3756+1161+1520*]. to treat with contempt, look down on, ridicule; (pass.) to be rejected, despised:– despised [3], despise [3], set at nought [3], contemptible [1], least esteemed [1]

1849 ἐξουσία, **exousia**, n. GK: *2026* [→ *1850, 2715*]. authority, power, the right to control or govern; dominion, the area or sphere of jurisdiction; a ruler, human or supernatural:– power [57], authority [28], powers [8], power over [4], right [2], authorities [1], jurisdiction [1], liberty [1], strength [1]

1850 ἐξουσιάζω, **exousiazō**, v. GK: *2027* [→ *1849*]. to have power over; (pass.) to be mastered:– hath power [2], brought under power [1], exercise authority upon [1]

1851 ἐξοχή, **exochē**, n. GK: *2029* [→ *1537+2192*]. leading, prominent:– principal [1]

1852 ἐξυπνίζω, **exypnizō**, v. GK: *2030* [→ *1537+5258*]. to wake up, arouse:– awake out of sleep [1]

1853 ἔξυπνος, **exypnos**, a. GK: *2031* [→ *1537+5258*]. awake, aroused:– awaking out of sleep (+*1096*) [1]

1854 ἔξω, **exō**, adv. GK: *2032* [→ *1537*]. out, outside:– without [23], of [10], forth [6], out of [6], out [5], away [1], outward [1], strange [1]

1855 ἔξωθεν, **exōthen**, adv. GK: *2033* [→ *1537*]. from the outside:– without [4], from without [2], outside [2], outward [2], outwardly [1]

1856 ἐξωθέω, **exōtheō**, v. GK: *2034* [→ *683; cf. 1537*]. to drive out, expel; to run aground:– drave out [1], thrust in [1]

1857 ἐξώτερος, **exōteros**, a. GK: *2035* [→ *1537*]. outside, farthest out (as a superlative):– outer [3]

1858 ἑορτάζω, **heortazō**, v. GK: *2037* [→ *1859*]. to celebrate a festival:– keep the feast [1]

1859 ἑορτή, **heortē**, n. GK: *2038* [→ *1858*]. feast, festival, in the NT this refers the joyous gathering of people for the celebrations of the Jewish calendar year, having a focus on ceremonial eating, such as Passover, Pentecost, and New Moon:– feast [26], holyday [1]

1860 ἐπαγγελία, **epangelia**, n. GK: *2039* [→ *1909*+*32*]. promise:– promise [40], promises [12], message [1]

1861 ἐπαγγέλλομαι, **epangellomai**, v. GK: *2040* [→ *1909*+*32*]. to promise; to profess, lay claim to:– promised [10], professing [2], made promise [1], promise made [1], promise [1]

1862 ἐπάγγελμα, **epangelma**, n. GK: *2041* [→ *1909*+*32*]. promise:– promises [1], promise [1]

1863 ἐπάγω, **epagō**, v. GK: *2042* [→ *1909*+*71*]. to bring upon; to make guilty:– bring upon [1], bringing in [1], bring [1]

1864 ἐπαγωνίζομαι, **epagōnizomai**, v. GK: *2043* [→ *1909*+*73*]. to contend, fight:– earnestly contend for [1]

1865 ἐπαθροίζω, **epathroizō**, v. GK: *2044* [→ *1909*; cf. *4867*]. (pass.) to increase; to be collected:– gathered thick together [1]

1866 Ἐπαίνετος, **Epainetos**, n.pr. GK: *2045* [→ *1909*+*136*]. Epenetus, "*praised*":– Epenetus [1]

1867 ἐπαινέω, **epaineō**, v. GK: *2046* [→ *1909*+*136*]. to praise, commend:– praise [4], commended [1], laud [1]

1868 ἔπαινος, **epainos**, n. GK: *2047* [→ *1909*+*136*]. praise, commendation:– praise [11]

1869 ἐπαίρω, **epairō**, v. GK: *2048* [→ *1909*+*142*]. to lift up; "to lift up the eyes" means "to look up"; "to lift up the voice" means "to shout" or "talk loudly"; "to lift up the heel" means "to oppose someone" (implying hostility):– lift up [13], exalteth [1], exalt [1], hoised up [1], lifted up [1], lifting up [1], taken up [1]

1870 ἐπαισχύνομαι, **epaischynomai**, v. GK: *2049* [→ *1909*+*150*]. to be ashamed of:– ashamed [11]

1871 ἐπαιτέω, **epaiteō**, v. GK: *2050* [→ *1909*+*154*]. to beg:– beg [1]

1872 ἐπακολουθέω, **epakoloutheō**, v. GK: *2051* [→ *1909*+*190*; cf. *1.3*]. to follow after, accompany; be devoted to:– diligently followed [1], follow after [1], following [1], follow [1]

1873 ἐπακούω, **epakouō**, v. GK: *2052* [→ *1909*+*191*]. to hear, listen to:– heard [1]

1874 ἐπακροάομαι, **epakroaomai**, v. GK: *2053* [→ *1909*+*202*]. to listen to:– heard [1]

1875 ἐπάν, **epan**, c.temp. GK: *2054* [→ *1909*+*302*]. when, as soon as:– when [3]

1876 ἐπάναγκες, **epanankes**, adv. GK: *2055* [→ *1909*+*318*]. necessarily:– necessary [1]

1877 ἐπανάγω, **epanagō**, v. GK: *2056* [→ *1909*+*303*+*71*]. to put out (to sea); to return:– launch out [1], returned [1], thrust out [1]

1878 ἐπαναμιμνήσκω, **epanamimnēskō**, v. GK: *2057* [→ *1909*+*303*+*3421*]. to remind again:– putting in mind [1]

1879 ἐπαναπαύομαι, **epanapauomai**, v. GK: *2058* [→ *1909*+*303*+*3973*]. to rest on, rely on:– restest [1], rest [1]

1880 ἐπανέρχομαι, **epanerchomai**, v. GK: *2059* [→ *1909*+*303*+*2064*]. to return (home):– come again [1], returned [1]

1881 ἐπανίστημι, **epanistēmi**, v. GK: *2060* [→ *1909*+*303*+*2476*]. to rebel against, rise up (in rebellion):– rise up against [1], rise up [1]

1882 ἐπανόρθωσις, **epanorthōsis**, n. GK: *2061* [→ *1909*+*303*+*3717*]. correcting:– correction [1]

1883 ἐπάνω, **epanō**, adv. GK: *2062* [→ *1909*+*507*]. above, on, upon; more than:– over [6], on [4], above [3], upon [3], thereon (+*846*) [2], more than [1], thereon [1]

1884 ἐπαρκέω, **eparkeō**, v. GK: *2064* [→ *1909*+*714*]. to help, aid:– relieve [2], relieved [1]

1885 ἐπαρχεία, **eparcheia**, n. GK: *2065* & *2066* [→ *1909*+*757*]. province:– province [2]

1886 ἔπαυλις, **epaulis**, n. GK: *2068* [→ *1909*+*833*]. place to live, residence:– habitation [1]

1887 ἐπαύριον, **epaurion**, adv. GK: *2069* [→ *839*; cf. *1909*]. the next day, tomorrow:– next day [7], on morrow [7], day following [2], morrow [1]

1888 ἐπαυτοφώρῳ, **epautophōrō**, a. GK: *2070* [→ *1909*+*846*]. pertaining to being caught in the act:– in the very act [1]

1889 Ἐπαφρᾶς, **Epaphras**, n.pr. GK: *2071*. Epaphras, "*handsome*":– Epaphras [3]

1890 ἐπαφρίζω, **epaphrizō**, v. GK: *576* & *2072* [→ *1909*+*876*]. to foam up:– foaming out [1]

1891 Ἐπαφρόδιτος, **Epaphroditos**, n.pr. GK: *2073*. Epaphroditus, "*handsome*":– Epaphroditus [3]

1892 ἐπεγείρω, **epegeirō**, v. GK: *2074* [→ *1909*+*1453*]. to stir up, arouse, excite:– raised [1], stirred up [1]

1893 ἐπεί, **epei**, c. GK: *2075* [→ *1909*]. since, because, for otherwise:– because [7], otherwise [4], seeing [3], else [2], then [2], else (+*686*) [1], for that [1], for then [1], forasmuch as [1], forasmuch [1], for [1], seeing that [1], since [1], when [1]

1894 ἐπειδή, **epeidē**, c. GK: *2076* [→ *1909*+*1211*]. when; since, because:– for [3], because [2], seeing [2], after that [1], forasmuch as [1], since [1]

1895 ἐπειδήπερ, **epeidēper**, c. GK: *2077* [→ *1909*+*1211*+*4007*]. inasmuch as, since, whereas:– forasmuch as [1]

1896 ἐπεῖδον, **epeidon**, v. GK: *2078* & *2393* [→ *1909*+*3708*]. to show favor, concern; to consider, look at:– behold [1], looked on [1]

1897 ἐπείπερ, **epeiper**, c. GK: *2080* [→ *1909*+*4007*]. since, indeed:– seeing [1]

1898 ἐπεισαγωγή, **epeisagōgē**, n. GK: *2081* [→ *1909*+*1519*+*71*]. introduction, bringing in:– bringing in [1]

1899 ἔπειτα, **epeita**, adv. GK: *2083* [→ *1909*+*1534*]. then, later, afterward:– then [9], after that [4], afterward [2], afterwards [1]

1900 ἐπέκεινα, **epekeina**, adv. GK: *2084* [→ *1909*+*1563*]. beyond, farther on:– beyond [1]

1901 ἐπεκτείνομαι, **epekteinomai**, v. GK: *2085* [→ *1614*; cf. *1909*]. to strain toward, stretch out:– reaching forth [1]

1902 ἐπενδύομαι, **ependyomai**, v. GK: *2086* [→ *1909*+*1722*+*1416*]. to be clothed with:– clothed upon with [1], clothed upon [1]

1903 ἐπενδύτης, **ependytēs**, n. GK: *2087* [→ *1909*+*1722*+*1416*]. outer garment, coat:– fisher's coat [1]

1904 ἐπέρχομαι, **eperchomai**, v. GK: *2082* & *2088* [→ *1909*+*2064*]. to come, come upon, happen to, with a possible implication that it will happen suddenly and forcibly:– come upon [5], come [2], came thither [1], come on [1], coming on [1]

1905 ἐπερωτάω, **eperōtaō**, v. GK: *2089* [→ *1909*+*2065*]. to ask, question:– asked [44], ask [8], demanded [2], asked after [1], askest [1], asking [1], desired [1], questioned [1]

1906 ἐπερώτημα, **eperōtēma**, n. GK: *2090* [→ *1909*+*2065*]. pledge; some translate "request, appeal":– answer [1]

1907 ἐπέχω, **epechō**, v. GK: *2091* [→ *1909*+*2192*]. (tr.) hold out, hold fast; (intr.) to give attention, watch, notice; to stay, stop:– heed [1], holding forth [1], marked [1], stayed [1], take heed [1]

1908 ἐπηρεάζω, **epēreazō**, v. GK: *2092*. to mistreat, speak maliciously against:– despitefully use [2], falsely accuse [1]

1909 ἐπί, **epi**, pp. GK: *2093* [→ *244*, *422*, *423*, *1860*, *1861*, *1862*, *1863*, *1864*, *1865*, *1866*, *1867*, *1868*, *1869*, *1870*, *1871*, *1872*, *1873*, *1874*, *1875*, *1876*, *1877*, *1878*, *1879*, *1880*, *1881*, *1882*, *1883*, *1884*, *1885*, *1886*, *1887*, *1888*, *1890*, *1892*, *1893*, *1894*, *1895*, *1896*, *1966*, *1897*, *1898*, *1899*, *1900*, *1901*, *1902*, *1903*, *1904*, *1905*, *1906*, *1907*, *1910*, *1911*, *1912*, *1913*, *1914*, *1915*, *1916*, *1917*, *1918*, *1919*, *1920*, *1921*, *1922*, *1923*, *1924*, *1925*, *1926*, *1927*, *1928*, *1929*, *1930*, *1931*, *1932*, *1933*, *1934*, *1935*, *1936*, *1937*, *1938*, *1939*, *1940*, *1941*, *1942*, *1943*, *1944*, *1945*, *1970*, *1946*, *1947*, *1948*, *1949*, *1950*, *1951*, *1952*, *1953*, *1954*, *1955*, *1956*, *1957*, *1958*, *1959*, *1960*, *1961*, *1962*, *1963*, *1964*, *1965*, *1967*, *1968*, *1969*, *1975*, *1976*, *1977*, *1978*, *1979*, *1980*, *1981*, *1982*, *1983*, *1984*, *1985*, *1986*, *1987*, *1988*, *1990*, *1991*, *1992*, *1993*, *1994*, *1995*, *1996*, *1997*, *1998*, *1999*, *2000*, *2001*, *2002*, *2003*, *2004*, *2005*, *2006*, *2007*, *2008*, *2009*, *2010*, *2011*, *2012*, *2013*, *2014*, *2015*, *2016*, *2017*, *2018*, *2019*, *2020*, *2021*, *2022*, *2023*, *2024*, *2025*, *2026*, *2027*, *2028*, *2029*, *2030*, *2032*, *2177*, *2178*, *2182*, *2183*, *2184*, *2185*, *2186*, *2721*, *3347*, *3927*, *4279*, *4901*, *4911*; cf. *1971*]. (gen.) on, over, when; (dat.) on, at, in, while; (acc.) across, over, on, to, for, while:– on [182], upon [148], in [122], over [49], unto [45], at [43], against [38], to [36], for [30], before [17], into [16], of [16], with [9], by [8], together (+*846*+*3588*) [7], above [5], toward [5], about [4], after [4], among [4], whereon (+*3739*) [4], as long as (+*3745*+*5550*) [3], besides [3], further (+*4183*) [3], of a truth (+*225*) [3], under [3], wherein (+*3739*) [3], as long as (+*3745*) [2], bountifully (+*2129*) [2], inasmuch as (+*3745*) [2], into one place (+*846*+*3588*) [2], throughout [2], through [2], towards [2], a great while (+*4183*) [1], about the time [1], as touching [1], because of [1], being [1], by the space of [1], chamberlain (+*2846*+*3588*) [1], charge of [1], come to ears (+*191*) [1], for the space of [1], in one place (+*846*+*3588*) [1], in the days of [1], in the time of [1], inasmuch as (+*3303*+*3745*+*3767*) [1], kept (+*2621*) [1], long (+*4183*) [1], long while (+*2425*) [1], longer (+*4183*) [1], on behalf [1], the space of [1], thereon (+*846*) [1], thereon [1], therewith (+*3778*) [1], three times (+*5151*) [1], thrice (+*5151*) [1], touching [1], truly (+*225*) [1], wherefore (+*3739*) [1], worse and worse (+*3588*+*5501*) [1]

1910 ἐπιβαίνω, **epibainō**, v. GK: *2094* [→ *1909*+*305*]. to go up, go upon, ride upon, board (a vessel):– came [1], come into [1], entering into [1], sitting [1], took [1], went aboard [1]

1911 ἐπιβάλλω, **epiballō**, v. GK: *2095* [→ *1909*+*906*]. (tr.) to throw over; to place; lay hold of, seize, arrest; to sew on; (intr.) to break over:– laid [6], lay on [3], putteth [2], beat [1], cast on [1], cast [1], falleth to [1], laid on [1], put to [1], stretched forth [1], thought thereon [1]

1912 ἐπιβαρέω, **epibareō**, v. GK: *2096* [→ *1909*+*922*]. to burden, weigh down excessively:– chargeable [2], overcharge [1]

1913 ἐπιβιβάζω, **epibibazō**, v. GK: *2097* [→ *1909*+*305*]. to put (someone) on (a mount):– set on [2], set thereon [1]

1914 ἐπιβλέπω, **epiblepō**, v. GK: *2098* [→ *1909*+*991*]. to look at, show special attention, consider, care about:– look upon [1], regarded [1], respect [1]

1915 ἐπίβλημα, **epiblēma**, n. GK: *2099* [→ *1909*+*906*]. patch:– piece [4]

1916 ἐπιβοάω, **epiboaō**, v. GK: *2100* [→ *1909*+*995*]. to cry out loudly:– crying [1]

1917 ἐπιβουλή, **epiboulē**, n. GK: *2101* [→ *1909*+*1014*]. plan, plot:– laid wait for (+*1096*) [1], laid wait [1], laying await [1], lying in wait [1]

1918 ἐπιγαμβρεύω, **epigambreuō**, v. GK: *2102* [→ *1909*+*1062*]. to marry (as next of kin):– marry [1]

1919 ἐπίγειος, **epigeios**, a. GK: *2103* [→ *1909*+*1093*]. being on the earth, earthly, that which is inferior when in contrast to heavenly or divine things:– earthly [4], terrestrial [2], in earth [1]

1920 ἐπιγίνομαι, **epiginomai**, v. GK: *2104* [→ *1909*+*1096*]. to come up, occur, happen:– blew [1]

1921 ἐπιγινώσκω, **epiginōskō**, v. GK: *2105* [→ *1909*+*1097*]. to know (fully), recognize, realize, come to understand:– knew [14], know [8], acknowledge [4], known [3], perceived [3], knoweth [2], knowing [2], acknowledged [1], had knowledge [1], knowest [1], knowledge [1], took knowledge [1], well known [1]

1922 ἐπίγνωσις, **epignōsis**, n. GK: *2106* [→ *1909*+*1097*]. knowledge, understanding, insight:– knowledge [16], acknowledging [3], acknowledgement [1]

1923 ἐπιγραφή, **epigraphē**, n. GK: *2107* [→ *1909*+*1125*]. inscription, superscription, written notice:– superscription [5]

1924 ἐπιγράφω, **epigraphō**, v. GK: *2108* [→ *1909*+*1125*]. (act.) to write; (pass.) to be written (upon), inscribed:– write [2], inscription [1], written over [1], written thereon [1]

1925 ἐπιδείκνυμι, **epideiknymi**, v. GK: *2109* [→ *1909*+*1166*]. to show, call attention to; to prove, point out:– shew [6], shewing [2], shewed [1]

1926 ἐπιδέχομαι, **epidechomai**, v. GK: *2110* [→ *1909*+*1209*]. to welcome, receive as a guest; to have to do with, accept, recognize:– receiveth [1], receive [1]

1927 ἐπιδημέω, **epidēmeō**, v. GK: *2111* [→ *1909*+*1218*]. to live as a visitor, foreigner:– strangers [1], were there [1]

1928 ἐπιδιατάσσομαι, *epidiatassomai*, v. GK: *2112* [→ *1909+1223+5021*]. to add to (a covenant):– added [1]

1929 ἐπιδίδωμι, *epididōmi*, v. GK: *2113* [→ *1909+1325*]. to give, deliver, hand over to:– give [5], delivered [2], gave [2], let drive (+*5342*) [1], offer [1]

1930 ἐπιδιορθόω, *epidiorthoō*, v. GK: *2114* [→ *1909+1223+3717*]. to straighten out, correct (in addition):– set in order [1]

1931 ἐπιδύω, *epidyō*, v. GK: *2115* [→ *1909+1416*]. to go down, set (of the sun):– go down [1]

1932 ἐπιείκεια, *epieikeia*, n. GK: *2116* [→ *1909+1503*]. gentleness, with an implication of tolerance and graciousness:– clemency [1], gentleness [1]

1933 ἐπιεικής, *epieikēs*, a. GK: *2117* [→ *1909+1503*]. gentle, considerate:– gentle [3], moderation [1], patient [1]

1934 ἐπιζητέω, *epizēteō*, v. GK: *2118* [→ *1909+2212*]. to look for, run after, seek earnestly:– seek [3], desire [2], seek after [2], seeketh after [2], after seek [1], desired [1], inquire [1], seeketh for [1], sought for [1]

1935 ἐπιθανάτιος, *epithanatios*, a. GK: *2119* [→ *1909+2348*]. condemned to die:– appointed to death [1]

1936 ἐπίθεσις, *epithesis*, n. GK: *2120* [→ *1909+5087*]. laying on:– laying on [3], putting on [1]

1937 ἐπιθυμέω, *epithymeō*, v. GK: *2121* [→ *1909+2372*]. to long for, desire; covet, lust:– desire [4], covet [2], desired [2], coveted [1], desireth [1], desiring [1], lust after [1], lusted [1], lusteth [1], lust [1], would fain [1]

1938 ἐπιθυμητής, *epithymētēs*, n. GK: *2122* [→ *1909+2372*]. one who desires, sets heart on (evil):– lust after [1]

1939 ἐπιθυμία, *epithymia*, n. GK: *2123* [→ *1909+2372*]. desire, longing (in contexts where the desire is positive and proper); coveting, craving, lusting (in contexts where the desire is immoral and sinful):– lusts [22], lust [9], concupiscence [3], desire [3], lusted after [1]

1940 ἐπικαθίζω, *epikathizō*, v. GK: *2125* [→ *1909+2523*]. to sit down (upon):– set [1]

1941 ἐπικαλέω, *epikaleō*, v. GK: *2126* [→ *1909+2564*]. (act./pass.) to call (upon), name, be named; (mid.) appeal to, call upon for aid:– surname [6], call on [5], surnamed [5], call upon [3], called [3], appeal unto [3], appealed unto [2], appealed to [1], appealed [1], call for [1], called on [1], calling on [1], calling upon [1]

1942 ἐπικάλυμμα, *epikalymma*, n. GK: *2127* [→ *1909+2572*]. cover-up, covering, veil:– cloke [1]

1943 ἐπικαλύπτω, *epikalyptō*, v. GK: *2128* [→ *1909+2572*]. (pass.) to be covered:– covered [1]

1944 ἐπικατάρατος, *epikataratos*, a. GK: *2063 & 2129* [→ *1909+2596+685*]. cursed:– cursed [3]

1945 ἐπίκειμαι, *epikeimai*, v. GK: *2130* [→ *1909+2749*]. to lay upon; to press, crowd upon, demand insistently:– imposed [1], instant [1], laid thereon [1], laid upon [1], lay on [1], lay [1], pressed upon [1]

1946 Ἐπικούρειος, *Epikoureios*, a.pr. or n.pr. GK: *2134* [→ *1909+2751*]. Epicurean, "*of Epicurus*":– Epicureans [1]

1947 ἐπικουρία, *epikouria*, n. GK: *2135* [→ *1909+2751*]. help:– help [1]

1948 ἐπικρίνω, *epikrinō*, v. GK: *2137* [→ *1909+2919*]. to decide, determine:– gave sentence [1]

1949 ἐπιλαμβάνομαι, *epilambanomai*, v. GK: *2138* [→ *1909+2983*]. to take hold, catch, trap, seize:– took [10], caught [2], lay hold on [2], take hold [2], took on [2], laid hold upon [1]

1950 ἐπιλανθάνομαι, *epilanthanomai*, v. GK: *2140* [→ *1909+2990*]. to forget:– forgotten [3], forget [2], forgetful [1], forgetteth [1], forgetting [1]

1951 ἐπιλέγω, *epilegō*, v. GK: *2141* [→ *1909+3004*]. (pass.) to be called; (mid.) to choose:– called [1], chose [1]

1952 ἐπιλείπω, *epileipō*, v. GK: *2142* [→ *1909+3007*]. to not have (time); to fail to have:– fail [1]

1953 ἐπιλησμονή, *epilēsmonē*, n. GK: *2144* [→ *1909+2990*]. forgetfulness:– forgetful [1]

1954 ἐπίλοιπος, *epiloipos*, a. GK: *2145* [→ *1909+3007*]. remaining, the rest:– rest [1]

1955 ἐπίλυσις, *epilysis*, n. GK: *2146* [→ *1909+3089*]. interpretation, explanation:– interpretation [1]

1956 ἐπιλύω, *epilyō*, v. GK: *2147* [→ *1909+3089*]. to explain; (pass.) to be settled, decided:– determined [1], expounded [1]

1957 ἐπιμαρτυρέω, *epimartyreō*, v. GK: *2148* [→ *1909+3144*]. to testify that, bear witness about:– testifying [1]

1958 ἐπιμέλεια, *epimeleia*, n. GK: *2149* [→ *1909+3199*]. needs, care, attention:– refresh (+*5177*) [1]

1959 ἐπιμελέομαι, *epimeleomai*, v. GK: *2150* [→ *1909+3199*]. to take care of, look after:– take care of [2], took care of [1]

1960 ἐπιμελῶς, *epimelōs*, adv. GK: *2151* [→ *1909+3199*]. carefully, diligently:– diligently [1]

1961 ἐπιμένω, *epimenō*, v. GK: *2152* [→ *1909+3306*]. to stay, remain; to continue in, keep on, persevere:– continue in [4], tarry [4], tarried [3], abide [2], continued [2], abode [1], bide still in [1], continue [1]

1962 ἐπινεύω, *epineuō*, v. GK: *2153* [→ *1909+3506*]. to accept, give consent:– consented [1]

1963 ἐπίνοια, *epinoia*, n. GK: *2154* [→ *1909+3563*]. thought, intention:– thought [1]

1964 ἐπιορκέω, *epiorkeō*, v. GK: *2155* [→ *1909+3727*]. to break an oath, swear falsely:– forswear [1]

1965 ἐπίορκος, *epiorkos*, a. GK: *2156* [→ *1909+3727*]. perjured; as a noun, perjurer:– perjured [1]

1966 ἔπειμι, *epeimi*, v. GK: *2079* [→ *1909*]. (ptcp.) the next day (from a verb that means "to follow, approach"):– next [3], following [2]

1967 ἐπιούσιος, *epiousios*, a. GK: *2157* [→ *1909+1510*]. what recurs on a day to day basis, daily:– daily [2]

1968 ἐπιπίπτω, *epipiptō*, v. GK: *2158* [→ *1909+4098*]. to fall upon, come eagerly, embrace; to come on:– fell on [5], fell [4], fallen upon [1], fell upon [1], lying [1], pressed upon [1]

1969 ἐπιπλήσσω, *epiplēssō*, v. GK: *2159* [→ *1909+4141*]. to rebuke, strike at:– rebuke [1]

1970 ἐπιπνίγω, *epipnigō*, v. GK: *4464* [→ *1909+4155*]. to overgrow, throttle, choke:–

1971 ἐπιποθέω, *epipotheō*, v. GK: *2160* [→ *1972, 1973, 1974; cf. 1909*]. to long for, crave, desire:– long after [2], desire [1], desiring greatly [1], earnestly desiring [1], greatly desiring [1], longed after [1], long [1], lusteth [1]

1972 ἐπιπόθησις, *epipothēsis*, n. GK: *2161* [→ *1971*]. longing (for):– earnest desire [1], vehement desire [1]

1973 ἐπιπόθητος, *epipothētos*, a. GK: *2162* [→ *1971*]. longed for:– longed for [1]

1974 ἐπιποθία, *epipothia*, n. GK: *2163* [→ *1971*]. longing, desire:– great desire [1]

1975 ἐπιπορεύομαι, *epiporeuomai*, v. GK: *2164* [→ *1909+4198*]. to come to, go to:– come out of [1]

1976 ἐπιράπτω, *epiraptō*, v. GK: *2165 & 2193* [→ *1909+4476*]. to sew on:– seweth [1]

1977 ἐπιρίπτω, *epiriptō*, v. GK: *2166* [→ *1909+4496*]. to throw on:– cast upon [1], casting [1]

1978 ἐπίσημος, *episēmos*, a. GK: *2168* [→ *1909+4592*]. notorious, prominent, outstanding:– notable [1], note [1]

1979 ἐπισιτισμός, *episitismos*, n. GK: *2169* [→ *1909+4621*]. food, something to eat:– victuals [1]

1980 ἐπισκέπτομαι, *episkeptomai*, v. GK: *2170* [→ *1909+4648*]. to visit, show concern, care for, come to help:– visited [5], visit [4], look out [1], visitest [1]

1981 ἐπισκηνόω, *episkēnoō*, v. GK: *2172* [→ *1909+4633*]. to rest upon, take up residence:– rest [1]

1982 ἐπισκιάζω, *episkiazō*, v. GK: *2173* [→ *1909+4639*]. to cast a shadow, overshadow; to envelope with a cloud:– overshadowed [3], overshadow [2]

1983 ἐπισκοπέω, *episkopeō*, v. GK: *2174* [→ *1909+4648*]. to see to, care for; to serve as an overseer:– looking diligently [1], taking the oversight [1]

1984 ἐπισκοπή, *episkopē*, n. GK: *2175* [→ *1909+4648*]. coming, visitation, the coming of divine power for recompense; an office of responsibility and place of leadership referring to an

office of apostle in Acts, and the office of overseer or bishop in the local church:– visitation [2], bishoprick [1], office of bishop [1]

1985 ἐπίσκοπος, *episkopos*, n. GK: *2176* [→ *1909+4648*]. overseer or bishop, a leader in a local church, an extension of one who guards, supervises, and helps:– bishop [5], bishops [1], overseers [1]

1986 ἐπισπάομαι, *epispaomai*, v. GK: *2177* [→ *1909+4685*]. to (attempt to) conceal circumcision, formally "to pull over (the foreskin to conceal circumcision)":– become uncircumcised [1]

1987 ἐπίσταμαι, *epistamai*, v. GK: *2179* [→ *1909+2476*]. to understand, know, be aware:– know [9], knowing [3], knoweth [1], understand [1]

1988 ἐπιστάτης, *epistatēs*, n. GK: *2181* [→ *1909+2476*]. master:– master [7]

1989 ἐπιστέλλω, *epistellō*, v. GK: *2182* [→ *1992*]. to write a letter:– write [1], written a letter [1], written [1]

1990 ἐπιστήμων, *epistēmōn*, a. GK: *2184* [→ *1909+2476*]. understanding, expert, learned:– knowledge [1]

1991 ἐπιστηρίζω, *epistērizō*, v. GK: *2185* [→ *1909+4741*]. to strengthen:– confirming [2], confirmed [1], strengthening [1]

1992 ἐπιστολή, *epistolē*, n. GK: *2186* [→ *1989*]. letter, epistle:– epistle [13], letters [6], letter [3], epistles [2]

1993 ἐπιστομίζω, *epistomizō*, v. GK: *2187* [→ *1909+4750*]. to silence, formally, "to stop the mouth":– mouths stopped [1]

1994 ἐπιστρέφω, *epistrephō*, v. GK: *2188* [→ *1909+4762*]. to turn (around, back, from), return:– converted [6], return [4], turned [4], turn [4], turn to [3], turned about [3], returned [2], turned to [2], came again [1], converteth [1], convert [1], go again [1], turn again [1], turn back [1], turn unto [1], turned again [1], turned unto [1], turning about [1], turning [1]

1995 ἐπιστροφή, *epistrophē*, n. GK: *2189* [→ *1909+4762*]. conversion, a fig. extension of *turning* an object, not found in the NT:– conversion [1]

1996 ἐπισυνάγω, *episynagō*, v. GK: *2190* [→ *1909+4862+71*]. to gather together:– gathered together [4], gather together [2], gathereth [1]

1997 ἐπισυναγωγή, *episynagōgē*, n. GK: *2191* [→ *1909+4864*]. gathering, meeting, assembling:– assembling together [1], gathering together [1]

1998 ἐπισυντρέχω, *episyntrechō*, v. GK: *2192* [→ *1909+4862+5143*]. to run together to:– came running together [1]

1999 ἐπίστασις, *epistasis*, n. GK: *2180 & 2194* [→ *1909+4862+2476*]. stirring up, disturbance, insurrection, rebellion; pressure:– cometh upon [1], raising up (+*4160*) [1]

2000 ἐπισφαλής, *episphalēs*, a. GK: *2195* [→ *1909; cf. 755*]. dangerous, unsafe:– dangerous [1]

2001 ἐπισχύω, *epischyō*, v. GK: *2196* [→ *1909+2479*]. to insist:– more fierce [1]

2002 ἐπισωρεύω, *episōreuō*, v. GK: *2197* [→ *1909+4987*]. to gather a great number, accumulate:– heap [1]

2003 ἐπιταγή, *epitagē*, n. GK: *2198* [→ *1909+5021*]. command, order; authority:– commandment [6], authority [1]

2004 ἐπιτάσσω, *epitassō*, v. GK: *2199* [→ *1909+5021*]. to command, order:– commanded [4], commandeth [3], charge [1], command [1], enjoin [1]

2005 ἐπιτελέω, *epiteleō*, v. GK: *2200* [→ *1909+5056*]. to finish, complete, end; to perfect, attain a goal; (mid.) to undergo:– perform [2], accomplished [1], accomplishing [1], do [1], finish [1], made perfect [1], make [1], perfecting [1], performance [1], performed [1]

2006 ἐπιτήδειος, *epitēdeios*, a. GK: *2201* [→ *1909+3588*]. needful, necessary, suitable:– needful [1]

2007 ἐπιτίθημι, *epitithēmi*, v. GK: *2202* [→ *1909+5087*]. to place, lay upon, put on:– laid on [7], put [4], laid [3], lay on [3], put upon [3], add [2], laid upon [2], lay [2], put on [2], putting on [2], laded with [1], lay upon [1], layeth [1], on laid [1], on lay [1], set on [1], set up [1], setteth on [1], set [1], surnamed (+*3686*) [1], surnamed [1], wounded (+*4127*) [1]

2008 ἐπιτιμάω, *epitimaō*, v. GK: *2203* [→ *1909+5092*]. to rebuke, warn:– rebuked [17], rebuke [6], charged [4], rebuking [1], straitly charged [1]

2009 ἐπιτιμία, *epitimia*, n. GK: 2204 [→ *1909+5092*]. punishment:– punishment [1]

2010 ἐπιτρέπω, *epitrepō*, v. GK: 2205 [→ *1909+5157*]. to let, allow, permit, give permission:– suffer [6], suffered [4], gave leave [2], permitted [2], permit [2], gave liberty [1], given licence [1], let [1]

2011 ἐπιτροπή, *epitropē*, n. GK: 2207 [→ *1909+5157*]. commission, permission:– commission [1]

2012 ἐπίτροπος, *epitropos*, n. GK: 2208 [→ *1909+5157*]. foreman, manager, guardian; derived from a Greek verb, "to instruct," not found in the NT:– steward [2], tutors [1]

2013 ἐπιτυγχάνω, *epitynchanō*, v. GK: 2209 [→ *1909+5177*]. to obtain, receive, gain:– obtained [4], obtain [1]

2014 ἐπιφαίνω, *epiphainō*, v. GK: 2210 [→ *1909+5316*]. (act.) to appear, make an appearance, show oneself; (pass.) shine:– appeared [3], give light [1]

2015 ἐπιφάνεια, *epiphaneia*, n. GK: 2211 [→ *1909+5316*]. appearing, appearance; usually referring to the return of Christ, cf. the English word "epiphany":– appearing [5], brightness [1]

2016 ἐπιφανής, *epiphanēs*, a. GK: 2212 [→ *1909+5316*]. glorious, splendid:– notable [1]

2017 ἐπιφαύσκω, *epiphauskō*, v. GK: 2213 [→ *1909+5316*]. to shine on:– give light [1]

2018 ἐπιφέρω, *epipherō*, v. GK: 2214 [→ *1909+5342*]. to bring upon, inflict:– brought [2], add [1], bring against [1], taketh [1]

2019 ἐπιφωνέω, *epiphōneō*, v. GK: 2215 [→ *1909+5456*]. to shout, cry out loudly:– cried against [1], cried [1], gave a shout [1]

2020 ἐπιφώσκω, *epiphōskō*, v. GK: 2216 [→ *1909+5316*]. to dawn, begin, shine forth:– dawn [1], drew on [1]

2021 ἐπιχειρέω, *epicheireō*, v. GK: 2217 [→ *1909+5495*]. to attempt, try to:– taken in hand [1], took upon [1], went about [1]

2022 ἐπιχέω, *epicheō*, v. GK: 2219 [→ *1632; cf. 1909*]. to pour on, pour over:– pouring in [1]

2023 ἐπιχορηγέω, *epichorēgeō*, v. GK: 2220 [→ *1909+5525+71*]. to support, supply; (pass.) to be supported, receive:– ministereth [2], add [1], ministered [1], nourishment ministered [1]

2024 ἐπιχορηγία, *epichorēgia*, n. GK: 2221 [→ *1909+5525+71*]. support, help:– supplieth [1], supply [1]

2025 ἐπιχρίω, *epichriō*, v. GK: 2222 [→ *1909+5548*]. to put on, anoint on, spread on:– anointed [2]

2026 ἐποικοδομέω, *epoikodomeō*, v. GK: 2224 [→ *1909+3624+1430*]. to build up, build on:– build [2], buildeth thereon [1], buildeth thereupon [1], building up [1], built thereupon [1], built up [1], built [1]

2027 ἐποκέλλω, *epokellō*, v. GK: 2131 & 2225 [→ *1909+2753*]. to run aground:– ran aground [1]

2028 ἐπονομάζω, *eponomazō*, v. GK: 2226 [→ *1909+3686*]. (pass.) to be called, named:– called [1]

2029 ἐποπτεύω, *epopteuō*, v. GK: 2227 [→ *1909+3708*]. to see, observe:– behold [2]

2030 ἐπόπτης, *epoptēs*, n. GK: 2228 [→ *1909+3708*]. eyewitness:– eyewitnesses [1]

2031 ἔπος, *epos*, n. GK: 2229. word:– so[S] [1]

2032 ἐπουράνιος, *epouranios*, a. GK: 2230 [→ *1909+3772*]. heavenly, celestial; heavenly realms:– heavenly [16], celestial [2], high [1], in heaven [1]

2033 ἑπτά, *hepta*, n.num. GK: 2231 [→ *1440, 1441, 1442, 2034, 2035*]. seven:– seven [86], seventh [1]

2034 ἑπτάκις, *heptakis*, adv. GK: 2232 [→ *2033*]. seven times:– seven times [4]

2035 ἑπτακισχίλιοι, *heptakischilioi*, a.num. GK: 2233 [→ *2033+5507*]. seven thousand:– seven thousand [1]

2036 ἔπω, *epō*, v. GK: 3306 [→ *3004*]. to speak, say:–

2037 Ἔραστος, *Erastos*, n.pr. GK: 2235. Erastus, "*beloved*":– Erastus [3]

ἐραυνάω, *eraunaō*. See *2045*.

2038 ἐργάζομαι, *ergazomai*, v. GK: 2237 [→ *2041*]. to work, be active, accomplish (something):– work [12], worketh [7], wrought [7], working [4], do [2], commit [1], doest [1], labouring [1], labour [1], minister [1], traded [1], trade [1]

2039 ἐργασία, *ergasia*, n. GK: 2238 [→ *2041*]. trade, business, making money; indulgence:– gain [2], craft [1], diligence [1], gains [1], work [1]

2040 ἐργάτης, *ergatēs*, n. GK: 2239 [→ *2041*]. worker, laborer, one who does (something):– labourers [8], workers [3], labourer [2], workman [2], workmen [1]

2041 ἔργον, *ergon*, n. GK: 2240 [→ *14, 289, 691, 692, 1090, 1091, 1092, 1217, 1753, 1754, 1755, 1756, 2038, 2039, 2040, 2108, 2109, 2110, 2418, 2557, 2673, 2716, 3008, 3009, 3010, 3011, 3834, 3835, 4020, 4021, 4333, 4903, 4904, 4943; cf. 4468*]. work, deed, activity, task, job:– works [103], work [47], deeds [16], deed [6], doing [1], labour [1], work's [1], works' [1]

2042 ἐρεθίζω, *erethizō*, v. GK: 2241. to stir up, provoke, arouse; embitter, provoke, irritate:– provoked [1], provoke [1]

2043 ἐρείδω, *ereidō*, v. GK: 2242. to stick fast, make immovable, jam:– stuck fast [1]

2044 ἐρεύγομαι, *ereugomai*, v. GK: 2243. to utter, proclaim:– utter [1]

2045 ἐραυνάω, *eraunaō*, v. GK: 2236 [→ *419, 1830; cf. 2065*]. to search, look into, try to find out:– searcheth [3], search [2], searching [1]

2046 ἐρευνάω, *ereunaō*, v. GK: 3306 [→ *3004*]. to utter, speak say:–

2047 ἐρημία, *erēmia*, n. GK: 2244 [→ *2048*]. remote place, desert, countryside, usually uninhabited areas:– wilderness [3], deserts [1]

2048 ἔρημος, *erēmos*, a. GK: 2245 [→ *2047, 2049, 2050*]. deserted, remote, solitary; as a noun, desert, uninhabited wilderness, or grasslands, implying in some contexts to be a forsaken, desolate place:– wilderness [32], desert [12], desolate [4], deserts [1], solitary [1]

2049 ἐρημόω, *erēmoō*, v. GK: 2246 [→ *2048*]. (pass.) to be brought to ruin, laid waste:– brought to desolation [2], come to nought [1], desolate [1], made desolate [1]

2050 ἐρήμωσις, *erēmōsis*, n. GK: 2247 [→ *2048*]. desolation, devastation, destruction. "The Abomination of Desolation" is a phrase derived from Hebrew, formally, "the detestable thing of desolation." This abomination is a person, thing, or event that defiles a holy place and thus causes it to be abandoned, implying God detests this thing or action. Many refer this to desecration of the temple by Antiochus Epiphanes as analogous to a future event predicted by Jesus:– desolation [3]

2051 ἐρίζω, *erizō*, v. GK: 2248 [→ *2054*]. to quarrel:– strive [1]

2052 ἐριθεία, *eritheia*, n. GK: 2249 [→ *2054*]. selfish ambition, faction, strife:– strife [4], contention [1], contentious [1], strifes [1]

2053 ἔριον, *erion*, n. GK: 2250. wool:– wool [2]

2054 ἔρις, *eris*, n. GK: 2251 [→ *2051, 2052*]. quarrel, strife, dissension, discord:– strife [4], contentions [1], debates [1], debate [1], variance [1]

2055 ἐρίφιον, *eriphion*, n. GK: 2252 [→ *2056*]. goat:– goats [1]

2056 ἔριφος, *eriphos*, n. GK: 2253 [→ *2055*]. (young) goat:– goats [1], kid [1]

2057 Ἑρμᾶς, *Hermas*, n.pr. GK: 2254. Hermas:– Hermas [1]

2058 ἑρμηνεία, *hermēneia*, n. GK: 1448 & 2255 [→ *2059*]. interpretation, translation of meaning from one language to another, in the NT a gift of the Spirit necessary for understanding the gift of tongues in assembly:– interpretation [2]

2059 ἑρμηνεύω, *hermēneuō*, v. GK: 2257 [→ *1328, 1329, 1421, 2058, 3177*]. to translate, give the meaning, interpret, explain:– by interpretation [3], interpreted [1]

2060 Ἑρμῆς, *Hermēs*, n.pr. GK: 2258. Hermes, "[poss.] *rock, cairn*":– Hermes [1], Mercurius [1]

2061 Ἑρμογένης, *Hermogenēs*, n.pr. GK: 2259. Hermogenes, "*born of Hermes*":– Hermogenes [1]

2062 ἑρπετόν, *herpeton*, n. GK: 2260. reptile:– creeping things [3], serpents [1]

2063 ἐρυθρός, *erythros*, a. GK: 2261. red:– Red [2]

2064 ἔρχομαι, *erchomai*, v. GK: 2262 [→ *424, 492, 565, 1330, 1525, 1660, 1831, 1880, 1904, 2718, 3922, 3928, 4022, 4281, 4334, 4339, 4897, 4905*]. to come, go:– come [289], came [197], cometh [98], coming [27], went [11], comest [2], entered [2], go [2], cometh [1], accompanied (+*4862*) [1], appear [1], be [1], brought [1], camest [1], fallen out [1], for to come (+*3195*) [1], grew (+*1519*) [1], lighting [1], next [1], passing by [1], set [1]

2065 ἐρωτάω, *erōtaō*, v. GK: 2263 [→ *1331, 1905, 1906; cf. 2045*]. to ask; beg, urge; pray:– ask [11], pray [10], besought [9], beseech [4], desired [4], prayed [4], asketh [1], asking [1], beseeching [1], desireth [1], desire [1], intreat [1]

2066 ἐσθής, *esthēs*, n. GK: 2264 [→ *2439*]. clothing, robe:– apparel [3], clothing [2], raiment [1], robe [1]

2067 ἔσθησις, *esthēsis*, n. GK: 2265 [→ *2439*]. government:– garments [1]

2068 ἐσθίω, *esthiō*, v. GK: 2266 & 2267 [→ *2068, 2719, 4906, 5315; cf. 3521, 5314*]. to eat, consume, devour:– eat [39], eateth [17], eating [6], devour [1], eaten [1], live [1]

2069 Ἑσλί, *Hesli*, n.pr. GK: 2268. Esli, "*Yahweh sets apart*":– Esli [1]

2070 ἐσμέν, *esmen*, v.1.pl. of 1510. GK: 1639 [→ *1510*]. we are; see *1510*:–

2071 ἔσομαι, *esomai*, v.1.s.fut. of 1510. GK: 1639 [→ *1510*]. will be; see *1510*:–

2072 ἔσοπτρον, *esoptron*, n. GK: 2269 [→ *1519+3708*]. mirror:– glass [2]

2073 ἑσπέρα, *hespera*, n. GK: 2270. evening:– evening [2], eventide [1]

2074 Ἑσρώμ, *Hesrōm*, n.pr. GK: 2272. Hezron, "*enclosure*":– Esrom [3]

2075 ἐστέ, *este*, v.2.pl. of 1510. GK: 1639 [→ *1510*]. you are; see *1510*:–

2076 ἐστί, *esti*, v.3.s. of 1510. GK: 1639 [→ *1510*]. he, she, it is; see *1510*:–

2077 ἔστω, *estō*, v.2.s.imper. of 1510. GK: 1639 [→ *1510*]. be; see *1510*:–

2078 ἔσχατος, *eschatos*, a. GK: 2274 [→ *1537*]. last (of a series), least, final:– last [48], lowest [2], ends [1], latter [1], uttermost part [1], uttermost [1]

2079 ἐσχάτως, *eschatōs*, adv. GK: 2275 [→ *1537*]. finally; at the point of death:– lieth at the point of death (+*2192*) [1]

2080 ἔσω, *esō*, adv. GK: 2276 [→ *1519*]. in, inner, inside, inwardly:– within [3], into [2], inner [1], inward [1]

2081 ἔσωθεν, *esōthen*, adv. GK: 2277 [→ *1519*]. from within, from inside, inwardly:– within [7], from within [3], inward part [1], inwardly [1], inward [1], out [1]

2082 ἐσώτερος, *esōteros*, a. GK: 2278 [→ *1519*]. inner:– inner [1], within [1]

2083 ἑταῖρος, *hetairos*, n. GK: 2279. friend, comrade, companion:– friend [3], fellows [1]

2084 ἑτερόγλωσσος, *heteroglōssos*, a. GK: 2280 [→ *2087+1100*]. speaking in a foreign language:– other tongues [1]

2085 ἑτεροδιδασκαλέω, *heterodidaskaleō*, v. GK: 2281 [→ *2087+1321*]. to teach false doctrine, teach heresy:– teach other doctrine [1], teach otherwise [1]

2086 ἑτεροζυγέω, *heterozygeō*, v. GK: 2282 [→ *2087+2218*]. to yoke together in a mismatch:– unequally yoked together [1]

2087 ἕτερος, *heteros*, a. GK: 2283 [→ *2084, 2085, 2086, 2088, 4200*]. other, different:– another [44], other [35], others [10], next [2], some [2], altered [1], another's [1], else [1], one [1], other's [1], strange [1]

2088 ἑτέρως, *heterōs*, adv. GK: 2284 [→ *2087*]. differently, other, otherwise:– otherwise [1]

2089 ἔτι, *eti*, adv. GK: 2285 [→ *3371, 3765*]. still, yet, again:– yet [42], more [16], while yet [7], any more [5], still [4], any further [3], longer [3], any longer [1], as yet [1], even [1], moreover (+*1161*) [1], moreover [1], no more (+*3367*) [1], now (+*3568*) [1], thenceforth [1], while as yet [1], yea (+*5037*) [1], yet a while [1]

2090 ἑτοιμάζω, *hetoimazō*, v. GK: 2286 [→ *2092*]. to prepare, be ready:– prepared [18], prepare [11], make ready [6], made ready [4], provided [1]

2091 ἑτοιμασία, **hetoimasia**, n. GK: 2288 [→ 2092]. readiness, preparation:– preparation [1]

2092 ἕτοιμος, **hetoimos**, a. GK: 2289 [→ 2090, 2091, 2093, 4282]. ready, prepared:– ready [14], made ready to hand (+1519) [1], prepared [1], readiness [1]

2093 ἑτοίμως, **hetoimōs**, adv. GK: 2290 [→ 2092]. readily:– ready [3]

2094 ἔτος, **etos**, n. GK: 2291 [→ 1332, 1333, 1541, 5063, 5148]. year:– years [40], years old [4], year [3], years of age [2]

2095 εὖ, **eu**, adv. GK: 2292 [→ 428, 1757, 2097, 2098, 2099, 2100, 2101, 2102, 2103, 2104, 2105, 2106, 2107, 2108, 2109, 2110, 2111, 2114, 2115, 2119, 2120, 2121, 2122, 2123, 2124, 2125, 2126, 2127, 2128, 2129, 2130, 2131, 2132, 2133, 2136, 2137, 2138, 2139, 2140, 2141, 2142, 2143, 2144, 2145, 2146, 2150, 2151, 2152, 2153, 2154, 2155, 2156, 2157, 2158, 2159, 2160, 2161, 2162, 2163, 2164, 2165, 2168, 2169, 2170, 2173, 2174, 2175, 2176, 4283, 4909, 4910]. well; well done!:– well [5], good [1]

2096 Εὔα, **Heua**, n.pr. GK: 2293. Eve, "*life*":– Eve [2]

2097 εὐαγγελίζω, **euangelizō**, v. GK: 2294 [→ 2095+32]. to preach (bring) the good news (gospel), often with a focus on the content of the message which is brought. In the NT it always refers to the death, burial, resurrection, and witness about Jesus Christ, including its implications for humankind's relationship to God:– preached [12], preach the gospel [10], preached the gospel [6], preach [6], preaching [5], the gospel preached [3], gospel preached [2], preach gospel [2], bring glad tidings [1], bring good tidings [1], brought good tidings [1], declare glad tidings [1], declared [1], preacheth [1], preaching the gospel [1], shew glad tidings [1], shewing the glad tidings [1]

2098 εὐαγγέλιον, **euangelion**, n. GK: 2295 [→ 2095+32]. gospel, good news; see also 2097:– gospel [74], gospel's [3]

2099 εὐαγγελιστής, **euangelistēs**, n. GK: 2296 [→ 2095+32]. evangelist, preacher of the gospel:– evangelist [2], evangelists [1]

2100 εὐαρεστέω, **euaresteō**, v. GK: 2297 [→ 2095+700]. to please:– pleased [1], please [1], well pleased [1]

2101 εὐάρεστος, **euarestos**, a. GK: 2298 [→ 2095+700]. pleasing, acceptable:– acceptable [4], well pleasing [3], accepted [1], please well (+1510) [1]

2102 εὐαρέστως, **euarestōs**, adv. GK: 2299 [→ 2095+700]. in an acceptable or pleasing manner:– acceptably [1]

2103 Εὔβουλος, **Euboulos**, n.pr. GK: 2300 [→ 2095+1014]. Eubulus, "*good counsel*":– Eubulus [1]

2104 εὐγενής, **eugenēs**, a. GK: 2302 [→ 2095+1096]. of noble birth, of noble character:– more noble than [1], nobleman (+444) [1], noble [1]

2105 εὐδία, **eudia**, n. GK: 2304 [→ 2095+2203]. fair weather:– fair weather [1]

2106 εὐδοκέω, **eudokeō**, v. GK: 2305 [→ 2095+1380]. to be well pleased, delight:– well pleased [7], pleased [5], pleasure [2], willing [2], good pleasure [1], had pleasure [1], have pleasure [1], take pleasure [1], thought good [1]

2107 εὐδοκία, **eudokia**, n. GK: 2306 [→ 2095+1380]. goodwill, good purpose, favor, pleasure, desire:– good pleasure [4], good will [2], good [2], desire [1]

2108 εὐεργεσία, **euergesia**, n. GK: 2307 [→ 2095+2041]. act of kindness, good deed:– benefit [1], good deed [1]

2109 εὐεργετέω, **euergeteō**, v. GK: 2308 [→ 2095+2041]. to do good to:– doing good [1]

2110 εὐεργέτης, **euergetēs**, n. GK: 2309 [→ 2095+2041]. benefactor; in context this is a title:– benefactors [1]

2111 εὔθετος, **euthetos**, a. GK: 2310 [→ 2095+5087]. fit, fit for service, useable, suitable:– fit [2], meet [1]

2112 εὐθέως, **eutheōs**, adv. GK: 2311 [→ 2117]. immediately, at once:– immediately [38], straightway [34], forthwith [8], by and by [3], anon [2], as soon as [2], shortly [1]

2113 εὐθυδρομέω, **euthydromeō**, v. GK: 2312 [→ 2117+5143]. to sail straight, run a straight course:– came with a straight course [1], straight course [1]

2114 εὐθυμέω, **euthymeō**, v. GK: 2313 [→ 2095+2372]. to keep up one's courage; to be happy, cheerful:– be of good cheer [2], merry [1]

2115 εὔθυμος, **euthymos**, a. GK: 2314 & 2315 [→ 2095+2372]. encouraged, cheerful, in good spirits:– more cheerfully [1], of good cheer [1]

2116 εὐθύνω, **euthynō**, v. GK: 2316 [→ 2117]. to make straight, straighten; to go straight:– listeth (+1014) [1], make straight [1]

2117 εὐθύς, **euthys**, a. GK: 2317 & 2318 [→ 2112, 2113, 2116, 2118, 2720]. straight, not crooked; by extension: right, upright, the moral quality of not being wrong or perverse to truth or purity:– straight [5], right [3]

2118 εὐθύτης, **euthytēs**, n. GK: 2319 [→ 2117]. righteousness, uprightness, a fig. extension of a straight (not crooked) object, not found in the NT:– righteousness [1]

2119 εὐκαιρέω, **eukaireō**, v. GK: 2320 [→ 2095+2540]. to have a chance to, have the opportunity to; to spend one's time:– had leisure [1], have convenient time [1], spent time [1]

2120 εὐκαιρία, **eukairia**, n. GK: 2321 [→ 2095+2540]. opportunity, the right moment:– opportunity [2]

2121 εὔκαιρος, **eukairos**, a. GK: 2322 [→ 2095+2540]. opportune, well timed, suitable; time of need:– convenient [1], time of need [1]

2122 εὐκαίρως, **eukairōs**, adv. GK: 2323 [→ 2095+2540]. opportunely, in season:– conveniently [1], in season [1]

2123 εὔκοπος, **eukopos**, a. GK: 2324 [→ 2095+2875]. easy; (compar.) easier:– easier [7]

2124 εὐλάβεια, **eulabeia**, n. GK: 2325 [→ 2095+2983]. reverence, reverent submission:– feared [1], godly fear [1]

2125 εὐλαβέομαι, **eulabeomai**, v. GK: 2326 [→ 2095+2983]. to have holy fear, reverence:– fearing [1], moved with fear [1]

2126 εὐλαβής, **eulabēs**, a. GK: 2327 [→ 2095+2983]. devout, godly, God-fearing:– devout [3]

2127 εὐλογέω, **eulogeō**, v. GK: 2328 [→ 2095+3004]. to praise, give thanks to, speak well of, extol; (pass.) to be blessed, receive blessing; in some contexts, to give a blessing is to act kindly and impart benefits to the one being blessed:– blessed [30], bless [10], blessing [3], praised [1]

2128 εὐλογητός, **eulogētos**, a. GK: 2329 [→ 2095+3004]. worthy of being praised, blessed, or commended:– blessed [8]

2129 εὐλογία, **eulogia**, n. GK: 2330 [→ 2095+3004]. blessing, praise, thanksgiving, the extolling of another; in some contexts, excessive praise is improper: flattery; by extension, generosity and (giving of) gifts:– blessing [10], bountifully (+1909) [2], bounty [2], blessings [1], fair speeches [1]

2130 εὐμετάδοτος, **eumetadotos**, a. GK: 2331 [→ 2095+3326+1325]. generous:– ready to distribute [1]

2131 Εὐνίκη, **Eunikē**, n.pr. GK: 2332 [→ 2095+3529]. Eunice, "*good victory*":– Eunice [1]

2132 εὐνοέω, **eunoeō**, v. GK: 2333 [→ 2095+3563]. to settle matters by coming to terms:– agree with [1]

2133 εὔνοια, **eunoia**, n. GK: 2334 [→ 2095+3563]. wholeheartedness, enthusiasm, eagerness:– benevolence [1], good will [1]

2134 εὐνουχίζω, **eunouchizō**, v. GK: 2335 [→ 2135; cf. 2192]. to emasculate, make (oneself) a eunuch; to be celibate, renounce marriage:– made eunuchs [2]

2135 εὐνοῦχος, **eunouchos**, n. GK: 2336 [→ 2134]. eunuch, court official:– eunuch [5], eunuchs [3]

2136 Εὐοδία, **Euodia**, n.pr. GK: 2337 [→ 2095+3598]. Euodia, "*good way* poss. *good fragrance*":– Euodias [1]

2137 εὐοδόω, **euodoō**, v. GK: 2338 [→ 2095+3598]. (pass.) to get along with; to have a way opened; to prosper, get along well:– have a prosperous journey [1], prospered [1], prospereth [1], prosper [1]

2138 εὐπειθής, **eupeithēs**, a. GK: 2340 [→ 2095+3982]. submissive, obedient, compliant:– easy to be intreated [1]

2139 εὐπερίστατος, **euperistatos**, a. GK: 2341 & 2342 [→ 2095+4012+2476]. easily entangling, constricting, obstructing:– easily beset [1]

2140 εὐποιΐα, **eupoiia**, n. GK: 2343 [→ 2095+4160]. doing good:– do good [1]

2141 εὐπορέω, **euporeō**, v. GK: 2344 [→ 2095+4198]. to have (financial) ability, have plenty, be well off:– ability [1]

2142 εὐπορία, **euporia**, n. GK: 2345 [→ 2095+4198]. prosperity, prosperous income:– wealth [1]

2143 εὐπρέπεια, **euprepeia**, n. GK: 2346 [→ 2095+4241]. beauty:– grace [1]

2144 εὐπρόσδεκτος, **euprosdektos**, a. GK: 2347 [→ 2095+4314+1209]. acceptable, favorable:– accepted [3], acceptable [2]

2145 εὐπρόσεδρος, **euprosedros**, a. GK: 2348 [→ 2095+4314+1476]. devoted, constant:– attend upon [1]

2146 εὐπροσωπέω, **euprosōpeō**, v. GK: 2349 [→ 2095+4383]. to make a good impression, make a good showing:– make a fair shew [1]

2147 εὑρίσκω, **heuriskō**, v. GK: 2351 [→ 429, 2182]. (act.) to find, discover, meet; (mid.) to obtain; (pass.) to be found:– found [112], find [46], findeth [12], finding [4], get [1], obtained [1], perceived [1]

2148 εὐροκλύδων, **euroklydōn**, n. GK: 2352 [→ 2830]. southeast wind, Euroclydon:– Euroclydon [1]

2149 εὐρύχωρος, **eurychōros**, a. GK: 2353 [→ 5562]. broad, spacious:– broad [1]

2150 εὐσέβεια, **eusebeia**, n. GK: 2354 [→ 2095+4576]. godliness, piety:– godliness [14], holiness [1]

2151 εὐσεβέω, **eusebeō**, v. GK: 2355 [→ 2095+4576]. to worship; to put religion into practice, show piety toward:– shew piety [1], worship [1]

2152 εὐσεβής, **eusebēs**, a. GK: 2356 [→ 2095+4576]. devout, godly, pious, reverent:– devout [3], godly [1]

2153 εὐσεβῶς, **eusebōs**, adv. GK: 2357 [→ 2095+4576]. in a godly manner:– godly [2]

2154 εὔσημος, **eusēmos**, a. GK: 2358 [→ 2095+4592]. intelligible, clear, distinct, easily recognizable:– easy to be understood [1]

2155 εὔσπλαγχνος, **eusplanchnos**, a. GK: 2359 [→ 2095+4698]. compassionate, tenderhearted:– pitiful [1], tenderhearted [1]

2156 εὐσχημόνως, **euschēmonōs**, adv. GK: 2361 [→ 2095+4976]. decently, fittingly, becomingly, properly:– honestly [2], decently [1]

2157 εὐσχημοσύνη, **euschēmosynē**, n. GK: 2362 [→ 2095+4976]. modesty, presentability:– comeliness [1]

2158 εὐσχήμων, **euschēmōn**, a. GK: 2363 [→ 2095+4976]. presentable, proper, right; prominent, of high standing:– honourable [3], comely [2]

2159 εὐτόνως, **eutonōs**, adv. GK: 2364 [→ 1614; cf. 2095]. vehemently, vigorously:– mightily [1], vehemently [1]

2160 εὐτραπελία, **eutrapelia**, n. GK: 2365 [→ 2095+5157]. coarse joking, vulgar jesting:– jesting [1]

2161 Εὔτυχος, **Eutychos**, n.pr. GK: 2366 [→ 2095+5177]. Eutychus, "*fortunate*":– Eutychus [1]

2162 εὐφημία, **euphēmia**, n. GK: 2367 [→ 2095+5346]. good report:– good report [1]

2163 εὔφημος, **euphēmos**, a. GK: 2368 [→ 2095+5346]. admirable, appealing, praiseworthy:– good report [1]

2164 εὐφορέω, **euphoreō**, v. GK: 2369 [→ 2095+5342]. to produce a good crop, be fruitful:– brought forth plentifully [1]

2165 εὐφραίνω, **euphrainō**, v. GK: 2370 [→ 2166, 2167]. (act.) to cause celebration, make glad; (mid./pass.) to celebrate, rejoice, be glad:– rejoice [5], make merry [3], merry [3], fared [1], maketh glad [1], rejoiced [1]

2166 Εὐφράτης, **Euphratēs**, n.pr. GK: 2371 [→ 2165]. Euphrates:– Euphrates [2]

2167 εὐφροσύνη, **euphrosynē**, n. GK: 2372 [→ 2165]. joy, gladness, cheerfulness:– gladness [1], joy [1]

2168 εὐχαριστέω, **eucharisteō**, v. GK: 2373 [→ 2095+5463]. to thank, give thanks, render gratitude; this can mean words that express gratitude or the emotion of gratitude:– thank [11], give thanks [8], gave thanks [6], given thanks [4], giving thanks [4], giveth thanks [1], givest thanks [1], thanked [1], thankful [1], thanks given [1]

2169 εὐχαριστία, **eucharistia**, n. GK: 2374 [→ 2095+5463]. expression of thanks, thanksgiving, gratitude:– thanksgiving [8], giving thanks [2], thanks [2], giving of thanks [1], thankfulness [1], thanksgivings [1]

2170 εὐχάριστος, **eucharistos**, a. GK: 2375 [→ 2095+5463]. thankful (in word and attitude):– thankful [1]

2171 εὐχή, **euchē**, n. GK: 2376 [→ 2172]. vow, oath; prayer:– vow [2], prayer [1]

Grk

2172 εὔχομαι, **euchomai**, v. GK: 2377 [→ 2171, 4335, 4336]. to pray for; wish for:– wish [3], pray [2], wished for [1], would (+302) [1]

2173 εὔχρηστος, **euchrēstos**, a. GK: 2378 [→ 2095+5530]. useful, helpful, serviceable:– profitable [2], meet for use [1]

2174 εὐψυχέω, **eupsycheō**, v. GK: 2379 [→ 2095+5594]. to be cheerful, glad:– of good comfort [1]

2175 εὐωδία, **euōdia**, n. GK: 2380 [→ 2095+3605]. aroma, fragrance:– sweet savour [1], sweet smell [1], sweetsmelling [1]

2176 εὐώνυμος, **euōnymos**, a. GK: 2381 [→ 2095+3686]. left (direction), south:– left [6], left hand [4]

2177 ἐφάλλομαι, **ephallomai**, v. GK: 2383 [→ 1909+242]. to jump on, leap upon:– leapt on [1]

2178 ἐφάπαξ, **ephapax**, adv. GK: 2384 [→ 1909+530]. once for all; at the same time:– once [3], at once [1], once for all [1]

2179 Ἐφεσῖνος, **Ephesinos**, a.pr.g. GK: 2385 [→ 2181]. Ephesian:– Ephesus [1]

2180 Ἐφέσιος, **Ephesios**, a.pr.g. GK: 2386 [→ 2181]. Ephesian, person of Ephesus:– Ephesians [5], Ephesian [1], of Ephesus [1]

2181 Ἔφεσος, **Ephesos**, n.pr. GK: 2387 [→ 2179, 2180]. Ephesus:– Ephesus [15]

2182 ἐφευρετής, **epheuretēs**, n. GK: 2388 [→ 1909+2147]. inventor, contriver:– inventors [1]

2183 ἐφημερία, **ephēmeria**, n. GK: 2389 [→ 1909+2250]. (priestly) division, group, class:– course [2]

2184 ἐφήμερος, **ephēmeros**, a. GK: 2390 [→ 1909+2250]. daily, for the day:– daily [1]

2185 ἐφικνέομαι, **ephikneomai**, v. GK: 2391 [→ 1909+2425]. to come (to), reach (to):– reached [1], reach [1]

2186 ἐφίστημι, **ephistēmi**, v. GK: 2392 [→ 1909+2476]. to approach, come near, stand beside, stop; to be imminent, at hand:– came upon [5], stood by [2], stood [2], assaulted [1], at hand [1], came [1], came [1], come upon [1], cometh upon [1], come [1], coming in [1], instant [1], present [1], standing by [1], stood before [1]

2187 Ἐφραίμ, **Ephraim**, n.pr. GK: 2394. Ephraim, "*doubly fruitful*":– Ephraim [1]

2188 ἐφφαθά, **ephphatha**, l.[v.]. GK: 2395. ephphatha!, be opened!:– ephphatha [1]

2189 ἔχθρα, **echthra**, n. GK: 2397 [→ 2190]. hostility, hatred, antagonism:– enmity [5], hatred [1]

2190 ἐχθρός, **echthros**, a. GK: 2398 [→ 2189]. (n.) enemy:– enemies [19], enemy [10], foes [2], enemy (+444) [1]

2191 ἔχιδνα, **echidna**, n. GK: 2399. viper, snake:– vipers [4], viper [1]

2192 ἔχω, **echō**, v. GK: 2400 [→ 183, 414, 420, 430, 463, 472, 566, 567, 568, 1758, 1777, 1836, 1838, 1851, 1907, 2517, 2558, 2697, 2722, 3348, 3352, 3353, 3562, 3794, 3930, 4023, 4042, 4122, 4123, 4124, 4284, 4337, 4465, 4778, 4830, 4910, 4912, 4928, 4975, 5242, 5247, 5254; cf. 2134, 4976]. (tr.) to have, hold, keep; (intr.) to be:– have [262], hath [131], had [111], having [84], hast [27], need (+5532) [10], are [5], were [5], with child (+1064+1722) [5], sick (+2560) [4], next [3], thank (+5485) [3], was [3], am [2], counted [2], count [2], holding [2], hold [2], is [2], must [2], needeth (+5532) [2], accompany [1], art [1], been [1], began to amend (+2866) [1], being [1], be [1], cannot (+3756) [1], could [1], diseased (+2560) [1], do [1], eat (+3542) [1], enjoy [1], fear (+5401) [1], following [1], go to law (+2917) [1], held [1], hold fast [1], is of [1], kept [1], lacked (+3361) [1], lieth at the point of death (+2079) [1], needed (+5532) [1], needest (+5532) [1], needful (+318) [1], possessed with [1], possessed [1], recover (+2573) [1], reigneth (+932) [1], rest (+372) [1], retain [1], sabbath day's journey (+3598+4521) [1], sick people (+2560) [1], took [1], trembled (+5156) [1], uncircumcised (+203) [1], using [1], with [1]

2193 ἕως, **heōs**, c.&pp.*. GK: 2401. up to, until:– unto [31], until [23], till (+302) [16], to [16], till [14], till (+3739) [9], how long (+4219) [7], until (+302) [5], until (+3739) [5], while [5], as far as [3], hitherto (+737) [2], till (+3748) [2], until (+3748) [2], while (+3739) [2], even (+2532) [1], even [1], no not one (+1520+3756) [1], thus far (+3778) [1], up to [1], whiles (+3748) [1]

2194 Ζαβουλών, **Zaboulōn**, n.pr. GK: 2404. Zebulun, "*honor*":– Zabulon [3]

2195 Ζακχαῖος, **Zakchaios**, n.pr. GK: 2405. Zacchaeus, "*righteous one, pure one*":– Zaccheus [3]

2196 Ζάρα, **Zara**, n.pr. GK: 2406. Zerah, "*dawning, shining*" or *flashing [red or scarlet] light*":– Zara [1]

2197 Ζαχαρίας, **Zacharias**, n.pr. GK: 2408. Zechariah, "*Yahweh remembers*":– Zacharias [11]

2198 ζάω, **zaō**, v. GK: 2409 [→ 326, 329, 2221, 2222, 2225, 2226, 2227, 4800, 4806]. to be alive, to live a life; in the NT this can also refer to the resurrection life, Jesus Christ is then "the Living One":– live [54], living [34], liveth [24], alive [15], lived [4], quick [4], lively [3], livest [2], lifetime [1], life [1]

2199 Ζεβεδαῖος, **Zebedaios**, n.pr. GK: 2411. Zebedee, "*Yahweh bestows*":– Zebedee [10], Zebedee's [2]

2200 ζεστός, **zestos**, a. GK: 2412 [→ 2204]. hot:– hot [3]

2201 ζεῦγος, **zeugos**, n. GK: 2414 [→ 2218]. yoke; by extension: a pair:– pair [1], yoke [1]

2202 ζευκτηρία, **zeuktēria**, n. GK: 2415 [→ 2218]. rope, band:– bands [1]

2203 Ζεύς, **Zeus**, n.pr. GK: 2416 [→ 1356, 1359, 1361, 2105, 2211]. Zeus, "*shine, bright*":– Jupiter [2]

2204 ζέω, **zeō**, v. GK: 2417 [→ 2200; cf. 2205, 2219]. to have great fervor, as a fig. extension something boiling or seething, not found in the NT:– fervent [2]

2205 ζῆλος, **zēlos**, n. GK: 2419 [→ 2206, 2207, 2208, 3863; cf. 2204]. zeal, ardent concern, enthusiasm, an attitude or emotion of deep, earnest concern; jealousy, envy, rage, morally corrupt zealous ill will:– zeal [6], envying [4], indignation [2], emulations [1], envyings [1], envy [1], fervent mind [1], jealousy [1]

2206 ζηλόω, **zēloō**, v. GK: 2418 & 2420 [→ 2205]. to desire, eagerly desire, show zeal, feel an attitude or emotion of deep concern; to be jealous, envious, to experience morally corrupt zealous ill will; covet, as a negative attitude of lust and desire for another's possessions:– desire [2], moved with envy [2], affect [1], covet earnestly [1], covet [1], envieth [1], jealous [1], zealously affected [1], zealously affect [1], zealous [1]

2207 ζηλωτής, **zēlōtēs**, n. GK: 2421 [→ 2205]. zealot, enthusiast, adherent, one who has the feelings or attitudes of deep commitment to a person or cause; in the NT this can technically refer to a person who belonged to a nationalist Jewish group that sought independence from Rome:– zealous [5]

2208 Ζηλωτής, **Zēlōtēs**, n. GK: 2421 [→ 2205]. same as 2207; zealot, enthusiast, adherent, one who has the feelings or attitudes of deep commitment to a person or cause; in the NT this can technically refer to a person who belonged to a nationalist Jewish group that sought independence from Rome:– Zelotes [2]

2209 ζημία, **zēmia**, n. GK: 2422 [→ 2210]. loss, damage:– loss [3], damage [1]

2210 ζημιόω, **zēmioō**, v. GK: 2423 [→ 2209]. (pass.) to forfeit, suffer loss or damage:– lose [2], cast away [1], receive damage [1], suffer loss [1], suffered loss [1]

2211 Ζηνᾶς, **Zēnas**, n.pr. GK: 2424 [→ 2203]. Zenas, "*gift of Zeus*":– Zenas [1]

2212 ζητέω, **zēteō**, v. GK: 2426 [→ 327, 1567, 1934, 2213, 2214, 4802, 4803, 4804]. to look for, seek out; to try to obtain, desire to possess, strive for:– seek [44], sought [31], seeking [11], seeketh [9], seek for [3], sought for [3], desiring [2], inquire [2], required [2], seekest [2], about [1], desired [1], endeavoured [1], go about [1], goeth about [1], going about [1], seek after [1], seeking for [1], sought out [1], went about [1]

2213 ζήτημα, **zētēma**, n. GK: 2427 [→ 2212]. question for discussion, point of dispute, controversy:– questions [3], question [2]

2214 ζήτησις, **zētēsis**, n. GK: 1700 & 2428 [→ 2212]. argument, debate, controversy, discussion:– questions [5], question [1]

2215 ζιζάνιον, **zizanion**, n. GK: 2429. weed, darnel, or some other troublesome weed:– tares [8]

2216 Ζοροβαβέλ, **Zorobabel**, n.pr. GK: 2431. Zerubbabel, "*offspring of Babylon*":– Zorobabel [3]

2217 ζόφος, **zophos**, n. GK: 2432. blackness, darkness, gloom:– darkness [2], blackness [1], mist [1]

2218 ζυγός, **zygos**, n. GK: 2433 [→ 2086, 2201, 2202, 4801, 4805, 5268]. yoke, a frame and cross bar placed on draft animals to pull various objects; pair of scales, ancient balance-pan scales. "To be under a yoke" means to be in an oppressed condition such as slavery:– yoke [5], pair of balances [1]

2219 ζύμη, **zymē**, n. GK: 2434 [→ 106, 2220; cf. 2204]. yeast, leaven:– leaven [13]

2220 ζυμόω, **zymoō**, v. GK: 2435 [→ 2219]. to leaven, ferment, work as yeast:– leavened [2], leaveneth [2]

2221 ζωγρέω, **zōgreō**, v. GK: 2436 [→ 2198+61]. to capture (alive):– catch [1], taken captive [1]

2222 ζωή, **zōē**, n. GK: 2437 [→ 2198]. life, physical or spiritual; with 166, "eternal life":– life [133], lifetime [1]

2223 ζώνη, **zōnē**, n. GK: 2438 [→ 2224]. belt, sash:– girdle [5], girdles [1], purses [1], purse [1]

2224 ζώννυμι, **zōnnymi**, v. GK: 2439 & 2440 [→ 328, 1241, 2223, 4024, 5269]. to dress, clothe oneself, put on a belt or sash:– girdedst [1], gird [1]

2225 ζωογονέω, **zōogoneō**, v. GK: 2441 [→ 2198+1096]. to give life, make alive; to preserve life, keep alive:– live [1], preserve [1]

2226 ζῷον, **zōon**, n. GK: 2442 [→ 2198]. living creature, animal:– beasts [16], beast [7]

2227 ζωοποιέω, **zōopoieō**, v. GK: 2443 [→ 2198+4160]. to make alive, give life to:– quickeneth [5], quickened [2], given life [1], giveth life [1], made alive [1], quickening [1], quicken [1]

2228 ἤ, **ē**, pt.disj. or comp. GK: 2445 [→ 2260, 2273]. or; (in a series) either…or; (in comparison) than:– or [260], than [36], either [8], before (+4250) [6], nor [5], or else [5], and [4], neither [3], what [3], but [2], rather than [2], but (+3756+4183) [1], except [1], rather [1], save [1], than (+235) [1], than (+3123) [1], yea [1]

2229 ἦ, **ē**, adv. GK: 2446. truly:– surely (+3375) [1]

 ἡ, **hē**. See 3588.

 ἥ, **hē**. See 3739.

 ᾗ, **ēi**. See 5600.

2230 ἡγεμονεύω, **hēgemoneuō**, v. GK: 2448 [→ 71]. to govern, lead, rule:– governor [2]

2231 ἡγεμονία, **hēgemonia**, n. GK: 2449 [→ 71]. reign, leadership, rulership:– reign [1]

2232 ἡγεμών, **hēgemōn**, n. GK: 2450 [→ 71]. ruler, prince, governor, prefect, procurator:– governor [16], governors [2], rulers [2], governor's [1], princes [1]

2233 ἡγέομαι, **hēgeomai**, v. GK: 2451 [→ 71]. to lead, rule, guide; to consider, think, regard:– count [7], chief [3], counted [2], have the rule over [3], esteem [2], governor [2], think [2], thought [2], account [1], esteeming [1], judged [1], supposed [1]

2234 ἡδέως, **hēdeōs**, adv. GK: 2452 [→ 2237]. gladly, with delight; in the superlative, most gladly, with utter delight:– gladly [3]

2235 ἤδη, **ēdē**, adv. GK: 2453. already, by this time, even now:– now [35], already [17], yet [2], by this time [1], far spent (+2827) [1], now about (+1161) [1], now already [1], now high time (+5610) [1], now ready [1]

2236 ἥδιστα, **hēdista**, adv.super. of 2234. GK: 2452 [→ 2237]. most gladly, with utter delight:– most gladly [1], very gladly [1]

2237 ἡδονή, **hēdonē**, n. GK: 2454 [→ 780, 829, 2234, 2236, 2238, 4913, 5369]. pleasure, desire, enjoyment, usually with a negative sense:– lusts [2], pleasures [2], pleasure [1]

2238 ἡδύοσμον, **hēdyosmon**, n. GK: 2455 [→ 2237+3605]. mint:– mint [2]

2239 ἦθος, **ēthos**, n. GK: 2456 [→ 1485]. character, habit and custom:– manners [1]

2240 ἥκω, **hēkō**, v. GK: 2457 [→ 433, 2520]. to come, to have come, be present:– come [24], came [3]

2241 ἠλί, **ēli**[1], l.[n.+p.]. GK: 2458 [cf. 1682]. Eli [Hebrew: my God]:– eli [2]

2242 Ἡλί[2], **Ēli**[2], n.pr. GK: 2459. Heli, "*ascent [to God]*":– Heli [1]

2243 Ἠλίας, **Ēlias**, n.pr. GK: 2460. Elijah, "*Yahweh is [my] God*":– Elias [30]

2244 ἡλικία, **hēlikia**, n. GK: 2461 [→ 2245]. life, time in life, age; stature, height:– stature [5], age [2], age (+2540) [1]

2245 ἡλίκος, *hēlikos*, a. GK: *2462* [→ *2244, 4080, 4915, 5082*]. how much, how great, how large:– how great [1], what great [1]

2246 ἥλιος, *hēlios*, n. GK: *2463* [cf. *1506*]. sun:– sun [30], east (+*395*) [2]

2247 ἧλος, *hēlos*, n. GK: *2464* [→ *4338*]. nail (used in crucifixion):– nails [2]

2248 ἡμᾶς, *hēmas*, p.pers.acc.pl. of *1473* GK: *1609* [→ *1473*]. us, to us; see *1473*:–

2249 ἡμεῖς, *hēmeis*, p.pers.nom.pl. of *1473* GK: *1609* [→ *1473*]. we, us, ourselves; see *1473*:–

2250 ἡμέρα, *hēmera*, n. GK: *2465* [→ *2183, 2184, 2522, 3314, 3574, 3637, 4594*]. day, time of the day, time, indefinite period of time. "The children of the day" means "God's people," who walk in light. "The day of the Lord" and "the day of Christ" are periods of judgment and vindication, longer than twenty-four hours:– day [199], days [154], daily (+*2596*) [15], this day (+*4594*) [3], time [3], years [2], a good while ago (+*575*+*744*) [1], age (+*1722*+*4260*) [1], alway (+*3588*+*3956*) [1], another[5] [1], at midday (+*3319*) [1], daily (+*1538*+*2596*) [1], daily (+*2596*+*3956*) [1], daily (+*3956*) [1], day by day (+*2596*) [1], day time [1], day's [1], ever (+*165*) [1], good while (+*2425*) [1], judgment [1], needeth (+*318*) [1]

2251 ἡμέτερος, *hēmeteros*, a. GK: *2466* [→ *1473*]. our, our own:– our [6], ours [2]

2252 ἤμην, *ēmēn*, v.1.imperf. of *1510*. GK: *1639* [→ *1510*]. I was; see *1510*:–

2253 ἡμιθανής, *hēmithanēs*, a. GK: *2467* [→ *2255*+*2348*]. half dead:– half dead [1]

2254 ἡμῖν, *hēmin*, p.pers.dat.pl. of *1473*. GK: *1609* [→ *1473*]. for us, to us, our; see *1473*:–

2255 ἥμισυς, *hēmisys*, a. GK: *2468* [→ *2253, 2256, 2256*]. half (temporal and spacial):– half [5]

2256 ἡμιώριον, *hēmiōrion*, n. GK: *2469 & 2470* [→ *2255*+*5610*]. half an hour:– half an hour [1]

2257 ἡμῶν, *hēmōn*, p.pers.gen.pl. of *1473*. GK: *1609* [→ *1473*]. our; see *1473*:–

2258 ἦν, *ēn*, v.3.imperf. of *1510*. GK: *1639* [→ *1510*]. he, she, it was; see *1510*:–

2259 ἡνίκα, *hēnika*, pt. GK: *2471*. when, whenever, at the time when:– when (+*302*) [2]

2260 ἤπερ, *ēper*, pt.comp. GK: *2472* [→ *2228*+*4007*]. than:– than [1]

2261 ἤπιος, *ēpios*, a. GK: *2473*. gentle, kind:– gentle [2]

2262 Ἤρ, *Ēr*, n.pr. GK: *2474*. Er, "*watcher, watchful*":– Er [1]

2263 ἤρεμος, *ēremos*, a. GK: *2475*. peaceful, quiet, tranquil:– quiet [1]

2264 Ἡρώδης, *Hērōdēs*, n.pr. GK: *2476* [→ *2265, 2266, 2267*]. Herod:– Herod [40], Herod's [4]

2265 Ἡρωδιανοί, *Hērōdianoi*, n.pr.g. GK: *2477* [→ *2264*]. Herodians:– Herodians [3]

2266 Ἡρωδιάς, *Hērōdias*, n.pr. GK: *2478* [→ *2264*]. Herodias:– Herodias [4], Herodias' [2]

2267 Ἡρωδίων, *Hērōdiōn*, n.pr. GK: *2479* [→ *2264*]. Herodion:– Herodion [1]

2268 Ἡσαΐας, *Ēsaias*, n.pr. GK: *2480*. Isaiah, "*Yahweh saves*":– Esaias [21]

2269 Ἡσαῦ, *Ēsau*, n.pr. GK: *2481*. Esau, "*hairy*":– Esau [3]

2270 ἡσυχάζω, *hēsychazō*, v. GK: *2483* [→ *2271, 2272*]. to be silent, have no objection; to rest; to lead a quiet life; to give up:– held peace [2], ceased [1], quiet [1], rested [1]

2271 ἡσυχία, *hēsychia*, n. GK: *2484* [→ *2270*]. quietness, silence; settling down, lack of disturbance:– silence [3], quietness [1]

2272 ἡσύχιος, *hēsychios*, a. GK: *2485* [→ *2270*]. quiet:– peaceable [1], quiet [1]

2273 ἤτοι, *ētoi*, pt.disj. GK: *2486* [→ *2228*+*5104*]. (in a series) whether...or:– whether [1]

2274 ἡττάομαι, *hēttaomai*, v. GK: *2273 & 2487* [→ *2276*]. to be inferior, lesser, worse off, with a focus on the manner in which someone is treated:– overcome [2], inferior [1]

2275 ἥττημα, *hēttēma*, n. GK: *2488* [→ *2276*]. loss, defeat:– diminishing [1], fault [1]

2276 ἥττων, *hēttōn*, a. GK: *2482 & 2489* [→ *2274, 2275*]. for the worse; (adv.) less:– less [1], worse [1]

2277 ἤτω, *ētō*, v.3.s.imper. of *1510*. GK: *1639* [→ *1510*]. let it be:–

2278 ἠχέω, *ēcheō*, v. GK: *2490* [→ *2279*]. to resound, ring out:– roaring [1], sounding [1]

2279 ἦχος[1], *ēchos*[1], n. GK: *2491 & 2492 & 2493* [→ *1837, 2278, 2727*]. sound, tone, blast (of a trumpet); news, report:– sound [2], fame [1]

2280 Θαδδαῖος, *Thaddaios*, n.pr. GK: *2497* [cf. *3002*]. Thaddaeus, "[poss.] *nipple*":– Thaddeus [2]

2281 θάλασσα, *thalassa*, n. GK: *2498* [→ *1337, 3864; cf. 217*]. sea, lake, a general term for any natural body of water:– sea [92]

2282 θάλπω, *thalpō*, v. GK: *2499*. to care for, cherish, comfort:– cherisheth [2]

2283 Θαμάρ, *Thamar*, n.pr. GK: *2500*. Tamar, "*date palm*":– Thamar [1]

2284 θαμβέω, *thambeō*, v. GK: *2501* [→ *2285*]. (pass.) to be amazed, astounded:– amazed [2], astonished [2]

2285 θάμβος, *thambos*, n. GK: *2502* [→ *1568, 1569, 2284*]. amazement, astonishment, wonder:– amazed [1], astonished (+*4023*) [1], wonder [1]

2286 θανάσιμος, *thanasimos*, a. GK: *2503* [→ *2348*]. deadly:– deadly [1]

2287 θανατηφόρος, *thanatēphoros*, a. GK: *2504* [→ *2348*+*5342*]. deadly:– deadly [1]

2288 θάνατος, *thanatos*, n. GK: *2505* [→ *2348*]. death:– death [116], deadly [2], deaths [1]

2289 θανατόω, *thanatoō*, v. GK: *2506* [→ *2348*]. to put to death, kill:– put to death [7], killed [2], dead [1], mortify [1]

θάνω, *thanō*. See *2348*.

2290 θάπτω, *thaptō*, v. GK: *2507* [→ *4916; cf. 5028*]. to bury, entomb:– buried [7], bury [4]

2291 Θάρα, *Thara*, n.pr. GK: *2508*. Terah:– Thara [1]

2292 θαρρέω, *tharreō*, v. GK: *2509* [→ *2294*]. to have confidence, be bold:– bold [2], confident [2], boldly [1], have confidence [1]

2293 θαρσέω, *tharseō*, v. GK: *2510* [→ *2294*]. take heart!, take courage!, cheer up!:– be of good cheer [5], be of good comfort [1]

2294 θάρσος, *tharsos*, n. GK: *2511* [→ *2292, 2293*]. encouragement, courage:– courage [1]

2295 θαῦμα, *thauma*, n. GK: *2512* [→ *2296*]. wonder, marvel, astonishment:– admiration [1]

2296 θαυμάζω, *thaumazō*, v. GK: *1703 & 2513* [→ *2295, 2297, 2298; cf. 2300*]. to be amazed (at), in wonder, astonished, surprised:– marvelled [21], wondered [11], marvel [9], wonder [2], admired [1], having in admiration (+*4383*) [1], wondering [1]

2297 θαυμάσιος, *thaumasios*, a. GK: *2514* [→ *2296*]. wonderful, remarkable:– wonderful [1]

2298 θαυμαστός, *thaumastos*, a. GK: *2515* [→ *2296*]. wonderful, marvelous, remarkable:– marvellous [6], marvel [1]

2299 θεά, *thea*, n. GK: *2516* [→ *2316*]. goddess:– goddess [3]

2300 θεάομαι, *theaomai*, v. GK: *2517* [cf. *2296, 2302, 2334*]. to see, look at; visit:– saw [8], seen [8], see [4], beheld [2], look on [1], looked upon [1]

2301 θεατρίζω, *theatrizō*, v. GK: *2518* [→ *2302*]. to publicly expose:– made a gazingstock [1]

2302 θέατρον, *theatron*, n. GK: *2519* [→ *2301; cf. 2300*]. theatre, spectacle, theatrical play:– theatre [2], spectacle [1]

2303 θεῖον, *theion*, n. GK: *2520* [→ *2306; cf. 2316 or 2380*]. sulfur:– brimstone [7]

2304 θεῖος, *theios*, a. GK: *2521* [→ *2316*]. divine:– divine [2], Godhead [1]

2305 θειότης, *theiotēs*, n. GK: *2522* [→ *2316*]. divine nature, divinity:– Godhead [1]

2306 θειώδης, *theiōdēs*, a. GK: *2523* [→ *2303*]. (yellow) as sulfur:– brimstone [1]

θελέω, *theleō*. See *2309*.

2307 θέλημα, *thelēma*, n. GK: *2525* [→ *2309*]. will, decision, desire:– will [62], desires [1], pleasure [1]

2308 θέλησις, *thelēsis*, n. GK: *2526* [→ *2309*]. will, decision:– will [1]

2309 θέλω, *thelō*, v. GK: *2527* [→ *1479, 2307, 2308*]. to will, decide, want to; wish, desire:– would [69], will [68], wilt [21], desire [9], willing [8], have [5], wouldest [4], desirous [3], desiring [2], listed [2], willingly [2], desired [1], desireth [1], disposed [1], forward [1], had rather [1], intending [1], it hath pleased [1], listeth [1], love [1], meaneth (+*1510*) [1], mean [1], pleased [1], so[5] [1], voluntary [1], will have [1], willeth [1], would have [1], would that [1]

2310 θεμέλιος, *themelios*, n. GK: *2528 & 2529* [→ *2311; cf. 5087*]. foundation:– foundation [12], foundations [4]

2311 θεμελιόω, *themelioō*, v. GK: *2530* [→ *2310*]. to lay a foundation; to make steadfast:– founded [2], grounded [2], laid the foundation [1], settle [1]

2312 θεοδίδακτος, *theodidaktos*, a. GK: *2531* [→ *2316*+*1321*]. taught by God:– taught of God [1]

2312' θεολόγος, *theologos*, n. GK: *2532* [→ *2316*+*3004*]. one who speaks of God or divine things:–

2313 θεομαχέω, *theomacheō*, v. GK: *2533* [→ *2316*+*3163*]. to fight against God:– fight against God [1]

2314 θεομάχος, *theomachos*, a. GK: *2534* [→ *2316*+*3163*]. fighting against God:– fight against God [1]

2315 θεόπνευστος, *theopneustos*, a. GK: *2535* [→ *2316*+*4154*]. God-breathed, inspired by God, referring to a communication from deity:– given by inspiration of God [1]

2316 θεός, *theos*, n. GK: *2536* [→ *112, 2299, 2304, 2305, 2312, 2312', 2313, 2314, 2315, 2317, 2318, 2319, 2320, 2321, 2333, 5095, 5377; cf. 2303*]. God, usually refers to the one true God; in a very few contexts it refers to a (pagan) god or goddess. The "Son of God" as a title of Jesus emphasizes his unique relationship to the Father. "The god of this age" refers to the devil:– God/god [1309], God's [15], gods [8], godly [6], Godward [1], exceeding fair (+*791*+*3588*) [1], godly (+*2596*) [1]

2317 θεοσέβεια, *theosebeia*, n. GK: *2537* [→ *2316*+*4576*]. worship of God, reverence for God:– godliness [1]

2318 θεοσεβής, *theosebēs*, a. GK: *2538* [→ *2316*+*4576*]. godly, God-fearing, devout:– worshipper of God [1]

2319 θεοστυγής, *theostygēs*, a. GK: *2539* [→ *2316*+*4767*]. God-hating:– haters of God [1]

2320 θεότης, *theotēs*, n. GK: *2540* [→ *2316*]. Deity, Divinity:– Godhead [1]

2321 Θεόφιλος, *Theophilos*, n.pr. GK: *2541* [→ *2316*+*5384*]. Theophilus, "*friend of God*":– Theophilus [2]

2322 θεραπεία, *therapeia*, n. GK: *2542* [→ *2324*]. service, care; (hence) healing:– healing [2], household [1]

2323 θεραπεύω, *therapeuō*, v. GK: *2543* [→ *2324*]. to serve, to give help, take care of another; by extension: to heal, cure; (pass.) to be healed:– healed [25], heal [10], cured [3], healing [3], cure [2], worshipped [1]

2324 θεράπων, *therapōn*, n. GK: *2544* [→ *2322, 2323*]. servant, a person who renders service:– servant [1]

2325 θερίζω, *therizō*, v. GK: *2545* [→ *2329*]. to reap, harvest:– reap [13], reapeth [3], reaped [2], reaping [2], reapest [1]

2326 θερισμός, *therismos*, n. GK: *2546* [→ *2329*]. harvest:– harvest [13]

2327 θεριστής, *theristēs*, n. GK: *2547* [→ *2329*]. harvester, reaper:– reapers [2]

2328 θερμαίνω, *thermainō*, v. GK: *2548* [→ *2329*]. (mid.) to keep warm, warm (oneself):– warmed [5], warming [1]

2329 θέρμη, *thermē*, n. GK: *2549* [→ *2325, 2326, 2327, 2328, 2330*]. heat:– heat [1]

2330 θέρος, *theros*, n. GK: *2550* [→ *2329*]. summer:– summer [3]

2331 Θεσσαλονικεύς, *Thessalonikeus*, n.pr.g. GK: *2552* [→ *2332*]. Thessalonian, "*from Thessalonica*":– Thessalonians [5], Thessalonica [1]

2332 Θεσσαλονίκη, *Thessalonikē*, n.pr. GK: *2553* [→ *2331*]. Thessalonica:– Thessalonica [5]

2333 Θευδᾶς, *Theudas*, n.pr. GK: *2554* [→ *2316*+*1435*]. Theudas, "*gift of God*":– Theudas [1]

θέω, *theō*. See *5087*.

2334 θεωρέω, **theōreō**, v. GK: 2555 [→ 333, 2335, 3865; cf. 2300]. to see, look at, watch closely; perceive, experience:– see [17], seeth [10], saw [9], beheld [4], beholding [4], perceive [4], behold [3], seen [1], consider [1], looking on [1], seeing [1], seest [1]

2335 θεωρία, **theōria**, n. GK: 2556 [→ 2334]. sight, spectacle:– sight [1]

2336 θήκη, **thēkē**, n. GK: 2557 [→ 5087]. sheath, scabbard:– sheath [1]

2337 θηλάζω, **thēlazō**, v. GK: 2558 [→ 330, 2338]. to nurse a baby; (n.) nursing infant:– give suck [3], gave suck [1], sucked [1], sucklings [1]

2338 θῆλυς, **thēlys**, a. GK: 2559 [→ 2337]. female, pertaining to women:– female [3], woman [1], women [1]

2339 θήρα, **thēra**, n. GK: 2560 [→ 2342]. trap, net:– trap [1]

2340 θηρεύω, **thēreuō**, v. GK: 2561 [→ 2342]. to catch in a mistake, a fig. extension of catching hunted prey, not found in the NT:– catch [1]

2341 θηριομαχέω, **thēriomacheō**, v. GK: 2562 [→ 2342+3163]. to fight wild animals:– fought with beasts [1]

2342 θηρίον, **thērion**, n. GK: 2563 [→ 2339, 2340, 2341]. (wild) animal, (fiendish) beast, snake:– beast [40], beasts [3], wild beasts [3]

2343 θησαυρίζω, **thēsaurizō**, v. GK: 2564 [→ 2344]. to store up, gather, reserve:– lay up [3], heaped treasure together [1], in store [1], kept in store [1], layeth up treasure [1], treasurest up [1]

2344 θησαυρός, **thēsauros**, n. GK: 2565 [→ 596, 597, 2343; cf. 5087]. treasure, what is stored up; storeroom:– treasure [13], treasures [5]

2345 θιγγάνω, **thinganō**, v. GK: 2566. to touch:– touch [2], handle [1]

2346 θλίβω, **thlibō**, v. GK: 2567 [→ 598, 2347, 4918]. (act.) to press upon, crowd up to; cause trouble; (pass.) to be narrow; to be pressed, troubled, persecuted:– afflicted [3], troubled [3], narrow [1], suffer tribulation [1], throng [1], trouble [1]

2347 θλῖψις, **thlipsis**, n. GK: 2568 [→ 2346]. trouble, distress, oppression, tribulation:– tribulation [18], affliction [11], afflictions [6], tribulations [3], trouble [3], afflicted [1], anguish [1], burdened [1], persecution [1]

2348 θνήσκω, **thnēskō**, v. GK: 2569 [→ 110, 599, 1935, 2253, 2286, 2287, 2288, 2289, 2349, 4880]. (perf.) to have died, be dead:– dead [11], dead man [1], died [1]

2349 θνητός, **thnētos**, a. GK: 2570 [→ 2348]. mortal:– mortal [5], mortality [1]

2350 θορυβέω, **thorybeō**, v. GK: 2572 [→ 2351]. to start a riot, throw into disorder; (pass.) to be alarmed, in commotion, distressed:– make ado [1], making noise [1], set on an uproar [1], trouble [1]

2351 θόρυβος, **thorybos**, n. GK: 2573 [→ 2350]. uproar, riot, commotion, disturbance:– tumult [4], uproar [3]

2352 θραύω, **thrauō**, v. GK: 2575. (pass.) to be oppressed, downtrodden, a fig. extension of an object broken in pieces:– bruised [1]

2353 θρέμμα, **thremma**, n. GK: 2576 [→ 5142]. livestock, domestic animal (usually a sheep or goat):– cattle [1]

2354 θρηνέω, **thrēneō**, v. GK: 2577 [→ 2355, 2360]. to sing a funeral dirge, lament, mourn:– mourned [2], lamented [1], lament [1]

2355 θρῆνος, **thrēnos**, n. GK: 2578 [→ 2354]. dirge, funeral song:– lamentation [1]

2356 θρησκεία, **thrēskeia**, n. GK: 2579 [→ 2357]. religion, worship:– religion [3], worshipping [1]

2357 θρῆσκος, **thrēskos**, a. GK: 2580 [→ 1479, 2356]. religious:– religious [1]

2358 θριαμβεύω, **thriambeuō**, v. GK: 2581. to lead in a triumphal procession:– causeth to triumph [1], triumphing over [1]

2359 θρίξ, **thrix**, n. GK: 2582 [→ 5155]. hair, a hair:– hair [10], hairs [5]

2360 θροέω, **throeō**, v. GK: 2583 [→ 2354]. (pass.) to be alarmed, disturbed:– troubled [3]

2361 θρόμβος, **thrombos**, n. GK: 2584. drop:– drops [1]

2362 θρόνος, **thronos**, n. GK: 2585. throne:– throne [50], seats [4], thrones [4], seat [3]

2363 Θυάτειρα, **Thyateira**, n.pr. GK: 2587. Thyatira:– Thyatira [4]

2364 θυγάτηρ, **thygatēr**, n. GK: 2588 [→ 2365]. daughter, by extension a term of endearment toward (younger) woman:– daughter [24], daughters [5]

2365 θυγάτριον, **thygatrion**, n. GK: 2589 [→ 2364]. little daughter:– little daughter [1], young daughter [1]

2366 θύελλα, **thyella**, n. GK: 2590 [→ 2372]. storm:– tempest [1]

2367 θύϊνος, **thyinos**, a. GK: 2591 [→ 2380]. citron, from the citron tree (a scented wood):– thyine [1]

2368 θυμίαμα, **thymiama**, n. GK: 2592 [→ 2380]. incense, burning incense, offering of incense:– incense [4], odours [2]

2369 θυμιατήριον, **thymiatērion**, n. GK: 2593 [→ 2380]. incense altar:– censer [1]

2370 θυμιάω, **thymiaō**, v. GK: 2594 [→ 2380]. to burn incense, offer incense:– burn incense [1]

2371 θυμομαχέω, **thymomacheō**, v. GK: 2595 [→ 2372+3163]. to quarrel, be fighting mad:– highly displeased [1]

2372 θυμός, **thymos**, n. GK: 2596 [→ 120, 1760, 1761, 1937, 1938, 1939, 2114, 2115, 2366, 2371, 2373, 3114, 3115, 3116, 3661, 4288, 4289, 4290]. wrath, fury, anger, rage, a state of intense displeasure based in some real or perceived wrong. "The anger of God" is due to moral offense and has a focus on righteous punishment:– wrath [14], fierceness [2], indignation [1], wraths [1]

2373 θυμόω, **thymoō**, v. GK: 2597 [→ 2372]. (pass.) to become angry:– wroth [1]

2374 θύρα, **thyra**, n. GK: 2598 [→ 2375, 2376, 2377]. door, gate, entrance:– door [29], doors [9], gate [1]

2375 θυρεός, **thyreos**, n. GK: 2599 [→ 2374]. (long, oblong) shield:– shield [1]

2376 θυρίς, **thyris**, n. GK: 2600 [→ 2374]. window:– window [2]

2377 θυρωρός, **thyrōros**, n. GK: 2601 [→ 2374]. doorkeeper, watcher (at door or gate):– kept the door [2], porter [2]

2378 θυσία, **thysia**, n. GK: 2602 [→ 2380]. sacrifice, offering:– sacrifice [17], sacrifices [12]

2379 θυσιαστήριον, **thysiastērion**, n. GK: 2603 [→ 2380]. altar:– altar [22], altars [1]

2380 θύω, **thyō**, v. GK: 2124 & 2604 [→ 1494, 2367, 2368, 2369, 2370, 2378, 2379; cf. 2303]. to kill, butcher; to offer sacrifice:– killed [5], kill [3], sacrifice [3], done sacrifice [1], sacrificed [1], slay [1]

2381 Θωμᾶς, **Thōmas**, n.pr. GK: 2605. Thomas, "*twin*":– Thomas [12]

2382 θώραξ, **thōrax**, n. GK: 2606. breastplate:– breastplates [3], breastplate [2]

2383 Ἰάϊρος, **Iairos**, n.pr. GK: 2608. Jairus, "*he gives light*":– Jairus [2]

2384 Ἰακώβ, **Iakōb**, n.pr. GK: 2609 [→ 2385]. Jacob, "*follower, replacer, one who follows the heel*":– Jacob [26], Jacob's [1]

2385 Ἰάκωβος, **Iakōbos**, n.pr. GK: 2610 [→ 2384]. James, "*follower, replacer, one who follows the heel*":– James [42]

2386 ἴαμα, **iama**, n. GK: 2611 [→ 2390]. healing:– healing [2], healings [1]

2387 Ἰαμβρῆς, **Iambrēs**, n.pr. GK: 2612. Jambres:– Jambres [1]

2388 Ἰανναί, **Iannai**, n.pr. GK: 2613. Jannai:– Janna [1]

2389 Ἰάννης, **Iannēs**, n.pr. GK: 2614. Jannes:– Jannes [1]

2390 ἰάομαι, **iaomai**, v. GK: 2615 [→ 2386, 2392, 2395]. (mid.) to heal; (pass.) to be healed, freed:– healed [18], heal [7], healing [1], made whole [1], maketh whole [1]

2391 Ἰάρετ, **Iaret**, n.pr. GK: 2616. Jared, "*servant*":– Jared [1]

2392 ἴασις, **iasis**, n. GK: 2617 [→ 2390]. healing, cure:– cures [1], healing [1], heal [1]

2393 ἴασπις, **iaspis**, n. GK: 2618. jasper:– jasper [4]

2394 Ἰάσων, **Iasōn**, n.pr. GK: 2619. Jason, "*to heal*":– Jason [5]

2395 ἰατρός, **iatros**, n. GK: 2620 [→ 2390]. doctor, physician:– physician [5], physicians [2]

2396 ἴδε, **ide**, pt. GK: 2623 [→ 1491]. see!, look!; here, there:– behold [24], lo [3], look [1], see [1]

2397 ἰδέα, **idea**, n. GK: 1624 & 2624 [→ 1491]. appearance (usually implies a condition of reality):– countenance [1]

2398 ἴδιος, **idios**, a. GK: 2625 [→ 2399]. one's own, private:– his own [47], their own [14], privately (+2596) [8], apart (+2596) [7], own [6], your own [6], his [5], due [3], her own [2], our own [2], their [2], acquaintance [1], alone (+2596) [1], aside (+2596) [1], his proper [1], his several [1], home (+1519+3588) [1], private [1], proper [1], severally [1], thine own [1]

2399 ἰδιώτης, **idiōtēs**, n. GK: 2626 [→ 2398]. ordinary, untrained person, one who does not understand, an inquirer:– unlearned [3], ignorant [1], rude [1]

2400 ἰδού, **idou**, pt. GK: 2627 [→ 1491]. look!, suddenly, now; here, there; this particle is used to enliven a Hebrew narrative style, by marking the change of a scene, or emphasize some detail or idea, and is not always translated:– behold [181], lo [29], see [3]

2401 Ἰδουμαία, **Idoumaia**, n.pr. GK: 2628. Idumea, "*[land of] Edom*":– Idumea [1]

2402 ἱδρώς, **hidrōs**, n. GK: 2629. sweat, perspiration:– sweat [1]

2403 Ἰεζάβελ, **Iezabel**, n.pr. GK: 2630. Jezebel, "*[poss.] unexalted, without a husband*":– Jezebel [1]

2404 Ἱεράπολις, **Hierapolis**, n.pr. GK: 2631 [→ 2413+4172]. Hierapolis, "*[pagan] sacred city*":– Hierapolis [1]

2405 ἱερατεία, **hierateia**, n. GK: 2632 [→ 2413]. priestly office, priesthood:– office of priesthood [1], priest's office [1]

2406 ἱεράτευμα, **hierateuma**, n. GK: 2633 [→ 2413]. priesthood:– priesthood [2]

2407 ἱερατεύω, **hierateuō**, v. GK: 2634 [→ 2413]. to serve as a priest:– executed the priest's office [1]

2408 Ἱερεμίας, **Ieremias**, n.pr. GK: 2635. Jeremiah, "*Yahweh loosens [the womb]; Yahweh lifts up, establishes*":– Jeremie [2], Jeremias [1]

2409 ἱερεύς, **hiereus**, n. GK: 2636 [→ 2413]. priest:– priest [17], priests [15]

2410 Ἱεριχώ, **Ierichō**, n.pr. GK: 2637. Jericho, "*moon city*":– Jericho [7]

2411 ἱερόν, **hieron**, n. GK: 2639 [→ 2413]. temple, sanctuary; of the temple in Jerusalem, it can denote the entire temple complex:– temple [71]

2412 ἱεροπρεπής, **hieroprepēs**, a. GK: 2640 [→ 2413+4241]. reverent, pertaining to proper reverence, worthy of reverence:– as becometh holiness [1]

2413 ἱερός, **hieros**, a. GK: 2641 [→ 748, 749, 2404, 2405, 2406, 2407, 2409, 2411, 2412, 2416, 2417, 2418, 2420]. sacred, holy, set apart for God; (pl.) the holy things:– holy [2]

2414 Ἱεροσόλυμα, **Hierosolyma**, n.pr. GK: 2642 [→ 2419]. Jerusalem:– Jerusalem [59]

2415 Ἱεροσολυμίτης, **Hierosolymitēs**, n.pr.g. GK: 2643 [→ 2419]. inhabitant of Jerusalem:– Jerusalem [1], of Jerusalem [1]

2416 ἱεροσυλέω, **hierosyleō**, v. GK: 2644 [→ 2413+4813]. to rob temples:– commit sacrilege [1]

2417 ἱερόσυλος, **hierosylos**, a. GK: 2645 [→ 2413+4813]. temple robber:– robbers of churches [1]

2418 ἱερουργέω, **hierourgeō**, v. GK: 2646 [→ 2413+2041]. to perform priestly duty, serve as a priest:– ministering [1]

2419 Ἱερουσαλήμ, **Ierousalēm**, n.pr. GK: 2647 [→ 2414, 2415]. Jerusalem, "*foundation of Shalem [peace]*":– Jerusalem [83]

2420 ἱερωσύνη, **hierōsynē**, n. GK: 2648 [→ 2413]. priesthood:– priesthood [4]

2421 Ἰεσσαί, **Iessai**, n.pr. GK: 2649. Jesse:– Jesse [5]

2422 Ἰεφθάε, **Iephthae**, n.pr. GK: 2650. Jephthah, "*Yahweh opens, frees*":– Jephthae [1]

2423 Ἰεχονίας, **Iechonias**, n.pr. GK: 2651. Jeconiah, "*Yahweh supports*":– Jechonias [2]

2424 Ἰησοῦς, *Iēsous*, n.pr. GK: *2652*. Jesus, Joshua, "*Yahweh saves*":– Jesus [964], Jesus' [10], him^S [1]

2425 ἱκανός, *hikanos*, a. GK: *2653* [→ *864, 867, 1338, 2185, 2426, 2427, 2428*]. sufficient, considerable, much; appropriate, competent, worthy, deserving:– many [11], much [6], long [5], worthy [5], sufficient [3], able [1], content (+*4160*) [1], enough [1], good while (+*2250*) [1], great number [1], great [1], large [1], long while (+*1909*) [1], meet [1], security [1], sore [1]

2426 ἱκανότης, *hikanotēs*, n. GK: *2654* [→ *2425*]. competence, fitness, capability:– sufficiency [1]

2427 ἱκανόω, *hikanoō*, v. GK: *2655* [→ *2425*]. to make competent, qualify one for, authorize:– made able [1], made meet [1]

2428 ἱκετηρία, *hiketēria*, n. GK: *2656* [→ *2425*]. petition, supplication:– supplications [1]

2429 ἱκμάς, *ikmas*, n. GK: *2657*. moisture:– moisture [1]

2430 Ἰκόνιον, *Ikonion*, n.pr. GK: *2658*. Iconium:– Iconium [6]

2431 ἱλαρός, *hilaros*, a. GK: *2659* [→ *2433*]. cheerful, without grudging, with an implication of a gracious attitude; note that the transliteration "hilarious" does not communicate the meaning of this attitude:– cheerful [1]

2432 ἱλαρότης, *hilarotēs*, n. GK: *2660* [→ *2433*]. cheerfully, not grudgingly, with an implication of a gracious attitude:– cheerfulness [1]

2433 ἱλάσκομαι, *hilaskomai*, v. GK: *2661* [→ *2431, 2432, 2434, 2435, 2436*]. (mid.) to make atonement for, with a focus on the means for accomplishing forgiveness, resulting in reconciliation; (pass.) to have mercy on, be merciful to:– make reconciliation [1], merciful [1]

2434 ἱλασμός, *hilasmos*, n. GK: *2662* [→ *2433*]. atoning sacrifice, the means of forgiveness; traditionally propitiation:– propitiation [2]

2435 ἱλαστήριον, *hilastērion*, n. GK: *2663* [→ *2433*]. atoning sacrifice; atonement cover, the place where sins are forgiven; traditionally propitiation or mercy seat:– mercy seat [1], propitiation [1]

2436 ἵλεως, *hileōs*, a. GK: *2664* [→ *2433*]. forgiving, gracious; (may God be) gracious!, God forbid!:– be it far from [1], merciful [1]

2437 Ἰλλυρικόν, *Illyrikon*, n.pr. GK: *2665*. Illyricum:– Illyricum [1]

2438 ἱμάς, *himas*, n. GK: *2666*. (leather) thong, strap:– latchet [3], thongs [1]

2439 ἱματίζω, *himatizō*, v. GK: *2667* [→ *2066, 2067, 2440, 2441; cf. 294*]. (pass.) to be dressed, clothed:– clothed [2]

2440 ἱμάτιον, *himation*, n. GK: *2668* [→ *2439*]. clothing, cloak, robe:– garments [15], garment [15], clothes [12], raiment [12], cloke [2], robe [2], vesture [2], apparel [1]

2441 ἱματισμός, *himatismos*, n. GK: *2669* [→ *2439*]. clothing:– vesture [2], apparelled [1], apparel [1], array [1], raiment [1]

2442 ἱμείρομαι, *himeiromai*, v. GK: *2670*. to desire, long for:– affectionately desirous [1]

2443 ἵνα, *hina*, c. GK: *2671* [→ *2444*]. a marker that shows purpose or result: in order that, in order to, so that, then; it can focus on the introduction of a discourse or on the content itself:– that [537], to [71], for to [5], after [1], albeit [1], because [1], must [1], so as [1], so that [1], to the intent that [1], to the intent [1], would [1]

 ἵνα μή, *hina mē*. See **3363**.

2444 ἱνατί, *hinati*, pt.inter. GK: *2672* [→ *2443*+*5101*]. why?:– why [5], wherefore [1]

2445 Ἰόππη, *Ioppē*, n.pr. GK: *2673*. Joppa, "*beautiful*":– Joppa [10]

2446 Ἰορδάνης, *Iordanēs*, n.pr. GK: *2674*. Jordan, "*descending*":– Jordan [15]

2447 ἰός, *ios*, n. GK: *2675* [→ *2728*]. poison, venom; corrosion, rust:– poison [2], rust [1]

2448 Ἰουδά, *Iouda*, n.pr. GK: *2676* [→ *2455*]. Judah, "*praised*":– Juda [3]

2449 Ἰουδαία, *Ioudaia*, n.pr. GK: *2677* [→ *2455*]. Judea, Judean, "*land of the Judahites*":– Judea [41], Jewry [2]

2450 ἰουδαΐζω, *ioudaizō*, v. GK: *2678* [→ *2455*]. to follow Jewish customs, live as a Jew:– live as do the Jews [1]

2451 Ἰουδαϊκός, *Ioudaikos*, a.pr. GK: *2679* [→ *2455*]. Jewish, "*Jewish*":– Jewish [1]

2452 Ἰουδαϊκῶς, *Ioudaikōs*, adv.pr. GK: *2680* [→ *2455*]. like a Jew, in a Jewish manner, "*Jewish*":– as do the Jews [1]

2453 Ἰουδαῖος, *Ioudaios*, a.pr.g. GK: *2681* [→ *2455*]. Jewish (people), "*Jewish*":– Jews [167], Jew [22], Jews' [4], Jewess [2], Judea [2]

2454 Ἰουδαϊσμός, *Ioudaismos*, n.pr. GK: *2682* [→ *2455*]. Judaism, "*Judaism*":– Jews' religion [2]

2455 Ἰούδας, *Ioudas*, n.pr. GK: *2683* [→ *2448, 2449, 2450, 2451, 2452, 2453, 2454*]. Judah, Judas, Jude, "*praised*":– Judas [33], Juda [8], Jude [1]

2456 Ἰουλία, *Ioulia*, n.pr. GK: *2684* [→ *2457*]. Julia, "*of Julian [the family of Julius Caesar]*":– Julia [1]

2457 Ἰούλιος, *Ioulios*, n.pr. GK: *2685* [→ *2456*]. Julius, "*of Julian [the family of Julius Caesar]*":– Julius [2]

2458 Ἰουνιᾶς, *Iounias*, n.pr. GK: *2687*. Junias:– Junia [1]

2459 Ἰοῦστος, *Ioustos*, n.pr. GK: *2688*. Justus, "*just*":– Justus [3]

2460 ἱππεύς, *hippeus*, n. GK: *2689* [→ *2462*]. horseman, cavalryman:– horsemen [2]

2461 ἱππικός, *hippikos*, a. GK: *2690* [→ *2462*]. mounted (troops), pertaining to a horseman:– horsemen [1]

2462 ἵππος, *hippos*, n. GK: *2691* [→ *67, 751, 2460, 2461, 5374, 5375, 5376*]. horse:– horse [8], horses [7], horses' [1]

2463 ἶρις, *iris*, n. GK: *2692*. rainbow; some translate as a brilliant halo or circle of light:– rainbow [2]

2464 Ἰσαάκ, *Isaak*, n.pr. GK: *2693*. Isaac, "*he [God] laughs*":– Isaac [20]

2465 ἰσάγγελος, *isangelos*, a. GK: *2694* [→ *2470*+*32*]. like an angel:– equal unto angels [1]

2466 Ἰσαχάρ, *Isachar*, n.pr. GK: *2695 & 2704*. Issachar, "*there is a reward [Ge. 30:18]; may [God] show mercy; hired hand*":– Isachar [1]

2467 ἵστημι, *isēmi*, v. GK: *3857* [cf. *1492*]. to know; presumed to be related to *1492*:– know [2]

2468 ἴσθι, *isthi*, v.2.s.imper. of *1510*. GK: *1639* [→ *1510*]. be; see *1510*:–

2469 Ἰσκαριώτης, *Iskariōtēs*, n.pr.[g.?]. GK: *2696 & 2697*. Iscariot, "*man of Kerioth* or *of the assassins*":– Iscariot [11]

2470 ἴσος, *isos*, a. GK: *2698* [→ *2465, 2471, 2472, 2473, 2481*]. equal, same; agreeable:– equal [4], agree together (+*1510*) [1], agreed together (+*1510*) [1], as much (+*3588*) [1], like [1]

2471 ἰσότης, *isotēs*, n. GK: *2699* [→ *2470*]. equality, fairness:– equality [2], equal [1]

2472 ἰσότιμος, *isotimos*, a. GK: *2700* [→ *2470*+*5092*]. as precious as, of equal value:– like precious [1]

2473 ἰσόψυχος, *isopsychos*, a. GK: *2701* [→ *2470*+*5594*]. like, of like soul, heart or mind:– likeminded [1]

2474 Ἰσραήλ, *Israēl*, n.pr. GK: *2702* [→ *2475*]. Israel, "*he struggles with God [El]*":– Israel [70]

2475 Ἰσραηλίτης, *Israēlitēs*, n.pr.g. GK: *2703* [→ *2474*]. Israelite, (one) of Israel:– of Israel [5], Israelites [2], Israelite [2]

2476 ἵστημι, *histēmi*, v. GK: *2705* [→ *181, 182, 386, 387, 436, 450, 478, 600, 605, 646, 647, 790, 868, 1292, 1339, 1370, 1611, 1764, 1815, 1817, 1839, 1881, 1987, 1988, 1990, 1999, 2139, 2186, 2525, 2688, 2721, 3179, 3936, 4026, 4291, 4368, 4414, 4712, 4713, 4714, 4715, 4739, 4911, 4921, 4955, 4956, 5287; cf. 4716, 4745*]. (intr.) to stand, to stand (firm), be present; to stop; (tr.) to make stand, place, put, establish:– stood [57], stand [34], standing [22], set [10], standeth [8], establish [3], stood still [3], appointed [2], established [2], standest [2], abode [1], brought [1], continue [1], covenanted [1], holden up [1], lay to charge [1], make stand [1], present [1], set up [1], setteth [1], stanched [1], stand still [1], standing up [1]

2477 ἱστορέω, *historeō*, v. GK: *2707*. to get acquainted with, visit:– see [1]

2478 ἰσχυρός, *ischyros*, a. GK: *2708* [→ *2479*]. powerful, strong, forceful:– strong [11], mighty [7], mightier than [3], stronger than [3], boysterous [1], powerful [1], valiant [1]

2479 ἰσχύς, *ischys*, n. GK: *2709* [→ *1340, 1765, 1840, 2001, 2478, 2480, 2729*]. strength, power:– strength [4], power [3], might [2], ability [1], mightily [1]

2480 ἰσχύω, *ischyō*, v. GK: *2710* [→ *2479*]. to be strong, powerful, able:– could [8], able [6], availeth [3], prevailed [3], whole [2], can do [1], cannot (+*3756*) [1], couldest [1], good [1], had much work (+*3433*) [1], might [1], strength [1]

2481 ἴσως, *isōs*, adv. GK: *2711* [→ *2470*]. perhaps:– it may be [1]

2482 Ἰταλία, *Italia*, n.pr. GK: *2712* [→ *2483*]. Italy:– Italy [5]

2483 Ἰταλικός, *Italikos*, a.pr.g. GK: *2713* [→ *2482*]. Italian:– Italian [1]

2484 Ἰτουραῖος, *Itouraios*, a.pr. GK: *2714*. Iturea, "*pertaining to Jetur*":– Iturea [1]

2485 ἰχθύδιον, *ichthydion*, n. GK: *2715* [→ *2486*]. little fish:– little fishes [1], small fishes [1]

2486 ἰχθύς, *ichthys*, n. GK: *2716* [→ *2485*]. fish:– fishes [15], fish [5]

2487 ἴχνος, *ichnos*, n. GK: *2717* [→ *421*]. step, footstep; course of action:– steps [3]

2488 Ἰωαθάμ, *Iōatham*, n.pr. GK: *2718*. Jotham, "*Yahweh will complete*":– Joatham [2]

2489 Ἰωαννά, *Iōanna*, n.pr. GK: *2720* [cf. *2491*]. Joanna, "*[prob.] Yahweh is gracious*":– Joanna [2]

2490 Ἰωαννᾶς, *Iōannas*, n.pr. GK: *2721* [cf. *2491*]. Joannas, "*[prob.] Yahweh is gracious*":– Joanna [1]

2491 Ἰωάννης, *Iōannēs*, n.pr. GK: *2722* [cf. *2489, 2490*]. John, "*Yahweh is gracious*":– John [131], John's [2]

2492 Ἰώβ, *Iōb*, n.pr. GK: *2724*. Job, "*where is my father poss. where is my father, O God?*":– Job [1]

2493 Ἰωήλ, *Iōēl*, n.pr. GK: *2727*. Joel, "*Yahweh is God*":– Joel [1]

2494 Ἰωνάμ, *Iōnam*; or Ἰωνάν, *Iōnan*, n.pr. GK: *2729 & 2730*. Jonam, Jonan:– Jonan [1]

2495 Ἰωνᾶς, *Iōnas*, n.pr. GK: *2731*. Jonah, "*dove*":– Jonas [12], Jona [1]

2496 Ἰωράμ, *Iōram*, n.pr. GK: *2732*. Jehoram, "*Yahweh exalts*":– Joram [2]

2497 Ἰωρίμ, *Iōrim*, n.pr. GK: *2733*. Jorim:– Jorim [1]

2498 Ἰωσαφάτ, *Iōsaphat*, n.pr. GK: *2734*. Jehoshaphat, "*Yahweh has judged*":– Josaphat [2]

2499 Ἰωσή, *Iōsē*, n.pr. GK: *2735* [cf. *2500*]. Jose, "*he will add*":– Jose [1]

2500 Ἰωσῆς, *Iōsēs*, n.pr. GK: *2736* [cf. *2499*]. Joses, Joseph, "*he will add*":– Joses [6]

2501 Ἰωσήφ, *Iōsēph*, n.pr. GK: *2737*. Joseph, "*he will add*":– Joseph [33], Joseph's [2]

2502 Ἰωσίας, *Iōsias*, n.pr. GK: *2739*. Josiah, "*let or may Yahweh give*":– Josias [2]

2503 ἰῶτα, *iōta*, n. GK: *2740*. smallest letter (of the Greek alphabet), which corresponds to the smallest letter of the Hebrew alphabet, *yodh*:– jot [1]

2504 κἀγώ, *kagō*, contr. [c.+p.]. GK: *2743* [→ *2532*+*1473*]. and I, I also, but I:– and I [43], I also [19], I [5], even I [5], me also [3], so I [3], and me [2], I in like wise [1], also [1], both me [1], but me [1], even I also [1], that I [1], when I [1]

2505 καθά, *katha*, c. or adv. GK: *2745* [→ *2596*+*3739*]. (just) as:– as [1]

2506 καθαίρεσις, *kathairesis*, n. GK: *2746* [→ *2596*+*138*]. tearing down, demolishment, destruction:– destruction [2], pulling down [1]

2507 καθαιρέω, *kathaireō*, v. GK: *2747* [→ *2596*+*138*]. to take down, demolish, overthrow; (pass.) to be robbed of, suffer the loss of:– took down [3], destroyed [2], casting down [1], pull down [1], put down [1], take down [1]

2508 καθαίρω, *kathairō*, v. GK: *2748* [→ *2513*]. to prune, clear unproductive wood, cleanse:– purged [1], purgeth [1]

2509 καθάπερ, *kathaper*, c. or adv. GK: *2749* [→ *2596*+*3739*+*4007*]. as, just as, like:– as [10], even as [2], as well [1]

2510 καθάπτω, *kathaptō*, v. GK: *2750* [→ *2596*+*681*]. to fasten, attach, take hold of, seize:– fastened [1]

2511 καθαρίζω, katharizō, v. GK: 2751 & 2760 [→ 2513]. to make clean, cleanse, purify:– cleansed [9], cleanse [6], make clean [5], clean [3], cleanseth [1], purged [1], purge [1], purging [1], purified [1], purifying [1], purify [1]

2512 καθαρισμός, katharismos, n. GK: 2752 [→ 2513]. cleansing, purification, washing:– cleansing [2], purifying [2], purged (+4160) [1], purged [1], purification [1]

2513 καθαρός, katharos, a. GK: 2754 [→ 167, 168, 169, 1245, 1571, 2508, 2511, 2512, 2514, 4027]. clean, pure, clear of responsibility, innocent:– pure [17], clean [10], clear [1]

2514 καθαρότης, katharotēs, n. GK: 2755 [→ 2513]. cleanness, purity:– purifying [1]

2515 καθέδρα, kathedra, n. GK: 2756 [→ 2516]. seat, bench:– seats [2], seat [1]

2516 καθέζομαι, kathezomai, v. GK: 2757 [→ 2515, 2521, 4410, 4775]. to sit down, be seated:– sat [4], sitting [2]

2517 καθεξῆς, kathexēs, adv. GK: 2759 [→ 2596+2192]. in order, in a sequence:– in order [2], afterward (+1722+3588) [1], by order [1], follow after [1]

2518 καθεύδω, katheudō, v. GK: 2761 [→ 2596]. to sleep, fall asleep:– sleep [8], asleep [5], sleepeth [3], sleepest [2], sleeping [2], slept [2]

2519 καθηγητής, kathēgētēs, n. GK: 2762 [→ 2596+71]. teacher; derivative of a verb "to guide, to explain," not found in the NT:– master [2], masters [1]

2520 καθήκω, kathēkō, v. GK: 2763 [→ 2596+2240]. to be fitting, (pcpl.) things that ought to be, that are proper:– convenient [1], fit [1]

2521 κάθημαι, kathēmai, v. GK: 2764 [→ 2516]. to sit, seat, ride; to live, stay, reside:– sat [41], sitting [20], sit [12], sitteth [10], sat down [2], dwell [1], set down [1], sittest [1], sitting down [1]

2522 καθημερινός, kathēmerinos, a. GK: 2766 [→ 2596+2250]. daily:– daily [1]

2523 καθίζω, kathizō, v. GK: 2767 [→ 339, 1940, 3869, 4776]. (tr.) to place, seat (someone), appoint; (intr.) to sit down, come to rest upon; stay, live. "To sit on the right side" means to be in a position of high status, "to sit on the left" is a lesser position. "To sit on the seat of Moses" means to have the capacity to interpret the Law of Moses with authority:– sit [14], sat down [11], sat [10], set [3], set down [2], sitteth down [2], continued [1], set to judge [1], sit down [1], sitteth [1], sitting [1], tarry [1]

2524 καθίημι, kathiēmi, v. GK: 2768 [→ 2596]. to let down, lower:– let down [3], let down (+5465) [1]

2525 καθίστημι, kathistēmi, v. GK: 2769 & 2770 [→ 2596+2476]. to put in charge, appoint; to escort, bring, take; (pass.) to be made, become, be appointed:– made [6], make ruler [5], is [2], ordained [2], appoint [1], conducted [1], made ruler [1], maketh [1], make [1], ordain [1], set [1]

2526 καθό, katho, adv. GK: 2771 [→ 2596+3739]. insofar as, to the degree that:– according to that (+1437) [1], according to that [1], as we [1], inasmuch as [1]

2526' καθολικός, katholikos, a. GK: 2772 [→ 2596+3650]. general, universal:–

2527 καθόλου, katholou, adv. GK: 2773 [→ 2596+3650]. at all, entirely, completely:– at all [1]

2528 καθοπλίζω, kathoplizō, v. GK: 2774 [→ 2596+3696]. (mid.) to fully arm or equip (oneself):– armed [1]

2529 καθοράω, kathoraō, v. GK: 2775 [→ 2596+3708]. (pass.) to be clearly seen, perceived:– clearly seen [1]

2530 καθότι, kathoti, c. GK: 2776 [→ 2596+3739+5101]. as, to the degree that; because:– according as [1], as (+302) [1], because that [1], because [1], forsomuch as [1]

2531 καθώς, kathōs, adv. GK: 2777 [→ 2596+5613]. as, just as, even as; in accordance with:– as [142], even as [27], according as [5], even [3], according to [1], as well as [1], how [1], seeing as [1], when [1]

2532 καί, kai, c. GK: 2779 [→ 2504, 2534, 2539, 2543, 2544, 2546, 2547, 2548, 2579, 4003, 5065]. (as a connective) and; (connecting and continuing) and then, then; (as a disjunctive) but, yet, however; (as an adv.) also, even, likewise:– and [8167], also [517], even [100], both [47], but [41], then [25], so [18], neither (+3756) [16], likewise [12], or [12], that [12], nor [11], yet [10], when [9], for [8], neither [8], with [6], yea [5], as [4], indeed [4], neither (+3361) [4], and also [3], eighteen (+1176+3638) [3], moreover [3], though [3], very [3], and yet [2], nor (+3756) [2], now [2], therefore [2], yet (+1063) [2],

also (+235) [1], also (+260) [1], although (+1487) [1], and (+5119) [1], and again [1], and no so much as (+3761) [1], and when [1], as well [1], at least (+1065) [1], beside [1], but though (+1161+1487) [1], by [1], else [1], even (+2193) [1], even all one as if (+846+1520+3588) [1], if [1], insomuch [1], moreover (+235) [1], neither (+3364) [1], neither (+3761) [1], neither any (+3762) [1], neither at any time (+3763) [1], nevertheless (+4133) [1], of either side (+1782+1782) [1], on either side one (+1782+1782) [1], so in like manner (+3779) [1], so that (+5620) [1], so that [1], therefore (+1352) [1], though (+1437) [1], though (+1487) [1], though (+1512) [1], thus [1], verily [1], wherefore (+1352) [1], wherefore (+5620) [1], which [1]

2533 Καϊάφας, Kaiaphas, n.pr. GK: 2780. Caiaphas:– Caiaphas [9]

2534 καίγε, kaige, pt. GK: 2781 [→ 2532+1065]. even, even though:–

2535 Κάϊν, Kain, n.pr. GK: 2782. Cain, "metal worker; brought forth, acquired [Ge. 4:1]":– Cain [3]

2536 Καϊνάμ, Kainam; or Καϊνάν, Kainan, n.pr. GK: 2783 & 2784. Cainam, Cainan, Kenan, "worker in iron, metal worker":– Cainan [1]

2537 καινός, kainos, a. GK: 2785 [→ 340, 341, 342, 1456, 1457, 2538]. new, latest, anew; in some contexts new is superior to old (Mt 9:17; Heb 8):– new [44]

2538 καινότης, kainotēs, n. GK: 2786 [→ 2537]. newness:– newness [2]

2539 καίπερ, kaiper, c. GK: 2788 [→ 2532+4007]. though, even though, although:– though [5], and yet [1]

2540 καιρός, kairos, n. GK: 2789 [→ 170, 171, 2119, 2120, 2121, 2122, 4340]. time (particular and general); right time, opportune time, proper time, appointed time:– time [53], times [11], season [8], seasons [4], always (+1722+3956) [2], due season [2], opportunity [2], age (+2244) [1], convenient season [1], due time [1], while [1]

2541 Καῖσαρ, Kaisar, n.pr. GK: 2790 [→ 2542]. Caesar:– Cesar [21], Cesar's [9]

2542 Καισάρεια, Kaisareia, n.pr. GK: 2791 [→ 2541]. Caesarea:– Cesarea [17]

2543 καίτοι, kaitoi, pt. GK: 2792 [→ 2532+5104]. and yet:– although [1]

2544 καίτοιγε, kaitoige, pt. GK: 2793 [→ 2532+5104+1065]. although, and yet:– though [2], nevertheless [1]

2545 καίω, kaiō, v. GK: 2794 [→ 1572, 2575, 2618, 2738, 2739, 2740, 2741, 2742, 2743, 3646]. to light (a wick), keep burning:– burning [6], burned [3], burneth [1], burn [1], light [1]

2546 κἀκεῖ, kakei, contr. [c.+adv.]. GK: 2795 [→ 2532+1563]. and there, and where:– and there [9], there also [1], thither also [1]

2547 κἀκεῖθεν, kakeithen, contr. [c.+adv.]. GK: 2796 [→ 2532+1563]. and from there:– and from thence [6], and thence [3], and afterward [1], thence also [1]

2548 κἀκεῖνος, kakeinos, contr. [c.+p.demo.]. GK: 2797 [→ 2532+1563]. and that one:– and he [4], and they [3], he also [3], and him [2], and the other [2], and them [2], they also [2], as them [1], even he [1], even they [1], him also [1], them also [1]

2549 κακία, kakia, n. GK: 2798 [→ 2556]. evil, wickedness, depravity, malice; in some contexts means an "evil" situation means a difficult and hard circumstance rather than a morally corrupt circumstance (Mt 6:34):– malice [6], maliciousness [2], evil [1], naughtiness [1], wickedness [1]

2550 κακοήθεια, kakoētheia, n. GK: 2799 [→ 2556+1485]. malice:– malignity [1]

2551 κακολογέω, kakologeō, v. GK: 2800 [→ 2556+3004]. to curse, malign, speak evil of:– curseth [2], spake evil [1], speak evil [1]

2552 κακοπάθεια, kakopatheia, n. GK: 2801 [→ 2556+3958]. suffering:– suffering affliction [1]

2553 κακοπαθέω, kakopatheō, v. GK: 2802 [→ 2556+3958]. to suffer trouble, endure hardship:– afflicted [1], endure afflictions [1], endure hardness [1], suffer trouble [1]

2554 κακοποιέω, kakopoieō, v. GK: 2803 [→ 2556+4160]. to do evil, do what is wrong:– do evil [2], doeth evil [1], evil doing [1]

2555 κακοποιός, kakopoios, a. GK: 2804 [→ 2556+4160]. wrongdoing:– evildoers [3], evildoer [1], malefactor [1]

2556 κακός, kakos, a. GK: 2805 [→ 172, 420, 1573, 2549, 2550, 2551, 2552, 2553, 2554, 2555, 2557, 2558, 2559, 2560, 2561, 4777, 4778]. evil, wicked, wrong, bad, a perversion of what pertains to goodness; as a noun, an evil thing can refer to any crime, harm, or moral wrong:– evil [45], harm [2], bad [1], ill [1], noisome [1], wicked [1]

2557 κακοῦργος, kakourgos, a. GK: 2806 [→ 2556+2041]. criminal, evildoer:– malefactors [3], evil doer [1]

2558 κακουχέω, kakoucheō, v. GK: 2807 [→ 2556+2192]. (pass.) to be mistreated, maltreated, tormented:– suffer adversity [1], tormented [1]

2559 κακόω, kakoō, v. GK: 2808 [→ 2556]. to harm, mistreat, oppress, persecute; poison, embitter:– entreat evil [1], evil entreated [1], harm [1], hurt [1], made evil affected [1], vex [1]

2560 κακῶς, kakōs, adv. GK: 2809 [→ 2556]. badly, wrongly, terribly:– sick (+2192) [4], sick [3], evil [2], amiss [1], diseased (+2192) [1], diseased [1], grievously [1], miserably [1], sick people (+2192) [1], sore [1]

2561 κάκωσις, kakōsis, n. GK: 2810 [→ 2556]. oppression, mistreatment:– affliction [1]

2562 καλάμη, kalamē, n. GK: 2811 [→ 2563]. straw; note some translate "stubble":– stubble [1]

2563 κάλαμος, kalamos, n. GK: 2812 [→ 2562]. reed, staff, stick, measuring rod, pen:– reed [11], pen [1]

2564 καλέω, kaleō, v. GK: 2813 [→ 410, 479, 1458, 1462, 1528, 1577, 1941, 2821, 2822, 3333, 3870, 3875, 4292, 4341, 4779, 4837]. to call, invite, summon. The authority of the speaker dictates the nature of the calling (friends invite; kings summon). This is also translated "to name," the giving of attribution to someone or something:– called [103], call [16], bidden [10], calleth [6], bade [4], bid [2], calling [1], named [1], name [1], surname [1]

2565 καλλιέλαιος, kallielaios, n. GK: 2814 [→ 2570+1636]. cultivated olive tree:– good olive tree [1]

2566 καλλίον, kallion, a.neut. of 2570. GK: 2819 [→ 2570]. good, right; beautiful, fine, excellent:–

2567 καλοδιδάσκαλος, kalodidaskalos, a. GK: 2815 [→ 2570+1321]. teaching what is good:– teachers of good things [1]

2568 Καλοὶ λιμένες, Kaloi limenes, n.pr. GK: 2816 [→ 2570+3040]. Fair Havens, "fair havens":– fair havens [1]

2569 καλοποιέω, kalopoieō, v. GK: 2818 [→ 2570+4160]. to do what is right or good:– well doing [1]

2570 καλός, kalos, a. GK: 2819 [→ 2565, 2566, 2567, 2568, 2569, 2573]. good, right; beautiful, fine, excellent:– good [82], better [6], honest [5], goodly [3], meet [2], better (+3123) [1], good thing [1], well [1], worthy [1]

2571 κάλυμμα, kalymma, n. GK: 2820 [→ 2572]. veil, covering:– vail [4]

2572 καλύπτω, kalyptō, v. GK: 2821 [→ 177, 343, 601, 602, 1942, 1943, 2571, 2619, 3871, 4028, 4780]. cover, veil, hide:– covered [2], cover [2], hid [2], covereth [1], hide [1]

2573 καλῶς, kalōs, adv. GK: 2822 [→ 2570]. rightly, well, sometimes with an implication of correctness:– well [30], good [3], full well [1], honestly [1], recover (+2192) [1], very well [1]

2574 κάμηλος, kamēlos, n. GK: 2823. camel:– camel [4], camel's [2]

2575 κάμινος, kaminos, n. GK: 2825 [→ 2545]. furnace, oven:– furnace [4]

2576 καμμύω, kammyō, v. GK: 2826. close, shut (the eyes):– closed [2]

2577 κάμνω, kamnō, v. GK: 2827. to grow weary; be sick:– fainted [1], sick [1], wearied [1]

2578 κάμπτω, kamptō, v. GK: 2828 [→ 344, 4781]. to bend, bow (on a knee):– bow [3], bowed [1]

2579 κἄν, kan, contr. [c.+pt.]. GK: 2829 [→ 2532+1487+302]. and if, even if:– and if [5], though [4], if but [2], also if [1], and though [1], at the least [1], yet [1]

2580 Κανά, Kana, n.pr. GK: 2830 [→ 2581]. Cana, "reed":– Cana [4]

2581 Κανανίτης, Kananitēs, n.pr.g. GK: 2832 [→ 2580]. Canaanite, from Cana:– Canaanite [2]

2582 Κανδάκη, *Kandakē*, n.pr. GK: *2833*. Candace, "[title?] *queen*":– Candace [1]

2583 κανών, *kanōn*, n. GK: *2834*. rule, standard; sphere of activity, limit:– rule [4], line [1]

2584 Καπερναούμ, *Kapernaoum*, n.pr. GK: *2835 & 3019*. Capernaum, "*village of Nahum*":– Capernaum [16]

2585 καπηλεύω, *kapēleuō*, v. GK: *2836*. to act as a peddler, trade in for profit:– corrupt [1]

2586 καπνός, *kapnos*, n. GK: *2837*. smoke:– smoke [13]

2587 Καππαδοκία, *Kappadokia*, n.pr. GK: *2838*. Cappadocia:– Cappadocia [2]

2588 καρδία, *kardia*, n. GK: *2840* [→ *2589, 4641*]. heart, mind (seat of thought and emotion). The heart was thought to be the seat of the inner self (composed of life, soul, mind, and spirit). "Heart" is similar in meaning to "soul," but often the "heart" has a focus on thinking and understanding (Mk 2:8; Lk 1:51; 24:38):– heart [101], hearts [57], heart's [1]

2589 καρδιογνώστης, *kardiognōstēs*, n. GK: *2841* [→ *2588+1097*]. knower of the heart:– knowest hearts [1], knoweth hearts [1]

2590 καρπός, *karpos*, n. GK: *2843* [→ *175, 2591, 2592, 2593*]. fruit, crop, harvest, produce of vegetation; by extension: deed, activity, produce of a person:– fruit [54], fruits [12]

2591 Κάρπος, *Karpos*, n.pr. GK: *2842* [→ *2590*]. Carpus, "*fruit(ful)*":– Carpus [1]

2592 καρποφορέω, *karpophoreō*, v. GK: *2844* [→ *2590+5342*]. to produce a crop, bear fruit:– bring forth fruit [4], bringeth forth fruit [1], beareth fruit [1], fruitful [1]

2593 καρποφόρος, *karpophoros*, a. GK: *2845* [→ *2590+5342*]. crop, fruitbearing:– fruitful [1]

2594 καρτερέω, *kartereō*, v. GK: *2846* [→ *4342, 4343; cf. 2904*]. to persevere, endure:– endured [1]

2595 κάρφος, *karphos*, n. GK: *2847*. speck, chip, particle:– mote [6]

2596 κατά, *kata*, pp. GK: *2848* [→ *176, 177, 178, 179, 180, 181, 182, 183, 478, 600, 604, 605, 843, 1246, 1455, 1459, 1460, 1944, 2505, 2506, 2507, 2509, 2510, 2516, 2517, 2518, 2519, 2520, 2522, 2524, 2525, 2526, 2526', 2527, 2528, 2529, 2530, 2531, 2597, 2598, 2599, 2600, 2601, 2602, 2603, 2604, 2605, 2606, 2607, 2609, 2610, 2611, 2612, 2613, 2614, 2615, 2616, 2653, 2617, 2618, 2619, 2620, 2621, 2622, 2623, 2624, 2625, 2626, 2627, 2628, 2629, 2630, 2631, 2632, 2633, 2634, 2635, 2636, 2637, 2638, 2639, 2640, 2641, 2642, 2643, 2644, 2645, 2646, 2647, 2648, 2649, 2650, 2651, 2652, 2653, 2654, 2655, 2656, 2657, 2658, 2659, 2660, 2661, 2662, 2663, 2664, 2665, 2666, 2667, 2668, 2669, 2670, 2671, 2672, 2673, 2674, 2675, 2676, 2677, 2678, 2679, 2680, 2681, 2682, 2683, 2684, 2685, 2686, 2687, 2688, 2689, 2690, 2691, 2692, 2693, 2694, 2695, 2696, 2697, 2698, 2699, 2700, 2701, 2702, 2703, 2704, 2705, 2706, 2708, 2709, 2710, 2711, 2712, 2713, 2714, 2715, 2716, 2718, 2719, 2720, 2721, 2722, 2723, 2726, 2727, 2728, 2729, 2730, 2731, 2732, 2733, 2734, 2735, 2736, 2737, 3872, 4293, 4294, 4782, 4783, 4784, 4785, 5270; cf. 2608*]. (gen.) against, contrary to, opposed; down, throughout; (acc.) in, by, with, in accordance with, for:– according to [104], after [59], against [58], in [32], by [28], daily (+*2250*) [15], as [10], every [10], at [8], of [8], privately (+*2398*) [8], apart (+*2398*) [7], throughout [7], through [4], to [4], about [3], according [3], concerning [3], down [3], every (+*3956*) [3], in divers [3], toward [3], with [3], after the manner [2], among [2], as concerning [2], as touching [2], before [2], from house to house (+*3624*) [2], inasmuch as (+*3745*) [2], into [2], natural (+*5449*) [2], on part [2], on [2], over against [2], upon [2], according as [1], affairs (+*3588*) [1], after a manner [1], after a sort [1], after the manner of [1], alone (+*1438*) [1], alone (+*2398*) [1], alone (+*3441*) [1], as (+*3739+5158*) [1], as (+*3745*) [1], as much as [1], as pertaining to [1], as wont (+*1485+3588*) [1], aside (+*2398*) [1], beyond measure (+*5236*) [1], cause [1], charitably (+*26*) [1], daily (+*1538+2250*) [1], daily (+*2250+3956*) [1], day by day (+*2250*) [1], deep (+*899*) [1], even as (+*3739+3779+5158*) [1], even thus (+*5024*) [1], every (+*1520+1538*) [1], every (+*3588*) [1], every house (+*3624*) [1], exceeding (+*5236*) [1], face to face (+*4383*) [1], far more exceeding (+*1519+5236+5236*) [1], for [1], godly (+*2316*) [1], in due [1], in every church (+*1577*) [1], in every house [1], every [1], in respect of [1], in the like manner (+*846+3588*) [1], in the presence (+*4383*) [1], like as (+*3665*) [1], matter (+*3588*) [1], mightily (+*2904*) [1], more excellent (+*5236*) [1], one by one (+*1520*) [1], out of measure (+*5236*) [1], particularly (+*1520+1538*) [1], particularly (+*3313*) [1], particular [1],

pertaining to [1], reason (+*3056*) [1], so (+*846+3588*) [1], state [1], the same (+*1565*) [1], together (+*846+3588*) [1], touching [1], unto [1], whereby (+*5101*) [1], where [1], willingly (+*1595*) [1], year by year (+*1763*) [1], your (+*4771*) [1], your own (+*4771*) [1]

2597 καταβαίνω, *katabainō*, v. GK: *2849* [→ *2596+305*]. to go down, descend:– come down [20], came down [16], went down [13], descended [7], descending [7], cometh down [4], descend [4], go down [2], coming down [1], falling down [1], fell [1], get down [1], goeth down [1], going down [1], steppeth down [1]

2598 καταβάλλω, *kataballō*, v. GK: *2850* [→ *2596+906*]. (pass.) to be struck down; (mid.) to lay (a foundation):– cast down [1], laying [1]

2599 καταβαρέω, *katabareō*, v. GK: *2851* [→ *2596+922*]. to burden, be a burden:– burden [1]

2600 κατάβασις, *katabasis*, n. GK: *2853* [→ *2596+305*]. place that goes down, slope, down-grade:– descent [1]

2601 καταβιβάζω, *katabibazō*, v. GK: *2854* [→ *2596+305*]. to bring down:– brought down [1], thrust down [1]

2602 καταβολή, *katabolē*, n. GK: *2856* [→ *2596+906*]. creation (of the world), beginning, foundation:– foundation [10], conceive [1]

2603 καταβραβεύω, *katabrabeuō*, v. GK: *2857* [→ *2596+1018*]. to disqualify for a prize, decide against:– beguile of reward [1]

2604 καταγγελεύς, *katangeleus*, n. GK: *2858* [→ *2596+32*]. advocate, proclaimer:– setter forth [1]

2605 καταγγέλλω, *katangellō*, v. GK: *2859* [→ *2596+32*]. to preach, proclaim, advocate, report:– preached [6], preach [4], shew [3], declare [1], declaring [1], spoken of [1], teach [1]

2606 καταγελάω, *katagelaō*, v. GK: *2860* [→ *2596+1070*]. to laugh at, mock:– laughed to scorn [3]

2607 καταγινώσκω, *kataginōskō*, v. GK: *2861* [→ *2596+1097*]. to condemn, convict; (pass.) to be in the wrong, condemned:– condemn [2], blamed [1]

2608 κατάγνυμι, *katagnymi*, v. GK: *2862* [→ *513, 3489; cf. 2596*]. to break:– brake [2], break [1], broken [1]

2609 κατάγω, *katagō*, v. GK: *2864* [→ *2596+71*]. to bring, bring down, land (on shore):– bring down [2], brought forth [1], brought [1], landed [1], landing [1], touched [1]

2610 καταγωνίζομαι, *katagōnizomai*, v. GK: *2865* [→ *2596+73*]. (mid.) to conquer, defeat, overcome:– subdued [1]

2611 καταδέω, *katadeō*, v. GK: *2866* [→ *2596+1210*]. to bandage, bind up:– bound up [1]

2612 κατάδηλος, *katadēlos*, a. GK: *2867* [→ *2596+1212*]. clear, quite plain:– evident [1]

2613 καταδικάζω, *katadikazō*, v. GK: *1463 & 2868* [→ *2596+1349*]. to judge, condemn:– condemned [4], condemn [1]

2614 καταδιώκω, *katadiōkō*, v. GK: *2870* [→ *2596+1377*]. to look for, search for:– followed after [1]

2615 καταδουλόω, *katadouloō*, v. GK: *2871* [→ *2596+1401*]. to make a slave, enslave:– bring into bondage [2]

2616 καταδυναστεύω, *katadynasteuō*, v. GK: *2872* [→ *2596+1410*]. (act.) to exploit, oppress, dominate; (pass.) to be under the power of, oppressed by:– oppressed [1], oppress [1]

2617 καταισχύνω, *kataischynō*, v. GK: *2875* [→ *2596+150*]. to dishonor, humiliate, shame, disappoint:– ashamed [6], confound [2], dishonoureth [2], confounded [1], maketh ashamed [1], shame [1]

2618 κατακαίω, *katakaiō*, v. GK: *2876* [→ *2596+2545*]. to burn up, consume:– burnt up [3], burnt [3], burn [3], burn up [1], burned [1], utterly burnt [1]

2619 κατακαλύπτω, *katakalyptō*, v. GK: *2877* [→ *2596+2572*]. (mid.) to cover (the head):– covered [2], cover [1]

2620 κατακαυχάομαι, *katakauchaomai*, v. GK: *1595 & 2878* [→ *2596+2744*]. to boast about; to triumph over:– boast against [1], boast [1], glory [1], rejoiceth against [1]

2621 κατάκειμαι, *katakeimai*, v. GK: *2879* [→ *2596+2749*]. to lie down (in bed); to recline (at dinner):– lay [5], sat at meat [2], kept (+*1909*) [1], lie [1], sat [1], sit at meat [1]

2622 κατακλάω, *kataklaō*, v. GK: *2880* [→ *2596+2806*]. to break in pieces:– brake [2]

2623 κατακλείω, *katakleiō*, v. GK: *1597 & 2881* [→ *2596+2808*]. to lock up:– shut up [2]

2624 κατακληροδοτέω, *kataklērodoteō*, v. GK: *2882 & 2883* [→ *2596+2819+3551*]. to parcel out by lot:– divided by lot [1]

2625 κατακλίνω, *kataklinō*, v. GK: *2884* [→ *2596+2827*]. (act.) to cause to sit; (pass.) to recline (at a table):– make sit down [1], sat at meat [1], sit down [1]

2626 κατακλύζω, *kataklyzō*, v. GK: *2885* [→ *2596+2830*]. (pass.) to be deluged, flooded:– overflowed [1]

2627 κατακλυσμός, *kataklysmos*, n. GK: *2886* [→ *2596+2830*]. flood, deluge:– flood [4]

2628 κατακολουθέω, *katakoloutheō*, v. GK: *2887* [→ *2596+190; cf. 1.3*]. to follow:– followed after [1], followed [1]

2629 κατακόπτω, *katakoptō*, v. GK: *2888* [→ *2596+2875*]. to cut:– cutting [1]

2630 κατακρημνίζω, *katakrēmnizō*, v. GK: *2889* [→ *2596+2910*]. to throw down a cliff:– cast down headlong [1]

2631 κατάκριμα, *katakrima*, n. GK: *2890* [→ *2596+2919*]. condemnation:– condemnation [3]

2632 κατακρίνω, *katakrinō*, v. GK: *2891* [→ *2596+2919*]. to condemn:– condemned [8], condemn [7], damned [2], condemnest [1], condemneth [1]

2633 κατάκρισις, *katakrisis*, n. GK: *2892* [→ *2596+2919*]. condemnation:– condemnation [1], condemn [1]

2634 κατακυριεύω, *katakyrieuō*, v. GK: *2894* [→ *2596+2962*]. to lord it over, gain dominion over, subdue; in some contexts there is an implication that this exercise of authority is harsh:– exercise dominion over [1], exercise lordship over [1], lords over [1], overcame [1]

2635 καταλαλέω, *katalaleō*, v. GK: *2895* [→ *2596+2980*]. to speak against, slander, accuse:– speak evil [2], speaketh evil [2], speak against [1]

2636 καταλαλιά, *katalalia*, n. GK: *2896* [→ *2596+2980*]. slander, defamation, evil speech:– backbitings [1], evil speakings [1]

2637 κατάλαλος, *katalalos*, a. GK: *2897* [→ *2596+2980*]. slanderous, defamatory:– backbiters [1]

2638 καταλαμβάνω, *katalambanō*, v. GK: *2898* [→ *2596+2983*]. to obtain, attain, take hold of; seize, overtake; (mid.) to grasp, understand, realize, find out:– apprehended [2], taken [2], apprehend [1], attained [1], come upon [1], comprehended [1], comprehend [1], found [1], obtain [1], overtake [1], perceived [1], perceive [1], taketh [1]

2639 καταλέγω, *katalegō*, v. GK: *2899* [→ *2596+3004*]. to put on a list, enroll, select:– taken into the number [1]

2640 κατάλειμμα, *kataleimma*, n. GK: *2900 & 5698* [→ *2596+3007*]. remnant:– remnant [1]

2641 καταλείπω, *kataleipō*, v. GK: *2901* [→ *2596+3007*]. to leave (behind), neglect; (pass.) remain (behind):– left [15], leave [6], forsaken [1], forsook [1], leaving [1], reserved [1]

2642 καταλιθάζω, *katalithazō*, v. GK: *2902* [→ *2596+3037*]. to stone to death:– stone [1]

2643 καταλλαγή, *katallagē*, n. GK: *2903* [→ *2596+236*]. reconciliation:– reconciliation [2], atonement [1], reconciling [1]

2644 καταλλάσσω, *katallassō*, v. GK: *2904* [→ *2596+236*]. to reconcile (among human beings or between human beings and God):– reconciled [5], reconciling [1]

2645 κατάλοιπος, *kataloipos*, a. GK: *2905* [→ *2596+3007*]. remaining, left over; (n.) remnant, the rest:– residue [1]

2646 κατάλυμα, *kataluma*, n. GK: *2906* [→ *2596+3089*]. guest room; inn:– guestchamber [2], inn [1]

2647 καταλύω, *katalyō*, v. GK: *2907* [→ *2596+3089*]. (tr.) throw down, abolish, destroy; (intr.) to be a guest, rest, find lodging:– destroy [6], thrown down [3], destroyest [2], come to nought [1], destroyed [1], dissolved [1], guest [1], lodge [1], overthrow [1]

2648 καταμανθάνω, *katamanthanō*, v. GK: *2908* [→ *2596+3129*]. notice carefully, consider closely:– consider [1]

2649 καταμαρτυρέω, *katamartyreō*, v. GK: *2909* [→ *2596+3144*]. to bring testimony against, bear testimony against:– witness against [4]

2650 καταμένω, *katamenō*, v. GK: *2910* [→ *2596+3306*]. to stay, live:– abode [1]

2651 καταμόνας, *katamonas*, a. GK: *2911* [→ *2596+3441*]. in private, alone:– alone [1]

2652 κατανάθεμα, *katanathema*, n. GK: *2873 & 2912* [→ *2596+331*]. curse, that which is under the ban (devoted exclusively to God):– curse [1]

2653 καταναθεματίζω, *katanathematizō*, v. GK: *2874 & 2913* [→ *2596+331*]. to (call down a) curse:– curse [1]

2654 καταναλίσκω, *katanaliskō*, v. GK: *2914* [→ *2596+303+259*]. to consume:– consuming [1]

2655 καταναρκάω, *katanarkaō*, v. GK: *2915* [→ *2596*]. to burden, be a burden:– burdensome [2], chargeable to [1]

2656 κατανεύω, *kataneuō*, v. GK: *2916* [→ *2596+3506*]. to signal, nod:– beckoned [1]

2657 κατανοέω, *katanoeō*, v. GK: *2917* [→ *2596+3563*]. to pay attention, notice, observe; consider, contemplate; this word has a strong implication that the attention paid is intense, and the contemplation is broad and thorough, resulting in complete understanding:– consider [4], behold [3], considered [2], beholdeth [1], beholding [1], considerest [1], discovered [1], perceived [1], perceivest [1]

2658 καταντάω, *katantaō*, v. GK: *2918* [→ *2596+473*]. to come to, arrive at; attain, reach:– came [8], come [3], attain [2]

2659 κατάνυξις, *katanyxis*, n. GK: *2919* [→ *2596+3572*]. stupor, bewilderment, unable to think:– slumber [1]

2660 κατανύσσομαι, *katanyssomai*, v. GK: *2920* [→ *2596+3572*]. to be pierced, stabbed:– pricked [1]

2661 καταξιόω, *kataxioō*, v. GK: *2921* [→ *2596+514*]. (pass.) to be counted worthy, considered worthy:– accounted worthy [2], counted worthy [2]

2662 καταπατέω, *katapateō*, v. GK: *2922* [→ *2596+3961*]. to trample (an action that can show disdain):– trodden under foot [2], trample [1], trodden down [1], trode upon [1]

2663 κατάπαυσις, *katapausis*, n. GK: *2923* [→ *2596+3973*]. rest:– rest [9]

2664 καταπαύω, *katapauō*, v. GK: *2924* [→ *2596+3973*]. to keep from, restrain; to give rest; to rest, cease:– ceased [1], given rest [1], restrained [1], rest [1]

2665 καταπέτασμα, *katapetasma*, n. GK: *2925* [→ *2596+4072*]. curtain:– vail [6]

2666 καταπίνω, *katapinō*, v. GK: *2927* [→ *2596+4095*]. to swallow, devour; (pass.) to be swallowed up, overwhelmed, drowned:– swallowed up [4], devour [1], drowned [1], swallow [1]

2667 καταπίπτω, *katapiptō*, v. GK: *2928* [→ *2596+4098*]. to fall down:– fallen down [1], fallen [1]

2668 καταπλέω, *katapleō*, v. GK: *2929* [→ *2596+4126*]. to sail to:– arrived [1]

2669 καταπονέω, *kataponeō*, v. GK: *2930* [→ *2596+4192*]. (pass.) to be oppressed, distressed:– oppressed [1], vexed [1]

2670 καταποντίζω, *katapontizō*, v. GK: *2931* [→ *2596*]. (pass.) to be drowned; to sink:– drowned [1], sink [1]

2671 κατάρα, *katara*, n. GK: *2932* [→ *2596+685*]. curse, imprecation:– curse [3], cursing [1], cursed [1]

2672 καταράομαι, *kataraomai*, v. GK: *2933* [→ *2596+685*]. (mid.) to curse:– curse [4], cursedst [1], cursed [1]

2673 καταργέω, *katargeō*, v. GK: *2934* [→ *2596+1.1+2041*]. to nullify, abolish, make ineffective; (pass.) cease, pass away:– done away [4], abolished [3], destroy [3], destroyed [2], become of no effect [1], bring to nought [1], ceased [1], come to nought [1], cumbereth [1], delivered [1], fail [1], loosed [1], made of none effect [1], make of none effect [1], make void [1], make without effect [1], put away [1], put down [1], vanish away [1]

2674 καταριθμέω, *katarithmeō*, v. GK: *2935* [→ *2596+706*]. (pass.) to be numbered among, belong to:– numbered [1]

2675 καταρτίζω, *katartizō*, v. GK: *2936* [→ *2596+737*]. to restore, put in order, mend; to make complete, equip, train; to prepare, ordain:– perfect [3], make perfect [2], mending [2], fitted [1], framed [1], perfected [1], perfectly joined together [1], prepared [1], restore [1]

2676 κατάρτισις, *katartisis*, n. GK: *2937* [→ *2596+737*]. perfection, completion:– perfection [1]

2677 καταρτισμός, *katartismos*, n. GK: *2938* [→ *2596+737*]. preparation, training, equipping:– perfecting [1]

2678 κατασείω, *kataseiō*, v. GK: *2939* [→ *2596+4579*]. to motion, signal by waving or shaking:– beckoned [2], beckoning [2]

2679 κατασκάπτω, *kataskaptō*, v. GK: *2940* [→ *2596+4626*]. (act.) to tear down; (pass.) to be ruined:– digged down [1], ruins [1]

2680 κατασκευάζω, *kataskeuazō*, v. GK: *2941* [→ *2596+4632*]. to prepare, make ready; to build, construct; to set up, arrange, furnish; there is a strong implication that the preparation is thorough, and a possible implication that the act of building may be for a special purpose:– prepare [3], builded [2], prepared [2], built [1], made [1], ordained [1], preparing [1]

2681 κατασκηνόω, *kataskēnoō*, v. GK: *2942* [→ *2596+4633*]. to perch, nest; to live, dwell:– lodge [2], lodged [1], rest [1]

2682 κατασκήνωσις, *kataskēnōsis*, n. GK: *2943* [→ *2596+4633*]. nest:– nests [1]

2683 κατασκιάζω, *kataskiazō*, v. GK: *2944* [→ *2596+4639*]. to overshadow:– shadowing [1]

2684 κατασκοπέω, *kataskopeō*, v. GK: *2945* [→ *2596+4648*]. to spy on, lie in wait for:– spy out [1]

2685 κατάσκοπος, *kataskopos*, n. GK: *2946* [→ *2596+4648*]. spy:– spies [1]

2686 κατασοφίζομαι, *katasophizomai*, v. GK: *2947* [→ *2596+4680*]. to deal treacherously with:– dealt subtilly with [1]

2687 καταστέλλω, *katastellō*, v. GK: *2948* [→ *2596+4724*]. (act.) to quiet, restrain:– appeased [1], quiet [1]

2688 κατάστημα, *katastēma*, n. GK: *2949* [→ *2596+2476*]. the way one lives, behavior:– behaviour [1]

2689 καταστολή, *katastolē*, n. GK: *2950* [→ *2596+4724*]. appearance, behavior:– apparel [1]

2690 καταστρέφω, *katastrephō*, v. GK: *2951* [→ *2596+4762*]. to overturn, upset:– overthrew [2]

2691 καταστρηνιάω, *katastrēniaō*, v. GK: *2952* [→ *2596+4764*]. to be filled with desires that conflict with dedication to someone:– wax wanton against [1]

2692 καταστροφή, *katastrophē*, n. GK: *2953* [→ *2596+4762*]. ruin, destruction:– overthrow [1], subverting [1]

2693 καταστρώννυμι, *katastrōnnymi*, v. GK: *2954* [→ *2596+4766*]. (pass.) to be scattered:– overthrown [1]

2694 κατασύρω, *katasyrō*, v. GK: *2955* [→ *2596+4951*]. to drag away (by considerable force):– hale [1]

2695 κατασφάττω, *katasphattō*, v. GK: *2956 & 2957* [→ *2596+4969*]. to kill, slaughter, strike down:– slay [1]

2696 κατασφραγίζω, *katasphragizō*, v. GK: *2958* [→ *2596+4973*]. (pass.) to be sealed up:– sealed [1]

2697 κατάσχεσις, *kataschesis*, n. GK: *2959* [→ *2596+2192*]. possession, taking into possession:– possession [2]

2698 κατατίθημι, *katatithēmi*, v. GK: *2960* [→ *2596+5087*]. (mid.) to grant a favor, do a favor:– do [1], laid [1], shew [1]

2699 κατατομή, *katatomē*, n. GK: *2961* [→ *2596+5114*]. mutilation, cutting away:– concision [1]

2700 κατατοξεύω, *katatoxeuō*, v. GK: *2962* [→ *2596+5115*]. to shoot down:– thrust through [1]

2701 κατατρέχω, *katatrechō*, v. GK: *2963* [→ *2596+5143*]. to run down:– ran down [1]

καταφάγω, *kataphagō*. See *2719*.

2702 καταφέρω, *katapherō*, v. GK: *2965* [→ *2596+5342*]. to cast (a vote) against; to bring (charges); (pass.) to be overwhelmed (by sleep):– fallen into [1], gave [1], sunk down [1]

2703 καταφεύγω, *katapheugō*, v. GK: *2966* [→ *2596+5343*]. to flee, take refuge:– fled for refuge [1], fled [1]

2704 καταφθείρω, *kataphtheirō*, v. GK: *2967* [→ *2596+5351*]. (pass.) to be depraved, corrupt:– corrupt [1], utterly perish [1]

2705 καταφιλέω, *kataphileō*, v. GK: *2968* [→ *2596+5384*]. to kiss:– kissed [5], kiss [1]

2706 καταφρονέω, *kataphroneō*, v. GK: *2969* [→ *2707*]. to despise, look down on, scorn, show contempt:– despise [7], despisest [1], despising [1]

2707 καταφρονητής, *kataphronētēs*, n. GK: *2970* [→ *2706*]. scoffer, despiser:– despisers [1]

2708 καταχέω, *katacheō*, v. GK: *2972* [→ *1632; cf. 2596*]. to pour out, pour down:– poured [2]

2709 καταχθόνιος, *katachthonios*, a. GK: *2973* [→ *2596*]. under the earth, subterranean; this may refer to the dead as a class of people, which generally are regarded as inhabiting the underworld. It is likely a more general term than the specific names for the abode of the dead: Hades, Gehenna, Tartaros, etc.:– under the earth [1]

2710 καταχράομαι, *katachraomai*, v. GK: *2974* [→ *2596+5530*]. to make full use of; to be engrossed in:– abuse [1], abusing [1]

2711 καταψύχω, *katapsychō*, v. GK: *2976* [→ *2596+5594*]. to cool off, refresh with:– cool [1]

2712 κατείδωλος, *kateidōlos*, a. GK: *2977* [→ *2596+1497*]. full of idols / images:– wholly given to idolatry (+*1510*) [1]

κατελεύθω, *kateleuthō*. See *2718*.

2713 κατέναντι, *katenanti*, adv. GK: *2978* [→ *2596+1725*]. ahead, before, in the sight of; opposite of:– over against [4], before [1]

κατενέγκω, *katenegkō*. See *2702*.

2714 κατενώπιον, *katenōpion*, adv.&pp.*. GK: *2979* [→ *2596+1722+3708*]. in the sight of, in the presence of; before:– before [2], before the presence [1], in the sight [1], sight [1]

2715 κατεξουσιάζω, *katexousiazō*, v. GK: *2980* [→ *1849; cf. 2596*]. to exercise authority over:– exercise authority upon [2]

2716 κατεργάζομαι, *katergazomai*, v. GK: *2981* [→ *2596+2041*]. to produce, accomplish, bring about, do:– worketh [7], wrought [6], do [3], done [2], working [2], causeth [1], doeth [1], perform [1], work out [1]

2717 , Not used in Strong's numbering system.

2718 κατέρχομαι, *katerchomai*, v. GK: *2982* [→ *2596+2064*]. to go down, come down:– came down [4], came [2], went down [2], come down [1], come [1], departed [1], descendeth [1], landed [1]

2719 κατεσθίω, *katesthiō*, v. GK: *2983 & 2984* [→ *2596+2068*]. to eat up, consume:– devour [6], devoured [3], devoured up [2], ate up [1], devoureth [1], eat up [1], eaten up [1]

2720 κατευθύνω, *kateuthynō*, v. GK: *2985* [→ *2596+2117*]. to guide, direct, lead:– direct [2], guide [1]

2721 κατεφίσταμαι, *katephistamai*, v. GK: *2987* [→ *2596+1909+2476*]. to make an attack upon, rise up against:– made insurrection against [1]

2722 κατέχω, *katechō*, v. GK: *2988* [→ *2596+2192*]. to hold back, suppress, restrain; hold fast, possess; (pass.) to be bound:– hold fast [3], hold [2], keep [2], had [1], held [1], keep in memory [1], letteth [1], made [1], possessed [1], possessing [1], retained [1], seize [1], stayed [1], take [1], withholdeth [1]

2723 κατηγορέω, *katēgoreō*, v. GK: *2989* [→ *2724, 2725*]. to accuse, bring charges against:– accuse [13], accused [6], accuseth [1], accusing [1], object [1]

2724 κατηγορία, *katēgoria*, n. GK: *2990* [→ *2723*]. (legal) charge, accusation:– accusation [2], accusation against [1], accused (+*1722*) [1]

2725 κατήγορος, *katēgoros*, n. GK: *2991 & 2992* [→ *2723*]. accuser:– accusers [6], accuser [1]

2726 κατήφεια, *katēpheia*, n. GK: *2993* [→ *2596+5316*]. gloominess, a feeling of dejection:– heaviness [1]

2727 κατηχέω, **katēcheō**, v. GK: 2994 [→ 2596+2279]. (act.) to instruct; (pass.) to be instructed, informed:– informed [2], instructed [2], instructed in [1], taught [1], teacheth [1], teach [1]

2728 κατιόω, **katioō**, v. GK: 2995 [→ 2596+2447]. (pass.) to become corroded, tarnished:– cankered [1]

2729 κατισχύω, **katischyō**, v. GK: 2996 [→ 2596+2479]. to overcome, prevail; to be able:– prevail against [1], prevailed [1]

2730 κατοικέω, **katoikeō**, v. GK: 2997 & 3001 [→ 2596+3624]. to live in, reside in, settle:– dwell [19], dwelt [11], dwelleth [7], inhabiters [3], dwellers [2], dwelling [2], dwellest [1], dwelling at [1], dwelt in [1]

2731 κατοίκησις, **katoikēsis**, n. GK: 2998 [→ 2596+3624]. where one lives, residence:– dwelling [1]

2732 κατοικητήριον, **katoikētērion**, n. GK: 2999 [→ 2596+3624]. dwelling place, home:– habitation [2]

2733 κατοικία, **katoikia**, n. GK: 3000 [→ 2596+3624]. where one lives, dwelling place:– habitation [1]

2734 κατοπτρίζω, **katoptrizō**, v. GK: 3002 [→ 2596+3708]. (mid.) to reflect or to look at, contemplate:– beholding as in a glass [1]

2735 κατόρθωμα, **katorthōma**, n. GK: 3003 [→ 2596+3717]. success, prosperity, good order:– very worthy deeds [1]

2736 κάτω, **katō**; or κατωτέρω, **katōterō**, adv. GK: 3004 & 3006 [→ 2596]. below; down, downward; bottom, under, lower:– down [5], beneath [3], bottom [2], under [1]

2737 κατώτερος, **katōteros**, a. GK: 3005 [→ 2596]. lower:– lower [1]

2738 καῦμα, **kauma**, n. GK: 3008 [→ 2545]. (scorching) heat:– heat [2]

2739 καυματίζω, **kaumatizō**, v. GK: 3009 & 3010 [→ 2545]. (act.) to scorch by heat, burn; (pass.) to be scorched, seared:– scorched [3], scorch [1]

2740 καῦσις, **kausis**, n. GK: 3011 [→ 2545]. burning:– burned [1]

2741 καυσόω, **kausoō**, v. GK: 3012 [→ 2545]. (pass.) to be consumed by fire, burned up:– fervent heat [2]

2742 καύσων, **kausōn**, n. GK: 3014 [→ 2545]. (scorching) heat, hot day:– heat [2], burning heat [1]

2743 καυτηριάζω, **kautēriazō**, v. GK: 3013 & 3015 [→ 2545]. (pass.) to be seared with a hot iron:– seared with a hot iron [1]

2744 καυχάομαι, **kauchaomai**, v. GK: 3016 [→ 2620, 2745, 2746]. to boast, brag about; to rejoice in, glory in; this can refer to proper or improper boasting, depending on the object of the boast:– glory [20], boast [6], rejoice [4], glorieth [2], makest boast [1], boasted [1], boasting [1], glorying [1], joy [1]

2745 καύχημα, **kauchēma**, n. GK: 3017 [→ 2744]. something to boast about, boasting; pride, joy:– rejoicing [4], glory [3], glorying [2], boasting [1], rejoice [1]

2746 καύχησις, **kauchēsis**, n. GK: 3018 [→ 2744]. boasting, pride; glorying in; this can refer to proper or improper boasting, depending on the object of the boast:– boasting [6], rejoicing [4], glorying [1], glory [1]

2747 Κεγχρεαί, **Kenchreai**, n.pr. GK: 3020. Cenchrea:– Cenchrea [3]

2748 Κεδρών, **Kedrōn**, n.pr. GK: 3022. Kidron:– Cedron [1]

2749 κεῖμαι, **keimai**, v. GK: 3023 [→ 345, 480, 606, 733, 1945, 2621, 2837, 2838, 2845, 2846, 3873, 4029, 4295, 4873]. to lay, lie, be laid, laid out; be destined, appointed:– laid [6], set [6], lying [4], lieth [2], appointed [1], is [1], laid up [1], lain [1], lay [1], lie [1], made [1], there [1]

2750 κειρία, **keiria**, n. GK: 3024 [→ 2751]. strip of linen, bandage, graveclothes:– graveclothes [1]

2751 κείρω, **keirō**, v. GK: 3025 [→ 1359, 1946, 1947, 2750, 2772, 2773, 2877]. (act.) to shear (another); (mid.) to have one's hair cut:– shorn [1], shearer [1]

2752 κέλευσμα, **keleusma**, n. GK: 3026 [→ 2753]. (loud) command, signal:– shout [1]

2753 κελεύω, **keleuō**, v. GK: 3027 [→ 2027, 2752]. to order, direct, command:– commanded [21], bid [1], commandest [1], commanding [1], commandment [1], command [1], gave commandment [1]

2754 κενοδοξία, **kenodoxia**, n. GK: 3029 [→ 2756+1391]. vain conceit, empty conceit, a state of pride that has no proper basis:– vainglory [1]

2755 κενόδοξος, **kenodoxos**, a. GK: 3030 [→ 2756+1391]. conceited, a state of pride that has no proper basis:– vain glory [1]

2756 κενός, **kenos**, a. GK: 3031 [→ 2754, 2755, 2757, 2758, 2761]. empty, empty-handed; by extension: vain, ineffective, useless, foolish:– vain [12], empty [4], in vain [2]

2757 κενοφωνία, **kenophōnia**, n. GK: 3032 [→ 2756+5456]. chatter, empty talk:– vain babblings [2]

2758 κενόω, **kenoō**, v. GK: 3033 [→ 2756]. to empty, deprive; (pass.) to be hollow, emptied, of no value:– in vain [1], made of no reputation [1], made of none effect [1], made void [1], make void [1]

2759 κέντρον, **kentron**, n. GK: 3034 [→ 1461, 1574]. sting, goad:– pricks [2], sting [2], stings [1]

2760 κεντυρίων, **kentyriōn**, n. GK: 3035. centurion, technically the commander of one hundred:– centurion [3]

2761 κενῶς, **kenōs**, adv. GK: 3036 [→ 2756]. without reason, in vain, to no purpose:– in vain [1]

2762 κεραία, **keraia**, n. GK: 3037 [→ 2768]. least stroke of a pen, projection [a portion of a letter of the alphabet], referring to the smallest detail of the Law:– tittle [2]

2763 κεραμεύς, **kerameus**, n. GK: 3038 [→ 2766]. potter:– potter's [2], potter [1]

2764 κεραμικός, **keramikos**, a. GK: 3039 [→ 2766]. pertaining to a potter:– potter [1]

2765 κεράμιον, **keramion**, n. GK: 3040 [→ 2766]. clay jar:– pitcher [2]

2766 κέραμος, **keramos**, n. GK: 3041 [→ 2763, 2764, 2765]. clay roof tile:– tiling [1]

2767 κεράννυμι, **kerannymi**, v. GK: 3042 [→ 185, 194, 4786]. to mix; (pass.) to be poured:– filled [1], fill [1], poured out [1]

2768 κέρας, **keras**, n. GK: 3043 [→ 2762, 2769]. horn, often a figure of power and position:– horns [10], horn [1]

2769 κεράτιον, **keration**, n. GK: 3044 [→ 2768]. carob pod:– husks [1]

 κεράω, **keraō**. See **2767**.

2770 κερδαίνω, **kerdainō**, v. GK: 2132 & 3045 [→ 2771]. to gain; make money; win over; spare:– gain [8], gained [5], get gain [1], win [1], won [1]

2771 κέρδος, **kerdos**, n. GK: 3046 [→ 146, 147, 2770]. gain, profit:– gain [2], lucre's [1]

2772 κέρμα, **kerma**, n. GK: 3047 [→ 2751]. coin:– money [1]

2773 κερματιστής, **kermatistēs**, n. GK: 3048 [→ 2751]. money exchanger:– changers of money [1]

2774 κεφάλαιον, **kephalaion**, n. GK: 3049 [→ 2776]. the (main) point; price, sum of money:– sum [2]

2775 κεφαλαιόω, **kephalaioō**, v. GK: 3050 & 3052 [→ 2776]. to strike on the head:– wounded in the head [1]

2776 κεφαλή, **kephalē**, n. GK: 3051 [→ 346, 607, 2774, 2775, 2777, 4030, 4344]. head (of a body); top (stone in a building); by extension: someone or something in the primary place, the point of origin:– head [57], heads [19]

2777 κεφαλίς, **kephalis**, n. GK: 3053 [→ 2776]. section of a scroll:– volume [1]

2778 κῆνσος, **kēnsos**, n. GK: 3056. (poll) tax:– tribute [4]

2779 κῆπος, **kēpos**, n. GK: 3057 [→ 2780]. garden, grove:– garden [5]

2780 κηπουρός, **kēpouros**, n. GK: 3058 [→ 2779]. gardener:– gardener [1]

2781 κηρίον, **kērion**, n. GK: 3059. wax, honeycomb:–

2782 κήρυγμα, **kērygma**, n. GK: 3060 [→ 2783]. preaching, proclamation, message, with a focus on the content of what is preached:– preaching [8]

2783 κῆρυξ, **kēryx**, n. GK: 3061 [→ 2782, 2784, 4296]. herald, preacher, proclaimer:– preacher [3]

2784 κηρύσσω, **kēryssō**, v. GK: 3062 [→ 2783]. to preach, proclaim, tell, often urging acceptance of the message, with warnings of consequences for not doing so:– preach [22], preached [20], preaching [8], published [3], preacheth [2],

publish [2], preacher [1], preachest [1], proclaimed [1], proclaiming [1]

2785 κῆτος, **kētos**, n. GK: 3063. huge fish:– whale's [1]

2786 Κηφᾶς, **Kēphas**, n.pr. GK: 3064. Cephas (Aramaic for Peter), "*rock*":– Cephas [6]

2787 κιβωτός, **kibōtos**, n. GK: 3066. ark, box, chest:– ark [6]

2788 κιθάρα, **kithara**, n. GK: 3067 [→ 2789, 2790]. harp, lyre:– harps [3], harp [1]

2789 κιθαρίζω, **kitharizō**, v. GK: 3068 [→ 2788]. to play the harp or lyre:– harped [1], harping [1]

2790 κιθαρῳδός, **kitharōdos**, n. GK: 3069 [→ 2788+5603]. harpist, lyre player:– harpers [2]

2791 Κιλικία, **Kilikia**, n.pr. GK: 3070. Cilicia:– Cilicia [8]

2792 κινάμωμον, **kinamōmon**, n. GK: 3072 & 3077. cinnamon:– cinnamon [1]

2793 κινδυνεύω, **kindyneuō**, v. GK: 3073 [→ 2794]. to be in danger:– in danger [2], in jeopardy [1], stand in jeopardy [1]

2794 κίνδυνος, **kindynos**, n. GK: 3074 [→ 2793]. danger, risk:– perils [8], peril [1]

2795 κινέω, **kineō**, v. GK: 3075 [→ 277, 2796, 3334, 4787]. to move, remove; to shake, stir up; (pass.) to be moved, removed; be aroused:– moved [2], move [2], wagging [2], mover [1], remove [1]

2796 κίνησις, **kinēsis**, n. GK: 3076 [→ 2795]. motion:– moving [1]

2797 Κίς, **Kis**, n.pr. GK: 3078. Kish, "*bow, power*":– Cis [1]

 κίχρημι, **kichrēmi**. See **5531**.

2798 κλάδος, **klados**, n. GK: 3080 [→ 2806]. branch, twig:– branches [9], branch [2]

2799 κλαίω, **klaiō**, v. GK: 3081 [→ 2805]. to weep, cry, wail, mourn:– weep [16], wept [11], weeping [9], weepest [2], bewail [1], weep (+4160) [1]

2800 κλάσις, **klasis**, n. GK: 3082 [→ 2806]. breaking:– breaking [2]

2801 κλάσμα, **klasma**, n. GK: 3083 [→ 2806]. broken piece, fragment:– fragments [7], broken [2]

2802 Κλαῦδα, **Klauda**; or Καῦδα, **Kauda**, n.pr. GK: 3007 & 3084 & 3085. Clauda, Cauda:– Clauda [1]

2803 Κλαυδία, **Klaudia**, n.pr. GK: 3086 [→ 2804]. Claudia, "[poss.] *lame*":– Claudia [1]

2804 Κλαύδιος, **Klaudios**, n.pr. GK: 3087 [→ 2803]. Claudius:– Claudius [3]

2805 κλαυθμός, **klauthmos**, n. GK: 3088 [→ 2799]. weeping, crying:– weeping [6], wailing [2], wept (+1096) [1]

2806 κλάω, **klaō**, v. GK: 3089 [→ 1575, 2622, 2798, 2800, 2801, 2814]. to break:– brake [9], broken [3], break [2], breaking [1]

2807 κλείς, **kleis**, n. GK: 3090 [→ 2808]. key:– key [4], keys [2]

2808 κλείω, **kleiō**, v. GK: 3091 [→ 608, 1576, 2623, 2807, 4788]. to close, shut, lock:– shut [10], shut up [3], shutteth [2], shutteth up [1]

2809 κλέμμα, **klemma**, n. GK: 3092 [→ 2813]. theft, stealing:– thefts [1]

2810 Κλεοπᾶς, **Kleopas**, n.pr. GK: 3093 [→ 2811+3962]. Cleopas, "*renowned father*":– Cleopas [1]

2811 κλέος, **kleos**, n. GK: 3094 [→ 2810]. credit, honor:– glory [1]

2812 κλέπτης, **kleptēs**, n. GK: 3095 [→ 2813]. thief:– thief [12], thieves [1]

2813 κλέπτω, **kleptō**, v. GK: 3096 [→ 2809, 2812, 2829]. steal:– steal [11], stole [2]

2814 κλῆμα, **klēma**, n. GK: 3097 [→ 2806]. branch (in context, vine branches):– branch [3], branches [1]

2815 Κλήμης, **Klēmēs**, n.pr. GK: 3098. Clement, "*mild*":– Clement [1]

2816 κληρονομέω, **klēronomeō**, v. GK: 3099 [→ 2819+3551]. to inherit, acquire; see also 2817:– inherit [14], heirs [1], heir [1], inheritance obtained [1], inherited [1]

Grk

2817 κληρονομία, *klēronomia*, n. GK: *3100* [→ *2819+3551*]. inheritance, transfer of property and possessions from one generation to another, usually within a family or clan and usually upon the death of the owner. This word often has an implication of a legitimate, historic right to the objects inherited. In some contexts this refers to salvation, an inheritance shared with Jesus Christ, the true heir:– inheritance [14]

2818 κληρονόμος, *klēronomos*, n. GK: *3101* [→ *2819+3551*]. heir, one who inherits:– heir [8], heirs [7]

2819 κλῆρος, *klēros*, n. GK: *3102* [→ *2624, 2816, 2817, 2818, 2820, 3490, 3647, 3648, 4345, 4789*]. (casting) lots; share, place, inheritance:– lots [6], inheritance [2], lot [2], part [2], heritage [1]

2820 κληρόω, *klēroō*, v. GK: *3103* [→ *2819*]. (pass.) to be chosen, appointed:– obtained an inheritance [1]

2821 κλῆσις, *klēsis*, n. GK: *3104* [→ *2564*]. call, calling; situation, station in life:– calling [10], vocation [1]

2822 κλητός, *klētos*, a. GK: *3105* [→ *2564*]. called, invited:– called [11]

2823 κλίβανος, *klibanos*, n. GK: *3106*. (fire of a) furnace, oven:– oven [2]

2824 κλίμα, *klima*, n. GK: *3107* [→ *2827*]. region:– regions [2], parts [1]

2825 κλίνη, *klinē*, n. GK: *3109* [→ *2827*]. bed, mat, stretcher:– bed [8], beds [1], tables [1]

2826 κλινίδιον, *klinidion*, n. GK: *3110* [→ *2827*]. bed, mat, stretcher (smaller and more temporary than a bed found in a home):– couch [2]

2827 κλίνω, *klinō*, v. GK: *3111* [→ *186, 347, 755, 1578, 2625, 2824, 2825, 2826, 2828, 4346, 4411*]. to bow down, lay down; to be over (late in the day):– lay [2], bowed down [1], bowed [1], far spent (+*2235*) [1], turned to flight [1], wear away [1]

2828 κλισία, *klisia*, n. GK: *3112* [→ *2827*]. group reclining for a meal:– company [1]

2829 κλοπή, *klopē*, n. GK: *3113* [→ *2813*]. theft, stealing:– thefts [2]

2830 κλύδων, *klydōn*, n. GK: *3114* [→ *2148, 2626, 2627, 2831*]. raging waters, waves:– raging [1], wave [1]

2831 κλυδωνίζομαι, *klydōnizomai*, v. GK: *3115* [→ *2830*]. to be tossed back and forth by waves:– tossed to and fro [1]

2832 Κλωπᾶς, *Klōpas*, n.pr. GK: *3116*. Clopas:– Cleophas [1]

2833 κνήθω, *knēthō*, v. GK: *3117* [cf. *1102*]. (pass.) to feel an itch:– itching [1]

2834 Κνίδος, *Knidos*, n.pr. GK: *3118*. Cnidus, "*age*":– Cnidus [1]

2835 κοδράντης, *kodrantēs*, n. GK: *3119*. penny, small Roman coin, about one-sixty-fourth of a denarius (a day's wage):– farthing [2]

2836 κοιλία, *koilia*, n. GK: *3120*. any and all internal organs, translated in context as: belly, stomach, womb, etc.; by extension: the source of feelings and emotions. "The fruit of the womb" means "a child.":– belly [11], womb [11], wombs [1]

2837 κοιμάω, *koimaō*, v. GK: *3121* [→ *2749*]. (pass.) to fall asleep, sleep; die:– sleep [4], slept [3], asleep [2], fallen asleep [2], fell asleep [2], sleeping [2], dead [1], fell on sleep [1], sleepeth [1]

2838 κοίμησις, *koimēsis*, n. GK: *3122* [→ *2749*]. (noun) sleep:– taking of rest [1]

2839 κοινός, *koinos*, a. GK: *3123* [→ *2840, 2841, 2842, 2843, 2844, 4790, 4791*]. common; (ceremonially) unclean, impure, unholy:– common [7], unclean [2], defiled [1], unholy [1]

2840 κοινόω, *koinoō*, v. GK: *3124* [→ *2839*]. to make (ceremonially) unclean, impure; to defile:– defile [6], defileth [5], call common [2], polluted [1], unclean [1]

2841 κοινωνέω, *koinōneō*, v. GK: *3125* [→ *2839*]. to share in, participate in:– partakers [2], partaker [2], communicated with [1], communicate [1], distributing [1], made partakers [1]

2842 κοινωνία, *koinōnia*, n. GK: *3126* [→ *2839*]. fellowship, the close association between persons, emphasizing what is common between them; by extension: participation, sharing, contribution, gift, the outcome of such close relationships:– fellowship [12], communion [4], communicate [1], communication [1], contribution [1], distribution [1]

2843 κοινωνικός, *koinōnikos*, a. GK: *3127* [→ *2839*]. willing to share, generous:– willing to communicate [1]

2844 κοινωνός, *koinōnos*, n. GK: *3128* [→ *2839*]. partner, participant, one who joins in with another in some enterprise or activity, in business or ministry:– partakers [4], partner [2], companions [1], fellowship [1], partaker [1], partners [1]

2845 κοίτη, *koitē*, n. GK: *3130* [→ *2749*]. (marriage) bed; conception; sexual immorality:– bed [2], chambering [1], conceived [1]

2846 κοιτών, *koitōn*, n. GK: *3131* [→ *2749*]. bedroom; trusted personal servant, chamberlain:– chamberlain (+*1909+3588*) [1]

2847 κόκκινος, *kokkinos*, a. GK: *3132* [→ *2848*]. scarlet, (bright) red; in some contexts, cloth that is scarlet or (bright) red (Rev 18:12,16):– scarlet [4], scarlet coloured [1], scarlet colour [1]

2848 κόκκος, *kokkos*, n. GK: *3133* [→ *2847*]. seed, kernel of grain:– grain of seed [5], corn [1], grain [1]

2849 κολάζω, *kolazō*, v. GK: *3134* [→ *2967*]. to punish:– punished [1], punish [1]

2850 κολακεία, *kolakeia*, n. GK: *3135*. flattery:– flattering [1]

2851 κόλασις, *kolasis*, n. GK: *3136* [→ *2967*]. punishment:– punishment [1], torment [1]

2852 κολαφίζω, *kolaphizō*, v. GK: *3139*. to strike with the fists, beat, torment; (pass.) receive a beating, be brutally treated:– buffeted [3], buffet [2]

2853 κολλάω, *kollaō*, v. GK: *3140* [→ *4347*]. (mid.) to join, associate with, cling to; (pass.) to be united, stuck to, piled up; to stay near, follow; to be hired out:– joined to [2], join [2], clave [1], cleaveth on [1], cleave [1], join to [1], joined [1], keep company [1]

2854 κολλούριον, *kollourion*, n. GK: *3141*. eye salve:– eyesalve [1]

2855 κολλυβιστής, *kollybistēs*, n. GK: *3142*. money exchanger:– moneychangers [2], changers' [1]

2856 κολοβόω, *koloboō*, v. GK: *3143* [→ *2967*]. to cut short, shorten:– shortened [4]

2857 Κολοσσαί, *Kolossai*, n.pr. GK: *3138 & 3145* [→ *2858*]. Colosse, "*punishment*":– Colosse [1]

2858 Κολοσσαεύς, *Kolossaeus*, n.pr.g. GK: *3137 & 3144* [→ *2857*]. Colossian:– Colossians [1]

2859 κόλπος, *kolpos*, n. GK: *3146*. lap area: side, bosom, chest; bay:– bosom [5], creek [1]

2860 κολυμβάω, *kolymbaō*, v. GK: *3147* [→ *1579, 2861*]. to swim:– swim [1]

2861 κολυμβήθρα, *kolymbēthra*, n. GK: *3148* [→ *2860*]. pool:– pool [5]

2862 κολωνία, *kolōnia*, n. GK: *3149*. Roman colony:– colony [1]

2863 κομάω, *komaō*, v. GK: *3150* [→ *2864*]. to have long hair:– have long hair [2]

2864 κόμη, *komē*, n. GK: *3151* [→ *2863*]. (long) hair:– hair [1]

2865 κομίζω, *komizō*, v. GK: *3152* [→ *2889*]. (act.) to bring; (mid.) to receive (what is due), reward, be repaid:– receive [6], received [3], brought [1], receiving [1]

2866 κομψότερον, *kompsoteron*, adv.comp. GK: *3153* [→ *2889*]. better:– began to amend (+*2192*) [1]

2867 κονιάω, *koniaō*, v. GK: *3154* [→ *2868*]. (pass.) to be whitewashed:– whited [2]

2868 κονιορτός, *koniortos*, n. GK: *3155* [→ *2867+3730*]. dust:– dust [5]

2869 κοπάζω, *kopazō*, v. GK: *3156* [→ *2875*]. to die down, abate:– ceased [3]

2870 κοπετός, *kopetos*, n. GK: *3157* [→ *2875*]. mourning, sorrowing, lamentation:– lamentation [1]

2871 κοπή, *kopē*, n. GK: *3158* [→ *2875*]. defeat, cutting down:– slaughter [1]

2872 κοπιάω, *kopiaō*, v. GK: *3159* [→ *2875*]. to work, labor, give effort; to become tired, grow weary:– labour [8], laboured [5], bestowed labour [3], laboureth [2], toil [2], labouring [1], toiled [1], wearied [1]

2873 κόπος, *kopos*, n. GK: *3160* [→ *2875*]. labor, work; bother, trouble, difficulty:– labour [8], labours [5], trouble (+*3930*) [4], troubleth (+*3930*) [1], weariness [1]

2874 κοπρία, *kopria*, n. GK: *3161 & 3162 & 3163*. manure pile, rubbish pile:– dung (+*906*) [1], dunghill [1]

2875 κόπτω, *koptō*, v. GK: *3164* [→ *348, 609, 677, 695, 1464, 1465, 1581, 2123, 2629, 2869, 2870, 2871, 2872, 2873, 2974, 4297, 4298, 4348, 4349, 4350*]. to cut; (mid.) to mourn, beat one's breast:– bewailed [2], cut down [2], lamented [1], lament [1], mourn [1], wail [1]

2876 κόραξ, *korax*, n. GK: *3165*. raven, crow:– ravens [1]

2877 κοράσιον, *korasion*, n. GK: *3166* [→ *2751*]. (little) girl:– damsel [6], maid [1]

2878 κορβᾶν, *korban*; or κορβανᾶς, *korbanas*, n. GK: *3167 & 3168*. Corban, a gift dedicated to God, temple treasury:– Corban [1], treasury [1]

2879 Κόρε, *Kore*, n.pr. GK: *3169*. Korah, "*shaven, bald*":– Core [1]

2880 κορέννυμι, *korennymi*, v. GK: *3170*. (pass.) to be filled to the full, have enough:– eaten enough (+*5160*) [1], full [1]

2881 Κορίνθιος, *Korinthios*, n.pr.g. GK: *3171* [→ *2882*]. Corinthian:– Corinthians [4]

2882 Κόρινθος, *Korinthos*, n.pr. GK: *3172* [→ *2881*]. Corinth, "*decoration*":– Corinth [6], Corinthus [1]

2883 Κορνήλιος, *Kornēlios*, n.pr. GK: *3173*. Cornelius, "*of a horn*":– Cornelius [10]

2884 κόρος, *koros*, n. GK: *3174*. cor (dry measure between ten and twelve bushels):– measures [1]

2885 κοσμέω, *kosmeō*, v. GK: *3175* [→ *2889*]. to make beautiful, decorate, dress; trim (a lamp); (pass.) to put in order; be adorned, decorated, beautifully dressed:– adorned [3], garnished [3], adorn [2], garnish [1], trimmed [1]

2886 κοσμικός, *kosmikos*, a. GK: *3176* [→ *2889*]. earthly, worldly:– worldly [2]

2887 κόσμιος, *kosmios*, a. GK: *3177 & 3178* [→ *2889*]. respectable, honorable:– good behaviour [1], modest [1]

2888 κοσμοκράτωρ, *kosmokratōr*, n. GK: *3179* [→ *2889+2904*]. (pl.) powers of the world:– rulers [1]

2889 κόσμος, *kosmos*, n. GK: *3180* [→ *1101, 1580, 2865, 2866, 2885, 2886, 2887, 2888, 4792*]. world: earth, world system, whole universe; adornment. In some contexts, the world is simply the place where people live, in other contexts (especially in John), the world is a system opposed to God:– world [185], adorning [1], world's [1]

2890 Κούαρτος, *Kouartos*, n.pr. GK: *3181*. Quartus, "*fourth [born]*":– Quartus [1]

2891 κοῦμι, *koumi*, l.[v.]. GK: *3182 & 3183*. koumi (Aramaic: stand up):– cumi [1]

2892 κουστωδία, *koustōdia*, n. GK: *3184*. guard:– watch [3]

2893 κουφίζω, *kouphizō*, v. GK: *3185*. to lighten, make lighter:– lightened [1]

2894 κόφινος, *kophinos*, n. GK: *3186*. basket of various sizes and considered typical of the Jews:– baskets [6]

2895 κράββατος, *krabbatos*, n. GK: *3187 & 3188*. bed, (sleeping) mat:– bed [9], beds [1], couches [1]

2896 κράζω, *krazō*, v. GK: *3189* [→ *349, 2905, 2906*]. call out, cry out, shout, exclaim:– cried [30], cried out [13], crying [6], crieth [3], crying out [3], cry out [2], crieth out [1], cry [1], out [1]

2897 κραιπάλη, *kraipalē*, n. GK: *3190*. dissipation:– surfeiting [1]

2898 κρανίον, *kranion*, n. GK: *3191* [→ *603*]. skull:– skull [3], Calvary [1]

2899 κράσπεδον, *kraspedon*, n. GK: *3192*. edge, border, hem; tassel:– border [2], hem [2], borders [1]

2900 κραταιός, *krataios*, a. GK: *3193* [→ *2904*]. mighty, powerful:– mighty [1]

2901 κραταιόω, *krataioō*, v. GK: *3194* [→ *2904*]. (pass.) to be strong, become strong:– waxed strong [2], strengthened [1], strong [1]

2902 κρατέω, *krateō*, v. GK: *3195* [→ *2904*]. to arrest, seize into custody; to take, grab, hold onto, obtain; (pass.) to be kept from, held:– took [10], hold [5], hold fast [3], holding [3], laid hold on [3], lay hold on [3], take [3], held [2], holden [2], laid [2], fast [1], holdest fast [1], holdeth [1], kept [1], laid hands on [1], laid hold upon [1], lay hands on [1], lay hold upon [1], obtained [1], retained [1], retain [1]

2903 κράτιστος, *kratistos*, a. GK: *3196* [→ *2904*]. most excellent, "your Excellency":– most excellent [2], most noble [2]

2904 κράτος, *kratos*, n. GK: *3197* [→ *192, 193, 1466, 1467, 1468, 2888, 2900, 2901, 2902, 2903, 2908, 2909, 3841, 4031; cf. 2594*]. power, strength:– power [5], dominion [4], mightily (+*2596*) [1], mighty [1], strength [1]

2905 κραυγάζω, *kraugazō*, v. GK: *3198* [→ *2896*]. to shout, cry out:– cried out [3], cried [3], cry [1]

2906 κραυγή, *kraugē*, n. GK: *3199* [→ *2896*]. crying out, shouting, verbal brawling:– cry [3], crying [2], clamour [1]

2907 κρέας, *kreas*, n. GK: *3200*. meat:– flesh [2]

2908 κρεῖσσον, *kreisson*, a.neut. of a form of *2909*. GK: *3201* [→ *2904*]. better, superior, greater:– better [1]

2909 κρείττων, *kreittōn*, a. GK: *3202* [→ *2904*]. better, superior, greater:– better [17], best [1], better than [1]

2910 κρεμάννυμι, *kremannymi*, v. GK: *3203* [→ *1582, 2630, 2911*]. to hang on, hang upon:– hanged [4], hang [2], hangeth [1]

2911 κρημνός, *krēmnos*, n. GK: *3204* [→ *2910*]. steep bank, cliff:– steep place [3]

2912 Κρής, *Krēs*, n.pr.g. GK: *3205* [→ *2914*]. Cretan:– Cretians [2], Cretes [1]

2913 Κρήσκης, *Krēskēs*, n.pr. GK: *3206*. Crescens, "*increasing*":– Crescens [1]

2914 Κρήτη, *Krētē*, n.pr. GK: *3207* [→ *2912*]. Crete:– Crete [5]

2915 κριθή, *krithē*, n. GK: *3208* [→ *2916*]. barley; barley flour was used in the preparation of cheaper kinds of bread:– barley [1]

2916 κρίθινος, *krithinos*, a. GK: *3209* [→ *2915*]. made of barley (flour):– barley [2]

2917 κρίμα, *krima*, n. GK: *3210* [→ *2919*]. judgment, condemnation; sentence, punishment:– judgment [12], damnation [7], condemnation [5], avenged (+*2919*) [1], condemned [1], go to law (+*2192*) [1], judgments [1]

2918 κρίνον, *krinon*, n. GK: *3211*. lily:– lilies [2]

2919 κρίνω, *krinō*, v. GK: *3212* [→ *87, 178, 350, 351, 470, 505, 610, 611, 612, 799, 843, 1252, 1253, 1341, 1469, 1506, 1948, 2631, 2632, 2633, 2917, 2920, 2922, 2923, 2924, 4299, 4793, 4942, 5271, 5272, 5273; cf. 1506*]. to decide, consider, as preferring one thing over another or determining the correctness of a matter; by extension: to judge, pass judgment on, condemn in a legal sense:– judge [45], judged [26], judgeth [9], determined [7], judgest [6], called in question [2], condemned [2], judging [2], avenged (+*2917*) [1], concluded [1], condemneth [1], condemning [1], condemn [1], damned [1], decreed [1], go to law [1], goeth to law [1], ordained [1], sentence [1], sue at the law [1], thought [1]

2920 κρίσις, *krisis*, n. GK: *3213* [→ *2919*]. judgment (human or divine), justice, the concept of determining the correctness of a matter; negatively: punishment, condemnation:– judgment [39], condemnation [3], damnation [3], accusation [2], judgments [2]

2921 Κρίσπος, *Krispos*, n.pr. GK: *3214*. Crispus, "*curled*":– Crispus [2]

2922 κριτήριον, *kritērion*, n. GK: *3215* [→ *2919*]. court of law; legal dispute, lawsuit:– judge [1], judgment seats [1], judgments [1]

2923 κριτής, *kritēs*, n. GK: *3216* [→ *2919*]. judge:– judge [13], judges [4]

2924 κριτικός, *kritikos*, a. GK: *3217* [→ *2919*]. able to discern or judge:– discerner [1]

2925 κρούω, *krouō*, v. GK: *3218*. to knock (on a gate or door):– knock [4], knocketh [3], knocked [1], knocking [1]

2926 κρύπτη, *kryptē*, n. GK: *3219* [→ *2928*]. hidden place:– *untranslated* [1]

2927 κρυπτός, *kryptos*, a. GK: *3220 & 3224 & 3226* [→ *2928*]. hidden, unseen, secret:– secret [10], hidden [3], hid [3], secrets [2], inwardly (+*1722+3588*) [1], secret place [1]

2928 κρύπτω, *kryptō*, v. GK: *3221* [→ *613, 614, 1470, 2926, 2927, 2931, 4032*]. to hide:– hid [10], hide [2], hidden [1], hideth [1], kept secret [1], secretly [1]

2929 κρυσταλλίζω, *krystallizō*, v. GK: *3222* [→ *2930*]. to be clear as crystal:– clear as crystal [1]

2930 κρύσταλλος, *krystallos*, n. GK: *3223* [→ *2929*]. rock crystal; some translate "ice":– crystal [2]

2931 κρυφῇ, *kryphē*, adv. GK: *3225* [→ *2928*]. in secret:– secret [1]

2932 κτάομαι, *ktaomai*, v. GK: *3227* [→ *2933, 2934, 2935*]. to get, gain, buy; take along; to control:– possess [3], purchased [2], obtained [1], provide [1]

2933 κτῆμα, *ktēma*, n. GK: *3228* [→ *2932*]. wealth, possessions; piece of property, field:– possessions [3], possession [1]

2934 κτῆνος, *ktēnos*, n. GK: *3229* [→ *2932*]. (domestic) animal: donkey, horse, cattle:– beasts [3], beast [1]

2935 κτήτωρ, *ktētōr*, n. GK: *3230* [→ *2932*]. (land) owner:– possessors [1]

2936 κτίζω, *ktizō*, v. GK: *3231* [→ *2937, 2938, 2939*]. to create; (ptcp) Creator:– created [12], creator [1], made [1], make [1]

2937 κτίσις, *ktisis*, n. GK: *3232* [→ *2936*]. creation, created thing, creature; governmental institution:– creature [11], creation [6], building [1], ordinance [1]

2938 κτίσμα, *ktisma*, n. GK: *3233* [→ *2936*]. creature, created thing:– creatures [2], creature [2]

2939 κτίστης, *ktistēs*, n. GK: *3234* [→ *2936*]. Creator:– creator [1]

2940 κυβεία, *kybeia*, n. GK: *3235*. cunning, craftiness, trickery:– sleight [1]

2941 κυβέρνησις, *kybernēsis*, n. GK: *3236* [→ *2942*]. administration; derived from a Greek verb meaning "to steer a ship, to guide," not found in the NT:– governments [1]

2942 κυβερνήτης, *kybernētēs*, n. GK: *3237* [→ *2941*]. sea captain, pilot:– master [1], shipmaster [1]

2943 κυκλόθεν, *kyklothen*, adv. GK: *3239* [→ *2945*]. (all) around; from all sides:– round about [3], about [1]

κυκλός, *kuklos*. See *2945*.

2944 κυκλόω, *kykloō*, v. GK: *3238 & 3240* [→ *2945*]. to surround: gather around, march around:– compassed about [2], came round about [1], compassed [1], stood round about [1]

2945 κύκλῳ, *kyklō*, adv. GK: *3241* [→ *2943, 2944, 4033*]. all around, in a circle, surrounding:– round about [7]

2946 κύλισμα, *kylisma*, n. GK: *3242 & 3243* [→ *2947*]. wallowing, rolling:– wallowing [1]

2947 κυλίω, *kyliō*, v. GK: *3244* [→ *617, 2946, 4351*]. (mid.) to roll around:– wallowed [1]

2948 κυλλός, *kyllos*, a. GK: *3245*. crippled, maimed:– maimed [4]

2949 κῦμα, *kyma*, n. GK: *3246* [→ *616, 1471*]. waves, surf:– waves [5]

2950 κύμβαλον, *kymbalon*, n. GK: *3247*. cymbal:– cymbal [1]

2951 κύμινον, *kyminon*, n. GK: *3248*. cummin:– cummin [1]

2952 κυνάριον, *kynarion*, n. GK: *3249* [→ *2965*]. (little or domesticated) dog:– dogs [4]

2953 Κύπριος, *Kyprios*, n.pr.g. GK: *3250* [→ *2954*]. from Cyprus:– Cyprus [3]

2954 Κύπρος, *Kypros*, n.pr. GK: *3251* [→ *2953*]. Cyprus, "*copper*":– Cyprus [5]

2955 κύπτω, *kyptō*, v. GK: *3252* [→ *352, 3879, 4794*]. to stoop down, bend down:– stooped [2], stoop down [1]

2956 Κυρηναῖος, *Kyrēnaios*, n.pr.g. GK: *3254* [→ *2957*]. from Cyrene:– Cyrenian [2], of Cyrene [2], Cyrene [1], Cyrenians [1]

2957 Κυρήνη, *Kyrēnē*, n.pr. GK: *3255* [→ *2956*]. Cyrene, "*wall*":– Cyrene [1]

2958 Κυρήνιος, *Kyrēnios*, n.pr. GK: *3256 & 3260*. Quirinius:– Cyrenius [1]

2959 κυρία, *kyria*, n. GK: *3257* [→ *2962*]. lady (female "lord"):– lady [2]

2960 κυριακός, *kyriakos*, a. GK: *3258* [→ *2962*]. pertaining to the Lord, the Lord's:– Lord's [2]

2961 κυριεύω, *kyrieuō*, v. GK: *3259* [→ *2962*]. to lord over; to be master of, have authority over, one who rules or exercises authority; note in some contexts there is an implication that the authority exercised is harsh:– Lord/lord [1], dominion over [1],

exercise lordship over [1], hath dominion over [1], have dominion over [1], lords [1], over [1]

2962 κύριος, *kyrios*, n. GK: *3261* [→ *2634, 2959, 2960, 2961, 2963; cf. 2964*]. lord, master. This can be a title of address to a person of higher status, "lord, sir"; a master of property or slaves; or a NT translation of the Hebrew 136 "Lord" or 3068 "LORD," that is "Yahweh," the proper name of God in the OT:– Lord/lord [703], Lord's/lord's [15], sir [11], masters [8], master [4], lords [3], God [1], masters' [1], owners [1], sirs [1]

2963 κυριότης, *kyriotēs*, n. GK: *3262* [→ *2962*]. authority, dominion, power, lordship:– dominion [2], dominions [1], government [1]

2964 κυρόω, *kyroō*, v. GK: *3263* [→ *208, 4300; cf. 2962*]. to reaffirm; to establish a covenant, ratify, validate:– confirmed [1], confirm [1]

2965 κύων, *kyōn*, n. GK: *3264* [→ *2952*]. dog:– dogs [4], dog [1]

2966 κῶλον, *kōlon*, n. GK: *3265*. dead body, corpse:– carcases [1]

2967 κωλύω, *kōlyō*, v. GK: *3266* [→ *209, 1254, 2849, 2851, 2856; cf. 1422*]. to hinder, stop, restrain, forbid; oppress; (pass.) to be prevented, kept from:– forbid [9], forbad [3], forbidding [3], forbidden [1], forbiddeth [1], hindered [1], hinder [1], kept from [1], let [1], not suffered [1], withstand [1]

2968 κώμη, *kōmē*, n. GK: *3267* [→ *2969, 2970*]. village, town:– village [15], town [8], villages [7], towns [3]

2969 κωμόπολις, *kōmopolis*, n. GK: *3268* [→ *2968+4172*]. village, market town:– towns [1]

2970 κῶμος, *kōmos*, n. GK: *3269* [→ *2968*]. orgy, revelry, carousing:– revellings [2], rioting [1]

2971 κώνωψ, *kōnōps*, n. GK: *3270*. gnat, mosquito:– gnat [1]

2972 Κῶς, *Kōs*, n.pr. GK: *3271*. Cos, "*summit*":– Cos [1]

2973 Κωσάμ, *Kōsam*, n.pr.k. GK: *3272*. Cosam, "*diviner*":– Cosam [1]

2974 κωφός, *kōphos*, a. GK: *3273* [→ *2875*]. unable to talk or speak, mute; deaf:– dumb [8], deaf [5], speechless [1]

2975 λαγχάνω, *lanchanō*, v. GK: *3275*. to choose by lot, decide by lot; receive (by lot or divine will):– obtained [2], cast lots [1], lot [1]

2976 Λάζαρος, *Lazaros*, n.pr. GK: *3276*. Lazarus, "*one whom God helps*":– Lazarus [15]

2977 λάθρα, *lathra*, adv. GK: *3277* [→ *2990*]. secretly, quietly:– privily [3], secretly [1]

2978 λαῖλαψ, *lailaps*, n. GK: *3278*. storm, hurricane, whirlwind:– storm [2], tempest [1]

2979 λακτίζω, *laktizō*, v. GK: *3280*. to kick:– kick [2]

2980 λαλέω, *laleō*, v. GK: *3281* [→ *215, 216, 412, 1255, 1583, 2635, 2636, 2637, 2981, 3424, 4354, 4814*]. to speak, talk:– speak [103], spake [72], spoken [33], speaketh [23], speaking [11], told [10], talked [8], said [7], say [6], preached [4], speakest [4], uttered [3], saith [2], tell [2], preaching [1], preach [1], talkest [1], talketh [1], talking [1], talk [1], utter [1]

2981 λαλιά, *lalia*, n. GK: *3282* [→ *2980*]. speech, a way of speaking, language:– speech [3], saying [1]

2982 λαμά, *lama*; or λεμά, *lema*, l.[pp.+p.inter.]. GK: *3283 & 3316*. lama (Hebrew: why?):– lama [1]

2983 λαμβάνω, *lambanō*, v. GK: *3284* [→ *353, 354, 423, 482, 484, 618, 678, 1187, 1949, 2124, 2125, 2126, 2638, 3028, 3335, 3336, 3880, 4301, 4355, 4356, 4380, 4381, 4382, 4815, 4838, 4843, 4878, 5274*]. to take, receive; (pass.) to be received, selected:– receive [61], received [57], took [55], take [32], receiveth [15], taken [12], taketh [4], taking [4], caught [3], had [2], obtain [2], took up [2], acceptest [1], accepteth [1], amazed (+*1611*) [1], attained [1], began [1], brought [1], call [1], came into room (+*1240*) [1], came [1], do [1], forgotten (+*3024*) [1], have [1], held [1], receiving [1]

2984 Λάμεχ, *Lamech*, n.pr. GK: *3285*. Lamech:– Lamech [1]

λαμμᾶ, *lamma*. See *2982*.

2985 λαμπάς, *lampas*, n. GK: *3286* [→ *2989*]. lamp, lantern, torch:– lamps [6], lamp [1], lights [1], torches [1]

2986 λαμπρός, *lampros*, a. GK: *3287* [→ *2989*]. bright, shining, splendorous, elegant:– bright [2], goodly [2], white [2], clear [1], gay [1], gorgeous [1]

2987 λαμπρότης, *lamprotēs*, n. GK: *3288* [→ *2989*]. brightness:– brightness [1]

2988 λαμπρῶς, *lamprōs*, adv. GK: *3289* [→ *2989*]. in luxury, splendidly:– sumptuously [1]

2989 λάμπω, *lampō*, v. GK: *3290* [→ *1584, 2985, 2986, 2987, 2988, 4034*]. to give light, shine:– shine [3], shined [2], giveth light [1], shineth [1]

2990 λανθάνω, *lanthanō*, v. GK: *3291* [→ *225, 226, 227, 228, 230, 1585, 1950, 1953, 2977, 3024*]. to keep secret, escape notice, be hidden:– hid [3], ignorant [2], hidden [1], unawares [1]

2991 λαξευτός, *laxeutos*, a. GK: *3292*. cut in rock:– hewn in stone [1]

2992 λαός, *laos*, n. GK: *3295* [→ *745, 2993, 2994, 3008, 3009, 3010, 3011, 3531, 3532*]. people, crowd; often denotes the people of God (either Israel or, by extension, the Christian church):– people [139], people's [2], peoples [2]

2993 Λαοδίκεια, *Laodikeia*, n.pr. GK: *3293* [→ *2992+1349*]. Laodicea:– Laodicea [6]

2994 Λαοδικεύς, *Laodikeus*, n.pr.g. GK: *3294* [→ *2992+1349*]. Laodicean:– Laodiceans [2]

2995 λάρυγξ, *larynx*, n. GK: *3296*. throat:– throat [1]

2996 Λασαία, *Lasaia*, n.pr. GK: *3297 & 3298*. Lasea:– Lasea [1]

2997 λάσκω, *laskō*, v. GK: *3279 & 3299*. to burst open:– burst asunder [1]

2998 λατομέω, *latomeō*, v. GK: *3300*. to cut, hew (rock):– hewn out [1], hewn [1]

2999 λατρεία, *latreia*, n. GK: *3301* [→ *1496, 1495, 3000*]. worship, ministry, service (to God):– service [4], divine service [1]

3000 λατρεύω, *latreuō*, v. GK: *3302* [→ *2999*]. to serve, minister (in religious duties):– serve [13], worship [3], served [2], service [1], serving [1], worshippers [1]

3001 λάχανον, *lachanon*, n. GK: *3303*. plant, herb, vegetable:– herbs [4]

3002 Λεββαῖος, *Lebbaios*, n.pr. GK: *3304* [cf. *2280*]. Lebbaeus, *"[one near to] my heart"*:– Lebbeus [1]

3003 λεγιών, *legiōn*, n. GK: *3305*. legion, technically an army unit of 6,000 with 6,000 support troops. Twice in the NT it is the proper name of a collective of demons (Mk 5:9; Lk 8:30):– legion [3], legions [1]

3004 λέγω, *legō*, v. GK: *3306* [→ *35, 148, 249, 356, 357, 379, 471, 483, 485, 550, 626, 627, 945, 1075, 1076, 1256, 1258, 1260, 1261, 1351, 1586, 1588, 1589, 1677, 1757, 1951, 2036, 2046, 2127, 2128, 2129, 2312', 2551, 2639, 3048, 3049, 3050, 3051, 3052, 3053, 3054, 3055, 3056, 3150, 3151, 3473, 3670, 3881, 3884, 4086, 4180, 4277, 4280, 4302, 4691, 4758, 4816, 4817, 4883, 4899, 5378, 5542, 5573; cf. 3670*]. say, said, the most general term for speaking in the NT, translated contextually with more specific words such as say, tell; ask, answer:– said [995], saying [403], say [398], saith [298], tell [59], spake [50], spoken [45], called [39], speak [38], sayest [21], told [18], commanded [6], speaketh [6], calleth [4], call [4], bade [3], bid [3], callest [3], command [3], named [2], speakest [2], answer [1], asked [1], biddeth [1], boasting [1], bring word [1], describeth [1], giving out [1], grant [1], made [1], put forth [1], saidst [1], sayings [1], seen [1], shew [1], speaking [1], telleth [1], uttered [1]

3005 λεῖμμα, *leimma*, n. GK: *3307* [→ *3007*]. remnant:– remnant [1]

3006 λεῖος, *leios*, a. GK: *3308*. smooth, level:– smooth [1]

3007 λείπω, *leipō*, v. GK: *3309* [→ *88, 89, 413, 620, 1257, 1459, 1587, 1952, 1954, 2640, 2641, 2645, 3005, 3062, 3063, 3064, 4035, 5275, 5277*]. to lack, fall short:– wanting [3], destitute [1], lackest [1], lack [1]

3008 λειτουργέω, *leitourgeō*, v. GK: *3310* [→ *2992+2041*]. to perform religious duties; serve:– ministered [1], ministering [1], minister [1]

3009 λειτουργία, *leitourgia*, n. GK: *3311* [→ *2992+2041*]. religious service, ceremony; service, ministry, help:– service [3], ministry [2], ministration [1]

3010 λειτουργικός, *leitourgikos*, a. GK: *3312* [→ *2992+2041*]. ministering, engaged in holy service:– ministering [1]

3011 λειτουργός, *leitourgos*, n. GK: *3313* [→ *2992+2041*]. servant, minister, one who cares for (another), often with a focus on a specific task or duty, which can be practical or spiritual:– ministers [2], minister [2], ministered [1]

3012 λέντιον, *lention*, n. GK: *3317*. towel, likely made of linen:– towel [2]

3013 λεπίς, *lepis*, n. GK: *3318* [→ *3014, 3015, 3016*]. scale, flake:– scales [1]

3014 λέπρα, *lepra*, n. GK: *3319* [→ *3013*]. leprosy:– leprosy [4]

3015 λεπρός, *lepros*, a. GK: *3320* [→ *3013*]. leprous; (n.) leper:– lepers [5], leper [4]

3016 λεπτός, *leptos*, a. GK: *3321* [→ *3013*]. very small copper coin, worth about 1/128th of a denarius (a day's wage):– mites [2], mite [1]

3017 Λευί, *Leui*, n.pr. GK: *3322* [→ *3018, 3019, 3020*]. Levi, "[perhaps] *wild cow* or *person pledged for a debt or vow*":– Levi [5]

3018 Λευίς, *Leuis*, n.pr. GK: *3323* [→ *3017*]. Levi, "[perhaps] *wild cow* or *person pledged for a debt or vow*":– Levi [3]

3019 Λευίτης, *Leuitēs*, n.pr.g. GK: *3324* [→ *3017*]. Levite:– Levite [2], Levites [1]

3020 Λευιτικός, *Leuitikos*, a.pr.g. GK: *3325* [→ *3017*]. Levitical:– Levitical [1]

3021 λευκαίνω, *leukainō*, v. GK: *3326* [→ *3022*]. to bleach, whiten:– made white [1], white [1]

3022 λευκός, *leukos*, a. GK: *3328* [→ *3021*]. white; bright, gleaming:– white [25]

3023 λέων, *leōn*, n. GK: *3329*. lion:– lion [6], lions [3]

3024 λήθη, *lēthē*, n. GK: *3330* [→ *2990*]. forgetfulness:– forgotten (+*2983*) [1]

3025 ληνός, *lēnos*, n. GK: *3332* [→ *5276*]. winepress:– winepress [4], winepress (+*3631*) [1]

3026 λῆρος, *lēros*, n. GK: *3333*. nonsense, idle talk:– idle tales [1]

3027 λῃστής, *lēstēs*, n. GK: *3334*. robber, bandit; rebel, revolutionary; this word is derived from the Greek verb, "to practice robbery or piracy," not found in the NT:– thieves [8], thief [3], robbers [2], robber [2]

3028 λῆμψις, *lēmpsis*, n. GK: *3331 & 3335* [→ *2983*]. receiving:– receiving [1]

3029 λίαν, *lian*, adv. GK: *3336*. very much, greatly, completely:– exceeding [5], greatly [4], chiefest [2], great while [1], sore [1], very [1]

3030 λίβανος, *libanos*, n. GK: *3337* [→ *3031*]. frankincense, incense, an aromatic resinous gum:– frankincense [2]

3031 λιβανωτός, *libanōtos*, n. GK: *3338* [→ *3030*]. censer (bowl for burning incense):– censer [2]

3032 Λιβερτῖνος, *Libertinos*, n.pr. GK: *3339*. Freedman, "*Freedman*":– Libertines [1]

3033 Λιβύη, *Libyē*, n.pr. GK: *3340*. Libya:– Libya [1]

3034 λιθάζω, *lithazō*, v. GK: *3342* [→ *3037*]. to stone:– stoned [4], stone [4]

3035 λίθινος, *lithinos*, a. GK: *3343* [→ *3037*]. made of stone:– stone [2], of stone [1]

3036 λιθοβολέω, *lithoboleō*, v. GK: *3344* [→ *3037+906*]. to throw stones:– stoned [5], stonest [2], cast stones [1], stone [1]

3037 λίθος, *lithos*, n. GK: *3345* [→ *2642, 3034, 3035, 3036, 3038, 5555*]. stone, boulder; this can refer to stone as a material or substance, and to a stone as a piece of rock. A "precious stone" is a "gem.":– stone [37], stones [15], another[S] [4], stumblingstone (+*4348*) [2], millstone (+*3457*) [1], stone's [1]

3038 λιθόστρωτος, *lithostrōtos*, a. GK: *3346* [→ *3037+4766*]. (n.) stone pavement; translated in the NIV as a place name:– pavement [1]

3039 λικμάω, *likmaō*, v. GK: *3347*. to crush:– grind to powder [2]

3040 λιμήν, *limēn*, n. GK: *3348* [→ *2568, 3041*]. harbor:– haven [2]

3041 λίμνη, *limnē*, n. GK: *3349* [→ *3040*]. lake:– lake [10]

3042 λιμός, *limos*, n. GK: *3350*. hunger, famine, starvation:– famine [4], famines [3], hunger [3], dearth [2]

3043 λίνον, *linon*, n. GK: *3351*. linen (garment); wick of a lamp:– flax [1], linen [1]

3044 Λίνος, *Linos*, n.pr. GK: *3352*. Linus:– Linus [1]

3045 λιπαρός, *liparos*, a. GK: *3353*. costly, rich; (n.) riches:– dainty [1]

3046 λίτρα, *litra*, n. GK: *3354*. (Roman) pound (about 12 oz. or 327 gr.):– pound [2]

3047 λίψ, *lips*, n. GK: *3355*. southwest:– south west [1]

3048 λογεία, *logeia*, n. GK: *3356* [→ *3004*]. collection:– collection [1], gatherings [1]

3049 λογίζομαι, *logizomai*, v. GK: *3357* [→ *3004*]. to credit, count, reckon; regard, think, consider:– think [7], imputed [5], counted [4], reckoned [4], accounted [2], reckon [2], suppose [2], accounting [1], account [1], conclude [1], count [1], despised (+*1519+3762*) [1], esteemeth [1], imputeth [1], impute [1], imputing [1], laid to charge [1], numbered [1], reasoned [1], thinkest [1], thinketh [1], thought [1]

3050 λογικός, *logikos*, a. GK: *3358* [→ *3004*]. spiritual, logical:– reasonable [1], word [1]

3051 λόγιον, *logion*, n. GK: *3359* [→ *3004*]. (pl.) words, sayings, oracles:– oracles [4]

3052 λόγιος, *logios*, a. GK: *3360* [→ *3004*]. learned, eloquent:– eloquent [1]

3053 λογισμός, *logismos*, n. GK: *3361* [→ *3004*]. thought; argument, reasoning:– imaginations [1], thoughts [1]

3054 λογομαχέω, *logomacheō*, v. GK: *3362* [→ *3004+3163*]. to quarrel about words:– strive about words [1]

3055 λογομαχία, *logomachia*, n. GK: *3363* [→ *3004+3163*]. quarrel about words:– strifes of words [1]

3056 λόγος, *logos*, n. GK: *3364* [→ *3004*]. word, spoken or written, often with a focus on the content of a communication (note the many contextual translations in NIV); matter, thing. "The Word" is a title of Christ (Jn 1:1), emphasizing his own deity and communication of who God is and what he is like:– word [175], words [48], saying [34], sayings [16], account [8], speech [8], matter [4], utterance [4], communication [2], things [2], thing [2], work [2], as concerning (+*1519*) [1], cause [1], communications [1], doctrine [1], fame [1], given exhortation (+*3870*) [1], have to do [1], intent [1], mouth [1], none (+*3762*) [1], preaching [1], question [1], reason (+*2596*) [1], reason [1], reckoneth (+*4868*) [1], rumour [1], say [1], shew [1], speaker [1], talk [1], tidings [1], treatise [1], word spoken [1], word's [1]

3057 λόγχη, *lonchē*, n. GK: *3365*. spear, lance:– spear [1]

3058 λοιδορέω, *loidoreō*, v. GK: *3366* [→ *3060*]. to insult, curse:– reviled [3], revilest [1]

3059 λοιδορία, *loidoria*, n. GK: *3367* [→ *3060*]. insult, slander, verbal abuse:– railing [2], speak reproachfully [1]

3060 λοίδορος, *loidoros*, n. GK: *3368* [→ *486, 3058, 3059*]. slanderer, verbal abuser:– railer [1], revilers [1]

3061 λοιμός, *loimos*, n.&a. GK: *3369*. pestilence; troublemaker, public menace:– pestilences [2], pestilent [1]

3062 λοιπός, *loipos*, a. GK: *3370* [→ *3063*]. remaining, left over, the rest; in some contexts a marker for a conclusion, "finally," or an adverb of time, "from now on," or "henceforth":– other [17], rest [12], others [6], finally (+*3588*) [4], remnant [4], now (+*3588*) [2], besides [1], finally [1], from henceforth (+*3588*) [1], furthermore [1], henceforth (+*3588*) [1], henceforth [1], moreover (+*1161+3739*) [1], remaineth (+*1510+3588*) [1], remain [1], residue [1], then [1]

3063 λοιπόν, *loipon*, a.neut.s. of *3062*. GK: *3370* [→ *3007, 3062, 3064*]. remaining, left over, the rest; see *3062*:–

3064 λοιποῦ, *loipou*, a.gen.s. of *3062*. GK: *3370* [→ *3063*]. remaining, left over, the rest; see *3062*:–

3065 Λουκᾶς, *Loukas*, n.pr. GK: *3371* [→ *3066*]. Luke:– Lucas [2], Luke [2]

3066 Λούκιος, *Loukios*, n.pr. GK: *3372* [→ *3065*]. Lucius:– Lucius [2]

3067 λουτρόν, *loutron*, n. GK: *3373* [→ *3068*]. washing, bath:– washing [2]

3068 λούω, *louō*, v. GK: *3374* [→ *628, 3067*]. to wash, have a bath:– washed [6]

3069 Λύδδα, **Lydda**, n.pr. GK: *3375*. Lydda:– Lydda [3]

3070 Λυδία, **Lydia**, n.pr. GK: *3376*. Lydia:– Lydia [2]

3071 Λυκαονία, **Lykaonia**, n.pr. GK: *3377* [→ *3072*]. Lycaonia:– Lycaonia [1]

3072 Λυκαονιστί, **Lykaonisti**, adv.pr. GK: *3378* [→ *3071*]. in (the) Lycaonian (language):– in the speech of Lycaonia [1]

3073 Λυκία, **Lykia**, n.pr. GK: *3379*. Lycia:– Lycia [1]

3074 λύκος, **lykos**, n. GK: *3380*. wolf:– wolves [4], wolf [2]

3075 λυμαίνω, **lymainō**, v. GK: *3381*. to destroy, damage, ruin:– made havock [1]

3076 λυπέω, **lypeō**, v. GK: *3382* [→ *3077*]. (act.) to cause sorrow, grief; (pass.) to be sorrowful, sad, distressed:– sorrowful [6], grieved [5], made sorry [5], sorry [3], sorrowed [2], caused grief [1], grieve [1], heaviness [1], make sorry [1], sorrow [1]

3077 λύπη, **lypē**, n. GK: *3383* [→ *253, 3076, 4036, 4818*]. sorrow, grief, pain:– sorrow [11], heaviness [2], grief [1], grievous [1], grudgingly (+*1537*) [1]

3078 Λυσανίας, **Lysanias**, n.pr. GK: *3384*. Lysanias:– Lysanias [1]

3079 Λυσίας, **Lysias**, n.pr. GK: *3385*. Lysias:– Lysias [3]

3080 λύσις, **lysis**, n. GK: *3386* [→ *3089*]. divorce:– loosed [1]

3081 λυσιτελέω, **lysiteleō**, v. GK: *3387* [→ *3089+5056*]. to be advantageous, (imper. form) it is better:– better [1]

3082 Λύστρα, **Lystra**, n.pr. GK: *3388*. Lystra:– Lystra [6]

3083 λύτρον, **lytron**, n. GK: *3389* [→ *3089*]. ransom, the price of release, thus making redemption possible:– ransom [2]

3084 λυτρόω, **lytroō**, v. GK: *3390* [→ *3089*]. to redeem, free a slave by paying a ransom; from the base meaning of slave redemption in the marketplace comes the figure of sinners redeemed by God from slavery to sin and death:– redeemed [2], redeem [1]

3085 λύτρωσις, **lytrōsis**, n. GK: *3391* [→ *3089*]. redemption, ransoming, releasing:– redemption [2], redeemed (+*4160*) [1]

3086 λυτρωτής, **lytrōtēs**, n. GK: *3392* [→ *3089*]. deliverer, redeemer:– deliverer [1]

3087 λυχνία, **lychnia**, n. GK: *3393* [→ *3088*]. lampstand (not a candlestick):– candlesticks [6], candlestick [6]

3088 λύχνος, **lychnos**, n. GK: *3394* [→ *3087*]. lamp, usually of clay or metal, with olive oil to fuel its wick (not a candle):– candle [8], light [5], lights [1]

3089 λύω, **lyō**, v. GK: *3395* [→ *179, 255, 359, 360, 487, 629, 630, 1262, 1590, 1955, 1956, 2646, 2647, 3080, 3081, 3083, 3084, 3085, 3086, 3885, 3886*]. to loose, release, untie; to break, destroy:– loose [15], loosed [10], broken [4], unloose [3], destroy [2], dissolved [2], loosing [2], break [1], broken down [1], broken up [1], melt [1], put off from [1]

3090 Λωΐς, **Lōis**, n.pr. GK: *3396*. Lois, "[perhaps] *more desirable, better*":– Lois [1]

3091 Λώτ, **Lōt**, n.pr. GK: *3397*. Lot:– Lot [3], Lot's [1]

3092 Μάαθ, **Maath**, n.pr. GK: *3399*. Maath, "*to be small*":– Maath [1]

3093 Μαγδαλά, **Magdala**, n.pr. GK: *3400 & 3401* [cf. *3094*]. Magdala:– Magdala [1]

3094 Μαγδαληνή, **Magdalēnē**, n.pr.g. GK: *3402* [cf. *3093*]. Magdalene, "*from Magdala*":– Magdalene [12]

3095 μαγεία, **mageia**, n. GK: *3404 & 3406* [→ *3096*]. magic:– sorceries [1]

3096 μαγεύω, **mageuō**, v. GK: *3405* [→ *3095, 3097*]. to practice sorcery, magic:– used sorcery [1]

3097 μάγος, **magos**, n. GK: *3407* [→ *3096*]. sorcerer; (pl.) Magi:– wise men [4], sorcerer [2]

3098 Μαγώγ, **Magōg**, n.pr. GK: *3408*. Magog, "[perhaps] *land of Gog*":– Magog [1]

3099 Μαδιάμ, **Madiam**, n.pr. GK: *3409*. Midian:– Madian [1]

3100 μαθητεύω, **mathēteuō**, v. GK: *3411* [→ *3129*]. (act./tr.) to teach; to make a disciple; (pass./intr.) to become a disciple:– disciple [1], instructed [1], taught [1], teach [1]

3101 μαθητής, **mathētēs**, n. GK: *3412* [→ *3129*]. disciple, student, follower; a committed learner and follower, in the NT usually of Jesus Christ:– disciples [240], disciple [27], disciples' [1]

3102 μαθήτρια, **mathētria**, n. GK: *3413* [→ *3129*]. (female) disciple, student, follower:– disciple [1]

3103 Μαθουσαλά, **Mathousala**, n.pr. GK: *3417*. Methuselah, "*man of the javelin*":– Mathusala [1]

3104 Μαϊνάν, **Mainan**, n.pr. GK: *3418*. Mainan:– Menan [1]

3105 μαίνομαι, **mainomai**, v. GK: *3419* [→ *1693, 3130, 3132*]. to rave, to be insane, out of one's mind, to think or reason in an irrational manner manifested by erratic actions or lack of reasonable speech:– mad [4], beside thyself [1]

3106 μακαρίζω, **makarizō**, v. GK: *3420* [→ *3107, 3108*]. to call blessed; to consider blessed:– call blessed [1], count happy [1]

3107 μακάριος, **makarios**, a. GK: *3421* [→ *3106*]. blessed (receiving God's favor), fortunate, good (in a position of favor), happy (feelings associated with receiving God's favor):– blessed [44], happy [5], happier [1]

3108 μακαρισμός, **makarismos**, n. GK: *3422* [→ *3106*]. blessedness, joy:– blessedness [3]

3109 Μακεδονία, **Makedonia**, n.pr. GK: *3423* [→ *3110*]. Macedonia:– Macedonia [24]

3110 Μακεδών, **Makedōn**, n.pr.g. GK: *3424* [→ *3109*]. Macedonian, "*from Macedonia*":– Macedonia [3], Macedonian [1], of Macedonia [1]

3111 μάκελλον, **makellon**, n. GK: *3425*. meat market, food market:– shambles [1]

3112 μακράν, **makran**, adv.&pp.*. GK: *3426* [→ *3372*]. far away, distant, long way off:– far [4], afar off (+*1519*) [1], afar off [1], far hence [1], far off [1], good way off [1], great way [1]

3113 μακρόθεν, **makrothen**, adv. GK: *3427* [→ *3372*]. from a distance, from far away:– afar off (+*575*) [5], afar [5], afar off [3], from far [1]

3114 μακροθυμέω, **makrothymeō**, v. GK: *3428* [→ *3372+2372*]. to have patience; to be patient; to exhibit internal and external control in a difficult circumstance, which control could exhibit itself by delaying an action:– patient [3], have patience [2], bear long [1], hath long patience [1], longsuffering [1], patiently endured [1], suffereth long [1]

3115 μακροθυμία, **makrothymia**, n. GK: *3429* [→ *3372+2372*]. patience, forbearance, internal and external control in a difficult circumstance, which control could exhibit itself by delaying an action:– longsuffering [12], patience [2]

3116 μακροθύμως, **makrothymōs**, adv. GK: *3430* [→ *3372+2372*]. patiently:– patiently [1]

3117 μακρός, **makros**, a. GK: *3431* [→ *3372*]. lengthy, long; distant, far away:– long [3], far [2]

3118 μακροχρόνιος, **makrochronios**, a. GK: *3432* [→ *3372+5550*]. pertaining to having a long life:– live long (+*1510*) [1]

3119 μαλακία, **malakia**, n. GK: *3433* [→ *3120*]. sickness, ailment:– disease [3]

3120 μαλακός, **malakos**, a. GK: *3434* [→ *3119*]. fine, soft; (n.) male prostitute, a male homosexual who is the passive sex partner:– soft [3], effeminate [1]

3121 Μαλελεήλ, **Maleleēl**, n.pr. GK: *3435*. Mahalalel, "*praise of God [El]*":– Maleleel [1]

3122 μάλιστα, **malista**, adv.super. GK: *3436* [→ *3123*]. especially:– specially [5], especially [4], chiefly [2], most [1]

3123 μᾶλλον, **mallon**, adv.comp. GK: *3437* [→ *3122*]. more, more than; rather, instead:– more [42], rather [34], better (+*2570*) [1], far (+*4183*) [1], more than [1], much more [1], much [1], than (+*2228*) [1]

3124 Μάλχος, **Malchos**, n.pr. GK: *3438*. Malchus, "*king*":– Malchus [1]

3125 μάμμη, **mammē**, n. GK: *3439*. grandmother:– grandmother [1]

3126 μαμωνᾶς, **mamōnas**, n. GK: *3440*. wealth, assets:– mammon [4]

3127 Μαναήν, **Manaēn**, n.pr. GK: *3441*. Manaen, "*comforter*":– Manaen [1]

3128 Μανασσῆς, **Manassēs**, n.pr. GK: *3442*. Manasseh, "*one that makes to forget*":– Manasses [3]

3129 μανθάνω, **manthanō**, v. GK: *3443* [→ *261, 2648, 3100, 3101, 3102, 4827*]. to learn, study, be instructed:– learn [13], learned [10], learning [1], understood [1]

3130 μανία, **mania**, n. GK: *3444* [→ *3105*]. insanity, madness:– make mad (+*1519+4062*) [1]

3131 μάννα, **manna**, n. GK: *3445*. manna, a food given by God to the generation of the Exodus: "the bread of heaven":– manna [5]

3132 μαντεύομαι, **manteuomai**, v. GK: *3446* [→ *3105*]. to fortune-tell, divine:– soothsaying [1]

3133 μαραίνω, **marainō**, v. GK: *3447* [→ *262, 263*]. (pass.) to fade away, disappear:– fade away [1]

3134 μαράνα θά, **marana tha**, i.[n.+v.]. GK: *3448*. maranatha (Aramaic: "Come, Lord!"):– Maranatha [1]

3135 μαργαρίτης, **margaritēs**, n. GK: *3449*. pearl:– pearls [7], pearl [2]

3136 Μάρθα, **Martha**, n.pr. GK: *3450*. Martha, "*lady [female lord]*":– Martha [13]

3137 Μαρία, **Maria**; or Μαριάμ, **Mariam**, n.pr. GK: *3451 & 3452*. Mary, "[perhaps] *beloved* or *plump*":– Mary [54]

3138 Μάρκος, **Markos**, n.pr. GK: *3453*. Mark, "*[Latin] large hammer*":– Mark [5], Marcus [3]

3139 μάρμαρος, **marmaros**, n. GK: *3454*. marble:– marble [1]

μάρτυρ, **martur**. See *3144*.

3140 μαρτυρέω, **martyreō**, v. GK: *3455* [→ *3144*]. to testify, give testimony; commend, speak well of, vouch for:– bear witness [15], testify [8], bear record [7], testified [6], bare record [5], bear witness [4], testifieth [4], beareth witness [1], witnessed [3], borne witness [2], gave testimony [2], obtained a good report [2], barest witness [1], bearest record [1], gave [1], give witness [1], hath good report [1], having a good report [1], obtained witness [1], of honest report [1], testifying [1], testimony [1], well reported of [1], well reported [1], witnesses [1], witnesseth [1], witnessing [1], witness [1]

3141 μαρτυρία, **martyria**, n. GK: *3456* [→ *3144*]. testimony, evidence; (good) reputation:– witness [15], testimony [14], record [7], report [1]

3142 μαρτύριον, **martyrion**, n. GK: *3457* [→ *3144*]. testimony, proof:– testimony [15], witness [4], testified [1]

3143 μαρτύρομαι, **martyromai**, v. GK: *3458* [→ *3144*]. to testify, declare; to insist on, urge:– testify [2], charged [1], take to record [1]

3144 μάρτυς, **martys**, n. GK: *3459* [→ *267, 1263, 1957, 2649, 3140, 3141, 3142, 3143, 4303, 4828, 4901, 5576, 5577, 5575*]. witness, testimony; martyr (one who witnessed unto death):– witnesses [21], witness [8], martyr [2], record [2], martyrs [1]

3145 μασσάομαι, **massaomai**, v. GK: *3460 & 3462* [→ *3146*]. to gnaw, bite:– gnawed [1]

3146 μαστιγόω, **mastigoō**, v. GK: *3463* [→ *631, 1591, 3145, 3147, 3148*]. to flog, whip, scourge; to punish, chastise:– scourge [5], scourged [1], scourgeth [1]

3147 μαστίζω, **mastizō**, v. GK: *3464* [→ *3146*]. to flog, scourge:– scourge [1]

3148 μάστιξ, **mastix**, n. GK: *3465* [→ *3146*]. flogging device, whip; suffering; disease, sickness:– plagues [2], plague [2], scourgings [1], scourging [1]

3149 μαστός, **mastos**, n. GK: *3410 & 3461 & 3466*. breast, chest:– paps [3]

3150 ματαιολογία, **mataiologia**, n. GK: *3467* [→ *3152+3004*]. meaningless talk, empty talk:– vain jangling [1]

3151 ματαιολόγος, **mataiologos**, a. GK: *3468* [→ *3152+3004*]. (n.) idle talker:– vain talkers [1]

3152 μάταιος, **mataios**, a. GK: *3469* [→ *3150, 3151, 3153, 3154, 3155*]. worthless, futile, useless, empty:– vain [5], vanities [1]

3153 ματαιότης, **mataiotēs**, n. GK: *3470* [→ *3152*]. emptiness, futility, frustration:– vanity [3]

3154 ματαιόω, **mataioō**, v. GK: *3471* [→ *3152*]. (pass.) to become futile, given over to worthlessness:– vain [1]

3155 μάτην, **matēn**, adv. GK: *3472* [→ *3152*]. in vain, to no end:– in vain [1]

3156 Ματθαῖος, **Matthaios**; or Μαθθαῖος, **Maththaios**, n.pr. GK: *3414 & 3473*. Matthew, "*gift of Yahweh*":– Matthew [5]

3157 Ματθάν, **Matthan**, n.pr. GK: *3474*. Matthan, "*gift*":– Matthan [2]

Grk

3158 Ματθάτ, *Matthat*; or Μαθθάτ, *Maththat*, n.pr. GK: *3415 & 3475*. Matthat, "*gift*":– Matthat [2]

3159 Ματθίας, *Matthias*, n.pr. GK: *3416 & 3476*. Matthias, "*gift of Yahweh*":– Matthias [2]

3160 Ματταθά, *Mattatha*, n.pr. GK: *3477*. Mattatha, "*gift*":– Mattatha [1]

3161 Ματταθίας, *Mattathias*, n.pr. GK: *3478*. Mattathias, "*gift of Yahweh*":– Mattathias [2]

3162 μάχαιρα, *machaira*, n. GK: *3479* [→ *3163*]. (short) sword:– sword [23], swords [6]

3163 μάχη, *machē*, n. GK: *3480* [→ *269, 1264, 2313, 2314, 2341, 2371, 3054, 3055, 3162, 3164*]. quarrel, conflict, fighting:– fightings [2], strifes [1], strivings [1]

3164 μάχομαι, *machomai*, v. GK: *3481* [→ *3163*]. to fight, quarrel, argue:– strove [2], fight [1], strive [1]

3165 μέ, *me*, p.pers.acc. of *1473*. GK: *1609* [→ *1473*]. me; see *1473*:–

3166 μεγαλαυχέω, *megalaucheō*, v. GK: *3482* [→ *3173*]. to become proud, boast:– boasteth [1]

3167 μεγαλεῖος, *megaleios*, a. GK: *3483* [→ *3173*]. (pl. n.) wonders, mighty deeds:– great things [1], wonderful works [1]

3168 μεγαλειότης, *megaleiotēs*, n. GK: *3484* [→ *3173*]. majesty, greatness, grandeur:– magnificence [1], majesty [1], mighty power [1]

3169 μεγαλοπρεπής, *megaloprepēs*, a. GK: *3485* [→ *3173+4241*]. majestic, magnificent:– excellent [1]

3170 μεγαλύνω, *megalynō*, v. GK: *3486* [→ *3173*]. to glorify, regard highly, praise, exalt; to lengthen, expand:– magnified [3], magnify [2], enlarged [1], enlarge [1], shewed great [1]

3171 μεγάλως, *megalōs*, adv. GK: *3487* [→ *3173*]. greatly:– greatly [1]

3172 μεγαλωσύνη, *megalōsynē*, n. GK: *3488* [→ *3173*]. majesty:– majesty [3]

3173 μέγας, *megas*, a. GK: *3489* [→ *3166, 3167, 3168, 3169, 3171, 3172, 3174, 3175, 3176, 3185, 3186, 3187*]. great; spatially: large; of quantity or degree: loud, intense, violent; of time: long (time); of position: great, important:– great [148], loud [33], greatest [2], high [2], large [2], come to years [1], exceedingly [1], great ones [1], great one [1], great things [1], mighty [1], sore [1], strong [1]

3174 μέγεθος, *megethos*, n. GK: *3490* [→ *3173*]. greatness:– greatness [1]

3175 μεγιστάν, *megistan*, n. GK: *3491* [→ *3173*]. great man, prince, high official:– great men [2], lords [1]

3176 μέγιστος, *megistos*, a.super. GK: *3492* [→ *3173*]. very great:– exceeding great [1]

3177 μεθερμηνεύω, *methermēneuō*, v. GK: *3493* [→ *3326+2059*]. to translate, give the meaning:– interpreted [6], by interpretation [1]

3178 μέθη, *methē*, n. GK: *3494* [→ *3184*]. drunkenness:– drunkenness [3]

3179 μεθίστημι, *methistēmi*; or μεθιστάνω, *methistanō*, v. GK: *3495 & 3496* [→ *3326+2476*]. to move, remove; bring, lead astray; (pass.) to lose, be discharged:– put out [1], removed [1], removed [1], translated [1], turned away [1]

3180 μεθοδεία, *methodeia*, n. GK: *3497* [→ *3326+3598*]. scheming, craftiness, strategy:– lie in wait [1], wiles [1]

3181 μεθόριον, *methorion*, n. GK: *3498* [→ *3326+3724*]. boundary; (pl.) region:– borders [1]

3182 μεθύσκω, *methyskō*, v. GK: *3499* [→ *3184*]. (pass.) to be or become drunk, intoxicated:– drunken [2], drunk [1], well drunk [1]

3183 μέθυσος, *methysos*, n. GK: *3500* [→ *3184*]. drunkard:– drunkards [1], drunkard [1]

3184 μεθύω, *methyō*, v. GK: *3501* [→ *271, 3178, 3182, 3183*]. to get drunk:– drunken [5], made drunk [1]

3185 μεῖζον, *meizon*, a.comp.n. of *3187*. GK: *3505* [→ *3173*]. greater, larger, older; louder; more:–

3186 μειζότερος, *meizoteros*, a.comp. GK: *3504* [→ *3173*]. greater:– greater than [1]

3187 μείζων, *meizōn*, a.comp. GK: *3505* [→ *3173*]. greater, larger, older; louder; more:– greater than [21], greater [13], greatest [9], more [2], elder [1]

3188 μέλαν, *melan*, a.neut. of *3189*. GK: *3506* [→ *3189*]. the color black; ink, made of soot or other carbon source mixed with oil or resin:– ink [3]

3189 μέλας, *melas*, a. GK: *3506* [→ *3188*]. the color black; ink, made of soot or other carbon source mixed with oil or resin:– black [3]

3190 Μελεᾶς, *Meleas*, n.pr. GK: *3507*. Meleas:– Melea [1]

μέλει, *melei*. See *3199*.

3191 μελετάω, *meletaō*, v. GK: *3509* [→ *3199*]. to plot, think about, meditate on; to give oneself wholly to, practice, cultivate:– imagine [1], meditate upon [1], premeditate [1]

3192 μέλι, *meli*, n. GK: *3510* [→ *3193*]. honey:– honey [4]

3193 μελίσσιος, *melissios*, a. GK: *3511 & 3512 & 3513* [→ *3192*]. pertaining to the bee, honeycomb:– honeycomb [1]

3194 Μελίτη, *Melitē*, n.pr. GK: *3514 & 3515*. Melita:– Melita [1]

3195 μέλλω, *mellō*, v. GK: *3516*. to be about to, on the point of; to be destined, must; to intend to; (what is) to come, the future:– should [21], shall [20], to come [14], will [7], would [7], about to [5], be [3], ready to [3], after [2], come [2], was to [2], would have [2], after that (+*1519+3588*) [1], afterwards [1], almost [1], at the point of [1], begin to [1], coming on [1], for to come (+*2064*) [1], hereafter [1], intending to [1], intend [1], meaning to [1], minding [1], ready [1], shall be [1], shalt [1], tarriest [1], time to come [1], to be [1], to [1], wilt [1], yet to [1]

3196 μέλος, *melos*, n. GK: *3517*. part, member, limb:– members [29], member [5]

3197 Μελχί, *Melchi*, n.pr. GK: *3518*. Melki, "*my king*":– Melchi [2]

3198 Μελχισέδεκ, *Melchisedek*, n.pr. GK: *3519*. Melchizedek, "*[my] king is Zedek [just]*":– Melchisedec [9]

3199 μέλω, *melō*, v. GK: *3508 & 3520* [→ *272, 278, 1958, 1959, 1960, 3191, 3338, 4304*]. to care, be concerned; (imper.) it is a care, it is a concern; (pers.) to trouble; to concern:– carest [3], careth [2], care for [1], cared for [1], cared [1], care [1], take care for [1]

3200 μεμβράνα, *membrana*, n. GK: *3521*. parchment, a fine animal leather specially prepared for use in making scrolls:– parchments [1]

3201 μέμφομαι, *memphomai*, v. GK: *3522* [→ *273, 274, 298, 299, 3202, 3437, 3469, 3470*]. to find fault with, blame:– find fault [1], finding fault with [1], found fault [1]

3202 μεμψίμοιρος, *mempsimoiros*, a. GK: *3523* [→ *3201*]. fault-finding, complaining:– complainers [1]

3203 through **3302** are not used in Strong's numbering system.

3303 μέν, *men*, pt.aff. GK: *3525* [→ *3304, 3305; cf. 3376*]. often untranslated; used with other particles to show contrast: on the one hand, one…or the other:– *usually untranslated* [121], indeed [22], verily [14], truly [12], some (+*3588*) [2], another (+*3739*) [1], as [1], even [1], for [1], furthermore (+*1534+3588*) [1], howbeit (+*235*) [1], inasmuch as (+*1909+3745+3767*) [1], one (+*3739*) [1], one [1], part (+*3588*) [1], partly (+*3778*) [1], some (+*243*) [1], some (+*3739*) [1], then [1]

3304 μενοῦν, *menoun*; or μενοῦνγε, *menounge*, pt. GK: *3528 & 3529* [→ *3303+3767+1065*]. rather, on the contrary, indeed:– doubtless [1], nay but [1], yea rather [1], yes verily [1]

3305 μέντοι, *mentoi*, pt. GK: *3530* [→ *3303+5104*]. but, yet, nevertheless, really:– yet [2], howbeit [1], if (+*1487*) [1], likewise (+*3668*) [1], nevertheless (+*3676*) [1], nevertheless [1]

3306 μένω, *menō*, v. GK: *3531* [→ *362, 1265, 1696, 1961, 2650, 3438, 3887, 4037, 4357, 4839, 5278, 5281*]. to stay, remain, live, dwell, abide; to be in a state that begins and continues, yet may or may not end or stop. "To abide in Christ" is to follow his example of a life obedient to the will of God:– abide [27], abideth [20], abode [12], dwelleth [10], remain [8], continue [7], tarry [7], remaineth [5], remained [3], abiding [2], continued [2], dwell [2], dwelt [2], endureth [2], tarried [2], continueth [1], continuing [1], dwellest [1], enduring [1], present [1], remaining [1], stand [1], tarried for [1]

3307 μερίζω, *merizō*, v. GK: *3532* [→ *3313*]. to give, assign; (mid.) to divide, share; (pass.) to be divided:– divided [8], distributed [2], dealt [1], difference between [1], divide [1], gave [1]

3308 μέριμνα, *merimna*, n. GK: *3533* [→ *275, 3309, 4305; cf. 3313*]. worry, concern, anxiety:– cares [3], care [3]

3309 μεριμνάω, *merimnaō*, v. GK: *3534* [→ *3308*]. to worry, have anxiety, be concerned:– take thought [9], careth for [4], careful [2], taking thought [2], care for [1], have care [1]

3310 μερίς, *meris*, n. GK: *3535* [→ *3313*]. district; part, share, what is common between:– part [4], partakers [1]

3311 μερισμός, *merismos*, n. GK: *3536* [→ *3313*]. dividing, separation; distribution, apportionment:– dividing asunder [1], gifts [1]

3312 μεριστής, *meristēs*, n. GK: *3537* [→ *3313*]. arbiter:– divider [1]

3313 μέρος, *meros*, n. GK: *3538* [→ *1266, 1267, 3307, 3310, 3311, 3312, 4181, 4829; cf. 3308*]. part, share, portion; (pl.) district, region:– part [17], parts [7], coasts [3], portion [3], behalf [2], respect [2], by course (+*303*) [1], craft [1], particularly (+*2596*) [1], particular [1], partly (+*5100*) [1], piece [1], side [1], somewhat (+*575*) [1], sort [1]

3314 μεσημβρία, *mesēmbria*, n. GK: *3540* [→ *3319+2250*]. (of time) noon, midday; (of place) south:– noon [1], south [1]

3315 μεσιτεύω, *mesiteuō*, v. GK: *3541* [→ *3319*]. to confirm, guarantee:– confirmed [1]

3316 μεσίτης, *mesitēs*, n. GK: *3542* [→ *3319*]. mediator:– mediator [6]

3317 μεσονύκτιον, *mesonyktion*, n. GK: *3543* [→ *3319+3571*]. midnight:– midnight [3], at midnight [1]

3318 Μεσοποταμία, *Mesopotamia*, n.pr. GK: *3544* [→ *3319+4215*]. Mesopotamia, "*[land] between rivers*":– Mesopotamia [2]

3319 μέσος, *mesos*, a. GK: *3545* [→ *3314, 3315, 3316, 3317, 3318, 3320, 3321, 3322*]. middle, center, among; between; in front of, before:– midst [39], among [6], among (+*1722*) [5], in the midst [2], way [2], among (+*303*) [1], at midday (+*2250*) [1], at midnight (+*3571*) [1], before (+*1722+3588*) [1], between (+*303*) [1], forth (+*1519+3588*) [1], midnight (+*3571+3588*) [1]

3320 μεσότοιχον, *mesotoichon*, n. GK: *3546* [→ *3319+5038*]. dividing wall:– middle wall [1]

3321 μεσουράνημα, *mesouranēma*, n. GK: *3547* [→ *3319+3772*]. midair:– midst of heaven [3]

3322 μεσόω, *mesoō*, v. GK: *3539 & 3548* [→ *3319*]. to be halfway through, at midpoint:– midst [1]

3323 Μεσσίας, *Messias*, n.pr. GK: *3549*. Messiah, Anointed One; see also *5547*, "*anointed*":– Messias [2]

3324 μεστός, *mestos*, a. GK: *3550* [→ *3325*]. full:– full [8]

3325 μεστόω, *mestoō*, v. GK: *3551* [→ *3324*]. (pass.) to be filled:– full [1]

3326 μετά, *meta*, pp. GK: *3552* [→ *276, 277, 278, 279, 2130, 3177, 3179, 3180, 3181, 3327, 3328, 3329, 3330, 3331, 3332, 3333, 3334, 3335, 3336, 3337, 3338, 3339, 3340, 3341, 3342, 3343, 3344, 3345, 3346, 3347, 3348, 3350, 3351, 3352, 3353, 3359, 4830*]. (gen.) with, among, a marker of association of various kinds and meanings; (acc.) after, later, a marker of time:– with [345], after [76], after (+*3588*) [12], among [5], afterward (+*3778*) [4], against [4], hereafter (+*3778*) [4], in [2], and [1], boldly (+*3954*) [1], foameth (+*876*) [1], followed (+*3588*) [1], freely (+*3954*) [1], hence (+*3778*) [1], joyfully (+*5479*) [1], of [1], on [1], setting [1], since [1], that should follow (+*3778*) [1], together (+*240*) [1], to [1], unto [1], upon [1], when (+*3588*) [1], when [1], without (+*3756*) [1]

3327 μεταβαίνω, *metabainō*, v. GK: *3553* [→ *3326+305*]. to go on, leave, move from:– departed [4], depart [3], passed [2], remove [2], go [1]

3328 μεταβάλλω, *metaballō*, v. GK: *3554* [→ *3326+906*]. (mid.) to change one's mind:– changed [1]

3329 μετάγω, *metagō*, v. GK: *3555* [→ *3326+71*]. to turn, steer:– turn about [1], turned about [1]

3330 μεταδίδωμι, *metadidōmi*, v. GK: *3556* [→ *3326+1325*]. to impart, share, contribute to needs:– impart [2], giveth [1], give [1], imparted [1]

3331 μετάθεσις, *metathesis*, n. GK: *3557* [→ *3326+5087*]. removal, taking up; change, transformation:– change [1], removing [1], translation [1]

3332 μεταίρω, *metairō*, v. GK: *3558* [→ *3326+142*]. to move on, leave:– departed [2]

3333 μετακαλέω, *metakaleō*, v. GK: *3559*
[→ *3326+2564*]. (mid.) to send for, summon, call to oneself:– called [2], call for [1], call hither [1]

3334 μετακινέω, *metakineō*, v. GK: *3560* [→ *3326+2795*]. (pass.) to be moved, removed, shifted from:– moved away [1]

3335 μεταλαμβάνω, *metalambanō*, v. GK: *3561* [→ *3326+2983*]. to share in, receive a share:– eat [1], have [1], partakers [1], partaker [1], receiveth [1], take [1]

3336 μετάλημψις, *metalēmpsis*, n. GK: *3562* [→ *3326+2983*]. receiving, sharing with:– received [1]

3337 μεταλλάσσω, *metallassō*, v. GK: *3563* [→ *3326+236*]. to exchange:– changed [1], change [1]

3338 μεταμέλομαι, *metamelomai*, v. GK: *3564* [→ *3326+3199*]. (mid.) to regret, repent; (pass.) to be repentant, changed of mind, remorseful:– repented [3], repent [3]

3339 μεταμορφόω, *metamorphoō*, v. GK: *3565* [→ *3326+3444*]. (pass.) to be transformed, transfigured, changed in form:– transfigured [2], changed [1], transformed [1]

3340 μετανοέω, *metanoeō*, v. GK: *3566* [→ *3326+3563*]. to repent, to change any or all of the elements composing one's life: attitude, thoughts, and behaviors concerning the demands of God for right living:– repent [21], repented [11], repenteth [2]

3341 μετάνοια, *metanoia*, n. GK: *3567* [→ *3326+3563*]. change of mind, repentance, the state of changing any or all of the elements composing one's life: attitude, thoughts, and behaviors concerning the demands of God for right living; note that this state can refer to the foundational salvation event in Christ, or to on-going repentance in the Christian life:– repentance [24]

3342 μεταξύ, *metaxy*, adv. GK: *3568* [→ *3326+4862*]. (spacial) between; (temporal) meanwhile, next:– between [6], mean while [1], next [1]

3343 μεταπέμπω, *metapempō*, v. GK: *3569* [→ *3326+3992*]. to summon, send for:– sent for [4], call for [2], send for [2]

3344 μεταστρέφω, *metastrephō*, v. GK: *3570* [→ *3326+4762*]. to pervert; to turn into, change:– turned [2], pervert [1]

3345 μετασχηματίζω, *metaschēmatizō*, v. GK: *3571* [→ *3326+4976*]. (act.) to transform, change (the form); (mid.) to masquerade, disguise (oneself):– transformed [2], change [1], in a figure transferred [1], transforming [1]

3346 μετατίθημι, *metatithēmi*, v. GK: *3572* [→ *3326+5087*]. to change (from one place or position to another); to bring back; to take away:– translated [2], carried over [1], changed [1], removed [1], turning [1]

3347 μετέπειτα, *metepeita*, adv. GK: *3575* [→ *3326+1909+1534*]. afterward:– afterward [1]

3348 μετέχω, *metechō*, v. GK: *3576* [→ *3326+2192*]. to share in, partake in, take part in:– partakers [3], partaker [2], pertaineth to [1], took part [1], useth [1]

3349 μετεωρίζομαι, *meteōrizomai*, v. GK: *3577*. to worry about, be anxious:– doubtful mind [1]

3350 μετοικεσία, *metoikesia*, n. GK: *3578* [→ *3326+3624*]. exile, deportation:– carrying away [2], brought [1], carried away [1]

3351 μετοικίζω, *metoikizō*, v. GK: *3579* [→ *3326+3624*]. to send to another place, exile, deport:– carry away [1], removed [1]

3352 μετοχή, *metochē*, n. GK: *3580* [→ *3326+2192*]. something in common, sharing, participation:– fellowship [1]

3353 μέτοχος, *metochos*, a. GK: *3581* [→ *3326+2192*]. sharing in, partners with:– partakers [4], fellows [1], partners [1]

3354 μετρέω, *metreō*, v. GK: *3582* [→ *3358*]. to measure:– measured [2], measure [3], mete [1], measuring [1]

3355 μετρητής, *metrētēs*, n. GK: *3583* [→ *3358*]. measure (about nine or ten gallons):– firkins [1]

3356 μετριοπαθέω, *metriopatheō*, v. GK: *3584* [→ *3358+3958*]. to deal gently:– have compassion [1]

3357 μετρίως, *metriōs*, adv. GK: *3585* [→ *3358*]. not greatly, moderately:– little [1]

3358 μέτρον, *metron*, n. GK: *3586* [→ *280, 488, 3354, 3355, 3356, 3357, 4620*]. measure, limit, what is apportioned:– measure [13]

3359 μέτωπον, *metōpon*, n. GK: *3587* [→ *3326+3708*]. forehead:– foreheads [6], forehead [2]

3360 μέχρι, *mechri*; or μέχρις, *mechris*, c.&pp.*. GK: *3588 & 3589*. until, to the point of:– until [7], unto [7], at [1], till (+*3739*) [1], till [1], to [1]

3361 μή, *mē*, pt.neg. GK: *3590* [→ *3365, 3366, 3367, 3368, 3369, 3371, 3379, 3380, 3381, 3383, 3385, 3387, 3386*]. no, not, absolutely not; a marker that negates a statement. At the beginning of a Greek question, it anticipates a negative response:– not [575], no [56], God forbid (+*1096*) [15], lest [14], never (+*165+1519+3588+3756*) [5], neither (+*2532*) [4], neither [3], no more [3], but [2], cannot (+*1410*) [2], cannot [2], no (+*3956*) [2], none (+*5100*) [2], nor [2], not (+*3756*) [2], nothing (+*5100*) [2], any [1], but (+*1437*) [1], but (+*1487+1622*) [1], but (+*1487*) [1], but that [1], except (+*1437*) [1], except (+*1487+1622*) [1], forbear [1], in no wise (+*1519+3588+3838*) [1], lacked (+*2192*) [1], lacketh (+*3918*) [1], lest (+*1519+3588*) [1], never (+*3756+4218*) [1], never (+*3756+4455*) [1], never [1], no (+*5100*) [1], no more at all (+*3756+3765*) [1], not withal [1], nothing (+*5101*) [1], nothing (+*846+1537*) [1], nothing [1], unless (+*1487+1622*) [1], untaken away (+*343*) [1], without [1]

3362 ἐὰν μή, *ean mē*, c.+pt.neg. GK: *1569 + 3590* [→ *1437+3361*]. if not, except, unless:– except [32], but [2], if not [1], not [1]

3363 ἵνα μή, *hina mē*, c.+pt.neg. GK: *2671 + 3590* [→ *2443+3361*]. that not, lest:– lest [42]

3364 οὐ μή, *ou mē*, pt.neg. GK: *4024 + 3590* [→ *3756+3361*]. intense negative: by no means, not at all, never:– not [58], no [7], in no wise [6], no at all [5], never [2], by any means [1], by no means [1], in no case [1], neither (+*2532*) [1], neither [1], nor ever [1], not at all [1], not in any wise [1], not one [1]

3365 μηδαμῶς, *mēdamōs*, adv. GK: *3592 & 3598* [→ *3361+1161+1473*]. surely not, by no means, certainly not:– not so [1], so [1]

3366 μηδέ, *mēde*, pt.neg.disj. GK: *3593* [→ *3361+1161*]. nor, or not, and not, but not:– neither [32], nor [17], not [4], nor yet [2], no not [1], not once [1], not so much as [1], or [1]

3367 μηδείς, *mēdeis*, a. GK: *3594 & 3599* [→ *3361+1161+1520*]. no one, not anyone, nobody, nothing:– no [46], nothing [27], none [6], any [4], not any [2], no man [1], no more (+*2089*) [1], not a whit [1], not at all [1], not [1], without any [1]

3368 μηδέποτε, *mēdepote*, adv. GK: *3595* [→ *3361+1161+4226*]. never:– never [1]

3369 μηδέπω, *mēdepō*, adv. GK: *3596* [→ *3361+1161*]. not yet:– not as yet [1]

3370 Μῆδος, *Mēdos*, n.pr.g. GK: *3597*. Mede:– Medes [1]

3371 μηκέτι, *mēketi*, adv. GK: *3600* [→ *3361+2089*]. no longer, never again:– no more [8], no longer [2], any longer [1], henceforth not [2], any longer [1], henceforth [1], hereafter [1], no henceforward [1], not any more [1], not henceforth [1], no [1]

3372 μῆκος, *mēkos*, n. GK: *3601* [→ *3112, 3113, 3114, 3115, 3116, 3117, 3118, 3373*]. length:– length [3]

3373 μηκύνω, *mēkynō*, v. GK: *3602* [→ *3372*]. (pass.) to grow (long), become long:– grow up [1]

3374 μηλωτή, *mēlōtē*, n. GK: *3603*. sheepskin:– sheepskins [1]

3375 μήν¹, *mēn*¹, n. GK: *3604* [→ *3561, 5072, 5150*]. month:– surely (+*2229*) [1]

3376 μήν², *mēn*², pt. GK: *3605* [cf. *3303*]. surely:– months [14], month [4]

3377 μηνύω, *mēnyō*, v. GK: *3606*. to inform, report, tell:– shewed [2], shew [1], told [1]

3378 μὴ οὐκ, *mē ouk*, pt.neg. GK: *3590 + 4024* [→ *3361+3756*]. intense negative: by no means, not at all, never:– not [4]

3379 μήποτε, *mēpote*, pt.&c. GK: *3607* [→ *3361+4226*]. never, otherwise, that…not:– lest [12], lest at any time [7], lest haply [2], if peradventure [1], no at all [1], whether or not [1]

3380 μήπω, *mēpō*, adv. GK: *3609* [→ *3361*]. not yet:– not yet [2]

3381 μήπως, *mēpōs*, adv. GK: *3610* [→ *3361+4226*]. so that…somehow, lest:– lest [5], lest by any means [3], lest by some means [1], lest haply [1], lest perhaps [1], lest that by any means [1]

3382 μηρός, *mēros*, n. GK: *3611*. thigh:– thigh [1]

3383 μήτε, *mēte*, c.neg. GK: *3612* [→ *3361+5037*]. and not, neither, nor:– neither [20], nor [15], so much as [1]

3384 μήτηρ, *mētēr*, n. GK: *3613* [→ *282, 3388, 3389, 3390*]. mother:– mother [76], mother's [7], mothers [2]

3385 μήτι, *mēti*, pt.inter.neut. of *3387*. GK: *3614* [→ *3361+5100*]. often not translated; expects a no answer to a question: surely not, unless:– any [3], doth [1], is [1], not [1]

3386 μήτιγε, *mētige*, pt.inter. GK: *3615* [→ *3361+5100+1065*]. how much more, not to speak of:– how much more [1]

3387 μήτι, *mēti*, pt.inter. GK: *3614* [→ *3361+5100*]. often not translated; expects a no answer to a question: surely not, unless:–

3388 μήτρα, *mētra*, n. GK: *3616* [→ *3384*]. womb:– womb [2]

3389 μητραλῴας, *mētralōas*; or μητρολῴας, *mētrolōas*, n. GK: *3617 & 3618* [→ *3384+248*]. one who kills a mother:– murderers of mothers [1]

3390 μητρόπολις, *mētropolis*, n. GK: *3619* [→ *3384+4172*]. capital city:– chiefest city [1]

3391 μία, *mia*, n.num.f. of *1520*. GK: *1651* [→ *1520*]. one, single; see *1520*.–

3392 μιαίνω, *miainō*, v. GK: *3620* [→ *283, 3393, 3394*]. to pollute, stain, defile; (pass.) to be defiled, corrupted, become ceremonially unclean; this refers to both ceremonial and moral uncleanness:– defiled [4], defile [1]

3393 μίασμα, *miasma*, n. GK: *3621* [→ *3392*]. corruption, defilement:– pollutions [1]

3394 μιασμός, *miasmos*, n. GK: *3622* [→ *3392*]. corruption, pollution, defilement:– uncleanness [1]

3395 μίγμα, *migma*, n. GK: *3623* [→ *3396*]. mixture, compound:– mixture [1]

3396 μίγνυμι, *mignymi*, v. GK: *3502 & 3503 & 3624* [→ *3395, 4874*]. to mix, mingle:– mingled [4]

3397 μικρόν, *mikron*, a.neut. of *3398*. GK: *3625* [→ *3398*]. little, small, short, lesser:–

3398 μικρός, *mikros*, a. GK: *3625* [→ *3397*]. little, small, short, lesser:– little [16], little while [8], least [6], little ones [6], small [6], less than [1], less [1], little while (+*3745+3745*) [1], while [1]

3399 Μίλητος, *Milētos*, n.pr. GK: *3626*. Miletus:– Miletus [2], Miletum [1]

3400 μίλιον, *milion*, n. GK: *3627*. (Roman) mile (about 4,854 feet):– mile [1]

3401 μιμέομαι, *mimeomai*, v. GK: *3628* [→ *3402, 4831*]. to imitate, follow an example, use as a model:– follow [4]

3402 μιμητής, *mimētēs*, n. GK: *3629* [→ *3401*]. imitator, an example:– followers [7]

3403 μιμνῄσκομαι, *mimnēskomai*, v. GK: *3630* [→ *3421*]. to remember, recall, bring to remembrance, often with an implication that a response or action of some kind will occur:– mindful [1], remember [1]

3404 μισέω, *miseō*, v. GK: *3631*. to hate; (pass.) to be hated, detestable:– hate [16], hated [12], hateth [10], hating [2], hateful [1], hatest [1]

3405 μισθαποδοσία, *misthapodosia*, n. GK: *3632* [→ *3408+575+1325*]. reward; punishment:– recompence of reward [2], reward [1]

3406 μισθαποδότης, *misthapodotēs*, n. GK: *3633* [→ *3408+575+1325*]. rewarder:– rewarder [1]

3407 μίσθιος, *misthios*, n. GK: *3634* [→ *3408*]. hired worker:– hired [2]

3408 μισθός, *misthos*, n. GK: *3635* [→ *489, 3405, 3406, 3407, 3409, 3410, 3411*]. wage; reward; what is paid back:– reward [24], hire [3], wages [2]

3409 μισθόω, *misthoō*, v. GK: *3636* [→ *3408*]. to hire:– hired [1], hire [1]

3410 μίσθωμα, *misthōma*, n. GK: *3637* [→ *3408*]. rented house, rented lodging:– hired house [1]

3411 μισθωτός, *misthōtos*, n. GK: *3638* [→ *3408*]. hired worker:– hireling [3], hired servants [1]

3412 Μιτυλήνη, *Mitylēnē*, n.pr. GK: *3639*. Mitylene:– Mitylene [1]

3413 Μιχαήλ, *Michaēl*, n.pr. GK: *3640*. Michael, "*Who is like God [El]?*":– Michael [2]

3414 μνᾶ, *mna*, n. GK: *3641*. mina (100 drachmas or denarii, about 100 days' wages):– pounds [5], pound [4]

3415 μνάομαι, *mnaomai*, v. GK: *3642* [→ *3423*]. be engaged, betrothed:– remember [9], remembered [6], mindful [1], remembrance [2], came in remembrance [1], rememberest [1]

3416 Μνάσων, *Mnasōn*, n.pr. GK: *3643*. Mnason:– Mnason [1]

3417 μνεία, *mneia*, n. GK: *3644* [→ *3421*]. remembrance, mention:– mention [4], remembrance [3]

3418 μνῆμα, *mnēma*, n. GK: *3645* [→ *3421*]. (burial) tomb:– sepulchre [4], tombs [2], graves [1]

3419 μνημεῖον, *mnēmeion*, n. GK: *3646* [→ *3421*]. tomb, grave:– sepulchre [26], graves [4], grave [4], sepulchres [3], tombs [3], tomb [2]

3420 μνήμη, *mnēmē*, n. GK: *3647* [→ *3421*]. remembrance, recalling, memory:– remembrance [1]

3421 μνημονεύω, *mnēmoneuō*, v. GK: *3648* [→ *363*, *364*, *1878*, *3403*, *3417*, *3418*, *3419*, *3420*, *3422*, *5279*, *5280*]. to remember; to think of:– remember [16], made mention [1], mindful [1], remembered [1], remembereth [1], remembering [1]

3422 μνημόσυνον, *mnēmosynon*, n. GK: *3649* [→ *3421*]. memory, remembrance; memorial offering:– memorial [3]

3423 μνηστεύω, *mnēsteuō*, v. GK: *3650* [→ *3415*]. (pass.) to be pledged to marriage, betrothed, become engaged:– espoused [3]

3424 μογιλάλος, *mogilalos*, a. GK: *3651* & *3652* [→ *3425*+*2980*]. hardly able to talk, speaking with difficulty; speaking in a hoarse or weak voice:– impediment in speech [1]

3425 μόγις, *mogis*, adv. GK: *3653* [→ *3424*, *3433*, *3449*]. scarcely ever:– hardly [1]

3426 μόδιος, *modios*, n. GK: *3654*. large bowl (holds about eight dry quarts):– bushel [3]

3427 μοί, *moi*, pers.p.dat. of *1473*. GK: *1609* [→ *1473*]. me, for me, to me; see *1473*:–

3428 μοιχαλίς, *moichalis*, n. GK: *3655* [→ *3432*]. adulteress; (a.) adulterous:– adulterous [3], adulteress [2], adulteresses [1], adultery [1]

3429 μοιχάω, *moichaō*, v. GK: *3656* [→ *3432*]. to commit adultery:– committeth adultery [4], commit adultery [2]

3430 μοιχεία, *moicheia*, n. GK: *3657* [→ *3432*]. (the state or condition of) adultery:– adulteries [2], adultery [2]

3431 μοιχεύω, *moicheuō*, v. GK: *3658* [→ *3432*]. (act.) to commit adultery; (pass.) to become an adulterer:– commit adultery [10], committeth adultery [2], adultery [1], committed adultery [1]

3432 μοιχός, *moichos*, n. GK: *3659* [→ *3428*, *3429*, *3430*, *3431*]. adulterer:– adulterers [4]

3433 μόλις, *molis*, adv. GK: *3660* [→ *3425*]. with difficulty, hardly; very rarely:– scarcely [2], scarce [2], had much work (+*2480*) [1], hardly [1]

3434 Μολόχ, *Moloch*, n.pr. GK: *3661*. Molech, "*shameful king*":– Moloch [1]

3435 μολύνω, *molynō*, v. GK: *3662* [→ *3436*]. to defile, soil, stain, make impure:– defiled [3]

3436 μολυσμός, *molysmos*, n. GK: *3663* [→ *3435*]. contamination, defilement:– filthiness [1]

3437 μομφή, *momphē*, n. GK: *3664* [→ *3201*]. grievance, cause for complaint:– quarrel [1]

3438 μονή, *monē*, n. GK: *3665* [→ *3306*]. room; dwelling place, abode:– abode [1], mansions [1]

3439 μονογενής, *monogenēs*, a. GK: *3666* [→ *3441*+*1096*]. one and only, unique:– only begotten [6], one only [1], only child [1], only [1]

3440 μόνον, *monon*, adv. GK: *3667* [→ *3441*]. only, alone; just, even, simply:– only [62], alone [3], but [1]

3441 μόνος, *monos*, a. GK: *3668* [→ *2651*, *3439*, *3440*, *3442*, *3443*]. only, alone, by oneself:– only [24], alone [21], by themselves [2], alone (+*2596*) [1]

3442 μονόφθαλμος, *monophthalmos*, a. GK: *3669* [→ *3441*+*3788*]. one-eyed:– one eye [2]

3443 μονόω, *monoō*, v. GK: *3670* [→ *3441*]. (pass.) to be left alone:– desolate [1]

3444 μορφή, *morphē*, n. GK: *3671* [→ *3339*, *3445*, *3446*, *4832*, *4833*]. form, outward appearance; nature, character:– form [3]

3445 μορφόω, *morphoō*, v. GK: *3672* [→ *3444*]. (pass.) to be formed, take on a form:– formed [1]

3446 μόρφωσις, *morphōsis*, n. GK: *3673* [→ *3444*]. embodiment, formulation; (outward) form, appearance:– form [2]

3447 μοσχοποιέω, *moschopoieō*, v. GK: *3674* [→ *3448*+*4160*]. to make an idol in the shape of a calf:– made a calf [1]

3448 μόσχος, *moschos*, n. GK: *3675* [→ *3447*]. calf, ox, young bull:– calf [4], calves [2]

3449 μόχθος, *mochthos*, n. GK: *3677* [→ *3425*]. toil, hardship, exertion:– travail [2], painfulness [1]

3450 μοῦ, *mou*, pers.p.gen. of *1473*. GK: *1609* [→ *1473*]. my, mine; see *1473*:–

3451 μουσικός, *mousikos*, a. GK: *3676*. (n.) musician:– musicians [1]

3452 μυελός, *myelos*, n. GK: *3678*. marrow:– marrow [1]

3453 μυέω, *myeō*, v. GK: *3679* [→ *3466*]. (pass.) to learn a secret:– instructed [1]

3454 μῦθος, *mythos*, n. GK: *3680* [→ *3888*, *3889*, *3890*]. myth, story, tale:– fables [5]

3455 μυκάομαι, *mykaomai*, v. GK: *3681*. to roar:– roareth [1]

3456 μυκτηρίζω, *myktērizō*, v. GK: *3682* [→ *1592*]. (pass.) to be mocked, treated with contempt:– mocked [1]

3457 μυλικός, *mylikos*, a. GK: *3683* [→ *3458*]. pertaining to a grinding mill:– millstone (+*3037*) [1]

3458 μύλος, *mylos*, n. GK: *3685* [→ *3457*, *3459*]. hand mill or millstone for grinding:– millstone (+*3684*) [2], millstone [2]

3459 μυλών, *mylōn*, n. GK: *3686* [→ *3458*]. millhouse:– mill [1]

3460 Μύρα, *Myra*, n.pr. GK: *3688* & *3694*. Myra:– Myra [1]

3461 μυριάς, *myrias*, n. GK: *3689* [→ *3463*]. myriad, ten thousand; thousands upon thousands, a practically uncountable number:– ten thousand [2], fifty thousand (+*4002*) [1], innumerable company [1], innumerable multitude [1], ten thousands [1], thousands [1], two hundred thousand thousand (+*1417*) [1]

3462 μυρίζω, *myrizō*, v. GK: *3690* [→ *3464*]. to pour perfume, anoint:– anoint [1]

3463 μύριοι, *myrioi*, a.num. GK: *3691* & *3692* [→ *3461*]. ten thousand; a practically uncountable number:– ten thousand [3]

3464 μύρον, *myron*, n. GK: *3693* [→ *3462*]. perfume, myrrh, ointment:– ointment [12], ointments [2]

3465 Μυσία, *Mysia*, n.pr. GK: *3695*. Mysia:– Mysia [2]

3466 μυστήριον, *mystērion*, n. GK: *3696* [→ *3453*]. mystery, secret; often refers to a misunderstood part of the OT that, with Christ's coming, is now unveiled:– mystery [22], mysteries [5]

3467 μυωπάζω, *myōpazō*, v. GK: *3697*. to be nearsighted:– cannot see far off [1]

3468 μώλωψ, *mōlōps*, n. GK: *3698*. wound, welt, bruise:– stripes [1]

3469 μωμάομαι, *mōmaomai*, v. GK: *3699* [→ *3201*]. (mid.) to criticize, find fault, blame; (pass.) to be discredited, have fault found with:– blamed [1], blame [1]

3470 μῶμος, *mōmos*, n. GK: *3700* [→ *3201*]. blemish:– blemishes [1]

3471 μωραίνω, *mōrainō*, v. GK: *3701* [→ *3474*]. (act.) to make foolish, show one foolish; (pass.) to become a fool, be made a fool; (pass.) to become saltless, tasteless, inert:– lost savour [2], fools [1], made foolish [1]

3472 μωρία, *mōria*, n. GK: *3702* [→ *3474*]. foolishness:– foolishness [5]

3473 μωρολογία, *mōrologia*, n. GK: *3703* [→ *3474*+*3004*]. foolish talk:– foolish talking [1]

3474 μωρός, *mōros*, a. GK: *3704* [→ *3471*, *3472*, *3473*]. foolish:– foolish [7], fools [3], fool [2], foolish man [1]

3475 Μωσεύς, *Mōseus*; or Μωσῆς, *Mōsēs*; or Μωϋσῆς, *Mōysēs*, n.pr. GK: *3705* & *3706* & *3707*. Moses, "*drawn out* [Ex. 2:10]; [Egyptian] *son*":– Moses [77], Moses' [3]

3476 Ναασσών, *Naassōn*, n.pr. GK: *3709*. Nahshon, "*small viper*":– Naasson [3]

3477 Ναγγαί, *Nangai*, n.pr. GK: *3710*. Naggai:– Nagge [1]

3478 Ναζαρέθ, *Nazareth*; or Ναζαρέτ, *Nazaret*, n.pr. GK: *3711* & *3712* & *3713* & *3714* & *3715* [→ *3479*, *3480*]. Nazareth, "[poss.] *sprout, branch* or *watchtower*":– Nazareth [12]

3479 Ναζαρηνός, *Nazarēnos*, a.pr.g. GK: *3716* [→ *3478*]. of Nazareth; (n.) Nazarene (in no way connected to the OT Nazirite):– Nazareth [2], of Nazareth [2]

3480 Ναζωραῖος, *Nazōraios*, n.pr.g. GK: *3717* [→ *3478*]. Nazarene, of Nazareth:– of Nazareth [13], Nazarenes [1], Nazarene [1]

3481 Ναθάν, *Nathan*; or Ναθάμ, *Natham*, n.pr. GK: *3718* & *3719*. Nathan, Natham, "*gift*":– Nathan [1]

3482 Ναθαναήλ, *Nathanaēl*, n.pr. GK: *3720*. Nathanael, "*gift of God [El]*":– Nathanael [6]

3483 ναί, *nai*, pt.aff. or emph. GK: *3721*. yes, indeed, a marker of strong agreement, affirmation, or emphasis:– yea [23], even so [5], yes [3], surely [1], truth [1], verily [1]

3484 Ναΐν, *Nain*, n.pr. GK: *3723*. Nain, "*pleasant, delightful*":– Nain [1]

3485 ναός, *naos*, n. GK: *3724* [→ *3511*]. temple; of the temple in Jerusalem, it generally denotes the temple building. Also used figuratively for the church as the dwelling place of the Holy Spirit:– temple [43], temples [2], shrines [1]

3486 Ναούμ, *Naoum*, n.pr. GK: *3725*. Nahum, "*comfort*":– Naum [1]

3487 νάρδος, *nardos*, n. GK: *3726*. nard, the oil of (spike)nard, extracted from the root:– spikenard (+*4101*) [2]

3488 Νάρκισσος, *Narkissos*, n.pr. GK: *3727*. Narcissus:– Narcissus [1]

3489 ναυαγέω, *nauageō*, v. GK: *3728* [→ *3491*+*2608*]. to be shipwrecked, have a shipwreck:– made shipwrack [1], suffered shipwrack [1]

3490 ναύκληρος, *nauklēros*, n. GK: *3729* [→ *3491*+*2819*]. ship owner or captain:– owner of the ship [1]

3491 ναῦς, *naus*, n. GK: *3730* [→ *3489*, *3490*, *3492*]. ship:– ship [1]

3492 ναύτης, *nautēs*, n. GK: *3731* [→ *3491*]. sailor:– shipmen [2], sailers [1]

3493 Ναχώρ, *Nachōr*, n.pr. GK: *3732*. Nahor:– Nachor [1]

3494 νεανίας, *neanias*, n. GK: *3733* [→ *3501*]. young man:– young man [4], young man's [1]

3495 νεανίσκος, *neaniskos*, n. GK: *3734* [→ *3501*]. young man:– young man [5], young men [5]

3496 Νεάπολις, *Neapolis*, n.pr. GK: *3735* & *3736* [→ *3501*+*4172*]. Neapolis, "*new city*":– Neapolis [1]

3497 Νεεμάν, *Neeman*; or Ναιμάν, *Naiman*, n.pr. GK: *3722* & *3737*. Naaman, "*pleasantness*":– Naaman [1]

3498 νεκρός, *nekros*, a. GK: *3738* [→ *3499*, *3500*]. dead (can be used physically or fig., of both persons and things); (n.) dead person, corpse:– dead [131], one dead [1]

3499 νεκρόω, *nekroō*, v. GK: *3739* [→ *3498*]. (act.) to put to death; (pass.) to be as good as dead:– as good as dead [1], dead [1], mortify [1]

3500 νέκρωσις, *nekrōsis*, n. GK: *3740* [→ *3498*]. death, deadness:– deadness [1], dying [1]

3501 νέος, *neos*, a. GK: *3742* [→ *365*, *3494*, *3495*, *3496*, *3502*, *3503*, *3504*, *3512*, *3555*, *3556*, *3561*]. new, fresh, young, younger:– new [12], younger [8], young [3], young men [1]

3502 νεοσσός, *neossos*, n. GK: *3743* & *3801* [→ *3501*]. the young (of a bird):– young [1]

3503 νεότης, *neotēs*, n. GK: *3744* [→ *3501*]. youth, childhood:– youth [5]

3504 νεόφυτος, *neophytos*, a. GK: *3745* [→ *3501*+*5453*]. newly converted, a fig. extension of a new plant, not found in the NT:– novice [1]

3505 Νέρων, *Nerōn*, n.pr. GK: *3746*. Nero, "[*family name*]":– Nero [1]

3506 νεύω, *neuō*, v. GK: *3748* [→ *1269, 1593, 1770, 1962, 2656*]. to motion, nod (as a signal):– beckoned [2]

3507 νεφέλη, *nephelē*, n. GK: *3749* [→ *3509*]. cloud:– cloud [18], clouds [8]

3508 Νεφθαλίμ, *Nephthalim*, n.pr. GK: *3750*. Naphtali:– Nephthalim [3]

3509 νέφος, *nephos*, n. GK: *3751* [→ *3507*]. cloud:– cloud [1]

3510 νεφρός, *nephros*, n. GK: *3752*. mind, the part of the inner person that feels, desires, and gives intent; a fig. extension of the kidney (not found in the NT):– reins [1]

3511 νεωκόρος, *neōkoros*, n. GK: *3753* [→ *3485*]. guardian of the temple:– worshipper [1]

3512 νεωτερικός, *neōterikos*, a. GK: *3754* [→ *3501*]. pertaining to youth, youthful:– youthful [1]

νεώτερος, *neōteros*. See **3501**.

3513 νή, *nē*, pt.aff. GK: *3755*. as surely as:– I protest [1]

3514 νήθω, *nēthō*, v. GK: *3756*. to spin (yarn):– spin [2]

3515 νηπιάζω, *nēpiazō*, v. GK: *3757* [→ *3516*]. to be (like) a child:– children [1]

3516 νήπιος, *nēpios*, a. GK: *3758* [→ *3515*]. (n.) child, infant; (a.) childlike, childish, infantile, with a negative implication of immaturity or positive implication of innocence, depending on the context:– babes [5], child [5], children [2], babe [1], childish [1]

3517 Νηρεύς, *Nēreus*, n.pr. GK: *3759*. Nereus:– Nereus [1]

3518 Νηρί, *Nēri*, n.pr. GK: *3760*. Neri, "*lamp of Yahweh*":– Neri [1]

3519 νησίον, *nēsion*, n. GK: *3761* [→ *3520*]. small island:– island [1]

3520 νῆσος, *nēsos*, n. GK: *3762* [→ *3519*]. island:– island [6], isle [3]

3521 νηστεία, *nēsteia*, n. GK: *3763* [→ *3522, 3523; cf. 2068*]. fasting, going without food:– fasting [4], fastings [3], fast [1]

3522 νηστεύω, *nēsteuō*, v. GK: *3764* [→ *3521*]. to fast, go without food:– fast [16], fasted [3], fastest [1], fasting [1]

3523 νῆστις, *nēstis*, n. GK: *3765* [→ *3521*]. hungry, without food:– fasting [2]

3524 νηφάλεος, *nēphaleos*; or νηφάλιος, *nēphalios*, a. GK: *3766 & 3767* [→ *3525*]. temperate (in the use of alcohol):– sober [2], vigilant [1]

3525 νήφω, *nēphō*, v. GK: *3768* [→ *366, 1594, 3524*]. to be self-controlled, clear-headed:– sober [4], watch [1]

3526 Νίγερ, *Niger*, n.pr. GK: *3769*. Niger, "*black*":– Niger [1]

3527 Νικάνωρ, *Nikanōr*, n.pr. GK: *3770* [→ *3529+435*]. Nicanor, "*victor*":– Nicanor [1]

3528 νικάω, *nikaō*, v. GK: *3771* [→ *3529*]. to overcome, overpower; to conquer, triumph:– overcometh [11], overcome [11], overcame [2], conquering [1], conquer [1], gotten the victory [1], prevailed [1]

3529 νίκη, *nikē*, n. GK: *3772* [→ *408, 959, 2131, 3527, 3528, 3530, 3531, 3532, 3533, 3534, 5245*]. victory:– victory [1]

3530 Νικόδημος, *Nikodēmos*, n.pr. GK: *3773* [→ *3529+1218*]. Nicodemus, "*victor over people*":– Nicodemus [5]

3531 Νικολαΐτης, *Nikolaitēs*, n.pr.g. GK: *3774* [→ *3529+2992*]. Nicolaitan, "*follower of Nicolas*":– Nicolaitans [2]

3532 Νικόλαος, *Nikolaos*, n.pr. GK: *3775* [→ *3529+2992*]. Nicolas, "*victor over people*":– Nicolas [1]

3533 Νικόπολις, *Nikopolis*, n.pr. GK: *3776* [→ *3529+4172*]. Nicopolis, "*victory city*":– Nicopolis [2]

3534 νῖκος, *nikos*, n. GK: *3777* [→ *3529*]. victory:– victory [4]

3535 Νινευΐ, *Nineui*, n.pr. GK: *3778 & 3779* [→ *3536*]. Nineveh:– Nineveh [1]

3536 Νινευΐτης, *Nineuitēs*, n.pr.g. GK: *3780* [→ *3535*]. Ninevite:– Ninevites [2], of Nineveh [1]

3537 νιπτήρ, *niptēr*, n. GK: *3781* [→ *3538*]. basin for washing:– bason [1]

3538 νίπτω, *niptō*, v. GK: *3782* [→ *449, 633, 3537*]. to wash; bathe:– wash [11], washed [6]

3539 νοέω, *noeō*, v. GK: *3783* [→ *3563*]. to understand, see with insight, reflect:– understand [8], perceive [2], consider [1], think [1], understanding [1], understood [1]

3540 νόημα, *noēma*, n. GK: *3784* [→ *3563*]. thought, mind; scheme, design, plot:– minds [4], devices [1], thought [1]

3541 νόθος, *nothos*, a. GK: *3785*. illegitimate, born out of wedlock:– bastards [1]

3542 νομή, *nomē*, n. GK: *3786* [→ *3551*]. pasture:– eat (+*2192*) [1], pasture [1]

3543 νομίζω, *nomizō*, v. GK: *3787* [→ *3551*]. to think, suppose, expect, consider:– supposed [4], supposing [4], think [4], suppose [1], thought [1], wont [1]

3544 νομικός, *nomikos*, a. GK: *3788* [→ *3551*]. pertaining to the law; (n.) expert in the law, lawyer:– lawyers [5], lawyer [3], about law [1]

3545 νομίμως, *nomimōs*, adv. GK: *3789* [→ *3551*]. properly, in accordance with the rules:– lawfully [2]

3546 νόμισμα, *nomisma*, n. GK: *3790* [→ *3551*]. coin:– money [1]

3547 νομοδιδάσκαλος, *nomodidaskalos*, n. GK: *3791* [→ *3551+1321*]. teacher of the law:– doctor of law [1], doctors of the law [1], teachers of the law [1]

3548 νομοθεσία, *nomothesia*, n. GK: *3792* [→ *3551+5087*]. law, legislation:– giving of the law [1]

3549 νομοθετέω, *nomotheteō*, v. GK: *3793* [→ *3551+5087*]. (pass.) to be given law; to be founded, enacted:– established [1], received law [1]

3550 νομοθέτης, *nomothetēs*, n. GK: *3794* [→ *3551+5087*]. lawgiver:– lawgiver [1]

3551 νόμος, *nomos*, n. GK: *3795* [→ *458, 459, 460, 632, 1268, 1772, 2624, 2816, 2817, 2818, 3542, 3543, 3544, 3545, 3546, 3547, 3548, 3549, 3550, 3621, 3622, 3623, 3891, 3892, 4789*]. law, regulation, principle; this has a broad range of meanings and referents, ranging from law as a principle revealed in nature or reason, to the OT Scriptures as a body, the first five books of the Scriptures, or any single command of the Scriptures:– law [195], laws [2]

3552 νοσέω, *noseō*, v. GK: *3796* [→ *3554*]. to be unhealthy, ill:– doting [1]

3553 νόσημα, *nosēma*, n. GK: *3797* [→ *3554*]. disease:– disease [1]

3554 νόσος, *nosos*, n. GK: *3798* [→ *3552, 3553*]. disease, illness:– diseases [6], sickness [3], sicknesses [2], infirmities [1]

3555 νοσσιά, *nossia*, n. GK: *3799* [→ *3501*]. chick, young (of a bird):– brood [1]

3556 νοσσίον, *nossion*, n. GK: *3800* [→ *3501*]. young (of a bird):– chickens [1]

3557 νοσφίζω, *nosphizō*, v. GK: *3802*. (mid.) to hold back for oneself, steal by misappropriating:– keep back [1], kept back [1], purloining [1]

3558 νότος, *notos*, n. GK: *3803*. south, south wind:– south [4], south wind [3]

3559 νουθεσία, *nouthesia*, n. GK: *3804* [→ *3563+5087*]. warning, admonition; instruction:– admonition [3]

3560 νουθετέω, *noutheteō*, v. GK: *3805* [→ *3563+5087*]. to warn, admonish; instruct:– admonish [3], warn [3], admonishing [1], warning [1]

3561 νουμηνία, *noumēnia*, n. GK: *3741 & 3806* [→ *3501+3375*]. New Moon Celebration:– new moon [1]

3562 νουνεχῶς, *nounechōs*, adv. GK: *3807* [→ *3563+2192*]. wisely, thoughtfully:– discreetly [1]

3563 νοῦς, *nous*, n. GK: *3808* [→ *279, 453, 454, 1270, 1271, 1425, 1771, 1963, 2132, 2133, 2657, 3340, 3341, 3539, 3540, 3559, 3560, 3562, 4306, 4307, 5282, 5283*]. mind, thinking; understanding, insight; "to open the mind" means "to understand something":– mind [15], understanding [7], minds [2]

3564 Νυμφᾶς, *Nymphas*, n.pr. GK: *3809 & 3810* [→ *3565*]. Nymphas:– Nymphas [1]

3565 νύμφη, *nymphē*, n. GK: *3811* [→ *3564, 3566, 3567*]. bride; daughter-in-law:– bride [5], daughter in law [3]

3566 νυμφίος, *nymphios*, n. GK: *3812* [→ *3565*]. bridegroom:– bridegroom [15], bridegroom's [1]

3567 νυμφών, *nymphōn*, n. GK: *3813* [→ *3565*]. bridegroom:– bridechamber [3]

3568 νῦν, *nyn*, adv. GK: *3814* [→ *3570, 3569, 5106*]. now, as it is; (with the art.) the present (time):– now [119], present [4], henceforth (+*3588*) [3], this time (+*3588*) [2], at this time [1], henceforth (+*575+3588*) [1], henceforth [1], hereafter (+*575+3588*) [1], now (+*2089*) [1], now henceforth [1], of late [1], this (+*3588*) [1], this [1], time [1]

3569 τανῦν, *tanyn*, contr. [art.+adv.] GK: *5422* [→ *3588+3568*]. concerning the present, now:– now [5]

3570 νυνί, *nyni*, adv. GK: *3815* [→ *3568*]. now, as it is; indeed, in fact:– now [21]

3571 νύξ, *nyx*, n. GK: *3816* [→ *1273, 1773, 3317, 3574*]. night, evening:– night [60], nights [3], at midnight (+*3319*) [1], midnight (+*3319+3588*) [1]

3572 νύσσω, *nyssō*, v. GK: *3817* [→ *2659, 2660*]. to pierce, stab:– pierced [1]

3573 νυστάζω, *nystazō*, v. GK: *3818*. to become drowsy; to sleep, be idle:– slumbered [1], slumbereth [1]

3574 νυχθήμερον, *nychthēmeron*, n. GK: *3819* [→ *3571+2250*]. a night and a day, about 24 hours:– a night and a day [1]

3575 Νῶε, *Nōe*, n.pr. GK: *3820*. Noah, "*rest, comfort*":– Noe [5], Noah [3]

3576 νωθρός, *nōthros*, a. GK: *3821*. slow to learn; lazy, sluggish:– dull [1], slothful [1]

3577 νῶτος, *nōtos*, n. GK: *3822*. back (of a human body); to have a "bent back" means to be "in trouble or oppression":– back [1]

3578 ξενία, *xenia*, n. GK: *3825* [→ *3581*]. place to stay, guest room:– lodging [2]

3579 ξενίζω, *xenizō*, v. GK: *3826* [→ *3581*]. to receive a guest, entertain; (pass.) to stay as a guest; to think of something as strange, be surprised, astonished:– lodged [4], think it strange [2], entertained [1], lodgeth [1], lodge [1], strange [1]

3580 ξενοδοχέω, *xenodocheō*, v. GK: *3827* [→ *3581+1209*]. to show hospitality:– lodged strangers [1]

3581 ξένος, *xenos*, a. GK: *3828* [→ *3578, 3579, 3580, 5381, 5382*]. strange, foreign, alien; (n.) foreigner, stranger, alien; host, one who shows hospitality:– strangers [6], stranger [4], strange [3], host [1]

3582 ξέστης, *xestēs*, n. GK: *3829*. pitcher, jug:– pots [2]

3583 ξηραίνω, *xērainō*, v. GK: *3830* [→ *3584*]. to wither, shrivel; become rigid:– withered away [6], dried up [3], withered [3], withereth [2], pineth away [1], ripe [1]

3584 ξηρός, *xēros*, a. GK: *3831* [→ *3583*]. dried up, (n.) dry land; shriveled, by extension: withered, paralyzed, of an atrophied limb of the body:– withered [4], dry [2], land [1]

3585 ξύλινος, *xylinos*, a. GK: *3832* [→ *3586, 3587*]. made of wood, wooden:– of wood [2]

3586 ξύλον, *xylon*, n. GK: *3833* [→ *3585*]. wood; tree; wooden club, stocks:– tree [10], staves [5], wood [3], stocks [1]

3587 ξυράω, *xyraō*, v. GK: *3834* [→ *3585*]. to have one's hair shaved:– shaven [2], shave [1]

3588 ὁ, *ho*, art. GK: *3836* [→ *2006, 3592, 3634, 3569, 5024, 5107, 5108, 5120, 5121, 5122, 5602*]. (often not translated) the, this, that, who:– *usually untranslated* [9495], the [7887], he [450], which [392], that [353], them [267], they [259], a [179], him [134], who [93], those [41], that (+*1519*) [27], to (+*1519*) [24], because (+*1223*) [24], she [18], what [18], as (+*1722*) [15], after (+*3326*) [12], an [12], their [12], when (+*1722*) [12], his [11], some [10]*

ὁ, *ho*. See **3739**.

3589 ὀγδοήκοντα, *ogdoēkonta*, n.num. GK: *3837* [→ *3638*]. eighty:– fourscore [2]

3590 ὄγδοος, *ogdoos*, a. GK: *3838* [→ *3638*]. eighth:– eighth [5]

3591 ὄγκος, *onkos*, n. GK: *3839* [→ *5246*]. hinderance, impediment:– weight [1]

3592 ὅδε, *hode*, p.demo. GK: *3840* [→ *3588*]. this (one); thus:– these [7], after this manner [1], he [1], she [1], such [1], thus [1]

3593 ὁδεύω, *hodeuō*, v. GK: *3841* [→ *3598*]. to travel:– journeyed [1]

3594 ὁδηγέω, *hodēgeō*, v. GK: *3842* [→ *3598+71*]. to lead, guide; explain, instruct:– lead [3], guide [2]

3595 ὁδηγός, *hodēgos*, n. GK: *3843* [→ *3598+71*]. guide, leader:– guides [2], guide [2], leaders [1]

3596 ὁδοιπορέω, *hodoiporeō*, v. GK: *3844* [→ *3598+4198*]. to be on a journey, travel:– went on journey [1]

3597 ὁδοιπορία, *hodoiporia*, n. GK: *3845* [→ *3598+4198*]. journey:– journeyings [1], journey [1]

3598 ὁδός, *hodos*, n. GK: *3847* [→ *296, 1327, 1353, 1529, 1841, 2136, 2137, 3180, 3593, 3594, 3595, 3596, 3597, 3938, 4922, 4923*]. road, path, a general term for a thoroughfare to get from one place to another; by extension: way, manner of life; "the Way" is a term for the Christian lifestyle (Ac 9:2; 19:9):– way [75], ways [11], journey [5], way side [5], highways [2], as went (+*4160*) [1], highway side [1], highways (+*1327+3588*) [1], sabbath day's journey (+*2192+4521*) [1]

3599 ὀδούς, *odous*, n. GK: *3848*. tooth:– teeth [10], tooth [2]

3600 ὀδυνάω, *odynaō*, v. GK: *3849* [→ *3601*]. to grieve, be anxious, in agony:– sorrowing [2], tormented [2]

3601 ὀδύνη, *odynē*, n. GK: *3850* [→ *3600*]. anguish, grief, pain:– sorrows [1], sorrow [1]

3602 ὀδυρμός, *odyrmos*, n. GK: *3851*. deep sorrow, mourning, lamentation:– mourning [2]

3603 ὅ ἐστι, *hō esti*; or ὅ ἐστιν, *hō estin*, p.rel.+v. GK: *4005* + *1639* [→ *3739+1510*]. that is, which is; see *1510* and *3739*:–

3604 Ὀζίας, *Ozias*, n.pr. GK: *3852*. Uzziah, "*Yahweh is [my] strength*":– Ozias [2]

3605 ὄζω, *ozō*, v. GK: *3853* [→ *2175, 2238, 3744, 3750*]. to give off a bad odor, stink, smell:– stinketh [1]

3606 ὅθεν, *hothen*, adv. GK: *3854* [→ *3739*]. from where, from there; therefore, this is why:– wherefore [4], whereupon [3], from whence [2], whence [2], where [2], from thence [1], whereby [1]

3607 ὀθόνη, *othonē*, n. GK: *3855* [→ *3608*]. linen sheet:– sheet [2]

3608 ὀθόνιον, *othonion*, n. GK: *3856* [→ *3607*]. (pl.) strips of linen, bandages:– linen clothes [5]

3609 οἰκεῖος, *oikeios*, a. GK: *3858* [→ *3624*]. belonging to the household, of the immediate family:– household [1], house [1], of household [1]

3610 οἰκέτης, *oiketēs*, n. GK: *3860* [→ *3624*]. house servant, domestic slave:– servant [3], household servants [1], servants [1]

3611 οἰκέω, *oikeō*, v. GK: *3861* [→ *3624*]. to live, dwell:– dwelleth [4], dwell [4], dwelling [1]

3612 οἴκημα, *oikēma*, n. GK: *3862* [→ *3624*]. cell, room in a prison:– prison [1]

3613 οἰκητήριον, *oikētērion*, n. GK: *3863* [→ *3624*]. dwelling, home:– habitation [1], house [1]

3614 οἰκία, *oikia*, n. GK: *3864* [→ *3624*]. house, home; family:– house [84], houses [8], from house to house (+*3588*) [1], home [1], household [1]

3615 οἰκιακός, *oikiakos*, n. GK: *3865* [→ *3624*]. member of a household:– of household [2]

3616 οἰκοδεσποτέω, *oikodespoteō*, v. GK: *3866* [→ *3624+1203*]. to manage one's home:– guide the house [1]

3617 οἰκοδεσπότης, *oikodespotēs*, n. GK: *3867* [→ *3624+1203*]. head or owner of the house, landowner:– goodman of the house [4], householder [3], master of the house [3], goodman [1], householder (+*444*) [1]

3618 οἰκοδομέω, *oikodomeō*, v. GK: *3868* [→ *3624+1430*]. to build, build up, rebuild, a physical edifice; by extension: to edify, strengthen, develop another person's life through acts and words of love and encouragement:– build [12], built [10], builders [5], edifieth [3], buildest [2], edified [2], edify [2], builded [1], building [1], emboldened [1]

3619 οἰκοδομή, *oikodomē*, n. GK: *3869* [→ *3624+1430*]. building, construction, a physical edifice; by extension: building up, edification, strengthening, developing another person's life through acts and words of love and encouragement:– edifying [7], edification [4], buildings [3], building [3], edify [1]

3620 οἰκοδομία, *oikodomia*, n. GK: *3870* [→ *3624+1430*]. edification:–

3621 οἰκονομέω, *oikonomeō*, v. GK: *3872* [→ *3624+3551*]. to manage:– steward [1]

3622 οἰκονομία, *oikonomia*, n. GK: *3873* [→ *3624+3551*]. management, administration, job of administration; what is put into effect, plan:– dispensation [4], stewardship [3], edifying [1]

3623 οἰκονόμος, *oikonomos*, n. GK: *3874* [→ *3624+3551*]. manager, administrator, director, trustee:– steward [5], stewards [3], chamberlain [1], governors [1]

3624 οἶκος, *oikos*, n. GK: *3875* [→ *456, 1460, 1774, 2026, 2730, 2731, 2732, 2733, 3350, 3351, 3609, 3610, 3611, 3612, 3613, 3614, 3615, 3616, 3617, 3618, 3619, 3620, 3621, 3622, 3623, 3625, 3626, 3832, 3939, 3940, 3941, 4039, 4040, 4924, 4925*]. house, home, a physical edifice; of royalty: palace; of deity: temple; by extension: family, lineage, people who live in or originated in a particular house:– house [96], home [5], houses [5], household [3], from house to house (+*2596*) [2], every house (+*2596*) [1], in every house (+*2596*) [1], temple [1]

3625 οἰκουμένη, *oikoumenē*, n. GK: *3876* [→ *3624*]. the (inhabited) world, (Roman) world; humankind:– world [14], earth [1]

3626 οἰκουρός, *oikouros*; or οἰκουργός, *oikourgos*, a. GK: *3877 & 3878* [→ *3624*]. staying at home, domestic:– keepers at home [1]

3627 οἰκτείρω, *oikteirō*, v. GK: *3879 & 3882* [→ *3628, 3629*]. to have compassion on:– have compassion [2]

3628 οἰκτιρμός, *oiktirmos*, n. GK: *3880* [→ *3627*]. compassion, mercy, pity:– mercies [4], mercy [1]

3629 οἰκτίρμων, *oiktirmōn*, a. GK: *3881* [→ *3627*]. merciful, compassionate:– merciful [2], tender mercy [1]

οἶμαι, *oimai*. See *3633*.

3630 οἰνοπότης, *oinopotēs*, n. GK: *3884* [→ *3631+4095*]. drunkard, wine-drinker:– winebibber [2]

3631 οἶνος, *oinos*, n. GK: *3885* [→ *3630, 3632, 3943*]. wine:– wine [32], winepress (+*3025*) [1]

3632 οἰνοφλυγία, *oinophlygia*, n. GK: *3886* [→ *3631+5397*]. drunkenness:– excess of wine [1]

3633 οἴομαι, *oiomai*; or οἶμαι, *oimai*, v. GK: *3883 & 3887*. to suppose, think, expect:– suppose [1], supposing [1], think [1]

3634 οἷος, *hoios*, p.rel. GK: *3888* [→ *4169*]. what sort of, what kind of:– such as [5], as [4], what manner [2], which [2], so as [1], what [1]

οἴω, *oiō*. See *5342*.

3635 ὀκνέω, *okneō*, v. GK: *3890* [→ *3636*]. to delay, hesitate:– delay [1]

3636 ὀκνηρός, *oknēros*, a. GK: *3891* [→ *3635*]. lazy, idle, not active; troublesome:– slothful [2], grievous [1]

3637 ὀκταήμερος, *oktaēmeros*, a. GK: *3892* [→ *3638+2250*]. eighth day:– eighth day [1]

3638 ὀκτώ, *oktō*, n.num. GK: *3893* [→ *3589, 3590, 3637*]. eight:– eight [6], eighteen (+*1176+2532*) [3]

3639 ὄλεθρος, *olethros*, n. GK: *3897* [→ *622, 623, 684, 1842, 3644, 3645, 4881*]. destruction, ruin:– destruction [4]

3640 ὀλιγόπιστος, *oligopistos*, a. GK: *3899* [→ *3641+4103*]. of little faith:– of little faith [5]

3641 ὀλίγος, *oligos*, a. GK: *3900* [→ *3640, 3642, 3643*]. little, small, short; (pl.) few:– few [20], little [9], small [5], almost (+*1722*) [2], short [2], while [2], briefly (+*1223*) [1], long (+*3756*) [1], season [1]

3642 ὀλιγόψυχος, *oligopsychos*, a. GK: *3901* [→ *3641+5594*]. timid, fainthearted, discouraged:– feebleminded [1]

3643 ὀλιγωρέω, *oligōreō*, v. GK: *3902* [→ *3641*]. to make light of, despise:– despise [1]

3644 ὀλοθρευτής, *olothreutēs*, n. GK: *3894 & 3904* [→ *3639*]. destroyer:– destroyer [1]

3645 ὀλοθρεύω, *olothreuō*, v. GK: *3895 & 3905* [→ *3639*]. to destroy:– destroyed [1]

3646 ὁλοκαύτωμα, *holokautōma*, n. GK: *3906* [→ *3650+2545*]. burnt offering, wholly consumed on the altar as dedicated to God:– burnt offerings [2], whole burnt offerings [1]

3647 ὁλοκληρία, *holoklēria*, n. GK: *3907* [→ *3650+2819*]. completeness, wholeness (in healing):– perfect soundness [1]

3648 ὁλόκληρος, *holoklēros*, a. GK: *3908* [→ *3650+2819*]. whole, complete:– entire [1], whole [1]

3649 ὀλολύζω, *ololyzō*, v. GK: *3909*. to wail, cry out:– howl [1]

3650 ὅλος, *holos*, a. GK: *3910* [→ *2526', 2527, 3646, 3647, 3648, 3651, 3654*]. all, whole, entire; throughout:– all [63], whole [43], every whit [2], all (+*1722*) [1], all long [1], altogether [1], throughout (+*1223*) [1]

3651 ὁλοτελής, *holotelēs*, a. GK: *3911* [→ *3650+5056*]. through and through, wholly, completely:– wholly [1]

3652 Ὀλυμπᾶς, *Olympas*, n.pr. GK: *3912*. Olympas:– Olympas [1]

3653 ὄλυνθος, *olynthos*, n. GK: *3913*. late fig:– untimely figs [1]

3654 ὅλως, *holōs*, adv. GK: *3914* [→ *3650*]. completely, (not) at all; actually:– at all [2], commonly [1], utterly [1]

3655 ὄμβρος, *ombros*, n. GK: *3915*. rainstorm (that may include thunder and lightning):– shower [1]

3656 ὁμιλέω, *homileō*, v. GK: *3917* [→ *3657, 3658, 4926*; cf. *3664*]. to talk, converse:– communed [2], talked [2]

3657 ὁμιλία, *homilia*, n. GK: *3918* [→ *3656*]. company, associations:– communications [1]

3658 ὅμιλος, *homilos*, n. GK: *3919* [→ *3656*]. crowd, throng:– company [1]

3659 ὄμμα, *omma*, n. GK: *3921* [→ *3708*]. eye:– eyes [1]

3660 ὀμνύω, *omnyō*, v. GK: *3922 & 3923* [→ *3728, 4945*]. to declare an oath, swear an oath, promise with an oath:– swear [13], sware [7], sweareth [4], sworn [1]

3661 ὁμοθυμαδόν, *homothymadon*, adv. GK: *3924* [→ *3664+2372*]. united, in togetherness, as one:– with one accord [11], one mind [1]

3662 ὁμοιάζω, *homoiazō*, v. GK: *3925* [→ *3664*]. to be like, resemble:– agreeth [1]

3663 ὁμοιοπαθής, *homoiopathēs*, a. GK: *3926* [→ *3664+3958*]. like, of the same quality or kind of desires:– of like passions with [1], subject to like passions [1]

3664 ὅμοιος, *homoios*, a. GK: *3927* [→ *871, 3661, 3662, 3663, 3665, 3666, 3667, 3668, 3669, 3670, 3673, 3674, 3675, 3676, 3945, 3946, 4927; cf. 3656, 3670*]. like, similar, of a same or similar nature or quality:– like [41], like unto [4], unto [2]

3665 ὁμοιότης, *homoiotēs*, n. GK: *3928* [→ *3664*]. similarity, likeness:– like as (+*2596*) [1], similitude [1]

3666 ὁμοιόω, *homoioō*, v. GK: *3929* [→ *3664*]. to make like, compare; (pass.) to be like, become like:– liken [5], likened [4], like [2], made like [2], likeness [1], resemble [1]

3667 ὁμοίωμα, *homoiōma*, n. GK: *3930* [→ *3664*]. likeness; looking like, image; form, appearance:– likeness [2], in likeness [1], like to [1], shapes [1], similitude [1]

3668 ὁμοίως, *homoios*, adv. GK: *3931* [→ *3664*]. likewise, in the same way, similarly:– likewise [27], likewise (+*3305*) [1], moreover [1], so [1]

3669 ὁμοίωσις, *homoiōsis*, n. GK: *3932* [→ *3664*]. likeness:– similitude [1]

3670 ὁμολογέω, *homologeō*, v. GK: *3933* [→ *437, 1843, 3671, 3672*]. to confess, acknowledge, agree, admit, declare; this can be a profession of allegiance, an admission of bad behavior, or an emphatic declaration of a truth:– confess [12], confessed [3], confesseth [2], profess [2], confession made [1], giving thanks [1], professed [1], promised [1]

3671 ὁμολογία, *homologia*, n. GK: *3934* [→ *3670*]. confession, profession, acknowledgment, to openly express commitment and allegiance:– profession [4], confession [1], professed [1]

3672 ὁμολογουμένως, *homologoumenōs*, adv. GK: *3935* [→ *3670*]. beyond all question, most certainly:– without controversy [1]

3673 ὁμότεχνος, *homotechnos*, a. GK: *3937* [→ *3664+5078*]. of the same trade:– same craft [1]

3674 ὁμοῦ, *homou*, adv. GK: *3938* [→ *3664*]. together:– together [3]

3675 ὁμόφρων, *homophrōn*, a. GK: *3939* [→ *3664+5424*]. living in harmony with, like-minded:– one mind [1]

ὁμόω, *omoō*. See *3660*.

3676 ὅμως, **homōs**, adv. GK: *3940* [→ *3664*]. just as; at the same time:– even [1], nevertheless (+*3305*) [1], though but [1]

3677 ὄναρ, **onar**, n. GK: *3941*. dream:– dream [6]

3678 ὀνάριον, **onarion**, n. GK: *3942* [→ *3688*]. young donkey:– young ass [1]

ὀνάω, **onaō**. See **3685**.

3679 ὀνειδίζω, **oneidizō**, v. GK: *3943* [→ *3681*]. to heap insults on, denounce, find fault, rebuke:– reproached [2], cast in teeth [1], reproach [1], reviled [1], revile [1], suffer reproach [1], upbraided [1], upbraideth [1], upbraid [1]

3680 ὀνειδισμός, **oneidismos**, n. GK: *3944* [→ *3681*]. disgrace, insult:– reproach [3], reproaches [2]

3681 ὄνειδος, **oneidos**, n. GK: *3945* [→ *3679, 3680*]. disgrace:– reproach [1]

3682 Ὀνήσιμος, **Onēsimos**, n.pr. GK: *3946* [→ *3685*]. Onesimus, "*useful*":– Onesimus [4]

3683 Ὀνησίφορος, **Onēsiphoros**, n.pr. GK: *3947* [→ *3685*+*5342*]. Onesiphorus, "*one bringing usefulness*":– Onesiphorus [2]

3684 ὀνικός, **onikos**, a. GK: *3948* [→ *3688*]. pertaining to a donkey, millstone worked by a donkey:– millstone (+*3458*) [1]

3685 ὀνίνημι, **oninēmi**, v. GK: *3949* [→ *3682, 3683*]. to have benefit or joy:– joy [1]

3686 ὄνομα, **onoma**, n. GK: *3950* [→ *2028, 2176, 3687, 5122, 5581*]. name; title; reputation:– name [172], named [28], name's [11], names [11], called [4], men (+*444*) [1], surnamed (+*2007*) [1]

3687 ὀνομάζω, **onomazō**, v. GK: *3951* [→ *3686*]. to give a name, designate a name; to confess; (mid.) to call oneself; (pass.) to be named; be known:– named [7], called [1], call [1], nameth [1]

3688 ὄνος, **onos**, n. GK: *3952* [→ *3678, 3684*]. donkey (female or male):– ass [5], ass's [1]

3689 ὄντως, **ontōs**, adv. GK: *3953* [→ *1510*]. really, certainly, surely:– indeed [6], certainly [1], clean [1], of a truth [1], verily [1]

3690 ὄξος, **oxos**, n. GK: *3954* [→ *3691*]. wine vinegar:– vinegar [7]

3691 ὀξύς, **oxys**, a. GK: *3955* [→ *3690, 3947, 3948*]. sharp; swift, quick:– sharp [7], swift [1]

3692 ὀπή, **opē**, n. GK: *3956*. hole, opening:– caves [1], place [1]

3693 ὄπισθεν, **opisthen**, adv. GK: *3957* [→ *3694*]. from behind; after:– behind [4], after [2], on the backside [1]

3694 ὀπίσω, **opisō**, adv. GK: *3958* [→ *3693*]. behind, after, following:– after [22], behind [6], back (+*1519*+*3588*) [3], again (+*1519*+*3588*) [1], backward (+*1519*+*3588*) [1], back [1], follow (+*1205*) [1], went back (+*565*+*1519*+*3588*) [1]

3695 ὁπλίζω, **hoplizō**, v. GK: *3959* [→ *3696*]. (mid.) to arm oneself with:– arm [1]

3696 ὅπλον, **hoplon**, n. GK: *3960* [→ *2528, 3695, 3833*]. instrument, weapon, armor:– armour [2], instruments [2], weapons [2]

3697 ὁποῖος, **hopoios**, a. GK: *3961* [→ *4226*]. what kind of, what sort of:– what manner of [2], of what sort [1], such as (+*5108*) [1], whatsoever [1]

3698 ὁπότε, **hopote**, pt.temp. GK: *3962* [→ *4226*]. when:– when [1]

3699 ὅπου, **hopou**, pt.pl. GK: *3963* [→ *4226*]. where, wherever; whenever:– where [58], whither [9], whithersoever (+*302*) [4], wheresoever (+*1437*) [3], whereas [2], wheresoever (+*302*) [2], in what place soever (+*1437*) [1], wheresoever [1], whithersoever (+*1437*) [1]

3700 ὀπτάνομαι, **optanomai**, v. GK: *3964* [→ *3708*]. (mid.) to appear:– see [29], appeared [15], seen [8], appear [2], look [2], shewed [1]

3701 ὀπτασία, **optasia**, n. GK: *3965* [→ *3708*]. (supernatural) vision:– vision [3], visions [1]

ὄπτομαι, **optomai**. See **3700**.

3702 ὀπτός, **optos**, a. GK: *3966*. broiled, roasted:– broiled [1]

3703 ὀπώρα, **opōra**, n. GK: *3967* [→ *5352*]. fruit:– fruits [1]

3704 ὅπως, **hopōs**, c.&adv. GK: *3968* [→ *4226*]. that, so that, (in order) to:– that [41], how [4], to [4], that (+*302*) [3], because [1], might [1], so that [1], when (+*302*) [1]

3705 ὅραμα, **horama**, n. GK: *3969* [→ *3708*]. (supernatural) vision; sight (from God):– vision [11], sight [1]

3706 ὅρασις, **horasis**, n. GK: *3970* [→ *3708*]. appearance; vision:– in sight [1], look [1], visions [1], vision [1]

3707 ὁρατός, **horatos**, a. GK: *3971* [→ *3708*]. pertaining to things visible, things seen:– visible [1]

3708 ὁράω, **horaō**, v. GK: *1625 & 3972* [→ *517, 542, 845, 872, 1799, 1896, 2029, 2030, 2072, 2529, 2714, 2734, 3359, 3659, 3700, 3701, 3705, 3706, 3707, 3799, 4275, 4308, 4383, 4659, 4893?, 4894?, 5299, 5432; cf. 3788, 4383*]. to see, notice; perceive; (pass.) to appear, be seen:– seen [33], see [12], saw [5], take heed [5], beholding [1], perceive [1], seeing [1], seeth [1]

3709 ὀργή, **orgē**, n. GK: *3973* [→ *3710, 3711, 3949, 3950; cf. 3713*]. wrath, anger, the feeling and expression of strong displeasure and hostility; this can range from petty human anger to the righteous anger of God toward sinful disobedience:– wrath [31], anger [3], indignation [1], vengeance [1]

3710 ὀργίζω, **orgizō**, v. GK: *3974* [→ *3709*]. (mid./pass.) to be angry, enraged, to feel and express strong displeasure and hostility; this can range from petty human anger to the righteous anger of God toward sinful disobedience:– angry [5], wroth [3]

3711 ὀργίλος, **orgilos**, a. GK: *3975* [→ *3709*]. quick-tempered, inclined to anger:– soon angry [1]

3712 ὀργυιά, **orgyia**, n. GK: *3976* [→ *3713*]. fathom (about six feet):– fathoms [2]

3713 ὀρέγω, **oregō**, v. GK: *3977* [→ *3712, 3715; cf. 3709*]. (mid.) to set one's heart on, strive for, aspire to, desire:– desire [2], coveted after [1]

3714 ὀρεινός, **oreinos**, a. GK: *3978* [→ *3735*]. hilly, (n.) hill country:– hill country [2]

3715 ὄρεξις, **orexis**, n. GK: *3979* [→ *3713*]. lust, desire:– lust [1]

3716 ὀρθοποδέω, **orthopodeō**, v. GK: *3980* [→ *3717*+*4228*]. to act in line with (the truth), act rightly:– walked uprightly [1]

3717 ὀρθός, **orthos**, a. GK: *3981* [→ *461, 1357, 1882, 1930, 2735, 3716, 3718, 3723*]. straight, level:– straight [1], upright [1]

3718 ὀρθοτομέω, **orthotomeō**, v. GK: *3982* [→ *3717*+*5114*]. to handle correctly, guide on a straight path:– rightly dividing [1]

3719 ὀρθρίζω, **orthrizō**, v. GK: *3983* [→ *3722*]. to get up early in the morning:– came early in the morning [1]

3720 ὀρθρινός, **orthrinos**, a. GK: *3984* [→ *3722*]. early in the morning:– morning [1]

3721 ὄρθριος, **orthrios**, a. GK: *3985* [→ *3722*]. early in the morning:– early [1]

3722 ὄρθρος, **orthros**, n. GK: *3986* [→ *3719, 3720, 3721*]. dawn, daybreak, early in the morning:– early in the morning (+*3588*+*5259*) [1], early in the morning [1], very early in the morning (+*901*) [1]

3723 ὀρθῶς, **orthōs**, adv. GK: *3987* [→ *3717*]. correctly, rightly, plainly:– rightly [2], plain [1], right [1]

3724 ὁρίζω, **horizō**, v. GK: *3988* [→ *592, 873, 3181, 3725, 3734, 4309, 4927*]. to determine, set, appoint, decree:– determined [3], ordained [2], declared [1], determinate [1], limiteth [1]

3725 ὅριον, **horion**, n. GK: *3990* [→ *3724*]. region, area, vicinity:– coasts [10], borders [1]

3726 ὁρκίζω, **horkizō**, v. GK: *1941 & 3991* [→ *3727*]. to command; implore, adjure:– adjure [2], charge [1]

3727 ὅρκος, **horkos**, n. GK: *3992* [→ *1844, 1845, 1964, 1965, 3726, 3728*]. oath:– oath [7], oaths' [2], oaths [1]

3728 ὁρκωμοσία, **horkōmosia**, n. GK: *3993* [→ *3727*+*3660*]. oath, taking of an oath:– oath [4]

3729 ὁρμάω, **hormaō**, v. GK: *3994* [→ *3730*]. to rush (as in a stampede):– ran violently [3], ran [1], rushed [1]

3730 ὁρμή, **hormē**, n. GK: *3995* [→ *874, 2868, 3729, 3731*]. plot, decision; impulse, desire:– assault [1], governor [1]

3731 ὅρμημα, **hormēma**, n. GK: *3996* [→ *3730*]. sudden violence:– violence [1]

3732 ὄρνεον, **orneon**, n. GK: *3997* [→ *3733*]. bird:– fowls [2], bird [1]

3733 ὄρνις, **ornis**, n. GK: *3989 & 3998* [→ *3732*]. hen, bird:– hen [2]

3734 ὁροθεσία, **horothesia**, n. GK: *3999* [→ *3724*+*5087*]. exact place, fixed boundary:– bounds [1]

3735 ὄρος, **oros**, n. GK: *4001* [→ *3714*]. hill, hillside, mountain, mountainside; this can refer to any elevated place from mounds to high mountains:– mountain [28], mount [21], mountains [13], hill [3]

3736 ὀρύσσω, **oryssō**, v. GK: *4002* [→ *1358, 1846*]. to dig up, dig out:– digged [3]

3737 ὀρφανός, **orphanos**, a. GK: *4003* [→ *642*]. (n.) an orphan:– comfortless [1], fatherless [1]

3738 ὀρχέομαι, **orcheomai**, v. GK: *4004*. to dance:– danced [4]

3739 ὅς, **hos**, p.rel. GK: *4005* [→ *1352, 1355, 1360, 1539, 2505, 2509, 2526, 2530, 3606, 3634, 3746, 3748, 3755, 3752, 3753, 3754, 3757, 3842, 4212, 5119*]. who, which, what, that; anyone, someone, a certain one:– which [452], whom [267], that [144], who [85], whose [53], what [45], whosoever (+*302*) [32], wherein (+*1722*) [23], whosoever (+*1437*) [19], whatsoever (+*1437*) [15], whereof [15], some [14], he [10], one [9], till (+*2193*) [9], wherewith [9], another [8], whatsoever (+*302*) [7], whereby (+*1722*) [6], whereunto (+*1519*) [6], until (+*2193*) [5], whereunto [5], because (+*473*) [4], since (+*575*) [4], the [4], till (+*891*) [4], until (+*891*) [4], whatsoever [4], when [4], where (+*1722*) [4], whereon (+*1909*) [4], whomsoever (+*1437*) [4], whomsoever (+*302*) [4], such [3], whatsoever (+*302*+*5100*) [3], whereby (+*1223*) [3], wherefore (+*156*+*1223*) [3], wherein (+*1519*) [3], wherein (+*1909*) [3], wherein [3], while (+*1722*) [3], whom (+*302*) [3], whoso (+*302*) [3], whosoever (+*302*+*4506*) [3], other [2], that (+*1437*) [2], when (+*1722*) [2], whereas (+*1722*) [2], wherefore (+*1223*) [2], whereof (+*4012*) [2], whereupon (+*1722*) [2], wherewith (+*1722*) [2], wherein [2], while (+*2193*) [2], while (+*891*) [2], whom (+*1437*) [2], another (+*3303*) [1], as (+*2596*+*5158*) [1], as (+*302*+*5100*) [1], as many as (+*3956*) [1], as [1], because (+*1752*) [1], called [1], even as (+*2596*+*3779*+*5158*) [1], even as (+*5158*) [1], he that (+*302*) [1], him [1], howbeit whereinsoever (+*302*+*1161*+*1722*) [1], in the mean time (+*1722*) [1], like [1], moreover (+*1161*+*3062*) [1], nothing (+*3756*) [1], once (+*302*+*575*) [1], one (+*3303*) [1], one man [1], others [1], since the time (+*575*) [1], soever (+*302*) [1], some (+*3303*) [1], that (+*1722*) [1], that (+*302*) [1], that (+*575*) [1], therefore (+*473*) [1], they [1], this [1], those [1], till (+*302*+*891*) [1], till (+*3360*) [1], what (+*1437*) [1], what (+*5101*) [1], whatsoever (+*1437*+*5100*) [1], whatsoever (+*302*+*302*+*5100*) [1], whatsoever (+*3956*) [1], whence [1], whereby (+*4012*) [1], whereby (+*4314*) [1], wherefore (+*1519*) [1], wherefore (+*1909*) [1], wherefore (+*5484*) [1], wherein (+*1223*) [1], wherein (+*1722*+*3778*) [1], wherein (+*4012*) [1], whereinto (+*1519*) [1], whereof (+*1537*) [1], whereon [1], whereto (+*1519*) [1], whereunto (+*3825*) [1], where [1], whether (+*1520*) [1], whither (+*1519*) [1], whomsoever (+*3956*) [1], whoso (+*1437*) [1], whosoever (+*3956*) [1]

3740 ὁσάκις, **hosakis**, adv. GK: *4006* [→ *3745*]. as often as, whenever:– as oft as (+*302*) [1], as often as (+*1437*) [1], as often as (+*302*) [1]

3741 ὅσιος, **hosios**, a. GK: *4008* [→ *462, 3742, 3743*]. holy, pious, devout; (n.) Holy One; divine decree (Ac 13:34):– holy [4], holy one [2], mercies [1]

3742 ὁσιότης, **hosiotēs**, n. GK: *4009* [→ *3741*]. holiness:– holiness [2]

3743 ὁσίως, **hosiōs**, adv. GK: *4010* [→ *3741*]. holy, in a devout manner:– holily [1]

3744 ὀσμή, **osmē**, n. GK: *4011* [→ *3605*]. fragrance, odor:– savour [4], odour [2]

3745 ὅσος, **hosos**, a. GK: *4012* [→ *3740, 4214*]. how great, how much, how far; as, just as:– as many as [25], whatsoever [7], that [9], whatsoever [6], how great [5], what [5], all that [4], as long as (+*1909*+*5550*) [3], as many as (+*302*) [3], as [3], how much [3], which [3], all [2], as long as (+*1909*) [2], inasmuch as (+*1909*) [2], inasmuch as (+*2596*) [2], little while (+*3398*+*3745*) [2], that ever [2], whatsoever (+*1437*) [2], whosoever (+*302*) [1], as (+*2596*) [1], as long as (+*5550*) [1], as many as (+*1437*) [1], as much as [1], ever [1], how many [1], inasmuch as (+*1909*+*3303*+*3767*) [1], more [1], so many as [1], what great [1], what soever [1], wherewith soever (+*302*) [1], who [1]

3746 ὅσπερ, **hosper**, p.rel.&pt. GK: *4013* [→ *3739*+*4007*]. whosoever:– whomsoever [1]

3747 ὀστέον, *osteon*; or ὀστοῦν, *ostoun*, n. GK: *4014 & 4016*. bone:– bones [4], bone [1]

3748 ὅστις, *hostis*, p.rel.&indef. GK: *4015 [→ 3739+5100]*. who, whoever, whatever; someone, anyone, everyone; a marker of time relationships: until, while:– which [82], who [30], whosoever [10], that [7], they [3], whosoever (+*302*) [3], till (+*2193*) [2], until (+*2193*) [2], whosoever (+*3956*) [2], as [1], a [1], he that [1], in that [1], such as [1], whatsoever (+*1437*+*3956*+*5100*) [1], whatsoever (+*302*) [1], what [1], whereas [1], which (+*302*) [1], whiles (+*2193*) [1]

3749 ὀστράκινος, *ostrakinos*, a. GK: *4017*. made of clay:– earthen [1], of earth [1]

3750 ὄσφρησις, *osphrēsis*, n. GK: *4018 [→ 3605]*. sense of smell:– smelling [1]

3751 ὀσφῦς, *osphys*, n. GK: *4019*. waist, loins, body; belt:– loins [8]

3752 ὅταν, *hotan*, pt.temp. GK: *4020 [→ 3739+5037+302]*. when, whenever; at once; as soon as:– when [115], as soon as [2], as long as [1], that [1], till (+*1508*) [1], whensoever [1], while [1]

3753 ὅτε, *hote*, pt.temp. GK: *4021 [→ 3739+5037]*. when, while, after; as, as soon as:– when [99], after [3], as soon as [2], that [1], while [1], whilst [1]

3754 ὅτι, *hoti*, c. GK: *4022 [→ 3739+5101]*. that; because, since; for:– that [622], for [265], *usually untranslated* [206], because [177], how that [20], how [11], because that [4], though [3], in that [1], seeing that [1], seeing [1], to [1], why [1]

3755 ὅτου, *hotou*, p.rel.&indef.gen. of *3748*. GK: *4015 [→ 3739+5100]*. a marker of time relationships: until, while; see *3748*:–

3756 οὐ, *ou*, adv.neg. GK: *4024 [→ 1847, 1848, 3760, 3761, 3762, 3763, 3764, 3765, 3766, 3768, 3777, 3780]*. no, not, not at all, in no way, absolutely not. At the beginning of a Greek question, it anticipates a positive response:– not [1209], no [140], cannot (+*1410*) [45], none [20], neither (+*2532*) [16], neither [12], nay [11], cannot [10], no (+*3956*) [7], never (+*165*+*1519*+*3361*+*3588*) [5], nothing [4], never [3], nothing (+*5101*) [3], neither (+*1161*) [2], nor (+*2532*) [2], nor [2], not (+*3361*) [2], but (+*2228*+*4183*) [1], cannot (+*1510*) [1], cannot (+*1735*) [1], cannot (+*2192*) [1], cannot (+*2480*) [1], long (+*3641*) [1], neither any (+*3762*) [1], never (+*165*+*1487*+*1519*+*3588*) [1], never (+*165*+*1519*+*3588*) [1], never (+*3361*+*4218*) [1], never (+*3361*+*4455*) [1], never before (+*3764*) [1], no more at all (+*3361*+*3765*) [1], no not one (+*1520*+*2193*) [1], none (+*3762*) [1], nothing (+*3739*) [1], nothing (+*3956*+*4487*) [1], nothing (+*5100*) [1], nothing at all (+*3762*) [1], special (+*3588*+*5177*) [1], unworthy (+*514*) [1], without (+*3326*) [1]

3757 οὗ, *hou*, adv.pl. GK: *4023 [→ 3739]*. where; to which:– where [22], whither [2], whence [1], when [1], wherein [1], whithersoever (+*1437*) [1]

3758 οὐά, *oua*, pt.interj. GK: *4025*. so!, aha!:– ah [1]

3759 οὐαί, *ouai*, pt.interj. GK: *4026*. woe!, how dreadful!, alas!:– woe [40], alas [6], woes [1]

3760 οὐδαμῶς, *oudamōs*, adv. GK: *4027 [→ 3756+1161]*. by no means:– not [1]

3761 οὐδέ, *oude*, c.neg. GK: *4028 [→ 3756+1161]*. and not, nor, neither, not either, not even:– neither [68], nor [30], not [17], no [3], nor yet [2], not so much as [2], then not [2], also not [1], and no so much as (+*2532*) [1], and not [1], even not [1], neither (+*2532*) [1], never [1], no more [1], no not so much [1], not even [1], not so much as (+*235*) [1], nothing (+*5100*) [1], yet not [1]

3762 οὐδείς, *oudeis*, a. GK: *4029 & 4032 [→ 3756+1161+1520]*. no one, not anyone, nothing:– no [116], nothing [68], none [26], any [7], man [2], not any [2], all [1], despised (+*1519*+*3049*) [1], neither any (+*1161*) [1], neither any (+*2532*) [1], neither any (+*3756*) [1], never (+*3768*) [1], none (+*3056*) [1], none (+*3756*) [1], not at all [1], nothing at all (+*3756*) [1], not [1], nought [1], ought [1], yet never (+*4455*) [1]

3763 οὐδέποτε, *oudepote*, adv. GK: *4030 [→ 3756+1161+4226+5037]*. never:– never [14], neither at any time (+*2532*) [1], nothing at any time (+*3956*) [1]

3764 οὐδέπω, *oudepō*, adv. GK: *4031 [→ 3756+1161]*. not yet, not ever:– as yet not [1], never before (+*3756*) [1], never yet [1], not yet [1], yet [1]

3765 οὐκέτι, *ouketi*, adv. GK: *4033 [→ 3756+2089]*. no longer, not again, not any more, no further:– no more [29], any more [3], after that [2], not [2], now not [2], any moe [1],

henceforth not [1], hereafter not [1], more [1], no longer [1], no more at all (+*3361*+*3756*) [1], not now [1], not yet [1], yet [1]

3766 οὐκοῦν, *oukoun*, adv. GK: *4034 [→ 3756+3767]*. so, then (to introduce a question):– then [1]

3767 οὖν, *oun*, pt.infer.&trans. GK: *4036 [→ 3304, 3766, 5105]*. therefore, then, so then:– therefore [257], then [195], so [16], and [9], now [9], wherefore [8], therefore (+*686*) [7], but [4], seeing then [3], then (+*5119*) [2], when [2], and so [1], forasmuch then as [1], forasmuch then [1], inasmuch as (+*1909*+*3303*+*3745*) [1], therefore seeing [1]

3768 οὔπω, *oupō*, adv. GK: *4037 [→ 3756]*. not yet, still not; not ever:– not yet [20], hitherto not [1], never (+*3762*) [1], no as yet [1], yet [1]

3769 οὐρά, *oura*, n. GK: *4038*. tail:– tails [4], tail [1]

3770 οὐράνιος, *ouranios*, a. GK: *4039 [→ 3772]*. heavenly, in heaven, from heaven:– heavenly [6]

3771 οὐρανόθεν, *ouranothen*, adv. GK: *4040 [→ 3772]*. from heaven:– from heaven [2]

3772 οὐρανός, *ouranos*, n. GK: *4041 [→ 2032, 3321, 3770, 3771]*. sky, air, firmament, any area above the earth; heaven(s), the place of sun, moon, and stars; heaven, in which God dwells. "The third heaven" may be a Jewish technical term for God's dwelling place; "heaven" in some contexts is a euphemism for "God" (Lk 15:18):– heaven [248], heavens [19], air [10], sky [5], heaven's [1], heavenly (+*1537*) [1]

3773 Οὐρβανός, *Ourbanos*, n.pr. GK: *4042*. Urbanus, "*refined, elegant*":– Urban [1]

3774 Οὐρίας, *Ourias*, n.pr. GK: *4043*. Uriah, "*Yahweh is [my] flame, light*":– Urias [1]

3775 οὖς, *ous*, n. GK: *4044 [→ 1801, 5621]*. ear; listening, responding:– ears [24], ear [13]

3776 οὐσία, *ousia*, n. GK: *4045 [→ 1510]*. wealth; estate, property:– goods [1], substance [1]

3777 οὔτε, *oute*, adv. [used as neg.]. GK: *4046 [→ 3756+5037]*. and not, neither, nor:– neither [45], nor [42], not [3], nor yet [2], none [1], nothing [1]

3778 οὗτος, *houtos*, p.demo. GK: *4047 [→ 3779, 5023, 5025, 5026, 5082, 5108, 5118, 5123, 5124, 5125, 5126, 5127, 5128, 5129, 5130]*. this, this one, these; (as object) him, her, it, them:– this [666], these [358], that [58], therefore (+*1223*) [43], the same [36], he [33], him [30], thus [21], for this cause (+*1223*) [14], they [13], those [13], she [12], them [11], it [9], such [9], hereby (+*1722*) [8], herein (+*1722*) [7], wherefore (+*1223*) [7], same [6], so [6], the [6], afterward (+*3326*) [4], hereafter (+*3326*) [4], therefore (+*1519*) [3], for this cause (+*1519*) [2], for this cause (+*1752*) [2], therefore (+*3844*) [2], therein (+*1722*) [2], thereunto (+*1519*) [2], to this end (+*1519*) [2], and partly (+*1161*) [1], by reason hereof (+*1223*) [1], from thenceforth (+*1537*) [1], hence (+*3326*) [1], hereby (+*1537*) [1], hereof [1], hereunto (+*1519*) [1], her [1], one [1], partly (+*3303*) [1], that same [1], that should follow (+*3326*) [1], the same (+*846*) [1], their [1], themselves [1], thereabout (+*4012*) [1], therein [1], thereunto (+*846*+*1519*) [1], therewith (+*1909*) [1], therewith [1], thus far (+*2193*) [1], wherein (+*1722*+*3739*) [1], which [1], who [1]

3779 οὕτως, *houtōs*, adv. GK: *4048 [→ 3778]*. in this manner, thus, in the same way, likewise:– so [171], thus [17], likewise [6], on this wise [6], after this manner [3], after that [1], as [1], can [1], even as (+*2596*+*3739*+*5158*) [1], for all that [1], in this manner [1], on this fashion [1], so in like manner (+*2532*) [1], what [1]

3780 οὐχί, *ouchi*, adv.neg. GK: *4049 [→ 3756]*. not, no!:– not [51], nay [5]

3781 ὀφειλέτης, *opheiletēs*, n. GK: *4050 [→ 3784]*. debtor, one who owes, is obligated, guilty:– debtors [3], debtor [2], ought [1], sinners [1]

3782 ὀφειλή, *opheilē*, n. GK: *4051 [→ 3784]*. debt; marital duty; (pl.) taxes:– debt [1], dues [1]

3783 ὀφείλημα, *opheilēma*, n. GK: *4052 [→ 3784]*. debt, obligation, what is owed:– debts [1], debt [1]

3784 ὀφείλω, *opheilō*, v. GK: *4053 [→ 3781, 3782, 3783, 3785, 4359, 5533]*. to owe, be in debt; be bound by oath; be obligated, ought, must:– ought [17], owest [3], bound [2], due [2], duty [2], behoved [1], debtor [1], debt [1], guilty [1], indebted [1], must needs [1], need [1], oweth [1], owe [1], should [1]

3785 ὄφελον, *ophelon*, pt. GK: *4054 [→ 3784]*. How I wish! How I hope!:– would [4]

3786 ὄφελος, *ophelos*, n. GK: *4055 [→ 5623]*. good, gain, benefit:– profit [2], advantageth [1]

3787 ὀφθαλμοδουλία, *ophthalmodoulia*, n. GK: *4056 [→ 3788+1401]*. eye-service, service performed to attract attention:– eyeservice [2]

3788 ὀφθαλμός, *ophthalmos*, n. GK: *4057 [→ 503, 3442, 3787; cf. 3708]*. eye, the organ of sight; by extension: the faculty of mental perception and understanding:– eyes [71], eye [30], sight [1]

3789 ὄφις, *ophis*, n. GK: *4058*. snake, serpent:– serpent [8], serpents [6]

3790 ὀφρῦς, *ophrys*, n. GK: *4059*. eyebrow, brow (of a hill):– brow [1]

3791 ὀχλέω, *ochleō*, v. GK: *4061 [→ 3793]*. (pass.) to be tormented, disturbed:– vexed [2]

3792 ὀχλοποιέω, *ochlopoieō*, v. GK: *4062 [→ 3793+4160]*. to form a mob:– gathered a company [1]

3793 ὄχλος, *ochlos*, n. GK: *4063 [→ 1776, 3791, 3792, 3926]*. crowd, people, multitude, mob, a gathering of any size, sometimes with the implication that these are common folk and not leaders or nobility:– people [83], multitude [59], multitudes [20], company [7], press [5], number [1]

3794 ὀχύρωμα, *ochyrōma*, n. GK: *4065 [→ 2192]*. stronghold, fortress; some translate as "prison":– strong holds [1]

3795 ὀψάριον, *opsarion*, n. GK: *4066 [→ 3800, 3953]*. (small) fish:– fish [3], fishes [1], small fishes [1]

3796 ὀψέ, *opse*, adv. GK: *4067 [→ 3797, 3798]*. in the evening, late in the day; (pp.) after:– at even [1], even [1], in the end [1]

3797 ὄψιμος, *opsimos*, a. GK: *4069 [→ 3796]*. late (in the season, April-May in the modern calendar), spring:– latter [1]

3798 ὄψιος, *opsios*, a. GK: *4070 [→ 3796]*. late; (n.) evening:– even [8], evening [5], at even (+*1096*) [1], eventide (+*3588*+*5610*) [1]

3799 ὄψις, *opsis*, n. GK: *4071 [→ 3708]*. face; appearance:– appearance [1], countenance [1], face [1]

3800 ὀψώνιον, *opsōnion*, n. GK: *4072 [→ 3795+5608]*. pay, wage; support, compensation:– wages [3], charges [1]

3801 ὁ ὢν καί ὁ ἦν καί ὁ ἐρχόμενος, *ho ōn kai ho ēn kai ho erchomenos*, rel.p.+v.+c. GK: *3836 + 1639 + 2779 + 2262 [→ 3588+1510+2064+2532]*. who is and who was and who is to come, a title of Christ:–

3802 παγιδεύω, *pagideuō*, v. GK: *4074 [→ 4078]*. to trap, entrap:– entangle [1]

3803 παγίς, *pagis*, n. GK: *4075 [→ 4078]*. trap, snare:– snare [5]

Πάγος, *Pagos*. See 697.

3804 πάθημα, *pathēma*, n. GK: *4077 [→ 3958]*. suffering, misfortune; passion:– sufferings [10], afflictions [3], affections [1], motions [1], suffering [1]

3805 παθητός, *pathētos*, a. GK: *4078 [→ 3958]*. subject to suffering:– suffer [1]

3806 πάθος, *pathos*, n. GK: *4079 [→ 3958]*. lust, sexual passion:– affections [1], inordinate affection [1], lust [1]

πάθω, *pathō*. See 3958.

3807 παιδαγωγός, *paidagōgos*, n. GK: *4080 [→ 3816+71]*. guardian, custodian, supervisor:– schoolmaster [2], instructors [1]

3808 παιδάριον, *paidarion*, n. GK: *4081 [→ 3816]*. little boy, child:– children [1], lad [1]

3809 παιδεία, *paideia*, n. GK: *4082 [→ 3816]*. discipline, training:– chastening [3], chastisement [1], instruction [1], nurture [1]

3810 παιδευτής, *paideutēs*, a. GK: *4083 [→ 3816]*. instructor, teacher; discipliner, corrector:– corrected [1], instructor [1]

3811 παιδεύω, *paideuō*, v. GK: *4084 [→ 3816]*. instruct, train, educate, as an on-going matter, in accord with rules and proper conduct; discipline, punish, for the purpose of better behavior:– chastened [3], chasteneth [2], chastise [2], chasten [1], instructing [1], learned [1], learn [1], taught [1], teaching [1]

3812 παιδιόθεν, *paidiothen*, adv. GK: *4085 & 4088 [→ 3816]*. from childhood:– of a child [1]

3813 παιδίον, *paidion*, n. GK: *4086 [→ 3816]*. child:– child [15], children [9], young child [8], little children [7], little

child [5], damsel [4], children's [1], young child's [1], young children [1]

3814 παιδίσκη, *paidiskē*, n. GK: *4087* [→ *3816*]. female servant, female slave, maidservant:– bondwoman [4], damsel [4], maid [2], bondmaid [1], maidens [1], maids [1]

3815 παίζω, *paizō*, v. GK: *4089* [→ *1701, 1702, 1703; cf. 3816*]. to indulge in revelry, play, amuse oneself, dance, sometimes a euphemism for sexual immorality:– play [1]

3816 παῖς, *pais*, n. GK: *4090* [→ *521, 3807, 3808, 3809, 3810, 3811, 3812, 3813, 3814; cf. 3815*]. boy, child, youth, usually below the age of puberty and not necessarily male; a personal servant, slave, attendant, with a possible implication of kind regard or close relationship; the word used in the Greek version of Isaiah, quoted in NT, for "servant" of the Lord:– servant [8], child [5], son [3], children [2], servants [2], maiden [1], maid [1], menservants [1], young man [1]

3817 παίω, *paiō*, v. GK: *4091*. to strike, hit (and so wound):– smote [4], striketh [1]

3818 Πακατιανός, *Pakatianos*, a.pr.g. GK: *4092*. Pacatian, "*in Pacatia*":– Pacatiana [1]

3819 πάλαι, *palai*, adv. GK: *4093* [→ *1597, 3820, 3821, 3822*]. long ago, in the past, already:– any while [1], great while ago [1], long ago [1], of old [1], old [1], past [1]

3820 παλαιός, *palaios*, a. GK: *4094* [→ *3819*]. old:– old [19]

3821 παλαιότης, *palaiotēs*, n. GK: *4095* [→ *3819*]. the old way, obsoleteness, age:– oldness [1]

3822 παλαιόω, *palaioō*, v. GK: *4096* [→ *3819*]. (act.) to make obsolete; (pass.) to wear out, become obsolete, become old:– wax old [1], decayeth [1], made old [1]

3823 πάλη, *palē*, n. GK: *4097*. struggle:– wrestle (+*1510*) [1]

3824 παλιγγενεσία, *palingenesia*, n. GK: *4098 & 4100* [→ *3825+1096*]. renewal; rebirth, regeneration:– regeneration [2]

3825 πάλιν, *palin*, adv. GK: *4099* [→ *3824*]. again, once more; furthermore; on the other hand:– again [141], whereunto (+*3739*) [1]

3826 παμπληθεί, *pamplēthei*, adv. GK: *4101 & 4113* [→ *3956+4130*]. with one voice, all together:– all at once [1]

3827 πάμπολυς, *pampolys*, a. GK: *4102* [→ *3956+4183*]. very great:– very great [1]

3828 Παμφυλία, *Pamphylia*, n.pr. GK: *4103* [→ *3956+5453*]. Pamphylia:– Pamphylia [5]

3829 πανδοχεῖον, *pandocheion*, n. GK: *4104 & 4106* [→ *3956+1209*]. inn:– inn [1]

3830 πανδοχεύς, *pandocheus*, n. GK: *4105 & 4107* [→ *3956+1209*]. innkeeper:– host [1]

3831 πανήγυρις, *panēgyris*, n. GK: *4108* [→ *3956+71*]. joyful assembly, festal gathering:– general assembly [1]

3832 πανοικεί, *panoikei*, adv. GK: *4109* [→ *3956+3624*]. with one's whole family:– all house [1]

3833 πανοπλία, *panoplia*, n. GK: *4110* [→ *3956+3696*]. full armor, worn by a heavily armed soldier:– whole armour [2], all armour [1]

3834 πανουργία, *panourgia*, n. GK: *4111* [→ *3956+2041*]. cunning, craftiness, deception, duplicity:– craftiness [3], cunning craftiness [1], subtilty [1]

3835 πανοῦργος, *panourgos*, a. GK: *4112* [→ *3956+2041*]. crafty, clever, sly:– crafty [1]

3836 πανταχόθεν, *pantachothen*, adv. GK: *4115* [→ *3956*]. from every direction:– from every quarter [1]

3837 πανταχοῦ, *pantachou*, adv. GK: *4114 & 4116* [→ *3956*]. everywhere; in all directions:– every where [6], in all places [1], throughout (+*1519*) [1]

3838 παντελής, *pantelēs*, a. GK: *4117* [→ *3956+5056*]. complete, perfect, absolute; at all:– in no wise (+*1519+3361+3588*) [1], uttermost [1]

3839 πάντη, *pantē*, adv. GK: *4118* [→ *3956*]. in every way:– always [1]

3840 πάντοθεν, *pantothen*, adv. GK: *4119* [→ *3956*]. from all directions; completely, entirely:– on every side [1], round about [1]

3841 παντοκράτωρ, *pantokratōr*, n. GK: *4120* [→ *3956+2904*]. Almighty; this title for God translates the Hebrew 7372, [Lord] "of Hosts" (the heavenly armies), and

Hebrew 8724, "Shaddai," (probably) God the Mountain, powerful and immovable:– Almighty [9], Omnipotent [1]

3842 πάντοτε, *pantote*, adv. GK: *4121* [→ *3956+3739+5037*]. always, at all times, forever:– always [29], ever [6], alway [5], evermore [2]

3843 πάντως, *pantōs*, adv. GK: *4122* [→ *3956*]. surely, certainly, by all possible means, quite:– altogether [1], by all means [2], at all [1], in no wise [1], must needs (+*1163*) [1], no doubt [1], surely [1]

3844 παρά, *para*, pp. GK: *4123* [→ *492, 531, 532, 3845, 3846, 3847, 3848, 3849, 3850, 3851, 3852, 3853, 3854, 3855, 3856, 3858, 3859, 3860, 3861, 3862, 3863, 3864, 3865, 3866, 3867, 3868, 3869, 3870, 3871, 3872, 3873, 3874, 3875, 3876, 3877, 3878, 3879, 3880, 3881, 3882, 3883, 3884, 3885, 3886, 3887, 3888, 3889, 3890, 3891, 3892, 3893, 3894, 3895, 3896, 3897, 3898, 3899, 3900, 3901, 3902, 3903, 3904, 3905, 3906, 3907, 3908, 3909, 3910, 3911, 3912, 3914, 3915, 3916, 3918, 3919, 3920, 3921, 3922, 3923, 3924, 3925, 3926, 3927, 3928, 3929, 3944, 3945, 3946, 3947, 3948, 3949, 3950, 3951, 3952, 3953, 3970, 4836, 4837, 4838, 4839, 4840*]. (gen.) from; (dat.) with, beside, among, in the sight of; (acc.) beside, along side, by, at:– of [53], with [42], from [24], by [14], at [12], by side [9], than [9], above [4], before [3], contrary to [3], against [2], among [2], any other than [2], in [2], more than [2], nigh unto [1], therefore (+*3778*) [2], amongst [1], friends (+*3588*) [1], had (+*3588*) [1], in the sight [1], past [1], save [1], such as give (+*3588*) [1]

3845 παραβαίνω, *parabainō*, v. GK: *4124* [→ *3844+305*]. to break, transgress; to leave, turn aside:– transgress [2], by transgression fell [1], transgresseth [1]

3846 παραβάλλω, *paraballō*, v. GK: *4125* [→ *3844+906*]. to come near (by ship); compare:– arrived [1], compare [1]

3847 παράβασις, *parabasis*, n. GK: *4126* [→ *3844+305*]. transgression, breaking, violation:– transgression [4], transgressions [2], breaking [1]

3848 παραβάτης, *parabatēs*, n. GK: *4127* [→ *3844+305*]. lawbreaker, transgressor:– transgressor [2], breaker [1], transgressors [1], transgress [1]

3849 παραβιάζομαι, *parabiazomai*, v. GK: *4128* [→ *3844+970*]. to urge strongly, persuade:– constrained [2]

3850 παραβολή, *parabolē*, n. GK: *4130* [→ *3844+906*]. parable, an illustration that teaches in a story or extended figure of speech; proverb, a short pithy saying:– parable [31], parables [15], figure [2], comparison [1], proverb [1]

3851 παραβουλεύομαι, *parabouleuomai*; or παραβολεύομαι, *paraboleuomai*, v. GK: *4131* [→ *3844+1014*]. to be careless, have no concern:– not regarding [1]

3852 παραγγελία, *parangelia*, n. GK: *4132* [→ *3844+32*]. order, command; instruction:– charge [2], commandments [1], commandment [1], straitly command (+*3853*) [1]

3853 παραγγέλλω, *parangellō*, v. GK: *4133* [→ *3844+32*]. to order, command, direct; to give instruction:– commanded [11], command [7], charged [3], charge [2], charging [1], commandeth [1], declare [1], gave commandment [1], give charge [1], give in charge [1], straitly command (+*3852*) [1]

3854 παραγίνομαι, *paraginomai*, v. GK: *4134* [→ *3844+1096*]. to come, arrive, be present; to appear:– came [16], come [15], cometh [3], coming [1], present [1], went [1]

3855 παράγω, *paragō*, v. GK: *4135* [→ *3844+71*]. to pass by, go on, walk beside; to pass away:– passed by [5], passeth away [2], departed [1], passed forth [1], past [1]

3856 παραδειγματίζω, *paradeigmatizō*, v. GK: *4136* [→ *3844+1164*]. to subject to public disgrace, hold up to contempt:– make a publick example [1], put to open shame [1]

3857 παράδεισος, *paradeisos*, n. GK: *4137*. paradise, a place of blessedness, from the base meaning of "garden":– paradise [3]

3858 παραδέχομαι, *paradechomai*, v. GK: *4138* [→ *3844+1209*]. to accept, welcome, receive:– receive [4], receiveth [1]

3859 παραδιατριβή, *paradiatribē*, n. GK: *4139* [→ *3844+1223+5147*]. useless occupation:– perverse disputings [1]

3860 παραδίδωμι, *paradidōmi*, v. GK: *4140* [→ *3844+1325*]. to hand over, betray, deliver to prison; to entrust, commit:– delivered [39], betrayed [19], betray [17], deliver [9], deliver up [6], delivered up [4], gave up [4], betrayeth [3], committed [2], deliveredst [2], gave [2], recommended [2], betrayest [1], brought forth [1], cast into prison [1], delivered into [1], delivering up [1], delivering [1], gave over [1], given over [1], given [1], give [1], hazarded [1], put in prison [1]

3861 παράδοξος, *paradoxos*, a. GK: *4141* [→ *3844+1391*]. remarkable, wonderful:– strange [1]

3862 παράδοσις, *paradosis*, n. GK: *4142* [→ *3844+1325*]. tradition; teachings:– tradition [10], traditions [2], ordinances [1]

3863 παραζηλόω, *parazēloō*, v. GK: *4143* [→ *3844+2205*]. to make envious, arouse jealousy:– provoke to jealousy [3], provoke to emulation [1]

3864 παραθαλάσσιος, *parathalassios*, a. GK: *4144* [→ *3844+2281*]. by the lake, by the sea:– upon the sea coast [1]

3865 παραθεωρέω, *paratheōreō*, v. GK: *4145* [→ *3844+2334*]. (pass.) to be overlooked, neglected:– neglected [1]

3866 παραθήκη, *parathēkē*, n. GK: *4146* [→ *3844+5087*]. deposit, thing entrusted to:– committed unto [1]

3867 παραινέω, *paraineō*, v. GK: *4147* [→ *3844+136*]. to warn, urge:– admonished [1], exhort [1]

3868 παραιτέομαι, *paraiteomai*, v. GK: *4148* [→ *3844+154*]. to request, beg; to make excuses; to refuse, reject:– refuse [4], excused [2], avoid [1], intreated [1], make excuse [1], refused [1], reject [1]

3869 παρακαθίζω, *parakathizō*, v. GK: *4149 & 4150* [→ *3844+2523*]. to sit down beside:– sat [1]

3870 παρακαλέω, *parakaleō*, v. GK: *4151* [→ *3844+2564*]. to ask, beg, plead; to comfort, encourage, exhort, urge; to call, invite:– besought [21], beseech [20], exhort [14], comforted [13], comfort [8], desired [5], pray [4], exhorted [3], exhorting [3], beseeching [2], comforteth [2], desiring [2], intreat [2], prayed [2], called for [1], desiredst [1], exhortation [1], exhorteth [1], given exhortation (+*3056*) [1], intreated [1], of good comfort [1]

3871 παρακαλύπτω, *parakalyptō*, v. GK: *4152* [→ *3844+2572*]. (pass.) to be hidden:– hid [1]

3872 παρακαταθήκη, *parakatathēkē*, n. GK: *4153* [→ *3844+2596+5087*]. deposit:– committed to trust [1], committed unto [1]

3873 παράκειμαι, *parakeimai*, v. GK: *4154* [→ *3844+2749*]. to be present, ready:– present [2]

3874 παράκλησις, *paraklēsis*, n. GK: *4155* [→ *3844+2564*]. encouragement, comfort, consolation, appeal:– consolation [14], exhortation [8], comfort [6], intreaty [1]

3875 παράκλητος, *paraklētos*, n. GK: *4156* [→ *3844+2564*]. counselor, intercessor, helper, one who encourages and comforts; in the NT it refers exclusively to the Holy Spirit and to Jesus Christ:– comforter [4], advocate [1]

3876 παρακοή, *parakoē*, n. GK: *4157* [→ *3844+191*]. disobedience, unwillingness to hear:– disobedience [3]

3877 παρακολουθέω, *parakoloutheō*, v. GK: *4158* [→ *3844+190; cf. 1.3*]. to follow, accompany; to know all about; to investigate:– attained [1], follow [1], fully known [1], understanding [1]

3878 παρακούω, *parakouō*, v. GK: *4159* [→ *3844+191*]. to refuse to listen, ignore:– neglect to hear [2]

3879 παρακύπτω, *parakyptō*, v. GK: *4160* [→ *3844+2955*]. to bend over; to look (intently):– looketh [1], look [1], stooped down and looked [1], stooping down and looking [1], stooping down [1]

3880 παραλαμβάνω, *paralambanō*, v. GK: *4161* [→ *3844+2983*]. to take with; take charge of; to receive, accept:– took [14], received [13], taketh [6], taken [5], take [4], took unto [2], receive [1], receiving [1], take unto [1], taketh to [1], taketh with [1], took with [1]

3881 παραλέγομαι, *paralegomai*, v. GK: *4162* [→ *3844+3004*]. to sail past, move along:– passing [1], sailed [1]

3882 παράλιος, *paralios*, a. GK: *4163* [→ *3844+217*]. (located) by the sea; (n.) seacoast:– sea coast [1]

3883 παραλλαγή, *parallagē*, n. GK: *4164* [→ *3844+236*]. change, variation:– variableness [1]

3884 παραλογίζομαι, *paralogizomai*, v. GK: *4165* [→ *3844+3004*]. to deceive, delude:– beguile [1], deceiving [1]

3885 παραλυτικός, *paralytikos*, a. GK: *4166 & 4167* [→ *3844+3089*]. (n.) paralytic, lame person:– sick of the palsy [7], had the palsy [1], man sick of the palsy [1], one sick of the palsy [1]

3886 παραλύω, *paralyō*, v. GK: *4168* [→ *3844+3089*]. (pass.) to be paralyzed, disabled; (n.) paralytic:– sick of the palsy [2], feeble [1], taken with a palsy [1], taken with palsies [1]

3887 παραμένω, *paramenō*, v. GK: *4169* [→ *3844+3306*]. to continue; to remain with:– abide [1], continueth [1], continue [1]

3888 παραμυθέομαι, *paramytheomai*, v. GK: *4170* [→ *3844+3454*]. to comfort, encourage, console:– comforted [2], comfort [2]

3889 παραμυθία, *paramythia*, n. GK: *4171* [→ *3844+3454*]. comfort, consolation:– comfort [1]

3890 παραμύθιον, *paramythion*, n. GK: *4172* [→ *3844+3454*]. comfort, consolation, encouragement:– comfort [1]

3891 παρανομέω, *paranomeō*, v. GK: *4174* [→ *3844+3551*]. to violate the law, act contrary to the law:– contrary to law [1]

3892 παρανομία, *paranomia*, n. GK: *4175* [→ *3844+3551*]. wrongdoing, lawlessness:– iniquity [1]

3893 παραπικραίνω, *parapikrainō*, v. GK: *4176* [→ *3844+4089*]. to rebel, disobey:– provoke [1]

3894 παραπικρασμός, *parapikrasmos*, n. GK: *4177* [→ *3844+4089*]. rebellion, revolt:– provocation [2]

3895 παραπίπτω, *parapiptō*, v. GK: *4178* [→ *3844+4098*]. to fall away, commit apostasy:– fall away [1]

3896 παραπλέω, *parapleō*, v. GK: *4179* [→ *3844+4126*]. to sail past:– sail by [1]

3897 παραπλήσιος, *paraplēsios*, a. GK: *4180* [→ *3844+4139*]. (adv.) almost, nearly:– nigh unto [1]

3898 παραπλησίως, *paraplēsiōs*, adv. GK: *4181* [→ *3844+4139*]. in just the same way:– likewise [1]

3899 παραπορεύομαι, *paraporeuomai*, v. GK: *4182* [→ *3844+4198*]. to pass by, go through:– passed by [3], passed [1], went [1]

3900 παράπτωμα, *paraptōma*, n. GK: *4183* [→ *3844+4098*]. trespass, transgression, sin against; to sin as a moral failure to keep a command, fig., stepping out of the bounds of God's law:– trespasses [9], offence [5], sins [3], fall [2], offences [2], faults [1], fault [1]

3901 παραρρέω, *pararreō*, v. GK: *4184* [→ *3844+4482*]. to drift away, flow past, slip away:– slip [1]

3902 παράσημος, *parasēmos*, a. GK: *4185* [→ *3844+4592*]. distinguished, marked; (n.) figurehead, emblem (on a ship):– sign [1]

3903 παρασκευάζω, *paraskeuazō*, v. GK: *4186* [→ *3844+4632*]. (act.) to prepare; (mid.) to get ready; (mid./pass.) to be ready:– ready [2], made ready [1], prepare [1]

3904 παρασκευή, *paraskeuē*, n. GK: *4187* [→ *3844+4632*]. Preparation Day:– preparation [6]

3905 παρατείνω, *parateinō*, v. GK: *4189* [→ *1614; cf. 3844*]. to keep on, prolong, extend:– continued [1]

3906 παρατηρέω, *paratēreō*, v. GK: *4190* [→ *3844+5083*]. to watch closely, observe:– watched [5], observe [1]

3907 παρατήρησις, *paratērēsis*, n. GK: *4191* [→ *3844+5083*]. careful observation:– observation [1]

3908 παρατίθημι, *paratithēmi*, v. GK: *4192* [→ *3844+5087*]. (act.) to set before; (mid.) to entrust, commit:– set before [8], commend [2], commit [2], put forth [2], alleging [1], commended [1], commit the keeping [1], committed [1], set meat before (+*5132*) [1]

3909 παρατυγχάνω, *paratynchanō*, v. GK: *4193* [→ *3844+5177*]. to happen to be there:– met with [1]

3910 παραυτίκα, *parautika*, adv. GK: *4194* [→ *3844+846*]. (a.) momentary:– for a moment [1]

3911 παραφέρω, *parapherō*, v. GK: *4195* [→ *3844+5342*]. to take away, remove; (pass.) to be carried away:– remove [1], take away [1]

3912 παραφρονέω, *paraphroneō*, v. GK: *4196* [→ *3913*]. to be out of one's mind, insane:– fool [1]

3913 παραφρονία, *paraphronia*, n. GK: *4197* [→ *3912*]. madness, insanity:– madness [1]

3914 παραχειμάζω, *paracheimazō*, v. GK: *4199* [→ *3844+5510*]. to spend the winter:– winter [3], wintered [1]

3915 παραχειμασία, *paracheimasia*, n. GK: *4200* [→ *3844+5510*]. spending the winter:– winter in [1]

3916 παραχρῆμα, *parachrēma*, adv. GK: *4202* [→ *3844+5530*]. immediately, instantly, at once:– immediately [13], straightway [3], forthwith [1], presently [1], soon [1]

3917 πάρδαλις, *pardalis*, n. GK: *4203*. leopard:– leopard [1]

3918 πάρειμι, *pareimi*, v. GK: *4205* [→ *3844+1510*]. to be present, here; to have come:– present [12], come [2], came [1], have [1], here present [1], here [1], lacketh (+*3361*) [1]

3919 παρεισάγω, *pareisagō*, v. GK: *4206* [→ *3844+1519+71*]. to bring in secretly:– privily bring in [1]

3920 παρείσακτος, *pareisaktos*, a. GK: *4207* [→ *3844+1519+71*]. brought in secretly, infiltrated:– unawares brought in [1]

3921 παρεισδύω, *pareisdyō*, v. GK: *4208* [→ *3844+1519+1416*]. to slip in secretly:– crept in unawares [1]

3922 παρεισέρχομαι, *pareiserchomai*, v. GK: *4209* [→ *3844+1519+2064*]. to come in, sneak in; to add to:– came in privily [1], entered [1]

3923 παρεισφέρω, *pareispherō*, v. GK: *4210* [→ *3844+1519+5342*]. to do one's best:– giving [1]

3924 παρεκτός, *parektos*, adv.&pp.*. GK: *4211* [→ *3844+1537*]. (adv.) besides; (pp.) except for, apart from:– except [1], saving for [1], without [1]

3925 παρεμβολή, *parembolē*, n. GK: *4213* [→ *3844+1722+906*]. camp, barracks; army:– castle [6], camp [3], armies [1]

3926 παρενοχλέω, *parenochleō*, v. GK: *4214* [→ *3844+1722+3793*]. to make difficult, trouble:– trouble [1]

3927 παρεπίδημος, *parepidēmos*, a. GK: *4215* [→ *3844+1909+1218*]. (n.) stranger:– pilgrims [2], strangers [1]

3928 παρέρχομαι, *parerchomai*, v. GK: *4216* [→ *3844+2064*]. to go by, pass by; (pass.) to pass away, come to an end, disappear; be taken away:– pass away [10], pass [8], past [3], came [1], come forth [1], go [1], pass over [1], passed away [1], passed by [1], passeth by [1], passing by [1], past away [1], transgressed [1]

3929 πάρεσις, *paresis*, n. GK: *4217* [→ *863; cf. 3844*]. leaving unpunished, passing over:– remission [1]

3930 παρέχω, *parechō*, v. GK: *4218* [→ *3844+2192*]. to present, give; to show, give proof; to cause, bring about, promote; (mid.) to set (an example); to provide; to get for oneself:– trouble (+*2873*) [4], brought [2], do [1], give unto [1], given [1], giveth [1], kept [1], minister [1], offer [1], shewed [1], shewing [1], troubleth (+*2873*) [1]

3931 παρηγορία, *parēgoria*, n. GK: *4219* [→ *3844+71*]. comfort:– comfort [1]

3932 παρθενία, *parthenia*, n. GK: *4220* [→ *3933*]. virginity:– virginity [1]

3933 παρθένος, *parthenos*, n. GK: *4221* [→ *3932*]. virgin (male and female), one who has never engaged in sexual relations:– virgin [7], virgins [6], virgin's [1]

3934 Πάρθοι, *Parthoi*, n.pr.g. GK: *4222*. Parthian:– Parthians [1]

3935 παρίημι, *pariēmi*, v. GK: *4223* [→ *863; cf. 3844*]. to leave undone, neglect; (pass.) to be feeble, weakened, listless:– hang down [1]

3936 παρίστημι, *paristēmi*, or παριστάνω, *paristanō*, v. GK: *4225* [→ *3844+2476*]. to place beside, put at disposal; to present, make an offering; (intr.) to stand before, provide, come to aid:– stood by [11], present [7], yield [4], brought before [2], stand [2], assist [1], come [1], commendeth [1], give [1], presented before [1], presented [1], prove [1], provide [1], shewed [1], shew [1], stand before [1], standing by [1], stood up [1], stood with [1], stood [1], yielded [1]

3937 Παρμενᾶς, *Parmenas*, n.pr.m. GK: *4226*. Parmenas, "*steady, reliable*":– Parmenas [1]

3938 πάροδος, *parodos*, n. GK: *4227* [→ *3844+3598*]. passing by:– way [1]

3939 παροικέω, *paroikeō*, v. GK: *4228* [→ *3844+3624*]. to live as a stranger, visit; to migrate:– sojourned [1], stranger [1]

3940 παροικία, *paroikia*, n. GK: *4229* [→ *3844+3624*]. residence as a stranger:– dwelt as strangers [1], sojourning [1]

3941 πάροικος, *paroikos*, a. GK: *4230* [→ *3844+3624*]. strange; (n.) alien, foreigner, stranger:– foreigners [1], sojourn (+*1510*) [1], strangers [1], stranger [1]

3942 παροιμία, *paroimia*, n. GK: *4231*. figure of speech, proverb, maxim:– proverbs [2], proverb [2], parable [1]

3943 πάροινος, *paroinos*, a. GK: *4232* [→ *3844+3631*]. drunken, given to drunkenness:– given to wine [2]

3944 παροίχομαι, *paroichomai*, v. GK: *4233* [→ *3844*]. to pass by:– past [1]

3945 παρομοιάζω, *paromoiazō*, v. GK: *4234* [→ *3844+3664*]. to be like:– like [1]

3946 παρόμοιος, *paromoios*, a. GK: *4235* [→ *3844+3664*]. like, similar:– like [2]

3947 παροξύνω, *paroxynō*, v. GK: *4236* [→ *3844+3691*]. (intr.) to be greatly distressed; to be angered, irritated:– easily provoked [1], stirred [1]

3948 παροξυσμός, *paroxysmos*, n. GK: *4237* [→ *3844+3691*]. sharp disagreement; spurring on, encouraging:– contention sharp [1], provoke unto [1]

3949 παροργίζω, *parorgizō*, v. GK: *4239* [→ *3844+3709*]. to anger, exasperate:– anger [1], provoke to wrath [1]

3950 παροργισμός, *parorgismos*, n. GK: *4240* [→ *3844+3709*]. anger:– wrath [1]

3951 παροτρύνω, *parotrynō*, v. GK: *4241* [→ *3844*]. to incite, arouse:– stirred up [1]

3952 παρουσία, *parousia*, n. GK: *4242* [→ *3844+1510*]. presence; coming, advent; in the NT usually of the second coming of the Son of Man, arriving as a conquering king:– coming [22], presence [2]

3953 παροψίς, *paropsis*, n. GK: *4243* [→ *3844+3795*]. dish:– platter [2]

3954 παρρησία, *parrēsia*, n. GK: *4244* [→ *3956+4487*]. boldness, confidence, frankness; public, openness (of speech):– boldness [8], confidence [6], openly [4], plainly [3], boldly (+*1722*) [1], boldly (+*3326*) [1], boldly [1], boldness of speech [1], bold [1], freely (+*3326*) [1], known openly (+*1722*) [1], openly (+*1722*) [1], plainly (+*1722*) [1], plainness of speech [1]

3955 παρρησιάζομαι, *parrēsiazomai*, v. GK: *4245* [→ *3956+4487*]. to speak boldly, preach fearlessly:– speak boldly [2], boldly [1], bold [1], freely [1], preached boldly [1], spake boldly [1], speaking boldly [1], waxed bold [1]

3956 πᾶς, *pas*, a. GK: *4246* [→ *537, 1275, 3826, 3827, 3828, 3829, 3830, 3831, 3832, 3833, 3834, 3835, 3836, 3837, 3838, 3839, 3840, 3841, 3842, 3843, 3954, 3955*]. all, every (thing, one), whole; always:– all [976], every [133], whosoever [31], every one [28], whole [12], any [9], no (+*3756*) [7], whatsoever [7], always (+*1223*) [3], every (+*2596*) [3], whosoever (+*302+3739*) [3], always (+*1722+2540*) [2], no (+*3361*) [2], whosoever (+*3748*) [2], all manner [1], alway (+*2250+3588*) [1], any one [1], as many as (+*3739*) [1], as many as [1], continually (+*1223*) [1], daily (+*2250+2596*) [1], daily (+*2250*) [1], ever (+*165+1519+3588*) [1], every man [1], every one's [1], every thing [1], every where [1], nothing (+*3756+4487*) [1], nothing at any time (+*3763*) [1], throughly (+*1722*) [1], whatsoever (+*1437+3748+5100*) [1], whatsoever (+*3739*) [1], whomsoever (+*3739*) [1], whosoever (+*3739*) [1]

3957 πάσχα, *pascha*, n. GK: *4247*. Passover, Passover week; Passover meal; Passover lamb:– passover [28], Easter [1]

3958 πάσχω, *paschō*, v. GK: *4248* [→ *2552, 2553, 3356, 3663, 3804, 3805, 3806, 4310, 4777, 4834, 4835, 4841*]. to experience, suffer, endure (almost always in NT with reference to unpleasant experiences):– suffer [21], suffered [17], felt [1], passion [1], suffering [1], vexed [1]

3959 Πάταρα, *Patara*, n.pr. GK: *4249*. Patara:– Patara [1]

3960 πατάσσω, *patassō*, v. GK: *4250*. to hit, strike; kill:– smite [5], smote [4], stroke [1]

3961 πατέω, *pateō*, v. GK: *4251* [→ *1704, 2662, 4043*]. to trample on, tread on:– tread under foot [1], treadeth [1], tread [1], trodden down [1], trodden [1]

3962 πατήρ, *patēr*, n. GK: *4252* [→ *493, 494, 540, 2810, 3964, 3965, 3966, 3967, 3968, 3969, 3970, 3971, 4986, 4989*]. father, a male parent or ancestor; by extension: an honorific title, leader, archetype; (pl.) parents, ancestors (of both

genders):– father [347], fathers [52], father's [17], fathers' [1], parents [1]

3963 Πάτμος, *Patmos*, n.pr. GK: *4253*. Patmos:– Patmos [1]

3964 πατραλῴας, *patraloas*, n. GK: *4254 & 4260* [→ *3962+248*]. one who kills one's father:– murderers of fathers [1]

3965 πατριά, *patria*, n. GK: *4255* [→ *3962*]. family, family line, clan; people, nation:– family [1], kindreds [1], lineage [1]

3966 πατριάρχης, *patriarches*, n. GK: *4256* [→ *3962+757*]. patriarch, father of a nation:– patriarchs [2], patriarch [2]

3967 πατρικός, *patrikos*, a. GK: *4257* [→ *3962*]. paternal, from one's ancestors:– fathers [1]

3968 πατρίς, *patris*, n. GK: *4258* [→ *3962*]. hometown, homeland, land of one's ancestors:– country [8]

3969 Πατροβᾶς, *Patrobas*, n.pr. GK: *4259* [→ *3962+979*]. Patrobas, "*father of existence*":– Patrobas [1]

3970 πατροπαράδοτος, *patroparadotos*, a. GK: *4261* [→ *3962+3844+1325*]. handed down from forefathers:– received by tradition from fathers [1]

3971 πατρῷος, *patroos*, a. GK: *4262* [→ *3962*]. ancestral, from forefathers:– fathers [3]

3972 Παῦλος, *Paulos*, n.pr. GK: *4263*. Paul, Paulus, "*little*":– Paul [157], Paul's [6], Paulus [1]

3973 παύω, *pauo*, v. GK: *4264* [→ *180, 372, 373, 1879, 2663, 2664, 4875*]. (act.) to cause to stop; (mid.) to stop, cease, finish:– ceased [7], cease [4], left [2], ceaseth [1], refrain [1]

3974 Πάφος, *Paphos*, n.pr. GK: *4265*. Paphos:– Paphos [2]

3975 παχύνω, *pachyno*, v. GK: *4266*. to become calloused of heart, make fat, and so unable to understand:– waxed gross [2]

3976 πέδη, *pede*, n. GK: *4267* [→ *3978*]. foot shackle, fetter:– fetters [3]

3977 πεδινός, *pedinos*, a. GK: *4268* [→ *3978*]. level, flat:– plain (+*5117*) [1]

3978 πεζεύω, *pezeuo*, v. GK: *4269* [→ *3976, 3977, 3979, 4759, 4760, 5132, 5133*]. to go on foot, travel by walking:– go afoot [1]

3979 πεζῇ, *peze*, adv. GK: *4270 & 4271* [→ *3978*]. on foot:– afoot [1], on foot [1]

3980 πειθαρχέω, *peitharcheo*, v. GK: *4272* [→ *3982+757*]. to obey; to take advice:– obey [2], hearkened [1], obey magistrates [1]

3981 πειθός, *peithos*, a. GK: *4273* [→ *3982*]. persuasive:– enticing [1]

3982 πείθω, *peitho*, v. GK: *4275* [→ *374, 543, 544, 545, 2138, 3980, 3981, 3988, 4006, 4086; cf. 4103*]. to convince, persuade; to trust in, have confidence in, be persuaded:– persuaded [16], trust [6], obey [5], believed [3], confidence [3], persuade [3], trusted [3], confident [2], having confidence [2], obeyed [2], persuading [2], agreed [1], assure [1], have confidence [1], made friend [1], persuadest [1], put trust [1], waxing confident [1], yield unto [1]

3983 πεινάω, *peinao*, v. GK: *4277* [→ *4361*]. to be hungry:– hungred [9], hunger [8], hungry [4], hungered [2]

3984 πεῖρα, *peira*, n. GK: *4278* [→ *551, 552, 1598, 3985, 3986, 3987*]. to try to do, attempt; to face, experience:– assaying [1], trial [1]

3985 πειράζω, *peirazo*, v. GK: *4279* [→ *3984*]. to test, tempt; to try to trap; to examine (oneself). The difference between a test and a temptation is found in the tester's motivations and expectations; the devil tempts that the believer might fail God's standards of faith and so sin; God tests that he might determine and sharpen true character, with no focus on making the believer fail:– tempted [15], tempting [7], tempt [6], tried [3], tempter [2], assayed [1], examine [1], gone about [1], prove [1], tempteth [1], try [1]

3986 πειρασμός, *peirasmos*, n. GK: *4280* [→ *3984*]. test; trial; temptation:– temptation [15], temptations [5], try [1]

3987 πειράω, *peirao*, v. GK: *4281* [→ *3984*]. to try, attempt:– assayed [1], went about [1]

3988 πεισμονή, *peismone*, n. GK: *4282* [→ *3982*]. persuasion:– persuasion [1]

3989 πέλαγος, *pelagos*, n. GK: *4283*. open sea; depths:– depth [1], sea [1]

3990 πελεκίζω, *pelekizo*, v. GK: *4284*. to behead, a derivative of the Greek noun "ax," not found in the NT:– beheaded [1]

3991 πέμπτος, *pemptos*, a. GK: *4286* [→ *4002*]. fifth:– fifth [4]

3992 πέμπω, *pempo*, v. GK: *4287* [→ *375, 1599, 3343, 4311, 4842*]. to send:– sent [52], send [25], thrust in [2], sending [1], sent forth [1]

3993 πένης, *penes*, a. GK: *4288* [→ *3998; cf. 4192*]. poor:– poor [1]

3994 πενθερά, *penthera*, n. GK: *4289* [→ *3995*]. mother-in-law:– mother in law [3], wife's mother [3]

3995 πενθερός, *pentheros*, n. GK: *4290* [→ *3994*]. father-in-law:– father in law [1]

3996 πενθέω, *pentheo*, v. GK: *4291* [→ *3997*]. to mourn, grieve (over):– mourn [5], mourned [2], wailing [2], bewail [1]

3997 πένθος, *penthos*, n. GK: *4292* [→ *3996*]. mourning, grief, sadness:– sorrow [3], mourning [2]

3998 πενιχρός, *penichros*, a. GK: *4293* [→ *3993*]. poor, needy:– poor [1]

3999 πεντάκις, *pentakis*, adv. GK: *4294* [→ *4002*]. five times:– five times [1]

4000 πεντακισχίλιοι, *pentakischilioi*, a.num. GK: *4295* [→ *4002+5507*]. five thousand:– five thousand [6]

4001 πεντακόσιοι, *pentakosioi*, a.num. GK: *4296* [→ *4002*]. five hundred:– five hundred [2]

4002 πέντε, *pente*, n.num. GK: *4297* [→ *1178, 3991, 3999, 4000, 4001, 4003, 4004, 4005*]. five:– five [36], fifty thousand (+*3461*) [1], threescore and fifteen (+*1440*) [1]

4003 πεντεκαιδέκατος, *pentekaidekatos*, a. GK: *4298* [→ *4002+2532+1176*]. fifteenth:– fifteenth [1]

4004 πεντήκοντα, *pentekonta*, n.num. GK: *4299* [→ *4002*]. fifty:– fifty [5], fifties [2]

4005 πεντηκοστή, *pentekoste*, n. GK: *4300* [→ *4002*]. Pentecost, fiftieth (day after Passover):– Pentecost [3]

4006 πεποίθησις, *pepoithesis*, n. GK: *4301* [→ *3982*]. confidence, trust:– confidence [5], trust [1]

4007 -περ, *-per*, pt.emph. GK: *4302* [→ *1355, 1512, 1895, 1897, 2260, 2509, 2539, 3746, 5618, 5619*]. an affix for various kinds of emphasis:– if (+*1437*) [3]

4008 πέραν, *peran*, adv. GK: *4305* [→ *495, 562, 1276, 4009, 4070, 4097; cf. 4198*]. on the other side; (n.) opposite side, region across:– other side [10], beyond [7], over [3], on the other side [1], farther side [1]

4009 πέρας, *peras*, n. GK: *4306* [→ *4008*]. end, limit:– ends [1], end [1], utmost parts [1], uttermost parts [1]

4010 Πέργαμος, *Pergamos*, n.pr. GK: *4307*. Pergamum:– Pergamos [2]

4011 Πέργη, *Perge*, n.pr. GK: *4308*. Perga:– Perga [3]

4012 περί, *peri*, pp. GK: *4309* [→ *563, 564, 1704, 2139, 4013, 4014, 681, 4015, 4016, 4017, 4018, 4019, 4020, 4021, 4022, 4023, 4024, 4025, 4026, 4027, 4028, 4029, 4030, 4031, 4032, 4033, 4034, 4035, 4036, 4037, 4038, 4039, 4040, 4041, 4042, 4043, 4044, 4045, 4046, 4047, 4048, 4049, 4059, 4060, 4061, 4062, 4063, 4064, 4065, 4066, 4067, 4843; cf. 4053*]. (gen.) about, concerning, in regard to; (acc.) around, about, nearby:– of [148], for [62], concerning [41], about [29], as touching [7], touching [4], at [3], against [2], as concerning [2], on [2], over [2], state (+*3588*) [2], whereof (+*3739*) [2], with [2], above [1], affairs (+*3588*) [1], affairs [1], among [1], company (+*3588*) [1], concern [1], estate [1], for sake [1], how it will go with (+*3588*) [1], in [1], of company [1], on behalf [1], pertaining [1], round about [1], same (+*1565*) [1], thereabout (+*3778*) [1], thereof [1], whereby (+*3739*) [1], wherein (+*3739*) [1], whereof (+*5101*) [1]

4013 περιάγω, *periago*, v. GK: *4310* [→ *4012+71*]. (tr.) to take (a wife); (intr.) to go about, travel about:– went about [3], compass [1], lead about [1], went [1]

4014 περιαιρέω, *periaireo*, v. GK: *4311* [→ *4012+138*]. to take away; (pass.) to be taken away; to cut loose, set sail; to be given up, abandoned:– taken away [2], take away [1], taken up [1]

4015 περιαστράπτω, *periastrapto*, v. GK: *4313* [→ *4012+796*]. to flash around, shine around:– shined round about [1], shone [1]

4016 περιβάλλω, *periballo*, v. GK: *4314* [→ *4012+906*]. to dress, clothe, wrap around:– clothed [8], arrayed in [4], clothed in [3], clothed with [3], arrayed [2], cast about [2], cast [1], put on [1]

4017 περιβλέπω, *periblepo*, v. GK: *4315* [→ *4012+991*]. to look around at:– looked round about [5], looked [1], looking round about [1]

4018 περιβόλαιον, *peribolaion*, n. GK: *4316* [→ *4012+906*]. covering, robe:– covering [1], vesture [1]

4019 περιδέω, *perideo*, v. GK: *4317* [→ *4012+1210*]. to wrap around:– bound about [1]

περιδρέμω, *peridremo*. See **4063**.

περιέλλω, *periello*. See **4014**.

περιέλθω, *perieltho*. See **4022**.

4020 περιεργάζομαι, *periergazomai*, v. GK: *4318* [→ *4012+2041*]. to be a busybody:– busybodies [1]

4021 περίεργος, *periergos*, a. GK: *4319* [→ *4012+2041*]. meddlesome, curious; (n.) busybody; (pl.) sorcery, magical arts:– busybodies [1], curious arts [1]

4022 περιέρχομαι, *perierchomai*, v. GK: *4320* [→ *4012+2064*]. to go around:– fet a compass [1], vagabond [1], wandered about [1], wandering about [1]

4023 περιέχω, *periecho*, v. GK: *4321* [→ *4012+2192*]. to seize, encircle; to contain, to say:– after [1], astonished (+*2285*) [1], contained [1]

4024 περιζώννυμι, *perizonnymi*, v. GK: *4322 & 4323* [→ *4012+2224*]. to buckle a belt around, gird, dress for service:– gird [3], girded about [1], girded [1], girt about [1], girt [1]

4025 περίθεσις, *perithesis*, n. GK: *4324* [→ *4012+5087*]. wearing, putting on:– wearing [1]

4026 περιΐστημι, *periistemi*, v. GK: *4325* [→ *4012+2476*]. to stand around; avoid, shun:– avoid [1], shun [1], stand by [1], stood round about [1]

4027 περικάθαρμα, *perikatharma*, n. GK: *4326* [→ *4012+2513*]. scum, refuse:– filth [1]

4028 περικαλύπτω, *perikalypto*, v. GK: *4328* [→ *4012+2572*]. to blindfold, cover the face or eyes; to cover (with gold):– blindfolded [1], cover [1], overlaid [1]

4029 περίκειμαι, *perikeimai*, v. GK: *4329* [→ *4012+2749*]. to surround, place or tie around; to be subject to:– bound with [1], compassed about [1], compassed with [1], hanged about [1], hanged [1]

4030 περικεφαλαία, *perikephalaia*, n. GK: *4330* [→ *4012+2776*]. helmet:– helmet [2]

4031 περικρατής, *perikrates*, a. GK: *4331* [→ *4012+2904*]. secure, having power, being in command of, getting under control:– come by (+*1096*) [1]

4032 περικρύπτω, *perikrypto*, v. GK: *4332* [→ *4012+2928*]. to seclude oneself, hide, conceal oneself:– hid [1]

4033 περικυκλόω, *perikykloo*, v. GK: *4333* [→ *4012+2945*]. to encircle, surround:– compass round [1]

4034 περιλάμπω, *perilampo*, v. GK: *4334* [→ *4012+2989*]. to shine around, blaze around:– shining round about [1], shone round about [1]

4035 περιλείπομαι, *perileipomai*, v. GK: *4335* [→ *4012+3007*]. to be left, remain:– remain [2]

4036 περίλυπος, *perilypos*, a. GK: *4337* [→ *4012+3077*]. overwhelmingly sorrowful; greatly distressing:– exceeding sorrowful [2], very sorrowful [2], exceeding sorry [1]

4037 περιμένω, *perimeno*, v. GK: *4338* [→ *4012+3306*]. to wait for:– wait for [1]

4038 πέριξ, *perix*, adv. GK: *4339* [→ *4012*]. around:– round about [1]

4039 περιοικέω, *perioikeo*, v. GK: *4340* [→ *4012+3624*]. to live in a neighborhood; (n.) neighbor:– dwelt round about [1]

4040 περίοικος, *perioikos*, a. GK: *4341* [→ *4012+3624*]. neighboring; (n.) neighbor:– neighbours [1]

4041 περιούσιος, *periousios*, a. GK: *4342* [→ *4012+1510*]. one's very own, special:– peculiar [1]

4042 περιοχή, *perioche*, n. GK: *4343* [→ *4012+2192*]. passage (of Scripture), portion:– place [1]

4043 περιπατέω, *peripateō*, v. GK: *4344* [→ *4012+3961*]. to walk (around); to live, conduct one's life:– walk [56], walked [18], walking [12], walketh [4], walkest [2], go [1], occupied therein [1], walkedst [1], walketh about [1]

4044 περιπείρω, *peripeirō*, v. GK: *4345* [→ *4012*]. to pierce:– pierced through [1]

4045 περιπίπτω, *peripiptō*, v. GK: *4346* [→ *4012+4098*]. to fall into the hands of; to strike; to face, be involved in:– fall into [1], falling [1], fell among [1]

4046 περιποιέω, *peripoieō*, v. GK: *4347* [→ *4012+4160*]. (mid.) to keep, save; to gain for oneself; to buy, acquire:– purchased [1], purchase [1]

4047 περιποίησις, *peripoiēsis*, n. GK: *4348* [→ *4012+4160*]. possession, property; sharing in, gaining; saving:– obtaining [1], obtain [1], peculiar (+*1519*) [1], purchased possession [1], saving [1]

4048 περιρήγνυμι, *perirēgnymi*, v. GK: *4351* [→ *4012+4486*]. to strip off, tear off:– rent off [1]

4049 περισπάω, *perispaō*, v. GK: *4352* [→ *4012+4685*]. (pass.) to be distracted:– cumbered [1]

4050 περισσεία, *perisseia*, n. GK: *4353* [→ *4053*]. abundance, prevalence:– abundance [2], abundantly (+*1519*) [1], superfluity [1]

4051 περίσσευμα, *perisseuma*, n. GK: *4354* [→ *4053*]. overflow, plenty; what is left over, scraps:– abundance [4], left [1]

4052 περισσεύω, *perisseuō*, v. GK: *4355* [→ *4053*]. to have abundance, more than enough, overflow, to have an excessive amount of something, ranging from moderate excess to a very great degree of excess:– abound [11], abounded [4], abundance [3], abounding [2], abundant [2], have abundance [2], remained [2], aboundeth [1], better [1], exceed (+*4183*) [1], exceed [1], excel [1], have enough and to spare [1], increased [1], increase [1], left [1], make abound [1], redound [1], remained over and above [1], remain [1]

4053 περισσός, *perissos*, a. GK: *4356* [→ *4050, 4051, 4052, 4054, 4055, 4056, 4057, 5248, 5249; cf. 4012*]. exceeding, going beyond; full, abundant; (compar.) more than; (n.) advantage:– greater [2], more than [2], abundantly (+*1537*) [1], abundantly [1], advantage [1], exceedingly (+*1537+5228*) [1], highly (+*1537*) [1], measure [1], more [1], superfluous [1], vehemently (+*1537*) [1]

4054 περισσότερον, *perissoteron*, adv. GK: *4357* [→ *4053*]. even more, so much more:– more [2], far more [1], great deal [1], greater [1], more abundantly than [1], more abundantly [1], much more than [1]

4055 περισσότερος, *perissoteros*, a. GK: *4358* [→ *4053*]. more than, even more; greater than; with special honor:– more abundant [3], more (+*5100*) [1], overmuch [1]

4056 περισσοτέρως, *perissoterōs*, adv. GK: *4359* [→ *4053*]. to a much greater degree; especially, frequently, extremely:– more abundantly [4], more abundant [2], more exceedingly [2], exceedingly [1], more earnest [1], more frequent [1], much more [1], rather [1]

4057 περισσῶς, *perissōs*, adv. GK: *4360* [→ *4053*]. even more, all the more:– exceedingly [1], more [1], out of measure [1]

4058 περιστερά, *peristera*, n. GK: *4361*. dove, pigeon:– doves [5], dove [4], pigeons [1]

4059 περιτέμνω, *peritemnō*, v. GK: *4362* [→ *4012+5114*]. to circumcise:– circumcised [13], circumcise [4], circumcising [1]

4060 περιτίθημι, *peritithēmi*, v. GK: *4363* [→ *4012+5087*]. to put on, set on; to treat with:– put on [3], bestow [1], put about [1], put upon [1], round about [1], set about [1]

4061 περιτομή, *peritomē*, n. GK: *4364* [→ *4012+5114*]. circumcision; fig., the Jews (as a group of people who adhered to the ritual of circumcision):– circumcision [35], circumcised [1]

4062 περιτρέπω, *peritrepō*, v. GK: *4365* [→ *4012+5157*]. to drive (to insanity):– make mad (+*1519+3130*) [1]

4063 περιτρέχω, *peritrechō*, v. GK: *4366* [→ *4012+5143*]. to run throughout, run about:– ran through [1]

4064 περιφέρω, *peripherō*, v. GK: *4367* [→ *4012+5342*]. to carry, carry around; (pass.) to be blown about, carried here and there:– carried about [3], bearing about [1], carry about [1]

4065 περιφρονέω, *periphroneō*, v. GK: *4368* [→ *4012+5424*]. to despise, look down on:– despise [1]

4066 περίχωρος, *perichōros*, a. GK: *4369* [→ *4012+5562*]. neighboring; (n.) surrounding country:– region round about [5], country round about [3], country about [1], region that lieth round about [1]

4067 περίψημα, *peripsēma*, n. GK: *4370* [→ *4012+5597*]. refuse, garbage, that which is removed in the process of cleaning:– offscouring [1]

4068 περπερεύομαι, *perpereuomai*, v. GK: *4371*. to boast, brag:– vaunteth [1]

4069 Περσίς, *Persis*, n.pr. GK: *4372*. Persis, "*female Persian*":– Persis [1]

4070 πέρυσι, *perysi*, adv. GK: *4373* [→ *4008*]. from last year, since last year:– a year ago (+*575*) [2]

πετάομαι, *petaomai*. See *4072*.

4071 πετεινόν, *peteinon*, n. GK: *4374* [→ *4072*]. bird:– fowls [9], birds [5]

4072 πέτομαι, *petomai*, v. GK: *4375* [→ *1600, 2665, 4071, 4419, 4420, 4421*]. to fly:– fly [3], flying [2]

4073 πέτρα, *petra*, n. GK: *4376* [→ *4074, 4075*]. rock, bedrock, rocky crag, or other large rock formation, in contrast to individual stones (cf. *4074*), with a focus that this is a suitable, solid foundation:– rock [13], rocks [3]

4074 Πέτρος, *Petros*, n.pr. GK: *4377* [→ *4073*]. Peter; this has the designative meaning "rock" or "individual stone", "*rock, stone*":– Peter [157], Peter's [4], stone [1]

4075 πετρώδης, *petrōdēs*, a. GK: *4378* [→ *4073+1491*]. rocky, stony; (n.) rocky place, thin soil with larger rocks or bedrock underneath:– stony ground [2], stony [2]

4076 πήγανον, *pēganon*, n. GK: *4379*. rue (a garden herb):– rue [1]

4077 πηγή, *pēgē*, n. GK: *4380*. spring, well (of water); flow (of blood):– fountains [4], fountain [4], well [3], wells [1]

4078 πήγνυμι, *pēgnymi*, v. GK: *4381* [→ *3802, 3803, 4362, 4634*]. to set up:– pitched [1]

4079 πηδάλιον, *pēdalion*, n. GK: *4382*. rudder, steering paddle:– helm [1], rudder [1]

4080 πηλίκος, *pēlikos*, a. GK: *4383* [→ *2245*]. how great, how large:– how great [1], how large [1]

4081 πηλός, *pēlos*, n. GK: *4384*. mud, lump of clay:– clay [6]

4082 πήρα, *pēra*, n. GK: *4385*. traveler's bag:– scrip [6]

4083 πῆχυς, *pēchys*, n. GK: *4388*. measure of length: cubit, or time: hour:– cubits [2], cubit [2]

4084 πιάζω, *piazō*, v. GK: *4389* [→ *4085*]. to seize, to grasp an object, usually with the hand; by extension: to arrest, capture, place in confinement:– take [4], caught [2], taken [2], apprehended [1], apprehend [1], laid hands on [1], took [1]

4085 πιέζω, *piezō*, v. GK: *4390* [→ *4084*]. (pass.) to be pressed down:– pressed down [1]

4086 πιθανολογία, *pithanologia*, n. GK: *4391* [→ *3982+3004*]. fine-sounding arguments, persuasive speech, a plausible yet false argument:– enticing words [1]

4087 πικραίνω, *pikrainō*, v. GK: *4393* [→ *4089*]. to turn sour, make bitter; to become sour, embittered:– bitter [2], made bitter [1], make bitter [1]

4088 πικρία, *pikria*, n. GK: *4394* [→ *4089*]. bitterness:– bitterness [4]

4089 πικρός, *pikros*, a. GK: *4395* [→ *3893, 3894, 4087, 4088, 4090*]. bitter, salty:– bitter [2]

4090 πικρῶς, *pikrōs*, adv. GK: *4396* [→ *4089*]. bitterly:– bitterly [2]

4091 Πιλᾶτος, *Pilatos*, n.pr. GK: *4276 & 4397*. Pilate, "*[family name]*":– Pilate [55]

πίμπλημι, *pimplēmi*. See *4130*.

4092 πίμπρημι, *pimprēmi*, v. GK: *4399* [→ *1714*]. to swell:– swollen [1]

4093 πινακίδιον, *pinakidion*, n. GK: *4400 & 4401* [→ *4094*]. (small) writing tablet:– writing table [1]

4094 πίναξ, *pinax*, n. GK: *4402* [→ *4093*]. platter, dish:– charger [4], platter [1]

4095 πίνω, *pinō*, v. GK: *4403* [→ *2666, 3630, 4188, 4213, 4221, 4222, 4224, 4844, 4849, 5202; cf. 4215*]. to drink:– drink [52], drinketh [8], drinking [6], drank [5], drunk [3], drunken [1]

4096 πιότης, *piotēs*, n. GK: *4404*. richness, nourishing sap:– fatness [1]

4097 πιπράσκω, *pipraskō*, v. GK: *4405* [→ *4008*]. to sell:– sold [9]

4098 πίπτω, *piptō*, v. GK: *4406* [→ *377, 496, 634, 1120, 1356, 1601, 1706, 1968, 2667, 3895, 3900, 4045, 4312, 4363, 4430, 4431*]. to fall, collapse; to bow down; to die:– fell [42], fall [20], fell down [14], fallen [5], falleth [3], fall down [2], fail [1], fallen down [1], falling down [1], light [1]

4099 Πισιδία, *Pisidia*, n.pr. GK: *4407 & 4408*. Pisidia:– Pisidia [2]

4100 πιστεύω, *pisteuō*, v. GK: *4409* [→ *4103*]. to believe, put one's faith in, trust, with an implication that actions based on that trust may follow; (pass.) entrust:– believe [115], believed [77], believeth [33], believest [8], believing [6], committed [3], believers [1], commit to trust [1], committed to trust [1], committed unto [1], commit [1], put in trust [1]

4101 πιστικός, *pistikos*, a. GK: *4410* [→ *4103*]. pure:– spikenard (+*3487*) [2]

4102 πίστις, *pistis*, n. GK: *4411* [→ *4103*]. faith, faithfulness, belief, trust, with an implication that actions based on that trust may follow; "the faith" often refers to the Christian system of belief and lifestyle:– faith [239], assurance [1], belief [1], believeth [1], believe [1], fidelity [1]

4103 πιστός, *pistos*, a. GK: *4412* [→ *569, 570, 571, 3640, 4100, 4101, 4102, 4104; cf. 3982*]. faithful, trustworthy, reliable, believing:– faithful [53], believed [2], believe [2], believing [2], true [2], believers [1], believeth [1], faithfully [1], man[s] [1], sure [1], woman that believeth [1]

4104 πιστόω, *pistoō*, v. GK: *4413* [→ *4103*]. (pass.) to be convinced of:– assured [1]

4105 πλανάω, *planaō*, v. GK: *4414* [→ *4106*]. to lead astray, cause to wander, deceive; (mid./pass.) to be deceived, deluded:– deceived [10], deceive [10], err [6], deceiveth [3], gone astray [3], seduce [2], deceiving [1], going astray [1], out of the way [1], wandered [1], went astray [1]

4106 πλάνη, *planē*, n. GK: *4415* [→ *635, 4105, 4107, 4108*]. error, delusion, deception:– error [7], deceit [1], deceive [1], delusion [1]

4107 πλανήτης, *planētēs*, n. GK: *4417* [→ *4106*]. wanderer; (a.) wandering:– wandering [1]

4108 πλάνος, *planos*, a. GK: *4418* [→ *4106*]. deceiving, leading astray; (n.) deceiver, imposter; fig. extensions of the base meaning "to wander off a path," not found in the NT:– deceivers [2], deceiver [2], seducing [1]

4109 πλάξ, *plax*, n. GK: *4419*. stone tablet:– tables [3]

4110 πλάσμα, *plasma*, n. GK: *4420* [→ *4111*]. what is formed, molded:– formed [1]

4111 πλάσσω, *plassō*, v. GK: *4421* [→ *4110, 4112*]. to form, mold:– formed [1]

4112 πλαστός, *plastos*, a. GK: *4422* [→ *4111*]. made up, fabricated, false:– feigned [1]

4113 πλατεῖα, *plateia*, n. GK: *4423* [→ *4116*]. (main) street, wide road:– streets [6], street [3]

4114 πλάτος, *platos*, n. GK: *4424* [→ *4116*]. width, breadth:– breadth [4]

4115 πλατύνω, *platynō*, v. GK: *4425* [→ *4116*]. to open wide, make wide:– enlarged [2], make broad [1]

4116 πλατύς, *platys*, a. GK: *4426* [→ *4113, 4114, 4115*]. wide, broad:– wide [1]

4117 πλέγμα, *plegma*, n. GK: *4427* [→ *4120*]. something braided or woven:– broided hair [1]

πλεῖον, *pleion*. See *4119*.

4118 πλεῖστος, *pleistos*, a.super. of *4183*. GK: *4498* [→ *4183*]. the most; very large:–

4119 πλείων, *pleiōn*, a.compar. of *4183* GK: *4498* [→ *4183*]. more than, greater than:–

4120 πλέκω, *plekō*, v. GK: *4428* [→ *1707, 1708, 4117*]. to twist together, weave, braid:– platted [3]

πλέον, *pleon*. See *4119*.

4121 πλεονάζω, *pleonazō*, v. GK: *4429* [→ *4137*]. to make increase; (intr.) to grow, increase, have abundance:– abound [4], abounded [1], aboundeth [1], abundant [1], had over [1], make to increase [1]

4122 πλεονεκτέω, *pleonekteō*, v. GK: *4430*
[→ *4137+2192*]. to exploit, take advantage of, outwit:– make a gain [2], defrauded [1], defraud [1], get an advantage [1]

4123 πλεονέκτης, *pleonektēs*, n. GK: *4431*
[→ *4137+2192*]. greedy person:– covetous [3], covetous man [1]

4124 πλεονεξία, *pleonexia*, n. GK: *4432* [→ *4137+2192*].
greediness, avarice:– covetousness [8], covetous practices [1], greediness [1]

4125 πλευρά, *pleura*, n. GK: *4433*. side (of the body):–
side [5]

4126 πλέω, *pleō*, v. GK: *4434* [→ *636, 1020, 1277, 1602,
2668, 3896, 4142, 4143, 4144, 5284*]. to travel by ship, sail:–
sailed [2], sail [2], sailing [1]

4127 πληγή, *plēgē*, n. GK: *4435* [→ *4141*]. plague:–
punishment: beating, flogging, wounding:– plagues [10],
stripes [5], wound [3], plague [2], wounded (+*2007*) [1]

4128 πλῆθος, *plēthos*, n. GK: *4436* [→ *4130*]. large
number, crowd, multitude, assembly:– multitude [29],
bundle [1], company [1], multitudes [1]

4129 πληθύνω, *plēthynō*, v. GK: *4437* [→ *4130*]. to
increase, grow in numbers, abound:– multiplied [8], multiply [2],
abound [1], multiplying [1]

4130 πίμπλημι, *pimplēmi*, v. GK: *4398* [→ *1705, 3826,
4128, 4129, 4132, 4140*]. to fill; (pass.) to be filled,
completed:– filled [18], accomplished [4], full came [1],
furnished [1]

4131 πλήκτης, *plēktēs*, n. GK: *4438* [→ *4141*]. violent
man, bully:– striker [2]

4132 πλήμμυρα, *plēmmyra*, n. GK: *4439* [→ *4130*]. flood,
high water; in context likely a flash flood in a narrow valley
(wadi):– flood [1]

4133 πλήν, *plēn*, c.&pp.*. GK: *4440* [→ *4137*]. but,
however, only, yet:– but [14], nevertheless [7],
notwithstanding [4], but rather [2], except [1], nevertheless
(+*2532*) [1], save [1], than [1]

4134 πλήρης, *plērēs*, a. GK: *4441* [→ *4137*]. full:– full [17]

4135 πληροφορέω, *plērophoreō*, v. GK: *4442*
[→ *4137+5342*]. to fulfill (completely); (pass.) to be fully
assured, convinced, persuaded:– fully persuaded [2], fully
known [1], make full proof [1], most surely believed [1]

4136 πληροφορία, *plērophoria*, n. GK: *4443*
[→ *4137+5342*]. full assurance, certainty, conviction:– full
assurance [3], assurance [1]

4137 πληρόω, *plēroō*, v. GK: *4444* [→ *378, 466, 1603,
1604, 4121, 4122, 4123, 4124, 4133, 4134, 4135, 4136,
4138, 4322, 4845, 5250*]. to fulfill, make full; (pass.) to be
filled, full, complete (often used with reference to the fulfillment
of the OT Scriptures):– fulfilled [45], filled [15], full [7], fulfil [6],
complete [2], ended [2], accomplish [1], after [1], expired [1], fill
up [1], fill with [1], filled with [1], filleth [1], fill [1], full come [1],
fully [1], make full [1], perfect [1], supply [1]

4138 πλήρωμα, *plērōma*, n. GK: *4445* [→ *4137*]. fullness,
fulfillment:– fulness [13], fulfilling [1], full [1], piece that filled
up [1], put in to fill up [1]

4139 πλησίον, *plēsion*, adv.&pp.*&n. GK: *4446* [→ *3897,
3808*]. near, close by; (n.) neighbor; (pp.) near:–
neighbour [16], near [1]

4140 πλησμονή, *plēsmonē*, n. GK: *4447* [→ *4130*].
indulgence, gratification:– satisfying [1]

4141 πλήσσω, *plēssō*, v. GK: *4448* [→ *1605, 1969, 4127,
4131*]. (pass.) to be struck:– smitten [1]

4142 πλοιάριον, *ploiarion*, n. GK: *4449* [→ *4126*]. (small)
boat:– boat [2], boats [1], little ships [1], little ship [1], small
ship [1]

4143 πλοῖον, *ploion*, n. GK: *4450* [→ *4126*]. boat, ship:–
ship [58], ships [8], took shipping (+*1519+1684+3588*) [1]

4144 πλόος, *ploos*, n. GK: *4452 & 4453* [→ *4126*]. voyage,
navigation:– course [1], sailing [1], voyage [1]

4145 πλούσιος, *plousios*, a. GK: *4454* [→ *4149*]. rich,
wealthy; (n.) rich person:– rich [28]

4146 πλουσίως, *plousiōs*, adv. GK: *4455* [→ *4149*]. richly,
generously, abundantly:– abundantly [2], richly [2]

4147 πλουτέω, *plouteō*, v. GK: *4456* [→ *4149*]. to be rich;
(pf.) to have acquired wealth:– rich [8], made rich [2], increased
with goods [1], waxed rich [1]

4148 πλουτίζω, *ploutizō*, v. GK: *4457* [→ *4149*]. to make
rich; (pass.) to be enriched:– enriched [2], making rich [1]

4149 πλοῦτος, *ploutos*, n. GK: *4458* [→ *4145, 4146, 4147,
4148*]. riches, wealth:– riches [22]

4150 πλύνω, *plynō*, v. GK: *4459* [→ *637*]. to wash (things):–
washed [1]

4151 πνεῦμα, *pneuma*, n. GK: *4460* [→ *4154*]. wind,
breath, things which are commonly perceived as having no
material substance; by extension: spirit, heart, mind, the
immaterial part of the inner person that can respond to God;
spirit being: (evil) spirit, ghost, God the Holy Spirit:– spirit [257],
ghost [92], spirits [32], life [1], spiritually [1], spiritual [1], wind [1]

4152 πνευματικός, *pneumatikos*, a. GK: *4461* [→ *4154*].
spiritual, pertaining to the Spirit; (n.) spiritual person:–
spiritual [26]

4153 πνευματικῶς, *pneumatikōs*, adv. GK: *4462*
[→ *4154*]. spiritually; figuratively:– spiritually [2]

4154 πνέω, *pneō*, v. GK: *4463* [→ *1606, 1709, 2315, 4151,
4152, 4153, 4157, 5285*]. to blow (of wind):– blew [3],
blow [2], bloweth [1], wind [1]

4155 πνίγω, *pnigō*, v. GK: *4464* [→ *638, 1970, 4156,
4846*]. to choke or strangle; drown:– choked [1], took by the
throat [1]

4156 πνικτός, *pniktos*, a. GK: *4465* [→ *4155*]. strangled,
choked; (n.) meat of strangled animals:– strangled [2], things
strangled [1]

4157 πνοή, *pnoē*, n. GK: *4466* [→ *4154*]. wind, breath:–
breath [1], wind [1]

4158 ποδήρης, *podērēs*, a. GK: *4468* [→ *4228*]. reaching to
the feet; (n.) robe reaching to the feet:– down to the foot [1]

4159 πόθεν, *pothen*, adv. GK: *4470*. from where, from
which:– whence [20], from whence [8]

4160 ποιέω, *poieō*, v. GK: *4472* [→ *15, 16, 17, 886, 1517,
1518, 2140, 2227, 2554, 2555, 2569, 3447, 3792, 4046,
4047, 4161, 4162, 4163, 4364, 4635, 4806, 5499*]. to do,
make, practice, produce, a generic term of action or
performance: note the many contextual translations in the
NIV:– do [196], did [54], done [52], made [50], make [47],
doeth [34], doest [1], doing [8], bringeth forth [7], maketh [6],
making [6], bring forth [5], wrought [5], cause [4], committed [4],
makest [4], shewed [4], causeth [3], committeth [3], bare [2],
bear [2], caused [2], commit [2], continue [2], dealt [2],
execute [1], fulfil [2], gave [2], keep [2], perform [2], put [2],
working [2], able [1], abode [1], agree (+*1106+1520*) [1],
appointed [1], as went (+*3598*) [1], avenge (+*1557+3588*) [1],
avenged (+*1557*) [1], banded together (+*4963*) [1], been [1],
bewrayeth (+*1212*) [1], bringing forth [1], bring [1], brought
forth [1], cast out (+*1570*) [1], content (+*2425*) [1], delay
(+*311*) [1], exerciseth [1], fulfilling [1], gained [1], held [1],
journeying (+*4197*) [1], keepeth [1], kept [1], laying wait
(+*1747*) [1], lightened the ship (+*1546*) [1], move [1],
observe [1], ordained [1], provide [1], purged (+*2512*) [1],
purposed [1], raising up (+*1999*) [1], redeemed (+*3085*) [1],
secure (+*275*) [1], shewest [1], shooteth out [1], spent [1], tarried
a space (+*5550*) [1], took [1], transgresseth law (+*458*) [1], weep
(+*2799*) [1], will [1], worketh [1], yield [1]

4161 ποίημα, *poiēma*, n. GK: *4473* [→ *4160*]. what is
made, workmanship, creation:– things that are made [1],
workmanship [1]

4162 ποίησις, *poiēsis*, n. GK: *4474* [→ *4160*]. doing,
working:– deed [1]

4163 ποιητής, *poiētēs*, n. GK: *4475* [→ *4160*]. doer,
keeper, obeyer; poet:– doer [3], doers [2], poets [1]

4164 ποικίλος, *poikilos*, a. GK: *4476* [→ *4182*]. of various
kinds, of all kinds:– divers [8], manifold [2]

4165 ποιμαίνω, *poimainō*, v. GK: *4477* [→ *4166*]. to
shepherd, take care of sheep; to rule, lead:– feed [4], rule [4],
feedeth [1], feeding cattle [1], feeding [1]

4166 ποιμήν, *poimēn*, n. GK: *4478* [→ *750, 4165, 4167,
4168*]. shepherd; pastor:– shepherd [13], shepherds [4],
pastors [1]

4167 ποίμνη, *poimnē*, n. GK: *4479* [→ *4166*]. flock:–
flock [4], fold [1]

4168 ποίμνιον, *poimnion*, n. GK: *4480* [→ *4166*]. flock:–
flock [5]

4169 ποῖος, *poios*, a. GK: *4481* [→ *3634*]. what?, which?,
of what kind?:– what [29], which [4], what manner [1]

4170 πολεμέω, *polemeō*, v. GK: *4482* [→ *4171*]. to fight,
make war:– make war [3], fought [2], fight [1], war [1]

4171 πόλεμος, *polemos*, n. GK: *4483* [→ *4170*]. war,
battle, fight:– wars [6], battle [5], war [5], fight [1], make war
against (+*1519+4820*) [1]

4172 πόλις, *polis*, n. GK: *4484* [→ *295, 1179, 2404, 2969,
3390, 3496, 3533, 4173, 4174, 4175, 4176, 4177, 4847*].
city, town, village:– city [145], cities [19]

4173 πολιτάρχης, *politarchēs*, n. GK: *4485*
[→ *4172+757*]. city official, formally, "politarch":– rulers of the
city [2]

4174 πολιτεία, *politeia*, n. GK: *4486* [→ *4172*].
citizenship:– commonwealth [1], freedom [1]

4175 πολίτευμα, *politeuma*, n. GK: *4487* [→ *4172*].
citizenship:– conversation [1]

4176 πολιτεύομαι, *politeuomai*, v. GK: *4488* [→ *4172*]. to
fulfill one's duty; to conduct oneself, lead one's life:–
conversation [1], lived [1]

4177 πολίτης, *politēs*, n. GK: *4489* [→ *4172*]. citizen,
subjects of a kingdom; neighbor:– citizen [2], citizens [1]

4178 πολλάκις, *pollakis*, adv. GK: *4490* [→ *4183*]. many
times, again and again, often, constantly:– often [7], oft [5],
oftentimes [3], ofttimes [3]

4179 πολλαπλασίων, *pollaplasiōn*, a. GK: *4491* [→ *4183*].
many times as much:– manifold more [1]

4180 πολυλογία, *polylogia*, n. GK: *4494* [→ *4183+3004*].
speaking many words, wordiness:– much speaking [1]

4181 πολυμερῶς, *polymerōs*, adv. GK: *4495*
[→ *4183+3313*]. at many times, in many ways:– times [1]

4182 πολυποίκιλος, *polypoikilos*, a. GK: *4497*
[→ *4183+4164*]. manifold, (very) many sided:– manifold [1]

4183 πολύς, *polys*, a. GK: *4498* [→ *3827, 4118, 4119, 4178,
4179, 4180, 4181, 4182, 4184, 4185, 4186, 4187*]. many,
great, large; (compar.) more than, greater than; (super.) the
most; very large:– many [221], much [74], great [59], more [11],
more than [7], greater than [4], greatly [4], long [4], moe [4],
most [4], further (+*1909*) [3], more part [2], straitly [2], a great
while (+*1909*) [1], above [1], abundant [1], altogether
(+*1722*) [1], but (+*2228+3756*) [1], common [1], exceed
(+*4052*) [1], far (+*3123*) [1], far passed [1], far [1], great deal [1],
greater part [1], greater [1], long (+*1909*) [1], longer (+*1909*) [1],
many moe [1], many things [1], moe than [1], more excellent [1],
oftentimes (+*5550*) [1], oft [1], plenteous [1], sore [1], very
great [1], very many [1]

4184 πολύσπλαγχνος, *polysplanchnos*, a. GK: *4492 &
4499* [→ *4183+4698*]. full of compassion, full of mercy:– very
pitiful [1]

4185 πολυτελής, *polytelēs*, a. GK: *4500* [→ *4183+5056*].
expensive, of great worth, costly:– costly [1], great price [1], very
precious [1]

4186 πολύτιμος, *polytimos*, a. GK: *4501* [→ *4183+5092*].
expensive, of great worth, valuable:– great price [1], very
costly [1]

4187 πολυτρόπως, *polytropōs*, adv. GK: *4502*
[→ *4183+5157*]. in various ways:– in divers manners [1]

4188 πόμα, *poma*, n. GK: *4503* [→ *4095*]. drink:– drinks [1],
drink [1]

4189 πονηρία, *ponēria*, n. GK: *4504* [→ *4190*]. evil,
wickedness, malice, in the NT always a negative moral quality
opposed to God and his goodness:– wickedness [6], iniquities [1]

4190 πονηρός, *ponēros*, a. GK: *4505* [→ *4189, 4191;
cf. 4192*]. bad, the negative quality of an object; evil, wicked,
crime, the negative moral quality of a person or action opposed
to God and his goodness; (n.) wicked deed, wicked thing; the
Evil One, a title of Satan:– evil [52], wicked [11], wicked one [6],
bad [1], evils [1], grievous [1], harm [1], lewd [1], malicious [1],
wickedness [1]

4191 πονηρότερος, *ponēroteros*, a.compar. of *4190* GK:
4505 [→ *4190*]. more evil, more wicked; see *4190*:– more
wicked than [2]

4192 πόνος, *ponos*, n. GK: *4506* [→ *1278, 2669; cf. 3993,
4190*]. pain, agony; hard work, toil:– pain [2], pains [1]

4193 Ποντικός, *Pontikos*, a.pr.g. GK: *4507*. from Pontus:–
Pontus [1]

4194 Πόντιος, *Pontios*, n.pr. GK: *4508*. Pontius, "*[tribal
name]*":– Pontius [4]

Grk

4195 Πόντος, *Pontos*, n.pr. GK: *4510*. Pontus, "*sea*":– Pontus [2]

4196 Πόπλιος, *Poplios*, n.pr. GK: *4511*. Publius, "*first*":– Publius [2]

4197 πορεία, *poreia*, n. GK: *4512 & 4515* [→ *4198*]. journey, trip; going about one's business, way of life, conduct:– journeying (+*4160*) [1], ways [1]

4198 πορεύομαι, *poreuomai*, v. GK: *4513* [→ *639, 640, 1279, 1280, 1531, 1607, 1710, 1711, 1712, 1713, 1820, 1975, 2141, 2142, 3596, 3597, 3899, 4197, 4200, 4313, 4365, 4848; cf. 4008*]. to come, go, travel:– go [74], went [44], goeth [7], departed [6], depart [5], walking [4], walk [4], gone [3], going [2], journeyed [2], made journey [1], take journey [1], walked [1]

4199 πορθέω, *portheō*, v. GK: *4514*. to destroy, annihilate; to raise havoc, pillage:– destroyed [2], wasted [1]

4200 πορισμός, *porismos*, n. GK: *4516* [→ *4198*]. means of gain:– gain [2]

4201 Πόρκιος, *Porkios*, n.pr. GK: *4517*. Porcius, "*[tribal name]*":– Porcius [1]

4202 πορνεία, *porneia*, n. GK: *4518* [→ *4204*]. sexual immorality, fornication, marital unfaithfulness, prostitution, adultery, a generic term for sexual sin of any kind:– fornication [24], fornications [1]

4203 πορνεύω, *porneuō*, v. GK: *4519* [→ *4204*]. to commit sexual immorality of any kind, adultery:– commit fornication [3], committed fornication [3], committed [1], committeth fornication [1]

4204 πόρνη, *pornē*, n. GK: *4520* [→ *1608, 4202, 4203, 4205*]. prostitute, a woman who practices sexual immorality for payment; this can refer to religious unfaithfulness:– harlots [4], harlot [4], whore [4]

4205 πόρνος, *pornos*, n. GK: *4521* [→ *4204*]. one who is sexually immoral (male or female), in some contexts distinguished from an adulterer (1Co 6:9):– whoremongers [4], fornicators [3], fornicator [1], whoremonger [1]

4206 πόρρω, *porrō*, adv. GK: *4522* [→ *4253*]. far, a long way off; (compar.) farther:– far [2], great way off [1]

4207 πόρρωθεν, *porrōthen*, adv. GK: *4523* [→ *4253*]. from a distance, at a distance:– afar off [2]

4208 πορρωτέρω, *porrōterō*, adv. GK: *4524* [→ *4253*]. farther:– further [1]

4209 πορφύρα, *porphyra*, n. GK: *4525* [→ *4210, 4211*]. purple (cloth or robe):– purple [5]

4210 πορφυροῦς, *porphyrous*, a. GK: *4526 & 4528* [→ *4209*]. purple, purple cloth, in some contexts implying royalty:– purple [3]

4211 πορφυρόπωλις, *porphyropōlis*, n. GK: *4527* [→ *4209+4453*]. dealer in purple cloth:– seller of purple [1]

4212 ποσάκις, *posakis*, adv. GK: *4529* [→ *3739*]. how many times?; how often!:– how often [2], how oft [1]

4213 πόσις, *posis*, n. GK: *4530* [→ *4095*]. drinking; a drink:– drink [3]

4214 πόσος, *posos*, a. GK: *4531* [→ *3745*]. how great?, how much?, how many?; how great!, how many!, how much!:– how much [13], how many [11], how great [1], how [1], what [1]

4215 ποταμός, *potamos*, n. GK: *4532* [→ *3318, 4216; cf. 4095*]. river, stream, torrent:– river [6], rivers [3], floods [2], flood [1], stream [2], waters [1]

4216 ποταμοφόρητος, *potamophorētos*, a. GK: *4533* [→ *4215+5342*]. swept away by a torrential flow of a river:– carried away of the flood [1]

4217 ποταπός, *potapos*, a. GK: *4467 & 4534* [→ *575+4226*]. of what kind?; how great!:– what manner [4], what manner of man [1], what manner of [1], what [1]

4218 ποτέ, *pote*, pt. GK: *4537* [→ *4226*]. once, at one time, formerly; now, now at last:– in time past [4], at any time [3], in times past [3], sometimes [3], sometime [3], in old time [2], once [2], aforetime [1], any time [1], at last [1], at length [1], ever yet [1], in time passed [1], never (+*3361+3756*) [1], were (+*1510*) [1], when [1]

4219 πότε, *pote*, adv.inter. GK: *4536* [→ *4226*]. when? how long?:– when [12], how long (+*2193*) [7]

4220 πότερον, *poteron*, a. or pt. GK: *4538* [→ *4226+2087*]. whether:– whether [1]

4221 ποτήριον, *potērion*, n. GK: *4539* [→ *4095*]. cup:– cup [31], cups [2]

4222 ποτίζω, *potizō*, v. GK: *4540* [→ *4095*]. to give or offer a drink; to water:– gave drink [3], gave to drink [2], give to drink [2], watereth [2], fed [1], give drink [1], made drink [1], made to drink [1], watered [1], watering [1]

4223 Ποτίολοι, *Potioloi*, n.pr. GK: *4541*. Puteoli, "*rotten [sulphur] smell* or *well, spring*":– Puteoli [1]

4224 πότος, *potos*, n. GK: *4542* [→ *4095*]. carousing, drinking party, orgy:– banquetings [1]

4225 πού, *pou*, adv. GK: *4543* [→ *4226*]. somewhere, a place where; about, approximately:– a certain place [2], about [1]

4226 ποῦ, *pou*, adv.inter.pl. GK: *4544* [→ *1221, 1222, 1513, 3368, 3379, 3381, 3697, 3698, 3699, 3704, 3763, 4217, 4219, 4218, 4220, 4225*]. where?, at what place?:– where [37], whither [10]

4227 Πούδης, *Poudēs*, n.pr. GK: *4545*. Pudens, "*modest*":– Pudens [1]

4228 πούς, *pous*, n. GK: *4546* [→ *405, 3716, 4158, 5074, 5286*]. foot; leg:– feet [76], foot [9]

4229 πρᾶγμα, *pragma*, n. GK: *4547* [→ *4238*]. thing, matter, practice:– things [4], matter [3], thing [2], business [1], work [1]

4230 πραγματεία, *pragmateia*, n. GK: *4548* [→ *4238*]. (pl.) affairs, concerns:– affairs [1]

4231 πραγματεύομαι, *pragmateuomai*, v. GK: *4549* [→ *4238*]. to put capital to work, do business:– occupy [1]

4232 πραιτώριον, *praitōrion*, n. GK: *4550*. Praetorium; palace (of the governor); palace guard:– judgment hall [4], Pretorium [1], common hall [1], hall of judgment [1], palace [1]

4233 πράκτωρ, *praktōr*, n. GK: *4551* [→ *4238*]. officer, a bailiff or constable in charge of a debtor's prison:– officer [2]

4234 πρᾶξις, *praxis*, n. GK: *4552* [→ *4238*]. deed, action, practice; function:– deeds [3], deed [1], office [1], works [1]

4235 πρᾶος, *praos*, a. GK: *4553* [→ *4239*]. gentle, humble, considerate:– meek [1]

4236 πραότης, *praotēs*, n. GK: *4554* [→ *4239*]. gentleness, humility, courtesy, considerateness:– meekness [9]

4237 πρασιά, *prasia*, n. GK: *4555* [→ *5556*]. group; in context this word is doubled: group by group:– in ranks (+*4237*) [1]

4238 πράσσω, *prassō*, v. GK: *4556* [→ *1281, 4229, 4230, 4231, 4233, 4234*]. to do, act, practice:– do [17], done [6], committed [3], doeth [3], commit [2], deeds [1], did [1], doest [1], exact [1], keep [1], required [1], used [1]

4239 πραΰς, *praus*, a. GK: *4558* [→ *4235, 4236, 4240*]. gentle, meek, the positive moral quality of dealing with people in a kind manner, with humility and consideration:– meek [3]

4240 πραΰτης, *prautēs*, n. GK: *4559* [→ *4239*]. gentleness, meekness, humility:– meekness [3]

4241 πρέπω, *prepō*, v. GK: *4560* [→ *2143, 2412, 3169*]. to be proper, appropriate, fitting:– becometh [3], became [2], become [1], comely [1]

4242 πρεσβεία, *presbeia*, n. GK: *4561* [→ *4245*]. delegation, ambassador:– ambassage [1], message [1]

4243 πρεσβεύω, *presbeuō*, v. GK: *4563* [→ *4245*]. to be an ambassador:– ambassadors [1], ambassador [1]

4244 πρεσβυτέριον, *presbyterion*, n. GK: *4564* [→ *4245*]. body or council of the elders, Sanhedrin:– elders [1], estate of the elders [1], presbytery [1]

4245 πρεσβύτερος, *presbyteros*, a. GK: *4565* [→ *4242, 4243, 4244, 4246, 4247, 4850*]. older; ancestral; (n.) in the Gospels and Acts, "elder," usually as an official leader of the Jewish community, in the epistles, "older man" and "older woman," who may or may not be official leaders of the church, depending on the context:– elders [58], elder [7], eldest [1], old men [1]

4246 πρεσβύτης, *presbytēs*, n. GK: *4562 & 4566* [→ *4245*]. older man, possibly an official of the church in some contexts:– aged men [1], aged [1], old man [1]

4247 πρεσβῦτις, *presbytis*, n. GK: *4567* [→ *4245*]. older woman, possibly an official of the church in context:– aged women [1]

πρήθω, *prēthō*. See *4092*.

4248 πρηνής, *prēnēs*, a. GK: *4568*. headlong, headfirst in prone position; some translate as "swollen, distended":– falling headlong (+*1096*) [1]

4249 πρίζω, *prizō*, v. GK: *4569 & 4573* [→ *1282*]. (pass.) to be sawn in two:– sawn asunder [1]

4250 πρίν, *prin*, adv. GK: *4570* [→ *4253*]. before:– before [7], before (+*2228*) [6], ere [1]

4251 Πρίσκα, *Priska*, n.pr. GK: *4571* [→ *4252*]. Prisca, Priscilla:– Prisca [1]

4252 Πρίσκιλλα, *Priskilla*, n.pr. GK: *4572* [→ *4251*]. Priscilla, Prisca:– Priscilla [5]

4253 πρό, *pro*, pp. GK: *4574* [→ *4206, 4207, 4208, 4250, 4254, 4255, 4256, 4257, 4258, 4259, 4260, 4261, 4262, 4263, 4264, 4265, 4266, 4267, 4268, 4269, 4270, 4271, 4272, 4273, 4274, 4275, 4276, 4277, 4278, 4279, 4280, 4281, 4282, 4283, 4284, 4285, 4286, 4287, 4288, 4289, 4290, 4291, 4292, 4293, 4294, 4295, 4296, 4297, 4298, 4299, 4300, 4301, 4302, 4303, 4304, 4305, 4306, 4307, 4308, 4309, 4310, 4311, 4312, 4313, 4315, 4368, 4372, 4373, 4384, 4385, 4386, 4387, 4388, 4389, 4390, 4391, 4392, 4393, 4394, 4399, 4400, 4401, 4402, 4408, 5432; cf. 4404, 4413*]. (of place) before, at; (of time) before, some time ago:– before [37], before (+*3588*) [6], before [3], before (+*4383*) [1], before that (+*3588*) [1], ever (+*3588*) [1]

4254 προάγω, *proagō*, v. GK: *4575* [→ *4253+71*]. to go on ahead, lead the way; to bring out, bring to trial:– went before [6], go before [5], brought forth [2], goeth before [2], going before [2], brought [1]

4255 προαιρέω, *proaireō*, v. GK: *4576* [→ *4253+138*]. (mid.) to decide, determine:– purposeth [1]

4256 προαιτιάομαι, *proaitiaomai*, v. GK: *4577* [→ *4253+156*]. to make a charge beforehand:– before proved [1]

4257 προακούω, *proakouō*, v. GK: *4578* [→ *4253+191*]. to hear about beforehand:– heard before [1]

4258 προαμαρτάνω, *proamartanō*, v. GK: *4579* [→ *4253+264*]. to sin earlier, to have sinned beforehand:– heretofore sinned [1], sinned already [1]

4259 προαύλιον, *proaulion*, n. GK: *4580* [→ *4253+833*]. entryway, gateway:– porch [1]

4260 προβαίνω, *probainō*, v. GK: *4581* [→ *4253+305*]. (spacial) to go on, go on farther; (temporal) to be well along (in years), advanced (in age):– well stricken [2], age (+*1722&2250*) [1], going on [1], gone further [1]

4261 προβάλλω, *proballō*, v. GK: *4582* [→ *4253+906*]. to push to the front, cause to come to the front; to sprout, put forth:– putting forward [1], shoot forth [1]

4262 προβατικός, *probatikos*, a. GK: *4583* [→ *4253+305*]. pertaining to sheep; (pr.n.) the Sheep (Gate):– sheep [1]

4263 πρόβατον, *probaton*, n. GK: *4585* [→ *4253+305*]. sheep:– sheep [39], sheep's [1], sheepfold (+*833+3588*) [1]

4264 προβιβάζω, *probibazō*, v. GK: *4586* [→ *4253+305*]. (pass.) to be prompted, caused to come forward:– before instructed [1], drew [1]

4265 προβλέπω, *problepō*, v. GK: *4587* [→ *4253+991*]. (mid.) to plan, select, provide:– provided [1]

4266 προγίνομαι, *proginomai*, v. GK: *4588* [→ *4253+1096*]. to commit beforehand, happen previously:– past [1]

4267 προγινώσκω, *proginōskō*, v. GK: *4589* [→ *4253+1097*]. to know beforehand, foreknow; (mid.) to choose beforehand:– foreknew [1], foreknow [1], foreordained [1], knew [1], know before [1]

4268 πρόγνωσις, *prognōsis*, n. GK: *4590* [→ *4253+1097*]. foreknowledge:– foreknowledge [2]

4269 πρόγονος, *progonos*, n. GK: *4591* [→ *4253+1096*]. (pl.) parents, forefathers, ancestors:– forefathers [1], parents [1]

4270 προγράφω, *prographō*, v. GK: *4592* [→ *4253+1125*]. to write beforehand; to show clearly, advertise, proclaim:– before ordained [1], evidently set forth [1], written aforetime [1], written [1], wrote afore [1]

4271 πρόδηλος, *prodēlos*, a. GK: *4593* [→ *4253+1212*]. obvious, clear, evident:– evident [1], manifest beforehand [1], open beforehand [1]

4272 προδίδωμι, *prodidōmi*, v. GK: *4594* [→ *4253+1325*]. to give beforehand:– first given [1]

4273 προδότης, *prodotēs*, n. GK: *4595* [→ *4253*+*1325*]. traitor, betrayer, treacherous one:– betrayers [1], traitors [1], traitor [1]

προδρέμω, *prodremō*. See **4390**.

4274 πρόδρομος, *prodromos*, a. GK: *4596* [→ *4253*+*5143*]. going before, forerunner:– forerunner [1]

4275 προείδω, *proeidō*, v. GK: *4632* [→ *4253*+*3708*]. to see previously; to see ahead, foresee:– foreseeing [1], seeing before [1]

προειρέω, *proeireō*. See **4280**.

4276 προελπίζω, *proelpizō*, v. GK: *4598* [→ *4253*+*1680*]. to be the first to hope, hope beforehand:– first trusted [1]

4277 προέπω, *proepō*, v. GK: *4625* [→ *4253*+*3004*]. to tell beforehand; to speak in the past:–

4278 προενάρχομαι, *proenarchomai*, v. GK: *4599* [→ *4253*+*1722*+*757*]. to begin beforehand, begin previously:– begun before [1], begun [1]

4279 προεπαγγέλλω, *proepangellō*, v. GK: *4600* [→ *4253*+*1909*+*32*]. (mid.) to promise beforehand; (pass.) to be promised previously:– promised afore [1]

4280 προερέω, *proereō*, v. GK: *4625* [→ *4253*+*3004*]. to tell beforehand; to speak in the past:–

4281 προέρχομαι, *proerchomai*, v. GK: *4601* [→ *4253*+*2064*]. to go on ahead; to lead; to visit in advance:– went before [2], go before [1], going before [1], go [1], outwent [1], passed on [1], went forward [1], went further [1]

4282 προετοιμάζω, *proetoimazō*, v. GK: *4602* [→ *4253*+*2092*]. to prepare in advance:– afore prepared [1], before ordained [1]

4283 προευαγγελίζομαι, *proeuangelizomai*, v. GK: *4603* [→ *4253*+*2095*+*32*]. to announce the gospel in advance:– preached before the gospel [1]

4284 προέχω, *proechō*, v. GK: *4604* [→ *4253*+*2192*]. (mid.) to be better off, have an advantage:– better [1]

4285 προηγέομαι, *proēgeomai*, v. GK: *4605* [→ *4253*+*71*]. to put above, go before:– preferring [1]

4286 πρόθεσις, *prothesis*, n. GK: *4606 & 4671* [→ *4253*+*5087*]. setting forth: plan, purpose, will; (a.) consecrated (bread):– purpose [8], shewbread (+*740*+*3588*) [3], shewbread (+*740*) [1]

4287 προθεσμία, *prothesmia*, n. GK: *4607* [→ *4253*+*5087*]. set time, fixed or limited time:– time appointed [1]

4288 προθυμία, *prothymia*, n. GK: *4608* [→ *4253*+*2372*]. eagerness, willingness, readiness:– forwardness of mind [1], readiness of mind [1], readiness [1], ready mind [1], willing mind [1]

4289 πρόθυμος, *prothymos*, a. GK: *4609* [→ *4253*+*2372*]. willing, eager:– ready [2], willing [1]

4290 προθύμως, *prothymōs*, adv. GK: *4610* [→ *4253*+*2372*]. eagerly, willingly:– of a ready mind [1]

4291 προΐστημι, *proistēmi*, v. GK: *4613* [→ *4253*+*2476*]. (act/mid) to manage, direct, lead; (mid.) to devote oneself, busy oneself to:– maintain [2], ruleth [2], rule [2], over [1], ruling [1]

4292 προκαλέω, *prokaleō*, v. GK: *4614* [→ *4253*+*2564*]. (mid.) to provoke, challenge:– provoking [1]

4293 προκαταγγέλλω, *prokatangellō*, v. GK: *4615* [→ *4253*+*2596*+*32*]. to foretell, predict, announce beforehand:– before shewed [1], foretold [1], had notice before [1], shewed before [1]

4294 προκαταρτίζω, *prokatartizō*, v. GK: *4616* [→ *4253*+*2596*+*737*]. to arrange for in advance, get ready beforehand:– make up beforehand [1]

4295 πρόκειμαι, *prokeimai*, v. GK: *4618* [→ *4253*+*2749*]. (pass.) to be set before, present:– set before [3], first [1], set forth for [1]

4296 προκηρύσσω, *prokēryssō*, v. GK: *4619* [→ *4253*+*2783*]. to preach beforehand:– before preached [1], first preached [1]

4297 προκοπή, *prokopē*, n. GK: *4620* [→ *4253*+*2875*]. progress, advancement:– furtherance [2], profiting [1]

4298 προκόπτω, *prokoptō*, v. GK: *4621* [→ *4253*+*2875*]. to go ahead, go forward, advance:– far spent [1], increased [1], increase [1], proceed [1], profited [1], wax [1]

4299 πρόκριμα, *prokrima*, n. GK: *4622* [→ *4253*+*2919*]. partiality, discrimination, prejudice:– preferring [1]

4300 προκυρόω, *prokyroō*, v. GK: *4623* [→ *4253*+*2964*]. to establish previously, ratify beforehand:– confirmed before [1]

4301 προλαμβάνω, *prolambanō*, v. GK: *4624* [→ *4253*+*2983*]. to take beforehand; to go on ahead; (pass.) to be caught, detected:– come aforehand [1], overtaken [1], taketh before [1]

4302 προλέγω, *prolegō*, v. GK: *4625* [→ *4253*+*3004*]. to tell beforehand; to speak in the past:– said before [4], told before [3], spoken before [2], foretell [1], foretold [1], forewarned [1], spake before [1], tell before [1], told in time past [1]

4303 προμαρτύρομαι, *promartyromai*, v. GK: *4626* [→ *4253*+*3144*]. to predict, bear witness to beforehand:– testified beforehand [1]

4304 προμελετάω, *promeletaō*, v. GK: *4627* [→ *4253*+*3199*]. to worry beforehand; some translate "to plan ahead":– meditate before [1]

4305 προμεριμνάω, *promerimnaō*, v. GK: *4628* [→ *4253*+*3308*]. to worry or be anxious beforehand:– take thought beforehand [1]

4306 προνοέω, *pronoeō*, v. GK: *4629* [→ *4253*+*3563*]. to provide for, care for; to consider, have regard for:– provide for [1], provide [1], providing [1]

4307 πρόνοια, *pronoia*, n. GK: *4630* [→ *4253*+*3563*]. foresight, provision, care:– providence [1], provision for [1]

4308 προοράω, *prooraō*, v. GK: *4632* [→ *4253*+*3708*]. to see previously; to see ahead, foresee; (mid.) to see in front of:– foresaw [1], seen before [1]

4309 προορίζω, *proorizō*, v. GK: *4633* [→ *4253*+*3724*]. to predestine, decide beforehand:– predestinated [2], predestinate [2], determined before [1], ordained [1]

4310 προπάσχω, *propaschō*, v. GK: *4634* [→ *4253*+*3958*]. to suffer previously:– suffered before [1]

4311 προπέμπω, *propempō*, v. GK: *4636* [→ *4253*+*3992*]. to accompany, escort; to send on one's way, help on one's journey:– brought on way [3], bring on journey [2], accompanied [1], bring forward on journey [1], brought on [1], conduct forth [1]

4312 προπετής, *propetēs*, a. GK: *4637* [→ *4253*+*4098*]. rash, reckless, thoughtless:– heady [1], rashly [1]

4313 προπορεύομαι, *proporeuomai*, v. GK: *4638* [→ *4253*+*4198*]. to go before:– go before [1], go [1]

4314 πρός, *pros*, pp. GK: *4639* [→ *676*, *677*, *1715*, *2144*, *2145*, *4316*, *4317*, *4318*, *4319*, *4320*, *4321*, *4322*, *4323*, *4324*, *4325*, *4326*, *4327*, *4328*, *4329*, *4330*, *4331*, *4332*, *4333*, *4334*, *4335*, *4336*, *4337*, *4338*, *4339*, *4340*, *4341*, *4342*, *4343*, *4344*, *4345*, *4346*, *4347*, *4348*, *4349*, *4350*, *4351*, *4354*, *4355*, *4356*, *4357*, *4358*, *4359*, *4360*, *4361*, *4362*, *4363*, *4364*, *4365*, *4366*, *4367*, *4369*, *4370*, *4371*, *4374*, *4375*, *4376*, *4377*, *4378*, *4379*, *4383*; cf. *4352*]. (gen.) to, for; (dat.) on, at, near, by; (acc.) to, toward; with; in order to; against:– unto [344], to [200], with [43], for [26], against [24], among [18], at [15], toward [8], by [4], according to [3], in [3], of [3], that (+*3588*) [3], about [2], amongst [2], before [2], between [2], pertaining to [2], that [2], to (+*3588*) [2], towards [2], as [1], because (+*3588*) [1], because of [1], belong unto [1], compared with [1], for (+*3588*) [1], nigh unto [1], pertain to [1], to do [1], together (+*240*) [1], whereby (+*3739*) [1], whereby [1], within [1]

4315 προσάββατον, *prosabbaton*, n. GK: *4640* [→ *4253*+*4521*]. day before the Sabbath (Friday):– day before the sabbath [1]

4316 προσαγορεύω, *prosagoreuō*, v. GK: *4641* [→ *4314*+*71*]. to designate:– called [1]

4317 προσάγω, *prosagō*, v. GK: *4642* [→ *4314*+*71*]. to bring to; to approach, come near:– bring [2], brought to [1], drew near [1]

4318 προσαγωγή, *prosagōgē*, n. GK: *4643* [→ *4314*+*71*]. access; approach:– access [3]

4319 προσαιτέω, *prosaiteō*, v. GK: *4644* [→ *4314*+*154*]. to beg:– begging [2], begged [1]

4320 προσαναβαίνω, *prosanabainō*, v. GK: *4646* [→ *4314*+*303*+*305*]. to move up, go up:– go up [1]

4321 προσαναλίσκω, *prosanaliskō*, v. GK: *4648 & 4649* [→ *4314*+*303*+*259*]. to spend lavishly or in addition:– spent [1]

4322 προσαναπληρόω, *prosanaplēroō*, v. GK: *4650* [→ *4314*+*303*+*4137*]. to supply, fill up:– supplied [1], supplieth [1]

4323 προσανατίθημι, *prosanatithēmi*, v. GK: *4651* [→ *4314*+*303*+*5087*]. to add; to consult, ask advice:– conferred [1], in conference added [1]

4324 προσαπειλέω, *prosapeileō*, v. GK: *4653* [→ *4314*+*547*]. to threaten further:– further threatened [1]

4325 προσδαπανάω, *prosdapanaō*, v. GK: *4655* [→ *4314*+*1160*]. to spend extra:– spendest more [1]

4326 προσδέομαι, *prosdeomai*, v. GK: *4656* [→ *4314*+*1189*]. to need:– needed [1]

4327 προσδέχομαι, *prosdechomai*, v. GK: *4657* [→ *4314*+*1209*]. to receive, welcome, accept; to wait for, anticipate:– looking for [3], receive [2], accepting [1], allow [1], looked for [1], receiveth [1], took [1], wait for [1], waited for [1], waited [1], waiting for [1]

4328 προσδοκάω, *prosdokaō*, v. GK: *4659* [→ *4314*+*1380*]. to look forward to, expect, wait for:– look for [5], looked [2], waited for [2], expecting to [1], in expectation [1], looketh for [1], looketh [1], looking for [1], tarried [1], waiting for [1]

4329 προσδοκία, *prosdokia*, n. GK: *4660* [→ *4314*+*1380*]. anticipation, expectation; apprehension:– expectation [1], looking after [1]

προσδρέμω, *prosdremō*. See **4370**.

4330 προσεάω, *proseaō*, v. GK: *4661* [→ *4314*+*1439*]. to allow to go farther:– suffering [1]

4331 προσεγγίζω, *prosengizō*, v. GK: *4662* [→ *4314*+*1451*]. to approach, come near:– come nigh [1]

4332 προσεδρεύω, *prosedreuō*, v. GK: *4663* [→ *4314*+*1476*]. to serve, wait upon:– wait at [1]

4333 προσεργάζομαι, *prosergazomai*, v. GK: *4664* [→ *4314*+*2041*]. to earn more:– gained [1]

4334 προσέρχομαι, *proserchomai*, v. GK: *4665* [→ *4314*+*2064*]. to come to, approach, draw near; to agree to:– came [35], came to [22], came unto [8], come unto [4], come [2], coming [2], went to [2], went unto [2], comers [1], cometh [1], coming to [1], consent to [1], draw near [1], drew near [1], go near [1], goeth [1], went [1]

4335 προσευχή, *proseuchē*, n. GK: *4666* [→ *4314*+*2172*]. prayer; place of prayer:– prayer [21], prayers [15], prayed earnestly (+*4336*) [1]

4336 προσεύχομαι, *proseuchomai*, v. GK: *4667* [→ *4314*+*2172*]. to pray:– pray [42], prayed [24], praying [12], prayeth [3], make prayers [2], prayest [2], make prayer [1], prayed earnestly (+*4335*) [1]

4337 προσέχω, *prosechō*, v. GK: *4668* [→ *4314*+*2192*]. to watch out, be on guard, beware; to pay attention, devote, apply oneself:– beware [7], take heed [6], gave heed [2], giving heed [2], attended unto [1], gave attendance at [1], give attendance [1], give heed to [1], give heed [1], given to [1], had regard [1]

4338 προσηλόω, *prosēloō*, v. GK: *4669* [→ *4314*+*2247*]. to nail to:– nailing [1]

4339 προσήλυτος, *prosēlytos*, n. GK: *4670* [→ *4314*+*2064*]. Gentile convert (to Judaism), transliterated as "proselyte":– proselytes [2], proselyte [2]

4340 πρόσκαιρος, *proskairos*, a. GK: *4672* [→ *4314*+*2540*]. lasting only for a short time, temporary:– for a time [1], for a while [1], season [1], temporal [1]

4341 προσκαλέω, *proskaleō*, v. GK: *4673* [→ *4314*+*2564*]. (mid.) to call, summon, send for; gather together:– called unto [16], called [6], calleth unto [2], calling unto [2], call for [1], called for [1], called to [1], call [1]

4342 προσκαρτερέω, *proskartereō*, v. GK: *4674* [→ *4314*+*2594*]. to join, adhere to; to be ready; to give attention, be faithful; to spend much time together:– continued [2], attending continually [1], continue in [1], continued stedfastly [1], continuing instant [1], continuing [1], give continually to [1], wait on [1], waited on continually [1]

4343 προσκαρτέρησις, *proskarterēsis*, n. GK: *4675* [→ *4314*+*2594*]. perseverance, patience:– perseverance [1]

4344 προσκεφάλαιον, *proskephalaion*, n. GK: *4676* [→ *4314*+*2776*]. cushion, pillow:– pillow [1]

4345 προσκληρόω, *prosklēroō*, v. GK: *4677*
[→ *4314+2819*]. (pass.) to be joined with, associated with:–
consorted with [1]

4346 πρόσκλισις, *prosklisis*, n. GK: *4680* [→ *4314+2827*].
favoritism, partiality:– partiality [1]

4347 προσκολλάω, *proskollaō*, v. GK: *4681*
[→ *4314+2853*]. (pass.) to be united to:– joined [2], cleave
to [1], cleave [1]

4348 πρόσκομμα, *proskomma*, n. GK: *4682*
[→ *4314+2875*]. stumbling block, something that causes one
to stumble:– stumblingblock [2], stumblingstone (+*3037*) [2],
offence [1], stumbling [1]

4349 προσκοπή, *proskopē*, n. GK: *4683* [→ *4314+2875*].
stumbling block, occasion for stumbling; fig. of sinning:–
offence [1]

4350 προσκόπτω, *proskoptō*, v. GK: *4684* [→ *4314+2875*].
to strike, beat; (intr.) to stumble, fall:– stumbleth [3], dash [2],
beat upon [1], stumbled [1], stumble [1]

4351 προσκυλίω, *proskyliō*, v. GK: *4685* [→ *4314+2947*].
to roll in front of, roll up to:– rolled [2]

4352 προσκυνέω, *proskyneō*, v. GK: *4686* [→ *4353*;
cf. *4314*]. to worship, pay homage, show reverence; to kneel
down (before):– worship [35], worshipped [24], worshipping [1]

4353 προσκυνητής, *proskynētēs*, n. GK: *4687* [→ *4352*].
worshiper:– worshippers [1]

4354 προσλαλέω, *proslaleō*, v. GK: *4688* [→ *4314+2980*].
to talk with:– speak with [1], speaking to [1]

4355 προσλαμβάνω, *proslambanō*, v. GK: *4689*
[→ *4314+2983*]. to take aside, take along; to partake; to
welcome, accept:– receive [4], took [4], received [3], taken [1],
take [1], took unto [1]

4356 πρόσλημψις, *proslēpsis*, n. GK: *4691 & 4692*
[→ *4314+2983*]. acceptance:– receiving [1]

4357 προσμένω, *prosmenō*, v. GK: *4693* [→ *4314+3306*].
to be with, continue in, remain, stay:– abide [1], been [1], cleave
unto [1], continueth [1], continue [1], tarried [1]

4358 προσορμίζω, *prosormizō*, v. GK: *4694* [→ *4314*].
(pass.) to be anchored, come into harbor:– drew to shore [1]

4359 προσοφείλω, *prosopheilō*, v. GK: *4695*
[→ *4314+3784*]. to owe (in addition):– owest besides [1]

4360 προσοχθίζω, *prosochthizō*, v. GK: *4696* [→ *4314*]. to
be angry, provoked:– grieved [2]

4361 πρόσπεινος, *prospeinos*, a. GK: *4698*
[→ *4314+3983*]. hungry:– hungry [1]

4362 προσπήγνυμι, *prospēgnymi*, v. GK: *4699*
[→ *4314+4078*]. to nail to (the cross):– crucified [1]

4363 προσπίπτω, *prospiptō*, v. GK: *4700* [→ *4314+4098*].
to fall down before; to beat against, strike against:– fell down
before [4], beat upon [1], falling down before [1], fell down at [1],
fell [1]

4364 προσποιέω, *prospoieō*, v. GK: *4701* [→ *4314+4160*].
to act as if, pretend:– made as though [1]

4365 προσπορεύομαι, *prosporeuomai*, v. GK: *4702*
[→ *4314+4198*]. to come to, approach:– come unto [1]

4366 προσρήγνυμι, *prosrēgnymi*, v. GK: *4703 & 4704*
[→ *4314+4486*]. to strike upon:– against beat vehemently [1],
beat vehemently upon [1]

4367 προστάσσω, *prostassō*, v. GK: *4705* [→ *4314+5021*].
(act./mid.) to command, order; (pass.) to be set, prescribed:–
commanded [6], bidden [1]

4368 προστάτις, *prostatis*, n. GK: *4706* [→ *4253+2476*].
helper:– succourer [1]

4369 προστίθημι, *prostithēmi*, v. GK: *4707*
[→ *4314+5087*]. to add to, increase ; (pass.) to be brought to,
given:– added [7], add [2], again [2], added to [1], added unto [1],
any more [1], increase [1], laid [1], more given [1], proceeded
further [1]

4370 προστρέχω, *prostrechō*, v. GK: *4708*
[→ *4314+5143*]. to run up to:– came running [1], ran to [1],
running to [1]

4371 προσφάγιον, *prosphagion*, n. GK: *4709*
[→ *4314+5314*]. (little) fish:– meat [1]

4372 πρόσφατος, *prosphatos*, a. GK: *4710* [→ *4253+5348
or* 5408]. new:– new [1]

4373 προσφάτως, *prosphatōs*, adv. GK: *4711*
[→ *4253+5348 or* 5408]. recently:– lately [1]

4374 προσφέρω, *prospherō*, v. GK: *4712* [→ *4314+5342*].
to bring to, present, offer; to treat as, deal with:– brought [12],
offered [12], offer [10], offered up [3], bring [2], brought unto [2],
offering [2], brought to [1], dealeth [1], doeth [1], presented [1],
put [1]

4375 προσφιλής, *prosphilēs*, a. GK: *4713* [→ *4314+5384*].
lovely, pleasing:– lovely [1]

4376 προσφορά, *prosphora*, n. GK: *4714* [→ *4314+5342*].
offering, presentation:– offering [7], offering up [1], offerings [1]

4377 προσφωνέω, *prosphōneō*, v. GK: *4715*
[→ *4314+5456*]. to call out; speak to, address:– spake [2],
called to [1], called unto [1], calling to [1], calling unto [1], spake
unto [1]

4378 πρόσχυσις, *proschysis*, n. GK: *4717* [→ *1632;
cf. 4314*]. sprinkling:– sprinkling [1]

4379 προσψαύω, *prospsauō*, v. GK: *4718* [→ *4314+5597*].
to touch:– touch [1]

4380 προσωπολημπτέω, *prosōpolēpteō*, v. GK: *4719 & 4722*
[→ *4383+2983*]. to show favoritism, partiality:– have respect
to persons [1]

4381 προσωπολήπτης, *prosōpolēptēs*, n. GK: *4720 & 4723*
[→ *4383+2983*]. one who shows favoritism, partiality:–
respecter of persons [1]

4382 προσωπολημψία, *prosōpolēpsia*, n. GK: *4721 & 4724*
[→ *4383+2983*]. favoritism, partiality:– respect of persons [4]

4383 πρόσωπον, *prosōpon*, n. GK: *4725* [→ *678, 2146,
4380, 4381, 4382*]. face, a part of the body; by extension: in
someone's presence, sight; (with various pp.) before, in front of,
on the surface of:– face [49], faces [6], person [5], presence [5],
countenance [3], appearance [1], before (+*1519*) [1], before
(+*4253*) [1], face to face (+*2596*) [1], fashion [1], having in
admiration (+*2296*) [1], in presence [1], in the presence
(+*2596*) [1], outward appearance [1], persons [1]

4384 προτάσσω, *protassō*, v. GK: *4726* [→ *4253+5021*]. to
determine beforehand, allot beforehand:– before appointed [1]

4385 προτείνω, *proteinō*, v. GK: *4727* [→ *1614; cf. 4253*].
to stretch out:– bound [1]

4386 πρότερον, *proteron*, n.neut. of *4387*. GK: *4728*
[→ *4253*]. before; (adv.) before, formerly, an earlier time:–

4387 πρότερος, *proteros*, a. GK: *4728* [→ *4253*]. before;
(adv.) before, formerly, an earlier time:– before [5], former [3],
first [2], at first [1]

4388 προτίθημι, *protithēmi*, v. GK: *4729* [→ *4253+5087*].
(mid.) to plan, purpose; to present, bring forth:– purposed [2],
set forth [1]

4389 προτρέπω, *protrepō*, v. GK: *4730* [→ *4253+5157*]. to
encourage, urge on:– exhorting [1]

4390 προτρέχω, *protrechō*, v. GK: *4731* [→ *4253+5143*].
to run ahead:– outrun (+*5030*) [1], ran before [1]

4391 προϋπάρχω, *prouparchō*, v. GK: *4732*
[→ *4253+5259+757*]. to exist formerly:– beforetime [1],
before [1]

4392 πρόφασις, *prophasis*, n. GK: *4733* [→ *4253+5316*].
excuse; pretense, show, cover:– pretence [3], cloke [2], shew [1],
under colour [1]

4393 προφέρω, *propherō*, v. GK: *4734* [→ *4253+5342*]. to
bring out:– bringeth forth [2]

4394 προφητεία, *prophēteia*, n. GK: *4735* [→ *4395, 4396,
4397, 4398, 5578*]. prophecy, an inspired message, sometimes
encouraging obedience to God, sometimes proclaiming the
future as a warning to preparedness and continued obedience:–
prophecy [14], prophecies [2], prophesying [2], prophesyings [1]

4395 προφητεύω, *prophēteuō*, v. GK: *4736* [→ *4394*]. to
prophesy, to speak an inspired message, sometimes encouraging
obedience to God, sometimes proclaiming the future as a
warning to preparedness and continued obedience:–
prophesy [14], prophesied [9], prophesieth [4], prophesying [1]

4396 προφήτης, *prophētēs*, n. GK: *4737* [→ *4394*].
prophet, one who speaks inspired utterances; the writings of the
OT prophets; see also *4394*:– prophets [81], prophet [67],
prophet's [1]

4397 προφητικός, *prophētikos*, a. GK: *4738* [→ *4394*].
prophetic, prophesy; see also *4394*:– of prophecy [1], prophets [1]

4398 προφήτις, *prophētis*, n. GK: *4739* [→ *4394*].
prophetess, a woman who speaks inspired utterances; see also
4394:– prophetess [2]

4399 προφθάνω, *prophthanō*, v. GK: *4740*
[→ *4253+5348*]. to anticipate, come before:– prevented [1]

4400 προχειρίζω, *procheirizō*, v. GK: *4741*
[→ *4253+5495*]. (mid.) to choose, appoint:– chosen [1],
make [1]

4401 προχειροτονέω, *procheirotoneō*, v. GK: *4742*
[→ *1614*]. to choose beforehand, appoint beforehand:– chosen
before [1]

4402 Πρόχορος, *Prochoros*, n.pr. GK: *4743*
[→ *4253+5525*]. Procorus:– Prochorus [1]

4403 πρύμνα, *prymna*, n. GK: *4744*. stern (of a vessel):–
hinder part of ship [1], hinder part [1], stern [1]

4404 πρωΐ, *prōi*, adv. GK: *4745* [→ *4405, 4406, 4407;
cf. 4253*]. early in the morning:– in the morning [4], early [2],
morning [2], early in the morning (+*260*) [1], early in the
morning [1]

4405 πρωΐα, *prōia*, n. GK: *4746* [→ *4404*]. early morning:–
morning [2], early [1], in the morning [1]

4406 πρώϊμος, *prōimos*, a. GK: *4611 & 4747* [→ *4404*].
early; (n.) autumn rains (in October of the modern calendar):–
early [1]

4407 πρωϊνός, *prōinos*, a. GK: *4612 & 4748* [→ *4404*].
early, pertaining to the morning:– morning [1]

4408 πρῴρα, *prōra*, n. GK: *4749* [→ *4253*]. bow (of a
vessel):– forepart [1], foreship [1]

4409 πρωτεύω, *prōteuō*, v. GK: *4750* [→ *4413*]. to be
supreme, first, have first place:– preeminence [1]

4410 πρωτοκαθεδρία, *prōtokathedria*, n. GK: *4751*
[→ *4413+2516*]. most important seat, seat of honor:– chief
seats [2], highest seats [1], uppermost seats [1]

4411 πρωτοκλισία, *prōtoklisia*, n. GK: *4752*
[→ *4413+2827*]. place of honor:– chief rooms [2], uppermost
rooms [2], highest room [1]

4412 πρῶτον, *prōton*, adv. GK: *4754* [→ *4413*]. first;
earlier; above all:– first [55], at first [2], at the beginning [1],
before [1], chiefly [1], first of all [1]

4413 πρῶτος, *prōtos*, a. GK: *4755* [→ *1207, 4409, 4410,
4411, 4412, 4414, 4415, 4416, 5383; cf. 4253*]. first
(chronologically or in order of importance):– first [86], chief [10],
before [2], former [2], beginning [1], best [1], chiefest [1], first
(+*1722*) [1]

4414 πρωτοστάτης, *prōtostatēs*, n. GK: *4756*
[→ *4413+2476*]. ringleader, leader:– ringleader [1]

4415 πρωτοτόκια, *prōtotokia*, n. GK: *4757*
[→ *4413+5088*]. inheritance rights (of the firstborn):–
birthright [1]

4416 πρωτότοκος, *prōtotokos*, a. GK: *4758*
[→ *4413+5088*]. firstborn (human or animal). In biblical
culture, the firstborn had higher status and received a greater
share of the inheritance. Jesus Christ, as the firstborn of God, is
of supreme status and inherits all things:– firstborn [7], first
begotten [1], firstbegotten [1]

4417 πταίω, *ptaiō*, v. GK: *4760* [→ *679*]. to stumble, fall,
trip:– offend [3], fall [1], stumbled [1]

4418 πτέρνα, *pterna*, n. GK: *4761*. heel:– heel [1]

4419 πτερύγιον, *pterygion*, n. GK: *4762* [→ *4072*]. highest
point:– pinnacle [2]

4420 πτέρυξ, *pteryx*, n. GK: *4763* [→ *4072*]. wing:–
wings [5]

4421 πτηνός, *ptēnos*, a. GK: *4764* [→ *4072*]. what is
winged or feathered; (n.) bird:– birds [1]

4422 πτοέω, *ptoeō*, v. GK: *4765* [→ *4423*]. (pass.) to be
startled, frightened:– terrified [2]

4423 πτόησις, *ptoēsis*, n. GK: *4766* [→ *4422*]. something
alarming:– amazement [1]

4424 Πτολεμαΐς, *Ptolemais*, n.pr. GK: *4767*. Ptolemais:–
Ptolemais [1]

4425 πτύον, *ptyon*, n. GK: *4768* [→ *4429*]. winnowing fork
or shovel:– fan [2]

4426 πτύρω, *ptyrō*, v. GK: *4769*. (pass.) to be frightened:–
terrified [1]

4427 πτύσμα, **ptysma**, n. GK: *4770* [→ *4429*]. saliva, spit:– spittle [1]

4428 πτύσσω, **ptyssō**, v. GK: *4771* [→ *380*]. to roll up:– closed [1]

4429 πτύω, **ptyō**, v. GK: *4772* [→ *1609, 1716, 4425, 4427*]. to spit (saliva):– spit [2], spat [1]

4430 πτῶμα, **ptōma**, n. GK: *4773* [→ *4098*]. dead body, carcass, corpse:– dead bodies [3], carcase [1], corpse [1]

4431 πτῶσις, **ptōsis**, n. GK: *4774* [→ *4098*]. falling, crash:– fall [2]

4432 πτωχεία, **ptōcheia**, n. GK: *4775* [→ *4434*]. poverty:– poverty [3]

4433 πτωχεύω, **ptōcheuō**, v. GK: *4776* [→ *4434*]. to be or become poor:– poor [1]

4434 πτωχός, **ptōchos**, a. GK: *4777* [→ *4432, 4433*]. poor; (n.) poor, beggar, a person of few resources, culturally considered oppressed, despised, and miserable. "The poor in spirit" are not lacking in spirit, but have the positive moral quality of humility, realizing they have nothing to offer God but are in need of his free gifts:– poor [31], beggar [2], beggarly [1]

4435 πυγμή, **pygmē**, n. GK: *4778* [→ *4437, 4438*]. fist; with a fist = NIV "ceremonial":– oft [1]

4436 πύθων, **pythōn**, n. GK: *4780*. spirit of divination:– of divination [1]

4437 πυκνός, **pyknos**, a. GK: *4781* [→ *4435*]. (a.) often, frequent, numerous; (adv.) often, as a comparative: quite often, as often as possible:– often [2], oftener [1]

4438 πυκτεύω, **pykteuō**, v. GK: *4782* [→ *4435*]. to fight with the fist, box:– fight [1]

4439 πύλη, **pylē**, n. GK: *4783* [→ *4440*]. (city) gate:– gate [8], gates [2]

4440 πυλών, **pylōn**, n. GK: *4784* [→ *4439*]. gate, door, entryway:– gates [11], gate [6], porch [1]

4441 πυνθάνομαι, **pynthanomai**, v. GK: *4785*. to ask, inquire, question:– asked [5], ask [2], demanded [2], inquired [1], inquire [1], understood [1]

4442 πῦρ, **pyr**, n. GK: *4786* [→ *329, 4443, 4445, 4446, 4447, 4448, 4449, 4450, 4451*]. fire, flames:– fire [73], fiery [1]

4443 πυρά, **pyra**, n. GK: *4787* [→ *4442*]. fire:– fire [2]

4444 πύργος, **pyrgos**, n. GK: *4788*. tower, watchtower:– tower [4]

4445 πυρέσσω, **pyressō**, v. GK: *4789* [→ *4442*]. to burn with a fever:– sick of a fever [2]

4446 πυρετός, **pyretos**, n. GK: *4790* [→ *4442*]. fever:– fever [6]

4447 πύρινος, **pyrinos**, a. GK: *4791* [→ *4442*]. fiery red, the color of fire:– fire [1]

4448 πυρόω, **pyroō**, v. GK: *4792* [→ *4442*]. to burn; to burn inwardly:– burn [2], burned [1], fiery [1], on fire [1], tried [1]

4449 πυρράζω, **pyrrazō**, v. GK: *4793* [→ *4442*]. to be red, the color of fire:– red [2]

4450 πυρρός, **pyrros**, a. GK: *4794* [→ *4442*]. fiery red, the color of fire:– red [2]

4451 πύρωσις, **pyrōsis**, n. GK: *4796* [→ *4442*]. burning, painful:– burning [2], fiery trial [1]

4452 -πω, **-pō**, pt. GK: * [→ *4458*]. an enclitic particle of indefiniteness; yet, even; used only in composition. See *3369, 3380, 3764, 3768, 4455*:–

4453 πωλέω, **pōleō**, v. GK: *4797* [→ *4211*]. to sell:– sold [14], sell [7], selleth [1]

4454 πῶλος, **pōlos**, n. GK: *4798*. colt:– colt [12]

4455 πώποτε, **pōpote**, adv. GK: *4799*. ever, at any time:– at any time [3], never (+*3361+3756*) [1], never [1], yet never (+*3762*) [1]

4456 πωρόω, **pōroō**, v. GK: *4800* [→ *4457*]. to harden, deaden, make dull:– hardened [3], blinded [2]

4457 πώρωσις, **pōrōsis**, n. GK: *4801* [→ *4456*]. hardening, stubbornness:– blindness [2], hardness [1]

4458 πώς, **pōs**, pt. GK: *4803* [→ *4452*]. somehow, in some way:–

4459 πῶς, **pōs**, pt.inter. GK: *4802*. how? in what way?; how!:– how [97], by what means [2], after what manner [1], how (+*302+1063*) [1], how can [1], that [1]

4460 Ῥαάβ, **Rhaab**, n.pr. GK: *4805*. Rahab, "*spacious, broad*":– Rahab [2]

4461 ῥαββί, **rhabbi**, l.[n.]. GK: *4806* [→ *4462*]. Rabbi, a title of a teacher:– master [9], Rabbi [8]

4462 ῥαββουνί, **rhabbouni**, or ῥαββουνεί, **rhabbounei**, l.[n.]. GK: *4807 & 4808 & 4809* [→ *4461*]. Rabboni, a title of a teacher:– Lord [1], Rabboni [1]

4463 ῥαβδίζω, **rhabdizō**, v. GK: *4810* [→ *4464*]. to beat with a rod:– beaten with rods [1], beat [1]

4464 ῥάβδος, **rhabdos**, n. GK: *4811* [→ *4463, 4465, 4474, 4475*]. rod, staff, stick; measuring rod; scepter:– rod [6], sceptre [2], staff [2], staves [1]

4465 ῥαβδοῦχος, **rhabdouchos**, n. GK: *4812* [→ *4464+2192*]. officer, the Roman *lictor*, a policeman:– sergeants [2]

4466 Ῥαγαύ, **Rhagau**, n.pr. GK: *4814*. Reu, "*friend [of God]*":– Ragau [1]

4467 ῥᾳδιούργημα, **rhadiourgēma**, n. GK: *4815* [→ *4468*]. crime, legal infraction:– lewdness [1]

4468 ῥᾳδιουργία, **rhadiourgia**, n. GK: *4816* [→ *4467; cf. 2041*]. trickery:– mischief [1]

4469 ῥακά, **rhaka**, l.[a.]. GK: *4819 & 4828*. Raca (a term of abuse, derived from Aramaic *rêqa'*, meaning "empty[-headed] one"), "*empty-headed [?]*":– Raca [1]

4470 ῥάκος, **rhakos**, n. GK: *4820*. piece of cloth:– cloth [2]

4471 Ῥαμά, **Rhama**, n.pr. GK: *4821*. Ramah, "*elevated spot*":– Rama [1]

4472 ῥαντίζω, **rhantizō**, v. GK: *4822* [→ *4473*]. to sprinkle:– sprinkled [3], sprinkling [1]

4473 ῥαντισμός, **rhantismos**, n. GK: *4823* [→ *4472*]. sprinkling:– sprinkling [2]

4474 ῥαπίζω, **rhapizō**, v. GK: *4824* [→ *4464*]. to strike, slap:– smite [1], smote with the palms of hands [1]

4475 ῥάπισμα, **rhapisma**, n. GK: *4825* [→ *4464*]. slap, strike:– smote with hands (+*1325*) [1], strike with the palms of hands (+*906*) [1], stroke with the palm of hand (+*1325*) [1]

4476 ῥαφίς, **rhaphis**, n. GK: *4827* [→ *729, 1976*]. needle:– needle [2], needle's [1]

4477 Ῥαχάβ, **Rhachab**, n.pr. GK: *4829*. Rahab, "*spacious, broad*":– Rachab [1]

4478 Ῥαχήλ, **Rhachēl**, n.pr. GK: *4830*. Rachel, "*ewe*":– Rachel [1]

4479 Ῥεβέκκα, **Rhebekka**, n.pr. GK: *4831*. Rebekah, "[poss.] *choice calf*":– Rebecca [1]

4480 ῥέδη, **rhedē**, n. GK: *4832*. carriage:– chariots [1]

4481 Ῥεμφάν, **Rhemphan**, or Ῥαιφάν, **Rhaiphan**, n.pr. GK: *4818 & 4833 & 4834 & 4854* [→ *4481, 4481, 4481*]. Rephan, Remphan:– Remphan [1]

4482 ῥέω, **rheō**, v. GK: *4835* [→ *131, 3901, 4511, 5493*]. to flow:– flow [1]

4483 ῥέω, **rheō**; and ἐρέω, **ereō**, v. GK: *3306* [→ *3004*]. to utter, speak, say:–

4484 Ῥήγιον, **Rhēgion**, n.pr. GK: *4836*. Rhegium:– Rhegium [1]

4485 ῥῆγμα, **rhēgma**, n. GK: *4837* [→ *4486*]. destruction, ruin:– ruin [1]

4486 ῥήγνυμι, **rhēgnymi**, or ῥήσσω, **rhēssō**, v. GK: *4838* [→ *1284, 4048, 4366, 4485*]. to burst, break forth; to tear to pieces; to throw violently:– burst [2], break forth [1], break [1], rent [1], teareth [1], threw down [1]

4487 ῥῆμα, **rhēma**, n. GK: *4839* [→ *368, 369, 731, 3954, 3955, 4489, 4490*]. word, saying; matter; thing:– words [31], word [25], saying [6], sayings [3], things [2], nothing (+*3756+3956*) [1], thing [1]

4488 Ῥησά, **Rhēsa**, n.pr. GK: *4840*. Rhesa:– Rhesa [1]

4489 ῥήτωρ, **rhētōr**, n. GK: *4842* [→ *4487*]. lawyer:– orator [1]

4490 ῥητῶς, **rhētōs**, adv. GK: *4843* [→ *4487*]. clearly, exactly:– expressly [1]

4491 ῥίζα, **rhiza**, n. GK: *4844* [→ *1610, 4492*]. root, rootstock:– root [16], roots [1]

4492 ῥιζόω, **rhizoō**, v. GK: *4845* [→ *4491*]. (pass.) to be rooted, with the associative meaning that a rooted object is strong and healthy:– rooted [2]

4493 ῥιπή, **rhipē**, n. GK: *4846 & 4856* [→ *4496*]. twinkling, rapid movement (of the eye); some translate as "the blink (of an eye)":– twinkling [1]

4494 ῥιπίζω, **rhipizō**, v. GK: *4847* [→ *4496*]. (pass.) to be tossed about:– tossed [1]

4495 ῥιπτέω, **rhipteō**, v. GK: *4848* [→ *4496*]. to throw off:– cast [1]

4496 ῥίπτω, **rhiptō**, v. GK: *4849* [→ *641, 1977, 4493, 4494, 4495*]. to throw, drop; to lay; (pass.) to be helpless, laid out:– cast [4], cast down [1], scattered abroad [1], thrown [1]

4497 Ῥοβοάμ, **Rhoboam**, n.pr. GK: *4850*. Rehoboam, "*[my] people will enlarge, expand*":– Roboam [2]

4498 Ῥόδη, **Rhodē**, n.pr. GK: *4851*. Rhoda, "*rose*":– Rhoda [1]

4499 Ῥόδος, **Rhodos**, n.pr. GK: *4852*. Rhodes, "*rose*":– Rhodes [1]

4500 ῥοιζηδόν, **rhoizēdon**, adv. GK: *4853*. with a roar; a derivative of a Greek noun meaning, "the noise made by a passing arrow," not found in the NT:– great noise [1]

4501 ῥομφαία, **rhomphaia**, n. GK: *4855*. (long) sword:– sword [7]

4502 Ῥουβήν, **Rhoubēn**, n.pr. GK: *4857*. Reuben, "*See, a son! [Ge. 29:32]; substitute a son*":– Reuben [1]

4503 Ῥούθ, **Rhouth**, n.pr. GK: *4858*. Ruth, "*friendship, poss. comrade, companion; refreshed*":– Ruth [1]

4504 Ῥοῦφος, **Rhouphos**, n.pr. GK: *4859*. Rufus, "*red-haired*":– Rufus [2]

4505 ῥύμη, **rhymē**, n. GK: *4860*. street, alley, lane:– street [2], lanes [1], streets [1]

4506 ῥύομαι, **rhyomai**, v. GK: *4861*. to rescue, deliver:– delivered [9], deliver [8], deliverer [1]

4507 ῥυπαρία, **rhyparia**, n. GK: *4864* [→ *4509*]. (moral) filth:– filthiness [1]

4508 ῥυπαρός, **rhyparos**, a. GK: *4865* [→ *4509*]. shabby, dirty; moral vileness, filthiness:– vile [1]

4509 ῥύπος, **rhypos**, n. GK: *4866* [→ *4507, 4508, 4510*]. dirt:– filth [1]

4510 ῥυπόω, **rhypoō**, v. GK: *4867* [→ *4509*]. to defile, pollute:– filthy [2]

4511 ῥύσις, **rhysis**, n. GK: *4868* [→ *4482*]. flow (of blood), bleeding:– issue [3]

4512 ῥυτίς, **rhytis**, n. GK: *4869*. wrinkle:– wrinkle [1]

4513 Ῥωμαϊκός, **Rhōmaikos**, a.pr. GK: *4870* [→ *4516*]. Roman, Latin:– Latin [1]

4514 Ῥωμαῖος, **Rhōmaios**, a.pr.g. GK: *4871* [→ *4516*]. Roman, from Rome; (n.) Roman citizen:– Romans [6], Roman [5], Romans (+*444*) [1], of Rome [1]

4515 Ῥωμαϊστί, **Rhōmaisti**, adv.pr. GK: *4872* [→ *4516*]. in Latin (language):– Latin [1]

4516 Ῥώμη, **Rhōmē**, n.pr. GK: *4873* [→ *4513, 4514, 4515*]. Rome:– Rome [14]

4517 ῥώννυμι, **rhōnnymi**, v. GK: *4874* [→ *732*]. to be strong; (pass.) farewell, goodbye, as the closing of a letter:– fare well [1], farewell [1]

4518 σαβαχθάνι, **sabachthani**, l.[v.+p.]. GK: *2407 & 4876*. sabachthani (Aramaic: "you have forsaken me"):– sabachthani [2]

4519 Σαβαώθ, **Sabaōth**, l.[pr.n.]. GK: *4877*. Almighty ["of Hosts"], a Greek transliteration of the Hebrew word *7372*, "armies, hosts." This title has the associative meanings of power and potent authority, and pictures the Lord as a great, powerful, supreme general:– sabaoth [1]

4520 σαββατισμός, **sabbatismos**, n. GK: *4878* [→ *4521*]. Sabbath-rest, Sabbath observance; "a sabbath's day journey" reckoned at 800 to 900 yards (2,000 cubits):– rest [1]

4521 σάββατον, **sabbaton**, n. GK: *4879* [→ *4315, 4520*]. Sabbath:– sabbath [57], week [9], sabbath day's journey (+*2192+3598*) [1], sabbath days [1]

4522 σαγήνη, **sagēnē**, n. GK: *4880*. (large) dragnet, a net with weights on the bottom and dragged through the water:– net [1]

4523 Σαδδουκαῖος, **Saddoukaios**, n.pr. GK: *4881* [cf. *4524*]. Sadducee, "[poss.] *followers of Zadok; righteous*":– Sadducees [14]

4524 Σαδώκ, **Sadōk**, n.pr. GK: *4882* [cf. *4523*]. Zadok, "*righteous one*":– Sadoc [2]

4525 σαίνω, **sainō**, v. GK: *4883*. (pass.) to be unsettled, disturbed:– moved [1]

4526 σάκκος, **sakkos**, n. GK: *4884*. sackcloth, a heavy coarse cloth used for making sacks, but worn by the penitent or mournful as a sign of contrition and sorrow:– sackcloth [4]

4527 Σαλά, **Sala**, n.pr. GK: *4885*. Sala, "*missile [a weapon], sprout*":– Sala [1]

4528 Σαλαθιήλ, **Salathiēl**, n.pr. GK: *4886*. Shealtiel, "*I have asked [him] of God [El]; poss. God [El] is a shield*":– Salathiel [3]

4529 Σαλαμίς, **Salamis**, n.pr. GK: *4887*. Salamis, "*peace*":– Salamis [1]

4530 Σαλίμ, **Salim**, n.pr. GK: *4890*. Salim:– Salim [1]

4531 σαλεύω, **saleuō**, v. GK: *4888* [→ *761, 4535*; cf. *242*]. to shake up; agitate; (pass.) to be shaken, swayed, unsettled:– shaken [11], moved [1], shake [1], shook [1], stirred up [1]

4532 Σαλήμ, **Salēm**, n.pr. GK: *4889*. Salem, "*peace*":– Salem [2]

4533 Σαλμών, **Salmōn**, n.pr. GK: *4891*. Salmon, "*little spark*":– Salmon [3]

4534 Σαλμώνη, **Salmōnē**, n.pr. GK: *4892*. Salmone:– Salmone [1]

4535 σάλος, **salos**, n. GK: *4893* [→ *4531*]. tossing motion, rolling motion (of the surging waves):– waves [1]

4536 σάλπιγξ, **salpinx**, n. GK: *4894* [→ *4537*]. trumpet:– trumpet [7], trumpets [2], trump [2]

4537 σαλπίζω, **salpizō**, v. GK: *4895* [→ *4536, 4538*]. to sound a trumpet, announce with a trumpet:– sounded [7], sound [3], sound a trumpet [1], trumpet sound [1]

4538 σαλπιστής, **salpistēs**, n. GK: *4896* [→ *4537*]. trumpeter:– trumpeters [1]

4539 Σαλώμη, **Salōmē**, n.pr. GK: *4897*. Salome, "*peaceful, prosperous one*":– Salome [2]

4540 Σαμάρεια, **Samareia**, n.pr. GK: *4899 & 4900* [→ *4541, 4542*]. Samaria, "*belonging to the clan of Shemer [1Ki 16:24]*":– Samaria [11]

4541 Σαμαρίτης, **Samaritēs**, n.pr.g. GK: *4901* [→ *4540*]. Samaritan:– Samaritans [6], Samaritan [3]

4542 Σαμαρῖτις, **Samaritis**, n.pr.g.&a. GK: *4902* [→ *4540*]. Samaritan:– Samaria [2]

4543 Σαμοθρᾴκη, **Samothrakē**, n.pr. GK: *4903*. Samothrace, "*Thracian Samos*":– Samothracia [1]

4544 Σάμος, **Samos**, n.pr. GK: *4904*. Samos, "*heights, lofty place*":– Samos [1]

4545 Σαμουήλ, **Samouēl**, n.pr. GK: *4905*. Samuel, "*his name is God [El]; heard of God [El]; the unnamed god is El*":– Samuel [3]

4546 Σαμψών, **Sampsōn**, n.pr. GK: *4907*. Samson, "*little one of Shemesh [pagan sun god] or sunny*":– Samson [1]

4547 σανδάλιον, **sandalion**, n. GK: *4908*. sandal:– sandals [2]

4548 σανίς, **sanis**, n. GK: *4909*. plank, board:– boards [1]

4549 Σαούλ, **Saoul**, n.pr. GK: *4910*. Saul, "*asked of God* or poss. *dedicated to God*":– Saul [9]

4550 σαπρός, **sapros**, a. GK: *4911* [→ *4595*]. bad, rotten, decayed; unwholesome:– corrupt [7], bad [1]

4551 Σάπφιρα, **Sapphira**, n.pr. GK: *4912* [→ *4552*]. Sapphira, "*beautiful*":– Sapphira [1]

4552 σάπφιρος, **sapphiros**, n. GK: *4913* [→ *4551*]. sapphire stone:– sapphire [1]

4553 σαργάνη, **sarganē**, n. GK: *4914*. (large flexible) basket, possibly made of ropes:– basket [1]

4554 Σάρδεις, **Sardeis**, n.pr. GK: *4915*. Sardis:– Sardis [3]

4555 σάρδινος, **sardinos**, n. GK: *4916* [→ *4556*]. carnelian, sard:– sardine [1]

4556 σάρδιον, **sardion**, n. GK: *4917* [→ *4555, 4557*]. carnelian (a reddish precious stone):– sardius [1]

4557 σαρδόνυξ, **sardonyx**, n. GK: *4918* [→ *4556*]. sardonyx (a variety of agate):– sardonyx [1]

4558 Σάρεπτα, **Sarepta**, n.pr. GK: *4919*. Zarephath, "*[poss.] smelting place; place of pigmenting, staining*":– Sarepta [1]

4559 σαρκικός, **sarkikos**, a. GK: *4920* [→ *4561*]. material; worldly, sinful; pertaining to the flesh; see also *4561*:– carnal [9], fleshly [1]

4560 σάρκινος, **sarkinos**, a. GK: *4921* [→ *4561*]. fleshly, made of flesh; human; worldly, unspiritual; see also *4561*:– fleshy [1]

4561 σάρξ, **sarx**, n. GK: *4922* [→ *4559, 4560*]. flesh, body, the soft tissue of a creature, often in contrast to bone, ligament, or sinew; by extension human, humankind, with a focus on the fallen human nature, which is frail and corrupt in contrast to immaterial (spiritual) things, thus the NIV translation "sinful nature":– flesh [147], carnal [2], carnally [1], fleshly [1]

4562 Σαρούχ, **Sarouch**; or Σερούχ, **Serouch**, n.pr. GK: *4923 & 4951 & 4952*. Serug, "*descendant, i.e., younger branch*":– Saruch [1]

4563 σαρόω, **saroō**, v. GK: *4924*. to sweep, sweep clean:– swept [2], sweep [1]

4564 Σάρρα, **Sarra**, n.pr. GK: *4925*. Sarah, "*princess*":– Sara [3], Sara's [1]

4565 Σαρών, **Sarōn**, n.pr. GK: *4926*. Sharon, "*plain, level country*":– Saron [1]

4566 Σατάν, **Satan**, n.pr. GK: *4927* [→ *4567*]. Satan, "*hostile opponent*":– Satan [1]

4567 Σατανᾶς, **Satanas**, n.pr. GK: *4928* [→ *4566*]. Satan, "*hostile opponent*":– Satan [35], Satan's [1]

4568 σάτον, **saton**, n. GK: *4929*. seah (dry measure of about 12 quarts):– measures [2]

4569 Σαῦλος, **Saulos**, n.pr. GK: *4930*. Saul, "*asked for* poss. *dedicated to God*":– Saul [17]

σαυτοῦ, **sautou**. See *4572*.

4570 σβέννυμι, **sbennymi**, v. GK: *4931* [→ *762*]. to extinguish, quench, snuff out:– quenched [4], quench [3], gone out [1]

4571 σέ, **se**, p.pers.a. of *4771*. GK: *5148* [→ *4771*]. you, thee; see *4771*:–

4572 σεαυτοῦ, **seautou**, p.reflex. GK: *4932* [→ *4771+846*]. yourself:– thyself [38], thine own self [2], thee [1], thy [1]

4573 σεβάζομαι, **sebazomai**, v. GK: *4933* [→ *4576*]. to worship:– worshipped [1]

4574 σέβασμα, **sebasma**, n. GK: *4934* [→ *4576*]. object of worship; some translate as a place of worship: sanctuary:– devotions [1], worshipped [1]

4575 σεβαστός, **sebastos**, a. GK: *4935* [→ *4576*]. (a.) revered, worthy of reverence, imperial (not found in the NT); (n.) Emperor, a title of reverence or veneration:– Augustus [2], Augustus' [1]

4576 σέβω, **sebō**, v. GK: *4936* [→ *763, 764, 765, 2150, 2151, 2152, 2153, 2317, 2318, 4573, 4574, 4575, 4586, 4587*]. (mid.) to worship, be devout, God-fearing:– devout [3], worship [3], worshipped [2], religious [1], worshippeth [1]

4577 σειρά, **seira**, n. GK: *4937*. chain:– chains [1]

4578 σεισμός, **seismos**, n. GK: *4939* [→ *4579*]. earthquake; storm:– earthquake [10], earthquakes [1], tempest [1]

4579 σείω, **seiō**, v. GK: *4940* [→ *383, 1286, 2678, 4578*]. to cause to shake; (pass.) to be shaken, stirred up:– shake [2], moved [1], quake [1], shaken [1]

4580 Σεκοῦνδος, **Sekoundos**, n.pr. GK: *4941*. Secundus, "*second*":– Secundus [1]

4581 Σελεύκεια, **Seleukeia**, n.pr. GK: *4942*. Seleucia:– Seleucia [1]

4582 σελήνη, **selēnē**, n. GK: *4943* [→ *4583*]. moon:– moon [9]

4583 σεληνιάζομαι, **selēniazomai**, v. GK: *4944* [→ *4582*]. (pass.) to have a seizure:– lunatick [2]

4584 Σεμεΐ, **Semei**; or Σεμεΐν, **Semein**, n.pr. GK: *4945 & 4946*. Semei, "*Yahweh has heard*":– Semei [1]

4585 σεμίδαλις, **semidalis**, n. GK: *4947*. finely ground flour:– fine flour [1]

4586 σεμνός, **semnos**, a. GK: *4948* [→ *4576*]. worthy of respect, noble:– grave [3], honest [1]

4587 σεμνότης, **semnotēs**, n. GK: *4949* [→ *4576*]. holiness, seriousness, respect:– gravity [2], honesty [1]

4588 Σέργιος, **Sergios**, n.pr. GK: *4950*. Sergius:– Sergius [1]

4589 Σήθ, **Sēth**, n.pr. GK: *4953*. Seth, "*determined, granted [Ge 4:25]; restitution*":– Seth [1]

4590 Σήμ, **Sēm**, n.pr. GK: *4954*. Shem, "*name, fame*":– Sem [1]

4591 σημαίνω, **sēmainō**, v. GK: *4955* [→ *4592*]. to make known; to indicate (beforehand), predict, foretell:– signifying [3], signified [2], signify [1]

4592 σημεῖον, **sēmeion**, n. GK: *4956* [→ *767, 1978, 2154, 3902, 4591, 4593, 4953*]. (miraculous) sign, signal, mark:– sign [29], signs [22], miracles [15], miracle [7], wonder [2], token [1], wonders [1]

4593 σημειόω, **sēmeioō**, v. GK: *4957* [→ *4592*]. (mid.) to take special note of:– note [1]

4594 σήμερον, **sēmeron**, adv. GK: *4958* [→ *2250*]. today, this day:– this day [19], to day [18], this day (+*2250*) [3], this day's [1]

4595 σήπω, **sēpō**, v. GK: *4960* [→ *4550*]. to rot, decay:– corrupted [1]

4596 σηρικός, **sērikos**; σιρικός, **sirikos**, a. GK: *4961 & 4986*. silken; (n.) silk (cloth):– silk [1]

4597 σής, **sēs**, n. GK: *4962* [→ *4598*]. moth:– moth [3]

4598 σητόβρωτος, **sētobrōtos**, a. GK: *4963* [→ *4597+977*]. moth-eaten:– motheaten [1]

4599 σθενόω, **sthenoō**, v. GK: *4964* [→ *769, 770, 771, 772*]. to strengthen, make strong:– strengthen [1]

4600 σιαγών, **siagōn**, n. GK: *4965*. cheek:– cheek [2]

4601 σιγάω, **sigaō**, v. GK: *4967* [→ *4602*]. to be or become silent; (pass.) to be hidden, concealed:– held peace [2], hold peace [2], keep silence [2], kept close [1], kept secret [1], kept silence [1]

4602 σιγή, **sigē**, n. GK: *4968* [→ *4601*]. silence:– silence [2]

4603 σιδήρεος, **sidēreos**, a. GK: *4969 & 4971* [→ *4604*]. made of iron:– of iron [4], iron [1]

4604 σίδηρος, **sidēros**, n. GK: *4970* [→ *4603*]. iron:– iron [1]

4605 Σιδών, **Sidōn**, n.pr. GK: *4972* [→ *4606*]. Sidon, "*fishery*":– Sidon [11]

4606 Σιδώνιος, **Sidōnios**, a.pr.g. GK: *4973* [→ *4605*]. Sidonian, a person of Sidon:– Sidon [1]

4607 σικάριος, **sikarios**, n. GK: *4974*. terrorist, assassin:– murderers [1]

4608 σίκερα, **sikera**, l.[n.]. GK: *4975*. fermented drink, beer:– strong drink [1]

4609 Σίλας, **Silas**, n.pr. GK: *4976* [→ *4610*]. Silas, "*asked for* poss. *dedicated to God*":– Silas [13]

4610 Σιλουανός, **Silouanos**, n.pr. GK: *4977* [→ *4609*]. Silas, Silvanus, "*asked for* poss. *dedicated to God*":– Silvanus [4]

4611 Σιλωάμ, **Silōam**, n.pr. GK: *4978*. Siloam, "*sent*":– Siloam [3]

4612 σιμικίνθιον, **simikinthion**, n. GK: *4959 & 4980*. apron:– aprons [1]

4613 Σίμων, **Simōn**, n.pr. GK: *4981* [→ *4826*]. Simon, "*he has heard* or *obedient one*":– Simon [68], Simon's [7]

4614 Σινά, **Sina**, n.pr. GK: *4982*. Sinai, "*Sin [pagan moon god]; glare [from white chalk]*":– Sinai [2], Sina [2]

4615 σίναπι, **sinapi**, n. GK: *4983*. mustard plant:– mustard [5]

4616 σινδών, **sindōn**, n. GK: *4984*. linen (cloth or garment):– linen cloth [3], linen [2], fine linen [1]

4617 σινιάζω, **siniazō**, v. GK: *4985*. to sift, shake in a sieve:– sift [1]

σῖτα, **sita**. See *4621*.

4618 σιτευτός, **siteutos**, a. GK: *4988* [→ *4621*]. fattened:– fatted [3]

4619 σιτιστός, **sitistos**, a. GK: *4990* [→ *4621*]. fattened; (n.) fattened cattle:– fatlings [1]

4620 σιτομέτριον, **sitometrion**, n. GK: *4991* [→ *4621+3358*]. measured allowance of food, ration of grain:– portion of meat [1]

4621 σῖτος, *sitos*, n. GK: 4992 [→ 776, 777, 1979, 4618, 4619, 4620]. wheat, grain:– wheat [12], corn [2]

4622 Σιών, *Sion*, n.pr. GK: 4994. Zion, "*citadel*":– Sion [7]

4623 σιωπάω, *siōpaō*, v. GK: 4995. to be quiet, remain silent; to be calm, not agitated:– hold peace [5], held peace [4], dumb [1], peace [1]

4624 σκανδαλίζω, *skandalizō*, v. GK: 4997 [→ 4625]. to cause to sin, cause to fall (into sin), offend; to fall away (from the faith), go astray; to take offense:– offended [16], offend [12], make to offend [2]

4625 σκάνδαλον, *skandalon*, n. GK: 4998 [→ 4624]. stumbling block, obstacle, offense; something that causes sin:– offence [5], offences [4], stumblingblock [3], occasion of stumbling [1], occasion to fall [1], things that offend [1]

4626 σκάπτω, *skaptō*, v. GK: 4999 [→ 2679, 4627]. to dig:– dig [2], digged [1]

4627 σκάφη, *skaphē*, n. GK: 5002 [→ 4626]. lifeboat, (small) boat:– boat [3]

4628 σκέλος, *skelos*, n. GK: 5003. leg:– legs [3]

4629 σκέπασμα, *skepasma*, n. GK: 5004. clothing, covering; this can refer to shelter or personal covering:– raiment [1]

4630 Σκευᾶς, *Skeuas*, n.pr. GK: 5005. Sceva:– Sceva [1]

4631 σκευή, *skeuē*, n. GK: 5006 [→ 4632]. (ship's) tackle, gear:– tackling [1]

4632 σκεῦος, *skeuos*, n. GK: 5007 [→ 384, 532, 643, 2080, 3903, 3904, 4631]. possession, merchandise, object, thing; jar, vessel, dish; a general term that can refer to a human being:– vessel [17], vessels [8], goods [2], sail [1], stuff [1]

4633 σκηνή, *skēnē*, n. GK: 5008 [→ 1981, 2681, 2682, 4634, 4635, 4636, 4637, 4638]. tabernacle; tent, shelter, dwelling:– tabernacle [15], tabernacles [4], habitations [1]

4634 σκηνοπηγία, *skēnopēgia*, n. GK: 5009 [→ 4633+4078]. (Feast of) Tabernacles:– tabernacles [1]

4635 σκηνοποιός, *skēnopoios*, n. GK: 5010 [→ 4633+4160]. tentmaker; some translate more generally: leather worker:– tentmakers [1]

4636 σκῆνος, *skēnos*, n. GK: 5011 [→ 4633]. tent:– tabernacle [2]

4637 σκηνόω, *skēnoō*, v. GK: 5012 [→ 4633]. to live, dwell; to spread a tent:– dwell [4], dwelt [1]

4638 σκήνωμα, *skēnōma*, n. GK: 5013 [→ 4633]. tent, dwelling place, lodging place:– tabernacle [3]

4639 σκιά, *skia*, n. GK: 5014 [→ 644, 1982, 2683]. shadow, shade:– shadow [7]

4640 σκιρτάω, *skirtaō*, v. GK: 5015. to leap, with an implication that the one leaping is joyful:– leaped [2], leap [1]

4641 σκληροκαρδία, *sklērokardia*, n. GK: 5016 [→ 4645+2588]. hardness of heart, stubbornness, obstinacy:– hardness of heart [2], hardness of hearts [1]

4642 σκληρός, *sklēros*, a. GK: 5017 [→ 4645]. hard, harsh:– hard [5], fierce [1]

4643 σκληρότης, *sklērotēs*, n. GK: 5018 [→ 4645]. hardness, stubbornness:– hardness [1]

4644 σκληροτράχηλος, *sklērotrachēlos*, a. GK: 5019 [→ 4645+5137]. stiff-necked, stubborn:– stiffnecked [1]

4645 σκληρύνω, *sklērynō*, v. GK: 5020 [→ 4641, 4642, 4643, 4644]. to harden (the heart), make obstinate, make stubborn; (pass.) to be hardened, become obstinate:– harden [3], hardened [2], hardeneth [1]

4646 σκολιός, *skolios*, a. GK: 5021. crooked; corrupt:– crooked [2], froward [1], untoward [1]

4647 σκόλοψ, *skolops*, n. GK: 5022. thorn; some translate this as a "splinter":– thorn [1]

4648 σκοπέω, *skopeō*, v. GK: 5023 [→ 244, 1980, 1983, 1984, 1985, 2684, 2685, 4649]. to watch out for, take notice of, look to:– mark [2], considering [1], look at [1], look [1], take heed [1]

4649 σκοπός, *skopos*, n. GK: 5024 [→ 4648]. goal:– mark [1]

4650 σκορπίζω, *skorpizō*, v. GK: 5025 [→ 1287, 4651]. to scatter, disperse:– scattereth [2], dispersed abroad [1], scattered [1], scattereth abroad [1]

4651 σκορπίος, *skorpios*, n. GK: 5026 [→ 4650]. scorpion:– scorpions [3], scorpion [2]

4652 σκοτεινός, *skoteinos*, a. GK: 5027 [→ 4655]. dark:– full of darkness [2], dark [1]

4653 σκοτία, *skotia*, n. GK: 5028 [→ 4655]. darkness, the dark:– darkness [14], dark [2]

4654 σκοτίζομαι, *skotizomai*, v. GK: 5029 [→ 4655]. (pass.) to be or become dark, be darkened:– darkened [8]

4655 σκότος, *skotos*, n. GK: 5030 [→ 4652, 4653, 4654, 4656]. darkness, the dark:– darkness [32]

4656 σκοτόω, *skotoō*, v. GK: 5031 [→ 4655]. (pass.) to be or become darkened:– full of darkness [1]

4657 σκύβαλον, *skybalon*, n. GK: 5032. rubbish, refuse, dung; this can refer to any of a number of rotten, decaying things, all that is worth getting rid of:– dung [1]

4658 Σκύθης, *Skythēs*, n.pr.g. GK: 5033. Scythian:– Scythian [1]

4659 σκυθρωπός, *skythrōpos*, a. GK: 5034 [→ 3708]. to look somber, appear downcast, implying a sad or sullen attitude:– sad countenance [1], sad [1]

4660 σκύλλω, *skyllō*, v. GK: 5035 [→ 4661]. to bother, annoy; (pass.) to be harassed; (mid.) to trouble oneself:– trouble [2], troublest [1]

4661 σκῦλον, *skylon*, n. GK: 5036 [→ 4660]. (pl.) spoils, booty:– spoils [1]

4662 σκωληκόβρωτος, *skōlēkobrōtos*, a. GK: 5037 [→ 4663+977]. eaten by worms:– eaten of worms [1]

4663 σκώληξ, *skōlēx*, n. GK: 5038 [→ 4662]. worm:– worm [3]

4664 σμαράγδινος, *smaragdinos*, a. GK: 5039 [→ 4665]. (of) emerald:– emerald [1]

4665 σμάραγδος, *smaragdos*, n. GK: 5040 [→ 4664]. emerald:– emerald [1]

4666 σμύρνα¹, *smyrna1*, n. GK: 5043 [→ 4667, 4668, 4669]. myrrh, an aromatic resinous gum:– myrrh [2]

4667 Σμύρνα², *Smyrna2*, n.pr.l. GK: 5044 [→ 4666]. Smyrna:– Smyrna [1]

4668 Σμυρναῖος, *Smyrnaios*, a.pr.g. GK: 5045 [→ 4666]. Smyrnaean:– Smyrna [1]

4669 σμυρνίζω, *smyrnizō*, v. GK: 5046 [→ 4666]. to mix with myrrh, referring to wine mixed with myrrh as a drug to deaden the senses and mind:– mingled with myrrh [1]

4670 Σόδομα, *Sodoma*, n.pr. GK: 5047. Sodom:– Sodom [9], Sodoma [1]

4671 σοί, *soi*, p.pers.dat. of 4771. GK: 5148 [→ 4771]. to you, for you, your; see *4771*:–

4672 Σολομών, *Solomōn*, n.pr. GK: 4898 & 5048. Solomon, "*peace, well being*":– Solomon [9], Solomon's [3]

4673 σορός, *soros*, n. GK: 5049. coffin, bier:– bier [1]

4674 σός, *sos*, a.poss. GK: 5050 [→ 4771]. (s.) your, yours:– thy [15], thine [9], thine own [3]

4675 σοῦ, *sou*, p.pers.gen. of 4771. GK: 5148 [→ 4771]. of you, your; see *4771*:–

4676 σουδάριον, *soudarion*, n. GK: 5051. piece of cloth, burial cloth, handkerchief:– napkin [3], handkerchiefs [1]

4677 Σουσάννα, *Sousanna*, n.pr. GK: 5052. Susanna, "*lily*":– Susanna [1]

4678 σοφία, *sophia*, n. GK: 5053 [→ 4680]. wisdom (either secular or divine). Christ is called "the wisdom of God" in 1Co 1:24, 30. On the basis of the OT, wisdom can be personified:– wisdom [51]

4679 σοφίζω, *sophizō*, v. GK: 5054 [→ 4680]. to make wise; (pass.) to be cleverly invented:– cunningly devised [1], make wise [1]

4680 σοφός, *sophos*, a. GK: 5055 [→ 781, 2686, 4678, 4679, 5385, 5386]. wise; expert, skilled; (n.) a person who is skilled or expert, often as a class or kind, a wise man or woman:– wise [21], wiser than [1]

4681 Σπανία, *Spania*, n.pr. GK: 5056. Spain:– Spain [2]

4682 σπαράσσω, *sparassō*, v. GK: 5057 [→ 4685]. to convulse, shake violently:– rent [1], tare [1], teareth [1], torn [1]

4683 σπαργανόω, *sparganoō*, v. GK: 5058. to wrap (in cloth), to bind a newborn infant in strips of long cloth, a normal act of child care for warmth, security, etc.:– wrapped in swaddling clothes [2]

4684 σπαταλάω, *spatalaō*, v. GK: 5059. to live in pleasure, in self-indulgence:– liveth in pleasure [1], wanton [1]

4685 σπάω, *spaō*, v. GK: 5060 [→ 385, 563, 645, 1288, 1986, 4049, 4682, 4952]. (mid.) to draw (a sword):– drew out [1], drew [1]

4686 σπεῖρα, *speira*, n. GK: 5061. company of soldiers, cohort; technically one tenth of a Roman legion: 600 fighting men:– band [7]

4687 σπείρω, *speirō*, v. GK: 5062 [→ 1289, 1290, 4690, 4691, 4701, 4702, 4703]. to sow seed, scatter seed:– sown [15], soweth [9], sowed [8], sow [8], sower [6], received seed [4], sowest [1]

4688 σπεκουλάτωρ, *spekoulatōr*, n. GK: 5063. executioner:– executioner [1]

4689 σπένδω, *spendō*, v. GK: 5064 [→ 786]. (pass.) to be poured out like a drink offering:– offered [2]

4690 σπέρμα, *sperma*, n. GK: 5065 [→ 4687]. seed, the part of a plant or animal that can propagate the species (cf. "sperm"); by extension: children, offspring, descendants:– seed [40], seeds [2], issue [1]

4691 σπερμολόγος, *spermologos*, a. GK: 5066 [→ 4687+3004]. babbler, chatterer, implying the person has low status, living by picking up scraps:– babbler [1]

4692 σπεύδω, *speudō*, v. GK: 5067 [→ 4704, 4705, 4706, 4707, 4708, 4709, 4710]. to hurry, hasten:– make haste [2], hasted [1], hasting [1], made haste [1], with haste [1]

4693 σπήλαιον, *spēlaion*, n. GK: 5068. den, cave, hideout:– den [1], dens [2], cave [1]

4694 σπιλάς, *spilas*, n. GK: 5069 [→ 4696]. blemish, spot:– spots [1]

4695 σπιλόω, *spiloō*, v. GK: 5071 [→ 4696]. to corrupt; (pass.) to be stained, defiled:– defileth [1], spotted [1]

4696 σπίλος, *spilos*, n. GK: 5070 [→ 784, 4694, 4695]. stain, blot:– spots [1], spot [1]

4697 σπλαγχνίζομαι, *splanchnizomai*, v. GK: 5072 [→ 4698]. to have compassion on, have pity on:– moved with compassion [5], had compassion [4], have compassion [3]

4698 σπλάγχνον, *splanchnon*, n. GK: 5073 [→ 2155, 4184, 4697]. inward parts of body: intestines; of emotion: *heart, affection, tenderness, compassion*:– bowels [9], inward affection [1], tender mercy (+*1656*) [1]

4699 σπόγγος, *spongos*, n. GK: 5074. sponge:– spunge [3]

4700 σποδός, *spodos*, n. GK: 5075. ashes:– ashes [3]

4701 σπορά, *spora*, n. GK: 5076 [→ 4687]. seed:– seed [1]

4702 σπόριμος, *sporimos*, a. GK: 5077 [→ 4687]. what is sown; (pl.n.) grainfield:– corn fields [2], corn [1]

4703 σπόρος, *sporos*, n. GK: 5078 [→ 4687]. seed:– seed [4], seed sown [1]

4704 σπουδάζω, *spoudazō*, v. GK: 5079 [→ 4692]. to be eager, make every effort, do one's best:– diligent [2], do diligence [2], endeavoured [1], endeavouring [1], endeavour [1], forward [1], give diligence [1], labour [1], study [1]

4705 σπουδαῖος, *spoudaios*, a. GK: 5080 [→ 4692]. zealous, eager, earnest; (compar.) more enthusiastic, very earnest:– diligent [1]

4706 σπουδαιότερον, *spoudaioteron*, a.compar.neut. of 4705. GK: 5080 [→ 4692]. (compar.) more enthusiastic, very earnest:– very diligently [1]

4707 σπουδαιότερος, *spoudaioteros*, a.compar. of 4705. GK: 5080 [→ 4692]. (compar.) more enthusiastic, very earnest:– diligent [1], more forward [1]

4708 σπουδαιοτέρως, *spoudaioterōs*, adv.compar. of 4709. GK: 5081 [→ 4692]. (compar.) all the more eager, with special urgency:– more carefully [1]

4709 σπουδαίως, *spoudaiōs*, adv. GK: 5081 [→ 4692]. earnestly, zealously, with vigor; (compar.) all the more eager, with special urgency:– diligently [1], instantly [1]

4710 σπουδή, *spoudē*, n. GK: 5082 [→ 4692]. hurry, haste; earnestness, diligence, zeal, eagerness:– diligence [5], haste [2], business [1], carefulness [1], care [1], earnest care [1], forwardness [1]

4711 σπυρίς, *spyris*, n. GK: 5083. basket:– baskets [4], basket [1]

4712 στάδιον, **stadion**, n. GK: *5084* [→ *2476*]. arena, stadium, race course; a unit of length: stade (about 200 yards):– furlongs [5], race [1]

4713 στάμνος, **stamnos**, n. GK: *5085* [→ *2476*]. jar:– pot [1]

4714 στάσις, **stasis**, n. GK: *5087* [→ *2476*]. continuance, state of existence; uprising, insurrection, riot; dispute, discord:– dissension [3], sedition [3], insurrection [1], standing [1], uproar [1]

4715 στατήρ, **statēr**, n. GK: *5088* [→ *2476*]. four-drachma coin, stater (four days' wages):– piece of money [1]

4716 σταυρός, **stauros**, n. GK: *5089* [→ *388, 4717, 4957*; *cf. 2476*]. cross:– cross [28]

4717 σταυρόω, **stauroō**, v. GK: *5090* [→ *4716*]. to crucify:– crucified [31], crucify [15]

4718 σταφυλή, **staphylē**, n. GK: *5091*. (bunch of) grapes:– grapes [3]

4719 στάχυς¹, **stachys¹**, n. GK: *5092* [→ *4720*]. head of grain:– ears of corn [3], ear [2]

4720 Στάχυς², **Stachys²**, n.pr. GK: *5093* [→ *4719*]. Stachys, "*head of grain*":– Stachys [1]

4721 στέγη, **stegē**, n. GK: *5094* [→ *4722*]. roof:– roof [3]

4722 στέγω, **stegō**, v. GK: *5095* [→ *648, 4721, 5152*]. to put up with, stand, endure; to protect, cover:– forbear [2], beareth [1], suffer [1]

4723 στεῖρα, **steira**, n. GK: *5096* [→ *4731*]. (state of) barrenness, infertility:– barren [4]

4724 στέλλω, **stellō**, v. GK: *5097* [→ *649, 1291, 1293, 1992, 2687, 2689, 4749, 4958, 5288, 5289*]. (mid.) to avoid, keep away from:– avoiding [1], withdraw [1]

4725 στέμμα, **stemma**, n. GK: *5098* [→ *4737*]. wreath, garland:– garlands [1]

4726 στεναγμός, **stenagmos**, n. GK: *5099* [→ *4728*]. groan, sigh:– groanings [1], groaning [1]

4727 στενάζω, **stenazō**, v. GK: *5100* [→ *4728*]. to groan, sigh; to grumble:– groan [2], grief [1], grudge [1], sighed [1]

4728 στενός, **stenos**, a. GK: *5101* [→ *389, 4726, 4727, 4729, 4730, 4959*]. narrow:– strait [3]

4729 στενοχωρέω, **stenochoreō**, v. GK: *5102* [→ *4728+5562*]. (pass.) to be crushed; to withhold, be restricted:– straitened [2], distressed [1]

4730 στενοχωρία, **stenochōria**, n. GK: *5103* [→ *4728+5562*]. distress, hardship, difficulty:– distresses [2], anguish [1], distress [1]

4731 στερεός, **stereos**, a. GK: *5104* [→ *4723, 4732, 4733*]. solid, strong; standing firm, steadfast:– strong [2], stedfast [1], sure [1]

4732 στερεόω, **stereoō**, v. GK: *5105* [→ *4731*]. to make strong; (pass.) to become strong, be strengthened:– established [1], made strong [1], received strength [1]

4733 στερέωμα, **stereōma**, n. GK: *5106* [→ *4731*]. firmness, steadfastness:– stedfastness [1]

4734 Στεφανᾶς, **Stephanas**, n.pr. GK: *5107* [→ *4737*]. Stephanas, "*victor's wreath*":– Stephanas [4]

4735 στέφανος², **stephanos²**, n. GK: *5109* [→ *4737*]. woven crown, wreath, victory garland; of various shapes and various materials, leaves, twigs, flowers, even metal, as a sign of victory, honor, and in some contexts, authority:– crown [15], crowns [3]

4736 Στέφανος¹, **Stephanos¹**, n.pr. GK: *5108* [→ *4737*]. Stephen, "*victor's wreath*":– Stephen [7]

4737 στεφανόω, **stephanoō**, v. GK: *5110* [→ *4725, 4734, 4736, 4735*]. to crown, present a wreath:– crowned [2], crownedst [1]

4738 στῆθος, **stēthos**, n. GK: *5111*. chest, breast:– breast [3], breasts [2]

4739 στήκω, **stēkō**, v. GK: *5112* [→ *2476*]. to stand, stand firm, be steadfast:– stand fast [6], standeth [1], stand [1]

4740 στηριγμός, **stērigmos**, n. GK: *5113* [→ *4741*]. security, firmness:– stedfastness [1]

4741 στηρίζω, **stērizō**, v. GK: *5114* [→ *793, 1991, 4740*]. to strengthen, establish, stand firm; to be resolute:– stablish [6], strengthen [2], established [1], establish [1], fixed [1], stablished [1], stedfastly set [1]

4742 στίγμα, **stigma**, n. GK: *5116* [→ *4743*]. mark, scar; in context Paul is likely referring to the scars he received in service to Jesus as marks of ownership by his master:– marks [1]

4743 στιγμή, **stigmē**, n. GK: *5117* [→ *4742*]. instant, moment:– moment [1]

4744 στίλβω, **stilbō**, v. GK: *5118*. to dazzle, be radiant:– shining [1]

4745 στοά, **stoa**, n. GK: *5119* [→ *4770; cf. 2476*]. covered colonnade, portico:– porch [3], porches [1]

4746 στοιβάς, **stoibas**; or στιβάς, **stibas**, n. GK: *5115 & 5120*. leafy branch:– branches [1]

4747 στοιχεῖον, **stoicheion**, n. GK: *5122* [→ *4748*]. principle, basic principle; element (of nature); elementary truths:– elements [4], rudiments [2], principles [1]

4748 στοιχέω, **stoicheō**, v. GK: *5123* [→ *4747, 4960*]. to follow, walk in, adhere to:– walk [4], walkest orderly [1]

4749 στολή, **stolē**, n. GK: *5124* [→ *4724*]. (flowing) robe:– robes [4], long clothing [1], long garment [1], long robes [1], robe [1]

4750 στόμα, **stoma**, n. GK: *5125* [→ *653, 1366, 1993, 4751*]. mouth; by extension: edge (of a sword):– mouth [69], face [4], mouths [4], edge [2]

4751 στόμαχος, **stomachos**, n. GK: *5126* [→ *4750*]. stomach:– stomach's [1]

4752 στρατεία, **strateia**, n. GK: *5127* [→ *4756*]. warfare; fight:– warfare [2]

4753 στράτευμα, **strateuma**, n. GK: *5128* [→ *4756*]. army, troops, soldiers:– armies [3], army [3], men of war [1], soldiers [1]

4754 στρατεύομαι, **strateuomai**, v. GK: *5129* [→ *4756*]. (mid.) to serve as a soldier; to wage war, fight, battle:– war [4], goeth a warfare [1], soldiers [1], warreth [1]

4755 στρατηγός, **stratēgos**, n. GK: *5130* [→ *4756+71*]. magistrate, praetor; captain, officer:– magistrates [5], captain [3], captains [2]

4756 στρατιά, **stratia**, n. GK: *5131* [→ *497, 4752, 4753, 4754, 4755, 4757, 4758, 4759, 4760, 4961*]. host, army (of heaven); (celestial) bodies:– host [2]

4757 στρατιώτης, **stratiōtēs**, n. GK: *5132* [→ *4756*]. soldier:– soldiers [21], soldier [4], soldiers' [1]

4758 στρατολογέω, **stratologeō**, v. GK: *5133* [→ *4756+3004*]. to gather an army; (ptcp.) commanding officer, with a focus on enlisting soldiers:– chosen to be a soldier [1]

4759 στρατοπεδάρχης, **stratopedarchēs**, n. GK: *5134 & 5135* [→ *4756+3978+757*]. military commander, commander of a camp:– captain of the guard [1]

4760 στρατόπεδον, **stratopedon**, n. GK: *5136* [→ *4756+3978*]. army:– armies [1]

4761 στρεβλόω, **strebloō**, v. GK: *5137* [→ *4762*]. to distort, twist:– wrest [1]

4762 στρέφω, **strephō**, v. GK: *5138* [→ *390, 391, 654, 1294, 1612, 1994, 1995, 2690, 2692, 3344, 4761, 4962, 4963, 5290*]. to turn, turn away, return; to change, repent, turn one's life:– turned [12], turn [4], converted [1], turning [1]

4763 στρηνιάω, **strēniaō**, v. GK: *5139* [→ *4764*]. to live in luxury, with an implication that this luxury contributes to improper sensuality and immorality:– lived deliciously [2]

4764 στρῆνος, **strēnos**, n. GK: *5140* [→ *2691, 4763*]. luxury:– delicacies [1]

4765 στρουθίον, **strouthion**, n. GK: *5141*. sparrow:– sparrows [4]

4766 στρώννυμι, **strōnnymi**; or στρωννύω, **strōnnyō**, v. GK: *5142 & 5143* [→ *2693, 3038, 5291*]. to spread out; (pass.) to be furnished:– furnished [2], spread [2], strawed [2], make bed [1]

4767 στυγητός, **stygētos**, a. GK: *5144* [→ *655, 2319, 4768*]. hated:– hateful [1]

4768 στυγνάζω, **stygnazō**, v. GK: *5145* [→ *4767*]. to be gloomy, sad, others translate "shocked, appalled"; (of weather) to be overcast, gloomy:– lowring [1], sad [1]

4769 στῦλος, **stylos**, n. GK: *5146*. pillar, column; (fig.) leader:– pillars [2], pillar [2]

4770 Στωϊκός, **Stōikos**, a.pr. GK: *5121 & 5147* [→ *4745*]. Stoic:– Stoicks [1]

4771 σύ, **sy**, p.pers. GK: *5148* [→ *4571, 4671, 4572, 4674, 4675, 5209, 5210, 5212, 5213, 5216*]. you, your:– you [1194], thee [453], your [375], thy [363], ye [282], thou [213], thine [49], yourselves [9], thine own [8], your own [4], yours [4], youward [2], on your part [1], you (+3588+5590) [1], your (+1537) [1], your (+2596) [1], your own (+2596) [1], yours (+3588) [1], youwards [1]

4772 συγγένεια, **syngeneia**, n. GK: *5149* [→ *4862+1096*]. family, relative, one's own people:– kindred [3]

4773 συγγενής, **syngenēs**, a. GK: *5150 & 5151* [→ *4862+1096*]. family, relative, one's own race or people:– kinsmen [5], kinsman [2], cousins [1], cousin [1], kinsfolks [1], kinsfolk [1], kin [1]

4774 συγγνώμη, **syngnōmē**, n. GK: *5152* [→ *4862+1097*]. concession:– permission [1]

4775 συγκάθημαι, **synkathēmai**, v. GK: *5153* [→ *4862+2516*]. to sit with:– sat with [1], sat [1]

4776 συγκαθίζω, **synkathizō**, v. GK: *5154* [→ *4862+2523*]. to sit down together; to be seated together:– made sit together [1], set down together [1]

4777 συγκακοπαθέω, **synkakopatheō**, v. GK: *5155* [→ *4862+2556+3958*]. to suffer together with, endure hardship with:– partaker of afflictions [1]

4778 συγκακουχέομαι, **synkakoucheomai**, v. GK: *5156* [→ *4862+2556+2192*]. (pass.) to be mistreated with:– suffer affliction with [1]

4779 συγκαλέω, **synkaleō**, v. GK: *5157* [→ *4862+2564*]. (act.) to call together; (mid.) to call to one's side, summon:– called together [5], calleth together [2], call together [1]

4780 συγκαλύπτω, **synkalyptō**, v. GK: *5158* [→ *4862+2572*]. to conceal:– covered [1]

4781 συγκάμπτω, **synkamptō**, v. GK: *5159* [→ *4862+2578*]. (pass.) to be bent over:– bow down [1]

4782 συγκαταβαίνω, **synkatabainō**, v. GK: *5160* [→ *4862+2596+305*]. to come, go down with:– go down with [1]

4783 συγκατάθεσις, **synkatathesis**, n. GK: *5161* [→ *4862+2596+5087*]. agreement:– agreement [1]

4784 συγκατατίθημι, **synkatatithēmi**, v. GK: *5163* [→ *4862+2596+5087*]. (mid.) to consent, agree with:– consented [1]

4785 συγκαταψηφίζομαι, **synkatapsēphizomai**, v. GK: *5164* [→ *4862+2596+5586*]. (pass.) to be added, chosen together with:– numbered [1]

4786 συγκεράννυμι, **synkerannymi**, v. GK: *5166* [→ *4862+2767*]. to combine, unite:– mixed [1], tempered together [1]

4787 συγκινέω, **synkineō**, v. GK: *5167* [→ *4862+2795*]. to stir up, arouse:– stirred up [1]

4788 συγκλείω, **synkleiō**, v. GK: *5168* [→ *4862+2808*]. to catch (fish hemmed up in a net); to confine, imprison, lock up:– concluded [2], inclosed [1], shut up [1]

4789 συγκληρονόμος, **synklēronomos**, a. GK: *5169* [→ *4862+2819+3551*]. inheriting together; (n.) co-heir:– fellowheirs [1], heirs together [1], heirs with [1], jointheirs with [1]

4790 συγκοινωνέω, **synkoinōneō**, v. GK: *5170* [→ *4862+2839*]. to share with, be connected with:– communicate with [1], have fellowship with [1], partakers [1]

4791 συγκοινωνός, **synkoinōnos**, n. GK: *5171* [→ *4862+2839*]. sharer, companion, participant, partner:– companion [1], partaker with [1], partakers [1], partakest (+1096) [1]

4792 συγκομίζω, **synkomizō**, v. GK: *5172* [→ *4862+2889*]. to bury, entomb:– carried [1]

4793 συγκρίνω, **synkrinō**, v. GK: *5173* [→ *4862+2919*]. to express, explain; to compare:– compare with [1], comparing amongst [1], comparing [1]

4794 συγκύπτω, **synkyptō**, v. GK: *5174* [→ *4862+2955*]. to bend over, be crippled:– bowed together [1]

4795 συγκυρία, **synkyria**, n. GK: *5175* [→ *4862*]. event that just happens, coincidence:– chance [1]

4796 συγχαίρω, **synchairō**, v. GK: *5176* [→ *4862+5463*]. to rejoice with:– rejoice with [5], rejoiced with [1], rejoiceth in [1]

4797 συγχέω, **syncheō**; or συγχύνω, **synchynō**, v. GK: 5177 & 5179 [→ 1632; cf. 4862]. to baffle, confuse; to stir up, cause trouble; (pass.) to be bewildered, confused; to be in an uproar, stirred up:– confounded [2], confused [1], in an uproar [1], stirred up [1]

4798 συγχράομαι, **synchraomai**, v. GK: 5178 [→ 4862+5530]. to associate with, have (friendly) dealings with:– have dealings with [1]

4799 σύγχυσις, **synchysis**, n. GK: 5180 [→ 1632; cf. 4862]. uproar, confusion:– confusion [1]

4800 συζάω, **syzaō**, v. GK: 5182 [→ 4862+2198]. to live with:– live with [3]

4801 συζεύγνυμι, **syzeugnymi**, v. GK: 5183 [→ 4862+2218]. to join together:– joined together [2]

4802 συζητέω, **syzēteō**, v. GK: 5184 [→ 4862+2212]. to discuss; to debate, argue:– disputed [1], disputing [1], inquire [1], question with [1], questioned [1], questioning with [1], questioning [1], question [1], reasoned [1], reasoning together [1]

4803 συζήτησις, **syzētēsis**, n. GK: 5185 [→ 4862+2212]. dispute, discussion:– disputation [1], disputing [1], reasoning [1]

4804 συζητητής, **syzētētēs**, n. GK: 5186 [→ 4862+2212]. philosopher, debater:– disputer [1]

4805 σύζυγος, **syzygos**, a. GK: 5187 [→ 4862+2218]. yokefellow, comrade:– yokefellow [1]

4806 συζωοποιέω, **syzōopoieō**, v. GK: 5188 [→ 4862+2198+4160]. to make alive with (someone):– quickened together with [1], quickened together [1]

4807 συκάμινος, **sykaminos**, n. GK: 5189. mulberry tree:– sycamine tree [1]

4808 συκῆ, **sykē**, n. GK: 5190 [→ 4810]. fig tree:– fig tree [16]

4809 συκομορέα, **sykomorea**, n. GK: 5191 [→ 4810]. sycamore-fig tree:– sycomore tree [1]

4810 σῦκον, **sykon**, n. GK: 5192 [→ 4808, 4809, 4811]. fig:– figs [4]

4811 συκοφαντέω, **sykophanteō**, v. GK: 5193 [→ 4810+5316]. to accuse falsely, oppress; to cheat, extort:– accuse falsely [1], taken by false accusation [1]

4812 συλαγωγέω, **sylagōgeō**, v. GK: 5194 [→ 4813+71]. to take captive:– spoil [1]

4813 συλάω, **sylaō**, v. GK: 5195 [→ 2416, 2417, 4812]. to rob:– robbed [1]

4814 συλλαλέω, **syllaleō**, v. GK: 5196 [→ 4862+2980]. to talk with, discuss with, confer with:– communed with [1], conferred [1], spake [1], talked with [1], talking with [1], talking [1]

4815 συλλαμβάνω, **syllambanō**, v. GK: 5197 [→ 4862+2983]. to seize, arrest, capture; to become pregnant, conceive; to help, come to the aid of:– conceived [4], take [3], took [3], help [1], taken [2], caught [1], conceive [1]

4816 συλλέγω, **syllegō**, v. GK: 5198 [→ 4862+3004]. to pick, pull up, collect:– gather [3], gather up [2], gathered [2], gather together [1]

4817 συλλογίζομαι, **syllogizomai**, v. GK: 5199 [→ 4862+3004]. to discuss together:– reasoned [1]

4818 συλλυπέω, **syllypeō**, v. GK: 5200 [→ 4862+3077]. (pass.) to be deeply distressed, grieved with:– grieved [1]

4819 συμβαίνω, **symbainō**, v. GK: 5201 [→ 4862+305]. to happen; to come about:– happened [5], befell [1], happen [1], so [1]

4820 συμβάλλω, **symballō**, v. GK: 5202 [→ 4862+906]. to dispute with; to confer with, meet with; to ponder; to engage in (war); (mid.) to help, assist:– conferred [1], encountered [1], helped [1], make war against (+1519+4171) [1], met with [1], pondered [1]

4821 συμβασιλεύω, **symbasileuō**, v. GK: 5203 [→ 4862+935]. to reign with, be king with:– reign with [2]

4822 συμβιβάζω, **symbibazō**, v. GK: 5204 [→ 4862+305]. (pass.) to be held together; to be united; (act.) to conclude; to prove; to instruct, teach, advise:– knit together [2], assuredly gathering [1], compacted [1], instruct [1], proving [1]

4823 συμβουλεύω, **symbouleuō**, v. GK: 5205 [→ 4862+1014]. to advise, counsel; (mid.) to plot, conspire, consult:– consulted [1], counsel [1], gave counsel [1], took counsel together [1], took counsel [1]

4824 συμβούλιον, **symboulion**, n. GK: 5206 [→ 4862+1014]. plan, plot; decision; council:– counsel [5], council [2], consultation [1]

4825 σύμβουλος, **symboulos**, n. GK: 5207 [→ 4862+1014]. counselor, advisor:– counseller [1]

4826 Συμεών, **Symeōn**, n.pr. GK: 5208 [→ 4613]. Simeon, Simon, "he has heard or obedient one":– Simeon [6], Simon [1]

4827 συμμαθητής, **symmathētēs**, n. GK: 5209 [→ 4862+3129]. fellow disciple:– fellowdisciples [1]

4828 συμμαρτυρέω, **symmartyreō**, v. GK: 5210 [→ 4862+3144]. to testify with; to confirm:– also bearing witness [2], beareth witness with [1], testify [1]

4829 συμμερίζομαι, **symmerizomai**, v. GK: 5211 [→ 4862+3313]. to share with:– partakers with [1]

4830 συμμέτοχος, **symmetochos**, a. GK: 5212 [→ 4862+3326+2192]. sharing with, being partner with, derived from the Greek verb "to share in the possession of something," not found in the NT:– partakers with [1], partakers [1]

4831 συμμιμητής, **symmimētēs**, n. GK: 5213 [→ 4862+3401]. fellow imitator:– followers together [1]

4832 σύμμορφος, **symmorphos**, a. GK: 5215 [→ 4862+3444]. conformed, being like:– conformed to [1], fashioned like unto [1]

4833 συμμορφόω, **symmorphoō**, v. GK: 5214 & 5216 [→ 4862+3444]. to give the same form:– made conformable [1]

4834 συμπαθέω, **sympatheō**, v. GK: 5217 [→ 4862+3958]. to sympathize with:– had compassion [1], touched with the feeling [1]

4835 συμπαθής, **sympathēs**, a. GK: 5218 [→ 4862+3958]. sympathetic:– compassion one of another [1]

4836 συμπαραγίνομαι, **symparaginomai**, v. GK: 5219 [→ 4862+3844+1096]. (mid.) to come together:– came together [1], stood with [1]

4837 συμπαρακαλέω, **symparakaleō**, v. GK: 5220 [→ 4862+3844+2564]. (pass.) to be mutually encouraged:– comforted together [1]

4838 συμπαραλαμβάνω, **symparalambanō**, v. GK: 5221 [→ 4862+3844+2983]. to take along with:– take with [2], took with [2]

4839 συμπαραμένω, **symparamenō**, v. GK: 5222 [→ 4862+3844+3306]. to stay with (someone) to help:– continue with [1]

4840 συμπάρειμι, **sympareimi**, v. GK: 5223 [→ 4862+3844+1510]. to be present with:– here present with [1]

4841 συμπάσχω, **sympaschō**, v. GK: 5224 [→ 4862+3958]. to suffer with, share in suffering:– suffer with [2]

4842 συμπέμπω, **sympempō**, v. GK: 5225 [→ 4862+3992]. to send with:– sent with [1], sent [1]

4843 συμπεριλαμβάνω, **symperilambanō**, v. GK: 5227 [→ 4862+4012+2983]. to put one's arms around, embrace:– embracing [1]

4844 συμπίνω, **sympinō**, v. GK: 5228 [→ 4862+4095]. to drink with:– drink with [1]

4845 συμπληρόω, **symplēroō**, v. GK: 5230 [→ 4862+4137]. (pass.) to be swamped, become full; to be fulfilled, come to an end:– come [1], filled [1], fully come [1]

4846 συμπνίγω, **sympnigō**, v. GK: 5231 [→ 4862+4155]. to choke; to crush:– choked [2], choke [2], thronged [1]

4847 συμπολίτης, **sympolitēs**, n. GK: 5232 [→ 4862+4172]. fellow citizen:– fellowcitizens with [1]

4848 συμπορεύομαι, **symporeuomai**, v. GK: 5233 [→ 4862+4198]. to go with, come together:– went with [3], resort [1]

4849 συμπόσιον, **symposion**, n. GK: 5235 [→ 4862+4095]. group:– by companies (+4849) [2]

4850 συμπρεσβύτερος, **sympresbyteros**, n. GK: 5236 [→ 4862+4245]. fellow elder:– also an elder [1]

συμφάγω, **sumphagō**. See **4906**.

4851 συμφέρω, **sympherō**, v. GK: 5237 [→ 4862+5342]. to bring together; to be helpful, be gained; (n.) common good; (imper. verb) it is good, better, beneficial:– expedient [7], profitable [3], profit [3], better [1], brought together [1], good [1], profit withal [1]

4852 σύμφημι, **symphēmi**, v. GK: 5238 [→ 4862+5346]. to agree with:– consent [1]

4853 συμφυλέτης, **symphyletēs**, n. GK: 5241 [→ 4862+5443]. (pl.) one's own countrymen, people:– countrymen [1]

4854 σύμφυτος, **symphytos**, a. GK: 5242 [→ 4862+5453]. united, being one with:– planted together [1]

4855 συμφύω, **symphyō**, v. GK: 5243 [→ 4862+5453]. to grow up with:– sprang up with [1]

4856 συμφωνέω, **symphōneō**, v. GK: 5244 [→ 4862+5456]. to agree with; to match, fit in with:– agree [2], agree with [1], agreed together [1], agreed [1], agreeth [1]

4857 συμφώνησις, **symphōnēsis**, n. GK: 5245 [→ 4862+5456]. harmony, agreement:– concord [1]

4858 συμφωνία, **symphōnia**, n. GK: 5246 [→ 4862+5456]. music:– musick [1]

4859 σύμφωνος, **symphōnos**, a. GK: 5247 [→ 4862+5456]. mutually consenting, agreeing; (n.) mutual agreement:– consent [1]

4860 συμψηφίζω, **sympsēphizō**, v. GK: 5248 [→ 4862+5586]. to calculate, compute:– counted [1]

4861 σύμψυχος, **sympsychos**, a. GK: 5249 [→ 4862+5594]. united in spirit, harmonious:– one accord [1]

4862 σύν, **syn**, pp. GK: 5250 [→ 799, 800, 801, 802, 1996, 1998, 1999, 3342, 4772, 4773, 4774, 4775, 4776, 4777, 4778, 4779, 4780, 4781, 4782, 4783, 4784, 4785, 4786, 4787, 4788, 4789, 4790, 4791, 4792, 4793, 4794, 4795, 4796, 4797, 4798, 4799, 4800, 4801, 4802, 4803, 4804, 4805, 4806, 4814, 4815, 4816, 4817, 4818, 4819, 4820, 4821, 4822, 4823, 4824, 4825, 4827, 4828, 4829, 4830, 4831, 4832, 4833, 4834, 4835, 4836, 4837, 4838, 4839, 4840, 4841, 4842, 4843, 4844, 4845, 4846, 4847, 4848, 4849, 4850, 4851, 4852, 4853, 4854, 4855, 4856, 4857, 4858, 4859, 4860, 4861, 4863, 4864, 4865, 4866, 4867, 4868, 4869, 4870, 4872, 4873, 4874, 4875, 4876, 4877, 4878, 4879, 4880, 4881, 4882, 4883, 4884, 4885, 4886, 4887, 4888, 4889, 4890, 4891, 4892, 4893, 4894, 4895, 4896, 4897, 4898, 4899, 4900, 4901, 4902, 4903, 4904, 4905, 4906, 4907, 4908, 4909, 4910, 4911, 4912, 4913, 4914, 4915, 4916, 4917, 4918, 4919, 4920, 4921, 4922, 4923, 4924, 4925, 4926, 4927, 4928, 4929, 4930, 4931, 4932, 4933, 4934, 4935, 4936, 4937, 4938, 4939, 4940, 4941, 4942, 4943, 4944, 4945, 4952, 4953, 4954, 4955, 4956, 4957, 4958, 4959, 4960, 4961, 4962, 4963, 4964]. with; as, besides, a marker which shows association with another thing or person:– with [121], accompanied (+2064) [1], and [1], beside [1], with also [1]

4863 συνάγω, **synagō**, v. GK: 5251 [→ 4862+71]. to gather together, assemble; invite, call together:– gathered together [20], gathered [8], gather [7], came together [6], assembled [4], gather together [3], gathereth [3], took in [3], assembled together [2], bestow [2], gather up [1], gathering [1], leadeth [1], resorted [1]

4864 συναγωγή, **synagōgē**, n. GK: 5252 [→ 656, 752, 1997]. synagogue, congregation, meeting, a gathering of worshipers, usually a Jewish congregation, though in some contexts it may refer to a Christian assembly; a synagogue building:– synagogue [33], synagogues [22], assembly [1], congregation [1]

4865 συναγωνίζομαι, **synagōnizomai**, v. GK: 5253 [→ 4862+73]. to join in a struggle, help, assist:– strive together with [1]

4866 συναθλέω, **synathleō**, v. GK: 5254 [→ 4862+118]. to contend at one's side, together:– laboured with [1], striving together [1]

4867 συναθροίζω, **synathroizō**, v. GK: 5255 [→ 4862; cf. 1865]. to bring together; (pass.) to be gathered:– gathered together [2], called together [1]

4868 συναίρω, **synairō**, v. GK: 5256 [→ 4862+142]. to settle (monetary accounts):– reckoneth (+3056) [1], reckon [1], take [1]

4869 συναιχμάλωτος, **synaichmalōtos**, n. GK: 5257 [→ 4862+164]. fellow prisoner:– fellowprisoner [2], fellowprisoners [1]

4870 συνακολουθέω, **synakoloutheō**, v. GK: 5258 [→ 4862+190; cf. 1.3]. to follow, accompany:– followed [1], follow [1]

4871 συναλίζω, **synalizō**, v. GK: *5259*. to eat with:–assembled together with [1]

4872 συναναβαίνω, **synanabainō**, v. GK: *5262* [→ *4862+303+305*]. to come with, travel with:– came up with [2]

4873 συνανάκειμαι, **synanakeimai**, v. GK: *5263* [→ *4862+303+2749*]. to eat with, have dinner with:– sat at meat with [2], sat with [2], sat also together with [1], sat at the table with [1], sat down with [1], sat with at meat [1], sit at meat with [1]

4874 συναναμείγνυμι, **synanameignymi**, v. GK: *5264* [→ *4862+303+3396*]. to associate with:– company with [1], have company with [1], keep company [1]

4875 συναναπαύομαι, **synanapauomai**, v. GK: *5265* [→ *4862+303+3973*]. to find rest together, be refreshed together:– with refreshed [1]

4876 συναντάω, **synantaō**, v. GK: *5267* [→ *4862+473*]. to meet; to happen to:– met [4], befall [1], meet [1]

4877 συνάντησις, **synantēsis**, n. GK: *5268* [→ *4862+473*]. meeting:– meet [1]

4878 συναντιλαμβάνομαι, **synantilambanomai**, v. GK: *5269* [→ *4862+473+2983*]. to help, come to the aid of:– helpeth [1], help [1]

4879 συναπάγω, **synapagō**, v. GK: *5270* [→ *4862+575+71*]. (pass.) to be led away, carried off; to associate with (the lowly):– carried away with [1], condescend to [1], led away with [1]

4880 συναποθνήσκω, **synapothnēskō**, v. GK: *5271* [→ *4862+575+2348*]. to die with:– dead with [1], die with [1], die [1]

4881 συναπόλλυμι, **synapollymi**, v. GK: *5272* [→ *4862+575+3639*]. (mid.) to die with, perish with:– perished with [1]

4882 συναποστέλλω, **synapostellō**, v. GK: *5273* [→ *4862+649*]. to send with:– sent [1]

4883 συναρμολογέω, **synarmologeō**, v. GK: *5274* [→ *4862+718+3004*]. (pass.) to be joined together, fit together:– fitly framed together [1], fitly joined together [1]

4884 συναρπάζω, **synarpazō**, v. GK: *5275* [→ *4862+726*]. to seize; (pass.) to be caught, seized:– caught [4]

4885 συναυξάνω, **synauxanō**, v. GK: *5277* [→ *4862+837*]. to grow together:– grow together [1]

4886 σύνδεσμος, **syndesmos**, n. GK: *5278* [→ *4862+1210*]. bond; sinew; captive:– bond [3], bands [1]

4887 συνδέω, **syndeō**, v. GK: *5279* [→ *4862+1210*]. (pass.) to be imprisoned with, bound with:– bound with [1]

4888 συνδοξάζω, **syndoxazō**, v. GK: *5280* [→ *4862+1391*]. (pass.) to be glorified with, share glory with:– glorified together [1]

4889 σύνδουλος, **syndoulos**, n. GK: *5281* [→ *4862+1401*]. fellow servant, fellow slave:– fellowservant [6], fellowservants [4]

συνδρέμω, **sundremō**. See **4936**.

4890 συνδρομή, **syndromē**, n. GK: *5282* [→ *4862+5143*]. running together:– ran together (+*1096*) [1]

4891 συνεγείρω, **synegeirō**, v. GK: *5283* [→ *4862+1453*]. to raise up with:– risen with [2], raised up with [1]

4892 συνέδριον, **synedrion**, n. GK: *5284* [→ *4862+1476*]. Sanhedrin; (local) council:– council [20], councils [2]

4893 συνείδησις, **syneidēsis**, n. GK: *5287* [→ *4862+1492 or 3708*]. conscience:– conscience [31], consciences [1]

4894 συνείδω, **syneidō**, v. GK: *5288* [→ *4862+1492 or 3708*]. to consider, know:– considered [1], know [1], privy [1], ware [1]

4895 σύνειμι¹, **syneimi**¹, v. GK: *5289* [→ *4862+1510*]. to be with; (n.) companion:– with [2]

4896 σύνειμι², **syneimi**², v. GK: *5290* [→ *4862*]. to gather together, come together:– gathered together [1]

4897 συνεισέρχομαι, **syneiserchomai**, v. GK: *5291* [→ *4862+1519+2064*]. to enter together with:– went in with [1], went with [1]

4898 συνέκδημος, **synekdēmos**, n. GK: *5292* [→ *4862+1537+1218*]. traveling companion:– companions in travel [1], travel with [1]

4899 συνεκλεκτός, **syneklektos**, a. GK: *5293* [→ *4862+1537+3004*]. chosen together with:– elected together with [1]

4900 συνελαύνω, **synelaunō**, v. GK: *5295* [→ *4862+1643*]. to drive, force, bring:– set at one (+*1515+1519*) [1]

4901 συνεπιμαρτυρέω, **synepimartyreō**, v. GK: *5296* [→ *4862+1909+3144*]. to testify at the same time:– also bearing witness [1]

4902 συνέπομαι, **synepomai**, v. GK: *5299* [→ *4862*]. to accompany:– accompanied [1]

4903 συνεργέω, **synergeō**, v. GK: *5300* [→ *4862+2041*]. to work together, work with; (n.) fellow worker:– helpeth with [1], work together [1], workers together [1], working with [1], wrought with [1]

4904 συνεργός, **synergos**, a. GK: *5301* [→ *4862+2041*]. fellow worker:– fellowlabourers [2], fellowlabourer [2], helpers [2], companion in labour [1], fellowhelpers [1], fellowhelper [1], fellowworkers [1], helper [1], labourers together with [1], workfellow [1]

4905 συνέρχομαι, **synerchomai**, v. GK: *5302* [→ *4862+2064*]. to come together, gather, assemble; to go along with, accompany:– come together [12], came together [4], came with [3], went with [3], come [2], accompanied [1], came [1], cometh together [1], companied with [1], go with [1], resorted [1], resort [1], with assembled [1]

4906 συνεσθίω, **synesthiō**, v. GK: *5303* [→ *4862+2068*]. to eat with:– eat [2], eat with [1], eateth with [1], with to eat [1]

4907 σύνεσις, **synesis**, n. GK: *5304* [→ *863; cf. 4862*]. understanding, insight; intelligence, the faculty of comprehension, often referring to wisdom and insight in spiritual matters:– understanding [6], knowledge [1]

4908 συνετός, **synetos**, a. GK: *5305* [→ *863; cf. 4862*]. intelligent, learned, with good sense:– prudent [4]

4909 συνευδοκέω, **syneudokeō**, v. GK: *5306* [→ *4862+2095+1380*]. to approve of, give approval; to be willing:– consenting [2], pleased [2], allow [1], pleasure [1]

4910 συνευωχέομαι, **syneuōcheomai**, v. GK: *5307* [→ *4862+2095+2192*]. to partake in a feast together:– feast with [2]

4911 συνεφίστημι, **synephistēmi**, v. GK: *5308* [→ *4862+1909+2476*]. to join in an attack:– rose up together [1]

4912 συνέχω, **synechō**, v. GK: *5309* [→ *4862+2192*]. to cover (ears); to crowd (against); to guard, hold in custody; to compel, urge on; (pass.) to suffer, be distressed; to be devoted to:– taken with [2], constraineth [1], held [1], in a strait [1], keep in [1], pressed [1], sick of [1], stopped [1], straitened [1], taken [1], throng [1]

4913 συνήδομαι, **synēdomai**, v. GK: *5310* [→ *4862+2237*]. to delight in agreement:– delight in [1]

4914 συνήθεια, **synētheia**, n. GK: *5311* [→ *4862+1485*]. custom, practice:– custom [2]

4915 συνηλικιώτης, **synēlikiōtēs**, n. GK: *5312* [→ *4862+2245*]. person of one's own age, contemporary:– equals [1]

4916 συνθάπτω, **synthaptō**, v. GK: *5313* [→ *4862+2290*]. (pass.) to be buried with:– buried with [2]

4917 συνθλάω, **synthlaō**, v. GK: *5314* [→ *4862*]. (pass.) to be broken to pieces:– broken [2]

4918 συνθλίβω, **synthlibō**, v. GK: *5315* [→ *4862+2346*]. to press around, crowd against:– thronged [1], thronging [1]

4919 συνθρύπτω, **synthryptō**, v. GK: *5316* [→ *4862*]. to break:– break [1]

4920 συνίημι, **syniēmi**, v. GK: *5317 & 5320* [→ *863; cf. 4862*]. to understand, realize:– understand [13], understood [7], understandeth [3], considered [1], understanding [1], wise [1]

4921 συνιστάω, **synistaō**; or συνίστημι, **synistēmi**, v. GK: *5318 & 5319* [→ *4862+2476*]. to commend, recommend; to demonstrate, bring out, prove to be; (intr.) to stand with; to hold together; to be formed:– commend [5], commendeth [3], approved [1], approving [1], commended [1], commending [1], consist [1], make [1], standing [1], stood with [1]

4922 συνοδεύω, **synodeuō**, v. GK: *5321* [→ *4862+3598*]. to travel with:– journeyed with [1]

4923 συνοδία, **synodia**, n. GK: *5322* [→ *4862+3598*]. company of travelers, caravan:– company [1]

4924 συνοικέω, **synoikeō**, v. GK: *5324* [→ *4862+3624*]. to live with:– dwell with [1]

4925 συνοικοδομέω, **synoikodomeō**, v. GK: *5325* [→ *4862+3624+1430*]. (pass.) to be built up together:– builded together [1]

4926 συνομιλέω, **synomileō**, v. GK: *5326* [→ *4862+3656*]. to talk with, converse with:– talked with [1]

4927 συνομορέω, **synomoreō**, v. GK: *5327* [→ *4862+3664+3724*]. to be next door to:– joined hard to [1]

4928 συνοχή, **synochē**, n. GK: *5330* [→ *4862+2192*]. anguish, distress:– anguish [1], distress [1]

4929 συντάσσω, **syntassō**, v. GK: *5332* [→ *4862+5021*]. to command, direct, instruct:– appointed [2]

4930 συντέλεια, **synteleia**, n. GK: *5333* [→ *4862+5056*]. end, close, completion:– end [6]

4931 συντελέω, **synteleō**, v. GK: *5334* [→ *4862+5056*]. to finish, accomplish; (pass.) to be fulfilled, be over, accomplished:– ended [4], finish [1], fulfilled [1], make [1]

4932 συντέμνω, **syntemnō**, v. GK: *5335* [→ *4862+5114*]. to cut short, speed up:– cut short [1], short [1]

4933 συντηρέω, **syntēreō**, v. GK: *5337* [→ *4862+5083*]. to protect, defend; to treasure, preserve in memory; (pass.) to be preserved:– preserved [1], kept [1], observed [1]

4934 συντίθημι, **syntithēmi**, v. GK: *5338* [→ *4862+5087*]. (mid.) to agree, decide:– agreed [2], assented [1], covenanted [1]

4935 συντόμως, **syntomōs**, adv. GK: *5339* [→ *4862+5114*]. briefly:– few words [1]

4936 συντρέχω, **syntrechō**, v. GK: *5340* [→ *4862+5143*]. to run together, go together; by extension, to be closely associated in a particular behavior or undertaking:– ran together [1], ran [1], run with [1]

4937 συντρίβω, **syntribō**, v. GK: *5341* [→ *4862+5147*]. to break, destroy; (pass.) to be broken, bruised, dashed to pieces:– brake [1], broken in pieces [1], broken to shivers [1], brokenhearted [1], broken [1], bruised [1], bruise [1], bruising [1]

4938 σύντριμμα, **syntrimma**, n. GK: *5342* [→ *4862+5147*]. ruin, destruction:– destruction [1]

4939 σύντροφος, **syntrophos**, a. GK: *5343* [→ *4862+5142*]. brought up with (in a family); this can refer to a foster sibling or an intimate friend:– brought up with [1]

4940 συντυγχάνω, **syntynchanō**, v. GK: *5344* [→ *4862+5177*]. to come together with, meet:– come at [1]

4941 Συντύχη, **Syntychē**, n.pr.f. GK: *5345* [→ *4862+5177*]. Syntyche, "*coincidence, success*":– Syntyche [1]

4942 συνυποκρίνομαι, **synypokrinomai**, v. GK: *5347* [→ *4862+5259+2919*]. to join in one's hypocrisy:– dissembled with [1]

4943 συνυπουργέω, **synypourgeō**, v. GK: *5348* [→ *4862+5259+2041*]. to join to help:– helping together [1]

4944 συνωδίνω, **synōdinō**, v. GK: *5349* [→ *4862+5604*]. to join in the pains of childbirth, suffer agony together:– travaileth in pain together [1]

4945 συνωμοσία, **synōmosia**, n. GK: *5350* [→ *4862+3660*]. plot, conspiracy:– conspiracy [1]

4946 Συράκουσαι, **Syrakousai**, n.pr. GK: *5352*. Syracuse:– Syracuse [1]

4947 Συρία, **Syria**, n.pr. GK: *5353* [→ *4948*]. Syria:– Syria [8]

4948 Σύρος, **Syros**, n.pr.g. GK: *5354* [→ *4947, 4949*]. Syrian:– Syrian [1]

4949 Συροφοίνισσα, **Syrophoinissa**, n.pr.g. GK: *5356* [→ *4948+5404*]. Syrophoenician:– Syrophenician [1]

4950 Σύρτις, **Syrtis**, n.pr. GK: *5358* [→ *4951*]. Syrtis, feared for its shifting sandbars and unpredictable currents:– quicksands [1]

4951 σύρω, **syrō**, v. GK: *5359* [→ *2694, 4950*]. to drag, tow; to sweep:– drew [3], dragging [1], haling [1]

4952 συσπαράσσω, **sysparassō**, v. GK: *5360* [→ *4862+4685*]. to cause to convulse:– tare [1]

4953 σύσσημον, **syssēmon**, n. GK: *5361* [→ *4862+4592*]. signal:– token [1]

4954 σύσσωμος, **syssōmos**, a. GK: *5362* [→ *4862+4983*]. co-member of a body:– of same body [1]

4955 συστασιαστής, **systasiastēs**, n. GK: *5363* [→ *4862+2476*]. fellow insurrectionist:– made insurrection with [1]

4956 συστατικός, **systatikos**, a. GK: *5364* [→ *4862+2476*]. commendatory, recommended:– commendation [1]

4957 συσταυρόω, **systauroō**, v. GK: *5365* [→ *4862+4716*]. (pass.) to be crucified with:– crucified with [5]

4958 συστέλλω, **systellō**, v. GK: *5366* [→ *4862+4724*]. to wrap up, cover up; (pass.) to be shortened, limited:– short [1], wound up [1]

4959 συστενάζω, **systenazō**, v. GK: *5367* [→ *4862+4728*]. to join in groaning, groan together:– groaneth [1]

4960 συστοιχέω, **systoicheō**, v. GK: *5368* [→ *4862+4748*]. to correspond:– answereth to [1]

4961 συστρατιώτης, **systratiōtēs**, n. GK: *5369* [→ *4862+4756*]. fellow soldier:– fellowsoldier [2]

4962 συστρέφω, **systrephō**, v. GK: *5370* [→ *4862+4762*]. to gather up, bring together:– gathered [1]

4963 συστροφή, **systrophē**, n. GK: *5371* [→ *4862+4762*]. commotion, disorderly gathering, mob; conspiracy, plot:– banded together (*+4160*) [1], concourse [1]

4964 συσχηματίζω, **syschēmatizō**, v. GK: *5372* [→ *4862+4976*]. (mid.) to conform to a pattern or mold; (pass.) to be conformed to a pattern or mold:– conformed to [1], fashioning according to [1]

4965 Συχάρ, **Sychar**, n.pr. GK: *4993 & 5373*. Sychar:– Sychar [1]

4966 Συχέμ, **Sychem**, n.pr. GK: *5374*. Shechem, "[poss.] *shoulder [saddle of a hill]; shoulders [and upper back]*":– Sychem [1]

4967 σφαγή, **sphagē**, n. GK: *5375* [→ *4969*]. slaughter:– slaughter [3]

4968 σφάγιον, **sphagion**, n. GK: *5376* [→ *4969*]. offering for slaughter:– slain beasts [1]

4969 σφάζω, **sphazō**, v. GK: *5377* [→ *2695, 4967, 4968*]. to kill, slay, murder:– slain [6], slew [2], kill [1], wounded [1]

4970 σφόδρα, **sphodra**, adv. GK: *5379* [→ *4971*]. very, greatly, exceedingly:– exceeding [4], very [3], greatly [2], exceedingly [1], sore [1]

4971 σφοδρῶς, **sphodrōs**, adv. GK: *5380* [→ *4970*]. violently:– exceedingly [1]

4972 σφραγίζω, **sphragizō**, v. GK: *5381* [→ *4973*]. to seal, to put a mark on an object to show possession, authority, identity, or security:– sealed [20], seal [2], sealing [1], set a seal [1], set to seal [1]

4973 σφραγίς, **sphragis**, n. GK: *5382* [→ *2696, 4972*]. seal:– seal [11], seals [5]

4974 σφυρόν, **sphyron**, n. GK: *5383 & 5384*. ankle or heel:– ankle [1]

4975 σχεδόν, **schedon**, adv. GK: *5385* [→ *2192*]. nearly, almost:– almost [3]

σχέω, **scheō**. See *2192*.

4976 σχῆμα, **schēma**, n. GK: *5386* [→ *807, 808, 809, 2156, 2157, 2158, 3345, 4964; cf. 2192*]. form, outward appearance:– fashion [1], in fashion [1]

4977 σχίζω, **schizō**, v. GK: *5387* [→ *4978*]. to tear, divide; (pass.) to be torn, divided, split (in opinion):– rent [5], divided [2], broken [1], maketh a rent [1], opened [1]

4978 σχίσμα, **schisma**, n. GK: *5388* [→ *4977*]. tear, split, divide an object into parts, with an implication that the object is now damaged; by extension: division, dissension, implying discord and damage to the unity of the original group:– division [3], divisions [2], rent [2], schism [1]

4979 σχοινίον, **schoinion**, n. GK: *5389*. (pl.) cords, ropes:– ropes [1], small cords [1]

4980 σχολάζω, **scholazō**, v. GK: *5390* [→ *4981*]. to devote oneself to; to be unoccupied, stand empty:– empty [1], give [1]

4981 σχολή, **scholē**, n. GK: *5391* [→ *4980*]. lecture hall, a building in which students meet for discussion and study, school:– school [1]

4982 σῴζω, **sōzō**, v. GK: *5392* [→ *810, 811, 1295, 4986, 4989, 4990, 4991, 4992*]. to save, rescue, deliver; to heal; by extension: to be in right relationship with God, with the implication that the condition before salvation was one of grave

danger or distress:– saved [53], save [41], made whole [9], healed [3], whole [2], do well [1], preserve [1]

4983 σῶμα, **sōma**, n. GK: *5393* [→ *4954, 4984, 4985*]. body, the mass of anything, usually a corporeal tissue, human, animal, or plant, though it can also refer to a heavenly body; the church is said to be like a (human) body, emphasizing its essential unity with very important diversities of function within the unity:– body [132], bodies [11], bodily [1], body's [1], slaves [1]

4984 σωματικός, **sōmatikos**, a. GK: *5394* [→ *4983*]. bodily, physical:– bodily [2]

4985 σωματικῶς, **sōmatikōs**, adv. GK: *5395* [→ *4983*]. in bodily form, corporeally:– bodily [1]

4986 Σώπατρος, **Sōpatros**, n.pr. GK: *5396* [→ *4982+3962*]. Sopater, "*saving one's father*":– Sopater [1]

4987 σωρεύω, **sōreuō**, v. GK: *5397* [→ *2002*]. to heap up, pile up; (pass.) to be loaded down:– heap [1], laden [1]

4988 Σωσθένης, **Sōsthenēs**, n.pr. GK: *5398*. Sosthenes:– Sosthenes [2]

4989 Σωσίπατρος, **Sōsipatros**, n.pr. GK: *5399* [→ *4982+3962*]. Sosipater, "*saving one's father*":– Sosipater [1]

4990 σωτήρ, **sōtēr**, n. GK: *5400* [→ *4982*]. Savior, one who delivers from grave danger; note that in the NT this always refers to God the Father and Jesus Christ as Savior of believers from righteous wrath in a proper relationship with God:– saviour [24]

4991 σωτηρία, **sōtēria**, n. GK: *5401* [→ *4982*]. salvation, rescue, deliverance, the state of not being in grave danger and so being safe; this can refer to ordinary dangers and conditions on earth, but it usually refers to the state of believers being safe from righteous wrath in a proper relationship with God:– salvation [40], saved [2], deliver (*+1325*) [1], health [1], saving [1]

4992 σωτήριον, **sōtērion**, n. GK: *5402* [→ *4982*]. salvation; this word can focus on the message or means of salvation:– salvation [5]

4993 σωφρονέω, **sōphroneō**, v. GK: *5404* [→ *4994, 4995, 4996, 4997, 4998; cf. 5424*]. to be in a right state of mind, have sober judgment; to be self-controlled:– right mind [2], sober [2], sober minded [1], soberly [1]

4994 σωφρονίζω, **sōphronizō**, v. GK: *5405* [→ *4993*]. to train, encourage, advise, urge:– teach to be sober [1]

4995 σωφρονισμός, **sōphronismos**, n. GK: *5406* [→ *4993*]. self-discipline, with an implication that this discipline demonstrates prudence and wisdom:– sound mind [1]

4996 σωφρόνως, **sōphronōs**, adv. GK: *5407* [→ *4993*]. in self-control:– soberly [1]

4997 σωφροσύνη, **sōphrosynē**, n. GK: *5408* [→ *4993*]. propriety, appropriateness; reasonableness, mental soundness:– sobriety [2], soberness [1]

4998 σώφρων, **sōphrōn**, a. GK: *5409* [→ *4993*]. self-controlled, implied to be wise and prudent in nature:– sober [2], discreet [1], temperate [1]

τά, **ta**. See *3588*.

4999 ταβέρναι, **tabernai**, n. GK: *5411* [→ *5140+4999*]. tavern, shop, store:– taverns [1]

5000 Ταβιθά, **Tabitha**, n.pr. GK: *5412*. Tabitha, "*gazelle*":– Tabitha [2]

5001 τάγμα, **tagma**, n. GK: *5413* [→ *5021*]. turn, order, arrangement:– order [1]

5002 τακτός, **taktos**, a. GK: *5414* [→ *5021*]. appointed, fixed:– set [1]

5003 ταλαιπωρέω, **talaipōreō**, v. GK: *5415* [→ *5005*]. to grieve, lament:– afflicted [1]

5004 ταλαιπωρία, **talaipōria**, n. GK: *5416* [→ *5005*]. misery, distress:– miseries [1], misery [1]

5005 ταλαίπωρος, **talaipōros**, a. GK: *5417* [→ *5003, 5004*]. wretched, miserable:– wretched [2]

5006 ταλαντιαῖος, **talantiaios**, a. GK: *5418* [→ *5007*]. weighing a talent (about 57 to 80 lbs.):– weight of a talent [1]

5007 τάλαντον, **talanton**, n. GK: *5419* [→ *5006*]. talent (weight and monetary unit; about 57 to 80 lbs.); a talent of silver was about 6,000 days' wages (denarii) of a common laborer and a talent of gold was about 180,000 days' wages, often implying a vast, unattainable amount:– talents [12], talent [3]

5008 ταλιθά, **talitha**, l.[n.]. GK: *5420*. talitha (Aramaic: "little girl"):– talitha [1]

5009 ταμεῖον, **tameion**, n. GK: *5421* [→ *5114*]. room, inner room, storeroom:– closets [1], closet [1], secret chambers [1], storehouse [1]

τανῦν, **tanun**. See *3568*.

5010 τάξις, **taxis**, n. GK: *5423* [→ *5021*]. order, succession; kind, nature:– order [10]

5011 ταπεινός, **tapeinos**, a. GK: *5424* [→ *5012, 5013, 5014*]. humble, lowly, downcast, timid:– humble [2], low degree [2], base [1], cast down [1], lowly [1], of low estate [1]

5012 ταπεινοφροσύνη, **tapeinophrosynē**, n. GK: *5425* [→ *5011+5424*]. humility, humbleness, modesty:– humility [3], humbleness of mind [1], humility of mind [1], lowliness of mind [1], lowliness [1]

5013 ταπεινόω, **tapeinoō**, v. GK: *5427* [→ *5011*]. (act.) to humble (oneself), lower (oneself); (pass.) to be humbled, brought low, in need:– humble [5], abased [4], humbleth [2], abasing [1], brought low [1], humbled [1]

5014 ταπείνωσις, **tapeinōsis**, n. GK: *5428* [→ *5011*]. humbleness, lowliness, humiliation:– humiliation [1], low estate [1], made low [1], vile [1]

5015 ταράσσω, **tarassō**, v. GK: *5429* [→ *1298, 1613, 5016, 5017*]. to trouble, disturb, throw into confusion; (pass.) to be disturbed, terrified, confused; to be stirred up:– troubled [15], troubleth [1], trouble [1]

5016 ταραχή, **tarachē**, n. GK: *5430* [→ *5015*]. disturbance:– troubles [1], troubling [1]

5017 τάραχος, **tarachos**, n. GK: *5431* [→ *5015*]. commotion; disturbance:– stir [2]

5018 Ταρσεύς, **Tarseus**, n.pr.g. GK: *5432* [→ *5019*]. Tarsus:– Tarsus [2]

5019 Ταρσός, **Tarsos**, n.pr. GK: *5433* [→ *5018*]. Tarsus:– Tarsus [3]

5020 ταρταρόω, **tartaroō**, v. GK: *5434*. to send to hell, hold captive in Tartarus; a derivative of the Greek noun "Tartarus," a place of torture and torment lower than Hades in Greek and Jewish apocalyptic literature, not found in the NT:– cast down to hell [1]

5021 τάσσω, **tassō**, v. GK: *5435* [→ *392, 498, 506, 657, 812, 813, 814, 1296, 1297, 1299, 1928, 2003, 2004, 4367, 4384, 4929, 5001, 5002, 5010, 5292, 5293*]. (act./mid.) to appoint, determine, arrange; devote; (pass.) to be established, appointed, assigned:– appointed [3], ordained [2], addicted [1], determined [1], set [1]

5022 ταῦρος, **tauros**, n. GK: *5436*. bull, ox:– bulls [2], oxen [2]

5023 ταῦτα, **tauta**, p.demo.neut.pl. of *3778*. GK: *4047* [→ *3778*]. these; see *3778*:–

5024 ταὐτά, **tauta**, contr. [art.+p.]. GK: *5437* [→ *3588+846*]. the same things:– even thus (*+2596*) [1], like [1]

5025 ταύταις, **tautais**, p.demo.fem.pl. of *3778*. GK: *4047* [→ *3778*]. to, for, by these; see *3778*:–

5026 ταύτη, **tautē**, p.demo.fem.s. of *3778*. GK: *4047* [→ *3778*]. to, for, by this; see *3778*:–

5027 ταφή, **taphē**, n. GK: *5438* [→ *5028*]. burial place:– bury [1]

5028 τάφος, **taphos**, n. GK: *5439* [→ *1779, 1780, 5027; cf. 2290*]. tomb, grave:– sepulchre [5], sepulchres [1], tombs [1]

5029 τάχα, **tacha**, adv. GK: *5440* [→ *5036*]. perhaps, possibly:– peradventure [1], perhaps [1]

5030 ταχέως, **tacheōs**, adv. GK: *5441* [→ *5036*]. quickly, in haste; very soon:– shortly [6], quickly [3], soon [2], hastily [1], outrun (*+4390*) [1], sooner [1], suddenly [1], with all speed (*+5613*) [1]

5031 ταχινός, **tachinos**, a. GK: *5442* [→ *5036*]. swift; soon, imminent:– shortly [1], swift [1]

5032 τάχιον, **tachion**, adv.compar.neut. of *5030*. GK: *5441* [→ *5036*]. very quickly, in haste; very soon:–

5033 τάχιστα, **tachista**, adv.super. of *5030*. GK: *5441* [→ *5036*]. most quickly, hastily; as soon as possible:–

5034 τάχος, **tachos**, n. GK: *5443* [→ *5036*]. quickness, immediateness; (in pp. phrase) quickly, immediately, soon:–

Grk

shortly (+*1722*) [4], quickly (+*1722*) [2], quickly [1], speedily (+*1722*) [1]

5035 ταχύ, *tachu*, a.neut.s. of *5036*. GK: *5444* [→ *5036*]. (adv.) quickly, momentarily, soon:–

5036 ταχύς, *tachys*, a. GK: *5444* [→ *5029, 5030, 5031, 5032, 5033, 5034, 5035*]. quick, swift; (adv.) quickly, momentarily, soon:– quickly [11], lightly [1], swift [1]

5037 τέ, *te*, pt. GK: *5445* [→ *1535, 1539, 3383, 3752, 3753, 3763, 3777, 3842, 5119, 5620*]. and, but (often not translated):– and [127], both [36], also [2], then [2], whether (+*1437*) [2], and whether (+*1437*) [1], between [1], even [1], inasmuch as both [1], or (+*1437*) [1], whether [1], yea (+*2089*) [1]

5038 τεῖχος, *teichos*, n. GK: *5446* [→ *3320, 5109*]. wall:– wall [8], walls [1]

5039 τεκμήριον, *tekmērion*, n. GK: *5447*. convincing proof:– infallible proofs [1]

5040 τεκνίον, *teknion*, n. GK: *5448* [→ *5088*]. dear children, little children:– little children [9]

5041 τεκνογονέω, *teknogoneō*, v. GK: *5449* [→ *5088+1096*]. to have children, bear a child:– bear children [1]

5042 τεκνογονία, *teknogonia*, n. GK: *5450* [→ *5088+1096*]. childbearing:– childbearing [1]

5043 τέκνον, *teknon*, n. GK: *5451* [→ *5088*]. child, son, daughter, offspring, descendant:– children [70], son [15], sons [6], child [5], children's [2], daughters [1]

5044 τεκνοτροφέω, *teknotropheō*, v. GK: *5452* [→ *5088+5142*]. to bring up children:– brought up children [1]

5045 τέκτων, *tektōn*, n. GK: *5454* [→ *5078*]. carpenter, woodworker; more generally: construction worker, including stonemason and metalworker:– carpenter's [1], carpenter [1]

5046 τέλειος, *teleios*, a. GK: *5455* [→ *5056*]. perfect, mature, finished:– perfect [16], full age [1], men [1], more perfect [1]

5047 τελειότης, *teleiotēs*, n. GK: *5456* [→ *5056*]. perfection, maturity, completeness:– perfection [1], perfectness [1]

5048 τελειόω, *teleioō*, v. GK: *5457* [→ *5056*]. to perfect, complete, finish; (pass.) to reach a goal, be fulfilled, completed, made perfect:– made perfect [9], perfected [4], finish [3], make perfect [3], fulfilled [2], consecrated [1], finished [1], perfect [1]

5049 τελείως, *teleiōs*, adv. GK: *5458* [→ *5056*]. fully, completely, perfectly:– end [1]

5050 τελείωσις, *teleiōsis*, n. GK: *5459* [→ *5056*]. perfection, accomplishment, fulfillment:– perfection [1], performance [1]

5051 τελειωτής, *teleiōtēs*, n. GK: *5460* [→ *5056*]. perfecter:– finisher [1]

5052 τελεσφορέω, *telesphoreō*, v. GK: *5461* [→ *5056+5342*]. to mature (to fruitfulness):– bring to perfection [1]

5053 τελευτάω, *teleutaō*, v. GK: *5462* [→ *5054; cf. 5056*]. to die:– dead [3], dieth [3], die [3], died [2], deceased [1]

5054 τελευτή, *teleutē*, n. GK: *5463* [→ *5053*]. death:– death [1]

5055 τελέω, *teleō*, v. GK: *5464* [→ *5056*]. to finish, complete, fulfill; (pass.) to be finished, be completed, fulfilled, perfected:– finished [8], accomplished [4], fulfilled [4], fulfil [3], pay [2], expired [1], filled up [1], gone over [1], made an end [1], performed [1]

5056 τέλος, *telos*, n. GK: *5465* [→ *255, 658, 1300, 1615, 2005, 3081, 3651, 3838, 4185, 4930, 4931, 5046, 5047, 5048, 5049, 5050, 5051, 5052, 5055; cf. 5053, 5057*]. end, result, outcome, finish, goal; revenue, tax, duty:– end [34], custom [3], by continual (+*1519*) [1], ending [1], ends [1], finally (+*3588*) [1], uttermost [1]

5057 τελώνης, *telōnēs*, n. GK: *5467* [→ *754, 5057, 5058*]. tax collector:– publicans [16], publican [6]

5058 τελώνιον, *telōnion*, n. GK: *5466 & 5468* [→ *5057*]. tax collector's booth:– receipt of custom [3]

5059 τέρας, *teras*, n. GK: *5469*. wonder, miracle, which is by implication a sign or portent:– wonders [16]

5060 Τέρτιος, *Tertios*, n.pr. GK: *5470*. Tertius, "*third*":– Tertius [1]

5061 Τέρτυλλος, *Tertyllos*, n.pr. GK: *5472*. Tertullus, "*third*":– Tertullus [2]

τέσσαρα, *tessara*. See *5064*.

5062 τεσσαράκοντα, *tessarakonta*, n.num. GK: *5473 & 5477* [→ *5064*]. forty:– forty [22]

5063 τεσσαρακονταετής, *tessarakontaetēs*, a.num. GK: *5474 & 5478* [→ *5064+2094*]. (of) forty years:– forty years [2]

5064 τέσσαρες, *tessares*, n.num. GK: *5475* [→ *1180, 5062, 5063, 5065, 5066, 5067, 5068, 5069, 5070, 5071, 5072, 5073, 5074, 5075, 5076, 5132, 5133*]. four:– four [42]

5065 τεσσαρεσκαιδέκατος, *tessareskaidekatos*, a.num. GK: *5476* [→ *5064+2532+1176*]. fourteenth:– fourteenth [2]

5066 τεταρταῖος, *tetartaios*, a. GK: *5479* [→ *5064*]. fourth (day):– four days [1]

5067 τέταρτος, *tetartos*, a. GK: *5480* [→ *5064*]. fourth in a series or collection; (n.) the fourth (fractional) part of something:– fourth [9], four [1]

5068 τετράγωνος, *tetragōnos*, a. GK: *5481* [→ *5064+1137*]. square, cubical:– foursquare [1]

5069 τετράδιον, *tetradion*, n. GK: *5482* [→ *5064*]. squad of four soldiers:– quaternions [1]

5070 τετρακισχίλιοι, *tetrakischilioi*, a.num. GK: *5483* [→ *5064+5507*]. four thousand:– four thousand [5]

5071 τετρακόσιοι, *tetrakosioi*, a.num. GK: *5484* [→ *5064*]. four hundred:– four hundred [4]

5072 τετράμηνος, *tetramēnos*, a. GK: *5485* [→ *5064+3375*]. (for) four months:– four months [1]

5073 τετραπλόος, *tetraploos*, a. [used as adv.]. GK: *5486 & 5487* [→ *5064*]. four times (as much):– fourfold [1]

5074 τετράπους, *tetrapous*, a. GK: *5488* [→ *5064+4228*]. four-footed; (n.) four-footed animal of any kind:– fourfooted beasts [1]

5075 τετραρχέω, *tetrarcheō*, v. GK: *5489* [→ *5064+757*]. to be a tetrarch:– tetrarch [3]

5076 τετράρχης, *tetrarchēs*, n. GK: *5490* [→ *5064+757*]. tetrarch, a ruler of less rank and authority than a king:– tetrarch [4]

τεύχω, *teuchō*. See *5177*.

5077 τεφρόω, *tephroō*, v. GK: *5491* [→ *5188*]. to reduce to ashes by fire:– turning into ashes [1]

5078 τέχνη, *technē*, n. GK: *5492* [→ *753, 3673, 5045, 5079; cf. 5088*]. skill, trade, craft:– art [1], craft [1], occupation [1]

5079 τεχνίτης, *technitēs*, n. GK: *5493* [→ *5078*]. craftsman, skilled worker, architect, designer, one who engages in a craft or trade, in some contexts with a focus or the design and planning of what is crafted:– craftsmen [2], builder [1], craftsman [1]

5080 τήκομαι, *tēkomai*, v. GK: *5494*. (pass.) to be melted:– melt [1]

5081 τηλαυγῶς, *tēlaugōs*, adv. GK: *5495* [→ *827*]. clearly, plainly:– clearly [1]

5082 τηλικοῦτος, *tēlikoutos*, p.demo. GK: *5496* [→ *2245+3778*]. so great, so large:– so great [2], great [1], mighty [1]

5083 τηρέω, *tēreō*, v. GK: *5498* [→ *1301, 3906, 3907, 4933, 5084*]. to keep, guard, obey, observe:– keep [32], kept [15], keepeth [10], reserved [7], observe [4], preserved [2], hold fast [1], keepers [1], reserve [1], watched [1], watching [1]

5084 τήρησις, *tērēsis*, n. GK: *5499* [→ *5083*]. jail, prison, custody; keeping, observance:– hold [1], keeping [1], prison [1]

τῇ, *tēi*, τήν, *tēn*, τῆς, *tēs*. See *3588*.

5085 Τιβεριάς, *Tiberias*, n.pr. GK: *5500* [→ *5086*]. Tiberias:– Tiberias [3]

5086 Τιβέριος, *Tiberios*, n.pr. GK: *5501* [→ *5085*]. Tiberius:– Tiberius [1]

5087 τίθημι, *tithēmi*, v. GK: *5502* [→ *113, 114, 115, 121, 276, 394, 428, 475, 477, 595, 659, 802, 1242, 1303, 1570, 1620, 1936, 2007, 2111, 2336, 2653, 2698, 3331, 3346, 3548, 3549, 3550, 3559, 3560, 3734, 3866, 3872, 3908, 4025, 4060, 4286, 4287, 4323, 4369, 4388, 4783, 4784, 4934, 5206, 2314, 3957; cf. 331, 2310, 2344, 2653*]. (act.) to place, put; (pass.) to be placed or put; (mid.) to set, appoint, decide, arrange:– laid [24], put [14], lay down [8], make [6], kneeled

down (+*1119+3588*) [5], lay [5], appointed [4], set [4], made [3], appoint [2], laid down [2], ordained [2], putteth [2], advised (+*1012*) [1], bowing [1], committed [1], conceived [1], giveth [1], laid aside [1], laid up [1], layedst down [1], making [1], purposed [1], put in way [1], putting [1], set forth [1], settle [1], sink down [1]

5088 τίκτω, *tiktō*, v. GK: *5503* [→ *815, 4415, 4416, 5040, 5041, 5042, 5043, 5044, 5110, 5388; cf. 5078*]. to give birth to; bear, produce:– brought forth [4], delivered [4], born [3], bring forth [3], bringeth forth [2], bearest [1], delivered of a child [1], in travail [1]

5089 τίλλω, *tillō*, v. GK: *5504*. to pick (heads of grain):– pluck [2], plucked [1]

5090 Τιμαῖος, *Timaios*, n.pr. GK: *5505* [→ *5092*]. Timaeus, "*precious, valuable*":– Timeus [1]

5091 τιμάω, *timaō*, v. GK: *5506* [→ *5092*]. to honor, show respect, give recognition:– honour [14], honoureth [4], honoured [1], valued [1], value [1]

5092 τιμή, *timē*, n. GK: *5507* [→ *818, 819, 820, 821, 927, 1784, 2008, 2009, 2472, 4186, 5090, 5091, 5093, 5094, 5095, 5096, 5097, 5098, 5389*]. honor, value, respect; nobility, specialness; money, cost:– honour [32], price [7], honours [1], precious [1], prices [1], sum [1]

5093 τίμιος, *timios*, a. GK: *5508* [→ *5092*]. precious, valuable, honored, costly:– precious [8], most precious [2], dear [1], honourable [1], more precious [1], reputation [1]

5094 τιμιότης, *timiotēs*, n. GK: *5509* [→ *5092*]. wealth:– costliness [1]

5095 Τιμόθεος, *Timotheos*, n.pr. GK: *5510* [→ *5092+2316*]. Timothy, "*precious one of God*":– Timotheus [19], Timothy [9]

5096 Τίμων, *Timōn*, n.pr. GK: *5511* [→ *5092*]. Timon, "*precious, valuable*":– Timon [1]

5097 τιμωρέω, *timōreō*, v. GK: *5512* [→ *5092+142*]. to punish:– punished [2]

5098 τιμωρία, *timōria*, n. GK: *5513* [→ *5092+142*]. punishment:– punishment [1]

5099 τίνω, *tinō*, v. GK: *5514* [→ *661*]. to pay (a price or penalty), in context the penalty is suffering:– punished (+*1349*) [1]

5100 τὶς, *tis*, p.indef. GK: *5516* [→ *3385, 3387, 3386, 3748, 3755*]. one, anyone, anything; some, someone, something:– any [131], certain [114], some [79], one [36], man [25], a [14], ought [7], somewhat [6], something [5], whatsoever (+*302+3739*) [3], divers [2], he [2], none (+*3361*) [2], nothing (+*3361*) [2], one (+*1520*) [2], somebody [2], what [2], whose [2], another (+*243*) [1], as (+*302+3739*) [1], broken⁵ pieces [1], every [1], kind [1], man's [1], matter [1], more (+*4055*) [1], no (+*3361*) [1], nothing (+*3756*) [1], nothing (+*3761*) [1], partly (+*3313*) [1], same [1], that [1], whatsoever (+*1437+3739*) [1], whatsoever (+*1437+3748+3956*) [1], whatsoever (+*302+302+3739*) [1], whatsoever [1], whomsoever (+*1437*) [1]

5101 τίς, *tis*, p.inter. GK: *5515* [→ *1302, 1360, 2444, 2530, 3754*]. who?, what?, which?, why?:– what [258], who [101], why [66], whom [25], which [16], how [10], whose [9], whether [8], whereunto [5], nothing (+*3756*) [3], what [+*302*] [3], wherefore [3], wherewith (+*1722*) [1], every [2], what (+*687*) [2], why (+*1519*) [2], any [1], how much [1], nothing (+*3361*) [1], one [1], that [1], what (+*3739*) [1], what have I to (+*1473*) [1], what man (+*687*) [1], what mean [1], what purpose [1], whereby (+*2596*) [1], wherefore (+*1519*) [1], wherefore (+*1752*) [1], wherefore (+*5484*) [1], whereof (+*4012*) [1], whereunto (+*302*) [1], wherewithal [1], wherewith [1], where [1], which (+*302*) [1], who (+*302*) [1]

5102 τίτλος, *titlos*, n. GK: *5518*. sign, prepared notice, inscription:– title [2]

5103 Τίτος, *Titos*, n.pr. GK: *5519*. Titus:– Titus [15]

τίω, *tiō*. See *5099*.

τό, *to*. See *3588*.

5104 τοί, *toi*, pt. GK: *5520* [→ *2273, 2543, 2544, 3305, 5105, 5106*]. surely (emphasizing reliability):–

5105 τοιγαροῦν, *toigaroun*, pt. GK: *5521* [→ *5104+1063+3767*]. therefore, then:– therefore [1], wherefore seeing [1]

τοίγε, *toige*. See *2544*.

5106 τοίνυν, *toinyn*, pt.infer. GK: *5523* [→ *5104+3568*]. then, therefore:– therefore [3], then [1]

5107 τοιόσδε, **toiosde**, a. GK: *5524* [→ *3588*]. such as this, of this kind:– such [1]

5108 τοιοῦτος, **toioutos**, a. GK: *5525* [→ *3588+3778*]. such, such as this, of such a kind:– such [51], such a one [8], like occupation [1], such as (+*3697*) [1]

5109 τοῖχος, **toichos**, n. GK: *5526* [→ *5038*]. wall:– wall [1]

5110 τόκος, **tokos**, n. GK: *5527* [→ *5088*]. interest (on a monetary loan):– usury [2]

5111 τολμάω, **tolmaō**, v. GK: *5528* [→ *662, 5112, 5113*]. to dare, be bold, courageous:– durst [7], bold [4], dare [4], boldly [1]

5112 τολμηρότερον, **tolmēroteron**, adv.comp. GK: *5530* [→ *5111*]. rather boldly:– more boldly [1]

5113 τολμητής, **tolmētēs**, n. GK: *5532* [→ *5111*]. bold man, daring man:– presumptuous [1]

5114 τομός, **tomos**, a. GK: *5533* [→ *564, 663, 664, 823, 1371, 2699, 3718, 4059, 4061, 4932, 4935, 5009*]. cutting, sharp; (compar.) sharper:– sharper [1]

5115 τόξον, **toxon**, n. GK: *5534* [→ *2700*]. bow (weapon):– bow [1]

5116 τοπάζιον, **topazion**, n. GK: *5535*. topaz (a bright yellow precious stone):– topaz [1]

5117 τόπος, **topos**, n. GK: *5536* [→ *824, 1786*]. place, location; passage (in a book); position; possibility, opportunity:– place [73], places [7], room [5], quarters [2], coasts [1], licence [1], plain (+*3977*) [1], rocks (+*5138*) [1], where [1]

5118 τοσοῦτος, **tosoutos**, a. GK: *5537* [→ *3778*]. so great, so many, so large, so long:– so much [7], so great [5], so many [4], so long [2], all so many [1], large [1], these many [1]

5119 τότε, **tote**, adv. GK: *5538* [→ *3739+5037*]. then, when, at that time:– then [147], that time [2], then (+*3767*) [2], after (+*5225*) [1], and (+*2532*) [1], that time forth [1], time [1], when [1]

5120 τοῦ, **tou**, art.gen.s. of *3588*. GK: *3836* [→ *3588*]. (often not translated) his, her, its; see *3588*:–

5121 τοὐναντίον, **tounantion**, contr. [art.+pp.*]. GK: *5539* [→ *3588+1725*]. but, on the contrary:– contrariwise [3]

5122 τοὔνομα, **tounoma**, contr. [art.+n.]. GK: *5540* [→ *3588+3686*]. named, by name:– named [1]

5123 τουτέστιν, **toutestin**, contr. [art.+v.]. GK: *5542* [→ *3778+1510*]. that is to say, by this we mean:–

5124 τοῦτο, **touto**, p.demo.neut.s. of *3778*. GK: *4047* [→ *3778*]. this; see *3778*:–

5125 τούτοις, **toutois**, p.demo.dat.pl. of *3778*. GK: *4047* [→ *3778*]. to, for, by these; see *3778*:–

5126 τοῦτον, **touton**, p.demo.acc.s. of *3778*. GK: *4047* [→ *3778*]. see *3778*:–

5127 τούτου, **toutou**, p.demo.gen.s. of *3778*. GK: *4047* [→ *3778*]. from, of this; see *3778*:–

5128 τούτους, **toutous**, p.demo.acc.pl. of *3778*. GK: *4047* [→ *3778*]. these; see *3778*:–

5129 τούτῳ, **toutō**, p.demo.dat.s. of *3778*. GK: *4047* [→ *3778*]. to, for, by this; see *3778*:–

5130 τούτων, **toutōn**, p.demo.gen.pl. of *3778*. GK: *4047* [→ *3778*]. from, of these; see *3778*:–

5131 τράγος, **tragos**, n. GK: *5543* [→ *5176*]. male goat:– goats [4]

5132 τράπεζα, **trapeza**, n. GK: *5544* [→ *5064+3978*]. table:– table [9], tables [4], bank [1], set meat before (+*3908*) [1]

5133 τραπεζίτης, **trapezitēs**, n. GK: *5545* [→ *5064+3978*]. banker:– exchangers [1]

5134 τραῦμα, **trauma**, n. GK: *5546* [→ *1626, 5135*]. (pl.) wounds:– wounds [1]

5135 τραυματίζω, **traumatizō**, v. GK: *5547* [→ *5134*]. to wound:– wounded [2]

5136 τραχηλίζω, **trachēlizō**, v. GK: *5548* [→ *5137*]. (pass.) to be laid bare:– opened [1]

5137 τράχηλος, **trachelos**, n. GK: *5549* [→ *4644, 5136*]. neck, throat:– neck [6], necks [1]

5138 τραχύς, **trachys**, a. GK: *5550* [→ *5139*]. rough, uneven:– rocks (+*5117*) [1], rough [1]

5139 Τραχωνῖτις, **Trachōnitis**, n.pr. GK: *5551* [→ *5138*]. Traconitis, "*rough, stony district*":– Trachonitis [1]

5140 τρεῖς, **treis**, n.num. GK: *5552* [→ *755, 5144, 5145, 5146, 5148, 5150, 5151, 5152, 5153, 5154*]. three:– three [69]

5141 τρέμω, **tremō**, v. GK: *5554* [→ *1790, 5156*]. to tremble, fear:– trembling [3], afraid [1]

5142 τρέφω, **trephō**, v. GK: *5555* [→ *397, 1305, 1361, 1625, 1789, 2353, 4939, 5044, 5160, 5161, 5162*]. to care for, feed, nurse; (pass.) to be nurtured, cared for:– nourished [3], feedeth [2], brought up [1], fed [1], feed [1]

5143 τρέχω, **trechō**, v. GK: *5556* [→ *1408, 1532, 1998, 2113, 2701, 4063, 4274, 4370, 4390, 4890, 4936, 5163, 5164, 5295*]. to run; to strive, give effort:– run [10], ran [6], runneth [2], course [1], running [1]

5144 τριάκοντα, **triakonta**, n.num. GK: *5558* [→ *5140*]. thirty:– thirty [9], thirtyfold [2]

5145 τριακόσιοι, **triakosioi**, a.num. GK: *5559* [→ *5140*]. three hundred:– three hundred [2]

5146 τρίβολος, **tribolos**, n. GK: *5560* [→ *5140+906*]. thistle:– briers [1], thistles [1]

5147 τρίβος, **tribos**, n. GK: *5561* [→ *1304, 3859, 4937, 4938, 5551*]. path:– paths [3]

5148 τριετία, **trietia**, n. GK: *5562* [→ *5140+2094*]. (for) three years:– three years [1]

5149 τρίζω, **trizō**, v. GK: *5563*. to gnash, grind:– gnasheth [1]

5150 τρίμηνος, **trimēnos**, a. GK: *5564* [→ *5140+3375*]. a period of three months:– three months [1]

5151 τρίς, **tris**, adv. GK: *5565* [→ *5140*]. three times:– thrice [10], three times (+*1909*) [1], thrice (+*1909*) [1]

5152 τρίστεγον, **tristegon**, n. GK: *5566* [→ *5140+4722*]. third story (of a building):– third loft [1]

5153 τρισχίλιοι, **trischilioi**, a.num. GK: *5567* [→ *5140+5507*]. three thousand:– three thousand [1]

5154 τρίτος, **tritos**, a. GK: *5568 & 5569* [→ *5140*]. third:– third [50], third time [5], third time (+*1537*) [1], thirdly [1]

τρίχες, **triches**. See *2359*.

5155 τρίχινος, **trichinos**, a. GK: *5570* [→ *2359*]. made of hair, hairy:– of hair [1]

5156 τρόμος, **tromos**, n. GK: *5571* [→ *5141*]. trembling, fear:– trembling [4], trembled (+*2192*) [1]

5157 τροπή, **tropē**, n. GK: *5572* [→ *396, 665, 1624, 1788, 1791, 2010, 2011, 2012, 2160, 4062, 4187, 4389, 5158, 5159*]. shifting, turning, variation, change:– turning [1]

5158 τρόπος, **tropos**, n. GK: *5573* [→ *5157*]. manner, way, kind; way of life:– as (+*3739*) [3], manner [2], means [2], way [2], as (+*2596+3739*) [1], conversation [1], even as (+*2596+3739+3779*) [1], even as (+*3739*) [1]

5159 τροποφορέω, **tropophoreō**, v. GK: *5574* [→ *5157+5342*]. to endure, put up with:– suffered manners [1]

5160 τροφή, **trophē**, n. GK: *5575* [→ *5142*]. food, nourishment:– meat [13], food [2], eaten enough (+*2880*) [1]

5161 Τρόφιμος, **Trophimos**, n.pr. GK: *5576* [→ *5142*]. Trophimus, "*nourished [child]*":– Trophimus [3]

5162 τροφός, **trophos**, n. GK: *5577* [→ *5142*]. mother, nurse:– nurse [1]

5163 τροχιά, **trochia**, n. GK: *5579* [→ *5143*]. path, course:– paths [1]

5164 τροχός, **trochos**, n. GK: *5580* [→ *5143*]. wheel; (fig.) whole course (of life):– course [1]

5165 τρύβλιον, **tryblion**, n. GK: *5581*. bowl:– dish [2]

5166 τρυγάω, **trygaō**, v. GK: *5582*. to gather or pick (grapes):– gather [2], gathered [1]

5167 τρυγών, **trygōn**, n. GK: *5583*. (pl.) doves, turtledoves:– turtledoves [1]

5168 τρυμαλιά, **trymalia**, n. GK: *5584* [→ *5169*]. eye (the tear-drop shaped hole of a needle through which thread is passed):– eye [2]

5169 τρύπημα, **trypēma**, n. GK: *5585* [→ *5168*]. eye (of a needle):– eye [1]

5170 Τρύφαινα, **Tryphaina**, n.pr. GK: *5586* [→ *5172*]. Tryphena, "*dainty*":– Tryphena [1]

5171 τρυφάω, **tryphaō**, v. GK: *5587* [→ *5172*]. to live in luxury, lead a life of self-indulgence:– lived in pleasure [1]

5172 τρυφή, **tryphē**, n. GK: *5588* [→ *1792, 5170, 5171, 5173*]. luxury, splendor; carousal, indulgence, reveling:– delicately [1], riot [1]

5173 Τρυφῶσα, **Tryphōsa**, n.pr. GK: *5589* [→ *5172*]. Tryphosa, "*delicate*":– Tryphosa [1]

5174 Τρῳάς, **Trōas**, n.pr. GK: *5590*. Troas:– Troas [6]

5175 Τρωγύλλιον, **Trōgyllion**, n.pr. GK: *5591*. Trogyllium:– Trogyllium [1]

5176 τρώγω, **trōgō**, v. GK: *5592* [→ *5131*]. to eat, feed on:– eateth [5], eating [1]

5177 τυγχάνω, **tynchanō**, v. GK: *5593* [→ *1783, 1793, 2013, 2161, 3909, 4940, 4941, 5190, 5241*]. to take part in; to obtain, provide; (intr.) to happen a certain way, to be extraordinary; perhaps:– obtain [3], obtained [2], enjoy [1], it may be (+*1487*) [1], it may be [1], it may chance (+*1487*) [1], little [1], refresh (+*1958*) [1], special (+*3588+3756*) [1]

5178 τυμπανίζω, **tympanizō**, v. GK: *5594* [→ *5180*]. (pass.) to be tortured, tormented:– tortured [1]

5179 τύπος, **typos**, n. GK: *5596* [→ *5180*]. pattern, model, example, type, a visual form to be copied, such as in crafting an idol; by extension: a pattern of behavior to be emulated:– ensamples [3], ensample [2], pattern [2], print [2], examples [1], example [1], fashion [1], figures [1], figure [1], form [1], manner [1]

5180 τύπτω, **typtō**, v. GK: *5597* [→ *499, 1795, 5178, 5179, 5296*]. to strike, beat, wound:– smote [4], smite [3], beat [2], beating [1], smiteth [1], smitten [1], stroke [1], wound [1]

5181 Τύραννος¹, **Tyrannos¹**, n.pr. GK: *5598*. Tyrannus, "*ruler*":– Tyrannus [1]

5182 τυρβάζω, **tyrbazō**, v. GK: *5600*. (mid.) trouble oneself; (pass.) to be troubled:– troubled [1]

5183 Τύριος, **Tyrios**, n.pr.g. GK: *5601* [→ *5184*]. Tyrian:– of Tyre [1]

5184 Τύρος, **Tyros**, n.pr. GK: *5602* [→ *5183*]. Tyre, "*rocky place*":– Tyre [11]

5185 τυφλός, **typhlos**, a. GK: *5603* [→ *5186*]. blind; (n.) blind person:– blind [43], blind man [7], blind men [3]

5186 τυφλόω, **typhloō**, v. GK: *5604* [→ *5185*]. to cause blindness, deprive of sight:– blinded [3]

5187 τυφόομαι, **typhoomai**, v. GK: *5605* [→ *5188*]. (pass.) to be or become conceited, implying foolishness:– highminded [1], lifted up with pride [1], proud [1]

5188 τύφω, **typhō**, v. GK: *5606* [→ *5077, 5187*]. (pass.) to smolder, smoke:– smoking [1]

5189 τυφωνικός, **typhōnikos**, a. GK: *5607*. of hurricane force:– tempestuous [1]

5190 Τυχικός, **Tychikos**, n.pr. GK: *5608* [→ *5177*]. Tychicus, "*good fortune*":– Tychicus [7]

5191 ὑακίνθινος, **hyakinthinos**, a. GK: *5610* [→ *5192*]. dark blue, *poss.* dark red:– jacinth [1]

5192 ὑάκινθος, **hyakinthos**, n. GK: *5611* [→ *5191*]. jacinth:– jacinth [1]

5193 ὑάλινος, **hyalinos**, a. GK: *5612* [→ *5194*]. of glass:– of glass [3]

5194 ὕαλος, **hyalos**, n. GK: *5613* [→ *5193*]. glass, some translate "crystal":– glass [2]

5195 ὑβρίζω, **hybrizō**, v. GK: *5614* [→ *5196*]. to insult, mistreat:– entreated spitefully [1], reproachest [1], shamefully entreated [1], spitefully entreated [1], use despitefully [1]

5196 ὕβρις, **hybris**, n. GK: *5615* [→ *1796, 5195, 5197*]. insult, mistreatment; disaster, damage:– harm [1], hurt [1], reproaches [1]

5197 ὑβριστής, **hybristēs**, n. GK: *5616* [→ *5196*]. insolent man, violent man:– despiteful [1], injurious [1]

5198 ὑγιαίνω, **hygiainō**, v. GK: *5617* [→ *5199*]. to be healthy, sound:– sound [8], whole [2], health [1], wholesome [1]

5199 ὑγιής, **hygiēs**, a. GK: *5618* [→ *5198*]. healthy, sound, well:– whole [13], sound [1]

5200 ὑγρός, **hygros**, a. GK: *5619* [→ *5205*]. moist, green:– green [1]

5201 ὑδρία, **hydria**, n. GK: *5620* [→ *5204*]. water jar:– waterpots [2], waterpot [1]

5202 ὑδροποτέω, **hydropoteō**, v. GK: *5621* [→ *5204+4095*]. to drink water (exclusively):– drink water [1]

5203 ὑδρωπικός, *hydrōpikos*, a. GK: *5622* [→ *5204*]. suffering from dropsy (edema, abnormal swelling from accumulated fluids):– had the dropsy [1]

5204 ὕδωρ, *hydōr*, n. GK: *5623* [→ *504, 5201, 5202, 5203*; cf. *5205*]. water:– water [64], waters [15]

5205 ὑετός, *hyetos*, n. GK: *5624* [→ *5200*; cf. *5204*]. rain:– rain [5], rain [+*1026*] [1]

5206 υἱοθεσία, *huiothesia*, n. GK: *5625* [→ *5207*+*5087*]. adoption as sons, sonship; in NT culture a son received greater inheritance and honor, but in Christ men and women inherit equally:– adoption [3], adoption of children [1], adoption of sons [1]

5207 υἱός, *huios*, n. GK: *5626* [→ *5206*]. son, child (of either gender), descendant (in any generation); by extension: a term of endearment; one of a class or kind, for example, a "son of the resurrection" is one who participates in the resurrection. "The Son of Man" is an OT phrase usually meaning "human being," that in the NT is used almost exclusively as a messianic title (see Da 7:13), emphasizing Jesus' humanity:– son [306], children [47], sons [24], child [3], foal [1]

5208 ὕλη, *hylē*, n. GK: *5627* [→ *1368*]. forest, wood:– matter [1]

5209 ὑμᾶς, *humas*, p.pers.acc.pl. of *4771*. GK: *5148* [→ *4771*]. you, your; see *4771*:–

5210 ὑμεῖς, *humeis*, p.pers.nom.pl. of *4771*. GK: *5148* [→ *4771*]. you, your; see *4771*:–

5211 Ὑμέναιος, *Hymenaios*, n.pr. GK: *5628*. Hymenaeus, "of [pagan god] Hymen":– Hymeneus [2]

5212 ὑμέτερος, *hymeteros*, a. GK: *5629* [→ *4771*]. (pl.) your, your own:– your [7], yours [2], your own [1]

5213 ὑμῖν, *humin*, p.pers.dat.pl. of *4771*. GK: *5148* [→ *4771*]. you, your; see *4771*:–

5214 ὑμνέω, *hymneō*, v. GK: *5630* [→ *5215*]. to sing hymns, sing praises:– sung a hymn [2], sang praises [1], sing praise [1]

5215 ὕμνος, *hymnos*, n. GK: *5631* [→ *5214*]. hymn, song of praise:– hymns [2]

5216 ὑμῶν, *humōn*, p.pers.gen.pl. of *4771*. GK: *5148* [→ *4771*]. you, your; see *4771*:–

5217 ὑπάγω, *hypagō*, v. GK: *5632* [→ *5259*+*71*]. to go (away):– go [53], goeth [9], goest [5], went [4], get [3], go away [2], departing [1], depart [1], get hence [1], going [1], went away [1]

5218 ὑπακοή, *hypakoē*, n. GK: *5633* [→ *5259*+*191*]. obedience:– obedience [11], obedient [2], obeying [1], obey [1]

5219 ὑπακούω, *hypakouō*, v. GK: *5634* [→ *5259*+*191*]. to obey, be obedient; to answer (the door):– obey [13], obeyed [5], obedient [2], hearken [1]

5220 ὕπανδρος, *hypandros*, a. GK: *5635* [→ *5259*+*435*]. married, legally bound to a man in marriage:– husband [1]

5221 ὑπαντάω, *hypantaō*, v. GK: *5636* [→ *5259*+*473*]. to go out to meet; to oppose:– met [4], went and met [1]

5222 ὑπάντησις, *hypantēsis*, n. GK: *5637* [→ *5259*+*473*]. meeting:– meet [1]

5223 ὕπαρξις, *hyparxis*, n. GK: *5638* [→ *5259*+*757*]. property, goods, possessions:– goods [1], substance [1]

5224 ὑπάρχοντα, *huparchonta*, v.ptcp. of *5225*. GK: *5639* [→ *5259*+*757*]. possessions, property:–

5225 ὑπάρχω, *hyparchō*, v. GK: *5639* [→ *5259*+*757*]. to have, possess; (n.) possessions; to be, exist:– being [13], was [8], be [7], goods [7], is [6], were [5], are [3], hath [2], have [2], after (+*5119*) [1], hast [1], live [1], possessed [1], possesseth [1], substance [1]

5226 ὑπείκω, *hypeikō*, v. GK: *5640* [→ *5259*+*1502*]. to submit, yield:– submit [1]

5227 ὑπεναντίος, *hypenantios*, a. GK: *5641* [→ *5259*+*1725*]. opposing, being against; (n.) enemy:– adversaries [1], contrary [1]

5228 ὑπέρ, *hyper*, pp. GK: *5642* [→ *5229, 5230, 5231, 5232, 5233, 5234, 5235, 5236, 5237, 5238, 5239, 5240, 5241, 5242, 5243, 5244, 5245, 5246, 5247, 5248, 5249, 5250, 5251, 5252, 5253*]. (acc.) above, beyond, more than; (gen.) for, in behalf of, for sake of; in place of:– for [104], above [12], of [12], for sake [7], more than [3], on behalf [3], very [3], than [2], beyond [1], by [1], hydrophobia [sic] [1], exceedingly (+*1537*+*4053*) [1], exceeding [1], for sakes [1], in behalf of [1], in

stead [1], more [1], on part [1], over [1], stead [1], toward [1], to [1]

5229 ὑπεραίρομαι, *hyperairomai*, v. GK: *5643* [→ *5228*+*142*]. to become conceited, exalt oneself:– exalted above measure [2], exalteth [1]

5230 ὑπέρακμος, *hyperakmos*, a. GK: *5644* [→ *5228*+*206*]. past one's prime, getting along in years:– pass the flower of age (+*1510*) [1]

5231 ὑπεράνω, *hyperanō*, adv. GK: *5645* [→ *5228*+*507*]. far above, high above:– far above [2], over [1]

5232 ὑπεραυξάνω, *hyperauxanō*, v. GK: *5647* [→ *5228*+*837*]. to grow more and more, increase abundantly:– groweth exceedingly [1]

5233 ὑπερβαίνω, *hyperbainō*, v. GK: *5648* [→ *5228*+*305*]. to wrong, transgress against, sin against:– go beyond [1]

5234 ὑπερβαλλόντως, *hyperballontōs*, adv. GK: *5649* [→ *5228*+*906*]. more severely, to a much greater degree:– above measure [1]

5235 ὑπερβάλλω, *hyperballō*, v. GK: *5650* [→ *5228*+*906*]. to go beyond, surpass, be incomparable:– exceeding [3], excelleth [1], passeth [1]

5236 ὑπερβολή, *hyperbolē*, n. GK: *5651* [→ *5228*+*906*]. all-surpassing, surpassing great, most excellent, beyond measure:– far more exceeding (+*1519*+*2596*+*5236*) [2], abundance [1], beyond measure (+*2596*) [1], exceeding (+*2596*) [1], excellency [1], more excellent (+*2596*) [1], out of measure (+*2596*) [1]

5237 ὑπερείδω, *hypereidō*, v. GK: *5653* [→ *5228*+*1491*]. to overlook, not punish:– winked at [1]

5238 ὑπερέκεινα, *hyperekeina*, adv. GK: *5654* [→ *5228*+*1563*]. beyond; (n.) regions beyond:– beyond [1]

5239 ὑπερεκτείνω, *hyperekteinō*, v. GK: *5657* [→ *1614*; cf. *5228*]. to go too far, overextend, stretch out beyond:– stretch beyond [1]

5240 ὑπερεκχύννω, *hyperekchynnō*, v. GK: *5658* [→ *1632*]. (pass.) to be running over, overflowing:– running over [1]

ὑπερεκπερισσοῦ, *huperekperissou*. See *5228* and **1537** and **4053**.

5241 ὑπερεντυγχάνω, *hyperentynchanō*, v. GK: *5659* [→ *5228*+*1722*+*5177*]. to intercede:– maketh intercession [1]

5242 ὑπερέχω, *hyperechō*, v. GK: *5660* [→ *5228*+*2192*]. to govern, have authority; to be better than, transcend; (n.) surpassing greatness:– better than [1], excellency [1], higher [1], passeth [1], supreme [1]

5243 ὑπερηφανία, *hyperēphania*, n. GK: *5661* [→ *5228*+*5316*]. arrogance, pride:– pride [1]

5244 ὑπερήφανος, *hyperēphanos*, a. GK: *5662* [→ *5228*+*5316*]. proud, arrogant:– proud [5]

ὑπερλίαν, *huperlian*. See *5228* and **3029**.

5245 ὑπερνικάω, *hypernikaō*, v. GK: *5664* [→ *5228*+*3529*]. to thoroughly conquer, go beyond conquest:– more than conquerors [1]

5246 ὑπέρογκος, *hyperonkos*, a. GK: *5665* [→ *5228*+*3591*]. boastful, bombastic:– great swelling [2]

5247 ὑπεροχή, *hyperochē*, n. GK: *5667* [→ *5228*+*2192*]. authority, superiority:– authority [1], excellency [1]

5248 ὑπερπερισσεύω, *hyperperisseuō*, v. GK: *5668* [→ *5228*+*4053*]. to increase all the more, exceed bounds, overflow:– exceeding [1], much more abound [1]

5249 ὑπερπερισσῶς, *hyperperissōs*, adv. GK: *5669* [→ *5228*+*4053*]. beyond all measure, exceedingly:– beyond measure [1]

5250 ὑπερπλεονάζω, *hyperpleonazō*, v. GK: *5670* [→ *5228*+*4137*]. to be (greatly) abundant:– exceeding abundant [1]

5251 ὑπερυψόω, *hyperypsoō*, v. GK: *5671* [→ *5228*+*5311*]. to exalt to the highest place:– highly exalted [1]

5252 ὑπερφρονέω, *hyperphroneō*, v. GK: *5672* [→ *5228*+*5424*]. to think too highly of oneself:– think highly [1]

5253 ὑπερῷον, *hyperōon*, n. GK: *5673* [→ *5228*]. upstairs room, upper story:– upper chamber [3], upper room [1]

5254 ὑπέχω, *hypechō*, v. GK: *5674* [→ *5259*+*2192*]. to experience:– suffering [1]

5255 ὑπήκοος, *hypēkoos*, a. GK: *5675* [→ *5259*+*191*]. obedient:– obedient [2], obey (+*1096*) [1]

5256 ὑπηρετέω, *hypēreteō*, v. GK: *5676* [→ *5257*]. to serve, care for needs:– ministered [1], minister [1], served [1]

5257 ὑπηρέτης, *hypēretēs*, n. GK: *5677* [→ *5256*; cf. *5259*]. servant, attendant, helper, one who serves or attends, not distinguished in status from other words for servant:– officers [10], servants [4], minister [3], ministers [2], officer [1]

5258 ὕπνος, *hypnos*, n. GK: *5678* [→ *69, 70, 879, 1797, 1798, 1852, 1853*]. sleep, slumber:– sleep [6]

5259 ὑπό, *hypo*, pp. GK: *5679* [→ *505, 506, 4391, 4942, 4943, 5217, 5218, 5219, 5220, 5221, 5222, 5223, 5224, 5225, 5226, 5227, 5254, 5255, 5260, 5261, 5262, 5263, 5264, 5265, 5266, 5267, 5268, 5269, 5270, 5271, 5272, 5273, 5274, 5275, 5276, 5277, 5278, 5279, 5280, 5281, 5282, 5283, 5284, 5285, 5286, 5287, 5288, 5289, 5290, 5291, 5292, 5293, 5294, 5295, 5296, 5297, 5298, 5299*; cf. *5257*]. (gen.) by, by means of; (acc.) under (in space as well as in status or authority); at (a time of day):– of [117], under [48], by [42], with [14], from [2], among [1], early in the morning (+*3588*+*3722*) [1], into [1], unto [1], whereof [1]

5260 ὑποβάλλω, *hypoballō*, v. GK: *5680* [→ *5259*+*906*]. to secretly persuade, instigate secretly:– suborned [1]

5261 ὑπογραμμός, *hypogrammos*, n. GK: *5681* [→ *5259*+*1125*]. example, model:– example [1]

5262 ὑπόδειγμα, *hypodeigma*, n. GK: *5682* [→ *5259*+*1164*]. example, model, pattern, copy:– example [4], ensample [1], patterns [1]

5263 ὑποδείκνυμι, *hypodeiknymi*, v. GK: *5683* & *5684* [→ *5259*+*1166*]. to show; to warn:– shew [2], warned [2], forewarn [1], shewed [1]

5264 ὑποδέχομαι, *hypodechomai*, v. GK: *5685* [→ *5259*+*1209*]. to welcome, receive as a guest:– received [4]

5265 ὑποδέω, *hypodeō*, v. GK: *5686* [→ *5259*+*1210*]. (mid.) to put on (sandals):– shod [2], bind on [1]

5266 ὑπόδημα, *hypodēma*, n. GK: *5687* [→ *5259*+*1210*]. sandal:– shoes [2], shoe's [1]

5267 ὑπόδικος, *hypodikos*, a. GK: *5688* [→ *5259*+*1349*]. accountable, answerable:– guilty before [1]

5268 ὑποζύγιον, *hypozygion*, n. GK: *5689* [→ *5259*+*2218*]. donkey:– ass [2]

5269 ὑποζώννυμι, *hypozōnnymi*, v. GK: *5690* [→ *5259*+*2224*]. to undergird, brace:– undergirding [1]

5270 ὑποκάτω, *hypokatō*, adv. GK: *5691* [→ *5259*+*2596*]. (pp.*) under:– under [9]

5271 ὑποκρίνομαι, *hypokrinomai*, v. GK: *5693* [→ *5259*+*2919*]. to pretend, make believe; see also *5273*:– feign [1]

5272 ὑπόκρισις, *hypokrisis*, n. GK: *5694* [→ *5259*+*2919*]. hypocrisy (an extension of an actor in a play, not found in the NT), implying arrogance and hardness of heart, utterly devoid of sincerity and genuineness:– hypocrisy [4], dissimulation [1], hypocrisies [1]

5273 ὑποκριτής, *hypokritēs*, n. GK: *5695* [→ *5259*+*2919*]. hypocrite (an extension of an actor in a play, not found in the NT), implying arrogance and hardness of heart, utterly devoid of sincerity and genuineness:– hypocrites [17], hypocrite [3]

5274 ὑπολαμβάνω, *hypolambanō*, v. GK: *5696* [→ *5259*+*2983*]. to take up; to show hospitality; to reply; to suppose, think, believe:– suppose [2], answering [1], received [1]

5275 ὑπολείπω, *hypoleipō*, v. GK: *5699* [→ *5259*+*3007*]. (pass.) to be left, remaining:– left [1]

5276 ὑπολήνιον, *hypolēnion*, n. GK: *5700* [→ *5259*+*3025*]. pit for a winepress:– winefat [1]

5277 ὑπολιμπάνω, *hypolimpanō*, v. GK: *5701* [→ *5259*+*3007*]. to leave behind:– leaving [1]

5278 ὑπομένω, *hypomenō*, v. GK: *5702* [→ *5259*+*3306*]. to stay behind; to stand firm, remain, persevere, endure:– endure [5], endured [3], endureth [3], take it patiently [2], abode still [1], patient [1], suffer [1], tarried behind [1]

5279 ὑπομιμνήσκω, *hypomimnēskō*, v. GK: *5703* [→ *5259*+*3421*]. to remind, call to mind; (pass.) to remember:– put in remembrance [3], bring to remembrance [1], put in mind [1], remembered [1], remember [1]

5280 ὑπόμνησις, **hypomnēsis**, n. GK: *5704* [→ *5259+3421*]. reminder, memory, remembrance:– remembrance [2], putting in remembrance [1]

5281 ὑπομονή, **hypomonē**, n. GK: *5705* [→ *5259+3306*]. perseverance, endurance, patience:– patience [29], enduring [1], patient continuance [1], patient waiting [1]

5282 ὑπονοέω, **hyponoeō**, v. GK: *5706* [→ *5259+3563*]. to think, suppose; expect; to sense, suspect:– deemed [1], supposed [1], think [1]

5283 ὑπόνοια, **hyponoia**, n. GK: *5707* [→ *5259+3563*]. suspicion:– surmisings [1]

5284 ὑποπλέω, **hypopleō**, v. GK: *5709* [→ *5259+4126*]. to sail to the lee of, to move to the side that offers protection or shelter:– sailed under [2]

5285 ὑποπνέω, **hypopneō**, v. GK: *5710* [→ *5259+4154*]. to blow gently (of wind):– blew softly [1]

5286 ὑποπόδιον, **hypopodion**, n. GK: *5711* [→ *5259+4228*]. footstool:– footstool [9]

5287 ὑπόστασις, **hypostasis**, n. GK: *5712* [→ *5259+2476*]. confidence, trust, being sure; being, essence:– confidence [2], confident [1], person [1], substance [1]

5288 ὑποστέλλω, **hypostellō**, v. GK: *5713* [→ *5259+4724*]. (act.) to draw back, withdraw; (mid.) to hesitate, shrink back:– draw back [1], kept back [1], shunned [1], withdrew [1]

5289 ὑποστολή, **hypostolē**, n. GK: *5714* [→ *5259+4724*]. shrinking back:– draw back [1]

5290 ὑποστρέφω, **hypostrephō**, v. GK: *5715* [→ *5259+4762*]. to turn back toward, return; to turn one's back on, turn away:– returned [24], return [5], returning [3], come again [1], turned back again [1], turned back [1]

5291 ὑποστρωννύω, **hypostrōnnyō**, v. GK: *5716* [→ *5259+4766*]. to spread out:– spread [1]

5292 ὑποταγή, **hypotagē**, n. GK: *5717* [→ *5259+5021*]. obedience, submission:– subjection [4]

5293 ὑποτάσσω, **hypotassō**, v. GK: *5718* [→ *5259+5021*]. to put in subjection, subject, subordinate; (pass.) to submit, be subject to:– subject [10], submit [6], put under [4], made subject [2], obedient [2], put in subjection [2], put [2], subject to [2], subjection [2], in subjection [1], put in subjection under [1], subdued [1], subdue [1], subjected [1], submitted [1], submitting [1], under obedience [1]

5294 ὑποτίθημι, **hypotithēmi**, v. GK: *5719* [→ *5259+5087*]. (act.) to risk, lay down (a life); (mid.) to point out, teach:– laid down [1], put in remembrance [1]

5295 ὑποτρέχω, **hypotrechō**, v. GK: *5720* [→ *5259+5143*]. to sail to the lee of, to move to the side that offers protection or shelter:– running under [1]

5296 ὑποτύπωσις, **hypotypōsis**, n. GK: *5721* [→ *5259+5180*]. example, pattern:– form [1], pattern [1]

5297 ὑποφέρω, **hypopherō**, v. GK: *5722* [→ *5259+5342*]. to endure, bear up under, stand up under:– bear [1], endured [1], endure [1]

5298 ὑποχωρέω, **hypochōreō**, v. GK: *5723* [→ *5259+5562*]. to withdraw, retreat:– went aside [1], withdrew [1]

5299 ὑπωπιάζω, **hypōpiazō**, v. GK: *5708 & 5724* [→ *5259+3708*]. to wear out, weaken; to beat up, treat roughly:– keep under [1], weary [1]

5300 ὗς, **hys**, n. GK: *5725*. female pig, sow:– sow [1]

5301 ὕσσωπος, **hyssōpos**, n. GK: *5727*. hyssop, highly aromatic leaves used in purification rites and at Passover:– hyssop [2]

5302 ὑστερέω, **hystereō**, v. GK: *5728* [→ *5306*]. to lack, be in need, destitute; to be inferior; to fall short:– behind [2], come short [2], lacked [2], wanted [2], come behind [1], destitute [1], fail [1], in want [1], lackest [1], lack [1], suffer need [1], worse [1]

5303 ὑστέρημα, **hysterēma**, n. GK: *5729* [→ *5306*]. what is lacking; poverty; what is needed:– lacking [3], want [3], behind [1], lack [1], penury [1]

5304 ὑστέρησις, **hysterēsis**, n. GK: *5730* [→ *5306*]. need, poverty, lack:– want [2]

5305 ὕστερον, **husteron**, a.neut. of *5306*. GK: *5731* [→ *5306*]. finally, last of all:–

5306 ὕστερος, **hysteros**, a. GK: *5731* [→ *5302, 5303, 5304, 5305*]. (comp.) later, second; (neu.) finally, last of all:– afterward [7], last [3], afterwards [1], at the last [1], latter [1]

5307 ὑφαντός, **hyphantos**, a. GK: *5733*. woven:– woven [1]

5308 ὑψηλός, **hypsēlos**, a. GK: *5734* [→ *5311*]. high, mighty; proud, arrogant; highly valued; (compar.) more exalted:– high [9], higher than [1], highly esteemed [1]

5309 ὑψηλοφρονέω, **hypsēlophroneō**, v. GK: *5735* [→ *5311+5424*]. to be arrogant, proud:– highminded [2]

5310 ὕψιστος, **hypsistos**, a. GK: *5736* [→ *5311*]. highest, most exalted; (as a title of God) the Most High:– highest [8], most high [5]

5311 ὕψος, **hypsos**, n. GK: *5737* [→ *5251, 5308, 5309, 5310, 5312, 5313*]. height, high position, heaven:– height [2], on high [2], exalted [1], high [1]

5312 ὑψόω, **hypsoō**, v. GK: *5738* [→ *5311*]. to lift up, elevate, exalt:– exalted [10], lift up [3], lifted up [3], exalteth [2], exalt [2]

5313 ὕψωμα, **hypsōma**, n. GK: *5739* [→ *5311*]. height; pretension:– height [1], high [1]

5314 φάγος, **phagos**, n. GK: *5741* [→ *4371; cf. 2068*]. glutton:– gluttonous [2]

5315 φάγω, **phagō**, v. GK: *2266* [→ *2068*]. to eat, consume, devour:– eat [88], eaten [5], meat [3], eating [1]

φαιλόνης, **phailonēs**. Alternate spelling of **5341**.

5316 φαίνω, **phainō**, v. GK: *5743* [→ *398, 852, 853, 854, 855, 1307, 1717, 1718, 2014, 2015, 2016, 2017, 2020, 2726, 4392, 4811, 5243, 5245, 5318, 5319, 5320, 5321, 5322, 5324, 5325, 5326, 5334?, 5335?, 5402, 5457, 5458, 5459, 5460, 5461, 5462*]. (act.) to shine, give light; (mid./pass.) to appear, be visible;:– appear [9], appeared [5], shineth [5], appeareth [3], shine [3], seen [2], seemed [1], shining [1], shone [1], think [1]

5317 Φάλεκ, **Phalek**, n.pr. GK: *5744*. Peleg, "*water canal*":– Phalec [1]

5318 φανερός, **phaneros**, a. GK: *5745* [→ *5316*]. visible, clear, plain, known:– manifest [9], known [3], openly (+*1722*) [3], abroad (+*1519*) [2], appear [1], outward (+*1722+3588*) [1], outwardly (+*1722+3588*) [1], spread abroad [1]

5319 φανερόω, **phaneroō**, v. GK: *5746* [→ *5316*]. (act.) to reveal, make known, show; (pass.) to appear, be disclosed, displayed, revealed:– made manifest [15], appear [9], manifested [9], shewed [4], appeared [3], make manifest [3], manifest [2], maketh manifest [1], manifested forth [1], manifestly declared [1], shew [1]

5320 φανερῶς, **phanerōs**, adv. GK: *5747* [→ *5316*]. openly, publicly:– openly [2], evidently [1]

5321 φανέρωσις, **phanerōsis**, n. GK: *5748* [→ *5316*]. manifestation, disclosure, revelation:– manifestation [2]

5322 φανός, **phanos**, n. GK: *5749* [→ *5316*]. torch, lantern:– lanterns [1]

5323 Φανουήλ, **Phanouēl**, n.pr. GK: *5750*. Phanuel, "*face of God [El]*":– Phanuel [1]

5324 φαντάζω, **phantazō**, v. GK: *5751* [→ *5316*]. (pass.) to become visible; (n.) a sight:– sight [1]

5325 φαντασία, **phantasia**, n. GK: *5752* [→ *5316*]. pomp, pageantry:– pomp [1]

5326 φάντασμα, **phantasma**, n. GK: *5753* [→ *5316*]. ghost, apparition, transliterated as "phantasm":– spirit [2]

5327 φάραγξ, **pharanx**, n. GK: *5754*. valley, ravine:– valley [1]

5328 Φαραώ, **Pharaō**, n.pr. GK: *5755*. Pharaoh, "*the great house*":– Pharaoh [3], Pharaoh's [2]

5329 Φαρές, **Phares**, n.pr. GK: *5756*. Perez, "*breaking out*":– Phares [3]

5330 Φαρισαῖος, **Pharisaios**, n.pr. GK: *5757*. Pharisee, "*separate ones*":– Pharisees [86], Pharisee [11], Pharisee's [2], Pharisees' [1]

5331 φαρμακεία, **pharmakeia**, n. GK: *5758* [→ *5332, 5333*]. witchcraft, magic, the use of spells and potions of magic, often involving drugs:– sorceries [2], witchcraft [1]

5332 φαρμακεύς, **pharmakeus**, n. GK: *5759* [→ *5331*]. magician, sorcerer:– sorcerers [1]

5333 φάρμακος, **pharmakos**, n. GK: *5761* [→ *5331*]. one who practices magical arts, magician:– sorcerers [1]

5334 φάσις, **phasis**, n. GK: *5762* [→ *5346 or 5316*]. news, report:– tidings [1]

5335 φάσκω, **phaskō**, v. GK: *5763* [→ *5346 or 5316*]. to claim, assert:– affirmed [1], professing [1], saying [1], say [1]

5336 φάτνη, **phatnē**, n. GK: *5764*. manger, stall:– manger [3], stall [1]

5337 φαῦλος, **phaulos**, a. GK: *5765*. evil, bad:– evil [4]

5338 φέγγος, **phengos**, n. GK: *5766*. light, radiance:– light [3]

5339 φείδομαι, **pheidomai**, v. GK: *5767* [→ *857, 5340*]. to spare, refrain from:– spared [4], spare [4], forbear [1], sparing [1]

5340 φειδομένως, **pheidomenōs**, adv. GK: *5768* [→ *5339*]. sparingly:– sparingly [2]

5341 φελόνης, **phelonēs**; or φαιλόνης, **phailonēs**, n. GK: *5742 & 5769*. cloak:– cloke [1]

5342 φέρω, **pherō**, v. GK: *5770* [→ *399, 667, 670, 959, 1308, 1313, 1336, 1533, 1627, 2018, 2164, 2287, 2592, 2593, 2702, 3683, 3911, 3923, 4064, 4135, 4136, 4216, 4374, 4376, 4393, 4851, 5052, 5159, 5297, 5409, 5411, 5412, 5413, 5414, 5459*]. to bring, bear, carry; lead:– brought [16], bring [14], bear [4], bringing [3], came [3], beareth [2], bring forth [2], bringeth forth [2], reach [2], bare [1], bearing [1], be [1], bring hither [1], brought forth [1], carry [1], driven [1], endured [1], endure [1], go on [1], laid [1], leadeth [1], let drive (+*1929*) [1], moved [1], rushing [1], upholding [1]

5343 φεύγω, **pheugō**, v. GK: *5771* [→ *668, 1309, 1628, 2703, 5437*]. flee, escape, elude:– flee [15], fled [11], escaped [2], fleeth [2], escape [1]

5344 Φῆλιξ, **Phēlix**, n.pr. GK: *5772*. Felix, "*fortunate, lucky*":– Felix [8], Felix' [1]

5345 φήμη, **phēmē**, n. GK: *5773* [→ *5346*]. news, report:– fame [2]

5346 φημί, **phēmi**, v. GK: *5774* [→ *1310, 2162, 2163, 4394, 4852, 5334?, 5335?, 5345; cf. 987, 1426, 4394*]. to say, declare, affirm:– said [47], saith [5], say [5], affirm [1]

5347 Φῆστος, **Phēstos**, n.pr. GK: *5776*. Festus, "*festal, joyful*":– Festus [12], Festus' [1]

5348 φθάνω, **phthanō**, v. GK: *5777* [→ *4372?, 4373?, 4399*]. to precede; to arrive, attain, come:– come [4], attained [2], prevent [1]

5349 φθαρτός, **phthartos**, a. GK: *5778* [→ *5351*]. perishable, not lasting, mortal:– corruptible [6]

5350 φθέγγομαι, **phthengomai**, v. GK: *5779* [→ *669, 5353*]. to speak, proclaim:– speak [2], speaking [1]

5351 φθείρω, **phtheirō**, v. GK: *5780* [→ *90, 861, 862, 1311, 1312, 2704, 5349, 5352, 5356*]. to destroy, corrupt; (pass.) to be corrupted, destroyed, perish; to be led astray:– corrupt [4], corrupted [2], defile [1], destroy [1]

5352 φθινοπωρινός, **phthinopōrinos**, a. GK: *5781* [→ *5351+3703*]. pertaining to the (late) autumn:– fruit withereth [1]

5353 φθόγγος, **phthongos**, n. GK: *5782* [→ *5350*]. voice, sound; note, musical tone:– sounds [1], sound [1]

5354 φθονέω, **phthoneō**, v. GK: *5783* [→ *5355*]. to envy, be jealous of:– envying [1]

5355 φθόνος, **phthonos**, n. GK: *5784* [→ *5354*]. envy:– envy [7], envies [1], envyings [1]

5356 φθορά, **phthora**, n. GK: *5785* [→ *5351*]. perishableness, destruction, corruption; depravity:– corruption [7], destroyed [1], perish [1]

5357 φιάλη, **phialē**, n. GK: *5786*. bowl:– vial [7], vials [5]

5358 φιλάγαθος, **philagathos**, a. GK: *5787* [→ *5384+18*]. loving what is good:– lover of good [1]

5359 Φιλαδέλφεια, **Philadelpheia**, n.pr. GK: *5788* [→ *5384+80; cf. 1.3*]. Philadelphia, "*love of brother/sister*":– Philadelphia [2]

5360 φιλαδελφία, **philadelphia**, n. GK: *5789* [→ *5384+80; cf. 1.3*]. brotherly love; brotherly kindness:– brotherly love [3], brotherly kindness [2], love of brethren [1]

5361 φιλάδελφος, **philadelphos**, a. GK: *5790* [→ *5384+80; cf. 1.3*]. loving as brothers:– love as brethren [1]

5362 φίλανδρος, **philandros**, a. GK: *5791* [→ *5384+435*]. loving one's husband:– love husbands (+*1510*) [1]

5363 φιλανθρωπία, **philanthrōpia**, n. GK: *5792* [→ *5384+444*]. love, kindness:– kindness [1], love toward man [1]

5364 φιλανθρώπως, *philanthrōpōs*, adv. GK: *5793* [→ *5384+444*]. in kindness, kindly:– courteously [1]

5365 φιλαργυρία, *philargyria*, n. GK: *5794* [→ *5384+696*]. love of money, avarice, greed:– love of money [1]

5366 φιλάργυρος, *philargyros*, a. GK: *5795* [→ *5384+696*]. money-loving, avaricious, greedy:– covetous [2]

5367 φίλαυτος, *philautos*, a. GK: *5796* [→ *5384+846*]. loving oneself, selfish:– lovers of own selves [1]

5368 φιλέω, *phileō*, v. GK: *5797* [→ *5384*]. to love, to have affection and regard of a very high order, not unlike *26*, and overlapping in meaning in some contexts:– love [10], loveth [6], kiss [3], loved [3], lovest [3]

5369 φιληδονος, *philēdonos*, a. GK: *5798* [→ *5384+2237*]. loving pleasure:– lovers of pleasures [1]

5370 φίλημα, *philēma*, n. GK: *5799* [→ *5384*]. kiss:– kiss [7]

5371 Φιλήμων, *Philēmōn*, n.pr. GK: *5800* [→ *5384*]. Philemon, "*beloved*":– Philemon [2]

5372 Φίλητος, *Philētos*, n.pr. GK: *5801* [→ *5384*]. Philetus, "*beloved*":– Philetus [1]

5373 φιλία, *philia*, n. GK: *5802* [→ *5384*]. friendship, love:– friendship [1]

5374 Φιλιππήσιος, *Philippēsios*, n.pr.g. GK: *5803* [→ *5384+2462*]. Philippian:– Philippians [2]

5375 Φίλιπποι, *Philippoi*, n.pr. GK: *5804* [→ *5384+2462*]. Philippi:– Philippi [6]

5376 Φίλιππος, *Philippos*, n.pr. GK: *5805* [→ *5384+2462*]. Philip, "*horse lover*":– Philip [33], Philip's [3], Philippi [2]

5377 φιλόθεος, *philotheos*, a. GK: *5806* [→ *5384+2316*]. loving God:– lovers of God [1]

5378 Φιλόλογος, *Philologos*, n.pr. GK: *5807* [→ *5384+3004*]. Philologus, "*lover of words [education]*":– Philologus [1]

5379 φιλονεικία, *philoneikia*, n. GK: *5808* [→ *5380*; cf. *5384*]. dispute, strife:– strife [1]

5380 φιλόνεικος, *philoneikos*, a. GK: *5809* [→ *5379*]. contentious, quarrelsome:– contentious [1]

5381 φιλοξενία, *philoxenia*, n. GK: *5810* [→ *5384+3581*]. hospitality, entertainment of strangers:– entertain strangers [1], hospitality [1]

5382 φιλόξενος, *philoxenos*, a. GK: *5811* [→ *5384+3581*]. hospitable:– given to hospitality [1], hospitality [1], lover of hospitality [1]

5383 φιλοπρωτεύω, *philoprōteuō*, v. GK: *5812* [→ *5384+4413*]. to love to be first:– loveth to have preeminence among [1]

5384 φίλος, *philos*, a. GK: *5813* [→ *865, 866, 2321, 2705, 4375, 5358, 5359, 5360, 5361, 5362, 5363, 5364, 5365, 5366, 5367, 5368, 5369, 5370, 5371, 5372, 5373, 5374, 5375, 5376, 5377, 5378, 5381, 5382, 5383, 5385, 5386, 5387, 5388, 5389, 5390, 5391; cf. 5379*]. (a.) friendly; (n.) friend (male or female):– friends [17], friend [12]

5385 φιλοσοφία, *philosophia*, n. GK: *5814* [→ *5384+4680*]. philosophy, human wisdom:– philosophy [1]

5386 φιλόσοφος, *philosophos*, n. GK: *5815* [→ *5384+4680*]. philosopher:– philosophers [1]

5387 φιλόστοργος, *philostorgos*, a. GK: *5816* [→ *5384*]. devoted, loving dearly:– kindly affectioned [1]

5388 φιλότεκνος, *philoteknos*, a. GK: *5817* [→ *5384+5088*]. loving one's children:– love children [1]

5389 φιλοτιμέομαι, *philotimeomai*, v. GK: *5818* [→ *5384+5092*]. to have an ambition, aspire to a goal:– labour [1], strived [1], study [1]

5390 φιλοφρόνως, *philophronōs*, adv. GK: *5819* [→ *5384+5424*]. hospitably, in a friendly manner:– courteously [1]

5391 φιλόφρων, *philophrōn*, a. GK: *5820* [→ *5384+5424*]. well disposed, friendly, kind:– courteous [1]

5392 φιμόω, *phimoō*, v. GK: *5821*. to muzzle; to silence; (pass.) to be quiet:– hold peace [2], muzzle [2], put to silence [2], speechless [1], still [1]

5393 Φλέγων, *Phlegōn*, n.pr.c. GK: *5823* [→ *5395*]. Phlegon, "*burning*":– Phlegon [1]

5394 φλογίζω, *phlogizō*, v. GK: *5824* [→ *5395*]. to set on fire:– set on fire [1], setteth on fire [1]

5395 φλόξ, *phlox*, n. GK: *5825* [→ *5393, 5394*]. flame, blaze:– flame [6], flaming [1]

5396 φλυαρέω, *phlyareō*, v. GK: *5826* [→ *5397*]. to gossip, talk nonsense:– prating against [1]

5397 φλύαρος, *phlyaros*, a. GK: *5827* [→ *3632, 5396*]. gossipy:– tattlers [1]

5398 φοβερός, *phoberos*, a. GK: *5829* [→ *5401*]. fearful, dreadful, terrible:– fearful [2], terrible [1]

5399 φοβέω, *phobeō*, v. GK: *5828 & 5830* [→ *5401*]. to fear, be afraid, alarmed, in some contexts improper and an impediment to faith and love; to reverence, respect, worship, in other contexts a proper fear for God, a deep reverence and awe:– fear [35], afraid [28], feared [17], fearing [6], feareth [4], afraid (+*5401*) [1], feared (+*5401*) [1], reverence [1]

5400 φόβητρον, *phobētron*, n. GK: *5831* [→ *5401*]. fearful event:– fearful sights [1]

5401 φόβος, *phobos*, n. GK: *5832* [→ *870, 1629, 1630, 1719, 5398, 5399, 5400*]. fear, terror; respect, reverence:– fear [40], terror [3], afraid (+*5399*) [1], fear (+*2192*) [1], feared (+*5399*) [1], fears [1]

5402 Φοίβη, *Phoibē*, n.pr. GK: *5833* [→ *5316*]. Phoebe, "*radiant*":– Phebe [2]

5403 Φοινίκη, *Phoinikē*, n.pr. GK: *5834* [→ *5404*]. Phoenicia, "*land of purple [dye]; poss. land of date palms*":– Phenice [2], Phenicia [1]

5404 φοῖνιξ¹, *phoinix¹*, n. GK: *5836* [→ *4949, 5403, 5405*]. palm tree, palm branch:– palm trees [1], palms [1]

5405 Φοῖνιξ², *Phoinix²*, n.pr. GK: *5837* [→ *5404*]. Phoenix:– Phenice [1]

5406 φονεύς, *phoneus*, n. GK: *5838* [→ *5408*]. murderer:– murderers [4], murderer [2], murderer (+*435*) [1]

5407 φονεύω, *phoneuō*, v. GK: *5839* [→ *5408*]. to commit murder, kill:– kill [8], killed [2], murder [1], slew [1]

5408 φόνος, *phonos*, n. GK: *5840* [→ *409, 4372?, 4373?, 5406, 5407*]. murder, killing:– murders [4], murder [4], slain (+*599*) [1], slaughter [1]

5409 φορέω, *phoreō*, v. GK: *5841* [→ *5342*]. to wear, bear:– beareth [1], bear [1], borne [1], weareth [1], wearing [1], wear [1]

5410 φόρον, *phoron*, n. GK: *5842*. forum, used only as a compound proper name "Forum of Appius," a market town south of Rome:– forum [1]

5411 φόρος, *phoros*, n. GK: *5843* [→ *5342*]. tax:– tribute [5]

5412 φορτίζω, *phortizō*, v. GK: *5844* [→ *5342*]. to load down (with a burden); (pass.) to be burdened:– heavy laden [1], lade [1]

5413 φορτίον, *phortion*, n. GK: *5845* [→ *5342*]. burden, load, cargo:– burdens [3], burden [2]

5414 φόρτος, *phortos*, n. GK: *5846* [→ *5342*]. cargo:– lading [1]

5415 Φορτουνᾶτος, *Phortounatos*, n.pr. GK: *5847*. Fortunatus, "*fortunate*":– Fortunatus [2]

5416 φραγέλλιον, *phragellion*, n. GK: *5848* [→ *5417*]. whip:– scourge [1]

5417 φραγελλόω, *phragelloō*, v. GK: *5849* [→ *5416*]. to flog:– scourged [1]

5418 φραγμός, *phragmos*, n. GK: *5850* [→ *5420*]. barrier, wall, country lane:– hedged [1], hedges [1], hedge [1], partition [1]

5419 φράζω, *phrazō*, v. GK: *5851*. to explain, interpret:– declare [2]

5420 φράσσω, *phrassō*, v. GK: *5852* [→ *5418*]. to shut; (pass.) to be stopped, silenced:– stopped [2], stop [1]

5421 φρέαρ, *phrear*, n. GK: *5853*. well, shaft, Abyss:– pit [5], well [2]

5422 φρεναπατάω, *phrenapataō*, v. GK: *5854* [→ *5424+539*]. to deceive:– deceiveth [1]

5423 φρεναπάτης, *phrenapatēs*, n. GK: *5855* [→ *5424+539*]. deceiver:– deceivers [1]

5424 φρήν, *phrēn*, n. GK: *5856* [→ *877, 878, 3675, 4065, 5012, 5252, 5309, 5390, 5391, 5422, 5423, 5426, 5427, 5428, 5429, 5430, 5431; cf. 2165, 2706, 3912, 4993*]. (pl.) thinking, understanding:– understanding [2]

5425 φρίσσω, *phrissō*, v. GK: *5857*. to shudder:– tremble [1]

5426 φρονέω, *phroneō*, v. GK: *5858* [→ *5424*]. to think, regard, hold an opinion; to set one's mind on; to have a (certain) attitude:– mind [9], think [4], minded [3], regardeth [3], likeminded (+*846+3588*) [2], savourest [2], careful [1], care [1], regard [1], set affection on [1], thinkest [1], understood [1]

5427 φρόνημα, *phronēma*, n. GK: *5859* [→ *5424*]. mind:– minded [2], mind [2]

5428 φρόνησις, *phronēsis*, n. GK: *5860* [→ *5424*]. wisdom, understanding:– prudence [1], wisdom [1]

5429 φρόνιμος, *phronimos*, a. GK: *5861* [→ *5424*]. wise, sensible, shrewd; conceited:– wise [13], wiser [1]

5430 φρονίμως, *phronimōs*, adv. GK: *5862* [→ *5424*]. shrewdly, wisely:– wisely [1]

5431 φροντίζω, *phrontizō*, v. GK: *5863* [→ *5424*]. to be careful, concerned:– careful [1]

5432 φρουρέω, *phroureō*, v. GK: *5864* [→ *4253+3708*]. to guard; (pass.) to be held prisoner; to be shielded:– kept [3], keep [1]

5433 φρυάσσω, *phryassō*, v. GK: *5865*. to rage, rave:– rage [1]

5434 φρύγανον, *phryganon*, n. GK: *5866*. brushwood, firewood:– sticks [1]

5435 Φρυγία, *Phrygia*, n.pr. GK: *5867*. Phrygia:– Phrygia [4]

5436 Φύγελος, *Phygelos*, n.pr. GK: *5869*. Phygelus, "*fugitive*":– Phygellus [1]

5437 φυγή, *phygē*, n. GK: *5870* [→ *5343*]. flight, fleeing:– flight [2]

5438 φυλακή, *phylakē*, n. GK: *5871* [→ *5442*]. prison, jail, haunt; guard; watch (of the night):– prison [33], watch [5], prisons [3], cage [1], hold [1], imprisonments [1], imprisonment [1], keeping watch (+*5442*) [1], ward [1]

5439 φυλακίζω, *phylakizō*, v. GK: *5872* [→ *5442*]. to imprison:– imprisoned [1]

5440 φυλακτήριον, *phylaktērion*, n. GK: *5873* [→ *5442*]. phylactery, a small box containing Scripture verses, traditionally bound on the forehead and arm by the Jews during prayer:– phylacteries [1]

5441 φύλαξ, *phylax*, n. GK: *5874* [→ *5442*]. guard, sentry:– keepers [3]

5442 φυλάσσω, *phylassō*, v. GK: *5875* [→ *1049, 1200, 1314, 5438, 5439, 5440, 5441*]. to obey, keep; to guard, watch; to keep away from, abstain:– keep [11], kept [8], beware [2], keep from [2], be ware [1], keepest [1], keepeth [1], keeping watch (+*5438*) [1], observed [1], observe [1], saved [1]

5443 φυλή, *phylē*, n. GK: *5876* [→ *246, 1429, 4853; cf. 5453*]. tribe; people, nation:– tribe [19], tribes [6], kindreds [4], kindred [2]

5444 φύλλον, *phyllon*, n. GK: *5877*. leaf:– leaves [6]

5445 φύραμα, *phyrama*, n. GK: *5878*. lump (of clay), batch (of dough); derived from a Greek verb, "to mix (wet or dry) substances," not found in the NT:– lump [5]

5446 φυσικός, *physikos*, a. GK: *5879* [→ *5453*]. pertaining to things of nature: natural, instinctive; (n.) creatures of instinct:– natural [3]

5447 φυσικῶς, *physikōs*, adv. GK: *5880* [→ *5453*]. by instinct, naturally:– naturally [1]

5448 φυσιόω, *physioō*, v. GK: *5881* [→ *5453*]. to puff up, inflate; (pass.) to be proud, arrogant:– puffed up [5], puffeth up [1], puft up [1]

5449 φύσις, *physis*, n. GK: *5882* [→ *5453*]. nature; natural state of being or characteristics:– nature [10], natural (+*2596*) [2], kind [1]

5450 φυσίωσις, *physiōsis*, n. GK: *5883* [→ *5453*]. arrogance, pride:– swellings [1]

5451 φυτεία, *phyteia*, n. GK: *5884* [→ *5453*]. plant:– plant [1]

5452 φυτεύω, *phyteuō*, v. GK: *5885* [→ *5453*]. to plant:– planted [8], planteth [3]

5453 φύω, *phyō*, v. GK: *5886* [→ *1631, 1720, 1721, 3504, 3828, 4854, 4855, 5446, 5447, 5448, 5449, 5450, 5451, 5452; cf. 5443*]. to grow up, come up, referring to plant growth:– sprang up [1], springing [1], sprung up [1]

5454 φωλεός, *phōleos*, n. GK: *5887*. hole (in the ground), den:– holes [2]

5455 φωνέω, *phōneō*, v. GK: *5888* [→ *5456*]. to call (out), summon:– called [16], crow [7], crew [5], cried [5], call [4], calleth [3], calleth for [1], calling [1]

5456 φωνή, *phōnē*, n. GK: *5889* [→ *219, 400, 800, 880, 2019, 2757, 4377, 4856, 4857, 4858, 4859, 5455*]. voice, sound, tone, noise of any kind; by extension: speaking, language:– voice [116], voices [15], sound [8], noise [1], was noised abroad (+*1096+3588*) [1]

5457 φῶς, *phōs*, n. GK: *5890* [→ *5316*]. light; daylight; firelight:– light [67], fire [2], lights [1]

5458 φωστήρ, *phōstēr*, n. GK: *5891* [→ *5316*]. star; brilliance, splendor:– lights [1], light [1]

5459 φωσφόρος, *phōsphoros*, a. GK: *5892* [→ *5316+5342*]. light-bearing; (n.) morning star, likely referring to the planet Venus:– day star [1]

5460 φωτεινός, *phōteinos*, a. GK: *5893* [→ *5316*]. full of light; bright:– full of light [4], bright [1]

5461 φωτίζω, *phōtizō*, v. GK: *5894* [→ *5316*]. to give light, shine; (pass.) to be enlightened, illuminated:– enlightened [2], bring to light [1], brought to light [1], give light [1], giveth light [1], illuminated [1], lightened [1], lighten [1], lighteth [1], make see [1]

5462 φωτισμός, *phōtismos*, n. GK: *5895* [→ *5316*]. light, illumination:– light [2]

5463 χαίρω, *chairō*, v. GK: *5897* [→ *884, 2168, 2169, 2170, 4796, 5479, 5483, 5484, 5485, 5486, 5487*]. to rejoice, be glad, delighted; (as a greeting) Hail!, Greetings!:– rejoice [26], glad [14], rejoiced [8], hail [6], rejoicing [5], greeting [3], joy [3], God speed [2], rejoiceth [2], farewell [1], joyed [1], joyfully [1], joying [1], rejoiceth greatly (+*5479*) [1]

5464 χάλαζα, *chalaza*, n. GK: *5898*. hail, hailstorm, hailstone:– hail [4]

5465 χαλάω, *chalaō*, v. GK: *5899* [→ *5468, 5469*]. to lower, let down:– let down [5], let down (+*2524*) [1], strake [1]

5466 Χαλδαῖος, *Chaldaios*, n.pr.g. GK: *5900*. Chaldean:– Chaldeans [1]

5467 χαλεπός, *chalepos*, a. GK: *5901*. difficult, harsh; violent:– fierce [1], perilous [1]

5468 χαλιναγωγέω, *chalinagōgeō*, v. GK: *5902* [→ *5465+71*]. to keep in check, keep a rein on one's mouth:– bridleth [1], bridle [1]

5469 χαλινός, *chalinos*, n. GK: *5903* [→ *5465*]. bit, bridle:– bits [1], bridles [1]

5470 χάλκεος, *chalkeos*, a. GK: *5905 & 5911* [→ *5475*]. made of bronze:– brass [1]

5471 χαλκεύς, *chalkeus*, n. GK: *5906* [→ *5475*]. metalworker:– coppersmith [1]

5472 χαλκηδών, *chalkēdōn*, n. GK: *5907* [→ *5475*]. chalcedony:– chalcedony [1]

5473 χαλκίον, *chalkion*, n. GK: *5908* [→ *5475*]. (copper or bronze) kettle:– brasen vessels [1]

5474 χαλκολίβανον, *chalkolibanon*, n. GK: *5909* [→ *5475*]. burnished bronze, fine bronze:– fine brass [2]

5475 χαλκός, *chalkos*, n. GK: *5910* [→ *5470, 5471, 5472, 5473, 5474*]. copper, bronze; objects of copper:– brass [3], money [2]

5476 χαμαί, *chamai*, adv. GK: *5912*. to the ground, on the ground:– on the ground [1], to the ground [1]

5477 Χανάαν, *Chanaan*, n.pr. GK: *5913* [→ *5478*]. Canaan, "*land of purple* hence *merchant trader*":– Canaan [2]

5478 Χαναναῖος, *Chananaios*, a.pr.g. GK: *5914* [→ *5477*]. Canaanite:– of Canaan [1]

5479 χαρά, *chara*, n. GK: *5915* [→ *5463*]. joy, rejoicing, happiness, gladness:– joy [52], gladness [3], joyfully (+*3326*) [1], joyfulness [1], joyful [1], joyous [1], rejoiceth greatly (+*5463*) [1]

5480 χάραγμα, *charagma*, n. GK: *5916* [→ *5481, 5482, 5489*]. mark, stamp; image, idol:– mark [8], graven [1]

5481 χαρακτήρ, *charaktēr*, n. GK: *5917* [→ *5480*]. exact representation, reproduction:– express image [1]

5482 χάραξ, *charax*, n. GK: *5918* [→ *5480*]. barricade, palisade (a defensive line or fence):– trench [1]

5483 χαρίζομαι, *charizomai*, v. GK: *5919* [→ *5463*]. to give grace; to forgive, cancel (a debt); to grant; to hand over into custody:– forgave [4], given [4], forgive [3], deliver [2],

forgiven [2], forgiving [2], gave [2], frankly forgave [1], freely given [1], freely give [1], granted [1]

5484 χάριν, *charin*, c. or pp.*. GK: *5920* [→ *5463*]. therefore, because of this, for this reason:– for cause [3], because of [2], for sake [1], to [1], wherefore (+*3739*) [1], wherefore (+*5101*) [1]

5485 χάρις, *charis*, n. GK: *5921* [→ *5463*]. grace, the state of kindness and favor toward someone, often with a focus on a benefit given to the object; by extension: gift, benefit; credit; words of kindness and benefit: thanks, blessing:– grace [130], favour [6], thanks [4], thank (+*2192*) [3], thank [3], pleasure [2], acceptable [1], benefit [1], gift [1], gracious [1], liberality [1], thanked [1], thankworthy [1]

5486 χάρισμα, *charisma*, n. GK: *5922* [→ *5463*]. gracious gift; see also *5485*:– gift [8], gifts [7], free gift [2]

5487 χαριτόω, *charitoō*, v. GK: *5923* [→ *5463*]. to give graciously, to show acts of kindness by freely giving; (n.) one highly favored; see also *5485*:– highly favoured [1], made accepted [1]

5488 Χαρράν, *Charran*, n.pr. GK: *5924*. Haran, "[earlier] *mountaineer*; perhaps *sanctuary*":– Charran [2]

5489 χάρτης, *chartēs*, n. GK: *5925* [→ *5480*]. (papyrus) paper:– paper [1]

5490 χάσμα, *chasma*, n. GK: *5926*. chasm:– gulf [1]

5491 χεῖλος, *cheilos*, n. GK: *5927*. lip; edge (of a shoreline):– lips [6], shore [1]

5492 χειμάζω, *cheimazō*, v. GK: *5928* [→ *5494*]. (pass.) to be battered in a storm:– tossed with a tempest [1]

5493 χείμαρρος, *cheimarros*, n. GK: *5929* [→ *5494+4482*]. valley, ravine, wadi:– brook [1]

5494 χειμών, *cheimōn*, n. GK: *5930* [→ *5492, 5493*]. winter; stormy weather:– winter [4], foul weather [1], tempest [1]

5495 χείρ, *cheir*, n. GK: *5931* [→ *849, 886, 1315, 2021, 4400, 5496, 5497, 5498, 5499; cf. 4401, 5500*]. hand, area or portion of the hand; power, control:– hands [90], hand [88], by (+*1223*) [1]

5496 χειραγωγέω, *cheiragōgeō*, v. GK: *5932* [→ *5495+71*]. to lead by the hand:– led by the hand [2]

5497 χειραγωγός, *cheiragōgos*, n. GK: *5933* [→ *5495+71*]. someone who leads by the hand, leader:– lead by the hand [1]

5498 χειρόγραφον, *cheirographon*, n. GK: *5934* [→ *5495+1125*]. written code, record of debt:– handwriting [1]

5499 χειροποίητος, *cheiropoiētos*, a. GK: *5935* [→ *5495+4160*]. hand-made, man-made:– made with hands [5], made by hands [1]

5500 χειροτονέω, *cheirotoneō*, v. GK: *5936* [→ *1614; cf. 5495*]. to appoint, choose:– ordained [3], chosen [1]

5501 χείρων, *cheirōn*, a. GK: *5937*. worse (than); more severe than:– worse than [5], worse [4], sorer [1], worse and worse (+*1909+3588*) [1]

5502 Χερούβ, *Cheroub*, n.pr. GK: *5938*. (pl.) cherubim:– cherubims [1]

5503 χήρα, *chēra*, n. GK: *5939*. widow:– widow [13], widows [11], widows' [3]

5504 χθές, *chthes*, adv. GK: *5940*. yesterday:– yesterday [3]

5505 χιλιάς, *chilias*, n. GK: *5942* [→ *5507*]. thousand:– thousand [21], thousands [2]

5506 χιλίαρχος, *chiliarchos*, n. GK: *5941* [→ *5507+757*]. military officer, commander; technically an officer of 1,000 soldiers; in the ancient Roman military an officer of a cohort, one tenth of a legion, about 600 soldiers:– chief captain [17], chief captains [2], captains [1], captain [1], high captains [1]

5507 χίλιοι, *chilioi*, a.num. GK: *5943* [→ *1367, 2035, 4000, 5070, 5153, 5506, 5505*]. thousand:– thousand [11]

5508 Χίος, *Chios*, n.pr. GK: *5944*. Kios:– Chios [1]

5509 χιτών, *chitōn*, n. GK: *5945*. tunic, robe, clothing, undergarment:– coats [5], coat [4], clothes [1], garment [1]

5510 χιών, *chiōn*, n. GK: *5946* [→ *3914, 3915*]. snow:– snow [3]

5511 χλαμύς, *chlamys*, n. GK: *5948*. robe, cloak, a heavy outer garment used by soldiers and travelers:– robe [2]

5512 χλευάζω, *chleuazō*, v. GK: *5949*. to sneer, mock, scoff:– mocked [1], mocking [1]

5513 χλιαρός, *chliaros*, a. GK: *5950*. lukewarm:– lukewarm [1]

5514 Χλόη, *Chloē*, n.pr. GK: *5951* [→ *5515*]. Chloe, "*tender shoot*":– Chloe [1]

5515 χλωρός, *chlōros*, a. GK: *5952* [→ *5514*]. light green; pale; (n.) green plant:– green [3], pale [1]

5516 χξϛ', *chi xi stigma*, n.num. GK: *5953*. 666:– six hundred threescore six [1]

5517 χοϊκός, *choikos*, a. GK: *5954* [→ *1632*]. made of dust, of the earth:– earthy [4]

5518 χοῖνιξ, *choinix*, n. GK: *5955*. (almost one liter or) quart:– measures [1], measure [1]

5519 χοῖρος, *choiros*, n. GK: *5956*. pig:– swine [14]

5520 χολάω, *cholaō*, v. GK: *5957* [→ *5521*]. to be angry:– angry [1]

5521 χολή, *cholē*, n. GK: *5958* [→ *5520*]. gall, bile:– gall [2]

5522 χόος, *choos*, n. GK: *5959* [→ *1632*]. dust:– dust [2]

5523 Χοραζίν, *Chorazin*, n.pr. GK: *5960 & 6002*. Korazin:– Chorazin [2]

5524 χορηγέω, *chorēgeō*, v. GK: *5961* [→ *5525+71*]. to supply, provide:– giveth [1], minister [1]

5525 χορός, *choros*, n. GK: *5962* [→ *2023, 2024, 4402, 5524*]. dance; (pl.) dancing:– dancing [1]

5526 χορτάζω, *chortazō*, v. GK: *5963* [→ *5528*]. to feed; (pass.) to be filled to satisfaction, eat one's fill:– filled [11], fed [1], fill [1], full [1], satisfy [1]

5527 χόρτασμα, *chortasma*, n. GK: *5964* [→ *5528*]. food:– sustenance [1]

5528 χόρτος, *chortos*, n. GK: *5965* [→ *5526, 5527*]. grass, plant; this can refer to plants in various forms and stages: hay, stalk, field, etc:– grass [12], blade [2], hay [1]

5529 Χουζᾶς, *Chouzas*, n.pr. GK: *5966*. Cuza, "*little judge*":– Chuza [1]

5530 χράομαι, *chraomai*, v. GK: *5968* [→ *671, 888, 889, 890, 2173, 2710, 3916, 4798, 5532, 5533, 5534, 5535, 5536, 5539, 5540, 5541, 5542, 5543, 5544; cf. 5531*]. to make use of, use; to do, act, proceed:– use [7], used [3], entreated [1]

5531 χράω, *chraō*, v. GK: *5969* [→ *5537, 5538; cf. 5530*]. to lend:– lend [1]

5532 χρεία, *chreia*, n. GK: *5970* [→ *5530*]. need, necessity:– need [25], need (+*2192*) [10], necessity [2], needeth (+*2192*) [2], business [1], lack [1], necessary [1], necessities [1], needed (+*2192*) [1], needest (+*2192*) [1], needful [1], uses [1], use [1], wants [1]

5533 χρεωφειλέτης, *chreōpheiletēs*, n. GK: *5971 & 5972* [→ *5530+3784*]. debtor:– debtors [2]

5534 χρή, *chrē*, pt. or v.imper. GK: *5973* [→ *5530*]. it should, it is necessary:– ought [1]

5535 χρήζω, *chrēzō*, v. GK: *5974* [→ *5530*]. to need, have need of:– have need [2], need [2], needeth [1]

5536 χρῆμα, *chrēma*, n. GK: *5975* [→ *5530*]. money, wealth, possessions:– money [4], riches [3]

5537 χρηματίζω, *chrēmatizō*, v. GK: *5976* [→ *5531*]. to warn; (pass.) to bear a name; to be warned, told about, revealed to:– warned of God [3], called [2], admonished of God [1], revealed [1], spake [1], warned from God [1]

5538 χρηματισμός, *chrēmatismos*, n. GK: *5977* [→ *5531*]. proclamation or answer from God:– answer of God [1]

5539 χρήσιμος, *chrēsimos*, a. GK: *5978* [→ *5530*]. pertaining to value, usefulness, advantage:– profit [1]

5540 χρῆσις, *chrēsis*, n. GK: *5979* [→ *5530*]. relations, functions:– use [2]

5541 χρηστεύομαι, *chrēsteuomai*, v. GK: *5980* [→ *5530*]. to be kind:– kind [1]

5542 χρηστολογία, *chrēstologia*, n. GK: *5981* [→ *5530+3004*]. smooth talk, attractive speech:– good words [1]

5543 χρηστός, *chrēstos*, a. GK: *5982* [→ *5530*]. easy, good; kind, loving, benevolent:– kind [2], better [1], easy [1], goodness [1], good [1], gracious [1]

5544 χρηστότης, *chrēstotēs*, n. GK: *5983* [→ *5530*]. kindness, goodness:– goodness [4], kindness [4], gentleness [1], good [1]

5545 χρῖσμα, *chrisma*, n. GK: *5984* [→ *5548*]. anointing:– anointing [2], unction [1]

5546 Χριστιανός, *Christianos*, n.pr.g. GK: *5985* [→ *5547*]. Christian:– Christian [2], Christians [1]

5547 Χριστός, *Christos*, n.pr. GK: *5986* [→ *500, 5546, 5580; cf. 5548*]. Christ, Anointed One, Messiah, the Greek translation of the Hebrew *4899* (cf. Greek *3323*). The Messiah is the Son of David, an anointed leader expected to bring in an age of peace and liberty from all oppression. In the NT, the Messiah is Jesus, who came first to bring liberty from sin and peace with God and who will come again to bring all things under his control:– Christ [553], Christ's [16]

5548 χρίω, *chriō*, v. GK: *5987* [→ *1472, 2025, 5545; cf. 5547*]. to anoint (physically, with oil; spiritually, with the Holy Spirit), to assign a person to a special task, implying a giving of power by God to accomplish the task:– anointed [5]

5549 χρονίζω, *chronizō*, v. GK: *5988* [→ *5550*]. to take a long time, delay; to stay a long time:– delayeth [2], tarried long [1], tarried [1], tarry [1]

5550 χρόνος, *chronos*, n. GK: *5989* [→ *3118, 5549, 5551*]. time, period of time:– time [28], times [5], while [4], as long as (+*1909*+*3745*) [3], season [3], world began (+*166*) [2], as long as (+*3745*) [1], long ago [1], oftentimes (+*4183*) [1], old [1], seasons [1], since world began (+*166*) [1], space [1], tarried a space (+*4160*) [1]

5551 χρονοτριβέω, *chronotribeō*, v. GK: *5990* [→ *5550*+*5147*]. to spend time:– spend time [1]

5552 χρύσεος, *chryseos*, a. GK: *5991 & 5997* [→ *5557*]. made of gold:– golden [15], gold [2], of gold [1]

5553 χρυσίον, *chrysion*, n. GK: *5992* [→ *5557*]. gold; gold jewelry or coins:– gold [9]

5554 χρυσοδακτύλιος, *chrysodaktylios*, a. GK: *5993* [→ *5557*+*1147*]. having or wearing a gold ring:– with a gold ring [1]

5555 χρυσόλιθος, *chrysolithos*, n. GK: *5994* [→ *5557*+*3037*]. chrysolite:– chrysolite [1]

5556 χρυσόπρασος, *chrysoprasos*, n. GK: *5995* [→ *5557*+*4237*]. chrysoprase (an apple-green quartz):– chrysoprasus [1]

5557 χρυσός, *chrysos*, n. GK: *5996* [→ *5552, 5553, 5554, 5555, 5556, 5558*]. gold:– gold [12], decked with gold (+*5558*) [1]

5558 χρυσόω, *chrysoō*, v. GK: *5998* [→ *5557*]. (pass.) to be adorned with gold:– decked with gold (+*5557*) [1], decked [1]

5559 χρώς, *chrōs*, n. GK: *5999*. skin, surface of the body:– body [1]

5560 χωλός, *chōlos*, a. GK: *6000*. lame, crippled:– lame [10], halt [4], cripple [1]

5561 χώρα, *chōra*, n. GK: *6001* [→ *5562*]. country, land, region; countryside, field:– country [13], region [4], land [3], fields [2], coasts [1], countries [1], field [1], ground [1], regions [1]

5562 χωρέω, *chōreō*, v. GK: *6003* [→ *402, 672, 1633, 2149, 4066, 4729, 4730, 5298, 5561, 5564*]. to go, come; to accept; to make room, have room:– receive [4], come [1], containing [1], contain [1], goeth [1], hath place [1], room [1]

5563 χωρίζω, *chōrizō*, v. GK: *6004* [→ *5565*]. to divide, separate, leave; (pass.) to be separated from, set apart:– depart [6], separate [3], departed [2], put asunder [2]

5564 χωρίον, *chōrion*, n. GK: *6005* [→ *5562*]. place, parcel of land, field:– field [3], land [2], place [2], lands [1], parcel of ground [1], possessions [1]

5565 χωρίς, *chōris*, adv. GK: *6006* [→ *673, 1316, 5563*]. (adv.) by itself, separately; (pp.*) without, besides, apart from, independent from:– without [36], beside [2], besides [1], by itself [1]

5566 χῶρος, *chōros*, n. GK: *6008*. northwest:– north west [1]

5567 ψάλλω, *psallō*, v. GK: *6010* [→ *5568*]. to sing hymns, sing songs of praise:– sing [3], making melody [1], sing psalms [1]

5568 ψαλμός, *psalmos*, n. GK: *6011* [→ *5567*]. Psalms (book of or section of OT); psalm, hymn of praise:– psalms [5], psalm [2]

5569 ψευδάδελφος, *pseudadelphos*, n. GK: *6012* [→ *5574*+*80; cf. 1.3*]. false brother:– false brethren [2]

5570 ψευδαπόστολος, *pseudapostolos*, n. GK: *6013* [→ *5574*+*649*]. false apostle:– false apostles [1]

5571 ψευδής, *pseudēs*, a. GK: *6014* [→ *5574*]. false, lying; (n.) liar:– liars [2], false [1]

5572 ψευδοδιδάσκαλος, *pseudodidaskalos*, n. GK: *6015* [→ *5574*+*1321*]. false teacher:– false teachers [1]

5573 ψευδολόγος, *pseudologos*, a. GK: *6016* [→ *5574*+*3004*]. false of speech; (n.) liar:– speaking lies [1]

5574 ψεύδομαι, *pseudomai*, v. GK: *6017* [→ *893, 5569, 5570, 5571, 5572, 5573, 5576, 5577, 5575, 5578, 5579, 5580, 5581, 5582, 5583*]. to lie, speak untruths:– lie [10], falsely [1], lied [1]

5575 ψευδόμαρτυς, *pseudomartys*, n. GK: *6020* [→ *5574*+*3144*]. false witness, one who gives false testimony:– false witnesses [3]

5576 ψευδομαρτυρέω, *pseudomartyreō*, v. GK: *6018* [→ *5574*+*3144*]. to give false testimony:– bear false witness [4], bare false witness [1]

5577 ψευδομαρτυρία, *pseudomartyria*, n. GK: *6019* [→ *5574*+*3144*]. false testimony:– false witness [2]

5578 ψευδοπροφήτης, *pseudoprophētēs*, n. GK: *6021* [→ *5574*+*4394*]. false prophet:– false prophets [7], false prophet [4]

5579 ψεῦδος, *pseudos*, n. GK: *6022* [→ *5574*]. lie, falsehood, deception:– lie [7], lying [2]

5580 ψευδόχριστος, *pseudochristos*, n. GK: *6023* [→ *5574*+*5547*]. (pl.) false Christos:– false Christs [2]

5581 ψευδώνυμος, *pseudōnymos*, a. GK: *6024* [→ *5574*+*3686*]. falsely called or identified:– falsely called [1]

5582 ψεῦσμα, *pseusma*, n. GK: *6025* [→ *5574*]. falsehood, untruth:– lie [1]

5583 ψεύστης, *pseustēs*, n. GK: *6026* [→ *5574*]. liar:– liar [8], liars [2]

5584 ψηλαφάω, *psēlaphaō*, v. GK: *6027* [→ *5597*]. to touch, handle:– feel after [1], handled [1], handle [1], touched [1]

5585 ψηφίζω, *psēphizō*, v. GK: *6028* [→ *5586*]. to calculate; to estimate:– counteth [1], count [1]

5586 ψῆφος, *psēphos*, n. GK: *6029* [→ *4785, 4860, 5585; cf. 5597*]. stone, vote (cast by stones); in NT times a white stone usually meant a vote for innocence, a black stone a vote for guilt; the white stone of Rev 2:17 may picture the innocence of its owner:– stone [2], voice against [1]

5587 ψιθυρισμός, *psithyrismos*, n. GK: *6030* [→ *5588*]. whispering gossip:– whisperings [1]

5588 ψιθυριστής, *psithyristēs*, n. GK: *6031* [→ *5587*]. gossip, whisperer:– whisperers [1]

5589 ψιχίον, *psichion*, n. GK: *6033*. crumb, very small piece:– crumbs [3]

5590 ψυχή, *psychē*, n. GK: *6034* [→ *5594*]. life, soul; heart, mind; a person; the immaterial (and eternal) part of inner person, often meaning the animate self, which can be translated by pronouns: "my soul" = "I, myself":– soul [39], life [35], souls [19], lives [5], minds [2], heartily (+*1537*) [1], heart [1], make to doubt (+*142*+*3588*) [1], mind [1], you (+*3588*+*4771*) [1]

5591 ψυχικός, *psychikos*, a. GK: *6035* [→ *5594*]. pertaining to the natural state: physical, unspiritual, without the Spirit:– natural [4], sensual [2]

5592 ψῦχος, *psychos*, n. GK: *6036* [→ *5594*]. cold:– cold [3]

5593 ψυχρός, *psychros*, a. GK: *6037* [→ *5594*]. cold:– cold [4]

5594 ψύχω, *psychō*, v. GK: *6038* [→ *403, 404, 674, 895, 1374, 1634, 2174, 2473, 2711, 5590, 5591, 5592, 5593*]. (pass.) to grow cold:– wax cold [1]

5595 ψωμίζω, *psōmizō*, v. GK: *6039* [→ *5596*]. to feed; to give to the poor:– bestow to feed [1], feed [1]

5596 ψωμίον, *psōmion*, n. GK: *6040* [→ *5595; cf. 5597*]. piece of bread:– sop [4]

5597 ψώχω, *psōchō*, v. GK: *6041* [→ *4067, 4379, 5584; cf. 5586, 5596*]. to rub:– rubbing [1]

5598 Ω¹, *Ō¹*, letter; n.pr. GK: *6042*. letter of the Greek alphabet; Omega:– Omega [4]

5599 ω², *ō²*, pt.interj. GK: *6043*. O!, Oh!:– O [16]

5600 ω, *ō*, v.subj. of *1510*. GK: *1639* [→ *1510*]. it may, might, could be; see *1510*:–

5601 Ὠβήδ, *Ōbēd*, n.pr. GK: *6044*. Obed, "*servant* or *worshiper*":– Obed [3]

5602 ὧδε, *hōde*, adv. GK: *6045* [→ *3588*]. here:– here [43], hither [13], here in a place [1], in this place [1], there [1], this place [1]

5603 ᾠδή, *ōdē*, n. GK: *6046* [→ *103, 2790*]. song:– song [5], songs [2]

5604 ὠδίν, *ōdin*, n. GK: *6047* [→ *4944, 5605*]. labor, birth pain; agony (of death):– sorrows [2], pains [1], travail [1]

5605 ὠδίνω, *ōdinō*, v. GK: *6048* [→ *5604*]. to suffer the pains of childbirth:– travail in birth [1], travailest [1], travailing in birth [1]

5606 ὦμος, *ōmos*, n. GK: *6049*. (pl.) shoulders:– shoulders [2]

5607 ὤν, *ōn*, v.ptcp. of *1510*. GK: *1639* [→ *1510*]. to be, exist, be present; all forms of this verb are indexed under *1510*:–

5608 ὠνέομαι, *ōneomai*, v. GK: *6050* [→ *3800; cf. 5057*]. to buy:– bought [1]

5609 ὠόν, *ōon*, n. GK: *6051*. egg:– egg [1]

5610 ὥρα, *hōra*, n. GK: *6052* [→ *2256, 2250, 5611*]. hour, portion of time, while, moment:– hour [86], time [11], hours [3], season [3], day [1], eventide (+*3588*+*3798*) [1], instant [1], now high time (+*2235*) [1], short [1]

5611 ὡραῖος, *hōraios*, a. GK: *6053* [→ *5610*]. beautiful:– beautiful [4]

5612 ὠρύομαι, *ōryomai*, v. GK: *6054*. to roar:– roaring [1]

5613 ὡς, *hōs*, pt.&c. GK: *6055* [→ *2531, 5615, 5616, 5618, 5619, 5620*]. as, that, how, about, when; like, as:– as [352], when [39], how [18], as though [16], about [14], like [9], as soon as [7], that [6], while [4], according as [3], like unto [3], after [2], as (+*302*) [2], as it were [2], for [2], after that [1], and [1], are [1], as if [1], even as [1], how that [1], since [1], so soon as (+*302*) [1], so that [1], so [1], to wit [1], unto [1], when (+*1063*) [1], when (+*1161*) [1], when (+*302*) [1], whensoever (+*1437*) [1], with all speed (+*5030*) [1]

5614 ὡσαννά, *hōsanna*, l.[v.+pt.]. GK: *6057*. Hosanna! (exclamation of praise, originally "Save [us]!"):– hosanna [6]

5615 ὡσαύτως, *hōsautōs*, adv. GK: *6058* [→ *5613*+*846*]. in the same way, so also, likewise, similarly:– likewise [13], in like manner [2], after the same manner [1], even so [1]

5616 ὡσεί, *hōsei*, pt.comp. GK: *6059* [→ *5613*+*1487*]. like, as; about (an approximation):– about [18], as [8], like [5], as it had been [1], as it were [1], like as [1]

5617 Ὡσηέ, *Hōsēe*, n.pr. GK: *6060*. Hosea, "*salvation*":– Osee [1]

5618 ὥσπερ, *hōsper*, pt.comp. GK: *6061* [→ *5613*+*4007*]. as, just as; like:– as [39], even as [2], like as [1]

5619 ὡσπερεί, *hōsperei*, pt.comp. GK: *6062* [→ *5613*+*4007*+*1487*]. like, as though, as it were:– as [1]

5620 ὥστε, *hōste*, pt. GK: *6063* [→ *5613*+*5037*]. a marker for introducing clauses: for this reason, therefore, so; so that, resulting in; to, for the purpose of:– so that [24], wherefore [16], insomuch that [15], therefore [9], that [7], so then [5], to [3], as [1], because [1], insomuch as [1], so that (+*2532*) [1], wherefore (+*2532*) [1]

5621 ὠτίον, *ōtion*, n. GK: *6065* [→ *3775*]. ear:– ear [5]

5622 ὠφέλεια, *ōpheleia*, n. GK: *6066* [→ *5623*]. value, advantage:– advantage [1], profit [1]

5623 ὠφελέω, *ōpheleō*, v. GK: *6067* [→ *512, 3786, 5622, 5624*]. to be of good use; to have value; to help; to devote (as a gift) to God:– profited [4], profit [4], profiteth [3], prevail [1], advantaged [1], bettered [1]

5624 ὠφέλιμος, *ōphelimos*, a. GK: *6068* [→ *5623*]. valuable, useful, profitable:– profitable [3], profiteth (+*1510*) [1]

NAVE'S TOPICAL BIBLE REFERENCE SYSTEM

ABBREVIATIONS AND OTHER SYMBOLS

Books of the Bible

1Ch	1 Chronicles
1Co	1 Corinthians
1Jn	1 John
1Ki	1 Kings
1Pe	1 Peter
1Sa	1 Samuel
1Th	1 Thessalonians
1Ti	1 Timothy
2Ch	2 Chronicles
2Co	2 Corinthians
2Jn	2 John
2Ki	2 Kings
2Pe	2 Peter
2Sa	2 Samuel
2Th	2 Thessalonians
2Ti	2 Timothy
3Jn	3 John
Ac	Acts
Am	Amos
Col	Colossians
Da	Daniel
Dt	Deuteronomy
Ecc	Ecclesiastes
Eph	Ephesians
Est	Esther
Ex	Exodus
Eze	Ezekiel
Ezr	Ezra
Gal	Galatians
Ge	Genesis
Hab	Habakkuk
Hag	Haggai
Heb	Hebrews
Hos	Hosea
Isa	Isaiah
Jas	James
Jdg	Judges
Jer	Jeremiah
Jn	John
Jnh	Jonah
Job	Job
Joel	Joel
Jos	Joshua
Jude	Jude
La	Lamentations
Lev	Leviticus
Lk	Luke
Mal	Malachi
Mic	Micah
Mk	Mark
Mt	Matthew
Na	Nahum
Ne	Nehemiah
Nu	Numbers
Ob	Obadiah
Phm	Philemon
Php	Philippians
Pr	Proverbs
Ps	Psalms
Rev	Revelation
Ro	Romans
Ru	Ruth
SS	Song of Songs / Song of Solomon
Tit	Titus
Zec	Zechariah
Zep	Zephaniah

Books of the Apocrypha

1Es	1 Esdras
1Mc	1 Maccabees
2Es	2 Esdras
2Mc	2 Maccabees
3Mc	3 Maccabees
4Mc	4 Maccabees
Bar	Baruch
Bel	Bel and the Dragon
Sir	Sirach
Tob	Tobit
Wis	Wisdom

Other

&	"and"; read this biblical text with the preceding
Antiq.	Josephus, *Antiquities of the Jews*.
BDB	Brown, Driver and Briggs *Hebrew and English Lexicon* (Oxford, 1907).
ISBE	*International Standard Bible Encyclopedia* (Eerdmans, 1979-88).
KB	Koehler and Baumgartner *Lexicon in Veteris Testamenti Libros* (Eerdmans, 1951-53).
JB	Jerusalem Bible
KJV	King James Version
NIV	New International Version
NRSV	New Revised Standard Version
w	"with"; read this biblical text with the preceding
ZPBE	*Zondervan Pictorial Bible Encyclopedia* (Zondervan, 1976).

A

A

AARON

Personal History:

Lineage of: a son of Amram of the Kohathites, and brother of Moses and Miriam (Ex 6:16-20; Nu 26:59-60; Jos 21:4, 10; 1Ch 6:2-3). His marriage to Elisheba, daughter of Amminadab (Ex 6:23). The children of: Nadab, Abihu, Eleazar and Ithamar (Ex 6:23, 25; 1Ch 6:3-4; 24:1-2). Descendants of (1Ch 6:3-15, 50-53; 24).

Character of (Ps 106:16).

As a Leader Ordained by God:

Meets Moses in the wilderness and is made spokesman for Moses (Ex 4:14-16, 27-31; 7:1-2, 6-7). Commissioned as a deliverer of Israel (Ex 6:13, 26-27; Dss 24:5; 1Sa 12:8; Ps 77:20; 105:26; Mic 6:4). Inspiration of (Ex 12:1; Lev 10:8; 11:1; 13:1; 15:1; Nu 2:1; 4:1, 17; 18:1; 19:1; 20:12). Summoned to Sinai with Nadab, Abihu, and seventy elders (Ex 19:24; 24:1, 9-10).

Events in the Life of:

Murmured against by the people (Ex 5:20-21; 16:2-12; Nu 14:2-5, 10; 16:3-11, 41; 20:2; Ps 106:16). Places pot of manna in the ark (Ex 16:34). With Hur supports the hands of Moses during battle (Ex 17:10-13). Judges Israel in the absence of Moses (Ex 24:13-14). Makes the golden calf (Ex 32; Dt 9:7-21; Ac 7:40-41).

His benedictions upon the people (Lev 9:22; Nu 6:23-26). Forbidden to mourn the death of his sons Nadab and Abihu (Lev 10:6, 19).

Gossips with Miriam about Moses because of jealousy (Nu 12:1). Intercedes for Miriam (Nu 12:11-12). Stops the plague started by Korah's rebellion, by priestly intercession (Nu 16:46-48). Rod of buds (Nu 17; Heb 9:4), preserved in the ark of the covenant (Nu 17; Heb 9:4).

He and Moses dishonor God in the presence of the Israelites when the rock is struck (Nu 20:12, 23-29). Moses and Aaron are not allowed to enter the land of Canaan because of this lack of faith at the waters of Meribah Kadesh in the Desert of Zin (Dt 32:51-52). Dies at 123 years of age on Mt. Hor (Nu 33:38-39). Death and burial of (Nu 20:27-28; Dt 10:6; 32:50).

As a Priest:

Priesthood of (Ex 28:1; 29:9; Nu 17; 18:1; Ps 99:6; Heb 5:4). Consecration of, to the priesthood (Ex 28; 29; Lev 8). Enters the priestly office (Lev 9).

Descendants of, ordained priests forever (Ex 28:40-43; 29:9; Nu 3:3; 18:1; 1Ch 23:13; 2Ch 26:18). See Priest, High Priest.

AARONITES Descendants of Aaron who were priests, numbering 3700 fighting men under Jehoiada who joined David at Hebron (1Ch 12:27). Their leader was Zadok (1Ch 27:17).

AB The Babylonian name of the fifth month in sacred sequence, month eleven in civil sequence. In the Bible it is referred to only as "the fifth month" (Nu 33:38; Ezr 7:8; Jer 1:3). The dry season (July-August); ripening season for grapes, figs, and olives. See Month, 5.

ABADDON (destruction). A Hebrew word for the underworld, meaning the place of destruction (Job 31:12, ftn), and in the OT is a synonym of death (Hell) and Sheol. The abode of the dead (Job 26:6, ftn; Pr 15:11, ftn; 27:20, ftn).

The name of the angel of the bottomless pit (Rev 9:11, ftn), whose Greek name is Apollyon which means destroyer.

ABAGTHA One of seven eunuchs that served King Xerxes (Est 1:10).

ABANA A river of Damascus mentioned by the leprous Naaman (2Ki 5:12).

ABARIM (geographic regions beyond). Either a region E of the Jordan and SE of the Dead Sea, or a mountain range NW of Moab (Nu 27:12; 33:47-48; Dt 32:49; Jer 22:20). See Nebo, 2.

ABBA An Aramaic word meaning father, which is a customary title of God in prayer. It is found in the Babylonian Talmud where it is used, of a child to his father, and also as a type of address to rabbis. It is equivalent to papa. This term conveys a sense of warm intimacy and also respect for the father. The Jews found it too presumptuous and nearly blasphemous; they would therefore never address God in this manner.

Jesus called God "Father" and gave that same right to his disciples (Mt 6:5-15). Paul sees this as symbolic of the Christian's adoption as a child of God and of possession of the Spirit (Mk 14:36; Ro 8:15; Gal 4:6).

ABDA (servant of Yahweh).
1. Father of Adoniram (1Ki 4:6).
2. A Levite of the family of Jeduthun, the son of Shammua (Ne 11:17).

ABDEEL (servant of God [El]). Father of Shelemiah, who was appointed by Jehoiakim, the king of Judah, "to arrest Baruch the scribe and Jeremiah the prophet" (Jer 36:26).

ABDI (servant of Yahweh or my servant).
1. A Levite in the reign of Hezekiah, the father of Kishi and grandfather of Ethan (1Ch 6:44; 2Ch 29:12).
2. A son of Elam (Ezr 10:26).

ABDIEL (servant of God [El]). A Gadite chief, the father of Ahi (1Ch 5:15).

ABDON (servant).
1. A Levitical city given to the tribe of Asher (Jos 19:28, ftn; 21:30; 1Ch 6:74).
2. A son of Hillel, from Pirathon in Ephraim, the hill country of the Amalekites; a judge of Israel for eight years (Jdg 12:13-15).
3. A son of Shashak (1Ch 8:23, 25, 28).
4. Firstborn son of Jeiel of Gibeon (1Ch 8:30; 9:35-36).
5. The son of Micah, an official of King Josiah (2Ch 34:20). Also called Acbor, son of Micaiah (2Ki 22:12).

ABEDNEGO (servant of Nego or Nebo). His Hebrew name was Azariah. He was taken as a captive to Babylon with Daniel, Hananiah, and Mishael, where each was given a Babylonian name (Da 1:6-20; 2:17, 49; 3:12-30). Azariah was given the Akkadian name Abednego, which was the Babylonian god of wisdom, connected with the planet Mercury.

Shadrach, Meshach, and Abednego were chosen to learn the language and the ways of the Chaldeans (Babylonians) so that they could enter the king's service (Da 1:3-5, 17-20). These three were eventually thrown into the king's furnace because they refused to bow down and worship Nebuchadnezzar's golden image (Da 3:1, 4-6, 8-30).

ABEL (proper name morning mist; place name meadow or stream).
1. The second son of Adam and Eve (Ge 4:1-2). The history of (Ge 4:1-15, 25). NT references to the death of (Mt 23:35; Lk 11:51; Heb 11:4; 12:24; 1Jn 3:12).
2. A city in Naphtali (2Sa 20:14, ftn; 20:18).
3. An element of certain place names. See seven place names following.

ABEL, GREAT STONE OF. KJV "the great stone of Abel" (1Sa 6:18) is "the large rock" in the NIV text; "Greater Abel" in the note.

ABEL BETH MAACAH (meadow of the house of Maacah [oppression]). Sheba son of Bicri fled there from King David (2Sa 20:14-22). A town in Naphtali (2Sa 20:15). Ben-Hadad later seized it (1Ki 15:20). Tiglath-Pileser, king of Assyria captured it (2Ki 15:29).

ABEL-CHERAMIM See Abel Keramim.

ABEL KERAMIM (meadow of vineyards). A place in Ammon, east of the Jordan, to which Jephthah pursued the Ammonites (Jdg 11:33).

ABEL MAIM (meadow of waters). A city conquered by Ben-Hadad (2Ch 16:4). Also known as Abel Beth Maacah (2Ch 16:4, ftn).

ABEL MEHOLAH (meadow of the round dance). A town probably in the Jordan Valley, named in conjunction with the retreat of the Midianites from Gideon (Jdg 7:22; 1Ki 4:12). Probably Elisha's birthplace (1Ki 19:16).

ABEL MIZRAIM (meadow of Egypt, or mourning of Egypt). The place was the threshing floor of Atad where the Israelites and all Pharaoh's officials mourned for Jacob (Ge 50:11).

ABEL SHITTIM (meadow of the acacia trees). A place where the Israelites made their final camp before crossing the Jordan into Canaan (Nu 33:49). See Shittim.

ABETTING See Complicity.

ABEZ See Ebez.

ABI See Abijah, 7.

ABIA, ABIAH See Abijah, 1 & 3.

ABI-ALBON ([my] father is Albon). Also called Abiel (1Ch 11:32). See Abiel. One of David's mighty men (2Sa 23:31).

ABIASAPH ([my] father has gathered). A Levite, and the last son of Korah (Ex 6:24). He is also identified as Ebiasaph (1Ch 6:23, 37; 9:19). See Ebiasaph.

ABIATHAR ([my] father gives abundance or the father is preeminent).
1. High priest under David.
He is the son of Ahimelech and, like his father, a high priest at Nob; he alone escaped from the massacre of his family and all the priests at Nob by Saul to join with David at Keilah, bringing an ephod with him (1Sa 22:6-23). Consults the ephod for David (1Sa 23:9; 30:7). David did not depose Zadok whom Saul had appointed to the priesthood; instead, the two constituted a double high priesthood (2Sa 15:35; 20:25; 1Ki 4:4; 1Ch 15:11). Abiathar was loyal to David when Absalom rebelled; leaves Jerusalem with the ark of the covenant, but is directed by David to return with the ark (2Sa 15:24-29). Helps David by sending his son Jonathan from Jerusalem to David with secret information concerning the counsel of Ahithophel (2Sa 15:35-36; 17:15-22; 1Ki 2:26).

Later he supports Adonijah's attempt to succeed David to the royal throne at David's death (1Ki 1:7). Because of this he is forced out of office by Solomon and is banished to Anathoth (1Ki 2:26-27). With this, the priestly line was confined to Zadok, an Aaronite, and the rule of Eli's house ended in fulfillment of prophecy (1Sa 2:31-35).

The reference to "Ahimelech son of Abiathar" as priest with Zadok is confusing because in other places "Abiathar son of Ahimelech" is known as the high priest. This problem is sometimes solved by saying that the names were transposed by a copyist error; many find this to be an improbable solution since the reference to Ahimelech, the son of Abiathar, as priest is too clear to make a mistake (2Sa 8:17; 1Ch 18:16; 24:3, 6, 31). One of the best explanations is that as the aged Abiathar came near to the end of David's reign, and his life, the responsibilities of office became heavy enough for him to shift many of those duties over to his oldest son Ahimelech; Ahimelech therefore became the functioning high priest.

When Jesus refers to "Abiathar as high priest" at Nob (instead of his father Ahimelech), it is perhaps best understood as Jesus referring to the "passage concerning Abiathar as high priest," by analogy with the way he refers to the burning bush (Mk 12:26).
2. See Ahimelech, 3.

ABIB (heads or spikes of grain). Hebrew name of the first month in sacred sequence, month seven in civil sequence (Ex 12:2). The name was changed to Nisan after the Exile (Ne 2:1; Est 3:7). The season of later rains (March-April); beginning of the barley and flax harvest.

The Passover and the Feast of Unleavened Bread were instituted, and the Israelites departed from Egypt in (Ex 13:4; 23:15; 34:18; Dt 16:1). It was to become a memorial month to the deliverance of the Israelites from Egypt (Ex 12, w 13:3-4; Dt 16:1-8, 16).

The order of events during the celebration month:
1. On the tenth day the Passover lamb was chosen.
2. On the fourteenth day the lamb was slain and eaten.
3. On the fifteenth day they began harvesting by gathering sheaves of the barley firstfruits.
4. On the sixteenth day they offered the sheaves.
The tabernacle, the Tent of Meeting, was set up in (Ex 40:2, 17). The Israelites arrived at the Desert of Zin, staying at Kadesh (Nu 20:1). Canaan entered in (Jos 4:19). Jordan's overflow in (1Ch 12:15).

See Month, 1; Nisan.

ABIDA ([my] father knows). Fourth of five sons of Midian, and the grandson of Abraham and Keturah (Ge 25:4; 1Ch 1:33).

ABIDAN ([my] father is judge). A son of Gideoni, and a prince of the tribe of Benjamin chosen to represent his tribe in the wilderness of Sinai (Nu 1:11; 2:22; 10:24). He was present at the dedication of the tabernacle (Nu 7:60, 65).

ABIEL ([my] father is God [El]).
1. The grandfather of Saul and Abner (1Sa 9:1; 14:51).
2. One of David's mighty men (1Ch 11:32), also called Abi-Albon (2Sa 23:31). Albon is a copyist's transference from the following verse; some mss of the LXX have Abiel here.

ABIEZER, ABIEZRITES ([my] father is help).
1. Founder of a clan of Manasseh (Jos 17:2; Jdg 6:34; 8:2). He was the second son of Hammoleketh, sister of Gilead and granddaughter of Manasseh (1Ch 7:17-18).
Also called Iezer, a shortened form, the progenitor of the Iezerites (Nu 26:30). See Iezer, Iezerites.
2. One of David's mighty men (2Sa 23:27; 1Ch 11:28; 27:12).

ABIGAIL ([my] father rejoices or father [cause] of joy).
1. The wife of Nabal of Carmel, a Calebite, and, after Nabal's death, of David (1Sa 25:3, 14-44; 27:3; 30:5; 2Sa 2:2), to whom she bore his second son, Kileab (2Sa 3:3), or Daniel (1Ch 3:1).
2. A sister of David, daughter of Nahash (Jesse), wife of Jether (Ithra, KJV an Israelite (some Hebrew mss have Ishmaelite), and mother of Amasa, commander of David's army (2Sa 17:25; 1Ch 2:16-17).

ABIHAIL ([my] father has strength/ wealth or cause of strength/wealth).
1. A Levite, the father of Zuriel, leader of the Merarite clans (Nu 3:35).
2. The wife of Abishur (1Ch 2:29).
3. A Gadite who lived in Gilead of Bashan and on the pasturelands of Sharon (1Ch 5:14).
4. The wife of Rehoboam, king of Judah. A daughter of Eliab, David's oldest brother (2Ch 11:18).
5. The father of Queen Esther (Est 2:15; 9:29).

ABIHU (he is [my] father). Son of Aaron (Ex 6:23; Nu 3:2). Summoned by God to Sinai (Ex 24:1, 9). Called to the priesthood (Ex 28:1). Died because he and Nadab offered unauthorized fire to the Lord (Lev 10:1-2; Nu 26:61). Died childless (Nu 3:4).

ABIHUD ([my] father has majesty). A son of Bela, the oldest son of Benjamin (1Ch 8:3).

ABIJAH ([my] father is Yahweh).
1. The second son of Samuel; appointed, with his brother Joel, as judges but did not follow in Samuel's ways. They followed after dishonest gains, bribes, and perverted justice. Because of this the Israelites demanded a king to lead them (1Sa 8:1-5; 1Ch 6:28).
2. A son of Jeroboam I of Israel (1Ki 14:1-18). He died of illness when still a child, in fulfillment of a prediction by the prophet Ahijah.
3. The wife of Judah's grandson Hezron and mother of Ashhur the father of Tekoa (1Ch 2:24).
4. The seventh son of Beker, the son of Benjamin (1Ch 7:8).
5. The second king of Judah, the son and successor of Rehoboam, and the grandson of Solomon (1Ch 3:10). Name is spelled "Abijam" in 1 Kings 14 and 15 (See NIV ftn). He reigned three years (2Ch 12:16). Prosperity tempted him to follow the evil ways of his father (1Ki 15:3). He had fourteen wives by whom he had twenty-two sons and sixteen daughters (2Ch 13:21).
He made war on Jeroboam I, the king of Israel, in an effort to recover the ten tribes of Israel (2Ch 13). Before the battle, Abijah condemns the apostasy of the Northern kingdom and at the same time affirms a theocratic institution; he shows the folly of opposing Yahweh's kingdom and concludes by urging Israel not to fight against Yahweh. Jeroboam I, with a numerically stronger army, was routed by Yahweh; the two nations were not allied as they once were, but Jeroboam never made war with Abijah again (1Ki 15:1-8; 2Ch 11:22; 13). He was succeeded by Asa his son (1Ki 15:8; 2Ch 14:1).
6. A descendant of Aaron. The ancestral head of the eighth of the 24 groups into which David had divided the priests (1Ch 24:10).

7. The daughter of Zechariah, and mother of king Hezekiah (2Ch 29:1). Also called Abi (2Ki 18:2, ftn).

8. A priest of Nehemiah's time (Ne 10:7).

9. A chief of the priests who returned from Babylon with Zerubbabel (Ne 12:4, 17). Probably the same as 8.

ABIJAM (*[my] father is the sea* or *father of the West*). See *Abijah, 5.*

ABILENE (probably *meadow*). A territory surrounding the city of Abila NW of Damascus (Lk 3:1).

ABIMAEL (*[my] father is God [El]*). The ninth of the thirteen sons or descendants of Joktan, who was descended from Shem (Ge 10:28; 1Ch 1:22).

ABIMELECH (*[my] father is a king* or *[my] father is Molech*).

1. A Philistine king of Gerar, S of Gaza in the foothills of the Judean mountains (Ge 20:1-18).

2. A second king of Gerar, probably the son of the one mentioned in 1, at whose court Isaac tried to pass off his wife Rebekah as his sister (Ge 26:1-11).

3. The son of Gideon by a concubine (Jdg 8:31; 9:1-57, w 6:32 & 7:1).

4. A Philistine king mentioned in the title of Psalm 34, who very likely is the same as Achish, king of Gath (1Sa 21:10-22:1), with whom David sought refuge when he fled from Saul.

5. A priest in the days of David. A son of Abiathar (2Sa 8:17; 1Ch 18:16). Also called Ahimelech in the LXX and in the Chronicles (1Ch 24:6).

6. See *Achish; Ahimelech.*

ABINADAB (*[my] father is generous* or *[my] father is Nadab*).

1. A Levite, in whose house the ark of God rested twenty years (1Sa 7:1-2; 2Sa 6:3-4; 1Ch 13:7).

2. The second son of Jesse (1Sa 16:8; 17:13).

3. Son of Saul (1Sa 31:2), also called Ishvi (1Sa 14:49).

4. Father of one of Solomon's governors who supplied provisions for the king and the royal household. Also called Ben-Abinadab (1Ki 4:11).

ABINOAM (*[my] father is graciousness*). The father of Barak (Jdg 4:6, 12; 5:1, 12).

ABIRAM (*[my] father is exalted*).

1. One of the sons of Eliab, a Reubenite, who conspired with Dathan and with On against Moses and Aaron; the earth opened and swallowed them (Nu 16; 26:9-10; Dt 11:6; Ps 106:17).

2. The son of Hiel of Bethel; in rebuilding Jericho, Hiel's firstborn, Abiram, died, as well as his youngest son, Segub, in accordance with the word of the Lord spoken to Joshua (1Ki 16:34, w Jos 6:26).

ABISHAG (*[my] father strays*). The Shunammite who looked after David in his old age (1Ki 1:3-4, 15). After David died, Adonijah, his oldest son, wished to marry Abishag. He tried using Bathsheba as leverage to gain Abishag as his wife. Solomon saw this as an attempt to gain the throne by controlling and possessing the king's harem which was a royal right. Solomon had him killed (1Ki 2:13-25).

ABISHAI (*[my] father is Jesse* or *father exists*). The son of Zeruiah, David's sister (1Sa 26:6; 1Ch 2:16). Became the chief of the Three, David's chief men, because he killed 300 men with his spear (2Sa 23:18-19).

Goes into Saul's camp with David; they find Saul asleep with his spear planted in the ground near his head; Abishai tells David that he will pin Saul to the ground with one thrust of the spear, which David does not allow (1Sa 26:6-8). Abishai and his brother Joab pursue Abner all day until they reach the hill of Ammah near Giah; later they murder Joab (2Sa 2:24; 3:30). Defeats the Ammonites (2Sa 10:10, 14). Defeats 18,000 Edomites in the Valley of Salt (1Ch 18:12).

Seeks the life of Shimei son of Gera (2Sa 16:5-9; 19:18-23). Leads a division of David's army against Absalom (2Sa 18:2, 5). Overthrows Sheba (2Sa 20:1-22). Saves David from being killed by Ishbi-Benob, one of the descendants of Rapha, a Philistine (2Sa 21:16-17). Obtains water from the well of Bethlehem for David (1Ch 11:15-20).

ABISHALOM (*[my] father is peace*). A longer form of Absalom (1Ki 15:2, 10). See *Absalom.*

ABISHUA (*[my] father is salvation*).

1. The son of Phinehas the priest (1Ch 6:4-5, 50; Ezr 7:5).

2. A Benjamite of the family of Bela (1Ch 8:4).

ABISHUR (*[my] father is a wall*). A man of Judah, the son of Shammai (1Ch 2:28-29).

ABITAL (*[my] father is [the] night dew*). The fifth wife of David and mother of Shephatiah (2Sa 3:4; 1Ch 3:3).

ABITUB (*[my] father is good*). A Benjamite, son of Shaharaim and Hushim (1Ch 8:8-11).

ABIUD (*[my] father has majesty*). The son of Zerubbabel (Mt 1:13).

ABLUTION See *Washings.*

ABNER (*[my] father is Ner [lamp]*). Son of Ner. Cousin of Saul (1Sa 14:50-51). Commander of the army of Saul (1Sa 14:50; 17:55; 26:5, 14). Abner breaks with Ish-Bosheth and the house of Saul (2Sa 3:6-11) and transfers his loyalty to the house of David (2Sa 3:12-21). Murdered by Joab; David's sorrow for (2Sa 3:22-39). Dedicated spoils of war to the tabernacle (1Ch 26:27-28).

ABOMINATION Activities that are offensive in a moral, religious, or even a natural sense of repulsion.

God's Law Regarding:

Sexual relations: incest (Lev 18:6-18; Dt 27:20), lying with a woman in her monthly period (Lev 18:19; 20:18), adultery (Dt 22:22), homosexuality (Lev 18:22; 20:13), bestiality (Lev 18:23; 20:15-16). Idolatry (Dt 7:25-26; 27:15; 32:16-42), divination, sorcery, interpreting omens, witchcraft, casting spells, mediums or spiritists, those who consult the dead (Dt 18:9-15), offering children in sacrifice by fire to Molech (Dt 18:10, w Lev 18:21). Wearing clothes of opposite sex (Dt 22:5), the earnings of a female or a male prostitute to pay a vow (Dt 23:18), remarriage of defiled wife (Dt 24:1-4). Unjust weights and measures (Dt 25:13-16; Pr 11:1; 20:10, 23).

See *Law.*

Idols:

(Dt 7:25-26; 27:15; 29:17-18; Eze 7:20-21). Solomon, in his old age, followed other gods and was punished (1Ki 11:1-12), Ashtoreth of the Sidonians, Molech of the Ammonites, Chemosh of the Moabites (1Ki 11:5-8; 11:33; 2Ki 23:13).

There are no gods apart from God (Dt 6:4; 1Ch 17:20; Isa 43:10-13; 44:6-28). Conditions for blessing: Return to God and turn from worthless gods (Jer 4:1-2), or receive disaster (Eze 5:5ff). Idols, the worship of, and related practices: (Eze 16:1-63; Hos 9:10).

See *Idol; Idolatry.*

Actions and Attitudes:

A false witness who pours out lies (Dt 19:15-21; Pr 6:19; 21:28), perverseness (Pr 3:32; 11:20), false pride (Pr 6:17; 16:5), murder (Pr 6:17), lying (Pr 6:17, 19; 12:22), one who devises wicked schemes (Pr 6:18), wicked imaginations, *i.e.*, the thoughts of the wicked (Pr 6:18; 15:26; 21:27), wickedness (Pr 8:7).

See *Falsehood.*

People, Types:

False witness (Pr 6:19; 17:15), trouble maker (Pr 6:19), mocker (Pr 24:9), dishonest (Pr 29:27).

Of Wicked:

Sacrifice (Pr 15:8; 21:27; Isa 1:13), ways (Pr 15:9), thoughts (Pr 15:26), prayer (Pr 28:9).

See *Wicked.*

ABOMINATION THAT CAUSES DESOLATION

An utterly abhorrent abomination (Da 9:27; 11:31; 12:11). Daniel's prophecies may refer to one or all of three events: to Antiochus' desecration of the temple in 167-169 B.C. (1Mc 1:21-61), to the destruction of Jerusalem in A.D. 70 (Mt 24:15; Mk 13:14), and to the setting up of the image of the beast (Rev 13:14-15). See *Antiochus, 4.*

ABORTION

Induced termination of pregnancy by killing the fetus. Clinical abortions are not addressed in the Bible. But the value of the unborn is clearly seen in texts that speak of their value and of judgments on those who kill them.

The value of the unborn (Job 31:15; Ps 139:13-16; Ecc 11:5; Isa 44:2, 24; 49:1, 5; Jer 1:4; Lk 1:41-45).

Punishment for injury to a pregnant mother and her unborn child (Ex 21:22-25). Punishment for the atrocity of ripping open pregnant women (2Ki 8:12; 15:16; Hos 13:16; Am 1:13-15).

See *Miscarry.*

ABRAHAM, ABRAM (*father of many* or *exalted father*).

Events in the Life of:

Called Abram, son of Terah (Ge 11:26-27). Abram marries Sarai (Ge 11:29). Dwells in Ur of the Chaldeans, but moves. Terah, his father, took Abram and the rest of the family, intending to move to Canaan. On the way they stop and settle in Haran in NW Mesopotamia, where Terah dies (Ge 11:31; Ne 9:7; Ac 7:4). Eventually Abram, at seventy-five, sets out from Haran for the land of Canaan (Ge 12:1-6; Ac 7:4).

The divine call of (Ge 12:1-3; Jos 24:3; Ne 9:7-8; Isa 51:2; Ac 7:2-4; Heb 11:8). See *Call.*

Canaan given to (Ge 12:1, 6-7; 15:7-21; Eze 33:24). Dwells in the hills E of Bethel and W of Ai (Ge 12:8). Relocates to Egypt because of a famine in Canaan (Ge 12:10-20; 26:1). Upon leaving Egypt, they travel to the Negev and on to Bethel; since there is not enough land in one place to support their large herds of sheep, Abram gives Lot his choice of land; Lot chooses the plain of Jordan, leaving Abram to live at the great trees of Mamre the Amorite at Hebron (Ge 13; 14:13; 35:27). Dwells in Gerar and Beersheba (Ge 20; 21:22-34).

Defeats Kedorlaomer king of Elam (Ge 14:5-16; Heb 7:1). Is blessed by Melchizedek (Ge 14:18-20; Heb 7:1-10). See *Melchizedek.*

God's covenant with (Ge 15; 17:1-22; Mic 7:20; Lk 1:73; Ro 4:13; 15:8; Heb 6:13-15; Gal 3:6-29; 4:22-31). See *Covenants, Major in the Old Testament.*

Ishmael born to (Ge 16:3, 7-16). Renamed Abraham by the Lord (Ge 17:5; Ne 9:7). Circumcision of (Ge 17:10-14, 23-27). See *Circumcision.* Angels appear to (Ge 18:1-16; 22:11-12, 15; 24:7). His questions and intercession concerning the destruction of the righteous and wicked in Sodom (Ge 18:23-32). Witnesses the destruction of Sodom (Ge 19:27-29). Dwells in Gerar; deceives Abimelech concerning Sarah, his wife (Ge 20). Isaac born to Abraham when he is 100 years old according to the promise of Yahweh (Ge 21:1-5; Gal 4:22-30). Sends Hagar and Ishmael away (Ge 21:10-14; Gal 4:22-30).

Trial of his faith in the offering of Isaac (Ge 22:1-19; Heb 11:17-19; Jas 2:21). See *Faith, Instances of trial of.* Sarah, his wife, dies (Ge 23:1-2). He purchases a place for her burial and buries her in a cave (Ge 23:3-20). See *Burial; Burying Places.* Provides a wife for Isaac (Ge 24). Marries Keturah (Ge 25:1). Death (Ge 15:15; 25:8-10). In Paradise (Mt 8:11; Lk 13:28; 16:22-31).

Wealth of (Ge 13:2; 24:35). Children of (Ge 16:15; 21:2-3; 25:1-4; 1Ch 1:32-34). Inheritance of (Ge 25:5-6). See *Inheritance.* Age of at different periods (Ge 12:4; 16:16; 21:5; 25:7).

Character Qualities of:

Personal piety of and promises to (Ge 12:7-8; 13:4, 18; 18:18-33; 20:7; 21:33; 22:3-13; 26:5; Ne 9:7-8; 2Ch 20:7; Isa 41:8; Ro 4:16-18; Jas 2:23). See *Worship.* Unselfishness of (Ge 13:9; 21:25-30). Independence of, in character (Ge 14:23; 23:6-16). Faith of (Ge 15:6; Ro 4:1-22; Gal 3:6-9; Heb 11:8-19; Jas 2:21-24). See *Faith, Instances of.* A prophet (Ge 20:7). Friend of God (2Ch 20:7; Isa 41:8; Jas 2:23).

How regarded by his descendants (Mt 3:9; Lk 13:16, 28; 19:9; Jn 8:33-40, 52-59).

ABRAHAM'S SIDE In the Lukan account of the rich man and Lazarus, Lazarus is being comforted at Abraham's side (KJV "bosom") while the rich man is being tormented in the fires of hell (Lk 16:22-23). See *Lazarus.*

In the Talmudic language, to sit in Abraham's side is to enter Paradise (compare 4Mc 13:17). It is the place where the righteous go at the moment of death and where judgment is enacted as preliminary and perhaps probationary until the Final Judgment at the end of the age.

See *Hades; Hell; Immortality; Paradise; Righteous, Promises to; Sheol; Spirit; Wicked, Punishment of.*

ABRAM See *Abraham, Abram.*

ABRECH, ABREK Transliteration of a term, perhaps of Egyptian origin, translated "make way" or "bow down" in the NIV (Ge 41:43; see NRSV ftn).

ABRONAH A place where the Israelites camped (Nu 33:34-35).

ABSALOM (*father is peace*).

1. The third son of David by Maacah, daughter of Talmai, king of Geshur (2Sa 3:3; 1Ch 3:2), also known as Abishalom (1Ki 15:2, 10, w 1Ch 11:20-21).

Absalom hates Amnon, one of his stepbrothers and David's first son, because Amnon had raped his sister Tamar; after two years, Absalom avenges Tamar (2Sa 13:1-29). He flees to Geshur and stays there three years (2Sa 13:37-38). He is permitted by David to return to Jerusalem (2Sa 14:1-24). He is more handsome than anyone in all Israel (2Sa 14:25). Children of (2Sa 14:27). Absalom is not allowed to see David for two years after his return from exile in Geshur (2Sa 14:28), at which time he forces Joab to get him an audience with the king (2Sa 14:31-33).

His popularity (2Sa 15:2-6, 13). Conspiracy (2Sa 15-17). Death and burial (2Sa 18:9-17). Pillar of (2Sa 18:18). David's mourning for (2Sa 18:33; 19:1-8).

2. Rehoboam's father-in-law (2Ch 11:20-21).

3. In the Apocrypha, an ambassador of Judas Maccabaeus, father of Mattathias and Jonathan (1Mc 11:70; 13:11; 2Mc 11:17).

ABSTEMIOUSNESS See *Abstinence; Temperance.*

ABSTINENCE

From Intoxicating Beverages:

Abuse of alcohol condemned (Pr 23:20, 31-35; Lk 21:34). Exemplified by Aaron and the Levitical priesthood, while on duty (Lev 10:8-11; Eze 44:21); Nazirites, while taking a special vow (Nu 6:2-4, 20); Manoah's wife, Samson's mother, during pregnancy (Jdg 13:2-5, 13-14); Kings and princes (Pr 31:4-5); John the Baptist (Lk 1:15).

Instances of:

Israelites in the wilderness (Dt 29:6). Samson (Jdg 16:17, w 13:3-5, 13-14 & Nu 6:3-4). Recabites, honoring an ancestral commitment (Jer 35:1-14). Daniel (Da 1:8, 12). John the Baptist (Mt 11:18; Lk 1:15; 7:33). See *Temperance.*

Other Things Abstained From:

Food, in fasting (Ne 1:4; 1Sa 7:6; Ne 9:1; Joel 2:12; Mt 6:16-18). See *Fasting.* Sexual contact within marriage, temporarily (Ex 19:15; 1Co 7:1-5).

In Israel—
The use of blood or fat (Ge 9:4; Lev 3:17). The tendon of the hip (Ge 32:32). Meat not properly bled and prepared (Ex 22:31; Dt 14:21). Whole groups of animals (Lev 11). Contact with unclean person (Lev 15). See *Unclean.*

Christians—
From evil and immorality (Ac 15:20, 29; Eph 4:17-5:21; Col 3:1-11; 1Pe 2:11-12). For the sake of a weaker brother (Ro 14; 1Co 8). Wrongly used as a form of self-righteousness (Col 2:20-23; 1Ti 4:1-3). From an appearance of evil (1Th 5:22).

ABUNDANCE

General:

(Ecc 5:9-20; Isa 15:7; Mt 13:12; 25:29; Mk 12:42-44; Lk 21:1-4; 2Co 8:12-15). Steadfast love (Ge 34:6-7; Ps 69:13; 103; Jnh 4:2). Peace (Lev 26:3, 6; Ps 37:10-11; Jer 33:6-9). Pardon (Nu 14:17-19; 2Ch 30:18-20; Isa 1:18; 55:7; Joel 3:20-21; Mic 7:18-20). Prosperity (Dt 28:47). Anguish (1Sa 1:16). Wealth (2Ch 17:3-6; 18:1; 20:25-27; 24:8-14; Ps 37:16; 52:6-7; Jer 48:36-38; 51:12-13). Honor (2Ch 17:5; 18:1; 1Co 12:23-24). Glory of Zion (Isa 66:11). Overflow of the heart (Mt 12:34; Lk 6:45). Life (Jn 5:39-40; 10:10; 20:30-31), is not in the abundance of possessions (Lk 12:15). Grace (Ro 5; 2Co 4:15), of giving (2Co 8:1-15), through the knowledge of our God and Savior Jesus Christ (2Pe 1:2). Affection, brotherly (2Co 7:15). Plunder (2Co 2:5). Immeasurably more than we ask (Eph 3:20). Holy Spirit (Tit 3:5-6).

From God:

Provisions, *i.e.* needs (Lev 26:3-5; Dt 30:9-10; Ps 132:13-15; Pr 3:9-10; Isa 30:23; Eze 36:29-30; Am 9:13; Zec 8:12; Php 4:19), grace (2Co 9:8), joys (Ps 36:8), life (Jn 10:10), power (Eph 3:20), participation in the divine nature and a rich welcome into the eternal kingdom (2Pe 1:3-11).

ABUSE

Substance Abuse: (1Co 6:12-13).

Of alcohol: Biblical condemnation of alcohol abuse may be generalized to apply to abuse of any mind- or behavior-altering

substance. Condemned (Pr 20:1; 21:17; 23:20, 30-35; Isa 5:22; Eph 5:18; 1Ti 3:8; Tit 2:3). Examples of (Ge 9:20-24; 19:30-36; Isa 28:7-8; 1Co 11:20-22). *See Abstinence; Temperance.*

Of food (Pr 23:1-3, 20-21; 25:16; 30:22; Isa 56:10-11; Am 6:4-7; 1Co 6:12-13; 1Co 11:20-22; Php 3:18-19).

Sexual Abuse:
Rape punished by death (Dt 22:25-27). Examples of: rape (Ge 34:1-7; Jdg 19:25-20:13; 2Sa 13:1-20; Zec 14:2), attempted homosexual rape (Ge 19:4-9; Jdg 19:22-24).

Abuse of Persons:
Physical injury: Punished in like kind (Ex 21:22-25; Lev 24:19-20).
Servants and slaves: Set free if physically abused (Ex 21:26-27).
Family: Under the law, an unfavored wife still had to be cared for (Ex 21:10-11; Dt 21:15-17). A child could be put to death for abuse of parents (Ex 21:15, 17; Dt 21:18-21). Corporal punishment, if done out of the motivation of love, is not abuse (Pr 3:11-12; 13:24; 29:15; Heb 12:7-11).

ABYSS (*unfathomable depth*). The abode of demons (Lk 8:31) and the place of the dead (Ro 10:7). The bottomless pit; a place of torment and of imprisoned demons (Rev 9:1-2, 11; 11:7; 17:8; 20:1-3).

ACACIA A tree (Isa 41:19). The ark of the covenant made of its wood (Ex 25:10), poles of the ark (Ex 25:13; 38:6), boards in the tabernacle (Ex 26:15-37), the altar of burnt offerings (Ex 38:1, 6).

ACBOR (*mouse or jerboa*).
1. The father of Baal-Hanan, a king of Edom (Ge 36:38-39; 1Ch 1:49).
2. The son of Micaiah, a messenger of King Josiah (2Ki 22:12-14). Also called Abdon the son of Micah (2Ch 34:20). *See Abdon, 5.*
3. The father of Elnathan (Jer 26:22; 36:12).

ACCAD *See Akkad.*

ACCEPTED BY GOD Lot's prayers (Ge 19:19-21), Job's prayers (Job 42:9), willing praise (Ps 119:108).

Israelites:
(Ex 28:38; Eze 20:40-41; 43:27). The OT prophets continually affirmed that offerings were only acceptable when the person was acceptable; the offerer never became acceptable to God by giving him gifts (Hos 8:13; Mal 1:6-14).

NT Believers:
People from every nation who fear God and do what is right (Ac 10:34-35). The believer's goal is to please God (2Co 5:9). Through Christ (Eph 1:4-6).

ACCEPTED TIME The time favorable for seeking God. When forgiven (Ps 32:5-6). When in trouble (Ps 69:13). Today, *i.e.,* now (Ps 95:7-8; Isa 49:8; 2Co 6:2).

ACCESS TO GOD Exemplified (Ex 24:2; 34:4-7). Typified (Lev 16:12-15, w Heb 10:19-22). In prayer (Dt 4:7; 2Ki 4:33; Mt 6:6; 1Pe 1:17). *See Prayer.* A privilege of believers (Dt 4:7; Ps 15; 23:6; 24:3-5). In his temple (Ps 15:1; 27:4-5; 43:3; 65:4). Blessedness of (Ps 16:11; 65:4; 73:28). Believers earnestly seek (Ps 27:4; 42:1-2; 43:3-4; 84:1-2). Is of God (Ps 65:4). Promises connected with (Ps 145:18-20; Isa 55:1-5; Mt 6:6; Jas 4:8). Urge others to seek (Isa 2:3; Jer 31:6). The wicked commanded to seek (Isa 55:6; Jas 4:8). Promised to repenting sinners (Hos 14:2; Joel 2:14). *See Repentance.* Is by Christ (Jn 10:7-10; 14:6-7; Ro 5:1-2; Eph 2:13; 3:12; Heb 7:18-19; 10:1-25; 1Pe 3:18). Obtained through faith (Ac 14:27; Ro 5:1-2; Eph 3:12; Heb 11:6). Is by the Holy Spirit (Eph 2:18). Believers have with confidence (Eph 3:12; Heb 4:16; 10:19-22). Follows upon reconciliation to God (Col 1:21-22). To obtain mercy and grace (Heb 4:16).

ACCESSORY *See Complicity.*

ACCO A town on the Mediterranean coast c. thirty miles south of Tyre, and ten from Mt. Carmel (Jdg 1:31, NIV). Also called Ptolemais by the ancient Greeks and Romans because Ptolemy, the Egyptian king, rebuilt the city in c. 100 B.C.; a town of Phoenicia (Ac 21:7, NIV, Ptolemais). *See Ptolemais.*

ACCOMPLICE *See Complicity.*

ACCOUNTABILITY *See Responsibility.*

ACCURSED People that are cursed (Dt 21:23; Jos 6:18; 7:1, 11, 13, 15; 1Ch 2:7; Isa 65:20; Ro 9:3; 1Co 12:3; Gal 1:8).
Things that are cursed (Jos 6:17-18; 7:12).
See Abomination; Anathema; Idolatry.

ACCUSATION, FALSE
Forbidden
(Ex 23:1, 7; Lev 19:16; Lk 3:14; Tit 2:3).
Consolation for falsely accused (Mt 5:11; Jn 15:19-21; 1Pe 4:14).

Instances of False Accusation:
Joseph by Potiphar's wife (Ge 39:7-20); Joseph's brothers by Joseph (Ge 42:6-14); Moses by Korah (Nu 16:1-3, 13); the prophet Ahimelech by Saul (1Sa 22:11-16); Abner by Joab (2Sa 3:24-27); Elijah by Ahab (1Ki 18:17-18); Naboth by Jezebel (1Ki 21:1-14); the Jews who returned under Ezra, accused by the men of Trans-Euphrates (Ezr 4:6-16; Ne 6:5-9); Job by Satan (Job 1:9-10; 2:4-5). David (Ps 41:5-9), by the princes of Ammon (2Sa 10:1-4; 1Ch 19:1-4); Jeremiah (Jer 26:8-15; 37:12-15; 43:1-4); Amos (Am 7:10-11); Mary (Mt 1:19); Jesus (Mt 9:34; 10:25; 12:2-14; 26:59-61; Mk 3:22; 14:53-65; Lk 23:2; Jn 18:30), Stephen (Ac 6:11-14), Paul (Ac 17:6-7; 21:27-29; 24:1-9, 12-13; 25:1-2, 7; Ro 3:8), Paul and Silas (Ac 16:19-21).
In last days, people will be slanderous (2Ti 3:3).
See Conspiracy; Evidence; False Witness; Persecution; Speaking; Evil; Talebearer.

ACELDAMA *See Akeldama.*

ACHAIA A region of Greece, on the S coast of the gulf of Corinth. Paul visits (Ac 18; 19:21; 1Co 16:15; 2Co 1:1). Generosity of the Christians in (Ro 15:26; 2Co 9:2; 11:10).

ACHAICUS (*belonging to Achaia*). A Corinthian Christian who helped Paul, visited him at Ephesus and was commended for his good will toward Paul (1Co 16:17-19).

ACHAN (a word play from Achar: *troubler*). The son of Carmi and a Judahite of Zerah's clan who participated in the assault upon Jericho; he also violated the sacrificial ban by stealing gold, silver, and a beautiful robe from the spoil taken. After Israel failed to take Ai, inquiry was made by lot, and Achan was found to be guilty. Sin and punishment of (Jos 7; 22:20; 1Ch 2:7).

ACHAR (*trouble*). A variant spelling of Achan (1Ch 2:7).

ACHAZ *See Ahaz.*

ACHBOR *See Acbor.*

ACHIM *See Akim.*

ACHISH (*the king gives*). King of the Philistines, also called Abimelech (Ps 34, title). David escapes to (1Sa 21:10-15; 27; 28:1-2; 29). Achish continues as king of Gath during the reign of Solomon (1Ki 2:39-40).

ACHMETHA *See Ecbatana.*

ACHOR (*trouble*). A valley near Jericho in which Achan was stoned (Jos 7:24-26; 15:7; Isa 65:10; Hos 2:15).

ACHSA, ACHSAH *See Acsah.*

ACHSHAPH *See Acshaph.*

ACHZIB *See Aczib.*

ACKNOWLEDGE
General (Isa 61:9; 63:16; 1Co 14:37-38).
Acknowledging, in an imperative sense, that the Lord is God and that there is no other (Dt 4:39; Pr 3:5-6), in an imprecatory sense (Ps 79:6-7; Jer 10:23-25).
We acknowledge our sins (Ps 32:5; 51:1-6; Isa 59:12-13), our rebellion, idolatry, and wickedness (Jer 3:13; 14:20).
Recognition (1Co 16:17-18).

ACRE The amount of land a pair of oxen could plow in a day (1Sa 14:14; Isa 5:10).

ACROPOLIS (*crest of city, high ground of city*). The upper or higher city, citadel, or castle of a Greek city. Especially the high rocky promontory in Athens where the treasury of the city and its finest temples were located.

ACROSTIC A literary device by which the first letter of each line of poetry forms either a word or the successive letters of the alphabet. An outstanding example is Psalm 119, in which each successive set of eight verses begins with a different letter of the Hebrew alphabet. The effect is not apparent in the English translation, but the Hebrew letters are given between the lines in order to show the construction. NIV notes identify other acrostic poems (Ps. 9-10; 24; 34; 37; 111; 112; 145; Pr 31:10-31; La 1; 2; 3; 4).

ACROSTIC POETRY *See Poetry.*

ACSAH (*decorative anklet*). Caleb's daughter (1Ch 2:49). Caleb offered her as a reward, to be married, to the man who would capture the city of Debir, which was formerly called Kiriath Sepher. Caleb's nephew, Othniel, took the city and won the prize (Jos 15:16-19; Jdg 1:9-15).

ACSHAPH (*fascination*). An important Canaanite city which Joshua captured with its king (Jos 11:1; 12:7, 20). It is named as being on the border of the lot assigned to Asher (Jos 19:24-25).

ACTIONS AT LAW Duty of defendant (Mt 5:40; 1Co 6:7). *See Adjudication at Law; Arbitration.*

ACTIVITY, EVIL Of sinners in general (Pr 1:10-16; 4:14-17; 6:18; Isa 59:7; Mic 2:1-2; 7:3; Ro 3:15-18). Of Pharisees (Mt 23:15). Of Paul in persecuting the church (Ac 9:2; 26:11; Gal 1:13; Php 3:6). Of busybodies in the church, stirring up strife (2Th 3:10-12; 1Ti 5:13; 1Pe 4:15). Of Satan (1Pe 5:8).

ACTS OF THE APOSTLES
Author: Anonymous; traditionally Luke, the companion of Paul
Date: Probably between A.D. 63 and 67
Outline:
I. Peter and the Beginnings of the Church in Israel (chs. 1-12).
 A. "Throughout Judea, Galilee and Samaria" (1:1-9:31; see 9:31).
 1. Introduction (1:1-2).
 2. Christ's post-resurrection ministry (1:3-11).
 3. The period of waiting for the Holy Spirit (1:12-26).
 4. The filling with the Spirit (ch. 2).
 5. The healing of the lame man and the resultant arrest of Peter and John (3:1-4:31).
 6. The community of goods (4:32-5:11).
 7. The arrest of the twelve apostles (5:12-42).
 8. The choice of the Seven (6:1-7).
 9. Stephen's arrest and martyrdom (6:8-7:60).
 10. The scattering of the Jerusalem believers (8:1-4).
 11. Philip's ministry (8:5-40).
 a. In Samaria (8:5-25).
 b. To the Ethiopian eunuch (8:26-40).
 12. Saul's conversion (9:1-31).

B. "As far as Phoenicia, Cyprus and Antioch" (9:32-12:25; see 11:19).
 1. Peter's ministry on the Mediterranean coast (9:32-11:18).
 a. To Aeneas and Dorcas (9:32-43).
 b. To Cornelius (10:1-11:18).
 2. The new Gentile church in Antioch (11:19-30).
 3. Herod's persecution of the church and his subsequent death (ch. 12).
II. Paul and the Expansion of the Church From Antioch to Rome (chs. 13-28).
 A. "Throughout the region of Phrygia and Galatia" (13:1-15:35; see 16:6).
 1. Paul's first missionary journey (chs. 13-14).
 2. The Jerusalem conference (15:1-35).
 B. "Over to Macedonia" (15:36-21; see 16:9).
 1. Paul's second missionary journey (15:36-18:22).
 2. Paul's third missionary journey (18:23-21:16).
 C. "To Rome" (21:17-28:31; see 28:14).
 1. Paul's imprisonment in Jerusalem (21:17-23:35).
 a. Arrest (21:17-22:29).
 b. Trial before the Sanhedrin (22:30-23:11).
 c. Transfer to Caesarea (23:12-35).
 2. Paul's imprisonment in Caesarea (chs. 24-26).
 a. Trial before Felix (ch. 24).
 b. Trial before Festus (25:1-12).
 c. Hearing before Festus and Agrippa (25:13-26:32).
 3. Voyage to Rome (27:1-28:15).
 4. Two years under house arrest in Rome (28:16-31).
See Missionary Journeys of Paul.

ACZIB (*deceit*).
1. A city of Judah in the Shephelah (Jos 15:44; Mic 1:14) perhaps the same as modern Tell el-Beida, which is SW of Adullam. Taken by Sennacherib, c. 701 B.C. Also called Kezib (Ge 38:5) and Cozeba (1Ch 4:22).
2. A town in Asher on the coast N of Acco (Jos 19:29; Jdg 1:31).

ADADAH A city in Judah (Jos 15:22).

ADAH (*adornment*).
1. The wife of Lamech and mother of Jabal (Ge 4:19-20, 23).
2. The daughter of Elon the Hittite, and the first of three wives of Esau; she was the mother of Eliphaz (Ge 36:2, 4, 10, 12, 16).

ADAIAH (*adornment of Yahweh*).
1. A native of Bozkath; the father of Jedidah, the mother of Josiah, the king of Judah (2Ki 22:1).
2. A Levite of the family of Gershom; the son of Ethni and father of Zerah, in the ancestry of Asaph (1Ch 6:41-43).
3. The son of Shimei and one of the chief Benjamites in pre-exilic Jerusalem (1Ch 8:1, 21).
4. A priest and a Levite; the son of Jeroham (1Ch 9:10-12), also in the parallel list in Nehemiah, although the genealogies do not agree in all details (Ne 11:12).
5. The father of Maaseiah, an army officer who helped make Joash king in the overthrow of Athaliah (2Ch 23:1).
6. A man who married a foreign wife during the Exile and divorced her after the Captivity (Ezr 10:29).
7. Another man who did the same thing (Ezr 10:39).
8. A descendant of Judah whose posterity lived in Jerusalem after the captivity (Ne 11:5).

ADALIA (possibly *honorable*). The fifth son of Haman (Est 9:8).

ADAM (*[red] earth*, or *[ruddy] skin color*).
1. The first man. His creation (Ge 1:26-28; 2:7; 1Co 15:45; 1Ti 2:13). The history of, before he sinned (Ge 1:26-30; 2:15-25). His temptation and sin (Ge 3; Job 31:33, ftn; Isa 43:27; Hos 6:7; Ro 5:14-21; 1Ti 2:14). The subsequent history of (Ge 3:20-24; 4:1-2, 25; 5:1-5). His death (Ge 5:5). Progenitor of the human race (Dt 32:8; Mal 2:10). A type of Christ (Ro 5:14). Brought sin and death into the world (1Co 15:22, 45).
2. Christ: the last Adam (1Co 15:45).
3. A city in the Jordan Valley where the Israelites entered the promised land (Jos 3:16).

ADAMAH (*[red] earth*). A city of Naphtali (Jos 19:36). The location is disputed, yet it may be the modern city of Tell ed-Damiyeh.

ADAMANT NIV "hardest stone" (Eze 3:9; Zec 7:12). *See Diamond; Flint, 2; Hardest Stone; Minerals of the Bible, 1; Stones.*

ADAMI NEKEB (*the ground of piercing*). A place on the border of Naphtali (Jos 19:33).

ADAR (possibly *dark, clouded*).
Month twelve in sacred sequence, six in civil sequence (Ezr 6:15; Est 3:7; 8:12; 9:1, 15-21). The rainy season (February-March); the season for harvesting citrus fruit. *See Month, 12.*

ADAR SHENI (*Second Adar*). This intercalary month (not in Bible) was added about every three years so the lunar calendar would correspond to the solar year. *See Month, 13.*

ADBEEL (*[the] grief of God [El]*). The third son of Ishmael (Ge 25:13; 1Ch 1:29).

ADDAN *See Addon.*

ADDAR (*glorious*).
1. Also called Ard (Ge 46:21; Nu 26:40).
A son of Bela, and grandson of Benjamin (1Ch 8:3). Counted as a son of Benjamin and head of a family in the tribe.
2. A place on the S border of Judah (Jos 15:3).
See Hazar Addar; Ataroth Addar.

ADDER A poisonous snake (Job 20:16; Isa 30:6; 59:5). *See Cobra; Serpent.*

A

ADDI (*my witness*, or *adorned*). An ancestor of Joseph, the husband of Mary (Lk 3:28).

ADDICTION (1Co 6:12-13; 2Pe 2:19; Ro 6:16-21). *See Abuse.*

ADDON The inhabitants of Addon came up after the Babylonian captivity, but were unable to prove their lineage as descendants of Israel (Ezr 2:59; Ne 7:61).

ADER *See Eder.*

ADIEL (*adornment of God [El]*).
1. A descendant of Simeon who gained more pastoral land for himself in the region of Gedor in the time of Hezekiah (1Ch 4:36).
2. A priest, son of Jahzerah and the father of Maasai; Maasai returned after the Babylonian captivity and was very active in reconstructing the temple (1Ch 9:12).
3. Father of Azmaveth, who was supervisor of David's treasuries (1Ch 27:25).

ADIN (*voluptuous, luxurious*).
1. One whose family returned from exile with Zerubbabel (Ezr 2:15; Ne 7:20).
2. One whose posterity came back with Ezra (Ezr 8:6).
3. The name of a family sealing the covenant (Ne 10:16).

ADINA (*adorned*). The son of Shiza, a Reubenite; one of David's mighty men (1Ch 11:42).

ADINO (*his adorned one*). KJV "Adino the Eznite" is a variant reading in the NIV (2Sa 23:8, ftn). *See Josheb-Basshebeth.*

ADITHAIM (*double [row] of adornments*). A city of Judah in the Shephelah (Jos 15:36).

ADJUDICATION AT LAW To be avoided (Pr 17:14; 20:3; 25:8-10; Mt 5:25, 40; Lk 12:58). *See Actions at Law; Arbitration; Compromise; Court, of Law; Justice; Litigation.*

ADJURATION KJV "adjure" is in the NIV to "pronounce" or "bind under oath," to "make someone swear an oath." It is an act or appeal in which a person in authority imposes some obligation upon another with the strength and solemnity of an oath (Jos 6:26; 1Sa 14:24; 1Ki 22:16; 2Ch 18:15). In the NT the high priest calls upon Jesus to acknowledge that he was the Messiah (Mk 5:7). The oath was binding and required a reply. *See Oath.*
It is also used to exorcise demons (Ac 19:13).

ADLAI (*be just*). The father of Shaphat, who was David's chief herdsman (1Ch 27:29).

ADMAH (*[red] earth*). A city near Gomorrah and Zeboiim (Ge 10:19). The king was Shinab (Ge 14:2, 8). Admah was destroyed along with Sodom and Gomorrah (Dt 29:23, w Ge 19:24-28; Hos 11:8).

ADMATHA (*unrestrained*). The third named prince of Persia and Media (Est 1:14).

ADMINISTRATORS Officers who ruled in Darius's kingdom; satraps report to (Da 6:2-7).

ADMONITION *See Wicked, Warned.*

ADNA (*delight*).
1. A son of Pahath-Moab who had married a foreign wife during the Exile (Ezr 10:30).
2. A chief priest, and the head of his father's house in the days of Joiakim (Ne 12:12-15).

ADNAH (*delight*).
1. One of the captains of the tribe of Manasseh who joined David at Ziklag (1Ch 12:20).
2. A man of Judah who held high military rank under Jehoshaphat (2Ch 17:14).

ADONI-BEZEK (*lord of Bezek*). The king of Bezek, who had the thumbs and big toes of 70 kings cut off: when the Israelites routed the Canaanites and Perizzites and captured Adoni-Bezek, they had his thumbs and big toes cut off (Jdg 1:4-7). *See Bezek.*

ADONIJAH (*[my] lord is Yahweh*).
1. The fourth son of David by his wife Haggith (2Sa 3:4; 1Ki 1:5-6; 1Ch 3:2). Usurpation of, and downfall (1Ki 1). Executed by Solomon (1Ki 2:13, 25).
2. A Levite whom Jehoshaphat sent to assist in teaching the law to the people of Judah (2Ch 17:8).
3. A leader who with Nehemiah sealed the covenant (Ne 10:16). *See Adonikam.*

ADONIKAM (*[my] lord arises*). One of the Jews who returned with Ezra from Babylon with Zerubbabel (Ezr 2:13). Later three of his descendants came with Ezra (Ne 7:18). Probably the same as Adonijah, 3 (Ne 10:16).

ADONIRAM (*[my] Lord is exalted*). A man in charge of forced labor during the reigns of David (2Sa 20:24), and later under Solomon (1Ki 4:6; 5:14), and then Solomon's son, Rehoboam (1Ki 12:18; 2Ch 10:18). He was stoned to death by the people of Israel as their first act of rebellion and revolt, which was lead by Jeroboam, son of Nebat, during the division of the monarchy. Also spelled Adoram (1Ki 12:18; 2Sa 20:24) and Hadoram (2Ch 10:18, ftn).

ADONI-ZEDEK (*[my] lord is righteousness*). The Amorite king of Jerusalem who with four other kings was defeated in battle and slain by Joshua at Gibeon (Jos 10:1-27).

ADOPTION
Explained: (2Co 6:18).
Of Children:
Instances of: Of one born in Abram's house (Ge 15:3), of Joseph's sons (Ge 48:5, 14, 16, 22), of Moses (Ex 2:5-10; Ac 7:20-21; Heb 11:24), of Esther (Est 2:7).
Spiritual Adoption:
Of Israel (Ex 4:22-23; Nu 6:27; Dt 14:1-2; 26:18-19; 27:9; 28:9-10; 32:5-6; 2Ch 7:14; Isa 63:8, 16; Jer 3:19; 31:9, 20; Hos 1:9-10; 11:1; Ro 9:4); of Solomon (2Sa 7:14; 1Ch 22:10; 28:6).
Of the righteous (Pr 14:26; Isa 43:1-6; 63:8, 16; Mt 5:9, 44-45; 12:50; 13:43; Lk 6:35; Jn 11:52; Ro 9:8, 26; 2Co 6:17-18; Eph 2:19; Php 2:15; Heb 12:6-7, 9; 1Jn 3:1-2, 10; 4:4).
Of the Gentiles promised (Hos 2:23; Ro 9:24-26; Eph 3:6, 14-15; Heb 2:10-11, 13); testified to by the Holy Spirit (Ro 8:14-17, 19, 21, 29; Gal 4:5-7); through the gospel (Eph 3:6).
The Means of Adoption:
By God's grace (Eze 16:3-6; Ro 4:16-17; Eph 1:5-6, 11); by faith (Jn 1:12-13; Gal 3:7, 26, 29; Eph 1:5); through Christ (Jn 1:12-13; Gal 3:26; 4:4-5; Eph 1:5; Heb 2:10-11, 13); according to promise (Ro 9:8; Gal 3:29; Eph 3:6); through the gospel (Eph 3:6).
Role of the Holy Spirit:
Witnessed by the Spirit (Ro 8:16); led by the Spirit as evidence of (Ro 8:14); the Spirit of sonship received (Ro 8:15; Gal 4:6).
Results:
A new name (Nu 6:27; Isa 62:2; Ac 15:17); disciplined by the Father (Dt 8:5; 2Sa 7:14; Pr 3:11-12; Heb 12:5-11); safety (Pr 14:26); God is Father-Redeemer (Isa 63:16); recipient of God's long-suffering mercy (Jer 31:1, 19-20); a new inheritance (Mt 13:43; Ro 8:17); the new birth (Jn 1:12-13); will become brothers and sisters of Christ (Jn 20:17; Heb 2:11-12).
A new lifestyle: A love of peace (Mt 5:9); desire for God's glory (Mt 5:16); likeness to God (Mt 5:44-45, 48); an avoiding of pretense (Mt 6:1-4); a forgiving spirit (Mt 6:14); confidence in God (Mt 6:25-34); a spirit of prayer (Mt 7:7-11); a merciful spirit (Lk 6:35-36); holiness (2Co 6:17-18; 7:1; Php 2:15); following God (Eph 5:1).
A new future: Gathered as one by Christ (Jn 11:52); final consummation (Ro 8:19, 23; 1Jn 3:2).

ADORAIM (*possibly pair of knolls*). A fortified city in SW Judah, five miles SW of Hebron, fortified by Rehoboam, son of Solomon (2Ch 11:9).

ADORAM *See Adoniram.*

ADORNING
Physical:
Bracelets (Ge 24:22; Nu 31:50; 2Sa 1:10). Earrings (Ge 35:4; Ex 32:2; 35:22; Nu 31:50; Jdg 8:24; Pr 25:12; Eze 16:12). Chains, used as ornaments (Ge 41:42; Pr 1:9; Eze 16:11; Da 5:29). Rings, for the fingers (Ge 41:42; Ex 35:22; Est 3:10; 8:8; Job 42:11; Isa 3:21; Hos 2:13; Lk 15:22). Ornaments, wearing of (Ex 33:4; Isa 3:18; Jer 2:32; 4:30; Eze 16:11; 23:40).
Jewels:
General references to (Ex 35:22; Nu 31:50). Discarded or refusal to wear (Ge 35:4; Ex 33:4; 1Pe 3:3). Brought as offerings to God (Ex 35:22; Nu 31:50; Mt 2:1-2, 9-11).
Spiritual:
Clothed in righteousness, salvation, strength (Job 29:14; Ps 132:16; Isa 52:1; 61:10; Zec 3:4; Mt 22:11). General references to (Ps 45:13; Pr 1:9; 4:9; SS 1:10; Isa 61:10; 1Pe 3:3-4; Rev 21:2). White clothing, the heavenly garment (Mt 17:2; Rev 3:5; 3:18; 4:4; 7:9; 19:8).

ADRAMMELECH (*nobility of Molech [king]*).
1. The name given to Adar, the god brought to Samaria from Assyria by the Sepharvites (2Ki 17:31).
2. One of the sons of Sennacherib, who along with his brother Sharezer, killed their father while he was worshiping in the temple of his god Nisroch (2Ki 19:37; Isa 37:38).

ADRAMYTTIUM (*the mansion of death*). A port city of Mysia, in the NW part of the Roman province of Asia (Ac 27:2).

ADRIATIC The Adriatic Sea, a body of water between Italy on the W and Dalmatia, Macedonia, and Achaia on the E (Ac 27:27).

ADRIEL (*[my] help is God [El]*). The son of Barzillai the Meholathite; Saul's son-in-law (1Sa 18:19; 2Sa 21:8-9).

ADULLAM, ADULLAMITE (*retreat* or *refuge; possibly [they are] just*).
1. A cave near the Dead Sea. David takes refuge in (1Sa 22:1; 2Sa 23:13; 1Ch 11:15). *See also the titles of Pss 57 and 142.*
2. An ancient city of Canaan (Ge 38:1; Jos 12:15; 15:35), fortified by Rehoboam (2Ch 11:5-7), inhabited after the Exile (Ne 11:25-30), referred to by Micah (Mic 1:15).
3. The people of Adullam, used of Hirah, Judah's friend (Ge 38:1, 12, 20).

ADULLAMITE *See Adullam, 3.*

ADULTERY
Defined:
(Mt 5:28, 32; 19:9; Mk 10:11-12; Lk 16:18; Ro 7:1-3). Laws concerning (Nu 5:11-31; Dt 22:13-29).
Repulsive to the righteous (Job 31:1-12; Eze 18:5-6, 9). Fatal consequences of (Pr 2:16-19; 5:3-4, 5-23; 6:23-35; 7:1-27; 9:13-18; 22:14; 23:26-28). Moral and spiritual corruption by (Jer 3:1-2; 5:7-8; Hos 4:1-2, 9-19). Source of: the heart (Mt 15:19; Mk 7:21-23), the sinful nature (Gal 5:19-21).
Figurative:
(Jer 3:1-2; 9:2; 23:10; Eze 16:15-16; Hos 1; 2:1-2; 3:1; 7:1-4; Ro 7:1-6).

ADOPTION

Forbidden:
(Ex 20:14; Lev 18:20; 19:29; Dt 5:18; 23:17; Pr 31:3; Mt 5:27-28; 19:16-19; Mk 10:17-19; Lk 18:18-20; Ac 15:20, 29; Ro 13:9, 13; 1Co 5:9-11; 6:13-16-18; 10:7-8; Eph 4:17-19; 5:3; Col 3:5; 1Th 4:3-7; 1Ti 1:9-10; Jas 2:10-11).
Forgiveness of:
(Jdg 19:1-4; Jn 4:16-26, 39-42; 8:10-11).
Lack of Repentance in:
(Pr 30:20; Isa 57:3-4; Jer 7:9-15; Ro 1:28-32; 2Co 12:21; 1Pe 4:3-4; Rev 9:20-21).
Instances of:
The Sodomites (Ge 19:4-8; Jude 7). Lot and his two daughters (Ge 19:31-38). Shechem (Ge 34:1-2). Reuben (Ge 35:22). Judah (Ge 38:1-26). Potiphar's wife (Ge 39:6-12). Israelites (Ex 32:6; Jer 23:10-11; 29:23; Eze 22:9-11; 33:26; Hos 7:4). Gilead, the father of Jephthah (Jdg 11:1). Samson (Jdg 16:1). The Levite's concubine (Jdg 19:1-2). The men of Gibeah (Jdg 19:22-25). The sons of Eli (1Sa 2:22). David (2Sa 11:1-5). Amnon, David's oldest son by Ahinoam (2Sa 13:1-20). Absalom, David's third son by Maacah (2Sa 16:22). Herod (Mt 14:3-4; Mk 6:17-18; Lk 3:19). The Samaritan woman (Jn 4:17-18). The woman brought to Jesus in the temple (Jn 8:3-11). The Corinthians (1Co 5:1-5). Gentiles (Eph 4:17-20; 1Pe 4:3-4). Those living in the last days (2Ti 3:6).
Penalties for:
Curses (Nu 5:11-31; Dt 27:20-23; Job 24:15-18). Death (Ge 20:3, 7; 26:11; 38:24; Lev 20:10-12; 21:9; Dt 22:13-27; 2Sa 12:7-14; Eze 23:45-48; Jn 8:4-5). Fines (Ex 22:16-17; Dt 22:19, 28-29). Make a guilt offering (Lev 19:20-22). Divine judgments (2Sa 12:10-12; Jer 29:22-23; Eze 16:38-41; Mal 3:5; 1Co 10:8; Heb 13:4; 2Pe 2:9-10, 14; Rev 2:20-22; 18:9-10). Excommunication (1Co 5:1-13; Eph 5:11-12). Exclusion from the kingdom of God (1Co 6:9-10; Gal 5:19, 21; Eph 5:5-6; Jude 7; Rev 21:8; 22:14-15).
See Fornication; Idolatry; Lasciviousness; Prostitute; Rape; Sensuality; Homosexual; Prostitute.

ADUMMIM (*red [streaks]*). A pass on the road between Jerusalem and Jericho (Jos 15:7; 18:17), on the north border of Judah and the south border of Benjamin. Held to be the scene of Jesus' parable of the Good Samaritan (Lk 10:30-35).

ADVENT *See Jesus the Christ, Second Coming; Millennium.*

ADVERSARY In general, an enemy; personal, national, or supernatural (Ex 23:22; 1Sa 2:10; Na 1:2; Mt 5:25). Specifically, Satan is the enemy of all mankind (1Pe 5:8).

ADVERSITY *See Afflictions.*

ADVICE *See Counsel.*

ADVOCATE (*helper, Paraclete*). An advocate is one who pleads the case or the cause of another. The Holy Spirit or Counselor (Jn 14:16-17, 26; 15:26; 16:7), Jesus Christ himself (1Jn 2:1).

AENEAS (*possibly praise*). A paralytic, healed at Lydda by Peter (Ac 9:32-35).

AENON (*spring*). A place probably N of Jerusalem to the W of the Jordan Valley because the Johannine account indicates that there was "plenty of water." Some scholars identify ancient Salim with present-day Salim, which is about three to four miles E of Nablus (Shechem). A place near Salim, W of the Jordan, where John the Baptist baptized (Jn 3:22-23).

AEON (*a segment of time, eternity*). A Greek word indicating a period of time, usually translated ever or forever (Eph 3:21; Jn 6:51, 58), age or ages (Eph 1:21; Col 1:26), world (Ro 12:2; 2Ti 4:10).

AFFECTIONS
Of Believers:
Supremely set on God (Dt 6:5; Ps 42:1; 73:23-26; 119:9-20; Mk 12:30). Should be zealous for God (Ps 69:9; 119:139; Gal 4:18). Should not grow cold (Ps 106:12-13; Mt 24:12; Gal 4:14-16; Rev 2:4). Should be set upon the house and worship of God (1Ch 29:3; Ps 26:8; 27:4; 84:1-2), the people of God (Ps 16:3; Ro 12:10; 2Co 7:13-16; 1Th 2:8), the commandments and statutes of God (Ps 19:8-10; 119), heavenly things (Col 3:1-2).
Blessedness of making God the object of our affections (Ps 91:14). Christ claims the first place in (Mt 10:37; Lk 14:26). Stirred up by communion with Christ (Lk 24:32).
Of the Wicked:
Not sincerely set on God (Isa 58:1-2; Eze 33:31-32; Lk 8:13), are unnatural and perverted (Ro 1:18-32; 2Ti 3:1-9; 2Pe 2:10-22). Desires of the flesh, crucified in believers (Ro 6:5-7; Gal 5:24), should be put to death by the Spirit (Ro 8:12-13; 13:14; 1Co 9:27; Col 3:5-6; 1Th 4:3-7). False teachers seek to captivate (Gal 1:9-10; 4:17; 2Ti 3:6; 2Pe 2:3, 18; Rev 2:14, 20).

AFFLICTED
In General:
Sympathy with (Job 6:14; Mt 25:34-40). Help for (Job 22:29; Isa 58:6-7; Lk 10:30-37; 1Ti 5:9-10). Rewards of service to (Isa 53:10; Mt 25:34-45). Exhorted to pray (Jas 5:13). Prayer for healing (Jas 5:14-15).
Duty to:
Pity (Job 6:14), comfort (Job 16:5; 29:25; 2Co 1:3-5; 1Th 4:18), relieve (Job 31:19-20; Isa 58:9-12; Php 4:14; 1Ti 5:10), protect the poor (Ps 82:3; Pr 22:22; 31:5), pray (Ac 12:5; Php 1:19; Jas 5:14-16), sympathize (Ro 12:15; Gal 6:2), remember those in prison and those who are mistreated (Heb 13:3).

AFFLICTED BELIEVERS
God's Relation to:
God is a refuge and strength to (Ps 27:5-6; Isa 25:4; Jer 16:19; Na 1:7), delivers (Ps 34:4, 19; Pr 12:13; Jer 39:17-18), protects (Ps

34:20), is with (Ps 46:5, 7; Isa 43:2-3), comforts (Isa 49:13; Jer 31:13; Mt 5:4; 2Co 1:3-5; 7:6).

Christ comforts (Isa 61:2, w Lk 4:18-19; Mt 11:28-30; Lk 7:13; Jn 14:1; 16:33), preserves (Isa 63:9; Lk 21:18), is with (Jn 14:18), supports (2Ti 4:17; Heb 2:18), delivers (Rev 3:10).

Attitudes and Actions of:

Should be resigned (1Sa 3:18; 2Ki 20:19; Job 1:21; Ps 39:9), acknowledge the justice of their discipline (Ne 9:33; Job 2:10; Isa 64:5-7; La 3:39; Mic 7:9), not despise discipline (Job 5:17-18; Pr 3:11-12; Heb 12:5-6), trust in the goodness of God (Job 13:15; Ps 71:20; 2Co 1:9), avoid sin (Job 34:31-32; Jn 5:14; 1Pe 2:12), praise God (Ps 13:5-6; 56:8-11; 57:6-7; 71:20-23), take encouragement from former mercy (Ps 27:9; 2Co 1:10), call upon God in the day of trouble (Ps 50:15; 55:16-17). *See Affliction, Prayer under.* Turn and devote themselves to God (Ps 116:7-9; Jer 50:3-5; Hos 6:1), be patient (Lk 21:19; Ro 12:12; 2Th 1:4-7; Jas 1:4; 1Pe 2:20), imitate Christ (Heb 12:1-3; 1Pe 2:21-23), imitate the prophets (Jas 5:10).

Examples of:

Joseph (Ge 39:20-23; Ps 105:17-19), Eli (1Sa 3:11-18), David (2Sa 12:15-23), Nehemiah (Ne 1:3-4), Job (Job 1:20-22), Paul (Ac 20:22-24; 21:13), the apostles (1Co 4:13; 2Co 6:4-10), Moses (Heb 11:24-29).

AFFLICTION

Consolation Under:

God is the Author and Giver of (Ps 23:4; Ro 15:5; 2Co 1:3-4; 7:6-7; Col 1:11; 2Th 2:16-17). Christ is the Author and Giver of (Isa 61:1-3; Jn 14:18; 2Co 1:5). The Holy Spirit is the Author and Giver of (Jn 14:16-17; 15:26; 16:7; Ac 9:31).

In the prospect of death (Job 19:25-27; Ps 23:4; Jn 14:1-3; 2Co 5:1; 1Th 4:12-13; Heb 4:9-10; Rev 7:14-17; 14:13). Through the Holy Scriptures (Ps 119:50, 76; Ro 15:4). Pray for (Ps 119:81-83). By ministers of the gospel (Isa 40:1-2; 1Co 14:3; 2Co 1:4, 6). Promised (Ps 119:76; Isa 51:3, 12; 66:13; Eze 14:22-23; Hos 2:14; Zec 1:17). Believers should administer to each other (1Th 4:18; 5:11, 14). Under the infirmities of age (Ps 71:9, 18).

Is sought in vain from the world (Ps 69:20; Ecc 4:1; La 1:2), abundant (Ps 71:21; Isa 66:10-11), a cause of praise (Isa 12:1; 49:13), everlasting (2Th 2:16-17), firm and secure (Heb 6:17-20).

To the persecuted (Dt 33:27), the poor (Ps 10:14; 34:6, 9-10), those deserted by friends or family (Ps 27:10; 41:9-12; Jn 14:18; 15:18-19), the sick (Ps 41:3), the troubled in mind (Ps 42; 94:19; Jn 14:1, 27; 16:20-22), those who mourn for sin (Ps 51:17; Isa 1:18; 40:1-2; 61:1-3; Mic 7:18-19; Lk 4:18-19), the tempted (Ro 16:17-20; 1Co 10:13; 2Co 12:9; Jas 1:12; 4:7-10; 2Pe 2:9; Rev 2:10).

Prayer Under:

For the presence and support of God (Ps 10:1; 102:2). Exhortation to (Jas 5:13). That, God would consider our trouble (2Ki 19:16; Ne 9:32; Ps 9:13; La 5), we may be taught the uncertainty of life (Ps 39:4), the Holy Spirit may not be withdrawn (Ps 51:11), we may be turned to God (Ps 51:12-15; 80:7; 85:4-7; Jer 31:18).

For protection and preservation from enemies (2Ki 19:19; 2Ch 20:12; Ps 17:8-9; 143:11-12), divine teaching and direction (Job 34:32; Ps 27:11; 143:10), divine comfort (Ps 4:6; 119:76-77), mercy (Ps 6:2; Hab 3:2), deliverance from troubles (Ps 25:17, 22; 39:10; Isa 64:9-12; Jer 17:14), pardon and deliverance from sin (Ps 39:8; 51:1-17; 79:8-9), relief from troubles (Ps 39:12-13), restoration of joy (Ps 51:8, 12; 69:29; 90:14-15), increase of faith (Mk 9:24).

AFFLICTIONS

In General:

God, determines the continuance of (Ge 15:13-14; Nu 14:33; Isa 10:25; Jer 29:10), appoints (2Ki 6:33; Job 5:6, 17; Ps 66:10-11; Am 3:6; Mic 6:9), dispenses as he will (Job 11:10; Isa 10:15-16; 45:7), regulates the measure of (Ps 80:5; Isa 9:1; Jer 46:28), does not willingly send (La 3:33).

Consequent upon the Fall (Ge 3:16-19). Frequently end in good (Ge 50:20; Ex 1:11-12; Dt 8:15-18; Jer 24:5-7; Eze 20:37). Sin visited with (2Sa 12:14; Ps 89:30-32; Isa 57:17; Ac 13:10-11). Sin produces (Job 4:8; 20:11; Pr 1:31).

Always less than we deserve (Ezr 9:13; Ps 103:10).Man is born to (Job 5:6-7; 14:1). Often severe (Job 16:7-16; Ps 42:7; 66:12; Rev 7:14). Tempered with mercy (Ps 78:38-39; 106:43-46; Isa 30:18-21; La 3:32; Mic 7:7-9; Na 1:12). Believers are to expect (Jn 16:33; Ac 14:22). Believers appointed to (1Th 3:3).

Of Believers:

Exhibit the love and faithfulness of God (Dt 8:5; Ps 119:75; Pr 3:11-12; 1Co 11:32; Heb 12:6-11; Rev 3:19-22). Believers have joy under (Job 5:17-18; Jas 5:11). Are but temporary (Ps 30:5; 103:9-10; Isa 54:7-8; Jn 16:20; 1Pe 1:6; 5:10). End in joy and blessedness (Ps 126:5-6; Isa 61:2-3; Mt 5:4; 1Pe 4:13-14). Often comes from the profession of the gospel (Mt 24:9; Jn 15:21; 2Ti 3:11-12). Are comparatively light (Ac 20:23-24; Ro 8:18; 2Co 4:17-18).

Benefits to Believers:

In, trying our faith and obedience (Ge 22:1-2, w Heb 11:17-18; Ex 15:23-25; Dt 8:2-3, 16; 1Pe 1:7; Rev 2:10), humbling us (Dt 8:3, 16; 2Ch 7:13-14; La 3:19-24; 2Co 12:7), leading us to confession of sin (Nu 21:7; Ps 32:4-5; 51:3-6), turning us to God (Dt 4:30-31; Ne 1:8-9; Ps 78:34-38; Isa 10:20-21; Hos 2:6-7), leading us to seek God in prayer (Jdg 4:3; Jer 31:18; La 2:17-19; Hos 5:14-15; Jnh 2:1), testing and exhibiting our sincerity (Job 23:10; Ps 66:10; Pr 17:3), keeping us from again departing from God (Job 34:31-32; Isa 10:20; Eze 14:10-11), convincing us of sin (Job 36:8-10; Ps 119:67; Lk 15:16, 18), exhibiting the power and faithfulness of God (Ps 34:19-20; 2Co 4:8-11), exercising our patience (Ps 40:1; Ro 5:3; Jas 1:3; 1Pe 2:20), teaching us the will of God (Ps 119:71; Isa 26:9), purifying us (Ecc 7:2-3; Isa 1:25-26; 48:10; Jer 9:6-7; Zec 13:9; Mal 3:2-3), promoting the glory of God (Jn 9:1-3; 11:3-4; 21:18-19), rendering us fruitful in good works (Jn 15:2; Heb 12:10-11), furthering the gospel (Ac 8:3-4; 11:19-21; Php 1:12-13; 2Ti 2:8-10; 4:16-18).

Examples of Benefits to Believers—

Joseph's brothers (Ge 42:21), Joseph (Ge 45:5-8), Israel (Dt 8:3-5), Josiah (2Ki 22:19), Hezekiah (2Ch 32:25-26), Manasseh (2Ch 33:12), Jonah (Jnh 2:7), Prodigal son (Lk 15:21).

Of the Wicked:

Are ineffective of themselves, for their conversion (Ex 9:30; Isa 9:13; Jer 2:30; Hag 2:17). God is glorified in (Ex 14:4; Eze 38:22-23). Their persecution of believers, a cause of (2Ki 30:7; Ps 55:19; Zec 2:9; 2Th 1:6). Are multiplied (Dt 31:17; Job 20:12-18; Ps 32:10). Sometimes humble them (1Ki 21:27). Frequently harden (Ne 9:28-31; Jer 5:3). Are continual (Job 15:20; Ecc 2:23; Isa 32:10). Produce slavish fear (Job 15:24; Ps 73:19; Jer 49:3, 5). Are often judicially sent (Job 21:17; Ps 107:17; Jer 30:15). God holds in derision (Ps 37:13; Pr 1:26-27). Are for examples to others (Ps 64:7-9; Zep 3:6-7; 1Co 10:5-13; 2Pe 2:6). Are often sudden (Ps 73:19; Pr 6:15; Isa 30:12-13; Rev 18:10). Failure to repent is a cause of (Pr 1:30-31; Eze 24:13; Am 4:6-12; Zec 7:11-12; Rev 2:21-22). Believers should not be alarmed at (Pr 3:25-26).

Examples of Afflictions of the Wicked—

Pharaoh and the Egyptians (Ex 9:14-15; 14:24-25), Ahaziah (2Ki 1:1-4), Gehazi (2Ki 5:27), Jehoram (2Ki 21:12-16), Uzziah (2Ch 26:19-21), Ahaz (2Ch 28:5-8, 22).

AFTERWARD (Ps 73:24; Pr 20:17; Mt 25:11; Jn 13:36; 1Co 15:46; Gal 3:23; Heb 12:11, 17).

AGABUS A prophet living in Jerusalem who prophesied a world-wide famine which was fulfilled during the reign of Claudius (Ac 11:27-30). He also met Paul in Caesarea and warned him that he would be arrested in Jerusalem (Ac 21:10-11).

AGAG (possibly *violent*).
1. The king of Amalek, referred to by Balaam (Nu 24:2-3, 7).
2. Another king of Amalek. Saul spared Agag when he should have killed him. When Samuel came into the camp, he rebuked Saul and ordered that Agag be brought to him. Samuel killed Agag as Saul should have according to God's command (1Sa 15:8-33).

AGAGITE (possibly *violent*). A description of Haman (Est 3:1, 10; 8:3, 5; 9:24). The LXX understood the term to mean "enemy." Josephus explains it as a synonym of Amalek, a descendant of Agag (Ant. xi, 6, 5). *See Agag, 2.*

AGAPE (*love; volitional and self-sacrificial love*). A Greek word meaning "love" and "love feasts." *See Love; Love Feast.*

AGAR See Hagar.

AGATE A precious stone used in the high priest's breastpiece (Ex 28:19; 39:12). KJV "agates" is also translated "rubies" in the NIV (Isa 54:12; Eze 27:16). *See Minerals of the Bible, 1; Ruby; Stones.*

AGE See Aeon.

AGE (OLD), AGED See Old Age.

AGEE (possibly *fugitive*). A Hararite and the father of Shammah (2Sa 23:11).

AGENCY Duties entrusted to God's servants.
In salvation of people (Job 33:14-30; Ps 8:2; Mt 4:19; 5:13-16; Lk 1:17; 5:10; 10:17; 1Co 1:26-29; 1Th 2:4; 1Ti 1:11; 6:20; Jas 5:20).
In executing judgments (Ge 3:15; 1Sa 15:18; 2Sa 7:14; 2Ki 9:6-9; 19:25-26; 2Ch 22:7; Ps 17:13-14; Isa 10:5-6; 13:5; 41:15; Jer 27:8; 51:20-23).

AGONY Under judgment of God (Eze 30:16; Mic 4:10; Rev 9:5; 16:10). Of the rich man (Lk 16:24-25). Of Jesus (Ac 2:24).

AGORA (*marketplace*). In ancient cities the town meeting place was the market where the public met for the exchange of merchandise, information, and ideas (Mk 6:56; Ac 17:17).

AGRAPHA (*unwritten things*). Sayings ascribed to Jesus transmitted to us outside of the canonical Gospels. The number is not large, and most are obviously apocryphal or spurious. They are found in the NT outside of the Gospels (Ac 1:4ff; 11:16; 20:35; 1Co 7:10), ancient manuscripts of the NT, patristic literature, papyri, and apocryphal gospels.

AGRICULTURE The occupation of man before the Fall (Ge 2:15). Rendered laborious by the curse on the earth (Ge 3:17-19). Man condemned to labor in, after the Fall (Ge 3:23). Contributes to the support of all (Ecc 5:9). The providence of God to be acknowledged in the produce of (Jer 5:24; Hos 2:8).

Requires:

Hard work will be abundantly recompensed (Pr 12:11; 13:23; 28:19; Heb 6:7). Diligence (Pr 27:23-27; Ecc 11:6). Wisdom (Isa 28:26). Hard work (2Ti 2:6). Patience in waiting (Jas 5:7).

Persons Engaged in, Called:

Workers of the ground (Ge 4:2). Workers or hired men (Mt 9:37; 20:1).

In General:

Patriarchs engaged in (Ge 4:2; 9:20). The labor of, supposed to be lessened by Noah (Ge 5:29, w Ge 9:20). Soil of Canaan suited to (Ge 13:10; Dt 8:7-10). Climate of Canaan favorable to (Dt 11:10-12). The Israelites loved and followed (2Ch 26:10). Peace favorable to (Jer 31:24). War destructive to (Jer 5:16-17; 51:23).

Was Promoted Among the Israelites by:

The prohibition against usury (Ex 22:25). The right of redemption (Lev 25:23-28). The promises of God's blessing on (Lev 26:4; Dt 7:13; 11:14-15). Allotments to each family (Nu 36:7-9).

Enactments to Protect:

Against, the trespass of cattle (Ex 22:5), injuring the produce of (Ex 22:6). Not to, be engaged in during the Sabbatical year (Ex 23:10-11), covet the fields of another (Dt 5:21), move landmarks (Dt 19:14; Pr 22:28), cut down crops of another (Dt 23:25).

Produce of, exported (1Ki 5:11; Eze 27:17). Often performed by hired help (1Ch 27:26; 2Ch 26:10; Mt 20:8; Lk 17:7). Produce of, often reduced in yield because of sin (Isa 5:10; 7:23; Jer 12:13; Joel 1:10-12). Grief resulted from the failure of the fruits of (Joel 1:11; Am 5:16-17).

Activities in:

Binding sheaves of grain or weeds into bundles (Ge 37:7; Mt 13:30). Stacking (Ex 22:6). Gleaning (Lev 19:9; Ru 2:3). Pruning (Lev 25:3; Isa 5:6; Jn 15:2). Watering (Dt 11:10; 1Co 3:6-8). Threshing (Dt 25:4; Jdg 6:11). Winnowing (Ru 3:2; Job 39:12; Mt 3:12). Plowing (Job 1:14). Harrowing (Job 39:10; Isa 28:24). Mowing (Ps 72:6; Am 7:1; Jas 5:4). Planting (Pr 31:16; Isa 44:14; Jer 31:5). Sowing (Ecc 11:4; Isa 32:20; Mt 13:3). Clearing out the stones (Isa 5:2). Hedging (Isa 5:2, 5; Hos 2:6). Digging (Lk 13:8; 16:3). Reaping (Isa 17:5). Fertilizing (Isa 25:10; Lk 14:34-35). Storing in barns (Mt 6:26; 13:30). Weeding (Mt 13:28). Grafting (Ro 11:17-19, 24).

Animals Used in:

The donkey (Dt 22:10), ox (Dt 22:10; 25:4), horse (Isa 28:28).

Tools of:

The sickle (Dt 16:9; 23:25), cart (1Sa 6:7; Isa 28:27-28), mattock (1Sa 13:20), ax (1Sa 13:20), plow (1Sa 13:20), fork (1Sa 13:21), iron pick (2Sa 12:31), hoe (Isa 7:25), pruning knives (Isa 18:5; Joel 3:10), rod (Isa 28:27), winnowing fork (Jer 15:7; Mt 3:12; Lk 3:17), shovel (Isa 30:24), threshing sledge (Isa 41:15), sieve (Am 9:9).

Illustrative of the:

Cultivating the heart (Jer 4:3; Hos 10:12). Cultivating the church (1Co 3:9).

AGRIPPA I Known in history as King Herod Agrippa I or Herod Agrippa, and in the NT as Herod, 10 B.C. to A.D. 44 He was the grandson of Herod the Great and ruled over the whole of Judea from A.D. 41 to 44. He killed James to please the Jews and intended to do the same to Peter (Ac 12:1-5). He died suddenly in Caesarea (Ac 12:19-23; Jos. Antiq. XIX.viii.2), A.D. 44.

AGRIPPA II Known in history as King Herod Agrippa II, Marcus Julius Agrippa, and in the NT as Agrippa, A.D. 28 to after A.D. 93, probably c. A.D. 100. He was the son of Agrippa I, and ruled over only a small part of his father's territory. Paul appeared before the tribunal of Agrippa and Festus (Ac 25:23-26). Died in c. A.D. 100.

AGUE NIV "fever"; a disease "that will destroy your sight and drain away your life" (Lev 26:16). *See Fever.*

AGUR (*gatherer, possibly wage earner*). The son of Jakeh; author or collector of the wise sayings of the Proverbs 30.

AHA A term of derision (Ps 35:21; 40:15; 70:3; Eze 25:3; 26:2).

AHAB (*brother of father*).
1. King of Israel for twenty-two years, reigning in Samaria (1Ki 16:29). Idolatry of (1Ki 16:30-33; 18:18-20; 21:25-26). Marries Jezebel (1Ki 16:31). Reproved by Elijah; assembles the prophets of Baal (1Ki 18:15-46). Defeats Ben-Hadad (1Ki 20). Illegally confiscates Naboth's vineyard (1Ki 21). Closing history and death of (1Ki 22:1-41; 2Ch 18). Succeeded by his son, Ahaziah (1Ki 22:40). Prophecies against (1Ki 20:42; 21:19-24; 22:19-28; 2Ki 9:8, 25-26). Other wickedness of (2Ki 3:2; 2Ch 21:6; 22:3-4; Mic 6:16). The seventy sons of, all his chief men, his close friends, and his priest were murdered (2Ki 10:1-11).
2. A false prophet (Jer 29:21-22).

AHARAH (*brother of Rah*). Also called Ashbel, Ahiram, and Aher, the third son of Benjamin (Ge 46:21; Nu 26:38; 1Ch 7:12; 8:1).

AHARHEL (*brother of Rachel*). A son of Harum, and the founder of a family enrolled in the tribe of Judah (1Ch 4:8).

AHASAI See Ahzai.

AHASBAI (*I seek refuge in Yahweh*). A Maacathite and the father of Eliphelet, one of David's heroes (2Sa 23:34). Possibly the same as Ur (1Ch 11:35). *See Ur.*

AHASUERUS Hebrew transliteration of the name of the Persian king Xerxes. *See Xerxes.*

AHAVA A Babylonian town on the Ahava Canal (Ezr 8:15, 21, 31).

AHAZ (*he has grasped*).
1. King of Judah, son and successor of Jotham (2Ki 15:38; 16:1; 2Ch 27:9; 28:1). Idolatrous abominations of (2Ki 16:3-4; 2Ch 28:2-4, 22-25). Kingdom of, invaded by the kings of Syria and Samaria (2Ki 16:5-6; 2Ch 28:5-8). Robs the temple to purchase aid from the king of Assyria (2Ki 16:7-9, 17-18; 2Ch 28:21). Visits Damascus, obtains a singular pattern of an altar, which he substitutes for the altar in the temple in Jerusalem and otherwise perverts the forms of worship (2Ki 16:10-16). Stairway of (2Ki 20:11; Isa 38:8). Prophets in the reign of (Isa 1:1; Hos 1:1; Mic 1:1). Prophecies concerning (Isa 7:13-25). Succeeded by Hezekiah (2Ki 16:20).
2. Son of Micah and great-grandson of Jonathan (1Ch 8:35; 9:41-42).

AHAZIAH (*Yahweh has upheld*).
1. King of Judah. Also called Azariah (2Ch 22:6, ftn) and Jehoahaz (2Ch 21:17, ftn). History of (2Ki 8:25-29; 9:16-29). Gifts of, to the temple (2Ki 12:18). Brothers of, slain (2Ki 10:13-14). Succeeded by Athaliah (2Ch 22:10-12).
2. King of Israel. History of (1Ki 22:40, 49, 51-53; 2Ch 20:35-37; 2Ki 1). Succeeded by Jehoram (2Ki 3:1).

AHBAN (*brother of intelligent one*). A Judahite, of the house of Jerahmeel (1Ch 2:29).

A

AHER (*another, a substitute*). A Benjamite (1Ch 7:12). *See Aharah.*

AHI (*my brother,* possibly *Yahweh is [my] brother*).
1. Chief of the Gadites in Gilead (1Ch 5:15).
2. A man of Asher, son of Shomer (1Ch 7:34).

AHIAH (*brother of Yahweh*).
1. A leader of Israel who agreed to the covenant of Nehemiah (Ne 10:26).
2. *See Ahijah.*

AHIAM (*brother of mother*). One of David's heroes (2Sa 23:33). The son of Sacar (1Ch 11:35).

AHIAN (*little brother*). Son of Shemida (1Ch 7:19).

AHIEZER (*[my] brother is a help*).
1. Captain of the tribe of Dan (Nu 1:12; 2:25-26). Contributes to the tabernacle (Nu 7:66-71).
2. One of David's valiant men (1Ch 12:3).

AHIHUD (*[my] brother has majesty*).
1. A prince of Asher, assists in allotting the land of Canaan among the tribes (Nu 34:27).
2. A son of Bela (1Ch 8:7).

AHIJAH (*[my] brother is Yahweh*).
1. Son of Bela (1Ch 8:7).
2. Son of Jerahmeel (1Ch 2:25).
3. A priest in Shiloh, probably identified with Ahimelech (1Sa 22:11). Was priest in Saul's reign (1Sa 14:3, 18). Killed (1Sa 22:11-19).
4. One of David's heroes (1Ch 11:36). Also called Eliam (2Sa 23:34).
5. A Levite who was treasurer in the tabernacle (1Ch 26:20).
6. Son of Shisha, secretary of Solomon (1Ki 4:3).
7. A prophet in Shiloh (1Ki 11:29-39; 12:15).
8. Father of Baasha (1Ki 15:27, 33; 2Ki 9:9).
See Ahiah.

AHIKAM (*[my] brother stands*). Son of Shaphan (2Ki 22:12-14; 25:22; 2Ch 34:20; Jer 26:24; 39:14; 40:5-16; 41:1-18; 43:6).

AHILUD (*[my] brother is born*). Father of: Baana (1Ki 4:12), Jehoshaphat (2Sa 8:16; 20:24; 1Ki 4:3; 1Ch 18:15).

AHIMAAZ (*[my] brother is fury*).
1. Father-in-law of king Saul (1Sa 14:50).
2. Son of Zadok, the high priest. Loyal to David (2Sa 15:36; 17:17-20; 18:19-33; 1Ch 6:8-9, 53).
3. One of Solomon's twelve district governors (1Ki 4:15). He married Basemath, the daughter of Solomon. Some suggest that he should be identified with the son of Zadok.

AHIMAN (possibly *[my] brother is a gift*).
1. One of the three giant sons of Anak seen in Mt. Hebron by the spies (Nu 13:22). Sheshai, Ahiman, and Talmai, were driven by Caleb from Hebron (Jos 15:14) and killed (Jdg 1:10).
2. A Levite gatekeeper (1Ch 9:17).

AHIMELECH (*[my] brother is king*).
1. Saul's high priest who helped David by giving him the bread of the Presence and Goliath's sword. Upon hearing this, Saul ordered the death of Ahimelech and the other priests with him (1Sa 21-22). Abiathar, son of Ahimelech, escaped.
2. A Hittite who, with Abishai, was asked to accompany David to Saul's camp (1Sa 26:6).
3. Son of Abiathar, and grandson of Ahimelech (2Sa 8:17; 1Ch 18:16; 24:6). *See Abiathar.*

AHIMOTH (*[my] brother is my support* possibly *my brother is Mot*). Son of Elkanah (1Ch 6:25), descendant of Kohath and a Levite.

AHINADAB (*[my] brother is willing*). Son of Iddo (1Ki 4:14).

AHINOAM (*[my] brother is pleasant*).
1. Wife of King Saul (1Sa 14:50).
2. One of David's wives, a Jezreelitess (1Sa 25:43), who lived with him at Gath (1Sa 27:3). Captured by the Amalekites at Ziklag (1Sa 30:5) but rescued by David (1Sa 30:18). Ahinoam bore Amnon, David's first son (2Sa 3:2).

AHIO (*[my] brother is Yahweh*).
1. A Levite, who drove the cart bearing the ark (2Sa 6:3-4; 1Ch 13:7).
2. A Benjamite (1Ch 8:14).
3. Son of Jeiel (1Ch 8:31; 9:37).

AHIRA (*[my] brother is my friend,* or *[my] brother is evil*). Prince captain of the tribe of Naphtali (Nu 1:15; 2:29; 7:78, 83; 10:27).

AHIRAM, AHIRAMITE (*[my] brother is exalted*). Son of Benjamin (Nu 26:38). *See Aharah.*

AHISAMACH (*[my] brother is a support*). A Danite, the father of Oholiab (Ex 31:6; 35:34; 38:23).

AHISHAHAR (*[my] brother was born at early dawn*). A descendant of Benjamin through Jediael and Bilhan (1Ch 7:10).

AHISHAR (*[my] brother is upright,* or *[my] brother has sung*). An official over Solomon's household (1Ki 4:6).

AHITHOPHEL (possibly *[my] brother is in the desert* or *[my] brother is foolishness*). One of David's counselors (2Sa 15:12; 1Ch 27:33). Joins Absalom (2Sa 15:31, 34; 16:15, 20-23; 17:1-23). Possibly referred to by David in Ps 55:12-14. Suicide of (2Sa 17:1-14, 23).

AHITUB (*[my] brother is goodness*).
1. High Priest, father of Ahiah (1Sa 14:3; 22:9, 11-12, 20).
2. Father of Zadok (2Sa 8:17; 1Ch 18:16).
3. Ruler of the house of God (1Ch 9:11; Ne 11:11).
4. The Ahitub mentioned (1Ch 6:8, 11-12) is probably identical with the last described above, or else he is confused with Azariah (2Ch 31:10).

AHLAB (*fat, fruitful, healthy*). A town of Asher from which the Israelites were not able to drive the inhabitants (Jdg 1:31).

AHLAI (*Alas! I wish that!*).
1. The father of Zabad, one of David's soldiers (1Ch 11:41).
2. A daughter of Sheshan who married her father's Egyptian slave Jarha. They had a son Attai (1Ch 2:31-35).

AHOAH (*brotherly*). A son of Bela (1Ch 8:4) and his descendants (2Sa 23:9, 28; 1Ch 11:12). *See Ahohite.* Also called Ahijah (1Ch 8:7) and Iri (1Ch 7:7).

AHOHITE A name given to the descendants of Ahoah, Dodo (2Sa 23:9), Zalmon (2Sa 23:28), Ilai (1Ch 11:29).

AHOLAH, AHOLA *See Oholah.*

AHOLIAB *See Oholiab.*

AHOLIBAH *See Oholah; Oholibah.*

AHOLIBAMAH *See Oholibamah.*

AHUMAI Son of Jahath (1Ch 4:2).

AHUZZAM (*possessor*). Son of Ashhur (1Ch 4:6).

AHUZZATH (*possession*). A "friend" of Abimelech, who made a peace treaty with Isaac at Beersheba after they saw that the Lord had blessed him (Ge 26:23-33).

AHZAI (*Yahweh has grasped*). A priest who lived in Jerusalem (Ne 11:13).

AI (*the ruin, the heap*).
1. A royal city of the Canaanites. Conquest and destruction of (Jos 7; 8). Population (Jos 8:25). Rebuilt (Ezr 2:28). Also called Aija (Ne 11:31) and Aiath (Isa 10:28).
2. A city of the Ammonites (Jer 49:3).

AIAH (*black kite [a type of hawk]*).
1. A Horite (Ge 36:24; 1Ch 1:40).
2. The father of Rizpah, Saul's concubine (2Sa 3:7; 21:8).

AIATH (possibly *ruin, heap*). Feminine form of the city Ai (Isa 10:28).

AIJA (*ruin, heap*). Another spelling of Ai (Ne 11:31). *See Ai, 1.*

AIJALON (*[the] place of the deer*).
1. A city of Dan (Jos 19:42). Assigned to the Levites (Jos 21:24; 1Sa 14:31; 1Ch 6:69). Amorites of, not exterminated (Jdg 1:35).
2. A city of Zebulun (Jdg 12:12).
3. A city of Judah (2Ch 28:18; 11:10).
4. A valley (Jos 10:12).

AIJELETH SHAHAR KJV title of Ps 22; NIV "The Doe of the Morning." A musical term which probably indicated the tune to which the psalm was sung. *See Music, Symbols Used in.*

AIN (*an eye/ball]* or *spring [of water]*).
1. A city of Simeon (Jos 19:7; 15:32; 21:16; 1Ch 4:32). Also called Ashan (1Ch 6:59). Possibly identical with En Rimmon (Ne 11:29).
2. A landmark on the northern boundary of Israel (Nu 34:11).

AIN FESHKA (*spring of Feshka*). Oasis on the W side of the Dead Sea, S of Khirbet Qumran. Used for farming by the community that produced the Dead Sea Scrolls.

AJAH *See Aiah.*

AJALON *See Aijalon.*

AKAN A Horite (Ge 36:27; 1Ch 1:42). Also spelled Jaakan (1Ch 1:42, ftn).

AKELDAMA (*field of blood*). The "Field of Blood" (Mt 27:8) purchased with money which Judas received for betraying Jesus (Ac 1:18-19).

AKHENATEN (*blessed spirit of [the god] Aten*). The name chosen by Amenhotep IV (1379-1362 B.C.), ruler in the Eighteenth Dynasty of Egypt, during the biblical era of the judges. He was a monotheist, demanding that all worship only the sun god under the name Aten. The Amarna Letters date from his era. *See Amarna, Tell El.*

AKIM (*Yahweh is my brother*). A descendant of Zerubbabel (Mt 1:14). Ancestor of Christ.

AKKAD An ancient center of Hamitic imperial power conquered by Nimrod (Ge 10:10). The city is evidently Agade which Sargon I brought into prominence as the capital of his Semitic empire, c. 2360-2180 B.C..

AKKUB (*guard*).
1. Son of Elioenai (1Ch 3:24).
2. A Levite who founded a family of temple gatekeepers (1Ch 9:17).
3. The head of a family of the temple servants (Ezr 2:45).
4. A Levite who helped expound the Law (Ne 8:7).

AKRABBIM (*scorpions*). See Scorpion Pass.

ALABASTER A white stone. Jars made of (Mt 26:7; Mk 14:3; Lk 7:37).

ALAMETH See Alemeth.

ALAMMELECH See Allammelech.

ALAMOTH A musical term (1Ch 15:20). In the title to Ps 46. See Music, Symbols Used in.

ALCOHOL See Abstinence; Abuse; Substance Abuse; Beer; Drunkenness; Fermented Drink; Wine.

ALEMETH (*concealment*).
1. Son of Beker and grandson of Benjamin (1Ch 7:8).
2. Son of Jehoaddah or Jadah (1Ch 8:36; 9:42).
3. A Levitical city (1Ch 6:60).
See Almon.

ALEXANDER (*man's defender*).
1. Son of Simon who carried the cross of Jesus (Mk 15:21).
2. A relative of the high priest, present at the defense of Peter and John (Ac 4:6).
3. A Jew of Ephesus (Ac 19:33).
4. A metalworker (1Ti 1:20; 2Ti 4:14).

ALEXANDER THE GREAT (*man's defender*). Son of Philip, King of Macedon. Lived from 356-323 B.C. He conquered the civilized world from Greece eastward to India. He is the "shaggy goat" of Da 8:5-8, 21. His hellenization of the world changed the trade language from Aramaic to Greek, the language of the NT. See Testaments, Time Between.

ALEXANDRA Wife of Aristobulus, King of the Jews (104-103 B.C.).

ALEXANDRIA A city of Egypt (Ac 6:9). Ships of (Ac 27:6; 28:11). Apollos born in (Ac 18:24).

ALGUM, ALGUMWOOD Probably a variant of almugwood (1Ki 10:11-12, ftn; 2Ch 2:8; 9:10-11). See Almug, Almugwood.

ALIAH See Alvah.

ALIAN See Alvan.

ALIENS (*sojourner, stranger, foreigner*). To be treated with justice (Ex 22:21; 23:9; Lev 19:33-34; Dt 1:16; 10:19 24:14, 17; 27:19; Jer 7:6; 22:3; Eze 22:29; Mal 3:5). Religious privileges of (Ex 12:48-49; Nu 9:14; 15:14-15). Kindness to Edomites, commanded (Dt 23:7).

Israelites Authorized:
To purchase, as slaves (Lev 25:44-45). To take usury from (Dt 15:3; 23:20). Not permitted to make kings of (Dt 17:15). Forbidden to eat the passover (Ex 12:45). Partially exempt from the law (Dt 14:21). Numerous in times of David and Solomon (2Sa 22:45-46; 2Ch 2:17; 15:9). Oppressed (Eze 22:29). Rights of (Nu 35:15; Jos 20:9; Eze 47:22-23). David's kindness to (2Sa 15:19-20). Hospitality to, required by Jesus (Mt 25:35, 38, 43).
See Glean; Heathen; Hospitality; Inhospitableness; Proselyte; Strangers.

ALL THINGS The whole created order. God created and rules over (1Ch 29:12; Ps 119:91; Ecc 11:5; Isa 44:24; Jer 10:16; 51:19; Jn 1:3; Ro 8:28; 1Co 8:6; Rev 4:11). Under Jesus' authority (Mt 11:27; 28:20; Lk 10:22; Jn 13:3; Eph 1:10, 22; Col 1:16, 17, 20; Heb 1:2, 3). All things are possible with God (Mt 19:26; Mk 10:27).

ALLAMMELECH (*oak of the king* or *oak of [the god] Molech*). A town of Asher (Jos 19:26).

ALLEGORY

Explained:
Allegory is a literary genre that attempts to explain spiritual truths in pictorial forms. Some parables, for example, are a type of allegory. Allegory is also a method of interpretation that searches for a mysterious, hidden meaning beyond the literal understanding of the text.

In the OT:
Of the trees seeking a king (Jdg 9:8-15). Israel is a vine brought from Egypt (Pr 80). Wisdom is pictured as a noble woman (Pr 1:2-33); folly as a harlot (Pr 9:13-18). Messiah's kingdom represented by the wolf and the lamb dwelling together (Isa 11:6-8).

In the NT:
Jesus used allegory, as in the interpretation of his parable of the sower (Mt 13:18-23; Mk 4:14-20; Lk 8:11-15). Paul used allegory in using Hagar and Sarah to represent the differences between the Old and New Covenants (Gal 4:21-31). Many events and characters in the book of Revelation are used allegorically; most are clear or explained in context. For example, the Lamb and the Lion of Judah are both Jesus (Rev 5:5-14); the dragon is Satan (Rev 12:9).

Allegory in Interpretation:
Allegory is used as a literary device in the Bible. But, with the exception of Gal 4:21-31, allegory is not used in the NT to interpret the OT. However, allegory became increasingly important during the Apostolic period and into the Ante-Nicene period. The Alexandrian Jews of this period wished to reconcile Christianity with Greek thought. Origen taught a threefold sense of Scripture, corresponding to the body, soul, and the spirit.
In the Middle Ages four senses were found: historical, allegorical, moral, and anagogical (mystical). Jerusalem is *literally* a city in Israel, *allegorically* the church, *morally* the believing soul, *anagogically* the heavenly Jerusalem. The conquests of Joshua have been understood to be an allegory of the soul's victory over sin and self. Many Jewish scholars understand the Song of Songs to be

allegorical, depicting God's love for Israel. On the other hand, many Christian scholars understand this as Christ's love for his church. *See Fable; Parable; Symbols and Similitudes.*

ALLELUIA *See Hallelujah.*

ALLIANCES

Forbidden:
(Ex 23:32; 34:12; Dt 7:2-3; 13:6, 8; Jos 23:6-7; Jdg 2:2; Ezr 9:12; Pr 1:10, 15; 2Co 6:14-17; Eph 5:11). Lead to idolatry (Ex 34:15-16; Nu 25:1-8; Dt 7:4; Jdg 3:5-7; Rev 2:20). Have led to murder and human sacrifice (Ps 106:37-38). Provoke the anger of God (Dt 7:4; 31:16-17; 2Ch 19:2; Ezr 9:13-14; Ps 106:29, 40; Isa 2:6). Provoke God to leave people to reap the fruits of them (Jos 23:12-13; Jdg 2:1-3).
Are ensnaring (Ex 23:33; Nu 25:18; Dt 12:30; 13:6; Ps 106:36). Are enslaving (2Pe 2:18-19). Are defiling (Ezr 9:1-2). Are degrading (Isa 1:23). Are ruinous to spiritual interests (Pr 29:24; Heb 12:14-15; 2Pe 3:17). Are ruinous to moral character (1Co 15:33). Are a proof of folly (Pr 12:11).
Children who enter into, bring shame upon their parents (Pr 28:7). Evil consequences of (Pr 28:19; Jer 51:7). The wicked are prone to (Ps 50:18; Jer 2:25). The wicked tempt believers to (Ne 6:2-4). Sin of, to be confessed, deeply repented of, and forsaken (Ezr 10).

Involve Believers:
In their guiltiness (2Jn 9-11; Rev 18:4). In their punishment (Nu 16:26; Jer 51:6; Rev 18:4). Unbecoming in those called believers (2Ch 19:2; 2Co 6:14, 16; Php 2:15). Exhortations to shun all inducements to (Pr 1:10-15; 4:14-15; 2Pe 3:17). Exhortations to hate and avoid (Pr 14:7; Ro 16:17; 1Co 5:9-11; Eph 5:6-7; 1Ti 6:5; 2Ti 3:5). A call to come out from (Nu 16:26; Ezr 10:11; Jer 51:6, 45; 2Co 6:17; 2Th 3:6; Rev 18:4). Means of preservation from (Pr 2:10-20; 19:27).
Blessedness of avoiding (Ps 1:1). Blessedness of forsaking (Ezr 9:12; Pr 9:6; 2Co 6:17-18). Believers grieve to meet with, in their dealings with the world (Ps 57:4; 120:5-6; 2Pe 2:7-8). Believers grieve to witness in their brothers (Ge 26:35; Ezr 9:3; 10:6). Believers hate and avoid (Ps 26:4-5; 31:6; 101:7; Rev 2:2). Believers deprecate (Ge 49:6; Ps 6:8; 15:4; 101:4, 7; 119:115; 139:19). Believers are separate from (Ex 33:16; Ezr 6:21). Believers should be careful when accidentally thrown into (Mt 10:16; Col 4:5; 1Pe 2:12). Pious parents prohibit, to their children (Ge 28:1). Persons in authority should denounce (Ezr 10:9-11; Ne 13:23-27). Punishment of (Nu 33:56; Dt 7:4; Jos 23:13; Jdg 2:3; 3:5-8; Ezr 9:7, 14; Ps 106:41-42; Rev 2:16, 22-23).

Exemplified:
Solomon (1Ki 11:1-8). Rehoboam (1Ki 12:8-9). Jehoshaphat (2Ch 18:3; 19:2; 20:35-38). Jehoram (2Ch 21:6). Ahaziah (2Ch 22:3-5). Israelites (Ezr 9:1-2). Israel (Eze 44:7). Judas Iscariot (Mt 26:14-16).

Examples of Avoiding—
Man of God (1Ki 13:7-10). Nehemiah (Ne 6:2-4; 10:29-31). David (Ps 101:4-7; 119:115). Jeremiah (Jer 15:17). Joseph of Arimathea (Lk 23:51). Church of Ephesus (Rev 2:6).

Examples of Forsaking—
Israelites (Nu 16:27; Ezr 6:21-22; 10:3-4, 16-17). Sons of the priests (Ezr 10:18-19).

Examples of God's Judgments Against—
Korah (Nu 16:32). Ahaziah (2Ch 22:7-8). Judas Iscariot (Ac 1:18).

ALLON *(oak).*
1. Son of Jedaiah (1Ch 4:37).
2. KJV Allon, a city of Naphtali (Jos 19:33), is "the large tree" in the NIV.

ALLON BACUTH *(oak of weeping).* Place where Rebekah was buried (Ge 35:8).

ALLOY *See Refining.*

ALMIGHTY (NIV rendering of *Shaddai* in the OT, *Pantokrator* in the NT). Used 56 times for: Identification (Ge 17:1). Invocation (Ge 28:3). Description (Eze 10:5). Praise (Rev 4:8). *See God, Names of.*

ALMODAD *(God [El] is loved).* First mentioned of Joktan's thirteen sons (Ge 10:26; 1Ch 1:20).

ALMON Levitical city of Benjamin (Jos 21:18). Called Alemeth (1Ch 6:60).

ALMON DIBLATHAIM *(way of the double fig cakes).* A stopping place in the wilderness journeys of the Israelites in Moab (Nu 33:46-47). Probably the same as Beth Diblathaim (Jer 48:22), and Diblah (Eze 6:14). *See Beth Diblathaim.*

ALMOND A tree (Ge 30:37). Fruit of (Ge 43:11). Aaron's rod of the (Nu 17:8). Bowls of lampstand in the tabernacle fashioned after the flowers of the (Ex 25:33-34; 37:19-20).

Figurative: Of old age (Ecc 12:5), of God's watching (Jer 1:11-12).

ALMS KJV "alms" is rendered "give (to the poor)" and "acts of righteousness" in the NIV.

To be Given:
Without public show (Mt 6:1-4; Ro 12:8). Freely (2Co 9:6-7). Commanded (Dt 15:7-11; Mt 5:42; 19:21; Lk 12:33; 2Co 9:5-7; Gal 2:10; 1Ti 6:18; Heb 13:16). Asked by the unfortunate (Jn 9:8; Ac 3:2). Withholding, not of love (1Jn 3:17).

Instances of Giving:
Zacchaeus (Lk 19:8). Dorcas (Ac 9:36). Cornelius (Ac 10:2). The early Christians (Ac 2:44-45; 4:34-37; 6:1-3; 11:29-30; 24:17; Ro 15:25-28; 1Co 16:1-4; 2Co 8:1-4; 9:1; Heb 6:10).
See Beneficence; Charitableness; Gifts From God; Giving; Liberality; Neighbor; Poor; Works, Good.

ALMUG, ALMUGWOOD Probably a variant of algum and algumwood (1Ki 10:11-12; 2Ch 2:8; 9:10-11, ftn). Trees of Ophir and Lebanon used in building the temple and musical instruments. *See Algum, Algumwood.*

ALOES Used as perfume (Ps 45:8; Pr 7:17; SS 4:14). In embalming the dead (Jn 19:39). Descriptive of the camping places of the Israelites (Nu 24:6).

ALOTH One of the districts in Israel during the reign of Solomon that shared the responsibility of supplying provisions for the king and the royal household for one month in the year (1Ki 4:16).

ALPHA AND OMEGA A title of Christ, meaning "First and Last" and "Beginning and End" (Rev 1:8, cf. 17; 21:6; 22:13; cf. Isa 41:4; 44:6; 48:12).

ALPHAEUS
1. Father of James (Mt 10:3; Mk 3:18).
2. Father of Levi (Mk 2:14).
3. Possibly Clopas, husband of the Mary at the cross (Jn 19:25; also Mk 15:40), as Clopas and Alphaeus are of Semitic derivation. Unlikely the Cleopas of the Emmaus road (Lk 24:18) since Clopas was a common Greek name.

ALTAR OF BURNT OFFERING Dimensions of (Ex 27:1; 38:1). Horns on the corners of (Ex 27:2; 38:2). Covered with bronze (Ex 27:2). All its vessels of bronze (Ex 27:3; 38:3). A network grating of bronze placed in the (Ex 27:4-5; 38:4). Furnished with rings and poles (Ex 27:6-7; 38:5-7). Made after a divine pattern (Ex 27:8).

Called:
The bronze altar (Ex 39:39; 1Ki 8:64). The altar of God (Ps 43:4). The altar of the Lord (Mal 2:13). Placed in the court before the door of the tabernacle (Ex 40:6, 29). Sanctified by God (Ex 29:44). Anointed and sanctified with holy oil (Ex 40:10; Lev 8:10-11). Cleansed and purified with blood (Ex 29:36-37). Was most holy (Ex 40:10). Sanctified whatever touched it (Ex 29:37). All sacrifices to be offered on (Ex 29:38-42; Isa 56:7). All gifts to be presented at (Mt 5:23-24). Nothing polluted or defective to be offered on (Lev 22:22; Mal 1:7-8). Offering at the dedication of (Nu 7).

The Fire Upon:
Came from before the Lord (Lev 9:24). Was continually burning (Lev 6:13). Consumed the sacrifices (Lev 1:8-9). Sacrifices bound to the horns of (Ps 118:27, ftn). The blood of sacrifices put on the horns and poured at the foot of (Ex 29:12; Lev 4:7, 18, 25; 8:15).

The Priests:
Alone to serve (Nu 18:3, 7). Derived support from (1Co 9:13). Ahaz removed and profaned (2Ki 16:10-16). The Jews were condemned for swearing lightly by (Mt 23:18-19). A type of Christ (Heb 13:10).

ALTAR OF INCENSE Dimensions of (Ex 30:1-2; 37:25). Covered with gold (Ex 30:3; 37:26). Top of, surrounded with a crown of gold (Ex 30:3; 37:26). Had four rings of gold under the crown for the poles (Ex 30:4; 37:27). Poles of, covered with gold (Ex 30:5). Called the golden altar (Ex 39:38). Placed before the veil in the outer sanctuary (Ex 30:6; 40:5, 26). Said to be before the Lord (Lev 4:7; 1Ki 9:25). Anointed with holy oil (Ex 30:25-27). The priest burned incense on, every morning and evening (Ex 30:7-8). No strange incense nor any sacrifice to be offered on (Ex 30:9). Atonement made for, by the high priest once every year (Ex 30:10; Lev 16:18-19). The blood of all sin offerings put on the horns of (Lev 4:7, 18). Covered by the priests before removal from the sanctuary (Nu 4:11). A type of Christ (Rev 8:3; 9:3).
Punishment for: Offering unauthorized fire on (Lev 10:1-2). Unauthorized offering on (2Ch 26:16-19).

ALTARS
Designed for sacrifice (Ex 20:24). To be made of earth or uncut stone (Ex 20:24-25; Dt 27:5-6). Of brick, detestable to God (Isa 65:3). Natural rocks sometimes used as (Jdg 6:19-21; 13:19-20). Were not to have steps up to them (Ex 20:26). For idolatrous worship, often built on roofs of houses (2Ki 23:12; Jer 19:13; 32:29). Idolaters raised Asherah poles near (Jdg 6:30; 1Ki 16:32-33; 2Ki 21:3). The Israelites not to raise Asherah poles (Dt 16:21). For idolatrous worship, to be destroyed (Ex 34:13; Dt 7:5). Probable origin of inscriptions on (Dt 27:8).

Mentioned in Scripture:
Of Noah (Ge 8:20). Of Abraham (Ge 12:7-8; 13:18; 22:9). Of Isaac (Ge 26:25). Of Jacob (Ge 33:20; 35:1, 3, 7). Of Moses (Ex 17:15; 24:4). Of Balaam (Nu 23:1, 14, 29). Of Joshua (Jos 8:30-31). Of the temple of Solomon (2Ch 4:1, 19). Of the second temple (Ezr 3:2-3). Of Reubenites, E of Jordan (Jos 22:10). Of Gideon (Jdg 6:26-27). Of the people of Israel (Jdg 21:4). Of Samuel (1Sa 7:17). Of David (2Sa 24:21, 25). Of Jeroboam at Bethel (1Ki 12:33). Of Ahaz (2Ki 16:10-12). Of the Athenians (Ac 17:23). For burnt offering (Ex 27:1-8). For incense (Ex 30:1-6). Protection afforded by (1Ki 1:50-51). Afforded no protection to murderers (Ex 21:14; 1Ki 2:18-34).

AL-TASCHITH *([do] not destroy).* In KJV titles of Pss 57-59; 75; NIV "Do Not Destroy." Probably the tune to which these psalms were sung. The phrase occurs in Isa 65:8, leading some to deduce it is the name of a vintage or wine-making song. *See Music, Symbols Used in.*

ALTRUISM *(concern and actions for the welfare of others).*

Jesus Commends:
By teaching (Mt 20:26-27; 23:11; Mk 9:35; 10:43-45; Lk 22:26-27; Jn 13:4-17; Ac 20:35). By example (Jn 13:4-17), came to serve (Mt 20:28; Php 2:7), went about doing good works (Ac 10:38), pleased not himself (Ro 15:3), became poor for others (2Co 8:9).

Paul Commends:
By teaching, to help the weak (Ac 20:33-35; Ro 15:1-2), to promote the welfare of others (1Co 10:24, 31-33; Gal 6:1-2, 10; Php 2:4-9). By example, became servant of all (1Co 9:18-22; 2Co 4:5), made many rich (2Co 6:10).

Motives Inspiring to:
Love of neighbor (Lk 10:25-37). To save people (1Co 9:22). For Jesus' sake (2Co 4:5). Example of Jesus (Php 2:3-8).
See Alms; Beneficence; Charitableness; Duty of People to People; Liberality; Love.

ALUSH Camping place of the Israelites (Nu 33:13).

ALVAH Chief of Edom, descended from Esau (Ge 36:40; 1Ch 1:51).

ALVAN (possibly *ascending one,* or *tall*). Son of Shobal, a descendant of Seir (Ge 36:23). Also spelled Alian (1Ch 1:40, ftn).

AMAD A town of Asher (Jos 19:26).

AMAL *(laborer, troubler).* Son of Helem (1Ch 7:35).

AMALEK Son of Eliphaz (Ge 36:12; 1Ch 1:36). Probably not the ancestor of the Amalekites mentioned in the time of Abraham (Ge 14:7).

AMALEKITE(S) Descent of (Ge 36:12, 16).

Character of:
Wicked (1Sa 15:18). Oppressive (Jdg 10:12). Warlike and cruel (1Sa 15:33). Governed by kings (1Sa 15:20, 32). A powerful and influential nation (Nu 24:7). Possessed cities (1Sa 15:5).

Country of:
In the south of Canaan (Nu 13:29; 1Sa 27:8). Extended from Havilah to Shur (1Sa 15:7). Was the scene of ancient warfare (Ge 14:7). Part of the Kenites dwelt among (1Sa 15:6).

Conflict With Israel:
Were the first to oppose Israel (Ex 17:8). Beaten at Rephidim, through the intercession of Moses (Ex 17:9-13). Doomed to utter destruction foretold (Nu 24:20). Presumption of Israel punished by (Nu 14:45). United with Eglon against Israel (Jdg 3:13). Part of their possessions taken by Ephraim (Jdg 5:14, w Jdg 12:15). With Midian, oppressed Israel (Jdg 6:3-5). Saul overcame, and delivered Israel (1Sa 14:48), commissioned to destroy (1Sa 15:1-3), massacred (1Sa 15:4-8), condemned for not utterly destroying (1Sa 15:9-26; 28:18). Agag, king of, slain by Samuel (1Sa 15:32-33). Invaded by David (1Sa 27:8-9). Pillaged and burned Ziklag (1Sa 30:1-2). Pursued and slain by David (1Sa 30:10-20). Spoil taken from, consecrated (2Sa 8:11-12). Confederated against Israel (Ps 83:5-7). Remnant of, completely destroyed during the reign of Hezekiah (1Ch 4:41-43).

AMAM A city of Judah (Jos 15:26). Probably within the district later assigned to Simeon (Jos 19:1-9).

AMANA *(constant).* A mountain near Lebanon (SS 4:8), from which flows the Abana River (2Ki 5:12). *See Abana.*

AMANUENSIS A secretary employed to write from dictation or to copy manuscripts.
Examples: Baruch (Jer 36:4; 45:1), Tertius (Ro 16:22), perhaps Silas (1Th 1:1; 1Pe 5:12) and Timothy (2Co 1:1; Php 1:1; Col 1:1; 1Th 1:1; 2Th 1:1; Phm 1:1).

AMARANTHINE A type of straw flower that does not shrivel when picked. NIV "can never fade" (1Pe 1:4; 5:4).

AMARIAH *(Yahweh has said).*
1. Two Levites (1Ch 6:7, 52; 23:19; 24:23).
2. Chief priest in the reign of Jehoshaphat (2Ch 19:11).
3. A high priest, father of Ahitub (1Ch 6:11; Ezr 7:3).
4. A Levite, who assisted in distributing temple gifts (2Ch 31:15-19).
5. Son of Hezekiah (Zep 1:1).
6. Father of Zechariah (Ne 11:4).
7. A priest, returned from exile (Ne 10:3; 12:2). Probably also in Ne 12:13.
8. A returned exile. Divorces his idolatrous wife (Ezr 10:42).

AMARNA, TELL EL *(the hill Amarna).* The modern name for the ancient capital of Amenhotep IV (c. 1379-1362 B.C.), where in 1887 a large number of clay tablets containing the private correspondence between the ruling Egyptian pharaohs and the political leaders in Canaan were discovered. *See Akhenaten; Texts, Ancient Near Eastern Non-Biblical Texts Relating to the Old Testament..*

AMASA *([my] people are from Jesse).*
1. Nephew of David (2Sa 17:25; 1Ch 2:17). Joins Absalom (2Sa 17:25). Returns to David and is made captain of the host (2Sa 19:13). Slain (2Sa 20:8-12; 1Ki 2:5, 32).
2. Son of Hadlai (2Ch 28:12).

AMASAI *([my] people are from Jesse).*
1. A Levite and ancestor of Samuel (1Ch 6:25, 35).
2. Leader of a body of men unhappy with Saul, who joined David (1Ch 12:18).
3. A priest and trumpeter (1Ch 15:24).
4. A Levite of the Kohathites (2Ch 29:12).

AMASHSAI Priest in Nehemiah's time (Ne 11:13).

AMASIAH *(Yahweh carries a load).* A captain under Jehoshaphat (2Ch 17:16).

AMAZIAH *(Yahweh is powerful).*
1. A Levite (1Ch 6:45).
2. King of Judah. History of (2Ki 14; 2Ch 25).
3. An idolatrous priest at Bethel (Am 7:10-17).
4. Father of Joshah (1Ch 4:34).

A

AMBASSADORS

Sent by:
Moses to Edom (Nu 20:14), to the Amorites (Nu 21:21), by Gibeonites to the Israelites (Jos 9:4), Israelites to various nations (Jdg 11:12-28).

Hiram to David (2Sa 5:11), Solomon (1Ki 5:1).

Ben-Hadad to Ahab (1Ki 20:2-6), Amaziah to Jehoash (2Ki 14:8), Ahaz to Tiglath-Pileser (2Ki 16:7), Hoshea to So, king of Egypt (2Ki 17:4), Sennacherib through the field commander, to Hezekiah (2Ki 19:9), Merodach-Baladan to Hezekiah (2Ki 20:12; 2Ch 32:31), Zedekiah to Egypt (Eze 17:15).

Other references to (Pr 13:17; Isa 18:2; 30:4; 33:7; 36:11; 39:1-2; Lk 14:32).

Figurative (Job 33:23; Ob 1; 2Co 5:20; Eph 6:20).

AMBER NIV "glowing metal" (Eze 1:4, 27; 8:2). See Glowing Metal; Minerals of the Bible, 1; Stones.

AMBITION

Worthy: (1Ti 3:1).

Worldly: (Jas 4:1-2; 1Jn 2:16).
Cursed (Isa 5:8; Heb 2:9). Insatiable (Hab 2:5-6, 9). Perishable (Job 20:6-7; Ps 49:11-13). False accusation against Moses (Nu 16:13). Parable illustrating (2Ki 14:9). Rebuked by Jesus (Mt 16:26; 18:1-3; 20:20-28; 23:5-7, 12; Mk 9:33-37; 10:35-45; 12:38-39; Lk 9:25, 46-48; 11:43; 22:24-30; Jn 5:44). Temptation by Satan (Mt 4:8-10; Lk 4:5-8).

Instances of:
King of Babylon (Isa 14:12-15). Eve (Ge 3:5-6). Korah and his followers (Nu 16:3-35). Abimelech (Jdg 9:1-6). Absalom (2Sa 15:1-13; 18:18). Haman (Est 5:9-13). Disciples of Jesus (Mt 18:1-3; 20:20-24; Mk 9:33-37; 10:35-45; Lk 9:46-48; 22:24-30). Diotrephes (3Jn 9-10).

Disappointed: Ahithophel (2Sa 17:23), Adonijah (1Ki 1:5), Haman (Est 6:6-9).

AMBUSH
Instances of: At Ai (Jos 8:2-22), Shechem (Jdg 9:25, 34), Gibeah (Jdg 20:29-41), near Zemaraim (2Ch 13:13). By Jehoshaphat (2Ch 20:21-22).

See Armies.
Figurative (Jer 51:12).

AMEN (so be it). A word used to reinforce a statement (Nu 5:22; Dt 27:12-26; Ne 5:13; 2Co 1:20; Rev 5:14; 22:20).

Used in prayer (1Ki 1:36; 1Ch 16:36; Ne 8:6; Ps 41:13; 72:19; 89:52; 106:48; Jer 28:6; Mt 6:13; 1Co 14:16; Rev 5:14; 19:4).

A title of Christ (Rev 3:14).

AMETHYST A precious stone (Ex 28:19; 39:12; Rev 21:20). See Minerals of the Bible, 1; Stones.

AMI (trustworthy, reliable, faithful). A servant of Solomon (Ezr 2:57). Also called Amon (Ne 7:59). See Amon.

AMINADAB See Amminadab.

AMITTAI (true). Father of Jonah (2Ki 14:25; Jnh 1:1).

AMMAH (cubit). A hill around Gibeon where Joab and Abishai halted in their pursuit of Abner and his forces after they defeated him in the battle of Gibeon (2Sa 2:24-32).

AMMI (my people). Name given to Israel symbolizing acceptance (Hos 2:1, KJV); opposite of Lo-Ammi, "not my people" (Hos 1:9).

AMMIEL (God [El] is my kinsman).
1. The son of Gemalli and spy sent out by Moses (Nu 13:12).
2. The father of Makir of Lo Debar (2Sa 9:4-5; 17:27).
3. The father of Bathsheba, one of David's wives (1Ch 3:5). Called also Eliam (2Sa 11:3).
4. The sixth son of Obed-Edom who, with his family, was associated with the temple gatekeepers (1Ch 26:5).

AMMIHUD ([my] people have majesty).
1. The father of Elishama, chief of Ephraim (Nu 1:10; 2:18; 7:48, 53), and the son of Ladan (1Ch 7:26).
2. A man of Simeon and father of Shemuel (Nu 34:20).
3. A Naphtalite whose son, Pedahel, also assisted in the division of the land (Nu 34:28).
4. Father of Talmai and king of Geshur. Absalom fled to Talmai after he killed his brother Amnon (2Sa 13:37).
5. Son of Omri, father of Uthai (1Ch 9:4).

AMMIHUR See Ammihud.

AMMINADAB (my people are generous).
1. A Levite. Aaron's father-in-law (Ex 6:23).
2. A prince of Judah (Nu 1:7; 2:3; 7:12, 17; 10:14; Ru 4:19-20; 1Ch 2:10; Mt 1:4; Lk 3:33).
3. A son of Kohath, son of Levi (1Ch 6:22). Perhaps the same as 1.
4. A Kohathite who assisted in the return of the ark from the house of Obed-Edom (1Ch 15:10-11).

AMMINADIB KJV "chariots of Amminadib" are "royal chariots of my people" in the NIV (SS 6:12, see also ftn). See Amminadab.

AMMISHADDAI (Shaddai is [my] kinsman). Father of Abiezer, captain of the tribe of Dan in Moses' time (Nu 1:12; 2:25; 7:66, 71; 10:25).

AMMIZABAD ([my] people have given a gift). Son of Benaiah, third of David's captains (1Ch 27:6).

AMMON (people). Ammon or Ben-Ammi is the name of one of the sons of Lot born to him by his youngest daughter in Zoar (Ge 19:38). See Ammonite(s).

AMMONI See Kephar Ammoni.

AMMONITE(S)

History of:
Descendants of Ben-Ammi, one of the sons of Lot (Ge 19:38). Character of (Jdg 10:6; 2Ki 23:13; 2Ch 20:22-23; Jer 27:3, 9; Eze 25:1-7; Am 1:13; Zep 2:10). Territory of (Nu 21:24; Dt 2:19; Jos 12:2; 13:10, 25; Jdg 11:13).

Israelites forbidden to disturb (Dt 2:19, 37). Excluded from the congregation of Israel (Dt 23:3-6). Confederated with Moabites and Amalekites against Israel (Jdg 3:12-13). Defeated by the Israelites (Jdg 10:7-18; 11:32-33; 12:1-3; 1Sa 11; 2Sa 8:12; 10; 11:1; 12:26-31; 17:27; 1Ch 18:1-2; 20:1-3; 2Ch 20; 26:7-8; 27:5). Conspired against the Jews (Ne 4:7-8).

Solomon took wives from (1Ki 11:1; Ne 13:26). Rehoboam took wives from (2Ch 12:13). Jews intermarried with (Ezr 9:1, 10-12; 10:10-44; Ne 13:23).

Kings of: Baalis (Jer 40:14; 41:10).

Idols of: Molech (2Ki 23:13). See Molech.

Prophecies Concerning:
(Isa 11:14; Jer 9:25-26; 25:15-21; 27:1-11; 49:1-6; Eze 21:20, 28-32; 25:1-11; Da 11:41; Am 1:13-15; Zep 2:8-11).

AMNESTY For political offenses: Shimei (2Sa 19:16-23). Amasa (2Sa 19:13, w 17:25).

AMNON (trustworthy).
1. Son of David (2Sa 3:2; 1Ch 3:1). Incest of, and death (2Sa 13).
2. Son of Shimon (1Ch 4:20).

AMOK (capable KB). Priest who returned with Zerubbabel from exile (Ne 12:7, 20).

AMON (trustworthy).
1. Governor of the city of Samaria (1Ki 22:26; 2Ch 18:25).
2. King of Judah (2Ki 21:18-26; 2Ch 33:21-25; Zep 1:1; Mt 1:10).
3. Ancestor of one of the families of the temple servants (Ne 7:59). Called Ami (Ezr 2:57). See Ami.
4. A city thought by most scholars to be the same as the city of No (Hebrew) (Jer 46:25). It was the capital of Egypt. Thebes is the Greek name.

AMORITE(S) (possibly hill dwellers BDB; westerners KB). Descendants of Canaan (Ge 10:15-6; 1Ch 1:13-14). Were giants (Am 2:9). Conquered by Kedorlaomer and rescued by Abraham (Ge 14).

Territory of (Ge 14:7; Nu 13:29; 21:13; Dt 1:4, 7, 19; 3:8-9; Jos 5:1; 10:5; 12:2-3; Jdg 1:35-36; 11:22), given to descendants of Abraham (Ge 15:21; 48:22; Dt 1:20; 2:26-36; 7:1; Jos 3:10; Jdg 11:23; Am 2:10), allotted to Reuben, Gad, and Manasseh (Nu 32:33-42; Jos 13:15-21), conquest of (Nu 21:21-30; Jos 10:11; Jdg 1:34-36).

Chiefs of (Jos 13:21). Wickedness of (Ge 15:16; 2Ki 21:11; Ezr 9:1). Idolatry of (Jdg 6:10; 1Ki 21:26). Judgments denounced against (Ex 23:23-24; 33:2; 34:10-11; Dt 20:17-18). Hornets sent among (Jos 24:12). Not exterminated (Jdg 1:34-36; 3:1-3, 5-8; 1Sa 7:14; 2Sa 2:2; 1Ki 9:20-21; 2Ch 8:7). Intermarry with Jews (Ezr 9:1-2; 10:18-44). Kings of (Jos 10:3-26).

AMOS (burden bearer). A prophet (Am 1:1). Forbidden to prophesy in Israel (Am 7:10-17). Vision of (Am 8:2).

AMOS, BOOK OF

Author: Amos of Tekoa

Date: Probably between 760-750 B.C.

Outline:
I. Superscription (1:1).
II. Introduction to Amos's Message (1:2).
III. Judgments on the Nations (1:3-2:16).
 A. Judgment on Aram (1:3-5).
 B. Judgment on Philistia (1:6-8).
 C. Judgment on Phoenicia (1:9-10).
 D. Judgment on Edom (1:11-12).
 E. Judgment on Ammon (1:13-15).
 F. Judgment on Moab (2:1-3).
 G. Judgment on Judah (2:4-5).
 H. Judgment on Israel (2:6-16).
 1. Ruthless oppression of the poor (2:6-7a).
 2. Unbridled profanation of religion (2:7b-8).
 3. Contrasted position of the Israelites (2:9-12).
 4. The oppressive system will perish (2:13-16).
IV. Oracles Against Israel (3:1-5:17).
 A. Judgment on the Chosen People (ch. 3).
 1. God's punishment announced (3:1-2).
 2. The announcement vindicated (3:3-8).
 3. The punishment vindicated (3:9-15).
 B. Judgment on an Unrepentant People (ch. 4).
 1. Judgment on the socialites (4:1-3).
 2. Perversion of religious life (4:4-5).
 3. Past calamities brought no repentance (4:6-11).
 4. No hope for a hardened people (4:12-13).
 C. Judgment on an Unjust People (5:1-17).
 1. The death dirge (5:1-3).
 2. Exhortation to life (5:4-6).
 3. Indictment of injustices (5:7-13).
 4. Exhortation to life (5:14-15).
 5. Prosperity will turn to grief (5:16-17).
V. Announcements of Exile (5:18-6:14).
 A. A Message of Woe Against Israel's Perverted Religion (5:18-27).
 B. A Message of Woe Against Israel's Complacent Pride (6:1-7).
 C. A Sworn Judgment on the Proud and Unjust Nation (6:8-14).
VI. Visions of Divine Retribution (7:1-9:10).
 A. Judgment Relented (7:1-6).
 1. A swarm of locusts (7:1-3).
 2. A consuming fire (7:4-6).
 B. Judgment Unrelented (7:7-9:10).
 1. The plumb line (7:7-17).
 a. The vision (7:7-9).
 b. Challenged and vindicated (7:10-17).
 2. The basket of ripe fruit (ch. 8).
 a. The vision (8:1-3).
 b. The exposition (8:4-14).
 3. The Lord by the altar (9:1-10).
 a. The vision (9:1-4).
 b. The exposition (9:5-10).
VII. Restored Israel's Blessed Future (9:11-15).
 A. Revival of the House of David (9:11-12).
 B. Restoration of Israel to an Edenic Promised Land (9:13-15).
See Prophets, The Minor.

AMOZ (strong). Father of Isaiah (2Ki 19:2, 20; 20:1; Isa 1:1; 13:1).

AMPHIPOLIS (a city surrounded or a city conspicuous). City of Macedonia not far from Philippi. Paul passed through it (Ac 17:1).

AMPLIATUS A Christian to whom Paul sent a greeting (Ro 16:8).

AMRAM, AMRAMITES (exalted people).
1. Father of Moses (Ex 6:18, 20; Nu 26:58-59; 1Ch 6:3, 18; 23:12-13). Head of one of the branches of Levites (Nu 3:19, 27; 1Ch 26:23). Age of, at death (Ex 6:20).
2. Son of Bani (Ezr 10:34).
3. See Hemdan.

AMRAPHEL King of Shinar (Ge 14:1, 9).

AMULET See Charmers and Charming.

AMUN See Amon.

AMUSEMENTS AND WORLDLY PLEASURES
Belong to the works of the flesh (Gal 5:19, 21). Are transitory (Ecc 2:11; Heb 11:25), meaningless (Ecc 2:11), choke the Word of God in the heart (Lk 8:14), formed a part of idolatrous worship (Ex 32:4, 6, 19, w 1Co 10:7; Jdg 16:23-25).

Lead to:
Rejection of God (Job 21:12-15), poverty (Pr 21:17), disregard of the judgments and works of God (Isa 5:12; Am 6:1-6), sorrow (Pr 14:13), greater evil (Job 1:5; Mt 14:6-8), attempting to find fulfillment in (Ecc 2:1-8).

Indulgence in:
A proof of folly (Ecc 7:4), a characteristic of the wicked (Isa 47:8; Eph 4:17, 19; 2Ti 3:4; Tit 3:3; 1Pe 4:3), a proof of spiritual death (1Ti 5:6), an abuse of riches (Jas 5:1, 5), wisdom of abstaining from (Ecc 7:2-3), shunned by the early believers (1Pe 4:3).

Abstinence From:
Seems strange to the wicked (1Pe 4:4), denounced by God (Isa 5:11-12), exclude from the kingdom of God (Gal 5:21), punishment of (Ecc 11:9; 2Pe 2:13), renunciation of, exemplified by Moses (Heb 11:25).

See Dancing; Games; Pleasure, Worldly; Worldliness.

AMZI (possibly Yahweh is my strength).
1. A descendant of Merari and of Levi, and progenitor of Ethan, whom David set over the service of song (1Ch 6:44-46).
2. An ancestor of Adaiah, a priest in the second temple (Ne 11:12).

ANAB (grape). A city of the Anakites taken by Joshua (Jos 11:21). It fell to Judah (Jos 15:50). SE of Debir, SW of Hebron. It retains its ancient name.

ANAH
1. Daughter of Zibeon and mother of Oholibamah, Esau's wife (Ge 36:2, 14, 25).
2. Son of Seir, chief of Edom (Ge 36:20, 29; 1Ch 1:38).
3. Son Zibeon (Ge 36:24; 1Ch 1:40-41). Also called Beeri (Ge 26:34).

ANAHARATH City on the border of Issachar (Jos 19:19). Modern en-Naura.

ANAIAH (Yahweh responds).
1. A leader or priest who assisted in the reading of the law to the people (Ne 8:4).
2. A returned exile who, with Nehemiah, sealed the covenant (Ne 10:22). Possibly the same as 1.

ANAK ([long] necked, tall). Descendant of Arba (Jos 15:13), and the ancestor of the Anakites (Nu 13:22, 28, 33). See Anakites.

ANAKITES ([long-] necked, tall). Descent of (Nu 13:22; Jos 15:13). Called the descendants of Anak (Nu 13:33), Anakites (Dt 1:28; 9:2).

Divided into three tribes (Jos 15:14). Inhabited the mountains of Judah (Jos 11:21). Hebron, chief city of (Jos 14:15, w 21:11). Of gigantic strength and stature (Dt 2:10-11, 21). Israel terrified by (Nu 14:1, w 13:33). Hebron a possession of, given to Caleb for his faithfulness (Jos 14:6-14). Driven from Hebron by Caleb (Jos 15:13-14). Driven from Kiriath Sepher or Debir by Othniel (Jos 15:15-17; Jdg 1:12-13). Almost annihilated (Jos 11:21-22).

ANAMITES A tribe descended from Mizraim (Ge 10:13; 1Ch 1:11).

ANAMMELECH (Anath is king). An Assyrian idol (2Ki 17:31).

ANAN (cloud). A Jew, returned from Babylonian captivity (Ne 10:26).

ANANI (Yahweh is a covering). A descendant of David (1Ch 3:24).

A

ANANIAH (*Yahweh is a covering*).
1. Son of Maaseiah (Ne 3:23).
2. Town of Benjamin (Ne 11:32).

ANANIAS (*Yahweh is gracious*).
1. High priest, before whom Paul was tried (Ac 23:2-5; 24:1; 25:2).
2. A covetous member of church at Jerusalem. Falsehood and death of (Ac 5:1-11).
3. A Christian in Damascus (Ac 9:10-18; 22:12-16).

ANARCHY
In Israel: (Jdg 17:6; 18:1; 19:1; 21:25; Isa 3:5-8).

In the Early Church: Warned against (Gal 5:13-14). Insubordinate members hostile to authority (2Pe 2:10-19; Jude 8-13).

ANATH (*a Semitic goddess*).
1. Father of the judge Shamgar (Jdg 3:31; 5:6).
2. A Canaanite goddess of war and of love, sometimes identified with Astarte, Asherah, and Ashtoreth. She was the sister and consort of Baal. The name is reflected in the city Beth Anath (Jos 19:38; Jdg 1:33). *See Asherah; Ashtoreth; Beth Anath.*

ANATHEMA (*devoted to destruction*).
A thing devoted to God becomes his and is therefore irrevocably withdrawn from common use (Lev 27:28-29; Ro 9:3; 1Co 12:3; 16:22; Gal 1:9).

ANATHEMA MARANATHA These words from 1Co 16:22 were formerly interpreted as a double curse. *Anathema* does mean cursed (1Co 12:3). *Marana tha* is Aramaic for "Come, O Lord!" (cf. Rev 22:20).
See Blasphemy; Cursing; God, Name of; Oath.

ANATHOTH, ANATHOTHITE (*plural of Anath*).
1. A Levitical city in Benjamin (Jos 21:18; 1Ch 6:60). Abiathar confined in (1Ki 2:26).
Birthplace of Jeremiah (Jer 1:1; 32:7-12), of Abiezer (2Sa 23:27), of Jehu (1Ch 12:3). Prophecies against (Jer 11:21-23). Inhabitants of, after Babylonian captivity (Ezr 2:23; Ne 7:27).
2. Son of Beker (1Ch 7:8).
3. A Jew, who returned from Babylon (Ne 10:19).

ANCHOR Literal (Ac 27:17, 29, 30, 40). Figurative (Heb 6:19).

ANCIENT OF DAYS A title of Yahweh (Da 7:9, 13, 22).

ANCIENT TEXTS RELATING TO THE OLD
TESTAMENT *See Texts, Ancient Near Eastern Non-Biblical Texts Relating to the Old Testament.*

ANCIENTS Those of the past (1Sa 24:13). *See Elders.*

ANDREW (*manly*). An apostle. A fisherman (Mt 4:18). Of Bethsaida (Jn 1:44). A disciple of John (Jn 1:40). Finds Peter, his brother, and brings him to Jesus (Jn 1:40-42). Call of (Mt 4:18; Mk 1:16). His name appears in the list of the apostles (Mt 10:2; Mk 3:18; Lk 6:14). Asks the Master privately about the destruction of the temple (Mk 13:3-4). Tells Jesus of the Greeks who wanted to see him (Jn 12:20-22). Reports the number of loaves at the feeding of the five thousand (Jn 6:8). Meets with the disciples after the Lord's ascension (Ac 1:13).

ANDRONICUS (*victor [over] man*). Relative of Paul; an apostle (Ro 16:7).

ANEM (*springs*). A Levitical city (1Ch 6:73).

ANER
1. A Canaanite chief and brother of Mamre (Ge 14:13, 24).
2. A Levitical city of Manasseh (1Ch 6:70).

ANGEL [OF THE LORD] (*messenger*). In addition to 54 occurrences of "the angel of the LORD" (Ex 3:2; Jdg 2:1), many uses of "angel" indicate a manifestation of God himself. These include: angel (Ac 7:30, 35 w Ex 3:2), my angel (Ex 23:20-23; 32:34), angel of God (Ex 14:19; Jdg 13:6; 2Sa 14:17, 20), angel of his Presence (Isa 63:9). *See Angels.*

ANGEL OF THE CHURCHES Heavenly messengers and guardians or earthly messengers and pastors (Rev 1:20; 2:1, 8, 18; 3:1, 7, 14).

ANGELS
Elect:
Created by God and Christ (Ne 9:6; Col 1:16). Worship God and Christ (Ne 9:6; Php 2:9-11; Heb 1:6). Are ministering spirits (1Ki 19:5; Ps 68:17; 104:4; Lk 16:22; Ac 12:7-11; 27:23; Heb 1:7, 14). Communicate the will of God and Christ (Da 8:16-17; 9:21-23; 10:11; 12:6-7; Mt 2:13, 20; Lk 1:19, 28; Ac 5:20; 8:26; 10:5; 27:23; Rev 1:1). Obey the will of God (Ps 103:20; Mt 6:10). Execute the purposes of God (Nu 22:22; Ps 103:21; Mt 13:39-42; 28:2; Jn 5:4; Rev 5:2). Execute the judgments of God (2Sa 24:16; 2Ki 19:35; Ps 35:5-6; Ac 12:23; Rev 16:1). Celebrate the praises of God (Job 38:7; Ps 148:2; Isa 6:3; Lk 2:13-14; Rev 5:11-12; 7:11-12). The law given by the mediation of (Ps 68:17; Ac 7:53; Heb 2:2).
Announced: The conception of Christ (Mt 1:20-21; Lk 1:31). The birth of Christ (Lk 2:10-12). The resurrection of Christ (Mt 28:5-7; Lk 24:23). The ascension and second coming of Christ (Ac 1:11). The conception of John the Baptist (Lk 1:13, 36).
Minister to Christ (Mt 4:11; Lk 4:11; Jn 1:51). Are subject to Christ (Eph 1:21; Col 1:16; 2:10; 1Pe 3:22). Shall execute the purposes of Christ (Mt 13:41; 24:31). Shall attend Christ at his second coming (Mt 16:27; 25:31; Mk 8:38; 2Th 1:7). Know and delight in the gospel of Christ (Eph 3:9-10; 1Ti 3:16; 1Pe 1:12). Mediation of, in response to prayer (Mt 26:53; Ac 12:5, 7). Rejoice over every repentant sinner (Lk 15:7, 10). Have charge over the

children of God (Ps 34:7; 91:11-12; Da 6:22; Mt 18:10). Are of different orders (Isa 6:2; 1Th 4:16; 1Pe 3:22; Jude 9; Rev 12:7). Not to be worshiped (Col 2:18; Rev 19:10; 22:9). Are examples of meekness (2Pe 2:11; Jude 9). Are wise (2Sa 14:20). Are mighty (Ps 103:20). Are holy (Mt 25:31). Are elect (1Ti 5:21). Are innumerable (Job 25:3; Heb 12:22).

Fallen: (Job 4:18; Mt 25:41; 2Pe 2:4; Jude 6; Rev 2:9). *See Demons.*

ANGER
Forbidden (Ecc 7:9; Mt 5:22; Ro 12:19). A work of the flesh (Gal 5:20). A characteristic of fools (Pr 12:16; 14:29; 27:3; Ecc 7:9).

Connected With:
Pride (Pr 21:24). Cruelty (Ge 49:7; Pr 27:3-4). Clamor and evil-speaking (Eph 4:31). Malice and blasphemy (Col 3:8). Strife and contention (Pr 21:19; 29:22; 30:33). Brings its own punishment (Job 5:2; Pr 19:19; 25:28). Grievous words stir up (Jdg 12:4; 2Sa 19:43; Pr 15:1). Should not betray us into sin (Ps 37:8; Eph 4:26). In prayer be free from (1Ti 2:8). May be averted by wisdom (Pr 29:8). Meekness pacifies (Pr 15:1; Ecc 10:4). Children should not be provoked to (Eph 6:4; Col 3:21). Be slow to (Pr 15:18; 16:32; 19:11; Tit 1:7; Jas 1:19). Avoid those given to (Ge 49:6; Pr 22:24).

Justifiable, Exemplified:
Our Lord (Mk 3:5). Jacob (Ge 31:36). Moses (Ex 11:8; 32:19; Lev 10:16; Nu 16:15). Nehemiah (Ne 5:6; 13:17, 25).

Sinful, Exemplified:
Cain (Ge 4:5-6). Esau (Ge 27:45). Simeon and Levi (Ge 49:5-7). Moses (Nu 20:10-11). Balaam (Nu 22:27). Saul (1Sa 20:30). Ahab (1Ki 21:4). Naaman (2Ki 5:11). Asa (2Ch 16:10). Uzziah (2Ch 26:19). Haman (Est 3:5). Nebuchadnezzar (Da 3:13). Jonah (Jnh 4:4). Herod (Mt 2:16). Jews (Lk 4:28). High Priest (Ac 5:17; 7:54).

ANGER OF GOD
Turned away by Christ (Lk 2:11, 14; Ro 5:9; 2Co 5:18-19; Eph 2:14, 17; Col 1:20; 1Th 1:10). Is turned away from them that believe (Jn 3:14-18; Ro 3:25; 5:1). Is turned away upon confession of sin and repentance (Job 33:27-28; Ps 106:43-45; Jer 3:12-13; 18:7-8; 31:18-20; Joel 2:12-14; Lk 15:18-20). Is slow (Ps 103:8; Isa 48:9; Jnh 4:2; Na 1:3). Is righteous (Ps 58:10-11; La 1:18; Ro 2:6, 8; 3:5-6; Rev 16:6-7). The justice of, not to be questioned (Ro 9:18, 20, 22). Manifested in terrors (Ex 14:24; Ps 76:6-8; Jer 10:10; La 2:20-22). Manifested in judgments and afflictions (Job 21:17; Ps 78:49-51; 90:7; Isa 9:19; Jer 7:20; Eze 7:19; Heb 3:17). Cannot be resisted (Job 9:13; 14:13; Ps 76:7; Na 1:6). Aggravated by continual provocation (Nu 32:14). Specially reserved for the day of wrath (Zep 1:14-18; Mt 25:41; Ro 2:5, 8; 2Th 1:8; Rev 6:17; 11:18; 19:15).

Against:
The wicked (Ps 7:11; 21:8-9; Isa 3:8; 13:9; Na 1:2-3; Ro 1:18; 2:8; Eph 5:6; Col 3:6). Those who forsake him (Ezr 8:22; Isa 1:4). Unbelief (Ps 78:21-22; Jn 3:36; Heb 3:18-19). Impenitence (Ps 7:12; Pr 1:30-31; Isa 9:13-14; Ro 2:5). Apostasy (Heb 10:26-27). Idolatry (Dt 29:20, 27-28; 32:19-20, 22; Jos 23:16; 2Ki 22:17; Ps 78:58-59; Jer 44:3). Sin, in believers (Ps 89:30-32; 90:7-9; 99:8; 102:9-10; Isa 47:6). Extreme, against those who oppose the gospel (Ps 2:2-3, 5; 1Th 2:16). Folly of provoking (Jer 7:19; 1Co 10:22). To be dreaded (Ps 2:12; 76:7; 90:11; Mt 10:28). To be deprecated (Ex 32:11; Ps 6:1; 38:1; 74:1-2; Isa 64:9). Removal of, should be prayed for (Ps 39:10; 79:5; 80:4; Da 9:16; Hab 3:2). Tempered with mercy to believers (Ps 30:5; Isa 26:20; 54:8; 57:15-16; Jer 30:11; Mic 7:11). To be borne with submission (2Sa 24:17; La 3:39, 43; Mic 7:9). Should lead to repentance (Isa 42:24-25; Jer 4:8).

Exemplified Against:
The old world (Ge 7:21-23). Builders of Babel (Ge 11:8). Cities of the plain (Ge 19:24-25). Egyptians (Ex 7:20; 8:6, 16, 24; 9:3, 9, 23; 10:13, 22; 12:29; 14:27). Israelites (Ex 32:35; Nu 11:1, 33; 14:40-45; 21:6; 25:9; 2Sa 24:1, 15). Enemies of Israel (1Sa 5:6; 7:10). Nadab (Lev 10:2). The Spies (Nu 14:37). Korah (Nu 16:31, 35). Aaron and Miriam (Nu 12:9-10). Five Kings (Jos 10:25). Abimelech (Jdg 9:56). Men of Beth Shemesh (1Sa 6:19). Saul (1Sa 31:6). Uzzah (2Sa 6:7). Saul's family (2Sa 21:1). Sennacherib (2Ki 19:28, 35, 37).

ANIAM (*I am kinsman*). A son of Shemida, a Manassehite (1Ch 7:19).

ANIM (*springs*). A city of Judah (Jos 15:50).

ANIMALS
Creation of:
(Ge 1:24-25; 2:19; Jer 27:5). Food of (Ge 1:30). Named (Ge 2:20). Ordained as food for man (Ge 9:2-3; Lev 11:3, 9, 21-22; Dt 14:4-6, 9, 11, 20). God's care of (Ge 9:9-10; Dt 25:4; Job 38:41; Ps 36:6; 104:11, 21; 145:15-16; 147:9; Jn 4:11; Mt 6:26; 10:29; Lk 12:6, 24; 1Co 9:9). Under the curse (Ge 3:14; 6:7, 17). Suffer under divine judgments sent upon man (Jer 7:20; 14:4; 21:6; Eze 14:13, 17, 19-21; Joel 1:18-20). Two of every kind preserved in the ark (Ge 6:19-20; 7:2, 9, 14-15; 8:19). Seven clean of every kind preserved in the ark (Ge 7:2-3). Suffered the plagues of Egypt (Ex 8:17; 9:9-10, 19; 11:5). Perish at death (Ecc 3:21). Possessed by demons (Mt 8:31-32; Mk 5:13; Lk 8:33). Clean and unclean (Ge 7:2, 8; 8:20; Lev 7:21; 11; 20:25; Dt 14:3-20; Ac 10:11-15; 1Ti 4:3-5).

God's Control of:
(Ps 91:13; Lk 10:19). Instruments of God's will (Ex 8; 10:4-15, 19; Nu 21:6; 22:28; Jos 24:12; Joel 1:4). Belong to God (Ps 50:10-12). Sent in judgment (Lev 26:22; Nu 21:6-7; Dt 8:15; Eze 5:17; 14:15; Rev 6:8).

Nature of:
(Job 41; Ps 32:9; Jas 3:7). Habits of (Job 12:7-8; 37:8; 39; 40:20-21; Ps 104:20-25; Isa 13:21-22; 34:14). Breeding of (Ge 30:35-43; 31:8-9). Instincts of (Dt 32:11; Job 35:11; 39; 40:15-24; Ps 104:11-30; Pr 6:5-8; 30:25-28; Isa 1:3; Jer 2:24; 8:7; La 4:3;

Mt 24:28). Abodes of (Job 24:5; 37:8; 39:5-10, 27-29; Ps 104:20, 22, 25; Isa 34:14-15; Jer 2:24; 50:39; Mk 1:13).

Cruelty to:
Of Balaam to his donkey (Nu 22:22-33). Hamstringing horses (2Sa 8:4; 1Ch 18:4).

Kindness to:
By the righteous (Pr 12:10). In not muzzling an ox while threshing (Dt 25:4; 1Ti 5:18). In relieving the overburdened (Ex 23:5; Dt 22:4). In rescuing from pits (Mt 12:11; Lk 13:15; 14:5). In feeding (Ge 24:32; 43:24; Jdg 19:21).
Instances of: Jacob in making shelters for his cattle (Ge 33:17). People of Gerar in providing tents for cattle (2Ch 14:15).

Laws Concerning:
Sabbath rest for (Ex 20:10; Dt 5:14). Treatment of vicious (Ex 21:28-32, 35-36). Penalty for injury of (Ex 21:33-34). Hybridizing of, forbidden (Lev 19:19). Working of (Dt 22:10). Mother birds and their young (Dt 22:6-7).

Names of:
Antelopes (Dt 14:5; Isa 51:20). Apes (1Ki 10:22). Baboons (1Ki 10:22; 2Ch 9:21). Donkeys, beasts of burden (Ge 22:3; Nu 22:28; Dt 22:10; Jdg 5:10; 10:4 1Sa 9:3; Mt 21:2). Bears (1Sa 17:34; 2Sa 17:8; 2Ki 2:24; Pr 17:12; 28:15; Isa 11:7). Behemoth (Job 40:15-24). Boars (Ps 80:13). Bull, as offerings (Ex 29:10-11, 36; Lev 4:4; Nu 15:8; 1Ki 18:33; 2Ch 13:9; Ezr 6:17; Ps 66:15). Calves (Ge 18:7; 1Sa 28:24; Am 6:4; Lk 15:23). Camels (Ge 12:16; 30:43; Lev 11:4; Jdg 6:5; 1Sa 30:17; 1Ch 5:21; Job 1:3; Mt 19:24; 23:24). Cattle, livestock (Ge 1:25; 31:18; Ex 9:4; 20:10; Nu 32:1; Jos 14:4; Eze 39:18; Am 4:1). Coneys, rock badgers (Lev 11:5; Ps 104:18; Pr 30:26). Cows (Ge 32:15; Dt 7:13; Isa 6:7). Deer (Dt 14:5; 2Sa 2:18; 22:34; 1Ch 12:8; Ps 42:1; Pr 5:19; 6:5; Isa 35:6; Jer 14:5). Dogs (1Ki 14:11; 22:38; Ps 59:6; Pr 26:17; Ecc 9:4; Lk 16:21). Dragons (Rev 12:3-17). Elephants (Job 40:15, ftn). Foxes (Jdg 15:4; Ne 4:3; Ps 63:10; SS 2:15; Mt 8:20). Gecko (Lev 11:30). Goats, as offerings (Ge 15:9; Lev 4:24; 16:15; Jdg 13:19; 2Ch 29:23). Heifers, offered as sacrifices (Ge 15:9; Nu 19:2; Dt 21:3; Heb 9:13). Horses (Dt 17:16; 2Ki 23:11; Job 39:19; Ps 32:9; 33:17; Isa 31:1). Lambs, for offerings (Ex 29:38-39; Lev 3:7; 4:32; 5:6; Nu 6:12). Leopards (SS 4:8; Isa 11:6; Jer 5:6; 13:23; Hos 13:7; Hab 1:8). Lions, general references to (Jdg 14:5; 1Sa 17:34; 1Ki 13:24; Da 6:19), characteristics of (Dt 33:22; Jdg 14:18; 2Sa 17:10; Job 10:16; Ps 17:12; Pr 30:30; Isa 31:4; Na 2:12). Lizards (Lev 11:30). Mountain sheep (Dt 14:5). Mules (2Sa 13:29; 18:9; 1Ki 1:33; Ps 32:9; Zec 14:15). Oxen, laws concerning (Ex 21:28; 22:1; 23:4; Lev 17:3; Dt 5:14; 22:1; 25:4; Lk 13:15; 1Co 9:9; 1Ti 5:18). Pigs (Lev 11:7; Isa 65:4; 66:17; Mt 7:6; 8:30; Lk 15:15; 2Pe 2:22). Rabbit (Lev 11:6). Rams, used in sacrifices (Ge 15:9; 22:13; Ex 29:15; Lev 5:15; Nu 5:8). Rats (Lev 11:29; 1Sa 6:4; Isa 66:17). Rooster (Pr 30:31). Sheep (Ge 4:4; 30:32; Dt 18:4; 32:14; 2Ch 7:5; 15:11; Job 1:3; 42:12; Mt 12:11). Wild oxen (Nu 23:22; Dt 33:17; Job 39:9; Ps 29:6; Isa 34:7). Vipers, poisonous serpents (Job 20:16; Isa 30:6; 59:5). Weasel (Lev 11:29). Wolves, illustrative of the wicked (Mt 7:15; 10:16; Jn 10:12; Ac 20:29).
See Birds; Insects.

ANISE *See Dill.*

ANKLET An ornament worn by women on the ankles (Isa 3:16, 20). *See Jewel, Jewelry.*

ANNA (*grace*). A widow and prophetess who at the age of 84 recognized Jesus as the Messiah when He was brought into the Temple (Lk 2:36-38).

ANNAS (*grace*). Associate high priest with Caiaphas (Lk 3:2; Jn 18:13, 19, 24; Ac 4:6).

ANNIHILATION The belief that there is no existence after death or that there is no existence for the wicked after death.
Some texts seem to imply death as final (Job 14:12, 18-22; Ps 6:5; 88:10; Isa 26:14). The resurrection is the hope of all believers (Ps 16:9-11; Isa 53:11; Da 12:1-3). In the teaching of Jesus (Mt 22:23-32; Lk 14:14; Jn 11:24-26), of the apostles (Ac 4:1-4, 33; 23:6-8; 24:10-21; 1Co 15). *See Resurrection.*
Eternal punishment of the wicked is also clearly taught (Da 12:2; Mt 18:8-9; Jn 3:36; 2Th 1:9; Rev 14:11; 20:4-15). *See Wicked, Punishment of.*

ANNUAL FEASTS All but Purim and Dedication instituted by Moses.

Designated as:
Solemn feasts (Nu 15:3; 2Ch 8:13; La 2:6; Eze 46:9). Set feasts (Nu 29:39; Ezr 3:5). Appointed feasts (Isa 1:14). Holy convocations (Lev 23:4). First and last days were Sabbatic (Lev 23:39-40; Nu 28:18-25; 29:12, 35; Ne 8:1-18). Kept with rejoicing (Lev 23:40; Dt 16:11-14; 2Ch 30:21-26; Ezr 6:22; Ne 8:9-12, 17; Ps 122:4; Isa 30:29; Zec 8:19). Divine protection given during (Ex 34:24).
All males were required to attend (Ex 23:17; 34:23; Dt 16:16; Eze 36:38; Lk 2:41-42; Jn 4:45; 7). Aliens permitted to attend (Jn 12:20; Ac 2:1-11). Attended by women (1Sa 1:3, 9; Lk 2:41).

Observed:
By Jesus (Mt 26:17-20; Lk 2:41-42; 22:15; Jn 2:13, 23; 5:1; 7:10; 10:22). By Paul (Ac 20:6, 16; 24:11, 17).

New Moon:
(Nu 10:10; 28:11-15; 1Ch 23:31; 2Ch 31:3; Ezr 3:5). Buying and selling at time of, suspended (Am 8:5).

The Passover:
Institution of (Ex 12:3-49; 23:15-18; 34:18; Lev 23:4-8; Nu 9:2-5, 13-14; 28:16-25; Dt 16:1-8, 16; Ps 81:3, 5). Design of (Ex 12:21-28).
Special Passover, for those who were unclean, or on journey to be held in second month (Nu 9:6-12; 2Ch 30:2-4). Lamb killed by Levites, for those who were ceremonially unclean (2Ch 30:17; 35:3-11; Ezr 6:20). Strangers authorized to celebrate (Ex 12:48-49; Nu 9:14).
Observed at place designated by God (Dt 16:5-7). With unleavened bread (Ex 12:8, 15-20; 13:3, 6; 23:15; Lev 23:6; Nu

A

9:11; 28:17; Dt 16:3-4; Mk 14:12; Lk 22:7; Ac 12:3; 1Co 5:8). Penalty for neglecting to observe (Nu 9:13).
Reinstituted by Ezekiel (Eze 45:21-24).

Observation of—
Renewed, by the Israelites on entering Canaan (Jos 5:10-11). By Hezekiah (2Ch 30:1). By Josiah (2Ki 23:22-23; 2Ch 35:1, 18). After return from captivity (Ezr 6:19-20). Observed by Jesus (Mt 26:17-20; Lk 22:15; Jn 2:13, 23; 13). Jesus when twelve years old, in the temple at time of (Lk 2:41-50). Jesus crucified at time of (Mt 26:2; Mk 14:1-2; Jn 18:28). Lord's Supper ordained at (Mt 26:26-28; Mk 14:12-25; Lk 22:7-20). The lamb of, a type of Christ (1Co 5:7).
Prisoners released at, by the Romans (Mt 27:15; Mk 15:6; Lk 23:16-17; Jn 18:39). Peter imprisoned at time of (Ac 12:3).

Christ Called—
Our Passover lamb (1Co 5:7; see also Jn 1:36; Rev 5:6-14).

Pentecost:
Called Feast of Weeks (Ex 34:22; Dt 16:10). Feast of Harvest (Ex 23:16). Day of First Fruits (Nu 28:26). Day of Pentecost (Ac 2:1; 20:16; 1Co 16:8).
Institution of (Ex 23:16; 34:22; Lev 23:15-21; Nu 28:26-31; Dt 16:9-12, 16).
Holy Spirit given to the apostles on the day of (Ac 2).

Purim:
Instituted by Esther and Mordecai to commemorate the deliverance of the Jews from the plot of Haman (Est 9:20-32).

Tabernacles:
Also called Feast of Ingathering. Instituted (Ex 23:16; 34:22; Lev 23:34-43; Nu 29:12-40; Dt 16:13-16). Design of (Lev 23:42-43). The law read in connection with, every seventh year (Dt 31:10-12; Ne 8:18).

Observance of—
After the captivity (Ezr 3:4; Ne 8:14-18). By Jesus (Jn 7:2, 14). Observance of, omitted (Ne 8:17). Penalty for not observing (Zec 14:16-19).
Jeroboam institutes an idolatrous feast parallel to, in the eighth month (1Ki 12:32-33).

Trumpets:
When and how observed (Lev 23:24-25; Nu 29:1-6). Celebrated after the captivity (Ne 8:2, 9-12).

Dedication or Hanukkah:
Instituted in the Intertestamental era, commemorating the dedication of the temple by Judas Maccabeus (1Mc 4:59). Observed by Jesus (Jn 10:22-39).
See Feasts; see also each feast by name.

ANOINTING
Of the body (Dt 28:40; Ru 3:3; Est 2:12; Ps 92:10; 104:15; 141:5; Pr 27:9, 16; Ecc 9:8; SS 1:3; 4:10; Isa 57:9; Am 6:6; Mic 6:15). Of guests (2Ch 28:15; Lk 7:46). The sick (Isa 1:6; Mk 6:13; Lk 10:34; Jas 5:14; Rev 3:18). The dead (Mt 26:12; Mk 14:8; 16:1; Lk 23:56). Of Jesus, as a token of love (Lk 7:37-38, 46; Jn 11:2; 12:3). Omitted in mourning (2Sa 12:20; 14:2; Isa 61:3; Da 10:3). God preserves those who receive (Ps 18:50; 20:6; 89:20-23). Believers receive (Isa 61:3; 1Jn 2:20).

In Consecration:
Of high priests (Ex 29:7, 29; 40:13; Lev 6:20; 8:12; 16:32; Nu 35:25; Ps 133:2).
Of priests (Ex 28:41; 30:30; 40:15; Lev 4:3; 8:30; Nu 3:3).
Of kings (Jdg 9:8, 15), Saul (1Sa 9:16; 10:1; 15:1), David (1Sa 16:3, 12-13; 2Sa 2:4; 5:3; 12:7; 9:21; 1Ch 11:3). Solomon (1Ki 1:39; 1Ch 29:22), Jehu (1Ki 19:16; 2Ki 9:1-3, 6, 12). Hazael (1Ki 19:15), Joash (2Ki 11:12; 2Ch 23:11), Jehoahaz (2Ki 23:30), Cyrus (Isa 45:1).
Of prophets (1Ki 19:16).
Of the tabernacle (Ex 30:26; 40:9; Lev 8:10; Nu 7:1), altars of (Ex 30:26-28; 40:10; Lev 8:11; Nu 7:1), vessels of (Ex 30:27-28; 40:9-10; Lev 8:10-11; Nu 7:1).
Jacob's pillar at Bethel (Ge 28:18; 31:13; 35:14).
See Dedication.

Figurative:
Of Christ's kingly and priestly office (Ps 45:7; 89:20; Isa 61:1; Da 9:24; Lk 4:18; 4:27; 10:38; Heb 1:9). Of spiritual gifts (2Co 1:21; 1Jn 2:20, 27). Of God's choice and enabling of leaders (Ex 40:13-15; Lev 8:12; 1Sa 16:13; 1Ki 19:16).
Symbolic of Jesus' death (Mt 26:7-12; Jn 12:3-7).

ANOINTING OIL
Formula of, given by Moses (Ex 30:22-25, 31-33). *See Oil; Ointment.*

ANOTH
See Beth Anoth.

ANT
Illustrate work ethic (Pr 6:6-8; 30:25).

ANTEDILUVIANS
(*those who lived before the flood*). Worship God (Ge 4:3-4, 26). Occupations of (Ge 4:2-3, 20-22). Arts of (Ge 4:2-3, 20-22; 6:14-22). Enoch prophesies to (Jude 14-15). Noah preaches to (2Pe 2:5). Wickedness of (Ge 6:5-7). Destruction of (Ge 7:1, 21-23; Job 22:15-17; Mt 24:37-39; Lk 17:26-27; 2Pe 2:5). *See Flood.*
Longevity of. *See Longevity.*
Giants among. *See Giants.*

ANTELOPE
(Dt 14:5; Isa 51:20). *See Deer.*

ANTHOTHIJAH
Son of Shashak, a Benjamite (1Ch 8:24-25).

ANTHROPOMORPHISMS
Figures of speech that attribute human anatomy, acts, and affections to God.

Anatomy:
Arm (Ps 89:13), body or form (Nu 11:25), ear (Ps 34:15), eye (2Ch 16:9; Isa 1:15), mouth (Ps 33:6), voice (Eze 1:24; 28), wings (Ps 36:7; 57:1).
See terms for body parts, e.g., Arm, Eye, Hand.

Intellectual Facilities:
Knowing (Ge 18:17-19), reason (Isa 1:18), remembering (Ge 9:16; 19:29; Ex 2:24; Isa 43:26; 63:11), understanding (Ps 147:5), will (Ro 9:19).

Actions:
Breathing (Ps 33:6), grasping, with hand (Ps 35:2), hearing (Ps 94:9), laughing (Ps 2:4; 37:13; 59:8; Pr 1:26), not tiring (Isa 40:28), resting (Ge 2:2-3, 19; Ex 20:11; 31:17; Dt 5:14; Heb 4:4, 10), seeing (Ge 18:21; Ex 14:24; Ps 94:9), sleeping (Ps 44:23; 78:65; 121:4), speaking (Ge 18:33; Nu 11:25; Ps 33:6), standing (Ps 35:2), walking (Ge 3:8; Lev 26:12; Dt 23:14; Job 22:14; Hab 3:15).

Affections and Emotions:
Amazement (Isa 59:16; 63:5; Mk 6:6), grief (Ge 6:6; Jdg 10:16; Ps 95:10; Heb 3:10, 17), jealousy (Ex 20:5; 34:13-14; Nu 25:11; Dt 29:20; 32:16, 21; 1Ki 14:22; Ps 78:58; 79:5; Isa 30:1-2; 31:1, 3; Eze 16:42; 23:25; 36:5-6; 38:19; Zep 1:18; 3:8; Zec 1:14; 8:2; 1Co 10:22), swearing an oath (Isa 62:8; Heb 6:16-17; 7:21, 28). *See Anger of God; Oath.*

ANTICHRIST(S)
(*against* or *substitute Christ*). (Mt 24:5, 23-24, 26; Mk 13:6, 21-22; Lk 21:8; 2Th 2:3-12; 1Jn 2:18, 22; 4:3; 2Jn 7). To be destroyed (Rev 19:20; 20:10, 15).

ANTI-LEBANON
See Lebanon.

ANTIOCH
1. A city of Syria. Disciples first called Christians in (Ac 11:19-30). Church in (Ac 13:1; 14:26-27). Barnabas and Paul make second visit to (Ac 14:26-28). Dissension in church of (Ac 15:22, w 15:1-35). Paul and Peter's controversy at (Gal 2:11-15).
2. A city of Pisidia. Persecutes Paul (Ac 13:14-52; Ac 14:19-22; 18:22; 2Ti 3:11).

ANTIOCHUS
(*opposer*). A favorite name of the Seleucid kings of Syria, referred to as the kings of the North in Da 11.
1. Antiochus II Theos (286-246 B.C.) married Berenice, daughter of Ptolemy II, the "king of the South" (Da 11:6).
2. Antiochus III, the Great (242-187 B.C.) gained control of Israel in 198 B.C. (Da 11:10-19).
3. Antiochus IV (Epiphanes), son of III (215-163 B.C.); his attempt to hellenize the Jews led to the Maccabean revolt (Da 8:9-12, 23-25; 11:21-35; see also 1 and 2Mc). *See Abomination That Causes Desolation; Testaments, Time Between.*

ANTIPAS
(possibly a contraction of *Antipater*).
1. A Christian martyr of Pergamum (Rev 2:13).
2. Herod Antipas, son of Herod the Great; ruled Galilee and Perea from 4 B.C. to A.D. 39. *See Herod.*

ANTIPATER
See Herod.

ANTIPATRIS
A city in Samaria (Ac 23:31).

ANTITYPE
See Types.

ANTONIA, TOWER OF
A fortress connected with temple at Jerusalem, built by Herod the Great. It was garrisoned by Roman soldiers who watched the temple area (Ac 21:30ff).

ANTOTHIJAH
See Anthothijah.

ANTOTHITE
See Anathoth, Anathothite.

ANUB
(*fruitful*). Son of Koz of the tribe of Judah (1Ch 4:8).

ANVIL
(Isa 41:7).

ANXIETY
Forbidden (Mt 6:25-34; Lk 12:11-12, 22-28; 1Co 7:32; Php 4:6; 1Pe 5:7).
Unavailing (Mt 39:6; Mt 6:27; Lk 12:25-26). Proceeds from unbelief (Mt 6:26, 28-30; Lk 12:24, 27-28). Martha rebuked for (Lk 10:40-41).
Remedy for (Ps 37:5; 55:22; Heb 13:5; 1Pe 5:6-7). *See Care, Worldly.*

APARTMENT
(Jer 36:22). *See Winter Apartment, Winter House.*

APES
In Solomon's zoological collections (1Ki 10:22; 2Ch 9:21).

APELLES
A disciple in Rome (Ro 16:10).

APHARSACHITES, APHARSATHCHITES, APHARSITES
Aramaic terms transliterated as proper names in the KJV are translated "officials" in the NIV (Ezr 5:6; 6:6).

APHEK
(*stronghold*).
1. A city of the tribe of Asher (Jos 19:30). A city whose inhabitants were not driven out by Asher (Jdg 1:31).
2. A city of the tribe of Issachar. Philistines defeat Israelites at (1Sa 4:1-11). Saul slain at (1Sa 29:1, w 1Sa 31). Probably the same as the royal city of the Canaanites (Jos 12:18).
3. A city between Damascus and Israel. Ben-Hadad defeated at (1Ki 20:26-30).

APHEKAH
(*the fortress*). A city in the mountains of Judah (Jos 15:53).

APHIAH
Ancestor of Saul (1Sa 9:1).

APHIK
See Aphek.

APHRAH
See Beth Ophrah; Ophrah.

APHSES
See Happizzez.

APOCALYPSE
(*disclosure*). Greek title of the book of Revelation. *See Apocalyptic Literature; Revelation, Book of.*

APOCALYPTIC LITERATURE
A type of prophetic literature that communicates the ultimate triumph of God over evil through dreams, visions, and symbols. Daniel and Revelation and parts of Ezekiel and Zechariah are canonical apocalypses. Many non-canonical apocalypses appeared between c. 200 B.C. and A.D. 200 in the style of Daniel, also claiming to have been written by a famous OT character. Major examples are 1 and 2 Enoch, Jubilees, Assumption of Moses, 2 Esdras, Apocalypse of Baruch, The Testaments of the Twelve Prophets, and the Psalms of Solomon.

APOCRYPHA
(*hidden, obscure*). Books and chapters interspersed among the canonical books of the OT in the LXX and Vulgate, but not found in the Hebrew OT. The Jewish people, who produced them, and Protestants do not consider them canonical. The Roman Catholic Church received the following as deuterocanonical at the Council of Trent (1546): Tobit, Judith, Additions to Esther, Wisdom of Solomon, Ecclesiasticus, Baruch, Letter of Jeremiah, The Prayer of Azariah and the Song of the Three Young Men, Susanna, Bel and the Dragon, and 1 and 2 Maccabees. Other works are considered deuterocanonical by the Orthodox Church: 1 and 2 Esdras, The Prayer of Manasseh, Psalm 151, 3 and 4 Maccabees. *See Testaments, Time Between.*

APOLLONIA
A city of Macedonia (Ac 17:1).

APOLLOS
An eloquent Christian convert at Corinth (Ac 18:24-28; 19:1; 1Co 1:12; 3:4-7). Refuses to return to Rome (1Co 16:12). Paul writes Titus about (Tit 3:13). Born in Alexandria (Ac 18:24).

APOLLYON
(*destroyer*). Angel of the bottomless pit (Rev 9:11).

APOSTASY
(*abandoning God*).

Described:
(Dt 13:13, 32; 32:15; Isa 65:11-12; Mt 12:45; Lk 11:24-26; Ac 7:39-43; 1Ti 4:1-3; 2Ti 3:6-9; 4:3-4; Heb 3:12; 2Pe 2:15-22; Jude 8). Foretold (Mt 24:12; 2Th 2:3; 1Ti 4:1-3; 2Ti 3:1-9; 4:3-4; 2Pe 2:1).
Admonitions against (Mt 24:4-5; Mk 13:5-6; Heb 3:12; 2Pe 3:17; 2Jn 8; Jude 4-6). No remedy for (Heb 6:4-8; 10:26-29).
Punishment (1Ch 28:9; Isa 1:28; 65:12-15; Jer 17:5-6; Eze 3:20; 18:24, 26; 33:12-13, 18; Zep 1:4-6; Jn 15:6; 2Th 2:11-12; Heb 10:25-31, 38-39; 2Pe 2:17-22; Jude 6).

Caused by:
Persecution (Mt 13:20-21; 24:9-12; Mk 4:5-17; Lk 8:13). Worldliness (2Ti 4:10).

Instances of:
Israelites (Ex 32; Nu 14; Ac 7:39-43), Saul (1Sa 15:26-29; 18:12; 28:15, 18), Amaziah (2Ch 25:14, 27), disciples (Jn 6:66), Judas (Mt 26:14-16; 27:3-5; Mk 14:10-11; Lk 22:3-6, 47-48; Ac 1:16-18), Hymenaeus and Alexander (1Ti 1:19-20), Phygelus and Hermogenes (2Ti 1:15).
See Antichrist(s); Apostates; Backsliding, Instances of Israel's Backsliding; Backsliders; Reprobacy; Reprobates.

APOSTATES

Described:
(Dt 13:13; Heb 3:12). Persecution tends to make (Mt 24:9-10; Lk 8:13). A worldly spirit tends to make (2Ti 4:10). Never belonged to Christ (1Jn 2:19). Believers do not become (Ps 44:18-19; Heb 6:9; 10:39). It is impossible to restore (Heb 6:4-6). Guilt and punishment of (Zep 1:4-6; Heb 10:25-31, 39; 2Pe 2:17, 20-22). Cautions against becoming (Heb 3:12; 2Pe 3:17). Shall abound in the latter days (Mt 24:12; 2Th 2:3; 1Ti 4:1-3).

Examples of:
Amaziah (2Ch 25:14, 27). Professed disciples (Jn 6:66). Hymenaeus and Alexander (1Ti 1:19-20). *See Apostasy.*

APOSTLE
(*to send off* or *out*). A title of Jesus (Heb 3:1). *See Apostles.*

APOSTLES
(*to send off* or *out*).

The Twelve:
In the Gospels, a title distinguishing the twelve disciples, whom Jesus selected to be intimately associated with himself (Lk 6:13). Names of the twelve (Mt 10:2-4; Mk 3:16-19; Lk 6:13-16; Ac 1:13, 26).
Selection of (Mt 4:18, 22; 9:9-10; 10:2-4; Mk 3:13-19; Lk 6:13-16; Jn 1:43).
Commission of (Mt 10; 28:19-20; Mk 3:14-15; 6:7-11; 16:15; Lk 9:1-5; 22:28-30; Jn 20:23; 21:15-19; Ac 1; 2; 10:42).
Uneducated (Mt 11:25; Ac 4:13). Miraculous power given to (Mt 10:1; Mk 3:15; 6:7; 16:17; Lk 9:1-2; 10:9; Ac 2:4, 43; 5:12-16; 1Co 14:18; 2Co 12:12). Authority of (Mt 16:19; 18:18; 19:28). Inspiration of (Mt 10:27; 16:17-19; Lk 24:45; Ac 1:2; 13:9). Duties of. *See above, Commission of.* For more information see Lk 24:48; Jn 15:27; Ac 1:8, 21-22; 2:32; 3:15; 4:33; 5:32; 10:39-41; 13:31; 2Pe 1:16, 18; 1Jn 1:1-3. *See Minister.*
Moral state of, before Pentecost (Mt 17:17; 18:3; 20:20-22; Lk 9:54-55). Slow to receive Jesus as Messiah (Mt 14:33). Forsake Jesus (Mk 14:50).
Fail to comprehend the nature and mission of Jesus, and the nature of the kingdom he came to establish (Mt 8:25-27; 15:23; 16:8-12, 21-22; 19:25; Mk 4:13; 6:51-52; 8:17-18; 9:9-10, 31-32; 10:13-14; Lk 9:44-45; 18:34; 24:19, 21; Jn 4:32-33; 10:6; 11:12-13; 12:16; 13:6-8; 14:5-9, 22; 16:6, 17-18, 32; 20:9; 21:12; Ac 1:6).

Other Than the Twelve:
Matthias (Ac 1:26), Paul and Barnabas (Ac 14:1-4, 14), Paul (Ro 1:1), Andronicus and Junias (Ro 16:7). A spiritual gift (1Co 12:28-31; Eph 4:11-13).
See Andronicus; Barnabas; Junias; Matthias; Minister; Paul.

False: (2Co 11:13; Rev 2:2).
See Teachers, False.

APOTHECARY
See Perfume, Perfumer.

APPAIM
(*[a pair of] nostrils*). Son of Nadab (1Ch 2:30-31).

APPAREL *See Dress.*

APPEAL Paul makes, to Caesar (Ac 25:10-11, 21-27; 26:32; 28:19). *See Change of Venue; Court, of Law.*

APPEAL TO GOD To witness (Ge 31:50; Dt 30:19; Jdg 11:10; 1Sa 12:5; Job 16:19; Ro 1:9; 2Co 1:23; Php 1:8; 1Th 2:5).

APPEARANCES Of God to people (Ge 12:7; 17:1; 18:1; 26:2; 35:9; Ex 3:16; 1Ki 3:5; 9:2; 2Ch 3:1).

APPEARING *See Eschatology.*

APPELLATIO The judicial process of appealing to a higher magistrate (Ac 25:1-12).

APPETITE Kept in subjection (Pr 23:1-2; Da 1:8-16; 1Co 9:27). *See Temperance.*

APPHIA Christian at Colosse (Phm 2).

APPIAN WAY An ancient Roman road on which Paul traveled (Ac 28:13-16).

APPIUS, FORUM OF A market town forty-three miles from Rome, where Paul met a delegation of Roman Christians (Ac 28:15).

APPLE A fruit (Pr 25:11; SS 2:3, 5; 7:8; 8:5; Joel 1:12).

APPLE OF THE EYE The eyeball; symbolizing that which is precious and protected (Dt 32:10; Ps 17:8; Pr 7:2; Zec 2:8).

APRON *See Dress.*

AQABAH, GULF OF The eastern arm of the Red Sea, where Solomon's seaport was located (1Ki 9:26). *See Ezion Geber.*

AQUEDUCT (*water channel*). A channel made of stone to convey water to places where the water is to be used (2Ki 18:17; Isa 7:3; 36:1). Many fine Roman aqueducts survive.

AQUILA (*eagle*). A Jewish Christian, a tentmaker by trade, who with his wife Priscilla labored with Paul at Corinth and was of help to Apollos and many others (Ac 18:2, 18, 26; Ro 16:3-4; 1Co 16:19; 2Ti 4:19).

AR (possibly *city*). A city of Moab (Nu 21:15; Dt 2:9, 18, 24, 29). Destruction of (Nu 21:26-30; Isa 15:1).

ARA Son of Jether (1Ch 7:38).

ARAB (*desert* or *steppe*).
1. A city of Judah (Jos 15:52).
2. *See Arabia; Arabians.*

ARABAH (*desert*). A name applying to the rift running from Mt. Hermon to the Gulf of Aqabah. It is a narrow valley of varying breadth and productivity. The Israelites made stops there in their wilderness wanderings, and Solomon got iron and copper from its mines (Dt 1:1, 7; 11:30; Jos 3:16; 1Sa 23:24; Jer 39:4).

ARABIA (*desert* or *steppe*). Paid tribute to Solomon (2Ch 9:14) and Jehoshaphat (2Ch 17:11). Exports of (Eze 27:21). Prophecies against (Isa 21:13; Jer 25:24). Paul visits (Gal 1:17).

ARABIANS, ARABS (*desert plateau dwellers*). Paid tribute to Solomon (2Ch 9:14) and Jehoshaphat (2Ch 17:11). Invade and defeat Judah (2Ch 21:16-17; 22:1). Defeated by Uzziah (2Ch 26:7). Oppose Nehemiah's rebuilding the walls of Jerusalem (Ne 2:19; 4:7). Commerce of (Eze 27:21). Gospel preached to (Ac 2:11; Gal 1:17). Prophecies concerning (Isa 21:13-17; 42:11; 60:7; Jer 25:24).

ARAD (*wild donkey*).
1. A city on the S of Canaan (Nu 21:1; 33:40). Subdued by Joshua (Jos 12:14; Jdg 1:16).
2. Son of Beriah (1Ch 8:15).

ARAH (*he wanders*).
1. An Asherite (1Ch 7:39).
2. Father of a family that returned from exile (Ezr 2:5; Ne 7:10).
3. Jew whose granddaughter became the wife of Tobiah the Ammonite (Ne 6:18).
4. Town in NE Palestine belonging to Sidonians (Jos 13:4).

ARAM
1. Son of Shem (Ge 10:22-23).
2. Son of Kemuel, Abraham's nephew (Ge 22:21).
3. An Asherite (1Ch 7:34).
4. Ancestor of Jesus (Mt 1:3-4; Lk 3:33). *See Ram, 1.*
5. Place in Gilead (1Ch 2:23).
6. Region corresponding to modern Syria (Nu 23:7; 2Sa 8:5; 1Ki 20:20; Am 1:5). The Aramean people spread from Phoenicia to the Fertile Crescent and were closely related to Israel, with whom their history was intertwined. *See Syria.*

ARAM MAACAH Also called Maacah. A small kingdom in Northwest Mesopotamia (1Ch 19:6, ftn). The states of Aram Maacah, Aram Rehob, and Zobah were N and NE of Israel and formed a solid block from the region of Lake Huleh through the Anti-Lebanons to beyond the Euphrates.
See Aram Naharaim; Aram Zobah; Zobah.

ARAM NAHARAIM A region in NW Mesopotamia (Ge 24:10; Dt 23:4; Jdg 3:8; 1Ch 19:6 and notes). *See Aram Maacah.*

ARAM ZOBAH Only in the Title of Ps 60 (Ps 60, ftn). *See Aram Maacah; Zobah.*

ARAMAIC A Semitic language closely related to Hebrew, which developed various dialects and spread to all of SW Asia. Aramaic portions in the OT are Da 2:4-7:28; Ezr 4:8-6:18; 7:12-26;

Jer 10:11. Aramaic words occur in the NT (Mk 5:41; 15:34; Mt 27:46; Ro 8:15; Gal 4:6; 1Co 16:22). Aramaic was the colloquial language of Israel from the time of the return from the Exile.

ARAN (*wild goat*). Son of Dishan (Ge 36:28; 1Ch 1:42).

ARARAT Modern Armenia (2Ki 19:37; Isa 37:38, KJV) and to its mountain range (Ge 8:4), the resting place of Noah's ark. The region is now part of Turkey.

ARATUS A Cilician poet (315-240 B.C.). Paul quotes from his *Phaenomena* (Ac 17:28). *See Asceticism; Cleanthes; Stoicism; Stoics.*

ARAUNAH (*strong*). A Jebusite from whom David bought a site for an altar (2Sa 24:16-24). Also spelled Ornan (1Ch 21:15 ftn, 18-28).

ARBA (*four*). Giant ancestor of Anak (Jos 14:15; 15:13; 21:11).

ARBATHITE (*person from Arabah*). A native of Beth Arabah (2Sa 23:31; 1Ch 11:32).

ARBEL *See Beth Arbel.*

ARBITE Paarai, one of David's mighty men (2Sa 23:35).

ARBITRATION The two prostitutes before Solomon (1Ki 3:16-28). Urged by Paul as a mode of action for Christians (1Co 6:1-8). *See Court, of Law.*

ARCH *See Architecture.*

ARCHAEOLOGY (*study of ancient things*). Study of the material remains of the past by excavating ancient buried cities and examining their remains; deciphering inscriptions; and evaluating the language, literature, art, architecture, monuments, and other aspects of human life and achievement. Biblical archaeology is concerned with Israel and the countries with which the Hebrews and early Christians came into contact. Modern archaeology began with Napoleon's expedition to Egypt, on which many scholars accompanied him to study Egyptian monuments (1798), and with the work of Edward Robinson in Palestine (1838, 1852). Discoveries of great importance which throw much light upon the patriarchal period are the Mari Tablets, the Nuzi Tablets, the Tell-el Amarna Tablets, and the Ras Shamra Tablets. The discovery of the Dead Sea Scrolls and the excavation of Qumran are among the more recent archaeological finds of importance. Archaeology is of great help in better understanding the Bible, in dealing with critical questions regarding the Bible, and in gaining an appreciation of the ancient world.

ARCHANGEL (*ruling angel*). A high order of angels (1Th 4:16). Michael called a "prince" (Da 10:13, 21; 12:1; Jude 9; Rev 12:7). *See Angels.*

ARCHELAUS (*ruler of people*). The son of Herod the Great. He ruled over Judea, Samaria, and Idumea from 4 B.C. to A.D. 6 (Mt 2:22).

ARCHERS Hunters or warriors with bow and arrow, weapons universally used in ancient times (Ge 21:20; 1Sa 20:17-42; Isa 21:17). "Arrow" is often used figuratively (Job 6:4; Jer 9:8), as is also "bow" (Ps 7:12). *See Archery.*

ARCHERY Practiced by Ishmael (Ge 21:20), Esau (Ge 27:3), Jonathan (1Sa 20:20, 36-37), Sons of Ulam (1Ch 8:40), Philistines (1Sa 31:1-3; 1Ch 10:3), Persians (Isa 13:17-18), people of Kedar (Isa 21:17), Syrians (1Ki 22:31-34), Israelites (2Sa 1:18; 1Ch 5:18; 12:2; 2Ch 14:8; 26:14; Ne 4:13; Zec 9:13), Lydians (Jer 46:9).
In war (Ge 49:23; Jdg 5:11; 1Sa 31:3; Isa 22:3; Jer 4:29; Zec 10:4).
See Archers; Armies; Arrows; Bow; War.

ARCHEVITES *See Erech, 2.*

ARCHI, ARCHITES *See Arkite(s).*

ARCHIPPUS (*master of the horse*). An office bearer in the church at Colosse (Col 4:17; Phm 2).

ARCHITECTURE The materials of architecture in antiquity were wood, clay, brick (formed of clay, whether sun-baked or kiln-fired), and stone. The determining factor in the choice of material used was local availability. The homes of the poor had no artistic distinction. The wealthy and the nobility, however, adorned their palatial homes ornately with gold and ivory. Architectural remains—temples, city gates, arches, ziggurats, pyramids—survive intact in great abundance, and archaeology has uncovered the foundations of countless buildings. Each country had its own distinctive style of architecture. No architecture has surpassed that of Greece, although the temple of Solomon and the one rebuilt by Herod were universally admired.

ARCHIVES Storage place for royal documents (Ezr 4:15; 5:17; 6:1).

ARCTURUS Constellation: the Bear (Job 9:9; 38:32). *See Astronomy; Bear, Illustrative of.*

ARD, ARDITE (*hunchbacked*).
1. Son of Benjamin (Ge 46:21).
2. Son of Bela and his clan (Nu 26:40).

ARDON (*hunchbacked*). Son of Caleb (1Ch 2:18).

ARELI, ARELITE Son of Gad (Ge 46:16) and his clan (Nu 26:17).

AREOPAGITE A member of the Areopagus (Ac 17:34).

AREOPAGUS (*hill of the Greek god, Ares*).
1. The rocky hill of the Greek god of war Ares (Mars) on the Acropolis at Athens.
2. The name of a council which met on Mars Hill. In NT times it was primarily concerned with morals and education. Paul was brought before it (Ac 17:19-34).

ARETAS (*virtuous*). A Nabataean king, father-in-law of Herod Antipas (2Co 11:32).

ARGOB (*mound*).
1. A region in Bashan taken by the Israelites under Moses (Dt 3:4) and given to the half-tribe of Manasseh (Dt 3:13).
2. Could also be a place or a person (2Ki 15:25). The Hebrew text is uncertain.

ARIDAI (perhaps *delight of Hari*). Son of Haman killed by the Jews (Est 9:9).

ARIDATHA (perhaps *given by Hari*). A son of Haman killed by the Jews (Est 9:8).

ARIEH (*lion*). Either a person or a place. The text is uncertain (2Ki 15:25).

ARIEL (*lioness of God [El]*).
1. Leader under Ezra (Ezr 8:16-17).
2. Figurative name for Jerusalem (Isa 29:1-2, 7).
3. In 2Sa 23:20 and 1Ch 11:22 "best men" (KJV "lionlike men") translates a word similar to Ariel.

ARIMATHEA Home of Joseph who buried Jesus in his own tomb (Mt 27:57; Mk 15:43; Lk 23:51; Jn 19:38). Its location is in doubt, but it is conjectured to be Ramathaim-Zophim, c. twenty miles NW of Jerusalem.

ARIOCH
1. King of Ellasar (Ge 14:1, 9).
2. Captain of Nebuchadnezzar's guard (Da 2:14-15, 24-25).

ARISAI Son of Haman (Est 9:9).

ARISTARCHUS (*best ruler*). A Thessalonian traveling companion of Paul (Ac 19:29; 20:4; 27:2; Col 4:10; Phm 24).

ARISTOBULUS (*best adviser*). A Roman Christian greeted by Paul (Ro 16:10).

ARK (*box*).
1. A boat. Directions for building of (Ge 6:14-16). Noah and family preserved in (Ge 6:18; 7:8; Mt 24:38; Heb 11:7; 1Pe 3:20). Animals saved in (Ge 6:19-20; 7:1-16).
2. A box or chest. *See Ark of the Covenant.*

ARK OF THE COVENANT

Description of:
Dimensions of (Ex 25:10; 37:1). Entirely covered with gold (Ex 25:11; 37:2). Surrounded with a crown of gold (Ex 25:11). Furnished with rings and poles (Ex 25:12-15; 37:3-5). Tables of testimony alone placed in (Ex 25:16, 21; 1Ki 8:9, 21; 2Ch 5:10; Heb 9:4). Atonement cover laid upon (Ex 25:21; 26:34). Placed in the Most Holy Place (Ex 26:33; 40:21; Heb 9:3-4). The pot of manna and Aaron's rod laid up before (Heb 9:4, w Ex 16:33-34; Nu 17:10). A copy of the law laid in the side of (Dt 31:26). Anointed with sacred oil (Ex 30:26). Covered with the veil by the priests before removal (Nu 4:5-6).
A symbol of the presence and glory of God (Nu 14:43-44; Jos 7:6; 1Sa 14:18-19; Ps 132:8). Considered the glory of Israel (1Sa 4:21-22). Was holy (2Ch 35:3). Sanctified its resting place (2Ch 8:11). The Israelites inquired of the Lord before (Jos 7:6-9; Jdg 20:27; 1Ch 13:3). Profanation of, punished (Nu 4:5, 15; 1Sa 6:19; 1Ch 15:13). Protecting of, rewarded (1Ch 13:14).

Was Called the:
Ark (Jos 3:3). Ark of God's might (2Ch 6:41; Ps 132:8). Ark of the covenant of the Lord (Nu 10:33). Ark of the testimony (Ex 30:6; Nu 7:89).

Was Carried:
By priests or Levites alone (Dt 10:8; Jos 3:14; 2Sa 15:24; 1Ch 15:2). Before the Israelites in their journeys (Nu 10:33; Jos 3:6). Sometimes to the camp in war (1Sa 4:4-5).

History and Miracles Connected With:
Jordan divided (Jos 4:7). Fall of the walls of Jericho (Jos 6:6-20). Captured by the Philistines (1Sa 4:11). Fall of Dagon (1Sa 5:1-4). Philistines plagued (1Sa 5:6-12). Manner of its restoration (1Sa 6:1-18). At Kiriath Jearim twenty years (1Sa 7:1-2). Removed from Kiriath Jearim to the house of Obed-Edom (2Sa 6:1-11). David made a tent for (2Sa 6:17; 1Ch 15:1). Brought into the city of David (2Sa 6:12-15; 1Ch 15:25-28). Brought by Solomon into the temple with great solemnity (1Ki 8:1-6; 2Ch 5:2-9). A type of Christ (Ps 40:8; Rev 11:19).

ARKITE(S) Descendants of Canaan (Ge 10:17; 1Ch 1:15). Member of a clan in Ephraim (Jos 16:2; 1Ch 27:33).

ARM Figurative of divine providence and salvation (Ex 6:6; 15:16; Dt 4:34; 5:15; 7:19; 9:29; 11:2; 26:8; 33:27; 1Ki 8:42; 2Ki 17:36; 2Ch 6:32; Ps 77:15; 89:10, 13, 21; 98:1; 136:12; SS 2:6; Isa 33:2; 40:10-11; 51:5, 9; 52:10; 59:16; 62:8; 63:5, 12; Jer 21:5; 27:5; 32:17; Eze 20:33; Lk 1:51; Ac 13:17). *See Anthropomorphisms.*

ARMAGEDDON (*Mount of Megiddo*). Found only in Rev 16:16; the final battlefield between the forces of good and evil. Located on the S rim of Esdraelon, the scene of many decisive battles in the history of Israel (Jdg 5:19-20; 6:33; 1Sa 31; 2Ki 23:29-30). *See Megiddo.*

ARMENIA *See Ararat.*

ARMIES
Those of the Israelites who were subject to service in (Nu 1:2-3; 26:2; 2Ch 25:5), who were exempt from service in (Nu 1:47-50; 2:33; Dt 20:5-9; Jdg 7:3). Numbering of Israel's military forces (Nu 1:2-3; 26:2; 1Sa 11:8; 2Sa 18:1-2; 24:1, 9; 1Ki 20:15; 2Ch 25:5). Levies for (Nu 31:4; Jdg 20:10). Compulsory service in (1Sa 14:52).
See Cowardice.

How Commanded:
Commander-in-chief (1Sa 14:50; 2Sa 2:8; 8:16; 17:25; 19:13; 20:23), Generals of corps and divisions (Nu 2:3-31; 1Ch 27:1-22; 2Ch 17:12-19), Captains of thousands (Nu 31:14, 48; 1Sa 17:18; 1Ch 28:1; 2Ch 25:5), of hundreds (Nu 31:14, 48; 2Ki 11:15; 1Ch 28:1; 2Ch 25:5), of fifties (2Ki 1:9; Isa 3:3). *See Cavalry; Chariot.*

Mustering of:
Methods employed in mustering: Sounding a trumpet (Nu 10:9; Jdg 3:27; 6:34; 1Sa 13:3-4), Cutting oxen in pieces, and sending the pieces throughout Israel (1Sa 11:7). Refusal to obey the summons, instance of (Jdg 21:5-11, w Jdg 20).

Tactics:
Camp and march (Nu 2). March in ranks (Joel 2:7). Move in attack in three divisions (Jdg 7:16; 9:43; 1Sa 11:11; 13:17, 18; 2Sa 18:2; Job 1:17). Flanks called wings (Isa 8:8). Orders delivered with trumpets (2Sa 2:28; 18:16; 20:1, 22; Ne 4:18, 20). *See Strategy.*

Strategies:
Ambushes at: Ai (Jos 8:2-22), Shechem (Jdg 9:25, 34), Gibeah (Jdg 20:29-43), Zemaraim (2Ch 13:4, 13). By Jehoshaphat (2Ch 20:20-22).

Reconnaissances:
Of Jericho (Jos 2:1-24), Ai (Jos 7:2-3), Bethel (Jdg 1:23-24), Laish (Jdg 18:2-10). Night attacks (Ge 14:15; Jdg 7:16-22). Decoy (Jos 8:4-22; Jdg 20:29-43; Ne 6). Delay (2Sa 17:7-14).

Speed of Action:
Abraham, in pursuit of Kedorlaomer (Ge 14:14-15). Joshua, against the Amorites (Jos 10:6, 9), the confederated kings (Jos 11:7). David's attack upon the Philistines (2Sa 5:23-25). Forced marches (Isa 5:26-27). Sieges (Jer 39:1), of Jericho (Jos 6), Samaria (2Ki 6:24-33:7), Jerusalem (2Ki 25:1-3).
Machines used (2Ch 26:15; Jer 6:6; Eze 26:9). Fortifications (Jdg 9:31; 2Sa 5:9; 2Ki 25:1; 2Ch 11:11; 26:9; Ne 3:8; 4:2; Isa 22:10; 25:12; 29:3; 32:14; Jer 6:6; 32:24; 33:4; 51:53; Eze 4:2; 17:17; 21:22; 26:8; 33:27; Da 11:15, 19; Na 2:1; 3:14). Standards (Nu 2:2-3, 10, 17-18, 25, 31, 34; 10:14, 18, 22, 25). Uniforms of (Eze 23:6, 12; Na 2:3). Standing armies (1Sa 13:2; 1Ch 27; 2Ch 1:14; 17:12-19; 26:11-15).

Religious Ceremonies Attending:
Seeking counsel from God before battle (Nu 27:21; Jdg 1:1; 1Sa 14:19, 37-41; 23:2-12; 30:8; 2Sa 2:1; 5:19, 23; 1Ki 22:7-28; 2Ki 3:11-19; 1Ch 14:10, 14; Jer 37:7-10). Sacrifices (1Sa 13:11-12). Purifications (Nu 31:19-24). Prophets prophesy before (2Ch 20:14-17). Holiness required (Dt 23:9). Officers consecrate themselves to God (2Ch 17:16). Army choir and songs (2Ch 20:21-22). Ark taken to battle (Jos 6:6-7, 13; 1Sa 4:4-11).

Divine Assistance to:
When Aaron and Hur held up Moses' hands (Ex 17:11-12). In siege of Jericho (Jos 6). Sun stands still (Jos 10:11-14). Gideon's victory (Jdg 7). Samaria's deliverances (1Ki 20; 2Ki 7). Jehoshaphat's victories (2Ki 3; 2Ch 20). Angel of the Lord puts to death the Assyrians (2Ki 19:35).
Determine royal succession (2Sa 2:8-10; 1Ki 16:16; 2Ki 11:4-12).
Composed of insurgents (1Sa 22:1-2). Mercenaries (2Sa 10:6; 1Ch 19:6-7; 2Ch 25:5-6). Confederated (Jos 10:1-5; 11:1-5; Jdg 1:3; 2Sa 10:6, 15-16, 19; 1Ki 15:20; 22:1-4; 2Ki 16:9; 18:19-21; 1Ch 19:6-7; 2Ch 16:2-9; 18:1, 3; 20:1; 22:5; 28:16, 20; Ps 83:1-12; Isa 7:1-9; 8:9-12; 54:15). Exhorted before battle (Dt 20:1-9). Battle shouts (Jdg 7:18; 1Sa 17:20, 52).

Triumphs of, Celebrated:
With songs (Jdg 5; 1Sa 18:6-7), music (2Ch 20:28), dancing (1Sa 18:6-7).

Rewards for Meritorious Conduct:
The general offers his daughter in marriage (Jos 15:16-17). King offers his daughter (1Sa 17:25; 18:17-28). Promotion (2Sa 23:8-39; 1Ch 11:6, 10-47). Share the spoils (Nu 31:25-47).
Insubordination in, punished, Achan (Jos 7). Check roll call (1Sa 14:17; Nu 31:48-49).
Panics (Isa 30:17): Among the Midianites (Jdg 7:21), Philistines (1Sa 14:15-19), Syrians (2Ki 7:7-15). Soldiers destroy each other to escape captivity (1Sa 14:20; 31:4-6).
Champions fight instead of (1Sa 17:8-53; 2Sa 2:14-17; 21:15-22). Confidence in vain (Ps 33:16; 44:6). Escort duty performed by (2Ki 1:9; Ac 23:23-24, 31-33).

Roman Army:
Commanders of (Ac 22:24-29). Centurions (Mt 8:5, 8; 27:54; Lk 7:2; 23:47; Ac 10:1, 7, 22; 21:32; 22:26; 23:17, 23; 24:23; 27:1, 11, 43; 28:16). Divided into regiments (Ac 10:1; 27:1).
For other than armies of the Israelites and Romans: *See Amalekite(s); Assyria; Babylon; Egyptians; Midianite(s); Persia; Syria.*
For commissaries of: *See Commissary.*
For weapons used: *See Armor.*
See Ambush; Cavalry; Fort; Garrison; Herald; Hostage; Navy; Reconnaissance; Siege; Soldiers; Spies; Standard; Strategy; Truce; War.

Figurative: (Dt 33:2; 2Ki 6:17; Ps 34:7; 68:17; Rev 9:16). *See Army.*

ARMLET, BRACELET
An ornament usually for the upper arm, worn by both men and women (Ex 35:22; Nu 31:50; 2Sa 1:10; Isa 3:20). *See Bracelet.*

ARMONI
(*[one] born in the dwelling tower, the palace*). A son of Saul by his concubine Rizpah, slain by the Gibeonites to satisfy justice (2Sa 21:8-11).

ARMOR
The equipment of a soldier (1Sa 13:22; Jer 46:3-4; Eph 6:14-17).

Defensive:
Helmet (1Sa 17:5, 38; 2Ch 17:17; 26:14; Jer 46:4; Eze 23:24). Breastplate (Rev 9:9-17). Coat of armor (1Sa 17:5, 38; 1Ki 22:34; 2Ch 18:33). Greaves, protection for the leg (1Sa 17:6). Shield (2Sa 1:21; 8:7; 1Ki 10:16, 17; 14:27; 2Ch 9:16; 26:14; Ne 2:3).

Offensive:
Bows (Ge 21:16, 20). Made of bronze (2Sa 22:35; Job 20; Ps 18:34). Of wood (Eze 39:9). David instructed the Israelites in the use of, by writing war song (2Sa 1:18). Arrows (1Sa 31:3; 2Sa 22:15; 1Ki 22:34; 2Ki 19:32; 2Ch 17:17; Ps 7:13; Isa 22:3; Jer 51:3).
War club (Job 41:29; Jer 51:20). Spear (Nu 25:7; 1Sa 18:10; 2Sa 18:14). Javelin, a heavy lance (Eze 39:9). Used by Goliath (1Sa 17:6). By Saul (1Sa 18:11; 19:9-10).
Sling, used for throwing stones (Pr 26:8). David slays Goliath with (1Sa 17:40-50). Skilled use of (Jdg 20:16). Used in war (Jdg 20:16; 2Ki 3:25; 2Ch 26:14).
Sword, use by Gibeon (Jdg 7:20). By Peter (Mt 26:51; Jn 18:10). David's army equipped with (1Ch 21:5).

Figurative: (Ro 13:12; 2Co 6:7; 10:4; Eph 6:11-17; 1Th 5:8).

ARMOR-BEARER
An attendant who carried a soldier's equipment.
Of Abimelech (Jdg 9:54), Jonathan (1Sa 14:6-7, 12, 14, 17), Saul (1Sa 16:21; 31:6), Goliath (1Sa 17:7), Joab (2Sa 18:15).

ARMORY
A place for the storage of armor (Ne 3:19; SS 4:4; Isa 22:8; 39:2). In different parts of the kingdom (1Ki 10:17; 2Ch 11:12). *See Jerusalem.*
Figurative: (Jer 50:25).

ARMY
In Israel males (except Levites) were subject to military duty at the age of twenty (Nu 1:3, 17). Army divisions were subdivided into thousands and hundreds, with respective officers (Nu 31:14). Until Israel got its first king it had no standing army, but whenever there was need, God raised up men of special ability to save the country from its enemies. Down to the time of Solomon, Israel's armies were composed mostly of footmen (1Sa 4:10); sire horsemen and chariots were added (2Sa 8:4; 1Ki 10:26, 28-29). The Roman army was composed of legions divided into cohorts, maniples, and centuries (Ac 10:1; 21:31).
See Armies.

ARNAN
Name of a family descended from David (1Ch 3:21).

ARNON
A river emptying into the Dead Sea from the east. Boundary between Moabites and Amorites (Nu 21:13-14, 26; 22:36; Dt 2:24, 36; 3:8, 16; Jos 12:1). Fords of (Isa 16:2). Miracles at (Nu 21:14).

ARODI, ARODITE
(*hunchbacked*). The sixth son of Gad (Ge 46:16) and his clan (Nu 26:17).

AROER, AROERITE
(*juniper*).
1. A city of the Amorites in the valley of the Arnon River (Dt 4:48). Conquered by Israelites (Dt 2:36; 3:12; Jdg 11:26). Taken by Hazael (2Ki 10:33).
2. A city built, or, probably more correctly, rebuilt, by the Gadites (Nu 32:34; Jos 13:25). Jephthah kills the Ammonites at (Jdg 11:33).
3. A city in Judah (1Sa 30:28). Birthplace of two of David's heroes (1Ch 11:44).

AROMATIC RESIN
Fragrant gum or resin listed with precious stones (Ge 2:12; Nu 11:7). *See Minerals of the Bible, 1; Resin.*

ARPAD
A fortified city of Syria, perhaps identical with Arvad (2Ki 18:34; 19:13). Idols of (Isa 36:19).

ARPHAXAD
Son of Shem (Ge 10:22; 11:10-13; 1Ch 1:17-18, 24; Lk 3:36).

ARREST
Of Jesus (Mt 26:57; Mk 14:46; Lk 22:54; Jn 18:12), apostles (Ac 5:17-18; 6:12), Paul and Silas (Ac 16:19), Paul (Ac 21:30). Paul authorized to arrest Christians (Ac 9:2).
See Extradition; Prison; Prisoners.

ARROGANCE
(1Sa 2:3; Pr 8:13; Isa 13:11). *See Pride.*

ARROWS

Described:
Deadly and destructive weapons (Pr 26:18). Sharp (Ps 120:4; Isa 5:28). Bright and polished (Isa 49:2; Jer 51:11). Sometimes poisoned (Job 6:4). Carried in a quiver (Ge 27:3; Isa 49:2; Jer 5:16; La 3:13). Swiftness of, alluded to (Zec 9:14). The ancients divined by (Eze 21:21).

Discharged:
From a bow (Ps 11:2; Isa 7:24). From machines (2Ch 26:15). At a mark for amusement (1Sa 20:20-22). At the beasts of the earth (Ge 27:3). Against enemies (2Ki 19:32; Jer 50:14). With great force (Nu 24:8; 2Ki 9:24).

Figurative:
Of Christ (Isa 49:2). Of the word of Christ (Ps 45:5). Of God's judgment (Dt 32:23-42; Ps 7:13; 21:12; 64:7; Eze 5:16). Of severe afflictions (Job 6:4; Ps 38:2). Of bitter words (Ps 64:3). Of slanderous tongues (Jer 9:8). Of false witnesses (Pr 25:18). Of devices of the wicked (Ps 11:2). Of young children (Ps 127:4). Of lightning (Ps 77:17-18; Hab 3:11). Broken, of destruction of power (Ps 76:3). Falling from the hand, of the paralyzing power (Eze 39:3).

ARSON
(Ps 74:7-8). Law concerning (Ex 22:6). Instances of: Samson (Jdg 15:4-5), Absalom (2Sa 14:30), Zimri (1Ki 16:18).

ART
Seen in the gifting of Bezalel and Oholiab to build the tabernacle and its furnishings (Ex 31:1-12; 35:30-39:43); of Huram(-abi) and his work on the temple of Solomon (1Ki 7:13-45; 2Ch 2:13-4:16).
Israel was not to apply artistic talents to create idols (Ex 20:4; 32:1-24; 34:17; Lev 26:1). *See Arts and Crafts; Bezalel; Huram; Tabernacle; Temple.*

ARTAXERXES
(*kingdom of righteousness*). There are three kings with the name of Artaxerxes.
1. Artaxerxes I (465-425 B.C.), son of Xerxes I; known as Macrocheir or Longimanus. He overcame revolts in Egypt, where, with Athenian support, unrest started in 460 and lasted until 454, and in other parts of the Persian Empire. During that time some of the eastern possessions were lost. By the peace treaty of Callias (449), signed at Susa, the relations between Athens and Persia were stabilized on a *status quo ante bellum* basis. Artaxerxes was buried at Naqsi Rustam next to the tombs of his father and grandfather.
Artaxerxes I authorized Ezra's mission to Jerusalem in 458 (Ezr 7:8, 11-26). He temporarily halted the reconstruction of Jerusalem (4:7-23). Nehemiah's two missions were under his reign and with his permission, the first in 445 (Ne 2:1ff; 13:6).
2. Artaxerxes II (404-359 B.C.), son of Darius II and grandson of Artaxerxes I; known as Mnemon. He crushed the rebellion of his brother Cyrus (Battle of Cunaxa, 401), as related by Xenophon in his *Anabasis*. He lost Egypt probably in 402 or 401, repelled the meddling of Sparta in the affairs of Asia Minor (Peace of Antalcidas, 386), and suppressed other rebellious movements led by local satraps. Several of his inscriptions refer to his building activities. The palace he built at Susa is considered by some authorities to be identical with the palace described in Esther (Est 1:5-6).
3. Artaxerxes III (359-338 B.C.), son of Artaxerxes II; known as Ochus. By the use of skillful diplomacy and military force he succeeded in maintaining a superficially strong empire, until the time when he was murdered as the result of a conspiracy led by Bagoas (338).

ARTEMAS
(*[given by] Artemis*). A companion of Paul (Tit 3:12).

ARTEMIS
The Greek goddess of hunting, corresponding to the Roman Diana. Her largest and most famous temple was at Ephesus; it was regarded as one of the wonders of the ancient world (Ac 19:23-41).

ARTIFICER
See Arts and Crafts; Occupations and Professions.

ARTILLERY
See Armory.

ARTISANS
See Occupations.

ARTS AND CRAFTS
Armorer (1Sa 8:12). Baker (Ge 40:1; 1Sa 8:13). Brickmaker (Ge 11:3; Ex 5:7-8, 18). Blacksmith (Ge 4:22; 1Sa 13:19). Carver (Ex 31:5; 1Ki 6:18). Carpenter (2Sa 5:11; Mk 6:3). Caulker (Eze 27:9, 27). Dyer (Ex 25:5). Embroiderer (Ex 35:35; 38:23). Embalmer (Ge 50:2-3, 26). Engraver (Ex 28:11; Isa 49:16; 2Co 3:7). Gardener (Ge 4:2; 9:20; Jer 29:5; Jn 20:15). Goldsmith (Ne 3:8, 31; Isa 40:19; Jer 10:9). Launderer (Ex 18:17; Mk 9:3). Mariner (Eze 27:8-9). Mason (2Sa 5:11; 2Ch 24:12). Musician (1Sa 18:6; 19:5; Ne 12:46; 1Sa 8:13). Perfumer (Ex 30:25, 35; 1Sa 8:13). Potter (Isa 64:8; Jer 18:3; La 4:2; Zec 11:13). Refiner of metals (1Ch 28:18; Mal 3:2-3). Rope-maker (Jdg 16:11). Silversmith (Jdg 17:4; Ac 19:24). Stonecutter (Ex 20:25; 1Ch 22:15). Shipbuilder (1Ki 9:26). Smelter of metals (Job 28:2). Spinner (Ex 35:25; Pr 31:19). Tailor (Ex 28:3). Tanner (Ac 9:43; 10:6). Tent maker (Ge 4:20; Ac 18:3). Tool maker (Ge 4:22; 2Ti 4:14). Weaver (Ex 35:35; Jn 19:23). Wine maker (Ne 13:15; Isa 63:3).

ARUBBOTH
A district laid under tribute to Solomon's governor (1Ki 4:10).

ARUMAH
(*lofty*). Place near Shechem where Abimelech lived (Jdg 9:41).

ARVAD, ARVADITES
Island off the coast of Phoenicia (Eze 27:8, 11). Its people were descendants of Ham (Ge 10:18; 1Ch 1:16; Eze 27:8, 11).

ARZA
(perhaps *gracious*). A steward of Elah (1Ki 16:9).

ASA
(possibly *healer* BDB; *myrtle* KB).
1. King of Judah (1Ki 15:8-24; 1Ch 3:10; 2Ch 14; 15; 16; Mt 1:7).
2. A Levite (1Ch 9:16).

ASAHEL
(*God [El] has made*).
1. Nephew of David and one of his captains (2Sa 2:18-24, 32; 3:27; 23:24; 1Ch 2:16; 11:26; 27:7).
2. A Levite commissioned by Jehoshaphat to teach the law to Judah (2Ch 17:8).
3. A Levite who had charge of tithes (2Ch 31:13).
4. Father of Jonathan (Ezr 10:15).

ASAIAH
(*Yahweh has made*).
1. An officer of King Josiah (2Ki 22:12-20; 2Ch 34:20-28).
2. A Simeonite (1Ch 4:36).
3. Levite in the time of David (1Ch 6:30).
4. A Shilonite (1Ch 9:5).
5. Chief Levite in David's day who helped bring the ark to Jerusalem (1Ch 15:6, 11).

ASAPH
(*gatherer*).
1. Father of Joah (2Ki 18:18; Isa 36:3, 22).
2. Son of Berekiah. One of the three leaders of music in David's organization of the tabernacle service (1Ch 15:16-19; 16:5-7; 25:1-9; 2Ch 5:12; 35:15; Ne 12:46). Appointed to sound the cymbals in the temple choir (1Ch 15:17, 19; 16:5, 7). A composer of sacred lyrics (2Ch 29:13-30). *See titles of Pss 50; 73-83.* Descendants of, in the temple choir (1Ch 25:1-9; 2Ch 20:14; 29:13; Ezr 2:41; 3:10; Ne 7:44; 11:22).

A

3. A Levite whose descendants lived in Jerusalem after the exile (1Ch 9:15).

4. A Kohath Levite (1Ch 26:1).

5. Keeper of forests (Ne 2:8).

ASAREL Son of Jehallelel (1Ch 4:16).

ASARELAH One of the temple choir (1Ch 25:2, 14), Probably identical with Azarel.

ASCENSION OF CHRIST Prophecies respecting (Ps 24:7; 68:18, w Eph 4:7-8). Foretold by himself (Jn 6:62; 7:33; 14:28; 16:5; 20:17). Forty days after his resurrection (Ac 1:3). Described (Ac 1:9). From Mount of Olives (Lk 24:50; w Mk 11:1; Ac 1:12). While blessing his disciples (Lk 24:50). When he had atoned for sin (Heb 9:12; 10:12). Was triumphant (Ps 68:18). Was to supreme power and dignity (Lk 24:26; Eph 1:20-21; 1Pe 3:22). As the Forerunner of His people (Heb 6:20). To intercede (Ro 8:34; Heb 9:24). To send the Holy Spirit (Jn 16:7; Ac 2:33). To receive gifts for people (Ps 68:18, w Eph 4:8-11). To prepare a place for his people (Jn 14:2). His second coming shall be in like manner as (Ac 1:10-11).

Typified (Lev 16:15, w Heb 6:20; 9:7, 9, 12).

ASCENTS, SONGS OF Title given Psalms 120 to 134. These psalms were, with 135 and 136, part of the liturgical collection "The Great Hallel." They were probably sung during the pilgrimage or "ascent" to Jerusalem required by the annual feasts.

ASCETICISM A philosophy that leads to severe self-discipline in subordinating the body to the control of the moral attributes of the mind. Extreme application of, rebuked by Jesus (Mt 11:19; Lk 7:34), by Paul (Col 2:20-23; 1Ti 4:1-4, 8). *See Stoicism; Stoics.*

Instances of the practice of: John the Baptist (Mt 11:18; Lk 7:33). Those who practiced celibacy for the kingdom of heaven (Mt 19:12).

ASENATH [*belonging to] the goddess Neith*]. Wife of Joseph and mother of Manasseh and Ephraim (Ge 41:45, 50; 46:20).

ASER See Asher.

ASH See Pine.

ASHAN (*smoke*). A Levitical city of Judah, later of Simeon (Jos 15:42; 19:7; 1Ch 4:32; 6:59). *See Ain, 1.*

ASHBEA See Beth Ashbea.

ASHBEL, ASHBELITE (possibly a form of *man of Baal* BDB; *having a long upper lip* KB). Son of Benjamin (Ge 46:21; 1Ch 8:1) and his clan (Nu 26:38).

ASHCHENAZ See Ashkenaz.

ASHDOD (perhaps *fortress*). A city of the Philistines (Jos 13:3; 1Sa 6:17; Am 3:9). Anakites inhabit (Jos 11:22). Assigned to Judah (Jos 15:47). Dagon's temple in, in which was deposited the ark (1Sa 5).

Conquest of: by Uzziah (2Ch 26:6), by Assyrian supreme commander (Isa 20:1).

People of, conspire against the Jews (Ne 4:7-8). Jews intermarry with (Ne 13:23-24). Prophecies concerning (Jer 25:20; Am 1:8; 3; Zep 2:4; Zec 9:6). Called Azotus in NT times (Ac 8:40).

ASHDOTH-PISGAH (*slopes of Pisgah*). See Pisgah.

ASHER [*Happy One!*].

1. Son of Jacob, by Zilpah (Ge 30:13; 35:26; 49:20; Ex 1:4; 1Ch 2:2). Descendants of (Ge 46:17; Nu 26:44-47; Lk 2:36).

2. Tribe of.
Census of, by families (Nu 1:40-41; 26:44-47; 1Ch 7:40; 12:36). Station of, in camp (Nu 2:25, 27). Prophecies concerning by Moses (Dt 33:24-25), by John (Rev 7:6). Allotment to, of land in Canaan (Jos 19:24-31; Eze 48:2). Criticized by Deborah (Jdg 5:17). Summoned by Gideon (Jdg 6:35; 7:23). Join Hezekiah (2Ch 30:11).

3. A city of Shechem (Jos 17:7; 1Ki 4:16).

ASHERAH

1. Canaanite goddess, sometimes identified with Anath and Ashtoreth. *See Anath; Ashtoreth.*

2. Asherah poles: images of or trees planted to the goddess Asherah. Forbidden to be established (Ex 34:13; Dt 7:5; 16:21; Isa 1:29; 17:8; 27:9; Mic 5:14). Worshiped by Israelites (Jdg 3:7; 1Ki 14:15, 23; 15:13; 2Ki 13:6; 17:10, 16; 21:3-7; 2Ch 24:18; Jer 17:2). Destroyed by Gideon (Jdg 6:28), Hezekiah (2Ki 18:4), Josiah (2Ki 23:14; 2Ch 34:3-4), Asa (2Ch 14:3), Jehoshaphat (2Ch 17:6; 19:3). *See High Places; Idolatry.*

ASHES Uses of, in purification (Nu 19:9-10, 17; Heb 9:13). A symbol of mourning (2Sa 13:19; Est 4:1, 3). Sitting in (Job 2:8; Isa 58:5; Jer 6:26; Eze 27:30; Jnh 3:6; Lk 10:13). Repenting in (Job 42:6; Da 9:3; Jnh 3:6; Mt 11:21; Lk 10:13). Disguises of (1Ki 20:38, 41).

ASHHUR (possibly *darkness, dawn* BDB; *a Babylonian goddess* KB). Son of Hezron (1Ch 2:24; 4:5).

ASHIMA An idol (2Ki 17:30).

ASHKELON One of the five chief cities of the Philistines (Jos 13:3). Captured by the people of Judah (Jdg 1:18). Samson slays thirty men of (Jdg 14:19). Tumors of (1Sa 6:17). Prophecies concerning (Jer 25:20; 47:5, 7; Am 1:8; Zep 2:4, 7; Zec 9:5).

ASHKENAZ Son of Gomer (Ge 10:3; 1Ch 1:6). Descendants of (Jer 51:27).

ASHNAH A name of two towns in Judah (Jos 15:33, 43).

ASHPENAZ (*guest*). A prince in Nebuchadnezzar's court (Da 1:3).

ASHRIEL See Asriel.

ASHTAROTH

1. Plural form of Ashtoreth. *See Ashtoreth.*

2. The capital city of Bashan (Dt 1:4; Jos 9:10). Giants dwell at (Jos 12:4). Allotted to Manasseh (Jos 13:31; 1Ch 6:71). Possibly identical with Ashteroth Karnaim (Ge 14:5).

ASHTERATHITE A native of Ashtaroth (1Ch 11:44).

ASHTEROTH KARNAIM (*Ashteroth of the pair of horns, [two peaks?]*). An ancient city of Palestine taken by Kedorlaomer (Ge 14:5).

ASHTORETH An idol of the Philistines, Sidonians, and Phoenicians, sometimes identified with Anath and Asherah. *See Anath; Asherah.* Probably identical with queen of heaven (Jer 7:18). Worshiped by Israelites (Jdg 2:13; 10:6; 1Sa 7:3-4; 12:10; 1Ki 11:5, 33; 2Ki 23:13). Temple of (1Sa 31:10). High places of, at Jerusalem, destroyed (2Ki 23:13).

ASHUR See Ashhur.

ASHURBANIPAL (*Ashur creates a son*). King of Assyria who colonized the cities of Samaria after the Israelites were taken captive to Assyria (Ezr 4:10). Reigned from 688-626 B.C. He was a great lover of learning—his library (over 22,000 tablets) survives.

ASHURI A tribal region, possibly Asher (2Sa 2:9).

ASHURNASIRPAL II Ruthless king of Assyria, reigned early in ninth century B.C.

ASHVATH (possibly *wrought iron*). Son of Japhlet (1Ch 7:33).

ASIA Inhabitants of, in Jerusalem, at Pentecost (Ac 2:9; 21:27; 24:19). Paul and Silas forbidden by the Holy Spirit to preach in (Ac 16:6). Gospel preached in, by Paul (Ac 19; 20:4). Paul leaves (Ac 20:16). Churches of (1Co 16:19; Rev 1:4, 11). High officials of Asia were friends of Paul (Ac 19:31).

ASIARCHS High officials of Asia. *See Asia.*

ASIEL [*God [El] has made*]. Grandfather of Jehu (1Ch 4:35).

ASKELON See Ashkelon.

ASNAH (possibly *thornbush* BDB; *he who belongs to [the god] Nah* IDB). Descendants of, return to Jerusalem (Ezr 2:50).

ASNAPPER See Ashurbanipal; Samaria.

ASP See Cobra; Serpent; Viper.

ASPATHA (possibly *given from a sacred horse*). Son of Haman (Est 9:7).

ASPHALTUM See Caulkers; Pitch; Tar.

ASRIEL (either *God has filled with joy*, or *[the object of] joy is God*).

1. Descendant of Manasseh (Nu 26:31; Jos 17:2).

2. Son of Manasseh, Asriel (1Ch 7:14).

ASS See Donkey, Domestic; Donkey, Wild.

ASSAR See Tel Assar.

ASSASSINATION David's abhorrence of (2Sa 4:9-12). Laws prohibiting (Dt 27:24).

Instances of:
Of Eglon, by Ehud (Jdg 3:15-22), Abner, by Joab (2Sa 3:27), Ish-Bosheth, by the sons of Rimmon (2Sa 4:5-7), Amnon, by Absalom (2Sa 13:28-29), Amasa, by Joab (2Sa 20:9-10), Joash, by his servants (Jer 12:19-20), Sennacherib, by his sons (2Ki 19:37; Isa 37:38).

ASSAULT AND BATTERY

Laws Concerning:
(Ex 21:15, 18-19, 22-27; Dt 17:8-12; Mt 5:39; Lk 6:29). Damages and compensation for (Ex 21:18-19, 22).

See Abuse; Bruise(s); Flog, Flogging; Scourging; Stripes, 1-3; Stoning.

The Beating of Jesus:
Prophecies of (Isa 50:6; La 3:30). The attacks upon (Mt 26:67; 27:30; Mk 14:65; Lk 22:63; Jn 19:3).

ASSHUR Son of Shem, and ancestor of the Assyrians (Ge 10:11, 22; 1Ch 1:17; Eze 32:22). *See Assyria.*

ASSHURITES Descendants of Dedan (Ge 25:3).

ASSIR (*prisoner*).

1. Son of Korah (Ex 6:24; 1Ch 6:22).

2. Son of Ebiasaph (1Ch 6:23, 37).

3. Son of Jehoiachin (1Ch 3:17).

ASSOCIATION-SEPARATION

Evil associations:
Warnings concerning (Ex 23:2; 34:12; Ps 1:1; Pr 4:14; 24:1; 1Co 5:11; 2Co 6:14). Results of (Nu 33:55; 1Ki 11:2; 2Ch 19:2; Pr 28:7; Jn 18:18; 18:25; 1Co 15:33).

Contact with impurity (Lev 5:2; 15:11; Nu 19:13; Isa 52:11; 2Co 6:17; Col 2:21).

Separation from unclean (Lev 13:5, 21, 33, 46; Nu 5:3). Israel from nations (Lev 20:26; Nu 23:9; Dt 7:2; Jos 23:7; Jdg 2:2; Ezr 9:12; 10:11; Isa 52:11; Jer 15:19). Believers from evil associations (Jn 15:19; Ac 2:40; Eph 5:11; 2Th 3:6). Final separation of evil from good (Mt 13:30, 49; 25:32; Lk 16:26; 17:34).

Good associations:
Companionship (Ps 119:63; Pr 2:20; 13:20; 2Th 3:14). Personal contact with Jesus (Mt 9:20, 25; 14:34-36; Mk 3:10; 9:27; Lk 6:19), Peter (Ac 3:7; 9:41).

ASSOS A seaport in Mysia (Ac 20:13-14).

ASSURANCE
Produced by faith (Eph 3:12; 2Ti 1:12; Heb 10:22). Made full by hope (Heb 6:11, 19). Confirmed by love (1Jn 3:14, 19; 4:18). Is the effect of righteousness (Isa 32:17). Is abundant in the understanding of the gospel (Col 2:2; 1Th 1:5).

Believers Privileged to Know:
Their election (Ps 4:3; 1Th 1:4). Their redemption (Job 19:25). Their adoption (Ro 8:16; 1Jn 3:2). Their salvation (Isa 12:2). Eternal life (1Jn 5:13). The unalienable love of God (Ro 8:38-39). Union with God and Christ (1Co 6:15; 2Co 13:5; Eph 5:30; 1Jn 2:5; 4:13). Peace with God by Christ (Ro 5:1). Preservation (Ps 3:6, 8; 27:3-5; 46:3). Answers to prayer (1Jn 3:22; 5:14-15). Continuance in grace (Php 1:6). Comfort in affliction (Ps 73:26; Lk 4:18-19; 2Co 4:8-10, 16-18). Support in death (Ps 23:4). A glorious resurrection (Job 19:26; Ps 17:15; Php 3:21; 1Jn 3:2). A kingdom (Heb 12:28; Rev 5:10). A crown (2Ti 4:7-8; Jas 1:12). Give diligence to attain to (2Pe 1:10-11). Strive to maintain (Heb 3:14, 18). Confident hope in God restores (Ps 42:11).

Exemplified:
David (Ps 23:4; 73:24-26). Paul (2Ti 1:12; 4:18).

ASSYRIA Antiquity and origin of (Ge 10:8-11). Situated beyond the Euphrates (Isa 7:20). Watered by the Tigris River (Ge 2:14).

Called:
The land of Nimrod (Mic 5:6). Shinar (Ge 11:2; 14:1). Asshur (Nu 24:22, 24). Nineveh, chief city of (Ge 10:11; 2Ki 19:36). Governed by kings (2Ki 15:19, 29).

Celebrated to Have:
Fertility (2Ki 18:32; Isa 36:17). Extent of conquests (2Ki 18:33-35; 19:11-13; Isa 10:9-14). Extensive commerce (Eze 27:23-24). Idolatry, the religion of (2Ki 19:37).

Described:
Most formidable (Isa 28:2). Intolerant and oppressive (Na 3:19). Cruel and warlike (Isa 10:7). Selfish and reserved (Hos 8:9). Unfaithful (2Ch 28:20-21). Proud and haughty (2Ki 19:22-24; Isa 10:8). An instrument of God's vengeance (Isa 7:18-19; 10:5-6). Chief men of, described (Eze 23:6, 12, 23). Armies of, described (Isa 5:26-29). Invaded Israel (2Ki 15:19). Bought off by Menahem (2Ki 15:19-20).

Tiglath-Pileser, King of:
Ravaged Israel (2Ki 15:29). Asked to aid Ahaz against Syria (2Ki 16:7-8). Took money from Ahaz, but did not strengthen him (2Ch 28:20-21). Conquered Syria (2Ki 16:9).

Shalmaneser, King of:
Reduced Israel to tribute (2Ki 17:3). Was conspired against by Hoshea (2Ki 17:4). Imprisoned Hoshea (2Ki 17:4). Carried Israel captive (2Ki 17:5-6). Repopulated Samaria from Assyria (2Ki 17:24).

Sennacherib, King of:
Invaded Judah (2Ki 18:13). Bought off by Hezekiah (2Ki 18:14-16). Insulted and threatened Judah (2Ki 18:17-32; 19:10-13). Blasphemed the Lord (2Ki 18:33-35). Prayed against by Hezekiah (2Ki 19:14-19). Reproved for pride and blasphemy (2Ki 19:20-34; Isa 37:21-29). His army destroyed by God (2Ki 19:35). Assassinated by his sons (2Ki 19:37). Condemned for oppressing God's people (Isa 52:4). Manasseh taken captive to (2Ch 33:11). The repopulation of Samaria from, completed by Ashurbanipal (Ezr 4:10). Idolatry of, brought into Samaria (2Ki 17:29). Judah condemned for trusting (Jer 2:18, 36). Israel condemned for trusting (Hos 5:13; 7:11; 8:9). The Jews condemned for following the idolatries of (Eze 16:28; 23:5, 7). The greatness, extent, duration, and fall of, illustrated (Eze 31:3-17).

Predictions Respecting:
Conquest of the Kenites by (Nu 24:22). Conquest of Syria by (Isa 8:4). Conquest and captivity of Israel by (Isa 8:4; Hos 9:3; 10:6; 11:5). Invasion of Judah by (Isa 5:26; 7:17-20; 8:8; 10:5-6, 12). Restoration of Israel from (Isa 27:12-13; Hos 11:11; Zec 10:10). Destruction of (Isa 10:12-19; 14:24-25; 30:31-33; 31:8-9; Zec 10:11). Participation in the blessings of the gospel (Isa 19:23-25; Mic 7:12).

ASTARTE See Anath; Ashtaroth, 1; Ashtoreth.

ASTONISHMENT Christ causes (Mt 13:54; 15:31; 22:22, 33; Mk 2:12; 4:41; 7:37; 10:24; Lk 2:48; 4:22, 26; 8:25).

ASTROLOGER, ASTROLOGY One who tries to find out the influence of the stars upon human affairs or to foretell events by their positions and aspects (Isa 47:13; Jer 10:1-2; Da 1:20; 2:27; 4:7; 5:7, 11; Isa 47:12-13). *See Astronomy; Sorcery.*

ASTRONOMY

Phenomena Concerning the Universe:
God the creator of (Job 9:6-9; 26:7, 13; 37:18; Ps 8:3; 136:5-9; Isa 40:22, 26). God the ruler of (Job 38:31-33; Ps 68:33; Eze 32:7-8; Am 5:8). Immeasurable (Jer 31:37; 33:22). Laws of, permanent (Ecc 1:5; Jer 31:35-36). Declares God's glory (Ps 19:1-6). Destruction of (Isa 34:4; Mt 24:35; 2Pe 3:10; Rev 6:12-14; 21:1).

Celestial Phenomena:
Fire from heaven, on the cities of the plain (Ge 19:24-25), on the two captains and their fifties (2Ki 1:10-14), on the flocks and servants of Job (Job 1:16).

Thunder and lightning on Mt. Sinai (Ex 19:16, 18; 20:18). Pillar of cloud and fire (Ex 13:21-22; 14:19, 24; 40:38; Nu 9:15-23; Ps 78:14). The sun and moon standing still (Jos 10:12-14). Hail on the Egyptians (Ex 9:22-34).

A

Darkness on the Egyptians (Ex 10:21-23), at the crucifixion of Christ (Mt 27:45; Lk 23:44-45).

Sun seemingly rotating (Ecc 1:5). Wandering stars (Jude 13).

Signs in the Sun, Moon and Stars:
(Joel 2:30-31; Isa 13:10). Foretold by Jesus as part of his second coming (Mt 24:29, 35; Mk 13:24-25; Lk 21:25; Ac 2:19-20). In the final judgments (Rev 8:10-12; 9:1-2; 10:1-2; 12:3-4; 13:13; 16:8-9; 19:11-14).

Constellations:Glory of (1Co 15:41). Darkened (Isa 13:10). The serpent (Job 26:13), Bear, Orion and Pleiades (Job 9:9; 38:31; Am 5:8).

See Constellations; Eclipse; Heaven; Meteorology; Moon; Stars; Sun.

ASUPPIM NIV "storehouses" at the S gate of the temple (1Ch 26:15, 17; Ne 12:25).

ASWAN Egyptian town on border of Egypt and Ethiopia (Isa 49:12; Eze 29:10; 30:6).

ASYNCRITUS (*incomparable*). A disciple at Rome (Ro 16:14).

ATAD (*thornbush*). The place where the sons of Jacob mourned for their father (Ge 50:10-11).

ATARAH (*circlet, wreath*). Wife of Jerahmeel (1Ch 2:26).

ATAROTH (*circlets, wreaths*). Also called Atroth.
1. A city E of Jordan (Nu 32:3, 34).
2. A city, or possibly two different cities, of Ephraim (Jos 16:2, 5, 7; 18:13).
3. A city of Judah (1Ch 2:54). Called Atroth Beth Joab. *See Atroth Beth Joab; Joab, 4.*
4. A city of Gad (Nu 32:35).

ATAROTH ADDAR (*wreaths of majesty*). See Ataroth, 2.

ATER (possibly *crippled one, left-handed one*, or the proper name *Etir*).
1. A descendant of Hezekiah who returned from Babylon (Ezr 2:16; Ne 7:21; 10:17).
2. A gatekeeper (Ezr 2:42; Ne 7:45).
3. An Israelite who agreed to Nehemiah's covenant (Ne 10:17).

ATHACH A city of Judah (1Sa 30:30).

ATHAIAH (possibly *[the] superiority of Yahweh*). Son of Uzziah (Ne 11:4).

ATHALIAH (possibly *Yahweh is exalted* BDB; *oldest of Yahweh* KB).
1. Wife of Jehoram, king of Judah (2Ki 8:18, 26; 11:1-3, 12-16, 20; 2Ch 22:10-12; 23:12-15, 21).
2. Son of Jehoram (1Ch 8:26).
3. Father of Jeshaiah (Ezr 8:7).

ATHARIM (traditionally *way of the spies*). The Israelites, under Moses, were attacked by the king of Arad, and some were taken captive (Nu 21:1ff).

ATHEISM Instances of (Ps 10:4; 14:1; 53:1). Arguments against (Job 12:7-25; Ro 1:19-20).
See God; Faith; Unbelief.

ATHENS, ATHENIANS A leading city of Greece and its inhabitants (Ac 17:15-34; 1Th 3:1).

ATHLAI (possibly *Yahweh is exalted* BDB; *oldest of Yahweh* KB). A son of Bebai (Ezr 10:28).

ATHLETE, ATHLETICS See Games.

ATOMS OF MATTER NIV "dust of the world" (Pr 8:26).

ATONEMENT
The divine act of grace in which God accepts an offering as a substitute for the punishment for sin. In the OT, the shed blood of sacrificial offerings effected atonement. The blood shed in the sacrifices was sacred. It epitomized the life of the sacrificial victim. Since life was sacred, blood (a symbol of life) had to be treated with respect (Ge 9:5-6). Eating blood was therefore strictly forbidden (Lev 7:26-27; Dt 12:16, 23-25; 15:23; 1Sa 14:32-34). Lev 17:14 stresses the intimate relationship between blood and life by twice declaring that "the life of every creature is its blood." Life is the precious and mysterious gift of God, and people are not to seek to preserve it or increase their life-force by eating "life" that is "in the blood" (Lev 17:11)—as many pagan peoples throughout history have thought they could do (Ge 9:4).

Practically every sacrifice included the sprinkling or smearing of blood on the altar or within the tabernacle (Lev 1:5; 3:2; 4:6, 25; 7:2; 17:6), thus teaching that atonement involves the substitution of life for life. The blood of the OT sacrifice pointed forward to the blood of the Lamb of God, who obtained for his people "eternal redemption" (Heb 9:12). "Without the shedding of blood there is no forgiveness" (Heb 9:22).

For tabernacle and furniture (Lev 16:15-20, 33). For the Levites (Nu 8:21). For those defiled by the dead (Nu 6:11). Made for houses (Lev 14:53). Sin. *See below, Sin.*

By:
Meat offerings (Lev 5:11-13), jewels (Nu 31:50), money (Ex 30:12-16; Lev 5:15-16; 2Ki 12:16), incense (Nu 16:46-50). By animals. *See below, Made by Animal Sacrifices.* By Jesus. *See below, Made by Jesus.*

Day of:
Time of (Ex 30:10; Lev 23:27; 25:9; Nu 29:7). How observed (Ex 30:10; Lev 16:2-34; 23:27-32; Nu 29:7-11; Heb 5:3; 9:7).

Made by Animal Sacrifices:
In the blood shed (Lev 17:11). In burnt offerings (Lev 1:4). For unintentional sin (Lev 4:13-21; Nu 15:22-28; 28:27-31; 29), for purification after childbirth (Lev 12:6-8).

In guilt offerings for sin (Lev 5:6-10; 6:7), for cleansing from a skin disease (Lev 14:12-32).

In sin offerings (Ex 29:36; Lev 4:20) for unintentional sins of a leader (Lev 4:22-35), of the descendants of Aaron (Lev 9:7; 10:17; 16:6-9). The scapegoat (Lev 16:10-34). On festival days (Nu 28:22; 29).

Forgiveness of sins through (Lev 5:10; 19:22).

Made by Jesus:
Through his blood shed (Lk 22:20; 1Co 1:23; Eph 2:13-15; Heb 9:12-15, 25-26; 12:24; 13:12, 20-21; 1Jn 5:6; Rev 1:5; 5:9; 7:14; 12:11), his death (Ro 3:24-26; 5:11-15; 1Th 1:10; Heb 13:12; 1Jn 2:2; 3:5-6; Rev 5:6, 9; 13:8).

Typified in Passover lamb (Ex 12:5, 11, 14; 1Co 5:7), in sacrifices (Ex 24:8; Lev 16:30, 34; 17:11; 19:22; Heb 9:11-28). Compare Ge 4:4, w Heb 11:4; Ge 22:2, w Heb 11:17, 19; Ex 12:5, 11, 14, w 1Co 5:7; Ex 24:8, w Heb 9:10; Lev 16:30, 34, w Heb 9:7, 12, 28; Lev 17:11, w Heb 9:22.

Divinely inspired (Lk 2:30-31; Gal 4:4-5; Eph 1:3-12, 17-22; 2:4-10; Col 1:19-20; 1Pe 1:20; Rev 13:8). A mystery (1Co 2:7; 1Pe 1:8-12). Once for all (Heb 7:27; 9:24-28; 10:10, 12, 14; 1Pe 3:18). Made on our behalf (Isa 53:4-12; Mt 20:28; Jn 6:51; 11:49-51; Gal 3:13; Eph 5:2; 1Th 5:9-10; Heb 2:9; 1Pe 2:24).

For reconciliation (Da 9:24-27; Ro 5:1-21; 2Co 5:18-21; Eph 2:16-17; Col 1:20-22; Heb 2:17). For remission of sins (Zec 13:1; Mt 26:28; Lk 22:20; 24:46-47; Jn 1:29; Ro 4:25; 1Co 15:3; Gal 1:3-4; Eph 1:7; Col 1:14; Heb 1:3; 10:1-20; 1Jn 1:7; 3:5). For redemption (Mt 20:28; Ac 20:28; Gal 3:13; 1Ti 2:6; Heb 9:12; Rev 5:9).

See Blood; Jesus the Christ, Death of, Mission of, Sufferings of; Redemption; Salvation.

ATONEMENT COVER KJV "mercy seat." Description of (Ex 25:17-22). Placed on the ark of the testimony (Ex 26:34; 30:6; 31:7; 40:20; Heb 9:5). Materials of, to be a freewill offering (Ex 35:4-12). Made by Bezalel (Ex 37:1, 6-9).

Sprinkled with blood (Lev 16:14-15). There God met with his people (Ex 25:22; 30:6, 36; Lev 16:2; Nu 7:89; 17:4; 1Sa 4:4; 2Sa 6:2; 2Ki 19:15; 1Ch 13:6; Ps 80:1; Ps 99:1; Isa 37:16; Heb 4:16). In Solomon's temple (1Ch 28:11).
See Tabernacle.

ATONEMENT, DAY OF *See Day of Atonement.*

ATONING SACRIFICE *See Propitiation.*

ATROPHY *See Disease; Shriveled Hand.*

ATROTH BETH JOAB (*circlets, folds of the house of Joab*). Descendants of Salma; the house of Joab, occurs in the genealogy of Judah (1Ch 2:54).

ATROTH SHOPHAN (*circlets, folds of Shophan*). Town built by Gadites E of Jordan (Nu 32:35).

ATTAI (*timely*, or perhaps *an abbreviation of Athaiah*).
1. A Gadite warrior (1Ch 12:11).
2. Son of Rehoboam (2Ch 11:20).
3. Grandson of Sheshan (1Ch 2:35-36).

ATTALIA A seaport of Pamphylia (Ac 14:25).

ATTORNEY *See Lawyer.*

ATTRIBUTES OF GOD *See God.*

AUGUSTUS (*reverent, holy*). A title of Roman emperors (Lk 2:1). "Emperor" and "Imperial" in Ac 25:21, 25; 27:1 are rendered Augustus in the KJV.

AUL *See Awl.*

AVA *See Avva.*

AVARICE Love of money: a root of evil (1Ti 6:10). Insatiable (Ecc 4:7-8; 5:10-11). Forbidden in overseer (1Ti 3:2-3; Tit 1:7). Instances of: Descendants of Joseph (Jos 17:14-18). *See Covetousness; Greed; Rich, The; Riches.*

AVEN (*evil power, wickedness*).
1. Valley of Aven (Am 1:5, ftn).
2. Bethel (Am 5:5, ftn).
3. Beth Aven (Hos 10:8, ftn). *See Beth Aven.*
4. A possible spelling for On or Heliopolis (Eze 30:17, ftn).

AVENGER OF BLOOD
Premosaic:
Cain fears (Ge 4:14-15), Lamech fears (Ge 4:24). Edict of God (Ge 9:5-6).
Mosaic Law Concerning:
Cities of refuge from (Nu 35:6-34; Dt 19:1-13; Jos 20:1-9; 21:13, 21, 27, 32, 38; 1Ch 6:57, 67). Set aside by David (2Sa 14:4-11).
Figurative: (Ps 8:2; 44:16; Ro 13:4; 1Th 4:6).
See Homicide.

AVITH Capital city of the Edomites (Ge 36:35; 1Ch 1:46).

AVVA Also called Ivvah. A district near Babylon (2Ki 17:24; 18:34; 19:13; Isa 37:13).

AVVIM
1. A city of Benjamin (Jos 18:23).
2. A tribe in southern Palestine. *See Avvites.*

AVVITES
1. A people driven out of Canaan by the Philistines (Dt 2:23; Jos 13:3).
2. Colonists of Samaria (2Ki 17:31).

AWAKENINGS, REFORMS
General references (1Ki 18:39; 2Ch 30:1; Ezr 10:1; Lk 3:7-10; Jn 4:39; Ac 2:40-41; 8:6; 9:35; 11:21; 13:48; 18:8; 19:18). Instances: Asa (1Ki 15:12). Jehu (1Ki 10:27). Jehoiada (2Ki 11:18). Josiah (2Ki 23:4). Jehoshaphat (2Ch 19:3). Hezekiah (2Ch 31:1). Manasseh (2Ch 33:15). Ezra (Ezr 10:3). Nehemiah (Ne 13:19).

AWL A sharp piercing tool (Ex 21:6; Dt 15:17).

AX, AXHEAD A tool for cutting wood (Dt 19:5; 20:19; 1Sa 13:20-21; 2Sa 12:31; Ps 74:5-6). A weapon of war (Jer 46:22). Elisha causes an axhead to float (2Ki 6:5-6).
Figurative of judgment (Jer 46:22; Mt 3:10).

AXLES Part of a wheeled vehicle, like the movable stands (1Ki 7:30-33).

AYYAH A city in Ephraim (1Ch 7:28).

AZAL *See Azel, 1.*

AZALIAH (*Yahweh is keeping in reserve*). Father of Shaphan (2Ki 22:3; 2Ch 34:8).

AZANIAH (*Yahweh has listened*). Father of Jeshua (Ne 10:9).

AZAREL (*God [El] has helped*).
1. Aaronite of the family of Korah (1Ch 12:6).
2. A musician in the temple (1Ch 25:18), also called Uzziel. *See Uzziel 4.*
3. A Danite prince (1Ch 27:22).
4. A son of Bani (Ezr 10:41).
5. A priest (Ne 11:13; 12:36).

AZARIAH (*Yahweh has helped*).
1. Man of Judah (1Ch 2:8).
2. King of Judah. See Uzziah, 1.
3. Son of Jehu (1Ch 2:38).
4. Son of Ahimaaz (1Ch 6:9).
5. Levite (1Ch 6:36).
6. Son of Zadok (1Ki 4:2).
7. High priest (1Ch 6:10).
8. Son of Nathan (1Ki 4:5).
9. Prophet (2Ch 15:1-8).
10. Son of King Jehoshaphat (2Ch 21:2).
11. Son of Jehoram (2Ch 22:6, ftn). See Ahaziah.
12. Son of Jehoram (2Ch 23:1).
13. Son of Johanan (2Ch 28:12).
14. Levite (2Ch 29:12).
15. High priest (2Ch 26:16-20).
16. Son of Hilkiah (1Ch 6:13-14).
17. Opponent of Jeremiah (Jer 43:2).
18. Jewish captive of Babylon (Da 1:7). See Abednego.
19. Son of Maaseiah (Ne 3:23).
20. Levite (Ne 8:7).
21. Priest (Ne 10:2).
22. Prince of Judah (Ne 12:32-33).

AZARIAHU A son of Jehoshaphat (2Ch 21:2).

AZAZ (*strong*). Father of Bela (1Ch 5:8).

AZAZEL NIV "scapegoat," one of the goats chosen for the service of the Day of Atonement (Lev 16:8, 10, 26). It has been interpreted both personally and impersonally as meaning: 1. remission of sin, 2. a place name, 3. an evil spirit, 4. the devil. *See Scapegoat.*

AZAZIAH (*Yahweh is strong*).
1. A harpist in the temple (1Ch 15:21).
2. Father of Hoshea (1Ch 27:20).
3. An overseer in the temple (2Ch 31:13).

AZBUK The father of Nehemiah (Ne 3:16).

AZEKAH (possibly *hoe [the ground]*). A town of Judah (Jos 10:10-11; 15:35; 1Sa 17:1; 2Ch 11:9; Ne 11:30; Jer 34:7).

AZEL (*noble*).
1. A place near Jerusalem (Zec 14:5).
2. A Benjamite (1Ch 8:37-38; 9:43-44).

AZEM *See Ezem.*

AZGAD (*strong is Gad*).
1. Ancestor of certain captives who returned from Babylon (Ezr 2:12; Ne 7:17).
2. A returned exile (Ezr 8:12).
3. A leader who signed Nehemiah's covenant (Ne 10:15).

AZIEL (*God is my strength*). A temple musician (1Ch 15:20).

AZIZA (*powerful*). Son of Zattu (Ezr 10:27).

AZMAVETH (*strong one of death* ISBE; *camel fodder, a plant of the plumose family* KB).
1. One of David's heroes (2Sa 23:31).
2. Benjamite (1Ch 12:3).
3. David's treasurer (1Ch 27:25).
4. Descendant of Jonathan (1Ch 8:36).
5. Place N of Anathoth (Ezr 2:24; Ne 12:29).

AZMON (*strongly [built body]*). A place on the S of Canaan (Nu 34:4, 5; Jos 15:4).

AZNOTH TABOR (possibly *peaks of Tabor*). A town in Naphtali (Jos 19:34).

AZOR (*help*). Ancestor of Jesus (Mt 1:13-14). Perhaps identical with Azrikam (1Ch 3:23).

AZOTUS The name of Ashdod in NT times (Ac 8:40). *See Ashdod.*

AZRIEL (*God [El] is [my] help*).
1. A chief of Manasseh (1Ch 5:24).
2. Father of Jerimoth (1Ch 27:19).
3. Father of Seraiah (Jer 36:26).

AZRIKAM (*[my] help arises*).
1. Son of Neariah (1Ch 3:23).
2. Son of Azel (1Ch 8:38; 9:44).
3. A Levite (1Ch 9:14; Ne 11:15).
4. Governor of the house of Ahaz (2Ch 28:7).

AZUBAH (*abandonment*).
1. Mother of Jehoshaphat (1Ki 22:42; 2Ch 20:31).
2. Wife of Caleb (1Ch 2:18-19).

AZUR See Azzur.

AZZAH See Gaza, 1.

AZZAN (*strong*). Father of Paltiel of the tribe of Issachar; chosen to help distribute the territory W of the Jordan among the various tribes who settled there (Nu 34:26).

AZZUR (*help*).
1. A leader who sealed Nehemiah's covenant (Ne 10:17).
2. A Gibeonite, the father of Hananiah, a false prophet in the days of King Zedekiah (Jer 28:1).
3. Father of Jaazaniah, an Israelite prince (Eze 11:1).

B

BAAL (*master, owner, lord*).
1. A god worshiped by the Canaanites and the Phoenicians; a god of storms and fertility. Often in the plural (Jdg 2:11; 3:7).
Wickedly worshiped by the Israelites in the time of the judges (Jdg 2:10-23; 1Sa 7:3-4), by the kingdom of Israel (2Ki 17:16; Jer 23:13; Hos 11:2; 13:1), under Ahab (1Ki 16:31-33; 18:18; 19:18), Jehoram (2Ki 3:2), by the Israelites (2Ki 21:3; 2Ch 22:2-4; 24:7; 28:2; 33:3). Jeremiah preaches against the worship of (Jer 2:8, 23; 7:9).
Altars of, destroyed by Gideon (Jdg 6:25-32), by Jehoiada (2Ki 11:18), by Josiah (2Ki 23:4-5).
Prophets of, slain by Elijah (2Ki 18:4). All worshipers of, destroyed by Jehu (2Ki 10:18-25).
2. A Benjamite (1Ch 8:30; 9:36).
3. A Reubenite (1Ch 5:5).
4. A city in the tribe of Simeon (1Ch 4:33). Called Baalath Beer (Jos 19:8).

BAAL-BERITH (*lord [Baal] of a covenant*). A god of the Shechemites (Jdg 9:4). Worshiped by Israelites (Jdg 8:33). Also called El-Berith (Jdg 9:46). *See El-Berith.*

BAAL GAD (*lord [Baal] of good luck*). A city of the Canaanites (Jos 11:17; 12:7; 13:5). Probably Baal Hermon (Jdg 3:3; 1Ch 5:23).

BAAL-GUR See Gur Baal.

BAAL HAMON (*lord [Baal] of Hamon*, or *possessor of abundance*). A place where Solomon had a vineyard (SS 8:11). Its location is unknown. Called Hammon (Jos 19:28).

BAAL-HANAN (*lord [Baal] is gracious*).
1. The son of Achbor and king of Edom (Ge 36:38; 1Ch 1:49).
2. An official under David (1Ch 27:28).

BAAL HAZOR (*lord [Baal] of Hazor*). Where Absalom had a sheep-range and where he brought about the death of Amnon in revenge for the rape of his sister (2Sa 13:23).

BAAL HERMON (*lord [Baal] of Hermon*).
1. A city near Mt. Hermon (1Ch 5:23). Probably identical with Baal Gad. *See Baal Gad.*
2. A mountain of Lebanon (Jdg 3:3).

BAAL MEON A city of the Reubenites (Nu 32:38; 1Ch 5:8; Eze 25:9). Also called: Beth Meon (Jer 48:23), Beth Baal Meon (Jos 13:17), Beon (Nu 32:3).

BAAL PEOR (*lord [Baal] of Peor*). An idol of Moab (Nu 25:3, 5; Dt 4:3; Ps 106:28; Hos 9:10).

BAAL PERAZIM (*lord [Baal] of making a breach, breaking through*). A place in the valley of Rephaim (2Sa 5:20; 1Ch 14:11). Called Mt. Perazim (Isa 28:21).

BAAL SHALISHAH (*lord [Baal] of Shalisha*). A place near Gilgal (1Sa 9:4; 2Ki 4:42).

BAAL TAMAR (*lord [Baal] of the palm tree*). A place near Gibeah (Jdg 20:33).

BAAL-ZEBUB (*lord [Baal] of the flies*). Name under which Baal was worshiped by the Philistines of Ekron (2Ki 1:2-3, 6). An intentional biblical corruption of the original name Baal-Zebul, "Baal the prince." *See Beelzebub.*

BAAL ZEPHON (*lord [Baal] of the North*). A place near which the Israelites encamped just before they crossed the Red Sea (Ex 14:2, 9; Nu 33:7). The site is unknown.

BAALAH ([feminine of Baal] *lady*).
1. A city in the S of Judah (Jos 15:29). Apparently identical with Balah (Jos 19:3) and Bilhah (1Ch 4:29).
2. A city in the N of Judah called also Kiriath Jearim. *See Kiriath Jearim.*
3. A mountain in Judah (Jos 15:11). Probably identical with Mt. Jearim.

BAALAH OF JUDAH (*lords [Baals] of Judah*). Town on N border of Judah; the same as Baalah and Kiriath Baal and Kiriath Jearim (2Sa 6:2; 1Ch 13:6).

BAALATH (feminine of Baal "lord" *lady*). A city of Dan (Jos 19:44; 1Ki 9:18; 2Ch 8:6).

BAALATH BEER (*lord [Baal] of the well*). A city in the tribe of Simeon (Jos 19:8). *See Baal, 4.*

BAALBEK (*city of Baal*). City of Coele-Syria, c. forty miles NW of Damascus, famous for its ruins.

BAALI (*my lord* or *my husband*). Name often given to Yahweh by Israel, no longer to be used when Baal worship is eradicated (Hos 2:16, ftn).

BAALIM Plural form of Baal in KJV (Jdg 2:11; 1Sa 7:4; Hos 2:13, 17; 11:2). *See Baal.*

BAALIS (possibly *son of delight*, or *Baals*). King of the Ammonites (Jer 40:14).

BAANA (*son of affliction*).
1. Son of Ahilud (1Ki 4:12).
2. Father of Zadok (Ne 3:4).
3. A son of Hushai (1Ki 4:16).

BAANAH (*son of affliction*).
1. A captain of Ish-Bosheth's army (2Sa 4:2, 5-6, 9).
2. Father of Heled (also Heleb) (2Sa 23:29, ftn; 1Ch 11:30).
3. Jewish leader of the Exile (Ezr 2:2; Ne 7:7; 10:27).
4. *See Baana, 3.*

BAARA (*passionate [burning] one*). Wife of Shaharaim (1Ch 8:8). Called Hodesh.

BAASEIAH (*the Lord is bold*). An ancestor of Asaph, the musician (1Ch 6:40).

BAASHA (*boldness*). King of Israel (1Ki 15:16-22, 27-34; 16:1-7; 21:22; 2Ki 9:9; 2Ch 16:1-6; Jer 41:9).

BABBLER A sarcastic title applied to Paul (Ac 17:18).

BABBLING Condemned (Mt 6:7; 1Ti 6:20; 2Ti 2:16).

BABEL (*gate of god[s]*; Ge 11:9 *confused*). A city in the plain of Shinar. Tower built and tongues confused at (Ge 11:1-9). *See Babylon.*

BABIES In the mouths of, praise is ordained (Mt 21:16).
Symbolize: Those without guile (Ps 8:2; Mt 11:25; Lk 10:21), the children of the kingdom of heaven (Mt 18:2-6; Mk 10:15; Lk 18:17), weak Christians (Ro 2:20; 1Co 3:1; Heb 5:13; 1Pe 2:2).
See Children; Parents.

BABOONS Imported by Solomon (1Ki 10:22; 2Ch 9:21).

BABYLON, BABYLONIA (*gate of god[s]*).
Described:
Origin of (Ge 10:8, 10). Origin of the name (Ge 11:8-9). Land of the Chaldeans (Eze 12:13). Land of Shinar in (Da 1:2; Zec 5:11, ftn). Land of Merathaim (Jer 50:21). Desert of the sea (Isa 21:1). Sheshach, a cryptic term for Babylon (Jer 25:12, 26, ftn). Lady of kingdoms (Isa 47:5). Situated beyond the Euphrates (Ge 11:31, w Jos 24:2-3). Formerly a part of Mesopotamia (Ac 7:2). Conquered by the Assyrians and a part of their empire (2Ki 17:24, w Isa 23:13). Watered by the rivers Euphrates and Tigris (Ps 137:1; Jer 51:13). Composed of many nations (Da 3:4, 29). Governed by Kings (2Ki 20:12; Da 5:1). Languages spoken in (Da 1:4; 2:4). With Media and Persia divided by Darius into 120 provinces (Da 6:1). Administrators placed over (Da 2:48; 6:2). Babylon the chief province of (Da 3:1).
Babylon the Capital of:
Its antiquity (Ge 11:4, 9). Enlarged by Nebuchadnezzar (Da 4:30). Surrounded with a great wall and fortified (Jer 51:53, 58). Called the jewel of kingdoms and the glory of Babylonians' pride (Isa 13:19), the golden city (Isa 14:4, KJV), the city of merchants (Eze 17:4), Babylon the great (Da 4:30).
Remarkable for:
Antiquity (Jer 5:15). Naval power (Isa 43:14). Military power (Jer 5:16; 50:23). National greatness (Isa 13:19; Jer 51:41). Wealth (Jer 50:37; 51:13). Commerce (Eze 17:4). Manufacture of garments (Jos 7:21). Wisdom of officials (Isa 47:10; Jer 50:35).
Inhabitants:
Idolatrous (Jer 50:38; Da 3:18). Addicted to magic (Isa 47:9, 12-13; Da 2:1-2). Profane and sacrilegious (Da 5:1-3). Wicked (Isa 47:10).
As a Power Was:
Arrogant (Isa 14:13-14; Jer 50:29, 31-32). Secure and self-confident (Isa 47:7-8). Grand and stately (Isa 47:1, 5). Covetous (Jer 51:13). Oppressive (Isa 14:4). Cruel and destructive (Isa 14:17; 47:6; Jer 51:25; Hab 1:6-7). An instrument of God's vengeance on other nations (Jer 51:7; Isa 47:6). Armies of, described (Hab 1:7-9).

Represented by:
A great eagle (Eze 17:3). A head of gold (Da 2:32, 37-38). A lion with eagle's wings (Da 7:4). Ambassadors of, sent to Hezekiah (2Ki 20:12). Figure of a woman (Rev 17).
Nebuchadnezzar, King of:
Made Jehoiakim vassal (2Ki 24:1). Besieged Jerusalem (2Ki 24:10-11). Took Jehoiachin captive to Babylon (2Ki 24:12, 14-16; 2Ch 36:10). Sacked the temple (2Ki 24:13). Made Zedekiah king (2Ki 24:17). Besieged and took Jerusalem (2Ki 24:20; 25:1-4). Burned Jerusalem (2Ki 25:7, 11, 18-21; 2Ch 36:20). Took Zedekiah captive to Babylon (2Ki 25:7). Sacked and burned the temple (2Ki 25:9, 13-17; 2Ch 36:18-19). Revolt of the Israelites from, and their punishment illustrated (Jer 27). The Israelites exhorted to be subject to, and settle in (Jer 27:17; 29:1-7). Treatment of the Israelites in (2Ki 25:27-30; Da 1:3-7). Grief of the Israelites in (Ps 137:1-6). Destroyed by the Medes (Da 5:30-31). Restoration of the Israelites from (2Ch 36:23; Ezr 1; 2:1-67). The gospel preached in (1Pe 5:13). A type of Antichrist (Rev 16:19; 17:5).
Predictions Respecting:
Conquests by (Jer 21:3-10; 27:2-6; 49:28-33; Eze 21:19-32; 29:18-20). Captivity of the Israelites by (Jer 20:4-6; 22:20-26; 25:9-11; Mic 4:10). Restoration of the Israelites from (Isa 14:1-4; 44:28; 48:20; Jer 29:10; 50:4, 8, 19). Destruction of (Isa 13; 14:4-22; 21:1-10; 47; Jer 25:12; 50; 51). Perpetual desolation of (Isa 13:19-22; 14:22-23; Jer 50:13, 39; 51:37). Acknowledgment of Yahweh (Ps 87:4).

BACA (*balsam tree*, or *weeping*). An unknown valley of Israel (Ps 84:6), figurative of an experience of sorrow turned into joy.

BACHRITES See Beker, Bekerite.

BACKBITING Evil of (Ps 15:1-3; Pr 25:23; Ro 1:29-30; 2Co 12:20).
See Accusation, False; Slander; Speaking, Evil.

BACKSLIDERS
Described as:
Blind (2Pe 1:9; Rev 3:17), godless (2Jn 9), idolaters (1Co 10:7), lukewarm (Rev 3:15-16), grumblers (Ex 17:7; 1Co 10:10), forsaking God (Jer 17:13), tempting Christ (1Co 10:9), forsaking God's covenant (Ps 78:10-11; Pr 2:17), turned aside to evil (Ps 125:5; 1Ti 5:15), unfit for God's kingdom (Lk 9:62).
God's Forbearance With:
(Dt 32:5-6, 26-27; Ezr 9:10, 14; Isa 42:3).
God's concern for (Dt 32:28-29; Ps 81:13-14; Isa 1:4-9, 21-22; 65:2-3; Jer 2:5, 11-13, 17, 31-32; 18:13-15; 50:6; Hos 6:4-11; 11:1-4; 11:7-9; Mt 23:37).
Called to repentance (Isa 30:9, 15; 31:6; Jer 3:4-7, 12-14, 21-22; 4:14; 6:16; Hos 14:1; Mal 3:7; Rev 2:4-5, 20-22; 3:2-3, 18-19).
Promises to penitent: Of finding the Lord (Dt 4:29-31; 2Ch 15:2-4). Of spiritual enlightenment (Isa 29:24; Jer 3:14-19; Hos 6:3). Of restoration (Dt 30:1-10; Pr 24:16; Isa 57:18-19; Hos 14:4; Zec 10:6). Of temporal prosperity (Lev 26:40-42; Dt 30:1-5, 7-10; Job 22:23-30). Return of (Jer 31:18-19; 50:4-5; Hos 3:5; Jnh 2:4).
Judgment of:
Warnings to (Dt 4:25-28; 28:58-59; 29:18; 31:16-18; 1Ki 9:6-9; 2Ch 7:19-22; Jer 7:13-34; 11:9-17; Mk 9:50).
Corrective judgments upon (Dt 32:16-25; 1Ki 8:33; 2Ch 7:19-22; Ne 9:26-30; Job 34:26-27; Isa 5:1; 8:1-15; 16:12; Eze 22:18-22; Hos 8:14; 9:1-17).
Punishment of: By temporal loss (Dt 28:15-68; Ezr 8:22; Jer 13:24-25; Eze 15; Am 2:4-6). By being overthrown by enemies (Nu 14:43; Dt 4:27-28; Jdg 2:12-15; 2Ki 18:11-12; 2Ch 29:6-8; Ps 78:40-43, 56-64). By being forsaken of God (2Ch 24:20; Isa 2:6; Jer 6:30; 12:7; 14:7, 10; 15:1; Hos 4:6, 10). By bearing the fruits of their sin (Pr 14:14; Eze 11:21; 16:43; 23:35).
Instances of:
Saul (1Sa 15:11, 26-28). Solomon (1Ki 11:4-40; Ne 13:26). Amon (2Ki 21:22-23). Rehoboam (2Ch 12:1-2). Joash (2Ch 24:24). Amaziah (2Ch 25:27). Jonah (Jnh 1:3). Disciples of Jesus (Jn 6:66). Peter (Mt 26:69-75). Corinthian Christians (1Co 5:1-8). Galatians (Gal 1:6; 3:1; 4:9-11; 5:6-7). Hymenaeus and Alexander (1Ti 1:20). Phygelus and Hermogenes (2Ti 1:15). Demas (2Ti 4:10). Churches of Asia (2Ti 1:15; Rev 2:4; 3:2-3, 15-18).
See Apostasy; Backsliding; Church, The Body of Believers, Evil Conditions of; Reprobacy.

BACKSLIDING Turning from God (1Ki 11:9). Leaving the first love (Rev 2:4). Departing from the simplicity of the gospel (2Co 11:3; Gal 3:1-3; 5:4, 7).
God is displeased at (Ps 78:57, 59). Despised by believers (Ps 101:3). Warnings against (Ps 85:8; 1Co 10:12). Guilt and consequences of (Nu 14:43; Ps 125:5; Isa 59:2, 9-11; Jer 5:6; 8:5, 13; 15:6; Lk 9:62). Brings its own punishment (Pr 14:14; Jer 2:19). A haughty spirit leads to (Pr 16:18). Leaning to (Pr 24:16; Hos 11:7). Liable to continue and increase (Jer 8:5; 14:7). Exhortations to return from (2Ch 30:6; Isa 31:6; Jer 3:12, 14, 22; Hos 6:1). Pray to be restored from (Ps 80:3; 85:4; La 5:21). Punishment of tempting others to the sin of (Pr 28:10; Mt 18:6). Not hopeless (Ps 37:24; Pr 24:16).
Attempt to bring back those guilty of (Gal 6:1; Jas 5:10, 20). Sin of, to be confessed (Isa 59:12-14; Jer 3:13, 14; 14:7-9). Pardon of, promised (2Ch 7:14; Jer 3:12; 31:20; 36:3). Healing of, promised (Jer 3:22; Hos 14:4). Afflictions sent to heal (Hos 5:15). Blessedness of those who keep from (Pr 28:15; Isa 26:3-4; Col 1:21-23).
Instances of Israel's Backsliding:
At Meribah (Ex 17:1-7), when Aaron made the golden calf (Ex 32), after Joshua's death (Jdg 2), during Asa's reign (2Ch 15), Hezekiah's reign (2Ch 30:2-12).
See Apostasy; Backsliders.

BACUTH See Allon Bacuth.

BAD COMPANY See Company, Evil.

BADGER See Sea Cow.

B

BAG Sack or pouch made for holding anything. Many kinds are mentioned in Scripture (Dt 25:13; 2Ki 5:23; Mt 10:10).

BAGPIPE (RSV); NIV "pipes." A musical instrument (Da 3:5, 7, 10, 15). *See Music, Instruments of.*

BAHURIM, BAHARUMITE (*young men*). A village between Jericho and Jerusalem, on the eastern slope of the Mount of Olives; modern Ras et-Tmim (2Sa 3:16; 16:5; 17:18; 19:16; 1Ki 2:8).

BAIL *See Creditor; Debt; Debtor; Security, For Debt.*

BAJITH NIV "temple"; a place of idolatrous worship in Moab (Isa 15:2). *See Idolatry; Sanctuary, 4; Shrine.*

BAKBAKKAR (*investigator*). A Levite (1Ch 9:15).

BAKBUK (*gurgling [sound coming out of a bottle]*). The founder of a family of temple servants who returned from the Captivity with Zerubbabel (Ezr 2:51; Ne 7:53).

BAKBUKIAH (*Yahweh pours out*). A name occurring three times in Nehemiah (Ne 11:17; 12:9, 25), a Levite in high office in Jerusalem right after the Exile.

BAKER (1Sa 8:13; Jer 37:21; Hos 7:4, 6). Pharaoh's chief baker (Ge 40). *See Bread.*

BALAAM (possibly *Baal [lord] of the people* BDB; possibly *the clan brings forth* IDB; *devourer, glutton* KB). Son of Beor. From Mesopotamia (Dt 23:4). A soothsayer (Jos 13:22). A prophet (Nu 24:2-9; 2Pe 2:15-16). Balak sends for, to curse Israel (Nu 22:5-7; Jos 24:9; Ne 13:2; Mic 6:5). Anger of, rebuked by his donkey (Nu 22:22-35; 2Pe 2:16). Counsel of, on occasion of Israel's corruption with the Midianites (Nu 31:16; Rev 2:14-15). Greed of (2Pe 2:15; Jude 11). Death of (Nu 31:8; Jos 13:22).

BALAC *See Balak.*

BALADAN Father of Merodach-Baladan (2Ki 20:12; Isa 39:1).

BALAH (*old, worn out*). A city of Simeon (Jos 19:3). Called Bilhah (1Ch 4:29).

BALAK (*devastator*). King of Moab (Nu 22:4; Jos 24:9; Jdg 11:25; Mic 6:5). Tried to bribe Balaam to curse Israel (Nu 22:5-7, 15-17). *See Balaam.*

BALANCES Used for weighing (Job 31:6; Isa 40:12, 15; Eze 5:1). Money weighed with (Isa 46:6; Jer 32:10). Must be just (Lev 19:36; Pr 16:11; Eze 45:10).
 False balance: Used (Hos 12:7; Am 8:5; Mic 6:11), an abomination (Pr 11:1; 20:23).
 Figurative (Job 6:2; 31:6; Ps 62:9; Isa 40:12; Da 5:27; Rev 6:5).

BALD LOCUST *See Insects.*

BALDNESS (Lev 13:40, 41). A judgment (Isa 3:24; Jer 47:5; 48:37; Eze 7:18). Artificial, a sign of mourning (Isa 22:12; Jer 16:6; Eze 27:31; 29:18; Am 8:10; Mic 1:16). Artificial, as an idolatrous practice, forbidden (Lev 21:5; Dt 14:1).
 Instance of: Elisha (2Ki 2:23).

BALL Playing at (Isa 22:18).

BALM A medicinal balsam (Ge 37:25; 43:11; Jer 8:22; 46:11; 51:8; Eze 27:17).

BALSAM TREES *See Tree.*

BAMAH (*high location [for cultic worship]*). A high place (Eze 20:29).

BAMOTH (*high locations [for cultic worship]*). A camping place of the Israelites (Nu 21:19-20).

BAMOTH BAAL (*high places for Baal [worship]*). A city assigned to Reuben as part of his inheritance (Jos 13:17).

BANI (*descendant*).
 1. KJV a Gadite; NIV "son of" (2Sa 23:36).
 2. Levite (1Ch 6:46).
 3. Descendant of Judah (1Ch 9:4).
 4. Levite (Ne 3:17).
 5. Levite (Ne 9:4).
 6. Levite (Ne 11:22).
 7. Levite (Ne 10:13).
 8. Man who signed covenant (Ne 10:14).
 9. Ancestor of Jews who returned from the Captivity (Ezr 10:29).
 10. KJV Bani; NIV "descendants of" (Ezr 10:38).

BANISHMENT (Ezr 7:26). Of Adam and Eve, from Eden (Ge 3:22-24). Of Cain, to be "a restless wanderer" (Ge 4:14). Of Jews, from Rome (Ac 18:2). Of John, to Patmos (Rev 1:9). *See Exile.*

BANK A primitive kind of banking was known in ancient times. Israelites could not charge each other interest (Ex 22:25) but could charge Gentiles (Dt 23:20). The concept of a bank as a savings institution was unknown. *See Borrowing; Interest; Lending.*

BANNER Banners, ensigns, or standards (not flags) were used in ancient times for military, national, and ecclesiastical purposes very much as they are today (Nu 2:2; Isa 5:26; 11:10; Jer 4:21).

BANQUET Social feasting was common among the Hebrews. There were feasts on birthdays (Ge 40:20), marriages (Ge 29:22), funerals (2Sa 3:35), grape-gatherings (Jdg 9:27), sheep-shearing (1Sa 25:2, 36), sacrifices (Ex 34:15), and on other occasions. Often a second invitation was sent on the day of the feast (Lk 7:45), and their feet were washed (Lk 7:44). Banquets were often invigorated with music, singing, and dancing (Lk 15:23-25).

BAPTISM (*dip*, or *immerse*).
 As administered by John (Mt 3:5-12; Jn 3:23; Ac 13:24; 19:4). Sanctioned by Christ's submission to it (Mt 3:13-15; Lk 3:21). Adopted by Christ (Jn 3:22; 4:1-2). Appointed an ordinance of the Christian church (Mt 28:19-20; Mk 16:15-16). To be administered in the name of the Father, the Son, and the Holy Spirit (Mt 28:19). Water, the outward and visible sign in (Ac 8:36; 10:47). Regeneration, the inward and spiritual grace of (Jn 3:3, 5-6; Ro 6:3-4, 11). Remission of sins, signified by (Ac 2:38; 22:16). Unity of the church effected by (1Co 12:13; Gal 3:27-28). Confession of sin necessary to (Mt 3:6). Repentance necessary to (Ac 2:38). Faith necessary to (Ac 8:37; 18:8). There is but one (Eph 4:5).
 Administered to: Individuals (Ac 8:38; 9:18). Households (Ac 16:15; 1Co 1:16). Emblematic of the influences of the Holy Spirit (Mt 3:11; Tit 3:5). Typified (1Co 10:2; 1Pe 3:20-21).

BAR An Aramaic word meaning "son"; in the NT used as a prefix (Mt 16:17, KJV). *See Barabbas; Barnabas; Barsabbas; Bartholomew; Bar-Jesus; Bar-Jona.*

BARABBAS (*son of a father*, possibly *son of a rabbi [teacher]*). A prisoner released by Pilate (Mt 27:16-26; Mk 15:7-15; Lk 23:18-25; Jn 18:40; Ac 3:14).

BARACHEL *See Barakel.*

BARACHIAH, BARAKIAH *See Berekiah, 5.*

BARAH *See Beth Barah.*

BARAK (*lightning*). Israelite who defeated Sisera at the command of Deborah the judge (Jdg 4-5; 1Sa 12:11; Heb 11:32).

BARAKEL (*God [El] blesses*). A Buzite, whose son Elihu was the last of Job's friends to reason with him (Job 32:2, 6).

BARBARIAN A foreigner (Ac 28:2-4; Ro 1:14; 1Co 14:11; Col 3:11). *See Strangers.*

BARBER A barber's razor (Eze 5:1).

BARHUMITE Azmaveth the Barhumite, one of the Thirty (2Sa 23:31).

BARIAH (possibly *board, bar; fugitive* ISBE; *descendant* KB). Son of Shecaniah (1Ch 3:22).

BAR-JESUS (*son of Joshua*). A false prophet (Ac 13:6).

BAR-JONA NIV "Simon son of Jonah," surname of Peter (Mt 16:17).

BARKOS (*son of [pagan god] Kos*). A Jew whose descendants returned from the Exile (Ezr 2:53; Ne 7:55).

BARLEY A product of: Egypt (Ex 9:31), Israel (Dt 8:8; 1Ch 11:13; Jer 41:8).
 Fed to horses (1Ki 4:28). Used in offerings (Nu 5:15; Eze 45:15). Selling of (2Ch 2:10; Hos 3:2). Tribute in (2Ch 27:5). Priests estimated value of (Lev 27:16; 2Ki 7:1; Rev 6:6). Absalom burns Joab's field of (2Sa 14:30).
 Loaves of (Jn 6:9, 13).

BARN A storehouse for crops (Dt 28:8; Ps 144:13; Pr 3:10; Hag 2:19; Mt 3:12; 6:26; 13:30; Lk 12:18, 24).
 See Granary; Storehouse.

BARNABAS (*son of comfort*). Also called Joseph (Ac 4:36). A prophet (Ac 13:1). An apostle (Ac 14:14). A Levite who gave his possessions to be owned in common with other disciples (Ac 4:36-37). Goes to Tarsus to find Paul, brings him to Antioch (Ac 11:25-26). Accompanies Paul to Jerusalem (Ac 11:30). Returns with Paul to Antioch (Ac 12:25).
 Goes With Paul to Seleucia (Ac 13), Iconium (Ac 14:1-7). Called Jupiter (Ac 14:12-18). Goes to Derbe (Ac 14:20). Is sent as delegate to Jerusalem (Ac 15; Gal 2:1-9). Estranged from Paul (Ac 15:36-39). Is reconciled to Paul (1Co 9:6). Piety of (Ac 11:22-24). Devotion of, to Jesus (Ac 15:25-26).

BARNEA *See Kadesh Barnea.*

BARREL A clay jar (1Ki 17:12, 14, 16; 18:33). *See Jar(s); Pottery.*

BARRENNESS Inability of women to bear children. A reproach (Ge 30:22-23; 1Sa 1:6, 7; 2:1-11; Isa 4:1; Lk 1:25). Sent as a judgment (Ge 20:17-18). *See Childlessness.*
 Barrenness miraculously removed: Sarai (Ge 17:15-21), Rebekah (Ge 25:21), Manoah's wife (Jdg 13), Hannah (1Sa 1:6-20), Elizabeth (Lk 1:5-25).

BARSABBAS (*son of the Sabbath* or *son of Saba*).
 1. Surname of Joseph (Ac 1:23).
 2. Judas (Ac 15:22).

BARTER (Job 6:27; 41:6; La 1:11). *See Commerce.*

BARTHOLOMEW (*son of Talmai*). One of the apostles (Mt 10:3; Mk 3:18; Lk 6:14; Ac 1:13).

BARTIMAEUS (*son of Timai*, or *son of uncleanness*). A blind man (Mt 20:29-34; Mk 10:46-52; Lk 18:35-43).

BARUCH (*be blessed*).
 1. An amanuensis of Jeremiah (Jer 32:12-16; 36:4-32; 43:3-6; 45:1-2).
 2. Son of Zabbai (Ne 3:20; 10:6).
 3. A descendant of Perez (Ne 11:5).

BARUCH, BOOK OF Jewish pseudepigraphal book found in the Apocrypha; alleging to be a treatise by Jeremiah's scribe Baruch to Jewish exiles in Babylon.

BARZILLAI (*[made] of iron*).
 1. A friend of David (2Sa 17:27-29; 19:31-39; 1Ki 2:7; Ezr 2:61; Ne 7:63).
 2. Father of Adriel (2Sa 21:8).
 3. A priest (Ezr 2:61; Ne 7:63).

BASE FELLOWS Derogatory term "sons of Belial"; NIV "evil" or "wicked men" (Dt 13:13; 1Sa 2:12; 10:27; 25:17; 30:22; 1Ki 21:10; 2Ch 13:7). *See Wicked.*

BASEMATH (*fragrant*).
 1. Wife of Esau (Ge 26:34).
 2. Ishmael's daughter (Ge 36:3-4, 13, 17). Also called Mahalath (Ge 28:9).
 3. Solomon's daughter (1Ki 4:15).

BASHAN (*fertile stoneless plain*). A region E of the Jordan and N of Arnon (Ge 14:5); modern Golan Heights. Og, king of (Jos 13:12). Allotted to the two and one half tribes, which had their possession E of the Jordan (Nu 32:33; Dt 3:10-14; Jos 12:4-6; 13:29-31; 17:1). Invaded and taken by Hazael, king of Syria (2Ki 10:32-33). Retaken by Jehoash (2Ki 13:25). Fertility and productivity of (Isa 33:9; Jer 50:19; Na 1:4). Forests of famous (Isa 2:13; Eze 27:6; Zec 11:2). Distinguished for its fine cattle (Dt 32:14; Ps 22:12; Eze 39:18; Am 4:1; Mic 7:14).
 See Argob; Ashtoreth; Edrei; Jair.

BASHAN-HAVOTH-JAIR *See Havvoth Jair.*

BASHEMATH, BASMATH *See Basemath.*

BASIC PRINCIPLES OF THIS WORLD Legalism and human traditions opposed to faith in Christ (Gal 4:3; Col 2:8, 20). *See Commandments and Statutes, of Men; Legalism.*

BASIN Made of gold (1Ki 7:50; 1Ch 28:17; 2Ch 4:8, 22; Ezr 1:10; 8:27), bronze (Ex 27:3; 38:3; 1Ki 7:45).
 See Bronze Basin; Bronze Sea; Tabernacle.

BASKET (Ge 40:16-17; Ex 29:3, 23, 32; Lev 8:2; Nu 6:15; Dt 26:2; 28:5, 17; 2Ki 10:7). Received the fragments after the miracles of the loaves (Mt 14:20; 15:37; 16:9-10). Paul let down from the wall in (Ac 9:25; 2Co 11:33).

BASON *See Basin.*

BASTARD *See Illegitimate.*

BAT Unclean for food (Lev 11:19; Dt 14:18; Isa 2:20).

BATH
 1. Bathing for physical cleanliness or refreshment is not often mentioned in the Bible, where most references to bathing are to partial washing. Bathing in the Bible stands primarily for ritual acts—purification of ceremonial defilement (Ex 30:19-21; Lev 16:4, 24; Mk 7:3-4).
 2. A Hebrew measure for liquids, containing about six gallons or twenty-two liters (1Ki 7:26, 38; Ezr 7:22; Isa 5:10; Eze 45:10-11, 14). *See Measure.*

BATH RABBIM (*daughter of a multitude*). A gate in the city of Heshbon (SS 7:4).

BATHSHEBA (*seventh daughter* or *daughter of an oath*). Wife of Uriah and later wife of David. Also spelled Bathshua (1Ch 3:5, ftn). Adultery of (2Sa 11:2-5). Solomon's mother (1Ki 1:11-31; 2:13-21; 1Ch 3:5).

BATHSHUA (possibly *daughter of opulence* BDB).
 1. The daughter of Shua (Ge 38:2; 1Ch 2:3).
 2. See Bathsheba.

BATTERING RAM (2Sa 20:15; Eze 4:2; 21:22).

BATTERY *See Assault and Battery.*

BATTLE Shouting in (Jdg 7:20; 1Sa 17:20). Priests in (2Ch 13:12). Prayer before: by Asa (2Ch 14:11), Jehoshaphat (2Ch 20:3-12). *See Armies; War.*

BATTLE OF LIFE

Ancient Heroes:
 Joshua (Jos 11:23). Gideon (Jdg 7:14). Jonathan (1Sa 14:6). David (1Sa 17:45). Elisha (2Ki 6:17). Jehoshaphat (2Ch 20:20).

The Spiritual Conflict:
 An inward battle (Ro 7:23). Spiritual weapons (2Co 10:4). Invisible foes (Eph 6:12). Young soldiers enlisted (1Ti 1:18). A fight of faith (1Ti 6:12). Demands entire consecration (2Ti 2:4).

The Soul's Enemies:
 (Ps 86:14; Jer 2:34; 18:20; Eze 13:18; 22:25; Lk 22:31; Eph 6:12; 1Pe 5:8).

Weapons and Armor:
 (1Sa 17:45; 2Co 10:4; Eph 6:17; Heb 4:12; Rev 12:11).

Divine Protection:
 Promised to believers (2Ch 16:9; Ps 34:7; 91:4; 125:2; Zec 2:5; Lk 21:18).

Examples of:
 (Ge 35:5; Ex 14:20; 2Ki 6:17; Ezr 8:31; Da 6:22; Rev 7:3).

The Victory:
 (Isa 53:12; Mt 12:20; Jn 16:33; 1Co 15:24; Rev 3:21; 6:2; 17:14).

BATTLE-AX *See Club.*

BATTLEMENTS Parapets on the tops of walls (Isa 54:11).

BAVAI *See Binnui, 1.*

BAY TREE NIV "tree" (Ps 37:35). *See Tree.*

BAZLUTH One of the temple servants (Ezr 2:52; Ne 7:54).

BDELLIUM See Aromatic Resin; Minerals of the Bible.

BE ESHTARAH A Levitical city (Jos 21:27). Called Ashtaroth (1Ch 6:71).

BEACON NIV "flagstaff" (Isa 30:17). See Ensign; Standard.

BEALIAH (Yahweh is Lord). A Benjamite soldier who joined David at Ziklag (1Ch 12:5).

BEALOTH (feminine plural of Baal "lord" lady). A town in Judah (Jos 15:24).

BEAM Large long piece of timber for use in houses (1Ki 6:9-10; 7:3). Used for impaling (Ezr 6:11). Used in figurative sense by Jesus; NIV "plank" (Mt 7:3; Lk 6:41).

BEANS Part of a simple diet (2Sa 17:28; Eze 4:9).

BEAR, THE

Described as:
Voracious (Da 7:5). Cunning (La 3:10). Cruel (Am 5:19). Often attacks men (2Ki 2:24; Am 5:19). Attacks the flock in the presence of the shepherd (1Sa 17:34). Particularly fierce when deprived of its young (2Sa 17:8; Pr 17:12). Growls when annoyed (Isa 59:11). Miraculously killed by David (1Sa 17:36-37).

Illustrative of:
God in his judgments (La 3:10; Hos 13:8). Peace in the Messianic era (Isa 11:7). Wicked rulers (Pr 28:15). The kingdom of the Medes (Da 7:5). The kingdom of Antichrist (Rev 13:2). A constellation (Job 9:9; 38:32).

BEARD Worn long by Aaron (Ps 133:2), Samson (Jdg 16:17), David (1Sa 21:13; Eze 5:1).
Shaven by Egyptians (Ge 41:14). Untrimmed in mourning (2Sa 19:24). Plucked (Ezr 9:3). Cut (Isa 7:20; 15:2; Jer 41:5; 48:37). Lepers required to shave (Lev 13:29-33; 14:9). Idolatrous practice of marring forbidden (Lev 19:27; 21:5). Beards of David's ambassadors half shaven by the king of the Amorites (2Sa 10:4).

BEAST
1. A mammal, not man, distinguished from birds and fish (Ge 1:29-30).
2. A wild, as distinguished from a domesticated animal (Lev 26:22; Isa 13:21-22).
3. Any of the inferior animals, as distinguished from man (Ps 147:9; Ecc 3:19).
4. Apocalyptic symbol of brute force—sensual, lawless, and God-opposing (Da 7; Rev 13:11-18).

BEATEN WORK Of metals (Ex 25:18; 37:17, 22; Nu 8:4).

BEATING As a punishment (Ex 5:14; Dt 25:3; Mk 13:9; Ac 5:40; 16:22, 37; 18:17; 21:32; 22:19).
See Assault and Battery; Punishment; Scourging.

BEATITUDES (divine favor). A word not found in the English Bible, but meaning either:
1. The joys of heaven.
2. A declaration of blessedness. Beatitudes occur frequently in the OT (Ps 32:1-2; 41:1). The Gospels contain isolated beatitudes by Christ (Mt 11:6; 13:16; Jn 20:29), but the word is most commonly used of those in Mt 5:3-11 and Lk 6:20-22, which set forth the qualities that should characterize his disciples. See Graces; Sermon on the Mount.

BEAUTY Vanity of (Ps 39:11; Pr 6:25; 31:30; Isa 3:24; Eze 16:14; 28:17). Consume away (Ps 39:11; 49:14).

Instances of:
Sarah (Ge 12:11). Rebekah (Ge 24:16). Rachel (Ge 29:17). Joseph (Ge 39:6). Moses (Ex 2:2; Heb 11:23). David (1Sa 16:12, 18). Bathsheba (2Sa 11:2). Tamar (2Sa 13:1). Absalom (2Sa 14:25). Abishag (1Ki 1:4). Vashti (Est 1:11). Esther (Est 2:7).

Spiritual:
(1Ch 16:29; Ps 27:4; 29:2; 45:11; 90:17; 110:3; Eze 16:14; Zec 9:17).

BEAUTY AND BANDS NIV "Favor" and "Union"; staffs representing God's favor and the union of Israel and Judah; broken (Zec 11:7-14).

BEBAI (child). The name of three Jews whose descendants came from exile (Ezr 2:11; 8:11; 10:28; Ne 7:16; 10:15).

BECHER See Beker, Bekerite.

BECORATH (firstborn). Son of Aphiah (1Sa 9:1).

BED Made of: iron (Dt 3:11), ivory (Am 6:4), gold and silver (Est 1:6). Used at meals (Am 6:4). Exempt from execution for debt (Pr 22:27). Perfumed (Pr 7:17).
Figurative (Ps 139:8).

BEDAD (solitary). Father of Hadad (Ge 36:35).

BEDAN (son of judgment).
1. In 1Sa 12:11 See Barak.
2. Son of Ulam (1Ch 7:17).

BEDEIAH (servant of Yahweh). A son of Bani who had taken a foreign wife (Ezr 10:35).

BEE In Israel (Dt 1:44; Jdg 14:8; Ps 118:12; Isa 7:18). Figurative of the Assyrians summoned for judgment (Isa 7:18). See Honey.

BEELIADA (the lord [Baal] knows). Son of David (1Ch 14:7). Called Eliada (2Sa 5:16; 1Ch 3:8).

BEELZEBUB (lord of the flies). The prince of demons (Mt 10:25; 12:24, 27; Mk 3:22; Lk 11:15, 18-19). See Baal-Zebub.

BEELZEBUL See Baal-Zebub.

BEER (as a place name cistern, well).
1. A stopping place of the Israelites (Nu 21:16-18).
2. A town in the tribe of Judah (Jdg 9:21).
3. A fermented, intoxicating beverage; its abuse condemned (1Sa 1:15; Pr 20:1; 31:4-6; Isa 28:7; 56:12; Mic 2:11). See Abuse, Substance Abuse; Drunkenness; Fermented Drink; Wine.

BEER ELIM (cistern, well of Elim).
A city of Moab (Isa 15:8).

BEER LAHAI ROI (well that belongs to the Living One seeing me).
A well, probably near Kadesh, where the Lord appeared to Hagar (Ge 16:7, 14) and where Isaac lived for some time (Ge 24:62; 25:11).

BEERA (cistern, well). Son of Zophah (1Ch 7:37).

BEERAH (cistern, well). A Reubenite (1Ch 5:6).

BEERI (/my] cistern, well).
1. A Hittite (Ge 26:34). See Anah.
2. Father of Hosea (Hos 1:1).

BEEROTH, BEEROTHITE (cisterns, wells).
1. NIV "wells" (Dt 10:6). See Bene Jaakan.
2. A city of the Hivites (Jos 9:17; 18:25; 2Sa 4:2; Ezr 2:25; Ne 7:29).
3. Inhabitants of Beeroth (2Sa 4:2, 5, 9; 23:37).

BEERSHEBA (the seventh well).
1. The most southern city of Israel (Jdg 20:1). Named by Abraham, who dwelt there (Ge 21:31-33; 22:19). The dwelling place of Isaac (Ge 26:23). Jacob went out from, toward Haran (Ge 28:10). Sacrifices offered at, by Jacob when traveling to Egypt (Ge 46:1). In the inheritance of Judah (Jos 15:20, 28; 2Sa 24:7). Afterward assigned to Simeon (Jos 19:2, 9; 1Ch 4:28). Two sons of Samuel were judges at (1Sa 8:2). Became a seat of idolatrous worship (Am 5:5; 8:14).
2. Well of, belonged to Abraham and Isaac (Ge 21:25-26).
3. Wilderness of, Hagar miraculously sees a well in (Ge 21:14-19). An angel fed Elijah in (1Ki 19:5, 7).

BEETLE NIV "cricket" (Lev 11:22). See Insects.

BEGGAR Set among princes (1Sa 2:8). Not the seed of the righteous (Ps 37:25). The children of the wicked (Ps 109:10; Pr 20:4; Lk 16:3).
Instances of: Bartimaeus (Mk 10:46), Lazarus (Lk 16:20-22), the blind man (Jn 9:8), the lame man (Ac 3:2-5).
See Poor.

BEHEADING Execution by: John the Baptist (Mt 14:10; Mk 6:27), James (Ac 12:2), martyrs (Rev 20:4). See Punishment.

BEHEMOTH The word is a Hebrew plural and means "beast par excellence," referring to a large land animal, possibly the hippopotamus or the elephant (Job 40:15, ftn). Much of the language used to describe it in vv. 16-24 is highly poetic and hyperbolic (Job 40:15-24).

BEKA A half shekel (Ex 38:26). See Measure.

BEKER, BEKERITE (young male camel).
1. Son of Benjamin (Ge 46:21; 1Ch 7:6, 8).
2. A family of Ephraim (Nu 26:35). Called Bered (1Ch 7:20).

BEL (Babylonian deity Bel). A Babylonian god (Isa 46:1; Jer 50:2; 51:44).

BELA, BELAITE (swallower, devourer).
1. A city called also Zoar (Ge 14:2, 8).
2. King of Edom (Ge 36:32-33; 1Ch 1:43-44).
3. Son of Benjamin (Ge 46:21; Nu 26:38, 40; 1Ch 7:6-7; 8:1, 3).
4. Son of Azaz (1Ch 5:8).

BELIAL (wicked, without use). A word meaning "worthlessness," "wickedness," "lawlessness" translated as a proper noun in the KJV (Dt 13:13; Jdg 19:22; 1Sa 25:25). Personified (2Co 6:15). See Base Fellows; Wicked.

BELIEVER See Righteous.

BELIEVING See Faith.

BELLOWS Used with the refiner's furnace (Jer 6:29).

BELLS Attached to the hem of the priest's robe (Ex 28:33-34; 39:25-26). On horses (Zec 14:20).

BELLY Used figuratively for the seat of the affections (Job 15:2, 35; 20:20; Ps 44:25; Pr 18:20; 20:27, 30; Hab 3:16; Jn 7:38; Tit 1:12).

BELOVED DISCIPLE Probably the apostle John (Jn 13:23; 19:26; 20:2; 21:7, 20).

BELSHAZZAR (Bel protect the king). King of Babylon (Da 5:1-30).

BELT Made of leather (2Ki 1:8; Mt 3:4), linen (Jer 13:1), gold (Da 10:5). Warrior's belt, used to bear arms (2Sa 18:11; 20:8), Jonathan gives his to David (1Sa 18:4).
Figurative (Isa 11:5; Eph 6:14).
Symbolic (Jer 13:1-11; Ac 21:11; Rev 15:6). See Dress; Sash.

BELTESHAZZAR (protect his life). His Hebrew name was Daniel. He was taken as a captive to Babylon with Hananiah, Mishael, and Azariah, where each one was given a Babylonian name (Da 1:6-20; 2:17, 49; 3:12-30). Daniel was given the name Belteshazzar. See Daniel.

BEMA See Judgment Seat.

BEN Hebrew word meaning "son" or "descendant"; possibly the name of a Levite (1Ch 15:18, ftn).

BEN-ABINADAB (son of Abinadab). See Abinadab.

BEN-AMMI (son of my people). Son of one of Lot's daughters; progenitor of Ammonites (Ge 19:38).

BEN-DEKER (son of Deker [pierces]). The father of one of Solomon's suppliers (1Ki 4:9).

BEN-GEBER (son of strength). See Geber.

BEN-HADAD (son of Hadad).
1. King of Syria (1Ki 15:18-20; 2Ch 16:2-4).
2. A king of Syria, who reigned in the time of Ahab, son of Ben-Hadad I (1Ki 20; 2Ki 5-7; 8:7-15).
3. Son of Hazael and king of Syria (2Ki 13:3, 24-25; Am 1:4).

BEN-HAIL (son of strength). A prince of Judah (2Ch 17:7).

BEN-HANAN (son of grace). A son of Shimon (1Ch 4:20).

BEN-HESED (loyal love). Father of one of Solomon's officers (1Ki 4:10).

BEN HINNOM (valley of the son [or sons] of Hinnom). A valley on the W and SW of Jerusalem which formed part of the border between Judah and Benjamin (Jos 15:8; 18:16; Ne 11:30-31). It later became the place of pagan sacrifice (2Ch 28:3; 33:6; Jer 32:35). Josiah defiled it by making it the city dump, where fires were kept constantly burning to consume the refuse (2Ki 23:10). Jewish apocalyptic writers called it the entrance to hell, and it became a figure of hell itself. Jesus used the term gehenna (NIV "hell") in this sense (Mt 5:22; 18:9; 23:15).
See Hades; Hell; Hinnom, Valley of; Topheth, Tophet.

BEN-HUR (son of Hur). See Hur, 4.

BEN-ONI (son of my sorrow). Name given Benjamin by Rachel (Ge 35:18). See Benjamin.

BEN-ZOHETH (son of Zoheth). Son of Ishi (1Ch 4:20).

BENAIAH (Yahweh has built).
1. Son of Jehoiada, commander of the Kerethites and Pelethites (2Sa 8:18; 1Ki 1:38). A distinguished warrior (2Sa 23:20-23; 1Ch 11:22-25; 27:5-6). Loyal to Solomon (1Ki 1:8, 10; 4:4).
2. An Ephraimite and distinguished warrior (2Sa 23:30; 1Ch 11:31; 27:14).
3. A Levitical musician (1Ch 15:18, 20; 16:5).
4. A priest (1Ch 15:24; 16:6).
5. Son of Jeiel (2Ch 20:14).
6. A Levite in time of Hezekiah (2Ch 31:13).
7. A chief of the Simeonites (1Ch 4:36).
8. Son of Parosh (Ezr 10:25).
9. Son of Pahath-Moab (Ezr 10:30).
10. Son of Bani (Ezr 10:35).
11. Son of Nebo (Ezr 10:43).
12. Father of Pelatiah (Eze 11:1, 13).

BENCHES Of those selling doves in the temple (Mt 21:12; Mk 11:15).

BENE BERAK (sons of Barak [lightning]). A city of Dan (Jos 19:45).

BENE JAAKAN (possibly son of Jaakan). A tribe that gave its name to certain wells in the wilderness (Nu 33:31-32; Dt 10:6). See Jaakan, Jaakanites.

BENEDICTIONS (pronouncements of blessing). Divinely appointed (Dt 10:8; 21:5; Nu 6:23-26).

By God:
Upon creatures he had made (Ge 1:22), mankind (Ge 1:28), Noah (Ge 9:1-2).

Instances of:
By Melchizedek upon Abraham (Ge 14:19-20; Heb 7:7). By Bethuel's household upon Rebekah (Ge 24:60). By Isaac upon Jacob (Ge 27:23-29, 37; 28:1-4), Esau (Ge 27:39-40). By Jacob upon Pharaoh (Ge 47:7-10), Joseph's sons (Ge 48), his own sons (Ge 49). By Moses upon the tribes of Israel (Dt 33). By Aaron (Lev 9:22-23), half the tribes who stood on Mt. Gerizim (Dt 11:29-30; 27:11-13; Jos 8:33). By Joshua upon Caleb (Jos 14:13), the Reubenites and Gadites, and the half tribe of Manasseh (Jos 22:6-7). By Naomi upon Ruth and Orpah (Ru 1:8-9). By the elders and people upon Ruth (Ru 4:11-12). By Eli upon Ruth (1Sa 1:17), upon Elkanah (1Sa 2:20). By David upon the people (2Sa 6:18), upon Barzillai (2Sa 19:39). By Araunah upon David (2Sa 24:23). By Solomon upon the people (1Ki 8:14, 55-58; 2Ch 6:3).
By Simeon upon Jesus (Lk 2:34). By Jesus (Lk 24:50).

Levitical: (Nu 6:23-26).

Apostolic: (Ro 1:7; 15:5, 13, 33; 16:20; 1Co 1:3; 16:23; 2Co 1:2; 13:14; Gal 1:3; 6:16, 18; Eph 1:2; 6:23-24; Php 1:2; 4:23; Col 1:2; 1Th 1:1; 5:23; 2Th 1:2; 3:16, 18; 1Ti 1:2; 6:21; 2Ti 1:2; 4:22; Tit 3:15; Phm 3, 25; Heb 13:20-21, 25; 1Pe 1:2; 5:10-11, 14; 2Pe 1:2-4; 2Jn 3; Jude 2; Rev 22:21).

BENEFACTOR A title of honor bestowed by ancient states upon those famous for notable deeds of benevolence (Lk 22:25).

B

BENEFICENCE (*goodness, kindness*).
Commanded:
(Lev 25:35-43; Dt 15:7-15, 18; Pr 3:27-28; 25:21-22; Mt 5:42; 19:21; 25:35-45; Mk 10:21; Lk 3:11; Ro 15:27; 1Co 13:3; 16:1-3; 2Co 8:7-15, 24; 9:1-15; Gal 2:10; 1Ti 5:8, 16; Heb 13:16; Jas 2:15-16; 1Jn 3:17).
Results:
Blessed (Ps 41:1; Pr 22:9). Rewarded (Ps 112:9; Pr 11:25; 28:27; Isa 58:6-11; Eze 18:5-9; Mt 19:21; Mk 9:41; 10:21; Heb 6:10).
Examples:
(Mt 25:35-45; Ac 11:29-30; Ro 15:25-27; 2Co 8:1-15; Php 4:10-18; 1Ti 6:18).
See Alms; Liberality; Poor, Duty to; Rich, The; Riches.
Instances of:
The old man of Gibeah (Jdg 19:16-21). Boaz (Ru 2). The Jews returned from Exile (Ne 5:8-12; 8:10-11). Job (Job 29:11-17; 31:16-23). The Temanites (Isa 21:14). The good Samaritan (Lk 10:33-35). Zacchaeus (Lk 19:8). The first Christians (Ac 2:44-46; 4:32-37). Cornelius (Ac 10:2, 4). Onesiphorus (2Ti 1:16-18).
See Alms; Poor, Duties to.

BENEVOLENCE *See Alms; Beneficence; Charitableness; Liberality; Love.*

BENINU (*our son*). A Levite (Ne 10:13).

BENJAMIN, BENJAMITE(S) (*son of [the] right hand* BDB; *southerner* KB).
1. Son of Jacob by Rachel (Ge 35:18, 24; 46:19). Taken into Egypt (Ge 42-45). Prophecy concerning (Ge 49:27). Descendants of (Ge 46:21; Nu 26:38-41).
2. Tribe of. Census of, at Sinai (Nu 1:37), in the plain of Moab (Nu 26:41). Clans of (Nu 26:38-40; 1Ch 7:6-12; 8:1). Position of, in camp and march (Nu 2:18, 22). Moses' benediction upon (Dt 33:12). Allotment in the land of Canaan (Jos 18:11-28). Reallotment (Eze 48:23). Did not exterminate the Jebusites (Jdg 1:21). Join Deborah in the war against Sisera (Jdg 5:14). Territory of, invaded by the Ammonites (Jdg 10:9). Did not avenge the crime of the Gibeonites against the Levite's concubine, the war that followed (Jdg 19-20). Saul, the first king of Israel, from (1Sa 9:1, 17; 10:20-21). Its rank in the time of Samuel (1Sa 9:21). Jerusalem within the territory of (Jer 6:1). A company of, joins David at Ziklag (1Ch 12:1-2, 16). Not enrolled by Joab when he took a census of the military forces of Israel (1Ch 21:6). Loyal to Ish-Bosheth, the son of Saul (2Sa 2:9, 15, 31; 1Ch 12:29). Subsequently joins David (2Sa 3:19; 19:16-17). Loyal to Rehoboam (1Ki 12:21; 2Ch 11:1). Military forces of, in the reign of Asa (2Ch 14:8), of Jehoshaphat (2Ch 17:17). Skill in archery and as slingers of stones (Jdg 3:15; 20:16; 1Ch 8:40; 12:2). Return to Israel from the Exile in Babylon (Ezr 1:5). Saints of, seen in John's vision (Rev 7:8). Paul, of the tribe of (Ro 11:1; Php 3:5).
See Israel.
3. Grandson of Benjamin (1Ch 7:10).
4. A son of Harim (Ezr 10:32). Probably identical with the man mentioned in Ne 3:23.
5. A Jew who assisted in purifying the wall of Jerusalem (Ne 12:34).
6. A gate of Jerusalem (Jer 20:2; 37:13; 38:7; Zec 14:10).

BENO (*his son*). A descendant of Merari (1Ch 24:26-27).

BENOTH *See Succoth Benoth.*

BEON A place E of Jordan, probably the same as Baal Meon (Nu 32:3, 38). *See Baal Meon.*

BEOR (perhaps *a burning*).
1. Father of Bela (Ge 36:32; 1Ch 1:43).
2. Father of Balaam (Nu 22:5; 24:3, 15; 31:8; Dt 23:4; Jos 13:22; 24:9; Mic 6:5; 2Pe 2:15).

BERA (*gift*). King of Sodom, defeated by Kedorlaomer in the days of Abraham (Ge 14:2, 8).

BERACAH (*blessing*).
1. An Israelite, who joined David at Ziklag (1Ch 12:3).
2. A valley in the S of Judah, where Jehoshaphat assembled the Israelites to offer praise to God for victory over the Ammonites and Moabites (2Ch 20:26). Between Bethlehem and Hebron.

BERACHIAH, BERECHIAH *See Berekiah.*

BERAIAH (*Yahweh creates*). Son of Shimei (1Ch 8:21).

BERAK *See Bene Berak.*

BEREA, BEREANS A city in the S of Macedonia (Ac 17:10, 13; 20:4). Its inhabitants are important as an example of comparing new teaching to the received Scriptures.

BEREAVEMENT From God (Hos 9:12). Mourning in, forbidden to Aaron, on account of his son's wickedness (Lev 10:6). To Ezekiel, for his wife (Eze 24:16-18).
Instances of:
Abraham, of Sarah (Ge 23:2). Jacob, of Joseph (Ge 37:34-35). Joseph, of his father (Ge 50:1, 4). The Egyptians, of their firstborn (Ex 12:29-33). Naomi, of her husband (Ru 1:3, 5, 20-21). David, of his child by Bathsheba (2Sa 12:15-23), of Absalom (2Sa 18:33; 19:4).
Resignation in:
Job (Job 1:18-21). David (2Sa 12:22, 30). Solomon (Ecc 7:2-4). Christians (1Th 4:13-18).
See Affliction, Consolation Under; Prayer Under; Resignation.

BERED (possibly *freezing rain*).
1. A town in the S of Israel (Ge 16:14).
2. A son of Shuthelah (1Ch 7:20). Probably the same as Beker (Nu 26:35).

BEREKIAH (*Yahweh blesses*).
1. Father of Asaph (1Ch 6:39; 15:17, 23).
2. A warrior of Ephraim (2Ch 28:12).
3. A brother of Zerubbabel (1Ch 3:20).
4. Son of Asa (1Ch 9:16).
5. Son of Iddo, father of Zechariah (Zec 1:1, 7; Mt 23:35).
6. Son of Meshullam (Ne 3:4, 30; 6:18).

BERI (*wisdom*). Son of Zophah (1Ch 7:36).

BERIAH, BERIITE (*prominent, excellent*).
1. Son of Asher (Ge 46:17; 1Ch 7:30) and his clan (Nu 26:44-45).
2. Son of Ephraim (1Ch 7:20-23).
3. A Benjamite (1Ch 8:13).
4. Son of Shimei (1Ch 23:10-11).

BERITES (*choice young men*). Followed Sheba in his rebellion against David (2Sa 20:14).

BERITH *See Baal-Berith.*

BERNICE (*victorious*). Daughter of Agrippa (Ac 25:13, 23; 26:30).

BERODACH-BALADAN *See Merodach-Baladan.*

BEROTHAH (*well*). Part of the northern boundary of Canaan (Eze 47:16).

BEROTHAI, BEROTHITE A city of Zobah (2Sa 8:8) and its inhabitants (1Ch 11:39).

BERYL (*yellow jasper*).
1. Set in the priestly breastplate (Ex 28:17; 39:10).
2. A precious stone (Eze 28:13).
3. John saw, in the foundation of the new Jerusalem (Rev 21:20).
See Minerals of the Bible, 1; Stones.

BESAI (*in secret council of Yahweh* KB). One of the temple servants (Ezr 2:49; Ne 7:52).

BESODEIAH (*in secret council of Yahweh*). Father of Meshullam (Ne 3:6).

BESOM *See Broom.*

BESOR A brook near Gaza (1Sa 30:9-10, 21).

BESTIALITY (*Sexual relations between a human and an animal*). (Ex 22:19; Lev 18:23; 20:16).

BETAH *See Tebah, 2.*

BETEN (*womb, bowels*). A city of Asher (Jos 19:25).

BETH The most common OT word for house, family or dynasty. Used in the more than fifty place names that follow.

BETH ANATH (*house of Anath*). A fortified city of Naphtali (Jos 19:38; Jdg 1:33).

BETH ANOTH (*house of Anath [plural]*). A city in Judah (Jos 15:59).

BETH ARABAH (*house of Arabah [desert plain]*). A city in the valley of the Dead Sea (Jos 15:6, 61; 18:22). Called Arabah (Jos 18:18).

BETH-ARAM *See Beth Haram.*

BETH ARBEL (*house of Arbel*). A city devastated by Shalman (Hos 10:14).

BETH ASHBEA (*house of Ashbea*). A descendant of Shelah (1Ch 4:21).

BETH AVEN (*house of idolatry*). A place on the mountains of Benjamin (Jos 7:2; 18:12; 1Sa 13:5; 14:23; Hos 4:15; 5:8; 10:5).

BETH AZMAVETH (*strong of death* ISBE; *house of Azmaveth [camel fodder, a plant of the plumose family]* KB). A town of Benjamin (Ne 7:28). Called Azmaveth (Ne 12:29; Ezr 2:24).

BETH BAAL MEON (*house of Baal Meon*). A place in the tribe of Reuben (Jos 13:17).
Called Baal Meon (Nu 32:38; Eze 25:9), Beon (Nu 32:3), Beth Meon (Jer 48:23).
Subdued by the Israelites (Nu 32:3-4). Assigned to the Reubenites (Jos 13:17).

BETH BARAH (*house of Barah [the river ford]*). A city E of the Jordan (Jdg 7:24).

BETH BIRI (*house of Biri* or *den of a lioness*). A town of Simeon S of Judah (1Ch 4:31). *See Beth Lebaoth.*

BETH CAR (*site [house] of a lamb*). A place W of Mizpah (1Sa 7:11).

BETH DAGON (*temple [house] of Dagon*).
1. A city of Judah (Jos 15:41).
2. A city of Asher (Jos 19:27).

BETH DIBLATHAIM (*house of Diblathaim*). A city of Moab (Jer 48:22). *See Almon Diblathaim.*

BETH EDEN (*house of Eden; garden place*). Probably another name for Damascus (Am 1:5). *See Damascus.*

BETH EKED Forty-two relatives of Ahaziah slaughtered there (2Ki 10:12-14).

BETH EMEK (*house of Emek* or *site of the valley*). A city of Asher (Jos 19:27).

BETH EZEL (*house of Ezel* or *site nearby*). A town of Judah (Mic 1:11).

BETH GADER (*house of Gader* or *site of a stone hedge*). A place in Judah (1Ch 2:51). Probably identical with Geder (Jos 12:13); and with Gedor (Jos 15:58).

BETH GAMUL (*house of recompense*). A city of Moab (Jer 48:23).

BETH GILGAL Perhaps an alternate name for Gilgal (Ne 12:29). *See Gilgal.*

BETH-HACCEREM *See Beth Hakkerem.*

BETH HAGGAN (*house of Haggan* or *site of the garden*). A garden house (2Ki 9:27). Probably identical with En Gannim (Jos 19:21).

BETH HAKKEREM (*house of Hakkerem* or *site of the vineyard*). A mountain in Judah (Ne 3:14; Jer 6:1).

BETH HARAM A fortified city of Gad, E of the Jordan (Jos 13:27).

BETH HARAN (*house of the mountaineer*). A fortified city E of Jordan (Nu 32:36).

BETH HOGLAH (*house of Hoglah* or *site of the partridge*). A place on the border of Judah (Jos 15:6; 18:19, 21).

BETH HORON (*house of Horon* or *site of a ravine*). Two ancient cities of Canaan, near which Joshua defeated the Amorites (Jos 10:10-11; 16:3, 5; 18:13-14; 1Sa 13:18; 1Ch 7:24). Solomon builds (1Ki 9:17; 2Ch 8:5). Taken from Judah by the ten tribes (2Ch 25:13).

BETH JESHIMOTH (*house of Jeshimoth* or *site of desolation*). A place in the plains of Moab, the S limit of Israel's encampment (Nu 33:49). It was assigned to the Reubenites (Jos 13:20), but was later in Moabite possession (Eze 25:9). Modern Tell el-Azeimeh, about twelve miles SE of Jericho (Jos 12:3).

BETH JOAB *See Atroth Beth Joab.*

BETH LEBAOTH (*house of Lebaoth* or *den of the lioness*). A town of Simeon in the S part of Judah (Jos 19:6). Called Lebaoth (Jos 15:32), and the same as Beth Biri (1Ch 4:31).

BETH-LEHEM-JUDAH *See Bethlehem; Judah.*

BETH-MAACHAH (*house of Maacah*). *See Abel Beth Maacah.*

BETH MARCABOTH (*site [house] of Marcaboth [chariots]*). A town of Simeon (Jos 19:5; 1Ch 4:31). Probably identical with Madmannah, which may have been its older name (Jos 15:31).

BETH MEON (*house of habitation*). A city of Moab (Jer 48:23); the same as Beth Baal Meon (Jos 13:17).

BETH MILLO (*house of Millo* or *site of earth fill*).
1. Beth Millo probably refers to the earthen fill used to erect a platform on which walls and other large structures were built (Jdg 9:6, 20). It may be identical with the "stronghold" of v. 46 (Jdg 9:46).
2. A name given to part of the citadel of Jerusalem, NIV "supporting terraces" (2Sa 5:9, ftn; 1Ch 11:8, ftn). King Solomon raised a levy to repair (1Ki 9:15, 24, ftn; 11:27, ftn). King Joash murdered at (2Ki 12:20). Repaired by King Hezekiah (2Ch 32:5, ftn).

BETH NIMRAH (*house of Nimrah [spotted leopard]* BDB; *house of a basin of clear, limpid water* KB). A fortified city E of Jordan (Nu 32:36; Jos 13:27).

BETH OPHRAH (*house of Ophrah* or *house of dust*). A city found in the Shephelah (Mic 1:10, ftn).

BETH-PALET *See Beth Pelet.*

BETH PAZZEZ A city in Issachar (Jos 19:21).

BETH PELET (*house of Pelet [escape]*). A city in Judah (Jos 15:27; Ne 11:26).

BETH PEOR (*house of Peor*). A place in the tribe of Reuben (Dt 3:29; 4:46; 34:6). Near the burial place of Moses (Jos 13:20).

BETH RAPHA (*house of Rapha [healing]*). Son of Eshton (1Ch 4:12).

BETH REHOB (*house of Rehob [main street, market]*). A place in Dan (Jdg 18:28; 2Sa 10:6). Called Rehob.

BETH SHAN (*site [house] of Shan [repose]*). A city of Manasseh (Jos 17:11; 1Ch 7:29). Not subdued (Jdg 1:27). Bodies of Saul and his sons exposed in (1Sa 31:10, 12). District of, under tribute to Solomon's governor (1Ki 4:12).

BETH-SHEAN *See Beth Shan.*

BETH SHEMESH (*temple [house] of Shemesh [pagan sun god]*).
1. A priestly city of Dan (Jos 21:16; 1Sa 6:15; 1Ch 6:59). On the northern border of Judah (Jos 15:10; 1Sa 6:9, 12). In later times transferred to Judah (2Ki 14:13). Mentioned in Solomon's governed districts (1Ki 4:9). Amaziah taken prisoner at (2Ki 14:11-13; 2Ch 25:21-23). Retaken by the Philistines (2Ch 28:18). Called Ir Shemesh (Jos 19:41).
2. A city near Jerusalem (Jos 19:22).

3. A fortified city of Naphtali (Jos 19:38; Jdg 1:33).

4. Literally "Beth Shemesh in Egypt," with the qualifying phrase being used to distinguish it from "Beth Shemesh in Judah" (2Ki 14:11). Called On (in Hebrew) in Egypt; also known as Heliopolis, about five miles NE of Cairo, where there was a temple of Ra (Jer 43:13, ftn).

BETH SHITTAH (*house of Shittah [acacias]*). A place near the Jordan (Jdg 7:22).

BETH TAPPUAH (*house of Tappuah [apricot;apple tree]*). A town of Judah (Jos 15:53).

BETH TOGARMAH A city in E Asia Minor (Eze 27:14; 38:6). See *Togarmah*.

BETH ZUR (*cliff house*). A town in Judah (Jos 15:58; 1Ch 2:45; 2Ch 11:7; Ne 3:16).

BETHANY (*house of Ananiah* or *poor ones* or *unripe figs*). A village on the eastern slope of the Mount of Olives (Jn 11:18). Mary, Martha, and Lazarus dwell at (Lk 10:38-41). Lazarus dies and is raised to life at (Jn 11). Jesus attends a feast in (Mt 26:6-13; Jn 12:1-9). The colt on which Jesus made his triumphal entry into Jerusalem obtained at (Mk 11:1-11). Jesus stays at (Mt 21:17; Mk 11:11-12, 19).

BETHEL (*temple [house] of God [El]*).

1. A city N of Jerusalem. The ancient city next to, and finally embraced in, was called Luz (Jos 18:13; Jdg 1:23-26). Abraham establishes an altar at (Ge 12:8; 13:3-4). The place where Jacob saw the vision of the stairway (Ge 28:10-22; 31:13; Hos 12:4), and builds an altar at (Ge 35:1-15). Deborah dies at (Ge 35:8). Conquered by Joshua (Jos 8:17, w 12:16), by the house of Joseph (Jdg 1:22-26). Allotted to Benjamin (Jos 18:13, 22). Court of justice held at, by Deborah (Jdg 4:5), by Samuel (1Sa 7:16).

Tabernacle at, and called House of God (Jdg 20:18, 31; 21:2). Jeroboam institutes idolatrous worship at (1Ki 12:25-33; 2Ki 10:29). Idolatry at (Jer 48:13; Am 4:4). Shalmaneser sends a priest to (2Ki 17:27-28). Prophecies against the idolatrous altars at (1Ki 13:1-6, 32; 2Ki 23:4, 15-20; Am 3:14). The company of prophets at (2Ki 2:3). Children of, mock Elisha (2Ki 2:23-24). People of, return from Babylon (Ezr 2:28; Ne 7:32). Prophecies against (Am 5:5).

2. A city in the S of Judah (1Sa 30:27).

3. A mountain (1Sa 13:2).

BETHER (perhaps *house [shrine] of the mountain*). Mountains of (SS 2:17, ftn, text "rugged hills").

BETHESDA (*site [house] of mercy*). A spring-fed pool in Jerusalem (Jn 5:1-16) into which the sick went for healing.

BETHHANAN See *Elon Bethhanan*.

BETHLEHEM (*house of bread;* possibly *temple [house] of Lakhmu [pagan deity]*).

1. A city SW of Jerusalem (Jdg 17:7; 19:18). Called Ephrathah and Ephrath (Ge 48:7; Ps 132:6; Mic 5:2), and Bethlehem in Judah (Jdg 17:7-9; 19:1, 18; Ru 1:1; 1Sa 17:12). Rachel dies and is buried at (Ge 35:16, 19; 48:7). The city of Boaz (Ru 1:1, 19; 2:4; 4). Taken and held by the Philistines (2Sa 23:14-16). Jeroboam converts it into a military stronghold (2Ch 11:6). The city of Joseph (Mt 2:5-6; Lk 2:4). Birthplace of Jesus (Mic 5:2; Mt 2; Lk 2:4, 15). Herod slays the children of (Mt 2:16-18).

2. A town of Zebulun, six miles W of Nazareth (Jos 19:15). Israel judged at (Jdg 12:10).

BETHPHAGE (*house of unripe figs*). A village on the Mount of Olives (Mt 21:1; Mk 11:1; Lk 19:29).

BETHSAIDA (*house of fishing*).

1. A city of Galilee. The city of Philip, Andrew, and Peter (Jn 1:44; 12:21). Jesus visits (Mk 6:45), cures a blind man in (Mk 8:22), prophesies against (Mt 11:21; Lk 10:13).

2. Secluded area E of the sea of Galilee; Jesus feeds five thousand people in (Mt 14:13; Mk 6:32; Lk 9:10).

BETHUEL (*man of God [El]*). Son of Nahor, father of Rebekah (Ge 22:22-23; 24:15, 24; 25:20; 28:2, 5).

BETHUL A city of Simeon (Jos 19:4). Called Kesil (Jos 15:30) and Bethuel (1Ch 4:30).

BETONIM (*pistachio nuts*). A town of Gad (Jos 13:26).

BETRAYAL Of Jesus (Mt 26:14-16, 45-50; Mk 14:10-11; Lk 22:3-6; 22:47-48; Jn 13:21). Of others, foretold (Mt 20:18; 24:10). Of David, by Doeg (1Sa 22:9-10, w 1Sa 21:1-10). Of cities (Jdg 1:24-25). See *Confidence, Betrayed*.

BETROTHAL Of Jacob (Ge 29:18-30). Exempts from military duty (Dt 20:7). A quasi-marriage (Mt 1:18; Lk 1:27).

Figurative (Isa 62:4; Hos 2:19-20; 2Co 11:2).

See *Marriage*.

BETTING By Samson (Jdg 14:12-19).

BEULAH (*married*). Poetic name for restored Israel (Isa 62:4).

BEZAI

1. Head of a Jewish family that returned from Babylon (Ezr 2:17; Ne 7:23).

2. A family that sealed the covenant with Nehemiah (Ne 10:18).

BEZALEL (*in the shadow of God [El]*).

1. A divinely inspired architect and master craftsman who built the tabernacle (Ex 31:2; 35:30-35; 36:1; 37:1; 38:1-7, 22).

2. Son of Pahath-Moab (Ezr 10:30).

BEZEK (*scattering, sowing*).

1. Residence of Adoni-Bezek (Jdg 1:5). See *Adoni-Bezek*.

2. A rendezvous of Israel under Saul (1Sa 11:8).

BEZER (*[metallic] ore,* or *place of refuge*).

1. A city of refuge, E of the Jordan (Dt 4:43; Jos 20:8; 21:36; 1Ch 6:78).

2. Son of Zophah (1Ch 7:37).

BIBLE, THE General references to (2Sa 22:31; Ps 12:6; 119:9, 50; 147:15; Mk 12:24; Lk 8:11; Eph 6:17). The Book of the ages (Ps 119:89; Mt 5:18; 24:35; 1Pe 1:25). Food for the soul (Dt 8:3; Job 23:12; Ps 119:103; Jer 15:16; 1Pe 2:2). Divinely inspired (Jer 36:2; Eze 1:3; Ac 1:16; 2Ti 3:16; 2Pe 1:21; Rev 14:13). Precepts written in the heart (Dt 6:6; 11:18; Ps 119:11; Ro 10:8; Col 3:16). Furnishes a light (Ps 19:8; 119:105, 130; Pr 6:23; 2Pe 1:19). Loved by the believers (Ps 119:47, 72, 82, 97, 140; Jer 15:16).

Mighty in its influence: a devouring flame (Jer 5:14), a crushing hammer (Jer 23:29), a life-giving force (Eze 37:7), a saving power (Ro 1:16), a penetrating sword (Eph 6:17; Heb 4:12).

Blessings to those who reverence it (Ps 19:11; Mt 7:24; Lk 11:28; Jn 5:24; 8:31; Rev 1:3). Purifies the life (Ps 119:9; Jn 15:3; 17:17; Eph 5:26; 1Pe 1:22). Written with a purpose (Jn 20:31; Ro 15:4; 1Co 10:11; 1Jn 5:13). The standard of faith (Pr 29:18; Isa 8:20; Jn 12:48; Gal 1:8; 1Th 2:13). Its words sacred (Dt 4:2; 12:32; Pr 30:6; Rev 22:19). The study of it commanded (Dt 17:19; Isa 34:16; Jn 5:39; Ac 17:11; Ro 15:4). Contains seed for the sower (Ps 126:6; Mk 4:14-15; 2Co 9:10). Absolutely trustworthy (Ps 18:56; Ps 111:7; Eze 12:25; Mt 5:18; Lk 21:33). Profitable for instruction (Dt 4:10; 11:19; 2Ch 17:9; Ne 8:13; Isa 2:3). Ignorance of, dangerous (Mt 22:29; Jn 20:9; Ac 13:27; 2Co 3:15).

See *Word of God*.

BICRI (*first born*). Father of Sheba (2Sa 20:1).

BIDKAR (*son of Deker [piercing]*). Jehu's captain (2Ki 9:25).

BIER (2Sa 3:31; Lk 7:14).

BIGAMY See *Polygamy*.

BIGOTRY

Condemned:

Exhibited: In self-righteousness (Isa 65:5; Mk 2:16; Lk 15:2; 18:9-14). In intolerance (Lk 9:49-50; Ac 18:12-13).

Rebuked (Ac 10:28, 45). Paul's argument against (Ro 3:1-23; 4:1-25).

Instances of:

Joshua (Nu 11:27-29). The Jews with, the Samaritans (Jn 4:9, 27), Jesus (Lk 4:28; 7:39; 11:38-39; 15:22; 19:5-7; Jn 5:18), the blind man (Jn 9:29-34), Paul (Ac 21:28-29; 22:22). John (Mk 9:38-40; Lk 9:49-50). James and John (Lk 9:51-56). The early Christians (Ac 10:45; 11:2-3; 15:1-10, 24; Gal 2:3-5). Paul (Ac 9:1-2; 22:3-4; 26:9-11; Gal 1:13-14; Php 3:6).

See *Intolerance; Persecution; Respect of Persons; Uncharitableness*.

BIGTHA (*gift of God*). Eunuch and servant of Xerxes (Est 1:10).

BIGTHANA (*gift of God*). A conspiring Persian officer (Est 2:21-23; 6:2).

BIGVAI (*fortunate*).

1. Man who returned from the Captivity (Ezr 2:2; Ne 7:19).

2. Ancestor of family that returned from the Captivity (Ezr 2:14; Ne 7:19).

3. Probably the same as 2 above (Ezr 8:14).

BILDAD (*Bel has loved*). One of Job's friends (Job 2:11; 8:1; 18:1; 25:1).

BILEAM (*[a gift] brought to the people*). A town of Manasseh (1Ch 6:70). Called Ibleam (Jos 17:11) and Gath Rimmon (Jos 21:25).

BILGAH (*gleam, smile*).

1. One of the chiefs of the priestly courses in the temple (1Ch 24:14).

2. A priest (Ne 12:5, 18), perhaps identical with Bilgai (Ne 10:8).

BILGAI (*gleam, smile*). A priest (Ne 10:8).

BILHAH (perhaps *simplicity,* or *modesty,* or *to be without concern*).

1. Rachel's servant, bears children by Jacob (Ge 29:29; 30:3-4; 37:2). Mother of Dan and Naphtali (Ge 30:1-8; 35:25; 46:23, 25). Reuben's incest with (Ge 35:22; 49:4).

2. A town in the land of Simeon (1Ch 4:29). Called Balah (Jos 19:3) and Baalah (Jos 15:29).

BILHAN (*foolish*).

1. A Horite chief (Ge 36:27; 1Ch 1:42).

2. A Benjamite (1Ch 7:10).

BILL OF DIVORCE See *Divorce*.

BILSHAN (*their Bel [lord]*). A Jew of the Captivity (Ezr 2:2; Ne 7:7).

BIMHAL (*son of circumcision*). Son of Japhlet (1Ch 7:33).

BINDING AND LOOSING The carrying of a key or keys was a symbol of the delegated power of opening and closing (Mt 16:19; Rev 1:18). See *Key*.

The apostles were given power to bind and to loose (Mt 16:19; 18:18). Peter loosed the feet of the lame man at the temple gate (Ac 3:1-10), and Paul bound the sight of Elymas (Ac 13:8-11). Peter was present when the Holy Spirit was poured out on the Jews (Ac 2), Samaritans (Ac 8:14-17), and Gentiles (Ac 10:34-48).

BINEA A descendant of King Saul (1Ch 8:37; 9:43).

BINNUI (*a son*).

1. Man who helped rebuild walls of Jerusalem (Ne 3:18, ftn).

2. A Jew of the Captivity (Ne 7:15). Called Bani (Ezr 2:10).

3. A Levite of the Captivity (Ne 3:24; 12:8; 10:9).

4. Father of Noadiah (Ezr 8:33).

5. Descendant of Pahath-Moab who married a foreign wife (Ezr 10:30).

6. KJV; NIV "descendants of" (Ezr 10:38).

BIRDS Creation of, on the fifth creative day (Ge 1:20-30). Mankind's rule over (Ge 1:26, 28; 9:2-3; Ps 8:5-8; Jer 27:6; Da 2:38; Jas 3:7). Given for food (Ge 9:2-3; Dt 14:11-20). What species were unclean (Lev 11:13-20; Dt 14:12-19).

Used for sacrifice. See *Dove; Pigeon*. Divine care of (Job 38:41; Ps 147:9; Mt 10:29; Lk 12:6, 24). Songs of, at the break of day (Ps 104:12; Ec 12:4; SS 2:12). Domesticated (Job 41:5; Jas 3:7). Solomon's proverbs of (1Ki 4:33). Nests of (Ps 104:17; Mt 8:20; 13:32). Instincts of (Pr 1:17). Habits of (Job 39:13-18, 26-30). Migrate (Jer 8:7).

Mosaic law protected the mother from being taken with the young (Dt 22:6-7). Cages of (Jer 5:27; Rev 18:2). See *Snare*.

Figurative (Isa 16:2; 46:11; Jer 12:9; Eze 39:4).

Symbolic (Da 7:6).

See *Cormorant; Dove; Eagle; Falcon; Gull; Hawk; Hen, 2; Heron; Hoopoe; Kite; Osprey; Ostrich; Owl; Partridge; Pigeon; Quail; Raven; Red Kite; Screech Owl; Sparrow; Stork; Swallow; Swift; Thrush; Vulture; White Owl*.

BIRSHA (*disagreeable in taste*). A king of Gomorrah (Ge 14:2-10).

BIRTH Pangs in giving (Ps 48:6; Isa 13:8; 21:3; Jer 4:31; 6:24; 30:6; 31:8). Giving, ordained to be in sorrow (Ge 3:16).

Famous births: Cain (Ge 4:1), Abel (Ge 4:2), Noah (Ge 5:28-29), Isaac (Ge 21:1-5), Esau and Jacob (Ge 25:24-26), the children of Jacob (Ge 29:31-30:24; 35:16-18), Moses (Ex 2:1-4), John the Baptist (Lk 1:5-25, 57), Jesus (Mt 1:18-25; Lk 1:26-38; 2:1-20).

See *Abortion; Children*.

BIRTHDAY Celebrated by feasts (Ge 40:20; Mt 14:6). Cursed (Job 3; Jer 20:14, 18).

BIRTHRIGHT

Described:

Belonged to the firstborn (Dt 21:15-16). Entitled the firstborn to a double portion of inheritance (Dt 21:15-17), a royal succession (2Ch 21:3). An honorable title (Ex 4:22; Ps 89:27; Jer 31:9; Ro 8:29; Col 1:15; Heb 1:6; 12:23; Rev 1:5).

Lost by Firstborn:

Sold by Esau (Ge 25:29-34; 27:36, w 25:33; Heb 12:16; Ro 9:12-13). Forfeited by Reuben (1Ch 5:1-2). Set aside: that of Manasseh (Ge 48:15-20), Adonijah (1Ki 2:15), Hosah's son (1Ch 26:10).

See *Firstborn*.

BIRZAITH (*well of olive oil*). A descendant of Asher (1Ch 7:31).

BISHLAM (*son of Shalom [peace]*). A Samaritan who obstructed the rebuilding of the temple at Jerusalem (Ezr 4:7-24).

BISHOP The same as elder or overseer (Ac 20:28; Php 1:1; 1Ti 3:1; Tit 1:7, ftns). See *Elders; Overseer*.

BIT Part of a bridle (Ps 32:9; Jas 3:3).

BITHIAH (possibly *worshiper of Yahweh* BDB; *[female pagan god] queen* KB). Daughter of Pharaoh; wife of Mered of Judah (1Ch 4:18).

BITHRON (*gully*). A district bordering on the Jordan (2Sa 2:29).

BITHYNIA A Roman province in Asia Minor (Ac 16:7; 1Pe 1:1).

BITTER HERBS Eaten symbolically with the Passover (Ex 12:8; Nu 9:11).

BITTER WATER At Marah (Ex 15:23). A ceremonial water used by the priest to determine marital faithfulness (Nu 5:18-27).

BITTERN See *Owl*.

BITTERNESS A poisonous and bitter plant (Hos 10:4; Am 6:12). See *Gall, 3*.

Of spirit (Dt 32:32; Jer 4:18; Ac 8:23; Ro 3:14; Eph 4:31; Heb 12:5; Jas 3:14).

BITUMEN See *Tar*.

BIZIOTHIAH (*contempt of Yahweh*). A town in Judah (Jos 15:28). Baalath Beer (Jos 19:8), and Balah (Jos 19:3).

BIZTHA (perhaps *eunuch,* or *bound*). A eunuch and servant of the Persian king Xerxes (Est 1:10).

BLACK VULTURE An unclean bird, not to be eaten under the law (Lev 11:13; Dt 14:13). See *Vulture*.

BLACKNESS Overcoming the day (Job 3:5). On the day of the LORD (Joel 2:6; Zep 1:15). God turning to dawn (Am 5:8).

See *Colors, Figurative and Symbolic*.

BLACKSMITH See *Smith*.

BLAIN See *Boil*.

BLASPHEMY (*speak against, revile*).

Described:

Reproaching God (2Ki 19:22; 2Ch 32:19; Ps 73:9, 11; 74:18; 139:20; Pr 30:9; Isa 5:19; 8:21-22; 37:23; 45:9; 52:5; Eze

B

35:12-13; Da 7:25; Mt 10:25). Defying God (Isa 29:15-16; 36:15-21; 37:10; Eze 8:12; 9:9; Mal 3:13-14). Denying God's word (Jer 17:15). Speaking lies against God (Hos 7:13). Attributing ignorance to God (Ps 10:11, 13; Isa 40:27). Exalting oneself above God (Da 11:36-37; 2Th 2:4). Calling Jesus accursed (1Co 12:3; Jas 2:7). Against the Holy Spirit (Mt 12:31-32; Mk 3:29-30; Lk 12:10). Occasioned by sins of believers (2Sa 12:14; Ro 2:24).

Foretold by Peter (2Pe 3:3-4). Foretold by John (Rev 13:1, 5-6; 16:9, 11, 21; 17:3).

Forbidden (Ex 20:7; 22:28; Lev 19:12; 22:32; Jas 3:10; 5:12). Punishment for (Lev 24:10-16; Isa 65:7; Heb 10:29).

Instances of:

The depraved son of Shelomith, who, in a fight with an Israelite, cursed God (Lev 24:10-16). Of the Israelites, in grumbling against God (Nu 21:5-6). Infidels who used the adultery of David as an occasion to blaspheme (2Sa 12:14). Shimei, in his malice toward David (2Sa 16:5). One of Sennacherib's field commanders, in the siege of Jerusalem (2Ki 18:22; 19; Isa 36:15-20; 37:10-33). Job's wife, when she exhorted Job to curse God and die (Job 2:9). Israel (Eze 20:27-28). Peter, when accused of being a disciple of Jesus (Mt 26:74; Mk 14:71). The revilers of Jesus, when He was crucified (Mt 27:40-44, 63). The early Christians, persecuted by Saul of Tarsus compelled to blaspheme the name of Jesus (Ac 26:11; 1Ti 1:13). Two disciples, Hymenaeus and Alexander, who were delivered to Satan that they might learn not to blaspheme (1Ti 1:20). Man of sin (2Th 2:3-4). Backslidden Ephesians (Rev 2:9).

False Accusations of:

Against Naboth (1Ki 21:13). Against Jesus (Mt 9:3; 26:65; Mk 2:7; 14:58; Lk 5:21; 22:70-71; Jn 5:18; 10:33; 19:7). Against Stephen (Ac 6:11, 13).

BLAST

1. From God's nostrils, figurative of judgment (Ex 15:8; 2Sa 22:16; Job 4:9; Ps 18:15).

2. From a horn, a call to assemble (Ex 19:13, 16; Lev 23:24) or to battle (Jos 6:5, 16; Job 39:25).

BLASTUS (*sprout [of a vine, branch]*). One of Herod's officers (Ac 12:20).

BLEEDING, SUBJECT TO A woman who had been bleeding for twelve years could not be healed by physicians (Mt 9:20; Mk 5:25; Lk 8:43, ftn). The precise nature of the woman's problem is not known. Her existence was wretched because she was shunned by people generally, since anyone having contact with her was made ceremonially unclean (Lev 15:25-33). Jesus healed her (both physically, "be freed from your suffering," and spiritually, "go in peace"; Mk 5:34) as a result of her simple act of faith.

BLEMISH A physical deformity. Barred sons of Aaron from exercise of priestly offices (Lev 21:17-23). Animals with, forbidden to be used for sacrifice (Lev 22:19-25).

Figurative (Eph 5:27; 1Pe 1:19).

BLESSING For blessing before eating, *See Benedictions; Prayer, Thanksgiving, and Before Taking Food.*

BLESSINGS, SPIRITUAL

From God:

(Dt 33:25, 27; Ps 18:28-36; 29:11; 37:6, 17, 24, 39; 63:8; 66:8-9; 68:18, 28, 35; 84:5, 11; Isa 40:11, 29, 31; 41:10, 13, 16; Ac 3:19; 1Co 2:9; Php 4:13; Jas 1:17; Jude 24).

Guidance (Ge 33:16; Ps 23:2-3; 119:102; Isa 40:11; 58:11).

Sanctification (Ex 31:13; Lev 21:8; Isa 1:25; 4:3-4; 6:6-7; 1Jn 1:9; Jude 1).

The perfecting of salvation (2Co 1:21; Php 1:6; 2:13; 4:19; Col 1:11-12; 1Th 5:24; Heb 13:20-21; 1Pe 1:5; 2Pe 1:2-4).

The deposit of the Spirit, guaranteeing what is to come (2Co 1:22; 5:5).

Peace (Isa 26:12; 57:19; Mal 4:2; Php 4:7).

From Christ:

(Jn 1:16; Ro 1:7; 16:20; 1Co 1:3; 16:23; 2Co 1:2; 13:14; Gal 1:3; 6:16, 18; Eph 1:2; 6:23-24; Php 1:2; 4:23; 1Th 5:28; 2Th 1:2; 3:16, 18; 1Ti 1:2; 2Ti 1:2; Phm 3, 25; 2Pe 1:1; 2Jn 3).

Contingent Upon Obedience; Resulting in:

Divine favor (Jn 19:5; Jer 7:23), mercy (Ex 20:6; Dt 5:10, 16; 7:9; 1Ki 8:23; 2Ch 30:9), holiness (Dt 28:9; 30:1-3, 6; Col 1:22-23), eternal salvation (Mt 10:22; 24:13; Mk 13:13; Heb 3:6, 14; 10:36; Rev 2:10).

See Contingencies; Faithfulness; Regeneration; Salvation.

BLESSINGS, TEMPORAL

From God: (Ps 136:25).

Rain (Dt 11:14; 28:12; Job 37:6; 38:25-27; Ps 68:9; 135:7; 147:8; Jer 10:13; 14:22; 51:16; Joel 2:23; Am 4:7; Zec 10:1, 12; Mt 5:45; Ac 14:17).

Seedtime and harvest (Ge 8:22; Lev 25:20-22; 26:4-5; Ps 107:35-38; Isa 55:10; Jer 5:24; Eze 36:30; Mal 3:11; Ac 14:17).

Food and clothing (Ge 1:3; 28:20-21; Dt 8:3-4; 10:18; 29:5; Ru 1:6; 2Ch 31:10; Ps 65:9; 68:1-10; 81:16; 104:14-15, 27-28; 111:5; 132:15; 145:15-16; 146:7; Ecc 2:24-25; 3:13; Isa 33:15-16; Joel 2:26; Mt 6:26, 30-33; Lk 12:22-31; Jn 6:31).

Preservation of life (Dt 4:1, 40; 5:33; 7:15; Ps 21:4; 23:6; 91:16; 103:2-5; Da 6:20, 22).

Children (Ps 113:9; Ps 127:3-5).

Prosperity (Ge 24:56; 26:24; 49:24-25; Nu 10:29; Dt 8:7-10, 18; 1Sa 2:7-8; 1Ch 29:12, 14, 16; 2Ch 1:12; Ezr 8:22; Ps 147:13-14; Ecc 5:19; Isa 30:23; Hos 2:8).

National greatness (Ge 22:17; 26:3-4; Dt 1:10; 7:13-14; 15:4, 6; 26:18-19; 32:13-14; Job 12:23; Ps 69:35-36; Isa 51:2; Jer 30:19; Eze 36:36-38; Da 5:18), social peace (Lev 26:6; 1Ch 22:9), victory over enemies (Ex 23:22; Lev 26:6-9; Dt 28:7; Ps 44:3), worldly honors (2Sa 7:8-9; 1Ch 17:7-8).

Exemplified to:

Noah at the time of the Flood (Ge 7:1). Abraham (Ge 24:1). Isaac (Ge 26:12-24, 28). Jacob (Ge 35:9-15). Israelites in Egypt (Ex 11:3), in the wilderness, supplying water (Ex 17:1-7; Nu 20:10-11;

Ps 78:15-20; 105:4), manna (Ex 16:14, 31; Nu 11:7-9; Ne 9:15; Ps 78:23-24), quail (Nu 11:31-33; Ps 78:23-30; 105:40). David (2Sa 5:10; 1Ch 14:2). Obed-Edom (2Sa 6:11). Solomon (1Ki 3:13; 1Ch 29:25; 2Ch 1:1). Elijah, fed by ravens (1Ki 17:2-7), by an angel (1Ki 19:5-8). The widow of Zarephath (1Ki 17:12-16). Hezekiah prospered (2Ki 18:6-7; 2Ch 32:29), restored to health (2Ki 20:1-7). Asa (2Ch 14:6-7). Jehoshaphat (2Ch 17:3-5; 20:30). Uzziah (2Ch 26:5-15). Jotham (2Ch 27:6). Job (Job 1:10; 42:10, 12). Daniel (Da 1:9).

Prayer for:

Rain (1Ki 8:36; 2Ch 6:27). Plentiful harvests (Ge 27:28; Dt 26:15; Dt 33:13-16). Daily bread (Mt 6:11; Lk 11:3), prosperity (Ge 28:3-4; 1Ch 4:10; Ne 1:11; 3Jn 2), providential guidance (Ge 24:12-14, 42-44; Ro 1:10; 1Th 3:11).

Instances of Prayer for:

Abraham (Ge 15:2-4). Abraham's servant (Ge 24:12). Laban (Ge 24:60). Isaac (Ge 25:21). Hannah (1Sa 1:11). Elijah (1Ki 17:20-21; 18:42, 44; Jas 5:17-18). Ezra (Ezr 8:21-23). Nehemiah (Ne 1:11; 2:4; 6:9).

Contingent Upon Obedience; Resulting in:

Longevity (Ex 20:12; Dt 4:40; 5:16; 1Ki 3:14; Pr 3:1-2). Deliverance from enemies (Ex 23:22; Lev 26:6-8; Dt 28:7; 30:1-4; Pr 16:7; Jer 15:19-21). Prosperity (Ge 26:3-5; Dt 7:12-14; 15:4-5; 28:2-12; 29:9; 30:1-5, 9-20; Jos 1:8; 1Ki 2:3-4; 9:3-9; 1Ch 22:13; 28:7-8; 2Ch 7:17-22; 26:5; 27:6; 31:10; Job 36:11; Isa 1:19; Jer 7:3-7; 11:1-5; 12:16; 17:24-27; 22:4-5, 15-16; Mal 3:10-12). Favors to children (Dt 4:1, 40; 5:29; 7:9; 12:25, 28). Preeminent honors (Dt 28:1, 13; Zec 3:7). Averted judgments (Ex 15:26; Dt 7:15).

See God, Goodness of, Providence of; Prosperity.

BLIGHT Destructive plant disease, sent as a judgment (Dt 28:22; 1Ki 8:37; Am 4:9; Hag 2:17).

BLIND Cruelty to, forbidden (Lev 19:14; Dt 27:18). Hated by David (2Sa 5:8). *See Blindness.*

BLINDNESS Disqualified for priestly office (Lev 21:18). Of animals, disqualified for a sacrifice (Lev 22:22; Dt 15:21; Mal 1:8). Miraculously inflicted upon the Sodomites (Ge 19:11), Syrians (2Ki 6:18-23), Saul of Tarsus (Ac 9:8-9), Elymas (Ac 13:11). Sent as a judgment (Dt 28:28).

Miraculous healing of (Mt 9:27-30; 11:5; 12:22; 21:14), Bartimaeus (Mt 20:30-34; Mk 10:46-52), a man of Bethsaida (Mk 8:22-25), a man born blind (Jn 9:1-7).

Instances of:

Isaac (Ge 27:1). Jacob (Ge 48:10). Eli (1Sa 4:14-15). Ahijah (1Ki 14:4).

Spiritual:

Instances of (Dt 29:4; Job 5:14; Isa 29:10-12; 56:10; 59:10; Jer 2:8; 5:21; 9:3; Eze 12:2; Ro 11:8). Foretold (Isa 60:2; Ro 2:4; 11:10).

Manifested:

In ignorance of God (Ex 5:2; Isa 1:3; Jer 4:22; Hos 4:1, 6; Jn 7:28; 15:21; 16:2-3; 17:25; Ac 17:23; 1Co 1:18-21; 2:8, 14-15; 15:34; Gal 4:8; Eph 4:17-19; 1Th 4:4-5; 1Jn 4:8; 3Jn 11), of Christ (Mt 16:3, 9; Lk 23:34; Jn 1:5, 10; 4:10-11, 15, 22; 8:15, 19, 27, 33, 42-43, 52-57; 9:29-39; Ac 3:14, 17; Ro 11:7-8, 25; 1Pe 1:14; 1Jn 3:1, 6), the Holy Spirit (Jn 14:17; Ac 19:2), of the Scriptures (Mt 22:29; Mk 12:24; Ac 13:27; 2Co 3:14-15; Heb 5:11-12; 2Pe 3:16).

In ignorance of moral truth (Dt 32:28; Pr 4:19; 28:5; Isa 5:13; Da 12:10; Mt 15:14, 16; 16:3, 9; 23:19, 24, 26; Mk 7:18; Lk 6:39; 12:48, 57; 2Ti 3:7; Jude 10), of the way of salvation (Lk 19:42; Jn 3:4; 6:52, 60; 2Pe 1:9; 1Jn 1:6, 8; 2:4, 9, 11; Rev 3:17), of God's ways (Ps 95:10; Jer 5:4; 8:7-9; Mic 4:12).

In unbelief (Ps 14:1, 4; Isa 15:1; Mk 16:14; Jn 12:35, 38; Ac 28:25, 27; 2Co 4:3-4, 6; 2Th 2:11-12). In insensibility (Dt 29:4; Jdg 16:20; Pr 7:7-23; 17:16; Isa 6:9-10; 42:18-20; 44:18-20; 48:8; Jer 16:10; Hos 7:11; Mt 6:23; 13:13-15; Mk 4:11-12; 6:52; 8:18; Lk 8:10; Jn 12:40; Ac 28:25-27). In presumption (Ps 10:5-6; 94:7-8; Isa 28:10-15; 40:21, 27-28; Jer 8:8-9; Am 9:10). In perversity (Job 21:14-15; Pr 1:7, 22, 29-30; 13:18; 19:2-3; Isa 5:20; 26:10-11; Jer 9:3, 6; Eze 12:2-3; Hos 5:4; Mt 21:32; Mk 3:5; Lk 11:52; Jn 3:19; Ro 1:19-23, 28-31). In hypocrisy (Tit 1:15-16).

Consequences of: (Pr 10:21; 14:12; Isa 27:11; Hos 4:6, 14; 2Th 1:8).

Remedy for: (Isa 9:2; 25:7; 35:5; 42:6-7; Lk 4:18; Jn 8:12; Ac 26:18; 2Co 4:6; Eph 5:8; Col 1:13; 1Pe 2:9).

See Affliction, Prayer Under; God, Providence of, Mysterious and Misinterpreted.

BLOOD Is the life (Ge 9:4; Lev 17:11, 14; 19:16; Dt 12:23; Mt 27:4, 24). Forbidden to be used as food (Ge 9:4; Lev 3:17; 7:26-27; 17:10-14; 19:26; Dt 12:16, 23; 15:23; Eze 33:25; Ac 15:20, 29; 21:25). Plague of (Ex 7:17-25; Ps 78:44; 105:29).

Sacrificial:

Sprinkled on altar and people (Ex 24:6-8; Eze 43:18, 20). Sprinkled on door posts (Ex 12:7-23; Heb 11:28). Without shedding of, no remission (Heb 9:22).

Of Sin Offering:

Sprinkled seven times before the veil (Lev 4;5-6, 17), on horns of altar of sweet incense, and at the bottom of the altar of burnt offering (Ex 30:10; Lev 4:7, 18, 25, 30; 5:9; 9:9, 12). Of bull of sin offering, put on the horns of the altar (Ex 29:12; Lev 8:15), poured at the bottom of the altar (Ex 29:12; Lev 8:15). See Offerings.

Of Trespass Offering:

Sprinkled on the altar (Lev 7:2). *See Offerings.*

Of Burnt Offering:

Sprinkled round about, and upon the altar (Ex 29:16; Lev 1:5, 11, 15; 8:19; Dt 12:27). *See Offerings.* Used for cleansing of leprosy (Lev 14:6-7, 17, 28, 51-52). *See Offerings.*

Of Peace Offering:

Sprinkled about the altar (Lev 3:2, 8, 13; 9:19). Blood of the ram of consecration put on tip of right ear, thumb, and large toe of, and sprinkled upon, Aaron and his sons (Ex 29:20-21; Lev 8:23-24, 30). *See Offerings.*

Blood of the Covenant: (Ex 24:5-8; Zec 9:11; Mt 26:28; Heb 9:18-19, 22; 10:29; 13:20).

See Offerings.

Of Atonement:

Sprinkled on atonement cover (Lev 16:14-15, 18-19, 27; 17:11).

Figurative:

Of victories (Ps 58:10), oppression and cruelty (Hab 2:12), destruction (Eze 35:6), guilt (Lev 20:9; 2Sa 1:16; Eze 18:13), judgments (Eze 16:38; Rev 16:6).

Of Jesus:

Shed on the Cross (Jn 19:18, 34). Atoning (Mt 26:28; Mk 14:24; Lk 22:20; Ro 3:24-25; 5:9; Eph 2:13, 16; Heb 9:14; 10:19; 12:24; 13:20; 1Jn 5:6, 8). Redeeming (Ac 20:28; Eph 1:7; Col 1:14, 20; Heb 9:12-14; 1Pe 1:18-19; Rev 1:5; 5:9; 7:14). Sanctifying (Heb 10:29; 13:12). Justification through (Ro 3:24-25; 5:9). Victory through (Rev 12:11). Eternal life by (Jn 6:53-56). Typified by the blood of sacrifices (Heb 9:6-28). Symbolized by the wine of the Lord's Supper (1Co 10:16; 11:25).

See Atonement; Jesus the Christ, Mission of, Sufferings of.

BLOOD, AVENGER One who took it upon himself to avenge the blood of a slain relative (Ge 9:6; Nu 35:6). *See Avenger of Blood.*

BLOOD, ISSUE OF See Bleeding, Subject to; Disease.

BLOOD MONEY Paid to Judas for betraying Jesus (Mt 27:6). *See Conscience Money.*

BLOODY SWEAT See Disease; Sweat, Bloody.

BLUE See Colors, Figurative and Symbolic.

BLUSHING With shame (Ezr 9:6; Jer 6:15; 8:12).

BOANERGES (*sons of thunder*). Surname of the sons of Zebedee (Mk 3:17).

BOARS, WILD (Ps 80:13). See Pig.

BOASTING Folly of (Ps 49:6-9; Pr 27:1; Isa 10:15; Jas 4:16). Deceitful (Pr 20:14; 25:14). Of the wicked (Ps 52:1; 94:4; Ro 1:30). Of the tongue (Jas 3:5). Forbidden (Jer 9:23).

Spiritual (Ps 52:1; 94:4; Ro 3:27; 11:17-21; 1Co 1:29; 4:6-7; 2Co 10:12-18; Eph 2:8-10).

Instances of:

Goliath (1Sa 17). Ben-Hadad (1Ki 20:10). Amaziah (2Ch 25:17-20). Sennacherib (2Ki 18:19, 28-35; 19:8-13; Isa 10:8-15). The disciples (Lk 10:17, 20).

See Ostentation.

BOAT See Ship.

BOAZ (perhaps *in him is strength*).

1. An ancestor of Jesus (Mt 1:5; Lk 3:32). History of, Ruth (Ru 2-4).

2. One of Solomon's bronze pillars erected at the temple. It stood on the left (north) side of the porch (1Ki 7:21; 2Ch 3:17).

BOAZ AND JAKIN See Boaz, 2; Jakin, 2; Temple, Solomon's.

BOCHERU See Bokeru.

BOCHIM See Bokim.

BODY

Called: house (2Co 5:1), house of clay (Job 4:19), golden bowl (Ecc 12:6), earthen vessel (2Co 4:7), tabernacle (2Pe 1:13), temple of God (1Co 3:16-17; 6:19), member of Christ (1Co 6:15).

Perishable (Job 17:14; 1Co 15:53-54). To be consecrated to God (Ro 12:1). To be kept unto holiness (1Co 6:13-20). Resurrection of, to a spiritual body (1Co 15:19-54; 2Co 5:14; Php 3:21). *See Resurrection.*

BOHAN (*thumb, big toe*). A Reubenite (Jos 15:6; 18:17).

BOIL A tumor or running sore. Plague of Egyptians (Ex 9:9-10; Dt 28:27, 35), of the Philistines, (1Sa 5:6, 9; 1Sa 6:5). Of Hezekiah, healed (2Ki 20:7; Isa 38:21). Of Job (Job 2:7-8). Levitical ceremonies prescribed for (Lev 13:18-23).

BOILING POT Parable of (Eze 24:3-5).

BOKERU (*his first born*). Son of Azel (1Ch 8:38; 9:44).

BOKIM (*weepings*). A place W of Jordan, near Gilgal (Jdg 2:1, 5).

BOLDNESS OF THE RIGHTEOUS

Exemplified (Pr 28:1; Ac 18:26; 19:8; Heb 13:6). In prayer (Heb 4:16; 10:19; 1Jn 3:21-22; 5:14-15). Inspired by, fear of the Lord (Pr 14:26). Faith in Christ (Eph 3:12).

Instances of boldness in prayer: Abraham (Ge 18:23-32). Moses (Ex 33:12-18). In the day of judgment (1Jn 2:28; 4:17). Its effect on others (Ac 4:13).

See Courage.

BOLSTER See Pillow.

BOLT, FIERY (Hab 3:5).

BOND Of the covenant (Eze 20:37), of peace (Eph 4:3). Posting bond (Ac 17:9).

B

BONDAGE Of Israelites, in Egypt (Ex 1:14; 2:23; 6:6), in Persia (Ezr 9:9). *See Emancipation; Servant.*

BONDMAN *See Servant.*

BONES Vision of the dry (Eze 37:1-14). None of Christ's broken (Ps 34:20; Jn 19:36).

BONNET *See Dress; Turban.*

BOOK Genealogies kept in (Ge 5:1). Law of Moses written in (Nu 5:23; Dt 17:18; 31:9, 24, 26; 2Ki 22:8). Topography of Israel, recorded in (Jos 18:9).

Non-biblical books cited in the Bible:
Book of Jashar (Jos 10:13; 2Sa 1:18), records of Samuel, Nathan, and Gad (1Sa 10:25; 1Ch 29:29), Iddo (2Ch 12:15; 13:22), Isaiah (2Ch 26:22; 32:32; Isa 8:1).

Annals of the Kings of Judah and Israel:
Of David (1Ch 27:24), Solomon (1Ki 11:41), Jehu (2Ch 20:34), other kings (2Ch 24:27; 16:11; 25:26; 27:7; 28:26; 35:27; 36:8), the kings of Israel (1Ki 14:19; 2Ch 20:34; 33:18).
Other records kept in (Ezr 4:15; 6:1-2; Est 6:1; 9:32; Jer 32:12; Ac 19:19). Prophecies written in, by Jeremiah (Jer 25:13; 30:2; 45:1; 51:60, 63; Da 9:2). Other prophecies written in (2Ch 33:18-19). Lamentations written in (2Ch 35:25). Numerous (Ecc 12:12). Eating of (Jer 15:16; Eze 2:8-10; 3:1-3; Rev 10:2-10). Of magic (Ac 19:19). Paul's left at Troas (2Ti 4:13).
Made in a roll (Jer 36:4; Zec 5:1). Sealed (Isa 29:11; Da 12:4; Rev 5:1-5).
Kiriath Jearim was called Kiriath Sepher, which signifies a city of books (Jos 15:15-16; Jdg 1:11-12).

Figurative:
Of Life: righteous written in (Ex 32:32; Da 12:1; Lk 10:20; Php 4:3; Heb 12:23; Rev 3:5; 21:27), wicked blotted out of (Ex 32:33; Rev 22:18-19), wicked not written in (Rev 13:8; 17:8; 20:15).
Of remembrance (Ps 56:8; 139:16; Mal 3:16; Rev 20:12).

BOOTH Made for shelter (Jnh 4:5), for cattle (Ge 33:17), watchmen (Job 27:18; Isa 1:8; 24:20). Prescribed for the Israelites to dwell in during the Feast of Tabernacles to remember their wanderings in the wilderness (Lev 23:40-43; Ne 8:15-16).

BOOTY Spoils of war. Property and persons were sometimes preserved and sometimes completely destroyed (Jos 6:18-21; Dt 20:14, 16-18). Abraham gave a tenth (Ge 14:20), David ordered that booty be shared with baggage guards (1Sa 30:21-25).

BOOZ *See Boaz, 1.*

BOR ASHAN (*pit of smoke*). A town in Judah (1Sa 30:30). Perhaps identical with Ashan (Jos 15:42). *See Ain, 1; Ashan.*

BORING THE EAR *See Piercing the Ear.*

BORN AGAIN *See New Birth.*

BORROWING Dishonesty in (Ps 37:21). Obligations in (Ex 22:14-15). Distress from (Ne 5:1-5; Pr 22:7). Compassion toward debtors commanded (Ne 5:6-13). Christ's rule concerning (Mt 5:42).
See Lending; Interest.
Instances of: Israelites from the Egyptians (Ex 3:22; 11:2; 12:35), iron axhead (2Ki 6:5); returned exiles from each other (Ne 5:1-13).
Borrowing trouble. *See Security, For Debt.*

BOSCATH *See Bozkath.*

BOSOM Used in the sense of sexual intimacy (Pr 5:20; Eze 23:8, 21). KJV "bosom" is NIV "arms" (Ge 16:5; Nu 11:12; 2Sa 12:3), "side" (Jn 1:18), "next to" (Jn 13:23).

BOSOR *See Beor; Bozrah.*

BOSS *See Shield.*

BOTANICAL GARDENS Garden of Eden (Ge 2:8-3:24), of Uzza (2Ki 21:18, 25), king's garden (2Ki 25:4; Ne 3:15 w Ecc 2:5), of Susa (Est 1:5-6;7:7-8).

BOTANY Laws of nature in the vegetable kingdom uniform in action (Mt 7:16-18, 20; Lk 6:43-44; 1Co 15:36-38; Gal 6:7). Lily, beauty of (Mt 6:28-29). The size of the harvest is related to the amount of seed sown (2Co 9:6).
See Algum; Almond; Aloes; Apple; Balm; Barley; Bay Tree; Beans; Bramble; Broom Tree; Bush; Cane; Caraway; Cassia; Cedar; Cinnamon; Citron Wood; Coriander; Cucumbers; Cummin; Cypress Wood; Date; Ebony; Fig Tree; Fir Tree; Flax; Frankincense; Galbanum; Gall, 3; Garlic; Gourd; Grain; Grass; Gum Resin; Hemlock; Henna Blossoms; Husk; Hyssop; Leek; Lentil(s); Lily; Mandrake; Melon; Millet; Mint; Mulberry Tree; Mustard Seed; Myrrh; Myrtle; Nard; Nettles; Nut; Oak; Olive; Onion; Palm Tree; Perfume; Pine; Plants of the Bible; Pomegranate; Poplar; Reed; Rose; Rue; Salt Herbs; Shittim; Spelt; Sycamore-Fig; Terebinth; Thistle; Thorn; Tree; Vine; Weeds; Wheat; Willow; Wormwood.

BOTCH *See Boil.*

BOTTLE Perfume bottles (Isa 3:20). *See Wine; Wineskin.*

BOTTOMLESS PIT *See Abyss.*

BOUNDARY STONES Stones used, to mark the boundary of property (Jos 13:21), to remove them was forbidden (Dt 27:17).

BOW

A Weapon:
(Ge 21:16, 20). Made of, bronze (2Sa 22:35; Job 20:24; Ps 18:34), wood (Eze 39:9). Used in war (Isa 13:18; La 2:4; Eze 39:3)

and in hunting (Ge 27:3). David's lament of the bow (2Sa 1:18-27). Used by the Elamites (Jer 49:35). *See Archery; Arrows.*

Figurative:
(Ge 49:24; Job 16:13; 29:20; Ps 78:57; La 3:12; Hos 1:5; Hab 3:9; Rev 6:2).

Rainbow:
A sign from God (Ge 9:8-16). A likeness of God's glory (Eze 1:28; Rev 4:3; 10:1).

BOWELS Diseased (2Ch 21:15-20). Judas's gushed out (Ac 1:18).
Figurative: Of the sensibilities (Ge 43:30; 1Ki 3:26; Job 30:27; Ps 22:14; SS 5:4; Jer 4:19; 31:20; La 1:20; Php 1:8; 2:1; Col 3:12; 1Jn 3:17).
See Heart.

BOWING In worship (2Ch 7:3). *See Obeisance; Worship, Attitudes in.*

BOWL Made of gold: for the tabernacle (Ex 25:29; 37:16), temple (1Ki 7:50; 1Ch 28:17; 2Ch 4:8). Of silver (Nu 4:7; 7:13, 19, 25, 31, 37, 43, 49, 55, 61, 67, 73, 79, 84). Stamped "HOLY TO THE LORD" (Zec 14:20-21). *See Basin.*
Figurative of fragile life (Ecc 12:6).
Symbolic: Of prayer (Rev 5:8). Seven bowls of judgment (Rev 15:7-16:17).

BOX Containing portions of Scripture (Mt 23:5, ftn). *See Jar(s).*

BOX TREE *See Cypress Wood.*

BOXING Figurative of personal discipline (1Co 9:26-27). *See Games.*

BOZEZ (*oozing place*). A rock near Gibeah (1Sa 14:4).

BOZKATH (*[swollen,] elevated spot*). A city of Judah (Jos 15:39; 2Ki 22:1).

BOZRAH (*enclosure [for sheep], fortress*).
1. A city of Edom (Ge 36:33). Prophecies concerning (Isa 34:6; 63:1; Jer 49:13, 22; Am 1:12).
2. A town of Moab (Jer 48:24).

BRACELET Present of (Ge 24:22). Worn by women (Ge 24:30; Isa 3:19); men, NIV "cord" (Ge 38:18, 25). Dedicated to the tabernacle (Ex 35:22; Nu 31:50). Taken as spoils (Nu 31:50; 2Sa 1:10).
Figurative of God's care for Israel (Eze 16:11).

BRAMBLE (Isa 34:13; Lk 6:44). Allegory of (Jdg 9:14-15).

BRANCH

Of Trees:
(Ge 30:37-43). Used in the Feast of Tabernacles (Lev 23:39-43; Ne 8:16-17). At the Triumphal Entry (Mt 21:6-9).

Figurative:
(Pr 11:28; Hos 14:6; Isa 60:21; Jn 15:2-5). Pruning of (Isa 18:5; Da 4:14; Jn 15:6; Ro 11:17, 21). Fruitless, cut off (Jn 15:2, 6). A title of Christ (Ps 80:15; Isa 4:2; 11:1; Jer 23:5; 33:15; Zec 3:8; 6:12). Symbolic name of Joshua (Zec 6:12).
See Graft.

BRASS *See Bronze.*

BRAVERY *See Boldness of the Righteous; Courage.*

BRAY The sound of a hungry donkey; a metaphor of humans crying out in need (Job 6:5; 30:7).

BRAZEN SEA *See Bronze Basin.*

BRAZEN SERPENT *See Bronze Snake.*

BRAZIER *See Coppersmith; Craftsman; Occupations and Professions.*

BREAD

Kinds of:
Bread of affliction (1Ki 22:27; Ps 127:2; Hos 9:4; Isa 30:20), leavened (Lev 7:13; 23:17; Hos 7:4; Am 4:5; Mt 13:33), unleavened (Ex 29:2; Jdg 6:19; 1Sa 28:24).
Made of wheat flour (Ex 29:2; 1Ki 4:22; 5:11; Ps 81:16), manna (Nu 11:8), meal (1Ki 17:12), barley (Jdg 7:13).

How Prepared:
Mixed with oil (Ex 29:2, 23), honey (Ex 16:31), with yeast. *See Yeast; see above, Kinds of.* Kneaded (Ge 18:6; Ex 8:3; 12:34; 1Sa 28:24; 2Sa 13:8; Jer 7:18; Hos 7:4).
Made into loaves (1Sa 10:3; 17:17; 25:18; 1Ki 14:3; Mk 8:14), cakes (Ge 6:19; 1Ki 14:3; 17:12), wafers (Ex 16:21; 29:23).
Baked in ovens (Ex 8:3; Lev 2:4; 7:9; 11:35; 26:26; Hos 7:4), in pans (Lev 2:5, 7; 2Sa 13:6-9), on hearths (Ge 18:6), on coals (1Ki 19:6; Isa 44:19; Jn 21:9).
Made by men (Ge 40:2), women (Lev 26:26; 1Sa 8:13; Jer 7:18). Trade in (Jer 37:21; Mk 6:35-37).
Offered in sacrifice (Lev 21:6, 8, 17, 21-22; 22:25; 1Sa 2:36; 2Ki 23:9). By idolaters (Jer 7:18; 44:19).
See Bread, Consecrated; Offerings.

Figurative:
(Isa 55:2; 1Co 10:17; 2Co 9:10). Christ: the bread of life (Jn 6:32-59).

Symbolic:
Of the body of Christ (Mt 26:26; Ac 20:7; 1Co 11:23-24).

BREAD, CONSECRATED (1Sa 21:4, 6; 1Ch 28:16; 2Ch 2:4; 29:18; Mt 12:4; Mk 2:26; Lk 6:4; Heb 9:2).
Required to be kept before the LORD continually (Ex 25:30; 2Ch 2:4). Placed on the table "in the Tent of Meeting" (Ex 40:22-23). *See Table of, below.* Ordinance concerning (Lev 24:5-9).

Unlawfully eaten by David (1Sa 21:6; Mt 12:3-4; Mk 2:25-26; Lk 6:3-4). Prepared by the Levites (1Ch 9:32; 23:29). Provided by a yearly per capita tax (Ne 10:32-33).

Table of:
(Heb 9:2). Ordinances concerning (Ex 25:23-28; 37:10-15). Its situation in the tabernacle (Ex 26:35; 40:22). Furniture of (Ex 25:29-30; 37:16; Nu 4:7). Consecration of (Ex 30:26-27, 29). How removed (Nu 4:7, 15). For the temple (1Ki 7:48, 50; 2Ch 4:19, 22).

BREAST Breast in the Bible can simply refer to the chest area of the body (Lk 18:13). It can also refer to the female mammary glands (Ge 49:25; La 4:3; Lk 23:29), both in nurturing (Ps 22:9; Joel 2:16; Isa 60:16) and erotic contexts (SS 4:5; 7:7; Eze 23:3, 21). To beat one's breast with a fist was a sign of sorrow or repentence (Eze 21:12; Lk 18:13; 23:48). *See Bosom.*

BREASTPLATE
1. For high priest (Ex 25:7). Directions for the making of (Ex 28:15-30). Made by Bezalel (Ex 31:2-5; 39:8, 21). Freewill offering of materials for (Ex 35:9, 27). Worn by Aaron (Ex 29:5; Lev 8:8).
2. Armor for soldiers (Rev 9:9, 17).
Figurative (Isa 59:17; Eph 6:14; 1Th 5:8).

BREATH Of life (Ge 2:7; 7:22; Ac 17:25). Of God (2Sa 22:16; Job 4:9; 15:30; 33:4; 37:10; Ps 18:15; 33:6; Isa 30:33).
Figurative (Eze 37:9).

BREECHES *See Dress; Undergarments.*

BRETHREN *See Brother; Brothers of Our Lord.*

BRIBERY (Ps 26:9-10; Pr 15:27; Isa 33:15-16). Corrupts conscience (Ex 23:8; Dt 16:18-19; Ecc 7:7). Perverts justice (1Sa 8:1-3; 12:3; Pr 17:23; 28:21; Isa 1:23; 5:22-23; Eze 22:12; Am 5:12; Mic 7:3). Destroys national welfare (Pr 29:4). Profanes God (Eze 13:19). Condemnation of (Job 15:34; Eze 22:12-13). Punishment for (Dt 27:25; Am 2:6).

Instances of:
Delilah (Jdg 16:4-5). Samuel's sons (1Sa 8:1-3). The false prophet, Shemaiah (Ne 6:10-13). Ben-Hadad (1Ki 15:18-19). Haman bribes Xerxes to destroy the Jews (Est 3:8-9). Chief priests bribe Judas (Mt 26:15; 27:3-9; Mk 14:11; Lk 22:5). Soldiers bribed to declare that the disciples stole the body of Jesus (Mt 28:12-15). Felix seeks a bribe from Paul (Ac 24:26).

BRICK Used in building: Babel (Ge 11:3), cities in Egypt (Ex 1:11, 14), houses (Isa 9:10), altars (Isa 65:3). Made by Israelites (Ex 5:7-19), slave labor (2Sa 12:31), Ninevites (Na 3:14).

BRICKKILN *See Brick.*

BRIDE Presents to (Ge 24:53). Maids of (Ge 24:59, 61; 29:24, 29). Ornaments of (Isa 49:18; 61:10; Jer 2:32; Rev 21:2).
Figurative (Ps 45:10-17; Eze 16:8-14; Rev 19:7-8; 21:2, 9; 22:17).

BRIDECHAMBER *See Bridegroom; Wedding.*

BRIDEGROOM Ornaments of (Isa 61:10). Exempt from military duty (Dt 24:5). Companions of (Jdg 14:11). Joy with (Mt 9:15; Mk 2:19-20; Lk 5:34-35).
Parable of (Mt 25:1-13; SS 4:7-16).
Figurative (Eze 16:8-14).

BRIDGE "River crossings" (Jer 51:32) may have included bridges or ferries. The Israelites generally crossed streams at a ford (Ge 32:22; 2Sa 19:18).

BRIDLE To control an animal (Ps 32:9; Pr 26:3; Rev 14:20). *See Bit.*
Figurative (2Ki 19:28; Ps 39:1; Jas 1:26).

BRIER Figurative (Isa 5:6; 55:13; Eze 2:6; 28:24).

BRIGANDINE *See Armor.*

BRIMSTONE *See Sulfur.*

BRONZE An alloy of copper and tin. Smelted (Eze 22:20; Job 28:2). Found in Canaan (Dt 8:9; Jos 22:8), Syria (2Sa 8:8). Tyrians traded in (Eze 27:13). Abundance of, for the temple (1Ki 7:47; 1Ch 22:14).

Articles made of:
Altar, vessels, and other articles of the tabernacle and temple (Ex 38:28-31; 1Ki 7:14-47; Ezr 8:27), cymbals (1Ch 15:19), trumpets (1Co 13:1), armor (1Sa 17:5-6; 2Ch 12:10), bows *See Bow,* fetters (Jdg 16:21; 2Ki 25:7), gates (Ps 107:16; Isa 45:2), bars (1Ki 4:13), idols (Da 5:4; Rev 9:20), mirrors (Ex 38:8), household vessels (Mk 7:4).
Workers in: Tubal-Cain (Ge 4:22), Hiram (1Ki 7:13-14), Alexander (2Ti 4:14).
See Bronze Basin; Bronze Sea; Copper; Molding.

Figurative:
(Lev 26:19; Dt 33:25; Isa 48:4; Jer 1:18; Eze 1:7; Da 2:32, 39; 7:19; 10:6; Zec 6:1; Rev 1:15).

BRONZE BASIN Directions for making (Ex 30:18-20). Situation of, in the tabernacle, tent of the congregation, and the altar (Ex 40:7). Sanctified (Ex 30:28; 40:11; Lev 8:11). Used for washing (Ex 40:30-32).
Figurative (Rev 4:6; 15:2, w Ex 38:8).
See Bronze Sea; Tabernacle.

BRONZE SEA Made by Solomon for the temple (1Ki 7:23-26, 30, 38-39; 2Ch 4:2-14). Altered by Ahaz (2Ki 16:17). Broken and carried to Babylon by the Chaldeans (2Ki 25:13, 16; Jer 52:17, 20).
Figurative (Rev 4:6; 15:2, w 1Ki 7:23).
See Bronze Basin; Temple.

BRONZE SNAKE Made by Moses for the healing of the Israelites (Nu 21:8-9). Worshiped by Israelites (2Ki 18:4). A symbol of Christ's crucifixion (Jn 3:14-15).

BROOK *See River; River of Egypt.*

BROOM A metaphor of Babylon swept away in judgment (Isa 14:23).

BROOM TREE A desert shrub (1Ki 19:4-5; Job 30:4; Ps 120:4).

BROTH (Jdg 6:19-20; 2Ki 4:38; Isa 65:4). Symbolic (Eze 24:5).

BROTHEL *See Groves; High Places; Idolatry; Prostitute.*

BROTHER

Signifies a relative (Ge 14:16; 29:12), a neighbor (Dt 23:7; Jdg 21:6; Ne 5:7), any Israelite (Jer 34:9; Ob 10), an inclusive term for all mankind (Ge 9:5; Mt 18:35; 1Jn 3:15), a companion (Jas 1:26; 1Ki 13:30; 20:33).

Love of (Pr 17:17; 18:24; SS 8:1). Unfaithful (Pr 27:10). Reuben's love for Joseph (Ge 37:21-22). Joseph's, for his brothers (Ge 43:30-34; 45:1-5; 50:19-25).

A fraternal title, especially among Christians. Instituted by Christ (Mt 12:50; 25:40; Heb 2:11-12). Used by disciples (Ac 9:17; 21:20; Ro 16:1; 1Co 7:12; 2Co 2:13), Peter (1Pe 1:22). Used among the Israelites (Lev 19:17; Dt 22:1-4).

Brother's widow, law concerning Levirate marriage of (Dt 25:5-10; Mt 22:24; Mk 12:19; Lk 20:28).

See Fraternity.

BROTHERLY KINDNESS *See Brother; Charitableness; Fellowship; Fraternity; Friendship; Love.*

BROTHERS OF OUR LORD James, Joseph, Simon, and Judas are called the Lord's brothers (Mt 13:55). He also had sisters (Mt 13:56). John records that his brothers did not believe in him (Jn 7:1-10). There are differences of opinion as to whether the "brothers" were full brothers, cousins, or children of Joseph by a former marriage.

BRUISE(S)

1. The so-called law of retaliation was meant to limit the punishment to fit the crime (Ex 21:25). By invoking the law of love, Jesus corrected the popular misunderstanding of the law of retaliation (Mt 5:38-42).

2. Castrated animals were not acceptable sacrifices (Lev 22:24).

3. Wounds inflicted, by shackles (Ps 105:18), because of drunkenness (physical and psychological effects) (Pr 29:35), by God upon Israel, because of the sins of the people, will be healed by the Lord (Isa 30:26). *See Bruised Reed, 1.*

BRUISED REED

1. Descriptive of someone who is weak; the "servant of the Lord" will mend broken lives (Isa 42:3; Mt 12:20).

2. NIV "splintered reed"; descriptive of depending on weak political alliances rather than relying on the Lord (2Ki 18:21; cf Isa 30:1-5; 31:1-3).

See Bruise(s).

BUBASTIS (*house of the cat goddess Bast*). One time capital of Lower Egypt; about forty miles NE of Cairo; modern Tel Basta. Prophesied against by Ezekiel (Eze 30:17, ftn). KJV Phi-Beseth.

BUCKET For water (Ex 7:19; Nu 24:7; Isa 40:15).

BUCKLER *See Shield.*

BUILDER Of the tabernacle. *See Bezalel; Master Craftsman.* Of the temple (2Ki 12:11; 22:6; Ezr 3:10). Of the wall of Jerusalem (Ne 4:18). Of the church (1Co 3:10). God (Heb 3:4; 11:10). Who rejected the capstone (Ps 118:22; Mt 21:42; Ac 4:11; 1Pe 2:7). *See Carpentry; Foundation.*

BUILDING The church as God's building (1Co 3:9; Eph 2:21). The eternal body compared to the earthly tent (2Co 5:1).

BUKKI (*proved of Yahweh BDB; mouth [gurgle sounds] of Yahweh ISBE*).

1. Son of Abishua (1Ch 6:5, 51; Ezr 7:4).

2. A prince of Dan (Nu 34:22).

BUKKIAH (*proved of Yahweh*). A Levite (1Ch 25:4, 13).

BUL Month eight in sacred sequence, month two in civil sequence. Also called Marcheshvan (not in Bible). The temple completed in (1Ki 6:38). Jeroboam institutes an idolatrous feast in, to correspond with the Feast of Tabernacles (1Ki 12:32-33). Time for planting wheat and barley (October–November). *See Month, 8.*

BULL

Uses of: For sacrifice (Ex 29:3, 10-14, 36; Lev 4:8, 16; Nu 7:87-88; 28:11-31; 29; Heb 9:13; 10:4), plowing (1Sa 14:14; 1Ki 19:19; Pr 14:4; Isa 32:20; Jer 31:18), treading out grain (Dt 25:4), with wagons (Nu 7:3-8; 2Sa 6:3-6).

Laws concerning: trespass by (Ex 21:28-36), theft of (Ex 22:1-10), rest for (Ex 23:12), not to be muzzled when treading grain (Dt 25:4; 1Co 9:9; 1Ti 5:18), not to be yoked with a donkey (Dt 22:10).

Twelve bronze, under the cast metal Sea in Solomon's temple (1Ki 7:25; 2Ch 4:4; Jer 52:20).

See Cattle; Offerings.

Symbolic (Eze 1:10; Rev 4:7).

BULRUSH *See Papyrus; Reed.*

BULWARK (Dt 20:20; 2Ch 26:15; Ecc 9:14). Figurative (Ps 48:13; Isa 26:1).

BUNAH Son of Jerahmeel (1Ch 2:25).

BUNNI

1. A Levite, a teacher with Ezra (Ne 9:4).

2. Ancestor of Shemaiah (Ne 11:15).

3. A family of Jews (Ne 10:15).

BURDEN Figurative: Of oppressions (Isa 58:6; Mt 23:4; Lk 11:46; Gal 6:2). Of the prophetic message (Isa 13:1; 15:1; 17:1; 19:1).

BURGLARY *See Theft.*

BURIAL Rites of (Jer 34:5). Soon after death (Dt 21:23; Jn 8:29; Jn 19:38-42; Ac 5:9-10). With spices (2Ch 16:14; Mk 16:1; Lk 23:56). Bier used at (2Sa 3:31; Lk 7:14).

Attended by relatives and friends: Of Jacob (Ge 50:5-9), Abner (2Sa 3:31), child of Jeroboam (1Ki 14:13), the son of the widow of Nain (Lk 7:12-13), Stephen (Ac 8:2).

Lack of, a disgrace (2Ki 9:10; Pr 30:17; Jer 16:4; 22:19; Eze 39:15). Directions given about, before death, by Jacob (Ge 49:29-30), Joseph (Ge 50:25). Burial of Gog (multitude) requiring 7 months (Eze 39:12-13).

BURNING As a punishment (Ge 19:28; Jos 6:24; 8:20; 11:13; Jdg 18:27; 1Sa 30:1; 1Ki 9:16; 2Ch 36:19; Job 1:16). *See Punishment.*

BURNING BUSH The LORD appears to Moses (Ex 3:2-5; Ac 7:30).

BURNT OFFERING *See Offerings, Burnt.*

BURYING PLACES Bought by Abraham (Ge 23; 25:9). Prepared by Jacob (Ge 50:5), Asa (2Ch 16:14), Joseph (Mt 27:60). On hills (2Ki 23:16; Jos 24:33). In valleys (Jer 7:32).

Family (Ge 47:30; 49:29; Ac 7:16). Of kings (1Ki 2:10; 2Ch 32:33), a place of honor (2Ch 24:16, 25; 21:20). For poor and strangers (Jer 26:23; Mt 27:7).

Tombs: In houses (1Sa 25:1; 1Ki 2:34), gardens (2Ki 21:18, 26; Jn 19:41), caves (Ge 23:9), under trees, Deborah's (Ge 35:8), King Saul's (1Sa 31:13).

Closed with stones (Mt 27:60, 66; Jn 11:38; 20:1). Sealed (Mt 27:66). Marked with pillars: Rachel's (Ge 35:20). Inscriptions (2Ki 23:17). Painted and decorated (Mt 23:27, 29).

Demon-possessed lived in (Mt 8:28). Any who touched were unclean (Nu 19:16, 18; Isa 65:4). Refused to the dead (Rev 11:9). Robbed (Jer 8:1).

See Cremation; Dead; Death, Physical; Elegy; Grave; Mourning.

Figurative (Isa 22:16; Ro 6:4; Col 2:12).

BUSH Desert shrubs (Ge 21:15; Jer 17:6). *See Burning Bush.*

BUSHELS (Lk 16:7). *See Measure.*

BUSINESS LIFE

Virtues Found in:

Diligence (Pr 10:4; 13:4; 22:29; 2Pe 3:14). Fidelity (Ge 39:6; 2Ch 34:11-12; Ne 13:13; Da 6:4; 1Co 4:2; Heb 3:5). Honesty (Lev 19:35-36; Dt 25:15; Pr 11:1; Ro 12:17; 13:8). Industry (Ge 2:15; Pr 6:6; 10:5; 12:11; 13:11; 20:13; Ro 12:11). Giving of just weights (Lev 19:36; Dt 25:13; Pr 11:1; 16:11; 20:10; Eze 45:10; Mic 6:11). Integrity (Ps 41:12; Pr 11:3; 19:1; 20:7).

Vices Found in:

Breach of trust (Lev 6:2; SS 1:6; Eze 16:17; Lk 16:12). Dishonesty (Dt 25:13; Pr 11:1; 20:14; 21:6; Hos 12:7). Extortion (Isa 16:2; Eze 22:12; Am 5:11; Mt 18:28; 23:25; Lk 3:13). Fraud (Lev 19:13; Mk 10:19; 1Co 6:8). Unjust gain (Pr 16:8; 21:6; 22:16; Jer 17:11; 22:13; Eze 22:13; Jas 5:4). Slothfulness (Pr 18:9; 24:30-31; Ecc 10:18; 2Th 3:11; Heb 6:12).

BUSYBODY Meddlers denounced (Pr 26:17; 1Ti 5:13; 2Th 3:11-12). Command against (Lev 19:16; 1Pe 4:15).

See Backbiting; Talebearer; Speaking, Evil.

BUTLER (1Ki 10:5; 2Ch 9:4; Ne 1:11; 2:1). Pharaoh's, imprisoned and released (Ge 40). *See Cupbearer.*

BUTTER (Ge 18:8; Dt 32:14; Job 5:25; 2Sa 17:29; Job 20:17; Isa 7:15, 22). Made by churning (Pr 30:33).

BUZ (*contempt*).

1. Son of Nahor (Ge 22:21).

2. Father of Jahdo (1Ch 5:14).

BUZI (*contempt*). The father of Ezekiel (Eze 1:3).

BYBLOS *See Gebal.*

BYWAYS NIV "winding paths," traveled to avoid danger (Jdg 5:6).

C

CAB A dry measure containing about two quarts (2Ki 6:25). *See Measure.*

CABBON A place in Judah (Jos 15:40).

CABINET Heads of departments in government. David's (2Sa 8:15-18; 15:12; 20:23-26; 1Ch 27:32-34), Solomon's (1Ki 4:1-7), Hezekiah's (Isa 36:3), Artaxerxes' (Ezr 7:14). *See Counselor.*

CABUL (*good for nothing*).

1. A city in the N of Israel (Jos 19:27).

2. Name given by Hiram to certain cities in Galilee (1Ki 9:13).

CAESAR

1. Augustus (Lk 2:1).

2. Tiberius (Lk 3:1; 20:22).

3. Claudius (Ac 11:28).

4. Nero (Php 4:22).

CAESAREA A seaport in Israel.

Home of Philip (Ac 8:40; 21:8), Cornelius, the centurion (Ac 10:1, 24), Herod (Ac 12:19-23), Felix (Ac 23:23-24).

Paul taken to, by the disciples to save him from his enemies (Ac 9:30), by Roman soldiers to be tried by Felix (Ac 23:23-35).

CAESAREA PHILIPPI A city in the N of Israel, visited by Jesus (Mt 16:13; Mk 8:27).

CAGE For birds (Jer 5:27; Rev 18:2).

CAIAPHAS High priest (Lk 3:2), son-in-law of Annas (Jn 18:13). Prophesies concerning Jesus (Jn 11:49-51; 18:14). Jesus tried before (Mt 26:2-3, 57, 63-65; Jn 18:24, 28). Peter and other disciples accused before (Ac 4:1-22).

CAIN (*metal worker* BDB KB; *brought forth, acquired* Ge 4:1).

1. Son of Adam (Ge 4:1). Jealousy and crime of (Ge 4:3-15; Heb 11:4; 1Jn 3:12; Jude 11). Settles in the land of Nod (Ge 4:16). Children and descendants of (Ge 4:17-18).

2. *See Kain, 1.*

CAINAN (*worker in iron, metal worker*).

1. Also called Kenan. Son of Enos (Ge 5:9-15; 1Ch 1:2; Lk 3:37).

2. Son of Arphaxad (Lk 3:36).

CAKES Of unleavened bread (Ex 12:39), mixed with oil for offerings (Ex 29:2), offered to the Queen of Heaven (Jer 7:18); of raisins and figs (1Sa 25:18); of dates (2Sa 6:19); of barley (Eze 4:12).

CALAH (*strength, vigor*). An ancient city of Assyria (Ge 10:11-12).

CALAMUS A sweet cane (SS 4:14; Eze 27:19). An ingredient of the holy ointment (Isa 43:24). Imported (Jer 6:20; Eze 27:19).

CALCOL Son of Mahol (1Ki 4:31). Son of Zerah (1Ch 2:6).

CALDRON In the tabernacle (1Sa 2:14), the temple (2Ch 35:13; Jer 52:18-19). Figurative of judgment (Eze 11:3-11).

CALEB (*dog* BDB; *snappish, warding off* KB).

1. Son of Jephunneh. Also spelled Kelubai (1Ch 2:9, ftn). One of the two survivors of the Israelites permitted to enter the land of promise (Nu 14:30, 38; 26:63-65; 32:11-13; Dt 1:34-36; Jos 14:6-15). Sent to Canaan as a spy (Nu 13:6). Brings favorable report (Nu 13:26-30; 14:6-9). Assists in dividing Canaan (Nu 34:19). Life of, miraculously saved (Nu 14:10-12). Leader of the Israelites after Joshua's death (Jdg 1:11-12). Age of (Jos 14:7-10). Inheritance of (Jos 14:6-15; 15:13-16). Descendants of (1Ch 4:15).

2. Third son of Hezron (1Ch 2:9). Ancestor of Bezalel the craftsman who built the tabernacle (1Ch 2:18-20).

3. Brother of Jerahmeel (1Ch 2:42, 50), possibly the same as 1.

CALEB EPHRATHAH A place near Bethlehem (1Ch 2:24).

CALENDAR In the biblical era, time was reckoned solely on astronomical observations. Days, months, and years were determined by the sun and moon.

1. Days of the week were not named by the Israelites, but were designated by ordinal numbers. Jewish day began in the evening with the appearance of the first stars. Days were subdivided into hours and watches. Israelites divided nights into three watches (Ex 14:24; Jdg 7:19; La 2:19), the Romans four (Mt 14:25).

2. Egyptians had a week of ten days. The seven-day week is of Semitic origin (the Creation account), and ran consecutively irrespective of lunar or solar cycles. This was done for man's physical and spiritual welfare. The biblical records are silent regarding the observance of the Sabbath day from creation to the time of Moses. Sabbath observance was either revived or given special emphasis by Moses (Ex 16:23; 20:8).

3. The Hebrew month began with the new moon. Before the Exile months were designated by numbers. After the Exile names adopted from the Babylonians were used.

4. The Jewish calendar had two concurrent years, the sacred year, beginning in the spring with the month Nisan, and the civic year, beginning with Tishri (see chart below). The sacred year was instituted by Moses and consisted of lunar months of twenty-nine or thirty days each, with an intercalary month called Adar Sheni added about every three years. Every seventh year was a sabbatical year for the Israelites—a year of solemn rest for landlords, slaves, beasts of burden, and land, and freedom for Hebrew slaves. Every fiftieth year was a Jubilee year, observed by family reunions, canceled mortgages, and return of lands to original owners (Lev 25:8-17).

C

Synchronized Jewish Sacred Calendar			
Sacred	Name	Modern Equivalent	Civic
1	Nisan	March-April	7
2	Iyyar	April-May	8
3	Sivan	May-June	9
4	Tammuz	June-July	10
5	Ab	July-August	11
6	Elul	August-September	12
7	Tishri	September-October	1
8	Bul	October-November	2
9	Kislev	November-December	3
10	Tebeth	December-January	4
11	Shebat	January-February	5
12	Adar	February-March	6

See Month; Time; also see each month under its respective topic heading.

CALF Offered in sacrifice (Mic 6:6). Golden idol, made by Aaron (Ex 32; Dt 9:16; Ne 9:18; Ps 106:19; Ac 7:41).
Images of, set up in Bethel and Dan by Jeroboam (1Ki 12:28-33; 2Ki 10:29). Worshiped by Jehu (2Ki 10:29). Prophecies against the golden calves at Bethel (1Ki 13:1-5, 32; Jer 48:13; Hos 8:5-6; 10:5-6, 15; 13:2; Am 3:14; 4:4; 8:14). Altars of, destroyed (2Ki 23:4, 15-20).

CALKERS *See Caulkers.*

CALL

Personal:
By Christ (Isa 55:5; Ro 1:6), his Spirit (Rev 22:17), his works (Ps 19:2-3; Ro 1:20), his ministers (Jer 35:15; 2Co 5:20), his gospel (2Th 2:14).
Is from darkness to light (1Pe 2:9). Addressed to all (Isa 45:22; Mt 20:16). Most reject (Pr 1:24; Mt 20:16). Effective to believers (Ps 110:3; Ac 13:48; 1Co 1:24). Not to many wise by human standards (1Co 1:26). To repentance (Isa 55:1).
To believers of grace (Gal 1:6; 2Ti 1:9), according to the purpose of God (Ro 8:28; 9:11, 23-24), without repentance (Ro 11:29), high (Php 3:14), holy (2Ti 1:9), heavenly (Heb 3:1), to fellowship with Christ (1Co 1:9), to holiness (1Th 4:7), to a prize (Php 3:14), to liberty (Gal 5:13), to peace (1Co 7:15; Col 3:15), to glory and virtue (2Pe 1:3), to the eternal glory of Christ (2Th 2:14; 1Pe 5:10), to eternal life (1Ti 6:12).
Partakers of justified (Ro 8:30), walk worthy of (Eph 4:1; 2Th 1:11), blessedness of receiving (Rev 19:9), is to be made sure (2Pe 1:10), praise God for (1Pe 2:9), illustrated (Pr 8:3-4; Mt 23:3-9).
Rejected (Jer 6:16; Mt 22:3-7).
Rejection of leads to judicial blindness (Isa 6:9, w Ac 28:24-27; Ro 11:8-10), delusion (Isa 66:4; 2Th 2:10-11), withdrawal of the means of grace (Jer 26:4-6; Ac 13:46; 18:6; Rev 2:5), temporal judgments (Jer 6:16, 19; 35:17; Zec 7:12-14), rejection by God (Pr 1:24-32; Jer 6:19, 30), condemnation (Jn 12:48; Heb 2:1-3; 12:25), destruction (Pr 29:1; Mt 22:3-7).

To Special Religious Duty:
Abraham (Ge 12:1-3; Isa 51:2; Heb 11:8). Moses (Ex 3:2, 4, 10; 4:1-16; Ps 105:26; Ac 7:34-35). Aaron and his sons (Ex 4:14-16; 28:1; Ps 105:26; Heb 5:4). Joshua (Nu 27:18-19, 22-23; Dt 31:14, 23; Jos 1:1-9). Gideon (Jdg 6:11-16). Samuel (1Sa 3:4-10). Solomon (1Ch 28:6, 10). Jehu (2Ki 9:6-7; 2Ch 22:7). Cyrus (Isa 45:1-4). Amos (Am 7:14-15). Apostles (Mt 4:18-22; 9:9; Mk 1:16-17; 2:14; 3:13-19; Lk 5:27; 6:13-16; Jn 15:16). The rich young ruler (Mk 10:21-22). Paul (Ac 9:4-6, 15-16; 13:2-3; Ro 1:1; 1Co 1:1; 2Co 1:1; Gal 1:1, 15-16; Eph 1:1; Col 1:1; 1Ti 1:1; 2Ti 1:1).

To All Believers:
(Ro 8:30; 1Co 1:2, 9, 24; 1Th 2:11-12; 2Th 2:13-14; 2Ti 1:9; Heb 3:1-2, 3:7-8; 1Pe 5:10; 2Pe 1:3, 10; Jude 1; Rev 17:14).
See Minister, Call of; Backsliders; Seekers.

CALLING, THE CHRISTIAN (1Co 1:26; Eph 1:18; 4:1; Php 3:14; 1Th 2:12; 2Th 2:14; 2Ti 1:9; Heb 3:1; 1Pe 5:10; 2Pe 1:10). *See Call.*

CALNEH (*all of them*). Also called Canneh and Calno, a city of Assyria (Ge 10:10; Isa 10:9; Eze 27:23; Am 6:2).

CALNO (*all of them*). City which tried to resist the Assyrians (Isa 10:9).

CALVARY *See Golgotha.*

CAMEL Herds of (Ge 12:16; 24:35; 30:43; 1Sa 30:17; 1Ch 27:30; Job 1:3, 17; Isa 60:6). Docility of (Ge 24:11).
Uses of: For riding (Ge 24:10, 61, 64; 31:17), posts (Est 8:10, 14; Jer 2:23), drawing chariots (Isa 21:7), for carrying burdens (Ge 24:10; 37:25; 1Ki 10:2; 2Ki 8:9; 1Ch 12:40; Isa 30:6), for cavalry (1Sa 30:17), for milk (Ge 32:15). Forbidden as food (Lev 11:4). Hair of, made into cloth (Mt 3:4; Mk 1:6). Ornaments of (Jdg 8:21, 26). Stables for (Eze 25:5).

CAMEL'S HAIR John the Baptist wore a garment made of camel's hair (Mt 3:4; Mk 1:6). Such garments are still used in the Near East.

CAMON *See Kamon.*

CAMP Of the Israelites around the tabernacle (Nu 2; 3). *See Itinerary.*

CAMPHIRE *See Henna Blossoms.*

CANA (*reed*). Marriage at (Jn 2:1-11). Nobleman's son healed at (Jn 4:46-47). Nathanael's home at (Jn 21:2).

CANAAN (*land of purple* hence *merchant, trader*).
1. Son of Ham (Ge 9:18, 22, 25-27). Descendants of (Ge 10:6, 15; 1Ch 1:8, 13).
2. Land of (Ge 11:31; 17:8; 23:2). Called Israel (Ex 15:14), the land of Israel (1Sa 13:19), of the Hebrews (Ge 40:15), of the Jews (Ac 10:39), of promise (Heb 11:9), the Beautiful Land (Da 8:9), the holy land (Zec 2:12), the Lord's land (Hos 9:3), Immanuel's land (Isa 8:8), Beulah (Isa 62:4).
Promised to Abraham and his seed (Ge 12:1-7; 13:14-17; 15:18-21; 17:8; Dt 12:9-10; Ps 105:11) and the promise renewed to Isaac (Ge 26:3). Extent of: According to the promise (Ge 15:18; Ex 23:31; Dt 11:24; Jos 1:4; 15:1), after the Conquest by Joshua (Jos 12:1-8), in Solomon's time (1Ki 4:21, 24; 2Ch 7:8; 9:26). Prophecy concerning, after the restoration of Israel (Eze 47:13-20). Fertility of (Dt 8:7-9; 11:10-13). Fruitfulness of (Nu 13:27; 14:7-8; Jer 2:7; 32:22). Products of: Fruits (Dt 8:8; Jer 40:10, 12), minerals (Dt 8:9). Exports of (Eze 27:17). Famines in (Ge 12:10; 26:1; 47:13; Ru 1:1; 2Sa 21:1; 1Ki 17). *See Famine.*
Spies sent into, by Moses (Nu 13:17-29). Conquest of, by the Israelites (Nu 21:21-35; Dt 3:3-6; Jos 6-12; Ps 44:1-3). Divided by lot among the twelve tribes and families (Nu 26:55-56; 33:54; 34:13), by Joshua, Eleazar, and a prince from each tribe (Nu 34:16-29; 35:1-8; Jos 14-19). Divided into twelve provinces by Solomon (1Ki 4:7-19). Into two kingdoms, Judah and Israel (1Ki 11:29-36; 12:16-21). Roman provinces of (Lk 3:1; Jn 4:3-4). *See Canaanite(s).*

CANAANITE, SIMON THE *See Simon, 2; Zealot, Simon the.*

CANAANITE(S) (*land of purple* hence *merchant, trader*).
Eleven nations descended from Canaan (Ge 10:15-19; Dt 7:1; 1Ch 1:13-16). Territory of (Ge 10:19; 12:6; 15:18; Ex 23:31; Nu 13:29; 34:1-12; Jos 1:4; 5:1), given to the Israelites (Ge 12:6-7; 15:18; 17:8; Ex 23:23; Dt 7:1-3; 32:49; Ps 135:11-12).
Wickedness of (Ge 13:13; Lev 18:25, 27-28; 20:23). To be expelled from the land (Ex 33:2; 34:11). To be destroyed (Ex 23:23-24; Dt 19:1; 31:3-5). Not expelled (Jos 17:12-18; Jdg 1:1-33; 3:1-3). Defeat the Israelites (Nu 14:45; Jdg 4:1-3). Defeated by the Israelites (Nu 21:1-3; Jos 11:1-16; Jdg 4:4-24), by the Egyptians (1Ki 9:16). Chariots of (Jos 17:18).
Isaac forbidden by Abraham to take a wife from (Ge 28:1). Judah marries a woman of (Ge 38:2; 1Ch 2:3). The Jews intermarry with after the Exile (Ezr 9:2).
Prophecy concerning (Ge 9:25-27).

CANANAEAN *See Zealot, Simon the.*

CANDACE (roughly *queen*). Queen of Ethiopia (Ac 8:27).

CANDIDATE Instance of Absalom, campaigning for popular favor (2Sa 15:1-6).

CANDLE *See Lamp.*

CANDLESTICK *See Lampstand.*

CANE Probably the sweet calamus (Isa 43:24; Jer 6:20).

CANKER *See Gangrene.*

CANKERWORM *See Locust.*

CANNEH An alternate form of Calneh. A city of Assyria (Eze 27:23). *See Calneh.*

CANNIBALISM (Lev 26:29; Dt 28:53-57; 2Ki 6:28-29; Jer 19:9; La 2:20; 4:10; Eze 5:10).

CANONICITY By the canon is meant the list of the books of the Bible recognized by the Christian church as genuine and inspired. The Protestant canon includes thirty-nine books in the OT and twenty-seven in the New. The Roman Catholic canon has fourteen more books and additions to the OT; the Orthodox as many as eighteen. *See Apocrypha.* The Jewish canon is the same as the Protestant OT. The OT canon was formed before the time of Christ, as is evident from Josephus (*Against Apion* 1:8), who wrote c. A.D. 90. We know very little of the history of the acceptance of the OT books as canonical. There is much more documentary evidence regarding the formation of the NT canon. The Muratorian Canon (c. A.D. 170), which survives only as a fragment, lists most of the NT books. Some of the books were questioned for a time for various reasons, usually uncertainty of authorship, but by the end of the fourth century our present canon was almost universally accepted, and this was done not by arbitrary decree of bishops, but by the general consensus of the church.

CANTICLES *See Song of Solomon.*

CAPERNAUM (*village of Nahum*). A city on the shore of the Sea of Galilee. Jesus chose, as the place of his abode (Mt 4:13; Lk 4:31). Miracles of Jesus performed at (Mt 9:1-26; 17:24-27; Mk 1:21-45; 2; 3:1-6; Lk 7:1-10; Jn 4:46-53; 6:17-25, 59).
Jesus' prophecy against (Mt 11:23; Lk 10:15).

CAPHTOR Place from which the Philistines originally came (Am 9:7), probably from the island of Crete (Jer 47:4; Am 9:7).

CAPHTORITES People of Caphtor (Ge 10:14; Dt 2:23; 1Ch 1:12).

CAPITAL The uppermost member of a column or pilaster crowning the shaft and taking the weight of the entablature (Ex 36:38; 1Ki 7:16-42; 2Ki 25:17; 2Ch 4:12-13; Jer 52:22).

CAPITAL AND LABOR Strife between (Mt 21:33-41; Mk 12:1-9; Lk 20:9-10). *See Employee; Employer; Master; Rich, The; Servant.*

CAPITAL PUNISHMENT *See Punishment.*

CAPPADOCIA Easternmost Roman province of Asia Minor (Ac 2:9; 1Pe 1:1).

CAPSTONE The keystone of an arch or the last stone put in place to complete a building. Figurative of Jesus: first rejected; finally taking his rightful place of supremacy (Ps 118:22; Zec 4:7; Mt 21:42; Mk 12:10; Lk 20:17; Ac 4:11; 1Pe 2:7). *See Cornerstone.*

CAPTAIN Commander-in-chief of an army (Dt 20:9; Jdg 4:2; 1Sa 14:50; 1Ki 2:35; 16:16; 1Ch 27:34). Of the tribes (Nu 2). Of thousands (Nu 31:48; 1Sa 17:18; 1Ch 28:1). Of hundreds (2Ki 11:15). *See Centurion.* Of fifties (2Ki 1:9; Isa 3:3). Of the guard (Ge 37:36; 2Ki 25:8). Of the ward (Jer 37:13).
Signifying any commander (Ac 5:16; 22:2; 2Ki 20:5), leader (1Ch 11:21; 12:34; 2Ch 17:14-19; Jn 18:12).
David's captains or chief heroes (2Sa 23; 1Ch 11; 12). King appoints (1Sa 18:13; 2Sa 17:25; 18:1).
Angel of the Lord called (Jos 5:14; 2Ch 13:12).
See Armies.

CAPTIVE Prisoner of war (Ge 14:12; 1Sa 30:1-2).
Cruelty to: Putting to death (Nu 31:9-20; Dt 20:13; 21:10; Jos 8:29; 10:15-40; 11:11; Jdg 7:25; 8:21; 21:11; 1Sa 15:32-33; 2Sa 8:2; 2Ki 8:12; Jer 39:6), 20,000 by Amaziah (2Ch 25:11-12), ripping open pregnant women (2Ki 8:12; 15:16; Am 1:13), enslaved or tortured with picks and axes (2Sa 12:31; 1Ch 20:3), blinded (Jdg 16:21; Jer 39:7), maimed (Jdg 1:6-7), ravished (La 5:11-13; Zec 14:2), enslaved (Dt 20:14; 2Ki 5:2; Ps 44:12; Joel 3:6), robbed (Eze 23:25-26), confined in pits (Isa 51:14). Other indignities to (Eze 20:4).
Kindness to (2Ki 25:27-30; Ps 106:46). Advanced to positions in state (Ge 41:39-45; Est 2:8; Da 1).

CAPTIVITY Of the, Israelites foretold (Lev 26:33; Dt 28:36), ten tribes (2Ki 17:6, 23-24; 18:9-12).
Of Judah in Babylon, prophecy of (Isa 39:6; Jer 13:19; 20:4; 25:2-11; 32:28), fulfilled (Ezr 1:11; 4:1-11-16; 25; 2Ch 36; Jer 52:28-30). Israelites, in promises to (Ne 1:9). Jews return from (Ezr 2; 3; 8).
As a judgment (Ezr 5:12; 9:7; Isa 5:13; Jer 29:17-19; La 1:3-5; Eze 39:23-24).
Figurative:
(Isa 61:1; Ro 7:23; 1Co 9:27; 2Co 10:5; 2Ti 2:26; 3:6). "Take captive your captives" (Jdg 5:12), "led captives in your train" (Ps 68:18; Eph 4:8).

CAR *See Beth Car.*

CARAVAN Company of travelers united together for a common purpose or for mutual protection and generally equipped for a long journey, especially in desert country or through foreign and presumably hostile territory (Ge 32-33; 1Sa 30:1-20).

CARAWAY (Isa 28:25-27).

CARBUNCLE NIV "sparkling jewels," (Isa 54:12), "beryl," and "chrysolite." *See Beryl; Chrysolite, 1; Minerals of the Bible, 1; Stones.*

CARCAS (perhaps *vulture*). A eunuch and servant of the Persian king Xerxes (Est 1:10).

CARCASS The dead body of a human or animal. Israelites were ceremonially unclean if they touched a carcass (Lev 11:8-40; Nu 6:6-7; 9:10; Dt 14:8).

CARCHEMISH A Babylonian city on the Euphrates, against which the king of Egypt made war (2Ch 35:20; Isa 10:9; Jer 46:2).

CARE
Worldly (Ecc 4:8; Mt 6:25-34; 13:22; Mk 4:19; Lk 8:14; 12:27; 14:18-19; 21:34; 1Co 7:32-33; Php 4:6; 2Ti 2:4). In vain (Ps 39:6; 127:2; Mt 6:27; Lk 12:25-26). Proceeds from unbelief (Mt 6:26, 28-30; Lk 12:24, 27-28), Martha rebuked for (Lk 10:40-41).
Remedy for (Ps 37:5; 55:22; Pr 16:3; Jer 17:7-8; Mt 6:26-34; Lk 12:22-32; Php 4:6-7; Heb 13:5; 1Pe 5:6-7).
Instances of: Martha (Lk 10:40-41). Certain ones who desired to follow Jesus (Mt 8:19-22; Lk 9:57-62).
See Anxiety; Carnal Mindedness; Rich, The; Riches; Worldliness.

CAREAH *See Kareah.*

CARITES Mercenary soldiers from Caria in SW Asia Minor (2Ki 11:4, 19).

CARMEL (*orchard planted with vine and fruit trees*).
1. A fertile and lovely mountain in Israel (SS 7:5; Isa 33:9; 35:2; Jer 46:18; 50:19; Am 1:2). Forests of (2Ki 19:23). Caves of (Am 9:3). An idolatrous high place upon; Elijah builds an altar upon, and confronts the worshipers of Baal, putting to death 450 of his prophets (1Ki 18:17-46). Elisha's abode at (2Ki 2:25; 4:25).
2. A city of Judah (Jos 15:55). Saul erects a memorial at (1Sa 15:12). Nabal's possessions at (1Sa 25:2). King Uzziah, who delighted in agriculture, had vineyards at (2Ch 26:10).

CARMELITE Hezro, one of David's mighty men, a native of Judean Carmel (1Sa 27:3; 1Ch 11:37).

CARMI, CARMITE (possibly *[fruitful] vine, vineyard owner* IDB).
1. Son of Reuben (Ge 46:9; Ex 6:14).
2. Son of Hezron (1Ch 4:1).
3. Father of Achan (Jos 7:1, 18; 1Ch 2:7) and his clan (Nu 26:6).

CARNAL MINDEDNESS Is in conflict with, the inner being (Ro 7:14-22), the Holy Spirit (Gal 5:17). Is at enmity with God (Ro 8:6-8; Jas 4:4). In the children of wrath (Eph 2:3). To be crucified (Ro 8:13; Gal 5:24). Excludes from kingdom of God (Gal 5:19-21). Reaps corruption (Gal 6:8).
See Care, Worldly; Flesh; Riches; Sin, Fruits of; Worldliness.

CARNELIAN Seen in John's vision of the glory of God (Rev 4:3) and the foundation of the New Jerusalem (Rev 21:20).
See Minerals of the Bible, 1; Stones.

CARPENTRY Building the ark (Ge 6:14-16). Tabernacle and furniture (Ex 31:2-9). *See Tabernacle.* David's palace (2Sa 5:11). Temple (2Ki 12:11; 22:6). *See Temple.* Making idols (Isa 41:7; 44:13). Carpenters (Jer 24:1; Zec 1:20), Joseph (Mt 13:55), Jesus (Mk 6:3).
See Carving; Master Craftsman.

CARPET See Tapestry.

CARPUS (*fruit(ful)*). A Christian at Troas (2Ti 4:13).

CARRIAGE A richly adorned royal means of transportation, a palanquin (SS 3:7, 9-10). In the description of fallen Babylon (Rev 18:13).

CARSHENA (possibly *black*). A Persian prince (Est 1:14).

CART(S) Vehicle(s) with wheels used for carrying goods as well as persons (Ge 45:19, 21; 46:5; 1Sa 6:7-14; 2Sa 6:3; Isa 28:27-28).

CARVING Woodwork of the temple was decorated with carvings of flowers, cherubim, and palm trees (1Ki 6:18, 29, 32, 35; Ps 74:6). Beds decorated with (Pr 7:16). Idols manufactured by (Dt 7:5; Isa 44:9-17; 45:20; Hab 2:18-19).
Persons skilled in: Bezalel (Ex 31:1-5), Huram (1Ki 7:13-51; 2Ch 2:13-14).

CASIPHIA A place in the Persian Empire (Ezr 8:17).

CASLUHITES A people whose progenitor was a son of Mizraim (Ge 10:14; 1Ch 1:12).

CASSIA An aromatic plant, probably cinnamon (Ps 45:8; Eze 27:19). An ingredient of the sacred oil (Ex 30:24).

CASTING See Molding.

CASTING LOTS To get a decision from God (Lev 16:8; Jos 18:6-10; 1Sa 14:42; 1Ch 24:31; 26:13-14; Jnh 1:7; Ac 1:26). To set a date (Est 3:7). To settle disputes (Pr 18:18). In divination (Eze 21:21). In gambling (Job 6:27; Ps 22:18; Mt 27:35). The decision is from the LORD (Pr 16:33). *See Lot, The.*

CASTLE See Fort; Tower. For the concept "My house is my castle" see Dt 24:10-11.

CASTOR AND POLLUX Twin sons of Zeus, Greek gods thought to have power over wind and wave (Ac 28:11).

CATACOMBS Subterranean burial places used by the early church. Most are in Rome, where they extend for 600 miles.

CATERPILLAR(S) See Grasshopper; Locust.

CATHOLIC EPISTLES See General Letters.

CATHOLICITY (liberality of religious sentiment, inclusiveness).
Taught:
In Christ's reproof of John (Mk 9:38-41; Lk 9:49-50). In Peter's vision of the sheet and visit to Cornelius (Ac 10:1-48). In Paul's commission (Ro 1:1-7, 14-16). In Paul's rebuke of Jewish exclusiveness (Ro 3:20-31; 4:1-25). In the judgment of apostolic church (Ac 15:1-31). In the unity of believers (Ro 5:1-2; Gal 3:27-28; Eph 2:14-17; Col 3:11-15). In the gifts of Holy Spirit to Gentiles as well as to Jews (Ac 10:44-48; 11:17-18).
See Heathen; Strangers.
Instances of:
Solomon, in his prayer (1Ki 8:41-43). Paul, in recognizing devout Gentiles (Ac 13:16, 26, 42-43). Peter (Ac 10:34-35). Rulers of the synagogue at Salamis, permitting the apostles to preach (Ac 13:5).

CATTLE Of the bovine species. Used for sacrifice (1Ki 8:63). *See Heifer; Offerings.* Sheltered (Ge 33:17). Pharaoh's dream of (Ge 41:2-7, 26-30). Stall-fed (Pr 15:17).
Gilead adapted to the raising of (Nu 32:1-4), and Bashan (Ps 22:12; Eze 39:18; Am 4:1).
See Animals; Bull; Cow; Heifer; Offerings.

CAUDA An island near Crete (Ac 27:16).

CAULKERS Those who drive some suitable substance into the seams of a ship's planking to render them watertight (Eze 27:9). *See Pitch; Tar.*

CAUL(S)
1. NIV "covering" of the liver. Burnt with sacrifice (Ex 29:13, 22; Lev 3:4, 10, 15; 4:9; 7:4; 8:16, 25; 9:10, 19).
2. NIV "headbands" (Isa 3:18). *See Headbands.*

CAUSE See Actions at Law.

CAUTION See Expediency; Prudence.

CAVALRY Mounted on, horses (Ex 14:23; 1Sa 13:5; 2Sa 8:4; 1Ki 4:26; 2Ch 8:6; 9:25; 12:3; Isa 30:16; 31:1; Jer 4:29; Zec 10:5; Rev 9:16-18), camels (1Sa 30:17).
See Armies.

CAVE Used as a dwelling: By Lot (Ge 19:30), Elijah (1Ki 19:9), Israelites (Eze 33:27), believers (Heb 11:38). Place of refuge (Jos 10:16-27; Jdg 6:2; 1Sa 13:6; 1Ki 18:4, 13; 19:9, 13). Burial place (Ge 23:9-20; 25:9; 49:29-32; 50:13; Jn 11:38).
Of Adullam (1Sa 22:1; 2Sa 23:13; 1Ch 11:15). En Gedi (1Sa 24:3-8).

CEDAR Valuable for building purposes (Isa 9:10). David's ample provision of, in Jerusalem, for the temple (2Ch 1:15; 22:4). Furnished by Hiram, king of Tyre, for Solomon's temple (1Ki 5:6-10; 9:11; 2Ch 2:16).
Used in rebuilding, the temple (Ezr 3:7), David's palace (2Sa 5:11; 1Ch 17:1), Solomon's palace (1Ki 7:2), masts of ships (Eze 27:5). Used in purifications (Lev 14:4, 6, 49-52; Nu 19:6).
Figurative (Ps 72:16; 92:12; Isa 2:13; 14:8; Jer 22:7; Eze 31:3; Zec 11:2).

CEDRON See Kidron.

CEILING A reference is to the walls of the temple (1Ki 6:15).

CELESTIAL PHENOMENA Fire from heaven, on the cities of the plain (Ge 19:24-25), on the two captains and their fifties (2Ki 1:10-14), on the flocks and servants of Job (Job 1:16). Hail, on the Egyptians (Ex 9:22-34).
Darkness, on the Egyptians (Ex 10:22-23), at the crucifixion of Jesus (Mt 27:45; Lk 23:44-45). Pillar of cloud and fire (Ex 13:21-22; 14:19, 24; 40:38; Nu 9:15-23; Ps 78:14). Thunder and lightning on Mt. Sinai (Ex 19:16, 18; 20:18). Sun stood still (Jos 10:12-13).
Prophecy of darkening of sun, moon, and stars (Joel 2:30, 32; Mt 24:29; Lk 21:25; Ac 2:19-20).
See Astronomy.

CELIBACY (*Abstaining from marriage and sexual activity*). Lamented by Jephthah's daughter (Jdg 11:38-39). Not obligatory (1Co 7:1-9, 25-26; 9:5; 1Ti 4:1-3). Practiced for kingdom of heaven's sake (Mt 19:10-12; 1Co 7:32-40). The 144,000 (Rev 14:1-4).

CELLAR See Storehouse.

CENCHREA A seaport near Corinth (Ac 18:18; Ro 16:1).

CENSER Used for offering incense (Lev 16:12; Nu 16:6-7, 16-18, 46; Rev 8:3). For the temple, made of gold (1Ki 7:50; 2Ch 4:22; Heb 9:4). Those which Korah used were converted into plates (Nu 16:37-39). Used in idolatrous rites (Eze 8:11).
Symbolic: (Rev 8:3, 5).

CENSORIOUSNESS See Charitableness; Speaking, Evil; Uncharitableness.

CENSUS Numbering of Israel by Moses (Ex 38:26; Nu 1; 3:14-43; 26), David (2Sa 24:1-9; 1Ch 21:1-8; 27:24).
A poll tax to be levied at each (Ex 30:12-16; 38:26).
Of the Roman Empire, by Caesar (Lk 2:1-3).

CENTURION (*ruler over 100*). A commander of 100 soldiers in the Roman army (Mk 15:44-45; Ac 21:32; 22:25-26; 23:17, 23; 24:23). Of Capernaum, comes to Jesus in behalf of his servant (Mt 8:5-13; Lk 7:1-10). In charge of the soldiers who crucified Jesus, testifies, "Truly this was the Son of God" (Mt 27:54; Mk 15:39; Lk 23:47).
See Cornelius; Julius.

CEPHAS (*rock*). See Peter, Simon.

CEREMONIAL WASHING The Mosaic Law, relative to cleansing, stresses that sin defiles. To keep this great truth constantly before the Israelites, specific ordinances concerning washings were given to Moses. The purpose was to teach, by this object lesson, that sin pollutes the soul, and that only those who were cleansed from their sins could be pure in the sight of the Lord (Heb 9:10; 10:22).
Of Garments (Ex 19:10, 14). Of priests (Ex 29:4; 30:18-21; 40:12, 31-32; Lev 8:6; 16:4, 24, 26, 28; Nu 19:7-10, 19; 2Ch 4:6). Of burnt offerings (Lev 1:9, 13; 9:14; 2Ch 4:6). Of the hands (Mt 15:2; Mk 7:2-5; Lk 11:38). Of the feet (1Ti 5:10).
For defilement (Lev 11:24-40). Of lepers (Lev 13:6; 14:9). Of those having bodily discharge (Lev 15:5-13). Of those having eaten or touched that which died (Lev 11:25, 40; 17:15-16).
Traditional forms of, not observed by Jesus (Lk 11:38-39).
See Defilement; Purification; Washings.

CERTIFICATE OF DIVORCE Given by the husband to his wife upon divorce (Dt 24:1-4; Mt 5:31; 19:7; Mk 10:4). Figurative of God's judgment on Israel (Isa 50:1; Jer 3:8). *See Divorce.*

CESAR See Caesar.

CESAREA See Caesarea.

CESAREA PHILIPPI See Caesarea Philippi.

CHAFF Winnowing of figurative of judgment (Job 21:18; Ps 1:4; 35:5; Isa 17:13; Da 2:35; Hos 13:3; Mt 3:12; Lk 3:17).

CHAINS Used as ornaments. Worn by princes (Ge 41:42; Da 5:7, 29), on ankles (Nu 31:50; Isa 3:19), on the breastplate of high priest (Ex 28:14; 39:15). As ornaments on camels (Jdg 8:26). A partition of, in the temple (1Ki 6:21; 7:17).
Used to confine prisoners (Ps 68:6; 149:8; Jer 40:4; Ac 12:6-7; 21:33; 28:20; 2Ti 1:16). *See Fetters.*
Figurative (Ps 73:6; Pr 1:9; La 3:7; Eze 7:23-27; Jude 6; 2Pe 2:4; Rev 20:1).

CHALCEDONY A precious stone (Rev 21:19). *See Minerals of the Bible, 1; Stones.*

CHALCOL See Calcol.

CHALDEA The southern portion of Babylonia. Often used interchangeably with Babylon as the name of the empire founded in the valley of the Euphrates. Abraham a native of (Ge 11:28, 31; 15:7). Founded by the Assyrians (Isa 23:13). Character of its people (Hab 1:6).
See Babylon; Chaldeans.

CHALDEAN ASTROLOGERS See Wise Men.

CHALDEANS
1. Virtually synonymous with the Babylonians (2Ki 25:4; 2Ch 36:17; Isa 13:19, ftns). See *Babylon; Chaldea.*
2. Learned and wise men of the east, NIV "astrologers" (Da 2:2, 4, 5, 10; 3:8; 4:7; 5:7).

CHALDEES See Chaldeans; Ur.

CHALK (Isa 27:9).

CHAMBERING See Adultery; Fornication.

CHAMBERLAIN See Eunuch.

CHAMBERS OF IMAGERY NIV "shrine of his own idol." Rooms in the temple where seventy elders of Israel worshiped idols (Eze 8:12).

CHAMELEON Forbidden as food (Lev 11:30).

CHAMOIS NIV "mountain sheep"; permitted as food (Dt 14:5). *See Animals.*

CHAMPAIGN Dt 11:30, KJV. See Arabah.

CHAMPIONSHIP Instances of battles decided by: Goliath and David (1Sa 17:8-53). Young men of David's and Abner's armies (2Sa 2:14-17). Representatives of the Philistines' and David's armies (2Sa 21:15-22).

CHANAAN See Canaan.

CHANCELLOR A state officer (Ezr 4:8-9, 17). *See Cabinet; Officer.*

CHANGE OF VENUE Granted Paul (Ac 23:17-35). Declined by Paul (Ac 25:9, 11).

CHANGERS OF MONEY See Money Changers.

CHAPITER See Capital.

CHAPMAN NIV "merchants" (2Ch 9:14). See *Merchant; Trade and Travel.*

CHARACTER
Of Believers:
Attentive to Christ's voice (Jn 10:3-4), blameless and harmless (Php 2:15), bold (Pr 28:1), contrite (Isa 57:15; 66:2), devout (Ac 8:2; 22:13), faithful (Rev 17:14), fearing God (Mal 3:16; Ac 10:2), following Christ (Jn 10:4, 27), godly (Ps 4:3; 2Pe 2:9), without falsehood (Jn 1:47), holy (Dt 7:6; 14:2; Col 3:12), humble (Ps 34:2; 1Pe 5:5), hungering for righteousness (Mt 5:6), just (Ge 6:9; Hab 2:4; Lk 2:25), led by the Spirit (Ro 8:14), generous (Isa 32:8; 2Co 9:13), loathing themselves (Eze 20:43), loving (Col 1:4; 1Th 4:9), lowly (Pr 16:19), meek (Isa 29:19; Mt 5:5), merciful (Ps 37:26; Mt 5:7), new creatures (2Co 5:17; Eph 2:10), obedient (Ro 16:19; 1Pe 1:14), poor in spirit (Mt 5:3), prudent (Pr 16:21), pure in heart (Mt 5:8; 1Jn 3:3), righteous (Isa 60:21; Lk 1:6), sincere (2Co 1:12; 2:17), steadfast (Ac 2:42; Col 2:5), taught of God (Isa 54:13; 1Jn 2:27), true (2Co 6:8), undefiled (Ps 119:1), upright (1Ki 3:6; Ps 15:2), watchful (Lk 12:37), zealous of good works (Tit 2:14). *See Righteous, Described.*
Of the Wicked:
Abominable (Rev 21:8), alienated from God (Eph 4:18; Col 1:21), blasphemous (Lk 22:65; Rev 16:9), blinded (2Co 4:4; Eph 4:18), boastful (Ps 10:3; 49:6), conspiring against believers (Ne 4:8; 6:2; Ps 38:12), corrupt (Mt 7:17; Eph 4:22), covetous (Mic 2:2; Ro 1:29), deceitful (Ps 5:6; Ro 3:13), delighting in the iniquity of others (Pr 2:14; Ro 1:32), despising believers (Ne 2:19; 4:2; 2Ti 3:3-4), destructive (Isa 59:7), disobedient (Ne 9:26; Tit 3:3; 1Pe 2:7), enticing to evil (Pr 1:10-14; 2Ti 3:6), envious (Ne 2:10; Tit 3:3), evildoers (Jer 13:23; Mic 7:3), fearful (Pr 28:1; Rev 21:8), fierce (Pr 16:29; 2Ti 3:3), foolish (Dt 32:6; Ps 5:5), forgetting God (Job 8:13), fraudulent (Pr 21:8; Isa 57:17), glorying in their shame (Php 3:19), hardhearted (Eze 3:7), hating the light (Job 24:13; Jn 3:20), heady and conceited (2Ti 3:4), hostile to God (Ro 8:7; Col 1:21), hypocritical (Isa 29:13; 2Ti 3:5), ignorant of God (Hos 4:1; 2Th 1:8), impudent (Eze 2:4), infidel (Ps 10:4; 14:1), loathsome (Pr 13:5), lovers of pleasure, not of God (2Ti 3:4), lying (Ps 58:3; 62:4; Isa 59:4), mischievous (Pr 24:8; Mic 7:3), murderous (Ps 10:8; 94:6; Ro 1:29), persecuting (Ps 69:26; 109:16), perverse (Dt 32:5), prayerless (Job 21:15; Ps 53:4), proud (Ps 59:12; Ob 3; 2Ti 3:2), rebellious (Isa 1:2; 30:9), rejoicing in the affliction of believers (Ps 35:15), reprobate (2Co 13:5; 2Ti 3:8; Tit 1:16), selfish (2Ti 3:2), sensual (Php 3:19; Jude 19), sold under sin (1Ki 21:20; 2Ki 17:17), stiff-hearted (Eze 2:4), stiff-necked (Ex 33:5; Ac 7:51), uncircumcised in heart (Jer 9:26), unclean (Isa 64:6; Eph 4:19), unjust (Pr 11:7; Isa 26:18), ungodly (Pr 16:27), unholy (2Ti 3:2), unmerciful (Ro 1:31), unprofitable (Mt 25:30; Ro 3:12), unruly (Tit 1:10), unthankful (Lk 6:35; 2Ti 3:2), unwise (Dt 32:6), without self-control (2Ti 3:3). *See Wicked, Described as.*
Good:
(Pr 22:1; Ecc 7:1). Defamation of, punished (Dt 22:13-19). Revealed in countenance (Isa 3:9).

C

Steadfastness of:
(Ps 57:7; 108:1; 112:7; Mk 4:20; 2Th 3:3). Exhortations to steadfastness (1Co 7:20; 15:58; 16:13; Eph 4:14-15; Php 1:27; 4:1; Col 1:23; 1Th 3:8; 2Th 2:15; Heb 3:6, 14; 10:23; 13:9; 1Pe 5:9; 2Pe 3:17; Rev 3:11). Reward of steadfastness (Mt 10:22; Jas 1:25). Continuing of (Rev 22:11).

Instances of Steadfastness:
Joseph (Ge 39:12). Moses (Heb 11:24-26). Joshua (Jos 24:15). Daniel (Da 1:8; 6:10). Three Hebrews (Da 3:16-18). Pilate (Jn 19:22). Peter and John (Ac 4:19-20). Paul (Ac 20:22-24; 21:13-14). See Decision; Stability.

Instability of:
(Pr 27:8; Jer 2:36; Hos 6:4; 7:8; 10:2; Mt 13:19-22; Mk 4:15-19; Lk 8:5-15; 2Pe 2:14; Rev 2:4). Warnings against (Pr 24:21-22; Lk 9:59-62; Eph 4:14; Heb 6:4-6; 13:9; Jas 1:6-8; 4:8; 2Pe 2:14).

Instances of Instability:
Reuben (Ge 49:3-4). Pharaoh (Ex 8:15, 32; 9:34; 14:5). Israelites (Ex 32:8; Jdg 2:17-19; 2Ch 11:17). Saul (1Sa 18:19). Solomon (1Ki 11:4-8). Rehoboam (2Ch 12:1). Pilate (Jn 18:37-40; 19:1-6). Demas (2Ti 4:10).

CHARASHIM See Craftsman; Ge Harashim.

CHARGE Delivered to ministers: See Ministers.

CHARGER See Plate, Platter.

CHARIOT For war (Ex 14:7, 9, 25; Jos 11:4; 1Sa 13:5; 1Ki 20:1, 25; 2Ki 6:14; 2Ch 12:2-3; Ps 20:7; Jer 46:9; 47:3; 51:21; Joel 2:5; Na 2:3-4; 3:2). Wheels of Pharaoh's, providentially taken off (Ex 14:25).
Commanded by captains (Ex 14:7; 1Ki 9:22; 22:31-33; 2Ki 8:21). Made of iron (Jos 17:18; Jdg 1:19). Introduced among Israelites by David (2Sa 8:4). Imported from Egypt by Solomon (1Ki 10:26-29). Cities for (1Ki 9:19; 2Ch 1:14; 8:6; 9:25). Royal (Ge 41:43; 46:29; 2Ki 5:9; 2Ch 35:24; Jer 17:25; Ac 8:29). Drawn by camels (Isa 21:7; Mic 1:13).
Kings ride in (2Ch 35:24; Jer 17:25; 22:4). Cherubim in Solomon's temple mounted on (1Ch 28:18).

Figurative:
Chariots of God (Ps 68:17; 104:3; 2Ki 6:17; Isa 66:15; Hab 3:8; Rev 9:9).

Symbolic: (Zec 6:1-8; 2Ki 2:11-12).

CHARISM, CHARISMA, CHARISMATA An inspired gift, bestowed on the apostles and early Christians without any claim of merit on the individual's part, for the good of the church (Mt 10:1, 8; Mk 16:17-18; Lk 10:1, 9, 17, 19; Ac 2:4; 10:44-46; 19:6; 1Co 12).
See Gifts From God; Miracles; Spiritual Gifts; Tongues, Gift of.

CHARITABLENESS Encouraged (Pr 10:12; 17:9). Commanded (Mt 5:23-24; 7:1-5; 18:21-22; Lk 6:36-42; 17:3-4; Jn 7:24; Ro 14:1-23; 15:1-2; 1Co 10:28-33; 16:14; 2Co 2:7; Gal 6:1; Eph 4:32; Col 3:13-14; 1Ti 1:5; 4:12; 2Ti 2:22; Jas 2:13; 4:11-12; 1Pe 3:9). Described (1Co 13:1-13). Covers sins (Pr 10:12; 17:9; 19:11; 1Pe 4:8). Pleases God (Mt 6:14-15; 18:23-35).
See Love; Uncharitableness.

CHARITY See Alms; Beneficence; Liberality; Love.

CHARMERS AND CHARMING Prohibited (Dt 18:11). Of serpents (Ps 58:4-5; Jer 8:17). Magic charms and amulets (Pr 17:8; Isa 3:20; Eze 13:18, 20). See Sorcery.

CHARRAN See Haran, 4.

CHASTISEMENT, FROM GOD A blessing (Job 5:17; Ps 94:12-13; Heb 12:11). Corrective (Dt 11:2-9; 2Sa 7:14-15; 2Ch 6:24-31; 7:13-14; Job 33:19; 34:31; Ps 73:14; 118:18; 119:67, 75; Isa 57:16-18; Jer 24:5-6; 46:28; 1Co 11:32).
Inflicted for sins (Lev 26:28; Ps 89:32; 107:10-12, 17; Isa 40:2; Jer 30:14; La 1:5; Hos 7:12; 10:10; Am 4:6). Administered in love (Dt 8:5; Pr 3:11-12; Heb 12:5-10; Rev 3:19).
Repentance under (Ps 106:43-44; 107:10-13, 17-19; Isa 26:16; Jer 31:18-19). Failure to repent under (Isa 42:25; Jer 2:30; Hag 2:17).
Prayer to be spared from (Ps 6:1; 38:1; 107:23-31). Vicariously borne by Jesus (Isa 53:4-5).
See Afflictions; Judgments; Punishment; Wicked, Punishment of.

CHASTITY

Commanded:
(Ex 20:14; Pr 2:10-11, 16-22; 5:3—21; 6:24-25; 7:1-5; 31:3; Mt 5:27-32; Ac 15:20; Ro 13:13; 1Co 6:13-19; 7:1-2, 7-9, 25-26, 36-37; Eph 5:3; Col 3:5; 1Th 4:3, 7).

Instances of:
Joseph (Ge 39:7-20). Boaz (Ru 3:6-13). Job (Job 31:1, 9-12). Paul (1Co 7). The 144,000 (Rev 14:1-5).
See Celibacy; Self-Control.

CHEATING See Dishonesty.

CHEBAR See Kebar.

CHEDORLAOMER See Kedorlaomer.

CHEERFULNESS See Contentment.

CHEESE (1Sa 17:18; 2Sa 17:29; Job 10:10).

CHELAL See Kelal.

CHELLUH See Keluhi.

CHELUB See Kelub.

CHELUBAI See Caleb, 1.

CHEMARIM NIV "pagan [priests]" (Zep 1:4). See Groves; High Places; Idol; Idolatry; Priest, Corrupt.

CHEMOSH An idol of the Moabites and Ammonites (1Ki 11:7, 33; 2Ki 23:13; Jer 48:7, 13, 46), and Amorites (Jdg 11:24).

CHENAANAH See Kenaanah.

CHENANI See Kenani.

CHENANIAH See Kenaniah.

CHEPHAR-HAAMMONAI See Kephar Ammoni.

CHEPHIRAH See Kephirah.

CHERAN See Keran.

CHERETHIMS, CHERETHITES See Kerethite(s).

CHERITH See Kerith.

CHERUB See Kerub.

CHERUBIM A classification or order of heavenly beings.
Eastward of the garden of Eden (Ge 3:24).
In the tabernacle (Ex 25:18-20; 37:7-9). Ark rested beneath the wings of (1Ki 8:6-7; 2Ch 5:7-8; Heb 9:5). Figures of, embroidered on walls of tabernacle (Ex 26:1; 36:8), and on the veil (Ex 26:31; 36:35).
In the temple (1Ki 6:23-29; 2Ch 3:10-13). Figures of, on the veil (2Ch 3:14), walls (1Ki 6:29-35; 2Ch 3:7), movable stands (1Ki 7:29, 36).
In Ezekiel's vision of the temple (Eze 41:18-20, 25).
Figurative (Eze 28:14, 16).
Symbolic (Eze 1; 10).

CHESALON See Kesalon.

CHESED See Kesed.

CHESIL See Kesil.

CHEST
1. The ark of the covenant (Ex 25:10-14; Dt 10:1-2).
2. For money (2Ki 12:9-10; 2Ch 24:8-11).
3. The torso (Job 41:24; Da 2:32; Rev 1:13).

CHESTNUT TREE See Plane Tree.

CHESULLOTH See Kesulloth.

CHEZIB See Kezib.

CHICKEN See Hen, 2.

CHIDING See Rebuke.

CHIDON See Kidon.

CHILDBEARING Pain of increased as part of the curse (Ge 3:16). Salvation through (1Ti 2:15), a verse of uncertain meaning.

CHILDLESSNESS A reproach (Ge 16:2; 29:32; 30:1-3, 13; 1Sa 1:6; Isa 4:1; Lk 1:25). See Barrenness.

CHILDREN

A Blessing:
[Ge 5:29; 30:1; Ps 127:3-5; Pr 17:6]. The gift of God (Ge 4:1, 25; 17:16, 20; 22:17; 28:3; 29:32-35; 30:2, 5-6, 17-20, 22-24; 48:9, 16; Ru 4:13; Job 1:21; Ps 107:38, 41; 113:9; 127:3). Promised to the righteous (Dt 7:12, 14; Job 5:25; Ps 128:2-4, 6). Given in answer to prayer, to Abraham (Ge 15:2-5; 21:1-2), Isaac (Ge 25:21), Leah (Ge 30:17-22), Rachel (Ge 30:22-24), Hannah (1Sa 1:9-20), Zechariah (Lk 1:13).

In Infancy:
Circumcision of. See Circumcision. Dedicated to God, Samson (Jdg 13:5, 7), Samuel (1Sa 1:24-28), Jesus (Lk 2:22). Nurses for (Ex 2:7-9; Ru 4:16; 2Sa 4:4; 2Ki 11:2; Ac 7:20). Treatment of (Eze 16:4-6; Lk 2:7, 12). Weaning of (Ge 21:8; 1Sa 1:22; 1Ki 11:20; Ps 131:2; Isa 28:9).

In Early Childhood:
Amusements of (Job 21:11; Zec 8:5; Mt 11:16-17; Lk 7:31-32). Early piety of, Samuel (1Sa 2:18; 3), Jeremiah (Jer 1:5-7), John the Baptist (Lk 1:15, 80), Jesus (Lk 2:40, 46-47, 52). Taught to walk (Hos 11:3). Tutored (2Ki 10:1; Ac 22:3; Gal 3:24; 4:1-2). See Tutor.

God's Care Of:
(Ex 22:22-24; Dt 10:18; 14:29; Job 29:12; Ps 10:14, 17-18; 27:10; 68:5; 146:9; Jer 49:11; Hos 14:3; Mal 3:5). Blessed by Jesus (Mt 19:13-15; Mk 10:13-16; Lk 18:15-17). Intercessional sacrifices in behalf of (Job 1:5).

Commandments to—
To honor and obey parents (Ex 20:12; Lev 19:3, 32; Dt 5:16; Pr 1:8-9; 6:20-23; 23:22; 30:11, 17; Mt 15:4; Mk 10:19; Lk 18:20; Eph 6:1, 2-3; Col 3:20; 1Ti 3:4). To seek wisdom (Pr 4:1-11, 20-22; 5:1-2; 8:21-33; 27:11). To praise the Lord (Ps 148:12-13). To remember their Creator (Pr 23:26; Ecc 12:1). To obey (Ps 119:9; Pr 3:1-3; 6:20-25). To be pure (Ecc 11:9-10; La 3:27; 1Ti 4:12; 2Ti 2:22; Tit 2:6). See Young Men.

Miracles on behalf of—
Raised from the dead, by Elijah (1Ki 17:17-23), Elisha (2Ki 4:17-36), Jesus (Mt 9:18, 24-26; Mk 5:35-42; Lk 7:13-15; 8:49-56). Healing of (Mt 15:28; 17:18; Mk 7:29-30; 9:23-27; Lk 8:42-56; 9:38-42; Jn 4:46-54).

Prayer in behalf of—
For healing (2Sa 12:16). For divine favor (Ge 17:18). For spiritual wisdom (1Ch 22:12; 29:19). For sins (Job 1:5).

Promises and assurances to—
Promise of divine instruction (Isa 54:13). Long life to the obedient (Ex 20:12; Dt 5:16; Pr 3:1-10; Eph 6:2-3). Love and peace (Pr 8:17, 32; Isa 40:11; 54:13). Acceptance by Jesus (Mt 18:4-5, 10; 19:14-15; Mk 9:37; 10:16; Lk 9:48; 18:15-16). Joy to parents of wise children (Pr 23:15-16, 24-25; 29:3). Forgiven sins (1Jn 2:12-13).

The righteous, blessed by God—
In escaping judgments (Ge 6:18; 7:1; 19:12, 15-16; Lev 26:44-45; 1Ki 11:13; 2Ki 8:19; Pr 11:21; 12:7). In temporal prosperity (Ge 12:7; 13:15; 17:7-8; 21:13; 26:3-4, 24; Dt 4:37; 10:15; 12:28; 1Ki 15:4; Ps 37:26; 102:28; 112:2-3; Pr 13:22). In divine mercy (Ps 103:17-18; Pr 3:33; 20:7; Isa 44:3-5; 65:23; Jer 32:39; Ac 2:39; 1Co 7:14).

Parental Relationships:
Love of, for parents: Ruth (Ru 1:16-18), Jesus (Jn 19:26-27). Counsel of parents to (1Ki 2:1-4; 1Ch 22:6-13; 28:9-10, 20). Of ministers (1Ti 3:4; Tit 1:6).

Instruction of—
The law (Dt 6:6-9; 11:19-20; 31:12-13; Jos 8:35; Ps 78:1-8). The fear of the Lord (Ps 34:11). The providence of God (Ex 10:2; 12:26-27; 13:8-10, 14-16; Dt 4:9-10; Joel 1:3). Righteousness (Pr 1:1, 4; 22:6; Isa 28:9-10; 38:19). The Scriptures (Ac 22:3; Eph 6:4; 2Ti 3:15).
See Instruction; Tutor; Young Men.

Correction and punishment—
By discipline (Pr 19:18; 23:13; 29:15; Eph 6:4; Col 3:2). By the rod (Pr 13:24; 22:15; 23:13-14; 29:15). By death (Ex 21:15; 21:17; Lev 20:9; Dt 21:21; 27:16; Pr 20:20; 22:15; 30:17; Mt 15:4; Mk 7:10).

Differences and partiality—
Differences made between male and female (Lev 12). Partiality of parents, Rebekah for Jacob (Ge 27:6-17), Jacob for Joseph (Ge 37:3-4). Partiality among, forbidden (Dt 21:15-17).

Death and Mistreatment—
Death, as a judgment upon parents: Firstborn of Egypt (Ex 12:29; Nu 8:17; Ps 78:5), sons of Eli (1Sa 3:13-14), sons of Saul (1Sa 28:18-19), David's child by Uriah's wife (2Sa 12:14-19). Eaten. See Cannibalism. Edict to murder: Of Pharaoh (Ex 1:22), Jehu (2Ki 10:1-8), Herod (Mt 2:16-18). Caused to pass through fire (2Ki 16:3; 17:7; Jer 32:35; Eze 16:21). Sacrificed (2Ki 17:31; Eze 16:20-21). Sold for debt (2Ki 4:1; Ne 5:5; Job 24:9; Mt 18:25). Sold in marriage, law concerning (Ex 21:7-11). Instance of Leah and Rachel (Ge 29:15-30).

Religious Involvement:
Attend divine worship (Ex 34:23; Jos 8:35; 2Ch 20:13; 31:16; Ezr 8:21; Ne 8:2-3; 12:43; Mt 21:15; Lk 2:46). Entitled to enjoy religious privileges (Dt 12:12-13). Illegitimate excluded from privilege of congregation (Dt 23:2; Heb 12:8).

Covenant involvement—
Bound by covenants of parents (Ge 17:9-14). Share benefits of parents' covenant privileges (Ge 6:18; 12:7; 13:15; 17:7-8; 19:12; 21:23; 26:3-5, 24; Lev 26:44-45; Isa 65:23; 1Co 7:14). Involved in guilt of parents (Ex 20:5; 34:7; Lev 20:5; 26:39-42; Nu 14:18, 33; 1Ki 16:12; 21:29; Job 21:19; Ps 37:28; Isa 14:20-21; 65:6-7; Jer 32:18; Da 6:24). Not punished for parent's sake (2Ki 14:6; Jer 31:29-30; Eze 18:1-30).

Character of:
Known by conduct (Pr 20:11). Future state (Mt 18:10; 19:14). Status of minors (Gal 4:1-2). Alienated: Ishmael, to gratify Sarah (Ge 21:9-15). Adopted. See Adoption; Parents.

Good—
Have Lord's presence (1Sa 3:19). Blessed of God (Pr 3:1-4; Eph 6:2-3). Honor the aged (Job 32:6-7). Honor father (Mal 1:6). A joy to parents (Pr 10:1; 15:20; 23:24; 29:3; 29:17). Keep the law (Pr 28:7). Know the scriptures (2Ti 3:15). Love parents (Ge 46:29). Obey parents (Ge 28:7; 47:30; Pr 13:1), which pleases God (Col 3:20). Attend to parental teaching (Pr 13:1). Partake of God's promises (Ac 2:39). Extol the Savior (Mt 21:15-16; Ps 8:2). Take care of parents (Ge 45:9-11; 47:12; Mt 15:5). Wise (Ecc 4:13). Illustrative of conversion (Mt 18:3), of a teachable spirit (Mt 18:4). Symbolic of regeneration (Mt 18:2-6, 10; 19:14-15; Mk 9:36-37; 10:13-15; Mk 10:16; Lk 9:46-48; 18:15, 17).

Good, Instances of—
Shem and Japheth (Ge 9:23). Isaac (Ge 22:6-12). Esau (Ge 28:6-9). Jacob (Ge 28:7). Judah (Ge 44:18-34). Joseph (Ge 45:9-13; 46:29; 47:11-12, 29-30; 48:12; 50:1-13). Moses (Ex 15:2; 18:7). Jephthah's daughter (Jdg 11:36-39). Ruth (Ru 1:15-17). Samuel (1Sa 2:26; 3:10). David (1Sa 22:3-4; Ps 71:5, 17). Solomon (1Ki 2:19-20; 3:3-13). Abijah (1Ki 14:13). Obadiah (1Ki 18:12). Jehoshaphat (1Ki 22:43; 2Ch 17:3). The captive maid (2Ki 5:2-4). Jewish children (2Ch 20:13; Ne 8:3; 12:43). Josiah (2Ch 34:1-3). Job (Job 29:4). Elihu (Job 32:4-7). Jeremiah (Jer 1:5-7). The Recabites (Jer 35:18-19). Daniel and the three Hebrews (Da 1:8-20). Children in the temple (Mt 21:15). John (Lk 1:80). Jesus (Lk 2:51-52). Timothy (2Ti 1:5; 3:15).

Wicked—
Disrespectful, to parents (Dt 27:16; Pr 15:20; 30:11; Eze 22:7; Mic 7:6; Job 19:18; 2Ki 2:23). Disobedient to parents (Dt 21:18-21; Pr 13:1; 15:5; 30:13; Ro 1:30; 2Ti 3:2). Defraud parents (Pr 28:7, 24; Mk 7:9-13). Disgrace parents (Pr 10:1; 17:2, 21, 25; 19:13, 26; 23:22). Betray parents (Mk 13:12).

Wicked, Instances of—
Canaan (Ge 4:25). Lot's daughters (Ge 19:14, 30-38). Ishmael (Ge 21:9). Eli's sons (1Sa 2:12, 22-25). Samuel's sons (1Sa 8:3). Absalom (2Sa 15). Adonijah (1Ki 1:5). Abijah (1Ki 15:33). Ahaziah (1Ki 22:52). Children at Bethel (2Ki 2:23-24). Samaritan's descendants (2Ki 17:41). Adrammelech and Sharezer (2Ki 19:37; 2Ch 32:31). Amon (2Ki 21:21).
See Babies; Young Men.

CHILDREN OF GOD See Righteous.

CHILEAB See Kileab.

CHILION See Kilion.

CHILMAD *See Kilmad.*

CHIMHAM *See Kimham.*

CHIMNEY NIV "window" (Hos 13:3). *See Window.*

CHINESE KJV "Sinim" is believed by some to be a reference to the Chinese; NIV has "Aswan" (Isa 49:12). *See Aswan.*

CHINNERETH, CHINNEROTH*See Kinnereth.*

CHIOS *See Kios.*

CHISLEU *See Kislev.*

CHISLON *See Kislon.*

CHISLOTH-TABOR *See Kisloth Tabor.*

CHITTIM *See Kittim.*

CHIUN NIV "pedestal"; perhaps the proper name "Kaiwan" (Am 5:26, ftn). *See Rephan.*

CHLOE (*tender shoot*). A Christian of Corinth (1Co 1:11).

CHOICE
Between life and death (Dt 30:19-20). God and false gods (Jos 24:15-18). Judgments by David (2Sa 24:12-14; 1Ch 21:11-13). Between God and Baal (1Ki 18:21, 39-40). Of Moses (Heb 11:24-25).
See Contingencies; Blessings, Spiritual Contingent Upon Obedience.

CHOIR Leaders of (1Ch 25:2-6; Ne 12:42). Presided over by chief musician (Ps 4; Hab 3:19). Instructed by teachers (1Ch 15:22, 27; 25:7-8).
In the tabernacle (1Ch 6:31-47). Composed of singers and instrumentalists (1Ch 15:16-21; 25:1-7; 2Ch 5:12-13; 23:13; Isa 38:20). Mixed choirs (2Ch 35:15, 25; Ezr 2:64-65). Sang every morning and evening (1Ch 9:33; 23:5, 30), during offering of sacrifices (1Ch 16:41-42; 2Ch 29:27-28), at restoration of the temple (Ezr 2:41; 3:10-11), at the dedication of the wall of Jerusalem (Ne 12:27-30). Appointed from the army to sing praises to God as a military strategy (2Ch 20:21).
See Music.

CHOOSING *See Choice.*

CHOR-ASHAN *See Bor Ashan.*

CHORAZIN *See Korazin.*

CHORUSES *See Music.*

CHOSEN Also referred to as elect (Mt 24:22, 24, 31). Few (Mt 20:16). Called (1Pe 2:9; Rev 17:14).
See Elect; Election; Foreknowledge of God; Predestination.

CHOZEBA *See Cozeba.*

CHRIST (*the Anointed One*). *See Jesus the Christ.*

CHRISTIAN (*follower of Christ*). Believers called (Ac 11:26; 26:28; 1Pe 4:16). *See Righteous.*

CHRISTIANITY The word does not occur in the Bible. It was first used by Ignatius, in the first half of the second century. It designates all that which Jesus Christ brings to people of faith, life, and salvation.

CHRISTMAS The anniversary of the birth of Christ and its observance. The date of the birth of Christ is not known. Celebrated by most Protestants and by Roman Catholics on December 25, by Eastern Orthodox churches on January 6, and by the Armenian church on January 19. The first mention of its observance on December 25 is in the time of Constantine, c. A.D. 325. The word *Christmas* is formed of *Christ* plus *Mass*, meaning a religious service in commemoration of the birth of Christ. It is not clear whether the early Christians thought of or observed Christmas, but once introduced, the observance spread throughout Christendom. Some Christian groups disapprove of the festival.

CHRONICLES, 1 and 2
Author: Anonymous; according to ancient Jewish tradition, Ezra
Date: Latter half of the fifth century B.C.
Outline:
I. Genealogies: Creation to Restoration (1Ch 1-9).
 A. The Patriarchs (ch. 1).
 B. The 12 Sons of Jacob/Israel (2:1-2).
 C. The Family of Judah (2:3-4:23).
 D. The Sons of Simeon (4:24-43).
 E. Reuben, Gad and the Half-Tribe of Manasseh (ch. 5).
 F. Levi and Families (ch. 6).
 G. Issachar, Benjamin, Naphtali, Manasseh, Ephraim and Asher (chs. 7-9).
II. The Reign of David (1Ch 10-29).
 A. Death of Saul (ch. 10).
 B. Capture of Jerusalem; David's Power Base (chs. 11-12).
 C. Return of the Ark; Establishment of David's Kingdom (chs. 13-16).
 D. Dynastic Promise (ch. 17).
 E. David's Conquest (chs. 18-20).
 F. The Census (ch. 21).
 G. Preparations for the Temple (ch. 22).
 H. Organization of the Temple Service (chs. 23-26).
 I. Administrative Structures of the Kingdom (ch. 27).
 J. David's Final Preparations for Succession and the Temple (28:1-29:20).
III. The Reign of Solomon (2Ch 1-9).
 A. The Gift of Wisdom (ch. 1).
 B. Building the Temple (2:1-5:1).

 C. Dedication of the Temple (5:2-7:22).
 D. Solomon's Other Activities (ch. 8).
 E. Solomon's Wisdom, Splendor and Death (ch. 9).
IV. The Schism, and the History of the Kings of Judah (2Ch 10-36).
 A. Rehoboam (chs. 10-12).
 B. Abijah (13:1-14:1).
 C. Asa (14:2-16:14).
 D. Jehoshaphat (17:1-21:3).
 E. Jehoram and Ahaziah (21:4-22:9).
 F. Joash (22:10-24:27).
 G. Amaziah (ch. 25).
 H. Uzziah (ch. 26).
 I. Jotham (ch. 27).
 J. Ahaz (ch. 28).
 K. Hezekiah (chs. 29-32).
 L. Manasseh (33:1-20).
 M. Amon (33:21-25).
 N. Josiah (34:1-36:1).
 O. Josiah's Successors (36:2-14).
 P. Exile and Restoration (36:15-23).

CHRONOLOGY, NEW TESTAMENT
In ancient times historians were not accustomed to recording history under exact dates, but were satisfied when some specific event was related to the reign of a noted ruler or a famous contemporary. Our method of dating events in reference to the birth of Christ was started by Dionysius Exiguus, a monk who lived in the sixth century, but who wrongly calculated Jesus' birth year. The birth of Christ must be dated in or before 5 B.C., as it is known that Herod the Great died in 4 B.C., and according to the Gospels Jesus was born some time before the death of the king. Luke gives the age of Jesus at his baptism as "about thirty years" (Lk 3:23). This would bring the baptism at c. A.D. 26 or 27. Since Herod began the reconstruction of the temple in 20 B.C., the "forty-six years" mentioned by the Jews during the first Passover of Jesus' public ministry (Jn 2:13-22), brings us to A.D. 27 for this first Passover. The ministry of John the Baptist began about the middle of A.D. 26. The time of the Crucifixion is determined by the length of the ministry of Jesus. Mark's Gospel seems to require at least two years. John's Gospel explicitly mentions three Passovers (Jn 2:23; 6:4; 11:55). If the feast (Jn 5:1) is also a Passover, as seems probable, then the length of the ministry of Jesus is a full three years and a little over. This places the Crucifixion at the Passover of A.D. 30.
As for the Apostolic Age the chronological data are very limited and uncertain. The death of Herod Agrippa I in A.D. 44 is one of the fixed dates of the NT. This was the year of Peter's arrest and miraculous escape from prison. The proconsulship of Gallio was between 51 and 53, and this would bring the beginning of Paul's ministry at Corinth to c. A.D. 50. The accession of Festus as governor, under whom Paul was sent to Rome, probably took place c. 59/60.

New Testament Chronology	
Birth of Jesus	7-5 B.C.
Baptism of Jesus	A.D. 26
Crucifixion of Jesus	30
Conversion of Saul	34/35
Death of Herod Agrippa I	44
James written	before 50 (?)
First Missionary Journey	46-48
Galatians written	48/49
Jerusalem Conference	49/50
Second Missionary Journey	50-52
Paul at Corinth	50-52
1 and 2 Thessalonians written	51
Arrival of Gallio as Proconsul	52
Third Missionary Journey	53-57
Paul at Ephesus	54-57
1 and 2 Corinthians written	55
Romans written	57
Paul's Arrest in Jerusalem	57
Imprisonment at Caesarea	57-59
On Island of Malta	59
Arrival at Rome	59
Roman Imprisonment	59-61/62
Colossians, Philemon, Ephesians	60
Philippians written	61
Paul's Release and Further Work	62-67
1 Timothy and Titus written	63-65
Synoptic Gospels and Acts written	before 67
1 and 2 Peter written	67/68
Peter's Death at Rome	67/68
Paul's Second Roman Imprisonment	67/68
2 Timothy written	67/68
Paul's Death at Rome	67/68
Jude written	c. 65-80
Writings of John	c. 90-100
Death of John	c. 100

CHRONOLOGY, OLD TESTAMENT
For the period from the Creation to the Flood the only Biblical data are the ages of the patriarchs in the genealogical tables of Genesis 5, 7, and 11. Extrabiblical sources for this period are almost completely lacking. For the period from the Flood to Abraham we are again dependent upon the genealogical data in the Bible. The numbers vary in the Masoretic text, the LXX, and the Samaritan Pentateuch. The construction of an absolute chronology from Adam to Abraham is not now possible on the basis of the available data.
The following chart is based on the early date of the Exodus. The later date (c. 1230 B.C.) only affects the dating of the patriarchs and judges.

Old Testament Chronology (From Abraham)	
Abram born	2166 B.C.
Abraham dies	1991
Jacob and family in Egypt	1876
Moses born	1526
The Exodus	1446
Moses dies; Israelites enter Canaan	1406
The Judges	1375-1050
Saul as king	1050-1010
David as king	1010-970
Solomon as king	970-930
Northern kingdom of Israel	930-722
Southern kingdom of Judah	930-586
Exile	586-538
First return under Zerubbabel	538
Temple rebuilt	536-516
Second return under Ezra	458
Wall of Jerusalem rebuilt	445
Third return under Nehemiah	432
Close of OT history and prophecy	c. 400

For the chronology of the kings, *See Kings.* For the approximate dates of OT books, see each by name.

CHRYSOLITE
1. One of the precious stones set in the priestly breastpiece (Ex 28:17; 39:10).
2. A precious stone used in poetic, prophetic, and apocalyptic literature (SS 5:14; Eze 1:16; 10:9; 28:13; Da 10:6; Rev 21:20). *See Minerals of the Bible, 1; Stones.*

CHRYSOPRASE A precious stone (Rev 21:20). *See Minerals of the Bible, 1; Stones.*

CHUB *See Libya.*

CHUN *See Cun.*

CHURCH, PLACE OF WORSHIP
Note: Nowhere in scripture does the word "church" identify a place of worship, but rather a group (or body) of believers, and only in the NT.
The Place Where God Was Worshiped:
Courts (Ps 65:4; 84:2, 10; 92:13; 96:8; 100:4; 116:19; Isa 1:12; 62:9; Zec 3:7). Holy Oracle (Ps 28:2). Holy place (Ex 28:29; 38:24;

Lev 6:16; 10:17; 14:13; 16:2-24; Jos 5:15; 1Ki 8:8; 1Ch 23:32; 2Ch 29:5; 30:27; 35:5; Ezr 9:8; Ps 24:3; 46:4; 68:17; Ecc 8:10; Isa 57:15; Eze 41:4; 42:13; 45:4; Mt 24:15; Ac 6:13; 21:28; Heb 9:12, 25). Holy temple (Ps 5:7; 11:4; 65:4; 79:1; 138:2; Jnh 2:4, 7; Mic 1:2; Hab 2:20; Eph 2:21; 3:17).

House of God (Ge 28:17, 22; Jos 9:23; Jdg 18:31; 20:18, 26; 21:2; 1Ch 9:11; 24:5; 2Ch 5:14; 22:12; 24:13; 33:7; 36:19; Ezr 5:8, 15; 7:20, 23; Ne 6:10; 11:11; 13:7, 11; Ps 42:4; 52:8; 55:14; 84:10; Ecc 5:1; Isa 2:3; Hos 9:8; Joel 1:16; Mic 4:2; Zec 7:2; Mt 12:4; 1Ti 3:15; Heb 10:21; 1Pe 4:17). House of the Lord (Ex 23:19; 34:26; Dt 23:18; Jos 6:24; Jdg 19:18; 1Sa 1:7, 24; 2Sa 12:20; 1Ki 3:1; 6:37; 7:40; 8:10, 63; 10:5; 2Ki 11:3-4, 15, 18-19; 12:4, 9-10, 13, 16; 16:18; 20:8; 23:2, 7, 11; 25:9; 1Ch 6:31; 22:1, 11, 14, 23:4; 26:12; 2Ch 8:16; 26:21; 29:5, 15; 33:15; 34:15; 36:14; Ezr 7:27; Ps 23:6; 27:4; 92:13; 116:19; 118:26; 122:1, 9; 134:1; Isa 2:2; 37:14; Jer 17:26; 20:1-2; 26:2, 7; 28:1, 5; 29:26; 35:2; 36:5-6; 38:14; 41:5; 51:51; La 2:7; Eze 44:4; Hag 1:2; Zec 8:9). House of Prayer (Isa 56:7; Mt 21:13; Mk 11:17; Lk 19:46). My Father's House (Jn 2:16; 14:2).

Sanctuary (Ex 25:8; Lev 19:30; 21:12; Nu 3:28; 4:12; 7:9; 8:19; 10:21; 18:1, 5; 19:20; 1Ch 9:29; 22:19; 24:5; 28:10; 2Ch 20:8; 26:18; 29:21; 30:8, 19; Ne 10:39; Ps 20:2; 28:2; 63:2; 68:24; 73:17; 74:3, 7; 77:13; 78:69; 150:1; Isa 16:12; 63:18; La 2:7, 20; 4:1; Eze 5:11; 42:20; 44:5, 27; 45:3; 48:8, 21; Da 8:11, 13-14; 9:17, 26; 11:31; Heb 8:2; 9:1-2; 13:11). Tabernacle (Lev 26:11; Jos 22:19; Ps 15:1; 61:4; 76:2; Heb 8:2, 5; 9:2, 11; Rev 13:6; 21:3). Temple (1Sa 1:9; 3:3; 2Ki 11:10, 13; Ezr 4:1; Ps 5:7; 11:4; 27:4; 29:9; 48:9; 68:29; Isa 6:1; Mal 3:1; Mt 4:5; 23:16; Lk 18:10; 24:53). Zion (Ps 9:11; 48:11; 74:2; 132:13; 137:1; Isa 35:10; Jer 31:6; 50:5; Joel 2:1, 15).

Buildings: *See Synagogue; Tabernacle; Temple.*

Nature:
Instituted by divine authority (Ex 25:8-9; Dt 12:11-14). Holy (Ex 30:26-29; 40:9; Lev 8:10-11; 16:33; 19:30; 21:12; 26:2; Nu 7:1; 8:19; 1Ki 9:3; 1Ch 29:3; 2Ch 3:8; Isa 64:11; Eze 23:39; 43:12). Should be shown reverence (Lev 19:30; 26:2). Figurative (1Co 3:17).

CHURCH, THE BODY OF BELIEVERS *(assembly)*.
"Church" in this entry encompasses organized bodies of believers in both testaments. In the OT, the church was a group of "gathered together" Hebrew believers, a congregation. In the NT, the church (technically) was a group of "called out" Christian believers.

Called:
In the OT, the congregation, congregation of Israel, or community of Israel (Ex 12:3, 6, 19, 47; 16:1, 2, 9-10, 22; Lev 4:13, 15; 10:17; 24:14). Zion (2Ki 19:21, 31; Ps 9:11; 48:2, 11-12; 74:2; 132:13; 137:1; Isa 35:10; Isa 40:9; 49:14; 51:16; 52:1-2, 7-8; 60:14; 62:1, 11; Jer 31:6; 50:5; La 1:4; Joel 2:1, 15). Also (Ro 9:33; 11:26; 1Pe 2:16). Daughter of Zion (Isa 62:11; Zec 9:9). Also (Mt 21:5; Jn 12:15). In the NT, church (Mt 16:18; 18:17; Ac 2:47; 7:38; 20:28; 1Co 11:18; 14:19, 23, 28, 33-34; 15:9; Gal 1:13; Eph 1:22; 1Ti 3:15).

Described as:
Assembly of believers (Ps 89:7). The upright (Ps 111:1). Body of Christ (1Co 12:27; Eph 1:22-23; 4:12; Col 1:24). Branch of God's planting (Isa 60:21). Bride (Gal 6:16). Bride of Christ (Rev 21:9). Christ's body (Ro 12:5; 1Co 12:12, 27; Eph 1:22-23; 4:12; Col 1:24). Church of God (Ac 20:28). Church of the living God (1Ti 3:15). Church of the firstborn (Heb 12:23). Congregation of Believers (Ps 149:1). Congregation of the Lord's Poor (Ps 74:19). Dove (SS 2:14; 5:2). Family in heaven and earth (Eph 3:15). Flock of God (Eze 34:15; 1Pe 5:2). Fold of Christ (Jn 10:16). General Assembly of the Firstborn (Heb 12:23). The God of Jacob (Isa 2:3). Golden lampstand (Rev 1:20). God's building (1Co 3:9). God's field (1Co 3:9). God's heritage (Joel 3:2; 1Pe 5:3). Habitation of God (Eph 2:22). Heavenly Jerusalem (Gal 4:26; Heb 12:22). Holy City (Rev 21:2). Holy Mountain (Zec 8:3). Holy hill (Ps 2:6; 15:1). House (Heb 3:6). House of God (1Ti 3:15; Heb 10:21). House of Christ (Heb 3:6). Household of God (Eph 2:19). Inheritance (Ps 28:9; Isa 19:25). Israel of God (Gal 6:16). Joy of the whole earth (Ps 48:1-2, 11-13). Kingdom of God (Mt 6:33; 12:28; 19:24; 21:31). Kingdom of heaven (Mt 3:2; 4:17; 5:3, 10, 19-20; 10:7). His kingdom (Ps 103:19; 145:12; Mt 16:28; Lk 1:33). My kingdom (Jn 18:36). Your kingdom (Ps 45:6; 145:11, 13; Mt 6:10; Lk 23:42). Lamb's bride (Eph 5:22-32; Rev 22:17). Lamb's wife (Rev 19:7-9; 21:9). The Lord's portion (Dt 32:9). Lot of God's inheritance (Dt 32:9). Mount Zion (Heb 12:22). New Jerusalem (Rev 21:2). Pillar and ground of the truth (1Ti 3:15). Place of God's throne (Eze 43:7). Pleasant portion (Jer 12:10). River of gladness (Ps 46:4-5). Sanctuary of God (Ps 114:2). Sought out, a city not forsaken (Isa 62:12). Spiritual house (1Pe 2:5). Strength and Glory of God (Ps 78:61). Temple of God (1Co 3:16-17). Temple of the Living God (2Co 6:16). Vineyard (Jer 12:10; Mt 21:41).

Discipline:

In the Mosaic Institution—
(Ge 17:14; Ex 12:15; 30:33, 37-38; Lev 7:27; 17:8-9; 19:5-8; 20:18; 22:3; Nu 9:13; 15:31; 19:13, 20; Dt 13:12-18; 17:2—13; 19:16-21; 21:1-9, 18-21; 22:13-29; Ezr 10:7-8).

In the Christian Church—
Designed to save the sinner (Mt 18:15; 1Co 5:1-13; 2Th 3:14). Designed to warn others (1Ti 5:20). Designed to preserve sound doctrine (Ro 16:17; Gal 5:10; 1Ti 1:19-20; Tit 1:13). Exercised with kindness (2Co 2:6-11; Gal 6:1; Jude 22-23). Exercised with forbearance (Ro 15:1-3). Reasons for discipline: Heresy (1Ti 6:3-5; Tit 3:10-11; 2Jn 10-11). Reasons for discipline: Immorality (Mt 18:17-18; 1Co 5:1-7, 11-13; 2Th 3:6). For schism (Ro 16:17). Discipline by reproof (2Co 7:8; 10:1-11; 13:2, 10; 1Th 5:14; 2Th 3:15; 1Ti 5:1-2; 2Ti 4:2; Tit 2:15). Witnesses required in (Mt 18:16; 2Co 13:1; 1Ti 5:19).

Evil Conditions of:
Backslidden (Rev 2:1-5, 12-25; 3:1-4, 14-20). *See Backsliders; Backsliding.* Barren (Mt 21:19-20; Mk 11:13-14; Lk 13:6-9). Corrupt (Isa 5:1-7; Mt 21:33-46; Mk 12:1-12; Lk 20:9-19). Corruption in (Hos 4:9; Mic 3:1-4, 9, 11; Mt 21:33-41; 23:2-7, 13,

15-33; 26:14-16, 59-68; Mk 12:1-12; 14:10-11; Lk 22:3-6). Dissensions in (1Co 1:11-13; 3:3-4; 11:18-19; 2Co 12:20-21). Divisions in, to be shunned (Ro 16:17; 1Co 1:10; 3:3). Persecution of (Ac 8:1-3; 1Co 15:9; 1Th 2:14-15). *See Persecution.*

God's Care for:
Clothed in righteousness (Rev 19:8). Defended by God (Ps 89:18; Isa 4:5; 49:25; Mt 16:18). Edified by the Word (Ro 12:6; 1Co 14:4, 13; Eph 4:15-16; Col 3:16). Is glorious (Ps 45:13; Eph 5:27). Growth of continuous (Ac 2:47; 5:14; 11:24). Harmonious fellowship (Ps 133:1-3; Jn 13:34; Ac 4:32; Php 1:4; 2:1; 1Jn 3:4). Indwelt by God (Ps 132:14). Loved. *See below, Loved.* Not to be Despised (1Co 11:22). Privileges of (Ps 36:8; 87:5). Provides leaders (Jer 3:15; Eph 4:11-12). Punishment for defiling (1Co 3:17). Safe under God's care (Ps 46:1-2, 5). Triumphant (Gal 4:26; Heb 12:22-23; Rev 3:12; 21:3, 10).

Qualifications for Elders/Overseers and Deacons:		
Self-controlled	Elder	1Ti 3:2; Tit 1:8
Hospitable	Elder	1Ti 3:2; Tit 1:8
Able to teach	Elder	1Ti 3:2; 5:17; Tit 1:9
Not violent but gentle	Elder	1Ti 3:3; Tit 1:7
Not quarrelsome	Elder	1Ti 3:3
Not a lover of money	Elder	1Ti 3:3
Not a recent convert	Elder	1Ti 3:6
Good reputation with outsiders	Elder	1Ti 3:7
Not overbearing	Elder	Tit 1:7
Not quick-tempered	Elder	Tit 1:7
Loves what is good	Elder	Tit 1:8
Upright, holy	Elder	Tit 1:8
Disciplined	Elder	Tit 1:8
Above reproach (blameless)	Elder / *Deacon*	1Ti 3:2; Tit 1:6 / *1Ti 3:9*
Husband of one wife	Elder / *Deacon*	1Ti 3:2; Tit 1:6 / *1Ti 3:12*
Temperate	Elder / *Deacon*	1Ti 3:2; Tit 1:7 / *1Ti 3:8*
Respectable	Elder / *Deacon*	1Ti 3:2 / *1Ti 3:8*
Not given to drunkenness	Elder / *Deacon*	1Ti 3:2; Tit 1:7 / *1Ti 3:8*
Manages his own family well	Elder / *Deacon*	1Ti 3:4 / *1Ti 3:12*
Sees that his children obey him	Elder / *Deacon*	1Ti 3:4-5; Tit 1:6 / *1Ti 3:12*
Does not pursue dishonest gain	Elder / *Deacon*	Tit 1:7 / *1Ti 3:8*
Keeps hold of the deep truths	Elder / *Deacon*	Tit 1:9 / *1Ti 3:9*
Sincere	*Deacon*	*1Ti 3:8*
Tested	*Deacon*	*1Ti 3:10*

Government:

Of the Mosaic Institution: (Dt 17:8-13).

Of the Christian Church:
Authority of apostles (Mt 16:19; Jn 20:23; Ac 1:15, 23-26; 5:1-11; Lk 7:17; 11:2, 33-34; Gal 2:9). Authority of apostolic council (Ac 15:1-31; 16:4-5). Authority of congregation (1Co 16:3, 16; Jude 22-23). Leadership by apostles. *See above, Authority of apostles.* Leadership by deacons (Ac 6:2-6; 1Ti 3:8-13). Leadership by elders (Ac 14:23; 20:17, 28; 1Ti 5:1, 17, 22; Tit 1:5; Jas 5:14-15; 1Pe 5:1-3). Leadership by overseers (1Ti 3:1-5). *See chart above: Qualifications for Elders/ Overseers and Deacons.* Leadership by prophets and teachers (Ac 13:1, 3, 5; 1Ti 4:14; 2Ti 1:6). Obedience to rulers (Heb 13:17, 24).

Responsibilities of Believers to Leaders—
To encourage (1Co 16:10-11). To esteem (Php 2:29; 1Th 5:12-13; 1Ti 5:17). To imitate the example of (1Co 11:1; Php 3:17; 2Th 3:7; Heb 13:7; 1Pe 5:3). To obey (Heb 13:17). To receive (Php 2:29). To reimburse (1Co 9:7-23; 2Co 12:13; Gal 6:6; Php 4:10-18; 2Th 3:7-9; 1Ti 5:17-18). To seek instruction from (Mal 2:7). Of leaders, to shepherd believers (Ac 20:28).

Loved:
By God (Isa 27:2-3; 43:1-7; 49:14-17; Jer 3:14-15; 13:11). By Christ (Jn 10:8, 11, 14; Eph 5:25-32; Rev 3:9). By believers (Ps 84:1-2; 87:7; 102:14; 137:5; 1Co 12:25; 1Th 4:9). Manifested, by prayer for (Ps 122:6; Isa 62:6). Manifested, by distress at misfortunes of (Ps 137:1-6; Isa 22:4; 14:17; 51:50-51; La 2:11; 3:48-51). Manifested, by joy at prosperity of (Isa 66:10, 13-14). Manifested, by zeal for (Isa 58:12; 62:1, 6-7).

New Testament Church:

List of NT Churches—
Antioch (Ac 13:1). Asia (1Co 16:19; Rev 1:4). Babylon (1Pe 5:13). Cenchrea (Ro 16:1). Caesarea (Ac 18:22). Cilicia (Ac 15:41). Corinth (1Co 1:2). Ephesus (Eph 1:22; Rev 2:1). Galatia (Gal 1:2). Galilee (Ac 9:31). Jerusalem (Ac 15:4). Joppa (Ac 9:42). Judea (Ac 9:31). Laodicea (Rev 3:14). Pergamum (Rev 2:12). Philadelphia (Rev 3:7). Samaria (Ac 9:31). Sardis (Rev 3:1). Smyrna (Rev 2:8). Syria (Ac 15:41). Thessalonica (1Th 1:1). Thyatira (Rev 2:18).

Described—
Beneficence of. *See Beneficence; Giving; Liberality.* Christ, the head of (Ps 118:22-23; Isa 28:16; 33:22; 55:4; Mt 12:6, 8; 21:42-43; 23:8, 10; Mk 2:28; 12:10; Lk 6:5; 20:17-18; Jn 13:13; 15:1-8; Ac 2:36; Ro 8:29; 9:5; 1Co 3:11; 11:3; 12:5; Eph 1:10, 22-23; 2:20-22; 4:15; 5:23-32; Col 1:13, 18; 2:10, 19; 3:11; Heb 3:3, 6; 1Pe 2:7; Rev 1:13; 2:1-28; 3:1, 7; 5:6; 21:22-23; 22:16). *See Jesus, Kingdom of.* Community in (Ac 4:32). Decrees of (Ac 15:28-29; 16:4). Design of (Ro 3:2; 9:4; Eph 2:20-22; 1Ti 3:15). Discipline. *See above, Discipline.* Diversity of callings in (1Co 12:5, 28; Eph 4:11-12). Divinely established or instituted (Mt 16:15-18; Eph 2:20-22; 1Th 1:1; 2Th 1:1; 1Ti 3:15). Founded on the lordship of Christ (Mt 16:18). Duty. *See Responsibilities below.* Edification, by teachers (Eph 4:11-12). By public worship (Col 3:16; Heb 10:25). Government. *See above, Government.* Growth of, rapid (Ac 2:41, 47; 4:4; 5:14; 6:7; 9:35; 11:21, 24; 14:1; 19:17-20). Growth of, cut back (Isa 2:2; Eze 17:22-24; Da 4:35). Holiness of (2Co 11:2; Eph 5:27; 2Pe 3:14; Rev 19:8). Loved. *See above, Loved.* Membership in (Mt 12:50; 19:14; Mk 10:14; Lk 18:16; Jn 15:5-6; Ac 2:41, 47; 4:4; 5:14; 9:35, 42; 11:21; Ro 12:4-5; 1Co 3:11-15; 12:12-28; Eph 4:25; 5:30; Php 4:3; Rev 21:27). Militancy of (SS 6:10; Php 2:25; 2Ti 2:3; 4:7; Phm 2). Mission of. *See below, Mission.* Pastoral care of (Ac 20:28). Responsibilities. *See below, Responsibilities.* Unity of (Ps 133:1; Jn 10:16; 17:11, 21-23; Ro 12:4-5; 1Co 10:17; 12:5, 12-27; Gal 3:26-28; Eph 1:10; 2:14-21; 3:6, 15; 4:4-6, 12-16, 25; Col 3:11, 15). Union of, with Christ (Jn 15:1-7; Ro 11:17; 2Co 11:2; Eph 5:30, 32; Rev 19:7; 21:9). Worship, to be attended (Heb 10:25). To be conducted with order (Ecc 5:1, 3; 1Co 11:4-5, 33; 14:26, 33, 40; 1Ti 3:15).

Mission of—
To be entrusted with the oracles of God (Ro 3:2; 9:4). To bring peace (Ps 22:27-31; Isa 2:2-5; 11:6-9; 52:1, 2, 7-8; 61:1-3; 65:25). To bring spiritual enlightenment (Isa 2:3; 29:18-19; Joel 2:26-32; Hab 2:14; Ac 2:16-21). To bring moral transformation (Isa 4:2-6; 32:3-4, 15-17; 35:1-2, 5-7; 44:3-5; 55:10-13; Zep 3:9). To be the salt and light of the world (Mt 5:13).

Prophecies Concerning—
Its universality (Ge 12:3; Isa 2:2; 40:5; 42:3-4; 45:23; 52:10, 15; 54:1-5; 56:7-8; 59:19; 60:1-9; 66:12, 19, 23; Jer 3:17; 4:2; 16:19; 31:7-9, 34; 33:22; Da 2:35, 44; 7:13-14, 18, 22, 27; Am 9:11-12; Zep 2:11; Zec 9:1, 10; 14:6-9, 16; Mal 1:11; Mt 8:11; Jn 10:16; Rev 11:15; 15:4).

Its prosperity (Ps 72:7-11, 16, 19; 86:9; 102:15-16, 18; 132:15-18; Isa 4:2-6; 25:6-8; 33:20-21; 49:6-12, 13-18; 51:3-8; 52:1-8, 10, 15; 54:1-5, 11-14; 55:5, 10-13; 60:1-9, 19-20; 61:1-11; 62:2-3, 12; 65:18-19, 23-25; 66:12, 19, 23; Jer 31:34; Eze 17:22-24; 34:26, 29-31; 47:3-12; Joel 2:26-32; Am 9:11-12; Mic 4:3-4; 5:2, 4, 7; Hab 2:14; Zep 3:9; Hag 2:7-9; Zec 2:10-11; 6:15; 8:20-23).

Its lasting (Isa 9:7; 33:20; Da 7:14, 27; Mt 16:18; Eph 1:10; Heb 12:23-24, 27-28; Rev 5:10, 13-14; 11:15; 12:10; 15:4; 20:4-6; 21:9-27; 22:1-5). *See Jesus the Christ, Kingdom of.*

State: Relationship of Church and State:

Ecclesiastical Power Superior to Civil—
Appoints kings (1Sa 10:1). Directs administration (1Sa 15:1-4). Reproves rulers (1Sa 15:14-35), withdraws support and anoints a successor (1Sa 16:1-13; 2Ki 9:1-26; 11:4-12). Attempted usurpation of ecclesiastical functions by civil authorities reproved (1Sa 13:8-14; 2Ch 26:16-21).

State Superior to Church—
Evident, in David's appointments (1Ch 23-25; 2Ch 35:4). In Solomon's power (1Ki 2:26-27; 5-8). In Hezekiah reorganizing temple service (2Ch 31:2-19). In Jeroboam subverting the Jewish religion (1Ki 12:26-33). In Manasseh subverting and restoring the true religion (2Ch 33:2-9, 15-17). In Joash supervising the repairs of the temple (2Ki 12:14-18). In Ahaz transforming the altars (2Ki 16:10-16). In Josiah exercising the function of a priest (2Ch 34:29-33).

State Favorable to the Church—
Cyrus, in proclamation to restore the temple (2Ch 36:22-23; Ezr 1:1-11). Darius, in edict to further restoration of the temple (Ezr 6:1-14). Artaxerxes, in exempting religious institution from taxes (Ezr 7:24).

See Ecclesiasticism; Jesus the Christ, Kingdom of; Ministers; Usurpation, in Ecclesiastical Affairs.

CHURNING (Pr 30:33). *See Butter.*

CHUSHAN-RISHATHAIM See *Cushan-Rishathaim.*

CHUZA *See Cuza.*

CILICIA Maritime province of Asia Minor. Jews dwell in (Ac 6:9). Churches of (Ac 15:23, 41; Gal 1:21). Sea of (Ac 27:5).

CINNAMON A spice (Pr 7:17; SS 4:14; Rev 18:13). An ingredient of the sacred oil (Ex 30:23).

C

CINNERETH, CINNEROTH *See Kinnereth; Galilee, Sea of.*

CIRCUMCISION

Institution of (Ge 17:10-14; Lev 12:3; Jn 7:22; Ac 7:8; Ro 4:11). A seal of righteousness (Ro 2:25-29; 4:11). Performed on all males on the eighth day (Ge 17:12-13; Lev 12:3; Php 3:5). Rite of, observed on the Sabbath (Jn 7:23). A prerequisite of the privileges of the Passover (Ex 12:48). Child named at the time of (Ge 21:3-4; Lk 1:59; 2:21). Neglected (Jos 5:7). Covenant promises of (Ge 17:4, 14; Ac 7:8; Ro 3:1; 4:11; 9:7-13; Gal 5:3). Necessity of, falsely taught by Judaizing Christians (Ac 15:1). Paul's argument against the continuance of (Ro 2:25, 28; Gal 6:13). Characterized by Paul as a yoke (Ac 15:10). Abrogated (Ac 15:5-29; Ro 3:30; 4:9-11; 1Co 7:18-19; Gal 2:3-4; 5:2-11; 6:12; Eph 2:11, 15; Col 2:11; 3:11).

Instances of:
Abraham (Ge 17:23-27; 21:3-4). Shechemites (Ge 34:24). Moses (Ex 4:25). Israelites at Gilgal (Jos 5:2-9). John the Baptist (Lk 1:59). Jesus (Lk 2:21). Paul (Php 3:5). Timothy (Ac 16:3).

Figurative:
(Ex 6:12, ftn; Dt 10:16; 30:6; Jer 4:4; 6:10, ftn; 9:26; Ro 2:28-29; 15:8, ftn; Php 3:3; Col 2:11; 3:11).
A designation of the Jews (Ac 10:45; 11:2; Ro 15:8, ftn; Eph 2:11; Col 4:11; Tit 1:10), of Christians (Php 3:3).

CIS *See Kish.*

CISTERN An artificial reservoir dug in the earth or rock for the collection and storage of water from rain or spring (Pr 5:15; Ecc 12:6; Isa 36:16; Jer 2:13). Cisterns were a necessity in Israel with its long, dry summers. Empty cisterns were sometimes used as prisons (Ge 37:22; Jer 38:6; Zec 9:11). *See Wells.*

Figurative:
(2Ki 18:31; Pr 5:15; Ecc 12:6).

CITIES Ancient (Ge 4:17; 10:10-12). Fortified (Nu 32:36; Dt 9:1; Jos 10:20; 14:12; 2Ch 8:5; 11:10-12; 17:2, 19; 21:3; Isa 23:11). Gates of. *See Gates.*

Designated as:
Royal (Jos 10:2; 1Sa 27:5; 2Sa 12:26; 1Ch 11:7), treasure (Ge 41:48; Ex 1:11; 1Ki 9:19; 2Ch 8:4; 16:4; 17:12), chariot (2Ch 1:14; 8:6; 9:25), merchant (Isa 23:11; Eze 17:4; 27:3). Town clerk of (Ac 19:35). Government of, by rulers (Ne 3:9, 12, 17-18; 7:2). *See Government.* Suburbs of (Nu 35:3-5; Jos 14:4). Watchmen of. *See Watchman.*

Figurative:
(Heb 11:10, 16; 12:22; 13:14).

CITIES OF REFUGE Six cities set apart by Moses and Joshua as places of asylum for those who had accidentally committed manslaughter: Bezer (Benjamin), Ramoth Gilead (Gad), Golan (Manasseh), Hebron (Judah), Shechem (Ephraim), Kedesh (Naphtali). There they remained until a fair trial could be held. If proved innocent of willful murder, they had to remain in the city of refuge until the death of the high priest (Nu 35; Dt 4:43; 9:1-13; Jos 20).

CITIES OF THE PLAIN Cities near the Dead Sea, including Sodom, Gomorrah, Admah, Zeboiim, and Zoar. Lot lived in Sodom (Ge 13:10-12). They were destroyed because of their wickedness (Ge 19). Josephus (Wars, 4.8.4) identified the area of the five cities at the "Lake Asphaltitus" (the Dead Sea) and said traces of the five cities were still visible. No archaeological evidence, however, backs up that siting and so the sites remain unidentified.

CITIZENS

Duties of:
Honors rulers (Ex 22:28; Nu 27:20; Job 34:18; Pr 16:14-15; 24:21; 25:6-7a, 15; Ecc 10:4, 20; Ac 23:5; 1Pe 2:17). Pray for rulers (Ezr 6:10; 1Ti 2:1-2). Promote peace (Jer 29:7). Obey the law (Ezr 7:26; 10:8; Ecc 4). Pay taxes (Mt 17:24-27; 22:17-21; Mk 12:14-17; Lk 20:22-25; Ro 13:5-7).

Rights of:
Public vindication when falsely accused (Ac 16:37). Protection from mob violence (Ac 19:36-41). Fair trial (Ac 22:25-29; 24:18-19; 25:5, 10-11, 16).

Loyal, Instances of:
Israelites (Jos 1:16-18; 2Sa 3:36-37; 15:23, 30; 18:3; 21:17; 1Ch 12:38). David (1Sa 24:6-11; 26:6-16; 2Sa 1:14). Hushai (2Sa 17:15-16). David's soldiers (2Sa 18:12-13; 23:15-16). Joab (2Sa 19:5-6). Barzillai (2Sa 19:32). Jehoiada (2Ki 11:4-12). Isaiah (Isa 22:4). Jeremiah (La 1-5). Mordecai (Est 2:21-23).

Wicked and Treacherous: (Pr 17:11; Pr 19:10, 12; 20:2; 2Ti 3:1-4; 2Pe 2:10; Jude 8).

Instances of—
Miriam and Aaron (Nu 12:1-11). Korah, Dathan, and Abiram (Nu 16:1-35; 26:9). Shechemites (Jdg 9:1-6, 22-25, 46-49). Ephraimites (Jdg 12:1-4). Israelites (1Sa 10:27; 1Ki 12:16-19). Absalom (2Sa 15:10-13). Ahithophel (2Sa 15:12; 17:1-4). Sheba (2Sa 20:1-2). Adonijah (1Ki 1:5-7). Jeroboam (1Ki 11:14-26; 12:20; 2Ch 13:5-9). Baasha (1Ki 15:27). Zimri (1Ki 16:9-10). Jozabad the son of Shimeath and Jehozabad the son of Shomer (2Ki 12:19-21; 14:5). Shallum (2Ki 15:10). Menahem (2Ki 15:14). Pekah (2Ki 15:25). Hoshea (2Ki 15:30). Sons of Sennacherib (2Ki 19:37; 2Ch 32:21). Ishmael (Jer 40:14-16; 41). Bigthana and Teresh (Est 2:21). Jews (Eze 17:12-20). Barabbas (Mk 15:7). Theudas and 400 (Ac 5:36-37). An Egyptian (Ac 21:38).

Figurative:
Citizenship in heaven (Eph 2:12, 19; Php 3:20; 1Pe 2:11).

CITRON WOOD An aromatic wood; KJV "thyine" (Rev 18:12).

CITY CLERK An official in Greco-Roman cities of the first century, as at Ephesus (Ac 19:35-41).

CITY OF DAVID

1. Jebusite stronghold of Zion captured by David and made by him his royal residence (2Sa 5:6-9).
2. Bethlehem, the home of David (Lk 2:4).

CITY OF DESTRUCTION A city of Egypt; exact location unknown (Isa 19:18, ftn). Some mss of the Massoretic Text, Dead Sea Scrolls, and the Vulgate have "City of the Sun" (Heliopolis). *See Heliopolis.*

CIVIL DAMAGES *See Damages and Compensations.*

CIVIL ENGINEERING (Jos 18:9; Job 28:9-11).

CIVIL SERVICE School for (Da 1:3-21). Appointment in, on account of merit (Ge 39:1-6, 17-21; 41:38-44; 1Ki 11:28; Est 6:1-11; Da 1:7, 17-21; 6:1-3; Mt 25:14-23, 29-30; Lk 19:12-27). Corruption in (Ne 5:15; Da 6:4-17; Mk 15:15; Ac 24:26). Reform in (Ne 4:14-15). Influence in (1Ki 1:5-40; 2Ki 4:13; Mt 20:20-23; Mk 10:35).

CLAIRVOYANCE *See Sorcery.*

CLAP Clapping hands in joy (2Ki 11:12), in praise (Ps 47:1), in astonishment (Job 21:5), in scorn (Job 27:23; 34:37), in praise (Ps 98:8; Isa 55:12).

CLASP
1. Used to fasten the curtains on the tabernacle (Ex 26:6, 11, 33; 35:11, 13, 18, 33).
2. To shake hands in agreement and pledge for some obligation (Isa 2:6 w Pr 6:1).
3. Worshipers clasped Jesus' feet (Mt 28:9).

CLAUDA *See Cauda.*

CLAUDIA (possibly *lame*). A female disciple (2Ti 4:21).

CLAUDIUS The fourth Roman emperor (c. A.D. 41-54). The famine foretold by Agabus took place in his reign (Ac 11:28). He banished all Jews from Rome (Ac 18:2).

CLAUDIUS LYSIAS A Roman military officer (Ac 21:31-40; 22:23-30). Had Paul transferred from Jerusalem to Caesarea and wrote a letter to Governor Felix in order to protect him from an assassination plot (Ac 23:10-35; 24:7, ftn; 24:22).

CLAY Man formed from (Job 33:6). Seals made of (Job 38:14). Used by a potter (Isa 29:16; 41:25; 45:9). Blind man's eyes anointed with (Jn 9:6).

Figurative (Job 4:19; Ps 40:2; Isa 45:9; 64:8; Jer 18:6; Ro 9:21). Symbolic (Da 2:33-41).

CLAY TABLETS Made of clay which, while still wet, had wedge-shaped letters imprinted on them with a stylus, and then were kiln-fired or sun-dried. They were made of various shapes, and were often placed in a clay envelope. Vast quantities have been excavated in the Near East. The earliest examples date to 3000 B.C.

CLEAN AND UNCLEAN ANIMALS *See Animals; Birds; Fish; Insects.*

CLEANLINESS Taught by frequent washings. *See Purification; Washing.* Regulation relating to, in camp (Dt 23:12-14).

Figurative (Ps 51:7, 10; 73:1; Pr 20:9; Isa 1:16; Eze 36:25; 1Jn 1:7, 9; Rev 1:5).
See Sanitation and Hygiene.

CLEANSING *See Washing.*

CLEANTHES The son of Phanius of Assos and head of the Stoic school in Athens from 263-232 B.C. His poem, *Hymn to Zeus,* is quoted by Paul before the Areopagus Court (Ac 17:28). He made Stoicism more religious in its orientation by teaching that the universe was a living being, that God was its soul, and that the sun was its heart. He taught detachment from moral concerns. Doing good for gain was like feeding cattle for meat. He also maintained that evil thoughts were worse than evil deeds, just as a tumor which does not break open is more dangerous than one which does.
See Aratus; Asceticism; Stoicism; Stoics.

CLEMENCY Of David toward disloyal subjects: Shimei (2Sa 16:5-13; 19:16-23), Amasa (2Sa 19:13, w 2Sa 17:25).
Divine. *See God, Longsuffering of, and Mercy of; Kindness.*

CLEMENT (*mild*). A disciple at Philippi (Php 4:3).

CLEOPAS (*renowned father*). A disciple to whom Jesus appeared after his resurrection (Lk 24:18).

CLEOPHAS *See Clopas.*

CLERGYMAN *See Deacon; Elders; Minister; Pastor; Overseer.*

CLERK Town (Ac 19:35).

CLOAK Outer garment, not to be taken in pledge for a loan (Ex 22:26-27). Elijah's (1Ki 18:46; 19:13); used in calling Elisha (1Ki 19:19); parting the Jordan (2Ki 2:8; 2Ki 2:14); passes to Elisha (2Ki 2:13). Jesus' touched by the woman; her bleeding healed (Mt 9:20-21). Paul's left at Troas (2Ti 4:13).
Figurative of a curse (Ps 109:19).

CLOPAS Husband of Mary (Jn 19:25). *See Mary, 2.*

CLOSET *See Room.*

CLOTH Parable of old and new (Mt 9:16). Burial (Mt 27:59; Mk 15:46).

CLOTHING Of the Israelites, did not wear out (Dt 8:4; 29:5; Ne 9:21). *See Dress.*

CLOUD

Pillar of, With Fire:
Symbolic of the Lord's presence (Ex 13:21-22; 16:10; 19:9, 16; 24:16-18; 33:9-10; 34:5; Lev 16:2; Nu 11:25; 12:5, 10; 14:10; 16:19, 42; Dt 31:15; 1Ki 8:10-11; 2Ch 7:1-3; Isa 6:1, 4; Mt 17:5; Lk 9:34-35; 1Co 10:1). A guide to Israel (Ex 14:19, 24; 40:36-38; Nu 9:15-23; 10:11-12, 33-36; Dt 1:33; Ne 9:12, 19; Ps 78:14; 105:39; Isa 4:5). In Isaiah's prophecy (Isa 4:5). In Ezekiel's vision (Eze 10:3-4, 18-19; 11:22-23).
Figurative (Jer 4:13; Hos 6:4; 13:3).
Symbolic (Rev 14:14).
See Celestial Phenomena.

CLOUT *See Dress.*

CLUB War club or club used by shepherds (2Sa 23:21; Job 41:29; Pr 25:18; Jer 51:20; Eze 39:9).

CNIDUS (*age*). A city in Asia Minor (Ac 27:7).

CO-HEIRS As God's children, Christians share in Christ's glory (Ro 8:17). *See Inheritance.*

COAL The Bible never refers to true mineral coal, which has not been found in Israel proper. The references are always either to charcoal or to live embers of any kind. Hebrews usually used charcoal for warmth or cooking (Isa 47:14; Jn 18:18; 21:9).
Figurative (Pr 25:22).
Symbolic (Isa 6:6-7; 2Sa 14:7).

COAL OIL *See Oil.*

COAT OF ARMOR (1Sa 17:5, 38; 1Ki 22:34; 2Ch 18:33). *See Armor.*

COBRA A poisonous snake (Dt 32:33; Pr 23:32). Venom of, illustrates the speech of the wicked (Ps 58:4). Child playing with illustrates Messianic age (Isa 11:8-9).
See Serpent; Viper.

COCK *See Birds; Rooster.*

COCK CROWING *See Rooster.*

COCKATRICE *See Viper.*

COCKLE *See Weeds.*

COELE-SYRIA (*hollow Syria*). A name for that part of Syria that lay between the Lebanon and Anti-Lebanon Mountains.

COERCION Religious: Penalty for (Ex 22:20). Oath against (2Ch 15:12-15).
Instances of (Da 3:2-6, 29; 6:26-27).
See Bigotry; Intolerance.

COFFER *See Chest, 2; Treasury.*

COFFIN Joseph placed in for burial (Ge 50:26). *See Burial.*

COIN *See Money.*

COL-HOZEH (*every seer*). Father of Baruch (Ne 11:5).

COLLAR *See Dress.*

COLLECTION Of money for the poor.
See Alms; Beneficence; Giving; Liberality.

COLLEGE NIV "Second District" of the city of Jerusalem (2Ki 22:14; 2Ch 34:22). *See School.*

COLLOP NIV "bulges" of fat (Job 15:27).

COLLUSION In Sin (Lev 20:4-5). *See Complicity; Connivance.*

COLONIZATION Of conquered countries and people (2Ki 17:6, 24; Ezr 4:9-10).

COLORS, FIGURATIVE AND SYMBOLIC

Black:
Of affliction (Job 3:5; Ps 107:10-11; 143:3; Isa 9:19; 24:11). Of calamity (Isa 5:30; 8:22; 50:3; Joel 2:6, 10; 3:14-15; Na 2:10). Of the day of wrath (Zep 1:14-15). Of death (Job 10:20-22; Am 5:8). Of the abode of the lost (Mt 8:12; 22:13; 25:30; 2Pe 2:4; Jude 13; Rev 16:10).

Blue:
Of deity (Ex 25:3-4; 26:1; 28:28, 37; 38:18; 39:1-5, 21, 24, 29, 31; Nu 4:5-12; 15:38-40; 2Ch 2:7, 14; 3:14). Of royalty (Est 8:15; Eze 23:6). Predominant color in drapery and furnishings of the tabernacle, and in clothing of the priests (Ex 24:10; Jer 10:9; Eze 1:26; 10:1).

Crimson, Red, Purple, and Scarlet:
Of iniquity (Isa 1:18; Rev 17:3-4; 18:12, 16). Of prosperity (2Sa 1:24; Pr 31:21; La 4:5). Of royalty (Jdg 8:26; Da 5:7, 16, 29; Mt 27:28). Types and shadows of the Atonement (Ex 25:3-5; 26:1, 14, 31, 36; 27:16; 28:4-6, 8, 15, 31, 33, 37; 35:5-7, 23-25, 35; 36:8, 19, 35, 37; 38:23; 39:1-43; Lev 14:4, 6, 49-52; Nu 4:7-8 13; 19:2, 5-6; Isa 63:1-3; Heb 9:19-23).

White:
Of Holiness (Lev 16:4, 32; Ps 51:7; Ecc 9:8; Isa 1:18; Da 7:9; 11:35; 12:10; Mt 17:2; 28:2-3; Mk 9:3; Rev 1:13-14; 2:17; 3:4-5, 18; 4:4; 6:2, 11; 7:9, 13-14; 15:6; 19:8, 11, 14; 20:11). Choir singers arrayed in white (2Ch 5:12).

COLOSSE (*punishment*). A city of Phrygia (Col 1:2, 7-8).

COLOSSIANS, BOOK OF

Author: The apostle Paul

Date: c. A.D. 60

Outline:

I. Introduction (1:1-14).
 A. Greetings (1:1-2).
 B. Thanksgiving (1:3-8).
 C. Prayer (1:9-14).
II. The Supremacy of Christ (1:15-23).
III. Paul's Labor for the Church (1:24-2:7).
 A. A Ministry for the Sake of the Church (1:24-29).
 B. A Concern for the Spiritual Welfare of His Readers (2:1-7).
IV. Freedom From Human Regulations Through Life With Christ (2:8-23).
 A. Warning to Guard Against the False Teachers (2:8-15).
 B. Pleas to Reject the False Teachers (2:16-19).
 C. An Analysis of the Heresy (2:20-23).
V. Rules for Holy Living (3:1-4:6).
 A. The Old Self and the New Self (3:1-17).
 B. Rules for Christian Households (3:18-4:1).
 C. Further Instructions (4:2-6).
VI. Final Greetings (4:7-18).

COLT

Ridden by Jesus (Mt 21:2, 5, 7; Mk 11:2; Jn 12:15).

COMFORT

See *Affliction, Consolation Under; Righteous, Promises to.*

COMFORTER

See *God, Grace of; Holy Spirit.*

COMMANDMENT

Used in the English Bible to translate a number of Hebrew and Greek words meaning law, ordinance, statute, word, judgment, precept, saying, charge, etc.

COMMANDMENTS AND STATUTES, OF GOD

Admonishing Against:

Backsliding (Dt 8:11-17; 28:18; Eze 33:12-13, 18; Lk 9:62; 1Co 10:12; Heb 3:12-13; 12:15; 2Pe 2:20-21). Conspiracy (Ex 23:1-2). Hypocrisy (Mt 6:1-5, 16; Lk 20:46-47; 1Pe 2:1). Lusts (Pr 31:3; Ro 13:13-14; Gal 5:16; 1Pe 2:11). Oppression of foreigners (Ex 22:21; 23:9; Dt 24:14; Zec 7:10). Popular corruption (Ex 23:2). Reviling rulers (Ex 22:28; Ac 23:5).

Concerning:

Children, commanding obedience to parents (Pr 6:20; 1Co 6:1-3; Col 3:20). *See below, Commanding Reverence for Parents.* Debtors' protection (Dt 24:10, 12-13). Father's concern for children (Eph 6:4; Col 3:21). A husband's love for his wife (Eph 5:23; Col 3:19), honor for his wife (1Pe 3:7). Permanence of marriage (Ge 2:24; Mt 19:6; Mk 10:9; 1Co 7:1-16). Judges' justice in court (Dt 1:16). Lost property (Ex 23:4; Dt 22:1-3). Man's supremacy over animals (Ge 9:2). Masters', equity (Col 4:1), humane treatment of servants (Eph 6:9). Ministers (Ac 20:31; 1Ti 1:4; 3:2-13; 4:12-16; 5:20-22; 2Ti 2:1-3, 14-16, 22-24; Tit 1:5-9; 2:1-10, 15; 1Pe 5:2-3). Faithfulness (Col 4:17; 1Ti 6:11-12, 14; 2Ti 1:8, 13). Fortitude (2Ti 2:3). Foolish questions (2Ti 2:23). Sanctification (1Th 4:3). Strife (2Ti 2:24). Places of public worship (Dt 12:11). Restitution (Ex 21:30-36; 22:1-15; Lev 6:4-5; 24:18; Nu 5:7). Servants' obedience (Eph 6:5-8; Col 3:22-25; Tit 2:9-10; 1Pe 2:18-19). Vicious animals (Ex 21:28-32, 35-36). Wives' obedience (Eph 5:22; Col 3:18; 1Pe 3:1-4). Women (Ex 5:22, 24; Tit 2:3-5; 1Pe 3:1-3). Young men's parental obedience (Pr 6:20; 23:22).

The Decalogue: (Ex 20:3-17; Dt 5:6-21). See *Decalogue; Tablets of the Law.*

Commanding:

Hate, of the abominations of the wicked (Dt 7:25-26). Hatred of evil (Ro 12:9-21). Abiding in Christ (Jn 15:4, 9; 1Jn 2:28). Abstinence from evil (1Th 5:22). Accord with Christ, and concord with one another (Php 2:2-5). Admonition and encouragement (1Th 5:14). Altruistic service (Mt 20:26; Mk 9:35; 10:42-45; Lk 22:26; Jn 13:14; Ro 15:1-2; 1Co 10:24; Gal 6:10; Php 2:3-4). Assistance to the distressed (Pr 82:4; Pr 24:11). Building a sanctuary (Ex 25:8). Casting anxiety upon the Lord (1Pe 5:7). Charitableness (Mt 18:10; Lk 6:37-38; Ro 14:1-3, 13, 19). Chastity (Pr 5:15-19; Mt 5:27-28). Cheerfulness (Ec 9:7-9). Choice of wise men for rulers (Ex 18:21; Dt 1:13). Christian graces (2Co 1:3-11; Col 3:12-17; 2Ti 2:22). Christian tolerance toward the weak (Ro 15:1). Confession of sin (Nu 8:12; Jas 5:16). Contentment (Lk 3:14; Heb 13:5). Courage (Dt 31:6-7; Jos 1:6-7, 9; 1Ki 2:2-3; 1Ch 28:20; Ne 4:14; Jer 1:8; Eze 2:6). Cross bearing (Mt 16:24; Mk 8:34). Destruction of idols (Ex 23:24; 34:13; Nu 33:52; Dt 7:25; 12:3). Diligence (Ecc 9:10; 11:6), in business (Pr 27:23). Discipleship (Mt 19:21; Mk 10:21; Lk 18:22). Discipline of, disorderly church members (2Th 3:6). Of Children (Mt 19:14; Mk 10:14; Lk 18:16-17). Discreet conduct (Co 12:17; Eph 4:1-3; 5:15-16; Php 1:27, 5; 1Pe 2:11-12). Doing all to the glory of God (1Co 10:31; Col 3:17, 23). Equity of servants (Col 4:1). Establishing and providing for the ordination of a holy ministry (Ex 28:1-3; 40:12-15; Lev 8:1-13). Esteem for pastors (1Th 5:12-13; 1Ti 5:17; Heb 13:7). Evangelism (Mt 28:19). Faith (Ex 14:13; 2Ch 20:20; Ps 37:3, 5; 62:8; 115:9, 11; Pr 3:5; Isa 26:4; 50:10; Jer 49:11; Mk 1:15; 5:36; 11:22; Jn 6:29; 12:36; 14:1, 11; 20:27), in Christ (1Jn 3:23). Faithfulness to ministers (Col 4:17; 1Ti 6:11-12, 14; 2Ti 1:8, 13), to friends (Pr 27:10). Family support (1Ti 5:8). Fear of God (Lev 19:14, 32; 25:17; Dt 6:13; 10:12, 20; 13:4; Jos 24:14; 1Sa 12:24; 2Ki 17:39; Pr 3:7; 23:17; 24:21; Ecc 12:13; Isa 8:13; 1Pe 2:17). Fidelity in marriage (Ge 2:24; Mt 19:6; Mk 10:8; 1Co 7:10-11), to God (1Sa 12:20; Mt 22:21), to God and government (Mt 22:21; Mk 12:17; Lk 20:25), to vows (Nu 30:2; Dt 23:21-23; Ps 50:14; Ecc 5:4). Forbearance (Eph 4:2; Col 3:13). Forgiveness (Mt 18:22; Mk 11:25; Lk 17:3-4; Ro 12:14; Eph 4:32; Col 3:13). Fortitude under persecution (Mt 10:26-28; Mk 13:9, 11-13; 2Ti 2:3; Rev 2:10). Fraternal reproof (Mt 18:15-17; Lk 17:3-4). Fruits of righteousness (Lk 3:11, 14).

Gentleness (Tit 3:2). Godliness (Eph 5:1). Golden Rule, in conduct (Mt 7:12; Lk 6:31). Good works (1Pe 3:21). Growth in grace (Heb 6:1; 2Pe 1:5-8; 3:18; Jude 20-21). Heed to instruction (Pr 4:10; 19:20; 22:17), to parental instruction (Pr 1:8; 23:22), to the truth (Mt 11:15; Mk 4:9; Rev 2:7). Helpfulness (1Co 10:24; Gal 6:1-2; Php 2:4; 1Th 5:11). Holiness (Ex 22:31; 30:29; Lev 11:44; 20:7, 25-26; 21:7; Nu 15:40; Dt 18:13; Jos 7:13; Isa 1:16-17; Jer 6:16; Am 5:14-15; 1Co 5:7; 2Co 7:1; Eph 4:22-32; Col 3:5, 8-9; 1Th 4:3-7; 2Ti 2:19, 22; Heb 12:14; Jas 1:21; 4:8; 1Pe 1:13-16; 2:11-12; 3:15; 3Jn 11). Holiness in ministers (Lev 21:6; Nu 8:14-15). Honesty (Lev 19:35-36; Dt 25:13-16; 1Th 4:12), in service (1Co 4:2; Eph 6:5-7; Col 3:22-23; Tit 2:9-10), in office (Lk 3:13). Honor, to civil rulers (1Pe 2:17), to wife (1Pe 3:7). Hospitality (Ro 12:13; Heb 13:2; 1Pe 4:9). Humane treatment of servants (Eph 6:9). Humility (Ro 12:16; Php 2:3; Jas 4:10; 1Pe 3:8; 5:6-7). Imitation of Christ (Ro 13:14; Col 2:6-7). Industry (Pr 6:6; Eph 4:28; 1Th 4:11; 2Th 3:12). Influence for righteousness (Mt 5:16; Php 2:15). Joyfulness (Ro 12:12; Php 3:1; 4:4; 1Th 5:16). Justice (Lev 19:15; Isa 56:1; Zec 7:9-10; Jn 7:24), in courts (Dt 1:17; 25:1-2), to foreigners (Lev 19:33-34; 24:22). Keeping the Sabbath holy (Ex 16:29; 20:8; 31:12-16; 35:2-3; Lev 19:3, 30; 26:2; Dt 5:12). Kindness (Pr 3:27-28; Eph 4:32; Col 3:12; 1Th 5:15). Kindness to animals (Dt 25:4). To enemies (Ex 23:4-5; Pr 25:21; Ro 12:20). Labor (Gen 3:19; 35:2; Dt 5:13). Laying up treasure in heaven (Mt 6:20). Liberality (Pr 3:9; Ecc 11:1; Mt 5:42; Lk 6:30; 12:33; 2Co 8:7; Heb 13:16). Liberality in God's service (Mal 3:10), in support of religion (Dt 15:19; 16:17), toward the house of God (Ex 22:29; 30:12-16; 34:26; 35:4-9), to the poor (Lev 19:9-10; 23:22; Dt 15:7-15; 24:19-21; Ro 12:13; Heb 13:16; 1Jn 3:17). Love, for enemies (Mt 5:44; Lk 6:27-29; Ro 12:14-15), for foreigners (Lev 19:34; Dt 10:19). Love for God (Dt 6:5; 10:12; 11:1, 8, 13; 30:16; Jos 22:5; 23:11; Mt 22:37; Mk 12:30; Lk 10:27). Love for other people (Lev 19:18, 33-34; Mt 19:19; 22:39; Mk 12:31; Lk 10:27; Jn 13:34; 15:12, 17; Ro 12:9-10; 13:8-10; 1Co 16:14; Gal 5:14; Eph 5:22; Col 3:14; 1Th 3:12; 4:9; Heb 13:1; Jas 2:8; 1Pe 2:17; 3:8; 4:8; 1Jn 3:11, 18, 23; 1Jn 4:7, 21; 2Jn 5). Love for wife (Eph 5:23; Col 3:19). Loving truth and peace (Zec 8:19). Maturity (1Co 16:13-14). Mature thinking (1Co 14:20; Tit 2:2). Meekness (Mt 5:39-40; Lk 6:29; Eph 4:2; Col 3:12; Tit 3:2). Mercy (Pr 3:3; Zec 7:9-10; Lk 6:36). Mercy to debtors (Dt 24:6). Oaths in God's name (Dt 6:13; 10:20). Obedience (Pr 7:1-4; Lev 18:4-5, 26, 30; 19:19, 37; 20:8, 22; 22:31; 25:18; Nu 15:40; Dt 4:1, 6, 23, 30; 5:32-33; 6:17-18; 7:11; 8:1, 6; 10:12-13; 11:1, 8, 13, 32; 12:28, 32; 13:4; 27:1, 10; 29:9; 30:2, 8, 16; 1Sa 15:1; 1Ki 2:2-3; 2Ki 17:37-38; 1Ch 28:20; Pr 3:6; 4:20-21; 5:7; 7:5-14; Ecc 12:13; Jn 13:15). Obedience of children (Pr 6:20; Eph 6:1-3; Col 3:20), of servants (Eph 6:5-8; Col 3:22-25; Tit 2:9-10; 1Pe 2:18-19), of soldiers (Dt 20:3; Lk 3:14), of wives (Eph 5:22; Col 3:18; 1Pe 3:1-4), of young men (Pr 6:20; 23:22). Obedience to Christ as Lord (1Pe 3:15), to civil government (Ecc 8:2; Mk 12:17; Lk 20:25; Ro 13:1, 7; Tit 3:1; 1Pe 2:13), to God's law (Dt 11:8, 13, 32; 30:16; Jos 22:5; 2Ki 17:37-38; 1Ch 28:8), to parents (Pr 6:20; Eph 6:1-3; Col 3:20). Orderly conduct of divine worship (1Co 14:26-33). Patience (Jas 1:4; 5:7-9). Patience under afflictions (Pr 3:11), under tribulations (Ro 12:12; Jas 1:2-4; 1Pe 4:1). Peaceableness (Ro 12:18; Col 3:15; 1Th 4:11; Heb 12:14). Perfection (Ge 17:1; Mt 5:48). Praise (Ps 146-150). *See Praise.* Prayer (Jer 33:3; Mt 7:7-11; Lk 11:9-13; Php 4:6; Col 4:2; 1Th 5:17-18; 1Ti 2:8), for more laborers in the Lord's vineyard (Mt 9:38), for rulers (1Ti 2:1-2). Prayerfulness (Lk 22:40; Ro 12:12; 1Th 5:17). Preparation for the Sabbath (Ex 16:23). Preparedness (Mt 24:44; 25:13, 1-12; 1Th 5:8). Propagation of children (Ge 9:1, 7). Propriety in worship (1Co 14:26-33, 40). Prudence (Col 4:5), in guests (Pr 23:1-2), in speech (Ecc 5:2, 6; 7:21; 10:20). Public instruction in the word of God (Dt 31:10-13). Worship (Ex 34:23; Dt 12:5-7, 11-14, 17-18, 26-27; 16:16). Pure conversation (Eph 4:29; 1Pe 3:10). Purity (2Co 7:1; Eph 5:1-4; 1Ti 5:22; Heb 13:4), in the family of a minister (Lev 21:9), of thought (Php 4:8). Quietness (1Th 4:11). Rebuke of sin (Lev 19:17; Eph 5:11). Reconciliation between Christian brothers (Mt 5:23-25). Regard for consciences of others (1Co 10:28). Regulated enjoyments (Ecc 11:9-10). Religious instruction of children (Dt 4:9; 6:7-9; 11:19-20; 32:46; Eph 6:4). Remembrance, of God in youth (Ecc 12:1), of God's mercies (Dt 5:15; 8:2). Of the law (Dt 6:6-9; 11:18; 32:46; 1Ch 16:15). Renunciation of sources of temptation (Mt 5:29-30; 18:8-9; Mk 9:43-48). Repentance (Pr 1:23; Eze 33:11; Mal 3:7; Mt 3:2; 7:13-14; Mk 1:15; Ac 2:38; 17:30; Rev 3:19). Reproof of the erring (1Ti 5:20). Resistance of evil (Jas 4:7). Respect for religious instruction (1Th 5:20). Rest on the Sabbath (Ex 20:10; 23:12; 32:21; 35:2-3; Lev 23:3, 24; Dt 5:14). Restraint of temper (Ecc 7:9; Eph 4:26, 31; Jas 1:19). Returning good for evil (Mt 5:4; 1Co 6:7; 1Pe 3:9). Reverence, for God's house (Lev 19:30; 26:2; Ecc 5:1), for holy places (Ex 3:5; Jos 5:15; Ac 7:33), for parents (Ex 20:12; Lev 19:3; 20:9; Dt 5:16; Pr 23:22; Mt 15:4; 19:19; Lk 18:20; Eph 6:1-2), for the aged (Lev 19:32). Right conduct (Dt 6:18; Pr 4:26-27; Php 1:27; Jas 1:19). Righteousness (Ex 23:7; Eze 45:9; Hos 12:6; Lk 13:24; Ro 13:7-8). Rulers to study God's law (Dt 17:18-20). Secrecy in giving alms (Mt 6:3). Seeking, the Lord (1Ch 16:11; Isa 55:6; Am 5:4, 6), the kingdom of God (Mt 6:24; Mk 8:34; 10:21; Lk 9:23; 18:22; Ro 15:2). Self-discipline (Mt 5:29-30; Mk 9:45-48). Self-examination (2Co 13:5). Service for God (Ex 23:25; Dt 6:13; 10:12, 20). Simplicity in worship (Mt 6:7). Six days of labor, and one day of rest (Ex 20:9-11; 35:2). Sobermindedness (Tit 2:6). Sobriety (1Th 5:8; 1Pe 1:13; 4:7; 5:8-9). Social peace (1Th 5:13). Spiritual diligence (Ro 12:11; 13:12; Heb 4:11; 2Pe 1:10; 3:14). Spirituality (Gal 5:16). Steadfastness (Dt 13:8, 10; Ro 12:21; 1Co 15:58; 16:13; Gal 5:1; Eph 6:11, 13-14, 18; Php 1:27; 4:1; 1Th 5:21; 2Th 2:15; 2Ti 1:13; 1Pe 1:13; Jude; Rev 3:11). Steadfastness in prayer (Ro 12:12; Eph 6:18; 1Th 5:17). Submission to God (2Ch 30:8; Pr 3:11; Jas 4:7), to fraternal counsel (Eph 5:21). Suffering, one for another (1Jn 3:16-17). Sympathy (Ro 12:15; Heb 13:3; 1Pe 3:8). Support of ministers (Dt 12:19; Gal 6:6; 1Ti 5:17-18).

Thankfulness (Dt 8:10; Col 2:6-7; 3:15). Thanksgiving (Eph 5:4, 20; Php 4:6; Col 3:17; 1Th 5:17-18; 1Ti 2:1; Heb 13:15). Tithing (Dt 12:6; 14:22). Truthfulness (Pr 3:3; Zec 8:16-17, 19; Eph 4:25). Various Christian duties (Ro 12:6-8; Eph 6:10-20; Jas 4:8-11; 5:7-9, 12, 14; 1Pe 1:13-17; 2:11-25; 3:8-9, 15; 4:7-15; 5:5-8; 2Pe 1:5-7). Watchfulness (Pr 4:23; Mt 24:42, 44; 25:13; Mk 13:35-37; Lk 12:35-40; 21:36; 1Co 16:13-14; Eph 5:15; Php 3:2; Col 4:2; 1Th 5:6; 1Pe 5:8-9; Rev 3:2). Watchfulness against backsliding (Dt 4:9; 8:11; 11:16, 28; 2Pe 3:17), against covetousness (Col 15:9; Lk 12:15), against false Christs (Mt 24:23-26; Mk 13:21-23; Lk 17:23). Wholehearted service (Jos 22:5; 24:14; 1Sa 12:24; 1Ch 28:9; Ecc 9:10). Wisdom (Pr 3:21; 4:5, 13; 5:1; 8:5-6, 32-33; 23:12, 23), in speech (Pr 23:9; 26:4-5; Col 4:6). Wise self-restraint (Ecc 7:16-18, 21). Witnessing for Christ (Mk 5:19; 1Pe 3:15). Worship (Ge 35:1; Ex 20:24; Rev 19:10; 22:9; Eph 5:19; Col 3:16). Zeal for righteousness (Jn 6:27; 1Co 15:58), for the faith (Jude 3), in one's calling (Ro 12:6-8).

Fixing Penalty for:

Adultery (Lev 20:10; 21:9; 1Co 6:9-10; Gal 5:19, 21). Arson (Ex 22:6). Bestiality (Ex 22:19; Lev 20:13, 15-16). Blasphemy (Lev 24:16). Carnality (Lev 19:20). Contempt of authority (Dt 17:12). Criminal neglect to safeguard life (Ex 21:28-36). Cursing parents (Ex 21:17; Lev 20:9). Destruction of neighbor's property (Lev 24:18). Disobedience (Nu 15:30-31). False Witness (Dt 19:18-19). Fornication (Ac 15:20; 1Co 6:18; 10:8). Idolatry (Lev 20:2-5; Dt 17:2-5), enticement to idolatry (Dt 13:5, 9-10, 15). Impenitence (Lev 23:29). Incest (Lev 20:11-12, 14, 17, 19-21). Kidnapping (Ex 21:16; Dt 24:7). Murder (Ex 21:12; Lev 24:17; Nu 35:31; Dt 19:11-13). Laziness (2Th 3:10). Loss of borrowed property (Ex 22:14-15), of property held in trust (Ex 22:7, 13). Personal injury (Ex 21:18-27; Lev 24:19-20). Sabbath breaking (Ex 31:14; 35:2). Seduction (Ex 22:16). Theft (Ex 21:1-4). Trespass (Ex 22:5). Untimely cohabitation (Lev 20:18). Witchcraft (Ex 22:18; Lev 20:27).

Forbidding:

Adultery (Ex 20:14; Lev 18:20; Dt 5:18; Mt 5:27; 19:18; Lk 18:20; Ro 13:9; 1Co 10:8). Anxiety (Mt 6:25-34; 10:19-23; Lk 12:11, 22-32; Jn 14:27; Php 4:6). Association with evil company (Pr 1:10-19), with harlots (Pr 2:16; 5:3-21; 6:20, 24-26; 7:1-27; 23:26-28). Bestiality (Lev 18:23; 20:13, 15-16). Boasting (Dt 9:4). Bribe taking (Ex 23:8; Dt 16:19; 27:25). Causeless strife (Pr 3:30). Change in God's law (Dt 4:2; 12:32). Class distinction (Ex 23:3; Lev 19:15; Nu 15:29; Dt 16:19), legislation (Lev 24:22). Company with drunkards (Pr 23:20). Conformity to the world (Lev 20:23). Contention (Ro 13:13; Php 2:14; 2Ti 2:14; Tit 3:2). Corrupt conversation (Eph 4:29; 5:4; Col 3:8). Covetousness (Ex 20:17; Dt 5:21; 7:25-26; Lk 12:15; Ro 13:9; Eph 5:3; Col 3:5; 1Ti 6:10-11; Heb 13:5). Dishonesty in business (Lev 19:13, 35; 25:14; Dt 25:13-15; Mic 10:19). Divorce (1Co 7:10-11, w Mt 5:32; 19:9; Mk 10:11-12; Lk 16:18). Drunkenness (Ro 13:13; Eph 5:18). Envy (Pr 3:31; 23:17; 24:1, 19; Ro 13:13; 1Pe 2:1). Evil speech (Ps 34:13; Pr 4:24; 30:10; Tit 3:2; 1Pe 3:10). Evil, to a neighbor (Ex 20:16; Lev 19:13, 16; Pr 3:29). False, dealing (Lev 6:1-5; 19:11), swearing (Lev 19:12), witness (Ex 20:16; 23:1; Lev 19:16; Dt 5:20; Pr 24:28; Mt 19:18; Lk 18:20). Falsehood (Lev 19:11; Eph 4:25; Col 3:9). Fellowship with the wicked (Pr 1:10-15; 4:14-15; Ro 16:17; 1Co 5:9-11; 2Co 6:14, 17; Eph 5:11; 2Th 3:6; 2Ti 3:5). Foolish, unlearned questions (2Ti 2:23). Fraud (Lev 19:11, 13, 35; 1Th 4:6). Giving cause for stumbling (1Co 8:9; 10:32). Grudges (Lev 19:18). Haste for riches (Pr 23:4), in litigation (Pr 25:8-9). Hatred (Lev 19:17; Eph 4:31; Col 3:8). Heed to false teachers (Dt 13:1-18). Idolatry (Ex 20:3-5, 23; Lev 18:21; 20:2-5; 26:1; Dt 4:16-19, 23; 5:7-9; 6:14; 13:2-3; 16:21-22; Jos 24:14; 2Ki 17:35; Eze 20:18; 1Co 10:7; 1Jn 5:21). Impure marriages (Lev 21:7). Incest (Lev 18:6; 20:11-12, 13, 17, 19-21; Dt 22:30). Indulgence in wine (Pr 23:31; Eph 5:18; Tit 2:3). Injustice (Ex 23:2-3; Lev 19:15; 25:17; Dt 16:19), to foreigners (Lev 12:49; 22:21; Lev 19:33-34; Dt 1:16; 24:14, 17), to the poor (Ex 23:6). Intolerance (Mk 9:39; Lk 9:49-50). Improper respect of persons (Jas 2:1-9). Labor on the Sabbath (Ex 20:10; 23:12; 34:21; 35:2-3; Lev 23:3; Dt 5:14). Lewdness (Pr 31:3; Ro 13:13; Eph 4:17-32; 5:3; 1Th 4:2-6; 2Ti 2:22). Lawlessness (2Ti 3:8). Laziness (2Th 3:10). Love of the world (1Jn 2:15). Malice (Lev 19:17-18; Eph 4:31; Col 3:8; 1Pe 2:1). Malicious mischief (Lev 19:14). Meddling (1Pe 4:15). Murder (Ex 20:13; Dt 5:17; Mt 5:21; 19:18; Ro 13:9; Jas 2:11; 1Pe 4:15). Murmuring (1Co 10:10; Php 2:14; Jas 5:9). Offerings with blemish implying insincere or imperfect service of God (Lev 1:3, 10; 3:1, 6; 4:3, 23, 28, 32; 5:15, 18; 6:6; 9:2-3; 22:18-22; Dt 15:21; 17:1). Oppression (Jer 19:13; Pr 22:22), of the poor (Dt 24:14), of the widows and orphans (Ex 22:22-24; Jer 22:3; Zec 7:10). Ostentation in giving, in fasting, and in prayer (Mt 6:1, 5-6, 17-18). Perjury (Lev 19:12). Perversion of justice (Dt 16:19-20; 24:17). Prejudice (Ex 23:3). Profane swearing (Mt 5:34-36; Jas 5:12). Profaning God's name (Lev 20:7; Lev 18:21; 19:12; 21:6; 22:32; Dt 5:11). Prostitution of a daughter (Lev 19:29). Putting a neighbor's life in peril by false witness (Lev 19:16). Removal of landmarks (Dt 19:14; Pr 22:28; 23:10). Resistance (Mt 5:39). Retaliation (Lev 19:18; Pr 24:29; Mt 5:38-42; Ro 12:17; 1Th 5:15; 1Pe 3:9). Robbery (Lev 19:13; Pr 22:22). Sabbath breaking (Ex 31:14; Jer 17:21-22). Self-confidence (Pr 3:5, 7). Self-pride (Ro 12:3). Self-praise (Pr 27:2). Selfishness (1Co 10:24; Php 2:4). Strife (2Ti 2:24). Homosexuality (Lev 18:22; 20:13). Taking of interest (Lev 22:25; Lev 25:35, 37). Talebearing (Lev 19:16). Theft (Ex 20:15; Lev 19:11; Dt 5:19; Mt 19:18; Lk 18:20; Ro 13:9; Eph 4:28; 1Pe 4:15).

Uncharitable judgments (Mt 7:1-5; Lk 6:37, 42; Ro 14:1-3, 13). Uncharitableness (Mt 24:17; Mt 18:10). Unholy ambition (Php 2:3). Unrighteous anger (Mt 5:22). Unrighteous judgments (Lev 19:15). Use of alcohol by priests on duty (Lev 10:9).

Vain repetitions in prayer (Mt 6:7-8). Various vices (Ro 13:12-13; Gal 5:19-21; Eph 4:28-31; 5:3-6, 11, 18; Col 3:5, 8-9; 1Th 4:3-6; 5:15, 22; 1Ti 3:3, 8; 6:17; 2Ti 3:2-5; Tit 2:3, 10; Heb 13:5; Jas 1:21; 2:11; 4:11; 5:9, 12; 1Pe 2:11; 3:9; 4:3).

Witchcraft (Lev 19:26, 31; 20:6). Withholding a servant's wages (Lev 19:13). Worldliness (Mt 6:19; Ro 12:2; 1Jn 2:15). Worldliness of ministers (2Ti 2:4-5).

Implied:
Commanding an exact conscience (Mt 6:22-24). Against self-righteousness (Mt 7:3).

Precepts of Jesus:
Stated or implied (Mt 5:16, 22-24, 27-48; 6:1-4, 6-8, 16-25, 31-34; 7:1-29; 10:5-42; 16:24; 18:8-10, 15-17; 18:21-22; 19:16-19; 20:25-28; 22:21, 34-40; 24:42-51; 25:34-46; Mk 6:7-11; 8:34; 9:35-50; 10:9-12, 17, 22; 11:22; 12:17; 13:33-37; Lk 6:27-42; 10:28-37; 12:1-2-31; 13:24; Jn 7:24; 13:34-35; 14:11, 15, 23-24; 15:2-12, 17, 20-22).

Prescribing:
Law of evidence (Dt 17:6; 19:15). Number of stripes in punishment (Dt 25:3). Priestly benedictions (Nu 6:23-26). Stimulants for the perishing (Pr 31:6).

Warning: The rich (1Ti 6:17-19).

Warning against:
Covetousness (Lk 12:15). False teachers (Mt 7:15; Eph 5:6-7; Col 2:8). Love of money (Heb 13:5). Quenching the Spirit (1Th 5:19). Sensuality (Pr 6:24-25). Sinful indulgence (Lk 21:34). Sinning against the Holy Spirit (Eph 4:30; 1Th 5:19). Temptations (Pr 1:10-15; 19:27).

See Adultery; Children; Citizens; Homicide; Instruction; Ministers; Obedience, Commanded; Servant; Theft; Wife; Women.

COMMANDMENTS AND STATUTES, OF MEN
Traditions (Isa 29:13; Ro 14:1-6, 10-21; Gal 1:14; Col 2:8; 1Ti 4:1-3). Rejected by Jesus (Mt 15:2-20; Mk 7:2-23).

COMMERCE
Laws concerning (Lev 19:36-37; 25:14, 17). Carried on by means of caravans (Ge 37:25, 27; Isa 60:6), ships (1Ki 9:27-28; 10:11; 22:48; Ps 107:23-30; Pr 31:14; Rev 18:19). Conducted in fairs (Eze 27:12, 19; Mt 11:16). Of the Arabs (Isa 60:6; Jer 6:20; Eze 27:21-24), Egyptians (Ge 42:2-34), Ethiopians (Isa 45:14), Ishmaelites (Ge 37:27-28), Israelites (1Ki 9:26-28; Ne 3:31-32; Eze 27:17), Ninevites (Na 3:16), Syrians (Eze 27:16, 18), Tyrians (2Sa 5:11; 1Ki 5:6; Isa 23:8; Eze 27; 28:5), Sidonians (Isa 23:2; Eze 27:8), Babylonians (Rev 18:3, 11-13), Israelites (Eze 27:17). From Tarshish (Jer 10:9; Eze 27:25).

Evil practices connected with (Pr 29:14; Eze 22:13; Hos 12:7).

Articles of:
Apes and baboons (1Ki 10:22), balm (Ge 37:25), blue cloth (Eze 27:24), bronze (Eze 27:13; Rev 18:12), cinnamon (Rev 18:13), cattle (Eze 27:21), chest of rich apparel (Eze 27:24), citron wood (Rev 18:12), clothes for chariots (Eze 27:20), embroidery (Eze 27:16, 24), frankincense (Jer 6:20; Rev 18:13), gold (1Ki 9:28; 10:22; 2Ch 8:18; Isa 60:6; Rev 18:12), honey (Eze 27:17), horses (1Ki 10:29; Eze 27:14; Rev 18:13), ivory (1Ki 10:22; 2Ch 9:21; Eze 27:15; Rev 18:12), iron (Eze 27:12, 19), land (Ge 23:13-16; Ru 4:3), lead (Eze 27:12), linen (Rev 18:12), oil (1Ki 5:11; Eze 27:17), pearls (Rev 18:12), perfumes (SS 3:6), precious stones (Eze 27:16, 22; 28:13, 16; Rev 18:12), sheep (Rev 18:13), slaves (Ge 37:28, 36; Dt 24:7), silk (Rev 18:12), silver (1Ki 10:22; 2Ch 9:21; Rev 18:12), sweet cane (Jer 6:20), timber (1Ki 5:6, 8), tin (Eze 27:12), wheat (1Ki 5:11; Eze 27:17; Rev 18:13), white wool (Eze 27:18), wine (2Ch 2:15; Eze 27:18; Rev 18:13), human bodies and souls (Rev 18:13).

Transportation of passengers (Jnh 1:3; Ac 21:2; 27:2, 6, 37). *See Merchant; Tarshish, 2, 3; Trade and Travel; Traffic.*

COMMISSARY
For armies, cattle driven with (2Ki 3:9). *See Armies.* For royal households (2Ki 4:7-19, 27-28).

COMMITMENT
Through the word of truth (Jn 17:17). To the Lord (Pr 16:3; 1Co 1:2; 2Co 7:1; 1Pe 1:15-16).

COMMONWEALTH
See Citizens.

COMMUNION
With God (Ps 16:7; Jn 14:23; 2Co 6:16; 1Jn 1:3). With Christ (Jn 14:23; 1Jn 1:3; Rev 3:20). With the Spirit (Jn 14:16-18; 2Co 13:14; Gal 4:6; Php 2:1-2). *See Fellowship.*

Instances of:
Enoch (Ge 5:22, 24). Noah (Ge 6:9, 13-22; 8:15-17). Abraham (Ge 12:1-3, 7; 17:1-2; 18:1-33; 22:1-2, 11-12, 16-18). Hagar (Ge 16:8-12). Isaac (Ge 26:2, 24, in dreams (Ge 28:13, 15; 31:3; 35:1, 7; 46:2-4). Moses (Ex 3; 4:1-17; 33:9, 11; 34:28-35; Nu 12:8). Joshua (Jos 6:11-24; 7:10-15). Gideon (Jdg 6:11-24). Solomon (1Ki 3:5-14; 2Ch 1:7-12).

Of Believers:
Unity (Ps 119:63; 133:1-3; Am 3:3; Jn 17:20-21; 1Co 10:16-17; 12:12-13). Commanded (Ro 12:15; 2Co 6:14-18; Eph 4:1-3; 5:11; Col 3:16; 1Th 4:18; 5:11, 14; Heb 3:13; 10:24-25; Jas 5:16). Exemplified (1Sa 23:16; Ps 55:14; Mal 3:16; Lk 22:32; 24:17, 32; Ac 2:42; 1Jn 1:3, 7). *See Eucharist; Fellowship.*

COMMUNITY
Christian (Ac 2:44-45; 4:32-37; 5:1-10).

COMPANY
Evil:
Perils of (Ge 19:14-15; Nu 16:21-26; 33:55; Jdg 2:1-3; 2Ch 19:2; Ezr 9:14; Ps 50:18; 106:35-36; Pr 13:20; Hos 7:5, 8-9; Mic 6:16). Seductive (Pr 12:11, 26; 16:29; Ecc 9:18; Mt 24:12; 1Co 15:33; 2Pe 2:7-8, 18). Shunned by the righteous (Ps 6:8; 26:4-5, 9; 28:3; 31:6; 84:10; 101:4, 7; 119:115; 120:5-7; 139:19-22; 141:4; Pr 14:7; 17:12; Jer 9:2; 15:17; Hos 4:17; Rev 2:2).

Warnings against (Ge 49:6; 2Sa 23:6-7; Pr 2:11-12, 16, 19; 4:14-15; 5:8; 9:6; 20:19; 22:5, 10; 22:24-25; 23:6, 20; 24:1; 28:7, 19; 29:24; 1Ti 6:5). Forbidden (Ex 23:2, 32-33; 34:12-15; Lev 18:3; 20:23; Dt 7:2-4; 12:30; Jos 23:6-13; Pr 1:10-15; Isa 8:11-12; Jer 51:6, 45; Ro 16:17-18; 1Co 5:6, 9-11; 2Co 6:14-17; Gal 5:9; Eph 5:6-7, 11; 2Th 3:6; 1Ti 5:22; 2Ti 3:4-5; 2Jn 10-11; Rev 18:4). *See Example; Influence, Evil.*

Good: (Ps 1:1; 15:1-5; Pr 13:20).
See Communion, Of Believers; Example; Fellowship; Influence, Good.

COMPASSES
Carpenter's (Isa 44:13).

COMPASSION
Of God: *See God, Mercy of.*
Of Christ: *See Jesus the Christ, Compassion of.*

COMPEL
By God (Ex 3:19; Ac 20:22; 1Co 9:16; 2Co 5:14). By people (Ezr 4:23; Gal 2:3; 6:12). By circumstances (1Sa 13:12; Ac 28:19).

COMPLACENCY
Indifference to God is judged (Pr 1:32-33; Isa 32:9, 11; Am 6:1; Zep 1:12; Lk 11:23). *See Lukewarmness.*

COMPLAINT
See Murmuring.

COMPLICITY
Warnings Against: (Ps 50:18; Pr 29:24; Ro 1:32; 2Jn 10-11).

Instances of:
Sarah, in deceiving Pharaoh (Ge 12:11-19), Abimelech (Ge 20:2-5, 11-14). Rebekah, in deceiving Isaac (Ge 27:5-17). The elders and nobles of Jezreel, in stoning Naboth (1Ki 21:7-14). Jews who opposed building the temple (Ne 6:10-19). Daughter of Herodias, in death of John the Baptist (Mt 14:8; Mk 6:25). Pilate, in the death of Christ (Mt 27:17-26; Mk 15:9-15; Lk 23:13-25; Jn 19:13-16). Paul, in death of Stephen (Ac 7:58). *See Collusion; Connivance; Conspiracy.*

COMPROMISE
Before litigation, commanded by Solomon (Pr 25:8-10), by Christ (Mt 5:25-26; Lk 12:58-59). *See Adjudication at Law; Arbitration; Court, Of Law; Justice.*

CONANIAH
(*Yahweh sustains*).
1. A Levite (2Ch 31:12-13).
2. Another Levite (2Ch 35:9).

CONCEALMENT, EXPOSURE
[*4059, 7621, 636, 649, 2821, 5158, 5745, 5746*].

Concealment of Sin:
(Ge 3:8; Jos 7:21; Pr 28:13; Isa 29:15; 30:1).

Secret Sins:
Warning against (2Ki 17:9; Job 24:16; Ps 19:12; 90:8; Eze 8:12; Eph 5:12). Called works of darkness (Job 24:14; Pr 7:8-9; Jn 3:20; Ro 13:12; Eph 5:11; 1Th 5:7).

Exposure of Sin:
Inevitable (Nu 32:23; Job 20:27; Pr 26:26; Ecc 12:14; Lk 12:2; 1Co 4:5). Rendered doubly certain (Job 10:14; 14:16; Jer 16:17; Eze 11:5; Hos 7:2; Am 5:12).

CONCEIT
Of the foolish (Pr 12:15; 26:5, 12, 16; 28:26; Ro 1:22). Of the rich (Pr 28:11). Of the self-righteous (Ps 36:2; Lk 18:11-12). Warnings against (Pr 3:5, 7; 23:4; Isa 5:21; Jer 9:23; Ro 11:25; 12:16; 2Ch 9:21; Isa 3:18; Gal 6:3). *See Hypocrisy; Pride; Self-Exaltation.*

CONCEPTION
Miraculous: By Sarah (Ge 21:1-2), Rebekah (Ge 25:21), Rachel (Ge 30:22), Manoah's wife (Jdg 13:3-24), Hannah (1Sa 1:19-20), Elizabeth (Lk 1:24-25, 36-37, 58), Mary (Mt 1:18, 20; Lk 1:31-35).

CONCISION
See Circumcision; Mutilators.

CONCUBINAGE
Laws concerning (Ex 21:7-11; Lev 19:20-22; Dt 21:10-14). Concubines might be dismissed (Ge 21:9-14). Called wives (Ge 37:2; Jdg 19:3-5). Children of, not heirs (Ge 15:4; 21:10).

Practiced by Abraham (Ge 16:3; 25:6; 1Ch 1:32). Nahor (Ge 22:23-24), Jacob (Ge 30:4), Eliphaz (Ge 36:12), Gideon (Jdg 8:31), a Levite (Jdg 19:1), Caleb (1Ch 2:46-48), Manasseh (1Ch 7:14), Saul (2Sa 3:7), David (2Sa 5:13; 15:16), Solomon (1Ki 11:3), Rehoboam (2Ch 11:21), Abijah (2Ch 13:21), Belshazzar (Da 5:2). *See Marriage; Polygamy.*

CONCUPISCENCE
Intense longing for what God would not have us to have (Ro 7:8; Col 3:5; 1Th 4:5). *See Covetousness.*

CONDEMNATION, SELF
See Self-Condemnation.

CONDESCENSION
Of God:
In Reasoning With His Creatures—
Sets forth his reasons for sending the flood (Ge 6:11-13). Enters into covenant with Abraham (Ge 15:1-21; 18:1-22). Indulges Abraham's intercession for Sodom (Ge 18:23-33). Warns Abimelech in a dream (Ge 20:3-7). Reasons with Moses (Ex 4:2-17). Sends quail to the Israelites in response to their murmuring (Ex 16:12). Indulges Moses' prayer to see his glory (Ex 33:18-23). Indulges Gideon's tests (Jdg 6:36-40). Reasons with Job (Job 38; 39; 40; 41). Invites sinners, "Come now, let us reason together" (Isa 1:18-20). Expostulates with backsliding Israel (Isa 41:21-24; 43:1-19; 65:1-16; Jer 3:1; 4:1-31; 7:1-34; Eze 18:25-32; 33:10-20; Hos 2; Mic 6:1-9; Mal 3:7-15).

In His Care—
For mankind (Ps 8:4-6; 144:3). For the world (Ps 113:5-6). In redemption (Isa 45:11; Jn 3:16; Ro 5:8; Heb 2:11; 6:17-18; 1Jn 4:10, 19).

Of Christ:
(Lk 22:27; Jn 13:5; 14; 2Co 8:9; Php 2:7-8; Heb 2:11).

CONDOLENCE
Instances of: David, to Hanun (2Sa 10:2). King of Babylon, to Hezekiah (2Ki 20:12-13). The three friends of, to Job (Job 2:11). Jesus, to Mary and Martha (Jn 11:23-35). *See Affliction, Consolation Under; Sympathy.*

CONDUCT, CHRISTIAN
Believing God (Mk 11:22; Jn 14:11-12). Fearing God (Ecc 12:13; 1Pe 2:17). Loving God (Dt 6:5; Mt 22:37). Following God (Eph 5:1; 1Pe 1:15-16). Obeying God (Lk 1:6; 1Jn 5:3). Rejoicing in God (Ps 33:1; Hab 3:18). Believing in Christ (Jn 6:29; 1Jn 3:23). Loving Christ (Jn 21:15; 1Pe 1:7-8). Following the example of Christ (Jn 13:15; 1Pe 2:21-24). Obeying Christ (Jn 14:21; 15:14).

Living:
To Christ (Ro 14:8; 2Co 5:15). To righteousness (Mic 6:8; Ro 6:18; 1Pe 2:24). Soberly, righteously, and godly (Tit 2:12).

Walking:
Honestly (1Th 4:12). Worthy of God (1Th 2:12). Worthy of the Lord (Col 1:10). In the Spirit (Gal 5:25). After the Spirit (Ro 8:1). In newness of life (Ro 6:4). Worthy of our vocation (Eph 4:1). As children of light (Eph 5:8). Rejoicing in Christ (Php 3:1; 4:4). Loving one another (Jn 15:12; Ro 12:10; 1Co 13; Eph 5:2; Heb 13:1). Striving for the faith (Php 1:27; Jude 3). Putting away all sin (1Co 5:7; Heb 12:1). Abstaining from all appearance of evil (1Th 5:22). Perfecting holiness (Mt 5:48; 2Co 7:1; 2Ti 3:17). Hating defilement (Jude 23). Following after that which is good (Php 4:8; 1Th 5:15; 1Ti 6:11). Overcoming the world (1Jn 5:4-5). Adorning the gospel (Mt 5:16; Tit 2:10). Showing a good example (1Ti 4:12; Tit 2:7; 1Pe 2:12). Abounding in the work of the Lord (1Co 15:58; 2Co 8:7; 1Th 4:1). Shunning the wicked (Ps 1:1; 2Th 3:6). Controlling the body (1Co 9:27; Col 3:5). Subduing the temper (Eph 4:26; Jas 1:19). Submitting to injuries (Mt 5:39-41; 1Co 6:7). Forgiving injuries (Mt 6:14; Ro 12:20). Living peaceably with all (Ro 12:18; Heb 12:14). Visiting the afflicted (Mt 25:36; Jas 1:27). Doing as we would be done by (Mt 7:12; Lk 6:31). Sympathizing with others (Gal 6:2; 1Th 5:14). Honoring others (Ps 15:4; Ro 12:10). Fulfilling domestic duties (Eph 6:1-8; 1Pe 3:1-7). Submitting to authorities (1Ch 13:17). Being liberal to others (Ac 20:35; Ro 12:13). Being contented (Php 4:11; Heb 13:4). Blessedness of maintaining (Ps 1:1-3; 19:9-11; 50:23; Mt 5:3-12; Jn 7:17; 15:10).

CONDUIT
See Aqueduct.

CONEY
Rock badger; unclean for food (Lev 11:5, ftn; Dt 14:7; Ps 104:18; Pr 30:26).

CONFECTION
A blend of incense or perfume (Ex 30:35; 1Sa 8:12). Difficult term transliterated "Pannag" in KJV (Eze 27:17). *See Perfume.*

CONFECTIONARY
A perfumer (1Sa 8:13). *See Perfume.*

CONFEDERACIES
Of kings (Ge 14:1-2; Jos 10:1-5; 11:1-5; 1Ki 20:1). *See Alliances.*

CONFESSION
To acknowledge one's faith in anything, as in the existence and authority of God, or the sins of which one has been guilty (Mt 10:32; Lev 5:5; Ps 32:5), to concede or allow (Jn 1:20; Ac 24:14; Heb 11:13), to praise God by thankfully acknowledging him (Ro 14:11; Heb 13:15).

Of Christ:
In baptism (Ac 19:4-5; Gal 3:27). To salvation (Mt 10:32; Lk 12:8; Ro 10:9-11). Inspired by the Holy Spirit (1Co 12:3; 1Jn 4:2-3). Fellowship with the Father through (1Jn 2:23; 4:15). Timid believers deterred from (Jn 12:42-43). Those refusing to make, rejected (Mt 10:33; Mk 8:38; Lk 12:9; 2Ti 2:12). Hypocritical (Mt 7:21-23; Lk 13:26; 1Jn 1:6; 2:4). Commanded (2Ti 1:8). Exemplified (Mt 3:11; 14:23; John 1:15-18; 6:29; 9:22-38; 11:27; Ac 8:35-37; 9:20; 18:5; Ro 1:16).

Of Sin: *See Sin, Confession of.*

CONFIDENCE
In People:
Warned against (Jer 9:4; 12:6; Mic 7:5).

Betrayed—
Joshua, by the Gibeonites (Jos 9:3-15). Eglon, by Ehud (Jdg 3:15-23). Sisera, by Jael (Jdg 4:17-22). Samson, by Delilah (Jdg 16:17-20). Ahimelech, by David (1Sa 21:1-9). Abner, by Joab (2Sa 3:27). Amasa, by Joab (2Sa 20:9-10). Worshipers of Baal, by Jehu (2Ki 10:18-28). *See Betrayal.*

False: *See False Confidence.*

In God:
(Ps 118:8; Pr 3:26; 14:26; Ac 28:31; Eph 3:12; Heb 3:16; 10:35; 1Jn 2:28; 3:21; 5:14). *See Faith.*

CONFISCATION
Of property: By David, that of Mephibosheth (2Sa 16:4). By Ahab, of Naboth's vineyard (1Ki 21:7-16). By Xerxes, of Haman's house (Est 8:1). As a penalty (Ezr 10:8).

CONFLAGRATIONS
See Burning.

CONFORMITY
Conformity to the world, condemned (Ro 12:1-2; Eze 5:7; 11:12; 1Pe 1:14-16).
Conformity to Christ, commanded (Ro 8:29; Eph 5:1-2; 1Co 4:16; 1Th 1:6; 2:14; Heb 6:12; 13:7; 3Jn 11).

CONFUSION
Of languages (Ge 11:1-9). Of Israel's enemies in battle (Ex 14:24; 23:27; Jos 10:10). Of Israel in judgment (Dt 28:20, 28; Jer 51:34). Of believers by false teachers (Gal 1:7; 5:10).

CONGESTION
NIV "swelling" (Lev 13:28) or "inflamation" (Dt 28:22). *See Disease.*

C

CONGREGATION, OF ISRAEL Collective term for God's chosen in the OT, or an assembly of the people summoned for a definite purpose (1Ki 8:65), either the whole assembly, or a part (Nu 16:3; Ex 12:6; 35:1; Lev 4:13).

Often considered in a non-technical sense, as a gathering of believers or chosen, the church of the OT. For that purpose. *See Church, The Body of Believers.*

CONIAH (*Yahweh sustains*). A name given to Jehoiachin, king of Judah, who was carried captive by Nebuchadnezzar (Jer 22:24, ftn; 22:28; 37:1, ftn), c. 597 B.C. *See Jehoiachin.*

CONNIVANCE Judged (Lev 20:4; 1Sa 3:11-13). Result (Pr 10:10).

CONONIAH *See Conaniah.*

CONQUESTS Of the Gentiles by Israel (Jos 6:20; 8:24; 10:28-29; 11:8, 23; 12:7; Jdg 1:8; 3:30; 4:16; 8:28; 9:45; 11:33).

CONSCIENCE Guide (Ps 51:3; Pr 20:12; Mt 6:22-23; Lk 11:33-36; Ro 2:14-15; 7:18, 22; 2Co 5:11). Approves (Job 27:6; Pr 21:2; Ac 23:1; 24:16; Ro 9:1; 1Co 4:4; 2Co 1:12; 1Ti 1:5, 19; 3:9; 2Ti 1:3; Heb 13:18; 1Pe 2:19; 3:16, 21; 1Jn 3:20-21). Struggle with (Job 15:21, 24; Ps 51:3; Mt 6:22-23; Lk 11:33-36; Ro 7:15-23). Purged (Heb 9:14; 10:22). *See Honesty; Integrity.* Of another, to be respected (Ro 14:2-20; 1Co 8:7-13; 10:27-32; 2Co 4:2).

Instances of Faithful:
Pharaoh, when he took Sarah into his harem (Ge 12:18-19). Abimelech, when he took Sarah for a concubine (Ge 26:9-11). Jacob, in his care of Laban's property (Ge 31:39), in his greeting of Esau (Ge 33:1-12). Joseph, with Potiphar's wife (Ge 39:7-12). Nehemiah, with taxes (Ne 5:15). Daniel, with the king's meat (Da 1:8). Peter, in his preaching (Ac 4:19-20; 5:29).

Unfaithful Conscience:
Corrupt (Mt 6:23; Lk 11:34; Jn 16:2-3). Dead (Pr 16:25; 30:20; Jer 6:15; Am 6:1-6; Ro 1:21-25; Eph 4:17-29). Defiled (Tit 1:15). Seared (1Ti 4:2). Guilty (Job 15:21, 24; Ps 51:1-14; 73:21; Pr 28:1; Isa 59:9-14; Mt 14:1-2; 27:3-5; Mk 6:14, 16; Jn 8:9; Ac 2:37; 1Ti 4:2; Tit 1:15; Heb 9:14; 10:26-27). *See Blindness, Spiritual.*

Instances of Guilty—
Adam and Eve, after they sinned (Ge 3:7-8). Jacob, after defrauding Esau (Ge 33:1-12). Joseph's brothers (Ge 42:21; 44:16). Pharaoh, after the plagues (Ex 9:27). Micah, after stealing (Jdg 17:2). David, for his indignity to Saul (1Sa 24:5), for his adultery and for his murder of Uriah (Ps 32; 38; 40:11-12; 51), for numbering Israel (2Sa 24:10; 1Ch 21:1-8). The old prophet of Bethel (1Ki 13:18, 29-32). The lepers of Samaria (2Ki 7:8-10). Jonah (Jnh 1:12). Herod, for beheading John the Baptist (Mt 14:2; Lk 9:7). Peter, after denying the Lord (Mt 26:75; Mk 14:72; Lk 22:62). Judas (Mt 27:3-5). The accusers of the women taken in adultery (Jn 8:9).

CONSCIENCE MONEY *See Money.*

CONSCIENTIOUSNESS *See Integrity.*

CONSCRIPTION Of soldiers (1Sa 14:52). Of forced labor (1Ki 5:13-18; 19:15-23; 2Ki 25:19).

CONSECRATED THINGS Laws regarding (Lev 27; Nu 18:8-32). *See Firstborn; Firstfruits.*

CONSECRATION Of Aaron. *See Aaron.* Of Priests. *See Priest.* Of the altar. *See Altar.* Of the temple. *See Temple, Solomon's; Offerings.*
Commanded (Ex 32:29). Personal (Ps 51:17; Mt 13:44-46; Ro 6:13, 16, 19; 12:1; 2Co 8:5). Conditional (Ge 28:20-22; 2Sa 15:7-8).
Instances of: Cain and Abel (Ge 4:4-7). Abraham, of Isaac (Ge 22:9-12). Jephthah, of his daughter (Jdg 11:30-40). Hannah, of Samuel (1Sa 1:11, 24-28). David consecrates the water (2Sa 23:16; 1Ch 11:18). Zicri, of himself (2Ch 17:16).
See Dedication; Offerings.

CONSERVATION *See Ecology.*

CONSISTENCY Encouraged (Ne 5:9; Mt 6:24; Lk 16:13; Ro 14:22; 1Co 10:21).
See Deceit; Expediency; Hypocrisy; Inconsistency; Obduracy; Prudence.

CONSOLATION *See Affliction, Consolation Under; Holy Spirit.*

CONSPIRACY Law against (Ex 23:1-2).

Instances of:
Joseph's brothers, against Joseph (Ge 37:18-20). Miriam and Aaron, against Moses (Nu 12; 14:4; 16:1-35). Abimelech, against Gideon's sons (Jdg 9:1-6). Gaal, against Abimelech (Jdg 9:23-41). Delilah, against Samson (Jdg 16:4-21). Abner, against Ish-Bosheth (2Sa 3:7-21). Of Absalom (2Sa 15:10-13). Of Jeroboam (1Ki 14:2). Of Baasha (1Ki 15:27). Of Zimri (1Ki 16:9). Of Jezebel, against Naboth (1Ki 21:8-13). Of Jehu (2Ki 9:14-26). Of Jehoiada (2Ki 11:4-16). Of servants, against Joash (2Ki 12:20).
People in Jerusalem, against Amaziah (2Ki 14:19). Shallum, against Zechariah (2Ki 15:10). Pekahiah (2Ki 15:23-25). Pekah (2Ki 15:30). Amon (2Ki 21:23). Sennacherib (2Ki 19:37). Amaziah (2Ch 25:27). Xerxes (Est 2:21-23). Jeremiah (Jer 18:18). Daniel (Da 6:4-17). Shadrach, Meshach, and Abednego (Da 3:8-18).
Against Jeremiah (Jer 11:9, 19). Jesus (Mt 12:14; 21:38-41; 26:3-4; 27:1-2; Mk 3:6). Paul (Ac 18:12; 23:12-15).

Falsely accused of: Jonathan (1Sa 22:8).

CONSTANCY In obedience (Ps 119:31, 33). In friendship (Pr 27:10). Under suffering (Mt 5:12; Heb 12:5; 1Pe 4:12-16). In

prayer (Lk 18:1; Ro 12:12; Eph 6:18; Col 4:2; 1Th 5:17). In beneficence (Gal 6:9). In profession (Heb 10:23).
Instances of: Ruth (Ru 1:14). Jonathan (1Sa 18:1; 20:16). Priscilla and Aquila (Ro 16:3-4).
See Character; Stability.

CONSTELLATIONS (2Ki 23:5; Job 9:9; 38:32; Isa 13:10). The serpent (Job 26:13). Orion (Job 9:9; Am 5:8).
See Astronomy.

CONSTITUTION Agreement between the ruler and the people. King commanded to study and obey the Mosaic Law (Dt 17:18-20). Made by David (2Sa 5:3; 1Ch 11:3). Made for Joash (2Ch 23:2-3, 11). Made by Zedekiah, proclaiming liberty (Jer 34:8-11). King of Medes and Persians bound by (Da 6:12-15). *See Covenant.*

CONSUMPTION NIV "wasting diseases" (Lev 26:16; Dt 28:22). *See Disease.*

CONTEMPT Sin of (Job 31:13-14; Pr 14:21). Folly of (Pr 11:12). A characteristic of the wicked (Pr 18:3; Isa 5:24; 2Ti 3:3).
Forbidden Toward:
Parents (Pr 23:22). Christ's little ones (Mt 18:10). Weak brothers (Ro 14:3). Young ministers (1Co 16:11). Believing masters (1Ti 6:2). The poor (Jas 2:1-3). Self-righteousness prompts to (Isa 65:5; Lk 18:9, 11). Pride and prosperity prompt to (Ps 123:4). Ministers should give no occasion for (1Ti 4:12). Of ministers, is a despising of God (Lk 10:16; 1Th 4:8).
Toward the Church:
Often turned into respect (Isa 60:14). Often punished (Eze 28:26). Causes believers to cry to God (Ne 4:4; Ps 123:3).
The Wicked Exhibit Toward:
Christ (Ps 22:6; Isa 53:3; Mt 27:29). Believers (Ps 119:141). Authorities (2Pe 2:10; Jude 8). Parents (Pr 15:5, 20). The afflicted (Job 19:18). The poor (Pr 14:6; Ecc 9:16). Believers sometimes guilty of (Jas 2:6).
Exemplified:
Hagar (Ge 16:4). Troublemakers (1Sa 10:27). Nabal (1Sa 25:10-11). Michal (2Sa 6:16). Sanballat (Ne 2:19; 4:2-3). False teachers (2Co 10:10).

CONTENTION *See Strife.*

CONTENTMENT Desirable (Pr 14:14; 15:13, 15, 30; 16:8; 17:1, 22; 30:8; Ecc 2:24; 4:6; 5:12; 6:9). Commanded (Ps 37:7; Ecc 9:7-9; Lk 3:14; 1Co 7:17, 20-24; Gal 5:26; 1Ti 6:6-8; Heb 13:5).
Instances of: Esau (Ge 33:9). Barzillai (2Sa 19:33-37). The Shunammite (2Ki 4:13). David (Ps 16:6). Paul (Php 4:11-12).
See Affliction, Consolation Under; Resignation.

CONTINENCE *See Chastity; Self-Control.*

CONTINENTS (Ge 1:9-10; Job 26:7, 10; 28:8-11; 38:4-18; Ps 95:5; 104:5-9; 136:6; Pr 8:29; 30:4). *See Geology.*

CONTINGENCIES
In Divine Government of Mankind:
Conditional Rewards (Ge 4:7; 18:19; Ex 19:5; Lev 26:3-4; Dt 7:12; 11:26-27; 30:15-16, 19; 1Ki 3:14; 1Ch 28:7; 2Ch 26:5; Job 36:11; Jer 11:4; 18:9-10; 22:4-5; Mt 19:17; 23:37; Jn 14:23; 15:7; Col 1:22-23; Heb 3:14; Rev 22:17). Conditional Punishment (Ge 2:16-17; 3:3; Lev 26:14-16; Dt 11:28; 30:15, 19; 1Ki 3:14; 20:42; Job 36:12; Jer 12:17; 18:8; Eze 33:14-16; Jnh 3:10; Mt 6:15; Jn 9:41; 15:6; 2Th 2:8-11; Rev 2:22; 3:3).
Instances of choice:
Joshua (Jos 24:15). David (2Sa 24:12-14). Jesus (Mt 26:39).
See Blessings, Spiritual; Contingent Upon Obedience; Predestination; Will.

CONTRACTS Binding force of (Jos 9:19; Pr 6:1-5; Mt 20:1-16; Gal 3:15). Penalty for breach of (Lev 6:1-7).
Dissolved:
By mutual consent (Ex 4:18), by blotting out (Col 2:14).
Ratified:
By giving presents (Ge 21:25-30; 1Sa 18:4), by consummating in the presence of the public at the gates of the city (Ge 23:17-18; Ru 4:1-11), by erecting a heap of stones (Ge 31:44-54), by oaths (Ge 26:3, 28, 31; Jos 9:15, 20; 1Ch 16:16; Heb 6:16-17), by joining hands (Pr 6:1; 17:18; 22:26), with salt (Nu 18:19), by taking off the sandal (Ru 4:6-8), by written instrument (Jer 32:10-15). By piercing the servant's ear (Ex 21:2-6).
Instances of:
Between Abraham and Abimelech, concerning wells of water (Ge 21:25-32), violated (Ge 26:15). Between Laban and Jacob, for Laban's daughter (Ge 29:15-20, 27-30), violated (Ge 29:23-27); regarding sharing flocks and herds (Ge 30:28-34), violated (Ge 30:27-43; 31:7). Between Joshua and Gibeonites (Jos 9:3-9, 15-19). Between Solomon and Hiram (1Ki 5:8-12; 9:11).
See Covenant; Land; Vows.

CONTRITION *See Repentance; Sin, Confession of.*

CONVENTION For counsel (Pr 15:22). *See Counsel.*

CONVERSATION Profane, forbidden (Mt 5:37; Jas 5:12). Corrupt, forbidden (Eph 4:29; Col 3:8). Edifying, commanded (Eph 4:29; Col 4:6). People judged by (Mt 12:36-37). *See Speaking.*
For KJV "conversation" *See Conduct, Christian.*

CONVERSION A turning, which may be literal or figurative, ethical or religious, either from God, or, more frequently, to God. It implies a turning from and a turning to something, and is therefore associated with repentance (Ac 3:19; 26:20), and faith (Ac 11:21). On its negative side it is turning from sin, and on its positive side it is faith in Christ (Ac 20:21). Although it is an act of man, it is done by the power of God (Ac 3:26). In the process of

salvation, it is the first step in the transition from sin to God. *See Converts.*

CONVERTS Parable illustrating four levels of receiving the Word: "Along the path" (Mt 13:4, 19). "Rocky places" (Mt 13:5, 20-21). "Choked" (Mt 13:7, 22). "Good soil" (Mt 13:8, 23; Lk 8:4-15).
See Backsliders; Conversion; Proselyte; Revivals.

Instances of:
Ruth (Ru 1:16). Nebuchadnezzar (Da 4). The mariners with Jonah (Jnh 1:5-6, 14, 16). Ninevites (Jnh 3). Gerasenes (Lk 8:35-39). The Samaritans (Jn 4:28-42). The thief on the cross (Lk 23:39-43). At Pentecost, three thousand (Ac 2:41). Post-Pentecostal (Ac 4:4). The eunuch (Ac 8:35-38). Saul of Tarsus (Ac 9:3-18). Sergius Paulus (Ac 13:7, 12; 26:12-23). Cornelius (Ac 10). Jews and Greeks at Antioch (Ac 13:43). Lydia (Ac 16:14-15). Jailer (Ac 16:27-34). Greeks (Ac 17:4, 12).

Zealous:
Instances of: Nebuchadnezzar (Da 3:29; 4:1-37). Andrew (Jn 1:40-41). Philip (Jn 1:43-45). The woman of Samaria (Jn 4:28-29). The man possessed of demons (Lk 8:39). The blind men (Mt 9:31; Jn 9:8-38). The mute man (Mk 7:36).

CONVEYANCE Of land: *See Land.*

CONVICTION, OF SIN To convince or prove guilty. The first stage of repentance.
Produced:
By dreams (Job 33:14-17). By visions (Ac 9:3-9). By adversity (Job 33:18-30; La 1:20; Lk 15:17-21). By the gospel (Ac 2:37; 1Co 14:24-25). By conscience (Jn 8:9; Ro 2:15). By the Holy Spirit (Jn 16:7-11). By God (Dt 28:65-67; Ps 38:1-22; 51:1-4, 7-17).
Instances of:
Adam and Eve, after their disobedience (Ge 3:8-10). Cain, after he killed Abel (Ge 4:13). Joseph's brothers, because of their cruelty to him (Ge 42:21-22; 44:16; 45:3; 50:15-21). Pharaoh, after the plague of hail (Ex 9:27-28), of locusts (Ex 10:16-17), after the death of the firstborn (Ex 12:31).
The Israelites, after worshiping the golden calf and being rebuked (Ex 33:4), after the death of ten spies and their sentence (Nu 14:39-40), after murmuring against God and being bitten by the serpents (Nu 21:7). After being judged for disobedience (Dt 28:65-67; Eze 33:10). In the last days (Eze 7:16-18, 25-26).
Saul, after sparing Agag and the best of the spoils (1Sa 15:24). David, after the pestilence sent because he numbered the people (1Ch 21:8, 30). After his sin with Bathsheba (2Sa 9:12-13; Ps 51:1-17). In penitential Psalms (Ps 31:10; 38:1-22). *See Psalms.* Widow of Zarephath, when her son died (1Ki 17:18). Job, in his distress (Job 40:4-5).
Isaiah, after his vision of God's throne (Isa 6:5). Belshazzar, after the handwriting on the wall (Da 5:6). Darius, when Daniel was in the lions' den (Da 6:18). Mariners, after casting Jonah into the sea (Jnh 1:16). Ninevites, at the preaching of Jonah (Jnh 3; Mt 12:41; Lk 11:32). Jonah, in the fish's belly (Jnh 2).
Herod, when he heard of the fame of Jesus (Mt 14:2; Mk 6:14; Lk 9:7). Jews, who condemned the woman taken in adultery (Jn 8:9). Judas, after his betrayal of Jesus (Mt 27:3-5). Peter, after the large catch of fish (Lk 5:8). Paul, on the way to Damascus (Ac 9:4-18). Felix, under the preaching of Paul (Ac 24:25). Philippian jailer, after the earthquake (Ac 16:29-30).
See Penitent; Remorse; Repentance; Sin, Confession of; Wicked.

CONVOCATION NIV "assembly"; a religious festival during which no work could be done (Ex 12:16; Lev 23:2-37; Isa 1:13).

COOKING Of the Passover lamb (Ex 12:9). A young goat might not be cooked in the mother's milk (Ex 23:19; Dt 14:21). Spice used in (Eze 24:10). Ephraim, a cake unturned (Hos 7:8). In the temple (Eze 46:19-24).
See Bread; Oven.

COOS *See Cos.*

COPING NIV "eaves"; a parapet on the temple roof (1Ki 7:9).

COPPER A mineral resource of Israel (Dt 8:9; Job 28:2). Refining, figurative of judgment (Eze 22:20; 24:11). Used as money (Mt 10:9; Mk 12:42). Alloyed with tin to make bronze. *See Bronze; Money.*

COPPERSMITH NIV Alexander the "metalworker" (2Ti 4:14).

COPULATION Forbidden between persons near of kin (Lev 18:6-16). During menses (Lev 15:19; 18:19), with animals (Ex 22:19).
See Adultery; Bestiality; Homosexual; Lasciviousness.

COR A measure of dry capacity, equal to the homer, containing ten ephahs or baths (1Ki 4:22; 5:11; 2Ch 2:10; 27:5; Ezr 7:22; Eze 45:14). *See Measure.*

CORAL Ranked by Hebrews with precious stones (Job 28:18; Eze 27:16).
See Minerals of the Bible, 1; Stones.

CORBAN (*gift*). An offering dedicated to God (Lev 1:2-3; 2:1; 3:1; Nu 7:12-17; Mk 7:11).

CORD
Ancient Uses of:
In casting lots (Mic 2:5), fastening tents (Ex 35:18; 39:40; Isa 54:2), leading or binding animals (Ps 118:27, ftn; Hos 11:4), hitching to a cast or plow (Job 39:10), binding prisoners (Jdg 15:13), measuring ground (2Sa 8:2; Jos 17:14; Ps 78:55; Am 7:17; Zec 2:1), worn on the head as a sign of submission (1Ki 20:31).

C

Figurative:
Of spiritual blessings (Ps 16:6). Of sin (Pr 5:22). Of life (Ecc 12:6). Of friendship (Ecc 4:12; Hos 11:4).

Symbolic Uses of:
Tassels of thread on the corners of garments served as a reminder to obey God's commands (Nu 15:38; cf Dt 6:4-9). Signifying an inheritance (Jos 17:14). Token in mourning (1Ki 20:31-33; Job 36:8). Ribbon used in poetic imagery (SS 4:3).

CORIANDER A spice (Ex 16:31; Nu 11:7).

CORINTH *(decoration).* A city of Achaia.

Visited:
By Paul (Ac 18; 2Co 12:14; 13:1, w 1Co 16:5-7 & 2Co 1:16). Apollos (Ac 19:1), Titus (2Co 8:16-17; 12:18). Erastus, a Christian of (Ro 16:23; 2Ti 4:20).

Church of:
Schism in (1Co 1:12; 3:4). Immoralities in (1Co 5; 11). Writes to Paul (1Co 7:1). Alienation of, from Paul (2Co 10). Abuse of ordinances in (1Co 11:22; 14). Heresies in (1Co 15:12; 2Co 11). Lawsuits in (1Co 6). Liberality of (2Co 9). Paul's letters to (1Co 1:2; 16:21-24; 2Co 1:1, 13).

CORINTHIANS, 1 and 2

1 Corinthians:

Author: The apostle Paul

Date: c. Spring A.D. 55

Outline:
I. Introduction (1:1-9).
II. Divisions in the Church (1:10-4:21).
 A. The Fact of the Divisions (1:10-17).
 B. The Causes of the Divisions (1:18-4:13).
 1. A wrong conception of the Christian message (1:18-3:4).
 2. A wrong conception of Christian ministry and ministers (3:5-4:5).
 3. A wrong conception of the Christian (4:6-13).
 C. The Exhortation to End the Divisions (4:14-21).
III. Moral and Ethical Disorders in the Life of the Church (chs. 5-6).
 A. Laxity in Church Discipline (ch. 5).
 B. Lawsuits Before Non-Christian Judges (6:1-11).
 C. Sexual Immorality (6:12-20).
IV. Instruction on Marriage (ch. 7).
 A. The Prologue: General Principles (7:1-7).
 B. The Problems of the Married (7:8-24).
 C. The Problems of the Unmarried (7:25-40).
V. Instruction on the Questionable Practices (8:1-11:1).
 A. The Principles Involved (ch. 8).
 B. The Principles Illustrated (ch. 9).
 C. A Warning From the History of Israel (10:1-22).
 D. The Principles Applied (10:23-11:1).
VI. Instruction on Public Worship (11:2-14:40).
 A. Propriety in Worship (11:2-16).
 B. The Lord's Supper (11:17-34).
 C. Spiritual Gifts (chs. 12-14).
 1. The test of the gifts (12:1-3).
 2. The unity of the gifts (12:4-11).
 3. The diversity of the gifts (12:12-31a).
 4. The necessity of exercising the gifts in love (12:31b-13:13).
 5. The superiority of prophecy over tongues (14:1-25).
 6. Rules governing public worship (14:26-40).
VII. Instruction on the Resurrection (ch. 15).
 A. The Certainty of the Resurrection (15:1-34).
 B. The Consideration of Certain Objections (15:35-37).
 C. The Concluding Appeal (15:58).
VIII. Conclusion: Practical and Personal Matters (ch. 16).

2 Corinthians:

Author: The apostle Paul

Date: c. Fall A.D. 55

Outline:
I. Primarily Apologetic: Paul's Explanation of His Conduct and Apostolic Ministry (chs. 1-7).
 A. Salutation (1:1-2).
 B. Thanksgiving for Divine Comfort in Affliction (1:3-11).
 C. The Integrity of Paul's Motives and Conduct (1:12-2:4).
 D. Forgiving the Offender at Corinth (2:5-11).
 E. God's Direction in the Ministry (2:12-17).
 F. The Corinthian Believers—a Letter from Christ (3:1-11).
 G. Seeing the Glory of God With Unveiled Faces (3:12-4:6).
 H. Treasure in Clay Jars (4:7-16a).
 I. The Prospect of Death and What It Means for the Christian (4:16b-5:10).
 J. The Ministry of Reconciliation (5:11-6:10).
 K. A Spiritual Father's Appeal to His Children (6:11-7:4).
 L. The Meeting With Titus (7:5-16).
II. Hortatory: The Collection for the Christians at Jerusalem (chs. 8-9).
 A. Generosity Encouraged (8:1-15).
 B. Titus and His Companions Sent to Corinth (8:16-9:5).
 C. Results of Generous Giving (9:6-15).
III. Polemical: Paul's Vindication of His Apostolic Authority (chs. 10-13).
 A. Paul's Defense of His Apostolic Authority and the Area of His Mission (ch. 10).
 B. Paul Forced Into Foolish Boasting (chs. 11-12).
 C. Final Warnings (13:1-10).
 D. Conclusion (13:11-14).

CORMORANT A bird forbidden as food (Lev 11:17; Dt 14:17). *See Birds.*

CORN *See Grain.*

CORNELIUS *(of a horn).* Roman centurion stationed at Caesarea, and the first Gentile convert (Ac 10:1).

CORNERSTONE Determined the design and structure of a building; the most important stone in the foundation (Isa 28:16). Figurative of Creation (Job 38:6). Of Christ (Isa 28:16; Zec 10:4; Eph 2:20; 1Pe 2:6).
See Capstone; Stones.

CORNET *See Music, Instruments of; Horn; Sistrums.*

CORPORAL PUNISHMENT *See Punishment.*

CORPULENCY Instances of: Eglon (Jdg 3:17), Eli (1Sa 4:18).

CORRECTION *See Afflictions, Of Believers; Chastisement, From God; Children, Correction of; Parents; Punishment; Reproof; Rod of Correction; Scourging.*

CORRUPTION

Physical Decomposition:
After death (Ge 3:19; Job 17:14; 21:26; 34:15; Ps 16:10; 49:9; 104:29; Ecc 3:20; 12:7; Jnh 2:6; Ac 2:27, 31; 13:34-37; 1Co 15:42, 50).

Figurative:
Of sin (Isa 38:17; Ro 8:21; Gal 6:8; 2Pe 1:4; 2:12, 19). Hill of (2Ki 23:13).

Judicial: *See Court, Of Law; Government; Judge.*

Ecclesiastical: *See Church, The Body of Believers, Corrupt; Ministers.*

Political: *See Bribery; Civil Service; Government; Politics.*

COS *(summit).* Island off the SW coast of Asia Minor (Ac 21:1).

COSAM *(diviner).* An ancestor of Christ (Lk 3:28).

COSMETICS Any of the various preparations used for beautifying the hair and skin (2Ki 9:30; Jer 4:30; Eze 23:40).

COTTON *See Linen.*

COUCH A piece of furniture for reclining, but sometimes only a rolled up mat (Am 6:4; Mt 9:6).

COULTER *See Plowshare.*

COUNCIL
1. Group of people gathered for deliberation (Ge 49:6; 2Ki 9:5).
2. The Jewish Sanhedrin (Mt 26:59; Ac 5:34) and lesser courts (Mt 10:17; Mk 13:9).

COUNSEL Wisdom in (Ex 18:14-23; Pr 1:5; 11:14; 15:22; 19:20; 20:18; 24:6). The wise profit by (Pr 1:5; 9:9; 12:15; 27:9). Rejected, by Rehoboam (1Ki 12:8-16), by rich young ruler (Mt 19:22). Consequences of rejecting divine (Pr 1:24-32).
See Prudence.

COUNSELOR A wise man, versed in law and diplomacy (1Ch 27:32-33). Ahithophel was, to David (2Sa 16:23; 1Ch 27:33), to Absalom (2Sa 16:23). A title of Christ (Isa 9:6). A title of the Holy Spirit (Jn 14:16, 26; 15:26; 16:7).

COUNTENANCE Angry (Pr 25:23). Cheerful (Job 29:24; Ps 4:6; 21:6; 44:3; Pr 15:13; 27:17). Fierce (Dt 28:50; Da 8:23). Guilty (Ge 4:5; Isa 3:9). Health indicated in (Ps 42:11; 43:5). Pride in (2Ki 5:1; Ps 10:4). Reading of (Ge 31:2, 5). Sad (1Sa 1:18; Ne 2:2-3; Ecc 7:3; Eze 27:35; Da 1:15; 5:6). Transfigured (Ex 34:29-35; Lk 9:29; 2Co 3:7, 13).
See Face.

COUNTRY Loved by Israelites in Exile (Ne 1; 2; 5; Ps 137:1-6). *See Church, The Body of Believers; Congregation, Of Israel; Patriotism.*

COURAGE Of the righteous (Pr 28:1; 2Ti 1:7). Exhortations to (Ps 31:24; Isa 51:7, 12-16; Eze 2:6; 3:9; Mt 10:28; Lk 12:4; 1Co 16:13; Php 1:27-28).

Commanded:
Upon Joshua (Dt 31:7-8, 22-23; Jos 1:1-9), the Israelites (Lev 26:6-8; Jos 23:6; 1Ch 19:13; 2Ch 32:7-8; Isa 41:10; 51:7, 12-16), Solomon (1Ch 22:13; 28:20), Asa (2Ch 15:1-7), the disciples (Mt 10:26, 28; Lk 12:4), Paul (Ac 18:9-10), other Christians (1Co 16:13; Php 1:27-28). By Jehoshaphat, upon judicial and executive officers (2Ch 19:11).

Instances of the Courage of Conviction:
Abraham, in leaving his fatherland (Ge 12:1-9), in offering Isaac (Ge 22:1-14). Gideon, in destroying the altar of Baal (Jdg 6:25-31). Ezra, in undertaking the perilous journey from Babylon to Israel without a guard (Ezr 8:22-23). The Jews, in returning answer to Tattenai (Ezr 5:11). The three Hebrews who refused to bow down to the image of Nebuchadnezzar (Da 3:16-18). Daniel, in persisting in prayer, regardless of the edict against praying (Da 6:10).
Peter and John, in refusing to obey men rather than God (Ac 4:19; 5:29).

Instances of Personal Bravery:
Joshua and Caleb, in advising that Israel go at once and possess the land (Nu 13:30; 14:6-12). Othniel, in killing Kiriath Sepher (Jos 15:16-17). Gideon, in attacking the confederate armies of the Midianites and Amalekites with 300 men (Jdg 7:7-23). Deborah, in leading Israel's armies (Jdg 4). Jael, in killing Sisera (Jdg 4:18-22). Agag, in the indifference with which he faced death (1Sa 15:32-33). David, in killing Goliath (1Sa 17:32-50), in entering the tent of Saul and carrying away Saul's spear (1Sa 26:7-12). David's captains (2Sa 23). Joab, in reproving King David (2Sa 19:5-7). Nehemiah, in refusing to take refuge in the temple (Ne 6:10-13). Esther, in going to the king to save her people (Est 4:8, 16; 5:7).
Joseph of Arimathea, in caring for the body of Jesus (Mk 15:43). Thomas, in being willing to die with Jesus (Jn 11:16). Peter and other disciples (Ac 3:12-26; 4:9-13, 19-20, 31). The apostles, under persecution (Ac 5:21, 29-32). Paul, in going to Jerusalem, despite his impressions that bonds and imprisonments awaited him (Ac 20:22-24; 24:14, 25).

See Boldness of the Righteous; Ministers; Reproof, Faithfulness in; Cowardice.

COURSE OF PRIESTS AND LEVITES David divided the priests and Levites into 24 groups, called courses (Lk 1:8), each with its own head (1Ch 24:1ff). Each course officiated a week at a time.

COURT, OF BUILDINGS

Of the Tabernacle:
(Ex 27:9, 12, 16-19; 35:17-18; 38:9, 15-20, 31; 39:40; 40:8, 33; Lev 6:16, 26; Nu 3:26, 37; 4:26).

Of the Temple:
(1Ch 28:12; 2Ch 4:9; 6:13; 23:5; 33:5). The inner court (1Ki 6:36; 7:12). The middle court (1Ki 8:64; 2Ch 7:7).

COURT, OF LAW

Ecclesiastical: (1Ch 26:29-32; 2Ch 19:8-11; Mt 18:15-17; Jn 20:23).
See Church, The Body of Believers, Discipline.

Civil:
Held, outside the camp (Lev 24:14), at the tabernacle (Nu 27:2), at the gates of the city (Dt 21:19; 22:15; 25:7; Jos 20:4; Ru 4:1; Zec 8:16), under a palm tree (Jdg 4:5). Circuit (1Sa 7:15-17).
Composition and, mode of procedure (Ex 18:25-26; Dt 1:15-17; 17:9; Ru 4:2-5; 1Ch 26:29; 2Ch 19:8-11; Mt 26:54-71; Mk 14:53, 55-65; 15:1; Lk 22:50-71; Jn 18:13-28; Ac 5:17-21, 25-28, 34, 38-41). Accused spoke in his own defense (Jer 26:11-16; Mk 15:3-5; Ac 4:8-12, 18-20, 29-32). Stephen before the Sanhedrin (Ac 7:1-60). Paul before the Sanhedrin (Ac 23:1-7), before Agrippa (Ac 26:1-32). *See Appeal; Punishment; Witness.* Superior and inferior (Ex 18:21-26; 24:14; Dt 1:15-17; 17:8-13; 2Ch 19:5-10).
Justice required of (Ex 23:2-3, 6-8; Dt 1:15-17; 25:1; 27:19; 2Ch 19:5-10; Ac 25:16). Sentence of, final and obligatory (Dt 17:8-12). Contempt of (Dt 17:8-13; Mic 5:1; Ac 23:1-5). *See Judge; Justice.*
Corrupt (Pr 17:15; 29:26; Isa 1:23; 5:23; 10:1-2; Mic 3:11; 7:3; Zep 3:3; Mt 26:59-62; 27:18-26; Mk 14:53-65; 15:10; Ac 4:15-18; 6:11-14; 24:26-27). *See Bribery.*
See Judge; Justice; Priest.

COURTESY *See Manners.*

COURTSHIP Ancient customs of: Suitor visited the woman (Jdg 14:7), women proposed marriage (Ru 3:9-13). *See Marriage.*

COVENANT *(agreement, contract).*

Of God With People:
See Covenants, Major in the Old Testament. Salt is an emblem of (Lev 2:13; Nu 18:19; 2Ch 13:5). Confirmed with an oath (Ge 22:16; 26:3; 50:24; Ex 34:27-28; Nu 32:11; Ps 89:35; 105:9; Lk 1:73; Heb 6:13, 17-18). Binding (Lev 26; Jer 11:2-3; Gal 3:15). Everlasting (Ge 8:20-22; 9:1-17; Ps 105:8, 10; Isa 54:10; 61:8). God faithful to (Lev 26:44-45; Dt 4:31; 7:8-9; Jdg 2:1; 1Ki 8:23; Ps 105:8-11; 106:45; 111:5; Mic 7:20).

Instances of, With Individuals and Groups—
With Adam (Ge 2:16-17), Noah (Ge 6:18; 8:16; 9:8-17), Abraham (Ge 12:1-3; 15; 17:1-22; Ex 6:4-8; Ps 105:8-11; Ro 9:7-13; Gal 3). *See Circumcision.* Isaac (Ge 17:19), Jacob (Ge 28:13-15). Israel, to deliver them from Egypt (Ex 6:4-8), to destroy Amalek (Ex 17:14-16). Phinehas (Nu 25:12-13). Levites (Ne 13:29; Mal 2:4-5).

Instances of, with Israel at Sinai—
At Horeb (Ex 34:27; Dt 5:2-3), in Moab (Dt 29:1-15). Blood of (Ex 24:8). *See Blood, Blood of the Covenant.* Book of (Ex 24:7). The Sabbath (Ex 31:16). The Ten Commandments (Ex 34:28; Dt 5:2-3; 9:9).

Major Social Concerns in the Covenant—
1. Personhood. Everyone's person is to be secure (Ex 20:13; 21:16-21, 26-31; Lev 19:14; 24:17; 27:18).
2. False Accusation. Everyone is to be secure against slander and false accusation (Ex 20:16; 23:1-3; Lev 19:16; Dt 5:20; 19:15-21).
3. Woman. No woman is to be taken advantage of within her subordinate status in society (Ex 21:7-11, 20, 26-32; 22:16-17; Dt 21:10-14; 22:13-30; 24:1-5).
4. Punishment. Punishment for wrongdoing shall not be excessive so that the culprit is dehumanized (Dt 25:1-5).
5. Dignity. Every Israelite's dignity and right to be God's freedman and servant are to be honored and safeguarded (Ex 21:2, 5-6; Lev 25; Dt 15:12-18).
6. Inheritance. Every Israelite's inheritance in the promised land is to be secure (Lev 25; Nu 27:5-7; 36:1-9; Dt 25:5-10).
7. Property. Everyone's property is to be secure (Ex 20:15; 21:33-36; 22:1-15; 23:4-5; Lev 19:35-36; Dt 5:19; 22:1-4; 25:13-15).
8. Fruit of Labor. Everyone is to receive the fruit of his labors (Lev 19:13; Dt 24:14; 25:4).
9. Fruit of the Ground. Everyone is to share the fruit of the ground (Ex 23:10-11; Lev 19:9-10; 23:22; 25:3-55; Dt 14:28-29; 24:19-21).
10. Rest on Sabbath. Everyone, down to the humblest servant and the resident alien, is to share in the weekly rest of God's Sabbath (Ex 20:8-11; 23:12; Dt 5:12-15).
11. Marriage. The marriage relationship is to be kept inviolate (Ex 20:14; Dt 5:18; see also Lev 18:6-23; 20:10-21; Dt 22:13-30).
12. Exploitation. No one, however disabled, impoverished or powerless, is to be oppressed or exploited (Ex 22:21-27; Lev 19:14, 33-34; 25:35-36; 23:19; 24:6, 12-15, 17; 27:18).
13. Fair Trial. Everyone is to have free access to the courts and is to be afforded a fair trial (Ex 23:6, 8; Lev 19:15; Dt 1:17; 10:17-18; 16:18-20; 17:8-13; 19:15-21).
14. Social Order. Every person's God-given place in the social order is to be honored (Ex 20:12; 21:15, 17; 22:28; Lev 19:3, 32; 20:9; Dt 5:16; 17:8-13; 21:15-21; 27:16).
15. Law. No one shall be above the law, not even the king (Dt 17:18-20).

16. **Animals.** Concern for the welfare of other creatures is to be extended to the animal world (Ex 23:5, 11; Lev 25:7; Dt 22:4, 6-7; 25:4).

Repudiated by God on account of Israelite's idolatry (Jer 44:26-27; Heb 8:9). Broken by the Israelites (Jer 22:9; Eze 16:59; Heb 8:9). Punishment for breaking (Lev 26:25-46).David (2Sa 7:12-16; 1Ch 17:11-14; 2Ch 6:16), David and his house (2Sa 23:5; Ps 89:20-37; Jer 33:21), God's people (Isa 55:3; 59:21).

Of People With God:
Jacob (Ge 28:20-22). Joshua (Jos 24:25). Absalom (2Sa 15:7-8). Jehoiada and Joash (2Ki 11:17). Josiah (2Ki 23:3). Asa (2Ch 15:12-15). Nehemiah (Ne 9:38; 10). Israelites (Ex 24:3, 7; 19:8; Dt 5:27; 26:17; Jer 50:5). See Vows.

Of People With People:
Sacred (Jos 9:18-21; Gal 3:15). Binding (Jos 9:18-20; Jer 34:8-21; Eze 17:14-18; Gal 3:15), on those represented as well (Dt 29:14-15). Breach of, punished (2Sa 21:1-6; Jer 34:8-22; Eze 17:13-19). National. See Alliances.

Ratified:
By giving the hand (Ezr 10:18; La 5:6; Eze 17:18), loosing the sandal (Ru 4:7-11), writing and sealing (Ne 9:38; Jer 32:10-12), giving presents (Ge 21:27-30; 1Sa 18:3-4), making a feast (Ge 26:30), erecting a monument (Ge 31:45-46, 49-53), offering a sacrifice (Ge 15:9-17; Jer 34:18-19), salting (Lev 2:13; Nu 18:19; 2Ch 13:5), taking an oath (Ge 21:23-24; 25:33; 26:28-31; 31:53; Jos 2:12-14; 14:9). See Oath.
See Contracts; Vows.

Instances of:
Abraham and Abimelech (Ge 21:22-32). Abimelech and Isaac (Ge 26:26-31). Jacob and Laban (Ge 31:44-54). Jonathan and David (1Sa 18:3-4; 20:16, 42; 2Sa 21:7). Jews with each other, to serve God (2Ch 15:12-15; Ne 10:28-32). King Zedekiah and his subjects (Jer 34:8). Ahab with Ben-Hadad (1Ki 20:34). Subjects with sovereign (2Ch 23:1-3, 16).

New Covenant:
Prophecy concerning (Jer 31:31-34; Isa 59:21; 61:8-9; Eze 16:59-63; 34:25-31; 37:24-28; Heb 8:4-13). Characterized by the Spirit rather than the letter (2Co 3:6-17). Purchased or ratified by the blood of Jesus (Mt 26:28; Mk 14:24; Lk 22:20; 1Co 11:25). Jesus the mediator (Heb 12:18-24). Everlasting (Heb 13:20).
See Covenants, Major in the Old Testament.

COVENANTS, MAJOR IN THE OLD TESTAMENT

Major Types:

Royal Grant (unconditional) —
A king's grant (of land or some other benefit) to a loyal servant for faithful or exceptional service. The grant was normally perpetual and unconditional, but the servant's heirs benefited from it only as they continued their father's loyalty and service (1Sa 8:14; 22:7; 27:6; Est 8:1).

Parity (conditional) —
A covenant between equals, binding them to mutual friendship or at least to mutual respect for each other's spheres and interests. Participants called each other "brothers" (Ge 21:27; 26:31; 31:44-54; 1Ki 5:12; 15:19; 20:32-34; Am 1:9).

Suzerain-vassal (unconditional) —
A covenant regulating the relationship between a great king and one of his subject kings. The great king claimed absolute right of sovereignty, demanded total loyalty and service (the vassal must "love" his suzerain) and pledged protection of the subject's realm and dynasty, conditional on the vassal's faithfulness and loyalty to him. The vassal pledged absolute loyalty to his suzerain—whatever service his suzerain demanded—and exclusive reliance on the suzerain's protection. Participants called each other "lord" and "servant" or "father" and "son" (Jos 9:6, 8; Eze 17:13-18; Hos 12:1).

Major Instances:

1. Noahic—Ge 9:8-17.
Type: Royal Grant.
Participant: Made with "righteous" (Ge 6:9) Noah (and his descendants and every living thing on earth—all life that is subject to man's jurisdiction).
Description: An unconditional divine promise never to destroy all earthly life with some natural catastrophe; the covenant "sign" being the rainbow in the storm cloud.

2. Abrahamic A—Ge 15:9-21.
Type: Royal (land) Grant.
Participant: Made with "righteous" (his faith was "credited to him as righteousness," v. 6) Abram (and his descendants, v. 16).
Description: An unconditional divine promise to fulfill the grant of the land; a self-maledictory oath symbolically enacted (v. 17).

3. Abrahamic B—Ge 17.
Type: Suzerain-vassal.
Participant: Made with Abraham as patriarchal head of his household.
Description: A conditional divine pledge to be Abraham's God and the God of his descendants (cf. "As for me," v. 4; "As for you," v. 9); the condition: total consecration to the Lord as symbolized by circumcision.

4. Sinaitic—Ex 19-24.
Type: Suzerain-vassal.
Participant: Made with Israel as the descendants of Abraham, Isaac and Jacob and as the people the Lord has redeemed from bondage to an earthly power.
Description: A conditional divine pledge to be Israel's God (as her Protector and the Guarantor of her blessed destiny); the condition: Israel's total consecration to the Lord as his people (his kingdom) who live by his rule and serve his purposes in history.

5. Phinehas—Nu 25:10-13.
Type: Royal Grant.
Participant: Made with the zealous priest Phinehas.
Description: An unconditionally divine promise to maintain the family of Phinehas in a "lasting priesthood" (implicitly a pledge to Israel to provide her forever with a faithful priesthood).

6. Davidic—2Sa 7:5-16.
Type: Royal Grant.
Participant: Made with faithful King David after his devotion to God as Israel's king and the Lord's vassal had come to special expression (v. 2).
Description: An unconditional divine promise to establish and maintain the Davidic dynasty on the throne of Israel (implicitly a pledge to Israel) to provide her forever with a godly king like David and through that dynasty to do for her what he had done through David—bring her into rest in the promised land (1Ki 4:20-21; 5:3-4).

7. New—Jer 31:31-34.
Type: Royal Grant.
Participant: Promised to rebellious Israel as she is about to be expelled from the promised land in actualization of the most severe covenant curse (Lev 26:27-39; Dt 28:36-37, 45-68).
Description: An unconditional divine promise to unfaithful Israel to forgive her sins and establish his relationship with her on a new basis by writing his law "on their hearts"—a covenant of pure grace.
See Covenant.

COVERING THE HEAD
A symbol of sorrow and/or shame (2Sa 15:30; Est 6:12; Jer 14:3-4).
A symbol of authority (1Co 11:10). In Corinth men are commanded to pray and prophesy only with uncovered heads; women with heads covered with a veil or long hair (1Co 11:3-16).

COVETOUSNESS
The Tenth Commandment against (Ex 20:17; Dt 5:21; Ro 13:9).
See Avarice; Bribery; Greed; Rich, The; Riches.

COW
Used for pulling carts (1Sa 6:7-12; Hos 10:11). Milk of, used for food. See Milk; Cattle.
Figurative (Am 4:1).

COWARDICE
Described (Jos 7:5). Disqualified for military service (Dt 20:8; Jdg 7:3). God inflicted on enemies (Jos 23:10). Inflicted as judgment (Lev 26:36-37; Dt 32:30). Rebuke for (Isa 51:12-13). Cause of adversity (Pr 29:25). Caused by adversity (Job 15:24; 18:11). Caused by wickedness (Pr 28:1).

Instances of:
Adam, in attempting to shift responsibility for his sin upon Eve (Ge 3:12). Abraham, in calling his wife his sister (Ge 26:7-9). Jacob, in flying from Laban (Ge 31:31). Aaron, in yielding to the Israelites when they demanded an idol (Ex 32:22-24). The ten spies (Nu 13:28, 31-33). Israelites, in fearing to attempt the conquest of Canaan (Nu 14:1-5; Dt 1:26-28), in the battle with the people of Ai (Jos 7:5), to meet Goliath (1Sa 17:24), to fight with the Philistines (1Sa 13:6-7). Twenty thousand of Gideon's army (Jdg 7:3). Ephraimites (Ps 78:9). Ephraimites and Manassites (Jos 17:14-18). Amorite kings (Jos 10:16). Canaanites (2Sa 2:11; 5:1). Samuel, fearing to obey God's command to anoint a king in Saul's place (1Sa 16:2). David, in fleeing from Absalom (2Sa 15:13-17). Nicodemus, in coming to Jesus by night (Jn 3:1-2). Joseph of Arimathea, secretly a disciple (Jn 19:38). Parents of the blind man, who was restored to sight (Jn 9:22). Early converts among the rulers (Jn 12:42-43). Disciples, in the storm at sea (Mt 8:26; Mk 4:38; Lk 8:25), when they saw Jesus walking on the water (Mt 14:25; Mk 6:50; Jn 6:19), when Jesus was apprehended (Mt 26:56). Peter, in denying the Lord (Mt 26:69-74; Mk 14:66-72; Lk 22:54-60; Jn 18:16-17, 25, 27). Pilate, in condemning Jesus, through fear of the people (Jn 19:12-16). Guards of the tomb of Jesus (Mt 28:4). The Philippian jailer (Ac 16:27). Peter and other Christians, at Antioch (Gal 2:11-14). False teachers (Gal 6:12). Companions of Paul (2Ti 4:16).

COZ
See Koz.

COZBI
(*deceitful* ISBE; *the luxuriant* KB). Daughter of Zur (Nu 25:15, 18).

COZEBA
(*liar*). A city of Judah (1Ch 4:22). See Kezib; Aczib.

CRACKNEL
See Cakes.

CRAFTINESS
Instances of: Satan, in the temptation of Eve (Ge 3:1-5). Jacob, in the purchase of Esau's birthright (Ge 25:31-33), obtaining Isaac's blessing (Ge 27:6-29), in management of Laban's flocks and herds (Ge 30:31-43). Gibeonites, in deceiving Joshua and the Israelites into a treaty (Jos 9:3-15). Sanballat, in trying to deceive Nehemiah into a conference (Ne 6). Jews, in seeking to entangle the Master (Mt 22:15-17, 24-28; Mk 12:13-14, 18-23; Lk 20:19-26), in seeking to slay Jesus (Mt 26:4; Mk 14:1).

CRAFTSMAN
Valley of (1Ch 4:14, ftn; Ne 11:35).
See Art; Ge Harashim; Master Craftsman.

CRANE
See Swift.

CREATION
The Bible clearly teaches that the universe, "all things," came into existence through the will of the eternal God (Ge 1; 2; Jn 1:1-3; Heb 11:3; Rev 4:11). The Bible gives no information as to how long ago the original creation of matter occurred, or when the first day of creation began, or the sixth day ended. The two Creation accounts supplement each other (Ge 1; 2). Genesis 1 describes the creation of the universe as a whole, while Genesis 2 gives a more detailed account of the creation of man and animals and says nothing about the creation of matter, light, heavenly bodies, plants, and animals, except to refer to the creation of animals as having taken place at an earlier time.

CREATOR
Creator of the universe, God as (Ge 1:1; Ne 9:6; Job 26:7; Ps 102:25; Ac 14:15; Heb 11:3). The Word (Jesus) as (Jn 1:1-3). Holy Spirit as (Ge 1:2; Job 26:13; 33:4; Ps 104:30). Creator of mankind, God as (Ge 1:26; 2:7; 5:2; Dt 4:32; Job 33:4; Ps 8:5; 100:3; Isa 51:13; Mal 2:10; Ac 17:28).

CREATURE
That which has been created (Ro 1:25; 8:39; Heb 4:13).

CREATURES, LIVING
Heavenly beings with four faces and four or six wings (Eze 1:5-24; 3:13; 10:15-22; Rev 4:6-9; 5:6-14; 6:1-7; 7:11; 14:3; 15:7; 19:4). Identified as cherubim (Eze 10:15).
See Cherubim.

CREDIT
See Borrowing; Creditor; Debt; Lending; Security, For Debt.

CREDITOR

Mosaic laws concerning:
Release of debtor-servants (Ex 21:2-6). Must return cloak left as a pledge (Ex 22:25-27; Dt 24:10-13). Must not take, widows' cloak for pledge (Dt 24:17). Nor millstones (Dt 24:6). Must not extort interest of the poor (Lev 25:35-37; Dt 15:2-3; 23:19-20). Must not oppress neighbor (Lev 25:14-17).

Christ's injunctions to: (Mt 5:42; Lk 6:34).

Oppression by:
Seizing debtor's personal property (Job 22:6; 24:3, 10; Pr 22:26-27). Seizing debtor's houses (Job 20:18-20). Imprisoning debtor (Mt 5:25-26; 18:28-35; Lk 12:58-59). Enslaving debtor's children (2Ki 4:1; Ne 5:1-13; Job 24:9).

Merciful: (Ps 112:5; Mt 18:23-27; Lk 7:41-43).
See Debt; Debtor; Jubilee; Security, For Debt.

CREDULITY
Willingness to trust too easily (Ge 3:6; Jos 9:14; Pr 14:15).

CREED
A succinct statement of faith epitomizing the basic tenets of religious faith (Dt 4:4-6; 26:5-9). Various NT passages give the biblical foundation for the Christian creeds: the Apostles' Creed, the Nicene Creed, and the Athanasian Creed (Mt 16:16; 1Ti 3:16).

CREEK
NIV "bay" (Ac 27:39). Identified as St. Paul's Bay, c. eight miles NW of the town of Zaletta on the island of Malta.

CREEPING THINGS
NIV "creatures that move along the ground." A general term for animals (Ge 1:26; Lev 11:20-23, 29-31, 42; Ps 104:20, 25; Ro 1:23). Unclean (Lev 5:2; 11:20, 29-44; Dt 14:19). Clean (Lev 11:21-22). Used in idolatrous worship (Eze 8:10).

CREMATION
(Jos 7:25; 1Sa 31:12; 2Ki 23:20; Am 2:1; 6:10).
See Burial.

CRESCENS
(*increasing*). A disciple with Paul at Rome (2Ti 4:10).

CRETE, CRETAN
An island in the Mediterranean, 165 miles long, 6 to 35 miles wide, forming a natural bridge between Europe and Asia Minor. It was the legendary birthplace of Zeus. Paul and Titus founded a church there (Tit 1:5-14). The Cretans in the OT are called Kerethites (1Sa 30:14; Eze 25:16). Cretans were in Jerusalem on the Day of Pentecost (Ac 2:11). According to Paul they were not of a high moral character (Tit 1:12).

CRIB
See Manger.

CRICKET
Permitted as food (Lev 11:22). See Insects.

CRIME
Some lists (Eze 22:8-12, 27-30; Hos 4:1-2; Mt 15:19; Mk 7:21-22; Ro 1:24, 29-32; 3:14-18; 13:9; 1Co 5:11; Gal 5:19-21).
See various crimes or sins, such as Adultery, Arson, Homicide. See also, Punishment.

CRIMINALS
Released at feasts (Mt 27:15, 21; Mk 15:6; Lk 23:17). Confined in prisons (Ge 39:20-23; Ezr 7:26; Ac 4:3; 12:4-5; 16:19-40), in dungeons (Ge 40:15; 41:14; Ex 12:29; Isa 24:22; Jer 37:16; 38:10; La 3:53, 55). Crucified with Jesus (Mt 27:38-44; Lk 23:32-39).
Cruelty to. See Scourging; Stoning; Mocking.
Punishment of. See various crimes, such as Adultery, Arson, Homicide. See also, Punishments.

CRIMINATION
See Self-Incrimination.

CRIMSON
Brilliant red dye obtained from an insect (2Ch 2:7, 14; Jer 4:30; Isa 1:18).

CRISPING PIN
NIV "purses" (Isa 3:22). See Purse.

CRISPUS
(*curled*). Former ruler of the Jewish synagogue at Corinth, converted by Paul (Ac 18:8; 1Co 1:14).

CRITICISM
Unjust. See Uncharitableness.

CROCODILE
See Leviathan.

CROCUS
A flower (Isa 35:1). See Plants of the Bible.

CROP
1. Pouch-like enlargement in the gullet of many birds in which food is partially prepared for digestion (Lev 1:16).
2. Produce of the land (Ge 26:12; Ex 23:10). Cursed (Ge 4:12). In the New Jerusalem (Rev 22:2).

CROSS
Jesus crucified on (Mt 27:32; Mk 15:21; Lk 23:26; Ac 2:23, 36; 4:10; 1Co 1:23; 2:2, 8; Eph 2:16; Php 2:8; Col 1:20; 2:14; Heb 12:2). Borne by Simon (Mt 27:32; Mk 15:21; Lk 23:26), by Jesus (Jn 19:17). Death on, a disgrace (Gal 3:13).

Figurative:
Of duty (Mt 10:38; 16:24; Mk 8:34; 10:21; Lk 9:23; 14:27). Of Christ's vicarious death (1Co 1:17-18; Gal 5:11; 6:14; Php 3:18).
See Crucifixion; Self-Denial.

CROSS-EXAMINED
Skill in cross-examining (Pr 20:5). Instance of (Ac 12:19). See Witness.

CROW
See Birds; Rooster.

CROWN Prescribed for priests (Ex 29:6; 39:30; Lev 8:9). Worn by kings (2Sa 1:10; 12:30; 2Ki 11:12; Est 6:8; SS 3:11; Rev 6:2), by queens (Est 1:11; 2:17; 8:15). Made of gold (Ps 21:3; Zec 6:11). An ornament (Eze 16:12; 23:42). Set with gems (2Sa 12:30; 1Ch 20:2; Zec 9:16; Isa 62:3). Given victor in games (1Co 9:25; 2Ti 2:5). Of thorns (Mt 27:29; Mk 15:17; Jn 19:5).

Figurative:
Of gracious visitation (Isa 28:5). Of heavenly reward (1Co 9:25; 2Ti 4:8; Jas 1:12; 1Pe 5:4; Rev 2:10; 3:11).

Symbolic: (Rev 4:4, 10; 6:2; 9:7; 12:1, 3; 13:1; 14:14; 19:12).

CRUCIBLE The crucible in which ore is melted to be purified and separated from dross (Pr 17:3; 27:21).

CRUCIFIXION The reproach of (Gal 3:13; 5:11). Of Jesus. *See Jesus the Christ, History of.* Of two criminals (Mt 27:38). Of disciples, foretold (Mt 23:34).

Figurative:
Of old nature (Ro 6:6; Gal 5:24). Of self-centered life (Gal 2:20; 6:14).
See Cross, Figurative.

CRUELTY
Instances of: Of Sarah to Hagar (Ge 16:6; 21:9-14). Egyptians to the Israelites (Ex 5:6-18). Peninnah to Hannah (1Sa 1:4-7; 2:3). Of Jews to Jesus (Mt 26:67; 27:28-31), soldiers to Jesus (Lk 22:64; Jn 19:3). In war (Isa 13:16, 18).
See Animals, Cruelty to; Kindness; Love; Malice; Prisoners, Of War.

CRUSE *See Jar(s).*

CRYING *See Mourning; Praise; Prayer; Weeping.*

CRYSTAL A precious stone (Job 28:17 Rev 4:6; 21:11; 22:1).
See Minerals of the Bible, 1; Stones.

CUB The young of a dog or a beast of prey; a cub (Ge 49:9; Dt 33:22; Jer 51:38; Na 2:11-12).

CUBIT A measure of distance, c. eighteen inches (Ge 6:16; Dt 3:11; Eze 40:5; 43:13; Rev 21:17). No one by worrying can add to his height (Mt 6:27; Lk 12:25 notes).

CUCKOO *See Gull.*

CUCUMBERS Vegetables enjoyed by Israel in Egypt (Nu 11:5).

CUD Chewing of, was one of the facts by which clean and unclean animals were distinguished (Lev 11:3-8; Dt 14:3-8).

CUMMIN A plant bearing a small aromatic seed (Isa 28:25, 27; Mt 23:23).

CUN (*chosen*). A Syrian city (1Ch 18:8). *See Tebah, 2; Berothai.*

CUNEIFORM A system of writing by symbolic wedge-shaped characters upon clay tablets used primarily in Mesopotamia in ancient times. More than half a million such clay tablets have been found.

CUP (Ge 40:11; 2Sa 12:3; 1Ki 7:26; Mt 23:25). Made of silver (Ge 44:2), gold (1Ch 28:17; Jer 52:19). Used in the institution of the Lord's Supper (Mt 26:27; Mk 14:23; Lk 22:20; 1Co 10:21). Of the table of demons (1Co 10:21).

Figurative:
Of sorrow (Ps 11:6; 73:10; 75:8; Isa 51:17, 22; Jer 25:15-28; Eze 23:31-34; Mt 20:22-23; 26:39; Mk 14:36; Lk 22:42; Jn 18:11; Rev 14:10). Of consolation (Jer 16:7). Of joy (Ps 23:5). Of salvation (Ps 116:13).

CUPBEARER A palace official who served wine at a king's table (Ge 40:11; 1Ki 10:5; 2Ch 9:4; Ne 1:11).

CUPIDITY *See Avarice; Covetousness; Lust.*

CURES Miraculous. *See Miracles; Disease; Physician.*

CURIOSITY Insatiable (Pr 27:20). Advised against (Ecc 7:21).
Instances of:
Of Eve (Ge 3:6). Of Abraham, to know whether God would destroy the righteous in Sodom (Ge 18:23-32). Of Jacob, to know the name of the angel (Ge 32:29). Of the Israelites, to see God (Ex 19:21, 24), to witness the offering in the Most Holy Place (Nu 4:19-20). Of Manoah, to know the name of an angel (Jdg 13:17-18). Of the people of Beth Shemesh, to see inside the ark (1Sa 6:19). Of the Babylonians, to see Hezekiah's treasures (2Ki 20:13). Of Daniel, to know a vision (Da 12:8-9).
Of Peter, to know what was being done with Jesus (Mt 26:58), to know what John would be appointed to do (Jn 21:21-22). A disciple, to know if there be few that be saved (Lk 13:23). Of Herod, to see Jesus (Lk 9:9; 23:8). Of the Jews, to see Lazarus, after he was raised from the dead (Jn 12:9), and to see Jesus (Jn 12:20-21). Of the disciples, to know whether Jesus would restore the kingdom of the Jews (Ac 1:6-7). Of the Athenians, to hear some new thing (Ac 17:19-21). Of angels, to look into the mysteries of salvation (1Pe 1:12).

CURSE Pronounced upon, the serpent (Ge 3:14-15), Adam and Eve (Ge 3:15-19), the ground (Ge 3:17-18), Cain (Ge 4:11-16), Canaan, Ham's son (Ge 9:24-27), the disobedient (Dt 28:15-68; Jer 11:3-17), Meroz (Jdg 5:23), Gehazi (2Ki 5:27). Barak commands Balaam to curse Israel (Nu 22:6; 23:11). Paternal (Ge 27:12-13; 49:5-7).
In the covenant with Abraham (Ge 12:3). Of the Mosaic law, enforcing the covenant (Dt 11:26-32; 27:12-26; 28:15-68; Jos 8:30-34).
Assumed for others (Mt 27:25). Rebekah for Jacob (Ge 27:13). Paul wishes he could assume for Israel (Ro 9:3). *See Blessings.*

Christ assumed the curse of the Mosaic law for us (Gal 3:13). *See Jesus the Christ, Vicarious Death of.*

CURSING Of God (Lev 24:11-16; Isa 8:21). Of parents (Ex 21:17; Mt 15:4; Mk 7:10). Shimei curses David (2Sa 16:5-8). The precepts of Jesus concerning (Mt 5:44; Lk 6:28). Apostolic (Ro 12:14).
See Anathema Maranatha; Blasphemy; God, Name of; Oath.

CURTAINS
Of the tabernacle:
Ten curtains formed the inner lining of the tabernacle, of embroidered linen (Ex 26:1-6). Eleven curtains of goat hair formed the tent over it (Ex 26:7-13). A single linen curtain covered the entrance (Ex 26:36-37). The courtyard was fenced by curtains (Ex 27:9-18). Made by Bezalel and Oholiab (Ex 36:8-38).
A single linen curtain divided the Most Holy Place from the Holy Place (Ex 26:31-33; 35:12; 39:34; 40:21), also in the temple (2Ch 3:14); called the second curtain (Heb 9:3); used to cover the ark (Nu 4:5). A type of the humanity or body of Christ (Heb 10:20). Figurative of the believer's access to God (Heb 6:19).

Of the temple:
Divided the Most Holy Place from the Holy Place (2Ch 3:14). Torn at the time of the crucifixion of Christ (Mt 27:51; Mk 15:38; Lk 23:45).
See Tabernacle; Tapestry.

CUSH
1. Son of Ham (Ge 10:6-8; 1Ch 1:8-10).
2. A Benjamite, the title of the Psalm (Ps 7).
3. Land of (Ge 2:13; Ps 68:31; Isa 18:1). *See Cushite; Ethiopia.*

CUSHAN Poetic form of Cush (Hab 3:7). *See Ethiopia.*

CUSHAN-RISHATHAIM (*man of Cush, doubly guilty*). King of Aram Naharaim; that is, NW Mesopotamia (Jdg 3:8-10).

CUSHI
1. See Cushite, 2.
2. Father of Shelemiah (Jer 36:14).
3. Father of Zephaniah (Zep 1:1).

CUSHITE
1. Moses' wife (Nu 12:1).
2. A messenger who brought news to David (2Sa 18:21-32).
3. Tirhakah, king of Egypt. *See Tirhakah.*
4. Zerah, perhaps Pharaoh Oskoron I. *See Zerah, 7.*
5. Ebed-Melech, who pulled Jeremiah from the cistern (Jer 38:7-13). *See Ebed-Melech.*
6. A people, probably Ethiopians (2Ch 12:3; 14:12-13). *See Ethiopia.*

CUSTOM When not referring to a tax, usually means "manner," "way," or "statute" (Ge 31:35; Jdg 11:39; Jer 32:11). In the NT it means "manner," "usage" (Lk 1:9; Ac 6:14), and "religious practices."

CUSTOM, RECEIPT OF *See Tax.*

CUTHAH A district of Asia, from which colonists were transported to Samaria (2Ki 17:24-30; Ezr 4:10).

CUTTINGS A heathen practice, including tattooings, gashes, castrations, usually done in mourning for the dead and to propitiate deities. Forbidden to the Israelites (Lev 19:28; 21:5; Dt 14:1; Jer 16:6).

CUZA (*little judge*). Herod's steward (Lk 8:3).

CYLINDER SEALS *See Seal.*

CYMBAL A musical instrument. Of bronze (1Ch 15:19, 28; 1Co 13:1).
Used in the tabernacle service (2Sa 6:5; 1Ch 13:8; 15:16, 19, 28), in the temple service (2Ch 5:12-13; 1Ch 16:5, 42; 25:1, 6; Ps 150:5).
Used on special occasions: the Day of Atonement (2Ch 29:25), laying of the foundation of the second temple (Ezr 3:10-11), dedication of the wall (Ne 12:27, 36).

CYPRESS WOOD (Isa 44:14; SS 1:14; 4:13). Probably the wood from which Noah's ark was made; KJV "gopher wood" (Ge 6:14). Used in making idols (Isa 44:12-17).

CYPRUS (*copper*). An island (Ac 21:3; 27:4). Barnabas born in (Ac 4:36). Persecuted Jews preached the gospel at (Ac 11:19-20). Visited by Barnabas and Saul (Ac 13:4-12). Barnabas and Mark visit (Ac 15:39). Mnason, a disciple of (Ac 21:16).

CYRENE, CYRENIAN (*wall*). A city in N Africa, W of Egypt, c. ten miles from the coast. Originally a Greek city, it passed into the hands of the Romans. Simon, who helped Jesus carry his cross, came from there (Lk 23:26). People from Cyrene were in Jerusalem on the Day of Pentecost (Ac 2:10). Jews from the synagogue of the Cyrenians disputed with Stephen (Ac 6:9).

CYRENIUS *See Quirinius.*

CYRUS King of Persia. Issued a decree for the emancipation of the Jews and rebuilding the temple (2Ch 36:22-23; Ezr 1; 3:7; 4:3; 5:13-14; 6:3). Prophecies concerning (Isa 13:17-22; 21:2; 41:2; 44:28; 45:1-4, 13; 46:11; 48:14-15).

D

DABAREH *See Daberath.*

DABBESHETH (*hump*). A place on the boundary line of Zebulun (Jos 19:11).

DABERATH (*pasture*). A town of Issachar (Jos 19:12; 21:28). Assigned to the Levites (1Ch 6:72).

DAGGER A short sword (Jdg 3:16-22).

DAGON (*[god of] grain* IDB; *fish* ISBE). A pagan deity with the body of a fish, head and hands of a man. Probably the god of agriculture. Worshiped in Mesopotamia and Canaan, with temples in Ashdod (1Sa 5:1-7), Gaza (Jdg 16:21-30), and in Israel (1Ch 10:10). Samson destroyed the temple in Gaza (Jdg 16:30).

DAILY SACRIFICE Ordained in Mt. Sinai (Nu 28:6). A lamb as a burnt offering, morning and evening (Ex 29:38-39; Nu 28:3-4). Doubled on the Sabbath (Nu 28:9-10). Required to be with a meat and drink offering (Ex 29:40-41; Nu 28:5-8). Slowly and entirely consumed (Lev 6:9-12). Perpetually observed (Ex 29:42; Nu 28:3, 6). Pleasing (Nu 28:8; Ps 141:2). Secured God's presence and favor (Ex 29:43-44). Times of offering, were seasons of prayer (Ezr 9:5; Da 9:20-21, w Ac 3:1). Restored after the Captivity (Ezr 3:3). The abolition of, foretold (Da 9:26-27; 11:31).

Illustrative of:
Christ (Jn 1:29, 36; 1Pe 1:19). Acceptable prayer (Ps 141:2).
See Sacrifices.

DALAIAH *See Delaiah.*

DALE, THE KING'S *See Valley, Vale.*

DALMANUTHA South of the Plain of Gennesaret a cave has been found bearing the name "Talmanutha," perhaps the spot where Jesus landed. Matthew says Jesus went to the vicinity of Magadan (Mt 15:39). Dalmanutha and Magadan (of Magdala), located on the western shore of the Sea of Galilee, may be names for the same place or for two places located close to each other (Mk 8:10). *See Magadan.*

DALMATIA (*deceitful*). Province on the NE shore of the Adriatic Sea also called Illyricum (Ro 15:19; 2Ti 4:10).

DALPHON (*crafty* ISBE; *sleepless* KB). The son of Haman (Est 9:7).

DAMAGES AND COMPENSATIONS Listed (Nu 5:5-8). For assault (Ex 21:18-19, 22). For personal injury (Ex 21:28-34). For deception (Lev 6:1-5). For slander (Dt 22:13-19). For seduction (Dt 22:28-29). *See Fine.*

DAMARIS A female convert of Athens (Ac 17:34).

DAMASCUS, DAMASCENES An ancient city (Ge 14:15; 15:2). The capital of Syria (1Ki 20:34; Isa 7:8; Jer 49:23-29; Eze 47:16-17). Laid under tribute to David (2Sa 8:5-6). Besieged by Rezon (1Ki 11:23-24). Recovered by Jeroboam (2Ki 14:28). Taken by the king of Assyria (2Ki 16:9). Walled (Jer 49:27; 2Co 11:33). Garrisoned (2Co 11:32). Luxury in (Am 3:12). Paul's experiences in (Ac 9; 22:5-16; 26:12-20; 2Co 11:32; Gal 1:17). Prophecies concerning (Isa 8:4; 17:1-2; Jer 49:23-29; Am 1:3, 5; Zec 9:1).
Wilderness of (1Ki 19:15).
See Syria.

DAMMIM *See Ephes Dammim, Pas Dammim.*

DAMNATION When referring to the future it means primarily eternal separation from God with accompanying punishments (Mt 5:29; 10:28; 23:33; 24:51). The severity of the punishment is determined by the degree of sin (Lk 12:36-48), and is eternal (Isa 66:24; Mk 3:29; 2Th 1:9; Jude 6-7). *See Punishment; Wicked, Punishment of.*

DAN, DANITE(S) (*judge*).
1. The fifth son of Jacob and Bilhah (Ge 30:6; 35:25). Descendants of (Ge 46:23; Nu 26:42-43). See below, Tribe of. Blessed of Jacob (Ge 49:16-17).
2. Tribe of: Census of (Nu 1:39; 26:42-43). Inheritance of, according to the allotment of Joshua (Jos 19:40-47), of Ezekiel (Eze 48:1). Position of, in journey and camp, during the exodus out of Egypt (Nu 2:25, 31; 10:25). Blessed by Moses (Dt 33:22). Fail to conquer the Amorites (Jdg 1:34-35). Conquests by (Jos 19:47; Jdg 18:27-29). Deborah rebukes for cowardice (Jdg 5:17). Idolatry of (Jdg 18). Commerce of (Jdg 5:17; Eze 27:19).
See Israel, Israelites.
3. A city of the tribe of Dan. Called Laish (Jdg 18:7, 13, 27, 29) and Leshem (Jos 19:47) and later known as Dan. *See Laish; Leshem.* Captured by the people of Dan (Jos 19:47). Idolatry established at (Jdg 18; 1Ki 12:28-29; Am 8:14). Captured by Ben-Hadad (1Ki 15:20; 2Ch 16:4).

DAN JAAN A place, probably in Dan, covered by David's census (2Sa 24:6).

DANCING Of children (Job 21:11). Of women (Ex 15:20; Jdg 11:34; 21:19-21; 1Sa 18:6; 21:11). Of David (2Sa 6:14-16; 1Ch 15:29). In the marketplace (Mt 11:16-17). At feasts (Jdg 21:19-21; Mt 14:6; Mk 6:22; Lk 15:23-25). As a religious ceremony (Ps 149:3; 150:4). Idolatrous (Ex 32:19; 32:25).
Figurative: Of joy (Ps 30:11; Ecc 3:4; Jer 31:4; 31:13; La 5:15).

DANIEL (*God [El] is my judge*).

1. An Israelite captive, also called Belteshazzar. *See Belteshazzar.* Educated at king's court (Da 1). Interprets visions (Da 2; 4; 5). Promotion and executive authority of (Da 2:48-49; 5:11, 29; 6:2). Conspiracy against, cast into the lions' den (Da 6).

Prophecies of (Da 4:8-9; 7-12; Mt 24:15).

Special diet (Da 1:8-16). Wisdom of (Da 1:17; Eze 28:3). Devoutness of (Da 2:18; 6; 9; 10; 12; Eze 14:14). Courage and fidelity of (Da 4:27; 5:17-23; 6:10-23). Worshiped by Nebuchadnezzar (Da 2:6).

2. David's son. Also called Kileab (Da 3:3; 1Ch 3:1).

3. A descendant of Ithamar, and a companion of Ezra (Ezr 8:2; Ne 10:6).

DANIEL, BOOK OF

Author: Daniel

Date: c. 530 B.C.

Outline:

I. Prologue: The Setting (ch. 1; in Hebrew).
 A. Historical Introduction (1:1-2).
 B. Daniel and His Friends Are Taken Captive (1:3-7).
 C. The Young Men Are Faithful (1:8-16).
 D. The Young Men Are Elevated to High Positions (1:17-21).

II. The Destinies of the Nations of the World (chs. 2-7, in Aramaic, beginning at 2:4b).
 A. Nebuchadnezzar's Dream of a Large Statue (ch. 2).
 B. Nebuchadnezzar's Making of a Gold Image and His Decree That It Be Worshiped (ch. 3).
 C. Nebuchadnezzar's Dream of an Enormous Tree (ch. 4).
 D. Belshazzar's and Babylon's Downfall (ch. 5).
 E. Daniel's Deliverance (ch. 6).
 F. Daniel's Dream of Four Beasts (ch. 7).

III. The Destiny of the Nation of Israel (chs. 8-12; in Hebrew).
 A. Daniel's Vision of a Ram and a Goat (ch. 8).
 B. Daniel's Prayer and His Vision of the 70 "Sevens" (ch. 9).
 C. Daniel's Vision of Israel's Future (chs. 10-12).
 1. Revelation of things to come (10:1-3).
 2. Revelation from the angelic messenger (10:4-11:1).
 3. Prophecies concerning Persia and Greece (11:2-4).
 4. Prophecies concerning Egypt and Syria (11:5-35).
 5. Prophecies concerning the antichrist (11:36-45).
 6. Distress and deliverance (12:1).
 7. Two Resurrections (12:2-3).
 8. Instruction to Daniel (12:4).
 9. Conclusion (12:5-13).

DANNAH (*stronghold*). A city in the mountains of Judah (Jos 15:49).

DARA *See Darda.*

DARDA Also called Dara. A famous wise man (1Ki 4:31; 1Ch 2:6).

DARIC Persian gold coin used in Israel after the return from the Captivity; said to have been named from the first Darius (1Ch 29:7; Ezr 8:27). Although the NIV uses "drachmas" for the following references, some believe that the coin intended was the daric (Ezr 2:69; Ne 7:70-72). *See Drachma.*

DARIUS (*Old Persian he who upholds the good*). A common name for Medo-Persian rulers.

1. Darius the Mede (Gubaru), the son of Xerxes (Da 5:31; 9:1), made governor of Babylon by Cyrus, but he seems to have ruled for only a brief time (Da 10:1; 11:1), prominent in the book of Daniel (Da 6:1, 6, 9, 25, 28; 11:1).

2. Darius I called the Great (spelled variously Hystaspos, Hystaspis, or Hystaspes), fourth and greatest of the Persian rulers (522-486 B.C.); reorganized the government into satraps and extended boundaries of the empire; a great builder; he was defeated by the Greeks at Marathon in 490 B.C.; renewed the edict of Cyrus and helped to rebuild the temple (Ezr 4:5, 24; 5:5-7; 6:1-12; Hag 1:1; 2:1, 10, 18; Zec 1:1, 7; 7:1). Died in 486 B.C. and was succeeded by Xerxes, the grandson of Cyrus the Great.

3. Darius, the Persian (spelled variously Codomanus or Codomannus), the last king of Persia (336-330 B.C.); defeated by Alexander the Great (330 B.C.) (Ne 12:22). Some scholars identify him with Darius II (Nothus), who ruled Persia and Babylon (423-404 B.C.).

DARKNESS Over the face of the earth (Ge 1:2; Job 38:9; Jer 4:23). Called "night" (Ge 1:5). God created (Isa 45:7). The NIV uses "[deep] darkness" to translate a word formerly translated "shadow of death", usually in a context of deep emotional despair or grief (Job 3:5; 10:21, 22; 12:22; 16:16; 24:17, 17; 28:3; 34:22; 38:17; Ps 23:4; 44:19; 107:10, 14; Isa 9:2; Jer 2:6; 13:16; Am 5:8).

Miraculous:

In Egypt (Ex 10:21-22; Ps 105:28), at Sinai (Ex 20:21; Heb 12:18), at the Crucifixion (Mt 27:45; Mk 15:33).

Figurative:

Of judgments (Pr 20:20; Isa 8:22; 13:10; Jer 4:28; 13:16; La 3:2; Eze 32:7-8; Joel 2:2, 10; Am 4:13; 5:18, 20; 8:9; Mic 7:8; Mt 24:29; Mk 13:24; Lk 23:45; Rev 8:12; 9:2). Of powers of evil (Lk 22:53; Eph 6:12; Col 1:13; 1Th 5:5; Rev 16:10).

Of the abode of the lost (Mt 8:12; 22:13; 25:30).

Of spiritual blindness (Isa 9:2; 42:16; 50:10; Mt 4:16; 6:22-23; Lk 1:79; 11:34; Jn 1:5; 3:19; 8:12; 11:9-10; Ac 26:18; Ro 1:21; 13:12-13; 1Co 4:5; 2Co 4:6; 6:14; Eph 5:8, 11; 1Th 5:4-5; 1Pe 2:9; 1Jn 1:5-7; 2:8-11). *See Blindness, Spiritual.*

Symbolic:

Of divine inscrutability (2Sa 22:10-12; Ps 18:11; 97:2). On Mt. Sinai (Ex 19:16; 20:21; Dt 4:11; 5:22; Heb 12:18). In the Sanctuary (1Ki 8:12; 2Ch 6:1). *See Tabernacle.*

DARKON (perhaps *rough*, or *stern*). A descendant of Solomon's servant, Jaala, who returned with Zerubbabel from Exile (Ezr 2:56; Ne 7:58).

DART A weapon (Job 41:26). *See Armor; Arrows.*

DATE A fruit (2Ch 31:5).

DATHAN (*strong*). A conspirator against Moses (Nu 16:1-35; 26:9; Dt 11:6; Ps 106:17).

DAUGHTER Daughter can refer to both persons and things, often without regard to relationship or gender.

1. Daughter (Ge 11:29) or other female descendant (Ge 24:48).
2. Women in general (Ge 28:6; Nu 25:1).
3. Worshipers of the true God (Ps 45:10; Isa 62:11; Mt 21:5; Jn 12:15).
4. City (Isa 37:22).
5. Citizens (Zec 2:10).

DAUGHTER-IN-LAW

Filial: Instance of, Ruth (Ru 1:11-18; 4:15).

Unfilial: Prophecy of (Mic 7:6; Mt 10:35).

DAVID (*beloved one*).

1. King of Israel. Genealogy of (Ru 4:18-22; 1Sa 16:11; 17:12; 1Ch 2:3-15; Mt 1:1-6; Lk 3:31-38). A shepherd (1Sa 16:11). Kills a lion and a bear (1Sa 17:34-36). Anointed king, while a youth, by the prophet Samuel, and inspired (1Sa 16:1, 13; Ps 89:19-37). Chosen of God (Ps 78:70).

Described to Saul (1Sa 16:18). Detailed as armor-bearer and musician at Saul's court (1Sa 16:21-23). Slays Goliath (1Sa 17). Love of Jonathan for (1Sa 18:1-4). Popularity and discretion of (1Sa 18). Saul's jealousy of (1Sa 18:8-30). Is defrauded of Merab and given Michal for his wife (1Sa 18:17-27). Jonathan intercedes for (1Sa 19:1-7). Probably writes Ps 11 at this period of his life.

Conducts a campaign against, and defeats, the Philistines (1Sa 19:8). Saul attempts to slay him; he escapes to Ramah and dwells at Naioth, where Saul pursues him (1Sa 19:9-24). About this time he writes Ps 59. He returns, and Jonathan makes a covenant with him (1Sa 20). He escapes by way of Nob, where he obtains some consecrated bread and Goliath's sword from Abimelech (1Sa 21:1-6; Mt 12:3-4), to Gath (1Sa 21:10-15). At this time he probably writes Pss 34, 35, 52, 56, and 120. He recruits an army of insurgents, goes to Moab, returning to Hereth (1Sa 22). Probably writes Pss 17, 58, 64, 109, and 142. He saves Keilah (1Sa 23:1-13). He makes a sacred covenant with Jonathan (1Sa 23:16-18). He goes to the wilderness of Ziph, and is betrayed to Saul (1Sa 23:13-26). He writes Ps 54 about the betrayal and probably Pss 22, 31, and 140. Saul is diverted from pursuit of (1Sa 23:27-28). At this time he probably writes Ps 12. Goes to En Gedi (1Sa 23:29). Writes Ps 57. Covenants with Saul (1Sa 26). Marries Nabal's widow, Abigail, and Ahinoam (1Sa 25). Dwells in the wilderness of Ziph, has the opportunity to kill Saul but takes his spear only, Saul is contrite (1Sa 26). Flees to Achish and dwells in Ziklag (1Sa 27). List of men who join him (1Ch 12:1-22). Conducts an expedition against Amalekites, misinforms Achish (1Sa 27:8-12). At this time probably writes Ps 141. Is refused permission to accompany the Philistines to battle against the Israelites (1Sa 28:1-2; 29). Rescues the people of Ziklag, who had been captured by the Amalekites (1Sa 30). Probably writes Ps 13. Death and burial of Saul and his sons (1Sa 31; 2Sa 1:1-14). Slays the murderer of Saul (2Sa 1:1-16). Lamentation over Saul (1:17-27).

After dwelling one year and four months at Ziklag (1Sa 27:7), goes to Hebron, and is anointed king by Judah (2Sa 2:1-4, 11; 5:5; 1Ki 2:11; 1Ch 3:4; 11:1-3). List of those who join him at Hebron (1Ch 12:23-40). Ish-Bosheth, the son of Saul, crowned (2Sa 2:4). David wages war against, and defeats, Ish-Bosheth (2Sa 2:13-32; 3:4). Demands the restoration of Michal, his wife (2Sa 3:14-16). Abner revolts from Ish-Bosheth, and joins David, but is slain by Joab (2Sa 3). David punishes Ish-Bosheth's murderers (2Sa 4).

Anointed king over all Israel, after reigning over Judah at Hebron seven years and six months, and reigns thirty-three years (2Sa 2:11; 5:5; 1Ch 3:4; 11:1-3; 12:23-40; 29:27). Makes a conquest of Jerusalem (2Sa 5:6; 1Ch 11:4-8; Isa 29:1). Builds a palace (2Sa 5:11; 2Ch 2:3). Friendship of, with Hiram, king of Tyre (2Sa 5:11; 1Ki 5:1). Prospered of God (2Sa 5:10, 12; 1Ch 11:9). Fame of (1Ch 14:17). Philistines make war against, and are defeated by him (2Sa 5:17, 25).

Assembles 30,000 men to escort the ark to Jerusalem with music and thanksgiving (2Sa 6:1-5). Uzzah is stricken when he attempts to steady the ark (2Sa 6:6-11). David is terrified and leaves the ark at the house of Obed-Edom (2Sa 6:9-11). After three months brings the ark to Jerusalem with dancing and great joy (2Sa 6:12-16; 1Ch 13). Organized the tabernacle service (1Ch 9:22; 15:16-24; 16:4-6, 37-43). Offers sacrifice, distributes gifts, and blesses the people (2Sa 6:17-19). Michal rebukes him for his religious enthusiasm (2Sa 6:20-23). Desires to build a temple, is forbidden, but receives promise that his seed should reign forever (2Sa 7:12-16; 23:5; 1Ch 17:11-14; 2Ch 6:16; Ps 89:3-4; 132:11-12; Ac 15:16; Ro 15:12). Interpretation and fulfillment of this prophecy (Ac 13:22-23). At this time, probably writes Ps 24, 101, and 138. Conquers the Philistines, Moabites, and Syria (2Sa 8).

Treats Mephibosheth, the lame son of Jonathan, with great kindness (2Sa 9:6; 19:24-30). Sends commissioners with a message of sympathy to Hanun, son of the king of Ammon; the message is misrepresented and commissioners treated with indignity; David retaliates by invading his kingdom and defeating the combined armies of the Ammonites and Syrians (2Sa 10; 1Ch 19). Probably writes Pss 18, 20, and 21.

Commits adultery with Bathsheba (2Sa 11:2-5). Wickedly causes the death of Uriah (2Sa 11:6-25). Takes Bathsheba to be his wife (2Sa 11:26-27). Is rebuked by the prophet Nathan (2Sa 12:1-14). Repents of his crime and confesses his guilt (Pss 6; 32; 38; 39; 40; 51). Is disciplined on account of his crime (Ps 38; 41; 69). His infant son by Bathsheba dies (2Sa 12:15-23). Solomon is born (2Sa 12:24-25).

Ammonites defeated and tortured (2Sa 12:26-31). Amnon's crime, his murder by Absalom, and Absalom's flight (2Sa 13). Absalom's return (2Sa 14:1-24). Absalom's usurpation (2Sa 14-15). David's flight from Jerusalem (2Sa 15:13-37). He probably writes, at this time Pss 5, 7, 26, 61, 69, 70, 86, and 143. Shimei curses him (2Sa 16). Crosses the Jordan (2Sa 17:21-29). Absalom's defeat and death (2Sa 18). Laments the death of Absalom (2Sa 18:33; 19:1-4). Reprimanded by Joab (2Sa 19:5-7). David reprimands the priests for not showing loyalty amid the murmurings of the people against him (2Sa 19:9-15). Shimei sues for clemency (2Sa 19:16-23). Mephibosheth sues for the king's favor (2Sa 19:24-30). Barzillai rewarded (2Sa 19:31-40). Judah accused by the ten tribes of stealing him away (2Sa 19:41-43). Returns to Jerusalem (2Sa 20:1-3). At this time, probably composes Pss 27, 66, 122, and 124. Sheba's conspiracy against David, and his death (2Sa 20). Makes Amasa general (2Sa 19:13). Amasa is slain (2Sa 20:4-10). Consigns seven sons of Saul to the Gibeonites to be slain to atone for Saul's persecution of the Gibeonites (2Sa 21:1-14). Buries the bones of Saul and his sons (2Sa 21:12-14).

Defeats the Philistines (2Sa 21:15-22; 1Ch 20:4-8). Takes the military strength of Israel without divine authority, and is reproved (2Sa 24; 1Ch 21; 27:24). Probably composes Pss 20, 131. Marries Abishag (1Ki 1:1-4). Probably composes Pss 19 and 111.

Reorganizes the tabernacle service (1Ch 22-26; 2Ch 7:6; 8:14; 23:18; 29:27-30; 35:15; Ezr 3:10; 8:20).

Adonijah usurps the scepter. Solomon is appointed to the throne (1Ki 1; 1Ch 23:1). Delivers his charge to Solomon (1Ki 2:1-11; 1Ch 22:6-19; 28; 29). Probably composes Pss 23 and 145.

Last words of (2Sa 23:1-7). Death probably (1Ki 2:10; 1Ch 29:28; Ac 2:29-30). Tomb of (Ac 2:29). Age of, at death (2Sa 5:4-5; 1Ch 29:28). Length of reign, forty years (1Ki 2:11; 1Ch 29:27-28). Wives of (2Sa 3:2-5; 11:3, 27; 1Ch 3:5). Children born at Hebron (2Sa 3:2-5; 1Ch 3:4), at Jerusalem (2Sa 5:14-16; 1Ch 3:5-8; 14:4-7). Descendants of (1Ch 3).

Civil and military officers of (2Sa 8:16-18). *See Cabinet.* List of his heroes and of their exploits (2Sa 23; 1Ch 11; 12:23-40).

Devoutness of (1Sa 13:14; 2Sa 6:5, 14-18; 7:18-29; 8:11; 24:25; 1Ki 3:14; 1Ch 17:16-27; 29:10; 2Ch 7:17; Zec 12:8; Ps 6; 7; 11; 13; 17; 22; 26; 27:7-14; 28; 31; 35; 37; 38; 39; 40:11-17; 42; 43; 51; 54; 55; 56; 57; 59; 60; 61; 62; 64:1-6; 66; 69; 70; 71; 86; 101; 108; 120:1-2; 140; 141; 142; 143; 144; Ac 13:22).

Justice in the administration of (2Sa 8:15; 1Ch 18:14). Discretion of (1Sa 18:14, 30). Meekness of (1Sa 24:7; 26:11; 2Sa 16:11; 19:22-23). Merciful (2Sa 19:23).

David as a musician (1Sa 16:21-23; 1Ch 15:16; 23:5; 2Ch 7:6; 29:26; Ne 12:36; Am 6:5), poet (2Sa 22). *See Psalms.* David as a prophet (2Sa 23:2-7; 1Ch 28:19; Mt 22:41-46; Ac 2:25-38; 4:25). Type of Christ (Ps 2; 16; 18:43; 69:7-9, 20-21, 26, 29; 89:19-37). Jesus called son of (Mt 9:27; 12:23; 15:22; 20:30-31; 21:9; 22:42; Mk 10:47-48; Lk 18:37, 39).

Prophecies concerning David and his kingdom (Nu 24:17, 19; 2Sa 7:11-16; 1Ch 17:9-14; 22; 2Ch 6:5-17; 13:5; 21:7; Ps 89:19-37; Isa 9:7; 16:5; 22:20-25; Jer 23:5; 33:15-26; Lk 1:32-33). Chronicles of, written by Samuel, Nathan, and Gad (1Ch 29:29-30).

2. A prophetic name for Christ (Jer 30:9; Eze 34:23-24; 37:24-25; Hos 3:5).

DAVID, CITY OF

1. Portion of Jerusalem occupied by David in c. 1003 B.C.; 2500 feet above sea level. Originally a Canaanite city (Eze 16:3), it dates back to the third millennium. Solomon enlarged the City of David for the temple and other buildings, and later kings enlarged the city still more (2Ch 32:4-5, 30; 2Ki 20:20; Isa 22:9-11).

2. Bethlehem (Lk 2:11).

DAY A creative period (Ge 1:5, 8, 13, 19, 23, 31; 2:2). Divided into twelve hours (Jn 11:9). Prophetic (Da 8:14, 26; 12:11-12; Rev 9:15; 11:3; 12:6). Six working days ordained (Ex 20:9; Eze 46:1). Sixth day of the week called preparation day (Mk 15:42; Jn 19:14, 31, 42). First day of the week called the Lord's Day (Rev 1:10). With the Lord as a thousand years (2Pe 3:8).

Day's journey, eighteen or twenty miles (Ex 3:18; 1Ki 19:4; Jnh 3:4). Sabbath day's journey, about two thousand paces (Ac 1:12). The seventh of the week ordained as a day of rest. *See Sabbath.*

DAY OF ATONEMENT An annual Hebrew feast when the high priest offered sacrifices for the sins of the nation (Lev 23:27; 25:9). It was the only fast required by Mosaic law (Lev 16:29; 23:31). The day marked the only entry of the high priest into the Most Holy Place (Lev 16). It was observed on the tenth day of the seventh month; a day of great solemnity and strictest conformity to the law.

DAY OF CHRIST The period connected with reward and blessing at the coming of Christ for believers (1Co 1:8; Php 1:6, 10; 2:16). *See below, Day of the Lord.*

DAY OF THE LORD

1. A "day" of God's judgment on the nations (Isa 13:6-9; Eze 30:3; Joel 3:14; Ob 1:15), on Israel (Joel 1:15; 2:1, 11, 31; Am 5:18-20).

2. The period commencing with the second advent of Christ and terminating with the making of a new heaven and a new earth (Isa 65:17-19; 66:22; 2Th 2:2; 2Pe 2:13; Rev 21:1). Preceded and introduced by apocalyptic judgments (Rev 4:1-19:6).

DAY'S JOURNEY Eighteen or twenty miles (Ex 3:18; 1Ki 19:4; Jnh 3:4). Sabbath day's journey, about two thousand paces (Ac 1:12).

DAYSMAN NIV "someone to arbitrate" (Job 9:33). *See Mediation.*

DAYSPRING NIV "dawn" (Job 38:12) and "rising sun" (Lk 1:78).

DAYSTAR *See Morning Star.*

DEACON (*serve*). An officer charged with the temporal affairs of the church. The seven men chosen to help the apostles are often considered deacons (Ac 6:1-6). Qualifications of (1Ti 3:8-13). The Greek word translated deacon signifies servant, and is so translated (Mt 23:11; Jn 12:26). Also translated minister (Mk 10:43; 1Co 3:5; 1Th 3:2).

DEACONESS (*serve*). Phoebe is called a "servant of the church," which could be translated a "deaconess" (Ro 16:1, ftn). 1Ti 3:1-13 lists character qualities of deacons. V. 11 refers either to deacons' wives or to special qualities required of deaconesses (see ftn). *See Women, In Leadership.*

DEAD

Raised to life, instances of:
Son of the widow of Zarephath (1Ki 17:17-23), Shunammite's son (2Ki 4:32-37), young man laid in Elisha's tomb (2Ki 13:21), widow's son (Lk 7:12-15), Jairus' daughter (Lk 8:49-55), Lazarus (Jn 11:43-44), Dorcas (Ac 9:37-40), Eutychus (Ac 20:9-12, w Heb 11:35).

Prepared for burial by washing (Ac 9:37), anointing (Mt 26:12), wrapping in linen (Mt 27:59). Burned. *See Cremation.* Burnings of incense made for (2Ch 16:14; 21:19; Jer 34:5).
See Burial; Cremation; Embalming.

Pictured as:
Rest (Job 3:13-19). Sleep (Job 14:11-15, 21; Da 12:12). Hopelessness (Job 17:13-15; Ecc 9:5-6; Eze 32:27, 30). Separation from God (Ps 6:5; 30:9; 88:10-12; 115:17).

Life after (Job 14:12-15; Ps 49:15; Da 12:2; Lk 20:35-36; Jn 11:25). Understanding after (Eze 32:31; Lk 16:19-31).

Abode of:
The pit (Job 17:13-15). Abraham's side (Lk 16:22), hell (Lk 16:23). *See Hades; Hell; Grave; Sheol.* Paradise (Lk 23:43).
See Burial; Death, Physical; Mourning; Resurrection; Righteous, Promises to; Wicked, Punishment of.

DEAD SEA Lies SE of Jerusalem. Called the Salt Sea (Ge 14:3; Nu 34:12), Sea of the Plain (Dt 3:17; 4:49; Jos 3:16), eastern sea (Joel 2:20; Zec 14:8). Prophecy concerning (Eze 47:7-10, 18).

DEAD SEA SCROLLS Discovered in 1947 by a Bedouin in caves a mile or so W of the NW corner of the Dead Sea, at Qumran. So far mss have been found in 11 caves, and they are mostly dated as coming from the last two centuries B.C. and the first century A.D. At least 382 mss are represented by the fragments of Cave Four alone, c. 100 of which are biblical mss. These include fragments of every book of the Hebrew Bible except Esther. Some of the books are represented in many copies. Not all the mss are in fragments; some are complete or nearly complete. In addition to biblical books, fragments of apocryphal and apocalyptic books, commentaries, psalms, and sectarian literature have been found. Near the caves are the remains of a monastery of huge size, possibly the headquarters of a monastic sect of Jews called the Essenes. The discoveries at Qumran are important for biblical studies in general. They are of great importance for a study of the OT text, both Hebrew and the LXX. They are also of importance in relation to the NT, as they furnish the background to the preaching of John the Baptist and Jesus. There is no evidence that either John the Baptist or Jesus was a member of the group. *See Testaments, Time Between.*

DEAFNESS Law concerning (Lev 19:14). Inflicted by God (Ex 4:11). Miraculous cure of (Mt 11:5; Mk 7:32; 9:25).
Figurative of moral insensitivity (Isa 6:10; 29:18; 35:5; Eze 12:2; Mt 13:15; Jn 12:40; Ac 28:26-27).
See Blindness, Spiritual; Conscience, Dead; Impenitence; Obduracy.

DEATH, PHYSICAL Universal to mankind (Ecc 3:2, 19-21; Ro 5:12, 14; 1Pe 1:24). Time of, unknown (Ge 27:2; Ps 39:4, 13). Nearness to (Jos 23:14; 1Sa 20:3). Separates spirit and body (Ecc 12:5, 7).
Does not end conscious existence (Lk 20:34-38; 23:39-43; Rev 20:12-13). Exemplified in the appearance of Moses and Elijah at the transfiguration of Jesus (Mt 17:2-3; Mk 9:4-5; Lk 9:30-33).
Not to be feared by the righteous (Mt 10:28). Brings rest to the righteous (Job 3:13, 17-19). Dispossesses of earthly goods (Job 1:21; Ps 49:17; Lk 12:16-20; 1Ti 6:7).
A judgment (Ge 2:17; 3:19; 6:7, 11-13; 19:12-13, 24-25; Jos 5:4-6; 1Ch 10:13-14). God's power over (Dt 32:39; 1Sa 2:6; Ps 68:20; 2Ti 1:10). Christ's power over (Heb 2:14-15; Rev 1:18). To be destroyed (Isa 25:8; Hos 13:14; 1Co 15:21-22, 26, 55-57; Rev 20:14; 21:4).
Preparation for (2Ki 20:1; Lk 12:35-37). By Moses (Nu 27:12-23), by David (1Ki 2:1-10), by Ahithophel (2Sa 17:23). Apostrophe to (Hos 13:14; 1Co 15:55).

Described as:
Sleep (Dt 31:16; 1Ki 14:31; 15:8, 24; 16:6, 28; Job 7:21; 14:12; Ps 76:5-6; Jer 51:39; Da 12:2; Jn 11:11; Ac 7:60; 13:36; 1Co 15:6, 18, 51; 1Th 4:13-15). "Breathing one's last" or "giving up one's spirit" (Ge 25:8; 35:29; La 1:19; Ac 5:10). King of terrors (Job 18:14). A change (Job 14:14). Going to your fathers (Ge 15:15; 25:8; 35:29). Putting off this tabernacle (2Pe 1:14). Requiring the soul (Lk 12:20). Going the way from which there is no return (Job 16:22). Being gathered to our people (Ge 49:33). In silence (Ps 94:17; 115:17). Returning to dust (Ge 3:19). Being cut down (Job 14:2). Fleeing as a shadow (Job 14:2). Departing (Php 1:23).

Desired:
(Jer 8:3; Rev 9:6). By Moses (Nu 11:15). By Elijah (1Ki 19:4). By Job (Job 3; 6:8-11; Job 7:1-3, 15-16; 10:1). By Jonah (Jnh 4:8). By Simeon (Lk 2:29). By Paul (2Co 5:2, 8; Php 1:20-23).

Exemption from:
Enoch (Ge 5:24; Heb 11:5). Elijah (2Ki 2). Promised to saints, when Christ returns for believers (1Co 15:51; 1Th 4:15, 17). No death in heaven (Lk 20:36; Rev 21:4).

Inevitable:
(2Sa 14:14; Job 7:1, 8-10, 21; 10:21-22; 14:2, 5, 7-12, 14, 19-21; 16:22; 21:23, 25-26, 32-33; 30:23; 34:15, 19; Ps 49:7-10; 82:7; 89:48; 144:4; Ecc 2:14-18; 5:15; 8:8; 9:5, 10; Isa 51:12; Jer 9:21; Zec 1:5; Jn 9:4; Heb 9:27; 13:14; Jas 1:10-11).

Of the Righteous:
A transition (Lk 16:22; 23:43). Balaam extols (Nu 23:10). Peaceful (Ps 37:37). Precious in the sight of the Lord (Ps 116:15). A merciful providence in (Isa 57:1-2). Anticipated with confidence (Pr 14:32; Lk 2:29; Ac 7:59; Ro 14:7-8; 1Co 3:21-23; 2Co 5:1, 4, 8; 1Th 5:9-10; 2Ti 4:6-8; Heb 11:13). Hope in (Da 12:13; 1Co 15:51-57; 2Co 1:9-10; 1Th 4:13-14; 2Pe 1:11, 14; Rev 14:13).

Of the Wicked:
(Job 18:14, 18; 20:4-5, 8, 11; 21:13, 17-18, 23-26; 24:20, 24; 27:8, 19-23; Ps 37:1-2, 9-10, 35-36; 49:7, 9-10, 14, 17, 19-20; Pr 5:22-23; 11:7, 10; 21:16; Ecc 8:10; Isa 14:11, 15). Sudden (Nu 16:32; Pr 10:25, 27; Isa 17:14; Ac 5:3-10). A judgment (Nu 16:29-30; 1Sa 25:38; Job 36:12, 14, 18, 20; Ps 55:23; 58:9; 78:50; 92:7; Pr 2:22; 14:32; Isa 26:14; Jer 16:3-4; Eze 28:8, 10; Am 9:10; Lk 12:20).

Scenes of:
Jacob blessing his sons (Ge 49:1-33; Heb 11:21). Moses (Dt 34:1-7). Samson (Jdg 16:25-30). Eli (1Sa 4:12-18). The wife of Phinehas (1Sa 4:19-21). Zechariah (2Ch 24:22). Jesus (Mt 27:34-53; Mk 15:23-38; Lk 23:27-49; Jn 19:16-30). Stephen (Ac 7:59-60).

Death Penalty:
Shall not be remitted (Nu 35:31). In the Mosaic law the death penalty was inflicted for murder (Ge 9:5-6; Nu 35:16-21, 30-33; Dt 17:6), adultery (Lev 20:10; Dt 22:24), incest (Lev 20:11-12, 14), bestiality (Ex 22:19; Lev 20:15-16), sodomy (Lev 18:22; 20:13), rape of a betrothed virgin (Dt 22:25), perjury (Zec 5:4), kidnapping (Ex 21:16; Dt 24:7), upon a priest's daughter, who committed immorality (Lev 21:9), witchcraft (Ex 22:18), offering human sacrifice (Lev 20:2-5), striking or cursing father or mother (Ex 21:15, 17; Lev 20:9), disobedience to parents (Dt 21:18-21), theft (Zec 5:3-4), blasphemy (Lev 24:23), Sabbath desecration (Ex 35:2; Nu 15:32-36), prophesying falsely or propagating false doctrines (Dt 13:10), sacrificing to false gods (Ex 22:20), refusing to abide by the decision of the court (Dt 17:12), treason (1Ki 2:25; Est 2:23), sedition (Ac 5:36-37).
Not inflicted on the testimony of less than two witnesses (Nu 35:30; Dt 17:6; 19:15).

Modes of Execution of the Death Penalty—
Burning (Ge 38:24; Lev 20:14; 21:9; Jer 29:22; Eze 23:25; Da 3:19-23). Stoning (Lev 20:2, 27; Nu 14:10; 15:33-36; Dt 13:10; 17:5; 22:21, 24; Jer 7:25; 1Ki 21:10; Eze 16:40). Hanging (Ge 40:22; Dt 21:22-23; Jos 8:29; Est 7:10). Beheading (Mt 14:10; Mk 6:16, 27-28). Crucifixion (Mt 27:35, 38; Mk 15:24, 27; Lk 23:33). The sword (Ex 32:27-28; 1Ki 2:25, 34, 46; Ac 12:2).

Executed By—
The witnesses (Dt 13:9; 17:7; Ac 7:58). The congregation (Nu 15:35-36; Dt 13:9).

Figurative:
(Ro 6:2-11; 7:1-11; 8:10-11; Col 2:20; 2Ti 2:11).
Symbolized by the pale horse (Rev 6:8).
See Dead; Regeneration; Second Death; Spiritual Death.

DEBAR *See Lo Debar.*

DEBIR (*back room [of a shrine temple for oracle pronouncement]*).
1. King of Eglon (Jos 10:3-27).
2. A town in the mountains of Judah. Also called Kiriath Sepher which signifies a city of books (Jos 15:15-16). Anakites expelled from, by Joshua (Jos 11:21). Taken by Othniel (Jos 15:15-17, 49; Jdg 1:12-13). Allotted to the Aaronites (Jos 21:15).
3. A place near the Valley of Achor (Jos 15:7).

DEBORAH (*hornet, wasp, wild honey bee*).
1. A nurse to Rebekah (Ge 24:59). Buried beneath an oak under Bethel (Ge 35:8).
2. The prophetess, a judge of Israel (Jdg 4:4-5; 5:7). Inspires Barak to defeat Sisera (Jdg 4:4-16). Triumphant song of (Jdg 5).

DEBT Teaching against (Ro 13:8).
Security for: Warnings against becoming a guarantor for others (Pr 11:15; 22:26). Clothing taken as, must be returned by sundown (Ex 22:25-27; Dt 24:10-13). Job 22:6; Am 2:8). Houses and property (Ne 5:3-4). Children (Job 24:9). Millstones forbidden (Dt 24:6).
See Debtor; Creditor; Security, For Debt.

DEBTOR Laws concerning (Ex 21:2-6; 22:10-15; Lev 25:14-17, 25-41, 47-55; Dt 24:10-13; Ne 10:31; Mt 5:25-26, 40; 18:25). Sold for debt (2Ki 4:1-7; Ne 5:3-5; Mt 18:25). Imprisoned for debt (Mt 18:30). Oppressed (2Ki 4:1-7; Ne 5:3-5; Job 20:18-19; Mt 18:28-30). Mercy toward, commanded (Mt 18:23-27). Wicked (Lk 20:9-16).
See Creditor; Debt; Security, For Debt.

DECALOGUE (*ten words*). Written by God (Ex 24:12; 31:18; 32:16; Dt 5:22; 9:10; Hos 8:12). Divine authority of (Ex 20:1; 34:27-28; Dt 5:4-22). Called the Words of the Covenant (Ex 34:28; Dt 4:13). Tables of Testimony (Ex 31:18; 34:29; 40:20). Listed (Ex 20:1-17; Dt 5:6-21). Confirmed, by Jesus (Mt 19:18-19; 22:34-40; Lk 10:25-28), by Paul (Ro 13:8-10).
See Commandments and Statutes, of God.

DECAPOLIS (*[league of] ten cities*). Ten cities situated in one district on the east of the Sea of Galilee (Mt 4:25; Mk 5:20; 7:31).

DECEIT Is falsehood (Ps 119:118). The tongue is an instrument of (Ro 3:13). Comes from the heart (Mk 7:22). Characteristic of the heart (Jer 17:9). God abhors (Ps 5:6). Forbidden (Pr 24:28; 1Pe 3:10). Christ was perfectly free from (Isa 53:9, w 1Pe 2:22).
Saints free from (Ps 24:4; Zep 3:13; Rev 14:5), purpose against (Job 27:4), avoid (Job 31:5), shun those addicted to (Ps 101:7),

pray for deliverance from those who use (Ps 43:1; 120:2), delivered from those who use (Ps 72:14), should beware of those who teach (Eph 5:6; Col 2:8), should lay aside, in seeking truth (1Pe 2:1). Ministers should lay aside (2Co 4:2; 1Th 2:3).
The wicked are full of (Ro 1:29), devise (Ps 35:20; 38:12; Pr 12:5), utter (Ps 10:7; 36:3), work (Pr 11:18), increase in (2Ti 3:13), use, to themselves (Jer 37:9; Ob 7), delight in (Pr 20:17).
False teachers are workers of (2Co 11:13), preach (Jer 14:14; 23:26), impose on others by (2Pe 2:13). Hypocrites practice (Hos 11:12). False witnesses use (Pr 12:17). A characteristic of Antichrist (2Jn 7). Characteristic of apostasy (2Th 2:10).
Evil of: Hinders knowledge of God (Jer 9:6). Keeps from turning to God (Jer 8:5). Leads to pride and oppression (Jer 5:27-28), to lying (Pr 14:25). Often accompanied by fraud and injustice (Ps 10:7; 43:1). Hatred often concealed by (Pr 26:24-26). The folly of fools is (Pr 14:8). The kisses of an enemy are (Pr 27:6). Punishment of (Ps 55:23; Jer 9:7-9).
Blessedness of being free from (Ps 24:4-5; 32:2).
See Confidence, False; Deception; Falsehood; Flattery; Hypocrisy.

DECEPTION
Instances of:
By Satan (Ge 3:4). Abraham, in saying that Sarah was his sister (Ge 12:13; 20:2). Isaac, in saying that his wife was his sister (Ge 26:7). Jacob and Rebekah, in imposing Jacob on his father, and Jacob's impersonating Esau (Ge 27:6-23). Jacob's sons, in entrapping the Shechemites (Ge 34:13-31), in representing to their father that Joseph had been destroyed by wild beasts (Ge 37:29-35). Joseph, in his ruse with his brothers (Ge 42-44). The Gibeonites, in misrepresenting their habitat (Jos 9:3-15). Ehud deceives Eglon, and slays him (Jdg 3:15-30). Delilah deceives Samson (Jdg 16:4-20). David feigns insanity (1Sa 21:10-15). Amnon deceives Tamar by feigning sickness (2Sa 13:6-14). Hushai deceives Absalom (2Sa 16:15-19). Sanballat tries to deceive Nehemiah (Ne 6). By Absalom, when he avenged his sister (2Sa 13:24-28), when he began his conspiracy (2Sa 15:7). The old prophet (1Ki 13:18). Gehazi (2Ki 5:20). Job's friends (Job 6:15). Doeg (Ps 52:2).
Herod (Mt 2:8). Pharisees (Mt 22:16). Chief priests (Mk 14:1). Lawyer (Lk 10:25). Ananias and Sapphira (Ac 5:1).
See Deceit; Hypocrisy; Falsehood; False Witness.

Self Deception: *See False Confidence; Flattery.*

DECISION
Teaching Concerning:
Choosing life (Dt 30:19). Committing to the Lord (Jos 24:15; 1Sa 12:20; 1Ki 18:21; Isa 50:7; Mt 6:24; 8:21-22; Lk 9:59-62; 1Co 15:58). Walking righteously (Jos 1:7; 2Ch 19:11; Pr 4:25-27; Mt 4:17; 2Th 3:13; 1Ti 6:11-14; Heb 12:1; 1Pe 1:13; 2Pe 1:10). Remaining in Christ (Jn 15:4-5, 7, 9; 1Jn 2:24, 28).
Endurance in:
Obedience (Jn 8:31; 1Co 15:58; Col 2:6-7; 2Th 2:15, 17; 2Pe 3:17-18; 2Jn 8), grace (Ac 13:43; 2Ti 2:1, 3), faith (Ac 14:22; 1Co 16:13; Php 1:27; Col 1:23; Heb 3:6-8, 14; 4:14; 10:23, 35; 1Pe 5:8-9; Jude 20-21), Christian service (Gal 5:1-26), the Lord (Php 4:1), holiness (1Th 3:8, 13), sound doctrine (Eph 4:14; 2Ti 1:13-14; Tit 1:7, 9; Heb 2:1; 13:9, 13).
Instances of:
Abel (Heb 11:4). Enoch (Heb 11:5-6). Noah (Heb 11:7). Abraham (Heb 11:8, 17-19). Jacob (Ge 28:20-22). Joseph (Ge 39:9). Moses (Nu 12:7; Heb 3:5; 11:24-26, 27). Israelites (Ex 19:7-8; 24:3, 7; Dt 4:4; 5:27; 26:17; Jos 22:34; 24:21-25; 1Ki 19:18; 2Ki 11:17; 2Ch 11:16; 13:10-11; 15:12, 15; 23:16; 29:10; Ezr 10:3-44; Ne 9:38; 10:28-31; Jer 34:15; 42:5-6; 50:5; Hos 11:12). Levites (Ezr 32:26). Caleb (Nu 14:6-10, 24; Dt 1:36; Jos 14:14). Balaam (Nu 22:15-18; 24:13). Phinehas (Nu 25:7-13). Joshua (Jos 24:15). Gideon (Jdg 6:25-28). Ruth (Ru 1:16).
Saul (1Sa 11:4-7). David (1Sa 17:32-37; 2Sa 22:22-24). Psalmist (Ps 17:3; 26:6, 11; 27:3-8; 40:9-10; 56:12; 57:7-8; 71:17; 86:11; 101:2-3; 108:1; 116:9, 13-14, 16; 119:8, 30-31, 33-36, 57, 94, 106, 115, 125, 145-146). A prophet of Judah (1Ki 13:8-10). Elijah (1Ki 18:22). Jehoshaphat (1Ki 22:7-8; 2Ch 18:6-7). Micaiah (1Ki 22:13-14; 2Ch 18:6-7). Naaman (2Ki 5:13-17). Hezekiah (2Ki 18:6; 2Ch 15:17). Josiah (2Ki 22:2-3; 23:25; 2Ch 34:31). Nehemiah (Ne 2; 4:6; 6:11). Esther (Est 4:16). Job (Job 2:9-10). Daniel (Da 1:8). The three Hebrews (Da 3:11-12, 16-18).
Matthew (Mt 9:9). Joseph (Mk 15:43). Nathanael (Jn 1:49). Martha (Jn 11:27). Disciples (Lk 18:28; Jn 6:68-69; Ac 2:42). Paul (Ac 9:29; Ro 1:16; 8:38-39; Php 1:20-21; 2Ti 4:7-8). Church, of Ephesus (Rev 2:2-3). Of Sardis (Rev 3:4, 8, 10). Saints (Rev 14:4).
See Character.

DECISION, VALLEY OF *See Jehoshaphat, Valley of.*

DECREE An official ruling or law (Da 2:9; Est 1:20; Jnh 3:7; Ac 16:4; Rev 13:8).

DEDAN
1. A son of Raamah (Ge 10:7; 1Ch 1:9).
2. A son of Jokshan (Ge 25:3; 1Ch 1:32).
3. A country, probably bordering on Edom (Jer 49:8; Eze 25:13; 27:15, 20; 38:13).

DEDANITES Descendants of Dedan (Isa 21:13).

DEDICATION Law concerning dedicated things (Lev 27; Nu 18:14; 1Ch 26:26-27). Must be without blemish (Lev 22:18-23; Mal 1:14). Not redeemable (Lev 27:28-29). Offering must be voluntary (Lev 1:3; 22:19). *See Offerings; Vows.* Of the tabernacle (Nu 7). Solomon's temple (1Ki 8; 2Ch 7:5). Second temple (Ezr 6:16-17). Of the wall of Jerusalem (Ne 12:27-43). Of houses (Dt 20:5). Of Samuel by his mother (1Sa 1:11, 22).
Of Self. *See Consecration.*
For instances of liberality in dedicated things. *See Liberality.*

DEDICATION, FEAST OF Annual Jewish feast celebrating the restoration of the temple following its desecration

by Antiochus Epiphanes. Jesus delivered a discourse at this feast (Jn 10:22ff).

See Feasts; Hanukkah; Kislev; Maccabees; Month, 9.

DEED To the land (Jer 32:12, 14, 44). *See Land.* For works. *See Works, Good.*

DEEP The ocean (Ne 9:11), chaos (Ge 1:2), the deepest part of the sea (Ge 49:25), Abyss (Lk 8:31; Rev 9:1; 11:7).

DEER Also called doe, roe deer. Designated among the clean animals, to be eaten (Dt 12:15; 14:5). Provided for Solomon's household (1Ki 4:23). Swiftness of (2Sa 2:18; 1Ch 12:8; Pr 6:5; SS 8:14; Isa 35:6). Surefootedness of (2Sa 22:34). Gentleness of (Pr 5:19).

DEFENSE An argument made before a court. Of Jeremiah (Jer 26:12-16), Peter (Ac 4:8-13; 5:23-29), Stephen (Ac 7), Paul (Ac 22; 23:1-6; 24:10-21; 26:1-23). Military defenses. *See Fort; Armies.*

DEFILEMENT Laws relating to (Lev 7:18-21; 11:43; 22:2-7). Caused by, leprosy (Lev 13:3, 44-46; 14; 22:4-7), copulation (Lev 15:17), discharges (Lev 15:1-17), childbirth (Lev 12:2-8; Lk 2:22), menses (Lev 15:19-33; 2Sa 11:4), touching the dead (Nu 19:11-22; 31:19-20), touching carcass of any unclean animal (Lev 11:39-40; 17:15-16; 22:8), touching carcass of any unclean thing (Lev 5:2-13; 11:8, 24-28, 31-38; 14:46-57; 15:5-11; Dt 23:10-11), slaying in battle (Nu 31:19-20). Contact with sinners falsely supposed to cause (Jn 18:28). Of priests (Lev 16:26, 28; Nu 19:7-10; Eze 44:25-26).

Egyptian perspective (Ge 43:32).

See Purification; Unclean, Uncleanness; Washings.

DEFORMITY *See Blemish.*

DEGRADATION Of God's people (Ex 32:25; Eze 16:6; 20:31; 2Pe 2:22).

DEGREES NIV "steps" on the stairway of Ahaz (2Ki 20:9-11).

DEGREES, SONGS OF Title of Pss 120 to 134 in the KJV. *See Ascents, Songs of.*

DEHAVITES At the end of Ezra 4:9 the KJV lists three peoples: "the Susanchites, the Dehavites, *and* the Elamites," while the NIV reads "the Elamites of Susa." The KJV transliterated "the Dehavites" from a difficult Aramaic term, rightly rendered "of" in the NIV.

DEITY OF JESUS *See Jesus the Christ, Deity of.*

DEKAR *See Ben-Deker, Ben-Dekar.*

DELAIAH (*Yahweh draws up [like water in a bucket]*).
1. Descendant of David (1Ch 3:1-24).
2. Head of the twenty-third course of priests (1Ch 24:18).
3. Prince who tried to save Jeremiah's roll from destruction (Jer 36:12, 25).
4. An ancestor of the tribe that returned under Zerubbabel (Ezr 2:60; Ne 7:62).
5. The father of Shemaiah (Ne 6:10).

DELIGHTING IN GOD Commanded (Ps 37:4). Reconciliation leads to (Job 22:21, 26). Observing the Sabbath leads to (Isa 58:13-14).

Saints' Experience in:
Communion with God (SS 2:3). The law of God (Ps 1:2; 119:24, 35). The goodness of God (Ne 9:25). The comforts of God (Ps 94:19). Promises to (Ps 37:4). Blessedness of (Ps 112:1).

Hypocrites:
Pretend to (Isa 58:2). In heart despise (Job 27:10; Jer 6:10).

DELILAH (*tease*). Philistine woman who lured Samson to his ruin (Jdg 16:4-20).

DELIVERANCE *See Affliction; God, Providence of; Prayer, Answer to.*

DELIVERER A title of Jesus (Ro 11:26). *See Titles and Names.*

DELUGE *See Flood.*

DELUSION, SELF *See Self-Delusion.*

DEMAGOGISM Instances of: Absalom (2Sa 15:2-6). Pilate (Mt 27:17-26; Mk 15:15; Lk 23:13-24; Jn 18:38-40; 19:6-13). Felix (Ac 24:27). Herod (Ac 12:3).

DEMAS (*[common] folks*). Fellow laborer with Paul (Col 4:14; Phm 24), who later deserted him (2Ti 4:10).

DEMETRIUS (*of Demeter*).
1. A disciple praised by John (3Jn 12).
2. A silversmith at Ephesus who made trouble for Paul (Ac 19:23-27).

DEMONS

General:
Worship of (Lev 17:7; Dt 32:17; 2Ch 11:15; Ps 106:37; Mt 4:9; Lk 4:7; 1Co 10:20-21; 1Ti 4:1; Rev 13:4). Worship of, forbidden (Lev 17:7; Zec 13:2; Rev 9:20).

Testify to the deity of Jesus (Mt 8:29; Mk 1:23-24; 3:11; 5:7; Lk 8:28; Ac 19:15).

Adversaries of men (Mt 12:45). Sent to cause trouble between Abimelech and the Shechemites (Jdg 9:23). Messages given false prophets by (1Ki 22:21-23).

Believe and tremble (Jas 2:19). To be judged at the general judgment (Mt 8:29, w 2Pe 2:4; Jude 6).

Punishment of (Mt 8:29; 25:41; Lk 8:28; 2Pe 2:4; Jude 6; Rev 12:7-9).

Possession By:

instances of—
Saul (1Sa 16:14-23; 18:10-11; 19:9-10). Two men of the Gadarenes (Mt 8:28-34; Mk 5:2-20). The mute man (Mt 9:32-33). The blind and mute man (Mt 12:22; Lk 11:14). The daughter of the Syrian Phoenician (Mt 15:22-29; Mk 7:25-30). The child with seizures (Mt 17:14-18; Mk 9:17-27; Lk 9:37-42). The man in the synagogue (Mk 1:23-26; Lk 4:33-35). Mary Magdalene (Mk 16:9; Lk 8:2-3). The herd of pigs (Mt 8:30-32).

Jesus falsely accused of being possessed of (Mk 3:22-30; Jn 7:20; 8:48; 10:20).

Exorcised—
Cast out by Jesus (Mt 4:24; 8:16; Mk 3:22; Lk 4:41). Power over, given the disciples (Mt 10:1; Mk 6:7; 16:17). Cast out by the disciples (Mk 9:38; Lk 10:17), by Peter (Ac 5:16), by Paul (Ac 16:16-18; 19:12), by Philip (Ac 8:7). The disciples could not expel (Mk 9:18, 28-29). Sceva's sons exorcise (Ac 19:13-16). The parable of the man repossessed (Mt 12:43-45).

See Devil; Satan.

DENARIUS *See Money.*

DENS Used as places of refuge (Jdg 6:2; Heb 11:38; Rev 6:15).

DENYING JESUS *See Jesus the Christ, Rejected.*

DEPRAVITY

In the Nature of Humanity: (Ge 6:5-8; 8:21; Job 4:17-19; 9:2-3, 20, 29-31; 11:12; 14:4; 15:14-16; 25:4-6; Ps 5:9; 51:5; 58:1-5; 94:11; 130:3; Pr 10:20; 20:6, 9; 21:8; Isa 1:5-6; 51:1; Jer 13:23; 16:12; 17:9; Hos 6:7; Mic 7:2-4; Mt 7:17; 12:34-35; 15:19; Mk 7:21-23; Jn 3:19; 8:23; 14:17; Ro 1:21-32; Ro 2:1; 6:6, 19-20; 7:5, 11-15, 18-25; 8:5-8, 13; 1Co 2:14; 3:3; 5:9-10; 2Co 5:14; Gal 5:17, 19-21; Eph 2:1-3, 12; 4:17-19, 22; Jas 4:5; 1Pe 1:18; 2:25; 1Jn 1:8, 10; 2:16).

Universal: (Ge 6:11-13; 2Ch 6:36; Ps 14:1-3; 53:1-3; 143:2; Ecc 7:20; Isa 53:6; 64:6; Mic 7:2-4; Ro 3:9-19, 23; 5:6, 12-14; 11:32; Gal 3:10-11, 22; Jas 3:2; 1Jn 5:19).

See Fall of Mankind, The; Sin.

DEPRESSION *See Despondency.*

DEPUTY An officer who administers the functions of a superior in his absence (1Ki 22:47; 2Ki 15:5; Ac 13:7-8; 18:12; 19:38).

DERBE A city of Lycaonia. Paul fled to (Ac 14:6, 20). Visited by Paul and Silas (Ac 16:1). Gaius born in (Ac 20:4).

DERISION The wicked held in, by God (Ps 2:4; Pr 1:26).
Instances of: Sarah, when the angels gave her the promise of a child (Ge 18:12). The evil children of Bethel deride Elisha (2Ki 2:23). The people of Israel scoff at Hezekiah (2Ch 30:1-10).

See Irony; Sarcasm; Scoffing.

DESERTS Vast barren plains (Ex 5:3; Jn 6:13). Uninhabited places (Mt 14:15; Mk 6:31).

Described as:
Uninhabited and lonesome (Jer 2:6). Uncultivated (Nu 20:5; Jer 2:2). Desolate (Eze 6:14). Dry and without water (Dt 8:15). Trackless (Isa 43:19). Great and terrible (Dt 1:19). Waste and howling (Dt 32:10). Infested with wild beasts (Isa 13:21; Mk 1:13). Infested with serpents (Dt 8:15). Infested with robbers (Jer 3:2; La 4:19). Danger of traveling in (Ex 14:3; 2Co 11:26). Guides required in (Nu 10:31; Dt 32:10).

Phenomena of, Alluded to:
Mirage or deceptive appearance of water (Jer 15:18). Scorching wind (Jer 4:11). Tornadoes or whirlwinds (Isa 21:1). Clouds of sand and dust (Dt 28:24; Jer 4:12-13).

Mentioned in Scripture:
Arabian or great desert (Ex 23:31). Beth Aven (Jos 18:12). Beersheba (Ge 21:14; 1Ki 19:3-4). Damascus (1Ki 19:15). Edom (2Ki 3:8). En Gedi (1Sa 24:1). Gibeon (2Sa 2:24). Judea (Mt 3:1). Jeruel (2Ch 20:16). Kedemoth (Dt 2:26). Kadesh (Ps 29:8). Maon (1Sa 23:24-25). Paran (Ge 21:21; Nu 10:12). Shur (Ge 16:7; Ex 15:22). Sin (Ex 16:1). Sinai (Ex 19:1-2; Nu 33:16). Ziph (1Sa 23:14-15). Zin (Nu 20:1; 27:14). Of the Red Sea (Ex 13:18). Near Gaza (Ac 8:26). Wastelands often found in (Jer 17:6). Parts of, afforded pasture (Ge 36:24; Ex 3:1). Inhabited by wandering tribes (Ge 21:20-21; Ps 72:9; Jer 25:24). The persecuted fled to (1Sa 23:14; Heb 11:38). The disaffected fled to (1Sa 22:2; Ac 21:38).

Illustrative of:
Barrenness (Ps 106:9; 107:33, 35). Those deprived of all blessings (Hos 2:3). The world (SS 3:6; 8:5). The Gentiles (Isa 35:1, 6; 41:19). What offers no support (Jer 2:31). Desolation by armies (Jer 12:10-13; 50:12).

DESIGN In nature, evidence of (Job 12:7-11; Pr 16:4).

DESIRED OF ALL NATIONS Some see as a title of Jesus (Hag 2:7). Others deny a messianic application and hold that it means the precious gifts of all nations (Hag 2:8 w Isa 60:5).

DESIRE, SPIRITUAL For divine piety (Ps 17:11; 51:1-4, 7-13; 119:82; Hab 3:2). For divine fellowship (Ps 62:1; 63:1, 8). For divine help (Ps 25:5, 15; 68:28; 119:77, 116-117).

Exhortations concerning (Ps 70:4; 105:4; Isa 55:1-2; 55:3, 6; Hos 10:12).

For God (Ps 24:6; 27:8; 33:20; 40:1; 42:1-11; 69:3; 73:26; 119:10, 12, 19-20, 25, 40, 81, 88, 123, 131-132, 135-136, 149, 156, 174; 123:1-2; 130:5-6; 143:6-12; 84:2; 26:8-9; Mt 13:17; Lk 10:42; Php 3:12-14; 1Pe 1:10). For his holy courts (Ps 84:2).

Reward of (Dt 4:29; Ps 34:10; 37:4, 9, 34; 107:9; 119:2; Pr 2:3-5; Isa 40:31; Jer 29:13; Mt 5:6; Lk 1:53; 6:21; Jn 6:35; Heb 11:6).

See Hunger, Figurative; Thirst.

Evil desire: *See Imagination; Lust.*

DESOLATION, ABOMINATION OF *See Abomination That Causes Desolation.*

DESPAIR *See Despondency.*

DESPISERS General references to (Pr 1:30; 9:8; Mt 7:6; Ac 13:41; Ro 2:4; 2Ti 3:3; Heb 10:28; 2Pe 2:10).

DESPONDENCY (Isa 35:3-4; Heb 12:12-13). Caused by corrective judgments (Nu 17:12-13; Dt 28:65-67; Isa 2:19; Hos 10:8; Mt 24:30; Lk 23:29-30; Rev 6:14-17; 9:5-6), deferred hope (Pr 13:12), adversity (Job 4:5; 9:16-35; 17:7-16).

Lament in (Job 3:1-26; 17:13-16; Ps 6:6; 22:1-2; 55:4-7; 77:7-9; 88:3-17; Ecc 2:20; Jer 8:20; La 3:1-20; 5:15-22; Mic 7:1-7).

Instances of:
Cain, when God pronounced judgment upon him (Ge 4:13-14). Hagar, when cast out of the household of Abraham (Ge 21:15-16). Moses, when sent on his mission to the Israelites (Ex 4:1, 10, 13; 6:12), at the Red Sea (Ex 14:15), when the people lusted for flesh (Nu 11:15). The Israelites, on account of the cruel oppressions of the Egyptians (Ex 6:9). Joshua, over the defeat at Ai (Jos 7:7-9). Elijah, when he fled from Jezebel to the wilderness and sat under the broom tree and wished to die (1Ki 19:4). Jonah, after he had preached to the Ninevites (Jnh 4:3, 8). The mariners with Paul (Ac 27:20).

See Affliction, Consolation Under; Righteous, Promises to.

DESPOTISM *See Government, Monarchical.*

DESTINY
1. Final determined end. Of all people (Ecc 7:2; 9:2-3; Heb 9:27). Of the wicked (Ps 73:17; Jer 15:2; 43:11). Of believers (1Co 2:7).
2. The pagan god of fate (Isa 65:11).

DETECTIVES *See Spies.*

DEUEL (*known of God [El]*). Also called Reuel (Nu 2:14, ftn). Captain of the tribe of Dan (Nu 1:14; 2:14; 7:42; 10:20).

DEUTERONOMY (*second [giving] of the law*).

Author: Moses, though the preamble (1:1-5) and report of Moses' death (ch. 34) were written by someone else.

Date: c. 1406 B.C.

Outline:
I. The Preamble (1:1-5).
II. The Historical Prologue (1:6-4:43).
III. The Stipulations of the Covenant (4:44-26:19).
 A. The Great Commandment: The Demand for Absolute Allegiance (4:44-11:32).
 B. Supplementary Requirements (chs. 12-26).
 1. Ceremonial consecration (12:1-16:17).
 2. Governmental leaders and a righteous nation (16:18-21:21).
 3. Sanctity of God's kingdom (21:22-25:19).
 4. Confession of God as Redeemer-King (ch. 26).
IV. Ratification; Curses and Blessings (chs. 27-30).
V. Covenant Leadership Succession (chs. 31-34).
 A. Change of Leadership (31:1-29).
 B. Song of Moses (31:30-32:47).
 C. Moses' Testamental Blessing on the Tribes (32:48-33:29).
 D. Death of Moses and Succession of Joshua (ch. 34).

Alternate Outline:
I. First Address (1:1-4:43).
II. Second Address (4:44-28:68).
III. Third Address (chs. 29-33).
IV. Moses' Death (ch. 34).

DEVIL (*slanderer* or *liar*). One of the principal titles of Satan, the archenemy of God and of mankind. It is not known how he originated, unless Isaiah and Ezekiel give us a clue (Isa 14:12-20; Eze 28:12-19), but it is certain that he was not created evil. He rebelled against God when in a state of holiness and apparently led other angels into rebellion with him (Jude 6; 2Pe 2:4). He is a being of superhuman power and wisdom but is not omnipotent or omniscient. He tries to frustrate God's plans and purposes for human beings. His principal method of attack is by temptation. His power is limited, and he can go only as far as God permits. On the Judgment Day he will be cast into hell to remain there forever.

See Satan.

DEVOTED THING That which is set apart to the Lord and therefore no longer belongs to the former owner (Lev 27:29, and ftn; Jos 7:1-15). *See Corban.*

DEVOTION

To God: *See Religion.*
For conspicuous instances of, study Enoch, Noah, Abraham, Moses, David, Solomon's early life, Josiah, Asa, Isaiah, Elijah, Jeremiah, Daniel, Shadrach, Meshach, and Abednego.

To Jesus: *See Peter, Simon; John; Paul; Mary.*
For elaborated topics covering the subject, *See Love, Of People for God; Consecration; Zeal.*

DEW A merciful providence (Dt 33:13). Forms imperceptibly (2Sa 17:12), in the night (Job 29:19). From the clouds (Pr 3:20). Called the dew of heaven (Da 4:15). Absence of (1Ki 17:1). Miraculous profusion and absence of (Jdg 6:36-40). *See Meteorology.*
Figurative (Ps 110:3; Isa 26:19; Hos 6:4; 13:3; 14:5).

DIADEM A golden plate worn on the turban of the high priest (Ex 29:6; 39:30; Lev 8:9). A royal crown (Isa 62:3). *See Crown.*

DIAL NIV "stairway" (2Ki 20:11; Isa 38:8). *See Stairs.*

D

D

DIAMOND *See Emerald; Flint; Minerals of the Bible, 1; Stones.*

DIANA Goddess of the Ephesians (Ac 19:24, 27-28, 35). *See Artemis.*

DIASPORA *(scattered [like] seed).* The name applied to the Jews living outside of Israel and maintaining their religious faith among the Gentiles (Jas 1:1; 1Pe 1:1). By the time of Christ the diaspora must have been several times the population of Israel. *See Dispersion; Testaments, Time Between.*

DIBLAH Probably an early copyist's error for Riblah, a town c. fifty miles S of Hamath (Eze 6:14).

DIBLAIM *(lump of [two dried fig] cakes).* Father of Hosea's wife (Hos 1:3).

DIBLATHAIM *See Almon Diblathaim; Beth Diblathaim.*

DIBON, DIBON GAD
1. Also called Dibon Gad and Dimon. A city on the northern banks of the Arnon (Nu 21:30). Israelites encamp at (Nu 33:45). Allotted to Gad and Reuben (Nu 32:3, 34; Jos 13:9, 17). Taken by Moab (Isa 15:2; Jer 48:18, 22).
2. A city in the tribe of Judah (Ne 11:25), probably identical with Dimonah (Jos 15:22).

DIBRI *(possibly speak).* The father of Shelomith (Lev 24:11).

DIDRACHMA *(two drachma).* The annual temple tax was two drachmas (Mt 17:24). *See Drachma; Money.*

DIDYMUS *(twin).* The surname of Thomas (Jn 11:16; 20:24; 21:2).

DIKLAH *([place of] date palms).* The son of Joktan, and the name of a district inhabited by his descendants (Ge 10:27; 1Ch 1:21).

DILEAN *(cucumber ISBE; protrude KB).* A city of Judah (Jos 15:38).

DILIGENCE Jesus as an example of (Mk 1:35; Lk 2:49).
Required:
By God in seeking him (1Ch 22:19; Heb 11:6), obeying him (Dt 6:17; 11:13), listening to him (Isa 55:2), striving after perfection (Php 3:13-14), developing Christian qualities (2Pe 1:5), keeping the soul (Dt 4:9), keeping the heart (Pr 4:23), labors of love (Heb 6:10-12), following every good work (1Ti 3:10), guarding against defilement (Heb 12:15), seeking to be found spotless (2Pe 3:14), making our calling sure (2Pe 1:10), self-examination (Ps 77:6), lawful business (Pr 27:23; Ecc 9:10), teaching religion (2Ti 4:2; Jude 3), instructing children (Dt 6:7; 11:19), discharging official duties (Dt 19:18), saints should abound in (2Co 8:7).
Required in the service of God (Jn 9:4; Gal 6:9). Is not in vain (1Co 15:58). Preserves from evil (Ex 15:26). Leads to assured hope (Heb 6:11). God rewards (Dt 11:14; Heb 11:6).
In temporal matters leads to favor (Pr 11:27), prosperity (Pr 10:4; 13:4), honor (Pr 12:24; 22:29).
Figurative: (Pr 6:6-8).
Exemplified:
Ruth (Ru 2:17). Hezekiah (2Ch 31:21). Nehemiah and his helpers (Ne 4:6). Psalmist (Ps 119:60). Apostles (Ac 5:42). Apollos (Ac 18:25). Titus (2Co 8:22). Paul (1Th 2:9). Onesiphorus (2Ti 1:17).
See Industry; Zeal; Idleness; Slothfulness.

DILL A plant whose aromatic seeds are used in cooking (Mt 23:23).

DIMNAH *(manure).* A Levite town in Zebulun (Jos 21:35). May be the same as Rimmono (1Ch 6:77).

DIMON A town in Moab, generally called "Dibon," but it is called Dimon two times (Isa 15:9, ftn), c. four miles N of Aroer.

DIMONAH A town in the S of Judah (Jos 15:22), probably the same as the "Dibon" of Nehemiah (Ne 11:25).

DINAH *(female judge).* The daughter of Jacob and Leah (Ge 30:21). Rape of (Ge 34).

DINAITES NIV "judges" (Ezr 4:9).

DINHABAH A city of Edom (Ge 36:32; 1Ch 1:43).

DINNER Eaten at noon (Ge 43:16). *See Feasts.*

DIONYSIUS, THE AREOPAGITE *(belonging to Dionysus).* A member of the Areopagus, Athenian supreme court; converted by Paul (Ac 17:34).

DIOSCURI *See Castor and Pollux.*

DIOTREPHES *(nurtured by Zeus).* A domineering Christian leader condemned by John (3Jn 9-10).

DIPLOMACY
Ecclesiastical:
Paul, in winning souls to Christ (1Co 9:20-23), in circumcising Timothy (Ac 16:3), in performing certain temple services to placate the Jews (Ac 21:20-25, w Gal 6:12).
Corrupt practices in:
The officers of Nebuchadnezzar's court to secure the destruction of Daniel (Da 6:4-15).
Instances of:
Abimelech (Ge 21:22-23; 26:26-31). The Gibeonites, in securing a league with the Israelites through deception (Jos 9:3-16). Of Jephthah, with the king of Moab, unsuccessful (Jdg 11:12-28).

Of Abigail (1Sa 25:23-31). Of Hiram, to secure the goodwill of David (2Sa 5:11). Of Tou, to promote the friendship of David (2Sa 8:10). David, in sending Hushai to Absalom's court (2Sa 15:32-37; 16:15-19; 17:1-14). The wise woman of Abel (2Sa 20:16-22). Absalom winning the people (2Sa 15:2-6). Solomon, in his alliance with Hiram (1Ki 5:1-12; 9:10-14, 26-27; 10:11), by intermarriage with other nations (1Ki 11:1). Ambassadors from Ben-Hadad to Ahab (1Ki 20:31-34). Jehoash purchases peace from Hazael (2Ki 12:18). Ahaz purchases aid from the king of Assyria (2Ki 16:7-9). The king of Assyria's field commander, in trying to entice Jerusalem to surrender by bombastic harangue (2Ki 18:17-37; 19:1-13; Isa 36:11-22). Sanballat, in an attempt to prevent the rebuilding of Jerusalem by Nehemiah (Ne 6).
The people of Tyre and Sidon, in securing the favor of Herod (Ac 12:20-22). Paul, in turning the Pharisees and Sadducees against each other at his trial (Ac 23:6-10).
See Prudence; Tact.

DISASTERS *See Burning.*

DISBELIEF *See Unbelief.*

DISCERNING OF SPIRITS The ability to discern between those who spoke by the Spirit of God and those who were moved by false spirits (1Co 12:10).

DISCHARGE, BODILY Caused ceremonial uncleanness. Of a male (Lev 15:2-15, 32). Of a female (Lev 15:25-33). Of a priest (Lev 22:3). *See Disease.*

DISCIPLE *(student).* A name given to the followers of any teacher. Of John the Baptist (Mt 9:14). Of the Pharisees (Lk 5:33). Of Jesus (Mt 10:1; 20:17; Ac 9:26; 14:20; 21:4). The seventy sent forth (Lk 10:1). First called Christians at Antioch (Ac 11:26).
See Apostles; Righteous.

DISCIPLESHIP Following Jesus.
Evangelism—Making Disciples: (Mt 28:18-20; Ac 6:7).
Personal Growth—Being a Disciple:
Characterized by putting Jesus first in all things (Mt 10:32-39; Mk 8:34-38; Lk 14:26-27, 33; Jn 21:15-19), by following Jesus' teaching (Jn 8:31-32), by fruitfulness (Jn 15:5-8), by love for other disciples (Jn 13:34-35).
See Commandments and Statutes, of God; Identification.

DISCIPLINE Of armies, for disobedience of orders (Jos 7:10-26; Jdg 21:5-12). *See Armies.*
Church Discipline: *See Church, The Body of Believers, Discipline.*
See Chastisement, From God; Graces; Self-Control; Self-Discipline.

DISCONTENTMENT *See Contentment; Murmuring.*

DISCOURAGEMENT *See Despondency.*

DISEASE Sent from God (Lev 14:34). As judgments (Ps 107:17; Isa 3:17).
Instances of:
Upon the Egyptians. *See Plague.* Upon Nabal (1Sa 25:38), David's child (2Sa 12:15), Gehazi (2Ki 5:27), Jeroboam (2Ch 13:20), Jehoram (2Ch 21:12-19), Uzziah (2Ch 26:17-20).
Threatened as judgments (Lev 26:16; Dt 7:15; 28:22, 27-28, 35; 29:22).
Healing of, from God (Ex 15:26; 23:25; Dt 7:15; 2Ch 16:12; Ps 103:3; 107:20).
In answer to prayer:
Of Hezekiah (2Ki 20:1-11; Isa 38:1-8), David (Ps 21:4; 116:3-8). Miraculous healing *see Miracles.*
Physicians employed for (2Ch 16:12; Jer 8:22; Mt 9:12; Mk 5:26; Lk 4:23). Remedies used (Pr 17:22; 20:30; Isa 38:21; Jer 30:13; 46:11), medicinal compress (2Ki 20:7), ointments (Isa 1:6; Jer 8:22), wine and oil (Lk 10:34).
Of the sexual organs (Lev 15; 22:4; Nu 5:2; Dt 23:10). *See Bleeding, Subject to; Circumcision; Menstruation.* Treatment of fractures (Eze 30:21).
See Affliction.
Figurative: (Ps 38:7; Isa 1:6; Jer 30:12). Various kinds of: *See Bleeding, Subject to; Blindness; Boil; Congestion; Consumption; Deafness; Demons; Discharge, Bodily; Dropsy; Dysentery; Fever; Gout; Hemorrhage; Hemorrhoids; Indigestion; Inflammation; Insanity; Itch; Lameness; Leprosy; Paralysis; Pestilence; Seizures; Sore; Stammering; Sunstroke; Tumor; Worm.*
Of the bowels. *See Bowels.*

DISFELLOWSHIP
From God and People:
Of the uncircumcised (Ge 17:14). Of violators of the law, of unleavened bread (Ex 12:15), of sacrifices (Lev 17:9; 19:5-7), of purification (Nu 19:20). Of those defiled, by eating prohibited food (Lev 7:25, 27; 17:10; 19:8), by touching the dead (Nu 19:13), by committing abominations (Lev 18:29; 20:3-6).
Commanded:
For blasphemy (Nu 15:31). For schism (Ro 16:17). For heresy (1Ti 6:3-5; Tit 3:10-11; 2Jn 10-11). For immorality (Mt 18:17-18; 1Co 5:1-7, 11, 13; 2Th 3:6).
See Excommunication.

DISGUISES Examples of (Ge 38:14; 1Sa 28:8; 1Ki 14:2; 20:38; 22:30; 2Ch 35:22).

DISH Usually made either of baked clay or of metal. Orientals ate from a central platter or dish (Mt 26:23). Dishes used in the tabernacle and temple were made of gold (Ex 37:16; Nu 7:14ff; 2Ch 4:22, 24:14) or bronze (1Ki 7:38-40; 2Ki 25:14).

DISHAN *(ibex [?]).* The son of Seir (Ge 36:21, 30; 1Ch 1:38).

DISHON *(ibex [?]).*
1. The son of Seir (Ge 36:21, 30; 1Ch 1:38).
2. The grandson of Seir (Ge 36:25; 1Ch 1:41).

DISHONESTY In not paying debts (Ps 37:12, 21; Jas 5:4). In collusion with thieves (Ps 50:18). In wicked devices for gain (Job 24:2-11; Pr 1:10-14; 20:14; Isa 32:7; Jer 22:13; Eze 22:29; Hos 12:7; Am 3:10; 8:5; Mic 6:10-11).
Denounced (Jer 7:8-10; 9:4-6; 9:8; Hos 4:1-2; Na 3:1). Forbidden (Lev 19:13, 35-36; Dt 25:13-16; Ps 62:10; Pr 3:27-28; 11:1; 20:10, 23; 1Th 4:6). Penalties for (Lev 6:2-7; Pr 20:17; Zep 1:9; Zec 5:3-4). Parable concerning (Lk 16:1-8).
Instances of:
Abimelech's servants usurp a well of water (Ge 21:25; 26:15-22). Jacob obtains his brother's birthright by unjust advantage (Ge 25:29-33), steals his father's blessing (Ge 27:6-29), Laban's flocks by skillful manipulation (Ge 30:31-43). Rebekah's guile in Jacob's behalf (Ge 27:6-17). Laban's treatment of Jacob (Ge 29:21-30; 31:36-42). Rachel steals the household gods (Ge 31:19). Simeon and Levi deceive the Shechemites (Ge 34:15-31). Achan hides the wedge of gold and the Babylonian garment (Jos 7:11-26). Micah steals eleven hundred pieces of silver (Jdg 17:2). Micah's priest steals his images (Jdg 18:14-21). Joab's guile in securing Absalom's return (2Sa 14:2-20). Ahab usurps Naboth's vineyard (1Ki 21:2-16). Judas's hypocritical sympathy for the poor (Jn 12:6).
See Diplomacy; Hypocrisy; Injustice; Treason.

DISOBEDIENCE TO GOD Originated in Adam (Ro 5:19). Characteristic of all (Ro 1:32; Eph 2:2; 5:6; Col 3:6; Tit 1:16; 3:3; Heb 2:2; 1Pe 2:8). Temptation to (Ge 3:1-5). Denunciations against (Nu 14:11-12, 22-23; 32:8-13; Dt 18:19).
Punishment of:
Of the Israelites by covenant curses (Lev 26:14-46; Dt 28:15-68). *See Wicked.* Of the Egyptians by plagues. *See Plague; Sin, Punishment of.*
Instances of:
Of Adam and Eve, eating the forbidden fruit (Ge 3:6-11). Of Lot, in refusing to go to the mountain, as commanded by the angels (Ge 19:19-20). Of Lot's wife, in looking back upon Sodom (Ge 19:26). Of Moses, in making excuses when commissioned to deliver Israel (Ex 4:13-14), when he struck the rock (Nu 20:11, 23-24). Of Aaron, at the striking of the rock by Moses (Nu 20:23-24). Of Pharaoh, in refusing to let the Israelites go (Ex 5:2; 7:13, 22-23; 8:15, 19, 32; 9:12, 34; 10:20, 27; 11:10; 14:8). Of the Israelites, in gathering excessive quantities of manna (Ex 16:19-20), in refusing to enter the promised land (Dt 1:26, w Nu 14:1-10; Jos 5:6; Ps 106:24-25). Of Nadab and Abihu, in offering unauthorized fire (Lev 10:1-2). Of Balaam, in accompanying the messengers from Balak (Nu 22:22). Of Achan, in hiding the wedge of gold and the Babylonian garment (Jos 7:15-26).
Of Saul, in offering a sacrifice (1Sa 13:13), in sparing Agag and the spoils of the Amalekites (1Sa 15; 28:18). Of David, in his adultery, and in the killing of Uriah (2Sa 12:9). Of Solomon, in building places for idolatrous worship (1Ki 11:7-10). Of the prophet of Judah, in not keeping the commandment to deliver his message to Jeroboam without delay (1Ki 13). Of a man of Israel, who refused to smite the prophet (1Ki 20:35-36). Of Ahab, in suffering the king of Assyria to escape out of his hands (1Ki 20:42). Of priests, in not performing their functions after the due order (1Ch 15:13). Of the people of Judah (Jer 43:7), in going to dwell in Egypt contrary to divine command (Jer 44:12-14). Of Jonah, in refusing to deliver the message to the Ninevites (Jnh 1).
Of the blind men Jesus healed, and commanded not to tell of their healing (Mt 9:30-31). Of the leper whom Jesus healed, and commanded not to tell of the fact (Mk 1:45). Of Paul, in going to Jerusalem contrary to repeated admonitions (Ac 21:4, 10-14).
Of the righteous. *See Commandments and Statutes, of God.* Of children. *See Children, Commandments to.*

DISPENSATION *(law or arrangement of a house).* The Greek word *oikonomia* means management or administration of a job or trust (Lk 16:2-4; 1Co 9:17; Eph 1:10; 3:2, 9; Col 1:25; 1Ti 1:4).

DISPENSATIONS An era of time during which mankind's obedience to God is tested according to the revelation of God available to him. From two dispensations (or covenants) to seven (innocence, conscience, human government, promise, law, grace, the kingdom) are held by various schools of interpretation.

DISPERSION Of the descendants of Noah (Ge 10). After building the tower of Babel (Ge 11:1-9; Dt 32:8). Of the Jews, foretold (Jer 16:15; 24:9; Jn 7:35). *See Diaspora.*

DISPLAY General references to (Est 1:4; 5:11; Isa 39:2; Lk 20:46; Ac 25:23).
In religious service (2Ki 10:16; Mt 6:2, 5, 16; 23:5).

DISPUTE About property. *See Property.*

DISSEMBLING *See Deception; Hypocrisy.*

DISSENSION In churches (1Co 1:10-13; 3:3-4; 11:18-19).

DISSIPATION Dangers of (Job 1:5). *See Drunkenness.*

DISTAFF Used in spinning thread (Pr 31:19).

DITCH *See Pit.*

DIVES *(rich).* In the Vulgate, the name given to the rich man in the parable of the rich man and Lazarus (Lk 16:19-31).

DIVIDING WALL The barrier between the Court of the Gentiles and the Court of the Jews in the temple in Jerusalem. For a Gentile to go beyond it meant death (Josephus, *Antiq.* 15.11.5). Figurative of Christ bringing Jews and Gentiles together as one in the church (Eph 2:14).

DIVINATION The practice of foreseeing or foretelling future events or discovering hidden knowledge; forbidden to Jews (Lev 19:26; Dt 18:10; Isa 19:3; Ac 16:16). Various means were used: reading omens, dreams, the use of the lot, astrology, necromancy, and others.

DIVINITY OF CHRIST *See Jesus the Christ, Deity of.*

DIVISIONS Forbidden in the church (1Co 1:10). Condemned in the church (1Co 1:11-13; 11:18). Improper in the church (1Co 12:24-25).

Are contrary to the: Unity of Christ (1Co 1:13; 12:13). Desire of Christ (Jn 17:21-23). Purpose of Christ (Jn 10:16). Spirit of the primitive church (1Co 11:16). Are a proof of a sinful spirit (1Co 3:3). Avoid those who cause (Ro 16:17). Evil of, illustrated (Mt 12:25).

DIVORCE Mosaic laws concerning (Ex 21:7-11; Dt 21:10-14; 24:1-4). Authorized for marital unfaithfulness (Mt 5:31-32; 19:3-11). Unjust reproved (Mal 2:14-16). From Gentile wives, required by Ezra (Ezr 10:1-16). Disobedience, a cause for, among the Persians (Est 1:10-22). Final, after remarriage of either party (Jer 3:1). Christ's injunctions concerning (Mk 10:2-12; Lk 16:18). Paul's injunctions concerning (1Co 7:10-17).

Figurative of God's judgment of Israel (Isa 50:1; 54:4-8; Jer 3:8). *See Certificate of Divorce; Marriage.*

DIZAHAB (*that which has gold*). A place in the region of Sinai where Moses gave a farewell address (Dt 1:1).

DOCTOR A physician (Mt 9:12; Mk 2:17; 5:26; Lk 5:31). Luke (Col 4:14).
See Physician; Disease.

DOCTRINES

Origin in God:
(Jn 7:16-17). Set forth by church councils (Ac 15:6-29).

False:
Jesus accuses scribes and Pharisees of false teaching (Mt 5:19-20; 15:9).

False teachers, to be avoided (Ro 16:17-18; 1Co 3:11, 21; 1Ti 1:3-7; 6:3-5, 20-21), accursed (Gal 1:6-8; Jude 4, 11), rejected (Tit 1:10-11, 14; 3:10-11; 2Jn 9-11). Admonitions against (Ro 16:17-18; Eph 4:14; Col 2:4, 8, 18-23; 1Ti 1:3-7; 4:7; 6:20-21; 2Ti 2:16; Tit 3:10-11; Heb 13:9).

False doctrine called: heresies (1Co 11:18-19; 2Pe 2:1-2), corruption (2Co 2:17; 11:3-4; Gal 1:6-8; 2Ti 2:14-18; 3:6-9; 2Pe 2:14-19).

Origin of false doctrine: people (Mt 15:9; Ro 16:17-18; 1Co 3:11, 21; 2Co 2:17; Eph 4:14; Col 2:4, 8, 18-23; 2Ti 3:6-9; Tit 1:10-11, 14; 2Pe 2:1-3), Satan (2Co 11:3-4; 1Ti 4:1-3), Antichrist (1Jn 4:3; 2Jn 7, 9-11).
See Minister, False and Corrupt; Schism; Teachers, False.

DODAI (*beloved*). An officer in David's army (1Ch 27:4).

DODANIM *See Rodanim.*

DODAVAHU (*beloved of Yahweh*). Eliezer's father (2Ch 20:37).

DODO (*beloved*).
1. The grandfather of Tola (Jdg 10:1).
2. The son of Ahohite (2Sa 23:9).
3. The father of one of David's mighty men (2Sa 23:24).

DOEG (*anxious*). An Edomite, present when Ahimelech helped David (1Sa 21:7; 22:9, 22; Ps 52:T). Killed eighty-five priests (1Sa 22:18-19).

DOER OF THE WORD Example of belief (Mt 7:21; 12:50; Lk 11:28; Ro 2:13-15; 2Co 8:11; Jas 1:22-27; 4:11). *See Hearers.*

DOG Among the Israelites (Ex 11:7; 22:31). Shepherd dogs (Job 30:1).

Habits of:
Licking blood (1Ki 21:19; 22:38), licking sores (Lk 16:21), returns to his vomit (Pr 26:11; 2Pe 2:22), lapping of (Jdg 7:5). Mute and sleeping (Isa 56:10-11).

Title of contempt (1Sa 17:43; 24:14; 2Sa 3:8; 9:8; 16:9; 2Ki 8:13; Isa 56:10-11; Mt 15:26).

Figurative:
Of sinners (Php 3:2; Rev 22:15). Of male prostitutes (Dt 23:18).

DOGMATISM *See Commandments and Statutes, of Men.*

DOMICILE Rights of (Dt 24:10-11).

DOMINION, OF MANKIND *See Mankind, Design of.*

DONATIONS *See Liberality.*

DONKEY, DOMESTIC Unclean for food (Lev 11:2-3, 26; Ex 13:13).

Described as:
Knowing its master (Isa 1:3). Strong (Ge 49:14). Fond of ease (Ge 49:14-15). Formed a part of patriarchal wealth (Ge 12:16; 30:43; Job 1:3; 42:12).

Was Used:
In agriculture (Isa 30:6, 24). For bearing burdens (Ge 42:26; 1Sa 25:18). For riding (Ge 22:3; Nu 22:21-23). In harness (Isa 21:7). In war (2Ki 7:7, 10). Governed by a bridle (Pr 26:3). Urged on with a staff (Nu 22:23, 27). Women often rode on (Jos 15:18; 1Sa 25:20). Persons of rank rode on (Jdg 10:3-4; 2Sa 16:2). Judges of Israel rode on white (Jdg 5:10). Young, most valued for labor (Isa 30:6, 24). Trustworthy persons appointed to take care of (Ge 36:24; 1Sa 9:3; 1Ch 27:30). Often taken unlawfully by corrupt rulers (Nu 16:15; 1Sa 8:16; 12:3). Sometimes counted an ignoble creature (Jer 22:19).

Laws Respecting:
Not to be coveted (Ex 20:17). Fall under a burden, to be assisted (Ex 23:5). Astray, to be brought back to its owner (Ex 23:4; Dt 22:1). Astray, to be taken care of till its owner appeared (Dt 22:2-3). Not to be yoked with an ox (Dt 22:10). To enjoy the Sabbath rest (Dt 5:14). Firstborn of, if not redeemed, to have its neck broken (Ex 13:13; 34:20). Christ entered Jerusalem on (Zec 9:9; Jn 12:14).

Miracles Connected With:
Mouth of Balaam's opened to speak (Nu 22:28; 2Pe 2:16). A thousand men slain by Samson with a jawbone of (Jdg 15:15-17). Not torn by a lion (1Ki 13:28). Eaten during famine in Samaria (2Ki 6:25).

DONKEY, WILD
Inhabits wild and solitary places (Job 39:6; Isa 32:14; Da 5:21). Ranges the mountains for food (Job 39:8). Brays when hungry (Job 6:5). Suffers in time of scarcity (Jer 14:6).

Described as:
Fond of liberty (Job 39:5). Intractable (Job 11:12). Unsocial (Hos 8:9). Despises his pursuers (Job 39:5-7). Supported by God (Ps 104:10-11).

Illustrative of:
Intractableness of natural man (Job 11:12). The wicked in their pursuit of sin (Job 24:5). Israel in their love of idols (Jer 2:23-24). The Assyrian power (Hos 8:9). The Ishmaelites (Ge 16:12).

DOOR Posts of, sprinkled with the blood of the Passover lamb (Ex 12:22), the law to be written on (Dt 11:20). Hinges for (Pr 26:14), made of gold (1Ki 7:5). Doors of the temple made of two leaves, cherubim and flowers carved upon, covered with gold (1Ki 6:31-35).

Figurative:
Door of hope (Hos 2:15), of opportunity (1Co 16:9; Rev 3:8), closed (Mt 25:10; Lk 13:25; Rev 3:7).

DOORKEEPER Keeper of doors and gates in public buildings, temples, walled cities, etc., often called "gatekeepers" (2Ki 7:10; 1Ch 23:5; Ps 84:10; Ezr 7:24; Mk 13:34). *See Gatekeepers.*

DOPHKAH (*drive [sheep]*). The first stopping place of the Israelites after they left the wilderness of Sin. It is usually identified with the Egyptian mining center at Serabit el-Khadim in Sinai (Nu 33:12).

DOR A town and district of Israel (Jos 11:2). Conquered by Joshua (Jos 12:23; 1Ki 4:11). Allotted to Manasseh, although situated in the territory of Asher (Jos 17:11; Jdg 1:27).

DORCAS (*gazelle*). A Christian woman living at Joppa whom Peter raised from the dead (Ac 9:36-43).

DOTHAN (*two wells*). A place c. thirteen miles N of Shechem near where Joseph was sold (Ge 37:17) and where Elisha saw a vision of angels (2Ki 6:13-23).

DOUBLE-MINDED One who is a doubter, unstable (Ps 119:113; Jas 1:8; 4:8).

DOUBTING In prayer (Mt 21:21; Jas 1:6-8). Admonishings against (Pr 24:10; Mt 8:26; 14:31; 17:17; Mk 4:40; 9:19; Lk 8:25; 9:40).

Instances of:
Job (Job 3; 4:3-6; 9:16-23; 30:20-21). Abraham (Ge 12:12-13; 15:8). Sarah (Ge 18:12-14). Lot (Ge 19:30). Moses (Ex 3:11; 4:1, 10, 13; 5:22-23; 6:12; Nu 11:21-22). Israelites (Ex 14:10-12, 15; 1Sa 17:11, 24; Isa 40:27-28; 49:14-15). Gideon (Jdg 6:13, 15). Samuel (1Sa 16:1-2). Psalmists (Ps 22:2; 42:5-6; 49:5; 73:13-17; 77:3, 7-9). Obadiah (1Ki 18:7-14). Elijah (1Ki 19:13-18). Jeremiah (Jer 1:6; 8:18; 32:24-25; 45:3; La 3:8, 17-18; 5:20). Christ's disciples (Mt 8:23-27; 14:29-31; 17:14-21; 28:17; Mk 4:38, 40; 9:14-29; 16:10-11; Lk 8:25; 9:40-41; Jn 14:8-11; 20:24-27). John the Baptist (Mt 11:2-3). Ananias (Ac 9:13-14). Peter (Mt 14:30-31). Thomas (Jn 20:25). Early believers (1Pe 1:6).
See Cowardice; Murmuring.

DOUGH First of, offered to God (Nu 15:19-21; Ne 10:37). Kneaded (Jer 7:18; Hos 7:4). Part of, for priest (Eze 44:30). *See Bread; Oven.*

DOVE Sent out from the ark by Noah (Ge 8:8-11). Mourning of (Isa 38:14; 59:11; Na 2:7). Domesticated (Isa 60:8). Nests of (Jer 48:28). Harmlessness of, typical of Christ's gentleness (Mt 10:16). Sacrificial uses of (Ge 15:9). Prescribed for purification, of women (Lev 12:6, 8; Lk 2:24), of Nazirites (Nu 6:10), of lepers (Lev 14:22). Burnt offering of (Lev 1:14-17). Trespass offering of, for the poor (Lev 5:7-10; 12:8). Sin offering, for those who touched any dead body (Nu 6:10). Market for, in the temple (Mt 21:12; Jn 2:14). Symbolic of the Holy Spirit (Mt 3:16; Lk 3:22; Jn 1:32). *See Pigeon.*

DOVE'S DUNG NIV "seed pods" (2Ki 6:25 and ftn). *See Plants of the Bible.*

DOWRY Sum paid to parents for a daughter taken as wife (Ex 22:16-17), by Shechem for Dinah (Ge 34:12), by Boaz for Ruth (Ru 4:3-9), by David to Saul for Michal (1Sa 18:25).

DOXOLOGY *See Praise.*

DRACHMA A Greek silver coin worth about a day's wages (Lk 15:8; Ac 19:19). The temple tax was two drachmas (Mt 17:24). In Ezr 2:69 and Ne 7:70-72 the term may refer to the Persian daric. *See Daric; Money.*

DRAGON Any terrible creature, as a venomous serpent (Dt 32:33; Ps 91:13), a sea monster (Ps 74:13; 148:7; Isa 27:1; Eze 29:3; 32:2). Figurative of forces opposed to God: Egypt (Isa 51:9), Satan (Rev 12; 13; 16:13; 20:2). *See Serpent.*

DRAM *See Daric.*

DRAMA *See Pantomime.*

DRAUGHT HOUSE *See Latrine.*

DRAWER OF WATER One who brought water from a well or a spring to a house (Dt 29:11; Jos 9:23-27).

DRAWING Of pictures on tile (Eze 4:1).

DREAM Transitory (Job 20:8). Vanity of (Ecc 5:3, 7).
Revelations by (Nu 12:6; Job 33:15-17; Jer 23:28; Joel 2:28; Ac 2:17). The dreams of the cupbearer and baker (Ge 40:8-23), of Pharaoh (Ge 41:1-36).
Interpreted by Joseph (Ge 40:12-13, 18-19; 41:25-32), by Daniel (Da 2:16-23, 28-30; 4). Delusive (Isa 29:7-8).
False prophets pretended to receive revelations through (Dt 13:1-5; Jer 23:25-32; 27:9; 29:8; Zec 10:2). *See Vision.*

Instances of:
Of Abimelech, concerning Sarah (Ge 20:3). Of Jacob, concerning the stairway (Ge 28:12), the speckled goats (Ge 31:10-13), concerning his going down into Egypt (Ge 46:2). Of Laban, concerning Jacob (Ge 31:24). Of Joseph, concerning the sheaves (Ge 37:5-10). Of the Midianite, concerning the cake of barley (Jdg 7:13). Of Solomon, concerning his choice of wisdom (1Ki 3:3-15). Of Eliphaz, of a spirit speaking to him (Job 4:12-21). Of Daniel, concerning the four beasts (Da 7). Of Joseph, concerning Mary's innocence (Mt 1:20-21), concerning the flight into Egypt (Mt 2:13), concerning the return into Israel (Mt 2:18-22). Of Pilate's wife, concerning Jesus (Mt 27:19). Cornelius's vision, concerning Peter (Ac 10:3-6). Peter's vision of the unclean beasts (Ac 10:10-16). Paul's vision of the man in Macedonia, crying, "Come over to Macedonia and help us" (Ac 16:9), relating to his going to Rome (Ac 23:11), concerning the shipwreck and the safety of all on board (Ac 27:23-24).

DRESS Of fig leaves (Ge 3:7). Of skins (Ge 3:21). Of other materials. *See also Hair; Goats' Hair; Leather; Linen; Sackcloth; Silk; Wool.* Mixed materials in, forbidden (Dt 22:11). Men forbidden to wear women's, and women forbidden to wear men's (Dt 22:5). Rules with respect to women's (1Ti 2:9-10; 1Pe 3:3). Not to be held over night as a pledge for debt (Ex 22:26). Ceremonial purification of (Lev 11:32; 13:47-59; Nu 31:20). Tearing of. *See Mourning.*

Of the head:
Turbans prescribed by Moses, for the priests (Ex 28:40; 29:9; 39:28), by Ezekiel (Eze 44:18). Turbans and headdresses worn by men (Da 3:21) and by women (Isa 3:20; Eze 24:17, 23). Shawls (Isa 3:23). Veils (Eze 13:18, 21).

Various articles of:
Mantle, robe, or cloak (Ezr 9:3; 1Ki 19:13; 1Ch 15:27; Job 1:20), richly ornamented (2Sa 13:18), purple (Jn 19:2, 5). Robe (Ex 28:4; 1Sa 18:4). Capes (Isa 3:22). Embroidered coat (Ex 28:4, 40; 1Sa 2:19; Da 3:21). Sleeveless shirt, called coat (Mt 5:40; Lk 6:29; Jn 19:23; 49:23). Cloak (2Ti 4:13; Jn 19:2, 5). Trousers (Da 3:21). Skirts (Eze 5:3). Sashes (Isa 3:20). *See Veil.*
Changes of clothing, the folly of excessive (Job 27:16). Uniform vestments kept in store for worshipers of Baal (2Ki 10:22-23; Zep 1:8), for wedding feast (Mt 22:11). Presents made of changes of clothing (Ge 45:22; 1Sa 18:4; 2Ki 5:5; Est 6:8; Da 5:7). Garments of priests. *See Priest.* Dress in mourning. *See Mourning.*

Symbolic:
Filthy, of unrighteousness and judgment (Isa 64:6; Zec 3:3-4). Clean, of acceptance (Zec 3:4-7).
See Colors, Figurative and Symbolic.

DRINK Beverages of the Israelites were water (Ge 24:11-18), wine (Ge 14:18; Jn 2:3), and milk (Jdg 4:19).

DRINK OFFERING *See Offerings, Drink; Libation.*

DRIVING Rapid, by Jehu (2Ki 9:20).

DROMEDARY *See Camel.*

DROPSY (Lk 14:2).

DROSS Refuse separated from molten ore or metal. Figurative of divine judgment (Ps 119:119; Pr 25:4; 26:23; Isa 1:22; Eze 22:18-19).

DROUGHT (Ge 31:40; 1Ki 17; 18; Jer 14:1-6). Sent by God as a judgment (Dt 28:23-24; 1Ki 8:35; 2Ch 6:26; 7:13; Hos 13:15). *See Famine; Meteorology; Rain.*
Figurative: (Ps 32:4; Isa 44:3).

DRUG ABUSE Not mentioned in the Bible, but the principles derived from alcohol abuse would apply to drugs. *See Abuse, Substance Abuse; Drunkenness.*

DRUNKARD

Described:
(Pr 23:29-35). The psalmist mocked by (Ps 69:12). Fellowship with, forbidden (1Co 5:11).

End Result:
Poverty (Pr 23:21; Isa 28:1, 3), cut off (Joel 1:5), destroyed (Na 1:10), trodden under feet (Isa 28:1, 3), shame (Hab 2:16), death (Dt 21:20-21). Insatiable appetite of (Hab 2:5-6). Excluded from the kingdom (1Co 6:9-10). Punishment of (Dt 21:20-21).
See Drunkenness; Wine; Temperance; Abstinence.

DRUNKENNESS

Condemned:
Repugnancy of (Isa 28:7-8; 56:12; Hos 7:5, 14; Joel 1:5; 3:3; Am 2:8, 12; Mt 24:49; Lk 12:45). Mockery of (Ps 69:12; Pr 20:1). Consequences of (Pr 21:17; 23:21, 29-35; Isa 5:11, 22; 24:9-11; 28:7; Hos 4:11). Death penalty for (Dt 21:20-21; 29:19-20; Jer 25:27). Excludes from the kingdom of God (1Co 6:9-10; Gal 5:19-21).

Forbidden (1Sa 1:14; Pr 23:20, 31-32; 31:4-7; Lk 21:34; Ro 13:13; 1Co 11:21-30; Eph 5:18; 1Th 5:7-8; 1Pe 4:3). Woes denounced against (Isa 5:11-12, 22; 28:1, 3, 7-8; Am 6:1, 6; Na 1:10; Hab 2:15-16).

Figurative:
(Isa 28:8; 51:17, 21-23; 63:6; Jer 25:15-16, 27-28; 51:7-9; La 3:15; Eze 23:31-34; Hab 2:15-16).
See Abstinence; Drunkard; Sobriety; Wine.

Instances of:
Noah (Ge 9:21). Lot (Ge 19:33). Nabal (1Sa 25:36). Uriah (2Sa 11:13). Amnon (2Sa 13:28). Elah (1Ki 16:9). Ben-Hadad and his thirty-two confederate kings (1Ki 20:16). Xerxes (Est 1:10-11). Belshazzar (Da 5:1-6). Believers (1Co 11:21).

Falsely Accused of:
Hannah (1Sa 1:12-16). Jesus (Mt 11:19). The apostles (Ac 2:13-15).

DRUSILLA Daughter of Herod Agrippa I; married first to Azizus, king of Emesa; later to Felix, procurator of Judea (Ac 24:24-25).

DRY PLACES (Nu 20:2; 2Ki 3:9; Ps 68:6; Isa 1:30; Jer 14:3; 17:6).

DUKE NIV "chief." Of Edom (Ge 36:15-43; Ex 15:15; 1Ch 1:51-54). Of the Midianites (Jos 13:21).

DULCIMER NIV "pipes" (Da 3:5, 10, 15). *See Music, Instruments of.*

DUMAH (*silence, name of underworld*).
1. Son of Ishmael (Ge 25:14; 1Ch 1:30; Isa 21:11-12).
2. A city of Canaan assigned to Judah (Jos 15:52).

DUMB *See Mute.*

DUNG Laws were made regarding excrement of human beings and animals used in sacrifice (Dt 23:12-14; Ex 29:14; Lev 8:17). Dry dung was often used as fuel (Eze 4:12-15), also fertilizer (Isa 25:10; Lk 13:8).

DUNG GATE A gate in the Jerusalem wall that led out to the Valley of Hinnom where rubbish was dumped (Ne 3:14).

DUNGEON In prisons (Jer 38:6; La 3:53). *See Prison.*

DURA A plain of Babylon where Nebuchadnezzar set up his image (Da 3:1).

DUST Man made from (Ge 2:7; 3:19, 23; Ecc 3:20). Casting of, in anger (2Sa 16:13). Shaking from feet (Mt 10:14; Ac 13:51). Put on the head in mourning (Jos 7:6; 1Sa 4:12; 2Sa 1:2; 15:30; Job 2:12; 42:6).

DUTY
1. Tribute levied on foreign commerce by Solomon (1Ki 10:15).
2. Escape from, sought by Moses (Ex 3:11; 4:1, 10, 13; 6:12, 30), by Jonah (Jnh 1:1-15), by Ananias (Ac 9:13-14).

Of People to God:
To love (Dt 6:5; 11:1; 30:15-20; Jos 23:11; Ps 31:23; Mt 22:37; Lk 12:27). To obey (Dt 10:12-13; 30:15-20; Jos 22:5; Pr 23:26; Mt 12:50; 22:21; 23:23; Lk 17:10; Jn 14:15, 21; 15:14; Ac 4:19-20; 5:29).

Of People to People:
To love (Lev 19:18; Mt 19:19; 22:39; Mk 12:31; Jn 13:34; Ro 13:8-10; Gal 5:14; Jas 2:8). To help (Isa 58:6-7; Mt 25:34-46; Lk 10:23-36). To forgive (Mt 18:21-35; Lk 17:3-4; Eph 4:32; Col 3:13). To practice "the golden rule" toward (Mt 7:12). To respect a brother's conscience (Ro 14:1-23; 1Co 8:1-13). To restore a sinning brother (Gal 6:1-2).
See Commandments and Statutes, of God; Children; Husband; Minister, Duties of; Parents; Wife.

DWARFED Could not officiate at the altar (Lev 21:20).

DYEING Of fabric (Ex 25:5; 26:14; Isa 63:1; Eze 23:15).

DYING *See Death, Physical.*

DYSENTERY (Ac 28:8).

DYSPEPSIA *See Indigestion.*

E

EAGLE

General:
As food: Forbidden as food, classified as detestable (Lev 11:13; Dt 14:12). *See Birds.*
Species of: Osprey (Lev 11:18; Dt 14:17). Vulture (Job 15:23; Pr 30:17; Mic 1:16; Mt 24:28; Lk 17:37).
Flight of: The swift flight of, as an analogy of the swiftness of destruction to come (Dt 28:49; Jer 4:13; 48:40; 49:22; La 4:19). Its soaring capability (Job 39:27; Isa 40:31; Jer 49:22; Ob 4). Their graceful flight as a simile for various themes (Pr 23:5; Isa 40:31; Ob 4).
Care of young: Nest of (Dt 32:11; Job 39:27-30; Jer 49:16). Bears young on her wings (Dt 32:11). Life is renewed like an eagle's (Ps 103:5; Isa 40:31).

Figurative:
Of God's care (Ex 19:4; Dt 32:11). Of warriors (2Sa 1:23; Jer 4:13; 48:40; Hos 8:1). Of the swiftness of life (Job 9:26). Of renewed life (Isa 40:31).

Symbolic:
Of the glory of God (Eze 1:10; 10:14). An allegory, the "seed of the land" (Zedekiah) is planted by a "great eagle" (Nebuchadnezzar) and grows up to be a "spreading vine"; this spreading vine is then transplanted by another eagle (Hophra) (Eze 17:1-8). A lion with wings of an eagle representing the majesty and strength of Babylon (Da 7:4). Of redeemed man (Rev 4:7). Of the church (Rev 12:14).

EAR

Attentiveness:
To what God says, to what is right, to his voice, to his commands, and to keep all his decrees (Ex 15:26; 23:22; Dt 11:13; 15:5; 28:1; Jer 11:6; Mt 13:23; Lk 8:15; Ac 17:11). To a truth worthy of attention (Mt 11:15; 13:9, 43; Mk 4:23; Lk 14:35). To Jesus' words (Lk 19:48). A stringent demand for attention to the utterances of prophets who were inspired by the Spirit (Rev 2:7, 11, 29; 3:6, 13, 22; 13:9).

Blocked:
God will listen to the righteous, not to sinners (Ge 18:23-32; 1Sa 8; Ps 34:15-16; 145:18-19; Pr 15:29; Isa 59:1; 15:7; Jas 5:16-18; 1Jn 5:14-15). *See God, Access to; Righteous, Promises to; Wicked, Prayers of.*
The result of ignoring, the law (Nu 15:30-31; Dt 1:43-46; Pr 28:9; Isa 1:10-15; 24:4-13). Ignoring the Lord (1Sa 2:27-33; 8; Isa 65:12-15; 66:4; Zec 7:11-14; Lk 9:26; 2Ti 2:11-13; Heb 6:4-6; 2Pe 2:1). *See God, Rejected; Jesus the Christ, Rejected.* The result of ignoring the plight of the poor (Dt 15:7-11; Pr 21:13; 22:16, 22-23; 28:8; Isa 10:1-4; Eze 16:49-50; Zec 7:9-14; Jas 2:13-15). Hearing blocked by life's troubles (Mt 13:18-23, esp. 22). *See Sower.*
See Poor, Warning Against Neglect; Poor, Oppression of.
The inability of idols to hear (1Ki 18:22-39; Ps 115:4-8; 135:15-18; Isa 46:7; Jer 10:2-5; 1Co 8:4-6; 12:2). *See Idol; Idolatry, Folly of.*

Ceremonies:
Pierced as a sign of servitude (Ex 21:5-6; Dt 15:16-17). Blood put upon, in consecration of priests (Ex 29:20; Lev 8:23), in cleansing lepers (Lev 14:14, 25). *See Leprosy.* Anointed with oil in purifications (Lev 14:17, 28).

Deaf:
Hearing closed to prevent obedience and subsequent salvation (Jos 11:20; Isa 6:10; 63:17; Jn 12:37-41; Ro 9:10-18; 11:25). *See Deafness.* The Lord, in refusing to listen to a petition (Dt 1:45), is petitioned to hear and to not refuse to answer (1Ki 8:28-53, esp. vv. 28-30, 32, 34, 36, 39, 43, 45, 49, 52; 2Ki 19:16; Ne 1:6).

Fearful:
The nations, because of reports of what God had accomplished (Ex 15:13-16; Dt 2:24-25; Jos 2:8-9; 1Sa 4:6-9; Est 8:15-17; Ps 48:4-7), from the knowledge of God's majesty (Ps 99:1-3; 114:7-8; Eze 38:20). *See Fear of God.* Of hearing God speak (Ex 20:19; Dt 5:25; Heb 12:18-21). *See Voice, of God; Anthropomorphisms, Acts.* Israel, from reports of punishment (Dt 13:11; 17:12-13; 19:18-21; 1Ti 5:20). *See Punishment.*

Figurative:
Anthropomorphic uses of: (Ps 17:6; 39:12; 77:1; 80:1; 84:8).

Misguided:
The value of listening to instruction (Pr 1:8-9; 2:1-22; 3:1-2; 4; 5:1-6; 6:20-29; 7:1-5; 19:27; 22:17-19). *See Counsel; Instruction; Knowledge; Wisdom.*
Listening to the advice of fools (Pr 13:20; Ecc 7:5-6). *See Speaking, Speech, Foolish.*

Misunderstood:
Taking the words of others too seriously (Ecc 7:21-22). Those listening to Jesus' words from the cross (Mt 27:46-47; Mk 15:34-35). Those who heard the voice of God (Jn 12:29).

Quick to hear:
Listening carefully to what others say (Jas 1:19).

Rational:
Words are tested by hearing (Job 12:11; 34:3). Powerful presentation (Job 29:21-25; 32:11-12). God will teach men (Isa 54:13; Jer 31:33-34; Jn 6:45; 1Co 2:13; 1Th 4:9; 1Jn 2:26-27).

Refusal to listen:
A rebellious people (Eze 12:2; Zec 7:11-14). The Jews (Jn 8:43; 10:20; Ac 13:44-50). The Sanhedrin (Ac 7:57). Men will reject the truth and accept a lie (2Ti 4:2-4).

Unconcerned:
People are not concerned with the pleading of God by his Spirit or by his prophets (Ne 9:29-30; Zec 7:11-12). *See Holy Spirit, Sin Against; Holy Spirit, Withdrawn From Unrepentant Sinners.* Idols, are absolutely indifferent to the prayers of people (Ps 115:6).
Israel, with ears which are open yet unable to hear (Isa 6:9-10; 42:18-20; 43:8). Those not concerned to take Jesus' words seriously (Mt 7:26-27). The reason Jesus speaks in parables (Mt 13:13). Those who hear the word but do not do what it says (Jas 1:22-25).

Worthless:
The parable of the sower (Mt 13:20-22; Mk 4:16-19; Lk 8:13-14). John the Baptist and Herod (Mk 6:20). Paul, in Athens at the Areopagus (Ac 17:19, 32), before Felix (Ac 24:24-26), before Agrippa and Festus (Ac 26:1-29).

EAR OF GRAIN *See Grain.*

EARLY RAIN *See Rain.*

EARLY RISING

General references to:
To rise early (Ge 19:27; 26:31; Ex 8:20; 34:4; Jos 3:1; Jdg 6:38; 1Sa 5:4; 15:12; 17:20; 2Ch 20:20). Daybreak (Jos 6:15; 1Sa 9:26;

Ps 46:5; 57:8; Da 6:19; Mk 16:2; Lk 24:22). Prior to daybreak (Ru 3:14; Pr 31:15). Morning (Ps 90:14; 101:8). *See Morning.*

To do evil: (Ex 32:6; Nu 14:40; Job 24:14; Isa 5:11).

EARNEST A pledge or token (Ps 86:17). The Spirit, as a guarantee of the future redemption of our bodies (Ro 8:23), of our inheritance (Ro 8:23; Eph 1:13-14), of the promise to come (2Co 1:22). *See Inheritance; Token, 1.*

EARNESTNESS An intense desire which results in repentance, produced by godly sorrow (2Co 7:11). Sincerity in your love (2Co 8:7-8). *See Sincerity; Zeal.*

EARRING

As an offering:
Offering of, for the golden calf (Ex 32:2-3). As a wave offering for the tabernacle (Ex 35:22). As an offering to the Lord to make atonement (Nu 31:50).

Types of:
Gold (Ex 32:2-3; Jdg 8:24; Pr 25:12). Gold studded with silver (SS 1:11).

Worn:
By the Israelites (Ex 32:2-3; Jdg 8:24). By Ishmaelites, as a cultural habit (Jdg 8:24). For idolatrous purposes (Ge 35:4; Isa 3:19).

EARTH

Creation of:
By God (Ge 1:1; Ex 20:11; 31:17; 2Ki 19:15; 2Ch 2:12; Ne 9:6; Job 38:4; Ps 90:2; 102:25; 104:5; 115:15; 124:8; 146:5-6; Pr 8:22-26; Isa 37:16; 45:18; 66:1-2; Jer 10:12; 27:5; 32:17; 51:15; Ac 14:15; Heb 11:3; 2Pe 3:5; Rev 10:6; 14:7). By Christ (Jn 1:3, 10; Heb 1:10). Primitive condition of (Ge 1:2, 6-7; Job 26:7; 38:4-7; Ps 104:5-9; Pr 3:19-20; Isa 40:22; 45:18; 48:13; Jer 4:23-26). *See Creation; God, Creator.* Created to be inhabited (Isa 45:18). By design (Isa 45:18).
Early divisions of (Ge 10-11; Dt 32:8; Ps 74:17).

Belongs to:
The Lord (Ex 9:29; 19:5; Dt 10:14; 1Sa 2:8; Ps 24:1; 50:12; Isa 66:1; 1Co 10:26). God controls (Job 9:6; Rev 7:1). God's footstool (Isa 66:1; La 2:1; Mt 5:35; Ac 7:49).

Cursed:
Cursed by God (Ge 3:17-19; 5:29; Ro 8:19-22).

Future of:
Perpetuity of (Ge 49:26; Dt 33:15; Ps 78:69; 104:5; Ecc 1:4; Hab 3:6). Will be judged (1Sa 2:10; Ps 96:13; 98:9). Destruction of, foretold (Ps 102:25-27; Isa 24:19-20; 51:6; Mt 5:17-18; 24:3, 6, 14, 29-31, 35-42; Mk 13:24-37; Lk 21:26-36; 2Pe 3:10-13; Rev 20:11; 21:1). A new earth (Isa 65:17; 66:22; 2Pe 3:13; Rev 21:1).

Residence of mankind: (Ps 115:16).

EARTHENWARE *See Pottery.*

EARTHQUAKES (*shaking, trembling*). (Job 9:6; Ps 18:7; 46:2-3; 104:32; Jer 4:24). *See Mountain.* As judgments (Ps 18:15; 60:2; Isa 13:13; 24:18-20; 29:6; Na 1:5; Rev 6:12-14; 11:13; 16:18, 20). *See Judgment.* Prophecies of (Eze 38:19-20; Zec 14:4; Mt 24:7; Mk 13:8; Lk 21:11; Rev 11:19).

Instances of:
At Sinai (Ex 19:18; Ps 68:8; 77:18; 114:4-7; Heb 12:26). When Korah, Dathan, and Abiram were swallowed up (Nu 16:31-34). When Jonathan and his armor-bearer attacked the garrison at Gibeah (1Sa 14:15). When the Lord revealed himself to Elijah in the still small voice (1Ki 19:11). In Canaan, in the days of Uzziah, king of Judah (Am 1:1; Zec 14:5). At the crucifixion of Jesus (Mt 27:51). At the resurrection of Jesus (Mt 28:2). When Paul and Silas were in prison at Philippi (Ac 16:26).

EAST

An Important Direction for God:
Glory of God from (Eze 43:2). Angel from (Rev 7:2).

An Important Direction for People:
The Garden of Eden (Ge 2:8; 3:24). *See Garden.* An east wind (Ge 41:6, 23, 27; Ex 10:13; 14:21; Job 15:2; 27:21; 38:24; Ps 48:7; 78:26; Isa 27:8; Jer 18:17; Eze 17:10; 19:12; 27:26; Hos 12:1; 13:15; Hab 1:9). *See Wind.* A significant direction for the Hebrews (Ex 38:13; Nu 3:38; 10:5; Eze 10:19; 11:23; 43:2, 4). God has removed our transgressions (Ps 103:12). Faces toward in worship (Eze 8:16).

People of:
Eastern people (Ge 29:1; Jdg 6:3, 33). Eastern people had a special reputation for wisdom (1Ki 4:30; Mt 2:1-12). "People of the east" denotes Arab groups who accompanied the Midianites and the Amalekites in attacking Israel (Job 1:3; Jer 49:28; Eze 25:4, 10). Kings of (Rev 16:12).

EAST WIND Hot, dry wind coming from the S and SE of Israel (Jer 4:11; Hos 13:15), destructive (Ge 41:6; Ps 48:7; Eze 17:10; 27:26), used as a means of salvation for Israel by God (Ex 14:21), used as a means of judgment by God (Isa 27:8; Jer 18:17; Jnh 4:8).

EASTER The day on which the church celebrates the resurrection of Jesus Christ. KJV "Easter" should be "Passover" as in NIV (Ac 12:4). *See Feasts; Passover.*

EASTERN SEA *See Dead Sea.*

EATING The host acting as waiter (Ge 18:8). Favored guests served an extra portion (Ge 43:34). *See Hospitality.* Sitting at table (Ex 32:6). *See Table.* Table used in (Jdg 1:7). Reclining on couches (Am 6:4, 7; Mt 26:7, 20; Mk 14:3, 18; Jn 12:2; 13:23). *See Couch.* Washing before (Mt 15:2).
See Feasts; Food; Gluttony.

EBAL
1. A Horite (Ge 36:23; 1Ch 1:40).

2. A mountain of Ephraim located N and directly opposite Mt. Gerizim. These two mountains form the two sides of an important E-W pass. Upon entering the land of Canaan, after the time of Moses, the Hebrews were to confirm their covenant with Yahweh. This required that half of the tribes were to be on Mt. Ebal to proclaim the blessings, the other half of the tribes were to stand on Mt. Ebal to proclaim the curses of the covenant with the ark of the covenant between them (Dt 11:29; 27:12-13; Jos 8:33). Altar built on (Dt 27:4-6; Jos 8:30). They were to sacrifice a fellowship offering there, eating and rejoicing in the presence of the Lord (Dt 27:7). Traditionally these were called peace offerings (Dt 27:7, ftn). All the words of this covenant were to be written very clearly on the stones of the altar that they set up (Dt 27:8). *See Gerizim.*

3. Son of Joktan (1Ch 1:22). *See Obal.*

EBED (*servant*).

1. Father of Gaal, who led the rebellion against Abimelech at Shechem (Jdg 9:26-45).

2. The son of Jonathan, one of those who returned to Israel with Ezra (Ezr 8:6).

3. The title *Ebed* was adopted, apparently by David, from an Akkadian practice, which was also used in Edom and Ammon. It was a designation of the class of court officials as distinguished from the older institution of tribal elders. In Ebed-Melech it becomes a proper name.

EBED-MELECH (*servant of Melek [king]*). An Ethiopian eunuch in Zedekiah's court who interceded on Jeremiah's behalf before King Zedekiah to have Jeremiah pulled out of a mud filled cistern (Jer 38:1-13). The prophecy concerning Ebed-Melech promised that he would survive the destruction of the kingdom as a reward for his efforts (Jer 39:16-18).

EBENEZER (*stone of help*). A town of Ephraim near Aphek where the Israelites fought two battles with the Philistines and were defeated, losing the ark in the second battle (1Sa 4:1-11; 5:1). Later, after defeating the Philistines, the Israelites erected a memorial stone, naming it Ebenezer (1Sa 7:12).

EBER (*[regions] beyond [the river]*, or source of the word *Hebrew*).

1. The probable founder of the Hebrew race (Ge 10:21-25; 11:14-17; 1Ch 1:18-19, 25; Lk 3:35). Prophecy concerning (Nu 24:24). Perhaps Eber in this passage should be understood not as a proper name but as the word for "region beyond" (here, beyond the Euphrates), which is the same as the name Eber in Hebrew.

2. A Gadite (1Ch 5:13).

3. A Benjamite (1Ch 8:12).

4. Another family of the tribe of Benjamin (1Ch 8:22).

5. A postexilic priest (Ne 12:20).

6. Father of Peleg and Joktan (Lk 3:35).

EBEZ A town given by lot to Issachar (Jos 19:20).

EBIASAPH (*[my] father has gathered*). A son of Korah (1Ch 6:23, 37; 9:19; 26:1). *See Korah, 4.* Abiasaph is an alternate form (Ex 6:24). Called also Asaph (1Ch 26:1). *See Asaph.*

EBONY A highly prized core wood of a tree imported from S India, Ceylon, and perhaps Ethiopia. It was valued by the Egyptians, Phoenicians, Babylonians, Greeks, and Romans for its use, along with ivory, in fine furniture, vessels, and turned objects. It was also used in the Near East for idols. *See Image; Idol; Idolatry; Temple, Idolatrous.* Merchandise in (Eze 27:15).

EBRONAH *See Abronah.*

ECBATANA (perhaps *place of gathering*). A city located at the foot of the Alvand Mountain which is now Hamadan. The capital of Media, where during the reign of Darius I, a copy of Cyrus's decree was found which authorized the rebuilding of the temple in Jerusalem (Ezr 6:2, 3-12). *See Cyrus; Darius; Medes; Persia; Temple, The Second.*

ECCLESIASTES

Author and Date:

Several passages strongly suggest that King Solomon is the author (1:1, 12, 16; 2:4-9; 7:26-29; 12:9; cf. 1Ki 2:9; 3:12; 4:29-34; 5:12; 10:1-8). On the other hand, the writer's title ("Teacher," Hebrew *Qoheleth*), his unique style of Hebrew and his attitude toward rulers (suggesting that of a subject rather than a monarch—see, e.g., 4:1-2; 5:8-9; 8:2-4; 10:20) may point to another person and a later period.

Outline:

I. Author (1:1).

II. Theme: The Meaninglessness of Man's Efforts on Earth Apart From God (1:2).

III. Introduction: The Profitlessness of Working to Accumulate Things to Achieve Happiness (1:3-11).

IV. Discourse, Part 1: In Spite of Life's Apparent Enigmas and Meaninglessness, It is to be Enjoyed as a Gift From God (1:12-11:6).

V. Discourse, Part 2: Since Old Age and Death Will Soon Come, Man Should Enjoy Life in His Youth, Remembering That God Will Judge (11:7-12:7).

VI. Theme Repeated (12:8).

VII. Conclusion: Reverently Trust in and Obey God (12:9-14).

ECCLESIASTICISM Jewish, rebuked by Jesus (Mt 9:10-13; 23:2-35), to be overthrown (Mt 21:19-20, 28-44). Arrogance of (Mt 12:2-8; 23:4). Traditional rules of the Jewish (Mt 15:1-20; Mk 7:2-23). *See Church, The Body of Believers; Commandments and Statutes, of Men; Minister, False and Corrupt; Usurpation, in Ecclesiastical Affairs.*

ECLIPSE Of the sun and moon (Isa 13:10; 60:19; Eze 32:7-8; Joel 2:10, 31; 3:15; Am 8:9; Mic 3:6; Mt 24:29; Mk 13:24; Ac 2:20; Rev 6:12; 8:12). *See Sun; Moon.*

ECOLOGY Mankind created to care for the earth (Ge 1:28, 2:15; Ps 8:6-8; 115:16). The land was to enjoy rest every seven

years (Lev 25:1-7); the land enjoyed its rest during Israel's exile (2Ch 36:20-21). Animals were to rest on the Sabbath (Ex 20:10). Fruit trees were not to be cut down in war time (Dt 20:19-20). A bird and its young were not to be caught together (Dt 22:6-7). Babylon judged for violence to the forests of Lebanon and its animals (Hab 2:17 w Isa 14:8).

ECONOMICS Political (Ge 41:33-57). Household (Pr 24:27; 31:10-31; Ecc 11:4-6; Jn 6:12-13). *See Family; Frugality; Industry.*

ECONOMY *See Economics; Government.*

ECUMENICISM (*the inhabited earth*). A movement among Christian religious groups—Protestant, Eastern Orthodox, Roman Catholic—to bring about a closer unity in work and organization. The word is not found in the NIV, but backing for the movement may be found in John 17 where Jesus prays for the unity of his church.

ED KJV transliterates the name of the altar erected by the tribes Reuben, Gad, and Manasseh at the fords of the Jordan (Jos 22:34); NIV "Witness."

EDAR *See Eder.*

EDEN (*paradise, delight,* possibly *flat land*).

1. The Garden of Eden (Ge 2:8-17; 3:23-24; 4:16; Isa 51:3; Eze 28:13; 31:9, 16, 18; 36:35; Joel 2:3).

2. Gods of (2Ki 19:12; Isa 37:12; Am 1:5).

3. A Gershonite (2Ch 29:12).

4. A Levite (2Ch 31:15).

5. A marketplace of costly merchandise (Eze 27:23-24).

EDER (*flock*).

1. A tower near Ephrath where Jacob encamped on the way back to Canaan (Ge 35:21).

2. A city of Judah (Jos 15:21).

3. A son of Beriah, grandson of Shaharaim, a Benjamite (1Ch 8:15).

4. A grandson of Merari (1Ch 23:23; 24:30).

EDICT A public proclamation, written and sealed with the king's signet and publicly read (Ezr 6:11-12; Est 2:8; 8:8-13; 9:1, 13). Penalties were severe for violating a Persian edict (Ezr 6:11). Moses' parents are listed as an example of those who were not afraid to transgress the royal edict (Heb 11:23).

EDIFICATION, EDIFY, EDIFYING (Latin *to build up*). The root of this Greek word is in various words and compound words in the NT, i.e., build (Mt 23:29; 26:61), building (Jn 2:20), builder (1Co 3:10; Heb 3:3-4), builds up (1Co 8:1), strengthen (1Co 8:10), edified (1Co 14:5, 17), edification (Ro 14:19).

Paul uses the word group frequently but never in the literal sense of "building" a building. He uses it often in the metaphorical sense of "building" or "building up" the church, and of "building up" fellow believers. Paul refers to the church as a building (1Co 3:9; Eph 2:21), and of building the church upon the foundation that he and the apostles and the prophets laid (1Co 3:10, 12, 14; Eph 2:20).

Paul uses the words more frequently in the sense of "strengthening, unifying, making for peace." Christians are to build up each other in this sense (1Th 5:11). It is primarily love that "builds up" (1Co 8:1).

EDOM (*red*).

1. A name of Esau, possibly on account of his being covered with red hair (Ge 25:25, 30; 36:1, 8, 19).

2. A name of the land occupied by the descendants of Esau. It extended from the Gulf of Aqabah to the Red Sea, and was also called Idumea (Ge 32:3; 36:16-17, 21; Jer 40:11).

Prophecies concerning (Jer 25:21-23; 27:1-11; Da 11:41). Noted for its wise men (Ob 8). Sins of (Ob 10-14). Wilderness of (2Ki 3:8).

See Edomite(s).

Figurative of the foes of Zion (Isa 63:1).

EDOMITE(S) (*red*). Called also Edom. Land of (Ge 32:3; Dt 2:4-5, 12). Descendants of Esau (Ge 36). Rulers of (Ge 36:9-43; Ex 15:15; 1Ch 1:51-54). Kings of (Ge 36:31-39; Nu 20:14; 1Ch 1:43-50; Eze 32:29; Am 2:1).

Prophecies concerning (Ge 25:23; 27:29, 37-40; Nu 24:18; Isa 11:14; 21:11-12; 34; 63:1-6; Jer 9:25-26; 27:1-11; 49:7-22; La 4:21-22; Eze 25:12-14; 32:29-30; 36:5; Joel 3:19; Am 1:11-12; 9:12; Ob 1-21; Mal 1:2-5).

Protected by divine command from desolation by the Israelites (Dt 2:4-6), from being held in abhorrence by the Israelites (Dt 23:7). Children of the third generation might be received into the congregation of Israel (Dt 23:8). Refuse the Israelites passage through their country (Nu 20:18-21). Saul makes war against (1Sa 14:47). Garrisons of (2Sa 8:14). David conquers (1Ki 11:14-16; 1Ch 18:11-13), writes battle songs concerning his conquest of (Ps 60:8-9; 108:9-10). Ruled by a deputy king (1Ki 22:47). Become confederates of Jehoshaphat (2Ki 3:9, 26). Revolt in the days of Jehoram (2Ki 8:20-22; 2Ch 21:8-10). Amaziah, king of Judah, invades the territory of Edom, defeating ten thousand Edomites (2Ki 14:7, 10; 2Ch 25:11-12; 28:17). The Lord delivers the army of, into the hands of Jehoshaphat (2Ch 20:20, 23). A Jewish prophet in Babylon denounces (Ps 137:7; Eze 25:12-14, 35). Join Babylon in the war against the Israelites (Eze 35:5; Am 1:9-11; Ob 11-16).

EDREI (*strong*).

1. A chief city of Og, king of Bashan (Dt 1:4; Jos 12:4). Assigned to Manasseh (Jos 13:12, 31). Located c. ten miles NE of Ramoth-Gilead.

2. A city of Naphtali, the location is unknown (Jos 19:37).

EDUCATION *See Instruction; Teachers; School.*

EGG (*whiteness*). (Job 6:6; Lk 11:12). Appears also in the plural (Dt 22:6; Job 39:14; Isa 10:14).

EGLAH (*heifer*). The wife of David (2Sa 3:5; 1Ch 3:3).

EGLAIM A city on the border of Moab (Isa 15:8).

EGLATH SHELISHIYAH (possibly *the third Eglath*). A town near Zoar mentioned in prophetic oracles of judgment on Moab (Isa 15:5; Jer 48:34).

EGLON (*circle* ISBE; *young bull* KB).

1. A city of Canaan located between Gaza and Lachish (Jos 10:3, 5, 23), captured by Joshua (Jos 10:36-37; 12:12), assigned to Judah (Jos 15:39).

2. The king of Moab who captured Jericho (the City of Palms) from the Israelites as a judgment against them, controlling it for eighteen years (Jdg 3:12-14). Eglon was assassinated by Ehud, a judge, because the Israelites cried out to the Lord (Jdg 3:15-23).

EGOTISM *See Conceit.*

EGYPT

The Country of:

Fertility of (Ge 13:10). Imports of (Ge 37:25, 36). Productions of (Nu 11:5; Ps 78:47; Pr 7:16; Isa 19:5-10). Irrigation employed in (Dt 11:10). Called, Rahab which is the poetic name for Egypt (Ps 87:4; 89:10), the land of Ham (Ps 105:23; 106:21-22). Exports of (Pr 7:16; Eze 27:7), of horses (1Ki 10:28-29). Limits of (Eze 29:10).

Abraham dwells in (Ge 12:10-20; 13:1). The king acquires title to land of (Ge 47:18-26). Joseph's captivity in and subsequent rule over. *See Joseph, 1.* Israelites in bondage in. *See Israel, Israelites.* Plagues in. *See Plague.* Civil war in (Isa 19:2). Overflowed by the Nile (Am 8:8; 9:5). Joseph takes Jesus to (Mt 2:13-20).

Prophecies against (Ge 15:13-14; Isa 19; 20:2-6; 45:14; Jer 9:25-26; 43:8-13; 44:30; 46; Eze 29-32; Hos 8:13; Joel 3:19; Zec 10:11).

See Egyptians.

Famine in (Ge 41; Ac 7:11). *See Famine.* Magi of (Ge 41:8; Ex 7:11; 1Ki 4:30; Ac 7:22). *See Magi.* Priests of (Ge 41:45; 47:22). Army of destroyed in the Red Sea (Ex 14:5-31; Isa 43:17). *See Army.* Armies of (Ex 14:7; Isa 31:1). Idols of (Eze 20:7-8).

River, or Brook of:

Perhaps identical with Shihor. *See River of Egypt; Shihor.* A small stream flowing into the Mediterranean Sea, the western boundary of the land promised to the Israelites (Ge 15:18; Nu 34:5; Jos 13:3; 15:4; 1Ki 8:65; 2Ki 24:7; Isa 27:12; Eze 47:19; 48:28).

Symbolic: (Rev 11:8).

EGYPTIANS Descendants of the Mizraim (Ge 10:6, 13-14, ftn). Hospitality of, to Abraham (Ge 12:10-20). Slaves bought by (Ge 37:36). The art of embalming the dead practiced by (Ge 50:2-3, 26). Oppressed the Israelites (Ex 1-2). Refuse to release the Israelites (Ex 5-10). Judged by plagues (Ex 7-12; Ps 78:43-51), firstborn of destroyed (Ex 12:29; Ps 78:51; 105:36; 136:10). Sent the Israelites away (Ex 12:31-42). Army pursued the Israelites, and was destroyed (Ex 14:5-31; Ps 106:7; Heb 11:29). Wisdom of (1Ki 4:30).

Refused to eat with the Hebrews (Ge 43:32). Abhorred shepherds (Ge 46:34). Eligible to membership in Israelite congregation in the third generation (Dt 23:7-8). Alliances with, without first consulting God, forbidden to the Israelites (Isa 30:1-5; 31:1-3; 36:6; Eze 17:15). Intermarry with the Israelites (1Ki 3:1). Invasions of Israel: Under Shishak (1Ki 14:25-26; 2Ch 12:2-9), Pharaoh Neco (2Ki 23:29-35; 2Ch 35:20-24; 36:2-4). Aid the Israelites against the Chaldeans (Jer 37:5-11). An enthusiastic Egyptian instigated a rebellion against the Roman government (Ac 21:38).

Conversion of, foretold (Isa 19:18). Prophecies of dispersion and restoration of (Eze 29:12-16; 30:23-26).

See Egypt.

EHI (*my brother [is exalted]*). A son of Benjamin (Ge 46:21).

EHUD (*united*).

1. A Benjamin judge, the assassin of Eglon (Jdg 3:15-30; 1Ch 8:6). *See Eglon, 2.*

2. Son of Bilhan (1Ch 7:10).

EKED *See Beth Eked.*

EKER (possibly *offspring*). The son of Ram, part of the postexilic clan of Jerahmeel (1Ch 2:27).

EKRON, EKRONITES (perhaps *barren place* or *fertile place*). One of the five chief cities of the Philistines (Jos 13:3). Conquered and allotted to Judah (Jos 15:11, 45; Jdg 1:18). Allotted to Dan (Jos 19:43). The ark of God taken to (1Sa 5:10). Temple of Baal-Zebub, the god of Ekron, at (2Ki 1:2). Prophecies against (Jer 25:20; Am 1:8; Zep 2:4; Zec 9:5).

EL (*God; Mighty One*). A generic word for God in the Semitic languages. The chief Canaanite god was El. The God of Israel is usually referred to in the plural form, *Elohim*, or in compound names, as in the following articles. *See Elohim.*

EL-BERITH (*a god of a covenant*). An alternate name for the god worshiped at Shechem, in whose temple some of the people of Shechem took refuge when Abimelech destroyed the city (Jdg 9:46). *See Baal-Berith.*

EL BETHEL (*God [El] of Bethel*). A name given by Jacob to Luz because God there revealed Himself to him (Ge 35:7).

EL ELOHE ISRAEL (*God, the God of Israel*). Name of an altar erected by Jacob near Shechem (Ge 33:20).

EL PARAN (*tree of Paran*). A place in the wilderness of Paran (Ge 14:6).

EL SHADDAI (*God of mountains* or *God who is self-sufficient* KB or in older etymology *God of breasts*). Translated "God Almighty" in the NIV following the NT rendering of *Shaddai* by *pantokrator*. The name by which God appeared to Abraham, Isaac, and Jacob (Ex 6:3).
See God, Names of; Shaddai.

ELA The father of Shimei, one of Solomon's district governors (1Ki 4:18).

ELAH (*a species of a mighty tree*).
1. A chief of Edom (Ge 36:41).
2. The valley (valley of the terebinth), in which David killed Goliath (1Sa 17:2, 19; 21:9).
3. The king of Israel, son of Baasha; killed by Zimri (1Ki 16:8-10).
4. The father of Hoshea, the last king of Israel (2Ki 15:30; 17:1; 18:1, 9).
5. The son of Caleb (1Ch 4:15).
6. The Benjamite, son of Uzzi (1Ch 9:8).
7. See Ela.

ELAM (*highland*).
1. The son of Shem (Ge 10:22; 1Ch 1:17).
2. The son of Shashak (1Ch 8:24).
3. The son of Meshelemiah (1Ch 26:3).
4. The ancestor of a family which returned from the Exile (Ezr 2:7; Ne 7:12).
5. Another ancestor of a returned family (Ezr 2:31; Ne 7:34).
6. The father of two sons returned from the Exile (Ezr 8:7).
7. The ancestor of a man who married a foreign woman (Ezr 10:2, 26).
8. A chief who sealed a covenant with Nehemiah (Ne 10:14).
9. A priest who took part in the dedication of the wall (Ne 12:42).
10. A country situated on the E side of the Tigris opposite Babylonia; was one of the earliest civilizations; figures prominently in Babylonian and Assyrian history. Some of its people were brought to Samaria by the Assyrians (Ezr 4:9-10). Elamites at Jerusalem on the Day of Pentecost (Ac 2:9).

ELAMITES (*highland*). Descendants of Shem (Ge 10:22). They were present at Pentecost (Ac 2:9).

ELASAH (*God has fashioned*).
1. The son of Pashhur the priest, and one of those with foreign wives (Ezr 10:22).
2. The son of Shaphan and one of Zedekiah's emissaries to Nebuchadnezzar who took a letter to the exiles in Babylon for Jeremiah (Jer 29:3).

ELATH (*grove of large trees*). A city on the coast of Edom situated at the head of the Gulf of Arabah (Dt 2:8; 1Ki 9:26; 2Ch 8:17). The conquest of, by the Edomites (2Ki 16:6), by Uzziah (2Ch 26:1-2).

ELDAAH (*God [El] is [my] desire*). A descendant of Abraham (Ge 25:4; 1Ch 1:33).

ELDAD (*beloved of God [El]; possibly Dadi [pagan god] is god*). One of Moses' 70 elders (Nu 11:24-29).

ELDERS

In the Mosaic System: *See Elders, Council of; Government, Mosaic.*

In the NT Church:
Received gifts on behalf of church (Ac 11:29-30). Ordained (Ac 14:23; Tit 1:5-9). Overseers of the church (Ac 15:1-29; 16:4-5; 20:17, 28-32; 21:18; 1Ti 5:17-19; 1Pe 5:1-5). Performed ecclesiastical duties (1Ti 4:14; Jas 5:14-15).

John's Vision of the Twenty-four Elders:
(Rev 4:4, 10; 5:5-6, 8, 11, 14; 7:11, 13; 11:16; 14:3; 19:4).
See Bishop; Church, Government of the Christian Church; Deacon; Overseer.

ELDERS, COUNCIL OF

Described:
Chosen elders of the nation, vested with representative, judicial, and executive authority (Ex 4:29; 5:15, 19; 6:14-25; 12:21; Nu 11:16-30). Called the council (Nu 16:2; Mk 15:43); council of the elders (Ps 107:32; Lk 22:66); elders of Israel (Ex 3:16, 18), of Judah (1Sa 30:26), of the people (Ex 19:7), of the community (Lev 4:15), of the Jews (Ezr 5:5); Sanhedrin (Mt 5:22; 26:59; Ac 4:15; 5:21-41).
Closely associated with Moses and subsequent leaders (Ex 3:16-18; 4:29; 12:21; 17:5-6; 18:12; 19:7; 24:1, 14; Nu 16:25; Dt 5:23; 27:1; 29:10; 31:9, 28; Jos 7:6; 8:10, 33; 23:2; 24:1; Jdg 11:5-11; Ac 5:17-18, 21). Made confession of sin in behalf of the nation (Lev 4:15; 9:1).
A similar council existed among the Egyptians (Ge 50:7), the Midianites and Moabites (Nu 22:4, 7-8), the Gibeonites (Jos 9:11).

Events Relating to:
Demands a king (1Sa 8:4-10, 19-22). Saul pleads to be honored before (1Sa 15:30). Chooses David as king (2Sa 3:17-21; 5:3; 1Ch 11:3). Closely associated with David (2Sa 12:17; 1Ch 15:25; 21:16). Joins Absalom in his usurpation (2Sa 17:4). David rebukes (2Sa 19:11). Assists Solomon at the dedication of the temple (1Ki 8:1-3; 2Ch 5:2-4). Counsels King Rehoboam (1Ki 12:6-8, 13). Counsels King Ahab (1Ki 20:7-8). Josiah assembles, to hear the law of the Lord (2Ki 23:1; 2Ch 34:29, 31).
Legislates with Ezra in reforming certain marriages with the Gentiles (Ezr 10:8-14). Legislates in later times (Mt 15:2, 7-9; Mk 7:1-13). Sits as a court (Jer 26:10-24). Constitutes, with priests and scribes, a court for the trial of both civil and ecclesiastical causes (Mt 21:23; 26:3-5, 57-68; 27:1-2; Mk 8:31; 14:53-65; 15:1; Lk 22:52-71; Ac 4:1-21; 6:12-15). Seeks counsel from prophets (Eze

8:1; 14:1; 20:1, 3). Corrupt (1Ki 21:8-14; Eze 8:11-12; Mt 26:14-15; 27:3-4).

ELEAD (*God [El] has testified*). A descendant of Ephraim (1Ch 7:21).

ELEADAH (*God [El] has adorned*). The son of Ephraim (1Ch 7:20).

ELEALEH (*God [El] is high*). A city in Transjordan, rebuilt by the tribe of Reuben (Nu 32:3, 37). Repossessed by the Moabites (Isa 15:4; 16:9; Jer 48:34).

ELEASAH (*God [El] has fashioned*).
1. A person or family of the clan of Jerahmeel of the tribe of Judah (1Ch 2:39-40).
2. A member of the tribe of Benjamin, descended from Saul (1Ch 8:37; 9:43).

ELEAZAR (*God [El] is a help*).
1. The son of Aaron (Ex 6:23; 28:1). He married a daughter of Putiel, who bore him Phinehas (Ex 6:25). After the death of Nadab and Abihu he is made the chief of the tribe of Levi (Nu 3:32). The duties of (Nu 4:16).
He succeeds Aaron as the high priest (Nu 20:26, 28; Dt 10:6). Assists Moses in the census (Nu 26:63). With Joshua, divides Israel (Nu 34:17). Death and burial of (Jos 24:33). Descendants of (1Ch 24:1-19).
2. An inhabitant of Kiriath Jearim who attended the ark (1Sa 7:1-2).
3. Son of Dodai the Ahohite, and one of David's three mighty men (2Sa 23:9-10, 13; 1Ch 11:12).
4. A Merarite Levite (1Ch 23:21-22; 24:28).
5. The son of Phinehas (Ezr 8:33; Ne 12:42).
6. A returned Israelite exile (Ezr 10:25).
7. The great-grandfather of Joseph, the husband of Mary (Mt 1:15).

ELECT (*chosen*). Those chosen by God for some special purpose (Ps 106:23; Isa 43:10; 45:4). Among the elect mentioned in Scripture are Moses, the Israelites, Christ, the angels, Christ's disciples.

ELECTION By grace (Mt 22:14; Jn 15:16; 17:6; Ro 11:5; Eph 1:4; 2:10; 2Th 2:13; 1Pe 2:9).
Of Israel (Dt 7:6; Isa 45:4). Of rulers (Ne 11:1). Of Christ as Messiah (Isa 42:1; 1Pe 2:6). Of ministers (Lk 6:13; Ac 9:15). Of good angels (1Ti 5:21). Of churches (1Pe 5:13).
See Chosen; Elect; Predestination.

ELECTIONEERING By Absalom (2Sa 15:1-6). Adonijah (1Ki 1:7). *See Candidate.*

ELEGY A song of sorrow. By David, on Saul and Jonathan (2Sa 1:17, 19-27), on Abner (2Sa 3:33-34).
See Lamentations, Book of; Poetry.

ELEMENTS (*rows, series, alphabet, first principles of a science, physical elements, heavenly bodies, planets, personal cosmic powers*). Heathen deities and practices (Gal 4:3, 9), rudiments (Col 2:8, 20), first principles (Heb 5:12). *See Basic Principles of this World.*

ELEPH *See Haeleph.*

ELEPHANT The Hebrew *behemoth* may be the elephant or hippopotamus (Job 40:15, ftn). *See Ivory.*

ELEVEN, THE The eleven apostles who remained after the defection of Judas (Mk 16:14; Lk 24:9, 33; Ac 2:14).

ELHANAN (*God [El] is gracious*).
1. The son of Dodo, one of David's heroes (2Sa 23:24; 1Ch 11:26).
2. A distinguished warrior in the time of David who killed Lahmi the brother of Goliath the Gittite (1Ch 20:5), or the Bethlehemite who killed Goliath (2Sa 21:19). The two accounts may be harmonized if an early copyist of Samuel misread "Lahmi the brother of" as "the Bethlehemite."

ELI (*Yahweh is exalted* IDB; *God [El] is exalted* KB). Misjudges and rebukes Hannah (1Sa 1:13-14). His benediction upon Hannah (1Sa 1:17-18; 2:20). Officiates when Samuel is presented at the tabernacle (1Sa 1:24-28). High priest (1Sa 1:25; 2:11; 1Ki 2:27). Judge of Israel (1Sa 4:18, ftn). Indulgent of his corrupt sons (1Sa 2:22-25, 29; 3:11-14). His concern for the ark (1Sa 4:11-18). Death of (1Sa 4:18).
Prophecies of judgments upon his house (1Sa 2:27-36; 3:11-14, w 1Ki 2:27).

ELI, ELI, LAMA SABACHTHANI *See Eloi, Eloi, Lama Sabachthani.*

ELIAB (*God [El] is [my] father*).
1. Son of Helon (Nu 1:9; 2:7; 7:24, 29; 10:16).
2. A Reubenite, progenitor of Dathan and Abiram (Nu 16:1, 12; 26:8-9; Dt 11:6).
3. The son of Jesse, and eldest brother of David (1Sa 16:6; 17:13, 28; 1Ch 2:13). Elihu, an officer over the tribe of Judah (1Ch 27:18).
4. An ancestor of Samuel (1Ch 6:27). Called also Elihu in the parallel genealogies (1Sa 1:1), and Eliel (1Ch 6:34).
5. A hero of the tribe of Gad (1Ch 12:9).
6. A Levite, a gatekeeper and musician (1Ch 15:18, 20; 16:5).

ELIADA (*God [El] knows*).
1. The son of David (2Sa 5:16; 1Ch 3:8).
2. Father of Rezon (1Ki 11:23).
3. Benjamite general (2Ch 17:17).

ELIAHBA (*God [El] hides*). The Shaalbonite, one of David's heroes (2Sa 23:32; 1Ch 11:33).

ELIAKIM (*God [El] establishes*).
1. The master of Hezekiah's household; sent by the king to negotiate with invading Assyrians (2Ki 18:17-37; Isa 36:1-22), and then to seek help of Isaiah the prophet (Isa 37:1-7).
2. The original name of King Jehoiakim (2Ki 23:34; 2Ch 36:4). *See Jehoiakim.*
3. Priest (Ne 12:41).
4. The ancestor of Jesus (Mt 1:13).
5. Another and earlier ancestor of Jesus (Lk 3:30).

ELIAM (*God [El] is [my] kinsman*).
1. The father of Bathsheba (2Sa 11:3). Called Ammiel (1Ch 3:5).
2. One of David's mighty men known as the "Thirty" (2Sa 23:34). Called Ahijah (1Ch 11:36).

ELIAS *See Elijah.*

ELIASAPH (*God [El] has added*).
1. The son of Deuel, a leader of the tribe of Gad (Nu 1:14; 2:14; 7:42, 47; 10:20).
2. The son of Lael, a leader of the families of the Gershonites (Nu 3:24).

ELIASHIB (*God [El] restores*).
1. A descendant of Zerubbabel and remotely related to David (1Ch 3:24).
2. A priest in the time of David (1Ch 24:12).
3. An ancestor of a man who helped Ezra (Ezr 10:6; Ne 12:10, 22-23).
4. A Levite who put away his foreign wife (Ezr 10:24).
5. A man who married a foreign woman (Ezr 10:27).
6. Another man who married a foreign woman (Ezr 10:36).
7. A high priest in the time of Nehemiah (Ne 3:1, 20-21; 13:4, 7, 28).

ELIATHAH (*God [El] comes*). A temple musician, the son of Heman (1Ch 25:4, 27).

ELIDAD (*God [El] is [my] beloved*). A Benjamite, the son of Kislon (Nu 34:21). Eleazar the priest and Joshua were appointed to assign the land west of the Jordan to the tribes who were to settle there. God also appointed one man from each of the tribes to help Eleazar and Joshua, Elidad being the leader from the tribe of Benjamin.

ELIEHOENAI (*my eyes [look] to Yahweh*).
1. A Korahite gatekeeper of the tabernacle (1Ch 26:3).
2. One of the family heads who returned with Ezra; the son of Zerahiah (Ezr 8:4). *See Elioenai.*

ELIEL (*God [El] is [my] God*).
1. The chief of Manasseh (1Ch 5:24).
2. The ancestor of Samuel (1Ch 6:34). Called Eliab (1Ch 6:27).
3. The son of Shimei (1Ch 8:20).
4. The son of Shashak (1Ch 8:22).
5. A Mahavite and a captain in David's army (1Ch 11:46).
6. One of David's heroes (1Ch 11:47).
7. A Gadite; perhaps the same as 5 or 6 (1Ch 12:11).
8. A chief Levite (1Ch 15:11).
9. A chief of Judah; perhaps the same as 5 (1Ch 15:9).
10. A Levite overseer (2Ch 31:13).

ELIENAI (*my eyes [look] to Yahweh*). A Benjamite citizen of Jerusalem (1Ch 8:20).

ELIEZER (*God [El] is [my] help*).
1. Steward of Abraham, who in place of a son, would have become Abraham's heir (Ge 15:2). Perhaps the same as the servant mentioned in (Ge 24).
2. The son of Moses and Zipporah (Ex 18:4; 1Ch 23:15, 17; 26:25).
3. The grandson of Benjamin (1Ch 7:8).
4. A priest (1Ch 15:24).
5. A Reubenite chief (1Ch 27:16).
6. A prophet who rebuked Jehoshaphat (2Ch 20:37).
7. A chieftain sent to induce the Israelites to return to Jerusalem (Ezr 8:16).
8. A priest who put away his foreign wife (Ezr 10:18).
9. A Levite who put away his foreign wife (Ezr 10:23).
10. A son of Harim who put away his foreign wife (Ezr 10:31).
11. An ancestor of Jesus (Lk 3:29).

ELIHOREPH A son of Shisha (1Ki 4:3).

ELIHU (*Yahweh is [my] God*).
1. The son of Tohu, an Ephraimite, an ancestor of Samuel (1Sa 1:1). Probably identical with Eliab (1Ch 6:27), and Eliel (1Ch 6:34).
2. A Manassite warrior, who joined David at Ziklag (1Ch 12:20).
3. A Korahite gatekeeper of the tabernacle (1Ch 26:7).
4. A chief of the tribe of Judah and one of David's brothers (1Ch 27:18). Possibly Eliab, the oldest brother of David (1Sa 16:6).
5. A son of Barakel the Buzite who speaks to Job when his three friends have failed to silence him (Job 32-37).

ELIJAH (*Yahweh is [my] God*).
1. The Tishbite, a Gileadite and prophet. Announces to Ahab the coming of a disastrous drought (1Ki 17:2-7). The severity of Ahab, which is noted in secular literature as well, i.e., Jos. *Antiq.* VIII.xiii.2, prompts Elijah to escape into the wilderness, where he is miraculously fed by ravens (1Ki 17:1-6). By divine direction, he goes to Zarephath of Sidon where he is sustained in the household of a widow (1Ki 17:8-16). The widow's son becomes fatally ill; Elijah prays over him with the result that his life is restored (1Ki 17:16-24). Paul has a similar experience with a young man named Eutychus (Ac 20:7-12). He returns and sends a message to Ahab through Obadiah, a devout believer in the Lord, who was in charge of Ahab's palace (1Ki 18:1-16). Meets Ahab and directs him to assemble the prophets of Baal (1Ki 18:17-20). Derisively challenges the priests of Baal to offer sacrifices (1Ki 18:25-29). Slays the prophets of Baal (1Ki 18:40). Escapes to the wilderness from the

E

fierceness of Jezebel (1Ki 19:1-18). Fasts forty days (1Ki 19:8). Despondency and murmuring of (1Ki 19:10, 14). Consolation given to (1Ki 19:11-18). Flees to the wilderness of Damascus; directed to anoint Hazael as king over Aram, Jehu son of Nimshi king over Israel, and Elisha to be a prophet in his own place (1Ki 19:9-21). Personal aspect of (1Ki 1:8).

Piety of (1Ki 19:10, 14; Lk 1:17; Ro 11:2; Jas 5:17). His translation to heaven in a whirlwind (2Ki 2:11). Antitype of John the Baptist (Mt 11:14; 17:10-13; Mk 9:11-13; Lk 1:17; Jn 1:21-25). Appears to Jesus at his transfiguration (Mt 17:1-4; Mk 9:2-5; Lk 9:28-33).

Miracles of:
Increases the oil of the widow of Zarephath (1Ki 17:14-16). Raises from the dead the son of the woman of Zarephath (1Ki 17:17-24). Causes fire to consume the sacrifice (1Ki 18:24, 36-38). Causes rain after a drought of three and a half years (1Ki 18:41-45; Jas 5:17-18). Calls fire down upon the soldiers of Ahaziah (2Ki 1:10-14; Lk 9:54, ftn).

Prophecies of:
Foretells a drought (1Ki 17:1), the destruction of Ahab and his house (1Ki 21:17-29; 2Ki 9:25-37), the death of Ahaziah (2Ki 1:2-17), the plague sent as a judgment upon the people in the time of Jehoram, king of Israel (2Ch 21:12-15).

2. A Benjamite chief, the son of Jeroham (1Ch 8:27).
3. A postexilic Jew who divorced his foreign wife; a descendant of Harim (Ezr 10:21).
4. A postexilic Jew who divorced his foreign wife; a descendant of Elam (Ezr 10:26).

ELIKA A Harodite, one of David's mighty men known as the "Thirty" (2Sa 23:25).

ELIM (big trees). The fourth stopping place of the Israelites after they crossed the Red Sea; they found twelve springs and seventy palm trees (Ex 15:27; 16:1; Nu 33:9-10).

ELIMELECH (God [El] is [my] king). An Ephrathite from Bethlehem of Judah who, with his wife, Naomi and his two sons, immigrated from Judah to Moab in the days of the judges to escape a famine in the land (Ru 1:2, 3; 2:1, 3; 4:3, 9).

ELIOENAI (my eyes [look] to Yahweh).
1. The son of Neariah (1Ch 3:23-24).
2. A Simeonite leader (1Ch 4:36).
3. A Benjamite (1Ch 7:8).
4. A man who divorced his foreign wife (Ezr 10:22).
5. A man who divorced his foreign wife (Ezr 10:27).
6. A priest, perhaps the same as 4 (Ne 12:41).

ELIPHAL ([my] God [El] sit in judgment). Perhaps the same as Eliphelet (2Sa 23:34). One of David's mighty men known as the "Thirty" (1Ch 11:35).

ELIPHAZ (God [El] is fine gold or God crushes).
1. The oldest son of Esau by his Hittite wife Adah (Ge 36:4, 10-12, 15-16; 1Ch 1:35-36).
2. One of Job's three friends; wise, rich, and a ruler of men. He was probably the leader of this trio (Job 42:7), and also the oldest. He took for granted that Job must have committed some major sin as the only explanation for his tremendous suffering. He tries to make it as easy as possible for Job to repent because of the powerful impact of the dream he had had concerning man's sinful condition in the presence of God (Job 4:12-21). In his second address, Eliphaz's point of view is that Job's problems stem from his strong sense of personal righteousness; that Job believes that he has all the wisdom that he needs, therefore, he has no need of input from God or wise men (Job 15). In his third address, Eliphaz condemns Job of many sins, calling him back to right relationship and the resultant blessing of God (Job 22).

ELIPHELEHU (God [El], distinguish him!). A Levite musician (1Ch 15:18, 21).

ELIPHELET (God [El] is [my] deliverance).
1. A son of David, probably identical with #2 (2Sa 5:16; 1Ch 3:8; 14:7).
2. One of David's mighty men known as the "Thirty" (2Sa 23:34).
3. A son of David (1Ch 3:6; 14:7). Called Elpelet (1Ch 14:5).
4. A descendant of Saul (1Ch 8:39).
5. A companion of Ezra (Ezr 8:13).
6. A priest from among the Israelites who had married a foreign woman and had pledged to divorce his wife (Ezr 10:33).

ELISABETH See Elizabeth.

ELISHA (God [El] is [my] salvation). The successor to Elijah the prophet . Elijah is instructed to anoint (1Ki 19:16). Called by Elijah (1Ki 19:19). Ministers to Elijah (1Ki 19:21). Witnesses Elijah's translation, receives a double portion of his spirit (2Ki 2:1-15; 3:11). Mocked by the children of Bethel (2Ki 2:23-24). Causes the king to restore the property of the hospitable Shunammite (2Ki 8:1-6). Instructs that Jehu be anointed the king of Israel (2Ki 9:1-3). Life of, sought by Jehoram (2Ki 6:31-33). The death of (2Ki 13:14-20). Bones of, restore a dead man to life (2Ki 13:21).

Miracles of:
Divides the Jordan (2Ki 2:14). Purifies the waters of Jericho by casting salt into the fountain (2Ki 2:19-22). Increases the oil of the woman whose sons were to be sold for debt (2Ki 4:1-7). Raises from the dead the son of the Shunammite (2Ki 4:18-37). Neutralizes the poison of the stew (2Ki 4:38-41). Increases the bread to feed one hundred men (2Ki 4:42-44). Heals Naaman the leper (2Ki 5:1-19; Lk 4:27). Sends leprosy as a judgment upon Gehazi (2Ki 5:26-27). Recovers the axhead that had fallen into a stream by causing it to float (2Ki 6:6). Reveals the counsel of the king of Syria (2Ki 6:12). Opens the eyes of his servant to see the hosts of the Lord (2Ki 6:17). Brings blindness upon the army of Syria (2Ki 6:18).

Prophecies of:
Foretells a son to the Shunammite woman (2Ki 4:16); plenty to the starving in Samaria (2Ki 7:1); death of the unbelieving prince (2Ki 7:2); seven years' famine in the land of Canaan (2Ki 8:1-3); death of Ben-Hadad, king of Syria (2Ki 8:7-10); elevation of Hazael to the throne (2Ki 8:11-15); the victory of Jehoash over Syria (2Ki 13:14-19). Elisha is referred to once in the NT (Lk 4:27).

ELISHAH (God [El] saves). The son of Javan, whose name was given to an ancient land and its people, not identified (Ge 10:4; 1Ch 1:7; Eze 27:7).

ELISHAMA (God [El] has heard).
1. A leader of the tribe of Ephraim during the census in the wilderness. The grandfather of Joshua (Nu 1:10; 2:18; 7:48, 53; 10:22; 1Ch 7:26).
2. A son of David (2Sa 5:16; 1Ch 3:8; 14:7).
3. KJV Elishama, another son of David, is NIV Elishua (1Ch 3:6, ftn). See Elishua.
4. The grandfather of the Ishmael who killed Gedaliah the governor of Israel appointed by Nebuchadnezzar (2Ki 25:25; Jer 41:1).
5. Of the tribe of Judah, descended from Sheshan (1Ch 2:41).
6. A priest sent by Jehoshaphat to teach the law in Judah (2Ch 17:8).
7. A secretary to Jehoiakim (Jer 36:12, 20-21).

ELISHAPHAT (God [El] is [my] judge). One of five Judean commanders who helped Jehoiada the priest in the overthrow of Athaliah to make Joash king (2Ch 23:1).

ELISHEBA (God [El] is an oath BDB; God [El] is [my] fill KB). The daughter of Amminadab and wife of Aaron (Ex 6:23).

ELISHUA (God [El] is [my] salvation). A son of David (2Sa 5:15; 1Ch 14:5). Elishama (1Ch 3:6, ftn) is probably a scribal error in Hebrew mss.

ELIUD (God [El] is [my] grandeur). An ancestor of Jesus; in the fifth generation before Jesus, he was the son of Akim and the father of Eleazar (Mt 1:14-15).

ELIZABETH (God is [my] oath). The wife of Zechariah and mother of John the Baptist (Lk 1:5-60).

ELIZAPHAN (God [El] is [my] hiding).
1. A Levite (Ex 6:22; Lev 10:4). The son of Uzziel, the leader of the families of the Kohathite clans who had the responsibility to take care of the ark, the table, the lampstand, and the vessels of the sanctuary (Nu 3:30; 1Ch 15:8; 2Ch 29:13).
2. A leader of Zebulun (Nu 34:25).

ELIZUR (God [El] is [my] rock). A leader of Reuben, the son of Shedeur; one of the leaders who helped Moses take the census in the wilderness (Nu 1:5; 2:10; 7:30, 35; 10:18).

ELKANAH (God [El] has possessed).
1. The grandson of Korah (Ex 6:24; 1Ch 6:23).
2. The father of Samuel (1Sa 1:1, 4, 8, 19, 21, 23; 2:11, 20; 1Ch 6:27, 34).
3. A Levite (1Ch 6:25, 36).
4. Possibly identical with 3 (1Ch 6:26, 35).
5. A Levite (1Ch 9:16).
6. A Levite who joined David at Ziklag (1Ch 12:6).
7. A doorkeeper for the ark, perhaps identical with 6 (1Ch 15:23).
8. A prince of Ahaz (2Ch 28:7).

ELKOSH The birthplace of Nahum the prophet (Na 1:1).

ELLASAR A city-state in Babylonia in the time of Abraham (Ge 14:1, 9).

ELM See Terebinth.

ELMADAM An ancestor of Jesus (Lk 3:28).

ELNAAM (God [El] is pleasantness). The father of two of David's mighty men known as the "Thirty" (1Ch 11:46).

ELNATHAN (God [El] has given).
1. The grandfather of Jehoiachin (2Ki 24:8).
2. Levites who helped Ezra (Ezr 8:16).
3. The son of Acbor and a high official of King Jehoiakim (Jer 26:22; 36:12, 25).

ELOHE See El Elohe Israel.

ELOHIM (a god, the God; Mighty One).

Used of the God of Israel:
The most frequent Hebrew word for God, gods, angels, or magistrates. The plural Elohim when used for God in the OT is singular in meaning, and is often called "plural of majesty." See God, Names of, Elohim; El.

Used of Pagan Gods:
The Philistine god Dagon (Jdg 16:23-24), the Sidonian goddess Ashtoreth (1Ki 11:5, 33), the Moabite god Chemosh (1Ki 11:33), the Ammonite god Chemosh (1Ki 11:33), and Baal-Zebub of Ekron (2Ki 1:2, 3, 6) are also referred to in the plural.

Used of Other Groups:
Judges (Ex 21:6; 22:8-9), heavenly beings (Ps 8:5), those high among people (Ps 36:7).

ELOI, ELOI, LAMA SABACHTHANI (My God, my God, why have you forsaken me?). One of the seven cries of Jesus from the cross (Mt 27:46; Mk 15:34 w Ps 22:1).

ELON, ELONITE (a species of a mighty tree).
1. The father-in-law of Esau (Ge 26:34; 36:2).
2. A son of Zebulun (Ge 46:14) and his clan (Nu 26:26).
3. A town of Dan (Jos 19:43).

4. A Hebrew judge (Jdg 12:11-12).

ELON BETHHANAN (tree of Bethhanan). A town of Dan (1Ki 4:9). Perhaps identical with Elon (Jos 19:43).

ELOTH See Elath.

ELPAAL (God [El] creates). A Benjamite (1Ch 8:11-12, 18).

ELPELET (God [El] is deliverance). A son of David (1Ch 14:5). Called Eliphelet (1Ch 3:6).

ELTEKEH (meeting place). A city of Dan (Jos 19:44; 21:23).

ELTEKON (God [El] has arranged). A city of Judah (Jos 15:59).

ELTOLAD (generation IDB; kindred of God [El] ISBE; God [El] + place where children could be obtained KB). A city of Judah (Jos 15:30; 19:4). Called Tolad (1Ch 4:29).

ELUL The sixth month in sacred sequence, month twelve in civil sequence. The returned Jews finish the wall of Jerusalem in (Ne 6:15). Zerubbabel builds the temple in (Hag 1:14-15).
A transitional season from dry to rainy (August-September). The season for processing grapes, figs, and olives. See Month, 6.

ELUZAI (God [El] is my strength). A Benjamite warrior who joined David while he was in exile from Saul at the Philistine city of Ziklag (1Ch 12:5). He was able to use a bow or sling with either hand.

ELYMAS (possibly wise one hence magician). A Jewish magician and false prophet associated with Proconsul Sergius Paulus at Paphos on Cyprus. He was punished with blindness when he opposed Paul and Barnabas and tried to turn the proconsul from the faith (Ac 13:8-11).

ELZABAD (God [El] has given).
1. A Gadite warrior who joined David at Ziklag (1Ch 12:12).
2. A Korahite gatekeeper (1Ch 26:7).

ELZAPHAN See Elizaphan.

EMANCIPATION Of all Hebrew servants (Ex 21:2; Lev 25:8-17, 39-41; Dt 15:12).
Proclamation of: By Cyrus (2Ch 36:23; Ezr 1:1-4), by Zedekiah (Jer 34:8-11). See Exodus; Jubilee.

EMBALMING Of Jacob (Ge 50:2-3), of Joseph (Ge 50:26), of Asa (2Ch 16:14), of Jesus (Mk 15:46; 16:1; Jn 19:39-40).

EMBEZZLEMENT (Lk 16:1-7). See Dishonesty.

EMBLEMS OF THE HOLY SPIRIT See Holy Spirit, Emblems of.

EMBROIDERY In blue, purple, and scarlet, on the curtains of the tabernacle (Ex 26:1, 36; 27:16), on the ephod and coat of the high priest, mingled with gold (Ex 28:4-5, 39). Bezalel and Oholiab divinely inspired for in the work of the tabernacle (Ex 35:30-35; 38:22-23). On the garments of Sisera (Jdg 5:30). On the garments of women (Ps 45:14; Eze 16:10, 13, 18). On the garments of princes (Eze 26:16).
See Tapestry.

EMEK See Beth Emek; Emek Keziz.

EMEK KEZIZ (valley of Keziz). A valley and city of Benjamin (Jos 18:21).

EMERALD One of the jewels in the priestly breastplate (Ex 28:18; 39:11; Jer 17:1).

Figurative:
Ezekiel uses imagery of the Creation and the Fall to picture the career of the king of Tyre; unlike Adam, who was naked, the king is pictured as a fully clothed priest, ordained to guard God's holy place; the nine stones listed are among the twelve worn by the priest (Eze 28:13).
Since God dwells in "unapproachable light" and is one "whom no one has seen or can see" (1Ti 6:16), he is described in terms of the reflected brilliance of precious stones—an emerald rainbow around the throne (Rev 4:3).

Symbolic:
In the foundation of the holy city (Rev 21:19).
See Minerals of the Bible, 1; Stones.

EMERGENCY See Decision.

EMERODS See Hemorrhoids.

EMITES (frightening beings). Early inhabitants of the area around Kiriathaim which is E of the Dead Sea. They were defeated in the time of Abraham by the four invading kings (Ge 14:5). A race of giants who were "strong and numerous, and as tall as the Anakites" (Dt 2:10-11). See Rephaites.

EMMANUEL See Immanuel.

EMMAUS (hot springs). A village seven miles from Jerusalem (Lk 24:7-35).

EMPLOYEE

Rights of an Employee:
Prompt payment (Lev 19:13). Participation of produce (Lev 25:6). Just compensation (Mt 10:10; Lk 10:7; Ro 4:4; Col 4:1; 1Ti 5:18). Oppression of (Dt 24:14-15; Pr 22:16; Mal 3:5; Lk 15:15-17; Jas 5:4). Kindness to exemplified (Ru 2:4; Lk 15:17, 19).

Character of Unrighteous: (Job 7:1-3; 14:1, 6; Mt 20:1-16; 21:33-41; Jn 10:12-13).
See Employer; Master; Servant; Slave.

E

EMPLOYER Required: To grant a Sabbath rest (Ex 20:10; Dt 5:14). To make prompt payment (Lev 19:13; Dt 24:15; Jas 5:4-5). To be kind (Lev 25:39-43; Job 31:13-15; Eph 6:9; Phm 15-16). Not to oppress (Dt 24:14-15; Pr 22:16; Mal 3:5). To accord just compensation (Jer 22:13; Mt 10:10; 20:1-15; Lk 10:7; Ro 4:4; Col 4:1; 1Ti 5:18).
 See Employee; Labor; Master; Servant.

EMULATION To create a desire for salvation (Ro 11:11, 14). To generosity in giving to aid others (2Co 8:1-8; 9:1-5). To love and good works (Heb 10:24).
 Illustrated: In Esau's marriages (Ge 28:6-9). In Jacob's household (Ge 30:1-24).

EN EGLAIM (*spring of two calves*). Possibly modern Ain Feshka at the NW corner of the Dead Sea (Eze 47:10).

EN GANNIM (*spring of gardens*).
 1. A city of Judah (Jos 15:34).
 2. A city of Issachar (Jos 19:21; 21:29).

EN GEDI (*spring of young goat*). Called Hazazon Tamar. Built by the Amorites (Ge 14:7; 2Ch 20:2). A city allotted to Judah (Jos 15:62). Famous for its vineyards (SS 1:14).
 Wilderness of, near the Dead Sea. David uses as a stronghold (1Sa 23:29; 24). Cave of (1Sa 24:3).

EN HADDAH (*spring of gladness*). A city of Issachar probably located c. six miles E of Mount Tabor (Jos 19:21).

EN HAKKORE (*spring of the partridge* or *spring of the caller*). A spring at Lehi from which Samson drank after slaughtering the Philistines (Jdg 15:19).

EN HAZOR (*spring of Hazor*). En Hazor was a fortified city assigned to Naphtali (Jos 19:37).

EN MISHPAT (*spring of judgment*). The ancient name of Kadesh (Ge 14:7). *See Kadesh.*

EN RIMMON (*spring of Rimmon*). A city of Judah in the Negev, later assigned to Simeon (Jos 19:7; 1Ch 4:32). Probably identical with Ain and Rimmon (Jos 15:32; 1Ch 4:32). Those returning from the Exile resettled at En Rimmon (Ne 11:29).

EN ROGEL (*spring of the fuller, or wanderer, or spy*). A spring near Jerusalem (Jos 15:7; 18:16; 2Sa 17:17), possibly the Jackal Well (Ne 2:13). A rebellious feast at (1Ki 1:9).

EN SHEMESH (*spring of Shemesh,* [sun or pagan god]). A place on the N boundary of Judah and the S boundary of Benjamin (Jos 15:7; 18:17). The last spring on the road between Jerusalem and the Jordan Valley was found there. En Shemesh has been called the "Spring of the Apostles" since the fifteenth century.

EN TAPPUAH (*spring of apple*). A spring of uncertain location at the S border of Manasseh (Jos 17:7); usually identified with modern Sheikh Abu Zarad c. eight miles S of Shechem. The town was a Canaanite stronghold that held out against the Israelites for a period of time during the conquest of the land by the Israelites.

ENAIM (*two springs*). It is most likely located in the high hill country SE of Jerusalem between Adullam and Timnah; KJV "open place" (Ge 38:14, 21).

ENAM A town in the western foothills of Judah (Jos 15:34).

ENAN (*spring*). The father of Ahira who was a military leader of the tribe of Naphtali and one who assisted in the Sinai census (Nu 1:15; 2:29; 7:78, 83; 10:27).

ENCAMPMENT Places where the Israelites encamped on the way from Egypt to Canaan (Nu 33). Also headquarters of armies (1Sa 13:16; 2Ch 32:1). *See Camp.*

ENCHANTMENT The use of any form of magic, including divination; forbidden to God's people (Dt 18:10; Ac 8:9, 11; 13:8, 10; 19:19). *See Divination; Magic; Sorcery.*

END OF THE WORLD Consummation of the age (Mt 13:39, 49; 24:3; 28:20; Heb 9:26). *See Eschatology.*

ENDOR (*spring of Dor*). A city of Issachar allotted to Manasseh (Jos 17:11). Deborah triumphs at, over Sisera (Jdg 4; Ps 83:10). The medium of, consulted by Saul (1Sa 28:7-25).

ENDURANCE *See Perseverance.*

ENEAS *See Aeneas.*

ENEMY
Kindness to:
 Commanded (Ex 23:4-5; Pr 25:21-22; Mt 5:43-48; Lk 6:27-36; Ro 12:14, 20).
Forgiveness of:
 Commanded (Mt 6:12-15; 18:21-35; Mk 11:25; Lk 17:3-4; Eph 4:31-32; Col 3:13; 1Pe 3:9).
 Instances of Forgiveness—
 Esau, of Jacob (Ge 33:4, 11). Joseph, of his brothers (Ge 45:5-15; 50:19-21). Moses, of Miriam and Aaron (Nu 12:1-13). David, of Saul (1Sa 24:10-12; 26:9, 23; 2Sa 1:14-17), of Shimei (2Sa 16:9-13; 19:23; 1Ki 2:8-9), of Absalom and his co-conspirators (2Sa 18:5, 12, 32-33; 19:6, 12-13). The prophet of Judah by Jeroboam (1Ki 13:3-6). Jesus, of his persecutors (Lk 23:34). Stephen, of his murderers (Ac 7:60).
Destruction of:
 Requested by David (Ps 35:1-7). The wickedness of David's enemies (Ps 56:2, 5-6; 57:4, 6; 62:4; 69:4; 71:10; 102:8; 109:2-5; 129:1-3). *See Prayer, Imprecatory.*
 Rejoicing at the destruction of, forbidden (Pr 24:17-18). Rejoicing at the destruction of, not practiced by Job (Job 31:29-30).

Figurative:
 Of the devil (Mt 13:25, 28, 39).

ENGAGEMENT *See Betrothal.*

ENGINE NIV "machines" of war (2Ch 26:15) or "battering rams" (Eze 26:9). *See Armies; Fort.*

ENGRAFTING *See Graft.*

ENGRAVING On the stones set in the priest's breastplate (Ex 28:9-11, 21, 36; 39:8-14). In making idols (Ex 32:4), in the priest's ephod (Ex 39:6), in the priest's crown (Ex 39:30).

ENOCH (*initiated* ISBE; *follower* KB).
 1. Cain's eldest son (Ge 4:17).
 2. A city built by Cain (Ge 4:17).
 3. The father of Methuselah (Ge 5:21-22). Walked with God and then was translated to heaven by God (Ge 5:24; Heb 11:5).

ENOCH, BOOKS OF Apocalyptic literature written by various authors and circulated under the name of Enoch; written c. 163 B.C. to A.D. 50. Possibly quoted in Jude 14-15.

ENON *See Aenon.*

ENOSH (*[mortal] man*). The son of Seth (Ge 4:26; 5:6-11; 1Ch 1:1; Lk 3:38).

ENQUIRING OF GOD *See Affliction, Prayer Under; Prayer.*

ENSIGN A standard or banner (Ps 74:4; Isa 5:26; 11:10, 12; 18:3; 30:17; 31:9; Zec 9:16). *See Banner; Standard.*

ENTERTAINMENTS Often great (Ge 21:8; Da 5:1; Lk 5:29). Preparations made for (Ge 18:6-7; Mt 22:4; Lk 15:23).
Given on Occasions of:
 Weaning children (Ge 21:8). Ratifying covenants (Ge 26:30; 31:54). Offering voluntary sacrifice (Ge 31:54; Dt 12:6-7; 1Sa 1:4-5). After wine was trodden (Jdg 9:27). Harvest home (Ru 3:2-7; Isa 9:3). Festivals (1Sa 20:5, 24-26). Sheepshearing (1Sa 25:2, 36; 2Sa 13:23). Return of friends (2Sa 12:4; Lk 15:23). Coronation of kings (1Ki 1:9, 18-19; 1Ch 12:39-40; Hos 7:5). Taking leave of friends (1Ki 19:21). National deliverance (Est 8:17; 9:17-19). Marriage (Mt 22:2). Birth days (Mt 6:21).
Kinds of, Mentioned in Scripture:
 Dinner (Ge 43:16; Mt 22:4; Lk 14:12). Banquet (Est 5:4-6). Served often by hired servants (Mt 22:3; Jn 2:5). Served often by members of the family (Lk 10:40; Jn 12:2). Supper (Lk 14:12; Jn 12:2). Under the direction of a master of the feast (Jn 2:8-9).
Invitations to:
 Should be sent to the poor (Dt 14:29, w Lk 14:13). Often by the master in person (2Sa 13:24; Est 5:4; Zep 1:7; Lk 7:36). Often only to relatives and friends (1Ki 1:9; Lk 14:16). Often addressed to many (Lk 14:16). Repeated through servants when all things were ready (Lk 14:17).
Often Given in:
 The house (Lk 5:29). Near landmarks (1Ki 1:9). The court of the house (Est 1:5-6; Est 1:7:36-37). The upper room or guest chamber (Mk 14:14-15). The house (Lk 5:29).
Guests at:
 Had their feet washed when they came a distance (Ge 18:4; 43:24; Lk 7:38, 44). Arranged according to rank (Ge 43:33; 1Sa 9:22; Lk 14:10). Often had separate dishes (Ge 43:34; 1Sa 1:4). A choice portion reserved for principal guests (Ge 43:34; 1Sa 1:5; 9:23-24). Began with thanksgiving (1Sa 9:13; Mk 8:6). Often scenes of great intemperance (1Sa 25:36; Da 5:3-4; Hos 7:5). Portions often sent to the absent (Ne 8:10; Est 9:19). None asked to eat more than he liked at (Est 1:8). Men and women did not usually meet at (Est 1:8-9; Mk 6:21, w Mt 14:11). Given by the guests in return (Job 1:4; Lk 14:12). Usually anointed (Ps 23:5; Lk 7:46). Music and dancing often introduced at (Am 6:5; Mk 6:22; Lk 15:25). Eager to take chief seats at, condemned (Mt 23:6; Lk 14:7-8). Often ate from the same dish (Mt 26:23). Concluded with a hymn (Mk 14:26). None admitted after the master had risen and shut the door (Lk 13:24-25). Offense given by refusing to go to (Lk 14:18, 24). Anxiety to have many guests at, alluded to (Lk 14:22-23). *See Feasts.*

ENTHUSIASM Instances of: Gideon (Jdg 6-7), Jehu (2Ki 9:1-14; 10:1-28). *See Zeal.*

ENUMERATION *See Census.*

ENVY
Characteristic of:
 Depravity (Ro 1:29; Tit 3:3). Worldliness (Ro 13:13; 1Co 3:3; 12:20; Gal 5:19-21; 1Ti 6:4; Jas 3:14, 16; 4:5). Not characteristic of love (1Co 13:4).
Described as:
 Destructive (Job 5:2). The cause of rotting bones (Pr 14:30). All consuming (Pr 27:4; SS 8:6). Drives people to achievement (Ecc 4:4). As unyielding as the grave (SS 8:6). Where envy and selfish ambition are found, disorder and every evil practice are found (Jas 3:16).
Forbidden: (Ps 37:1, 7; 49:16-20; Pr 3:31-32; 23:17-18; 24:1-2, 19-20; Ro 13:13; Gal 5:25-26; Jas 5:8-9; 1Pe 2:1-2).
Punishment for: (Eze 35:11).
Instances of:
 Cain, of Abel (Ge 4:4-8). Sarah, of Hagar (Ge 16:5-6; 21:9-10). Philistines, of Isaac because of the large number of flocks and herds he owned (Ge 26:14). Rachel, of Leah (Ge 30:1). Leah, of Rachel (Ge 30:15). Laban's sons, of Jacob (Ge 31:1). Joseph's brothers, of Joseph (Ge 37:4-11, 18-20; Ac 7:9). Joshua, of Eldad and Medad (Nu 11:28-30). Miriam and Aaron, of Moses (Nu 12:1-10). Korah, Dathan, and Abiram, of Moses (Nu 16:3; Ps 106:16-18). Saul, of

David (1Sa 18:8-9, 29; 1Sa 20:31). Haman, of Mordecai (Est 5:13). Asaph, at prosperity of wicked (Ps 73:2-3). The wicked, at the prosperity of the righteous (Ps 112:10; Isa 26:11). The princes of Babylon, of Daniel (Da 6:3-4).
 Priests, of Jesus (Mt 27:18; Mk 15:10; Jn 11:47-48). Jews, of Paul and Barnabas (Ac 13:45; 17:5).
 See Jealousy.

EPAENETUS *See Epenetus.*

EPAPHRAS (*handsome*). A co-worker with Paul (Col 1:7; 4:12; Phm 23).

EPAPHRODITUS (*handsome*). A messenger of Paul (Php 2:25; 4:18). Sick at Rome (Php 2:26-27, 30).

EPENETUS (*praised*). A convert to Christ in the province of Asia (Ro 16:5).

EPHAH (*darkness*).
 1. A son of Midian (Ge 25:4; 1Ch 1:33; Isa 60:6).
 2. Caleb's concubine (1Ch 2:46).
 3. A son of Jahdai (1Ch 2:47).
 4. A measure of about 3/5 bushel. *See Measure, Dry Capacity.*

EPHAI (*my bird*). A Netophathite (Jer 40:8). Sons warned Gedaliah (Jer 40:8-16; 41:3).

EPHER (*[small] gazelle*).
 1. A son of Midian (Ge 25:4; 1Ch 1:33).
 2. A son of Ezra (1Ch 4:17).
 3. A chief of Manasseh (1Ch 5:24).

EPHES DAMMIM (*border of Dammim [blood]*). A place between Socoh and Azekah in Judah, where David killed Goliath (1Sa 17:1). Called Pas Dammim (1Ch 11:13).

EPHESIANS, EPISTLE TO THE
Author: The apostle Paul
Date: c. A.D. 60
Outline:
I. Greetings (1:1-2).
II. The Divine Purpose: The Glory and Headship of Christ (1:3-14).
III. Prayer That Christians May Realize God's Purpose and Power (1:15-23).
IV. Steps Toward the Fulfillment of God's Purpose (chs. 2-3).
 A. Salvation of Individuals by Grace (2:1-10).
 B. Reconciliation of Jew and Gentile Through the Cross (2:11-18).
 C. Uniting of Jew and Gentile in One Household (2:19-22).
 D. Revelation of God's Wisdom Through the Church (3:1-13).
 E. Prayer for Deeper Experience of God's Fullness (3:14-21).
V. Practical Ways to Fulfill God's Purpose in the Church (4:1-6:20).
 A. Unity (4:1-6).
 B. Maturity (4:7-16).
 C. Renewal of Personal Life (4:17-5:20).
 D. Deference in Personal Relationships (5:21-6:9).
 1. Principle (5:21).
 2. Husbands and wives (5:22-33).
 3. Children and parents (6:1-4).
 4. Slaves and masters (6:5-9).
 E. Strength in the Spiritual Conflict (6:10-20).
VI. Conclusion, Final Greetings and Benediction (6:21-24).

EPHESUS Paul visits and preaches in (Ac 18:19-21; 19; 20:16-38). Apollos visits and preaches in (Ac 18:18-28). Sceva's sons attempt to expel a demon in (Ac 19:13-16). Timothy directed by Paul to remain at (1Ti 1:3). Onesiphorus lives at (2Ti 1:18). Paul sends Tychicus to (2Ti 4:12). Church at (Rev 1:11). Apocalyptic message to (Rev 2:1-7).
 See Ephesians, Epistle to the.

EPHLAL (*judgment, arbitration*). A descendant of Judah through Perez and the family of Jerahmeel (1Ch 2:37).

EPHOD
 1. A sacred vestment worn by the high priest. Described (Ex 25:7; 28:6-14, 31-35). Breastplate attached to (Ex 28:22-30). Making of (Ex 39:2-26). Worn by Aaron (Ex 39:5).
 An ephod made by his mother was worn by Samuel as a young boy ministering before the Lord (1Sa 2:18), by the common priests (1Sa 22:18), by David (2Sa 6:14). Used as an oracle (1Sa 23:9, 12; 30:7-8).
As an idol—
 Gideon made an ephod out of gold, placing it in his hometown of Ophrah, the ephod subsequently becoming an idol to Israel (Jdg 8:27). Micah from the hill country of Ephraim made one of gold (Jdg 17:5; 18:14). Prophecy concerning the absence of an ephod from Israel (Hos 3:4).
 2. A man of Manasseh (Nu 34:23).

EPHPHATHA (*to open*). An Aramaic passive imperative transliterated into the Greek (Mk 7:34).

EPHRAIM (*doubly fruitful*).
 1. The second son of Joseph (Ge 41:52). Adopted by Jacob (Ge 48:5). Blessed before Manasseh; prophecies concerning (Ge 48:14-20). Descendants of (Nu 26:35-37; 1Ch 7:20-27). Mourns for his sons (1Ch 7:21-22).
 2. A tribe of Israel. Prophecy concerning (Ge 49:25-26; Isa 7; 9:18-21; 11:13; 28:1-6; Jer 31; Hos 5:13-14; Zec 9:10-13; 10:7-12). Numbered at Sinai and in the plains of Moab (Nu 1:33; 26:37). Place in camp and march (Nu 2:18, 24; 10:22). Blessed by Moses (Dt 33:13-17).
 Territory allotted to, after the conquest of Canaan (Jos 16:5-9; 17:9-10, 15-18; 1Ch 7:28-29). Fail to expel the Canaanites (Jos 16:10). Take Bethel in battle (Jdg 1:22-25). Join Gideon against the Midianites (Jdg 7:24-25). Rebuke Gideon for not summoning them to join the war against the Midianites (Jdg 8:1). Their jealousy of Jephthah (Jdg 12:1). Defeated by him (Jdg 12:4-6). Receive

Ish-Bosheth as king (2Sa 2:8-9). Revolt from the house of David (1Ki 12:25; 2Ch 10:16). Jeroboam set up a golden calf in Bethel (1Ki 12:29). Some of the tribe join Judah under Asa (2Ch 15:9). Chastise Ahaz and Judah (2Ch 28:7). Join Hezekiah in reinstituting the Passover (2Ch 30:18). Join in the destruction of idols in Jerusalem (2Ch 31:1). Submit to the scepter of Josiah (2Ch 34:1-6). Envied other tribes (Isa 11:13). Reallotment of territory to, by Ezekiel (Eze 48:5). Worshiped Baal (Hos 13:1). Sin of, remembered by God (Hos 13:12).

Name of, applied to the ten tribes (2Ch 17:2; 25:6-7; Isa 7:8-9; 11:12-13; 17:3; Jer 31:18, 20; Hos 4:17; 5:3, 5; 6:4, 10; 8:11; 12:14). Tribe of, called Joseph (Rev 7:8).

3. Mount of. A range of low mountains (Jos 17:15-18). Joshua has his inheritance in (Jdg 2:9). Residence of Micah (Jdg 17:8). A place of hiding for the Israelites (1Sa 14:22). Sheba resides in (2Sa 20:21). Prophecy concerning its conversion (Jer 31:6). Noted for rich pastures (Jer 50:19).

4. A wood E of the Jordan. Absalom killed in (2Sa 18:6-17).

5. A gate of Jerusalem (2Ki 14:13; 2Ch 25:23; Ne 8:16; 12:39).

6. A city in the territory of Ephraim to which Jesus escapes to evade the persecution of Caiaphas (Jn 11:54).

EPHRAIMITE (*doubly fruitful*). A member of the tribe of Ephraim (Jos 16:5-10; Jdg 12).

EPHRATH, EPHRATHAH (*fruitful land*).
1. A place near Bethel where Rachel died and was buried (Ge 35:16, 19; 48:7).
2. A name of Bethlehem (Ru 4:11; Mic 5:2).
3. The second wife of Caleb, mother of Hur (1Ch 2:19, 50; 4:4).
4. An area associated with Kiriath Jearim (Ps 132:6, ftn).

EPHRON (*gazelle*).
1. The son of Zohar; the Hittite from whom Abraham purchased the field containing the cave of Machpelah, to the E of Mamre (Ge 23:8-17; 25:9; 49:29-30; 50:13).
2. Mount Ephron, a district whose cities were on the border of Judah (Jos 15:9).
3. A city near Bethel from which Abijah took Jeroboam I (2Ch 13:19).
4. A strongly fortified city between Karnaim and Beth Shan (Scythopolis) in the Maccabean period. It tried to prevent the passage of Judas and the Israelites with him, but Judas took the city, plundered it, and killed all its male inhabitants (1Mc 5:46-52; 2Mc 12:27-29).

EPIC Heroic poetry. Miriam's song (Ex 15:1-19, 21). Deborah's song (Jdg 5). *See Poetry.*

EPICUREANS A style of life familiar to Solomon long before Epicurus (341-270 B.C.) defined the doctrine through his school of philosophy in Athens (Ecc 2:1-10). Paul confronts a group of Epicurean and Stoic philosophers at a meeting of the Court of the Areopagus (Mars Hill) which is NW of the Acropolis and connected to it (Ac 17:16-34). *See Aratus; Cleanthes; Stoicism; Stoics.* It is suspected that by the Christian era the responsibility of the Court of the Areopagus was to censor the religious life of the community, and because of Paul's teaching concerning Jesus and the Resurrection they were exercising that right of censor.
See Sensuality.

EPILEPSY *See Seizures.*

EPISTLE (*letter*). Formal letters containing Christian doctrine and exhortation, referring particularly to the twenty-one epistles of the NT, divided into Pauline and General epistles. Not all the letters of the apostles have survived (1Co 5:9; Col 4:16).

EPISTLES, GENERAL *See General Letters.*

EPISTLES, PASTORAL *See Pastoral Epistles.*

EQUALITY *See Mankind, Equality of All People.*

EQUITY *See Justice.*

ER (*watcher, watchful*).
1. The eldest son of Judah (Ge 38:3, 6-7; 46:12; Nu 26:19; 1Ch 2:3).
2. A son of Judah's son Shelah (1Ch 4:21).
3. An ancestor of Jesus (Lk 3:28).

ERAN, ERANITE (*watcher, watchful*). A grandson of Ephraim and his clan (Nu 26:36).

ERASTUS (*beloved*).
1. A convert of Paul sent with Timothy from Ephesus into Macedonia on an errand (Ac 19:22).
2. The "city treasurer" or the "city director of public works" of Corinth; a Christian (Ro 16:23).
3. A companion of Paul who remained in Corinth (2Ti 4:20). Possibly the same as 1 above.

ERECH
1. A Babylonian city founded by Nimrod (Ge 10:10), located forty miles NW of Ur toward Babylon.
2. The men of Erech along with the men of Tripolis, Persia, and Babylon were settled in the cities of Samaria and elsewhere in Trans-Euphrates by Ashurbanipal (Ezr 4:9-10).

ERI, ERITE (*watcher*). The fifth son of Gad, the grandson of Jacob (Ge 46:16) and his clan (Nu 26:16).

ERRORS In teachers and doctrines. *See Teachers, False.*

ESAIAS *See Isaiah.*

ESARHADDON (*Ashur has given a brother [for a lost son]*). The son and successor of Sennacherib after Sennacherib was murdered by his sons Adrammelech and Sharezer in 681 B.C.; ruled Assyria 681-669 B.C. (2Ki 19:37; 2Ch 32:21; Isa 37:38); restored

the city of Babylon; conquered Egypt; brought deportees into Samaria (Ezr 4:2); took Manasseh captive (2Ch 33:11).

ESAU (*hairy*). The eldest of twin sons born to Isaac and Rebekah. Birth of (Ge 25:19-26; 1Ch 1:34). A hunter (Ge 25:27-28). Beloved by Isaac (Ge 25:27-28). Sold his birthright for a single meal of stew (Ge 25:29-34; 27:36; Heb 12:16). He was alternately called Edom because he had red coloring; Edom means red (Ge 25:25, 30). Married two Hittite women (Ge 26:34). Polygamy of (Ge 26:34; 28:9; 36:2-3). His marriages a grief to Isaac and Rebekah (Ge 26:35). Was defrauded of his father's blessing by Jacob (Ge 27; Heb 11:20). Met Jacob on the return of the latter from Haran (Ge 33:1). With Jacob, buried his father (Ge 35:29).

Descendants of (Ge 36; 1Ch 1:35-57). Called Edom (Ge 25:30; 36:1, 8). His name used to denote his descendants and their country (Dt 2:5; Jer 49:8, 10; Ob 6). Ancestor of Edomites (Jer 49:8). Enmity of descendants of, toward descendants of Jacob (Ob 10-14). Prophecies concerning (Ob 18).

ESCAPE

God Provides for the Righteous:
Noah and his family (Ge 7:7). The infant Jesus (Mt 2:13). By salvation (Ps 68:20). From temptation (Ecc 7:26; 1Co 10:13; 2Ti 2:26; 2Pe 1:4).

No Escape From the Judgment of God:
Adam and Eve (Ge 3:7-11). Cain (Ge 4:9-12). Mankind (Job 34:21-30; Ps 56:7; Isa 10:1-3; Mt 23:33; Ro 2:3; 1Th 5:2-3; Heb 2:2-3; 12:25-26; Rev 6:15-17).
See Sin, Fruits of, Punishment of; Judgment; Judgments.

ESCHATOLOGY (*study of last events*). Division of systematic theology dealing with the doctrine of last things such as death, resurrection, second coming of Christ, end of the age, divine judgment, and the future state. The OT teaches a future resurrection and judgment day (Job 19:25-27; Isa 25:6-9; 26:19-21; Da 12:2-3).

The NT interprets, enlarges, and completes the OT eschatology. It stresses the Resurrection (Ro 8:11; 1Co 15), the second coming of Christ (Mt 16:27; Lk 17:30; 1Co 1:7; 4:5; 1Th 2:19; 3:13; 4:13-18; 2Th 1:7-10; 2:1-6; 1Pe 1:7; 1Jn 2:28), the final judgment when the unsaved are cast into hell (Rev 20), and the righteous enter heaven (Mt 25:31-46). Christians differ on how the Millennium is to be interpreted, dividing themselves into amillennialists, postmillennialists, and premillennialists (Rev 20:1-6). *See Millennium.*

ESCHEAT *See Confiscation.*

ESDRAELON (*the valley of God's sowing* or *God will sow*). Mentioned as "Esdraelon" only in the Apocrypha. The Valley of Jezreel which lies between Galilee on the N and Samaria on the S (Jos 17:16; Jdg 6:33). Assigned to Issachar (Jos 15:56). Known as the "fertile valley."

ESDRAS, BOOKS OF *See Apocrypha.*

ESEK (*dispute*). A well dug by Isaac's servants in the valley near Gerar. A dispute arose between Isaac's herdsmen and the herdsmen of Gerar over rights to the water, so he named it Esek which means *dispute*. Isaac's men moved to another place and found the same problem, so he named it Sitnah which means *opposition*. Finally they dug a third well that no one quarreled over, so he named Rehoboth, which means *room* (Ge 26:19-22).

ESHAN (*support*). A city in Judah (Jos 15:52).

ESH-BAAL (*man of Baal*). Ish-Bosheth, the youngest son of Saul; he was made king over Israel by Abner to repudiate David's claim to the throne, he ruled two years and then was murdered by David's men (2Sa 2:8-10; 4:5-12). He was originally called Esh-baal (1Ch 8:33; 9:39).

ESHBAN (*man of understanding*). A son of Dishon, a Horite chief from the region of Mt. Seir (Ge 36:26; 1Ch 1:41).

ESHCOL (*[grape] cluster*).
1. An Amorite, and ally of Abraham (Ge 14:13, 24).
2. A valley or brook near Hebron (Nu 13:23-24; 32:9; Dt 1:24).

ESHEK (*oppressor*). A descendant of Jonathan (1Ch 8:38-40).

ESHTAOL, ESHTAOLITES (*[place of oracles] inquiry*). A town of Judah (Jos 15:33). Allotted to Dan (Jos 19:41; Jdg 18:2, 8, 11). Samson moved by the Spirit of the Lord near (Jdg 13:25). Samson buried near (Jdg 16:31).

ESHTEMOA, ESHTEMOH (*[place where oracle is] heard*).
1. A town of Canaan assigned to Judah (Jos 15:50). Allotted to the Aaronites (Jos 21:14; 1Ch 6:57). David shared the spoil with (1Sa 30:28).
2. A descendant of Ezra (1Ch 4:17, 19).

ESHTON (*possibly hen-pecked [husband]* or *effeminate*). A son of Mehir, the son of Kelub (1Ch 4:11-12).

ESLI (*Yahweh sets apart*). An ancestor of Jesus (Lk 3:25).

ESROM *See Hezron.*

ESSENES An important Jewish community which was flourishing in Israel during the lifetime of Jesus. They were not mentioned in the Bible, but described in Josephus and Philo, and are presumed to be the inhabitants of Qumran, where Dead Sea Scrolls were discovered. Most lived communal, celibate lives. They observed the law strictly; they practiced ceremonial baptisms; they were apocalyptic; they opposed the temple priesthood. *See Testaments, Time Between.*

ESTATE *See Land.*

ESTHER (Persian *star*, possibly *[Babylonian goddess] Ishtar*). Called also Hadassah (Est 2:7). The cousin of Mordecai (Est 2:7, 15). Chosen to be queen (Est 2:17). Tells the king of the plot against his life (Est 2:22). Fasts on account of the decree to destroy the Israelites; accuses Haman to the king; intercedes for her people (Est 4-9).

ESTHER, BOOK OF
Author: Anonymous
Date: Shortly after the events narrated, c. 460 B.C.
Outline:
I. The Feasts of Xerxes (1:1-2:18).
 A. Vashti Deposed (ch. 1).
 B. Esther Made Queen (2:1-18).
II. The Feasts of Esther (2:19-7:10).
 A. Mordecai Uncovers a Plot (2:19-23).
 B. Haman's Plot (ch. 3).
 C. Mordecai Persuades Esther to Help (ch. 4).
 D. Esther's Request to the King: First Banquet (5:1-8).
 E. A Sleepless Night (5:9-6:14).
 F. Haman Hanged: The Second Banquet (ch. 7).
III. The Feasts of Purim (chs. 8-10).
 A. The King's Edict in Behalf of the Jews (ch. 8).
 B. The Institution of Purim (ch. 9).
 C. The Promotion of Mordecai (ch. 10).

ETAM (*possibly place of birds of prey*).
1. A rock where Samson was bound and delivered to the Philistines (Jdg 15:8, 11-13).
2. A name in the list of Judah's descendants, but probably referring to 4 (1Ch 4:3).
3. A village of Simeon (1Ch 4:32).
4. A city in Judah (2Ch 11:6).

ETERNAL LIFE Participation in the life of Jesus Christ, the eternal Son of God (Jn 1:4; 10:10; 17:3; Ro 6:23), which reaches its fruition in the life to come (Mt 25:46; Jn 6:54; Ro 2:7; Tit 3:7). It is endless in its duration and divine in quality. *See Immortality; Life, Everlasting.*

ETERNAL PUNISHMENT *See Punishment, Eternal.*

ETERNITY God inhabits (Isa 57:15; Mic 5:2), rules (Jer 10:10). God, adoration for (Ps 30:12; 41:13), steadfastness of (Ps 72:17; 90:2; Mt 6:13), righteousness of (Ps 119:142; 2Co 9:9). *See God, Eternity of.*
Priestly order of Melchizedek (Ps 110:4). *See Christ, Eternity of.*
Angels (Jude 6). *See Life, Everlasting; Punishment, Eternal.*

ETH KAZIN A landmark in the boundary line of Zebulun (Jos 19:13).

ETHAM (*possibly fort*). The second camping place of Israel (Ex 13:20; Nu 33:6-8).

ETHAN (*long lived, ever-flowing [streams]*).
1. An exceptionally wise man in Solomon's time; an Ezrahite (1Ki 4:31; Ps 89:T).
2. A son of Zerah (1Ch 2:6, 8).
3. A descendant of Gershon (1Ch 6:42-43).
4. A Levite singer (1Ch 6:44; 15:17, 19).

ETHANIM (*ever-flowing [streams]*). Seventh month in sacred sequence, First in civil sequence. The Feast of Trumpets on (Lev 23:23-25). The Day of Atonement, on the tenth day of (Lev 23:26-32). The Feast of Tabernacles, beginning on the fifteenth day of (Lev 23:33-43). The Jubilee proclaimed on the tenth day of the fiftieth year (Lev 25:9). The temple dedicated in and the ark restored (1Ki 8:2). The altar restored in, after the Captivity (Ezr 3:1, 6). Called Tishri in current Jewish calendar.
Beginning of the early rains (September-October), the time of plowing. *See Month, 7.*

ETHBAAL (*with [him is] Baal*). The king of Sidon; the father of Jezebel (1Ki 16:31).

ETHER (*perhaps perfume*). A city of Canaan. Assigned to Judah (Jos 15:42). Subsequently allotted to Simeon (Jos 19:7). Called Token in the parallel passage (1Ch 4:32).

ETHIOPIA A region in Africa, inhabited by the descendants of Ham, S of Egypt. Was called the land of Cush (Ge 10:6; 1Ch 1:9; Isa 11:11). Rivers of (Ge 10:6; Isa 18:1). Moses marries a Cushite woman (Nu 12:1). Tirhakah, the king of Ethiopia, attempted to stop Sennacherib's invasion of Israel in the time of Hezekiah (2Ki 19:9). Zerah was defeated by Asa in the Valley of Zephathah near Mareshah (2Ch 14:9-15; 16:8). Was ruled by Xerxes as a part of the Babylonian Empire (Est 1:1). Prophecies concerning the submission of (Ps 68:31; 87:4; Isa 45:14; Da 11:43). Desolation of (Isa 20:2-6; 43:3; Eze 30:4-9; Hab 3:7; Zep 2:12). Merchandise of (Isa 45:14). Ebed-Melech, an official in the royal palace, probably a eunuch and keeper of the royal harem, a native of; treats Jeremiah with kindness by interceding on his behalf before Zedekiah (Jer 38:7-13; 39:15-18). Warriors of (2Ch 12:3; 16:8; Jer 46:9; Eze 38:5). Bordered Egypt on the S (Eze 29:10). Candace, queen of (Ac 8:27). A eunuch from, becomes a disciple under the preaching of Philip (Ac 8:27-39).

ETHIOPIAN EUNUCH Treasurer of Candace, queen of the Ethiopians (Ac 8:26-39), became a Christian through Philip.

ETHNAN (*gift* or *hire*). One of the sons of Helah, of the tribe of Judah (1Ch 4:7); some identify him with Ithnan, a town in S Judah in the Negev (Jos 15:23).

ETHNI (*gift* or *hire*). An ancestor of Asaph, a musician (1Ch 6:41).

ETIQUETTE *See Manners.*

E

EUBULUS (*good counsel*). A Roman Christian who was a friend of Paul's during his second Roman imprisonment; he sent greetings with Paul's letter to Timothy (2Ti 4:21). His name is common in papyri and inscriptions.

EUCHARIST (*thanksgiving*). One name for the Lord's Supper, meaning "giving of thanks." *See Lord's Supper.*

Instituted (Mt 26:17-29; Mk 14:22-25; Lk 22:19-20; Jn 13:1-4). Celebrated by the early Church (Ac 2:42, 46; 20:7; 1Co 11:26). Bread and cup of, symbols of the body and blood of Christ (Mt 26:26-28; 1Co 10:16-17, 21-22; 11:23-25). Profanation of, forbidden (1Co 11:20-22, 33-34). Self-examination before taking, commanded (1Co 11:27-32).

EUNICE (*good victory*). The daughter of Lois, Timothy's mother, and the wife of a Gentile (Ac 16:1; 2Ti 1:5).

EUNUCH (*one emasculated*). Castrated males, used as custodians of royal harems and court officials (2Ki 20:18; Est 1:10-15; 2:21; Jer 41:16; Da 1:3; Ac 8:27). Not practiced by Israelites; eunuchs not allowed to enter the assembly of the Lord (Dt 23:1). *See Ethiopian Eunuch.*

Figurative of those who stay unmarried for the sake of the kingdom (Mt 19:10-12).

EUODIA (*good fragrance*). A Christian woman at Philippi (Php 4:2).

EUPHRATES (*to break forth*). A river in the Garden of Eden (Ge 2:14). The eastern limit of the kingdom of Israel (Ge 15:18; Ex 23:31; Dt 1:7; 11:24; Jos 1:4; 2Sa 8:3; 1Ki 4:21; 1Ch 5:9; 18:3). Pharaoh Neco, king of Egypt, made conquest to (2Ki 24:7; Jer 46:2-10). On the banks of, Jeremiah symbolically buries his belt (Jer 13:1-7; see v.4, ftn). Jeremiah instructs staff officer Seraiah son of Neriah to cast the roll containing prophecies against Babylon into the Euphrates (Jer 51:59-64).

Symbolic: Of the extension of the empire of Assyria (Isa 8:6-8). In the Apocalypse (Rev 9:14; 16:12).

EUROCLYDON, EURAQUILOSee *Northeaster.*

EUTYCHUS (*fortunate*). A youth who fell asleep and fell out of the window to his death while Paul preached; was restored to life by Paul (Ac 20:9-10).

EVANGELISM See *Minister, Duties of; Zeal.*

EVANGELIST (*[a bringer of] good news*).
1. A Church leader (Eph 4:11). One who preached the good news of Jesus Christ from place to place (Ac 8:12, 26-39; 14:7; 1Co 1:17; 3:6). Philip is a typical example (Ac 21:8). Timothy was encouraged by Paul to do the work of an evangelist (2Ti 4:5).
2. In biblical studies: the author of a Gospel.

EVAPORATION (Ps 135:7; Jer 10:13; 51:16; Am 5:8; 9:6).

EVE (*life*). Creation of (Ge 1:26-28; 2:21-24; 1Ti 2:13). Named by Adam (Ge 2:23; 3:20). Deceived by Satan (Ge 3; 2Co 11:3; 1Ti 2:14). Clothed with fig leaves (Ge 3:7), with skins (Ge 3:21). Messiah promised to (Ge 3:15). Curse denounced against (Ge 3:16). Children of (Ge 4:1-2, 25; 5:3-4).

EVENING SACRIFICE One of two daily offerings prescribed in the Mosaic ritual (Ex 29:38-42; Nu 28:3-8).

EVENING, THE The day originally began with (Ge 1:5). Divided into two, commencing at 3 o'clock, and sunset (Ex 12:6; Nu 9:3).

Called the cool of the day (Ge 3:8). People cease from labor in (Ru 2:17; Ps 104:23). Wild beasts come forth in (Ps 59:6, 14). Where morning dawns and evening fades God calls forth songs of joy (Ps 65:8). The enemies of Jerusalem were so zealous to attack and defeat her that the soldiers encouraged each other to do battle at times of the day when attacks were rarely made, i.e., noon and evening (Jer 6:4-5).

A Time For:
Custom of sitting at the gates in (Ge 19:1). Meditation (Ge 24:63). Passover lamb killed in (Ex 12:6, 18). The golden lampstand lighted in (Ex 27:21, w Ex 30:8). Part of the daily sacrifice offered in (Ex 29:41; Ps 141:2; Da 9:21). All defiled persons unclean until (Lev 11:24-28; 15:5-7; 17:15; Nu 19:19). Humiliation often continued until (Jos 7:6; Jdg 20:23, 26; 21:2; Ezr 9:4-5). Exercise (2Sa 11:2). Prayer (Ps 55:17; Mt 14:15, 23). Taking food (Mk 14:17-18; Lk 24:29-30). The sky red in, a token of fair weather (Mt 16:2).

EVERLASTING ARMS (Dt 33:27).

EVERLASTING FIRE See *Fire, Figurative.*

EVERLASTING LIFE See *Life, Everlasting.*

EVERLASTING PUNISHMENTSee *Punishment, Eternal.*

EVI (*desire*). One of five Midianite kings killed by the Israelites under Moses (Nu 31:8; Jos 13:21).

EVICTION Of tenants (Mt 21:41; Mk 12:9).

EVIDENCE False, forbidden (Ex 20:16; 23:1, 7; Pr 24:28; Mt 19:18). Concealment of, punished (Lev 5:1). The entire community involved in (Lev 24:14). Two or more witnesses required in to sustain an allegation (Nu 35:30; Dt 17:6-7; 19:15; Mt 18:16; Heb 10:28). Punishment for falsehood in (Dt 19:16-21). Self-incriminating, demanded (Jos 7:19-21).

See Witness; False Witness; Accusation, False; Self-Incrimination.

EVIL Tree of the knowledge of good and evil (Ge 2:9, 17). Knowledge of (Ge 3:5, 22). In the heart (Ge 6:5; 8:21; Lk 6:45). To be forsaken (Ps 34:14; 37:27; Pr 3:7; 1Pe 3:11). To be abhorred (Ps 97:10; Am 5:15; Ro 12:9). You are not to repay evil for evil done to you (Ro 12:17; 1Th 5:15; 1Pe 3:9).

Appearance of to be avoided (Ro 14:1-23; 1Co 8:7-13; 10:28-33; 1Th 4:11-12; 5:22), exemplified by Paul, refusing to eat that which was offered to idols (1Co 8:13), in supporting himself (1Co 9:7-23).

See Company, Evil; Imagination, Of Mankind, Evil; Nonresistance.

EVIL-MERODACH (*worshiper of Marduk[s]* changed in textual transmission to read *fool of [blessing]*). Son and successor of Nebuchadnezzar. Released Jehoiachin from prison (2Ki 25:27-30; Jer 52:31-34).

EVIL FOR EVIL See *Retaliation.*

EVIL FOR GOOD (Ps 7:4-5; 35:12; 109:5; Pr 17:13).
Instances of:
Joseph accuses his brothers of rendering (Ge 44:4). Israelites, to Moses (Ex 5:21; 14:11; 15:24; 16:2-3; 17:3-4). Saul returns, to David (1Sa 19:1, 4-5, 10). Nabal returns, to David (1Sa 25:21), David, to Uriah (2Sa 11), to Joab (1Ki 2:4-6).
See Enemy; Good for Evil.

EVIL PUT AWAY (Dt 13:5; 17:7; 19:19; 21:21; 22:21; 24:7; Job 22:23; 1Co 5:13).

EVIL SPEAKING See *Speaking, Evil.*

EVIL SPIRITS See *Demons.*

EVILDOERS Warnings to (Ps 34:16; 37:9; 94:16; 119:115; Isa 9:17; 14:20; 31:2). Examples of (Jdg 2:11; 3:7; 4:1; 6:1; 10:6; 13:1; 1Ki 14:22; 15:26; 16:7; 2Ki 8:27; 13:2; 14:24; 15:9, 28; 17:2; 21:2; 23:32; 24:9; Ne 9:28; Isa 65:12; 2Ti 4:14).

EWE Female sheep.

EXALTATION
Of Christ See *Jesus the Christ, Exaltation of.*
Of Self See *Self-Exaltation.*

EXAMPLE
Bad:
Admonitions against (Lev 18:2-3; 20:23; Dt 18:9; 2Ch 30:7; Isa 8:11; Hos 4:9, 15; Zec 1:4; Mt 23:1-3; 1Co 8:9-13; 10:6; Eph 4:17; 3Jn 11). Corrupting (Pr 22:24-25; Jer 16:12; 17:1-2; Eze 20:18; Hos 4:9; 5:5).
Good:
Commanded (1Ti 4:12; Tit 2:7-8; 1Pe 5:3). Inspiring (Ne 5:8-19; 1Th 1:6-8; 1Pe 2:11-25). To be imitated (Heb 13:7; Jas 5:10-11). Illustrated (Ps 101:2; 1Pe 3:5-6).
God, our:
In holiness (Lev 11:44; 19:2). In perfection (Mt 5:48). In mercy (Lk 6:36). In not discriminating (Eph 6:9).
Christ, our:
In service (Mt 20:28; Mk 10:43-45; Lk 22:27; Jn 13:13-17, 34; Php 2:5-8). In meekness (2Co 10:1; 1Pe 2:20-25). In self-renunciation (Ro 15:2-7; 2Co 8:7; Eph 5:1-2; 1Jn 3:16). In enduring persecution (1Pe 3:17-18; 4:1). In forgiving (Col 3:13). In obedience (1Jn 2:6). In steadfastness (Heb 12:2-3). In perseverance (Rev 3:21). *See Jesus the Christ, Our Example.*
Paul, our:
Commanded (1Co 4:16; 11:1; Php 3:17; 4:9; 1Ti 1:16; 2Ti 1:13). In self-control (1Co 7:7-8). In self-maintenance (1Th 3:7-10). In beneficence (Ac 20:35).
See Influence.

EXCHANGERS See *Money Changers.*

EXCOMMUNICATION Disciplinary exclusion from church fellowship. Jews had temporary and permanent excommunication (Jn 9:22; 12:42; 16:2). Early church practiced it (1Co 5:5; 1Ti 1:20). *See Disfellowship.*

EXCUSES For disobedience (Ge 3:12-13; Ex 32:22-24; Dt 30:11-14). For rejecting salvation (Lk 14:18-20; Jn 15:22; Ac 24:25; Ro 1:20-21; 3:19). Inexcusable (Ro 2:1).
Examples:
For release from duty: By Moses, when commissioned to deliver Israel (Ex 3:11; 4:1, 10-14), by Gideon (Jdg 6:12-17), by Jesus' disciples (Mt 8:21; Lk 9:59-62).
When called to be a prophet: Elisha (1Ki 19:19-21), Isaiah (Isa 6:5-8), Jeremiah (Jer 1:5-10).
For physical healing: Naaman, the leper (2Ki 5:10-14).

EXECUTION See *Death, Death Penalty.*

EXECUTIONER (*punishment*). (Ge 37:36; Pr 16:14; Jer 39:9; Da 2:14; Mt 14:10). *See Punishment.*

EXHORTATIONS, SPECIAL To avoid various forms (Pr 4:15; Ro 16:17; 1Ti 6:20; 2Ti 2:16, 23; Tit 3:9). To choose between good and evil (Ex 32:26; Dt 30:19; Jos 24:15; 1Ki 18:21).

EXILE Usually refers to the period of time during which the Southern Kingdom (Judah) was detained in Babylon. Began in the reign of Jehoiakim (609-598 B.C.), culminating in the fall of Jerusalem (c. 586 B.C.). It ended with the decree of Cyrus permitting Jews to return to Israel c. 536 B.C. *See Diaspora; Outcasts.*

EXODUS (*a going out*). Departure of Israel from Egypt under Moses (Heb 11:22). *See Exodus, Book of.*

EXODUS, BOOK OF
Author: Moses
Date: c. 1445-1406 B.C.
Outline:
I. Divine Redemption (chs. 1-18).
　A. Fulfilled Multiplication (ch. 1).
　　1. The promised increase (1:1-7).
　　2. The first pogrom (1:8-14).
　　3. The second pogrom (1:15-21).
　　4. The third pogrom (1:22).
　B. Preparations for Deliverance (2:1-4:26).
　　1. Preparing a leader (2:1-10).
　　2. Extending the time of preparation (2:11-22).
　　3. Preparing the people (2:23-25).
　　4. Calling a deliverer (3:1-10).
　　5. Answering inadequate objections (3:11-4:17).
　　6. Preparing a leader's family (4:18-26).
　C. First Steps in Leadership (4:27-7:5).
　　1. Reinforced by brothers (4:27-31).
　　2. Rebuffed by the enemy (5:1-14).
　　3. Rebuffed by the enslaved (5:15-23).
　　4. Revisited by old objections (5:22-23).
　　5. Reinforced by the name of God (6:1-8).
　　6. Reminded of one's lowly origins (6:9-7:5).
　D. Judgment and Salvation Through the Plagues (7:6-11:10).
　　1. Presenting the signs of divine authority (7:6-13).
　　2. First plague: water turned to blood (7:14-24).
　　3. Second plague: frogs (7:25-8:15).
　　4. Third plague: gnats (8:16-19).
　　5. Fourth plague: flies (8:20-32).
　　6. Fifth plague: against livestock (9:1-7).
　　7. Sixth plague: boils (9:8-12).
　　8. Seventh plague: hail (9:13-35).
　　9. Eighth plague: locusts (10:1-20).
　　10. Ninth plague: darkness (10:21-29).
　　11. Tenth plague announced: death of the firstborn (ch. 11).
　E. The Passover (12:1-28).
　　1. Preparations for the Passover (12:1-13).
　　2. Preparations for Unleavened Bread (12:14-20).
　　3. Celebration of the Passover (12:21-28).
　F. The Exodus From Egypt (12:29-51).
　　1. Death at midnight (12:29-32).
　　2. Expulsion from Egypt (12:33-42).
　　3. Regulations for the Passover (12:43-51).
　G. The Consecration of the Firstborn (13:1-16).
　H. Crossing the "Red Sea" (13:17-15:21).
　　1. Into the wilderness (13:17-22).
　　2. At the "Red Sea" (14:1-14).
　　3. Across the "Red Sea" (14:15-31).
　　4. Song at the sea (15:1-21).
　I. Journey to Sinai (15:22-18:27).
　　1. The waters of Marah (15:22-27).
　　2. The manna and the quail (ch. 16).
　　3. The waters of Meribah (17:1-7).
　　4. The war with Amalek (17:8-16).
　　5. The wisdom of Jethro (ch. 18).
II. Covenant at Sinai (chs. 19-24).
　A. The Covenant Proposed (ch. 19).
　B. The Decalogue (20:1-17).
　C. The Reaction of the People to God's Fiery Presence (20:18-21).
　D. The Book of the Covenant (20:22-23:33).
　　1. Prologue (20:22-26).
　　2. Laws on slaves (21:1-11).
　　3. Laws on homicide (21:12-17).
　　4. Laws on bodily injuries (21:18-32).
　　5. Laws on property damage (21:33-22:15).
　　6. Laws on society (22:16-31).
　　7. Laws on justice and neighborliness (23:1-9).
　　8. Laws on sacred seasons (23:10-19).
　　9. Epilogue (23:20-33).
　E. Ratification of the Covenant (ch. 24).
III. Divine Worship (chs. 25-40).
　A. Instructions Concerning the Tabernacle (chs. 25-31).
　　1. Collection of the materials (25:1-9).
　　2. Ark and atonement cover (25:10-22).
　　3. Table of the bread of the Presence (25:23-30).
　　4. Gold lampstand (25:31-40).
　　5. Curtains and frames (ch. 26).
　　6. Altar of burnt offering (27:1-8).
　　7. Courtyard (27:9-19).
　　8. Priesthood (27:20-28:5).
　　9. Garments of the priests (28:6-43).
　　10. Ordination of the priests (ch. 29).
　　11. Altar of incense (30:1-10).
　　12. Census tax (30:11-16).
　　13. Bronze basin (30:17-21).
　　14. Anointing oil and incense (30:22-38).
　　15. Appointment of craftsmen (31:1-11).
　　16. Sabbath rest (31:12-18).
　B. False Worship (chs. 32-34).
　　1. The golden calf (32:1-29).
　　2. Moses' mediation (32:30-35).
　　3. Threatened separation and Moses' prayer (ch. 33).
　　4. Renewal of the covenant (ch. 34).
　C. The Building of the Tabernacle (chs. 35-40).
　　1. Summons to build (35:1-19).
　　2. Voluntary gifts (35:20-29).
　　3. Bezalel and his craftsmen (35:30-36:7).
　　4. Progress of the work (36:8-39:31).
　　5. Moses' blessing (39:32-43).
　　6. Erection of the tabernacle (40:34-38).
　　7. Dedication of the tabernacle (40:34-38).

EXORCISM (*to bind with an oath, to conjure*). The casting out of demons by means of magical formulas and ceremonies (Mt 12:27; Mk 9:38; Ac 19:13). *See Demons.*

EXPANSE The heavens above the earth (Ge 1:6-8, 14-17, 20).

EXPECTATION Of the righteous (Ps 62:5; Pr 24:14; Php 1:20). Of the wicked (Pr 10:28; 11:7, 23; Zec 9:5; Ac 12:11).

EXPEDIENCY To avoid offending others (Ro 14:1-2, 14-22; 1Co 6:12; 8:8-13; 9:22-23; 10:23-29, 32-33). To save people (1Co 9:19-23). Rule governing (1Co 10:30-31). Exemplified by Paul, in circumcising Timothy (Ac 16:3), in purifying himself at the temple (Ac 21:23-27).
See Evil; Prudence.

EXPERIENCE Solomon's (Ecc 1:2). Religious, relating of. *See Testimony, Religious.*

EXPERIMENT In worldly pleasure, Solomon's (Ecc 1; 2).

EXPIATION The act or means of making amends or reparation for sin. *See Atonement.*

EXPORTS From Egypt: horses and chariots, and linen yarn (1Ki 10:28-29; 2Ch 1:16-17), grain (Ge 42; 43).
 From Gilead: spices (Ge 37:25).
 From Ophir: gold (1Ki 10:11; 22:48; 1Ch 29:4).
 From Tarshish: gold (1Ki 10:22), ivory, apes, and baboons (1Ki 10:22), silver, iron, tin, lead, bronze, slaves (Eze 27:12-13).
 From Arabia: sheep and goats (Eze 27:21).
 From Israel: honey (Eze 27:17).
See Imports; Commerce.

EXPOSTULATION *See Reproof.*

EXTERMINATION *See War.*

EXTORTION Prayed upon the wicked by David (Ps 109:11). Warning against (Pr 22:16). Purged out of the land (Isa 16:4). Judged by God (Eze 22:12). Cruel (Mic 2:3).
 Scribes and Pharisees accused of by Christ (Mt 23:25). Pharisee judges himself not guilty of (Lk 18:11).
 Forbidden (Lk 3:13-14). Cause for disfellowship (1Co 5:10-11). Excludes from the kingdom of God (1Co 6:10).

Instances of:
 Jacob, in demanding Esau's birthright for a bowl of stew (Ge 25:31). Pharaoh in exacting of the Egyptians lands and persons for grain (Ge 47:13-26). The Jews after the Captivity (Ne 5:1-13).
See Interest; Usury.

EXTRADITION Instances of: Elijah from hiding to Ahab by Obadiah (1Ki 18:7, 10). Uriah from Egypt to Jehoiakim by Elnathan and company (Jer 26:21-23). Early believers from Damascus chief priests, in Jerusalem by Paul (Ac 9:2, 14; 22:5).

EXTRAVAGANCE Not to be pursued (Pr 21:17, 20; Lk 16:19). *See Gluttony.*

EYE Anthropomorphisms, figurative of God's omniscience (Ps 11:4; Pr 15:3), justice (Am 9:8), holiness (Hab 1:13), care (Ps 33:18-19; 34:15; 121:3-5; Isa 1:15; 1Pe 3:12), glory (Isa 3:8). *See Anthropomorphisms.*

Figurative:
 Of the moral state (Mt 7:3-5; 13:15-16; Mk 7:22). Of moral perception (Mt 6:22-23; Mk 8:18; Lk 10:23; Ac 26:18). Of insatiable desire (Pr 27:20; Ecc 1:18; 2Pe 2:14; Hos 2:16). Of evil pleasure (Mt 5:29; 18:9; Mk 9:27).

EYE FOR EYE *See Retaliation.*

EYES, OPENED (Ge 21:19; Nu 22:31; 2Ki 6:17; Lk 24:31).

EYES, PAINTING OF *See Cosmetics.*

EYESALVE Used figuratively for restoration of spiritual vision (Rev 3:18).

EZBAI Father of Naarai (1Ch 11:37). Possibly identical with Paarai (2Sa 23:35).

EZBON
 1. A son of Gad (Ge 46:16). Called Ozni (Nu 26:16).
 2. A son of Bela (1Ch 7:7).

EZEKIAS *See Hezekiah.*

EZEKIEL (*God [El] strengthens*). A priest. The time of his prophecy (Eze 1:1-3). Persecution of (Eze 3:25). Visions of: Of God's glory (Eze 1; 8; 10; 11:22), of Israelites' abominations (Eze 8:5-6), of their punishment (Eze 9:10), of the valley of dry bones (Eze 37:1-14), of a man with a measuring line (Eze 40-48), of the river (Eze 47:1-5).
 Teaches by pantomime: Feigns muteness (Eze 3:26; 24:27; 33:22), symbolizes the siege of Jerusalem by drawings on a tile (Eze 4), shaves himself (Eze 5:1-4), removes his belongings to illustrate the approaching Israelite captivity (Eze 12:3-7), sighs (Eze 21:6-7), employs a boiling pot to symbolize the destruction of Jerusalem (Eze 24:1-14), omits mourning at the death of his wife (Eze 24:16-27), prophesies by parable of an eagle (Eze 17:2-10). Other parables (Eze 15; 16; 19; 23).
 Prophecies of concerning various nations (Eze 25-29). His popularity (Eze 33:31-32).

EZEKIEL, BOOK OF
Author: Ezekiel
Date: See chart below
Outline:
I. Oracles of Judgment Against Israel (chs. 1-24).
 A. Ezekiel's Inaugural Vision (chs. 1-3).
 1. The divine overwhelming (ch. 1).
 2. The equipping and commissioning (2:1-3:15).
 3. The watchman 3:16-21).
 4. Further stipulations (3:22-27).

B. Symbolic Acts Portraying the Siege of Jerusalem (chs. 4-5).
 1. The city of Jerusalem on a clay tablet (4:1-3).
 2. Prophetic immobility (4:4-8).
 3. Diet for the siege and exile (4:9-17).
 4. The divine razor and its consequences (ch. 5).
C. Oracles Explaining Divine Judgment (chs. 6-7).
 1. Doom for the mountains of Israel (ch. 6).
 2. The end (ch. 7).
D. Vision of the Corrupted Temple (chs. 8-11).
 1. Four abominations (ch. 8).
 2. Destruction of the city (ch. 9).
 3. God's glory leaves Jerusalem (ch. 10).
 4. Conclusion of the vision (ch. 11).
E. Symbolic Acts Portraying Jerusalem's Exile (ch. 12).
 1. An exile's baggage (12:1-16).
 2. Anxious eating (12:17-20).
 3. The nearness of judgment (12:21-28).
F. Oracles Explaining Divine Judgment (chs. 13-24).
 1. False prophets and magic charms (ch. 13).
 2. The penalty for idolatry (14:1-11).
 3. Noah, Daniel and Job (14:12-23).
 4. Jerusalem as a burnt vine branch (ch. 15).
 5. Jerusalem as a wayward founding (16:1-43).
 6. Jerusalem compared to other cities (16:44-63).
 7. Jerusalem's kings allegorized (17:1-21).
 8. The new tree (17:22-24).
 9. The lesson of three generations (ch. 18).
 10. The twofold lament (ch. 19).
 11. Israel as a hardened repeater (ch. 20).
 12. The sword of the Lord (ch. 21).
 13. Jerusalem the city of blood (ch. 22).
 14. Oholah and Oholibah (ch. 23).
 15. The final fire: Jerusalem's end (24:1-14).
 16. The death of Ezekiel's wife and the destruction of the temple (24:15-27).
II. Oracles of Judgment Against the Nations (chs. 25-32).
 A. Against Ammon (25:1-7).
 B. Against Moab (25:8-11).
 C. Against Edom (25:12-14).
 D. Against Philistia (25:15-17).
 E. Against Tyre (26:1-28:19).
 1. The end of the city (ch. 26).
 2. A lament for Tyre (ch. 27).
 3. Against the king of Tyre (28:1-19).
 F. Against Sidon (28:20-24).
 G. A Note of Promise for Israel (28:25-26).
 H. Against Egypt (chs. 29-32).
 1. As a doomed monster (29:1-16).
 2. As a payment to Nebuchadnezzar (29:17-21).
 3. The approaching day (30:1-19).
 4. Pharaoh's arms are broken (30:20-26).
 5. As a felled cedar (ch. 31).
 6. A lament over Pharaoh (32:1-16).
 7. As consigned to the pit among the uncircumcised (32:17-32).
III. Oracles of Consolation for Israel (chs. 33-48).
 A. The Watchman (33:1-20).
 B. Jerusalem's Fall Reported and Explained (33:21-33).
 C. The Lord as the Good Shepherd (ch. 34).
 D. Oracles Against Edom (ch. 35).
 E. Consolations for the Mountains of Israel (36:1-15).
 F. Summary of Ezekiel's Theology (36:16-38).
 G. Vision of National Restoration (ch. 37).
 1. National resurrection (37:1-14).
 2. National reunification (37:15-28).
 H. The Final Battle (chs. 38-39).
 I. Vision of Renewed Worship (chs. 40-48).
 1. Wall around the temple (40:1-47).
 2. Temple exterior (40:48-41:26).
 3. Temple interior (ch. 42).
 4. The return of God's glory (ch. 43).
 5. The priesthood (ch. 44).
 6. Land allotment (ch. 45).
 7. The duties of the prince (ch. 46).
 8. Life-giving water (47:1-12).
 9. Land allotment (47:13-48:35).

EZEL *See Beth Ezel.*

EZEM (*bone [strength]*). A city in the S of Judah (Jos 15:29; 19:3; 1Ch 4:29).

EZER (*help*).
 1. The sixth son of Seir; a clan chief of the native Horite inhabitants of Edom (Ge 36:21, 27, 30; 1Ch 1:38, 42).
 2. A Judahite, father of Hushah (1Ch 4:4).
 3. An Ephraimite slain by the men of Gath (1Ch 7:21).
 4. A Gadite warrior who went over to David (1Ch 12:9).
 5. A Levite, son of Jeshua, who repaired a section of the wall of Jerusalem under Nehemiah's direction (Ne 3:19).
 6. A priest who participated in the dedication of the wall (Ne 12:42).

EZION GEBER (*giant, the giant backbone*). The last encampment of Israel before coming to the wilderness of Zin (Nu 33:35-36; Dt 2:8). Solomon, built a navy at (1Ki 9:26), visited (2Ch 8:17). Jehoshaphat's ships built at (2Ch 20:36), wrecked at (1Ki 22:48).

EZRA (*help*). A famous scribe and priest (Ezr 7:1-6, 10-12, 21; Ne 12:36). Appoints a fast (Ezr 8:21). Commissioned by Artaxerxes to rebuild the temple in Jerusalem which he directs (Ezr 7:8). Persecuted by Tattenai the governor (Ezr 6:3-17). Darius renews the decree of Cyrus for rebuilding the temple which he directs to completion (Ezr 6:1-15). His charge to the priests (Ezr 8:29). Exhorts people to put away heathen wives (Ezr 10:1-17). Reads the law (Ne 8). Reforms corruption (Ezr 10; Ne 13). Participates in the dedication of the wall of Jerusalem (Ne 12:27-43).

EZRA, BOOK OF
Author: According to Jewish tradition Ezra wrote Ezra and Nehemiah and also 1 and 2 Chronicles.
Date: c. 440 B.C.
Outline:
I. First Return From Exile and Rebuilding of the Temple (chs. 1-6).
 A. First Return of the Exiles (ch. 1).
 1. The edict of Cyrus (1:1-4).
 2. The return under Sheshbazzar (1:5-11).
 B. List of Returning Exiles (ch. 2).
 C. Revival of Temple Worship (ch. 3).
 1. The rebuilding of the altar (3:1-3).
 2. The Feast of Tabernacles (3:4-6).
 3. The beginning of temple reconstruction (3:7-13).
 D. Opposition to Rebuilding (4:1-23).
 1. Opposition during the reign of Cyrus (4:1-5).
 2. Opposition during the reign of Xerxes (4:6).
 3. Opposition during the reign of Artaxerxes (4:7-23).
 E. Completion of the Temple (4:24-6:22).
 1. Resumption of work under Darius (4:24).
 2. A new beginning inspired by Haggai and Zechariah (5:1-2).
 3. Intervention of Tattenai (5:3-5).
 4. Report to Darius (5:6-17).
 5. Search for the decree of Cyrus (6:1-5).
 6. Darius's order for the rebuilding of the temple (6:6-12).
 7. Completion of the temple (6:13-15).
 8. Dedication of the temple (6:16-18).
 9. Celebration of Passover (6:19-22).
II. Ezra's Return and Reforms (chs. 7-10).
 A. Ezra's Return to Jerusalem (chs. 7-8).
 1. Introduction (7:1-10).
 2. The authorization by Artaxerxes (7:11-26).
 3. Ezra's doxology (7:27-28).
 4. List of those returning with Ezra (8:1-14).
 5. The search for Levites (8:15-20).
 6. Prayer and fasting (8:21-23).
 7. The assignment of the sacred articles (8:24-30).
 8. The journey and arrival in Jerusalem (8:31-36).
 B. Ezra's Reforms (chs. 9-10).
 1. The offense of mixed marriages (9:1-5).
 2. Ezra's confession and prayer (9:6-15).
 3. The people's response (10:1-4).
 4. The public assembly (10:5-15).
 5. Investigation of the offenders (10:16-17).
 6. The list of offenders (10:18-43).
 7. Dissolution of mixed marriages (10:44).

EZRAH A Judahite (1Ch 4:17).

EZRAHITES The family or clan of Ethan and Heman, legendary wise men and poets (1Ki 4:31; Ps 88:T; 89:T). The word is probably a gentilic form of "Zerah," since 1Ch 2:6 designates Ethan and Heman as sons of Zerah.

EZRI (*my help*). Son of Kelub; the steward in charge of the agriculture of the crown lands in the time of David (1Ch 27:26).

F

FABLE (*talk, tale, legend, myth*). A type of literary genre in which animals and inanimate objects are used as persons or actors, speaking and using human behavior as if they actually were human beings. The fable is akin to the *allegory* and the *parable*. The fable is distinguished from the others in that there is a moral to the story; while the primary point of the allegory and the parable is to teach spiritual virtues.
 There are two fables in the OT. In the first, the people of Shechem are warned by Jotham, the sole survivor of Abimelech's coup, that Abimelech is treacherous and will provide certain tyranny (Jdg 9:7-15). In the second, Jehoash, king of Israel, snubs Amaziah, king of Judah, with an insult, warning that he is courting disaster (2Ki 14:9).
 In the NT, the debate among the parts of the body may be considered a fable (1Co 12:14-26). For KJV "fable" (1Ti 1:4; 4:7; 2Ti 4:4; Tit 1:14; 2Pe 1:16). *See Myths.*
See Allegory; Parable.

FACE
General References to:
Refers to the face of the waters (Ge 1:2), the earth (Ge 1:29), a man (Ge 3:19; Jas 1:23), flocks (Ge 30:40), God (Nu 6:25), the moon (Job 26:9), the seraphs (Isa 6:2), and the sky (Mt 16:3), Christ (2Co 4:6), the living creatures around the throne (Rev 4:7). The man himself may be meant (Dt 7:10), as in the Oriental circumlocution for "I." Character revealed in (Isa 3:9). Disfiguring of, in fasting (Mt 6:16).

Reflects Feelings:
(Ge 4:5; Pr 15:13). Moses in the presence of God (Ex 3:6). Favors are granted when the face is lifted up (Nu 6:25). Ruth bowed with her face to the ground in humility (Ru 2:10). Mourning (2Sa 19:4). To turn away or to hide the face is rejection (Pr 13:1). To seek the face is a desire for an audience (Ps 105:4). To harden the face is to promise no appeal (Pr 21:29). To spit on the face is a serious insult (Mt 26:67). Determination was evident when Jesus set his face to go to Jerusalem (Lk 9:51).

F

Covered:

By a harlot (Ge 38:15). Moses, when talking to the people after he was in the presence of God (Ex 34:29-35; 2Co 3:13-18). David (2Sa 19:4). In the doom of Haman (Est 7:8).

Of God:

Applied to God, it denotes his presence. Jacob struggles with God until daybreak and lives; he names the place where he fought, Peniel, which means "face of God," because "I saw God face to face, and yet my life was spared" (Ge 32:30). God himself or his glory which could not be seen by Moses (or by any man) or he would die (Ex 33:20). God hides his face when angry (Job 13:24). God also hides his face from sin to show his displeasure (Pr 27:9) and to show that he has forgiven sin (Ps 51:9). John says that the Son of God alone has ever seen God face to face (Jn 1:18). The literal translation for the "bread of the Presence" would be the "bread of the face" (Ex 25:30).

Transfigured:

Moses (Ex 34:29-35), Jesus (Mt 17:2; Lk 9:29).
See Countenance.

FAIR

Has the meaning of, just (Jdg 16:9; Pr 1:3; 2:9; 2Co 6:13; Col 4:1), clear skies (Job 26:13; Mt 16:2), persuasive (Pr 7:21), clean (Zec 3:5), beautiful (Hos 10:11; Ac 7:20).

It is not used to describe complexion.

FAIR HAVENS

A small bay near Lasea on the S coast of Crete, about five miles E of Cape Matala. Paul stayed here for a short time on his way to Rome (Ac 27:8-12).

FAITH

General Explanation of:

Faith has both an active and a passive sense in the Bible. The former meaning relates to one's loyalty to a person or fidelity to a promise; the latter confidence in the word or assurance of another. Faith is not merely *what* a person believes, i.e., accurate doctrine or creed, but also and more importantly, that the object of his faith is valid. A man's life is governed by his thoughts; he will ultimately become that which he dwells most upon in his mind. This is the reason for Paul's instruction to the Romans, "Do not conform any longer to the pattern of this world, but be transformed by the renewing of your mind" (Ro 12:2). He wrote similar instruction to the Philippians, "Finally, brothers, whatever is true, whatever is noble, whatever is right, whatever is pure, whatever is lovely, whatever is admirable—if anything is excellent or praiseworthy—think about such things" (Php 4:8).

The Value of:

People are kept secure by (2Ch 20:20; Ro 11:20; 2Co 1:24; 1Jn 5:4), are established by (Isa 7:9), are saved by (Jn 3:15; Ac 16:31; Ro 9:30-32; Gal 2:16; Eph 2:8-9; Php 3:9), healed by (Ac 14:9; Jas 5:15), are sanctified by (Ac 26:18), receive the Holy Spirit by (Gal 3:5, 14), live by (2Co 5:7). Causes men to be a blessing to others (Jn 7:38). Disbelieving God is a great sin (Jn 16:9; Ro 14:23). Faith is necessary to please God (Heb 11:6).

The Gift of God:

The apostles ask Jesus to increase (Lk 17:5). God gives a certain measure of (Ro 12:3; 1Co 2:4-5). Given by the Spirit (1Co 12:8-9).

The Purpose of:

To gain understanding and to grow in the truth (Ps 119:97-105, 129-131; Jn 8:31-32; 2Ti 2:15; 1Jn 2:5, 14). To grow in the grace of God (Ac 2:42-47; Ro 4:4-5; 5:2; 1Co 15:10; Eph 4:15; Heb 4:16). To help us to rejoice through our faith (Ro 5:2-5, 11; 15:13; Php 1:18-19; 2:17-18). To strengthen the man of faith (Ro 6:12-14; 11:20; 1Co 9:27; Php 4:6-7; 2Th 3:3; 2Ti 4:7-8; 1Pe 1:3-5). To be transformed into the image of Christ (Ro 8:29; 1Co 15:49; 2Co 3:18; 4:3-6). To become strong people of faith (Eph 4:1-3, 11-13, 15-16).

The Effect of:

Faith not works (Gal 5:5-6). Produces good works (1Th 1:3; 2Th 1:11), internal changes (1Th 2:13), perseverance (Jas 1:3).

The Righteousness of:

The true righteousness of God comes from (Ro 1:17; 3:21-30; 4:3, 11; 9:31-33; 10:4-11; Gal 2:16; Php 3:9; Heb 11:7).

The Biblical Position Concerning:

Credited as righteousness (Ge 15:6; Ro 4:3; Gal 3:6; Jas 2:23). Inspired by God's goodness (Ps 36:7, 9). Inspired by the Holy Spirit (1Co 12:8-9). Explained (Ps 118:8-9; Lk 17:6; 18:8; 1Ti 4:12; Heb 11:1-3, 6). Worry, doubt, and the lack of faith (Mt 6:25-34; 14:31; Lk 9:40; 17:5). Prayer for increase of (Mk 9:24; Lk 17:5). The gift of God (Ro 12:3). The righteous live by (Hab 2:4; Ro 1:17; Gal 3:11; Heb 10:38). Miracles accomplished by (Mt 17:18-20; 21:21-22; Mk 9:23; 11:23-24). Secures salvation (Col 2:12; 2Th 2:13; Heb 4:1-11; 6:1, 12, 18).

The Old Testament Use:

In the OT, the word "faith" in the sense of belief occurs only five times (2Ch 20:20, 20; Isa 7:9; 26:2; Hab 2:4). Faith is also communicated by words such as "believe," "fear," "hope," "love," and "trust." Faith is seen in the examples of the servants of God who committed their lives to him in unwavering trust and obedience. OT faith is never mere assent to a set of doctrines or outward acceptance of the Law, but absolute confidence in the faithfulness of God and a loving obedience to his will.

The New Testament Use:

In the NT "faith" and "believe" occur almost 500 times. The NT makes the claim that the promised Messiah had come and that Jesus of Nazareth was this promised Messiah. To believe on him meant to become a Christian, and was pivotal in the experience of the individual. Jesus offered himself as the object of faith and made plain that faith in him was necessary for eternal life.

The first Christians called themselves believers (Ac 2:44) and endeavored to persuade others to believe in Jesus (Ac 6:7; 28:24). In the epistles of Paul, faith is contrasted with works as a means of salvation (Ro 3:20-22). Faith is trust in the person of Jesus, the truth of his teaching, and the redemptive work which he accomplished at Calvary.

Faith may also refer to the body of truth which constitutes the whole of the Christian message (Jude 3).

Examples in the NT: In God (Lk 1:38-55; Ac 27:25; Ro 4:24; Heb 6:1; 1Pe 1:21; 4:19; 1Jn 3:21).

Strengthened by Miracles:

Of Abraham (Ge 15:8-18), of Gideon (Jdg 6:17, 36-40), of Hezekiah (2Ki 20:8-11), of Zechariah (Lk 1:18-20, 64).

In Affliction:

Exemplified by Job (Job 13:15-16; 14:15; 16:19; 19:25-27).

In Adversity:

Exemplified by, Hagar (Ge 16:15), Moses (Nu 14:8-9), Asa (2Ch 14:11), Jehoshaphat (2Ch 20:12), Hezekiah (2Ch 32:7-8), Nehemiah (Ne 1:10; 2:20), the psalmist (Ps 3:3, 5-6; 4:3, 8; 6:8-9; Ps 7:1, 10; 9:3-4; 11:1; 13:5; 17:6; 20:5-7; 31:1, 3-6, 14-15; 32:7; 33:20-22; 35:10; 38:9, 15; 42:5-6, 8; 43:5; 44:5, 8; 46:1-3, 5, 7; 54:4; 55:16-17, 23; 56:3-4, 8-9; 57:1-3; 59:9, 17; 60:9-10, 12; 61:2, 4, 6-7; 62:1, 5-7; 63:6-7; 69:19, 35-36; 70:5; 71:1, 3, 5-7, 14, 16, 20-21; 73:23-24, 26, 28; 86:2, 7; 89:18, 26; 91:1-2, 9-10; 92:10, 15; 94:14-15, 17-18, 22; 102:13; 108:10-13; 118:6-7, 10, 14, 17; 119:42, 57, 74, 81, 114, 166; 121:2; 138:7-8; 140:6-7, 12; 142:3, 5; 143:8-9), Jeremiah (La 3:24), Daniel (Da 3:16-17), Jonah (Jnh 2:2), Micah (Mic 7:7-9, 20), Paul (Ac 27:25; 2Co 1:10; 4:8-9, 13, 16-18; Php 1:19-21; 1Ti 4:10; 2Ti 1:12-13; 4:7-8, 18), the author of the letter to the Hebrews (Heb 10:34).

Commanded:

(Ps 4:5; 115:9, 11; Ecc 11:1; Isa 26:4; Mt 6:25-34; Mk 1:15; 11:22; Lk 12:32; 1Ti 6:11-12; 1:7; Jas 1:6). In time of public danger (Ex 14:13; Nu 21:34; Dt 1:21, 29-30; 3:2, 22; 7:17-21; 20:1; 31:8, 23; Jos 10:25; Jdg 6:14-16; 2Ki 19:6-7; 2Ch 20:15, 17, 20; 32:7-8; Ne 4:14; Isa 37:6; Jer 42:11). In time of adversity (Ps 37:3, 5, 7; 55:22; 62:8; Isa 43:1-2, 5, 10; 44:2, 8).

Commanded upon public leaders (Jos 1:5-9; 2Ch 15:7). Upon the young (Pr 3:5-6, 24-26). Upon the discouraged (Isa 35:3-4; 41:10, 13-14; 50:10). Upon widows (Jer 49:11).

Exemplified:

By Asa (2Ch 14:11). By Jehoshaphat (2Ch 20:12). By Hezekiah (2Ch 32:8). By Job (Job 1:21-22; 2:10; 5:8-9; 19:25-27). By the psalmists, setting forth supreme confidence in God (Ps 4:3, 8; 11:1; 13:5-6; 16:1-2, 5, 8-11; 18:1-3, 30-50; 20:5-8; 23:1-6; 25:1-15; 27:1-14; 31:1-5, 22-23, 24; 40:1-11; 46:1-11; 56:10-13; 57:1-11; 60:6-12; 61:1-8; 62:5-12; 63:1-8). By the following Psalms in their entirety (Ps 91; 95; 105-108; 115-118; 121; 123-126; 130; 135-136; 138-140; 145-150). By Isaiah (Isa 8:10, 17; 12:2; 17:13-14; 25:9; 26:1, 8; 33:1, 22; 50:7-9; 63:16; 64:8). By Jeremiah (Jer 14:9, 22; 16:19; 17:17; 20:11).

Instances of:

Abel (Heb 11:4). Noah, in building the ark (Ge 6:14-22; Heb 11:7). Abraham, in forsaking the land of his birth at the command of God (Ge 12:1-4; Heb 11:8), in believing the promise of many descendants (Ge 12:7; 15:4-6; Ro 4:18-21; Heb 11:11-12), in the offering up of Isaac (Ge 22:1-10; Heb 11:17-19). Jacob, in blessing Joseph's sons (Ge 48:8-21; Heb 11:21). Joseph, concerning God's providence in his being sold into Egypt, and the final deliverance of Israel (Ge 50:20, 24; Heb 11:22). Job (Job 1:21-22; 2:10). Eliphaz, in the overruling providence of God, that afflictions are for the good of the righteous (Job 5:6-27).

Jochebed, in caring for Moses (Ex 2:2-3; Heb 11:23). Pharaoh's servants, who obeyed the Lord (Ex 9:20). Moses, in espousing the cause of his people (Heb 11:24-28), at the death of Korah (Nu 16:28-29). Israelites (Ps 22:4-5), when Aaron declared the mission of himself and Moses (Ex 4:31), for forty years wanderings (Dt 8:2), in the battle with the Canaanites (1Ch 5:20), and other conquests (2Ch 13:8-18), by the waters of Meribah (Ps 81:7). Caleb, in advising to take the land of promise (Nu 13:30; 14:6-9), when he asked for Hebron (Jos 14:12). Rahab, in hospitality to the spies (Jos 2:9, 11; Heb 11:31). The spies sent to look over Jericho (Jos 2:24). Conquest of Jericho (Jos 6; Heb 11:30). Manoah's wife (Jdg 13:23). Hannah (1Sa 1). Jonathan, in killing the Philistines (1Sa 14:6).

David, in killing Goliath, the hero of the Philistines (1Sa 17:37, 45-47), in choosing to fall into the hands of the Almighty in his punishment for numbering Israel (2Sa 24:14), in believing God's promise that his kingdom would be a perpetual kingdom (Ac 2:30). The widow of Zarephath, in feeding Elijah (1Ki 17:13-15). Elijah, in his controversy with the priests of Baal (1Ki 18:32-38). Hezekiah (2Ki 18:5, 19). Amaziah, in dismissing the Ephraimites in obedience to the command of God, and going alone to battle against the Edomites (2Ch 25:7-10).

The three Hebrews who refused to worship Nebuchadnezzar's idol (Da 3:13-27). Daniel, in the lions' den (Da 6). Nebuchadnezzar (Da 6:16). The Ninevites, in obeying Jonah (Jnh 3:5). Habakkuk (Hab 3:17-19). Ezra, in making the journey from Babylon to Jerusalem without a military escort (Ezr 8:22). Mordecai, in the deliverance of the Jews (Est 4:14). Esther, in going before the king (Est 4:9-5:4).

Joseph, in obeying the vision about Mary and to flee into Egypt (Mt 1:18-24; 2:13-14). Mary, in believing the angel of the Lord, and in submitting to the Lord's will (Lk 1:38). Simeon, when he saw Jesus in the temple (Lk 2:25-35). Paul (Ro 8:18, 28, 38-39; 1Co 9:24-27; 2Co 5:7; Gal 5:5). The great people of faith (Heb 11:32-34).

The Trial of:

To prove depth of faith (Dt 8:2; 1Ch 29:17; Ps 26:2). To test spirituality (Mt 13:9-22; Lk 8:13-14). By tribulations (Mt 24:21-25; 2Th 1:3-5). By deferred hope (Heb 6:13-15). By trials (Jas 1:3, 12). Is precious (1Pe 1:7).

Instances of—

Noah (Ge 6:14-22; Heb 11:7). Abraham, when commanded to leave his native land (Ge 12:1-4; Heb 11:8), when commanded to offer Isaac (Ge 22:1-19; Heb 11:17-19). Moses, when sent to Pharaoh (Ex 3:11-12; 4:10-17; Heb 11:25-29), at the Red Sea, by the murmurings of the people (Ex 14:15; Heb 11:29). Joshua and the Israelites, in the method of taking Jericho (Jos 6; Heb 11:30). Gideon, when commanded to deliver Israel (Jdg 6:36-40; Heb 11:32). Ezra, in leaving Babylon without a military escort (Ezr 8:22). Job, by affliction and adversity (Job 1; 2). The three Hebrews, when commanded to worship Nebuchadnezzar's image (Da 3:8-30; Heb 11:32-34). Daniel, when forbidden by decree to pray to Yahweh (Da 6:4-23; Heb 11:32-33).

The two blind men who appealed to Jesus for sight (Mt 9:28). The Syrian Phoenician woman (Mt 15:21-28; Mk 7:24-30). The disciples, by the question of Jesus, in the storm at sea (Mt 8:23-27; Mk 4:36-41; Lk 8:22-26), as to who he was (Mt 16:15-20; Lk 9:20-21), by their inability to cast out the evil spirit from the boy (Mt 17:14-21; Mk 9:14-29; Lk 9:37-42). Of Philip, when questioned by Jesus as to how the multitude would be fed (Jn 6:5-6). Of Peter, when asked whether he loved Jesus (Jn 21:15-17).
See Tribulation.

Rewards of:

Protection (2Sa 22:31; Ps 5:11; 9:9-10; 18:30; 33:18-20; Pr 29:25; 30:5; Jer 39:18; Na 1:7; Heb 13:5-6). Spiritual peace (Ps 2:12; 32:10; 40:4; 84:5, 12; Isa 26:3; Ro 15:13). Prosperity (Pr 28:25; Isa 57:13; Jer 17:7-8). Eternal life (2Ti 1:1, 8).
See Faith in Christ.

FAITH, TEACHINGS OF JESUS

Beliefs held in common by apostles and early believers (Ac 6:7; 16:5; 1Co 16:13; Gal 1:23; 3:23, 25; 6:10; Php 1:27; 1Ti 3:9; 4:1; 5:8; 6:10, 21; 2Ti 3:8; 4:7; Tit 1:1, 4, 13; 3:15; Jude 3; Rev 2:13).

FAITH IN CHRIST

General References Concerning:

Commanded (Mt 17:7; Jn 6:20; 20:27, 29; 1Jn 3:23). All things possible by (Mt 21:22; Mk 9:23; Lk 17:6). Prayer for increase of (Mk 9:24).

Leads to salvation (Jn 1:12; 3:14-18, 36; 5:24; 6:40, 47; 7:38; 12:36, 46; 20:31; Ac 10:43; 13:48; 15:9, 11; 16:31; 20:21; 26:18; Ro 1:16-17; 3:22-28; 4:1-25; 5:1-2; 9:31-33; 10:4-10; 11:20; 1Co 1:21; 2:5; Gal 2:16; Gal 3:1-29; 5:5-6; Eph 2:8; 3:12, 17; 1Ti 1:16; 2Ti 1:13; 3:15; 1Pe 1:9; 2:6-7; 2Pe 1:1; Rev 3:20). Will result in good works (Jn 14:12; Jas 2:1-26).

Christ, the focus of faith (Ps 2:12; Heb 12:2). The Christian triumphs by (Ro 8:35, 37; 2Co 1:24; Eph 4:13; 6:16; Php 3:9; Col 1:23; 2:7; Heb 10:22, 38-39; 13:7; 1Pe 1:5, 7-9; 1Jn 5:4-5, 10, 14).

Exemplified by:

The wise men of the East as they worship the infant King Jesus (Mt 2:1-2, 11). The disciples in response to the call of Jesus (Mt 4:18-22; Mk 1:16-20; Lk 5:4; Lk 5:5-11; Jn 1:35-49; 6:68-69; 16:27, 30, 33). Peter (Mt 4:18-22; 16:16; Mk 1:16-20; Lk 5:4-5; Jn 6:68-69). Andrew (Mt 4:18-22; Mk 1:16-20; Jn 1:41). James and John (Mt 4:21-22; Mk 1:19-20). Philip (Jn 1:43-46). Nathanael (Jn 1:46-49). The disciples, through the miracle at Cana of Galilee (Jn 2:11). Jews at Jerusalem (Jn 2:23; 8:30; 11:45; 12:11). The Samaritans, who believed through the preaching of Jesus (Jn 4:39-42), of Philip (Ac 8:9-12).

Those who were healed by Jesus: the leper (Mt 8:2; Mk 1:40; Lk 5:12-13). The centurion, for the healing of his servant (Mt 8:5-10, 13; Lk 7:3-9). Those who brought the paralytic to Jesus (Mt 9:1-2; Mk 2:1-5; Lk 5:18-20). Jairus, for the healing of his daughter (Mt 9:18, 23-25; Mk 5:22-43; Lk 8:41-56). The woman subject to bleeding (Mt 9:20-22; Mk 5:25-34; Lk 8:43-48). Two blind men (Mt 9:27-30). The disciples in the storm (Mt 14:33). The sick of Gennesaret (Mt 14:36; Mk 3:10; 6:54-56). The Syrian Phoenician woman (Mt 15:22-28; Mk 7:25-30). The people of Decapolis (Mt 15:30). The father of the demon-possessed child (Mt 17:14-15; Mk 9:24; Lk 9:38, 42). Blind Bartimaeus, and a fellow blind man (Mt 20:30-34; Mk 10:46-52; Lk 18:35-43). Those who brought the deaf and mute man to Jesus (Mk 7:32). The woman who was a sinner (Lk 7:38, 44-48, 50). Mary, the sister of Martha (Lk 10:38-42; Jn 11:32). The Samaritan leper (Lk 17:11-19).

The nobleman, for the healing of his son (Jn 4:46-47, 50). The people who saw the feeding of the five thousand (Jn 6:14). The blind man whom Jesus healed on the Sabbath (Jn 9:13-38). The people in Bethany beyond the Jordan (Jn 10:41-42). Zacchaeus (Lk 19:1-6). The thief, on the cross (Lk 23:42). John, the disciple, after the resurrection (Jn 20:8). Thomas, after the resurrection (Jn 20:28).

Those in the early church. By three thousand, at Pentecost (Ac 2:41). By five thousand (Ac 4:4). By multitudes (Ac 5:14). By Stephen (Ac 6:8; 7:55-56). By the Ethiopian eunuch (Ac 8:36, 38). By the cripple at Lystra (Ac 14:8-10). Paul (Ro 7:24-25; 2Co 12:9-10; Gal 2:20; Php 4:13; 2Ti 1:12; 4:18). Expressed as a response to the preaching of the gospel. Of Lydda and Sharon (Ac 9:35), of Joppa (Ac 9:42), of Antioch (Ac 11:21-24). Barnabas (Ac 11:24). Eunice, Lois, and Timothy (Ac 16:1; 2Ti 1:5). Lydia (Ac 16:14). Philippian jailer (Ac 16:31-34). Crispus (Ac 18:8). The Corinthians (Ac 18:8; 1Co 15:11). Jews at Rome (Ac 28:24). Ephesians (Eph 1:13, 15). Colossians (Col 1:2, 4). Thessalonians (1Th 1:6; 3:6-8; 2Th 1:3-4). Philemon (Phm 5). Church at Thyatira (Rev 2:19).

FAITHFUL SAYINGS

These are trustworthy statements; words that you may depend upon as truthful and everlasting (1Ti 1:15; 3:1; 4:9; 2Ti 2:11; Tit 3:8).

FAITHFULNESS

Described:

Scarce (Ps 12:1; Pr 20:6). Tested (Lk 16:10-12). A fruit of the Spirit (Gal 5:22). Rewards of (Ps 31:23; Pr 28:20; Mt 10:22; 13:12; 25:29; Mk 13:13; Heb 10:34; Rev 2:10).

Required:

(Mt 24:45-51, w Lk 12:36-48; Mt 25:14-30, w Lk 19:12-27). Of those who are trusted (1Co 4:2). Of servants (Eph 6:5-9; Col 3:22).

Instances of:

Abraham's servant (Ge 24:33). Moses (Nu 12:7; Heb 3:3, 5). Ruth (Ru 1:15-18). Ittai the Gittite (2Sa 15:19-22). David (2Sa 22:22-25). Elijah (1Ki 19:10, 14). Workmen in temple repairs (2Ki 12:15; 2Ch 34:12). Josiah (2Ki 22:2). Abijah (2Ch 13:10-12). Jehoshaphat (2Ch 20:1-30). Hanani and Hananiah (Ne 7:2). Abraham (Ne 9:7-8; Gal 3:9). Nehemiah's treasurer (Ne 13:13). Job (Job 1:21-22; 2:9-10). The three Hebrew captives (Da 3:16-18). Daniel (Da 6:10). Jesus (Jn 4:34; Heb 3:2). Abraham (Gal 3:9). Paul (1Ti 1:12; 2Ti 4:7).
See Reward, A Motive, To Faithfulness.

See also, Jesus the Christ, Faithfulness of; God, Faithfulness of; Minister, Faithful.

FALCON A bird of prey (Job 28:7; Isa 34:15), unclean for food (Dt 14:13). *See Birds.*

FALL OF MANKIND, THE The fall of mankind as related in Genesis 3 is the historical choice by which Adam and Eve sinned voluntarily, and consequently involved all the human race in sin. Since the Fall, there is no person who continually does what is right and never sins (1Ki 8:46; Ps 130:3; 143:2; Pr 20:9; Ecc 7:20; Ro 3:8-10; 5:12; 1Co 15:22; 1Jn 1:8). By the Fall mankind was alienated from God. Mankind was created in God's own image, with a rational and moral nature like God's, with no inner impulse to sin, and with a will free to choose the will of God. Yielding to the outward temptation turned mankind from God and created an environment in which sin became a potent factor. Redemption from the Fall is accomplished through the second Adam, Jesus Christ (Ro 5:12-21; 1Co 15:21-22, 45-49).

Consequences of:
Knowledge of, nakedness (Ge 3:7). Guilt (Ge 3:8-10). Cursing of, the serpent (Ge 3:14-15). Cursing of the ground (Ge 3:17-18). Multiplying of sorrows (Ge 3:16-19). Death, physical (Ge 3:19; Ro 5:12, 14; 1Co 15:21-22). Spiritual (Ro 5:12, 14, 18-19, 21).

Means of:
By transgression of commandments (Ge 2:16-17; 3:1-3, 6, 11-12; Job 31:33; Isa 43:27; Hos 6:7). Through deception of Satan (Ge 3:4-5, 13; 2Co 11:3; 1Ti 2:14). Through evil desire (Ge 3:6; Ecc 7:29).
See Depravity.

FALLOW DEER *See Animals; Deer.*

FALLOW GROUND Land that is left idle for a growing season, after plowing and harrowing, so that weeds and insects are killed while the soil regains its fertility. *See Agriculture.*

Practical Application:
Israel is instructed to follow this practice every seventh year (Ex 23:11), but through much of its history, they failed to allow their land a sabbath rest (Lev 26:34-35).

Spiritual Application:
Israel is encouraged to seek God and to become spiritually active (Jer 4:3; Hos 10:12).

FALSE ACCUSATION *See Accusation, False.*

FALSE APOSTLES Paul speaks of false apostles in 2 Corinthians only. These people "masquerade as apostles of Christ" (2Co 11:13). Paul denounces them as servants of Satan (2Co 11:14), "masquerading as servants of righteousness," which is not surprising, since their master "masquerades as an angel of light" (2Co 11:14-15). Yet they claim to be servants of Christ (2Co 11:23). Apparently they boasted of their Jewish heritage, using this to help justify their self-proclaimed position as "apostle of Christ" (2Co 11:22).

FALSE CHRISTS These are people who make a false claim to be the Messiah. Jesus warned his disciples that imitators and pretenders would follow him who would try to deceive his followers (Mt 24:5-11, 23-25; Mk 13:6, 21, 23; Lk 21:8). False Christs are to be distinguished from the Antichrist. The false Christ is an impostor while the latter is one who opposes Christ. His opposition is mainly through the doctrines about Jesus' person and work which are contrary to the truth.

FALSE CONFIDENCE

Described:
In self (Dt 29:19; 1Ki 20:11; Pr 3:5, 7; 26:5, 12; 28:26; Isa 5:21; Ro 12:16; 2Co 1:9). In outward resources (Ps 20:7; 33:17; 44:6; 49:6; Pr 11:28; Isa 22:9-11; 31:1-3; Jer 48:7; Zec 4:6; Mk 10:24, ftn). In man (Ps 33:16; 62:9; 118:8; 146:3-4; Isa 2:22; Jer 17:5; Hos 5:13; 7:11).

Instances of:
At the tower of Babel (Ge 11:4). Sennacherib, in the siege of Jerusalem (2Ki 19:23). Asa, in relying on Syria rather than on God (2Ch 16:7-9). Hezekiah, in the defenses of Jerusalem (Isa 22:11). Peter, in asserting his devotion to Jesus (Mt 26:35; Lk 22:33-34; Jn 13:37-38).
See Confidence.

FALSE PROPHET Any person pretending to possess a message from God, but not possessing a divine commission (Jer 29:9). Test for (Dt 13:1-5; 18:20-22).

The False Prophet of the Apocalypse:
The false prophet is mentioned in the book of Revelation (Rev 19:20) and is usually identified with the two-horned beast of Revelation (Rev 13:11-18).

FALSE TEACHERS *See Teachers, False.*

FALSE WITNESS

Described:
Punishment for (Dt 19:16-20; Pr 19:5, 9; 21:28; Zec 5:3-4). Innocent suffer from (Ps 27:12; 35:11). Proverbs concerning (Pr 6:16-19; 12:17; 14:5, 8, 25; 19:5, 9; 21:28; 24:28; 25:18). God hates (Pr 6:16-19). Results from a corrupt heart (Mt 15:19).
See Evidence; Falsehood; Perjury; Witness.

Forbidden:
(Ex 20:16; 23:1-3; Lev 6:1-5; 19:11-12, 16; Dt 5:20; Pr 24:28; Mt 19:18; Lk 3:14; 18:20; 1Ti 1:9-10).

Instances of:
Witnesses against, Naboth (1Ki 21:13), Jesus (Mt 26:59-61; Mk 14:54-59), Stephen (Ac 6:11-13), Paul (Ac 16:20-21; 17:5-7; 24:5; 25:7-8).

FALSEHOOD

Described:
Atonement for (Lev 6:2-7). Punishment for (Ps 12:2-4; 52:4-5; 55:23; 63:11; Pr 10:10, 31; 12:19; 14:5, 25; 19:5, 9; Rev 21:8, 27; 22:15). Falsehood will be found out (Pr 10:9; 28:18). Destructive (Pr 11:9; 26:18-19, 24-26, 28; Isa 32:7).
See Accusation, False; Conspiracy; Deceit; Deception; False Witness; Flattery; Hypocrisy; Perjury; Teachers, False.
All guilty of (Job 13:4; Ps 116:11; Jer 9:3-5; Hos 7:13; Mic 6:12; Ro 3:4). Refrained from by the righteous (Job 27:4; 31:5-6, 33; 36:4; Pr 14:5, 25; Isa 63:8). Practiced by the wicked (Ps 10:7; 28:3; 36:3; 50:19-20; 52:2-4; 58:3; 62:4; 109:2; Pr 2:12-15; 12:17, 20; 21:6; Isa 28:15; 57:11; 59:3-4, 12-13; Jer 7:28, 28; 9:3, 5-6, 8; 12:6; Hos 4:1-2; Ob 7; Mic 6:12; Na 3:1; Jn 8:44-45; 1Ti 4:2; 1Pe 3:16). Wicked easily misled by (Pr 14:8; 17:4). An abomination to the Lord (Ps 5:6, 9; Pr 6:12-13, 16-19; 12:22). Abhorred by the righteous (Ps 31:18; 59:12; 101:5, 7; 119:29, 69, 163; 120:2-4; 144:8, 11; Pr 10:18; 13:5; 20:17).

Forbidden:
(Ex 20:16; 23:1; Lev 19:11-12, 16; Ps 34:13, w 1Pe 3:10; Pr 17:7; Ecc 5:6; Zep 3:13; Eph 4:25, 29; Col 3:9; 1Ti 1:9-10).

Instances of:
Satan, in deceiving Eve (Ge 3:4-5), in impugning Job's motives for being righteous (Job 1:9-10; 2:4-5), in his tempting of Jesus (Mt 4:8-9; Lk 4:6-7). Adam and Eve, in attempting to avoid responsibility (Ge 3:12-13). Cain, in denying knowledge of his brother (Ge 4:9). Abraham, in denying that Sarah was his wife (Ge 12:11-19; 20:2). Sarah, to the angels, denying her laugh of unbelief (Ge 18:15), in denying to the king of Gerar, that she was Abraham's wife (Ge 20:5, 16). Isaac, denying that Rebekah was his wife (Ge 26:7-10). Rebekah and Isaac, in the conspiracy against Esau (Ge 27:6-24, etc). Jacob's sons, in the scheme to destroy the Shechemites by first having them circumcised (Ge 34). Joseph's brothers in deceiving their father into a belief that Joseph was killed by wild beasts (Ge 37:29-35). Potiphar's wife, in falsely accusing Joseph (Ge 39:14-17). Joseph, in the deception he carried on with his brothers (Ge 42-44).
Pharaoh, in dealing deceitfully with the Israelites (Ex 7-12). Aaron, in attempting to shift responsibility for the making of the golden calf (Ex 32:1-24). Rahab, in denying that the spies were in her house (Jos 2:4-6). The Gibeonites' ambassadors, in the deception they perpetrated upon Joshua and the elders of Israel in leading them to believe that they came from a distant region, in fact they dwelt in the immediate vicinity (Jos 9). Ehud, in pretending to bear secret messages to Eglon, king of Moab, while his object was to assassinate him (Jdg 3:16-22). Sisera, who instructed Jael to mislead his pursuers (Jdg 4:20).
Saul, in professing to Samuel to have obeyed the commandment to destroy all spoils of the Amalekites, when in fact he had not obeyed (1Sa 15:1-20), in accusing Ahimelech of conspiring with David against himself (1Sa 22:11-16), in deceiving the medium of Endor as to his identity (1Sa 28:7-12). Michal, in the false statement that David was sick, in order to save him from Saul's violence (1Sa 19:12-17).
David, who lied to Ahimelech, professing to have a mission from the king, in order that he might obtain provisions and armor (1Sa 21), in feigning madness (1Sa 21:13-15), and other deceits with the Philistines (1Sa 27:8-12), the falsehood he put in the mouth of Hushai, of friendship to Absalom (2Sa 15:34-37). The Amalekite who claimed to have slain Saul (2Sa 1:10-12). Hushai, in false professions to Absalom (2Sa 16:16-19), in his deceitful counsel to Absalom (2Sa 17:7-14). The wife of the Baharumite who saved the lives of Hushai's messengers, sent to inform David of the movements of Absalom's army (2Sa 17:15-22).
The old prophet of Bethel who misguided the prophet of Judah (1Ki 13:11-22), Jeroboam's wife, pretending to be another woman (1Ki 14:1-6). Jezebel, Ahab, and the conspirators against Naboth (1Ki 21:7-13). Gehazi, when he ran after Naaman and misrepresented that Elisha wanted a talent of silver and two changes of clothing (2Ki 5:20-24). Hazael, servant of the king of Syria, lied to the king in misrepresenting the prophet Elisha's message in regard to the king's recovery (2Ki 8:7-15). Jehu lied to the worshipers of Baal in order to gain advantage over them and destroy them (2Ki 10:18-28). Zedekiah, in violating his oath of allegiance to Nebuchadnezzar (2Ch 36:13; Eze 16:59; 17:13-20).
Samaritans, in their efforts to hinder the rebuilding of the temple at Jerusalem (Ezr 4). Sanballat, in trying to obstruct the rebuilding of Jerusalem (Ne 6). Haman, in his conspiracy against the Jews (Est 3:8). In the answers of Job's friends (Job 21:34). Jeremiah's adversaries in accusing him of joining the Chaldeans (Jer 37:13-15). Princes of Israel, when they went to Jeremiah for a vision from the Lord (Jer 42:20).
Herod, to the wise men, in professing to desire to worship Jesus (Mt 2:8). Jews, in falsely accusing Jesus of blasphemy, when he forgave sin (Mt 9:2-8; Mk 2:5-12; Lk 5:21-26), in falsely accusing Jesus of being a glutton and a drunkard (Mt 11:19), in refusing to bear truthful testimony concerning John the Baptist (Mt 21:24-27), when he announced that he was the Son of God (Mt 26:65; Mk 14:64; Jn 10:33-38). The disobedient son who promised to work in the vineyard but did not (Mt 21:30). Peter, in denying Jesus (Mt 26:69-75; Mk 14:66-72; Jn 18:16-18, 25-27). The Roman soldiers, who said the disciples stole the body of Jesus (Mt 28:13, 15).
Ananias and Sapphira falsely state that they had sold their land for a given sum (Ac 5:1-10). Stephen's accusers, who falsely accused him of blaspheming Moses and God (Ac 6:11-14). Paul's opponents, falsely accusing him of treason to Caesar (Ac 16:20-21; 17:5-7; 24:5; 25:7-8). The Cretans, who are always liars, evil brutes, lazy gluttons (Tit 1:12).
See Accusation, False; Conspiracy; False Witness; Hypocrisy; Perjury; Teachers, False.

FAME OF JESUS (Mt 4:24-25; 9:26, 31; 14:1; Mk 1:28, 45; Lk 4:14, 37; 5:15; 7:17).

FAMILIAR SPIRITS *See Spiritists.*

FAMILY The concept of the family in the Bible differs from the modern institution. The Hebrew family was larger than families

today, including the father of the household, his parents, if living, his wife or wives and children, his daughters and sons-in-law, slaves, guests, and foreigners under his protection. Marriage was arranged by the father of the groom, and the family of the bride, for whom a dowry or purchase money was paid to her father (Ge 24). Polygamy and concubinage were practiced, though not favored by God. A husband could divorce his wife, but she could not divorce him.
The father of a family had the power of life and death over his children. To dishonor a parent was punishable by death (Ex 21:15, 17).
The NT concept followed that of the OT. Parents and children, husbands and wives, masters and slaves were commanded to live together in harmony and love (Eph 5:22-6:9; Col 3:18-4:1).

Good, Exemplified:
Abraham (Ge 18:19). Jacob (Ge 35:2). Joshua (Jos 24:15). David (2Sa 6:20). Job (Job 1:5). Lazarus of Bethany (Jn 11:1-5). Cornelius (Ac 10:2, 33). Lydia (Ac 16:15). The Philippian jailer (Ac 16:31-34). Crispus (Ac 18:8). Lois (2Ti 1:5).

Unhappiness in:
Caused, by indiscreetness (Pr 11:22; 12:4; 14:1; 30:21, 23). By hatred (Ps 15:17). By contention (Pr 18:19; 19:13; 21:9, 19; 25:24; 27:15-16).

Instances of –
Of Abraham, on account of Hagar (Ge 16:5; 21:10-11). Of Isaac, on account of disagreement between Jacob and Esau (Ge 27:4-46). Of Jacob, polygamous jealousy between Leah and Rachel (Ge 29:30-34; 30:1-25). Moses and Zipporah (Ex 4:25-26). Elkanah, on account of feuds (1Sa 1:4-7). David and Michal (2Sa 6:16, 20-23). Xerxes, on account of Vashti's refusing to appear before his drunken officials (Est 1:10-22).

Instituted:
(Ge 2:23-24). Government of (Ge 3:16; 18:19; Est 1:20, 22; 1Co 7:10; 11:3, 7-9; Eph 5:22-24; Col 3:18; 1Ti 3:2, 4-5, 12; 1Pe 3:1, 6). Husband should provide for (Ge 30:30; 1Ti 5:8). Duty to (Isa 58:7). Idolatrous (Jer 7:18).
Persian customs in (Est 1:10-22). *See Harem.*
See Children; Husband; Orphan; Widow; Wife.

Of Saints:
Live in unity (Ge 45:24; Ps 133:1). Live in mutual forbearance (Ge 50:17-21; Mt 18:21-22). Should be taught God's Word (Dt 4:9-10). Rejoice together before God (Dt 14:26). Warned against departing from God (Dt 29:18). Deceivers and liars should be removed from (Ps 101:7). Blessed (Ps 128:3, 6). Should be managed wisely (Pr 31:27; 1Ti 3:4-5, 12). Punishment of irreligious (Jer 10:25). Worship God together (1Co 16:19).

Religion in:
Purpose: To keep the way of the Lord (Ge 18:19), to keep children from sinning (Job 1:5), to be an example to the household (Ps 101:2).
Observed by: Abraham (Ge 12:7-8; 13:3-4; 18:19), Joshua (Jos 24:15), Job (Job 1:5), David (Ps 101:2).
Manifested in observance of religious rites (Ge 17:12-14; 35:2-4, 7; Lk 2:21; Ac 10:2, 47-48; 16:15; 16:25-34; 1Co 1:16), in religious instruction of children (Dt 4:9-10; 11:19-20), in household consecration (Dt 12:5-12; Jos 24:15; Ac 10:1-2; 18:8).

FAMINE

Described:
Pharaoh forewarned of, in dreams (Ge 41). Sent as a judgment (Lev 26:19-29; Dt 28:23-24, 38-42; 1Ki 17:1; 2Ki 8:1; 1Ch 21:12; Ps 105:16; 107:33-34; Isa 3:1-8; 14:30; Jer 14:15-22; 19:9; 29:17, 19; La 5:4-5, 10; Eze 4:16-17; 5:16-17; 14:13-14; Joel 1:15-16; Am 4:6-9; 5:16-17; Hag 1:10-11; Mt 24:7; Lk 21:11; Rev 6:5-8). Description of (Dt 28:53-57; Isa 5:13; 9:18-21; 17:11; Jer 5:17; 14:1-6; 48:33; La 1:11, 19; 2:11-22; 4:4-10; Joel 1:17-20). Righteous delivered from (Job 5:20; Ps 33:19; 37:19). Cannibalism in (Dt 28:53; 2Ki 6:28).

Instances of:
In Canaan (Ge 12:10; 26:1; 2Sa 21:1; 1Ki 17; 18:1; 2Ki 6:25-29; 7:4). In Egypt (Ge 41:53-57). In Jerusalem, from siege (2Ki 25:3; Jer 52:6). Universal (Ac 11:28).

Figurative:
God will withdraw from those who will not listen to the words of his prophets in the same way that food and water is scarce during famine (Am 8:11).

FAN *See Winnow; Winnowing.*

FANATICISM Absolute and aggressive devotion to religion. The prophets of Baal (1Ki 18:28). The Jews against Christ (Jn 19:15). The Jews in stoning Stephen (Ac 7:57). Saul in persecuting the church (Ac 9:1). The Jews in their rage against Paul (Ac 21:36; 22:23).

FAREWELLS Allusions to (Ru 1:14; Lk 9:61; Ac 18:21; 20:38; 21:6; 2Co 13:11).

FARMER An agriculturalist (Isa 28:24; Jer 14:4; Mt 21:33-46; Mk 12:1-9; Jn 15:1; 1Co 3:9).
Parables of, describing the spread of the gospel (Mt 13:3-23); describing the unfaithful Jews, given over to corruption and hypocrisy (Mt 21:33-46; Mk 12:1-12; Lk 20:9-19).

Figurative:
Of God as the master gardener (Jn 15:1). Of the spread of the gospel (Mt 13:3-23); of Paul and Apollos 1Co 3:5-9). *See Agriculture; Farming.*

FARMING Was the chief occupation of the people of Israel after the conquest of Canaan. Each family received a piece of ground marked by boundaries that could not be removed (Dt 19:14). Plowing took place in the autumn when the ground was softened by the rain. Grain was sown during the month of February; harvest began in the spring and usually lasted from Passover to Pentecost. The grain was cut with a sickle, and gleanings were for the poor (Ru 2:2). The grain was threshed out on the threshing floor, a saucer-shaped area of beaten clay 25 or more feet in

diameter, on which animals dragged a sledge over the sheaves to beat out the grain. The grain was winnowed by tossing it into the air to let the chaff blow away and was then sifted to remove impurities (Ps 1:4). Wheat and barley were the most important crops, but other grains and vegetables were cultivated as well. *See Agriculture; Fallow Ground.*

FARTHING
NIV "penny." *See Money.*

FASTING
Described:
Accompanied by self-denial (Dt 9:18; Ne 9:1), confession of sin (1Sa 7:6; Ne 9:1-2), reading of the Scriptures (Jer 36:6), prayer (Da 9:3; Mt 17:21).

Commanded (Joel 1:14; 2:12-13). Precepts concerning (Mt 6:16-18).

Of the disobedient, unacceptable (Isa 58:3-7; Jer 14:12; Zec 7:5; Mt 6:16).

Observed:
In times of bereavement, of the people of Jabesh Gilead, for Saul and his sons (1Sa 31:13; 1Ch 10:12), of David, at the time of Saul's death (2Sa 1:12), of Abner's death (2Sa 3:35), of his child's sickness (2Sa 12:16, 21-23).

On occasions of, public calamities (2Sa 1:12; Ac 27:33), private afflictions (2Sa 12:16), approaching danger (Est 4:16; Ac 27:9, 33-34), afflictions (Ps 35:13; Da 6:18), religious observances (Zec 8:19), ordination of ministers (Ac 13:3; 14:23).

Habitual, of the Israelites (Zec 8:19), by John's disciples (Mt 9:14), by Pharisees (Mt 9:14; Mk 2:18; Lk 18:12), by Anna (Lk 2:37), by Cornelius (Ac 10:30), by Paul (2Co 6:5; 11:27).

Prolonged, forty days and nights, by Moses (Ex 24:18; 34:28; Dt 9:9, 18), forty days and nights, by Elijah (1Ki 19:8), three weeks, by Daniel (Da 10:2-3), forty days and nights, by Jesus (Mt 4:2; Mk 1:12-13; Lk 4:1-2).

See Humiliation and Self-Affliction; Humility.

Instances of:
Of the Israelites, in the conflict between the other tribes with the tribe of Benjamin, on account of the wrong suffered by a Levite's concubine (Jdg 20:26), when they went to Mizpah for the ark (1Sa 7:6).

Of David, at the death of Saul (2Sa 1:12), during the sickness of the child born to him by Bathsheba (2Sa 12:16-22), while interceding in prayer for his friends (Ps 35:13), in his zeal for Zion (Ps 69:10), in prayer for himself and his adversaries (Ps 109:4, 24). Of Ahab, when Elijah prophesied the destruction of himself and his house (1Ki 21:27, w 21:20-29). Of Jehoshaphat, at the time of the invasion of the confederated armies of the Canaanites and Syrians (2Ch 20:3).

Of the Jews, in Babylon, with prayer for divine deliverance and guidance (Ezr 8:21, 23), when Jeremiah prophesied against Judea and Jerusalem (Jer 36:9). Of Ezra, on account of the idolatrous marriages of the Jews (Ezr 10:6). Of Nehemiah, on account of the desolation of Jerusalem and the temple (Ne 1:4). Of Darius, when he put Daniel in the lions' den (Da 6:18). Of Daniel, on account of the captivity of the people, with prayer for their deliverance (Da 9:3), at the time of his vision (Da 10:1-3). Of the Ninevites, when Jonah preached to them (Jnh 3:5-10).

Of Paul, at the time of his conversion (Ac 9:9). Of the disciples, at the time of the consecration of Barnabas and Saul (Ac 13:2-3). Of the consecration of the elders (Ac 14:23).

FAT
Offered in Sacrifices:
The layer of fat around the kidneys and other viscera of sacrificial animals which was forbidden for food, but which was burned as an offering to Yahweh (Lev 4:31). Offered in sacrifice (Ex 23:18; 29:13, 22; Lev 1:8; 3:3-5, 9-11, 14-17; 4:8-10; 7:3-5; 8:16, 25-26; 10:15; 17:6; 1Sa 2:15-16; Isa 43:24). Belonged to the Lord (Lev 3:16). Forbidden as food (Lev 3:16-17; 7:23). Idolatrous sacrifices of (Dt 32:38).

Instances of Fat People:
Eglon king of Moab (Jdg 3:17, 22). Eli the priest (1Sa 4:18). *See Corpulency.*

FATHER
Described:
Has various meanings in the Bible:
1. The originator of a way of life (Ge 4:20).
2. A male ancestor, immediate or remote, the father of nations or peoples (Ge 17:4; Ro 9:5).
3. An immediate male progenitor (Ge 42:13).
4. An adviser (Jdg 17:10), or a source (Job 38:28).
5. A spiritual ancestor (Jn 8:44; Ro 4:11).

God is the Creator of the human race (Mal 2:10) and is called the Father of the universe (Jas 1:17).

FATHERHOOD, OF GOD *See God, Fatherhood of.*

FATHER-IN-LAW
Unjust, Laban to Jacob (Ge 29:21-23; 31:7, 39-42). Hospitable to son-in-law, a man of Bethlehem in Judah (Jdg 19:3-9).

FATHERLESS *See Orphan.*

FATHERS' GOD
(Ex 3:13; Dt 1:11; 4:1; Jos 18:3; 2Ch 28:9; 29:5). *See God.*

FATHOM *See Sounding.*

FATTENED CALF
A clean animal fattened for offering to God (1Sa 28:24; 2Sa 6:13; Lk 15:23).

FAULT FINDING
(Jude 16). *See Murmuring; Rebuke; Uncharitableness.*

FAVOR *See God, Grace of.*

FAVORITISM
Instances of: Rebekah, for her son Jacob (Ge 27:6-17). Jacob, for Rachel (Ge 29:30, 34). Israel (Jacob), for Joseph

(Ge 37:3-4). Joseph, for Benjamin (Ge 43:34). Forbidden in parents (Dt 21:15-17). Elkanah, for Hannah (1Sa 1:4-5).
See Partiality.

FEAR *See Cowardice; Fear of God.*

FEAR OF GOD
Described:
As, wisdom (Job 28:28; Pr 15:33), pure (Ps 19:9), the beginning of wisdom (Ps 111:10; Pr 9:10; 15:33), the beginning of knowledge (Pr 1:7), hating evil (Pr 8:13), adding length to life (Pr 10:27), a fountain of life (Pr 14:27), leading to life (Pr 19:23).

Commanded (Lev 19:14, 32; 25:36, 43; Dt 6:13; 10:20; 13:4; Jos 24:14; 1Sa 12:24; 2Ki 17:36; 1Ch 16:30; 2Ch 19:7; Ne 5:9; Ps 2:11; 22:23; 34:9; 96:4; Pr 3:7; 23:17; 24:21; Ecc 5:7; 12:13; Isa 8:13; 29:23; Ro 11:20-21; Col 3:22; 1Pe 2:17; Rev 14:7). Cultivated by God (Ex 3:5; 19:12-13; Heb 12:18-24).

Deters from sin (Ex 20:18-20; Pr 16:6; Jer 32:39-40). Averts temporal calamity (Dt 28:47-49; 28:58-68; 2Ki 17:36-39). Secures divine blessing (Dt 5:29; Ps 25:12-14; 31:19-20; 33:18-19; 34:7, 9; 85:8-9; 103:11, 13, 17; 111:5; 112:1; 115:11, 13; 128:1-4; 145:18-19; Pr 22:4; Ecc 7:18; 8:12-13; Mal 4:2; Lk 1:50; Ac 10:34-35).

Universality of, foretold (Ps 76:11-12; 102:15). A bond of fellowship among righteous (Mal 3:16-18).

Instances of Guilty Fear:
Adam and Eve (Ge 3:8-13). The wicked (Job 15:20-25; 18:11; Pr 10:24). Those without moral direction (Pr 1:24-27). Those without God in general (Isa 2:19-21; 33:14). King Belshazzar (Da 5:6). The nations (Mic 7:17). Judas (Mt 27:3-5). The guards at Jesus' tomb (Mt 28:4). Christians no longer fear (Ro 8:15; 2Ti 1:7). Demons (Jas 2:19). The nations in the day of wrath (Rev 6:16).

Instances of Godly Fear:
Noah, in preparing the ark (Heb 11:7). Abraham, tested in the offering of his son Isaac (Ge 22:12). Jacob, in the vision of the stairway, and the covenant of God (Ge 28:16-17; 42:18). The midwives of Egypt, in refusing to take the lives of the Hebrew children (Ex 1:17, 21). The Egyptians, at the time of the plague of thunder and hail and fire (Ex 9:20).

Phinehas, in turning away the anger of God at the time of the plague (Nu 25:11, w 25:6-15). The nine-and-one-half tribes of Israel west of the Jordan (Jos 22:15-20). Obadiah, in his devotion to God, sheltered one hundred prophets against Jezebel because he feared God more than he feared the wrath of Jezebel (1Ki 18:3-4). Jehoshaphat, in proclaiming a fast when the land was about to be invaded by the armies of the Ammonites and Moabites (2Ch 20:3).

Nehemiah, in his reform of the public administration which had heavily taxed the people and lorded their rule over the people (Ne 5:15). Hanani, which qualified him to be ruler over Jerusalem (Ne 7:2). Job, according to the testimony of Satan (Job 1:8). David (Ps 119:38). Hezekiah, in his treatment of the prophet Micah, who prophesied evil against Jerusalem (Jer 26:19). The Israelites, in obeying the voice of the Lord (Hag 1:12).

The women of the tomb (Mt 28:8). Cornelius, who feared God with all his house (Ac 10:2).

Motivates God's:
Power (Jos 4:24; Ps 99:1; Jer 5:22; Mt 10:28; Lk 12:5), providence (1Sa 12:2-4), power and justice (Job 37:19-24), wrath (Ps 90:11), forgiveness (Ps 130:4), majesty (Jer 10:7).
See Conviction, of Sin; Faith.

Motivates People:
To respect others (Lev 19:14, 30; 25:17, 36, 43). To obedience (Nu 32:15; Dt 6:13-15; 7:1-4; 8:5-6; 10:12-13, 20; 13:4, 6-11; 17:11-13; 21:18-21; 28:14-68; 31:11-13; 1Sa 12:24-25; Job 13:21; 31:1-4, 13-23; Isa 1:20; Jer 4:4; 22:5; Mt 10:28; Lk 12:4-5; 2Co 5:10-11; 2Ti 4:1-2; 2Pe 3:10-12; Rev 14:9-10). To truthfulness (Dt 15:9; 19:16-20). To filial obedience (Dt 21:21).

Reverence:
Expressed in the Old Testament (Ge 35:5; Ex 18:21; 20:18-26; Lev 22:32; Dt 4:10; 5:29; 6:2; 10:12-13, 20-21; 14:23; 17:13; 28:58; Jos 24:14-15; 1Sa 12:14-15, 23-25; 2Sa 23:3-4; 1Ki 8:40; 2Ki 17:36-39; 1Ch 16:30; 2Ch 19:7, 9-10; Ezr 10:3; Job 28:28; 37:24; Ps 2:11; 15:4; 19:9; 22:23, 25; 31:19; 33:8, 18; 34:11; 37:7, 9, 11; 46:10; 52:6; 60:4; 64:9; 67:7; 72:5; 76:7, 11; 85:9; 86:11; 89:7; 90:11; 96:4, 9; 99:1; 102:15; 103:11, 13, 17; 111:5, 10; 112:1; 115:11, 13; 118:4; 119:63, 74, 79; 128:1, 4; 130:4; 135:20; 145:19; 147:11; Pr 1:7; 2:5; 3:7; 8:13; 9:10; 10:27; 14:2, 16, 26-27; 15:16, 33; 16:6; 19:23; 22:4; 23:17; 24:21; 28:14; 31:30; Ecc 3:14; 7:18; 8:12-13; 12:13; Isa 2:10, 19-21; 25:3; 33:6, 13; 50:10-11; 59:19; 60:5; Jer 5:22; 10:7; 32:39, 40; 33:9; Hos 3:5; Mic 7:16-20; Zep 3:7; Zec 2:13; Mal 1:6; 4:2).

Expressed in the New Testament (Mt 10:28; Lk 1:50; 12:5; 23:40; Ac 10:34-35; 13:26; Ro 11:20; 2Co 5:11; 7:1; Eph 5:21; 6:5; Php 2:12-13; Col 3:22; Heb 5:7; 12:28-29; Jas 2:19; 1Pe 1:17; 3:1-2; 1Jn 4:16-18; Rev 11:18; 14:7; 19:5).

See Punishment, Design of, to Secure Obedience; Reward, A Motive, To Faithfulness.

FEASTS
Described:
The host serves his guests (Ge 18:8). Men alone present at (Ge 40:20; 43:32, 34; 1Sa 9:22; Est 1:8; Mk 6:21; Lk 14:24), women alone (Est 1:9). Guests arranged according to age (Ge 43:33), rank (1Sa 9:22; Lk 14:8-10). Men and women attend (Ex 32:6, w 2-3; Da 5:1-4). Marriage feasts provided by the bridegroom (Jdg 14:10, 17). Given by kings (1Sa 20:5; 25:36; 2Sa 9:10; 1Ki 2:7; Est 1:3-8; Da 5:1-4). Drunkenness at (1Sa 25:36; Est 1:10; Da 5:1-4). Wine served at (Est 5:6; 7:7; Isa 5:12). Music at (Isa 5:12; Am 6:4-5; Lk 15:25). Reclined on couches (Am 6:4, 7; Jn 13:23, 25). Dancing at (Mt 14:6; Lk 15:25). Served in one dish (Mt 26:23). Were presided over by a master of the banquet (Jn 2:8-9). *See Entertainments.*

Covenants ratified by (Ge 26:28-31).

Annual Festivals:
Instituted by Moses: Divine protection given during (Ex 34:24). Designated as, sacred assemblies (Lev 23:4). First and last days

were sabbatic (Lev 23:39-40; Nu 28:18-25; 29:12, 35; Ne 8:1-18). Kept with rejoicing (Lev 23:40; Dt 16:11-14; 2Ch 30:21-26; Ezr 6:22; Ne 8:9-12, 17; Ps 42:4; Isa 30:29; Zec 8:19). Solemn feasts (Nu 15:3; 2Ch 8:13; La 2:6; Eze 46:9), Appointed feasts (Nu 29:39; Ezr 3:5; Isa 1:14).

The three principal festivals were Passover, Pentecost, and Tabernacles. All males were required to attend (Ex 23:17; 34:23; Dt 16:16; Ps 42:4; 122:4; Eze 36:38; Lk 2:41; Jn 4:45; 7). Attended by women (1Sa 1:3, 9; Lk 2:41). Aliens permitted to attend (Jn 12:20; Ac 2:1-11).

Celebrations for:
Birthdays (Ge 40:20; Mk 6:21), coronations (1Ki 1:25; 1Ch 12:38-40), national deliverances (Est 8:17; 9:17-19).

Figurative:
(Mt 22:1-14; Lk 14:16-24; Rev 19:9, 17).

Observed:
By Jesus (Mt 26:17-20; Lk 2:41-42; 22:15; Jn 2:13, 23; 5:1; 7:10; 10:22-23), by Paul (Ac 20:6, 16; 24:11, 17).

See for full treatment of annual feasts: Dedication; Hanukkah; Kislev; Passover; Pentecost; Purim; Tabernacles, Feast of; Trumpets, Feast of.

FEET
Sitting at (Lk 8:35; 10:39; Jas 2:3). Washing of, as an example, by Jesus (Jn 13:4-14). *See Washings.*

FELIX
(*fortunate, lucky*). Governor of Judea. Paul tried before (Ac 23:24-35; 24). Trembles under Paul's preaching (Ac 24:25). Leaves Paul in bonds (Ac 24:26-27; 25:14).

FELLOES *See Rim.*

FELLOW
A term of reproach (Ge 19:9; 1Sa 21:15; Mt 12:24; 26:61).

FELLOWSHIP
Defined (Ecc 4:9, 12; Am 3:3).
Of the Righteous:
In brotherhood (Lev 18:19; 1Sa 23:16-18; Mt 23:8; Jn 13:34-35; 15:17; Ro 14:1-4, 10, 13; 1Co 1:10; 12:13; 16:19-20; Gal 6:10; Eph 2:14-21; 5:30; 1Th 4:9-10; Heb 13:1; 1Pe 1:22-23). In worship (Ps 55:13-14; 1Co 10:16-17; Eph 5:19; Col 3:16). In unity of purpose (Ps 119:63; 133:1-3; Am 3:3; Mal 3:16; Jn 17:11, 21-23; Ac 1:14; 2:1, 42, 44-47; Ro 15:6-7; 1Co 1:10; Php 1:3-6, 27-30; 2:1-4; Col 2:2; 1Pe 3:8-9). In ministry (Mt 20:25-28; Mk 10:42-45; Lk 22:32; Ac 20:34-35; Ro 1:12; 15:1-7; Gal 6:2, 10; 1Th 4:18; 5:11, 14; Heb 3:13; 10:24-25; 1Pe 2:17; 1Jn 3:14; 4:7-8, 11-13). Exemplified (Gal 2:9).

With God:
Signified in people walking with God (Ge 5:22, 24; 6:9). Signified in God dwelling with people (Ex 29:45; Ps 101:6; Isa 57:15; Zec 2:10; Jn 14:23; 2Co 6:16; 1Jn 3:24; 4:13; Rev 21:3-4). General (Ex 33:11, 14-17; Lev 26:12; Am 3:3; 2Co 13:11; 1Jn 1:3, 5-7). Possible only through Christ (Mk 9:37; Jn 17:21, 23). *See Communion, With God.*

With Christ:
Attained, by receiving Christ (Mk 9:37; Rev 3:20). By doing God's will (Mt 12:48-50; Lk 8:21). Through a gathering of believers (Mt 18:20; 28:20), commemorating Christ's death (1Co 10:16-17), by walking in the light (1Jn 1:3, 5-7). By abiding in Christ (1Jn 2:6, 24, 28; 3:6, 24). By keeping God's commandments (1Jn 3:6, 24). By continuing in his teaching (2Jn 9). General (Mt 18:20; Lk 24:32; 1Co 1:9; 10:16-17; Jn 1:3, 5-7; Rev 3:20). Signified in Christ dwelling with people (Jn 6:56; 14:23; Eph 3:17; Col 1:27; 1Jn 3:24; 4:13). Signified in our union with Christ (Jn 15:1-8; 17:21-23, 26; Ro 7:4; 8:1, 10, 17; 11:17; 12:5; 1Co 6:13-15, 17; 12:12, 27; 2Co 11:2; 13:5; Eph 5:30; Col 3:3; 1Th 5:9-10; Heb 2:11; 1Jn 5:12, 20). Through the Spirit (Jn 14:16; 1Jn 3:6, 24; 4:13). *See Communion, With the Spirit.*

With the Holy Spirit:
General (Jn 14:16-17; Ro 8:9; 1Co 3:16; 2Co 13:14; Gal 4:6; Php 2:1). *See Communion, With the Spirit.*

With the Wicked:
Abhorred by the righteous (Ge 49:6; Ex 33:15-16; Ezr 6:21-22; 9:14; Ps 6:8; 26:4-5). Implicating (Ps 50:18). Revelry (Ps 50:18; Pr 12:11; 29:24; 1Co 15:33; 2Pe 2:18-19). Impoverishing (Pr 28:19). Forbidden with those who provide the wrong type of influence (Ex 23:32-33; 34:12-16; Nu 16:26; Dt 7:2-3; 12:30; 13:6-11; Jos 23:6-8, 13; Ezr 9:12; 10:11; Ps 1:1; Pr 1:10-16; 4:14-17; 14:7; Mt 18:17; Ro 16:17; 1Co 5:9-13; 2Co 6:14-17; Eph 5:11; 2Th 3:6, 14-15; 1Ti 6:3-5; 2Ti 3:2-9; 2Pe 3:17-18; 2Jn 9-11; Rev 18:1-4). Punishment for fellowship with the wicked (Nu 25:1-8; 33:55-56; Dt 31:16-17; Jos 23:12-13; Jdg 3:5-8; Ezr 9:7, 14; Ps 106:34-35, 41-42; Rev 2:16, 22-23).

Instances of Evil Fellowship With the Wicked—
By Solomon (1Ki 11:1-8), Rehoboam (1Ki 12:8-9), Jehoshaphat (2Ch 18:3; 19:2; 20:35-37), Jehoram (2Ch 21:6), Ahaziah (2Ch 22:3-5), Israelites (Ezr 9:1-2), Israel (Eze 44:7), Judas Iscariot (Mt 26:14-16).

Instances of Avoiding Fellowship With the Wicked—
The man of God (1Ki 13:7-10). Nehemiah (Ne 6:2-4; 10:29-31). David (Ps 101:4-7; 119:115). Jeremiah (Jer 15:17). Joseph of Arimathea (Lk 23:51). Church of Ephesus (Rev 2:6).
See Company, Evil; Influence, Evil.

FELLOWSHIP OFFERINGS
Traditionally "peace" offerings (Ex 20:24; 24:5; Lev 3:6; 7:11; 19:5). Offered by the leaders (Nu 7:17), by Joshua (Jos 8:31), by David (2Sa 6:17; 24:25). *See Offerings.*

FENCE
Walls made of stone enclosing a field, town, etc. (Nu 22:24; Ps 62:3; Pr 24:30-31; Isa 5:2; Mic 7:11). Hedge (Job 1:10; Isa 5:5; Mic 7:4; Hos 2:6). Figurative (Ps 22:30).

FENCED CITY *See Walled Cities.*

FERMENTED DRINK
Intoxicating beverages, usually other than grape wine (Dt 14:26). Used in drink offerings (Nu 28:7).

Forbidden to priests on duty (Lev 10:9), to Nazirites while under a vow (Nu 6:3; cf. Jdg 13:4, 7, 14; Lk 1:15). *See Abstinence; Beer; Drunkenness; Wine.*

FERRET *See Gecko.*

FERTILE CRESCENT
A modern description of the territory from the Persian Gulf to Egypt, which is watered by the Euphrates, Tigris, Orontes, Jordan, and Nile rivers. *See Canaan; Mesopotamia; Palestine.*

FESTIVALS *See Feasts.*

FESTUS, PORCIUS
(festal, joyful). Was the Roman governor who succeeded Felix in the province of Judea (Ac 24:27). He presided at the hearing of the apostle Paul when he made his defense before Herod Agrippa II (Ac 24:27; 26:32). When Paul appealed to Caesar, Festus sent him to Rome. The date of Festus's accession is uncertain, probably A.D. 59/60. He died in office in A.D. 62.

FETTERS
A translation of words which have the general meaning "anything that restricts or restrains" as well as those which bear the specific definition "shackle for the foot." Fetters were made from wood, bronze, or iron. The prisoner would have manacles on his wrists which were suspended from his neck by a rope. His feet would have been shackled and connected by a short piece of rope or chain so that the hobbled prisoner could take only short steps (2Sa 3:34; Job 36:13; Ps 2:3; 105:18; 149:8). Used for securing prisoners (2Ch 33:11; 36:6; Mk 5:4). *See Chains; Shackles.*

FEVER
(Lev 26:16; Dt 28:22; Job 30:30; Mt 8:14; Ac 28:8).

FEW SAVED
The number saved spoken of as few (Mt 7:14; 22:14; Lk 13:24; 1Pe 3:20; Rev 3:4).

FICKLENESS *See Instability.*

FIELD
The biblical field was generally not enclosed, but was marked off from its neighbors by boundary markers (Dt 19:14; 27:17; Job 24:2; Pr 22:28; 23:10; Hos 5:10). A cultivated area where crops are grown (Ru 2:2; Ps 107:37), a place where herds could graze (Ge 34:5; Ex 9:21; Nu 22:24).

FIG
Aprons made of fig leaves, by Adam and Eve (Ge 3:7). Common to Palestine (Nu 13:23; Dt 8:8), to Egypt (Ps 105:33). Two hundred cakes of, sent by Abigail to David (1Sa 25:18, 19:35). Dried and preserved (1Sa 30:12). Employed as a remedy (2Ki 20:7; Isa 38:21). Trade in (Ne 13:15).

FIG TREE
In an allegory (Jdg 9:11). Jeremiah's parable of (Jer 24:1-10). Jesus' cursing of (Mt 21:18-22; Mk 11:12-14, 20-26). Barren, parable of (Lk 13:6-9; 21:29-31).
Figurative of signs of the end times (Mt 24:32; Rev 6:13).

FIGHT OF FAITH
(1Ti 6:12; 2Ti 4:7; Heb 10:32; 11:32-34).

FIGURE
See "Figurative" under principal topics throughout the work. *See also, Allegory; Pantomime; Parable; Symbols and Similitudes; Types.*

FILIGREE
Ornate gold settings for the jewels of the ephod and breastpiece (Ex 28:13, 20; 39:6, 13, 16).

FINANCES
Methods of raising money. *See Money; Temple; Tribute.*

FINE
For personal injury (Ex 21:22, 30). For theft (Ex 22:4, 7-9; Pr 6:30-31). When sinning unknowingly (Lev 5:15-16; 22:14). For deception (Lev 6:2-6). Restitution for any wrongdoing (Nu 5:5-8). *See Damages and Compensations.*

FINGER
Used in priestly service (Ex 29:12; Lev 4:6, 17, 25, 30, 34). Six on one hand (2Sa 21:20; 1Ch 20:6).

FINGER OF GOD
Anthropomorphism, indicating God's interaction with his creation. Creation (Ps 8:3). Miracles (Ex 8:19). Writing the tablets of the law (Ex 31:18; Dt 9:10). Exorcism (Lk 11:20). *See Anthropomorphisms.*

FINGERS, FINGERBREADTH
A unit of measurement. The two bronze pillars of Solomon's temple were four fingers thick and hollow in the center (Jer 52:21). *See Measure.*

FINING POT *See Crucible.*

FIR TREE
Wood of, used for building (SS 1:17).

FIRE
Children sacrificed in (2Ki 16:3; 17:17). Used as a signal in war (Jer 6:1). Men were burned in a furnace (Jer 29:22; Heb 11:34). The threat of being thrown into a furnace is used by Nebuchadnezzar for all those who would not fall down and worship the image that he set up of (Da 3:6, 11, 15, 21).

Figurative:
Of judgments (Dt 4:24; 32:22; Isa 33:14; Jer 23:29; Am 1:4, 7, 10, 12, 14; 2:2; Mal 3:2; Lk 12:49; Rev 20:9), spiritual power (Ps 104:4; Jer 20:9; Mt 3:11; Lk 3:16), cleansing (Isa 6:6-7), of the destruction of the wicked (Mt 13:42, 50; 25:41; Mk 9:48; Rev 9:2; 21:8).
Everlasting fire (Isa 33:14; Mt 18:8; 25:41; Mk 9:48).

Miracles Connected With:
Miraculously descends upon and consumes Abraham's sacrifice (Ge 15:17), Elijah's (1Ki 18:38), David's (1Ch 21:26), Solomon's, at dedication of the temple (2Ch 7:1-3). Pillar of fire (Ex 13:21-22; 14:19, 24; 40:38; Nu 9:15-23).
Display of, at Elijah's translation (2Ki 2:11). Consumes, the conspirators with Korah, Dathan, and Abiram (Nu 16:35), the captains and their fifties (2Ki 1:9-15).
Torture by (Jer 29:22; Eze 23:25, 47; Da 3).
See Celestial Phenomena; Cloud, Pillar of.

Symbolic:
Of God's presence, with Abram in the covenant (Ge 15:17), in the burning bush (Ex 3:2), on Sinai (Ex 19:18).
Tongues of, on the disciples (Ac 2:3).
See Arson.

FIREBRAND
Burning wood used for light (Jdg 7:16), torches used as weapons (Pr 26:18), a remnant of a burnt stick (Am 4:11). *See Torches.*

FIREPAN
(*to rake together*). A vessel for carrying live coals (Ex 27:3; 38:3).

FIRKIN *See Gallon.*

FIRMAMENT *See Expanse.*

FIRST BEGOTTEN *See Firstborn.*

FIRST DAY OF THE WEEK *See Sunday.*

FIRSTBORN
The first male born, whether man or animal, was reserved by God for himself (Ex 13:2, 12-16; 22:29-30; 34:19-20; Lev 27:26; Nu 3:13; 8:17-18; Dt 15:19-23; Ne 10:36).
Redemption of (Ex 13:13; 34:20; Lev 27:26-27; Nu 3:40-51; 18:15-17). Levites taken instead of firstborn of the families of Israel (Nu 3:12, 40-45; 8:16-18).

Birthright of:
Had precedence over other sons of the family (Ge 4:1, 5-7; Dt 21:15-17), a double portion of inheritance (Dt 21:15-17), royal succession (2Ch 21:3). Sold by Esau (Ge 25:29-34; 27:36; Ro 9:12-13; Heb 12:16). Set aside, that of Manasseh (Ge 48:15-20; 1Ch 5:1), Adonijah (1Ki 2:13-15), Hosah's son (1Ch 26:10). Forfeited by Reuben (Ge 49:3-4; 1Ch 5:1-2). Honorable distinction of (Ex 4:22; Ps 89:27; Jer 31:9; Ro 8:29; Col 1:15; Heb 1:6; 12:23; Rev 1:5).
See Birthright.

Jesus as Firstborn:
Among many brothers (Ro 8:29), over all creation (Col 1:15), from the dead (Col 1:18; Rev 1:5), God's firstborn (Heb 1:6).

FIRSTFRUITS
Offerings of:
First ripe of fruits, grain, oil, wine, and first of the fleece, required as an offering (Ex 22:29; Lev 2:12-16; Nu 18:12; Dt 18:4; 2Ch 31:5; Ne 10:35, 37, 39; Pr 3:9; Jer 2:3; Ro 11:16).
Offerings of, presented at the tabernacle (Ex 22:29; 23:19; 34:26; Dt 26:3-10), belonged to the priests (Lev 23:20; Nu 18:12-13; Dt 18:3-5), must be free from blemish (Lev 22:21; Nu 18:12). Freewill offerings of, given to the prophets (2Ki 4:42).

Offerings described:
Drink (Ge 35:14; Ex 29:40-41; 30:9; 37:16; Lev 23:13, 18, 37; Nu 4:7; Nu 6:15, 17; 15:5, 7, 10, 24; 28:7-31; 29:6, 11, 16, 18-39; Dt 32:38; 2Ki 16:13-15; 1Ch 29:21; 2Ch 29:35; Ezr 7:17; Isa 57:6; Jer 7:18; 19:13; 32:29; 44:17-25; 52:19; Eze 20:28; 45:17; Joel 1:9, 13; 2:14; Php 2:17; 2Ti 4:6). Freewill (Ex 35:29; 36:3; Lev 7:16; 22:18, 21, 23; 23:37-38; Nu 15:3; 29:39; Dt 12:6, 17; 16:10; 2Ch 31:14; Ezr 1:4, 6; 2:68; 3:5; 7:16; 8:28; Ps 54:6; Eze 46:12; Am 4:5). Burnt (Lev 1; 6:8-13). Grain (Lev 2; 6:14-23). Fellowship (Lev 3; 7:11-21). Sin (Lev 4:5-13; 6:24-30). Guilt (Lev 5:14-6:7; 7:1-10). Wave offering (Ex 29:22-26; 35:22; Lev 7:30; 23:10-14, 17). To be offered as a thank offering upon entrance into the Land of Promise (Dt 26:3-10; 2Ch 29:31; 33:16; Ps 50:14, 23; 56:12; 107:22; 116:17; Jer 17:26; 33:11; Am 4:5).

Figurative:
(Ro 8:23; 11:16; 1Co 15:20, 23; Jas 1:18).
See Offerings.

FIRSTLING *See Firstborn.*

FISH
Creation of (Ge 1:20-22). Appointed for food (Ge 9:2-3). Clean and unclean (Lev 11:9-12; Dt 14:9-10). Broiled (Jn 21:9-13; Lk 24:42).
Caught with, spears (Job 41:7), nets (Ecc 9:12; Hab 1:14-17; Lk 5:2-6; Jn 21:6-8), hooks (Isa 19:8; Am 4:2; Hab 1:15; Mt 17:27). Sold by men from Tyre living in Jerusalem (Ne 13:16).

Figurative:
(Eze 47:9-10).

Miracles Connected With:
Jonah swallowed by (Jnh 1:17; 2; Mt 12:40). The loaves and fishes (Mt 14:19; 15:36-38; Lk 9:13-17). Coin obtained from mouth of (Mt 17:27). Overflowing nets (Lk 5:6-7; Jn 21:6, 8, 11). Furnished for the disciples by Jesus after his resurrection (Lk 24:42; Jn 21:9-13).

FISH GATE
An ancient gate on the E side of Jerusalem near Gihon where Tyrians held a fish market (2Ch 33:14; Ne 3:3; 12:39; 13:16; Zep 1:10).

FISH POOL *See Pool.*

FISH SPEAR *See Spear.*

FISHERMEN
Certain apostles (Mt 4:18-21; Mk 1:16-20; Jn 21:2-3).
Figurative (Jer 16:16; Mt 4:19).

FISHHOOK *See Hooks.*

FITCH *See Caraway.*

FLAG *See Ensign; Reed.*

FLAGON *See Wine.*

FLATTERY
Condemned and rebuked (Job 32:21-22; Ps 12:2-4; Pr 28:23; Lk 6:26). Deceives, self (Ps 36:2). The simple (Ro 16:18).
Practiced by enemies (Ps 12:2; Pr 26:28; 29:5; Jude 16). Against God (Ps 78:36). By seducing women (Pr 5:3; 6:24; 7:5, 21). Not practiced by Paul (1Th 2:4-6).

F

Instances of:
Jacob (Ge 33:10). Gideon (Jdg 8:1-3). Mephibosheth (2Sa 9:8). Woman of Tekoa (2Sa 14:17-20). Absalom (2Sa 15:2-6). Israel and Judah (2Sa 19:41-43). Adonijah (1Ki 1:42). Ahab (1Ki 20:4). False prophets (1Ki 22:1-13). Darius's officials (Da 6:1-9). Herodians (Lk 20:21). Tyrians (Ac 12:22). Tertullus flatters Felix (Ac 24:2-4). Paul flatters Felix (Ac 24:10). Agrippa (Ac 26:2-3).

FLAX
In Egypt (Ex 9:31). In Palestine (Jos 2:6). Linen made from (Pr 31:13; Isa 19:9). *See Linen.*

FLEA
(*mosquito*). (1Sa 24:14; 26:20).

FLEECE *See Prayer; Token, 1; Wool.*

FLESH
1. The physical part of the body of people or animals (Ge 17:13-14; 1Co 15:39).
2. Human nature, deprived of the Holy Spirit, and dominated by sin (Ro 7:5, ftn); usually "sinful [nature]" in the NIV. *See Body; Carnal Mindedness.*

FLESHHOOK *See Meat Forks.*

FLIES
Plague of (Ex 8:21-31; Ps 78:45; 105:31). Common sense analogy (Ecc 10:1). Figurative (Isa 7:18).

FLINT
1. Knives of flint used for circumcision (Ex 4:25; Jos 5:2-3).
2. Judah's heart had been inscribed with the point of a flint (Jer 17:1). The Israelites make their hearts harder than flint (Zec 7:12). Figurative (Isa 5:28; 50:7; Jer 17:1; Eze 3:9; Zec 7:12). *See Hardest Stone; Minerals of the Bible, 1; Stones.*

FLOCK
A collection of sheep under the care of a shepherd, sometimes including goats as well (Ge 27:9; 30:32). Used figuratively of Christ's disciples (Lk 12:32; 1Pe 5:2-3).

FLOG, FLOGGING
Described:
The practice or system of punishment by repeated lashes or blows, usually with a rod or whip; or an instance of such punishment.
1. Beating is recognized as a legitimate form of punishment (Dt 25:1-3). According to Proverbs, hasty and poor judgments, like careless talk, often lead to strife; the settling of strife involves punishment for those who have been wrong, and it should be recognized that flogging (beating) is "for the back of fools" (Pr 19:29, w 18:6; 20:3).
It is permissible to discipline a child, and parents are encouraged to apply the rod of punishment to drive out folly (Pr 22:15) so that the child will not follow a path of destruction (Pr 19:18; 23:13-14). The rod "imparts wisdom" (Pr 29:15) and promotes a healthy and happy family (Pr 29:17). Discipline is rooted in love not anger (Pr 3:11-12). *See Abuse.*
2. Elsewhere in the OT it is recognized that even the innocent may sometimes be scourged and crushed by evil individuals (Isa 52:13-53:12, esp 53:5). The suffering of the innocent, often at the hands of evildoers, is a common theme in the Psalms (13; 22; 28; 31:9-24; 35; 38; 41; 69; 71; 86; 102; 109).
3. Jesus warned certain of his disciples that they would be beaten in the synagogues if they continued to preach the gospel (Mk 13:9). According to Ac 5:40, the apostles were beaten by representatives of the Sanhedrin and ordered not to speak in the name of Jesus, but only after Gamaliel had pleaded with his fellow members not to put the defendants to death (Ac 5:33-39). Paul, who himself had beaten and imprisoned many Christians (Ac 22:19-20), was flogged with rods three times (2Co 11:25). In Ac 16:11-24, both Paul and Silas were involved.

Flogging of Jesus:
Prophesied (Isa 50:6). Described (Mt 20:19; 26:67-68; 27:26, 30; Mk 10:34; 15:15, 19; Lk 22:63-64; 23:16; Jn 18:22; 19:1).
See Assault and Battery; Bruise(s); Lashes; Scourging; Stoning; Stripes.

FLOOD
Foretold (Ge 6:13, 17). History of (Ge 6-8). The promise that it should not recur (Ge 8:20-22; Isa 54:9). References to (Job 22:16; Mt 24:38-39; Lk 17:26-27; Heb 11:7; 1Pe 3:20; 2Pe 2:5).
See Meteorology.

FLOUR
Finely crushed and sifted grain, generally wheat, rye, or barley (Jdg 6:19).

FLOWER *See Plants of the Bible.*

FLUTE
A wind instrument (Da 3:5, 7, 10, 15). *See Music, Instruments of.*

FOAL *See Animals.*

FODDER
(*mix, mingle*). Food for animals consisting of a mixture of grains (Ge 24:25, 32; 43:24; Jdg 19:19; Job 6:5; 24:6; Isa 30:24).

FOLLY *See Fool.*

FOOD
Articles of:
Bread (Ge 18:5-6; 1Sa 17:17), milk (Ge 49:12; Pr 27:27), vinegar (Nu 6:3; Ru 2:14), oil (Dt 12:17; Pr 21:17, 20; Eze 16:13, 18-19), butter (Ps 55:21; Pr 30:33), roasted grain (Ru 2:14; 1Sa 17:17; 25:18), cheese (1Sa 17:18; Job 10:10), dried fruit (1Sa 25:18; 30:12), meat (Pr 9:2), wine (Jn 2:3-10), fruit (2Sa 16:2), herbs (Ex 12:8; Nu 9:11; 2Ki 4:39; Job 30:4; La 3:15; Lk 11:42), honey (SS 5:1; Isa 7:15), fish (Mt 7:10; Lk 24:42).
From God (Ge 1:29-30; 9:3; Job 36:31; Ps 23:5; 104:14-15; 111:5; 136:25; 145:15; 147:9; Pr 30:8; Isa 3:1; Mt 6:11; Ac 14:17; Ro 14:14, 21; 1Ti 4:3-5).

F

Practices Concerning:

Men and women did not partake together (Ge 18:8-9; Est 1:3, 9). Prepared by females (Ge 27:9; 1Sa 8:13; Pr 31:15). A hymn sung after (Mt 26:30). Thanks given before (Mk 8:6; Ac 27:35). Things prohibited as (Ex 22:31; Lev 11:4-8, 10-20, 41-42; 17:13-15). Peter's vision concerning (Ac 10:10-16). Paul's teaching concerning the eating of food offered to idols (Ro 14:2-23; 1Co 8:4-13; 10:18-32). Flesh unwarrantedly forbidden as (1Ti 4:3-4).

See Bread; Eating; Oven.

FOOL In Scripture connotes conceit and pride, or deficiency in judgment rather than mental inferiority.

Described as:

Arrogant (Ps 5:5). Iniquitous (Ps 107:17; Tit 3:3). Atheistic (Ps 14:1; 53:1). A reproach (Ps 74:18, 22). Despising wisdom (Pr 1:7, 22; 18:2). Deceitful (Pr 1:14, 18). Contentious (Pr 1:18; 18:6-7; 29:9). Clamorous (Pr 9:13). An embarrassment to his father (Pr 10:1; 15:20; 17:25; 19:13). Excessively talkative (Pr 10:8, 10; 29:11; Ecc 10:12-14). A mocker (Pr 14:9). A dreamer (Pr 17:24). Quarrelsome (Pr 20:3). Wasteful (Pr 21:20). Idle (Ecc 4:5). Willful (Pr 1:7; 27:22). Lacking in understanding (Pr 9:13; 10:13; 15:21; 26:1, 3-12; Ecc 7:4-6). Deficient in conscience (Pr 10:23). Practice deception (Pr 14:8). Gullible (Pr 14:15). Unknowledgeable (Pr 15:7). Angry (Ecc 7:9). Unperceptive (Mt 7:26-27).

General:

Causes sorrow (Pr 10:1; 17:25; 19:13). To be forsaken (Pr 9:6). To be avoided (Pr 14:8). Some suffer affliction because of (Ps 107:17).

Parables of:

The foolish virgins (Mt 25:1-13). The rich fool (Lk 12:16-20).

FOOT Washing the feet, of the disciples by Jesus (Jn 13:4-16), by disciples (1Ti 5:10). *See Purification; Washing.*

Figurative (Mt 18:8).
For footwear: *See Sandal.*

FOOTMAN *See Runner.*

FOOTSTOOL A literal support for the feet (2Ch 9:18), a figure of subjection (Ps 110:1; Isa 66:1; Mt 5:35).

FORD (*pass over, through*). A shallow place in a stream where people and animals could cross on foot (Ge 32:22; Isa 16:2).

FOREHEAD The part of the face above the eyes. Often revealing the character of the person— Shamelessness (Jer 3:3), courage (Eze 3:9), or godliness (Rev 7:3).

FOREIGNER Among the Jewish people, anyone outside the nation was regarded as inferior (Ge 31:15) and possessed restricted rights.

He could not eat the Passover (Ex 12:43), intermarry on equal terms (Ex 34:12-16), become king (Dt 17:15), enter the sanctuary (Eze 44:9; Ac 21:28-29). They could be included in the nation by accepting the law and its requirements.

In the NT the word is applied to those who are not members of God's kingdom (Eph 2:19).

FOREKNOWLEDGE OF GOD *See God, Foreknowledge of, Wisdom of.*

FOREMAN *See Master Craftsman.*

FOREORDINATION *See Predestination.*

FORERUNNER Figurative of Christ, "who went before us" (Heb 4:14; 6:20).

FORESKIN The fold of skin cut off in the process of circumcision (Ge 17:11, 14; Ex 4:25; 1Sa 18:25, 27; 2Sa 3:14). *See Circumcision.*

FORESTS

Described:

Abounded with wild honey (1Sa 14:25-26). Populated by wild beasts (Ps 50:10; 104:20; Isa 56:9; Jer 5:6; Mic 5:8). Undergrowth often in (Isa 9:18). Tracts of land covered with trees (Isa 44:14). Often afforded pasture (Mic 7:14).

Were places of refuge (1Sa 22:5; 23:16). Hereth (1Sa 22:5). Ephraim (2Sa 18:6, 8). Supplied timber for building (1Ki 5:6-8). Lebanon (1Ki 7:2; 10:17). Carmel (Isa 33:9; 35:1-2; Na 1:4). Often destroyed by enemies (2Ki 19:23; Isa 37:24; Jer 46:23). Jotham built towers in (2Ch 27:4). Owned by King Artaxerxes and kept by Asaph (Ne 2:8). The power of God extends over (Ps 29:9). The oaks of Bashan (Isa 2:13; Eze 27:6; Zec 11:2). Arabia (Isa 21:13). Called on to rejoice at God's mercy (Isa 44:23).

Illustrative:

Prophecies concerning the coming invasion of Jerusalem by Sennacherib, its failure to withstand the invasion, and the unbelief of the Jews. The moral change in the Jewish nation shall be as great as if the wooded Lebanon were to become a fruitful field and vice versa (Isa 29:17). These prophecies are illustrative of those accustomed to a life of self-indulgence, who because of the devastations of the enemy would now go without (Isa 32:15, 19). Illustrative of the southern kingdom (Eze 20:46-47).

Destruction of illustrates the destruction of the wicked (Isa 9:18; 10:17-18; Jer 21:14).

FORGERY *See Seal.*

FORGETTING GOD A characteristic of the wicked (Pr 2:17; Isa 65:11). Backsliders guilty of (Jer 2:32; 3:21).

Is forgetting his covenant (Dt 4:23; 2Ki 17:38), past deliverances (Jdg 8:34; Ps 78:42-43), what he has done (Ps 78:7, 11; 106:13), benefits (Ps 103:2), kindnesses (Ps 106:7), law (Ps 119:153, 176; Hos 4:6), Jerusalem (Ps 137:5), power to deliver (Isa 51:13-15), word of encouragement (Heb 12:5), Word of God (Jas 1:22-25).

Cautions against (Dt 6:12; 8:11). Prosperity leads to (Dt 8:11-20; Hos 13:6). Trials should not lead to (Ps 44:17-22).

Exhortation to those guilty of (Ps 50:22). Resolve against (Ps 119:16, 93). Encouraged by false teachers (Jer 23:27).

Punishment of (Job 8:12-13; Ps 9:17; Isa 17:10-11; Eze 23:35; Hos 8:11-14), threatened (Ps 50:22).

See Apostasy; Backsliders; Forsaking God.

FORGIVENESS

Of Enemies:

By showing kindness to enemy's animal (Ex 23:4-5). By giving (Pr 25:21-22; Mt 5:39-41; Ro 12:20). Commanded (Pr 24:17; Mt 5:38-48; 18:21-35; Mk 11:25; Lk 6:27-37).

See Enemy.

Each Other:

(Lk 17:3-4; Eph 4:32; Col 3:13; Phm 10, 18). A condition of divine forgiveness (Mt 6:12-15; 18:21-35; Mk 11:25; Lk 11:4). Spirit of, disallows rejoicing (Pr 24:17-18). Disallows retaliation (Pr 24:29; Ro 12:17, 19). Blesses (Ro 12:14; 1Co 4:12-13; 1Pe 3:9).

FORM In religious service (1Ch 15:13-14; 2Ch 29:34). Irregularity in (2Ch 30:2-5, 17, 20; Mt 12:3-4).

See Church, The Body of Believers; State.

FORMALISM Despised by God (Isa 1:11-15; 29:13-16; Ps 50:8-15; Jer 6:20; 14:12; Am 5:21-23; Mal 1:6-14; Lk 13:24-27; 2Ti 3:1-5). Empty (Mt 15:8-9; Ro 2:17-29; 1Co 7:19; Php 3:4-7).

Rejected by God for presenting sacrifices rather than, obedience (1Sa 15:22-23; Ecc 5:1; 1Co 7:19; 1Jn 2:3-11), thanksgiving (Ps 50:8-15; 69:30-31), repentance (Ps 51:16-17), mercy (Hos 6:6; Mic 6:6-8; Mt 9:13; 12:7), justice, mercy, and humility (Mic 6:6-8), a pure heart (Mt 15:8-9; Ro 2:17-29).

FORNICATION Instructions concerning illicit sexual intercourse (Ac 15:20, 29; 21:25; 1Co 5:1; 6:13, 18; 7:2). More specifically and primarily unlawful intercourse of an unwed person (Mt 15:19; Mk 7:21; 1Co 6:9, 18; Gal 5:19). It was commonly associated with heathen worship (Jer 2:20; 3:6) and was used as a figure of disloyalty to God (Eze 16:3-22).

See Adultery; Prostitute.

FORSAKING GOD

Exemplified:

The wicked guilty of (Dt 28:20). Idolaters guilty of (1Sa 8:8; 1Ki 11:33). Backsliders guilty of (Jer 15:6).

Israelites (1Sa 12:10). Saul (1Sa 15:11). Ahab (1Ki 18:18). Amon (2Ki 21:22). Kingdom of Judah (2Ch 12:1, 5; 21:10; Isa 1:4; Jer 15:6). Kingdom of Israel (2Ch 13:11, w 2Ki 17:7-18). Many disciples (Jn 6:66). Phygelus and Hermogenes (2Ti 1:15). Balaam son of Beor (2Pe 2:15).

Condemned:

Forsaking the covenant (Dt 29:25; 1Ki 19:10; Jer 22:9; Da 11:30). Prosperity tempts to (Dt 31:20; 32:15). Provokes God to forsake people (Jdg 10:13; 2Ch 15:2; 24:20, 24). Resolve against (Jos 24:16; Ne 10:29-39).

Warnings against (Jos 24:20; 1Ch 28:9). His house (2Ch 29:6). His commandments (Ezr 9:10). Sin of, to be confessed (Ezr 9:10). Unreasonableness and ingratitude of (Jer 2:5-6). Leads men to follow their own devices (Jer 2:13). Wickedness of (Jer 2:13; 5:7). Trusting in man is (Jer 17:5). Curse pronounced upon (Jer 17:5). Brings confusion (Jer 17:13). Brings down his wrath (Ezr 3:12). Followed by remorse (Eze 6:9). The right way (2Pe 2:15).

See Forgetting God; Apostasy.

FORT, FORTIFICATION

A Military Defense:

Caves used for (Jdg 6:2; 1Sa 23:26). Field-made during military operations (Dt 20:19-20; 2Ki 25:1; Jer 6:6; 32:24; 33:4; Eze 4:2; 17:17; 26:8; Da 11:15). Defenses of cities (2Sa 5:9; 2Ch 11:10-11; 26:9, 15; Ne 3:8; 4:2; Isa 22:10; 25:12; 29:3; Jer 51:53; Na 3:14). Erected in, vineyards and herding grounds (Isa 5:2; Mt 21:33; Mk 12:1), the desert (2Ch 26:10).

Figurative:

Of God's care (2Sa 22:2-3, 47; Ps 18:2; 31:3; 71:3; 91:2; 144:2; Pr 18:10; Na 1:7).

FORTITUDE *See Courage.*

FORTUNATUS (*fortunate*). A Corinthian Christian, a friend of Paul (1Co 16:17).

FORTUNE

1. Changes of. See illustrated in lives of Joseph, from slave to prime minister. See *Joseph, 1.* Pharaoh's butler and baker (Ge 40). David, from shepherd boy to king, noting the changes (1Sa 15:3; 7:16-13; 2Sa 2:1-7). See *David;* also *Jeroboam; Haman; Mordecai; Esther; Job; Daniel.*

2. A pagan god (Isa 65:11).

FORTUNE-TELLING *See Sorcery.*

FORTY A significant number.

Days:

Of rain, at the time of the flood (Ge 7:17), of flood, before sending forth the raven (Ge 8:6). For embalming (Ge 50:3). Jesus in the desert (Mt 4:2; Mk 1:15; Lk 4:2), compare to Israel's forty years in the desert. Spies in the land of promise (Nu 13:25). Goliath challenged Israel (1Sa 17:16). Symbolic (Eze 4:6). Of probation, given to the Ninevites (Jn 3:4). Christ's stay after the Resurrection (Ac 1:3).

Days of fasting:

By Moses (Ex 24:18; 34:28; Dt 9:9, 25), Elijah (1Ki 19:8), Jesus (Mt 4:2).

Years:

Isaac's and Esau's age at time of marriages (Ge 25:20; 26:34). Wandering of the Israelites in the desert (Ex 16:35; Nu 14:34). Caleb's age when he spied out the land (Jos 14:7). Peace in Israel (Jdg 3:11; 5:31; 8:28). Eli as judge (1Sa 4:17), Saul as king (Ac 31:21), David as king (2Sa 5:4), Solomon (1Ki 11:42), Joash (2Ki

12:1). Egypt, to be desolated (Eze 29:11), to be restored after (Eze 29:13).

Lashes:

Administered as punishment for criminals (Dt 25:3; 2Co 11:24).

FORUM OF APPIUS A place forty-three miles SE of Rome, where Paul was met by friends (Ac 28:15).

FOUNDATION The lowest part of a building, and on which it rests (Lk 14:29; Ac 16:26).

Described:

Of stone (1Ki 5:17). Joined together by cornerstones (Ezr 4:12, w 1Pe 2:6, & Eph 2:20). Strongly laid (Ezr 6:3). Security afforded by (Mt 7:25; Lk 6:48). Deep laid (Lk 6:48).

Figuratively Applied to:

Kingdoms (Ex 9:18). The mountains (Dt 32:22). The heavens (2Sa 22:8). The earth (Job 38:4; Ps 104:5). The world (Mt 13:35). The ocean (Ps 104:8).

Illustrative of:

Hope of saints (Ps 87:1). The righteous (Pr 10:25). Christ (Isa 28:16; 1Co 3:11). Doctrines of the apostles (Eph 2:20). Decrees and purposes of God (2Ti 2:19). First principles of the gospel (Heb 6:1-2). Security of saints' inheritance (Heb 11:10).

Laid for:

Cities (Jos 6:26; 1Ki 16:34). Temples (1Ki 6:37; Ezr 3:10). Walls (Ezr 4:12; Rev 21:14). Houses (Lk 6:48). Towers (Lk 14:28-29).

FOUNDING *See Molding.*

FOUNTAIN Fountain of life (Ps 36:9; Pr 10:11; 13:14; 14:27; 16:22). Figurative of faithful wife (Pr 5:18; SS 4:12, 15). Prophetic life-giving and cleansing fountain from the temple (Joel 3:18; Zec 13:1, w Rev 22:1-2).

See Fountain of Life; Spring; Wells.

FOUNTAIN GATE A gate in the walls of Jerusalem (Ne 2:14; 3:15; 12:37).

FOUNTAIN OF LIFE (Ps 36:9; Pr 13:14; 14:27; Jer 2:13; 17:13; Zec 13:1; Rev 7:17).

FOWL *See Birds.*

FOWLER, FOWLER'S SNARE A bird-catcher (Ps 91:3; 124:7).

Figurative:

1. Of the calamities and plots which await (Job 22:10; Ps 91:3; 124:7; Pr 22:5; Isa 24:17; Jer 48:43; Hos 9:8).

2. As the source or agent of calamity (Jos 23:13; Ps 69:22; Isa 8:14; Hos 5:1).

FOX Samson uses, to burn the field of the Philistines (Jdg 15:4-5). Depreciations of (SS 2:15). Dens of (Mt 8:20; Lk 9:58).

Figurative: Of heretics (SS 2:15). Of unfaithful prophets (Eze 13:1-7). Of craftiness (Lk 13:32).

See Jackal.

FRACTURES Treatment of (Eze 30:21).

Figurative: David calling for God to break the arm of the wicked man (Ps 10:15). David claiming that the power of the wicked will be broken (Ps 37:17). The strength of Moab is broken (Jer 48:25).

FRAGRANCE Fragrant offerings (Lev 4:7; Nu 4:16). Metaphorical of acceptable service to God (2Co 2:14, 16; Eph 5:2; Php 4:18).

FRANKINCENSE A fragrant gum resin consisting of small, white chunks and beads which are easily ground into a powder; this powder emits a sweet odor when burned. An ingredient of the sacred oil (Ex 30:34). Commerce in (Rev 18:11-13).

FRATERNITY (*mutual, familial love*).

Commanded by:

Moses to the Israelites (Dt 15:7-15; Jos 1:14-15). David (Ps 22:22; 133:1-3). Malachi (Mal 2:10). Jesus (Ps 22:22; Mt 5:22-26; 18:15-18, 21-22, 35; 23:8; 25:40; Jn 13:34-35; 15:12-14; 21:17). Paul (Ro 12:10; 1Co 6:1-8; Gal 6:1-5; 1Th 4:9; 2Th 3:14-15). Peter (1Pe 1:12; 2:17; 3:8; 2Pe 1:5, 7). John (1Jn 2:9-11).

Nazirites, vows of (Nu 6:1-21; La 4:7; Am 2:11-12; Ac 21:24-31). See *Nazirite(s), Nazirite(s).*

Unity (Ps 133:1-3). Broken (Zec 11:14). Incompatible with, pride of title (Mt 23:8). Indifference to another's conscience (1Co 8:1-13; 10:28-29). Selfishness (1Jn 3:17).

Exemplified:

By Abraham and Lot (Ge 13:8). By Jonathan and David (1Sa 18:1; 19:2-7; 20:17, 41-42; 23:16-18). By early Christians (Ac 2:42-47). By Paul (Ro 9:2-3; 10:1-4; 1Co 9:20-23). By James, Peter, and John (Gal 2:9). By Epaphroditus (Php 2:25-26). By the Thessalonian church (2Th 1:3).

See Brother; Church, The Body of Believers; Fellowship; Friendship; Love.

FRATRICIDE One who kills or murders his own brother or sister. Instances of Cain (Ge 4:8). Abimelech (Jdg 9:5). Absalom (2Sa 13:28-29). Solomon (1Ki 2:23-25). Jehoram (2Ch 21:4). See *Homicide; Murder.*

FRAUD *See Dishonesty.*

FREEDMAN A slave who has been granted his freedom (1Co 7:22), or a free man as contrasted with a slave (Gal 4:22-23), among Christians (Col 3:11).

FREEDMEN One of a number of synagogues at Jerusalem, conducted for Jews who spoke Greek rather than Aramaic, the latter being the native language of Palestinian Jews (Ac 6:9).
 See Emancipation.

FREEDOM From servitude. See Emancipation; Jubilee.

FREEWILL See Blessings, Spiritual, Contingent Upon Obedience.

FREEWILL OFFERINGS In the category of gifts, freewill offerings were voluntary offerings prompted solely by the impulse of the donor (Lev 22:21, 23; 23:38; Nu 29:39; Dt 12:6, 17; 2Ch 31:14; Ezr 3:5; 7:16; 8:28; Ps 119:108; 2Co 8:1-15).
 See Beneficence; Gift, Giving; Liberality; Offerings.

FRET The verb means to be irritated, angry, or nervous (Ps 37:1, 7-8; Pr 24:19).

FRIENDS

General:
 Affectionate (Dt 13:6; 1Sa 18:1; 20:17; Jn 15:9-17). Sympathetic (Job 2:11; 6:14; Ps 35:14). Mercenary (Pr 14:20; 19:4, 6). Forsaken (Pr 17:9; 27:14). Faithful (Pr 17:17; 18:24; 27:6). Of mutual help (Pr 27:9, 19). Cause rejoicing (Pr 27:9). Not to forsake (Pr 27:10). *See Friendship.*
 Jesus calls his disciples (Lk 12:4; Jn 15:14-15).

False: (Ps 41:9; 88:18; Zec 13:6).
 Instances of: Pharaoh's chief cupbearer to Joseph (Ge 40:23). Delilah to Samson (Jdg 16:4-21). The wife of a Levite living in the hill country of Ephraim (Jdg 19:1-2). David, to Uriah (2Sa 11), to Joab (1Ki 2:5-6). Ahithophel to David (2Sa 15:12). Job's friends (Job 6:14-30; 19:13-22). David's friends to David (Ps 31:11-12; 35:11-16; 41:9; 55:12-14, 20-21; 88:8). Judas (Mt 26:48-49; Mk 14:43-50; Lk 22:47-48; Ac 1:16-17). Jesus' disciples (Mt 26:56, 58). Paul's friends (2Ti 4:16).
 See Hypocrisy.

FRIENDSHIP

General:
 Value of (Ecc 4:9-12). Faithfulness in (Ps 35:13-14; Pr 17:9, 17; 27:6, 9-10, 14, 17, 19). Trials growing out of (Dt 13:6-9; Pr 22:24-25).
 Promoted by, sympathy (Job 6:14-15). Fidelity (Pr 11:13). Not wearing out one's welcome (Pr 25:17). Mutual understanding (Am 3:3).
 See Friends.

Instances of:
 Abraham and Lot (Ge 14:14-16). Ruth and Naomi (Ru 1:16-17). David and Jonathan (1Sa 18:1-4; 20; 23:16-18; 2Sa 1:17-27; 9:1-13). David and Abiathar (1Sa 22:23). David and Mephibosheth (2Sa 9). David and Nahash (2Sa 10:2). David and Ittai (2Sa 15:19-22). David and Hushai (2Sa 15:32-37; 16; 17:1-22). David and Hiram (1Ki 5:1). Joram and Ahaziah (2Ki 8:28-29; 9:16). Jehu and Jehonadab (2Ki 10:15-27). Job and his three friends (Job 2:11-13). Daniel and his three companions (Da 2:49).
 The Marys, and Joseph of Arimathea, for Jesus (Mt 27:55-61; 28:1-8; Lk 24:10; Jn 20:11-18). Mary, Martha, and Lazarus, and Jesus (Lk 10:38-42; Jn 11:1-46). Luke and Theophilus (Ac 1:1). Paul and his nephew (Ac 23:16). Paul, Priscilla, and Aquila (Ro 16:3-4). Paul, Timothy, and Epaphroditus (Php 2:19-20, 22, 25).

FRINGES See Tassel(s).

FROGS Plague of (Ex 8:2-14; Ps 78:45; 105:30).
 Symbolic (Rev 16:13).

FRONTLETS A leather band worn on the forehead (Ex 13:6-16; Dt 6:1-8; 11:18). See Phylactery.

FROST Appeared in winter on the high elevations in Bible lands (Job 37:10; 38:29).

FROWARDNESS See Disobedience to God.

FRUGALITY

General:
 Diligent (Pr 12:27). Good (Pr 13:22). Wise (Pr 21:17; 21:20). Prudent (Pr 22:3). Industrious (Eph 4:28). The mark of a virtuous woman (Pr 31:27).
 Admonition regarding (Pr 23:20-21). Commanded by Jesus (Jn 6:12).
 Pretense of to cover greed (Mk 14:4-5).

Instances of:
 The provisions made by the Egyptians against famine (Ge 41:48-54), the gathering of manna (Ex 16:17-18, 22-24). The gathering of bread and fish after the feeding of the multitudes (Mt 14:20; 15:37).
 See Extravagance; Industry.

FRUIT TREES Planting and first harvest (Lev 19:23-25). Care for (Dt 20:19-20). In Ezekiel's vision, evergreen and with healing properties (Eze 47:12). See Tree.

FRUITS

Natural: Created (Ge 1:11-12, 27-29).
 See the list of various fruit-producing trees at Tree.

Spiritual: (Gal 5:22-23). See Righteousness, Fruits of; Sin, Fruits of; Holy Spirit, Fruit of.

FRYING PAN See Pan(s).

FUEL Wood, charcoal, dried grass, and even the dung of animals and humans was used for fuel (Eze 4:12, 15; Mt 6:30; Jn 18:18).

FUGITIVES

From Servitude:
 Not to be returned (Dt 23:15-16).

From Justice:
 Moses (Ex 2:15), Absalom (2Sa 13:34-38).

From the Avenger of Blood:
 See Avenger of Blood; Cities of Refuge.

From the Wrath of the King:
 David (1Sa 21:10), Jeroboam (1Ki 11:40), Joseph, to Egypt (Mt 2:13-15).

Instances of:
 From slavery, Shimei's servants (1Ki 2:39), Onesimus (Phm 10).
 See Exodus.

FULLER NIV "launderer"; one who cleans or dyes cloth or garments. The word is also used at times for one who thickens and shrinks newly shorn wool and newly woven cloth after cleansing it of natural oils. He may also have traded in textiles (Mal 3:2; Mk 9:3). *See Soap.*

FULLER'S FIELD See Washerman's Field.

FULLNESS OF TIME The time appointed when God's purposes for mankind and history for a particular event have been fulfilled (Mk 1:15; Gal 4:4; Eph 1:10; 1Ti 2:6; Tit 1:3; Heb 9:26).

FUNERAL The ceremonies used in disposing of a dead human body. In Palestine the body was buried within a few hours after death in a tomb or cave. The body was washed, anointed with spices, and wrapped in cloths (Jn 12:7; 19:39-40). Refusal of proper burial was utter disgrace (Jer 22:19).

FURLONG See Stadia.

FURNACE Furnaces of the biblical period were made of brick or stone and were designed for different purposes, from small domestic types to large commercial smelters as those at Ezion Geber.

Figurative:
 Of affliction (Dt 4:20; 1Ki 8:51; Ps 12:6; Isa 48:10; Jer 11:4). Of the Lord who refines the heart (Pr 17:3). Of lust (Hos 7:4). Of hell (Mal 4:1; Mt 13:42, 50; Rev 9:2).

Uses of:
 For refining gold (Pr 17:3), silver (Eze 22:22; Mal 3:3). For melting lead and tin (Eze 22:20). For capital punishment, Shadrach, Meshach, and Abednego cast into by Nebuchadnezzar (Da 3:6-26).

FURNITURE The principle reference to furniture in the Bible concerns the articles in the tabernacle and temple. Common people had little furniture; kings had beds (Dt 3:11) and tables (Jdg 1:7).

FUTURE See Immortality; Eschatology.

FUTURE PUNISHMENT See Punishment, Eternal.

G

GAAL (loathing). Son of Ebed, who led the men of Shechem in a revolt against Abimelech, the son of Gideon (Jdg 9:26-41).

GAASH (rumble, quake). A foothill of Mt. Ephraim. Joshua's inheritance embraced (Jos 24:30). Joshua buried on the north side of (Jos 24:30; Jdg 2:9). Brooks of (2Sa 23:30).

GABA See Geba.

GABBAI (collector). A chief of Benjamin (Ne 11:8).

GABBATHA (possibly height, ridge). The place called "the Stone Pavement" (Jn 19:13), where Jesus was tried before Pilate.

GABRIEL [strong] man of God [El]). A messenger of God. Appeared to Daniel (Da 8:16; 9:21), to Zechariah (Lk 1:11-19), to Mary (Lk 1:26-29).

GAD, GADITES (fortune).
 1. Jacob's seventh son (Ge 30:11; 35:26; Ex 1:4). Children of (Ge 46:16; Nu 26:15-18; 1Ch 5:11). Prophecy concerning (Ge 49:19).
 2. A tribe of Israel. Blessed by Moses (Dt 33:20). Enumeration of, at Sinai (Nu 1:14, 24-25), in the plains of Moab (Nu 26:15-18), in the reign of Jotham (1Ch 5:11-17). Place of, in camp and march (Nu 2:10, 14, 16). Wealth of, in cattle, and spoils (Nu 32:1; Jos 22:8). Petition for their portion of land E of the Jordan (Nu 32:1-5; Dt 3:12, 16-17; 29:8). Boundaries of territory (Jos 13:24-28; 1Ch 5:11). Aid in the conquest of the region W of the Jordan (Nu 32:16-32; Jos 4:12-13; 22:1-8). Erect a monument to signify the unity of the tribes E of the Jordan with the tribes W of the river (Jos 22:10-14).
 Disaffected toward Saul as king and joined the faction under David in the wilderness of Hebron (1Ch 12:8-15, 37-38). Join the Reubenites in the war against the Hagrites (1Ch 5:10, 18-22). Smitten by the king of Syria (2Ki 10:32-33). Carried into captivity to Assyria (1Ch 5:26). Land of, occupied by the Ammonites, after the tribe is carried into captivity (Jer 49:1). Reallotment of territory to, by Ezekiel (Eze 48:27, 29).
 3. A prophet of David (1Sa 22:5). Requests David leave Adullam (1Sa 22:5). Bears the divine message to David offering choice between three evils, for his presumption in numbering Israel (2Sa 24:11-14; 1Ch 21:9-13). Requests David build an altar on threshing floor of Arnaunah (2Sa 24:18-19; 1Ch 21:18-19). Assists

David in organizing temple service (2Ch 29:25). Writings of (1Ch 29:29).

GADARENES The region around the city of Gadara is six miles SE of the S end of the Sea of Galilee (Mt 8:28). Mark and Luke identify the region by the capital city Gerasa, located about thirty-five miles southeast of the Sea (Mk 5:1; Lk 8:26 and ftns). *See Gerasenes.*

GADDAH See Hazar Gaddah.

GADDI (my fortune). A chief of Manasseh. One of the twelve spies who explored Canaan (Nu 13:11).

GADDIEL (God [El] is my fortune BDB; [pagan god] Gad is [my] god KB). A chief of Zebulun. One of the twelve spies (Nu 13:10).

GADER See Beth Gader.

GADI (my fortune). Father of Menahem, a king of Israel (2Ki 15:14-20).

GAHAM (burning brightly). A son of Nahor by his concubine Reumah (Ge 22:24).

GAHAR ([born in the] year of little rain). One of the temple servants (Ezr 2:47; Ne 7:49).

GAIUS
 1. A Macedonian and companion of Paul. Seized at Ephesus (Ac 19:29).
 2. A man of Derbe. Accompanied Paul from Macedonia (Ac 20:4).
 3. A Corinthian, whom Paul baptized (Ro 16:23; 1Co 1:14).
 4. Man to whom 3 John was addressed (3Jn 1).

GALAL (possibly tortoise IDB; roll away KB).
 1. A Levite (1Ch 9:15).
 2. Son of Jeduthun (1Ch 9:16; Ne 11:17).

GALATIA A province of Asia Minor. Its churches visited by Paul (Ac 16:6; 18:23). Collection taken in, for Christians at Jerusalem (1Co 16:1). Peter's address to (1Pe 1:1). Churches in (Gal 1:2). *See Galatians, Epistle to the.*

GALATIANS, EPISTLE TO THE

Author: The apostle Paul

Date:
 If the letter was addressed to churches located in north-central Asia Minor (Pessinus, Ancyra and Tavium), Galatians was written between A.D. 53 and 57.
 If the letter was addressed to churches in the southern area of the Roman province of Galatia (Antioch, Iconium, Lystra and Derbe), Galatians was written A.D. 48 or 49.

Outline:
I. Introduction (1:1-9).
 A. Salutation (1:1-5).
 B. Denunciation (1:6-9).
II. Personal: Authentication of the Apostle of Liberty and Faith (1:10-2:10).
 A. Paul's Gospel Was Received by Special Revelation (1:10-12).
 B. Paul's Gospel Was Independent of the Jerusalem Apostles and the Judean Churches (1:13-2:21).
 1. Evidenced by his early activities as a Christian (1:13-17).
 2. Evidenced by his first post-Christian visit to Jerusalem (1:18-24).
 3. Evidenced by his visit to Jerusalem fourteen years later (2:1-10).
 4. Evidenced by his rebuke of Peter at Antioch (2:11-21).
III. Doctrinal: Justification of the Doctrine of Liberty and Faith (chs. 3-4).
 A. The Galatians' Experience of the Gospel (3:1-5).
 B. The Experience of Abraham (3:6-9).
 C. The Curse of the Law (3:10-14).
 D. The Priority of the Promise (3:15-18).
 E. The Purpose of the Law (3:19-25).
 F. Sons, Not Slaves (3:26-4:11).
 G. Appeal to Enter Into Freedom From Law (4:12-20).
 H. The Allegory of Hagar and Sarah (4:21-31).
IV. Practical: Practice of the Life of Liberty and Faith (5:1-6:10).
 A. Exhortation to Freedom (5:1-12).
 B. Life by the Spirit, Not by the Flesh (5:13-26).
 C. Call for Mutual Help (6:1-10).
V. Conclusion (6:11-18).

GALBANUM A fragrant gum used in the sacred oil (Ex 30:34).

GALEED (heap of [stones that are a] witness). The name given by Jacob to the heap of stones which he and Laban raised as a memorial of their compact (Ge 31:47-48).

GALILEAN A native of Galilee (Mt 26:69; Jn 4:45; Ac 1:11; 5:37).

GALILEE (ring, circle, hence region). The northern district of Israel. A city of refuge in (Jos 20:7; 21:32; 1Ch 6:76). Cities in, given to Hiram (1Ki 9:11-12). Taken by king of Assyria (Isa 9:29). Prophecy concerning (Isa 9:1; Mt 4:15). Called Galilee of the nations (Isa 9:1). Herod, tetrarch of (Mk 6:21; Lk 3:1; 23:6-7). Jesus resides in (Mt 17:22; 19:1; Jn 7:1, 9). Teaching and miracles of Jesus in (Mt 4:23, 25; 15:29-31; Mk 1:14, 28, 39; 3:7; Lk 4:14, 44; 5:17; 23:5; Jn 1:43; 4:3, 43-45; Ac 10:37). People of, receive Jesus (Jn 4:45, 53). Disciples were chiefly from (Ac 1:11; 2:7). Women from, ministered to Jesus (Mt 27:55-56; Mk 15:41; Lk 23:49, 55). Jesus appeared to his disciples in, after his resurrection (Mt 26:32; 28:7, 10, 16-17; Mk 14:28; 16:7; Jn 21).
 Routes from, to Judea (Jdg 21:19; Jn 4:3-5). Dialect of (Mk 14:70). Called Gennesaret (Mt 14:34; Mk 6:53). Churches in (Ac 9:31).

G

G

GALILEE, SEA OF Also called the Lake of Gennesaret (Lk 5:1), the Sea of Kinnereth (Nu 34:11, ftn; Dt 3:17), and the Sea of Tiberias, because Herod's capital was on its shores (Jn 6:1; 21:1). The lake is thirteen miles long and eight miles wide, filled with fresh and clear water, and full of fish. Because it was located in a pocket in the hills, it was subject to sudden violent storms. *See Gennesaret, 2; Kinnereth, 3; Tiberias.*

GALL
1. The secretion of the human gall bladder (Job 16:13).
2. The poison of serpents (Job 20:14).
3. A bitter and poisonous herb (Jer 9:15; Hos 10:4; Am 6:12), perhaps used to deaden pain (Mt 27:34).
Figurative of the bitter end of immorality (Pr 5:4).

GALLERY A balcony of the temple in Ezekiel's vision (Eze 41:16; 42:3, 5-6).

GALLEY *See Ship.*

GALLIM (*heaps*). A town of Benjamin (Isa 10:30; 1Sa 25:44).

GALLIO Proconsul of Achaia. Dismisses complaint of Jews against Paul (Ac 18:12-17).

GALLON A unit of liquid measure. Six gallons is equal to the biblical measure known as a bath. Four quarts (one gallon), which is one sixth of a bath, is known as a hin. John records that the water jars used to hold water for ceremonial washing would hold twenty to thirty gallons of water; Jesus used this water to replenish the wine supply at the marriage celebration at Cana in Galilee (Jn 2:6).

GALLOWS Used for execution of criminals (Est 2:23; 5:14; 6:4; 7:9-10; 9:13, 25). Reproach of being hanged upon (Gal 3:13). *See Punishment.*

GAMALIEL (*recompense of God [El]*).
1. Chief of tribe of Manasseh (Nu 1:10; 2:20; 10:23).
2. An eminent Pharisee and teacher of the law, the teacher of Paul (Ac 22:3). He was broadminded and tolerant toward early Christians (Ac 5:34-39).

GAMBLING *See Betting; Lot, The.*

GAMES Footraces (1Co 9:24, 26; Gal 2:2; Php 2:16; Heb 12:1). Gladiatorial (1Co 4:9; 9:26; 15:32; 2Ti 4:7).
Figurative:
Of the Christian life (1Co 9:24, 26; Gal 5:7; Php 2:16; 3:14; Heb 12:1). Of a successful ministry (Ge 23:10, 16; Php 2:16). Fighting wild beasts, of spiritual conflict (1Co 4:9; 9:26; 15:32; 2Ti 4:7).

GAMMAD (probably *valiant men*). Men of in the watchtowers of Tyre (Eze 27:11).

GAMUL (*weaned*). The head of the twenty-second course of priests (1Ch 24:17).

GANGRENE Perhaps in a running or festering sore (Ex 9:9-10; Lev 21:20, 22:22; Dt 28:27; Job 7:5). False teaching spreads like gangrene (2Ti 2:17).

GANNIM *See En Gannim.*

GARDEN A cultivated piece of ground planted with flowers, vegetables, shrubs, or trees, fenced with a mud or stone wall (Pr 24:31) or with thorny hedges (Isa 5:5). Gardens were sometimes used for burial places (Ge 23:17; 2Ki 21:18, 26; Jn 19:41). The future state of the saved is figuratively represented by a garden (Rev 22:1-5).

GARDENER *See Occupations and Professions.*

GAREB (*scabby*).
1. One of David's warriors (2Sa 23:38; 1Ch 11:40).
2. A hill near Jerusalem (Jer 31:39).

GARLAND A crown or wreath for the head; figurative of the rewards of wisdom (Pr 1:9; 4:9). *See Crown.*

GARLIC (Nu 11:5).

GARMENT Of righteousness (Isa 61:10; Mt 22:11; 2Co 5:3; Rev 3:18; 7:14; 16:15; 19:8). *See Dress; Robe.*

GARMITE (*bone, bony*). A title applied to Keilah (1Ch 4:19).

GARNER *See Barn; Granary; Storehouse.*

GARRISON A fortress manned by soldiers, used chiefly for the occupation of a conquered country (1Sa 10:5; 13:3; 14:1, 6; 2Sa 8:6, 14). *See Fort.*

GASHMU *See Geshem.*

GATAM Grandson of Esau (Ge 36:11, 16; 1Ch 1:36).

GATE, INSPECTION Name of one of the gates of Jerusalem (Ne 3:31).

GATEKEEPERS Guards at the city gates, the doors of the king's palace, and doors of the temple (1Ch 9:17-32; 2Ch 34:13; 35:15). Lodged round about the temple in order to be present for opening the doors (1Ch 9:27). One-third were gatekeepers at the temple (2Ch 23:4), one-third were gatekeepers of the king's house (2Ch 23:5), one-third were gatekeepers of the gate of foundation (2Ch 23:5). They served, also, as gatekeepers of the gates of the walls (Ne 12:25). They served in twenty-four courses (1Ch 26:13-19). Their posts were determined by lot (1Ch 24:31; 26:13-19).

GATES Of cities (Dt 3:5; Jos 6:26; 1Sa 23:7; 2Sa 18:24; 2Ch 8:5). Made of iron (Ac 12:10; Ps 107:16; bronze (Ps 107:16; Isa 45:2). Double doors (Isa 45:1; Eze 41:24).
The open square of, a place for idlers (Ge 19:1; 1Sa 4:18; Ps 69:12; Pr 1:21; Jer 17:19-20). Religious services held at (Ac 14:13). The law read at (Ne 8). Place for the transaction of public business, announcement of legal transactions (Ge 23:10, 16), conferences on public affairs (Ge 34:20), holding courts of justice (Dt 16:18; 21:19; 22:15; Jos 20:4; Ru 4:1; 2Sa 15:2; Pr 22:22; Zec 8:16). Place for public concourse (Ge 23:10; Pr 1:21; 8:3; Jer 14:2; 22:2). Thrones of kings at (1Ki 22:10; 2Ch 18:9; Jer 38:7; 39:3). Punishment of criminals outside of (Dt 17:5; Jer 20:2; Ac 7:58; Heb 13:12). Closed at night (Jos 2:5, 7), on the Sabbath (Ne 13:19). Guards at (2Ki 7:17; Ne 13:19, 22). Jails made in the towers of (Jer 20:2). Bodies of criminals exposed to view as (Jos 8:2-9; 2Ki 10:8).
Figurative:
Of the people of a city (Isa 3:26). Of the gospel (Isa 60:11). Of the powers of hell (Mt 16:18). Of death (Job 38:17; Ps 9:13; Isa 38:10). Of the grave (Isa 38:10). Of righteousness (Ps 118:19). Of salvation (Ge 28:17; Ps 24:7; 118:19-20; Isa 26:2). Narrow gate, of the way to life (Mt 7:13-14).
Symbolic: (Rev 21:12-13, 21, 25).
See Jerusalem, Gates of.

GATH (*winepress*). One of the five chief cities of the Philistines (Jos 13:3; 1Sa 6:17; Am 6:2; Mic 1:10). Anakites, a race of giants, inhabitants of (Jos 11:22). Goliath dwelt in (1Sa 17:4; 1Ch 20:5-8). Obed-Edom belonged to (2Sa 6:10). The ark taken to (1Sa 5:8). Inhabitants of, called Gittites (Jos 13:3). David takes refuge at (1Sa 21:10-15; 27:2-7). Band of Gittites, attached to David (2Sa 15:18-22). Taken by David (1Ch 18:1). Shimei's servants escape to (1Ki 2:39-41). Fortified by Rehoboam (2Ch 11:8). Taken by Hazael (2Ki 12:17). Recovered by Jehoash (2Ki 13:25). Besieged by Uzziah (2Ch 26:6). Called Metheg Ammah (2Sa 8:1).

GATH HEPHER (*winepress water pit*). A town on the border of Zebulun (Jos 19:12-13) and birthplace of Jonah the prophet (2Ki 14:25).

GATH RIMMON (*winepress of pomegranate*).
1. A city of Dan on the Philistine plain (Jos 19:45).
2. A town of Manasseh, W of Jordan, assigned to Levites (Jos 21:25).

GAULANITIS A province NE of the Sea of Galilee, ruled by Herod Antipas. It encompassed the region of OT Golan. *See Golan.*

GAZA (*strong*).
1. A city of the Philistines (Jos 13:3; Jer 25:20). One of the border cities of the Canaanites (Ge 10:19). A city of the Avvim and Anakim (Dt 2:23; Jos 11:22). Allotted to Judah (Jos 15:47; Jdg 1:18). A temple of Dagon, situated at (Jdg 16:23). Samson dies at (Jdg 16:21-31). On the western boundary of the kingdom of Israel in the time of Solomon (1Ki 4:24). Smitten by Pharaoh (Jer 47:1). Prophecies relating to (Am 1:6-7; Zep 2:4; Zec 9:5). Desert of (Ac 8:26-39).
2. A city of Ephraim (Jdg 6:4; 1Ch 7:28).

GAZATHITES, GAZITES NIV "[people of] Gaza" (Jos 13:3; Jdg 16:2). *See Gaza, 1.*

GAZELLE *See Animals.*

GAZER *See Gezer.*

GAZEZ (possibly *sheep shearer* IDB; possibly *one born at the time of shearing* KB). The name of the son and of the grandson of Ephah (1Ch 2:46).

GAZZAM (*some kind of bird or insect*). One of the temple servants (Ezr 2:48; Ne 7:51).

GE HARASHIM It may be the broad valley between Lod and Ono (1Ch 4:14, ftn; Ne 11:35).

GEBA (*hill*). A town in the territory of Benjamin (Jos 18:24; Ezr 2:26; Ne 7:30), assigned to the Levites (Jos 21:17). Jonathan defeated the Philistines at Geba (1Sa 13:3). Asa fortified the city (1Ki 15:22), and in Hezekiah's time it was the northern most city of Judah (2Ki 23:8). Men from Geba returned after the Exile (Ezr 2:26).

GEBAL (possibly *border* BDB; *hill* KB).
1. A seaport of Phoenicia N of Sidon, also known as Byblos. Modern Jebeil, twenty-five miles N of Beirut. The land of the Gebalites is mentioned (Jos 13:5). The town was renowned for its expert stonemasons (1Ki 5:17-18) and for shipbuilding (Eze 27:9).
2. A land between the Dead Sea and Petra (Ps 83:6-8).

GEBALITES The inhabitants of Gebal or Byblos (Jos 13:5). *See Gebal.*

GEBER (*[strong young] man*).
1. One of Solomon's suppliers in Ramoth Gilead (1Ki 4:13). Called Ben-Geber.
2. The son of Uri (1Ki 4:19).

GEBIM (*ditches*). A place near Anathoth (Isa 10:31).

GECKO (Lev 11:30). *See Animals, Names of.*

GEDALIAH (*great is Yahweh*).
1. Governor appointed by Nebuchadnezzar after carrying the Israelites into captivity (2Ki 25:22-24). Jeremiah committed to the care of (Jer 39:14; 40:5-6). Warned of the conspiracy of Ishmael by Johanan and the captains of his army (Jer 40:13-16). Slain by Ishmael (2Ki 25:25-26; Jer 41:1-10).
2. A musician (1Ch 25:3, 9).
3. A priest, who divorced his Gentile wife after the Exile (Ezr 10:18).

4. Ancestor of Zephaniah (Zep 1:1).
5. A prince who caused imprisonment of Jeremiah (Jer 38:1).

GEDEON *See Gideon.*

GEDER (*wall [of stones]*). An ancient city of Canaan (Jos 12:13). Possibly identical with Gedor, 2 or 3.

GEDERAH (*stone pen, sheep corral*). Located between the valleys of Sorek and Aijalon in the hills of Judah (Jos 15:36). Often identified as modern Jedirah, though others identify it with Khirbet Judraya.

GEDEROTH (*stone pens, sheep corrals*). A city in the plain of Judah (Jos 15:41; 2Ch 28:18).

GEDEROTHAIM (*two stone pens, two sheep corrals*). A city in the plain of Judah (Jos 15:36).

GEDI *See En Gedi.*

GEDOR (*wall* BDB; *pock-marked* KB).
1. A city in mountains of Judah (Jos 15:58).
2. The town of Jeroham (1Ch 12:7). Possibly identical with Geder.
3. Valley of, taken by Simeonites (1Ch 4:39). *See Geder.*
4. An ancestor of Saul (1Ch 8:31; 9:37).
5. Either a place or a person, authorities disagree (1Ch 4:4, 18).

GEHAZI (possibly *valley of vision*). The servant of Elisha (2Ki 4:8-37; 5:1-27; 8:4-6). He was punished for greed by becoming a leper.

GEHENNA (*valley of Hinnom*). See Ben Hinnom; Hell.

GELILOTH (*region*). A place mentioned (Jos 18:17), as marking the boundary of Benjamin. Gilgal is substituted (Jos 15:7).

GEMALLI (*my reward* KB). Father of Ammiel, and one of the twelve spies (Nu 13:12).

GEMARIAH (*Yahweh has accomplished*).
1. Son of Shaphan the scribe and friend of Jeremiah (Jer 36:10-25).
2. A son of Hilkiah, sent as ambassador to Nebuchadnezzar (Jer 29:3).

GENEALOGY (*account of one's descent*). (Nu 1:18; 2Ch 12:15; Ezr 2:59; Ne 7:5; Heb 7:3). Of no spiritual significance (Mt 3:9; 1Ti 1:4; Tit 3:9).
From Adam to Noah (Ge 4:16-22; 5; 1Ch 1:1-4; Lk 3:36-38), to Abraham (Ge 11:10-32; 1Ch 1:4-27; Lk 3:34-38), to Jesus (Mt 1:1-16; Lk 3:23-38). Of the descendants of Noah (Ge 10), of Nahor (Ge 22:20-24), of Abraham, by his wife Keturah (Ge 25:1-4; 1Ch 1:32-33), of Ishmael (Ge 25:12-16; 1Ch 1:28-31), of Esau (Ge 36; 1Ch 1:35-54), of Jacob (Ge 35:23-26; Ex 1:5; 6:14-27; Nu 26; 1Ch 2-9), of Perez to David (Ru 4:18-22). Of the Jews who returned from the Captivity (Ezr 7:1-5; 8:1-15; Ne 7; 11:12). Of Joseph (Mt 1; Lk 3:23-38).

GENEALOGY OF JESUS CHRIST Two genealogies are given in the NT (Mt 1:1-17; Lk 3:23-28). Matthew traces the descent of Jesus from Abraham and David, and divides it into three sets of fourteen generations. He omits three generations after Joram, namely Ahaziah, Joash, and Amaziah (1Ch 3:11-12). Contrary to Hebrew practice, he names five women: Tamar, Rahab, Ruth, Bathsheba, and Mary. The sense of "became the father of" in Hebrew genealogies is not exact; it includes immediate or remote descent, an adoptive relation, or legal heirship. Luke's genealogy moves from Jesus to Adam, agreeing with the accounts in 1 Chronicles between Abraham and Adam (1Ch 1:1-7, 24-28). From David to Abraham he agrees with Matthew; from Jesus to David he differs from Matthew. Perhaps Matthew gives the line of legal heirship, while Luke gives the line of physical descent.

GENERAL LETTERS The seven letters following Hebrews—James; 1 and 2 Peter; 1, 2, and 3 John and Jude—have often been designated as the General Letters. This term goes back to the early church historian Eusebius (c. A.D. 265-340), who in his *Ecclesiastical History* (2.23-25) first referred to these seven letters as Catholic Letters, using the word "catholic" to mean "universal."
The letters so designated may be said to be, for the most part, addressed to general audiences rather than to specific persons or localized groups. 2 and 3 John, the two letters that seem most obviously addressed to individuals, have long been viewed as appendages of 1 John, which is clearly general in its address. However, when compared with Paul's letters, all these letters except 3 John are clearly general in nature. By contrast, Paul addresses his letters to such recipients as the saints at Philippi, or the churches of Galatia, or Timothy or Titus.
As Eusebius noted long ago, one interesting fact connected with the General Letters is that most of them were at one time among the disputed books of the NT. James, 2 Peter, 2 John, 3 John, and Jude were all questioned extensively before being admitted to the canon of Scripture.

GENERALS Roman military leaders (Rev 6:15; 19:18). *See Captain.*

GENERATION A period of time (Ex 3:15; Da 4:3; Lk 1:50), or all the people living in a given period (Jdg 2:10; Mt 11:16), or a class of people having a certain quality (Dt 32:5, 20; Mt 8:38), or a company gathered together (Ps 49:19).

GENERATION, EVIL (Dt 32:5; Pr 30:12; Mt 3:7; 12:39, 45; Lk 9:41; Ac 2:40).

GENEROSITY *See Beneficence; Giving; Liberality.*

GENESIS (beginning).

Author: Historically, Jews and Christians alike have held that Moses was the author/compiler of the first five books of the OT.

Date: c. 1446 to 1406

Outlines:

Literary Outline:
I. Introduction (1:1-2:3).
II. Body (2:4-50:26).
 A. "The account of the heavens and the earth" (2:4-4:26).
 B. "The written account of Adam's line" (5:1-6:8).
 C. "The account of Noah" (6:9-9:29).
 D. "The account of Shem, Ham and Japheth" (10:1-11:9).
 E. "The account of Shem" (1:10-26).
 F. "The account of Terah" (11:217-25:11).
 G. "The account of Abraham's son Ishmael" (25:12-18).
 H. "The account of Abraham's son Isaac" (25:19-35:29).
 I. "The account of Esau" (36:1-37:1).
 J. "The account of Jacob" (37:2-50:26).

Thematic Outline:
I. Primeval History (1:1-11:26).
 A. Creation (1:1-2:3).
 1. Introduction (1:1-2).
 2. Body (1:3-31).
 3. Conclusion (2:1-3).
 B. Adam and Eve in Eden (2:4-25).
 C. The Fall and Its Consequences (3:1-24).
 D. The Rapid "Progress" of Sin (4:1-16).
 E. Two Genealogies (4:17-5:32).
 1. The genealogy of pride (4:17-24).
 2. The genealogy of death (4:25-5:32).
 F. The Extent of Sin Before the Flood (6:1-8).
 G. The Great Flood (6:9-9:29).
 1. Preparing for the Flood (6:9-7:10).
 2. Judgment and redemption (7:11-8:19).
 a. The rising of the waters (7:11-24).
 b. The receding of the waters (8:1-19).
 3. The flood's aftermath (8:20-9:29).
 a. A new promise (8:20-22).
 b. New ordinances (9:1-7).
 c. A new relationship (9:8-17).
 d. A new temptation (9:18-23).
 e. A final word (9:24-29).
 H. The Spread of the Nations (10:1-11:26).
 1. The diffusion of nations (10:1-32).
 2. The confusion of tongues (11:1-9).
 3. The first Semitic genealogy (11:10-26).
II. Patriarchal History (11:27-50:26).
 A. The Life of Abraham (11:27-25:11).
 1. Abraham's background (11:27-32).
 2. Abraham's land (12:1-14:24).
 3. Abraham's people (15:1-24:67).
 4. Abraham's last days (25:1-11).
 B. The Descendants of Ishmael (25:2-18).
 C. The Life of Jacob (25:19-35:29).
 1. Jacob at home (25:19-27:46).
 2. Jacob abroad (28:1-30:43).
 3. Jacob at home again (31:1-35:29).
 D. The Descendants of Esau (36:1-37:1).
 E. The Life of Joseph (37:2-50:26).
 1. Joseph's career (37:2-41:57).
 2. Jacob's migration (42:1-47:31).
 3. Jacob's last days (48:1-50:14).
 4. Joseph's last days (50:15-26).

GENIUS Mechanical, a divine inspiration (Ex 28:3; 31:2-11; 35:30-35; 36:1). See Inspiration.

GENNESARET
1. "The land of Gennesaret" is a plain on the NW shore of the Sea of Galilee (Mt 14:34; Mk 6:53).
2. "The Lake of Gennesaret" is the same as the Sea of Galilee (Lk 5:1). See Galilee, Sea of.

GENTILES (nation, people). Usually meaning non-Israelite people. See Heathen.

General:
Ways of, condemned (Jer 10:2-3; Eph 4:17-19). God's forbearance toward (Ac 14:16). Impartiality toward (Ro 2:9-11). Ignorant worship practices of (Mt 6:7-8, 31-32; Ac 17:4, 16, 22-27; 1Co 10:20; 12:2). Wicked practices of (Ro 1:18-32; Gal 2:15; Eph 5:12; 1Th 4:5; 1Pe 4:3-4). Moral responsibility of (Ro 2:14-15).
See Idolatry; Missions.

Prophecies of the Conversion of:
(Ge 12:3; 22:18; 49:10; Dt 32:21; Ps 2:8; 22:27-31; 46:4, 10; 65:2, 5; 66:4; 68:31-32; 72:8-11, 16, 19; 86:9; 102:15, 18-22; 145:10-11; Isa 2:2-4; 9:2, 6-7; 11:6-10; 18:7; 24:16; 35:1-2, 5-7; 40:5; 42:1-12; 45:6, 8, 22-24; 49:1, 5-6, 18-23; 54:1-3; 55:5; 56:3, 6-8; 60:1-14; 65:1; 66:12, 19, 23; Jer 3:17; 4:2; 16:19-21; Da 2:35, 44-45; 7:13-14; Hos 2:23; Joel 2:28-32; Am 9:11-12; Mic 4:3-4; Hag 2:7; Zec 2:10-11; 6:15; 8:20-23; 9:1, 10; 14:8-9, 16; Mal 1:11; Mt 3:9; 8:11; 12:17-21; 19:30; Mk 10:31; Lk 13:29-30; 21:24; Jn 10:16; Ac 9:15).
See Church, The Body of Believers, Prophecies Concerning.

Conversion of:
(Ac 10:45; 11:1-8; 13:2, 46-48; 14:27; 15:7-31; 18:4-6; 26:16-18; 28:28; Ro 1:5-7; 9:22-30; 10:19-20; 11:11-13, 17-21; 15:9-12; Eph 3:1-8; Col 3:11; 1Th 2:16; 1Ti 3:16; 2Ti 1:11; Rev 11:15; 15:4).
See Jesus the Christ, Kingdom of.

GENTILES, COURT OF THE The part of Herod's temple which the Gentiles could enter (not mentioned in the Bible). In the temple of Revelation (Rev 11:2).

GENTILES, INCLUSION OF See Catholicity.

GENTLENESS

Of Christ: (Isa 40:11; Mt 11:29; 2Co 10:1).
 See Jesus the Christ, Compassion of, Humility of, Meekness of.

Of God: (2Sa 22:36; Ps 18:35; Isa 40:11).
 See God, Compassion of, Longsuffering of.

Of Paul: (1Th 2:7).

Exhortations to:
A fruit of the Spirit (Gal 5:22; Jas 3:17). Required in the Lord's servants (2Ti 2:24-26). Required in all Christians (Tit 3:1-2).
See Humility; Kindness; Meekness; Patience.

GENUBATH (thief). A son of Hadad the Edomite (1Ki 11:20).

GEOLOGY Origin, in God (Ge 1:9-10; 1Sa 2:8; 2Sa 22:16; Job 12:8-9; Ps 18:15; 24:1-2; 104:5; 136:6; Pr 30:4; 2Pe 3:5-7). Control, by God (Job 28:9-11; Ps 104:5-13; Pr 30:4; Hab 3:9). Infinity of (Jer 31:37). Destruction of (2Pe 3:5-7).
See Astronomy; Creation; Earth; Hot Springs; Meteorology.

GERA (perhaps sojourner). A name common to the tribe of Benjamin.
1. A son of Benjamin (Ge 46:21).
2. A grandson of Benjamin (1Ch 8:3, 5).
3. The father of Ehud (Jdg 3:15).
4. A son of Ehud (1Ch 8:7).
5. Father of Shimei (2Sa 16:5).

GERAH A weight equal about 1/20 of a shekel or 1/2 gram (Ex 30:13; Lev 27:25; Nu 3:47). See Measure.

GERAR (circle, region).
1. A city of the Philistines (Ge 10:19). Abimelech, king of (Ge 20:1; 26:6). Visited by Abraham (Ge 20:1), by Isaac (Ge 26:1; 2Ch 14:13-14).
2. A valley (Ge 26:17-22).

GERASENES The region around Gerasa, one of the cities of the Decapolis near the SE end of the Sea of Galilee, in which the demoniacs lived whom Jesus healed (Mt 8:28, ftn; Mk 5:1; Lk 8:26, 37). See Gadarenes.

GERGESENES A variant reading probably harmonizing Gadarenes and Gerasenes, the region in which Jesus exorcized demons (Mt 8:28; Mk 5:1; Lk 8:26, ftns). See Gadarenes; Gerasenes.

GERIZIM Mount of blessing (Dt 11:29; 27:12; Jos 8:33). Jotham addresses the Shechemites from, against the conspiracy of Abimelech (Jdg 9:7). Samaritans worship at (Jn 4:20).

GERSHOM (traveler there).
1. Son of Moses (Ex 2:22; 18:3; 1Ch 23:15-16; 26:24).
2. See Gershon.
3. A descendant of Phinehas (Ezr 8:2).
4. A Levite (Jdg 18:30).

GERSHON, GERSHONITES Also called Gershom. Son of Levi (Ge 46:11; Ex 6:16-17; Nu 3:17-26; 4:22-28, 38; 7:7; 26:57; Jos 21:6; 1Ch 6:1, 16-17, 20, 43, 62, 71; 15:7; 23:6). Descendants of Gershon (Nu 3:25; 4:24, 38; 7:7).

GERUTH KIMHAM (lodging place of Kimham). An unidentified place near Bethlehem, at which Ishmael and his fellow assassins stopped during their flight to Egypt (Jer 41:17).

GESHAN A descendant of Caleb (1Ch 2:47).

GESHEM (rain shower). An Arab who opposed the work of Nehemiah (Hebrew Gashmu, a variant of Geshem) (Ne 2:19; 6:1-2, 6, ftn).

GESHUR, GESHURITES (bridge).
1. District E of the sources of the Jordan. The inhabitants of, not subdued by the Israelites (Dt 3:14; Jos 12:5; 1Ch 2:23). David marries a princess of (2Sa 3:3; 1Ch 3:2). Absalom takes refuge in, after the murder of Amnon (2Sa 13:37-38; 15:8).
2. A people living S of the Philistines near Sinai. Their land was not taken at the time of the Conquest (Jos 13:2-13). Inhabitants of one of the villages of, exterminated, and the spoils taken by David (1Sa 27:8).

GETHER The third son of Aram (Ge 10:23; 1Ch 1:17).

GETHSEMANE (olive oil press). A garden near Jerusalem. Jesus betrayed in (Mt 26:36-50; Mk 14:32-46; Lk 22:39-49; Jn 18:1-2).

GEUEL (splendor of God [El]). A representative from the tribe of Gad sent to spy out Canaan (Nu 13:15).

GEZER (possibly pieces). A Canaanite royal city perhaps also called Gob (2Sa 21:18 w 1Ch 20:4). The king of, defeated by Joshua (Jos 10:33; 12:12). Canaanites not all expelled from, but made to pay tribute (Jos 16:10; Jdg 1:29). Allotted to Ephraim (Jos 16:10; 1Ch 7:28). Assigned to Levites (Jos 21:21). Battle with Philistines at (1Ch 20:4; 2Sa 21:18). Struck by David (2Sa 5:25; 1Ch 14:16). Fortified by Solomon after Pharaoh, king of Egypt, drives out Canaanites, making Gezer a dowry for Pharaoh's daughter (1Ki 9:15-17). Pharaoh Shishak, invaded the land in Rehoboam's fifth year as king. He launched an attack from Gezer, and was able to threaten and plunder Jerusalem from there (1Ki 14:25-28; 2Ch 12:1-12). Gezer was twelfth on a list of 156 cities captured by Shishak in his twentieth year. This record is found on a huge relief in the Egyptian stele at Karnak. Shishak's raids went as far N as the Sea of Galilee.

GHOR, THE The Arabic name for the Jordan Valley, biblical Arabah. See Arabah.

GHOST An apparition (Isa 29:4); Jesus mistaken for (Mt 14:26; Mk 6:49; Lk 24:37-39). KJV "give up the ghost," means to breathe one's last, to die (Ge 25:8; 35:29; 49:33; Job 11:20; Mt 27:50; Jn 19:30). KJV "Holy Ghost" is NIV "Holy Spirit." See Holy Spirit; Spirit.

GIAH (bubbling spring). A place on the way to the wilderness of Gibeon (2Sa 2:24).

GIANTS People of exceptional height and strength, such as Og, king of Bashan (Jos 12:4; 13:12), and Goliath, whom David killed (1Sa 17). The Nephilim and descendants of Anak were giants to the Israelites (Ge 6:4; Nu 13:33) as were the Rephaites (Dt 2:11, 20; 3:11). See Anakites; Nephilim; Rephaites.

GIBBAR ([young vigorous] man, hero). A man whose children returned from captivity with Zerubbabel (Ezr 2:20).

GIBBETHON (mound, hill). A city of Dan (Jos 19:44). Allotted to the Levites (Jos 21:23). Besieged by Israel, while in possession of Philistines (1Ki 15:27; 16:15, 17).

GIBEA (mound, hill). A Judah ite (1Ch 2:49).

GIBEAH (mound, hill).
1. Of Judah (Jos 15:57).
2. Of Saul. Also called Gibeah of Benjamin. The people's wickedness (Jdg 19:12-30; Hos 9:9; 10:9). Destroyed by the Israelites (Jdg 20). The city of Saul (1Sa 10:26; 15:34; 22:6). The ark of the covenant conveyed to, by the Philistines (1Sa 7:1; 2Sa 6:3). Deserted (Isa 10:29).
3. Another town in Benjamin, also called Gibeah (Jos 18:28).
4. Gibeah in the field (Jdg 20:31). Probably identical with Geba.
See Geba.

GIBEATH HAARALOTH (hill of foreskins). Place where the Israelites were circumcised after the wilderness wanderings (Jos 5:3).

GIBEATHITE (of Gibeah). Shemaah, two of whose sons were among David's warriors (1Ch 12:3).

GIBEON (mound, hill).
1. A city of the Hivites (Jos 9:3, 17; 2Sa 21:2). The people of deceive Joshua into a treaty (Jos 9). Made servants by the Israelites when their deception was discovered (Jos 9:27). The sun stands still over, during Joshua's battle with the five confederated kings (Jos 10:12-14). Allotted to Benjamin (Jos 18:25). Assigned to the Aaronites (Jos 21:17). The tabernacle located at (1Ki 3:4; 1Ch 16:39; 21:29; 2Ch 1:2-3, 13). Smitten by David (1Ch 14:16). Seven sons of Saul slain at, to avenge the inhabitants of (2Sa 21:1-9). Solomon worships at, and offers sacrifices (1Ki 3:4), God appears to him in dreams (1Ki 3:5; 9:2). Abner slays Asahel at (2Sa 2:18-32; 3:30). Ishmael, the son of Nethaniah, defeated at, by Johanan (Jer 41:11-16).
2. Pool of (2Sa 2:13; Jer 41:12).

GIBEONITE(S) (people from Gibeon). Descended from the Hivites and Amorites (Jos 9:3, 7, w 2Sa 21:2). A mighty and warlike people (Jos 10:2). Cities of (Jos 9:17).
Israel deceived by (Jos 9:4-13), made a league with (Jos 9:15). Spared on account of their oath (Jos 9:18-19). Appointed woodcutters (Jos 9:20-27). Attacked by the kings of Canaan (Jos 10:1-5). Delivered by Israel (Jos 10:6-10).
Saul sought to destroy (2Sa 21:2). Israel plagued for Saul's cruelty to (2Sa 21:1). Effected the destruction of the remnant of Saul's house (2Sa 21:4-9). The office of the temple servants probably originated in (1Ch 9:2, ftn). Part of, returned from the captivity (Ne 7:25).

GIBLITES See Gebalites.

GIDDALTI (I pronounce [God as] Great ISBE; I reared up KB). A son of Heman (1Ch 25:4, 29).

GIDDEL (big).
1. One of the temple servants (Ezr 2:47; Ne 7:49).
2. One of Solomon's servants (Ezr 2:56; Ne 7:58).

GIDEON (one who cuts, hacks). Call of, by an angel (Jdg 6:11, 14). His excuses (Jdg 6:15). Promises of the Lord to (Jdg 6:16). Angel attests the call to, by miracle (Jdg 6:21-24). He destroys the altar of Baal and builds one to the Lord (Jdg 6:25-27). Tests God's word with a fleece (Jdg 6:36-40). Leads an army against and defeats the Midianites (Jdg 6:33-35; 7; 8:4-12). Ephraimites rebuke, for not inviting them to join in the campaign against the Midianites (Jdg 8:1-3). Avenges himself upon the people of Succoth (Jdg 8:14-17). Israel desires to make him king; he refuses (Jdg 8:22-23). Makes an ephod which becomes a snare to the Israelites (Jdg 8:24-27). Had seventy sons (Jdg 8:30). Death of (Jdg 8:32). Faith of (Heb 11:32).

GIDEONI (one who cuts, hacks). Father of Abidan (Nu 1:11; 2:22; 7:60, 65; 10:24).

GIDOM (a cutting off, stop pursuit). Limit of pursuit after battle of Gibeah (Jdg 20:45).

GIER EAGLE See Birds; Osprey.

GIFT, GIVING A gift can be a blessing (1Sa 25:27), given to gain a favor (Ge 34:12), as an act of submission (Ps 68:29), an offering (Ex 28:38), a bribe (Pr 18:16). In the NT, anything given (Lk 21:1; Jas 1:17), a present (Mt 7:11), special spiritual endowment (Ro 1:11; 1Ti 4:14). See Gifts From God.

GIFTS FROM GOD

Himself:
In Christ, the Savior (Isa 42:6; 55:4; Jn 3:16; 4:10; 6:32-33), in the Holy Spirit, the Comforter. See Holy Spirit.

G

Temporal:

Food and clothing (Mt 6:25, 33). Rain and fruitful seasons (Ge 8:22; 27:28; Lev 26:4-5; Isa 30:23). Wisdom (2Ch 1:12). Peace (Lev 26:6; 1Ch 22:9). Gladness (Ps 4:7). Strength and power (Ps 29:11; 68:18). Wisdom and knowledge (Ecc 2:26; Da 2:21-23; 1Co 1:5-7). Talents, figurative of gifts and abilities (Mt 25:14-30). All good things (Ps 21:2; 34:10; 84:11; Isa 42:5; Eze 11:19; Jn 16:23-24; Ro 8:32; 1Ti 6:17; Jas 1:17; 2Pe 1:3).

To be used and enjoyed (Ecc 3:13; 5:19-20; 1Ti 4:4-5). Should cause us to remember God (Dt 8:18). All creatures partake of (Ps 136:25; 145:15-16). Prayer for (Zec 10:1; Mt 6:11). *See Presents.*

Spiritual:

Of the Spirit (Ro 11:29; 12:6-8; 1Co 7:7; 12:4-11; 13:2; Eph 4:7; 1Pe 4:10). Life, eternal (Isa 42:5; Eze 11:19; Jn 3:16-17, 36; 6:27; Ro 5:16-18; 6:23). Grace (Jas 4:6). Wisdom (Pr 2:6; Jas 1:5). Repentance (Ac 11:28). Faith (Eph 2:8; Php 1:29). Rest (Mt 11:28). Glory (Jn 17:22).

See Blessings, Spiritual, From God; Charism, Charisma, Charismata; Miracles, Miraculous Gifts of the Spirit; Tongues, Gift of.

GIHON (*to gush forth*).

1. A river in Egypt (Ge 2:13).

2. Pools near Jerusalem (1Ki 1:33, 38, 45). Hezekiah brings the waters of the upper pool by an aqueduct into the city of Jerusalem (2Ch 32:4, 30; 33:14; Ne 2:13-15; 3:13-16; Isa 7:3; 22:9-11; 36:2).

GILALAI A priest and musician (Ne 12:36).

GILBOA (*bubbling*). A hill S of Jezreel, where Saul was defeated by the Philistines and died (1Sa 28:4; 31:1-8; 1Ch 10:1-8).

GILEAD (perhaps *monument of stones*).

1. A region E of the Jordan allotted to the tribes of Reuben and Gad and the half tribe of Manasseh (Nu 32:1-30; Dt 3:13; 34:1; 2Ki 10:33). Reubenites expel the Hagrites from (1Ch 5:9-10, 18-22). Ammonites make war against; defeated by Jephthah (Jdg 11; Am 1:13). The prophet Elijah a native of (1Ki 17:1). David retreats to, at the time of Absalom's rebellion (2Sa 17:16, 22, 24). Pursued into, by Absalom (2Sa 17:26). Absalom defeated and slain in the forests of (2Sa 18:9).

Hazael, king of Syria, attacks the land of (2Ki 10:32-33; Am 1:3). Invaded by Tiglath-Pileser, king of Syria (2Ki 15:29). A grazing country (Nu 32:1; 1Ch 5:9). Exported spices, balm, and myrrh (Ge 37:25; Jer 8:22; 46:11).

Figurative of prosperity (Jer 22:6; 50:19).

2. A mountain (Jdg 7:3; SS 4:1; 6:5).

3. A city (Hos 6:8; 12:11).

4. Grandson of Manasseh (Nu 26:29-30; 27:1; 36:1; Jos 17:1; 1Ch 2:21, 23; 7:14, 17).

5. Father of Jephthah (Jdg 11:1-2).

6. A chief of Gad (1Ch 5:14).

GILGAL (*circle of stones*).

1. Place of the first encampment of the Israelites W of the Jordan (Jos 4:19; 9:6; 10:6, 43; 14:6). Monument erected in, to commemorate the passage of the Jordan by the Israelites (Jos 4:19-24). Circumcision renewed at (Jos 5:2-9). Passover kept at (Jos 5:10-11). Manna ceased at, after the Passover (Jos 5:12). Quarries at (Jdg 3:19). Eglon, king of Moab, resides and is slain at (Jdg 3:14-26). A judgment seat, where Israel, in that district, came to be judged by Samuel (1Sa 7:16). Saul proclaimed king over all Israel at (1Sa 11:15; 13:4-15; 15:6-23). Agag, king of the Amalekites, slain at, by Samuel (1Sa 15:33). Tribe of Judah assembles at, to proceed to the E side of the Jordan to conduct King David back after the defeat of Absalom (2Sa 19:14-15, 40-43). A school of the prophets (2Ki 4:38-40).

Prophecies concerning (Hos 4:15; 9:15; 12:11; Am 4:4; 5:5).

2. A royal city in Canaan. Conquered by Joshua (Jos 12:23).

GILOH A town near Hebron in the western foothills of Judah (Jos 15:51; 2Sa 15:12).

GILONITE Ahithophel, one of David's counselors from the town of Giloh (2Sa 15:12; 23:34).

GIMZO (*place of sycamore trees*). A town off the Jerusalem Highway, three miles SW of Lydda (2Ch 28:18).

GIN See Snare; Trap.

GINATH (*protector*). The father of Tibni (1Ki 16:21).

GINNETHO See Ginnethon.

GINNETHON A priest who returned to Jerusalem with Zerubbabel (Ne 10:6; 12:4).

GIRDLE See Belt; Sash.

GIRGASHITES A Canaanite people (Ge 10:15). Land of, given to Abraham and his descendants (Ge 15:21; Dt 7:1; Jos 3:10; Ne 9:8). Driven out before the Israelites (Jos 24:11).

GIRZITES (*people from Gezer*). A tribe named with the Geshurites and the Amalekites (1Sa 27:8).

GISHPA (*listener*). An overseer of the temple servants (Ne 11:21).

GITTAH-HEPHER See Gath Hepher.

GITTAIM (*two winepresses*). A town of Benjamin to which the Beerothites fled (Ne 11:31, 33; 2Sa 4:3). The site is unknown.

GITTITE(S) (*of Gath*). Natives of Gath (Jos 13:1-3; 2Sa 6:8-11; 15:18; 21:19).

GITTITH In the titles of Psalms 8, 81, 84. It may denote a musical instrument imported from Gath or may be the title of a tune.

GIVING Rules for: Without ostentation (Mt 6:1-4). Regularly (1Co 16:2). Liberally (2Co 9:6-15). Cheerfully (2Co 8:11-12; 9:7).

See Alms; Beneficence; Liberality.

GIZONITE The title of the sons of Hashem, among David's bodyguards (1Ch 11:34).

GLADIATOR One who contends with wild beasts (1Co 15:32). *See Games.*

GLADNESS See Joy.

GLASS Was manufactured as early as 2500 B.C. by the Egyptians, and later by the Phoenicians, who promoted its commercial use, especially in jewelry. In the KJV, the glass mentioned by Paul (2Co 3:18) and by James (Jas 1:23-24) was a mirror of polished bronze. *See Mirror.* The references in Revelation to the sea of glass (Rev 4:6; 15:2) and the new Jerusalem (Rev 21:18, 21) emphasize the purity and clarity of crystal.

GLEAN, GLEANING

Laws concerning

The Hebrew custom of allowing the poor to follow the reapers, and to gather the grain or grapes that remained after the harvest (Lev 19:9-10; 23:22; Dt 24:19-20). *See Orphan; Strangers; Widow.*

Figurative:

(Jdg 8:2; Isa 17:6; Jer 49:9; Mic 7:1).

Instances of:

Ruth in the field of Boaz (Ru 2:2-3).

GLEDE See Red Kite.

GLORIFIED SAINTS Great cloud of witnesses (Heb 12:1), righteous people made perfect (Heb 12:23; Rev 6:11), 144,000 (Rev 14:1-5). Under the altar (Rev 6:9), before the throne (Rev 14:3). Sing song of redemption (Rev 14:3), of worship (Rev 15:2-4).

GLORIFYING GOD Commanded (1Ch 16:28; Ps 22:23; Isa 42:12). Due to him (1Ch 16:29) for his holiness (Ps 99:9; Rev 15:4), mercy and truth (Ps 115:1; Ro 15:9), faithfulness and truth (Isa 25:1), wondrous works (Mt 15:31; Ac 4:21), judgments (Isa 25:3; Eze 28:22; Rev 14:7), deliverances (Ps 50:15), grace to others (Ac 11:18; 2Co 9:13; Gal 1:24).

Accomplished by:

Relying on his promises (Ro 4:20), praising him (Ps 50:23), doing all to glorify him (1Co 10:31), dying for him (Jn 21:19), suffering for Christ (1Pe 4:14, 16), glorifying Christ (Ac 19:17; 2Th 1:12), bringing forth fruits of righteousness (Jn 15:8; Php 1:11), patience in affliction (Isa 24:1-3, 15), faithfulness (1Pe 4:11). Required in body and spirit (1Co 6:20). Shall be universal (Ps 86:9; Rev 5:13).

Believers:

Should resolve on (Ps 69:30; 118:28), unite in (Ps 34:3; Ro 15:6), persevere in (Ps 86:12). All the blessings of God are designed to lead to (Isa 60:21; 61:3). The holy example of the believers may lead others to (Mt 5:16; 1Pe 2:12).

All, by nature, fail in (Ro 3:23). The wicked averse to (Da 5:23; Ro 1:21). Punishment for not (Da 5:23, 30; Mal 2:2; Ac 12:23; Ro 1:21). Heavenly hosts engaged in (Rev 4:11).

Exemplified:

By David (Ps 57:5), the multitude (Mt 9:8; 15:31), the virgin Mary (Lk 1:46), the angels (Lk 2:14), the shepherds (Lk 2:20), by Jesus (Jn 17:4), the paralyzed man (Lk 5:25), the woman with infirmity (Lk 13:13), the leper whom Jesus healed (Lk 17:15), the blind man (Lk 18:43), the centurion (Lk 23:47), the church at Jerusalem (Ac 11:18), the Gentiles at Antioch (Ac 13:48), Abraham (Ro 4:20), Paul (Ro 11:36).

See Praise.

GLORY Concerning God, the exhibition of his divine attributes and perfections (Ps 19:1) or the radiance of his presence (Lk 2:9). Concerning people, the manifestation of their commendable qualities, such as wisdom, righteousness, self-control, ability, etc. Glory is destiny of believers (Php 3:21; Ro 8:21; 1Co 15:43).

Spiritual:

Is given by God (Ps 84:11), is the work of the Holy Spirit (2Co 3:18).

Eternal:

Secured by the death of Christ (Heb 2:10), accompanies salvation by Christ (2Ti 2:10), inherited by believers (1Sa 2:8; Ps 73:24; Pr 3:35; Col 3:4; 1Pe 5:10), believers called to (2Th 2:14; 1Pe 5:10), enhanced by afflictions (2Co 4:17), present afflictions not worthy to be compared with (Ro 8:18), of the church shall be rich and abundant (Isa 60:11-13), the bodies of believers shall be raised in (1Co 15:43; Php 3:21), believers shall be glory of their ministers (1Th 2:19-20), afflictions of ministers are glory to believers (Eph 3:13).

Temporal:

Is given by God (Da 2:37), passes away (1Pe 1:24). The devil tries to seduce by (Mt 4:8). Of hypocrites turned to shame (Hos 4:7). Seek not, from man (Mt 6:2; 1Th 2:6). Of the wicked is in their shame (Php 3:19). Ends in destruction (Isa 5:14).

Of God:

Exhibited in Christ (Jn 1:14; 2Co 4:6; Heb 1:3). Ascribed to God (Gal 1:5).

Exhibited in his name (Dt 28:58; Ne 9:5), his majesty (Job 37:22; Ps 93:1; 104:1; 145:5, 12; Isa 2:10), his power (Ex 15:1, 6; Ro 6:4), his works (Ps 19:1; 111:3), his holiness (Ex 15:11). Described as great (Ps 138:5), eternal (Ps 104:31), rich (Eph 3:16), highly exalted (Ps 8:1; 113:4).

Exhibited to Moses (Ex 34:5-7, w 33:18-23). Stephen (Ac 7:55), his church (Dt 5:24; Ps 102:16).

Enlightens the church (Isa 60:1-2; Rev 21:11, 23). Believers desire to behold (Ps 63:2; 90:16). God is jealous of (Isa 42:8). The earth is full of (Isa 6:3). The knowledge of, shall fill the earth (Hab 2:14).

GLOWING METAL

1. *Glowing metal* used to describe the color of divine glory (Eze 1:4, 27; 8:2).

2. *Bronze glowing in a furnace* used in John's description of the King of Glory (Rev 1:15).

See Amber; Minerals of the Bible, 1; Stones.

GLUTTONY

General:

Impoverishes (Pr 23:21). Deadens moral sensibilities (Am 6:4-7; Lk 12:19-20, 45-46; Php 3:19). Loathsome (Pr 30:21-22).

Warnings against (Pr 30:21-22; Lk 21:34; Ro 13:13-14; 1Pe 4:2-3). Punished, by death (Dt 21:20-21), plagues (Nu 11:32-33). Associated with drunkenness (Dt 21:20-21; Pr 23:21; Ecc 10:17; Lk 12:45-46; Ro 13:13; 1Pe 4:3). Proverb relating to (Isa 22:13; 1Co 15:32).

Instances of:

Israelites (Ex 16:20-21; Nu 11:4, 32-35; Ps 78:18). Sons of Eli (1Sa 2:12-17). Belshazzar (Da 5:1). Jesus falsely accused of (Mt 11:19; Lk 7:34).

See Pleasure, Worldly.

GNASH To grind the teeth together as an expression of rage (Job 16:9), hatred (Ps 37:12), frustration (Ps 112:10). In the NT it expresses anguish and failure rather than anger (Mt 8:12; 13:42, 50; 25:30).

GNASHING OF TEETH Of the enemy, in maliciousness (Job 16:9; Ps 35:16; 37:12; 112:10; La 2:16). Of the lost, from anguish of spirit (Mt 8:12; 13:42; 22:13; 24:51; 25:30; Lk 13:28).

GNAT Plague of (Ex 8:16-19; Ps 105:31). See Insects.

GNOSTICISM A second-century heresy that was a mixture of Judaism, Christianity, and Greek mystery religions. Its forerunners are seen in the errors refuted in the books of Colossians, 1 and 2 Timothy, 2 Peter, and 1 John. Some of its major tenets were:

1. The human body is matter, and therefore is evil. It is to be contrasted with God, who is wholly spirit and therefore good.

2. Salvation is the escape from the body, achieved not by faith in Christ but by special knowledge (the Greek word for "knowledge" is *gnosis,* from which comes Gnosticism).

3. Christ's true humanity was denied in two ways: (1) Some said that Christ only seemed to have a body, a view called Docetism, and (2) others said that the divine Christ joined the man Jesus at baptism and left him before he died, a view called Cerinthianism, after its most prominent spokesman, Cerinthus. This view is the background of much of 1 John (see 1Jn 1:1; 2:22; 4:2-3).

4. Since the body was considered evil, it was to be treated harshly. This ascetic form of Gnosticism is the background of part of Colossians (Col 2:21-23).

5. Paradoxically, this dualism also led to immorality. Since matter (and not the breaking of God's law) was considered evil, breaking his law was of no moral consequence.

GOAD An instrument for prodding animals (1Sa 13:21; Ac 26:14). Six hundred men slain with by Shamgar, a judge of Israel (Jdg 3:31). See Oxgoad.

Figurative of mental incentive (Ecc 12:11).

GOAH A place near Jerusalem (Jer 31:39).

GOAT Designated as one of the clean animals to be eaten (Lev 11:1-8; Dt 14:4). Used for food (Ge 27:9; 1Sa 16:20), for the passover feast (Ex 12:5; 2Ch 35:7), as a sacrifice by Abraham (Ge 15:9), by Gideon (Jdg 6:19), Manoah (Jdg 13:19).

Milk of, used for food (Pr 27:27). Hair of, used for clothing (Nu 31:20), pillows (1Sa 19:13), curtains of the tabernacle (Ex 26:7; 35:23; 36:14). Used for tents. *See Curtains; Tabernacle.* Mosaic law required that a kid should not be killed for food before it was eight days old (Lev 22:27), nor should it be boiled in its mother's milk (Ex 23:19). Numerous (Dt 32:14; SS 4:1; 6:5; 1Sa 25:2; 2Ch 17:11). Wild, in Israel (1Sa 24:2; Ps 104:18).

GOATS' HAIR (Ex 25:4; 26:7; 35:6; 36:14; Nu 31:20).

GOB (*cistern*). Site of two of David's battles with the Philistines (2Sa 21:18-19).

GOBLET See Cup.

GOD

Access to:

Israel (Dt 4:7). The pure of heart (Ps 24:3-4). The thirsty (Isa 55:3). Gentiles (Ac 14:27). Enemies of God (Col 1:21-22). Believers (Heb 4:16; 1Pe 1:17). The cleansed (Jas 4:8).

Through hope (Ps 27:4; 43:2), fear (Ps 145:18-19; 1Pe 1:17), prayer (Mt 6:6; Heb 4:10), faith (Heb 11:6), love (1Jn 4:16), Christ (Jn 10:7, 9; 14:6; Ro 5:2; Eph 2:13, 18; 3:12; Col 1:21-22; Heb 7:19, 25; 10:19, 22; 1Pe 1:17). Satisfying (Ps 65:4).

Anger of: *See Anger of God.*

Appearance of:

To Adam (Ge 3:8-21). To Abraham (Ge 17:1; 18:2-33). To Jacob, at Peniel (Ge 32:30), at Bethel (Ge 35:7, 9). To Moses, in the burning bush (Ex 3:2; Dt 33:16; Mk 12:26; Lk 20:37; Ac 7:30), at Sinai (Ex 19:16-24; 24:10; 33:18-23). To Moses and Joshua (Dt 31:14-15). To princes of Israel, at Sinai (Ex 24:9-11). To Gideon (Jdg 6:11-24). To Solomon (1Ki 3:5; 9:2; 11:9; 2Ch 1:7-12; 7:12-22). To Isaiah (Isa 6:1-5). To Ezekiel (Eze 1:26-28).

Compassion of: *See below, Longsuffering of; Mercy of.*

Condescension of:

(Ps 113:5-6). Manifested: In reasoning, with Noah (Ge 6:11-13), with Moses (Ex 4:2-17), with sinners (Isa 1:18-20). In entering into a covenant with Abraham (Ge 15:1-21; 18:1-22). In indulging Abraham's intercession for Sodom (Ge 18:2-33). In indulging Moses' prayer to behold his glory (Ex 33:18-23). In indulging

Gideon's tests (Jdg 6:36-40). In his care of man (Ps 8:4-6; 144:3). In redemption (Jn 3:16; Ro 5:8; Heb 6:17-18).

Creator:
(Ps 148:3-5; Pr 16:4; Isa 45:7; 66:2; Jer 51:19; Am 4:13; Mk 13:19; Ac 7:50; Ro 1:20; 1Co 11:12; Heb 2:10; 3:4; Rev 4:11). Of the earth (Ge 1:1-2, 9-10; 2:1-4; Ex 20:11; 1Sa 2:8; 2Ki 19:15; Ne 9:6; Job 38:4, 7-10; Ps 24:1-2; 89:11; 90:2; 95:5; 102:25; 104:2-3, 5-6, 24, 30; 119:90; 121:2; 124:8; 136:5-9; 146:5-6; Pr 3:19; 8:26-29; Isa 37:16; 40:28; 42:5; 44:24; 45:12, 18; 48:13; 51:13, 16; Jer 10:12; 27:5; 32:17; 51:15; Jnh 1:9; Ac 4:24; 14:15; 17:24-25; Rev 10:6; 14:7). Of the heavens (Ge 1:1, 6-8; 2:1-4; Ex 20:11; 2Ki 19:15; 1Ch 16:26; Ne 9:6; Job 9:8-9; 37:16, 18; Ps 8:3; 19:1, 4; 96:5; 102:25; 104:2-3, 5-6, 24, 30; 121:2; 124:8; 136:5; 146:5-6; Pr 3:19; 8:26-28; Isa 37:16; 42:5; 44:24; 45:18; Jer 32:17; Am 5:8; Ac 4:24; 14:15; Rev 10:6; 14:7). Of the sun, moon, and stars (Ge 1:14-19; Ps 136:7-9). Of the seas (Ge 1:9-10; Ex 20:11; Ne 9:6; Ps 95:5; 146:5-6; Pr 8:26-29; Jnh 1:9; Ac 4:24; 14:15; Rev 10:6; 14:7). Of vegetation (Ge 1:11-12). Of animals (Ge 1:20-25; Job 12:7-9; Jer 27:5).
Creator of mankind (Ge 1:26-28; 2:7; 5:1-2; 9:6; Ex 4:11; Dt 4:32; 32:6, 15, 18; Job 10:3, 8-9, 11-12; 31:15; 33:4; 34:19; Ps 94:9; 95:6; 100:3; 119:73; 149:2; Pr 20:12; 22:2; Ecc 7:29; 12:1; Isa 17:7; 42:5; 43:1, 7, 15; 44:2, 24; 45:12; 51:13; 64:8; Jer 27:5; Zec 12:1; Mal 2:10; Mk 10:6; Ac 17:24-29; 1Co 12:18, 24-25; Heb 12:9; 1Pe 4:19). Through Christ (Ro 11:36; 1Co 8:6; Eph 3:9; Heb 1:1-2). *See Jesus the Christ, Creator.* By his word (Ps 33:6-7, 9; 2Co 4:6; Heb 11:3; 2Pe 3:5). By his will (Rev 4:11).

Dissertations on:
His works and providence (Job 5:8-20). The administration of his government (Job 9:2-35; 10:1-22). His providence and grace (Job 33:4-30; Ps 107). His righteousness (Job 34:10-30; 35:1-16; Na 1:2-9). His majesty and justice (Job 36:30-33). His majesty and works (Ps 104:10-15).

Dwells With the Righteous:
(Ex 25:8; 29:45; Lev 26:11-12; 1Ki 6:13; Eze 37:26-27; 2Co 6:16; Rev 21:3).

Eternity of:
(Ge 21:33; Ex 3:15; 15:18; Dt 32:40; 33:27; 1Ch 16:36; 29:10; Ne 9:5; Job 36:26; Ps 9:7; 41:13; 90:1-2, 4; 92:8; 93:2; 102:12, 24-27; 145:13; 146:10; Isa 40:28; 44:6; 57:15; 63:16; Jer 10:10; La 5:19; Da 4:3, 34; Hab 1:12; Ro 1:20; 16:26; Eph 3:21; 1Ti 1:17; 6:15-16; 2Pe 3:8; Rev 4:8-10; 11:17).

Faithfulness of:
(Ge 9:16; 28:15; Lev 26:44-45; Dt 4:31; Jdg 2:1; 1Sa 12:22; Isa 42:16; 44:21; 49:7, 14-16; Jer 29:10; 31:36-37; 32:40; 33:14, 20-21, 25-26; Eze 16:60; Hos 2:19-20; Ro 3:3-4; Heb 6:10, 13-19). Confidence in (Nu 23:19; Dt 32:4; 2Sa 7:28; 1Ch 28:20; Ne 1:5; Ps 36:5; 40:10; 89:1-2, 5, 8, 14, 24, 28, 33, 34; 92:1-2, 15; 94:14; 105:8, 42; 111:5, 7-9; 119:90-91; 132:11; Isa 25:1; La 3:23; Da 9:4; Mic 7:20; 1Co 1:9; 10:13; 2Co 1:18-20; 1Th 5:24; 2Th 3:3; 2Ti 2:13, 19; Tit 1:2; Heb 10:23; 11:11; 1Pe 4:19; 2Pe 3:9; 1Jn 1:9).
Exemplified (Ge 21:1; 24:27; Ex 2:24; 6:4-5; Dt 7:8-9; 9:5; Jos 21:45; 23:14; 1Ki 8:15, 20, 23-24, 56; 2Ki 8:19; 13:23; 2Ch 6:4-15; 21:7; Ne 1:5; 9:7-8; Ps 98:3; Hag 2:5; Lk 1:54-55, 68-70, 72-73; Ac 13:32-33; Heb 6:10, 13-19).

Fatherhood of:
Taught in the Old Testament (Ex 4:22; Dt 14:1; 32:5-6; 2Sa 7:14; 1Ch 28:6; 29:10; Ps 68:5; 89:26; Isa 1:2; 9:6; 63:16; 64:8; Jer 3:19; Hos 1:10; 11:1). Taught by Jesus (Mt 5:45; 6:4, 8-9; 7:11; 10:20, 29, 32-33; 11:25-27; 12:50; 13:43; 15:13; 16:17, 27; 18:10, 14, 19; 20:23; 26:29, 39; Mk 8:38; 11:25; 13:32; Lk 2:49; 10:21-22; 11:2; 11:13; 22:29; 23:46; 24:49; Jn 1:14, 18; 2:16; 4:21, 23; 5:17-23, 36-37, 43; 6:27, 32, 44-46; 8:19, 27, 38, 41-42, 49; 10:15, 29-30, 32-33, 36-38; 12:26-28, 50; 13:1, 3; 14:2, 6-13, 20-21, 23-24, 26, 31; 15:8-10, 16, 23-24, 26; 16:3, 10, 15, 23, 25-28; 17:1, 5, 11, 21, 24; 20:17, 21). Taught by the apostles (Ac 1:4; 2:33; Ro 1:3-4, 7; 8:14-16; 1Co 1:3; 8:6; 15:24; 2Co 1:3; 6:18; Gal 1:1, 3-4; 4:4-7; Eph 1:2-3, 17; 2:18; 3:14; 4:6; 5:20; 6:23; Php 1:2; Col 1:2-3, 12; 3:17; 1Th 1:1, 3; 3:11, 13; 2Th 1:1-2; 2:16; 1Ti 1:2; 2Ti 1:2; Tit 1:4; Heb 1:5-6; 12:9; Jas 1:17, 27; 3:9; 1Pe 1:2-3, 17; 1Jn 1:2; 2:1, 13, 15, 22-24; 3:1; 4:14; 2Jn 3-4, 9; Jude 1; Rev 1:5-6; 3:5; 14:1). *See Adoption, Spiritual Adoption.*

Favor of: *See below, Grace of.*

Foreknowledge of:
(Ac 15:18). Of contingencies (1Sa 23:10-12). Of future events (Isa 42:9; 44:7; 45:11; 46:9-10; 48:5-6; Jer 1:5; Da 2:28-29; Ac 2:23). Of human needs (Mt 6:8). Of the day of judgment (Mt 24:36; Mk 13:32). Of the redeemed (Ro 8:29; 11:2; 1Pe 1:2).

Glory of:
(Ps 24:8-10; 57:5, 11; 72:18-19; Isa 40:5; Php 1:11). Described (Eze 1:26-28; Hab 3:3-6). Transcendent (Ps 113:4). Shall endure forever (Ps 104:31). Ascribed by angels (Lk 2:14). To be ascribed by people (Ps 29:2; Ro 11:36).
Manifested in the burning bush (Ex 3:2). In Mount Sinai (Ex 19:18; 20:18-19; 24:10, 17; 33:18-23; 34:5, 29-35; Dt 4:11-12, 33, 36; 5:5, 24-25; Heb 12:18-21). In the tabernacle (Ex 40:34-35). In the heavens (2Sa 22:10-15; Ps 18:9-14; 19:1). In his sovereignty (Ps 97:2-6; 145:5, 11-12; Isa 6:1-5; 24:23; Jude 24-25). In the church (Isa 35:2; 60:1-2, 19-21; 61:3; Eph 3:21). In Christ (Jn 13:31-32; 14:13; 17:1). To Ezekiel (Eze 3:12, 23; 8:4). To Stephen (Ac 7:55).

Goodness of:
(Ex 33:19; Dt 30:9; Ps 25:8-10; 31:19; 33:5; 36:7; 86:5; 100:5; 106:1; 119:68; Na 1:7; Mt 5:45; Ac 14:17; Jas 1:17). Enduring (Ps 52:1). Leads to repentance (Ro 2:4). Gratefully acknowledged (1Ch 16:34; 2Ch 5:13; 7:3; Ps 68:19; 107:8-9, 43; 118:29; 135:3; 136:1; 145:7, 9; Isa 63:7).
Manifested: In gracious providence (Mt 7:11). To the righteous (Ps 31:19; La 3:25; Ro 11:22). To the wicked (Lk 6:35).

Grace of:
Unmerited favor (Dt 7:7-8; 2Ch 30:9; Eph 1:6; Tit 2:11; Heb 4:16). Divine help (Ps 84:11; 1Co 10:13; 2Co 1:12; 12:9; 1Pe 1:5). No warrant for sinful indulgence (Ro 6:1, 15). Intercessory prayer for (Jn 17:11-12, 15; 1Th 1:1; 5:28; 2Pe 1:2). Exhortation against

rejecting (2Co 6:1-2). Exemplified with respect to Jacob and Esau (Ro 9:10-16).
Manifested: In drawing men to Christ (Jn 6:44-45), in redemption (Eph 1:5-9, 11-12), in justification (Ge 15:6; Ro 3:22-24; 4:4-5, 16; 5:2, 6-8, 15-21; Tit 3:7). In passing over transgression (Nu 23:20-21; Ne 9:17; Ro 3:25). In salvation (Ro 11:5-6; Eph 2:8-9; 2Ti 1:9), in calling to service (Gal 1:15-16), in spiritual growth (Eph 3:16). In spiritual gifts (1Co 1:4-8; Eph 4:7, 11).
Manifested: In character and conduct (2Co 1:12; Php 2:13), in the character and conduct of the righteous (1Co 15:10; 2Co 1:12; Php 2:13), in sustaining the righteous (1Ch 17:8; 2Co 12:9; 1Pe 1:5; Jude 24), in sustaining in temptation (1Co 10:13; Rev 3:10).
Manifestation of: To Enoch (Ge 5:24). To Noah (Ge 6:8, 17-18). To Abraham (Ge 12:2; 21:22). To Ishmael (Ge 21:20). To Isaac (Ge 26:24). To Jacob (Ge 46:3-4; 48:16). To Joseph (Ge 39:2-3, 23). To Moses (Ex 3:12; 33:12-17). To Israel (Dt 4:7). To Naphtali (Dt 33:23). To Joshua (Jos 1:5, 9). To Job (Job 10:12). To David (1Sa 25:26, 34; 2Sa 7:8-16). To Jeremiah (Jer 15:20). To the righteous (Ps 5:12; Ac 4:33).

Guidance of:
(Ge 12:1; 24:27; Ps 23:2-3; 48:14; 73:24; Pr 3:6; Jer 3:4; 32:19; Lk 1:79; Jn 10:3-4). By pillars of cloud and fire (Ex 13:21; Ne 9:19). By his presence (Ex 15:13; 33:13-15; Dt 32:10, 12; Ps 78:52; 80:1; 107:7). By the ark of the covenant (Nu 10:33). By his counsel (2Sa 22:29; Ps 5:8; 25:9; Isa 48:17). By his Spirit (Jn 16:13). Prayed for (Ps 25:5; 27:11; 31:3; 61:2). Promised (Ps 32:8; Isa 40:11; 42:16; 58:11).

Holiness of:
(Jos 24:19; 1Sa 6:20; 1Ch 16:10; Job 6:10; 15:15; 25:5; Ps 11:7; 22:3; 36:6; 47:8; 60:6; 89:35; 98:1; 105:3; 111:9; 119:142; 145:17; Pr 9:10; Isa 5:16; 6:3; 29:19, 23; 41:14; 43:14-15; 45:19; 47:4; 49:7; 52:10; 57:15; Eze 36:21-22; 39:7, 25; Da 4:8; Hos 11:9; Hab 1:12-13; Lk 1:49; Jn 17:11; Ro 1:23; 1Jn 2:20; Rev 4:8; 6:10; 15:4).
Incomparable (Ex 15:11; 1Sa 2:2; Job 4:17-19). Without iniquity (Dt 32:4; 2Ch 19:7; Job 34:10; 36:23; Ps 92:15; Jer 2:5; La 3:38; Mt 19:17; Mk 10:18; Lk 18:19; Jas 1:13). A reason for personal holiness (Lev 11:44; 19:2; 20:26; 21:8; 2Ch 19:7; Mt 5:48; 1Pe 1:15-16). A reason for thanksgiving (Ps 30:4; 99:3, 5, 9; Isa 12:6). A reason for reverent approach to God (Ex 3:5; Jos 5:15).
Light, figurative of. *See below, Light.*
See Sin, Separates from God; below, God, Perfections of, Righteousness of.

Human Forms and Appearances of: *See Anthropomorphisms.*

Immanence of:
(Ge 26:24; 28:15; Ex 3:12; Dt 4:7; Jos 3:7; Ac 17:27-28).

Immutable:
(Nu 23:19-20; 1Sa 15:29; Ps 102:27; Isa 40:28; Jas 1:17). In purpose (Job 23:13; Ps 33:11; Pr 19:21; Ecc 3:14; 7:13; Isa 31:2; Heb 6:17-18). In faithfulness (Ps 119:89-91). In mercy (Isa 59:1; Hos 13:14; Mal 3:6; Ro 11:29).

Impartial:
(Dt 10:17). Despises none (Job 36:5). Does not show favoritism (2Ch 19:7; Job 34:19; 37:24; Ac 10:34-35; Ro 2:6, 11; Eph 6:8-9; Col 3:25; 1Pe 1:17).

Incomparable:
(Ex 16:11; Dt 33:26; 2Sa 7:22; 1Ki 8:23; Ps 35:10; 71:19; 89:6-8; 113:5; Mic 7:18).

Incomprehensible:
(Job 15:8; 37:1-24; Isa 40:12-31; 55:8-9; Mt 11:27; 1Co 2:16).

Infinite:
(1Ki 8:27; 2Ch 2:6; 6:1, 18; Ps 147:5; Jer 23:24).

Invisible:
(Ex 20:21; 33:20; Dt 4:11-12; 4:15; 5:22; 1Ki 8:12; 2Ch 6:1; Job 9:11; 23:8-9; Ps 18:11; 97:2; Jn 1:18; 5:37; 6:46; Ro 1:20; Col 1:13-15; 1Ti 1:17; 6:16; Heb 11:27; 1Jn 4:12).

Jealous:
(Ex 20:5, 7; 34:14; Dt 4:24; 5:9, 11; 6:15; 29:20; 32:16, 21; Jos 24:19; 2Ki 19:31; Ps 30:1-2; Eze 23:25; 36:5; 39:25; Joel 2:18; Na 1:2; Zec 1:14; 1Co 10:22).

Judge:
(Ge 16:5; Jdg 11:27; 1Sa 2:3, 10; 24:12, 15; 1Ch 16:33; Job 21:22; Ps 11:4-5; 26:1-2; 35:24; 43:1; 50:4, 6; 58:11; 75:7; 76:8-9; 82:8; 94:1-2; 135:14; Pr 16:2; 29:26; Ecc 3:17; 11:9; 12:14; Isa 3:13-14; 28:17, 21; 30:18, 27; 33:22; Jer 32:19; Da 7:9-10; Na 1:3; Mal 3:5; Ac 17:31; 1Co 5:13; Heb 10:30-31; 12:22-23; Rev 6:16-17; 11:18; 16:5; 18:8).
Just Judge (Ge 18:21, 25; Nu 16:22; Dt 32:4; Ne 9:33; Job 4:17; 8:3; 34:10-12; Ps 7:9, 11; 9:4, 7-8; 67:4; 96:10, 13; 98:9; Isa 26:7; 45:21; Jer 32:19; Ro 2:2, 5-16; 3:4-6, 26; 11:22, 23; Eph 6:8-9; 1Pe 1:17; Rev 19:2). Incorruptible Judge (Dt 10:17; 2Ch 19:7; Job 8:3; 34:19).

Justice of:
(Dt 32:4; 2Sa 22:25; 1Ki 8:32; Job 31:13-15; Ps 51:4; 62:12; 89:14; 97:2; 145:17; Pr 21:2-3; 24:12; Isa 61:8; Jer 9:24; 11:20; 20:12; 32:19; 50:7; Eze 14:23; 18:25, 29-30; 33:7-19; Da 9:7, 14; Na 1:3, 6; Zep 3:5; Ac 17:31; Ro 2:2, 5-16; Heb 6:10; 1Pe 1:17; 2Pe 2:9; 1Jn 1:9; Jude 6; Rev 11:18; 15:3).

Knowledge of:
(Ge 6:5; 1Sa 2:3; Job 12:13, 22; 21:22; 22:13-14; 26:6; 28:23-24; 36:4-5; 37:16; Ps 147:4-5; Pr 3:19-20; Isa 40:13-14, 26-28; 46:9-10; Mt 24:36; Mk 13:32; Ro 11:33-34; 1Co 1:25; 1Jn 1:5).
Knows the human state and condition (Ge 16:13; Ex 3:7; Dt 2:7; 2Ki 19:27; 2Ch 16:9; Job 23:10; 31:4; 34:21, 25; Ps 1:6; 33:13-15; 37:18; 38:9; 66:7; 69:19; 103:14; 119:168; 139:1-4, 6, 12, 14-16; 142:3; Pr 5:21; 15:3, 11; Jer 29:15-16; 37:28; 66:18; Jer 23:22, 32:19; Am 9:2-4; Mt 10:29-30; 1Co 8:3).
Knows the human heart (Ge 20:6; Dt 31:21; 1Sa 16:7; 2Sa 7:20; 1Ki 8:39; 1Ch 28:9; 29:17; 2Ch 6:30; Job 11:11; Ps 7:9; 44:21; 94:9-11; Pr 15:11; 16:2; 17:3; 21:2; 24:12; Jer 11:20; 16:17;

17:10; 20:12; Eze 11:5; Am 4:13; Mt 6:4, 8, 18, 32; Lk 16:15; Ac 1:24; 15:8; 1Co 3:20; 1Th 2:4; Heb 4:13; 1Jn 3:20). *See above, Foreknowledge of; below, Wisdom of.*

Light:
(Da 2:22; Jas 1:17; 1Jn 1:5).

Longsuffering:
(Ge 6:3; 15:16; Ex 34:6; Nu 14:18; Ps 86:15; 103:8-10; Isa 5:1-4; 30:18; 48:9, 11; 57:16; Jer 7:13, 23-25; 9:24; Eze 20:17; Joel 2:13; Hab 1:2-4; Mt 21:33-41; Mk 12:1-9; Lk 20:9-16; Ac 14:16; Ro 3:25; 15:5; 1Pe 3:20).
Abused by people (Ne 9:28-31; Pr 1:24-27; 29:1; Ecc 8:11; Isa 5:1-4; Jer 7:13, 23-25; Mt 24:48-51). *See below, Mercy of.*
Manifested in deferring judgments (Mic 7:18; Lk 13:6-9; Ac 17:30; Ro 9:22-23; 2Pe 3:9, 15). In giving time for repentance (Jer 11:7; Mt 23:37; Lk 13:34; Ro 2:4).

Love of:
(Dt 4:37; 7:7-8, 13; 10:15, 18; 23:5; 33:3, 12; 2Sa 12:24; Job 7:17; Ps 42:8; 47:4; 69:16; Hos 11:1; Mal 1:2; 2Co 13:11, 14; 1Jn 3:1; 4:12, 16, 19; Jude 21). Everlasting (2Ch 20:21; Jer 31:3). Better than life (Ps 63:3).
For the wicked (Mt 18:12-14; Lk 15:4-7, 11-27; Ro 5:8; Eph 2:4-5). For the righteous (Ps 103:13; 146:8; Pr 15:9; Jn 14:21, 23; 16:27; 17:10, 23, 26; Ro 1:7; 9:13; 11:28; 2Th 2:16). For the cheerful giver (2Co 9:7).
Exemplified (Ex 19:4-6; Lev 20:24, 26; Dt 32:9-12; 2Sa 7:23-24; Ps 48:9, 14; Isa 43:1-4; 49:13-16; 54:5-6, 10; 62:4-5; 63:7-9; 66:13; Jer 3:14-15; Eze 16:8; Hos 2:19-20, 23; Zec 2:8). In forgiveness of sins (Isa 38:17; Tit 3:4-5). In the gift of his Son (Jn 3:16; 1Jn 4:8-10). In chastisements (Heb 12:6).

Mercy of:
(Ex 20:2, 6; Dt 5:10; Ex 33:19; Dt 4:31; 7:9; 1Ki 8:23; 2Ch 30:9; Ezr 9:9; Ps 18:50; 25:6, 8; 31:7; 32:10; 36:5; 57:10; 62:12; 69:16; 98:3; 108:4; 111:4; 116:5; 117:2; 119:64, 156; 138:2; 146:7-8; Isa 60:10; Jer 9:24; 31:20; 32:18; Da 9:4; Hos 2:23; Zec 10:6; Lk 6:36; Ac 17:30; Ro 9:15; 11:32; 15:9; 2Co 1:3; Heb 4:16; 1Pe 1:3; 2Pe 3:9). Everlasting (1Ch 16:34, 41; 2Ch 5:13; 7:3, 6, 14; Ezr 3:11; Ps 89:1-2, 28; 100:5; 103:17; 106:1; 107:1; 118:1-4, 29; 136:1-26).
Manifested: In withholding punishment (Ge 8:21; 18:26, 30-32; Ex 32:14; Nu 16:48; 2Sa 24:14, 16; 2Ki 13:23; Ezr 9:13; Job 11:6; Isa 12:1; 54:9; Eze 16:6, 42, 63; 20:17; Hos 11:8-9; Joel 2:13, 18; Jnh 4:2, 10-11; Mal 3:6). In rescuing from destruction (Ge 19:16; Nu 21:8; Jdg 2:18; 2Ki 14:26-27; Ne 1:10; 9:17-20, 27-31). In leading his people (Ex 15:13). In comforting the afflicted (2Co 12:9). In hearing prayer (Ex 22:27; Heb 4:16). In desire to save sinners (Ps 5:29; 32:29; Jdg 10:16; 2Ch 36:15; Isa 65:2, 8; Jer 2:9; Eze 18:23, 31-32; 33:11; Mt 18:12-14; Lk 15:4-7; 1Ti 2:4, 6). In forbearance toward sinners (2Ch 24:18-19; Ps 145:8-9; La 3:22-23, 31-33; Da 4:22-27; Na 1:3). In granting forgiveness (Ex 34:6-7; Nu 14:18-20; 2Sa 12:13; 2Ch 7:14; Job 33:14-30; Ps 32:1-2, 5; 65:3; 78:38-39; 85:2-3; 86:5, 13, 15; 99:8; 103:3, 8-14; 130:3-4; 130:7-8; Pr 16:6; 28:13; Isa 55:7-9; Jer 3:12, 22; 31:20, 34; 33:8, 11; 36:3; 50:20; Eze 36:25; Da 9:9; Hos 14:4; Mic 7:18-19; Mt 6:14; 18:23-27; Lk 1:50, 77-78; Ac 26:18; Ro 10:12-13; 2Co 5:19; Eph 1:6-8; 2:4-7; 1Ti 1:13; Tit 3:5; Heb 8:12; 1Jn 1:9).
Symbolized: In the atonement cover (Ex 25:17-22; 37:6-9; Lev 16:1-14; Nu 7:89; Heb 9:5).

Name of:
To be revered (Ex 20:7; Dt 5:11; 28:58; Ps 111:9; Mic 4:5; 1Ti 6:1). To be praised (Ps 34:3; 72:17). Not to be profaned (Ex 20:7; Lev 18:21; 19:12; 20:3; 21:6; 22:2, 32; Dt 5:11; Ps 139:20; Isa 52:5; Ro 2:24; Rev 16:9). Profaned (Ps 139:20).

Names of:
In the ancient world a name was not merely a label but the meaning of the name was virtually equivalent to whoever or whatever bore it (1Sa 25:25). Giving a name to anyone or anything was tantamount to owning or controlling it (Ge 1:5, 8, 10; 2:19-20; 2Sa 12:28). Changing a name could signify a promotion to a higher status (Ge 17:5; 32:28) or a demotion (2Ki 23:34-35; 24:17), and blotting out or cutting off the name of a person or thing meant that that person or thing was destroyed (2Ki 14:27; Isa 14:22; Zep 1:4; cf. Ps 83:4).
The name and being of God are often used in parallelism with each other (Ps 18:49; 68:4; 74:18; 86:12; 92:1; Isa 25:1; Mal 3:16), which stresses their essential identity. Believing in Jesus' name (Jn 3:18) is therefore the same as believing in Jesus himself. Prayer in his name would be prayer in concert with his character, mind, and purpose.
The name Jesus is the Greek form for the Hebrew Joshua or "*salvation of Yahweh.*" As Yahweh's Savior his name accurately describes his work and purpose (Mt 1:21).

El **and its compounds—**
El is the generic Semitic name for "God" or "deity." *El* is one of the oldest designations for deity in the ancient world. The word is found in several Semitic languages such as Akkadian, Phoenician, and South Arabic. Even though the derivation of the word is uncertain, the root meaning is "power and authority" (Ge 1:1; Ps 19:1).
El Berith means "god of the covenant" (Jdg 9:46) and is an alternate form of the name *Baal-Berith* (Jdg 8:33; 9:4). These are names of pagan gods and not the God of Israel. The remains of the Canaanite temple to Baal-Berith at Shechem, has been recovered.
El Bethel means "God of Bethel," but is a place name, not a name of God. God directs Jacob to return to Bethel and build an altar there (Ge 35:1, 6-7).
El Elohe Israel means "God [El], the God of Israel" or "mighty is the God of Israel." Though a statement about God, it is actually the name of an altar, also associated with the travels of Jacob (Ge 33:18-20).
El Elyon; See below Elyon.
El Olam means "God the Everlasting One" or "God of Eternity." While living among the Philistines, Abraham calls upon the name of Yahweh, the Eternal God (Ge 21:33). Isaiah quotes God as saying, "The LORD is the everlasting God, the Creator of the ends of the earth" (Isa 40:28). The Psalmist expresses that, "from

everlasting to everlasting you are God" (Ps 90:1-2; cf 93:2; Isa 26:4).

El Roi means "God who sees me." As Hagar wandered in the desert, the angel of the LORD appeared to her (Ge 16:7-12). After his appearance she gave Yahweh this name saying, "You are the One who sees me." The well at that place was named "Beer Lahai Roi," which means "well of the Living One who sees me" (Ge 16:14).

El Shaddai appears seven times (Ge 17:1; 28:3; 35:11; 43:14; 48:3; Ex 6:3; Eze 10:5). It probably means "God the Mountain," similar to "God the Rock" (Dt 32:4). Older etymology defined it as "God the Provider," understanding *Shaddai* to be derived from the word for "breast." *See below Shaddai.*

Eloah—
Eloah is thought to be a singular form of "Elohim." It is used primarily in Job (42 times) as a way to refer to God, but without referring to him as the "God of Israel." In other references it is usually synonymous in meaning with *Elohim* (Ps 50:22-23), or *Yahweh* (Ps 139:19, 21), or *Adonay* (Ps 114:7). It also appears in the exilic and postexilic periods (2Ch 32:15; Ne 9:17; Da 11:37-39).

Elohim **(and its compounds) and** *Theos*—
Elohim, the plural form of *El*, *Eloah* is used as a plural to refer to the many gods of the nations. But *Elohim* is used in a singular sense in the great majority of instances, and is thus referred to as "plural of majesty." In the singular sense *Elohim* is sometimes applied to the god of another people as in Chemosh, the god of the Amorites (Jdg 11:24), or Ashtoreth (Ishtar), the goddess of Sidon (1Ki 11:5), or Baal-Zebub, the god of Ekron (2Ki 1:2), but is used overwhelmingly (over 2300 times) in the OT to refer to Israel's God, meaning "the true God."

Theos is the NT counterpart of *Elohim* (Mt 22:32 w Ex 3:6). It usually refers to the true God, but can refer to pagan deities (Ac 17:18, 23; 1Co 8:5).

Yahweh, Yah, **and Compounds**—
Yahweh is the personal covenant name of Israel's God, the most common name for God in the OT (6829 times). *Yah* is its shortened form. The NIV consistently renders Yahweh as LORD. The name sounds like and may be derived from the Hebrew for the word "I AM" (Ex 3:14-15). The basic meaning of his name is "He who is" or "He who is truly present." or "I will be to you all that I am." For Israel, Yahweh is not merely one god among many; he is the Creator and Ruler of heaven and earth, who is worthy of and demands the exclusive homage of his people. It is important to understand that this is God's intensely personal name. The respect with which it was treated bears witness to the national feeling of Israel and also their fear of the God who is among them. This was recognized by the scribes who even avoided pronunciation of the name. They would use circumlocutions and alternate names where possible. *See below on Adonay.* In the NT, John records that Jesus made seven self-descriptions (Jn 6:35; 8:12 w 9:5; 10:7, 9; 10:11, 14; 11:25; 14:6; 15:1, 5), each one being introduced by "I am." The Greek text makes this statement solemnly emphatic and echoes God's self-revelation to Moses (Ex 3:14). In a similar fashion, Jesus expressed the eternity of his being and his oneness with the Father by saying, "I tell you the truth," Jesus answered, "before Abraham was born, I am!" (Jn 8:58). The people listening knew exactly what he meant by what he said: I AM GOD. The penalty for such blasphemy was stoning (Lev 24:16), which they fully intended to carry out (Jn 8:59).

Yahweh Nissi means "Yahweh is my banner or standard." This was the name given to the altar which Moses erected to commemorate the defeat of the Amalekites at Rephidim (Ex 17:8-15).

Yahweh Rapha. At Marah, on the way to Sinai, the LORD promised Israel that if they fully obeyed him, he would not bring on them the diseases he brought on Egypt. His name of assurance means "[I am] Yahweh who heals you" (Ex 15:26).

Yahweh Shalom means "Yahweh is peace." The angel of the LORD appeared to Gideon to commission him to liberate Israel from the Midianites (Jdg 6:1-22). The LORD greeted him with peace, so Gideon built an altar and named it "The LORD is Peace" (Jdg 6:23-24).

Yahweh Shammah means "The LORD is There." Not a name of God, this is the name given to the restored Jerusalem (Eze 48:35). The glory of God will return and Messiah will rule from New Jerusalem forever (Eze 43; cf. Rev 21). God's name is inseparably linked with Jerusalem.

Yahweh Tsabbaoth means "LORD of Hosts" and is consistently translated "LORD Almighty" in the NIV (e.g., 1Sa 1:3, 11). "Hosts" can refer to, human armies (Ex 7:4; Ps 44:9), celestial bodies (Ge 2:1; Dt 4:19; Isa 40:26), or heavenly creatures such as angels (Jos 5:14; 1Ki 22:19; Ps 148:2). This title is probably best understood as a general reference to the sovereignty of God over all powers in the universe. In the NT *Tsabbaoth* is twice transliterated by the Greek "Sabaoth" (Ro 9:29; Jas 5:4), but is usually *Pantokrator* (2Co 6:18; Rev 1:8; 4:8).

Yahweh Tsidkenu means "Yahweh our Righteousness." This is the designation of the future king who will rise up from the line of David to rule over Israel (Jer 23:5-6). Righteousness is the divine attribute of the Messiah who imputes his righteousness to his followers and therefore is able to reconcile them to God (2Co 5:21). In a second reference, Jeremiah directs attention to Jerusalem, the capital of the King, which because of her intimate relationship to Messiah, will be given the same name and nature of the righteous monarch (Jer 33:15-16).

Yahweh Yireh means "Yahweh will provide," "Yahweh will see [to it]." *Yireh* comes from the same Hebrew root as *Moriah*, the name of the region to which God sent Abraham to sacrifice Isaac (Ge 22:2; 2Ch 3:1). Both words are place names that confess Yahweh as the provider of a substitutionary sacrifice (Ge 22:14, cf. v. 8).

Adon, Adonay, **and** *Kurios*
Adon or *Adonay* is a title for God that emphasizes his sovereignty, that is "Lord." *Adon* is basically a title of honor. Out of respect one might address a superior with this title in the same way that we would say "sir" or "your honor." It would be used by a subject addressing a king (1Sa 24:8), a wife to her husband (Ge

18:12), a daughter or son to their father (Ge 31:35), a slave to his master (Ge 24:12; Ex 21:5), a subordinate to his leader (Nu 11:28). It therefore refers to one's position of authority and prestige (Ge 23:6; 45:8). The special spelling *Adonay* belongs preeminently to Yahweh, because he alone is the "Lord of the earth" (Jos 3:11, 13; Ps 97:5; Mic 4:13; Zec 4:14; 6:5). In the years after the Exile (after 538 B.C.), with reverence for the name of God increasing, the name *Yahweh* began to be pronounce as *Adonay* in the reading of the Scriptures. The LXX translators, out of fear of profaning the name of God, were led to translate *Yahweh* as *kurios* or "Lord." The Massoretic pronunciation of the Hebrew text continued this tradition by using the vowels of *Adonay* with the consonants of *Yahweh* as a signal that the proper name of God should be pronounced as *Adonay*. The misreading of this convention led to the mispronunciation of the name of God as *Jehovah*.

Kurios is the NT counterpart of both *Adonay* (Mt 22:44 w Ps 110:1) and *Yahweh* (Mt 4:10 w Dt 6:13). It is used as a term of respect (Mt 13:27) and submission (Jn 13:16; 15:20) as well as the title "Lord" (Mt 1:20, 22).

Shaddai—
Shaddai is used forty-eight times as a name of God, thirty-two times in Job (Job 5:17; 6:4, 14; etc.), seven times in the compound name *El Shaddai. See above EL.*. It probably means "[God] the Mountain," similar to "God the Rock" (Dt 32:4). Older etymology defined it as "[God] the Provider," understanding *Shaddai* to be derived from the word for "breast." The NIV consistently translates *Shaddai* as "Almighty" (Ge 17:1; Ps 91:1).

Elyon **and** *Hupsistos*—
Elyon means "the Most High" or "the exalted One" (Ge 14:17-20; Ps 18:13; Isa 14:13-14). The NT Greek uses the form *hupsistos* meaning "highest," or "most exalted." Jesus was known as, and called, the Son of the Most High God (Mk 5:7; Lk 1:32-33; 6:28). The Holy Spirit is the power of the Most High (Lk 1:35). John the Baptist would be known as a prophet of the Most High God (Lk 1:76). Jesus taught his disciples to "love your enemies, do good to them, and lend to them without expecting to get anything back," because in so doing, their reward will be great and they will prove that they are "sons of the Most High, because he is kind to the ungrateful and wicked" (Lk 6:35). The Most High God is far too great and magnificent to be limited to houses made by men (Ac 7:48-50). The early apostles were known as servants of the Most High God (Ac 16:17). Melchizedek was king of Salem and priest of the Most High God (Heb 7:1 w Ge 14:17-20).

Other descriptive titles—
The Ancient of Days (Da 7:9, 13, 22). Deliverer (2Sa 22:2; Ps 18:2). Father (Ps 89:26; Mt 16:17; Mk 14:36; Lk 22:29; Jn 5:17; 8:54; 10:29; 14:23; Ro 8:15; Gal 4:6), Everlasting Father (Isa 9:6). The First and the Last (Isa 44:6; 48:12; Rev 1:17; 2:8; 22:13). God of gods (Dt 10:17; Ps 136:2; Da 2:47; 11:36), the God of heaven and earth (Ge 24:3, 7). The Holy One (Isa 41:14; 43:14-15; 48:17), a God whose name is Holy (Isa 57:15). A Jealous God (Ex 34:14). Judge (Ge 18:25; Dt 32:36; Jdg 11:26). King of kings (1Ti 6:15; Rev 17:14; 19:16). The Living God (Jer 10:10; Da 6:26; Hos 1:10; Mt 16:16). Lord of lords (Dt 10:17; Ps 136:3; 1Ti 6:15; Rev 17:14; 19:16). Lord of kings (Da 2:47). The Mighty One (Isa 49:26; 60:16), Mighty God (Isa 9:6; 10:21; Lk 22:69). Prince (Ac 5:31), Prince of Peace (Isa 9:6). Redeemer (Job 19:25; Ps 19:14; 78:35; Isa 41:14; 43:14; 44:6; Jer 50:34). Righteous One (1Sa 45:21; Ps 4:1; 7:9). Rock appears five times in the Song of Moses (Dt 32:4, 15, 18, 30, 31), and several times in the Psalms (Ps 18:2, 31, 46; 19:14; 28:1; 78:35; 89:26), Isaiah (Isa 17:10; 26:4; 30:29; 44:8), and Habakkuk (Hab 1:12); in the NT Paul says that the Rock of Israel was Christ (1Co 10:4). The blessed and only Ruler (1Ti 6:15). Savior (Dt 32:15; 1Ch 16:35; Ps 89:26; Isa 43:3; Jn 4:42; Lk 1:47; Ac 5:31; 1Ti 1:1; 2:3; 4:10; Tit 1:3). Shield (Ps 3:3; 18:30). Strength (Ps 22:19). A Warrior (Ex 15:3). Wonderful Counselor (Isa 9:6).

Omnipotent:
(Ge 17:1; 18:14; Job 42:2; Ac 26:8; Rev 19:6; 21:22). *See below, Power of.*

Omnipresent:
(Ge 28:16; 1Ki 8:27; 2Ch 2:6; Ac 7:48-49; Ps 139:3, 5, 7-10; Jer 23:23-24; Ac 17:24, 27-28). *See below, Presence of.*

Omniscient: *See above, Knowledge of; below, Wisdom of.*

Perfection of:
(Dt 32:4; 2Sa 22:31; Ps 18:30; Mt 5:48; Ro 12:2; Jas 1:17; 1Jn 1:5; Rev 15:3). *See above, Holiness of; below, Righteousness of.*

Personality of: *See below, Unity of.*

Power of:
(Ex 9:16; 15:6-7, 11-12; Nu 11:23; Dt 7:21; 11:2; Job 37:1-23; Ps 21:13; 29:3-9; 62:11; 68:34-35; 74:13, 15; 77:14, 16, 18; 78:12-51; 79:11; 89:8, 13; 93:1, 4; 105:26-41; 106:8; 111:6; 135:6, 8-12; 147:5, 16-18; Isa 26:4; 40:12, 22, 24, 26, 28; 51:10, 15; 63:12; Jer 5:22; 27:5; 32:17, 27; Da 2:20; Mt 19:26; Mk 10:27; 14:36; Lk 1:49, 51; 18:27; 22:29; 1Co 6:14; Rev 19:1). Supreme (Dt 32:39; Jos 4:24; 1Sa 2:6-7; 14:6; 1Ch 29:11-12; 2Ch 14:11; 25:8-9; Job 5:9; 23:13-14; 26:7-14; 36:5, 22, 27-33; 38:8, 11; 40:9; 42:2; Ps 104:7, 9, 29-30, 32; Da 4:35). Irresistible (Dt 32:39; Job 10:7; 1Sa 2:10; 2Ch 20:6; Job 9:4-7, 10, 12-13, 19; 11:10; 12:14-16; 14:20; 41:10-11; Ps 66:3, 7; 76:7; Isa 14:24, 27; 31:3; 43:13, 16-17; 46:10-11; 50:2-3; Na 1:3-6). Incomparable (Dt 3:24; Job 40:9; Ps 89:8). Omnipotent (Ge 18:14; Jer 32:27; Mt 19:26). Everlasting (Ro 1:20). Creation by (Jer 10:12). The resurrection of Christ by (1Co 6:14; 2Co 13:4). The resurrection of believers by (1Co 6:14). Manifested in behalf of believers (Dt 33:26-27; 2Ch 16:9; Ezr 8:22; Ne 1:10; Jer 20:11; Da 3:17). Manifested in his works (Dt 3:24; Ps 33:9; 107:25, 29; 114:7-8; Pr 30:4; Isa 48:13; Jer 10:12-13; 51:15; Ro 1:20). *See above, Omnipotent.*

Presence of:
(Ge 16:13; 28:16; Ex 20:24; 29:42-43; 30:6; 33:14; Dt 4:34-36, 39; 1Ki 8:27; Ps 139:3, 5, 7-10; Isa 57:15; 66:1; Jer 23:23-24; 32:18-19; Jnh 1:3-4; Ac 17:24, 27-28; 1Co 12:6).

Manifested above the atonement cover. *See Shekinah.*

Preserver:
(Ne 9:6; Job 33:18; Ps 3:3; 12:7; 17:7; 68:6; 73:23; Isa 27:3; 49:8; Jer 2:6; Da 5:23; Mt 10:29-31; Lk 12:6-7; 21:18; Jn 17:11, 15; 1Pe 3:12-13; 2Pe 2:9).

Of the righteous (Ge 15:1; 28:15; 49:24-25; Ex 8:22-23; 9:26; 11:7; 12:13, 17, 23; 15:2, 13, 16-17; 19:4; 23:20-31; Dt 1:30-31; 32:10; 33:12, 25-28; Jos 23:10; 1Sa 2:9; 2Sa 22:1-51; 2Ch 16:9; Job 1:10; 5:11, 18-24; 10:12; Ps 9:9; 18:14; 23:1-6; 31:20, 23; 32:6, 8; 34:7, 15, 17, 19-22; 37:17, 23-24, 28, 32-33; 41:1-3; 46:1, 7; 50:15; 84:11; 91:1, 3-4, 7, 9-10, 14-15; 102:19-20; 103:2-5; 107:9-10, 13; 116:6; 118:13; 121:3-4, 7-8; 125:1-3; 145:14, 19-20; 146:7-8; Pr 2:7-8; 10:3, 30; Isa 25:4; 30:21, 26; 33:16; 40:11, 29, 31; 42:16; 43:2; 46:3-4; 52:12; 58:11; 63:9; Jer 31:9-10, 28; Eze 11:16; 34:11-16, 22, 31; Da 3:27-28; Joel 2:18; Zec 2:5, 8; Mt 4:6; 1Co 10:13; 2Ti 4:17-18; 2Th 3:3; Jas 4:15).

His Preserving Care Exemplified—
To Noah and his family, at the time of the flood (Ge 6:8, 13-21; 7; 8:1, 15-16). To Abraham and Sarah, in Egypt (Ge 12:17), in Gerar (Ge 20:3). To Lot, when Sodom was destroyed (Ge 19). To Hagar, when Abraham cast her out (Ge 21:17, 19). To Jacob, when he fled from home (Ge 35:3), when he fled from Laban, his father-in-law (Ge 31:24, 29), when he met Esau (Ge 33:3-10), as he journeyed in the land of Canaan (Ge 35:3). To Joseph, in Egypt (Ge 39:2, 21). To Moses, in his infancy (Ex 2:1-10).

To the Israelites: In bringing about their deliverance from bondage (Ex 1:9-12; 2:23-25; 3:7-9). In exempting the land of Goshen from the plague of flies (Ex 8:22). In preserving their cattle from the plague (Ex 9:4-7). In exempting the land of Goshen from the plague of darkness (Ex 10:21-23). In saving the firstborn, when the plague of death destroyed the firstborn of Egypt (Ex 12:13, 23). In deliverance from Egypt (Ex 13:3, 17-22; 14; 19:4; Lev 26:13). In the wilderness (Ex 40:36-38; Nu 9:17-23; 10:33; 22:12; 23:8; Dt 1:31; 23:5; 26:7-9).

In victories under Joshua, over the Canaanites (Jos 6-11; 24:11-13), under Othniel (Jdg 3:9-11), under Ehud (Jdg 3:15-30), under Shamgar (Jdg 3:31), under Deborah (Jdg 4:5), under Gideon (Jdg 7; 8:1-23), under Jephthah (Jdg 11:29-40), under David (1Sa 17:45-49), under Ahab (1Ki 20). In delivering the kingdom of Israel from Syria (2Sa 8). In delivering Israel by Jeroboam II (2Ki 14:26-27), by Abijah (2Ch 13:4-18). In delivering from the oppressions of the king of Syria (2Ki 13:2-5). To the kingdom of Judah: In delivering from Egypt (2Ch 12:2-12), from the Ethiopians (2Ch 14:11-14). In giving peace with other nations (2Ch 17). In delivering them from the army of the Assyrians (2Ki 19). To David (1Sa 17:32, 45-47; 2Sa 7; 1Ch 11:13-14). To Hezekiah (2Ki 19). To Job (Job 1:9-12; 2:6). To Jeremiah and Baruch (Jer 36:26). To Daniel and the three Hebrew captives (Da 2:18-23; 3:27-28; 6). To Jonah (Jnh 1:17).

To the wise men of the east (Mt 2:12). To Jesus and his parents (Mt 2:13, 19-22). To Peter (Ac 12:3-17). To Paul and Silas (Ac 16:26-39). To Paul (Ac 27:24; 28:5-6, w Mk 16:18). *See below, Providence of; See Poor, God's Care.*

Providence of:
(Ge 24:7, 40-50, 56; 26:24; Lev 26:4-6, 10; Dt 8:18; 11:12-15; 15:4-6; 32:11-14; 1Sa 2:6-9; 1Ki 11:14-40; 1Ch 29:14, 16; Ps 23:1-6; 34:7, 9-10; 71:6-7, 15; Ps 107:1-43; 127:1-5; 136:5-25; 144:12-15; 147:8-9, 13-14; Pr 16:33; Ecc 2:24; 3:13; 5:19; Isa 46:4; 51:2; 55:10; Eze 36:28-38; Joel 2:18-26; Mt 5:45; Ro 8:28; Jas 4:15).

In providing for temporal necessities (Ge 1:29-30; 2:16; 8:22; 9:1-3; 28:20-21; 48:15-16; 49:24-25; Ex 16:15; Lev 25:20-22; Dt 2:7; 7:13-15; 8:4; 10:18; 28:2-13; 29:5; Ru 1:6; Ne 9:24-25; Job 5:8-11; 22:18, 25; Ps 36:6-7; 37:3, 19, 22, 25, 34; 65:9-13; 67:6; 85:12; 104:10-15; 111:5; 136:25; 145:15-16; Isa 43:20; 48:21; Jer 5:24; 27:6; Hos 2:8; Jnh 4:6; Zec 10:1; Mt 6:26, 30-33; 10:29-31; Lk 12:6-7, 24-28; 22:35; Jn 6:31; Ac 14:17; 2Co 9:10).

In sending prosperity (Ps 75:7; 127:1-2; Isa 48:14-15; 54:16-17; Eze 29:19-20). In sending adversity (1Sa 2:6-9; 2Sa 17:14; Ps 75:7; Ecc 3:10). In saving from adversity (Ge 7:1; Ps 9:26; 15:26; 23:25-26; Ps 103:3-5; 116:1-15; 118:5-6, 13-14; 146:7-9; Da 6:20-22).

In delivering from enemies (Ge 14:20; Ex 3:17; 6:7; 14:29-30; 23:22; 34:24; Dt 20:4; 23:14; 30:4, 20; 31:3, 8; 2Ki 20:6; 2Ch 20:3-30; 32:8; Ezr 8:22-23; Ps 18:17, 27; 44:1-3; 61:3; 78:52-55; 97:10; 105:14-45; Ac 7:34-36; 12:1-12; Pr 16:7). In thwarting evil purpose (Ge 37:5-20, w 45:5-7 & Ps 105:17 & Ac 7:9-10; Ex 14:4; Nu 23:7-8, 23, w 22:12-18; 24:10-13; Ezr 5:5; Ne 6:16; Est 7:10, w 6:1-12 & 9:25; Job 5:12-13, w Isa 8:9-10; Ps 33:10; Ac 5:38-39). In turning the curse into blessing (Dt 23:4, 6; Php 1:12, 19). In exalting the lowly (2Sa 7:8-9; 1Ch 17:7-8; Ps 68:6; 113:7-8). In leading people to repentance (Am 4:7-12).

In punishing evildoers (Dt 2:30; Jos 10:10-11, 19; Jdg 9:23-24; 1Ch 5:26; Isa 41:2, 4). In punishing rulers (Da 5:18, 22). In punishing nations (Dt 9:4-5; Job 12:23; Eze 29:19-20). In ordaining instruments of discipline (Isa 13:3-5). In using the Gentiles to execute his purpose (Ezr 6:22; Isa 44:28; 45:1-6, 13). In fulfilling prophecy (1Ki 12:15; 2Ch 10:15; 36:22-23; Ezr 1:1; Ac 3:17-18).

In nature (Job 12:7-20; 37:6-24; 38:25-27, 41; 39:5-6; Ps 104:16-19, 24-30; 135:7; Jer 10:13; 51:16; 14:22; 31:35).

Instances of—
Saving Noah (Ge 7:1; 2Pe 2:5). The call of Abraham (Ge 12:1). Protecting Abraham, Sarah, and Abimelech (Ge 20:3-6). Deliverance of Lot (Ge 19). Care of Isaac (Ge 26:2-3), of Jacob (Ge 31:7). The mission of Joseph (Ge 37:5-10; 39:2-3, 21, 23; 45:7-8; 50:20; Ps 105:17-22). Warning Pharaoh of famine (Ge 41).

Delivering the Israelites (Ex 3:8; 11:3; 13:18; Ac 7:34-36). The pillar of cloud (Ex 13:21; 14:19-20). Dividing the Red Sea (Ex 14:21). Delaying and destroying Pharaoh (Ex 14:25-30). Purifying the waters of Marah (Ex 15:25). Supplying manna and quail (Ex 16:13-15; Nu 11:31-32). Supplying water at Meribah (Nu 20:7-11; Ne 9:10-25). Protection of homes while at feasts (Ex 34:24). In the conquest of Canaan (Ge 15:18). Saving David's army (2Sa 5:23-25). The revolt of the ten tribes (1Ki 12:15, 24; 2Ch 10:15). Fighting the battles of Israel (2Ch 13:12, 18; 14:9-14; 16:7-9; 20:15, '17; 22; 23; 32:21-22). Restoring Manasseh after his conversion (2Ch 33:12-13). Feeding Elijah and the widow (1Ki 17; 19:1-8). In prospering Hezekiah (2Ki 18:6-7; 2Ch 32:29), and Asa

(2Ch 14:6-7), and Jehoshaphat (2Ch 17:3, 5; 20:30), and Uzziah (2Ch 26:5-15), and Jotham (2Ch 27:6), and Job (Job 1:10; 42:10, 12), and Daniel (Da 1:9).

In turning the heart of the king of Assyria to favor the Jews (Ezr 6:22). In rescuing Jeremiah (La 3:52-58; Jer 38:6-13). Restoration of the Jews (2Ch 36:22-23; Ezr 1:1). Rescuing the Jews from Haman's plot (Esther). Rebuilding the walls of Jerusalem (Ne 6:16).

Warning Joseph in dreams (Mt 1:20; 2:13, 19-20), and the wise men of the east (Mt 2:12-13). Deliverance of Paul (2Co 1:10). Restoring Epaphroditus (Php 2:27). Banishment of John to Patmos (Rev 1:9).

Mysterious and Misinterpreted—
The silence of God (Job 33:13). The adversity of the righteous (Ecc 7:15; 8:14). The prosperity of the wicked (Job 12:6; 21:7; 24:1; Ps 73:2-5, 12-17; Ecc 7:15; 8:14; Jer 12:1-2; Mal 3:14-15). Likeness in the lot of the righteous and the wicked (Ecc 9:2, 11). Permitting the violence of the wicked toward the righteous (Job 24:1-12; Hab 1:2-3, 11, 13-14).

Rejected:
By Israel (1Sa 8:7-8; Isa 65:12; 66:4). By Saul (1Sa 15:26). *See Jesus the Christ, Rejected.*

Repentance Attributed to:
(Ge 6:6-7; Ex 32:14; Jdg 2:18; 1Sa 15:35; 2Sa 24:16; 1Ch 21:15; Ps 106:45; Jer 26:19; Am 7:3; Jnh 3:10). *See Anthropomorphisms; Relent.*

Righteousness of:
(Ge 18:25; Jdg 5:11; Ps 7:9; 72:1; 88:12; 89:16; 119:40; 143:1; Isa 41:10; 56:1; Jer 4:2; 9:24; Mic 7:9; Ac 17:31).
Ascribed by people (Ex 9:27; Ezr 9:15; Job 36:3; Ps 5:8; 48:10; 71:15, 19; 89:14; 97:2; 116:5; 145:17; Jer 12:1; Da 9:7, 14; 2Ti 4:8). Ascribed by Jesus (Jn 17:25). Ascribed by the angel (Rev 16:5). Revealed in the heavens (Ps 50:6). Revealed in the gospel (Ro 1:17; 3:4-6, 21-22; 10:3-4; 2Pe 1:1).
Endures forever (Ps 119:142, 144; Isa 51:8). *See above, Holiness of, Perfection of.*

Savior:
(Ex 6:6-7; Ps 3:8; 18:30; 28:8; 31:5; 33:18-19; 34:22; 37:39-40; 74:12; 76:8-9; 85:9; 96:2; 98:2-3; 111:9; 118:14; 121:7; 149:4; Isa 26:1; 33:22; 35:4; 43:3, 11-12, 14; 45:15, 17, 21-22; 46:12-13; 49:25; 50:2; 59:1; 60:16; 63:8, 16; Jer 3:23; 14:8; 33:6; Eze 37:23; Hos 1:7; 13:4; Joel 3:16; Jnh 2:9; Lk 1:68; Jn 3:16-17; Ro 8:30-32; 1Ti 2:3-4; 4:10; Tit 1:2-3; 2:10-11; 3:4-5; 1Jn 4:9-10).
Called Redeemer (Ps 19:14; Isa 41:14; 47:4; 48:17; Jer 50:34). Salvation (Ps 27:1; 62:1-2; 62:6-7; Isa 12:2). God of salvation (Ps 25:5; 65:5; 68:19-20; 88:1). Rock of salvation (Dt 32:15, 31). Shield (Dt 33:29).
Salvation from national adversity (Ex 15:2; Isa 25:4, 9; 52:3, 9-10), from sin (Job 33:24, 27-30; 44:22-24; Ro 1:16), through Christ (2Ti 1:9).

Self-Existent:
Has life in himself (Jn 5:26). Is the I am that I am (Ex 3:14). Is the first and the last (Isa 44:6). Is the living God (Jer 10:10). Lives forever (Dt 32:40). Needs nothing (Ac 17:24-25).

Sovereign:
(Ex 20:3; Job 25:2; 33:13; 41:11; Ps 44:4; 47:8; 59:13; 74:12; 82:1, 8; 83:18; 93:1-2; 95:3-5; 96:10; 97:1, 5, 9; 98:6; 103:19; 105:7; 113:4; 115:3, 16; 136:2-3; Isa 24:23; 33:22; 40:22-23; 43:15; 44:6; 52:7; 66:1; La 3:37; Mic 4:7, 13; Mal 1:14; Jn 10:29; 19:11; Ac 7:49; Ro 9:19; 11:36; Eph 4:6; 1Ti 6:15-16; Heb 1:3; Jas 4:12; Rev 4:11; 19:6).
Over heaven (Dt 26:15). Over earth (Ex 9:29; Jos 3:11; Ps 24:1, 10; 47:2, 7-8; 50:10-12; Isa 54:5; Jer 10:10; 1Co 10:26). Over heaven and earth (Ge 14:18-20, 22; 24:3; Ex 19:5; Dt 4:39; 10:14, 17; Jos 2:11; 2Ki 19:15; 1Ch 29:11-12; Ne 9:6; Ps 89:11; 135:5-6; Mt 6:10; 11:25; Lk 10:21; Ac 17:24-26; Rev 11:4, 13, 17).
Over the spirits of all mankind (Nu 27:16; Dt 32:39; Job 12:9-10, 16-17; Ps 22:28-29; Ecc 9:1; Isa 45:23; Jer 18:1-23; Eze 18:4; Ro 14:11). In human affairs (Ps 75:6-7; Jer 27:5-7; 32:27-28; Eze 16:50; 17:24; Da 2:20-21, 47; 4:3, 17, 25, 34-35, 37; 5:18, 26-28).
Everlasting (Ex 15:18; Ps 10:16; 29:10; 66:7; 145:11-13; 146:10; La 5:19; Da 6:26).

Spirit:
(Jn 4:24; Ac 17:29). *See Holy Spirit.*

Teacher:
(Job 36:22; Ps 94:10, 12; 119:135, 171; Isa 28:26; 54:13; Jn 6:45; 1Th 4:9).

Truth:
(Ge 24:27; Ex 34:6; Nu 23:19; 1Sa 15:29; Ps 25:10; 31:5; 33:4; 43:3; 57:3, 10; 71:22; 86:11, 15; 89:14; 108:4; 132:11; 138:2; Isa 25:1; 65:16; Da 4:37; Jn 8:26; Ro 3:4, 7; Tit 1:2; Rev 6:10; 15:3).
Endures to all generations (Ps 117:2; 146:10).

Ubiquitous: *See above, Omnipresent.*

Unchangeable: *See above, Immutable.*

Unity of:
(Dt 4:35; 6:4; 2Sa 7:22; Isa 42:8). Taught by Jesus (Mk 12:29, 32; Jn 17:3). Taught by Paul (1Co 8:4, 6; Gal 3:20; Eph 4:6; 1Ti 2:5). Disbelieved in by Syrians (1Ki 20:28). Believed in by demons (Jas 2:19).

Unsearchable:
Dt 29:29; Job 5:8-9; 9:10; 11:7-9; 26:9, 14; 36:26; 37:5, 23; 77:19; 139:6; 145:3; Pr 30:4; Ecc 3:11; 11:5; Isa 40:28; 45:15; 55:8-9; Ro 11:33-34; 1Co 2:10-11, 16).
Symbolized by darkness (Ex 20:21; Dt 4:11; 5:22; 1Ki 8:12; Ps 18:11; 97:2). By the cloud upon the atonement cover (Lev 16:2). Name of, secret (Jdg 13:18). Dwells in thick darkness (1Ki 8:12; Ps 97:2). Known only to Christ, and to those to whom Christ reveals him (Mt 11:27).
See Mysteries.

Voice of: *See Anthropomorphisms.*

Wisdom of:
(Ezr 7:25; Job 9:4; 12:13, 16; Isa 31:2; Da 2:20-22, 28; Ro 11:33; 16:27; 1Co 1:24-25). Infinite (Ps 147:5). Manifold (Eph 3:10). Ascribed by angels (Rev 7:12). Works made in (Ps 104:24; 136:5; Pr 3:19-20; Jer 10:12). *See above, Knowledge of.*

Works of:
In creation (Job 9:8-9; Ps 8:3-5; 89:11; 136:5-9; 139:13-14; 148:4-5; Ecc 3:11; Jer 10:12). Good (Ge 1:10, 18, 21, 25). Faithful (Ps 33:4). Wonderful (Ps 26:7; 40:5). Incomparable (Ps 86:8). In his overruling providence in the human affairs (Ps 26:7; 40:5; 66:3; 75:1; 111:2, 4, 6; 118:17; 145:4-17). *See Creation.*

GODLESSNESS

Described as:
Destitute of the love of God (Jn 5:42, 44). Forgetting God (Job 8:11-13; Ps 9:17; 50:22; Isa 17:10; Jer 2:32). Ignoring God (Job 35:10; Ps 28:5; 52:7; 53:2-3; 54:3; 55:19; 86:14; Isa 5:12; 22:11; 30:1; 31:1; Hos 7:2-4). Forsaking God (Dt 32:15). Despising God (1Sa 2:30; Ps 36:1; Pr 14:2; Jn 15:23-25). Loving deceit (Isa 30:9-11). Devoid of understanding (Ps 14:2-3; 53:4; Isa 1:3; Ro 1:21-22; 3:11; Eph 4:18).
Rebellious (Ps 2:2; Isa 30:2; Da 5:23). Haters of God (Dt 7:10). Enemies of God (Ro 1:21; Jas 4:4). Sinfulness (Ro 8:6-8). Impugning God's justice (Eze 33:17-20; Mal 2:17). Atheistic rejecting God (Ps 10:4; 14:1; 53:1). Willfully sinning (Heb 10:26-27).
See Impenitence; Obduracy; Prayerlessness; Reprobacy; Unbelief; Wicked.

GODLINESS See Holiness; Righteousness.

GODLY See Righteous.

GODS See Idol; Idolatry; Image.

GOG (*precious golden object*).
1. A Reubenite (1Ch 5:4).
2. A Scythian prince. Prophecy against (Eze 38; 39; Rev 20:8).

GOIIM (*nations, Gentiles*). A people who, led by King Tidal, along with three Eastern kings, Amraphel king of Shinar, Arioch king of Ellasar, and Kedorlaomer king of Elam, went to war against Bera king of Sodom, Birsha king of Gomorrah, Shinab king of Admah, Shemeber king of Zeboiim, and the king of Bela (that is, Zoar) (Ge 14:1-2, 9). This latter group of kings joined forces in the Valley of Siddim (the Salt Sea, which is the Dead Sea) (Ge 14:3).
The Goiim may have been non-Semitic tribes who lived to the N. They have been identified with the Hittites because of the resemblance of the name Tidal to the royal Hittite name Tudhaliash, and less reasonably to the Guti (in NE Mesopotamia). Goiim may be the generic Hebrew term for "nations." *See Goyim.*

GOLAN A town in Bashan. Given to Manasseh as a city of refuge (Dt 4:43; Jos 20:8). A Levitical city (Jos 21:27; 1Ch 6:71). *See Gaulanitis.*

GOLD Exported from Havilah (Ge 2:11-12). From Ophir (1Ki 9:28; 10:11; 1Ch 29:4; 2Ch 8:18; Job 22:24), Tarshish (1Ki 22:48), Parvaim (2Ch 3:6), Sheba (1Ki 10:10; 2Ch 9:9; Ps 72:15), Uphaz (Jer 10:9).
Refined (Job 28:19; 31:24; Pr 8:19; 17:3; 27:21; Zec 13:9; Mal 3:3).

Used in the Arts:
Beaten work (2Ch 9:15), made into wire threads and wrought into embroidered tapestry (Ex 39:3), apparel (Ps 45:9, 13), in ornamenting the priests' garments (Ex 39), modeled into forms of fruits (Pr 25:11), into ornaments (Ge 24:22; Ex 3:22; 11:2; 28:11; Nu 31:50-51; SS 1:10; 5:14; Eze 16:17), crowns made of (Ex 25:25; 37:2-11; 39:30; Est 8:15; Ps 21:3; Zec 6:11), lampstands made of, for the tabernacle (Ex 25:31-38; 37:17-24), shields of (1Ki 10:16-17), overlaying with (Ex 25:11, 13, 24, 28; 26:27, 29; 30:5; 36:34, 36, 38; 37:2-4, 11, 15; 1Ki 6:20-22; 28, 30, 32, 35), beds made of (Est 1:6). Wedge of (Jos 7:21; Isa 13:12).
Used as money (Ge 44:1, 8; 1Ch 21:25; Ezr 8:25-28; Isa 13:17; 60:9; Eze 7:19; 28:4; Mt 2:11; 10:9; Ac 3:6; 20:33; 1Pe 1:18). Solomon rich in (1Ki 10:2, 14, 21).
Vessels and utensils made of, for the tabernacle (Ex 25:26, 29, 38-39; 37:16), for the temple (1Ch 18:11; 22:14, 16; 29:2-7). Altar, lamps, and other articles made of (1Ki 7:49-51; 2Ki 25:15; Jer 52:19; Ezr 8:27; Da 5:3). *See above, Overlaying with.*
Belongs to God (Hag 2:8).

Figurative: (Ecc 12:6; Jer 51:7; La 4:1; 1Co 3:12).

Symbolic: (Da 2:32-45; Rev 21:18, 21).
See Goldsmith.

GOLDEN CANDLESTICK See Lampstand.

GOLDEN RULE (Mt 7:12; Lk 6:31; also Lev 19:18; Ro 13:9; Gal 5:14). *See Love.*

GOLDSMITH (2Ch 2:7, 14; Ne 3:8, 31-32; Isa 40:19; 41:7; 46:6).

GOLGOTHA (*skull*). The place of the crucifixion of Christ, located outside of Jerusalem (Mt 27:33; Mk 15:22) on the public road (Jn 19:20).

GOLIATH (*exile*). A giant champion of Gath. Defied the armies of Israel and is slain by David (1Sa 17; 21:9; 22:10). His sons (2Sa 21:15-22; 1Ch 20:4-8).

GOMER (*complete*).
1. Son of Japheth (Ge 10:2-3; 1Ch 1:5-6).
2. A people descended from Gomer (Eze 38:6).
3. Wife of Hosea (Hos 1:3).

GOMORRAH (*to overwhelm with water*). One of the "cities of the plain" (Ge 10:19; 13:10). Its king defeated by Kedorlaomer

(Ge 14:2, 8-11). Wickedness of (Ge 18:20). Destroyed (Ge 19:24-28; Dt 29:23; 32:32; Isa 1:9-10; 13:19; Jer 23:14; 49:18; 50:40; Am 4:11; Zep 2:9; Mt 10:14-15; Mk 6:11; Lk 9:5; Ro 9:29; 2Pe 2:6; Jude 7). *See Cities of the Plain.*

GONORRHEA Possibly among the bodily discharges of Lev 15. *See Discharge, Bodily; Disease.*

GOOD AND EVIL Choice between, by Adam and Eve (Ge 3). Exhortation to choose between (Jos 24:15). Conflict between (Rev 16:13-21). Subjective conflict between (Ro 7:9-25).

GOOD FOR EVIL Injunctions by Christ concerning (Mt 5:44-48; Lk 6:27-36).
Instances of: Abraham, to Abimelech (Ge 20:14-18). David, to Saul (1Sa 24:17; 26), to his enemies (Ps 35:12-14). Elisha, to the Syrians (2Ki 6:22-23). Jesus, to his crucifiers (Lk 23:34). Stephen (Ac 7:60).
See Golden Rule; Evil for Good; Nonresistance.

GOOD NEWS (Pr 15:30; 25:25). *See Gospel.*

GOPHER WOOD See Cypress Wood.

GOSHEN (*mound of earth*).
1. A district in Egypt especially adapted to herds and flocks. Israelites dwelt in (Ge 45:10; 46:28; 47). Exempted from plagues (Ex 8:22; 9:26).
2. A town and district of Judah (Jos 10:41; 11:16; 15:51).

GOSPEL (*good news*). From God (Jn 17:7-8, 14; 2Th 2:14). Contrasted with the law (Lk 16:16; Jn 1:16-17; Ac 12:24; 19:20; 2Co 3:6-13; 9:8-15; 10:9; 12:22-24). Called the New Covenant (Jer 31:31-34; Heb 7:22; 8:6-13; 9:8-15; 10:9; 12:22-24).

Described as:
Dispensation of grace (Eph 3:2). Doctrine according to godliness (1Ti 6:3). Everlasting gospel or eternal good tidings (Rev 14:6). The faith (Jude 3). Glorious gospel (1Ti 1:11). Pattern of sound teaching (2Ti 1:13). Gospel of the glory of Christ (2Co 4:4). Good tidings or good news (Isa 40:9; 41:27; 52:7; 61:1; Mt 11:5; Lk 7:22; Ac 13:32-33; 1Pe 1:25). Gospel, of Christ (Ro 1:16; 1Co 9:12, 18; Gal 1:7; Php 1:27; 1Th 3:2), of God (Ro 1:1; 15:16; 1Th 2:8; 1Pe 4:17), of grace of God (Ac 20:24), of Jesus Christ (Mk 1:1), of the kingdom (Mt 4:23; 24:14), of peace (Eph 6:15), of salvation (Eph 1:13).
The kingdom (Lk 16:16). The law of liberty (Jas 1:25). Ministration of the Spirit (2Co 3:8). Mystery, of Christ (Eph 3:4), of the gospel (Eph 6:19). Power of God (Ro 1:16; 1Co 1:18). Preaching of Jesus Christ (Ro 16:25). Word of Christ (Col 3:16), of faith (Ro 10:8), of God (1Th 2:13; 1Pe 1:23), of life (Php 2:16), of the Lord (1Pe 1:25), of reconciliation (2Co 5:19), of salvation (Ac 13:26), of truth (Eph 1:13). Words of this life (Ac 5:20).
Likened to:
A mustard seed (Mt 13:31-32; Mk 4:30-33; Lk 13:18-19), good seed (Mt 13:24-30, 36-43), yeast (Mt 13:33), a pearl of great price (Mt 13:45-46; Lk 13:20-21), a treasure hidden in a field (Mt 13:44), a householder (Mt 20:1-6), a feast (Lk 14:16-24).
Dissemination of (Ac 14:3; 16:17; 20:24), commanded (Mt 24:14; 28:18-20; Mk 13:10; 16:15; Ac 5:20; Ro 10:15-18; 16:25-26; 1Co 1:18, 21, 24-25; 9:16-18; 2Pe 3:8-11). Desired by prophets, righteous, kings (Mt 13:17; Lk 23:34). Hid from the lost (2Co 4:3-4). Comes in power, word, assurance (1Th 1:5).
Proclaimed to Abraham (Gal 3:8), by angels (Lk 2:10-11; Rev 14:6). Preached by Jesus (Mt 4:23; Mk 1:14-15), by Peter (Ac 10:36), by Paul (Ac 13:32-33; 20:24; Ro 15:29; 1Co 9:16-18; Gal 2:2; Col 1:5-6, 23), to the Gentiles (Gal 2:2; Eph 3:8; Col 1:23, 26-29), to both Jews and Gentiles (Ro 1:16; 1Co 1:24), to the poor (Mt 11:4-6; Lk 7:22), to the dead (1Pe 3:19; 4:6), to every nation (Lk 2:10-11; Ro 16:26; Rev 14:6).
Life and immortality brought to light in (2Ti 1:10). Salvation through (Ro 1:16-17; 1Co 15:1-2; Eph 1:13-14; Jas 1:21; 1Pe 1:23).

Prophecies concerning:
(Isa 2:3-5; 4:2-6; 9:2, 6-7; 25:7-9; 29:18, 24; 32:3-4; 35:5-10; 40:9; 41:27; 42:6-7; 46:13; 49:13; 51:4-6; 52:7; 55:1-5; 60:1-22; 61:1-3; Jer 31:31-34; Eze 34:23-31; 47:1-12; Joel 2:28-32; Mic 4:1-7; Mt 24:14; Lk 1:67-79; 2:12-14, 34). Fulfilled by Christ (Lk 4:18-19).
See Church, The Body of Believers, Prophecies Concerning; Jesus the Christ, Kingdom of, Mission of; Kingdom of God, of Heaven; Synoptic Gospels, The.

GOSSIP Proverbs concerning (Pr 11:13; 16:28; 17:9; 26:20). Forbidden (Lev 19:16; Ps 50:20; Pr 11:3; 20:19; Eze 22:9).
See Slander; Speaking, Evil; Talebearer.

GOURD Carvings of decorated the temple (1Ki 6:18) and its cast metal Sea (1Ki 7:24). Elisha purifies stew made with poisonous gourds (2Ki 4:38-41).

GOUT Perhaps Asa's disease in the feet (2Ch 16:12). *See Disease.*

GOVERNMENT Paternal functions of (Ge 41:25-57). Civil service school provided by (Da 1:3-20). Maintains a system of public instruction (2Ch 17:7-9).

Constitutional:
It was provided in the law of Moses that in the event of the establishment of a monarchy a copy of the law of Moses should be made and the king should be required to study this law all the days of his life and conform his administration to it (Dt 17:18-20). This constituted the fundamental law and had its likeness to the constitution of modern governments. When David was crowned king of all Israel he made a league in the nature of a constitution which was a basis of good understanding between himself and the people (2Sa 5:3). When Joash was enthroned a covenant was made between him and the people (2Ch 23:3, 11). This no doubt refers to the law of Moses (Dt 17:18-20), which had been preserved by Jehoiada, the priest. Zedekiah made a covenant with the people proclaiming liberty (Jer 34:8-11). That the king of the Medes and

Persians was restricted by a constitution "which cannot be annulled," is evident from Da 6:12-15.

See Constitution; Israel, Israelites; Judge; Kings; Nation.

Corruption in: (1Ki 21:5-13; Pr 25:5; Mic 3:1-4, 9-11).

Instances of Corruption in: Pilate, in delivering Jesus to death to please the noisy crowd (Mt 27:24; Jn 19:12-16). Felix, who hoped for money from Paul (Ac 24:26).

See Court, Of Law, Corrupt; Church, The Body of Believers, Evil Conditions of; Corrupt; Rulers; Wicked.

Duty of Citizens to:
To pay taxes (Mt 22:17-21; Lk 20:22-25). To render obedience to civil authority (Ro 13:1-7; Tit 3:1; 1Pe 2:13-17).

God in:
(2Ch 22:7; Jer 18:6; Eze 21:25-27; 29:19-20). In appointment of Saul as king (1Sa 9:15-17; 10:1). In Saul's rejection (1Sa 15:26-28; Ac 13:22). In appointment of David (1Sa 16:1, 7, 13; 2Sa 7:13-16; Ps 89:19-37; Ac 13:22). In counseling Solomon (1Ki 9:2-9). In magnifying Solomon (1Ch 29:25). In reproving Solomon's wickedness (1Ki 11:9-13). In raising adversaries against Solomon (1Ki 11:14, 23). In tearing the nation of Israel in two (1Ki 11:13; 12:1-24; 2Ch 10:15; 11:4). In blotting out the house of Jeroboam (1Ki 14:7-16; 15:27-30). In appointment of kings (1Ki 14:14; 16:1-2; 1Ch 28:4-5; Da 2:20-21, 37; 4:17; 5:18-23). In destruction of nations (Jer 25:12-17; Am 9:8; Hag 2:22).

Relation of God to: (Ps 22:28; Pr 8:15-16; Isa 9:6-7; Jer 1:9-10; 18:6-10; 25:12-17; Eze 21:25-27; 29:19-20; Da 2:20-21, 37; 4:17; 5:18-28; 10:13; Hos 8:4; Am 9:8; Hag 2:21-22; Jn 19:10-11).

See God, Sovereign; Jesus the Christ, Kingdom of.

Mosaic:
Administrative and judicial system (Ex 18:13-26; Nu 11:16-17, 24-25; Dt 1:9-17).

Popular Government, by a National Assembly, or Its Representatives—
Accepted the law given by Moses (Ex 19:7-8; 24:3, 7; Dt 29:10-15). Refused to make conquest of Canaan (Nu 14:1-10). Chose, or ratified, the chief ruler (1Sa 10:24; 8:4-22; 11:14-15; 2Sa 3:17-21; 5:1-3; 1Ch 29:22; 2Ch 23:3). Possessed veto power over king's purposes (1Sa 14:44-45). Constituted the court in certain judicial cases (Nu 35:12, 24-25).

Delegated, Council of Elders—
Closely associated with Moses and subsequent leaders (Ex 3:16, 18; 4:29-31; 12:21; 17:5-6; 18:12; 19:7-8; 24:1, 14; Lev 4:15; 9:1; Nu 11:16-17, 30; 16:25; Dt 1:13-15; 5:23; 27:1; 29:10-15; 31:9, 28; Jos 7:6; 8:10, 32-33; 23:2-3, 6; 24:1, 24-25; Jdg 21:16-25; Ac 5:17-18, 21-41).

Miscellaneous Facts Relating to the Council—
Demands a king (1Sa 8:4-10, 19-22). Saul pleads to be honored before (1Sa 15:30). Chooses David as king (2Sa 5:3; 1Ch 11:3). Closely associated with David (2Sa 12:17; 1Ch 15:25; 21:16). Joins Absalom in his usurpation (2Sa 17:4). David rebukes (2Sa 19:11). Assists Solomon at the dedication of the temple (1Ki 8:1-3; 2Ch 5:2-4). Counsels King Rehoboam (1Ki 12:6-8, 13). Counsels King Ahab (1Ki 20:7-8). Josiah assembles, to hear the law of the Lord (2Ki 23:1; 2Ch 34:29-30).

Legislates with Ezra in reforming certain marriages with the heathen (Ezr 9:1; 10:8-14). Legislates in later times (Mt 15:2, 7-9; Mk 7:1-13). Sits as a court (Jer 26:10-24). Constitutes, with priests and scribes, a court for the trial of both civil and ecclesiastical causes (Mt 21:23; 26:3-5, 57-68; 27:1-2; Mk 8:31; 14:43, 53-65; 15:1; Lk 22:52-54, 66-71; Ac 4:1-21; 6:9-15). Unfaithful to the city (La 1:19). Seeks counsel from prophets (Eze 8:1; 14:1; 20:1, 3). Corrupt (1Ki 21:8-14; Eze 8:11-12; Mt 26:14-15, w Mt 27:3-4).

A similar council existed among the Egyptians (Ge 50:7) and among the Midianites and Moabites (Nu 22:4, 7, and Gibeonites (Jos 9:11).

Executive officers of tribes and cities, called princes or nobles, members of the national assembly (Nu 1:4-16, 44; 7:2-3, 10-11, 18, 24, 54, 84; 10:4; 16:2; 17:2, 6; 27:2; 31:13-14; 32:2; 34:18-29; 36:1; Jos 9:15-21; 17:4; 22:13-32; 1Ki 21:11-14; Ne 3:9, 12, 16, 18-19).

The Mosaic judicial system. *See Court, Of Law; Judge; Levites; Priest; Rulers; Sanhedrin; Synagogue.*

Ecclesiastical: *See Church, The Body of Believers, Government of; Church, The Body of Believers, State; Priest.*

Imperial: (Ge 14:1; Jos 11:10; 1Ki 4:21; Est 1:1; Da 4:1; 6:1-3; Lk 2:1).

Monarchical:
Tyranny in: By Pharaoh (Ex 1:8-22; 2:23-24; 3:7; 5:1-10). By Saul (1Sa 22:6-19). By David (2Sa 11:14-17). By Solomon (1Ki 2:23-25, 28-34, 36-46). By Rehoboam (1Ki 12:1-16). By Ahab and Jezebel (1Ki 21:7-16). By Jehu (2Ki 10:1-14). By Xerxes (Est 1:11-12, 19-22; 3:6-15; 8:8-13). By Nebuchadnezzar (Da 1:10; 2:5-13; 5:19). By Herod (Mk 6:27-28).

Municipal:
Based on a local council and executive officers (Dt 19:12; 21:2-8, 18-21; 22:13-21; 25:7-9; Jos 20:4; Jdg 8:14-16; 11:5-11; Ru 4:2; 1Sa 11:3; 16:4; 30:26; 1Ki 21:8-14; 2Ki 10:1-7; Ezr 10:8, 14; Ne 3:9, 12, 16, 18-19; La 5:14).

Patriarchal: (Ge 27:29, 37).

Provincial:
(Ezr 4:8-9; 5:3, 6; 6:6; 8:36; Ne 2:7, 9; 5:14; Da 6:1-3; Mt 27:2; 28:14; Lk 2:2; 3:1; Ac 24:1).

Representative:
(Dt 1:13-15; Jos 9:11). *See above, Delegated, Council of Elders.*

Theocratic:
(Ex 19:3-8; Dt 26:16-19; 29:1-13; Jdg 8:23; 1Sa 8:6-7; 10:19; 12:12; Isa 33:22).

See God, Sovereign; Jesus the Christ, Kingdom of.

GOVERNOR A provincial or city ruler (1Ki 4:7; 10:15; Ezr 2:63; Jn 18:28). Joseph (Ge 42:6), Zebul (Jdg 9:30), Gedaliah (2Ki

25:23). Tattenai (Ezr 5:3, 6). Sheshbazzar (Ezr 5:14). Nehemiah (Ne 7:65, 70; 8:9; 10:1; 12:26).

GOYIM (*nations, Gentiles*). A people, where the king of Goyim in Gilgal, was among those defeated by Joshua (Jos 12:23). Goyim may be the generic Hebrew word for "nations." *See Goiim.*

GOZAN A city in NE Mesopotamia on the Habor River, to which the Israelites were deported by the Assyrians (2Ki 17:6; 18:11; 19:12; 1Ch 5:26).

GRACE A term employed by the Biblical writers with a wide variety of meaning: charm, sweetness, loveliness (Ps 45:2), the attitude of God toward men (Tit 2:11), the method of salvation (Eph 2:5), the opposite of legalism (Gal 5:4), the impartation of spiritual power or gifts (1Co 2:6; 2Ti 2:1), the liberty which God gives to men (Jude 4).

Before meals. *See Prayer, Thanksgiving, and Before Taking Food.*

GRACE OF GOD Unmerited favor (Dt 7:7-8; 2Ch 30:9; Eph 1:6; Tit 2:11; Heb 4:16). Abundant (1Ti 1:14). Divine help (Ge 20:6; Job 10:12; Ps 84:11; 94:17-19; 138:3; 2Co 10:13; 2Co 1:12; 12:9; 1Pe 1:5).

Growth in (Ps 84:7; Pr 4:18; Php 1:6, 9-11; 3:12-15; Col 1:10-11; 2:19; 1Th 3:10, 12-13; 2Th 1:3; Heb 6:1-3; 1Pe 2:1-3; 2Pe 3:18). Believers to be stewards of (1Pe 4:10). Intercessory prayer for (Ps 143:11; Da 9:18; Jn 17:11-12, 15; 1Th 1:1; 5:28; 2Pe 1:2). No warrant for sinful indulgence (Ro 6:1, 15). Exhortation against rejecting (2Co 6:1-2). With respect to Jacob and Esau (Ro 9:10-16).

Manifested:
In drawing people to Christ (Jn 6:44-45). In redemption (Eph 1:5-9, 11-12). In justification (Ge 15:6; Ro 3:22-24; 4:4-5, 16; 5:2, 6-8, 15-21; Tit 3:7). In passing over transgressions (Nu 23:20-21; Ne 9:17; Ro 3:25). In salvation (Ro 11:5-6; Eph 2:8-9; 2Ti 1:9). In calling to service (Gal 1:15-16). In spiritual growth (Eph 3:16). In spiritual gifts (1Co 1:4-8; Eph 4:7, 11).

In the character and conduct of the righteous (1Co 15:10; 2Co 1:12; Php 2:13). In sustaining the righteous (1Ch 17:8; Da 10:18-19; 2Co 12:9; 1Pe 1:5; 5:10; Jude 24). In sustaining in temptation (Ge 20:6; 1Co 10:13; Rev 3:10).

Manifested to:
Enoch (Ge 5:24). Noah (Ge 6:8, 17-18). Abraham (Ge 12:2; 21:22). Ishmael (Ge 21:20). Isaac (Ge 26:24). Jacob (Ge 46:3-4; 48:16). Joseph (Ge 39:2-3, 23). Moses (Ex 3:12; 33:12-17). Israel (Dt 4:7). Naphtali (Dt 33:23). Joshua (Jos 1:5, 9). Job (Job 10:12). David (1Sa 25:26, 34; 2Sa 7:8-16). Daniel (Da 10:18-19). Jeremiah (Jer 15:20). The righteous (Ps 5:12; Ac 4:33).

See God, Grace of.

GRACES Christian (Mt 5:3-11; Ro 5:3-5; 1Co 13:1-8, 13; Gal 5:22-23; 1Pe 1:5-9).

See Beatitudes; Character; Charitableness; Courage; Gentleness; Hope; Kindness; Knowledge; Longsuffering; Love; Meekness; Mercy; Patience; Peace; Perseverance; Purity; Righteousness, Fruits of; Stability; Temperance; Wisdom.

GRAFT A horticultural process by which the branches of a cultivated tree may be inserted into the trunk of a wild tree. Figurative of Gentiles partaking of Israel's covenants and blessings (Ro 11:17ff.).

GRAIN In valleys (Ps 65:13; Mk 4:28). A product of Egypt (Ge 41:47-49), Israel (Dt 33:28; Eze 27:17). Roasted (Ru 2:14; 1Sa 17:17; 25:18; 2Sa 17:28). Ground (2Sa 17:19). Eaten by the Israelites (Jos 5:11-12). Shocks of, burnt (Jdg 15:5). Mosaic laws concerning (Ex 22:6; Dt 23:25).

Individual heads of grain (Ge 41:5-7, 22-27; Lev 23:14; Ru 2:2; Job 24:24; Isa 17:5; Mk 4:26-29). Grain that is ripe but soft, which is roasted and eaten (Lev 2:14). The poor may pick what they can eat on the spot; refers to grain rubbed between the hands (Dt 23:25). Picked by Christ's disciples (Mt 12:1; Mk 2:23; Lk 6:1). Newly ripened heads of grain (2Ki 4:42).

Figurative: (Ps 72:16; Hos 14:7; Jn 12:24).

Symbolic: (Ps 72:16).
See Barley; Barn; Bread; Firstfruits; Glean, Gleaning; Harvest; Plants of the Bible; Reaping; Rye; Threshing; Tithes; Wheat.

GRANARY A storehouse for grain and other dry crops (Ex 22:29; Jer 50:26; Joel 1:17).
See Barn; Storehouse.

GRANDFATHER Called Father (Ge 10:21).

GRAPE Cultivated in vineyards, by Noah (Ge 9:20), Canaanites (Nu 13:24; Dt 6:11; Jos 24:13), Edomites (Nu 20:17), Amorites (Nu 21:22; Isa 16:8-9), Philistines (Jdg 15:5). Grown, at Baal Hamon (SS 8:11), Carmel (2Ch 26:10), En Gedi (SS 1:14), Jezreel (1Ki 21:1), Lebanon (Hos 14:7), Samaria (Jer 31:5), Shechem (Jdg 9:27), Shiloh (Jdg 21:20-21), Timnath (Jdg 14:5).

Culture of (Lev 25:3, 11; Dt 28:39; 2Ch 26:10; SS 6:11; Isa 5:1; Jer 31:5).

Wine made of (Jer 25:30). Wine of, forbidden to Nazirites (Nu 6:4). *See Nazirite(s).*

See Vine; Vineyards; Wine.

Figurative (Dt 32:32; Ps 128:3; Jer 2:21; Eze 15; Hos 10:1; Rev 14:18-20).

Fable of (Jdg 9:12-13). Parables of the vine (Ps 80:8-14; Eze 17:6-10; 19:10-14; Jn 15:1-5). Proverb of (Eze 18:2).

See Vine; Vineyards; Wine.

GRASS Created on the third creative day (Ge 1:11). Mown (Ps 72:6). God's care of (Mt 6:30; Lk 12:28). On roofs of houses (Ps 129:6).

Figurative (Ps 90:5-6; Isa 40:6; 1Pe 1:24; Jas 1:10-11).

GRASSHOPPER (Nu 13:33; Ecc 12:5; Isa 40:22; Na 3:17). *See Locust.*

GRATE A copper network, placed under the top of the great altar, to hold the sacrifice while burning (Ex 27:4; 35:16; 38:4-5).

GRATITUDE *See Thankfulness.*

GRAVE Prepared by Jacob (Ge 50:5). Defilement from touching (Nu 19:16, 18). Weeping at (2Sa 3:32; Jn 11:31; 20:11). Of parents, honored (2Sa 19:37). Welcomed (Job 3:20-22).

Resurrection From:
Of Lazarus (Jn 11:43-44; 12:17), of Jesus (Mt 28:5-6; 1Co 15:12-20), of believers after Jesus' resurrection (Mt 27:52-53), of all the dead foretold (Jn 5:28; 1Co 15:22-54).

See Burial; Sheol; Tomb.

GRAVE CLOTHES Preparatory to burial, the body was washed and anointed with spices, then wrapped in a winding sheet, bound with strips of cloth, and the head wrapped in a square cloth (Jn 11:44; 19:40).

GRAVEL Figurative of food gained by fraud (Pr 20:17), of judgment (La 3:16).

GRAVEN IMAGE NIV "carved image" or "idol" of wood, stone, or metal (Dt 7:5; Isa 44:9-17; 45:20). *See Carving; Groves; High Places; Iconoclasm; Idol; Idolatry.*

GRAVING *See Engraving.*

GREAT OWL *See Birds.*

GREAT SEA *See Mediterranean Sea.*

GREATER SIDON *See Sidon.*

GREATNESS Of God (Dt 3:24; Ps 77:13; 95:3; 104:1; 135:5; 145:3; Isa 12:6; Jer 32:18; Mal 1:11). Of Christ (Isa 53:12; 63:1; Mt 12:6; Lk 11:31; Php 2:9-10).

GREAVES Leg armor worn below the knee (1Sa 17:6).

GREECE Inhabitants of, called Gentiles (Mk 7:26; Jn 7:35; Ro 2:10; 3:9; 1Co 10:32; 12:13), desire to see Jesus (Jn 12:20-23), marry among the Jews (Ac 16:1), accept the Messiah (Ac 17:2-4, 12, 34), persecute the early Christians (Ac 6:9-14; 9:29; 18:17). Gentiles called Greeks (Ro 10:12; Gal 3:28; Col 3:11).

Schools of philosophy in Athens (Ac 19:9). Philosophy of (1Co 1:22-23). Poets of (Ac 17:28).

See Asceticism; Athens; Epicureans; Stoicism; Stoics.

GREED
Described:
Greed is idolatry (Col 3:5). Insatiable (Pr 1:19; 21:26; Ecc 1:8; 4:8; 5:10-11; Isa 56:11). Root of evil (1Ti 6:9-11). Tends to poverty (Pr 11:24, 26; 22:16). Gains of, unstable (Job 20:15; Pr 23:4-6; Jer 17:11). Disqualifies from sacred office (Ex 18:21; 1Ti 3:3; Tit 1:7, 11; 1Pe 5:2). Disqualifies from kingdom of God (Mt 19:23-24; 22:25; Lk 18:24-25; 1Co 6:10; Eph 5:3, 5; Php 3:18-19). Denounced (Ps 10:3; Pr 1:19; Isa 5:8; Jude 11).

Forbidden:
Warnings against (Dt 15:9-10; Pr 1:19; 15:27; Hos 4:18; Hab 2:5-9; Mt 6:19-21, 24-25, 31-33; 13:22; 16:26; Mk 4:19; 7:21-23; Lk 8:14; 12:16-21; Jn 6:26-27; 1Co 5:11; 1Th 2:5; 1Ti 6:5-8; 2Ti 3:2, 5; Heb 13:5; Jas 4:2; 1Jn 2:15-17). Commandments against (Ex 20:17; Dt 5:21; Ro 13:9; Col 3:2; 1Ti 3:8). Prayer against (Ps 119:36).

Reproof for (Ne 5:7; Isa 1:23; Jer 6:13; 22:17; Eze 33:31; Hos 10:1; Mic 2:2; 3:11; 7:3; Hag 1:6; Ro 1:29). Punishment for (Ex 18:21; Job 31:24-25, 28; Isa 57:17; Jer 8:10; 51:13; Eze 22:12-13; Col 3:5-6; 2Pe 2:3, 14-17).

See Avarice; Greed; Rich, The; Riches; Worldliness.

Instances of:
Eve, in desiring the forbidden fruit (Ge 3:6). Lot, in choosing the plain of the Jordan (Ge 13:10-13). Laban, in giving Rebekah to be Isaac's wife (Ge 24:29-51), in deceiving Jacob when he served him seven years for Rachel (Ge 29:15-30), in deceiving Jacob in wages (Ge 31:7, 15, 41-42). Jacob, in defrauding Esau of his father's blessing (Ge 27:6-29), in defrauding Laban of his flocks and herds (Ge 30:35-43), in buying Esau's birthright (Ge 25:31). Balaam, in loving the wages of unrighteousness (2Pe 2:15, w Nu 22).

Achan, in hiding the treasure (Jos 7:21). Eli's sons, in taking the flesh of the sacrifice (1Sa 2:13-17). Samuel's sons, in taking bribes (1Sa 8:3). Saul, in sparing Agag and the booty (1Sa 15:8-9). David, of Bathsheba (2Sa 11:2-5). Ahab, in desiring Naboth's vineyard (1Ki 21:2-16). Gehazi, in taking a gift from Naaman (2Ki 5:20-27). Israelites, in exacting usury of their brothers (Ne 5:1-11), in keeping back the portion of the Levites (Ne 13:10), in building fine houses while the house of the Lord lay waste (Hag 1:4-9), in following Jesus for the loaves and fishes (Jn 6:26).

Money changers in the temple (Mt 21:12-13; Lk 19:45-46; Jn 2:14-16). The rich young ruler (Mt 19:16-22). The rich fool (Lk 12:15-21). Judas, in betraying Jesus for thirty pieces of silver (Mt 26:15-16; Mk 14:10-11; Lk 22:3-6; Jn 12:6). The unjust steward (Lk 16:1-8). The Pharisees (Lk 16:14).

Simon Magus, in trying to buy the gift of the Holy Spirit (Ac 8:18-23). The sorcerers, in filing complaint against Paul and Silas (Ac 16:19). Demetrius, in raising a riot against Paul and Silas (Ac 19:24, 27). Felix, in hoping for a bribe from Paul (Ac 24:26). Demas, in forsaking Paul for love of the world (2Ti 4:10).

See Avarice; Bribery; Covetousness; Rich, The; Riches.

GREEK LANGUAGE Was a branch of the Indo-European family from which most of the languages of Europe are descended. The Attic dialect spoken in Athens and its colonies on the Ionian coast was combined with other dialects in the army of Alexander the Great and was spread by his conquests through the East. A kind of "Jewish Greek," influenced by semitic thought and culture, was widely spoken in Israel and became the chief language of the early church (Ac 21:37).

GREEK VERSIONS There were several early translations of the Hebrew OT into Greek. Some of the major versions were:

1. The Septuagint, originating in Alexandria in the third and second centuries B.C.. This was the Bible of the early church.

2. The version of Aquila in the early second century A.D. 125) was a word-for-word rendering of the Hebrew produced for the Jewish people when Christians took over the Septuagint.

3. The version of Theodotion, a late second-century revision of the Septuagint.

4. The version of Symmachus, an idiomatic translation probably of the second century.

GREETINGS Antiquity of (Ge 18:2; 19:1).

Given:

By brothers to each other (1Sa 17:22). By inferiors to their superiors (Ge 47:7). By superiors to inferiors (1Sa 30:21). By all passersby (1Sa 10:3-4; Ps 129:8). On entering a house (Jdg 18:15; Mt 10:12; Lk 1:40-41, 44). Often sent through messengers (1Sa 25:5, 14; 2Sa 8:10). Often sent by letter (Ro 16:21-23; 1Co 16:21; Col 4:18; 2Th 3:17). Denied to persons of bad character (2Jn 10). Persons in haste excused from giving or receiving (2Ki 4:29; Lk 10:24).

Expressions Used as:

"You are welcome at my house" (Jdg 19:20).

"Long life to you! Good health to you and your household! And good health to all that is yours" (1Sa 25:6).

"Peace to this house" (Lk 10:5).

"The LORD be with you! The LORD bless you!" (Ru 2:4).

"The blessing of the LORD be upon you; we bless you in the name of the LORD" (Ps 129:8).

"The LORD bless you! I have carried out the [LORD's] instructions" (1Sa 15:13).

"God be gracious to you my son" (Ge 43:29).

"How are you, my brother?" (2Sa 20:9).

"Greetings, Rabbi!" (Mt 26:49).

"Greetings, you who are highly favored! The Lord is with you" (Lk 1:28).

"Greetings" (Mt 28:9).

Sometimes insincere (2Sa 20:9; Mt 26:49). Given to Christ in derision (Mt 27:29, w Mk 15:18).

Often Accompanied by:

Embracing and kissing (Ge 33:4; 45:14-15; Lk 15:20). Taking hold of the beard with the right hand (2Sa 20:9). Bowing frequently to the ground (Ge 33:3). Embracing and kissing the feet (Mt 28:9; Lk 7:38, 45). Touching the hem of the garment (Mt 14:36). Falling prostrate on the ground (Est 8:3; Mt 2:11; Lk 8:41). Kissing the dust (Ps 72:9; Isa 49:23). The Jews are condemned for giving only to their own countrymen (Mt 5:47). The Pharisees condemned for seeking, in public (Mt 23:7; Mk 12:38).

GREYHOUND NIV "strutting rooster" (Pr 30:31). *See Animals.*

GRIEF Attributed to the Holy Spirit (Eph 4:30; Heb 3:10, 17). *See Affliction; Sorrow.*

GRIND To pulverize grain between two millstones (Mt 24:41; Lk 17:35). *See Mill; Millstone.*

GROUND Man made from (Ge 2:7; 3:19, 23; Job 4:19; 33:6). Animals from (Ge 2:19). Vegetables from (Ge 2:9). Cursed (Ge 3:17; 5:29).

GROVES

1. Groups of fruit trees (Dt 6:11; Ecc 2:6). *See Tree.*

2. NIV "Asherah [poles]"; an image of the Canaanite goddess Asherah. *See Asherah, 2; High Places; Idolatry.*

GROWTH *See Conformity; Discipleship; Grace of God, Growth in; Holiness; Sanctification.*

GRUMBLING

Condemned:

Forbidden (1Co 10:10; Php 2:14*; Jas 5:9*). Rebuked (Job 15:11-13*; Ecc 7:10*; La 3:39*; Ro 9:19-20*). Punishment for (Nu 14:26-37*; 17:10-11). Foolish (Pr 19:3*).

Against Others:

Cain (Ge 4:13-14). Moses (Ex 5:22-23*; Nu 11:11-15). Israelites (Ex 16:8*, 12*; 17:2-3; Nu 11:1-10; 14; 16:41; 20:2-5; 21:5-6; Dt 1:26-28; Ps 44:9-26*; 106:24-26; Mal 3:14*). Korah (Nu 16:8-11). Job (Job 3; 6; 7; 9:10; 13; 16:6-14; 19:7-20; 30; 33:12-13*). David (2Sa 6:8; Ps 116:10-11). The psalmist (Ps 73:13-22*). Elijah (1Ki 19:4, 10). Jonah (Jnh 4). Jews, against Jesus (Jn 6:41-43, 52).

Against Moses:

By the Israelites (Ex 5:21; 14:11-12; 15:24; 16:2-3; 17:2-3; Nu 14; 16:2-3, 14, 41; 20:2-5).

Against Others:

Rachel (Ge 30:1). Asaph (Ps 73:3). Solomon (Ecc 2:17-18). Hezekiah (Isa 38:10-18). Jeremiah (Jer 20:14-18; La 3). Martha (Lk 10:40*).

See Doubt; Envy; Ingratitude; also Contentment; Resignation.

GUARD Imperial guard (Ge 37:36; 2Ki 25:8; Da 2:14), runner, trusted messengers of a king (1Ki 14:27-28), bodyguard (2Sa 23:23), executioner (Mk 6:27), Roman guard (Mt 27:65).

GUDGODAH (*cleft*). A station of the Israelites in the wilderness (Dt 10:7), probably identical with Hor Haggidgad (Nu 33:32-33).

GUEST Greetings to (Ge 18:2). Abraham's hospitality to. *See Hospitality.*

Rules for the conduct of (Pr 23:1-3, 6-8; 25:6-7, 17; Lk 10:5-7; 14:7-11; 1Co 10:27). *See Hospitality.*

GUEST ROOM According to Jewish custom an extra or upper room was offered to those who had come to Jerusalem to celebrate the Passover (Mk 14:14; Lk 22:11).

GUIDANCE *See God, Guidance of.*

GUILE *See Conspiracy; Deceit; Hypocrisy.*

GUILELESSNESS Truthfulness; without deceit. Commanded (Ps 34:13; 1Pe 2:1; 3:10). Of Jesus (1Pe 2:22). Of Nathanael (Jn 1:47). A grace of the righteous (Ps 32:2). *See Truthfulness.*

GUILT The deserving of punishment because of infraction of a law. Guilt could be the result of unconscious sin (Lev 5:17) or could be incurred by the group for the sin of an individual (Jos 7:10-15). There are degrees of guilt (Lk 12:47-48; Ac 17:30), but in the sight of God all people are guilty of sin (Ro 3:19).

See Conviction, of Sin.

GUILT OFFERING Sacrifice of a ram for the purpose of expiation of sins against others; in addition to the sacrifice, restitution had to be made (Lev 5:16-19; 6:5-18; 7:1-10; Nu 5:7-8). Of the Servant's self-sacrifice (Isa 53:10 w Mt 20:28; Mk 10:45). *See Offerings.*

GULL A bird. Forbidden as food (Lev 11:16; Dt 14:15).

GUM RESIN Fragrant ingredient used in incense (Ex 30:34). *See Aromatic Resin; Incense.*

GUNI (*spotted sand grouse*).

1. Son of Naphtali (Ge 46:24; 1Ch 7:13) and his clan (Nu 26:48).

2. Father of Abdiel (1Ch 5:15).

GUR Place where Jehu slew Ahaziah (2Ki 9:27).

GUR BAAL (*sojourn of Baal*). A town probably located S of Beersheba (2Ch 26:7).

GUTTER Of the temple in Ezekiel's vision (Eze 43:13, 14, 17).

H

HAAHASHTARI (*the Ahashtarites*). Son of Naarah (1Ch 4:6).

HAARALOTH *See Gibeath Haaraloth.*

HABAIAH *See Hobaiah.*

HABAKKUK (*garden plant* KB). Prophet of the book which bears his name; wrote when the temple was still standing (Hab 2:20; 3:19), between c. 605-587 B.C., probably during the reign of the Judean king Jehoiakim.

HABAKKUK, BOOK OF (*garden plant* KB).

Author: Habakkuk

Date: Close to the battle of Carchemish (605 B.C.)

Outline:

I. Title (1:1).

II. Habakkuk's First Complaint: Why Does the Evil in Judah Go Unpunished? (1:2-4).

III. God's Answer: The Babylonians Will Punish Judah (1:5-11).

IV. Habakkuk's Second Complaint: How Can a Just God Use Wicked Babylon to Punish a People More Righteous Than Themselves? (1:12-2:1).

V. God's Answer: Babylon Will Be Punished, and Faith Will Be Rewarded (2:2-20).

VI. Habakkuk's Prayer: After Asking for Manifestations of God's Wrath and Mercy (as in the past), He Closes With Confession of Trust and Joy in God (ch. 3).

See Prophets, The Minor.

HABAZZINIAH (possibly *exuberant in Yahweh*). Head of the family of Recabites (Jer 35:3).

HABERGEON NIV "(coat of) armor," "javelin." *See Armor; Breastplate; Coat of Mail.*

HABIRU A people mentioned in Mari, Nuzi, and Amarna tablets; fundamental meaning seems to be "wanderers"; of mixed racial origin, including both Semites and non-Semites. Connection with Hebrews is obscure.

HABIT (Ex 21:29, 36; Nu 22:30; Jer 13:23; 22:21; Mic 2:1; 1Ti 5:13; Heb 10:25).

HABOR A river of Mesopotamia (2Ki 17:6; 18:11; 1Ch 5:26).

HACALIAH (*dark*). Father of Nehemiah (Ne 1:1; 10:1).

HACHILAH *See Hakilah.*

HACMONI, HACMONITE (*wise*). Father of Jehiel and Jashobeam (2Sa 23:8, ftn; 1Ch 11:11; 27:32). *See Tahkemonite.*

HADAD (*thunderer [Semitic storm god]*).

1. Grandson of Abraham (Ge 25:15).

2. A king of Edom (Ge 36:35-36; 1Ch 1:46-47).

3. Another king of Edom (Ge 36:39, ftn; 1Ch 1:50-51).

4. A member of the royal house of Edom who escaped to Egypt when David conquered Edom and then later returned to his homeland to revolt against Solomon (1Ki 11:14-25). The Hebrew actually reads "Adad" for the first "Hadad" in 1Ki 11:17, and it has been conjectured that 1Ki 11:14ff. combines two accounts, one of Hadad the Edomite and the other of Adad the Midianite. Convincing reasons have been given for identifying this Hadad with 3 above.

5. The ancient Semitic storm god who as the great Baal of the Ugaritic pantheon figured in the struggle of the religion of Israel against Canaanite religion.

HADAD RIMMON A place in the valley of Megiddo (Zec 12:11).

HADADEZER (*[pagan god] Hadad is a help*). Son of Rehob, king of Zobah, vanquished by David (2Sa 8:3-13; 10:15-19; 1Ki 11:23; 1Ch 18:3-10; 19:6-19).

HADAR (*thunderer, Semitic storm god*).

1. Son of Ishmael (Ge 25:15 KJV). *See Hadad, 1.*

2. King of Edom (Ge 36:39, ftn.). *See Hadad, 3.*

HADAREZER *See Hadadezer.*

HADASHAH (*new*). A town in Judah (Jos 15:37).

HADASSAH (*myrtle* BDB and KB; possibly *myrtle* or *bride* IDB). The Hebrew name of Esther (Est 2:7). *See Esther.*

HADATTAH *See Hazor Hadattah.*

HADES (*the underworld*). The unseen world (Mt 11:23; 16:18; Lk 10:15; 16:23; Ac 2:27, 31; Rev 1:18; 6:8; 20:13-14). The realm (or state) of the dead is usually expressed in Hebrew by *sheol* and in Greek by *hades* (2Sa 22:6; Job 26:5; Ps 6:5; 17:15; 30:9; 49:15; 86:13; 88:10-12; 115:17; 116:3; Pr 15:24; 21:16; 27:20; Ecc 9:4-6; Isa 5:14; Jnh 2:2; Lk 23:42-43; Jn 8:22; 2Co 12:4).

See Grave; Hell; Immortality; Paradise; Righteous, Promises to; Sheol; Spirit; Wicked, Punishment of.

HADID (*sharp*). A city of Benjamin. Captive of, returned from Babylon (Ezr 2:33; Ne 7:37; 11:34).

HADLAI (*resting* ISBE; *fat* IDB; *be stout* KB). Father of Amasa (2Ch 28:12).

HADORAM (*Hadad is exalted*).

1. Descendant of Shem (Ge 10:27; 1Ch 1:21).

2. Son of Tou (1Ch 18:10). Called Joram (2Sa 8:10).

3. Hebrew *Adoram* (2Sa 20:24, ftn) or *Hadoram* (2Ch 10:18, ftn), a variant of *Adoniram*. An officer in charge of forced labor during the reigns of David and then Solomon. He then held the same office under Rehoboam, Solomon's son. *See Adoniram.*

HADRACH A district of Syria (Zec 9:1).

HAELEPH A town of Benjamin, near Jerusalem (Jos 18:28).

HAGAB (*locust*). Ancestor of the temple servants who returned with Zerubbabel (Ezr 2:46).

HAGABA, HAGABAH (*locust*). One of the temple servants (Ezr 2:45; Ne 7:48).

HAGAR (*emigration, flight*). A servant of Abraham and handmaid of Sarah. Given by Sarah to Abraham to be his wife (Ge 16). Descendants of (Ge 25:12-15; 1Ch 5:10, 19-22; Ps 83:6, ftn). Allegorically identified with slavery to the law (Gal 4:24-25).

HAGARENES *See Hagar.*

HAGARITES, HAGERITES *See Hagrite(s).*

HAGGAI (*festal* BDB; *born on the feast day* KB). Haggai was a prophet who, with Zechariah, encouraged the returned exiles to rebuild the temple (Ezr 5:1-2; 6:14). The prophet's name ("festal, ") may indicate he was born during one of the three pilgrimage feasts (Unleavened Bread, Pentecost or Weeks, and Tabernacles; cf. Dt 16:16). Based on 2:3 Haggai may have witnessed the destruction of Solomon's temple. If so, he must have been in his early 70s during his ministry.

HAGGAI, BOOK OF

Author: Haggai

Date:

The messages of Haggai were given during a four-month period in 520 B.C., the second year of King Darius. The first message was delivered on the first day of the sixth month (Aug. 29), the last on the 24th day of the ninth month (Dec. 18).

Outline:

I. First Message: The Call to Rebuild the Temple (1:1-11).

 A. The People's Lame Excuse (1:1-4).

 B. The Poverty of the People (1:5-6).

 C. The Reason God Has Cursed Them (1:7-11).

II. The Response of Zerubbabel and the People (1:12-15).

 A. The Leaders and Remnant Obey (1:12).

 B. The Lord Strengthens the Workers (1:13-15).

III. Second Message: The Temple to Be Filled With Glory (2:1-9).

 A. The People Encouraged (2:1-5).

 B. The Promise of Glory and Peace (2:6-9).

IV. Third Message: A Defiled People Purified and Blessed (2:10-19).

 A. The Rapid Spread of Sin (2:10-14).

 B. Poor Harvests Because of Disobedience (2:15-17).

 C. Blessing to Come as the Temple Is Rebuilt (2:18-19).

V. Fourth Message: The Promise to Zerubbabel (2:20-23).

 A. The Judgment of the Nations (2:20-22).

 B. The Significance of Zerubbabel (2:23).

See Prophets, The Minor.

H

HAGGAN *See Beth Haggan.*

HAGGEDOLIM (*the great ones*). The father of Zabdiel, a priest (Ne 11:14).

HAGGI, HAGGITE (*festal* BDB; *born on the feast day* KB). Son of Gad (Ge 46:16) and his clan (Nu 26:15).

HAGGIAH (*feast of Yahweh*). A Levite (1Ch 6:30).

HAGGIDGAD *See Hor Haggidgad.*

HAGGITH (*festal* BDB; *born on the feast day* KB). Wife of David. Mother of Adonijah (2Sa 3:4; 1Ki 1:5, 11; 2:13; 1Ch 3:2).

HAGGOYIM *See Harosheth Haggoyim.*

HAGIOGRAPHA (*holy writings*). The third division of the Hebrew OT: Psalms, Proverbs, Job, Song of Solomon, Ruth, Lamentations, Ecclesiastes, Esther, Daniel, Ezra, Nehemiah, 1 and 2 Chronicles.

HAGRI (*wanderer*). Father of Mibhar (2Sa 23:36; 1Ch 11:38).

HAGRITE(S) (possibly *people from Hagar*). Descendants of Hagar, mother of Ishmael with whom Saul made war (1Ch 5:10, 19-21; 27:31; Ps 83:6, ftn).

HAHIROTH *See Pi Hahiroth.*

HAI *See Ai.*

HAIL (Job 38:22; Hag 2:17). Plague of, in Egypt (Ex 9:18-29; Ps 78:48; 105:32). Destroys army of the Amorites (Jos 10:11).
Figurative: (Isa 28:2; Rev 8:7; 11:19; 16:21).

HAIR Numbered (Mt 10:30; Lk 12:7). Worn long by women (Isa 3:24; Lk 7:38; 1Co 11:5-6, 15; 1Ti 2:9; 1Pe 3:3; Rev 9:8), by Absalom (2Sa 14:26). Worn short by men (1Co 11:14). Symbolic dividing of (Eze 5:1-2).
See Baldness; Leprosy; Mourning; Nazirite(s), Nazarite(s).

HAKILAH A hill in Judah where David and his followers hid from Saul (1Sa 23:19; 26:3).

HAKKATAN (*the small one*). Father of Johanan (Ezr 8:12).

HAKKEREM *See Beth Hakkerem.*

HAKKORE *See En Hakkore.*

HAKKOZ (*the thorn*).
1. The eponym of a family of priests in David's time (1Ch 24:10). Members of this family were among those unable to document their claim to priestly rank after the Exile and so were suspended from office (Ezr 2:61; Ne 7:63).
2. Ancestor of Meremoth, who helped repair the wall of Jerusalem (Ne 3:4, 21).

HAKUPHA (*crooked*). One of the temple servants (Ezr 2:51; Ne 7:53).

HALAH A place to which Israelite captives were transported (2Ki 17:6; 18:11; 1Ch 5:26).

HALAK, MOUNT OF (*bare, bald*). A mountain, the southern limit of Joshua's conquests (Jos 11:17; 12:7).

HALF-HOMER *See Homer; Measure.*

HALF-TRIBE *See Manasseh, 2.*

HALHUL A city in Judah (Jos 15:58).

HALI (*adornment*). A border town of Asher (Jos 19:25).

HALL
1. Court of the high priest's palace (Lk 22:55).
2. Official residence of a Roman governor (Mt 27:27; Mk 15:16).

HALLEL (*praise*). Two liturgical collections of Psalms read at Passover. Psalms 113-118 called the "Egyptian Hallel"; Psalm 136, "the Hallel"; Psalms 120-136 are often called the "Great Hallel." *See Passover.*

HALLELUJAH (*praise Yahweh*). Liturgical exclamation urging all to praise Yahweh. Occurs at the beginning of Psalms 106, 111-113, 117, 135, 146-150 and at the close of 104-106, 113, 115-117, 135, 146-150. *See Praise.*

HALLOHESH (*the whisperer*). Father of Shallum (Ne 3:12). Sealed the covenant with Nehemiah (Ne 10:24).

HALLOW, HALLOWED (*to render as holy*). To set apart for sacred use; to hold sacred; to reverence as holy (Ex 20:11; Mt 6:9).

HAM
1. Son of Noah (Ge 5:32; 9:18, 24; 1Ch 1:4). Provokes Noah's wrath, resulting in curse on Ham's son Canaan (Ge 9:18-27). His children (Ge 10:6-20; 1Ch 1:8-16).
2. Family name of the descendants of Ham (1Ch 4:40; Ps 78:51; 105:23, 27; 106:22).
3. Place where Kedorlaomer killed the Zuzites (Ge 14:5).

HAMAN Prime minister of Xerxes, king of Persia (Est 3:1, 10; 7:7-10).

HAMATH, HAMATHITES (*fortress*). A city of upper Syria; the N border of the ideal limits of the Promised Land (Nu 13:21; 34:8; Jos 13:5; Eze 47:16). Solomon's kingdom extended from the Wadi of Egypt to the entrance of Hamath (1Ki 8:65), and

the kingdom of Israel at the time of Jeroboam reached northward to the entrance of Hamath (2Ki 14:25; Am 6:14). Inhabited by Canaanites (Ge 10:18). Prosperity of (Am 6:2). David receives gifts of gold and silver from Tou, king of (2Sa 8:9-10; 1Ch 18:3, 9-10). Conquest of, by Jeroboam (2Ki 14:25, 28), by the Chaldeans (2Ki 25:20-21). Israelites taken captive to (Isa 11:11). Prophecy concerning (Jer 49:23). Solomon builds store cities in (2Ch 8:4).

HAMATH ZOBAH (*fortress of Zobah*). A town on the border of Israel. Subdued by Solomon (2Ch 8:3).

HAMMAHLEKOTH *See Sela Hammahlekoth.*

HAMMATH (*hot springs*).
1. Fortified city of Naphtali, c. one mile S of Tiberias (Jos 19:35).
2. Founder of Recabites (1Ch 2:55).

HAMMEDATHA (*given by the moon [god]*). Father of Haman (Est 3:1, 10; 8:5; 9:10, 24).

HAMMELECH NIV "the king" (Jer 36:26; 38:6).

HAMMER A tool used for a variety of purposes: Smoothing metals (Isa 41:7), driving tent pins (Jdg 4:21), forging (Isa 44:12). Sometimes used figuratively for any crushing power (Jer 23:29; 50:23).

HAMMOLEKETH (*the queen*). Daughter of Makir (1Ch 7:17-18).

HAMMON (*hot springs*).
1. A city of Asher (Jos 19:28).
2. A Levitical city of Naphtali (1Ch 6:76). Possibly identical with Hammath and Hammoth Dor.

HAMMOTH DOR (*hot spring of Dor*). Naphtali (Jos 21:32). Possibly identical with Hammath (Jos 19:35). Called Hammon (1Ch 6:76).

HAMMUEL (*God [El] of Ham* KB). A Simeonite (1Ch 4:26).

HAMMURABI King of Babylon (c. 1704-1662 B.C.). Not the same as Amraphel (Ge 14:1-12). He was a great builder and lawgiver (Code of Hammurabi). *See Texts, Ancient Near Eastern Non-Biblical Texts Relating to the Old Testament.*

HAMON *See Baal Hamon; Hamon Gog.*

HAMON GOG, VALLEY OF (*multitude of Gog*). Prophetic name for place E of Dead Sea where the "multitude of Gog" will be buried (Eze 39:11-15).

HAMONAH (*multitude*). Prophetic name of city near which Gog is defeated (Eze 39:16).

HAMOR (*male donkey*). Father of Shechem. Jacob buys ground from (Ge 33:19; Jos 24:32; Jdg 9:28). Murdered by the sons of Jacob (Ge 34:26; 49:6). Called Hamor (Ac 7:16).

HAMSTRING Disabling an animal by cutting the large tendon at the back of the knee, usually to render it useless for military service. Of horses (Jos 11:6, 9; 2Sa 8:4; 1Ch 18:4). Of oxen (Ge 49:6).

HAMUL, HAMULITE (*pitied*). Son of Perez (Ge 46:12; 1Ch 2:5) and his clan (Nu 26:21).

HAMUTAL (*my husband's father is like dew*). Wife of Josiah. Mother of Jehoahaz and Zedekiah (2Ki 23:31; 24:18; Jer 52:1).

HANAMEL (*God [El] is gracious*). Cousin of Jeremiah, to whom he sold a field in Anathoth (Jer 32:7-12).

HANAN (*gracious*).
1. Son of Shashak (1Ch 8:23).
2. Son of Azel (1Ch 8:38; 9:44).
3. One of David's mighty men (1Ch 11:43).
4. One of the temple servants (Ezr 2:46; Ne 7:49).
5. A Levite (Ne 8:7; 10:10). Probably identical with the one mentioned in Ne 13:13.
6. A chief who sealed the covenant with Nehemiah (Ne 10:22, 26).
7. An officer in the temple (Jer 35:2-10).

HANANEL, TOWER OF (*God [El] is gracious*). Name of a tower forming part of the wall of Jerusalem (Ne 3:1; 12:39; Jer 31:38; Zec 14:10).

HANANI (*gracious*).
1. Son of Heman (1Ch 25:4, 25).
2. A prophet who rebuked Asa, king of Judah (2Ch 16:7).
3. Father of Jehu the prophet (1Ki 16:1, 7; 2Ch 19:2; 20:34). Possibly identical with 2.
4. A priest (Ezr 10:20).
5. A brother of Nehemiah and keeper of the gates of Jerusalem (Ne 1:2; 7:2).
6. A priest and musician (Ne 12:36).

HANANIAH (*Yahweh is gracious*).
1. Son of Heman (1Ch 25:4, 23).
2. A captain of Uzziah's army (2Ch 26:11).
3. Father of Zedekiah (Jer 36:12).
4. A prophet of Gibeon who uttered false prophecies in the temple during the reign of Zedekiah (Jer 28).
5. Grandfather of Irijah (Jer 37:13).
6. Son of Shashak (1Ch 8:24).
7. Hebrew name of Shadrach. *See Shadrach.*
8. Son of Zerubbabel (1Ch 3:19, 21).
9. Son of Bebai (Ezr 10:28).
10. A priest (Ne 3:8).
11. Son of Shelemiah (Ne 3:30).
12. A keeper of the gates of Jerusalem (Ne 7:2).

13. One who sealed the covenant (Ne 10:23).
14. A priest in time of Jehoiakim (Ne 12:12, 41).

HAND

Ceremonial:
Laying on of hands (Heb 6:2), in consecration (Ge 48:14; Ex 29:10, 15, 19; Lev 1:4; 3:2, 8, 13; 4:15, 24, 33; 16:21), in ordaining the Levites (Nu 8:10-11), Joshua (Nu 27:18-23; Dt 34:9), Timothy (1Ti 4:14; 2Ti 1:6), in healing (Mk 6:5; 7:32; 16:18; Lk 4:40; Ac 28:8), in blessing children (Mt 19:13; Mk 10:16); in solemnizing testimony (Lev 24:14). Lifted up in benediction (Lev 9:22; Lk 24:50), in prayer. *See Hands, Laying on of; Prayer, Attitudes in.*
Ceremonial washing of (Mt 15:2; Mk 7:2-5). *See Washings; Cleanliness.*

Symbolic:
Symbol of righteousness (Job 17:9). Washing of, a symbol of innocence (Dt 21:6; Mt 27:24).
Clasping of, in token of contract (Ezr 10:19; Pr 6:1; 17:18; Eze 17:18), of friendship (2Ki 10:15; Job 17:3). Right hand lifted up in swearing (Ge 14:22; Ps 106:26; Isa 62:8), symbol of power (Isa 23:11; 41:10), place of honor (Ps 45:9; 80:17).

Figurative:
(Mt 5:30; 18:8; Mk 9:43).

Anthropomorphic Use of:
Hand of the Lord considered limited in power (Nu 11:23), is mighty (Jos 4:24), was heavy (1Sa 5:6), against the Philistines (1Sa 7:13), on Elijah (1Ki 18:46), not limited in power (Isa 59:11), was with the early Christians (Ac 11:21). *See Anthropomorphisms.*

HANDBREADTH A measure, about four inches (Ex 25:25; 1Ki 7:26; 2Ch 4:5; Ps 39:5; Isa 48:13; Eze 40:5, 43; Jer 52:21). *See Fingers, Fingerbreadth; Span.*

HANDKERCHIEF Sometimes translated "cloth," used for a variety of purposes (Lk 19:20-23; Jn 11:44; 20:7; Ac 19:12).

HANDLE Door knob (SS 5:5).

HANDMAID, HANDMAIDEN Female slave or servant. *See Maid(s); Maidservant(s); Servant.*

HANDS, LAYING ON OF Ceremony having the idea of transference, identification, and devotion to God (Ex 29:10, 15, 19; Lev 16:21; Ac 8:14-17; 2Ti 1:6). *See Hand.*

HANDSTAFF NIV "war clubs" (Eze 39:9). *See Club.*

HANES A place in Egypt (Isa 30:4).

HANGING Not a form of capital punishment in Bible times. Where used, except 2Sa 17:23; Mt 27:5, it refers to the suspension of a body from a tree or post after the criminal had been put to death (Ge 40:19, 22; Dt 21:22).

HANGINGS Material hung in the tabernacle so as to preserve the privacy and sacredness of that which was within (Ex 27:9-19; Mt 27:51).

HANIEL *See Hanniel, 2.*

HANNAH (*favor*). Mother of Samuel. Her trials, prayer, and promise (1Sa 1:1-18). Samuel born to, dedicates him to God, leaves him at the temple (1Sa 1:19-28). Her hymn of praise (1Sa 2:1-10). Visits Samuel at the temple(annually Sa 2:18-19). Children of (1Sa 2:20-21).

HANNATHON A city of Zebulun (Jos 19:14).

HANNIEL (*favor of God [El]*).
1. A son of Ephod, appointed by Moses to divide the land among the several tribes (Nu 34:23).
2. A son of Ulla (1Ch 7:39).

HANOCH, HANOCHITE (*initiation*).
1. Grandson of Abraham by Keturah (Ge 25:4; 1Ch 1:33).
2. Son of Reuben (Ge 46:9; Ex 6:14; 1Ch 5:3) and his clan (Nu 26:5).

HANUKKAH (*dedication*). The Feast of Rededication. After Judas Maccabeus had cleansed the temple from the pollution of pagan worship (c. 165 B.C.), the twenty-fifth of Kislev (December) was kept annually in memory of this.
See Dedication; Feasts; Kislev; Maccabees; Month, 9.

HANUN (*favored*).
1. King of Ammon who provoked David to war (2Sa 10:1-5; 1Ch 19:1-5).
2. Two men who helped repair wall of Jerusalem (Ne 3:13, 30).

HAPHARAIM, HAPHRAIM (*place of two trenches*). A city of Issachar (Jos 19:19).

HAPPINESS

Of the Wicked:
Limited to this life (Ps 17:14; Lk 16:25), short (Job 20:5), uncertain (Lk 12:20), vain (Ecc 2:1; 7:6).
Is derived from their wealth (Job 21:13; Ps 52:7), their power (Job 21:7; Ps 37:35), their worldly prosperity (Ps 17:14; 73:3-4, 7), gluttony (Isa 22:13; Hab 1:16), drunkenness (Isa 5:11; 56:12), vain pleasure (Job 21:12; Isa 5:12), successful oppression (Hab 1:15). Marred by jealousy (Est 5:13), often interrupted by judgments (Nu 11:33; Job 15:21; Ps 73:18-20; Jer 25:10-11). Leads to sorrow (Pr 14:13). Leads to recklessness (Isa 22:12). Sometimes a stumbling block to saints (Ps 73:3, 16; Jer 12:1; Hab 1:13). Saints often permitted to see the end of (Ps 73:17-20), envy not (Ps 37:1). Woe against (Am 6:1; Lk 6:25).
Illustrated (Ps 37:35-36; Lk 12:16-20; 16:19-25).
Exemplified: Israel (Nu 11:33). Haman (Est 5:9-11). Belshazzar (Da 5:1). Herod (Ac 12:21-23).

Of the Righteous:

In the Lord, through abundance (Ps 36:8; Ecc 2:24-26; 3:12-13, 22). In chastisement (Job 5:17-27). In fellowship (Ps 133:1). In good works (Pr 14:21; Ecc 3:12; Mt 5:3-9). In hope (Ro 5:2). In obedience (Ps 40:8; 128:1-2; 144:15; 146:5; Pr 16:20; 28:14; 29:18). In peace (Php 4:7). In persecution (Mt 3:10-11; 2Co 12:10; 1Pe 3:14; 4:12). In protection (Dt 33:29; Isa 12:2-3). In satisfaction (Ps 63:5). Trust (Pr 16:20). In wisdom (Pr 3:13-18).

Beatitudes (Mt 5:3-12).

See Joy; Peace; Praise.

HAPPIZZEZ A governor of the temple (1Ch 24:15).

HARA (*hill, highland*). Place in Assyria to which Israelites were exiled by Assyrians (1Ch 5:26).

HARADAH (*place of fear*). One of the camps of Israel (Nu 33:24-25).

HARAM *See Beth Haram.*

HARAN (earlier *mountaineer,* but perhaps *sanctuary*).
1. Father of Lot and brother of Abraham (Ge 11:26-31).
2. Son of Caleb (1Ch 2:46).
3. A Levite (1Ch 23:9).
4. A place in Mesopotamia to which Terah and Abraham migrated (Ge 11:31; 12:4-5; Ac 7:2, 4). Death of Terah at (Ge 11:32). Abraham leaves, by divine command (Ge 12:1-5). Jacob flees to (Ge 27:43; 28:7; 29), returns from, with Rachel and Leah (Ge 31:17-21). Conquest of, by king of Assyria (2Ki 19:12). Merchants of (Eze 27:23). Idolatry in (Jos 24:2, 14; Isa 37:12).

HARARITE (*mountain dweller*). A place or family name (2Sa 23:11, 33; 1Ch 11:34).

HARASHIM *See Ge Harashim.*

HARBONA (*donkey driver*). Eunuch of Xerxes (Est 1:10; 7:9).

HARD, HARD-HEARTED *See Obduracy.*

HARDEST STONE The Lord makes Ezekiel's forehead harder than "the hardest stone" (Eze 3:9). *See Adamant; Diamond; Flint; Minerals of the Bible, 1; Stones.*

HARE *See Animals; Rabbit.*

HAREM The wives and concubines of a king (Ecc 2:8; Est 2:3, 13-14).

HAREPH (*autumn,* or *sharp* IDB; *scornful* ISBE). Son of Caleb (1Ch 2:51).

HARESETH *See Kir Hareseth.*

HARHAIAH Father of Uzziel (Ne 3:8).

HARHAS Grandfather of the husband of Huldah, the prophetess (2Ki 22:14). Called Hasrah (2Ch 34:22).

HARHUR (possibly *fever* BDB; possibly *raven* IDB; *one born during his mother's fever* KB). Head of a family that returned with Zerubbabel (Ezr 2:51; Ne 7:53).

HARIM (*consecrated [to Yahweh]*).
1. Priest (1Ch 24:8).
2. Family that returned with Zerubbabel (Ezr 2:39; Ne 7:35).
3. Family of priests (Ezr 2:39; 10:21; Ne 7:42; 12:15).
4. Family that married foreign wives (Ezr 10:31).
5. Father of a worker on the wall (Ne 3:11).
6. A man who sealed the covenant (Ne 10:27).

HARIPH (*one born at harvest time*).
1. One of the exiles (Ne 7:24). Probably the same as Jorah (Ezr 2:18).
2. One who sealed the covenant (Ne 10:19).

HARLOT *See Adultery; Prostitute..*

HARLOTRY *See Adultery; Prostitute.*

HARMON Possibly a place name (Am 4:3, ftn.).

HARNEPHER (*[pagan god] Horus is merciful*). Asherite (1Ch 7:36).

HAROD, HARODITE (*trembling*). Spring beside which Gideon encamped (Jdg 7:1). Family name of Shammah and Elika (2Sa 23:25).

HAROEH (*the seer*). Grandson of Caleb (1Ch 2:52).

HARORITE Shammoth, one of David's mighty men (1Ch 11:27).

HAROSHETH HAGGOYIM (*Harosheth of the nations*). Town in N Israel c. sixteen miles NW of Megiddo; home of Sisera (Jdg 4:2, 13, 16).

HARP A stringed instrument of music (Isa 38:20; Eze 33:32; Hab 3:19). With three strings (1Sa 18:6), ten strings (Ps 33:2; 92:3; 144:9; 150:4). Originated with Jubal (Ge 4:21). Made of almugwood (1Ki 10:12). David skillful in playing (1Sa 16:16, 23). Used in worship (1Sa 10:5; 1Ch 16:5; 25:1-7; 2Ch 5:12-13; 29:25; Ps 33:2; 43:4; 49:4; 57:8; 71:22; 81:2; 93:3; 98:5; 108:2; 147:7; 149:3; 150:3). Used, in national jubilees, after the triumph over Goliath (1Sa 18:6), over the armies of Ammon and Moab (2Ch 20:20-29), when the new walls of Jerusalem were dedicated (Ne 12:27, 36). Used in festivities (Ge 31:27; Job 21:11-12; Isa 5:12; 23:16; 24:8; 30:32; Eze 26:13; Rev 18:22), in mourning (Job 30:31). Discordant (1Co 14:7). Hung on the willows by the captive Israelites (Ps 137:2). Heard in heaven, in John's apocalyptic vision (Rev 5:8; 14:2; 15:2). The symbol used in the Psalms to indicate

when the harp was to be introduced in the music was *neginah* or *neginoth.* See titles of Pss 4; 6; 54; 55; 61; 67; 76.

See Music, Instruments of, Symbols Used in.

HARROW Instrument for dragging or leveling off a field (Job 39:10), "breaking up the soil" (Isa 28:24; Hos 10:11). *See Picks, Iron.*

HARSHA (*deaf*). One of the temple servants (Ezr 2:52; Ne 7:54).

HART *See Deer.*

HARUM (*consecrated*). A descendant of Judah (1Ch 4:8).

HARUMAPH (*disfigured nose*). Father of Jedaiah (Ne 3:10).

HARUPHITE (*sharp* or *autumn*). Designation of Shephatiah (1Ch 12:5).

HARUZ (perhaps *gold,* or *eager*). Father-in-law of King Manasseh (2Ki 21:19).

HARVEST Sabbath to be observed in (Ex 34:21). Sabbath desecrated in (Ne 13:15-22).
Of wheat at Pentecost, in Israel (Ex 34:22; Lev 23:15-17), and before vintage (Lev 26:5). Of barley, before wheat (Ex 9:31-32).
Celebrated with joy (Jdg 9:27; Isa 9:3; 16:10; Jer 48:33). Promises of plentiful (Ge 8:22; Jer 5:24; Joel 2:23-24).

Figurative: (Job 24:5; Ps 10:5; Jer 8:20; Joel 3:13; Mt 9:37; 13:39; Lk 10:2; Rev 14:15).

See Pentecost, 1; Tabernacles, Feast of; Firstfruits; Reaping; Glean, Gleaning.

HASADIAH (*Yahweh is faithful*). Son of Zerubbabel (1Ch 3:20).

HASENUAH *See Hassenuah.*

HASHABIAH (*Yahweh has reckoned*).
1. Ancestor of Ethan (1Ch 6:45).
2. Ancestor of Shemaiah (1Ch 9:14; Ne 11:15).
3. Son of Jeduthun (1Ch 25:3).
4. Civil official in David's time (1Ch 26:30).
5. Overseer of tribe of Levi (1Ch 27:17).
6. Chief of Levites (2Ch 35:9).
7. Levite teacher (Ezr 8:19).
8. Chief priest (Ezr 8:24).
9. Worker on the wall (Ne 3:17).
10. Priest (Ne 12:21).
11. Ancestor of Uzzi (Ne 11:22).
12. Chief of Levites (Ne 3:17; 12:24).

HASHABNAH (probably *Yahweh has considered me*). Man who sealed covenant with Nehemiah (Ne 10:25).

HASHABNEIAH (probably *Yahweh has considered me*).
1. Father of Hattush (Ne 3:10).
2. A Levite (Ne 9:5).

HASHBADDANAH (probably *Yahweh has considered me*). A man who stood by Ezra as he read the law (Ne 8:4).

HASHEM Father of several members of David's guard (1Ch 11:34).

HASHMONAH A camp of the Israelites (Nu 33:29-30).

HASHUBAH (*consideration*). A descendant of King Jehoiakim (1Ch 3:20).

HASHUM (*broad-nosed*).
1. Family which returned from the Exile (Ezr 2:19; 10:33; Ne 7:22).
2. Priest who stood at side of Ezra when he read the law (Ne 8:4).
3. Chief of people who sealed the covenant (Ne 10:18). May be the same as 2.

HASHUPHA *See Hasupha.*

HASMONEANS *See Maccabees.*

HASRAH Grandfather of Shallum (2Ch 34:22), "Harhas" (2Ki 22:14).

HASSENAAH Father of sons who built fish gate in Jerusalem (Ne 3:3).

HASSENUAH (*the hated women*). A Benjamite and the father of Judah, a governor of Jerusalem (1Ch 9:7; Ne 11:9).

HASSHUB (*considerate*).
1. Son of Pahath-Moab (Ne 3:11).
2. One of the Captivity who assisted in repairing the wall of Jerusalem (Ne 3:23).
3. Head of a family (Ne 10:23).
4. A Levite (1Ch 9:14; Ne 11:15).

HASSOPHERETH (*the scribes*). May have once been an official title (Ezr 2:55).

HASTE In judgment, by Moses and the Israelites (Nu 32:1-19; Jos 22:10-34). *See Rashness.*

HASUPHA Family that returned from exile with Zerubbabel (Ezr 2:43; Ne 7:46).

HAT *See Dress; Headdress; Turbans.*

HATHACH (*good*). A eunuch in the court of Xerxes (Est 4:5-6, 9-10).

HATHATH (possibly *terror* BDB and KB; possibly *weakness* IDB). A son of Othniel (1Ch 4:13).

HATIPHA (*taken captive*). One of the temple servants (Ezr 2:54; Ne 7:56).

HATITA A gatekeeper of the temple (Ezr 2:42; Ne 7:45).

HATRED Is blinding (1Jn 2:9, 11). Carnal (Gal 5:19-20). Murderous (1Jn 3:15). Unforgiving (Mt 6:15). Leads to deceit (Pr 26:24-26). Opposite of love (Pr 15:17). Prevents from loving God (1Jn 4:20). Produces strife (Pr 10:12).
Toward the righteous (Ps 25:19; 35:19; Mt 10:22; Jn 15:18-19, 23-25; 17:14).
Forbidden (Eph 4:31; Col 3:8). Toward a brother (Lev 19:17). Toward an enemy (Mt 5:43-44).
Justified against iniquity (Ps 97:10; 101:3; 119:104, 128, 163; 139:21-22). Of God (Ps 5:5; 45:7; Isa 61:8; Mal 2:16).

See Envy; Jealousy; Malice; Revenge.

HATTAAVAH *See Kibroth Hattaavah.*

HATTIL (*talkative*). A returned exile (Ezr 2:57; Ne 7:59).

HATTIN, HORNS OF (*hollows*). Hill near village of Hattin on which, tradition says, Christ delivered the Sermon on the Mount.

HATTUSH
1. Descendant of Zerubbabel (1Ch 3:22).
2. Man who returned from Babylon (Ezr 8:2).
3. Worker on the wall (Ne 3:10). May be the same as 2.
4. Man who sealed the covenant (Ne 10:4). May be the same as 2 or 3.
5. Priest who returned with Zerubbabel (Ne 12:2).

HAUGHTINESS *See Pride.*

HAURAN (*black*). Plateau E of the Jordan and N of Gilead (Eze 47:16, 18). Called Bashan in ancient times; in the time of the Romans, Auranitis.

HAVENS *See Fair Havens.*

HAVILAH (*stretch of sand*).
1. Son of Cush (Ge 10:7; 1Ch 1:9).
2. Son of Joktan (Ge 10:29; 1Ch 1:23).
3. Land encompassed by Pishon River (Ge 2:11-12).
4. One of the boundaries of the Ishmaelites (Ge 25:18; 1Sa 15:7).

HAVVOTH JAIR (*villages of Jair*). A group of unwalled towns in the NW part of Bashan (Nu 32:41; Dt 3:14; Jos 13:30; Jdg 10:4).

HAWK A carnivorous and unclean bird (Lev 11:16; Dt 14:15; Job 39:26).

HAY (Pr 27:25; Isa 15:6; 1Co 3:12).

HAZAEL (*God [El] sees*). King of Syria. Anointed king by Elijah (1Ki 19:15). Conquests by (2Ki 8:28-29; 9:14; 10:32-33; 12:17-18; 13:3, 22; 2Ch 22:5-6). Conspires against, murders, and succeeds to the throne of Ben-Hadad (2Ki 8:8-15). Death of (2Ki 13:24).

HAZAIAH (*Yahweh sees*). A man of Judah (Ne 11:5).

HAZAR (*a settlement*). Often prefixed to descriptive place names. Also used for encampments of nomads.

HAZAR ADDAR (*settlement of Addar*). Also called Addar, a place on the southern boundary of Canaan (Nu 34:4; Jos 15:3).

HAZAR ENAN (*settlement of Enan*). The NE boundary point of the promised land (Nu 34:9-10; Eze 47:17; 48:1).

HAZAR GADDAH (*settlement of [pagan god] Gad*). A town in the southern district of Judah (Jos 15:27).

HAZAR HATTICON *See Hazer Hatticon.*

HAZAR SHUAL (*settlement of Shual [jackal]*). Town in S Judah (Jos 15:28; 19:3; 1Ch 4:28; Ne 11:27).

HAZAR SUSAH, HAZAR SUSIM (*settlement of Susah [horse]*). A city of Judah (Jos 19:5; 1Ch 4:31).

HAZARMAVETH (*village of [pagan god] Maveth*). Son and descendants of Joktan (Ge 10:26; 1Ch 1:20).

HAZAZON TAMAR (*Hazazon of the palm trees*). The ancient name of En Gedi, a town on W coast of Dead Sea (Ge 14:7; 2Ch 20:2).

HAZEL *See Almond.*

HAZER HATTICON (*place of Hatticon*). A place on the boundary of Hauran, probably E of Damascus (Eze 47:16).

HAZERIM (*unwalled settlements*). A district in the S of Canaan (Dt 2:23).

HAZEROTH (*settlements*). A station in the travels of the Israelites (Nu 11:35; 12:16; 33:17-18; Dt 1:1).

HAZEZON-TAMAR *See Hazazon Tamar.*

HAZIEL (*vision of God [El]*). A Levite (1Ch 23:9).

HAZO A son of Nahor (Ge 22:22).

HAZOR (*an enclosure*).
1. City c. five miles W of waters of Merom, ruled by Jabin (Jos 11:1, 10), conquered by Joshua and, later, by Deborah and Barak

(Jdg 4; 1Sa 12:9), fortified by Solomon (1Ki 9:15), its inhabitants taken into exile by Assyria (2Ki 15:29).

 2. Town in S of Judah (Jos 15:23).
 3. Another town in S Judah (Jos 15:25).
 4. Town N of Jerusalem (Ne 11:33).
 5. Region in S Arabia (Jer 49:28-33).

HAZOR HADATTAH (*new Hazor*). Probably an adjective qualifying Hazor, making it equivalent to New Hazor. A city of Judah (Jos 15:25).

HAZZELELPONI Daughter of Etam (1Ch 4:3).

HAZZOBEBAH Daughter of Koz (1Ch 4:8).

HAZZURIM See *Helkath Hazzurim*.

HEAD Shaven when vows were taken (Ac 21:24). Diseases of (Isa 3:17). Anointed (Lev 14:18, 29).

HEAD OF THE CHURCH Christ, who gives the church life, direction, strength (Eph 1:22; 5:23; Col 1:18).

HEADBANDS Head coverings worn by priests (Ex 28:40; 29:9; Lev 8:13), by women (Isa 3:18, 20). Used in disguise (1Ki 20:38-41). See *Dress; Turban*.

HEADSTONE See *Cornerstone*.

HEALING
In the Old Testament:
 The LORD the healer (Ge 20:17; Ex 15:26; Ps 6:2; 30:2; 103:3; Ac 4:30).
 In answer to prayer (Jas 5:14-16), of Miriam (Nu 12:10-15), of Jeroboam (1Ki 13:1-6), of Hezekiah (2Ki 20:1-7). By Elisha, of Naaman (2Ki 5:1-14).
By Jesus:
 The nobleman's son (Jn 4:46-53). The disabled man (Jn 5:2-9). A leper (Mt 8:2-4; Mk 1:40-45; Lk 5:12-13). Peter's mother-in-law (Mt 8:14-15). Paralyzed man (Mt 9:2-8; Mk 2:1-12; Lk 5:17-26). The man with the withered hand (Mt 12:9-13; Mk 3:1-5; Lk 6:6-10). The centurion's servant (Mt 8:5-13; Lk 7:1-10). Demoniacs (Mt 8:28-34, w Mk 5:1-20, & Lk 8:26-36; Mt 12:22; 17:14-18; Mk 9:14-27; Lk 9:38-42; 11:14). Blind and mute (Mt 9:27-33; 12:22; 20:30-34; Mk 8:22-25; 10:46-52; Lk 18:35-43). Woman with issue of blood (Mt 9:20-22; Mk 5:25-34; Lk 8:43-48). Many sick (Mt 8:16; 9:35; 14:14, 35-36; 15:30-31; 19:2; Mk 6:5, 53-56; Lk 4:40; 9:11). Daughter of the Syrian Phoenician woman (Mt 15:22-28; Mk 7:25-30). Woman with an infirmity (Lk 13:10-13). Ten lepers (Lk 17:12-14). See *Miracles, of Jesus*.
 Power of, given to the apostles (Mt 10:1, 8; Mk 3:13-15; 6:7, 13; Lk 9:1-2, 6), to the Seventy (Lk 10:9, 17), to all believers (Mk 16:18). Special gifts of (1Co 12:9, 28, 30).
By the Apostles:
 The lame man, in Jerusalem (Ac 3:2-10), in Lystra (Ac 14:8-10). Sick, in Jerusalem (Ac 5:15-16), on the island of Malta (Ac 28:8-9). Aeneas (Ac 9:34).
Figurative:
 Healing of disease a metaphor for forgiving of sins (Ps 103:3; Hos 7:1).
 See *Miracles*.

HEALTH Health was a promised blessing of the Old Covenant (Ex 15:26; Dt 7:12-16), as diseases were part of its curse (Lev 26:14-16; Dt 28:20-29, 58-63). Health can be affected by sin (Ps 38:3, 7), but not all disease is the result of sin (Jn 9:1-3).
 The wish for health and wholeness (Hebrew *shalom*) was part of standard greetings (Ge 29:6; 43:27, 28; 1Sa 25:4-6; 3Jn 2). The fear of the LORD brings health (Pr 3:7-8), words of wisdom (Pr 4:20-22), good news (Pr 15:30).
 See *Healing*.

HEAR See *Obedience*.

HEARERS Unresponsive (Eze 33:30-32; Mt 7:26-27; 13:14-15, 19-22; Lk 6:49; 8:11-14; Ro 2:13; Jas 1:22-24). Obedient (Mt 7:24-25; 13:23; Lk 6:47-48; 8:15; Jas 1:25).

HEART Seat of affection and source of action (Dt 5:29; 6:5-6; 2Ch 12:14; Ps 57:7; 112:7; Pr 4:23; 14:30; 15:13-15; 16:1; Mt 9:4; 12:33, 35; 15:18-20; 23:26; Mk 7:21-23). Lives forever (Ps 22:26). Of the Gentiles, taught of God (Ro 2:14-16).
Changed:
 (Ps 51:10). Instances of: Saul (1Sa 10:9), Solomon (1Ki 3:11-12), Paul (Ac 9:1-18).
Hardening of:
 Forbidden (Heb 3:8, 15; 4:7). Instances of: Pharaoh (Ex 4:21; 7:3, 13, 22; 8:15, 32; 9:12, 35; 10:1; 14:8), Sihon (Dt 2:30), king of Canaan (Jos 11:20), Philistines (1Sa 6:6).
Known to God:
 (Dt 31:21; 1Sa 16:7; 2Sa 7:20; 1Ki 8:39; 1Ch 28:9; 2Ch 6:30; Job 11:11; 16:19; 31:4; Ps 1:6; 44:21; 51:10; 94:11; 139:1-12; Pr 5:21; 16:2; 21:2; Isa 66:18; Jer 12:13; 17:10; Eze 11:5; 19:21; 36:25-26; Lk 16:15; Ac 1:24; 15:8; Ro 8:27; 1Co 3:20; Heb 4:12; Rev 2:23).
 To Christ (Ro 8:27; Rev 2:23).
Regenerate:
 Is penitent (Ps 34:18; 51:10, 17; 147:3; Pr 15:3). Renewed (Dt 30:6; Ps 51:10; Eze 11:19; 18:31; 36:26; Jn 3:3, 7; Ro 2:29; Eph 4:22-24; Col 3:9-10; Heb 10:22; Jas 4:8). Pure (Ps 24:4; 66:18; Pr 20:9; Mt 5:8; 2Ti 2:22; 1Pe 3:15). Enlightened (2Co 4:6). Established (Ps 57:7; 108:1; 112:7-8; 1Th 3:13). Refined by affliction (Pr 17:3). Tried or tested (1Ch 29:17; Ps 7:9; 26:2; Pr 17:3; Jer 11:20; 12:3; 20:12; 1Th 2:4; Heb 11:17; Rev 2:2, 10). Strengthened (Ps 27:14; 112:8; 1Th 3:13). Graciously affected of God (1Sa 10:26; 1Ch 29:18; Ezr 6:22; 7:27; Pr 16:1; 21:1; Jer 20:9; Ac 16:14).

Should Render to God:
 Obedience (Dt 10:12; 11:13; 26:16; 1Ki 2:4; Ps 119:1, 12; Eph 6:6). Faith (Ps 27:3; 112:7; Ac 8:37; Ro 6:17; 10:10). Trust (Pr 3:5). Love (Dt 6:5-6; Mt 22:37). Fear (Ps 119:161; Jer 32:40). Fidelity (Ne 9:8). Zeal (2Ch 17:16; Jer 20:9). Seeking God (2Ch 19:3; 30:19; Ezr 7:10; Ps 10:17; 84:2).
Should Be:
 Joyful (1Sa 2:1; Ps 4:7; 97:11; Isa 65:14; Zec 10:7). Perfect (1Ki 8:61; Ps 101:2). Upright (Ps 97:11; 125:4). Clean (Ps 51:10; 73:1). Pure (Ps 24:4; Pr 22:11; Mt 5:8; 1Ti 1:5; 2Ti 2:22; Jas 4:8; 1Pe 1:22). Sincere (Lk 8:15; Ac 2:46; Eph 6:5; Col 3:22; Heb 10:22). Repentant (Dt 30:2; Ps 34:18; 51:17). Devout (1Sa 1:13; Ps 4:4; 9:1; 27:8; 77:6; 119:10, 69, 145). Wise (1Ki 3:9, 12; 4:29; Job 9:4; Pr 8:10; 10:8; 11:29; 14:33; 23:15). Tender (1Sa 24:5; 2Ki 22:19; Job 23:16; Ps 22:14; Eph 4:32). Holy (Ps 66:18; 1Pe 3:15). Compassionate (Jer 4:19; La 3:51). Lowly (Mt 11:29).
The Unregenerate Heart:
 Is full of iniquity (Ge 6:5; 8:21; 1Sa 17:28; Pr 6:14, 18; 11:20; Pr 20:9; Ecc 8:11; 9:3; Jer 4:14, 18; 17:9; Ac 8:21-23; Ro 1:21). Loves evil (Dt 19:18; Ps 95:10; Jer 17:5). A fountain of evil (Mt 12:34-35; Mk 7:21). See *Depravity*. Wayward (2Ch 12:14; Ps 101:4; Pr 6:14; 11:20; 12:8; 17:20; Jer 5:23; Heb 3:10). Blind (Ro 1:21; Eph 4:18). See *Blindness, Spiritual*. Is double (1Ch 12:33; Ps 12:2; Pr 28:14; Isa 9:9; 10:12; Hos 10:2; Jas 1:6, 8). See *Instability*. Is hard (Ps 76:5; Eze 2:4; 3:7; 11:19; 36:26; Mk 6:52; 10:5; 16:14; Jn 12:40; Ro 1:21; 2:5). See *Impenitence; Obduracy*. Is deceitful (Jer 17:9). Proud (2Ch 32:25-26; Ps 101:5; Pr 18:12; 28:25; Jer 48:29; 49:16). See *Pride*. Is subtle (Pr 7:10). See *Hypocrisy*. Is sensual (Eze 6:9; Hos 13:6; Ro 8:7). See *Lasciviousness*. Is worldly (2Ch 26:16; Da 5:20; Ac 8:21-22). Judicially hardened (Ex 4:21; Jos 11:20; Isa 6:10; Ac 28:26-27). Malicious (Ps 28:3; 140:2; Pr 24:2; Ecc 7:26; Eze 25:15). See *Malice*. Is impenitent (Ro 2:5). See *Impenitence*. Is diabolical (Jn 13:2; Ac 5:3). Is covetous (Jer 22:17; 2Pe 2:14). See *Covetousness*. Is foolish (Pr 12:23; 22:15; Ecc 9:3). Under the wrath of God (Ro 1:18-19, 31; 2:5-6).
 See *Regeneration; Sanctification*.

HEARTH Of an altar (Lev 6:9; Isa 30:14; Eze 43:15-16). Figurative (Isa 29:2).

HEAT Jonah overcome with (Jnh 4:8). See *Sunstroke*.

HEATH See *Bush*.

HEATHEN Gentiles, pagans. Under this head are all who are not descendants of Abraham, Isaac and Jacob.
Described:
 Cast out of Canaan (Lev 18:24-25; Ps 44:2) and their land given to Israel (Ps 78:55; 105:44; 135:12; 136:21-22; Isa 54:1-3). Excluded from the temple (La 1:10).
 Wicked practices of. See *Idolatry*.
Divine Revelations Given to:
 Abimelech (Ge 20:3-7), Nebuchadnezzar (Da 4:1-18), Belshazzar (Da 5:5, 24-29), Cyrus (2Ch 36:23; Ezr 1:1-4), the Magi (Mt 2:1-11), the centurion (Mt 8:5-13; Lk 7:2-9), Cornelius (Ac 10:1-7).
Pious People Among:
 (Isa 65:5; Ac 10:35). Melchizedek (Ge 14:18-20). Abimelech (Ge 20). Balaam (Nu 22). Jethro (Ex 18). Eliphaz (Job 4). Bildad (Job 8). Zophar (Job 11). Elihu (Job 32). Nebuchadnezzar, after his restoration (Da 4). The Ninevites (Jnh 3:5-10). The Magi (Mt 2:1-12). The centurion of Capernaum (Mt 8:5-13; Lk 7:2-9), of Caesarea (Ac 10). Believed in Christ (Mt 8:5-13; Lk 7:2-9).
 See *Gentiles*.

HEAVE OFFERING See *Offerings*.

HEAVE SHOULDER See *Offerings*.

HEAVEN
God's Dwelling Place:
 (Dt 26:15; 1Ki 8:30, 39, 43, 49; 1Ch 16:31; 21:26; 2Ch 2:6; 6:21, 27, 30, 33, 35, 39; 7:14; 30:27; Ne 9:27; Job 22:12, 14; Ps 2:4; 11:4; 20:6; 33:13; 102:19; 103:19; 115:3-6; 123:1; Ecc 5:2; Isa 57:15; 63:15; 66:1; Jer 23:24; La 3:41, 50; Da 5:23; Zec 2:13; Mt 5:34, 45; 6:9; 10:32-33; 11:25; 12:50; 16:17; 18:10, 14; Mk 11:25-26; 16:19; Ac 7:49, 55-56; Ro 1:18; Heb 8:1; Rev 8:1; 12:7-9; 21:22-27; 22:1-5).
Figurative:
 Of divine government (Mt 16:19; 18:18; 23:22). Of God (Mt 21:25).
The Future Home of the Righteous:
 (2Ki 2:11; Mt 5:12; 13:30, 43; Lk 16:22; Jn 12:8, 26; 13:36; 17:24; 2Co 5:1; Php 3:20; Col 1:5-6, 12; 3:9; 1Th 4:17; Heb 10:34; 11:10, 16; 12:22; 1Pe 1:4; Rev 2:7; 3:21).
Called:
 A city (Heb 11:10, 16), a garden (Mt 3:12), a house (Jn 14:2-3; 2Co 5:1), a kingdom (Mt 25:34; Lk 12:32; 22:29-30), the kingdom of Christ and of God (Eph 5:5), a heavenly country (Heb 11:16), a rest (Heb 4:9; Rev 14:13), glory (Col 3:4), paradise (Lk 23:43; 2Co 12:2, 4; Rev 2:7).
 Everlasting (2Co 5:1; Heb 10:34; 13:14; 1Pe 1:4; 2Pe 1:11). Allegorical representatives of (Rev 4:1-11; 5:1-14; 7:9-17; 14:1-3; 15:1-8; 21; 22:1-5). No marriage in (Mt 22:30; Lk 20:34-36). Names of the righteous written in (Lk 10:20; Heb 12:22-24). Treasures in (Mt 6:20; 19:21; Lk 12:33). Joy in (Ps 16:11; Lk 15:6-7, 10). Righteousness dwells in (2Pe 3:13). No sorrow in (Rev 7:16-17; 21:4). The wicked excluded from (Gal 5:21; Eph 5:5; Rev 22:15).
 See *Righteous, Promises to*.

HEAVEN OPENED (Mt 3:16; Ac 7:56; 10:11; Rev 19:11).

HEAVENLY PLACES (Eph 1:3, 20; 2:6; 3:10).

HEAVENS, NEW To be created (Isa 65:17; 66:22; 2Pe 3:13; Rev 21:1-4).

HEAVENS, PHYSICAL (Ge 1:1; 2Ch 2:6; 6:18; Job 38:31-33; Ps 19:1; 50:6; 68:33; 89:29; 103:11; 113:4; 115:16; 136:5; Jer 31:37; Eze 1:1; Mt 24:29-30; Ac 2:19-20).
 Created by God (Ge 1:1; 2:1; Ex 20:11; 1Ch 16:26; 2Ch 2:12; Ne 9:6; Job 9:8; Ps 8:3; 19:1; 33:6, 9; 102:25; 148:4-6; Pr 8:27; Isa 37:16; 40:22; 42:5; 45:12, 18; Jer 10:12; 32:17; 51:15; Ac 4:24; 14:15; Heb 1:10; Rev 10:6; 14:7). See *Creation; God, Creator; Heavens, New*.
 Destruction of (Job 14:12; Ps 102:25-26; Isa 51:6; Mt 5:18; 24:35; Heb 1:10-12; 2Pe 3:10-12; Rev 6:12-14; 20:11; 21:1, 4). Figurative of divine judgment (Isa 34:4).
 See *Sky*.

HEAVING AND WAVING See *Offerings*.

HEBER, HEBERITE (*associate*).
 1. An Asherite, the son of Beriah; great-grandson of Jacob (Ge 46:17; Nu 26:45; 1Ch 7:31-32).
 2. Kenite whose wife Jael killed Sisera (Jdg 4:11-21; 5:24).
 3. A Judahite, the father of Soco and son of Ezrah (1Ch 4:18).
 4. A Benjamite and son of Elpaal (1Ch 8:17).

HEBREW A word supposed to be a corruption of the name of Eber, who was an ancestor of Abraham (Ge 10:24; 11:14-26). See *Genealogy*. Applied to Abraham (Ge 14:13) and his descendants (Ge 39:14; 40:15; 43:32; Ex 2:6; Dt 15:12; 1Sa 4:9; 29:3; Jnh 1:9; Ac 6:1; 2Co 11:22; Php 3:5). Used to denote the language of the Jews (Jn 5:2; 19:20; Ac 21:40; 22:2; 26:14; Rev 9:11).
 See *Israel, Israelites; Jews*.

HEBREW LANGUAGE The NW branch of the Semitic language family; has close affinity to Ugaritic, Phoenician, Moabitic, and the Canaanite dialects; sister languages include Arabic, Akkadian, and Aramaic. Except for a few Aramaic passages in Ezra, Daniel, and Jeremiah, it is the language of the OT.

HEBREW OF THE HEBREWS A Jew of pure blood, very strict in observing the law (Php 3:4-6).

HEBREWS, EPISTLE TO THE
Author: Anonymous. Historical speculations as to authorship include Paul, Barnabas, Apollos, and Priscilla.
Date: Before the destruction of Jerusalem and the temple in A.D. 70
Outline:
I. Prologue: The Superiority of God's New Revelation (1:1-4).
II. The Superiority of Christ to Leaders of the Old Covenant (1:5-7:28).
 A. Christ Is Superior to the Angels (1:5-2:18).
 1. Scriptural proof of superiority (1:5-14).
 2. Exhortation not to ignore the revelation of God in his Son (2:1-4).
 3. Further Scriptural proof of superiority over the angels (2:5-18).
 B. Christ Is Superior to Moses (3:1-4:13).
 1. Demonstration of Christ's superiority (3:1-6).
 2. Exhortation to enter salvation-rest (3:7-4:13).
 C. Christ Is Superior to the Aaronic Priests (4:14-7:28).
 1. Exhortation to hold fast (4:14-16).
 2. Qualifications of a priest (5:1-10).
 3. Exhortation to abandon spiritual lethargy (5:11-6:12).
 4. Certainty of God's promise (6:13-20).
 5. Christ's superior priestly order (ch. 7).
III. The Superior Sacrificial Work of Our High Priest (chs. 8-10).
 A. A Better Covenant (ch. 8).
 B. A Better Sanctuary (9:1-12).
 C. A Better Sacrifice (9:13-10:18).
 D. Exhortations (10:19-39).
IV. Final Plea for Persevering Faith (chs. 11-12).
 A. Examples of Past Heroes of the Faith (ch. 11).
 B. Encouragement for Persevering Faith (12:1-11).
 C. Exhortations for Persevering Faith (12:12-17).
 D. Motivation for Persevering Faith (12:18-29).
V. Conclusion (ch. 13).
 A. Practical Rules for Christian Living (13:1-17).
 B. Request for Prayer (13:18-19).
 C. Benediction (13:20-21).
 D. Personal Remarks (13:22-23).
 E. Greetings and Final Benediction (13:24-25).

HEBRON (*association*).
 1. For Jos 19:28 See *Abdon, 1*.
 2. A city of Judah, S of Jerusalem. When built (Nu 13:22). Fortified (2Ch 11:10). Also called Kiriath Arba (Ge 23:2; 35:27; Jos 15:13). Abraham dwells and Sarah dies at (Ge 23:2). Hoham, king of, confederated with other kings of the Canaanites against Joshua (Jos 10:3-39). Children of Anakim dwell at (Nu 13:22; Jos 11:21). Conquest of, by Caleb (Jos 14:6-15; Jdg 1:10, 20). A city of refuge (Jos 20:7; 21:11, 13). David crowned king of Judah at (2Sa 2:1-11; 3), of Israel (2Sa 5:1-5). The burial place of Sarah (Ge 23:2), Abner (2Sa 3:32), Ish-Bosheth (2Sa 4:12). The conspirators against Ish-Bosheth hanged at (2Sa 4:12). Absalom made king at (2Sa 15:9-10). Jews of the Babylonian captivity dwell at (Ne 11:25). Pool of (2Sa 4:12).
 3. Son of Kohath (Ex 6:18; Nu 3:19; 1Ch 6:2, 18; 23:12, 19).
 4. The family name of Mareshah (1Ch 2:42-43; 15:9).

HEDGE Protecting a vineyard (Isa 5:5). Of thorns (Mic 7:4; Mk 12:1). Figurative of divine protection (Job 1:10), of divine entrapment (Job 3:23). See *Fence*.

HEEDFULNESS Commanded (Ex 23:13; Pr 4:25-27).
 Necessary: In the care of the soul (Dt 4:9). In the house and worship of God (Ecc 5:1). In what we hear (Mk 4:24). In how we hear (Lk 8:18). In keeping God's commandments (Jos 22:5). In conduct (Eph 5:15). In speech (Pr 13:3; Jas 1:19). In worldly company (Ps 39:1; Col 4:5). In giving judgment (2Ch 19:6-7).

Against sin (Heb 12:15-16). Against unbelief (Heb 3:12). Against idolatry (Dt 4:15-16). Against false Christs, and false prophets (Mt 24:4-5, 23-24). Against false teachers (Php 3:2; Col 2:8; 2Pe 3:16-17). Against presumption (1Co 10:12).
Promises to (1Ki 2:4; 1Ch 22:13).
See Obedience.

HEGAI Eunuch in charge of Xerxes' harem (Est 2:3, 8, 15).

HEIFER When used as sacrifice, must be without blemish and must not have come under the yoke (Nu 19:2; Dt 21:3). An atonement for murder (Dt 21:1-9). The red heifer used for the water of separation (Nu 19; Heb 9:13).
Used for plowing (Jdg 14:18), for treading out wheat (Hos 10:11). Tractable (Hos 10:11). Intractable (Hos 4:16).
See Cattle; Offerings.
Figurative: Of backsliders (Hos 4:16). Of the obedient (Hos 10:11).

HEIFER, RED *See Animals.*

HEIR
Literal:
Mosaic law relating to inheritance of (Nu 27:8-11; 36:1-8; Jos 17:3-6). Prescribing right of, to redeem alienated land (Lev 25:25; Ru 4:1-12). To inherit slaves (Lev 25:45-46). Firstborn son to have double portion (Dt 21:15-17). Children of wives and concubines are (Ge 15:3; 21:10; 25:5-6; Gal 4:30). All possessions left to (Ecc 2:18-19). Minor, under guardians (Gal 4:1-2).
See Birthright; Firstborn; Inheritance; Orphan; Will.
Figurative:
Of spiritual adoption (Ro 8:14-17; Gal 3:29; 4:6-7; Tit 3:7; Jas 2:5). *See Adoption.*

HELAH (*necklace* IDB; *rust* KB). A wife of Asher (1Ch 4:5).

HELAM Place in Syrian desert E of Jordan where David defeated forces of Hadadezer (2Sa 10:16-17).

HELBAH (*a fertile region*). A town of Asher (Jdg 1:31).

HELBON (*fertile*). A village near Damascus, noted for fine wines (Eze 27:18).

HELDAI (*mole*).
1. The Netophathite. One of David's heroes (1Ch 27:15). Heled is a variant spelling (2Sa 23:29; 1Ch 11:30).
2. A leader among those returned from the Exile (Zec 6:10, 14).

HELECH Possibly Cilicia, an area in SE (modern day) Turkey (Eze 27:11).

HELED *See Heldai, 1.*

HELEK, HELEKITE (*portion, lot*). Son of Gilead (Jos 17:2) and his clan (Nu 26:30).

HELEM (*health*).
1. A descendant of Asher (1Ch 7:35).
2. Probably the same as Heldai (Zec 6:10, 14).

HELEPH (possibly *sharp, cutting*). A town of Naphtali (Jos 19:33).

HELEZ (*vigor* BDB).
1. One of David's mighty men (2Sa 23:26; 1Ch 11:27; 27:10).
2. A man of Judah (1Ch 2:39).

HELI (*ascent [to God]*). Father of Joseph, the husband of Mary (Lk 3:23), or perhaps the father of Mary, the mother of Jesus.

HELIOPOLIS (*sun [god] city*). City near S end of the Nile Delta called "On" in the Bible (Ge 41:45; 46:20; Isa 19:18, ftn). *See City of Destruction.*

HELKAI (*Yahweh is [my] portion*). A priest (Ne 12:15).

HELKATH (*portion*). A Levitical town (Jos 19:25; 21:31), also spelled Hukok (1Ch 6:75). *See Hukok.*

HELKATH HAZZURIM (possibly *portion [field] of rock,* or *swords* IDB; *portion [field] of snare* KB). Plain near pool of Gibeon where soldiers of Joab and Abner fought (2Sa 2:12-16).

HELL In the NIV, "hell" usually translates the Greek *geena* and *hades,* but is conceptually the same as the Hebrew *Sheol,* usually rendered "grave," the unseen world and abode of the dead (Ge 37:35; 42:38; 44:29, 31; Dt 32:22; 1Sa 2:6; 2Sa 22:6; 1Ki 2:6, 9; Job 7:9; 11:8; 14:13; 17:13; 21:13; 24:19; 26:6; Ps 9:17; 16:10; 18:5; 55:15; 86:13; 116:3; 139:8; Pr 5:5; 7:27; 9:18; 15:11, 24; 23:14; 27:20; Isa 5:14; 14:9, 15; 28:15, 18; 57:9; Eze 31:16-17; 32:21, 27; Am 9:2; Jnh 2:2; Hab 2:5). In the NT hell is the unseen world (Mt 11:23; 16:18; Lk 10:15; 16:23; Ac 2:27, 31; Rev 1:18; 6:8; 20:13-14), a place of torment (Mt 5:22, 29-30; 10:28; 18:9; 23:15, 33; Lk 12:5; Jas 3:6) and of captivity for fallen angels (2Pe 2:4).
Figurative:
Of divine judgments (Dt 32:22; Eze 31:15-17).
The Future State, or Abode, of the Wicked:
(Ps 9:17; Pr 5:5; 9:18; 15:24; 23:14; Isa 30:33; 33:14; Mt 3:12; 5:22, 29-30; 7:13; 8:11-12; 10:28; 13:30, 38-42, 49-50; 16:18; 18:8-9, 34-35; 22:13; 25:30, 41, 46; Mk 9:43-48; Lk 3:17; 16:23-28; Ac 1:25; 2Th 1:9; 2Pe 2:4; Jude 6, 23; Rev 2:11; 9:1-2; 11:7; 14:10-11; 19:20; 20:10, 15; 21:8).
See Grave; Hades; Sheol; Wicked, Punishment of.

HELLENISTS NIV "Grecian Jews"; Jews of the Dispersion who spoke Greek and followed some aspects of Greek culture (Ac 6:1; 9:29).

HELM *See Rudder(s).*

HELMET A defensive headgear worn by soldiers (1Sa 17:5, 38; 2Ch 26:14; Jer 46:4; Eze 23:24).
Figurative: (Isa 59:17; Eph 6:17; 1Th 5:8).

HELON (*strength, power*). Father of Eliab (Nu 1:9; 2:7; 7:24, 29; 10:16).

HELPER Woman created as a helper suitable for man (Ge 2:18, 20). Yahweh is the helper of Israel (Dt 33:29; Hos 13:9), of the fatherless (Ps 10:14), of David (Ps 27:9). Eliezer means "God is my helper" (Ex 18:4, ftn.).

HELPMEET *See Helper.*

HELPS One of the gifts of the Spirit, probably the ability to perform helpful works in a gracious manner (1Co 12:7-11, 28-31).

HEM OF A GARMENT Fringes or tassels on the borders of the Israelite outer garment (Nu 15:38-39).

HEMAM *See Homam.*

HEMAN (*faithful*).
1. A man noted for wisdom, to whom Solomon is compared (1Ki 4:31; 1Ch 2:6).
2. "The Singer," a chief Levite, and musician (1Ch 6:33; 15:17, 19; 16:41). The king's seer (1Ch 25:5). His sons and daughters temple musicians (1Ch 6:33; 25:1-6). "Maskil of," title of Psalm 88. *See Maskil.*

HEMATH
1. *See Hamath.*
2. *See Hammath, 2.*

HEMDAN (*desirable*). Son of Dishon (Ge 36:26).

HEMLOCK A poisonous and bitter plant (Hos 10:4; Am 6:12). *See Gall, 3; Plants of the Bible; Poison.*

HEMORRHAGE Menstruation (Lev 15:19; Mt 9:20; Lk 8:43). A woman subject to bleeding for twelve years (Mk 5:25-29; Mk 5:24-34; Lk 8:). *See Bleeding, Subject to; Menstruation.*

HEMORRHOIDS NIV "tumors" (Dt 28:27); a disease with which the Philistines were afflicted (1Sa 5:6, 12; 6:4; 5:11). *See Disease; Tumor.*

HEN (proper name: *gracious*).
1. Son of Zephaniah (Zec 6:14).
2. Hen protecting her chicks figurative of Jesus' desire for Jerusalem (Mt 23:37; Lk 13:34).

HENA (*[pagan god] Anath*). A city on the Euphrates (2Ki 18:34; 19:13; Isa 37:13).

HENADAD (*favor of Hadad [pagan god]*). A Levite (Ezr 3:9; Ne 3:18, 24; 10:9).

HENNA BLOSSOMS A shrub of Israel (perhaps the cypress) with tightly clustered, aromatic blossoms (SS 1:14; 4:13).

HENOCH *See Enoch.*

HEPHER, HEPHERITE (perhaps *help*).
1. Son of Gilead, and ancestor of Zelophehad (Nu 26:32-33; 27:1; Jos 17:2-3).
2. Son of Naarah (1Ch 4:6).
3. One of David's heroes (1Ch 11:36).
4. A city W of the Jordan (Jos 12:17; 1Ki 4:10).

HEPHZIBAH (*my pleasure is in her*).
1. Wife of Hezekiah (2Ki 21:1).
2. Symbolic name given to Zion (Isa 62:4).

HERALD (Isa 40:3; Da 3:4). Signified by the word "preacher" (1Ti 2:7; 2Ti 1:11; 2Pe 2:5).

HERBS Given for food (Ge 1:29-30; Pr 15:17). *See Vegetation.*

HERD Herds of cattle were used in plowing, threshing, and sacrifice (Ge 18:7; Job 1:3; 42:12).

HERDSMAN Person in charge of cattle (Ge 13:7) or pigs (Mt 8:33), despised in Egypt (Ge 46:34) but honored in Israel (Ge 47:6; 1Ch 27:29).

HEREDITY Like gives birth to like (Ge 5:3; Job 14:4; Jn 3:6-7).
Results of:
Natural, depravity (Job 21:19; Ps 51:5; 58:3; Isa 48:8; Jn 9:2; Ro 5:12; Eph 2:3).
Judicial, ordained consequences of parental conduct (Ex 20:5-6; 34:7; Nu 14:18, 33; Dt 5:9; Ps 37:28; Isa 14:20-21; 65:6-7; Jer 32:18; Ro 5:12; 1Co 15:22). Does not determine moral status (Jer 31:29-30; Eze 18:1-32; Mt 3:9).

HERES (*sun*).
1. District around Aijalon (Jdg 1:35).
2. Place E of the Jordan (Jdg 8:13).
3. Egyptian city, translated "city of destruction" (Isa 19:18), undoubtedly Heliopolis.

HERESH (*deaf, silent*). A Levite (1Ch 9:15).

HERESY Propagandism of, forbidden under severe penalties (Dt 13; Tit 3:10-11; 2Jn 10-11). Teachers of, among early Christians (Ac 15:24; 2Co 11:4; Gal 1:7; 2:4; 2Pe 2; Jude 3-16; Rev 2:2). Paul and Silas accused of (Ac 16:20-21, 23). Paul accused of (Ac 18:13). Disavowed by Paul (Ac 24:13-17). *See Teachers, False.*

HERETH A forest in which David found refuge from Saul (1Sa 22:5).

HERMAS Friend of Paul in the church at Rome (Ro 16:14).

HERMES (possibly *rock, cairn*).
1. Greek god (messenger), the same as Mercury in Latin. Paul mistaken for (Ac 14:12).
2. Friend of Paul in the church at Rome (Ro 16:14).

HERMOGENES (*born of Hermes*). A Christian who deserted Paul (2Ti 1:15).

HERMON, MOUNT (*consecrated place*). Mountain marking S end of Anti-Lebanon range; thirty miles SW of Damascus; 9000 ft. above sea level; marks N boundary of Israel; has three peaks. Has borne several names: the Amorites call it "Senir," (Dt 3:9), the Sidonians call it "Sirion" (Dt 3:9), "Siyon," (Dt 4:48). Probably the Mount of Transfiguration (Mt 17:1). Seat of Baal worship (Jdg 3:3). Modern Jebel es-Sheikh.

HEROD Idumean rulers of Israel (37 B.C. to A.D. 100). Line started with Antipater, whom Julius Caesar made procurator of Judea in 47 B.C.
1. Herod the Great, first procurator of Galilee, then king of the Jews (37-4 B.C.); built Caesarea, temple at Jerusalem; slaughtered children at Bethlehem (Mt 2:1-18). At his death his kingdom was divided among his three sons: Archelaus, Herod Antipas, and Philip.
2. Archelaus ruled over Judea, Samaria, and Idumea (4 B.C. to A.D. 6), and was removed from office by the Romans (Mt 2:22).
3. Herod Antipas ruled over Galilee and Perea (4 B.C. to A.D. 39); killed John the Baptist (Mt 14:1-12); called "fox" by Jesus (Lk 13:32).
4. Philip, tetrarch of Batanaea, Trachonitis, Gaulanitis, and parts of Jamnia (4 B.C. to A.D. 34). Best of the Herods.
5. Herod Agrippa I; grandson of Herod the Great; tetrarch of Galilee; king of Israel (A.D. 37-44); killed James the apostle (Ac 12:1-23).
6. Herod Agrippa II. King of territory E of Galilee (A.D. 50-100); Paul appeared before him (Ac 25:13-26:32).

HERODIANS They are mentioned as enemies of Jesus once in Galilee, and again at Jerusalem (Mt 22:15-22; Mk 3:6; 12:13-17; Lk 20:20-26). The Pharisees were ardent nationalists, opposed to Roman rule, while the hated Herodians, as their name indicates, supported the Roman rule of the Herods. Now, however, the Pharisees enlisted the help of the Herodians to trap Jesus in his words. After trying to put him off guard with flattery, they sprang their question: "Is it right to pay taxes to Caesar or not?" (Mt 22:17). If he said "no," the Herodians would report him to the Roman governor and he would be executed for treason. If he said "yes," the Pharisees would denounce him to the people as disloyal to his nation.

HERODIAS (feminine form of Herod). Granddaughter of Herod the Great who had John the Baptist put to death (Mt 14:3-6; Mk 6:17; Lk 3:19).

HERODION A Roman Christian (Ro 16:11).

HERON Large aquatic bird Israelites could not eat (Lev 11:19; Dt 14:18).

HESED *See Ben-Hesed.*

HESHBON (*reckoning*). A city of the Amorites (Nu 21:25-35; Dt 1:4). Built by Reuben (Nu 32:37). Allotted to Gad (Jos 21:38-39). Pools at (SS 7:4). Prophecy concerning (Isa 16:8; Jer 48:2, 34-35; 49:1-3).

HESHMON A town in the S of Judah (Jos 15:27).

HETH Son of Canaan and ancestor of the Hittites (Ge 10:15; 23:3, ftn, 5, 7, 10, 16, 18; 27:46; 49:32; 1Ch 1:13). *See Hittite(s).*

HETHLON A place on the northern frontier of Israel (Eze 47:15; 48:1).

HEXATEUCH (*six books*). A term referring to the Pentateuch and Joshua as though it were a literary unit.

HEZEKIAH (*Yahweh is [my] strength*).
1. King of Judah (2Ki 16:20; 18:1-2; 1Ch 3:13; 2Ch 29:1; Mt 1:9). Religious zeal of (2Ch 29; 30; 31). Purges the nation of idolatry (2Ki 18:4; 2Ch 31:1; 33:3). Restores the true forms of worship (2Ch 31:2-21). His piety (2Ki 18:2, 5-6; 2Ch 29:2; 31:20-21; 32:32; Jer 26:19). Military operations of (2Ki 18:19; 1Ch 4:39-43; 2Ch 32; Isa 36; 37). Sickness and restoration of (2Ki 20:1-11; 2Ch 32:24; Isa 38:1-8). His psalm of thanksgiving (Isa 38:9-22). His lack of wisdom in showing his resources to commissioners of Babylon (2Ki 20:12-19; 2Ch 32:25-26, 31; Isa 39). Prospered of God (2Ki 18:7; 2Ch 32:27-30). Conducts the Brook Gihon into Jerusalem (2Ki 18:17; 20:20; 2Ch 32:4, 30; 33:14; Ne 2:13-15; 3:13, 16; Isa 7:3; 22:9-11; 36:2). Scribes of (Pr 25:1). Death and burial of (2Ki 20:21; 2Ch 32:33). Prophecies concerning (2Ki 19:20-34; 20:5-6, 16-18; Isa 38:5-8; 39:5-7; Jer 26:18-19).
2. One of the exiles (Ezr 2:16; Ne 7:21; 10:17).
3. An ancestor of the prophet Zephaniah (Zep 1:1).
4. *See Hizkiah, 1.*

HEZION (*vision* BDB; *one with floppy ears* IDB). Grandfather of Ben-Hadad (1Ki 15:18).

HEZIR (*boar*).
1. A Levite (1Ch 24:15).
2. A prince of Judah (Ne 10:20).

HEZRAI *See Hezro.*

HEZRO Also called Hezrai. A Carmelite (2Sa 23:35; 1Ch 11:37).

HEZRON, HEZRONITE (*enclosure*).
1. A son of Perez (Ge 46:12). Ancestor of the Hezronites (Nu 26:6). An ancestor of Jesus (Mt 1:3; Lk 3:33).

H

2. A son of Reuben (Ge 46:9; Ex 6:14; 1Ch 4:1; 5:3). Ancestor of the Hezronites (Nu 26:21).

HIDDAI One of David's heroes (2Sa 23:30). Called Hurai (1Ch 11:32).

HIDDEKEL *See Tigris.*

HIEL (*God [El] lives*). Rebuilder of Jericho (1Ki 16:34). In him was fulfilled the curse pronounced by Joshua (Jos 6:26).

HIERAPOLIS (*[pagan] sacred city*). Ancient Phrygian city near Colosse (Col 4:13).

HIEROGLYPHICS *See Writing.*

HIGGAION A musical term probably meaning "solemn sound" or "meditation." It occurs in Ugaritic as with the meaning "to utter." According to Gesenius, it signifies the murmuring tone of a harp and therefore should be rendered in a melancholy manner (Ps 92:3). Combined with *Selah*, it may have been intended to indicate a pause in the vocal music while the instruments played an interlude (Ps 9:16, ftn). Mendelssohn translates it "meditation, thought" (Ps 19:14). Therefore, the music was to be rendered in a mode to promote devout meditation.

See Music, Symbols Used in.

HIGH PLACES A term used to describe places of worship (Ge 12:8; 22:2, 14; 31:54; 1Sa 9:12; 2Sa 24:25; 1Ki 3:2, 4; 18:30, 38; 1Ch 16:39; 2Ch 1:3; 33:17). Signify a place of idolatrous worship (Nu 22:41; 1Ki 11:7; 12:31; 14:23; 15:14; 22:43; 2Ki 17:9, 29; Jer 7:31). Licentious practices at (Eze 16:24-43). The idolatrous, to be destroyed (Lev 26:30; Nu 33:52). Asa destroys (2Ch 14:3; Jehoshaphat (2Ch 17:6), Hezekiah (2Ki 18:4), Josiah (2Ki 23:8).

See Groves; Idolatry; Shrine.

HIGH PRIEST *See Priest.*

HIGHWAYS (*a built up road*). From, Gibeon to Beth Horon (Jos 10:10), Bethel to Shechem (Jdg 21:19), Judea to Galilee, by way of Samaria (Jn 4:3-5, 43). To Bethel (Jdg 20:31), to Gibeah (Jdg 20:31), to cities of refuge (Dt 19:3). Built by rulers (Nu 20:17; 21:22).

Figurative (Pr 16:17; Isa 11:16; 35:8-10; 40:3-4; Mt 3:3; 7:13-14).

See Roads.

HILEN A city of Judah. Assigned to the priests (1Ch 6:58). Called Holon (Jos 15:51; 21:15).

HILKIAH (*Yahweh is [my] portion*).
1. Father of Eliakim (2Ki 18:18).
2. Merarite Levite (1Ch 6:45).
3. Merarite Levite (1Ch 26:11).
4. High priest who found book of the Law and sent it to Josiah (2Ki 22-23; 2Ch 34:14).
5. Priest who returned with Zerubbabel (Ne 12:7).
6. Father of Jeremiah (Jer 1:1).
7. Father of Gemariah who stood by Ezra at Bible reading (Ne 8:4).

HILL COUNTRY Any region of hills and valleys, but in Scripture generally the higher part of Judea (Lk 1:39, 65).

HILLEL (*he has praises*). Father of Abdon (Jdg 12:13, 15).

HILLS Perpetual (Ge 49:26; Hab 3:6).

HIN A measure for liquids, and containing one-sixth or one-seventh of a bath. Probably equivalent to about four quarts (Ex 29:40; Lev 19:36; 23:13). *See Measure.*

HIND *See Deer.*

HINGE A fitting enabling a door or window to swing in its place (1Ki 7:50), often used figuratively for something of great importance.

HINNOM, VALLEY OF A valley W and SW of Jerusalem (Jos 15:8; 18:16; 2Ki 23:10; Ne 11:30). Children offered in sacrifice in (2Ch 28:3; 33:6; Jer 7:31-32; 19:2, 4, 6; 32:35). Possibly valley of vision identical with (Isa 22:1, 5).

See Ben Hinnom; Topheth, Tophet.

HIP AND THIGH Hebrew idiom denoting thoroughness with which Samson slew Philistines (Jdg 15:8, KJV).

HIPPOPOTAMUS *See Behemoth.*

HIRAH An Adullamite (Ge 38:1, 12).

HIRAM (*[my] brother is elevated*). Hiram (Hebrew *Huram*, a variant of *Hiram*), was a Phoenician king who was the first to accord the newly established King David international recognition. It was vital to him that he have good relations with the king of Israel since Israel dominated the inland trade routes to Tyre, and Tyre was dependent on Israelite agriculture for much of its food. A close relationship existed between these two realms until the Babylonian invasions. Builds a palace for David (2Sa 5:11; 1Ch 14:1; 2Ch 2:3). Aids Solomon in building the temple (1Ki 5; 2Ch 2:3-16). Dissatisfied with cities given by Solomon (1Ki 9:11-13). Makes presents of gold and seamen to Solomon (1Ki 9:14, 26-28; 10:11).

HIRE Law concerning hired property (Ex 22:14-15).

See Employer; Master; Servant; Wages.

HIRED SERVANT Jacob (Ge 29:15; 30:26), re-employed (Ge 30:27-34; 31:6-7, 41). Laborers for a vineyard (Mt 20:1-15).

The prodigal (Lk 15:15-19). Kindness to (Ru 2:4). Treatment of, more considerate than that accorded slaves (Lev 25:53).

Rights to:
To receive wages (Mt 10:10; Lk 10:7; Ro 4:4; 1Ti 5:18; Jas 5:4), daily (Lev 19:13; Dt 24:15). To share in spontaneous products of land in Sabbatic year (Lev 25:6). Wages of, paid in portion of flocks or products (Ge 30:31-32; 2Ch 2:10), or in money (Mt 20:2, 9-10). Oppression of, forbidden (Dt 24:14; Col 4:1). Oppressors of, punished (Mal 3:5).

Mercenary (Job 7:2). Unfaithful (Jn 10:12-13).

See Employee; Master; Servant; Wages.

HIRELING *See Hired Servant.*

HISTORY (Job 8:8-10). *See Genesis; Joshua; Judges; Ruth; Samuel, 1 and 2; Kings, 1 and 2; Chronicles, 1 and 2; Ezra; Nehemiah; Esther; Israel, Israelites; Jesus the Christ, History of.*

HITTITE(S) (*descendants of Heth*). A tribe of Canaanites. Sons of Heth (Ge 10:15; 23:3, ftn, 5, 7, 10, 16, 18). Sell a burial site to Abraham (Ge 23). Esau intermarries with (Ge 26:34; 36:2). Dwelling place of (Ge 23:17-20; Nu 13:29; Jos 1:4; Jdg 1:26). Their land given to the Israelites (Ex 3:8; Dt 7:1; Jos 1:4). Conquered by Joshua (Jos 9:1-2; 10; 11; 12; 24:11). Intermarry with Israelites (Jdg 3:5-7; Ezr 9:1). Solomon intermarries with (1Ki 11:1; Ne 13:26). Pay tribute to Solomon (1Ki 9:20-21). Retain their own kings (1Ki 10:29; 2Ki 7:6; 2Ch 1:17). Officers from, in David's army (1Sa 26:6; 2Sa 11:3; 23:39).

HIVITE(S) A tribe of Canaanites (Ge 10:17; 1Ch 1:15). Shechemites and Gibeonites were families of (Ge 34:2; Jos 9:7; 11:19). Esau intermarries with (Ge 26:34; 36:2). Dwelling place of (Jos 11:3; Jdg 3:3; 2Sa 24:7). Their land given to the Israelites (Ex 23:23, 28; Dt 20:17; Jdg 3:5). Conquered by Joshua (Jos 9:1; 12:8; 24:11). Pay tribute to Solomon (1Ki 9:21; 2Ch 8:8).

HIZKI (*Yahweh is [my] strength*, or *my strength*). A Benjamite (1Ch 8:17).

HIZKIAH (*Yahweh is [my] strength*).
1. A son of Neariah (1Ch 3:23).
2. *See Hezekiah, 3.*

HIZKIJAH *See Hezekiah, 2.*

HOBAB (*beloved*, possibly *deceit*). Brother-in-law of Moses (Nu 10:29; Jdg 4:11).

HOBAH A place N of Damascus (Ge 14:15).

HOBAIAH (*Yahweh has hidden*). Priest whose descendants were excluded from priesthood (Ezr 2:61; Ne 7:63).

HOD (*grandeur*). A son of Zophah (1Ch 7:37).

HODAVIAH (*give thanks to Yahweh*).
1. Chief in Manasseh (1Ch 5:24).
2. Benjamite (1Ch 9:7).
3. Levite whose descendants returned with Zerubbabel (Ezr 2:40; 3:9; Ne 7:43).
4. Son of Elioenai (1Ch 3:24).

HODESH (*new moon*). Wife of Shaharaim (1Ch 8:9).

HODEVAH *See Hodaviah, 3.*

HODIAH (*grandeur is Yahweh*).
1. Wife of Ezra (1Ch 4:19).
2. A Levite (Ne 8:7; 9:5; 10:10, 13).
3. An Israelite chief (Ne 10:18).

HODSHI *See Tahtim Hodshi.*

HOGLAH (*partridge*). A daughter of Zelophehad (Nu 26:33; 27:1; 36:11; Jos 17:3).

HOHAM Amorite king who entered a league against Joshua (Jos 10:3).

HOLIDAY (*a good day*). For rest. *See Sabbath.* One year in seven (Lev 25:2-7). *See Jubilee.*

HOLINESS

Defined:
Sin and holiness, sinful man and the holy Yahweh, are the dominant ideas in the Mosaic law. The supreme purpose of the system of Mosaic ordinances was to impress Israel as a separated people and through Israel to impress all people for all time that a holy God can be pleased by none but holy people. This is a central truth of the true religion. The student must, therefore, seek for this spiritual purpose through all the ordinances of the law. Defilement and uncleanness, exclusion of the unclean from the congregation atonements and atoning sacrifices, washings and purifications, whole burnt offerings, unblemished priests and unblemished offerings, typifying unblemished and uncorrupted motives in worship and service— all these were ordained as object lessons to teach that there is a difference between unholiness and holiness and thus to exalt holiness as the supreme lesson of life.

As in the books of the Mosaic law, so throughout the Holy Scriptures, the attainment of holiness is a dominant theme.

Attribute of God:
(Jos 24:19; 1Sa 6:20; Job 6:10; Ps 22:3; 47:8; 60:6; 89:35; 111:9; 145:17; Isa 5:16; 6:3; 29:19, 23; 41:14; 43:14-15; 47:4; 49:7; 57:15; Eze 36:21-22; 39:7, 25; Hos 11:9; Hab 1:12-13; Lk 1:49; Jn 17:11; Ro 1:23; Rev 4:8; 6:10; 15:4).

Described:
(Ro 14:17). As walking in uprightness (Isa 57:2). As a highway (Isa 35:8). As departing from evil (Ps 34:14; 37:27). As satisfying (Jn 6:35). As crucifying the sinful nature (Gal 5:24). As a new creature (Gal 6:15). As a new self (Eph 4:24; Col 3:10). As a rest (Heb 4:3, 9). As pure, peaceable, gentle (Jas 3:17).

Commanded:
(Ge 17:1; Ex 22:31; Lev 10:8-10; 11:44-45; 19:2; 20:7, 26; Nu 15:40; Dt 13:17; 18:13; Jos 7:13; 2Ch 20:21; Job 5:24; Ps 4:4; 97:10; Isa 52:1, 11; Mic 6:8; Zep 2:3; Mt 5:19-30, 48; 12:33; Jn 5:14; Ro 6:1-23; 1Co 3:16; 5:7; 15:34; 2Co 6:14-17; 7:1; Eph 1:4; 5:1, 3, 8-11; 1Th 4:3-4, 7; 5:22-23; 2Th 2:13; 1Ti 4:12; 5:22; 6:11-12; 2Ti 2:19, 21-22; 1Pe 1:5; 2Pe 1:5-8; 1Jn 2:1, 5, 29; 2Jn 4; Rev 18:4).
Commanded upon Israel (Ex 19:6; 22:31; Dt 7:6; 26:19; 28:9; Isa 4:3; 52:1, 11; 60:1, 21; Zec 8:3; 14:20-21).
Commanded upon the church (2Co 11:2; 1Pe 2:5, 9; Rev 19:8).

Exhortations to:
(Mt 5:30; Jn 5:14; Ro 6:13, 19; 12:1-2; 13:12-14; 1Co 6:13, 19-20; 10:31; 2Co 13:7-8; Eph 4:22-24; Col 3:5, 12-15; 1Th 2:12; 3:13; 1Ti 4:12; Tit 2:9-10, 12; 1Pe 4:1; 2Pe 3:11-12, 14; 3Jn 11).

Motives to:
God's holiness (Ge 17:1; Lev 11:44-45; 19:2; 20:26; Isa 6:1-8; Mt 5:48; 1Pe 1:15-16). God's mercies (Ro 12:1).

Taught:
By figures (Isa 61:9-11; Mt 12:33; 1Co 3:17; Eph 2:21). By inscriptions (Ex 28:36; Zec 14:20).
By disfellowship: Of the uncircumcised (Ge 17:14). Of those who violated the law, of unleavened bread (Ex 12:15), of sacrifices (Lev 17:9; 19:5-7), or purification (Nu 19:20). Of those who were defiled (Lev 7:25, 27; 13:5, 21, 26; 17:10; 18:29; 19:8; 20:3-6; Nu 5:2-3; 19:13). Of those who were guilty of blasphemy (Nu 15:31).
As a condition of fellowship: (Heb 12:14).

Typified:
In unblemished offerings (Ex 12:5; Lev 1:3, 10; 3:1, 6; 4:3, 23; 5:15; 6:6; 9:2-3; 22:19, 21; Nu 28:3, 9, 11, 19, 31; 29:2, 8, 13, 17, 20, 23, 26, 29, 32, 36). In washing of offerings (Lev 1:9, 13). In washing of priests (Ex 29:4; Lev 8:6; 1Ch 15:14). In washing of garments (Lev 11:28, 40; 13:6, 34; 14:8-9, 47; 15:5-13; Nu 19:7-8, 10, 19, 21). In purifications (Lev 12:4, 6-8; 15:16-18, 21-22, 27; 16:4, 24, 26, 28; 17:15-16). By differentiating between clean and unclean animals (Lev 11:1-47; 20:25; Dt 14:3-20).

See God, Holiness of; Sanctification.

HOLM NIV "cypress" (Isa 44:14, RSV). *See Cypress Wood.*

HOLON (perhaps *sandy*).
1. Levitical city in hill country of Judah (Jos 15:51), called Hilen (1Ch 6:58).
2. Moabite town (Jer 48:21).

HOLY *See Holiness; Sanctification.*

HOLY DAY *See Holiday.*

HOLY GHOST *See Holy Spirit.*

HOLY OF HOLIES Most holy place, in the tabernacle (Lev 4:6), in the temple (1Ki 6:16). Separated from the holy place by the veil (Ex 26:33; Heb 9:3). Contained atonement cover and ark of the testimony (Ex 26:34; 40:20-21; 1Ki 8:6), the cherubim (Ex 25:18-20; 26:34; 37:7-9; Heb 9:3-5).
Divine dwelling place (Ex 25:8, 21-22; 26:34; Lev 16:2). Entered by the high priest on the Day of Atonement (Ex 26:34; Lev 16:12-13; Heb 9:6-7). Atonement made for (Ex 26:34; Lev 16:15-17, 33).

See Holy Place; Tabernacle.

HOLY PLACE In the tabernacle and the temple. Separated from the most holy place by the veil (Ex 26:33).
Contents of: Altar of incense (Ex 30:1-6; 40:5, 26), the table of the bread of the Presence (Ex 40:4, 24; Heb 9:2), the lampstand (Ex 26:35; 40:4, 24; Heb 9:2). *See various items by name.*
Priests ministered in (Ex 29:30; 39:1, 41; Heb 9:6), required to eat sin offering in (Lev 6:25-26; 10:17).

See Sanctuary; Tabernacle; Temple.

HOLY SPIRIT (Ge 1:2; Ps 51:11; Mt 1:18, 20; Gal 3:2-3, 14; 6:8; Col 1:8; Heb 6:4).

Activities:
Convinces of sin (Ge 6:3; Jn 16:8-11). Comforts (Jn 14:16-17, 26; 15:26; 16:7-14; Ac 9:31). Guides (Jn 16:13; Ac 13:2-4; 15:8, 28; 16:6-7; Ro 8:4, 14; Gal 5:16, 18, 25). Helps our infirmities (Ro 8:26). Regenerates (Jn 3:5-6; 2Co 3:3, 18; Tit 3:5-6). Sanctifies (Ro 15:16; 1Co 6:11; 2Th 2:13; 1Pe 1:2). Dwells in believers (Ro 8:11). Invites to salvation (Rev 22:17). Communion with (2Co 13:14; Php 2:1).
Given to every Christian (1Co 12:7). Given in answer to prayer (Lk 11:13; Ac 8:15), through laying on of hands (Ac 8:17-19; 19:6). Access to the Father by (Eph 2:18). Prayer in (Eph 6:18; Jude 20). Wisdom and strength from (Ne 9:20; Zec 4:6; Eph 3:16). Liberty from (2Co 3:17). Love of God given by (Ro 5:5).
Ministers commissioned by (Ac 20:28). Christian baptism in the name of, with the name of Father and son (Mt 28:19). Gospel preached in power of (1Co 2:4, 10; 1Pe 1:5; 1Pe 1:12). Word of God, sword of (Eph 6:17). Water, a symbol of (Jn 7:38-39). Demons cast out by (Mt 12:28). Power to bestow, not for sale (Ac 8:18-20).
Poured Upon: Israel (Isa 32:15; Eze 39:29). The Gentiles (Ac 10:19-20, 44-47; 11:15-16). All people (Joel 2:28-29; Ac 2:17).

Jesus and the Spirit:
Immaculate conception of Jesus by (Mt 1:20; Lk 1:35). Jesus anointed and led by (Isa 61:1; Mt 3:16; 4:1; Mk 1:10; Lk 3:22; 4:18; Jn 1:32-33; Ac 10:38; Heb 9:14). Sent in Jesus' name (Jn 14:15-17; 15:26).

Christians:
Are temples of (1Co 3:16; 6:19). Are filled with (Ac 2:4, 33; 4:8, 31; 6:5; 8:17; 11:24; 13:9, 52; Eph 5:18; 2Ti 1:14). Have fellowship with (Ro 8:9, 11; 1Co 3:16; 6:19; 2Co 13:14; Php 2:1). Receive deposit of (2Co 1:22; 5:5; Eph 1:13-14). Are sealed with (2Co 1:22; Eph 1:13; 4:30). Have righteousness, peace, and joy in (Ro 14:17; 15:13; 1Th 1:6). Are unified by (1Co 12:13). Testify that Jesus is Lord by (Jn 15:26; 16:14; 1Co 12:3).

Baptism of:
(Mt 3:11; Mk 1:8; Lk 3:16; Jn 1:33; 20:22; Ac 1:5; 11:16; 19:2-6; 1Jn 2:20, 27).

Deity of: See Trinity, Holy.

Fruit of: (Ro 8:23; Gal 5:22-23).

Gifts of:
Foretold (Isa 44:3; Joel 2:28-29). Of different kinds (1Co 12:4-6, 8-10, 28). Bestowed for the confirmation of the gospel (Ro 15:19; Heb 2:4). See Gifts From God.

Inspiration of:
(Mt 10:20; Mk 13:11; Lk 12:12; 1Co 2:4, 10-14; 1Ti 4:1).

Instances of : Joseph (Ge 41:38). Bezalel (Ex 31:3; 35:31). The seventy elders (Nu 11:17). Balaam (Nu 24:2). Judges Othniel (Jdg 3:10), Gideon (Jdg 6:34), Jephthah (Jdg 11:29). King Saul (1Sa 11:6). King David (1Ch 28:11-12). The prophets (2Pe 1:21). Azariah (2Ch 15:1). Zechariah (2Ch 24:20).
Zechariah (Lk 1:67). Elizabeth (Lk 1:41). Simeon (Lk 2:25-26). John the Baptist (Lk 1:15). The disciples (Ac 6:3; 7:55; 8:29; 9:17; 10:45).

Intercession of: (Ro 8:26-27).

Power of:
Promised (Lk 24:49; Ac 1:8; 2:38). On Christ (Mt 12:28; Lk 4:14). On ministers (Ac 2:4; Ro 15:19). On the righteous (Ro 15:13; Eph 3:16).

Revelations from:
(Mk 12:36; Lk 2:26-27; Jn 16:13; 1Co 2:10-11; Eph 3:5; 1Ti 4:1; Heb 3:7; 2Pe 1:21; Rev 2:7, 11, 29; 14:13).

Sin Against:
(Ac 8:18-22; 1Jn 5:16). By grieving (Isa 63:10-11, 14; Eph 4:30). By resisting (Ac 5:9; 7:51; Eph 4:30; 1Th 5:19; Heb 10:29). By blaspheming (Mt 12:31-32; Mk 3:29; Lk 12:10). By lying to (Ac 5:3).

Withdrawn From Unrepentant Sinners:
(Ge 6:3; Dt 32:30; Jer 7:29; Hos 4:17-18; 9:12; Ro 1:24, 26, 28).

Instances of: Antediluvians (Ge 6:3-7). Israelites (Dt 1:42; 28:15-68; 31:17-18). Saul (1Sa 16:14; 18:12; 28:15-16; 2Sa 7:15).

Witness of:
(Ac 5:32; Ro 8:15-16; 9:1; 2Co 1:22; 5:5; Gal 4:6; Eph 1:13-14; Heb 10:15; 1Jn 3:24; 4:13; 5:6-8).

Emblems of:

Water—
(Jn 3:5; 7:38-39). Fertilizing (Ps 1:3; Isa 27:3; 44:3-4; 58:11). Refreshing (Ps 46:4; Isa 41:17-18). Freely given to those who are thirsty (Isa 55:1; Jn 4:14; Rev 22:17). Cleansing (Eze 16:9; 36:25; Eph 5:25-27; Heb 10:22). Abundant (Jn 7:37-38).

Fire—
As a guiding light as the Israelites traveled at night (Ex 13:21; Ps 78:14). Purifying (Isa 4:4; Mal 3:2-3). Searching (Zep 1:12, w 1Co 2:10).

Wind—
Powerful (1Ki 19:11, w Ac 2:2). Reviving (Eze 37:9-10, 14). Independent (Jn 3:8). The coming of the promised Holy Spirit at Pentecost (Ac 2:2).

Oil—
Consecrating (Isa 61:1). Comforting (Isa 61:3; Heb 1:9). Illuminating (Mt 25:3-4; 1Jn 2:20, 27). Healing (Lk 10:34; Jas 5:14).

Rain and Dew—
Blessing (Ps 133:3; Hos 14:5). Righteousness (Hos 10:12).

A Dove—
(Mt 3:16).

A Voice—
Guiding (Isa 30:21, w Jn 16:13). Speaking through the Twelve as they were to go out (Mt 10:20). Warning (Heb 3:7-11).

A Seal—
(Rev 7:2). Authenticating (Jn 6:27; 2Co 1:22). Securing (Eph 1:13-14; 4:30).

Tongues of Fire—
(Ac 2:3-4, 6-11).
See Titles and Names, Titles and Names of the Holy Spirit.

HOLY TRINITY See God; Jesus the Christ; Holy Spirit; Trinity, Holy.

HOMAGE Rendered, to Joseph (Ge 41:43), to kings (1Ki 1:16, 23, 31), to princes (Est 3:2, 5), to Mordecai (Est 6:11), to Daniel (Da 2:46). Refused, by Peter (Ac 10:25-26), by Paul and Barnabas (Ac 14:11-18), by the angel seen by John in his vision (Rev 10:10; 22:8-9).
See Worship.

HOMAM An Edomite and a son of Lotan (Hebrew *Hemam*, a variant of *Homam*) (Ge 36:22, ftn; 1Ch 1:39).

HOME See Family.

HOMELESS (Job 24:8; La 4:5; Lk 9:58; 1Co 4:11).

HOMER (*the load a donkey can carry*). A measure. See Measure.

HOMESTEAD Mortgaged (Ne 5:3). When alienable, and when inalienable (Lev 25:25-34). See Land.

HOMICIDE

Accidental:
(Ex 21:13; Nu 35:11-15, 22-28, 32; Dt 4:41-43; 19:1-10; Jos 20:1-9). See Cities of Refuge.

Murder:
(Job 24:14; Ps 10:8; 38:12; 94:3, 6; Pr 12:6; 28:17; Isa 59:3; Jer 2:34; 7:9-10; 19:4; Eze 22:9; Hos 4:1-3; Hab 2:10, 12). God's abhorrence of (Ps 5:6; 9:12; Pr 6:16-17).
Forbidden (Ex 20:13; Dt 5:17; Pr 1:15-16; Jer 22:3; Mt 5:21; 19:18; Mk 10:19; Lk 18:20; Ro 13:9; 1Ti 1:9; Jas 2:11; 1Pe 4:15; 1Jn 3:12, 15).
Through conspiracy (Ps 37:32; Pr 1:11-12). In hearts of the wicked (Mt 15:19; Mk 7:21). Impenitence for (Rev 9:21). Penitence for (Ps 51:1-17). Inquest over suspected (Dt 21:1-9).

Instances of:
Cain (Ge 4:8). Lamech (Ge 4:23-24). Simeon and Levi (Ge 34:25-31). Pharaoh (Ex 1:16, 22). Moses (Ex 2:12). Ehud (Jdg 3:16-23). Abimelech (Jdg 9:5, 18, 56). Joab (2Sa 3:24-27; 20:9-10; 1Ki 2:5). Solomon (1Ki 2:23-46). Recab and Baanah (2Sa 4:5-8). David (2Sa 11:14-17; 12:9). Absalom (2Sa 13:22-29). Baasha (1Ki 15:27-29). Zimri (1Ki 16:9-11). Ahab and Jezebel (1Ki 21:1024). Hazael (2Ki 8:15). Jehu (2Ki 9:24-37). Athaliah (2Ki 11:1). Of Joash by his servants (2Ki 12:20-21). Menahem (2Ki 15:16). Of Sennacherib, by his sons (2Ki 19:37; Isa 37:38). Manasseh (2Ki 21:16; 24:4). Of Amon, by his servants (2Ki 21:23). Jehoram (2Ch 21:4). Joash (2Ch 24:21). Amaziah's soldiers (2Ch 25:12). Nebuchadnezzar (Jer 39:6). Ishmael (Jer 41:1-7).
Herod the Great (Mt 2:16). Herod the tetrarch (Mt 14:10; Mk 6:27). Barabbas (Mk 15:7; Ac 3:14).

Punishment for:
(Lev 24:17; Dt 19:11-13; Ps 55:23). By a curse (Ge 4:9-12; 49:7; Dt 27:24-25). By death (Ge 9:5-6; Ex 21:12, 14; Nu 35:16-21, 30-33; Dt 17:6; 1Ki 21:19; Eze 35:6; Hos 1:4). By everlasting punishment (Rev 21:8; 22:15).

Instances Of Punishment For—
Cain (Ge 4:11-15). The murderer of Saul (2Sa 1:15-16). David (2Sa 12:9-18). Joab (1Ki 2:31-34). Haman (Est 7:10). The murderers of Ish-Bosheth (2Sa 4:11-12), of Joash (2Ki 14:5).

HOMOSEXUAL Sexual activity between members of the same sex is universally condemned in Scripture. Male homosexuality forbidden by law and punished by death (Lev 18:22; 20:13). Male and female homosexuality condemned (Ro 1:26). With other sexually immoral persons excluded from the kingdom of God (1Co 6:9-11). Male shrine prostitution was practiced even in the temple (1Ki 14:24; 15:12; 2Ki 23:7). Male prostitutes also translates the derogatory term "dog" (Dt 23:17-18; possibly Rev 22:15). See Dog.
Instances of: the men of Sodom (Ge 19:4-5; Jude 7) and Gibeah (Jdg 19:22).

HONESTY

General:
Prayer of (Ps 7:3-4). Promises for (Ps 15:5; 24:4). Pleases God (Pr 11:1; 12:22). Proceeds from God (Pr 16:11; 20:10). Golden rule of (Mt 7:12; Lk 6:31).

Commanded:
(Lev 19:35-36; Dt 16:20; 25:13-16; Pr 4:25; Eze 45:10; Mk 10:19; Lk 3:12-13; Ro 13:13; Php 4:8; Col 3:22; 1Th 4:11-12; 1Ti 2:2; 1Pe 2:11-12).

Instances of:
Jacob, returning money placed in sacks (Ge 43:12). Samuel, incorruptible in his judicial duties (1Sa 12:3-5). Overseers of temple repairs, with whom no reckoning was kept (2Ki 12:15; 22:4-7). Treasurers of the temple (Ne 13:13).
Paul, in all his actions (Ac 24:16; 2Co 4:1-2; 7:2; 8:21). The writer of Hebrews (Heb 13:18).
See Integrity; Righteousness; Dishonesty.

HONEY (Ex 16:31; 2Sa 17:29; Pr 25:27; SS 4:11; Isa 7:15; Mt 3:4). Not to be offered with sacrifices (Lev 2:11). Found in rocks (Dt 32:13; Ps 81:16), upon the ground (1Sa 14:25). Samson's riddle concerning (Jdg 14:14). Sent as a present by Jacob to Egypt (Ge 43:11). Plentiful in Israel (Ex 3:8; Lev 20:24; Dt 8:8; Eze 20:6), in Assyria (2Ki 18:32). An article of merchandise from Israel (Eze 27:17).

HOOD NIV "tiaras" (Isa 3:23). See Crown.

HOOF Parting of, one of the physical marks for distinguishing clean and unclean animals (Lev 11:3-8; Dt 14:3-8).

HOOKS For tabernacle, made of gold (Ex 26:32, 37; 36:36), silver (Ex 27:10; 38:10-12, 17, 19). In the temple, seen in Ezekiel's vision (Eze 40:43). Used for catching fish (Eze 29:4). For pruning (Isa 2:4; 18:5; Joel 3:10). See Meat Forks.

Figurative: (Ex 38:4).

HOOPOE A bird forbidden as food (Lev 11:19; Dt 14:18). See Birds.

HOPE

Godly:
In God (Ps 31:24; 33:22; 38:15; 39:7; 43:5; 71:5, 14; 78:7; 130:7; 146:5; Jer 17:7; La 3:21, 24, 26; 1Pe 1:21). A helmet (1Th 5:8). An anchor (Heb 6:18-19). Joy in (Pr 10:28; Ro 5:2; 12:12; Heb 3:6).
Of God's calling (Eph 1:18; 4:4). Of eternal life (Col 1:5-6, 23, 27; Tit 1:2; 3:7; 1Pe 1:3, 13; 1Jn 3:3). Of the resurrection (Ac 23:6; 24:14-15; 26:6-7; 28:20). Deferred (Pr 13:12).
Of wicked shall perish (Job 8:13; 11:20; 27:8; Pr 10:28; 11:7, 23).

Grounds of:
God's Word (Ps 119:74, 81; Ro 15:4). God's mercy (Ps 33:18). Jesus Christ (1Th 1:3; 1Ti 1:1).

Instances of:
(Job 31:24, 28; Ps 9:18; 16:9; 119:116; Pr 14:32; 23:18, 22; 24:14; Hos 2:15; Zec 9:12; Ro 4:18; 5:3-5; 15:13; 1Co 13:13; 2Co 3:12; Gal 5:5; Eph 2:12; Php 1:20; 2Th 2:16; Heb 6:11; 1Pe 3:15).
See Faith.

HOPHNI (*tadpole*). Son of Eli (1Sa 1:3). Sin of (1Sa 2:12-36; 3:11-14). Death of (1Sa 4:4, 11, 17).

HOPHRA A pharoah who ruled Egypt from 589-570 B.C. (Jer 44:30).

HOR (perhaps *mountain*). Mountain on which Aaron died (Nu 20:22-29; 21:4; 33:38-39; 34:7-8; Dt 32:50).

HOR HAGGIDGAD (*cavern of the Gidgad*). Israelite encampment (Nu 33:32-33), called Gudgodah (Dt 10:7).

HORAM (*height* ISBE). King of Gezer (Jos 10:33).

HOREB (*dry, desolate*). A range of mountains of which Sinai is chief (Ex 3:1; 17:6; 33:6; Dt 1:2, 6, 19; 4:10, 15; 5:2; 9:8; 29:1; 1Ki 8:9; 19:8; 2Ch 5:10; Ps 106:19; Mal 4:4). See Sinai, Mount of, Desert of.

HOREM (*consecrated*). A fortification in Naphtali (Jos 19:38).

HORESH A stronghold in the Desert of Ziph (1Sa 23:15-19).

HORI (*cave-dweller*).
1. Son of Lotan (Ge 36:22, 30; 1Ch 1:39).
2. A Simeonite (Nu 13:5).

HORITE(S) People conquered by Kedorlaomer (Ge 14:6), may be the same as the Hivites (Ge 34:2; Jos 9:7), thought to be Hurrians, from highlands of Media.

HORMAH (*consecration*). A city SW of the Dead Sea (Nu 14:45; 21:1-3; Dt 1:44). Taken by Judah and Simeon (Jdg 1:17; Jos 12:14). Allotted to Simeon (Jos 19:4; 1Ch 4:30). Within the territory allotted to Judah (Jos 15:30; 1Sa 30:30).

HORN Used to hold the anointing oil (1Sa 16:1; 1Ki 1:39). Used for a trumpet. See Trumpet.

Figurative:
Of divine protection (2Sa 22:3). Of power (1Ki 22:11; Ps 89:24; 92:10; 132:17).

Symbolic:
(Da 7:7-24; 8:3-9, 20; Am 6:13, ftn.; Mic 4:13; Zec 1:18-21; Rev 5:6; 12:3; 13:1, 11; 17:3-16).

HORNET (*depression, discouragement*). A hornet or wasp (Ex 23:28; Dt 7:20; Jos 24:12).

HORON See Beth Horon.

HORONAIM (*twin hollows, twin caves*). A town of Moab (Isa 15:5; Jer 48:3, 5, 34).

HORONITE (*citizen of Horonaim*, or more probably *of Beth Horon*). Sanballat the Horonite, who opposed Nehemiah in the restoration of Jerusalem (Ne 2:10, 19; 13:28).

HORSE

Description of:
Great strength (Job 39:19-25), swifter than eagles (Jer 4:13), snorting and neighing of (Isa 5:28; Jer 8:16), a vain thing for safety (Ps 33:17; Pr 21:31).
Used by the Egyptians in war (Ex 14:9; 15:19), the Israelites (1Ki 22:4). Used for cavalry (2Ki 18:23; Jer 47:3; 51:21). Egypt famous for (Isa 31:1). Forbidden to kings of Israel (Dt 17:16). Hamstrung by Joshua (Jos 11:6, 9), David (2Sa 8:4). Israel reproved for keeping (Isa 2:7; 3:1; Eze 17:15; Hos 14:3). Exported from Egypt (1Ki 10:28-29; 2Ch 9:25, 28), from Babylon (Ezr 2:66; Ne 7:68). Bits for (Jas 3:3), bells for (Zec 14:20), harness for (Jer 46:4). Commerce in (Rev 18:13). See above, Exported. Dedicated to religious uses (2Ki 23:11).

Symbolic:
(Zec 1:8; Rev 6:2-8; 9:17; 19:11-21).

HORSE GATE One of the gates of Jerusalem (Ne 3:28-32; Jer 31:38-40).

HORSE LEECH See Leech.

HORTICULTURE Encouraged (Lev 19:23-25; Dt 20:19-20). See Agriculture; Graft; Pruning.

HOSAH (*refuge*).
1. A city of Asher (Jos 19:29).
2. A Levite (1Ch 16:38; 26:10-11).

HOSANNA (*save now*). Originally a prayer, "O LORD, save us" (Ps 118:25), chanted when Jesus entered Jerusalem (Mt 21:9-15; Mk 11:9-10; Jn 12:13).

HOSEA (*salvation*).

Author: Hosea son of Beeri

Date: About the middle of the eighth century B.C.

Outline:
I. Superscription (1:1).
II. The Unfaithful Wife and the Faithful Husband (1:2-3:5).
 A. The Children as Signs (1:2-2:1).
 B. The Unfaithful Wife (2:2-23).
 1. The Lord's judgment of Israel (2:2-13).
 2. The Lord's restoration of Israel (2:14-23).
 C. The Faithful Husband (ch. 3).
III. The Unfaithful Nation and the Faithful God (chs. 4-14).
 A. Israel's Unfaithfulness (4:1-6:3).
 1. The general charge (4:1-3).
 2. The cause declared and the results described (4:4-19).
 3. A special message to the people and leaders (ch. 5).
 4. A sorrowful plea (6:1-3).
 B. Israel's Punishment (6:4-10:15).
 1. The case stated (6:4-7:16).
 2. The judgment pronounced (chs. 8-9).

3. Summary and appeal (ch. 10).
C. The Lord's Faithful Love (chs. 11-14).
1. The Lord's fatherly love (11:1-11).
2. Israel's punishment for unfaithfulness (11:12-13:16).
3. Israel's restoration after repentance (ch. 14).
See Prophets, The Minor.

HOSHAIAH (*Yahweh has saved*).
1. One of the returned exiles (Ne 12:32).
2. A distinguished Israelite captive (Jer 42:1; 43:2).

HOSHAMA (*Yahweh has heard*). Son of Jehoiachin, king of Judah (1Ch 3:18).

HOSHEA (*salvation*).
1. The original name of Joshua (Nu 13:8, 16; Dt 32:44). *See Joshua.*
2. A chief of Ephraim (1Ch 27:20).
3. King of Israel. Assassinates Pekah and usurps the throne (2Ki 15:30). Evil reign of (2Ki 17:1-2). Becomes subject to Assyria (2Ki 17:3). Conspires against Assyria and is imprisoned (2Ki 17:4). Last king of Israel (2Ki 17:6; 18:9-12; Hos 10:3, 7).
4. A Jewish exile (Ne 10:23).

HOSPITALITY Unselfish (Lk 14:12-14). Deceitful guise of (Pr 9:1-5; 23:6-8). Parable of (Mt 22:2-10).
Commanded:
(Isa 58:6-7; Mt 25:34-39; Ro 12:13; 1Ti 3:2; 5:10; Tit 1:7-8; Heb 13:2; 1Pe 4:9-11; 3Jn 5-8). Toward strangers (Ex 22:11; 23:9; Lev 19:10, 33-34; 24:22; Dt 10:18-19; 26:12-13; 27:19).
Instances of:
Pharaoh to Abraham (Ge 12:16). Melchizedek to Abraham (Ge 14:18). Abraham to angels (Ge 18:1-8). Lot to an angel (Ge 19:1-11). Abimelech to Abraham (Ge 20:14-15). Hittites, to Abraham (Ge 23:3, ftn, 6, 11). Laban, to Abraham's servant (Ge 24:31-33), to Jacob (Ge 29:13-14). Isaac to Abimelech (Ge 26:30). Joseph to his brothers (Ge 43:31-34). Pharaoh to Jacob (Ge 45:16-20; 47:7-12). Jethro to Moses (Ex 2:20). Rahab to the spies (Jos 2:1-16). Man of Gibeah to the Levite (Jdg 19:16-21). Pharaoh to Hadad (1Ki 11:17, 22). Jeroboam to the prophet of Judah (1Ki 13:7). The widow of Zarephath to Elijah (1Ki 17:10-24). The Shunammite to Elisha (2Ki 4:8). Elisha to the Syrian spies (2Ki 6:22). Job to strangers (Job 31:32). David to Mephibosheth (2Sa 9:7-13). King of Babylon to Jehoiachin (2Ki 25:29-30). Nehemiah to rulers and Jews (Ne 5:17-19).
Martha to Jesus (Lk 10:38; Jn 12:1-2). Pharisees to Jesus (Lk 11:37-38). Zacchaeus to Jesus (Lk 19:1-10). Disciples to Jesus (Lk 24:29). The tanner to Peter (Ac 10:6, 23). Lydia to Paul and Silas (Ac 16:15). Barbarians to Paul (Ac 28:2). Publius to Paul (Ac 28:7). Phoebe to Paul (Ro 16:2). Onesiphorus to Paul (2Ti 1:16). Gaius (3Jn 5, 8).
Rewarded:
Rahab (Jos 6:17, 22-25). Widow of Zarephath (1Ki 17:10-24).
See Feasts; Guest; Inhospitableness; Strangers.

HOST (*army*). Army (Ge 21:22), angels (Ps 103:21; Jos 5:14). Heavenly bodies (Dt 4:19), creation (Ge 2:1). LORD of hosts (1Sa 17:45). *See Almighty; God, Names of, Yahweh Tsabbaoth..* One who shows hospitality (Ro 16:23; Lk 10:35). *See Hospitality.*

HOSTAGES (2Ki 14:14; 2Ch 25:24).

HOSTILITY To the Righteous (Mic 7:6; Mt 10:21, 35-36; Mk 13:12; Lk 12:53).

HOT SPRINGS (Ge 36:24).

HOTHAM (*signet ring, seal*).
1. Son of Heber an Asherite (1Ch 7:32).
2. An Aroerite and father of two of David's mighty men (1Ch 11:44).

HOTHAN See Hotham, 2.

HOTHIR (*one who remains*). Son of Heman (1Ch 25:4, 28).

HOUGHING See Hamstring.

HOURS A division of time. Twelve, in the day (Jn 11:9; Mt 20:3-12; 27:45-46), in the night (Ac 23:23). Symbolic (Rev 8:1; 9:15).

HOUSE Built of stone (Lev 14:40-45; Isa 9:10; Am 5:11), brick (Ge 11:3; Ex 1:11-14; Isa 9:10), wood (SS 1:17; Isa 9:10). Built into city walls (Jos 2:15).
Used for worship (Ac 1:13-14; 12:12; Ro 16:5; 1Co 16:19; Col 4:15; Phm 2).
"A man's castle" (Dt 24:10-11).
Architecture of:
Foundations of stone (1Ki 5:17; 7:9; Ezr 6:3; Jer 51:26). Figurative (Ps 87:1; Isa 28:16; 48:13; Ro 15:20; 1Co 3:11; Eph 2:20; 1Ti 6:19; Heb 6:1; Rev 21:14). Cornerstone (Job 38:6; Ps 144:12). Figurative (Ps 118:22; Isa 28:16; Eph 2:20; 1Pe 2:6).
Porches (Jdg 3:23; 1Ki 7:6-7), courts (Est 1:5), summer apartment (Jdg 3:20, w Am 3:15; 1Ki 17:19), inner chamber (1Ki 22:25), chambers (Ge 43:30; 2Sa 18:33; 2Ki 1:2; 4:10; Ac 1:13; 9:37; 20:8), guest chamber (Mk 14:14), pillars (Pr 9:1), with courts (Ne 8:16), lattice (Jdg 5:28), windows (Jdg 5:28; Pr 7:6), walls plastered (Da 5:5), hinges (Pr 26:14).
Roofs, flat (Jos 2:6; Jdg 16:27; 1Sa 9:25; 2Sa 11:2; 16:22; Isa 15:3; 22:1; Mt 24:17; Lk 12:3), battlements required in Mosaic law (Dt 22:8). Prayer on (Ac 10:9). Altars on (2Ki 23:12; Jer 19:13; 32:29; Zep 1:5). Booths on (Ne 8:16), used as place to sleep (Jos 2:8; Ac 10:9), as dwelling place (Pr 21:9; 25:24).
Painted (Jer 22:14; Eze 8:10, 12). Windows of (Hos 13:3). Laws regarding sale of (Lev 25:29-33; Ne 5:3). Dedicated (Dt 20:5; Ps 30 [title]).
Figurative:
(2Sa 7:18; Ps 23:6; 36:8; Jn 14:2; 2Co 5:1; 1Ti 3:15; Heb 3:2).

HOUSE OF GOD A place of prayer (Mt 21:13; Mk 11:17; Lk 19:46). Holy (Ecc 5:1; Isa 62:9; Eze 43:12; 1Co 3:17).
See Synagogue; Tabernacle; Temple.

HOUSEHOLD GODS Used by Laban, stolen by Rachel (Ge 31:19, 30-35), by Micah, stolen by the Danites (Jdg 17:5; 18:14, 17-20). Condemned and disposed of by Jacob (Ge 35:2-4, w Ge 31:35-39). Destroyed by Josiah (2Ki 23:24). *See Idol.*

HOUSETOPS As places of resort (Jos 2:6; 1Sa 9:25; Ne 8:16; Pr 21:9; Mt 10:27; 24:17; Lk 5:19; Ac 10:9).

HUBBAH (*God has hidden [someone from danger?]*). An Asherite (1Ch 7:34).

HUKKOK A place on the boundary line of Naphtali (Jos 19:34).

HUKOK The name of a Levitical city in Asher (1Ch 6:75), a variant spelling of Helkath (Jos 31:21). *See Helkath.*

HUL Son of Aram (Ge 10:23; 1Ch 1:17).

HULDAH (*weasel*). A prophetess. Foretells the destruction of Jerusalem (2Ki 22:14-20; 2Ch 34:22-28).

HUMAN SACRIFICE See Offerings, Human Sacrifices.

HUMILIATION AND SELF-AFFLICTION
Commanded (Lev 16:29-31; 23:26-32; Ezr 8:21-23; 2Ch 7:14).
See Fasting; Humility.

HUMILITY (Ps 51:17; 69:32; 138:6; Pr 3:34; 11:2; 12:15; 16:19; Isa 57:15; 66:2; Lk 10:21; 2Co 7:6; Gal 6:14; Jas 4:6).
Commanded:
(Dt 15:15; Pr 25:6-7a; 27:2; 30:32; Ecc 5:2; Jer 45:5; Mic 6:8; Mt 18:2-4; 20:26-27; Mk 9:33-37; 10:43-44; Lk 9:46-48; 14:10; 17:10; 22:24-27; Jn 13:14-16; Ro 11:18-20, 25; 12:3, 10, 16; 1Co 3:18; 4:6; 10:12; Gal 5:26; Eph 4:1-2; 5:21; Php 2:3-11; Col 3:12; Jas 1:9-10; 4:10; 1Pe 5:3, 5-6).
Feigned, forbidden (Col 2:18-23).
Rewards of:
(Job 5:11; 22:29; Ps 138:6; Pr 15:33; 18:12; 22:4; 29:23; Mt 5:3; 23:12; Lk 1:52; 14:11; 18:13-14).
Exemplified by:
Abraham (Ge 18:27, 32). Jacob (Ge 32:10). Joseph (Ge 41:16). Moses (Ex 3:11; 4:10). David (1Sa 18:18-23; 23:14; 26:20; 2Sa 7:18-20; 1Ch 17:16-18; 29:14). The Psalmist (Ps 8:3-4; 73:22; 131:1-2; 141:5; 144:3). Solomon (1Ki 3:7; 2Ch 1:10; 2:6). Mephibosheth (2Sa 9:8). Ahab (1Ki 21:29). kings and princes of Israel (2Ch 12:6-7, 12). Josiah (2Ki 22:18-19; 2Ch 34:26, 27). Job (Job 7:17-18; 9:14-15; 40:4-5; 42:2-6). Elihu (Job 32:4-7; 33:6). Ezra (Ezr 9:13, 15). Agur (Pr 30:2-3). Isaiah (Isa 6:5). Hezekiah (Isa 38:15). Jeremiah (Jer 1:6; 10:23-24). Daniel (Da 2:30). Ezra and the Jews (Ezr 8:21, 23).
Elizabeth (Lk 1:43). John the Baptist (Mt 3:14; Mk 1:7; Lk 3:16; Jn 1:27; 3:29-30). Jesus (Mt 11:29; 13:4-16). Woman of Canaan (Mt 15:27). The righteous (Mt 25:37-40). The tax collector (Lk 18:13). Centurion (Mt 8:8; Lk 7:6-7). Peter (Ac 2:12). Paul (Ac 20:19; Ro 7:18; 1Co 2:1-3; 15:9-10; 2Co 3:5; 11:30; 12:5-12; Eph 3:8; Php 3:12-13; 4:12; 1Ti 1:15).

HUMTAH (*an [unclean] reptile*). A city of Judah (Jos 15:54).

HUNGER
General:
"Man does not live on bread alone" (Dt 8:3; Mt 4:4; Lk 4:3). Labor excites (Pr 16:26). Source of temptation (Ge 25:29-34; Ex 16:2-3; Heb 12:16). An occasion of the temptation of Jesus (Mt 4:3-4; Lk 4:2-3). Of an enemy, an opportunity for good works (Pr 25:21-22; Ro 12:20).
Experienced by Jesus (Mt 21:18; Mk 11:12). Endured, by Jesus during his temptation (Mt 4:2:4; Lk 4:2-4), by Paul for Christ's sake (1Co 4:11). Foretold as a judgment upon the Israelites (Isa 8:21; 9:20).
Figurative:
Of spiritual desire (Ps 107:9; Pr 2:3-5; Isa 55:1-2; Am 8:11-13; Mt 5:6; Lk 1:53; 6:21; Jn 6:35; 1Pe 2:2).
See Appetite; Famine; Desire, Spiritual; Thirst.

HUNTING Authorized in the Mosaic law (Lev 17:13). By Nimrod (Ge 10:9). By Esau (Ge 27:3, 5, 30, 33). By Ishmael (Ge 21:20). Of lion (Job 10:16). Fowling (1Sa 26:20; Ps 140:5; 141:9-10; Pr 1:17; Ecc 9:12; La 3:52; Am 3:5).
Figurative: (Jer 16:16).

HUPHAM, HUPHAMITE Son of Benjamin and his clan (Nu 26:39).

HUPPAH (*canopy*, hence *protection*). Priest in David's time (1Ch 24:13).

HUPPIM, HUPPITES (*coast people*). Descendants of Benjamin (Ge 46:21; 1Ch 7:12, 15).

HUR (perhaps *child*).
1. An Israelite who assisted in supporting Moses' hands during battle (Ex 17:10, 12; 24:14).
2. A son of Caleb (Ex 31:2; 35:30; 38:22; 1Ch 2:19-20; 2Ch 1:5).
3. A king of Midian (Nu 31:8; Jos 13:21).
4. Called Ben-Hur, an officer of Solomon's commissary (1Ki 4:8).
5. Father of Caleb (1Ch 2:50; 4:4).
6. A son of Judah (1Ch 4:1).
7. A ruler (Ne 3:9).

HURAI One of David's heroes (1Ch 11:32). Also called Hiddai (2Sa 23:30).

HURAM, HURAM-ABI (*brother of the exalted one*).
1. Benjamite (1Ch 8:5).

2. King of Tyre (2Ch 2:3, ftn, 11-12). Usually called Hiram (Hebrew *Huram*, a variant of *Hiram*). *See Hiram.*
3. Tyrian craftsman whose full name is Huram-Abi, is sent by King Hiram to execute the artistic work of the interior of the temple (1Ki 7:13-45; 2Ch 2:13; 4:11-16).

HURI (*linen weaver* ISBE). Father of Abihail (1Ch 5:14).

HURRIANS See Horite(s), Horim.

HUSBAND
Relation to His Wife:
In general (Ge 2:23-24; Mt 19:5-6; Mk 10:7; 1Co 7:3-5). Love for (Eph 5:22-33; Col 3:19). Headship of (1Co 11:3). Chastity of (Pr 5:15-20; Mal 2:14-16). Rights of (1Co 7:3, 5). Sanctified in the wife (1Co 7:14, 16).
May give wife certificate of divorce (Dt 24:1-4). Law relating to, in cases where wife's virtue is questioned (Nu 5:11-31; Dt 22:13-21). Exemptions for (Dt 24:5).
Duties of (Ecc 9:9; Col 3:19; 1Pe 3:7). Family provider (Ge 30:30; 1Ti 5:8).
Examples:
Faithful: Isaac (Ge 24:67), Joseph (Mt 1:19-20). Unreasonable and oppressive (Est 1:10-22).
Figurative:
(Isa 54:5-6; Jer 3:14; 31:32; Hos 2:19-20).
See Family; Marriage.

HUSBANDMAN See Agriculture; Farmer.

HUSBANDRY See Agriculture; Animals; Farmer.

HUSHAH (perhaps *haste*). Son of Ezer (1Ch 4:4). Probably called Shuah (1Ch 4:11).

HUSHAI An Arkite. A counselor of David who overthrew counsels of Ahithophel (2Sa 15:32, 37; 16:16-18; 17:5-15; 1Ch 27:33).

HUSHAM A Temanite (Ge 36:34-35; 1Ch 1:45-46).

HUSHATHITE Family name of Sibbecai, one of David's heroes (2Sa 21:18; 1Ch 11:29; 20:4; 27:11).

HUSHIM
1. Son of Dan (Ge 46:23). Also called Shuham (Nu 26:42). *See Shuham, Shuhamite.*
2. Wife of Shaharaim (1Ch 8:8, 11).

HUSHITES Benjamites; descendants of Aher (1Ch 7:12).

HUSK The skin or heads of grain (Nu 6:4; 2Ki 4:42). *See Pods.*

HUZ Son of Nahor (Ge 22:21). *See Uz.*

HUZOTH See Kiriath Huzoth.

HYACINTH See Colors, Figurative and Symbolic.

HYBRIDIZING Forbidden (Lev 19:19).

HYENA A scavenging wild dog that roams the desert (Isa 13:22; 34:14; Jer 50:39). *See Animals.*

HYGIENE (1Co 6:18; 9:25). *See Sanitation and Hygiene.*

HYKSOS A W Semitic people who ruled an Egyptian empire embracing Syria and Palestine; the core of their rule over Egypt was from 1648-1540.

HYMENAEUS (*of [pagan god] Hymen*). Apostate Christian excommunicated by Paul (1Ti 1:19-20; 2Ti 2:16-18).

HYMN See Psalms; Song.

HYPOCRISY (*pretender, pretentious*).
Described:
(Job 31:33-34; Ps 5:6, 9; 52:4; 78:34-37; Isa 29:13; 32:5-6; 48:1-2; 58:2-5; Jer 12:2; 17:9; Eze 33:30-32; Hos 6:4; 10:1, 4; Zec 7:5-6; Mt 15:3-9; 21:28-32; Mk 7:5-13; 9:50; 14:34-35; Lk 18:11-12; Ro 9:6-7; 1Co 5:8; 13:1; 2Co 4:2; 1Jn 1:6, 10; 2:4, 9, 19; 4:20; Rev 3:1).
Betrays friends (Ps 55:12-14, 20-23; Pr 11:9; 25:19; Ob 7; Zec 13:6).
Hypocrisy of prostitutes (Pr 7:10-21), of false teachers (Mic 3:11; Ro 16:17-18; 2Pe 2:1-3, 17, 19), of dishonest buyers (Pr 20:14).
Condemned:
Abhorred by God (Job 13:16; Ps 50:16-17; Pr 15:8; 21:27; Isa 1:9-15; 9:17; 10:6; 58:2-5; 61:8; 65:2-5; 66:3-5; Jer 5:2; 6:20; 7:4, 8-10; Eze 5:11; 20:39; Hos 8:13; 9:4; 11:12; Am 5:21-27; Zec 7:5-6; Mal 1:6-14; 2:13).
Rebuked by Jesus (Mt 3:7-8; 7:7-8; 9:13; 15:7-9; 16:3; 23:2-33; Lk 6:46; 11:39, 42, 44; 12:54-56; 13:13-17; Jn 6:26, 70; 7:19; 15:2, 6; Rev 2:9; 3:9).
Exposed by Paul (Ro 2:1, 3, 17-29; 2Co 5:12; Gal 6:3; Php 3:2, 18-19; 1Ti 4:2; 2Ti 3:5, 13; Tit 1:16).
Warning to (Job 15:31, 33-34; 17:8; 20:4-5; 27:8-10; 34:30). Warning against (Pr 23:6-8; 26:18-19, 23-26; Jer 9:8; Mic 7:5; Mt 6:1-2, 5, 16, 24; 7:5, 15, 21-23; 16:6; 23:14; Mk 8:15; 12:38-40; Lk 12:1-2; 13:26-27; 16:13, 15; 20:46-47; Jas 1:8, 22-24, 26; 3:17; 4:8; 1Pe 2:1, 16; Jude 12-13).
Punishment for (Job 8:13-15; 36:13-14; Ps 55:23; 101:7; Isa 29:15-16; 33:14; 42:21-22; Eze 5:11; 14:3-4, 7-8; Hos 8:13; 9:4; Mt 22:12-13; 24:50-51; 25:41-45; Ro 1:18).
See Deceit; Deception.
Instances of:
Jacob, in impersonating Esau and deceiving his father (Ge 27). Joseph's sons, in deception of their father concerning Joseph (Ge 37:29-35). Joseph's deception of his brothers (Ge 42-44). Pharaoh (Ex 8:15, 28-29, 32; 9:27-35; 10:8-29). Balaam (Jude 11, w Nu

22-24). Delilah, the wife of Samson (Jdg 16). Jael (Jdg 4:8-21). Ehud (Jdg 3:15-25). The Assyrian field commander (2Ki 18:17-37). Ahaz (Isa 7:12, w 17-25). Johanan (Jer 42:1-12, 20, 22). Ishmael (Jer 41:6-7). The false prophets (Eze 13:1-23).

Herod (Mt 2:8). Judas (Mt 26:25, 48; Jn 12:5-6). Pilate (Mt 27:24). Pharisees (Mt 15:1-9; 22:18; Mk 12:13-14; Jn 8:4-9; 9:24; 19:15). The ruler (Lk 13:14-17). Spies sent to entrap Jesus (Lk 20:21). Priests and Levites (Lk 10:31-32). Chief priests (Jn 18:28). Ananias and Sapphira (Ac 5:1-10). Simon (Ac 8:18-23). Peter and others at Antioch (Gal 2:11-14). Judaizing Christians in Galatia (Gal 6:13). False teachers at Ephesus (Rev 2:2).

See Conspiracy; Treachery.

HYSSOP A plant indigenous to western Asia and northern Africa (1Ki 4:33).

Ceremonial Use:
The Israelites used, in sprinkling the blood of the Passover lamb upon the frames of their doors (Ex 12:22), in sprinkling blood in purifications (Lev 14:4, 6, 51-52; Heb 9:19). Used in the sacrifices of separation (Nu 19:6). Used in giving Jesus vinegar on the cross (Jn 19:29).

Figurative of spiritual cleansing (Ps 51:7).

I

I AM WHO I AM A name of God (Ex 3:14; Rev 1:4, 11, 17). *See God, Names of, Yahweh; Yahweh.*

IBEX Probably a species of antelope (Dt 14:5).

IBHAR (*he chooses*). Son of David (2Sa 5:15; 1Ch 3:6; 14:5).

IBLEAM A town given to the tribe of Manasseh (Jos 17:11). Ahaziah slain there (2Ki 9:27). Generally identified with Bileam (1Ch 6:70).

IBNEIAH (*Yahweh built*). A Benjamite (1Ch 9:8).

IBRI (*Hebrew*). A Levite (1Ch 24:27).

IBSAM (*fragrance*). Son of Tola (1Ch 7:2).

IBZAN (*swift*). The tenth judge of Israel (Jdg 12:8-10), had thirty sons and thirty daughters.

ICE (Job 6:16; 37:10; 38:29; Ps 147:17; Eze 1:22).

ICHABOD (*where is the glory?*). Son of Phinehas, Eli's son (1Sa 4:18-22).

ICONIUM A city of Asia Minor. Paul preaches in (Ac 13:51; 14:21-22; 16:2), is persecuted by the people of (Ac 14:1-6; 2Ti 3:11).

ICONOCLASM Idols to be destroyed (Ex 23:24; 34:13; Nu 33:52; Dt 7:5, 25-26; 12:1-4; Jdg 2:2; Jer 50:2). Destroyed by, Jacob (Ge 35:2-4), Moses (Ex 32:19-20), Gideon (Jdg 6:28-32), David (2Sa 5:21; 1Ch 14:12), Jehu (2Ki 10:26-28), Jehoiada (2Ki 11:18), Hezekiah (2Ki 18:3-6), Josiah (2Ki 23:4-20), Asa (2Ch 14:3-5; 15:8-16), Jehoshaphat (2Ch 17:6; 19:3), Jews (2Ch 30:14), Manasseh (2Ch 33:15).

See Idolatry.

IDALAH A town of Zebulun (Jos 19:15).

IDBASH (*honey*). A descendant of Judah (1Ch 4:3).

IDDO (probably *Yahweh has adorned*).
1. Father of Ahinadab (1Ki 4:14).
2. A descendant of Gershom (1Ch 6:21).
3. A son of Zechariah (1Ch 27:21).
4. A prophet (2Ch 9:29; 12:15; 13:22).
5. Ancestor of Zechariah (Ezr 5:1; 6:14; Zec 1:1, 7).
6. A priest (Ne 12:4, 16).
7. The chief of the Jews established at Casiphia (Ezr 8:17).

IDENTIFICATION With Jesus, price of (Mt 4:19; 8:22; 9:9; 16:24; 19:21; Mk 2:14; 8:34; 10:21; Lk 5:27; 9:23; 18:22; Jn 15:14, 18-19; 16:2). Indication of (Jn 10:27; 12:26; Ac 11:26). *See Discipleship.*

IDLENESS Comparisons regarding (Pr 15:19; 18:9; 22:13; 26:13-16; Ecc 4:5). Poverty from (Pr 6:6-11; 10:4-5; 12:9, 24, 27; 13:4; 14:23; 19:15; 20:4, 13; 23:21; 24:30-34; Ecc 10:18). Denounced (Pr 21:25-26; Isa 56:10; Lk 19:20-24; 2Th 3:10-11; 1Ti 5:13).

A sin of Sodom (Eze 16:49). Other instances of (Mt 20:6-7; Ac 17:21).

See Laziness; Slothfulness; Industry.

IDOL (*image*).
Manufacture of (Ex 20:4; 32:4, 20; Dt 4:23; Isa 40:19-20; 44:9-12, 17; Hab 2:18; Ac 19:24-25). Manufacture of forbidden (Ex 20:4; 34:17). Made of gold (Ex 32:3-4; Ps 115:4-7; 135:15-17; Isa 2:20; 30:22; 31:7; Hos 8:4), silver (Isa 2:20; 30:22; 31:7; Hos 8:4), wood and stone (Lev 26:1; Dt 4:28; 2Ki 19:18; Isa 37:19; 41:6; 44:13-19; Eze 20:32). Coverings of (Isa 30:22).

Prayer to, unanswered (1Ki 18:25-29). Falls down before the ark of Yahweh (1Sa 5:1-5). Used by Michal to save the life of David (1Sa 19:13-17). Derided (Ps 115:4-8; 135:15-18; Isa 44:9-17). To be abandoned (Isa 2:20). To be destroyed (Dt 12:3). Things offered

to, not to be eaten (Ex 34:15). Paul's instructions concerning eating things offered to (1Co 8; 10:25-33).

See Iconoclasm; Idolatry.

IDOLATRY (*image*).

Wicked Practices of:
Human sacrifices (Lev 18:21; 20:2-5; Dt 12:31; 18:10; 2Ki 3:26-27; 16:3; 17:17-18; 21:6; 23:10; 2Ch 28:3; 33:6; Ps 106:37-38; Isa 57:5; Jer 7:31; 19:4-7; 32:35; Eze 16:20-21; 20:26, 31; 23:37, 39; Mic 6:7), practices of, relating to the dead (Dt 14:1), licentiousness of (Ex 32:6, 25; Nu 25:1-3; 1Ki 14:24; 15:12; 2Ki 17:30; 23:7; Eze 16:17; 23:1-44; Hos 4:12-14; Am 2:8; Mic 1:7; Ro 1:24, 26-27; 1Co 10:7-8; 1Pe 4:3-4; Rev 2:14, 20-22; 9:20-21; 14:8; 17:1-6).

Other Customs of:
Offered burnt offerings (Ex 32:6; 1Ki 18:26; Ac 14:13), libations (Isa 57:6; 65:11; Jer 7:18; 19:13; 32:29; 44:17, 19, 25; Eze 20:28), of wine (Dt 32:38), of blood (Ps 16:4; Zec 9:7), meat offerings (Isa 57:6; Jer 7:18; 44:17; Eze 16:19), peace offerings (Ex 32:6).

Incense burned on altars (1Ki 12:33; 2Ch 30:14; 34:25; Isa 65:3; Jer 1:16; 11:12, 17; 44:3; 48:35; Eze 16:18; 23:41; Hos 11:2). Prayers to idols (Jdg 10:14; Isa 44:17; 45:20; 46:7; Jnh 1:5). Praise (Jdg 16:24; Da 5:4).

Singing and dancing (Ex 32:18-19). Music (Da 3:5-7). Cutting the flesh (1Ki 18:28; Jer 41:5). Kissing (1Ki 19:18; Hos 13:2; Job 31:27). Bowing (1Ki 19:18; 2Ki 5:18). Tithes and gifts (2Ki 23:11; Da 11:38; Am 4:4-5).

Annual Feasts:
(1Ki 12:32; Eze 18:6, 11-12, 15; 22:9; Da 3:2-3).

Objects of:
Sun, moon, and stars (Dt 4:19; 2Ki 17:16; 21:3, 5; 2Ch 33:3, 5; Job 31:26-28; Jer 7:17-20; 8:2; Eze 8:15-16; Zep 1:4-5; Ac 7:42). Images of angels (Col 2:18), animals (Ro 1:23). Gods of Egypt (Ex 12:12). Golden calf (Ex 32:4). Bronze serpent (2Ki 18:4). Net and dragnet (Hab 1:16). Pictures (Nu 33:52; Isa 2:16). Pictures on walls (Eze 8:10). Earrings (Ge 35:4).

See Artemis; Shrine.

Folly of:
(Dt 4:28; 32:37-38; Jdg 6:31; 10:14; 1Sa 5:3-4; 12:21; 1Ki 18:25-29; 19:18; 2Ch 25:15; Ps 106:19-20; 115:4-5, 8; 135:15-18; Isa 37:19; 44:9-20; 45:20; 46:1-2, 6-7; Jer 2:28; 11:12; 16:19-20; 48:13; 51:17; Hos 8:5-6; Zec 10:2; Ac 14:13, 15; 17:22-23, 29; Ro 1:22-23; 1Co 8:4; 10:5; 12:2; Gal 4:8; Rev 9:20).

Illustrated by contrast of idols with the true God (Ps 96:5; Isa 40:12-26; 41:23-29; Jer 10:5; 14:22; Da 5:23; Hab 2:18-20). Exemplified in the ruin of Israel (2Ch 28:22-23).

Denounced:
(Dt 12:31; 27:15; Job 31:26-28; Ps 44:20-21; 97:7; Isa 42:17; 45:16; Jer 3:1-11; 32:34-35; Eze 16:16-63; 43:7-9; Hos 1:2; 2:2-5; 4:12-19; 5:1-3; 9:10; 13:2-3; Jnh 2:8; Am 4:4-5; Hab 1:16; Ac 17:16-29; Ro 1:25; 1Co 6:9-10).

Forbidden:
(Ge 35:2; Ex 20:3-6, 23; 23:13, 24, 32-33; 34:14, 17; Lev 19:4; 26:1, 30; Dt 4:15-28; 5:7-9; 7:2-5, 16; 11:16-17; 16:21-22; Ps 81:9; Eze 8:8-18; 14:1-8; 16:15-63; 20:7-8, 16, 18, 24, 27-32, 39; 23:7-49; Ac 15:20-29; 1Co 10:14, 20-22; 1Jn 5:21).

Prophecies Relating to:
(Isa 46:1-2). Its punishments (Nu 33:4; Dt 31:16-21, 29; Isa 21:9; Jer 51:44, 47, 52). Its end (Isa 2:8, 18, 20; 17:7-8; 27:9; Jer 10:11, 15; Hos 10:2; 14:8; Mic 5:13-14; Zep 2:11; Zec 13:2).

Punishment of:
(Dt 8:19; 11:28; 13:6-9; 17:2-5; 28:14-18; 30:17-18; 32:15-26; Jdg 2:3; 1Ki 9:6-9; Ne 9:27-37; Ps 16:4; 59:8; 78:58-64; 106:34-42; Isa 1:29-31; 2:6-22; 30:22; 65:3-7; Jer 1:15-16; 5:1-17; 7; 8:1-2, 19; 13:9-27; 16; 17:1-6; 18:13-17; 19; 22:5-9; 44; Eze 6; 8:8-18; 9; 14:1-8; 16:15-63; 20:7-8, 24-39; 22:4; 23:9-10, 22-49; 44:10-12; Hos 8:5-14; 10; 13:14; 5:5; Mic 1:1-9; 5:12-14; 6:16; Zep 1; Mal 2:11-13; Rev 21:8; 22:15).

See Groves; High Places; Iconoclasm; Idol; Prostitute.

IDUMEA (*land of Edom*). Greek and Roman name for Edom (Mk 3:8).

IEZER, IEZERITE (*my [father] is help*). Chief in the tribe of Manasseh (Nu 26:30). Also called Abiezer (Jos 17:2). *See Abiezer, 1.*

IFS OF THE BIBLE *See Blessings, Spiritual, Contingent Upon Obedience.*

IGAL (*he redeems*).
1. Spy of Issachar (Nu 13:7).
2. One of David's heroes (2Sa 23:36).
3. Descendant of Jehoiachin (1Ch 3:22).

IGDALIAH (*Yahweh is great*). Father of Hanan (Jer 35:4).

IGEAL (*he redeems*). Son of Shemaiah (1Ch 3:22).

IGNORANCE

Characteristic of Mankind:
(Job 8:9; 28:12-13, 20-21; Pr 8:5; 19:2; Ecc 7:23-24; Jer 10:23; Hos 4:14; Jn 13:7).

Concerning God (1Sa 3:7; Job 11:7-8, 12; 36:26, 29; 37:5, 15-16, 19, 23; Ps 139:6; Pr 30:3-4; Ac 17:23, 30), his works (Ecc 3:11; 8:17; 11:5), his wisdom (1Co 2:7-10).

Concerning the Holy Spirit (Ac 19:2).

Concerning the Scripture (Mt 22:29; Mk 12:24; Jn 20:9; 1Ti 1:7).

Concerning the future (Pr 27:1; Ecc 8:6-7; Ac 1:7; 1Co 13:9, 12).

Concerning snares of the wicked (Pr 7:6-23; 9:14-18; 22:3; 27:12).

Remedy for (Jas 1:5-6).

Sins of:
Sacrifices for: Unintentional sin by the anointed priest (Lev 4:1-12), by the whole community of Israel (Lev 4:13-21; Nu 15:22-26), by a leader (Lev 4:22-26), by a member of the community (Lev 4:27-35; 5:1-19; Nu 15:27-29; Eze 45:20). Forgiven (1Ti 1:12-13; Heb 5:2). Forgiven on account of reparation (Ge 20:1-7).

Evil consequences of:
(Isa 5:13; Hos 4:6). Alienates from God (Eph 4:18-19). Darkens understanding (Lk 23:34; Jn 16:2-3; 1Co 2:8).

Punishment of:
(Eze 3:18; 8, Lk 12:48). By fines (Lev 22:14). Instances of: Pharaoh (Ge 12:11-17). Abimelech (Ge 20:1-18).

See Knowledge; Wisdom.

IIM (*heaps, ruins*).
1. For KJV Nu 33:45, *See Iyim.*
2. A town in the extreme S of Judah (Jos 15:29).

IJE-ABARIM *See Iye Abarim.*

IJON (*place of heaps [of stone]*). A town of Naphtali (1Ki 15:20; 2Ki 15:29; 2Ch 16:4).

IKKESH (*crooked, perverted*). Father of Iri (2Sa 23:26; 1Ch 11:28; 27:9).

ILAI One of David's heroes (1Ch 11:29), called Zalmon (2Sa 23:28).

ILLEGITIMATE Excluded from the assembly of the Lord to the tenth generation (Dt 23:2). Had no claim to paternal care or the usual privileges and discipline of legitimate children.

Instances of:
Ishmael (Ge 16:3, 15; Gal 4:22), Moab and Ammon (Ge 19:36-37), Jephthah (Jdg 11:1), David's child by Bathsheba (2Sa 11:2-5). Jesus slanderously accused of being (Jn 8:41).

Figurative: (Heb 12:8).

ILLYRICUM Also called Dalmatia. Visited, by Paul (Ro 15:19), by Titus (2Ti 4:10). Now part of Yugoslavia.

IMAGE

Manufactured Images: *See Idol; Idolatry.*

Figurative:
Mankind created in, of God (Ge 1:26-27; 5:1; 9:6; Jas 3:9). Regenerated into (Ro 17:15; Ro 8:29; 2Co 3:18; Eph 4:24; Col 3:10; 1Jn 3:1-3). Christ, of God (Col 1:15; Heb 1:3). *See Image of God.*

IMAGE, NEBUCHADNEZZAR'S Symbolic figure seen by Nebuchadnezzar in a dream, the meaning of which Daniel interpreted (Da 2).

IMAGE OF GOD Mankind is created in God's image (Ge 1:26-27; 5:1, 3; 9:6; 1Co 11:7; Eph 4:24; Col 3:10; Jas 3:9). The image is not corporeal but rational, spiritual, and social. The fall of man destroyed, but did not obliterate the image. Restoration of the image begins with regeneration.

IMAGE WORSHIP *See Idol.*

IMAGINATION Of mankind: Evil (Ge 6:5; 8:21; Dt 29:19-20; Pr 6:16-18). Vain (Ro 1:21). An abomination to God (Pr 6:16-18). Condemned, as equal to act (Mt 5:28).

Known by God (1Ch 28:9). To be subjected (2Co 10:3-5).

IMLAH (*fullness*). Father of Micaiah the prophet (1Ki 22:8-9; 2Ch 18:7-8).

IMMANENCE OF GOD *See Condescension of God.*

IMMANUEL (*God with us*). Isaiah foretold the birth of this child, a sign to Ahaz that God would come near in judgment (Isa 7:14-25). Isaiah's son is called Immanuel (Isa 8:8, 10) and might be the immediate fulfillment. The prophecy is applied to Jesus, whose name means "Yahweh is salvation." He is God come near to save (Mt 1:22-23). *See Jesus the Christ, Prophecies Concerning; Messianic Hope.*

IMMER (*lamb* KB).
1. A family of priests (1Ch 9:12; Ezr 2:37; 10:20; Ne 7:40; 11:13).
2. Head of a division of priests (1Ch 24:14).
3. Name of a man or town (Ezr 2:59; Ne 7:61).
4. Father of Zadok (Ne 3:29).
5. Father of Pashhur (Jer 20:1-2).

IMMORTALITY The biblical concept of immortality is not simply the survival of the soul after bodily death, but the self-conscious continuance of the whole person, body and soul together, in a state of blessedness, due to the redemption of Christ and the possession of "eternal life." The Bible nowhere attempts to prove this doctrine but everywhere assumes it as an undisputed postulate. The condition of believers in their state of immortality is not a bare endless existence but a communion with God in eternal satisfaction and blessedness.

Exemption from death and annihilation. *See Annihilation.*

Apparently Understood:
By David (2Sa 12:23; Ps 21:4; 22:26; 23:6; 37:18, 27; 86:12; 133:3; 145:1-2). By Nehemiah (Ne 9:5). By Job (Job 14:13). By the psalmists (Ps 49:7-9; 73:26; 121:8). By Moses (Ex 3:6; Mt 22:32; Mk 12:26-27; Lk 20:36-38; Ac 7:32). By Abraham (Heb 11:10).

Implied:
In the translation of Enoch (Ge 5:24; Heb 11:5). In the translation of Elijah (2Ki 2:11). In redemption from Sheol (Ps 16:10-11). In the spirit returning to God (Ecc 3:21; 12:7). In the soul surviving the death of the body (Mt 10:28). In the appearance of Moses and Elijah at the transfiguration of Jesus (Mt 17:2-9; Mk

9:2-10; Lk 9:29-36). In the abolition of death (Isa 25:8). In the Savior's promise to his disciples (Jn 14:2-3). In the resurrection (Isa 26:19; Da 12:2-3; Jn 6:40; 1Co 15:12-25; 1Th 4:13-18; 5:10). In eternal inheritance (Ac 20:32; 26:18; Heb 9:15; 1Pe 1:3-5). In the everlasting punishment of the wicked (2Th 1:7-9). In the Judgment (2Pe 3:7).

Taught:
By Christ (Mt 16:26; 19:16-17; 25:46; Mk 10:30; Lk 9:25; 10:25-28; Jn 3:14-16, 36; 5:39-40; 6:39-40, 44, 47, 50-58; 10:28; 11:25-26; 14:19; 17:2-3; Rev 3:4). By Paul (Ro 2:7; 6:22-23; 1Co 15:12-25; 2Co 5:1; Gal 6:8; Col 1:5-6; 2Th 2:16; 1Ti 4:8; 6:12, 19; 2Ti 1:9-10; Tit 1:2; 3:7). By John (1Jn 2:17, 25; 5:13; Rev 1:7; 22:5). By Jude (Jude 21). In Hebrews (Heb 9:15; 10:34; 11:5, 10, 13-16; 13:14).
See Eternal Life; Resurrection; Righteous, Promises to; Judgment; Wicked, Punishment of.

IMMUTABILITY (*not changeable*). The perfection of God by which he is devoid of all change in essence, attributes, consciousness, will, and promises (Mal 3:6; Ps 33:11; 102:26).

IMNA (possibly *he is withheld* BDB; *luck, fortune* IDB). Son of Helem (1Ch 7:35).

IMNAH, IMNITE (*good fortune*).
1. Firstborn of Asher (Ge 46:17; Nu 26:44; 1Ch 7:30).
2. A Levite (2Ch 31:14).

IMPENITENCE Leads to destruction (Mt 24:38-39, 48-51; Lk 13:3; 13:5; Rev 16:9-21).

Admonitions Against:
(Ps 95:8; Jer 6:16-19; 2Co 12:21; Heb 3:8; Rev 2:5, 16, 21-22; 3:3).

Judgments:
Denounced against (Lev 23:29; 26:22-43; Dt 29:19-21; 1Sa 15:23; Ps 7:11-13; 50:17, 21; 68:21; 81:11-12; 107:11-12; Pr 1:24-31; 11:3; 15:10, 32; 19:16; 28:13-14; 29:1; Eze 3:19; 20:36; 33:4-5, 9; Hos 7:13-14; Mt 11:16-21; 12:41-42; 13:15; 23:37-38; Lk 7:35; 10:13; 13:34; Ro 2:4-5).
Denounced against Israel's (Isa 65:12, 15; 66:4; Jer 12:11; 13:17, 27; 14:10; 15:6-7; 19:15; 26:4-6; Eze 3:19, 26; 20:8, 13, 21; Da 9:13; Zec 7:11-13; Mal 2:2).

Reason Given for Impenitence:
Evil company (Jer 2:25). Hypocrisy (Jer 3:10). Idolatry (Isa 46:12-13; Jer 44:17; Eze 20:8; Hos 4:17; 11:2, 7; Rev 9:20-21). Lack of understanding or spiritual blindness (Job 33:14; Ps 32:9; 82:5; Pr 26:11; Hos 5:4). Leniency (Ecc 8:11; Isa 26:10). Material abundance (Ps 52:1; Isa 32:9-11). Obstinacy (Isa 48:4, 8; Jer 8:5-7; Eze 2:4; Ac 7:51). Rebellion (Job 9:2, 4; 24:13; Ps 10:3; 50:7; 78:8; Pr 21:29; Isa 57:11; Jer 5:21-24; 6:10, 16-19; 44:10; Eze 2:4-5; 12:2; 22:8, 13, 21). Refusal to listen (Ps 58:3-5; 106:24-25; Isa 28:12; 42:22-25; Jer 6:16-19; 7:13-14, 24, 28; 11:8; 16:12; 17:23; 22:21; 25:4; 26:4-6; 29:19; 32:33; 35:14-17; 44:16-17; Eze 3:5-7; 20:8; Zec 1:4; 7:11-13; Mt 13:15; Lk 16:31). Seeming lack of hope (Jer 2:25; 18:12).

Instances of:
Pharaoh (Ex 9:30, 34; 10:27; 14:5-9). Israelites (Nu 14:22-23; 2Ki 17:14; 2Ch 24:19; 36:16-17; Ne 9:16-17, 29-30; Jer 36:31). Eli's sons (1Sa 2:25). Amaziah (2Ch 25:16). Manasseh (2Ch 33:10). Amon (2Ch 33:23). Zedekiah (2Ch 36:12-13; Jer 37:2). Jehoiakim and his servants (Jer 36:22-24). Belshazzar (Da 5:22-23). The rich young man (Mt 19:22). Jews who opposed Jesus (Mt 27:4, 25; Mk 3:5).
See Affliction, Of the Wicked; Backsliders; Blindness, Spiritual; Infidelity; Obduracy; Unbelief; Reprobates.

IMPORTS
Of Israel:
From Egypt: Horses, chariots, and linen (1Ki 10:28-29; 2Ch 1:16).
From Gilead: Spices, balm, and myrrh (Ge 37:25).
From Ophir: Gold (1Ki 10:11; 22:48; 1Ch 29:4).
From Tarshish: Gold, silver, ivory, apes, and baboons (1Ki 10:22; 2Ch 9:21), silver, iron, tin, lead, bronze, and slaves (Eze 27:12-13).
From Arabia: Sheep and goats (Eze 27:21).

Of Egypt:
From Gilead: Spices, balm, and myrrh (Ge 37:25).

Of Tyre:
All commodities from and of the trade world (Eze 27:12-25).

IMPORTUNITY *See Prayer.*

IMPOSTORS Deceivers who lead others astray (2Co 6:8); a general word for evil men, cheaters, who also lead others astray (2Ti 3:13).

IMPRECATION Instances of: Ruth (Ru 1:17). Samuel (1Sa 3:17). David (2Sa 1:21; 3:28-29). Shimei (2Sa 16:5, 13).

IMPRECATORY PSALMS 35, 58, 69, 70, 83, 109, 137, 140, among others. These contain expressions of an apparent vengeful attitude towards enemies. For some people these psalms constitute one of the "moral difficulties" of the OT. In his covenant with Abraham, God promises to curse those who curse his people (Ge 12:3). *See Curse; Psalms.*

IMPRISONMENT
Of Joseph (Ge 39:20). Jeremiah (Jer 38:6). John the Baptist (Mt 11:2; 14:3). Apostles (Ac 5:18). Paul and Silas (Ac 16:24). Peter (Ac 12:4).
Debtors (Mt 5:26; 18:30).
See Prison; Prisoners; Punishment.

IMPUTATION *See Impute.*

IMPUTE To attribute something to a person, or reckon something to the account of another.

Aspects of the Doctrine Found in the NT:
1. The imputation of Adam's sin to his posterity.
2. The imputation of the sin of man to Christ.
3. The imputation of Christ's righteousness to the believer (Ge 2:3; Ro 3:24; 5:15; Gal 5:4; Tit 3:7; 1Pe 2:24).

IMRAH (*he rebels*). A chief of the tribe of Asher (1Ch 7:36).

IMRI (*Yahweh spoke*).
1. A man of Judah (1Ch 9:4).
2. Father of Zaccur (Ne 3:2).

INCARNATION (*taking on flesh*). The doctrine that the eternal son of God became human, and that he did so without in any manner or degree diminishing his divine nature (Jn 1:4; Ro 8:3; 1Ti 3:16). *See Jesus the Christ, Incarnation of.*

INCENDIARISM *See Arson.*

INCENSE
General:
Formula for compounding (Ex 30:34-35). Uses of (Ex 30:36-38; Lev 16:12; Nu 16:17, 40, 46; Dt 33:10). Compounded by Bezalel (Ex 37:29), by priests (1Ch 9:30). Offered, morning and evening (Ex 30:7-8; 2Ch 13:11), on the golden altar (Ex 30:1-7; 40:5, 27; 2Ch 2:4; 32:12), in making atonement (Lev 16:12-13; Nu 16:46-47; Lk 1:10). Unlawfully offered by Nadab and Abihu (Lev 10:1-2), Korah, Dathan, and Abiram (Nu 16:16-35), by Uzziah (2Ch 26:16-21). Offered in idolatrous worship (1Ki 12:33; Jer 41:5; Eze 8:11). Presented by the wise men to Jesus (Mt 2:11).
See Altar of Incense.

Figurative:
Of prayer (Ps 141:2). Of praise (Mal 1:11). Of an acceptable sacrifice (Eph 5:2).

Symbolic:
Of the prayers of saints (Rev 5:8; 8:3-4).

INCEST
Defined and Forbidden:
(Lev 18:6-18; 20:11-12, 17-21; Dt 22:30; 27:20-23; Eze 22:11; 1Co 5:1).

Instances of:
Lot with his daughters (Ge 19:31-36). Abraham (Ge 20:12-13). Nahor (Ge 11:29). Reuben (Ge 35:22; 49:4). Amram (Ex 6:20). Judah (Ge 38:16-18; 1Ch 2:4). Amnon (2Sa 13:14). Absalom (2Sa 16:21-22). Israel (Am 2:7). Herod (Mt 14:3-4; Mk 6:17-18; Lk 3:19).

Instances of Marriage of Near Relatives:
Abraham with Sarah (Ge 20:11-13). Isaac with Rebekah (Ge 24:15, 67). Jacob with Leah and Rachel (Ge 29:23, 30). Rehoboam (2Ch 11:18).

INCINERATION *See Cremation.*

INCOMPARABILITY OF GOD *See God, Incomparable; None Like God.*

INCONSISTENCY Hypocritical (Mt 7:3-5; 23:3-4). Inexcusable (Ro 2:1, 21-23).
Instances of: Jehu (2Ki 10:16-31). The Jews, in oppressing the poor (Ne 5:8-9), in accusing Jesus of violating the Sabbath (Jn 7:22-23). Peter and the other disciples, in requiring of the Gentiles that which they did not require of themselves (Gal 2:11-14).
See Deceit; Deception; Hypocrisy.

INDECISION About God (1Ki 18:21; Hos 10:2; Mt 6:24). About ethics (Mt 26:41; Jas 1:8; 4:17; Rev 3:15).
See Decision; Instability; Lukewarmness.
Instances of: Moses at the Red Sea (Ex 14:15). Joshua at Ai (Jos 7:10). Esther (Est 5:8). Rulers, who believed in Jesus (Jn 12:42). Felix (Ac 24:25).

INDIA Probably the eastern limit of the kingdom of Xerxes (Est 1:1; 8:9).

INDICTMENTS
Instances of:
Naboth on charge of blasphemy (1Ki 21:13, w 21:1-16). Jeremiah of treasonable prophecy, but of which he was acquitted (Jer 26:1-24), a second indictment (Jer 37:13-15). Three Hebrew captives on the charge of resistance to authority (Da 3:12, w 3:1-28; 6:13, w 6:1-24).
Jesus, under two charges, first, of blasphemy (Mt 26:61, w Mk 14:58; Mt 26:63-65, w Mk 14:61-64; Lk 22:67-71; Jn 19:7), second, of treason (Mt 27:11, 37; Mk 15:2, 26; Lk 23:2-3, 38; Jn 18:30, 33; 19:12, 19-22).
Stephen for blasphemy (Ac 6:11, 13). Paul (Ac 17:7; 18:13; 24:5; 25:18-19, 26-27). Paul and Silas (Ac 16:20-21).
Indictment rejected (Ac 18:14-16).

INDIGESTION Of Timothy (1Ti 5:23). *See Disease.*

INDUSTRY Brings prosperity (Pr 10:4-5; 12:11, 24, 27; 13:4, 11; 21:5; 22:29; 28:19). Commanded (Ge 2:15; Ex 23:12; 35:2; Dt 5:13; Pr 20:13; 27:23-27; Ecc 9:10; 11:4, 6; Ro 12:11; Eph 4:28; 1Th 4:11-12; 2Th 3:10-12; 1Ti 5:8). Instigated (Pr 16:26). Profitable (Pr 14:4, 23). Reflections concerning (Ecc 1:3; 2:10-11, 17-22).

Exemplified:
By ants and conies (Pr 30:25-26). By prudent wife (Pr 31:13-27).

Instances of:
Jeroboam (1Ki 11:28). Paul (Ac 18:3; 20:33-34; 1Co 4:12; 1Th 2:9; 2Th 3:8).
See Frugality; Idleness; Labor; Slothfulness; Work.

INFANTICIDE The killing of children. Commanded by Pharaoh (Ex 1:15-16; Ac 7:19); by God concerning Midianite boys (Nu 31:17); by Herod (Mt 2:16-18).

INFANTS *See Children.*

INFERTILITY *See Barrenness.*

INFIDELITY
Relating to God:
Disbelief in God (Nu 15:30-31; 2Ch 32:14-19; Isa 29:16). Prosperity tempts to (Dt 32:15). Arguments against (Job 12:7-25; Ps 94:8-9; Isa 10:15; 19:16; 45:9, 18; Ro 1:20; 9:20-21).

Exemplified—
In mocking God (Ps 14:1, 6; 50:21; Isa 57:4-11; Eze 36:2; Da 3:15; Ac 17:18; 2Pe 3:3-4; Jude 18-19). In mocking God's servants (1Ki 22:24; 2Ki 2:23; 2Ch 30:6, 10; 36:16; Jer 17:15; 43:2; Eze 20:49; Ac 2:13).
In rejecting God (Ex 5:2; Job 15:25-26; 21:14-15; Ps 14:1; 53:1; 106:24-25; Jer 2:31). In rejecting Christ (Mt 12:24; 27:39-44; Mk 3:22; Lk 11:15; 19:14, 27). By Antichrist (Da 7:25; 8:25; 11:36-37).
In doubting God's help (Ex 17:7; Ps 3:2; 78:19-20, 22; 107:11-12). In impugning God's holiness (Job 35:3; Ps 10:11, 13; Eze 18:2, 29; Mal 1:7; 3:14), God's knowledge (Job 22:13-14, 17; Ps 59:7; 64:5; 73:11; Isa 29:15; Eze 8:12), God's mercy (Ps 42:3), God's righteousness (Eze 18:2, 29).

Punishment for—
(Nu 15:31; Dt 29:19-21; Ps 12:3-4; Pr 3:34; 9:12; 19:29; 24:9; Isa 3:8; 5:18-19, 24-25; 28:9-10, 14-22; 47:10-11; Jer 5:12, 14; 48:42; 50:24, 29; Eze 9:9-10; 32:20; Hos 7:5, 13, 15; Am 5:18; 7:16-17; Mic 7:10; Zep 1:12; Lk 19:14, 27; Heb 10:28-29; 2Pe 2:1).

Relating to Friends:
(Ps 41:9; Mt 26:14-16, 47-50; Mk 14:10-11, 43-46; Lk 22:3-6, 47-48; Jn 13:18; 18:2-5).
See Presumption; Skepticism; Unbelief.

INFINITY *See God, Infinite.*

INFIRMITY Physical (Ecc 12:3). Of Isaac (Ge 27:1). Of Jacob (Ge 48:10). Moses exempt from (Dt 34:7). Caleb exempt from (Jos 14:11). Of Eli (1Sa 3:2). Of Barzillai (2Sa 19:32).
See Affliction; Blindness; Deafness; Lameness; Old Age; Taste.

INFLAMMATION Disease brought as a curse for unfaithfulness to Yahweh (Dt 28:22). *See Disease.*

INFLUENCE
Intercession in Behalf of Friends:
Of Jonathan for David (1Sa 19:1-6; 20:4-9). Solicited, Bathsheba for Adonijah (1Ki 2:13-18). Offered, Elisha for Shunammite woman (2Ki 4:12-13). Of nobles of Judah in behalf of Tobiah (Ne 6:17-19). Of mother of Zebedee's children for sons (Mt 20:20-24). Of Blastus for Tyre and Sidon (Ac 12:20).

Good Influences:
Injunctions concerning (Mt 5:13-16; Mk 4:21-22; 11:33-36; Jn 7:38; 1Co 7:14, 16; Php 2:15; 1Th 1:7-8; 1Ti 6:1; Heb 11:4; 1Pe 2:11-12; 3:1-2, 15-16).

Instances of—
David over his successors (1Ki 3:3; 2Ki 18:3; 22:2; 2Ch 29:2; 34:2). Asa over Jehoshaphat (1Ki 22:42-43). Joash over Amaziah (2Ki 14:3). Amaziah over Azariah (2Ki 15:1-3). Uzziah over Jotham (2Ki 15:34). Josiah, in religious zeal (2Ki 22:1-20; 2Ch 34:33). Hezekiah, for religious reform (2Ch 29:1-31). Ezra, against marriage with idolaters (Ezr 10:1, 9). Nehemiah, during the rebuilding of the walls of Jerusalem (Ne 4:7-23; 5).

Evil Influences:
Of ruler over servants (Pr 22:12). Of wicked parents over children (Jer 17:1-2). Of wicked priest and people (Hos 4:9). Warnings against (Pr 22:24-25; Lk 12:1; 1Co 5:6-8; Gal 5:7-9; 2Ti 2:14, 17-18; Heb 12:15). Parable of (Mt 13:24-25).

Instances of—
Eve over Adam (Ge 3:6). Solomon's wives (1Ki 11:3-4). The young men over Rehoboam (1Ki 12:8-14; 2Ch 10:8-14). Rehoboam over Abijah (1Ki 15:3). Jeroboam over Nadab (1Ki 15:25-26). Jezebel over Ahab (1Ki 21:4-16, 25). Ahab over Ahaziah (1Ki 22:52-53; 2Ki 8:25-27). Ahab over Jehoram (2Ki 8:16, 18; 2Ch 21:5-6; 22:3-5). Jeroboam over Israel (2Ki 17:21-22). Manasseh over Judah (2Ki 21:9; 2Ch 33:9). Manasseh over Amon (2Ki 21:20-21). Jehoiakim over Jehoiachin (2Ki 24:9).

Political Influence:
(1Ki 2:13-18; 2Ki 4:12-13; Ne 6:17-19; Pr 19:6; 29:26; Da 5:10-12; Mt 20:20-24; Ac 12:20).
See Example; Politics.

INGATHERING, FEAST OF *See Tabernacles, Feast of.*

INGRAFTING *See Graft.*

INGRATITUDE
To God:
(Ro 1:21; 2Ti 3:2). Prosperity tempts to (Dt 6:10-12; 8:12-14; 32:6, 13, 15, 18; 2Ch 26:15-16; Jer 5:7-9, 24; Hos 13:6). Punishment for (Dt 28:47-48; 1Ki 16:1-3; 2Ch 32:25; Ps 78:16-17, 27-32, 42-68; Da 5:18, 20-21).

Instances of—
(Nu 16:9-10). Israel (Dt 31:16; Jdg 2:10-12; 8:34-35; 10:11, 13-14; 1Sa 8:7-8; 10:19; Ne 9:25-26, 35; Ps 106:7, 21; Isa 1:2; Jer 2:6-9, 17, 31; 4:7; 7:13, 19; 11:1, 3; Am 3:1-2; Mic 6:3-4). Saul (1Sa 15:17, 19). David (2Sa 12:7-9). Baasha (1Ki 16:1-2). Jerusalem (Eze 16:17). Humanity (Ro 1:21; 2Ti 3:2).

Ingratitude to Jesus:
The nine lepers (Lk 17:12-18). His own people (Jn 1:11).

Ingratitude of Person to Person:
(Pr 17:13; 2Ti 3:2).

Instances of—
Laban to Jacob (Ge 31). Pharaoh's cupbearer to Joseph (Ge 40:23). Israelites to Moses (Ex 16:3; 17:2-4; Nu 16:12-14), to Gideon (Jdg 8:35). Shechemites (Jdg 9:17-18). Men of Keilah to David (1Sa 23:5-12). Saul to David (1Sa 24). Nabal (1Sa 25:21). David to Joab (1Ki 2:5-6), with the history of Joab's services to David. *See Joab.* David to Uriah (2Sa 11:6-17). David's companions to David (Ps 35:11-16; 38:20; 41:9; 109:4-5). Citizens (Ecc 9:14-16). Joash (2Ch 24:22). Jeremiah's enemies (Jer 18:20).

INHERITANCE Of children (Ge 24:36; 25:5; 2Ch 21:3). Of children of concubines (Ge 15:3; 21:9-11; 25:6). Of children of polygamous marriages (Dt 21:15). Of daughters (Nu 27:8; Job 42:15). Of all mankind (Ecc 2:18-19). Of servants (Pr 17:2). Of real estate inalienable (1Ki 21:3; Jer 32:6-8; Eze 46:16-18).
Law concerning (Nu 27:6-11). Lesson concerning, of prodigal (Lk 15:12, 25-31). Proverbs concerning (Pr 17:2; 20:21).
Instance of Israel to Joseph (Ge 48:21-22).
Figurative: Spiritual (Mt 25:34; Ac 20:32; 26:18; Ro 8:16-17; Gal 4:7; Eph 1:11-14; Col 3:24; Tit 3:7; Heb 1:14; 9:15-17).
See Firstborn; Heir; Testament; Will.

INHOSPITABLENESS Instances of: Toward the Israelites: Edom (Nu 20:1, 18-21), Sihon (Nu 21:22-23), Ammonites and Moabites (Dt 23:3-6). Men of Gibeah toward a Levite (Jdg 19:15). Nabal toward David (1Sa 25:10-17). Samaritans toward Jesus (Lk 9:53). *See Hospitality.*

INIQUITIES, OUR (Job 14:17; Ps 40:12; 90:8; 130:3; Isa 59:2; 64:6; Jer 2:22; Mic 7:10). *See Sin.*

INIQUITY General references to (Job 15:16; Ps 41:6; 53:1; Isa 5:18; Jer 30:14; Eze 9:9; Hos 14:1; Mic 2:1; Mt 23:28; 24:12; Ro 6:19). *See Sin.*

INJUSTICE An abomination to God (Pr 17:15). To the righteous (Pr 29:27).
In civil administration (Ps 82:2; Ecc 5:8; La 3:34-36). In gains, unstable (Pr 28:8; Am 5:11-12). Judged (Pr 11:7; Ecc 3:16; Lk 16:10; 1Th 4:7; Rev 22:11). Practiced by the wicked (Isa 26:10), without shame (Zep 3:5). Protection from, given (Ps 12:5), interceded (Ps 43:1).
God innocent of (2Ch 19:7; Eze 18:25-29; Ro 3:5-8; 9:14-18; Heb 6:10). Job innocent of (Job 16:16-17; 31:13-15).

INK Any liquid used with pen or brush to form written characters (Jer 36:18; 2Co 3:3; 2Jn 12; 3Jn 13).

INKHORN See Writing Kit.

INN A lodging place for travelers. Inns in the modern sense were not very necessary in ancient times, since travelers found hospitality the rule (Ex 2:20; Jdg 19:15-21; 2Ki 4:8; Ac 28:7; Heb 13:2). Ancient inns were usually mere shelters for man and beast, although often strongly fortified.

INNOCENCE Signified by washing the hands (Dt 21:6; Ps 26:6; Mt 27:24). Found in Daniel (Da 6:22), Jeremiah (Jer 2:35). Professed by Pilate (Mt 27:24). Contrasted with guilt (Ge 2:25; 3:7-11).

INNOCENT Not to suffer for guilty (Dt 24:16; 2Ki 14:6; 2Ch 25:4; Jer 31:29-30; Eze 18:20).

INNOCENTS, SLAUGHTER OF The slaughter, by Herod the Great, of children in Bethlehem (Mt 2:16-18). *See Infanticide; Murder.*

INNUENDO (Ps 35:19; Pr 6:13; 10:10). *See Accusation, False.*

INQUEST Into an unsolved murder (Dt 21:1-9).

I.N.R.I The initials of the Latin superscription on the cross of Jesus, standing for IESUS NAZARENUS, REX IUDAEORUM, "Jesus of Nazareth, King of the Jews" (Mt 27:37; Mk 15:26; Lk 23:38; Jn 19:19).

INSANITY (Pr 26:18). Sent as a judgment from God (Dt 28:28; Zec 12:4).
Feigned by David (1Sa 21:13-15). Nebuchadnezzar's (Da 4:32-34). Jesus accused of (Mk 3:21; Jn 10:20). Paul (Ac 26:24-25). Cured by Jesus (Mt 4:24; 17:15).
Demonic:
Saul (1Sa 16:14; 18:10).
False accusation of:
Against Jesus (Mk 3:21; Jn 10:20), against Paul (Ac 26:24-25; 2Co 5:13).
See Demons, Possession by.

INSCRIPTIONS On gravestones (2Ki 23:17). On the turban of the high priest (Ex 28:36). On the sacred diadem (Ex 39:30). On the bells of horses (Zec 14:20).
Over Jesus at the Crucifixion (Mt 27:37; Mk 15:26; Lk 23:38; Jn 19:19). Precepts written on the doorframes and gates and worn on the hand and forehead (Dt 6:6-9; 11:18-20; Isa 57:8).

INSECTS Created by God (Ge 1:24-25). Fed by God (Ps 104:25, 27; Ps 145:9, 15).
Divided Into:
Clean and fit for food (Lev 11:21-22). Unclean and abominable (Lev 11:23-24).
Mentioned in Scripture:
Ant (Pr 6:6; 30:25). Bee (Jdg 14:8; Ps 118:12; Isa 7:18). Cricket (Lev 11:22). Flea (1Sa 24:14). Fly (Ex 8:22; Ecc 10:1; Isa 7:18). Gnat (Ex 8:16; Ps 105:31; Mt 23:24). Grasshopper (Lev 11:22; Jdg 6:5; Job 39:20; Ps 78:46; Isa 33:4; Na 3:15-16). Hornet (Dt 7:20). Katydide (Lev 11:22). Locust (Ex 10:12-13; Joel 1:4; 2:25). Maggot (Ex 16:20). Moth (Job 4:19; 27:18; Isa 50:9). Spider (Job 8:14; Isa 59:5). Worm (Job 25:6; Mic 7:17).

INSINCERITY See Hypocrisy.

INSINUATION See Innuendo.

INSOMNIA Instances of: Xerxes (Est 6:1). Nebuchadnezzar (Da 6:18).

INSPECTION GATE One of the gates of Jerusalem (Ne 3:31). See Miphkad.

INSPIRATION (breathed into).
Claims that the Scriptures are Inspired:
(2Ti 3:16; 1Ki 13:20; 2Ch 33:18; 36:15; Ne 9:30; Job 33:14-16; Isa 51:16; Jer 7:25; 17:16; Da 9:6, 10; Hos 12:10; Joel 2:28; Am 3:7-8; Zec 7:12; Lk 1:70; Ac 3:18; Ro 1:1-2; 1Co 12:7-11; Heb 1:1; 2Pe 1:21; Rev 10:7; 22:6, 8).
Instances of People Inspired by God:
Enoch (Jude 14). Joseph (Ge 40:8; 41:16, 38-39). Moses (Ex 3:14-15; 4:12, 15, 27; 6:13, 29; 7:2; 19:9-19; 24:16; 25:22; 33:9, 11; Lev 1:1; Nu 11:17; 7:89; 9:8-10; 11:17, 25; 12:6-8; 16:28-29; Dt 1:5-6; 5:4-5, 31; 34:10-11; Ps 103:7). Aaron (Ex 6:13; 12:1). The tabernacle workers (Ex 28:3; 31:3, 6; 35:31; 36:1). The seventy elders (Nu 11:16-17, 24-25). Eldad and Medad (Nu 11:26-29). Balaam (Nu 23:5, 16, 20, 26; 24:2-4, 15-16). Joshua (Dt 34:9; Jos 4:15).
Samuel (1Sa 3:1, 4-10, 19-21; 9:6, 15-20; 15:16). Saul (1Sa 10:6-7, 10-13; 19:23-24). Messengers of Saul (1Sa 19:20, 23). David (2Sa 23:2-3; 1Ch 28:19; Mk 12:36). Nathan (1Ki 14:5). Elijah (1Ki 17:1, 24; 19:15; 2Ki 10:10). Micaiah (1Ki 22:14, 28; 2Ch 18:27). Elisha (2Ki 2:9; 3:11-12, 15; 6:8-12, 32; 15:8). Jahaziel (2Ch 20:14). Azariah (2Ch 15:1-2). Zechariah, the son of Jehoiada (2Ch 24:20; 26:5). Isaiah (2Ki 20:4; Isa 6:1-9; 8:11; 44:26; Ac 28:25). Jeremiah (2Ch 26:12; Jer 1:9; 2:1; 7:1; 11:1, 18; 13:1-3; 16:1; 18:1; 20:9; 23:9; 24:4; 25:3; 26:1-2, 12; 27:1-2; 29:30; 33:1; 34:1; 42:4, 7; Da 9:2). Ezekiel (Eze 1:1, 3; 2:1-2, 4-5; 3:10-12, 16, 24; 8:1; 11:1, 4-5, 24; 33:22; 37:1; 40:1; 43:5-6). Daniel (Da 2:19; 7:16; 8:16; 9:22; 10:7-9). Hosea (Hos 1:1-2). Joel (Joel 1:1). Amos (Am 3:7-8; 7:14-15). Obadiah (Ob 1). Jonah (Jnh 1:1; 3:1-2). Micah (Mic 1:1; 3:8). Habakkuk (Hab 1:1). Haggai (Hag 1:13). Zechariah (Zec 2:9; 7:8).
Elizabeth (Lk 1:41). Zechariah (Lk 1:67). Simeon (Lk 2:26-27). Disciples (Mt 10:19; Mk 13:11; Lk 12:11-12; 21:14-15; Ac 2:1-4). The apostles (Ac 2:4). Philip (Ac 8:29). Agabus (Ac 11:28; 21:10-11). John the apostle (Rev 1:10-11).
See Genius; Prophecy; Prophets; Revelation; Word of God, Inspiration of.

INSTABILITY
Warnings Against:
(Pr 24:21-22; 27:8; Mt 6:24; 8:19-22; 12:25; 13:20-21; Mk 4:16-17; Lk 8:13; 9:57-62; Eph 4:14; Heb 13:9; Jas 1:6-8; 4:8; 2Pe 2:14; Rev 2:4; 3:2).
Instances of:
Reuben (Ge 49:4). Pharaoh (Ex 8:15, 32; 9:34; 10:8-11, 16-20; 14:5). Israel (Ex 19:8; 24:3, 7; 32:8-10; Jdg 2:17; 1Ki 18:21; Ps 106:12-13; Jer 2:36). Saul in his feelings toward David (1Sa 18:19). David, in yielding to lust (2Sa 11:2-4). Solomon, in yielding to his idolatrous wives (1Ki 11:1-8). Ephraim and Judah (Hos 6:4). Jews (Hos 6:4-5; Jn 5:35). Lot's wife (Lk 17:32). Disciples (Jn 6:66). Mark (Ac 15:38). Galatians (Gal 1:6; 4:9-11).
See Backsliding; Hypocrisy; Indecision.

INSTINCT Of animals (Pr 1:17; Isa 1:3). Of birds (Jer 8:7). *See Animals; Birds.*

INSTRUCTION Provision for, made by the state (2Ch 17:7-9; Da 1:3-5, 17-20). Sought (Pr 9:9-12; 119:12; 143:8, 10). Paying attention to, commanded (Pr 4:1-2, 10, 13, 20; 5:1-2; 22:17; 23:12, 23). Lack of (2Ch 15:3; Pr 24:30-34). Hatred (Ps 50:17; Pr 1:29-30; 5:12-13; Jer 32:33; Lk 20:1-2). From nature (Pr 24:30-34; Ecc 1:13-18; 3; 4:1; Mt 6:25-30). From the study of human nature (Ecc 3-12).
In religion:
(Ex 24:12; Lev 10:11; Dt 24:8; 27:14-26; 31:9-13; 33:10; 2Ch 17:8-9; 35:3; Ne 8:7-13; Mal 2:6-7). By means of the law (Dt 27:1-26; Ro 2:18; Gal 3:24-25). By means of proverbs (Pr 1:1-6, 20-30). By means of the song of Moses (Dt 31:19; 32:1-44). By priests (Ezr 7:10; Mal 2:7). By Jesus (Mt 5:1-2; Mk 6:2; 12:35; Lk 4:16-21; 19:47; 20:1-8; 21:37-38; 24:27; Jn 7:14; 8:2). By preachers (2Ki 23:2; Ne 8:7-8; 1Co 12:28-29; Eph 4:11). By teachers (2Ki 23:2; Ne 8:7-8; 1Co 12:28-29; Eph 4:11).
By symbols. *See Symbols and Similitudes.* By parables. *See Parable.* Inscriptions on doors and gates (Dt 11:20-21), on monuments (Jos 8:30-35). The public reading of the law (Dt 31:9-13; Jos 8:34-35; Ne 8:2-3).
By Object Lessons:
Passover feast (Ex 12:26-27). Dedication of firstlings (Ex 13:8-10). Phylacteries (Ex 13:9, 16). Inscriptions (Ex 28:36; 39:30; Dt 6:6-9; 11:18-20; Zec 14:20; Mt 27:37). The pot of manna, a reminder of God's care (Ex 16:32). The sacred oil, a symbol of holiness (Ex 30:31). The pillar of twelve stones at the fords of the Jordan (Jos 4:7, 19-24). Tassels on the borders of garments (Nu 15:38-39). The garment torn in pieces (1Ki 11:30-32). The symbolic wearing of sackcloth and going barefoot (Isa 20:2-3). The linen belt (Jer 13:1-11). Potter's vessel (Jer 19:1-12). Basket of figs (Jer 24). Bonds and yokes (Jer 27:2-11; 28). By stones being put in a brick pavement (Jer 43:8-13). Illustrations on a tile (Eze 4:1-3). Lying on one side in public view for a long period (Eze 4:4-8). Eating bread baked with dung (Eze 4:9-17). Shaving the head (Eze 5). Moving household goods (Eze 12:3-16). Eating and drinking sparingly (Eze 12:18-20). Sighing (Eze 21:6-7). The boiling pot (Eze 24:1-14). Widowhood (Eze 24:16-27). Two sticks joined together (Eze 37:16-22).
Of Children:
By parents, commanded (Ex 10:2; 12:26-27; 13:8-10, 14-16; Dt 4:9-10; 6:6-9; 11:18-19; Ps 78:5-8; Pr 22:6; Isa 38:19; Eph 6:4). Law concerning (Dt 31:9-13; Jos 8:35). Exemplified (Ps 34:11; Pr 20:7; Ac 22:3; 2Ti 3:15).

See Children.
By Types:
See Washings; Blemish; Defilement; Disfellowship; Types. See Firstborn; Holiness; Passover; Pillar; Purification.

INSTRUMENTALITY See Agency.

INSTRUMENTS, MUSICAL See Music.

INSURGENTS Army of, David's (2Sa 22:1-2).

INSURRECTION (Ps 64:2). Described by David (Ps 55). Led by Bicri (2Sa 20), Absalom. *See Absalom.* Barabbas (Mk 15:7).

INTEGRITY
General:
Essential (Ex 18:21; Lk 16:10; 2Co 8:21). Commanded (Dt 16:19-20; Pr 4:25-27; Isa 56:1; Mic 6:8; Zec 7:9; Lk 3:13-14; 6:31; 11:42; Ro 13:5; 14:5, 14, 22; Eph 6:6; Php 4:8; Col 3:22-23; 1Ti 1:5; 3:9; Tit 1:7-8; 1Pe 2:12; 3:16).
Rewards of (2Sa 22:21; Ps 15:1-5; 18:20; 24:3-5; Pr 10:9; 20:7; 28:20; Isa 26:7; 33:15-16; Jer 7:5, 7; Eze 18:5, 7-9).
Proverbs concerning (Pr 2:2, 5, 9; 3:3-4; 4:25-27; 10:9; 11:3, 5; 12:22; 14:30; 15:21; 16:11; 19:1; 20:7; 21:3, 15; 22:11; 28:6, 20).
Instances of:
Pharaoh, when he learned that Sarah was Abraham's wife (Ge 12:18-20). Abraham, in instructing his family (Ge 18:19). Abimelech, when warned of God that the woman he had taken into his household was Isaac's wife (Ge 26:9-11). Jacob, in the care of Laban's property (Ge 31:39). Joseph, in resisting Potiphar's wife (Ge 39:8-12), in his innocence of the charge on which he was cast into the dungeon (Ge 40:15). Moses, in taking nothing from the Israelites in consideration of his services (Nu 16:15). Samuel, in exacting nothing from the people on account of services (1Sa 12:4-5). Workmen, who repaired the temple (1Ki 12:15; 22:7).
Priests who received the offerings of gold and other gifts for the renewing of the temple under Ezra (Ezr 2:24-30, 33-34). Nehemiah, in his reforms and in receiving no compensation for his own services (Ne 5:14-19). Job (Job 1:8; 10:7; 13:15; 16:17; 27:4-6; 29:14; 31:1-40). The psalmist (Ps 7:3-5, 8; 17:3; 26:1-3; 69:4; 73:15; 119:121). The Recabites, in keeping the Nazirite vows (Jer 35:12-19). Daniel, in maintaining uprightness of character (Da 6:4). The three Hebrews, who refused to worship Nebuchadnezzar's idol (Da 3:16-21, 28). Levi, in his life and service (Mal 2:6).
Joseph, the husband of Mary, in not jealously accusing her of immorality (Mt 1:19). Zacchaeus (Lk 19:8). Nathanael, in whom was no guile (Jn 1:47). Joseph, a counselor (Lk 23:50-51). Peter, when offered money by Simon (Ac 8:18-23). Paul and Barnabas (Ac 14:12-15). Paul (Ac 23:1; 24:16; Ro 9:1; 2Co 4:2; 5:11; 7:2; 1Th 2:4). The author of Hebrews (Heb 13:18).
See Character; Dishonesty; Honesty; Justice; Righteousness.

INTEMPERANCE See *Abstinence; Drunkard; Drunkenness; Temperance; Wine.*

INTERCESSION
Of People With God:
(Jer 27:18). Priestly (Ex 28:12, 29-30, 38; Lev 10:17). For spiritual blessing (Nu 6:23-26; 1Sa 12:23; Job 1:5; 42:8-10). To avert judgment (Ge 20:7; Ex 32:9-14; Nu 14:11-21; 16:45-50; Dt 9:18-29; Isa 65:8). For deliverance from enemies (1Sa 7:5-9; Isa 37:4). For healing of disease (Jas 5:14-16). For stubborn sinners, unavailing (Jer 7:16; 11:14; 14:11).
Commanded—
(Jer 29:7; Joel 2:17; Mt 5:44; Eph 6:18; 1Ti 2:1-2; 1Jn 5:16).
Examples of—
(Ge 48:16; Ex 32:31-32; 34:9; Nu 10:35-36; 27:16-17; Jos 7:8-9; Jdg 5:31; Ru 2:12; 1Sa 1:17; 12:23; 2Sa 24:17; 1Ki 8:29, 38-39, 44-45; 1Ch 29:18-19; 2Ch 6:40-41; 30:18-19; Ps 7:9; 12:1; 20:1-4; 25:22; 28:9; 36:10; 51:18; 80:1-2, 14-19; 122:7-8; 125:4; 132:9-10; 134:3; 141:5; Isa 62:1; 63:17-19; 64:8-12; Jer 18:20; Eze 9:8; 11:13; Da 9:3-19; Joel 2:17; Mic 7:14; Mt 5:44; 6:10; Ac 7:60; 8:15; Ro 1:9; 10:1; 1Co 1:3; 2Co 9:10, 14; 13:7; Gal 1:3; 6:16; Eph 1:15-19; 3:14-19; Php 1:3-5, 9; Col 1:3-4, 9; 2:1-2; 4:12; 1Th 1:2; 3:10, 12-13; 5:23; 2Th 1:11; 2:16-17; 3:5, 16; 2Ti 1:3; 4:16; Phm 4, 6; Heb 13:20-21; 1Pe 5:10).
Instances of—
Abraham, in behalf of Sodom (Ge 18:23-32), in behalf of Abimelech (Ge 20:17-18). Abraham's servant, in behalf of his master (Ge 24:12). Jacob, in behalf of his children (Ge 49). Moses, in behalf of Pharaoh (Ex 8:12-13, 30-31; 9:33; 10:18-19). Moses for Israel (Nu 16:20-22; 21:7; Dt 33:6-17; Ps 106:23), for Miriam (Nu 12:13-15). David, for Israel (2Sa 24:17). Solomon, for Israel (1Ki 8:29-53). Ezra, for Israel (Ezr 9:5-15). Nehemiah, in behalf of Judah and Jerusalem (Ne 1:4-9). Asaph, for the church (Ps 80-83). The "Sons of Korah," for the church (Ps 85:1-7). Jeremiah, for Israel (Am 7:5-6). Syrian Phoenician woman, for her daughter (Mt 15:22). Disciples, in behalf of Peter's wife's mother (Lk 4:38-39). Parents, for demon-possessed son (Mt 17:15; Mk 9:17-27). Others, who sought Jesus in behalf of the afflicted (Mt 12:22; 15:22, 30; 17:14-18; Mk 1:32; 2:3; Lk 5:18-20; Jn 4:47, 49). Paul for the church (Ac 20:32). Onesiphorus (2Ti 1:16, 18). For the church (Ac 14:26; 15:40).
Requested—
By Pharaoh, of Moses (Ex 8:8, 28; 9:28; 10:17; 12:32), and by the Israelites (Nu 21:7). By Samuel (1Sa 12:19). By Jeroboam, of a prophet (1Ki 13:6). By Hezekiah, of Isaiah (2Ki 19:1-4). By Zedekiah, of Jeremiah (Jer 37:3), and by Johanan (Jer 42:1-6). By Daniel, of Shadrach, Meshach, and Abednego (Da 2:17-18). By Darius, of the Jews (Ezr 6:10). By Simon the sorcerer, of Peter (Ac 8:24). By Paul, of the churches (Ro 15:30-32; 2Co 1:11; Eph 6:19-20; 1Th 5:25; 2Th 3:1; Heb 13:18).
Answered—
Of Moses in behalf of Pharaoh, for the plague of frogs to be ended (Ex 8:12, 15), the plague of flies (Ex 8:30-32), the plague of rain,

thunder, and hail (Ex 9:27-35), plague of locusts (Ex 10:16-20), plague of darkness (Ex 10:21-23); for the Israelites, during the battle with the Amalekites (Ex 17:11-14), after the Israelites had made the golden calf (Ex 32:11-14, 31-34; Dt 9:18-29; 10:10; Ps 106:23), after the murmuring of the people (Ex 33:15-17), when the fire of the Lord consumed the people (Nu 11:1-2), when the people murmured on account of the report of the spies (Nu 14:11-20), that the poisonous snakes might be taken away (Nu 21:4-9); that Miriam's leprosy might be healed (Nu 12:13); in behalf of Aaron, on account of his sin in making the golden calf (Dt 9:20). Of Samuel, for deliverance from the oppressions of the Philistines (1Sa 7:5-14). The prophet of Israel, for the restoration of Jeroboam's shriveled hand (1Ki 13:1-6). Of Elijah, for the raising from the dead the son of the hospitable widow (1Ki 17:20-23). Of Elisha, for the raising from the dead the son of the Shunammite woman (2Ki 4:33-36). Of Isaiah, in behalf of Hezekiah and the people, to be delivered from Sennacherib (2Ki 19).

Intercessional Influence of the Righteous—

(Ge 18:26-32; 19:22; 26:4-5, 24; 1Ki 11:12-13, 34; 15:4; 2Ki 8:19; 2Ch 21:7; Ps 103:17-18; Isa 37:35; Jer 5:1; Eze 14:14, 16, 18, 20; Mt 24:22; Ro 11:27-28; Rev 5:8; 8:3-4).

Intercession of People With Jesus: *See Mediation.*

Intercession of People with People:

Instances of: Reuben for Joseph (Ge 37:21-22). Judah for Joseph (Ge 37:26-27). Judah with Joseph (Ge 44:18-34). Pharaoh's chief baker for Joseph (Ge 41:9-14). Rahab for her people (Jos 2:12-13). Aaron for Miriam (Nu 12:12). Jonathan for David (1Sa 19:1-7). Abigail for Nabal (1Sa 25:23-35). Joab for Absalom (2Sa 14:1-24). Bathsheba, for Solomon (1Ki 1:11-22, 28-31), for Adonijah (1Ki 2:13-25). Esther for her people (Est 7:2-6). Ebed-Melech for Jeremiah (Jer 38:7-13). Elisha offers to see the king for the Shunammite (2Ki 4:13). The king of Syria for Naaman (2Ki 5:6-8). Paul for Onesimus (Phm 10-21).

Intercession of Jesus:

(Lk 22:31-32; 23:33-34; Jn 14:16; 17:9, 11, 15-17, 20-22; Ro 8:34; Heb 7:25; 9:24; 1Jn 2:1-2). *See Jesus the Christ, Mediation of.*

See *Children, Of the Righteous, Blessed of God; Prayer, Intercessory.*

INTEREST Income from lending money.

Charging Interest:

From a poor Israelite, forbidden (Ex 22:25; Lev 25:36-37; Dt 23:19). From a stranger, authorized (Dt 23:20). Unprofitable (Pr 28:8). Rebuked (Ne 5:1-13; Eze 22:12).

Charging No Interest:

Rewarded (Ps 15:5; Eze 18:8-9, 17). Lender and borrower equal before God (Isa 24:2).

See *Borrowing; Debt; Debtor; Lending; Money; Usury.*

INTERMARRY The patriarchs did not allow marriage outside their clan: Abraham (Ge 24:3), Jacob (Ge 28:1). Exceptions: Esau (Ge 26:34-35), Judah and his sons (Ge 38), Joseph (Ge 41:45, 50), Moses (Nu 12:1). Aaron and Miriam judged for criticizing Moses' intermarriage (Nu 12:1-15).

Israel was forbidden to intermarry with the Canaanites for religious reasons, not racial (Dt 7:1-6; Jos 23:12-13). Negative results of (Jdg 3:6-7), Solomon (1Ki 11:1-6), returned exiles (Ezr 9:14-15).

There are no racial barriers in the church (Col 3:11). Even marriage between believers and unbelievers does not have to end in divorce (1Co 7:12-16), though is not recommended (2Co 6:14-18). *See Marriage.*

INTERMEDIATE STATE Period of time which elapses between death and the resurrection. For the righteous it is one of blessedness (2Co 5:8); for the wicked it is one of conscious suffering (Lk 16:19-31).

INTERPRETATION Of dreams. *See Dream.* Of foreign tongues (1Co 14:9-19). *See Tongues, Gift of.*

INTERPRETER Of dreams (Ge 40:8; 41:16; Da 2:18-30). Of languages (Ge 42:23; 2Ch 32:31; Ne 8:8; Job 33:23). In Christian churches (1Co 12:10, 30; 14:5, 13, 26-28).

Figurative (Job 33:23).

INTOLERANCE

Religious:

Exemplified by Cain (Ge 4:8), Joshua (Nu 11:24-28), James and John (Mk 9:38-39; Lk 9:49), the Jews, in persecuting Jesus. *See Jesus the Christ, Rejected.*

History of:

In persecuting the disciples (Ac 4:1-3, 15-21; 17:13), Stephen (Ac 6:9-15; 7:57-59; 8:1-3), Paul (Ac 13:50; 17:5; 18:13; 21:28-31; 22:22-23; 23:2).

Of Idolatrous Religions:

Taught by Moses (Ex 22:20; Dt 13; 17:1-7).
Exemplified by Elijah (1Ki 18:40), Jehu (2Ki 10:18-31), by the Jews, at the time of the religious revival under the leadership of Azariah (2Ch 15:12-13).
See Persecution.

INTOXICANTS *See Beer; Fermented Drink; Wine.*

INTOXICATION *See Abstinence; Drunkenness.*

INTRIGUE *See Conspiracy.*

INVECTIVE *See Satire.*

INVENTION Of musical instruments: By Jubal (Ge 4:21), by David (1Ch 23:5; 2Ch 7:6; 29:26; Am 6:5).

The use of metals (Ge 4:22). Machines of war (2Ch 26:15).

INVESTIGATION By Solomon, into nature and design of things (Ecc 1:13-18; 2:1-12; 7:25; 8:17; 12:9-14).

INVITATIONS The "Comes" of God's Word (Ge 7:1; Nu 10:29; Isa 1:18; 55:1; Mt 11:28; 22:4; Lk 14:17; Rev 22:17).

Divine pleading (Pr 1:24; Isa 1:18; 55:1; Eze 18:31; Mic 6:3; Mt 23:37; Ro 10:21; 2Co 5:20).

Divine call: To repentance (Jer 35:15; Eze 33:11; Hos 6:1; Mt 22:3; 2Co 5:20; Rev 3:20). To leadership (Ge 12:1; Ex 3:10; Jdg 6:14; 1Ki 19:19; Isa 6:8; Ac 26:16). Universality of (Isa 45:22; 55:1; Mt 22:9; Jn 7:37; Ro 10:12; 1Ti 2:4; Rev 22:17).

Refused by people (Ps 81:11; Isa 65:12; Jer 7:13; Hos 9:17; Mt 22:3; Jn 5:40; Ro 10:21). Warnings (Ge 19:17; Dt 29:20; Jos 24:20; 1Sa 12:15; Isa 28:14; Jer 13:16; Jnh 3:4; Heb 12:25; 2Pe 3:17).

IPHDEIAH (*Yahweh redeems*). A Benjamite (1Ch 8:25).

IPHTAH (*he opens*). A city of Judah (Jos 15:43).

IPHTAH EL (*God [El] opens*). A valley in Zebulun (Jos 19:14, 27).

IR (possibly *stallion donkey*). A Benjamite (1Ch 7:12).

IR NAHASH (*city of Nahash*). Whether a man or a town is not clear (1Ch 4:12, ftn). *See Nahash.*

IR SHEMESH (*city of Shemesh*). A city of Dan (Jos 19:41).

IRA (possibly *stallion donkey*).

1. The Jairite, David's priest (2Sa 20:26).
2. The Ithrite, one of David's heroes (2Sa 23:38; 1Ch 11:40).
3. From Tekoa, one of David's heroes (2Sa 23:26; 1Ch 11:28; 27:9).

IRAD Son of Enoch (Ge 4:18).

IRAM A chief of Edom (Ge 36:43; 1Ch 1:54).

IRI (perhaps *donkey's colt*). A son of Bela (1Ch 7:7).

IRIJAH (*Yahweh sees*). A captain of the guard who imprisoned the prophet Jeremiah (Jer 37:13-14).

IRON

1. First recorded use of (Ge 4:22). Ore of (Dt 8:9; Job 28:2). Melted (Eze 22:20). Used in the temple (1Ch 22:3; 29:2, 7).

Articles Made of—

Ax (2Ki 6:6; 2Ch 18:10; Ecc 10:10; Isa 10:34), bed (Dt 3:11), breastplate (Rev 9:9), chariot (Jos 17:16, 18; Jdg 1:19; 4:3), fetters (Ps 105:18; 107:10, 16; 149:8), file (Pr 27:17), furnace (Dt 4:20; 1Ki 8:51; Jer 11:4), gate (Ac 12:10), harrow (2Sa 12:31), horn (1Ki 22:11; 2Ch 18:10; Mic 4:13), idols (Da 2:33; 5:4, 23), pans (Eze 4:3; 27:19), pen (Job 19:24; Jer 17:1), pillars (Jer 1:18), rods (Ps 2:9; Rev 2:27; 12:5; 19:15), threshing instruments (Am 1:3), tools (1Ki 6:7), vessels (Jos 6:24), weapons (Nu 35:16; 1Sa 17:7; Job 20:24; 41:7), yokes (Dt 28:48; Jer 28:13-14).

See *Steel.*

Figurative (2Sa 23:7; Jer 15:12; 1Ti 4:2).

2. A city of Naphtali (Jos 19:38).

IRONY Instances of: Michal to David (2Sa 6:20). Elijah to the priests of Baal (1Ki 18:27). Job to his accusers (Job 12:2). Ezekiel to the prince of Tyre (Eze 28:3-5). Micaiah (1Ki 22:15). Amos to the Samaritans (Am 4:4). Jesus to Pharisees (Mk 2:17). Pharisees and Herodians to Jesus (Mt 22:16). Roman soldiers to Jesus (Mt 27:29; Mk 15:17-19; Lk 23:11; Jn 19:2-3). Pilate, calling Jesus king (Mk 15:19; Jn 19:15). Superscription of Pilate over Jesus (Mt 27:37; Mk 15:26; Lk 23:38; Jn 19:19). Agrippa to Paul (Ac 26:28).

See *Sarcasm; Satire.*

IRPEEL (*God [El] heals*). A city of Benjamin (Jos 18:27).

IRRIGATION Of gardens (Dt 11:10; Pr 21:1; Ecc 2:6; Isa 58:11).

Figurative (1Co 3:6, 8).

IRU Eldest son of Caleb (1Ch 4:15).

ISAAC (*he laughs, he will laugh,* some contexts *mock*; other contexts *El [God] laughs*).

1. Miraculous son of Abraham (Ge 17:15-19; 18:1-15; 21:1-8; Jos 24:3; 1Ch 1:28; Gal 4:28; Heb 11:11). Ancestor of Jesus (Mt 1:2). Offered in sacrifice by his father (Ge 22:1-19; Heb 11:17; Jas 2:21). Is provided a wife from among his kindred (Ge 24; 25:20). Abrahamic covenant confirmed in (Ge 26:2-5; 1Ch 16:15-19). Dwells in the south country at the well Beer Lahai Roi (Ge 24:62; 25:11). With Ishmael, buries his father in the cave of Machpelah (Ge 25:9). Esau and Jacob born to (Ge 25:19-26; 1Ch 1:34; Jos 24:4). Dwells in Gerar (Ge 26:7-11). Prospers (Ge 26:12-14). Possesses large flocks and herds (Ge 26:14). Digs wells, and is defrauded of them by the herdsmen of Abimelech (Ge 26:15, 21). Removes to the valley of Gerar, afterward called Beersheba (Ge 26:22-33). His old age, last blessing upon his sons (Ge 27:18-40). Death and burial of (Ge 35:27-29; 49:31). His filial obedience (Ge 22:9). His peaceableness (Ge 26:14-22). Was a prophet (Ge 27:28-29, 39-40; Heb 11:20). Has devoutness (Ge 24:63; 25:21; 26:25; Mt 8:11; Lk 13:28). Prophecies concerning (Ge 17:16-21; 18:10-14; 21:12; 26:2-5, 24; Ex 32:13; 1Ch 16:16; Ro 9:7).

2. A designation of the ten tribes (Am 7:9).

ISAIAH, BOOK OF

Author: Isaiah son of Amoz

Date: Between c. 701 and 681 B.C.

Outline:

Part 1: The Book of Judgment (chs. 1-39):

I. Messages of Rebuke and Promise (chs. 1-6).
 A. Introduction: Charges Against Judah for Breaking the Covenant (ch. 1).
 B. The Future Discipline and Glory of Judah and Jerusalem (chs. 2-4).
 1. Jerusalem's future blessings (2:1-5).

 2. The discipline of Judah (2:6-4:11).
 3. The restoration of Zion (4:2-6).
 C. The Nation's Judgment and Exile (ch. 5).
 D. Isaiah's Unique Commission (ch. 6).
II. Prophecies Occasioned by the Aramean and Israelite Threat Against Judah (chs. 7-12).
 A. Ahaz Warned Not to Fear the Aramean and Israelite Threat (chs. 7).
 B. Isaiah's Son and David's Son (8:1-9:7).
 C. Judgment Against Israel (9:8-10:4).
 D. The Assyrian Empire and the Davidic Kingdom (10:5-12:6).
 1. The destruction of Assyria (10:5-34).
 2. The establishment of the Davidic king and his kingdom (ch. 11).
 3. Songs of joy for deliverance (ch. 12).
III. Judgment Against the Nations (chs. 13-23).
 A. Against Assyria and Its Ruler (13:1-14:27).
 B. Against Philistia (14:28-32).
 C. Against Moab (chs. 15-16).
 D. Against Aram and Israel (ch. 17).
 E. Against Cush (ch. 18).
 F. Against Egypt and Cush (chs. 19-20).
 G. Against Babylon (21:1-10).
 H. Against Dumah (Edom) (21:11-12).
 I. Against Arabia (21:13-17).
 J. Against the Valley of Vision (Jerusalem) (ch. 22).
 K. Against Tyre (ch. 23).
IV. Judgment and Promise (the Lord's Kingdom) (chs. 24-27).
 A. Universal Judgments for Universal Sin (ch. 24).
 B. Deliverance and Blessing (ch. 25).
 C. Praise for the Lord's Sovereign Care (ch. 26).
 D. Israel's Enemies: Punished but Israel's Remnant Restored (ch. 27).
V. Six Woes: Five on the Unfaithful in Israel and One on Assyria (chs. 28-33).
 A. Woe to Ephraim (Samaria)—and to Judah (ch. 28).
 B. Woe to David's City, Jerusalem (29:1-14).
 C. Woe to Those Who Rely on Foreign Alliances (29:15-24).
 D. Woe to the Obstinate Nation (ch. 30).
 E. Woe to Those Who Rely on Egypt (chs. 31-32).
 F. Woe to Assyria—but Blessing for God's People (ch. 33).
VI. More Prophecies of Judgment and Promise (chs. 34-35).
 A. The Destruction of the Nations and the Avenging of God's People (ch. 34).
 B. The Future Blessings of Restored Zion (ch. 35).
VII. A Historical Transition From the Assyrian Threat to the Babylonian Exile (chs. 36-39).
 A. Jerusalem Preserved From the Assyrian Threat (chs. 36-37).
 1. The siege of Jerusalem by Sennacherib and the Assyrian army (ch. 36).
 2. The Lord's deliverance of Jerusalem (ch. 37).
 B. The Lord's Extension of Hezekiah's Life (ch. 38).
 C. The Babylonian Exile Predicted (ch. 39).

Part 2: The Book of Comfort (chs. 40-66):

VIII. The Deliverance and Restoration of Israel (chs. 40-48).
 A. The Coming of the Victorious God (40:1-26).
 B. Unfailing Strength for the Weary Exiles (40:27-31).
 C. The Lord of History (41:1-42:9).
 D. Praise and Exhortation (42:10-25).
 E. The Regathering and Renewal of Israel (43:1-44:5).
 F. The Only God (44:6-45:25).
 G. The Lord's Superiority over Babylon's Gods (ch. 46).
 H. The Fall of Babylon (ch. 47).
 I. The Lord's Exhortations to His People (ch. 48).
IX. The Servant's Ministry and Israel's Restoration (chs. 49-57).
 A. The Call and Mission of the Servant (49:1-13).
 B. The Repopulation of Zion (49:14-26).
 C. Israel's Sin and the Servant's Obedience (ch. 50).
 D. The Remnant Comforted Because of Their Glorious Prospect (51:1-52:12).
 E. The Sufferings and Glories of the Lord's Righteous Servant (52:13-53:12).
 F. The Future Glory of Zion (ch. 54).
 G. The Lord's Call to Salvation and Covenant Blessings (55:1-56:8).
 H. The Condemnation of the Wicked in Israel (56:9-57:21).
X. Everlasting Deliverance and Everlasting Judgment (chs. 58-66).
 A. False and True Worship (ch. 58).
 B. Zion's Confession and Redemption (ch. 59).
 C. Zion's Peace and Prosperity (ch. 60).
 D. The Lord's Favor (ch. 61).
 E. Zion's Restoration and Glory (62:1-63:6).
 F. Prayer for Divine Deliverance (63:7-64:12).
 G. The Lord's Answer: Mercy and Judgment (ch. 65).
 H. Judgment for False Worshipers and Blessing for True Worshipers (ch. 66).

ISAIAH (*Yahweh saves*).

The Prophet:

Son of Amos (Isa 1:1). Prophecies in the days of Uzziah, Jotham, Ahaz, and Hezekiah, kings of Judah (Isa 1:1; 6:1; 7:1, 3; 14:27; 20:1; 36:1; 38:1; 39:1), at the time of the invasion by the Assyrian supreme commander (Isa 20:1). Symbolically wears sackcloth, and walks barefoot, as a sign to Israel (Isa 20:2-3). Comforts and encourages Hezekiah and the people in the siege of Jerusalem by Sennacherib, king of Assyria (2Ki 18; 19; Isa 37:6-7). Comforts Hezekiah in his affliction (2Ki 20:1-11; Isa 38). Performs the miracle of the returning shadow to confirm Hezekiah's faith (2Ki 20:8-11). Reproves Hezekiah's folly in exhibiting his resources to the commissioners from Babylon (2Ki 20:12-19; Isa 39). Is chronicler of the times of Uzziah and Hezekiah (2Ch 26:22; 32:32).

The Prophecies:

Foretells punishment of the Jews for idolatry, and reproves self-confidence and distrust of God (Isa 2:6-20). Foretells the destruction of the Jews (Isa 3). Promises to the remnant restoration of divine favor (Isa 4:2-6; 6). Delineates in the parable of the

vineyard the ingratitude of the Jews, and reproves it (Isa 5:1-10). Denounces existing corruption (Isa 5:8-30).

Foretells the ill success of the plot of the Israelites and Syrians against Judah (Isa 7:1-6). Pronounces calamities against Israel and Judah (Isa 7:16-25; 9:2-6). Foretells prosperity under Hezekiah, and the manifestation of the Messiah (Isa 9:1-7). Pronounces vengeance upon the enemies of Israel (Isa 9:8-12). Denounces the wickedness of Israel, and foretells the judgments of God (Isa 9:13-21). Pronounces judgments against false prophets (Isa 10:1-4). Foretells the destruction of Sennacherib's armies (Isa 10:5-34), the restoration of Israel and the triumph of the Messiah's kingdom (Isa 11).

The burden of Babylon (Isa 13; 14:1-28). Denunciation against the Philistines (Isa 14:9-32). Burden of Moab (Isa 15-16). Burden of Damascus (Isa 17). Obscure prophecy, supposed by some authorities to be directed against the Assyrians, by others against the Egyptians, and by others against the Ethiopians (Isa 18). The burden of Egypt (Isa 19-20). Denunciations against Babylon (Isa 21:1-10). Prophecy concerning Seir (Isa 21:11-12), Arabia (Isa 21:13-17), concerning the conquest of Jerusalem, the captivity of Shebna, and the promotion of Eliakim (Isa 22:1-22), the overthrow of Tyre (Isa 23), the judgments upon the land, but that a remnant of the Jews would be saved (Isa 25-27).

Reproves Ephraim for his wickedness, and foretells the destruction by Shalmaneser (Isa 28:1-5). Declares the glory of God upon the remnant who are saved (Isa 28:5-6). Exposes the corruption in Jerusalem and exhorts to repentance (Isa 28:7-29). Foretells the invasion of Sennacherib, the distress of the Jews and the destruction of the Assyrian army (Isa 29:1-8). Denounces the hypocrisy of the Jews (Isa 29:9-17). Promises a reformation (Isa 29:18-24). Reproves the people for their confidence in Egypt, and their contempt of God (Isa 30:1-17; 31:1-6). Declares the goodness and patience of God toward them (Isa 30:18-26; 32-35).

Reproves the Jews for their spiritual blindness and infidelity (Isa 42:18-25). Promises ultimate restoration of the Jews (Isa 43:1-13). Foretells the ultimate destruction of Babylon (Isa 43:14-17; 47). Exhorts the people to repent (Isa 43:22-28). Comforts the church with promises, exposes the folly of idolatry, and their future deliverance from captivity by Cyrus (Isa 44; 45:1-5; 48:20). Foretells the conversion of the Gentiles, and triumph of the gospel (Isa 45:5-25). Denounces the evils of idolatry (Isa 46). Reproves the Jews for their idolatries and other wickedness (Isa 48). Exhorts to sanctification (Isa 56:1-8). Foretells calamities to Judah (Isa 57-58; 59:9-12).

Foreshadows the person and the kingdom of the Messiah (Isa 32-35; 42; 45; 49-56; 59:15-21; 60-66).

ISCAH Daughter of Haran and sister of Lot (Ge 11:29).

ISCARIOT (*man of Kerioth* or *of the assassins*). See Judas.

ISHBAH (*he boasts, congratulates*). Father of Eshtemoa (1Ch 4:17).

ISHBAK Son of Abraham and Keturah (Ge 25:2; 1Ch 1:32).

ISHBI-BENOB A giant warrior slain by Abishai (2Sa 21:16).

ISH-BOSHETH (*man of shame*). Son of Saul. Called Esh-Baal (1Ch 8:33; 9:39). Made king by Abner (2Sa 2:8-10). Deserted by Abner (2Sa 3:6-12). Restores Michal, David's wife, to David (2Sa 3:14-16). Assassinated (2Sa 4:5-8). Avenged by David (2Sa 4:9-12).

ISHHOD (*man of grandeur*). One of the tribe of Manasseh (1Ch 7:18).

ISHI (*God has saved*).
1. A play on the two Hebrew words for husband. In this verse the first is "husband"; the second is "master" which is identical with the name of the god Baal. There will be such a vigorous reaction against Baal worship that this Hebrew word for "master" will no longer be used of the Lord (Hos 2:16, ftn).
2. A son of Appaim (1Ch 2:31).
3. A descendant of Judah (1Ch 4:20).
4. A Simeonite (1Ch 4:42).
5. One of the heads of Manasseh (1Ch 5:24).

ISHIAH See Isshiah.

ISHIJAH (*Yahweh forget*). One of the sons of Harim (Ezr 10:31).

ISHMA (*desolate* ISBE; *God [El] he heard* KB). A descendant of Judah (1Ch 4:3).

ISHMACHIAH See Ismakiah.

ISHMAEL (*God [El] he heard*).
1. Son of Abraham (Ge 16:11, 15-16; 1Ch 1:28). Prayer of Abraham for (Ge 17:18, 20). Circumcised (Ge 17:23-26). Promised to be the father of a nation (Ge 16:11-12; 17:20; 21:12-13, 18). Sent away by Abraham (Ge 21:6-21). With Isaac buries his father (Ge 25:9). Children of (Ge 25:12-18; 1Ch 1:29-31). Daughter of, marries Esau (Ge 28:9; 36:2-3). Death of (Ge 25:17-18).
2. Father of Zebadiah (2Ch 19:11).
3. A son of Azel (1Ch 8:38; 9:44).
4. One of the captains of hundreds (2Ch 23:1).
5. A priest of the Exile (Ezr 10:22).
6. A son of Nethaniah. Assassinated Gedaliah, governor of Judah under king of Babylon, and takes captive many Jews (Jer 40:8-16; 41:1-11; 2Ki 25:23-25). Defeated by Johanan and put to flight (Jer 41:12-15).

ISHMAELITE(S) (*one from Ishmael*). Descended from Abraham's son, Ishmael (Ge 16:15-16; 1Ch 1:28). Divided into twelve tribes (Ge 25:16). Heads of tribes of (Ge 25:13-15; 1Ch 1:29-31).

Original possessions of (Ge 25:18). Governed by kings (Jer 25:24). Dwelt in tents (Isa 13:20). Rich in cattle (1Ch 5:21). Wore ornaments of gold (Jdg 8:24). Were the merchants of the east (Ge 37:25; Eze 27:20-21). Traveled in large companies or caravans (Ge

37:25; Job 6:19). Waylaid and plundered travelers (Jer 3:2). Often confederate against Israel (Ps 83:6).

Called:
Hagrites, either Ishmaelites (descendants of Hagar; Ge 16) or a group mentioned in Assyrian inscriptions as an Aramean confederacy (1Ch 5:10, 19-22; 27:31), are named among the enemies of Israel (Ps 83:6). Arabs (Isa 13:20).

Overcome by:
Gideon (Jdg 8:10-24). Reubenites and Gadites (1Ch 5:10, 18-20). Uzziah (2Ch 26:7). Sent presents to Solomon (1Ki 10:15; 2Ch 9:14). Sent flocks to Jehoshaphat (2Ch 17:11).

Prophecies Concerning:
To be numerous (Ge 16:10; 17:20). To be wild and savage (Ge 16:12). To be warlike and predatory (Ge 16:12). To be divided into twelve tribes (Ge 17:20). To continue independent (Ge 16:12). To be a great nation (Ge 21:13, 18). To be judged with the nations (Ge 25:23-25). Their glory to be diminished (Isa 21:13-17). Their submission to Christ (Ps 72:10, 15). Probably preached to by Paul (Gal 1:17).

ISHMAIAH (*Yahweh heard*).
1. Gibeonite (1Ch 12:4).
2. Chief of Zebulunites (1Ch 27:19).

ISHMEELITE See Ishmaelite(s).

ISHMERAI (*Yahweh guards*). A chief Benjamite (1Ch 8:18).

ISHOD See Ishhod.

ISHPAH (*he judged*). A Benjamite (1Ch 8:16).

ISHPAN (possibly *may God judge*). Son of Shashak (1Ch 8:22).

ISHTAR Semitic goddess worshiped in Phoenicia, Canaan, Assyria, and Babylonia, and sometimes even by the Israelites. Some identify her with Ashtoreth or Ashtaroth (Jdg 2:13; 10:6; 1Ki 11:5; 2Ki 23:13).

ISHTOB (*man of Tob*). See Tob, 2.

ISHUAH See Ishvah.

ISHUAI See Ishvi, Ishvite.

ISHVAH (*he will level*). Son of Asher (Ge 46:17; 1Ch 7:30).

ISHVI, ISHVITE
1. Son of Asher (Ge 46:17; 1Ch 7:30) and his clan (Nu 26:44).
2. Son of Saul (1Sa 14:49).

ISLAND, ISLE
1. Dry land, as opposed to water (Isa 42:15).
2. Body of land surrounded by water (Jer 2:10).
3. Coastland (Ge 10:5; Isa 20:6).
4. The farthest regions of the earth (Isa 41:5; Zep 2:11).

ISMAIAH See Ishmaiah.

ISMAKIAH (*Yahweh sustains*). Overseer of the temple (2Ch 31:13).

ISPAH See Ishpah.

ISRAEL, ISRAELITES (*he struggles with God [El]*).
1. A name given to Jacob (Ge 32:24-32; 2Ki 17:34; Hos 12:3-4).
2. A name of the Christ in prophecy (Isa 49:3).
3. A name given to the descendants of Jacob, a nation. Also called Israelites and Hebrews (Ge 43:32; Ex 1:15; 9:7; 10:3; 21:2; Lev 23:42; Jos 13:6; 1Sa 4:6; 13:3, 19; 14:11, 21; Php 3:5).

Tribes of:
Tribes of Israel were named after the sons of Jacob. In lists usually the names Levi and Joseph, two sons of Jacob, do not appear. The descendants of Levi were consecrated to the rites of religion, and the two sons of Joseph, Ephraim and Manasseh, were adopted by Jacob in Joseph's stead (Ge 48:5; Jos 14:4), and their names appear in the lists of tribes instead of those of Levi and Joseph, as follows: Asher, Benjamin, Dan, Ephraim, Gad, Issachar, Judah, Manasseh, Naphtali, Reuben, Simeon, Zebulun.

Names of, seen in John's vision, on the gates of the New Jerusalem (Rev 21:12).

Prophecies, concerning (Ge 15:5, 13; 25:23; 26:4; 27:28-29, 40; 48:19; 49:1-28), of the multitude of (Ge 13:16; 15:5; 22:17; 26:4; 28:14), of their captivity in Egypt (Ge 15:13-14; 46:7:6-7).

Divided into families, each of which had a chief (Nu 25:14; 26; 36:1; Jos 7:14; 1Ch 4-8).

Number of, who went into Egypt (Ge 46:8-27; Ex 1:5; Dt 10:22; Ac 7:14). Number of, at the time of the Exodus (Ex 12:37-38, w Ge 47:27; Ex 1:7-20; Ps 105:24; Ac 7:17). Number of, fit for military service when they left Egypt (Ex 12:37), at Sinai, by tribes (Nu 1:1-50), after the plague (Nu 26), when David numbered (2Sa 24:1-9; 1Ch 21:5-6; 27:23-24), after the Captivity (Ezr 2:64; Ne 7:66-67), in John's apocalyptic vision (Rev 7:1-8).

Early History:
Dwelt in Goshen (Ge 46:28-34; 47:4-10, 27-28). Dwelt in Egypt 430 years (Ge 15:13; Ex 12:40-41; Ac 7:6; Gal 3:17). Enslaved and oppressed by the Egyptians (Ex 1-2; 5; Ac 7:18-36). Their groaning heard by God (Ex 2:23-25). Moses commissioned as deliverer (Ex 3:2-22; 4:1-17). The land of Egypt plagued on their account. See *Egypt*. Exempt from the plagues (Ex 8:22-23; 9:4-6, 26; 10:23; 11:7; 12:13). Children were spared when the firstborn of Egypt were slain (Ex 12:13, 23). Instituted the Passover (Ex 12:1-28). Borrowed jewels from the Egyptians (Ex 11:2-3; 12:35-36; Ps 105:37). Urged by the Egyptians to depart (Ex 12:31-39). Journey from Rameses to Succoth (Ex 12:37-39). Made the journey by night (Ex 12:42). The day of their deliverance to be a memorial (Ex 12:42; 13:3-16). Led of God (Ex 13:18, 21-22). Providentially cared for (Dt 8:3-4; 29:5-6; 34:7; Ne 9:21; Ps 105:37). See *Manna*; *Cloud, Pillar of.*

Journey from Succoth, to Etham (Ex 13:20), to Pi Hahiroth (Ex 14:2; Nu 33:5-7). Pursued by the Egyptians (Ex 14:5-31). Pass through the Red Sea (Ex 14:19-22; Dt 11:4; Ps 78; 105-107; 136). Order of march (Nu 2). Journey to Marah (Ex 15:23-25; Nu 33:8). Murmur on account of the bitter water (Ex 15:23-25; water of sweetened (Ex 15:25). Journey to Elim (Ex 15:27; Nu 33:9). The itinerary (Nu 33).

Murmured for food (Ex 16:2-3). Provided with manna and quails (Ex 16:4-36). Murmured for want of water at Rephidim (Ex 17:2-7), water miraculously supplied from the rock at Meribah (Ex 17:5-7). Defeat the Amalekites (Ex 17:13; Dt 25:17-18). Arrive at Sinai (Ex 19:1; Nu 33:15). At the suggestion of Jethro, Moses' father-in-law, they organize a system of government (Ex 18:25; Dt 1:9-18). The message of God to them, requiring that they shall be obedient to his commandments, and as a reward they would be to him a holy nation, and their reply (Ex 19:3-8). Sanctify themselves for receiving the law (Ex 19:10-15). The law delivered to (Ex 20-23; 24:1-4; 25:31; Lev 1:25; 27; Dt 5; 15:16). The people receive it and covenant obedience to it (Ex 24:3, 7). Idolatry of (Ex 32; Dt 9:17-21). The anger of the Lord in consequence (Ex 32:9-14). Moses' indignation; breaks the tables of stone; enters the camp; commands the Levites; three thousand slain (Ex 32:19-35). Visited by a plague (Ex 32:35). Obduracy of (Ex 33:3; 34:9; Dt 9:12-29). God withdraws his presence (Ex 33:1-3). The mourning of, when God refused to lead them (Ex 33:4-10). Tablets renewed (Ex 34). Pattern for the tabernacle and its furnishings, and forms of worship to be observed (Ex 25-31). Gifts consecrated for the creation of the tabernacle (Ex 35; 36:1-7; Nu 7). The building of the tabernacle; the manufacture of its furnishings, including the garments of the priests; and their sanctification (Ex 36:8-38; 37-40). First sacrifice offered by under the law (Lev 8:14-36; 9:8-24). Second Passover observed (Nu 9:1-5).

March out of the wilderness (Nu 10:11-36). Itinerary (Nu 33). Order of camp and march (Nu 2). Arrive at the border of Canaan (Nu 12:16). Send twelve spies to view the land (Nu 13; 32:8; Dt 1:22, 25; Jos 14:7). Return with a majority and minority report (Nu 13:26-33; 14:6-10). Murmuring over the report (Nu 14:1-5). The judgment of God upon them in consequence of their unbelief and murmuring (Nu 14:13-39). Reaction, and their purpose to enter the land; are defeated by the Amalekites (Nu 14:40-45; Dt 1:41-45). Stay at Kadesh (Dt 1:46). Return to the wilderness, where they remain thirty-eight years, and all die except Joshua and Caleb (Nu 14:20-39). Rebellion of Korah, Dathan, and Abiram (Nu 16:1-40; Dt 11:6). Murmur against Moses and Aaron; are plagued; 14, 700 die; plague stayed (Nu 16:41-50). Murmur for want of water in Meribah; the rock is struck (Nu 20:1-13). Are refused passage through the country of Edom (Nu 20:14-21). The death of Aaron (Nu 20:22, 29; 33:38-39; Dt 10:6).

Defeat the Canaanites (Nu 21:1-3). Are scourged with serpents (Nu 21:4-9). Defeat Sihon, king of the Amorites (Nu 21:21-32; Dt 2:24-35), and Og, the king of Bashan (Nu 21:33-35; Dt 3:1-17). Arrive in the plains of Moab, at the fords of the Jordan (Nu 22:1; 33:48-49). Commit idolatry with the people of Moab (Nu 25:1-5). Visited by a plague in consequence; 24,000 die (Nu 25:6-15; 26:1). The people numbered for the allotment of the land (Nu 26). The daughters of Zelophehad sue for an inheritance (Nu 27:1-11; Jos 17:3-6). Conquest of the Midianites (Nu 31). Nations dread (Dt 2:25). Renew the covenant (Dt 29). Moses dies, and people mourn (Dt 34). Joshua appointed leader (Nu 27:18-23; Dt 31:23). See *Joshua, 1.*

All who were numbered at Sinai perished in the wilderness except Caleb and Joshua (Nu 26:63, 65; Dt 2:14-16). Piety of those who entered Canaan (Jos 23:8; Jdg 2:7-10; Jer 2:2-3). Men chosen to allot the lands of Canaan among the tribes and families (Nu 34:17-29). Remove from Shittim to Jordan (Jos 3:1). Cross Jordan (Jos 4). Circumcision observed and Passover celebrated (Jos 5). Jericho taken (Jos 6). Ai taken (Jos 7-8). Make a covenant with the Gibeonites (Jos 9). Defeat the five Amorite kings (Jos 10). Conquest of the land (Jos 21:43-45, w Jdg 1). The land allotted (Jos 15-21).

Two-and-a-half tribes return from west side of the Jordan; erect a memorial to signify the unity of the tribes; the memorial misunderstood; the controversy which followed; its amicable adjustment (Jos 22). Joshua's exhortation immediately before his death (Jos 23). Covenant renewed, death of Joshua (Jos 24; Jdg 2:8-9). Religious fidelity during the life of Joshua (Jos 24:31; Jdg 2:7).

Under the Judges:
Public affairs administered 450 years by the judges (Jdg 2:16-19; Ac 13:20). The original inhabitants not fully expelled (Jdg 1:27-36; 3:1-7). Reproved by an angel for not casting out the original inhabitants (Jdg 2:1-5). People turn to idolatry (Jdg 2:10-23). Delivered for their idolatry to the king of Mesopotamia during eight years; their repentance and deliverance (Jdg 3:8-11). Renew their idolatry, and are put under tribute to the king of Moab during eighteen years; repent and are delivered by Ehud; eighty years of peace follow (Jdg 3:12-30). Shamgar resists a foray of the Philistines and delivers Israel (Jdg 3:31). People again do evil and are put under bonds for twenty years to the king of Syria (Jdg 4:1-3). Delivered by Deborah, a prophetess, and judged (Jdg 4-5). Seven years of bondage to the Midianites; delivered by Gideon (Jdg 6-7; 8:1-28). See *Gideon*. Return to idolatry (Jdg 8:33-34).

Abimelech foments an intertribal war (Jdg 9). Judged, by Tola twenty-three years (Jdg 10:1-2), by Jair twenty-two years (Jdg 10:3-4). People backslide, and are given over to the Philistines for discipline eighteen years; repent and turn to the Lord; delivered by Jephthah (Jdg 10:6-18; 11). Ephraimites go to war against other tribes; defeated by Jephthah (Jdg 12:1-7). Judged, by Ibzan seven years (Jdg 12:8-10), by Elon ten years (Jdg 12:11-12), by Abdon eight years (Jdg 12:13-15). Backslide again and are disciplined by the Philistines forty years (Jdg 13:1). Judged by Samson twenty years (Jdg 15:20, w Jdg 13-16). Scandal of the Bethlehemite's concubine, and the consequent war between the Benjamites and the other tribes (Jdg 19-21). Judged by Eli forty years (1Sa 4:18, w 1Sa 1-4). Smitten by the Philistines at Ebenezer (1Sa 4:1-2, 10-11). Demand a king (1Sa 8:5-20; Hos 13:10).

The United Kingdom:
Saul anointed king (1Sa 10; 11:12-15; 12:13). Ammonites invade Israel, are defeated (1Sa 11). Philistines smitten (1Sa 14). Amalekites defeated (1Sa 15). David anointed king (1Sa 16:11-13).

Goliath slain (1Sa 17). Israel defeated by the Philistines, and Saul and his sons killed (1Sa 31). *See Saul.* David defeats the Amalekites (1Sa 30; 2Sa 1:1), made king (2Sa 2:4, 11). Ish-Bosheth made king (2Sa 2:8-10).

The conflict between the two political factions (2Sa 2:12-32; 3:1).

David made king over all Israel (2Sa 5:1-5). Conquests of David (2Sa 8), Absalom's rebellion (2Sa 15-18). *See David.*

Solomon anointed king (1Ki 1:32-40). Temple built (1Ki 6). Solomon's palace built (1Ki 7). Solomon's death (1Ki 11:41-43). *See Solomon.*

The Revolt of the Ten Tribes:

Foreshadowing circumstances indicating the separation: Disagreement after Saul's death (2Sa 2; 1Ch 12:23-40; 13). Lukewarmness of the ten tribes, and zeal of Judah for David in Absalom's rebellion (2Sa 19:41-43). The rebellion of Sheba (2Sa 20). The two factions are distinguished as Israel and Judah during David's reign (2Sa 21:2). Providential (Zec 11:14).

Revolt consummated under Rehoboam, son and successor of Solomon (1Ki 12). The ten tribes that revolted from the house of David also called Ephraim (Hos 7:8, 11), Jacob (Hos 12:2).

Israel (The Ten Tribes):

War continued between the two kingdoms all the days of Rehoboam and Jeroboam (1Ki 14:30), and between Jeroboam and Abijah (1Ki 15:7), and between Baasha and Asa (1Ki 15:16, 32). Famine prevails in the reign of Ahab (1Ki 18:1-6). Israel, also called Samaria, invaded by, but defeats, Ben-Hadad, king of Syria (1Ki 20). Moab rebels (2Ki 1:1; 3). Army of Syria invades Israel, but peacefully withdraws through the tact of the prophet Elisha (2Ki 6:8-23). Samaria besieged (2Ki 6:24-33; 7), city of, taken, and the people carried to Assyria (2Ki 17). The land repopulated (2Ki 17:24).

The remnant that remained after the able-bodied were carried into captivity associated with the kingdom of Judah (2Ch 30:18-26; 34:6; 35:18).

The Kings of Israel

	Names	Ruled	Dates B.C.
1.	Jeroboam I	22 years	930-909
2.	Nadab	2 years	909-908
3.	Baasha	24 years	908-886
4.	Elah	2 years	886-885
5.	Zimri	7 days	885
6.	Omri	12 years	885-874
7.	Ahab	22 years	874-853
8.	Ahaziah	2 years	853-852
9.	Joram	12 years	852-841
10.	Jehu	28 years	841-814
11.	Jehoahaz	17 years	814-798
12.	Jehoash	16 years	798-782
13.	Jeroboam II	41 years	793-753
14.	Zechariah	6 months	753
15.	Shallum	1 month	752
16.	Menahem	10 years	752-742
17.	Pekahiah	2 years	742-740
18.	Pekah	20 years	752-732
19.	Hoshea	9 years	732-722

Note: Some kings, such as Jehoash and Jeroboam II, had overlapping reigns.

See also the chart at Kings; each king by name.

Prophecies Concerning—

Of captivity, famine, and judgments (1Ki 14:15-16; 17:1; 20:13-28; 21:17; 8:1; Isa 7:8; 8:4-7; 9:8-21; 17:3-11; 28:1-8; Hos 1:1-9; 2:1-13; 4:10; 11:5-6; 12:7-14; 13; Am 2:6-16; 3-9).

Of restoration (Hos 2:14-23; 11:9-11; 13:13-14; 14:8). Of the reunion of the ten tribes and Judah (Jer 3:18; Eze 37:16-22).

Judah:

The nation composed of the tribes of Judah and Benjamin, called Judah (Isa 11:12-13; Jer 4:3), and Jews ruled by the descendants of David. *See Jews.*

In the historical books of the Kings and the Chronicles the nation is called Judah, but in the prophecies it is frequently referred to as Israel (Isa 8:14; 49:7).

Rehoboam succeeds Solomon. In consequence of his arbitrary policy ten tribes rebel (1Ki 12). Other circumstances of his reign (1Ki 14:21-31; 2Ch 10-12). Death of Rehoboam (1Ki 14:31). Abijah's wicked reign (1Ki 15:1-8; 2Ch 13), Asa's good reign (1Ki 15:9-24; 2Ch 14-16). Asa makes a league with Ben-Hadad, king of Syria , to make war against Israel (1Ki 15:16-24). Jehoshaphat succeeds Asa (1Ki 15:24; 2Ch 17-20; 21:1), joins Ahab against the king of Syria (1Ki 22). *See Jehoshaphat.* Jehoram, also called Joram, reigns in the place of his father, Jehoshaphat (1Ki 8:16-24; 2Ch 21). Edom revolts (2Ki 8:20-22). Ahaziah also called Azariah (2Ch 22:6) and Jehoahaz (2Ch 21:17; 25:23), succeeds Jehoram (2Ki 8:24-29; 2Ch 22); slain by Jehu (2Ki 9:27-29; 2Ch 22:8-9); Athaliah, his mother, succeeds him (2Ki 11:1-16; 2Ch 22:10-12; 23:1-15).

The Kings (and Queen) of Judah

	Name	Ruled	Dates B.C.
1.	Rehoboam	17 years	930-913
2.	Abijah	3 years	913-910
3.	Asa	41 years	910-869
4.	Jehoshaphat	25 years	872-848
5.	Jehoram	8 years	848-841
6.	Ahaziah	1 year	841
7.	Queen Athaliah	6 years	841-835
8.	Joash	40 years	835-796
9.	Amaziah	29 years	796-767
10.	Uzziah / Azariah	52 years	792-740
11.	Jotham	16 years	750-735
12.	Ahaz	16 years	732-715
13.	Hezekiah	29 years	715-686
14.	Manasseh	55 years	697-642
15.	Amon	2 years	642-640
16.	Josiah	31 years	640-609
17.	Jehoahaz	3 months	609
18.	Jehoiakim	11 years	609-598
19.	Jehoiachin	3 months	598-597
20.	Zedekiah / Mattaniah	11 years	597-586

Note: Some kings, such as Uzziah and Jotham, had overlapping reigns.

See also the chart at Kings; each king by name.

Jehoash, also called Joash, succeeds Athaliah (2Ki 11:21; 12:1-21; 2Ch 24). The temple repaired (2Ki 12). Amaziah reigns, and Judah is invaded by the king of Israel; Jerusalem is taken and the sacred things of the temple carried away (2Ki 14:1-20; 2Ch 25). Azariah, also called Uzziah, succeeds him (2Ki 14:21-22; 15:1-7; 2Ch 26). Jotham succeeds Uzziah (2Ki 15:7, 32-38; 2Ch 27). Rezin, king of Syria, invades Judah (2Ki 15:37). Jotham is succeeded by Ahaz (2Ki 16:1; 2Ch 28). Judah is invaded by kings of Samaria and Syria; Ahaz hires the king of Assyria to make war on the king of Syria (2Ki 16:5-9). Ahaz changes the fashion of the altar in the temple (2Ki 16:10-18). Hezekiah succeeds Ahaz (2Ki 16:19-20; 2Ch 29-32). His good reign (2Ki 18:1-8). He revolts from the sovereignty of the king of Assyria (2Ki 18:7). King of Assyria invades Judah and blasphemes the God of Judah; his army overthrown (2Ki 18:9-37; 19). Hezekiah's sickness and miraculous restoration (2Ki 20). Succeeded by Manasseh (2Ki 20:21; 2Ch 33:1-20). Manasseh's wicked reign (2Ki 21:1-18). Amon succeeds Manasseh on the throne (2Ki 21:18-26; 2Ch 33:20-25).

Josiah succeeds Amon; the temple is repaired; the Book of the Law recovered; religious revival follows; and the king dies (2Ki 22; 23:1-30; 2Ch 34-35). Josiah is succeeded by Jehoahaz, who reigns three months, is dethroned by the king of Egypt, and the land put under tribute (2Ki 23:30-35; 2Ch 36:1-3). Jehoiakim is elevated to the throne; becomes tributary to Nebuchadnezzar for three years; rebels; is conquered and carried to Babylon (2Ki 24:1-6; 2Ch 36:4-8). Jehoiachin is made king, suffers invasion, and is carried to Babylon (2Ki 24:8-16; 2Ch 36:9-10). Zedekiah is made king by Nebuchadnezzar; rebels; Nebuchadnezzar invades Judah, takes Jerusalem, and carries the people to Babylon, despoiling the temple (2Ki 24:17-20; 25; 2Ch 36:11-21). The poorest of the people are left to occupy the country and are joined by fragments of the army of Judah, the dispersed Israelites in other lands, and the king's daughters (2Ki 25:12, 22-23; Jer 39:10; 40:7-12; 52:16). Gedaliah

appointed governor over (2Ki 25:22). His administration favorable to the people (2Ki 25:23-24; Jer 40:7-12). Conspired against and slain by Ishmael (2Ki 25:25; Jer 40:13-16; 41:1-3). Ishmael seeks to betray the people to the Ammonites (Jer 41:1-18). The people take refuge in Egypt (2Ki 25:26; Jer 41:14-18; 42:13-18).

Captivity of Judah—

Great wickedness the cause of their adversity (Eze 5-7; 16; 23:22-44). Dwell in Babylon (Da 5:13; 6:13; Jer 52:28-30) by the Kebar River (Eze 1:1; 10:15). Patriotism of (Ps 137). Plotted against, by Haman (Est 3). Are saved by Esther (Est 4-9). Cyrus decrees their restoration (2Ch 36:22-23; Ezr 1:1-4). Cyrus directs the rebuilding of the temple and the restoration of the vessels that had been carried to Babylon (2Ch 36:23; Ezr 1:3-11). Proclamation renewed by Darius and Artaxerxes (Ezr 6:1-14). Ezra returns with 1, 754 of the captives to Jerusalem (Ezr 2). Temple rebuilt and dedicated (Ezr 3-6). Artaxerxes issues proclamation to restore the temple service (Ezr 7). Priests and Levites authorized to return (Ezr 8). Corruption among the returned captives; reform (Ezr 9-10). Nehemiah leads 49, 942 captives back to the land (Ne 2; 7:5-67; Ps 85; 87; 107; 126). Wall of Jerusalem rebuilt and dedicated (Ne 2-6; 12). The law read and expounded (Ne 8). Solemn feast is kept, priests are purified; and the covenant sealed (Ne 8-10). One-tenth of the people, to be determined by lot, volunteer to dwell in Jerusalem, and the remaining nine parts dwell in other cities (Ne 11). Catalog of the priests and Levites who came up with Zerubbabel (Ne 12). Nehemiah reforms various abuses (Ne 13). Expect a Messiah (Lk 3:15). Many accept Jesus as the Christ (Messiah) (Jn 2:23; 10:42; 11:45; 12:11; Ac 21:20). Reject Jesus. *See Jesus the Christ, Rejected.*

Rejected by God (Mt 21:43; Lk 20:16).

Prophecies Concerning Israel and Judah:

Of their rejection of the Messiah (Isa 8:14-15; 49:5, 7; 52:14; 53:1-3; Zec 11; 13; Mt 21:33; 22:1).

Of war and other judgments (Dt 28:49-57; 2Ki 20:17-18; 21:12-15; 22:16-17; 23:26-27; Isa 1:1-24; 3; 4:1; 5; 6:9-13; 7:17-25; 8:14-22; 9; 10:12; 22:1-14; 28:14-22; 29:1-10; 30:1-17; 31:1-3; 32:9-14; Jer 1:11-16; 4:5-31; 6; 7:8-34; 8; 9:9-26; 10:17-22; 11:9-23; 13:9-27; 14:14-18; 15:1-14; 16; 17:1-4; 18:15-17; 19; 20:5; 21:4-7; 22:24-30; 25:8-38; 34; 37; 38:1-3; 42:13-22; 43-45; La 5:6; Eze 4-5; 11:7-12; 12; 15-17; 19; 22:13-22; 23:22-35; 24; 33:21-29; Da 9:26-27; Joel 2:1-17; Am 2:4-5; Mic 2:10; 3; 4:8-10; Hab 1:6-11; Zep 11; Zec 11; 14:1-3; Mal 4:1; Mt 21:33-34; 23:35-38; 24:2, 14-42; Mk 13:1-13; Lk 13:34-35; 19:43-44; 21:5-25; 23:28-31; Rev 1:7).

Dispersion of (Isa 24:1; Jer 9:16; Hos 9:17; Joel 3:6, 20; Am 9:9; Eze 4:13; 5:10, 12; 20:23; 36:19; Da 9:7; Jn 7:35; Ac 2:5).

Of blessing and restoration (Isa 1:25-27; 2:1-5; 4:2-6; 11:11-13; 25; 26:1-2, 12-19; 27:13; 29:18-24; 30:18-26; 32:15-20; 33:13-24; 35; 37:31-32; 40:2, 9; 41:27; 44; 49:13-23; 51; 52:1-12; 60; 61:4-9; 62; 66:5-22; Jer 3:14-18; 4:3-18; 12:14-16; 23:3; 24:1-7; 29:1-14; 30:3-22; 32:36-44; 33; 44:28; Eze 14:22-23; 16:60-63; 20:40-41; 36:1-38; 37:12, 21; Da 11:30-45; 12:1; Joel 3; Am 9:9-15; Ob 17-21; Mic 2:12-13; 5:3; Zep 2:7; Zec 1:14-21; 2:8; 10:5-12; 12:1-14; 13; 14:3-21; Mal 3:4; Ro 11; 2Co 3:16; Rev 7:15).

ISRAELITES See Israel, Israelites.

ISSACHAR (*there is reward, Ge. 30:18; may [God] show mercy* IDB; *hired hand* KB).

1. Fifth son of Jacob (Ge 30:18; Ex 1:3; 1Ch 2:1). Jacob's prophetic benedictions upon (Ge 49:14-15). In the time of David (1Ch 7:1-5).

2. Tribe of. Descended from Jacob's son (Ge 30:17-18). Prophecies concerning (Ge 49:14-15; Dt 33:18-19).

Persons selected from to number the people (Nu 1:8), to spy out the land (Nu 13:7). To divide the land (Nu 34:26). Strength of, on leaving Egypt (Nu 1:28-29; 2:6). Encamped under the standard of Judah east of the tabernacle (Nu 2:5). Next to and under the standard of Judah in the journeys of Israel (Nu 10:14-15). Offering of, at the dedication (Nu 7:18-23). Families of (Nu 26:23-24). Strength of, on entering Canaan (Nu 26:25). On Gerizim said amen to the blessings (Dt 27:12). Bounds of their inheritance (Jos 19:17-23). Assisted Deborah against Sisera (Jdg 5:15). Officers of, appointed by David (1Ch 27:18), appointed by Solomon (1Ki 4:17). Some of, at David's coronation (1Ch 12:32). Number of warriors belonging to, in David's time (1Ch 7:2, 5). Many of, at Hezekiah's Passover (2Ch 30:18). Remarkable persons of (Jdg 10:1; 1Ki 15:27).

ISSHIAH (*Yahweh forgets*).

1. Man of Issachar (1Ch 7:3).

2. A disaffected Israelite who joined David at Ziklag; one of David's heroes (1Ch 12:6).

3. A Kohathite Levite (1Ch 23:20).

4. A Levite (1Ch 24:21).

ISSUE OF BLOOD See Bleeding, Subject to; Hemorrhage.

ISUAH See Ishvah.

ISUI See Ishvi.

ITALIAN REGIMENT Cohort of Italian soldiers stationed in Caesarea when Peter preached to Cornelius (Ac 10:1).

ITALY (Ac 27:1; Heb 13:24). Aquila and Priscilla expelled from (Ac 18:2).

ITCH A skin disease (Lev 13:30-37; 14:54; Dt 28:27). *See Disease; Scall.*

ITHAI One of David's valiant men (2Sa 23:29; 1Ch 11:31).

ITHAMAR (possibly *[is]land of palms* BDB; *[father] of Tamar* KB). Son of Aaron (Ex 6:23; 28:1; 1Ch 6:3). Entrusted with money of the tabernacle (Ex 38:21). Charged with duties of the tabernacle (Nu 4:28; 7:8). Forbidden to lament the death of his brothers, Nadab and Abihu (Lev 10:6-7). Descendants of (1Ch 24:1-19).

ITHIEL (*God [El] is with me*).
1. A Benjamite (Ne 11:7).
2. An unidentified person (Pr 30:1).

ITHLAH (*hanging, lofty place*). A city of Dan (Jos 19:42).

ITHMAH (*fatherless* KB; *purity* ISBE). A Moabite (1Ch 11:46).

ITHNAN A town in the extreme S of Judah (Jos 15:23).

ITHRA (*abundance* BDB; *what remained* KB). Hebrew Ithra is a variant of Jether (2Sa 17:25, ftn). Father of Amasa (2Sa 17:25; 1Ch 2:17). *See Jether, 3.*

ITHRAN (*what is over, profit* KB; *excellent* ISBE).
1. Son of Dishon (Ge 36:26; 1Ch 1:41).
2. Son of Zophah (1Ch 7:37).

ITHREAM (*remainder of the people*). Son of David (2Sa 3:5; 1Ch 3:3).

ITHRITE(S) (*excellence,* or *preeminence* ISBE; *remainder* KB). Family of two of David's heroes (2Sa 23:38; 1Ch 11:40).

ITINERARY Of the Israelites (Nu 33; Dt 10:6-7). *See Israel, Israelites.*

ITTAH-KAZIN See Eth Kazin.

ITTAI (*possibly with me* BDB).
1. Gittite who became a loyal follower of David (2Sa 15:18-22; 18:2, 5).
2. See Ithai.

ITUREA (*pertaining to Jetur*). Region NE of Israel; its people descended from Jetur, son of Ishmael, and from whom the name Iturea is derived (Ge 25:15), ruled by Philip (Lk 3:1).

IVAH See Ivvah.

IVORY (SS 5:1, 4; 7:4; Eze 27:15). Exported from, Tarshish (1Ki 10:22; 2Ch 9:21), the coasts of Cyprus, the Hebrew is Kittim (Eze 27:6).
Ahab's palace made of (1Ki 22:39). Other houses made of (Ps 45:8; Am 3:15). Other articles made of: Stringed instruments (Ps 45:8), thrones (1Ki 10:18; 2Ch 9:17), benches (Eze 27:6), beds (Am 6:4), vessels (Rev 18:12).

IVVAH District in Babylon conquered by the Assyrians (2Ki 18:34; 19:13; Isa 37:13).

IYE ABARIM (*heaps of Abarim [regions beyond]*). One of the places where Israel camped in the desert (Nu 21:11; 33:44). Also called Iyim (Nu 33:45, ftn).

IYIM (Nu 33:45). See Iye Abarim.

IYYAR See Month, 2; Ziv.

IZHAR, IZHARITES (*the shining one*). Son of Kohath (Ex 6:18, 21; 1Ch 6:2, 18, 38; 23:12, 18) and his descendants (Nu 3:27; 1Ch 24:22; 26:23, 29).

IZLIAH (*long living, eternal* IDB; *Yahweh delivers* ISBE). A Benjamite son of Elpaal (1Ch 8:18).

IZRAHIAH (*Yahweh, he shines*). Grandson of Tola (1Ch 7:3).

IZRAHITE (*shining*). Family name of Shamhuth (1Ch 27:8).

IZRI (*Yahweh designs*). Perhaps the same as Zeri. Leader of the fourth division of Levitical singers (1Ch 25:11).

IZZIAH (*may Yahweh sprinkle [in atonement]* BDB; *Yahweh unites* ISBE). An Israelite of the Parosh family who marries an idolatrous wife (Ezr 10:25).

J

JAAKAN, JAAKANITES Son of Ezer (Ge 36:20-21, 27; Dt 10:6; 1Ch 1:42). A Horite (1Ch 1:42), and the same as Akan (Ge 36:27). *See Akan; Bene Jaakan.*

JAAKOBAH (*may [deity] protect* IDB). Descendant of Simeon (1Ch 4:36).

JAALA One of the servants of Solomon returned from exile (Ezr 2:56; Ne 7:58).

JAALAM See Jalam.

JAAN See Dan Jaan.

JAANAI See Janai.

JAAR An alternate name for Kiriath Jearim (Ps 132:6, ftn). *See Kiriath Jearim.*

JAARE-OREGIM Father of Elhanan, who slew the giant brother of Goliath (2Sa 21:19). Spelled Jair (1Ch 20:5).

JAARESHIAH (*Yahweh plants*). Son of Jeroham (1Ch 8:27).

JAASAU See Jaasu.

JAASIEL (*God [El] does*). One of David's warriors (1Ch 11:47). Son of Abner (1Ch 27:21).

JAASU Of the family of Bani (Ezr 10:37).

JAAZANIAH (*Yahweh listens*).
1. Also called Jezaniah (Jer 40:8, ftn). A Maacathite captain who joined Gedaliah at Mizpah (2Ki 25:23; Jer 42:1).
2. A Recabite (Jer 35:3).
3. An idolatrous zealot (Eze 8:11).
4. A wicked prince of Judah (Eze 11:1-13).

JAAZER See Jazer.

JAAZIAH (*may Yahweh nourish* IDB). A descendant of Merari (1Ch 24:26-27).

JAAZIEL (*God [El] strengthens* ISBE). A Levite musician (1Ch 15:18).

JABAL Son of Lamech. A shepherd (Ge 4:20).

JABBOK (*flowing*). A stream on the E of the Jordan, the northern boundary of the possessions of the Ammonites (Nu 21:24; Jdg 11:13), of the Reubenites and the Gadites (Jos 12:2; Dt 3:16). The northern boundary of the Amorites (Jdg 11:22).

JABESH (*dry*).
1. Father of King Shallum (2Ki 15:8-13).
2. Short term for Jabesh-Gilead (1Ch 10:12).

JABESH GILEAD (*dry Gilead*). A city E of the Jordan (Jdg 21:8-15). Besieged by the Ammonites (1Sa 11:1). Saul and his sons buried at (1Sa 31:11-13; 2Sa 2:4; 1Ch 10:11-12). Bones of Saul and his son removed from, by David, and buried at Zela (2Sa 21:12-14).

JABEZ (*to grieve*).
1. A city of Judah (1Ch 2:55).
2. The head of a family (1Ch 4:9-10).

JABIN (*perceptive*).
1. King of Hazor, defeated and slain by Joshua (Jos 11).
2. Another king of Hazor, defeated by Barak (Jdg 4; 1Sa 12:9; Ps 83:9).

JABNEEL (*God [El] will build*).
1. Town in N border of Judah, just S of Joppa (Jos 15:11), modern Yebna. Called Jabneh (2Ch 26:6). Later called Jamnia.
2. Frontier town of Naphtali (Jos 19:33), modern Tell en-Naam.

JABNEH A Philistine city (2Ch 26:6). See Jabneel, 1.

JACAN A Gadite (1Ch 5:13).

JACHIN, JACHINITES See Jakin.

JACINTH (*hyacinth*). A precious stone in the high priest's breastpiece (Ex 28:19; 39:12), in the foundation of New Jerusalem (Rev 21:20). *See Minerals of the Bible, 1; Stones.*

JACKAL A carnivorous scavenger, inhabiting the desert. Often translated "dragon" in the KJV (Job 30:29; Ps 44:19; Isa 13:21, 22; Jer 9:11; Mal 1:3).

JACKAL WELL Named only in Ne 2:13; possibly En Rogel or the Pool or Siloam. *See En Rogel; Siloam, Pool of.*

JACOB (*follower, replacer, one who follows the heel*). Son of Isaac and twin brother of Esau (Ge 25:24-26; Jos 24:4; 1Ch 1:34; Ac 7:8). Ancestor of Jesus (Mt 1:2). Given in answer to prayer (Ge 25:21). Obtains Esau's birthright for a bowl of stew (Ge 25:29-34; Heb 12:16). Fraudulently obtains his father's blessing (Ge 27:1-29; Heb 11:20). Esau seeks to kill, escapes to Paddan Aram (Ge 27:41-46; 28:1-5; Hos 12:12). His vision of the stairway (Ge 28:10-22). God confirms the covenant of Abraham to (Ge 28:13-22; 35:9-15; 1Ch 16:13-18).
Lives in Haran with his uncle, Laban (Ge 29; 30; Hos 12:12). Serves fourteen years for Leah and Rachel (Ge 29:15-30; Hos 12:12). Sharp practice of, with the flocks and herds of Laban (Ge 30:32-43). Dissatisfied with Laban's treatment and returns to the land of Canaan (Ge 31). Meets angels of God on the journey and calls the place Mahanaim (Ge 32:1-2). Dreads to meet Esau; sends him presents; wrestles with an angel (Ge 32). Name of, changed to Israel (Ge 32:28; 35:10). *See Israel.* Reconciliation of, with Esau (Ge 33:4). Journeys to Succoth (Ge 33:17). Goes to Shechem where he purchases a parcel of ground from Hamor, and erects an altar (Ge 33:18-20). His daughter, Dinah, raped and avenged (Ge 34).
Returns to Bethel, where he builds an altar and dedicates a pillar (Ge 35:1-7). Deborah, Rebekah's nurse, dies, and is buried at Bethel (Ge 35:8). Journeys to Ephrath; Benjamin is born to; Rachel dies, and is "buried on the way to Ephrath (that is, Bethlehem)" (Ge 35:16-19; 48:7). Erects a monument at Rachel's grave (Ge 35:20). The incest of his son, Reuben, and his concubine, Bilhah (Ge 35:22). List of the names of his twelve sons (Ge 35:23-26). Returns to Kiriath Arba, the city of his father (Ge 35:27). Lives in the land of Canaan (Ge 37:1).
His partiality for his son, Joseph, and the consequent jealousy of his other sons (Ge 37:3-4). Joseph's prophetic dream concerning (Ge 37:9-11). His grief over the loss of Joseph (Ge 37:34-35). Sends into Egypt to buy grain (Ge 42:1-2; 43:1-14). His grief over the detention of Simeon and the demand for Benjamin to be taken into Egypt (Ge 42:36). His love for Benjamin (Ge 43:14; 44:29). Hears that Joseph still lives (Ge 45:26-28).
Moves to Egypt (Ge 46:1-7; 1Sa 12:8; Ps 105:23; Ac 7:14-15). List of his children and grandchildren who went down into Egypt (Ge 46:8-27). Meets Joseph (Ge 46:28-34). Pharaoh receives him and is blessed by Jacob (Ge 47:1-10). The land of Goshen assigned to (Ge 47:11-12, 27). Lives in Egypt seventeen years (Ge 47:28). Exacts promise from Joseph to bury him with his fathers (Ge 47:29-31). His benediction upon Joseph and his two sons (Ge

48:15-22). Gives the land of the two Amorites to Joseph (Ge 48:22; Jn 4:5).
His final prophetic benedictions upon his sons: Reuben (Ge 49:3-4), Simeon and Levi (Ge 49:5-7), Judah (Ge 49:8-12), Zebulun (Ge 49:13), Issachar (Ge 49:14-15), Dan (Ge 49:16-18), Gad (Ge 49:19), Asher (Ge 49:20), Naphtali (Ge 49:21), Joseph (Ge 49:22-26), Benjamin (Ge 49:27). Charges his sons to bury him in the field of Machpelah (Ge 49:29-30). Death of (Ge 49:33). Body of, embalmed (Ge 50:2). Forty days mourning for (Ge 50:3). Burial of (Ge 50:4-13). Descendants of (Ge 29:31-35; 30:1-24; 35:18, 22-26; 46:8-27; Ex 1:1-5; 1Ch 2-9).
Prophecies concerning himself and descendants (Ge 25:23; 27:28-29; 28:10-15; Ge 31:3; 35:9-13; 46:3; Dt 1:8; Ps 105:10-11). His wealth (Ge 36:6-7). Well of (Jn 4:5-30).

JACOB'S WELL Well near base of Mt. Gerizim where Jesus talked with a Samaritan woman (Jn 4).

JADA (*shrewd one* BDB; *[God] has cared* IDB). A Judahite, son of Onam (1Ch 2:26, 28).

JADAH (*honeycomb*). Most Hebrew manuscripts have Jarah. Descendant of Gibeon (1Ch 9:42, ftn), Jehoaddah (1Ch 8:36).

JADAU See Jaddai.

JADDAI An Israelite who married a foreign woman during the Captivity (Ezr 10:43).

JADDUA (*one known*).
1. Prince who sealed covenant (Ne 10:21).
2. Son of Jonathan; priest who returned from Babylon (Ne 12:11).

JADON (*frail one* or *Yahweh rules* IDB). One who helped in rebuilding of Jerusalem wall (Ne 3:7).

JAEL (*mountain goat*). Wife of Heber and killer of Sisera (Jdg 4:17-22; 5:6, 24).

JAGUR A town of Judah (Jos 15:21).

JAHATH (*snatch up*).
1. Grandson of Judah (1Ch 4:1-2).
2. Great-grandson of Levi (1Ch 6:16-20).
3. Levite (1Ch 23:10-11).
4. Levite (1Ch 24:22).
5. Merarite Levite (2Ch 34:8-12). See Merari.

JAHAZ (*perhaps a trodden* or *open place*). Also called Jahzah. A Levitical city in Reuben, taken from the Moabites (Jos 13:18; 21:36; Isa 15:4; Jer 48:21). Sihon defeated at (Nu 21:23; Dt 2:32; Jdg 11:20).

JAHAZIAH See Jahzeiah.

JAHAZIEL (*God [El] will see*).
1. A disaffected Israelite who joined David at Ziklag (1Ch 12:4).
2. A priest (1Ch 16:6).
3. Son of Hebron (1Ch 23:19; 24:23).
4. A Levite, and prophet (2Ch 20:14).
5. A chief, or the father of a chief, among the exiles, who returned from Babylon (Ezr 8:5).

JAHDAI (*Yahweh lead*). A descendant of Caleb (1Ch 2:47).

JAHDIEL (*God [El] gives joy*). Head of a family of Manasseh (1Ch 5:24).

JAHDO (*[God] gives joy*). Son of Buz (1Ch 5:14).

JAHLEEL, JAHLEELITE (*wait for God [El]* BDB; possibly *may God [El] show himself friendly* IDB). Son of Zebulun (Ge 46:14; Nu 26:26).

JAHMAI (*protect*). Son of Tola (1Ch 7:2).

JAHZAH A city of Reuben (1Ch 6:78). See Jahaz.

JAHZEEL, JAHZEELITE (*God [El] apportions*). A son of Naphtali and his clan (Nu 26:48). Also spelled Jahziel (Ge 46:24; 1Ch 7:13).

JAHZEIAH (*Yahweh sees*). Israelite who opposed Ezra in the matter of divorcing wives (Ezr 10:15).

JAHZERAH (possibly *prudent*). A priest (1Ch 9:12).

JAHZIEL See Jahzeel.

JAILER Of Philippi, converted (Ac 16:27-34).

JAIR, JAIRITE (*he gives light*).
1. Son of Manasseh. Founder of twenty-three cities in Gilead (Nu 32:41; Dt 3:14; Jos 13:30; 1Ki 4:13; 1Ch 2:22-23).
2. A judge of Israel (Jdg 10:3-5).
3. A Benjamite (Est 2:5).
4. Father of Elhanan (1Ch 20:5).

JAIRUS (*he gives light*). A ruler of the synagogue in Capernaum (Mt 9:18). Daughter of, restored to life (Mt 9:18, 23-26; Mk 5:22-43; Lk 8:41-56).

JAKAN See Akan; Jaakan, Jaakanites.

JAKEH (*prudent*). Father of Agur, a writer of proverbs (Pr 30:1).

JAKIM (*he will establish*).
1. Son of Shimei (1Ch 8:19).
2. Head of a priestly division in the tabernacle service (1Ch 24:12).

JAKIN, JAKINITE (*he establishes*).
1. Son of Simeon (Ge 46:10; Ex 6:15; Nu 26:12). Called Jarib (1Ch 4:24).
2. One of Solomon's bronze pillars erected at the temple. It stood on the right (south) side of the porch (1Ki 7:21; 2Ch 3:17). *See Boaz, 2.*
3. A priest who returned from exile to Jerusalem (1Ch 9:10; Ne 11:10).
4. A priest, head of one of the courses (1Ch 24:17).

JALAM Son of Esau (Ge 36:5, 14, 18; 1Ch 1:35).

JALON Son of Ezra (1Ch 4:17).

JAMBRES An Egyptian magician (Ex 7:11; 2Ti 3:8).

JAMES (*follower, replacer, one who follows the heel*; same as Jacob).
1. An apostle. Son of Zebedee and Salome (Mt 4:21; 27:56). *See Salome.* Brother of John, and a fisherman (Lk 5:10). Called to be an apostle (Mt 4:21-22; 10:2; Mk 1:19-20; Lk 6:14; Ac 1:13). Surnamed Boanerges by Jesus (Mk 3:17).
A close companion of Jesus, and present at the large catch of fish (Lk 5:10), the healing of Peter's mother-in-law (Mk 1:29), the raising of Jairus' daughter (Mk 5:37; Lk 8:51), the transfiguration of Jesus (Mt 17:1; Mk 9:2; Lk 9:28), in Gethsemane (Mt 26:37; Mk 14:33), at the sea of Tiberias when Jesus revealed himself to the disciples after his resurrection (Jn 21:2; 1Co 15:7). Asks Jesus concerning his second coming (Mk 13:3). Civil ambitions (Mt 20:20-23; Mk 10:35-41). Martyred (Ac 12:2).
2. The younger, an apostle. Son of Alphaeus (Mt 10:3; Mk 3:18; 15:45; Lk 12:17).
3. Brother of Jesus (Mt 13:55; Mk 6:3; Gal 1:19; 2:9, 12). The brother of Judas (Jude) and Joseph (Mt 13:55; Mk 6:3; Jude 1). A witness of Christ's resurrection (1Co 15:7). Addresses the council at Jerusalem in favor of liberty for the Gentile converts (Ac 15:13-21). Disciples sent by, to Antioch (Gal 2:12). Hears of the success attending Paul's ministry (Ac 21:18-19). Epistle of (Jas 1:1).
4. Father of apostle Judas (not Iscariot) (Lk 6:16; Ac 1:13).

JAMES, EPISTLE OF

Author: James, brother of Jesus. *See James, 3.*

Date: In the early 60s, possibly before A.D. 50

Outline:
I. Greetings (1:1).
II. Trials and Temptations (1:2-18).
 A. The Testing of Faith (1:2-12).
 B. The Source of Temptation (1:13-18).
III. Listening and Doing (1:19-27).
IV. Favoritism Forbidden (2:1-13).
V. Faith and Deeds (2:14-26).
VI. Taming the Tongue (3:1-12).
VII. Two Kinds of Wisdom (3:13-18).
VIII. Warning Against Worldliness (ch. 4).
 A. Quarrelsomeness (4:1-3).
 B. Spiritual Unfaithfulness (4:4).
 C. Pride (4:5-10).
 D. Slander (4:11-12).
 E. Boasting (4:13-17).
IX. Warning to Rich Oppressors (5:1-6).
X. Miscellaneous Exhortations (5:7-20).
 A. Concerning Patience in Suffering (5:7-11).
 B. Concerning Oaths (5:12).
 C. Concerning the Prayer of Faith (5:13-18).
 D. Concerning Those Who Wander from the Truth (5:19-20).
 See General Letters.

JAMES THE YOUNGER, THE LESS *See James, 2.*

JAMIN, JAMINITE (possibly *right hand* BDB; *south, an indication of [good] fortune* KB).
1. Son of Simeon (Ge 46:10; Ex 6:15; Nu 26:12; 1Ch 4:24).
2. Descendants of Hezron (1Ch 2:27).
3. A priest who expounded the law to the exiles who returned to Jerusalem (Ne 8:7).

JAMLECH (*he will reign*). Descendant of Simeon (1Ch 4:34).

JANAI (*he will answer*). A Gadite chief (1Ch 5:12).

JANIM A city of Judah (Jos 15:53).

JANNAI (*he will answer?*). Ancestor of Joseph (Lk 3:24).

JANNES An Egyptian magician (Ex 7:11; 2Ti 3:8).

JANOAH (*resting place*).
1. Town of Naphtali (2Ki 15:29).
2. Town on boundary of Ephraim (Jos 16:6-7).

JANUM See Janim.

JAPHETH (*enlarge*). Son of Noah (Ge 5:32; 6:10; 7:13; 10:21); had seven sons (Ge 10:2), descendants were maritime peoples (Ge 10:5); blessed by Noah (Ge 9:20-27).

JAPHIA (perhaps *may the deity shine*).
1. King of Lachish killed by Joshua (Jos 10:3).
2. Son David (2Sa 5:15; 1Ch 3:7).
3. City in E border of Zebulun (Jos 19:12).

JAPHLET (*he delivers* IDB; possibly *he escapes* ISBE). Grandson of Beriah (1Ch 7:33).

JAPHLETITES (*of Japhlet*). Clan on W border of Ephraim (Jos 16:1-3).

JAPHO See Joppa.

JAR(S) For holding water (Ge 24:14-26; Ru 2:9; Jn 2:6-7), flour (1Ki 17:10-16). Containing manna, kept in the ark (Ex 16:33; Heb 9:4). Figurative of fragile human body in which believers minister the New Covenant (2Co 4:7).

JARAH (*honeycomb*). See Jadah.

JAREB NIV "great king" of Assyria (Hos 5:13; 10:6).

JARED (*servant* KB).
1. A descendant of Seth (Ge 5:15-16, 18-20; 1Ch 1:2).
2. An ancestor of Jesus (Lk 3:37).
3. Son of Mahalalel (1Ch 1:2).

JARESIAH See Jaareshiah.

JARHA Egyptian slave of Sheshan (1Ch 2:34-35).

JARIB (*Yahweh contends*).
1. Son of Simeon (1Ch 4:24).
2. A chief among the Captivity (Ezr 8:16).
3. A priest who married an idolatrous wife (Ezr 10:18).

JARKON See Me Jarkon.

JARMUTH (*height*).
1. City of Judah sixteen miles W by S of Jerusalem (Jos 15:35), modern Tell Yarmuk.
2. Levite city of Issachar (Jos 21:28-29). Ramoth (1Ch 6:73), Remeth (Jos 19:21).

JAROAH (*soft, delicate*). A descendant of Gad (1Ch 5:14).

JASHAR, BOOK OF (*upright, straight*). Author of book quoted (Jos 10:13; 2Sa 1:18), in LXX version (1Ki 8:53).

JASHEN (possibly *asleep*). Father of some of David's heroes (2Sa 23:32), Hashem (1Ch 11:34).

JASHER, BOOK OF See Jashar, Book of.

JASHOBEAM (*the people return*).
1. Hero who joined David at Ziklag (1Ch 12:6).
2. One of David's leaders (1Ch 11:11), Adino the Eznite in Hebrew and Septuagint (2Sa 23:8, ftn).
3. Hacmoni (1Ch 27:2-3). *See above, 2.* May be the same.

JASHUB, JASHUBITE (*he returns*).
1. Son of Issachar (Ge 46:13; Nu 26:24).
2. Shear-Jashub, a son of Isaiah (Isa 7:3).
3. Man who married foreign wife (Ezr 10:29).

JASHUBI LEHEM (*[they] returned to Lehem*). A descendant of Shelah (1Ch 4:22).

JASIEL See Jaasiel.

JASON (*to heal*). A Christian at Thessalonica (Ac 17:5-7, 9) and possibly Paul's relative (Ro 16:21).

JASPER A precious stone set in the high priest's breastplate (Ex 28:20; 39:13; Job 28:18; Eze 28:13; Rev 4:3; 21:11, 18-19). *See Minerals of the Bible, 1; Stones.*

JATHNIEL (*God [El] hires* BDB; *God [El] is forever* KB). Son of Meshelemiah (1Ch 26:2).

JATTIR (possibly *preeminence* IDB). A Levitical city (Jos 15:48; 21:14; 1Sa 30:27; 1Ch 6:57).

JAVAN
1. A son of Japheth. Father of Elishah, Tarshish, Kittim, and Rodanim (Ge 10:4; 1Ch 1:7). Javan is same as Greek Ionia, with whom the Hebrews traded (Isa 66:19; Joel 3:4-6).
2. A city in Arabia in which the Phoenicians traded (Eze 27:13, 19).

JAVELIN A heavy lance (Eze 39:9), used by Goliath (1Sa 17:6), by Saul (1Sa 18:11; 19:9-10).

JAZER (*he helps*).
1. Taken from the Amorites (Nu 21:32; 32:1, 3, 35). Ammonite stronghold E of the Jordan, probably c. fourteen miles N of Heshbon; assigned to Gad (Jos 13:24-25), later given to Levites; a city of refuge E of the Jordan (Jos 21:39).
2. Sea of (Jer 48:32).

JAZIZ Overseer of David's flocks (1Ch 27:31).

JEALOUSY (Pr 6:34; 27:4; Ecc 4:4; SS 8:6). Law concerning, when husband is jealous of his wife (Nu 5:12-31). Image of (Eze 8:3-4). Forbidden (Ro 13:13).
Attributed to God (Ex 20:5; 34:13-14; Nu 25:11; Dt 29:20; 32:16, 21; 1Ki 14:22; Ps 78:58; 79:5; Isa 30:1-2; 31:1, 3; Eze 16:42; 23:25; 36:5-6; 38:19; Zep 1:18; 3:8; Zec 1:14; 8:2; 1Co 10:22).
See Anthropomorphisms.
A desire to emulate (Ro 10:19; 11:11).
See Emulation; Envy.

Figurative: (2Co 11:2).

Instances of:
Cain, of Abel (Ge 4:5-6, 8). Sarah, of Hagar (Ge 16:5). Joseph's brothers, of Joseph (Ge 37:4-11, 18-28). Saul, of David (1Sa 18:8-30; 19:8-24; 20:24-34). Joab, of Abner (2Sa 3:24-27). Nathan, of Adonijah (1Ki 1:24-26). Ephraimites, of Gideon (Jdg 8:1), of Jephthah (Jdg 12:1). The brother of the prodigal son (Lk 15:25-32). Sectional, between Israel and the tribe of Judah (2Sa 19:41-43).

JEALOUSY, WATER OF See Water of Bitterness.

JEARIM (*timberlands*). Hill on N border of Judah (Jos 15:10).

JEATHERAI Descendant of Gershom (1Ch 6:21).

JEBEREKIAH (*Yahweh blesses*). Father of Zechariah (Isa 8:2).

JEBUS Name of Jerusalem when in possession of Jebusites (Jos 15:63; Jdg 19:10), taken by Israelites (Jdg 1:8), but stronghold not captured until David's time (2Sa 5:7-8).

JEBUSITE(S) (*of Jebus*). One of the tribes of Canaan (Dt 7:1). Land of, given to Abraham and his descendants (Ge 15:21; Ex 3:8, 17; 23:23-24; Dt 20:17; Ex 33:2; 34:10-11). Conquered by Joshua (Jos 10-12; 24:11), by David (2Sa 5:6-9). Jerusalem within the territory of (Jos 18:28). Not exterminated, but intermarry with the Israelites (Jdg 3:5-6; Ezr 9:1-2; 10:18-44). Pay tribute to Solomon (1Ki 9:20-21).

JECAMIAH See Jekamiah.

JECOLIAH (*Yahweh is able*). Mother of King Uzziah (2Ch 26:3; 2Ki 15:2).

JECONIAH Variant of Jehoiachin (Jer 22:24, 28; 37:1). *See Jehoiachin.* King of Judah, captured by Nebuchadnezzar (2Ki 24:1-12).

JEDAIAH (*Yahweh has favored* IDB, or *Yahweh knows*).
1. Descendant of Simeon (1Ch 4:37).
2. A returned exile (Ne 3:10).
3. A priest of the Captivity (1Ch 9:10; 24:7; Ezr 2:36; Ne 7:39).
4. A priest who lived in Jerusalem after the return of the Captivity (Ne 11:10; 12:6, 19; Zec 6:10, 14).
5. Another priest, who returned from Babylon with Nehemiah (Ne 12:7, 21).

JEDIAEL (*known of God [El]*).
1. Son of Benjamin (1Ch 7:6, 10-11).
2. Son of Shimri (1Ch 11:45).
3. A Manassite chief who joined David at Ziklag (1Ch 12:20).
4. Son of Meshelemiah (1Ch 26:2).

JEDIDAH (*beloved* BDB; *lovely, beloved* KB). Mother of King Josiah (2Ki 22:1).

JEDIDIAH (*beloved of Yahweh*). Name that Nathan gave to Solomon (2Sa 12:24-25).

JEDUTHUN A musician of the temple (1Ch 16:41; 25:1). Called Ethan (1Ch 6:44; 15:17). *See titles of Psalms 39, 62, 77.*

JEEZER, JEEZERITES See Abiezer, 1; Iezer.

JEGAR SAHADUTHA (*witness heap*). Name given by Laban to heap of stones set up as memorial of covenant between him and Jacob; called Galeed by Jacob (Ge 31:47-48).

JEHALLELEL (*he shall praise God [El]* BDB; *God [El] shines forth* IDB).
1. Descendant of Judah (1Ch 4:16).
2. Merarite Levite (2Ch 29:12).

JEHATH Son of Gershon (1Ch. 6:20).

JEHDEIAH (*Yahweh rejoices [in his works]*).
1. Descendant of Moses (1Ch 24:20).
2. Man in charge of David's donkeys (1Ch 27:30).

JEHEZKEL (*God [El] gives strength*). Priest in David's time (1Ch 24:16).

JEHIAH (*Yahweh lives*). A Levite, and doorkeeper of the ark (1Ch 15:24).

JEHIEL (*God [El] lives*).
1. A Levite gatekeeper (1Ch 15:18). Probably identical with Jehiah. *See Jehiah.*
2. A Gershonite Levite (1Ch 23:8; 29:8).
3. A companion of David's sons (1Ch 27:32).
4. Son of Jehoshaphat (2Ch 21:2).
5. Son of Heman (2Ch 29:14).
6. A Levite overseer in the temple (2Ch 31:13).
7. A priest who gave extraordinary offerings for the Passover (2Ch 35:8).
8. Father of Obadiah (Ezr 8:9).
9. Father of Shecaniah (Ezr 10:2).
10. Name of two priests who married idolatrous wives (Ezr 10:21, 26).

JEHIELI (*of Jehiel*). Son of Ladan (1Ch 26:21-22).

JEHIZKIAH (*Yahweh gives strength*). Israelite chief in days of Ahaz, king of Judah (2Ch 28:12).

JEHOADDAH Descendant of King Saul (1Ch 8:36), Jadah (1Ch 9:42).

JEHOADDIN (probably *Yahweh is delight*). Wife of King Joash of Judah (2Ch 25:1), Jehoaddin (2Ki 14:2).

JEHOAHAZ (*Yahweh holds*).
1. Son of Jehu and king of Israel (2Ki 10:35; 13:1-9).
2. Son of Jehoram, king of Judah (2Ch 21:17). *See Ahaziah.*
3. Also called Shallum. King of Judah and successor of Josiah (2Ki 23:30-31; 1Ch 3:15; 2Ch 36:1; Jer 22:11). Wicked reign of (2Ki 23:32). Pharaoh Neco, king of Egypt, invades the kingdom of, defeats him, and takes him captive to Egypt (2Ki 23:33-35; 2Ch 36:3-4). Prophecies concerning (Jer 22:10-12).

JEHOASH, JOASH (*Yahweh bestows* ISBE; *man of Yahweh* KB).
1. Grandson of Benjamin (1Ch 7:8).
2. Descendant of Judah (1Ch 4:22).
3. Father of Gideon (Jdg 6:12).
4. Keeper of David's supply of oil (1Ch 27:28).

5. Israelite who joined David at Ziklag (1Ch 12:3).
6. Son of King Ahab (1Ki 22:26).
7. King of Judah (2Ki 11-13; 2Ch 24-25).
8. King of Israel (2Ki 13:10-13; 14:8-16; 2Ch 25:17-24).

JEHOHANAN (*Yahweh has been gracious*).
1. A gatekeeper of the tabernacle (1Ch 26:3).
2. A military chief under Jehoshaphat, whose corps consisted of 280,000 men (2Ch 17:15). Probably identical with a captain of a hundred (2Ch 23:1).
3. Son of Bebai (Ezr 10:28).
4. A priest among the exiles who returned from Babylon (Ne 12:13).
5. A choir member in the temple (Ne 12:42).

JEHOIACHIN (*Yahweh supports*). (Jer 22:24; 37:1). King of Judah and successor to Jehoiakim (2Ki 24:6-8; 1Ch 3:16; 2Ch 36:8-9; Jer 24:1). Wicked reign of (2Ki 24:9; 2Ch 36:9). Nebuchadnezzar invades his kingdom, takes him captive to Babylon (2Ki 24:10-16; 2Ch 36:10; Est 2:6; Jer 27:20; 29:1-2; Eze 1:2). Confined in prison thirty-seven years (2Ki 25:27). Released from prison by Evil-Merodach and promoted above other kings, and honored until death (2Ki 25:27-30; Jer 52:31-34). Prophecies concerning (Jer 22:24-30; 28:4). Sons of (1Ch 3:17-18). Ancestor of Jesus, called Jeconiah (Mt 1:11, 12).

JEHOIADA (*Yahweh has known*).
1. Father of Benaiah, one of David's officers (2Sa 8:18).
2. A high priest. Overthrows Athaliah, the usurping queen of Judah, and establishes Jehoash upon the throne (2Ki 11; 2Ch 23). Salutary influence of, over Joash (Hebrew *Jehoash*, a variant of *Joash*) (2Ki 12:2, ftn; 2Ch 24:2, 22). Directs the repairs of the temple (2Ki 12:7-16; 2Ch 24:4-14). Death of (2Ch 24:15-16).
3. A priest who led 3, 700 priests armed for war (1Ch 12:27).
4. Son of Benaiah (1Ch 27:34).
5. A returned exile (Ne 3:6).
6. A priest mentioned in Jeremiah's letter to the captive Israelites (Jer 29:26).

JEHOIAKIM (*Yahweh lifts up, establishes*). Also called Eliakim. King of Judah (1Ch 3:15). Wicked reign and final overthrow of (2Ki 23:24-37; 24:1-6; 2Ch 36:4-8; Jer 22:13-19; 26:22-23; 36; Da 1:1-2). Dies and is succeeded by his son, Jehoiachin (2Ki 24:6).

JEHOIARIB (*Yahweh argues [for me]*).
1. Priest in days of David (1Ch 24:7).
2. Priest who returned from exile (1Ch 9:10). *See Joiarib.*

JEHONADAB *See Jonadab, 2.*

JEHONATHAN (*Yahweh has given*).
1. Overseer of David's property (1Ch 27:25).
2. Levite (2Ch 17:8).
3. Priest (Ne 12:18).

JEHORAM (*Yahweh exalts*).
1. King of Judah (1Ki 22:50; 2Ki 8:16; 1Ch 3:11; 2Ch 21:5). Ancestor of Jesus (Mt 1:8). Marries Athaliah, whose wicked counsels influence his reign for evil (2Ki 8:18-19; 2Ch 21:6-13). Slays his brothers to strengthen himself in his sovereignty (2Ch 21:4, 13). Edom revolts from (2Ki 8:20-22; 2Ch 21:8-10). Philistines and Arabs invade his territory (2Ch 21:16-17). Death of (2Ch 21:18-20; 2Ki 8:24). Prophecy concerning (2Ch 21:12-15).
2. A son of Ahab. *See Joram.*
3. A priest commissioned to go through Israel and instruct the people in the law (2Ch 17:8).

JEHOSHABEATH *See Jehosheba.*

JEHOSHAPHAT (*Yahweh has judged*).
1. David's recorder (2Sa 8:16; 20:24; 1Ki 4:3; 1Ch 18:15).
2. One of Solomon's district officers (1Ki 4:17).
3. King of Judah. Succeeds Asa (1Ki 15:24; 22:41; 1Ch 3:10; 2Ch 17:1; Mt 1:8). Strengthens himself against Israel (2Ch 17:2). Inaugurates a system of public instruction in the law (2Ch 17:7-9). His wise reign (2Ch 17:7-9; 19:3-11). His system of tribute (2Ch 17:11). His military forces and armament (2Ch 17:12-19). Joins Ahab in an invasion of Ramoth Gilead (1Ki 22; 2Ch 18). Rebuked by the prophet Jehu (2Ch 19:2). The allied forces of the Amorites, Moabites, and other tribes invade his territory and are defeated by (2Ch 20). Builds ships for commerce with Tarshish; ships are destroyed (1Ki 22:48-49; 2Ch 20:35-37). Joins Jehoram, king of Israel, in an invasion of the land of Moab, and defeats the Moabites (2Ki 3). Makes valuable gifts to the temple (2Ki 12:18). Death of (1Ki 22:50; 2Ch 21:1). Religious zeal of (1Ki 22:43, 46; 2Ch 17:1-9; 19; 20:1-32; 22:9). Prosperity of (1Ki 22:45, 48; 2Ch 17-20). Bequests of, to his children (2Ch 21:2-3).
4. Father of Jehu (2Ki 9:2, 14).
5. A priest who assisted in bringing the ark from Obed-Edom (1Ch 15:24).

JEHOSHAPHAT, VALLEY OF (*valley of Yahweh's judgment*). Symbolic name for a valley where all nations will be gathered by Yahweh for judgment (Joel 3:2, 12), also called "the valley of decision" (Joel 3:14).

JEHOSHEBA (*Yahweh is an oath* ISBE; *Yahweh gives plenty, satisfies* KB). Daughter of King Jehoram; wife of high priest Jehoiada; hid Joash from Athaliah (2Ki 11:2). Also spelled Jehoshabeath (1Ch 22:11, ftn).

JEHOSHUA, JEHOSHUAH *See Joshua, 1.*

JEHOVAH A misreading of the name of God, Yahweh. Hebrew was originally written using only consonants. The pronunciation (and vowels) of the Hebrew Bible was handed down orally. When the vowels were eventually added to the Hebrew text, the name Yahweh was no longer pronounced. Instead, out of reverence, the title Adonay (Lord) was substituted. In keeping with this oral tradition, the Jewish scribes inserted into Yahweh the vowels for

Adonay, resulting in the spelling Yehowah, though the name was still pronounced Adonay in oral reading. In c. 1520 the Christian scholar Petrus Galatinus introduced the hybrid spelling Jehovah, which became widely used in English versions, literature, and hymns. In the NIV, Yahweh is represented by LORD.
 See God, Names of; Yahweh.

JEHOVAH-JIREH *See God, Names of, Yahweh Yireh.*

JEHOVAH-NISSI *See God, Names of, Yahweh Nissi.*

JEHOVAH-RAPAH *See God, Names of, Yahweh Raphah.*

JEHOVAH-SHALOM *See God, Names of, Yahweh Shalom.*

JEHOVAH-SHAMMAH *See God, Names of, Yahweh Shammah.*

JEHOVAH-TSIDKENU *See God, Names of, Yahweh Tsidkenu.*

JEHOZABAD (*Yahweh endows*).
1. Son of Shomer, and one of the assassins of King Jehoash (2Ki 12:21; 2Ch 24:26).
2. Son of Obed-Edom (1Ch 26:4).
3. A Benjamite chief who commanded 180,000 men (2Ch 17:18).

JEHOZADAK (*Yahweh is just*). Also called Jozadak. A priest of the Exile (1Ch 6:14-15; Hag 1:1, 12, 14; 2:2, 4; Zec 6:11).

JEHU (*Yahweh is he*).
1. The prophet who announced the wrath of Yahweh against Baasha, king of Israel (1Ki 16:1, 7, 12; 2Ch 19:2; 20:34).
2. Son of Nimshi, king of Israel (1Ki 19:16; 2Ki 9:1-4). Religious zeal of, in killing idolaters (2Ki 9:14-37; 10:1-28; 2Ch 22:8-9). His territory invaded by Hazael, king of Syria (2Ki 10:32-33). Prophecies concerning (1Ki 19:17; 2Ki 10:30; 15:12; Hos 1:4). Death of (2Ki 10:35).
3. Son of Obed (1Ch 2:38).
4. Son of Joshibiah (1Ch 4:35).
5. A Benjamite (1Ch 12:3).

JEHUBBAH *See Hubbah.*

JEHUCAL (*Yahweh is capable*). Man sent by King Zedekiah to Jeremiah for prayers (Jer 37:3). Prince who put Jeremiah in prison (Hebrew *Jucal*, a variant of *Jehucal*) (Jer 38:1, ftn).

JEHUD (*declare*). Town in Dan, c. seven miles E of Joppa (Jos 19:45).

JEHUDI (*Jew*). Prince in Jehoiakim's court (Jer 36:14, 21).

JEHUDIJAH NIV "Judean" wife of Mered (1Ch 4:18).

JEHUSH *See Jeush, 4.*

JEIEL (*God [El] has preserved* IDB; possibly *God [El] sweeps up* KB).
1. Also called Jehiel. A Reubenite (1Ch 5:7).
2. A Benjamite (1Ch 9:35).
3. One of David's heroes (1Ch 11:44).
4. A Levite and singer in the tabernacle service (1Ch 15:18, 21; 16:5).
5. A Levite, ancestor of Jahaziel, who encouraged Judah against their enemies (2Ch 20:14).
6. A scribe during the reign of Uzziah (2Ch 26:11).
7. A Levite who cleansed the temple (2Ch 29:13).
8. A chief of the Levites whom David gave, with other chiefs, "five thousand Passover offerings and five hundred head of cattle for the Levites" for sacrifice (2Ch 35:9).
9. A son of Adonikam, an exile who returned to Jerusalem with Ezra (Ezr 8:13).
10. A priest who was defiled by marriage to an idolatrous woman (Ezr 10:43).

JEKABZEEL (*God [El] gathers*). A city in the S of Judah (Ne 11:25).

JEKAMEAM (*[my] kinsman establishes*). Son of Hebron (1Ch 23:19; 24:23).

JEKAMIAH (*Yahweh will establish*).
1. Judahite (1Ch 2:41).
2. Son of King Jehoiachin (Jehoiachin) (1Ch 3:18).

JEKUTHIEL (*God [El] will nourish*). Son of Ezra (1Ch 4:18).

JEMIMAH (*dove*). Daughter of Job born after restoration from affliction (Job 42:14).

JEMUEL Son of Simeon (Ge 46:10; Ex 6:15). Also called Nemuel (Nu 26:9, 12; 1Ch 4:24). *See Nemuel, 1.*

JEPHTHAH (*Yahweh opens, frees*). A judge of Israel. Illegitimate and therefore not entitled to inherit his father's property (Jdg 11:1-2). Escapes the violence of his half-brothers, lives in the land of Tob (Jdg 11:3). Recalled from the land of Tob by the elders of Gilead (Jdg 11:5). Made captain of the host (Jdg 11:5-11) and made head of the land of Gilead (Jdg 11:7-11). His message to the king of the Ammonites (Jdg 11:12-28). Leads the host of Israel against the Ammonites (Jdg 11:29-33). His rash vow concerning his daughter (Jdg 11:31, 34-40). Falsely accused by the Ephraimites (Jdg 12:1). Leads the army of the Gileadites against the Ephraimites (Jdg 12:4). Judges Israel six years, dies, and is buried in Gilead (Jdg 12:7). Faith of (Heb 11:32).

JEPHUNNEH (perhaps *may he [God] turn* or *turned*).
1. Father of Caleb (Nu 13:6).
2. Son of Jether (1Ch 7:38).

JERAH (*moon [god?]*). Son of Joktan (Ge 10:26; 1Ch 1:20).

JERAHMEEL, JERAHMEELITE (*God [El] will have compassion*).
1. Son of Hezron (1Ch 2:9).
2. Son of Kish (1Ch 24:29).
3. An officer of Jehoiakim, king of Judah (Jer 36:26).

JERASH *See Gerasenes.*

JERED (*rose* IDB; *servant* KB). A Judahite (1Ch 4:18).

JEREMAI (possibly *fat*). Of the family of Hashum (Ezr 10:33).

JEREMIAH, BOOK OF

Author: Jeremiah, son of Berekiah

Date: Between 626 and 586 B.C.

Outline:
I. Call of the Prophet (ch. 1).
II. Warnings and Exhortations to Judah (chs. 2-35).
 A. Earliest Discourses (chs. 2-6).
 B. Temple Message (chs. 7-10).
 C. Covenant and Conspiracy (chs. 11-13).
 D. Messages Concerning the Drought (chs. 14-15).
 E. Disaster and Comfort (16:1-17:18).
 F. Command to Keep the Sabbath Holy (17:19-27).
 G. Lessons from the Potter (chs. 18-20).
 H. Condemnation of Kings, Prophets and People (chs. 21-24).
 I. Foretelling the Babylonian Exile (chs. 25-29).
 J. Promises of Restoration (chs. 30-33).
 K. Historical Appendix (chs. 34-35).
III. Suffering and Persecutions of the Prophet (chs. 36-38).
 A. Burning Jeremiah's Scroll (ch. 36).
 B. Imprisoning Jeremiah (chs. 37-38).
IV. The Fall of Jerusalem and Its Aftermath (chs. 39-45).
 A. The Fall Itself (ch. 39).
 B. Accession and Assassination of Gedaliah (40:1-41:15).
 C. Migration to Egypt (41:16-43:13).
 D. Prophecy Against Those in Egypt (ch. 44).
 E. Historical Appendix: Promise to Baruch (ch. 45).
V. Judgment Against the Nations (chs. 46-51).
 A. Against Egypt (ch. 46).
 B. Against Philistia (ch. 47).
 C. Against Moab (ch 48).
 D. Against Ammon (49:1-6).
 E. Against Edom (49:7-22).
 F. Against Damascus (49:23-27).
 G. Against Kedar and Hazor (Arabia) (49:28-33).
 H. Against Elam (49:34-39).
 I. Against Babylon (chs. 50-51).
VI. Historical Appendix (ch. 52).

JEREMIAH (*Yahweh loosens [the womb]* BDB; *Yahweh lifts up* IDB; possibly *Yahweh shoots, establishes* KB). One of the greatest Hebrew prophets (c. 640-587 B.C.); born into priestly family of Anathoth, two-and-a-half miles NE of Jerusalem; called to prophetic office by a vision (Jer 1:4-10), and prophesied during last five kings (Josiah, Jehoahaz II, Jehoiakim, Jehoiachin, Zedekiah), probably helped Josiah in his reforms (2Ki 23), warned Jehoiakim against Egyptian alliance, prophetic roll destroyed by king (Jer 36), persecuted by nobility in days of the last king (Jer 36-37), Nebuchadnezzar kind to him after the destruction of Jerusalem (Jer 39:11-12), compelled to go to Egypt with Israelites who slew Gedaliah, and there he died (Jer 43:6-7).
Six other Jeremiahs are briefly mentioned in the OT:
1. Benjamite who came to David at Ziklag (1Ch 12:4).
2. A Gadite (1Ch 12:10).
3. A Gadite (1Ch 12:13).
4. A Manassite (1Ch 5:24).
5. Father of the wife of King Josiah (2Ki 23:30-31).
6. A Recabite (Jer 35:3).

JEREMOTH (*swollen* or *obese*).
1. A Benjamite (1Ch 7:8).
2. A Benjamite (1Ch 8:14).
3. Descendant of Elam who put away foreign wife (Ezr 10:26).
4. Descendant of Zattu who put away foreign wife (Ezr 10:27).
5. Descendant of Bani who put away foreign wife (Ezr 10:29).

JERIAH (*Yahweh founds*). A descendant of Hebron (1Ch 23:19; 24:23; 26:31).

JERIBAI (*Yahweh pleads*). A valiant man of David's guard (1Ch 11:46).

JERICHO (*moon city*).
1. A city E of Jerusalem and near the Jordan (Nu 22:1; 26:3; Dt 34:1). Called the City of Palm Trees (Dt 34:3). Situation of, pleasant (2Ki 2:19). Rahab the harlot lived in (Jos 2; Heb 11:31). Joshua sees the "captain of the host" of the Lord near (Jos 5:13-15). Besieged by Joshua seven days; fall and destruction of (Jos 6; 24:11). Situated within the territory allotted to Benjamin (Jos 18:12, 21). The Kenites lived at (Jdg 1:16). King of Moab makes conquest of, and establishes his capital at (Jdg 3:13). Rebuilt by Hiel (1Ki 16:34). Company of "the sons of the prophets," lived at (2Ki 2:4-5, 15, 18). Captives of Judah, taken by the king of Israel, released at, on account of the denunciation of the prophet Obed (2Ch 28:7-15). Inhabitants of, taken captive to Babylon, return to, with Ezra and Nehemiah (Ezr 2:34; Ne 7:36), assist in repairing the walls of Jerusalem (Ne 3:2). Blind men healed at, by Jesus (Mt 20:29-34; Mk 10:46; Lk 18:35). Zacchaeus lived at (Lk 19:1-10).
2. Plain of (2Ki 25:5; Jer 52:8).
3. Waters of (Jos 16:1). Purified by Elisha (2Ki 2:18-22).

JERIEL (*founded of God [El]* BDB; *God [El] will see* IDB). Son of Tola (1Ch 7:2).

JERIJAH *See Jeriah.*

J

JERIMOTH (*swollen or obese*). See also Jeremoth.
1. Son of Bela (1Ch 7:7).
2. A disaffected Israelite, who denounced Saul and joined David at Ziklag (1Ch 12:5).
3. Son of Mushi (1Ch 23:23; 24:30).
4. Son of Heman (1Ch 25:4, 22).
5. A ruler of the tribe of Naphtali (1Ch 27:19).
6. A son of David (2Ch 11:18).
7. A Levite (2Ch 31:13).

JERIOTH (*tents*). Wife of Caleb. Probably identical with Azubah (1Ch 2:18).

JEROBOAM (*the people increase* BDB).
1. First king of Israel after the revolt. Promoted by Solomon (1Ki 11:28). Ahijah's prophecy concerning (1Ki 11:29-39; 14:5-16). Flees to Egypt to escape from Solomon (1Ki 11:26-40). Recalled from Egypt by the ten tribes on account of disaffection toward Rehoboam, and made king (1Ki 12:1-20; 2Ch 10:12-19). Subverts the religion of Moses (1Ki 12:25-33; 13:33-34; 14:9, 16; 16:2, 26, 31; 2Ch 11:14; 13:8-9). Hand of, paralyzed (1Ki 13:1-10). His wife sent to consult the prophet Ahijah concerning her child (1Ki 14:1-18). His wars with Rehoboam (1Ki 14:19, 30; 15:6; 2Ch 11:1-4). His war with Abijah (1Ki 15:7; 2Ch 13). Death of (1Ki 14:20; 2Ch 13:20).
2. King of Israel. Successor to Jehoash (2Ki 14:16, 23). Makes conquest of Hamath and Damascus (2Ki 14:25-28). Wicked reign of (2Ki 14:24). Prophecies concerning (Am 7:7-13). Death of (2Ki 14:29). Genealogies written during his reign (1Ch 5:17).

JEROHAM (*he will be compassionate*).
1. A Levite, and grandfather of Samuel (1Sa 1:1; 1Ch 6:27, 34).
2. A chief of the tribe of Benjamin (1Ch 8:27).
3. A descendant of Benjamin (1Ch 9:8).
4. A priest, and father of Adaiah, who lived in Jerusalem after the Exile (1Ch 9:12; Ne 11:12).
5. Father of two Israelites who joined David at Ziklag (1Ch 12:7).
6. The father of Azarel (1Ch 27:22).
7. Father of Azariah (2Ch 23:1).

JERUB-BAAL (*Baal contends*). See Gideon.

JERUB-BESHETH (*Shame [Baal] contends*). See Gideon.

JERUEL (*God [El] is a foundation*). A wilderness in the S of Judah (2Ch 20:16).

JERUSALEM (*foundation of Shalem [peace]*).
Called:
Jebus (Jos 18:28; Jdg 19:10), Zion (1Ki 8:1; Zec 9:13), City of David (2Sa 5:7; Isa 22:9), Salem (Ge 14:18; Ps 76:2), Ariel (Isa 29:1), City of God (Ps 46:4), City of the Great King (Ps 48:2), City of Judah (2Ch 25:28), The Perfection of Beauty, The Joy of the Whole Earth (La 2:15), The Throne of the Lord (Jer 3:17), Holy Mountain (Da 9:16, 20), Holy City (Ne 11:1, 18; Mt 4:5), City of our festivals (Isa 33:20), City of Truth (Zec 8:3), to be called "The LORD Our Righteousness" (Jer 33:16), Yahweh Shammah (Eze 48:35), *See God, Names of: Yahweh Shammah.* New Jerusalem (Rev 21:2, 10-27).
Situation and appearance of (Ps 122:3; 125:2; SS 6:4; Mic 4:8). Walls of (Jer 39:4).
Gates of:
Benjamin Gate (Jer 37:13; 38:7; Zec 14:10). Corner Gate (2Ki 14:13; 2Ch 25:23; 26:9; Jer 31:38; Zec 14:10). Dung Gate (Ne 2:13; 3:13, 14; 12:31). East Gate (1Ch 26:14; 2Ch 31:14; Ne 3:29). Ephraim Gate (2Ki 14:13; 2Ch 25:23; Ne 8:16; 12:39). First Gate (Zec 14:10). Fish Gate (2Ch 33:14; Ne 3:3; 12:39; Zep 1:10). Fountain Gate (Ne 2:14; 3:15; 12:37). Foundation Gate (2Ch 23:5). Gate of Joshua (2Ki 23:8). Gate of the guards (2Ki 11:19). Horse Gate (Ne 23:15; Ne 3:28; Jer 31:40). Inspection Gate (Ne 3:31). Jeshanah [Old] Gate (Ne 3:6; 12:39). King's Gate (1Ch 9:18). Middle Gate (Jer 39:3). New Gate (Jer 26:10; 36:10). North Gate (1Ch 26:14). Potsherd Gate (Jer 19:2). Shallecketh Gate (1Ch 26:16). Sheep Gate (Ne 3:1, 32; 12:39; Jn 5:2). South Gate (1Ch 26:15). Sur Gate (2Ki 11:6). Upper Gate (Jer 15:35; 2Ch 23:20; 27:3). Upper Gate of Benjamin (Jer 20:2). Valley Gate (2Ch 26:9; Ne 2:13, 15; 3:13). Water Gate (Ne 3:26; 8:1, 3, 16; 12:37). West Gate (1Ch 26:16).
Gates of the twelve tribes in Ezekiel's vision (Eze 48:31-34). Measurement of (Eze 45:6).
Buildings:
High priest's palace (Jn 18:15). Barracks (Ac 21:34). Stairway of Ahaz (2Ki 20:11). Stairs (Ne 9:4).
Squares and Streets:
Square on the east side (2Ch 29:4). Square before the house of God (Ezr 10:9). Square before the Water Gate (Ne 8:1, 3, 16), by the Gate of Ephraim (Ne 8:16). Street of the bakers (Jer 37:21). Streets of Jerusalem (Jer 5:1; 7:17, 34; 11:6, 13; 14:16; 33:10; 44:6, 9, 17, 21; Zec 8:4).
Towers:
See Beth Millo; Hananel, Tower of; Meah; Ophel; Siloam, Tower of.
Places in and Around:
Moriah (2Ch 3:1). The tomb of Jesus (Jn 19:41). *See Gethsemane; Golgotha; Jehoshaphat, Valley of; Olives, Mount of; Topheth, Topheth.*
History of:
Melchizedek ancient king and priest of (Ge 14:18). King of, confederated with the four other kings of the Amorites, against Joshua and the hosts of Israel (Jos 10:1-5). Confederated kings defeated, and the king of Jerusalem slain by Joshua (Jos 10:15-26). Fell to Benjamin in the allotment of the land of Canaan (Jos 18:28). Conquest of, made by David (2Sa 5:7). The inhabitants of, not expelled (Jos 15:63; Jdg 1:21). Conquest of Mount Zion in, made by David (1Ch 11:4-6). The citadel of Mount Zion, occupied by David, and called the City of David (2Sa 5:5-9; 1Ch 11:7). Ark brought to, by David (2Sa 6:12-19). The threshing floor of Araunah within the citadel (2Sa 24:16). David purchased and built an

altar upon it (2Sa 24:16-25). The city built around the citadel (1Ch 11:8). The capital of David's kingdom by divine appointment (1Ki 15:4; 2Ki 19:34; 2Ch 6:6; 12:13).
Fortified by Solomon (1Ki 3:1; 9:15). The temple built within the citadel. *See Temple.*
The chief Levites lived in (1Ch 9:34). The high priest lived at (Jn 18:15). Annual feasts kept at (Eze 36:38, w Dt 16:16, & Ps 122:3-5; Lk 2:41; Jn 4:20; 5:1; 7:1-14; 12:20; Ac 18:21). Prayers of the Israelites made toward (1Ki 8:38; Da 6:10). Beloved (Ps 122:6; 137:1-7; Isa 62:1-7). *See Country, Love of; Patriotism.* Oaths taken in the name of (Mt 5:35).
Captured and pillaged by: Shishak, king of Egypt (1Ki 14:25-26; 2Ch 12:9), Jehoash, king of Israel (2Ki 14:13-14; 2Ch 25:23-24), Nebuchadnezzar, king of Babylon (2Ki 24:8-16; 25:1-17; 2Ch 36:17-21; Jer 1:3; 32:2; 39; 52:4-7, 12-24; La 1:5-8). Walls of, restored and fortified by: Uzziah (2Ch 26:9-10), Jotham (2Ch 27:3), Manasseh (2Ch 33:14). Water supply brought in from the Gihon by Hezekiah (2Ki 18:17; 20:20; 2Ch 32:3-4, 30; Ne 2:13-15; Isa 7:3; 22:9-11; 36:2). Besieged by: Pekah (2Ki 16:5), the Philistines (2Ch 21:16-17), Sennacherib (2Ki 18:13-37; 19:20-37; 2Ch 32). Rebuilding of ordered by proclamation of Cyrus (2Ch 36:23; Ezr 1:1-4). Rebuilt by Nehemiah under the direction of Artaxerxes (Ne 2-6). Wall of, dedicated (Ne 12:27-43). Temple restored. *See Temple.*
Roman rulers resided at: Herod I (Mt 2:3), Pontius Pilate (Mt 27:2; Mk 15:1; Lk 23:1-7; Jn 18:28-29), Herod III (Ac 12:1-23).
Life and miracles of Jesus connected with: *See Jesus the Christ, History of.*
Gospel preached first preached at (Mic 4:2; Lk 24:47; Ac 1:4; 2:14). Day of Pentecost at (Ac 2). Stephen martyred at (Ac 6:8-7:60). Disciples persecuted and dispersed from (Ac 8:1-4; 11:19-21).
For personal incidents occurring there: *See biographies of individuals; Israel, Israelites.*
Prophecies Concerning:
Prophecies against (Isa 3:1-8; Jer 9:11; 19:6, 15; 21:10; 26:9, 11; Da 9:2, 27; Mic 1:1; 3:12); of pestilence, famine, and war in (Jer 34:2; Eze 5:12; Joel 3:2-3; Am 2:5); of the destruction of (Jer 7:32-34; 26:18; 32:29, 31-32; Da 9:24-27). Destruction of, foretold by Jesus (Mt 23:37-38; 24:15; Mk 13:14-23; Lk 13:35; 17:26-37; 19:41-44; 21:20-24).
Prophecies of the rebuilding of (Isa 44:28; Jer 31:38-40; Eze 48:15-22; Da 9:25; Zec 14:8-11). Of final restoration of (Joel 3:20-21; Zec 2:2-5; 8).
Sins of:
Wickedness (Lk 13:33-34). Catalog of abominations in (Eze 22:3-12, 25-30, 23; 33:25-26). Led Judah to sin (Mic 1:5).

JERUSALEM, NEW City of God referred to as coming down out of heaven from God (Rev 3:12; 21:2). Described as the mother of believers (Gal 4:26).

JERUSHA (*possession*). Wife of King Uzziah and mother of King Jotham (2Ki 15:33; 2Ch 27:1).

JESARELAH Ancestral head of a course of musicians (1Ch 25:14, ftn). Also called Asarelah (1Ch 25:2).

JESHAIAH (*Yahweh saves*).
1. Grandson of Zerubbabel (1Ch 3:21).
2. Son of Jeduthun (1Ch 25:3, 15).
3. Grandson of Eliezer (1Ch 26:25).
4. A Jew of the family of Elam, who returned from exile (Ezr 8:7).
5. A Levite who joined Ezra to return to Jerusalem (Ezr 8:19).
6. A Benjamite, detailed by lot to live in Jerusalem after the Exile (Ne 11:7).

JESHANAH (*old*).
1. A city on the N of Benjamin (2Ch 13:19).
2. Gate in NW corner of Jerusalem in Nehemiah's time (Ne 3:6).

JESHEBEAB (*father lives*). Priest, and head of the fourteenth course (1Ch 24:13).

JESHER (perhaps *the deity shows himself just*). Son of Caleb (1Ch 2:18).

JESHIMON (*a waste, a desert*).
1. A place in the Sinai peninsula, E of the Jordan (Nu 21:20; 23:28).
2. A place in the desert of Judah (1Sa 23:24; 26:1).

JESHIMOTH See Beth Jeshimoth.

JESHISHAI (*aged*). A Gadite (1Ch 5:14).

JESHOHAIAH (possibly *Yahweh humbles*). A descendant of Simeon (1Ch 4:36).

JESHUA (*Yahweh saves*).
1. A priest, head of the ninth course (1Ch 24:11). Nine hundred and seventy-three of his descendants returned from Babylon (Ezr 2:36; Ne 7:39).
2. A Levite, had charge of the tithes (2Ch 31:15). His descendants returned with Ezra from Babylon (Ezr 2:40; Ne 7:43).
3. Also called Joshua. A priest who accompanied Zerubbabel from Babylon (Ezr 2:2; Ne 7:7; 12:1). Descendants of (Ne 12:10). He rebuilt the altar (Ezr 3:2). Assisted Zerubbabel in restoring the temple (Ezr 3; 4:1-6; 5; Hag 1:1, 12-14; 2:2). Contended with those who sought to defeat the rebuilding (Ezr 4:1-3; 5:1-2). Symbolic of the restoration of Israel (Zec 3; 6:9-15).
4. Father of Jozabad (Ezr 8:33).
5. Son of Pahath-Moab (Ezr 2:6; Ne 7:11).
6. Father of Ezer (Ne 3:19).
7. A Levite who explained the law to the people when Ezra read the law (Ne 8:7; 12:8).
8. A Levite who sealed Nehemiah's covenant (Ne 10:9).
9. A city of Judah (Ne 11:26).

JESHURUN (*upright*). A name used poetically for Israel (Dt 32:15; 33:5, 26; Isa 44:2).

JESIAH See Isshiah, 2 & 3.

JESIMIEL (*God [El] will establish*). A descendant of Simeon (1Ch 4:36).

JESSE Father of David (Ru 4:17; 1Sa 17:12). Ancestor of Jesus (Mt 1:5-6). Samuel visits, under divine command, to select from his sons a successor to Saul (1Sa 16:1-13). Saul asks, to send David to become a member of his court (1Sa 16:19-23). Sons in Saul's army (1Sa 17:13-28). Lives with David in Moab (1Sa 22:3-4). Descendants of (1Ch 2:13-17).

JESTING Foolish, forbidden (Eph 5:4; Mt 12:36).

JESUI, JESUITES See Ishvi, 1; Ishvites.

JESUS THE CHRIST (*Yahweh Saves, Anointed One*).
History of:
Birth and Childhood—
Genealogy of (Mt 1:1-17; Lk 3:23-38).
The angel Gabriel appears to Mary (Lk 1:26-38). Mary visits Elizabeth (Lk 1:39-56). Mary's *magnificat* (Lk 1:46-55). An angel appears to Joseph concerning Mary (Mt 1:18-25).
Birth of (Lk 2:1-7). Angels appear to the shepherds (Lk 2:8-20). Magi visit (Mt 2:1-12). Circumcision of (Lk 2:21). Is presented in the temple (Lk 2:21-38). Flight into, and return from, Egypt (Mt 2:13-23). Disputes with the doctors in the temple (Lk 2:41-52).
Ministry—
Is baptized by John (Mt 3:13-17; Mk 1:9-11; Lk 3:21-23). Temptation of (Mt 4:1-11; Mk 1:12-13; Lk 4:1-13). John's testimony concerning him (Jn 1:1-18). Testimony of John the Baptist concerning (Jn 1:19-34). Disciples adhere to (Jn 1:35-51). Miracles at Cana of Galilee (Jn 2:1-12). Drives the money changers from the temple (Jn 2:13-25). Nicodemus comes to (Jn 3:1-21). Baptizes (Jn 3:22; 4:2). Returns to Galilee (Jn 4:12; Mk 1:14; Lk 4:14; Jn 4:1-3). Visits Sychar, and teaches the Samaritan woman (Jn 4:4-42). Teaches in Galilee (Mt 4:12; 4:17; Lk 4:14-15; Jn 4:43-45). Heals a nobleman's son of Capernaum (Jn 4:46-54). Is rejected by the people of Nazareth, lives at Capernaum (Mt 4:13-16; Lk 4:16-31). Chooses Peter, Andrew, James, and John as disciples, miracle of the catch of fishes (Mt 4:18-22; Mk 1:16-20; Lk 5:1-11).
Preaches throughout Galilee (Mt 4:23-25; Mk 1:35-39; Lk 4:42-44). Heals a demoniac (Mk 1:21-28; Lk 4:31-37). Heals Peter's mother-in-law (Mt 8:14-17; Mk 1:29-34; Lk 4:38-41). Heals a leper in Galilee (Mt 8:2-4; Mk 1:40-45; Lk 5:12-16). Heals a paralytic (Mt 9:2-8; Mk 2:1-12; Lk 5:17-26). Calls Matthew (Mt 9:9; Mk 2:13-14; Lk 5:27-28). Heals an invalid at the pool of Bethesda on the Sabbath day, is persecuted, and makes his defense (Jn 5:1-47). Defines the law of the Sabbath on the occasion of his disciples picking the heads of grain (Mt 12:1-14; Mk 3:1-6; Lk 6:6-11). Withdraws from Capernaum to the Sea of Galilee, where he heals many (Mt 12:15-21; Mk 3:7-12).
Goes up onto a mountain, and calls and ordains twelve disciples (Mt 10:2-4; Mk 3:13-19; Lk 6:12-19). Delivers the "Sermon on the Mount" (Mt 5-7; Lk 6:20-49). Heals the centurion's servant (Mt 8:5-13; Lk 7:1-10). Raises from the dead the son of the widow of Nain (Lk 7:11-17). Receives the message from John the Baptist (Mt 11:2-19; Lk 7:18-35). Rebukes the unbelieving cities about Capernaum (Mt 11:20-30). Anointed by a sinful woman (Lk 7:36-50). Preaches in the cities of Galilee (Lk 8:1-3).
Heals a demoniac, and denounces the scribes and Pharisees (Mt 12:22-37; Mk 3:19-30; Lk 11:14-20). Replies to the scribes and Pharisees who seek a sign from him (Mt 12:38-45; Lk 11:16-36). Denounces the Pharisees and other hypocrites (Lk 11:37-54). Discourses to his disciples (Lk 12:1-59). Parable of the barren fig tree (Lk 13:6-9). Parable of the sower (Mt 13:1-23; Mk 4:1-25; Lk 8:4-18). Parable of the weeds, and other teachings (Mt 13:24-53; Mk 4:26-34).
Crosses the Sea of Galilee, and stills the tempest (Mt 8:18-27; Mk 4:35-41; Lk 8:22-25). Casts out the legion of demons (Mt 8:28-33; Mk 5:1-21; Lk 8:26-40). Returns to Capernaum (Mt 9:1; Mk 5:21; Lk 8:40). Eats with tax collectors and sinners, and speaks on fasting (Mt 9:10-17; Mk 2:15-22; Lk 5:29-39). Raises to life the daughter of Jairus, and heals the woman who has the issue of blood (Mt 9:18-26; Mk 5:22-43; Lk 8:41-56). Heals two blind men and casts out a mute spirit (Mt 9:27-34). Returns to Nazareth (Mt 13:53-58; Mk 6:1-6). Teaches in various cities in Galilee (Mt 9:35-38).
Instructs his disciples and empowers them to heal diseases and cast out unclean spirits (Mt 10; Mk 6:6-13; Lk 9:1-6). Herod falsely supposes him to be John, whom he had beheaded (Mt 14:1-2, 6-12; Mk 6:14-16, 21-29; Lk 9:7-9). The Twelve return; he goes to the desert; multitudes follow him; he feeds five thousand (Mt 14:13-21; Mk 6:30-44; Lk 9:10-17; Jn 6:1-14). Walks on the water (Mt 14:22-36; Mk 6:45-56; Jn 6:15-21). Teaches in the synagogue in Capernaum (Jn 6:22-65). Disciples forsake him (Jn 6:66-71).
He justifies his disciples in eating without washing their hands (Mt 15:1-20; Mk 7:1-23). Heals the daughter of the Syrian Phoenician woman (Mt 15:21-28; Mk 7:24-30). Heals a mute man (Mt 15:29-31; Mk 7:31-37). Feeds four thousand (Mt 15:32-39; Mk 8:1-9). Refuses to give a sign to the Pharisees (Mt 16:1-4; Mk 8:10-12). Cautions his disciples against the yeast of hypocrisy (Mt 16:4-12; Mk 8:13-21). Heals a blind man (Mk 8:22-26). Foretells his death and resurrection (Mt 16:21-28; Mk 8:31-38; 9:1; Lk 9:21-27).
Is transfigured (Mt 17:1-13; Mk 9:2-13; Lk 9:28-36). Heals a demoniac (Mt 17:14-21; Mk 9:14-29; Lk 9:37-43). Foretells his death and resurrection (Mt 17:22-23; Mk 9:30-32; Lk 9:43-45). Miracle of tribute money in the fish's mouth (Mt 17:24-27). Reproves the ambition of his disciples (Mt 18:1-35; Mk 9:33-50; Lk 9:46-50). Reproves the intolerance of his disciples (Mk 9:38-39; Lk 9:49-50).
Journeys to Jerusalem to attend the Feast of Tabernacles, passing through Samaria (Lk 9:51-62; Jn 7:2-11). Commissions the Seventy (Lk 10:1-19). Heals ten lepers (Lk 17:11-19). Teaches in

Jerusalem at the Feast of Tabernacles (Jn 7:14-53; 8). Answers a lawyer, who tests his wisdom with the question, "What must I do to inherit eternal life?" by the parable of the good Samaritan (Lk 10:25-37). Hears the report of the Seventy (Lk 10:17-24). Teaches in the house of Mary, Martha, and Lazarus, in Bethany (Lk 10:38-42).

Teaches his disciples to pray (Lk 11:1-13). Heals a blind man, who, because of his faith in Jesus, was excommunicated (Jn 9). Teaches in Jerusalem (Jn 9:39-41; 10:1-21). Teaches in the temple at Jerusalem, at the Feast of Dedication (Jn 10:22-39). Goes across the Jordan to escape violence from the rulers (Jn 10:40-42; 11:3-16).

Returns to Bethany and raises Lazarus from the dead (Jn 11:1-46). Escapes to the city of Ephraim from the conspiracy led by Caiaphas, the high priest (Jn 11:47-54). Journeys toward Jerusalem to attend the Passover; heals many who are diseased and teaches the people (Mt 19:1-2; Mk 10:1; Lk 13:10-35). Dines with a Pharisee on the Sabbath (Lk 14:1-24). Teaches the multitude the conditions of discipleship (Lk 14:25-35).

Tells the parables of the lost sheep, the lost piece of silver, prodigal son, unjust steward (Lk 15:1-32; 16:1-13). Reproves the hypocrisy of the Pharisees (Lk 16). Tells the parable of the rich man and Lazarus (Lk 16:19-31). Teaches his disciples concerning offenses, meekness, and humility (Lk 17:1-10). Teaches the Pharisees concerning the coming of his kingdom (Lk 17:20-37). Tells the parables of the unjust judge, and the Pharisee and tax collector praying in the temple (Lk 18:1-14).

Interprets the law concerning marriage and divorce (Mt 19:3-12; Mk 10:2-12). Blesses little children (Mt 19:13-15; Mk 10:13-16; Lk 18:15-17). Receives the rich young ruler, who asks what he must do to inherit eternal life (Mt 19:16-22; Mk 10:17-22; Lk 18:18-24). Tells the parable of the vineyard (Mt 20:1-16). Foretells his death and resurrection (Mt 20:17-19; Mk 10:32-34; Lk 18:31-34). Listens to the mother of James and John in behalf of her sons (Mt 20:20-28; Mk 10:35-45). Heals two blind men at Jericho (Mt 20:29-34; Mk 10:46-50; Lk 18:35-43). Visits Zaccheus (Lk 19:1-10). Tells the parable of the pounds (Lk 19:11-28).

Final Week in Jerusalem—

Goes to Bethany six days before the Passover (Jn 12:1-9). Triumphal entry into Jerusalem, while the people throw palm branches in the way (Mt 21:1-11; Mk 11:1-11; Lk 19:29-44; Jn 12:12-19). Enters the temple (Mt 21:12; Mk 11:11; Lk 19:45). Drives the money changers out of the temple (Mt 21:12-13; Lk 19:45-46). Heals the sick in the temple (Mt 21:14). Teaches daily in the temple (Lk 19:47-48).

Performs the miracle of causing the barren fig tree to wither (Mt 21:17-22; Mk 11:12-14, 20-22). Tells the parable of the two sons (Mt 21:28-31), the parable of the wicked farmers (Mt 21:33-46; Mk 12:1-12; Lk 20:9-19), of the marriage (Mt 22:1-14; Lk 14:16-24). Tested by the Pharisees and Herodians and enunciates the duty of the citizen to his government (Mt 22:15-22; Mk 12:13-17; Lk 20:20-26). Tried by the Sadducees concerning the resurrection of the dead (Mt 22:23-33; Mk 12:18-27; Lk 20:27-40) and by a lawyer (Mt 22:34-40; Mk 12:28-34). Exposes the hypocrisies of the scribes and Pharisees (Mt 23; Mk 12:38-40; Lk 20:45-47).

Extols the widow who casts two small copper coins into the treasury (Mk 12:41-44; Lk 21:1-4). Verifies the prophecy of Isaiah concerning the unbelieving Jews (Jn 12:37-50). Foretells the destruction of the temple and of Jerusalem (Mt 24; Mk 13; Lk 21:5-36). Laments over Jerusalem (Mt 23:37; Lk 19:41-44). Tells the parables of the ten virgins and of the talents (Mt 25:1-30). Foretells the scenes of the Day of Judgment (Mt 25:31-46).

Anointed with precious ointment (Mt 26:6-13; Mk 14:3-9; Jn 12:1-8). Last Passover, and institution of the Lord's Supper (Mt 26:17-30; Mk 14:12-25; Lk 22:7-20). Washes the disciples' feet (Jn 13:1-17). Foretells his betrayal (Mt 26:23; Mk 14:18-21; Lk 22:21; Jn 13:18). Accuses Judas of his betrayal (Mt 26:21-25; Mk 14:18-21; Lk 22:21-23; Jn 13:21-30). Teaches his disciples, and comforts them with promises, including the gift of the Holy Spirit (Jn 14-16). Last prayer (Jn 17).

Arrest, Crucifixion, Resurrection—

Moves to Gethsemane (Mt 26:30, 36-46; Mk 14:26, 32-42; Lk 22:39-46; Jn 18:1). Is betrayed and apprehended (Mt 26:47-56; Mk 14:43-54, 66-72; Lk 22:47-53; Jn 18:2-12).

Trial of, before Caiaphas (Mt 26:57-58, 69-75; Mk 14:53-54, 66-72; Lk 22:54-62; Jn 18:13-18, 25-27). Led by the council to Pilate (Mt 27:1-2, 11-14; Mk 15:1-5; Lk 23:1-5; Jn 18:28-38). Arraigned before Herod (Lk 23:6-12). Tried before Pilate (Mt 27:15-26; Mk 15:6-15; Lk 23:13-25; Jn 18:39-40; 19:1-16). Mocked by the soldiers (Mt 27:27-31; Mk 15:16-20). Is led away to be crucified (Mt 27:31-34; Mk 15:20-23; Lk 23:26-32; Jn 19:16-17).

Crucified (Mt 27:35-56; Mk 15:24-41; Lk 23:33-49; Jn 19:18-30). Taken from the cross and buried (Mt 27:57-66; Mk 15:42-47; Lk 23:50-56; Jn 19:31-42).

Arises from the dead (Mt 28:2-15; Mk 16:1-11; Lk 24:1-12; Jn 20:1-18). Is seen by Mary Magdalene (Mt 28:1-10; Mk 16:9; Jn 20:11-17), by Peter (Lk 24:34; 1Co 15:5). Appears to two disciples who journey to Emmaus (Mk 16:12-13; Lk 24:13-35). Appears in the midst of the disciples, when Thomas is absent (Mk 16:14-18; Lk 24:36-49; Jn 20:19-23), when Thomas was present (Jn 20:26-29), at the Sea of Galilee (Mt 28:16; Jn 21:1-14), to the apostles and five hundred believers on a mountain in Galilee (Mt 28:16-20, w Ac 10:40-42; 13:31; 1Co 15:6-7). Appears to James, and also to all the apostles (Ac 1:3-8; 1Co 15:7).

Ascension and Additional Appearances—

Ascends to heaven (Mk 16:19-20; Lk 24:50-53; Ac 1:9-12). Appears to Paul (Ac 9:3-17; 18:9-10; 23:11; 26:16; 1Co 9:1; 15:8). Stephen's vision of (Ac 7:55-56). Appears to John on Patmos (Rev 1:10-18).

Miscellaneous Facts Concerning:

Was with the Israelites in the wilderness (1Co 10:4, 9; Heb 11:26; Jude 5).

Brothers of (Mt 13:55; Mk 6:3; 1Co 9:5; Gal 1:19). Sisters of (Mt 13:56; Mk 6:3).

Appearances of, After His Resurrection:

To Mary Magdalene and other women (Mt 28:1-10; Mk 16:9; Lk 24:1-10; Jn 20:11-17). To Peter (Lk 24:34; 1Co 15:5). To two disciples who journey to Emmaus (Mk 16:12-13; Lk 24:13-31). In the midst of the disciples, when Thomas is absent, in Jerusalem (Jn 20:19-23), when Thomas is present (Mk 16:14-18; Lk 24:36-49; Jn 20:26-29; 1Co 15:5). To certain disciples, Sea of Galilee (Jn 21:1-14). To the eleven disciples, mountain in Galilee (Mt 28:16). To upwards of five hundred (1Co 15:6). To James, and also all the apostles, Jerusalem (Ac 1:3-8; 1Co 15:7). To Paul (Ac 9:3-6; 23:11; 26:13-18; 1Co 9:1; 15:8).

In Stephen's vision (Ac 7:55-56). To John, in a vision, on Patmos (Rev 1:10-18).

Ascension of:

(Mk 16:19; Lk 24:50-51; Jn 14:2-4; Ac 1:9; 3:21; Eph 1:20; 4:8-10; 1Ti 3:16; Heb 1:3; 4:14; 9:24). Foretold (Ps 47:5; 68:18; Lk 24:26, 50; Jn 1:51; 6:62; 7:33; 14:2-3, 12, 28; 16:5, 7, 10, 16, 28; 17:13; 20:17).

Atonement by:

(Ro 3:24-26; 5:11, 15; 1Th 1:10; Heb 13:12; 1Jn 2:2; 3:5; 4:10; Rev 5:6, 9; 13:8).

Made once for all (Heb 7:27; 9:24-28; 10:10, 12, 14; 1Pe 3:18). Vicarious (Isa 53:4-12; Mt 20:28; Jn 6:51; 11:49-51; Gal 1:4; 3:13; Eph 5:2; 1Th 5:9-10; Heb 2:9; 1Pe 2:24).

Through his blood (Lk 22:20; 1Co 1:23; Eph 2:13-15; Heb 9:12-15, 25-26; 12:24; 13:12, 19-21; 1Jn 5:6; Rev 1:5; 5:9; 7:14; 12:11).

For reconciliation (Ro 5:1-21; 2Co 5:18-19, 21; Eph 2:6-17; Col 1:20-22; Heb 2:17).

For remission of sins (Zec 13:1; Mt 26:28; Lk 24:46-47; Jn 1:29; Ro 4:25; 1Co 15:3; Gal 1:3-4; Eph 1:7; Col 1:14; Heb 1:3; 10:1-20; 1Jn 1:7; 3:5).

Atonement Typified—

(Ex 29:36-37; 30:10, 15-16; Lev 1:4; 5:6, 16, 18; 6:7; 8:34; 9:2-3, 7; 10:17; 12:7-8; 14:18-20; 31, 53; 15:14-15, 29-30; 16:6, 10-11, 16-18, 24, 27, 30, 32-34; 17:11; 23:27-28; 25:9; Nu 8:19, 21; 16:46; 25:13; 28:22, 30; 29:5; 31:50).

Atoning blood (Mt 26:28; Mk 14:24; Lk 22:20; Eph 1:7; 2:13; Heb 9:14; 10:19; 1Jn 1:7). Atoning blood of, typified (Ex 12:7, 13, 22-23; 24:6, 8; 29:12, 15, 20-21; 30:10; Lev 1:5, 10-11; 3:2, 8, 13; 4:5-7, 17-18, 25, 30, 34; 5:8-9; 6:30; 7:2; 8:2, 15, 19, 23-24; 9:9, 18; 14:6, 14-15, 25; 16:14-15, 18-19, 27; 17:6, 11; Nu 18:17; 19:2-4; Dt 12:27; 2Ki 16:13, 15; 2Ch 29:22; 30:16; 35:11; Eze 43:20; 45:19-20; 1Pe 1:19).

Benevolence of:

Manifested in his companionship with sinners (Mt 9:10-12; Mk 2:14-17; Lk 5:30; 15:2; 19:10-12). See below, Compassion of; Love of.

Compassion of:

For those who were in spiritual distress (Isa 42:3; Mt 9:36; 12:20; 18:12-13; 23:37; Mk 1:41; 6:34; Lk 7:13; 13:34; 15:4-9, 20-24; 19:41-42; Jn 11:33-38; 18:8-9; 2Co 8:9; Heb 4:15; 5:2). For those who were in temporal adversity (Isa 53:4; 63:9; Mt 8:3, 16-17; 14:14; 15:32; 20:34; Mk 8:2-3). For his sheep (Isa 40:11; Mk 6:34).

Condescension of:

(Lk 22:27; Jn 13:5, 14; 2Co 8:9; Php 2:7-8; Heb 2:11).

Confessing: See Confession, of Christ; Testimony, Religious.

Creator:

(Jn 1:3, 10; 1Co 8:6; Eph 3:9; Col 1:16-17; Heb 1:2, 10; Rev 3:14).

Death of:

(Jn 12:32-33; Ac 5:30; 7:52; Heb 2:14; 12:2, 24; Rev 5:12; 13:8).

Death foretold by God (Ge 3:15; Heb 2:14). By the psalmist (Ps 22:1, 17-18; Mt 27:46; Mk 15:34; Ps 22:17; Mt 27:36; Lk 23:35; Ps 22:18; Mt 27:35; Mk 15:24; Lk 23:34; Jn 19:23-24; Ps 34:20; Jn 19:36; Ps 69:21; Mt 27:34, 48; Mk 15:36; Lk 23:36; Jn 19:28-30). By Isaiah (Isa 52:14; 53:7-12). By Zechariah (Zec 13:7; Mt 26:31). By Jesus himself (Mt 12:40; 16:4, 21; 17:12-13, 22-23; 20:17-19; 21:33-39; 26:2, 12, 18; Mk 8:31; 9:31; 10:32-34; 14:8-9; Lk 9:22, 44; 12:50; 17:25; 18:31-33; 22:15, 21, 37; Jn 2:19, 21; 10:11, 15, 17-18; 12:7, 24, 32-34; 14:19; 18:11).

Paul's testimony concerning Jesus' death (Ac 17:3; 26:22-23; 1Co 1:17-18, 23-24; 2:2; 15:3-4; 2Co 4:10-11; 13:4; Gal 3:1; 1Th 2:15; 4:14).

See above, History of, for Circumstances of the Death of.

Purpose of His Death—

To make reconciliation (Ro 5:6-11; Eph 2:13-16).

To redeem (Isa 53:4-6, 8, 10-12; Mt 20:28; 26:28; Mk 10:45; 14:24; Jn 6:51; 10:11, 17; 11:49-52; Ac 20:28; 26:23; Ro 3:24-25; 8:3, 32; 1Co 5:7; 6:20; 8:11; 15:3; Gal 1:4; 3:13; 4:4-5; Eph 1:6-7; 5:2, 25-27; Col 1:14, 20, 22; 2:14-15; 1Th 1:10; 2:6; Tit 2:14; Heb 2:9-10, 14-15, 18; 7:27; 9:12-17, 25-26, 28; 10:10, 12, 14, 17-20; 1Pe 1:18-19; 2:21, 24; 3:18; 1Jn 2:2; 3:16; 4:10; Rev 1:5-6; 5:9-10; 13:8).

To purge sins (Zec 13:1; Lk 24:46-47; Jn 1:29; Heb 1:3; 13:11-12; 1Jn 1:7; Rev 7:14-15).

To secure forgiveness (Ac 5:30-31; Ro 4:25).

To save (Jn 3:14-17; Ro 6:3-5, 9-10; 14:9, 15; 2Co 5:14-15, 19, 21; 8:9; Gal 2:20; 1Th 5:9-10).

Vicarious Death of—

(Isa 53:4-12; Mt 20:28; Jn 6:51; 11:49, 51; Gal 3:13; Eph 5:2; 1Th 5:9-10; Heb 2:9; 1Pe 2:24).

Vicarious death of, typified (Ex 29:11, 15-16, 20; 29:38-42; Lev 1:5, 11, 15; 3:2, 8, 13; 4:4, 15, 24, 29; 6:25; 7:2; 8:15, 19; 9:8, 15, 18-19, 23-24; 14:13, 19, 25; 2Ch 29:22, 24; 30:15; 35:1). See Atonement; Redemption.

Voluntary Death of—

(Isa 50:6; 53:12; Lk 9:51; 12:50; 22:15, 42; Jn 10:17-18; 18:5, 8, 11; Php 2:8; Heb 7:27; 9:26; 1Jn 3:16).

Divine Sonship of:

Testified to—

By God, at his baptism (Mt 3:17; Mk 1:11; Lk 3:22), at the transfiguration (Mt 17:5; Mk 9:7; Lk 9:35; 2Pe 1:17), in his commandment to believe in (1Jn 3:23).

By Jesus himself (Mt 11:27; Mt 26:63-64; 27:43; Mk 14:61-62; Lk 10:22; 22:70; Jn 3:16-18, 34-36; 6:27, 40, 46, 57; 9:35-37; 11:4; 19:7).

By the disciples (Mt 14:33; 1Jn 4:14), unclean spirits (Mt 8:29; Mk 3:11; 5:7, w Lk 8:28; Lk 4:41), Mark (Mk 1:1), John the Baptist (Jn 1:34), John the apostle (Jn 1:14, 18; 1Jn 1:7; 2:22-24; 3:8, 23; 4:9, 10, 14; 5:5, 9-13, 20; 2Jn 3; Rev 2:18), Nathanael (Jn 1:49), Martha (Jn 11:27), the centurion (Mt 27:54; Mk 15:39), Peter (Ac 3:13; 13:33), Paul (Ro 1:3-4, 9; 8:3, 29, 32; 1Co 1:9; 15:24, 27-28; 2Co 1:3, 19; Gal 1:16; 4:4; Eph 1:3; Col 1:3; 1Th 1:10), the author of Hebrews (Heb 1:1-3, 5; 4:14; 5:5, 8; 6:6; 7:3; 10:29).

Other Evidences—

Declared God to be his Father (Mt 15:13; 18:10, 19; 20:23; 26:53, 63-64; Lk 10:22; 22:29; Jn 5:19-21, 23, 26-27, 30, 36-37; 8:16, 19, 26-29, 38, 49, 54; 10:15, 17-18, 29-30, 36-38; 11:41; 12:49-50; 13:3; 14:7, 9-11, 13, 16, 20-21, 23-24, 28, 31; 15:1, 8-10, 15, 23-24; 16:15, 27-28, 32; 17:1-26; 20:17, 21).

Peter's confession of (Mt 16:15-17).

Prophecies concerning (Ps 2:7; Lk 1:32, 35).

Worshiped by the disciples as the Son of God (Mt 14:33).

See below, Deity of; Relation of, to the Father; Son of God; Son of Man.

Deity of:

Indicated by the Titles Ascribed to Him—

Immanuel (Isa 7:14, w Mt 1:23). First and Last (Rev 1:17; 22:13). God (Ps 102:24-27, w Heb 1:10-13; Jn 1:1; 20:28; Ro 9:5; 1Jn 5:20-21), God and Savior Jesus Christ (2Pe 1:1). God our Savior (Tit 2:13). Holy One (Ac 3:14). Lord of lords and King of kings (Rev 17:14). Lord (Ps 110:1 w Mt 22:42-45; Isa 40:3 w Mt 3:3; Ac 20:28). Lord Almighty (Isa 8:13-14; 1Pe 2:8). My Lord and My God (Jn 20:28). Lord of all (Ac 10:36; Ro 10:12). Mighty God (Isa 9:6). Only born of the Father (Jn 1:14, 18; 3:16, 18; 1Jn 4:9), Son of God (Mt 26:63-67; Mk 1:1; 15:39; 1Co 1:9; 2Co 1:19; Gal 2:20; Eph 4:13; Heb 1:2; 2Pe 1:17; 1Jn 1:3; 3:23; 5:10, 12-13, 20), Son of Man (Da 7:13-14; Mt 11:19; 12:8). See above, Divine Sonship of; below, Son of God; Son of Man.

Addressed as Yahweh (Lord)—

(Isa 40:3 w Mt 3:3). King or LORD of glory (Ps 24:7, 10; 1Co 2:8; Jas 2:1). The LORD our righteousness (Jer 23:5-6; 1Co 1:30), The LORD all (Ps 97:9; Jn 3:31), The First and the last, the Alpha and the Omega (Isa 44:6, w Rev 1:17; Isa 48:12-16, w Rev 22:13). Yahweh's fellow and equal (Zec 13:7; Php 2:6). LORD Almighty (Isa 6:1-3 w Jn 12:41; Isa 8:13-14 w 1Pe 2:8). LORD (Ps 110:1; Mt 22:42-45). Yahweh the Shepherd (Isa 40:10-11; Heb 13:20). LORD, for whose glory all things were created (Pr 16:4; Col 1:16). Lord the messenger of the covenant (Mal 3:1; Lk 7:27). Invoked as LORD (Joel 2:32; 1Co 1:2).

Equality With God—

As the eternal God and Creator (Ps 102:24-27; Heb 1:8, 10-12). The Mighty God (Isa 9:6), the great God and Savior (Hos 1:7, w Tit 2:13), God over all (Ro 9:5), God the Judge (Ecc 12:14, w 1Co 4:5; 2Co 5:10; 2Ti 4:1), Immanuel (Isa 7:14, w Mt 1:23), Lord of lords and King of kings (Da 10:17, w Rev 1:5; 17:14), the Holy and Righteous One (1Sa 2:2, w Ac 3:14).

The Lord from heaven (1Co 15:47). Lord of the Sabbath (Ge 2:3, w Mt 12:8), Lord of all (Ac 10:36; Ro 10:11-13). Son of God (Mt 26:63-67), the only born Son of the Father (Jn 1:14, 18; 3:16, 18; 1Jn 4:9). His blood is called the blood of God (Ac 20:28). One with the Father (Jn 10:30, 38; 12:45; 14:7-10; 17:10). As sending the Spirit equally with the Father (Jn 14:16, w Jn 15:26). As unsearchable equally with the Father (Pr 30:4; Mt 11:27). As Creator of all things (Isa 40:28; Jn 1:3; Col 1:16), supporter and preserver of all things (Ne 9:6, w Col 1:17; Heb 1:3). Acknowledged by Old Testament saints (Ge 17:1, w 48:15-16; 32:24-30, w Hos 12:3-5; Jdg 6:22-24; 13:21-22; Job 19:25-27). Is one with the Father (Jn 5:17-18, 23; 10:30, 33, 38; 12:45; 14:7-11; 17:11, 21-23). Sends the Holy Spirit equally with the Father (Jn 14:16). Identical with the Adonay (Lord) of the Old Testament (Jn 12:40-41, w Isa 6:8-11), and the Yahweh (LORD) of the Old Testament (Jn 19:37, w Zec 12:10).

Has power to forgive sins (Mt 1:21; 9:6; Mk 2:5; Lk 5:20; Col 3:13). Paul's apostleship from (Gal 1:1). Invoked with the Father and the Spirit in benedictions (Ro 1:7; 1Co 1:3; 2Co 1:2; Gal 1:3; Eph 1:2; 6:23-24; 1Ti 1:1; 3:11; 2Th 1:1-2; 2:16-17; 2Ti 1:2). All power given to (Mt 28:17-18). Eternity ascribed to (Jn 1:1-2; 1Jn 1:1). See below, Eternity of. Is judge (2Co 5:10). See below, Judge.

Testimony Concerning His Deity—

By the Father (Jn 5:32, 34, 37; 6:27; 8:18; Ac 13:33; 1Jn 5:9), at his baptism (Mt 3:16-17; Mk 1:11; Lk 3:22), at his transfiguration (Mt 17:5; Mk 9:7; Lk 9:35; 2Pe 1:17).

By Jesus concerning himself (Jn 5:18, 31, 36; 8:18, 42; 10:33, 36, 38; 12:45; 14:11-13; 16:27-28; 17:5, 8, 24-25; 19:7), to Peter and other disciples (Mt 16:16-17; Mk 8:29-30; Lk 9:20-21), to the Jews (Mt 22:43-44; Jn 5:23; 10:30, 33, 36, 38; 12:45), to his disciples (Jn 16:27-28), to the restored blind man (Jn 9:35-37), to Philip (Jn 14:7-11, 20), to Caiaphas (Mt 26:63-64; Mk 14:61-62; Lk 22:67-70), to Pilate (Jn 18:36-37; 1Ti 6:13).

By the angel, to Joseph (Mt 1:23), to Mary (Lk 1:32, 35). John the Baptist (Jn 1:29-34; 5:33). John, the apostle (Jn 1:14, 18; 13:3; 1Jn 2:22-24). The disciples (Jn 16:30). Paul (Ac 9:20). The author of the epistle to the Hebrews (Heb 11:26). The Scriptures (Jn 5:39). Thomas (Jn 20:28). Demons (Mt 8:29; Mk 1:23-24; 3:11; 5:6-7; Lk 4:34, 41).

Eternity of:

Called everlasting Father (Isa 9:6). Was before creation (Jn 1:1-2, 15; 17:5, 24; Col 1:17; 2Ti 1:9). Was from the beginning (1Jn 2:13). Was from everlasting (Mic 5:2). Continues forever (Ps 102:24-27 w Heb 1:10-13; Ps 110:4; Heb 3:21; Heb 7:16, 24-25; Rev 5:13-14). The same yesterday and today and forever (Heb 13:8).

J

Exaltation of:
(Ps 2:8-9; 68:18; Eph 4:8). In glory (Mt 26:64; Mk 16:19; Lk 22:69; 24:26; Jn 7:39; Ac 2:33-34; 3:20-21; 7:55-56; Ro 8:17, 34; Eph 1:20-22; 4:10; Col 3:1; 1Ti 3:16; Heb 1:3; 10:12-13; 12:2; 1Pe 3:22; Rev 3:21). As Lord of heaven and earth (Php 2:9-11; Col 2:15). As Savior (Ac 5:31). As priestly mediator (Heb 4:10, 14; 6:20; 7:26; 8:1; 9:24).

An Example:
Claimed himself (Mt 11:29; 20:28; Mk 10:43-45; Lk 22:26-27; Jn 10:4; 13:13-15, 34; 17:14, 18, 21-22; Rev 3:21). Referred to by Paul (Ro 8:29; 13:14; 15:2-7; 2Co 4:10; 8:9; 10:1; Gal 3:27; 6:2; Eph 4:13, 15, 24; 5:2; 6:9; Php 2:5-8; Col 3:10-11, 13; 1Th 1:6). Referred to by other apostles (Heb 3:1; 12:2-4; 1Pe 1:15; 2:21-24; 3:17-18; 1Jn 2:6; 3:1-3, 16; 4:17).

Faith in: *See Faith in Christ; Salvation, Conditions of.*

Faithfulness of:
(Isa 11:5; Lk 4:43; Jn 7:18; 8:29; 9:4; 14:3; 17:8; Heb 3:2; Rev 1:5; 3:14). In mediation (Heb 2:17).

Genealogy of: *See above, History of.*

Glorification of:
(Jn 7:39; 12:16; 17:1; Ac 7:55-56; Heb 8:1).

Head of the Church:
(Ps 118:22-23, w Mt 21:42-43, & Mt 12:10; Isa 28:16, w Eph 2:2-22, & 1Pe 2:6; Col 2:10-18, w 1Pe 2:7; Jn 15:1-8; 1Co 3:11; Eph 1:22-23; 4:15; 5:23-32; Col 1:18; 2:10, 19; 3:11; Rev 2:2-28; 3:1, 7; 22:16).

Holiness of:
Foretold (Ps 45:7; Isa 11:4-5; Jer 23:5; Zec 9:9). Professed by himself (Jn 5:30; 7:18; 8:46; 14:30; Rev 3:7).
Testified to: By the angel to his mother (Lk 1:35). By demons (Mk 1:24; Lk 4:34). By the centurion at the Crucifixion (Lk 23:47). By Stephen (Ac 7:52). By Peter (Jn 6:69; Ac 3:14; 4:27-30; 1Pe 1:19; 2:22). By John (1Jn 2:1, 29; 3:5). By Paul (Ac 13:35; 2Co 5:21). By the author of Hebrews (Heb 1:9; 4:15; 7:26-28; 9:14).

Humanity of:
(Ps 22:22; Jn 1:14). Took on himself human nature (Php 2:7-8; Heb 2:9-10, 14-18). Was born of flesh (Isa 9:6; Mt 1:18-25; Lk 2:11-14; 1Jn 4:2; 2Jn 7).
Called: Seed of the woman (Ge 3:15; Gal 4:4), son of David (Mt 20:30-31; 21:9; 22:42; Mk 12:35; Lk 18:38), a prophet like Moses (Dt 18:15-19; Ac 3:22-23; 7:37).
See above, Humanity of; below, Relation of, to the Father.

Humility of:
(2Co 8:9; Php 2:7-8). Became a servant (Lk 22:27; Jn 13:5, 14). *See below, Meekness of.*

Impeccability of: *See above, Holiness of; below, Temptation of.*

Incarnation of:
(Jn 16:28; 1Ti 3:16). Foretold (Ge 3:15; Dt 18:15-18; Ps 2:7; Isa 7:14-16; 9:6; 11:1; Jn 7:42; Ac 13:33; Heb 1:5). Accomplished through the generation of the Holy Spirit (Mt 1:1, 16-18, 23; Lk 1:26-56). Was made a little lower than the angels (Heb 2:9, 14). Was made flesh (Lk 24:39; Jn 1:14; 20:27; Ro 8:3; 1Co 15:47; 2Co 5:16; Gal 4:4; Php 2:7-8; Heb 1:3, 6; 2:9-18; 10:5; 1Jn 1:1-3; 4:2; 2Jn 7). Came in the lineage of Judah (Heb 7:14). Was of the seed of David (Mt 22:45; Ro 1:3; 9:5; Rev 22:16). Was the son of Mary (Mt 13:55; Lk 2:1-21).
See above, Humanity of; below, Relation of, to the Father.

Intercession of: *See below, Mediation of.*

Judge:
(Mt 3:12 w Lk 3:17; Mt 25:31-34; Ac 10:42; Ro 2:16; 1Co 4:4-5; 2Co 5:10; 2Ti 4:1, 8; Rev 2:23). Prophecy concerning (Isa 2:4 w Mic 4:3; Isa 11:3-4; Mic 5:1). Ordained of God (Jn 5:22; Ac 17:31). Righteous (2Ti 4:8).

Justice of:
(2Sa 23:3; Zec 9:9; Mt 27:19; Lk 5:30; Ac 3:14; 22:14).

King:
Prophecies concerning (Ge 49:10; 1Sa 2:10; 2Sa 7:12 w Ac 2:30; Ps 2:6; 18:43-44; 45:3-7; 72:5, 8, 11; 89:3-4, 19-21, 23, 27, 29, 36-37; 110:1-2; 132:11, 17-18; Isa 9:6-7; 22:22; 32:1; 52:7, 13; Jer 23:5; 30:9; 33:17; Eze 37:24-25; Da 2:35, 44; 7:13-14; Hos 3:5; Mic 5:2, 4; Zec 6:12-13; 9:9-10; Mt 2:2, 6; 21:5; 22:42-45; Lk 1:32-33; Ac 2:30). Appointed by the Father as King (Lk 22:29-30; Ac 2:30, 36 w 2Sa 7:12; Ac 5:31; Eph 1:20-22; Heb 2:7-8).
Authority of Jesus as King (Mk 2:28; Jn 5:27). Universal kingdom (Mt 11:27 w Lk 10:22; Mt 28:18; Lk 19:27; Jn 3:31, 33; 13:3; 17:2; Ro 9:5; 10:12; 14:9; Col 2:10; Heb 1:2-13; 2:7-8; 1Pe 3:22; Rev 3:7, 14, 21).
Dominion of Jesus, universal (Ac 10:36; 1Co 15:23-28; Eph 1:20-22; Php 2:9-11; Rev 1:5-7, 18; 11:15). Future glory of Jesus as King (Mt 19:28; 25:31-34; 26:64; Mk 14:62; Lk 22:69; Heb 10:12-13; Rev 5:13).
Kingship of: Avowed by himself (Mt 21:5; 27:11; Lk 23:2; Jn 18:36-37). Ascribed, by disciples (Lk 19:38; Jn 1:49; 12:13, 15; Ac 17:7). In superscription on the cross (Jn 19:12, 19). Symbolic statements concerning (Rev 5:5, 12; 6:2, 15-17; 14:14; 17:14; 19:11-12, 15-16).
See below, Lordship of.

Kingdom of:
Brings joy and gladness (Ps 46:4; Isa 25:6; 35; 52:9; 55:12). Brings peace (Ps 46:9; Isa 11:6-9). Is within us (Lk 17:21). Truth (Jn 18:37). Is not of this world (Jn 18:36).
Keys of (Mt 16:19). Glad tidings of (Lk 8:1). Mysteries of (Lk 8:10). Is not meat and drink (Ro 14:17).

Likened to—
A man who sowed good seed (Mt 13:24-30, 38-43; Mk 4:26-29). A mustard seed (Mt 13:31-32; Mk 4:30-31; Lk 13:18-19). Yeast (Mt 13:33; Lk 13:21). A treasure (Mt 13:44). A pearl (Mt 13:45). A net (Mt 13:47-50). A king who called his servants to account (Mt 18:23-35). A landowner (Mt 20:1-16). A king who made a marriage feast for his son (Mt 22:1-14; Lk 14:16-24). Ten virgins (Mt 25:1-13). A man who entrusted property to his servants (Mt 25:14-30; Lk 19:12-27).

Prophecies Concerning—
Its character: To enlighten (Jer 31:34; Heb 8:11). To bring peace (Ps 46:9; Isa 65:25; Mic 4:3-7). To bring salvation (Isa 62:11). To bring joy (Isa 25:6; 35:1-10; 42:1-7, 18-21; Lk 2:10). Shall be a river of salvation (Eze 47:1-12; Zec 14:8-9, 16, 20-21).
Will be forever (Isa 51:6, 8; Lk 1:33; Heb 1:8; 2Pe 1:11). Transforms (Isa 11:10; 55:12-13; 65:17-25). Future glory and greatness (Isa 49:22-23; Hag 2:7-9; Rev 21:9-27).
Universality of the kingdom (Ge 12:3; 22:18; 49:10; Ps 72:5, 8-11, 16-17, 19; 89:1-37; 113:3; Isa 9:6-7; 40:4-11; 42:1-7; 49:1-26; 52:10; 54:1-3; 59:19-21; Jer 3:14-19; Da 2:35, 44; 7:13-14, 18, 22, 27; Hab 2:14; Zec 9:1, 10; Mt 8:11; Lk 13:29-30; Rev 14:6). Unity of the kingdom (Jn 10:16).
Growth of the kingdom (Mt 13:31-33; Lk 13:21). Ends of earth shall turn to him (Ps 66:4; 86:9; Isa 2:2-4; 45:14; 60:1-9; Jer 3:17; 16:19-21; 33:16; Eze 17:22-23; Mic 4:1-4; Zep 2:11; Zec 2:10-11; 6:15; 8:20-23). Shall include all nations (Ps 2:8; 68:31-32; 110:4-6; Hos 2:23; Am 9:11-12; Mal 1:11).
Final triumph of the kingdom (Ge 3:15; Ps 2:9; Isa 11:1-13; Da 2:44; 7:9-14, 27; Mt 16:18; Ac 2:34-35; 1Co 15:24-28; Eph 1:10; Php 2:10-11; Heb 10:13; 12:23-24, 27-28; Rev 5:9-10, 13-14; 6:2; 11:15; 12:10; 19:11-21; 20:1-3).
Secular notions concerning: To restore the kingdom of Israel (Mk 11:9-10; Jn 6:14-15; Ac 1:6-7). Rank of princes in the kingdom of (Mt 20:20-23; Mk 10:35-40; Lk 9:46-48).

Love of:
(Ps 69:9; Rev 3:9, 19). Jesus' love compels us (2Co 5:13-14), surpasses knowledge (Eph 3:17-19).
Jesus' love for his disciples (Jn 10:3-4, 11, 14-16; 13:1, 23; 14:1-3, 18, 21, 27; 15:9-13, 15; 17:6-26; Ro 8:35, 37-39; 2Th 2:13). For children (Mt 19:13-15; Mk 10:13-14, 16; Lk 18:15-16). For his mother (Jn 19:26-27). For the lost (Isa 40:11; Mt 18:12-13; Mk 8:12; Lk 13:34).
Jesus' love exemplified: In renunciation (2Co 8:9; Php 2:6-8). In compassion (Isa 42:3; Mt 9:36; 14:14; 15:32; Lk 7:13; 22:31-32; Jn 11:5, 33-36; Ac 10:38; Heb 4:15). In his heart for others (Mt 23:37; Lk 23:28, 34; Jn 18:8-9). In his sacrifice (Gal 2:20; Eph 5:2, 25, 29-30; 1Jn 3:16; Rev 1:5). In his vicarious suffering (Isa 53:4; Mt 8:17; Ro 15:3). In redemption (Ps 72:14; Isa 63:9).

Lordship of:
The sovereignty of the Messiah, as conceived by Old Testament writers, seems best described by the word "King," but New Testament writers use the word "Lord." *See above, King.* Jesus said of himself, the Son of Man is Lord even of the Sabbath (Mt 12:8; Mk 2:28).
The student will find suggestions for profitable reflection in a study of the various forms of expression used by the authors of the epistles in which they attribute Lordship to our Savior (Mt 12:8; Ac 2:36; Ro 1:7; 5:1, 11, 21; 6:23; 7:25; 8:39; 10:9; 13:14; 14:14; 15:6, 30; 16:20; 1Co 1:2-3, 7-10; 5:4; 6:11; 8:6; 9:1; 11:25; 12:3; 15:31, 57; 16:23; 2Co 1:2-3, 14; 4:5, 14; 8:9; 11:31; 13:14; Gal 1:3; 6:14, 18; Eph 1:2-3, 17; 3:11; 5:20; 6:23-24; Php 1:2, 11; 2:19; 3:20; 4:23; Col 1:3; 2:6; 3:17, 24; 1Th 1:1, 3; 4:1; 5:10, 24, 28; 2Th 1:1-2, 7, 12; 2:1, 8, 15-16; 3:6, 12, 18; 1Ti 1:2, 12; 6:3, 14; 2Ti 1:2; Phm 1, 3, 5, 25; Jas 1:1; 2:1; 1Pe 1:3; 3:15; 2Pe 1:2, 8, 14, 16; 2:20; 3:18; Jude 4, 18, 21, 25).

Mediation of:
(Jn 14:6, 14; 16:23-24, 26; 20:31; Ro 1:8; 5:1-2; 6:23; 1Co 6:11; 15:57; 2Co 1:20; Eph 3:12; 4:32; 5:20; Col 3:17; 1Ti 2:1, 3, 5; Heb 9:11-28; Eph 2:5; 1Jn 2:1-2, 12).
As a priest (Ps 110:4; Zec 6:13; Heb 2:17; 3:1-2; 4:14-15; 5:5-6, 10; 6:19-20; 7:1, 3, 19, 21, 24-28; 8:1-2, 6; 9:11; 10:19-21). Through his sacrifice (Eph 2:13-18; Heb 10:11-12; 12:24).
Exemplified in his intercession (Isa 53:12; Lk 13:8-9; 22:31-32; 23:33-34; Jn 14:16; 17:1-14, 15-17, 19-22; Ro 8:34).
See below, Priesthood of.

Meekness of:
(Mt 11:29; Mk 14:60-61; 15:3-5; 2Co 10:1; Php 2:8). Prophecies concerning (Ps 45:4; Isa 42:1-3; 50:5-6; 52:1, 14; 53:7; Mt 12:19-20; 21:5; Ac 8:32).
Exemplified in not resenting false accusation (Mk 2:6-11). In submitting to enemies (Mt 26:47-63; 27:12-14; Jn 8:48-50; Heb 12:2-3; 1Pe 2:23). In praying for enemies (Lk 23:34). In becoming a servant (Php 2:7).
See above, Humility of; Meekness.

Messiah:
Messianic Psalms (Ps 2:1-12; 67:1-7; 68:1-35; 69:1-36; 72:1-20; 96:1-13; 98:1-9; 110:1-7). Prophecies concerning the Messiah (Da 9:25-26; Ac 3:18-20).
Simeon's testimony to the Messiah (Lk 2:28-32). Andrew's belief in the Messiah (Jn 1:41, 45). Peter's confession of the Messiah (Mt 16:15-16; Mk 8:29; Lk 9:20; Jn 6:69). Was proclaimed as Messiah by apostles (Ac 9:22; 13:27; 17:2-3; 26:6-7, 22-23; 28:23; Ro 1:1-3; 1Co 1:5:23; 1Pe 1:10-11; 2Pe 1:16-18; 1Jn 5:6-9).
Jesus' own testimony to his messiahship (Mt 11:3-6; 26:63-64; Lk 24:27; Jn 4:25-26, 29, 42; 5:33, 36-37, 39, 46; 6:27; 8:14, 17-18, 25, 28, 56; 13:19).
Was called David's son (Mt 22:42-45; Mk 12:35-37; Lk 20:41-44). Is the anointed of God (Ps 2:2; Ac 4:26-27).
See above, King; Lordship of; below, Son of Man. See also, Messianic Hope.

Miracles of:
Water made wine (Jn 2:1-11).
First miraculous catch of fishes (Lk 5:1-11).
Demoniac in the synagogue healed (Mk 1:23-26; Lk 4:33-36).
Heals Simon's wife's mother (Mt 8:14-15; Mk 1:29-31; Lk 4:38-39).
Heals diseases in Galilee (Mt 4:23-24; Mk 1:34).
Miracles at Jerusalem (Jn 2:23).
Cleanses the leper (Mt 8:1-4; Mk 1:40-45; Lk 5:12-16).
Heals the paralytic (Mt 9:1-8; Mk 2:1-12; Lk 5:17-26).
Heals the crippled man (Jn 5:1-16).
Restores the withered hand (Mt 12:9-13; Mk 3:1-5; Lk 6:6-11).
Heals multitudes from Judah, Jerusalem, and coasts of Tyre and Sidon (Lk 6:17-19).

Heals the centurion's servant (Mt 8:5-13; Lk 7:1-10).
Heals demoniacs (Mt 8:16-17; Lk 4:40-41).
Raises the widow's son (Lk 7:11-16).
Heals in Galilee (Lk 7:21-22).
Heals a demoniac (Mt 12:22-37; Mk 3:20-30; Lk 11:14-15, 17-23).
Healing of the diseased in the land of Gennesaret (Mt 14:34-36).
The demoniacs in Gadarenes healed (Mt 8:28-34; Mk 5:1-20; Lk 8:26-39).
Raises Jairus' daughter (Mt 9:18-19, 23-26; Mk 5:22-24, 35-43; Lk 8:41-42, 49-56).
Heals the woman with the issue of blood (Mt 9:20-22; Mk 5:25-34; Lk 8:43-48).
Opens the eyes of two blind men in the house (Mt 9:27-31).
A demon cast out and a mute man cured (Mt 9:32-33).
Five thousand fed (Mt 14:15-21; Mk 6:35-44; Lk 9:12-17; Jn 6:5-14).
Heals sick in Galilee (Mt 14:14).
Walking on the sea (Mt 14:22-33; Mk 6:45-52; Jn 6:14-21).
The daughter of the Syrian Phoenician healed (Mt 15:21-28; Mk 7:24-30).
Healing of the lame, blind, mute, and maimed, near the Sea of Galilee (Mt 15:30).
Four thousand fed (Mt 15:32-39; Mk 8:1-9).
One deaf and mute cured (Mk 7:31-37).
One blind cured (Mk 8:22-36).
Child healed (Mt 17:14-21; Mk 9:14-29; Lk 9:37-43).
Piece of money in the fish's mouth (Mt 17:24-27).
The ten lepers cured (Lk 17:11-19).
Opening the eyes of one born blind (Jn 9).
Raising of Lazarus (Jn 11:1-54).
Woman with the spirit of infirmity cured (Lk 13:10-17).
The dropsy cured (Lk 14:1-6).
Two blind men cured near Jericho (Mt 20:29-34; Mk 10:46-52; Lk 18:35-43).
The fig tree blighted (Mt 21:17-22; Mk 11:12-14, 20-24).
Healing of Malchus' ear (Lk 22:49-51).
Second catch of fishes (Jn 21:6).
Not particularly described (Mt 4:23-24; 14:14; 15:30; Mk 1:34; Lk 6:17-19; 7:21-22; Jn 2:23; 3:2). Resurrection (Mt 28:6; Mk 16:6; Lk 24:6; Jn 20:1-18). Holds the vision of his disciples, that they should not recognize him (Lk 24:16, 31, 35). His appearances and disappearings (Lk 24:15, 31, 36-45; Jn 20:19, 26). Opening the understanding of his disciples (Lk 24:45). His Ascension (Lk 24:51; Ac 1:9).
See Miracles.

Mission of:
(Isa 42:7; Mt 18:12-14; Lk 12:49-53; Jn 4:25, 34; 18:37). To fulfill the Law and the Prophets (Mic 5:2; Mt 5:17; Ro 10:4). To be Lord of all (Ro 14:9; 15:8-9; 2Co 5:15; Eph 4:10). To glorify the Father (Jn 17:4).
To preach the gospel (Isa 61:1; Mt 4:23; 9:13; Mk 1:38; Lk 4:18-19, 43; 5:31-32; 8:1). To preach repentance (Lk 5:30-32; 24:47; Ac 3:26; 5:31). To bring life (Jn 6:51; 10:10; 2Co 5:14, 21). To give light (Isa 9:2; 42:6; Lk 1:78-79; 2:30-32, 34; Jn 1:1-9; 9:39; 12:46-47).
To condemn sin (Ro 8:3-4). To die for sinners (Ro 5:6-8). To be propitiation for sin (Mt 20:28; Mk 10:45; Lk 24:26, 46; Jn 6:51; Ac 26:23; Ro 4:24-25; 5:6-8; 2Co 5:18; Gal 1:3-4; 4:4-5; Heb 2:9, 14; 9:26; 1Jn 3:5, 8; 4:8, 10). To purge sins (Zec 13:1; Mal 3:2-3). To give remission of sins (Ac 10:43; Ro 4:25). To destroy the works of the devil (Ge 3:15; Jn 3:8).
To bring salvation (Mt 1:21; 15:24; 18:12-14; Lk 19:10; Jn 3:13-17; Ro 14:15; 1Ti 1:15). To deliver from fear of death (Heb 2:15). To deliver from temptation (Heb 2:18). To comfort the contrite (Isa 61:1-3). To baptize with the Holy Spirit and with fire (Mt 3:11-12; Lk 3:16). To preach to spirits in prison (1Pe 3:19; 4:6, cf. Eph 4:9).

Names, Appellations, and Titles of:
Adam (1Co 15:45). Advocate (1Jn 2:1). Almighty (Rev 1:8). Alpha and Omega (Rev 22:13). Amen (Rev 3:14). Angel (Ge 48:16; Ex 23:20). Angel of his presence (Isa 63:9). Anointed (Ps 2:2). Apostle (Heb 3:1). Arm of the Lord (Isa 51:9-10). Atoning sacrifice (1Jn 2:2). Author of life (Ac 3:15). Author of salvation (Heb 2:10). Author and perfecter of our faith (Heb 12:2).
Banner for the peoples (Isa 11:10). Beginning and End (Rev 22:13). Blessed and only Ruler (1Ti 6:15). Branch (Jer 23:5; Zec 3:8). Bread of life (Jn 6:48). Bridegroom (Mt 9:15). Bright Morning Star (Rev 22:16).
Capstone (Mt 21:42). Carpenter (Mk 6:3). Carpenter's son (Mt 13:55). Chief Shepherd (1Pe 5:4). Child (Isa 9:6; Lk 2:27). Chosen one (Isa 42:1). Chosen by God (1Pe 2:4). Chosen and precious cornerstone (1Pe 2:6). Christ (Mt 1:16). The Christ (Mt 16:20; Mk 14:61, 62; Lk 9:20). Christ, a king (Lk 23:2). Christ Jesus (Ro 3:24; 8:1; 1Co 1:2, 30). Christ Jesus our Lord (1Ti 1:12; Ro 8:39). Christ of God (Lk 9:20). Christ of God, the Chosen One (Lk 23:35). Christ the Lord (Lk 2:11). Christ the power of God and the wisdom of God (1Co 1:24). Christ, the Son of God (Jn 11:27). Christ, the Son of the Blessed One (Mk 14:61). Commander (Isa 55:4). Commander of the LORD's army (Jos 5:14). Consolation of Israel (Lk 2:25). Cornerstone (Eph 2:20). Counselor (Isa 9:6). Covenant for the people (Isa 42:6).
David (Jer 30:9). Deliverer (Ro 11:26). Desired of all nations (Hag 2:7). Doctor (Mt 9:12). Eternal life (1Jn 5:20). Everlasting Father (Isa 9:6). Exact representation of God's being (Heb 1:3).
Faithful and True (Rev 19:11). Faithful witness (Rev 1:5). Faithful and true witness (Rev 3:14). The First and the Last (Rev 1:17; 2:8; 22:13). Firstborn (Heb 1:6). Firstborn from the dead (Rev 1:5). Foundation (Isa 28:16). Fountain (Zec 13:1). Friend of tax collectors and sinners (Mt 11:19).
Gate (Jn 10:7). Gift of God (Jn 4:10). Glorious Lord Jesus Christ (Jas 2:1). Glory of Israel (Lk 2:32). God (Jn 20:28). God and Savior of Israel (Isa 45:15). God of all the earth (Isa 54:5). God over all, forever praised (Ro 9:5). God the One and Only (Jn 1:18). God with us (Mt 1:23). Good Shepherd (Jn 10:11, 14). Good Teacher (Mk 10:17). Great God and Savior (Tit 2:13). Great high priest

(Heb 4:14). Great Shepherd of the sheep (Heb 13:20). Guarantee (Heb 7:22).

Head of every man (1Co 11:3). Head of the body, the church (Col 1:18). Head of the church (Eph 5:23). Heir of all things (Heb 1:2). High priest (Heb 4:15). Holiness (1Co 1:30). Holy One (Ps 16:10). Holy One of God (Mk 1:24). Holy One of Israel (Isa 41:14; 54:5). Holy and Righteous One (Ac 3:14). Holy servant Jesus (Ac 4:30). Our Hope (1Ti 1:1). Horn of salvation (Lk 1:69).

I am (Jn 8:58). Immanuel (Isa 7:14; Mt 1:23). Indescribable gift (2Co 9:15). Innocent man (Mt 27:19). Israel (Isa 49:3).

Jesus (Mt 1:21). Jesus Christ (Mt 1:1; Jn 1:17; 17:3; Ac 2:38; 4:10; 9:34; 10:36; 16:18; Ro 1:6; 2:16; 5:15, 17; 1Co 2:2; 2Co 1:19; 4:5; Gal 2:16; Php 1:11; 2:11; 2Ti 2:8; Heb 13:8; 1Jn 1:3; 2:1). Jesus Christ our Lord (Ro 5:21; 7:25; 1Co 1:9; Jude 25). Jesus Christ our Savior (Tit 3:6). Jesus of Nazareth (Mk 1:24; Lk 24:19). Jesus of Nazareth, the King of the Jews (Jn 19:19). Jesus, the King of the Jews (Mt 27:37). Jesus the Son of God (Heb 4:14). Jesus, the Son of Joseph (Jn 6:42). Judge (Ac 10:42).

King (Mt 21:5). King of Israel (Jn 1:49). King of kings (1Ti 6:15; Rev 17:14). King of glory (Ps 24:7-10). King of the ages (Rev 15:3). King of the Jews (Mt 2:2). King over the whole earth (Zec 14:9).

Lamb (Rev 5:6, 8; 6:16; 7:9-10, 17; 12:11; 13:8; 14:1, 4; 15:3; 17:14; 19:7, 9; 21:9, 14, 22-23, 27). Lamb of God (Jn 1:29). Lawgiver (Isa 33:22). Leader (Isa 55:4). Life (Jn 14:6). Light, everlasting (Isa 60:20). Light of the world (Jn 8:12). Light for the Gentiles (Isa 42:6). Light, true (Jn 1:9). Living bread (Jn 6:51). Living Stone (1Pe 2:4). Lion of the tribe of Judah (Rev 5:5). Lord (Jn 20:28). Lord Almighty (Jas 5:4). Lord of all (Ac 10:36; Ro 10:12). Lord of lords (Rev 17:14; 19:16). LORD Our Righteousness (Jer 23:6). Lord God Almighty (Rev 15:3). Lord and Savior Jesus Christ (2Pe 1:11; 3:18). Lord Christ (Col 3:24). Lord Jesus (Ac 7:59; Col 3:17; 1Th 4:2). Lord Jesus Christ (Ac 11:17; 15:26; 28:31; Ro 5:1, 11; 13:14). LORD mighty in battle (Ps 24:8). Lord of the dead and the living (Ro 14:9). Lord of the Sabbath (Mk 2:28). Lord's Christ (Lk 2:26). LORD, your holy one (Isa 43:15). LORD, your redeemer (Isa 43:14).

Man Christ Jesus (1Ti 2:5). Man of sorrows (Isa 53:3). Man who is close to me [the LORD] (Zec 13:7). Master (Mt 23:8). Mediator (1Ti 2:5). Messenger of the covenant (Mal 3:1). Messiah (Jn 1:41). Mighty God (Isa 9:6). Mighty One of Israel (Isa 1:24). Mighty one of Jacob (Isa 49:26). Mighty to save (Isa 63:1). Morning star (2Pe 1:19; Rev 22:16).

Nazarene (Mt 2:23).

Offspring of David (Rev 22:16). Offspring of the woman (Ge 3:15). The One and Only (Jn 1:14). One and only Son (Jn 3:16, 18). One he [the Father] loves (Eph 1:6). Only God our Savior (Jude 25). Overseer (1Pe 2:25).

Passover lamb (1Co 5:7). Perfecter of faith (Heb 12:2). Power of (1Co 1:24). Physician (Lk 4:23). Precious cornerstone (Isa 28:16). Priest (Heb 7:17). Prince (Ac 5:31). Prince of Peace (Isa 9:6). Prophet (Dt 18:15, 18; Mt 21:11; Lk 24:19).

Rabbi (Jn 1:49). Rabboni (Jn 20:16). Radiance of God's glory (Heb 1:3). Ransom (1Ti 2:6). Redeemer (Isa 59:20). Resurrection and life (Jn 11:25). Redemption (1Co 1:30). Righteous Branch (Jer 23:5). Righteous Judge (2Ti 4:8). Righteous One (Ac 7:52; 22:14). Righteous servant (Isa 53:11). Righteousness (1Co 1:30). Rising sun (Lk 1:78). Rock (1Co 10:4). Rock that makes them fall (1Pe 2:8). Root of David (Rev 5:5; 22:16). Root of Jesse (Isa 11:10). Rose of Sharon (SS 2:1). Ruler (Mt 2:6; 1Ti 6:15). Ruler of God's creation (Rev 3:14). Ruler of the kings of the earth (Rev 1:5). Ruler over Israel (Mic 5:2).

Sacrifice (Jn 2:2). Salvation (Lk 2:30). Sanctuary (Isa 8:14). Savior (Lk 2:11). Savior Christ Jesus (2Ti 1:10). Savior Jesus Christ (Tit 2:13; 2Pe 1:1). Savior of the body (Eph 5:23). Savior of the world (1Jn 4:14). Scepter (Nu 24:17). Second man from heaven (1Co 15:47). Seed of Abraham (Gal 3:16). Servant (Isa 42:1). Servant of rulers (Isa 49:7). Serves in the sanctuary (Heb 8:2). Shepherd (Mk 14:27). Shepherd and Overseer of souls (1Pe 2:25). Shepherd, Chief (1Pe 5:4). Shepherd, good (Jn 10:11). Shepherd, great (Heb 13:20). Shepherd of Israel (Ps 80:1). Shiloh (Ge 49:10, ftn). Son he [God] loves (Col 1:13). Son of Abraham (Mt 1:1). Son of David (Mt 9:27). Son of the Father (2Jn 3). Son of God. *See Jesus the Christ, Son of God.* Son of Man. *See Jesus the Christ, Son of Man.* Son of the Blessed One (Mk 14:61). Son of the Most High (Lk 1:32). Star (Nu 24:17). Stone (Mt 21:42). Stone that causes men to stumble (1Pe 2:8). Sun of righteousness (Mal 4:2). Sure foundation (Isa 28:16).

Teacher (Jn 3:2). Tested stone (Isa 28:16). True God (1Jn 5:20). True vine (Jn 15:1). Truth (Jn 14:6).

Vine (Jn 15:1).

Way (Jn 14:6). Who is, who was, and who is to come (Rev 1:4). Wisdom (Pr 8:12). Wisdom of God (1Co 1:24). Witness (Isa 55:4; Rev 1:5). Wonderful Counselor (Isa 9:6). Word (Jn 1:1). Word of God (Rev 19:13). Word of life (1Jn 1:1).

Yahweh. *See in list above: I am, Lord, and LORD* 61.

In His Name:
(1Co 6:11; Php 2:9; Col 3:17; Rev 19:16). Baptism (Mt 28:19; Ac 2:38). Life (Jn 20:31). Miracles performed (Ac 3:6; 4:10; 19:13). Prayer (Jn 14:13; 16:23-24, 26; Eph 5:20; Col 3:17; Heb 13:15). Preaching (Lk 24:47). Faith (Mt 12:21; Jn 1:12; 2:23). Remission of sins (Lk 24:47; Ac 10:43; 1Jn 2:12). Salvation (Ac 4:12; 10:43). Those who use his name must turn away from wickedness (2Ti 2:19).

See above, Intercession of; below, Priesthood of.

Obedience of:
Foretold (Ps 40:8; Isa 11:5-6; Heb 10:7-9). To his parents (Lk 2:51). To God (Lk 2:49; 4:34; 5:30, 36; 6:38; 8:29, 46, 55; 9:4; 14:31; 15:10; 17:4).

Exemplified: In his baptism (Mt 3:15). Sufferings (Mt 26:39, 42; Mk 14:36; Lk 22:42; Heb 5:8). Death (Jn 19:30; Php 2:8).

Omnipotence of:
(Ps 45:3-5; 110:3; Isa 9:6; 40:10; 50:2-3; 63:1; Mt 6:7; 12:13, 28-29; 28:18; Mk 3:27; Lk 5:17; 9:1; 11:20-22; Jn 2:10; 5:21, 28-29; 10:17-18, 28; Php 3:20-21; Col 1:17; 2Th 1:9; 1Ti 6:16; Heb 1:3; 7:25; 2Pe 1:16; Rev 1:8; 3:7; 5:12).

Omnipresence of:
(Mt 18:20; 28:20; Jn 3:13; Eph 1:23).

Omniscience of:
(Col 2:3; Rev 2:18, 23; 5:5, 12). Manifested in his knowledge, of the Father (Mt 11:27; Jn 7:29). Knowledge of human hearts (Mt 9:4; 12:25; 17:27; 22:18; Mk 2:8; Lk 5:22; 6:8; 9:46-48; 11:17; 22:10-12 w Mk 14:13-15; Jn 1:48; 2:24-25; 4:16-19, 28-29; 5:42; 6:64; 13:11; 21:17). Knowledge of future events (Mt 24:25; Jn 13:1, 3, 10; 16:30, 32; 18:4; 21:6). The coin in the fish's mouth (Mt 17:27), the presence of schools of fish (Lk 5:4-7; Jn 21:6).

Our example:
(Jn 10:4; Heb 3:1-2; 1Jn 2:6; Rev 14:4). In meekness (Mt 11:29; Heb 12:2-4; 1Pe 2:21-24). Humility (Lk 22:26-27; Jn 13:13-15, 34; 2Co 10:1; Php 2:5-8). Ministering (Mt 20:28; Mk 10:43-45; 2Co 8:9, w 8:5-11; Gal 6:2). Loving others (Jn 13:34; Eph 5:2). Character (Ro 8:29; 15:2-3, 5, 7; 1Pe 1:15-16; 1Jn 3:1-3, 16; 4:17). Enduring suffering (1Pe 3:17-18).

Parables of:
The wise and foolish builders (Mt 7:24-27; Lk 6:47, 49). Two debtors (Lk 7:41-47).
The rich fool (Lk 12:16-21).
The servants waiting for their lord (Lk 12:35-40).
Barren fig tree (Lk 13:6-9).
The sower (Mt 13:3-9, 18-23; Mk 4:1-9, 14-20; Lk 8:5-8, 11-15).
The weeds (Mt 13:24-30, 36-43).
Seed growing secretly (Mk 4:26-29).
Mustard seed (Mt 13:31-32; Mk 4:30-32; Lk 13:18-19).
Yeast (Mt 13:33; Lk 13:20-21).
Hid treasure (Mt 13:44).
Pearl of great price (Mt 13:45-46).
Fishing net (Mt 13:47-50).
Unmerciful servant (Mt 18:23-35).
Good Samaritan (Lk 10:30-37).
Friend at midnight (Lk 11:5-8).
Good shepherd (Jn 10:1-16).
Great supper (Lk 14:15-24).
Lost sheep (Mt 18:12-14; Lk 15:3-7).
Lost piece of money (Lk 15:8-10).
The prodigal and his brother (Lk 15:11-32).
The unjust steward (Lk 16:19-31).
Rich man and Lazarus (Lk 16:19-31).
Importunate widow (Lk 18:1-8).
Pharisee and tax collector (Lk 18:9-14).
Laborers in the vineyard (Mt 20:1-16).
The pounds (Lk 19:11-27).
The two sons (Mt 21:28-32).
Wicked farmers (Mt 21:33-44; Mk 12:1-12; Lk 20:9-18).
Marriage of the king's son (Mt 22:1-14).
Fig tree in leaf (Mt 24:32; Mk 13:28-29).
Man taking a far journey (Mt 13:34-37).
Ten virgins (Mt 25:1-13).
Talents (Mt 25:14-30).
The vine (Jn 15:1-5).

Passion of: *See below, Sufferings of.*

Possibility of Sinning: *See below, Temptation of.*

Perfections of:
(Col 2:3). Is the image of God (2Co 4:4; Col 1:15). All the fullness of the Father lived in him (Col 1:19; 2:9). Righteous (Isa 11:5; Jn 7:18; 2Co 1:19). Without deceit (Isa 53:9). Sinless (Mt 27:3-4; Ac 13:28; 2Co 5:21). Faithful (2Th 3:3; 2Ti 2:13; Heb 3:2). Full of grace and truth (Jn 1:14, 18; Col 2:3). Just in judgment (Jn 5:30).

Perfected through sufferings (Heb 2:10). Perfections of typified (Lev 24:17-21).

Persecutions of: *See Persecution.*

Popularity of:
(Mt 4:24; 8:1; 13:2; 14:13, 35; 19:1-2; 21:8-11; Mk 1:33; 2:2; 3:7, 20; 6:33, 55-56; 10:1; 11:8-10; 12:37; Lk 4:14-15, 42; 5:1; 9:11; 12:1; 19:35-38; Jn 6:15; 12:12-13, 19).

Power of:
(Ps 110:3; 1Co 1:24). Called Mighty God (Isa 9:6). Has all power (Mt 28:18; Jn 10:17-18, 28; 17:2; Php 3:20-21; 2Th 1:9; 1Ti 6:16; 2Pe 1:16; Rev 3:7; 5:12).

Manifested: In creation (Jn 1:3, 10; Col 1:16). Salvation of men (Heb 7:25). Upholding all things (Col 1:17; Heb 1:3). In forgiving sins (Mt 9:2, 6; Mk 2:5, 10; Lk 5:20, 24; Col 3:13). In healing diseases (Mt 8:3, 16; 9:6-7; 12:13; Mk 5:27-34; Lk 5:17; 6:19; Ac 10:38). Casting out demons (Mt 8:16; 12:28-29; Mk 3:27; Lk 11:20-22). Stilling the tempest (Mt 8:27). Giving the apostles power to heal (Mt 10:1; Mk 6:7; Lk 9:11). Resurrection (Jn 2:19; 10:17-18).

Prayers of:
(Mt 11:25-26; Lk 3:21; 11:1). In secret (Mt 14:23; Mk 1:35; 6:46; Lk 5:16; 6:12; 9:18, 28-29). At the grave of Lazarus (Jn 11:41-42). For Peter (Lk 22:32). For believers (Jn 17:1-26). In Gethsemane (Mt 26:36-39; Mk 14:32-35; Lk 22:42-44; Heb 5:7). On the cross (Mt 27:46; Lk 23:34, 46).

Preexistence of:
Was in the beginning (Jn 1:1-3; 1Jn 2:13-14; Rev 3:14). Came from heaven (Jn 3:13; 6:62; Php 2:5-7). Came from the Father (Jn 13:3; 16:28). Was before creation (Jn 17:5, 24; 2Ti 1:9; 1Jn 1:1-2; 1Pe 1:20). Maker of all things (Jn 1:3; Col 8:6; Col 1:15-17; Heb 1:1-2, 8-12; Rev 4:11). Was before Abraham (Jn 8:56-58). With the Israelites in the wilderness (1Co 10:4, 9; Jude 5).

Prescience of: *See above, Omniscience of.*

Priesthood of:
Appointed and called by God (Heb 3:1-2; 5:4-5), after the order of Melchizedek (Ps 110:4; Heb 5:6; 6:20; 7:15-17), superior to Aaron and the Levitical priests (Heb 7:11, 16, 22; 8:1-2, 6). Consecrated with an oath (Heb 7:20-21). Has an unchangeable priesthood (Heb 7:23, 28). Is of unblemished purity (Heb 7:26, 28), faithful (Heb 3:2). Needed no sacrifice for himself (Heb 7:27).

Offered himself as a sacrifice (Heb 9:14, 26). His sacrifice superior to all others (Heb 9:13-14, 23). Offered sacrifice but once (Heb 7:27). Made reconciliation (Heb 2:17). Obtained redemption for us (Heb 9:12). Entered into heaven (Heb 4:14; 10:12).

Sympathizes with saints (Heb 2:18; 4:15). Intercedes (Heb 7:25; 9:24). Blesses (Ac 3:26). On his throne (Zec 6:13). Appointment of, an encouragement to steadfastness (Heb 4:14).

Typified: Melchizedek (Ge 14:18-20). Aaron and his sons (Ex 40:12-15).

Promises of, to his disciples:
Of everlasting life (Mt 19:28; Mk 10:29-30; Lk 18:29-30; 23:43; Jn 5:25-29; 6:54, 57-58; 12:25-26). Of power (Lk 24:49; Jn 7:38-39; Ac 1:4-8). Of the Counselor (Jn 14:16, 26; 15:26-27; 16:7-14). Of his mediatorship (Jn 16:23-24, 26).

Prophecies Concerning:
(Ge 18:18; 22:18; 26:4; 28:14; Isa 53:2-12; Mt 8:17; Gal 3:8, 16).

Described in Prophecy as—
The branch (Isa 11:1; Jer 23:5-6; 33:15; Zec 3:8; Ro 15:12). Capstone and Cornerstone (Ps 118:22; Isa 28:16). Banner for the peoples (Isa 11:10). Fountain for sin (Zec 13:1). King (Zec 9:9). Leader and commander (Isa 55:4-5). Light to the Gentiles (Isa 42:6-7; 49:6; 52:10, 15; Lk 2:31-32). Lord (Isa 40:3, 5; 35:2; Jer 31:34; Mal 3:1-3; Lk 3:4). God's chosen one (Isa 42:1). Priest (Ps 110:4). Prophet (Dt 18:15, 18; Ac 3:22-24). Redeemer (Isa 59:20). Ruler over Israel (Mic 5:2). Savior (Isa 62:10-11; Mt 1:21; Lk 1:31). Seed of woman (Ge 3:15). Shepherd (Isa 40:11; Eze 34:23). Son of man (Da 7:13-14).

Future Glory and Power—
(Rev 19:11-12, 15). To have universal dominion (Ps 72:5, 8-11, 17, 19; Isa 2:2-4; 9:6-7; 60:1-9; Da 2:35, 44; 7:18, 22, 27; Mic 4:1-4). To be King of kings (Ps 72:5, 8-11, 17, 19; Rev 1:5-7; 11:15; 12:10; 17:14; 19:16; 20:4, 6). To sit at right hand of God (Mk 14:62; 1Pe 3:22). To be judge (Jude 14-15; Rev 2:23; 6:16-17; 14:14-16).

Prophet:
(Dt 18:15, 18; Mt 21:11, 46; Lk 7:16; 13:33; 24:19; Jn 4:19; 6:14; 7:40; 9:17; Ac 3:22-23; 7:37). Foretold (Isa 52:7; Na 1:15). Anointed with the Holy Spirit (Isa 42:1; 61:1, w Lk 4:18; Jn 3:34). Reveals God (Mt 11:27; Jn 3:2, 13, 34; 17:6, 14, 26; Heb 1:1-2). Declared his doctrine to be that of the Father (Jn 8:26, 28; 12:49-50; 14:10, 24; 15:15; 17:8, 26). Foretold things to come (Mt 24:3-35; Lk 19:41-44). Faithful (Heb 4:43; Jn 17:8; Heb 3:2; Rev 1:5; 3:14). Abounded in wisdom (Lk 2:40, 47, 52; Col 2:3). Mighty in deed and word (Mt 13:54; Mk 1:27; Lk 4:32; Jn 7:46). Humble in his teaching (Mt 12:17-20). God commands us to hear (Dt 18:15; Ac 3:22). God will severely visit neglect of (Dt 18:15, 18-19; Ac 3:23; Heb 2:3).

Received:
Crowds attend his ministry (Mt 8:1; 13:2; 14:13, 35; 19:1-2; Mk 1:37, 45; 2:2, 15; 3:7, 20-21; 4:1; 5:21; 10:1; 11:18; 12:37; Lk 9:11; 12:1; 19:48; 21:38; Jn 6:2; 8:2).

Many believe on him (Mt 4:24; 21:8-11, 15; Jn 6:2; 6:55-56; 11:8-10; Lk 6:17-19; 7:16-17; 19:36-38, 47-48; 23:27; Jn 2:11, 23; 4:45; 8:30; 10:41-42; 11:45-48; 12:9, 11-13, 18-21, 42).

Authority of his teaching confessed (Mt 1:22; Lk 4:32; Jn 3:2; 7:46).

With astonishment and gladness (Mt 9:8, 27-28, 33; 13:54; 15:31; Mk 1:27; 2:12; 5:42; 7:37; Lk 4:36-37, 42; 5:26; 13:17; 18:43; Jn 7:31, 40-44; 9:17, 24-25, 29-30, 33; 11:37).

Instances of his being received: By Matthew (Mt 9:9), by Peter and other fishermen (Mk 1:16-20; Lk 5:3-11), by Philip (Jn 1:43, 45), by Nathanael (Jn 1:45-50), by Zacchaeus (Lk 19:1-10), by thief on the cross (Lk 23:40-42), by three thousand at Pentecost (Ac 2:41; 4:4).

Redeemer: *See below, Savior. See Redemption.*

Rejected:
(Lk 9:26; 10:16; 11:23; Heb 6:4-6; 1Pe 2:4, 7-8; 1Jn 2:22-23; 4:3; 2Jn 7).

Rejected by the Jews (Mt 13:54-58 w Isa 6:9-10; Mt 23:37; Mk 6:3-6; Lk 7:34; 13:34; 19:27, 42; 22:67; Jn 1:11; 5:38, 40, 43; 7:3-5, 12-13, 15, 25-27; 8:13, 21-22, 24, 45-47, 53; 9:16-17, 24; 10:20-21, 24, 33; 11:46-48; 12:37, 48; Ac 13:46; 18:5-6; 22:18; 28:24-25, 27; Ro 3:3; 9:31-32; 10:16, 21; 1Co 1:8). By Gadarenes or Gerasenes (Mt 8:34; Mk 5:17; Lk 8:37). By Gentiles (1Co 1:23). By followers (Jn 6:36, 60-66).

Prophecies concerning his rejection (Ps 2:1-3; 118:22; Isa 53:1-4; Lk 9:44). Foretold by himself (Mt 11:16-19; Mk 9:12; Lk 4:23-29; 7:31-35; 17:25; Jn 15:18, 20, 24). In the parable of the house built on the sand (Mt 7:26; Lk 6:46-49).

Punishment for rejection, foretold (Mt 8:12; 10:14-15, 33; 12:38-45; Mk 12:1-12; 16:16; Lk 20:9-18; 2Ti 2:12; Heb 6:6; 10:29; 2Pe 2:1).

Relation of, to the Father:
(Ps 110:1; Mt 17:1; 1Th 5:18; Heb 2:9). Called God his Father (Jn 20:23; 26:39; Mk 13:32; Rev 2:27). With God in the beginning (Jn 1:1-2, 14). Was sent by God (Jn 3:34-35; 4:34; 6:27, 32-33, 38-40, 44-46; 7:16, 28-29, 33; 8:16, 19, 28-29, 38, 40, 42, 49, 54-55; 9:4; 11:41-42; 12:44, 49-50; 17:1-10, 24-26; 1Co 3:23). Endued with the Holy Spirit (Isa 42:1; 61:1; Mic 5:4; Ac 10:38).

Is the Son of God (Lk 5:19-26, 37, 45; Ro 8:32; 15:6; Heb 1:2-3; 5:5-10; 2Pe 1:17). Is one with the Father (Jn 10:18, 25, 30, 32-33, 36-38; 14:7, 9-14, 20, 24; 15:23-26). Is subject to the Father (Ps 110:1; Mk 10:40; Jn 20:17; Ac 2:22, 33, 36; 3:13, 26; 4:27; 1Co 15:24, 27-28). Is the image of God (2Co 4:4, 6; Php 2:6; Col 1:15, 19).

God raised him from the dead (Ac 13:37; Ro 1:4; Eph 1:17, 20-22; 1Pe 1:21). Ascended to the Father (Jn 24:51; Jn 16:5, 10, 28; Ac 1:9-11; Rev 3:12, 21).

See above, Deity of; Humanity of; Divine Sonship of.

Resurrection of:
Prophecies concerning (Ps 2:7; 16:9-10; Isa 55:3; Ac 13:13-34). Foretold by himself (Mt 12:40; 16:4, 21; 17:23; 20:19; 26:32; 27:52-53, 63; Mk 8:31; 9:9-10; 10:34; 14:58; Lk 9:22; 18:33; 24:7, 46; Jn 2:19, 21-22).

Certified by angels (Mt 28:6-7; Mk 16:6-7; Lk 24:5-7). Mary Magdalene (Mt 28:1-8; Mk 16:10; Lk 24:10; Jn 20:18). Clopas and his fellow disciple on the road to Emmaus (Mk 16:12-13; Lk

24:13-35). Luke (Ac 1:3, 22). Peter (Ac 2:24, 31-32 w Ps 16:9-10; Ac 3:15; 4:10, 33; 5:30-32; 10:40-41; 1Pe 1:3, 21; 3:18, 21). Paul (Ac 13:30-34 w Ps 2:7; Ac 17:2-3, 31; 26:23; 26:26; Ro 1:4; 4:24-25; 5:10; 6:4-5, 9-10; 8:11, 34; 1Co 6:14; 15:3-8, 12-19; 15:20-23; 2Co 4:10-11, 14; 5:15; 13:4; Gal 1:1; Eph 1:20; Php 3:10; Col 1:18; 2:12; 1Th 1:10; 4:14; 2Ti 2:8). The author of Hebrews (Heb 13:20). John (Rev 1:5, 18). Appeared to the eleven apostles after his resurrection (Mk 16:14; Lk 24:36-51; Jn 20:19-29).

Rose for our justification (Ro 4:25). Rose for our salvation (Ro 5:10; 10:9). An earnest of the general resurrection (1Co 6:14; 15:21-23; 2Co 4:14; 1Th 4:14; 1Pe 1:3). The theme of apostolic preaching (Ac 2:24, 31-32; 3:15; 4:10, 33; 5:30-32; 10:40-41; 17:2-3).

See Resurrection.

Reticence of:
(Isa 53:7; Mt 26:63; 27:12, 14; Mk 14:61; 15:4-5; Jn 19:9; 1Pe 2:23).

Revelation by:
Concerning his kingdom (Mt 8:11-12; 10:23, 34; 13:24-50; 16:18, 28; 21:43-44; 24:14; Mk 9:1; 16:17-18; Lk 9:27; 12:40-53; 13:24-35; 17:20-37; Jn 4:21, 23; 5:25-29; 6:39, 54; 12:35; 13:19; 14:29; 16:4). His rejection by the Jews (Mt 21:33-44; Lk 17:25). His crucifixion (Jn 3:14; 8:28; 12:32, w Lk 24:6-7). Judgments upon the Jews (Mt 23:37-39). The destruction of the temple, and Jerusalem (Mt 24; Mk 13; Lk 19:41-44). The destruction of Capernaum (Mt 11:23; Lk 10:15).

Concerning persecutions of Christians (Mt 23:34-36). His being forsaken by his disciples (Jn 16:32). Lazarus (Jn 11:4, 11, 23, 40). Peter (Jn 21:18-23). Fame of the woman who anointed his head (Mt 26:13; Mk 14:8-9). False Christs (Mt 24:4-5, 23-26; Mk 13:5-6, 21-23; Lk 17:23-24; 21:8). Things to come (Rev 1:1).

Concerning his death and resurrection (Mt 12:39-40; 16:21; 17:12, 22-23; 20:18-19; 21:33-39; 26:2, 18, 21, 23-24, 45-46; 27:63; Mk 8:31; 9:31; 10:32-34; Lk 9:22-24; 17:25; 18:31-33; 22:15, 37; Jn 2:19; 10:15, 17; 12:7, 23, 32; 13:18-27; 14:19; 16:20, 32). His ascension (Jn 7:33-34; 8:21; 13:33; 16:10, 16).

Righteousness of: *See above, Holiness of.*

Salvation by: *See Salvation.*

Savior:
(Mt 1:21; Ac 5:31; 13:23, 38-39, 47; 15:11; 16:31; 1Co 1:30; 15:57; Eph 5:23; Php 3:20; 1Ti 1:1, 15; 2Ti 1:9-10, 12; 2:10; 3:15; Tit 1:4; Heb 2:3; 5:9; 2Pe 1:11; 2:20; 1Jn 3:5; 4:9, 14; 5:11-13).

Savior through his death (Ro 3:25; 4:25; 5:1, 6, 8-10; Gal 1:4; 2:20; Eph 2:13-18, 20; 5:2, 25-26; Col 1:12-14; 1Th 1:10; 5:9-10; Tit 2:13-14; 1Pe 1:18-19; 3:18; 1Jn 4:10). Through his resurrection (Ac 3:26; Ro 10:9; 1Co 15:17; 1Pe 3:21).

Savior by his intercession (Heb 7:22, 25). By redemption (Ro 3:24). By reconciliation (Ro 5:15, 17-19, 21; 2Co 5:18-19, 21; Eph 2:7, 13-18, 20; Heb 2:17).

The only Savior (Ac 4:12; 1Co 3:11).

Prophecies concerning his Savior (Ps 72:4, 12-14, 17; Isa 42:6-7; 49:6, 8-9, 16-17; 59:20; 61:1-3; Zec 9:9; Mal 4:2; Lk 1:68-77; 4:18-19).

Illustrated: By parables of lost sheep and lost coin (Mt 18:12-13; Lk 15:1-10).

Testified to by angels (Lk 2:11). By Simeon (Lk 2:30-32). By himself (Mt 9:12-13; Lk 5:31-32; 19:10; Jn 5:33-34, 40; 6:27, 32-33, 35, 37, 39, 51, 53-58; 7:37-39; 8:12; 9:5, 39; 10:7, 9-11, 14-16, 27-28; 11:25-26; 12:47; 14:6; 17:2-3, 12). By John (Jn 1:29). By the people of Sychar (Jn 4:42). By the heavenly host (Rev 5:5-14).

See above, Death of; Purpose of His Death.

Second Coming:
(Mt 26:64; Jn 14:28-29; 21:22; Ac 1:11; 3:20-21; 1Co 11:26; Php 3:20-21; 1Th 1:10; 2:19; 3:13; 4:15-17; 2Th 2:1-5; 2:8; 1Ti 6:14-15; Tit 2:13; 2Pe 3:3-4).

At an unexpected time (Mt 24:3, 27, 30-31, 36-39, 42-44; 25:6, 10, 13, 19; Mk 13:13-37; Lk 12:37-40; 17:22-30; 21:5-35; 1Th 5:2-3, 23; 2Pe 3:8-14; Rev 16:15; 22:20).

Coming in heavenly glory (Mt 16:27; 25:31; Mk 8:38; 13:26-27; 14:62; Lk 9:26; 21:27).

Coming to judge the world (Mt 16:27; 25:31-46; Lk 19:12-13, 15; 1Co 1:7-8; 4:5; 2Th 1:7-10; 2Ti 4:1; Rev 22:12).

Coming to receive his saints (Jn 14:3; Lk 15:23; Col 3:4; 2Th 1:10; 2Ti 4:8; Heb 9:28; 1Pe 5:4; 1Jn 3:2).

Exhortations in view of his coming (Jas 5:7-9; 1Pe 1:7, 13; 4:13; 1Jn 2:28; Rev 3:11).

Shepherd:
Jesus the true shepherd: Foretold (Ge 49:24; Isa 40:11; Eze 34:23; 37:24). The chief (1Pe 5:4). The good (Jn 10:11, 14). The great (Mic 5:4; Heb 13:20).

His sheep he knows (Jn 10:14, 27). He calls (Jn 10:3). He gathers (Isa 40:11; Jn 10:16). He guides (Ps 23:3; Jn 10:3-4). He feeds (Ps 23:1-2; Jn 10:9). He cherishes tenderly (Isa 40:11). He protects and preserves (Jer 31:10; Eze 34:10; Zec 9:16; Jn 10:28). He laid down his life for (Zec 13:7; Mt 26:31; Jn 10:11, 15; Ac 20:28). He gives eternal life to (Jn 10:28).

Typified: David (1Sa 16:11).

Son of God:
Acclaimed by God (Ps 2:4 w Ac 13:13; Ps 89:26-27; Mt 3:17; 17:5; Mk 1:11; 9:7; Lk 3:22; 9:35; 2Pe 1:17).

Proclaimed by angels (Lk 1:32, 35; Rev 2:18).

Claimed by Christ (Mt 10:40; 11:27; 16:13; 18:10, 19; 20:23; 21:37; 26:53, 63-64; 27:43; Mk 14:61-62; Lk 10:22; 20:13; 22:29, 70; Jn 5:17-37; 6:27, 38, 40, 46, 57, 69; 7:17, 28-29; 8:16, 19, 26-29, 38-42, 49, 54; 9:35-37; 10:15-18, 29-30, 36-38; 11:4, 27, 41; 12:49-50; 14:7-13, 16, 20, 24, 28, 31; 15:23-24; 16:15). As equality with the Father (Mt 10:40; 11:27; Lk 10:22; Jn 1:1-2; 8:16, 19; 10:15-18, 29-30, 36-38; 14:7-13, 16, 20, 24, 28, 31; 15:23-24; 16:15).

Sonship recognized by the disciples (Mt 14:33; 16:15-17). By Peter (Mt 16:15-17). By the centurion (Mt 27:54; Mk 15:39). By Nathanael (Jn 1:49-50). By Martha (Jn 11:27). By Satan, who tempted him (Mt 4:3, 6; Lk 4:3, 9). By demons (Mk 3:11; 5:7; Lk 4:41; 8:28).

Claim to sonship recognized by the Jews (Mt 27:43; Jn 19:7). By the high priest (Mk 14:61-62).

Testified by Mark (Mk 1:1). By Luke (Ac 3:13). By John (Jn 1:1-2, 14, 18, 34; 3:16-18, 34-36; 13:3; 1Jn 1:7; 2:22-24; 3:8, 23; 4:9-10, 14; 5:5, 9-10, 13, 20; 2Jn 3). By Paul (Ro 1:3-4, 9; 8:3, 29, 32; 1Co 1:9; 15:24, 27-28; 2Co 1:3, 19; Gal 1:16; 4:4; Eph 1:3; 3:14; Col 1:3, 15, 19; 1:17; 1Th 1:10). In Hebrews (Heb 1:1-3, 5; 4:14; 5:5, 8; 6:6; 7:3; 10:29).

Belief in, basis of eternal life (Jn 1:1-2, 12; 3:16-18, 34-36; 6:40; 20:31; 1Jn 2:22-24; 3:23; 5:5, 9-10, 13, 20), for growth and purity (Jn 15:1, 8-10; 1Jn 1:7).

Denial of, basis of antichrist (1Jn 2:22-24).

See above, Deity of; Relation of, to the Father. See Son of God.

Son of Man:
Used in a messianic sense (Da 7:13-14).

Used by Jesus: Of himself (Mt 11:19, 27; 16:13; Mk 14:21, 41; Lk 6:22; 7:34; 18:31; Jn 1:51; 3:13). In a messianic sense, of his coming (Mt 10:23; 16:27-28; 24:27, 30, 37, 44; 25:13, 31; Mk 13:26; Lk 9:26; 12:40; 17:22, 24, 26, 30; 18:8; 21:27), his kingdom (Mt 16:28; 19:28; Mk 8:38; 14:62), his judgment (Mt 24:29-30; Mk 8:38; Lk 9:26; 12:8-10; 21:36), his lordship or deity (Mt 12:8; 13:37, 41; 16:13, w 16:16, 27-28; 19:28; 24:27; Mk 2:28; Lk 6:5; 12:8, 10; 17:22, 24; 21:36; 22:69; Jn 12:23; 13:31), his suffering and death (Mt 12:40; 17:9, 12, 22; 20:18, 28; 26:2, 24-25; Mk 8:31; 9:9, 12, 31; 10:33-34, 45; 14:21, 41; Lk 9:22, 44; 11:30; 17:22-26; 18:31; 22:22, 48; 24:7; Jn 3:14; 8:28; 12:23; 13:31), his resurrection (Mt 12:40; 17:9, 22-23; 20:18-19; Mk 8:31; 9:9, 31; 10:33-34; Jn 6:62; 12:23; 13:31).

Of himself, as the supreme human (Mt 8:20; 12:32), a servant of mankind (Mt 20:28; Mk 10:45; Lk 9:56, 58), the forgiver of sins (Mt 9:6; Mk 2:10; Lk 5:24; 12:10), the Redeemer (Mt 18:11; 20:28; Lk 19:10; 6:27, 53).

Used by the angel at the empty tomb, in quoting Christ (Lk 24:7); Stephen, in his vision of Jesus (Ac 7:56); John, in his vision of Jesus (Rev 1:13; 14:14).

Synonymous with *Christ*, as used by, Caiaphas the high priest (Mt 26:63, w 26:65; Mk 14:61-62), the religious leaders (Lk 22:70, w 22:66-71, & 23:35), the people in questioning him (Jn 12:34).

The title is a reference to the human nature of Jesus, designating him as the God-Man (Mt 8:20; 12:32).

See Son of Man.

Sovereignty of: *See above, King; Lordship of.*

Sufferings of:
Foretold: By the psalmist (Ps 22:6-8, 11-13, 17-21, w Mt 27:35 & Mk 15:24 & Lk 23:34 & Jn 19:23-24; Ps 69:7-9, 20), by prophets (Isa 50:6; 52:13-14; 53:1-12, w Mt 26:67 & 27:26 & Lk 22:37 & Jn 12:38; Mic 5:1; Zec 11:12-13; Lk 24:26, 46; 1Pe 1:11), by himself (Mt 16:21; 17:12, 22-23; 20:17-19; Mk 8:31; 9:12; 10:32-34; Lk 9:22; 18:31-33; Jn 3:14; 13:21).

In Gethsemane (Mt 26:38-45; Mk 14:34-39; Lk 22:42-44; Jn 18:11). In Pilate's judgment hall (Mt 27:24-30; Mk 15:15-20; Jn 19:16-18). At his crucifixion (Mt 27:31-50; Mk 15:34, 36; Lk 23:33-46; Jn 19:28).

Apostolic teaching concerning his suffering (Ac 3:18; 17:3; 2Co 1:5; Php 2:8; 3:10; Heb 2:9; 4:15; 5:7-8; 12:2-3; 1Pe 1:11; 2:21-23; 3:18; 4:1, 13; Rev 5:6; 19:13).

See above, Death of.

Sympathy of: *See above, Compassion of, Love of.*

Teacher:
(Mt 5:1-2; Jn 7:46; Ac 1:1). From God (Jn 3:2).

Taught with authority (Mt 7:29; 23:8; Mk 1:22). Without respect of persons (Mt 22:16; Mk 12:14; Lk 20:21). By the lake shore (Mk 4:1). In cities and villages (Mt 11:1; Mk 6:6; Lk 23:5). In synagogues (Mt 4:23; Mk 1:21; Lk 4:15; 6:6). In the temple (Mt 21:23; 26:55; Mk 12:35; Lk 21:37; Jn 8:2). In the wilderness (Mk 6:34).

Temptation of:
(Lk 22:28). By the devil (Mt 4:1-11; Mk 1:12-13; Lk 4:1-13). In all points as we are (Heb 4:15).

Typified:
In offerings (Ge 4:4; 8:20; 22:13; Ex 12:5-7; 24:5; 29:36-37; Lev 1:4, 10-12; 3:6, 12; 4:3-7, 14-18, 20, 23-25, 28-30, 32-34; 5:6-11, 16, 18; 6:6-7; 7:2; 8:14-15, 18-19, 22-24; 9:2, 7-9, 18; 12:6-8; 14:12-14, 25, 30-31; 15:15, 29-30; 16:3, 5, 9, 11, 14-16, 21-22; 19:21-22; 22:18-19; 23:12, 18-19, 27-28; Nu 6:10-11, 14, 16-17; 8:8, 12; 15:24-25, 27; 28:3-4, 9, 11, 15, 19, 22-23, 27, 30; 29:5, 8, 11, 13, 16-34, 38; 1Ch 29:21; 2Ch 7:5; 29:21-24; Ezr 6:17, 20; 8:35; Eze 43:18-27; 45:15, 18-23).

In the Passover (Ex 12:3, 5; Nu 28:16). In the cornerstone (Isa 28:16; Mk 12:10-11).

In David (Eze 34:23-24; 37:24-25; Hos 3:5). Solomon (Ps 72). Hezekiah (Isa 32:1).

Unchangeable: (Heb 13:8).

Union of, With the Righteous: *See Righteous, Union of, with Christ.*

Wisdom of:
(Mk 6:2; Lk 2:40, 46-47, 52; Jn 7:15). *See above, Omniscience.*

Worship of:
(1Co 1:2; 2Co 12:8-9; Php 2:10-11). John's vision of (Rev 5:8-9, 12-14; 7:10).

Worship commanded (Jn 5:23; Heb 1:6).

Instances of: By the wise men (Mt 2:2). By the disciples (Mt 14:33). By the Canaanite woman (Mt 15:25). By a leper (Mt 8:2). By women after his resurrection (Mt 28:9). By the eleven disciples after his resurrection (Mt 28:17; Lk 24:52). By the multitudes (Mk 11:9-10 w Mt 21:9). By Simon Peter (Lk 5:8). By the blind man whom Jesus healed (Jn 9:38). By evil spirits (Mk 3:11). By a demon-possessed man (Mk 5:6-7). By Stephen (Ac 7:59-60). By Paul (1Ti 1:12; 2Pe 3:18).

Zeal of:
For God's house (Lk 2:49; Jn 2:17; Ps 69:9). In obedience to God (Jn 4:32, 34; 9:4; Ro 15:3). In doing good (Ac 10:38). In preaching the gospel (Mt 4:23; 9:35; Mk 6:6; Lk 4:43 w Mk 1:38; 8:1). In giving himself as a sacrifice (Lk 9:51; 12:50; 13:32-33; 1Ti 6:13).

JESUS, JUSTUS *See Justus, 3.*

JETHER (*abundance*).
1. Jethro is the father-in-law of Moses (Ex 4:18).
2. Gideon's eldest son (Jdg 8:20-21).
3. Father of Amasa (2Sa 17:25; 1Ch 2:17).
4. Judahite (1Ch 2:32).
5. Judahite (1Ch 4:17).
6. Asherite, same as Ithran (1Ch 7:37, w 7:38).

JETHETH Edomite chieftain (Ge 36:40; 1Ch 1:51).

JETHLAH *See Ithlah.*

JETHRO (*remainder* KB). A priest of Midian and father-in-law of Moses (Ex 3:1), personal name probably Reuel (Ex 2:18; 3:1), father of Zipporah, whom Moses married (Ex 3:1-2), advised Moses (Ex 18:14-24).

JETUR Son of Ishmael and descendants (Ge 25:15; 1Ch 1:31), Itureans of NT times.

JEUEL (*God [El] has preserved*).
1. Judahite (1Ch 9:6).
2. Levite (2Ch 29:13).
3. Leader in Ezra's company (Ezr 8:13).

JEUSH (perhaps *may God aid*).
1. Son of Esau (Ge 36:5).
2. Benjamite (1Ch 7:10).
3. Gershonite Levite (1Ch 23:10-11).
4. Descendant of Jonathan (1Ch 8:39).
5. Son of Rehoboam (2Ch 11:19).

JEUZ (*he comes to help* BDB; possibly *encouraged* IDB). Head of a Benjamite family (1Ch 8:10).

JEWEL, JEWELRY Articles of jewelry in OT times: diadems, bracelets, necklaces, anklets, rings for fingers, gold nets for hair, pendants, amulets and pendants with magical meanings, jeweled perfume and ointment boxes, crescents for camels; used for personal adornment and utility and for religious festivals. Not much said about jewelry in NT; most condemnatory (1Ti 2:9; Jas 2:2). The New Jerusalem is adorned with jewels (Rev 21:19).

See Minerals of the Bible, 1; Stones.

JEWS (*from Judah*). A corrupted form of Judah, and applied to the people of the kingdom of Judah and Benjamin (2Ki 16:6; 25:25; 2Ch 32:18). After the dissolution of the kingdom of Israel, the name was applied to all Israelites as well as to those of the two tribes (Mt 27:11; Ac 2:5).

Sins attached to the Captivity (Isa 1:4-25; 2:6-10; 3:9; 59:2-15; 65:2-7; Jer 5:1; 6:21-28; 44:1-3; Eze 5:6; 12:2; 16:2, 15-47, 57-63). See the book of Jeremiah, which deals chiefly with the sins of and the corrective judgments of God to be inflicted upon.

Captive in Babylon (2Ki 24:1-20; 25:1, 21). Haman's plot against (Est 3:6-15). Feast of Purim instituted to commemorate their deliverance from Haman's plot (Est 9:26-32).

The proclamation of Cyrus authorizing their return to the land of Canaan (2Ch 36:22-23; Ezr 1:2-4), and of Artaxerxes (Ezr 7:11-26).

After the Captivity:
Return from Babylon (Ezr 7:1-9; 8:31-32). Lists of those who returned from Babylon (Ezr 2:1-67; 8:1-20; Ne 7:6-69; 12:1-21). Rebuild the temple (Ezr 3:8-13). Rebuilding suspended during the reign of Artaxerxes (Ezr 4:1-24). Resumption of the rebuilding interfered with by Tattenai, governor of the province, by protest followed by a letter to Darius (Ezr 5). Darius' reply to Tattenai authorizing the rebuilding of the temple; temple completed (Ezr 6:1-15).

Vessels of the temple, that were taken to Babylon by Nebuchadnezzar, returned by command of Cyrus (Ezr 1:7-11; 6:5). Liberality of Artaxerxes toward the temple (Ezr 7:14-23). Made marriages among the Canaanites: Ezra instituted reforms (Ezr 10). Rebuilt the walls of Jerusalem under proclamation of Artaxerxes (Ne 2; 3; 4; 5; 6). Walls dedicated (Ne 12:27-43). Mission of Jesus to (Mt 10:5-6; 15:24; Mk 7:27). Some accept Jesus (Jn 2:23; 10:42; 11:45; 12:11; Ac 21:20). Others disbelieve in Jesus (Mt 13:5-8; Jn 5:38, 40, 43; 6:36; 12:37). Reject Jesus (Lk 13:34; 17:25; Jn 1:11). See *Crucifixion.* Devout, among them (Ac 2:5). Spurned Paul's preaching (Ac 13:46; 18:5-6; 28:24-27). Persecuted Paul (Ac 9:22-23; 13:50; 20:3, 19; 23:12-30; 2Co 11:24). Entrusted with the oracles of God (Ac 7:38; Ro 3:1-2).

Prophecies Concerning:
Their rejection of the Messiah (Isa 49:5, 7; 52:14; 53:1-3; Zec 13; Mt 21:33-39; 22:1-5).

War and other judgments (Isa 3; 4:1; 5; 6:9-13; 7:17-25; 8:14-22; 10:12; 22:1-14; 28:14-22; 29:1-10; 30:1-17; 31:1-3; 32:9-14; Jer 1:11-16; 4:5-31; 6; 7:8-34; 8; 9:9-26; 10:17-22; 11:9-23; 13:9-27; 14:14-18; 15:1-14; 16; 17:1-4; 18:15-17; 19; 20:5; 21:4-7; 22:24-30; 25:8-38; 28; 34; 37; 38:1-3; 42:13-22; 43-45; La 5:6; Eze 4; 5; 11:7-12; 12; 15-17; 19; 22:13-22; 23:22-35; 24; 33:21-29; Da 9:26-27; Joel 2:1-11; Am 2:4-5; Mic 3; 4:8-10; Hab 1:6-11; Zep 1; Zec 14:1-3; Mal 4:1; Mt 21:33-45; 23:35-38; 24:2, 14-42; Mk 13:1-13; Lk 13:34-35; 19:43-44; 21:5-25; 23:28-31; Rev 1:7).

Dispersion (Isa 24:1; Jer 9:16; Hos 9:17; Joel 3:6, 20; Am 9:9; Eze 4:13; 5:10, 12; 20:23; 36:19; Da 9:7).

Blessing and restoration of (Isa 1:25-27; 2:1-5; 4:2-6; 11:11-13; 25; 26:1-2, 12-19; 27:13; 29:18-24; 30:18-26; 32:15-20; 33:13-24; 35; 37:31-32; 40:2, 9; 41:27; 44; 49:13-23; 51; 52:1-12; 60; 61:4-9; 62; 66:5-22; Jer 3:14-18; 4:3-18; Joel 3; Am 9:9-15; Ob 17-21; Mic 2:12-13; 5:3; Zep 2:7; Zec 1:14-21; 2; 8; 10:5-12; 12:1-14; 13; 14:3-21; Mal 3:4; Ro 11).

See Israel, Israelites; Judah.

JEZANIAH (*Yahweh gives ear*). Also known as Azariah (Jer 42:1, ftn), as was King Uzziah (2Ki 14:21, ftn; 2Ch 26:1, ftn). *See also, Jaazaniah, 1.*

JEZEBEL (possibly *unexalted, unhusbanded* BDB). Daughter of Ethbaal, a Sidonian, and wife of Ahab (1Ki 16:31). Worshiped idols and persecuted the prophets of God (1Ki 18:4, 13, 19; 2Ki 3:2, 13; 9:7, 22). Vowed to kill Elijah (1Ki 19:1-3). Wickedly accomplishes the death of Naboth (1Ki 21:5-16). Death of, foretold (1Ki 21:23; 2Ki 9:10). Death of, at the hand of Jehu (2Ki 9:30-37).
Figurative (Rev 2:20).

JEZER, JEZERITE (*formed, fashioned*). Son of Naphtali (Ge 46:24; Nu 26:49; 1Ch 7:13).

JEZIAH *See Izziah.*

JEZIEL A disaffected Israelite who joined David at Ziklag (1Ch 12:3).

JEZLIAH *See Izliah.*

JEZOAR *See Zohar, 3.*

JEZRAHIAH (*Yahweh will arise* or *shine*).
1. Descendant of Issachar called Izrahiah (1Ch 7:3).
2. Musician (Ne 12:42).

JEZREEL, JEZREELITE (*God [El] will sow* or *scatter*).
1. A city in the S of Judah (Jos 15:56; 1Sa 25:43; 27:3; 29:1, 11).
2. A city of Issachar (Jos 19:18; 2Sa 2:9). Ahab's residence in (1Ki 18:45-46; 21:1). Naboth's vineyard in (1Ki 21:1). Joram's residence in (2Ki 8:29). Jehu kills King Ahab, his wife, and friends at (2Ki 9:15-37; 10:11). Prophecies concerning (Hos 1:4-5, 11).
3. A valley (Jos 17:16). Place of Gideon's battle with the Midianites (Jdg 6:33). Place of the defeat of the Israelites under Saul and Jonathan (1Sa 29:1, 11; 31:1-6; 2Sa 4:4).
4. A descendant of Etam (1Ch 4:3).
5. Figurative of Israel (Hos 1:4-5, 11).

JIBSAM *See Ibsam.*

JIDLAPH (*he weeps*). Son of Nahor (Ge 22:22).

JIMNA, JIMNAH *See Imnah.*

JIPHTAH *See Iphtah.*

JIPHTHAH-EL *See Iphtah El.*

JOAB (*Yahweh is father*).
1. Son of David's sister (1Ch 2:16). Commander of David's army (2Sa 8:16; 20:23; 1Ch 11:6; 18:15; 27:34). Dedicated spoils of his battles (1Ch 26:28). Defeated the Jebusites (1Ch 11:6). Defeats and slays Abner (2Sa 2:13-32; 3:27; 1Ki 2:5). Destroys all the males in Edom (1Ki 11:16). *See Psalm 60, title.* Defeats the Ammonites (2Sa 10:7-14; 1Ch 19:6-15). Captures Rabbah (2Sa 11:1, 15-25; 12:26-29; 1Ch 20:1-2).
Secures the return of Absalom to Jerusalem (2Sa 14:1-24). Barley field of, burned by Absalom (2Sa 18). Rebukes David for lamenting the death of Absalom (2Sa 19:1-8). Replaced by Amasa as commander of David's army (2Sa 17:25; 19:13). Kills Amasa (2Sa 20:8-13; 1Ki 2:5). Causes Sheba to be put to death (2Sa 20:16-22). Opposes the numbering of the people (2Sa 24:3; 1Ch 21:3). Numbers the people (2Sa 24:4-9; 1Ch 21:4-5; 27:23-24). Supports Adonijah as successor to David (1Ki 1:7; 2:28). Slain by Benaiah, under Solomon's order (1Ki 2:29-34).
2. A grandson of Kenaz (1Ch 4:14).
3. An Israelite (or the name of two Israelites) whose descendants returned from Babylon to Jerusalem (Ezr 2:6; 8:9; Ne 7:11).
4. "House of Joab" (1Ch 2:54). Probably identical with 1. *See Atroth Beth Joab.*

JOAH (*Yahweh is brother*).
1. Son of Asaph (2Ki 18:18, 26; Isa 36:3, 11, 22).
2. A descendant of Gershom (1Ch 6:21; 2Ch 29:12).
3. A son of Obed-Edom (1Ch 26:4).
4. A Levite, who repaired the temple (2Ch 34:8).

JOAHAZ (*Yahweh grips*). Father of Joah, recorder of King Josiah (2Ch 34:8).

JOANAN An ancestor of Jesus (Lk 3:27).

JOANNA (probably feminine form of *John*). Wife of Cuza, the steward of Herod Agrippa, and a disciple of Jesus (Lk 8:3; 24:10).

JOASH (*Yahweh has bestowed*).
1. Son of Beker (1Ch 7:8).
2. Keeper of the stores of oil (1Ch 27:28).
3. Father of Gideon (Jdg 6:11, 29, 31; 7:14; 8:13, 29-32).
4. Son of Ahab, king of Israel (1Ki 22:26; 2Ch 18:25).
5. Also called Jehoash, Joash. Son of Ahaziah and king of Judah. Saved from his grandmother by Jehosheba, his aunt, and hidden for six years (2Ki 11:1-3; 2Ch 22:11-12). Anointed king by the priest, Jehoiada (2Ki 11:12-21; 2Ch 23:1-21). Righteousness of, under influence of Jehoiada (2Ki 12:2; 2Ch 24:2). Repaired the temple (2Ki 12:4-16; 2Ch 24:4-14, 27). Wickedness of, after Jehoiada's death (2Ch 24:17-22). Secured peace from Hazael, king of Syria, by gift of dedicated treasures from the temple (2Ki 12:17-18; 2Ch 24:23-24). Prophecy against (2Ch 24:19-20). Put Jehoiada's son to death (2Ch 24:20-22; Mt 23:35). Diseases of (2Ch 24:25). Conspired against and slain (2Ki 12:20-21; 2Ch 24:25-26).
6. A king of Israel. *See Jehoash, Joash.*
7. A descendant of Shelah (1Ch 4:22).
8. One of David's officers (1Ch 12:3).

JOATHAM *See Jotham, 3.*

JOB (*where is my father,* or perhaps *where is my father, O God?*).
1. A man who lived in Uz (Job 1:1). Righteousness of (Job 1:1, 5, 8; 2:3; Eze 14:14, 20). Riches of (Job 1:3). Trial of, by affliction of Satan (Job 1:13-19; 2:7-10). Fortitude of (Job 1:20-22; 2:10; Jas 5:11). Visited by Eliphaz, Bildad, and Zophar as comforters (Job 2:11-13). Complaints of, and replies by his three friends (Job 3-37). Replied to by God (Job 38-41). Submission of, to God (Job 40:3-5; 42:1-6). Later blessings and riches of (Job 42:10-16). Death of (Job 42:16-17).
2. *See Jashub.*

JOB, BOOK OF

Author: Anonymous

Date: Anytime from the reign of Solomon to the Exile.

Outline:
I. Prologue (chs. 1-2).
 A. Job's Happiness (1:1-5).
 B. Job's Testing (1:6-2:13).
 1. Satan's first accusation (1:6-12).
 2. Job's faith despite loss of family and property (1:13-22).
 3. Satan's second accusation (2:1-6).
 4. Job's faith during personal sufferings (2:7-10).
 5. The coming of the three friends (2:11-13).
II. Dialogue-Dispute (chs. 3-27).
 A. Job's Opening Lament (ch. 3).
 B. First Cycle of Speeches (chs. 4-14).
 1. Eliphaz (chs. 4-5).
 2. Job's reply (chs. 6-7).
 3. Bildad (ch. 8).
 4. Job's reply (chs. 9-10).
 5. Zophar (ch. 11).
 6. Job's reply (chs. 12-14).
 C. Second Cycle of Speeches (chs. 15-21).
 1. Eliphaz (ch. 15).
 2. Job's reply (chs. 16-17).
 3. Bildad (ch. 18).
 4. Job's reply (ch. 19).
 5. Zophar (ch. 20).
 6. Job's reply (ch. 21).
 D. Third Cycle of Speeches (chs. 22-26).
 1. Eliphaz (ch. 22).
 2. Job's reply (chs. 23-24).
 3. Bildad (ch. 25).
 4. Job's reply (ch. 26).
 E. Job's Closing Discourse (ch. 27).
III. Interlude on Wisdom (ch. 28).
IV. Monologues (29:1-42:6).
 A. Job's Call for Vindication (chs. 29-31).
 1. His past honor and blessing (ch. 29).
 2. His present dishonor and suffering (ch. 30).
 3. His protestations of innocence and final oath (ch. 31).
 B. Elihu's Speeches (chs. 32-37).
 1. Introduction (32:1-5).
 2. The speeches themselves (32:6-37:24).
 a. First speech (32:6-33:33).
 b. Second speech (ch. 34).
 c. Third speech (ch. 35).
 d. Fourth speech (chs. 36-37).
 C. Divine Discourses (38:1-42:6).
 1. God's first discourse (38:1-40:2).
 2. Job's response (40:3-5).
 3. God's second discourse (40:6-41:34).
 4. Job's repentance (42:1-6).
V. Epilogue (42:7-17).
 A. God's Verdict (42:7-9).
 B. Job's Restoration (42:10-17).

JOBAB (*howl*).
1. Son of Joktan (Ge 10:29; 1Ch 1:23).
2. Second king of Edom (Ge 36:33; 1Ch 1:44-45).
3. King of Madon (Jos 11:1; 12:19).
4. Benjamite (1Ch 8:9).
5. Benjamite (1Ch 9:18).

JOCHEBED (*Yahweh is glorious*). Mother of Miriam, Aaron, and Moses (Ex 6:20; Nu 26:59). Nurses Moses when he is adopted by Pharaoh's daughter (Ex 2:1-9).

JODA An ancestor of Joseph, the father (so it was thought) of Jesus (Lk 3:26).

JOED (*Yahweh is witness*). A Benjamite (Ne 11:7).

JOEL (*Yahweh is God [El]*).
1. Son of Samuel (1Sa 8:2; 1Ch 6:33; 15:17).
2. A Simeonite (1Ch 4:35).
3. A Reubenite (1Ch 5:4, 8).
4. A Gadite (1Ch 5:12).
5. A Kohathite Levite (1Ch 6:36).
6. Descendant of Issachar (1Ch 7:3).
7. One of David's valiant men (1Ch 11:38). Called "Igal son of Nathan" (2Sa 23:36).
8. Name of two Gershonites (1Ch 15:7, 11; 23:8; 26:22).
9. Prince of Manasseh (1Ch 27:20).
10. A Kohathite who assisted in the cleansing of the temple (2Ch 29:12).
11. One of Nebo's family (Ezr 10:43).
12. Son of Zicri (Ne 11:9).
13. One of the twelve minor prophets, probably lived in the days of Uzziah (Joel 1:1; Ac 2:16).

JOEL, BOOK OF

Author: Joel

Date: As early as the ninth century B.C. to as late as the postexilic period (sixth century), after Haggai and Zechariah. In either case, its message is not significantly affected by its dating.

Outline:
I. Title (1:1).
II. Judah Experiences a Foretaste of the Day of the Lord (1:2-2:17).
 A. A Call to Mourning and Prayer (1:2-14).
 B. The Announcement of the Day of the Lord (1:15-2:11).
 C. A Call to Repentance and Prayer (2:12-17).
III. Judah Is Assured of Salvation in the Day of the Lord (2:18-3:21).
 A. The Lord's Restoration of Judah (2:18-27).
 B. The Lord's Renewal of His People (2:28-32).
 C. The Coming of the Day of the Lord (ch. 3).
 1. The nations judged (3:1-16).
 2. God's people blessed (3:17-21).
 See Prophets, The Minor.

JOELAH (*let him help*). One of David's recruits at Ziklag (1Ch 12:7).

JOEZER (*Yahweh is help*). A Korahite, who joined David at Ziklag (1Ch 12:6).

JOGBEHAH (*height*). City in Gilead assigned to Gad (Nu 32:35; Jdg 8:11).

JOGLI (perhaps *may God reveal*). A prince of Dan (Nu 34:22).

JOHA
1. A Benjamite (1Ch 8:16).
2. One of David's valiant men (1Ch 11:45).

JOHANAN (*Yahweh is gracious*).
1. Jewish leader who tried to save Gedaliah from plot to murder him (Jer 40:13-14), took Jews, including Jeremiah, to Egypt (Jer 40:43).
2. Son of King Josiah (1Ch 3:15).
3. Son of Elioenai (1Ch 3:24).
4. Father of Azariah, high priest in Solomon's time (1Ch 6:9-10).
5. Benjamite; joined David at Ziklag (1Ch 12:4).
6. Gadite; warrior in David's army (1Ch 28:12).
7. Ephraimite chief (2Ch 28:12).
8. Exile who left Babylon with Ezra (Ezr 8:12).
9. Son of Tobiah, who married a Jewess in days of Nehemiah (Ne 6:18).
10. Son of Eliashib (Ezr 10:6).
11. High priest, grandson of Eliashib (Ne 12:22).

JOHN (*Yahweh is gracious*).
1. John the Baptist. *See John the Baptist.*
2. The apostle, the son of Zebedee, and brother of James. *See John, the Apostle.*
3. John Mark. *See Mark.*
4. Father of Simon Peter (Jn 1:42; 21:15, 17).
5. Jewish religious dignitary who called Peter and John to account for their preaching about Jesus (Ac 4:6).
6. Father of Mattathias (1Mc 2:1).
7. Eldest son of Mattathias (1Mc 9:36).
8. Father of Eupolemus (2Mc 4:11).
9. John Hyrcanus, son of Simon (1Mc 13:53; 16:1).
10. Jewish envoy (2Mc 11:17).

JOHN, 1, 2 and 3

Author: The apostle John, son of Zebedee

Date: Between A.D. 85 and 95

Outline of 1 John:
I. Introduction: The Reality of the Incarnation (1:1-4).
II. The Christian Life as Fellowship With the Father and the Son (1:5-2:28).
 A. Ethical Tests of Fellowship (1:5-2:11).
 1. Moral likeness (1:5-7).
 2. Confession of sin (1:8-2:2).
 3. Obedience (2:3-6).
 4. Love for fellow believers (2:7-11).
 B. Two Digressions (2:12-17).
 C. Christological Test of Fellowship (2:18-28).
 1. Contrast: apostates versus believers (2:18-21).
 2. Person of Christ: the crux of the test (2:22-23).
 3. Persistent belief: key to continuing fellowship (2:24-28).
III. The Christian Life as Divine Sonship (2:29-4:6).
 A. Ethical Tests of Sonship (2:29-3:24).
 1. Righteousness (2:29-3:10a).
 2. Love (3:10b-24).
 B. Christological Tests of Sonship (4:1-6).
IV. The Christian Life as an Integration of the Ethical and the Christological (4:7-5:12).
 A. The Ethical Test: Love (4:7-5:5).
 1. The source of love (4:7-16).
 2. The fruit of love (4:17-19).
 3. The relationship of love for God and love for one's spiritual brother (4:20-5:1).
 4. Obedience: the evidence of love for God's children (5:2-5).
 B. The Christological Test (5:6-12).
V. Conclusion: Great Christian Certainties (5:13-21).
 See General Letters.

Outline of 2 John:
I. Salutation (1-3).
II. Commendation (4).
III. Exhortation and Warning (5-11).
IV. Conclusion (12-13).
 See General Letters.

Outline of 3 John:
I. Salutation (1-2).
II. Commendation of Gaius (3-8).
III. Condemnation of Diotrephes (9-10).
IV. Exhortation to Gaius (11).
V. Example of Demetrius (12).
VI. Conclusion (13-14).
 See General Letters.

JOHN MARK *See Mark, John.*

JOHN, THE APOSTLE Son of Zebedee and Salome, and brother of James (Mt 4:21; 27:56; Mk 15:40; Ac 12:1-2), lived in Galilee, probably in Bethsaida (Lk 5:10; Jn 1:44), fisherman (Mk 1:19-20), became disciple of Jesus through John the Baptist (Jn 1:35), called as an apostle (Mk 1:19-20; Lk 5:10), one of three apostles closest to Jesus (the others are Peter and James), at raising of Jairus' daughter (Mk 5:37; Lk 8:51), transfiguration (Mt 17:1; Mk 9:2; Lk 9:28), Gethsemane (Mt 26:37; Mk 14:33), asked Jesus to call fire down on Samaritans, and given name Boanerges (sons of thunder) (Mk 3:17; Lk 9:54), mother requested that John and James be given places of special honor in coming kingdom (Mk 10:35), helped Peter prepare Passover (Lk 22:8), lay close to Jesus' breast at Last Supper (Jn 13:25), present at trial of Jesus (Jn 18:15-16), witnessed crucifixion of Jesus (Jn 19:26-27), recognized Jesus at Sea of Galilee (Jn 21:1-7), active with Peter in apostolic church (Ac 3:1-4:22; 8:14-17). Lived to an old age; fourth Gospel, three letters and Revelation attributed to him. *See John, 1, 2 and 3; John, the Gospel of; Revelation.*

JOHN THE BAPTIST Forerunner of Jesus; son of Zechariah and Elizabeth, both of priestly descent (Lk 1:5-25, 56-58), lived as Nazirite in desert (Lk 1:15; Mt 11:12-14, 18), began ministry beyond Jordan in the fifteenth year of Tiberias Caesar (Lk 3:1-3), preached baptism of repentance in preparation of coming of Messiah (Lk 3:4-14), baptized Jesus (Mt 3:13-17; Mk 1:9-10; Lk 3:21; Jn 1:32), bore witness to Jesus as Messiah (Jn 1:24-42), imprisoned and put to death by Herod Antipas (Mt 11:7-14; Lk 7:24-28), disciples loyal to him long after his death (Ac 18:25).

JOHN, THE GOSPEL OF

Author: The apostle John, son of Zebedee

Date: Traditionally toward the end of the first century, c. A.D. 85 or later. More recently, some scholars have suggested a date as early as the 50s and no later than 70.

Outline:
I. Prologue (1:1-18).
II. Beginnings of Jesus' Ministry (1:19-51).
 A. The Ministry of His Forerunner (1:19-34).
 B. Jesus' Introduction to Some Future Disciples (1:35-51).
III. Jesus' Public Ministry: Signs and Discourses (chs. 2-11).
 A. Changing Water to Wine (2:1-11).
 B. Cleansing the Temple (2:12-25).
 C. Interview with Nicodemus (3:1-21).
 D. Parallel Ministry With John the Baptist (3:22-4:3).
 E. Journey Through Samaria: The Woman at the Well (4:4-42).
 F. Healing of the Official's Son (4:43-54).
 G. To Jerusalem for an Annual Feast (ch. 5).
 H. The Feeding of the 5000 and the Sermon on the Bread of Life (ch. 6).
 I. Jesus at the Feast of Tabernacles (chs. 7-8).
 J. Healing of the Man Born Blind (ch. 9).
 K. Parable of the Good Shepherd (10:1-21).
 L. Debating at the Feast of Dedication (10:22-39).
 M. Ministry in Perea (10:40-42).
 N. The Raising of Lazarus (ch. 11).
IV. The Passion Week (chs. 12-19).
 A. The Anointing of Jesus' Feet (12:1-11).
 B. The Triumphal Entry (12:12-19).
 C. The Coming of the Greeks (12:20-36).
 D. Continued Jewish Unbelief (12:37-50).
 E. Farewell Discourses (chs. 13-17).
 1. Discourse at the Last Supper (chs. 13-14).
 2. Discourse on the way to Gethsemane (chs. 15-16).
 3. Jesus' prayer of intercession (ch. 17).
 F. Jesus' Betrayal and Arrest (18:1-12).
 G. The Trials of Jesus (18:13-19:15).
 H. The Crucifixion and Burial (19:16-42).
V. The Resurrection (20:1-29).
VI. The Statement of Purpose (20:30-31).
VII. Epilogue (ch. 21).
 See Synoptic Gospels, The.

JOIADA (*Yahweh knows*).
1. Repaired walls of Jerusalem (Ne 3:6).
2. Son of Eliashib (Ne 12:10; 13:28).

JOIAKIM (*Yahweh lifts up*). Father of Eliashib (Ne 12:10, 12, 26).

JOIARIB (*Yahweh contends, pleads [your case]*).
1. A returned exile (Ezr 8:16).
2. A descendant of Judah (Ne 11:5).
3. A priest who returned from Babylon (Ne 12:6, 19). *See Jehoiarib.*

JOKDEAM A city in Judah (Jos 15:56).

JOKIM (*Yahweh lifts up*). A descendant of Shelah (1Ch 4:22).

JOKMEAM (*let the people arise*). A Levitical city of Ephraim (1Ch 6:68).

JOKNEAM A Levitical city of Zebulun (Jos 12:22; 19:11; 21:34). *See Jokmeam.*

JOKSHAN Son of Abraham, by Keturah (Ge 25:2-3, 6; 1Ch 1:32).

JOKTAN (*smaller*). Son of Eber (Ge 10:25-26, 29; 1Ch 1:19-20, 23).

JOKTHEEL
1. A city of Judah (Jos 15:38).
2. A name given by Amaziah to Sela, stronghold of Edom (2Ki 14:7; 2Ch 25:11-12). *See Sela.*

JONA *See Jonah.*

JONADAB (*Yahweh is generous, noble*).
1. The son of Shimeah, David's brother (2Sa 13:3). His complicity with Amnon in his rape of Tamar (2Sa 13:3-5). Comforts David on death of Amnon (2Sa 13:32-35).
2. A Kenite who helped Jehu abolish Baal worship (temporarily) in Samaria (2Ki 10:15-27). *Jonadab* is spelled "Jehonadab" in this passage (2Ki 10:15-23). He was also a leader of a conservative movement that was characterized by various practices of a settled agricultural society, including the building of houses, the sowing of crops, and the use of wine. *See Nazirite(s).*
His followers still adhered to these principles nearly 250 years later and were known as Recabites (Jer 35:5-10, 16-19). *See Recabite(s).*

JONAH (*dove*). Prophet of Israel; son of Amittai; predicted victory over Syria through Jeroboam II, who reigned c. 793-753 B.C.; author of book of Jonah (2Ki 14:25; Jnh 1:1).

JONAH, BOOK OF

Author: Traditionally the prophet Jonah

Date: Before the fall of Samaria in B.C. 722-721

Outline:
I. Jonah Flees His Mission (chs. 1-2).
 A. Jonah's Commission and Flight (1:1-3).
 B. The Endangered Sailors' Cry to Their Gods (1:4-6).
 C. Jonah's Disobedience Exposed (1:7-10).
 D. Jonah's Punishment and Deliverance (1:11-2:1; 2:10).
 E. Jonah's Prayer of Thanksgiving (2:2-9).
II. Jonah Reluctantly Fulfills His Mission (chs. 3-4).
 A. Jonah's Renewed Commission and Obedience (3:1-4).
 B. The Endangered Ninevites' Repentant Appeal to the Lord (3:5-9).
 C. The Ninevites' Repentance Acknowledged (3:10-4:4).
 D. Jonah's Deliverance and Rebuke (4:5-11).
 See Prophets, The Minor.

JONAM (*Yahweh is gracious*). An ancestor of Christ (Lk 3:30).

JONAN *See Jonam.*

JONAS *See Jonah; John, 4.*

JONATH-ELEM-RECHOKIM NIV "To [the tune of] A Dove on Distant Oaks" (Ps 56:T). Probably the melody to which Ps 56 was sung. *See Music, Symbols Used in.*

JONATHAN (*gift of Yahweh*).
1. A Levite of Bethlehem, who becomes a priest for Micah, accepts idolatry, joins the Danites (Jdg 17:7-13; 18:1-30).
2. Son of Saul (1Sa 14:49). Victory of, over the Philistine garrison of Geba (1Sa 13:3-4, 16), over Philistines at Micmash (1Sa 14:1-18). Under Saul's curse pronounced against any who might take food before he was avenged of his enemies (1Sa 14:24-30, 43). Rescued by the people (1Sa 14:43-45). Love of, for David (1Sa 18:1-4; 19:1-7; 20; 23:16-18). Killed in battle with Philistines (1Sa 31:2, 6; 2Sa 21:12-14; 1Ch 10:2). Buried by inhabitants of Jabesh Gilead (1Sa 31:11-13). Mourned by David (2Sa 1:12, 17-27). Son of, cared for by David (2Sa 4:4; 9; 1Ch 8:34).
3. Son of Abiathar (2Sa 15:27). Acts as spy for David (2Sa 15:27-28; 17:17-22). Informs Adonijah of Solomon's succession to David (1Ki 1:42-48).
4. Nephew of David, slays a giant and becomes one of David's chief warriors (2Sa 21:21; 1Ch 20:7).
5. One of David's heroes (2Sa 23:32; 1Ch 11:34).
6. A son of Jada (1Ch 2:32-33).
7. Secretary of the cabinet of David (1Ch 27:32).
8. Father of Ebed (Ezr 8:6).
9. Son of Asahel (Ezr 10:15).
10. Also called Johanan. A descendant of Jeshua (Ne 12:11-12).
11. Name of two priests (Ne 12:14, 35).
12. A scribe (Jer 37:15, 20; 38:26).
13. Son of Kareah (Jer 40:8).

JOPPA (*beautiful*). An ancient walled town on coast of Israel, c. thirty-five miles NW of Jerusalem; assigned to Dan; mentioned in Amarna letters; seaport for Jerusalem. In NT times Peter raised Dorcas to life there (Ac 9:36ff) and received the vision of a sheet filled with animals (Ac 10:1ff; 11:5ff). Modern Jaffa.

JORAH (*one born during harvest*). Family which returned with Zerubbabel (Ezr 2:18). Also called Hariph (Ne 7:24).

JORAI (possibly *Yahweh sees* IDB; *whom Yahweh teaches* ISBE). A Gadite (1Ch 5:13).

JORAM (*Yahweh is exalted*). Short form of Jehoram. *See Jehoram.*
1. Son of king of Hamath (2Sa 8:10).
2. Levite (1Ch 26:25).
3. Son of Ahab, king of Israel (2Ki 8:29).
4. King of Judah (2Ki 8:21-24; 11:2; 1Ch 3:11; Mt 1:8).
5. Priest (2Ch 17:8).

JORDAN (*descent*).
River of:
A river in Israel. Empties into the Dead Sea (Jos 15:5). Fords of (Ge 32:10; Jos 2:7; Jdg 3:28; 7:24; 8:4; 10:9; 12:5-6; 2Sa 2:29; 17:22, 24; 19:15, 31; Jn 1:28). Swelling of, at harvest time (Jos 3:15; Jer 12:5), and in the early spring (1Ch 12:15). The waters of, miraculously separated for the passage of the Israelites (Jos 3; 4; 5:1; Ps 114:3), of Elijah (2Ki 2:6-8), of Elisha (2Ki 2:14). Crossed at a ford (2Sa 19:18). Naaman washes in, for the healing of his leprosy (2Ki 5:10-14). John the Baptist baptizes in (Mt 3:6; Mk 1:5), baptizes Jesus in (Mt 3:13; Mk 1:9).
Plain of:
(Ge 13:10-12). Israelites camped in (Nu 22:1; 26:3, 63). Solomon's foundry in (1Ki 7:46; 2Ch 4:17).

JORIM Ancestor of Jesus (Lk 3:29).

JORKEAM Descendant of Caleb (1Ch 2:44).

JOSABAD *See Jozabad, 1.*

JOSAPHAT *See Jehoshaphat.*

JOSE *See Joshua, 5.*

JOSECH Father of Semein; ancestor of Jesus (Lk 3:26).

JOSEDECH *See Jozadak.*

JOSEPH (*he will add*).
1. Son of Jacob (Ge 30:24). Personal appearance of (Ge 39:6). His favorite child (Ge 33:2; 37:3-4, 35; 48:22; 1Ch 5:2; Jn 4:5). His father's partiality for, excites the jealousy of his brothers (Ge 37:4, 11, 18-28; Ps 105:17; Ac 7:9). His prophetic dreams of his fortunes in Egypt (Ge 37:5-11). Sold into Egypt (Ge 37:27-28). Is falsely reported to his father as killed by wild beasts (Ge 37:29-35). Is bought by Potiphar, an officer of Pharaoh (Ge 37:36). Is prospered of God (Ge 39:2-5, 21, 23). Is falsely accused, and cast into prison; is delivered by the friendship of another prisoner (Ge 39; 40; Ps 105:18). Is an interpreter of dreams: of the two prisoners (Ge 40:5-23); of Pharaoh (Ge 41:1-37). His name is changed to Zaphenath-Paneah (Ge 41:45). Is promoted to authority next to Pharaoh at thirty years of age (Ge 41:37-46; Ps 105:19-22). Takes as his wife the daughter of the priest of On (Ge 41:45). Provides against the years of famine (Ge 41:46-57). Exports the produce of Egypt to other countries (Ge 41:57). Sells the stores of food to the people of Egypt, exacting of them all their money, flocks and herds, lands and lives (Ge 47:13-26). Exempts the priests from the exactions (Ge 47:22, 26).
His father sends down into Egypt to buy grain (Ge 42-44). Reveals himself to his brothers, sends for his father, provides the land of Goshen for his people, and sustains them during the famine (Ge 45; 46; 47:1-13). His two sons (Ge 41:50, 52; Dt 33:13-17). Mourns the death of his father (Ge 50:1-14). Exacts a pledge from his brothers to convey his remains to Canaan (Ge 50:24-25; Heb 11:22, w Ex 13:19; Jos 24:32; Ac 7:16). Death of (Ge 50:22-26).
Kindness of heart (Ge 40:7-8). His integrity (Ge 39:7-12), humility (Ge 41:16; 45:7-9), wisdom (Ge 41:33-57), piety (Ge 41:51-52), faith (Ge 45:5-8). Was a prophet (Ge 41:38-39; 50:25; Ex 13:19). God's providence with (Ge 39:2-5; Ps 105:17-22). Descendants of (Ge 46:20; Nu 26:28-37).
2. Father of Igal the spy (Nu 13:7).
3. Of the sons of Asaph (1Ch 25:2, 9).
4. A returned exile (Ezr 10:42).
5. A priest (Ne 12:14).
6. Husband of Mary (Mt 13:55; Mk 6:3; Mt 1:18-25; Lk 1:27). His genealogy (Mt 1:1-16; Lk 3:23-38). An angel appears and testifies to the innocency of his betrothed (Mt 1:19-24). Lives at Nazareth (Lk 2:4). Belongs to the city of Bethlehem (Lk 2:4). Goes to Bethlehem to be enrolled (Lk 2:1-4). Jesus born to (Mt 1:25; Lk 2:7). Presents Jesus in the temple (Lk 2:22-39). Returns to Nazareth (Lk 2:39). Warned in a dream to escape to Egypt in order to save the child's life (Mt 2:13-15). Warned in a dream to return to Nazareth (Mt 2:19-23). Attends the annual feast at Jerusalem with his family (Lk 2:42-51).
7. Of Arimathea. Requests the body of Jesus for burial in his own tomb (Mt 27:57-60; Mk 15:42-47; Lk 23:50-56; Jn 19:38-42).
8. Three ancestors of Joseph, 6 (Lk 3:24, 26, 30).
9. One of the brothers of Jesus (Mt 13:55; Mk 6:3).
10. Also called Barsabbas and Justus. One of the two persons nominated in place of Judas (Ac 1:21-23).
11. A Levite, called Barnabas by the apostles (Ac 4:36). *See Barnabas.*
12. A designation of the ten tribes of Israel (Am 5:6).

JOSES
1. Son of Mary, 2; brother of the younger James (Mt 27:56; Mk 15:40, 47).
2. *See Joseph, 9.*
3. *See Joseph, 11.*

JOSHAH (*gift of Yahweh*). A descendant of Simeon (1Ch 4:34).

JOSHAPHAT (*Yahweh judges*).
1. One of David's mighty men (1Ch 11:43).
2. Priest (1Ch 15:24).

JOSHAVIAH (*Yahweh places*). One of David's bodyguards (1Ch 11:46).

JOSHBEKASHAH (*one sitting in request [prayer?]*). Leader of the seventeenth course of musicians (1Ch 25:4, 24).

JOSHEB-BASSHEBETH (*one sitting in the seat*). A Tahkemonite, who was the chief of the Three; one of David's mighty men (2Sa 23:8). This is probably a corruption of Jashobeam, a Hacmonite (1Ch 11:11).

JOSHIBIAH (*Yahweh places*). A Simeonite (1Ch 4:35).

JOSHUA (*Yahweh saves*).
1. Also called Hoshea (Nu 13:8). Son of Nun (1Ch 7:27). Intimately associated with Moses (Ex 24:13; 32:17; 33:11). A religious zealot (Nu 11:28). Sent with others to view the promised land (Nu 13:8). Makes favorable report (Nu 14:6-10). Rewarded for his courage and fidelity (Nu 14:30, 38; 32:12). Commissioned, ordained, and charged with the responsibilities of Moses' office (Nu 27:18-23; Dt 1:38; 3:28; 31:3, 7, 23; 34:9). Divinely inspired (Nu 27:18; Dt 34:9; Jos 1:5, 9; 3:7; 8:8). His life miraculously preserved when he made a favorable report of the land (Nu 14:10). Promises to (Jos 1:5). Leads the people into the land of Canaan (Jos 1-4; Ac 7:45; Heb 4:8). Renews circumcision of the Israelites; reestablishes the Passover; has a vision of the angel of God (Jos 5). Besieges and takes Jericho (Jos 6). Takes Ai (Jos 7-8). Makes a league with the Gibeonites (Jos 9:3-27). The kings of the six nations of the Canaanites confederate against him (Jos 9:1-2), make war upon the Gibeonites, are defeated and slain (Jos 10). Defeats seven

other kings (Jos 10:28-43). Makes conquest of Hazor (Jos 11). Completes the conquest of the whole land (Jos 11:23). List of the kings whom Joshua killed (Jos 12). Allots the land (Jos 13-19). Sets the tabernacle up in Shiloh (Jos 18:1). Sets apart cities of refuge (Jos 20), forty-eight cities for the Levites (Jos 21). Exhortation of, before his death (Jos 23-24). Survives the Israelites who refused to enter Canaan (Nu 26:63-65). His portion of the land (Jos 19:49-50). Death and burial of (Jos 24:29-30). Esteem in which he was held (Jos 1:16-18). Faith of (Jos 6:16). Military genius of, as exhibited at the defeat of the Amalekites (Ex 17:13), at Ai (Jos 8), in Gibeon (Jos 10), at Hazor (Jos 11). Age of, at death (Jdg 2:8).

2. An Israelite (1Sa 6:14, 18).
3. A governor of Jerusalem (2Ki 23:8).
4. The postexilic high priest. *See Jeshua, 3.*
5. An ancestor of Jesus (Lk 3:29).

JOSHUA, BOOK OF

Author: Traditionally Joshua the son of Nun

Date: Traditionally before 1375 B.C.

Outline:
I. The Entrance into the Land (1:1-5:12).
 A. The Exhortations to Conquer (ch. 1).
 B. The Reconnaissance of Jericho (ch. 2).
 C. The Crossing of the Jordan (chs. 3-4).
 D. The Consecration at Gilgal (5:1-12).
II. The Conquest of the Land (5:13-12:24).
 A. The Initial Battles (5:13-8:35).
 1. The victory at Jericho (5:13-6:27).
 2. The failure at Ai because of Achan's sin (ch. 7).
 3. The victory at Ai (8:1-29).
 4. The covenant renewed at Shechem (8:30-35).
 B. The Campaign in the South (chs. 9-10).
 1. The treaty with the Gibeonites (ch. 9).
 2. The long day of Joshua (10:1-15).
 3. The southern cities conquered (10:16-43).
 C. The Campaign in the North (ch. 11).
 D. The Defeated Kings of Canaan (ch. 12).
III. The Distribution of the Land (chs. 13-21).
 A. Areas Yet to Be Conquered (13:1-7).
 B. The Land East of the Jordan for Reuben, Gad and Half of Manasseh (13:8-33).
 C. The Lands Given to Judah and "Joseph" at Gilgal (chs. 14-17).
 D. The Lands Given to the Remaining Tribes at Shiloh (chs. 18-19).
 1. The tabernacle at Shiloh (18:1-10).
 2. The allotments for Benjamin, Simeon, Zebulun, Issachar, Asher, Naphtali, and Dan (18:1-10).
 3. The town given to Joshua (19:49-51).
 E. The Cities Assigned to the Levites (chs. 20-21).
 1. The six cities of refuge (ch. 20).
 2. The forty-eight cities of the priests (ch. 21).
IV. Epilogue: Tribal Unity and Loyalty to the Lord (chs. 22-24).
 A. The Altar of Witness by the Jordan (ch. 22).
 B. Joshua's Farewell Exhortation (ch. 23).
 C. The Renewal of the Covenant at Shechem (24:1-28).
 D. The Death and Burial of Joshua and Eleazar (24:29-33).

JOSIAH (*let or may Yahweh give*).
1. King of Judah (2Ki 21:24-26; 22:1; 1Ch 3:14; 2Ch 33:25). Ancestor of Jesus (Mt 1:10-11). Slain in battle with Pharaoh Neco (2Ki 23:29-30; 2Ch 35:20-24). Lamentations for (2Ch 35:25). Piety of, exemplified in his repairing the temple (2Ki 22:3-7; 2Ch 34:1-4). Anxiety, when the copy of the law was discovered and read to him (2Ki 22:8-20; 2Ch 34:14-33), in keeping a solemn Passover (2Ki 23:21-23; 2Ch 35:1-19). Prophecies concerning (1Ki 13:1-3). Destroys the altar and high places of idolatry (2Ki 23:3-20, 24-25).

2. Son of Zephaniah (Zec 6:10).

JOSIAS *See Josiah.*

JOSIPHIAH (*Yahweh will add*). Ancestor of family which returned with Ezra (Ezr 8:10).

JOT NIV "the smallest letter" of the Hebrew alphabet (Mt 5:17-18). Used figuratively to emphasize the importance of the smallest details of the law.

JOTBAH (*good, pleasant*). A place in Judah (2Ki 21:19). Possibly the same as Jotbathah (Dt 10:7).

JOTBATHAH (*good, pleasant*). The twentieth encampment of Israel (Nu 33:33-34; Dt 10:7). Possibly the same as Jotbah (2Ki 21:19).

JOTHAM (*Yahweh completes*).
1. Son of Gideon; speaker of the first biblical parable (Jdg 9:5-57).
2. Judahite (1Ch 2:47).
3. Eleventh king of Judah; son of Uzziah, whose regent he was for a time; successful, righteous king (2Ki 15:5-38; 2Ch 27); contemporary of Isaiah (Isa 1:1), Hosea (Hos 1:1), Micah (Mic 1:1), ancestor of Jesus (Mt 1:9).

JOURNEY, SABBATH DAY'S Three thousand feet (Ac 1:12).

JOY (Ps 30:5; Ps 30:11; Ps 33:21; Ps 97:11; Ps 132:16; Pr 29:6).

General:
From God (Ecc 2:26; Ro 15:13). In the Lord (Ps 9:2; 104:34; Isa 9:3; 29:19; 41:16; 61:10; Lk 1:47; Ro 5:11). In Christ (Php 3:3; 4:4; 1Pe 1:8). In the word of God (Ps 19:8; 119:14, 16, 111, 162; Jer 15:16). In worship (2Ch 7:10; Ezr 6:22; Ne 12:43; Ps 42:4; 43:4; 71:23; Isa 56:7; Zep 3:14; Zec 2:10; 9:9).
A fruit of the Spirit (Gal 5:22; Eph 5:18-19). For salvation (Ps 13:5; 20:5; 21:1, 6; 35:9; Isa 12:2-3; 25:9; 35:1-2, 10; 55:12; Ro 5:2; 14:17). On account of a good conscience (2Co 1:12). Over a sinner's repentance (Lk 15:6-10, 22-32).
Under adversity (Ps 126:5-6; Isa 61:3; Mt 5:12; Ac 5:41; 2Co 6:10; 7:4; 8:2; 12:10; Col 1:11; 1Th 1:6; Heb 10:34; Jas 1:2; 1Pe

4:13). Fullness of (Ps 16:11; 36:8; 63:5; Jn 15:11; 16:24; Ac 2:28; 1Jn 1:4). Everlasting (Isa 51:11; 61:7). In heaven (Mt 25:21; Lk 15:7, 10).
Attributed to God (Dt 28:63; 30:9; Jer 32:41).

Commanded:
(Dt 12:18; Ne 8:10; Ps 2:11; 5:11; 32:11; 68:3; 97:12; 100:1-2; 105:3, 43; 149:2, 5; Joel 2:23; Lk 2:10; 6:23; 10:20; Ro 12:12; 1Th 5:16).

Instances of:
Moses and the Israelites, when Pharaoh and his army were destroyed (Ex 15:1-22). Deborah and the Israelites, when Sisera was overthrown (Jdg 5). Jephthah's daughter, when he returned from his victory over the Ammonites (Jdg 11:34). Hannah, when Samuel was born (1Sa 2:1-11). Naomi, when Boaz showed kindness to Ruth (Ru 2:20; 4:14). David, over the offerings of the princes and people for the house of God (1Ch 29:10-19). Jews, over the hanging of Haman (Est 8:15-16, w Est 7:10).
The Israelites: When Saul was presented as their king (1Sa 10:24), when David killed Goliath (1Sa 18:6-7), when they repaired to David to Hebron to make him king (1Ch 12:40), when they took the ark from Kiriath Jearim (1Ch 13:8), when they brought the ark from the house of Obed-Edom to Jerusalem (1Ch 15:16, 25, 28), when they made gifts to the house of God (1Ch 29:9), when they turned away from idolatry (2Ch 15:14-15; 23:18, 21; 29:30, 36; 30:21, 23, 26), when the foundation of the second temple was laid (Ezr 3:11-13), when they kept the dedication of the temple, and the feast of tabernacles under Ezra (Ezr 6:16, 22), after hearing again the word of God (Ne 8:9-18). when the Wall of Jerusalem was dedicated (Ne 12:43).
Elizabeth, when Mary visited her (Lk 1:5-44). Mary, when she visited Elizabeth (Lk 1:46-56). Zechariah, when John was born (Lk 1:67-79). The angels, when Jesus was born (Lk 2:13-14). The shepherds when they saw the infant Jesus (Lk 2:20). The Magi (Mt 2:10). Simeon, when Jesus was presented in the temple (Lk 2:28-32).
The disciples, because the demons were subject to them (Lk 10:17). The father, when his prodigal son returns (Lk 15:20-32). The angels, when sinners repent (Lk 15:7, 10). The disciples, when Jesus triumphantly entered Jerusalem (Mt 21:8-9; Mk 11:8-9; Mk 11:8-10). The women who returned from the Lord's tomb (Mt 28:8). The disciples, after the resurrection of Jesus (Lk 24:41), in the temple after the Ascension of Jesus (Lk 24:53), in the temple because they had received the gift of the Holy Spirit (Ac 2:46-47).
The crippled man, healed by Peter (Ac 3:8). Paul, when he went up to Jerusalem (Ac 20:22-24). Paul and Silas, in the jail at Philippi (Ac 16:25). Rhoda, when she heard Peter at the gate (Ac 12:14). The disciples at Jerusalem, when Peter told them about the conversion of Cornelius and other Gentiles (Ac 11:18). Barnabas, when he saw the success of the gospel at Antioch (Ac 11:22-23).
Paul and the Corinthians, because the excommunicated member repented (2Co 1:24; 2:3). Paul and Titus, because of the hospitality of the Corinthians (Ro 15:32; 1Co 16:18 2Co 7:13, w 2Co 8:6). The Macedonians, when he prayed for the Philippians (Php 1:4). The Thessalonians, when they believed Paul's gospel (1Th 1:6). Paul, rejoicing over his converts (1Th 2:19-20; 3:9; Phm 7). Early Christians, when they believed in Jesus (1Pe 1:8-9).
See Happiness; Praise; Thanksgiving.

Of the Wicked:
Short (Job 20:5). Meaningless (Ecc 2:10; 7:6; 11:8-9). Shallow (Pr 14:13; 15:21). Overshadowed by impending judgment and sorrow (Pr 14:13; Ecc 11:8-9; Isa 16:10; Jas 4:10).

JOZABAD (*Yahweh bestowed*).
1. One of the two servants of Joash, who killed him in Millo (2Ki 12:21).
2. Gederathite; joined David at Ziklag (1Ch 12:4).
3. Two Manassites who also joined David (1Ch 12:20).
4. Levites (2Ch 31:13).
5. Chief Levite (2Ch 35:9).
6. Levite who assisted Ezra (Ezr 8:33).
7. Man who put foreign wife away (Ezr 10:22).
8. Another such man (Ezr 10:23).
9. Levite who helped Nehemiah (Ne 8:7).
10. Chief Levite in Nehemiah's time (Ne 11:16).

JOZACHAR (*Yahweh remembered*). *See Jehozabad, 1; Jozabad, 1; Zabad, 4.*

JOZADAK (*Yahweh is righteous*). Father of Jeshua the high priest who returned with Zerubbabel (Ezr 3:2, 8; 5:2; 10:18; Ne 12:26). Called Jehozadak in Haggai and Zechariah. *See Jehozadak.*

JUBAL Son of Lamech. Inventor of harp and flute (Ge 4:21).

JUBILEE Called: Year of the Lord's favor (Isa 61:2). The year of freedom (Eze 46:17).
Laws concerning (Lev 25:8-55; 27:17-24; Nu 36:4).
See Emancipation; Sabbatic Year.

JUBILEES, BOOK OF Jewish apocalyptic book written in intertestamental period.

JUCAL *See Jehucal.*

JUDA *See Judah.*

JUDAEA *See Judea.*

JUDAH (*praised*).
1. Son of Jacob (Ge 35:23). Intercedes for Joseph's life when his brothers were about to slay him, and proposes that they sell him to the Ishmaelites (Ge 37:26-27). Takes two wives (Ge 38:1-6). Lives at Kezib (Ge 38:5). His incest with his daughter-in-law (Ge 38:12-26). Goes down into Egypt for grain (Ge 43:1-10; 44:14-34; 46:28). Prophetic benediction of his father upon (Ge 49:8-12). The ancestor of Jesus (Mt 1:2-3; Rev 5:5).
2. Tribe of: Prophecies concerning (Ge 49:10). Enrollment of the military forces of, at Sinai (Nu 1:26-27; 2:4), at Bezek (1Sa 11:8; 2Sa 24:9), in the plain of Moab (Nu 26:22). Place of, in camp and march (Nu 2:3, 9; 10:14). By whom commanded (Nu 2:3;

Moses' benediction upon (Dt 33:7). Commissioned of God to lead in the conquest of the promised land (Jdg 1:1-3, w Jdg 1:4-21). Make David king (2Sa 2:1-11; 5:4-5). Rebuked by David for lukewarmness toward him after Absalom's defeat (2Sa 19:11-15). Accused by the other tribes of stealing the heart of David (2Sa 19:41-43). Loyal to David at the at the time of the insurrection led by Sheba (2Sa 20:1-2). Is accorded the birthright forfeited by Reuben (1Ch 5:1-2; 28:4; Ps 60:7). Loyal to the house of David at the time of the revolt of the ten tribes (1Ki 12:20). Inheritance of (Jos 15; 18:5; 19:1, 9).
3. Name of two exiled priests (Ezr 10:23; Ne 12:8).
4. A Benjamite (Ne 11:9).
5. A prince or priest who assisted in the dedication of the walls of Jerusalem (Ne 12:34, 36).

JUDAISM
1. The religion of the Jews in NT times (Gal 1:13-14).
2. "Converts to Judaism" (Ac 2:11; 6:5; 13:43). Gentiles who adopted the religious beliefs and customs of the Jews.

JUDAS (Greek for *Judah*).
1. Surnamed Iscariot. Chosen as an apostle (Mt 10:4; Mk 3:19; Lk 6:16; Ac 1:17). Treasurer of the disciples (Jn 12:6; 13:29). His greed exemplified by his protest against the breaking of the box of ointment (Jn 12:4-6), by his bargain to betray Jesus for a sum of money (Mt 26:14-16; Mk 14:10-11; Lk 22:3-6; Jn 13:2). His apostasy (Jn 17:12). Betrays the Lord (Mt 26:47-50; Mk 14:43-45; Lk 22:47-49; Jn 18:2-5; Ac 1:16-25). Returns the money to the rulers of the Jews (Mt 27:3-10). Hangs himself (Mt 27:5; Ac 1:18). Prophecies concerning (Mt 26:21-25; Mk 14:18-21; Lk 22:21-23; Jn 13:18-26; 17:12; Ac 1:16, 20, w Ps 41:9; 109:8; Zec 11:12-13).
2. One of the brothers of Jesus (Mt 13:55; Mk 6:3) and writer of the epistle of Jude (Jude 1).
3. Brother of James (Lk 6:16; Ac 1:13).
4. An apostle, probably identical with Lebbaeus, or Thaddaeus (Jn 14:22).
5. Of Galilee, who stirred up a sedition among the Jews soon after the birth of Jesus (Ac 5:37).
6. A disciple who entertained Paul (Ac 9:11).
7. Surnamed Barsabbas. A Christian sent to Antioch with Paul and Barnabas (Ac 15:22-32).

JUDE (*Judah*). The writer of the last of the NT epistles. The brother of James (Jude 1:1), probably brother of Jesus (Mk 6:3).

JUDE, EPISTLE OF

Author: Jude the brother of Jesus and James

Date: Probably c. A.D. 65

Outline:
I. Salutation (1-2).
II. Occasion for the Letter (3-4).
 A. The Change of Subject (3).
 B. The Reason for the Change: The Presence of Godless Apostates (4).
III. Warning Against the False Teachers (5-16).
 A. Historical Examples of the Judgment of Apostates (5-7).
 1. Unbelieving Israel (5).
 2. Angels who fell (6).
 3. Sodom and Gomorrah (7).
 B. Description of the Apostates of Jude's Day (8-16).
 1. Their slanderous speech deplored (8-10).
 2. Their character graphically portrayed (11-13).
 3. Their destruction prophesied (14-16).
IV. Exhortation to Believers (17-23).
V. Concluding Doxology (24-25).
 See General Letters.

JUDEA (*land of the Judahites, Jews*).
1. Greek spelling of Judah. The southern division of Israel. It extended from the Jordan and Dead Sea to the Mediterranean, and from Shiloh on the N to the wilderness on the S (Mt 4:25; Lk 5:17; Jn 4:47, 54). The term is applied to all of Israel (Lk 1:5). The term is applied to the territory E of Jordan (Mt 19:1; Mk 10:1; Lk 23:5).
2. Wilderness of. Called Beth Arabah (Jos 18:22). John the Baptist preaches in (Mt 3:1; Lk 3:3).

JUDGE

Character of and Precepts Relating to:
Must be righteous (Ex 18:21-22; Lev 19:15; Dt 16:18-20; 1Ki 3:9; Ps 58:1-2; 72:1-2, 4), intelligent (Dt 1:12-13; Isa 28:6). Must judge righteously (Dt 1:16-17).
Jurisdiction of as judge (1Sa 2:25). Inferior and superior judges (Dt 17:8-11). Held circuit courts (1Sa 7:16). Rules for guidance of (Ex 18:22; Dt 19:16-19; 25:1-3; 2Ch 19:5-10; Pr 24:23; Eze 44:24; Jn 7:24).
Kings and other rulers as (2Sa 8:15; 15:2; 1Ki 3:16-28; 10:9; 2Ki 8:1-6; Ps 72:1-4; Mt 27:11-26; Ac 23:34-35; 24; 25:11-12). Priests and Levites as (Dt 17:9; 1Ch 23:4; 2Ch 19:8; Eze 44:23-24; Mt 26:57-62). Women as: Deborah (Jdg 4:4).
Persian government provided (Ezr 7:25).

Corrupt:
(1Sa 8:3; Ps 82:2-4; Isa 5:22-23; Da 9:12; Mic 7:3; Zep 3:3).
Instances of: Eli's sons (1Sa 2:12-17, 22-25). Samuel's sons (1Sa 8:1-5). The judges of Jezreel (1Ki 21:8-13). Pilate (Mt 27:24, 26; Mk 15:15, 19-24). Felix (Ac 24:26-27).

Of Israel:
Executives and leaders of the nation. During the time when the land was ruled by judges (Jdg 2:16-19; Ac 13:20).
Othniel (Jdg 3:9-11). Ehud (Jdg 3:15, 30). Shamgar (Jdg 3:31). Deborah (Jdg 4:4-5). Gideon (Jdg 6:11-40; 7:8). Abimelech (Jdg 9:1-54). Tola (Jdg 10:1-2). Jair (Jdg 10:3-5). Jephthah (Jdg 12:7). Ibzan (Jdg 12:8-10). Elon (Jdg 12:11-12). Abdon (Jdg 12:13-14). Samson (Jdg 15:20; 16:31).
Eli (1Sa 4:18). Samuel (1Sa 7:6, 15-17). The sons of Samuel (1Sa 8:1-5).
See Court, Of Law; God, Judge; Justice; Witness.

JUDGES, BOOK OF

Author: Anonymous; traditionally Samuel

Date: Possibly between 1040 and 1000 B.C.

Outline:
I. Prologue: Incomplete Conquest and Apostasy (1:1-3:6).
 A. First Episode: Israel's Failure to Purge the Land (1:1-2:5).
 B. Second Episode: God's Dealings with Israel's Rebellion (2:6-3:6).
II. Oppression and Deliverance (3:7-16:31).
 Major Judges (A-F) *Minor Judges* (1-6)
 A. Othniel Defeats Aram Naharaim (3:7-11).
 B. Ehud Defeats Moab (3:12-30).
 1. Shamgar (3:31).
 C. Deborah Defeats Canaan (chs. 4-5).
 D. Gideon Defeats Midian (chs. 6-8).
 (Abimelech, the anti-judge, ch. 9).
 2. Tola (10:1-2).
 3. Jair (10:3-5).
 E. Jephthah Defeats Ammon (10:6-12:7).
 4. Ibzan (12:8-10).
 5. Elon (12:11-12).
 6. Abdon (12:13-15).
 F. Samson Checks Philistia (chs. 17-21).
III. Epilogue: Religious and Moral Disorder (chs. 17-21).
 A. First Episode (chs. 17-18; see 17:6; 18:1).
 1. Micah's corruption of religion (ch 17).
 2. The Danites' departure from their tribal territory (ch. 18).
 B. Second Episode (chs. 19-21; see 19:1; 21:25).
 1. Gibeah's corruption of morals (ch. 19).
 2. The Benjamites' removal from their tribal territory (chs. 20-21).

JUDGING See *Uncharitableness.*

JUDGMENT

General:
Forewarned (Ecc 11:9; 12:14; Mt 8:29 w 2Pe 2:4 & Jude 6; Mt 13:30, 40-43, 49-50; Mt 25:31-46; Mk 8:38; Ac 24:25; 2Th 1:7-8; Heb 6:2).
Fierce and fiery (Mt 3:12; 10:15; 11:22; 12:36-42; Lk 3:17; 10:10-14; 11:31-32; 13:24-29; Ac 2:19-20).
According to opportunity and works (Ge 4:7; 1Sa 26:23; Job 34:11-12; Ps 62:12; Pr 12:14; 24:11-12; Isa 3:10-11; 59:18; Jer 17:10; 32:19; Eze 7:3-4, 27; 18:4-9; 18:19-32; 33:18-20; Hos 4:9; 12:2; Zec 1:6; Mt 25:31; Lk 12:47-48; 13:6-9; 19:12-27; Jn 3:19-20; Ro 2:5-12; 1Co 3:8, 12:15; 2Co 11:15; Gal 6:7-8; Eph 6:7-8; Col 3:25; Heb 10:26-30; 12:25; Jas 2:13; 1Pe 1:17; 2Pe 2:20-21; Rev 2:23; 20:12-13).

Design of:
To exhibit a basis for rewards and punishments (2Co 5:10; 2Ti 4:8; Rev 11:18; 22:12). To reveal secrets (Ecc 12:14; Lk 12:2-3; Ro 2:16; 1Co 3:13).

Who Will Be the Judge:
God as Judge (1Ch 16:33; Ps 9:7; 50:4, 6; 96:13; 98:9; Ecc 12:14; Da 7:9-10; Ro 2:5, 16; 3:6; 2Ti 4:8; Heb 10:30; 12:23; 13:4; 1Pe 4:5; Rev 20:11-15).
Jesus Christ as Judge (Mt 7:22-23; 13:30, 40-43, 49-50; 16:25, 27; 25:31-46; Mk 8:38; Jn 5:22; 12:48; Ac 10:42; 17:31; Ro 2:16; 14:10; 1Co 4:5; 2Co 5:10; 2Th 1:7-8; 2Ti 4:1; 2Pe 2:9; 3:10; Rev 1:7; 6:15-17).
The saints as judges (Mt 19:28; 1Co 6:2; Jude 14).

Time of:
Appointed (Mt 13:30; Ac 17:31; Heb 9:27; 2Pe 3:7, 10-12). Known to God only (Mk 13:32).

Who Will Be Judged:
The righteous and wicked (Ecc 3:17; Mt 25:31-46; Jude 14-15; Rev 11:18). The wicked (Job 21:30; Eze 18:20-28; 2Pe 2:9; 3:7). The living and the dead (Ac 10:42; 2Ti 4:1; 1Pe 4:5). All must be made manifest (Mk 4:22; Ac 17:31; 2Co 5:10). Kings and princes, slaves and freemen (Rev 6:15-16). Fallen angels (2Pe 2:4; Jude 6). *See God, Judge; Jesus the Christ, Judge; Punishment, According to Deeds.*

JUDGMENT, HALL OF See *Praetorium.*

JUDGMENT SEAT (Mt 27:19; Ac 18:12; 25:10). Of Christ (Ro 14:10).

JUDGMENTS Denounced against Solomon (1Ki 11:9-14, 23), Jeroboam (1Ki 14:7-15), Ahab and Jezebel (1Ki 21:19-24), Ahaziah (2Ch 22:7-9), Manasseh (2Ch 33:11). Against disobedience (Lev 26:14-39; Dt 28:15-68; 29:1-29; 32:19-43).

Design of:
To correct (Dt 30:1-2; 1Ki 8:33-34; 2Ch 7:13; Job 5:17; 23:10; 34:31-32; Ps 94:12-13; 107:10-14, 17; Pr 3:11; Isa 9:13-14; 26:9; Jer 24:5; 30:11; La 1:5, 12; Eze 20:37, 43; Hos 2:6-7; 5:15; 1Co 11:32; Heb 12:5-11). To humble (2Co 12:7).

Misunderstood:
(Jer 16:10; Joel 2:17). No escape from (Ex 20:7; 34:7; Isa 2:10, 12-19, 21; Eze 14:13-14; Am 5:16-20; 9:1-4; Mt 23:33; Heb 2:1-3; 10:28-29; 12:25; Rev 6:16-17). *See Escape.* Executed by human instrumentality (Jer 51:2). Delayed (Ps 10:6; 50:21; 55:19). *See Punishment, Delayed.*

Instances of:
On the serpent (Ge 3:14-15), Eve (Ge 3:16), Adam (Ge 3:17-19), Cain (Ge 4:11-15), the Antediluvians (Ge 6-7), Sodomites (Ge 19:23-25).
Egyptians, the plagues and overthrow (Ex 7-13; 14:1-31). Nadab and Abihu (Lev 10:1-3). Miriam (Nu 12:1-15).
Upon the Israelites: For worshiping Aaron's calf (Ex 32:35), for murmuring (Nu 11:1, 33-34; 14:22-23, 32, 35-37; 21:6; 25:4-5, 9). The forty years wandering, a judgment (Nu 14:26-39; 26:63-65; Dt 2:14-17), delivered into the hands of the Assyrians (2Ki 17:6-41), Chaldeans (2Ch 36:14-21).
Upon the Canaanites (Lev 18:25; Dt 7; 12:29-32), with the conquest of, by Joshua. *See Canaanite(s).*

Upon Abimelech (Jdg 9:52-57), Uzzah (2Sa 6:7), Eli's house (1Sa 2:27-36, w 1Sa 4:10-22), the prophet of Judah, for disobedience (1Ki 13:1-24), Zimri (1Ki 16:18-19), Gehazi (2Ki 5:27), Sennacherib (2Ki 19:35-37), Hananiah, the false prophet (Jer 28:15, 17).
See Chastisement, From God; Punishment; Sin, Punishment of.

JUDITH (*Jewess* or *Judahite*).
1. Wife of Esau (Ge 26:34).
2. Heroine of the apocryphal book of Judith.

JULIA (*of Julian [the family of Julius Caesar]*). A Christian woman in Rome (Ro 16:15).

JULIUS (*of Julian [the family of Julius Caesar]*). Roman centurion to whom Paul was entrusted (Ac 27:1, 3).

JUNIAS A relative or countryman of Paul (Ro 16:7). Possibly a feminine name and an apostle.

JUNIPER See *Broom Tree.*

JUPITER Latin for the god Zeus. See *Zeus.*

JURISDICTION See *Church, The Body of Believers, State.*

JURY Of ten elders (Ru 4:2). Of seventy elders (Nu 11:16-17, 24-25).

JUSHAB-HESED (*loyal love will be returned*). Son of Zerubbabel (1Ch 3:20).

JUST, THE See *Righteous.*

JUST SHALL LIVE BY FAITH (Hab 2:4; Ro 1:17; Gal 3:11; Heb 10:38).

JUSTICE From God (Ps 72:1-2; Pr 29:26).
Commanded (Ex 23:1-3, 6-8; Lev 19:13-15; Dt 16:18-20; 25:1-4; Ps 82:3-4; 106:3; Pr 18:5; Isa 1:17; Jer 7:5, 7; La 3:35-36; Mic 6:8; Zec 7:9; 8:16; Jn 7:24, 51).
Must be impartial (Pr 24:23; 28:21). Can be perverted (Ecc 3:16; 5:8; Isa 59:14-15; Jer 22:3; Am 5:7, 11-12; Mic 7:3; Hab 1:4; Mt 12:7). Will be rewarded (Jer 22:4, 15-16; Eze 18:5-9).
Of God: *See God, Justice of.*
See Court, Of Law; Injustice; Judge.

JUSTIFICATION The act of divine grace which restores the sinner to the relationship with God that he would have had if he had not sinned; pardon of sin. The word is used also to denote the state of the sinner after he is restored to divine favor.
Not imputing guilt to the sinner (Ps 32:2; Isa 53:11; Zec 3:4; Jn 5:24; Ro 4:6; 8:1).
Comes from God (Isa 45:24-25; 50:8; 54:17; 61:10; Ro 3:25; 8:30, 33; 2Co 5:19, 21; Tit 3:7). Achieved through Christ (Isa 53:11; Jer 23:6; Ac 13:39; Ro 3:20-25; 5:9, 11, 16-18, 21; 1Co 1:30; 6:11; Col 2:13-14). Is based on his righteousness (Ps 71:16; 89:16; Isa 42:21; 46:12-13; 51:5-6; 56:1; Ro 1:16-17; Gal 5:4-6).
Is not by the law (Ro 3:20; Gal 2:16; 3:11; 5:4-6). Is by faith (Ge 15:6; Hab 2:4; Ro 1:16-17; 3:20-22, 24, 28, 30; 4:2-25; 5:1; 9:30-32; 10:4, 6, 8-11; Gal 2:14-21; 3:6, 8-9, 21-22, 24; 5:4-6; Php 3:8-9; Heb 11:4, 7; Jas 2:20-23, 26).
Fruits of: Peace (Ro 5:1). Holiness (Ro 6:22).
Example of: Abraham (Ge 15:6; Ro 4:3).
See Adoption; Forgiveness; Regeneration; Sanctification; Sin, Confession of, Forgiveness of.

JUSTUS (*just*).
1. A disciple nominated with Matthias to succeed Judas Iscariot (Ac 1:23).
2. A believer in Corinth (Ac 18:7).
3. Also called Jesus. A disciple in Rome (Col 4:11).

JUTTAH (*extended, inclined*). A Levitical city in Judah (Jos 15:55; 21:16).

K

KAB See *Cab; Measure.*

KABZEEL (*God [El] collects*). A city of Judah (Jos 15:21; 2Sa 23:20; 1Ch 11:22).

KADESH (*sacred place*). Also known as En Mishpat (Ge 14:7). A place c. seventy miles S of Hebron, in the vicinity of which Israel wandered for thirty-seven years (Dt 1:46; Nu 33:37-38; Dt 2:14). Miriam died there (Nu 20:1), Moses sent spies to Israel from there (Nu 13:21-26; Dt 1:19-25), Moses displeased God there by striking the rock instead of speaking to it (Nu 20:2-13). Often called Kadesh Barnea (Nu 32:8; Dt 2:14).

KADESH BARNEA (*sacred place of Barnea*). See *Kadesh.*

KADMIEL (*[stand] before God [El]*).
1. A Levite (Ezr 2:40; 3:9; Ne 7:43; 12:8, 24).
2. A Levite who assisted in leading the worship of the people (Ne 9:4-5; 10:9).

KADMONITES (*easterners*). Ancient Arab tribe between Egypt and Euphrates (Ge 15:18-21).

KAIN (*smith*).
1. Town in Judah (Jos 15:57).
2. Tribal name (Nu 24:22; Jdg 4:11). See *Kenite(s).*

KALLAI (*swift*). A priest (Ne 12:20).

KAMAI See *Leb Kamai.*

KAMON Place where Jair was buried (Jdg 10:5).

KANAH (*reed*).
1. Brook flowing between Ephraim and Manasseh into the Mediterranean (Jos 16:8; 17:9).
2. City c. eight miles SE of Tyre, near boundary of Manasseh (Jos 19:28).

KAREAH (*bald head*). Father of Johanan, governor of Judah in the time of Gedaliah (2Ki 25:23; Jer 40:8, 13; 41:11, 13-14, 16).

KARKA (*floor, ground*). A city of Judah (Jos 15:3).

KARKOR Place E of Jordan where Gideon defeated Midianites (Jdg 8:10). Exact location unknown.

KARNAIM (*horns*). A city conquered by Israel (Am 6:13).

KARTAH (*city*). A city of Zebulun (Jos 21:34).

KARTAN A Levitical city in Naphtali (Jos 21:32).

KATTATH A city in Zebulun (Jos 19:15).

KATYDID An insect permitted as food (Lev 11:22). See *Insects.*

KAZIN See *Eth Kazin.*

KEBAR A river of Mesopotamia (Eze 1:1, 3; 3:15, 23; 10:15, 22; 43:3).

KEDAR (*mighty*).
1. Son of Ishmael (Ge 25:13; 1Ch 1:29).
2. A nomadic clan of the Ishmaelites (Ps 120:5; SS 1:5; Isa 21:16; 42:11; 60:7; Jer 49:28). Flocks of (Isa 60:7; Jer 49:28). Princes and commerce of (Eze 27:21).

KEDEMAH (*east*). Son of Ishmael (Ge 25:15; 1Ch 1:31).

KEDEMOTH (*east*). A city of Moab, allotted to Reuben and the Merarite Levites (Jos 13:18; 1Ch 6:79). Encircled by a wilderness of same name (Dt 2:26).

KEDESH (*sacred place*).
1. A city of Judah (Jos 15:23). Possibly identical with Kadesh Barnea.
2. Called also Kishion and Kishon. A Canaanite city taken by Joshua (Jos 12:22; 19:20; 21:28; 1Ch 6:72).
3. Called also Kedesh in Naphtali. A city of refuge (Jos 20:7; 21:32). Home of Barak and Heber (Jdg 4:6, 9, 11). Captured by Tiglath-Pileser (2Ki 15:29).

KEDESH NAPHTALI (*sacred place of Naphtali*). See *Kedesh, 3.*

KEDORLAOMER (*servant of [the deity] Lagamar*). King of Elam (Ge 14:1-16).

KEDRON See *Kidron.*

KEEPERS Of the prison (Ge 39:22; Ac 5:23; 12:6; 16:27, 36).

KEHELATHAH (*assembly*). An encampment of Israel (Nu 33:22-23).

KEILAH
1. One of a group of nine cities in the southern part of Israel allotted to Judah (Jos 15:44). Philistines make a predatory excursion against, after harvest (1Sa 23:1). David rescues (1Sa 23:2-13). Rulers of, aid in restoring the wall of Jerusalem after the Captivity (Ne 3:17-18).
2. A descendant of Caleb (1Ch 4:19).

KELAIAH (perhaps *Yahweh has dishonored*). Called also Kelita. A Levite who divorced his Gentile wife after the Captivity and assisted Ezra in expounding the law (Ezr 10:23; Ne 8:7; 10:10).

KELAL (*perfection, completeness*). Son of Pahath-Moab (Ezr 10:30).

KELITA See *Kelaiah.*

KELUB (*basket*).
1. A descendant of Caleb (1Ch 4:11).
2. Father of Ezri (1Ch 27:26).

KELUBAI See *Caleb, 1.*

KELUHI Son of Bani (Ezr 10:35).

KEMUEL (*God's [El's] mound* ISBE).
1. Son of Nahor; uncle of Laban and Rebekah (Ge 22:21).
2. Prince of Ephraim (Nu 34:24).
3. Father of Hashabiah, leading Levite (1Ch 27:17).

KENAANAH (*toward Canaan*).
1. Father of the false prophet Zedekiah (1Ki 22:11, 24; 2Ch 18:10, 23).
2. Brother of Ehud (1Ch 7:10).

KENAN Great-grandson of Adam (1Ch 1:2). Enosh is the father of Kenan (Ge 5:9-14).

KENANI (*Yahweh strengthens*). A Levite (Ne 9:4).

KENANIAH (*Yahweh strengthens*).
1. A Levite (1Ch 15:22, 27).
2. An Izharite (1Ch 26:29).

KENATH (*possession*). Amorite city in region of Bashan in kingdom of Og (Nu 32:42; 1Ch 2:22-23).

KENAZ (*hunting*).
1. Grandson of Esau (Ge 36:11, 15; 1Ch 1:36).
2. A chief of Edom (Ge 36:42; 1Ch 1:53).
3. Brother of Caleb (Jos 15:17; Jdg 1:13; 3:9, 11; 1Ch 4:13).
4. Grandson of Caleb (1Ch 4:15).

KENITE(S) (*of the [copper] smiths*).
1. A Canaanite tribe whose country was given to Abraham (Ge 15:19; Nu 24:21-23).
2. The descendants of Jethro, a Midianite, father-in-law of Moses. Joined the Israelites and lived at Jericho (Jdg 1:16; 4:11; 1Ch 2:55), later in the wilderness of Judah (Jdg 1:16-17). Jael, one of the, betrayed and killed Sisera (Jdg 4:17-21).

KENIZZITE(S) Descendants of Kenaz (Ge 15:19). Caleb (Nu 32:12) and Othniel (Jos 15:17) were Kenizzites.

KENOSIS (*emptying*). A term applied to Christ's taking of form of a servant in the Incarnation (Php 2:7).

KEPHAR AMMONI (*village of Ammonites*). A town of Benjamin (Jos 18:24).

KEPHIRAH (*village*). A city of the Hivites (Jos 9:17; 18:26; Ezr 2:25; Ne 7:29).

KERAMIM See Abel Keramim.

KERAN A Horite (Ge 36:26; 1Ch 1:41).

KERCHIEF See Handkerchief.

KEREN-HAPPUCH (*horn of [cosmetic] eyeshadow*; i.e., *cosmetic case*). Youngest daughter of Job (Job 42:14).

KERETHITE(S) (possibly *Cretans* BDB KB; *executioners* ISBE). A Philistine tribe, which allied with David and, with the Pelethites, formed his bodyguard (1Sa 30:14, 16; 2Sa 8:18; 15:18; 20:7, 23; 1Ki 1:38, 44; 1Ch 18:17; Eze 25:16; Zep 2:5). Solomon's escort at his coronation (1Ki 1:38).

KERIOTH, KERIOTH HEZRON (*town of Hezron*).
1. A city of Judah (Jos 15:25).
2. A city of Moab (Jer 48:24, 41; Am 2:2).

KERITH (*cut off, perish*). A brook near Jericho (1Ki 17:3-7).

KEROS Ancestor of the temple servants who returned with Zerubbabel (Ezr 2:44; Ne 7:47).

KERUB Name of a place or person (Ezr 2:59; Ne 7:61).

KESALON A landmark in the N boundary of Judah (Jos 15:10).

KESED (*Chaldean [Babylonian]*). Son of Nahor (Ge 22:22).

KESIL A town in the S of Israel (Jos 15:30). Probably identical with Bethul (Jos 19:4), and Bethuel (1Ch 4:30).

KESULLOTH (*loins or flanks [of Mt. Tabor]* BDB). A city of Issachar (Jos 19:18). Probably identical with Kisloth Tabor (Jos 19:12) and Tabor (1Ch 6:77).

KETTLE Cooking vessel or basket (1Sa 2:14).

KETURAH (*incense, scented one*). Abraham's second wife. Mother of six sons, ancestors of Arabian tribes (Ge 25:1-6; 1Ch 1:33).

KEY (Jdg 3:25). A symbol of authority (Isa 22:22; Mt 16:19; Rev 1:18; 3:7; 9:1; 20:1). See Binding and Loosing.
Figurative: key of knowledge (Lk 11:52).

KEZIAH (*cassia [cinnamon]*). Second daughter of Job (Job 42:14).

KEZIB (*deceit*). Birthplace of Shelah (Ge 38:5), probably identical with Cozeba (1Ch 4:22), and Aczib (Jos 15:44).

KEZIZ See Emek Keziz.

KIBROTH HATTAAVAH (*graves of lust, greed*). A station where the Israelites were miraculously fed with quail (Nu 11:31-35; 33:16-17; Dt 9:22).

KIBZAIM A Levitical city in Ephraim (Jos 21:22).

KID See Animals; Goats.

KIDNAPPING Forbidden (Ex 21:16; Dt 24:7).
Instance of (Jdg 21:20-23).

KIDNEY Used with surrounding fat as a burnt offering (Ex 29:13, 22; Lev 3:4, 10, 15; 4:9). Regarded as the seat of the emotions; usually translated "heart" (Ps 7:9; 16:7).

KIDON Place where Uzzah was stricken to death because he had put his hand on the ark (1Ch 13:9-11). Called Nacon's threshing floor (2Sa 6:6).

KIDRON Brook of, running S under the eastern wall of Jerusalem between Jerusalem and the Mount of Olives (1Ki 2:37; Ne 2:15; Jer 31:40). David flees from Absalom across (2Sa 15:23). Destruction of idols at, by Asa, Josiah, and the Levites (1Ki 15:13; 2Ki 23:6, 12; 2Ch 29:16). Source of, closed by Hezekiah (2Ch 32:1-4). Jesus crossed, on the night of his agony (Jn 18:1).

KILEAB A son of David (2Sa 3:3). Also called Daniel (1Ch 3:1).

KILION (*annihilation*). Son of Elimelech and Naomi, married Orpah (Ru 1:2-5; 4:9-10).

KILLING See Homicide.

KILMAD Merchants of (Eze 27:23).

KIMHAM A Gileadite (2Sa 19:37-38, 40; Jer 41:17).

KINAH (*lament, dirge*). A city of Judah (Jos 15:22).

KINDNESS
Commanded: (Zec 7:9-10; Mt 5:42; Lk 6:30; 6:34-35; Ac 20:35; Ro 12:15; 15:1-2; Gal 6:1-2, 10; Eph 4:32; Col 3:12; 1Pe 3:8-9; 1Jn 3:17-18). To enemies (Ex 23:4-5; Lk 6:34-35). To strangers (Lev 19:34). To a brother (Dt 22:1).
Inspired by love (1Co 13:4-7). Commends ministers (2Co 6:6). Rewards of (Pr 14:21; Mt 5:7; 25:34-35).
Of God (Lk 6:35). Of good women (Pr 31:26; 1Ti 5:9-10). Of good men (Ps 112:5; Heb 5:2). Of Jesus. See Jesus the Christ, Compassion of.
Instances of:
Hittites to Abraham (Ge 23:6, 11). Keeper of the prison to Joseph (Ge 39:21-23). Pharaoh to Jacob (Ge 45:16-20; 47:5-6). Pharaoh's daughter to Moses (Ex 2:6-10). Moses to Jethro's daughters (Ex 2:17, 19). Jethro to Moses (Ex 2:20). Rahab to the spies (Jos 2:4-16). Boaz to Ruth (Ru 2:8-16; 3:15). David to Nabal (1Sa 25:15-16). Abigail to David (1Sa 25:14-35). David to Mephibosheth (2Sa 9:1-13). Joab to Absalom (2Sa 14:1-24). Obadiah to the prophets of the Lord (1Ki 18:4). Ahab to Ben-Hadad (1Ki 20:32-34). The Shunammite woman to Elisha (2Ki 4:8-10). Elisha to the Shunammite woman (2Ki 4:13-17, 28-37; 8:1). Evil-Merodach to Jehoiachin (2Ki 25:28-30). Jehosheba to Joash (2Ch 22:11). Nehemiah and the nobles to the people (Ne 5:8-19). Mordecai to Esther (Est 2:7). Ebed-Melech to Jeremiah (Jer 38:7-13). Nebuchadnezzar to Jeremiah (Jer 39:11-12).
Joseph to Mary (Mt 1:19, 24). Centurion to his servant (Lk 7:2-6). Jews to Mary and Martha (Jn 11:19, 33). John to Mary (Jn 19:27). Felix to Paul (Ac 24:23). Julius to Paul (Ac 27:3, 43). Barbarians to Paul (Ac 28:2, 7). Onesiphorus to Paul (2Ti 1:16-18).

KINE See Cattle.

KINGDOM OF GOD, OF HEAVEN The sovereign rule of God manifested in Christ to defeat His enemies, creating a people over whom He reigns, and issuing in a realm or realms in which the power of His reign is experienced. All they are members of the kingdom of God who voluntarily submit to the rule of God in their lives. Entrance into the kingdom is by the new birth (Jn 3:3-5); two stages in the kingdom of God; present and future in an eschatological sense; Jesus said that his ability to cast out demons was evidence that the kingdom of God had come among men (Mt 12:28). "Kingdom of heaven" is used exclusively in Matthew (33 times). Likened to, a man who sowed good seed (Mt 13:24-30, 38-43; Mk 4:26-29), a grain of mustard seed (Mt 13:31-32; Mk 4:30-31; Lk 13:18-19), leaven (Mt 13:33; Lk 13:21), a treasure (Mt 13:44), a pearl (Mt 13:45), a net (Mt 13:47-50), a king who called his servants to a reckoning (Mt 18:23-35), a house owner (Mt 20:1-16), a king who made a marriage feast for his son (Mt 22:2-14; Lk 14:16-24), ten virgins (Mt 25:1-13), a man traveling into a far country, who called his servants, and delivered to them his goods (Mt 19:12-27).
"My kingdom is not of this world" (Jn 18:36).
Children of the (Mt 18:3; 19:14; Mk 10:14; Lk 18:16). Rich cannot enter (Mt 19:23-24; Mk 10:23-25; Lk 18:24-25, 29-30). Keys of (Mt 16:19). Glad tidings of (Lk 8:1). Mysteries of (Lk 8:10). Is not eating and drinking (Ro 14:17).
See Church, The Body of Believers; Jesus, Kingdom of.

KINGDOM OF ISRAEL See Israel.

KINGDOM OF JUDAH See Judah.

KINGDOM OF SATAN The realm of Satan's influence (Mt 12:26; Lk 11:18).

KINGS
In Israel:
Israel warned against seeking (1Sa 8:9-18). Sin of Israel in seeking (1Sa 12:17-20). Israel in seeking, rejected God as their king (1Sa 8:7; 10:19). Israel asked for, that they might be like the nations (1Sa 8:5, 19-20). First given to Israel in anger (Hos 13:11). God reserved to himself the choice of (Dt 17:14-15; 1Sa 9:16-17; 16:12). When first established in Israel, not hereditary (Dt 17:20, w 1Sa 13:13-14; 15:28-29). Rendered hereditary in the family of David (2Sa 7:12-16; Ps 89:35-37). Of Israel not to be foreigners (Dt 17:15). Laws for the government of the kingdom by, written by Samuel (1Sa 10:25).
Forbidden to accumulate: Horses (Dt 17:16). Wives (Dt 17:17). Treasure (Dt 17:17).
Required to write and keep a copy of the divine law (Dt 17:18-20). Had power to make war and peace (1Sa 11:5-7). Often exercised power arbitrarily (1Sa 22:17-18; 2Sa 1:15; 4:9-12; 1Ki 2:23, 25, 31). Sometimes nominated their successors (1Ki 1:33-34; 2Ch 11:22-23). Punished for transgressing the divine law (2Sa 12:7-12; 1Ki 21:18-24).
Called the Lord's anointed (1Sa 16:6; 24:6; 2Sa 19:21).
Ceremonies at Inauguration of:
Anointing (1Sa 10:1; 16:13; Ps 89:20). Crowning (2Ki 11:12; 2Ch 23:11; Ps 21:3). Proclaiming with trumpets (2Sa 15:10; 1Ki 1:34; 2Ki 9:13; 11:14). Enthroning (1Ki 1:35, 46; 2Ki 11:19). Strapping on the sword (Ps 45:3). Putting into their hands the books of the law (2Ki 11:12; 2Ch 23:11). Covenanting to govern lawfully (2Sa 5:3). Receiving homage (1Sa 10:1; 1Ch 29:24). Shouting "Long live the King!" (1Sa 10:24; 2Sa 16:16; 1Ki 1:25; 2Ch 23:11). Offering sacrifice (1Sa 11:15). Feasting (1Ch 12:38-39; 29:22). Dwelt in royal palaces (2Ch 9:11; Ps 45:15). Arrayed in

royal apparel (1Ki 22:30; Mt 6:29). Names of, often changed at their accession (2Ki 23:34; 24:17).
Officers of:
Prime minister (2Ch 19:11, w 2Ch 28:7). First Counselor (1Ch 27:33). Confident or king's special friend (1Ki 4:5; 1Ch 27:33). Comptroller of the household (1Ki 4:6; 2Ch 28:7). Scribe or secretary (2Sa 8:17; 1Ki 4:3). Captain of the host (2Sa 8:16; 1Ki 4:4). Captain of the guard (2Sa 8:18; 20:23). Recorder (2Sa 8:16; 1Ki 4:3). Providers for the king's table (1Ki 4:7-19). Master of the wardrobe (2Ki 22:14; 2Ch 34:22). Treasurer (1Ch 27:25). Storekeeper (1Ch 27:25). Overseer of, the tribute (1Ch 4:6; 12:18), royal farms (1Ch 27:26), royal vineyards (1Ch 27:27), royal plantations (1Ch 27:28), royal herds (1Sa 21:7; 1Ch 27:29), royal camels (1Ch 27:30), royal flocks (1Ch 27:31). Armor-bearer (1Sa 16:21). Cupbearer (1Ki 10:5; 2Ch 9:4). Approached with greatest reverence (1Sa 24:8; 2Sa 9:8; 14:22; 1Ki 1:23). Presented with gifts by strangers (1Ki 10:2, 10, 25; 2Ki 5:5; Mt 2:11). Right hand of, the place of honor (1Ki 2:19; Ps 45:9; 110:1). Attendants of, stood in their presence (1Ki 10:8; 2Ki 25:19). Exercised great hospitality (1Sa 20:25-27; 2Sa 9:7-13; 19:33; 1Ki 4:22-23, 28).
Their Revenues Derived From:
Voluntary contributions (1Sa 10:27, w 1Sa 16:20; 1Ch 12:39-40). Tribute from foreign nations (1Ki 4:21, 24-25; 2Ch 8:8; 17:11). Tax on produce of the land (1Ki 4:7-19). Tax on foreign merchandise (1Ki 10:15). Their own flocks and herds (2Ch 32:29). Produce of their own lands (2Ch 26:10).
Conspiracies Against:
Absalom against David (2Sa 15:10). Adonijah against Solomon (1Ki 1:5-7). Jeroboam against Rehoboam (1Ki 12:12, 16). Baasha against Nadab (1Ki 15:27). Zimri against Elah (1Ki 16:9-10). Omri against Zimri (1Ki 16:17). Jehu against Joram (2Ki 9:14). Shallum against Zechariah (2Ki 15:10). Menahem against Shallum (2Ki 15:14). Pekah against Menahem (2Ki 15:25).
The Kings of Israel and Judah:
See chart on the following page. See also each king by name and the outlines of the books of Kings and Chronicles.
Relation to God:
God chooses (Dt 17:15; 1Ch 28:4-6). God ordains (Ro 13:1). God anoints (1Sa 16:12; 2Sa 12:7). Set up by God (1Sa 12:13; Da 2:21). Removed by God (1Ki 11:11; Da 2:21). Christ is the Prince of (Rev 1:5). Christ is the King of (Rev 17:14). Reign by direction of Christ (Pr 8:15). Supreme judges of nations (1Sa 8:5). Resistance to, is resistance to the ordinance of God (Ro 13:2). Able to enforce their commands (Ecc 8:4). Numerous subjects the honor of (Pr 14:28). Not saved by their armies (Ps 33:16). Dependent on the earth (Ecc 5:9). Throne of, established by righteousness and justice (Pr 16:12; 29:14).
Should:
Fear God (Dt 17:19). Serve Christ (Ps 2:10-12). Keep the law of God (1Ki 2:3). Study the Scriptures (Dt 17:19). Promote the interests of the Church (Ezr 1:2-4; 6:1-12). Nourish the Church (Isa 49:23). Rule in the fear of God (2Sa 23:3). Maintain the cause of the poor and oppressed (Pr 31:8-9). Investigate all matters (Pr 25:2). Not pervert judgment (Pr 31:5). Prolong their reign by hating greed (Pr 28:16).
Specially Warned Against:
Impurity (Pr 31:3). Lying (Pr 17:7). Listening to lies (Pr 29:12). Intemperance (Pr 31:4-5). The gospel is to be preached to (Ac 9:15; 26:27-28). Without understanding, are oppressors (Pr 28:16). Often reproved by God (1Ch 16:21). Judgments upon, when opposed to Christ (Ps 2:2, 5, 9).
When Good:
Regard God as their strength (Ps 99:4). Speak righteously (Pr 16:10). Love righteous lips (Pr 16:13). Abhor wickedness (Pr 16:12). Reject evil (Pr 20:8). Punish the wicked (Pr 20:26). Favor the wise (Pr 14:35). Honor the diligent (Pr 22:29). Befriend the good (Pr 22:14). Are pacified by submission (Pr 16:14; 25:15). Evil counselors should be removed from (2Ch 22:3-4; Pr 25:5).
Good exemplified: David (2Sa 8:15). Asa (1Ki 15:11). Jehoshaphat (1Ki 22:43). Amaziah (2Ki 15:3). Uzziah (2Ki 15:34). Hezekiah (2Ki 18:3). Josiah (2Ki 22:2).
Should Be:
Honored (Ro 13:7; 1Pe 2:17). Feared (Pr 24:21). Revered (1Sa 24:8; 1Ki 1:23, 31). Obeyed (Ro 13:1, 5; 1Pe 2:13). Prayed for (1Ti 2:1-2). Folly of resisting (Pr 19:12; 20:2). Punishment for resisting the lawful authority of (Ro 13:2). Guilt and danger of stretching out the hand against (1Sa 26:9; 2Sa 1:14). Curse not, even in thought (Ex 22:28; Ecc 10:20). Speak no evil of (Job 34:18; 2Pe 2:10). Pay tribute to (Mt 22:21; Ro 13:6-7). Be not presumptuous before (Pr 25:6). Wicked despise (2Pe 2:10; Jude 8).

KING'S GARDEN Near the Pool of Siloam (2Ki 25:4; Jer 39:4; 52:7; Ne 3:15).

KING'S HIGHWAY Ancient N and S route E of the Jordan through Edom and Moab (Nu 20:17; 21:22). The road is still in use.

KING'S VALLEY Valley of Shaveh E of Jerusalem (Ge 14:17; 2Sa 18:18).

KINGS, 1 and 2

Author: Anonymous; Jewish tradition credits Jeremiah

Date: Between 562 B.C. and 538

Outline:
I. The Solomonic Era (1:1-12:24).
 A. Solomon's Succession to the Throne (1:1-2:12).
 B. Solomon's Throne Consolidated (2:13-46).
 C. Solomon's Wisdom (ch. 3).
 D. Solomon's Reign Characterized (ch. 4).
 E. Solomon's Building Projects (5:1-9:9).
 1. Preparation for building the temple (ch. 5).
 2. Building the temple (ch. 6).
 3. Building the palace (7:1-12).
 4. The temple furnishings (7:13-51).

KINNERETH (*zithers, lyres*).
1. A district in the N of Israel (Jos 11:2; 1Ki 15:20).
2. A city in Naphtali (Jos 19:35).
3. The sea of (Nu 34:11; Jos 12:3; 13:27). *See Galilee, Sea of.*

KINSMAN Family or friends (Job 19:14), of same tribe (1Ch 12:2, 29; 2Ch 29:34; Ezr 8:17), fellow Israelites (2Ch 28:8). Figurative of wisdom (Pr 7:4). *See Kinsman-Redeemer.*

KINSMAN-REDEEMER A close relative responsible for protecting the interests of needy members of the extended family. To provide an heir for a brother who had died (Ge 38:6-11; Dt 25:5-10; Ru 3-4). *See Levirite Marriage.* To redeem land that a poor relative had sold outside the family (Lev 25:25-28). To redeem a relative who had been sold into slavery (Lev 25:47-49). To avenge the killing of a relative (Nu 35:19-21). *See Avenger of Blood.*

KIOS An island W of Smyrna (Ac 20:15).

The Kings of the United Kingdom				
	Name	Ruled	Dates B.C.	Biblical References
1.	Saul	40 years	1050–1010	1Sa 11:15,31; 1Ch 10
2.	David	40 years	1010–970	2Sa 2:4; 1Ki 2:11; 1Ch 11–29
3.	Solomon	40 years	970–930	1Ki 1:39; 11:43; 2Ch 1–9

The Kings (and Queen) of Judah				
1.	Rehoboam	17 years	930–913	1Ki 12:1–24; 14:21–31; 2Ch 10:1–17; 12
2.	Abijah	3 years	913–910	1Ki 15:1–8; 2Ch 13
3.	Asa	41 years	910–869	1Ki 15:9–24; 2Ch 14; 16:14
4.	Jehoshaphat	25 years	872–848	1Ki 22:41–50; 2Ch 17; 21:1
5.	Jehoram	8 years	848–841	2Ki 8:16–24; 21
6.	Ahaziah	1 year	841	2Ki 8:25–29; 9:16–29; 2Ch 22:1–9
7.	Queen Athaliah	6 years	841–835	2Ki 11:1–3; 2Ch 22:10–12
8.	Joash	40 years	835–796	2Ki 11:4; 12; 2Ch 23–24
9.	Amaziah	29 years	796–767	2Ki 14:1–20; 2Ch 25
10.	Uzziah / Azariah	52 years	792–740	2Ki 14:21–22; 15:1–7; 2Ch 26
11.	Jotham	16 years	750–735	2Ki 15:32–38; 2Ch 27
12.	Ahaz	16 years	732–715	2Ki 16; 2Ch 28
13.	Hezekiah	29 years	715–686	2Ki 18–20; 2Ch 29–32
14.	Manasseh	55 years	697–642	2Ki 21:1–18; 2Ch 33:1–20
15.	Amon	2 years	642–640	2Ki 21:19–26; 2Ch 33:21–25
16.	Josiah	31 years	640–609	2Ki 22; 23:1–30; 2Ch 34–35
17.	Jehoahaz	3 months	609	2Ki 23:31–33; 2Ch 36:1–4
18.	Jehoiakim	11 years	609–598	2Ki 23:34–37; 24:1–6; 2Ch 36:5–8
19.	Jehoiachin	3 months	598–597	2Ki 24:8–16; 2Ch 36:9–10
20.	Zedekiah / Mattaniah	11 years	597–586	2Ki 24:17–20; 25:1–7; 2Ch 36:11–21

The Kings of Israel				
1.	Jeroboam I	22 years	930–909	1Ki 12:20,25; 14:20
2.	Nadab	2 years	909–908	1Ki 15:25–27,31
3.	Baasha	24 years	908–886	1Ki 15:28–34; 16:1–7
4.	Elah	2 years	886–885	1Ki 16:8–14
5.	Zimri	7 days	885	1Ki 16:11–12,15–20
6.	Omri	12 years	885–874	1Ki 16:23–28
7.	Ahab	22 years	874–853	1Ki 16:29–22:40
8.	Ahaziah	2 years	853–852	1Ki 22:51–53; 2Ki 1
9.	Joram	12 years	852–841	2Ki 3–9:26
10.	Jehu	28 years	841–814	2Ki 9:3–10; 36
11.	Jehoahaz	17 years	814–798	2Ki 13:1–9
12.	Jehoash	16 years	798–782	2Ki 13:10–25; 14:8–16
13.	Jeroboam II	41 years	793–753	2Ki 14:23–29
14.	Zechariah	6 months	753	2Ki 15:8–12
15.	Shallum	1 month	752	2Ki 15:13–15
16.	Menahem	10 years	752–742	2Ki 15:16–22
17.	Pekahiah	2 years	742–740	2Ki 15:23–26
18.	Pekah	20 years	752–732	2Ki 15:27–31; 16:5
19.	Hoshea	9 years	732–722	2Ki 17:1–6

Note: Some kings, such as Jehoash and Jeroboam II, had overlapping reigns.

KIR (*walled enclosure*). The inhabitants of Damascus carried into captivity to, by the king of Assyria (2Ki 16:9). Prophecies concerning (Isa 22:6; Am 1:5; 9:7).

KIR HARESETH (*walled [city] of pottery fragments*). A city of Moab (2Ki 3:25; Isa 16:7, 11; Jer 48:31, 36). Called Kir of Moab (Isa 15:1).

KIR OF MOAB *See Kir.*

KIRIATH (*city of*). City of Benjamin (Jos 18:28).

KIRIATH ARBA (*city of four*). Ancient name for Hebron (Ge 23:2; Jos 14:15; 15:54; 20:7).

KIRIATH BAAL *See Kiriath Jearim.*

KIRIATH HUZOTH (*city of Huzoth [outside spaces]*). A residence of Balak (Nu 22:39).

KIRIATH JEARIM (*city of timberlands*). Called also Baalah, one of the four cities of the Gibeonites. Inhabitants of, not destroyed, on account of the covenant made by the Israelites with the Gibeonites (Jos 9:17, w Jos 9:3-27).

In the territory allotted to Judah (Jos 15:9, 60; 18:14). The Philistines bring the ark to (1Sa 6:21, w 1Sa 6:1-21), ark remains twenty years at (1Sa 7:1-2; 1Ch 13:5-6). David brings the ark from (2Sa 6:1-11; 1Ch 13:5-8; 2Ch 1:4). Inhabitants of, who were taken into captivity to Babylon, returned (Ezr 2:25; Ne 7:29). Uriah, the prophet, an inhabitant of (Jer 26:20).

KIRIATH SANNAH (*city of Sannah*). A city of Judah (Jos 15:49); also called Kiriath Sepher and Debir. *See Debir; Kiriath Sepher.*

KIRIATH SEPHER (*city of scribe*). A city of Judah (Jos 15:15-16); also called Kiriath Sannah; Debir. *See Debir; Kiriath Sannah.*

KIRIATHAIM (*two cities*).
1. Town in Moab N of Arnon. Assigned to Reuben (Nu 32:37; Jos 13:19).
2. City of Gershonite Levites in Naphtali (1Ch 6:76). Called Kartan (Jos 21:32).

KIRIOTH *See Kerioth, Kerioth Hezron.*

KIRJATH-ARIM *See Kiriath Jearim.*

KISH (*bow, power*).
1. Father of Saul (1Sa 9:1-3; 10:21; 2Sa 21:14). Called Kish (Ac 13:21).
2. A Benjamite (1Ch 8:30; 9:36).
3. A Levite (1Ch 23:21-22; 24:29).
4. A Levite (2Ch 29:12).
5. Great-grandfather of Mordecai (Est 2:5).

KISHI (possibly *gift* IDB; *snarer* ISBE). Also called Kushaiah. Father of Ethan, a chief assistant in the temple music (1Ch 6:44; 15:17).

KISHION City of Issachar (Jos 19:20). Also called Kedesh (1Ch 6:72).

KISHON (*cunning*). A river of Israel emptying into the Mediterranean near the northern base of Mount Carmel. Sisera defeated here, and his army destroyed (Jdg 4:7, 13; 5:21; Ps 83:9). Prophets of Baal destroyed by Elijah at (1Ki 18:40).

KISLEV Month nine in sacred sequence, month three in civil sequence (Ezr 10:9; Jer 36:9, 22; Zec 7:1). The rainy season (November-December); the season for planting. The Feast of Dedication (Jn 10:22).
See Dedication; Feasts; Hanukkah; Maccabees; Month, 9.

KISLON (*slow*IDB; *strength* ISBE). Father of Eldad (Nu 34:21).

KISLOTH TABOR A place on the border of Zebulun (Jos 19:12). Called Tabor (1Ch 6:77). Probably the same as Kesulloth (Jos 19:18).

KISS Of affection (Ge 27:26-27; 31:55; 33:4; 48:10; 50:1; Ex 18:7; Ru 1:14; 2Sa 14:33; 19:39; Lk 15:20; Ac 20:37). The feet of Jesus kissed by the penitent woman (Lk 7:38).
Deceitful (Pr 27:6), of Joab, when he killed Amasa (2Sa 20:9-10), of Judas, when he betrayed Jesus (Mt 26:48; Lk 22:48). Holy (Ro 16:16; 2Co 13:12; 1Th 5:26; 1Pe 5:14).

KITE A bird forbidden as food (Lev 11:14; Dt 14:13).

KITLISH Town in lowlands of Judah (Jos 15:40), site unknown.

KITRON (*incense, [sacrificial] smoke*). A city of Zebulun (Jdg 1:30).

KITTIM
1. Descendants of Javan (Ge 10:4; 1Ch 1:7).
2. The Hebrew name for Cyprus; probably inhabited islands of the Mediterranean (Isa 23:1, 12; Jer 2:10; Eze 27:6).
3. Prophecies concerning (Nu 24:24; Da 11:30).

KNEADING TROUGH Shallow vessel for kneading dough with hands (Ex 8:3; 12:34).

KNEE Bowing the knee or kneeling as an act of reverence (Ge 41:43; 2Ki 1:13), and subjection (Isa 45:23; Php 2:10).

KNIFE An edged tool used by Abraham in offering Isaac (Ge 22:6, 10). Of flint, used in circumcision (Ex 4:25; Jos 5:2, 3). Used for pruning (Isa 18:5), by scribes (Jer 36:23).

KNOB *See Capital.*

KNOWLEDGE Of good and evil (Ge 2:9, 17; 3:22). Is power (Pr 3:20; 24:5). Desire for (1Ki 3:9; Ps 119:66; Pr 2; 3; 12:1; 15:14; 18:15). Rejected (Hos 4:6). Those who reject are destroyed (Hos 4:6). Fools hate (Pr 1:22, 29). A divine gift (1Co 12:8). Is pleasant (Pr 2:10). Shall be increased (Da 12:4).
The earth shall be full of (Isa 11:9). Fear of the Lord is the beginning of (Pr 1:7). Of more value than gold (Pr 8:10). The priest's lips should keep (Mal 2:7).
Of salvation (Lk 1:77). Key of (Lk 11:52). Now we know in part (1Co 13:9-12). Of God more than burnt offering (Hos 6:6). Of Christ (Php 3:8).
See God, Knowledge of; Jesus the Christ, Omniscience of; Wisdom.

KOA People E of Tigris, between Elam and Media (Eze 23:23).

KOHATH Second son of Levi (Ge 46:11; Ex 6:16). Grandfather of Moses, Aaron, and Miriam (Nu 26:58-59). Father of the Kohathites, one of the divisions of the Levites (Ex 6:18; Nu 3:19, 27).
See Levites.

KOLAIAH (*Yahweh's voice*).
1. A Benjamite and ancestor of Sallu (Ne 11:7).
2. Father of the false prophet Ahab (Jer 29:21).

KORAH, KORAHITE(S) (*shaven, bald*).
1. Son of Esau (Ge 36:5, 14, 18; 1Ch 1:35).
2. Grandson of Esau (Ge 36:16).
3. Descendant of Caleb (1Ch 2:43).
4. Levite from whom the Korahites were descended (Ex 6:24; 1Ch 6:22).

KORAZIN Denunciation against (Mt 11:21; Lk 10:13).

KORE (*proclaimer*).
1. A Korahite (1Ch 9:19; 26:1).
2. A Levite, keeper of the East Gate (2Ch 31:14).

KORHITE(S) *See Korah, Korahite(s), 4; Levites.*

KOZ (*thorn*). The father of Anub and Hazzobebah (1Ch 4:8).

KUE Probably Cilicia in SE Asia Minor (1Ki 10:28; 2Ch 1:16).

KUSHAIAH Merarite Levite (1Ch 15:17). Also called Kishi (1Ch 6:44).

L

LAADAH (perhaps *having a fat neck or throat*). Son of Shelah (1Ch 4:21).

LAADAN *See Ladan.*

LABAN (*white*).
1. Son of Bethuel (Ge 28:5). Brother of Rebekah (Ge 22:23; 24:15, 29). Receives the servant of Abraham (Ge 24:29-33). Receives Jacob and gives him his daughters in marriage (Ge 29:12-30). Jacob becomes his servant (Ge 29:15-20, 27; 30:27-43). Outwitted by Jacob (Ge 30:37-43; 31:1-21). Pursues Jacob, overtakes him in hill country of Gilead, and covenants with him (Ge 31:22-55).
2. Place in Plains of Moab (Dt 1:1).

LABOR Honorable (Ps 128:2; Pr 21:25; 1Th 4:11). Laborers protected by laws (Dt 24:14). Creative work of God described as labor (Ge 2:2). Difficult labor the result of the curse (Ge 3:17-19). Sleep of laborer sweet (Ecc 5:12).
Labor commanded (Ge 3:19; Ex 20:9-11; 23:12; 34:21; Lev 23:3; Lk 13:14; Ac 20:35; Eph 4:28; 1Th 4:11; 2Th 3:10-12).
Compensation for (Lev 19:13; Dt 25:4; 1Co 9:9; 1Ti 5:18; Jer 22:13; Mal 3:5; Mt 20:1-15; Lk 10:7; Jas 5:4). Of servants must not be oppressive (Dt 24:14-15).
Paul, an example (2Th 3:8-13).
See Capital and Labor; Employee; Employer; Idleness; Industry; Master; Servant.

LACE Cord used to bind high priest's breastplate to the ephod (Ex 28:28, 37; 39:21, 31).

LACHISH Canaanite royal city and Judean border fortress, occupying a strategic valley twenty-five miles SW of Jerusalem. It is identified with Tell ed-Duweir (Tell Lakhish). Joshua captured it (Jos 10:31-33); destroyed by Nebuchadnezzar along with Jerusalem (2Ki 24:25; Jer 34:7), resettled after the Exile (Ne 11:30). Lachish Letters (ostraca) from the time of Jeremiah reveal much about the city.

LACHRYMATORY A container for holding the tears of mourners (Ps 56:8, ftn).

LADAN
1. A descendant of Ephraim (1Ch 7:26).
2. A Levite, called also Libni (1Ch 6:17; 23:7-9; 26:21).

LADDER (Ge 28:12, ftn). *See Stairs.*

LAEL (*[belonging] to God [El]*). Father of Eliasaph (Nu 3:24).

LAHAD (perhaps *slow, indolent*). A descendant of Judah (1Ch 4:2).

LAHAI-ROI *See Beer Lahai Roi.*

LAHMAS Town in Judean Shephelah (Jos 15:40). Probably modern Khirbet el-Lahm.

LAHMI Brother of Goliath. Slain by Elhanan (2Sa 21:19; 1Ch 20:5).

LAISH (*lion*).
1. A Sidonian city at the N. extremity of Israel (Jdg 18:7, 14, 27, 29). Called also Leshem (Jos 19:47), and afterwards Dan. *See Dan, 3; Leshem.*
2. A native of Gallim; a Benjamite, whose son became the husband of Michal, David's wife (1Sa 25:44; 2Sa 3:15).
3. *See Laishah.*

LAISHAH (*lion*). A town near Jerusalem (Isa 10:30).

LAKE OF FIRE Place of final judgment (Rev 19:20; 20:10, 14-15; 21:8).

LAKKUM Town of Naphtali (Jos 19:33), location unknown.

LAMA SABACHTHANI *See Eloi, Eloi, Lama Sabachthani.*

LAMB Used, for food (Dt 32:14; Am 6:4), for sacrifices (Ge 4:4; 22:7), especially at Passover (Ex 12:3-5). Sacrificial lambs typical of Christ (Jn 1:29; Rev 5:6, 8).
Offering of (Lev 3:7; 5:6; 22:23; 23:12; Nu 7:15, 21; 28:3-8), at the daily morning and evening sacrifices (Ex 29:38-42). Offering of, at the Feast of Passover (Ex 12:15), Pentecost (Lev 23:18-20), Tabernacles (Nu 29:13-40), the New Moon (Nu 28:11), trumpets (Nu 29:2). Offering of, on the Sabbath day (Nu 28:9), at

purifications (Lev 12:6; 14:10-25), by the Nazirite (Nu 6:12), for sin of ignorance (Lev 4:32).

Figurative:
The wolf living with, a figure of Messiah's reign (Isa 11:6; 65:25). A type of young believers (Jn 21:15).
A name given to Christ (Jn 1:29, 36; Rev 5:6, 8, 12-13; 6:1, 16; 7:9-10, 14; 12:11; 13:8; 14:4, 10; 17:14; 19:7, 9; 21:9, 14, 22-23, 27; 22:1, 3). Jesus compared to (Isa 53:7; Ac 8:32; 1Pe 1:19).

LAMB OF GOD A title of Jesus (Jn 1:29; Rev 6:16; 7:9-10, 14, 17; 12:11; 13:8; 14:1, 4; 15:3; 17:14; 19:7; 21:9, 14, 22-23, 27; 22:1, 3).

LAME *See Disease.*

LAMECH
1. Father of Jabal, Jubal, and Tubal-Cain (Ge 4:18-24).
2. Son of Methuselah, and father of Noah, lived 777 years (Ge 5:25-31; 1Ch 1:3). Ancestor of Jesus (Lk 3:36).

LAMENESS Disqualified priest from exercising the priestly office (Lev 21:18). Disqualified animals for sacrificial uses (Dt 15:21). Hated by David (2Sa 5:8). Healed by Jesus (Mt 11:5; 15:31; 21:14; Lk 7:22), by Peter (Ac 3:2-11).

LAMENTATIONS Of David (Ps 60:1-3). Of Jeremiah (La 1-5). Of Ezekiel (Eze 19; 28:12-19). *See Elegy.*

LAMENTATIONS, BOOK OF
Author: Anonymous, traditionally Jeremiah
Date: Shortly after the fall of Jerusalem in 586 B.C.
Outline:
I. Jerusalem's Misery and Desolation (ch. 1).
II. The Lord's Anger Against His People (ch. 2).
III. Judah's Complaint—and Basis of Consolation (ch. 3).
IV. The Contrast Between Zion's Past and Present (ch. 4).
V. Judah's Appeal for God's Forgiveness (ch. 5).

LAMP
Figurative: Of joy (Jer 25:10). Life (Job 18:5-6; 21:17; Pr 13:9; 20:20). The word of God (Ps 119:105; Pr 6:23; 2Pe 1:19). Spiritual illumination (Mt 6:22). Religious influence (Mt 5:15; Mk 4:21; Lk 8:16; 11:33). Jesus is the lamp of the New Jerusalem (Rev 21:23).
Symbolic (Rev 4:5; 8:10).
See Lampstand.

LAMPSTAND
Of the Tabernacle:
Made of gold after divine pattern (Ex 25:31-40; 37:17-24; Nu 8:4), burned olive oil (Ex 27:20). Place of (Ex 26:35; 40:24-25; Heb 9:2). Furniture of (Ex 25:38; 37:23; Nu 4:9-10). Burned every night (Ex 27:20-21). Trimmed every morning (Ex 30:7). Carried by Kohathites (Nu 4:4, 15). Called the lamp of God (1Sa 3:3).
Of the Temple:
Ten branches of (1Ki 7:49-50). Of gold (1Ch 28:15; 2Ch 4:20). Taken with other spoils to Babylon (Jer 52:19).
Symbolic (Zec 4:2, 11; Rev 1:12-13, 20; 2:5; 11:4).

LANCE *See Javelin; Spear.*

LAND Appeared on third creative day (Ge 1:9). Original title to, from God (Ge 13:14-17; 15:7; Ex 23:31; Lev 25:33). Bought and sold (Ge 23:3-18; 33:19; Ac 4:34; 5:1-8).
Sale and redemption of, laws concerning (Lev 25:15-16, 23-33; 27:17-24; Nu 36:4; Jer 32:7-16, 25, 44; Eze 46:18). Conveyance of, by written deeds and other forms (Ge 23:3-20; Ru 4:3-8, 11; Jer 32:9-14), witnessed (Ge 23:10-11; Ru 4:9-11; Jer 32:9-14).
Sold for debt (Ne 5:3-5). Rights in, alienated (2Ki 8:1-6). Leased (Lk 20:9-16; Mt 21:33-41).
Priest's part in (Ge 47:22; Eze 48:10). King's part in (Eze 48:21). Widow's share in (Ru 4:3-9). Unmarried woman's rights in (Nu 27:1-11; 36:1-11).
To rest every seventh year for the benefit of the poor (Ex 23:11). Products of, for all (Ecc 5:9). Monopoly of (Ge 47:20-26; Isa 5:8; Mic 2:1-2). *See Mortgage.*
Rules for apportioning Canaan among the tribes (Eze 47:22). *See Canaan.*

LANDMARKS (*border*). Protected from fraudulent removal (Dt 19:14; 27:17; Job 24:2; Pr 22:28; 23:10; Hos 5:10). *See Boundary Stones.*

LANES Country lanes (Lk 14:21). *See Streets.*

LANGUAGE Unity of (Ge 11:1, 6). Confusion of (Ge 11:1-9; 10:5, 20, 31). Dialects of the Jews (Jdg 12:6; Mt 26:73). Many spoken at Jerusalem (Jn 19:20; Ac 2:8-11).
Gift of (Mk 16:17; Ac 2:7-8; 10:46; 19:6; 1Co 12:10; 14). *See Tongues, Gift of.*

Mentioned in Scripture:
Aramaic (2Ki 18:26; Ezr 4:7; Da 2:4). Of Ashdod (Ne 13:24). Babylonian [or Chaldean] (Da 1:4). Canaanite (Isa 19:18). Egyptian (Ac 2:10; Ps 81:5). Greek (Jn 19:20; Ac 21:37). Hebrew (Rev 9:11; 16:16). Of Judah (Ne 13:24). Latin (Jn 19:20). Lycaonia (Ac 14:11). Parthia and other lands (Ac 2:9-11).

LANTERN (Jn 18:3).

LAODICEA A Phrygian city. Paul's concern for (Col 2:1). Epaphras' zeal for (Col 4:13). Epistle to the Colossians to be read in (Col 4:15-16). Message to, through John (Rev 1:11; 3:14-22).

LAODICEA, CHURCH AT *See Laodicea.*

LAODICEANS, EPISTLE TO Letter mentioned by Paul (Col 4:16). This is probably a letter of Paul that was not preserved for the canon. Some theorize it may be the letter to the Ephesians as a circular letter. An apocryphal epistle to the Laodiceans exists in Latin.

LAPIDARY One who cuts precious stones (Ex 31:5; 35:33).

LAPPED A Hebrew verb used to indicate alertness (Jdg 7:5-7) and disgust (1Ki 21:19; 22:38).

LAPPIDOTH (*flames*). Husband of Deborah (Jdg 4:4).

LAPWING See Hoopoe.

LARCENY See Theft.

LASCIVIOUSNESS Unbridled lust, licentiousness, wantonness.

Condemned:
Forbidden (Col 3:5; 1Th 4:3-6). Warnings against (Pr 2:16-18; 5:3-5, 8-13; 7:6-27; 9:13-18; 30:18-20; 31:3; Ro 13:13; 1Co 6:13, 15-18; 1Pe 4:2-3; Jude 4, 7).
Sinful practices in (Joel 3:3; Ro 1:22-29). Proceeds from unregenerate heart (Mk 7:21-23; Gal 5:19; Eph 4:17-19). Impenitence in (2Co 12:21). Excludes from the kingdom of God (1Co 6:9-10, 13, 15-18; 9:27; Gal 5:19, 21; Eph 5:5).
Lascivious practices in idolatrous worship. See Idolatry, Wicked practices of.
See Adultery; Homosexual; Incest; Lust; Prostitute; Rape; Sensuality.

Figurative: (Eze 16:15-59). See Prostitute.

Instances of:
Sodomites (Ge 19:5). Lot's daughters (Ge 19:30-38). Judah (Ge 38:15-16). The Gibeahites (Jdg 19:22-25). Eli's sons (1Sa 2:22). David (2Sa 5:13; 11:2-27). Amnon (2Sa 13:1-14). Solomon (1Ki 11:1-3). Rehoboam (2Ch 11:21-23). Persian kings (Est 2:3, 13-14, 19).

LASEA Seaport on S coast of Crete. Visited by Paul (Ac 27:8).

LASHA Place near Sodom and Gomorrah (Ge 10:19). Site not identified.

LASHARON ([*belonging to*] *Sharon*). King of, killed by Joshua (Jos 12:18).

LASHES
1. Beating could subject the culprit to abuse, so the law kept the punishment from becoming inhumane (Dt 25:2-3). Solomon uses hyperbole to illustrate that a rebuke has greater influence on a wise man than a hundred lashes will have on a fool (Pr 17:10). Compare Paul's experience (2Co 11:24). See Stripes.
2. A figurative description of Jerusalem experiencing the wrath of God finally being rebuilt into the Holy City, the New Jerusalem (Isa 54:11-12, w Rev 21:10, 18-21).
See Assault and Battery; Bruise(s); Flog, Flogging; Scourging; Stoning.

LAST First and last: a title of Yahweh (Isa 44:6; 48:12), of Jesus (Rev 1:17; 2:8; 22:13). See Titles and Names.
The first will be last and the last first (Nu 24:20; Mt 19:30; 20:16; Mk 9:35; 10:31; Lk 13:30).

LAST DAYS The days before the final judgment (Jn 12:48), when God's kingdom is established on earth (Isa 2:2-4; Mic 4:1-8), and Israel is restored to her God (Hos 3:5). Began with the coming of Jesus and of the Spirit (Ac 2:16-21; Heb 1:2; 1Pe 1:20). The time of the resurrection (Jn 6:39-44, 54; 11:24). A time of great trouble and deception (2Ti 3:1-17; 2Pe 3:3-17; Jude 18-19), culminating in the Second Coming of Christ (1Pe 1:5). See Day of the Lord; Eschatology.

LATCHET See Thong.

LATIN The language of the Roman Empire, used in Israel in NT times (Jn 19:20).

LATRINE Temple of Baal used as (2Ki 10:27).

LATTICE Latticework used for privacy, ventilation, decoration (Jdg 5:28; 2Ki 1:2; Pr 7:6).

LAUGHTER Used to express joy (Ge 21:6; Lk 6:21), derision (Ps 2:4), disbelief (Ge 18:13).

LAUNDERER See Fuller.

LAVER See Bronze Basin; Bronze Sea.

LAW
1. Ten Commandments given to Moses (Ex 20:3-17; Dt 5:6-21), summarizing God's requirements of mankind.
2. The Torah, first five books of OT (Mt 5:17; Lk 16:16).
3. The whole OT (Jn 10:34; 12:34).
4. God's will in words, acts, precepts (Ex 20:1-17; Ps 19:1-14).

The Purpose of the Law—
Under the old covenant, believers manifested their faith in Yahweh by observing the law for their own good (Dt 6:4-9; 10:12-13; 30:1-16). Christ fulfilled the law; respected, loved it, and showed its deeper significance (Mt 5:17-48). The law prepared the way for the coming of Christ (Gal 3:24). The law could not bring victory over sin (Ro 3-8; Gal).
Jesus' summary of the law: It demands perfect love for God, and love for one's neighbor comparable to that which one has for oneself (Mt 22:35-40).
Made for the lawless (1Ti 1:8-10). Must be obeyed (Mt 22:21; Lk 20:22-25).

Law of God:
(Ps 119:1-8; Jas 1:25). Spiritual (Ro 7:14). Must be obeyed (1Jn 5:3). Love, the fulfilling of (Ro 13:10; 1Ti 1:5).
See Litigation; Commandments and Statutes, Of God; Duty, Of People to God.

Law of Moses:
Contained in the books of Exodus, Leviticus, Numbers, and Deuteronomy. Divine authority for (Ex 19:16-24; 20:1-2;

24:12-18; 32:15-16; 34:1-4, 27-28; Lev 26:46; Dt 4:10-13, 36; 5:1-22; 9:10; 10:1-5; 33:2-4; 1Ki 8:9; Ezr 7:6; Ne 1:7; 8:1; 9:14; Ps 78:5; 103:7; Isa 33:22; Mal 4:4; Ac 7:38, 53; Gal 3:19; Heb 9:18-21).
Given at Sinai (Ex 19; Dt 1:1; 4:10-13, 44-46; 32:2; Hab 3:3). Received by the disposition of angels (Dt 32:2; Ps 68:17; Ac 7:53; Gal 3:19; Heb 2:2). Was given because of transgression until the Messiah came (Gal 3:19). Engraved on stone (Ex 20:3-17; 24:12; 31:18; 32:16; 34:29; 40:20; Dt 4:13; 5:22; 9:10), on monuments (Dt 27:2-8; Jos 8:30-35).
See Tablets of the Law; Commandments and Statutes, Of God.
Preserved in the ark of the covenant (Ex 25:16; Dt 31:9, 26). To be written on doorframes (Dt 6:9; 11:20) and as a symbol on the forehead and a sign on the hand (Ex 13:9, 16; Dt 6:4-9; 11:18-21), meaning the law was to govern society, home, personal thoughts and actions. Children instructed in. See Children; Instruction.
Expounded by priests and Levites (Lev 10:11; Dt 33:10; 2Ch 35:3), by princes, priests, and Levites (Ezr 7:10; Ne 8:1-18), from city to city (2Ch 17:7-10), in synagogues (Lk 4:16; Ac 13:14-52; 15:21, w Ac 9:20, & 14:1; 17:1-3; 18:4, 26). Expounded to the assembled nation at the feast of tabernacles in the sabbatic year (Dt 31:10-13). Rehearsed by Moses, with many admonitions (Dt 4:44-46; 5-34).
Obedience to, commanded (Dt 4:40; 5:32; 6:17; 7:11; 8:1, 6; 10:12-13; 11:1, 8, 32; 13:4; 16:12; 27:1; 30:16; 32:46; Jos 1:7; 22:5; 1Ki 2:3; 8:61; 2Ki 17:37). Found by Hilkiah in the house of the Lord (2Ki 22:8; 2Ch 34:14).
Blessings and curses of, responsively read by Levites and people at Ebal and Gerizim (Dt 27:12-26; Jos 8:33-35).
Formed a constitution on which the civil government of the Israelites was founded, and according to which rulers were required to rule (Dt 17:18-20; 2Ki 11:12; 2Ch 23:11). See Constitution; Government.
Was given because of transgressions until the coming of the Messiah (Gal 3:19). Was committed to the Jews (Ro 3:1-2). Brings the knowledge of sin (Ro 3:20; 7:7).
Prophecies in, of the Messiah (Lk 24:44; Jn 1:45; 5:46; 12:34; Ac 26:22-23; 28:23; Ro 3:21-22). See Jesus the Christ, Prophecies Concerning.
Epitomized by Jesus (Mt 22:40; Mk 12:29-33; Lk 10:27).
Temporary (Jer 3:16; Da 9:27; Heb 10:1-18). Weakness of the law (Ro 8:3, 6).
Fulfilled by Christ (Mt 5:17-45; Ac 6:14; 13:39; Ro 10:3-4; Eph 2:15; Heb 8:4-13; 9:8-24; 10:3-9).
Superseded by the gospel (Lk 16:16-17; Jn 1:17; 4:20-24; 8:35; Gal 4:30-31; Ac 10:28; 15:1-20; 21:20-25; Ro 7:1-6; 2Co 3:7-14; Gal 2:3-9, 19; 4:4-31; 5:1-18; Col 2:14-23; Heb 7:5-9).

LAW OF MOSES See Law.

LAWGIVER God is the only absolute lawgiver (Jas 4:12), instrumentally, Moses bears this description (Jn 1:17; 7:19).

LAWSUITS To be avoided (Pr 25:8-10; Mt 5:25-26; 1Co 6:1-8).
See Actions at Law; Adjudication at Law; Arbitration; Compromise; Court, Of Law; Justice.

LAWYER One versed in the law of Moses. Test Jesus with questions (Mt 22:35; Lk 10:25-37). Jesus' satire against (Lk 11:45-52). Tertullus presents case against Paul (Ac 24:1-2). Zenas (Tit 3:13). See Litigation.

LAYING ON OF HANDS Symbolic act signifying impartation of inheritance rights (Ge 48:14-20), gifts and rights of an office (Nu 27:18, 23), dedication of animals (Lev 1:4), priests (Nu 8:10), people for special service (Ac 6:6; 13:3).

LAZARUS (*one whom God helps*).
1. Brother of Martha and Mary; raised from the dead by Jesus (Jn 11:1-12:19).
2. Beggar who died and went to Abraham's side (Lk 16:19-31). See Abraham's Side.

LAZINESS (Pr 12:27; 18:9; 19:24; 21:25; 22:13; 26:13-16). Brings adversity (Pr 12:24; Ecc 10:18), destruction (Pr 13:4; 19:15; 20:4; 23:21; 24:30-34).
Admonitions against (Pr 6:6-11; 10:4-5, 26; 15:19). Denounced (Mt 25:26-27). Of ministers, denounced (Isa 56:10). Forbidden (Ro 12:11; Heb 6:12).
See Idleness; Slothfulness.

LEAD A mineral (Ex 15:10). Purified by fire (Nu 31:22; Jer 6:29; Eze 22:18, 20). Used in making inscriptions on stone (Job 19:24). Refining (Jer 6:29; Eze 22:18, 20). Trade in (Eze 27:12). Used for weighing (Zec 5:7-8).

LEADERSHIP Instances of: Abraham, Moses, Joshua, Gideon, Deborah. See each under its own entry.

LEAF Leaf of a tree, page of a book, leaf of a door. Metaphorically, green leaves symbolize prosperity, and dry leaves ruin and decay (Ps 1:3; Pr 11:28; Job 13:25; Isa 1:30).

LEAGUE See Alliances; Treaty.

LEAH (possibly *wild cow* BDB; *wild cow, gazelle* IDB; *cow* KB [cf. Rachel = *ewe*]). Daughter of Laban (Ge 29:16). Married to Jacob (Ge 29:23-26). Children of (Ge 29:31-35; 30:9-13, 17-21). Flees with Jacob (Ge 31:4, 14, 17; 33:2-7). "Built up the house of Israel" (Ru 4:11).

LEANNOTH (*the suffering of affliction*, NIV; *sickness or suffering poem*, JB). See Music, Symbols Used in.

LEARNING See Instruction; Knowledge.

LEASE See Land; Renting.

LEASING An obsolete word for falsehood (Ps 4:2; 5:6).

LEATHER (*skin*). Designates the tanned hide of animals. Skins were used for rough clothing as well as for armor, bags, sandals, and writing materials (Lev 13:48; Eze 16:10; Mt 3:4; Heb 11:37).

LEAVEN (*piece of fermented dough*). For bread (Ex 12:34, 39; Hos 7:4; Mt 13:33). Leavened bread used with peace offering (Lev 7:13; Am 4:5), with wave offering (Lev 23:15-17). Leavened bread forbidden with meat offerings (Lev 2:11; 6:17; 10:12; Ex 23:18; 34:25), at the Passover (Ex 12:19-20; 13:3-4, 7; 23:18), with blood (Ex 23:18; 34:25).
A type of sin (1Co 5:6-8).

Figurative:
Of the hypocrisy of the Pharisees (Mt 16:6-12; Mk 8:15; Lk 12:1). Of other evils (1Co 5:6-8; Gal 5:9). Parable of (Mt 13:33; Lk 13:21).

LEB KAMAI (*the heart of my attackers*). A cryptogram (hidden code) for Babylon (Jer 51:1 ftn). See Babylon.

LEBANA, LEBANAH (*white*). Ancestor of a family which returned from the Exile (Ezr 2:45; Ne 7:48).

LEBANON (*white, snow*). A mountain range. Northern boundary of the land of Canaan (Dt 1:7; 3:25; 11:24; Jos 1:4; 9:1). Early inhabitants of (Jdg 3:3). Snow of (Jer 18:14). Streams of (SS 4:15). Cedars of (Jdg 9:15; 2Ki 19:23; 2Ch 2:8; Ps 29:5; 104:16; Isa 2:13; 14:8; Eze 27:5). Other trees (2Ki 19:23; 2Ch 2:8). Flower of (Na 1:4). Beasts of (Isa 40:16). Fertility and productiveness of (Hos 14:5-7). "Palace of the Forest of," (1Ki 7:2-5). Valley of (Jos 11:17; 12:7). Tower of (SS 7:4). Solomon had store cities (1Ki 9:19). Figurative: (Isa 29:17; Jer 22:6).

LEBAOTH (*lionesses*). Town in S Judah (Jos 15:32), also called Beth Lebaoth (Jos 19:6), and probably Beth Biri (1Ch 4:31).

LEBBAEUS ([*one near to*] *my heart*). An alternate reading in some mss for Thaddaeus, one of Christ's apostles (Mt 10:3). See Thaddaeus.

LEBO HAMATH (*the entrance to Hamath*). A city located on the Orontes River of Northern Syria, though it might be "the entrance to Hamath" rather than a main city (Nu 13:21; 34:8 and ftns). See Hamath.

LEBONAH (*frankincense*). A city on the highway from Bethel to Shechem (Jdg 21:19).

LECAH (*to you*). A town or person in Judah (1Ch 4:21).

LEECH Bloodsucking parasite, personifying greed (Pr 30:15). See Animals.

LEEK A herb of the lily family, similar in flavor to the onion (Nu 11:5).

LEES (*something preserved*). Sediment of wine (Isa 25:6). Also used figuratively to describe blessings of messianic times, spiritual lethargy, inevitability of God's judgment (Jer 48:11; Ps 75:8).

LEFT Used with a variety of meanings. Simple direction; North (Ge 14:15). Lesser blessing (Ge 48:13-19). Characteristic of Benjamites (Jdg 3:15, 21; 20:16).

LEFT-HANDED Characteristic of Benjamites (Jdg 3:15; 20:16; 1Ch 12:2).

LEGALISTIC Seeking God's favor by keeping the letter of the law without keeping its spirit (Mt 23:23-24). Legalists in the early church required circumcision for salvation (Ac 15:1-29). Paul's first letter, Galatians, was written to combat legalistic teaching about the Christian life (Gal 3:2, 10-14; 4:9-11).
The Christian lives a life of grace, not works (Eph 2:8-9) and is not judged by ritual observance of special diet or holy days (Ro 14:1-18; Col 2:16-19; Heb 13:9). See Commandments and Statutes, Of Men; Grace.

LEGENDS See Inscriptions.

LEGION (*military company*).
1. Largest unit in the Roman army, including infantry and cavalry.
2. Vast number (Mt 26:53; Mk 5:9).

LEGISLATION Class, forbidden (Ex 12:49; Lev 24:22; Nu 9:14; 15:15, 29; Gal 3:28). Supplemental, concerning Sabbath-breaking (Nu 15:32-35), inheritance (Nu 27:1-11). See Government; Law.

LEGS Of the crucified broken (Jn 19:31-32).

LEHABITES Descendants of Mizraim (Ge 10:13; 1Ch 1:11).

LEHEM See Jashubi Lehem.

LEHI (*jawbone*). Place where Samson killed a thousand Philistines with a jawbone of a donkey (Jdg 15:9, 14).

LEMUEL ([*belonging*] *to God* [*El*]). A king, otherwise unknown, to whom his mother taught the maxims in Pr 31:1-9.

LENDING

To the Poor, Commanded:
(Lev 25:35; Dt 15:7, 11). Commanded by Christ (Mt 5:42; Lk 6:34-35). Encouraged (Ps 112:5; Pr 19:17). God, the merciful Lender (Ps 37:25-26). Borrower to be released in the year of release (Dt 15:1-6).

Things Forbidden as Security of Loans:
Millstones (Dt 24:6). Widow's cloak (Dt 24:17).

Lender:
Forbidden to take interest from poor Hebrews (Ex 22:25-27; Lev 25:36-37; Dt 23:19-20). Forbidden to enter debtor's house for

security (Dt 24:10-11). Forbidden to keep overnight clothing left in pledge (Dt 24:12-13).

Oppression of borrower (Ne 5:1-13). Is master of borrower (Pr 22:7). Lender and borrower will be equal (Isa 24:1-2). Wicked, punished (Pr 28:8; Eze 18:13).

See Borrowing; Interest; Money.

LENTIL(S) (Ge 25:34; 2Sa 17:28; 23:11; Eze 4:9).

LEOPARD
A carnivorous animal (SS 4:8). Fierceness of (Jer 5:6; 13:23; Hos 13:7; Hab 1:8).

Figurative: (Da 7:6). Taming of, the triumph of the gospel (Isa 11:6).

LEPROSY
The word is used for various diseases affecting the skin—not necessarily leprosy (Hansen's disease).

General:
Law concerning (Lev 13-14; 22:4; Nu 5:1-3; 12:14; Dt 24:8; Mt 8:4; Lk 5:14; 17:14). Entailed (2Ki 5:27). Isolation of lepers (Lev 13:46; Nu 5:2; 12:14; 2Ki 15:5; 2Ch 26:21). Separate burial (2Ch 26:23).

Sent as a judgment. On Miriam (Nu 12:1-10), Gehazi (2Ki 5:27), Azariah/Uzziah (2Ki 15:5; 2Ch 26:20-21). Other instances: Four lepers outside Samaria (2Ki 7:3), Simon (Mk 14:3).

Healed:
Miriam (Nu 12:13-14), Naaman (2Ki 5:8-14), by Jesus (Mt 8:3; Mk 1:40-42; Lk 5:13; 17:12-14). Disciples empowered to heal (Mt 10:8).

LESBIAN
Sexual activity between females is condemned (Ro 1:26). *See Homosexual.*

LESHEM
(*lion*). City renamed Dan, at extreme N of Israel (Jos 19:47), variant of Laish. *See Dan, 3; Laish.*

LETHEK
About 10 bushels (330 liters) (Hos 3:2). *See Measure.*

LETTER
Designates an alphabetical symbol, rudimentary education (Jn 7:15), written communication, the external (Ro 2:27, 29), Jewish legalism (Ro 7:6; 2Co 3:6). In ancient times correspondence was privately delivered. Archaeology has uncovered many different kinds of letters. *See Writing.*

LETTERS
Written by David to Joab (2Sa 11:14), king of Syria to king of Israel (2Ki 5:5-6), the field commander to Hezekiah (Isa 37:9-14), king of Babylon to Hezekiah (Isa 39:1), Sennacherib to Hezekiah (2Ki 19:14). Of Artaxerxes to Nehemiah (Ne 2:7-9). Open letter from Sanballat to Nehemiah (Ne 6:5). Luke to Theophilus, the books of Luke and Acts (Ac 1:1). Claudius Lysias to Felix (Ac 23:25-30). Letter of intercession by Paul to Philemon in behalf of Onesimus (Phm 1), of recommendation (2Co 3:1). In the NT, the books of Romans through Jude and Rev 1-3. *See Writing.*

LETUSHITES
(*sharpened*). Descendants of Dedan, grandson of Abraham (Ge 25:3).

LEUMMITES
(perhaps *peoples* or *hordes*). Descendants of Dedan (Ge 25:3).

LEVI
(perhaps *wild cow* or *person pledged for a debt or vow*). Son of Jacob (Ge 29:34; 35:23; 1Ch 2:1). Avenges the seduction of Dinah (Ge 34; 49:5-7). Jacob's prophecy regarding (Ge 49:5-7). His age at death (Ex 6:16). Descendants of, made ministers of religion. *See Levites.*

LEVIATHAN
(*coiled one [like a serpent]*). Possibly a crocodile (Job 41; Ps 104:26). A sea monster figurative of forces of chaos opposed to Yahweh (Job 3:8; Ps 74:14; Isa 27:1). *See Dragon; Serpent.*

LEVIRATE MARRIAGE
Jewish custom according to which when an Israelite died without male heirs, his nearest relative married the widow, and their firstborn son became the heir of the first husband (Dt 25:5-10; Ru 3-4). *See Kinsman-Redeemer.*

LEVITES
(*of Levi*). The descendants of Levi. Set apart as ministers of religion (Nu 1:47-54; 3:6-16; 16:9; 26:57-62; Dt 10:8; 1Ch 15:2). Substituted in the place of the firstborn (Nu 3:12, 41-45; 8:14, 16-18; 18:6). Religious zeal of (Ex 32:23-28; Dt 33:9-10; Mal 2:4-5). Consecration of (Nu 8:6-21). Sedition among, led by Korah, Dathan, Abiram, and On, on account of jealousy toward Moses and Aaron (Nu 16, w 4:19-20).

Three Divisions of:
Each having the name of one of its progenitors. Gershon, Kohath, and Merari (Nu 3:17). Gershonites and their duties (Nu 3:18-26; 4:23-26; 10:17). Ruling chief over the Gershonites was the second son of the ruling high priest (Nu 4:28). Kohathites, consisting of the families of the Amramites, Izharites, Hebronites, Uzzielites (Nu 3:27; 4:18-20). Of the Amramites, Aaron, and his family were set apart as priests (Ex 28:1; 29:9; Nu 3:38; 8:1-14; 17; 18:1), the remaining families appointed to take charge of the ark, table, lampstand, altars and vessels of the sanctuary, the hangings, and all the service (Nu 3:27-32; 4:2-15). The chief over the Kohathite was the oldest son of the ruling high priest (Nu 3:32; 1Ch 9:20). Merarites (Nu 3:20, 33-37; 4:31-33; 7:8; 10:17; 1Ch 6:19, 29-30; 23:21-23). The chief over the Merarites was the second son of the ruling high priest (Nu 4:33).

Place of, in camp and march (Nu 1:50-53; 2:17; 3:23-35). Cities assigned to, in the land of Canaan (Jos 21). Lodged in the chambers of the temple (1Ch 9:27, 33; Eze 40:44). Resided also in villages outside of Jerusalem (Ne 12:29).

Age of, when inducted into office (Nu 4:3, 30, 47; 8:23-26; 1Ch 23:3, 24, 27; Ezr 3:8), when retired from office (Nu 4:3, 47; 8:25-26).

Functions of:
Had charge of the tabernacle in camp and on the march (Nu 1:50-53; 3:6-9, 21-37; 4:1-15, 17-49; 8:19, 22; 18:3-6), and of the temple (1Ch 9:27-29; 23:2-32; Ezr 8:24-34).

Bore the ark of the covenant (Dt 10:8; 1Ch 15:2, 26-27). Ministered before the ark (1Ch 16:4). Custodians and administrators of the tithes and other offerings (1Ch 9:26-29; 26:28; 29:8; 2Ch 24:5, 11; 31:11-19; 34:9; Ezr 8:29-30, 33; Ne 12:44). Prepared the bread of the Presence (1Ch 23:28-29). Assisted the priests in preparing the sacrifice (2Ch 29:12-36; 2Ch 35:1-18). Killed the Passover for the children of the Captivity (Ezr 6:20-21). Teachers of the law (2Ch 33:10; 2Ch 17:8-9; 30:22; 35:3; Ne 8:7-13; Mal 2:6-7). Were judges (Dt 17:9; 1Ch 23:4; 26:29; 2Ch 19:8-11; Ne 11:16). *See Judge.*

Were scribes of the sacred books. *See Scribe.* Pronounced the blessings of the law in the responsive service at Mount Gerizim (Dt 27:12; Jos 8:33). Were gatekeepers of the temple. *See Gatekeepers.* Were overseers in building and the repairs of the temple (1Ch 23:2-4; Ezr 3:8-9). Were musicians of the temple service. *See Music.* Supervised weights and measures (1Ch 23:29).

List of those who returned from the Captivity (Ezr 2:40-63; 7:7; 8:16-20; Ne 7:43-73; 12). Sealed the covenant with Nehemiah (Ne 10:9-28).

Privileges of:
In lieu of landed inheritance, forty-eight cities with suburbs were assigned to them (Nu 35:2-8, w 18:24 & 26:62; Dt 10:9; 12:12, 18-19; 14:27-29; 18:1-8; Jos 13:14; 14:3; 18:7; 1Ch 6:54-81; 13:2; 2Ch 23:2; Eze 34:1-5). Assigned to, by families (Jos 21:4-40). Suburbs of their cities were inalienable for debt (Lev 25:32-34). Tithes and other offerings (Nu 18:24, 26-32; Dt 18:1-8; 26:11-13; Jos 13:14; Ne 10:38-39; 12:44, 47). Firstfruits (Nu 18:12, 19). Spoils of war, including captives (Nu 31:30, 42-47). *See Tithes.* Tithes withheld from (Ne 13:10-13; Mal 3:10). Pensioned (2Ch 31:16-18). Owned lands (Dt 18:8, w 1Ki 2:26). Land allotted to, by Ezekiel (Eze 48:13-14).

Enrollment of, at Sinai (Nu 1:47-49; 2:33; 3:14-39; 4:2-3; 26:57-62; 1Ch 23:3-5). Degraded from the Levitical office by Jeroboam (2Ch 11:13-17; 13:9-11). Loyal to the ruler (2Ki 11:7-11; 2Ch 23:7).

Intermarry with Canaanites (Ezr 9:1-2; 10:23-24). Exempt from enrollment for military duty (Nu 1:47-54, w 1Ch 12:26). Subordinate to the sons of Aaron (Nu 3:9; 8:19; 18:6).

Prophecies Concerning:
(Jer 33:18; Eze 44:10-14; Mal 3:3), of their repentance of the crucifixion of the Messiah (Zec 12:10-13). John's vision concerning (Rev 7:7).

LEVITICUS (*relating to the Levites*).

Author: Moses

Date: Between 1445 and 1406 B.C.

Outline:
I. The Five Main Offerings (chs. 1-7).
 A. Their Content, Purpose and Manner of Offering (1:1-6:7).
 B. Additional Regulations (6:8-7:38).
II. The Ordination, Installation and Work of Aaron and His Sons (chs. 8-10).
III. Laws of Cleanness—Food, Childbirth, Infections, etc. (chs. 11-15).
IV. The Day of Atonement and the Centrality of Worship at the Tabernacle (chs. 16-20).
V. Moral Laws Covering Incest, Honesty, Thievery, Idolatry, etc. (chs. 18-20).
VI. Regulations for the Priests, the Offerings and the Annual Feasts (21:1-24:9).
VII. Punishment for Blasphemy, Murder, etc. (24:10-23).
VIII. The Sabbath Year, Jubilee, Land Tenure and Reform of Slavery (ch. 25).
IX. Blessings and Curses for Covenant Obedience and Disobedience (ch. 26).
X. Regulations for Offerings Vowed to the Lord (ch. 27).

LEVY
A tribute imposed by a conquering king (2Ki 23:33; 2Ch 36:3).

LEX TALIONIS See Retaliation.

LIARS
All people are liars (Ps 116:11). Satan the father of lies (Jn 8:44, 55). Ungodly (1Ti 1:10). Characteristc of Cretans (Tit 1:12). Eternally punished (Rev 21:8).

God cannot lie (Nu 23:19; Tit 1:2; Heb 6:18).

See Deceit; Deception; False Witness; Falsehood; Hypocrisy.

LIBATION
(*pour [as an offering]*). Pouring out of wine or some other liquid as an offering to a deity as an act of worship (Ex 29:40-41; Jer 44:17-25). *See Offerings, Drink.*

LIBERALITY

Commanded:
(Ex 22:29-30; 23:15; 34:20; Lev 23:22; 25:35-43; Dt 12:11-12, 17-19; Pr 3:27-28; Mt 5:42; Ac 20:35; Ro 12:8; 2Co 8:7, 9, 11-14, 24; 1Ti 6:18; Heb 13:16).

In offerings, for tabernacle (Ex 25:1-8; 35:4-29; 36:3-6; 38:8). For the temple (Hag 1:8). With the Levites (Dt 12:11-12, 17-19; 18:1-8). For the temple commanded by Cyrus (Ezr 1:2-4). In offerings for sacrifice (2Sa 24:24).

In paying tithes (Dt 14:27-29). In gifts to God (Ps 76:11).

In gifts to the poor (Dt 15:7-11; 24:19-22; Ne 8:10; Ps 41:1-3; Isa 58:6-7; Mt 19:21-22; Mk 10:21; Lk 3:10-11; Ro 12:13; 15:27; 16:1-2; 2Co 9:5; Gal 2:10; Eph 4:28; 1Ti 5:16; 6:17-19; Jas 2:15-16; 1Jn 3:17-18). By the noble woman (Pr 31:20). In gifts to liberated Hebrew slaves (Dt 15:12-18).

Giving according to ability (Nu 35:8; Dt 16:10, 17; 1Co 16:1-3; 2Co 8:12). Giving without a show (Mt 6:1-4). Giving of freewill (Lev 19:5; 22:9; 1Ch 29:5; Pr 21:26; 2Co 8:12; 9:1-6; Phm 14). Giving with love (1Co 13:3).

Rewards for giving (Ps 112:5, 9; Pr 3:9-10; 11:24-25; 13:7; 14:21; 19:6, 17; 22:9; 28:27; Ecc 11:1-2; Isa 32:8; 58:10-12; Eze 18:7-16; Mal 3:10-12; Mt 5:42; 25:34-40, 46; Lk 6:30-38; 12:33-34; Heb 6:10).

See Alms; Beneficence; Charitableness; Giving; Minister; Poor, Duty to; Rich, The; Riches; Tithes.

Instances of:
King of Sodom to Abraham (Ge 14:21). Jacob, consecrating the tenth of his income (Ge 28:22). Pharaoh to Joseph's people (Ge 45:18-20). Israelites at the building of the tabernacle (Ex 35:21-29; 36:3-7; 38:8; Nu 7; 31:48-54; Jos 18:1). Reubenites (Jos 22:24-29). David (2Sa 5:1; 2Sa 7:2; 1Ch 17:1; 2Sa 8:11; 1Ki 7:51; 8:17-18; 1Ch 21:24; 22; 26:26; 28:2; 29:2-5, 17). Barzillai and others to David (2Sa 17:27-29; 19:32). Araunah for sacrifice (2Sa 24:22-23). Joab to David (2Sa 12:26-28).

Israelites' offerings for the temple 1Ch 29:6-9, 16-17). Samuel (1Ch 26:27-28). Solomon (2Ch 5:4-5; 2Ch 2:1-6; 1Ki 6:7; 5:17; 8:13). Queen of Sheba to Solomon (1Ki 10:10). Asa and Abijah (1Ki 15:15). Elisha toward Elijah (1Ki 19:21). Jehoshaphat (2Ch 12:18). Joash and his people (2Ki 12:4-14; 2Ch 24:4-14). David (1Ch 16:3). Hezekiah (2Ch 29; 30:1-12; 31:1-10, 21). Manasseh (2Ch 33:16). Josiah (2Ki 22:3-6; 2Ch 34:8-13; 35:1-19).

Jews after the Captivity (Ezr 1:5-6; 2:68-69; 3:2-9; 5:2-6; 6:14-22; 8:25-35; Ne 3; 4:6; 6:3; 7:70-72; 10:32-39; 13:12, 31; Hag 1:12-19). Cyrus (Ezr 1:2-4, 7-11; 3:7; 5:13-15; 6:3). Darius (Ezr 6:7-12). Artaxerxes (Ezr 7:13-27; 8:34-36).

The Magi (Mt 2:11). Centurion (Lk 7:4-5). Mary Magdalene (Lk 8:2-3). The good Samaritan (Lk 10:33-35). Poor widow (Lk 21:2-4). Christians in Jerusalem (Ac 2:44-45; 4:32-37), in Antioch (Ac 11:29), at Philippi (Php 4:18), Corinth (2Co 8:19; 9:1-13), Macedonia (2Co 8:1-4). People of Malta to Paul (Ac 28:10).

LIBERTINES See Freedman.

LIBERTY
Freedom, whether physical, moral, or spiritual. Israelites who had becomes slaves were freed in the Year of Jubilee (Lev 25:8-17). Through Christ's death and resurrection the believer is free from sin's dominion (Jn 1:29; 8:36; Ro 6-7), Satan's control (Ac 26:18), the law (Gal 3), fear, the second death, future judgment.

Of Hebrew Servants:
In the seventh year (Ex 21:2; Dt 15:12; Jer 34:14), in Year of Jubilee (Lev 25:10, 40).

Political: (Ac 22:28).

Religious: In Rome (Ac 28:31).

Spiritual: (Ps 119:45; Isa 61:1; Lk 4:18; Jn 8:32-33, 36; Ro 6:6, 22; 8:1-2; 1Co 7:22; 2Co 3:17; Gal 2:4; 1Pe 2:16).

Figurative: Of the gospel (Jas 1:25; 2:12).

LIBNAH (*white*).
1. A station of the Israelites in the desert (Nu 33:20).
2. A city of Judah, captured by Joshua (Jos 10:29-32, 39; 12:15). Allotted to the priests (Jos 21:13; 1Ch 6:57). Sennacherib besieged; his army defeated near (2Ki 19:8, 35; Isa 37:8-36).

LIBNATH See Shihor Libnath.

LIBNI, LIBNITE(S) (*[descendant of] Libni* or *white*).
1. Son of Gershon (Ex 6:17; Nu 3:18; 1Ch 6:17, 20). Descendants called Libnites (Nu 3:21; 26:58).
2. Grandson of Merari (1Ch 6:29).

LIBRARIES
Libraries, both public and private, were not uncommon in ancient times in the Oriental, Greek, and Roman worlds. The Dead Sea Scrolls are one example of an ancient library that has survived to modern times.

LIBYA, LIBYANS
A people of N Africa, W of Egypt, who were allies of Egypt (2Ch 12:3; 16:8; Eze 30:5; 38:5; Da 11:43; Ac 2:10). Also called Put. *See Put, 2.*

LICE See Gnat.

LICENTIOUSNESS See Adultery; Lasciviousness.

LIEUTENANTS See Satrap; Secretary.

LIFE
Breath of (Ge 2:7). Called breath of God (Job 27:3). Tree of (Ge 2:9; 3:22, 24; Pr 3:18; 13:12; Rev 2:7). Sacredness of, an inference from what is taught in the law concerning murder. *See Homicide.* Meaninglessness of (Ecc 1-7).

Length of:
Long life promised (Ge 6:3; Ps 91:16), to Solomon (1Ki 3:11-14), to the wise (Pr 3:16; 9:11), to the obedient (Dt 4:40; 22:7; Pr 3:1-2), to those who honor parents (Ex 20:12; Dt 5:16), to those who show kindness to animals (Dt 22:7), given to those who fear God (Pr 10:27; Isa 65:20).

See Longevity.

Brevity of (Ge 47:9; Job 10:9, 20-21; 13:12, 25, 28; Ps 89:47-48; 90:10; 146:4; Isa 2:22). Compared, to a shadow (1Ch 29:15; Job 8:9; 14:1-2; Ps 102:11; 144:3; 144:4; Ecc 6:12). To a weaver's shuttle (Job 7:6-10). To a courier (Job 9:25-26). To a handbreadth (Ps 39:4-5, 11). To a wind (Ps 78:39). To grass (Ps 90:3, 5-6, 9-10; 102:11; 103:14-16; Isa 40:6-8, 24; 51:12; Jas 1:10-11; 1Pe 1:24). To a leaf (Isa 64:6). To a vapor (Jas 4:14).

Weary of: Job (Job 3; 7:1-3; 10:18-19). Jeremiah (Jer 20:14-18), Elijah (1Ki 19:1-4), Jonah (Jnh 4:8), Paul (Php 1:21-24).

See Suicide.

Hated (Ecc 2:17). To be hated for Christ's sake (Lk 14:26). What shall a man give in exchange for (Mt 16:26; Mk 8:37). He that loses it for Christ's sake shall save it (Mt 10:39; 16:25-26; Lk 9:24; Jn 12:25).

Uncertainty of (1Sa 20:3; Job 4:19-21; 17:1; Pr 27:1; Lk 12:20). End of, certain (2Sa 14:14; Ps 22:29; Ecc 1:4; Isa 38:12).

See Death, Physical.

Comes From God:
(Ge 2:7; 8:3; 30:20; 32:39; 1Sa 2:6; Job 27:3; Ps 30:3; 104:30; Ecc 12:7; Isa 38:16; Ac 17:25, 28; Ro 4:17; 1Ti 6:13; Jas 4:15).

Spiritual Life:
(Dt 8:3). From Christ (Jn 1:4; 6:27, 33, 35; 10:10; 17:2-3; Ro 6:11; 8:10; Col 3:4). Through faith (Jn 3:14-16; 5:24-26; 40; 6:40, 47; 11:25-26; 20:31; Gal 2:19-20). Signified, in figure of new birth

(Jn 3:3-8; Tit 3:5). In figure of death, burial, and resurrection (Ro 6:4-8).

Everlasting Life:
(Ps 21:4; 121:8; 133:3; Isa 25:8; Da 12:2; Mt 19:16-21, 29; 25:46; Mk 10:17-21, 29-30; Lk 18:18-22, 29-30; Jn 3:14-16, 36; 4:14; 5:24-25, 29, 39; 6:27, 40, 47, 50-58, 68; 10:10, 27-28; 12:25, 50; 17:2-3; Ac 13:46, 48; Ro 2:7; 5:21; 6:22-23; 1Co 15:53-54; 2Co 5:1; Gal 6:8; 1Ti 1:16; 4:8; 6:12, 19; 2Ti 1:10; Tit 1:2; 3:7; 1Jn 2:25; 3:15; 5:11-13, 20; Jude 21; Rev 1:18).
See Immortality.

LIFE, THE BOOK OF Figurative expression denoting God's record of those who inherit eternal life (Php 4:3; Rev 3:5; 21:27).

LIGHT

Physical:
Created (Ge 1:3-5; Ps 74:16; Isa 45:7; 2Co 4:6). Miraculous (Ex 13:21; Dt 1:33; Mt 17:2; Mk 9:3; Lk 9:29; Ac 9:3; 12:7; 26:13).

Figurative:
(1Ki 11:36). Of the Lord (Ps 27:1; Isa 60:19-20; Jas 1:17; 1Jn 1:5, 7; 2:8-10). Of the Lord's word (Ps 119:105; Pr 6:23). Of personal influence for righteousness (Mt 5:14-16; Mk 4:21; Lk 8:16). Of the righteous (Lk 16:8; Eph 5:8, 14; Php 2:15; 1Th 5:5). Of John the Baptist (Jn 5:35). Of spiritual understanding (Isa 8:20; Lk 1:33-36; 2Co 4:6). Of the gospel (2Co 4:4, 6). Of spiritual wisdom (Ps 119:130; Isa 2:5; 2Pe 1:19). Of righteousness (Mt 5:16; Ac 26:18; 1Pe 2:9). Of heavenly glory (Rev 21:23).

Of Christ's heavenly glory (1Ti 6:16). Of Christ's kingdom (Isa 58:8). Of the Savior (Isa 49:6; Mal 4:2; Mt 4:16; Lk 2:32; Jn 1:4-5, 7-9; 3:19-21; 8:12; 9:5; 12:35-36, 46; Rev 21:23).

LIGHTNING (Job 28:26; 37:3; 38:25, 35; Ps 18:14; 77:18; 78:48; 97:4; 135:7; 144:6; Jer 10:13; 51:16; Eze 1:13-14; Da 10:6; Na 2:4; Zec 9:14; 10:1; Mt 24:27; 28:3; Lk 10:18; Rev 4:5; 8:5; 11:19; 16:18). Plague of, sent upon Egypt (Ex 9:23; Ps 77:18; 78:48; 105:32).

LIGN ALOES *See Aloes.*

LIGURE *See Jacinth.*

LIKHI (*take, marry*). Manassite (1Ch 7:19).

LILY The principal capitals of the temple ornamented with carvings of (1Ki 7:19, 22, 26). Molded on the rim of the bronze Sea in the temple (1Ki 7:26; 2Ch 4:5). Lessons of trust gathered from (Mt 6:28-30; Lk 12:27).
Figurative of the lips of the beloved (SS 5:13).

LIME (Isa 33:12; Am 2:1).

LINE Usually a measuring line (2Sa 8:2; Ps 78:55), a portion (Ps 16:6), sound made by a musical chord (Ps 19:4).

LINE OF JUDGMENT The divine (2Ki 21:13; Isa 28:17; 34:11; La 2:8; Am 7:8).

LINEN Exported from Egypt (1Ki 10:38; Eze 27:7), from Syria (Eze 27:16). Curtains of the tabernacle made of (Ex 26:1; 27:9). Robes of priests made of (Ex 28:5-8, 15, 39-42), of royal households made of (Ge 41:42; Est 8:15). Garments for men made of (Ge 41:42; Eze 9:2; Lk 16:19), for women (Isa 3:23; Eze 16:10-13). Bedding made of (Pr 7:16). Mosaic law forbade its being mingled with wool (Lev 19:19; Dt 22:11). The body of Jesus wrapped in (Mk 15:46; Jn 20:5).

Figurative:
Pure and white, of righteousness (Rev 15:6; 19:8, 14).

LINTEL Horizontal beam forming the upper part of the doorway (Ex 12:22-23).

LINUS A Christian at Rome (2Ti 4:21).

LION

General:
King of beasts (Mic 5:8). Fierceness of (Job 4:10; 28:8; Ps 7:2; Pr 22:13; Jer 2:15; 49:19; 50:44; Hos 13:8). The roaring of (Ps 22:13; Pr 20:2). Strength of (Pr 30:30; Isa 38:13; Joel 1:6). Instincts of, in taking prey (Job 38:39-40; 41:14; La 3:10; Am 3:4; Na 2:12). Lair of, in the jungles (Jer 4:7; 25:38).

Kept in captivity (Da 6). Sent as judgment upon the Samaritans (2Ki 17:25-26). Slain by Samson (Jdg 14:5-9), David (1Sa 17:34, 36), Benaiah (2Sa 23:20), saints (Heb 11:33). Disobedient prophet slain by (1Ki 13:24-28), an unnamed person slain by (1Ki 20:36). Used for the torture of criminals (Da 6:16-24; 7:12; 2Ti 4:17).

The bases in the temple ornamented by moldings of (1Ki 7:29, 36). Twelve statues of, on the stairs leading to Solomon's throne (1Ki 10:19-20). Samson's riddle concerning (Jdg 14:14, 18). Proverb of (Ecc 9:4). Parable of (Eze 19:1-9).

Figurative:
Of a ruler's wrath (Pr 19:12; Jer 5:6; 50:17; Hos 5:14), of Satan (1Pe 5:8), of divine judgments (Isa 15:9).

Symbolic:
(Ge 49:9; Isa 29:1; Eze 1:10; 10:14; Da 7:4; Rev 4:7; 5:5; 9:8, 17; 13:2).

LITIGATION To be avoided (Mt 5:25; Lk 12:58; 1Co 6:1-8). *See Actions at Law; Adjudication at Law; Arbitration; Compromise.*

LITTER *See Wagon.*

LITTLE EVILS So called (Pr 6:10; Ecc 10:1; SS 2:15; 1Co 5:6).

LITTLE OWL *See Birds.*

LIVER Considered center of life and feeling (Pr 7:23), used especially for sacrifice (Ex 29:13) and divination (Eze 21:21).

LIVERY *See Dress; Land, Conveyance of.*

LIVING CREATURES Possibly identical with cherubim (Eze 1:5-22; 3:13; Rev 4:6-9).

LIVING GOD Title emphasizing the reality and existence of the true God (Dt 5:26; Jos 3:10; 1Sa 17:26; Ps 42:2; 84:2; Isa 37:17; Jer 23:36; Da 6:26; Mt 26:63; Ac 14:15; 1Th 1:9; Heb 10:31; Rev 7:2).

LIZARD Unclean; not permitted as food (Lev 11:29-30; Pr 30:28).

LO-AMMI (*not my people*). Symbolic naming for Hosea's third child to represent a break in the covenant relationship between the Lord and Israel (Ex 6:7; Jer 7:23). This break would later be restored (Hos 1:9-10, ftn; 2:1, 23). The warnings became more severe in moving from the first to the third child. *See Lo-Ruhamah; Ruhamah.*

LO DEBAR (*no pasture*). A city in Manasseh (2Sa 9:4-5; 17:27). Home of Mephibosheth, the lame son of Jonathan (2Sa 9:3-5).

LOAVES Miracle of the five (Mt 14:15-21; 16:9; Mk 6:37-44; Lk 9:12-17; Jn 6:5-13), of the seven (Mt 15:34-38; 16:10; Mk 8:1-10). *See Bread.*

LOBBYING To frustrate rebuilding the temple (Ezr 4:4-5).

LOCK Beams of wood or iron used for fastening gates or doors (SS 5:5; Lk 11:7).

LOCUST Authorized as food (Lev 11:22), used as (Mt 3:4; Mk 1:6). Plague of (Ex 10:1-19; Ps 105:34-35). Devastation by (Dt 28:38; 1Ki 8:37; 2Ch 7:13; Isa 33:4; Joel 1:4-7; Rev 9:7-10). Sun obscured by (Joel 2:2, 10). Instincts of (Pr 30:27).
See Grasshopper.
Figurative (Jer 46:23).
Symbolic (Rev 9:3-10).

LOD A city in Benjamin (1Ch 8:12; Ezr 2:33; Ne 7:37; 11:35). Called Lydda (Ac 9:38).

LODGE Temporary shelter built in a garden for a watchman guarding ripening fruit (Isa 1:8).

LOFT *See Upper Chamber, Upper Room.*

LOG A measure for liquids, holding about a pint (Lev 14:10, 12, 15, 24).

LOGIA Greek word for the nonbiblical sayings of Christ, such as those in the so-called Gospel of Thomas discovered in 1945.

LOGOS Usually rendered "word," in the Johannine writings it also appears as a title of Jesus: "The Word" (Jn 1:1ff; 1Jn 1:1; Rev 19:13). In the OT God creates by the word (Ge 1:3; Ps 33:9). In the Judaism of NT times, "word" was used as a way of referring to God himself. In Greek philosophy, "word" refers to the dynamic principle of reason operating in the world and forming a medium of communion between God and man. *See Jesus the Christ, Names, Appellations, and Titles of; Logos.*

LOIN Part of the body between the ribs and thighs (Lev 3:4, 10, 15), vulnerable (Dt 33:11), a seat of strength (Job 40:16).

LOIS (perhaps *more desirable, better*). Grandmother of Timothy, commended by Paul for her faith (2Ti 1:5).

LONGEVITY (Ge 6:3; Ps 90:10).

Promised:
To the obedient under the old covenant (Ex 20:12; Dt 4:40; 22:7). To the righteous (Job 5:26; Ps 21:4; 34:11-13; 91:16; Pr 3:2, 16; 9:11; 10:27; Isa 65:20; 1Pe 3:10-11). To Solomon (1Ki 3:11-14).

Instances of:
Adam, 930 years (Ge 5:5). Seth, 912 years (Ge 5:8). Enos, 905 years (Ge 5:11). Kenan, 910 years (Ge 5:14). Mahalalel, 895 years (Ge 5:17). Jared, 962 years (Ge 5:20). Enoch, 365 years (Ge 5:23). Methuselah, 969 years (Ge 5:27). Lamech, 777 years (Ge 5:31). Noah, 950 years (Ge 9:29). Shem (Ge 11:11). Arphaxad (Ge 11:13). Shelah (Ge 11:15). Eber (Ge 11:17). Peleg (Ge 11:19). Reu (Ge 11:21). Serug (Ge 11:23). Nahor (Ge 11:25). Terah, 205 years (Ge 11:32). Sarah, 127 years (Ge 23:1). Abraham, 175 years (Ge 25:7). Isaac, 180 years (Ge 35:28). Jacob, 147 years (Ge 47:28). Joseph, 110 years (Ge 50:26). Amram, 173 years (Ex 6:20). Aaron, 123 years (Nu 33:39). Moses, 120 years (Dt 34:7). Joshua, 110 years (Jos 24:29). Eli, 98 years (1Sa 4:15). Barzillai, 80 years (2Sa 19:32). Job, 140 years (Job 42:16). Jehoiada, 130 years (2Ch 24:15). Anna, 84 years (Lk 2:36-37). Paul (Phm 9).
See Life; Old Age.

LONGSUFFERING (1Ti 1:16). A Christian grace (1Co 13:4, 7; 2Co 6:4-6; Gal 5:22; Col 1:11; 2Ti 3:10; 4:2). Commanded (Eph 4:2; Col 3:12-13).
See Charitableness; God, Longsuffering of; Patience.

LOOKING BACKWARD Toward the old life (Ge 19:17, 26; Nu 11:5; 14:4; Lk 9:62).

LOOKING GLASS *See Mirror.*

LORD A term applied to both men and God, expressing varied degrees of honor, dignity, and majesty; applied also to idols (Ex 22:8; Jdg 2:11, 13), used of Jesus as Messiah (Ac 2:36; Php 2:9-11; Ro 1:4; 14:8). *See God, Names of; Titles and Names; Yahweh.*

LORD'S DAY The day especially associated with the Lord Jesus Christ; a day consecrated to the Lord; the first day of the week, commemorating the resurrection of Jesus (Jn 20:1-25; Rev

1:10) and the pouring out of the Spirit (Ac 2:1-41), set aside for worship (Ac 20:7).

LORD'S PRAYER Prayer taught by Jesus as a model of how his disciples should pray (Mt 6:9-13; Lk 11:2-4).

LORD'S SUPPER Instituted by Christ on the night of his betrayal immediately after the Passover Feast to be a memorial of his death and a visible sign of the blessings of the new covenant.

Variously called: Body and blood of Christ (Mt 26:26, 28), communion of the body and blood of Christ (1Co 10:16), bread and cup of the Lord (1Co 11:27), breaking of bread (Ac 2:42; 20:7), Lord's Supper (1Co 11:20).

Not to be observed unworthily (1Co 11:27-32).
See Eucharist.

LO-RUHAMAH (*no compassion*). Symbolic name given to Hosea's daughter (Hos 1:6, 8; 2:4, 23). The naming represents a reversal of the love (compassion) that God had earlier shown to Israel (Ex 33:19; Dt 7:6-8) but was later promised again (Hos 2:23). *See Lo-Ammi; Ruhamah.*

LOST SHEEP Parable of (Mt 18:12-13; Lk 15:4-7).

LOST, THE *See Wicked, Punishment of.*

LOT The son of Haran. Accompanies Terah from Ur of the Chaldeans to Haran (Ge 11:31). Migrates with Abraham to the land of Canaan (Ge 12:4). Accompanies Abraham to Egypt; returns with him to Bethel (Ge 13:1-3). Rich in flocks, herds, and servants; separates from Abraham and locates in Sodom (Ge 13:5-14). Taken captive by Kedorlaomer; rescued by Abraham (Ge 14:1-16). Providentially saved from destruction in Sodom (Ge 19; Lk 17:28-29). Righteous (2Pe 2:7-8). Disobediently protests against going to the mountains, and chooses Zoar (Ge 19:17-22). His wife disobediently longs after Sodom, and becomes a pillar of salt (Ge 19:26; Lk 17:32). Commits incest with his daughters (Ge 19:30-38). Descendants of. *See Ammonite(s); Moabite(s).*

LOT, THE (Pr 16:33; 18:18; Isa 34:17; Joel 3:3). The scapegoat chosen by (Lev 16:8-10).

The land of Canaan divided among the tribes by (Nu 26:55; Jos 15; 18:10; 19:51; 21; 1Ch 6:61, 65; Eze 45:1; 47:22; 48:29; Mic 2:5; Ac 13:19). Saul chosen king by (1Sa 10:20-21). Priests and Levites designated by, for sanctuary service (1Ch 24:5-31; 26:13; Ne 10:34; Lk 1:9). Used after the Captivity (Ne 11:1). An apostle chosen by (Ac 1:26). Achan's guilt discovered by (Jos 7:14-18), Jonathan's (1Sa 14:41-42), Jonah's (Jnh 1:7). Used to fix the time for the execution of condemned persons (Est 3:7; 9:24). The garments of Jesus divided by (Ps 22:18; Mt 27:35; Mk 15:24; Jn 19:23-24).

For Feast of, *See Casting Lots; Purim.*

LOTAN (*of Lot*). Son of Seir (Ge 36:20, 22, 29).

LOTS, CASTING *See Casting Lots; Lot, The.*

LOTUS A water plant (Job 40:21-22). *See Plants of the Bible.*

LOVE (1Co 13; 14:1; Col 1:8; 2:2; 1Th 1:3; 5:8; 1Ti 6:11; 2Ti 1:7; Phm 5; Heb 10:24; 1Jn 4:7, 16-18).

The theme of the Song of Songs, and often allegorized representing the love of God for Israel, of the Messiah for the church and of his church for the Messiah (SS 1-8). *See Church, Loved.*

Love of Person for Person:
(Ro 5:7; Jas 1:27). Defined (1Co 13:1-13). In the parable of the good Samaritan (Lk 10:25-37). Is edifying (1Co 8:1). Is precious (Pr 15:17). Is unquenchable (Pr 17:17; SS 8:6-7). Is a fruit of the Spirit (Gal 5:22). Promotes peace (Pr 10:12; 17:9). A proof, of discipleship of Jesus (Jn 13:34-35), of regeneration (1Jn 3:14, 19).

Commanded—
(Lev 19:18; Mt 5:40-42; 7:12; 19:19; 22:39-40; Mk 12:30-33; Lk 6:30-38; Ro 12:9, 15; 13:8-10; 1Co 10:24; 16:14; Gal 6:1-2, 10; Eph 4:2, 32; 5:2; Php 1:9; Col 3:14; 1Th 3:12; 1Ti 1:5; 4:12; 6:11; 2Ti 2:22; Jas 2:8; 2Pe 1:7; 1Jn 4:20-21). Toward strangers (Lev 19:34; Dt 10:19). Toward enemies (Pr 24:17; Mt 5:43-48; Lk 6:35; Ro 12:14, 20). Toward fellow Christians (Jn 13:14-15, 34-35; 15:12-13, 17; Ro 12:9-10, 15-16; 14:19, 21; 15:1-2, 5, 7; 16:1-2; 1Co 14:1; 2Co 8:7-8; Gal 5:13-14; 6:1-2, 10; Eph 4:2, 32; Php 2:2; Col 2:2; 3:12-14; 1Th 3:12; 5:8, 11, 14; 1Ti 6:2; Phm 16; Heb 10:24; 13:1, 3; 1Pe 1:22; 2:17; 3:8-9; 4:8; 2Pe 1:7; 1Jn 3:11, 14, 16-18, 19, 23; 4:7, 11-12, 20-21; 2Jn 5). Demonstrated by obedience (1Jn 5:1-2).
Rewards of (Mt 10:41-42; 25:34-40, 46; Mk 9:41; 1Jn 2:10).

Instances of—
Abraham for Lot (Ge 14:14-16). Moses for Israel (Ex 32:31-32). David and Jonathan (1Sa 18:1; 20:17). Israel for David (1Sa 18:16). David's subjects for David (2Sa 15:30; 17:27-29). Hiram for David (1Ki 5:1). Obadiah for the prophets (1Ki 18:4). Nehemiah for Israelites (Ne 5:10-18). Job's friends (Job 42:11). Centurion for his servant (Lk 7:2-6). Good Samaritan (Lk 10:29-37). Stephen (Ac 7:60). Roman Christians for Paul (Ac 28:15). Priscilla and Aquila for Paul (Ro 16:3-4).

Exemplified by Paul (Ac 26:29; Ro 1:11-12; 9:1-3; 1Co 4:9-16; 8:13; 2Co 1:3-6, 14, 23-24; 2:4; 3:2; 4:5; 6:4-6, 11-13; 7:1-4; 11:2; 12:14-16, 19-21; 13:9; Gal 4:19-20; Eph 3:13; Php 1:3-5, 7-8, 23-26; 2:19; 4:1; Col 1:3-4, 24, 28-29; 2:1, 5; 4:7; 1Th 2:7-8, 11-12, 17-20; 3:5, 7-10, 12; 2Th 1:4; 2Ti 1:3-4, 8; 2:10; Tit 3:15; Phm 9, 12, 16).
See Brother; Fraternity; Friendship; Golden Rule.

Love of Man for Woman:
Isaac for Rebekah (Ge 24:67). Jacob for Rachel (Ge 29:20, 30). Shechem for Dinah (Ge 34:3, 12). Boaz for Ruth (Ru 2-4).

Love of People for God:
Defined (1Jn 5:3; 2Jn 6). Incompatible with love of the world (1Jn 2:15), with hatred of brother (1Jn 4:20-21), with guilty fear (2Ti 1:7; 1Jn 4:18). Reasons for (Ps 116:1; 1Jn 4:19).

L

The gift of God (Dt 30:6; 2Ti 1:7). Through the Holy Spirit (Ro 5:5).

Commanded (Dt 6:5; 10:12; 11:1, 13, 22; 19:9; 30:16, 19-20; Jos 22:5; 23:11; Ps 31:23; Pr 23:26; Mt 22:37-38; Mk 12:29-30, 32-33; Lk 11:42; 2Th 3:5; Jude 21). Tested (Dt 13:3). Obedience proof of (1Jn 2:5; 5:1-2; 2Jn 6).

Leads to generosity (1Jn 3:17-18), hate of evil (Ps 97:10), love from God (Ps 8:1-8). Rewards of (Ex 20:6; Dt 5:10; 7:9; Ps 37:4; 69:35-36; 91:14; 145:20; Isa 56:6-7; Jer 2:2-3; Ro 8:28; 1Co 8:3). Exemplified (Ps 18:1; 63:5-6; 73:25-26; 103).

Love of People for Jesus:
Commanded (Mt 10:37-38; Jn 15:9; 1Co 16:22). Love of God produces (Jn 8:42). Obedience results from (Jn 14:15, 21, 23; 2Co 5:6, 8, 14-15).

Rewards of (Mt 25:34-40, 46; Mk 9:41; Lk 7:37-50; Jn 16:27; Eph 6:24; 2Ti 4:8; Heb 6:10; Jas 1:12; 2:5).

Instances of—
Mary (Mt 26:6-13; Lk 10:39; Jn 12:3-8). Peter (Mt 17:4; Jn 13:37; 18:10; 20:3-6; 21:15-17). The healed demoniac (Mk 5:18; Lk 8:38). Thomas (Jn 11:16). The disciples (Mk 16:10; Lk 24:17-41; Jn 16:27; 20:20). Mary Magdalene and other disciples (Mt 27:55-56, 61; 28:1-9; Lk 8:2-3; 23:27, 55-56; 24:1-10; Jn 20:1-2, 11-18). Joseph of Arimathea (Mt 27:57-60). Nicodemus (Jn 19:39-40). Women of Jerusalem (Lk 23:27). Paul (Ac 21:13; Php 1:20-21, 23; 3:7-8; 2Ti 4:8). Philemon (Phm 5). Early Christians (1Pe 1:8; 2:7), lost that love (Rev 2:4).

Of Children for Parents: *See Children.*

Of God: *See God, Love of.*

Of Jesus: *See Jesus the Christ, Love of.*

Of Money:
A root of all kinds of evil (1Ti 6:10). *See Avarice; Riches.*

Of Parents for Children: *See Parents.*

LOVE FEAST (*agape feast*). A common meal eaten by early Christians in connection with the Lord's Supper to express and deepen brotherly love (1Co 11:18-22, 33-34; Jude 12).

LOVERS

Instances Within or Resulting in Marriage:
Isaac and Rebekah (Ge 24:67). Jacob and Rachel (Ge 29:20, 30). Boaz and Ruth (Ru 2-4). The beloved and her lover (SS 1-8).

Instances Outside of Marriage:
Shechem and Dinah (Ge 34:3, 12). Gomer and her lovers (Hos 1-3).

Figurative of Disloyalty to Yahweh:
Israel and pagan gods (Jer 3:1-2; Hos 2). Jerusalem and political allies (La 1:2; Eze 16:33-42; 23).

LOVING-KINDNESS The kindness and mercy of God toward people (Ps 17:7; 26:3).

LOYALTY Commanded (Ex 22:28; Nu 27:20; Ezr 6:10; 7:26; Job 34:18; Pr 24:21; Ecc 8:2; 10:4; Ro 13:1; Tit 3:1). Enforced (Ezr 10:8; Pr 17:11). Disloyalty (2Pe 2:10). *See Patriotism.*

Instances of:
Israelites (Jos 1:16-18; 2Sa 3:36-37; 15:23, 30; 18:3; 21:17; 1Ch 12:38). David (1Sa 24:6-10; 26:6-16; 2Sa 1:14). Uriah (2Sa 11:9). Ittai (2Sa 15:21). Hushai (2Sa 17:15-16). David's soldiers (2Sa 18:12-13; 23:15-16). Joab (2Sa 19:5-6). Barzillai (2Sa 19:32). Jehoiada (2Ki 11:4-12). Mordecai (Est 2:21-23).

LUBIM(S) *See Libya, Libyans; Put, 2.*

LUCAS *See Luke.*

LUCIFER Latin for "morning star" (Isa 14:12); a title of the king of Babylon, often understood as a reference to the devil. *See Devil; Satan.*

LUCIUS
1. A Christian at Antioch (Ac 13:1).
2. A relative of Paul (Ro 16:21).

LUD A son of Shem (Ge 10:22; 1Ch 1:17).

LUDITES Descendants of Mizraim (Ge 10:13; 1Ch 1:11). Perhaps the same as the Lydians. *See Lydia, Lydians.*

LUHITH A city of Moab (Isa 15:5; Jer 48:5).

LUKE A disciple. A physician (Col 4:14). Wrote to Theophilus (Lk 1:1-4; Ac 1:1-2). Accompanies Paul in his tour of Asia and Macedonia (Ac 16:10-13; 20:5-6), to Jerusalem (Ac 21:1-18), to Rome (Ac 27:28; 2Ti 4:1; Phm 24).

LUKE, GOSPEL OF
Author: Traditionally Luke, the companion of Paul

Date: The two most commonly suggested periods for dating the Gospel of Luke are: (1) A.D. 59-63, and (2) the 70s or the 80s.

Outline:
I. The Preface (1:1-4).
II. The Coming of Jesus (1:5-2:52).
 A. The Annunciations (1:5-56).
 B. The Birth of John the Baptist (1:57-80).
 C. The Birth and Childhood of Jesus (ch. 2).
III. The Preparation of Jesus for His Public Ministry (3:1-4:13).
 A. His Forerunner (3:1-20).
 B. His Baptism (3:21-22).
 C. His Genealogy (3:23-38).
 D. His Temptation (4:1-13).
IV. His Ministry in Galilee (4:14-9:9).
 A. The Beginning of the Ministry in Galilee (4:14-41).
 B. The First Tour of Galilee (4:42-5:39).
 C. A Sabbath Controversy (6:1-11).
 D. The Choice of the Twelve Apostles (6:12-16).
 E. The Sermon on the Plain (6:17-49).

F. Miracles in Capernaum and Nain (7:1-18).
G. The Inquiry of John the Baptist (7:19-29).
H. Jesus and the Pharisees (7:30-50).
I. The Second Tour of Galilee (8:1-3).
J. The Parables of the Kingdom (8:4-21).
K. The Trip Across the Sea of Galilee (8:22-39).
L. The Third Tour of Galilee (8:40-9:9).
V. His Withdrawal to Regions Around Galilee (9:10-50).
 A. To the Eastern Shore of the Sea of Galilee (9:10-17).
 B. To Caesarea Philippi (9:18-50).
VI. His Ministry in Judea (9:51-13:21).
 A. Journey Through Samaria to Judea (9:51-62).
 B. The Mission to the Seventy (10:1-24).
 C. The Lawyer and the Parable of the Good Samaritan (10:25-37).
 D. Jesus at Bethany With Mary and Martha (10:38-42).
 E. Teachings in Judea (11:1-13:21).
VII. His Ministry in and Around Perea (13:22-19:27).
 A. The Narrow Door (13:22-30).
 B. Warning Concerning Herod (13:31-35).
 C. At a Pharisee's House (14:1-23).
 D. The Cost of Discipleship (14:24-35).
 E. The Parables of the Lost Sheep, the Lost Coin and the Prodigal Son (ch. 15).
 F. The Parable of the Shrewd Manager (16:1-18).
 G. The Rich Man and Lazarus (16:19-31).
 H. Miscellaneous Teachings (17:1-10).
 I. Ten Healed of Leprosy (17:11-19).
 J. The Coming of the Kingdom (17:20-37).
 K. The Persistent Widow (18:1-8).
 L. The Pharisee and the Tax Collector (18:9-14).
 M. Jesus and the Children (18:15-17).
 N. The Rich Young Ruler (18:18-30).
 O. Christ Foretells His Death (18:31-34).
 P. A Blind Beggar Given His Sight (18:35-43).
 Q. Jesus and Zacchaeus (19:1-10).
 R. The Parable of the Ten Minas (19:11-27).
VIII. His Last Days: Sacrifice and Triumph (19:28-24:53).
 A. The Triumph Entry (19:28-44).
 B. The Cleansing of the Temple (19:45-48).
 C. The Last Controversies With the Jewish Leaders (ch. 20).
 D. The Olivet Discourse (ch. 21).
 E. The Last Supper (22:1-38).
 F. Jesus Praying in Gethsemane (22:39-46).
 G. Jesus' Arrest (22:47-65).
 H. Jesus on Trial (22:66-23:25).
 I. The Crucifixion (23:26-56).
 J. The Resurrection (24:1-12).
 K. The Post-Resurrection Ministry (24:13-49).
 L. The Ascension (24:50-53).
See Acts of the Apostles; Synoptic Gospels, The.

LUKEWARMNESS Instances of: The Reubenites and other tribes, when Deborah called on them to assist Sisera (Jdg 5:16-17). Israel (Hos 10:2). The Jews (Ne 3:5; 13:11; Hag 1:2-11). The church, at Pergamum (Rev 2:14-16), Thyatira (Rev 2:20-24), Sardis (Rev 3:1-3), Laodicea (Rev 3:14-16).
See Backsliding; Blindness, Spiritual; Complacency.

LUNACY *See Insanity; Demons.*

LUST (*evil desires*). Sinful (Job 31:9-12; Mt 5:28). Worldly (1Jn 2:16-17). Chokes the word (Mk 4:19). Tempts to sin (Ge 3:6; Jas 1:14-15; 2Pe 2:18).

Forbidden (Ex 20:17; Pr 6:24-25; Ro 13:14; Eph 4:22; Col 3:5; 1Th 4:5; Tit 2:12; 1Pe 2:11). Warnings against (1Co 10:6-7; 2Ti 2:22). Wicked under power of (Jn 8:44; Ro 1:24, 26-27; 1Ti 6:9; Jas 4:1-3; 1Pe 4:3; 2Pe 3:3; Jude 16, 18). Of Israelites (Ps 106:13-14).

The righteous restrain (1Co 9:27).
See Adultery; Covetousness; Homosexual; Incest; Lasciviousness; Sensuality.

LUTE Stringed instrument used to accompany songs of praise (1Sa 18:6; 2Ch 20:28). *See Music, Instruments of.*

LLUZ
(*almond tree*).
1. Town on N boundary of Benjamin (Jos 16:2; 18:13).
2. Hittite town (Jdg 1:26).

LYCAONIA A province of Asia Minor. Paul visits towns of (Ac 14:6-21; 16:1-2).

LYCIA A province of Asia Minor. Paul visits (Ac 27:5).

LYDDA Called also Lod. A city of Benjamin (1Ch 8:12; Ezr 2:33; Ne 11:35). Peter heals Aeneas in (Ac 9:32-35).

LYDIA, LYDIANS
1. A woman of Thyatira, who with her household, was converted through the preaching of Paul (Ac 16:14-15). Entertains Paul and Silas (Ac 16:15, 40).
2. A country and people in the N Africa or Asia Minor; mercenary warriors (Isa 66:19; Jer 46:9; Eze 27:10; 30:5). Perhaps the same as the Ludites. *See Ludites.*

LYING Lying spirit from God (1Ki 22:21-23; 2Ch 18:20-22). *See Falsehood; Hypocrisy; Liars.*

LYRE Used in religious services (2Sa 6:5; 1Ch 13:8; 16:5; 25:1, 5-6; 2Ch 29:25; Ps 33:2; 57:8; 71:22; 81:2; 92:3; 108:2; 144:9; 150:3). At the dedication of the new wall when the captives returned (Ne 12:27). Used in idolatrous worship (Da 3:5, 7, 10, 15).
See Music, Instruments of.

LYSANIAS A tetrarch (Lk 3:1).

LYSIAS Chief captain of Roman troops in Jerusalem (Ac 24:7, ftn; 24:22). *See Claudius Lysias.*

LYSTRA A city of Lycaonia to which Paul and Barnabas fled from persecutions in Iconium (Ac 14:6-23; 2Ti 3:11). Church of, elders ordained for, by Paul and Barnabas (Ac 14:23). Timothy a resident of (Ac 16:1-4).

M

MAACAH
(perhaps *dull, stupid*).
1. Son of Nahor (Ge 22:24).
2. Mother of Absalom (2Sa 3:3; 1Ch 3:2).
3. Father of Achish, king of Gath (1Sa 27:2). Possibly the same as Maoch. (1Ki 2:39).
4. Mother of Abijah and grandmother of Asa (1Ki 15:2, 10-13; 2Ch 11:20-23; 15:16). Also called Micaiah (2Ch 13:2, ftn).
5. Wife of Makir (1Ch 7:15-16).
6. Concubine of Caleb (1Ch 2:48).
7. Wife of Jeiel (1Ch 8:29; 9:35).
8. Father of Hanan (1Ch 11:43).
9. Father of Shephatiah (1Ch 27:16).
10. A small kingdom E of Bashan. *See Maacathite(s).*

MAACATHITE(S) People of the nation of Maacah, in the region of Bashan (Dt 3:14; Jos 12:5; 13:11; 2Sa 10:6, 8; 23:34; 1Ch 4:19; 19:6-7).

MAADAI (*ornaments*). Israelite who married a foreign woman (Ezr 10:34).

MAADIAH *See Moadiah.*

MAAI (*to be compassionate*). Priest who blew trumpet at dedication of wall (Ne 12:36).

MAALEH-ACRABBIM *See Scorpion Pass.*

MAARATH (*barren*). A city of Judah (Jos 15:59).

MAASAI (*work of Yahweh*). Priestly family after the Exile (1Ch 9:12).

MAASEIAH, MAHSEIAH (*Yahweh is a refuge*).
1. Levite musician (1Ch 15:18, 20).
2. Army captain who assisted Jehoiada in overthrowing Athaliah (2Ch 23:1).
3. Officer of Uzziah (2Ch 26:11).
4. Son Ahaz, king of Judah (2Ch 28:7).
5. Governor of Jerusalem in Josiah's reign (2Ch 34:8).
6. A priest who married a foreigner (Ezr 10:18).
7. A priest who married a foreigner (Ezr 10:21).
8. A priest who married a foreigner (Ezr 10:22).
9. Israelite who married a foreigner (Ezr 10:30).
10. Father of Azariah (Ne 3:23).
11. Priest; assistant of Ezra (Ne 8:4).
12. Man who explained law to people (Ne 8:7).
13. Chief who sealed covenant with Nehemiah (Ne 10:25).
14. Descendant of son of Baruch (Ne 11:5).
15. Benjamite (Ne 11:7).
16. Priest who blew trumpet at dedication of temple (Ne 12:41).

MAATH (*to be small*). An ancestor of Jesus (Lk 3:26).

MAAZ (perhaps *angry* or *wrath*). A son of Ram (1Ch 2:27).

MAAZIAH (*Yahweh is a refuge*).
1. A priest (1Ch 24:18).
2. A priest who sealed the covenant with Nehemiah (Ne 10:8).

MACBANNAI (*clad with a cloak*). A Gadite warrior (1Ch 12:13).

MACBENAH (*bond*). A descendant of Caleb (1Ch 2:49). "Father of" may mean "founder of" or "leader of" a city.

MACCABEES (*hammer*). Hasmonean Jewish family of Modein (or Modin) that led revolt against Antiochus Epiphanes, king of Syria, and won freedom for the Jews. The family consisted of the father, Mattathias, an aged priest, and his five sons: Johanan, Simon, Judas, Eleazar, and Jonathan. The name Maccabee was first given to Judas, perhaps because he inflicted sledgehammer blows against the Syrian armies, and later was also used for his brothers. The revolt began in 168 B.C. The temple was recaptured and sacrifices were resumed in 165 B.C. The cleansing of the temple and resumption of sacrifices have been celebrated annually ever since in the Feast of Dedication. The Maccabees served as both high priests and kings. The story of Maccabees is told in two books of the Apocrypha, I and II Maccabees.

The following were the most prominent of the Maccabees: Judas (166-160 B.C.), Jonathan (160-142 B.C.), Simon (142-134 B.C.), John Hyrcanus (134-104 B.C.), Aristobulus (104-103 B.C.), Alexander Jannaeus (103-76 B.C.), Alexandra (76-67 B.C.), Aristobulus II (66-63 B.C.). In 63 B.C. the Romans took over when Pompey conquered the Israelites.
See Dedication; Feasts; Hanukkah; Kislev; Month, 9; Testaments, Time Between.

MACEDONIA A province in N Greece. Paul has a vision concerning (Ac 16:9), preaches in, at Philippi (Ac 16:12), revisits (Ac 20:1-6; 2Co 2:13; 7:5). Church at, sends contributions to the poor in Jerusalem (Ro 15:26; 2Co 8:1-5). Timothy visits (Ac 19:22). Disciples in (Ac 19:22; 27:2).

M (side tab marker)

MACEDONIAN EMPIRE, THECalled the kingdom of Greece (Da 11:2).

Illustrated by the:
Bronze part of the image in Nebuchadnezzar's dream (Da 2:32, 39). Leopard with four wings and four heads (Da 7:6, 17). Shaggy goat with notable horn (Da 8:5-8, 21). Philippi the chief city of (Ac 16:12).

Predictions Respecting:
Conquest of the Medo-Persian kingdom (Da 8:6-7; 11:2-3). Power and greatness of Alexander its last king (Da 8:8; 11:3). Division of it into four kingdoms (Da 8:8, 22). Divisions of it ruled by strangers (Da 11:4). History of its four divisions (Da 11:4-29). The little horn to arise out of one of its divisions (Da 8:8-12). Gospel preached in, by God's desire (Ac 16:9-10). Liberality of the churches of (2Co 8:1-5).

MACHAERUS Fortress stronghold built by Alexander Janneus (c. 90 B.C.) and used as a citadel by Herod Antipas; located on E of Dead Sea; John the Baptist was put to death there (Mt 14:3ff).

MACHI *See Maki.*

MACHIR *See Makir.*

MACHPELAH (*double [cave]*). The burying place of Sarah, Abraham, Isaac, Rebekah, Leah, and Jacob (Ge 23:9, 17-20; 25:9; 49:30-31; 50:13; Ac 7:16).

MACNADEBAI (possibly *possession of Nebo*). Israelite who divorced foreign wife (Ezr 10:40).

MADAI (*Medes*). People descended from Japheth (Ge 10:2; 1Ch 1:5).

MADMANNAH (*dung place*).
1. Town in S Judah eight miles S of Kiriath Sepher (Jos 15:31).
2. Grandson of Caleb (1Ch 2:48-49).

MADMEN (sounds like *be silenced*).
1. A place (Jer 48:2).
2. A maniac, of insane persons (1Sa 21:15). *See Insanity.*

MADMENAH (*dunghill*). City of Benjamin (Isa 10:31).

MADNESS *See Insanity; Madmen.*

MADON (*contention*). Canaanite city near modern Qarn Hattin (Jos 11:1; 12:19).

MAGADAN Town on the NW shore of Sea of Galilee, three miles N of Tiberias. Also called Magdala, the home of Mary Magdalene (Mt 15:39). Mark (8:10) has "Dalmanutha." *See Dalmanutha.*

MAGBISH (perhaps *thick*). Name of man or place (Ezr 2:30).

MAGDALA *See Dalmanutha; Magadan.*

MAGDALENE (*of Magdala*). *See Mary, 3.*

MAGDIEL (*choice gift of God [El]*). Chief of Edom (Ge 36:43; 1Ch 1:54).

MAGGOT Infested leftover manna (Ex 16:20, 24). Synonymous with "worm" (Job 25:6). *See Animals.*

MAGI Originally a religious caste among the Persians; devoted to astrology, divination, and interpretation of dreams. Later the word came to be applied generally to fortune-tellers and exponents of esoteric religious cults throughout the Mediterranean world (Ac 8:9; 13:6, 8). Nothing is known of the Magi of the Nativity story (Mt 2); they may have come from S Arabia.

MAGIC The art or science of influencing or controlling the course of nature, events, and supernatural powers through occult science of mysterious arts (Ge 41:8; Ex 7:11, 22; 8:7, 18; Ac 19:19). Includes necromancy, exorcism, dreams, shaking arrows, inspecting entrails of animals, divination, sorcery, astrology, soothsaying, divining by rods, witchcraft (1Sa 28:8; Eze 21:21; Ac 16:16).

MAGICIAN A person who claims to understand and explain mysteries by magic (Da 1:20). Failed to interpret Pharaoh's dreams (Ge 41:8, 24), Nebuchadnezzar's (Da 2:2-13; 4:7). Worked apparent miracles (Ex 7:11-12, 22; 8:7, 18).

MAGISTRATE(S) An officer of civil law (Jdg 18:7; Ezr 7:25; Lk 12:11, 58; Ac 16:20, 22, 35, 38). Obedience to, commanded (Tit 3:1).
See Government; Rulers.

MAGNA CARTA *See Constitution.*

MAGNANIMITY Instances of: Joshua and the elders of Israel to the Gibeonites who had deceived the Israelites (Jos 9:3-27). Of Moses. *See Moses.* David to Saul (1Sa 24:3-11). Ahab to Ben-Hadad (1Ki 20:32-34).
See Charitableness.

MAGNIFICAT Song of praise by Mary (Lk 1:46-55).

MAGOG (perhaps *land of Gog*).
1. Son of Japheth (Ge 10:2; 1Ch 1:5).
2. Land of God.
Various identifications: Scythians, Lydians, Tartars of Russia. Used symbolically for forces of evil (Rev 20:7-9).

MAGOR-MISSABIB (*terror on every side*). A symbolic name given by Jeremiah to Pashhur (Jer 20:3-6).

MAGPIASH (*moth killer*). Israelite who sealed covenant with Nehemiah (Ne 10:20).

MAGUS, SIMON *See Simon, 8.*

MAHALAH *See Mahlah, 2.*

MAHALALEL (*praise of God [El]*).
1. Son of Kenan (Ge 5:12-17; 1Ch 1:2; Lk 3:37).
2. A man of Judah (Ne 11:4).

MAHALATH (*the suffering of affliction* NIV; *sickness or suffering poem*, JB).
1. Daughter of Ishmael (Ge 28:9).
2. Wife of Rehoboam (2Ch 11:18).
3. Musical term in the titles of Pss 53 and 88. Possibly the name of a tune. The Hebrew appears to be the word for "suffering" or "sickness." Perhaps the Hebrew phrase indicates here that the psalm is to be used in a time of affliction, when the godless mock. *See Music, Symbols Used in.*

MAHALI *See Mahli, 1.*

MAHANAIM (*double camp*). The place where Jacob had the vision of angels (Ge 32:2). The town of, allotted to Gad (Jos 13:26, 30). One of the Levitical cities (Jos 21:38). Ish-Bosheth establishes himself at, when made king over Israel (2Sa 2:8-12). David lodges at, during Absalom's rebellion (2Sa 17:27-29; 1Ki 2:8).

MAHANEH DAN (*camp of Dan*).
1. Place between Zorah and Eshtaol (Jdg 13:25).
2. Place W of Kiriath Jearim (Jdg 18:12).

MAHARAI (*impetuous* ISBE). One of David's warriors (2Sa 23:28; 1Ch 11:30; 27:13).

MAHATH (perhaps *tough*).
1. Kohathite; ancestor of Heman (1Ch 6:35).
2. Levite who helped Hezekiah (2Ch 29:12; 31:13).

MAHAVITE (*villagers*). Family name of Eliel, one of David's warriors (1Ch 11:46).

MAHAZIOTH (*visions*). Son of Heman (1Ch 25:4, 30).

MAHER-SHALAL-HASH-BAZ (*quick to the plunder, swift to the spoil*). Symbolic name Isaiah gave his son (Isa 8:1, 3).

MAHLAH (perhaps *weak one*).
1. Daughter of Zelophehad (Nu 26:33; 27:1ff; 36; Jos 17:3ff).
2. Grandson of Manasseh (1Ch 7:18).

MAHLI (perhaps *shrewd, cunning*).
1. Son of Merari (Ex 6:19; 1Ch 6:19; Ezr 8:18).
2. Son of Mushi (1Ch 6:47; 23:23; 24:30).

MAHLITE(S) Descendant of Mahli, son of Merari (Nu 3:33; 26:58; 1Ch 23:22).

MAHLON (*sick*). Son of Naomi and first husband of Ruth (Ru 1:2, 5; 4:9-10).

MAHOL (*place of round-dancing*). Father of Heman, Calcol, and Darda (1Ki 4:31).

MAID(S), MAIDSERVANT(S)
1. Female slave or servant (Ge 12:16; 16:1; Lk 12:45).
2. Female personal servant or attendant (Ge 24:61; 1Sa 25:42; Est 2:9).
See Servant.

MAIDEN(S)
1. Young woman (Ps 68:25; 148:12).
2. Young woman of marriageable age, probably a virgin (Ge 24:43; Ps 78:63; Isa 62:5; Jer 2:32).

MAIL
1. Sending of letters (2Sa 11:14-15; 1Ki 21:8-11; 2Ki 5:5-7; Est 3:13; 8:10; 2Pe 3:16). *See Letter; Letters.*
2. Armor (1Sa 17:5). *See Armor.*

MAIMED Not acceptable as sacrifices (Lev 22:22). *See Disease.*

MAJESTY Name of God (Heb 1:3; 8:1). *See God.*

MAJORITY AND MINORITY REPORTS Of the spies (Nu 13:26-33; 14:6-10).

MAKAZ A place in Judah (1Ki 4:9).

MAKHELOTH (*assemblies*). An encampment of Israel (Nu 33:25-26).

MAKI (perhaps *reduced* or *bought*). Gadite; father of Geuel, one of 12 spies (Nu 13:15).

MAKIR, MAKIRITE (*bought*).
1. One of the sons of Manasseh (Ge 50:23). Father of the Makirites (Nu 26:29; 36:1). The land of Gilead allotted to (Nu 32:39-40; Dt 3:15; Jos 13:31). Certain cities of Bashan given to (Jos 13:31; 17:1).
2. A man of Lo Debar who took care of Jonathan's lame son, Mephibosheth (2Sa 9:4-5; 17:27).

MAKKEDAH (*locality of shepherds*). A city in Judah, conquered by Joshua (Jos 10:28; 12:16). Five kings of the Amorites hide in a cave of, and are slain by Joshua (Jos 10:5, 16-27).

MAKTESH (*mortar*). A district where merchants traded (Zep 1:11, ftn). *See Agora; Market.*

MALACHI (*my messenger* or *messenger of Yahweh*). Prophet of Judah who lived c. 450-400 B.C.; author of OT book which bears

his name; nothing known of him beyond what is said in his book; contemporary of Nehemiah (Mal 2:11-17; Ne 13:23-31).

MALACHI, BOOK OF
Author: The prophet Malachi
Date: c. 433 to 400 B.C.
Outline:
I. Title (1:1).
II. Introduction: God's Covenant Love for Israel Affirmed (1:2-5).
III. Israel's Unfaithfulness Rebuked (1:6-2:16).
 A. The Unfaithfulness of the Priests (1:6-2:9).
 1. They dishonor God in their sacrifices (1:6-14).
 2. They do not faithfully teach the law (2:1-9).
 B. The Unfaithfulness of the People (2:10-16).
IV. The Lord's Coming Announced (2:17-4:6).
 A. The Lord Will Come to Purify the Priests and Judge the People (2:17-3:5).
 B. A Call to Repentance in View of the Lord's Coming (3:6-18).
 1. An exhortation to faithful giving (3:6-12).
 2. An exhortation to faithful service (3:13-18).
 C. The Day of the Lord Announced (ch. 4).
See Prophets, The Minor.

MALCAM (*their king* ISBE KB; or *[servant of] Malk [pagan god]*).
1. A Benjamite (1Ch 8:9).
2. Either Molech, a god of the Moabites and Ammonites (Jer 49:1, 3; Am 1:15; Zep 1:5, ftns) or their king; maybe both. *See Molech.*

MALCHIAH, MALCHIJAH *See Malkijah.*

MALCHIEL *See Malkiel.*

MALCHIJAH *See Malkijah, 2, 3, 4, 7, 11, 12.*

MALCHIRAM *See Malkiram.*

MALCHI-SHUA *See Malki-Shua.*

MALCHUS (*king*). Servant of the high priest; Peter assaults in Gethsemane; healed by Jesus (Mt 26:51; Mk 14:47; Lk 22:50-51; Jn 18:10).

MALEFACTOR *See Criminals.*

MALELEEL *See Mahalalel, 1.*

MALFEASANCE IN OFFICEIllustrated in the Parables of Jesus: The tenants of the vineyard (Mk 12:1-8; Lk 20:9-15). The rich man's manager (Lk 16:1-7).

MALICE
Characteristics:
Outgrowth of original sin (Ge 3:15). Is hated by God (Pr 6:16-19). Reacts (Job 15:35; Ps 7:15-16; 10:7, 14; Jer 20:10). Blinds those possessed of (1Jn 2:9-11; 4:20). Is murderous (1Jn 3:13-15). Preludes divine forgiveness (Mt 6:15; 18:28-35).
Is forbidden (Lev 19:14, 17-18; 2Ki 6:21-22; Pr 20:22; 24:17-18, 29; Zec 7:10; 8:17; Mt 5:38-41; Lk 6:29; Ro 12:19; 1Co 5:8; 14:20; Eph 4:31; Col 3:8; 1Th 5:15; 1Pe 2:1; 3:9). The wicked filled with (Pr 4:16-17; Ps 10:7-10, 14; Pr 4:16-17; 6:14; 21:10; 30:14; Isa 59:4-6; Mt 13:25, 28; Jn 8:44; Ro 1:29-32; Gal 5:19-21; Tit 3:3; 3Jn 10). Punishment for (Dt 27:17-18; Pr 6:14-15; 17:5; 28:10; Isa 29:20-21; 32:6; Eze 18:18; 26:2-3; 28:3, 6-7, 12-17; Am 1:11; Mic 2:1; Mt 26:52; Jas 2:13).
Proverbs concerning (Pr 4:16-17; 6:14-16, 18-19; 10:6, 12; 11:17; 12:10; 14:17, 22; 15:17; 16:30; 17:5; 20:22; 21:10; 24:8, 17-18, 29; 26:2, 27; 28:10; 30:14).

Instances of:
Cain toward Abel (Ge 4:8; 1Jn 3:12). Ishmael toward Sarah (Ge 21:9). Sarah toward Hagar (Ge 21:10). Philistines toward Isaac (Ge 26:12-15, 18-21). Esau toward Jacob (Ge 27:41-42). Joseph's brothers toward Joseph (Ge 37:2-28; 42:21; Ac 7:9-10). Potiphar's wife toward Joseph (Ge 39:14-20). Ammonites toward the Israelites (Dt 23:3-4). Saul toward David (1Sa 18:8-29; 19; 20:30-33; 22:6-23; 23:7-28; 26:1-2, 18). David toward Michal (2Sa 6:21-23), toward Joab (1Ki 2:5-6), toward Shimei (1Ki 2:8-9). Shimei toward David (2Sa 16:5-8). Ahithophel toward David (2Sa 17:1-3). Jezebel toward Elijah (1Ki 19:1-2). Ahaziah toward Elijah (2Ki 1:7-15). Jehoram toward Elisha (2Ki 6:31). Samaritans toward the Jews (Ezr 4; Ne 2:10; 4:6). Haman toward Mordecai (Est 3:5-15; 5:9-14). Not practiced by Job (Job 31:29-30). The psalmist's enemies (Ps 22:7-8; 35:15-16, 19-21; 38:16, 19; 41:5-8; 55:3; 56:5-6; 57:4, 6; 59:3-4, 7; 62:3-4; 64:2-6; 69:4, 10-12, 26; 86:14; 102:8; 109:2-5, 16-18; 140:1-4); the psalmist demands retribution (Ps 10:7-10, 14; 70:2-3; 71:10-13, 24). Jeremiah's enemies (Jer 26:8-11; 38:1-6). Nebuchadnezzar toward Zedekiah (Jer 52:10-11). Daniel's enemies (Da 6:4-15).
Herodias toward John (Mt 14:3-11; Mk 6:24-28). James and John toward the Samaritans (Lk 9:54). Enemies of Jesus (Ps 22:11; Mt 27:18, 27-30, 39-43; Mk 12:13; 15:10-11, 16-19, 29-32; Lk 11:53-54; 23:10-11, 39; Jn 18:22-23). Paul's enemies (Ac 14:5, 19; 16:19-24; 17:5; 19:24-35; 21:27-31, 36; 22:22-23; 23:12-15; 25:3; Php 1:15-17).
See Conspiracy; Hatred; Homicide; Jealousy; Persecution; Retaliation; Revenge.

MALINGERING Instances of: David feigning madness (1Sa 21:13-15), the sluggard (Pr 6:9-11).

MALKIEL, MALKIELITE (*God [El] is [my] king*). An Asherite; son of Beriah (Ge 46:17; Nu 26:45; 1Ch 7:31).

MALKIJAH (*Yahweh is [my] king*).
1. Gershonite (1Ch 6:40).
2. Ancestor of Adaiah (1Ch 9:12; Ne 11:12).
3. Priest (1Ch 24:9).
4. Israelite who married a foreigner (Ezr 10:25).
5. Another who married a foreigner (Ezr 10:25).

M

6. Another who married a foreigner (Ezr 10:31).
7. Son of Harim (Ne 3:11).
8. Son of Recab (Ne 3:14).
9. Goldsmith (Ne 3:31).
10. Man who assisted Ezra (Ne 8:4).
11. Israelite who sealed covenant with Nehemiah (Ne 10:3).
12. Priest (Ne 12:42). May be same as 11.
13. Father of Pashhur who helped arrest Jeremiah (Jer 21:1; 38:1).

MALKIRAM (/*my*/ *king is exalted*). Son of Jehoiachin (1Ch 3:18).

MALKI-SHUA (/*my*/ *king saves*). Son of King Saul (1Sa 14:49; 31:2; 1Ch 8:33; 9:39; 10:2).

MALLOTHI (*my expression*). Son of Heman, a singer (1Ch 25:4, 26).

MALLOWS See *Salt Herbs*.

MALLUCH (*counselor* ISBE; *king* KB).
1. Levite; ancestor of Ethan (1Ch 6:44).
2. Man who married foreign woman (Ezr 10:29).
3. Another such man (Ezr 10:32).
4. Priest who returned with Zerubbabel (Ne 10:4; 12:2).
5. Chief of people who sealed covenant (Ne 10:27).
6. Head of a priestly family (Ne 12:14).

MALTA An island in the Mediterranean. Paul shipwrecked there (Ac 28:1-10).

MAMMON (*wealth*). Aramaic word for riches (Mt 6:24; Lk 16:11, 13).

MAMRE (*strength*).
1. A plain near Hebron. Abraham resides in (Ge 13:18; 14:13), entertains three angels and is promised a son (Ge 18:1-15). Isaac lives in (Ge 35:27).
2. An Amorite and confederate of Abraham (Ge 14:13, 24).

MAN See *Mankind*.

MAN OF SIN See *Antichrist(s)*.

MAN, SON OF A phrase used by God in addressing Daniel (Da 8:17) and Ezekiel (over eighty times), by Daniel in describing a person he saw in a night vision (Da 7:13-14), and many times by Jesus when referring to himself, undoubtedly identifying himself with the Son of Man of Daniel's prophecy and emphasizing his union with mankind (Lk 9:26; 19:10; 22:48; Jn 6:62).
See *Jesus the Christ, Son of Man; Son of Man*.

MANAEN (*comforter*). An associate of Herod in his youth, and a Christian teacher (Ac 13:1).

MANAHATH (*resting place*).
1. Son of Shobal (Ge 36:23; 1Ch 1:40).
2. A city in Benjamin (1Ch 8:6).

MANAHATHITES (*of Manahath*).
1. Descendants of Shobal, son of Caleb (1Ch 2:52).
2. Descendants of Salma, son of Caleb (1Ch 2:54).

MANASSEH (*one that makes to forget*).
1. Son of Joseph and Asenath (Ge 41:50-51; 46:20), adopted by Jacob on his deathbed (Ge 48:1, 5-20).
2. Tribe of. Descendants of Joseph. The two sons of Joseph, Ephraim and Manasseh, were reckoned among the primogenitors of the twelve tribes, taking the places of Joseph and Levi.
Adopted by Jacob (Ge 48:5). Prophecy concerning (Ge 49:25-26). Enumeration of (Nu 1:34-35; 26:29-34). Place of in camp and march (Nu 2:18, 20; 10:22-23). Blessing of Moses on (Dt 33:13-17). Inheritance of one-half of the tribe E of the Jordan (Nu 32:33, 39-42). One-half of the tribe W of the Jordan (Jos 16:9; 17:5-11). The eastern half assist in the conquest of the country W of the Jordan (Dt 3:18-20; Jos 1:12-15; 4:12-13). Join the other eastern tribes in erecting a monument to testify to the unity of all Israel; misunderstood; makes satisfactory explanation (Jos 22). Join Gideon in war with the Midianites (Jdg 6-7). Malcontents of, join David (1Ch 12:19, 31). Smitten by Hazael (2Ki 10:33). Return from the Captivity (1Ch 9:3). Reallotment of territory to, by Ezekiel (Eze 48:4). Affiliate with the Israelites in the reign of Hezekiah (2Ch 30). Incorporated into kingdom of Judah (2Ch 15:9; 34:6-7). 144,000 from (Rev 7:6).
See *Israel, Tribes of*.
3. The father of Gershom (Jdg 18:30).
4. King of Judah. History of (2Ki 21:1-18; 2Ch 33:1-20; Mt 1:10).
5. Two Jews who put away their Gentile wives after the Captivity (Ezr 10:30, 33).

MANASSES See *Manasseh*.

MANASSITES (*forgetting*). Descendants of Joseph's son Manasseh (Ge 41:51).

MANDRAKE (Ge 30:14-16; SS 7:13).

MANEH See *Mina*.

MANGER Stall or trough for feeding livestock (Job 39:9; Pr 14:4; Isa 1:3; Lk 2:7-16).

MANKIND
Created:
Male and Female (Ge 1:26-27; 2:7; 5:1-2; Dt 4:32; Job 4:17; 10:2-3, 8-9; 31:15; 33:4; 34:19; 35:10; 36:3; Ps 8:5; 100:3; 119:73; 138:8; 139:14-15; Ecc 7:29; Isa 17:7; 42:5; 43:7; 45:12; 64:8; Jer 27:5; Zec 12:1; Mal 2:10; Mt 19:4; Mk 10:6; Heb 2:7).
A little lower than the angels (Job 4:18-21; Ps 8:5; Heb 2:7-8), than God (Ps 8:5). Above other creatures (Mt 10:31; 12:12).

Design of:
To have dominion over all creation (Ge 1:26, 28; 2:19-20; 9:2-3; Ps 8:6-8; Da 2:38; Heb 2:7-8; Jas 3:7). For the glory and pleasure of God (Pr 16:4; Isa 43:7).
Equality of all people (Job 21:26; 31:13-15; Ps 33:13-15; Pr 22:2; Mt 20:25-28; 23:8-10; 23:11; Mk 10:42-44; Ac 10:28, 34-35; 17:26). Equality under the gospel (Gal 3:28). See *Race, 1.*
Mortal (Job 4:17; Ecc 2:14-15; 3:20; 1Co 15:21-22; Heb 9:27). See *Immortality*. Insignificance of (Ge 6:3; 18:27; Job 4:18-19; 7:17; 15:14; 22:2-5; 25:2-6; 35:2-8; 38:4, 12-13; Ps 8:3-4; 78:39; 144:3-4).
A spirit (Job 4:19; 14:10; 32:8; Ps 31:5; Pr 20:27; Ecc 1:8; 3:21; 12:7; Isa 26:9; Zec 12:1; Mt 4:4; 10:28; 26:41; Mk 14:38; Lk 22:40; 23:46; 24:39; Jn 3:3-8; 4:24; Ac 7:59; Ro 1:9; 2:29; 7:14-25; 1Co 2:11; 6:20; 7:34; 14:14; 2Co 4:6-7, 16; 5:1-9; Eph 3:16; 4:4; 1Th 5:23; Heb 4:12; Jas 2:26).
See *Duty; Ignorance; Neighbor; Women; Young Men.*

MANNA (*What is it?*; possibly *food*). Miraculously given to Israel for food in the wilderness (Ex 16:4, 15; Ne 9:15).

Called:
God's manna (Ne 9:20). Bread of heaven (Ps 105:40). Bread from heaven (Ps 78:24). Angel's food (Ps 78:25). Spiritual food (1Co 10:3). Previously unknown (Dt 8:3, 16).

Described as:
Like coriander seed (Ex 16:31; Nu 11:7). White (Ex 16:31). Like in, color to resin (Nu 11:7), taste to wafers made with honey (Ex 16:31), taste to oil (Nu 11:8). Like frost (Ex 16:14). Fell after the evening dew (Nu 11:9). None fell on the Sabbath (Ex 16:26-27). Gathered every morning (Ex 16:21). An omer of, gathered for each person (Ex 16:16). Two portions of, gathered the sixth day on account of the Sabbath (Ex 16:5, 22-26). He that gathered much or little had sufficient and nothing left over (Ex 16:18). Melted away by the sun (Ex 16:21).

Given:
When Israel murmured for bread (Ex 16:2-3). In answer to prayer (Ps 105:40). Through Moses (Jn 6:31-32). To exhibit God's glory (Ex 16:7). As a sign of Moses' divine mission (Jn 6:30-31). For forty years (Ne 9:21). As a test of obedience (Ex 16:4). To teach that man does not live by bread only (Dt 8:3, w Mt 4:4). To humble and prove Israel (Dt 8:16). If kept longer than a day (except on the Sabbath) began to spoil (Ex 16:19-20).

The Israelites:
At first covetous of (Ex 16:17). Ground, made into cakes and baked in pans (Nu 11:8). Counted, inferior to food of Egypt (Nu 11:4-6). Loathed (Nu 21:5). Punished for despising (Nu 11:10-20). Punished for loathing (Nu 21:6). Ceased when Israel entered Canaan (Ex 16:35; Jos 5:12).

Illustrative of:
Christ (Jn 6:32-35). Blessedness given to saints (Rev 2:17). A golden pot of, laid up in the holiest for a memorial (Ex 16:32-34; Heb 9:4).

MANNERS Polite social customs. Obeisance to strangers (Ge 18:2; 19:1). Standing while guests eat (Ge 18:8), in presence of superiors (Ge 31:35; Job 29:8), of the aged (Lev 19:32). Courteousness commanded (1Pe 3:8). Rule for guests (Pr 23:1-2; 1Co 10:27). See *Salutations.*

MANOAH (*rest*). A Danite of Zorah and father of Samson (Jdg 13:2-24).

MANSERVANT See *Servant*.

MANSIONS Spacious homes of the rich that offer no protection from God's judgment (Ps 49:14; Isa 5:9; Am 3:15; 5:11).

MANSLAUGHTER See *Fratricide; Homicide; Infanticide; Regicide.*

MANSLAYER A person who has killed another human being accidentally; the manslayer could find asylum in cities of refuge (Nu 35; Dt 4:42; 19:3-10; Jos 20:3). See *Cities of Refuge.*

MANTLE Torn in token of grief (Ezr 9:3; Job 1:20; 2:12). Of Elijah (1Ki 19:19; 2Ki 2:8, 13-14). See *Dress.*

MANURE Used as fertilizer (Isa 25:10; Lk 13:8; 14:34-35).

MANUSCRIPTS, DEAD SEA See *Dead Sea Scrolls*.

MAOCH (*a poor one*). The father of Achish, king of Gath, who protected David (1Sa 27:2; 29:1-11). Possibly the same as Maacah, 2. See *Maacah, 2.*

MAON (*dwelling*).
1. Descendant of Caleb (1Ch 2:42-45).
2. Town S of Hebron (1Sa 23:24-28; 25:1-3).

MAONITES Enemies of Israel (Jdg 10:11-12), possibly from Maon 2, also called Meunim or Meunites. See *Meunim, Meunites.*

MARA (*bitter*). Name Naomi called herself (Ru 1:20).

MARAH (*bitter*). The first station of the Israelites, where Moses made the bitter waters sweet (Ex 15:22-25; Nu 33:8-9).

MARALAH A landmark on the boundary of Zebulun (Jos 19:11).

MARANATHA (*our Lord has come* or *our Lord, come!*). An expression of greeting and encouragement, marking the desire of Christians for the Lord's return (1Co 16:22).

MARBLE (*marble* or *alabaster*). In the temple (1Ch 29:2). Pillars of (Est 1:6; SS 5:15). Merchandise of (Rev 18:12). Mosaics of (Est 1:6).

MARCABOTH See *Beth Marcaboth*.

MARCHESHVAN See *Bul; Month, 8.*

MARCUS See *Mark, John.*

MARDUK Marduk, the chief god of the Babylonians (Jer 50:2).

MARESHAH (perhaps *head place*).
1. A city of Judah (Jos 15:44; 2Ch 11:8; 14:9-10). Birthplace of Eliezer the prophet (2Ch 20:37). Prophecy concerning (Mic 1:15).
2. Father of Hebron (1Ch 2:42).
3. A son of, or possibly a city founded by, Laadah (1Ch 4:21).

MARI Ancient city of Euphrates Valley, discovered in 1933 and subsequently excavated. Twenty thousand cuneiform tablets have been found, throwing much light upon ancient Syrian civilization. Mari kingdom was contemporary with Hammurabi of Babylon and the Amorite tribes of Canaan, ancestors of the Hebrews.

MARINER (1Ki 9:27; 2Ch 8:18; Isa 42:10; Eze 27:27). Perils of (Ps 107:23-30; Jnh 1:5; Ac 27:17-44). Cowardice of (Ac 27:30). See *Commerce; Ship.*

MARK A word with various meanings: a special sign of ownership (Eze 9:4, 6; Rev 7:2-8), signature (Job 31:35), a target (1Sa 20:20), a form of tattooing banned by the Lord (Lev 19:28), a goal to be attained (Php 3:14), a particular brand denoting the name or rank of men (Rev 13:16).
See *Mark, John.*

MARK, GOSPEL OF
Author: Anonymous, traditionally John Mark
Date : Possibly in the 50s or early 60s A.D.
Outline:
I. The Beginnings of Jesus' Ministry (1:1-13).
 A. His Forerunner (1:1-8).
 B. His Baptism (1:9-11).
 C. His Temptation (1:12-13).
II. Jesus' Ministry in Galilee (1:14-6:29).
 A. Early Galilean Ministry (1:14-3:12).
 1. Call of the first disciples (1:14-20).
 2. Miracles in Capernaum (1:21-34).
 3. A tour of Galilee (1:21-34).
 4. Ministry in Capernaum (2:1-22).
 5. Sabbath controversy (2:23-3:12).
 B. Later Galilean Ministry (3:13-6:29).
 1. Selection of the twelve apostles (3:13-19).
 2. Teachings in Capernaum (3:20-35).
 3. Parables of the kingdom (4:1-34).
 4. Trip across the Sea of Galilee (4:35-5:20).
 5. More Galilee miracles (5:21-43).
 6. Unbelief in Jesus' hometown (6:1-6).
 7. Six apostolic teams tour Galilee (6:7-13).
 8. King Herod's reaction to Jesus' ministry (6:14-29).
III. Withdrawals From Galilee (6:30-9:32).
 A. To the Eastern Shore of the Sea of Galilee (6:30-52).
 B. To the Western Shore of the Sea of Galilee (6:53-7:23).
 C. To Phoenicia (7:24-30).
 D. To the Region of the Decapolis (7:31-8:10).
 E. To the Vicinity of Caesarea Philippi (8:11-9:32).
IV. Final Ministry in Galilee (9:33-50).
V. Jesus' Ministry in Judea and Perea (ch. 10).
 A. Teaching Concerning Divorce (10:1-12).
 B. Teaching Concerning Divorce (10:13-16).
 C. The Rich Young Man (10:17-31).
 D. Prediction of Jesus' Death (10:32-34).
 E. A Request of Two Brothers (10:35-45).
 F. Restoration of Bartimaeus's Sight (10:46-52).
VI. The Passion of Jesus (chs. 11-15).
 A. The Triumphal Entry (11:12-19).
 B. The Cleansing of the Temple (11:12-19).
 C. Concluding Controversies With Jewish Leaders (11:20-12:44).
 D. The Olivet Discourse Concerning the End of the Age (ch. 13).
 E. The Anointing of Jesus (14:1-11).
 F. The Arrest, Trial and Death of Jesus (14:12-15:47).
VII. The Resurrection of Jesus (ch. 16).
 See *Synoptic Gospels, The.*

MARK, JOHN (Mark [Latin] *large hammer*; John [Hebrew] *Yahweh is gracious*). Author of the second Gospel. John was his Jewish name, Mark (Marcus) his Roman; called John (Ac 13:5, 13), Mark (Ac 15:39), "John, also called Mark" (Ac 12:12), relative of Barnabas (Col 4:10), accompanied and then deserted Paul on first missionary journey (Ac 12:25; 13:13), went with Barnabas to Cyprus after Paul refused to take him on his second missionary journey (Ac 15:36-39), fellow-worker with Paul (Phm 24), recommended by Paul to church at Colosse (Col 4:10), may have been the young man of Mark 14:51-52. Early tradition makes him the "interpreter" of Peter in Rome and founder of the church in Alexandria.

MARKET A place for general merchandise. Held at gates. See *Gates*. Judgment seat at (Ac 16:19). Trade of, in Tyre, consisted of horses, horsemen, mules, horns, ivory, and ebony, emeralds, purple, embroidered wares, linen, coral, agate, honey, balm, wine, wool, oil, cassia, calamus, charioteers' clothing, lambs, rams, goats, precious stones, and gold, spices, and costly apparel (Eze 27:13-25). See *Agora.*

MAROTH (*bitterness*). A city of Judah (Mic 1:12).

MARRIAGE
General:
Divine institution of (Ge 2:18, 20-24; Mt 9:4-6; Mk 10:7-8; 1Co 6:16; Eph 5:31). Based on principle of creation (1Co 11:11-12; Ge 2:18).
Unity of husband and wife in (Ge 2:23-24; Mt 19:5-6; Mk 10:2-10; 1Co 6:16; Eph 5:31, 33). Obligations under, inferior to duty to God (Dt 13:6-10; Mt 19:29; Lk 14:26). Indissoluble except

for adultery (Mal 2:13-16; Mt 5:31-32; Mk 10:11-12; Lk 16:18; Ro 7:1-3; 1Co 7:39-40). Dissolved by death (Mt 22:29-30; Mk 12:24-25; Ro 7:1-3).

Commended (Pr 18:22; Heb 13:4). Commanded of exiled Israelites (Jer 29:6). Commanded because of immorality (1Co 7:1-7).

None in the resurrection state (Mt 22:29-30; Mk 12:24-25). Levirate (the brother required to marry a brother's widow) (Ge 38:8, 11; Dt 25:5-10; Ru 4:5; Mt 22:24-27; Mk 12:19-23; Lk 20:28-33).

Mosaic Laws Concerning:

Of priests (Lev 21:1, 7, 13-15). Captives (Dt 21:10-14). Divorced persons (Dt 24:1-5). A virgin, not pledged to be married, who has been seduced (Ex 22:16-17). Within tribes (Nu 36:8). Incestuous, forbidden (Lev 18:6-18 w Dt 22:30; Lev 20:14, 17, 19-21; Mk 6:17-18).

Among antediluvians (Ge 6:2). Among relatives, Abraham and Sarah (Ge 11:29; 12:13; 20:2, 9-16), Isaac and Rebekah (Ge 24:3-4, 67), Jacob and his wives (Ge 28:2; 29:15-30). Levirate (the brother required to marry a brother's widow) (Ge 38:8, 11; Dt 25:5-10; Ru 4:5; Mt 22:24-27; Mk 12:19-23; Lk 20:28-33).

Intermarriage. See Intermarry.

Various Principles:

Parents contract for their children: Hagar selects a wife for Ishmael (Ge 21:21). Abraham for Isaac (Ge 24). Laban arranges for his daughters' marriage (Ge 29). Samson asks his parents to procure him a wife (Jdg 14:2). Parents' consent required in the Mosaic law (Ex 22:17). Presents given to parents to secure their favor (Ge 24:53; 34:12; 1Sa 18:25). Nuptial feasts (Ge 29:22; Jdg 14:12; Est 2:18; Mt 22:11-12). Jesus present at (Jn 2:1-5). Ceremony attested by witnesses (Ru 4:1-11; Isa 8:1-3). Bridegroom exempt one year from military duty (Dt 24:5). Bridal ornaments (Isa 49:18; Jer 2:32). Bridal presents (Ge 24:53). Herald preceded the bridegroom (Mt 25:6). Wedding robes adorned with jewels (Isa 61:10). Festivities attending (Jer 7:34; 16:9; 25:10; Rev 18:23).

Wives obtained by purchase (Ge 29:20, 27-29; 31:41; Ru 4:10; 2Sa 3:14; Hos 3:2; 12:12), by kidnapping (Jdg 21:21-23). Given by kings (1Sa 17:25; 18:17, 27). Daughters given in, as rewards of valor (Jdg 1:12; 1Sa 17:25; 18:27).

Wives taken by edict (Est 2:2-4, 8-14). David gave 100 foreskins for a wife (2Sa 3:14).

Wives among the Israelites must be Israelites (Ex 34:16; Dt 7:3-4; Ezr 9:1-2, 12; Ne 10:30; 13:26-27; Mal 2:11). Betrothal a quasi-marriage (Mt 1:18; Lk 1:27).

Discouraged among the Corinthians (1Co 7:1, 8-9, 25-40). Celibacy deplored (Jdg 11:38; Isa 4:1). Unhappiness in (Pr 21:9, 19).

Marriage of widows (Ro 7:1-3; 1Co 7:39-40; 1Ti 5:14). Marriage of ministers (Lev 21:7-8, 13-14; Eze 44:22; 1Co 9:5; 1Ti 3:2, 12). Prophecies concerning the forbidding of (1Ti 4:1, 3).

Figurative:

(Isa 54:5; 62:4-5; Jer 3:14; 31:32; Eze 16:8; Hos 2:19-20; Eph 5:23-32; Rev 19:7-9) Parables of (Mt 22:2-10; 25:1-10; Mk 2:19-20; Jn 3:29; 2Co 11:2).

See Bride; Bridegroom; Divorce; Husband; Intermarry; Wife.

MARROW Heart of the bone (Job 21:24), used figuratively of good things (Ps 63:5; Isa 25:6).

MARS HILL See Areopagus.

MARSENA Counselor of King Xerxes (Est 1:10-14).

MARSH Swamp lands (Eze 47:11).

MARTHA (a lady, [female] lord). Sister of Mary and Lazarus (Jn 11:1). Ministers to Jesus (Lk 10:38-42; Jn 12:2). Beloved by Jesus (Jn 11:5).
See Lazarus; Mary, 4.

MARTYR (witness). One who dies to bear witness to a cause (Ac 22:20; Rev 17:6).

MARTYRDOM Of prophets (Mt 23:34; Lk 11:50; Rev 16:6). Followers of Jesus exposed to (Mt 10:21-22, 39; 23:34; 24:9; Mk 13:12; Lk 21:16-17). Spirit of, required by Jesus (Mt 16:25; Lk 9:24; Jn 12:25). Possessed by the righteous (Ps 44:22; Ro 8:36; Rev 12:11). Must be based on love (1Co 13:3).
Prophetic reference to (Rev 6:9-11; 11:7-12; 17:6).
See Persecution.

Instances of:

Abel (Ge 4:3-8). Prophets slain by Jezebel (1Ki 18:4, 13). Zechariah (2Ch 24:21-22). John the Baptist (Mk 6:18-28). Jesus. See Jesus the Christ, Death of. Stephen (Ac 7:58-60). James the apostle (Ac 12:2). The prophets (Mt 22:6; 23:35; Ro 11:3; 1Th 2:15; Heb 11:32-37).

MARY (perhaps fat one; See Miriam).
1. See Mary, The Virgin.
2. Mother of James and Joses (Mt 27:56; Mk 15:40; Lk 24:10), probably the wife of Clopas (Jn 19:25), witnessed Crucifixion and visited grave on resurrection morning (Mt 27:56; 28:1).
3. Mary Magdalene; Jesus cast seven demons out of her (Mk 16:9; Lk 8:2), appears at Jesus' crucifixion (Mt 27:55-56; Mk 15:40-41; Jn 19:25), followed body of Jesus to grave (Mt 27:61) and was first to learn of the Resurrection (Mt 28:1-8; Mk 16:9; Lk 24:1-12; Jn 20:1-9, 18). See Dalmanutha; Magadan.
4. Mary of Bethany; sister of Lazarus and Martha; lived in Bethany (Jn 11:1), commended by Jesus (Lk 10:42), anointed feet of Jesus (Jn 12:3).
5. Mother of John Mark; sister of Barnabas (Col 4:10), home in Jerusalem meeting place of Christians (Ac 12:12).
6. Christian at Rome (Ro 16:6).

MARY, THE VIRGIN (perhaps fat one; See Miriam). Wife of Joseph (Mt 1:18-25), relative of Elizabeth, the mother of John the Baptist (Lk 1:36), of the seed of David (Ac 2:30; Ro 1:3; 2Ti 2:8), mother of Jesus (Mt 1:18, 20; Lk 2:1-20), attended to ceremonial purification (Lk 2:22-38), fled to Egypt with Joseph and

Jesus (Mt 2:13-15), lived in Nazareth (Mt 2:19-23), took twelve-year-old Jesus to temple (Lk 2:41-50), at wedding in Cana of Galilee (Jn 2:1-11), concerned for Jesus' safety (Mt 12:46; Mk 3:21, 31ff; Lk 8:19-21), at the cross of Jesus (Jn 19:25ff) where she was entrusted by Jesus to the care of John (Jn 19:25-27), in the Upper Room (Ac 1:14).

Distinctive Roman Catholic doctrines about Mary: Perpetual Virginity, Intercession, Immaculate Conception (1854), and Assumption of Mary (1950).

MASCHIL See Maskil.

MASH Variant spelling of Meshech, son of Aram (Ge 10:22-23, ftn). See Meshech.

MASHAL Also called Mishal (Jos 19:26; 21:30). See Mishal. A Levitical city in Asher (1Ch 6:74).

MASKIL Occurs in the titles of several psalms (Pss 32; 42; 44-45; 52-55; 74; 78; 88-89; 142). The Hebrew word perhaps indicates that these psalms contain instruction in godliness (14:2; 53:2, "any who understand"; 41:1, "he who has regard"; 47:7, ftn).
See Music, Symbols Used in.

MASKING See Disguises.

MASON A trade in the time of David (2Sa 5:11), of later times (2Ki 12:12; 22:6; 1Ch 14:1; Ezr 3:7).

MASREKAH (perhaps vineyard). Royal city of King Samlah, in Edom (Ge 36:31, 36-37; 1Ch 1:47-48).

MASSA (burden, oracle). Tribe descended from Ishmael near Persian Gulf (Ge 25:14; 1Ch 1:30).

MASSACRE Authorized by Moses (Dt 20:13, 16). Decree to destroy the Jews (Est 3).
Instances of: Inhabitants of Heshbon (Dt 2:34), of Bashan (Dt 3:6), of Ai (Jos 8:24-26), of Hazor (Jos 11:11-12), of the cities of the seven kings (Jos 10:28-40). Midianites (Nu 31:7-8). Prophets of Baal (1Ki 18:40). Worshipers of Baal (2Ki 10:18-28). Sons of Ahab (2Ki 10:1-8). Royal family of Athaliah (2Ki 11:1). Inhabitants of Tiphsah (2Ki 15:16). Edomites (2Ki 14:7).
See Captive.

MASSAH (test, try). Site of rock in Horeb from which Moses drew water (Ex 17:1-7; Dt 6:16; 9:22), connected with Meribah (Dt 33:8).

MASTER Yahweh called (Jer 31:32, ftn; Hos 2:16). See Baali. Jesus called (Mt 8:19; 10:25; 23:8; 26:18, 25, 49; Mk 14:45; Lk 8:24; Jn 13:13-14). Jesus spoke against abuse of the title (Mt 23:8). See Lord.

MASTER, OF SERVANTS

Duties to Servants:

Must allow Sabbath rest (Dt 5:14). Compensate (Jer 22:13; Ro 4:4; Col 4:1; 1Ti 5:18). Pay promptly (Lev 19:13; Dt 24:15; Jas 5:4). Forbidden to oppress (Lev 19:13; 25:43; Dt 24:14; Job 31:13-14; Pr 22:16; Mal 3:5). Forbidden to threaten (Eph 6:9). Exhorted to show kindness (Phm 10-16). Exhorted to show wisdom (Pr 29:12, 21).
See Employer; Employee; Hired Servant; Servant.

Good Masters:

Abraham (Ge 18:19). Job (Job 31:13-15). The centurion (Lk 7:2).

Unjust Masters:

Instances of: Sarah to Hagar (Ge 16:6). Laban to Jacob (Ge 31:7). Potiphar's wife to Joseph (Ge 39:7-20). Violent, to be punished (Ex 21:20-21, 26-27).

MASTER CRAFTSMAN Instances of: Tubal-Cain (Ge 4:22), Bezalel (Ex 31:2-11; 35:30-35), Huram or Huram-Abi (1Ki 7:13-50; 2Ch 2:13-14; 4:11-18), Wisdom (Pr 8:30), Paul (1Co 3:10). See Art.

MATERIALISM Love of possessions.

Love of money:

A root of all kinds of evil (1Ti 6:10). Insatiable (Ecc 4:7-8; 5:10-11). Forbidden in overseer (1Ti 3:2-3; Tit 1:7). Materialists do not love God (Mt 6:24; 1Jn 2:15-17; 3:17).

Treasures in Heaven Versus Materialism:

(Mt 6:19-21; 1Ti 6:17-19).
See Avarice; Greed; Love, Of Money; Rich, The; Riches.

MATHUSALA See Methuselah.

MATRED (perhaps spear). Mother of Mehetabel, wife of Hadad (Ge 36:39), who is called "Hadad" (1Ch 1:50).

MATRI (rainy). Head of Benjamite family (1Sa 10:21).

MATTAN (gift).
1. A priest of Baal slain in the idol temple at Jerusalem (2Ki 11:18; 2Ch 23:17).
2. Father of Shephatiah (Jer 38:1).

MATTANAH (gift). Encampment of Israel in wilderness (Nu 21:18-19).

MATTANIAH (gift of Yahweh).
1. Original name of King Zedekiah (2Ki 24:17).
2. Chief choir leader and watchman (Ne 11:17; 12:8, 25).
3. Levite (2Ch 20:14).
4. Son of Elam (Ezr 10:26).
5. Son of Zattu (Ezr 10:27).
6. Son of Pahath-Moab (Ezr 10:30).
7. Son of Bani (Ezr 10:37).
8. Grandfather of Hanan (Ne 13:13).

9. Son of Heman; head musician (1Ch 25:4-5, 7, 16).
10. Levite who assisted Hezekiah (2Ch 29:13).

MATTATHA An ancestor of Jesus (Lk 3:31).

MATTATHAH See Mattattah.

MATTATHIAS (gift of Yahweh).
1. Assistant of Ezra, spelled Mattithiah (Ne 8:4).
2. Name borne by two ancestors of Christ (Lk 3:25-26).
3. Priest; founder of Maccabee family (1Mc 2). See also, 1Mc 11:70; 16:14-16; 2Mc 14:19.

MATTATTAH (gift). One of the family of Hashum (Ezr 10:33).

MATTENAI (gift).
1. Two Israelites who put away their Gentile wives after the Captivity (Ezr 10:33, 37).
2. A priest in the time of Joiakim (Ne 12:19).

MATTHAN (gift). Grandfather of Joseph, Mary's husband (Mt 1:15).

MATTHAT (gift of God).
1. Father of Heli, ancestor of Joseph (Lk 3:23).
2. Father of Jorim, and ancestor of Joseph (Lk 3:29).

MATTHEW (gift of Yahweh). Son of Alphaeus (Mk 2:14), tax collector, also called Levi (Mk 2:14; Lk 5:27), called by Jesus to become disciple (Mt 9:9; Mk 2:14; Lk 5:27) and gave feast for Jesus; appointed apostle (Mt 10:3; Mk 3:18; Lk 6:15; Ac 1:13).

MATTHEW, GOSPEL OF

Author: Anonymous, traditionally the apostle Matthew

Date: Probably in the late 60s A.D.

Outline:
I. The Birth and Early Years of Jesus (chs. 1-2).
 A. His Genealogy (1:1-17).
 B. His Birth (1:18-2:12).
 C. His Sojourn in Egypt (2:13-23).
II. The Beginnings of Jesus' Ministry (3:1-4:11).
 A. His Forerunner (3:1-12).
 B. His Baptism (3:13-17).
 C. His Temptation (4:1-11).
III. Jesus' Ministry in Galilee (4:12-14:12).
 A. The Beginning of the Galilean Campaign (4:12-25).
 B. The Sermon on the Mount (chs. 5-7).
 C. A Collection of Miracles (chs. 8-9).
 D. The Commissioning of the Twelve Apostles (ch. 10).
 E. Ministry Throughout Galilee (11-12).
 F. The Parables of the Kingdom (ch. 13).
 G. Herod's Reaction to Jesus' Ministry (14:1-12).
IV. Jesus' Withdrawals From Galilee (14:13-17:20).
 A. To the Eastern Shore of the Sea of Galilee (14:13-15:20).
 B. To Phoenicia (15:21-28).
 C. To the Decapolis (15:29-16:12).
 D. To Caesarea Philippi (16:13-17:20).
V. Jesus' Last Ministry in Galilee (17:22-18:35).
 A. Prediction of Jesus' Death (17:22-23).
 B. Temple Tax (17:24-27).
 C. Discourse on Life in the Kingdom (ch. 18).
VI. Jesus' Ministry in Judea and Perea (chs. 19-20).
 A. Teaching Concerning Divorce (19:1-12).
 B. Teaching Concerning Little Children (19:13-15).
 C. The Rich Young Man (19:16-30).
 D. The Parable of the Workers in the Vineyard (20:1-16).
 E. Prediction of Jesus' Death (20:17-19).
 F. A Mother's Request (20:20-28).
 G. Restoration of Sight at Jericho (20:29-34).
VII. Passion Week (chs. 21-27).
 A. The Triumphal Entry (21:1-11).
 B. The Cleansing of the Temple (21:12-17).
 C. The Last Controversies With the Jewish Leaders (21:18-23:39).
 D. The Olivet Discourse Concerning the End of the Age (chs. 24-25).
 E. The Anointing of Jesus' Feet (26:1-13).
 F. The Arrest, Trials and Death of Jesus (26:14-27:66).
VIII. The Resurrection (ch. 28).
See Synoptic Gospels, The.

MATTHIAS (gift of Yahweh). Apostle chosen by lot to take place of Judas (Ac 1:15-26), had been follower of Christ (Ac 1:21-22).

MATTITHIAH (gift of Yahweh).
1. A Levite who had charge of the baked offerings (1Ch 9:31).
2. A Levite musician (1Ch 15:18, 21; 16:5).
3. A chief of the fourteenth division of temple musicians (1Ch 25:3, 21).
4. An Israelite who divorced his Gentile wife after the Captivity (Ezr 10:43).
5. A prince who stood by Ezra when he read the law to the people (Ne 8:4).

MATTOCK (cut in, plow). Single-headed farming tool with point on one side and broad edge on other side (1Sa 13:20-21; Isa 7:25).

MAUL See Club.

MAW One of the stomachs of a ruminating animal (Dt 18:3).

MAZZAROTH See Constellations.

ME JARKON (waters of Jarkon [greenish?]). A city in Dan (Jos 19:46).

MEADOW
1. Place where reeds grow (Ge 41:2, 18).
2. Pastureland (Jdg 20:33).

MEAH NIV "Hundred" (Ne 3:1; 12:38). *See Tower, Of the Hundred.*

MEAL *See Grain.*

MEAL OFFERING *See Offerings.*

MEANINGLESS *See Vanity, 1.*

MEARAH (*cave*). *See Arah, 4.*

MEASURE

False and Just:
Just (Lev 19:35-36; Dt 25:13-16; Pr 16:11).
False (Hos 12:7-9). An abomination (Pr 11:1; 20:10, 23; Mic 6:10-12). *See Dishonesty; Integrity.*

Table of Measures:
See chart to the right.

MEAT *See Food.*

MEAT FORKS Used in the tabernacle (Ex 27:3; 38:3; Nu 4:14; 1Sa 2:13-14). Made of gold (1Ch 28:17), of bronze (2Ch 4:16).

MEAT OFFERING *See Offerings, Meat.*

MEBUNNAI (*well built*). One of David's bodyguards (2Sa 23:27), called Sibbecai (2Sa 21:18).

MECHANIC *See Art; Master Craftsman.*

MECHERATHITE *See Mekerathite.*

MECONAH (*foundation*). A city in Judah (Ne 11:28).

MEDAD (*beloved*). One of the seventy elders who did not go to the tabernacle with Moses, but prophesied in the camp (Nu 11:26-29).

MEDAN (*dissension*). Son of Abraham and Keturah (Ge 25:2; 1Ch 1:32).

MEDDLING *See Busybody; Talebearer.*

MEDEBA A city of Moab (Nu 21:30). An idolatrous high place (Isa 15:2). Allotted to Reuben (Jos 13:9, 16). David defeats army and the Ammonites at (1Ch 19:7-15).

MEDES Inhabitants of Media. Israelites distributed among, when carried to Assyria (2Ki 17:6; 18:11). Palace in the Babylonian province of (Ezr 6:2). An essential part of the Medo-Persian Empire (Est 1:1-19). Supremacy over the Babylonian Empire (Da 5:28, 31; 9:1; 11:1).

MEDIA *See Medes.*

MEDIATION

Between People and God:
(Ex 18:19; Job 9:33; Gal 3:19). Solicited by Israel (Ex 20:19-20; Dt 5:27).
Instances of: By Moses (Ex 32:11-13; 34:9; Nu 14:13-19; 27:5; Dt 5:5; 9:18-20, 25-29). Aaron (Nu 16:47-48). Joshua (Jos 7:6-9). Samuel (1Sa 8:10, 21). David (2Sa 24:17).

Between People and Jesus:
In behalf of the afflicted (Mt 12:22; 15:30; Mk 1:32). The four friends for the paralytic (Mt 2:3-12; 9:2-8; Lk 5:18-20). Jairus (Mt 9:18; Mk 5:23; Lk 8:41). The nobleman for his son (Jn 4:47, 49). The father of the demoniac for his son (Mt 17:15; Mk 9:17-18). The Syrian Phoenician woman for her daughter (Mt 15:22; Mk 7:24-26). The disciples for Peter's mother-in-law (Mk 1:30; Lk 4:38-39).

Between Persons:
Reuben for Joseph (Ge 37:21-22). Judah for Joseph (Ge 37:26-27). Pharaoh's chief baker for Joseph (Ge 41:9-13, w 40:14). Jonathan for David (1Sa 19:1-7). Abigail for Nabal (1Sa 25:23-35). Joab for Absalom (2Sa 14:1-24). Bathsheba for Solomon (1Ki 1:15-31), for Adonijah (1Ki 2:13-25). Ebed-Melech for Jeremiah (Jer 38:7-13). Elisha offers to see the king for the Shunammite (2Ki 4:13). The king of Syria for Naaman (2Ki 5:6-8). Paul for Onesimus (Phm 10-21).
See Intercession; Jesus, Mediation of.

MEDICINE Used (Isa 38:21; Lk 10:34; 1Ti 5:23). *See Disease; Physician.*
Figurative (Pr 17:22; Isa 1:6; Jer 8:22; 30:13; 46:11; 51:8-9; Eze 47:12; Rev 22:2).

MEDITATION On the Lord (Ps 63:5-6; 104:34; 139:17-18). On the law of the Lord (Ps 1:2; 19:14; 49:3; 119:11, 15-16, 23, 48, 55, 59, 78, 97-99; 119:148). Commanded (Jos 1:8). On the works of the Lord (Ps 77:10-12; 143:5).
Instances of: Isaac (Ge 24:63). David (Ps 4:4; 39:3).

MEDITERRANEAN SEA Mentioned in Scripture as: The Sea (Nu 34:5; Ps 80:11). The Great Sea (Nu 34:6-7; Jos 1:4; 9:1; 15:12, 47; 23:4; Eze 47:10, 15, 20; 48:28). Sea of the Philistines (Ex 23:31). The western sea (Dt 11:24; Joel 2:20; Zec 14:8).

MEDIUM A spiritist; one who consults the dead (Lev 19:31; 20:6; Dt 18:9-13; Isa 8:19-22). Punished by death in the law (Lev 20:27). Saul and the medium at Endor (1Sa 28:3-25; 1Ch 10:13-14). *See Necromancer, Necromancy; Sorcery; Spiritists.*

MEEKNESS

Described:
Advantageous (Ps 25:9; Pr 14:29; 17:1; 19:11; Ecc 7:8; 10:4; Am 3:3; 1Co 13:4-5, 7). Honorable (Pr 20:3). Potent (Pr 15:1, 18; 16:32; 25:15; 29:8). A fruit of the Spirit (Gal 5:22-23, 26).

Commanded (Zep 2:3; Mt 5:38-41 w Lk 6:29; Mt 11:29; Mk 9:50; Ro 12:14, 18; 14:19; 1Co 6:7; 7:15; 10:32; 2Co 13:11; Gal 6:1; Eph 4:1-2; Php 2:14-15; Col 3:12-13; 1Th 5:14-15; 1Ti 3:3; 6:11; 2Ti 2:24-25; Tit 2:2, 9; 3:2; Heb 10:36; 12:14; Jas 1:4, 19, 21; 3:13; 1Pe 2:18-23; 3:4, 11, 15; 2Pe 1:5-7).
Rewards of (Ps 22:26; 37:11; 76:8-9; 147:6; 149:4; Isa 29:19; Mt 5:5; 11:29).

Instances of:
God (La 3:22, 28-30).
Abraham (Ge 13:8-9). Isaac (Ge 26:20-22). Moses (Ex 16:7-8; 17:2-7; Nu 12:3; 16:4-11). Gideon (Jdg 8:2-3). Hannah (1Sa 1:13-16). Saul (1Sa 10:27). David (1Sa 17:29; 2Sa 16:9-14; Ps 38:13-14). Psalmist (Ps 120:5-7).
Jesus (Isa 11:4; 42:1-4; 53:7; La 3:28-30; Mt 11:29; 12:19-20; 26:47-54; 27:13-14; Mk 15:4-5; Lk 23:34; 2Co 10:1; 1Pe 2:21-23). *See Jesus the Christ, Humility of; Meekness of.* Stephen (Ac 7:60). Paul (Ac 21:20-26; 1Co 4:12-13; 2Co 12:10; 1Th 2:7; 2Ti 4:16). The Thessalonians (2Th 1:4). Job (Jas 5:11). The archangel (Jude 9).
See Humility; Kindness; Patience.

MEGIDDO (*place of troops*). City on the Great Road linking Gaza and Damascus, connecting the coastal plain and the Plain of Esdraelon or Megiddo (Jos 12:21; 17:11; Jdg 1:27; 5:19), fortified by Solomon (1Ki 9:15), wounded Ahaziah died there (2Ki 9:27), Josiah lost life there in battle with Pharaoh Neco (2Ki 23:29-30; 2Ch 35:20-27). Large-scale excavations have revealed a great deal of material of great archaeological value.

MEGIDDON *See Megiddo.*

MEHETABEEL *See Mehetabel, 2.*

MEHETABEL (*God [El] does good*).
1. Wife of Hadad (Ge 36:39; 1Ch 1:50).
2. A person whose grandson tried to intimidate Nehemiah (Ne 6:10).

MEHIDA (possibly *bought as slave*). A person whose descendants returned from Babylon (Ezr 2:52; Ne 7:54).

MEHIR (*hired hand*). Son of Kelub (1Ch 4:11).

MEHOLAH, MEHOLATHITE A city in Issachar, probably the same as Abel Meholah. Barzillai and his son Adriel lived there (1Sa 18:19; 2Sa 21:8). *See Abel Meholah.*

MEHUJAEL Descendant of Cain; father of Methushael (Ge 4:18).

MEHUMAN Eunuch of Xerxes, king of Persia (Est 1:10).

MEHUNIM *See Maonites; Meunim, Meunites, 2.*

MEKERATHITE (*one of Mekerath*). Description of Hepher (1Ch 11:36).

MEKONAH *See Meconah.*

MELAH *See Tel Melah.*

MELATIAH (*Yahweh sets free*). A Gibeonite who assisted in repairing the wall of Jerusalem (Ne 3:7).

MELCHESEDEC *See Melchizedek.*

MELCHI *See Melki.*

MELCHIAH *See Malkijah.*

MELCHISHUA, MELCHI-SHUA *See Malki-Shua.*

MELCHIZEDEK (*[my] king is Zedek [just]*). Priest and king of Salem (Jerusalem); blessed Abram in the name of Most High God and received tithes from him (Ge 14:18-20), type of Christ, the Priest-King (Ps 110:4; Heb 5:6-10; 6:20; 7).

MELEA Ancestor of Jesus (Lk 3:31).

MELECH (*king*). Son of Micah (1Ch 8:35; 9:41).

MELICU *See Malluch, 6.*

MELITA *See Malta.*

MELKI (*my king*).
1. Ancestor of Jesus (Lk 3:24).
2. Remote ancestor of Jesus (Lk 3:28).

Biblical Weights and Measures and Approximate Equivalents

Dry Capacity:

1.	Cor or homer	10 ephahs	6 bushels	220 liters	1Ki 4:22; 5:11; 2Ch 2:10; 27:5; Ezr 7:22
2.	Lethek	5 ephahs	3 bushels	110 liters	Hos 3:2
3.	Ephah	10 omers	3/5 bushel	22 liters	Ex 16:36; Lev 5:11; Nu 5:15; Jdg 6:19; Ru 2:17; 1Sa 1:24; Isa 5:10; Eze 45:10-11,13,24; Am 8:5
4.	Seah	1/3 ephah	7 quarts	7.3 liters	Ge 18:6; 1Sa 25:18; 1Ki 18:32; 2Ki 7:1,16,18
5.	Omer	1/10 ephah	2 quarts	2 liters	Ex 16:16,18,22,32-33,36
6.	Cab	1/18 ephah	1 quart	1 liter	2Ki 6:25

Liquid Capacity:

1.	Bath	1 ephah	6 gallons	22 liters	1Ki 7:26,38; 2Ch 2:10; 4:5; Ezr 7:22; Isa 5:10; Eze 45:10-11,14; Lk 16:6
2.	Hin	1/6 bath	4 quarts	4 liters	Ex 29:40; 30:24; Lev 19:36; 23:13; Nu 15:4-10; 28:5,7,14; Eze 4:11; 45:24; 46:5,7,11,14
3.	Log	1/72 bath	1/3 quart	0.3 liter	Lev 14:10,12,14,21,24

Weight:

1.	Talent	60 minas	75 pounds	34 kilograms	Ex 25:39; 38:27
2.	Mina	50 shekels	1.25 pounds	0.6 kilogram	1Ki 10:17; Ezr 2:69; Da 5:26-28
3.	Shekel	2 bekas	2/5 ounce	11.5 grams	Ge 20:16; Eze 45:12
4.	Pim	2/3 shekel	1/3 ounce	7.6 grams	1Sa 13:21, ftn
5.	Beka	10 gerahs	1/5 ounce	5.5 grams	Ge 24:22; Ex 38:26
6.	Gerah	1/20 shekel	1/50 ounce	0.6 gram	Ex 30:13; Lev 27:25

Length:

1.	Cubit		18 inches	0.5 meter	Ge 6:15-16; Rev 21:17
2.	Span		9 inches	23 cm.	Ex 28:16; 1Sa 17:4; Isa 40:12; La 2:20; Eze 43:13
3.	Handbreadth		3 inches	8 centimeters	Ex 25:25; 1Ki 7:26; 2Ch 4:5; Ps 39:5; Eze 43:13
4.	Finger		0.75 inch	1.85 cm.	Jer 52:21

M

MELODY See Music.

MELON (Nu 11:5).

MELZAR NIV "guard" (Da 1:11, 16). See Guard.

MEMBER Any feature or part of the body (Job 17:7; Jas 3:5).

MEMORIAL Passover (Ex 12:14). See Passover.
Firstborn set apart as a (Ex 13:12-16). Pot of manna (Ex 16:32-34). Feast of Tabernacles (Lev 23:43). Shoulder stones of the ephod (Ex 28:12). Atonement money (Ex 30:16). The twelve stones of Jordan (Jos 4:1-9).
The Lord's Supper (Lk 22:19; 1Co 11:24-26).
See Pillar.

MEMPHIS Capital city of Egypt, on W bank of Nile, c. twenty miles S of modern Cairo; its destruction foretold (Isa 19:13; Jer 2:16; 44:1; 46:14, 19; Eze 30:13, 16).

MEMUCAN One of the seven nobles of Xerxes who counseled the king to divorce Queen Vashti (Est 1:14-21).

MENAHEM (comforter). Sixteenth king of Israel; evil; slew his predecessor, Shallum (2Ki 15:13-22).

MENAN See Menna.

MENE, MENE, TEKEL, PARSIN Four Aramaic words, probably meaning "numbered, numbered, weighed, and divided," which suddenly appeared on the walls of Belshazzar's banquet hall (Da 5:25-28).

MENI See Destiny, 2.

MENNA An ancestor of Jesus (Lk 3:31).

MENSES See Menstruation.

MENSTRUATION Law relating to (Lev 15:19-30; 20:18; Eze 18:6). Cessation of, in old age (Ge 18:11). Immunities of women during (Ge 31:35). Uncleanness of (Isa 30:22).
Figurative (Isa 30:22; La 1:17; Eze 36:17).
See Bleeding, Subject to.

MEON See Baal Meon; Beth Baal Meon; Beth Meon.

MEONENIM See Soothsayers' Tree.

MEONOTHAI (my dwellings). Father of Ophrah (1Ch 4:14).

MEPHAATH (splendor). A Levitical city in Reuben (Jos 13:18; 21:37; 1Ch 6:79; Jer 48:21).

MEPHIBOSHETH (from the mouth of shame [a derogatory term for Baal]).
1. Son of Saul, whom David surrendered to the Gibeonites to be slain (2Sa 21:8-9).
2. Son of Jonathan (2Sa 4:4). Also called Merib-Baal (1Ch 8:34; 9:40). Was lame (2Sa 4:4). David entertains him at his table (2Sa 9:1-7; 21:7). Property restored to (2Sa 9:9-10). His ingratitude to David at the time of Absalom's usurpation (2Sa 16:1-4; 19:24-30). Property of, confiscated (2Sa 16:4; 19:29-30).

MERAB (abundant). Daughter of King Saul (1Sa 14:49). Betrothed to David by Saul (1Sa 18:17-18), but given to Adriel as his wife (1Sa 18:19).

MERAIAH (loved by Yahweh). A priest (Ne 12:12).

MERAIOTH (rebellious).
1. High priest (1Ch 6:6-7).
2. Priest; ancestor of Hilkiah (1Ch 9:11).
3. Another priestly ancestor of Helkai (Ne 12:15). May be same as "Meremoth" (Ne 12:3).

MERARI, MERARITE(S) (bitter). Youngest son of Levi; progenitor of Merarites (Nu 3:17, 33-37; Jos 21:7, 34-40).

MERATHAIM (double rebellion). Symbolic name for Babylon (Jer 50:21).

MERCENARIES See Soldiers.

MERCHANDISE See Commerce.

MERCHANT (Ge 23:16; 37:28; 1Ki 10:15, 28; 2Ch 9:14; Ne 3:32; 13:20; Job 41:6; SS 3:6; Isa 23:2; 47:15; Eze 17:4; 27:13, 17, 21-36; 38:13; Hos 12:7; Na 3:16; Mt 13:45; Rev 18:3, 11, 23). See Commerce.

MERCURIUS, MERCURY See Hermes, 1.

MERCY (Ps 85:10; Pr 20:28; Hos 4:1; Jas 2:13).
A grace of the godly (Ps 37:25-26; Pr 11:17; 12:10; 14:22, 31; Ro 12:8). Iniquity atoned by (Pr 16:6). Of the wicked, cruel (Pr 12:10).
Commanded (Pr 3:3; Hos 12:6; Mic 6:8; Mt 9:13; 12:7; 23:23; Lk 6:36; Col 3:12-13). To be shown with cheerfulness (Ro 12:8).
Rewards of (2Sa 22:26; Ps 18:25; 37:25-26; Pr 14:21; 21:21; Mt 5:7).
See God, Mercy of; Kindness.
Instances of: The prison keeper, to Joseph (Ge 39:21-23). Joshua to Rahab (Jos 6:25). The Israelites to the man of Bethel (Jdg 1:23-26). David to Saul (1Sa 24:10-13, 17).

MERCY SEAT See Atonement Cover; Tabernacle.

MERED (rebel). Son of Ezra (1Ch 4:17-18).

MEREMOTH (elevations).
1. Priest who returned from the Exile (Ne 12:3).
2. Another priest who returned from the Exile (Ezr 8:33; Ne 3:4, 21).

3. Man who divorced foreign wife (Ezr 10:36).
4. Priest who signed covenant with Nehemiah (Ne 10:5).

MERES (worthy). One of the princes of Persia (Est 1:14).

MERIBAH (to strive, contend).
1. Place NW of Sinai where God gave Israelites water from a rock (Ex 17:1-7).
2. Place near Kadesh Barnea where God also gave Israelites water from a rock. Because of Moses' loss of temper God did not permit him to enter the Promised Land (Nu 20:1-13). Also called Meribah Kadesh (Nu 27:14; Dt 32:51).

MERIBAH KADESH See Meribah, 2.

MERIB-BAAL (Baal contends). Son of Jonathan (1Ch 8:34; 9:40). See Mephibosheth, 2.

MERIT Personal. See Grace.

MERODACH See Marduk.

MERODACH-BALADAN (Marduk has given a son). Twice king of Babylon (722-710; 703-702 B.C.), invited Hezekiah to join conspiracy against Assyria (2Ki 20:12-19; Isa 39:1-8).

MEROM (high place). Place near headwaters of Jordan river where Joshua defeated N coalition (Jos 11:5, 7). Possibly identified with Tell el-Khirba.

MERON See Shimron Meron.

MERONOTH, MERONOTHITE A place near Gibeon (Ne 3:7) and its inhabitants (1Ch 27:30).

MEROZ A place N of Mount Tabor. Deborah and Barak curse the inhabitants of, in their song of triumph (Jdg 5:23).

MESECH See Meshech.

MESHA
1. Place in S Arabia (Ge 10:30).
2. Benjamite (1Ch 8:9).
3. Descendant of Judah (1Ch 2:42).
4. King of Moab in days of Ahab, Ahaziah, and Jehoram (2Ki 3:4).

MESHACH (perhaps I have become weak). His Hebrew name was Mishael. He was taken as a captive to Babylon with Daniel, Hananiah, and Azariah, where each one was given a Babylonian name (Da 1:6-20; 2:17, 49; 3:12-30). Mishael was given the Akkadian name Meshach.
Shadrach, Meshach, and Abednego were chosen to learn the language and the ways of the Babylonians so that they could enter the king's service (Da 1:3-5, 17-20), c. 605 B.C. These three were eventually thrown into Nebuchadnezzar's furnace because they refused to bow down and worship the huge golden image that he had made (Da 3:1, 4-6, 8-30).

MESHECH
1. Son of Japheth (Ge 10:2; 1Ch 1:5).
2. Son of Shem (Ge 10:23; 1Ch 1:17).
3. A tribe (Ps 120:5; Eze 27:13; 32:26; 38:2-3); descendants of 1.

MESHELEMIAH (Yahweh repays). Father of Zechariah (1Ch 9:21; 26:1-2, 9), "Shelemiah" (1Ch 26:14).

MESHEZABEL (God delivers).
1. Ancestor of Meshullam (Ne 3:4).
2. Covenanter with Nehemiah (Ne 10:21).
3. Judahite (Ne 11:24).

MESHILLEMITH (restitution). A priest (1Ch 9:12).

MESHILLEMOTH (restitution).
1. Father of an Ephraimite who protested against the attempt of the Israelites to enslave their captive brothers (2Ch 28:12-13).
2. A priest (Ne 11:13).

MESHOBAB A Simeonite (1Ch 4:34).

MESHULLAM (restitution KB).
1. Grandfather of Shaphan (2Ki 22:3).
2. Son of Zerubbabel (1Ch 3:19).
3. Leading Gadite (1Ch 5:13).
4. Chief Benjamite (1Ch 8:17).
5. Father of Sallu (1Ch 9:7).
6. Benjamite of Jerusalem (1Ch 9:8).
7. Priest (1Ch 9:11; Ne 11:11).
8. Ancestor of priest (1Ch 9:12).
9. Kohathite (2Ch 34:12).
10. Israelite who returned with Ezra (Ezr 8:16).
11. Opposed divorcing foreign wives (Ezr 10:15).
12. Divorced foreign wife (Ezr 10:29).
13. Son of Berekiah; helped rebuild Jerusalem wall (Ne 3:4, 30; 6:18).
14. Another repairer of wall (Ne 3:6).
15. Helper of Ezra (Ne 8:4).
16. Priest (Ne 10:7).
17. Priest who sealed covenant (Ne 10:20).
18. Benjamite (Ne 11:7).
19. Priest (Ne 12:13).
20. Possibly the same man (Ne 12:33).
21. Another priest (Ne 12:16).
22. Levite (Ne 12:25).

MESHULLEMETH (restitution). Wife of Manasseh and mother of Amon (2Ki 21:19).

MESOBAITE See Mezobaite.

MESOPOTAMIA ([land] between rivers). The country between the Tigris and the Euphrates. Abraham a native of (Ac 7:2). Nahor lived in (Ge 24:10). People who lived in, called Syrians (Ge 25:20). Balaam from (Dt 23:4). The Israelites subjected to, eight years under the judgments of God (Jdg 3:8), delivered from, by Othniel (Jdg 3:9-10). Chariots hired from, by the Ammonites (1Ch 19:6-7). People of, present at Pentecost (Ac 2:9).
See Babylon; Chaldea.

MESS Any dish of food sent to the table (Ge 43:34; 2Sa 11:8; Heb 12:16).

MESSENGER (send). Figurative (Hag 1:13; Mal 2:7; 3:1; 4:5-6; Mt 11:10; Mk 1:2; Lk 7:27). Of Satan (2Co 12:7).

MESSIAH (anointed). The basic meaning of the Hebrew mashiah and the Greek christos is "anointed one."
In the OT the word is used of prophets, priests, and kings who were consecrated to their office with oil. The expression "the Lord's anointed" and its equivalent is not used as a technical designation of the Messiah, but refers to the king of the line of David ruling in Jerusalem and anointed by the Lord through the priest. With the possible exception of Da 9:25-26, the title "Messiah" as a reference to Israel's eschatological king does not occur in the OT. It appears in this sense later in the NT, where he is almost always called "the Christ." The OT pictures the Messiah as one who will put an end to sin and war and usher in universal righteousness and through his death will make vicarious atonement for the salvation of sinful people.
The NT concept of the Messiah is developed directly from the teaching of the OT. Jesus of Nazareth is the Messiah; he claimed to be the Messiah (Mt 26:63-64; Mk 14:61-62; Lk 22:67-70; Jn 4:25-26) and the claim was acknowledged by his disciples (Mt 16:16; Mk 8:29; Lk 9:20; Ac 4:27; 10:38).
See Jesus the Christ, Messiah.

MESSIANIC HOPE (Mt 13:17; Jn 8:56; Ac 9:22; Heb 11:13; 1Pe 1:10-12). Created by prophecy (Ge 49:10; Nu 24:17; 1Sa 1:10; 2Sa 7:12-13; Isa 9:6-7; 11:1-9; 33:17; 40:3-5; 55:3-5; 62:10-11; Jer 23:5-6; 33:15-17; Da 2:44; 7:13-14; 9:24-27; Mic 5:2; Zec 9:9; Mal 3:1-3; Ac 13:27), by the covenant with David to establish his throne forever (2Sa 7:12-16; 1Ch 17:11-14; 22:10; 28:7), by the messianic psalms (Pss 2; 16; 21; 22; 45; 72; 87; 89; 96; 110; 132:11, 17-18).
Confirmed in the vision of Mary (Lk 1:30-33). Exemplified by the priest Zechariah (Lk 1:68-79), by the prophet Simeon (Lk 2:25, 29-32), by the prophetess Anna (Lk 2:36-38), by the wise men of the East (Mt 2:1-12), by John the Baptist (Mt 11:3), by the people (Jn 7:31, 40-42; 12:34), by Caiaphas (Mt 26:63; Mk 14:61), by Joseph of Arimathea (Mk 15:43; Lk 23:51), by the disciples on the way to Emmaus (Lk 24:21), by Paul (Ac 26:6-7).
See Jesus the Christ, Prophecies Concerning.

MESSIAS See Messiah.

METAL See Bronze; Copper; Gold; Iron; Lead; Silver; Tin.

METAPHOR A figure of speech that describes by comparison without using the word "like" or "as." Used extensively in the Song of Songs, for example "How beautiful you are, my darling! Oh, how beautiful! Your eyes are doves" (SS 1:15). Jesus spoke in metaphors (Mt 5:13-16). See Parable.

METEOROLOGY

Weather Described:
Controlled by God (Ge 2:5-6; 27:39; Job 9:7; 26:7-8, 11; Ps 19:2-6; 104:2-3, 7, 13, 19-20; 107:25; Ecc 11:3; Isa 13:13; 24:18; 50:3; Jer 4:11-12; 10:13; 51:16; Da 2:21; Hos 8:7; Joel 2:30-31; Am 9:6; Na 1:3; Mt 24:27; 24:29; 21:25; Jn 3:8; Ac 2:19-20; 2Pe 2:17; Jude 12). Tempest stilled by Jesus (Mt 8:24-27; Lk 8:22-25).
Weather, affected by godly prayers (1Sa 12:16-18; 1Ki 18:41-45; Isa 5:5-6; Jas 5:17-18). Forecast of weather (Mt 16:2-3; Lk 12:54-56).
Weather in the land of Uz (Job 27:20-21; 28:24-27; 29:19; 36:27-33; 37:6-22; 38:8-11, 22, 24-37). Weather in Israel (Ps 18:10-15; 29:3-10; 48:7; 65:8-12; 133:3; 135:6-7; 147:7-8; 148:7-8; Pr 25:23; 26:1; 30:4; Ecc 1:6-7; Hos 6:4; 13:15). The autumnal storms of the Mediterranean (Ac 27:9-20, 27).

Phenomena of:
The deluge (Ge 7:8). Fire from heaven on the cities of the plain (Ge 19:24-25). Plagues of hail, thunder, and lightning in Egypt (Ex 9:22-29; Ps 78:17-23), of darkness (Ex 10:22-23). East wind that divided the Red Sea (Ex 14:21), that brought the quails (Nu 11:31-32; Ps 78:26-28). Pillar of cloud and fire. See Pillar. Sun stood still (Jos 10:12-13). Dew on Gideon's fleece (Jdg 6:36-40). Stars in their courses fought against Sisera (Jdg 5:20). Stones from heaven (Jos 10:11). Fire from heaven at Elijah's command (2Ki 1:10-14). The whirlwind which carried Elijah to heaven (2Ki 2:1, 11).
Wind under God's control (Ps 107:25). East wind (Ps 48:7). Rain, formation of (Ps 135:6-7). Dew, copious (Ps 133:3). Rain in answer to Samuel's prayer (1Sa 12:16-18), Elijah's prayer (1Ki 18:41-45). Rain discomfits the Philistine army (1Sa 7:10). Wind destroyed Job's children (Job 1:18-19). Darkness at the Crucifixion (Mt 27:45; Lk 23:44-45).
See Astronomy; Celestial Phenomena; Dew; Hail; Rain; Weather.

Symbolic:
Used in the Revelation (Rev 6:12-14; 7:1; 8:3-12; 9:1-2, 17-19; 10:1-6; 11:6; 12:1-4, 7-9; 14; 15:1-4; 16:8, 17-21; 19:11-18; 20:11; 21:1).

METEYARD Archaic word for "measures of length" (Lev 19:35).

METHEG AMMAH (the bridle of the metropolis). A town David took from the Philistines (2Sa 8:1).

METHUSAEL See Methushael.

M

METHUSELAH (*man of the javelin*). Son of Enoch and grandfather of Noah (Ge 5:21-27; 1Ch 1:3).

METHUSHAEL (perhaps *man of God*). Father of Lamech (Ge 4:18).

MEUNIM, MEUNITES (*the people of Maon*).
1. People conquered by the Simeonites (1Ch 4:41); fought against Jehoshaphat (2Ch 20:1) and Uzziah (2Ch 26:7).
2. Counted among the temple servants (Ezr 2:50; Ne 7:52). May be the descendants of 1.
See Maonites.

ME-ZAHAB (*waters of gold*). Grandfather of Mehetabel (Ge 36:39; 1Ch 1:50).

MEZOBAITE Name of place otherwise unknown (1Ch 11:47).

MIAMIN *See Mijamin.*

MIBHAR (*choice*). One of David's valiant men (1Ch 11:38).

MIBSAM (*sweet odor*).
1. Son of Ishmael (Ge 25:13; 1Ch 1:29).
2. Son of Shallum (1Ch 4:25).

MIBZAR (*bastion*). Chief of Edom (Ge 36:42; 1Ch 1:53).

MICA (*who is like Yahweh?*).
1. Grandson of Jonathan (2Sa 9:12). *See Micah,* 9.
2. A Levite; descendant of Asaph (1Ch 9:15; Ne 11:17, 22).
3. A Levite covenanter (Ne 10:11), possibly the same as 2.

MICAH (*who is like Yahweh?*).
1. Ephraimite whose mother made an image for which he secured a priest; both image and priest were later stolen by the tribe of Dan (Jdg 17-18).
2. Reubenite (1Ch 5:5).
3. Grandson of Jonathan (1Ch 8:34; 9:40). *See Mica,* 1.
4. Levite (1Ch 23:20).
5. Father of Abdon, one of Josiah's officers (2Ch 34:20). *See Micaiah,* 2.
6. Prophet Micah, the Moreshethite; prophesied in the reigns of Jotham, Ahaz, and Hezekiah (Mic 1:1; Jer 26:18).

MICAH, BOOK OF
Author: The prophet Micah of Moresheth
Date: Sometime between 750 and 686 B.C.
Outline:
I. Superscription (1:1).
II. Judgment Against Israel and Judah (1:2-3:12).
 A. Introduction (1:2).
 B. The Predicted Destruction (1:3-7).
 C. Lamentation for the Destruction (1:8-16).
 D. Corruption in Micah's Society (2:1-11).
 E. Hope in the Midst of Gloom (2:12-13).
 F. The Leaders Condemned (ch. 3).
III. Hope for Israel and Judah (chs. 4-5).
 A. The Coming Kingdom (ch. 4).
 B. The Coming King (5:1-5a).
 C. Victory for the People of God (5:5b-15).
IV. The Lord's Case Against Israel (ch. 6).
 A. The Lord's Accusation (6:1-8).
 B. The Coming Judgment (6:9-16).
V. Gloom Turns to Triumph (ch. 7).
 A. Micah Laments the Corruption of His Society (7:1-6).
 B. Micah's Assurance of Hope (7:7).
 C. A Bright Future for God's People (7:8-13).
 D. Victory for God's Kingdom (7:14-20).
See Prophets, The Minor.

MICAIAH (*who is like Yahweh?*).
1. A prophet living in Samaria who predicted the death of King Ahab (1Ki 22; 2Ch 18).
2. Father of Acbor, one of Josiah's officers (2Ki 22:12-14). *See Micah,* 5.
3. Daughter of Uriel of Gibeah (2Ch 13:2).
4. Offical of Jehoshaphat; a teacher (2Ch 17:7).
5. Ancestor of priest in Nehemiah's time (Ne 12:35).
6. Priest (Ne 12:41).
7. Grandson of Shaphan (Jer 36:11-13).
8. *See Maacah,* 4.

MICE *See Rat(s).*

MICHA *See Mica.*

MICHAEL (*who is like God [El]?*).
1. An Asherite (Nu 13:13).
2. Two Gadites (1Ch 5:13-14).
3. A Gershonite Levite (1Ch 6:40).
4. A descendant of Issachar (1Ch 7:3).
5. A Benjamite (1Ch 8:16).
6. A captain of the thousands of Manasseh who joined David at Ziklag (1Ch 12:20).
7. Father of Omri (1Ch 27:18).
8. Son of Jehoshaphat. Slain by his brother, Jehoram (2Ch 21:2-4).
9. Father of Zebadiah (Ezr 8:8).
10. The archangel. His message to Daniel (Da 10:13, 21; 12:1). Contention with the devil (Jude 9). Fights with the dragon (Rev 12:7).

MICHAH *See Micah.*

MICHAIAH *See Micaiah.*

MICHAL (*who is like God [El]?*). Daughter of Saul. Given to David as a reward for slaying Goliath (1Sa 18:22-28). Rescues David from death (1Sa 19:9-17). Saul forcibly separates them, and

she is given in marriage to Paltiel (1Sa 25:44). David recovers her to himself (2Sa 3:13-16). Ridicules David on account of his religious zeal (2Sa 6:16, 20-23).

MICHMASH *See Micmash.*

MICHRI *See Micri.*

MICHTAM *See Miktam.*

MICMASH (perhaps *hidden place*). A place in Benjamin c. eight miles NE of Jerusalem; Jonathan led Israelites to victory over Philistines there (1Sa 14:31; Ne 11:31).

MICMETHATH A city between Ephraim and Manasseh (Jos 16:6; 17:7).

MICRI A Benjamite (1Ch 9:8).

MIDDIN A city in Judah in the wilderness just W of the Dead Sea (Jos 15:61).

MIDDLE WALL *See Dividing Wall.*

MIDIAN Son of Abraham by Keturah (Ge 25:2, 4 ; 1Ch 1:32-33).

MIDIANITE(S) Descendants of Midian, son of Abraham by Keturah (Ge 25:1-2, 4; 1Ch 1:32-33). Called Ishmaelites (Ge 37:25, 28; Jdg 8:24). Were merchants (Ge 37:28). Buy Joseph and sell him to Potiphar (Ge 37:28, 36). Defeated by the Israelites under Phinehas; five of their kings slain, the women taken captives, their cities burned, and rich spoils taken (Nu 31). Defeated by Gideon (Jdg 6-8). Owned multitudes of camels and large quantities of gold (Isa 60:6). A snare to the Israelites (Nu 25:16-18). Prophecies concerning (Isa 60:6; Hab 3:7).

MIDNIGHT Scenes at (Ex 11:4; Mt 25:6; Ac 16:25; 20:7).

MIDWIVES Assist in childbirth (Ge 35:17; 38:28). Save Israelite boys in Egypt (Ex 1:15-21).

MIGDAL EDER *See Eder,* 1.

MIGDAL EL (*tower of God [El]*). A city of Naphtali (Jos 19:38).

MIGDAL GAD (*tower of Gad*). A city of Judah (Jos 15:37).

MIGDOL (*tower*).
1. A place near the Red Sea where the Israelites encamped (Ex 14:2; Nu 33:7-8).
2. A city on the NE border of lower Egypt (Jer 44:1; 46:14).

MIGRON (*precipice*). A city in Benjamin. Saul encamps near, under a pomegranate tree (1Sa 14:2). Prophesy concerning (Isa 10:28).

MIJAMIN (*from the right hand*).
1. Priest in David's time (1Ch 24:9).
2. A man who divorced his foreign wife (Ezr 10:25).
3. Covenanter priest (Ne 10:7).
4. Priest who returned from the Exile (Ne 12:5).

MIKLOTH (*rods*).
1. A Benjamite of Jerusalem (1Ch 8:32; 9:37-38).
2. A ruler in the reign of David (1Ch 27:4).

MIKNEIAH (*Yahweh acquires*). A doorkeeper of the temple and musician (1Ch 15:18, 21).

MIKTAM The term always stands in the superscription of Davidic prayers occasioned by great danger (Ps 16, 56-60). Variously related to words for "golden," "inscription," and "atonement." *See Music, Symbols Used in.*

MILALAI A priest who took part in the dedication of the walls of Jerusalem (Ne 12:36).

MILCAH (*queen*).
1. Wife of Nahor and mother of Bethuel (Ge 11:29; 22:20-23; 24:15, 24, 47).
2. Daughter of Zelophehad. Special legislation in regard to the inheritance of (Nu 26:33; 27:1-7; 36:1-12; Jos 17:3-4).

MILCOM *See Molech.*

MILDEW (*yellow, pale*). Fungus growth destructive of grains and fruits (Dt 28:22; 1Ki 8:37; Am 4:9; Hag 2:17).

MILE Equal to about 3, 500 cubits or 8.6 stadia (Eze 45:3; Mt 5:41; Lk 24:13).

MILETUS A seaport in Asia Minor. Paul visits (Ac 20:15), and sends to Ephesus for the elders of the church, and addresses them here (Ac 20:17-38). Trophimus left sick at (2Ti 4:20).

MILITARY INSTRUCTION Of children (2Sa 1:18). *See Armies.*

MILK Used for food (Ge 18:8; Jdg 4:19; SS 5:1; Eze 25:4; 1Co 9:7). Of goats (Pr 27:27), sheep (Dt 32:14; Isa 7:21-22), camels (Ge 32:15), cows (Dt 32:14; Isa 6:7, 10). Churned (Pr 30:33). Kid not to be cooked in its mother's milk (Ex 23:19; Dt 14:21).
 Figurative (Ex 3:8, 17; 13:5; 33:3; Nu 13:27; Dt 26:9, 15; Isa 55:1; 60:16; Jer 11:5; 32:22; Eze 20:6; Joel 3:18; 1Co 3:2; Heb 5:12-13; 1Pe 2:2).

MILL (Jer 25:10). Upper and lower stones of (Dt 24:6; Job 41:24; Isa 47:2). Used in Egypt (Ex 11:5). Operated by women (Mt 24:41), and captives (Jdg 16:21; La 5:13). Manna ground in (Nu 11:8). Sound of, to cease (Rev 18:22). *See Grind; Millstone.*

MILLENNIUM The Latin for a thousand years, from (Rev 20:1-15).
 It refers to a period when Christ rules and Satan is bound; when Jesus shall have triumphed over all forms of evil (1Co 15:24-28; 2Th 2:8; Rev 14:6-18; 19:11-16). At the restoration of all things (Ac 3:21). When the creation shall be delivered from the corruption of evil (Ro 8:19-21). When the Son of Man shall sit on the throne of his glory (Mt 19:28; Lk 22:28-30), and the righteous shall be clothed with authority (Da 7:22; Mt 19:28; Lk 22:28-30; 1Co 6:2; Rev 2:5), and possess the kingdom (Mt 25:34; Lk 12:32; 22:29).
 Christ rules from his throne in Zion or Jerusalem (Isa 65:17-25; Zep 3:11-13; Zec 9:9-10; 14:16-21). Christ fulfills the promise of the kingdom of God on earth (Mt 16:18-19; 26:29; Mk 14:25; Heb 8:11).
 Amillenialists believe Jesus is reigning now. *Premillenialists* believe Jesus will literally reign on earth for a thousand years after his second coming. *Postmillenialists* believe the Church will Christianize the world for a long period of time after which Christ will return.
 See Church, The Body of Believers, Prophecies Concerning; Jesus the Christ, Kingdom of; Second Coming of.

MILLET (Eze 4:9).

MILLO *See Beth Millo.*

MILLSTONE Not to be taken in pledge (Dt 24:6). Probably used in executions by drowning (Mt 18:6; Mk 9:42; Lk 17:2). Abimelech killed by one being hurled upon him (Jdg 9:53). Figurative of the hard heart (Job 41:24). *See Grind; Mill.*

MINA In the sexagesimal system (based on the number 60) that originated in Mesopotamia, there were 60 shekels in a mina and 60 minas in a talent. A shekel, which was about two-fifths of an ounce of silver, was the average wage for a month's work. Thus a mina would be the equivalent of five years' wages, and a talent would be 300 years' wages (1Ki 10:17, ftn, w 2Ch 9:16, ftn; Ezr 2:69; Ne 7:71-72, ftn). *See Measure.*

MINCING (*to go like a little child, i.e., to trip along*). To speak, walk, or behave in an affectedly elegant, dainty, or nice manner. Used of the haughty women of Zion (Isa 3:16).

MIND In Scripture it often means "heart" or "soul." In the NT it is often used in an ethical sense (Ro 7:25; Col 2:18).

MINERALS OF THE BIBLE The science of mineralogy is a recent one, and did not exist in ancient times. It is often impossible to be certain that when a mineral name is used in the Bible, it is used with the same meaning as that attached in modern mineralogy. The following minerals are mentioned in the Bible:

Precious Stones:
 Agate (Ex 28:19; 39:12), amethyst (Ex 28:19; 39:12; Rev 21:20), aromatic resin or resin (Ge 2:12; Nu 11:7), beryl (Ex 28:17; 39:10; Eze 28:13; Rev 21:20), carnelian (Rev 4:3; 21:20), chalcedony (Rev 21:19), chrysolite (Da 10:6; Rev 21:20), chrysoprase (Rev 21:20), coral (Job 28:18; Eze 27:16), crystal (Job 28:17; Rev 4:6; 21:11; 22:1), emerald (Ex 28:18; 39:11), glowing metal (Eze 1:4, 27; 8:2; Rev 1:15), hardest stone (Eze 3:9; Zec 7:12), jacinth (Ex 28:19; 39:12; Rev 9:17), jasper (Ex 28:20; 39:13; Job 28:18; Eze 28:13; Rev 4:3; 21:11, 18, 19), onyx (Ge 2:12; Ex 25:7; 28:9, 20; 35:9, 27; 39:6, 13; 1Ch 29:2; Job 28:16; Eze 28:13, 16), pearl (Rev 21:21), ruby (Ex 28:17; 39:10; Job 28:18; Eze 28:13, 16), sapphire (Ex 24:10; 28:18; 39:11; Eze 1:26; 10:1; 28:13; Rev 21:19), sardonyx (Rev 21:20), sparkling jewels (Isa 54:12), topaz (Ex 28:17; 39:10; Job 28:19; Eze 28:13; Rev 21:20), turquoise (Ex 28:18; Eze 27:16).

Metals:
 Gold (Ge 2:11-12), silver (Mt 10:9), iron (Nu 31:22), bronze (Ge 4:22; Ezr 8:27), lead (Ex 15:10), tin (Nu 31:22), glowing metal (Eze 1:4, 27; 8:2), dross (Ps 119:119; Pr 25:4; Isa 1:22, 25; Eze 22:18-19).

Common Minerals:
 Alabaster (Mt 26:7; Mk 14:3; Lk 7:37), flint (Isa 5:28; 50:7; Jer 17:1; Eze 3:9; Zec 7:12), marble (1Ch 29:2; Est 1:6; SS 5:15; Rev 18:12), soda (Pr 25:20; Jer 2:22), sulfur (Ge 19:24; Dt 29:23; Job 18:15; Ps 11:6; Isa 30:33; 34:9; Eze 38:22; Lk 17:29; Rev 9:17-18; 14:10; 19:20; 20:10; 21:8), water.
 See Stones.

MINES, MINING An ancient occupation; described in (Job 28:1-11; Dt 8:9; 1Ki 7:13-50).

MINGLED PEOPLE Non-Israelite people who left Egypt with the Israelites (Ex 12:38). The term is also used for the mixed blood of certain of Israel's enemies (Jer 25:20; 50:37).

MINIAMIN (*from the right, good fortune*).
1. Levite (2Ch 31:15).
2. Head of a family of priests (Ne 12:17).
3. A priest in Nehemiah's time (Ne 12:41).

MINISTER (*servant*).
1. An officer in civil government. Joseph (Ge 41:40-44), Iri (2Sa 20:26), Zabud (1Ki 4:5), Ahithophel (1Ch 27:33), Zebadiah (2Ch 19:11), Elkanah (2Ch 28:7), Haman (Est 3:1), Mordecai (Est 10:3, w Est 8; 9), Daniel (Da 2:48; 6:1-3).
 See Cabinet.
2. A sacred teacher.

Good Ministers:
 Likened to sowers (Ps 126:6; Mt 13:3-8; Mk 4:3-8; Lk 8:5-8). Teachers of schools (1Sa 19:20; 2Ki 2:3, 5, 15; 4:38; 2Ch 15:3; 17:7-9; Ac 13:1).
 Hired (Jdg 17:10; 18:4). Exempt from taxation (Ezr 7:24). In politics (2Sa 15:24-27). In war (2Ch 13:12-14).
 Influential in public affairs (1Sa 12:6-10), designate kings (1Sa 9:15-16; 10:1; 16:1-13), recommend civil and military appointments (2Ki 4:13).

M

In vigorous opposition with rulers: Samuel with Saul (1Sa 13:11-14; 15:10-31), Nathan with David (2Sa 12:1-4), Elijah with Ahab (1Ki 18:17-18).

Recreation for (Mk 6:31-32). Take leave of congregations (Ac 20:17-38). Personal bearing of (Tit 2:7-8). Preach with ecclesiastical authority (Gal 1:15-24; 2:1-9). Work of, will be tried (1Co 3:12-15). Responsibility of (Eze 3:17-21; 33:8; Mt 10:14-40; Ac 18:6; 20:26-27; 1Co 1:23; 2Co 1:23-15; 5:11, 18-19; 1Ti 6:20). Speaking evil of, forbidden (Jude 8, 10). Clothed with authority (1Th 5:12; Tit 1:13-14; 2:15; 3:1-2, 8-9; Heb 13:6-7, 17). *See the epistles to Timothy and Titus in their entirety.* Clothed with salvation (2Ch 6:41). Exhorted to grow in grace (1Ti 6:11; 2Ti 2:22).

Marriage of (Lev 21:7-15; Mt 8:14; Mk 1:30; 1Co 9:5; 1Ti 3:2, 12; Tit 1:5-7).

Incorruptible: Balaam (Nu 22:18, 37-38; 23:8, 12; 24:12-14, w 2Pe 2:15-16), Micaiah (1Ki 22:13-14), Peter (Ac 8:18-23). Patience of (Jas 5:10). Inconsistent (Mt 27:3-7).

Love of, for the church, exemplified by Paul (Php 1:7; 1Th 1:2-4; 2:8, 11). Kindness to, Ebed-Melech to Jeremiah (Jer 38:7-13). Fear of (1Sa 16:4). Example to the flock (Php 3:17; 2Th 3:9; 1Ti 4:12; Tit 2:1, 7-8; 1Pe 5:3). Intolerance of (Mt 15:23; 19:13; Mk 10:13; Lk 18:15). Message of, rejected (Jer 7:27; Eze 33:30-33). God's care of (1Ki 17:1-16; 19:1-8; Mt 10:29-31; Lk 12:6-7). Their calling, glorious (2Co 3:7-11). Discouragements of (Isa 30:10-11; 53:1; Eze 3:8-9, 14; Hab 1:2-3; Mt 13:57; Mk 6:3-4; Lk 4:24; Jn 4:44).

Defended (Jer 26:16-24; Ac 23:9). Beloved (Ac 20:37-38; 21:5-6).

Sent out in teams of two: Disciples (Mk 6:7), Paul and Barnabas (Ac 13:2-3), Judas and Silas (Ac 15:27), Barnabas and Mark (Ac 15:37, 39), Paul and Silas (Ac 15:40), Paul and Titus (2Co 8:19, 23), Timothy and Erastus (Ac 19:22), Titus and a companion (2Co 12:18).

Call of—
(Am 2:11; Mt 9:38; Ro 10:14-15; Eph 4:11-12; Heb 5:4). Aaron and his sons (Ex 28:1; 1Ch 23:13; Heb 5:4). Levites (Nu 3:5-13; 16:5, 9). Samuel (1Sa 3:4-10). Elisha (1Ki 19:16, 19). Isaiah (Isa 6:8-10). Jeremiah (Jer 1:5). Jonah (Jnh 1:1-2; 3:1-2).

The twelve apostles (Mt 4:18-22 w Mk 1:17-20; Mt 9:9; Mk 2:14; Lk 5:27 w Mt 10:1-5; Jn 1:43). The seventy-two disciples (Lk 10:1-2). Paul (Ac 13:2-3; 20:24; 22:12-15; 26:14-18; Ro 1:1; 1Co 1:1, 27-28 w 2Co 1:1 & Col 1:1; 1Co 9:16-19; 2Co 5:20; Gal 1:15-16; Eph 3:7-8; Col 1:25-29; 1Ti 1:11; Tit 1:5). Barnabas (Ac 13:2-3). Archippus (Col 4:17).
See Call, Personal; Excuses.

Character and Qualifications of—
(Lev 10:3-11). Blameless (1Ti 3:2-4, 7-13; Tit 1:5-9). Compassionate (Heb 5:2). Consecrated (Nu 16:9-10). Consistent (Ro 2:21-23). Courageous (Jer 1:7-8, 17-19; Ac 20:22, 24; 2Ti 1:7). Diligent (2Ch 29:11; 1Co 15:10). Eager to serve (Isa 6:8). Endued with power (Lk 24:49; Ac 1:8; 4:8, 31; Gal 2:8). Gentle (2Ti 2:24-25). A good example (Tit 2:1, 7-8, 15; Jas 3:1, 13, 16-18). Holy (Lev 21:6; Isa 6:7; 52:11; Mal 2:6; Jn 17:17; 1Co 9:27; 2Ti 2:21; Tit 1:5-9). Humble (Mt 20:25-28; 23:8, 10-11; Lk 22:27; Jn 13:13-17; 15:20; 2Co 4:5). Meek (1Co 4:12-13; 2Co 10:1). Patient (Jas 5:10). Persevering (Mt 10:22-24; 2Co 4:1, 8-10). Prepared (Ezr 7:10). Responsible (1Pe 4:10-11). Saved (2Ch 6:41). Sincere (2Co 4:1-2). Strong (2Ti 2:1). Tactful (1Co 9:18-23; 10:23, 28-33; 2Co 6:3; 12:16). Willing to suffer hardship (2Ti 2:3; 4:5). Wise (Mal 2:7; Pr 11:30; Mt 10:16; Lk 6:39; 2Co 4:6; 2Ti 2:7; 3:14, 16-17).

Not quarrelsome (2Ti 2:14, 23-24; Tit 3:9). Not of the world (Jn 15:19; 17:14). Not entangled with the world (2Ti 2:4-5).

Zealous (Jer 20:9; Eze 34:1-31; 2Ti 1:6-8; 4:2). *See Zeal.* Instances of: Titus (2Co 8:16-17), Epaphroditus (Php 2:25-30), Epaphras (Col 4:12-13), John, in his vision (Rev 5:4-5).

Faithful (1Sa 2:35; Mt 24:45; Lk 12:42-44; Ac 20:22, 24; 1Co 2:2; 2Co 6:4-7). Instances of: Moses (Dt 4:26; 30:19; Heb 3:2, 5), Micaiah (2Ch 18:12-13), Azariah (2Ch 26:16-20), Balaam (Nu 22:18, 38; 23:8, 12; 24:12-14), Nathan (2Sa 12:1-14), Isaiah (Isa 22:4-5; 39:3-7), Jeremiah (Jer 17:16; 26:1-15; 28; 37:9-10, 16-18), John the Baptist (Mt 3:2-12; Mk 6:18; Lk 3:7-19), the apostles (Ac 4:19-20, 31; 5:21, 29-32), Peter (Ac 2:14-40; 3:12-26; 4:8-12; 8:18-23), Paul (Ac 15:25-26; 17:16-17; 19:8; 20:26-27), Tychicus (Col 4:7).
See the epistles to Timothy and Titus in their entirety.

Described as—
Administering God's grace (1Pe 4:10). Ambassadors for Christ (2Co 5:20; Eph 6:20). Angels of the church (Rev 1:20; 2:1, 8, 12, 18; 3:1, 7, 14). Apostles (Lk 6:13; Rev 18:20). Apostles of Jesus Christ (Tit 1:1). Defenders of the gospel (Php 1:7). Elders (1Ti 5:17; 1Pe 5:1). Entrusted with God's work (Tit 1:7), with the secret things of God (1Co 4:1). Evangelists (Eph 4:11; 2Ti 4:5). Fishers of men (Mt 4:19; Mk 1:17). God's fellow workers (1Th 3:2). Lights (Jn 5:35). Men of God (Dt 33:1; 1Ti 6:11). Messengers of the Church (2Co 8:23), of the LORD Almighty (Mal 2:7). Ministers of God (Isa 61:6), before the LORD (Joel 2:17), of Christ (Ro 15:16; 1Ti 4:6), of a new covenant (2Co 3:6), in the Sanctuary (Eze 45:4). Overseers (Ac 20:28). Pastors (Eph 4:11). Preachers (Ro 10:14; 1Ti 2:7), of righteousness (2Pe 2:5). Servants of the Church (2Co 4:5), of God (Tit 1:1; Jas 1:1), of the gospel (Eph 3:7; Col 1:23), of Jesus Christ (Php 1:1; Jude 1), of the Lord (2Ti 2:24), of the Word (Lk 1:2). Shepherds (Jer 23:4). Soldiers of Christ (Php 2:25; 2Ti 2:3-4). Stars (Rev 1:20; 2:1). Teachers (Isa 30:20; Eph 4:11). Watchmen (Isa 62:6; Eze 33:7). Witnesses (Ac 1:8; 5:32; 26:16). Workers (Mt 9:38; Phm 1), together with God (2Co 6:1).

Duties of—
(Eph 4:11-12). To preach (Mt 10:7; Ro 1:14-15). To preach the unsearchable riches of Christ (Eph 3:8-12). To admonish (Isa 58:1; 62:6-7). To exhort (2Co 5:20; 1Ti 4:13; 6:17-18; 2Pe 1:12-16). To warn (Jer 7:25; Eze 33:1-9). To reprove (Eze 6:11; 34; Jnh 1:2; 2Co 7:8). *See Reproof.* To teach (Lev 10:11; 2Ki 17:27-28; 2Ch 15:3; Ezr 7:10; Jer 26:2; Eze 44:23; Mt 10:7, 27; 28:19-20; Mk 10:43-45; Ac 5:20; 6:4; 16:4; 18:9-10; 26:16-18; Ro 1:15; 12:6-7; 2Co 10:8; Eph 3:8-10; 4:11-12; 1Ti 2:7; 4:13-16; 2Ti 2:2, 14-15, 24-25; 4:1-2, 5). To teach the lordship of Jesus (2Co 4:5). To serve (Mt 20:25-28; Mk 10:43-45; 2Co 4:5). To make disciples of Christ

(Mt 28:19-20). To win souls (Pr 11:30; Jn 4:35-38; 2Co 5:18, 20). To witness for Christ (Lk 24:48; Jn 15:27; Ac 1:22; 10:42; 22:15). To do the work of an evangelist (2Ti 4:5). To give himself continually to prayer (Ac 6:4). To lament over the worldliness and sins of the church (Joel 1:13-15; 2:17). To speak boldly (Eph 6:20). To minister to all without respect of persons or races (Ro 1:14-15). To exercise authority in the church (Mt 16:19; 18:18; 1Co 4:19-21; 2Co 7:8-9, 12, 15; 13:2-3; 13:10; 2Th 3:4; 1Ti 1:3-4, 11, 18; 5:19-22; 1Pe 5:1-3). To feed the flock (Jer 3:15; 23:4, 22, 28; Jn 21:15-17; Ac 20:28; 1Co 14:1-33; 1Pe 5:2-4). To strengthen the discouraged (Lk 22:32). To comfort the people (Isa 40:1-2, 9, 11; 1Th 3:2).

Charges delivered to: (Nu 18:1-7; 27:18-23; Dt 31:7-8, 14-23; Jos 1:1-9; Jer 1:18-19; Eze 3:4). Jesus to the twelve (Mt 10:5-42), to the seventy-two (Lk 10:1-16). Paul charges Timothy (1Ti 1:18-20; 2; 3; 4; 5; 6; 2Ti 1:6-13; 2; 3; 4).

Duty of the Church to—
To esteem (1Th 5:12-13). To pray for (Heb 13:18; 2Ch 6:41; Ps 132:9; Mt 9:37-38; Ac 4:29; 12:5; Ro 15:30-32; 2Co 1:11; Eph 6:18-20; Php 1:19; Col 4:2-4; 1Th 5:25; 2Th 3:1-2; Phm 22; Heb 13:19). To imitate the example of (1Co 11:1; Php 3:17; 2Th 3:7; Heb 13:7). To submit to the authority of (1Co 11:2; 16:16; 1Th 5:12-13; 2Th 3:4; Heb 13:7, 17). To provide for the support, of priest and Levite (Nu 18:20-21; Dt 10:9; 14:27; 18:1-4; Jos 13:14; 18:7; Jer 31:14; Eze 44:28), of the twelve apostles (Mt 10:9-10; Mk 6:8; Lk 22:35), of the seventy-two disciples (Lk 10:7-8), of Christian preachers (1Co 9:3-4, 7-14; Gal 6:6; Php 4:10-18; 1Ti 5:18). Right of support, waived by Paul (Ac 20:33-35; 1Co 9:15-18; 2Co 11:7-10; 12:13-18; 1Th 2:5-6, 9; 2Th 3:7-9).
See Church, The Body of Believers, Responsibilities and Duties.

Hospitality to—
Woman of Zarephath to Elijah (1Ki 17:10-16). The Shunammite to Elisha (2Ki 4:8-10). The barbarians to Paul (Ac 28:1-10). Simon the tanner to Peter (Ac 9:43). The Philippian jailer (Ac 16:33-34). Aquila and Priscilla to Paul (Ac 18:3), to Apollos (Ac 18:26). Justus to Paul (Ac 18:7). Philip the evangelist to Paul (Ac 21:8-10).

Joys of—
(Jn 4:36-38; 2Co 2:14; 7:6-7; Php 2:16; 1Th 2:13, 19-20; 3:8-9; 2Jn 4; 3Jn 4).

Ordination of—
Matthias (Ac 1:26), seven deacons (Ac 6:5-6), Paul and Barnabas (Ac 13:3), Timothy (1Ti 4:14).
See Levites; Priest.

Prayer for—
Commanded (Mt 9:37-38; Lk 10:2; Ro 15:30-32; 2Co 1:11; Eph 6:18-20; Php 1:19; Col 4:2-4; 1Th 5:25; 2Th 3:1-2; Phm 22; Heb 13:18-19). Exemplified (2Ch 6:41; Ps 132:9; Ac 1:24-25; 4:29; 6:6; 12:5; 14:23).

Precepts for Guidance of—
(Jer 1:7-8, 17-19; Eze 2:6-8; Mt 7:6; 10:7-8, 11-13, 16, 25-28; Lk 10:1-11; Col 4:17; 1Ti 1:3-4, 11, 18-19; 4:6-7, 12-16; 5:1-3; 7-11, 19-22; 6:3-4, 10-14, 17-21; 2Ti 1:6-8; 2:2-7, 14-16, 23-25; 4:1-2, 5; 1Pe 5:1-4; 2Pe 1:12-16).

Promises to—
(2Sa 23:6-7; Ps 126:5-6; Jer 1:7-10, 17-19; 15:20-21; 20:11; Da 12:3; Mt 10:28-31; 28:20; Lk 10:19; 12:11-12; 24:49; Jn 4:36-38; Ac 1:4-5, 8; 18:9-10; 1Co 3:8; 9:9-10; 2Co 2:14-16; 7:6-7; Php 2:16; 1Th 2:13, 19-20; 3:8-9; 1Pe 5:4; 3Jn 4). *See Righteous, Promises to.*

Success Attending—
Jonah (Jnh 1:5-6, 9, 14, 16; 3:4-9). Apostles (Ac 2:1-4, 41). Philip (Ac 8:6, 8, 12). Peter (Ac 9:32-35). Paul (Ac 13:16-43; 1Co 4:15; 9:2; 15:11; 2Co 3:2-3; 12:12; 13:4; Php 2:16; 1Th 1:5). Apollos (Ac 18:24-28). *See Revivals.*

Trials and Persecutions of—
Foretold (Mt 10:16-27 w Jn 13:16; Mt 23:34). Rehearsed (Mt 23:34).

Instances of: Elijah (1Ki 22:24-27; 2Ch 18:23-26). Hanani (2Ch 16:10). Zechariah (2Ch 24:20-22, 25; Mt 23:35; Lk 11:51). Isaiah (Isa 20:2-3). Jeremiah (Jer 11:19-21; 15:10, 15; 17:15-18; 18:18-23; 20:1-3, 7-18; 32:2-3; 33:1; 37:15-21; 38:6-13; 39:15; 43:1-7; La 3:53-55). Ezekiel (Eze 3:24-25; 24:15-18). Hosea (Hos 1:2). Amos (Am 5:10; 7:10-17). The apostles (Ac 5:17-42). Peter (Ac 12:3-19). Paul (Ac 9:23-25, 29-30; 14:4-6, 11-20; 16:16-24; 17:5-10, 13-14; 18:12-13; 20:3; 21:27-40; 22:22-30; 23:10-35; 24:26-27; 27:9-44; 1Co 2:1-4; 4:9-13; 2Co 6:4-10; 7:5; 11:23-33; 12:7-10; Eph 3:1, 13; 2Ti 1:8, 16; 2:9; 4:16-17).
See Paul, Persecutions of; also, Accusation, False; Persecution.

Zealous—
Titus (2Co 8:16-17). Epaphroditus (Php 2:25-30). Epaphras (Col 4:12-13). Tychicus (Col 4:7). John, in his vision (Rev 5:4-5). *See Zeal.*

False and Corrupt:
(1Ki 12:31; Ne 13:29; Jer 2:8; 6:13-14; 8:10-11; 12:10; 14:14; Eze 22:25, 28; 44:8, 10; Hos 9:7-8; Zep 3:4; Mal 1:6-10; 2Ti 4:3). Mercenary (Isa 8:3; Isa 56:11; Mic 3:11). Presumptuous (Dt 18:20-22; Jn 5:43). Insincere (Php 1:15-16). Senseless (Jer 10:21). Adulterous (Isa 2:22; Jer 23:14; Hos 6:9). Murderous (Hos 6:9). Pervert the truth (2Co 2:17; 11:3-4, 13-15; Gal 1:6-8; 1Ti 4:1-3, 7). Lead the people astray (Isa 3:12; Jer 50:6). Addicted to alcohol (Isa 28:7; 56:12). Indifferent to good and evil (Isa 56:10; Eze 22:26). Desired by the wicked (Isa 30:10-11; Jer 5:13-14, 30-31; Am 2:11-12; Mic 2:11).

Condemned—
Denunciations against false ministers (Isa 5:20; Jer 23:11-40; La 4:13-14; Eze 13:1-23; 34:1-10, 16-22; Mt 23:4-7, 13-14, 36; 2Pe 2:1-22).

Warnings against false ministers (Dt 13:1-4; Isa 8:19-20; Jer 14:13-16; 27:9-18; Mt 5:19; 7:15-23; 15:9, 13-14 w Lk 6:39; Mt 23:3-4, 13; 24:4-5, 11, 24, 26, 48-51; Mk 13:21-22; Lk 21:8; Jn 10:1, 5, 8, 10, 12-13; Ac 20:20, 30; Eph 4:14; Php 3:2; Col 2:4, 8, 18-19; 1Ti 1:3-7; 6:3-5; 2Ti 2:17-18; Tit 1:10-14; 1Jn 2:18-19, 22-23, 26; 4:1-3, 5; 2Jn 7, 10-11; Rev 2:12, 14-15, 18, 20-23).

Judgments upon false ministers (Isa 29:10-11; Hos 5:1; Gal 5:10).

Punishment of false ministers (Dt 13:1, 5; 18:20; Isa 43:27-28; Jer 14:15; 23:1-2, 11, 15, 21; 27:9-18; La 4:13-14; Eze 14:9-10; Hos 4:5-6, 8-13; Mic 3:5-7; Zec 10:3; 13:2-5; Mal 2:1-3, 8-9; Lk 12:45-46; 2Pe 2:3; Jude 4, 11).

Instances of—
Nadab and Abihu (Lev 10:1-2). Korah, Dathan, and Abiram (Nu 16:1-40). Eli's sons (1Sa 2:12-17, 22, 25, 29, 34; 3:13; 4:11). Samuel's sons (1Sa 8:1-3). The old prophet of Bethel (1Ki 13:11-32). Jonathan (Jdg 17:7-13; 18). Noadiah (Ne 6:14). Priests under, Jehoash (2Ki 12:7; 2Ch 24:5-6), Hezekiah (2Ch 30:3, 5). Priests and Levites (Ezr 2:61-62; 9:1-2; 10:18-24; Ne 13:4-9, 28-29; Zec 7:5-6). Hananiah (Jer 28). Jonah (Jnh 1:1-6). Scribes and Pharisees (Mt 23:15-16), Caiaphas (Mt 26:2-3, 57, 63-65; Jn 11:49-51; 18:14). Judas (Mt 26:14-16, 21-25, 47-50; 27:3-5; Jn 12:4-6; Ac 1:18). Judaizing Christians (Gal 3:1-2; 4:17; 6:12-13). Hymenaeus (1Ti 1:20; 2Ti 2:17-18). Alexander (1Ti 1:20). Philetus (2Ti 2:17-18).

MINNI A district of Armenia (Jer 51:27).

MINNITH A place E of the Jordan (Jdg 11:33; Eze 27:17).

MINOR PROPHETS, THE See Prophets, The Minor.

MINORITY REPORT See Reports.

MINORS Legal status of (Gal 4:1-2). See Orphan; Young Men.

MINSTREL NIV "harpist" (1Sa 16:23); "flute players" (Mt 9:23). See Flute; Harp.

MINT (sweet odor). (Mt 23:23; Lk 11:42).

MIPHKAD See Gate, Inspection.

MIRACLES
General:
Called: Marvelous things (Ps 78:12), marvelous works (Ps 105:5; Isa 29:14), signs and wonders (Jer 32:21; Jn 4:48; 2Co 12:12).

Performed through the power of God (Jn 3:2; Ac 14:3; 15:12; 19:11), of the Holy Spirit (Mt 12:28; Ro 15:19; 1Co 12:9-10, 28-30), in the name of Christ (Mk 16:17; Ac 3:16; 4:30). Faith required in those who perform (Mt 17:20; 21:21; Jn 14:12; Ac 3:16; 6:8). Faith required in those for whom they were performed (Mt 9:28; Mk 9:22-24; Ac 14:9). Power to work, given the disciples (Mk 3:14-15; 16:17-18, 20). Demanded by unbelievers (Mt 12:38-39; 16:1; Lk 11:16, 29; 23:8).

Alleged miracles performed by magicians (Ex 7:10-12, 22; 8:7), by other impostors (Mt 7:22). Performed through the powers of evil (2Th 2:9; Rev 16:14). Done in support of false religions (Dt 13:1-2), by false Christs (Mt 24:24), by false prophets (Mt 24:24; Rev 19:20), by the medium of Endor (1Sa 28:7-14), by Simon (Ac 8:9-11). Not to be regarded (Dt 13:3). Deceive the ungodly (2Th 2:10-12; Rev 13:14; 19:20). A mark of apostasy (2Th 2:3, 9; Rev 13:13).

List of Miracles and Supernatural Events:

In the Old Testament—
Creation (Ge 1). Flood (Ge 7-8). Confusion of tongues (Ge 11:1-9). Fire on Abraham's sacrifice (Ge 15:17). Conception of Isaac (Ge 17:17; 18:12; 21:2). Destruction of Sodom (Ge 19). Lot's wife turned to salt (Ge 19:26). Closing of the wombs of Abimelech's household (Ge 20:17-18). Opening of Hagar's eyes (Ge 21:19). Conception of Jacob and Esau (Ge 25:21). Opening of Rachel's womb (Ge 30:22).

Burning bush (Ex 3:2). Transformation of Moses' rod into a serpent (Ex 4:3-4, 30; 7:10, 12). Moses' leprosy (Ex 4:6-7, 30). Plagues in Egypt. *See Plague.* Pillar of cloud and fire (Ex 13:21-22; 14:19-20). Passage of the Red Sea (Ex 14:22). Destruction of Pharaoh and his army (Ex 4:23-30). Sweetening the waters of Marah (Ex 15:25). Manna (Ex 16:4-31). Quail (Ex 16:13). Defeat of Amalek (Ex 17:9-13). Transfiguration of the face of Moses (Ex 34:29-35). Water from the rock (Ex 17:5, 7). Thundering and lightning on Sinai (Ex 19:16-20; 24:10, 17; Dt 4:33). Miriam's leprosy (Nu 12:10-15). Judgments by fire (Nu 11:1-3). Destruction of Korah (Nu 16:31-35; Dt 11:6-7). Plague (Nu 16:46-50). Aaron's rod buds (Nu 17:1-9). Waters from the rock in Kadesh (Nu 20:8-11). Plague of serpents (Nu 21:6-9). Destruction of Nadab and Abihu (Lev 10:1-2). Balaam's donkey speaks (Nu 22:23-30). Preservation of Moses (Dt 34:7).

Jordan divided (Jos 3:14-17; 4:16-18). Fall of Jericho (Jos 6:20). Midianites destroyed (Jdg 7:16-22). Hail on the confederated kings (Jos 10:11). Sun and moon stand still (Jos 10:12-14).

Dew on Gideon's fleece (Jdg 6:37-40). Samson's strength (Jdg 14:6; 16:3, 29-30). Samson supplied with water (Jdg 15:19).

Fall of Dagon (1Sa 5:1-14). Tumors (1Sa 5:9-12; 6:1-18). Destruction of the people of Beth Shemesh (1Sa 6:19-20). Thunder (1Sa 12:16-18). Destruction of Uzzah (2Sa 6:1-8). Plague in Israel (1Ch 21:14-26).

Fire on the sacrifices of Aaron (Lev 9:24), of Gideon (Jdg 6:21), of Manoah (Jdg 13:19-20), of Solomon (2Ch 7:1), of Elijah (1Ki 18:38).

Jeroboam's hand withered (1Ki 13:3-6). Appearance of blood (2Ki 3:20-22). Panic of the Syrians (2Ki 7:6-7). Elijah is fed by ravens (1Ki 17:6), by an angel (1Ki 19:1-8), increases the widow's meal and oil (1Ki 17:9-16; Lk 4:26), raises the widow's son (1Ki 17:17-24). Rain in answer to Elijah's prayer (1Ki 18:41-45). Elijah brings fire on Ahaziah's army (2Ki 1:10-12), divides Jordan (2Ki 2:8). Elijah's translation (2Ki 2:11).

Elisha divides Jordan (2Ki 2:14), sweetens the waters of Jericho (2Ki 2:19-22), increases a widow's oil (2Ki 4:1-7), raises the Shunammite's child (2Ki 4:18-37), renders the poisoned stew harmless (2Ki 4:38-41), feeds one hundred men (2Ki 4:42-44), cures Naaman (2Ki 5:1-19), strikes Gehazi with leprosy (2Ki 5:26-27), causes the ax to float (2Ki 6:6), reveals the counsel of the king of Syria (2Ki 6:12), causes the eyes of his servant to be opened (2Ki 6:17), strikes with blindness the army of the king of Syria (2Ki 6:18), the dead man restored to life (2Ki 13:21).

Destruction of Sennacherib's army (2Ki 19:35; Isa 37:36), return of the shadow on the stairway (2Ki 20:9-11), Hezekiah's cure (Isa 38:21), deliverance of Shadrach, Meshach, and Abednego (Da 3:23-27), of Daniel (Da 6:22), the sea calmed on Jonah being cast into it (Jnh 1:15), Jonah in the fish's belly (Jnh 1:17; 2:10), his plant (Jnh 4:6-7).

Surrounding the Birth of Jesus—
Conception by Elizabeth (Lk 1:18, 24-25). The incarnation of Jesus (Mt 1:18-25; Lk 1:26-80). The appearance of the star of Bethlehem (Mt 2:1-9). The deliverance of Jesus (Mt 2:13-23).

Of Jesus—
Water changed into wine (Jn 2:1-11). Heals the nobleman's son (Jn 4:46-54). Catch of fish (Lk 5:1-11). Heals the demoniac (Mk 1:23-26; Lk 4:33-36). Heals Peter's mother-in-law (Mt 8:14-17; Mk 1:29-31; Lk 4:38-39). Cleanses the leper (Mt 8:1-4; Mk 1:40-45; Lk 5:12-16). Heals the paralytic (Mt 9:1-8; Mk 2:1-12; Lk 5:17-26). Heals the crippled man (Jn 5:1-16). Restores the withered hand (Mt 12:9-13; Mk 3:1-5; Lk 6:6-11). Restores the centurion's servant (Mt 8:5-13; Lk 7:1-10). Raises the widow's son to life (Lk 7:11-16). Heals a demoniac (Mt 12:22-37; Mk 3:11; Lk 11:14-15). Stills the tempest (Mt 8:23-27; 14:32; Mk 4:35-41; Lk 8:22-25). Casts demons out of two men of Gadara (Mt 8:28-34; Mk 5:1-20; Lk 8:26-39). Raises from the dead the daughter of Jairus (Mt 9:18-19, 23-26; Mk 5:22-24, 35-43; Lk 8:41-42, 49-56). Cures the woman with the issue of blood (Mt 9:20-22; Mk 5:25-34; Lk 8:43-48). Restores two blind men to sight (Mt 9:27-31). Heals a demoniac (Mt 9:32-33). Feeds five thousand people (Mt 14:15-21; Mk 6:35-44; Lk 9:12-17; Jn 6:5-14). Walks on the sea (Mt 14:22-33; Mk 6:45-52; Jn 6:16-21). Heals the daughter of the Syrian Phoenician woman (Mt 15:21-28; Mk 7:24-30). Feeds four thousand people (Mt 15:32-39; Mk 8:1-9). Restores one deaf and mute (Mk 7:31-37). Restores a blind man (Mk 8:22-26). Restores a possessed child (Mt 17:14-21; Mk 9:14-29; Lk 9:37-43). Tribute money obtained from a fish's mouth (Mt 17:24-27). Restores ten lepers (Lk 17:11-19). Opens the eyes of a man born blind (Jn 9). Raises Lazarus from the dead (Jn 11:1-46). Heals the woman with the spirit of infirmity (Lk 13:10-17). Cures a man with dropsy (Lk 14:1-6). Restores two blind men near Jericho (Mt 20:29-34; Mk 10:46-52; Lk 18:35-43). Curses a fig tree (Mt 21:17-22; Mk 11:12-14, 20-24). Heals the ear of Malchus (Lk 22:49-51). Second catch of fish (Jn 21:6).

Of the Disciples of Jesus—
By the seventy-two (Lk 10:17-20), by other disciples (Mk 9:39; Jn 14:12), by the apostles (Ac 3:6, 12-13, 16; 4:10, 30; 9:34-35; 16:18). Peter cures the sick (Ac 5:15-16), Aeneas (Ac 9:34), raises Dorcas (Ac 9:40), announces the death of Ananias and Sapphira (Ac 5:5, 10). Peter and John cure a lame man (Ac 3:2-11). Peter and other apostles delivered from prison (Ac 5:19-23; 12:6-11; 16:26). Philip carried away by the Spirit (Ac 8:39). Paul strikes Elymas with blindness (Ac 13:11), heals a cripple (Ac 14:10), casts out evil spirits and cures sick (Ac 16:18; 19:11-12; 28:8-9), raises Eutychus to life (Ac 20:9-12), shakes a viper off of his hand (Ac 28:5). Paul cured of blindness (Ac 9:3-6, 17-18).

Convincing Effect of, on:
The Israelites (Ex 4:28-31; 14:31; Nu 17:1-13). Pharaoh's servants (Ex 10:7). Pharaoh (Ex 10:16-17; 12:31-32). Egyptians (Ex 12:33; 1Sa 6:6). The Canaanites (Jos 2:9-11; 5:1). Gideon (Jdg 6:17-22, 36-40; 7:1). People who witnessed Elijah's (1Ki 18:24, 37-39). Naaman (2Ki 5:14-15). Nebuchadnezzar (Da 2:47; 3:28-29; 4:2-3). Darius (Da 6:20-27).
Simon Peter (Lk 5:4-11). Disciples of Jesus (Jn 2:11, 22-23; 20:30-31). The nobleman whose child Jesus healed (Jn 4:48-53). People who witnessed Christ's (Jn 7:31; 11:43-45; 12:10-11). People who witnessed Philip's (Ac 8:6). People who witnessed Peter's (Ac 9:32-42). Sergius Paulus, the deputy (Ac 13:8-12). Gentiles (Ro 15:18-19).
Resisted by the hard-hearted (Ne 9:17; Ps 78:10-32; Jn 9:24-28; 15:24-25).

Design of:
To reveal God (Ex 7:5, 17; 8:8-10, 22; 9:4-16, 29; 10:1-2; 14:4, 18; Dt 4:33-39; Jos 4:23-24; 1Ki 18:24, 37-39; Jer 32:20). Produce faith in God (Ex 14:31; Nu 14:11; Jos 3:7-17; 2Ch 7:1-3; Ps 106:9-12). Produce the fear of God (1Sa 12:17-18; Da 6:20-27; Jnh 1:14-16). Encourage obedience (Ex 16:4-6; 19:4-5; Dt 11:1-8; 29:1-9; Jdg 2:7; Ps 78:10-32). Glorify God (Lk 5:26; Jn 11:4; Ac 4:21-22). Testify to the messiahship of Jesus (Mt 11:2-5 w Lk 7:19-22; Mk 2:9-12; Lk 5:24-26; 18:42-43; Jn 2:11; 4:48; 5:36; 11:4, 40-42; 14:11; 15:24). Glorify Jesus (Ac 3:1-10, 12-13). Testify to God's servants (Ex 4:2-9; 19:9; Nu 16:28-35; 1Sa 12:17-18; Zec 2:9; Ac 2:22; Heb 2:4). Preserve the righteous (Da 3:28-29; 6:20-27). Change wicked purposes (Ex 3:19-20; 9:16-17; 10:16-17; 11:1-10; 12:29-33; 14:24-25).

Miraculous Gifts of the Spirit:
Foretold (Isa 35:4-6; Joel 2:28-29). Of different kinds (1Co 12:4-6). Enumerated (1Co 12:8-10, 28). Christ was endued with (Mt 12:28). Poured out on Pentecost (Ac 2:1-4). Communicated on preaching the gospel (Ac 10:44-46), by laying on of the apostles' hands (Ac 8:17-18; 19:6), for the confirmation of the gospel (Mk 16:20; Ac 14:3; Ro 15:19; Heb 2:4), for the edification of the church (1Co 12:7; 14:12-13). To be sought after (1Co 12:31; 14:1). Temporary nature of (1Co 13:8). Not to be neglected (1Ti 4:14; 2Ti 1:6), or despised (1Th 5:20), or purchased (Ac 8:20).
See Gifts From God, Spiritual.

MIRE Figurative of distress (Ps 40:2; 69:2).

MIRIAM (variously *bitterness, plump one, the wished-for child, one who loves or is loved*).
1. Sister of Aaron and Moses; saved life of the baby Moses (Ex 2:4, 7-8), prophetess (Ex 15:20), criticized Moses for his marriage (Nu 12), buried at Kadesh (Nu 20:1).
2. Judahite (1Ch 4:17).

MIRMAH (*deceit*). A Benjamite (1Ch 8:10).

MIRROR Ancient mirrors were made of polished metal (Ex 38:8; Job 37:18; 1Co 13:12; 2Co 3:18; Jas 1:23). *See Glass.*

MISCARRY Of people, a judgment of God (Hos 9:14). Lack of in people and in animals, a sign of God's blessing (Ge 31:38; Ex 23:25-26; Job 21:10). *See Abortion.*

MISCEGENATION *See Intermarry.*

MISER (Ecc 4:7-8).

MISGAB NIV "stronghold"; a place otherwise unknown (Jer 48:1).

MISHAEL (*who belongs to God [El]?*).
1. A son of Uzziel, helps carry the bodies of Nadab and Abihu out of the camp (Ex 6:22; Lev 10:4).
2. A Jew who stood by Ezra when he read the law to the people (Ne 8:4).
3. Also called Meshach. *See Meshach.*

MISHAL Levitical city in Asher (Jos 19:26; 21:30), also called Mashal (1Ch 6:74). *See Mashal.*

MISHAM Son of Elpaal (1Ch 8:12).

MISHMA (*rumor*).
1. Son of Ishmael (Ge 25:14; 1Ch 1:30).
2. Of the tribe of Simeon (1Ch 4:25-26).

MISHMANNAH (*fatness*). A Gadite who joined David at Ziklag (1Ch 12:10).

MISHPAT *See En Mishpat.*

MISHRAITES Clan of Kiriath Jearim in Judah (1Ch 2:53).

MISJUDGMENT Instances of: Of the Reubenites and Gadites (Nu 32:1-33; Jos 22:11-31). Of Hannah (1Sa 1:14-17). *See Accusation, False; Uncharitableness.*

MISPAR (*number*). Coworker of Zerubbabel (Ezr 2:2). "Mispereth" (Ne 7:7).

MISPERETH Also called Mizpar. A Jew who returned with Zerubbabel from Babylon (Ezr 2:2; Ne 7:7).

MISREPHOTH MAIM (*waters of Misrephoth [lime burning]*). Place near Sidon and Tyre (Jos 11:8; 13:6).

MISSIONARY JOURNEYS OF PAUL
I. The First Missionary Journey, c. A.D. 46-48 (Ac 13:1-14:28).
 A. Barnabas and Saul are Sent From Antioch (13:1-3).
 B. Ministry at Cyprus (13:4-13).
 1. Preaching in the synagogues (13:4-5).
 2. Controversy with Bar-Jesus (13:6-13).
 C. Ministry at Antioch (13:14-50).
 1. Paul preaches on first Sabbath (13:14-43).
 2. Paul preaches on second Sabbath (13:44-50).
 D. Ministry at Iconium (13:51-14:5).
 E. Ministry at Lystra (14:6-20).
 1. A lame man is healed (14:6-10).
 2. Paul and Barnabas are deified (14:11-18).
 3. Paul is stoned (14:19-20).
 F. Ministry on the Return Trip (14:21-25).
 G. Report on the First Missionary Journey (14:26-28).
II. The Jerusalem Council (15:1-35).
 A. Debate Over Gentiles Keeping the Law (15:1-5).
 B. Peter Preaches Salvation Through Grace (15:6-11).
 C. Paul and Barnabas Testify (15:12).
 D. James Proves Gentiles Are Free From the Law (15:13-21).
 E. The Council Sends an Official Letter (15:22-29).
 F. Report to Antioch (15:30-35).
III. The Second Missionary Journey, c. A.D. 49-52 (Ac 15:36-18:22).
 A. Contention Over John Mark (15:36-41).
 B. Derbe and Lystra: Timothy is Circumcised (16:1-5).
 C. Troas: Macedonian Call (16:6-10).
 D. Philippi: Extensive Ministry (16:11-40).
 1. Lydia is converted (16:11-15).
 2. Spirit of divination is cast out (16:16-24).
 3. Philippian jailer is converted (16:25-34).
 4. Paul is released from prison (16:35-40).
 E. Thessalonica: "Turn the World Upside Down" (17:1-9).
 F. Berea: Many Receive the Word (17:10-15).
 G. Athens: Paul's Sermon on Mars' Hill (17:16-34).
 H. Corinth: One-and-a-Half Years of Ministry (18:1-17).
 1. Paul works with Aquila and Priscilla (18:1-3).
 2. Jews reject Paul (18:4-6).
 3. Crispus, the Gentile, is converted (18:7-11).
 4. Gallio will not try Paul (18:12-17).
 I. Return Trip to Antioch (18:18-22).
IV. The Third Missionary Journey, c. A.D. 53-57 (Ac 18:23-21:16).
 A. Galatia and Phrygia: Strengthening the Disciples (18:23).
 B. Ephesus: Three Years of Ministry (18:24-19:41).
 1. Apollos teaches effectively (18:24-28).
 2. Disciples of John receive the Holy Spirit (19:1-7).
 3. Paul teaches in Tyrannus' school (19:8-10).
 4. Miracles are performed at Ephesus (19:11-20).
 5. Timothy and Erastus are sent to Macedonia (19:21-22).
 6. Demetrius causes uproar at Ephesus (19:23-41).
 C. Macedonia: Three Months of Ministry (20:1-5).
 D. Troas: Eutychus Falls From Loft (20:6-12).
 E. Miletus: Paul Bids Farewell to Ephesian Elders (20:13-38).
 F. Tyre: Paul is Warned About Jerusalem (21:1-6).
 G. Caesarea: Agabus's Prediction (21:7-16).
V. The Trip to Rome, c. A.D. 57-59 (Ac 21:17-28:31).
 A. Paul Witnesses in Jerusalem (21:17-23:33).
 1. Paul conforms to Jewish customs (21:17-26).
 2. Paul's arrest (21:27-39).
 3. Paul's defense before the crowd (21:40-22:23).
 4. Paul's defense before the centurion (22:24-29).
 5. Paul's defense before the Sanhedrin (22:30-23:11).
 6. Jews' plan to kill Paul (23:12-22).

 7. Paul's rescue (23:23-33).
 B. Paul's Witnesses in Caesarea (23:34-28:31).
 1. Paul is tried before Felix (23:34-24:27).
 2. Paul is tried before Festus (25:1-22).
 3. Paul is tried before Agrippa (25:23-26:32).
 C. Paul Witnesses in Rome (27:1-28:31).
 1. Paul's witness during the shipwreck (27:1-44).
 2. Paul's witness on Malta (28:1-15).
 3. Paul's witness in Rome (28:16-31).
VI. The Fourth Missionary Journey, c. A.D. 62-68.
It is clear from Ac 13:1-21:17 that Paul went on three missionary journeys. There is also reason to believe that he made a fourth journey after his release from the Roman imprisonment recorded in Ac 28. The conclusion that such a journey did indeed take place is based on: (1) Paul's declared intention to go to Spain (Ro 15:24, 28), (2) Eusebius's implication that Paul was released following his first Roman imprisonment (*Ecclesiastical History*, 2.22.2-3) and (3) statements in early Christian literature that he took the gospel as far as Spain (Clement of Rome, *Epistle to the Corinthians*, ch. 5; *Actus Petri Vercellenses*, chs. 1-3; Muratorian Canon, lines 34-39).
The places Paul may have visited after his release from prison are indicated by statements of intention in his earlier writings and by subsequent mention in the Pastoral Letters. The order of his travel cannot be determined with certainty, but the itinerary that follows seems likely.
 1. Rome: released from prison in c. A.D. 62.
 2. Spain: c. A.D. 62-64 (Ro 15:24, 28).
 3. Crete: c. A.D. 64-65 (Tit 1:5).
 4. Miletus: c. A.D. 65 (2Ti 4:20).
 5. Colosse: c. A.D. 66 (Phm 22).
 6. Ephesus: c. A.D. 66 (1Ti 1:3).
 7. Philippi: c. A.D. 66 (Php 2:23-24; 1Ti 1:3).
 8. Nicopolis: c. A.D. 66-67 (Tit 3:12).
 9. Rome: c. A.D. 67.
 10. Martyrdom: c. A.D. 67/68.
 See Paul; Pastoral Epistles.

MISSIONS Spreading the good news throughout the world.
General:
Religious propagandism (2Ki 17:27-28; 1Ch 16:23-24). Commanded (Ps 96:3, 10; Mt 28:19; Mk 16:15; Lk 24:47-48). Prophecy concerning (Mt 24:14; Mk 13:10). Peter's vision concerning (Ac 10:9-20).
Ordained by Jesus (Mt 24:14; 28:19; Mt 16:15-16; Lk 24:47-49). Saul and Barnabas ordained for (Ac 13:2-4, 47). Paul appointed to (Ac 26:14-18; 1Co 16:9). Practiced by the psalmist (Ps 18:49). Practiced by Jonah (Jnh 3:1-9). Symbolized by the flying angel (Rev 14:6-7).
Missionary hymn (Ps 96).
The first to do homage to the Messiah were Gentiles (Mt 2:11).
See Gentiles, Conversion of; Heathen; Jesus the Christ, King; Jesus the Christ, Kingdom of.

Missionaries, All Christians Should Be:
After the example of Christ (Ac 10:38). Women and children as well as men (Ps 8:2; Pr 31:26; Mt 21:15-16; Php 4:3; 1Ti 5:10; Tit 2:3-5; 1Pe 3:1). The zeal of idolaters should provoke to (Jer 7:18). The zeal of hypocrites should provoke to (Mt 23:15). An imperative duty (Jdg 5:23; Lk 19:40). The principle on which (2Co 5:14-15). However weak they may be (1Co 1:27). From their calling as saints (Ex 19:6; 1Pe 2:9). As faithful stewards (1Pe 4:10-11).
In youth (Ps 71:17; 148:12-13). In old age (Dt 32:7; Ps 71:18). In the family (Dt 6:7; Ps 78:5-8; Isa 38:19; 1Co 7:16; 1Pe 2:12). In first giving their own selves to the Lord (2Co 8:5). In declaring what God has done for them (Ps 66:16; 116:16-19). In hating one's life for Christ (Lk 14:26). In openly confessing Christ (Mt 10:32). In following Christ (Lk 14:27; 18:22). In preferring Christ above all relations (Lk 14:26; 1Co 2:2). In joyfully suffering for Christ (Heb 10:34). In forsaking all for Christ (Lk 10:34). In a holy example (Mt 5:16; Php 2:15; 1Th 1:7). In holy conduct (1Pe 2:12). In holy boldness (Ps 119:46). In dedicating themselves to the service of God (Ps 27:4). In devoting all property to God (1Ch 29:2-3, 14, 16; Ecc 11:1; Mt 6:19-20; Mk 12:44; Lk 12:33; 18:22, 28; Ac 2:45; 4:32-34).
In holy conversation (Ps 37:30, w Pr 10:31; Pr 15:7; Eph 4:29; Col 4:6). In talking of God and His works (Ps 71:24; 77:12; 119:27; 145:11-12). In showing forth God's praises (Isa 43:21).
In inviting others to embrace the gospel (Ps 34:8; Isa 2:3; Jn 1:46; 4:29). In seeking the edification of others (Ro 14:19; 15:2; 1Th 5:11). In admonishing others (1Th 5:14; 2Th 3:15). In reproving others (Lev 19:17; Eph 5:11). In teaching and exhorting (Ps 34:11; 51:13; Col 3:16; Heb 3:13; 10:25). In interceding for others (Col 4:3; Heb 13:18; Jas 5:16). In aiding ministers in their labors (Ro 16:3, 9; 2Co 11:9; Php 4:14-16; 3Jn 6). In giving a reason for their faith (Ex 12:26-27; Dt 6:20-21; 1Pe 3:15). In encouraging the weak (Isa 35:3-4; Ro 14:1; 15:1; 1Th 5:14). In visiting and relieving the poor and sick (Lev 25:35; Ps 112:9, w 2Co 9:9; Mt 25:36; Ac 20:35; Jas 1:27). With a willing heart (Ex 35:29; 1Ch 29:9, 14). With great generosity (Ex 36:5-7; 2Co 8:3). Encouragement to (Pr 11:25, 30; 1Co 1:27; Jas 5:19-20). Blessedness of (Da 12:3). Illustrated (Mt 25:14; Lk 19:13).
See Minister.

MIST
1. Steamy vapor rising from the ground (Ge 2:6).
2. Dimness of vision (Ac 13:11).
3. Description of false teachers (2Pe 2:17).

MITE(S) *See Money; Penny.*

MITHCAH (*sweetness*). An encampment of the Israelites (Nu 33:28-29).

MITHNITE Family name of Joshaphat (1Ch 11:43).

MITHRAISM Cult of Mithras, Persian sun-god, widely disseminated in the Roman Empire in the first century A.D.

MITHREDATH (*gift to [pagan deity] Mithra*).
1. Treasurer of Cyrus (Ezr 1:8).

2. A Persian officer who joined in writing a letter hostile to the Jews (Ezr 4:7).

MITRE See Turban.

MITYLENE Capital of Lesbos. Paul visits (Ac 20:14-15).

MIXED MARRIAGE See Intermarry.

MIXED MULTITUDE Non-Israelites who traveled and associated with the Israelites (Nu 11:4-6; Ne 13:3).

MIZAR (small). A hill near Mt. Hermon (Ps 42:6).

MIZPAH (lookout point).
1. A city allotted to Benjamin (Jos 18:26). The Israelites assemble at (Jdg 20:1-3), and decree the penalty to be executed upon the Benjamites for their mistreatment of the Levite's concubine (Jdg 20:10). Assembled by Samuel that he might reprove them for their idolatry (1Sa 7:5). Crown Saul king of Israel at (1Sa 10:17-25). A judgment seat of Samuel (1Sa 7:16). Walled by Asa (1Ki 15:22; 2Ch 16:6). Temporarily the capital of the country after the Israelites had been carried away captive (2Ki 25:23, 25; Jer 40:6-15; 41:1-14). Captivity returned to (Ne 3:7, 15, 19).
2. A valley near Lebanon (Jos 11:3, 8).
3. A city in Moab. David gives his parents to the care of the king of (1Sa 22:3-4).
4. A city in the lowland of Judah (Jos 15:38).
5. A town in Gilead (Jos 10:17; Jdg 11:34). May be the location of a treaty between Jacob and Laban (Ge 31:48-49).

MIZPAR See Mispar.

MIZPEH See Mizpah.

MIZRAIM (Hebrew word for Egypt). Son of Ham (Ge 10:6, 13; 1Ch 1:8, 11), progenitor of the Egyptians, a people of N Africa, Hamitic people of Canaan.

MIZZAH (terror). Son of Reuel (Ge 36:13, 17; 1Ch 1:37).

MNASON A native and Christian of Cyprus who entertained Paul (Ac 21:16).

MOAB (seed).
1. Son of Lot (Ge 19:37).
2. Plains of. Israelites come in (Dt 2:17-18). Military forces numbered in (Nu 26:3, 63). The law rehearsed in, by Moses (Nu 35-36; Dt 29-33). The Israelites renew their covenant in (Dt 29:1). The land of promise allotted in (Jos 13:32).

MOABITE STONE Black basalt stele, two by four feet, inscribed by Mesha king of Moab, with thirty-four lines in the Moabite language (practically a dialect of Hebrew), giving his side of the story (2Ki 3).

MOABITE(S) Descendants of Lot through his son Moab (Ge 19:37). Called the people of Chemosh (Nu 21:29). The territory E of Jordan, bounded on the N by the Arnon River (Nu 21:13; Jdg 11:18). Israelites commanded not to distress the Moabites (Dt 2:9). Refuse passage of Jephthah's army through their territory (Jdg 11:17-18). Balak was king of (Nu 22:4), calls for Balaam to curse Israel (Nu 22-24; Jos 24:9; Mic 6:5). Are a snare to the Israelites (Nu 25:1-3; Ru 1:4; 1Ki 11:1; 1Ch 8:8; Ezr 9:1-2; Ne 13:23). Land of, not given to the Israelites as a possession (Dt 2:9, 29). David takes refuge among, from Saul (1Sa 22:3-4). David conquers (2Sa 8:2; 23:20; 1Ch 11:22; 18:2-11). Israelites had war with (2Ki 3:5-27; 13:20; 24:2; 2Ch 20:1). Prophecies concerning judgments upon (Jer 48).

MOADIAH (perhaps Yahweh assembles or Yahweh promises). A chief priest who returned from the Exile with Zerubbabel at the time of Joiakim (Ne 12:5, 17).

MOB At Thessalonica (Ac 17:5), Jerusalem (Ac 21:28, 30), Ephesus (Ac 19:29-40).

MOCKING Ishmael mocks Sarah (Ge 21:9). Elijah mocks the priests of Baal (1Ki 18:27). Zedekiah mocks Micaiah (1Ki 22:24). Children mock Elisha (2Ki 2:23). The tormentors of Job mock (Job 15:12; 30:1). The persecutors of Jesus mock him (Mt 26:67-68; 27:28-31, 39-44; Mk 10:34; 14:65; 15:17-20, 29-32; Lk 23:11; Jn 19:2-3, 5; 1Pe 2:23). The Ammonites mock God (Eze 25:3). Tyre mocks Jerusalem (Eze 26:2). The wicked mock (Isa 28:15, 22; 2Pe 3:3).
See Scoffing.
Figurative (Ecc 7:16; 1Co 7:31).

MODESTY Of women (1Ti 2:9).
Instances of: Moses (Nu 12:3). Saul (1Sa 9:21). Vashti (Est 1:11-12). Elihu (Job 32:4-7).
See Humility.

MOLADAH (generation). Town c. ten miles E of Beersheba (Ne 11:26).

MOLDING (wreath or border). (Job 28:2; Eze 24:11). The decorative ledge of gold around the ark of the covenant (Ex 25:11; 37:2), the table (Ex 25:24-25; 37:11-12), and the incense altar (Ex 30:3-4; 37:26-27). Of images (Ex 32:4, 8; 34:17; Lev 19:4; Dt 9:12), pillars (1Ki 7:15), bronze Sea (1Ki 7:23), done in the plain of Jordan (1Ki 7:46; 2Ch 4:17), mirrors (Job 37:18).

MOLECH ("shameful" king) Molech is the deliberate misvocalization of the name of a pagan god. The consonants for the word king, melek, are combined with the vowels for shame, bosheth.
An idol of the Ammonites (Ac 7:43). Worshiped by the wives of Solomon, and by Solomon (1Ki 11:1-8). Children sacrificed to (2Ki 23:10, w Jer 32:35; 2Ki 16:3; 21:6; 2Ch 28:3; Isa 57:5; Jer 7:31; Eze 16:20-21; 20:26, 31; 23:37, 39, w Lev 18:21; 20:2-5). See Malcam, 2.

MOLE(S) NIV "chameleon" (Lev 11:30), "rodent" (Isa 2:20). See Animals; Chameleon.

MOLID (descendant). A descendant of Judah, the son of Abishur and his wife Abihail (1Ch 2:29).

MOLTEN IMAGE See Tabernacle.

MONARCHY Described by Samuel (1Sa 8:11-18). See Government; Kings.

MONEY Silver used as (Ge 17:12-13, 23, 27; 20:16; 23:9, 13; 31:15; 37:28; 42:25-35; 43:12-23; 44:1-8; 47:14-18; Ex 12:44; 21:11, 21, 34-35; 22:7, 17, 25; 30:16; Lev 22:11; 25:37, 51; 27:15, 18; Nu 3:48-51; 18:16; Dt 2:6, 28; 14:25-26; 21:14; 23:19; Jdg 5:19; 16:18; 17:4; 1Ki 21:2, 6, 15; 2Ki 5:26; 12:4, 7-16; 15:20; 22:7, 9; 23:35; 2Ch 24:5, 11, 14; 34:9, 14, 17; Ezr 3:7; 7:7; Ne 5:4, 10-11; Est 4:7; Job 31:39; Ps 15:5; Pr 7:20; Ecc 7:12; 10:19; Isa 43:24; 52:3; 55:1-2; Jer 32:9-10, 25, 44; La 5:4; Mic 3:11; Mt 25:18, 27; 28:12, 15; Mk 14:11; Lk 9:3; 19:15, 23; 22:5; Ac 7:16; 8:20).
Gold used as (Ge 13:2; 24:35; 44:8, w 44:1; 1Ch 21:25; Ezr 8:25-27; Isa 13:17; 46:6; 60:9; Eze 7:19; 28:4; Mt 2:11; 10:9; Ac 3:6; 20:33; 1Pe 1:18).
Copper used as (Mt 10:9; Mk 6:8; 12:42; Lk 21:2).
Weighed (Ge 23:16; 43:21; Job 28:15; Jer 32:9-10; Zec 11:12). Image on (Mt 22:20-21). Conscience (Jdg 17:2; Mt 27:3, 5). Ransom atonement (Ex 30:12-16; Lev 5:15-16). Sin offering (2Ki 12:16). Value of, varied corruptly (Am 8:5). Love of, the root of evil (1Ti 6:10). See Materialism.
See Daric; Drachma; Gerah; Penny; Pound; Shekel; Silver; Talent.

MONEY CHANGERS Those who changed foreign currency into sanctuary money at a profit (Mt 21:12; Mk 11:15; Jn 2:14-15).

MONITOR LIZARD Unclean for food (Lev 11:30). See Animals.

MONOPOLY Of lands (Isa 5:8; Mic 2:2), by Pharaoh (Ge 47:19-26), of food (Pr 11:26).

MONOTHEISM (one God). Belief that there is but one God.

MONSTERS See Animals; Behemoth; Leviathan; Serpent.

MONTH Sun and moon for signs and seasons (Ge 1:14). The beginning and ending of the Flood (Ge 7:11; 8:4).
Twelve months reckoned to a year (1Ki 4:7; 1Ch 27:1-15; Est 2:12). Time computed by months (Ge 29:14; Nu 10:10; Jdg 11:37; 1Sa 6:1; Ps 81:3; Rev 22:2). Months in prophecy (Rev 11:2).

1. Abib (Post-Exilic name: Nisan)
March-April
Month 7 in civil sequence. The Jewish calendar began with (Ex 12:2; 13:4; Dt 16:1). Passover instituted and celebrated in (Ex 12:1-28; 23:15). Israelites left Egypt in (Ex 13:4). Tabernacle set up in (Ex 40:2, 17). Israelites arrive at Zin in (Nu 20:1). Cross Jordan in (Jos 4:19). Jordan overflows in (1Ch 12:15). After the Captivity called Nisan (Ne 2:1; Est 3:7). Decree to put the Jews to death in (Est 3:12). The death of Jesus in (Mt 26:27).
Season: Spring; Later rains.
Agriculture: Barley and flax harvest begin.
Feasts: 14th, Passover (Ex 12:18; Lev 23:5); 15-21st, Unleavened Bread (Lev 23:6); 16th, Firstfruits (Lev 23:10f).

2. Ziv (Post-Exilic name: Iyyar) April-May
Month 8 in civil sequence. Israel numbered in (Nu 1:1, 18). Passover to be observed in, by the unclean and others who could not observe it in the first month (Nu 9:10-11). Israel departed from the wilderness of Zin in (Nu 10:11). Temple begun in (1Ki 6:1; 2Ch 3:2). An irregular Passover celebrated in (2Ch 30:1-27). Rebuilding of the temple begun in (Ezr 3:8).
Season: Dry season begins.
Agriculture: Barley harvest.
Feasts: 14th, Later Passover (Nu 9:10-11).

3. Sivan (Post-Exilic name) May-June
Month 9 in civil sequence. Asa renews the covenant of himself and people in (2Ch 15:10).
Agriculture: Early figs begin; Wheat harvest.
Feasts: 6th, Pentecost or Feast of Weeks (Lev 23:15ff); Harvest.

4. Tammuz (Post-Exilic name) June-July
Month 10 in civil sequence. The number only appears in the Bible. Jerusalem taken by Nebuchadnezzar in (Jer 39:2; 52:6-7).
Agriculture: Tending vines.
Feasts: None.

5. Ab (Post-Exilic name) July-August
Month 11 in civil sequence. Number only mentioned. Aaron died on the first day of (Nu 33:38). Temple destroyed in (2Ki 25:8-10; Jer 1:3; 52:12-30). Ezra arrived at Jerusalem in (Ezr 7:8-9).
Agriculture: Ripening of grapes, figs, and olives.
Feasts: None.

6. Elul (Post-Exilic name)
August-September
Month 12 in civil sequence. Wall of Jerusalem finished in (Ne 6:15). Temple built in (Hag 1:14-15).
Agriculture: Processing grapes, dates, summer figs, and olives.
Feasts: None.

7. Ethanim (Post-Exilic name: Tishri)
September-October
Month 1 in civil sequence. Feasts held in (Lev 23:24, 27; Ne 8:13-15). Jubilee proclaimed in (Lev 25:9). Solomon's temple dedicated in (1Ki 8:2). Altar rebuilt and offerings renewed in (Ezr 3:1, 6).
Season: Autumn (early) rains begin.
Agriculture: Plowing.

Feasts: 1st, Trumpets (Nu 29:1; Lev 23:24); 10th, Atonement (Lev 16:29ff; 23:27ff); 15-21st, Tabernacles or Booths (Lev 23:34ff); 22nd, Solemn assembly (Lev 23:36).

8. Bul (Post-Exilic name: **Marchesvan**)
October-November
Month 2 in civil sequence. The temple finished in (1Ki 6:38). Jeroboam's idolatrous feast in (1Ki 12:32-33; 1Ch 27:11).
Season: Plowing.
Agriculture: Winter figs; sowing of wheat and barley.
Feasts: None.

9. Kislev (Post-Exilic name)
November-December
Month 3 in civil sequence.
Agriculture: Sowing.
Feasts: 25th, Hanukkah or Dedication (1Mc 4:52f; Jn 10:22).

10. Tebeth (Post-Exilic name)
December-January
Month 4 in civil sequence. Nebuchadnezzar besieges Jerusalem in (2Ki 25:1; Jer 52:4). Esther chosen queen (Est 2:16).
Season: Winter rains begin (snow on high ground).
Agriculture: None.
Feasts: None.

11. Shebat (Post-Exilic name)
January-February
Month 5 in civil sequence. Moses probably died in (Dt 1:3).
Agriculture: None.
Feasts: None.

12. Adar (Post-Exilic name)
February-March
Month 6 in civil sequence. Second temple finished in (Ezr 6:15). Feast of Purim (Est 9:1-26).
Agriculture: Almond trees bloom; citrus fruit harvest.
Feasts: Purim.

13. Adar Sheni (not in Bible)
Second Adar is an intercalary month added about every three years so the lunar calendar would correspond to the solar year. See Calendar; Time. See also each month by name.

MONUMENT See Pillar.

MOON Created by God (Ge 1:16; Ps 8:3; 136:7-9). Its light (Job 31:26; Ecc 12:2). Its influences (Dt 33:14; Ps 121:6). Seasons of (months) (Ps 104:19). Joseph's dream concerning (Ge 37:9). Stand still (Jos 10:12-13; Hab 3:11). Worship of, forbidden (Dt 4:19; 17:3). Worshiped (2Ki 23:5; Job 31:26-27; Jer 7:18; 8:2; 44:17-19, 25). No light of, in eternity (Rev 21:23).

Figurative:
Shining of (Isa 30:26; 60:19; Rev 21:23). Darkening of (Job 25:5; Isa 13:10; 24:23; Eze 32:7; Joel 2:10, 31; 3:15; Mt 24:29; Mk 13:24; Lk 21:25; Ac 2:20; Rev 6:12; 8:12).
Symbolic: (Rev 12:1).

Feast of the New Moon:
(Nu 10:10; 28:11-15; 1Ch 23:31; 2Ch 31:3; Ezr 3:5). Trade at time of, prohibited (Am 8:5).

MORAL AGENCY See Contingencies.

MORAL LAW See Law.

MORALITY See Duty of People to People; Integrity; Neighbor.

MORASTHITE See Moresheth.

MORDECAI (pagan Babylonian god Marduk). A Jewish captive in Persia (Est 2:5-6). Foster father of Esther (Est 2:7). Informs Xerxes of a conspiracy against his life, and is rewarded (Est 2:21-23; 6:1-11). Promoted in Haman's place (Est 8:1-2, 15; 10:1-3). Intercedes with Xerxes for the Jews; establishes the festival of Purim in commemoration of their deliverance (Est 8-9).

MOREH (|place of] instructor).
1. A plain near Shechem and Gilgal (Ge 12:6; Dt 11:30).
2. A hill in the plain of Jezreel where the Midianites encamped (Jdg 7:1, 12).

MORESHETH (possession of Gath). Hometown of Micah; probably Moresheth Gath (Jer 26:18; Mic 1:1).

MORESHETH GATH (possession of Gath). Town c. five miles W of Gath in the Shephelah (Mic 1:14). See Moresheth.

MORIAH Place to which Abraham to offer up Isaac (Ge 22:2). Solomon built temple on Mt. Moriah (2Ch 3:1), but it is not certain whether it is the same place.

MORNING The second part of the day at the Creation (Ge 1:5, 8, 13, 19, 23, 31). The first part of the natural day (Mk 16:2). Ordained by God (Job 38:12). Began with first dawn (Jos 6:15; Ps 119:147). Continued until noon (1Ki 18:26; Ne 8:3). Dawning of calls for rejoicing (Ps 65:8).

The Jews:
Generally rose early in (Ge 28:18; Jdg 6:28). Eat but little in (Ecc 10:16). Went to the temple in (Lk 21:38; Jn 8:2). Offered a part of the daily sacrifice in (Ex 29:38-39; Nu 28:4-7). Devoted a part to prayer and praise (Ps 5:3; 59:16; 88:13). Gathered the manna in (Ex 16:21). Began their journeys in (Ge 22:3). Held courts of justice in (Jer 21:12; Mt 27:1). Contracted covenants in (Ge 26:31). Transacted business in (Ecc 11:6; Mt 20:1). Was frequently cloudless (2Sa 23:4). A red sky in, a sign of bad weather (Mt 16:3). Ushered in by the morning stars (Job 38:7).

Illustrative:
Of the resurrection day (Ps 49:14). Breaking forth, of the glory of the church (SS 6:10; Isa 58:8). Star of, of the glory of Christ (Rev 22:16). Star of, of reward of saints (Rev 2:28). Clouds in, of the short-lived profession of hypocrites (Hos 6:4). Wings of, of rapid

movements (Ps 139:9). Spread upon the mountains, of heavy calamities (Joel 2:2).

MORNING SACRIFICE *See Offerings.*

MORNING STAR Figurative of the glory of the king of Babylon (Isa 14:12). Of Jesus (2Pe 1:19; Rev 2:26; 22:16).

MORSEL A choice bit of food (Pr 18:8; 26:22).

MORTAL, MORTALITY A mortal is a being subject to death (Ro 8:11; 1Co 15:53-54).

MORTAR
1. An instrument for crushing grain (Nu 11:8; Pr 27:22). *See Grinding; Mill.*
2. A cement (Ex 1:14). Tar used as, in building tower of Babel (Ge 11:3). Used to plaster houses (Lev 14:42-45). Untempered, not enduring (Eze 13:10-15; 22:28). To be trodden to make firm (Na 3:14).
 Figurative (Isa 41:25).

MORTGAGE *(take on pledge, give in pledge, exchange)*. On land (Ne 5:3). *See Land.*

MORTIFICATION *(self-denial)*. Instances of: David's ambassadors, sent to Hanun (2Sa 10:1-5). Judas (Mt 27:3-5). *See Humility.*

MOSAIC Picture or design made by setting tiny squares or cones of varicolored marble, limestone, or semiprecious stones in some medium such as plaster to tell a story or to form a decoration (Est 1:6).

MOSERAH *(possession)*. An encampment of the Israelites where Aaron died (Dt 10:6). Probably identical with Moseroth, below.

MOSEROTH *(possession)*. An encampment of the Israelites (Nu 33:30-31).

MOSES *(drawn out* Ex 2:10; Egyptian for *son)*.
Personal History:
 A Levite and son of Amram (Ex 2:1-4; 6:20; Ac 7:20; Heb 11:23). Hidden in an basket (Ex 2:3). Discovered and adopted by the daughter of Pharaoh (Ex 2:5-10). Learned in all the wisdom of Egypt (Ac 7:22). His loyalty to his race (Heb 11:24-26). Takes the life of an Egyptian; flees from Egypt; finds refuge among the Midianites (Ex 2:11-22; Ac 7:24-29). Joins himself to Jethro, priest of Midian; marries Jethro's daughter Zipporah; has two sons (Ex 2:15-22; 18:3-4). Is herdsman for Jethro in the desert of Horeb (Ex 3:1). Has the vision of the burning bush (Ex 3:2-6). God reveals to him his purpose to deliver the Israelites and bring them into the land of Canaan (Ex 3:7-10). Commissioned as a leader of the Israelites (Ex 3:10-22; 6:13). His rod miraculously turned into a serpent, his hand made leprous, and each restored (Ex 4:1-9, 28). With his wife and sons leaves Jethro to perform his mission (Ex 4:18-20). His controversy with his wife on account of circumcision (Ex 4:20-26). Meets Aaron in the wilderness (Ex 4:27-28).
 With Aaron assembles the leaders of Israel (Ex 4:29-31). With Aaron goes before Pharaoh, in the name of Yahweh demands the liberties of his people (Ex 5:1). Rejected by Pharaoh; hardships of the Israelites increased (Ex 5). People murmur against Moses and Aaron (Ex 5:20-21; 15:24; 16:2-3; 17:2-3; Nu 14:2-4; 16:41; 20:2-5; 21:4-6; Dt 1:12, 26-28). *See Israel.* Receives comfort and assurance from the Lord (Ex 6:1-8). Unbelief of the people (Ex 6:9). Renews his appeal to Pharaoh (Ex 6:11). Under divine direction brings plagues upon the land of Egypt (Ex 7-12). Secures the deliverance of the people and leads them out of Egypt (Ex 13). Crosses the Red Sea; Pharaoh and his army are destroyed (Ex 14). Composes a song for the Israelites on their deliverance from Pharaoh (Ex 15). Joined by his family in the wilderness (Ex 18:1-12).
 Institutes a system of government (Ex 18:13-26; Nu 11:16-30; Dt 1:9-18). Receives the law and ordains various statutes. *See Law of Moses.* Face of, transfigured (Ex 34:29-35; 2Co 3:13). Sets up the tabernacle. *See Tabernacle.* Reproves Aaron for making the golden calf (Ex 32:22-23), for irregularity in the offerings (Lev 10:16-20). Jealousy of Aaron and Miriam toward (Nu 12). Rebellion of Korah, Dathan, and Abiram against (Nu 16). Appoints Joshua as his successor (Nu 27:22-23; Dt 31:7-8, 14, 23; 34:9).
 Not permitted to enter Canaan, but views the land from the top of Pisgah (Nu 27:12-14; Dt 3:17; 3:23-29; 32:48-52; 34:1-8). Death and burial of (Nu 31:2; Dt 32:50; 34:1-6). Body of, disputed over (Jude 9). 120 years old at death (Dt 31:2). Mourning for, thirty days in the plains of Moab (Dt 34:8). His virility (Dt 31:2; 34:7).
 Present with Jesus on the Mount of Transfiguration (Mt 17:3-4; Mk 9:4; Lk 9:30).
 Type of Christ (Dt 18:15-18; Ac 3:22; 7:37).

Benedictions of:
 Upon the people (Lev 9:23; Nu 10:35-36; Dt 1:11). Last benediction upon the tribes (Dt 33).

Character of:
 Murmurings of (Ex 5:22-23; Nu 11:10-15). Impatience of (Ex 5:22-23; 6:12; 32:19; Nu 11:10-15; 16:15; 20:10; 31:14). Respected and feared (Ex 33:8). Faith of (Nu 10:29; Dt 9:1-3; Heb 11:23-28). Called the man of God (Dt 33:1). God spoke to, as a man to his friend (Ex 33:11). Magnified of God (Ex 19:9; Nu 14:12-20; Dt 9:13-29, w Ex 32:30). Magnanimity of, toward Eldad and Medad (Nu 11:29). Meekness of (Ex 14:13-14; 15:24-25; 16:2-3, 7-8; Nu 12:3; 16:4-11). Obedience of (Ex 7:6; 40:16, 19, 21). Unspiring (Nu 14:12-20; w Dt 9:13-29, w Ex 32:30).

Intercessory Prayers of: *See Intercession, Instances of; Intercession, Solicited; Intercession, Answered, .*

Miracles of: *See Miracles.*

Prophecies of:
 (Ex 3:10; 4:5, 11-12; 6:13; 7:2; 17:16; 19:3-9; 33:11; Nu 11:17; 12:7-8; 36:13; Dt 1:3; 5:31; 18:15, 18; 34:10, 12; Hos 12:13; Mk 7:9-10; Ac 7:37-38).

MOSES, ASSUMPTION OF Pseudonymous Jewish apocalyptic book, probably written early in the early first century A.D.; gives prophecy of future of Israel. Possibly quoted in Jude 9.

MOSES, LAW OF *See Law.*

MOST HIGH Title of God (Ge 14:18-19, 20, 22; Ps 7:17). *See God, Names of, Elyon.*

MOST HOLY PLACE *See Holy of Holies.*

MOTE *See Speck.*

MOTH An insect (Job 4:19; 27:18; Ps 39:11). Destructive of garments (Job 13:28; Isa 50:9; 51:8; Hos 5:12). Figurative (Mt 6:19-20; Jas 5:2).

MOTHER
Relationship With:
 Reverence for, commanded (Ex 20:12; Lev 19:3; Dt 5:16; Pr 23:22; Mt 15:4; 19:19; Mk 7:10; 10:19; Lk 18:20; Eph 6:2). To be obeyed (Dt 21:18; Pr 1:8; 6:20). Love for (1Ki 19:20). Must be subordinate to love for Christ (Mt 10:37).— Dishonoring of, to be punished (Ex 21:15; Lev 20:9; Pr 20:20; 28:24; 30:11, 17; Mt 15:4-6; Mk 7:10-12). Incest with, forbidden (Lev 18:7).
 Sanctifying influence of (1Co 7:14; 2Ti 1:5). Wicked (Ge 27:6-17; 2Ki 11:1-3).

Love of:
 (Isa 49:15; 66:13). Exemplified by: Hagar (Ge 21:14-16). The mother of Moses (Ex 2:1-3). Hannah (1Sa 1:20-28). Rizpah (2Sa 21:8-11). Bathsheba (1Ki 1:16-21). The mother whose child was brought to Solomon (1Ki 3:16-26). The woman whose sons were to be taken for debt (2Ki 4:1-7). The Shunammite (2Ki 4:18-37). Mary the mother of Jesus (Lk 2:41-50). The bereaved mothers of Bethlehem (Mt 2:16-18). The Syrian Phoenician woman (Mt 15:21-28; Mk 7:24-30).
 Grieves over wayward children (Pr 10:1; 19:26; 29:15). Rejoices over good children (Pr 23:23-25).

MOTHER-IN-LAW Not to be defiled (Lev 18:17; 20:14; Dt 27:23). Conflict with (Mic 7:6; Mt 10:35). Beloved by Ruth (Ru 1:14-17). Peter's, healed by Jesus (Mk 1:30-31).

MOTIVE Ascribed to God (Ps 106:8; Eze 36:21-22, 32). Right, required (Mt 6:1-18). Sinful, illustrated by Cain (Ge 4:7; 1Jn 3:12).
 Misunderstood: The tribes of Reuben and Gad, in asking inheritance E of Jordan (Nu 32:1-33), when they built the memorial (Jos 22:9-34). David's, by King Hanun (2Sa 10:2-3; 1Ch 19:3-4). The king of Syria, in sending presents to the king of Israel by Naaman (2Ki 5:5-7). Job in his righteousness (Job 1:9-11; 2:4-5).

MOTTO *See Inscriptions.*

MOUNT EPHRAIM *See Ephraim.*

MOUNT OF BEATITUDES Site of the Sermon on the Mount (Mt 5-7), exact location unknown. *See Beatitudes; Hattin, Horns of; Sermon on the Mount.*

MOUNTAIN Melted (Ps 97:5; Dt 4:11; 5:23; Jdg 5:5; Isa 64:1-3; Mic 1:4; Na 1:5). Overturning and removing of (Job 9:5; 14:18; 28:9; Eze 38:20), by faith (Mt 17:20; 21:21; Mk 11:23). Abraham offers Isaac upon Mount Zion, the site of the temple (Ge 22:2). *See Zion.* Horeb appointed as a place for the Israelites to worship (Ex 3:12). Signals from (Isa 13:2; 18:3; 30:17). Used for idolatrous worship (Dt 12:2; 1Sa 10:5; 1Ki 14:23; Jer 3:6; Hos 4:13).
 Jesus tempted upon (Mt 4:8; Lk 4:5). Jesus preaches from (Mt 5:1). Jesus goes up into, for prayer (Mt 14:23; Lk 6:12; 9:28), is transfigured upon (Mt 17:1-9; Mk 9:2-10; Lk 9:28-36), meets his disciples on, after his resurrection (Mt 28:16-17).
 Burning mountains. *See Volcanoes.*

MOURNING
For the Dead:
 Head uncovered (Lev 10:6; 21:10), lying on the ground (2Sa 12:16), personal appearance neglected (2Sa 14:2), cutting the flesh (Lev 19:28; 21:1-5; Dt 14:1; Jer 16:6-7; 41:5), lamentations (Ge 50:10; Ex 12:30; 1Sa 30:4; Jer 22:18; Mt 2:17-18), fasting (1Sa 31:13; 2Sa 1:12; 3:35). Priests prohibited, except for nearest of kin (Lev 21:1-11). For Nadab and Abihu forbidden (Lev 10:6). Sexes separated in (Zec 12:12, 14).
 Hired mourners (2Ch 35:25; Ecc 12:5; Jer 9:17; Mt 9:23).
 Abraham mourned for Sarah (Ge 23:2), Egyptians, for Jacob seventy days (Ge 50:1-3), Israelites, for Aaron thirty days (Nu 20:29).
 David's lamentations over the death of Saul and his sons (2Sa 1:17-27), the death of Abner (2Sa 3:33-34), the death of Absalom (2Sa 18:33).
 Jeremiah and the singing men and singing women lament for Josiah (2Ch 35:25).

For Calamities and Other Sorrows:
 Tearing the garments (Ge 37:29, 34; 44:13; Nu 14:6; Jdg 11:35; 2Sa 1:2, 11; 3:31; 13:19, 31; 15:32; 2Ki 2:12; 5:8; 6:30; 11:14; 19:1; 22:11, 19; Ezr 9:3, 5; Job 1:20; 2:12; Isa 37:1; Jer 41:5; Mt 26:65; Ac 14:14). Wearing mourning garb (Ge 38:14; 2Sa 14:2). *See Sackcloth.* Cutting or plucking off the hair and beard (Ezr 9:3; Jer 7:29). *See Baldness.* Covering the head and face (2Sa 15:30; 19:4; Est 6:12; Jer 14:3-4), and the upper lip (Lev 13:45; Eze 24:17, 22; Mic 3:7). Laying aside ornaments (Ex 33:4, 6). Walking barefoot (2Sa 15:30; Isa 20:2). Laying the hand on the head (2Sa 13:19; Jer 2:37). Ashes put on the head (2Sa 13:19; Eze 27:30). Dust on the head (Jos 7:6). Dressing in black (Jer 14:2). Sitting on the ground (Isa 3:26).
 Caused ceremonial defilement (Nu 19:11-16; 31:19; Lev 21:1). Prevented offerings from being accepted (Dt 26:14; Hos 9:4).
 See Elegy.

MOUSE *See Rat(s).*

MOUTH Has various connotations: literal mouth, language, opening; sometimes personified (Ps 119:108; Pr 15:14; Rev 19:15).

MOWING This was done by hand with a short sickle—originally of flint, later of metal (Ps 72:6; Jas 5:4). The king's share were the portion of the harvest taken as taxes (Am 7:1).

MOZA *(sunrise)*.
1. A son of Caleb (1Ch 2:46).
2. A Benjamite (1Ch 8:36-37; 9:42-43).

MOZAH A Benjamite city (Jos 18:26).

MUFFLER *See Veil.*

MULBERRY TREE (Lk 17:6).

MULE Uses of: For royal riders (2Sa 13:29; 18:9; 1Ki 1:33, 38), by saints in Isaiah's prophetic vision of the kingdom of Christ (Isa 66:20), as pack animals (2Ki 5:17; 1Ch 12:40). Tribute paid in (1Ki 10:25). Used in barter (Eze 27:14), by the exiles returning from Babylon (Ezr 2:66; Ne 7:68), in war (Zec 14:15).

MULTITUDE FED Miraculously (Ex 16:13; Nu 11:31; 2Ki 4:43; Mt 14:21; 15:38).

MUMMIFICATION *See Embalming.*

MUNITIONS Fortifications (Na 2:1).

MUPPIM Son or descendant of Benjamin (Ge 46:21). Called Shupham (Nu 26:39) and Shuppim (1Ch 7:12, 15). Shephuphan may be the same person (1Ch 8:5).

MURDER Forbidden on penalty of death (Ge 9:4-6; Ex 21:14; Lev 24:17; Dt 19:11-13), a murdered man's nearest relative had the duty to pursue the slayer and kill him (Nu 35:19), but the slayer could flee to a city of refuge, where he would be tried and then either turned over to the avenger or be protected (Nu 35:9-34; Dt 19:1-10). *See Homicide; Infanticide; Regicide.*

MURMURING *See Grumbling.*

MURRAIN A plague of Egypt (Ex 9:3, 6; Ps 78:50).

MUSHI, MUSHITE(S) Merarite Levite; progenitor of Mushites (Ex 6:19; Nu 3:20; 26:58; 1Ch 6:19, 47; 23:21, 23).

MUSIC
Used:
 At the crowning of kings (1Ki 1:39-40; 2Ch 23:13, 18). In national triumphs (Ex 15:1-21; Nu 21:17-18; Jdg 5:1-31; Jdg 11:34; 1Sa 18:6-7). In worship (1Ch 6:31-32; 15:16-22, 24, 27-28; 16:4-42; 23:5; 25:1-7; 2Ch 5:12-13; 20:19, 21-22, 28; 29:25-30; 35:15; Ezr 2:64-65; 3:10-11; Ne 12:27-47; Ps 33:1-3; 68:4, 25-26, 32; 81:1-3; 87:7; 92:1-3; 95:1-2; 98:1-8; 104:33; 105:2; 135:1-3; 144:9; 149:1-3, 6; 150:1-6; Mk 14:26; Lk 14:15; Eph 5:19; Col 3:16; Heb 2:12). At the offering of sacrifices (2Ch 29:27-28). In idolatrous worship (Da 3:4-7, 10, 15). For dancing (Mt 11:17). In joy (Ge 31:27; 2Sa 19:35; Job 21:12; Ecc 2:8; Isa 5:12). In revelry (Am 5:23; 6:5). In mourning (2Ch 35:25). In preparing for funerals (Mt 9:23).
 Refrained from in sorrow (Job 30:31; Pr 25:20; Isa 16:10; 24:8-9; Eze 26:13; Rev 18:22). Captive Jews refrained from (Ps 137:1-4).
 Teachers of (1Ch 15:22; 25:7-8; 2Ch 23:13). Physical effect of, on people (1Sa 16:15-16, 23; Eze 33:32). Choir director (Ne 12:42). Chief musician (Ne 12:42; Hab 3:19). Chambers for musicians in the temple (Eze 40:44). In heaven (Rev 5:8-9; 14:2-3; 15:2-3).
 Allegorical (Rev 5:8-9; 14:2-3; 15:2-3; 18:22). Symbolic of judgment (Isa 3:16). Of God's emotions (Isa 30:29, 32; Jer 31:4).

Instruments of:
 Invented by Jubal (Ge 4:21), David (1Ch 23:5; 2Ch 7:6; 29:26; Am 6:5). Made by Solomon (1Ki 10:12; 2Ch 9:11; Ecc 2:8), Tyrians (Eze 28:13).

 Kinds—
 Horn (Da 3:5, 7, 10). *See Trumpet.* Cymbal (1Ch 15:19, 28; 1Co 13:1). *See Cymbal.* Flute (Ge 4:21; Da 3:5, 7, 10, 15). Gittith, possibly a stringed instrument (Ps 8; 81; 84, T). Harp (1Sa 10:5; 16:16, 23; 1Ch 16:5). *See Harp.* Lyre (1Ch 16:5). *See Lyre.* Pipe (1Sa 10:5; Isa 30:20; Da 3:5, 10, 15). *See Pipe.* Sistrum (2Sa 6:5). Tambourine (Ps 15:20). *See Tambourine.* Trumpet (Jos 6:4). *See Trumpet.* Zither (Da 3:5, 7, 10, 15).

Symbols Used in:
 Many of psalm titles contain terms that may indicate the tunes of songs popular at the time of the psalmists. This practice of setting new words to an old tune is common to the hymnology of every age.
 Aijeleth Shahar, NIV "To [the tune of] The Doe of the Morning" (Ps 22:T). This is probably a tune designation.
 Alamoth (1Ch 15:20; Ps 46:T). The Hebrew word means "maidens." It may refer to "maidens playing tambourines" to accompany the music.
 Al-taschith, NIV "[To the tune of] Do Not Destroy" (Titles of Ps 57-59; 75). The phrase also occurs in Isa 65:8, leading some to deduce it is the name of a vintage or wine-making song.
 Gittith (Titles of Pss 8; 81; 84). This may mean a Gittite lyre or the name of a tune.
 Higgaion (Ps 9:16). The word is also translated "meditation" (Ps 19:14), "melody" (Ps 92:3), and "mutter" (La 3:62). Combined with "Selah," it may have been intended to indicate a pause in the vocal music while the instruments played an interlude, a time for devout meditation.
 Jonath-elem-rechokim, NIV "To [the tune of] A Dove on Distant Oaks" (Ps 56:T). This is probably a tune designation.

Mahalath (Ps 53:T), *Mahalath Leannoth* (Ps 88:T). The Hebrew appears to be the word for "suffering" or "sickness." Perhaps it indicates that the psalms are to be used in a time of affliction, such as when the godless mock.

Maskil (Titles of Pss 32; 42; 44; 45; 52; 53; 54; 55; 74; 79; 88; 89; 142). Related to a word meaning "to instruct" or "to become wise by instruction," it may indicate a psalm that instructs or that is skillfully made.

Miktam (Titles of Pss 16; 56-60). Variously related to words for "golden," "inscription," and "atonement."

Muth-Labben, NIV "To [the tune of] The Death of the Son" (Ps 9:T). This may be a variant of *alamoth* or a funeral song.

Neginah and *Neginoth*, NIV "stringed instruments" (Titles of Pss 4; 54-55; 61; 67; Hab 3:19). This seems to indicate that the song should be accompanied by stringed instruments.

Nehiloth, NIV "flutes" (Ps 5:T). This seems to indicate accompaniment (perhaps exclusively) by wind instruments (Ps 5).

Selah. This term appears seventy-one times in the Psalms and in Hab 3:3, 9, 13. Its meaning is not clear. Possibly it signified a pause in the vocal music while an instrumental interlude played.

Sheminith. (1Ch 15:21; Ps 6:T; 12:T). Related to the word for "eighth," this may have indicated an octave or accompaniment by a eight-stringed instrument.

Shiggaion (Ps 7:T) and *Shigionoth* (Hab 3:1). These could be tune designations or literary categories.

Shoshannim NIV "To [the tune of] Lilies" (Ps 45; 69:T) and *Shushan-eduth*, NIV "To [the tune of] The Lily of the Covenant" (Ps 60:T; 80:T). Again, these are probably tune designations.

MUSTARD SEED Kingdom of heaven compared to (Mt 13:31-32; Mk 4:31-32; Lk 13:19). Faith compared to (Mt 17:20).

MUSTER Of troops (1Sa 14:17; 2Sa 20:4; 1Ki 20:26; 2Ki 25:29; Isa 13:4). *See Armies.*

MUTE Stricken of God (Ex 4:11; Lk 1:20, 64), miraculous healing of, by Jesus (Mt 9:32-33; 12:22; 15:30-31; Mk 7:37; 9:17, 25-26). *See Deafness.*

MUTH-LABBEN NIV "To [the tune of] The Death of the Son" (Ps 9:T). Probably name of the tune to which the psalm was sung. *See Music, Symbols Used in.*

MUTILATORS Sarcastic term for Judaizers who required circumcision for salvation (Php 3:2). *See Circumcision.*

MUTINY Israelites against Moses (Nu 14:4). *See Conspiracy; Rebellion.*

MUZZLE Mosaic law forbade muzzling of oxen when they were treading out the grain (Dt 25:4).

MYRA A city of Lycia. Paul visits (Ac 27:5-6).

MYRRH A fragrant gum. A product of the land of Canaan (SS 4:6, 14; 5:1). One of the compounds in the anointing oil (Ex 30:23). Used as a perfume (Est 2:12; Ps 45:8; Pr 7:17; SS 3:6; 5:13). Brought by wise men as a present to Jesus (Mt 2:11). Offered to Jesus on the cross (Mk 15:23). Used for embalming (Jn 19:39). Trade in (Ge 37:25; 43:11).

MYRTLE (Ne 8:15; Isa 41:19; 55:13; Zec 1:8). *See Plants of the Bible; Tree.*

MYSIA District occupying NW end of Asia Minor bounded by the Aegean, the Hellespont, the Propontis, Bithynia, Phrygia, and Lydia. In 133 B.C. it fell to the Romans and they made it a part of the province of Asia. Traversed by Paul (Ac 16:7-8).

MYSTERIES
Of God (Dt 29:29; Job 15:8; Ps 25:14; Pr 3:32; Am 3:5; Heb 5:11).
Of redemption (Mt 11:25; 13:11, 35; Mk 4:11; Lk 8:10; Ro 16:25-26; 1Co 2:7-10; 2Co 3:12-18; Eph 1:9-10; 3:3-5, 9, 18-19; 6:19; Col 1:25-27; 2:2; 4:3; 1Ti 3:9, 16; 1Pe 1:10-12; Rev 10:7).
Of regeneration (Jn 3:8-12).
Of iniquity (2Th 2:7).

MYSTERY RELIGIONS Greco-Roman religious movement that thrived from c. 700 B.C. to A.D. 400. To gain access to the divine mysteries, specially appointed priests carefully prepared individuals through stages of initiation, instruction, and secret revelation. The enlighted were then joined with the divine and could receive healing, success, and immortality. Though the word "mystery" is used in the NT (Ro 11:25; 16:25; 1Co 15:51; Eph 3:3-9), the openness of the preaching of the gospel makes it clear that Christianity is not a mystery religion. *See Mysteries.*

MYTHS Untrue stories or speculations about religion that are contrary to sound doctrine and godliness (1Ti 1:4; 4:7; 2Ti 4:4; Tit 1:14).

N

NAAM (*pleasant*). Son of Caleb (1Ch 4:15).

NAAMAH (*pleasant*).
1. Daughter of Lamech and Zillah (Ge 4:22).
2. Wife of Solomon; mother of Rehoboam (1Ki 14:21, 31).
3. Town in Judah (Jos 15:41), site unknown.

NAAMAN, NAAMITE (*pleasantness*).
1. Son of Benjamin (Ge 46:21).
2. Son of Bela and his clan (Nu 26:40; 1Ch 8:4).
3. Son of Ehud (1Ch 8:7).
4. A Syrian general healed of leprosy by Elisha (2Ki 5:1-23; Lk 4:27).

NAAMATHITE (*of Naamath*). Designation of Zophar (Job 2:11; 11:1; 20:1; 42:9).

NAARAH (*[young] woman*).
1. Wife of Ashhur (1Ch 4:5f).
2. Place on border of Ephraim (Jos 16:7).

NAARAI (*young man of Yahweh*). Also called Paarai. One of David's heroes (1Ch 11:37).

NAARAN A city in the eastern limits of Ephraim (1Ch 7:28).

NAARATH *See Naarah, 2.*

NAASHON, NAASSON *See Nahshon.*

NABAL (*fool*). Rich shepherd of Maon in Judah who insulted David and was saved from vengeance by his wife Abigail, who after Nabal's death became David's wife (1Sa 25:1-42).

NABATEA, NABATEANS Arabian tribe named in the Apocrypha but not in Bible. Their king, Aretas IV, controlled Damascus when Paul was there (2Co 11:32). Capital was Petra. *See Petra; Sela.*

NABONIDAS, NABONIDUS (*[pagan god] Nabu is wonderful*). Last ruler of Neo-Babylonian Empire (556-539 B.C.), his son Belshazzar (Da 5; 7:1; 8:1) was coregent with him from the third year of his reign.

NABOPOLASSAR (*[pagan god] Nabu protect the son!*). First ruler of the Neo-Babylonian Empire (626-605 B.C.). Allied with Medes and Scythians, he overthrew the Assyrian Empire, destroying Nineveh in 612 B.C., as prophesied (Zep 2:13-15).

NABOTH (*a sprout*). A Jezreelite. His vineyard forcibly taken by Ahab; stoned at the instigation of Jezebel (1Ki 21:1-19). His murder avenged (2Ki 9:21-36).

NACHOR *See Nahor, 1.*

NACON (*established*). Benjamite at whose threshing floor Uzzah was killed for touching the ark (2Sa 6:6). Also called Kidon (1Ch 13:9, ftn). The place was subsequently called Perez Uzzah. *See Perez Uzzah.*

NADAB (*volunteer, free will offering*).
1. Son of Aaron (Ex 6:23). Called to Mount Sinai with Moses and Aaron to worship (Ex 24:1, 9-10). Set apart to priesthood (Ex 28:1, 4, 40-43). Offers unauthorized fire to God and is destroyed (Lev 10:1-2; Nu 3:4; 26:61). Buried (Lev 10:4-5). His family forbidden to mourn (Lev 10:6-7).
2. Son and successor of Jeroboam (1Ki 14:20). His wicked reign; murdered by Baasha (1Ki 15:25-31).
3. Great-grandson of Jerahmeel (1Ch 2:28, 30).
4. A Benjamite (1Ch 8:30; 9:36).

NAGGAI An ancestor of Jesus (Lk 3:25).

NAGGING Proverbs concerning (Pr 19:13; 21:9, 19; 25:24; 26:21; 27:15). Jezebel's destroys Samson (Jdg 16:16).

NAHALAL (*watering place*). Also spelled Nahalol (Jdg 1:30). A Levitical city within Zebulun's territory (Jos 19:15; 21:35; Jdg 1:30).

NAHALIEL (*wadi of God [El]*). A station of the Israelites (Nu 21:19).

NAHALOL, NAHALLAL *See Nahalal.*

NAHAM (*repent, console*). Descendant of Judah through Caleb (1Ch 4:19).

NAHAMANI (*Yahweh has consoled*). A Jewish exile (Ne 7:7).

NAHARAI Beerothite, Joab's armor-bearer (2Sa 23:37).

NAHARAIM *See Aram Naharaim.*

NAHASH (*viper* or *copper*).
1. Ammonite king defeated by Saul (1Sa 11:1-2; 12:12).
2. Ammonite king whose son insulted David's messengers, and David avenged the insult (2Sa 10; 1Ch 19).
3. Father of Abigail and Zeruiah (2Sa 17:25).
See also Ir Nahash.

NAHATH (*descent; possibly rest*).
1. Son of Reuel (Ge 36:13, 17; 1Ch 1:37).
2. A Levite, grandson of the Kohathite Elkanah (1Ch 6:26); probably the same as Tohu (1Sa 1:1), and Toah (1Ch 6:34).
3. A Levite and overseer of the sacred offerings in the time of Hezekiah (2Ch 31:13).

NAHBI (perhaps *hidden* or *timid*). A leader of Naphtali and one of the twelve spies (Nu 13:14).

NAHOR (apparently from Assyrian place name Til-Nahiri, *the mound of Nahuru*).
1. Grandfather of Abraham (Ge 11:22-26; 1Ch 1:26). In the lineage of Christ (Lk 3:34).
2. Brother of Abraham (Ge 11:26; Jos 24:2). Marriage and descendants of (Ge 11:27, 29; 22:20-24; 24:15, 24).

NAAMAN, NAAMITE (*pleasantness*).
1. Son of Benjamin (Ge 46:21).
2. Son of Bela and his clan (Nu 26:40; 1Ch 8:4).
3. Son of Ehud (1Ch 8:7).
4. A Syrian general healed of leprosy by Elisha (2Ki 5:1-23; Lk 4:27).

NAHSHON (*small viper*). A captain of Judah's host (Ex 6:23; Nu 1:7; 2:3; 7:12, 17; 10:14). In the lineage of Christ (Mt 1:4; Lk 3:32).

NAHUM (*comfort*).
1. Author of book of Nahum; native of Elkosh; prophesied 663-612 B.C. (Na 1:1; 3:8-11).
2. An ancestor of Jesus (Lk 3:25).

NAHUM, BOOK OF
Author: The prophet Nahum
Date: Between 663 and 612 B.C.
Outline:
I. Title (1:1).
II. Nineveh's Judge (1:2-15).
 A. The Lord's Kindness and Sternness (1:2-8).
 B. Nineveh's Overthrow and Judah's Joy (1:9-15).
III. Nineveh's Judgment (ch. 2).
 A. Nineveh Besieged (2:1-10).
 B. Nineveh's Desolation Contrasted With Her Former Glory (2:11-13).
IV. Nineveh's Total Destruction (ch. 3).
 A. Nineveh's Sins (3:1-4).
 B. Nineveh's Doom (3:5-19).
See Prophets, The Minor.

NAIL
1. Fingernail (Dt 21:12; Da 4:33; 7:19).
2. Tent peg (Jdg 4:21-22; 5:26), peg driven into wall to hang things on (Ezr 9:8; Isa 22:23-25).
3. Nails of metal: iron, bronze, gold (1Ch 22:3; 2Ch 3:9).

NAIN (*pleasant, delightful*). A city in Galilee. Jesus restores to life a widow's son in (Lk 7:11).

NAIOTH (*dwellings*). Place in or near Ramah of Benjamin where Samuel lived with a band of prophets (1Sa 19:18-20:1).

NAKED
1. Without any clothing (Ge 2:25; 3:7-11).
2. Poorly clad (Job 22:6).
3. Without an outer garment (Jn 21:7). Often used figuratively for spiritual poverty (Rev 3:17) and a lack of power (Ge 42:9).

NAME Value of a good (Pr 22:1; Ecc 7:1). A new name given, to persons who have spiritual adoption (Isa 62:2), to Abraham (Ge 17:5), Sarah (Ge 17:15), Jacob (Ge 32:28), Peter (Mt 16:18), Paul (Ac 13:9). Intercessional influence of the name of Jesus. *See Jesus the Christ, In His Name.*
Symbolic (Hos 1:3-4, 6, 9; 2:1), of prestige (1Ki 1:47).

NAMES OF GOD *See God, Names of; Titles and Names.*

NAMES OF JESUS *See Jesus the Christ, Names, Appellations, and Titles of; Titles and Names.*

NANNAR (*lightgiver*). Name given at Ur to Babylonian moon-god Sin.

NAOMI (*my joy*). Wife of Elimelech; mother-in-law of Ruth; lived in Moab; returns to Bethlehem; kinswoman of Boaz (Ru 1-4).

NAPHISH (*refreshed*). The eleventh son of Ishmael; progenitor of a tribe, probably the Nephussim (Ge 25:15; 1Ch 1:31; 5:19).

NAPHOTH (*heights*). A town assigned to Manasseh, also called Dor and Naphoth Dor (Jos 17:11, ftn). Conquered by Joshua (Jos 11:2; 12:23). *See Dor; Naphoth Dor.*

NAPHOTH DOR (*heights of Dor*). A town assigned to Manasseh, also called Dor and Naphoth (Jos 17:11, ftn). *See Dor; Naphoth.*

NAPHTALI, NAPHTALITES (*wrestling*).
1. Son of Jacob and Bilhah (Ge 30:7-8; 35:25). Jacob blesses (Ge 49:21). Sons of (Ge 46:24; 1Ch 7:13).
2. Tribe of. Census of (Nu 1:42-43; 26:48-50). Position assigned to, in camp and march (Nu 2:25-31; 10:25-27). Moses' benediction on (Dt 33:23). Inheritance of (Jos 19:32-39; Jdg 1:33; Eze 48:3). Defeat Sisera (Jdg 4:6, 10; 5:18). Follow Gideon (Jdg 6:35; 7:23). Aid in conveying the ark to Jerusalem (Ps 68:27). Military operations of (1Ch 12:34, 40), against (1Ki 15:20; 2Ki 15:29; 2Ch 16:4).
Prophecies concerning (Isa 9:1-2; Rev 7:6).

NAPHTUHITES The inhabitants of central Egypt (Ge 10:13; 1Ch 1:11).

NAPKIN Cloth for wiping perspiration off (Lk 19:20; Jn 11:44; 20:7).

NARCISSUS A believer at Rome (Ro 16:11).

NARD An aromatic plant (SS 4:13-14). *See Perfume; Plants of the Bible.*

NATHAN (*gift*).
1. Prophet during reigns of David and Solomon; told David that not he but Solomon was to build the temple (2Sa 7; 1Ch 17), rebuked David for sin with Bathsheba (2Sa 12:1-25), helped get throne for Solomon (1Ki 1:8-53), wrote chronicles of reign of David (1Ch 29:29) and Solomon (2Ch 9:29), associated with David in arranging musical services for house of God (2Ch 29:25).
2. Son of David (2Sa 5:14; 1Ch 14:4).
3. Father of Igal (2Sa 23:36).
4. Judahite (1Ch 2:36).
5. Israelite who returned from the Exile (Ezr 8:16).
6. Man who put away his foreign wife (Ezr 10:39).

NATHANAEL (*gift of God [El]*). Disciple of Jesus (Jn 1:45-51), identified commonly with Bartholomew. Church Fathers use the two names interchangeably.

NATHAN-MELECH (*gift of king* or *gift of Melek, Molech, Malk [pagan god]*). Officer of Josiah (2Ki 23:11).

NATION People divided into nations after the Flood (Ge 10:1-32). Ordained of God (Ac 17:26). Righteousness exalts (Pr 14:34).

Peace of:
(Job 34:29; Ps 33:12; 89:15-18). Promises of peace to (Lev 26:6; 1Ki 2:33; 2Ki 20:19; 1Ch 22:9; Ps 29:11; 46:9; 72:3, 7; 128:6; Isa 2:4; 14:4-7; 60:17-18; 65:25; Jer 30:10; 50:34; Eze 34:25-28; Hos 2:18; Mic 4:3-4; Zec 1:11; 3:10; 8:4-5; 9:10; 14:11). Prayer for peace (Jer 29:7; 1Ti 2:1-2). Peace given by God (Jos 21:44; 1Ch 22:18; 23:25; Ps 147:13-14; Ecc 3:8; Isa 45:7). Instances of national peace (Jos 14:15; Jdg 3:11, 30; 1Ki 4:24-25). *See War.*

Sins of:
Involved in sins, of rulers (Ge 20:4, 9; 2Sa 24:10-17; 1Ki 15:26, 30, 34; 2Ki 24:3; 1Ch 21:7-17; Jer 15:4), of other individuals, as Achan (Jos 7:1, 11-26).
Atonement made for (2Ch 29:21). Penitent, promises to (Lev 26:40-42; Dt 4:29-31; 5:29; 30:1-10; 2Ch 7:13-14; Jer 3:22).
In adversity, prayer of (Jdg 6:7; 10:10; 21:2-4; 2Ch 7:13-14; Ps 74; Jer 3:21; 31:18; Joel 2:12), prayer for (Ezr 9:6-15; Ne 1:4-11; Ps 74; 84:1-7; Isa 63:7-19; Jer 6:14; 8:11, 20-21; 9:1-2; 14:7, 20; La 2:20-22; Da 9:3-21). *See Sin, National.*

Judgments Against:
Chastisement of (Lev 18:24-30; 26:28; Dt 11:2; 2Ch 6:24, 26, 28; 7:13-14; Ps 106:43; Isa 14:26-27; Jer 2:30; 5:29; 18:6-10; 25:12-33; 30:14; 31:18-20; 46:28; Eze 2:3-5; 39:23-24; Da 7:9-12; 9:3-16; La 1:5; Hos 7:12; 10:10; Joel 1:1-20; Am 9:9; Zep 3:6, 8; Hag 2:17). Perish (Ps 9:17; Isa 60:12).
Judgments denounced against, on account of its unrighteousness (Dt 9:5; Ps 9:17; Isa 3:4-8; 14:24-27; 19:4; 59:1-15; 60:12; Jer 2:19, 35-37; 5:6-29; 6; 9:7-26; 12:14, 17; 18:6-10; 25:12-33; 50:45-46; 51; Eze 2:9-10; 7; 22:12-31; 24:6-24; 33:25-29; Hos 4:1-10; 7:12-13, 16; 13; Am 2; 3; 5; 9:8-10; Mic 6:13-16; Zep 3:8).
Instances of punishment of: The Canaanites (Dt 9:5). The Sodomites (Ge 19:24-25, 28-29; La 4:6). The Egyptians (Ex 7-11; 12:1-36; 14). The Israelites (2Sa 21:1; 24:14-16; 2Ki 24:2-4, 20; 2Ch 28:1, 5-8, 16-19; 29:8-9; 30:7; 36:16-20; Ezr 9:7; Ne 9:36-37; Jer 2:15-16; 30:11-15; La 1:3, 8, 14; Eze 36:16-20; 39:17-24; Joel 1:1-20; Am 4:6-11).
See Government; Kings; Rulers.

NATIONAL RELIGION Supported by taxes (Ex 30:11-16; 38:26). Ministers of, supported by state (1Ki 18:19; 2Ch 11:13-15). Subverted by Jeroboam (1Ki 12:26-33; 2Ch 11:13-15). Idolatrous, established by Jeroboam (1Ki 12:26-33).

NATIONS BLESSED BY ABRAHAM (Ge 12:2; 18:18; 22:18; 26:4; Ac 3:25; Gal 3:8).

NATURAL Natural death (Nu 16:29; 19:16, 18), sleep (Jn 11:13), physical relations (Ro 1:26-27), body (1Co 15:44, 46), instincts (Jude 1:19).

NATURAL RELIGION *See Religion, Natural.*

NATURALIZATION Giving rights of citizenship to aliens (Ac 22:28).
Figurative (Eph 2:12-13, 19).

NATURE The entire compass of one's life (Jas 3:6). The inherent character of a person or thing (Ro 1:26; 2:14; 11:21-24). Disposition (2Pe 1:4). Sinful nature (Ro 7:18, 25; 1Co 5:5; Gal 5:13).
Laws of, uniform in operation: In the vegetable kingdom (Ge 1:11, 12; Mt 7:16-18; Lk 6:43-44; 1Co 15:36-38; Gal 6:7; Jas 3:12), animal kingdom (Ge 1:21, 24-25; Jer 13:23), succession of seasons (Ge 8:22), succession of day and night (Ge 8:22; Jer 33:20).

NAUGHTINESS *See Sin.*

NAUM *See Nahum.*

NAVE *See Rim.*

NAVEL "Belly button" (SS 7:2).

NAVIGATION Sounding in (Ac 27:28). *See Commerce; Mariner; Navy.*

NAVY Solomon's (1Ki 9:26), Hiram's (1Ki 10:11), of Kittim (Da 11:30, ftn, 40).
See Commerce; Mariner.

NAZARENE (possibly *sprout, branch*).
1. Inhabitant of Nazareth (Mt 2:23); possibly a wordplay on the Hebrew *nezer*, "branch," a messianic title (cf. Isa 11:1). *See Branch.*
2. A Christian (Ac 24:5).

NAZARETH (possibly *sprout, branch* or *watchtower*). A village in Galilee. Joseph and Mary live at (Mt 2:23; Lk 1:26-27, 56; 2:4, 39, 51). Jesus from (Mt 21:11; Mk 1:24; 10:47; Lk 4:34; 18:37; 24:19). People of, reject Jesus (Lk 4:16-30). Its name infamous (Jn 1:46).

NAZARETH DECREE An inscription on a slab of white marble, dating c. A.D. 40-50, by Claudius Caesar, found in Nazareth, decreeing capital punishment for anyone disturbing graves and tombs.

NAZIRITE(S) (*one under sacred vow*). An Israelite who consecrated himself or herself and took a vow of separation and self-imposed abstinence for the purpose of some special service. The Nazirite vow included a renunciation of wine, prohibition of

the use of the razor, and avoidance of contact with a dead body. The period of time for the vow was anywhere from 30 days to a lifetime (Nu 6:1-21; Jdg 13:5-7; Am 2:11, 12).
Instances of: Samson (Jdg 13:5, 7; 16:17). Samuel (1Sa 1:11). Recabites (Jer 35). John the Baptist (Mt 11:18; Lk 1:15; 7:33).
See Abstinence; Wine.

NEAH A border town in Zebulun (Jos 19:13). The site is unknown.

NEAPOLIS (*new city*). A seaport of Macedonia. Paul visits (Ac 16:11).

NEARIAH (*[young] man of Yahweh*).
1. Son of Shemaiah (1Ch 3:22-23).
2. A Simeonite leader (1Ch 4:42).

NEBAI (*thrive*). Signer of the covenant with Nehemiah (Ne 10:19).

NEBAIOTH Son of Ishmael (Ge 25:13; 28:9; 36:3; 1Ch 1:29). Prophecies concerning (Isa 60:7).

NEBALLAT A town occupied by the Benjamites after the Captivity (Ne 11:34).

NEBAT (*look to, regard [approvingly]*). Father of Jeroboam (1Ki 11:26; 12:2).

NEBO (*height* or *Mount of Nabu [Nebo]*).
1. A city allotted to Reuben (Nu 32:3, 38; 1Ch 5:8). Prophecies concerning (Isa 15:2; Jer 48:1, 22).
2. A mountain range E of the Jordan. Moses views Canaan from (Dt 32:49-50), dies on (Dt 34:1).
3. A city in Judah (Ezr 2:29; Ne 7:33).
4. The ancestor of certain Jews (Ezr 10:43).
5. A Babylonian idol (Isa 46:1).

NEBO-SARSEKIM A prince of Nebuchadnezzar who entered Jerusalem when it fell (Jer 39:3, ftn).

NEBUCHADNEZZAR (*Nebo protect my boundary stone* BDB and IDB; *Nebo protect my son!* KB).
1. The fourth Dynasty ruler of the Old Babylonian Empire (c. 1140 B.C.).
2. Ruler of the Neo-Babylonian Empire (605-562 B.C.); son of Nabopolassar; conquered Pharaoh Neco at Carchemish (605 B.C.); destroyed Jerusalem and carried Israelites into captivity (587 B.C.) (2Ki 25:1-21); succeeded by son Evil-Merodach. Often mentioned in OT (1Ch 6:15; 2Ch 36; Ezr 1:7; 2:1; 5:12, 14; 6:5; Ne 7:6; Est 2:6; Jer 21:2; 52:4; Da 1-5).

NEBUSHAZBAN (*Nebo [Nabu] save me!*). Chief officer of Nebuchadnezzar (Jer 39:11-14).

NEBUZARADAN (*Nebo [Nabu] has given seed [offspring]*). Nebuchadnezzar's general when the Babylonians besieged Jerusalem (2Ki 25:1, 11-12, 20; Jer 52:12ff), conducted captives to Babylon.

NECK Term often used in Bible with literal and figurative meanings (Ex 32:9; Dt 9:13; Ps 75:5; Ac 7:51).

NECKLACE Ornamental chain worn around the neck (Isa 3:19).

NECO Pharaoh of Egypt (609-595 B.C.); defeated Josiah at battle of Megiddo (2Ki 23:29; 2Ch 35:20ff); defeated by Nebuchadnezzar at battle of Carchemish (2Ki 24:7; Isa 10:9; Jer 46:2).

NECROMANCER, NECROMANCY Consulting with the dead; forbidden by Mosaic law (Dt 18:10-11), King Saul consulted with the medium of Endor (1Sa 28:7-25). Judgment upon (Isa 8:19; 29:4).
See Medium; Sorcery; Witchcraft.

NEDABIAH (*Yahweh volunteers*). A son of Jehoiachin (1Ch 3:18).

NEEDLE'S EYE Figure used by Jesus (Mt 19:24; Mk 10:25; Lk 18:25). Jesus does not say that salvation is threatened by possessing riches but that those who are wealthy will have great difficulty subordinating their riches to the will of God; in addition, a wealthy man will not enter the kingdom of God based on his riches, but only on the saving grace of God and the finished work of Jesus Christ (Mt 19:25-26).

NEEDLEWORK Art of working in with the needle various kinds of colored threads in cloth (Jdg 5:30; Ps 45:14).

NEESING NIV "snorting" (Job 41:18).

NEGEV (*dry [land]*, hence *south country*). The desert region lying to the S of Judea, sometimes translated "the south" (Ge 12:9; 13:1; 20:1; Nu 13:29; 1Sa 27:5-6).

NEGINAH *See Music, Symbols Used in.*

NEGINOTH *See Music, Symbols Used in.*

NEHELAMITE (perhaps *of Nehelam* or a play on the word for *dream*). Designation of Shemaiah, a false prophet (Jer 29:24, 31-32).

NEHEMIAH (*Yahweh has comforted*).
1. Leader of Jews who returned with Zerubbabel (Ezr 2:2; Ne 7:7).
2. Son of Azbuk; helped rebuild walls of Jerusalem (Ne 3:16).
3. Son of Hacaliah; governor of Persian province of Judah after 444 B.C.; cupbearer to King Artaxerxes of Persia (Ne 1:11; 2:1); rebuilt walls of Jerusalem (Ne 1:4-6); cooperated with Ezra in numerous reforms (Ne 8); nothing known of the end of his life.

NEHEMIAH, BOOK OF

Author: Nehemiah

Date: c. 430 B.C.

Outline:
I. Nehemiah's First Administration (chs. 1-12).
 A. Nehemiah's Response to the Situation in Jerusalem (ch. 1).
 1. News of the plight of Jerusalem (1:1-4).
 2. Nehemiah's prayer (1:5-11).
 B. Nehemiah's Journey to Jerusalem (ch. 2).
 1. The king response (2:1-8).
 2. The journey itself (2:9-10).
 3. Nehemiah's nocturnal inspection of the walls (2:11-16).
 4. His exhortation to rebuild (2:17-18).
 5. The opposition of Sanballat, Tobiah and Geshem (2:19-20).
 C. List of the Builders of the Wall (ch. 3).
 1. The northern section (3:1-7).
 2. The western section (3:8-13).
 3. The southern section (3:14).
 4. The eastern section (3:15-32).
 D. Opposition to Rebuilding the Wall (ch. 4).
 1. The derision of Sanballat and Tobiah (4:1-5).
 2. The threat of attack (4:6-15).
 3. Rebuilding the wall (4:16-23).
 E. Social and Economic Problems (ch. 5).
 1. The complaints of the poor (5:1-5).
 2. The cancellation of debts (5:6-13).
 3. Nehemiah's unselfish example (5:14-19).
 F. The Wall Rebuilt Despite Opposition (ch. 6).
 1. Attempts to snare Nehemiah (6:1-9).
 2. The hiring of false prophets (6:10-14).
 3. The completion of the wall (6:15-19).
 G. List of Exiles (7:1-73a).
 1. Provisions for the protection of Jerusalem (7:1-3).
 2. Nehemiah's discovery of the list of returnees (7:4-5).
 3. The returnees delineated (7:6-72).
 4. Settlement of the exiles (7:73a).
 H. Ezra's Preaching and the Outbreak of Revival (7:73b-10:39).
 1. The public exposition of the Scriptures (7:73b-8:12).
 2. The Feast of Tabernacles (8:13-18).
 3. A day of fasting, confession and prayer (9:1-5a).
 4. A recital of God's dealings with Israel (9:5b-31).
 5. Confession of sins (9:32-37).
 6. A binding agreement (9:38).
 7. A list of those who sealed it (10:1-29).
 8. Provisions of the agreement (10:30-39).
 I. New Residents of Judah and Jerusalem (ch. 11).
 1. New residents for Jerusalem (11:1-24).
 a. Introductory remarks (11:1-2).
 b. Residents from Judah (11:4b-6).
 c. From Benjamin (11:7-9).
 d. From the priests (11:10-14).
 e. From the Levites (11:15-18).
 f. From the temple staff (11:25-36).
 2. New residents for Judah (11:25-36).
 a. Places settled by those from Judah (11:25-30).
 b. Places settled by those from Benjamin (11:31-35).
 c. Transfer of Levites from Judah to Benjamin (11:36).
 J. Lists of Priests and the Dedication of the Wall (ch. 12).
 1. Priests and Levites from the first return (12:1-9).
 2. High priests and Levites since Joiakim (12:10-26).
 3. Dedication of the wall of Jerusalem (12:27-43).
 4. Regulation of the temple offerings and services (12:44-47).
II. Nehemiah's Second Administration (ch. 13).
 A. Abuses During His Absence (13:1-5).
 1. Mixed marriages (13:1-3).
 2. Tobiah's occupation of the temple quarters (13:4-5).
 B. Nehemiah's Return (13:6-9).
 1. His arrival (13:6-7).
 2. His expulsion of Tobiah (13:8-9).
 C. Reorganization and Reforms (13:10-31).
 1. Offerings for the temple staff (13:10-14).
 2. The abuse of the Sabbath (13:15-22).
 3. Mixed marriages (13:23-29).
 4. Provisions of wood and firstfruits (13:30-31).

NEHILOTH *See Music, Symbols Used in.*

NEHUM (*comfort*). Chief of Judah who returned with Zerubbabel; also called "Rehum" (Ezr 2:2; Ne 7:7).

NEHUSHTA (*[strong as* or *color of] bronze*). Wife of Jehoiakim, king of Judah, and mother of Jehoiachin (2Ki 24:6, 8).

NEHUSHTAN (combination of *bronze* and *viper*). The bronze serpent (2Ki 18:4).

NEIEL A landmark on the boundary of Asher (Jos 19:27).

NEIGHBOR Defined (Lk 10:25-37). Duty to, defined in the Golden Rule (Mt 7:12).
Love does no harm to (Ro 13:10). Love for, commanded (Lev 19:18; Mt 19:19; 22:39; Mk 12:31-33; Lk 10:25-37; Ro 13:9-10; Gal 5:14; Jas 2:8-9). Kindness to, commanded (Ex 23:4-5; Dt 22:1-4; Isa 58:6-7; Gal 6:10). Charitableness toward, commanded (Ro 15:2). Benevolence toward, commanded (Pr 3:28-29). Righteous treatment of, commanded (Zec 8:16-17). Honesty toward, commanded (Lev 19:13). Kindness to, rewarded (Isa 58:8-14; Mt 25:34-46). Righteous treatment of, rewarded (Ps 15:1-3).
False witness against, forbidden (Ex 20:16; Lev 19:16). Hatred of, forbidden (Lev 19:17). Oppression of, denounced (Jer 22:13). Penalty for violation of the rights of (Lev 6:2-5).
See Duty; Mankind.

NEKEB *See Adami Nekeb.*

NEKODA Head of a family of temple servants who could not prove Israelite descent (Ne 7:50, 62; Ezr 2:60).

N

NEMUEL, NEMUELITE
1. Brother of Dathan and Abiram (Nu 26:9).
2. Son of Simeon (Nu 26:12; 1Ch 4:24). Also called Jemuel (Ge 46:10; Ex 6:15). *See Jemuel.*

NEPHEG (*sprout, shoot*).
1. Brother of Korah, Dathan, and Abiram (Ex 6:21).
2. Son of David (2Sa 5:15; 1Ch 3:7; 14:6).

NEPHEW Grandson (Jdg 12:14), descendant (Job 18:19; Isa 14:22), grandchild (1Ti 5:4).

NEPHILIM (*ones falling [upon], hence violent ones, possibly giants*). Antediluvians (Ge 6:4), aboriginal dwellers in Canaan (Nu 13:32-33), not angelic fallen beings (Dt 1:28).

NEPHISH *See Naphish.*

NEPHISHESIM *See Nephussim.*

NEPHTHALIM, NEPTHALIM *See Naphtali.*

NEPHTOAH (*an opening*). Spring and town on the border of Judah and Benjamin (Jos 15:9; 18:15), two miles NW of Jerusalem; modern Lifta.

NEPHUSSIM A family of the temple servants (Ezr 2:50; Ne 7:52).

NEPOTISM Of Joseph (Ge 47:11-12). Of Saul (1Sa 14:50). Of David (2Sa 8:16; 19:13). Of Nehemiah (Ne 7:2).

NER (*lamp*).
1. Father of Abner (1Sa 14:50; 26:14).
2. Grandfather of King Saul (1Ch 8:33).

NEREUS (*pagan Greek deity*). A Christian at Rome (Ro 16:15).

NERGAL (*pagan deity*). Babylonian deity of destruction (2Ki 17:30).

NERGAL-SHAREZER (*Nergal protect the prince!*). The name of princes of Babylon (Jer 39:3, 13).

NERI (*lamp of Yahweh*). An ancestor of Jesus (Lk 3:27).

NERIAH (*lamp of Yahweh*). Father of Baruch (Jer 32:12).

NERIGLISSAR *See Nergal-Sharezer.*

NERO (*family name*). The fifth Roman emperor (A.D. 54-68); killed many Christians when Rome burned in A.D. 64; called "Caesar" (Ac 25:11; Php 4:22).

NEST Bird's (Nu 24:21; Mt 8:20). Birds stir up (Dt 32:11).

NET Of interwoven chains (1Ki 7:17). Hidden in a pit (Ps 35:7-8). Set for birds (Pr 1:17), wild animals (Isa 51:20). Fish caught in (Mt 4:18-21; 13:47; Lk 5:4; Jn 21:6-11).
See Snare.
Figurative (Job 18:8; 19:6; Ps 9:15; 10:9; 25:15; 31:4; 35:7-8; 57:6; 66:11; 140:5; 141:10; Pr 12:12; 29:5; Ecc 7:26; 9:12; Isa 19:8; Eze 26:5, 14; 47:10; Hos 7:12).

NETAIM Residence of Judahite potters (1Ch 4:23).

NETHANEL (*God [El] has given*).
1. The prince of Issachar. Numbers the tribe (Nu 1:8). Captain of the host of Issachar (Nu 2:5; 10:15). Liberality of, for the tabernacle (Nu 7:18-23).
2. A priest and doorkeeper for the ark (1Ch 15:24).
3. A Levite (1Ch 24:6).
4. Son of Obed-Edom and gatekeeper of the temple (1Ch 26:4).
5. A prince sent by Jehoshaphat to teach the law in the cities of Judah (2Ch 17:7).
6. A Levite (2Ch 35:9).
7. A priest who divorced his Gentile wife (Ezr 10:22).
8. A priest (Ne 12:21).
9. A Levite and musician (Ne 12:36).

NETHANIAH (*Yahweh has given*).
1. Father of Ishmael (2Ki 25:23, 25; Jer 40:8, 14-15; 41:1-2, 6-7, 9-12).
2. A singer and chief of the temple musicians (1Ch 25:2, 12).
3. A Levite appointed by Jehoshaphat to accompany the princes who were to teach the law in Judah (2Ch 17:8).
4. Father of Jehudi (Jer 36:14).

NETHINIM *See Temple Servants.*

NETOPHAH, NETOPHATHITE(S) (*trickle, drip*). Village of Judah and its inhabitants; c. three miles S of Jerusalem (2Sa 23:28-29; 1Ch 2:54; 9:16; Ne 12:28).

NETTLES A stinging plant (Pr 24:31; Isa 34:13).
Figurative (Job 30:7; Hos 9:6; Zep 2:9).

NETWORK White cloth (Isa 19:9), ornamental carving upon pillars of Solomon's temple (1Ki 7:18, 42), a grate for the great altar of burnt offerings at the tabernacle (Ex 27:4; 38:4).

NEW BIRTH The corruption of human nature requires (Jn 3:6; Ro 8:7-8). None can enter heaven without (Jn 3:3). Is of the will of God (Jas 1:18). Is of the mercy of God (Tit 3:5). Is for the glory of God (Isa 43:7).

Effected by:
God (Jn 1:13; 1Pe 1:3). Christ (1Jn 2:29). The Holy Spirit (Jn 3:6; Tit 3:5). By means of: The word of God (Jas 1:18; 1Pe 1:23). The resurrection of Christ (1Pe 1:3). The ministry of the gospel (1Co 4:15).

Described as:
A new creation (2Co 5:17; Gal 6:15; Eph 2:10). Newness of life (Ro 6:4). A spiritual resurrection (Ro 6:4-6; Eph 2:1, 5; Col 2:12; 3:1). A new heart (Eze 36:26). A new spirit (Eze 11:19; Ro 7:6). Putting on the new man (Eph 4:24). The inward man (Ro 7:22; 2Co 4:16). Circumcision of the heart (Dt 30:6, w Ro 2:29; Col 2:11). Partaking of the divine nature (2Pe 1:4). The washing of regeneration (Tit 3:5). All saints partake of (Ro 8:16-17; 1Pe 2:2; 1Jn 5:1).

Produces:
Likeness to God (Eph 4:24; Col 3:10). Likeness to Christ (Ro 8:29; 2Co 3:18; 1Jn 3:2). Knowledge of God (Jer 24:7; Col 3:10). Hatred of sin (1Jn 3:9; 5:18). Victory over the world (1Jn 5:4). Delight in God's law (Ro 7:22).

Evidenced by:
Faith in Christ (1Jn 5:1). Righteousness (1Jn 2:29). Brotherly love (1Jn 4:7). Connected with adoption (Isa 43:6-7; Jn 1:12-13). Literalistic objection to (Jn 3:4). Manner of effecting illustrated (Jn 3:8). Preserves from Satan's devices (1Jn 5:18).

NEW COVENANT *See Covenants, Major in the Old Testament.*

NEW CREATION *See Regeneration.*

NEW MOON Feast of (Nu 10:10; 28:11-15; 1Ch 23:31; 2Ch 31:3). Commerce at time of, suspended (Am 8:5).

NEW TESTAMENT A collection of twenty-seven documents regarded by the church as inspired and authoritative, consisting of four Gospels, the Acts of the Apostles, twenty-one letters, and the book of Revelation. All were written during the apostolic period, either by apostles or by men closely associated with the apostles. The Gospels tell the story of the coming of the Messiah, God in the flesh, to become the Savior of the world. Acts describes the beginnings and growth of the church. The letters set forth the significance of the person and work of Christ and rules for the Church. Revelation tells of the consummation of all things in Jesus Christ. The formation of the NT canon was a gradual process, the Holy Spirit working in the church and guiding it to recognize and choose those Christian books God wanted brought together to form the Christian counterpart of the Jewish OT. By the end of the fourth century, the NT canon was basically settled.

NEW THINGS (Isa 42:9; 43:19; 48:6; 65:17; 2Co 5:17; Rev 21:5).

NEW YEAR *See Feasts; Trumpets, Feast of.*

NEZIAH (*director [of worship]*). One of the temple servants (Ezr 2:54; Ne 7:56).

NEZIB (*pillar, garrison*). A city in Judah (Jos 15:43).

NIBHAZ An idol (2Ki 17:31).

NIBSHAN A city of Judah (Jos 15:62).

NICANOR (*victor*). A deacon of the church at Jerusalem (Ac 6:5).

NICODEMUS (*victor over people*). Pharisee; member of the Sanhedrin; came to Jesus at night for conversation (Jn 3); spoke up for Jesus before the Sanhedrin (Jn 7:25-44); brought spices for burial of Jesus (Jn 19:39-42).

NICOLAITANS (*follower of Nicolas*). A heretical sect with immoral practices (Rev 2:6, 15).

NICOLAS (*victor over people*). A proselyte of Antioch and deacon of the church at Jerusalem (Ac 6:5-6).

NICOPOLIS (*victory city*). City in Epirus in NW Greece, founded by Augustus Caesar (Tit 3:12).

NIGER (*black*). Surname of Simeon, leader of the church at Antioch (Ac 13:1-3).

NIGHT (Ge 1:5, 16, 18). Meditations in (Ps 19:2; 77:6; 119:148; 139:11). Worship in (Ps 134:1). Jesus prays all night (Lk 6:12). No night in heaven (Rev 21:25; 22:5). Divided into hours (Ac 23:23). Used figuratively (Isa 15:1; 21:11-12; Jn 9:4; Ro 13:12; 1Th 5:5).

NIGHT HAWK *See Screech Owl.*

NILE The main river of Egypt and of Africa, 4,050 miles long; it begins at Lake Victoria and flows northward to the Mediterranean; the annual overflow deposits sediment which makes N Egypt one of the most fertile regions in the world. Moses was placed on the Nile in a basket of papyrus (Ex 2:3); the turning of the Nile into blood was one of the ten plagues (Ex 7:20-21); on its bank grows the reed from which the famous papyrus writing material is made. *See River of Egypt.*

NIMRAH (*spotted leopard* BDB; *basin of limpid [clear] water* KB). A city of Gad (Nu 32:3).

NIMRIM, WATERS OF (*limpid [clear] waters* KB; *wholesome waters* BDB; possibly *waters of leopards* IDB). Waters on the borders of Gad and Moab (Isa 15:6; Jer 48:34).

NIMROD (perhaps *to rebel*, or *the Arrow, the mighty hero*). Son of Cush. "A mighty hunter before the LORD" (Ge 10:8-9; 1Ch 1:10). Founder of Babylon. *See Babylon.*

NIMRUD Ancient Calah in Assyria, founded by Nimrod (Ge 10:11, 12).

NIMSHI Father of Jehu (2Ki 9:2, 20).

NINEVEH A capital of the Assyrian Empire (Ge 10:11-12). Nineveh and its surrounding region had a population of upwards of 120,000 when Jonah preached (Jnh 4:11). Extent of (Jnh 3:4). Sennacherib in (2Ki 19:36-37; Isa 37:37-38). Jonah preaches to (Jnh 1:1-2; 3). Nahum prophesies against (Na 1-3). Zephaniah foretells the desolation of (Zep 2:13-15).

NISAN Babylonian name for Abib (Ne 2:1; Est 3:7). *See Abib; Month, 1.*

NISROCH An idol (2Ki 19:36-37; Isa 37:37-38).

NITRE *See Soda.*

NO *See Thebes.*

NOADIAH (*meet with Yahweh*).
1. Levite who returned to Jerusalem after the Exile (Ezr 8:33).
2. False prophetess who tried to terrorize Nehemiah (Ne 6:14).

NOAH (*rest, comfort*).
1. Son of Lamech (Ge 5:28-29), righteous in a corrupt age (Ge 6:8-9; 7:1; Eze 14:14), warned people of the Flood 120 years (Ge 6:3), built an ark (Ge 6:12-22), saved from the Flood with wife and family, together with beasts and fowl of every kind (Ge 7:8), repopulated earth (Ge 9:10), lived 950 years.
God establishes a covenant with (Ge 9:8-17). *See Covenants, Major in the Old Testament.*
2. Daughter of Zelophehad (Nu 26:33; 27:1; 36:11; Jos 17:3).

NOB A city of Benjamin (Ne 11:31-32). Called "the town of the priests" (1Sa 22:19). Home of Ahimelech the priest (1Sa 21:1; 22:11). Probable seat of the tabernacle in Saul's time (1Sa 21:4, 6, 9). David flees to, and is aided by Ahimelech (1Sa 21:1-9; 22:9-10). Destroyed by Saul (2Sa 22:19). Prophecy concerning (Isa 10:32).

NOBAH (*barking*).
1. Manassite; took Kenath from Amorites (Nu 32:42).
2. Town near which Gideon defeated the Midianites (Jdg 8:11).

NOBAI *See Nebai.*

NOBLE A word which is used to describe people who were renowned for deeds performed or in some other way were distinguished for skills or genius; people of high rank, position, title, or one well born (Jdg 5:13; Ezr 4:10; Est 6:9; Pr 17:26; Lk 19:12-27; 1Co 1:26), persons who possess high moral qualities or ideals (Ps 16:3; Isa 32:5; Ac 17:11), anything having qualities of a very high order (Eze 17:8, 23; 1Ti 3:1; Lk 21:5).
A nobleman supports and defends his community. He has a generous heart (Ex 35:5, 22; 2Ch 29:31; Nu 21:18; 1Ch 28:21). He is one belonging to a king (Jn 4:46-53). The noble wife is praised in Pr 31:10-31.

NOD (*wandering*). Region E of Eden to which Cain went (Ge 4:16).

NODAB Tribe of Arabs, probably Ishmaelites E of the Jordan (1Ch 5:19).

NOE *See Noah.*

NOGAH (*joy, splendor*). Son of David (1Ch 3:7; 14:6).

NOHAH (*rest*). Son of Benjamin (1Ch 8:2).

NOLLE PROSEQUI The complaint against Paul (Ac 18:12-17).

NON *See Nun.*

NONCONFORMITY *See Church, The Body of Believers, State; Form; Formalism.*

NONE LIKE GOD (Ex 8:10; 15:11; Dt 33:26; 2Sa 7:22; 1Ki 8:23; 1Ch 17:20; Ps 89:6; Isa 40:18; Mk 12:32).

NONRESISTANCE Commanded (Mt 5:38-41; Ro 12:17-21; 1Th 5:15; 1Pe 2:19-23). Forgive those who wrong you (Mt 18:15, 21-35; Lk 6:36-37; Eph 4:32; Jas 2:13; 1Pe 3:9). Love your enemies (Ex 23:4-5; Job 31:29-30; Pr 25:21-22; Mt 5:43-48; 6:14-15; Lk 6:27-36; 10:30-37; Ro 12:17-21; 13:10; 1Jn 3:10-11). Return good for evil (Pr 15:1; 25:21-22; Mt 5:38-41; 6:14-15; Ro 12:17-21; 1Th 5:15; 1Pe 3:9). Seek peace (Ps 34:14; 133:1-3; Mt 5:9; 18:15; 2Co 13:11; Gal 5:22; Col 3:12-13; Heb 12:14; Jas 3:17-18; 1Pe 3:11). Suffer gladly for Christ (Mt 5:10-12; Lk 6:22-23; Jn 15:20; Ac 5:41; Ro 12:14; 1Co 4:12-13; 13:7; Gal 5:22; Col 3:12-13; 1Pe 2:19-23; 3:14). Christ, our example (Lk 23:34; 1Pe 2:19-23; 1Jn 2:6). Exemplified by Stephen (Ac 7:60).
See Revenge; Good for Evil; Evil for Good.

NOON (Dt 28:29; Job 11:17; Ps 55:17; 91:6; Isa 58:10; Ac 22:6).

NOPH *See Memphis.*

NOPHAH A city of Sihon (Nu 21:30).

NORTH Often merely as a point of the compass; but sometimes a particular country, usually Assyria or Babylonia (Jer 3:18; 46:6; Eze 26:7; Zep 2:13).

NORTHEASTER A hurricane-force E wind the Mediterranean; shipwrecked Paul (Ac 27:14).

NOSE Jewels for (Pr 11:22; Isa 3:21; Eze 16:12). Mutilated (Eze 23:25).

NUBIANS An African people (Da 11:43).

NUCLEAR WAR Some see a reference to nuclear war in predictions of the fiery destruction of the earth (Zep 1:18; 2Pe 3:7, 10) and in the seven trumpets of Revelation (Rev 8:5-9:19).

NUMBERS Hebrews did not use figures to denote numbers. They spelled numbers out in full; from second century B.C. they used Hebrew letters of the alphabet for numbers. Numbers were often used symbolically; some had special religious significance (Ge 2:2; Ex 20:3-17; Dt 6:4), especially 1, 3, 7, 10, 12, 40, 70, 666, 1000.

NUMBERS, BOOK OF

Author: Traditionally ascribed to Moses

Date: 1445 to 1406 B.C.

Outline:

I. Israel at Sinai, Preparing to Depart for the Promised Land (1:1-10:10).
 A. The Commands for the Census of the People (chs. 1-4).
 1. The numbers of men from each tribe mustered for war (ch. 1).
 2. The placement of the tribes around the tabernacle and their order for march (ch. 2).
 3. The placement of the Levites around the tabernacle, and the numbers of the Levites and the firstborn of Israel (ch. 3).
 4. The numbers of the Levites in their tabernacle service for the Lord (ch. 4).
 B. The Commands for Purity of the People (5:1-10:10).
 1. The test for purity in the law of jealousy (ch. 5).
 2. The Nazirite vow and the Aaronic benediction (ch. 6).
 3. The offerings of the twelve leaders at the dedication of the tabernacle (ch. 7).
 4. The setting up of the lamps and the separation of the Levites (ch. 8).
 5. The observance of the Passover (9:1-14).
 6. The covering cloud and the silver trumpets (9:15-10:10).
II. The Journey From Sinai to Kadesh (10:11-12:16).
 A. The Beginning of the Journey (10:11-36).
 B. The Beginning of the Sorrows: Fire and Quail (ch. 11).
 C. The Opposition of Miriam and Aaron (ch. 12).
III. Israel at Kadesh, the Delay Resulting From Rebellion (14:1-20:13).
 A. The Twelve Spies and Their Mixed Report of the Good Land (ch. 13).
 B. The People's Rebellion Against God's Commission, and Their Defeat (ch. 14).
 C. A Collection of Laws on Offerings, the Sabbath and Tassels on Garments (ch. 15).
 D. The Rebellion of Korah and His Allies (ch. 16).
 E. The Budding of Aaron's Staff: A Sign for Rebels (ch. 17).
 F. Concerning Priests, Their Duties and Their Support (ch. 18).
 G. The Red Heifer and the Cleansing Water (ch. 19).
 H. The Sin of Moses (20:1-13).
IV. The Journey From Kadesh to the Plains of Moab (20:14-22:1).
 A. The Resistance of Edom (20:14-21).
 B. The Death of Aaron (20:22-29).
 C. The Destruction of Arad (21:1-3).
 D. The Bronze Snake (21:4-9).
 E. The Song of the Well (21:10-20).
 F. The Defeat of Sihon and Og (21:21-30).
 G. Israel Enters Moab (21:31-22:1).
V. Israel on the Plains of Moab, in Anticipation of Taking the Promised Land (22:2-32:42).
 A. Balak of Moab Hires Balaam to Curse Israel (22:2-41).
 B. Balaam Blesses Israel in Seven Oracles (chs. 23-24).
 C. The Baal of Peor and Israel's Apostasy (ch. 25).
 D. The Second Census (ch. 26).
 E. Instructions for the New Generation (chs. 27-30).
 1. The inheritance for women (27:1-11).
 2. The successor to Moses (27:12-23).
 3. Commands regarding offerings (28:1-15).
 4. Commands regarding festivals (28:16-29:40).
 5. Commands regarding vows (ch. 30).
 F. The War Against Midian (ch. 31).
 G. The Settlement of the Transjordan Tribes (ch. 32).
VI. Appendixes Dealing With Various Matters (chs. 33-36).
 A. The Stages of the Journey (ch. 33).
 B. The Land of Inheritance (chs. 34-35).
 C. The Inheritance for Women (ch. 36).

NUN (*fish* hence *fertile, productive*). Father of Joshua (Ex 33:11).

NURSE (Ge 24:59; 35:8; Ex 2:7; Ru 4:16; 2Ki 11:2; Isa 60:4; 1Th 2:7). Careless (2Sa 4:4).

NUT Pistachio and almond (Ge 43:11), perhaps walnut (SS 6:11).

NYMPHA A Christian of Laodicea. House of, used as a place of worship (Col 4:15).

O

OAK A tree. Grew in Israel (Ge 35:4). Absalom hung in the boughs of (2Sa 18:9, 14). Deborah buried under (Ge 35:8). Oars made of (Eze 27:6).
Figurative (Am 2:9).

OAR For propelling boats (Isa 33:21; Eze 27:6, 29).

OATH A solemn and binding promise.

Used In Solemnizing Covenants:
Between Abraham and the king of Sodom (Ge 14:22-23), and Abimelech (Ge 21:22-23), between Isaac and Abimelech (Ge

26:26-29, 31). Abraham requires oath of his servant Eliezer (Ge 24:2-3, 9). Esau confirms the sale of his birthright by (Ge 25:33). Jacob confirms the covenant between him and Laban by (Ge 31:53), requires Joseph to swear that he would bury Jacob with his fathers (Ge 47:28-31). Joseph requires a like oath (Ge 50:25). Rahab requires an oath from the spies (Jos 2:12-14; 6:14). The Israelites confirm the covenant with the Hivites (Jos 9:3-20). Moses covenants with Caleb by (Jos 14:9). The elders of Gilead confirm their pledge to Jephthah by (Jdg 11:10). The Israelites swear in Mizpah (Jdg 21:5). Ruth swears to Naomi (Ru 1:17). Boaz swears to Ruth (Ru 3:13). Saul swears to Jonathan (1Sa 19:6). Jonathan and David confirm a covenant by (1Sa 20:3, 13-17). David swears to Saul (1Sa 24:21-22; 2Sa 21:7). Saul swears to the medium of Endor (1Sa 28:10). David swears not to eat until the sun goes down (2Sa 3:35). Joab confirms his word by (2Sa 19:7). David swears to Bathsheba that Solomon confirms his word by (1Ki 2:23), so also does Shimei (1Ki 2:42). Elisha seals his vow to follow Elijah by (2Ki 2:2). King of Samaria confirms his word with an (2Ki 6:31). Gehazi confirms his lie by (2Ki 5:20). Jehoiada requires an oath from the rulers (2Ki 11:4). Zedekiah violates (2Ch 36:13). Ezra requires, of the priests and Levites (Ezr 10:5, 19), so also does Nehemiah (Ne 5:12-13). Zedekiah swears to Jeremiah (Jer 38:16). Gedaliah confirms his word by (Jer 40:9).
Peter confirms his denial of Jesus by (Mk 14:71). Used to cast out demons (Ac 19:13); used by Gadarene demoniac in an attempt to keep Jesus from casting out the legion (Mk 5:7).
Used in solemnizing testimony (Ex 22:10-11; Nu 5:19-24; Dt 6:13; 10:20; 1Ki 8:31-32; Ps 15:1-4; Heb 6:16). Used in confirming allegiance to sovereigns (Ecc 8:2). Used as a result of returning to God (Jer 4:2).
Attributed to God (Ge 22:16; Ps 89:35; 95:11; 105:9; 132:11; Isa 14:24; 45:23; Jer 11:5; 22:5; 49:13; 51:14; Lk 1:73; Heb 3:11, 18; 4:3; 6:13-14, 17; 7:21, 28; Rev 10:6).
Christ's teachings concerning (Mt 23:18-22). Required of Christ (Mt 26:63).
Paul confirms certain statements by (2Co 1:23; Gal 1:20).
Written in the law of Moses (Da 9:11). Mosaic law concerning (Ex 23:1). Samuel affirms his honesty of administration by (1Sa 12:5).
Heard, in Daniel's vision (Da 7:2). In John's vision (Rev 10:5-6).

Profane and Wicked:
Forbidden (Ex 20:7; Lev 19:12; Dt 5:11; Mt 5:33-37; Jas 5:12). Unrighteous, forbidden (Lev 19:12; Hos 4:15). Punishment for (Lev 6:2-5).
Made by Israelites (Isa 48:1; Jer 5:2, 7; 7:8-9). By Herod (Mt 14:7, 9; Mk 6:23, 26). By enemies of Paul (Ac 23:12-14).

Idolatrous: (Jer 12:16).

See Covenant; False Witness; God, Name of; Perjury.

OBADIAH (*servant [worshiper] of Yahweh*).
1. Governor of Ahab's household (1Ki 18:3-16).
2. Judahite (1Ch 3:21).
3. Chief of Issachar (1Ch 7:3).
4. Son of Azel (1Ch 8:38).
5. Levite who returned from captivity (1Ch 9:16). Also called Abda (Ne 11:17).
6. Gadite soldier (1Ch 12:9).
7. Father of Ishmaiah, prince of Zebulun (1Ch 27:19).
8. Prince of Judah (2Ch 17:7).
9. Merarite Levite (2Ch 34:12).
10. Jew who returned from captivity (Ezr 8:9).
11. Priestly covenanter with Nehemiah (Ne 10:5).
12. Gatekeeper in Jerusalem (Ne 12:25).
13. A prophet who wrote the book of Obadiah.

OBADIAH, BOOK OF

Author: The prophet Obadiah

Date:
If Obadiah relates to the invasion of Jerusalem by Philistines and Arabs during the reign of Jehoram (853-841 B.C.) (2Ki 8:20-22; 2Ch 21:8-20), the prophet would be a contemporary of Elisha.
If Obadiah relates to the Babylonian attacks on Jerusalem (605-586), the prophet would be a contemporary of Jeremiah. This alternative seems more likely.

Outline:
I. Title and Introduction (1).
II. Judgment on Edom (2-14).
 A. Edom's Destruction Announced (2-7).
 1. The humbling of her pride (2-4).
 2. The completeness of her destruction (5-7).
 B. Edom's Destruction Reaffirmed (8-14).
 1. Her shame and destruction (8-10).
 2. Her crimes against Israel (11-14).
III. The Day of the Lord (15-21).
 A. Judgment on the Nations but Deliverance for Zion (15-18).
 B. The Lord's Kingdom Established (19-21).

See Prophets, The Minor.

OBAL Called also Ebal. A son of Joktan (Ge 10:28; 1Ch 1:22).

OBDURACY Callousness, hardness. Angers God (Ps 78:31; Isa 57:17). Warnings against (Ps 95:8-11; Heb 3:8, 15; 4:7). Punishment for (Lev 26:23-25; Ps 78:31-32; Pr 1:24-31; 29:1; Jer 3:2; Am 4:6-11).
Instances of: The antediluvians (Ge 6:3, 5, 7). Sodomites (Ge 19:14). Pharaoh (Ex 7:14, 22-23; 8:15, 19, 32; 9:7, 12, 35; 10:20, 28; 11:10; 14:5-8). Israelites (Nu 14:22; Ne 9:28-29; Ps 78:32; Isa 9:13-14; Jer 2:20; 5:3; Am 4:6-12; Zec 7:11-12). Sons of Eli (1Sa 2:22-25). Brothers of a rich man (Lk 16:31). Mankind in the last days (Rev 9:20-21).

See Afflictions, Of the Wicked; Impenitence; Reprobacy.

OBED (*servant [worshiper]*).
1. Son of Boaz and grandfather of David (Ru 4:17-22; 1Ch 2:12; Mt 1:5; Lk 3:32).
2. Son of Ephlal and grandson of Zabad (1Ch 2:37-38).
3. One of David's heroes (1Ch 11:47).

4. Son of Shemaiah. A gatekeeper of the temple (1Ch 26:7).
5. Father of Azariah (2Ch 23:1).

OBED-EDOM (*servant [worshiper] of Edom*).
1. A Korahite Levite. Doorkeeper of the ark (1Ch 15:18, 24; 26:4-8). David leaves the ark with (2Sa 6:10; 1Ch 13:13-14). Ark removed from (2Sa 6:12; 1Ch 15:25). Appointed to sound with harps (1Ch 15:21). Appointed to minister before the ark (1Ch 16:4-5, 37-38).
2. A doorkeeper of the temple (1Ch 16:38).
3. A caretaker of the vessels of the temple in time of Amaziah (2Ch 25:24).

OBEDIENCE

General:
Better than sacrifice (1Sa 15:22; Ps 40:6-9; Pr 21:3; Jer 7:22-23; Hos 6:6; Mic 6:6-8; Mt 9:13; 12:7; Mk 12:33; Heb 10:8-9).
Commanded (Ge 17:9; Ex 23:22; Lev 19:19, 36-37; 20:8, 22; 22:31; Nu 15:38-40; 30:2; Dt 4:1-40; 5:1-33; 6:1-25; 8:1-6, 11-20; 10:12-13; 11:1-3, 8-9, 13-28, 32; 13:4; 26:16-18; 27:1-10; 32:46; Jos 22:5; 23:6-7; 24:14-15; 1Sa 12:14, 20, 24; 15:22; 2Ki 17:37-38; 1Ch 16:15; 28:9-10, 20; Ezr 7:23; Ps 76:11; Pr 7:1; Ecc 12:13; Jer 26:13; 38:20; Da 7:27; Mal 4:4; Eph 6:6-8; Php 2:12; 1Ti 6:14, 18; Jas 1:22-25; 2:10-12; 1Pe 1:2, 14).
Proof of love (Jn 14:15, 21; 1Jn 2:5-6; 5:2-3; 2Jn 6, 9), under Mosaic law (Lev 18:5; Eze 20:11, 13, 21; Lk 10:28; Ro 10:5; Gal 3:10, 12). Proof that we know God (1Jn 2:3-4).
Vows of (Ex 24:7; Jos 24:24; Ps 119:15, 106, 109). Prayer for guidance in (Ps 143:10).
Cannot be rendered to two masters (Mt 6:24).

Rewards:
(Ge 18:19; Lev 26:3-13; Nu 14:24; Dt 7:12-15; 28:1-15; Jos 14:6-14; 2Ki 18:3; Isa 1:19).
Rewarded by: Prosperity (Dt 7:9, 12-15; 15:4; Jos 1:8; 1Ki 2:3-4; 9:3-5; 1Ch 22:13; 28:7-8; 2Ch 26:5; 27:6; Job 36:11; Pr 28:7; Jer 7:3-7; 11:1-5; 22:16; Mal 3:10-12; 1Jn 3:22). Long life (Dt 4:1, 40; 32:47; 1Ki 3:14; Pr 3:1-2; 19:16). Victory over enemies (Ex 23:22; Pr 16:7). Triumph over adversities (Mt 7:24-25; Lk 6:46-48). Divine favor (Ex 19:5; 20:6; Dt 5:10; 11:26-27; 12:28; 1Ki 8:23; Ne 1:5; Ps 25:10; 103:17-18, 20; 112:1; 119:2; Pr 1:33; Jer 7:23; 11:4; Mt 5:19; 25:20-23; Lk 11:28; 12:37-38; Jn 12:26; 13:17; Jas 1:25; Rev 22:7). Fellowship with Christ (Mt 12:50; Mk 3:35; Lk 8:21; Jn 14:23; 15:10, 14; 1Jn 3:24). Everlasting life (Mt 19:17, 29; Jn 8:51; 1Jn 2:17; Rev 2:10).

Exemplified:
(Dt 33:9; Ps 1:2; 103:1-22; 1Th 1:9; Rev 2:19). Noah (Ge 6:9, 22; 7:5; Heb 11:7). Abraham (Ge 12:1-4; 17:23; 18:19; 21:4; 22:12, 18; 26:3-5; Ne 9:8; Ac 7:3-8; Heb 11:8-17; Jas 2:21). Bethuel and Laban (Ge 24:50). Jacob (Ge 35:1, 7). Laban (Ge 31:29). Moses (Nu 27:12-22; Heb 3:2-3). Moses and Aaron (Ex 7:6; 40:16, 21, 23, 32). Israelites (Ex 12:28; 32:25-29; 39:42-43; Nu 9:20-21, 23; Dt 33:9). Jos 22:2-3; Jdg 2:7; Ps 99:7). Israelites under the preaching of Haggai (Hag 1:12). Caleb (Nu 14:24; Dt 1:36; Jos 14:6-14). Joshua (Jos 10:40; 11:15). Reubenites (Jos 22:2-3). Gibeon (Jdg 6:25-28). David (1Ki 11:6, 34; 15:5; 2Ch 29:2; Ac 13:22). Elijah (1Ki 17:5).
The psalmist (Ps 17:3; 26:3-6; 119:30-31, 40, 44, 47-48, 51, 55-56, 59-60, 67, 69, 100, 102, 105-106, 110, 112, 119, 166-168). Elisha (1Ki 19:19-21). Hezekiah (2Ki 18:6; 20:3; 2Ch 31:20-21; Isa 38:3). Josiah (2Ki 22:2; 23:24-25). Asa (2Ch 14:2). Jehoshaphat (2Ch 17:3-6; 20:32; 22:9). Uzziah (2Ch 26:4-5). Jotham (2Ch 27:2). Levites (2Ch 29:34). Cyrus (Ezr 1:1-4). Ezra (Ezr 7:10). Hanani (Ne 7:2). Job (Job 1:8). The three Hebrews (Da 3). Jonah (Jnh 3:3). Ninevites (Jnh 3:5-10).
Zechariah (Lk 1:6). Simeon (Lk 2:25). Joseph (Mt 1:24; 2:14). Mary (Lk 1:38). Jesus (Mt 3:15; 26:39, 42; Lk 22:42; Jn 4:32, 34; 5:30; 6:38; 8:28-29; 9:4; 12:49-50; 14:31; 17:4; Php 2:8; Heb 3:2). By, John the Baptist (Mt 3:15). John and James (Mk 1:19-20). Matthew (Mt 9:9). Simon and Andrew (Mk 1:16-18). Levi (Mk 2:14). The rich young man (Mt 19:20; Mk 10:20; Lk 18:21). The disciples (Jn 17:6; Ac 4:19-20; 5:29). Cornelius (Ac 10:2). Paul (Ac 23:1; 24:17; 26:4-5; Php 3:7-14; 2Ti 1:3). Paul and Timothy (2Co 1:12; 6:3). Paul, Timothy, and Silas (1Th 2:1). The Christians at Rome (Ro 6:17).
To Civil Law. *See Citizens.*
Filial. *See Children.*

See Blessings, Spiritual, Contingent Upon Obedience; Commandments and Statutes, Of God; Duty; Faithfulness; Law.

OBEISANCE The act of bowing low or of prostrating oneself in token of respect or submission (Ge 43:28; Ex 18:7; 2Sa 1:2). *See Worship, Attitudes in.*

OBIL (*camel driver*). An Ishmaelite. Camel-keeper for David (1Ch 27:30).

OBJECT TEACHING *See Instruction.*

OBLATION *See Offerings.*

OBLIGATION A motive of obedience (Dt 4:32-40; 6-11; 26:16; 32:6; 1Sa 12:24; 1Ch 16:12; Ro 2:4; 2Co 5:15). Acknowledgment of (Ps 116:12-14, 17). *See Duty.*

OBLIQUITY *See Depravity.*

OBOTH (*fathers*). A camping place of Israel in the forty years' wandering (Nu 21:10-11; 33:43-44).

OBSEQUIOUSNESS *See Tact.*

OBSTETRICS (Eze 16:4). *See Midwives.*

OCCULTISM *See Sorcery.*

OCCUPATIONS AND PROFESSIONS Artisan—a worker with any materials, as carpenter, smith, engraver, etc.—author; baker; barber; beggar; carpenter; clerk; coppersmith; counselor; cupbearer; doctor; diviner; dyer; farmer; fisherman; gatekeeper; herdsman; hunter; judge; launderer; lawyer; magician;

mason; medium; musician; nurse; perfumer; physician; plowman; potter; preacher; priest; prophet; rabbi; recorder; robber; ruler; sailor; scribe; seer; servant; sheepshearer; shepherd; silversmith; singer; slave; smith; soldier; sorcerer; spinner; steward; tanner; taskmaster; tax collector; teacher; tentmaker; tiller; town clerk; treasurer; watchman; weaver; witch; writer.
See each occupation by name.

OCRAN (*trouble*). An Asherite and the father of Pagiel who numbered Israel (Nu 1:13; 2:27; 10:26).

ODED (*restorer*).
1. A prophet in Samaria (2Ch 28:9).
2. Father of the prophet Azariah (2Ch 15:1).

ODOR Pleasant or unpleasant smell (Ge 8:21; Lev 1:9-17; Jn 11:39). Also used figuratively (Ro 5:8).

OFFENSE Used in a variety of ways: Injury, hurt, damage, occasion of sin, stumbling block, infraction of the law, sin, transgression, state of being offended.

OFFERINGS Holy (Lev 2:3; 6:17, 25, 27, 29; 7:1, 6; 10:12; Nu 18:9-10). Offered at door of the tabernacle (Lev 1:3; 3:2; 17:4, 8-9), of the temple (1Ki 8:62; 12:27; 2Ch 7:12).
All animal sacrifices, must be eight days old or over (Lev 22:27), must be without blemish (Ex 12:5; 29:1; Lev 1:3, 10; 22:18-25; Dt 15:21; 17:1; Eze 43:23; Mal 1:8, 14; Heb 9:14; 1Pe 1:19). *See Bruise(s)*, *2*, must be salted (Lev 2:13; Eze 43:24; Mk 9:49), accompanied with leaven (Lev 7:13; Am 4:5), without leaven (Ex 23:18; 34:25), eaten (1Sa 9:13). Ordinance relating to scapegoat (Lev 16:7-26). Atonement for sin made by. *See Atonement.*

Figurative:
(Ps 51:17; Jer 33:11; Ro 12:1; Php 4:18; Heb 13:15).

Animal Sacrifices:
A type of Christ (Ps 40:6-8, w Heb 10:1-14; Isa 53:11-12, w Lev 16:21; Jn 1:29; 1Co 5:7; 2Co 5:21; Eph 5:2; Heb 9:19-28; 10:1, 11-12; 13:11-13; Rev 5:6).

Burnt:
(Lev 9:2). Its purpose was to make an atonement for sin (Lev 1:4; 7). Ordinances concerning (Ex 29:15-18; Lev 1; 5:7-13; 6:9-13; 17:8-9; 23:18, 26-37; Nu 15:24-25; 19:9; 28:26-31; 29). Accompanied by other offerings (Nu 15:3-16). Skins of, belonged to priests (Lev 7:8). Offered daily, morning and evening (Ge 15:17; Ex 29:38-42; Lev 6:20; Nu 28; 29:6; 1Ch 16:40; 2Ch 2:4; 13:11; Ezr 3:3; Eze 46:13-15). Music with (Nu 10:10).
Offered, by Noah (Ge 8:20), in idolatrous worship (Ex 32:6; 1Ki 18:26; 2Ki 10:25; Ac 14:13). For cleansing leprosy (Lev 14).

Daily:
Sacrificial (Ex 29:38-42; Lev 6:20; Nu 28:3-8; 29:6; 1Ki 18:29; 1Ch 16:40; 2Ch 2:4; 13:11; Ezr 3:3-6; 9:4-5; Ps 141:2; Eze 46:13-15; Da 9:21, 27; 11:31).

Drink:
Libations of wine offered with the sacrifices (Ge 35:14; Ex 29:40-41; 30:9; Lev 23:13, 18; Nu 6:17; 15:24; 28:5-15, 24-31; 29:6-11, 18-40; 2Ki 16:13; 1Ch 29:21; 2Ch 29:35; Ezr 7:17).

Fellowship:
Laws concerning (Ex 20:24; 24:5; Lev 3:6; 7:11-18; 9:3-4, 18-22; 19:5; 23:10; Nu 6:14; 10:10). Offered, by the tribal leaders (Nu 7:17, 23, 29, 35, 41, 47, 53, 59, 65, 71, 77, 83, 88), by Joshua (Jos 8:31), by David (2Sa 6:17; 24:25).
Offered in idolatrous worship (Ex 32:6). Offered by harlots (Pr 7:14).

Free Will:
(Lev 23:38; Nu 29:39; Dt 12:6; 2Ch 31:14; Ezr 3:5). Must be perfect (Lev 22:17-25). To be eaten, at tabernacle (Dt 12:17-18), by priests (Lev 7:16-17). With meat and drink offerings (Nu 15:1-16). Obligatory (Dt 16:10), when signified in a vow (Dt 23:23).

Guilt:
Ordinances concerning (Lev 5; 6:1-7; 7:1-7; 14:10-22; 15:15, 29-30; 19:21-22; Nu 6:12; Ezr 10:19). To be eaten by the priests (Lev 7:6-7; 14:13; Nu 18:9-10). Offered by idolaters (1Sa 6:3, 8, 17-18). *See below, Sin.*

Heave: *See below, Presentation or Wave.*

Human Sacrifices:
Forbidden (Lev 18:21; 20:2-5; Dt 12:31). Offered by Abraham (Ge 22:1-19; Heb 11:17-19), by Canaanites (Dt 12:31), Moabites (2Ki 3:27), Israelites (2Ki 16:3; 2Ch 28:3; 2Ki 23:10; Isa 57:5; Jer 7:31; 19:5; 32:35; Eze 16:20-21; 20:26, 31; 23:37, 39), by the Sepharvites to idols (2Ki 17:31). To demons (Ps 106:37-38), to Baal (Jer 19:5-6).

Meat:
Ordinances concerning (Ex 29:40-41; 30:9; 40:29; Lev 2; 5:11-12; 6:14-23; 7:9-13, 37; 9:17; 23:13, 16-17; Nu 4:16; 5:15, 18, 25-26; 8:8; 15:3-16, 24; 18:9; 28:5, 9, 12-13, 20-21, 26-31; 29:3-4, 14). To be eaten in the Holy Place (Lev 10:13; Nu 18:9-10). Offered with animal sacrifices (Nu 15:3-16). Not mixed with leaven (Lev 2:4, 11; 6:14-18; 10:12-13; Nu 6:15, 17). Storerooms for, in the temple (Ne 12:44; 13:5-6), provided for in the vision of Ezekiel (Eze 42:12).

Peace: *See above, Fellowship.*

Presentation or Wave:
Given to the priests' families as part of their share (Lev 10:14; Nu 5:9; 18:10-19, 24). Consecrated by being elevated by the priest (Ex 29:27). Consisted of the right thigh or hindquarter (Ex 29:27-28; Lev 7:12-14, 32, 34; 10:15), spoils, including captives and other articles of war (Nu 31:29, 41). When offered (Lev 7:12-14; Nu 6:20; 15:19-21). In certain instances this offering was brought to the tabernacle, or temple (Dt 12:6, 11, 17-18). To be offered on taking possession of the land of Canaan (Nu 15:18-21).

Sin:
Ordinances concerning (Ex 29:10-14, w Heb 13:11-13; Lev 4; 5; 6:1-7, 26-30; 9:1-21; 12:6-8; 14:19, 22, 31; 15:30; 23:19; Nu

6:10-11, 14, 16; 8:8, 12; 15:27; 28:15, 22-24, 30; 29:5-6, 11, 16-38). Temporary (Da 11:31; Heb 9-10).

Special Sacrifices:
In consecration of the altar. *See Altar.* Of priests. *See Priest.* Of the temple. *See Temple, Solomon's.* For leprosy. *See Leprosy.* For defilement. *See Defilement.*

Thank:
Ordinances concerning (Lev 7:11-15; 22:29; Dt 12:11-12).

Trespass: *See above, Guilt.*

Vow:
(Lev 7:16-17; 22:17-25; Dt 23:21-23).

Wave:
Ordinances concerning (Ex 29:22, 26-28; Lev 7:29-34; 8:25-29; 9:19-21; 10:14-15; 23:10-11, 17, 20; Nu 5:25; 6:19-20). Belonged to the priests (Ex 29:26-28; Lev 7:31, 34; 8:29; 9:21; 23:20; Nu 18:11, 18). To be eaten (Lev 10:14-15; Nu 18:11, 18-19, 31).

Wood:
Fuel for the temple (Ne 10:34; 13:31).

Insufficiency of:
(Heb 8:7-13; 9:1-15; 10:1-12, 18-20). Unavailing, when not accompanied by piety (1Sa 15:22; Ps 40:6; 50:8-14; 51:16-17; Pr 21:3, 27; Isa 1:11-14; 66:3; Jer 6:20; 7:21-23; 14:12; Hos 6:6; 8:13; Am 5:21-24; Mic 6:6-8; Mt 9:13; 12:7; Mk 12:33).

OFFICER
Civil:
Chosen by the people (Dt 1:13-16), appointed by kings (2Sa 8:16-18; 20:23-26; 1Ki 4:1-19; 9:22; Ezr 7:25). *See Government; Judge; Rulers.*

Ecclesiastical: *See Priest; Levites; Apostle; Elders; Deacon; Minister.*

OFFSCOURING Term of contempt; NIV "scum" (La 3:45; 1Co 4:13).

OG King of Bashan. A man of gigantic stature (Nu 21:33; Dt 3:11; Jos 12:4; 13:12). Defeated and slain by Moses (Nu 21:33-35; Dt 1:4; 3:1-7; 29:7; 31:4; Jos 2:10; 9:10; Ps 135:11-20; 136:18-20). Land of, given to Gad, Reuben, and Manasseh (Nu 32:33; Dt 3:8-17; 4:47-49; 29:7-8; Jos 12:4-6; 13:12, 30-31; 1Ki 4:19; Ne 9:22; Ps 136:20-21).

OHAD Son of Simeon (Ge 46:10; Ex 6:15).

OHEL (*[skin] tent*). Son of Zerubbabel (1Ch 3:20).

OHOLAH (*she who has a tent*). In God's parable to Ezekiel (ch. 23), Oholah is a woman representing Samaria, who with her sister Oholibah (Jerusalem) was accused of being unfaithful to Yahweh. Imaginary characters, figurative of idolatry (Eze 23:4-5, 36, 44).

OHOLIAB (*tent of [my] Father*). A craftsman of the tabernacle (Ex 31:6; 35:34; 36:1-2; 38:23).

OHOLIBAH (*my tent is in her*). *See Oholah.*

OHOLIBAMAH (*[my] tent is a high place*).
1. One of Esau's three wives (Ge 36:2, 18, 25). Also called Judith the daughter of Beeri (Ge 26:34).
2. An Edomite chief (Ge 36:41; 1Ch 1:52), probably so named from the district of his possession.

OIL Sacred (Ex 30:23-25; 31:11; 35:8, 15, 28; 37:29; 39:38; Nu 4:16; 1Ch 9:30). Compounded by Bezalel (Ex 37:1, 29). Punishment for profaning (Ex 30:31-33). Used for idols (Eze 23:41). Illuminating, for tabernacle (Ex 25:6; 27:20; Lev 24:2-4). Of olives (Ex 25:6).
For domestic use (Mt 25:3). Used for food (Lev 2:4-5; 14:10, 21; Dt 12:17; 1Ki 17:12-16; Job 29:6; Pr 21:17; Eze 16:13; Hos 2:5). For the head (Ps 23:5; 105:15; Lk 7:46). For anointing kings (1Sa 10:1; 16:1, 13; 1Ki 1:39).
Tribute paid in (Hos 12:1). Commerce in (2Ki 4:1-7).
See Anointing; Ointment.

OIL TREE *See Plants of the Bible.*

OINTMENT (Job 41:31). Used in care of newborns (Eze 16:9).

OLD AGE Wise (1Ki 12:6-8; 2Ch 10:6-8; Job 12:12). Devout (Lk 2:37). Exemplary, commanded (Tit 2:2-3). Deference toward (Lev 19:32; Job 32:4-9). Righteous, is glorious (Pr 16:31). Wasted, is bitter (Ge 47:9; Ecc 6:3, 6; 12:1-7).
Promised to the righteous (Job 5:26; Ps 34:12-14; 91:14, 16; Pr 3:1-2). God's care in (Isa 46:4). Psalmist prays not to be forsaken in (Ps 71:9, 18). David enjoys (1Ch 29:28). Paul, the aged (Phm 9).
Infirmities in (2Sa 19:34-37; Ps 90:10). Vigor in (Dt 34:7; Ps 92:12-14). Join in praise to the Lord (Ps 148:12-13).
See Longevity; Infirmity.

OLD GATE *See Jeshanah, 2.*

OLD TESTAMENT In Protestant Bibles, thirty-nine books from Genesis to Malachi: Five of law, twelve of history, five of poetry, five of major prophets, and twelve of minor prophets. In the Hebrew Bible, the same contents are organized into twenty-four books from Genesis to Chronicles: Five of law, eight of the prophets, and eleven of miscellaneous writings. All of these books were regarded by Israelites as Scripture, inspired and authoritative, before the first century A.D. (Mt 5:17-20; Lk 24:44; Jn 17:17; 2Ti 3:16). They appeared over a period of c. 1000 years. The authors of many of them are unknown.

OLIVE A fruit tree. Branch of, brought by the dove to Noah's ark (Ge 8:11). Common to the land of Canaan (Ex 23:11; Dt 6:11; 8:8), Israelites commanded to cultivate in the land of promise (Dt

28:40). Branches of, used for booths (Ne 8:15). Produces blooms (Job 15:33). Precepts concerning gleaning the fruit of (Dt 24:20; Isa 17:6). Cherubim made of the wood of (1Ki 6:23, 31-33). Fable of (Jdg 9:8).

Figurative:
Of prosperity (Ps 128:3). The wild, a figure of the Gentiles; the cultivated, of the Jews (Ro 11:17-21, 24).

Symbolic: (Zec 4:2-12; Rev 11:4).

Fruit of:
Oil extracted from, used as illuminating oil in the tabernacle (Ex 39:37; Lev 24:2; Zec 4:12).
See Oil.

OLIVES, MOUNT OF A ridge, c. one mile long, with four identifiable summits, E of Jerusalem, beyond the Valley of Jehoshaphat, through which flows the Kidron stream. Gethsemane, Bethphage, and Bethany are on its slopes (2Sa 15:30; Zec 14:4; Mt 21:1; 24:3; 26:30; Mk 11:1; 13:3; 14:26; Lk 19:29, 37; 22:39; Jn 8:1; Ac 1:12).

OLIVET *See Olives, Mount of.*

OLYMPAS A believer at Rome (Ro 16:15).

OMAR (*speaker*). Son of Eliphaz, grandson of Esau (Ge 36:11, 15; 1Ch 1:36).

OMEGA Alpha and Omega, a title of Christ, meaning he is the beginning and end of all things (Rev 1:8, 11; 21:6; 22:13). *See Jesus the Christ, Names of; Titles and Names.*

OMER One-tenth part of an ephah. A dry measure containing, according to the Rabbis, two quarts, but according to Josephus, three and one-half quarts (Ex 16:16-18, 36).

OMNIPOTENCE (*all power*). The attribute of God which describes his ability to do whatever he wills. He cannot do anything contrary to his nature as God, such as to ignore sin, to sin, or to do something absurd or self-contradictory. God is not controlled by his power, but has complete control over it; otherwise he would not be a free being. Although the word "omnipotence" is not found in the Bible, the Scriptures clearly teach the omnipotence of God (Job 42:2; Jer 32:17; Mt 19:26; Lk 1:37; Rev 19:6).
See God, Omnipotent; Jesus the Christ, Power of.

OMNIPRESENCE (*all presence*). The attribute of God by virtue of which he fills the universe in all its parts and is present everywhere at once. Not a part, but the whole of God is present in every place. The Bible teaches the omnipresence of God (Ps 139:7-12; Jer 23:23-24; Ac 17:27-28). This is true of all three members of the Trinity.
See God, Omnipresent.

OMNISCIENCE (*all knowing*). The attribute by which God perfectly and eternally knows all things which can be known, past, present, and future. God's omniscience is clearly taught in Scripture (Ps 147:5; Pr 15:11; Isa 46:1).
See God, Knowledge of; Jesus the Christ, Omniscience of.

OMRI (*thrive, live long* ISBE).
1. King of Israel. Was commander of the army of Israel, and was proclaimed king by the army upon news of the assassination of King Elah (1Ki 16:16). Defeats his rival, Tibni, and establishes himself (1Ki 16:17-22). Surrendered cities to the king of Syria (1Ki 20:34). Wicked reign and death of (1Ki 16:23-28). Denounced by Micah (Mic 6:16).
2. Son of Beker, grandson of Benjamin (1Ch 7:8).
3. A descendant of Perez (1Ch 9:4).
4. Son of Michael, and ruler of tribe of Issachar in time of David (1Ch 27:18).

ON (*sun [god] city*).
1. Capital of lower Egypt (Ge 41:45; 46:20).
2. A leader of the Reubenites who rebelled against Moses (Nu 16:1).

ONAM (*intense, strong*). A son of Shobal (Ge 36:23; 1Ch 1:40).

ONAN (*powerful, intense*). Son of Judah. Slain for his refusal to raise seed to his brother (Ge 38:4, 8-10; 46:12; Nu 26:19; 1Ch 2:3).

ONE AND ONLY A title applied to Jesus by John (Jn 1:14, 18; 3:16, 18; 1Jn 4:9), and once in Hebrews (Heb 11:17). It emphasizes the unique relationship of Jesus to God the Father. In ancient mss in Jn 1:18, Jesus is called God the One and Only, a clear reference to his deity.

ONE ANOTHER Responsibilities of fellow believers to (1Pe 4:7-10). All believers members of (Ro 12:5; Eph 4:25).

Commanded to:
Admonish (Ro 15:14; Col 3:16, w 2Th 3:15). Assemble together with (Heb 10:24). Bear burdens of (Gal 6:2). Comfort (1Th 4:18; 5:11, w 14). Confess faults to (Jas 5:16). Consider above self (Heb 10:24). Be courteous (1Pe 3:8). Edify (Ro 14:18; 1Th 5:11). Encourage (Heb 10:24). Equality with (2Co 12:16; 15:5, 7; 1Co 11:33; 12:25; Php 2:3). Exhort daily (Heb 3:13). Have fellowship with (1Jn 1:7). Forgive (Eph 4:32; Col 3:13). Do good to (1Th 5:15). Be hospitable to (1Pe 4:9), in greeting (Ro 16:16; 1Co 16:20; 2Co 13:12; 1Pe 5:5). Be kind to (Eph 4:32). Love (Jn 13:34-35; 15:12, 17; Ro 12:10; 13:8; 1Co 12:25; Gal 5:13; Eph 4:2; 1Th 3:12; 4:9; 1Pe 1:22; 2:17; 3:8; 1Jn 3:11, 23; 4:7, 11-12; 2Jn 5). Minister to (1Pe 4:10). Be patient with (Col 3:13). Be at peace with (Mk 9:50; 1Th 5:13). Pray for (Jas 5:16). Prefer (Ro 12:10; Php 2:3; 1Ti 5:21). Provoke to love and good works (Heb 10:24). Serve (Gal 5:13; 1Pe 4:10), by washing feet of (Jn 13:14). Be subject to (1Pe 5:5), husband and wife, each to be subject to (Eph 5:21). Teach (Col 3:16). Wait for (1Co 11:33).
Love of, exemplified (2Th 1:3).

Commanded Not to:
Deceive (1Co 7:5), devour and consume (Gal 5:15), do evil to (1Th 5:5), envy (Gal 5:26), grudge (Jas 5:9), judge (Ro 14:13), lie to (Lev 19:11; Col 3:9), owe anything to (Ro 13:8), provoke (Gal 5:26), speak evil of (Jas 4:11).

ONE GOD
(Dt 4:35; 6:4; 32:39; 2Sa 7:22; 1Ch 17:20; Ps 83:18; 86:10; Isa 43:10; 44:6; 45:18; Mk 12:29; 1Co 8:4; Eph 4:6; 1Ti 2:5; 1Jn 5:7). That God is one (Dt 6:4) does not deny the doctrine of the Trinity, for the same word is used of husband and wife as "one flesh" (Ge 2:24).

ONESIMUS
(*useful*). Runaway slave of Philemon of Colosse; converted through Paul, who wrote the letter to Philemon in his behalf (Col 4:9; Phm).
See Philemon, Epistle to.

ONESIPHORUS
(*one bringing usefulness*). A Christian of Ephesus (2Ti 1:16-17; 4:19).

ONION
Enjoyed by Israel in Egypt (Nu 11:5).

ONLY-BEGOTTEN
See One and Only.

ONO
(*strong*). Town in Benjamin, c. six miles SE of Joppa (1Ch 8:12; Ne 6:2; 11:35).

ONYCHA
A component of the sacred perfume, made from the shells of a species of mussel, possessing an odor (Ex 30:34).

ONYX
Exported from Havilah (Ge 2:12). Contributed by Israelites to the priests' garments (Ex 25:7; 35:9). Used in the breastplate (Ex 28:9-12, 20; 39:6, 13). Used in building the temple (1Ch 29:2). Precious stone (Job 28:16; Eze 28:13). Seen in the foundations of the city of the New Jerusalem in John's apocalyptic vision (Rev 21:20).
See Minerals of the Bible, 1; Stones.

OPHEL
(*mound, hill*). A gate in the wall of the city and the temple (2Ch 27:3; 33:14; Ne 3:26-27).

OPHIR
1. Son of Joktan (Ge 10:29; 1Ch 1:23).
2. A country celebrated for its gold and other valuable merchandise. Products of, used by Solomon and Hiram (1Ki 9:28; 10:11; 2Ch 8:18; 9:10). Jehoshaphat sends ships to, which are wrecked (1Ki 22:48). Gold of, proverbial for its fineness (1Ch 29:4; Job 22:24; 28:16; Ps 45:9; Isa 13:12).

OPHNI
A town of the Benjamites (Jos 18:24).

OPHRAH
(*young gazelle*).
1. A city in Benjamin (Jos 18:23; 1Sa 13:17). Possibly identical with Ephron (2Ch 13:19) and Ephraim (Jn 11:54).
2. A city in Manasseh, home of Gideon (Jdg 6:11, 24; 8:27, 32; 9:5).
3. Son of Meonothai and descendant of Judah through Kenaz and Othniel (1Ch 4:14).

OPINION

Public:
Kings influenced by. *See Kings.* Jesus inquires about (Mt 16:13; Lk 9:18). Feared by Nicodemus (Jn 3:2), Joseph of Arimathea (Jn 19:38), the parents of the man who was born blind (Jn 9:21-22), rulers who believed in Jesus but feared the Pharisees (Jn 12:42-43), chief priests who feared to answer the questions of Jesus (Mt 21:26; Mk 11:18, 32; 12:12), and to further persecute the disciples (Ac 4:21; 5:26).

Concessions to:
By Paul in circumcising Timothy (Ac 16:3). James and the Christian elders who required Paul to observe certain rites (Ac 21:18-26). Disciples who urged circumcision (Gal 6:12). Peter and Barnabas with others (Gal 2:11-14).
See Prudence.

Corrupt Yielding to:
By Herod, in the case of John the Baptist (Mk 6:26), of Peter (Ac 12:3), by Peter, concerning Jesus (Mt 26:69-75), by Pilate (Mt 27:23-27; Mk 15:15; Lk 23:13-25; Jn 18:38-39; 19:4-16), by Felix and Festus, concerning Paul (Ac 24:27; 25:9).

OPPORTUNITY
Providential (1Co 16:9; 2Co 2:12). Neglected (Lk 12:47). Spurned (Pr 1:24-25; Mt 23:34-38; Lk 14:16-24). Lost (Nu 14:40-43; Pr 1:28; Jer 8:20; Hos 5:6; Mt 24:50-51; 25:1-10, 24-28; Lk 19:20-24; 13:25-28). Terrible consequences of neglecting (Ps 3:19; Mt 25:3-13, 24-30, 41-46).
Terrible consequences of spurning (Pr 1:24-32; Mt 10:14-15; 11:20-24).
The measure of responsibility (Pr 1:24-30; Jer 8:20; Eze 3:19; 33:1-17; Hos 5:6; Mt 10:14-15; 11:20-24; Mt 23:34-38; 25:1-46 w Lk 19:20-24; Lk 12:47; 13:25-28; 14:16-24).
See Judgment, According to Opportunity and Works; Responsibility.

OPPRESSION
Seeming hopelessness under (Ecc 4:1). Proverbs concerning (Pr 3:31; 14:31; 22:16, 22; 28:3; 30:14; Ecc 4:1; 5:8; 7:7).

God:
A refuge from (Ps 9:9; 12:5). Promises aid against (Ps 12:5; 72:4, 14; Isa 58:6; Jer 50:34). God will judge (Ps 10:17-18; 103:6; Ecc 5:8; Isa 10; Jer 21:12; 22:17; Eze 22:7; Am 4:1; Mic 2:2; Hab 2:5-11; Mal 3:5; Jas 5:4). God will reward those who fight against (Isa 33:15-16).

National:
God judges (Ac 7:7), relieved (Ex 3:9; 12:30-39; Dt 26:7-8; Jdg 2:14; 6:8; 10:11; 2Ki 13; Isa 52:4). Prayer for deliverance from (Ps 17:8-9; 44:24; 74:21; 119:121, 134; Isa 38:14).

Oppressors:
Punished (Job 27:13-23; Ps 72:4; 103:6; Isa 10). Oppression forbidden (Ex 22:21-24; Dt 23:15-16; 24:14-15; Pr 22:22; Zec

7:10). Oppression warned against (Ps 62:10; Eze 45:9; Jas 2:6). Command to relieve the oppressed (Isa 1:17).

Instances of:
Hagar, by Sarah (Ge 16:6). Jacob, by Laban (Ge 31:39). Israelites, by Egyptians (Ex 1:10-22; 5), by Assyrians (Isa 52:4). Rehoboam resolves to oppress the Israelites (1Ki 12:14). Strangers and the poor and needy, by Israelites (Eze 22:29; Am 5:11-12; 8:4-6). Of people, by the scribes and Pharisees (Mt 23:2-4).

ORACLE
(*speak*). Utterance of prophecy. KJV "burden," (Isa 14:28; 15:1; Eze 12:10; Na 1:1) or "parable" (Nu 23:7, 18; 24:3, 4, 15, 16, 20, 21, 23) or "prophecy" (Pr 30:1; 31:1).

ORACLES
NIV "words" of God. Scriptures called (Ac 7:38; Ro 3:2; Heb 5:12; 1Pe 4:11).

ORATOR
A public speaker. Instances of: Judah (Ge 44:18-34). Aaron (Ex 4:14-16). Moses (Dt 1-4:40). Jonah (Jnh 3:4-10). Peter (Ac 2:14-40; 3:12-26; 4:8-12; 10:34-48; 11:4-17). Stephen (Ac 7:2-60). Paul and Barnabas (Ac 14:14-17). Paul (Ac 13:16-41; 17:22-31; 22:1-21; 24:10-21; 26:1-29; 27:21-25). James (Ac 15:13-21). Apollos (Ac 18:24-28). Herod (Ac 12:21). The city clerk (Ac 19:35-41). Tertullus (Ac 24:1).

ORDAIN, ORDINATION
An act of conferring a sacred office upon someone, as: Deacons (Ac 6:6), missionaries (Ac 13:3), elders (Ac 14:23). OT priests were ordained to office (Ex 28:41; 29:9).
Instances of: Priests (Ex 29:1-9, 19-35; 40:12-16; Lev 8:6-35; Heb 7:21). Apostles (Mk 3:14). Ministers: the seven (Ac 6:5-6), Paul and Barnabas (Ac 13:2-3), Timothy (1Ti 4:14).

ORDINANCE
A decree of the Law (Ex 12:14, 24, 43; 13:10; 15:25; Nu 9:14; 10:8; 15:15; 18:8; Isa 24:5; Mal 4:4; Ro 13:2; 1Pe 2:13).
Insufficiency, in salvation (Isa 1:10-17; Gal 5:6; 6:15; Eph 2:15; Col 2:14, 20-23; Heb 9:1, 8-10).
See Form; Formalism.

OREB
(*raven*).
1. A prince of Midian, overcome by Gideon and killed by the Ephraimites (Jdg 7:25; 8:3; Ps 83:11).
2. A rock E of the Jordan, where Oreb was slain (Jdg 7:25; Isa 10:26).

OREN
(*fir or cedar* BDB IDB; *laurel* KB). Son of Jerahmeel (1Ch 2:25).

ORGAN
See Flute; Music, Instruments of.

ORION
The constellation of (Job 9:9; 38:31; Isa 13:10; Am 5:8).

ORNAN
See Araunah.

ORONTES
The chief river of Syria, c. 400 miles long, rises in Anti-Lebanon range and flows N for most of its course.

ORPAH
(*neck, the girl with a full mane[?], or rain cloud*). Daughter-in-law of Naomi (Ru 1:4, 14).

ORPHAN
To be visited (Jas 1:27). Beneficent provision for (Dt 14:28-29; 16:10-11, 14; 24:19-22; 26:12-13). Kindness toward (Job 29:12-13; 31:16-18, 21). God the friend of (Ex 22:22-24; Dt 10:18; Ps 10:14; 10:17-18; 27:10; 68:5; 146:9; Pr 23:10-11; Jer 49:11; Hos 14:3; Mal 3:5). Justice to, required (Dt 24:17-22; 27:19; Ps 82:3; Isa 1:17, 23; Jer 7:6-7; 22:3). Oppressed (Job 6:27; 22:9; 24:3, 9; Isa 10:1-2; Jer 5:28).
See Adoption; Children; Widow.
Instances of: Lot (Ge 11:27-28). Daughters of Zelophehad (Nu 27:1-5). Jotham (Jdg 9:16-21). Mephibosheth (2Sa 9:3). Joash (2Ki 11:1-12). Esther (Est 2:7). A type of Zion in affliction (La 5:3).

OSEE
See Hosea.

OSHEA
See Joshua.

OSNAPPAR
See Ashurbanipal.

OSPRAY
See Vulture.

OSPREY
A carnivorous bird. Forbidden as food (Lev 11:13; Dt 14:12).

OSSIFRAGE
See Vulture.

OSTENTATION
In prayer and almsgiving (Mt 6:1; Pr 25:14; 27:2). *See Boasting.*

OSTIA
The port of Rome on the Tiber, some sixteen miles from the city.

OSTRACA
Inscribed fragments of pottery, or potsherds. Some important ancient documents have come down to us in this form, i.e., the Lachish Letters.

OSTRICH
A large, flightless bird that does not take care of its young well (Job 39:13-18; La 4:3).

OTHNI
Son of Shemaiah (1Ch 26:7).

OTHNIEL
Son of Kenaz and nephew of Caleb. Conquers Kiriath Sepher, and as reward secures Caleb's daughter as his wife (Jos 15:16-20; Jdg 1:12-13). Becomes deliverer and judge of Israel (Jdg 3:8-11). Death of (Jdg 3:11). Descendants of (1Ch 4:13-14).

OUCHES
See Filigree.

OUTCASTS
General references to (Isa 11:12; 16:3; 27:13; Jer 30:17).

OVEN
Ancient ovens were primitive, often a hole in the ground coated with clay and in which a fire was made. The dough was

spread on the inside and baked. Sometimes ovens were made of stone, from which the fire was raked when the oven was very hot and into which the unbaked loaves were placed (Ex 8:3; Lev 2:4; 7:9; 11:35; 26:26; Hos 7:4-7).
Figurative (Ps 21:9; Mal 4:1; Mt 6:30; Lk 12:28).

OVERCOMING
See Perseverance.

OVERSEER
Ruler (Pr 6:7). Office of church leadership, traditionally "bishop," (Ac 20:28; Php 1:1; 1Ti 3:1-7) same as an elder (Tit 1:5-9; 1Pe 5:1-4). A title of Christ (1Pe 2:25). *See Elders.*

OVERWEIGHT
See Corpulency.

OWL
Several kinds of carnivorous birds (Isa 14:23; 34:11; Zep 2:14). Unclean for food (Lev 11:16-18; Dt 14:15-17). Lives in the desert (Job 30:29; Ps 102:6; Isa 13:21; 34:11-15; 43:20; Jer 50:39; Mic 1:8).

OWNER OF A SHIP
Usually captained his ship or contracted to state service (Ac 27:11).

OX
See Bull; Cattle; Wild Ox.

OXGOAD
A pointed stick used to prod the ox on to further effort. Used by Shamgar to kill six hundred Philistines (Jdg 3:31).

OZEM
1. Son of Jesse (1Ch 2:15).
2. Son of Jerahmeel (1Ch 2:25).

OZIAS
See Uzziah, 1.

OZNI, OZNITE
(*my ear, my hearing*). Son of Gad and his clan (Nu 26:16).

P

PAARAI
(*devotee of Peor*). One of David's valiant men (2Sa 23:35). Called Naarai (1Ch 11:37).

PACK ANIMALS
Used for transporting army supplies (1Ch 12:40).

PADDAN ARAM
(*plain of Aram*).
1. Region near the head of the fertile crescent; sometimes called simply "Paddan," (Ge 48:7, ftn). Another name for Aram Naharaim (Ge 24:10). Literally "Aram of the two rivers"—the Euphrates and the Tigris. Naharaim was the northern part of the area called later by the Greeks "Mesopotamia"—literally "between the rivers." It was located NE of Canaan, the area known today as Syria.
2. A town near Shechem (Ge 33:18, ftn).

PADON
(*ransom*). One of the temple servants (Ezr 2:44; Ne 7:47).

PAGIEL
(perhaps *fortune of God* or *God is entreated*, less probably *God has met his worshiper*). Son of Ocran and leader of the tribe of Asher at the time of the Exodus (Nu 1:13; 2:27; 7:72, 77; 10:26).

PAHATH-MOAB
(*supervisor of Moab*). The ancestor of an influential family of Judah, which returned to Jerusalem from the Captivity (Ezr 2:6; 10:30; Ne 3:11; 7:11).

PAI
See Pau.

PAIN
Experienced on earth (Job 14:22; 30:17-18; La 3:5; Rev 16:10). Chastens (Job 33:19). None in Heaven (Rev 21:4).
See Afflictions.

PAINTING
Around the eyes, to enhance their appearance (2Ki 9:30; Jer 4:30; Eze 23:40). Of rooms (Jer 22:14). Of portraits (Eze 23:14).

PALACE
For kings (1Ki 21:1; 2Ki 15:25; Jer 49:27; Am 1:12; Na 2:6). Of David (2Sa 7:2). Of Solomon (1Ki 7:1-12). At Babylon (Da 4:29; 5:5; 6:18). At Susa (Ne 1:1; Est 1:2; 7:7; Da 8:2).
Archives kept in (Ezr 6:2). Proclamations issued from (Am 3:9). Figurative of a government (Am 1:12; 2:2; Na 2:6).

PALAL
(*he has judged*). Son of Uzai. One of the workmen in rebuilding the walls of Jerusalem (Ne 3:25).

PALE HORSE
Symbol of death (Rev 6:8).

PALESTINE
The name is derived from Philistia, an area along the S seacoast occupied by the Philistines (Ps 60:8). The original name was Canaan (Ge 12:5); after the Conquest it came to be known as Israel (1Sa 13:19), and in the Greco-Roman period, Judea, Samaria, and Galilee. The land was c. seventy miles wide and 150 miles long, from the Lebanon mountains in the N to Beersheba in the S. The area W of the Jordan was 6000 miles; E of the Jordan, 4000 miles. In the N, from Acco to the Sea of Galilee was twenty-eight miles. From Gaza to the Dead Sea in the S, fifty-four miles.
Physically, the land is divided into five parts: the Plain of Sharon and the Philistine Plain along the coast; adjoining it, the Shephelah, or foothills region; then the central mountain range; after that the Jordan valley; and E of the Jordan the Transjordan plateau.
The varied configuration of Palestine produces a great variety of climate. The Maritime Plain has an annual average temperature of 57 degrees at Joppa; Jerusalem averages 63 degrees; while Jericho

and the Dead Sea area have a tropical climate. As a result, plants and animals of varied latitudes may be found.

Before the Conquest the land was inhabited by Canaanites, Amorites, Hittites, Horites, and Amalekites. These were conquered by Joshua, the judges, and the kings. The kingdom was split in 931 B.C.; the N kingdom was taken into captivity by the Assyrians in 722 B.C.; the S kingdom by the Babylonians in 587 B.C. From 587 B.C. to the time of the Maccabees the land was under foreign rule by the Babylonians, Persians, Alexander the Great, Egyptians, and Syrians. In 63 B.C. the Maccabees lost control of the land to the Romans, who held it until the time of Mohammed.

In NT times Palestine W of the Jordan was divided into Galilee, Samaria, and Judea; and E of the Jordan into the Decapolis and Perea.

See Philistia; Philistines.

PALLU, PALLUITE (*wonderful*). Son of Reuben (Ge 46:9; Ex 6:14; Nu 26:5, 8; 1Ch 5:3).

PALM SUNDAY See *Triumphal Entry of Jesus.*

PALM TREE Deborah judged Israel under (Jdg 4:5). Wood of, used in the temple (1Ki 6:29, 32, 35; 2Ch 3:5). In the temple seen in the vision of Ezekiel (Eze 40:16; 41:18). Branches of, thrown in the way when Jesus made his triumphal entry into Jerusalem (Jn 12:13). Jericho was called the City of Palm Trees (Dt 34:3).

Figurative: Of the prosperity of the righteous (Ps 92:12). Used as a symbol of victory (Rev 7:9).

PALMER WORM See *Locust.*

PALMS, CITY OF See *Jericho.*

PALSY See *Paralysis.*

PALTI (*[God (El)] is [my] deliverance*).
1. Spy from Benjamin (Nu 13:9).
2. See *Paltiel, 2.*

PALTIEL (*God [El] is [my] deliverance*).
1. Prince of Issachar (Nu 34:26).
2. Son-in-law of Saul (1Sa 25:44; 2Sa 3:15).

PALTITE (*delivered*). One of David's mighty men (2Sa 23:26). "Pelonite" (1Ch 11:27; 27:10).

PAMPHYLIA A province in Asia Minor. Men of, in Jerusalem (Ac 2:10). Paul goes to (Ac 13:13-14; 14:24). John, surnamed Mark, in (Ac 13:13; 15:38). Sea of (Ac 27:5).

PAN(S) Clay pan for cooking the grain offering (Lev 2:7; 7:9). For baking bread (2Sa 13:9). Silver pans of the temple (Ezr 1:9). Iron (Eze 4:3).

PANIC In armies (Lev 26:17; Dt 32:30; Jos 23:10; Ps 35:5). From God (Ge 35:5; Ex 15:14-16; Jdg 7:22; 1Sa 14:15-20; 2Ki 7:6-7; 2Ch 20:22-23).
See Armies.

PANNAG See *Confection.*

PANTOMIME By Isaiah (Isa 20:2-3). By Ezekiel (Eze 4:1-8; 12:18). Agabus (Ac 21:11).

PAPER (2Jn 12). See *Parchment.*

PAPHOS A city of Cyprus. Paul blinds a sorcerer in (Ac 13:6-13).

PAPS NIV "breasts" (Lk 23:28) or "chest" (Rev 1:13). See *Breast.*

PAPYRUS (*reed plant*). A reed which grows in swamps and along rivers or lakes, especially along the Nile; from eight to twelve feet tall; used to make baskets, sandals, boats, and especially paper, the most common writing material of antiquity (Job 8:11; Isa 18:2). The NT books were undoubtedly all written on papyrus. Moses' basket of (Ex 2:3).

PARABLE (*to be similar, to be comparable*).

Defined:
1. Proverbial saying used in wisdom and prophetic discourse (Ps 78:2; Pr 1:6).
2. A story in which things in the spiritual realm are compared with events that could happen in the temporal realm; or, an earthly story with a heavenly meaning (Eze 17; 24; Mt 13; Lk 13). Differs from a fable, myth, allegory, or proverb. A characteristic teaching method of Jesus.

Listing of:
Of the trees (Jdg 9:8-15). Of the lamb (2Sa 12:1-6). Of the woman of Tekoa (2Sa 14:5-12). Of the garment torn to pieces (1Ki 11:30-32). Of the prisoner of war (1Ki 20:39-42). Of the thistle and cedar (2Ki 14:9). Of a vine of Egypt (Ps 80:8-16). Of the vineyard (Isa 5:1-7; 27:2-3). Of the farmer (Isa 28:23-29). Of the skins filled with wine (Jer 13:12-14). Of the two eagles (Eze 17). Of lions' cubs (Eze 19:1-9). Of Oholah and Oholibah (Eze 23). The boiling pot (Eze 24:3-5). The plant (Jnh 4:10-11).

The sheet let down from heaven in Peter's vision (Ac 10:10-16). The two covenants (Gal 4:22-31). The mercenary soldier (2Ti 2:3-4). Husbandman (2Ti 2:6). Furnished house (2Ti 2:20-21). The athlete (2Ti 2:5). Mirror (Jas 1:23-25).

See Jesus the Christ, Parables of; Symbols and Similitudes; Types.

PARACLETE (*comforter, exhorter*). One who pleads another's cause. Used by Christ of the Holy Spirit in John's Gospel (Jn 14:16, 26; 15:26; 16:7), and of Christ (1Jn 2:1).

PARADISE (*park* or *garden*). Park (Ecc 2:5), forest (Ne 2:8), orchard (SS 4:13), home of those who die in Christ (Lk 23:43).

PARADOX Of wealth (Pr 13:7). Wisdom (1Co 3:18). Life (Mt 10:39; 16:25; Mk 8:35; Lk 17:33; Jn 12:25). Christian life (2Co 6:4, 8-10; 12:4, 10-11; Eph 3:17-19; Php 3:7). New Jerusalem (Rev 21:18, 21).

PARAH (*cow*). A Benjamin city (Jos 18:23).

PARALLELISM A characteristic of OT Hebrew poetry. Rather that rhyming words as in English poetry, Hebrew poetry rhymes thoughts by comparison and contrast of two or three lines. Two major categories of parallelism are "synonymous," in which the parallel lines echo similar ideas, and "antithetical," in which the parallel lines contrast. In the NIV, parallelism is shown by indentation: the indented line is parallel to the preceding line.

Examples of Synonymous Parallelism—
1Why do the nations conspire
 and the peoples plot in vain?
2The kings of the earth take their stand
 and the rulers gather together
against the LORD
 and against his Anointed One.
3"Let us break their chains," they say,
 "and throw off their fetters."
4The One enthroned in heaven laughs;
 the Lord scoffs at them. (Ps 2:1-4)

Examples of Antithetical Parallelism—
For the LORD watches over the way of
 the righteous,
but the way of the wicked will perish. (Ps 1:6)
The fear of the LORD is the beginning of
 knowledge,
but fools despise wisdom and discipline.
 (Pr 1:7)
See Poetry; Psalms.

PARALYSIS (*lame*). Cured by Jesus (Mt 4:24; 8:6, 13; 9:2, 6), by Philip (Ac 8:7), by Peter (Ac 9:33-34).

PARAMOUR See *Lovers.*

PARAN, MOUNT PARAN, DESERT OF PARAN (*plain*). Desert or wilderness of (Ge 21:21; Nu 10:12; 12:16; 13:3, 26; Dt 1:1). Mountains of (Dt 33:2; Hab 3:3). Israelites encamp in (Nu 12:16). David takes refuge in (1Sa 25:1). Hadad flees to (1Ki 11:17-18).

PARBAR NIV "the court to the west" of the temple (1Ch 26:18).

PARCHED LAND Symbolic of loss of strength or blessing (Job 30:1; Ps 143:6). Changed to flowing springs, symbolic of blessing (Ps 107:35; Isa 35:1).

PARCHMENT Writing material made of animals skins, probably copies of books of the OT in 2Ti 4:13.

PARDON Forgiveness. God demands a righteous ground for pardoning the sinner—the atoning work of Christ (Ex 34:9; 1Sa 15:25-26; Isa 55:7). See *Atonement; Forgiveness.*

PARENTAL BLESSINGS Very important in OT times; often prophetic of a child's future (Ge 27:4, 12, 27-29).

PARENTS

General:
To be revered (Ex 20:12; Lev 19:3; Dt 5:16; Mt 15:4; 19:19; Mk 7:10; 10:19; Lk 18:20). Obeyed (Pr 1:8; 6:20; 23:22; Eph 6:1; Col 3:20).

Covenant blessings of, entailed upon children (Ge 6:18; Ex 20:6; Ps 103:17). Curses upon, entailed upon children (Ex 20:5; Lev 20:5; Isa 14:20; Jer 9:14; La 5:7). Involved in children's wickedness (1Sa 2:27-36; 4:10-18). Cursing of, to be punished (Ex 21:17; Lev 20:9).

Beloved:
By Joseph (Ge 46:29). Rahab (Jos 2:12-13). Ruth (Ru 1:16-17). Elisha (1Ki 19:20).
Mother, beloved (Pr 31:28).

Duties of:
Fathers to direct household (Ge 18:19; Lev 20:9; Pr 3:12; 13:24; 19:18; 1Ti 3:4-5, 12; Tit 1:6; Heb 12:7). To govern with kindness (Eph 6:4; Col 3:21). A prerequisite to church leadership (1Ti 3:4-5, 12). To provide for children (2Co 12:14; 1Ti 5:8). To instruct children in righteousness (Ex 10:2; 12:27; 13:8, 14; Dt 4:9-10; 6:7, 20-25; 11:18-21; 32:46; Ps 78:5-6; Pr 22:6, 15; 27:11; Isa 38:19; Joel 1:3; Eph 6:4; 1Th 2:11). To discipline children (Pr 19:8; 22:6, 15; 23:13-14; 29:15, 17).

Indulgent:
Eli (1Sa 2:27-36; 3:13-14), David (1Ki 1:6).

Influence of:
Evil (1Ki 15:26; 22:52-53; 2Ki 8:27; 21:20; 2Ch 21:6; 22:3). Good (1Ki 22:43; 2Ki 15:3, 34). See *Influence.*

Love of:
Reflection of God's love (Ps 103:13; Pr 3:12; Isa 49:15; 66:13; Mt 7:9-11; Lk 11:11-13). Must be exceeded by love for Christ (Mt 10:37). To be taught (Tit 2:4).

Love Exemplified:
By Hagar (Ge 21:15-16), Rebekah's mother (Ge 24:55), Isaac and Rebekah (Ge 25:28), Isaac (Ge 27:26-27), Laban (Ge 31:26-28), Jacob (Ge 37:3-4; 42:4, 38; 43:13-14; 45:26-28; 48:10-11), Moses' mother (Ex 2), Naomi (Ru 1:8-9), Hannah (1Sa 2:19), David (2Sa 12:18-23; 13:38-39; 14:1, 33; 18:5, 12-13, 33; 19:1-6), Rizpah (2Sa 21:10), the mother of the infant brought to Solomon by the harlots (1Ki 3:22-28), Mary (Mt 12:46; Lk 2:48; Jn 2:5; 19:25), Jairus (Mk 5:23), father of the demoniac (Mk 9:24), nobleman (Jn 4:49).

Paternal Blessings:
Of Noah (Ge 9:24-27), Abraham (Ge 17:18), Isaac (Ge 27:10-40; 28:3-4), Laban (Ge 31:55), Jacob (Ge 48:15-20; 49:1-28), reproaches (Ge 9:24-25; 49:3-7).

Partiality of:
Isaac for Esau (Ge 25:28), Rebekah for Jacob (Ge 25:28; 27:6-17), Jacob for Joseph (Ge 33:2; 37:3; 48:22), for Benjamin (Ge 42:4). See *Partiality.*

Prayers in Behalf of Children:
Of Hannah (1Sa 1:27), David (2Sa 7:25-29; 1Ch 17:16-27; 2Sa 12:16; 1Ch 22:12; 29:19), Job (Job 1:5).
See *Children, Instruction of.*

PARLOR See *Upper Room.*

PARMASHTA (*the very first*). Son of Haman (Est 9:9).

PARMENAS (*steady, reliable*). One of seven men chosen for daily ministration to the poor (Ac 6:5).

PARNACH Father of Elizaphan (Nu 34:25).

PAROSH (*flea*). The ancestor of one of the families which returned to Jerusalem from captivity in Babylon (Ezr 2:3; 8:3; Ne 7:8; 10:14).

PAROUSIA (*presence, coming*). A Greek word frequently used in NT of our Lord's return (Mt 24:3; 1Co 15:23; 1Th 3:13; 4:15; 2Pe 1:16).

PARRICIDE One who murders his father, mother, or a close relative (2Ki 19:37; 2Ch 32:21; Isa 37:38).

PARSHANDATHA One of the ten sons of Haman (Est 9:7).

PARSIMONY Stinginess with money or resources. Of the Jews toward the temple (Hag 1:2, 4, 6, 9), toward God (Mal 3:8-9). Punishment of (Hag 1:9-11). See *Liberality.*

PARSIN Aramaic for "divided," symbolic of the division of Babylon between the Medes and Persians (Da 5:24-28).

PARTHIANS The inhabitants of Parthia, a country NW of Persia (Ac 2:9).

PARTIALITY Forbidden, among Christians (1Ti 5:21), by parents (Dt 21:15-17). Effects upon children (Ge 37:4). See *Parents.*

Instances of:
Of Brothers: Joseph for Benjamin (Ge 43:30, 34).
Of parents: Isaac for Esau (Ge 25:25), Rebekah for Jacob (Ge 25:28; 27:6-17), Jacob, for Joseph (Ge 33:2; 37:3-4; 48:22), for Benjamin (Ge 42:4).
Of husbands: Jacob for Rachel (Ge 29:30), Elkanah for Hannah (1Sa 1:4-5).
See Respect of Persons.

PARTICEPS CRIMINIS Participating in evil (2Jn 11). See *Collusion.*

PARTITION, MIDDLE WALL OF See *Dividing Wall.*

PARTNERSHIP With God (1Co 3:7, 9; 2Co 6:1; Php 2:13).

PARTRIDGE (1Sa 26:20; Jer 17:11).

PARUAH (*blooming* ISBE; *cheerful* KB). Father of Jehoshaphat (1Ki 4:17).

PARVAIM An unknown gold region (2Ch 3:6).

PAS DAMMIM (*place of blood*). A battle between David and the Philistines, fought at (1Ch 11:13). Called Ephes Dammim (1Sa 17:1).

PASACH (*to divide*). Son of Japhlet (1Ch 7:33).

PASCHAL LAMB See *Passover.*

PASEAH (*hobbling one*).
1. A son of Eshton (1Ch 4:12).
2. Ancestor of a family which returned to Jerusalem from captivity in Babylon (Ezr 2:49; Ne 7:51).
3. Father of Jehoiada, probably identical with preceding (Ne 3:6).

PASHHUR (*perhaps be quiet, and round about*).
1. A priest, son of Malkijah (1Ch 9:12). An influential man and ancestor of an influential family (Jer 21:1; 38:1; Ezr 2:38; 10:22; Ne 7:41; 10:3; 11:12).
2. Son of Immer and governor of the temple. Beats and imprisons Jeremiah (Jer 20:1-6).
3. Father of Gedaliah, who persecuted Jeremiah (Jer 38:1).

PASSAGE Ford of a river (Ge 32:23), mountain pass (1Sa 13:23), a crossing (Jos 22:11).

PASSENGERS See *Commerce.*

PASSION
1. Lust or desire (Hos 7:6; 1Co 7:9).
2. Often used as a technical term of the suffering of Jesus. See *Jesus the Christ, Sufferings of.*

PASSIVITY See *Nonresistance.*

PASSOVER (*pass over, spare*). Institution of (Ex 12:3-49; 23:15-18; 34:18; Lev 23:4-8; Nu 9:2-5, 13-14; 28:16-25; Dt 16:1-8, 16; Ps 81:3, 5). Design of (Ex 12:21-28). Special Passover, for those who were unclean, or on a journey, to be held in the second month (Nu 9:6-12; 2Ch 30:2-4). Lamb killed by Levites, for those who were ceremonially unclean (2Ch 30:17; 35:3-11;

Ezr 6:20). Strangers authorized to celebrate (Ex 12:48-49; Nu 9:14).

Observed at place designated by God (Dt 16:5-7), with unleavened bread (Ex 12:8, 15-20; 13:3, 6; 23:15; Lev 23:6; Nu 9:11; 29:17; Dt 16:3-4; Mk 14:12; Lk 22:7; Ac 12:3; 1Co 5:8). Penalty for neglecting to observe (Nu 9:13).

Reinstituted by Ezekiel (Eze 45:21-24).

Observation of, renewed by the Israelites on entering Canaan (Jos 5:10-11), by Hezekiah (2Ch 30:1), by Josiah (2Ki 23:22-23; 2Ch 35:1, 18), after return from captivity (Ezr 6:19-20). Observed by Jesus (Mt 26:17-20; Lk 22:15; Jn 2:13, 23; 13). Jesus in the temple at the time of (Lk 2:41-50). Jesus crucified at the time of (Mt 26:2; Mk 14:1-2; Jn 18:28). The lamb of, a type of Christ (1Co 5:7). Lord's supper ordained at (Mt 26:26-28; Mk 14:12-25; Lk 22:7-20).

Prisoner released at, by the Romans (Mt 27:15; Mk 15:6; Lk 23:16-17; Jn 18:39). Peter imprisoned at the time of (Ac 12:3).

Christ called our Passover (1Co 5:7).

See Feasts; Hallel.

PASSPORTS *See Safe-Conduct.*

PASTOR A leader of the church (Eph 4:11), possibly the same as elder and overseer. *See Elders; Overseer.*

PASTORAL EPISTLES A common title for 1 and 2 Timothy and Titus, which were written by the apostle Paul to his special envoys sent on specific missions in accordance with the needs of the hour. They give instruction to Timothy and Titus concerning the pastoral care of churches. Though some date the Pastorals within the framework of Acts, most scholars believe all three were written not long after the events of Ac 28. After his imprisonment in Rome (c. A.D. 60-62), Paul most likely began his fourth missionary journey. *See Missionary Journeys of Paul.*

First Timothy was written to Timothy at Ephesus while Paul was still traveling in the coastal regions of the Aegean Sea. Titus was written to Titus in Crete (c. A.D. 63-65), probably from Nicopolis or some other city in Macedonia. Second Timothy was written from Rome toward the end of Paul's second imprisonment shortly before he was executed (A.D. 67 or 68).

The epistles concern church organization and discipline, including such matters as the appointment of bishops and deacons, the opposition of heretical or rebellious members, and the provision for maintenance of doctrinal purity.

Certain themes and phrases recur throughout the Pastoral Letters: (1) *God the Savior.* Three times in 1 Timothy and three times in Titus God the Father is called Savior (1Ti 1:1; 2:3; 4:10; Tit 1:3; 2:10; 3:4). Once in 2 Timothy and three times in Titus Jesus is also called Savior (2Ti 1:10; Tit 1:4; 2:13; 3:6). (2) *Sound doctrine, faith, and teaching.* Correct teaching, in keeping with that of the apostles (1Ti 1:10; 6:3; 2Ti 1:13; 4:3; Tit 1:9). The teaching is called "sound" not only because it builds up in the faith, but because it protects against the corrupting influence of false teachers. (3) *Godliness.* A key word (along with "godly") in the Pastorals, occurring eight times in 1 Timothy (2:2; 3:16; 4:7-8; 6:3, 5-6, 11), once in 2 Timothy (3:5) and once in Titus (1:1), but nowhere else in the writings of Paul. (4) *Controversies.* Appearing in (1Ti 1:4; 6:4; 2Ti 2:23; Tit 3:9); (5) *Trustworthy sayings.* A clause found nowhere else in the NT but used five times in the Pastorals (1Ti 1:15; 3:1; 4:9; 2Ti 2:11; Tit 3:8).

The authorship of these letters has been disputed because of differences in vocabulary and style from the other epistles ascribed to Paul, and because their references to his travels do not accord with the itineraries described in Acts. The differences though real, have been exaggerated, and can be explained on the basis of a change of time, subject matter, scribes, and destination.

See also Church, New Testament Church, Qualifications for Elders/Overseers and Deacons; Timothy, 1 and 2; Titus.

PASTURE A place to graze sheep (Jn 10:9; Ge 29:7); essential for survival of flocks (Ge 47:4; 1Ch 4:39-41; Job 39:8; Isa 14:30; Jer 14:6); where David worked (2Sa 7:8; 1Ch 17:7); for cattle (1Ki 4:23); a figure of peace (Ps 23:2; Ps 37:3); a figure of God's flock (Ps 74:1; 79:13; 83:12; 95:7; 100:3; Jer 23:1-3; 50:7, 19; Eze 34:14); for camels (Eze 25:5). Pasturelands were the environs around towns and villages (Nu 35).

PATARA A Lycian city in Asia Minor. Visited by Paul (Ac 21:1-2).

PATHROS *See Upper Egypt.*

PATHRUSITES *(of Pathros).* A descendant of Mizraim and ancestor of the Philistines (Ge 10:14; 1Ch 1:12).

PATHS, RIGHT (Ps 16:11; 23:3; 25:10; 119:35; Pr 2:9; 4:11, 18; Isa 2:3; 26:7; Heb 12:13).

PATHWAY OF SIN General references to (Pr 2:15; 12:15; 13:15; 14:12; 15:9; Isa 49:8; Mt 7:13). Walking in (Dt 29:19; Jer 7:24; Eph 2:2; Php 3:18; 1Pe 4:3; 2Pe 2:10; 3:3; Jude 18).

PATIENCE Commended (Ecc 7:8-9; La 3:26-27). Commanded (Ps 37:7-9; Eph 4:2; Col 3:12-13; 1Th 5:14; 1Ti 6:11; 2Ti 2:24-25; Tit 2:2; Heb 12:1; Jas 5:7-8; 2Pe 1:5-6). A fruit of tribulation (Ro 5:3-4; Rev 1:9). A grace of the righteous (Ec 8:15; 21:19; Ro 2:7; 8:25; 12:12; 15:4-5; 1Co 13:4-5; 2Co 6:4-6; 12:12; Col 1:10-11; 1Th 1:3; 2Th 3:5; Heb 6:12; 10:36; Jas 1:3-4, 19; 1Pe 2:19-23; Rev 14:12). Prerequisite of a overseer (1Ti 3:3). Propagates peace (Pr 15:18). Possible because of God's righteousness (Rev 13:10).

Instances of: Isaac toward the people of Gerar (Ge 26:15-22). Moses (Ex 16:7-8). Job (Job 1:21; Jas 5:11). David (Ps 40:1). Simeon (Lk 2:25). Paul (2Ti 3:10). Prophets (Jas 5:10). The Thessalonians (2Th 1:4). The church at Ephesus (Rev 2:2-3) and Thyatira (Rev 2:19). John (Rev 1:9).

Of Jesus (1Pe 2:21-23; Rev 1:9). *See Jesus the Christ. See Longsuffering; Meekness.*

PATMOS An island in the Aegean Sea. John an exile on (Rev 1:9).

PATRIARCHAL GOVERNMENT *See Government.*

PATRIARCHS, PATRIARCHAL AGE *(first father [of a nation, tribe]).* Name given in NT to those who founded the Hebrew race and nation: Abraham (Heb 7:4), sons of Jacob (Ac 7:8-9), David (Ac 2:29). The term is now commonly used to refer to the persons whose names appear in the genealogies and covenant-histories before the time of Moses (Ge 5, 11).

PATRICIDE Killing one's father. Of Sennacherib (2Ki 19:37; Isa 37:38; 1Ti 1:9).

PATRIOTISM Commanded (Ps 51:18; 122:6-7). Exhortation concerning (2Sa 10:12). Religious ceremony for the fostering of, commanded (Dt 26:1-11). Appealed to in battle (2Sa 10:12). Songs of: Deborah (Jdg 5:1-31), Israel (Ps 85:1-13; 137:1-6). Lack of, lamented (La 5:1-22).

Instances of: Moses (Heb 11:24-26). Deborah and Barak (Jdg 4:5). The tribes of Zebulun and Naphtali (Jdg 5:18-20). Eli (1Sa 4:17-18). Phinehas' wife (1Sa 4:19-22). Joab (2Sa 10:12). Uriah (2Sa 11:11). The Psalmist (Ps 51:18; 85:1-13). Hadad (1Ki 11:21-22). The lepers of Samaria (2Ki 7:9). Israelite exiles (Ne 1:1-11; 2:1-20; Ps 137:1-6). Nehemiah (Ne 1:2, 4-11; 2:3). The Jews in public defense (Ne 2:3; 4:1-23). Isaiah (Isa 62:1). Jeremiah (Jer 8:11, 21-22; 9:1-2; La 5:1-22).

Lacking in: The tribes of Reuben, Asher, and Dan (Jdg 5:15-17). Inhabitants, of Meroz (Jdg 5:23), of Succoth and Peniel (Jdg 8:4-17).

See Country, Love of.

PATROBAS *(father of existence).* A believer at Rome (Ro 16:14).

PATROS *See Upper Egypt.*

PATTERN Of the tabernacle (Heb 8:5-9:23). *See Tabernacle.*

PAU *(groaning, bleating).* A city of Edom (Ge 36:39; 1Ch 1:50).

PAUL *(little).*

Background and conversion:

Also called Saul (Ac 8:1; 9:1; 13:9). Of the tribe of Benjamin (Ro 11:1; Php 3:5). Personal appearance of (2Co 10:1, 10; 11:6). Born in Tarsus (Ac 9:11; 21:39; 22:3). Educated at Jerusalem in the school of Gamaliel (Ac 22:3; 26:4). A zealous Pharisee (Ac 22:3; 23:6; 26:5; 2Co 11:22; Gal 1:14; Php 3:5). A Roman (Ac 16:37; 22:25-28). Persecutes the Christians; present at and gives consent to the stoning of Stephen (Ac 7:58; 8:1, 3; 9:1; 22:4). Sent to Damascus with letters for the arrest and return to Jerusalem of Christians (Ac 9:1-2).

His vision and conversion (Ac 9:3-22; 22:4-19; 26:9-15; 1Co 9:11; 15:8; Gal 1:13; 1Ti 1:12-13). Is baptized (Ac 9:18; 22:16). Called to be an apostle (Ac 22:14-21; 26:14-21; 26:6-18; Ro 1:1; 1Co 1:1; 9:1-2; 15:9; Gal 1:1, 15-16; Eph 1:1; Col 1:1; 1Ti 1:1; 2:7; 2Ti 1:1, 11; Tit 1:1, 3). Preaches in Damascus (Ac 9:20, 22). Is persecuted by the Jews (Ac 9:23-24). Escapes by being let down from the wall in a basket; goes to Arabia (Gal 1:17), Jerusalem (Ac 9:25-26; Gal 1:18-19). Received by the disciples in Jerusalem (Ac 9:26-29). Goes to Caesarea and returns to Tarsus (Ac 9:30; 18:22).

Brought to Antioch by Barnabas (Ac 11:25-26). Teaches at Antioch one year (Ac 11:26). Brings the contributions of the Christians in Antioch to the Christians in Jerusalem (Ac 11:27-30). Returns with John to Antioch (Ac 12:25).

First Missionary Journey:

See Missionary Journeys of Paul. Sent to the Gentiles (Ac 13:2-3, 47-48; 22:17-21; Ro 11:13; 15:16; Gal 1:15-24). Visits Seleucia (Ac 13:4), Cyprus (Ac 13:4). Preaches at Salamis (Ac 13:5), at Paphos (Ac 13:6). Sergius Paulus the proconsul is converted (Ac 13:7-12). Contends with Elymas the sorcerer (Ac 13:6-12). Visits Perga in Pamphylia (Ac 13:13). John, a companion of, departs for Jerusalem (Ac 13:13). Visits Antioch in Pisidia and preaches in the synagogue (Ac 13:14-41). His message received gladly by the Gentiles (Ac 13:42, 49). Persecuted and expelled (Ac 13:50-51). Visits Iconium and preaches to the Jews and Greeks; is persecuted; escapes to Lystra; goes to Derbe (Ac 14:1-6). Heals an crippled man (Ac 14:8-10). The people attempt to worship him (Ac 14:11-18). Is persecuted by Jews from Antioch and Iconium and is stoned (Ac 14:19; 2Co 11:25; 2Ti 3:11). Escapes to Derbe, where he preaches the gospel, and returns to Lystra, Iconium, and to Antioch, encourages the disciples, and ordains elders (Ac 14:19-23). Revisits Pisidia, Pamphylia, Perga, Attalia, and returns to Antioch (Ac 14:24-28).

Contends with the Judaizing Christians against circumcision (Ac 15:1-2). Refers the question of circumcision to the apostles and elders at Jerusalem (Ac 15:2, 4). He declares to the apostles at Jerusalem the miracles and wonders God had done among the Gentiles by them (Ac 15:12). Returns to Antioch, accompanied by Barnabas, Judas, and Silas, with letters to the Gentiles (Ac 15:22, 25).

Second Missionary Journey:

See Missionary Journeys of Paul. Makes his second tour of the churches (Ac 15:36). Chooses Silas as his companion, and passes through Syria and Cilicia, confirming the churches (Ac 15:36-41). Visits Lystra; circumcises Timothy (Ac 16:1-5). Goes through Phrygia and Galatia; is forbidden by the Holy Spirit to preach in Asia; visits Mysia; desires to go to Bithynia, but is restrained by the Spirit; goes to Troas, where he has a vision of a man saying, "Come over into Macedonia, and help us"; he immediately proceeds to Macedonia (Ac 16:6-10). Visits Samothrace and Neapolis; comes to Philippi, the chief city of Macedonia; visits a place of prayer at the riverside; preaches the Word; the merchant, Lydia of Thyatira, is converted and baptized (Ac 16:11-15). Exorcizes a demon from a fortune-teller (Ac 16:16-18). Persecuted, beaten, and cast into prison with Silas; sings songs of praise in the prison; an earthquake shakes the prison; he preaches to the alarmed jailer, who believes and is baptized with his household (Ac 16:19-34). Is released by the civil authorities on the ground of his being a Roman citizen (Ac 16:35-39; 2Co 6:5; 11:25; 1Th 2:2). Is received at the house of Lydia (Ac 16:40). Visits Amphipolis, Apollonia, and Thessalonica;

preaches in the synagogue (Ac 17:1-4). Is persecuted (Ac 17:5-9; 2Th 1:1-4). Escapes to Berea by night; preaches in the synagogue; many honorable women and men believe (Ac 17:10-12). Persecuted by the Jews who come from Thessalonica; is conducted by the brothers to Athens (Ac 17:13-15). Disputes on Mars' Hill with philosophers (Ac 17:16-34).

Visits Corinth; lives with Aquila and his wife, Priscilla, who were tentmakers; joins in their trade; reasons in the synagogue every Sabbath; is rejected by the Jews; turns to the Gentiles; stays there one year and six months, teaching the word of God (Ac 18:1-11). Persecuted by Jews, taken before the proconsul; accusation dismissed; takes his leave many days, and sails to Syria, accompanied by Aquila and Priscilla (Ac 18:12-18). Visits Ephesus, where he leaves Aquila and Priscilla; enters a synagogue, where he reasons with the Jews; starts on his return journey to Jerusalem; visits Caesarea, and returns to Antioch (Ac 18:19-22).

Third Missionary Journey:

See Missionary Journeys of Paul. Returning to Ephesus, passes through Galatia and Phrygia, strengthening the disciples (Ac 18:18-23). Baptizes disciples of John in the name of the Lord Jesus; preaches in the synagogue, remains in Ephesus for two years; heals the sick (Ac 19:1-12). Jewish exorcists are beaten by a demon and many Ephesians believe, bringing their books of sorcery to be burned (Ac 19:13-20; 1Co 16:8-9). Sends Timothy and Erastus into Macedonia, but he himself remains in Asia for a period of time (Ac 19:21-22). The spread of the gospel through his preaching interferes with the idol-makers; he is persecuted, and a great uproar of the city is created; the city clerk appeases the people; dismisses the accusation against Paul, and disperses the people (Ac 19:23-41; 2Co 1:8; 2Ti 4:14).

Proceeds to Macedonia after encouraging the churches in those parts; comes into Greece and stays three months; returns through Macedonia, accompanied by Sopater, Aristarchus, Secundus, Gaius, Timothy, Tychicus, and Trophimus (Ac 20:1-6). Visits Troas, preaches until the break of day; restores to life Eutychus, who fell from the window (Ac 20:6-12). Visits Assos, Mitylene, Kios, Samos, and Miletus, hurrying to Jerusalem, to be there at Pentecost (Ac 20:13-16). Sends for the elders of the church of Ephesus; tells them of how he had preached in Asia, and of his tests and afflictions testifying repentance toward God; declares he was compelled by the Spirit to go to Jerusalem; exhorts them to watch over themselves and their flock; kneels down, prays, and departs (Ac 20:17-38). Visits Cos, Rhodes, Patara; takes a ship for Tyre; stays seven days; is brought on his way by the disciples to the outskirts of the city; kneels, prays, and leaves; comes to Ptolemais; greets the brothers and stays one day (Ac 21:1-7). Departs for Caesarea; enters the house of Philip the evangelist; is warned by Agabus not to go to Jerusalem; proceeds to Jerusalem (Ac 21:8-16).

Arrest and Trials:

See Missionary Journeys of Paul. Is received warmly by the brothers; talks of the things that had been done among the Gentiles by his ministry; enters the temple; the people are stirred against him by the Jews from Asia; an uproar is created; he is thrown out of the temple; the commander of the troops interposes and arrests him (Ac 21:17-33). His defense (Ac 21:33-40; 22:1-21). Is confined in the barracks (Ac 22:24-30). Is brought before the Sanhedrin; his defense (Ac 22:30; 23:1-5). Is returned to the barracks (Ac 23:10). Is encouraged by a vision, promising him that he must testify in Rome (Ac 23:11). Jews conspire against his life (Ac 23:12-15). Thwarted by his nephew (Ac 23:16-22). Is escorted to Caesarea by a military guard (Ac 23:23-33). Is confined in Herod's palace in Caesarea (Ac 23:35). His trial before Felix (Ac 24). Remains in custody for two years (Ac 24:27). His trial before Festus (Ac 25:1-12). Appeals to Caesar (Ac 25:10-12). His examination before Agrippa (Ac 25:13-27; 26).

Is taken to Rome in custody of Julius, a centurion, and guard of soldiers; boards the ship, accompanied by other prisoners, and sails along the coast of Asia; stops at Sidon and Myra (Ac 27:1-5). Transferred to a ship of Alexandria; sails past Cnidus, Crete, and Salmone to Fair Havens (Ac 27:6-8). Predicts loss of the ship; his advice not heeded, the voyage resumed (Ac 27:9-13). The ship encounters a hurricane; Paul encourages and comforts the officers and crew; the soldiers advise putting the prisoners to death; the centurion interferes, and all 276 on board are saved (Ac 27:14-44). The ship is wrecked, and all on board take refuge on the island of Malta (Ac 27:14-44). Kind treatment by the inhabitants of the island (Ac 28:1-2). Is bitten by a viper and miraculously preserved (Ac 28:3-6). Heals the chief official's father and others (Ac 28:7-10). Is delayed in Malta three months; proceeds on the voyage; delays at Syracuse; sails by Rhegium and Puteoli; meets brothers who accompany him to Rome from the Forum of Appius; arrives at Rome and is permitted to live by himself in custody of a soldier (Ac 28:11-16). Calls the chief Jews together; states his situation; is kindly received; expounds the gospel; testifies to the kingdom of heaven (Ac 28:17-29). Lives two years in his own hired house, preaching and teaching (Ac 28:30-31).

Sickness in Asia (2Co 1:8-11). Caught up to the third heavens (2Co 12:1-4). Has "a thorn in the flesh" (2Co 12:7-9; Gal 4:13-14). His independence of character (1Th 2:9; 2Th 3:8).

Persecutions of:

(Ac 9:16, 23-25, 29; 14:19; 16:19-39; 20:22-24; 21:13, 27-33; 22:22-24; 23:10, 12-15; Ro 8:35-37; 1Co 4:9, 11-13; 2Co 1:8-10; 4:8-9; 6:4-5, 8-10; 11:23-27, 32-33; 12:10; Gal 5:11; 6:17; Php 1:30; Col 1:24; 1Th 2:2, 14-15; 3:4; 2Ti 1:12; 2:9-10; 3:11-12; 4:16-17).

Character of:

(2Co 10:1, 10; 11:6; Gal 4:13). Cheerful in adversity (Ac 10:25; Ro 8:35-37; 2Co 4:8-10; 12:10; 2Ti 2:10; 3:11-12; 4:16-17). Courageous (Ac 9:29; 20:22-24; 21:13; Eph 6:20; 1Th 2:2). Purposeful, even when the Holy Spirit warns him not to go to Jerusalem (Ac 20:22-23; 21:4, 10-14). Indomitable (Ro 8:35-37; 1Co 4:9-13; 2Co 4:8-12; 6:4-10; 11:23-33; 12:10; 1Th 2:2; 2Ti 1:12; 3:11; 4:7). Joyous in suffering (Ac 16:25; Php 2:17; Col 1:24; 2Ti 2:9). Meek (1Co 4:12-13; 2Ti 4:16). Self-forgetful (1Co 4:9, 11-13). Self-supporting (Ac 18:3; 20:33-35; 2Co 11:7, 9; 1Th 2:9; 2Th 3:8). Tactful (1Co 9:19-22; 10:33; Phm 8-21). Zealous (Ro 9:3; 2Co 5:11-14; 6:4-10; 11:22-33; 12:10, 14-15; Php 3:6-16; Col 1:29). Ready for death (2Ti 4:6-8).

PAULUS, SERGIUS Roman proconsul of Cyprus; became a Christian through Paul (Ac 13:6-12).

PAVEMENT, STONE The courtyard outside the palace in Jerusalem where Pilate passed public sentence on Jesus (Jn 19:13).

PAVILION (*booth, tent*). Movable tent or canopy (1Ki 20:12; Jer 43:10). Figuratively of God's protection (Ps 27:5) or majesty (Job 36:29).

PAWN See Surety.

PAZZEZ See Beth Pazzez.

PEACE

From God:
(Nu 6:26; Ps 29:11; 85:8; Isa 26:12; 57:19; 1Co 14:33).

Social:
Beneficence of (Ps 133:1; Pr 15:17; 17:1, 14; Ecc 4:6). Honorable (Pr 20:3).
Commanded (Ge 45:24; Ps 34:14; Jer 29:7; Mk 9:50; Ro 12:18; 14:19; 2Co 13:11; Eph 4:3, 31-32; 1Th 5:13; 1Ti 2:2; 2Ti 2:22; Heb 12:14; 1Pe 3:10-11). Love of, commanded (Zec 8:19). Promised (Lev 26:6; Job 5:23-24; Isa 2:4; 11:6-9, 13; 60:17-18; Hos 2:18). The righteous assured of (Pr 16:7). Broken by the gospel (Mt 10:21-22, 34-36; Lk 12:51-53). Moses' efforts in behalf of, resented (Ex 2:13-14; Ac 7:26-29).
Promoters of peace promised: Joy (Pr 12:20). Adoption (Mt 5:9). Fruit of righteousness (Jas 3:17-18). God's favor (Lk 2:14).
Instances of promoters of peace: Abraham (Ge 13:8-9), Abimelech (Ge 26:29), Mordecai (Est 10:3). David (Ps 120:6-7).
See Charitableness; Nation, Peace of.

Spiritual:
Through Christ (Isa 2:4; 9:6-7; 11:6, 13; Mic 4:3, 5; Lk 1:79; Jn 7:38; 14:27; Ac 10:36; Ro 5:1; 10:15). To the world (Isa 2:4; 11:6-9; Lk 2:14). To God's children (Isa 54:10, 13).
From God (Nu 34:29; Ps 29:11; 72:3, 7; 85:8; Jer 33:6; Eze 34:25; Hag 2:9; Mal 2:5; Ro 15:13, 33; 16:20; 1Co 1:3; 14:33; 2Co 1:2; Gal 1:3; Php 4:7, 9; 1Th 1:1; 5:23; 2Th 3:16; 1Ti 1:2; 2Ti 1:2; Tit 1:4; Phm ; Heb 13:20; Rev 1:4). From Christ (Mt 11:29; Jn 14:27; 16:33; 20:19; Eph 2:14-17; Col 3:15; Rev 1:4-5).
A fruit of the Spirit (Ro 14:17; Gal 5:22). A fruit of righteousness (Ro 2:10). Assured to the righteous (Ps 37:4, 11, 37; 125:1, 5; Pr 3:17, 24; Isa 26:3, 12; 32:2, 17-18; 55:2, 12; 57:1-2, 19; Ro 8:6).
Through the reconciliation of Christ (Isa 53:5; Jn 7:38; Ro 5:1; Col 1:20), acquaintance with God (Job 22:21, 26; Ps 4:8; 17:15; 73:25-26; Isa 12:1-2; 25:8; 28:12; Lk 2:29), loving God's law (Ps 1:1-2; 119:165), obedience (Pr 25:12-13; Isa 48:18; Jer 6:16).
No peace to the wicked (Isa 48:22; 57:21). To be made with God (Isa 27:5).
See Charitableness; Joy; Praise.

PEACE OFFERINGS See Fellowship Offerings; Offerings.

PEACOCK See Baboons; Ostrich.

PEARL (Rev 17:4; 18:12, 16). "Pearl of great price" (Mt 13:45-46). Ornaments made of (1Ti 2:9).

Figurative:
Teaching should be given in accordance with the spiritual capacity of the learners (Mt 7:6).

Symbolic:
The twelve gates of the Holy City, the New Jerusalem, are each made of a single pearl (Rev 21:21).
See Minerals of the Bible, 1; Stones.

PECULIAR PEOPLE See Saints.

PEDAHEL (*God [El] ransoms*). Chief of Naphtali (Nu 34:28).

PEDAHZUR (*the Rock ransoms*). Father of Gamaliel (Nu 1:10; 2:20; 7:54, 59; 10:23).

PEDAIAH (*Yahweh ransoms*).
1. Grandfather of Jehoiakim (2Ki 23:36).
2. Father of Zerubbabel (1Ch 3:18).
3. Father of Joel, chief of Manasseh (1Ch 27:20).
4. Man who helped build the wall of Jerusalem (Ne 3:25).
5. A Benjamite, the father of Joed (Ne 11:7).
6. Levite; temple treasurer (Ne 13:13).

PEEP NIV "chirp" of a bird (Isa 10:14); "whisper" of a medium supposed to come from the dead (Isa 8:19).

PEKAH (*he has opened*). The son of Remaliah the eighteenth king of Israel; murdered Pekahiah; reigned from 752-732 B.C. (2Ki 15:27); made a league with Damascus against Judah (2Ki 15:37-38); became subject to Assyria (2Ki 15:29); murdered by Hoshea (2Ki 15:25-31; 2Ch 28:5-15).

PEKAHIAH (*Yahweh opens*). Israel's seventeenth king; son of Menahem; wicked and idolatrous (2Ki 15:24); murdered by Pekah (2Ki 15:22-25).

PEKOD (*visitation*). Aramean tribe living to the E and near the mouth of the Tigris (Jer 50:21; Eze 23:23).

PELAIAH (*Yahweh is spectacular*).
1. Son of Elioenai (1Ch 3:24).
2. A Levite who assisted Ezra in instructing the people in the law (Ne 8:7; 10:10).

PELALIAH (*Yahweh intercedes in arbitration*). A priest; the father of Jeroham and Amzi (Ne 11:12).

PELATIAH (*Yahweh rescues*).
1. Grandson of Zerubbabel (1Ch 3:21).
2. A Simeonite military leader (1Ch 4:42).
3. A man who sealed a covenant with Nehemiah (Ne 10:22).

4. A prince of Israel; Ezekiel prophesied against him (Eze 11:2, 13).

PELEG (*water canal*). The son of Eber (Ge 10:25; 11:16-19; 1Ch 1:19, 25; Lk 3:35).

PELET (*rescue*).
1. Son of Jahdai (1Ch 2:47).
2. Son of Azmaveth (1Ch 12:3).

PELETH (perhaps *swift*, or *swiftness*).
1. A Reubenite (Nu 16:1).
2. Son of Jonathan (1Ch 2:33).

PELETHITES (*courier*). A part of David's bodyguard (1Ki 1:38; 2Sa 8:18; 20:7, 23; 1Ch 18:17). Absalom's escort (2Sa 15:18).

PELICAN See Owl.

PELLA A city E of the Sea of Galilee; one of the cities forming the Decapolis.

PELONITE(S) (*separates*). Designation of two of David's mighty men: Helez (1Ch 11:27; 27:10) and Ahijah (1Ch 11:36).

PELUSIUM An Egyptian city on the E arm of the Nile, KJV "Sin" (Eze 30:15-16).

PEN (Jdg 5:14; Ps 45:1; Isa 8:1; Jer 8:8; 3Jn 13). Made of iron (Job 19:24; Jer 17:1).

PENALTY

Vicariously assumed:
By Rebekah (Ge 27:13), Abigail (1Sa 25:24), the woman of Tekoa (2Sa 14:9), the persecutors of the Jews (Mt 27:25), Jesus for the human race (Gal 3:13). Paul desires to assume for Israel (Ro 9:3). *See Suffering, Vicarious.*
See Fine; Judgments; Punishment; Sin, Punishment of; Wicked, Punishment of. See also penalties under various crimes, such as Murder.

PENCE See Money; Penny.

PENDANTS Articles of jewelry (Jdg 8:26). *See Dress.*

PENIEL (*face of God [El]*). The place where Jacob wrestled with the angel of Yahweh (Ge 32:24-32), not far from Succoth (Jdg 8:8-9, 17). Also spelled Penuel (Ge 32:31; Jdg 8:8; 1Ki 12:25, ftns).

PENINNAH (possibly *pearls, coral branches* KB; *woman with rich hair* KB). One of the wives of Elkanah (1Sa 1:2).

PENITENCE See Repentance; Sin, Confession of.

PENITENT

Promises to:
Of mercy (Lev 26:40-42; Dt 4:29-31; 30:1-10; 2Ki 22:19; 1Ch 28:9; Job 22:23-29; 33:26-28; Ps 6:8-9; 9:10; 22:26; 90:14-15; 145:18-19; 147:3; Isa 27:5; Mt 5:4; 7:7-11 w Lk 11:9-13; Mt 12:20, 31; Lk 12:10).
Of forgiveness (Ps 32:5-6; 34:18; 51:17; 86:5; Isa 55:7; Eze 18:21-23; 33:10-16; Mt 6:14-15; 11:28-30; Lk 6:37; 15:4-32 w Mt 18:12-14; Lk 18:10-14; Jn 6:37; Ac 13:38-39; 1Jn 1:9).
Of salvation (Ps 145:18-19; Lk 4:18; 19:10; Ro 10:9-13; Heb 7:25).
Of divine favor (Nu 5:6-7; Isa 66:2).
See Forgiveness; Repentance; Sin, Confession of. See also, Obduracy; Reprobacy.

PENKNIFE See Knife.

PENNY The smallest Roman copper coin (Mt 5:26; Mk 12:42; Lk 12:6, 59). *See Money.*

PENS
1. Walled enclosure for livestock (Nu 32:16, 24, 36; Jn 10:1, 16).
2. Instrument for writing (Ps 45:1; Isa 8:1; Jer 8:8; 3Jn 13).

PENSION Of Levites (2Ch 31:16-18).

PENTATEUCH, THE (*five books*, i.e., the *torah* or law). The first five books of the Bible; covers the period of time from the creation to the end of the Mosaic era; authorship is attributed to Moses in Scripture.

Outline:
1. Era of beginnings (Ge 1:1-11:32).
2. Patriarchal period (Ge 12:1-50:26).
3. Emancipation of Israel (Ex 1:1-19:2).
4. Religion of Israel (Ex 19:3-Lev 27:34).
5. Organization of Israel (Nu 1:1-10:10).
6. Wilderness wanderings (Nu 10:11-22:1).
7. Preparations for entering Canaan (Nu 22:2-36:13).
8. Retrospect and prospect (Dt 1-34).

PENTECOST (*fiftieth [day]*).
1. The Israelite Feast of Weeks (Ex 34:22; Dt 16:9-11), also called the Feast of Harvest (Ex 23:16) and the day of firstfruits (Nu 28:26), which fell on the fiftieth day after Passover. The feast originally celebrated the dedication of the firstfruits of the wheat harvest, the last crop to ripen. The ritual of the feast is described (Lev 23:15-21). Institution of (Ex 23:16; 34:22; Lev 23:15-21; Nu 28:26-31; Dt 16:9-12, 16). Called in the NT the Day of Pentecost (Ac 2:1; 20:16; 1Co 16:8). *See Annual Feasts; Feasts.*
2. The Christian Pentecost fell on the same day as the Israelite Feast of Weeks. The coming of the Holy Spirit (Ac 2) transformed the Israelite festival into a Christian anniversary, marking the beginning of the Christian church.

PENUEL (*face of God [El]*).
1. Son of Hur and chief of Gedor (1Ch 4:4).
2. Son of Shashak (1Ch 8:25).

3. Variant spelling of Peniel. See Peniel.

PENURIOUSNESS See Parsimony.

PEOPLE Common. Heard Jesus gladly (Mt 7:28; 9:8, 33; 13:54; Mk 6:2).

PEOR (*opening*).
1. A mountain in Moab near the town of Beth Peor (Dt 3:29).
2. Contraction for Baal Peor (Nu 25:18; 31:16; Jos 22:17). *See Baal Peor.*

PERAEA See Perea.

PERATH In Hebrew it has the same spelling as Euphrates (Jer 13:4-7, ftn). Some identify it with Wadi Farah (Parah, Jos 18:23) near Anathoth.

PERAZIM, MOUNT (*breaking out*). Usually identified with Baal Perazim, where David obtained a victory over the Philistines (2Sa 5:20; 1Ch 14:11).

PERDITION (*ruin, destruction*). In the NT the word refers to the final state of the wicked, one of loss or destruction (Jn 17:12; Php 1:28; 2Th 2:3; 1Ti 6:9).

PERDITION, SON OF A phrase used to designate Judas Iscariot (Jn 17:12) and the "man of lawlessness" who is the Antichrist (2Th 2:3).

PEREA (*beyond the Jordan*). The name given by Josephus to the region E of the Jordan; known in the Gospels as "across the Jordan" (Mt 4:15, 25; Mk 3:7-8).

PERES (*divided*). One of the words written on a wall for Belshazzar and interpreted by Daniel (Da 5:1-29).

PERESH (*offal eviscerated* BDB; *dung* ISBE; *contents of stomach [not intestine]* KB). Son of Makir (1Ch 7:16).

PEREZ, PEREZITE (*breaking out*). A son of Judah by Tamar (Ge 38:29; 1Ch 2:4), descendants of (Ge 46:12; Nu 26:20-21; 1Ch 2:5; 9:4), return from the Captivity (Ne 11:4, 6). In the lineage of David and Jesus (Ru 4:12; Mt 1:3; Lk 3:33).

PEREZ UZZAH (*breaking out of Uzzah*). The name of the place where Uzzah was struck dead for touching the ark of God (2Sa 6:8, ftn). Perez Uzzah means *outbreak against Uzzah;* the place name memorialized a divine warning that was not soon forgotten.
See Nacon.

PERFECTION Major idea: complete or whole, rather than without fault or shortcoming. None without sin (1Ki 8:46; 2Ch 6:36; Ecc 7:20).
From God (Ps 18:32; 1Pe 5:10). Through Christ (Col 1:21-22, 28; 2:9-11; Heb 10:14; 13:20-21; 1Pe 5:10; 1Jn 3:6-10). Through God's love (1Jn 4:12).

Ascribed to:
Noah (Ge 6:8-9), Jacob (Nu 23:21), David (1Ki 11:4, 6), Asa (1Ki 15:14), Job (Job 1:1), Zechariah and Elizabeth (Lk 1:6), Nathanael (Jn 1:47). The peaceful (Ps 37:31, 37). The wise (1Co 2:6). Man of God (2Ti 3:17). The self-controlled (Jas 3:2). Those who obey God's word (1Jn 2:5).

Blessings of:
(Ps 106:3; 119:1-3, 6; Mt 5:6). Reward of (Ps 37:31, 37; Pr 2:21; Lk 6:40; 1Jn 5:18).

Commanded:
(Ge 17:1; Dt 5:32; 18:13; Jos 23:6; 1Ki 8:61; 1Ch 28:9; Mt 5:48; 2Co 7:1; 13:11; Php 1:10; 2:15; Col 3:14; Jas 1:4). Requirements for (Dt 5:32; Jos 23:6; 1Ki 8:61; 1Ch 29:19; Mt 19:21; 2Co 7:1). Program for (Eph 4:11-13; Heb 6:1; 1Jn 2:5).

Desire for:
(Mt 5:6; 2Ti 3:17). In Job (Job 9:20-21). In David (Ps 101:2). In Paul (Php 3:12-15).

Prayer for:
(1Ch 29:19; 2Co 13:9; Col 4:12; 1Th 3:10, 13; Heb 13:20-21).

God is Perfect:
(Dt 32:4; 2Sa 22:31; Ps 18:30; 19:7; 50:2).
See God, Perfection of; Holiness; Sanctification.

PERFIDY See Conspiracy; Hypocrisy; Treachery.

PERFUME, PERFUMER
1. For personal use (Pr 7:17; 27:9; SS 1:12; 3:6; Isa 3:20, 24), burial (2Ch 16:14).
2. For sacred incense (Ex 30:34-38; 37:29).
See Nard.

PERGA The capital of Pamphylia. Paul preaches in (Ac 13:13-14; 14:25).

PERGAMUM A city of Mysia. One of the "seven churches" (Rev 1:11; 2:12-17).

PERIDA (*single, unique*). One of the servants of Solomon. Descendants of, returned to Jerusalem, from captivity in Babylon (Ne 7:57). Called Peruda (Ezr 2:55).

PERIZZITES (*villager*). One of the seven nations in the land of Canaan (Ge 13:7). Territory of, given to Abraham (Ge 15:20; Ex 3:8; 23:23). Doomed to destruction (Dt 20:17). Not all destroyed; Israelites marry among (Jdg 3:5-7; Ezr 9:1-2).
See Canaanite(s).

PERJURY (Isa 48:1; Jer 5:2; 7:9; 1Ti 1:9-10).

Condemned:
Forbidden (Lev 19:12; Zec 8:17; Mt 5:33). Penalty for (Lev 6:2-7). Judgments upon perjurers (Hos 10:4; Zec 5:3-4; Mal 3:5).

Instances of:

Zedekiah (2Ch 36:13). Witnesses against Naboth (1Ki 21:8-13), against David (Ps 35:11), against Jesus (Mt 26:59-61; Mk 14:56-59), against Stephen (Ac 6:11, 13-14). Peter, when he denied Jesus with an oath (Mt 26:74; Mk 14:71).

See Falsehood; False Witness; Oath.

PERSECUTION

Of Jesus:

(Ac 4:27; Heb 12:2-3; 1Pe 4:1). Meekly endured (Isa 50:6). Foretold (Ge 3:15; Isa 49:7; 50:6; 52:14; 53:2-10; Mic 5:1; Zec 12:10; Mt 2:13). Typified, in the persecutions of Israel's kings (Ps 2:1-5; 22:1-2, 6-8, 11-21; 109:25; Ro 15:3).

Persecution by the Jews (Mt 12:14; 22:15; 26:3-4; Mk 12:13; 15:14; Lk 6:11; 11:53-54; 20:20; 22:2-5, 52-53; 23:23; Jn 5:16; 7:1, 7, 19; 11:57; 15:18, 20-21; 18:22-23; 19:6, 15; Ac 2:23). In making false imputation (Mt 12:24; Mk 3:22; Lk 11:15; Jn 10:20). In bringing false accusation (Mt 11:19; Lk 7:34; Jn 8:29-30). In acts of violence (Lk 4:28-29; 22:63-65 w Mt 26:67; Mk 14:65). In seeking false testimony (Mt 26:59). In seeking his death (Mt 26:14-16; Mk 3:6, 21; 14:1, 48; 11:18; Lk 19:47; Jn 7:20, 30, 32; 8:37, 40, 48, 52, 59; 10:31). In crucifying him (Ac 3:13-15; 7:52; 13:27-29; 1Co 2:8).

Persecution by Herod (Lk 13:31; 23:11). Persecution by the Roman soldiers (Mt 27:25-30; Mk 15:15-20; Jn 19:2-3). Forsaken by God (Mk 15:34).

Of the Righteous:

(Ge 49:23; Ps 11:2; 37:32; 38:20; 74:7-8; 119:51, 61, 69, 78, 85-87, 95, 110, 157, 161; Pr 29:10, 27; Isa 26:20; 29:20-21; 59:15; Jer 11:19; 15:10; 18:18; Am 5:10; Ro 8:35; 2Co 12:10; Gal 4:29; 6:17).

By mocking (Ps 42:3, 10; 69:9-12; 119:51; Jer 20:7-8). By violence (Ps 94:5; Jer 2:30; 50:7; Ac 5:29, 40-42; 7:52; Gal 6:12, 17; 1Th 2:2, 14-15; Jas 2:6). By ecclesiastical censure (Jn 9:22, 34; 12:42; 2Ti 4:16-17).

Divine permissions of, mysterious (Hab 1:13). The mode of divine chastisement (La 1:3). Done to church members (Ac 8:1, 4; 11:19-21; Php 1:12-14, 18). Powerless to separate from the love of Christ (Ro 8:17, 35-39).

Exhortations to courage under (Isa 51:12, 16; Heb 12:3-4; 13:13; 1Pe 3:14, 16-17; 4:12-14, 16, 19). Courageously endured (Jer 26:11-14; 1Co 4:9-13; 2Co 4:8-12; 6:4-5, 8-10; 11:23-27; 12:10; 2Th 1:4; 2Ti 1:8, 12; 2:9-10; Heb 11:25-27; 11:33-38; Jas 5:6, 10). Rejoicing under (Ro 5:3; Col 1:24; 1Th 1:6; Heb 10:32-34). Perseverance under (Ps 44:15-18, 22).

Prayer for deliverance from (Ps 70:1-5; 83:1; 140:1, 4; 142:6). Deliverance from (Ps 124; 129:1-2). John's vision concerning (Rev 2:3, 10, 13; 6:9-11; 7:13-17; 12:10-11; 17:6; 20:4).

Of Christians, foretold (Mt 20:22; 23:34-35; 24:8-10; Mk 13:9-13; Lk 21:12-19; Jn 15:18-21; 16:1-2; 2Ti 3:2-3, 12-13; 1Jn 3:1, 13). Christ offers consolation (Mk 8:38; 9:42; Lk 6:22-23; 17:33; Jn 17:14). Promises to those who endure (Mt 5:10-12; 10:16-18, 21-23, 28-31; Lk 6:22-23). Should provoke love (1Co 13:3).

Instances of:

Abel (Ge 4:8; Mt 23:35; 1Jn 3:12). Lot (Ge 19:9). Moses (Ex 2:15; 17:4). David (Ps 31:13; 56:5; 59:1-2). Prophets martyred by Jezebel (1Ki 18:4). Gideon (Jdg 6:28-32). Elijah (1Ki 18:10; 19; 2Ki 1:9; 2:23). Micaiah (1Ki 22:26; 2Ch 18:26). Elisha (2Ki 6:31). Hanani (2Ch 16:10). Zechariah (2Ch 24:21; Mt 23:35). Job (Job 1:9; 2:4-5; 12:4-5; 13:4-13; 16:1-4; 17:2; 19:1-5; 30:1-10). Jeremiah (Jer 11:19; 15:10, 15; 17:15-18; 18:18-23; 26; 32:2; 33:1; 36:26; 37; 38:1-6). Uriah (Jer 26:23). The prophets (2Ch 36:16; Mt 21:35-36; 1Th 2:15). The three Hebrews of the Captivity (Da 3:8-23). Daniel (Da 6). The Jews (Ezr 4; Ne 4).

John the Baptist (Mt 14:3-12). James (Ac 12:2). Simon (Mk 15:21). The disciples (Jn 9:22, 34; 20:19). Lazarus (Jn 9:22, 34; 12:10; 20:19). The apostles (Ac 4:3-16, 18; 5:18-42; 12:1-19; Rev 1:9). Stephen (Ac 6:9-15; 7:1-60). The church (Ac 8:1; 9:1-14; Gal 1:13). Timothy (Heb 13:23). John (Rev 1:9). Antipas (Rev 2:13). The church of Smyrna (Rev 2:8-10).

Paul (2Ti 2:9-10; 4:16-17; Ac 9:16, 23-25, 29; 16:19-25; 21:2-33; 22:22-24; 23:10, 12-15; 1Co 4:9, 11-13; 2Co 1:8-10; 4:8-12; 6:4-5, 8-10; 11:23-27, 32-33; Col 1:24; 1Th 2:2, 14-15; 2Ti 1:8, 12; 3:11-12). *See Paul.*

PERSEPOLIS Capital of Persia, thirty miles NE of modern Shiraz; founded by Darius I (521-486 B.C.); destroyed by Alexander the Great in 331 B.C.

PERSEVERANCE

From the Lord:

(Ps 37:24, 28; Ro 8:30, 33-35; 1Co 1:8-9; 2Co 1:21-22). Acknowledged (Ps 73:24; 138:8; Ro 8:37-39; Col 2:7; 2Ti 4:18). Promised (Jer 32:40; Jn 6:34-40; 10:28-29).

Commanded:

(1Ch 16:11; Hos 12:6; 1Th 5:21; 2Th 2:15-17; 2Ti 2:1, 3, 12; 3:14; Tit 1:9; Jas 1:4, 25; 1Pe 4:16; 5:8-9; Rev 22:11). Exhortations to (Ac 11:23; 13:43; 14:21-22; 1Co 15:58; 16:13; Gal 5:1, 10; Eph 4:14-15; 6:13, 18; Php 1:27; 3:16; 4:1; Col 1:10, 22-23; 1Th 3:8; 2Th 3:15; 2Ti 1:13; Heb 2:1; 6:1, 11-12, 15; 10:23, 35-36; 12:5-15; 13:9, 13; 2Pe 3:17-18; Rev 16:15).

A proof of discipleship (Jn 8:31-32). A condition of fruitfulness (Jn 15:4-5, 7, 9). Intercessory prayer for (Lk 22:31-32).

Motives to:

The example, of Moses (Heb 3:5). Of the prophets (Jas 5:10-11). Of Christ (Heb 3:6, 14; 12:2-4). The intercession of Christ (Heb 4:14). The heavenly witnesses (Heb 12:1). Acceptance by Christ (2Co 5:9, 15; 1Pe 1:4-7).

Rewards contingent upon (Gal 6:9; Jas 1:12; Rev 2:7, 10-11, 17, 25-28; 3:5, 11, 21; 14:12; 21:7). Eternal life contingent upon (Mt 10:22; 24:13; Mk 13:13; Ro 2:6-7; 2Pe 1:10-11).

Lacking in:

The wayside and other hearers (Mk 4:3-8). Churches of Asia (Rev 2:5; 3:1-3, 14-18).

Instances of:

Caleb and Joshua, in representing the land of promise (Nu 14:24, 38). The righteous (Job 17:9; Pr 4:18).

In prayer, Abraham in interceding for Sodom (Ge 18:23-32), Jacob (Ge 32:24-26), Elijah for rain (1Ki 18:42-45), Paul for the removal of the thorn in his flesh (2Co 12:7-9).

See Character; Instability; Stability.

PERSIA

In Biblical History:

An empire which extended from India to Ethiopia, comprising 127 provinces (Est 1:1; Da 6:1). Government of, restricted by constitutional limitations (Est 8:8; Da 6:8-12). Municipal governments in, provided with dual governors (Ne 3:9, 12, 16-18). The princes advisory in matters of administration (Da 6:1-7). Status of women in, queen sat on the throne with the king (Ne 2:6). Vashti divorced for refusing to appear before the king's courtiers (Est 1:10-22; 2:4).

Israel captive in (2Ch 36:20), captivity foretold (Hos 13:16). Men of in the Syrian army (Eze 27:10).

Rulers of:

Xerxes (Est 1:3). Darius (Da 5:31; 6; 9:1). Artaxerxes I (Ezr 4:7-24). Artaxerxes II (Ezr 7; Ne 2; 5:1). Cyrus (2Ch 36:22-23; Ezr 1; 3:7; 4:3; 5:13-14, 17; 6:3; Isa 41:2-3; 44:28; 45:1-4, 13; 46:11; 48:14-15). Princes of (Est 1:14).

System of justice (Ezr 7:25). Prophecies concerning (Isa 13:17; 21:1-10; Jer 49:34-39; 51:11-64; Eze 32:24-25; 38:5; Da 2:31-45; 5:28; 7; 8; 11:1-4).

See Babylon; Chaldea.

PERSIS (*female Persian*). A Christian woman in Rome (Ro 16:12).

PERSONAL CALL *See Call, Personal; Minister, Call of.*

PERSONIFICATION Of wisdom (Pr 1; 2:1-19; 8-9). Of the Israel and/or the Church, in allegorical interpretation (SS 1-8). *See Pantomime.*

PERUDA (*single, unique*). One of the servants of Solomon. Descendants of, return to Jerusalem from captivity in Babylon (Ezr 2:55). Called Perida (Ne 7:57).

PERVERSENESS (Pr 11:3; 12:8; 15:4; 28:6; Eze 9:9; Mt 17:17; 1Ti 6:5).

PESHITTA (*simple*, i.e., no marginal notes). Ancient Syriac translation of the Bible.

PESTILENCE Sent as a judgment (Lev 26:16, 25). Sent upon the Egyptians. *See Egypt; Plague.*

PESTLE An instrument used to grind in a mortar (Pr 27:22).

PETER, 1 and 2

1 Peter:

Author: The apostle Peter

Date: In the early 60s A.D.

Outline:

I. Salutation (1:1-2).
II. Praise to God for His Grace and Salvation (1:3-12).
III. Exhortations to Holiness of Life (1:13-5:11).
 A. The Requirement of Holiness (2:4-12).
 B. The Position of Believers (2:4-12).
 1. A spiritual house (2:4-8).
 2. A chosen people (2:9-10).
 3. Aliens and strangers (2:11-12).
 C. Submission to Authority (2:13-3:7).
 1. Submission to rulers (2:13-17).
 2. Submission to masters (2:18-20).
 3. Christ's example of submission (2:21-25).
 4. Submission of wives to husbands (3:1-6).
 5. The corresponding duty of husbands (3:7).
 D. Duties of All (3:8-17).
 E. Christ's Example (3:18-4:6).
 F. Conduct in View of the End of All Things (4:7-11).
 G. Conduct of Those Who Suffer for Christ (4:12-19).
 H. Conduct of Elders (5:1-4).
 I. Conduct of Young Men (5:5-11).
IV. The Purpose of the Letter (5:12).
V. Closing Greetings (5:13-14).
 See General Letters.

2 Peter:

Author: The apostle (Simon) Peter

Date: Probably between 65 and 68.

Outline:

I. Introduction (1:1-2).
II. Exhortation to Growth in Christian Virtues (1:3-11).
 A. The Divine Enablement (1:3-4).
 B. The Call for Growth (1:5-7).
 C. The Value of Such Growth (1:8-11).
III. The Purpose and Authentication of Peter's Message (1:12-21).
 A. His Aim in Writing (1:12-15).
 B. The Basis of His Authority (1:16-21).
IV. Warning Against False Teachers (ch. 2).
 A. Their Coming Predicted (2:1-3a).
 B. Their Judgment Assured (2:3b-9).
 C. Their Characteristics Set Forth (2:10-22).
V. The Fact of Christ's Return (3:1-16).
 A. Peter's Purpose in Writing Restated (3:1-2).
 B. The Coming of Scoffers (3:3-7).
 C. The Certainty of Christ's Return (3:8-10).
 D. Exhortations Based on the Fact of Christ's Return (3:11-16).
VI. Concluding Remarks (3:17-18).
 See General Letters.

PETER, SIMON (*rock, stone*). Also called Simon and Cephas (Mt 16:16-19; Mk 3:16; Jn 1:42). Simeon (Ac 15:14, ftn). A fisherman (Mt 4:18; Lk 5:1-7; Jn 21:3). Call of (Mt 4:18-20; Mk 1:16-18; Lk 5:1-11). His wife's mother healed (Mt 8:14; Mk 1:29-30; Lk 4:38). An apostle (Mt 10:2; 16:18-19; Mk 3:16; Lk 6:14; Ac 1:13). An evangelist (Mk 1:36-37). Confesses Jesus as Christ (Mt 16:16-19; Mk 8:29; Lk 9:20; Jn 6:68-69). His presumption in rebuking Jesus (Mt 16:22-23; Mk 8:32-33), when the throng was pressing Jesus and the woman touched him (Lk 8:45), when Jesus foretold his persecution and death (Mt 16:21-23; Mk 8:31-33), in refusing to let Jesus wash his feet (Jn 13:6-11). Present at the healing of Jairus's daughter (Mk 5:37; Lk 8:51), at the transfiguration (Mt 17:1-4; Mk 9:2-6; Lk 9:28-33; 2Pe 1:16-18), in Gethsemane (Mt 26:36-46; Mk 14:33-42; Lk 22:40-46). Seeks the interpretation of the parable of the manager (Lk 12:41), of the law of forgiveness (Mt 18:21), of the law of defilement (Mt 15:15), of the prophecy of Jesus concerning his second coming (Mk 13:34). Walks upon the water of the Sea of Galilee (Mt 14:28-31). Sent with John to prepare the Passover (Lk 22:8). Calls attention to the withered fig tree (Mk 11:21). His failure foretold by Jesus, and his profession of fidelity (Mt 26:33-35; Mk 14:29-31; Lk 22:31-34; Jn 13:36-38). Cuts off the ear of Malchus (Mt 26:51; Mk 14:47; Lk 22:50). Follows Jesus to the high priest's palace (Mt 26:58; Mk 14:54; Lk 22:54; Jn 18:15). His denial of Jesus and his repentance (Mt 26:69-75; Mk 14:66-72; Lk 22:55-62; Jn 18:17-18, 25-27). Visits the tomb (Lk 24:12; Jn 20:2-6). Jesus sends message to, after the Resurrection (Mk 16:7). Jesus appears to (Lk 24:34; 1Co 15:4-5). Present at the Sea of Tiberias when Jesus appeared to his disciples; leaps into the sea, and comes to land when Jesus is recognized, is commissioned to feed the flock of Christ (Jn 21:1-23).

Remains in Jerusalem (Ac 1:13). His statement before the disciples concerning the death of Judas, and his recommendation that the vacancy in the apostleship be filled (Ac 1:15-22). Preaches at Pentecost (Ac 2:14-40). Heals the crippled man in the portico of the temple (Ac 3). Accused by the council; his defense (Ac 4:1-23). Foretells the death of Ananias and Sapphira (Ac 5:1-11). Imprisoned and scourged; his defense before the council (Ac 5:17-42). Goes to Samaria (Ac 8:14). Prays for the baptism of the Holy Spirit (Ac 8:15-18). Rebukes Simon, the sorcerer, who desires to purchase like power (Ac 8:18-24). Returns to Jerusalem (Ac 8:25). Receives Paul (Gal 1:18; 2:9). Visits Lydda; heals Aeneas (Ac 9:32-34). Visits Joppa; stays with Simon the tanner; raises Dorcas from the dead (Ac 9:36-43). Has a vision of a sheet containing clean and unclean animals (Ac 10:9-16). Receives the servant of the centurion; goes to Caesarea; preaches and baptizes the centurion and his household (Ac 10). Advocates, in the council of the apostles and elders, the preaching of the gospel to the Gentiles (Ac 11:1-18; 15:7-11). Imprisoned and delivered by an angel (Ac 12:3-19). Writes two letters (1Pe 1:1; 2Pe 1:1).

Miracles of. *See Miracles, Of the Disciples of Jesus.*

PETHAHIAH (*Yahweh opens*).
1. A priest in the reign of David (1Ch 24:16).
2. A Levite who divorced his Gentile wife (Ezr 10:23).
3. A Levite, probably identical with 2 (Ne 9:5).
4. A counselor of Artaxerxes (Ne 11:24).

PETHOR A city in Mesopotamia. Home of the prophet Balaam (Nu 22:5; Dt 23:4).

PETHUEL (*God's opening*). Father of the prophet Joel (Joel 1:1).

PETITION Right of, recognized by Pharaoh (Ex 5:15-18), Israel (Nu 27:1-5; 32:1-5; 36:1-5; Jos 17:4, 14, 16; 21:1-2), David (1Ki 1:15-21), Rehoboam (1Ki 12:1-17; 2Ch 10), Jehoram (2Ki 8:3, 6).

PETRA (*rock, cliff, rock grotto*). OT Sela (Jdg 1:36; 2Ki 14:7; Isa 16:1). Capital city of the Nabateans. *See Nabatea, Nabateans; Sela.*

PEULLETHAI (*worker, wage earner*). A gatekeeper of the tabernacle (1Ch 26:5).

PHALEC *See Peleg.*

PHALLU *See Pallu.*

PHALTI *See Palti.*

PHALTIEL *See Paltiel.*

PHANUEL (*face of God [El]*). Father of Anna the prophetess (Lk 2:36).

PHARAOH (*the great house*).
1. King of Egypt at the time of Abraham (Ge 12:14-20; Ps 105:14).
2. Ruler of Egypt at the time of the famine. *See Egypt; Israel, Israelites.*
3. Ruler of Egypt at the time of the deliverance and exodus of the Israelites. *See Israel, Israelites.*
4. Father-in-law of Mered (1Ch 4:18).
5. Ruler of Egypt at the time of David (1Ki 11:17-22).
6. Father-in-law of Solomon (1Ki 3:1; 9:16).
7. At the time of Hezekiah (2Ki 18:21).
8. Pharaoh Neco. His invasion of Assyria, Josiah's death (2Ki 23:29-35; 24:7; 2Ch 35:20-24; 36:3-4; Jer 46:2; 47:1).
9. Pharaoh. (Jer 37:4-7; 44; Eze 17:15-17). Prophecies concerning (Jer 44:30; 46:25-26; Eze 29; 30:21-26).

PHARES, PHAREZ *See Perez.*

PHARISEES (*separate ones*). A sect of the Jews (Ac 15:5). Doctrines of (Mt 15:9), concerning the Resurrection (Ac 23:6, 8), association with tax collectors and sinners (Mt 9:11-13).

Traditions of, in regard to fasting (Mt 9:14; Lk 18:12), the washing of hands (Mt 15:1-3; Mk 7:1-15), the duties of children to parents (Mt 15:4-9), the Sabbath (Mt 12:2-8). Denounced by Jesus (Mt 23:2-36; Lk 11:39-44). Hypocrisy of, reproved by John (Mt 3:7-10), by Jesus (Mt 6:2-8, 16-18; 15:1-9; 16:1-12; 21:33-46;

P

23:2-33; Lk 11:14-54; 12:1; 15:1-9). Reject John (Lk 7:30), Christ (Mt 12:38-39; 15:12; Jn 7:48). Come to Jesus with questions (Mt 19:3; 22:15-22).

Minister to Jesus (Lk 7:36; 11:37; 14:1). Become disciples of Jesus (Jn 3:1; Ac 15:5; 22:5).

Paul a Pharisee (Ac 23:6; 26:5).

See Herodians; Sadducees; Testaments, Time Between.

PHAROSH *See Parosh.*

PHARPAR A river of Damascus. Referred to by Naaman (2Ki 5:12).

PHARZITES *See Perez, Perezite.*

PHASEAH *See Paseah.*

PHASELIS Rhodian colony in Lycia (1Mc 15:23).

PHASELUS Latinization of Phasael, the son of Antipater the Idumean, and brother of Herod the Great.

PHEBE *See Phoebe.*

PHENICE *See Phoenicia; Phoenix.*

PHENICIA *See Phoenicia.*

PHICOL Chief captain of the Philistines (Ge 21:22, 32; 26:26).

PHILADELPHIA (*love of brother, sister*). A city of Lydia. One of the seven churches (Rev 1:11; 3:7-13).

PHILANTHROPY *See Alms; Beneficence; Charitableness; Giving; Liberality; Neighbor; Poor.*

PHILEMON (*beloved*). Convert of Paul at Colosse; Epistle to Philemon written to him.

PHILEMON, EPISTLE TO

Author: The apostle Paul

Date: c. A.D. 60

Outline:
I. Greetings (1-3).
II. Thanksgiving and Prayer (4-7).
III. Paul's Plea for Onesimus (8-21).
IV. Final Request, Greetings and Benedictions (22-25).

PHILETUS (*beloved*). False teacher in the church at Ephesus (2Ti 2:17).

PHILIP (*horse lover*).
1. King of Macedonia; father of Alexander the Great; founder of city of Philippi in Macedonia (1Mc 1:1).
2. Philip V, king of Macedonia (1Mc 8:5).
3. Governor of Jerusalem under Antiochus, regent of Syria (2Mc 5:22).
4. Herod Philip. Married Herodias (Mt 14:3; Mk 6:17; Lk 3:19).
5. Herod Philip II, tetrarch of Batanaea, Trachonitis, Gaulanitis, and parts of Jamnia. Best of Herods (Lk 3:1).

PHILIP THE APOSTLE Native of Bethsaida, the same town as Andrew and Peter (Jn 1:44), undoubtedly first a disciple of John the Baptist (Jn 1:43), brought his friend Nathanael to Jesus (Jn 1:45), called to apostleship (Mt 10:3; Mk 3:18; Lk 6:14), faith tested by Jesus before feeding of the 5000 (Jn 6:5-6), brought Greeks to Jesus (Jn 12:20-23), asked to see the Father (Jn 14:8-12), in the Upper Room with 120 (Ac 1:13).

PHILIP THE EVANGELIST Chosen one of the seven (Ac 6:5). A Hellenist, or Greek-speaking Jew, preached in Samaria (Ac 8). Ethiopian eunuch converted through him (Ac 8:26-40). Paul stayed at his home in Caesarea, where he lived with his four unmarried daughters who were prophetesses (Ac 21:8-9).

PHILIPPI A city of Macedonia. Paul preaches in (Ac 16:12-40; 20:1-6; 1Th 2:1-2). Contributes to the maintenance of Paul (Php 4:10-18). Paul sends Epaphroditus to (Php 2:25). Paul writes a letter to the Christians of (Php 1:1).

PHILIPPIANS, EPISTLE TO

Author: The apostle Paul

Date: c. A.D. 61

Outline:
I. Salutation (1:1-2).
II. Thanksgiving and Prayer for the Philippians (1:3-11).
III. Paul's Personal Circumstances (1:12-26).
IV. Exhortations (1:27-2:18).
 A. Living a Life Worthy of the Gospel (1:27-30).
 B. Following the Servant Attitude of Christ (2:1-18).
V. Paul's Associates in the Gospel (2:19-30).
 A. Timothy (2:19-24).
 B. Epaphroditus (2:25-30).
VI. Warnings Against Judaizers and Antinomians (3:1-4:1).
 A. Against Judaizers or Legalists (3:1-16).
 B. Against Antinomians or Libertines (3:17-4:1).
VII. Final Exhortations, Thanks and Conclusion (4:2-23).
 A. Exhortations Concerning Various Aspects of the Christian Life (4:2-9).
 B. Concluding Testimony and Repeated Thanks (4:10-20).
 C. Greetings and Benediction (4:21-23).

PHILISTIA The seacoast in the W of Dan and Simeon (Ps 60:8; 87:4; 108:9).

PHILISTINES Descendants of Mizraim (Ge 10:14; 1Ch 1:12; Jer 47:4; Am 9:7). Called Kerethites (1Sa 30:14-16; Eze 25:16; Zep

2:5), Casluhites (Ge 10:14; 1Ch 1:12), Caphtor (Jer 47:4; Am 9:7). Territory of (Jos 13:3; Jdg 3:3; Dt 2:23; Jos 13:3; 15:47).

Rulers of (Jos 13:3; Jdg 3:3; 16:5, 30; 1Sa 5:8, 11; 6:4, 12; 7:7; 29:2, 6-7). Kings of: Abimelech I (Ge 20), Abimelech II (Ge 26), Achish (1Sa 21:10-15; 27:2-12; 28:1-2; 29).

Allowed to remain in Canaan (Jdg 3:3-4). Shamgar slays six hundred with an oxgoad (Jdg 3:31). For their history during the leadership of Samson (Jdg 13-16). Defeat the Israelites; take the ark; suffer plagues, and return the ark (1Sa 4-6). Army of (1Sa 13:5). Defeated by Samuel (1Sa 7), by Saul and Jonathan (1Sa 9:16; 13-14). Their champion, Goliath, slain by David (1Sa 17). David slays two hundred (1Sa 18:22-30). David finds refuge among (1Sa 27). Defeat the Israelites and slay Saul and his sons (1Sa 31; 1Ch 10:1). Defeated by David (2Sa 5:17-25; 23:9-16; 1Ch 14:8-16). Pay tribute to Jehoshaphat (2Ch 17:11). Defeated by Hezekiah (2Ki 18:8).

Prophecies against (Isa 9:11-12; 14:29-31; Jer 25:17-20; 47; Eze 25:15-17; Am 1:6-8; Zep 2:4-7; Zec 9:5-7).

PHILOLOGUS (*lover of words [education]*). Christian in Rome to whom Paul sent a salutation (Ro 16:15).

PHILOSOPHY (*lover of discernment, lover of wisdom*). The nature of things (Ecc 1-7). A philosophical discourse on wisdom (Job 28). Philosophical inductions and deductions relating to God and his providence (Job 5:8-20; 9; 10:2-21; 12:6-24; 33:12-30; 37). Reveals the mysteries of providence (Pr 25:2; Ro 1:19-20). Is not sufficient for an adequate knowledge of God (1Co 1:21-22), or of salvation through the atonement of Jesus Christ (1Co 2:6-10). Employment of, was not Paul's method of preaching the gospel (1Co 1:17, 19, 21; 2:1-5, 13). Greek schools of (Ac 17:18). Rabbinical (Col 2:8, 16-19; 1Ti 6:20).

See Aratus; Asceticism; Epicureans; Gnosticism; Stoicism; Stoics; Reasoning; Wisdom.

PHINEHAS (*the Negro*).
1. Son of Eleazar and grandson of Aaron (Ex 6:25; 1Ch 6:4, 50; 9:20; Ezr 7:5; 8:2), who slew Zimri and Cozbi at God's command (Nu 25:6-15; Ps 106:30).

God establishes a covenant with (Nu 25:10-13). *See Covenants, Major in the Old Testament.*

2. Son of Eli; sinful priest (1Sa 1:3; 2:12-17, 22-25, 27-36; 3:11-13). He and his brother were killed by Philistines (1Sa 4).
3. Father of Eleazar who returned from exile (Ezr 8:33).

PHLEGON (*burning*). A disciple in Rome (Ro 16:14).

PHOEBE (*radiant*). A deaconess of the church at Cenchrea (Ro 16:1).

PHOENICIA (*land of purple [dye for trading], possibly land of date palms*). Country along Mediterranean coast, c. 120 miles long, extending from Arvad (Arados, 1Mc 15:23) to Dor, just S of Carmel. The Semitic name for the land was Canaan. The term Phoenicia is from a Greek word meaning "purple-red," perhaps because the Phoenicians were the discoverers of the crimson-purple dye derived form the murex shellfish. The people were Semites who came in a migration from the Mesopotamian region during the second millennium B.C. They became great seafarers, establishing colonies at Carthage and Spain, and perhaps even reached England. Inhabitants of, descended from Canaan (Ge 10:15, 18-19). Called Sidonians (Jdg 18:7; Eze 32:30). They were famous shipbuilders (Eze 27:9) and carpenters (1Ki 16:31; 18:19). Hiram, one of their kings was friendly with David and Solomon (2Sa 5:11; 1Ki 5:1-12; 2Ch 2:3-16), and another Hiram helped Solomon in the building of the temple in Jerusalem (1Ki 7:13-47; 2Ch 2:13-14). Jews from, hear Jesus (Mk 3:8). Jesus healed a Syrian Phoenician woman's daughter in its regions (Mk 7:24-30). Paul visited Christians there (Ac 15:3; 21:2-7; 27:3).

PHOENIX Town on the S coast of Crete (Ac 27:12).

PHRYGIA An inland province of Asia Minor. People from, in Jerusalem (Ac 2:10). Paul in (Ac 16:6; 18:23).

PHURAH *See Purah.*

PHUT *See Put.*

PHUVAH *See Puah.*

PHYGELUS (*fugitive*). A Christian in Asia. Turns from Paul (2Ti 1:15).

PHYLACTERY (*safeguard, means of protection*). A small box containing slips of parchment on which were written portions of the law (Ex 13:9, 16; Dt 6:4-9; 11:18). Worn ostentatiously on the forehead and left arm (Mt 23:5).

PHYSICIAN (2Ch 16:12; Mt 9:12; Mk 5:26; Lk 8:43). Proverbs about (Mk 2:17; Lk 4:23). Luke a physician (Col 4:14). Figurative (Job 13:4; Jer 8:22; Lk 5:31).

PHYSIOGNOMY The art of discovering temperament and character from outward appearance. Character revealed in (Isa 3:9). *See Countenance; Face.*

PHYSIOLOGY The human body (Job 10:11; Ps 139:14-16; Pr 14:30). *See Hygiene.* Figurative of the Church (Eph 4:16; Col 2:19).

PI-BESETH (*temple [house] of Bastet [pagan goddess]*). *See Bubastis.*

PI HAHIROTH (*temple [house] of Hathor [pagan goddess]; possibly mouth of canals*). The place on the W shore of the Red Sea where Pharaoh overtook the Israelites (Ex 14:2, 9; Nu 33:7-8).

PICKS, IRON An instrument of iron used by prisoners of war (2Sa 12:31; 1Ch 20:3), who were used by victorious kings as menial laborers in royal building projects (1Ki 9:20-21; cf. also Ex 1:11).

PICTURES *See Idol; Idolatry.*

PIECE OF SILVER *See Silver.*

PIERCING THE EAR A token of servitude for life (Ex 21:6; Dt 15:17; Ps 40:6).

PIETY Religious duty.

PIG An unclean animal (Lev 11:7; Dt 14:8; Isa 65:4; 66:3, 17). Possessed by demons (Mt 8:30-33). *See Animals.*

PIGEON (*young bird*). Used as sacrifice (Ge 15:9; Lev 1:14; 5:7; 12:8; 14:22; Lk 2:24). *See Dove.*

PILATE, PONTIUS (*family name*). Roman governor of Judea (Mt 27:2; Lk 3:1). Causes slaughter of certain Galileans (Lk 13:1). Tries Jesus and orders his crucifixion (Mt 27; Mk 15; Lk 23; Jn 18:28-40; 19; Ac 3:13; 4:27; 13:28; 1Ti 6:13). Allows Joseph of Arimathea to take Jesus' body (Mt 27:57-58; Mk 15:43-45; Lk 23:52; Jn 19:38).

PILDASH (*steely* ISBE; *spider* KB). Son of Nahor (Ge 22:22).

PILEHA *See Pilha.*

PILGRIM *See Sojourners.*

PILGRIMAGE
1. Jews were expected to make pilgrimages to the temple in Jerusalem for the great feasts (Ps 120-134; Ac 2:5-11).
2. The NT describes Christians as pilgrims or aliens (Heb 11:13; 1Pe 2:11).

PILHA (*millstone* IDB; *plowman* ISBE; *harelip* KB). One of those who sealed the covenant with Nehemiah (Ne 10:24).

PILLAR Of Solomon's temple (1Ki 7:13-22; 2Ki 25:17). Broken and carried to Babylon (2Ki 25:13; Jer 52:17, 20-21). Of Solomon's palaces (1Ki 7:6). Pillar of salt, Lot's wife turned to (Ge 19:26; Lk 17:32).

Used to mark roads (Jer 31:21).

Monuments erected to commemorate events: By Jacob, his vision of angels (Ge 28:18, w 31:13; 35:14), his covenant with Laban (Ge 31:45); by Moses, the covenant between Yahweh and Israel (Ex 24:4); by Joshua, the passing over Jordan (Jos 4:1-9, w Dt 27:2-6; Jos 8:30), at Shechem (Jos 24:25-27, w Jdg 9:6); by Samuel, the discomfiture of the Philistines (1Sa 7:12); by Absalom, to keep his name in remembrance (2Sa 18:18). As a boundary (Jos 15:6, w 18:17), a marker (1Sa 20:19), a landmark (2Sa 20:8; 1Ki 1:9). Prophecy of one in Egypt (Isa 19:19). Monuments of idolatry, to be destroyed (Dt 12:3).

Figurative (Rev 3:12).

PILLAR OF CLOUD AND FIRE God guided Israel out of Egypt and through the wilderness by a pillar of cloud by day and fire by night (Ex 13:21-22). The pillar of cloud rested over the tent of meeting outside the camp whenever the Lord met Moses there (Ex 33:7-11). The cloud and fire were divine manifestations. *See Celestial Phenomena.*

PILLOW
1. A support for the head (Ge 28:11, 18; 1Sa 26:7, 11, 16).
2. NIV "magic charms" (Eze 13:18, 20).

PILOT Captain or operator of a ship (Ac 27:11; Jas 3:4).

PILTAI (*Yahweh rescues*). A priest who returned to Jerusalem from captivity in Babylon (Ne 12:17).

PIM *See Measure.*

PIN Tent peg (Jdg 4:21; 5:26), stick for beating wool in the loom (Jdg 16:13-14). KJV "crisping pins" (Isa 3:22) are NIV "purses."

PINE A tree (Ne 8:15; Isa 41:19; 60:13).

PINING AWAY (Lev 26:39; La 4:9; Eze 4:17; 24:23; 33:10).

PINNACLE (*sun*, or *a little wing*). On a building, a turret, battlement, pointed roof or peak. Satan tried to get Jesus to throw himself down from the pinnacle of the temple (Mt 4:5-6; Lk 4:9).

PINON (*darkness* ISBE; *name related to famous copper mines* KB). Chief of Edom of the family of Esau (Ge 36:40-41; 1Ch 1:52).

PIPE A wind instrument of music. Used in religious services (1Sa 10:5; Isa 30:29). *See Music, Instruments of.*

PIRAM (*possibly wild donkey* IDB; *indomitable* ISBE; *possibly zebra* KB). A king of the Amorites. Overcome and slain by Joshua (Jos 10:3, 16-18, 24-27).

PIRATHON, PIRATHONITE A place in the land of Ephraim (Jdg 12:15). Men of (Jdg 12:13; 2Sa 23:30; 1Ch 11:31; 27:14).

PISGAH A ridge or mountain E of the Jordan, opposite to Jericho. The Israelites come to (Nu 21:20). The water courses flowing from Mount Pisgah were a boundary of the country assigned to the Reubenites and Gadites (Dt 3:17; 4:49; Jos 12:3). Balaam prophesies on (Nu 23:14-24). Moses views Israel from (Dt 3:27; 34:1-4).

PISHON One of the rivers of Eden (Ge 2:11).

PISIDIA A province in Asia Minor. Paul visits (Ac 13:14; 14:24).

PISIDIAN ANTIOCH *See Antioch, 2; Pisidia.*

PISON *See Pishon.*

PISPAH An Asherite (1Ch 7:38).

P

PISTACHIO Nuts, in a gift sent by Jacob to Joseph (Ge 43:11). *See Plants of the Bible; Tree.*

PIT Bitumen deposit "tar pits" (Ge 14:10), deep place (Ge 37:20-29; Mt 12:11), well or cistern (Jer 14:3; Lk 14:5), earthen vessel (Lev 11:33), death, grave, or Sheol (Job 33:18; Isa 14:15; Nu 16:30, 33).

PITCH
1. Pitch or tar (Ge 14:10; Ex 2:3). *See Caulkers; Tar.*
2. To encamp (Ge 12:8; 31:25; Ex 17:1; Nu 1:51; Jos 8:11).

PITCHER Jars for temple service and personal use (Ex 25:29; 37:16; 1Ch 28:17; Ecc 12:6; Mk 7:4).

PITHOM (*temple [house] of [pagan god] Atum*). Egyptian store city in a valley between the Nile and Lake Timsah; dedicated to the sun god Atum (Ex 1:11).

PITHON Son of Micah (1Ch 8:35; 9:41).

PITY Tender, considerate, compassionate feeling for others.
Commanded (Job 6:14; 1Pe 3:8). For the poor (Pr 19:17; 28:8). Forbidden, to Canaanites (Dt 7:16), to idolatrous proselytizers (Dt 13:8), to murderers (Dt 19:13), to false witnesses (Dt 19:21), to wife in certain situations (Dt 25:12).
Withholding of, from Jesus, prefigured in David (Ps 69:20). Of God (Ps 103:13; Isa 63:9; Joel 2:18; Jnh 4:11; Jas 5:11), withheld from reprobates (Jer 13:14; 21:7; Eze 5:11; 7:4; 8:18; 9:5, 10; Zec 11:6).
Required of believers (Isa 1:17; Mt 18:28-35).
See God, Mercy of; Jesus the Christ, Compassion of; Mercy.

PLACE OF ATONEMENT *See Atonement Cover.*

PLAGUE As a judgment on the Egyptians (Ps 105; 135:8-9; Ac 7:36). The plague of blood (Ex 7:14-25), frogs (Ex 8:1, 15), lice (Ex 8:16-19), flies (Ex 8:20). On cattle (Ex 9:1-7). Of boils and blains (Ex 9:8-12), hail (Ex 9:18-34), locusts (Ex 10:1-20), darkness (Ex 10:21-23). Death of the firstborn (Ex 11:4-7; 12:17, 29-30).
On the Israelites: On account of idolatry (Ex 32:35), after eating quail (Nu 11:33), after refusing to enter the promised land (Nu 14:37), after murmuring on account of the destruction of Korah (Nu 16:41-50), of serpents (Nu 21:6), for the sin of Peor (Jos 22:17), on account of David's sin (2Sa 24:10-25).
On the Philistines (1Sa 6:4-5).
Denounced as a judgment (Lev 26:21; Dt 28:59). Foretold (Rev 11:6; 15:1, 6-8; 16; 22:18-19).
See Judgments; Pestilence.

PLAIN Broad stretch of level land (Ge 11:2; Eze 3:22).

PLAN OF SALVATION *See Jesus Christ, Mission of; Redemption; Salvation.*

PLANE A tool (Isa 44:13). *See Tools.*

PLANE TREE Possibly a chestnut tree (Ge 30:37; Eze 31:8).

PLANET *See Astronomy; Stars.*

PLANTS OF THE BIBLE The following plants are mentioned in the Bible. Some of them are not identifiable with certainty.
Acacia tree (Ex 25:10ff), algum tree (2Ch 2:8; 9:11), almond (tree) (Ge 30:37; Ex 25:33-36; Ecc 12:5; Jer 1:11), almugwood (1Ki 10:11, 12; 2Ch. 2:8, 9:10 ftn.), aloes (Nu 24:6; Ps 45:8; Pr 7:17; SS 4:14; Jn 19:39), apple tree (SS 2:3; 8:5; Joel 1:12).
Balm (Ge 37:25; 43:11; 2Ch 28:15; Jer 8:22; 46:11; Eze 27:17), barley (Hos 3:2), beans (2Sa 17:28; Eze 4:9), brambles (Isa 34:13; Jdg 9:14-15), briers (Isa 63:9; Eze 2:6), broom tree (1Ki 19:3-4; Job 30:4; Ps 120:4), bush (burning bush) (Ex 3:2-3).
Calamus (SS 4:14; Isa 43:24; Jer 6:20; Eze 27:19), caraway (Isa 28:25-27), cassia (Ex 30:22-25; Ps 45:8; Eze 27:19), cedar (Lev 14:4, 6, 49; Nu 19:6; 2Sa 5:11; 1Ki 5:8), cedars of Lebanon (1Ki 4:33; Eze 31:3, 5), cinnamon (Ex 30:23; Pr 7:17; SS 4:14; Rev 18:13), citron wood (Rev 18:12), coriander (Ex 16:31; Nu 11:7), crocus (Isa 35:1), cucumber (Nu 11:5), cummin (Isa 28:26-27; Mt 23:23), cypress (Ge 6:14; Isa 41:19, 44:14, 60:13; Eze 27:6).
Date (Nu 33:9), dill (Mt 23:23), ebony (Eze 27:15), fig (Ge 3:6-7; Dt 8:8; Jdg 9:10-11; 1Ki 4:25; Isa 41:19; 60:13), flax (Ex 9:31; Jos 2:6; Jdg 15:14), frankincense (Eze 30:34; Rev 18:13), galbanum (Ex 30:34-36), garlic (Nu 11:5), gourd (1Ki 6:18; 7:24; 2Ki 4:39), grain (Lev 23:14), grape (Ge 40:10-11), green tree (Ps 37:35), gum resin (Ex 30:34).
Henna blossoms (SS 1:14; 4:13), herbs, bitter herbs (Ex 12:8), hyssop (Ex 12:22; Lev 14:4; Ps 51:7; 1Ki 4:33), leeks (Nu 11:5), lentils (Ge 25:29-30, 34; 2Sa 17:28), lilies (1Ki 7:19, 22, 26; SS 5:13; Mt 6:28; Lk 12:27), linen (Est 1:5-6).
Mandrakes (Ge 30:14-16; SS 7:13), melon (Nu 11:5; Isa 1:8; Jer 10:5), millet (Eze 4:9; 27:17), mint (Mt 23:23; Lk 11:42), mulberry tree (Lk 17:6), mustard (Mt 13:31-32; 17:20; Mk 4:31; Lk 13:19), myrrh (Ge 37:25-27, 43:11; Est 2:12; Pr 7:17; SS 5:13; Mt 2:11), myrtle (Isa 41:19, 55:13; Zec 1:7-10), nettles (Isa 34:13), nut trees (SS 6:11), nuts [pistachio] (Ge 43:11).
Oak (Ge 35:4; Zec 11:2), olive tree (Jdg 9:8; Job 15:33; Ps 52:8; Isa 17:6; Isa 24:13), onion (Nu 11:5), onycha (Ex 30:34-35), palm (Nu 33:9), pine tree (1Ki 5:10; Isa 60:13), plane tree (Ge 30:37; Eze 31:8), poisonous weeds (Hos 10:4), pomegranate (Dt 8:8; 1Sa 14:2), poplars (Ge 30:37; Hos 4:13), reed (Job 40:15, 20-22), reeds (Ex 2:3; Job 8:11), resin (Ge 2:12; Nu 11:6-7), rose of Sharon (SS 2:1-2), rue (Lk 11:42), rush (Isa 9:6).
Saffron (SS 4:14), salt herbs (Job 30:1, 3-4), seaweed (Jnh 2:5), seed pods (2Ki 6:25, ftn.), spelt (Ex 9:32; Isa 28:5; Ezr 4:9), spices (Ge 37:25; 43:11; Ex 25:6; Mt 23:23), sycamore (1Ki 10:27; 1Ch 27:28; 2Ch 1:15; Am 7:14; Lk 19:4), terebinth (Isa 6:13; Hos 4:13), thistles (Ge 3:18; 2Ki 14:9; Heb 6:8), thorns (Isa 7:19; Mt 27:29; Mk 15:17; Jn 19:5), tumbleweed (Ps 83:13; Isa 17:13), vine (Ge 9:20, 40:9-11; Jnh 4:5-7), weeds (Job 31:40; Pr 24:31; Mt

13:25), wheat (Ge 30:14; Dt 8:8), wild vine (2Ki 4:39; Jer 2:21), willow (Eze 17:5), wormwood (Rev 8:11).
See Tree.

PLASTER In Egypt stone buildings, even the finest granite, were plastered, inside and out, to make a smooth surface for decoration (Dt 27:2, 4). The poor used a mixture of clay and straw. In Israel an outside clay coating would have to be renewed after the rainy season.

PLASTER, MEDICINAL A cake of figs applied to a boil (Isa 38:21).

PLATE, PLATTER Dedicated to the tabernacle (Nu 7:13, 19, 25, 31, 37, 43, 49, 55, 61, 67, 73, 79, 84-85). John the Baptist's head carried on (Mt 14:8, 11).

PLEADING (Dt 17:8). Of the guilty (Jos 7:19-21). Jesus declined to plead (Mt 26:62; Mk 15:2; Lk 23:3; Jn 18:33-34). Prisoners required to plead (Ac 7:1). *See Defense.*

PLEASANT LAND The land of Israel (Ps 106:24; Zec 7:14; cf. Jer 3:19; 12:10; Dt 8:7-9). *See Israel.*

PLEASING AROMA Of sacrifices (Ge 8:21; Ex 29:18, 25, 41; Lev 1:9, 13, 17; 2:2, 9, 12; 3:5, 16; 4:31; 6:15, 21; 8:21, 28; 23:13, 18; 26:31; Nu 15:3, 7, 10, 13, 14, 24; 18:17; 28:2, 6, 8, 13, 24, 27; 29:2, 6, 8, 13, 36; Eze 6:13; 16:19; 20:28, 41). Of Christian service (2Co 2:15; Eph 5:2; Php 4:18). *See Offerings.*

PLEASURE, WORLDLY Unfulfilling (Job 21:12-13; Ecc 1:17; 2:1-13; 1Ti 5:6). Proverbs and parables concerning (Pr 9:17; 15:21; 21:17; Lk 8:14).
Rejected and judged by God (Job 20:12-16; Isa 5:11-12; 22:12-13; 47:8-9; Am 6:1; Ro 1:32; 2Th 2:12). Rejected by Moses (Heb 11:25-26), by Paul (2Ti 3:4; Tit 3:3), by Peter (2Pe 2:13).
See Gluttony; Happiness; Joy; Worldliness.

PLEDGE
1. Personal property of a debtor held to secure a payment (Ge 38:17-18). Law of Moses was concerned with protection of the poor. A pledged outer garment had to be restored at sunset for a bed covering (Ex 22:26-27), a widow's clothing could not be taken (Dt 24:17), a handmill or its upper millstone could not be taken (Dt 24:6).
2. In marriage *See Betrothal.*

PLEIADES (*heap, group [of stars]*). Stars in the constellation Taurus (Job 9:9; 38:31).

PLINY Gaius Plinius Caecilius Secundus, called "the Younger," Roman governmental official, famous as the author of literary letters covering all types of subjects, one of which contains a description of the Christian church in Bithynia, a province which Pliny governed in A.D. 112. The letter, together with the reply of the emperor Trajan are important evidence for the official attitude towards the Christians.

PLOTTING General references to (Est 3:9; Ps 36:4; 37:12; Pr 6:14; Isa 32:7; Mic 2:1). Against Christ (Mt 12:14; 26:4; 27:1; Lk 6:11; 19:47; 22:4; Jn 5:16; 11:47, 53).
General examples of (Ge 37:18; Nu 16:3; Jdg 9:1; 2Ki 12:20; 14:19; Da 6:4; Mt 12:14; Ac 23:13).

PLOW The ancient plow consisted of a forked stick, the trunk hitched to the animals which drew it, the branch braced and terminating in the share, which was at first the sharpened end of the branch, later a metal point. It was ordinarily drawn by a yoke of oxen (Job 1:14; Am 6:12). Such a plow did not turn over the soil; it did little more than scratch the surface.
Figurative of afflictions (Ps 129:3).

PLOWSHARE (*the blade of a plow*). To beat swords into plowshares was symbolic of an age of peace (Isa 2:4), to beat plowshares into swords portended coming war (Joel 3:10).

PLUMB LINE A cord with a weight, the plummet, tied to one end; used in testing whether a wall is perpendicular (Am 7:7-9; 2Ki 21:13; Isa 28:17).

PLUMMET *See Plumb Line.*

POCHERETH *See Pokereth-Hazzebaim.*

PODS Seed pods eaten in famine (2Ki 6:24). Perhaps carob, eaten by the prodigal son and the pigs (Lk 15:16). *See Plants of the Bible.*

POET (*doer, or a maker*). Paul quotes from pagan poets (Ac 17:28; 1Co 15:32; Tit 1:12). A great deal of the OT is written in the form of poetry.

POETRY

Acrostic:
(Ps 25; 34; 37; 111; 112; 119; 145; Pr 31:10-31; La 1-5).

Didactic:
Moses' song (Dt 32). The book of Job, the Proverbs, the Song of Songs, much of the books of prophecy. *See Psalms, Topically Arranged.*

Elegy:
On the death of Saul (2Sa 1:19-27). Of Abner (2Sa 3:33-34). *See Elegy.*

Epic:
Moses' song (Ex 15:1-19). Miriam's song (Ex 15:21). Deborah's song (Jdg 5) David's song of praise (2Sa 22).

Lyrics, Sacred:
Moses' and Miriam's songs (Ex 15). Hannah's song (1Sa 2:1-10). The song of Elizabeth (Lk 1:42-45). Of Mary (Lk 1:46-55). Of Zechariah (Lk 1:68-79). The Psalms. *See Psalms.*
See Parallelism

POETS, PAGAN, QUOTATIONS FROM Paul quotes pagan poets in arguments. Examples include: Cleanthes (Ac 17:28), Epimenides (Tit 1:12), Menander (1Co 15:33).

POISON A substance producing a deadly effect, like the venom of reptiles (Dt 32:24, 33; Job 20:16; Job 6:4; Ps 58:4). Vegetable poisons were known in antiquity: poisonous weeds (Hos 10:4), wild gourd (2Ki 4:39-40). A poisoned drink is referred to in Mark (Mk 16:18).

POKERETH-HAZZEBAIM (*pitfall of gazelles, i.e., gazelle hunter*). The ancestor of a family which returned to Jerusalem from captivity in Babylon (Ezr 2:57; Ne 7:59).

POLE Used to carry the ark (Ex 24:13-15), the table of the bread of the Presence (Ex 25:27-28), the bronze altar (Ex 27:6-7), the incense altar (Ex 30:4-5). Standard on which the bronze serpent was displayed (Nu 21:8-9).

POLICY *See Diplomacy.*

POLITARCH City magistrate of Thessalonica (Ac 17:6, 8). Sixteen epigraphical inscriptions with the word have been discovered.

POLITICS Statecraft.

Corruption in:
(Ps 12:8), in the court of Xerxes (Est 3), of Darius (Da 6:4-15).

Instances of:
Absalom, electioneering for the throne (2Sa 15:2-6). Pilate, condemning Jesus to gratify popular clamor (Mt 27:23-27; Mk 15:15; Lk 23:13-25; Jn 18:38-39; 19:4-13).

Ministers:
Zadok the priest, a partisan of David (2Sa 15:24-29). Nathan the prophet influences the selection of David's successor (1Ki 1:11-40).

Women in:
The wise woman of Abel, who saved the city through diplomacy (2Sa 20:16-22). Bathsheba, in securing the crown for Solomon (1Ki 1:15-21). Herodias, in influencing the administration of Herod (Mt 14:3-11; Mk 6:17-28). Mother of Zebedee's children, in seeking favor for her sons (Mt 20:20-23).
Influence in. *See Influence, Political.*
See Diplomacy; Government.

POLL TAX *See Tax.*

POLLUTION Ceremonial or moral defilement, profanation, and uncleanness (Eze 20:25; 2Pe 2:20). *See Corruption; Defilement; Unclean, Uncleanness; Sanitation and Hygiene.*

POLLUX With Castor, one of the twin gods, sons of Zeus and patrons of sailors (Ac 28:11).

POLYGAMY (*many marriages*). Forbidden (Dt 17:17; Lev 18:18; Mal 2:14-15; Mt 19:4-5; Mk 10:2-8; 1Ti 3:2, 12; Tit 1:6). Authorized (2Sa 12:8).

Examples of:
Tolerated (Ex 21:10; 1Sa 1:2; 2Ch 24:3). Practiced by, (Job 27:15), Lamech (Ge 4:19), Abraham (Ge 16), Esau (Ge 26:34; 28:9), Jacob (Ge 29:30), Ashhur (1Ch 4:5), Gideon (Jdg 8:30), Elkanah (1Sa 1:2), David (1Sa 25:39-44; 2Sa 3:2-5; 5:13; 1Ch 14:3), Solomon (1Ki 11:1-8), Rehoboam (2Ch 11:18-23), Abijah (2Ch 13:21), Jehoram (2Ch 21:14), Joash (2Ch 24:3), Ahab (2Ki 10:1), Jehoiachin (2Ki 24:15), Belshazzar (Da 5:2, w 1Ch 2-8), Hosea (Hos 3:1-2). Mosaic law respecting the firstborn in (Dt 21:15-17).
Sought by women [polyandry] (Isa 4:1).

The Evil Effects of:
Husband's favoritism in (Dt 21:15-17), Jacob's (Ge 29:30; 30:15), Elkanah's (1Sa 1:5), Rehoboam's (2Ch 11:21). Domestic infelicity, in Abraham's family (Ge 16; 21:9-16), Jacob's (Ge 29:30-34; 30:1-23), Elkanah's (1Sa 1:4-7). Upon Solomon (1Ki 11:4-8).
See Concubinage; Marriage.

POLYTHEISM (Ge 31:19; 35:2, 4; Jos 24:2, 23; Jdg 2:13; 3:7; 10:16; 17:5; Jer 2:28; 11:13; Da 4:8; 1Co 8:5).

POMEGRANATE A fruit. Abounded in the land of Canaan (1Sa 14:2). Brought by the spies to show the fruitfulness of the land of Canaan (Nu 13:23). Figures of the fruits of, were embroidered on the ephod (Ex 28:33-34; 39:24), carved on the pillars of the temple (1Ki 7:18, 20, 42; Jer 52:22-23). Wine made of (SS 8:2).

POMMEL *See Capital.*

PONTIUS PILATE *See Pilate, Pontius.*

PONTUS (*sea*). A province of Asia Minor (Ac 2:9; 1Pe 1:1). Aquila lived in (Ac 18:2).

POOL Of Gibeon (2Sa 2:13; Jer 41:12). Of Hebron (2Sa 4:12). Of Samaria (1Ki 22:38). Of Heshbon (SS 7:4).
Of Jerusalem: Upper pool (2Ki 18:17; Isa 36:2), lower pool (Isa 22:9), Siloam (Jn 9:7, 11), called Siloam (Ne 3:15, ftn), and probably identical with the king's pool (Ne 2:14).

POOR

Proverbs Concerning:
(Ps 37:16 w Isa 29:19; Pr 10:15; 13:7-8, 23; 18:23; 19:1, 4, 7, 17, 22; 20:13; 21:13; 22:2, 9; 23:21; 24:20-21, 31; 28:6, 8, 11, 19; 29:14; Ecc 4:6, 13; 6:8; 9:15-16). Always part of the society (Mt 26:11; Mk 14:7; Jn 12:8).

Attitudes toward:
Job (Job 30:25). Jesus and the poor widow (Mk 12:43-44). Lazarus (Lk 16:20-21). Judas (Jn 12:6). James (Jas 1:9-10).

Duty to:
(Ex 22:25-27; 23:11; Lev 19:9-10; 25:25-28, 35-43; Dt 14:28-29; 15:2-14; 24:12-21; 26:12-13; Ne 8:10; Ps 37:21, 26;

41:1-3; 112:4-5, 9; Pr 28:27; 29:7; 31:9, 20; Isa 1:7; 16:3-4; 58:7, 10; Eze 18:7; Da 4:27; Zec 7:10; Mt 5:42; 19:21; 25:35-36; Mk 14:7; Lk 3:11; 6:30; 11:41; 12:33; 14:12-14; 18:22; 19:8; Ac 20:35; Ro 12:8, 13, 20; 1Co 13:3; 16:1-2; 2Co 6:10; 8:9; 9:5-7; Gal 2:10; 6:10; Eph 4:28; 1Ti 5:9-10, 16; Heb 13:3; Jas 1:27; 2:2-9, 15-16; 5:4; 1Jn 3:17-19).

God's care of:
(1Sa 2:7-8; Job 5:15-16; 31:15; 34:18-19, 28; 36:6, 15; Ps 9:18; 10:14; 12:5; 14:6; 34:6; 35:10; 68:10; 69:33; 72:2, 4, 12-14; 74:21; 102:17; 107:9, 36, 41; 109:31; 113:7-8; 132:15; 140:12; 146:5, 7; Pr 22:2, 22-23; 29:13; Ecc 5:8; Isa 11:4; 14:30, 32; 25:4; 29:19; 41:17; Jer 20:13; Zep 3:12; Zec 11:7; Mt 11:5; Lk 4:18; 7:22; 16:22; Jas 2:5).

See God, Goodness of, Providence of.

The Poor, Without Friends:
(Pr 14:20; 19:4, 7). Wisdom of, despised (Ecc 9:15-16). Warning against neglect of (Pr 20:13; 21:13; 22:16; Eze 16:49). Neglect of, by the disciples (Ac 6:1-6). Neglect of, denounced (Mt 25:42, 45).

Kindness to:
Commanded (Ne 8:10, 12). Rewarded (Ps 41:1-3; Isa 58:10; Lk 14:12-14).
Righteous treatment of, required (Ps 82:3-4; Pr 22:22; 31:9; Isa 1:17). Rewarded (Pr 29:14; Jer 22:16; Eze 18:7, 16-17; Da 4:27). Compassion toward (Job 30:25; Pr 14:21; 29:7; Heb 13:3; Jas 1:27).
Liberality to (Pr 31:20; Isa 58:7; Mt 5:42, w Lk 6:30; Lk 3:11; 19:8; Ro 12:8, 13, 20; 1Co 13:3; 16:1-2; 2Co 9:5-15; Gal 2:10; Eph 4:28; 1Ti 5:9-10, 16; Jas 2:15-16; 1Jn 3:17). Liberality to, rewarded (Pr 19:17; 22:9; 28:27; Ps 112:9; Mt 19:21; 25:34-36; Lk 6:35; 12:33; 18:22; Ac 20:35).

Instances of Kindness—
Ruth, to Naomi (Ru 2:2, 11). Boaz, to Ruth (Ru 2:8-16; 3:15). Elijah, to the widow of Zarephath (1Ki 17:12-24). Elisha, to the prophet's widow (2Ki 4:1-7). The Jews (Est 9:22). Job (Job 29:11-17; 31:16-22, 38-40). The Temanites (Isa 21:14). Nebuzaradan (Jer 39:10).
The good Samaritan (Lk 10:33-35). Zacchaeus (Lk 19:8). Dorcas (Ac 9:36). Cornelius (Ac 10:2, 4). Christian church, at Jerusalem (Ac 6:1), at Antioch (Ac 11:29-30). Churches of Macedonia and Achaia (Ro 15:25-26; 2Co 8:1-5). By Paul (Ro 15:25).

Oppression of:
(Ne 5:1-13; Job 20:19-21; 22:6-7, 9-11; 24:4, 7-12; Ps 10:2, 8-10; 37:14; 109:16; Pr 14:31; 17:5; 19:7; 22:7, 16; 28:3, 15; 30:14; Ecc 5:8; Isa 3:14-15; 10:1-2; 32:6-7; Eze 18:12; 22:29; Am 2:6; 4:1; 5:11-12; 8:4-6; Hab 3:14; Jas 2:6; 5:4). Oppression forbidden (Dt 24:14; Zec 7:10).
Instances of oppression of (2Ki 4:1; Ne 5:1-5).

Mosaic laws concerning:
Atonement money of, must be uniform with that of the rich (Ex 30:15). Inexpensive offerings authorized for (Lev 5:7; 12:8; 14:21-22).
Discrimination, in favor of, forbidden (Ex 23:3; Lev 19:15); against, forbidden (Ex 23:6; Jas 2:2-9).
Exactions of interest from, forbidden (Ex 22:25; Lev 25:35-37). Garments of, taken in pledge, to be restored (Ex 22:26; Dt 24:12-13). To participate triennially in the tithes (Dt 14:28-29; 26:12-13). Gleanings reserved for (Lev 19:9-10; 23:22; Dt 24:19-21). To share the products of the land in the seventh year (Ex 23:11). To be released from servitude, in seventh year (Dt 15:12), in Jubilee (Lev 25:39-43). Alienated lands of, to be restored in Jubilee (Lev 25:25-28).

Figurative:
Poor in spirit (Isa 66:2; Mt 5:3; Lk 6:20).
See Alms; Beneficence; Creditor; Debtor; Employee; Employer; Liberality; Orphans; Poverty; Rich, The; Riches; Servants; Wages; Widow.

POPLAR (*white*). A tree (Ge 30:37; Hos 4:13).

POPLARS, RAVINE OF A brook, probably on the boundary between Moab and Edom (Isa 15:7).

POPULARITY Instances of: David (2Sa 3:36). Absalom (2Sa 15:2-6, 13). Job (Job 29).

POPULARITY OF JESUS (Mt 4:24; 8:1; 13:2; 14:13, 35; 19:1-2; 21:8-9; Mk 1:33; 2:2; 3:7, 20; 5:21; 6:33, 55-56; 10:1; 11:8-10; 12:37; Lk 4:14-15, 42; 5:1; 9:11; 12:1; 19:35-38; Jn 6:2, 15; 12:12-13, 19).

PORATHA Son of Haman (Est 9:8).

PORCH An area with a roof supported by columns: colonnade (1Ki 7:6ff), porch (Jdg 3:23, ftn), place before a court (Mk 14:68), gateway (Mt 26:71).

PORCIUS *See Festus, Porcius.*

PORPHYRY A purple stone used in mosaics (Est 1:6).

PORPOISE *See Sea Cow.*

PORTERS *See Gatekeepers.*

PORTION A part; less than the whole of anything; share (Nu 31:30, 47; Ne 8:10, 12).

POST
1. Of the tabernacle (Ex 26:32, 37; 27:1-17). Of a city gate (Jdg 16:3).
2. Of a watchman (Ne 7:3; 13:11; Ecc 10:4; Isa 62:6).

POSTERITY PROMISED (Ge 15:5, 18; 17:20; 22:17; 26:14; Lev 26:9; Dt 7:13; Ro 4:18).

POT Utensil of metal or clay for holding liquids or other substances (2Ki 4:38).

POTENTATE *See Rulers.*

POTIPHAR (*he whom [pagan god] Ra gives*). An officer of Pharaoh. Joseph's master (Ge 37:36; 39:1).

POTIPHERA (*he whom [pagan god] Ra gives*). A priest of On. Joseph's father-in-law (Ge 41:45, 50; 46:20).

POTSHERD A fragment of earthenware (Job 2:8; Isa 45:9).

POTTAGE *See Stew.*

POTTER *See Occupations and Professions.*

POTTER'S FIELD Piece of ground which the priests bought with the money Judas received for betraying our Lord (Mt 27:7).

POTTER'S GATE Of Jerusalem (Jer 19:2).

POTTERY One of the oldest crafts in the Bible lands. The place where potter's clay was dug was called "potter's field" (Mt 27:7). Pottery was shaped by hand on a potter's wheel, powered by foot or by an apprentice (Jer 18:3-6), then dried and baked in a kiln.
Many different items were made: basins, bowls, cups, dishes, flasks, jars, lamps, ovens, pots. Thousands of objects have been found by the archaeologists. Careful study has been made of the historical development of pottery styles, so that experts can date and place pottery with considerable accuracy.

POUND A talent equaled about seventy-five pounds (Ex 25:39, ftn), a mina about 1.25 pounds (1Ki 10:17, ftn), forty shekels about one pound (Ge 3:15, ftn). *See Measure.*

POVERTY (1Sa 2:7). Destructive (Pr 10:15). A source of temptation (Pr 30:8-9). To be preferred over wealth, with trouble (Pr 15:16), without right (Pr 16:8; Ecc 4:6). *See Poor.*
Caused by laziness (Pr 6:11; 20:13; 24:33-34), by drunkenness (Pr 23:21), by evil associations (Pr 28:19).

POWER

Of Christ:
As the Son of God, is the power of God (Jn 5:17-19; 10:28-30), as man, is from the Father (Ac 10:38).
Described as supreme (Eph 1:20-21; 1Pe 3:22), unlimited (Mt 28:18), over all flesh (Jn 17:2), over all things (Jn 3:35; Eph 1:22), glorious (2Th 1:9), everlasting (1Ti 6:16). Is able to subdue all things (Php 3:21).
Exemplified in, creation (Jn 1:3, 10; Col 1:16), upholding all things (Col 1:17; Heb 1:3), salvation (Isa 63:1; Heb 7:25), His teaching (Mt 7:28-29; Lk 4:32), working miracles (Mt 8:27; Lk 5:17), enabling others to work miracles (Mt 10:1; Ac 5:31), giving spiritual life (Jn 5:21, 25-26), giving eternal life (Jn 17:2), raising the dead (Jn 5:28-29), rising from the dead (Jn 2:19; 10:18), overcoming the world (Jn 16:33), overcoming Satan (Col 2:15; Heb 2:14), destroying the works of Satan (1Jn 3:8), ministers should make known (2Pe 1:16).
Saints made willing by (Ps 110:3), aided by (Heb 2:18), strengthened by (Php 4:13; 2Ti 4:17), preserved by (2Ti 1:12; 4:18), bodies of, shall be changed by (Php 3:21), rests upon saints (2Co 12:9). Present in the assembly of saints (1Co 5:4). Shall be specially manifested at his second coming (Mk 13:26; 2Pe 1:16). Shall subdue all power (1Co 15:24). The wicked shall be destroyed by (Ps 2:9; Isa 11:4; 63:3; 2Th 1:9).
See Jesus the Christ, Omnipotence of; Power of.

Of God:
One of his attributes (Ps 62:11).
Expressed by the voice of God (Ps 29:3, 5; 68:33), finger of God (Ex 9:3, 15; Isa 48:13), arm of God (Job 40:9; Isa 52:10), thunder of his power (Job 26:14).
Described as, great (Ps 79:11; Na 1:3), strong (Ps 89:13; 136:12), glorious (Ex 15:6; Isa 63:12), mighty (Job 9:4; Ps 89:13), everlasting (Isa 26:4; Ro 1:20), sovereign (Ro 9:21), effectual (Isa 43:13; Eph 3:7), irresistible (Dt 32:39; Da 4:35), incomparable (Ex 15:11-12; Dt 3:24; Job 40:9; Ps 89:8), unsearchable (Job 5:9; 9:10), incomprehensible (Job 26:14; Ecc 3:11).
All things possible to (Mt 19:26). Nothing too hard for (Ge 18:14; Jer 32:27). Can save by many or by few (1Sa 14:6). Is the source of all strength (1Ch 29:12; Ps 68:35).
Exemplified in, the creation (Ps 102:25; Jer 10:12), in establishing and governing all things (Ps 65:6; 66:7), in the miracles of Christ (Lk 11:20), in the resurrection of Christ (2Co 13:4; Col 2:12), in the resurrection of saints (1Co 6:14), in making the gospel effectual (Ro 1:16; 1Co 1:18, 24), in delivering his people (Ps 106:8), in the destruction of the wicked (Ex 9:16; Ro 9:22).
Saints, long for exhibitions of (Ps 63:1-2), have confidence in (Jer 20:11), receive increase of grace by (2Co 9:8), strengthened by (Eph 6:10; Col 1:11), upheld by (Ps 37:17; Isa 41:10), supported in affliction by (2Co 6:7; 2Ti 1:8), delivered by (Nu 1:10; Da 3:17), exalted by (Job 36:22), kept by, for salvation (1Pe 1:5). Exerted in behalf of saints (1Ch 16:9). Works in and for saints (2Co 13:4; Eph 1:19; 3:20). The faith of saints stands in (1Co 2:5).
Should be acknowledged (1Ch 29:11; Isa 33:13), pleaded in prayer (Ps 79:11; Mt 6:13), feared (Jer 5:22; Mt 10:28), magnified (Ps 21:13; Jude 25). Efficiency of ministers is through (1Co 3:6-8; Gal 2:8; Eph 3:7). Is a ground of trust (Isa 26:4; Ro 4:21).
The wicked do not know (Mt 22:29), have it against them (Ezr 8:22), shall be destroyed by it (Lk 12:5).
The heavenly host magnified (Rev 4:11; 5:13; 11:17).
See God, Omnipotent, Power of.

Of the Holy Spirit:
Is the power of God (Mt 12:28, w Lk 11:20). Christ worked his miracles by (Mt 12:28).
Exemplified in creation (Ge 1:2; Job 26:13; Ps 104:30), the conception of Christ (Lk 1:35), raising Christ from the dead (1Pe 3:18), giving spiritual life (Eze 37:11-14, w Ro 8:11), working miracles (Ro 15:19), making the gospel efficacious (1Co 2:4; 1Th 1:5), overcoming all difficulties (Zec 4:6-7). Promised by the Father (Lk 24:49). Promised by Christ (Ac 1:8).
Saints upheld by (Ps 51:12), strengthened by (Eph 3:16), enabled to speak the truth boldly by (Mic 3:8; Ac 6:5, 10; 2Ti

1:7-8), helped in prayer by (Ro 8:26), abound in hope by (Ro 15:13). Qualifies ministers (Lk 24:49; Ac 1:8-9). God's word the instrument of (Eph 6:17).
See Holy Spirit.

Spiritual:
From God (Isa 40:29-31; Lk 24:49; 1Co 1:24-28; Php 2:13; 2Ti 1:7). From Christ (2Co 12:9; Eph 1:19-20). From the Holy Spirit (Jn 7:38-39; Ac 1:8; 2:2-4). On believers (Ac 6:8, 10; 1Co 4:19-20; Heb 6:5). In the spirit of Elijah (Lk 1:17).
In preaching (Ac 4:33; 6:10; 1Th 1:5), of Christ (Lk 4:32). Through prayer (Ge 32:28; Mk 9:29; Lk 24:49; Ac 1:14; 2:1; 2:2-4).

PRAETOR Originally the highest Roman magistrate; later, officials elected to administer justice; under the principate the office declined in prestige, power, and functions.

PRAETORIAN GUARD (*residence of the Praetor [leader]*). Guard of imperial palace or provincial governor; NIV "palace guard" (Php 1:13) and "Caesar's household" (Php 4:22).

PRAETORIUM (*residence of the Praetor [leader]*). In the Gospels it refers to the temporary palace or headquarters of the Roman governor while in Jerusalem (Mt 27:27; Mk 15:16), the palace of Herod at Caesarea (Ac 23:35).

PRAISE

Examples of:
(Ps 7:17; 22:22-23; 28:6-7; 32:11; 34:1-3; 41:13; 42:4; 51:15; 65:1; 71:8, 14-15; 75:1; 79:13; 81:1; 84:4; 86:12; 89:95; 104:33-34; 109:30; 113:1-2; 115:18; 118:15; 140:13; 145:1-21; 146:1-10; 148:1-14; 149:1-9; 150; Isa 24:15-16; 25:1; 35:10; 38:19; 43:21; 49:13; 51:3; 52:7-10; Jer 31:7; Ro 11:36; 16:27; 1Co 15:57; Eph 3:20-21; Heb 2:12; Jude 25; Rev 1:6; 14:7).
With music (Ps 33:2-3; 43:3-4; 47:1, 6-7; 57:7-9 w 108:1-3; 66:1-2, 4; 67:4; 68:4; 32-34; 69:30; 71:22; 81:1; 92:1-3; 95:1-2; 98:4-6; 104:33; 144:9; 149:2-3; 150:3-5; Jas 5:13).
Daily (1Ch 23:30; Ps 92:1-2; 145:2). In the night (Ps 42:8; 63:5-6; 77:6; 92:1-3; 119:62; 134:1; 149:5; Ac 16:25). Seven times a day (Ps 119:164).
Congregational (Ps 22:22; 26:12; 68:26; 111:1; 116:18-19; 134:1-2; 135:2; 149:1).
For God's goodness and mercy (Ps 13:6; 63:3-6; 100:5; 101:1; 106:1, 48; 107:8-9, 15, 21, 31; 117:2; 118:29; 136; 138:2; 144:1-2; 145:7-9, 14-21; 146:7-9; Isa 12:1-6; Jer 33:11). For God's greatness (Ps 48:1; 145:3, 10-12; 147:1-20; Isa 24:14). For God's holiness (Ps 99:2, 5, 9). For God's works (Ps 9:1-2; 107:8-9, 15, 21, 31-32; 145:4-6, 10-13; 147:12-18; 150:2). For deliverance from enemies (Ge 14:20; Ps 44:7-8; 54:6-7; 69:16). For salvation (Isa 61:3).

Commanded:
(Dt 8:10; Ps 9:11; 30:4; 32:11; 33:1-3; 69:34; 70:4; 95:1-2, 6-7a; 96:1-4, 7-9; 97:12; 100:1-5; 105:1-5; 117:1; 134:1-2; 135:1-3, 19-21; Isa 42:10-12; Eph 5:19; Heb 13:15; 1Pe 4:11; 5:11). All nations to praise God (Ps 69:34; 103:22; 148:1-14).
Angels exhorted to (Ps 103:20-21; 148:2). In heaven (Ne 9:6; Job 38:7; Ps 103:20-21; 148:2-4; Isa 6:3; Eze 3:12; Lk 2:13-14; 15:7, 10; Rev 1:6; 4:8-11; 5:9-14; 7:9-12; 11:16-17; 14:2-3; 15:3-4; 19:1-6).

Instances of:
Song of Moses, after the passage of the Red Sea (Ex 15:1-19). Miriam (Ex 15:21). Deborah, after defeating the Canaanites (Jdg 5:1-31). Hannah (1Sa 2:1-10). David, celebrating his deliverance from the hand of Saul (2Sa 22 w Ps 18). On bringing the ark to Zion (1Ch 16:8-36). At the close of his reign (1Ch 29:10-19). The choir when Solomon brought the ark into the temple (2Ch 5:13). Israelites (2Ch 7:2-3; Ne 9:5-6). Daniel (Da 2:20, 23). Nebuchadnezzar (Da 4:37). Jonah (Jnh 2:9).
Mary (Lk 1:46-55). Shepherds (Lk 2:20). The leper (Lk 17:15). Jesus and his disciples (Mt 26:30; Mk 14:26). Disciples (Ac 2:46-47; 4:24). Paul and Silas, in prison (Ac 16:25).

Psalms of:
For God's goodness to Israel (Pss 46; 48; 65-66; 68; 76; 81; 85; 98; 105; 124; 126; 129; 135; 136). For God's goodness to the righteous (Pss 23; 34; 36; 91; 100; 103; 107; 117; 121). For God's goodness to individuals (Pss 9; 18; 22; 30; 40; 75; 103; 108; 116; 118; 138; 144). For God's attributes (Pss 8; 19; 22; 24; 29; 33; 47; 50; 65-66; 76-77; 92-93; 95-99; 104; 111; 113-115; 134; 139; 147-148; 150).
See Glorifying God; Hallelujah; Prayer; Thankfulness.

PRAYER (Ps 17:1, 6; 22:1-2, 19; 28:1-2; 35:22; 55:1-2, 16-17; 57:2; 61:1-2; 70:5; 102:1-2; 130:1-2; 141:1-2; 142:1-2).

General:
Attitudes in: *See Worship.*
Boldness in: Commanded (Heb 4:16). Exemplified by Abraham in his inquiry concerning Sodom (Ge 18:23-32), by Moses, supplicating for assistance in delivering Israel (Ex 33:12, 18). Secret (Ge 24:63; Mt 6:6). Silent (Ps 5:1). Weeping in (Ezr 10:1). In a loud voice, satirized by Elijah (1Ki 18:27).
Long: Of Pharisees (Mt 23:14), scribes (Mk 12:40; Lk 20:47). Profuse, to be avoided (Ecc 5:2; Mt 6:7). Vain repetitions of, to be avoided (Mt 6:7).
Daily: In the morning (Ps 5:3; 88:13; 143:8; Isa 32:2). Morning and evening (Ps 92:2). Twice daily (Ps 88:1). Three times a day (Ps 55:17; Da 6:10). In the night (Ps 119:55, 62). All night (Lk 6:12). Without ceasing (1Th 5:17).
Disbelief in: (Job 21:15).
Family: By Abraham (Ge 12:7-8; 13:4, 8). By Jacob (Ge 35:3, 7). Cornelius (Ac 10:2).
Hypocritical, forbidden (Mt 6:5). Discreet (Ecc 5:2; Mt 6:6).
"Lord's prayer": A model taught to the disciples (Mt 6:9-12; Lk 11:2-4). *See below, Of Jesus.*
Of the righteous, acceptable (Pr 15:8, 29). Spirit of, from God (Zec 12:10). Divine help in (Ro 8:26).
Postures in: Bowing (Ge 24:26, 48, 52; Ex 4:31; 34:8-9; 2Ch 29:29). Kneeling (1Ki 8:54; 2Ch 6:13; Ezr 9:5; Ps 95:6; Da 6:10;

Lk 22:41; Ac 20:36; 21:5). Hands uplifted (1Ki 8:22; 2Ch 6:12-13; Ezr 9:5; Isa 1:15; La 3:41; 1Ti 2:8). Standing (Lk 18:11, 13).

Power of (Mk 9:28-29; Jas 5:16-18). Accompanied by works (Ne 4:9). Kept in divine remembrance (Ne 8:3-4).

Prayer contest: Proposed by Elijah (1Ki 18:24-39).

Public, should edify (1Co 14:14-15). Social (Mt 18:19; Ac 1:13-14; 16:16, 25; 20:36; 21:5). Held in private houses (Ac 1:13-14; 12:12), in the temple (Ac 2:46; 3:1). Perseverance in (Ro 12:12; Eph 6:18). Evils averted by (Jer 26:19).

Private commanded (Mt 6:6). Exemplified by Lot (Ge 19:20), Eliezer (Ge 24:12), Jacob (Ge 32:9-12), Gideon (Jdg 6:22, 36, 39, Hannah (1Sa 1:10), David (2Sa 7:18-29), Hezekiah (2Ki 20:2), Isaiah (2Ki 20:11), Manasseh (2Ch 33:18-19), Ezra (Ezr 9:5-6), Nehemiah (Ne 2:4), Jeremiah (Jer 32:16-25), Daniel (Da 9:3, 19), Jonah (Jnh 2:1), Habakkuk (Hab 1:2), Anna (Lk 2:37), Jesus (Mt 14:23; 26:36, 39; Mk 1:35; Lk 9:18, 29), Paul (Ac 9:11), Peter (Ac 9:40; 10:9), Cornelius (Ac 10:30).

Rebuked: Of Moses, at the Red Sea (Ex 14:15), when he prayed to see Canaan (Dt 3:23-27). Of Joshua (Jos 7:10).

Submissiveness in: Exemplified by Jesus (Mt 26:39; Mk 14:36; Lk 22:42), David (2Sa 12:22-23), Job (Job 1:20-21).

Signs asked for, as assurance of answer: By Abraham's servant (Ge 24:14, 42-44). By Gideon (Jdg 6:36-40).

Answer to:

Promised—
(Ex 33:17-20; 1Ki 8:22-53; 1Ch 28:9; 2Ch 6; Job 8:5-6; 12:4; 22:27; 33:26; Ps 10:17; 81:10; Pr 10:24; 15:8, 29; 16:1; Isa 58:9; 65:24; Eze 36:37; Mt 6:5-8; 18:19-20; 21:22; Mk 11:24-25; Lk 11:9-13; 18:6-8; 21:36; 4:10, 23-24; Jn 16:23-27; Ro 8:26; 10:12-13; Eph 2:18; 3:20; Heb 4:16; 10:22-23; Jas 1:5-7; 1Jn 3:22; 5:14-15).

Promised to those in adversity (Ex 6:5-6 w Ac 7:34; Ex 22:23, 27; Ps 9:10, 12; 18:3; 32:6; 34:15, 17; 37:4-5; 38:15; 50:15; 55:16-17; 56:9; 65:2, 5; 69:32-33; 86:7; 91:15; 102:17-20; Isa 19:20; 30:19; 31:9; Joel 2:18-19, 32; Zec 10:1, 6; 13:9). Promised to those who diligently seek God (2Ch 7:14; Ps 145:18-19; Pr 2:3, 5-6; Isa 55:6; Jer 29:12-13; 33:3; La 3:25; Am 5:4-6; Zep 2:3; Zec 13:9; Mt 7:7-11; Jn 9:31; 15:7, 16; Heb 11:6; Jas 4:8, 10; 5:16). Promised to the meek (Mk 11:25). Promised to the penitent (Dt 4:30-31; 2Ch 7:13-15).

Delayed—
(Ps 22:1-2; 40:1; 80:4; 88:14; Jer 42:2-7; Hab 1:2; Lk 18:7).
Withheld: Of Balaam (Dt 23:5; Jos 24:10). Of Job (Job 30:20, w 42:12). Of the Israelites, when attacked by the Amorites (Dt 1:45). The prayer of Jesus, "Let this cup pass" (Mt 26:39, 42, 44, w 45-75 & Mt 27).

Differs From Request—
Exceeds petition (Eph 3:20). Solomon asked wisdom; the answer included wisdom, riches, honor and long life (1Ki 3:7-14; 2Ch 1:7-12). Disciples prayed for Peter, the answer included Peter's deliverance (Ac 12:15, w v.5).

Moses asked to see God's face; God revealed his goodness (Ex 33:18-20). Moses asked to be permitted to cross the Jordan; the answer was permission to view the land of promise (Dt 3:23-27). Martha and Mary asked Jesus to come and heal their brother Lazarus; Jesus delayed, but raised Lazarus from the dead (Jn 11). Paul asked that the thorn in the flesh be removed; the answer was a promise of grace to endure it (2Co 12:8-9).

Answered—
(Job 34:28; Ps 3:4; 4:1; 6:8-9; 18:6; 21:2, 4; 22:4-5, 24; 28:6; 30:2-3; 31:22; 34:4-6; 40:1; 66:19-20; 77:1-2; 81:7; 99:6-8; 106:44; 107:6, 13; 116:1-8; 118:5, 21; 119:26; 120:1; 138:3; La 3:57-58; Hos 12:4; Jnh 2:1-2, 7; Lk 23:42-43; Ac 4:31; 2Co 12:8-9; Jas 5:17-18).

Instances of—
Cain (Ge 4:13-15). Abraham, for a son (Ge 15), entreating for Sodom (Ge 18:23-33), for Ishmael (Ge 17:20), for Abimelech (Ge 20:17). Hagar, for deliverance (Ge 16:7-13). Abraham's servant, for guidance (Ge 24:12-52). Rebekah, concerning her pains in pregnancy (Ge 25:22-23). Jacob, for deliverance from Esau (Ge 32:9-32; 33:1-17).

Moses, for help at the Red Sea (Ex 14:15-16), at the waters of Marah (Ex 15:25), at Horeb (Ex 17:4-6), in the battle with the Amalekites (Ex 17:8-14), concerning the murmuring of the Israelites for flesh (Nu 11:11-35), in behalf of Miriam's leprosy (Nu 12:13-15). Moses, Aaron, and Samuel (Ps 99:6).

Israelites: For deliverance from bondage (Ex 2:23-25; 3:7-10; Ac 7:34), from Pharaoh's army (Ex 14:10-30), from the king of Mesopotamia (Jdg 3:9, 15), Sisera (Jdg 4:3, 23-24; 1Sa 12:9-11), Ammon (Jdg 10:6-18; 11:1-33), for God's favor under the reproofs of Azariah (2Ch 15:1-15), from Babylonian bondage (Ne 9:27).

Gideon, asking the token of dew (Jdg 6:36-40). Manoah, asking about Samson (Jdg 13:8-9). Samson, asking for strength (Jdg 16:28-30). Hannah, asking for a child (1Sa 1:10-17, 19-20). David, asking whether Keilah would be delivered into his hands (1Sa 23:10-12), and Ziklag (1Sa 30:8), whether he should go into Judah after Saul's death (2Sa 2:1), whether he should go against the Philistines (2Sa 5:19-25). David, in adversity (Ps 118:5; 138:3). Solomon, asking wisdom (1Ki 3:1-13; 9:2-3).

Elijah, raising the widow's son (1Ki 17:22), asking fire on his sacrifice (1Ki 18:36-38), rain (1Ki 17:1; 18:1, 42-45; Jas 5:17). Elisha, leading the Syrian army (2Ki 6:17-20). Jabez, asking for prosperity (1Ch 4:10). Abijah, for victory over Jeroboam (2Ch 13:14-18). Asa, for victory over Zerah (2Ch 14:11-15). The people of Judah (2Ch 15:15). Jehoshaphat, for victory from the Canaanites (2Ch 18:31; 20:6-7). Jehoahaz, for victory over Hazael (2Ki 13:4). Priests and Levites, when blessing the people (2Ch 30:27). Hezekiah and Isaiah, for deliverance from Sennacherib (2Ki 19:14-20; 2Ch 32:20-23), to save Hezekiah's life (2Ki 20:1-7, 11; 2Ch 32:24). Manasseh, for deliverance from the king of Babylon (2Ch 33:13, 19). Reubenites, for deliverance from the Hagrites (1Ch 5:20). The Jews, returning from the Captivity (Ezr 8:21, 23). Ezekiel, to have the baking of his bread of affliction changed (Eze 4:12-15). Daniel, for the interpretation of Nebuchadnezzar's dream (Da 2:19-23), interceding for the people (Da 9:20-23), in a vision (Da 10:12).

Zechariah, for a son (Lk 1:13). The leper, for healing (Mt 8:2-3; Mk 1:40-43; Lk 5:12-13). Centurion, for his servant (Mt 8:5-13;

Lk 7:3-10; Jn 4:50-51). Peter, asking that Tabitha be restored (Ac 9:40). The disciples, for Peter (Ac 12:5-17). Paul, to be restored to health (2Co 1:9-11).

Confession in:
(Lev 26:40; Ezr 10:1; Lk 15:21; 16:13). Commanded (Lev 5:5; Nu 5:6-7; Jer 3:13, 25). A condition of forgiveness (1Ki 8:47, 49-50; Pr 28:13; 1Jn 1:9).

Instances of—
(Jdg 10:10, 15; 1Sa 12:10; Ne 9:2-3, 33-35; Ps 31:10; 32:5; 38:4, 18; 40:11-12; 41:4; 51:2-5; 69:5; 106:6; 119:176; 130:3). Moses for Israel (Ex 32:31-32; 34:9). Ezra confesses for Judah (Ezr 9:6-15). Nehemiah confesses for Judah (Ne 1:4-11). Isaiah confesses for Judah (Isa 14:20-21; 59:12-15; 64:5-7). Jeremiah confesses for Judah (Jer 14:7, 20; La 1:18, 20; 3:42). Daniel confesses for Judah (Da 9:5-15).

Commanded:
(1Ch 16:11, 35; Ps 105:3-4; Isa 55:6; La 3:1; Lk 18:1; Eph 1:18; Php 4:6; Col 4:2; 1Th 5:17-18; 1Ti 2:8; Heb 4:16).

Exemplified:
By Eliezer (Ge 24:12). Jacob (Ge 32:9-12). Gideon (Jdg 6:22, 36, 39). Hannah (1Sa 1:10, 13). David (2Sa 7:18-29). Solomon at the dedication of the temple (1Ki 8:23-53; 2Ch 6:14-42). Hezekiah (2Ki 20:2). Isaiah (2Ki 20:11). Manasseh (2Ch 33:18-19). Ezra (Ezr 9:5-15). Nehemiah (Ne 2:4). Jeremiah (Jer 32:16-25). Daniel (Da 9:3-19). Jonah (Jnh 2:1-9). Habakkuk (Hab 1:2). Anna (Lk 2:37). Jesus (Mt 14:23; 26:36, 39; Mk 1:35; 6:46; Lk 5:16; 6:12; 9:18, 28-29). Paul (Ac 9:11). Peter (Ac 9:40; 10:9). Cornelius (Ac 10:30).

Persistence in:
(Ps 17:1-6; 22:1-2, 19; 28:1-2; 35:22-23; 55:1-2, 16-17; 57:2; 61:1-2; 70:5; 86:3, 6; 88:1-2, 9, 13; 102:1-28; 119:145-147; 130:1-2; 141:1-2; 142:1-2). Isa 62:7; Hos 12:4; Lk 11:5-8; 18:1-7).

Instances of—
Abraham (Ge 18:23-32). Jacob (Ge 32:24-30). Moses (Ex 32:32; 33:12-16; 34:9; Dt 9:18, 25). Gideon (Jdg 6:36-40). Samson (Jdg 16:28). Hannah (1Sa 1:10-11). Elijah (1Ki 18:24-44; Jas 5:17-18). Hezekiah (2Ki 19:15-19; Isa 38:2-3). Asa (2Ch 14:11). Ezra (Ezr 9:5). Nehemiah (Ne 1:4-11; 9:32). Isaiah (Isa 64:12). Daniel (Da 9:3, 17-19). Sailors (Jnh 1:14). Habakkuk (Hab 1:2).

Two blind men of Jericho (Mt 20:30-31; Mk 10:48; Lk 18:39). The Syrian Phoenician woman (Mt 15:22-28; Mk 7:25-30). The centurion (Mt 8:5; Lk 7:3-4). Jesus (Mt 26:39, 42; Mk 14:36, 39; Lk 22:42-44; Heb 5:7). Paul (2Co 12:8). Believers (Ro 8:26; Eph 6:18).

Imprecatory:
Asking for vengeance against enemies (Nu 16:15; 22:6-11; 23:7-8; 24:9-10; Dt 11:29-30; 27:11-13; 33:11; Jos 8:33-34; Jdg 16:28; 2Sa 16:10-12; Ne 4:4-5; 5:13; Job 3:1-10; 27:7; Ps 5:10; 6:10; 9:20; 10:2, 15; 25:3; 28:4; 31:17-18; 35:4, 8, 26; 40:14-15; 54:5; 55:9, 15; 56:7; 58:7; 59:5, 11, 15; 68:1-2; 69:23-24, 27-28; 70:2-3; 71:13; 79:10, 12; 83:13-17; 94:2; 109:7, 9-20, 28-29; 119:78, 84; 129:5; 140:9-10; 143:12; 144:6; Jer 11:20; 12:3; 15:15; 17:18; 18:21-23; 20:12; La 1:22; 3:64-66; Gal 1:8-9; 2Ti 4:14-15). *See Imprecation.*

In Adversity:
By Jacob (Ge 43:14). Moses (Ex 32:32). The Israelites (Nu 20:16; Dt 26:7; Jdg 3:9). David (2Sa 22:7). Hezekiah (2Ki 19:16, 19). Jehoshaphat (2Ch 20:4-13). Manasseh (2Ch 33:12-13). The Psalmist (Ps 5:1-2; 7:1-2, 6-7; 13:1-4; 22:1-21; 25:2, 16-19, 22; 27:11-12; 28:1; 31:1-4, 9, 14-18; 35:1-28; 38:1-22; 43:1-5; 44:4, 23-26; 54:1-3; 55:1-17; 56:1-13; 57:1-2; 59:1-17; 64:1-2; 69:1-36; 70:1-5; 71:1-24; 74:1-23; 79:1-13; 94:1-23; 102; 108:6, 12; 109:1-2, 21, 26-28; 120:2; 140:1-13; 142:1-2, 5-7; 143:1-12). Jeremiah (Jer 15:15). Jonah (Jnh 2:1-9). Stephen (Ac 7:59-60). Paul and Silas (Ac 16:25).

In Behalf of the Nations: *See Nation, Sin of.*

Intercessory:
(Ge 20:7; Jer 27:18; 29:7; Mt 5:44; Eph 6:18-19; 1Ti 2:1; Heb 13:20-21; Jas 5:14-16).

Priestly (Ex 28:12, 29-30, 38; Lev 10:17). For spiritual blessing (Nu 6:23-26; 1Sa 12:23; Job 1:5; 42:8-10). To avert judgments (Ge 20:7; Ex 32:9-14; Nu 14:11-21; 16:45-50; Dt 9:18-20, 25-29; 1Sa 65:8). For deliverance from enemies (1Sa 7:5-9; Isa 37:4). For healing disease (Jas 5:14-16).

For the unrepentant, unavailing (Jer 7:16; 11:14; 14:11).

Of Moses for Israel (Ex 32:11-14, 31-32; 34:9; Nu 14:19; 21:7; Dt 9:18-20, 24-29). Of Joshua for Israel (Jos 7:6-7). Of Boaz for Ruth (Ru 2:12). Of Eli for Hannah (1Sa 1:17). Of Samuel for Israel (1Sa 7:9; 12:23). Of David, for Israel (2Sa 24:17; 1Ch 29:18), for Solomon (1Ch 29:19). Of Solomon (1Ki 8:31-53; 2Ch 6:22-42). Of Hezekiah for transgressors (2Ch 30:18-19). Of Job for his three friends (Job 42:8-10). Of the Psalmist for the righteous (Ps 7:9; 28:9; 36:10; 80:14-15). Of Daniel for Israel (Da 9:3-19). Of Jesus for his murderers (Lk 23:34). Of Stephen for his murderers (Ac 7:60). Of Peter and John for Samaritan believers (Ac 8:15). Of the recipients of bounty for Corinthian donors (2Co 9:14).

Of Paul, for unbelieving Jews (Ro 10:1), for Roman Christians (Ro 1:9), for Ephesian Christians (Eph 1:15-19; 3:14-19), for Philippian Christians (Php 1:3-5, 9), for Colossian Christians (Col 1:3, 9), for Thessalonian Christians (1Th 1:2; 3:10, 12-13; 5:23; 2Th 1:11-12; 2:16-17; 3:5, 16), for Onesiphorus (2Ti 1:16, 18), for Philemon (Phm 4). Of Philemon for Paul (Phm 22).

See Intercession; Jesus the Christ, Mediation of; Mediation.

Requested (Nu 21:7; Ro 15:30-32; 2Co 1:11; Eph 6:19; Col 4:3; 1Th 5:25; 2Th 3:1; Heb 13:18). *See Intercession, Solicited.*

Of Jesus:
(Mt 6:9-13; 11:25-26; Lk 11:1-4; Jn 12:27-28). Before day (Mk 1:35). In secret (Mt 14:23; Mk 1:35; 6:46; Lk 5:16; 6:12; 9:18, 28-29). In a mountain (Mt 14:23; Mk 6:46; Lk 6:12; 9:28). In the wilderness (Lk 5:16). Thanksgiving before eating (Mt 14:19; 15:36; 26:26-27; Mk 6:41; 8:6; 1Co 11:24). In distress (Jn 12:27; Heb 5:7). In blessing children (Mt 19:13, 15; Mk 10:16). At the grave of Lazarus (Jn 11:41-42). For Peter (Lk 22:31-32). For believers (Jn 17:1-26). For the Comforter, the Holy Spirit (Jn 14:16). In Gethsemane (Mt 26:36-44; Mk 14:32-35; Lk 22:41-44;

Heb 5:7). On the cross (Mt 27:46; Lk 23:34, 46). Present ministry, at the right hand of the Father (Heb 7:25), Of his apostles (Ac 1:24-25).

See Jesus the Christ, Prayers of.

Of the Wicked, Not Heard:
(Dt 1:45; 2Sa 22:42; Job 35:12-13; Ps 18:41; 66:18; Pr 1:24-28; 15:8, 29; 21:13, 27; 28:9; Isa 1:15; 45:19; 59:2; Jer 11:11; 14:12; 15:1; 18:17; La 3:8, 44; Eze 8:18; 20:8, 31; Hos 5:6; Mic 3:4; Zec 7:12-13; Mal 2:11-13; Jn 9:31; Jas 1:6-7; 4:3). *See Wicked, Prayers of.*

To idols (1Ki 18:26-29). *See Idolatry.*

Penitential:
Of David (Ps 51:1-17), the tax collector (Lk 18:13). *See above, Confession in; See Sin, Confession of.*

Pleas Offered in:
(Ex 33:13; Nu 14:13-19; 16:22; Dt 3:24-25; 9:26-29; Jos 7:7-9; 2Sa 7:25-29; Ezr 9:15-19; 2Ch 14:11; Ne 9:32; Ps 9:19-20; 38:16; 71:18; 74:10-11, 18, 20-23; 79:10-12; 83:1-2, 18; 119:42, 73, 146, 149, 153; 143:11-12; Isa 37:15-20; 63:17-19; La 3:56-63; Joel 2:17).

Pleas based on God's mercy (Ps 69:13, 16; 109:21, 26-27; 115:1; 119:124). God's providence (Ps 4:1; 27:8). God's promises (Ge 32:9-12; Ex 32:13; 1Ki 8:25-26, 59-60; Ne 1:8-9; Ps 89:49-51; 119:43, 49, 116; Jer 14:21). Personal consecration (Ps 119:94). Personal righteousness (Ps 86:1-2, 4-5, 17; 119:38, 145, 173-176; Jer 18:20).

Thanksgiving, and Before Taking Food:
(Jos 9:14; 1Sa 9:13; Ro 14:6; 1Co 10:30-31; 1Ti 4:3-5).
See Praise; Thankfulness.

Exemplified—
By Jesus (Mt 14:19; 15:36; 26:26-27; Mk 6:41; 8:6-7; 14:22-23; Lk 9:16; 22:19; Jn 6:11, 23; 1Co 11:24). By Paul (Ac 27:35).

PRAYERFULNESS
Commanded (Ro 12:12; Col 4:2; 1Th 5:17). Spirit of, from God (Zec 12:10).

Exemplified by: The psalmist (Ps 5:1-3; 42:8; 109:4; 116:2). Daniel (Da 6:10). Anna (Lk 2:37). The apostles (Ac 6:4). Cornelius (Ac 10:2). Peter (Ac 10:9). Paul (Ro 1:9; Eph 1:15-16; Col 1:9; 1Th 3:10; 2Ti 1:3). Widows (1Ti 5:5).

See Prayer; Prayerlessness.

PRAYERLESSNESS
(Jos 9:14; Job 15:4; 21:14-15; Ps 14:4; 53:4; 79:6; Isa 43:22; 64:7; Jer 10:21, 25; Da 9:13; Hos 7:7; Jnh 1:6; Zep 1:6). *See Prayer.*

PREACHING
The act of exhorting, prophesying, reproving, teaching.

General:
Noah called preacher (2Pe 2:5). Solomon called preacher (Ecc 1:1, 12). Sitting while (Mt 5:1; Lk 4:20; 5:3). Moses slow to (Ex 4:10-12).

Appointed and practiced by Jesus as the method of promulgating the gospel (Mt 4:17; 11:1; Mk 16:15, 20; Lk 4:18-19, 43). Attested to by Paul (Tit 1:3). Grave responsibility of (2Co 2:14-17).

Repentance, the subject, of John the Baptist's (Mt 3:2; Mk 1:4, 15; Lk 3:3), of Christ's (Mt 4:17; Mk 1:15), the apostles' (Mk 6:12). The gospel of the kingdom of God, the subject of Christ's (Mk 1:14-15; 2:2; Lk 8:1). Christ crucified and risen, the burden of Paul's (Ac 17:3).

Jesus preaches to the spirits in prison (1Pe 3:19; 4:9, w Eph 4:9).

Preaching Should:
Edify (1Co 14:1-25). Be skillful (2Ti 2:15-16). Be in power (1Th 1:5). Be with boldness (Ac 13:46; 2Co 3:12-13). Not be, with mere human strategy (Mt 26) with deceit or flattery (1Th 2:3-6).

Effective Preaching:
By Azariah (2Ch 15:1-15), Jonah (Jnh 3), Haggai (Hag 1:7-12), Peter (Ac 2:14-41), Philip (Ac 8:5-12, 27-38), Paul (Ac 9:20-22; 13:16-43). *See Revivals.*

Impenitence Under:
Asa (2Ch 16:7-10), Ahab (2Ch 18:7-26), the Jews (Ac 13:46). *See Obduracy.*

See Minister; Call, Personal.

PRECEPTS *See Commandments and Statutes, Of God; Law.*

PRECIOUS STONES
In the breastpiece of the high priest the stones were set, probably, in the order of the tribes of the Israelites. The first stone, ruby, was probably the tribal stone for Reuben; topaz for Simeon; beryl for Levi; turquoise for Judah; sapphire for Issachar; emerald for Zebulun; jacinth for Dan; agate for Naphtali; amethyst for Asher; chrysolite for Gad; onyx for Joseph; jasper for Benjamin (Ex 28:9-21; 39:6-14). Voluntary offerings of, by the Israelites for the breastpiece and ephod (Ex 35:27). Exported, from Sheba (1Ki 10:2, 10; 2Ch 9:1, 9; Eze 27:22), from Ophir (1Ki 10:11; 2Ch 9:10).

Partial catalog of (Eze 28:13). Seen in the foundation of the New Jerusalem in John's apocalyptic vision (Rev 21:19-21). In kings' crowns (2Sa 12:30; 1Ch 20:2).

Figurative (Isa 54:11-12).

See Stones; Agate; Amethyst; Beryl, 1; Carbuncle; Crystal; Diamond; Emerald; Jasper; Ruby; Sapphire; Sardis; Topaz.

PREDESTINATION
According to the purpose of grace (Ex 33:19; Isa 44:1-2, 7; Mal 1:2-3; Ac 13:48; Ro 8:28-30, 33; 9:11-29; 11:5, 7-8; 1Co 1:26-29; Eph 1:4-5, 9-11; 3:11; 2Th 2:13; 2Ti 1:9; Tit 1:1-2; 1Pe 1:2, 20).

Of prosperity to Abraham (Ge 21:12; Ne 9:7-8). Of Joseph's mission to Egypt (Ge 45:5-7; Ps 105:17-22). Of Israel as a nation (Ge 21:12; Dt 4:37; 7:7-8; 10:15; 32:8; 1Sa 12:22; Ps 33:12; 135:4). Of Ishmael as a nation (Ge 21:12-13; 25:12-18). Of famine in Egypt (Ge 41:30-32). Of judgment to Pharaoh (Ex 9:16). Of David as king (2Ch 6:6; Ps 78:67-68, 70-72). Of Jehu's dynasty (2Ki 10:30; 15:12). Of the dividing of Solomon's kingdom (1Ki 11:11-12, 31-39; 12:15). Of mercy to the widow at Sidon (Lk 4:25-27).

Of the destruction of the Canaanites (Jos 11:20), of Ben-Hadad (1Ki 20:42), of Ahaziah (2Ch 22:7), of Amaziah and the idolatrous Israelites (2Ch 25:20).

Acknowledged by Job (Job 23:13-14). Of agent to execute divine judgments (2Ki 19:25; 2Ch 22:7; Hab 1:12). Of Jeremiah as prophet (Jer 1:4-5). Of revelation to a chosen people (Mt 11:25-26; Lk 8:10; 1Co 2:7).

Of the death of Jesus (Mt 26:24; Mk 14:21; Lk 22:22; 24:26-27; Ac 2:23; 3:18; 4:28; Rev 13:8).

Of Paul to the ministry (Ac 9:15; Gal 1:15-16; 1Ti 2:7).

Of the times and bounds of nations (Ac 17:26). Of times and seasons (Ac 1:7).

Of the standard of righteousness (Eph 2:10). Of the kingdom prepared for the righteous (Mt 25:34).

Of salvation and election (Mt 20:16; 20:23; 24:22, 40; Mk 13:20, 22; Lk 10:20; 17:34-36; 18:7; Jn 6:37, 39, 44-45; 15:16, 19; 17:2, 6, 9; Ac 2:39, 47; 13:48; 22:14; Ro 1:6; 8:28-30, 33; 11:5, 7-8; 1Co 1:26-29; Eph 1:9-11; Col 3:12; 1Th 1:4; 2:12-13; 2Ti 1:9; Tit 1:1-2; Jas 1:18; 1Pe 1:2, 20; 2Pe 1:10).

Of the wicked, to the day of evil (Pr 16:4), to condemnation (Jude 4). Of the day of judgment (Ac 17:31).

See Election.

PREJUDICE *See Respect of Persons.*

PREPAREDNESS (Mt 24:44; 25:1-13; Mk 13:32-37; Lk 12:35-48; 19:41-44). *See Faithfulness.*

PRESBYTERY *See Elders.*

PRESCIENCE *See God, Foreknowledge of.*

PRESENTS To Abraham, by Pharaoh (Ge 12:16), by Abimelech (Ge 20:14). To Rebekah (Ge 24:22). To Esau (Ge 32:13-15). To prophets (1Ki 14:3; 2Ki 4:42). To those in adversity (Job 42:10-11).

Betrothal (Ge 24:53). Marriage (Est 2:18). Propitiatory (Ge 32:20; 33:8-11; 1Sa 25:27-35; Pr 21:14). To confirm covenants (Ge 21:28-30; 1Sa 18:3-4). Rewards of service (Da 5:7). Kings to kings (2Sa 8:10; 1Ki 10:10, 13; 15:18-19).

To corrupt courts, forbidden (Ex 23:8; Dt 16:19; 27:25; Isa 5:23). *See Bribery; Liberality.*

PRESIDENTS *See Administrators.*

PRESS Crowd (Mk 2:4; Lk 8:19).

PRESSVAT NIV "wine vat" (Hag 2:16). *See Wine.*

PRESUMPTION (Dt 29:19-20; Ps 10:6; 19:13; 73:8-9).

Admonitions Against:
(Pr 25:6-7; Lk 14:7-11). Warning against (1Co 10:9-12). Excommunication for (Nu 15:30). Proverbs concerning (Pr 18:12-13; 25:6-7a). Punishment for (Jer 23:34).

Sins of:
The self-righteous (Isa 65:5; Lk 18:11-12). The selfish rich, in forgetting God (Lk 12:18-20). Temptation to (Dt 6:16; Mt 4:5-7; Lk 4:9-11).

In ignoring God (Lk 10:15; 29:16; 37:23-25; Ro 9:23-25, 20-21; Jas 4:13-15). Questioning God's righteousness (Isa 58:3; Ro 9:20-21). Defying God (Job 15:25; Ps 94:7; Isa 5:18-25; 14:13-14; 28:14-18, 22; 29:15-16, 20; 40:27; 45:9-10; Ro 1:32; 9:20-21; 2Th 2:3). Reviling God's prophet (1Ki 22:24). Despising the lordship of Christ, and the authority of the Church (2Pe 2:10-11).

Instances of:
Satan, when he said to Eve, "You will not surely die" (Ge 3:1-5). Builders of Babel (Ge 11:4). Abraham, in questioning about Sodom (Ge 18:23-32). Pharaoh (Ex 5:2). Moses, in scolding Yahweh (Nu 11:11-15, 22). Nadab and Abihu (Lev 10:1-2). Israelites, in ascending to the top of the hill against the Amalekites (Nu 14:44-45, w Dt 1:43). Murmuring (Ex 14:11-12; 17:2, 7; Nu 16:41; 21:5; 1Co 10:9-12). In reviling God (Mal 1:6-7, 12; 3:7-8, 13). Korah, Dathan, and Abiram (Nu 16:3).

Saul, in sacrificing (1Sa 13:8-14), sparing the Amalekites (1Sa 15:3, 9-23). Men of Beth Shemesh (1Sa 6:19). Uzzah, in steadying the ark (2Sa 6:6-7). David's anger at Uzzah's death (2Sa 6:8). David, in numbering Israel (2Sa 24:1-17). Jeroboam (1Ki 13:4). Ben-Hadad (1Ki 20:10). The Syrians, in limiting the sovereignty of God (1Ki 20:23, 28). Zedekiah (1Ki 22:24-25; 2Ch 18:23-24). Uzziah (2Ch 26:16). Sennacherib (2Ki 19:22; 2Ch 32:13-14). Isa 37:23-25). Job, in cursing the day of his birth (Job 3), reproved by Eliphaz (Job 4:5). Jonah (Jnh 4:1-8).

Peter, in objecting to Jesus' statement that he must be killed (Mt 16:21-23; Mk 8:32), in reflecting on his knowledge when he asked, amid a throng, who touched him (Lk 8:45), in objecting to Jesus washing his feet (Jn 13:8), in asking Jesus, "What shall this man do?" (Jn 21:20-22). The disciples, in rebuking those who brought little children to Jesus (Mt 19:13; Mk 10:13-14; Lk 18:15), in their indignation at the anointing of Jesus (Mt 26:8-9; Mk 14:4-5; Jn 12:5), reproving Jesus (Jn 7:3-5). The brothers of Jesus (Jn 7:3-5). James and John, in desiring to call down fire on the Samaritans (Lk 9:54). Those who reviled Jesus (Mt 27:42-43; Mk 15:29-32). Theudas (Ac 5:36). Sons of Sceva (Ac 19:13-14). Diotrephes (3Jn 9).

See Blasphemy; Mocking; Pride.

PRETORIUM *See Praetorium.*

PRICK *See Goad; Thorn.*

PRIDE

Condemned:
Admonitions against (Dt 8:11-14, 17-20; Ps 49:11; 75:4-6; Jer 9:23; Mt 23:5-7; Lk 14:8-9; 20:46-47; Ro 11:17-21, 25; 12:3, 16; 1Co 4:6-8, 10; 5:2, 6; 8:1-2; 10:12; 13:4; 14:38; 2Co 10:5, 12, 18; Gal 6:3; Eph 4:17; Php 2:3; 1Ti 2:9; 6:3-4, 17; 2Ti 3:2, 4; 1Pe 5:3; Rev 3:17-18).

Prayer regarding (Ps 9:20; 10:2-6, 11). Prevented by divine discipline (2Co 12:7). Proceeds from the carnal mind (Mk 7:21-22; 1Jn 2:16). Leads, to strife (Pr 13:10; 28:25), to destruction (Pr

15:25; 16:18; 17:19; 18:11-12; Isa 14:12-16; 26:5; 28:3; Da 11:45; Zep 3:11; Mal 4:1; 1Ti 3:6; Rev 18:7-8).

Rebuked (1Sa 2:3-5; 2Ki 14:9-10; 2Ch 25:18-19; Job 12:2; Jer 13:9, 15, 17; Hab 2:4-5, 9). Repugnant to God (Job 37:24; Ps 12:3; 18:27; 31:23; 101:5; 138:6; Pr 6:16-17; 8:13; 16:5; Jer 50:31-32; Lk 1:51; Jas 4:6).

The proud shall be humbled (Lev 26:19; Ps 52:6-7; Pr 11:2; Isa 2:11-17; 3:16-26; 5:13; 13:11; 22:16, 19; 23:7, 9; 24:4, 21; Jer 49:4, 16; Da 4:37; Ob 3-4; Mt 23:12; Mk 10:43; Lk 1:52; 9:46; 18:14; Rev 18:7-8).

Pride discussed with Job (Job 11:12; 12:2-3; 13:2, 5; 15:1-13; 18:3-4; 21:31-32; 32:9-13; 37:24). Proverbs concerning (Pr 3:34; 6:16-17; 8:13; 10:17; 11:2; 12:9, 15; 13:10; 14:21; 15:5, 10, 12, 25, 32; 16:5, 18-19; 17:19; 18:11-12; 21:4, 24; 25:14, 27; 26:5, 12, 16; 27:2; 28:11, 25; 29:8, 23; 30:12-13). Cited by the psalmists (Ps 10:2-6, 11; 49:11; 52:7; 73:6, 8-9; 119:21, 69-70, 78).

See Rich, The.

Instances of:
Pharaoh (Ex 7-11; 12:29-36; 14). Ahithophel (2Sa 17:23). Naaman (2Ki 5:11-13). Hezekiah (2Ki 20:13; 2Ch 32:25-26, 31; Isa 39:2). Uzziah (2Ch 26:16-19). Haman (Est 3:5; 5:11, 13; 6:6; 7:10).

Moab (Isa 16:6-7; Jer 48:7, 14-29; Zep 2:9). Israel (Isa 9:9-10; Hos 5:5; 7:10). Assyria (Isa 10:5-16; Eze 31:10-11). Jerusalem (Eze 16:56). Tyre (Eze 28:2-9, 17). Egypt (Eze 30:6). Nebuchadnezzar (Da 4:30-34; 5:20). Moab and Ammon (Zep 2:9). Nineveh (Zep 2:15).

The Scribes and Pharisees (Mt 20:6; 23:6-8, 11-12; Mk 10:43; 12:38-39; Lk 9:46; 11:43; 18:14; 20:45-47). Herod (Ac 12:21-23).

See Ambition.

PRIEST

Before the Mosaic Covenant:
Melchizedek (Ge 14:18; Heb 5:6, 10-11; 6:20; 7:1-21). Jethro (Ex 2:16). Priests in Israel before the giving of the law (Ex 19:22, 24).

Mosaic:
(Ex 28:1-4; 29:9, 44; Nu 3:10; 18:7; 1Ch 23:13). Hereditary descent of office (Ex 27:21; 28:43; 29:9). Consecration of (Ex 29:1-9, 19-35; 40:12-16; Lev 6:20-23; 8:6-35; Heb 7:21). Is holy (Lev 21:6-7; 22:9, 16). Washings of (Ex 40:30-32; Lev 16:24). Must be without blemish (Lev 21:17-23). Vestments of (Ex 28:2-43; 39:1-29; Lev 6:10-11; 8:13; Eze 44:17-19). Put on vestments in the temple (Eze 42:14; 44:19). Atonement for (Lev 16:6, 24; Eze 44:27). Defilement and purification of (Eze 44:25-26). Marriage of (Lev 21:7-15; Eze 44:22). Chambers for, in the temple (Eze 40:45-46). Exempt from tax (Ezr 7:24). Armed and organized for war at the time of the disaffection toward Saul (1Ch 12:27-28). Beard and hair of (Eze 44:20).

Twenty-four courses of (1Ch 24:1-19; 28:13, 21; 2Ch 8:14; 31:2; 35:4-5; Ezr 2:36-39; Ne 13:30). Chosen by lot (Lk 1:8-9, 23).

Usurpations of the office of (Nu 3:10; 16; 18:7; 2Ch 26:18). Jeroboam appointed priests who were not of the sons of Levi (1Ki 12:31; 13:33).

See Levites; Minister.

Compensation for—
No part of the land of Canaan allowed to (Nu 18:20; Dt 10:9; 14:27; 18:1-2; Jos 13:14, 33; 14:3; 18:7; Eze 44:28). Provided with cities and suburbs (Lev 25:32-34; Nu 35:2-8; Jos 21:1-4, 13-19, 41-42; 1Ch 6:57-60; Ne 11:3, 20; Eze 45:1-6; 48:8-20). Own lands sanctified to the Lord (Lev 27:21). Tithes of the tithes (Nu 18:8-18, 26-32; Ne 10:38). Part of the spoils of war, including captives (Nu 31:25-29). Firstfruits (Lev 23:20; 24:9; Nu 18:12-13, 17-18; Dt 18:3-5; Ne 10:36). Redemption money (Nu 27:23), of the firstborn (Nu 3:46-51; 18:15-16). Things devoted (Lev 27:21; Nu 5:9-10; 18:14). Fines (Lev 5:16; 22:14; Nu 5:8). Trespass money and other trespass offerings (Lev 5:15, 18; Nu 5:5-10; 18:9; 2Ki 12:16). The bread of the Presence (Ex 25:30; Lev 24:5-9; 2Ch 2:4; 13:11; Ne 10:33; Mt 12:4; Heb 9:2). *See Bread, Consecrated.* Portions of sacrifices and offerings (Ex 29:27-34; Lev 2:2-3, 9-10; 5:12-13, 16; 6:15-18, 26; 7:6-10, 31-34; 10:12-14; 14:12-13; Nu 6:19-20; 18:8-19; Dt 18:3-5; 1Sa 2:13-14; Eze 44:28-31; 45:1-4; 1Co 9:13; 10:18).

Regulations by Hezekiah concerning compensation (2Ch 31:4-19). Portion of the land allotted to, in redistribution in Ezekiel's vision (Eze 48:8-14). For sustenance of their families (Lev 22:11-13; Nu 18:11, 19).

Duties of—
To offer sacrifices (Lev 1:4-17; 2:2, 16; 3:5, 11, 13, 16; 4:5-12, 17, 25-26, 30-35; 1Ch 16:40; 2Ch 13:11; 29:34; 35:11-14; Ezr 6:20; Heb 10:11). *See Offerings.* To offer the first fruits (Lev 23:10-11; Dt 26:3-4). To pronounce benedictions (Nu 6:22-27; Dt 21:5; 2Ch 30:27). Teach the law (Lev 10:11; Dt 24:8; 27:14; 31:9-13; 33:10; Jer 2:8; Mal 2:7). Light the lamps in the tabernacle (Ex 27:20-21; 2Ch 13:11; Lev 24:3-4). Keep the sacred fire always burning (Lev 6:12-13). To furnish a quota of wood for the sanctuary (Ne 10:34). Responsible for the sanctuary (Nu 4:5-15; 18:1, 5, 7). To act as scribes (Ezr 7:1-6; Ne 8:9). Be present at and supervise the tithing (Ne 10:38). Sound the trumpet in calling assemblies and in battle (Nu 10:2-10; 31:6; Jos 6; 2Ch 13:12). Examine lepers. *See Leprosy.* Purify the unclean (Lev 15:31). *See Defilement.* Value things devoted (Lev 27:8, 12). Officiated in the holy place (Heb 9:6). Chiefs of Levites (Nu 3:9, 32; 4:19, 28, 33; 1Ch 9:20). To act as magistrates (Nu 5:14-31; Dt 17:8-13; 19:17; 21:5; 2Ch 19:8; Eze 44:23-24). To encourage the army on the eve of battle (Dt 20:2-4). Bear the ark through the Jordan (Jos 3; 4:15-18), in battle (1Sa 4:3-5).

Figurative (Ex 19:6; Isa 61:6; 1Pe 2:9; Rev 1:6; 5:10; 20:6).

High Priest:
Moses did not designate Aaron chief or high priest. The function he served was superior to that of other priests. The title appears after the institution of the office (Lev 21:10-15; Nu 3:32). Qualifications of, consecration of, etc. *See above, Mosaic.*

Clothing of (Ex 28:2-43; 39:1-31; Lev 8:7-9). Respect due to (Ac 23:5).

Duties of—
Had charge of the sanctuary and altar (Nu 18:2, 5, 7). To offer sacrifices (Heb 5:1; 8:3). To designate subordinate priests for duty (Nu 4:19; 1Sa 2:36). To officiate in consecrations of the Levites (Nu 8:11-21). To have charge of the treasury (2Ki 12:10; 22:4; 2Ch 24:6-14; 34:9). To light the lamps of the tabernacle (Ex 27:20-21; 30:8; Lev 24:4; Nu 8:3). To burn incense (Ex 30:7-8; 1Sa 2:28; 1Ch 23:13). To place bread of the Presence on the table every Sabbath (Lev 24:8). To offer for his own sins of ignorance (Lev 4:3-12).

On the Day of Atonement (Ex 30:10; Lev 16; Heb 5:3; 9:7, 22-23).

Judicial (Nu 5:15; Dt 17:8-13; 1Sa 4:18; Hos 4:4; Mt 26:3, 50, 57, 62; Ac 5:21-28; 23:1-5). To number the people (Nu 1:3). Officiate at the choice of the ruler (Nu 27:18-19, 21). To distribute the spoils of war (Nu 31:26-29).

Compensation. See above, Compensation for.

A second priest, under the high priest (Nu 3:32; 4:16; 31:6; 1Ch 9:20; 2Sa 15:24; 2Ki 25:18; Lk 3:2).

Miscellaneous Facts Concerning:
Priestly office performed by prophets (1Sa 16:5). Loyal to Rehoboam at the time of the revolt of the ten tribes (2Ch 11:13). Zeal of (1Ch 9:10-13), in purging the temple (2Ch 29:4-17). Wickedness of (2Ch 36:14). Taken with the captives to Babylon (Jer 29:1). Return from the Captivity (Ezr 1:5; 2:36-39, 61, 70; 3:8; 7:7; 8:24-30; Ne 7:39-42, 63-73; 10:1-8; 12:1-7). Polluted by marrying idolatrous wives (Ezr 9:1-2; 10:5, 18-19; Ne 10:28). Restore the altar and offer sacrifices (Ezr 3:1-7). Supervise the building of the temple (Ezr 3:8-13). Inquire of John the Baptist whether he was the Christ (Jn 1:19). Conspire to destroy Jesus (Mt 26:3-5, 14-15, 47, 51; Mk 14:10-11, 43-47, 53-66; 15:1; Lk 22:1-6, 50, 54, 66-71; 23:1-2; Jn 11:47; 19:15-16, 18). Try and condemn Jesus (Mt 26:57-68; 27:1-2; Mk 14:53-65; Lk 22:54-71; 23:13-24; Jn 18:15-32). Incite the people to ask that Barabbas be released and Jesus destroyed (Mt 27:20; Mk 15:11; Lk 23:18). Persecute the disciples (Ac 22:5). Reprove and threaten Peter and John (Ac 4:6-21; 5:17-41). Try, condemn, and stone Stephen (Ac 6:12-15; 7). Paul brought before (Ac 22:30; 23:1-5). Many converts among (Ac 6:7).

Corrupt:
(Jer 23:11-12; Eze 22:26; Lk 10:31). Instances of: Eli's sons (1Sa 2:12-17, 22), of the returned exiles (Ezr 9:1-2; 10:18-22; Ne 13:4-9, 13, 28-29).

Idolatrous (1Ki 12:32; 2Ki 10:19; 11:18; 23:5; 2Ch 23:17; 34:4-5; Jer 48:35; Hos 10:5; Zep 1:4).

PRIMOGENITURE *See Birthright; Firstborn.*

PRINCE OF PEACE *See Jesus.*

PRINCE, PRINCESS A prince is a leader, an exalted person clothed with authority. A princess is the daughter or wife of a chief or king. The prince may be the head of a family or tribe, a ruler, governor, magistrate, satrap, or royal descendant (Nu 22:8; 1Sa 18:30). He may also be a spiritual ruler (Isa 9:6) or the ruler of demons (Mt 9:34).

PRINCIPALITIES
1. Rule; ruler (Eph 1:21; Tit 3:1).
2. Order of powerful angels and demons (Ro 8:38; Eph 3:10; 6:12). *See Demons.*

PRINT A mark made by pressure (Lev 19:28; Jn 20:25).

PRISCILLA, PRISCA Priscilla (diminutive of Prisca) was the wife of the Jewish Christian Aquila, with whom she is always mentioned in the NT; tentmakers; had a church in their house; taught Apollos; assisted Paul (Ac 18:2, 26; Ro 16:3; 1Co 16:19; 2Ti 4:19).

PRISON Prisoners were often put in dry wells or cisterns (Ge 37:24; Jer 38:6-13), or dungeons which were part of a palace (1Ki 22:27). The Herods and the Romans had royal prisons (Lk 3:20; Ac 12:4; 23:10, 35). Jesus foretells imprisonment for his disciples (Lk 21:12). Disobedient spirits are now in prison (1Pe 3:19). Satan will be imprisoned (Rev 20:7).

PRISONERS

General:
Required to labor (Jdg 16:21). Kept on bread and water of affliction (1Ki 22:27; 2Ch 18:26; Isa 30:20), in chains (Ac 12:6), in stocks (Pr 7:22; Jer 29:26; Ac 16:24).

Confined in the court of the palace (Jer 32:2), house of the scribe (Jer 37:15), house of captain of the guard (Ge 40:3). Visited by friends (Mt 11:2; Ac 24:23). Bound to soldiers (Ac 12:6).

Severe hardships of, mitigated (Jer 37:20-21). Cruelty to (Jer 38:6; La 3:53-54). *See Captive.* Keepers responsible for (Ac 12:18-19). Tortured to extort self-incriminating testimony (Ac 22:24). Flogged (Mt 27:26; Mk 15:15; Ac 16:23, 33; 2Co 6:5; 11:23-24). Permitted to make defense (Ac 24:10; 25:8, 16; 26:1; 2Ti 4:16). *See Flog, Flogging; Scourging.*

Kindness to: By the prison keeper to Jeremiah (Jer 38:7-28), by Philippian jailer to Paul (Ac 16:33), by Felix (Ac 24:23), by Julius, the centurion (Ac 27:1, 3; 28:16, 30-31). To be visited and ministered to (Mt 25:35-46). Released at feasts (Mt 27:15-17; Mk 15:6; Lk 23:17; Jn 18:39).

Of War:
Put to death (Jos 10:16-27; 1Sa 15:33; 27:11; 2Sa 12:31; 2Ki 25:7; 1Ch 20:3; Hos 13:16; Am 1:13; La 3:34), by divine command (Nu 31:9, 17). Thumbs and toes cut off (Jdg 1:6-7). Blinded (2Ki 25:7). Kept captive.

Consolations for (Ps 69:33; 79:11; 102:19-20; 146:7).

See Captive; Imprisonment.

Examples of—
Joseph (Ge 39:20-23; 40; 41:14-44). Jeremiah (Jer 38:6-28; 39:14). John the Baptist (Mt 11:2; 14:3-12; Mk 6:17; Lk 3:20). Jesus (Mt 26:47-75; 27; Mk 14:43-72; 15; Lk 22:47-71; 23; Jn 18:3-40; 19). Apostles (Ac 5:17-42). Peter (Ac 12:3-19). Paul (Ac 16:19-40; 21:27-40; 22:28). Silas (Ac 16:19-40).

Figurative: (Isa 61:1; Lk 4:18).

PRIVILEGE *See Judgment, According to Opportunity and Works; Responsibility.*

PRIZE A reward of competition according to the rules (1Co 9:24-27), figurative of living the Christian life by faith (Php 3:14; Col 2:18).

PROBATION A period of critical examination and evaluation (Ro 5:3-4).
Adam on (Ge 2:15-17; 3:3). Amorites (Ge 15:16). Solomon (1Ki 3:14; 9:4-9, w 11:9-12). Taught in parables of the talents and minas (Mt 25:14-30; Lk 19:12-27), the fig tree (Lk 13:6-9), embezzling steward (Lk 16:1-12). Taught by the author of Hebrews (Heb 6).
None after death (Mt 12:32; 25:10-13; 26:4).
See Perseverance.

PROCHORUS *See Procorus.*

PROCLAMATION Imperial (2Ch 30:1-10; Est 1:22; 6:9; 8:10-14; Isa 40:3, 9; Da 3:4-7; 4:1; 5:29). Emancipation (2Ch 36:23; Ezr 1:1-4).

PROCONSUL (*for the consul*). Roman official who served as deputy consul in a Roman province; term of the office was usually one year; Sergius Paulus and Gallio were proconsuls (Ac 13:7; 18:12).

PROCORUS An early Christian deacon (Ac 6:5).

PROCRASTINATION (Eze 11:2-3; 12:22, 27-28). Rebuked (Mt 8:21-22; Lk 9:59, 61). Admonition against (1Th 5:2-3). Forbidden (Ex 22:29). Warning against (Heb 3:7-19).
Parables of: Evil servant (Mt 24:48-51). The five foolish virgins (Mt 25:2-13).
See Excuses.
Instances of: Pharaoh (Ex 8:10). Elisha (1Ki 19:20-21). Esther (Est 5:8). Disciple of Christ whose father died (Mt 8:21; Lk 9:59, 61). Felix (Ac 24:25).

PROCURATOR The governor of a Roman province appointed by the emperor; often subject to the imperial legate of a larger political area. Pilate, Felix, and Festus were procurators (Mt 27:2; Ac 23:24; 26:30).

PRODIGAL SON Parable of (Lk 15:11-32).

PRODIGALITY *See Extravagance; Frugality; Industry.*

PROFANATION Of God's name (Lev 20:3; Pr 30:9), forbidden (Ex 20:7; 18:21; 19:12; 21:6; 22:2-3; Dt 5:11).
Instances of: (Ps 139:20; Isa 52:5; Ro 2:24). Of the Sabbath (Ne 13:15-22; Eze 20:12-13, 16; 22:8; 23:38). Of the house of God (2Ch 33:7; Ne 13:7; Jer 7:11; Mt 21:13; Mk 11:17; Lk 19:46). Of holy things: Forbidden (Lev 22:15).
See Profane; Profanity.

PROFANE (*unloose, set free*). To desecrate or defile (Ex 31:14; Lev 19:8, 12; Eze 22:26; Mt 12:5), common as opposed to holy (Eze 28:16; 42:20), godless, unholy (Heb 12:16). *See Sacrilege.*

PROFANITY Of the name of God. *See God, Name of.* Of the Sabbath. *See Sabbath.*
See Blasphemy; Oath.

PROFESSION False (Pr 20:6; Hos 8:2). Of faith in Jesus. *See Confession; Testimony, Religious.*

PROGNOSTICATION By astrologers (Isa 47:13). *See Prophecy; Prophets.*

PROHIBITION Of the use of intoxicating beverages. To priests on duty (Lev 10:9). To Nazirites (Nu 6:3-4).
See Abstinence; Commandments and Statutes, Of God; Drunkenness.

PROMISCUITY Punished by death under the law (Dt 22:20-21).
Figurative of Israel's alliances with the nations and their gods (Eze 16; 23).
See Adultery; Bestiality; Fornication; Homosexual; Prostitute.

PROMISE First promise of the Redeemer (Ge 3:15), promise repeated to Abraham (Ge 12:2, 7), promise made to David that his house would continue forever (2Sa 7:12-13, 28). Jesus' promise of the Spirit fulfilled at Pentecost. There are hundreds of promises made to believers (Jas 2:5; 1Ti 4:8; 2Pe 3:9).

PROMISES To the afflicted. *See Afflictions, Consolation Under.* To backsliders. *See Backsliders.* To children. *See Children.* To orphans. *See Orphans.* To the righteous. *See Righteous.* To seekers. *See Seekers.*

PROMISES, OR GROUND OF ASSURANCE

General:
(Heb 6:12; Jas 2:5; 2Pe 1:4; 3:13). Against the recurrence of universal flood (Ge 9:11). Of answer to prayer (2Ch 7:14; Job 22:27; Ps 2:8; 145:19; Isa 58:9; 65:24; Jer 29:12; 33:3; Mt 6:6; 7:7-8, 11; 17:20; 18:19; 21:22; Mk 11:24; Lk 11:13; Jn 14:13-14; 16:23-24; Jas 1:5; 5:15-16; 1Jn 5:14-15). Of blessings upon worshipers (Ex 20:24; Isa 40:31). Of comfort in sorrow (Ps 46:1; 50:15; 146:8; 147:3; Isa 43:2; Lk 6:21; 2Co 1:3-4; 7:6). Of spiritual enlightenment (Isa 29:18, 24; 35:5-6; 42:16; Mt 10:19; Lk 21:14-15; Jn 7:17; 8:12, 32; Heb 8:10). Of God's presence (Ex 3:12; Dt 31:8; 1Sa 10:7). Of Christ's presence with believers (Mt 18:20; 28:20). Of forgiveness (Ps 130:4; Isa 1:18; 43:25; 55:7; Jer 31:34; 33:8; Mt 6:14; 12:31-32; Mk 3:28; Lk 12:10; Ac 10:43; 13:38-39; Jas 5:15-16; 1Jn 1:9). Of healing (Jas 5:15). Of the Holy Spirit (Joel 2:28; Lk 11:13; 24:49; Jn 7:38-39; 14:16-17, 26; 15:26; 16:7; Ac 2:38). Of spiritual adoption (Lev 26:12; 2Co 6:17-18; Heb 8:10). Of victory of the Messiah over Satan (Ge 3:15).

Given:
To believers (Jer 17:7-8; Mk 16:16-18; Jn 3:15-16; 5:24; 6:35, 40, 47; 7:38; 11:25; 14:12; Ro 9:33; 10:9, 11). Backsliders (Lev 26:40-42; Dt 30:1-3; 2Ch 30:9; Jer 3:12-15; Hos 14:4; Mal 3:7). Children (Ex 20:12; Dt 5:16; Mt 19:14; Mk 10:14; Lk 18:15-16; Eph 6:3).
To the burdened (Mt 11:28-29). The afflicted (Job 33:24-28; 36:15; Ps 9:9; 12:5; 18:27; 41:3; La 3:31). Orphans and widows (Dt 10:18; Ps 68:5; 146:9; Pr 15:25; Jer 49:11).
To seekers (Dt 4:29; 1Ch 28:9; 2Ch 15:2; Ezr 8:22; Ps 34:10; 145:18; Jer 29:13; Mt 5:6; 6:33; Lk 6:21; Jn 6:37; Ro 10:13; Heb 11:6).
To the faithful (Mt 25:21; Lk 12:42-44; 19:16-19; Ro 2:7, 10; Rev 2:10). The forgiving, of divine forgiveness (Mt 6:14; Mk 11:25; Lk 6:37). The humble (Isa 57:15; Mt 5:3; 18:4; 23:12; Lk 6:20; 14:11; 18:14; Jas 4:6; 1Pe 5:5-6). The compassionate giver (Ps 41:1-3; 112:9; Pr 3:9-10; 11:25; 22:9; 28:27; Ecc 11:1; Isa 58:10-11; Mt 6:4; Lk 6:38; 2Co 9:6, 8). The meek (Ps 10:17; 22:26; 25:9; 37:11; 147:6; 149:4; Pr 29:23; Isa 29:19; Mt 5:5). The merciful (2Sa 22:26; Ps 18:25; 41:1-3; Mt 5:7). Ministers (Ps 126:5-6; Jer 1:8; 20:11; Da 12:3; Mt 28:20; Jn 4:36-37; 1Pe 5:4).
To the obedient (Ex 15:26; 19:5-6; 20:6, w Dt 5:11; Ex 23:22, 25-26; Dt 4:40; 6:2-3; 12:28; 28:1-6; 30:2-10; 1Ki 3:14; Ne 1:5; Ps 1:1, 3; 25:10; 103:17-18; 119:1-2; Pr 1:33; Isa 1:19; Jer 7:23; Eze 18:19; Mal 3:10-11; Mt 5:19; 12:50; Mk 3:35; Lk 8:21; 11:28; Jn 8:51; 12:26; 14:21, 23; 15:10; 1Jn 2:5, 17; 3:24).
To those who fear the Lord (Ps 34:7; 103:11-13, 17; 112:1; 115:13; 128:1-6; 145:19; Pr 10:27; 19:23; Ecc 7:18; 8:12). Those who have spiritual desire (Isa 55:1; Mt 5:6; Lk 6:21). Those who endure to the end (Mt 10:22; 24:13; Mk 13:13; Rev 2:7, 11, 17, 26-28; 3:5, 12, 21; 21:7). Those who love their enemies (Mt 5:44-45). Those who rebuke the wicked (Pr 24:25). Those who confess Christ (Mt 10:32; Ro 10:9; 1Jn 2:23; 4:15). Peacemakers, of sonship (Mt 5:9). Penitents (Lev 26:40-42; Dt 4:20-31; 2Ch 7:14; 30:9; Ps 34:18; 147:3; Isa 1:18; 55:7; Mt 5:4). The poor (Ex 22:27; Job 36:15; Ps 12:5; 35:10; 69:33; 72:2, 4, 12-14; 109:31; 132:15; Pr 22:22-23; Isa 41:17). The pure in heart (Mt 5:8). Persecuted saints (Mt 5:10-11; Lk 6:22-23; 21:12-18; 1Pe 4:14).
To the righteous (Job 17:9; 36:11; Ps 1:1-3; 34:7, 22; 37:4-5; 55:22; 119:1, 105; 138:8; 145:20; 146:8; Pr 25:22; Isa 58:8; Jer 17:7; Mt 6:30, 33; 10:22, 42; 24:13; Lk 6:35; 18:6-8; Ro 5:9; 8:30-31; 1Co 2:9; 3:21-22; Gal 6:9; Php 4:7; 2Th 3:3; Rev 2:17, 26, 28; 3:5; 14:13). The wise of heart (Pr 2:10-21).

Concerning:
Answer to prayer (Pr 15:29; Mk 11:23-24; Jn 14:13-14; Ac 10:4; 1Pe 3:12; 1Jn 3:22). Blessings upon their children (Ps 103:17; 112:2-3; Isa 59:21). Comfort (Isa 25:8; 66:13-14; Mt 5:4; Jn 14:16-18; Rev 21:4).
Deliverance, from temptation (1Co 10:13; Jas 4:7; 2Pe 2:9), from trouble (Job 5:19-24; Ps 33:18-19; 34:15, 17; 50:15; 97:10-11; Pr 3:25-26; Isa 41:10-13; 43:2). Divine help (Ps 55:22; Isa 41:10-11, 13; 2Co 12:9; Php 4:19; Heb 13:5-6). Divine guidance (Ps 25:12; 32:8; 37:23-24; 48:14; 73:24; Pr 3:5-6; 58:11). Divine mercy (Ps 32:10; 103:17-18; Mal 3:17). Divine presence (Ge 26:3, 24; 28:15; 31:3; Ex 33:14; Dt 31:6, 8; Jos 1:5; 1Ki 6:13; Hag 1:13; 2:4-5; Mt 18:20; 28:20; Jn 14:17, 23; 2Co 6:16; 13:11; Php 4:9; Heb 13:5; Jas 4:8; Rev 21:3). Divine likeness (1Jn 3:2). The ministry of angels (Heb 1:14).
Peace (Isa 26:3; Jn 16:33; Ro 2:10). Providential care (Ge 15:1; Ex 23:22; Lev 26:5-6, 10; Dt 33:27; 1Sa 2:9; 2Ch 16:9; Ezr 8:22; Job 5:15; Ps 34:9-10; 37:23-26; 121:2-8; 125:1-3; 145:19-20; Pr 1:33; 2:7; 3:6; 10:3; 16:7; Isa 49:9-11; 65:13-14; Eze 34:11-17, 22-31; Lk 12:7; 21:18; 1Pe 5:7). Overruling providence (Ro 8:28; 2Co 4:17). Spiritual enlightenment (Isa 2:3; Jn 8:12). Seeing God (Mt 5:8). Spiritual blessings (Isa 64:4; 1Co 2:9).
Refuge in adversity (Ps 33:18-19; 62:8; 91:1, 3-7, 9-12; Pr 14:26; Na 1:7). Strength in adversity (Ps 29:11). Security (Ps 32:6-7; 84:11; 121:3-8; Isa 33:16). Temporal blessings (Lev 25:18-19; 26:5; Dt 28:1-13; Ps 37:9; 128:1-6; Pr 2:21; 3:1-4, 7-10; Mt 6:26-33; Mk 10:30; Lk 18:29-30). Wisdom (Jas 1:5).
The rest of faith (Heb 4:9). Heavenly rest (Heb 4:9). Eternal life (Da 12:3; Mt 19:29; 25:46; Mk 10:29-30; Lk 18:29-30; Jn 3:15-16, 36; 4:14; 5:24, 29; 6:40; 10:28; 12:25; 17:2; Ro 2:7; 6:22-23; Gal 6:8; 1Th 4:15-17; 1Ti 1:16; 4:8; Tit 1:2; 1Jn 2:25; 5:13; Rev 22:5). Living with Christ (Jn 14:2-3; 17:24; Col 3:4; 1Th 4:17; 5:10). Everlasting remembrance (Ps 112:6). Names written in heaven (Lk 10:20).
Resurrection (Jn 5:29; 1Co 15:48-57; 2Co 4:14; 1Th 4:16). Future glory (Mt 13:43; Ro 8:18; Col 3:4; 2Ti 2:10; 1Pe 1:5; 5:4; Rev 7:14-17). Treasure in heaven (Mt 10:21; Lk 18:22). Inheritance (Mt 25:34; Ac 20:32; 26:18; Col 1:12; 3:24; Tit 3:7; Heb 9:15; Jas 2:5; 1Pe 1:4). Heavenly reward (Mt 5:12; 13:43; 2Ti 4:8; Heb 11:16; Jas 1:12; 2Pe 1:11; Rev 2:7, 10; 22:5, 12, 14). Reigning forever (Rev 22:5, w 1Co 4:8; Rev 5:10; 11:15).
See Blessings, Spiritual; God, Goodness of; Jesus the Christ, Compassion of, Love of.

PROMOTION (Ps 75:6-7; 78:70-71; 113:7-8). As a reward of merit (1Ch 11:6).
Instances of: Abraham (Ge 12:2). Joseph, from imprisoned slave to prince (Ge 41:1-45). Moses, from exile to lawgiver. *See Moses.* Aaron, from slave to high priest. *See Aaron.* Saul, from obscurity to a scepter. *See Saul.* David, from shepherd to throne. *See David.* Jeroboam, from slave to the throne (1Ki 11:26-35). Baasha, "out of dust" to the throne (1Ki 16:1-2). Daniel, from captive to premier (Da 2:48). *See Daniel.* Shadrach, Meshach, and Abednego (Da 3:30).

PROPAGATION Of species, commanded (Ge 1:11-12, 21-25, 28; 9:1, 7). *See Barrenness.*

PROPERTY

In Real Estate:
(Ge 23:17-18; 26:20). Rights in, violated (Ge 21:25-32; 26:18-22). Dedicated (Lev 27:16-25). *See Land.*

Dwellings:
Alienated for debt (Lev 25:14-15). Confiscation of Naboth's vineyard (1Ki 21:15-16). Priests exempt from taxes (Ge 47:22).

Restriction of to lineal descendants (Nu 27:1-11; 36:1-9). Inherited (Ecc 2:21). Landmarks of, not to be removed (Dt 19:14; 27:17).

Personal:
Rights in, sacred (Ex 20:17; Dt 5:21). Laws concerning trespass of, and violence to (Ex 21:28-36; 22:9; Dt 23:25). Strayed, to be returned to owner (Lev 6:3-4; Dt 22:1-3). Hired (Ex 22:14-15), or loaned (Ex 22:10-15). Sold for debt (Pr 22:26-27), rights of redemption of (Jer 32:7). Dedicated to God, redemption of (Lev 27:9-13, 26-33). In slaves (Ex 21:4).

PROPHECY (*speak before*). Concerning the Church. *See Church, The Body of Believers, Prophecies Concerning.* Relating to various countries, nations, and cities. *See under their respective names.* Respecting individuals. *See individuals by name.*

Concerning Jesus the Messiah:
The first messianic prophecy (Ge 3:15), concerns the announcement of the victor over Satan, the victor described as "the seed of the woman."

Messianic Prophecies and Fulfillments	
Ge 12:3; 18:18; 22:18	Ac 3:25; Gal 3:8
Ge 17:7, 19; 22:16-17	Lk 1:55, 72-74
Dt 18:15, 18	Ac 3:22-23
Ps 2:1-2	Ac 4:25-26
Ps 2:7	Ac 13:33; Heb 1:5; 5:5
Ps 8:2	Mt 21:16
Ps 8:4-6	Heb 2:6-8
Ps 16:8-11	Ac 2:25-28, 31
Ps 16:10	Ac 13:35
Ps 22:1	Mt 27:46; Mk 15:34
Ps 22:18	Mt 27:35; Mk 15:24; Lk 23:34; Jn 19:24
Ps 22:22	Heb 2:12
Ps 31:5	Lk 23:46
Ps 41:9	Jn 13:18; Ac 1:16
Ps 45:6-7	Heb 1:8-9
Ps 68:18	Eph 4:8-13
Ps 69:21	Mt 27:34, 48; Mk 15:23, 36; Lk 23:36; Jn 19:28-29
Ps 69:25; 109:8	Ac 1:20
Ps 78:2	Mt 13:35
Ps 95:7-11	Heb 3:7-11; 4:3, 5-7
Ps 102:25-27	Heb 1:10-12
Ps 110:1	Mt 22:43-44; Mk 12:36-37; Lk 20:42-44; Ac 2:34-36; Heb 1:13
Ps 110:4	Heb 5:6; 7:15-17, 21
Ps 118:22-23	Mt 21:42; Mk 12:10-11; Lk 20:17; Ac 4:11; Eph 2:20; 1Pe 2:7
Ps 118:25-26	Mt 21:9; Mk 11:9; Lk 13:35; Jn 12:13
Ps 132:11, 17	Lk 1:69; Ac 2:30
Isa 7:14	Mt 1:23
Isa 9:1-2	Mt 4:15-16
Isa 9:7; Da 7:14, 27	Lk 1:32-33
Isa 11:10	Ro 15:12
Isa 25:8	1Co 15:54-55

P

Isa 28:16	Ro 9:33; 10:11; 1Pe 2:6
Isa 40:3-5	Mt 3:3; Mk 1:3; Lk 3:4-6; Jn 1:23
Isa 42:1-4	Mt 12:17-21
Isa 49:6	Lk 2:32; Ac 13:47-48; 26:23
Isa 53:1	Jn 12:38; Ro 10:16
Isa 53:3-6	Ac 26:22-23
Isa 53:4-6, 11	1Pe 2:24-25
Isa 53:4	Mt 8:17
Isa 53:9	1Pe 2:22
Isa 53:12	Mk 15:27-28; Lk 22:37
Isa 54:13	Jn 6:45
Isa 55:3	Ac 13:34
Isa 59:20-21	Ro 11:26-27
Jer 31:31-34	Heb 8:8-12; 10:16-17
Hos 1:10	Ro 9:26
Hos 2:23	Ro 9:25; 1Pe 2:10
Joel 2:28-32	Ac 2:16-21; Ro 10:13
Am 9:11-12	Ac 15:16-17
Mic 5:2	Mt 2:5-6; Jn 7:42
Hab 1:5	Ac 13:40-41
Hag 2:6	Heb 12:26
Zec 9:9	Mt 21:4-5; Jn 12:14-15
Zec 11:13	Mt 27:9-10
Zec 12:10	Jn 19:34
Zec 13:7	Mt 26:31, 56; Mk 14:27, 50
Mal 3:1	Mt 11:10; Mk 1:2; Lk 7:27
Mal 4:5-6	Mt 11:13-14; 17:10-13; Mk 9:11-13; Lk 1:16-17

See Jesus the Christ, Prophecies Concerning; Jesus the Christ, King, Prophecies Concerning.

General:
Inspired (Isa 28:22; Lk 1:70; 2Ti 3:16; 2Pe 1:21). "The word of the Lord came to," Elijah (1Ki 17:8; 21:17, 28), Isaiah (Isa 2:1; 8:5; 13:1; 14:28; 38:4), Jeremiah (Jer 1:4; 7:1; 11:1; 13:8; 16:1; 18:1; 25:1-2; 26:1; 27:1; 29:30; 30:1, 4; 32:1, 6, 26; 33:1, 19, 23; 34:12; 35:12; 36:1; 37:6; 40:1; 43:8; 44:1; 46:1; 49:34; 50:1), Ezekiel (Eze 3:16; 6:1; 7:1; 11:14; 12:1, 8, 17, 21; 13:1; 14:12; 15:1; 16:1; 17:1; 18:1; 20:45; 21:1, 8, 18; 22:1, 17, 23; 23:1; 24:1, 5, 20; 25:1; 26:1; 27:1; 28:1, 11, 20; 29:1, 17; 30:1, 20; 31:1; 32:1, 17; 33:1, 23; 34:1; 35:1; 36:16; 37:15; 38:1), Amos (Am 7:14-15), Jonah (Jnh 3:1), Haggai (Hag 2:1, 10, 20), Zechariah (Zec 1:7; 4:8; 6:9; 7:1, 4, 8; 8:1, 18).
Publicly proclaimed (Jer 11:6). Exemplified in pantomime (Eze 4; 5:1-4; Ac 21:11). Written, by an amanuensis (Jer 45:1), in books (Jer 45:1; 51:60).
Proof of God's foreknowledge (Isa 43:9). Sure fulfillment of (Eze 12:22-25, 28; Hab 2:3; Mt 5:18; 24:35; Ac 13:27, 29). Cessation of (La 2:9).
Of apostasy (1Jn 2:18; Jude 17-18), false teachers (2Pe 2:3). Tribulations of the righteous (Rev 2:10).

Miscellaneous, Fulfilled:
The birth and zeal of Josiah (1Ki 13:2; 2Ki 23:1-20). Death of the prophet of Judah (1Ki 13:21-22, 24-30). Extinction of Jeroboam's house (1Ki 14:5-17), of Baasha's house (1Ki 16:2-3, 9-13). Concerning the rebuilding of Jericho (Jos 6:26; 1Ki 16:34). The drought, foretold by Elijah (1Ki 17:14). Destruction of Ben-Hadad's army (1Ki 20:13-30). The death of a man who refused to kill a prophet (1Ki 20:35-36). The death of Ahab (1Ki 20:42; 21:18-24; 22:31-38). The death of Ahaziah (2Ki 1:3-17). Elijah's translation (2Ki 2:3-11). Cannibalism among the Israelites (Lev 26:29; Dt 28:53; 2Ki 6:28-29; Jer 19:9; La 4:10). The death of the Samaritan lord (2Ki 7:2, 19-20). The end of the famine in Samaria (2Ki 7:1-18). Jezebel's tragic death (1Ki 21:23; 2Ki 9:10, 33-37). The killing of Syria by Joash (2Ki 13:16-25). Conquests of Jeroboam (2Ki 14:25-28). Four generations of Jehu to sit upon the throne of Israel (2Ki 10:30, w 15:12). Destruction of Sennacherib's army,

and his death (2Ki 19:6-7, 20-37). The captivity of Judah (2Ki 20:17-18; 24:10-16; 25:11-21).
Concerning Christ. *See Jesus the Christ, Prophecies Concerning. See above, Concerning Jesus the Messiah.*
Concerning John (Mt 3:3). Rachel weeping for her children (Jer 31:15; Mt 2:17-18). Deliverance of Jeremiah (Jer 39:15-18). Invasion of Judah by the Chaldeans (Hab 1:6-11), fulfilled (2Ki 25; 2Ch 36:17-21), betrayal of Jesus by Judas, prophecy (Ps 41:9), fulfillment (Jn 13:18; 18:1-9), Judas' self-destruction (Ps 69:25; Ac 1:16, 20), fulfilled (Mt 27:5; Ac 1:16-20). Outpouring of the Holy Spirit (Joel 2:28-29), fulfilled (Ac 2:16-21). Spiritual blindness of the Israelites (Isa 6:9; 29:13), fulfilled (Mk 7:6-7; Ac 28:25-27). Mission of Jesus (Ps 68:18), fulfilled (Eph 4:8, 10). *See Jesus the Christ, Mission of.* Captivity of the Israelites (Jer 25:11-12; 29:10, 14; 32:3-5; Da 9:2, w 2Ki 25:1-8; Ezr 1). Of the destruction of the ship in which Paul sailed (Ac 27:10, 18-44). *See Prophetesses; Prophets.*

PROPHETESSES *(speak before).* Miriam (Ex 15:20).
Deborah (Jdg 4:4). Huldah (2Ki 22:14). False (Eze 13:17-19). Isaiah's wife (Isa 8:3). All the daughters of Israel (Joel 2:28-29). Noadiah (Ne 6:14). Elizabeth (Lk 1:41-45). Anna (Lk 2:36-38). Daughters of Philip (Ac 21:9). Jezebel (Rev 2:20).
See Women.

PROPHETS *(speak before).*

General:
Called seers (1Sa 9:19; 2Sa 15:27; 24:11; 2Ki 17:13; 1Ch 9:22; 29:29; 2Ch 9:29; 12:15; 29:30; Isa 30:10; Mic 3:7). Schools of (1Ki 20:35; 2Ki 2:3-15; 4:1, 38; 9:1). Kept the chronicles or records (1Ch 29:29; 2Ch 9:29; 12:15). Not honored in their own country (Mt 13:57; Lk 4:24-27; Jn 4:44). Officiate at installation of kings (1Ki 1:32-35). Counselors to kings (1Ki 22:6-28; 2Ki 6:9-12; Isa 37:2-3; Jer 27:12-15).
Inspired by angels (Zec 1:9, 13-14, 19; Ac 7:53; Gal 3:19; Heb 2:2). Persecutions of (2Ch 36:16; Am 2:12). Martyrs (Jer 2:30; Mt 23:37; Mk 12:5; Lk 13:34; 1Th 2:15; Heb 11:37; Rev 16:6). Compensation of: Presents (1Sa 9:7-8; 1Ki 14:3; 2Ki 4:42; 8:8-9; Eze 13:19). Presents refused by (Nu 22:18; 1Ki 13:7-8; 2Ki 5:5, 16).
Inspiration of: (1Ki 13:20; 2Ch 33:18; 36:15; Ne 9:30; Job 33:14-16; Jer 7:25; Da 9:6, 10; Hos 12:10; Joel 2:28; Am 3:7-8; Zec 7:12; Lk 1:70; Ac 3:18; Ro 1:1-2; 1Co 12:7-11; Heb 1:1; 2Pe 1:21; Rev 10:7; 22:6, 8).

Examples of Prophets:
Enoch (Jude 14). Joseph (Ge 40:8; 41:16, 38-39). Moses (Ex 3:14-15; 4:12, 15, 27; 6:13, 29; 7:2; 19:9-19; 24:16; 25:22; 33:9, 11; Lev 1:1; Nu 1:1; 7:89; 9:8-10; 11:17, 25; 12:6-8; 16:28-29; Dt 1:5-6; 5:4-5, 31; 34:10-11; Ps 103:7). Aaron (Ex 6:13; 12:1). Eleazar (Nu 26:1). Balaam (Nu 23:5, 16, 20, 26; 24:2-4, 15-16). Joshua (Jos 4:15).
Samuel (1Sa 3:1, 4-10, 19-21; 9:6, 15-20; 15:16). Saul (1Sa 10:6-7, 10-13; 19:23). Saul's men (1Sa 19:20). David (2Sa 23:2-3; Mk 12:36). Nathan (2Sa 7:3-4; 2Sa 7:8). Gad (2Sa 24:11). Ahijah (1Ki 14:5). Elijah (1Ki 17:1, 24; 19:15; 2Ki 10:10). Micaiah (1Ki 22:14, 28; 2Ch 18:27). Elisha (2Ki 2:9; 3:11-12, 15; 5:8; 6:8-12, 32). Jahaziel (2Ch 20:14). Azariah (2Ch 15:1-2). Zechariah, the son of Jehoiada (2Ch 24:20; 26:5).
Isaiah (2Ki 20:4; Isa 6:1-9; 8:11; 44:26; Ac 28:25). Jeremiah (2Ch 36:12; Jer 1:1-19; 2:1; 7:1; 11:1, 18; 13:1-3; 16:1; 18:1; 20:9; 23:9; 24:4; 25:3; 26:1-2; 27:1-2; 29:30; 33:1; 34:1; 42:4, 7; Da 9:2). Ezekiel (Eze 1:1, 3; 2:1-2, 4-5; 3:10-12, 14, 16-17, 22, 24, 27; 8:1; 11:1, 4-5, 24; 33:22; 37:1; 40:1; 43:5-6). Daniel (Da 2:19; 7:16; 8:16; 9:22; 10:7-9). Hosea (Hos 1:1-2). Joel (Joel 1:1). Amos (Am 3:7-8; 7:14-15). Obadiah (Ob 1). Jonah (Jnh 1:1; 3:1-2). Micah (Mic 1:1; 3:8). Habakkuk (Hab 1:1). Haggai (Hag 1:13). Zechariah, the son of Berekiah (Zec 2:9; 7:8).
Elizabeth (Lk 1:41). Zechariah (Lk 1:67). Simeon (Lk 2:26-27). John the Baptist (Lk 3:2). The apostles (Ac 2:4). Philip (Ac 8:29). Agabus (Ac 11:28; 21:10-11). Disciple at Tyre (Ac 21:4), John the apostle (Rev 1:10-11).
See Revelation; Word of God, Inspiration of.

False:
(Dt 18:21-22; 1Ki 13:18; Ne 6:12; Jer 23:16-27, 30-32; La 2:14). Warnings against (Dt 13:1-3; Mt 24:5, 23-24, 26; Mk 13:6, 21-22; Lk 21:8). Denunciations against (Dt 18:20; Jer 14:15). Punishment of (Dt 18:20; Jer 14:13-16; 20:6; 28:16-17; 29:32; Zec 13:3). Drunken (Isa 28:7).

Instances of —
Noadiah (Ne 6:14), four hundred in Samaria (1Ki 22:6-12; 2Ch 18:5), Pashhur (Jer 20:6), Hanani (Jer 28; Ro 15:16).

Idolatrous:
(1Ki 18:19, 22, 25-28, 40).
See Minister, False and Corrupt.

PROPHETS, THE MINOR Also known as "The Book of the Twelve." In Ecclesiasticus (an Apocryphal book written c. 190 B.C.), Jesus ben Sirach spoke of "the twelve prophets" (Sir 49:10) as a unit parallel to Isaiah, Jeremiah and Ezekiel. He thus indicated that these twelve prophecies were at that time thought of as a unit and were probably already written together on one scroll, as is the case in later times. Josephus (*Against Apion*, 1.8.3) also was aware of this grouping. Augustine (*The City of God*, 18.25) called them the "Minor Prophets," referring to the small size of these books by comparison with the major prophetic books and not at all suggesting that they are of minor importance.
In the tradition of the Jewish canon these works are arranged in what was thought to be their chronological order:
(1) the books that came from the period of Assyrian power (Hosea, Joel, Amos, Obadiah, Jonah, Micah);
(2) those written about the time of the decline of Assyria (Nahum, Habakkuk, Zephaniah) and
(3) those dating from the postexilic era (Haggai, Zechariah, Malachi).
On the other hand, their order in the Septuagint (the earliest Greek translation of the OT) is: Hosea, Amos, Micah, Joel, Obadiah, Jonah, Nahum, Habakkuk, Zephaniah, Haggai, Zechariah, Malachi (the order of the first six was probably determined by length, except

for Jonah, which is placed last among them because of its different character).
In any event, it appears that within a century after the composition of Malachi the Jews had brought together the twelve shorter prophecies to form a book (scroll) of prophetic writings, which was received as canonical and paralleled the three major prophetic books of Isaiah, Jeremiah and Ezekiel. The great Greek manuscripts Alexandrinus and Vaticanus place the minor prophets before the major prophets, but in the traditional Jewish canon and in all modern versions they appear after them.

PROPITIATION *(to cover).* To appease the wrath of God so that his justice and holiness will be satisfied and he can forgive sin. Propitiation does not make God merciful; it makes divine forgiveness possible. An atonement must be provided; in OT times, animal sacrifices; now, the death of Christ for man's sin. Through Christ's death propitiation is made for man's sin (Ro 3:25; 5:1, 10-11; 2Co 5:18-19; Col 1:20-22; 1Jn 2:2; 4:10; Heb 9:5).
See Atonement.

PROSELYTE A person of Gentile origin who had accepted the Jewish religion, whether living in Israel or elsewhere (Mt 23:15; Ac 2:10; 6:5; 13:43). A distinction was apparently made between uncircumcised proselytes, i.e., those who had not fully identified themselves with the Jewish nation and religion; and circumcised proselytes, those who identified themselves fully with Judaism. *See Converts.*

PROSPERITY From God (Ge 33:11; 49:24-26; Ps 127:1; 128:1-2). Design of (Ecc 7:14). Promised to the righteous (Job 22:23-27).
Evil effects of: Pride (in 2Ch 32:25). Forgetfulness of God in (2Ch 12:1; 26:16; Hos 4:7). The prosperous despise the unfortunate (Job 12:5). Dangers of (Dt 8:10-18; 31:20; 32:15; Jer 5:7; Hos 13:6).
Instances of wisdom in: Joseph and Daniel as deduced from their general conduct. *See Joseph, 1; Daniel.*
See Blessings, Temporal; Rich, The; Riches.

PROSTITUTE Forbidden (Lev 19:29; Dt 23:17). Punishment of (Lev 21:9). Shamelessness of (Pr 2:16; 7:11-27; 9:13-18). Schemes of (Pr 7:10; 9:14-17; Isa 23:15-16; Hos 2:13). To be shunned (Pr 5:3-20; 7:25-27).
In ancient heathen worship a special class of prostitutes was connected with shrines and temples (Ge 38:15, 21, 22), male (1Ki 14:24; 15:12). *See Shrine.* Their earnings were not to be received at the temple (Dt 23:17-18). The term is often used in the OT to refer to religious unfaithfulness (Ex 34:15-16; Isa 1:21; Jer 2:20; Eze 23).
Rahab (Jos 2:3-6; 6:17, 23, 25; Heb 11:31). Jephthah, the son of (Jdg 11:1). Gomer (Hos 1:2-3; 3:3). Babylon (Rev 17).

PROSTRATION *See Obeisance; Worship, Attitude in.*

PROTRACTED MEETINGS (1Ki 8:65; 2Ch 7:8-10; 30:23). *See Revivals.*

PROUD *See Pride.*

PROVENDER *See Fodder.*

PROVERB Pithy saying, comparison or question expressing a familiar or useful truth (Ge 10:9; 1Sa 10:12; Proverbs). Design of (Pr 1:1-4). Written and compiled by Solomon (Pr 1:1; 25:1).

Miscellany of:
(1Sa 10:12; 24:13-14; 2Sa 3:8; 20:18; 1Ki 20:11; Pr 1:17; Eze 12:22-23; 16:44; 18:2-4, w Jer 31:29; Hos 4:9; Mt 12:33, w Lk 6:44; Lk 4:23; 14:34; Jn 1:46; 1Co 15:33; Gal 6:7).
See Proverbs, The Book of Proverbs Arranged Topically.

PROVERBS, BOOK OF

Authors: Although the book begins with a title ascribing these proverbs to Solomon, it is clear from later chapters that he was not the only author of the book. Pr 22:17 and 24:23 refer to the "sayings of the wise." Ch. 30 is attributed to Agur son of Jakeh and 31:1-9 to King Lemuel.

Date: If Solomon is granted a prominent role in the book, most of Proverbs would stem from the tenth century B.C. The role of Hezekiah's men (25:1) indicates that important sections of Proverbs were compiled and edited from 715 to 686 B.C. Perhaps it was also at this time that the sayings of Agur (ch. 30) and Lemuel (31:1-9) and the other "sayings of the wise" (22:17-24:22; 24:23-34) were added to the Solomonic collections.

Outline:
I. Prologue: Purpose and Theme (1:1-7).
II. The Superiority of the Way of Wisdom (1:8-9:18).
 A. Appeals and Warnings Confronting Youth (1:8-33).
 1. Enticements to secure happiness by violence (1:8-19).
 2. Warnings against rejecting wisdom (1:20-33).
 B. Commendation of Wisdom (chs. 2-4).
 1. Benefits of accepting wisdom's instructions (ch. 2).
 2. Wisdom's instructions and benefits (3:1-20).
 3. Wisdom's instructions and benefits (3:21-35).
 4. Challenge to hold on to wisdom (ch. 4).
 C. Warnings Against Folly (chs. 5-7).
 1. Warning against adultery (ch. 5).
 2. Warning against perverse ways (6:1-19).
 3. Cost of committing adultery (6:20-35).
 4. Warning against the enticements of an adulteress (ch. 7).
 D. Appeals Addressed to Youth (chs. 8-9).
 1. Wisdom's appeal (ch. 8).
 2. Invitations of wisdom and folly (ch. 9).
III. The Main Collection of Solomon's Proverbs (10:1-22:16).
IV. The Thirty Sayings of the Wise (22:17-24:22).
V. Additional Sayings of the Wise (24:23-34).
VI. Hezekiah's Collection of Solomon's Proverbs (chs. 25-29).
VII. The Words of Agur (ch. 30).
VIII. The Words of King Lemuel (31:1-9).
IX. Epilogue: The Ideal Wife (31:10-31).

P

The Book of Proverbs Arranged Topically:

Introduction to Wisdom—
The call of Wisdom (8:1-36; 9:1-6). Benefits of following Wisdom (2:1-22; 3:13-24). Dangers of rejecting Wisdom (1:20-33; 9:13-18). Solomon' personal plea (4:1-27).

Proverbs of Solomon and Sayings of the Wise—
Value of wise sayings (22:17-21). Purpose of the Proverbs (1:1-7).
Preeminence of God: Fear of the Lord (9:10-12; 10:27; 14:2, 26-27; 15:33; 19:23; 28:14). Trust in God or self (3:5-8; 14:12, & 16:25; 16:3, 20; 18:2, 4, 10; 19:3; 20:24; 21:22; 26:12; 28:26; 29:25). Divine providence (15:3; 16:1, 4, 9, 33; 19:21; 21:30-31; 22:12; 27:1).
Insight and Ignorance: Wisdom and folly (13:14; 14:24; 15:24; 16:22; 17:12; 24:7, 13-14). Dealing with fools (26:4-11; 27:22; 29:9). Discernment and understanding (10:13, 23; 13:15; 14:6, 8, 15, 33; 15:21; 16:16; 17:24; 19:8; 20:5; 20:12). Knowledge (10:14; 13:16; 14:18; 15:14; 18:15; 19:2; 20:15; 21:11-12; 23:3-4).
Sharing and Responding to Wisdom: Advice and rebuke (3:1-2; 9:7-9; 10:8; 12:15; 13:1; 13:13; 15:31; 17:10; 19:16, 20, 25, 27; 23:9; 25:12; 27:5-6; 27:17; 29:1). Value of Advisors (11:14; 15:22; 20:18; 24:5-6). Discipline (3:11-12; 10:17; 12:1; 13:18, 24; 15:5, 10, 12, 32; 19:18; 20:30; 22:6, 15; 23:13-14; 29:15, 17, 19, 21). Lawkeeping (28:4, 7, 9; 29:18). Repentance (14:9; 28:13).
Good and Evil: Righteousness and wickedness (10:6-7, 16, 28-30; 11:5-10, 18-20, 23; 12:2-3, 5-8, 12, 21, 28; 13:9, 21, 25; 14:11, 19, 23; 15:6, 9; 20:7; 21:18; 24:15-16; 28:12, 28; 29:2, 16, 27). Integrity and perversion (10:9; 13:6; 15:26; 21:8; 24:8-9; 28:18; 29:10). Appropriate consequences (3:33-35; 10:3, 22; 10:24-25; 11:21, 27, 30-31; 14:14, 22; 16:7; 17:13; 18:3; 19:29; 21:12, 16, 21; 22:8; 26:1, 3, 27).
Sincere Motivation: Motive and the heart (15:11; 16:2; 17:3; 20:11, 27; 21:2; 27:19). False worship (15:8, 29; 21:3, 27). Duplicity (6:12-15; 10:10-11; 11:3; 16:30; 20:14; 23:6-8; 26:23-26).
Concern for others: Love and faithfulness (3:3-4; 16:6; 20:6; 25:19). Love, hatred, and compassion (10:12; 15:17; 17:5; 24:17-18; 25:21-22). Kindness and mercy (11:16-17; 12:10, 25; 21:10). Overstaying welcome (25:16-17).
Concern for Self: Pride and humility (11:2; 12:9; 13:7, 10; 15:25; 16:5, 18-19; 18:12; 19:10; 20:9; 21:4, 24; 22:4; 25:27; 26:16; 27:2; 27:21; 29:23). Selfishness (18:1). Jealousy (27:4). Envy (14:30; 24:19-20). Greed (28:25).
Control of Self: Self-control (25:28; 29:11). Rashness (20:25; 21:5; 25:8; 29:20). Temper and patience (12:16; 14:16-17, 29; 15:18; 16:32; 19:11, 19; 22:24-25; 29:8, 22). Drunkenness and gluttony (20:1; 23:19-21; 23:29-35). Adultery (5:1-23; 6:20-35; 7:1-27; 22:14). Prostitution (23:26-28; 29:3).
Control of the Tongue: Wise and foolish talk (14:3; 15:2, 7; 16:23; 18:6-7; 19:1; 23:15-16). Righteous and wicked talk (10:20-21, 31-32; 11:11; 12:13-14; 13:2, 3; 15:28; 17:4). Appropriate speech (15:23; 16:21, 24; 25:11; 27:14). Maintaining silence (10:19; 12:23; 13:3; 17:28; 18:13; 21:23). Controlled speech (15:1; 17:27; 25:15). Flattery (26:28; 28:23; 29:5). Slander and gossip (10:18; 11:13; 16:28; 17:9; 18:8, & 26:22; 20:19; 26:20). Hurtful talk (11:12; 12:18; 15:4; 16:27; 25:23; 26:2). Quarreling (17:14, 19; 20:3; 22:10; 26:21). Lying (12:19, 22; 17:20; 19:5, 22; 21:6). Power of tongue (18:20-21).
Disharmony and Strife: Solicitation to evil (1:10-19; 16:29; 25:26; 27:3; 28:10). Violence (3:31-32; 21:7; 21:29). Murderers (28:17). Causing others harm (3:29-30). Revenge (20:22; 24:28-29). Dissension and strife (6:16-19; 17:1; 18:18-19). Meddling (26:17).
Honesty: Truthfulness (12:20; 13:5; 24:26; 26:18-19). Accurate weights (11:1; 16:11; 20:10, 23). Boundary stones (22:28; 23:10-11). Wrongfully obtained gains (10:2; 13:11; 20:17, 21). Bribery (15:27; 17:8, 23; 21:14).
Justice: False witnesses (12:17; 14:5, 25; 19:9, 28; 21:28; 25:18). Open-mindedness (18:17). Judicial justice (17:15, 26; 18:5; 21:15; 24:11-12, 23-25; 28:5; 29:26).
Economic Well-Being: Wealth and poverty (3:9-10; 10:15; 11:4, 28; 13:8; 14:20; 15:16; 17:16; 18:11, 23; 19:4, 6-7; 22:2, 7; 23:4-5; 27:7; 28:6, 8, 11, 20-22). Benevolence and generosity (3:27-28; 11:24-26; 13:22; 14:21; 18:16; 19:17; 21:13; 22:9; 25:14; 28:27). Oppression of the poor (13:23; 14:31; 15:15; 16:8; 22:16, 22-23; 29:7, 13). Industriousness (6:6-11; 10:4-5, 26; 12:11, 24, 27; 13:4; 14:4, 23; 15:19; 16:26; 18:9; 19:15; 19:24, & 26:15; 20:4, 13, 17; 21:25-26; 22:29; 24:27, 30-34; 26:14; 27:18, 23-27; 28:19). Conservation (21:20). Surety for another (6:1-5; 11:15; 17:18; 20:16, & 27:13; 22:26-27).
Persons and Attributes: Parents and children (1:8-9; 10:1; 11:29; 15:20; 17:2, 6, 21, 25; 19:26; 20:20; 23:22-25; 28:24). The elderly (16:31; 20:29). Women and wives (11:22; 12:4; 14:1; 18:22; 19:13-14; 21:9, & 25:24; 21:19; 27:15-16). Kings and rulers (14:28, 35; 16:10, 12-15; 17:7, 11; 19:12; 20:2, 8, 26, 28; 21:1; 22:11; 23:1-3; 24:21-22; 25:2-7; 28:2-3; 28:15-16; 29:4, 12, 14). Messengers (13:17; 25:13). Companions (12:26; 13:20; 14:7; 17:17; 18:24; 24:1-2; 27:8-10; 29:24).
Various Concerns: Caution (16:17; 22:3, & 27:12; 22:5). Reputation (22:1; 25:9-10). Courage (3:25-26; 14:32; 22:13; 24:10; 26:13; 28:1). Hope (13:12; 13:19; 23:17-18).
Various Observations: Joy and grief (14:10, 13; 15:13; 17:22; 18:14; 25:20; 27:11; 29:6). Good news (15:30; 25:25). Curiosity (27:20).
The sayings of Agur son of Jakeh (30:1-33).
The sayings of King Lemuel (31:1-9).
A wife of noble character (31:10-31).

PROVIDENCE The universal sovereign reign of God; God's preserving and governing all his creatures, and all their actions (Job 9:5-6; 28:25; Ps 104:10-25; 145:15; 147:9; Mt 4:4; 6:26-28; Lk 12:6-7; Ac 17:25-28). General providence includes the government of the entire universe, especially the affairs of men. Special providence is God's particular care over the life and activity of the believer (Ro 8:28).
See God, Providence of.

PROVINCE Unit of an empire, like those of the Roman Empire. In Persia they were called satrapies. Rome's provinces were divided into two categories: imperial, those requiring a frontier army, and ruled by a legate appointed by the emperor; senatorial, those presenting no major problems and ruled by someone appointed by the Senate—a proconsul (Ac 13:7).

PROVOCATION Any cause of God's anger at sin (1Ki 15:30; 21:22; Eze 20:28; Ne 9:18, 26).

PROXY In priest's service (2Ch 30:17). *See Substitution; Suffering, Vicarious.*

PRUDENCE

General:
(Job 34:3-4; Ps 112:5; Hos 14:9; Mt 7:6).
In restraining speech (Pr 39:1; Pr 12:8; 21:23; 23:9; 26:4; 29:11; Am 5:13). In heeding counsel (Pr 15:5; 20:18). In restraining appetite (Pr 23:1-2). In avoiding strife (Pr 25:8-10; 29:8). In refraining from making a guarantee (Pr 6:1-2).
Proverbs concerning (Pr 8:12; 11:13, 15, 29; 12:8, 16, 23; 13:16; 14:8, 15-16, 18; 15:5, 22; 16:20-21; 17:2, 18; 18:15-16; 19:2; 20:5, 16, 18; 21:5, 20, 23; 22:3, 7, 26-27; 23:1-3, 9; 24:6, 27; 25:8-10; 26:4-5; 27:12; 29:8, 11; Ecc 7:16-17; 8:2-3; 10:1, 10). Illustration of (Lk 14:28-32). Injunctions concerning (Ro 14:16; 1Co 6:12; 8:8-13; 10:25-33; Col 4:5; Jas 1:19).
See Diplomacy; Gentleness; Wisdom.

Instances of:
Jacob, in his conduct toward Esau (Ge 32:3-21), toward his sons, after Dinah's defilement (Ge 34:5, 30). Joseph, in the affairs of Egypt (Ge 41:33-57). Jethro's advice to Moses (Ex 18:17-23). The Israelites, in the threatened war with the two-a-one-half tribes (Jos 22:10-34). Saul, in not slaying the Jabesh Gileadites (1Sa 11:13). David, in his overthrowing Ahithophel's counsel (2Sa 15:33-37). Abigail, in averting David's wrath (1Sa 25:18-31). Achish, in dismissing David (1Sa 29). Elijah, in his flight from Jezebel (1Ki 19:3-4). Rehoboam's counselors (1Ki 12:7). Jehoram, in suspecting a Syrian stratagem (2Ki 7:12-13). Nehemiah, in conduct of affairs at Jerusalem (Ne 2:12-16; 4:13-23). Daniel (Da 1:8-14). Certain elders of Israel (Jer 26:17-23).
Jesus, in charging those who were healed not to advertise his miracles (Mt 9:30; 16:20; Mk 3:12; 5:43; 7:36; 8:30; 9:9), going to the feast secretly (Jn 7:10), in restricting his public appearances (Jn 11:54; 12:36), in avoiding his enemies (Mt 12:14-16; Mk 3:7; Jn 11:47-54). Joseph, in his conduct toward Mary (Mt 1:19). Peter, in escaping Herod (Ac 12:17). Paul, in circumcising Timothy (Ac 16:3), in performing temple rites (Ac 21:20-26), in setting the Jewish sects on each other (Ac 23:6), avoiding suspicion in administering the gifts of the churches (2Co 8:20), his lack of, in his persistence in going to Jerusalem despite the warnings of the Spirit and his friends (Ac 20:22-25, 37-38; 21:10-14), Paul and Barnabas, in escaping persecution (Ac 14:6), Paul and Silas, in escaping from Berea (Ac 17:10-15). The town clerk of Ephesus, in averting a riot (Ac 19:29-41).
See Diplomacy; Tact.

PRUNING To care for and increase productivity of vines (Lev 25:3-4; Isa 5:6; 18:5). Pruning hook (Isa 2:4; 18:5; Joel 3:10; Mic 4:3). Figurative of discipline (Jn 15:2-6).

PSALMODY *See Music.*

PSALMS

Psalms Outside the Book of:
Of Moses celebrating the deliverance at the Red Sea (Ex 15:1-19). Didactic songs composed by Moses, celebrating the providence, righteousness, and judgments of God (Dt 32:1-43; Ps 90). Song of Deborah, celebrating Israel's victory over Sisera (Jdg 5). Of Hannah, in thankfulness for a son (1Sa 2:1-10). Of David, celebrating his deliverance (2Sa 22), on the occasion of removing the ark (1Ch 16:7-36), at the close of his reign (2Sa 23:2-7; 1Ch 29:10-19). Of Isaiah (Isa 12: 25-26). Of Hezekiah, celebrating deliverance from death (Isa 38:9-20). Of Mary (Lk 1:46-55). Elizabeth (Lk 1:42-45). Zechariah (Lk 1:68-79).

Book of Psalms:
Collection and Structure—
The Hebrew Psalter is divided into five books:
1. Psalms 1-41.
2. Psalms 42-72.
3. Psalms 73-89.
4. Psalms 90-106.
5. Psalms 107-150.
The formation of psalters probably goes back to the early days of the first (Solomon's) temple or even to the time of David. The Psalter was put into its final form by postexilic temple personnel, who completed it probably in the third century B.C.

Topically Arranged—
Psalms of affliction (Ps 3-5; 11; 13; 16-17; 22; 26-28; 31; 35; 41-42; 44; 54-57; 59-64; 69-71; 74; 77; 79-80; 83-84; 86; 88-89; 102; 109; 120; 123; 129; 137; 140-143). Didactic psalms (Ps 1; 5; 7; 9-12; 14-15; 17; 24-25; 32; 34; 36-37; 39; 49; 50; 52-53; 58; 73; 75; 82; 84; 90-92; 94; 101; 112; 119; 121; 125; 127-128; 131; 133). Historical psalms (Ps 78; 105-106). Imprecatory psalms. *See Prayer, Imprecatory.* Intercessional psalms (Ps 20; 67; 122; 132; 144). Messianic Psalms. *See Jesus the Christ, Messiah, Messianic Psalms.* Penitential psalms (Ps 6; 25; 32; 38; 51; 102; 130; 143). Psalms of praise (Ps 8; 19; 24; 29; 33; 47; 50; 65-66; 76-77; 93; 95-97; 99; 104; 111; 113-115; 134; 139; 147-148). Prophetic psalms (Ps 2; 16; 22; 40; 68-69; 72; 87; 97; 110; 118). Psalms of thanksgiving: For God's goodness to Israel (Ps 21; 46; 48; 65-66; 76; 81; 85; 98; 105; 124; 126; 129; 135-136; 149). For God's goodness to good people (Ps 23; 34; 36; 91; 100; 103; 107; 117; 121; 145-146). For God's mercies to individuals (Ps 9; 18; 30; 34; 40; 75; 103; 108; 118; 138; 144).

Superscriptions and authorship—
Of the 150 psalms, only 34 lack superscriptions of any kind (only 17 in the Septuagint). If the superscriptions refer to authorship, authors include Moses (Ps 90), David (Ps 3-9; 11-32; 34-41; 51-65;

68-70; 86; 101; 103; 108-110; 122; 124; 131; 133; 138-145), Solomon (Ps 72; 127), Asaph (Ps 50; 73-83), sons of Korah (Ps 42; 44-49; 84-85; 87-88), Heman (Ps 88), Ethan (Ps 89). Many of the psalm titles include musical terms in Hebrew, some designating ancient melodies, others preserving musical instructions. The meaning of some of these terms is uncertain or unknown. *See Music, Symbols Used in.*

PSALMS OF SOLOMON One of the pseudepigrapha, consisting of 18 psalms in imitation of the canonical psalms, probably written between 64 and 46 B.C.

PSALTERY *See Harp; Lyre.*

PSEUDEPIGRAPHA (*writing under a false name*). Books not in the Hebrew canon or the Apocrypha, ascribed to earlier biblical authors. They were written chiefly during the intertestamental, apostolic, and post-apostolic periods.

PTOLEMAIS A seaport in Asher, formerly called Acco. Paul visits (Ac 21:7).
See Acco.

PTOLEMY Common name of the fifteen Macedonian kings of Egypt whose dynasty extended from the death of Alexander the Great in 323 B.C. to the murder of Ptolemy XV, son of Julius Caesar and Cleopatra in 30 B.C.; Ptolemy I, Soter (323-285 B.C.); Ptolemy II, Philadelphus (285-246 B.C.); LXX translated, Golden Age of Ptolemaic Egypt; Ptolemy III (c. 246-221 B.C.); Ptolemy IV, Philopator (221-203 B.C.); Ptolemy V, Epiphanes (203-181 B.C.); Ptolemy VI, Philometor (181-146 B.C.); Ptolemy VII, Neos Philopator (146-117 B.C.); Ptolemy XI was the last of the male line of Ptolemy I, killed by Alexandrians; Ptolemy XII (51-47 B.C.) fled to Rome; Ptolemy XIII had Cleopatra as his wife.
See Testaments, Time Between.

PUAH (perhaps from the Ugaritic meaning *girl*).
1. Son of Issachar (Ge 46:13; Nu 26:23, ftn; 1Ch 7:1).
2. A Hebrew midwife (Ex 1:15).
3. Father of Tola (Jdg 10:1).

PUBLIC OPINION Jesus inquires about (Mt 16:13; Mk 8:27; Lk 9:18).

Feared By:
Nicodemus (Jn 3:2), by Joseph of Arimathea (Jn 19:38), by the parents of the man who was born blind (Jn 9:21-22), by rulers who believed in Jesus but feared the Pharisees (Jn 12:42-43), by Herod (Mt 14:5), by chief priests (Mt 21:26; Mk 11:18, 32; Lk 12:12; 20:6), by those who feared to further persecute the disciples (Ac 4:21; 5:26).

Kings Influenced By:
Saul (1Sa 14:45; 15:24), David (2Ch 20:21), Hezekiah (2Ch 30:2), Zedekiah (Jer 38:19, 24-27), Herod (Mt 14:5; Ac 12:2-3), Pilate (Jn 19:6-13).

Concessions to:
By Paul in circumcising Timothy (Ac 16:3). By James and the Christian elders who required Paul to observe certain rites (Ac 21:18-26). By disciples who urged circumcision (Gal 6:12). By Peter and Barnabas with others (Gal 2:11-14).

Corrupt Yielding to:
By Herod in the case of John the Baptist (Mk 6:26), Peter (Ac 12:3). By Peter concerning Jesus (Mt 26:69-75; Mk 14:66-72; Lk 22:54-62). By Pilate (Mt 27:23-27; Mk 15:15; Lk 23:13-25; Jn 18:38-39; 19:4-16). By Felix and Festus concerning Paul (Ac 24:27; 25:9).

PUBLICANS *See Tax Collectors.*

PUBLIUS (*first*). Chief man in the island of Malta. Father of, healed by Paul (Ac 28:7-8).

PUDENS (*modest*). A Christian in Rome (2Ti 4:21).

PUHITES *See Puthites.*

PUITE The descendants of Puah, of the tribe of Issachar (Nu 26:23, ftn; 1Ch 7:1). *See Puah.* The Masoretic Text has "through Puvah, the Punite."

PUL
1. King of Assyria. Forced tribute from Menahem, king of Israel (2Ki 15:19; 1Ch 5:26).
2. A place or tribe in Africa (Isa 66:19).

PULPIT NIV "platform" used primarily as a position from which to speak (Ne 8:4).

PULSE NIV "lentils" (2Sa 17:28) and "vegetables" (Da 1:12, 16). *See Vegetarians; Vegetation.*

PUNISHMENT Assumed for others (Ge 27:13; 1Sa 25:24; 2Sa 14:9; Mt 27:25).
See Affliction; Afflictions; Chastisement, From God; Fine; Judgments; Penalty; Retaliation; Wicked, Punishment of.

Death Penalty:
Shall not be remitted (Nu 35:31). In the Mosaic law the death penalty was inflicted for murder (Ge 9:5-6; Nu 35:16-21, 30-33; Dt 17:6), adultery (Lev 20:10; Dt 22:24), incest (Lev 20:11-12, 14), bestiality (Ex 22:19; Lev 20:15-16), sodomy (Lev 18:22; 20:13), promiscuity (Dt 22:21-24), rape of an engaged virgin (Dt 22:25), perjury (Zec 5:4), kidnapping (Ex 21:16; Dt 24:7), a priest's daughter who became a prostitute (Lev 21:9), witchcraft (Ex 22:18), offering human sacrifice (Lev 20:2-5), striking or cursing father or mother (Ex 21:15, 17; Lev 20:9), disobedience to parents (Dt 21:18-21), theft (Zec 5:3-4), blasphemy (Lev 24:11-14, 16, 23), Sabbath desecration (Ex 35:2; Nu 15:32-36), prophesying falsely or propagating false doctrines (Dt 13:1-10), sacrificing to false gods (Ex 22:20), refusing to abide by the decision of a court (Dt 17:12), treason (1Ki 2:25; Est 2:23), sedition (Ac 5:36-37).

P

Я

Modes of execution of Death Penalty —

Burning (Ge 38:24; Lev 20:14; 21:9; Jer 29:22; Eze 23:25; Da 3:19-23), stoning (Lev 20:2, 27; 24:14; Nu 14:10; 15:33-36; Dt 13:10; 17:5; 22:21, 24; Jos 7:25; 1Ki 21:10; Eze 16:40), hanging (Ge 40:22; Dt 21:22-23; Jos 8:29), beheading (Mt 14:10; Mk 6:16, 27-28), crucifixion (Mt 27:35, 38; Mk 15:24, 27; Lk 23:33), the sword (Ex 32:27-28; 1Ki 2:25, 34, 46; Ac 12:2). Executed by the witnesses (Dt 13:9; 17:7; Ac 7:58), by the congregation (Nu 15:35-36; Dt 13:9).

Not inflicted on testimony of less than two witnesses (Nu 35:30; Dt 17:6; 19:15).

Minor Offenses:

Punishable by scourging (Lev 19:20; Dt 22:18; 25:2-3; Pr 17:10; 19:29; 20:30; Mt 27:26; Mk 15:15; Lk 23:16; Jn 19:1; Ac 22:24, 29), imprisonment (Ge 39:20; 40). See Prison. Confinement within limits (1Ki 2:26, 36-38).

By God:

According to deeds (Job 34:11; Ps 62:12; Pr 12:14; 24:12; Isa 59:13; Jer 17:10; Eze 7:3, 27; 16:59; 39:24; Zec 1:6; Mt 5:22; 16:27; 25:14-30; Mk 12:40; Lk 12:47-48; 2Pe 3:7).
See Judgment, According to Opportunity and Works.
See parables of the vineyard (Isa 5:1-7), landowner (Mt 21:33-41), talents (Mt 25:14-30), servants (Lk 12:47-48).
Imposed on children (Ex 34:7; Jer 31:29; La 5:7). Not imposed on children (Dt 24:16; 2Ch 25:4).
Delayed (Ps 50:21; 55:19; Pr 1:24-31; Ecc 8:11-13; Hab 1:2-4).
Design of, to secure obedience (Ge 2:17; Ex 20:3-5; Lev 26:14-39; Dt 13:10-11; 17:13; 19:19-20; 21:21-22; Pr 19:25; 21:11; 26:3). See Judgments, Design of.
No escape from (Ge 3:7-19; 4:9-11; Job 11:20; 34:21-22; Pr 1:24-31; 11:21; 16:5; 29:1; Isa 10:3; Jer 11:11; 15:1; 25:28-29; Eze 7:19; Am 2:14-16; 9:1-4; Zep 1:18; Mt 10:28; 23:33; Ro 2:3; 1Th 5:2-3; Col 3:25; Heb 2:3; 12:25-26; Rev 6:15-17).
Eternal (Isa 34:8-10; Da 12:2; Mt 3:12; 10:28; 18:8; 25:41, 46; Mk 3:29; Lk 3:17; Jn 5:29; Heb 6:2; 10:28-31; Rev 14:10-11; 19:3; 20:10).
See Wicked, Punishment of.

PUNISHMENT, EVERLASTING Is taught in Scripture for those who reject God's love revealed in Christ (Mt 25:46; Da 12:2). The final place of everlasting punishment is called the "lake of fire" (Rev 19:20; 20:10, 14-15), also called "the second death" (Rev 14:9-11; 20:6). "Hell" in Scripture translates the word Hades, the unseen realm where the souls of all the dead are. Gehenna is the place of everlasting punishment of Hades; paradise is the place of blessing of Hades (Lk 16:19-31). The reason for eternal punishment is man's rejection of God's provision for the forgiveness of sin through the life and work of Jesus Christ, God's Son (Jn 3:16-18).
See Hades; Hell.

PUNITE See Puite.

PUNON A city of Edom. A camping ground of the Israelites, in their forty years' wandering (Nu 33:42-43).

PUR (lots). Lot cast to destroy Jews in the time of Esther (Est 3:7; 9:24, 26). Feast of Purim is a Jewish festival commemorating the deliverance of the Jews from mass murder by Haman. See Lot, The; Purim.

PURAH (branch ISBE; imposing KB). A servant of Gideon (Jdg 7:10-11).

PURIFICATION In studying the Mosaic law relating to purifications, it must be kept in mind that sin defiles. To keep this great truth constantly before the mind of the Israelites, specific ordinances concerning purifications were given to Moses; the purpose being, by this object lesson, to teach that sin defiles and only the pure in heart can see God. Therefore, certain incidents, such as eating that which had died of itself, touching the dead, etc., were signified as defiling, and definite ceremonies were prescribed for persons who were defiled. During the period of defilement, and when performing the ceremonies required of them, the defiled were expected to contemplate the defilement of sin and the need of purification of the heart.

Required:

Sanitary and symbolic (Ex 19:10, 14; Heb 9:10). For women after childbirth (Lev 12:6-8; Lk 2:22). After menstruation (Lev 15:19-33; 2Sa 11:4). After intercourse (Lev 15:16-18). For a discharge (Lev 15:4-18). For those cleansed of leprosy (Lev 14:8-9). For eating that which died of itself (Lev 17:15). For those who had slain in battle (Nu 31:19-24).
Of priests (Ex 29:4; 30:18-21; 40:12, 30-32; Lev 8:6; 16:4, 24, 26, 28; 22:3; Nu 19:7-8; 2Ch 4:6). Of Levites (Nu 8:6-7, 21). Of lepers. See Leprosy. Of the Jews before the Passover (Jn 11:55).
By fire, for things that resist fire (Nu 31:23). By blood (Lev 14:6-7; Heb 9:12-14, 19-22). By abstaining from sexual intercourse (Ex 19:15). By washing in water, parts of animal sacrifices (Lev 1:9, 13; 9:14; 2Ch 4:6).
Penalty to be imposed upon those who do not observe the ordinances concerning (Lev 7:20-21; 22:3; Nu 19:13, 20).
Water of (Nu 19:17-21; 31:23). Washing hands in water, symbolic of innocence (Dt 21:6; Ps 26:6). Traditions of the elders concerning (Mt 15:2; Mk 7:2-5, 8-9; Lk 11:38).
See Washing; Defilement; Sanitation and Hygiene; Spiritual Purification.

Practiced by:

Jacob (Ge 35:2). Moses (Ex 19:10, 14). Aaron (Ex 29:4; 30:18-21; 40:12, 30-32; Lev 8:6). Paul, to show his fidelity to the law (Ac 21:24, 26).

Figurative:

(Ps 26:6; 51:7; Eze 36:25). See Spiritual Purification.

PURIM (lots). A feast instituted to commemorate the deliverance of the Jews from the plot of Haman (Est 9:20-32). See Annual Feasts; Lot, The; Pur.

PURITY A Christian virtue (1Ti 4:12; 5:22; Tit 1:15). Word of God pure (Ps 12:6; 19:8; 119:140).
Of the human heart (Ps 24:3-5; 65:3; Pr 15:26; 20:9; 21:8; 30:12; Isa 1:18, 25; 6:7; Mic 6:11; 1Ti 1:5; 2Ti 2:21-22; Heb 10:2). Blessedness of (Mt 5:8). Prayer for (Ps 51:7; Da 12:10; Heb 9:13-14). Through divine discipline (Mal 3:2-3; Jn 15:2), the blood of Christ (Heb 9:13-14).
Commanded (1Ti 3:9; 5:22; 2Ti 1:3; 2:21-22; Jas 4:8; 1Pe 1:22). Meditation upon, commanded (Php 4:8).
Jesus our pattern in (1Jn 3:3). Exemplified by Paul (2Ti 1:3).
See Holiness; Sanitation and Hygiene; Spiritual Purification.
For symbolisms of purity, See Colors, Figurative and Symbolic, White; Defilement; Purification; Washings.

PURPLE A color highly esteemed in ancient times; because of its costliness, it became a mark of distinction to wear robes of purple. Royalty was so dressed. The color included various shades between crimson and violet (Ex 25:4; 26:36; 28:15; 35:6; Jdg 8:26; 2Ch 2:14).
See Colors, Figurative and Symbolic.

PURSE A bag for holding money (Pr 1:14; 7:20; Hag 1:6; Lk 10:4).

PURTENANCE Entrails (Lev 1:9).

PURVEYOR Those providing supplies to Solomon (1Ki 4:7-19, 27).

PUT
1. Son of Ham (Ge 10:6; 1Ch 1:8).
2. The descendants of Put, or the country inhabited by them; Put has also been taken to signify Egypt and is often associated with the Libyans (Isa 66:19, ftn; Eze 27:10; 30:5; 38:5; Jer 46:9; Na 3:9). See Libya.

PUTEOLI (Latin rotten [sulfur] smell or well, spring). Seaport of Italy, eight miles W of Naples; nearest harbor to Rome (Ac 28:13-14).

PUTHITES (simple). Family descended from Caleb (1Ch 2:50, 53).

PUTIEL (he whom God [El] gives). The father-in-law of Eleazar the priest (Ex 6:25).

PUVAH See Puah.

PYGARG See Ibex.

PYRAMIDS (possibly pointed [like a flame tongue, or a wheat tip]). Tombs with superstructures of triangular form made for the interment of royalty in Egypt. About eighty survive. See Ziggurat.

PYRRHUS (fiery red). Father of Sopater (Ac 20:4).

Q

QUAIL Miracle of, in the wilderness of Sin (Ex 16:13), Kibroth Hattaavah (Nu 11:31-32; Ps 105:40).

QUARANTANIA The mountain where according to tradition Satan tempted Jesus to worship him (Mt 4:8-10), Tell el-Sultan, a short distance W of OT Jericho.

QUARANTINE For prevention of the spread of disease. See Sanitation and Hygiene.

QUARRIES A place to remove building stone (Jos 7:5; 1Ki 5:17, 6:7; Ecc 10:9; Isa 51:1).

QUARTUS (fourth [born]). A Christian in Corinth (Ro 16:23).

QUATERNION (four). A squad of four soldiers (Ac 12:4).

QUEEN The wife of a king (1Ki 11:19). Crowned (Est 1:11; 2:17). Divorced (Est 1:10-22). Sits on the throne with the king (Ne 2:6). Makes feasts for the women of the royal household (Est 1:9). Exerts an evil influence in public affairs. See Jezebel. Counsels the king (Da 5:10-12). Queen of Sheba visits Solomon (1Ki 10:1-13). Candace, of Ethiopia (Ac 8:27).
Queen Athaliah was the only independent female ruler of Israel or Judah. See Athaliah.
Queen of Heaven (Jer 7:18; 44:7-19, 25). See Idolatry; Queen of Heaven.

QUEEN OF HEAVEN Probably Ishtar, Babylonian female deity (Jer 7:18; 44:17-25). See Idolatry.

QUICKENING Coming to life. Of the church: By the Father (Ps 71:20; 80:18; Ro 4:17; 8:11; Eph 2:1; 1Pe 6:13), by the Holy Spirit (Jn 6:63; Ro 8:11; 2Co 3:6; 1Pe 3:18). See Life; Regeneration; Resurrection.

QUICKSANDS NIV "sandbars" (Ac 27:17). See Sandbars.

QUIRINIUS Governor of Syria A.D. 6-9. His census of A.D. 6 at the request of the emperor Augustus is referred to in Ac 5:37. Another census, in which Joseph and Mary were registered, is mentioned in Lk 2:2. This may indicate Quirinius served an earlier term as governor of Syria and Luke mentions his "first" (NIV) and otherwise unknown census. Or the verse may be translated "This

was before the census that took place while Quirinius was governor of Syria."

QUIVER (from a root meaning to hang, suspend). For arrows (Ge 27:3; Isa 22:6).

R

RA Egyptian sun-god. Joseph married a daughter of the priest of On, center of the cult of Ra (Ge 41:45, 50). The plague of darkness was an insult against (Ex 10:21-23).

RAAMAH
1. Son of Cush (Ge 10:7; 1Ch 1:9).
2. A place in Arabia (Eze 27:22).

RAAMIAH (Yahweh has thundered). An Israelite who returned from captivity with Zerubbabel (Ne 7:7).

RAAMSES See Rameses.

RABBAH (chief, capital [city]).
1. A town in Judah (Jos 15:60), not now identifiable.
2. Capital of Ammon, represented today by Amman, the capital of Jordan, twenty-two miles E of Jordan (Jos 13:25; 2Sa 11:1; 12:27-29; 1Ch 20:1; Jer 49:2-3). Subsequently captured by Ptolemy Philadelphus (285-247 B.C.), who changed its name to Philadelphia; became one of the cities of the Decapolis. Twice spelled "Rabbath" (Dt 3:11; Eze 21:20).

RABBATH-AMMON (chief city of Ammon). See Rabbah.

RABBI, RABBONI ([my] great one, [my] master). The title of a teacher (Mt 23:7-8; Jn 3:2). Ostentatiously used by the Pharisees (Mt 23:7). Used in addressing John the Baptist (Jn 3:26), in addressing Jesus (Mt 26:25, 49; Mk 9:5; 10:51; 11:21; 14:45; Jn 4:31; 9:2; 11:8 Jn 1:38, 49; 3:2; 6:25). Jesus called "Rabboni" (Jn 20:16). Forbidden by Jesus as a title to his disciples (Mt 23:8).

RABBIM See Bath Rabbim.

RABBIT Forbidden as food (Lev 11:6; Dt 14:7). See Animals.

RABBITH (great). A city in Issachar (Jos 19:20).

RABBLE (Ex 12:38; Nu 11:4; Mt 26:47; Ac 16:22; 17:5).

RABBONI ([my] great one, [my] master). Variant of Rabbi, the Aramaic word for Teacher (Jn 20:16).

RABMAG NIV "high official"; the Babylonian title of Nergal-Sharezer (Jer 39:3, 13).

RABSARIS NIV "chief officer"; a title used of Assyrian (2Ki 18:17) and Babylonian officials (Jer 39:3, 13).

RABSHAKEH NIV "field commander"; a title of a Assyrian officer sent by Sennacherib against Jerusalem. He speaks publicly in Hebrew to cause disloyalty to Hezekiah and a surrender of the city (2Ki 18:17-37; 19:4, 8; Isa 36; 37:4, 8).

RACA (empty [headed]). A term of contempt and scorn (Mt 5:22).

RACAL (trade). A city in Judah (1Sa 30:29).

RACE
1. Human. Unity of (Ge 3:20; Mal 2:10; Ac 17:26). See Mankind.
2. Foot race. Figurative: (Ps 19:5; Ecc 9:11; 1Co 9:24; Gal 5:7; Php 2:16; Heb 12:1-2).

RACHAB See Rahab.

RACHAL See Racal.

RACHEL (ewe). Daughter of Laban and wife of Jacob. Meets Jacob at the well (Ge 29:9-12). Jacob serves Laban fourteen years to secure her for his wife (Ge 29:15-30). Sterility of (Ge 29:31). Her grief in consequence of her sterility; gives her maid to Jacob in order to secure children in her own name (Ge 30:1-8, 15, 22-34). Later fertility of; becomes the mother of Joseph (Ge 30:22-25), of Benjamin (Ge 35:16-18, 24). Steals the household images of her father (Ge 31:4, 14-19, 33-35). Her death and burial (Ge 35:18-20; 48:7; 1Sa 10:2).

RADDAI (possibly beating down ISBE; Yahweh rules KB). Son of Jesse (1Ch 2:14).

RAGAU See Reu.

RAGUEL See Jethro; Reuel, 2.

RAHAB (spacious, broad).
1. A prostitute of Jericho who hid Israelites spies (Jos 2:1), mother of Boaz; great-grandmother of King David (Mt 1:5; Ru 4:18-21), shining example of faith (Heb 11:31).
2. Mythical monster of the deep; enemy of Yahweh (Job 9:13; Ps 89:10), applied to Egypt (Ps 87:4; Isa 30:7; 51:9).

RAHAM (compassion). Son of Shema (1Ch 2:44).

RAHEL See Rachel.

RAIL Taunts of the enemy (Ps 102:6). *See Slander; Speaking or Speech, Evil.*

RAIMENT *See Cloth; Clothing; Dress; Garment; Robe.*

RAIN Forty days of, at the time of the Flood (Ge 7:4, 10-12, 17-24). The plague of, upon Egypt (Ex 9:22-26, 33-34). Miraculously caused by Samuel (1Sa 12:16-19), by Elijah (1Ki 18:41-45). David delivered by (2Sa 5:17-21; Isa 28:21). North wind unfavorable to (Pr 25:23). Withheld as judgment (Dt 11:17; 28:24; 1Ki 8:35; 2Ch 7:13; Jer 3:3; Am 4:7; Zec 14:17). The earth shall no more be destroyed by (Ge 9:8-17). Sent by God (Dt 11:13-14; Job 37:6; Isa 30:23; Jer 5:24; 14:22). Contingent upon obedience (Lev 26:3-4; Dt 11:13-14). Prayer for (1Ki 8:35-36; 2Ch 6:26-27). Answer to prayer for, promised (2Ch 7:13-14; Zec 10:1). Withheld, in answer to prayer (Jas 5:17-18).

In Israel the rainy season extends from October to April; the dry season, from May to September. The early rain occurs in October and November (Ps 84:6; Isa 30:23; Jer 5:24); the latter rain in March and April (Job 29:23; Pr 16:15; Jer 3:3; 5:24; Zec 10:1). Crops are therefore planted so that they will grow during the rainy season.

"Rain" is often used in the OT in a figurative sense. An abundance of rain denotes the rich blessing of Yahweh upon his people (Dt 28:12); lack of rain is a sign of God's displeasure (Dt 28:23-24). In Canaanite religion, Baal was conceived of as the god of rain, and was therefore ardently worshiped.

RAINBOW A token that the earth shall never again be destroyed by flooding (Ge 9:8-16; Eze 1:28). *See Meteorology.* Symbolic (Rev 4:3; 10:1).

RAISIN Preserved grapes. Given by Abigail to David (1Sa 25:18). Given to the famished Egyptian to revive him (1Sa 30:12). Given by Ziba to David (2Sa 16:1). Given to David at Ziklag (1Ch 12:40).

RAISING From the dead. *See Dead; Resurrection.*

RAKEM (*weaver, embroider*). A descendant of Makir, son of Manasseh (1Ch 7:16).

RAKKATH (*narrow place*). A fortified city in Naphtali (Jos 19:35), probably near the Sea of Galilee on the site of Tiberias.

RAKKON (*narrow place*). A city in Dan (Jos 19:46).

RAM (As a proper name *high, exalted*).
1. The son of Hezron and an ancestor of Jesus (Ru 4:19; 1Ch 2:9-10). Called Aram (Mt 1:3-4; Lk 3:33).
2. The son of Jerahmeel (1Ch 2:25, 27).
3. An ancestor, probably of Elihu (Job 32:2).
4. A sheep. Skins of, used for the roof of the tabernacle (Ex 26:14; 39:34). Seen in Daniel's vision (Da 8:3, 20). Used in sacrifice. *See Offerings.*
Trumpets made of the horns of. *See Horn; Trumpet.*
5. A weapon used to break down doors and gates. *See Battering Ram.*

RAMAH (*elevated spot*).
1. A city allotted to Benjamin (Jos 18:25; Jdg 19:13). Attempted fortification of, by King Baasha; destruction of, by Asa (1Ki 15:17-22; 2Ch 16:1-6). People of, return from the Babylonian Captivity (Ezr 2:26; Ne 7:30; 11:33). Jeremiah imprisoned in (Jer 40:1). Prophecies concerning (Isa 10:29; Jer 31:15; Hos 5:8; Mt 2:18).
2. A city of S Judah allotted to the tribe of Simeon (Jos 19:8).
3. A city of Asher (Jos 19:29).
4. A city of Naphtali (Jos 19:36).
5. Also called Ramathaim. A city in the hill country of Ephraim (Jdg 4:5; 1Sa 1:1). Home of Elkanah (1Sa 1:1, 19; 2:11), and of Samuel (1Sa 1:19-20; 7:17; 8:4; 15:34; 16:13). David flees to (1Sa 19:18). Samuel dies and is buried in (1Sa 25:1; 28:3).
See Ramoth Gilead.

RAMATH *See Ramah, 2.*

RAMATH LEHI (*height [hill] of Lehi*). The place where Samson killed a thousand Philistines with the jawbone of a donkey (Jdg 15:17).

RAMATH MIZPAH (*height [hill] of Mizpah [watch tower]*). Northern boundary line of Gad (Jos 13:26). Also called Mizpah, Galeed, and Jegar Sahadutha (Ge 31:47-49).

RAMATHAIM-ZOPHIM, RAMATHAIM ZUPHIM (*two heights of Zophim*). *See Ramah, 5.*

RAMATHITE (*of Ramah*). Designation of Shimei, King David's overseer in charge of the vineyards (1Ch 27:27).

RAMESES (*Ra [pagan sun god] created him*).
1. Egyptian store city built by Israelites (Ex 1:11), possibly the modern San el-Habar in the NE part of the Delta.
2. The name of eleven Egyptian pharaohs, of whom Rameses II (c. 1301-1234 B.C.) was the most famous, many scholars holding that he was the pharaoh of the Exodus. Some of these pharaohs must have had at least an indirect influence on Israelite life, but none of them is mentioned in the OT.

RAMIAH (*Yahweh is exalted*). An Israelite in the time of Ezra who married a foreign wife (Ezr 10:25).

RAMOTH (*height*).
1. Ramoth in Gilead. *See Ramoth Gilead.*
2. Ramoth Negev. A place probably in the south of Simeon (Jos 19:8; 1Sa 30:27). *See Ramah, 2.*
3. A city of Issachar, allotted to the Levites (1Ch 6:73).
4. *See Jeremoth, 6.*

RAMOTH GILEAD (*heights in Gilead*). A city of Gad, and a city of refuge (Dt 4:43; Jos 20:8; 1Ch 6:80). One of Solomon's

district governors at (1Ki 4:13). In the possession of the Syrians (1Ki 22:3). Besieged by Israel and Judah; Ahab slain at (1Ki 22:29-36; 2Ch 18). Recovered by Joram; Joram wounded at (2Ki 8:28-29; 9:14-15; 2Ch 22:5-6). Elisha anoints Jehu king at (2Ki 9:1-6).

RAMS' HORNS *See Shofar; Trumpet.*

RAMS' SKINS Skins of sheep; used for clothing of shepherds and covering for the tabernacle (Ex 25:5).

RANSOM Of a human life (Ex 21:30; 30:12; Job 36:18; Ps 49:7-8; Pr 6:35; 13:8; Hos 13:14).
Jesus as (Mt 20:28; Mk 10:45; 1Ti 2:5-6; Heb 9:15).
Figurative (Job 33:24; Isa 35:10; 51:10).
See Jesus the Christ, Redeemer; Savior, Saviour; Redemption.

RAPACITY Of the wicked (Lk 11:39; 20:14, 47; Jn 10:12; Ac 20:29; Gal 5:15; Jas 4:2; 1Pe 5:8). *See Greed; Wicked.*

RAPE Law imposes death penalty for (Dt 22:25-27). Captives afflicted with (Isa 13:16; La 5:11; Zec 14:2).
Instances of: Dinah by Shechem (Ge 34:1-2). The servant of a Levite by Benjamites; tribe of Benjamin nearly exterminated by the army of the other tribes as punishment (Jdg 19:22-30; 20:35). Tamar by Amnon; avenged in the death of Amnon at the hand of Absalom, Tamar's brother (2Sa 13:6-29, 32-33).

RAPHA, RAPHAH (possibly *one healed*).
1. Son of Benjamin (1Ch 8:2).
2. A descendant of Jonathan also called Rephaiah (1Ch 9:43) and Raphah (1Ch 8:37). *See Rephaiah, 4.*
3. An ancestor of certain Philistine warriors (2Sa 21:16, 20, 22; 1Ch 20:4, 6, 8). *See Rephaites.*

RAPHU (*healed*). The father of Palti, who was sent from the tribe of Benjamin to spy out the land of Canaan (Nu 13:9).

RAPTURE Theological term not used in the Bible. The imminent translation or removal from earth of the Church at the second coming of Christ (Mt 24:36-42; Mk 13:32; Ac 1:7, 11; 1Co 15:50-52; 1Th 4:14-18; Tit 2:13; 1Pe 3:12; Rev 1:7). Includes both living and dead (1Co 15:50-52; Php 3:20-21; 1Th 4:13-17; 1Jn 3:2). Followed by the marriage of the Church to Christ (Mt 25:1-10; 2Co 11:2; Eph 5:23, 32; Rev 19:6-9), believers being rewarded (Mt 25:19; 1Co 3:12-15; 2Co 5:10; 2Ti 4:8; 1Pe 5:2).
See Second Coming of Christ, The.

RAS SHAMRA (*fennel mound*). The modern name of the mound marking the site of the ancient city of Ugarit, located on the Syrian coast opposite the island of Cyprus; an important commercial center; destroyed by Sea Peoples who overran the area c. 1200 B.C.; reached the peak of prosperity in 1500-1200 B.C. Several hundred clay tablets, forming part of a scribal library, were found from 1929 through 1936; personal and diplomatic correspondence; business, legal, and governmental records; veterinary texts, and most importantly, religious literature. These throw a great deal of light upon Canaanite religion and culture, and Hebrew literary style; they show striking similarities between Canaanite and Hebrew systems of worship. They clarify our knowledge of the world in which Israel developed. *See Texts, Ancient Near Eastern Non-Biblical Texts Relating to the Old Testament.*

RASH Regulations for determining whether clean or unclean (Lev 13-14). *See Disease.*

RASHNESS (Ps 116:11; Pr 19:2). Admonitions against (Pr 25:8; Ecc 5:2; 7:9). Folly of (Pr 14:29; 29:20). Leads to poverty (Pr 21:5).

Instances of:
Moses, in slaying the Egyptian (Ex 2:11-12; Ac 7:24-25), when he struck the rock (Nu 20:10-12). Jephthah's vow (Jdg 11:31-39). Israel's vow to destroy the Benjamites (Jdg 21:2-23). Uzzah, in steadying the ark (2Sa 6:6-7). David, in his generosity to Ziba (2Sa 16:4, w 19:26-29). Rehoboam, in forsaking the counsel of the old men (1Ki 12:8-15). Josiah, in fighting against Neco (2Ch 35:20-24). Naaman, in refusing to wash in the Jordan (2Ki 5:11-12).
Peter, in cutting off the ear of Malchus (Mt 26:51; Mk 14:47; Lk 22:50). James and John, in desiring to call down fire on the Samaritans (Lk 9:54). Paul, in persisting to go to Jerusalem against the repeated admonitions of the Holy Spirit (Ac 21:4, 10-15). The centurion, in rejecting Paul's counsel (Ac 27:11).

RAT(S) Forbidden as food (Lev 11:29), used as food (Isa 66:17). Images of (1Sa 6:4-5, 11, 18).

RAVEN (*crow, raven*). A black carnivorous bird (Pr 30:17; SS 5:11). Forbidden as food (Lev 11:15; Dt 14:14). Preserved by Noah in the ark (Ge 8:7). Fed Elijah (1Ki 17:4-6). Cared for by divine providence (Lk 12:24).

RAVISHMENT *See Rape.*

RAZOR (*any instrument of iron*). Priests of Israel were not permitted to cut their beard (Lev 21:5). Nazirites could not use the razor as long as they were under vows (Nu 6:5).

READING Taught (Dt 6:9; 11:20).

READINGS, SELECT
Judah's Defense (Ge 44:18-34). Joseph Revealing His Identity (Ge 45:1-15). The Deliverance of the Israelites From Pharaoh (Ex 14:5-30). Song of Moses When Pharaoh and His Army Were Overthrown (Ex 15:1-19). David's Lament Over Absalom (2Sa 18:19-33). Lights and Shadows (Ru 1:1-22). Elijah's Miraculous Preservation (1Ki 17:1-16). Elisha and the Widow's Oil (2Ki 4:1-7). Naaman the Leper (2Ki 5:1-14). Esther's Triumph (Est 4:1-17; 7:1-10).
The Brevity of Life (Job 14:1-10). Nature's Testimony (Job 28:1-28). God's Challenge to Job (Job 38). The Beasts of the Field (Job 39).

The Righteous and the Wicked in Contrast (Ps 1). The Triumphant King (Ps 2). Mankind in Nature (Ps 8). Mankind in Extremity (Ps 18:1-19). Confidence in God (Ps 23). The King of Glory (Ps 24). The Glory of God (Ps 29). Our Refuge (Ps 46). The Majesty of God (Ps 77:13-20). The Joy of the Righteous (Ps 84). The State of the Glory (Ps 91). The New Song (Ps 98). The Majesty and Providence of God (Ps 104). In Captivity (Ps 137). The Omnipresence of God (Ps 139). Old Age (Ecc 12:1-7).
Christ's Kingdom Foreshadowed (Isa 35:1-10). The Omnipotence and Incomparableness of God (Isa 40:1-30). The Wrath of God (Am 9:1-6). The Majesty of God (Hab 3:3-13).
Mary's Magnificat (Lk 1:46-56). The Prophetic Blessing of Zechariah (Lk 1:67-80). The Beatitudes (Mt 5:1-16). God's Providence (Mt 6:26-34). Wise and Foolish Builders (Mt 7:21-27). The Good Samaritan (Lk 10:25-37). The Prodigal Son (Lk 15:11-32). The Raising of Lazarus (Jn 11:1-45). The Betrayal (Lk 22:47-62). The Resurrection (Lk 24:1-12).
Peter at Pentecost (Ac 2:1-36). Stephen's Defense (Ac 7). Paul and Silas in Prison (Ac 16:16-40). Paul on Mars' Hill (Ac 17:22-31). Paul Before Felix (Ac 24:1-27). Paul Before Agrippa (Ac 26:1-32). Love (1Co 13). The New Heaven and the New Earth (Rev 21:1-7). The River of Life (Rev 22:1-21).

REAIA *See Reaiah, 2.*

REAIAH (*Yahweh has seen*).
1. A man of Judah, son of Shobal (1Ch 4:2). Apparently called Haroeh (1Ch 2:52).
2. Son of Micah, a Reubenite (1Ch 5:5).
3. Ancestor of a family that returned to Jerusalem from captivity in Babylon (Ezr 2:47; Ne 7:50).

REAPING In ancient times done either by pulling up grain by roots or cutting with a sickle. The stalks are then bound into bundles and taken to threshing floor (Ps 129:7).
Laws concerning gleaning at the time of reaping (Lev 19:9-10; 23:22; Dt 24:19-20).
Figurative (Ps 126:6; Hos 10:12-13; Jn 4:35-38), of deeds that produce own harvest (Pr 22:8; Hos 8:7; 1Co 9:11; Gal 6:7-8).

REASONING With God (Job 13:3, 17-28). God reasons with people (Ex 4:11; 20:5, 11; Isa 1:18; 5:3-4; 43:26; Hos 4:1; Mic 6:2).
Natural understanding (Da 4:36). To be applied to religion (1Co 10:15; 1Pe 3:15). Not a sufficient guide in human affairs (1Co 12:8; Pr 3:5; 14:12). Of the Pharisees (Lk 5:21-22; 20:5). Of Paul from the Scriptures (Ac 17:2; 18:4, 19; 24:25). The gospel cannot be explained by human wisdom (1Co 1:18-2:14).
See Investigation; Philosophy; Wisdom.

REBA (*fourth part*). A king of Midian. Slain by the Israelites (Nu 31:8; Jos 13:21).

REBECCA *See Rebekah.*

REBEKAH (possibly *choice calf*). Daughter of Bethuel, grand-niece of Abraham (Ge 22:20-23). Becomes Isaac's wife (Ge 24:15-67; 25:20). Mother of Esau and Jacob (Ge 25:21-28; Ro 9:10). Passes as Isaac's sister (Ge 26:6-11). Displeased with Esau's wives (Ge 26:34-35). Prompts Jacob to deceive Isaac (Ge 27:5-29). Sends Jacob to Laban (Ge 27:42-46). Burial place of (Ge 49:31).

REBELLION Treasonable (Pr 17:11).
Instances of: Absalom (2Sa 15-18). Sheba (2Sa 20). Revolt of the ten tribes (1Ki 12:16-20; 2Ch 10; 13:5-12).
See Sin.

REBUKE Cain rebukes God (Ge 4:13-14). Pharaoh rebukes Abraham for calling his wife his sister (Ge 12:18-19). Abimelech rebukes Abraham for a like offense (Ge 20:9-10). Abimelech rebukes Isaac for similar conduct (Ge 26:9-10). Isaac and Laban rebuke each other (Ge 31:26-42). Jacob rebukes Simeon and Levi for killing Hamor and Shechem (Ge 34:30). Reuben rebukes his brothers for their treatment of Joseph (Ge 42:22). Israelites rebuke Moses and tempt God (Ex 17:7). Deborah rebukes Israel in her poem (Jdg 5:16-23). David rebukes Joab for killing Abner (2Sa 3:28-31). Joab rebukes David for lamenting the death of Absalom (2Sa 19:5-7).
Jesus rebukes his disciples because of their unbelief (Mt 8:26; 14:31; 16:8-11; 17:17; Mk 4:40; Lk 8:25), for slowness of heart (Mt 15:16; 16:8-9, 11; Mk 7:18; Lk 24:25; Jn 14:9), for sleeping in Gethsemane (Mt 26:40; Mk 14:27), for forbidding children to be brought to him (Mt 19:14; Mk 10:14; Lk 18:16).
David prays to escape Yahweh's rebuke (Ps 6:1; 38:1). Do not rebuke a mocker (Pr 9:8), an older man (1Ti 5:1).

RECAB (probably *rider* or *horseman*, from *to mount, ride*).
1. Son of Rimmon. Murders Ish-Bosheth, son of Saul; put to death by David (2Sa 4:5-12).
2. Father of Jehonadab (2Ki 10:15, 23; 1Ch 2:55; Jer 35:6, 8, 16, 19). Ancestor of the Recabites (Jer 35).
3. Father of Malkijah (Ne 3:14).

RECABITE(S) A family of Kenites descended from Recab, through Jonadab (1Ch 2:55; Jer 35:6). Commanded by Jonadab to drink no wine (Jer 35:6); perpetuation of the family promised as a reward (Jer 35).
See Abstinence; Nazirite(s).

RECAH Unknown place in tribe of Judah (1Ch 4:12).

RECHAB *See Recab.*

RECHABITE(S) *See Recabite(s).*

RECHAH *See Recah.*

RECIPROCITY Returning good for good (Ro 15:27; 1Co 9:11; Gal 6:6). *See One Another.*

RECONCILIATION

Between People:
(Mt 5:23-26). Between Esau and Jacob (Ge 33:4, 11). Between Saul and David (1Sa 19:7). Between Pilate and Herod (Lk 23:12).

Between God and People:
Through atonement of animal sacrifices (Lev 8:15; Eze 45:15). After the seventy weeks of Daniel's vision (Da 9:24).
Through Christ (Ro 5:1, 10; 11:15; 2Co 5:18-21; Eph 2:15-18; Col 1:20-22; Heb 2:17).
See Atonement; Jesus the Christ, Mission of; Propitiation; Redemption.

RECONNAISSANCE
Of Jericho (Jos 2:1-24), Bethel (Jdg 1:23), Laish (Jdg 18:2-10). *See Spies.*

RECORDER
See Occupations and Professions.

RECREATION
See Rest.

RED
Bloodlike or blood-red color (Ex 25:5; 26:14; 35:7; Zec 1:8; Rev 6:4).

RED HEIFER
Ashes of red heifer were used for removal of certain types of ceremonial uncleanness (Nu 19:9).

RED KITE
A carnivorous bird, unclean for food (Dt 14:13).

RED SEA
"Sea of Reeds" in NIV ftns. The locusts that devastated Egypt destroyed in (Ex 10:19). Israelites cross; Pharaoh and his army drowned in (Ex 14; 15:1, 4, 11, 19; Nu 33:8; Dt 11:4; Jos 2:10; 4:23; 24:6-7; Jdg 11:16; 2Sa 22:16; Ne 9:9-11; Ps 66:6; 78:13, 53; 106:7-11, 22; 136:13-15; Isa 43:16-17; Ac 7:36; 1Co 10:1-2; Heb 11:29). Israelites camp by (Ex 14:2, 9; Nu 14:25; 21:4; 33:10-11; Dt 1:40; 2:1-3). Boundary of the promised land (Ex 23:31). Solomon builds ships on (1Ki 9:26).

REDEEMED, THE
(Isa 35:9; 51:11; Mt 8:11; Rev 5:9; 7:9; 14:4; 19:6).

REDEEMER
See Jesus the Christ, Savior; Redemption.

REDEMPTION
(*to tear loose; a ransom*). Deliverance from the enslavement of sin and release to a new freedom by the sacrifice of the Redeemer, Jesus Christ. The death of Christ is the redemptive price. The word contains both the ideas of deliverance and the price of that deliverance, or ransom (Ro 3:24; Gal 3:13; Eph 1:7; 1Pe 1:18-19).

Of Person or Property:
(Ex 13:13; Lev 25:25-34; 27:2-33; Ro 4:3-10). Redemption money paid to priests (Nu 3:46-51). Of the firstborn (Ex 13:13; 34:20; Lev 27:27; Nu 3:40-51; 18:15-17).

Of Land:
(Lev 27:19-20; Jer 32:7). In Hebrew society, any land that was forfeited through economic distress could be redeemed by the nearest of kin. If not so redeemed, it returned to its original owner in the Year of Jubilee (Lev 25:24-34).

Of Our Souls:
(Ps 111:9; 130:7). Through Christ (Mt 20:28; Mk 10:45; Lk 2:38; Ac 20:28; Ro 3:24-26; 1Co 1:30; 6:20; 7:23; Gal 1:4; 2:20; 4:4-5; Eph 1:7; 5:2; Col 1:14, 20-22; 1Ti 2:6; Tit 2:14; Heb 9:12, 15; 1Pe 1:18-19; Rev 5:9-10).
See Atonement; Ransom; Redeemer.

REED
A water plant (Isa 19:6-7; 35:7; Jer 51:32). Used as a measuring device of six cubits (Eze 40:3-8; 41:8; 42:16-19; 45:1; Rev 11:1; 21:15-16). Mockingly given to Jesus as a symbol of royalty (Mt 27:29). Jesus struck with (Mt 27:30; Mk 15:19).
Figurative of weakness (1Ki 14:15; 2Ki 18:21; Isa 36:6; 42:3; Eze 29:6; Mt 11:7; 12:20).

REEDS, SEA OF
See Red Sea.

REELAIAH
A returned captive from Babylon (Ezr 2:2).

REFINING
The process of eliminating by fire the dross of metals. Of gold (1Ch 28:18). Of silver (1Ch 29:4). Of wine (Isa 25:6).
Figurative: Of the corrective judgments of God (Isa 1:25; 48:10; Jer 9:7; Zec 13:9; Mal 3:2-3). Of the purity of the word of God (Ps 18:30; 119:140).

REFUGE, CITIES OF
See Cities of Refuge.

REFUGEE SLAVES
Laws concerning (Dt 23:15-16). Onesimus (Phm 1). *See Servant.*

REGEM
(*friend*). Son of Jahdai (1Ch 2:47).

REGEM-MELECH
(*friend of king*, possibly *chief of troops of the king*). A captive sent as a messenger from the Jews in Babylon to Jerusalem (Zec 7:2).

REGENCY
See Deputy.

REGENERATION
The new birth, the inner recreating of fallen human nature by the gracious working of the Holy Spirit. It changes human disposition from godlessness, lawlessness, rebellion, self-seeking, and unbelief to a desire to love and serve God.
Necessity of (Jer 13:23; Mt 12:33-35; 18:3; Mk 10:15; Lk 18:17; Jn 3:3, 5; Tit 3:5-6).
Parables of (Mt 13:23, 33; Mk 4:20, 26-29; Lk 13:21).

Also Called:
Born again or born from above (Jn 3:3-8; 1Pe 1:2-3, 22-23). Born of God (Jn 1:12-13, 16; Jas 1:18; 1Jn 2:27, 29; 3:9, 14; 4:7; 5:1, 4-5, 11-12, 18). Born by the Spirit (Jn 3:5-6; Gal 4:29), through the Holy Spirit (Eze 12:10; Jn 3:5-8; 1Co 12:13; 2Th 2:13; 1Pe 1:2-3, 22-23).
Circumcision of the heart (Dt 29:4; 30:6; Eze 44:7, 9; Ro 2:28; Col 2:11-13). Change of heart (Ps 51:2, 7, 10; Jer 24:7; 31:33-34

w Heb 8:10-11; Jer 32:28-40; Eze 11:19-20; 18:31; 36:26-27, 29; Ro 12:2). New creature (2Co 5:17; Gal 6:15; Eph 4:22-24; Col 3:9-10). Spiritual cleansing (Jn 15:3; Ac 15:9; 1Co 6:11). Spiritual illumination (Jn 6:44-45; 8:12; Ac 26:18; 1Co 2:11-16; 2Co 4:6; Eph 5:14; Heb 10:16). To make spiritually alive (Heb 6:21). Spiritual resurrection (Jn 5:24; Ro 6:3-23; 8:2-4; Gal 2:20).

Other Scriptures Related to:
(1Ki 8:58; Ps 36:9; 65:3; 68:18; 110:3; Pr 4:23; 12:28; 14:27; Isa 1:16-17, 25; 4:4; 12:3; 26:12; 32:3-4, 15, 17; 35:5-6; 42:16; 43:7; 44:3-5; 55:1-3; Jer 13:13-14; 24:7; 31:3; 33:6; Eze 16:9; Lk 1:16-17; Jn 4:10, 14; 10:9-10; 13:8; 17:2; Ac 2:38, 47; 3:26; 11:17, 21; 16:14; Ro 7:6, 24; 15:16; 1Co 1:24, 30; 3:6-7, 9; 15:10; 2Co 1:21-22; 3:3, 18; Php 1:6; Heb 4:12; Jas 5:19-20; 1Pe 2:3, 9; 2Pe 1:3-4).
See Atonement; Conversion; Reconciliation; Redemption; Righteous; Salvation; Sanctification; Sin, Forgiveness of.

REGICIDE
(*murder of a king.*) Of Ehud (Jdg 3:16-23). Of Saul (2Sa 1:16). Of Ish-Bosheth (2Sa 4:5-8). Of Nadab (1Ki 15:25-30). Of Elah (1Ki 16:9-11). Of Joram (2Ki 9:24). Of Ahaziah (2Ki 9:27). Of Joash (1Ki 12:20-21). Of Amaziah (2Ki 14:19-20). Of Zechariah (2Ki 15:10). Of Shallum (2Ki 15:14). Of Pekahiah (2Ki 15:25). Of Pekah (2Ki 15:30). Of Sennacherib (2Ki 19:36-37; Isa 37:37-38).
See Homicide.

REGISTRATION
Of citizens (Isa 4:3). *See Census.*

REHABIAH
(*Yahweh has enlarged*). Son of Eliezer (1Ch 23:17; 24:21; 26:25).

REHOB
(*broad, wide [place, market]*).
1. Father of Hadadezer, king of Zobah (2Sa 8:3, 12).
2. A Levite who sealed the covenant with Nehemiah (Ne 10:11).
3. A town in northern Israel. The limit of the investigation made by the twelve spies (Nu 13:21). Possessed by the Syrians (2Sa 10:6, 8). Called Beth Rehob (2Sa 10:6).
4. A town of Asher (Jos 19:28).
5. A Levitical city of Asher (Jos 19:30; 21:31; 1Ch 6:75). Canaanites not driven from (Jdg 1:31).

REHOBOAM
(*[my] people will enlarge, expand*). Successor to Solomon as king (1Ki 11:43; 2Ch 9:31). Refuses to reform abuses (1Ki 12:1-15; 2Ch 10:1-15). Ten tribes, under the leadership of Jeroboam, who successfully revolt from (1Ki 12:16-24; 2Ch 10:16-19; 11:1-4). Builds fortified cities; is temporarily prosperous (2Ch 11:5-23). Invaded by the king of Egypt and despoiled (1Ki 14:25-28; 2Ch 12:1-12). Death of (1Ki 14:31; 2Ch 12:16). Genealogy and descendants of (1Ch 3; Mt 1:7).

REHOBOTH
(*broad, wide [places, markets]*).
1. A city built by Asshur (Ge 10:11).
2. A city of the Edomites (Ge 36:37; 1Ch 1:48).
3. The name given to a well dug by Isaac (Ge 26:22).

REHUM
(*[he] is compassionate*).
1. A captive who returned to Jerusalem from Babylon (Ezr 2:2). Called Nehum (Ne 7:7).
2. An official who wrote a letter to Artaxerxes, influencing him against the Jews (Ezr 4:8-9, 17, 23).
3. A Levite who repaired part of the wall of Jerusalem (Ne 3:17).
4. A Jew of the Exile who signed the covenant with Nehemiah (Ne 10:25).
5. A priest who returned to Jerusalem from the Captivity in Babylon (Ne 12:3).

REI
(*friendly* or *[my] friend*). An Israelite loyal to David at the time of the usurpation of Adonijah (1Ki 1:8).

REINS
KJV word for internal parts; kidneys as the seat of the emotions (Ps 7:9; 26:2; Jer 17:10; Job 19:27). *See Heart; Kidney.*

REJECTION
Of God (1Sa 8:7; 10:19; 2Ki 17:15; Lk 7:30). *See God, Rejected.*
Of Israel by God (Nu 14:12, 26-37; 2Ki 17:20; Jer 6:30; 7:29; 14:19; La 5:22). Of Saul by God (1Sa 15:23, 26).
Of Jesus. *See Jesus the Christ, Rejected.*

REKEM
(*friendship*).
1. A king of the Midianites, slain by the Israelites (Nu 31:8; Jos 13:21).
2. A son of Hebron (1Ch 2:43-44).
3. A city in Benjamin (Jos 18:27).

RELEASE
Year of: *See Jubilee; Sabbatic Year.*

RELENT
God relents, or changes his mind, in response to change in his people (Jer 18:5-10; 26:1-6, 12-13, 17-19). In response to the intercession of Moses, when Israel sinned with the golden calf (Ex 32:11-14); of Amos (Am 7:1-6). Because of his covenant love (Ps 106:44-45; Joel 2:13-14; Jnh 3:8-4:2).
Requests for God to relent (Job 6:29; Ps 90:13-16).
God will not relent when his people deserve his judgment (Jer 4:27-28; Eze 24:14).
See Repentance.

RELIGION

False: (Dt 32:31-33).
See Idolatry; Intolerance; Teachers, False.

Family: *See Family.*

National:
Supported by taxes (Ex 30:11-16; 38:26). Priests supported by the state (1Ki 18:19; 2Ch 11:13-15). Subverted by Jeroboam (1Ki 12:26-33; 2Ch 11:13-15). Idolatrous established by Jeroboam (1Ki 12:26-33).

Natural:
(Job 12:7-16; 37:1-24; Ps 8:1-9; 19:1-6; Ac 14:17; 17:23-28; Ro 1:18-20; 10:16-18). *See Revivals.*

True, As Presented By:
Jesus (Mt 22:36-40). In the "Sermon on the Mount": True blessedness (Mt 5:2-16), fulfillment of the law (Mt 5:17-48), "acts of righteousness" (Mt 6:1-18), service and treasure (Mt 6:19-21), judgment (Mt 7:1-6), asking (Mt 7:7-11), the "golden rule" (Mt 7:12), wholehearted commitment to God (Mt 7:13-29; Mt 22:26-35).
Paul (Ro 8:18; 10:1-13; 12:1-21; 1Co 13:1-13; Gal 5:22-25; 1Th 5:23). James (Jas 1:27; 2:8-26). Peter (1Pe 2:5-9). Jude (Jude 20-21).
See Blessings, Spiritual; Commandments and Statutes, Of God; Duty; Graces; Regeneration; Repentance; Sanctification; Sin, Forgiveness of.

Instances of Properly Religious Persons:
Abel (Ge 4:4-8; Heb 11:4). Noah (Ge 6-9). Abraham (Ge 12:1-8; 15; 17; 18:22-33). Jacob (Ge 28:10-22; 32:24-32). Moses (Ex 3:2-22; Dt 32-32). Jethro (Ex 18:12). Joshua (Jos 1). Gideon (Jdg 6-7). Samuel (1Sa 3). David. *See Psalms.* Solomon (1Ki 5:3-5; 2Ch 6). Jehu (2Ki 10:16-30). Hezekiah (2Ki 18:3-7; 19:14-19). Jehoshaphat (2Ch 17:3-9; 19:20). Jabez (1Ch 4:9-10). Asa (2Ch 14-15). Josiah (2Ki 22-23). Daniel (Da 6:4-22). The three Hebrews (Da 3). Zechariah (Lk 1:13, 67-79). Simeon (Lk 2:25-35). Anna the prophetess (Lk 2:36-37). The centurion (Lk 7:1-10). Cornelius (Ac 10). Eunice and Lois (2Ti 1:5).
See for additional instances John, Paul, Peter, Simon, Stephen, and other apostles and disciples, also each of the prophets.

RELIGIOUS

Coercion:
(Ex 22:20; 2Ch 15:12-15; Da 3:2-6; 6:26-27). *See Intolerance.*

Revivals:
(Zec 8:20-23). Prayer for (Hab 3:2). Prophecies concerning (Isa 32:15; Joel 2:28; Mic 4:1-8). *See Revivals.*

Testimony:
(Ps 18:49; 22:22; 26:12; 34:8-9; Isa 45:24; 1Co 13:1; Rev 12:11). *See Testimony, Religious.*

REMALIAH
(*Yahweh has adorned*). Father of Pekah, king of Israel (2Ki 15:25, 27, 30; 16:1, 5; 2Ch 28:6; Isa 7:1, 4; 8:6).

REMETH
(*heights*). A city in Issachar (Jos 19:17-21), probably, Ramoth (1Ch 6:73), and Jarmuth (Jos 21:29).

REMMON
See Rimmon, 2.

REMMON-METHOAR
See Rimmon, 3.

REMNANT
1. People who survived political or military crises (Jos 12:4; 13:12).
2. Spiritual core of Israel who would survive God's judgment and become the seed of the new people of God (Isa 10:20-23; 11:11-12; Jer 32:38-39; Zep 3:13; Zec 8:12).

REMORSE
(Pr 1:25-27). Of the promiscuous (Pr 5:7-13). Of the lost (Lk 13:28). Of the wicked (Pr 28:1; Isa 2:19; 57:20-21; Eze 7:16-18, 25-26). Of Israelites (Eze 33:10). Of believers (1Jn 3:20).
Instances of: David (Ps 31:10; 38:2-6; 51:1-19). Isaiah (Isa 6:5). Jeremiah (La 1:20). Peter (Mt 26:75). Judas (Mt 27:3-5). The Jews (Ac 2:37). Paul (Ac 9:6).
See Conviction, of Sin; Penitent; Repentance; Sin, Confession of.

REMPHAN
See Rephan.

RENDING
Of garments, a token of affliction (Ge 37:29, 34; 44:13; Nu 14:6; Jdg 11:35; 2Sa 1:2, 11; 3:31; 13:19, 31; 15:32; 2Ki 2:12; 5:8; 6:30; 11:14; 19:1; Ezr 9:3, 5; Job 1:20; 2:12; Isa 36:22; 37:1; Jer 41:5; Mt 26:65; Ac 14:14).
Figurative (Joel 2:13). Symbol of dividing of a kingdom (1Sa 15:27-28).

RENTING
Land (Mt 21:33-41; Lk 20:9-16). Houses (Ac 28:30).

RENUNCIATION
(Php 3:7-8). Of self for others, exemplified, by Moses (Ex 32:32), Jesus (Php 2:7), Paul (Ro 9:3; 2Co 13:7). Of self for Christ (Mt 16:25; Lk 14:26-33; 17:33; Jn 12:25). Of business for Christ (Mt 4:20; 9:9; Mk 1:18-20; 2:14; Lk 5:27-28).
Of possessions for Christ (Mt 19:21-29; Mk 10:21-30; Lk 18:22-30). Of one's all for Christ, illustrated by parable (Mt 13:44-46).
Of the will, to the Father, exemplified by Jesus (Mk 14:36; Lk 22:42; Jn 5:30; 6:38).
See Self-Denial.

REPENTANCE
(Ps 34:14, 18; Isa 22:12).

Exhortations to:
(Pr 1:22-23; Jer 6:16-18; 7:3; 26:3; Hos 6:1; 14:1-3; Am 5:4-6; Mt 3:2).
Commanded (Dt 32:29; 2Ch 30:6-9; Job 36:10; Isa 22:12; 31:6; 44:22; 55:6-7; Jer 3:4, 12-14, 19, 22; 18:11; 25:5-6; 26:13; 35:15; Eze 12:1-5; 14:6; 18:30-32; 33:10-12, 14-16, 19; Da 4:27; Hos 10:12; 14:1-2; Joel 1:14; 2:12-13, 15-17; Am 4:12; Jnh 3:8-9; Hag 1:7; Zec 1:3; Mt 4:17; Mk 1:4, 15; 6:12; Lk 3:3; Ac 2:38; 3:19; 8:22; 17:30; Rev 2:5, 16; 3:2-3, 19).

Source:
Gift of God (2Ti 2:25). Gift of Christ (Ac 5:31). Goodness of God leads to (Ro 2:4). Tribulation leads to (Dt 4:30; 30:1-3; 1Ki 8:33-50; 2Ch 6:36-39; Job 34:31-32).

Condition:
Of forgiveness (Lev 26:40-42; Dt 4:29-31; 30:1-3, 8; 1Ki 8:33-50; 2Ch 6:36-39; 7:14; Ne 1:9; Job 11:13-15; 22:23; Ps 34:18; Pr 28:13; Isa 55:7; Jer 3:4, 12-14; 18:7-8; 36:3; Eze 18:21-23, 27-28, 30-31; Am 5:6; Mal 3:7; Mt 5:4; Lk 13:1-5; 1Jn 1:9). Of divine favor (Lev 26:40-42; 2Ch 7:14; Isa 57:15).

Foretold:
Of Israel (Jer 50:4-5; Eze 11:18-20; Hos 3:5; Zec 12:10). Universal (Ps 22:27; Ro 14:11).

Rewards of:
(Isa 59:20; Pr 1:23; Jer 7:3, 5, 7; 24:7; Eze 18:21-23, 27-28).

Preached by:
John the Baptist (Mt 3:2, 7-8; Mk 1:4, 15; Lk 3:3). Jesus (Mt 4:17; Mk 1:15; Lk 5:32). Peter (Ac 2:38, 40; 3:19; 8:22). Paul (Ac 17:30; 20:21; 26:20). The apostles (Mk 6:12).
To be preached to all nations (Lk 24:47). Joy in heaven over (Lk 15:1-10).
Unavailing, to Israel (Nu 14:39-45), to Esau (Heb 12:16-17).

Attributed to God:
God relents, or changes his mind, in response to change in his people (Ge 6:6-7; Ex 32:14; Dt 32:36; Jdg 2:18; 1Sa 15:11, 35; 2Sa 24:16; 1Ch 21:15; Ps 106:45; 110:4; 135:14; Jer 15:6; 18:1-10; 26:3; 42:10; Joel 2:13; Am 7:3, 6; Jnh 3:9-10). *See Relent.*
God will not repent (Nu 23:19; 1Sa 15:29; Ps 110:4; Ro 11:29).

Exemplified:
By Job (Job 7:20-21; 9:20; 13:23; 40:4; 42:5-6), David (Ps 32:5; 38:3-4, 18; 40:12; 41:4; 51:1-4, 7-17), the Israelites (Nu 21:7; 2Ch 29:6; Jer 3:21-22, 25; 14:7-9, 20; 31:18-19; La 3:40-41), Daniel for the Jews (Da 9:5-7; 10:12), the prodigal son (Lk 15:17-20).

Instances of:
Joseph's brothers, for their ill treatment of Joseph (Ge 42:21; 50:17-18). Pharaoh, for his hardness of heart (Ex 9:27; 10:16-17). Balaam, for his spiritual blindness (Nu 22:34, w 22:24-35). Israelites, for worshiping the golden calf (Ex 33:3-4), for their murmuring on account of the lack of bread and water, when the plague of fiery serpents came upon them (Nu 21:4-7), when rebuked by an angel for not expelling the Canaanites (Jdg 2:1-5), for their idolatry, when afflicted by the Philistines (Jdg 10:6-16; 1Sa 7:3-6), for asking for a king (1Sa 12:16-20), in the time of Asa, under the preaching of Azariah (2Ch 15:1-15), under the preaching of Oded (2Ch 28:9-15), under the influence of Hezekiah (2Ch 30:11). Achan, for his theft (Jos 7:19-21). Saul, at the reproof of Samuel for not destroying the Amalekites (1Sa 15:24, w 15:6-11). Job (Job 42:6).
David, at the rebuke of Nathan, the prophet (2Sa 12:11, 13, w 12:7-14; Ps 32:5; 38:3-4, 18; 40:12; 41:4; 51:1-4, 7-17), for numbering Israel (2Sa 24:10, 17). The psalmist (Ps 106:6; 119:59-60, 176; 130:1-3). *See Psalms, Topically Arranged.*
Rehoboam, when his kingdom was invaded, and Jerusalem besieged (2Ch 12:1-12). Isaiah (Isa 6:5). Hezekiah, for his pride (Isa 38:15), at the time of his sickness (2Ch 32:26), when reproved by the prophet Micah (Jer 26:18-19). Ahab, when reproved by Elijah for his idolatry (1Ki 21:27). Jehoahaz (2Ki 13:4). Josiah, when he heard the law which had been discovered in the temple (2Ki 22:11-20). Manasseh, when he was carried captive to Babylon by the king of Assyria (2Ch 33:12-13). Jonah, after his punishment (Jnh 2:2-9). The Ninevites, at the preaching of Jonah (Jnh 3:5, 9-10).
The Jews of the Exile, at the dedication of the temple (Ezr 6:21; 9:4, 6, 10, 13-14), for their idolatrous marriages (Ezr 10), for their oppressive usury (Ne 5:1-13), after hearing the law expounded by Ezra (Ne 9:1-3), under the preaching of Haggai (Hag 1).
The Jews under the preaching of John the Baptist (Mt 3:6). The woman who anointed Jesus with oil (Lk 7:37-48). The disobedient son (Mt 21:29). The prodigal son (Lk 15:17-21). The tax collector (Lk 18:13). Peter, of his denial of Jesus (Mt 26:75; Mk 14:72; Lk 22:62). The Ephesians, under the preaching of Paul (Ac 19:18).
See Conviction, of Sin; Penitence; Remorse; Sin, Confession of; Sin, Forgiveness of.

REPETITION
In Prayers: *See Babbling; Prayer, Persistence in.*

REPHAEL
(*God [El] heals*). A gatekeeper of the temple in the time of David (1Ch 26:7).

REPHAH
(possibly *rich* IDB; *easy [life]* KB). A grandson of Ephraim (1Ch 7:25).

REPHAIAH
(*Yahweh heals*).
1. A descendant of David (1Ch 3:21).
2. A Simeonite captain (1Ch 4:42).
3. Son of Tola, of the tribe of Issachar (1Ch 7:2).
4. A descendant of Jonathan (1Ch 9:43). Also called Raphah (1Ch 8:37).
5. Governor over half of Jerusalem in the time of Nehemiah (Ne 3:9).

REPHAIM
See Rephaites.

REPHAIM, VALLEY OF
(*sunken, powerless ones [giants]* BDB; possibly *shades, ghosts of the dead [giants]* KB). Fertile plain S of Jerusalem, three miles from Bethlehem (Jos 15:8; 18:16; 2Sa 5:18, 22; 23:13; 1Ch 11:15; 14:9; Isa 17:4-5).

REPHAITES
(*mighty*). Giant people who lived in Canaan even before Abraham's time (Ge 14:5; 15:20; Dt 2:11, 20; 3:11, 13; Jos 12:4; 13:12; 17:15; 1Ch 20:4). *See Giants.*

REPHAN
A pagan god noted in Ac 7:43 quoting the LXX (Am 5:26, ftn). In Am 5:26, the NIV translates the Hebrew word "pedestal," though the ftn offers the proper name "Kaiwan." The Egyptian *repa* and the Assyrian "Kaiwan" both refer to the planet Saturn, which may harmonize the two texts. *See Chiun.*

REPHIDIM
(possibly *supports, rests* BDB; *resting place* KB). Encampment of Israelites in the wilderness; there Moses struck a rock to secure water (Ex 17:1-7; 19:2), battle with Amalekites took place there (Ex 17:8-16).

REPORTS
Majority and minority, of spies (Nu 13:26-33; 14:6-10).

REPROBACY
Admonitions against (2Co 13:5-7; Heb 3:10-12, 17-19; 6:4-9; 12:15-17). Curses denounced against (Dt 28:15-68; 31:17-18; Isa 65:12; Hos 9:12; Mk 3:29; Heb 10:26-31). *See Reprobates.*

REPROBATE
Moral corruption, unfitness, disqualification, disapproved (Ro 1:28; 1Co 9:27). *See Reprobacy; Reprobates.*

REPROBATES
(Jer 6:30; Ro 1:21-32; 2Ti 3:8; 1Jn 5:16; Jude 4-13; Rev 22:4).

Described as:
Men of corrupt minds (2Ti 3:8), vessels of wrath (Ro 9:22). Moral insensibility of (Isa 22:12-14; 28:13; 29:9-12; Mt 13:14-15; 15:14; Ro 11:7-8). Rejected of God (Ps 81:11-12; Pr 1:24-28; Jer 6:30; 7:16; 15:1; Hos 5:6; Mt 15:14; 25:8-13; Lk 13:24-28; 14:24; Jn 10:26; Ro 1:21-26, 28; 2Th 2:10-11; Heb 3:10-12, 17-19; 6:4-8; 10:26-31).
Admonitions against (Heb 12:15-17).

Instances of:
Antediluvians (Ge 6:5-7). Sodomites (Ge 13:13; 19:13; Jude 7). Jannes and Jambres (2Ti 3:8). Eli's house (1Sa 3:14). Saul (1Sa 15:23; 16:14; 18:12; 28:15). Judas (Jn 17:12). Angels (Jude 6). Antichrist (2Th 2:7-12).
In Israel (Nu 14:26-48; Dt 1:42; Isa 6:9-10; Heb 3:10-12, 17-19; Jude 5). In the Church (2Co 13:5-7; Heb 3:10-12, 17-19; 6:4-9; Jude 4-13).
See Obduracy; Reprobacy.

REPRODUCTION
See Propagation.

REPROOF, REPROVE

Commanded:
(Lev 19:17; Ps 141:5; Pr 9:7-8; 10:17; 26:5; Mt 18:15-17; Lk 17:3-4; Eph 5:11; 1Th 5:14, 20; 2Ti 4:2; Tit 1:13; Heb 3:13). Of elders, forbidden (1Ti 5:1-2).

Profitable:
(Pr 13:18; 15:5, 31-32; 27:5-6; 28:23; Ecc 7:5). Wise profit by (Pr 17:10; 19:25; 21:11; 25:12).

Needed in the Church:
(Eph 4:15; Php 3:1; 1Th 5:14; 1Ti 5:1-2, 20; 2Ti 4:2; Tit 1:13; Heb 3:13).

Hated:
(Pr 10:17; 12:1; 15:10, 12; Am 5:10; Jn 7:7; Gal 4:16). By the Israelites (Nu 14:9-10; Jer 26:11). By Ahab (1Ki 18:17; 21:20; 22:8). By Asa (2Ch 16:10). By Herodias (Mk 6:18-19). By people of Nazareth (Lk 4:28-29). Jews (Ac 5:33; 7:54).

Faithfulness in:
Instances of: Moses, of Pharaoh (Ex 10:29; 11:8), of the Israelites (Ex 16:6-7; 32:19-30; Nu 14:41; 20:10; 32:14; Dt 1:12, 26-43; 9:16-24; 29:2-4; 31:27-29; 32:15-18), of Eleazar (Lev 10:16-18), of Korah (Nu 16:9-11). Israelites, of the two-a-one-half tribes (Jos 22:15-20), of the tribe of Benjamin (Jdg 20:12-13).
Samuel, of Saul (1Sa 15:14-35). Jonathan, of Saul (1Sa 19:4-5). Nathan, of David (2Sa 12:1-9). Joab, of David (2Sa 19:1-7; 24:3; 1Ch 21:3). The prophet Gad, of David (2Sa 24:13). Shemaiah, of Rehoboam (2Ch 12:5). A prophet of Judah, of Jeroboam (1Ki 13:1-10; 2Ch 13:8-11). Elijah, of Ahab (1Ki 18:18-21; 21:20-24), of Ahaziah (2Ki 1:3). Micaiah, of Ahab (1Ki 22:14-28). Elisha, of Jehoram (2Ki 3:13-14), of Gehazi (2Ki 5:26), of Hazael (2Ki 8:11-13), of Jeroboam (2Ki 13:19).
Amos, of the Israelites (Am 7:12-17). Isaiah, of Hezekiah (2Ki 20:17). Jehoash, of Jehoiada (2Ch 24:20). Azariah, of Asa (2Ch 15:2), of Uzziah (2Ch 26:17-18). Hanani, of Asa (2Ch 16:7-9). Jehu, of Jehoshaphat (2Ch 19:2). Zechariah, of the princes of Judah (2Ch 24:20). Oded, of the people of Samaria (2Ch 28:9-11). Jeremiah, of the cities of Judah (Jer 26:8-11). Ezra, of the men of Judah and Benjamin (Ezr 10:10). Nehemiah, of the Jews (Ne 5:6-13), of the corruptions in the temple, and of the violation of the Sabbath (Ne 13). Daniel, of Nebuchadnezzar (Da 4:27), of Belshazzar (Da 5:17-24).
Jesus, of the Jews: When Pharisees and Sadducees came to him desiring a sign (Mt 16:1-4; Mk 8:11-12), of the scribes and Pharisees (Mt 23; Lk 11:37-54), of the Pharisees (Lk 16), when they brought the woman to him who was caught in adultery (Jn 8:7).
Jesus, in his parables: Of the king's feast (Lk 14:16-24), of the two sons (Mt 21:28-32), of the vineyard (Mt 21:33-46; Mk 12:1-12; Lk 20:9-20), of the barren fig tree (Lk 13:6-9), the withering of the fig tree (Mt 21:17-20; Mk 11:12-14).
John the Baptist, of the Jews (Mt 3:7-12; Lk 3:7-9), of Herod (Mt 14:3; Mk 6:17; Lk 3:19-20). Peter, of Simon, the sorcerer (Ac 8:20-23). Stephen, of the high priest (Ac 7:51-53). Paul, of Elymas, the sorcerer (Ac 13:9-11), of Ananias, the high priest (Ac 23:3). Paul and Silas, of the magistrates of Philippi (Ac 16:37-40).
See One Another; Reprobacy.

REPTILES
(1Ki 4:33; Ac 10:12; 11:6; Ro 1:23). Adder (Job 20:16). Cobra (Isa 11:8). Chameleon (Lev 11:30). Frog (Ex 8:2). Gecko (Lev 11:30). Lizards (Lev 11:29-30). Serpent (Job 20:14, 16). Skink (Lev 11:30). Snake (Ex 7:9-12). Viper (Ge 49:17; Isa 59:5). *See Animals.*

REPUTATION, GOOD
(Pr 3:4; 22:1; Ecc 7:1). Of Mordecai (Est 9:4). Of overseers (1Ti 3:7). *See Character; Name.*

RESEN
A town founded by Nimrod (Ge 10:8-12), between Nineveh and Calah.

RESERVOIR
A place where water is collected and kept for use when wanted, chiefly in large quantities. Because most of W Asia was subject to periodic droughts, and because of frequent sieges, reservoirs and cisterns were a necessity (2Ch 26:10; 18:31; Ecc 2:6).

RESHEPH
(*flame, flash of fire*). Grandson of Ephraim (1Ch 7:25).

RESIGNATION

Commanded:
(Ps 4:4; 46:10; Lk 21:19; Ro 12:12; Php 2:14; Col 1:10-11; Jas 1:9-10; 4:7; 1Pe 4:12-13, 19). Under chastisement and afflictions (Job 5:17; Pr 3:11; 18:14; Jer 51:50; La 3:39; Mic 6:9; 1Th 3:3; 2Ti 2:3; 4:5; Heb 2:6-12; 12:5, 9; Jas 5:11, 13; 1Pe 1:6). Under bereavement (1Th 4:13-18).

Exemplified by:
Aaron (Lev 10:1-3). The Israelites (Jdg 10:15). Eli (1Sa 3:18). David (2Sa 12:23; 15:26; 16:10-11; 24:14). The Shunammite (2Ki 4:26). Hezekiah (2Ki 20:19; Isa 39:8). Nehemiah (Ne 9:33). By Esther (Est 4:16). Job (Job 1:13-22; 2:9-10; 34:31; Jas 5:11). The psalmists (Ps 39:9; 103:10; 119:75). Jeremiah (Jer 10:19; La 1:18). Daniel (Da 9:14). Micah (Mic 7:9).
Jesus (Mt 26:39; Mk 14:36; Lk 22:42; Jn 18:11). The thief on the cross (Lk 23:40-41). Stephen (Ac 7:59-60). Agabus, Luke, and others when Paul insisted on going to Jerusalem (Ac 21:14). Paul (Ro 5:3-5; 2Co 6:4-10; 7:4; Php 1:20-24; 4:11-12; 2Ti 4:6). Paul and Silas (Ac 16:25). Thessalonian believers (2Th 1:4). Hebrew believers (Heb 10:34).
See Afflicted Believers; Affliction; Afflictions, Made Beneficial.

RESIN
See Aromatic Resin; Gum Resin.

RESPECT
To the aged (Lev 19:32). To rulers (Pr 25:6). To a host (Lk 14:10). To one another (Ro 12:10; Php 2:3; 1Pe 2:17).

RESPECT OF PERSONS
Favoritism (Pr 24:23; 28:21; Jas 2:1-9). God does not have (Dt 10:17; 2Ch 19:7; Job 31:13-15; 34:19; Ac 10:34; 15:9; Ro 2:11-12; 10:12; Eph 6:8-9; Col 3:25; 1Pe 1:17). *See God, Justice of; Justice.*

RESPONSIBILITY
Attempts to shift: Adam (Ge 3:12-13), Eve (Ge 3:13), Sarah (Ge 16:5, w 16:2), Esau (Ge 27:36, w Ge 25:29-34), Aaron (Ex 32:22-24), Saul (1Sa 15:20-21), Pilate (Mt 27:24). Assumed by the Jews for the death of Jesus (Mt 27:25).
Personal (Eze 14:14-20; 18:20, 30; Mt 12:37; Jn 9:41; 15:22-24; Ro 14:12; 1Co 3:8, 13-15; Gal 6:5; 1Pe 4:5; Rev 2:23).
According to privilege (Eze 18:10; 33:1-19; Mt 10:11-15; 11:20-24; 12:41-42; 23:31-35; 25:14-30; Mk 6:11; Lk 9:5; 10:10-15; 11:31-32, 49-51; 13:6-9; 19:12-27; 21:1-4; Jn 3:18-19; 12:48; 15:22, 24; Ac 17:30-31; Ro 12:3, 6-8; Eph 4:7; 1Ti 6:20).
See Judgment, According to Opportunity and Works.

RESPONSIVE RELIGIOUS SERVICE
Reciting the curses of the covenant (Dt 27:14-26). In worship (Ps 48; 118:2-4; 124:1; 129:1). At the dedication of the wall of Jerusalem (Ne 12).

REST
Divine institution for. *See Sabbath.* Commanded (Ex 16:23; 20:10; 23:12; 31:15; 34:21; 35:2; Dt 5:12, 14).
The annual feasts added rest days: First and last days of feasts of Passover and Tabernacles (Ex 12:16; Lev 23:5-8, 39-40; Nu 28:18, 25; 29:12, 35), Pentecost (Nu 28:26), Trumpets (Lev 23:24-25; Nu 29:1), Atonement (Lev 16:29-31; 23:27-28; Nu 29:7). In seventh year (Ex 23:11; Lev 25:1-4). In the Year of Jubilee (Lev 25:11-12).
Recommended by Jesus (Mk 6:31-32; 7:24, w Mt 8:18, 24). Heavenly (2Th 1:7). Spiritual (Mt 11:29; Heb 4:1-11).
See Peace, Spiritual; Resignation.

RESTITUTION
To be made for injury to life, limb, or property (Ex 21:30-36; Lev 24:18), for theft (Ex 22:1-4; Pr 6:30-31; Eze 33:15), for dishonesty (Lev 6:2-5; Nu 5:7; Job 20:18; Eze 33:15; Lk 19:8).

RESTORATION
Of the Jews. *See Israel; Israelites.* Of all things (Ac 3:21; Rev 21:1-5).

RESURRECTION

In the Old Testament:
As understood by Job (Job 14:12-15; 19:25-27). By the psalmists (Ps 16:9-10; 17:15; 49:15). By the prophets (Isa 25:8; 26:19; Da 12:2-3, 13; Hos 13:14).

In the New Testament:
Debated by the Pharisees and Sadducees (Ac 23:6, 8; 24:14-15; 26:6-8; Mt 22:23-32).
Taught by Jesus (Mt 22:30-32; 24:31; Mk 12:25-27; Lk 14:14; 20:27-38; Jn 5:21, 25, 28-29; 6:39-40, 44, 54; 11:23-25). By the apostles (Ac 4:1-2; 17:18, 31-32; 23:6-8; 24:14-15; Ro 4:16-21; 8:10-11, 19, 21-23; 1Co 6:14; 15:12-57; 2Co 4:14; 5:1-5; Php 3:10-11, 21; Rev 20:5-6; Heb 6:2; 11:35).
Error in the early church (2Ti 2:18; 1Co 15:12-58).

Of Jesus:
Typified by Isaac (Ge 22:13; Heb 11:19), by Jonah (Jnh 2:10, w Mt 12:40). Foretold (Ps 16:9-10), by himself (Mt 16:21; 17:9, 23; 20:19; 26:61; 27:63; Mk 8:31; 9:9-10, 31; 10:34; Lk 9:22; 18:33; 24:7, 46; Jn 2:19-21; 10:17-18; 14:19).
Appearances after the resurrection (Mt 27:53; 28:2-15; Mk 16:1-11; Lk 24:1-12; Jn 20:1-18; Rev 1:18). Denied by the Jews (Mt 28:12-15).
Raised by the power of God (Ac 2:24, 32; 3:15, 26; 4:10; 5:30; 10:40; 15:20, 30, 33-34, 37; 17:31; Ro 4:24; 8:11; 10:9; 1Co 6:14; 15:15; 2Co 4:14; Gal 1:4; Eph 1:20; Col 2:12; 2Ti 1:10; 1Pe 1:21), for our justification (Ro 4:25; 1Pe 3:21). Guarantee of general resurrection (1Co 15:12-15; 1Pe 1:3).
The theme of apostolic preaching (Ac 2:24, 31-32; 3:15; 4:10, 33; 5:30; 10:40-41; 17:2-3, 18).
See Grave; Jesus the Christ, Resurrection of.

Special Resurrections:
Of saints after Christ's resurrection (Mt 27:52-53). The two witnesses (Rev 11:11).
See Dead, Raised to Life.

At Christ's Second Coming:
(1Th 4:14, 16). The first resurrection (Rev 20:4-6). Of all the dead (Jn 5:28-29; Ac 24:15; 1Co 15:20-21; Rev 20:13).

R

Figurative:
Of the restoration of Israel (Eze 37:1-14). Of regeneration (Ro 6:4; Eph 2:1, 5-6; Col 2:12; 3:1).

RETALIATION (Ps 10:2). Judicial, ordained in Mosaic law (Ex 21:23-25; Lev 24:17-22; Dt 19:19-21). Malicious, forbidden (Lev 19:18; Pr 20:22; 24:29; Mt 5:38-44; 7:1-2; Lk 9:54; Ro 12:17, 19; 1Co 6:7-8; 1Th 5:15; 1Pe 3:9). Warning against (Pr 26:27; Isa 33:1; Mt 7:1-2).
See Avenger of Blood; Hatred; Malice; Revenge.
Instances of: Israelites on the Amalekites (Dt 25:17-19, w 1Sa 15:1-9). Gideon on the princes of Succoth (Jdg 8:7, 13-16), kings of Midian (Jdg 8:18-21), Peniel (Jdg 8:8, 17). Joab on Abner (2Sa 3:27, 30). David upon Michal (2Sa 6:21-23), on Joab (1Ki 2:5-6), Shimei (1Ki 2:8-9). Jews on their enemies (Est 9).

RETICENCE OF JESUS (Isa 53:7; Mt 26:63; 27:12, 14; Mk 14:61; 15:4-5; Jn 19:9; 1Pe 2:23). *See Jesus the Christ, Reticence of.*

RETRIBUTION *See Sin, Punishment of.*

REU (*friend [of God]*). Son of Peleg and ancestor of Abraham and of Jesus (Ge 11:18-21; 1Ch 1:25; Lk 3:35).

REUBEN (*see, a son!* [Ge. 29:32]; *substitute a son* IDB). Son of Jacob (Ge 29:32; 1Ch 2:1). Brings mandrakes to his mother (Ge 30:14). Commits incest with one of his father's concubines, and, in consequence, forfeits the birthright (Ge 35:22; 49:4; 1Ch 5:1). Tactfully seeks to save Joseph from the conspiracy of his brothers (Ge 37:21-30; 42:22). Offers to become surety for Benjamin (Ge 42:37). Jacob's prophetic benediction upon (Ge 49:3-4). His children (Ge 46:9; Ex 6:14; 1Ch 5:3-6; Nu 16:1).

REUBENITE(S) (*of Reuben*). The descendants of Reuben. Military enrollment of, at Sinai (Nu 1:20-21), in Moab (Nu 26:7). Place of, in camp and march (Nu 2:10). Standard of (Nu 10:18). Have their inheritance east of the Jordan (Nu 32; Dt 3:1-20; Jos 13:15-23; 18:7). Assist the other tribes in conquest of the region west of the Jordan (Jos 1:12-18; 22:1-6). Unite with the other tribes in building a monument to signify the unity of the tribes on the east of the Jordan with the tribes on the west of the river; monument misunderstood; the explanation and reconciliation (Jos 22:10-34). Reproached by Deborah (Jdg 5:15-16). Taken captive into Assyria (2Ki 15:29; 1Ch 5:26).
See Israel.

REUEL (*friend of God [El]*).
1. Son of Esau (Ge 36:4, 10).
2. Father-in-law of Moses (Ex 2:16-22), probably the same as Jethro (Ge 3:1). *See Jethro.*
3. The father of Eliasaph (Nu 2:14). Called Deuel (Nu 1:14).
4. Benjamite (1Ch 9:8).

REUMAH A concubine of Nahor (Ge 22:24).

REVELATION The doctrine of God's making himself and relevant truths known to mankind. Revelation is of two kinds: general and special. General revelation is available to all people, and is communicated through nature, conscience, and history. Special revelation is revelation given to particular people at particular times (although it may be intended for others as well), and comes chiefly through the Bible and Jesus Christ.
God reveals himself to Moses (Ex 3:1-6, 14; 6:1-3). The law is revealed (Ex 20-35; Lev 1-7). The pattern of the temple (1Ch 28:11-19). The sonship of Jesus (Mt 3:17; 16:17; 17:5). The nature of the Father through the Son (Jn 1:18; 14:8).
See Inspiration; Prophecy; Prophets; Word of God, Inspiration of.

REVELATION, BOOK OF THE

Author: The apostle John

Date: Probably in the latter part of Nero's reign (A.D. 54-68) or the latter part of Domitian's reign (81-96).

Outline:
I. Introduction (1:1-8).
 A. Prologue (1:1-3).
 B. Greetings and Doxology (1:4-8).
II. Jesus Among the Seven Churches (1:9-20).
III. The Letters to the Seven Churches (chs. 2-3).
 A. Ephesus (2:1-7).
 B. Smyrna (2:8-11).
 C. Pergamum (2:12-17).
 D. Thyatira (2:18-29).
 E. Sardis (3:1-6).
 F. Philadelphia (3:7-13).
 G. Laodicea (3:14-22).
IV. The Throne, the Scroll and the Lamb (chs. 4-5).
 A. The Throne in Heaven (ch. 4).
 B. The Seven-Sealed Scroll (5:1-5).
 C. The Lamb Slain (5:6-14).
V. The Seven Seals (6:1-8:1).
 A. First Seal: The White Horse (6:1-2).
 B. Second Seal: The Red Horse (6:3-4).
 C. Third Seal: The Black Horse (6:5-6).
 D. Fourth Seal: The Pale Horse (6:7-8).
 E. Fifth Seal: The Souls Under the Altar (6:9-11).
 F. Sixth Seal: The Great Earthquake (6:12-17).
 G. The Sealing of the 144,000 (7:1-8).
 H. The Great Multitude (7:9-17).
 I. Seventh Seal: Silence in Heaven (8:1).
VI. The Seven Trumpets (8:2-11:19).
 A. Introduction (8:2-5).
 B. First Trumpet: Hail and Fire Mixed With Blood (8:6-7).
 C. Second Trumpet: A Mountain Thrown in the Sea (8:8-9).
 D. Third Trumpet: The Star Wormwood (8:10-11).
 E. Fourth Trumpet: A Third of the Sun, Moon and Stars Struck (8:12-13).
 F. Fifth Trumpet: The Plague of Locusts (9:1-12).
 G. Sixth Trumpet: Release of the Four Angels (9:13-21).

H. The Angel and the Little Scroll (ch. 10).
I. The Two Witnesses (11:1-14).
J. Seventh Trumpet: Judgments and Rewards (11:15-19).
VII. Various Personages and Events (chs. 12-14).
 A. The Woman and the Dragon (ch. 12).
 B. The Two Beasts (ch. 13).
 C. The Lamb and the 144,000 (14:1-5).
 D. The Harvest of the Earth (14:6-20).
VIII. The Seven Bowls (chs. 15-16).
 A. Introduction: The Song of Moses and the Seven Angels with the Seven Plagues (ch. 15).
 B. First Bowl: Ugly and Painful Sores (16:1-2).
 C. Second Bowl: Sea Turns to Blood (16:3).
 D. Third Bowl: Rivers and Springs of Water Become Blood (16:4-7).
 E. Fourth Bowl: Sun Scorches People With Fire (16:8-9).
 F. Fifth Bowl: Darkness (16:10-11).
 G. Sixth Bowl: Euphrates River Dries Up (16:12-16).
 H. Seventh Bowl: Tremendous Earthquake (16:17-21).
IX. The Great Prostitute (17:1-19:5).
 A. Babylon Described (ch. 17).
 B. The Fall of Babylon (ch. 18).
 C. Praise for Babylon's Fall (19:1-5).
X. Praise for the Wedding of the Lamb (19:6-10).
XI. The Return of Christ (19:11-21).
XII. The Thousand Years (20:1-6).
XIII. Satan's Doom (20:7-10).
XIV. Great White Throne Judgment (20:11-15).
XV. New Heaven, New Earth, New Jerusalem (21:1-22:5).
XVI. Conclusion (22:6-21).

REVELING Any extreme intemperance and lustful indulgence, usually accompanying pagan worship (Gal 5:21; 1Pe 4:3).

REVENGE Forbidden (Lev 19:18; Pr 24:29; Ro 12:17, 19; 1Th 5:15; 1Pe 3:9). Jesus an example of forbearing (1Pe 2:23). Rebuked by Jesus (Lk 9:54-55). Inconsistent with a Christian spirit (Lk 9:55). Proceeds from a spiteful heart (Eze 25:15). Punishment for (Eze 25:15-17; Am 1:11-12).
Exemplified:
By Simeon and Levi (Ge 34:25). By Samson (Jdg 15:7-8; 16:28-30). By Joab (2Sa 3:27). By Absalom (2Sa 13:23-29). By Jezebel (1Ki 19:2). By Ahab (1Ki 22:27). By Haman (Est 3:8-15). By the Edomites (Eze 25:12). By the Philistines (Eze 25:15). By Herodias (Mk 6:19-24). By James and John (Lk 9:54). By the chief priests (Ac 5:33). By the Jews (Ac 7:54-59; 23:12).
See Retaliation; Vengeance.

REVENUE Solomon's (2Ch 9:13-14).
See Tax.

REVERENCE For God (Ge 17:3; Ex 3:5; 19:16-24; 34:29-35; Isa 45:9). *See Fear of God.* For God's house (Lev 19:30; 26:2). For ministers (1Sa 16:4; Ac 28:10; 1Co 16:18; Php 2:29; 1Th 5:12-13; 1Ti 5:17; Heb 13:7, 17). *See Minister.* For Kings (1Sa 24:6; 26:9, 11; 2Sa 1:14; 16:21; Ecc 10:20; 1Pe 2:17). *See Rulers.* For magistrates (Ex 22:28; 2Pe 2:10; Jude 8). *See Rulers.* For parents (Ex 20:12; Lev 19:3; Isa 45:10). *See Parents.* For the aged (Lev 19:32; Job 32:4-7).

REVILE, REVILING To revile is to address or speak of someone abusively; to reproach (Ex 21:17; Zep 2:8; Mk 15:32; 1Co 6:10).

REVIVALS
Religious:
(Zec 8:20-23). Prayer for (Hab 3:2). Prophecies concerning (Isa 32:15; Joel 2:28; Mic 4:1-8; Hab 3:2).
Instances of:
Under Joshua (Jos 5:2-9), Samuel (1Sa 7:1-6), Elijah (1Ki 18:17-40), Jehoash and Jehoiada (2Ki 11-12; 2Ch 23-24), Hezekiah (2Ki 18:1-7; 2Ch 29-31), Josiah (2Ki 22-23; 2Ch 34-35), Asa (2Ch 14:2-5; 15:1-14), Manasseh (2Ch 33:12-19). In Nineveh (Jnh 3:4-10). At Pentecost and post-Pentecostal times (Ac 2:1-42, 46-47; 4:4; 5:14; 6:7; 9:35; 11:20-21; 12:24; 14:1; 19:17-20).
See Religion.

REVOLT Of the ten tribes (1Ki 12:1-24).

REWARD (Isa 40:10-11). In Moses' choice (Heb 11:26). For bravery (1Sa 17:25; Jdg 1:13).
A Motive:
To repentance (Lev 26:40-45; Isa 1:16-20; Ac 26:18). To obedience (Ex 20:6; Lev 25:18-19; 26:3-13; Dt 4:40; 6:3, 18; 11:13-16, 18-21, 26-29; 27:12-26; Jos 8:33; Isa 1:16-20; 3:10; Eph 6:1-3; Heb 12:28). To faithfulness (Mt 24:45-47; 25:14-33; Lk 12:42-44; 19:12-27; 1Co 3:8; Rev 2:10; 22:12). To righteous conduct (Ro 2:10; 1Pe 3:9-12). To perseverance (Mt 10:22; 24:13; Mk 13:13; Ro 2:6-7; Gal 6:9; Rev 2:17, 25-27; 3:5, 11-12, 21; 21:7). To honesty (Dt 25:15).
To follow Christ (Mt 10:32; 16:24-27; 20:1-16; 25:34-46; Mk 10:21; Lk 12:8; 2Pe 1:10-11). To endure persecution (Lk 6:22-23; Heb 10:34). To endure tribulation (Rev 2:7, 10; 7:17). To love enemies (Lk 6:35). To deliver the oppressed (Jer 17:24-26; 22:3-4). To honor parents (Ex 20:12; Eph 6:1-3). To honor the Sabbath (Jer 17:24-26). To give generously (Dt 15:9-11; 24:19). To show kindness to animals (Pr 12:6-7).
See Blessings, Spiritual, Contingent Upon Obedience; Punishment; Righteous, Promises to; Sin, Separates From God; Wicked, Punishment of.

REZEPH (*heated stones, live coals*). A city destroyed by the Assyrians (2Ki 19:12; Isa 37:12).

REZIA *See Rizia.*

REZIN
1. A king of Syria who harassed the kingdom of Judah (2Ki 15:37; 16:5-9). Prophecy against (Isa 7:1-9; 8:4-8; 9:11).
2. A returned Babylonian captive (Ezr 2:48; Ne 7:50).

REZON (*prince* IDB; *high official* KB). King of Damascus. An adversary of Solomon (1Ki 11:23-25).

RHEGIUM A city of Italy. Touched by Paul on the way to Rome (Ac 28:13).

RHESA An ancestor of Jesus (Lk 3:27).

RHODA (*rose*). A servant or slave girl in the home of Mary, John Mark's mother (Ac 12:13).

RHODES (*rose*). An island on the SW tip of Asia Minor; commercial center until crippled by Rome is 166 B.C.; famous for Colossus, a statue of Helios; Paul stopped off there (Ac 21:1).

RIBAI (*opponent*). A Benjamite. The father of Ittai (2Sa 23:29; 1Ch 11:31).

RIBBON Ribbon used in poetic imagery (SS 4:3). Tassels of thread on the corners of garments; NIV "cord" (Nu 15:38).

RIBLAH
1. A city on the boundary of Canaan and Israel, N of the Sea of Galilee (Nu 34:11).
2. An important town on the E bank of the Orontes River fifty miles S of Hamath. There Pharaoh Neco (609 B.C.) put King Jehoahaz II of Judah in chains. Also in this place, Nebuchadnezzar killed the sons of King Zedekiah of Judah (587 B.C.) and put out his eyes. Following this, Zedekiah was carried off in chains to Babylon (2Ki 25:6f; Jer 39:5-7). It is possible that the two Riblahs may be the same.

RICH, THE
Admonitions to:
(Jer 9:23; 1Ti 6:17-19; Jas 1:9-11). Not to trust riches for divine favor (Ps 49:16-18; Ecc 7:19; Zep 1:18).
Characteristics of:
Wicked (Job 21:7-15; Ps 73:3-9; Pr 28:8, 20, 22; Jer 5:27-28; Lk 12:15-21; 16:19-31; Jas 2:6-7). Immoral (Jer 5:7-8). Deluded (Pr 11:28; 13:7; 18:11). Conceited (Pr 28:11). Proud (Ps 73:3, 6, 8-9; Eze 28:5). Arrogant (Ps 73:8). Oppressive (Ne 5:1-13; Mic 6:10-13; Jas 2:6). Cruel to the poor (Pr 18:23). Envied (Ps 73:3-22). Hated (Job 27:19, 23). Denounced (Isa 5:8; Jer 17:11; 22:13-15; Am 6:1-6; Lk 6:24-25; Jas 5:1-4).
Have many friends (Pr 14:20; 19:9). Made so by God (Ecc 5:19-20). Difficult to enter the kingdom (Mt 19:24; Mk 10:17-27; Lk 18:24-25). Unscrupulous methods of (Jer 5:26-28). Discrimination in favor of, in the church, forbidden (Jas 2:1-9). Divine judgments against (Job 27:13-23; Ps 52:1-7; 73:18-20).
Instances of Righteous Rich:
Abraham (Ge 13:2; 24:35). Isaac (Ge 26:12-14). Solomon (1Ki 10:23; 2Ch 9:22). Jehoshaphat (2Ch 18:1). Hezekiah (2Ki 20:12-13). Job (Job 1:3; 31:24-25, 28). Joseph of Arimathea (Mt 27:57). Zacchaeus (Lk 19:2).
See Riches.

RICHES (1Sa 2:7; Ps 37:16; 52:7; Pr 11:4; 14:24; 15:6, 16-17; 16:8; 19:4; Ecc 4:8; 5:11-14; 6:1-2; 7:11-12; 10:19; Isa 5:8; Jer 48:36). Delusive (Pr 11:28; Lk 12:16-21). Unstable (Pr 23:5; 27:24).
Unsatisfying to the covetous (Ecc 5:10-12). A snare (Dt 6:10-12; 8:7-17; 31:20; 32:15; Pr 30:8-9; Jer 5:7-8; Hos 12:8; Mt 13:22; 19:16-24; Mk 4:19; 10:17-25; Lk 16:19-26; 18:18-25; 1Ti 6:9-11, 17).
Worthless in the day of calamity (Eze 7:17, 19; Zep 1:18). Fraudulently gotten, unprofitable (Pr 10:2; 21:6; 28:8; Jer 17:11). Admonitions against the desire for (Pr 23:4; 28:20, 22; 1Ti 6:9-11, 17). The heart not to be set upon (Ps 62:10; Mt 6:19-21). Liberality with (Pr 13:7-8). Benevolent use of, required (1Jn 3:17).
Figurative (Rev 3:17-18).
See Covetousness; Rich, The.

RIDDLE (*hidden saying, proverb*). Any "dark saying" of which the meaning is not immediately clear and must be found by shrewd thought (Nu 12:8; Pr 1:6). It may be a parable (Ps 49:4), or something for men to guess (Jdg 14:12-19), or just a hard question (1Ki 10:1; 2Ch 9:1).

RIGHTEOUS
Compared with:
The sun (Jdg 5:31; Mt 13:43), stars (Da 12:3), lights (Mt 5:14; Php 2:15). Mount Zion (Ps 125:1-2), Lebanon (Hos 14:5-7). Treasure (Ex 19:5; Ps 135:4), treasured possession (Mal 3:17). Gold (Job 23:10; La 4:2), vessels of gold and silver (2Ti 2:20), stones of a crown (Zec 9:16), living stones (1Pe 2:5).
Babies (Mt 11:25; 1Pe 2:2), little children (Mt 18:3; 1Co 14:20), obedient children (1Pe 1:14), members of the body (1Co 12:20, 27), soldiers (2Ti 2:3-4), runners in a race (1Co 9:24; Heb 12:1), wrestlers (2Ti 2:5), good servants (Mt 25:21), strangers and pilgrims (1Pe 2:11).
Sheep (Ps 78:52; Mt 25:33; Jn 10), lambs (Isa 40:11; Jn 21:15), calves of the stall (Mal 4:2), lions (Pr 28:1; Mic 5:8), eagles (Ps 103:5; Isa 40:31), doves (Ps 68:13; Isa 60:8), thirsty deer (Ps 42:1), good fish (Mt 13:48).
Dew and showers (Mic 5:7), watered gardens (Isa 58:11), unfailing springs (Isa 58:11), vines (SS 6:11; Hos 14:7), branches of a vine (Jn 15:2, 4-5), pomegranates (SS 4:13), good figs (Jer 24:2-7), lilies (SS 2:2; Hos 14:5), poplars by flowing streams (Isa 44:4), trees planted by rivers (Ps 1:3), cedars in Lebanon (Ps 92:12), palm trees (Ps 92:12), green olive trees (Ps 52:8; Hos 14:6), fruitful trees (Ps 1:3; Jer 17:8), grain (Hos 14:7), wheat (Mt 3:12; 13:29-30), salt (Mt 5:13).

Relation to God:
(Lev 20:24-26). Access to God (Ps 31:19-20; Isa 12:6). Few (Mt 7:14; 22:14). Righteous and wicked, circumstances of, contrasted (Job 8; Ps 17:14-15). *See below, Contrasted With the Wicked.*
At the judgment. *See Judgment.*
Fellowship of. *See Fellowship.*

Hatred toward. *See Persecution.*
Joy of. *See Joy.*
Perseverance of. *See Perseverance.*

Contrasted With the Wicked:
(Ps 1:1-6; 11:5; 17:14-15; 32:10; 37:17-22, 37-38; 73:1-28; 75:10; 91:7-8; Pr 2:21-22; 3:32-33; 4:16-19; 10:3, 6, 9, 11, 16, 20-21, 23-25, 28-32; 11:3, 5-6, 8-11, 18-21, 23, 31; 12:3, 5-7, 10, 12-13, 21, 26; 13:5-6, 9, 17, 21-22, 25; 14:2, 11, 19, 22-32; 15:6, 8-9, 28-29; 22:5, 8-9; 24:16; 28:1, 4-5, 13-14, 18; 29:2, 6-7, 27; Isa 32:1-8; 65:13-14; Ro 2:7-10; Eph 2:12-14; Php 2:15; 1Th 5:5-8; Tit 1:15; 1Pe 4:17-18; 1Jn 3:3-17).

See Wicked, Contrasted With the Righteous; Described as.

Described:
(Ps 1:1-3; 15:1-5; 24:3-5; 37:26, 30-31; 84:7; 112:1-10; 119:1-3; Isa 33:15-16; 51:1; 62:12; 63:8; Jer 17:7-8; 31:12-14, 33-34; Eze 18:5-9; Zec 3:2, 7-8. As dead to sin (Ro 6:2, 11; Col 3:3). Freed from sin (Ro 6:7, 18, 22; 1Jn 3:6, 9).
Good (Lk 6:45). Pure (Mt 5:8; 1Jn 3:3; 2Ti 2:21-22). Holy (Dt 7:6; Eph 1:4; 4:24; Col 1:22; 3:12; 1Pe 1:15; 2Ti 2:19; Heb 3:1). Sanctified (1Co 1:2; 6:11). Godly (Ps 4:3; 2Pe 2:9). Wise (Ps 37:30; Pr 2:9-12). Faithful (Mt 24:45; 25:21, 23; Lk 19:17; Eph 1:1; Col 1:2; Rev 17:14). Merciful (Mt 5:7). Meek (Mt 5:5; 2Ti 2:25). Industrious (Eph 4:28; 2Jn 9). Stable (Mt 7:24-27; Eph 4:14). Saved (Ac 2:47). Saints (Ro 1:7; 1Co 1:2; Eph 1:1). Chosen (1Pe 2:9; Rev 17:14). Spotless (Jas 1:27). Separate (Ex 33:16). Obedient (Mt 12:50; Jn 15:14; 1Jn 2:3, 5). New creature (2Co 5:17; Eph 2:10; 4:23-24; Col 3:9-10). Spiritually minded (Ro 8:4, 6). Patient, long-suffering, joyful (Col 1:11; 1Th 1:3). Peaceful, meek, gentle, patient (2Ti 2:21-25). Blameless, harmless, and without blemish (Eph 1:4; Php 2:15). Kind, tenderhearted, forgiving (Eph 4:32).
Servants of Christ (Eph 6:6). Servants of righteousness (Ro 6:19). Children of light (1Th 5:5). Children of God (Ro 8:14, 16; 1Jn 3:2). A temple of God (2Co 6:16). Beloved of God (Ro 1:7). Poor in spirit (Mt 5:3). Hungering and thirsting after righteousness (Mt 5:6). Growing in grace (Ps 84:7; Eph 4:13). Imitators of Christ (1Pe 4:1-2; 1Jn 2:6). Salt of the earth (Mt 5:13). City set on a hill (Mt 5:14). Led by the spirit (Ro 8:14; Gal 5:18). Filled with goodness and knowledge (Ro 15:14; Col 1:9-13). Grounded in love (Eph 3:17). Following Christ (Mt 10:38; 16:24; Mk 8:34; Lk 9:23). Rooted in Christ (Col 2:7).
Hating falsehood (Pr 13:5), abhorring wickedness (Ps 101:3-4), having renounced dishonesty (2Co 4:2). Without bitterness, wrath, anger, clamor, evil speaking, malice (Eph 4:31). Grieved by the wickedness of the wicked (Ps 119:158; Ac 17:16; 2Pe 2:7-8).

Happiness of:
(Job 5:17-27; Pr 3:13-18; 16:20; Mt 4:3-12). Satisfying (Ps 36:8; 63:5). Under fiery trials (1Pe 4:12-13). Under persecution (Mt 5:10-12).

Promises to and Comfort of:
Deliverance from temptation (1Co 10:13; 2Pe 2:9). Deliverance from trouble (Ps 5:19-24; Ps 34:15, 17; 50:15; 91:15; 97:10-11; Pr 3:25-26; Isa 41:10-13; 43:2). Refuge in adversity (Ps 33:18-19; 62:8; 91:1-15; Pr 14:26; Na 1:7). Strength in adversity (Ps 29:11). Security (Ps 32:6-7; 84:11; 121:3-8; Isa 33:16). Providential care (Ge 15:1; Ex 23:22; Lev 26:5-6, 10; Dt 33:27; 1Sa 2:9; 2Ch 16:9; Ezr 8:22; Job 5:15; Ps 34:9-10; 125:1-3; 145:19-20; Pr 1:33; 2:7; 3:6; 10:3; 16:7; Isa 49:9-11; 65:13-14; Eze 34:11-17, 22-31; Lk 12:7, 32; 21:18; 1Pe 5:7). Overruling providence (Ro 8:28; 2Co 4:17).
Answer to prayer (Pr 15:29; Mk 11:23-24; Jn 14:13-14; Ac 10:4; 1Pe 3:12; 1Jn 3:22). Temporal blessings (Lev 25:18-19; 26:5; Dt 28:1-13; Ps 37:9; 128:1-6; Pr 2:21; 3:1-4, 7-10; Mt 6:26-33; Mk 10:30; Lk 18:29-30). Blessings upon their children (Ps 103:17; 112:2-3).

Righteous Receive—
Comfort in tribulation (Isa 25:8; 66:13-14; Mt 5:4; Jn 14:16-18; Rev 21:4). Joy (Isa 35:10; 51:11). Spiritual enlightenment (Isa 2:3; Jn 8:12). Peace (Isa 26:3; Ro 2:10). Seeing God (Mt 5:8). Inconceivable spiritual blessings (Isa 64:4; 1Co 2:9). The rest of faith (Heb 4:9). Wisdom (Jas 1:5). Divine help (Ps 55:22; Isa 41:10-13; Heb 13:5-6). Divine guidance (Ps 25:12; 32:8; 37:23-24; 48:14; 73:24; Pr 3:5-6). Divine mercy (Ps 32:10; 103:17-18; Mal 3:17). The divine presence (Ge 26:3, 24; 28:15; 31:3; Ex 33:14; Dt 31:6, 8; Jos 1:5; 1Ki 6:13; Hag 1:13; 2:4-5; Mt 28:20; Jn 14:17, 23; 2Co 6:16; 13:11; Php 4:9; Heb 13:5; Jas 4:8; Rev 21:3). The divine likeness (1Jn 3:2). The ministry of angels (Heb 1:14). Dwelling with Christ (Jn 14:2-3; Col 3:4; 1Th 4:17; 5:10). Everlasting remembrance (Ps 112:6). Having names written in heaven (Lk 10:20).
Resurrection (Jn 5:29; 1Co 15:48-57; 2Co 4:14; 1Th 4:16). Future glory (Ro 8:18; Col 3:4; 2Ti 2:10; 1Pe 1:4). Inheritance (Mt 25:34; Ac 20:32; 26:18; Col 1:12; 3:24; Tit 3:7; Heb 9:15; Jas 2:5; 1Pe 1:4). Heavenly reward (Mt 5:12; 13:43; 2Ti 4:8; Heb 11:16; Jas 1:12; 2Pe 1:11; Rev 2:7, 10; 22:5, 12, 14). Eternal life (Da 12:2-3; Mt 19:29; 25:46; Mk 10:29-30; Lk 18:29-30; Jn 3:15-18, 36; 4:14; 5:24, 29; 6:39-40; 10:28; 12:25-26; Ro 2:7; 6:22-23; Gal 6:8; 1Th 4:15-17; 1Ti 1:16; 4:8; Tit 1:2; 1Jn 2:25; 5:13; Rev 7:14-17).
Contingent upon perseverance (Heb 10:36; Rev 2:7, 10-11, 17, 26-28; 3:4-5, 10, 12, 21; 21:7).
See Adoption; Affliction, Comfort in; God, Preserver, Providence of.
Promises in specific areas. *See the specific topic.*

Union:
With God (1Jn 3:24; 4:13, 15-16; 2Jn 9).
With Christ (Jn 6:51-58; 14:20; 15:1-11; 17:21-23, 26; Ro 8:1; 12:5; 1Co 6:13-20; 10:16; 2Co 13:5; Gal 2:20; Col 1:27; 2:6-7; 1Jn 2:6, 24, 28; 3:6, 24; 5:12, 20; 2Jn 9).
See Adoption; Communion; Fellowship, with Christ.

RIGHTEOUSNESS (Ps 15:1-5; 24:3-5; 106:3; Pr 11:5-6, 18, 30; Hos 10:12; Mt 5:20; Lk 1:75; Jn 16:8, 10; Ro 6:19-22; 8:4; Eph 4:24; Jas 1:27).

Required:
(Isa 28:17; Hos 10:12; Mic 6:8; Zec 7:9-10; 8:16-17; Mal 3:3; Mt 5:20; 23:23; Lk 3:10-14; 13:6-9; Ro 6:19-22; 7:4-6; 8:4;

14:17-19; 2Ti 2:22; 1Jn 3:10). Commanded in official administration (Jer 22:3, 6).

Imputed:
On account of obedience (Rev 6:25; Ps 106:31; Eze 18:9), on account of faith (Ge 15:6; Ro 4:3, 5, 9, 11, 13, 20, 22, 24; Gal 3:6; Jas 2:23). Proof of regeneration (1Jn 2:29). Exalts a nation (Pr 14:34). Safeguards life (Pr 10:2, 16; 11:19; 12:28; 13:6). Winning others to, rewarded (Da 12:3).

Fruits of:
(Ps 1:3; Mt 7:16-18; 12:35; Lk 6:43; Jn 15:4-8; 2Co 9:10; Gal 5:22-23; Php 1:11; Col 3:12-15; 1Th 1:3; Tit 2:2-6, 11-12; 1Pe 3:8-14; 2Pe 1:5-8; 1Jn 3:7). Generosity (Ac 11:29). Peace (Isa 32:17; Jas 3:8).

Symbolized:
(Eze 47:12; Rev 22:2). Figuratively described as a garment (Job 29:14; Isa 61:10; Zec 3:4; Mt 22:11-14; Rev 6:11; 7:9; 19:8).

Of God: *See God, Righteousness of.*

Of Jesus: *See Jesus the Christ, Holiness of, Righteousness of. See also, Sin, Fruits of; Works, Good.*

RIM The rim of a wheel (1Ki 7:33; Eze 1:18).

RIMMON (*pomegranate,* or *Rimmon [pagan thunder, storm god]*).
1. Father of the murderers of Ish-Bosheth (2Sa 4:2, 5, 9).
2. A city S of Jerusalem (Zec 14:10). Allotted to Judah (Jos 15:32; Ne 11:29), afterward to Simeon (Jos 19:7; 1Ch 4:32). Also called En Rimmon (Ne 11:29).
3. A city of Zebulun (Jos 19:13). Also called Rimmono (1Ch 6:77).
4. A rock in Benjamin (Jdg 20:45, 47; 21:13).
5. A Syrian idol (2Ki 5:18).

RIMMON-METHOAR *See Rimmon, 3.*

RIMMON PEREZ (*pomegranate pass [breach]*). A camping place of the Israelites (Nu 33:19-20).

RIMMON, ROCK OF (*pomegranate rock*). The fortress to which 600 Benjamites fled after escaping slaughter (Jdg 20:45, 47; 21:13), near Gibeah.

RIMMONO *See Rimmon, 3.*

RING Of gold (Nu 31:50). Worn as a sign of office (Ge 41:42). Given as a token (Est 3:10, 12; 8:2-10). Worn in the nose (Pr 11:22; Isa 3:21). Offerings of, to the tabernacle (Ex 35:22; Nu 31:50).

RINGSTRAKED *See Streaked.*

RINNAH (*ringing cry [of joy] to Yahweh*). A son of Shimon (1Ch 4:20).

RIOT To squander in evil ways (Pr 23:20; 28:7), waste (Tit 1:6; 1Pe 4:4), revelry (Ro 13:13), luxury (2Pe 2:13).

RIPHATH A son of Gomer (Ge 10:3; 1Ch 1:6).

RISING

Early:
(Pr 31:15). For devotions (Ps 5:3; 59:16; 63:1; 88:13; SS 7:12; Isa 26:9). Practiced by the wicked (Pr 27:14; Mic 2:1; Zep 3:7), by drunkards (Isa 5:11). Illustrates spiritual diligence (Ro 13:11-12).

Instances of:
Lot (Ge 19:23). Abraham (Ge 19:27; 21:14; 22:3). Isaac (Ge 26:31). Abimelech (Ge 20:8). Jacob (Ge 28:18; 32:31). Laban (Ge 31:55). Moses (Ex 8:20; 9:13). Joshua (Jos 3:1; 6:12, 15; 7:16). Gideon (Jdg 6:38). Elkanah (1Sa 1:19). Samuel (1Sa 15:12). David (1Sa 17:20). Mary (Mk 16:2; Lk 24:1). Apostles (Ac 5:21).
See Industry.

Late:
Consequences of (Pr 6:9-11; 24:33-34).
See Idleness; Slothfulness.

RISSAH (*dew* ISBE). Encampment of Israelites in the wilderness (Nu 33:21-22), site unknown.

RITHMAH (*[place of] broom plants*). A camping place of the Israelites (Nu 33:18-19).

RIVER May refer to large streams (Ge 2:10-14), the Nile (Ge 41:1; 2Ki 19:24), a winter torrent, the bed of which is dry during summer (Am 6:14), fountain stream (Ps 119:136).
Figurative: Of salvation (Ps 36:8; 46:4; Isa 32:2; Eze 47:1-12; Rev 22:1-2). Of grief (Ps 119:136; La 3:48).

RIVER OF EGYPT
1. The Brook or Wadi of Egypt on the SW border of Israel, flowing into the Mediterranean Sea (Ge 15:18; Nu 34:5; 2Ki 24:7; Isa 27:12), probably modern Wadi el-Arish, though some identify it with the Nile.
2. The Nile (Am 8:8; 9:5).
See Egypt; Nile.

RIVERS Names of: Abana (2Ki 5:12). Arnon (Dt 2:36). Kebar (Eze 1:1). Euphrates (Ge 2:14). Gozan (2Ki 17:6; 1Ch 5:26). Jordan. *See Jordan.* Kanah (Jos 16:8). Kishon (Jdg 5:21). Of Egypt (Ex 1:22). Pharpar (2Ki 5:12). Pishon (Ge 2:11). Tigris (Ge 2:14). Ulai (Da 8:16).

RIZIA (possibly *pleasant one* KB). An Asherite (1Ch 7:39).

RIZPAH (*heated stones, live coals*). Concubine of Saul (2Sa 3:7). Guards the bodies of her sons hanged by command of David (2Sa 21:8-11).

ROADS May refer to paths or highways; hundreds of allusions to roads in the Bible; road robbers quite common (Mt 11:10; Lk 10:30), Romans built highways throughout the empire, some of

which are still in use; used by traders, travelers, and armies; Paul used Roman roads on his missionary journeys; the statement "All roads lead to Rome" shows how well provided the Roman empire was with roads. *See Highways.*

ROBBERS (Pr 1:11-16). Dens of (Jer 7:11). Bands of (Hos 6:9; 7:1).

ROBBERY
Illegal seizure of another's property; forbidden by law (Lev 19:13); highways unsafe (Jdg 5:6; Lk 10:30; 2Co 11:26); houses built to resist robbers; even priests sometimes turned to pillage (Hos 6:9); denounced by prophets (Isa 61:8; Eze 22:29); withholding tithes and offerings from God's storehouse regarded as robbery (Mal 3:8). *See Theft.*

ROBE Of righteousness (2Ch 6:41; Isa 61:10; Rev 6:11; 7:9, 13). Parable of the man who was not dressed in a wedding garment (Mt 22:11).
See Dress.

ROBINSON'S ARCH The remains of ancient Jerusalem masonry, named for the American archaeologist Edward Robinson, who discovered it in 1838. Giant stones, projecting from the SW wall of the temple enclosure are evidently part of an arch that in Herod's time supported a monumental stairway.

ROBOAM *See Rehoboam, 2.*

ROCK Struck by Moses for water (Dt 8:15; Ps 78:15-16, 20). Houses in (Jer 49:16; Ob 3; Mt 7:24-25). Oil from (Job 29:6; Dt 32:13). Name of deity (Dt 32:4). *See God, Names of.*
Figurative (2Sa 22:32, 47; 23:3; Ps 18:2; 31:2; 40:2; Isa 17:10; 32:2; Mt 16:18; 1Co 10:4).

ROD Branch, stick, staff; symbol of authority (Ex 4:2, 17, 20; 9:23; 14:16), discipline symbolized by rod (Mic 5:1); messianic ruler (Isa 11:1); affliction (Job 9:34).

ROD OF AARON (Ex 7:9-10, 12, 15, 19-20; 8:5, 16-17; Nu 17:6, 8, 10; Heb 9:4).

ROD OF CORRECTION (Ps 89:32; Pr 10:13; 13:24; 22:15; 23:14; 26:3; 29:15; La 3:1).

ROD OF MOSES (Ex 4:2, 17, 20; 7:19; 8:16; 9:23; 10:13; 14:16; 17:5, 9).

RODANIM (*people of Rhodes*). The son of Javan; most manuscripts of the Masoretic Text have *Dodanim* (Ge 10:4, ftn). Tribe descended from Javan, son of Japheth (1Ch 1:7).

RODENTS (Isa 2:20). *See Animals; Rat(s).*

ROE DEER Permitted as food (Dt 14:5). *See Deer.*

ROGELIM (*[place of] treaders, fullers [one who cleans clothes by kneading with no soap]*). A town near Mahanaim whose citizens assisted David (2Sa 17:27, 29; 19:31).

ROHGAH Son of Shomer (1Ch 7:34).

ROI *See Beer Lahai Roi.*

ROLL Sheets of papyrus or parchment (made of skin) sewn together to make a long sheet of writing material which was wound around a stick to make a scroll (Isa 34:4; Jer 36; Eze 3:1-3; Rev 5; 10:1-10).

ROLLER NIV "splint" (Eze 30:21).

ROMAMTI-EZER (*[he is my] highest help*). Son of Heman (1Ch 25:4, 31).

ROMAN EMPIRE City of Rome founded in 753 B.C.; a monarchy until 509 B.C.; a republic from 509 to 31 B.C.; the empire began in 31 B.C., fell in the fifth century A.D. Rome extended its hold over all Italy and eventually over the whole Mediterranean world, Gaul, half of Britain, the Rhine-Danube rivers, and as far as Parthia.
Augustus, the first Roman emperor, divided the Roman provinces into senatorial districts, which were ruled by proconsuls (Ac 13:7; 18:12; 19:38), and imperial districts ruled by governors (Mt 27:2; Lk 2:2; Ac 23:24). Moral corruption was among the causes of the decline and fall of the Roman Empire. Roman reservoirs, aqueducts, roads, public buildings, statues survive.
Many Roman officials are referred to in the NT, including the emperors Augustus (Lk 2:1), Tiberius (Lk 3:1), Claudius (Ac 11:28), and Nero (Ac 25:11-12).

ROMANS, EPISTLE TO THE

Author: The apostle Paul

Date: Probably written in the early spring of A.D. 57

Outline:
I. Introduction (1:1-15).
II. Theme: Righteousness From God (1:16-17).
III. The Unrighteousness of All Mankind (1:18-3:20).
 A. Gentiles (1:18-32).
 B. Jews (2:1-3:8).
 C. Summary: All People (3:9-20).
IV. Righteousness Imputed: Justification (3:21-5:21).
 A. Through Christ (3:21-26).
 B. Received by Faith (3:27-4:25).
 1. The principle established (3:27-31).
 2. The principle illustrated (ch. 4).
 C. The Fruits of Righteousness (5:1-11).
 D. Summary: Man's Unrighteousness Contrasted With God's Gift of Righteousness (5:12-21).
V. Righteousness Imparted: Sanctification (chs. 6-8).
 A. Freedom From Sin's Tyranny (ch. 6).
 B. Freedom From the Law's Condemnation (ch. 7).

C. Life in the Power of the Holy Spirit (ch. 8).
VI. God's Righteousness Vindicated: The Problem of the Rejection of Israel (chs. 9-11).
 A. The Justice of the Rejection (9:1-29).
 B. The Cause of the Rejection (9:30-10:21).
 C. Facts That Lessen the Difficulty (ch. 11).
 1. The rejection is not total (11:1-10).
 2. The rejection is not final (11:11-24).
 3. God's ultimate purpose is mercy (11:25-36).
VII. Righteousness Practiced (12:1-15:13).
 A. In the Body—the Church (ch. 12).
 B. In the World (ch. 13).
 C. Among Weak and Strong Christians (14:1-15:13).
VIII. Conclusion (15:14-33).
IX. Commendation and Greetings (ch. 16).

ROME

ROME The capital of the Roman Empire. The Jews were excluded from Rome by Claudius (Ac 18:2). Paul's visit to Rome. *See Paul.* Visited by Onesiphorus (2Ti 1:16-17). Paul desires to preach in (Ro 1:15). Abominations in (Ro 1:18-32). Christians in (Ro 16:5-17; Php 1:12-18; 4:22; 2Ti 4:21).

ROOF

See House, Architecture of.

ROOM

1. Chamber in a house (Ac 1:13). Used as a place for private prayer (Mt 6:6).
2. Place or position in society (Mt 23:6; Lk 14:7-8; 20:46).

ROOSTER

Stately in its stride (Pr 30:31). Its crowing a sign of Peter's denial of Jesus (Mt 26:34, 74-75; Mk 13:35; 14:30, 68, 72).

ROOT

Usually used in a figurative sense.
1. Essential cause of something (1Ti 6:10).
2. Foundation or support of something (2Ki 19:20; Job 5:3).
3. Injured roots means loss of life or vitality (Job 31:12; Isa 5:24).
4. Root of Jesse and Root of David, messianic titles (Isa 11:10; Ro 15:12; Rev 5:5; 22:16). *See Titles and Names, Of Jesus.*

ROPE

Threefold (Ecc 4:12). Worn on the head as an emblem of servitude (1Ki 20:31-32). Used in casting lots (Mic 2:5).
Figurative: Of love (Hos 11:4). Of affliction (Job 36:8). Of temptations (Ps 140:5; Pr 5:22).

ROSE

Or "crocus" (SS 2:1; Isa 35:1).

ROSETTA STONE

Inscribed basalt slab, found on Rosetta branch of the Nile in 1799, with text in hieroglyphics, demotic (a cursive Egyptian language), and Greek. It furnished the key for the decipherment of hieroglyphics.

ROSH

(*head, leader*).
1. Son of Benjamin (Ge 46:21).
2. Chief of three nations that are to invade Israel during the latter days (Eze 38:2; 39:1).

ROW, ROWERS

See Ship.

RUBY

A precious stone (Job 28:18; Pr 20:15; 31:10; La 4:7; Eze 27:16). In the priestly breastplate (Ex 28:17; 39:10). In the Garden of Eden (Eze 28:13).
See Minerals of the Bible, 1; Sardius; Stones.

RUDDER(S)

Used to steer a ship (Ac 27:40; Jas 3:4).

RUDDY

Red or fair complexion (1Sa 16:12).

RUDE

(*untrained, ignorant of rules*). Technically not trained (2Co 11:6).

RUDIMENTS

(*first principles or elements of anything*). Elements (Gal 4:3, 9; 2Pe 3:10, 12), first principles (Heb 5:12), physical elements of the world (2Pe 3:10, 12).

RUE

(Lk 11:42).

RUFUS

(*red haired*).
1. Brother of Alexander and son of Simon of Cyrene who bore the cross (Mk 15:21).
2. Friend of Paul (Ro 16:13).

RUHAMAH

(*pitied*). A symbolic name of Israel used to indicate the return of God's mercy (Hos 2:1; cf Ro 9:25-26; 1Pe 2:10). A play on words is involved, for the second child of Gomer, wife of Hosea, was called Lo-Ruhamah, denoting a time when God had turned his back on Israel because of her apostasy. The NT references apply to Gentiles coming into the Church (Ro 9:25-26; 1Pe 2:10).
See Lo-Ammi; Lo-Ruhamah.

RULERS

General:
Appointed and removed by God. *See Government, God in.*
Chastised (Da 4). *See Nation.*
Monarchical. *See Kings.*
Patriarchal (Ge 27:29, 37). Instances of: Nimrod (Ge 10:8-10). Abraham (Ge 14:13-24; 17:6; 21:21-32). Melchizedek (Ge 14:18). Isaac (Ge 26:26-31). Judah (Ge 38:24). Heads of families (Ex 6:14). Ishmael (Ge 17:20). Esau and the chiefs of Edom (Ge 36).
Theocratic. *See Government.*
Ordained of God (2Ch 9:8; Ro 13:1-2, 4; 1Pe 2:14). Appointed by God (1Sa 9:15-17; 10:1; 15:17; 16:1, 7, 13; 2Sa 7:13-16; 1Ki 14:14; 16:1-4; 1Ch 28:4-5; 29:25; Ps 89:19-37; Da 2:21, 37; 5:21; Ac 13:22). Accountable to God (2Ch 1:7).
Servants of the people (1Ki 12:7; 2Ch 10:7; Eze 34:2-4). Loyalty to, commanded (Ecc 7:26). Must not be reviled (Ex 22:28; 2Sa 16:9; 19:21; Ecc 10:20; Ac 23:5; 2Pe 2:10-11; Jude 8).
Righteous, beloved (Pr 29:2, 14). A terror to evildoers (Pr 14:35; Ro 13:3). Incompetent, oppress (Pr 28:16). Corrupted, by evil

counselors (Pr 25:5), by gifts (Pr 29:4; Isa 1:23; Am 5:11-12; Mic 7:3).
Mosaic law concerning atonement for sins of (Lev 4:22-26).

Character and Qualifications of:
(Nu 27:16-17; 2Sa 23:4; Pr 20:8, 26, 28). Diligent (Ro 12:8). Wise (Ge 41:33; Dt 1:13; Ps 2:10; Pr 20:26; 28:2). Merciful (Isa 16:5; Zec 7:9).
Required to know the law (Jos 1:8; Ezr 7:25), to fear the Lord (Ps 2:11), to be truthful (Pr 17:7), to be righteous (Ex 18:21; Dt 16:19; 27:19; 2Sa 23:3-4; Pr 16:12, 13), to judge justly (Ex 18:16, 20-21; 23:3, 6-7, 9; Lev 19:15; 24:22; Dt 1:16-17; 25:1; 2Ch 9:8; Ps 82:2-4; Pr 31:9; Isa 16:5; 58:6; Jer 22:2-3; Zec 7:9-10; 8:16). Should not drink wine (Pr 31:4-5). Forbidden to take bribes (Ex 23:8; Dt 16:19), to show partiality (Lev 19:15; Dt 1:17; 16:19; Pr 24:23).

Duties of:
To rule in righteousness (Isa 58:6; Jer 22:1-3). To be judges (2Ch 9:8). To judge according to law (Dt 17:18-19; Jos 1:7-8). In judicial functions to make thorough investigations (Dt 19:18-19).

Righteous, Instances of:
Pharaoh, in his treatment of Abraham (Ge 12:15-20). Abimelech, in his treatment of Abraham (Ge 20), of Isaac (Ge 26:6-11). Joseph, in his conduct of the affairs of Egypt (Ge 41:37-57). Pharaoh, in his treatment of Jacob and his family (Ge 47:5-10; 50:1-6). Moses, in his administration of the affairs of the Israelites (Nu 16:15). *See Government, Mosaic.* Samuel, in not taking reward for judgment (1Sa 12:3-4). Saul, after the defeat of the Ammonites (1Sa 11:12-13).
Solomon, in his judgment between the two women who claimed the same child (1Ki 3:16-28), according to the testimony of the queen of Sheba (1Ki 10:6-9). Asa, in abolishing sodomy and other abominations of idolatry (1Ki 15:11-15; 2Ch 14:2-5). Jehoshaphat, in walking in the ways of the Lord (1Ki 22:41-46; 2Ch 17:3-10; 19; 20:3-30). Hezekiah, in his fear of the Lord (2Ki 18:3; 20:1-11; 2Ch 30; 31). Josiah, in repairing the temple and in other good works (2Ki 22; 23; 2Ch 34; 35). Cyrus, in emancipating the Jews (Ezr 1). Darius, in advancing the rebuilding of the temple (Ezr 6:1-12). Artaxerxes, in commissioning Ezra to restore the forms of worship at Jerusalem (Ezr 7; Ne 2; 5:14). Nehemiah (Ne 4; 5). Daniel. *See Daniel.* King of Nineveh, in repenting and proclaiming a fast (Jnh 3:6-9).

Wicked:
(Ne 9:34-37; Ps 58:1-2; 82:2; 94:20-21; Ecc 3:16-17; 5:8; Isa 5:7; 28:14-15; Hos 7:3). Oppress the people (Ex 3:9; 1Sa 8:10-18; Job 35:9; Pr 28:15-16; Am 4:1; 5:11-12). Pervert justice (Dt 27:19). Cause people to mourn (Pr 29:2; Ecc 4:1). A public calamity (Ecc 10:16; Isa 5:22-23). An abomination to God (Pr 17:15). Abhorred by men (Pr 21:24; 29:2).
Admonitions to (Eze 34:2-4, 7-10; 45:9). Denounced (Eze 34:2-4, 7-10; Am 4:1-2; Mic 3:1-5, 9-11; Zep 3:3). Divine judgment upon (Isa 3:14-15; 10:1-3; 30:33; 40:23; Jer 5:28-29; Eze 21:25-26; Hos 5:10; Am 5:11-12; Zep 1:8).

Instances of—
Potiphar, putting Joseph into prison (Ge 39:20, w 40:15). Pharaoh, oppressing the Israelites (Ex 1-11). Adoni-Bezek, torturing seventy kings (Jdg 1:7). Abimelech, slaying his seventy brothers (Jdg 9:1-5). Eli's sons, desecrating the sacrifices (1Sa 2:12-17), debauching themselves and the worshipers (1Sa 2:22). Samuel's sons, taking bribes (1Sa 8:1-5).
Saul, sparing Agag and the best of the booty (1Sa 15:8-35), in jealousy plotting against David (1Sa 18:8-29), seeking to slay David (1Sa 19), slaying Ahimelech and the priests (1Sa 22:7-19), Hanun, mistreating David's servants (2Sa 10:4; 1Ch 19:2-5). David, numbering Israel and Judah (2Sa 24:10; 1Ch 21:1-7; 27:23-24). Solomon, luxurious and idolatrous (1Ki 11:1-13), oppressing the people (1Ki 12:4; 4:7-23). Rehoboam, making the yoke heavy (1Ki 12:8-11; 2Ch 10:1-15).
Jeroboam, perverting the true worship (1Ki 12:26-33; 13:1-5; 14:16), exalting wicked persons to the priesthood (1Ki 12:31; 13:33; 2Ki 17:32; 2Ch 11:14-15; Eze 44:7, w Nu 3:10). Abijah, walking in the sins of Rehoboam (1Ki 15:3). Nadab, walking in the ways of Jeroboam (1Ki 15:26). Baasha, walking in the ways of Jeroboam (1Ki 15:33-34). Asa, imprisoning the seer and oppressing the people (2Ch 16:10). Zimri, walking in the ways of Jeroboam (1Ki 16:19). Omri, walking in the ways of Jeroboam (1Ki 16:25-29). Ahab, serving Baal (1Ki 16:30-33; 21:21-26), confiscating Naboth's vineyard (1Ki 21, w 1Sa 8:14; 1Ki 22:38; 2Ki 9:26). Jehoram, following the sins of Jeroboam (2Ki 3:2). Hazael, committing atrocities (2Ki 8:12; 10:32; 12:17; 13:3-7). Jehoram, walking in the ways of the kings of Israel (2Ki 8:18; 2Ch 21:13). Jehu, did not depart from the sins of Jeroboam (2Ki 10:29). Jehoahaz, in following the sins of Jeroboam (2Ki 13:1-2). Jehoash, in following the wicked example of Jeroboam (2Ki 13:10-11). Jeroboam II, not departing from the sins of Jeroboam (2Ki 14:23-24). Zechariah, Menahem, Pekahiah, and Pekah, following the sins of Jeroboam (2Ki 15:9, 18, 24, 28), conspiring against and slaying Pekahiah (2Ki 15:25). Hoshea, who conspired against Pekah (2Ki 15:30), in permitting Baal worship (2Ki 17:1-2, 7-18). Ahaz, burning his children in idolatrous sacrifice (2Ki 16:3; 2Ch 28:2-4).
Manasseh, who committed the abominations of the heathen (2Ki 21:1-17; 2Ch 33:2-7). Amon, who followed the evil example of Manasseh (2Ki 21:19-22). Jehoahaz, who followed in the ways of his fathers (2Ki 23:32). Jehoiakim, in walking in the ways of his fathers (2Ki 23:37), and Jehoiachin (2Ki 24:9). Zedekiah, following the evil example of Jehoiakim (2Ki 24:19; 2Ch 36:12-13) and persecuting Jeremiah (Jer 38:5-6). Joash, killing Zechariah (2Ch 24:2, 17-25). Ahaziah, doing evil like the house of Ahab (2Ch 22:1-9). Amaziah, worshiping the gods of Seir (2Ch 25:14). Uzziah, invading the priest's office (2Ch 26:16).
Xerxes and Haman, decreeing the death of the Jews (Est 3). Nebuchadnezzar, commanding to destroy the wise men (Da 2:1-13), and committing the three Hebrews to the furnace (Da 3:1-23). Belshazzar, in drunkenness and committing sacrilege (Da 5:22-23). Darius, in deifying himself (Da 6:7, 9). The princes, conspiring against Daniel (Da 6:1-9).
Herod the Great, slaying the children in Bethlehem (Mt 2:16-18). Herod Antipas, in beheading John the Baptist (Mt

14:1-11), in craftiness and tyranny (Lk 13:31-32; 23:6-15). Herod Agrippa, persecuting the church (Ac 12:1-19). Pilate, delivering Jesus for crucifixion (Mt 27:11-26; Mk 15:15). Chief priests, elders, and all the council, seeking false witness against Jesus (Mt 26:59). Ananias, commanding that Paul be struck (Ac 23:2).
See Government; Judge; Kings.

RUMAH

(*height*). Home of Pedaiah, whose daughter Zebidah bore Jehoiakim to Josiah, king of Judah (2Ki 23:36), perhaps Arumah near Shechem, or Rumah in Galilee.

RUNNER

A bodyguard running before kings and princes (1Sa 8:11; 2Sa 15:1; 1Ki 1:5). An athlete (Job 9:25; 1Co 9:24). *See Army; Games.*

RUSH

A water plant (Isa 19:6). *See Plants of the Bible; Reed.*

RUTH

(*friendship* BDB; *refreshed [as with water]* IDB; possibly *comrade, companion* ISBE). A Moabitess who married a son of Elimelech and Naomi of Bethlehem (Ru 1:1-4), ancestor of Christ (Mt 1:5), the Book of Ruth is about her.

RUTH, BOOK OF

Author: Anonymous, Jewish tradition points to Samuel
Date: During the period of the monarchy
Outline:
I. Introduction: Naomi Emptied (1:1-5).
II. Naomi Returns From Moab (1:6-22).
 A. Ruth Clings to Naomi (1:6-18).
 B. Ruth and Naomi Return to Bethlehem (1:19-22).
III. Ruth and Boaz Meet in the Harvest Fields (ch. 2).
 A. Ruth Begins Work (2:1-7).
 B. Boaz Shows Kindness to Ruth (2:8-16).
 C. Ruth Returns to Naomi (2:17-23).
IV. Ruth Goes to Boaz at the Threshing Floor (ch. 3).
 A. Naomi Instructs Ruth (3:1-5).
 B. Boaz Pledges to Secure Redemption (3:6-15).
 C. Ruth Returns to Naomi (3:16-18).
V. Boaz Arranges to Marry Ruth (4:1-12).
 A. Boaz Confronts the Unnamed Kinsman (4:1-8).
 B. Boaz Buys Naomi's Property and Announces His Marriage to Ruth (4:9-12).
VI. Conclusion: Naomi Filled (4:13-17).
VII. Epilogue: Genealogy of David (4:18-22).

RYE

See Spelt.

S

SABACHTHANI

See Eloi, Eloi, Lama Sabachthani.

SABAEANS

See Sabeans; Seba.

SABAOTH, LORD OF

(*Yahweh of [angelic] armies*). Regularly translated "LORD Almighty" in the NIV. *See Almighty; God, Names of; Yahweh Tsabbaoth.*

SABBATH

(*cease, rest*).
A Time of Rest:
(Ge 2:2-3; Lev 23:25; 26:34-35). Holy (Ex 16:23; Ex 20:8, 11; 31:14-15; 35:2; Dt 5:12; Ne 9:14; Isa 58:13-14; Eze 44:24). A sign (Ex 31:13, 16-17; Eze 20:12-13, 16, 20-21, 24). The Lord is represented as resting on (Ge 2:2-3; Ex 31:17; Heb 4:4).
Rest on, commanded (Ex 16:28-30; 23:12; 31:15; 34:21; 35:2-3; Lev 6:29-31; 19:3, 30; 23:1-3, 27-32; 26:2; Dt 5:12; 2Ch 36:21; Jer 17:21-22, 24-25, 27; Lk 23:56), of servants and animals (Ex 16:5, 23-30; 20:10; Mk 16:1; Lk 23:56).

Observation of:
Offerings prescribed for (Lev 24:8; Nu 28:9-10; 1Ch 9:32; 23:31; 2Ch 2:4; Eze 46:4-5). Song for (Ps 92:1-15; 118:24). Preparation for (Ex 16:5, 22; Mt 27:62; Mk 15:42; Lk 23:54; Jn 19:31). Religious usages on (Ge 2:3; Mk 6:2; Lk 4:16, 31; 6:6; 13:10; Ac 13:14).
Worship on (Eze 46:1, 3; Ac 15:21; 16:13). Commanded (Eze 46:1, 3). Religious instruction on (Mk 6:2; Lk 4:16, 31; 6:6; 13:10; Ac 13:14, 27, 42, 44; 15:21; 17:2; 18:4). Apostles taught on (Ac 13:14-43, 44-48; 17:2; 18:4). Hypocritical observance, provokes divine displeasure (Isa 1:13; La 2:6; Eze 20:12-13, 16, 21, 24; Am 8:5). Rewards for observance of (Isa 56:2, 4-7; 58:13-14; Jer 17:21-22, 24-25).
Observed by: Moses (Nu 15:32-34). Nehemiah (Ne 13:15, 21). The women preparing to embalm the body of Jesus (Lk 23:56). Paul (Ac 13:14). The disciples (Ac 16:13). John (Rev 1:10).

Violations of:
Punished, by death (Ex 35:2; Nu 15:32-36), by judgments (Jer 17:27). Instances of: Gathering manna (Ex 16:27). Gathering sticks (Nu 15:32). By men from Tyre (Ne 13:16). Inhabitants of Jerusalem (Jer 17:21-23). Profanation of (Ex 16:27-28; Nu 15:32-36; Ne 10:31; 13:15, 21; Jer 17:21-23; Eze 22:8; 23:38).

Christ's Interpretation of:
(Mt 12:1-8, 10-13; Lk 6:1-10; Mk 2:23-28; 13:10-17; 14:1-5; Jn 7:21-24; 9:14). Christ is Lord of (Mt 12:8; Mk 2:28; Lk 6:5). Christ performed miracles on (Mt 12:10-13; Mk 3:1-5; Lk 6:1-10; Lk 13:10-17; Jn 5:5-14; 7:21-24). Christ taught on (Mk 1:21-22; 6:2; Lk 4:16, 31; 6:6; 13:10-17).

The Christian and the Sabbath:
Christian not to be judged regarding (Col 2:16; Ro 1:1-12).

The first day of the week is called the Lord's day (Mt 28:1, 5-7; Mk 16:9; Jn 20:1, 11-16, 19, 26; Ac 20:7; 1Co 16:2; Rev 1:10).

SABBATH, COVERT FOR THE NIV "Sabbath canopy" (2Ki 16:18).

SABBATH, DAY AFTER THE The waving of the sheaf in Lev 23:11 may be on the day after the ordinary weekly Sabbath or after the first day of the Passover.

SABBATH DAY'S JOURNEY A limited journey (c. 3000 feet) which Rabbinic scholars thought a Jew might travel on the Sabbath without breaking the law (Ac 1:12; cf. Ex 16:29; Nu 35:5; Jos 3:4).

SABBATIC YEAR A rest recurring every seventh year. Called the Year of Release (Dt 15:9; 31:10). Ordinances concerning (Ex 23:9-11; Lev 25). Israelite servants set free in (Ex 21:2; Dt 15:12; Jer 34:14). Creditors required to release debtors in (Dt 15:1-6, 12-18; Ne 10:31). Ordinances concerning instruction in the law during (Dt 31:10-13; Ne 8:18). Punishment to follow a violation of the ordinances concerning (Lev 26:34-35, w 32-41; Jer 34:12-22). See Jubilee.

SABBEUS See Shemaiah, 17.

SABEANS One of the Sabean monarchs was the famous Queen of Sheba (1Ki 10:1, 4, 10, 13; 2Ch 9:1, 3, 9, 12). See Sheba, 7. The Sabeans were a merchant people from Sheba who in early times lived in SW Arabia (modern Yemen) in a region bordering Ophir and Havilah (Isa 45:14; Eze 23:42 cf. Eze 27:20-22). Romans called it Arabia Felix. Sabean raiders invaded the land of Uz and killed Job's flocks and servants (Job 1:15; Isa 43:3). Prophecies concerning (Isa 43:3; Joel 3:8). Giants among (Isa 45:14). Proverbial drunkards (Eze 23:42, ftn). They were slave traders (Joel 3:8). See Seba.

SABTA, SABTAH A son of Cush (Ge 10:7; 1Ch 1:9), perhaps also a place in S Arabia.

SABTECA A son of Cush (Ge 10:7; 1Ch 1:9).

SACAR (reward [given by God], possibly hired hand).
1. Father of Ahiam (1Ch 11:35), "Sharar" (2Sa 23:33, ftn). See Sharar.
2. Son of Obed-Edom (1Ch 26:4).

SACKBUT See Lyre.

SACKCLOTH A symbol of mourning (1Ki 20:31-32; Job 16:15; Isa 15:3; Jer 4:8; 6:26; 49:3; La 2:10; Eze 7:18; Da 9:3; Joel 1:8). Worn by Jacob when it was reported to him that Joseph had been devoured by wild beasts (Ge 37:34). Animals covered with, at the time of national mourning (Jnh 3:8).
See Mourning.

SACRAMENT (something obligated [to do]). A symbolic rite instituted by Christ setting forth the central truths of the Christian faith: death and resurrection with Christ and participation in the redemptive benefits of Christ's mediatorial death. The Roman Catholic Church has seven sacraments; the Protestant Church two, often called ordinances: baptism and the Lord's Supper.

SACRED PLACES (Dt 12:5, 11; 14:23; 15:20; 16:2; 17:8; Jos 9:27; 18:1; 1Ch 22:1; 2Ch 7:15; Ps 78:68). See Tabernacle; Temple.

SACRIFICES
Figurative:
(Isa 34:6; Eze 39:17; Zep 1:7-8; Ro 12:1; Php 2:17; 4:18). Of self-denial (Php 3:7-8). Of praise (Ps 116:17; Jer 33:11; Hos 14:2; Heb 13:15). "Fruit of the lips" signifies praise (Hos 14:2).
See Bruise(s), 2; Offerings.

SACRILEGE (stealing, hence, profaning something sacred). Profaning holy things. Forbidden (Lev 19:8; 1Co 3:17; Tit 1:11; 1Pe 5:2).

Instances of:
Esau sells his birthright (Ge 25:33). Nadab and Abihu offer unauthorized fire (Lev 10:1-7; Nu 3:4). Of Uzzah (2Sa 6:6-7). Of Uzziah (2Ch 26:16-21). Of Korah and his company (Nu 16:40). Of the people of Beth Shemesh (1Sa 6:19). Of Ahaz (2Ch 28:24). Of money changers in the temple (Mt 21:12-13; Lk 19:45; Jn 2:14-16). Of those who profaned the Lord's Supper (1Co 11:29).

SADDLE (to ride, riding seat). Getting a beast ready for riding (Ge 22:3; Nu 22:21; Jdg 19:10; 2Sa 16:1; 17:23). Donkeys were not ridden with saddles; when carrying heavy burdens they had a thick cushion on their backs.

SADDUCEES (followers of Zadok; possibly righteous). A Jewish religious sect in the time of Christ. Beliefs: Acceptance only of the Law and rejection of oral tradition; denial of the Resurrection, immortality of the soul, and the spirit world (Mk 12:18; Lk 20:27; Ac 23:8); they supported the Maccabees; a relatively small group, but generally held the high priesthood; they were denounced by John the Baptist (Mt 3:7-8) and Jesus (Mt 16:6, 11-12); they opposed Christ (Mt 21:12f; Mk 11:15f; Lk 19:47) and the apostles (Ac 5:17, 33). See Testaments, Time Between.

SADOC See Zadok.

SAFE-CONDUCT Letters or passports provided to Nehemiah (Ne 2:7).

SAFFRON See Plants of the Bible.

SAHADUTHA See Jegar Sahadutha.

SAIL See Ship.

SAILORS See Mariner; Occupations and Professions.

SAINTS (unique, consecrated, holy ones).
1. A member of God's covenant people Israel, whether a layman (Ps 34:9; 79:1; 85:8), or a leader (2Ch 6:41; Ps 16:3).
2. A NT believer (Ac 9:13; 2Co 1:1). The saints are the Church (2Co 1:1), people called out of the world to be God's own people. Throughout the Bible the saints are urged to live lives befitting their position (Eph 4:1; Col 1:10), for even saints can sin (1Jn 1:10-2:2). See Sanctification; Holiness.

SAKIA (possibly one who looks to Yahweh KB). Son of Shaharaim (1Ch 8:10).

SALAH, SALA (missile or petition ISBE; possibly javelin KB). See Shelah, 1.

SALAMIS (peace). A city of Cyprus. Paul and Barnabas preach in (Ac 13:4-5).

SALATHIEL See Shealtiel, 2.

SALECAH A city on the NE boundary of Bashan (Dt 3:10; Jos 12:5; 13:11; 1Ch 5:11); possibly identified with Salkhad.

SALEM (peace). Name of a city of which Melchizedek was king (Ge 14:18; Ps 76:2; Heb 7:1-2), probably Jerusalem.

SALIM A place near Aenon W of Jordan (Jn 1:28; 3:23, 26; 10:40).

SALLAI (possibly God had restored).
1. A Benjamite dwelling in Jerusalem (Ne 11:8).
2. See Sallu.

SALLU (possibly he restores).
1. A Benjamite dwelling in Jerusalem (1Ch 9:7; Ne 11:7).
2. A priest who returned to Jerusalem with Zerubbabel (Ne 12:20).

SALMA (little spark KB).
1. A son of Caleb (1Ch 2:51, 54).
2. See Salmon.

SALMON (little spark KB). The father of Boaz, the husband of Ruth (Ru 4:20-21; 1Ch 2:11), in the lineage of Joseph (Mt 1:4-5; Lk 3:32). Also spelled Salma (Ru 4:20, ftn).

SALMONE A promontory of Crete (Ac 27:7).

SALOME (peaceful, prosperous one).
1. The wife of Zebedee and the mother of James and John (Mt 27:56; Mk 15:40; 16:1), ministered to Jesus (Mk 15:40-41), present at the crucifixion of Jesus (Mt 27:56), came to the tomb to anoint the body of Jesus (Mk 16:1).
2. The daughter of Herodias; as a reward for her dancing she obtained the head of John the Baptist (Mt 14:3-11; Mk 6:17-28). Her name is not given in the Gospels, but in Josephus.

SALT Lot's wife turned into a pillar of (Ge 19:26). The city of Salt (Jos 15:62). The valley of salt (2Sa 8:13; 2Ki 14:7). Salt sea (Ge 14:3; Nu 34:12; Dt 3:17; Jos 3:16; 12:3; 15:2). Salt pits (Zep 2:9). All animal sacrifices were required to be seasoned with (Lev 2:13; Ezr 6:9; Eze 43:24; Mk 9:49). Used in ratifying covenants (Nu 18:19; 2Ch 13:5). Elisha casts, into the pool of Jericho, to purify it (2Ki 2:20-21).
Symbolic: Of fidelity (Nu 18:19; 2Ch 13:5), of barrenness and desolation (Dt 29:23; Jdg 9:45; Jer 17:6; Zep 2:7).
Figurative: Of the saving efficacy of the church (Mt 5:13; Mk 9:49-50; Lk 14:34). Of wise conversation (Col 4:6).

SALT, CITY OF A city in the wilderness of Judah, between Nibshan and En Gedi (Jos 15:62), the site of which is uncertain; possibly Qumran.

SALT, COVENANT OF A covenant confirmed with sacrificial meals at which salt was used (Lev 2:13; Nu 18:19).

SALT HERBS A plant that grows in harsh terrain (Job 30:4).

SALT SEA See Dead Sea.

SALT, VALLEY OF A valley between Jerusalem and Edom in which great victories were won over the Edomites (2Sa 8:13; 2Ki 14:7; 2Ch 25:11).

SALU (restored IDB). Father of Zimri (Nu 25:14).

SALUTATIONS See Greetings.

SALVATION
Call to:
(Dt 30:19-20; Isa 55:1-3, 6-7; Lk 3:6; Ac 16:31; Heb 2:3).
Signifying:
Gracious providence (Dt 32:15; Ps 68:19-20; 91:16; 95:1; 116:13; 149:4; Isa 12:2-3). Personal deliverance from enemies (2Sa 22:36; Ps 3:8; 18:2; 37:39; Isa 1:18; 32:1-4). National deliverance from enemies (Ex 15:2; 1Ch 16:35; Ps 98:2-3; 106:8; Isa 46:12-13; Jer 3:23). A divine standard of righteousness (Isa 56:1), the saving power of divine truth (Isa 45:17), the light and glory of Zion (Isa 62:1). The promised Messiah (Jn 4:22). Personal righteousness (2Ch 6:41; Ps 132:16). Eternal life (1Th 5:8-9; 1Pe 1:5, 9; 1Jn 5:11). Everlasting (Isa 45:17; 52:10). Liberty (Isa 61:1-3; Mt 11:28-30).
To be developed (Php 2:12; 1Th 5:8-10; Jude 3).
From God:
(Ps 3:8; 36:8-9; 37:39; 68:18-20; 91:16; 98:2-3; 106:8; 121:1-8; Isa 46:12-13; 51:4-5; 63:9; Jer 3:23; 21:8; Eze 18:32; Joel 2:32; 1Pe 1:5; 1Jn 2:25).
Through Jesus Christ—
(Isa 61:10; Mt 1:21; Lk 19:10; 24:46-47; Jn 3:14-17; 11:51-52; Ac 4:12; 13:26, 38-39, 47; 16:30-31; Ro 5:15-21; 7:24-25; 9:30-33; 1Co 6:11; Gal 1:4; 3:13-14; Eph 1:9-10, 13; 2Ti 1:9-10;

2:10; Tit 3:5-7; Heb 2:3, 10; 5:9; 7:25; 1Jn 4:9-10; 5:11; Jude 3; Rev 3:20; 5:9).
By—
The atonement (1Co 1:18, 21, 24-25; Gal 1:4; 3:8, 13-14, 21, 26-28; Col 1:20-23, 26-27; 1Ti 2:6; Rev 5:9), the Resurrection (Ro 5:10), the gospel (Ro 1:16; Jas 1:21), the grace of God (Eph 2:8-9; Tit 2:11; 2Pe 3:15), the word of God (Jas 1:21), the power of God (1Co 1:18).
Message of:
Foretold by the prophets (Isa 29:18-19, 24; 35:8; Lk 2:31-32; 1Pe 1:10). By angels (Lk 2:9-14). From the seed of Abraham (Ge 12:13). Proclaimed by Christ (Lk 19:10; Jn 12:32). Preached by the apostles (Ac 11:17-18; 16:17). Wisdom for, derived from the Scriptures (2Ti 3:15). Praise for, ascribed to God and the Lamb (Rev 7:9-10).
For:
Israel (Isa 45:17; 46:12-13; Ac 13:26, 38-39, 47; Ro 1:16). The Gentiles (1Ki 8:41-43; Isa 52:10, 15; 56:1, 6-8; Mt 21:31; 24:14; Jn 10:16; Ac 11:17-18; 15:7-9, 11; 28:28; Ro 11:11-12; 15:9, 16; Gal 3:8, 14; Eph 3:6, 9).
All people (Mt 18:14; 22:9-10; 22:14; Lk 2:10, 31-32; 3:6; 13:29; Gal 3:28; Eph 2:14, 17; Col 3:11; 1Ti 2:3-4; 4:10; 2Pe 3:9; Rev 5:9; 7:9-10; 14:6; 22:17).
Experienced by Moses (Ex 15:2). Priests clothed with (2Ch 6:41; Ps 132:16).
From:
From sin (Mt 1:21; Mk 2:17; Lk 5:31-32). From spiritual hunger and thirst (Jn 4:14; 6:35; 7:37-38).
See Adoption; Redemption; Regeneration; Sanctification.
Conditions of:
Repentance (Mt 3:2; Mk 1:4; Lk 3:8; Ac 2:38; 3:19; 2Co 7:10). Faith in Christ (Mk 16:15-16; Jn 3:14-18; 5:24; 6:47; 9:35; 11:25-26; 12:36; 20:31; Ac 2:21; 15:9, 11; 20:21; Ro 1:16-17; 3:21-30; 4:1-25; 5:1-2; 10:4, 8-13; Gal 2:16; 3:8, 26-28; Eph 2:8; Php 3:9; 2Th 2:13; 1Ti 1:15-16; Heb 4:1-2; 1Pe 1:9). Supreme love to Christ (Lk 14:25-27). Renunciation of the world (Mt 19:16-21; Lk 14:33; 18:18-26). Choice (Dt 30:19-20; Ps 65:4; Jos 1:4-5). Seeking God (Am 5:4). Fear of God (Pr 14:27; 15:23; 16:6; Mal 4:2).
Not by works (Ro 3:28; 4:1-25; 9:30-33; Ro 11:6; Gal 2:16; Eph 2:8-9; 2Ti 1:9-10; Tit 3:5-7).
See Blessings, Spiritual, Contingent Upon Obedience; Faith; Obedience; Perseverance; Repentance.
Plan of:
(Jn 17:4; Heb 6:17-20). Foreordained (Eph 1:4-6; 3:11). Described as a mystery (Mt 13:11; Mk 4:11; Lk 8:10; Ro 16:25-26; 1Co 2:7-9; Eph 1:9-10, 13; 3:9-10; 6:19; Col 1:26-27; 1Ti 3:16; Rev 10:7).
Includes—
The incarnation of Christ (Gal 4:4-5). The atonement by Christ (Jn 18:11; 19:28-30; Ac 3:18; 17:3; Ro 16:25-26; 1Co 1:21-25; 2:7-9; Eph 1:7-11; 3:18; 6:19; Col 1:26-27; Heb 2:9-18; 10:10). Initial grace (Jn 6:37, 44-45, 65; Eph 2:5; Tit 2:11). The election of grace (2Th 2:13-14; 2Ti 1:9-10). Inheritance (Heb 1:14). Regeneration (Jn 3:3-12).
Sets Forth—
Reconciliation to God through Christ (2Co 5:18-19; Col 1:9, 19-23; Heb 2:14-18). Righteousness by faith in the atonement of Christ, as opposed to righteousness by works (Ro 10:3-9; 16:25-26; Eph 2:6-10).
Offered and Rejected—
(Dt 32:15; Mt 22:3-13; 23:37; Lk 14:16-24; Jn 5:40).
Parables of: (Lk 15:2-32).
Illustrated by:
A horn (Ps 18:2; Lk 1:69), a tower (2Sa 22:51), a helmet (Isa 59:17; Eph 6:17), a shield (2Sa 22:36), a lamp (Isa 62:1), a cup (Ps 116:13), clothing (2Ch 6:41; Ps 132:16; 149:4; Isa 61:10), wells (Isa 12:3), walls and bulwarks (Isa 26:1; 60:18), chariots (Hab 3:8), a victory (1Co 15:57).
Typified by the bronze snake (Nu 21:4-9, w Jn 3:14-15).
See Atonement; Jesus the Christ, Mission of; Redemption; Regeneration; Sanctification; Sin, Forgiveness of.

SAMARIA (belonging to clan of Shemer, 1Ki. 16:24, BDB).
1. City of, built by Omri (1Ki 16:24). Capital of the kingdom of the ten tribes (1Ki 16:29; 22:51; 2Ki 13:1, 10; 15:8). Besieged by Ben-Hadad (1Ki 20; 2Ki 6:24-33; 7). The king of Syria is led into, by Elisha, who miraculously blinds him and his army (2Ki 6:8-23). Ahab ruled in. See Ahab; Jezebel. Besieged by Shalmaneser, king of Assyria, three years; taken; the people carried away to Halah and Habor, cities of the Medes (2Ki 17:5-6; 18:9-11). Idolatry of (1Ki 16:32; 2Ki 13:6). Temple of, destroyed (2Ki 10:17-28; 23:19). Paul and Barnabas preach in (Ac 15:3). Visited by Philip, Peter, and John (Ac 8:5-25).
2. Country of (Isa 7:9). Foreign colonies distributed among the cities of, by the king of Assyria (2Ki 17:24-41; Ezr 4:9-10). Roads through, from Judea into Galilee (Lk 17:11; Jn 4:3-8). Jesus journeys through (Jn 4:1-42), heals lepers in (Lk 17:11-19). The good Samaritan from (Lk 10:33-35). No dealings between the Jews and the inhabitants of (Jn 4:9). Expect the Messiah (Jn 4:25). Disciples made from the inhabitants of (Jn 4:39-42; Ac 8:5-8, 4-17, 25). Jesus forbids the apostles to preach in the cities of (Mt 10:5).

SAMARITAN PENTATEUCH See Samaritan(s), 2.

SAMARITAN(S) (of Samaria).
1. The inhabitants of the region of Samaria (2Ki 17:26; Mt 10:5; Lk 9:52; 10:33; Jn 4:9, 30, 40; Ac 8:25). After the captivity of the N kingdom colonists from Babylonia, Syria, Elam, and other Assyrian territories (2Ki 17:24-34), intermarried with remnants of Jews in Samaria; held in contempt by the Jews (Ne 4:1-3; Mt 10:5; Jn 4:9-26).
2. The sect which derived its name from Samaria, a term of contempt with the Jews (Jn 8:48). Religion of the Samaritans was based on the Pentateuch alone.

SAMGAR, SAMGAR-NEBO Depending on word division, Samgar is the city of Nergal-Sharezer, a Babylonian official at the siege of Jerusalem, or Samgar-Nebo is himself an official (Jer 39:3 and ftn).

See Nebo-Sarsekim.

SAMLAH (*a garment*). One of the ancient kings of Edom (Ge 36:36-37; 1Ch 1:47-48).

SAMOS (*heights, lofty place*). An island in the Aegean Sea. Visited by Paul (Ac 20:15).

SAMOTHRACE (*Thracian Samos*). An island in the Aegean Sea. Visited by Paul (Ac 16:11).

SAMSON (*little one of Shemesh [pagan sun god] or sunny* IDB KB; *strong,* Josephus *Antiq.* 5.8.4). A judge of Israel (Jdg 16:31). A Danite, son of Manoah; miraculous birth of; a Nazirite from his mother's womb; the mother forbidden to drink wine or strong drink, or to eat any unclean thing during gestation (Jdg 13:2-7, 24-25). Desires a Philistine woman for his wife; slays a lion (Jdg 14:1-7). His marriage feast and the riddle propounded (Jdg 14:8-19). Wife of, estranged (Jdg 14:20; 15:1-2). Is avenged for the estrangement of his wife (Jdg 15:3-8). His great strength (Jdg 15:7-14; Heb 11:32). Slays a thousand Philistines with the jawbone of a donkey (Jdg 15:13-17). Miraculously supplied with water (Jdg 15:18-19). Consorts with Delilah, a harlot; who plots with the Philistines to overcome him (Jdg 16:4-20). Is blinded by the Philistines and confined to hard labor in prison; pulls down the pillars of the temple, killing himself and many Philistines (Jdg 16:21-31; Heb 11:32).

SAMUEL (*his name is God [El]* BDB IDB ISBE; *heard of God,* KD; *the unnamed god is El* KB).
1. Last of the judges (1Sa 7:15), and first of the prophets after Moses (2Ch 25:18; Jer 15:1). A seer (1Sa 9:9) and priest (1Sa 2:18, 27, 35). The son of Elkanah and Hannah (1Sa 1:19-20), birth the result of special providence. Brought up by Eli (1Sa 3), anointed Saul (1Sa 10) and David (1Sa 16:13). Traditional author of biblical books which bear his name, died at Ramah (1Sa 25:1).
2. Descendant of Issachar (1Ch 7:2).

SAMUEL, 1 and 2

Author: Anonymous, some have suggested Zabud, son of Nathan the prophet, who is referred to in 1Ki 4:5 as the "personal adviser" to King Solomon.

Date: Probably shortly after Solomon's death (930 B.C.)

Chronology of the Books of Samuel
(all dates B.C.):
1105: Birth of Samuel (1Sa 1:20).
1080: Birth of Saul.
1050: Saul anointed to be king (1Sa 10:1).
1040: Birth of David.
1025: David anointed to be Saul's successor (1Sa 16:1-13).
1010: Death of Saul and beginning of David's reign over Judah in Hebron (2Sa 1:1; 2:1, 4, 11).
1003: Beginning of David's reign over all Israel and capture of Jerusalem (2Sa 5).
997-992: David's wars (2Sa 8:1-14).
991: Birth of Solomon (2Sa 12:24; 1Ki 3:7; 11:42).
980: David's census (2Sa 24:1).
970: End of David's reign (2Sa 5:4-5; 1Ki 2:10-11).

Outline:
I. Historical Setting for the Establishment of Kingship in Israel (1Sa 1-7).
 A. Samuel's Birth, Youth and Calling to Be a Prophet; Judgment on the House of Eli (1Sa 1-3).
 B. Israel Defeated by the Philistines, the Ark of God Taken and the Ark Restored; Samuel's Role as Judge and Deliverer (1Sa 4-7).
II. The Establishment of Kingship in Israel Under the Guidance of Samuel the Prophet (1Sa 8-12).
 A. The People's Sinful Request for a King and God's Intent to Give Them a King (1Sa 8).
 B. Samuel Anoints Saul Privately to Be King (1Sa 9:1-10:16).
 C. Saul Chosen to Be King Publicly by Lot at Mizpah (1Sa 10:17-27).
 D. The Choice of Saul as King Confirmed by Victory Over the Ammonites (1Sa 11:1-13).
 E. Saul's Reign Inaugurated at a Covenant Renewal Ceremony Convened by Samuel at Gilgal (1Sa 11:14-12:25).
III. Saul's Kingship a Failure (1Sa 13-15).
IV. David's Rise to the Throne; Progressive Deterioration and End of Saul's Reign (1Sa 16:1-2Sa 5:5).
 A. David Is Anointed Privately, Enters the Service of King Saul and Flees for His Life (1Sa 16-26).
 B. David Seeks Refuge in Philistia, and Saul and His Sons Are Killed in Battle (1Sa 27-31).
 C. David Becomes King Over Judah (2Sa 1-4).
 D. David Becomes King Over All Israel (2Sa 5:1-5).
V. David's Kingship in Its Accomplishments and Glory (2Sa 5:6-9:12).
 A. David Conquers Jerusalem and Defeats the Philistines (2Sa 5:6-25).
 B. David Brings the Ark to Jerusalem (2Sa 6).
 C. God Promises David and Everlasting Dynasty (2Sa 7).
 D. The Extension of David's Kingdom Externally and the Justice of His Rule Internally (2Sa 8).
 E. David's Faithfulness to His Covenant With Jonathan (2Sa 9).
VI. David's Kingship in Its Weaknesses and Failures (2Sa 10-20).
 A. David Commits Adultery and Murder (2Sa 10-12).
 B. David Loses His Sons Amnon and Absalom (2Sa 13-20).
VII. Final Reflections on David's Reign (2Sa 21-24).

SANBALLAT (*Sin [pagan moon god] has given life*). A very influential Samaritan who tried unsuccessfully to defeat Nehemiah's plans for rebuilding the walls of Jerusalem (Ne 4:1ff; 6:1-14; 13:28).

SANCTIFICATION Separated, set apart, made holy: For God (Ex 33:16; Dt 7:6). From iniquity (2Ti 2:21).

By:
God (Ex 29:44; 31:13; Lev 20:8; 21:8, 15, 23; 22:9, 16; Jer 1:5; Eze 20:12; 37:28). In Christ (1Co 1:2, 30; 6:11; Eph 5:25-27; Heb 2:11; 10:10, 14; 13:12). By the Holy Spirit (Ro 15:16; 2Th 2:13-14; 1Pe 1:2).
By the blood of Christ (Heb 9:14; 13:12). By faith in Christ (Ac 26:17-18). By the truth (Jn 17:17, 19). By confession of sin (1Jn 1:9). By intercessory prayer for (1Th 5:23). Sanctification is the will of God (1Th 4:3-4).

Instances of:
The altar sanctifies the gift (Ex 29:37; 30:29; Mt 23:19).
The Sabbath (Ge 2:3; Dt 5:12; Ne 13:22). Mount Sinai (Ex 19:23). The tabernacle (Ex 29:43-44; 30:26, 29; 40:34-35; Lev 8:10; Nu 7:1). The furniture of the tabernacle (Ex 30:26-29; Nu 7:1). The altar of burnt offerings (Ex 29:36-37; 40:10-11; Lev 8:11, 15; Nu 7:1). The basin (Ex 30:23; Lev 8:11). The temple (2Ch 29:5, 17, 19).
Houses (Lev 27:14-15). Land (Lev 27:16-19, 22). Offerings (Ex 29:27). Material things by anointing (Ex 40:9-11).
The firstborn of Israelites (Ex 13:2; Lev 27:26; Nu 8:17; Dt 15:19). Eleazar to get the ark (1Sa 7:1). Jesse to offer a sacrifice (1Sa 16:5). Job's children, by Job (Job 1:5).
Of Levites (1Ch 15:12, 14; 2Ch 29:34; 30:15), commanded (1Ch 15:12; 2Ch 29:5). Of priests (1Ch 15:14; 2Ch 5:11; 30:24), commanded (2Ch 29:5). Of Aaron and his sons (Ex 28:41; 29:33, 44; 40:13; Lev 8:12, 30). Of Israel (Ex 29:10, 14)], commanded (Ex 19:10; Lev 11:44; 20:7; Nu 11:18; Jos 3:5; 7:13; Joel 2:16). Of the Corinthian Christians (1Co 1:2; 6:11; 7:14). Of the church (Eph 5:26; 1Th 5:23; Jude 24).

See Holiness; Purity; Sin, Forgiveness of; Spiritual Purification.

SANCTUARY (*sacredness, apartness, place apart, sacred place, holy place*).
1. The tabernacle or temple, where God established his earthly abode.
2. Judah (Ps 114:2).
3. Place of asylum (1Ki 2:28f).
4. In plural, idolatrous shrines (Am 7:9).
5. Earthly sanctuary a type of the heavenly sanctuary, in which Christ is high priest and sacrifice (Heb 10:1-18).

SAND Found in the desert and on the shores of large bodies of water; symbolic of numberlessness, vastness (Ge 22:17; Jer 33:22; 1Ki 4:29), weight (Job 6:3), and instability (Mt 7:26).

SANDAL Taken off on holy ground (Ex 3:5; Jos 5:15; Ac 7:33), in mourning (Eze 24:17), in token of refusal to observe the Levirate marriage (Dt 25:9; Ru 4:7-8). (Of the Israelites did not wear out (Dt 29:5). Poor sold for a pair of (Am 2:6; 8:6). Made of leather (Eze 16:10), thong of (Ge 14:23; Isa 5:27; Mk 1:7), untying of, a humble service (Lk 3:16).

See Dress.

SANDBARS Off the shores of N Africa S of Crete; site of Paul's shipwreck (Ac 27:17, 41).

SANHEDRIN (*sit together*). Highest Jewish tribunal during Greek and Roman periods; its origin is unknown; lost its authority when Jerusalem fell to the Romans in A.D. 70; in the time of Jesus it had authority only in Judea, but its influence was recognized even in the Diaspora (Ac 9:2; 22:5; 26:12). Composed of seventy members, plus the president, who was the high priest; members drawn from chief priests, scribes, and elders (Mt 16:21; 27:41; Mk 8:31; 11:27; 14:43, 53; Lk 9:22); the secular nobility of Jerusalem; final court of appeal for all questions connected with the Mosaic law; could order arrests by its own officers of justice (Mt 26:47; Mk 14:43; Ac 4:3; 5:17f; 9:2); did not have the right of capital punishment in the time of Christ (Jn 18:31-32). *See Elders, Council of.*

SANITATION AND HYGIENE

Relating to:
Carcasses (Lev 5:2; 10:4-5; 11:24-40; 22:4, 6; Nu 9:6, 10; 19:11-16; 31:19; Dt 21:22-23). Childbirth (Lev 12:3; Eze 16:4). Circumcision. *See Circumcision.* Contagion (Lev 5:2-3; 7:19, 21; 11:24-40; Nu 9:6, 10; 19:11-16, 22; 31:19-20). Infectious skin diseases (Lev 13-14; Nu 5:2-4; Dt 24:8). Bodily discharges (Lev 15:2-33; 22:4-8).

For Prevention of the Spread of Disease:
By washing (Lev 13:6, 34, 53-54, 58-59; 14:8-9, 46, 48, 54-57; 15:2-28; Nu 31:19-20, 22-24; Dt 23:10-11). By burning (Lev 7:19; 13:51-52, 55-57; Nu 31:19-20, 22-23). By isolation, *i.e.,* quarantine (Lev 13:2-5, 31-33, 45-50; 14:34-38; 15:19; Nu 5:2-3; 12:10, 14-15; 2Ki 7:3; 15:5; 2Ch 26:21; Lk 17:12). By demolishing infected houses (Lev 14:39-45).

Food:
Acceptable: Animals with split hoof that chew cud (Lev 11:2-3; Dt 14:6). Aquatic animals having fins and scales (Lev 11:9; Dt 14:9). Certain insects (Lev 11:22).
Forbidden: Fat (Lev 3:17; 7:23-25). Blood (Lev 3:17; 7:26-27; 17:10-14; 19:26; Dt 12:16, 20-25; 15:23). Meat that touched anything unclean (Lev 7:19). Meat of fellowship and thank offerings remaining until the second day (Lev 7:15; 22:30). Meat of vow or voluntary offerings left until the third day (Lev 7:16, 18; 19:5-8). Animals that only chew cud or only have a split hoof (Lev 11:4, 8, 26; Dt 14:7-8). Aquatic animals without fins and scales (Lev 11:10-12; Dt 14:10). Animals dying of themselves or torn by beasts (Lev 22:31; Lev 17:15; 22:8; Dt 14:21). Certain insects (Lev 11:23). Certain creatures that move on the ground (Lev 11:20-21, 28-31, 41). Certain birds (Lev 11:13-18).

Waste Products:
Disposition (Ex 29:14, 34; Lev 4:11-12, 21; 6:30; 7:17, 19; 8:17, 32; 9:11; 16:27-28; 19:6; Dt 23:12-13; Heb 13:11).

Women in Childbirth: (Lev 12:2, 4-5).

Penalties Concerning:
(Dt 28:15, 21-22, 27, 35, 45, 59-62).
See Defilement; Leprosy; Purification; Unclean, Uncleanness; Washings.

SANNAH See Kiriath Sannah.

SANSANNAH (*a palm branch*). A city of Judah (Jos 15:31).

SAPH (*a basin, threshold*). A Philistine giant, slain by one of David's heroes (2Sa 21:18; 1Ch 20:4).

SAPHIR See Shaphir.

SAPPHIRA (*beautiful*). The wife of Ananias; struck dead at Peter's feet because she lied (Ac 5:1-10).

SAPPHIRE
1. A precious stone (Ex 24:10; Eze 28:13).
2. Set in the priestly breastplate (Ex 28:18; 39:11).

Symbolic:
Throne of God (Ex 24:10; Eze 1:26; 10:1). Seen in the foundation of the Holy City, the New Jerusalem in John's apocalyptic vision (Rev 21:19).

Figurative:
Ezekiel uses imagery of the Creation and the Fall to picture the career of the king of Tyre; unlike Adam, who was naked, the king is pictured as a fully clothed priest, ordained to guard God's holy place; the nine stones listed are among the twelve worn by the priest (Eze 28:13).
See Minerals of the Bible, 1; Stones.

SARAH, SARAI (*princess*).
1. .The wife of Abraham (Ge 11:29-31; 12:5). Near of kin to Abraham (Ge 12:10-20; 20:12). Abraham represents her as his sister, and Abimelech, king of Gerar, takes her; she is restored to Abraham by means of a dream (Ge 20:1-14). Is sterile; gives her maid, Hagar, to Abraham as a wife to bear his child (Ge 16:1-3). Her jealousy of Hagar (Ge 16:4-6; 21:9-14). Her miraculous conception of Isaac (Ge 17:15-21; 18:9-15). Name changed from Sarai to Sarah (Ge 17:15). Gives birth to Isaac (Ge 21:3, 6-8). Death and burial of (Ge 23; 25:10). Character of (Heb 11:11; 1Pe 3:5-6).
2. The daughter of Asher (Ge 46:17; Nu 26:46; 1Ch 7:30).

SARAPH (*burning one, serpent*). A descendant of Shelah (1Ch 4:22).

SARCASM

Instances of:
Cain's self-justifying argument when God asked him where Abel was (Ge 4:9). Israelites reproaching Israel (Nu 11:20; Jdg 10:14). Balak reproaching Balaam (Nu 24:11). Joshua to descendants of Joseph (Jos 17:15). By Jotham (Jdg 9:7-19), Samson (Jdg 14:18). The men of Jabesh to Nahash (1Sa 11:10). Eliab to David (1Sa 17:28). Elijah to the priests of Baal (1Ki 18:27). David's reply to Michal's irony (2Sa 6:21). Ahab's reply to Ben-Hadad (1Ki 20:11). Jehoash to Amaziah (2Ki 14:9-10; 2Ch 25:18-19). The field commander to Hezekiah (2Ki 18:23-24). Sanballat's address to the army of Samaria (Ne 4:2-3). Zophar to Job (Job 11:12). Job to Zophar (Job 12:2-3). Of Solomon (Pr 26:16). The persecutors of Jesus (Mt 27:28-29; Lk 23:11; Jn 19:2-3, 5, 15). Paul (1Ti 4:7). Agrippa to Paul (Ac 26:28).
See Irony; Satire.

SARDINE See Carnelian; Minerals of the Bible.

SARDIS Chief city of Lydia; famous for arts and crafts; patron of mystery cults (Rev 1:11; 3:1-6).

SARDITE See Sered, Seredite.

SARDIUS See Carnelian; Minerals of the Bible, 1; Ruby; Stones.

SARDONYX A precious stone seen in the foundation of the Holy City, the New Jerusalem (Rev 21:20). *See Minerals of the Bible, 1; Stones.*

SAREPTA See Zarephath.

SARGON (*firm, faithful king* BDB; *the king is legitimate* IDB).
1. Sargon I, king and founder of early Babylonian Empire (2400 B.C.). Not referred to in the Bible.
2. Sargon II (722-705 B.C.), an Assyrian king (Isa 20:1), successor of Shalmaneser who captured Samaria (2Ki 17:1-6), defeated Egyptian ruler So (2Ki 17:4), destroyed the Hittite Empire; succeeded by his son Sennacherib.

SARID (*survivor*). A village on the boundary of Zebulun (Jos 19:10, 12); modern Tel Shadud, N of Megiddo.

SARON See Sharon.

SARSECHIM See Nebo-Sarsekim.

SARUCH See Serug.

SASH A belt or waistband. Worn by the high priest (Ex 28:4, 39; 39:29; Lev 8:7; 16:4), by other priests (Ex 28:40; 29:9; Lev 8:13), by women (Isa 3:18-24), by Jesus in John's vision (Rev 1:13). Commerce in (Pr 31:24). *See Belt; Dress.*

SATAN (*hostile opponent*).
1. As a common noun; enemy or adversary (1Sa 29:4; 1Ki 5:4; 11:14; Ps 38:20; 109:6).
2. As a proper noun; the chief of the fallen spirits, the grand adversary of God and man (Job 1:6, 12; 2:1; Zec 3:1), hostile to everything good. Not an independant rival of god, but is able to go only as far as God permits (Job 1:12; 2:6; Lk 22:31). Basically evil; story of his origin not told, but he was originally good; fell as

a star out of heaven because of pride (possibly Isa 14:12; Eze 29:12-19; Lk 10:18; 1Ti 3:6). Ruler of a powerful kingdom standing in opposition to God (Mt 12:26; Lk 11:18); continually seeks to defeat the divine plans of grace toward mankind (1Pe 5:8); defeated by Christ at Calvary (Ge 3:15; Jn 3:8).

Sterilizes the heart (Mt 13:19, 38-39; Mk 4:15; Lk 8:12). Causes spiritual blindness (2Co 4:4), physical infirmities (Lk 13:16).

Devices of (2Co 2:11; 12:7; Eph 6:11-12, 16; 1Th 2:18; 1Ti 3:6-7).

Hymenaeus and Alexander delivered to (1Ti 1:20). Contends with Michael (Jude 9). Ministers of, masquerade as apostles of Christ (2Co 11:15).

To be resisted (Eph 4:27; Jas 4:7; 1Pe 5:8-9). Resistance of, effectual (1Jn 2:13; 5:18). Gracious deliverance from the power of (Ac 27:18; Col 1:13). Persecutes the church (Rev 2:10, 13-14).

Christ accused of being (Mt 9:34; Mk 2:22-26; Lk 11:15, 18). Paul accuses Elymas the sorcerer of being (Ac 13:10).

Called:
Beelzebub (Mt 12:24; Mk 3:22; Lk 11:15). Belial (2Co 6:15). The devil (Mt 4:1; 13:39; Lk 4:2-6; Rev 20:2). Satan (1Ch 21:1; Job 1:6; Zec 3:1; Lk 22:31; Jn 13:27; Ac 5:3; 26:18; Ro 16:20). Possibly Apollyon (Rev 9:11) and Lucifer (Isa 14:12, KJV). See *Titles and Names, Of the Devil.*

Character of:
Accuser (Job 1:6-7, 9-12; 2:3-7). Adversary (Lk 22:31, 53; 1Pe 5:8). Deceiver of the whole world (Rev 12:9). Murderer and liar (Jn 8:44; Ac 5:3). Sinned from the beginning (1Jn 3:8). Subtle (Ge 3:1; 2Co 11:3). Tempter (Mt 4:3; 1Co 7:5; 1Th 3:5; 1Ti 5:15). Transforms himself into an angel of light (2Co 11:14).

Described as:
Accuser of our brothers (Rev 12:10). Ancient serpent (Rev 12:9; 20:2). Angel of the bottomless pit (Rev 9:11). Father of lies (Jn 8:44). Great dragon (Rev 12:9). Evil one (Mt 13:19, 38). Power of darkness (Col 1:13). Prince of this world (Jn 12:31; 14:30; 16:11), of demons (Mt 12:24), of the power of the air (Eph 2:2). Ruler of the darkness of this world (Eph 6:12). Spirit that works in the children of disobedience (Eph 2:2). The god of this world (2Co 4:4).

Instances of Temptations of:
Eve (Ge 3:1, 4-5, 14-15; 2Co 11:3). Job (Job 1:13-22; 2:7-10). David (1Ch 21:1). Jesus (Mt 4:1-11; Mk 1:13; Lk 4:1-13; Jn 14:30). Judas (Jn 13:2, 27).

Kingdom of:
Called gates of hell (Mt 16:18). To be destroyed (Ge 3:15; Mt 13:30; Ro 16:20; 1Jn 3:8).

Symbolized:
By the serpent (Ge 3:13; 2Co 11:3). By the dragon (Rev 12:3-4).

Synagogue of: (Rev 2:9; 3:9).
See *Demons.*

Destiny of:
A conquered enemy of believers (Jn 12:31; 16:9-10; 1Jn 3:8; Col 2:15). Judged already (Jn 16:11). Under perpetual curse (Ge 3:14; Isa 65:25). To be cast out of this world (Jn 12:31), bound (Rev 20:1-3), cast into the lake of fire (Mt 25:41; Rev 20:10).

SATIRE Hannah's song of exultation over Peninnah (1Sa 2:1-10, w 1:5-10). Of Jesus against hypocrites (Mt 23:2-33; Mk 12:13-40; Lk 11:39-54). See *Irony; Sarcasm.*

SATRAP (*protector of the land*). An official in the Persian Empire who ruled several small provinces (satraps), each having its own governor. (Ezr 8:36; Est 3:12; 8:9; 9:3; Da 3:2-3, 27; 6:1-7).

SATYR NIV "goat idols" (Lev 17:7; 2Ch 11:15); "wild goats" (Isa 34:14).

SAUL (*asked, possibly dedicated to God*).
1. Also called Shaul. King of Edom (Ge 36:37-38; 1Ch 1:48-49).
2. King of Israel. A Benjamite, son of Kish (1Sa 9:1-2). Sons of (1Ch 8:33). His personal appearance (1Sa 9:2; 10:23). Made king of Israel (1Sa 9; 10; 11:12-15; Hos 13:11). Dwells at Gibeah of Saul (1Sa 14:2; 15:34; Isa 10:29). Defeats the Philistines (1Sa 13; 14:46, 52). Kills the Amalekites (1Sa 15). Is reproved by Samuel for usurping the priestly functions (1Sa 13:11-14), for disobedience in not slaying the Amalekites; the loss of his kingdom foretold (1Sa 15). Dedicates the spoils of war (1Sa 15:21-25; 1Ch 26:28). Sends messengers to Jesse, asking that David be sent to him as musician and armor-bearer (1Sa 16:17-23). Defeats the Philistines after Goliath is slain by David (1Sa 17). His jealousy of David; gives his daughter, Michal, to David to be his wife; becomes David's enemy (1Sa 18). Tries to slay David; Jonathan intercedes and incurs his father's displeasure; David's loyalty to him; Saul's repentance; prophesies (1Sa 19). Hears Doeg against Ahimelech and slays the priest and his family (1Sa 22:9-19). Pursues David to the wilderness of Ziph; the Ziphites betray David to (1Sa 23). Pursues David to En Gedi (1Sa 24:1-6). His life saved by David (1Sa 24:5-8). Saul's contribution for his bad faith (1Sa 24:16-22). David is again betrayed to, by the Ziphites; Saul pursues him to the hill of Hakilah; his life spared again by David; his confession and his blessing upon David (1Sa 26). Slays the Gibeonites; crime avenged by the death of seven of his sons (2Sa 21:1-9). His kingdom invaded by Philistines; seeks counsel of the medium of Endor, who foretells his death (1Sa 28:3-25; 29:1). Is defeated and with his sons is slain (1Sa 31); their bodies exposed in Beth Shan; rescued by the people of Jabesh and burned; bones of, buried under a tree at Jabesh (1Sa 31, w 2Sa 1; 2; 1Ch 10). His death a judgment on account of his sins (1Ch 10:13).
3. Of Tarsus. See *Paul.*

SAVIOR (*deliverer*). One who saves, delivers, or preserves from any evil or danger, whether physical or spiritual, temporal or eternal; term applied both to people (Jdg 3:9, 15; 2Ki 13:5; Ne 9:27; Ob 21) and to God (Ps 44:3, 7; Isa 43:11; 45:21; 60:16; Jer 14:8; Hos 13:4). In NT it is never applied to people, but only to God and Christ (Lk 1:47; 1Ti 1:1; 2:3; 4:10; Tit 1:3). Savior is

preeminently the title of the Son (2Ti 1:10; Tit 1:4; 2:13; 3:6; 2Pe 1:1; 1Jn 4:10).
See *God, Savior; Jesus the Christ, Savior.*

SAVOR Taste (Mt 5:13; Lk 14:34), smell (Joel 2:20). Also used metaphorically (2Co 2:14; Eph 5:2; Php 4:18).

SAVORY MEAT NIV "tasty food." Meals made by Jacob and Esau for their father Isaac prior to receiving his blessings (Ge 27:4, 9, 14, 17, 31).

SAW Used as an instrument of torture (Heb 11:37), for cutting stone (2Sa 12:31; 1Ki 7:9).
Figurative (Isa 10:15).

SCAB Disease of the skin (Lev 13:2, 6-8; 14:56; 21:20; 22:22; Dt 28:27; Isa 3:17).
See *Disease; Sanitation and Hygiene.*

SCAFFOLD NIV "platform" (2Ch 6:13).

SCALE
1. Only fish having fins and scales were permitted as food for Hebrews (Lev 11:9-12).
2. Instrument for weighing (Isa 40:12; Pr 16:11; 20:23).

SCALL NIV "itch," an infectious skin disease (Lev 13:30-37; 14:54; Dt 28:27). See *Disease; Leprosy; Sore.*

SCAPEBIRD (Lev 14:4-7, 53).

SCAPEGOAT The second of two goats for which lots were cast on the Day of Atonement (Lev 16:8, 10, 26). The first was sacrificed as a sin offering, but the second had the people's sins transferred to it by prayer and was then taken into the wilderness and released.
See *Azazel.*

SCARLET Probably a bright rich crimson. Scarlet cloth was used for the hangings of the tabernacle (Ex 25:4), high priest's vestments (Ex 39:1), royal or expensive apparel (2Sa 1:24). Sins are "as scarlet" (Isa 1:18).
See *Colors, Figurative and Symbolic.*

SCEPTER (*royal staff*). A staff used by kings to signify favor or disfavor to those who desired audience (Est 5:2; 8:4). A symbol of authority (Nu 24:17; Isa 14:5). Made of gold (Est 4:11), of iron (Ps 2:9; Rev 2:27; 12:5).
Figurative (Ge 49:10; Nu 24:17; Isa 9:4).

SCEVA Chief priest living in Ephesus whose seven sons were exorcists (Ac 19:14-17).

SCHISM (*division*). A formal division inside a religious group (1Co 12:25). See *Divisions.*

SCHOOL Company of the prophets at Naioth (1Sa 19:20), Bethel (2Ki 2:3), Jericho (2Ki 2:5, 15), Gilgal (2Ki 4:38), Jerusalem, probably (2Ki 22:14; 2Ch 34:22). Crowded attendance at (2Ki 6:1). In the home (Dt 4:9-10; 6:7, 9; 11:19-20; Ps 78:5-8). Assembly to hear public reading of the law (Dt 31:10-13). State (2Ch 17:7-9; Da 1:3-21). Of Gamaliel (Ac 5:34; 22:3). Of Tyrannus (Ac 19:9).
See *Instruction; Psalms, Topically Arranged; Sons of the Prophets.*

SCIENCE Observations of, and deductions from, facts (Job 26:7-14; 28; Ecc 1:13-17). The key of knowledge (Lk 11:52; Ro 2:20). See *Astronomy; Geology; Philosophy.*

SCOFFER One who derides, mocks (2Pe 3:3).

SCOFFING
By:
The people of Israel (2Ch 30:6-10; 36:16; Ps 78:19-20; 107:11-12; Hos 7:5). Unbelievers (Ps 42:3, 10; 73:8-9, 11-12; Pr 1:22, 25; Jer 17:15; 43:2; La 1:7; Eze 8:12; 9:9; 12:22; 2Pe 3:3-4). The Wicked, at God's requirements (Job 21:14-15; Isa 10:15; 57:4; Eze 11:2-3; 33:20).
Against:
Christ (Mt 12:24; Mk 3:22; Lk 4:23; 11:15; 16:14). The first Christians (Ac 2:13). Paul (Ac 13:45; 17:18, 32).
Proverbs Concerning:
(Pr 1:22, 25; 3:34; 9:12; 13:1; 14:6, 9; 19:29; 21:11, 24; 22:10; 24:9).
Punishment for:
(Pr 3:24; 9:12; 19:29; Isa 5:18-19, 24-25; 29:20; Heb 10:29).
See *Hatred; Malice; Unbelief.*
Instances of:
Ishmael (Ge 21:9). Children at Bethel (2Ki 2:23). Ephraim and Manasseh (2Ch 30:10). Chiefs of Judah (2Ch 36:16). Sanballat (Ne 4:1). Enemies of Job (Job 30:1, 9). Enemies of David (Ps 35:15-16). Rulers of Israel (Isa 28:14). Ammonites (Eze 25:3). Tyrians (Eze 26:2). Heathen (Eze 36:2-3). Soldiers (Mt 27:28-30; Lk 23:36). Chief priests (Mt 27:41). Pharisees (Lk 16:14). The men who held Jesus (Lk 22:63-64). Herod (Lk 23:11). People and rulers (Lk 23:35). Some of the multitude (Ac 2:13). Athenians (Ac 17:32).

SCORNERS (Ps 1:1; Pr 9:12; 21:11, 24). An abomination (Pr 24:9). Admonitions to (Pr 1:22-23). Punishment of (Pr 19:29; Isa 29:20). Warnings against (Pr 3:34; 13:1; 14:6; 19:29; 22:10; 29:8).
See *Mocking; Scoffing.*

SCORPION A venomous insect common in the wilderness through which the Israelites journeyed (Dt 8:15). Power over, given to the seventy-two (Lk 10:19). Unfit for food (Lk 11:12). Sting of in the tail (Rev 9:10).
Symbolic (Rev 9:3, 5, 10).
Figurative: Of enemies (Eze 2:6). Of cruelty (1Ki 12:11, 14).

SCORPION PASS A chain of hills in the south of Israel (Nu 34:4; Jdg 1:36). Area assigned to tribe of Judah (Jos 15:3).

SCOURGING Corporal punishment by stripes. Prescribed in the Mosaic law for fornication (Lev 19:20; Dt 22:18), for other offenses (Dt 25:2). Forty stripes the maximum limit (Dt 25:3). Fatal (Job 9:23), of servants avenged (Ex 21:20). Foretold by Jesus as a persecution of the Christians (Mt 10:17).
Of children. See *Children, Correction and Punishment; Punishment.*
Instances of:
Of Jesus (Mt 20:19; 27:26; Mk 15:15; Jn 19:1). Of Paul and Silas (Ac 16:23). Of Paul (Ac 21:32; 22:24; 2Co 11:24-25). Of Sosthenes (Ac 18:17).
Figurative:
Of the oppressions of rulers (1Ki 12:11). Of the evil tongue (Job 5:21).
See *Assault and Battery; Bruise(s); Lashes; Stoning; Stripes.*

SCREECH OWL Forbidden as food (Lev 11:16; Dt 14:15). See *Birds.*

SCRIBE (*write, copy*). A writer and transcriber of the law (2Sa 8:17; 20:25; 1Ki 4:3; 2Ki 12:10; 18:37; 19:2; 1Ch 24:6; 27:32; Ne 13:13; Jer 36:12). King's secretary (2Ki 12:10-12; 22:1-14; Est 3:12; 8:9). Mustering officer of the army (2Ki 25:19; 2Ch 26:11). Instructors in the law (Mt 7:29; 13:52; 17:10; 23:2-3). See *Levites.* Test Jesus with questions, bringing to Jesus a woman taken in adultery (Jn 8:3). Members of the council (Mt 2:4). Conspire against Jesus (Mt 26:3, 57; 27:41; Mk 14:1; Lk 22:66). Hypocrisy of, reproved by Jesus (Mt 15:20; 9:3; 12:38; 15:1; 16:21; 20:18; 21:15).

SCRIPTURES (*writing*). The Word of God (Jer 30:2). Interpreted by doctors (Jn 3:10; 7:52). Inspired (2Ti 3:16).
See *Word of God.*

SCROLL A document made of papyrus or smoothed skins of animals sewn together to make a long strip which was wound around sticks at both ends (Isa 34:4; Jer 36; Eze 3:1-3; Rev 5; 10:1-10). They varied in length from a few feet to thirty-five feet. The codex form of a book was not used until the second century A.D.

SCROLLS, DEAD SEA See *Dead Sea Scrolls.*

SCULPTURE See *Art.*

SCURVY See *Disease; Scab; Sore.*

SCYTHIAN A nomadic people, savage and uncivilized, living N and E of the Black Sea (Col 3:11).

SEA Creation of (Ge 1:9-10; Ps 95:5; 148:4-5). Limits of, established by God (Ge 1:9; Job 26:10; 38:8; Ps 33:7; Jer 5:22). Calmed by Jesus (Mt 8:24-26; Mk 4:37-39). Jesus walked on (Mt 14:25-31). Dead, to be given up by, at the Resurrection (Rev 20:13).
Symbolic:
In Daniel's vision (Da 7:2-3). In John's apocalyptic vision (Rev 4:6; 8:8-9; 10:2, 5-6, 8; 13:1; 15:2; 16:3; 21:1).
Waves of:
Reuben is as turbulent as (Ge 49:3-4). God walks on (Job 9:8). God controls (Job 38:8, 11; Ps 65:7; 89:9; 93:3-4; Jer 5:22). The wicked are like (Isa 57:20-21; Jude 13). Jesus controls (Mt 8:23-26; 14:32; Mk 4:35-41). Jesus walks through on the surface of the sea of Galilee (Mt 14:22-33). When God's people are built up and become mature, attaining to the whole measure of the fullness of Christ, they will no longer be tossed back and forth by every deceitful doctrine and scheme like the waves of the sea (Eph 4:14). Doubters are like (Jas 1:6).

SEA, BRONZE The great basin in Solomon's temple where the priests washed their hands and feet preparatory to temple ministry (1Ki 7:23-26; 2Ch 4:2-6).

SEA COW Native to the Red Sea. Skins of, used for covering of tabernacle (Ex 25:5; 26:14; 35:7, 23; 36:19; 39:34; Nu 4:6, 8, 10-12, 14, 25). For sandals (Eze 16:10).

SEA MEW See *Birds.*

SEA MONSTER Figurative of forces of chaos opposed to God (Job 7:12; Ps 74:13; Isa 27:1; Eze 32:2). See *Dragon; Leviathan.*

SEA OF GALILEE Called Sea of Kinnereth (Nu 34:11; Dt 3:17; Jos 12:3; 13:27). Lake of Gennesaret (Lk 5:1). Sea of Tiberias (Jn 21:1). Jesus calls disciples on the shore of (Mt 4:18-22; Lk 5:1-11). Jesus teaches from a boat on (Mt 13:13). Miracles of Jesus on (Mt 8:24-32; 14:22-33; 17:27; Mk 4:37-39; Lk 5:1-9; 8:22-24; Jn 12:1-11).

SEA OF GLASS A crystalline pavement or basin before the throne of God (Rev 4:6; 15:2).

SEA OF JAZER Perhaps the Dead Sea (Jer 48:32).

SEAL
1. A stamp used for signifying documents. Given as a pledge (Ge 38:18). Engraved (Ex 28:11, 21, 36; 39:6, 14, 30; 2Ti 2:19). Decrees signified by (1Ki 21:8; Est 8:8).
Documents sealed with: Ahab's letter, under false pretenses (1Ki 21:8), covenants (Ne 9:38; 10:1; Isa 8:16), decrees (Est 8:8; Da 6:9), deeds (Jer 32:10). Treasures secured by (Dt 32:34). Lion's den made sure by (Da 6:17), tomb of Jesus (Mt 27:66).
Circumcision a seal of righteousness (Ro 4:11).
Figurative: Of secrecy (Da 12:9; Rev 5:1). Of certainty of divine approval (Jn 6:27; 2Co 1:22; Eph 1:13; 4:30; Rev 7:3-4). In John's vision (Rev 6; 8:1; 10:4).

S

2. An amphibious animal. Skins of were used as a covering of the tabernacle (Ex 25:5; 26:14; 35:7, 23; 36:19; 39:34; Nu 4:25).

SEAMEN *See Mariner.*

SEASONS (Ge 1:14; 8:22; Ps 104:19; Jer 33:20; Da 2:21; Mt 21:41; 24:32; Mk 12:2; Ac 1:7; 1Th 5:1).

SEAT Chair, stool, throne (1Sa 20:18; Lk 1:52).

SEBA
1. Son of Cush (Ge 10:7; 1Ch 1:9).
2. A region in Ethiopia (Ps 72:10; Isa 43:3).
 See Sabeans; Sheba.

SEBAM (*sweet smell*). A town in Reuben (Nu 32:3), also called Sibmah (Nu 32:38), E of the Dead Sea, but the exact location is unknown.

SEBAT *See Shebat.*

SECACAH (*thicket, cover*). A village in the wilderness of Judah (Jos 15:61), location unknown.

SECHU *See Secu.*

SECOND ADAR This intercalary month (not in the Bible) was added about every three years so the lunar calendar would correspond to the solar year.
 See Adar Sheni; Month, 13.

SECOND COMING OF CHRIST
Called the:
 Times of refreshing from the presence of the Lord (Ac 3:19). Times of restitution of all things (Ac 3:21, w Ro 8:21). Last time (1Pe 1:5). Appearing of Jesus Christ (1Pe 1:7). Revelation of Jesus Christ (1Pe 1:13). Glorious appearing of the great God and our Savior (Tit 2:13). Coming of the day of God (2Pe 3:12). Day of our Lord Jesus Christ (1Co 1:8).

Foretold by:
 Prophets (Da 7:13; Jude 14). Jesus (Mt 25:31; Jn 14:3). Apostles (Ac 3:20; 1Ti 6:14). Angels (Ac 1:10-11). Signs preceding (Mt 24:3).
 The time of, unknown (Mt 24:36; Mk 13:32).

The Manner of:
 In clouds (Mt 24:30; 26:64; Rev 1:7). In the glory of his Father (Mt 16:27). In his own glory (Mt 25:31). In flaming fire (2Th 1:8). With power and great glory (Mt 24:30). As he ascended (Ac 1:9, 11). With a shout and the voice of the archangel (1Th 4:16). Accompanied by angels (Mt 16:27; 25:31; Mk 8:38; 2Th 1:7). With his saints (1Th 3:13; Jude 14). Suddenly (Mk 13:36). Unexpectedly (Mt 24:44; Lk 12:40). As a thief in the night (1Th 5:2; 2Pe 3:10; Rev 16:15). As the lightning (Mt 24:27). The heavens and earth shall be dissolved (2Pe 3:10, 12). They who shall have died in Christ shall rise first at (1Th 4:16). The saints alive at, shall be caught up to meet him (1Th 4:17). It is not to make atonement (Heb 9:28, w Ro 6:9-10; Heb 10:14).

The Purposes of:
 To complete the salvation of saints (Heb 9:28; 1Pe 1:5). Be glorified in his saints (2Th 1:10). Be marveled at among those who believe (2Th 1:10). Bring to light the hidden things of darkness (1Co 4:5). Judge (Ps 50:3-4, w Jn 5:22; 2Ti 4:1; Jude 15; Rev 20:11-13). Reign (Isa 24:23; Da 7:14; Rev 11:15). Destroy death (1Co 15:25-26). Every eye shall see him at (Rev 1:7). Should be always considered as at hand (Ro 13:12; Php 4:5; 1Pe 4:7). Blessedness of being prepared for (Mt 24:46; Lk 12:37-38).

The Saints:
 Assured of (Job 19:25-26). Love (2Ti 4:8). Look for (Php 3:20; Tit 2:13). Wait for (1Co 1:7; 1Th 1:10). Speed its coming (2Pe 3:12). Pray for (Rev 22:20). Should be ready for (Mt 24:44; Lk 12:40). Should watch for (Mt 24:42; Mk 13:35-37; Lk 21:36). Should be patient unto (2Th 3:5; Jas 5:7-8). Shall be preserved at (1Jn 2:28; 1Jn 4:17). Shall be blameless at (1Co 1:8; 1Th 3:13; 5:23; Jude 24). Shall be like him at (Php 3:21; 1Jn 3:2). Shall see him as he is (1Jn 3:2). Shall appear with him in glory at (Col 3:4). Shall receive a crown of glory at (2Ti 4:8; 1Pe 5:4). Shall reign with him at (Da 7:27; 2Ti 2:12; Rev 5:10; 20:6; 22:5). Faith of, will be praised at (1Pe 1:7).

The Wicked:
 Scoff at (2Pe 3:3-4). Presume upon the delay of (Mt 24:48). Shall be surprised by (Mt 24:37-39; 1Th 5:3; 2Pe 3:10). Shall be punished at (2Th 1:8-9). The man of sin to be destroyed at (2Th 2:8). Illustrated (Mt 25:6; Lk 12:36, 39; 19:12, 15).
 See Jesus the Christ, Second Coming.

SECOND DEATH (Rev 19:20; 20:14; 21:8). Righteous exempt from (Rev 2:11). *See Punishment, Eternal; Wicked, Punishment of.*

SECRET Alms to be given in (Mt 6:4). Prayer to be offered in (Mt 6:6). Of others not to be divulged (Pr 25:9; Mt 18:15).
 Belong to God (Dt 29:29; Ps 25:14). God knows secrets of the heart (Dt 31:21; 1Sa 16:7; 2Sa 7:20; 2Ki 19:27; Ps 44:21; 90:8; Heb 4:12-13).
 Shall be revealed and judged (Ecc 12:14; Da 2:28, 47; Am 3:7; Mk 4:22; Lk 8:16-17; Ro 2:16; 1Co 4:5).
 See Mysteries.

SECRETARY (2Sa 8:17; 20:24; 1Ki 4:3; 2Ki 12:10-12; 18:18, 37; 22:1-14; 1Ch 27:32; Est 3:12; 8:9). Military (2Ki 25:19; 2Ch 26:11). *See Amanuensis; Scribe.*

SECT (*sect, party, school*). Religious group with distinctive doctrine: Sadducees (Ac 5:17), Pharisees (Ac 15:5; 26:5), Christians (Ac 24:5; 28:22).

SECU (*lookout point*). Village near Ramah (1Sa 19:22).

SECUNDUS (*second*). A Thessalonian Christian. Accompanies Paul from Corinth (Ac 20:4-6).

SECURITY
In Salvation:
 The theological teaching which maintains the certain continuation of the salvation of those who are saved; also known as the perseverance of the saints (Jn 10:28; Ro 8:38-39; Php 1:6; 2Th 3:3; 1Pe 1:5).

False:
 From the evils of sin. Promises peace and long life (Job 29:18). Is ignorant of God and truth (Pr 10:4; 50:21). Trusts in lies (Isa 28:15; Rev 3:17). Is inconsiderate and forgetful (Isa 47:7). Relies on earthly treasures (Jer 49:4, 16). Is deceived by pride (Ob 3; Rev 18:7). Puts off the evil day (Am 6:3). Leads to increased guilt (Ecc 8:11). Its refuge will be swept away (Isa 28:17). Ruin shall overtake it (Isa 47:9; Am 9:10). God is against it (Jer 21:13; Eze 39:6; Am 6:1).
 See Confidence, False; Self-Deception; Self-Delusion.

For Debt:
 A guarantee to pay: not to be taken if essential to life (garments) or livelihood (millstones) (Ex 22:26; Dt 24:6, 6, 17); not to be used as unreasonable leverage upon the disadvantaged (Job 22:6; 24:3, 9; Eze 18:16; Am 2:8).
 Instances of: Judah (Ge 43:9; 44:32); fields and vineyards (Ne 5:3).
 Warnings against: (Pr 6:1; 11:15; 17:18; 20:16).
 See Debt.

SEDITION Charged against Paul (Ac 24:5). How punished (Ac 5:36-37).

SEDUCER *See Impostors.*

SEDUCTION (2Ti 3:6, 13). Laws concerning (Ex 22:16-17; Dt 22:23-29). *See Rape.*
 Instances of: Of Dinah (Ge 34:2). Tamar (2Sa 13:1-14).

SEED Every herb, tree, and grass, yields its own (Ge 1:11-12, 29). Each kind has its own body (1Co 15:38). Not to be mingled in sowing (Lev 19:19; Dt 22:9).
 Parables concerning (Mt 13; Lk 8).
 Illustrative (Ecc 11:6; Hos 10:12; 2Co 9:6; Gal 6:7-8).
 Sowing of, type of burial of the body (1Co 15:36-38).

SEEDTIME *See Agriculture.*

SEEKERS
Must:
 Have faith (Heb 11:6). Remember God's mercies (Isa 51:1). Count the cost (Lk 14:26-33).

Seeking God:
 Commanded (1Ch 16:11; 22:19; Ps 105:4; Isa 26:8-9; Hos 10:12; Joel 2:12-13; Am 5:4-6, 8, 14; Zep 2:3; Mt 6:33; Jas 4:8; Rev 22:17). For salvation (Ge 49:18). To sacrifice (2Ch 11:16). The result of adversity (Ps 78:34; 83:16; Hos 5:15). Prophesied (Jer 50:4; Hos 3:5; Zec 8:20-23). Punishment for not seeking (2Ch 15:13; Isa 8:19). Not of self (Ro 3:11). By unrepentant sinners, vain (Am 8:12; Lk 13:24).
 See Seeking God.

Promises:
 (Jn 6:37). Of finding God (Dt 4:29; 1Ch 28:9; 2Ch 15:2, 12; Pr 8:17, 34-35; Isa 45:19, 22; Jer 29:13; Ac 17:27). Of pardon (2Ch 30:18-19; Ps 69:32; Eze 18:27; Ac 2:21). Of salvation (Heb 9:28). Of providential care (2Ch 26:5; Ezr 8:22; Ps 34:4; 81:10; 145:19; Isa 49:9-12, 23; Mt 6:33). Of spiritual blessings (Job 8:5-6; Ps 9:10; 22:26; 24:3-6; 40:1-4; 63:1-8; 70:4-5; 119:2; 145:18-19; Pr 2:3-5; 28:5; Isa 44:3-4; 45:19, 22; 55:6-7; 61:1-3; La 3:25-26, 41; Mt 5:6; 6:33; 7:7-11; Lk 6:21; 11:9-13; Ac 2:21; Ro 10:12-13; Heb 7:25; Rev 3:20; 21:6).

Instances of:
 Asa (2Ch 14:7). Jehoshaphat (2Ch 17:3-4). Uzziah (2Ch 26:5). Hezekiah (2Ch 31:21). Josiah and Ahaz. Ezra (Ezr 7:10). Job (Job 5:8). David (Ps 17:1-2; 25:5, 15; 27:4, 8; 34:4; 40:1-2; 63:1-8; 143:6). The psalmists (Ps 33:20; 42:1-4; 77:1-9; 84:2; 119:10; 130:5-6). The beloved for her lover (SS 3:1-4). Daniel (Da 9:3). The Magi (Mt 2:1-2). Cornelius, the Centurion (Ac 10:7, 30-33).
 See Backsliders; Penitent; Sin, Confession of; Sin, Forgiveness of; Zeal.

SEEKING GOD Commanded (Isa 55:6; Mt 7:7).

Includes Seeking:
 His name (Ps 83:16). His Word (Isa 34:16). His strength (1Ch 16:11; Ps 105:4). His commandments (1Ch 28:8; Mal 2:7). His precepts (Ps 119:45, 94). His kingdom (Mt 6:33; Lk 12:31). His righteousness (Mt 6:33). Christ (Mal 3:1; Lk 2:15-16). Honor which comes from him (Jn 5:44). Justification by Christ (Gal 2:16-17). The city which God has prepared (Heb 11:10, 16; 13:14). By prayer (Job 8:5; Da 9:3). In his house (Dt 12:5; Ps 27:4).

Should Be:
 Immediate (Hos 10:12). Evermore (Ps 105:4). While he may be found (Isa 55:6). With the heart (Dt 4:29; 1Ch 22:19). In the day of trouble (Ps 77:2).

Ensures:
 His being found (Dt 4:29; 1Ch 28:9; Pr 8:17; Jer 29:13). His favor (La 3:25). His protection (Ezr 8:22). His not forsaking us (Ps 9:10). Life (Ps 69:32; Am 5:4, 6). Prosperity (Job 8:5-6; Ps 34:10). Being heard by him (Ps 34:4). Understanding all things (Pr 28:5). Gifts of righteousness (Hos 10:12). Imperative upon all (Isa 8:19). Afflictions designed to lead to (Ps 78:33-34; Hos 5:15). None, by nature, are found to be engaged in (Jas 4:2, w Ro 3:11; Lk 12:23, 30).

The Saints:
 Specially exhorted to (Zep 2:3). Desirous of (Job 5:8). Purpose, in heart (Ps 27:8). Prepare their hearts for (2Ch 30:19). Set their hearts to (2Ch 11:16). Engage in, with the whole heart (2Ch 15:12;

Ps 119:10). Early in (Job 8:5; Ps 63:1; Isa 26:9). Earnest in (SS 3:2, 4). Characterized by (Ps 24:6). Is never in vain (Isa 45:19). Blessedness of (Ps 119:2). Leads to joy (Ps 70:4; 105:3). Ends in praise (Ps 22:26). Promise connected with (Ps 69:32). Shall be rewarded (Heb 11:6).

The Wicked:
 Are gone out of the way of (Ps 14:2-3, w Ro 3:11-12). Do not prepare their hearts for (2Ch 12:14). Refuse, through pride (Ps 10:4). Not led to, by affliction (Isa 9:13). Sometimes pretend to (Ezr 4:2; Isa 58:2). Rejected, when too late in (Pr 1:28). They who neglect are denounced (Isa 31:1). Punishment of those who neglect (Zep 1:4-6).

Exemplified:
 Asa (2Ch 14:7). Jehoshaphat (2Ch 17:3-4). Uzziah (2Ch 26:5). Hezekiah (2Ch 31:21). Josiah (2Ch 34:3). Ezra (Ezr 7:10). David (Ps 34:4). Daniel (Da 9:3-4).

SEER An older term for prophet (1Sa 9:9). *See Prophets.*

SEGUB (*exalted*).
1. Son of Hiel, the rebuilder of Jericho (1Ki 16:34).
2. Grandson of Judah (1Ch 2:4-5, 21-22).

SEIR (*hairy, shaggy, covered with trees* BDB IDB; possibly *the place of the goats* or *the place of Esau* [Ge 25:25, BDB]; *small forest, rich forest* KB). A Horite; an ancestor of the inhabitants of the land of Seir (Ge 26:20; 1Ch 1:38).

SEIR, LAND OF and MOUNT
1. Alternate names for the region occupied by the descendants of Edom or Esau. Originally called the land of Seir (Ge 32:3), later called Edom (Ge 36:8-9), extends S from Moab on both sides of the Arabah c. one hundred miles; mountainous; in the Greek period it was called Idumea. Mt. Seir c. 3, 500 feet high. "Seir" also used for people who lived in Mt. Seir (Eze 25:8).
2. Region on the border of Judah W of Kiriath Jearim (Jos 15:10).

SEIRAH (*place of the goats* BDB possibly *woody hills* IDB KB; *shaggy forest* ISBE). A town in Ephraim, probably in the SE part (Jdg 3:26).

SEIZING Of property. *See Land.*

SEIZURES An affliction resulting from demon possession (Mt. 4:24; 17:5). Some feel this is a reference to epilepsy. *See Disease.*

SELA (*rocky crags, cliffs*). An Edomite city (Isa 16:1; 42:11), also called Joktheel (2Ki 14:7). *See Joktheel.* Later the capital of the Nabateans, called Petra by the Greeks. *See Nabatea, Nabateans; Petra.*

SELA HAMMAHLEKOTH (*slippery rock* BDB). A cliff in the wilderness of Maon (1Sa 23:28).

SELAH This term appears seventy-one times in the Psalms and in Hab 3:3, 9, 13. Its meaning is not clear. Possibly it signified a pause in the vocal music while an instrumental interlude played.
 See Music, Symbols Used in.

SELED (*jump for joy*). A descendant of Jerahmeel (1Ch 2:30).

SELEUCIA A seaport of Syrian Antioch, founded by Seleucus I in 300 B.C. (Ac 13:4).

SELEUCIDS A dynasty of rulers of the kingdom of Syria (it included Babylonia, Bactria, Persia, Syria, and part of Asia Minor), descended from Seleucus I, a general of Alexander the Great. It lasted from 312 to 64 B.C., when the Romans took it over. One of them, Antiochus Epiphanes, precipitated the Maccabean War by trying forcibly to Hellenize the Jews. *See Testaments, Time Between.*

SELF-CONDEMNATION (1Ki 8:31-32; Job 9:20; Pr 5:12-13; Mt 23:31; Ro 2:1; 1Jn 3:20; Rev 1:7).
 Parables of (Mt 21:33-41; 25:24-27; Mk 12:1-12; Lk 19:21-23).
 Instances of: Achan (Jos 7:19-25). David (1Sa 24:1-15; 26:1-20; 2Sa 12:5-7; 24:17). Ahab (1Ki 20:39-42). Jonah (Jnh 1:12). Those who condemned the woman (Jn 8:9).
 See Self-Incrimination; Remorse; Repentance.

SELF-CONFIDENCE *See Confidence, False.*

SELF-CONTROL
A Virtue:
 Without self-control temptation and evil may freely assault a person (Pr 25:28). Of Saul (1Sa 10:27). Of David (1Sa 24:1-15; 26:1-20). Of Jesus (Mt 26:62-63; 27:12-14).
 Paul instructed concerning self-control in relation to righteousness (Ac 24:25), the marriage bed (1Co 7:5); as a fruit of the Spirit (Gal 5:23); in contrast to the godlessness of the last days (1Th 5:8; 2Ti 3:3; 2Th 1:6). Overseers and deacons must have a life that is characterized by self-control (1Ti 3:2; Tit 1:8). Taught by leaders and exemplified by older believers (Tit 2:2, 5-6); taught by the grace of God (Tit 2:12).
 Peter lists self-control as one of the qualities of a godly life (2Pe 1:6). A believer should continually be prepared for Christ's return, exhibiting a self-controlled life (1Pe 1:13; 4:7). Be self-controlled and prepared for the devil, who prowls about looking for those who have a false sense of security which therefore make them prime candidates for his trap in the world's system (1Pe 4:7).

Sexual Self-control:
 Vow of (Job 31:1). Commanded (Mt 5:27-28; Ro 13:13; 1Co 7:1-9, 25-29, 36-38; Col 3:5; 1Ti 4:12; 5:1-2).

 Instances of Sexual self-control:
 Joseph (Ge 39:7-12). Uriah (2Sa 11:8-13). Boaz (Ru 3:6-13). Joseph, husband of Mary (Mt 1:24-25). Eunuchs (Mt 19:12). Paul (1Co 7:8; 9:27). Believers (Rev 14:1, 4-5).
 See Abstinence; Chastity; Discipline; Graces, Christian; Patience; Rashness; Self-Discipline; Tact.

SELF-DECEPTION (Jas 1:26). *See Confidence, False; Security, False.*

SELF-DEFENSE Accused heard in (Mt 27:11-14; Mk 15:2-5; Lk 23:3; Jn 7:51; Ac 2:37-40; 22; 23; 24:10-21; 26). *See Defense.*

SELF-DELUSION A characteristic of the wicked (Ps 49:18). Prosperity frequently leads to (Ps 30:6; Hos 12:8; Lk 12:17-19). Obstinate sinners often given up to (Ps 81:11-12; Hos 4:17; 2Th 2:10-11).

Exhibited In Thinking That:
Our own ways are right (Pr 14:12), we should adhere to established wicked practices (Jer 44:17), we are pure (Pr 30:12), we are better than others (Lk 18:11), we are rich in spiritual things (Rev 3:17), we may have peace while in sin (Dt 29:19), we are above adversity (Ps 10:6), gifts entitle us to heaven (Mt 7:21-22), privileges entitle us to heaven (Mt 3:9; Lk 13:25-26), God will not punish our sins (Jer 5:12), Christ will not come to judge (2Pe 3:4), our lives will be prolonged (Isa 56:12; Lk 12:19; Jas 4:13).
Frequently persevered in to the last (Mt 7:22; 25:11-12; Lk 13:24-25). Fatal consequences of (Mt 7:23; 24:48-51; Lk 12:20; 1Th 5:3).

Exemplified:
Ahab (1Ki 20:27, 34). Israelites (Hos 12:8). Jews (Jn 8:33, 41). Church of Laodicea (Rev 3:17).
See Confidence, False; Security, False.

SELF-DENIAL (Lk 21:2-4; 1Co 6:12; 9:12, 15, 18-19, 23, 25-27; 10:23-24; 2Co 6:3; Php 2:4-8; 3:7-9; 2Ti 2:4; Tit 2:12; Heb 13:13; Rev 12:11).

In Respect to:
Appetite (Pr 23:2; Da 10:3). Sinful pleasures (Mt 5:29-30; 18:8-9; Mk 9:43). Carnality (Ro 6:6; 8:12-13, 35-36; 13:14; 1Co 9:27; Gal 5:16-17, 24; Col 3:5; Tit 2:12; 1Pe 2:11-12, 14-16).

Required of Christ's Disciples:
(Mt 8:19-22; 10:37-39; 16:24-25; 19:12, 21; Mk 2:14; 8:34-35; 10:29; Lk 5:11; 9:23-24, 57-58; 12:33; 14:26-27, 33; 18:27-30; Jn 12:25; 2Ti 2:4; Heb 13:13; 1Pe 4:1; 3Jn 7). For a brother's sake (Ro 14:1-22; 15:1-5; 1Co 8:10-13; 10:23-24; Php 2:4). For the sake of the ministry (2Co 6:3). Christ's teachings concerning (Mk 12:43-44; Lk 21:2-4).

Parables of:
(Mt 13:44-46; 18:8-9; Mk 9:43).

Instances of:
Abraham, when he accorded to Lot his preference for the grazing lands of Canaan (Ge 13:9; 17:8), in offering Isaac (Ge 22:12). Moses, in choosing suffering over pleasure (Heb 11:25), in taking no compensation from the Israelites (Nu 16:15). Samuel, in his administration of justice (1Sa 12:3-4). The widow of Zarephath, in sharing with Elijah the last of her sustenance (1Ki 17:12-15).
David, in paying for the threshing floor (2Sa 24:24). The psalmist (Ps 132:3-5). Daniel, in refusing royal food (Da 1:8), in refusing rewards from Belshazzar (Da 5:16-17). Esther, in risking her life for her people (Est 4:16). The Recabites, in refusing wine or fermented drink, or even to plant vineyards (Jer 35:6-7).
Peter and other apostles, in abandoning their vocations to follow Jesus (Mt 4:20; 9:9; Mk 1:16-20; 2:14; Lk 5:11, 27-28), in forsaking all (Mt 19:27; Mk 10:28; Lk 5:28). The widow, who cast all into the treasury (Lk 21:4). The early Christians, in having everything in common (Ac 2:44-45; 4:34). Joseph, in selling his possessions and giving all to the apostles (Ac 4:36-37).
Paul (1Co 10:23-24; Gal 2:20; 6:14), in not counting even his life valuable to himself (Ac 20:24; 21:13; Php 3:7-8), in laboring for his own support while he taught (Ac 20:34-35; 1Co 4:12; 10:33), in not exercising his authority (1Co 6:12; 9:12, 15, 18-19, 23-27).
See Cross; Humility.

SELF-DISCIPLINE Needed: Not to give in to sin (Ro 6:12-14); to "run the race" of life according to the rules (1Co 9:24-27; 2Ti 2:1-7). Contrasted to timidity (2Ti 1:7). *See Self-Control.*

SELF-EXALTATION Christian attitude toward (2Co 10:5, 17-18). Christ's teaching concerning (Mk 12:38). Parables of (Lk 14:7-11).
Self-deception (Isa 5:21; 1Co 3:18; 8:2; Gal 6:3). Punishment for (Eze 31:10-14; Ob 3-4).
Instances of: Job (Job 12:3). Pharaoh (Ex 9:17). Korah, Dathan, and Abiram (Nu 16:1-11). Sennacherib (2Ch 32:9-19). Prince of Tyre, making himself God (Eze 28:2, 9-10). Nebuchadnezzar (Da 4:30; 5:20). Belshazzar (Da 5:22-23). Simon the sorcerer (Ac 8:9-11). Herod, when deified by the people (Ac 12:20-23). The man of lawlessness (2Th 2:4).
See Pride; Self-Righteousness.

SELF-EXAMINATION

Commanded:
(Ps 4:4; Hag 1:7; 1Co 11:28, 31; 2Co 13:5; Gal 6:4). By inference (Jer 17:9).
Conversion as a result of (Ps 119:59; La 3:40).

Exemplified by:
Job (Job 13:23). David (Ps 19:2; 26:2; 139:23-24). The psalmist (Ps 77:6; 119:59). The disciples (Mt 26:22; Mk 14:19).
See Meditation; Repentance; Sin, Confession of.

SELF-INCRIMINATION Under ancient customs, accused persons were required to give self-incriminating testimonies of guilt of the offense charged and were, on occasions, scourged to force self-incriminating testimony whether guilty or innocent (Nu 5:11-27; 2Sa 1:10, 16; 1Ki 8:31-32; 2Ch 6:22; Ac 22:24). Instances of: Achan (Jos 8:19-25). *See Self-Condemnation.*

SELF-INDULGENCE Instances of: Solomon (Ecc 2:10). The rich fool (Lk 12:16-20). The rich man as contrasted to Lazarus (Lk 16:19). *See Gluttony; Idleness; Slothfulness; also, Self-Denial.*

SELFISHNESS

Denounced:
Admonitions against (Lk 6:32-34; Ro 14:15; 15:1-3; 1Co 10:24; Gal 6:2; Php 2:4). Christ's example against (Ro 15:3; 2Co 5:15; Php 2:5-8). Judged (Pr 18:17; 24:11-12; Hag 1:4, 9-10).

Exemplified by:
Corrupt officials (Mic 3:11). Corrupt priests and prophets (Eze 34:18; Zec 7:6). Those who accumulate too much (Pr 11:26; Isa 5:8; Mt 19:21-22). The self-indulgent (Ro 14:15; 2Ti 3:2-4). Those unsympathetic with the unfortunate (Pr 28:27; Jas 2:15-16; 1Jn 3:17). Cain (Ge 4:9). The Gadites and Reubenites (Nu 32:6). David's friends (Ps 38:11). The Israelites (Hag 1:4; Mal 1:10). Early Christians (Php 2:20-21).
See Liberality; Poor; Unselfishness.

SELF-RIGHTEOUSNESS

Described as:
Assertive (Pr 20:6; Mt 7:22-23). Delusive (Pr 12:15; 16:2; 21:2; 28:26; Isa 28:20; 50:11; 64:6; Hos 12:8; Mt 7:22-23; 22:12-13; Gal 6:3).

Denounced:
(Job 12:2; Pr 25:14, 27; 26:12; 30:12-13; Isa 5:21; 65:3-5; Jer 2:13, 22-23, 34-35; 8:8; Eze 33:24-26; Am 6:13; Mt 9:10-13; Mk 2:16; 8:15; Lk 5:30; 16:14-15; 18:9-14; 22:12-13; 23:29-31; Ro 11:19-21).
Admonitions against (Dt 9:4-6; 1Sa 2:9; Pr 27:2, 21; Jer 7:4; Hab 2:4; 2Co 1:9; 10:17-18).
Judgments against (Pr 14:12; Isa 28:17; 50:11; Jer 8:8; 49:4, 16; Zep 3:11).
Proverbs concerning (Pr 12:15; 14:12; 16:2; 20:6; 21:2; 25:14, 27; 26:12; 27:2, 21; 28:13, 26; 30:12-13).
Parables concerning (Lk 7:36-50; 10:25-37; 15:25-32; 18:9-14). Paul's instruction regarding (Ro 2:17-20; 3:27; 10:3; 11:19-21; 2Co 1:9; 10:17-18; Gal 6:3).

Instances of:
Job accused of (Job 11:4; 32:1-2; 33:8-9; 35:2, 7-8). Israelites (Nu 16:3; Ro 2:17-20; 10:3). Saul (1Sa 15:13-21). The wicked (Ps 10:5-6).
Pharisees (Mt 9:10-13; Mk 2:16-17; Lk 5:30; 7:39; 15:2; 16:14-15; 18:9-14; Jn 9:28-41). The rich young ruler (Mt 19:16-22; Mk 10:17-22; Lk 18:18-23). The lawyer (Lk 10:25-29). Church of Laodicea (Rev 3:17-18).
See Hypocrisy; Self-Exaltation.

SELF-WILL Stubbornness.

Forbidden:
(2Ch 30:8; Ps 75:5). Ministers should be without (Tit 1:7), warn their people against (Heb 3:7-12), pray that their people may be forgiven for (Ex 34:9; Dt 9:27). Characteristic of the wicked (Pr 7:11; 2Pe 2:10). The wicked will not cease from (Jdg 2:19). Punishment for (Dt 21:21; Pr 29:1).

Proceeds From—
Unbelief (2Ki 17:14), pride (Ne 9:16, 29), an evil heart (Jer 7:24). God knows (Isa 48:4). Exhibited in refusing to listen to God (Pr 1:24), refusing to listen to the messengers of God (1Sa 8:19; Jer 44:16; Zec 7:11), refusing to walk in the ways of God (Ne 9:17; Isa 42:24; Ps 78:10), refusing to listen to parents (Dt 21:18-19), refusing to receive correction (Dt 21:18; Jer 5:3; 7:28), rebelling against God (Dt 31:27; Ps 78:8), resisting the Holy Spirit (Ac 7:51), walking in the counsels of an evil heart (Jer 7:24, w Jer 23:17), hardening the neck (Ne 9:16), hardening the heart (2Ch 36:13), going backward and not forward (Jer 7:24), heinousness of (1Sa 15:23).

Illustrated: (Ps 32:9; Jer 31:18).

Exemplified:
Simeon and Levi (Ge 49:6). Israelites (Ex 32:9; Dt 9:6, 13). Saul (1Sa 15:19-23). David (2Sa 24:4). Josiah (2Ch 35:22). Zedekiah (2Ch 36:13).
See Obduracy.

SELVEDGE NIV the "edge" of each of the two curtains which covered the boards of the tabernacle (Ex 26:4; 36:11).

SEM *See Shem.*

SEMAKIAH (*Yahweh sustains, consecrates*). The son of Shemaiah (1Ch 26:7).

SEMEI *See Shimei, 18.*

SEMEIN (*Yahweh has heard*). An ancestor of Christ (Lk 3:26).

SEMITES (*of Shem*). A diverse group of ancient peoples whose languages were related, belonging to the Semitic family of languages; their world was the Fertile Crescent. The principal Semitic peoples of ancient times: Akkadians—including Babylonians and Assyrians; Arameans—including Edomites, Ammonites, and Moabites; Hebrews; Arabs; Ethiopians (Ge 10:22-31).

SENAAH Descendants of Senaah (sometimes spelled Hassenaah), returned with Zerubbabel (Ezr 2:35; Ne 7:38).

SENATE *See Elders, Council of.*

SENATOR *See Elders; Occupations and Professions.*

SENEH (*thorny* BDB; possibly *[cliff shaped like] a tooth* IDB). A rock protecting the garrison of the Philistines at Micmash (1Sa 14:5).

SENIR The Amorite name of Mt. Hermon (Dt 3:9; 1Ch 5:23; SS 4:8; Eze 27:5).

SENNACHERIB (*[pagan moon god] Sin has increased the brothers* BDB ISBE; *Sin replace the [lost] brothers!* IDB). The king of Assyria (705-681 B.C.), the son and successor of Sargon II; a great builder and warrior; invaded Judah in the time of Hezekiah, but

his army was miraculously destroyed (2Ki 18; 19; Isa 36; 37). Accounts of his campaigns recorded on clay prisms survive.

SENSUALITY (Ecc 2:24; 8:15; 11:9).
Of the glutton (Isa 22:13). Of the drunkard (Isa 56:12). Of the selfish (Lk 12:19-20; 16:25). Epicurean Philosophy Justifies (Isa 22:13; 1Co 15:32).
Admonition against (Jas 5:5). Warning against (Jude 18-19).
See Adultery; Drunkenness; Fornication; Gluttony; Homosexual; Lasciviousness; Self-Indulgence; also, Abstinence; Continence; Self-Denial; Temperance.

SENTRY *See Watchman.*

SENUAH (*sons of the hated [rejected] woman, i.e., the poor class* BDB). *See Hassenuah.*

SEORIM (*one born at the time of the barley [harvest]*). A descendant of Aaron; head of the fourth course of priests (1Ch 24:1-8).

SEPHAR A mountain in Arabia (Ge 10:30).

SEPHARAD A place to which the inhabitants of Jerusalem were exiled (Ob 20); possibly Sardis or Sparta.

SEPHARVAIM An Assyrian city, from which the king of Assyria colonized Samaria (2Ki 17:24, 31; 18:34; 19:13; Isa 36:19; 37:13).

SEPHARVITES The people of Sepharvaim (2Ki 17:31).

SEPHER *See Kiriath Sepher.*

SEPTUAGINT (*seventy*). A translation of the OT into Greek, prepared in Alexandria in the second and third centuries B.C. *See Testaments, Time Between; Texts and Versions.*

SEPULCHRE *See Burial.*

SEPULCHRE, CHURCH OF THE HOLY One of two main sites identified as the tomb of Jesus; built by Constantine in A.D. 325.

SERAH (*one who explains, opens, extends* IDB; *abundance* ISBE KB). *See Sarah, 2.*

SERAIAH (*Yahweh persists* BDB ISBE; *Yahweh is prince* IDB; *Yahweh contends* KB).
1. David's secretary. Probably the same as Sheva, Shisha, and Shavsha. (2Sa 8:17; 20:25; 1Ki 4:3; 1Ch 18:16).
2. Chief priest at the time of the taking of Jerusalem (2Ki 25:18). Father of Ezra (Ezr 7:1). Slain by Nebuchadnezzar (2Ki 25:18-21; Jer 52:24-27).
3. An Israelite captain who surrendered to Gedaliah (2Ki 25:23; Jer 40:8).
4. The son of Kenaz (1Ch 4:13-14).
5. A Simeonite (1Ch 4:35).
6. A priest who returned from the Babylonian captivity (Ezr 2:2; Ne 12:1, 12). Called Azariah (Ne 7:7).
7. One who sealed the covenant with Nehemiah (Ne 10:2). Possibly identical with 6, above.
8. A ruler of the temple after the Captivity (Ne 11:11).
9. The son of Azriel. Commanded by King Jehoiakim to seize Jeremiah (Jer 36:26).
10. A servant of Zedekiah (Jer 51:59, 61).

SERAPHS (*burning ones, [winged] serpents*). Celestial beings whom Isaiah saw standing before the enthroned Lord (Isa 6:2-3, 6-7). Possibly the same as the "living creatures" (Rev 4:6-9).

SERED, SEREDITE The son of Zebulun and his descendants (Ge 46:14; Nu 26:26).

SERGEANTS NIV "officers." *See Occupations and Professions.*

SERGIUS PAULUS A Roman deputy and convert of Paul (Ac 13:7-12).

SERMON ON THE MOUNT
The Sermon on the Mount is the first of five great discourses in Matthew (chs. 5-7; 10; 13; 18; 24-25). It contains three types of material: (1) beatitudes, or declarations of blessedness (5:1-12), (2) ethical admonitions (5:13-20; 6:1-7:23) and (3) contrasts between Jesus' ethical teaching and Jewish legalistic traditions (5:21-48). The sermon ends with a short parable stressing the importance of practicing what has just been taught (7:24-27) and an expression of amazement by the crowds at the authority with which Jesus spoke (7:28-29).
Opinion differs as to whether the sermon is a summary of what Jesus taught on one occasion or a compilation of teachings presented on numerous occasions. Matthew possibly took a single sermon and expanded it with other relevant teachings of Jesus. Thirty-four of the verses in Matthew's account of the sermon occur in different contexts in Luke than the so-called "Sermon on the Plain" (Lk 6:17-49).
The Sermon on the Mount's call to moral and ethical living is so high that some have dismissed it as being completely unrealistic or have projected its fulfillment to the future kingdom. There is no doubt, however, that Jesus (and Matthew) gave the sermon as a standard for all Christians, realizing that its demands cannot be met in our own power. It is also true that Jesus occasionally used hyperbole to make his point. For example, Jesus is not teaching self-mutilation (Mt 5:29-30), for even a blind man can lust. The point is that we should deal as drastically with sin as necessary.

SERPENT Satan appears in the form of, to Eve (Ge 3:1-15; 2Co 11:3). Subtlety of (Ge 3:1; Ecc 10:8; Mt 10:16). Curse upon (Ge 3:14-15; 49:17). Metaphorically feeds on the dust (Ge 3:14; Isa 65:25; Mic 7:17). Unfit for food (Mt 7:10). Venom of (Dt 32:24, 33; Job 20:16; Ps 58:4; 140:3; Pr 23:31-32; Ac 28:5-6). The staff

S

of Moses transformed into (Ex 4:3; 7:15). Poisonous, sent as a plague upon the Israelites (Nu 21:6-7; Dt 8:15; 1Co 10:9); the wound of miraculously healed by looking upon the bronze image set up by Moses (Nu 21:8-9). Charming of (Ps 58:4-5; Ecc 10:11; Jer 8:17). Mentioned in Solomon's riddle (Pr 30:19). Constriction of (Rev 9:19). Sea serpent (Am 9:3). The seventy-two given power over (Lk 10:19). The apostles given power over (Mk 16:18; Ac 28:5).

 Figurative (Pr 23:32; Isa 14:29).
 See Adder; Cobra; Dragon; Viper.

SERUG (*descendant* i.e., *younger branch* BDB). An ancestor of Abraham (Ge 11:20-23; 1Ch 1:26). Called Serug (Lk 3:35).

SERVANT Distinguished as a bond servant (who was a slave) and hired servant.

Bond Servant:
 Laws of Moses concerning (Ex 20:10; 21:1-11, 20-21, 26-27, 32; Lev 19:20-22; 25:6, 10, 35-55; Dt 5:14; 15:12, 14, 18; 24:7). Kidnapping and slave trading forbidden (Dt 21:10-14; 24:7; 1Ti 1:10; Rev 18:13).
 Fugitive, not to be returned to master (Dt 23:15-16). David erroneously supposed to be a fugitive slave (1Sa 25:10). Instances of fugitive: Hagar, commanded by an angel to return to her mistress (Ge 16:9). Sought by Shimei (1Ki 2:39-41). Interceded for, by Paul (Phm 10-21).
 Bought and sold (Ge 17:13, 27; 37:28, 36; 39:17; Lev 22:11; Dt 28:68; Est 7:4; Eze 27:13; Joel 3:6; Am 8:6; Rev 18:13). Captives of war made (Dt 20:14; 21:10-14; 2Ki 5:2; 2Ch 28:8, 10; La 5:13), captive bondservants shared by priests and Levites (Nu 31:28-47). Thieves punished by being made (Ge 43:18; Ex 22:3). Defaulting debtors made (Lev 25:39; Mt 18:25). Children of defaulting debtors sold for (2Ki 4:1-7).
 Voluntary servitude (Lev 25:47; Dt 15:16-17; Jos 9:11-21). Given as dowry (Ge 29:24, 29). Owned by priests (Lev 22:11; Mk 14:66). Slaves owned slaves (2Sa 9:10). The master might marry or give in marriage (Ex 21:7-10; Dt 21:10-14; 1Ch 2:34-35). Taken in concubinage (Ge 16:1-2, 6; 30:3, 9). Used as soldiers by Abraham (Ge 14:14). Rights of those born to a master (Ge 14:14; 17:13, 27; Ex 21:4; Pr 29:21; Ecc 2:7; Jer 2:14).
 Must be circumcised (Ge 17:13, 27; Ex 12:44). Must enjoy religious privileges with the master's household (Dt 12:12, 18; 16:11, 14; 29:10-11). Must have rest on the Sabbath (Ex 20:10; 23:12; Dt 5:14).
 Servitude threatened, as a national punishment, for disobedience of Israel (Dt 28:68; Joel 3:7-8). Degrading influences of bondage exemplified by cowardice (Ex 14:11-12; 16:3; Jdg 5:16-18, 23).
 Social status of (Mt 10:24-25; Lk 17:7-9; 22:27; Jn 13:16). Equal status of, with other disciples of Jesus (1Co 7:21-22; 12:13; Gal 3:28; Eph 6:8).
 Proverbs concerning (Pr 12:9; 13:17; 17:2; 19:10; 25:13; 26:6; 27:18, 27; 29:19, 21; 30:10, 21-23).
 Parables of (Mt 24:45-51; Lk 12:35-48; 16:1-13).
 Conspiracy by. *See Conspiracy.*

Cruelty to—
 Hagar (Ge 16:1-21; Gal 4:22-31). Joseph (Ge 37:26-28, 36). The Israelites (Ex 1:8-22; 2:1-4; 5:7-9; Dt 6:12, 21; Ac 7:19, 34). Sick, abandoned (1Sa 30:13). Gibeonites (Jos 9:22-27). Canaanites (1Ki 9:21). Jews in Babylon (2Ch 36:20; Est 1:1-10), freeing of (2Ch 36:23; Ezr 1:1-4).
 Admonitions against cruelty to (Jer 22:13).

Kindness to—
 (Ps 123:2; Pr 29:21). Commanded (Lev 25:43; Eph 6:9). Exemplified by Job (Job 19:15-16; 31:13-14), by Boaz (Ru 2:4), by the centurion (Mt 8:8-13; Lk 7:2-10), by Paul (Phm 1-21).

Duties of—
 To be faithful (1Co 4:2). Obedient (Mt 8:9; Eph 6:5-9; Col 3:22-25; Tit 2:9-10; 1Pe 2:18-20). To honor masters (Mal 1:6; 1Ti 6:1-2).
 Warning to (Zep 1:9).
 Figurative (Lev 25:42, 55; Ps 116:16; Isa 52:3; Mt 24:45, 51; Lk 12:35-48; 16:1-13; 17:7-9; Jn 8:32-35; Ro 6:16-22; 1Co 4:1-2; 7:21-23; Gal 5:13; 1Pe 2:16; 2Pe 2:19; Rev 7:3).

Good, Instances of—
 Joseph (Ge 39:2-20; 41:9-57; Ac 7:10), Elisha (2Ki 2:1-6). Servants of Abraham (Ge 24), of Boaz (Ru 2:4), of Jonathan (1Sa 14:7), of Abigail (1Sa 25:14-17), of David (2Sa 12:18; 15:15, 21), of Ziba (2Sa 9), of Naaman (2Ki 5:2-3, 13), of Nehemiah (Ne 4:16, 23), of centurion (Mt 8:9), of Cornelius (Ac 10:7), Onesimus (Phm 11). Servants in the parable of the pounds and talents (Mt 25:14-23; Lk 19:12-19).
 Redeemed (Ne 5:8). Freed (2Ch 36:23; Ezr 1:1-4; Jer 34:8-22; Ac 6:9; Co 7:21). Called Freedmen (Ac 6:9). Tact in management of (Ecc 7:21).

Wicked and Unfaithful, Instances of—
 Jeroboam (1Ki 11:26), Gehazi (2Ki 5:20-27), Zimri (1Ki 16:9-10; 2Ki 9:31), Onesimus (Phm 11).
 Servants of Abraham and Lot (Ge 3:7), of Abimelech (Ge 21:25), of Ziba (2Sa 16:1-4, w 2Sa 19:26-27), of Absalom (2Sa 13:28-29; 14:30), of Shimei (1Ki 2:39), of Joash (2Ki 12:19-21), of Amon (2Ki 21:23), of Job (Job 19:15-16). In the parable of the talents and pounds (Mt 25:24-30; Lk 19:20-26). In the parable of the vineyard (Mt 21:33-41; Mk 12:1-9).
 See Employee; Employer; Master.

Hired Workers:
 Jacob (Ge 29:15; 30:26), reemployed (Ge 30:27-34; 31:6-7, 41). Parable of laborers for a vineyard (Mt 20:1-15). Of the father of the prodigal son (Lk 15:17, 19), of the prodigal son (Lk 15:5-19). Kindness to (Ru 2:4). Treatment of, more considerable than that accorded slaves (Lev 25:53). Await employment in the marketplace (Mt 20:1-3).
 Mercenary (Job 7:2). Unfaithful (Jn 10:12-13).

Rights of—
 Receive wages (Mt 10:10; Lk 10:7; Ro 4:4; 1Ti 5:18; Jas 5:4). Daily payment of wages (Lev 19:13; Dt 24:15). Share in spontaneous products of land in the seventh year (Lev 25:6). Wages

of, paid in a portion of the flocks or products (Ge 30:31-32; 2Ch 2:10), or in money (Mt 20:2, 9-10).
 Oppression of, forbidden (Dt 24:14; Col 4:1), punished (Mal 3:5).
 See Master, of Servants; Wages.

SERVANT OF THE LORD Agent for such as the patriarchs (Ex 32:13), Moses (Nu 12:7f), and the prophets (Zec 1:6).
 Used as a title for the Messiah in Isaiah 40-66. The NT applies Isaiah's Servant passages to Jesus (Isa 42:1-4; Mt 12:16-21).
 See Jesus the Christ, Messiah; Obedience of.

SERVICE Refers to all sorts of work from the most inferior and menial to the most honored and exalted (Lev 23:7f; Nu 3:6ff).

SERVITOR See Occupations and Professions; Servant.

SETH (*determined, granted,* Ge 4:25; *restitution* KB).
 1. The third son of Adam and Eve, born after the murder of Abel. Name is a play on "granted," Eve said, "God has granted me another child in place of Abel, since Cain killed him" (Ge 4:25). It was through Seth that the genealogy of Noah passed (Ge 4:25-26; 5:3, 8; 1Ch 1:1; Lk 3:38).
 2. *See Sheth.*.

SETHUR (*concealed [by deity]* IDB). One of the twelve spies (Nu 13:13).

SEVEN Interesting facts concerning the number.

Days:
 Week consists of (Ge 2:3; Ex 20:11; Dt 5:13-14). Noah in the ark before the Flood (Ge 7:4, 10), remains in the ark after sending out the dove (Ge 8:10-12). Mourning for Jacob lasted (Ge 50:10), of Job (Job 2:13). The plague of bloody waters in Egypt lasted (Ex 7:25). The Israelites circled Jericho (Jos 6:4). The Passover lasted (Ex 12:15). Saul directed by Samuel to wait at Gilgal for the prophet's command (1Sa 10:8; 13:8). The elders of Jabesh Gilead ask for a truce of (1Sa 10:8; 13:8). Dedication of the temple lasted double (1Ki 8:65). Ezekiel sits by the Kebar River in astonishment (Eze 3:15). The Feast of Tabernacles lasted (Lev 23:34, 42). Consecration of priests and altars lasted (Ex 29:30, 35; Eze 43:25-26). Defilements lasted (Lev 12:2; 13:4). Fasts of (1Sa 31:13; 2Sa 12:16, 18, 22). The firstborn of flocks and sheep shall remain with the mother before being offered (Ex 22:30). The feast of Xerxes continued (Est 1:5). Paul stayed at Tyre (Ac 21:4), at Puteoli (Ac 28:14).

Weeks:
 In Daniel's vision concerning the coming of the Messiah (Da 9:25). Ten times (Da 9:24-27). The period between the Passover and Pentecost (Lev 23:15).

Months:
 Holy convocations in the seventh month (Lev 23:24-44; Nu 29; Eze 45:25).

Years:
 Jacob serves for each of his wives (Ge 29:15-30). Of plenty (Ge 41:1-32, 53). Famine lasted in Egypt (Ge 41:1-32, 54-56), in Canaan (2Sa 24:13; 2Ki 8:1). Insanity of Nebuchadnezzar (Da 4:32). Seven times, the period between the Jubilees (Lev 25:8).

Miscellaneous Sevens:
 Of clean beasts taken into the ark (Ge 7:2). Abraham gives Abimelech seven lambs (Ge 21:28). Rams and bulls required in sacrifices (Lev 23:18; Nu 23:1; 29:32; 1Ch 15:26; Eze 45:23). Blood sprinkling seven times (Lev 4:6; 14:7), oil (Lev 14:16). Seven cows and seven heads of grain in Pharaoh's vision (Ge 41:2-7). Israelites marched around Jericho seven times, on the seventh day sounding seven trumpets (Jos 6:4). Elisha's servant looked seven times for the appearance of rain (1Ki 18:43). Naaman was required to wash in the Jordan seven times (2Ki 5:10).
 Seven steps in the temple seen in Ezekiel's vision (Eze 40:22, 26). The heat of Nebuchadnezzar's furnace intensified sevenfold (Da 3:19). The light of the sun intensified sevenfold (Isa 30:26). The threatened sevenfold punishment of Israel (Lev 26:18-21). Silver purified seven times (Ps 12:6). Worshiping seven times a day (Ps 119:164). Seven eunuchs at the court of Xerxes (Est 1:10), seven princes (Est 1:14). Seven counselors at the court of Artaxerxes (Ezr 7:14). Seven maidens given to Esther (Est 2:9). Symbolic of many sons (Ru 4:15; 1Sa 2:5; Jer 15:9), of liberality (Ecc 11:1-2). Seven wise men (Pr 26:16). Seven women shall seek polyandrous marriage (Isa 4:1). Seven shepherds to be sent forth against Assyria (Mic 5:5-6). Seven lamps and pipes (Zec 4:2).
 See Seven Words From the Cross.
 Seven ministers in the apostolic church (Ac 6:3). Seven churches in Asia (Rev 1:4, 20). Seven seals (Rev 5:1). Seven thunders (Rev 10:3). Seven heads and seven crowns (Rev 12:3; 13:1; 17:9). Seven kings (Rev 17:10). Seven stars (Rev 1:16, 20; 3:1; Am 5:8). Seven spirits (Rev 1:4; 3:1; 4:5; 5:6). Seven eyes of the Lord (Zec 3:9; 4:10; Rev 5:6). Seven golden lampstands (Rev 1:12). Seven angels with seven trumpets (Rev 8:2). Seven plagues (Rev 15:1). Seven horns and seven eyes (Rev 5:6). Seven angels with seven plagues (Rev 15:6). Seven golden bowls (Rev 15:7). Scarlet colored beast having seven heads (Rev 17:3, 7).

SEVEN WORDS FROM THE CROSS The seven statements Jesus made from the cross. No single Gospel account recounts them all:
 "Father, forgive them, for they do not know what they are doing." (Lk 23:34).
 "I tell you the truth, today you will be with me in paradise." (Lk 23:43).
 "Dear woman, here is your son," and to the disciple "Here is your mother." (Jn 19:26-27).
 "My God, my God, why have you forsaken me?" (Mt 27:46-47; Mk 15:34-36).
 "I am thirsty." (Jn 19:28).
 "It is finished." (Jn 19:30).
 "Father, into your hands I commit my spirit." (Lk 23:46; cf.Mt 27:50; Mk 15:37).

SEVENTY Seventy descendants of Jacob in Egypt (Ex 1:5; Dt 10:22). The council of the Israelites composed of seventy elders (Ex 24:1, 9; Nu 11:16, 24-25). Seventy-two (KJV seventy) disciples sent forth by Jesus (Lk 10:1-17). The Jews in captivity in Babylon seventy years (Jer 25:11-12; 29:10; Da 9:2; Zec 1:12; 7:5). *See Israel.*

SEVENTY WEEKS, THE The name applied to a period of time (probably 490 years) referred to in Daniel (Da 9:24-27).

SEVENTY-TWO, THE Seventy-two (KJV seventy) disciples were sent on a preaching mission by Jesus (Lk 10:1-17).

SEXUAL PURITY See Chastity; Self-Control.

SEXUAL RELATIONS See Adultery; Bestiality; Fornication; Homosexual; Incest; Prostitute; Rape.

SHAALABBIN (*site of foxes*). Town between Ir Shemesh and Aijalon (Jos 19:42).

SHAALBIM (site of foxes). A town, probably in central Israel, won by Danites from Amorites (Jdg 1:35).

SHAALBONITE Designation of Eliahba, one of David's mighty men (2Sa 23:32; 1Ch 11:33).

SHAALIM, LAND OF (possibly *[land of] hollow depth* KB). A region probably near the N boundary of Benjamin's territory (1Sa 9:4).

SHAAPH
 1. Son of Jahdai (1Ch 2:47).
 2. Son of Caleb (1Ch 2:49).

SHAARAIM (*double gates*).
 1. A town in Judah (Jos 15:36; 1Sa 17:52).
 2. A town in Simeon (1Ch 4:31), "Sharuhen" (Jos 19:6), and "Shilhim" (Jos 15:32).

SHAASHGAZ A eunuch of Xerxes' court (Est 2:14).

SHABBETHAI (*one born at Sabbath* ISBE KB).
 1. A Levite, assistant to Ezra (Ezr 10:15).
 2. An expounder of the Law (Ne 8:7).
 3. A chief Levite, attendant of the temple (Ne 11:16).

SHACHIA See Sakia.

SHACKLES Made of bronze (Jdg 16:21; 2Ki 25:7; 2Ch 33:11; 36:6; Jer 39:7; 52:11). Used for securing prisoners (2Ch 33:11; 36:6; Mk 5:4). See Chains; Fetters.

SHADDAI (*the Mountain One* IDB; other suggestions: 1. *mountain* 2. *maternal goddess of many breasts* 3. *self-sufficient* 4. *an Akkadian spirit, Shad* 5. *almighty, omnipotent* KB). *Shaddai* is used forty-eight times as a name of God, thirty-two times in Job (Job 5:17; 6:4, 14; etc.), seven times in the compound name *El Shaddai*. The NIV consistently translates *Shaddai* as "Almighty" (Ge 17:1; Ps 91:1).
 See God, Names of, Shaddai.

SHADOW Used literally, figuratively (1Ch 29:15; Ps 17:8; Isa 30:3), theologically (Col 2:17; Heb 8:5; 10:1).

SHADOW OF DEATH See Darkness.

SHADRACH (*servant of [pagan moon god] Aku*). His Hebrew name was Hananiah. He was taken as a captive to Babylon with Daniel, Mishael, and Azariah, each of whom was given a Babylonian name (Da 1:6-20; 2:17, 49; 3:12-30). Hananiah was renamed Shadrach.
 Shadrach, Meshach, and Abednego were chosen to learn the language and the ways of the Chaldeans (Babylonians) so that they could enter the king's service (Da 1:3-5, 17-20), c. 605 B.C. These three were eventually thrown into Nebuchadnezzar's furnace because they refused to bow down and worship the huge golden image he had made (Da 3:1, 4-6, 8-30).

SHAFT
 1. Stem of the gold lampstand (Ex 25:31; 37:17).
 2. Shaft of a spear (1Sa 17:7).
 3. Water (2Sa 5:8) or mine shaft (Job 28:4).

SHAGEE (*wanderer, meanderer [like feeding sheep]*). The father of Jonathan, one of David's guard (1Ch 11:34).

SHAHAR See Zereth Shahar.

SHAHARAIM (*one born at early [reddish] dawn* KB). A Benjamite (1Ch 8:8).

SHAHAZUMAH (*elevated place*). A city in Issachar (Jos 19:22).

SHALEM (*peace or safe*). See Paddan Aram, 2.

SHALIM, LAND OF See Shaalim, Land of.

SHALISHA (*a third part*). A district bordering on the Mount Ephraim (1Sa 9:4).

SHALISHAH See Baal Shalishah.

SHALLEKETH (possibly *[gate of] sending forth* BDB). One of the gates of the temple (1Ch 26:16).

SHALLUM (*peace, well being, prosperity*).
 1. The son of Naphtali (1Ch 7:13), "Shillem" (Ge 46:24; Nu 26:48-49). See Shillem, Shillemite.
 2. The son of Shaul (1Ch 4:25).
 3. The son of Sismai (1Ch 2:40-41).

4. The son of Korah chief of the gatekeepers (1Ch 9:17, 19, 31; Ne 7:45), "Meshelemiah" (1Ch 26:1), "Shelemiah" (1Ch 26:14).

5. The son of Zadok (1Ch 6:12f), "Meshullam" (1Ch 9:11; Ne 11:11).

6. A king of Israel (2Ki 15:10-15).

7. The father of Jehizkiah (2Ch 28:12).

8. Husband of the prophetess Huldah (2Ki 22:14).

9. The king of Judah (1Ch 3:15), better known as Jehoahaz II.

10. The uncle of Jeremiah (Jer 32:7).

11. The father of Maaseiah (Jer 35:4).

12. A Levite who divorced his foreign wife (Ezr 10:24).

13. A man who divorced his foreign wife (Ezr 10:42).

14. A ruler who helped build Jerusalem's walls (Ne 3:12).

SHALLUN (recompense). A Jew who repaired a gate of Jerusalem (Ne 3:15).

SHALMAI (perhaps Yahweh is well-being). An ancestor of the temple servants that returned with Zerubbabel (Ezr 2:46; Ne 7:48).

SHALMAN (abbreviation of Shalmaneser IDB ISBE). Either a contraction of Shalmaneser or the Moabite king Salamanu (Hos 10:14).

SHALMANESER (the god Shulman is chief, or Sulmanu is leader). The title of five Assyrian kings, of whom one is mentioned in the OT, another refers to an Israelite king.

1. Shalmaneser III (859-824 B.C.), the son of Ashurnasirpal; inscription left by him says that he opposed Ben-Hadad of Damascus and Ahab of Israel, and made Israel tributary.

2. Shalmaneser V (726-722 B.C.), the son of Tiglath-Pileser; received tribute from Hoshea; besieged Samaria and carried the N tribes of Israel into captivity (2Ki 17:3; 18:9), "Shalman" (Hos 10:14).

SHAMA (one obedient [to Yahweh]). One of David's heroes (1Ch 11:44).

SHAMARIAH See Shemariah, 2.

SHAMBLES NIV "meat market" (1Co 10:25).

SHAME Of Adam and Eve: no shame before the Fall (Ge 2:25), but after (Ge 3:10). Jesus is ashamed of those who deny him (Mk 8:38; Lk 9:26). Of believers who do not continue in Christ (1Jn 2:28). Of the cross (Heb 12:2).

Destitute of the Israelites when they worshiped the golden calf (Ex 32:25), the unjust (Zep 3:5).

SHAMED See Shemed.

SHAMELESSNESS Of the wicked (Jer 6:15; 8:12; Zep 3:5).

SHAMER
1. See Shemer.
2. See Shemer; Shomer, 2.

SHAMGAR ([the pagan Hurrian god] Shimke gave [a son] IDB). The son of Anath; judge; killed 600 Philistines with an oxgoad (Jdg 3:31; 5:6).

SHAMHUTH (possibly one born at a time of a horrible event KB). David's fifth divisional army commander (1Ch 27:8). See Shammah, 4.

SHAMIR (possibly thorny or emery [flint]).
1. A town in Judah c. thirteen miles SW of Hebron (Jos 15:48).
2. A town in Ephraim; the home of Tola (Jdg 10:1f).
3. A temple attendant (1Ch 24:24).

SHAMMA (astonishment). The son of Zophah, an Asherite (1Ch 7:37).

SHAMMAH (waste).
1. The grandson of Esau (Ge 36:13, 17; 1Ch 1:37).
2. The brother of David (1Sa 16:9; 17:13), also called Shimea (1Ch 20:7) and Shimeah (2Sa 13:3, 32).
3. One of David's mighty men (2Sa 23:11), also called Shagee (1Ch 11:34).
4. Another of David's mighty men (2Sa 23:33), also called Shammoth (1Ch 11:27) and Shamhuth (1Ch 27:8). May be the same as 3.

SHAMMAI (Yahweh has heard).
1. The son of Onam (1Ch 2:28, 32).
2. The father of Maon (1Ch 2:44-45).
3. The son of Ezra (1Ch 4:17).

SHAMMOTH (desolation). One of David's mighty men (1Ch 11:27), apparently the same as Shammah, 4 (2Sa 23:25) and Shamhuth (1Ch 27:8).

SHAMMUA (possibly [Yahweh] hears KB; rumor, ZPEB).
1. The son of Zaccur; Reubenite spy (Nu 13:4).
2. The son of David and Bathsheba (2Sa 5:14; 1Ch 14:4).
3. A Levite; the father of Abda (Ne 11:17), also called Shemaiah (1Ch 9:16).
4. A priest (1Ch 24:14; Ne 12:6, 18).

SHAMMUAH See Shammua, 2.

SHAMSHERAI (a combination of Shemesh [pagan sun god] and Shamar [guard]). The son of Jeroham (1Ch 8:26).

SHAN See Beth Shan.

SHAPHAM A chief of Gad (1Ch 5:12).

SHAPHAN (rock badger).
1. A secretary of King Josiah (2Ki 22:3-14; 2Ch 34:8-20). The father of Gemariah (Jer 36:10-12).

2. The father of Ahikam and the grandfather of Gedaliah (2Ki 22:12; 25:22; 2Ch 34:20; Jer 26:24; 39:14; 40:5, 9, 11; 41:2; 43:6).

3. The father of Elasah (Jer 29:3).

4. The father of Jaazaniah (Eze 8:11).

SHAPHAT (he judges).
1. A Simeonite spy (Nu 13:5).
2. The father of Elisha the prophet (1Ki 19:16, 19).
3. A Gadite chief in Bashan (1Ch 5:12).
4. A herdsman of David (1Ch 27:29).
5. The son of Shemaiah (1Ch 3:22).

SHAPHER See Shepher, Mount.

SHAPHIR (lovely). A town probably in SW Israel (Mic 1:10-15).

SHARAI A descendant of Bani who divorced his Gentile wife (Ezr 10:40).

SHARAIM See Shaaraim, 1.

SHARAR (firm). The father of one of David's mighty men (2Sa 23:33), "Sacar" (1Ch 11:35). See Sacar, 1.

SHARE Plowshare (1Sa 13:20).

SHAREZER ([pagan god] protect the king!).
1. The son of the Assyrian king Sennacherib (2Ki 19:37; Isa 37:38).
2. Contemporary of Zechariah the prophet (Zec 7:2).

SHARON (plain, level country).
1. Israel coastal plain between Joppa and Mount Carmel (1Ch 27:29; Isa 35:2; Ac 9:35).
2. Suburbs of Sharon possessed by the tribe of Gad (1Ch 5:16).
3. See Lasharon.
4. Figurative of fruitfulness, glory, peace (Isa 35:2; 65:10).

SHARONITE (of Sharon). Shitrai, in charge of David's herds in Sharon (1Ch 27:29).

SHARUHEN A Simeonite town in Judah's territory (Jos 19:6). Apparently the same as Shilhim (Jos 15:32), and Shaaraim (1Ch 4:31); possibly identified with Tell el-Farah.

SHASHAI (noble). A descendant of Bani, who put away his Gentile wife (Ezr 10:40).

SHASHAK A Benjamite (1Ch 8:14, 25).

SHAUL, SHAULITE (asked, possibly dedicated to God).
1. The son of Simeon and his descendants (Ge 46:10; Ex 6:15; Nu 26:13; 1Ch 4:24).
2. An ancient king of Edom (Ge 36:37; 1Ch 1:48-49).
3. Son of Uzziah (1Ch 6:24).

SHAVEH KIRIATHAIM (level plain of two towns). The plain where Kedorlaomer defeated the Emites (Ge 14:5), probably on the E of the Dead Sea (Nu 32:37).

SHAVEH, VALLEY OF (level valley). The valley where, after rescuing his nephew Lot, Abraham met the king of Sodom (Ge 14:17).

SHAVING The priests and Nazirites were prohibited from shaving (Lev 21:5; Nu 6:5), Hebrews generally wore beards. Shaving was often done for religious reasons, as an act of contrition (Job 1:20), consecration for Levites (Nu 6:9; 8:7), cleansing for lepers (Lev 14:8f; 13:32ff), also as an act of contempt (2Sa 10:4).

SHAVSHA David's secretary (1Ch 18:16), also called Shisha (1Ki 4:3), Seraiah (2Sa 8:17), and Sheva (2Sa 20:25).

SHEAF A handful of grain left behind by the reaper, gathered and bound by women and children, and later taken to the threshing-floor (Jer 9:22; Ru 2:7, 15). Some sheaves were left behind for the poor (Dt 24:19).

SHEAL (May God grant!, asking). A descendant of Bani, who put away his Gentile wife (Ezr 10:29).

SHEALTIEL (I have asked [him] of God [El] BDB ISBE KB; possibly God [El] is a shield, God [El] is a victor IDB).
1. Father of Zerubbabel and an ancestor of Jesus (1Ch 3:17; Ezr 3:2, 8; 5:2; Ne 12:1; Hag 1:1, 12, 14; 2:2, 23).
2. A son of Jehoiachin, king of Judah (Mt 1:12), or of Neri (Lk 3:27). He may have been the real son of Neri, but only the legal heir of Jehoiachin.

SHEARIAH (possibly Yahweh breaks). The son of Azel; descendant of Jonathan (1Ch 8:38; 9:44).

SHEARING HOUSE See Beth Eked.

SHEAR-JASHUB (a remnant will return). The symbolic name of Isaiah's oldest son (Isa 7:3; 8:18).

SHEBA (seven or oath).
1. The son of Raamah (Ge 10:7; 1Ch 1:9).
2. The son of Joktan (Ge 10:28; 1Ch 1:22).
3. The son of Jokshan (Ge 25:3; 1Ch 1:32).
4. A Benjamite who led an insurrection against David (2Sa 20).
5. A Gadite (1Ch 5:13).
6. A city of Simeon (Jos 19:2).
7. Queen of, visits Solomon (1Ki 10:1-13; 2Ch 9:1-12). Kings of, bring gifts to Solomon (Ps 72:10). Rich in gold (Ps 72:15), incense (Jer 6:20). Merchandise of (Eze 27:22-23; 38:13). Prophecies concerning the people of, coming into the kingdom of Messiah (Isa 60:6).

See Sabeans; Seba.

SHEBAH See Shibah.

SHEBAM See Sebam.

SHEBANIAH
1. Trumpeter priest (1Ch 15:24).
2. Levite who signed covenant with Nehemiah (Ne 9:4-5; 10:10).
3. Another Levite who signed a covenant (Ne 10:12).
4. A priest who signed a covenant (Ne 10:4).
5. Priest (Ne 12:14).

SHEBARIM (quarry). A place, called the "stone quarries" in the NIV, near Ai to which Israelite soldiers were chased (Jos 7:5, ftn).

See Quarries; Stones.

SHEBAT ([the month of] destroying [rain]). Month eleven in sacred sequence (Zec 1:7), month five in civil sequence. Winter (January-February). See Month, 11.

SHEBER (possibly lion IDB; possibly breaking or crushing or roughly broken grain KB). The son of Caleb (not the Israelite spy of the land of Canaan) (1Ch 2:48).

SHEBNA ([Yahweh] return now IDB).
1. A scribe of Hezekiah (2Ki 18:18, 26, 37; 19:2; Isa 36:3, 11, 22; 37:2).
2. An official of the king (Isa 22:15-19).

SHEBUEL (possibly captive of God [El] or God [El] restores). See Shubael.

SHECANIAH (Yahweh has taken up his abode).
1. The head of the tenth course of priests in the days of David (1Ch 24:11).
2. Levite (2Ch 31:15).
3. Descendant of David (1Ch 3:21-22).
4. Man who returned with Ezra (Ezr 8:3).
5. Another man who returned with Ezra (Ezr 8:5).
6. Man who proposed to Ezra that foreign wives be put away (Ezr 10:2-4).
7. Keeper of E gate of Jerusalem in the time of Nehemiah (Ne 3:29).
8. The father-in-law of Tobiah the foe of Nehemiah (Ne 6:18).
9. The chief priest who returned with Zerubbabel (Ne 12:3).

SHECHEM, SHECHEMITE (possibly shoulder [saddle of a hill] BDB; shoulders [and upper part of the back] KB).
1. A district in the central part of the land of Canaan. Abraham dwells in (Ge 12:6). Jacob buys a piece of ground in, and builds an altar (Ge 33:18-20). The flocks and herds of Jacob kept in (Ge 37:12-14). Joseph buried in (Jos 24:32). Jacob buried in (Ac 7:16, w Ge 50:13).
2. Also called Sychar, a city of refuge in Mount Ephraim (Jos 20:7; 21:21; Jdg 21:19). Joshua assembled the tribes of Israel at, with all their elders, chiefs, and judges, and presented them before the Lord (Jos 24:1-28). Joshua buried at (Jos 24:30-32). Abimelech made king at (Jdg 8:31; 9). Rehoboam crowned at (1Ki 12:1). Destroyed by Abimelech (Jdg 9:45), rebuilt by Jeroboam (1Ki 12:25). Men of, slain by Ishmael (Jer 41:5). Jesus visits; disciples made in (Jn 4:1-42).
3. Son of Hamor; seduces Jacob's daughter; slain by Jacob's sons (Ge 33:19; 34; Jos 24:32; Jdg 9:28).
4. Descendant of Manasseh and his clan (Nu 26:31; Jos 17:2).
5. Son of Shemida (1Ch 7:19).

SHECHINAH See Shekinah.

SHEDEUR (Shaddai is light, or Shaddai is fire). Reubenite; father of Elizur (Nu 1:5; 2:10; 7:30; 10:18).

SHEEP Offered in sacrifice, by Abel (Ge 4:4), by Noah (Ge 8:20), by Abraham (Ge 22:13). See Offerings. Required in the Mosaic offerings. See Offerings.

The land of Bashan adapted to the raising of (Dt 32:14), Bozrah (Mic 2:12), Kedar (Eze 27:21), Nebaioth (Isa 60:7), Sharon (Isa 65:10). Jacob's management of (Ge 30:32-40). Milk of, used for food (Dt 32:14). Shearing of (Ge 31:19; 38:12-17; Isa 53:7), feasting at the time of shearing (1Sa 25:11, 36; 2Sa 13:23). First fleece of, belonged to priests and Levites (Dt 18:4). Tribute paid in (2Ki 3:4; 1Ch 5:21; 2Ch 17:11).

Figurative:
(1Ch 21:17; Ps 74:1; Jer 13:20). Of backsliders (Jer 50:6). Of lost sinners (Mt 9:36; 10:6). Of the righteous (Jer 50:17; Eze 34; Mt 26:31; Mk 14:27; Jn 10:1-16). Of the defenselessness of ministers (Mt 10:16).

Parable of the lost (Mt 18:11-13; Lk 15:4-7).

SHEEP GATE An ancient gate of Jerusalem (Ne 3:1, 32; 12:39; Jn 5:2).

SHEEP MARKET NIV "Sheep Gate" (Jn 5:2).

SHEEP PEN Enclosure for protection of sheep (Nu 32:16; Jdg 5:16; 1Sa 24:3; Jn 10:1, 16).

SHEEPMASTER See Occupations and Professions; Shepherd.

SHEEP-SHEARER See Occupations and Professions.

SHEERAH (blood relationship or female relative IDB; remainder KB). The daughter of Ephraim; the descendants built three villages (1Ch 7:24).

SHEET A large piece of linen (Ac 10:11; 11:5).

SHEHARIAH (he seeks Yahweh). The son of Jeroham; Benjamite (1Ch 8:26).

SHEKEL (*weight*). A weight, equal to twenty gerahs (Ex 30:13; Nu 3:47; Eze 45:12). Used to weigh silver (Jos 7:21; Jdg 8:26; 17:2-3). Fractions of, used in currency (Ex 30:13; 1Sa 9:8; Ne 10:32). Used to weigh gold (Ge 24:22; Nu 7:14, 20-86; Jos 7:21; 1Ki 10:16), cinnamon (Ex 30:23), hair (2Sa 14:26), iron (1Sa 17:7), myrrh (Ex 30:23), rations (Eze 4:10). Fines paid in (Dt 22:19, 29). Fees paid in (1Sa 9:8). Sanctuary revenues paid in (Ex 30:13; Ne 10:32).

Of different standards: Of the sanctuary (Ex 30:13), of the king's weight (2Sa 14:26). Corrupted (Am 8:5).

SHEKINAH Jewish term for the dwelling presence of God's glory (Ex 25:22; Lev 16:2; 2Sa 6:2; 2Ki 19:14-15; Ps 80:1; Isa 37:16; Eze 9:3; 10:18; Heb 9:5). Not used in the Bible.

SHELAH (*missile [a weapon], sprout* ISBE).
1. Son of Arphaxad and ancestor of Joseph (Ge 10:24; 11:12-15; 1Ch 1:18, 24; Lk 3:35).
2. Son of Judah (Ge 38:5, 11, 14, 26; 46:12; Nu 26:20; 1Ch 2:3; 4:21).
3. The father of Zechariah (Ne 11:5).

SHELANITE (*missile [a weapon], sprout* ISBE). Descendants of Shelah (Nu 26:20). See Shelah, 2. Apparently called Shilonites (1Ch 9:5). See Shilonite(s), 2.

SHELEMIAH (*Yahweh pays back*, possibly *restores peace offering of Yahweh*).
1. Doorkeeper of tabernacle (1Ch 26:14); in previous verses of this chapter he is called "Meshelemiah."
2. Son of Cushi (Jer 36:14).
3. Man sent to arrest Jeremiah (Jer 36:26).
4. Father of a man whom Zedekiah sent to Jeremiah to ask his prayers (Jer 37:3).
5. The son of Hananiah (Jer 37:13).
6. Two men who divorced foreign wives (Ezr 10:39, 41).
7. Father of Hananiah (Ne 3:30).
8. Priest; treasurer (Ne 13:13).

SHELEPH (*one plucked out, drawn out*). The son of Joktan (Ge 10:26; 1Ch 1:20).

SHELESH (*triplet* KB; possibly *obedient* or *gentle* IDB). The son of Helem (1Ch 7:35).

SHELISHIYAH See Eglath Shelishiyah.

SHELOMI (*at peace*). The father of Ahihud, Asherite prince (Nu 34:27).

SHELOMITH (*at peace*).
1. Daughter of Dibri; her son was killed for blasphemy (Lev 24:10-12, 23).
2. The daughter of Zerubbabel (1Ch 3:19).
3. Cousin of Moses (1Ch 23:18).
4. A descendant of Moses (1Ch 26:25).
5. Child of Rehoboam (2Ch 11:20).
6. An ancestor of a family that returned with Ezra (Ezr 8:10).

SHELOMOTH (*at peace*).
1. Gershonite Levite (1Ch 23:9).
2. Izharite Levite (1Ch 24:22).

SHELUMIEL (*God [El] is [my] peace*). The son of Zurishaddai and leader of Simeon in the time of Moses (Nu 1:6; 2:12; 7:36, 41; 10:19).

SHEM (*name, fame*). The son of Noah. Preserved in the ark (Ge 5:32; 6:10; 7:13; 9:18; 1Ch 1:4). His filial conduct (Ge 9:23-27). The descendants of (Ge 10:1, 21-31; 11:10-29; 1Ch 1:17-54). In genealogy of Jesus (Lk 3:36).

SHEMA (*he hears*).
1. A town in S Judah (Jos 15:26).
2. The son of Hebron (1Ch 2:43-44).
3. The son of Joel (1Ch 5:8).
4. A Benjamite (1Ch 8:13).
5. An assistant of Ezra (Ne 8:4).
6. The Hebrew name for, "Hear, O Israel: The LORD our God, the LORD is one" (Dt 6:4, ftn).

SHEMAAH (possibly *Yahweh hears*). The father of Ahiezer and Joash, soldiers of David (1Ch 12:3).

SHEMAIAH (*Yahweh hears*).
1. Simeonite prince (1Ch 4:37).
2. Reubenite (1Ch 5:4), possibly the same as Shema of (1Ch 5:8).
3. The chief Levite (1Ch 15:8, 11).
4. A Levite scribe (1Ch 24:6).
5. The son of Obed-Edom (1Ch 26:4, 6-7).
6. A prophet who forbade Rehoboam to war against Israel (1Ki 12:22-24).
7. A descendant of David (1Ch 3:22).
8. A Merarite Levite (1Ch 9:14; Ne 12:18).
9. A Levite who returned from exile (1Ch 9:16). Also called Shammua (Ne 11:17).
10. A Levite (1Ch 17:8).
11. A Levite who cleansed the temple (2Ch 29:14).
12. A Levite who assisted in the distribution of food (2Ch 31:15).
13. A Levite in the days of Josiah (2Ch 35:9).
14. A Levite who returned with Ezra (Ezr 8:13).
15. One whom Ezra sent back for ministers (Ezr 8:16), possibly the same as (Ezr 8:13).
16. A priest who divorced his foreign wife (Ezr 10:21).
17. Another priest who divorced his foreign wife (Ezr 10:31).
18-23. Men who played various roles in Nehemiah's rebuilding and in the dedication of the Jerusalem wall (Ne 3:29; 6:10ff; 10:8; 12:6, 18, 34, 35, 36, 42).
24. The father of Uriah the prophet (Jer 26:20).

25. A false prophet who fought against Jeremiah (Jer 29:24-32).
26. The father of Delaiah, a prince in the days of Jehoiakim (Jer 36:12).

SHEMARIAH (*Yahweh guards, preserves*).
1. One of David's mighty men (1Ch 12:5).
2. The son of Rehoboam, king of Judah (2Ch 11:19).
3. A man who put away his foreign wife (Ezr 10:32).
4. Another man who put away his foreign wife (Ezr 10:41).

SHEMEBER The king of Zeboiim, a city near the Dead Sea (Ge 14:2).

SHEMED (*destruction*). The son of Elpaal (1Ch 8:12).

SHEMER (possibly *watch* IDB; possibly *sediment of wine from which clear wine is made* KB). See Shomer, 1, 3, 4.

SHEMESH See Beth Shemesh; En Shemesh; Ir Shemesh.

SHEMIDA, SHEMIDAITE (possibly *the name knows* BDB KB; possibly *[pagan god] Eshmun has known* IDB). The son of Gilead; a family descended from Shemida (Nu 26:32; Jos 17:2; 1Ch 7:19).

SHEMINITH (*eight [strings]*). A musical term of uncertain meaning, possibly "octave" (1Ch 15:21; Ps 6; 12, titles).
See Music, Symbols Used in.

SHEMIRAMOTH (*heights, heavens* BDB; possibly *proper name of a pagan goddess* KB).
1. A Levite musician (1Ch 15:18, 20; 16:5).
2. A Levite sent by Jehoshaphat to instruct the people in the law (2Ch 17:8).

SHEMUEL (possibly *his name is God [El]* BDB IDB ISBE; *the unnamed god is El* KB; *heard of God [El]* KD).
1. A Simeonite leader (Nu 34:20).
2. See Samuel, 2.

SHEN (*tooth, crag [of rock]*). An unidentified site near which Samuel erected the stone "Ebenezer" (1Sa 7:12).

SHENAZZAR (*may [the moon god] Sin protect*). The son of Jehoiachin (1Ch 3:18).

SHENIR See Senir.

SHEOL (possibly *place of inquiry [of the dead]* BDB; *desolate place, no-country underworld* KB). The OT name for the place of departed souls, corresponding to the NT word "Hades." When translated "hell" it refers to the place of punishment, but when translated "grave" the reference is to the place of the dead in general. It often means the place or state of the soul between death and resurrection. The clearest indication of different conditions in Sheol is in Christ's parable of the rich man and Lazarus (Lk 16:19-31).

See Grave; Hades; Hell.

SHEPHAM (*nakedness*). A place in NE of Canaan, near Sea of Galilee (Nu 34:10-11).

SHEPHATIAH (*Yahweh has judged*).
1. The son of David (2Sa 3:4).
2. The son of Reuel (1Ch 9:8).
3. One of David's mighty men (1Ch 12:5).
4. A Simeonite prince (1Ch 27:16).
5. The son of King Jehoshaphat (2Ch 21:2).
6. The founder of a family which returned with Zerubbabel (Ezr 2:4).
7. One of the children of Solomon's servants whose descendants returned with Zerubbabel (Ezr 2:57).
8. One whose descendants returned with Ezra (Ezr 8:8). May be the same as (Ezr 2:57).
9. The son of Mahalalel (Ne 11:4).
10. The prince who wanted Jeremiah to be put to death for prophesying (Jer 38:1).

SHEPHELAH, THE (*lowland*). Hilly country between the mountains of Judah and the maritime plain S of the plain of Sharon, extending through the country of Philistia along the Mediterranean (Jos 12:8).

SHEPHER, MOUNT A mountain, camping place of the Israelites in the desert (Nu 33:23-24).

SHEPHERD

General:
One who cares for flocks (Ge 31:38-40; Ps 78:52-53; Jer 31:10; Am 3:12; Lk 2:8). David defends his flock against a lion and a bear (1Sa 17:34-35). Causes the flock to rest (Ps 23; SS 1:7; Jer 33:12). Numbers the flock (Lev 27:32; Jer 33:13). Knows his flock by name (Jos 10:3-5). Keeps the sheep and goats apart (Mt 25:32). Waters the flocks (Ge 29:2-10). Keeps the flocks in folds (Nu 32:16; Isa 24:3; 2Sa 7:8; Jn 10:1). Watch towers of (2Ch 26:10; Mic 4:8). Dogs of (Job 30:1). Was an abomination to the Egyptians (Ge 46:34). Angels appeared to (Lk 2:8-20).

Instances of:
Abel (Ge 4:2). Rachel (Ge 29:9). Daughters of Jethro (Ex 2:16). Moses (Ex 3:1). David (1Sa 16:11; 2Sa 7:8; Ps 78:70).

Figurative:
(Ge 49:24). Of prophets, priests, Levites, and civil authorities (Eze 34). Of Cyrus (Isa 44:28). Of Yahweh (Ps 23; Isa 40:11). Of Christ (Zec 13:7; Mt 26:31; Mk 14:27; Jn 10:1-16; Heb 13:20; 1Pe 2:25).

SHEPHI See Shepho.

SHEPHO (possibly *track, bare ways formed without human work by the traffic caravans* KB). Early descendant of Seir (Ge

36:23; 1Ch 1:40). Lesser known brother of Groucho, Harpo, and Chico.

SHEPHUPHAN (perhaps *serpent*). The son of Bela (1Ch 8:5).

SHERAH See Sheerah.

SHERD See Potsherd

SHEREBIAH (possibly *Yahweh has sent burning heat* BDB).
1. A prominent Levite in Ezra's time (Ezr 8:18, 24).
2. Covenanter with Nehemiah (Ne 10:12).
3. Levite who returned with Zerubbabel (Ne 12:8).
4. The chief Levite (Ne 12:24).

SHERESH (*root, rootstock, sucker [of a plant]*). The son of Makir (1Ch 7:16).

SHEREZER See Sharezer.

SHERIFF (Da 3:2-3). See Magistrates.

SHESHACH (cryptogram for *Babel [Babylon]*). Perhaps a cryptogram for "Babel" or "Babylon" (Jer 25:26, ftn; 51:41, ftn).

SHESHAI (possibly *sixth [child]*). The son of Anak (Nu 13:22; Jos 15:14; Jdg 1:10).

SHESHAN A descendant of Jerahmeel (1Ch 2:31, 34-35).

SHESHBAZZAR (*may [the pagan moon god named] Sin protect [the father]*). A Jewish official whom Cyrus made deputy governor of Judah and who helped lay the foundation of the temple (Ezr 1:8, 11; 5:14, 16). Some believe that Sheshbazzar and Zerubbabel were the same person for the following reasons:
1. Both were governors (Ezr 5:14; Hag 1:1; 2:2).
2. Both are said to have laid the foundation of the temple (Ezr 3:2-8; 5:16; Hag 1:14-15; Zec 4:6-10).
3. Jews in Babylon were often given "official" Babylonian names (cf. Da 1:7).
4. Josephus (*Antiq.*, 11.1.3) seems to identify Sheshbazzar with Zerubbabel.

Others point out, however:
1. The Apocrypha distinguishes between the two men (1Es 6:18).
2. Sheshbazzar was likely an elderly man at the time of the return, while Zerubbabel was probably a younger contemporary.
3. Sheshbazzar may have been viewed as the official governor, while Zerubbabel served as the popular leader (Ezr 3:8-11).
4. Whereas the high priest Jeshua is associated with Zerubbabel, no priest is associated with Sheshbazzar.
5. Although Sheshbazzar presided over the foundation of the temple in 536 B.C., so little was accomplished that Zerubbabel had to preside over a second foundation sixteen years later (Hag 1:14-15; Zec 4:6-10).

Others identify Sheshbazzar with Shenazzar (1Ch 3:18), the fourth son of King Jehoiachin. Zerubbabel would then have been Sheshbazzar's nephew (compare 3:2 with 1Ch 3:18). See Zerubbabel.

SHETH (*sons of tumult*, or *sons of pride, compensation*). A designation for Moab (Nu 24:17).

SHETHAR A prince of Persia (Est 1:14).

SHETHAR-BOZENAI (*delivering the kingdom*). Persian official who tried to hinder Jews (Ezr 5:3, 6).

SHEVA (*vanity, emptiness* IDB; *one who will emulate* IDB KB).
1. David's scribe (2Sa 20:25), perhaps the same as "Seraiah" (1Ch 2:49). See Seraiah, 1.
2. The son of Caleb (1Ch 2:49).

SHEWBREAD See Bread, Consecrated.

SHIBAH (possibly *seven* BDB ISBE; possibly *oath* BDB IDB; *plenty* KB). The name of the well dug by Isaac's servants. A town of Beersheba named from this well (Ge 26:31-33, ftn). Called Beersheba in NIV.

SHIBBOLETH (*flowing stream* BDB KB; or *ear of grain* IDB). A word differently pronounced on the two sides of the Jordan, and was used by the men of Gilead to determine whether the speaker was of Ephraim or not. Those who said "Sibboleth" instead of "Shibboleth" were killed. Forty-two thousand Ephraimites were killed at the fords of the Jordan at that time (Jdg 12:5-6).

SHIBMAH See Sibmah.

SHICRON See Shikkeron.

SHIELD

Defensive Armor:
Different kinds of (Ps 35:2; Eze 38:4). Used by Saul (2Sa 1:21), by the Benjamites (2Ch 14:8; 17:17). Uzziah equipped the Israelites with (2Ch 26:14). Made of bronze (1Ki 14:27), of gold (2Sa 8:7; 1Ki 10:16-17; 2Ch 9:15-16), of wood (Eze 39:9-10). Stored in armories (1Ki 10:17; 2Ch 11:12; 32:5, 27), in the tabernacle (2Ki 11:10; 2Ch 23:9). Covered when not in use (Isa 22:6). Painted red (Na 2:3). See Armor.

Figurative:
Of God's protection (Ge 15:1; Dt 33:29; 2Sa 22:3, 36; Ps 5:12; 18:2, 35; 33:20; 59:11; 84:9, 11; 89:18; Pr 30:5). Of God's truth (Ps 91:4). Of kings (Ps 47:9). Of an entire army (Jer 46:3).

SHIGGAION (*go astray, wander [i.e., a wild, passionate song, with rapid changes in rhythm]* BDB; possibly Akkadian for *dirge* KB). A musical term of unknown meaning found in the heading of (Ps 7).
See Music, Symbols Used in.

SHIGIONOTH (*go astray, wander [i.e., a wild, passionate song, with rapid changes in rhythm]* BDB; possibly Akkadian for *dirge* KB). The plural of *shiggaion*. The heading of Habakkuk's psalm (Hab 3:1).
See *Music, Symbols Used in.*

SHIHON See *Shion.*

SHIHOR (possibly *black water* BDB; Egyptian *Canal of [pagan god] Horus* KB). May refer to the Nile, a stream which separated Egypt from Israel, or a branch of the Nile (Jos 13:3; 1Ch 13:5; Isa 23:3; Jer 2:18).

SHIHOR LIBNATH A small stream on the S border of Asher (Jos 19:26).

SHIKKERON (possibly *drunkenness* IDB; *hog bean plant* IDB). A town on the N boundary of Judah (Jos 15:11).

SHILHI (possibly *[my] javelin [thrower?]* IDB KB). Father-in-law of Jehoshaphat, king of Judah (1Ki 22:42; 2Ch 20:31).

SHILHIM A city of Judah (Jos 15:32).

SHILLEM, SHILLEMITE (*recompense* BDB IDB; possibly *whole, healthy, complete* KB). The son of Naphtali (Ge 46:24; 1Ch 7:13), and his descendants (Nu 26:49).

SHILOAH A stream or pool (Isa 8:6). Probably identical with Siloah and Siloam. See *Siloam, Pool of.*

SHILOH
1. A city in Ephraim, c. twelve miles N and E of Bethel where the tabernacle remained from the time of Joshua to the days of Samuel (Jos 21:19; 1Sa 4:3), Benjamites kidnapped wives (Jdg 21:15-24), residence of Eli and Samuel (1Sa 3:21), home of the prophet Ahijah (1Ki 14:3), a ruin in Jeremiah's time (Jer 7:12, 14).
2. A word of uncertain meaning regarded by many Jews and Christians as a reference to the Messiah; the NIV has "until he comes to whom it belongs" (Ge 49:10, ftn).

SHILONI See *Shelah, 3.*

SHILONITE(S) (*of Shiloh*).
1. A man of Shiloh (1Ki 12:15; 15:29; 2Ch 9:29; 10:15).
2. Apparently denotes a descendant of Shelah (1Ch 9:5). See *Shelanite.*

SHILSHAH (possibly *obedient* or *gentle* IDB; *third [part, child?], triplet* KB). An Asherite; the son of Zophah (1Ch 7:37).

SHIMEA (*he has heard* or *he is obedient*).
1. Brother of David (1Ch 20:7). Perhaps the same as "Shammah" (1Sa 16:9), "Shimeah" (2Sa 21:21).
2. The son of David and Bathsheba (1Ch 3:5).
3. A Merarite Levite (1Ch 6:30).
4. A Gershonite Levite (1Ch 6:39).

SHIMEAH (*he has heard* or *he is obedient*).
1. The brother of David (2Sa 13:3, 32; 21:21).
2. A Benjamite (1Ch 8:32), "Shimeam" (1Ch 9:38).

SHIMEAM See *Shimeah, 2.*

SHIMEATH (*guardian, watcher*). The mother of an assassin of King Joash (2Ki 12:21; 2Ch 24:26).

SHIMEATHITES A family of scribes (1Ch 2:55).

SHIMEI, SHIMEITES (*Yahweh has heard, or famous*).
1. Son of Gershon (Ex 6:17; Nu 3:18; 1Ch 6:17; 23:7, 10) and his descendants (Nu 3:21).
2. A Benjamite. Curses David; David's magnanimity toward (2Sa 16:5-13; 19:16-23, w 1Ki 2:36-46).
3. An officer of David (1Ki 1:8).
4. One of Solomon's district governors (1Ki 4:18).
5. A son of Jesse (1Ch 2:13).
6. The grandson of Jehoiachin (1Ch 3:19).
7. The son of Zaccur (1Ch 4:26-27).
8. A Reubenite. The son of Gog (1Ch 5:4).
9. A Merarite. The son of Libni (1Ch 6:29).
10. A Gershonite. The son of Jahath (1Ch 6:42).
11. The father of a family in Benjamin (1Ch 8:21).
12. A Levite (1Ch 23:9).
13. A leader of singers in the time of David (1Ch 25:17).
14. David's overseer of vineyards (1Ch 27:27).
15. A son of Heman (2Ch 29:14).
16. A Levite. The treasurer of tithes and offerings in the time of Hezekiah (2Ch 31:12-13).
17. A Levite who put away his Gentile wife (Ezr 10:23).
18. The name of two Israelites who put away Gentile wives (Ezr 10:33, 38).
19. A Benjamite. The grandfather of Mordecai (Est 2:5).
20. The ancestor of a family (Zec 12:13). Possibly identical with 1.

SHIMEON (possibly *offspring of hyena and wolf* BDB KB). An Israelite who divorced his Gentile wife (Ezr 10:31).

SHIMHI See *Shimei, 11.*

SHIMI See *Shimei, 1.*

SHIMMA See *Shimea, 1.*

SHIMON A man of Judah (1Ch 4:20).

SHIMRATH (*guardian, watchman*). The son of Shimei (1Ch 8:21).

SHIMRI (*Yahweh guards, preserves*).
1. The son of Shemaiah; a Simeonite (1Ch 4:37).

2. The father of Jediael and Joha, two of David's mighty men (1Ch 11:45).
3. A Merarite Levite doorkeeper (1Ch 26:10).
4. A Levite who assisted in cleansing the temple (2Ch 29:13).

SHIMRITH (*guardianess, watch woman*). A Moabitess; the mother of Jehozabad who helped kill Joash, king of Judah (2Ch 24:26), "Shomer" (2Ki 12:21).

SHIMROM See *Shimron, 1.*

SHIMRON, SHIMRONITE (*guardian, watchman*).
1. The son of Issachar (Ge 46:13; 1Ch 7:1) and his descendants (Nu 26:24).
2. A town in N Canaan whose king fought Joshua (Jos 11:1ff); probably Shimron Meron. See *Shimron Meron.*

SHIMRON MERON A city conquered by Joshua (Jos 12:20). Probably identical with Shimron, 2. See *Shimron, 2.*

SHIMSHAI (*one given to [pagan sun god] Shemesh*). A scribe who tried to hinder the Jews in rebuilding the temple (Ezr 4:8-9, 17, 23).

SHINAB (*[pagan god] Sin is his father*). The king of Admah. A Canaanite city, later destroyed (Ge 14:2).

SHINAR An alluvial plain of Babylonia in which lay the cities of Babel, Erech, Akkad, and Calneh (Ge 10:10), the Tower of Babel was built there (Ge 11:1-9), Amraphel, king of Shinar, invaded Canaan (Ge 14:1, 9). Elsewhere rendered Babylon(ia): Nebuchadnezzar transported the temple treasures to (Da 1:2, ftn), Jews exiled to (Zec 5:11, ftn).

SHION A town in Issachar near Nazareth (Jos 19:19).

SHIP Built, by Noah (Ge 6:13-22), by Solomon (1Ki 9:26; 2Ch 8:17), by Jehoshaphat (1Ki 22:48; 2Ch 20:35-36), of cypress wood (Ge 6:14), of fir wood (Eze 27:5), of papyrus (Isa 18:2), sealed with pitch (Ge 6:15).
Equipped with, rudder (Ac 27:40; Jas 3:4), rigging (Isa 33:23; Ac 27:19), sails (Isa 33:23; Ac 27:1, 9, 17, 40), embroidered sails (Eze 27:7), masts (Isa 33:23; Eze 27:5), oars (Jnh 1:13; Mk 6:48), figurehead (Ac 28:11), anchor (Ac 27:29-30, 40; Heb 6:19), lifeboats (Ac 27:30, 32).
Used, in commerce (Ac 21:3; 27:10), in commerce with Tarshish (1Ki 22:48; Isa 60:9; Jnh 1:3), with Ophir (1Ki 10:11; 2Ch 8:18), with Adramyttium (Ac 27:2), for passenger traffic (Isa 60:9; Jnh 1:3; Ac 20:13; 27:2, 37; 28:11).
Repaired by caulking (Eze 27:9).
Wrecked, at Ezion Geber (1Ki 22:48; 2Ch 20:35-37), at Malta (Ac 27:14-44).
Warships used by Kittim (Nu 24:24; Da 11:30).
See *Mariner.*

SHIPHI (*flowing abundance*). The father of Ziza (1Ch 4:37).

SHIPHMITE (*family name of Zabdi*). Vineyard overseer (1Ch 27:27).

SHIPHRAH (*beautiful, fair*). A Hebrew midwife who saved Hebrew boy babies (Ex 1:15-21).

SHIPHTAN (*he has judged*). The father of the representative of Ephraim on the committee which divided the promised land among the Israelites (Nu 34:24).

SHISHA The father of two of Solomon's secretaries (1Ki 4:3), may be identical with Seraiah (2Sa 8:17), Sheva (2Sa 20:25), and Shavsha (1Ch 18:16).

SHISHAK The first Egyptian Pharaoh mentioned by name in the Bible; the founder of the twenty-second dynasty (945-924 B.C.), gave refuge to Jeroboam (1Ki 11:40), invaded Jerusalem in the reign of Rehoboam (1Ki 14:25f).

SHITRAI (*scribe, officer*). A chief shepherd of David (1Ch 27:29).

SHITTAH See *Beth Shittah.*

SHITTAH TREE NIV "acacia." See *Acacia Wood; Plants of the Bible; Tree.*

SHITTIM (*acacia trees*).
1. Also called Abel Shittim (Nu 33:49). A camping place of Israel (Nu 25:1; 33:49). Joshua sends spies from (Jos 2:1). Valley of (Joel 3:18). Balaam prophesies in (Mic 6:5). See *Abel Shittim.*
2. Hebrew for acacia (Joel 3:18).
See *Acacia Wood.*

SHIZA A Reubenite. The father of one of David's mighty men (1Ch 11:42).

SHOA (*rich*). People mentioned in association with the Babylonians, Chaldeans, and Assyrians (Eze 23:23). May be Sutu of Amarna letters.

SHOBAB (*one who turns back, repents*).
1. The grandson for Hezron (1Ch 2:18).
2. The son of David (2Sa 5:14; 1Ch 3:5; 14:4).

SHOBACH The captain of the host of Hadadezer. Slain by David's army (2Sa 10:16, 18). Also called Shophach (1Ch 19:16, 18).

SHOBAI (possibly *captive* or *Yahweh returns*). A gatekeeper, whose descendants returned to Jerusalem with Zerubbabel (Ezr 2:42; Ne 7:45).

SHOBAL (perhaps a nickname *basket*).
1. Chief of the Horites (Ge 36:20, 23, 29).
2. Ephrathite; founder of Kiriath Jearim (1Ch 2:50, 52).

3. Grandson of Judah (1Ch 4:1-2).

SHOBEK (*victor* IDB). A Jew who sealed the covenant with Nehemiah (Ne 10:24).

SHOBI (possibly *captive* or *Yahweh returns*). The son of Nahash. Brought supplies to David in his flight from Absalom (2Sa 17:27).

SHOCHO See *Soco, 2.*

SHOE See *Sandal.*

SHOFAR (*ram horn*). A trumpet of ram's horn (Jos 6:4-6, 8, 13). See *Trumpet.*

SHOHAM (*carnelian [precious stone]*). A Merarite (1Ch 24:27).

SHOMER (*guardian, watchman*).
1. A man who sold the hill of Samaria to Omri, king of Israel (1Ki 16:24).
2. The father of Jehozabad, conspirator of Joash of Judah (2Ki 12:20-21).
3. A Merarite Levite (1Ch 6:46).
4. The great-grandson of Asher (1Ch 7:32, 34).

SHOPHACH A Syrian general slain by David (1Ch 19:16, 18), "Shobach" (2Sa 10:16).

SHOPHAN See *Atroth Shophan.*

SHORE Coast line or beach (Jos 15:2; Jdg 5:17; Mt 13:2).

SHOSHANNIM NIV "Lilies." See *Music, Symbols Used in.*

SHOULDER The shoulder of a sacrificed ox or sheep went to the priest as his portion (Dt 18:8), the sacred furniture of the tabernacle had to be carried upon the shoulders (Nu 7:6-9).

SHOULDER PIECE
1. Part of the ephod in which the front and the back were joined together (Ex 28:7-8).
2. A piece of meat taken from the shoulder of an animal (Eze 24:4).

SHOUTING In joy and praise (1Ch 15:28; 2Ch 15:12-14; Ezr 3:11-13; Ps 47:1; Isa 12:6; Lk 17:15; 19:37-41; Ac 3:8-9; Rev 5:12-14).
See *Clap; Praise; Worship.*
In battle (Jos 6:20; Jdg 7:18; 1Sa 17:20, 52; 2Ch 13:15).

SHOVEL A utensil in the tabernacle (Ex 27:3; 38:3; Nu 4:14), temple (1Ki 7:40; Jer 52:18).

SHOWBREAD See *Bread, Consecrated.*

SHRINE Places of idolatrous worship, often a high place (Eze 16:24-25, 31, 39). Frequented by temple prostitutes (Ge 38:21-22; Dt 23:17; Hos 4:14), including male prostitutes (1Ki 14:24; 15:12; 22:46; 2Ki 23:7; Job 36:14). A shrine also refers to an idolatrous symbol, certain small idol houses, made by the silversmith, Demetrius, and sold to the worshipers of the Temple of Diana (Ac 19:24).
See *Artemis; Groves; High Places; Idolatry; Prostitute.*

SHRIVELED HAND As a judgment (1Ki 13:4). Jesus heals on the Sabbath (Mt 12:10-13 w Mk 3:1-6; Lk 6:6-11). See *Disease.*

SHROUD A sheet to cover the dead (Isa 25:7).

SHRUB See *Plants of the Bible.*

SHUA (*prosperity* ISBE).
1. A Canaanite whose daughter became Judah's wife (Ge 38:2, 12).
2. Heber's daughter (1Ch 7:32).

SHUAH (*depression, lowland [an Aramean land on the Euphrates River]*).
1. The son of Abraham by Keturah (Ge 25:2; 1Ch 1:32).
2. See *Shua, 1.*
3. See *Shuhah.*

SHUAL (*fox* or *jackal*).
1. District near Micmash (1Sa 13:17).
2. The son of Zophah (1Ch 7:36).

SHUBAEL (possibly *captive of God [El]*, or *God [El] restores*).
1. The son of Gershom son of Moses (1Ch 23:16; 26:24).
2. The son of Amram (1Ch 24:20).
3. A singer, the son of Heman (1Ch 25:4, 20).

SHUHAH (*pit, depression*). Kelub's brother (1Ch 4:11).

SHUHAM, SHUHAMITE The son of Dan and his clan (Nu 26:42-43); also called Hushim (Ge 46:23). See *Hushim, 1.*

SHUHITE (*of Shuah*). Bildad, one of Job's friends (Job 2:11; 8:1; 18:1; 25:1); possibly a descendant of Shuah, 1.

SHULAMMITE (*peaceful*). A designation of the beloved in the Song of Songs (SS 6:13); possibly the same as Shunammite.

SHUMATHITES (*garlic*). Family of Kiriath Jearim (1Ch 2:53).

SHUNAMMITE
1. A person from Shunem. Abishag, the woman who nourished David (1Ki 1:3), desired by Adonijah as wife (1Ki 2:13-25).
2. A woman who gave hospitality to Elisha and whose son he raised to life (2Ki 4:8-37).

SHUNEM A city of Issachar (Job 19:18), three-and-a-half miles N of Jezreel; the site of a Philistine encampment before battle (1Sa

S

28:4), the home of Abishag, David's nurse (1Ki 1:3), home of a woman who befriended Elisha (2Ki 4:8-37).

SHUNI, SHUNITE The son of Gad (Ge 46:16) and his clan (Nu 26:15).

SHUPHAM, SHUPHAMITE The son of Benjamin and progenitor of Shuphamites (Nu 26:39). May be the same as Shephuphan (1Ch 8:5).

SHUPPIM
1. A Levite (1Ch 26:16).
2. See Shuppites.

SHUPPITES Descendants of Ir (1Ch 7:12, 15).

SHUR (wall). A wilderness southwest of Israel (Ge 16:7; 20:1; 25:18; Ex 15:22; 1Sa 15:7; 27:8).

SHUSHAN See Susa.

SHUSHAN-EDUTH (lily of testimony). See Music, Symbols Used in.

SHUTHELAH, SHUTHALHITE
1. The son of Ephraim and his clan (Nu 26:35-36).
2. The son of Zabad; father of Ezer and Elead (1Ch 7:21).

SHUTTLE Part of a weaving loom; used as a figure of the shortness of life (Job 7:6).

SIA (assembly). Progenitor of the temple servants that returned with Zerubbabel (Ne 7:47), "Siaha" (Ezr 2:44).

SIAHA See Sia.

SIBBECAI One of David's mighty men, designated "Hushathite" (2Sa 21:18; 1Ch 11:29; 20:4; 27:11), killed the Philistine "Saph" (2Sa 21:18).

SIBBOLETH See Shibboleth.

SIBMAH A city of Reuben (Nu 32:38; Jos 13:19; Isa 16:8-9; Jer 48:32). Apparently also called Sebam (Nu 32:3).

SIBRAIM A place on the N boundary of Israel (Eze 47:16).

SICHEM See Shechem, 1.

SICILY An island lying off the "toe" of Italy, visited by Paul (Ac 28:12). See Syracuse.

SICK, THE Visiting (Ps 41:6). Visiting, a duty (Mt 25:36, 43; Jas 1:27). See Afflicted; Affliction; Disease.

SICKLE (reaping hook). A tool used for cutting grain, sometimes also for pruning (Dt 16:9; Joel 3:13; Mk 4:29). Used figuratively for God's judgment (Joel 3:13; Rev 14:14).

SICKNESS Figurative of sin and judgment (Isa 1:5-6; Hos 5:13). See Affliction; Disease; Sick, The.

SIDDIM, VALLEY OF (possibly valley of furrows, valley of demons BDB; valley of bordering furrows KB). Vale of, a valley of uncertain location. Scene of the king of Sodom (Ge 14:3, 8, 10).

SIDON (fishery).
1. The son of Canaan (Ge 10:15; 1Ch 1:13).
2. A city on the northern boundary of the Canaanites, twenty-two miles N of Tyre (Ge 10:19). Designated by Jacob as the border of Zebulun (Ge 49:13). Was on the northern boundary of Asher (Jos 19:28; 2Sa 24:6). Belonged to the land of Israel according to the promise (Jos 13:6). Inhabitants of lived in security (Jdg 18:7). Israelites failed to make the conquest of (Jdg 1:31; 3:3). The inhabitants of, contributed cedar for the first and second temple (1Ki 5:6; 1Ch 22:4; Ezr 3:7). Solomon marries a woman of (1Ki 11:1). Chief gods were Baal and Ashtoreth (1Ki 11:5, 33; 2Ki 23:13). Jezebel, wife of King Ahab, was a daughter of a king of Sidon (1Ki 16:31). People of, come to hear Jesus (Mk 3:8; Lk 6:17). Inhabitants of, offend Herod (Ac 12:20-23).
Commerce of (Isa 23:2, 4, 12). Seamen of (Eze 27:8). Prophecies concerning (Jer 25:15-22; 27:3-11; 47:4; Eze 28:21-23; 32:30; Joel 3:4-8). Jesus visits the region of, and heals the daughter of the Syrian Phoenician woman (Mt 15:21-28; Mk 7:24-31). Visited by Paul (Ac 27:3).

SIEGE An offer of peace must be made to the city before beginning (Dt 20:10-12). Conducted by erecting embankments parallel to the walls of the besieged city (Dt 20:19-20; Isa 29:3; 37:33). Battering rams used in. See Battering Ram. Distress of the inhabitants during (2Ki 6:24-29; 25:3; Isa 9:20; 36:12; Jer 19:9). Cannibalism in (2Ki 6:28-29).

Instances of:
Of Jericho (Jos 6). Rabbah (2Sa 11:1). Abel (2Sa 20:15), Gibbethon (1Ki 15:27), Tirzah (1Ki 16:17). Jerusalem, by the children of Judah (Jdg 1:8), by David (2Sa 5:6, 9), by Rezin, king of Syria, and Pekah, son of Remaliah, king of Israel (2Ki 16:5), by Nebuchadnezzar (2Ki 24:10-11; Da 1:1; 2Ki 25:1-3; Jer 52), by Sennacherib (2Ch 32:1-23). Samaria (1Ki 20:1; 2Ki 6:24; 17:5; 18:9-11).

SIEVE A sifting device for grain; made of reeds, horsehair, or strings (Isa 30:28; Am 9:9). Also used figuratively (Lk 22:31).

SIGN A miracle to confirm faith (Mt 12:38; 16:4; 24:30; Mk 8:11-12; 13:4; Jn 2:11; 3:2; 4:48). Asked for by, and given to Abraham (Ge 15:8-17), Moses (Ex 4:1-9), Gideon (Jdg 6:17, 36-40), Hezekiah (2Ki 20:8), Zechariah (Lk 1:18). Given to Jeroboam (1Ki 13:3-5).
A token of coming events (Mt 16:3-4; 24:3). See Miracles.

SIGNAL Used in war (Isa 18:3). See Armies; Ensign; Trumpet.

SIGNET See Seal.

SIHON King of the Amorites. His seat of government at Heshbon (Nu 21:26). The proverbial chant celebrating the victory of Sihon over the Moabites (Nu 21:26-30). Conquest of his kingdom by the Israelites (Nu 21:21-25; Dt 2:24-37; 3:2, 6, 8).

SIHOR See Shihor.

SILAS (asked, possibly dedicated to God). Also called Silvanus (1Th 1:1, ftn). Sent to Paul, in Antioch, from Jerusalem (Ac 15:22-34). Becomes Paul's companion (Ac 15:40-41; 2Co 1:19; 1Th 1:1; 2Th 1:1). Imprisoned with Paul in Philippi (Ac 16:19-40). Driven, with Paul, from Thessalonica (Ac 17:4-10). Left by Paul at Berea (Ac 17:14). Rejoins Paul at Corinth (Ac 17:15; 18:5). Carries Peter's epistle to Asia Minor (1Pe 5:12).

SILENT YEARS, FOUR HUNDRED See Testaments, Time Between.

SILK Wearing apparel made of (Pr 31:22; Eze 16:10, 13). Merchandise of (Rev 18:22). See Linen.

SILLA (embankment). A place of uncertain location (2Ki 12:20).

SILOAH See Siloam.

SILOAM, POOL OF (sent). A reservoir located within the city walls of Jerusalem at the S end of the Tyropean Valley; receives water through a 1,780-foot tunnel from En Rogel (Ne 3:15; Lk 13:4; Jn 9:7, 11), constructed by Hezekiah in the late eighth century B.C. "Shiloah" (Isa 8:6). The pool today is called Birket Silwan and a nearby village is Silwan. See Siloam, Village of.

SILOAM, TOWER OF Probably part of the fortification system of the Jerusalem wall, near the pool of Siloam (Lk 13:4).

SILOAM, VILLAGE OF Not mentioned in the Bible; the modern village (Silwan) situated across the valley E of the Gihon Spring.

SILVANUS See Silas.

SILVER (pale, white). From Tarshish (Eze 27:12). Refining of (Pr 17:3; 25:4; 26:23; Eze 22:18-22; Jer 6:29-30; Zec 13:9; Mal 3:3). See Refining.
Used for money (Ge 13:2; 17:12; 20:16; 23:13-16; Am 8:6; Mt 10:9; 26:15; Mk 14:11; Ac 19:19). See Money. For ornamentation of, and in the manufacture of, the utensils for the tabernacle (Ex 26:19; 27:17; 35:24; 36:24; 38:25; Nu 7:13, 19, 25, 31, 37, 43, 49, 55, 61, 67, 73, 79, 85), of the temple (1Ch 28:14; 29:2-5; Ezr 5:14; 6:5; 8:26; Da 5:2). Cups made of (Ge 44:2), trumpets (Nu 10:2), cords (Ecc 12:6), chains (Isa 40:19), shrines (Ac 19:24), idols (Ex 20:23; Isa 30:22; Hos 13:2), baskets, or filigree (Pr 25:11), jewels (SS 1:11). See Jewel, Jewelry. Towers, figurative (SS 8:9). Vessels of (Nu 7:85; 1Ki 10:25; 2Sa 8:10; 2Ki 12:13; 1Ch 18:10; 2Ch 24:14; Ezr 1:6; 5:14; 6:5; 8:26; Da 5:2; 11:8).
Abundance of (1Ki 10:27; 1Ch 22:14; 29:2-7; 2Ch 1:15; Ecc 2:8; Isa 2:7). Dross from (Pr 25:4; 26:23). Rejected (Jer 6:30). Workers in (2Ch 2:14; Ac 19:24). See Smith.
Symbolic (Da 2:32, 35).

SILVERSMITH (Ac 19:24). See Smith.

SIMEON (he has heard or obedient one).
1. The son of Jacob (Ge 29:33; 35:23; Ex 1:1-2; 1Ch 2:1). With Levi avenges upon the Shechemites the seduction of Dinah (Ge 34; 49:5-7). Goes down to Egypt to buy grain; is bound by Joseph and detained (Ge 42:24, 36; 43:23). His sons (Ge 46:10; Ex 6:15; 1Ch 4:24-37). Descendants of (Nu 26:12-14).
See below, Tribe of.
2. Tribe of: Military enrollment of, at Sinai (Nu 1:22-23; 2:13), in the plains of Moab (Nu 26:14). Place of, in camp and march (Nu 2:12; 10:18-19). Inheritance allotted to (Jos 19:1-9; Jdg 1:3-17; 1Ch 4:24-43). Stood on Mount Gerizim to bless at the time of the rehearsal of the law (Dt 27:12). Joined with the people of Judah and Benjamin in the renewal of the Passover (2Ch 15:9, w 15:1-15). Idolatry of (2Ch 34:6, w 34:1-7).
See Israel.
3. A devout man in Jerusalem. Blesses Jesus in the temple (Lk 2:25-35).
4. An ancestor of Jesus (Lk 3:30).
5. A disciple. Also called Niger (Ac 13:1).
6. Hebrew name of Peter (Ac 15:14, ftn). See Peter, Simon.

SIMEONITE(S) (of Simeon). A member of the tribe of Simeon.

SIMILITUDE (likeness). Pattern, resemblance, similarity (Nu 12:8; 2Ch 4:3; Ps 106:20; Heb 7:15).

SIMON (he has heard or obedient one).
1. See Peter, Simon.
2. One of the twelve apostles. Called the Zealot (Mt 10:4; Mk 3:18; Lk 6:15; Ac 1:13). See Zealot.
3. A brother of Jesus (Mt 13:55; Mk 6:3).
4. A leper. Jesus dines with (Mt 26:6; Mk 14:3).
5. A man of Cyrene. Compelled to carry Jesus' cross (Mt 27:32; Mk 15:21; Lk 23:26).
6. A Pharisee. Jesus dines with (Lk 7:36-44).
7. The father of Judas Iscariot (Jn 6:71; 12:4; 13:2, 26).
8. A sorcerer. Converted by Philip; rebuked by Peter (Ac 8:9-13, 18-24).
9. A tanner. Peter lodges with (Ac 9:43; 10:6, 17, 32).

SIMON MACCABEUS Hasmonean ruler in Israel (143-134 B.C.).

SIMONY Ecclesiastical corruption, named after Simon the sorcerer (Ac 8:9-19).

SIMPLE Naive; easily led into wrong-doing (Ps 19:7; 119:130; Pr 7:7).

SIMRI See Shimri, 3.

SIN

Adamic:
Original, of Adam (Ge 3:6; Hos 6:7; Ro 5:12, 15-19).

Sin Nature:
The inherited tendencies to evil (Mt 7:17-18; 12:33-35; Mk 7:20-23; Lk 6:45; Ro 6:6; 7:17, 20, 23, 25; 8:3, 5-7; Gal 5:16-17; Eph 2:3; Jas 1:14; 4:17).

Defined:
Transgressing the law (Hos 6:8; Mt 5:28; 1Co 8:12; Heb 12:15; Jas 2:10-11; 4:17; 1Jn 3:4; 5:17). Turning away from God (Dt 29:18; Ps 95:10). Not seeking God (2Ch 12:14). Foolish thoughts (Pr 24:8-9). Self-deception (Isa 42:20). That which is not of faith (Ro 14:23).
See Atonement; Conviction, of Sin; Depravity; Regeneration; Repentance; Reprobacy; Salvation; Sanctification; Wicked, Punishment of.
Against the body (Ecc 5:6). Against conscience (Ro 14:23). Against knowledge (Pr 26:11; Lk 12:47-48; Jn 9:41; 15:22; Ro 1:21, 32; 2:17-23; Heb 10:26; Jas 4:17; 2Pe 2:21-22). See Ignorance, Sins of. Attempts to cover, vain (Ge 3:10; Job 31:33; Isa 29:15; 59:6).
Christ's description of (Mt 5:2-20; Jn 8:34, 44).
Deceitful (Heb 3:13). Defiles (Ps 51:2, 7; Isa 1:18; Heb 12:15; 1Jn 1:7). See Defilement. Degrees in (Lk 7:41-47; 12:47-48). Dominion of (Ro 3:9). Enslaves (Jn 8:34; Ro 6:16; 2Pe 2:19). From the heart (Isa 44:20; Jer 7:24; 17:9; Eze 20:16; Mt 5:28; 7:17-18; 12:33-35; 15:8, 11, 16-19; Lk 6:45). Of the tongue (Ecc 5:6). In thought (Pr 24:9). Fools mock at (Pr 14:9). Little sins (SS 2:15). Magnitude of (Job 22:5; Ps 25:11).
None in heaven (Rev 22:3-4).
Parable of (Mt 13:24-25, 33, 39). Paul's discussion of the responsibility for (Ro 2). Pleasures of (Jn 20:12-16; 21:12-13; Lk 8:14; Heb 11:25). See Pleasure, Worldly.
Reproach to God (2Sa 12:14).
Secret sins (Ps 19:12; 44:22; 64:2; 90:8; Ecc 12:14; Eze 8:12; 11:5; Mt 10:26; Lk 8:17; 12:2-3; Jn 3:20; Ro 2:16; Eph 5:12).
Sinfulness of (Job 22:5; Ps 51:1; Isa 1:18; Ro 7:13).
To be hated (Dt 7:26; Ps 119:113).

Confession of:
(1Ki 8:47; Pr 28:13). Signified by placing hands on the head of the offering (Lev 3:2, 13; 4:4, 15, 24, 29, 33; 16:21; Nu 8:12). Illustrated in parables, of the prodigal son (Lk 15:17-21). Of the Pharisee and the tax collector (Lk 18:13).
To God, commanded (Lev 5:5-10; 16:21). Exemplified by Israel (Nu 14:40; Jdg 10:10; 1Sa 7:6), by Saul (1Sa 15:2, 4), by David (2Sa 12:13; 24:10, 17; 1Ch 21:17), by the psalmist (Ps 32:5; 38:3-4, 18; 40:11-12; 41:4; 51:2-5; 69:5; 73:21-22; 119:59-60, 176), by the Jews (2Ch 29:6; Ezr 9:4-7, 10-15; Ne 9:2-38; Ps 106:6; Isa 26:13; 59:12-15; 64:5-7; Jer 3:21-22, 25; 8:14-15; 14:7, 20; 31:18-19; La 3:40-42; Da 9:5-6, 8-11, 15, 20), by Job (Job 7:20; 9:20; 13:23; 40:4; 42:5-6), by Isaiah (Isa 6:5), by Jeremiah (La 1:18-20), by Paul (1Co 15:9).
To believers, commanded (Jas 5:16; 1Jn 1:8-10).

Consequences of:
Look on the face (Isa 3:9). Guilty fear (Ge 3:7-10; Pr 10:24; 25:1). Depraved conscience (Pr 30:20). Judgment (Jer 5:25). Trouble (Isa 57:20-21; Jer 4:18).
Effects upon children (Ex 20:5; 34:7; Lev 26:39-40; Nu 14:33; Dt 5:9; Ps 21:10; 37:28; 109:9-10; Pr 14:11; Isa 14:20-22; 65:7; Jer 32:18; La 5:7; Ro 5:12-21). Attributed to Job's children because of Job's alleged wickedness (Job 5:4; 18:19; 21:19). Punishment for, not brought upon children (Dt 24:16; 2Ki 14:6; 2Ch 25:4; Jer 31:29-30; Eze 18:2-4, 20).
No escape from (Ge 3:8-19; Isa 28:18-22; Am 9:2-4; Mt 23:33; Heb 2:3). See Punishment, No Escape From; Wicked.

Conviction of:
Produced by dreams (Job 33:14-17), by visions (Ac 9:3-9), by afflictions (Job 33:18-20; La 1:20; Lk 15:17-21), by adversity (Ps 107:4-6, 10-14, 17-20, 23-30), by the gospel (Ac 2:37), by religious testimony (1Co 14:24-25), by the conscience (Jn 8:9; Ro 2:15), by the Holy Spirit (Jn 16:7-11). See Conviction, of Sin; Repentance; Instances of.

Forgiveness of:
(Ac 26:18; Eph 1:7). Promised (Ex 34:6-7; Lev 4:20, 26, 31, 35; 5:4-13; Nu 14:18; 15:25; Dt 4; Ps 130:4; Isa 1:6-18; 43:25-26; 44:21-22; 55:6-7; Jer 31:34; 33:8; Eze 18:21-22; 33:14-16; Mt 12:31; Mk 3:28; Heb 8:12; 10:17; Jas 5:15; 1Jn 1:7, 9). Blessedness of (Ps 32:1-2; Ro 4:7-8).

Instances of Forgiveness:
Israelites (Nu 14:20; Ps 85:2-3; 99:8; 103:12). David (2Sa 12:13; Ps 32:5). Isaiah (Isa 6:7). Paralytic (Mt 9:2, 6; Mk 2:5; Lk 5:20, 24). The prostitute (Lk 7:48; Jn 8:11). Believers (Col 2:13).

Conditions of Forgiveness—
Repentance (Mt 3:6; Lk 3:3; 13:3, 5; Ac 2:38; 3:19). Faith (Ac 10:36, 43; 13:38-39; 26:16-18). Confession of sins (1Jn 1:7, 9). Parable of (Mt 18:23-27).
Through the shedding of blood (Heb 9:22). The mission of Christ to secure (Mt 1:21; 26:28; Lk 24:47; 1Jn 2:1-2, 12; Rev 1:5).
Prayer for (Ps 19:12; 25:7, 11; 51:9; 79:9). Spirit of (Mt 6:12, 14-15; 18:35; Mk 11:25). Intercessory prayer for (1Ki 8:22-50). Apostolic (Jn 20:23).
See Atonement; Conviction, of Sin; Offerings; Repentance.

Fruits of:
(Dt 29:18; Mk 7:21-23; 1Co 3:3; 6:9-11; Gal 5:19-21; 1Pe 4:3; Jas 5:11). Fruits of original sin (Ge 3:7-24; 4:9-13; Ro 5:12-21). God's anger (Jer 7:19). Moral insensibility (Pr 30:20). No peace (Isa 57:20-21). Shame (Pr 3:35). Withholding of God's goodness (Jer 7:19).

S

Destruction and death (Ge 6:5-7; 1Ki 13:33-34; Job 5:2; Ps 5:10; 94:23; Pr 5:22-23; 10:24, 29-31; 11:18-19, 27, 29; Isa 3:9, 11; 9:18; 14:21; Jer 14:16; 21:14; Eze 11:21; 22:31; 23:31-35; Hos 12:14; 13:9; Ro 6:23).

The same as sown (Job 4:8; 13:26; 20:11; Ps 9:15-16; 10:2; 141:10; Pr 1:31; 11:5-7; 12:13, 14-21, 26; 22:8; Isa 50:11; Jer 4:18; 21:14; Eze 11:21; Hos 8:7; 10:13; Mic 7:13; Ro 7:5; Gal 6:7-8).

Proverbs concerning (Pr 1:31; 3:35; 5:22-23; 8:36; 10:24, 29-31; 11:5-7, 18-19, 27, 29; 12:13-14, 21, 26; 13:5-6, 15; 22:8; 28:1; 29:6; 30:20).

Known:

To God (Ge 3:11; 4:10; 18:13; Ex 16:8-9, 12; Nu 12:2; 14:26-27; Dt 1:34; 31:21; 32:34; Jos 7:10-15; 10:14; 11:11; 13:27; 14:16-17; 20:27; 24:23; 34:21-22, 25; Ps 44:20-21; 69:5; 90:8; 94:11; Ecc 5:8; Isa 29:15; Jer 2:22; 16:17; 29:23; Eze 21:24; Hos 5:3; 7:2; Am 5:12; 9:1-4, 8; Hab 2:11; Mal 2:17; Mt 10:26).

To Jesus (Mt 26:46; Lk 6:8; Jn 4:17-19; 5:42; 6:64; 13:11; Rev 2:23).

To the Holy Spirit (Ac 5:3-11).

See God, Omniscient; Jesus the Christ, Omniscience of.

Love of:

(Job 15:16; 20:12-13; Pr 2:14; 4:16-17; 10:23; 16:30; 26:11; Jer 14:10; Eze 20:16; Hos 4:8; 9:10; Mic 7:3; Jn 3:19-20; 12:43; 1Pe 3:19-20; 2Pe 2:22).

See Reprobacy; Wicked, Described As.

Moved to:

By the devil (Mt 13:24-25, 38-39; Jn 8:34, 44; Eph 2:1-2; 1Jn 3:6, 8-10, 15). By the fallen nature (Gal 5:16-17; Eph 2:3; Jas 1:14-15; 4:1-3).

National, Punishment of:

(Ge 6:5-7; 7:21-22; Lev 26:14-38; Dt 9:5; Job 34:29-30; Isa 19:4; Jer 12:17; 25:31-38; 46:28; Eze 16:49-50; Jnh 1:2).

See Government; Nation.

Instances of—

The Sodomites (Ge 18:20). Egyptians (Ex 7-14). See Egypt. Israelites (Lev 26:14-39; Dt 32:30; 2Sa 21:1; 24:1; 2Ki 24:3-4, 20; 2Ch 36:21; Ezr 9; Ne 9:36-37; Isa 1:21-23; 3:4, 8, 5; 59:1-15; Jer 2; 5; 6; 9; 23; 30:11-15; La 1:3, 8, 14; 4:6; Eze 2; 7; 22; 24:6-14; 28:18; 33:25-26; 36:16-20; 39:23-24; 44:4-14; Hos 4:1-11; 6:8-10; 7:1-7, 13; Am 2; 5; Mic 6; 7:2-6). Babylon (Jer 50:45-46; 51). See Babylon; See also prophecies cited under Assyria; Damascus; Edom; Elam; Ethiopia; Philistines; Syria.

Not imputed:

To righteous (Ps 32:2; Ro 4:6-8), to ignorant (Ro 4:15; 5:13), to redeemed (2Co 5:19).

Progressive:

(Dt 29:19; 1Ki 16:31; Ps 1:1; Isa 5:18; 30:1; Jer 9:3; 16:11-12; Hos 13:2; 2Ti 3:13; Jas 1:14-15). Progressiveness exemplified in Joseph's brothers, from jealousy (Ge 37:4), to conspiracy (Ge 37:18), to murder (Ge 37:20). See also, Cain; Abel. Retroactive (Ps 7:15-16; 9:15-16; 10:2; 94:23; Pr 1:31; 5:22-23; 8:36; 11:5-6, 27, 29; Isa 3:9, 11; Jer 2:19; 4:8; 7:19). A root of bitterness (Dt 29:18; Heb 12:15).

Punishment of:

(Ge 2:17; 3:16-19; 4:10-14; 6:5-7; 18:20; 19:13; Ex 32:33-34; 34:7; Lev 19:8; 26:14-21; Nu 15:30-31; 32:23; Dt 28:15-68; 1Ki 13:33-34; 1Ch 21:7-27; Job 21:17; Ps 95:10-11; Pr 1:24-32; Jer 44:2-6; Eze 18:4; Mt 25:41, 46; Ro 6:23).

See Punishment; Wicked, Punishment of.

Pollution of:

Typified, by the defilement caused by touching any unclean thing (Lev 5:2-3; 11:24-28, 31; 22:5), by eating any unclean thing (Lev 11:41-47), by touching a dead body (Lev 21:1; Nu 5:2; 9:6, 10; 19:11, 13, 16; 31:19), by skin diseases (Lev 13:3, 8, 11, 20, 25, 27, 30, 36, 44-46, 51, 55; 14:44; Nu 5:2-3), by sexual impurities (Lev 15:1-33; 22:4; Dt 23:10-11).

Repentance for:

Commanded (2Ch 30:7-9; Job 36:10; Ps 34:14; Pr 1:22-23; Isa 22:12; 31:6; 44:22; 55:6-7; Jer 3:4, 12-14, 19; 6:8, 16; 18:11; 25:5; 26:13; 35:15; Eze 14:6; 18:30-32; 33:10-12; Da 4:27; Hos 6:1; 10:12; 14:1-2; Joel 1:14; 2:12-13, 15-18; Am 4:12; Jnh 3:8-9; Zec 1:3; Mt 4:17; Mk 1:15; 6:12; Ac 2:38, 40; 3:19; 8:22; 17:30; 20:21; Jas 4:8-10; Rev 2:5, 16; 3:2-3, 19).

Gift, of God (2Ti 2:25), of Christ (Ac 5:31). Tribulation leads to (Dt 4:30; 1Ki 8:33-50; 2Ch 6:36-39; Ps 107:4-6, 10-14, 17-20, 23-30). Goodness of God leads to (Ro 2:4).

A condition of pardon (Lev 26:40-42; Dt 4:29-31; 30:1-3; 2Ch 7:14; Ne 1:9; Pr 28:13; Jer 7:5-7; 36:3; Eze 18:21-23, 27-28, 30-31; Mal 3:7; 1Jn 1:9).

Repugnant:

To God (Ge 6:6-7; Lev 18:24-30; Nu 22:32; Dt 25:16; 32:19; 2Sa 11:27; 1Ki 14:22; Ps 5:4-6; 10:3; 11:5; 78:59; 95:10; 106:40; Pr 3:32; 6:16-19; 11:20; 15:8-9, 26; 21:27; Isa 43:24; Jer 25:7; 44:4, 21-22; Hab 1:13; Zec 8:17; Lk 16:15). See God, Holiness of.

To Christ (Rev 2:6, 15).

To the righteous (Ge 39:7-9; Dt 7:26; Job 1:1; 21:16; 22:18; Ps 26:5, 9; 84:10; 101:3-4, 7; 119:104, 113, 128, 163; 120:2, 5-7; 139:19-22; Pr 8:13; 29:27; Jer 9:2; Ro 7:15, 19, 23-24; 2Pe 2:7-8; Jude 23; Rev 2:2). See Holiness.

Separates From God:

(Dt 31:17-18; Jos 7:12; 2Ch 24:20; Ps 78:59-61; Isa 59:1-2; 64:7; Eze 23:18; Hos 9:12; Am 3:2-3; Mic 3:4; Mt 7:23; 25:41; Lk 13:27; Ro 8:7; Heb 12:14). See God, Holiness of; Wicked, Punishment of.

Works spiritual death (Ro 5:12, 21; 6:21, 23; 7:13; Eph 2:1; Jas 1:15).

By the righteous, dishonors God (2Sa 12:14), a reproach (2Sa 12:14).

Against the Holy Spirit, unpardonable (Mt 12:31; Mk 3:29; Lk 12:10; 1Jn 5:16-17).

Typified:

The design of the Mosaic ordinances was to impress the Israelites, and through them the consciences of all people for all

time, with the offensiveness of sin. To produce this effect the Mosaic law contained numerous types of sin, the design of which was to teach that sin is repugnant to God, and that it separates from God and from the righteous. Hence, we find many object lessons about uncleanness and defilement, blemishes, separation from the congregation, atonements from the congregation, atonements and atoning sacrifices, washings and purifications; all of which were designed to typify the corruption of sin and the necessity, in order to please a holy Yahweh, that sin must be purged and the heart purified.

By blemishes that disqualified animals for sacrifices (Ex 12:5; Lev 1:10; 3:1, 6; 4:3, 23; 5:15; 6:6; 9:2-3; 22:19-22; Nu 28:3, 9, 11, 19, 31; 29:2, 8, 13, 17, 20, 23, 26, 29, 32, 36). By blemishes of priests, disqualifying them from performing sacred offices (Lev 21:17-23). By unclean animals (Lev 11:1-47; 20:25; Dt 14:3-20).

Its effect, in separating the wicked from God and from the righteous, by excluding the defiled and unclean from the congregation (Lev 7:20, 25, 27; 13:5, 26, 33; 15:19; 17:9-10, 15; 18:29; 19:8; 20:3-6; Nu 5:2-3; 19:20; Dt 23:10-11).

Words for:

Missing the mark (Ro 5:12). Overstepping the boundary, or trespassing (Ro 4:15). Blunder, or offense (Ro 5:15). Disobedience, or disregard (Ro 5:19). Unrighteousness (Ro 1:18). Ungodliness (Ro 1:18). Lawlessness (Tit 2:14).

SIN, CITY OF See Pelusium.

SIN, DESERT OF (desert of clay or possibly desert of Sin [pagan moon god]). The wilderness through which the Israelites passed; between Elim and Mount Sinai (Ex 16:1; 17:1; Nu 33:11-12).

SIN MONEY NIV "money from ... sin offerings" (2Ki 12:16). See Blood Money.

SINA See Sinai.

SINAI, MOUNT OF; DESERT OF (Sin [pagan moon god]; glare [from white chalk] ISBE).

1. A mountain in the peninsula E of the Red Sea. Israelites arrive at in their wanderings in the wilderness (Ex 19:2; Dt 1:2). The law delivered to Moses upon (Ex 19:3-25; 20; 24:12-18; 32:15-16; 34:2-4; Lev 7:38; 25:1; 26:46; 27:34; Nu 3:1; Dt 4:15; 5:26; 29:1; 33:2; Ne 9:13; Ps 68:8, 17; Mal 4:4; Ac 7:30, 38).

God establishes a covenant (Ex 19-24). See Covenants, Major in the Old Testament.

Figurative of the law (Gal 4:24-25).

See Horeb; Israel, Israelites.

2. Desert of. Israelites journeyed in (Nu 10:12), kept the Passover in (Nu 9:1), numbered in (Nu 26:64).

SINCERITY Does not exempt from guilt (Ge 20). See Ignorance, Sins of. Forgiveness of enemies must be sincere (Mt 18:35). Servants must render honest service (Eph 6:5-7). Whatever is done must be in (1Co 10:31). Jesus was an example of (1Pe 2:22). Ministers should be examples of (Tit 2:7). Opposed to human wisdom (2Co 1:12).

Should characterize our love to God (2Co 8:8, 24), our love to Jesus (Eph 6:24), our service to God (Jos 24:14), our faith (1Ti 1:5), our love to one another (Ro 12:9; 1Pe 1:22; 1Jn 3:18), our whole conduct (2Co 1:12), the preaching of the gospel (2Co 2:17; 1Th 2:3-5).

A characteristic of the doctrines of the gospel (1Pe 2:2). The gospel sometimes preached without (Php 1:16). The wicked devoid of (Ps 5:9; 55:21). Exhortations to (1Co 5:8; 1Pe 2:1). Blessedness of (Ps 32:2).

Exemplified:

By men of Zebulun (1Ch 12:33). By Hezekiah (Isa 38:3). By Nathanael (Jn 1:47). By Paul (2Co 1:12). By Timothy (2Ti 1:5). By Lois and Eunice (2Ti 1:5).

SINEW Tendon, in contrast to bone structure (Ge 32:32; Job 40:17; Eze 37:6-8).

SINFULNESS Universal (1Ki 8:46; 2Ch 6:36; Ps 14:3; Ecc 7:20; Ro 3:23; 11:32; 1Jn 1:8, 10). See Depravity; Sin.

SINGERS See Music.

SINGLE EYE NIV "good eye"; connotes generosity (Mt 6:22). See Eye.

SINIM See Aswan.

SINITES A tribe of Canaanites (Ge 10:17; 1Ch 1:15).

SINLESSNESS (Ps 119:3). The believer's goal (Php 1:9-11; 1Th 3:13; 5:23; 1Pe 4:1-2; 1Jn 3:6, 9; 5:18). Impossible to attain (1Jn 1:8, 10).

SINNER See Wicked.

SIN OFFERING

Offered:

For sins of ignorance (Lev 4:2, 13, 22, 27). At the consecration of priests (Ex 29:10, 14; Lev 8:14). At the consecration of Levites (Nu 8:8). At the expiration of a Nazirite's vow (Nu 6:14). On the Day of Atonement (Lev 16:3, 9). Was a most holy sacrifice (Lev 6:25, 29). Probable origin of (Ge 4:4, 7).

Consisted of:

A young bull for priests (Lev 4:3; 9:2, 8; 16:3, 6). A young bull or he-goat for the congregation (Lev 4:14; 16:9; 2Ch 29:23). A male goat for a ruler (Lev 4:23). A female goat or female lamb for a private person (Lev 4:28, 32). Sins of the offerer transferred to, by laying on of hands (Lev 4:4, 15, 24, 29; 2Ch 29:23). Was killed in the same place as the burnt offering (Lev 4:24; 6:25).

The blood of:

For a priest or for the congregation, brought by the priest into the tabernacle (Lev 4:5, 16). For the priest or for the congregation, sprinkled seven times before the Lord, outside the veil, by the priest

with his finger (Lev 4:6, 17). For a priest or for the congregation, put upon the horns of the altar of incense (Lev 4:7, 18). For a ruler or for a private person put upon the horns of the altar of burnt offering by the priest with his finger (Lev 4:25, 30). In every case poured at the foot of the altar of burnt offering (Lev 4:7, 18, 30; 9:9). Fat, kidneys, etc. burned on the altar of burnt offering (Lev 4:8-10, 19, 26, 31; 9:10).

When for a priest or the congregation, the skin, carcass, burned without the camp (Lev 4:11-12, 21; 6:30; 9:11). Was eaten by the priests in a holy place when its blood had not been brought into the tabernacle (Lev 6:26, 29, w 30). Meant for burning and not eating that of the congregation, its blood not having been brought into the tabernacle (Lev 10:16-18, w 9:9, 15). Whatever touched the flesh of, was rendered holy (Lev 6:27). Garments sprinkled with the blood of, to be washed (Lev 6:27). Laws respecting the vessels used for boiling the flesh of (Lev 6:28). Was typical of Christ's sacrifice (2Co 5:21; Heb 13:11-13).

SION See Siyon, Mount; Zion.

SIPHMOTH A city of Judah (1Sa 30:28).

SIPPAI A Philistine giant (1Ch 20:4). Called Saph (2Sa 21:18).

SIRACH, SON OF The author of Ecclesiasticus also known as the Wisdom of Jesus ben Sirach; wrote c. 190-170 B.C. See Apocrypha.

SIRAH A well, c. one mile N of Hebron (2Sa 3:26).

SIRION (coat of mail). A Sidonian name of Mount Hermon (Dt 3:9; Ps 29:6). See Hermon, Mount; Siyon, Mount.

SISAMAI See Sismai.

SISERA

1. Captain of the army of Jabin, king of Hazor; defeated in battle by Barak; slain by Deborah (Jdg 4-5; 1Sa 12:9; Ps 83:9).

2. Ancestor of the temple servants who returned with Zerubbabel (Ezr 2:53; Ne 7:55).

SISMAI (possibly belonging to Sisam [pagan god]). The son of Eleasah (1Ch 2:40).

SISTER

1. A full or half-sister (Ge 20:12; Dt 27:22).

2. Wife (SS 4:9).

3. A woman of the same country or tribe (Nu 25:18).

4. Blood relatives (Mt 13:56; Mk 6:3).

5. Female fellow Christian (Ro 16:1; 2Jn 15).

SISTRUMS Percussion instruments (2Sa 6:5). See Music, Instruments of.

SITHRI (possibly Yahweh is my hiding place). Kohathite Levite; cousin of Aaron and Moses (Ex 6:22).

SITNAH (hostility). A well dug by Isaac between Gerar and Rehoboth (Ge 26:21).

SIVAN Month three in sacred sequence (Est 8:9), month nine in civil sequence. Time of the wheat harvest (May-June) and the Feast of Weeks or Pentecost (Dt 16:9-12). See Month, 3.

SIYON, MOUNT A name of Mount Hermon (Dt 4:48, ftn w 3:9). See Hermon, Mount; Sirion.

SKEPTICISM (Job 21:15; 22:17; Ps 14:1; 53:1; Zep 1:12; Mal 3:14). Of Pharaoh (Ex 5:2). Of Thomas (Jn 20:25-28). See Unbelief.

SKILL Examples of (Ex 28:3; 31:3; 35:35; 38:23; 1Ki 7:14; 1Ch 22:15; 2Ch 2:13; 26:15).

SKIN Clothes of (Ge 3:21). For covering the tabernacle (Ex 25:5; Nu 4:8-10, 19, 26, 31; 9:10). Diseases of (Lev 13:38-39; Dt 28:27, 35; Job 7:5). See Boil; Leprosy.

SKINK Unclean for food (Lev 11:30). See Animals.

SKIRT See Dress.

SKULL See Golgotha.

SKY Clouds, firmament; also used figuratively (Dt 33:26).

SLANDER

Characteristics of:

Comes from the evil heart (Lk 6:45). Often arises from hatred (Ps 109:3). Idleness leads to (1Ti 5:13).

The wicked addicted to (Ps 50:20). Hypocrites addicted to (Pr 11:9). A characteristic of the devil (Rev 12:10). The wicked love (Ps 52:4). They who indulge in, are fools (Pr 10:18).

Women warned against (Tit 2:3). Ministers' wives should avoid (1Ti 3:11).

Christ was exposed to (Ps 35:11; Mt 26:60). Rulers exposed to (Jude 8). Ministers exposed to (Ro 3:8; 2Co 6:8). The nearest relations exposed to (Ps 50:20). Saints exposed to (Ps 38:12; 109:2; 1Pe 4:4).

Saints should, keep their tongues from (Ps 34:13, w 1Pe 3:10), lay aside (Eph 4:31), be warned against (Tit 3:1-2), give no occasion for (1Pe 2:12; 3:16), return good for (1Co 4:13), blessed in enduring (Mt 5:11), characterized as avoiding (Ps 15:1, 3).

Should not be listened to (1Sa 24:9). Causes anger (Pr 25:23). A fruit of wickedness (Ro 1:29-30; 2Co 12:20; 2Pe 2:10).

Forbidden (Ex 23:1; 1Ti 3:11; Tit 2:3; 3:2; Jas 4:11; 1Pe 2:1). Punishment for (Dt 19:16-21; 22:13-19; Ps 101:5; 1Co 6:10).

Instances of:

Joseph, by Potiphar's wife (Ge 39:14-18). Land of Canaan misrepresented by the spies (Nu 14:36). Of Mephibosheth, by Ziba (2Sa 16:3; 19:24-30). Of David, by his enemies (Ps 31:13; 35:21; 41:5-9; 64:3; 140:3). Of Naboth, by Jezebel (1Ki 21:9-14). Of

Jeremiah, by the Jews (Jer 6:28; 18:18). Of the Jews, of one another (Jer 9:4).

Of Jesus, by the Jews falsely charging that he was a drunkard (Mt 11:19), that he blasphemed (Mk 14:64; Jn 5:18), that he had a demon (Jn 8:48, 52; 10:20), that he was seditious (Lk 22:65; 23:5), that he was a king (Lk 23:2; Jn 18:37, w 19:1-5). Of Paul. *See Paul.*

Effects of:
Separating friends (Pr 16:28; 17:9), deadly wounds (Pr 18:8; 26:22), strife (Pr 26:20), discord among brothers (Pr 6:19), murder (Ps 31:13; Eze 22:9). End of, is wicked madness (Ecc 10:13). People shall give account for (Mt 12:36).

The Tongue:
(Job 5:21). Is venomous (Ps 140:3; Ecc 10:11), is destructive (Pr 11:9).

See Accusation, False; Backbiting; False Witness; Falsehood; Speaking or Speech, Evil.

SLAVE, SLAVERY Both the OT and the NT included regulations for societal situations such as slavery and divorce (Dt 24:1-4), which were the results of the hardness of hearts (Mt 19:8). Such regulations did not encourage or condone such situations but were divinely given, practical ways of dealing with the realities of the day. *See Servant.*

SLAYER, THE NIV "one accused of murder" (Nu 35:11-28; Dt 4:42; 19:3-6; Jos 20:3). *See Cities of Refuge.*

SLEEP From God (Ps 127:2). Of the sluggard (Pr 6:9-10). Of Jesus (Mt 8:24; Mk 4:38; Lk 8:23). A symbol of death (Job 14:12; Mt 9:24; Mk 5:39; Lk 8:52; Jn 11:11-12; 1Th 4:14). *See Death, Physical.*

SLIME Slime pit (Job 9:31; Ps 40:2). *See Caulkers; Pitch; Tar.*

SLING Used for throwing stones (Pr 26:8). David slays Goliath with (1Sa 17:40-50). Dexterous use of (Jdg 20:16; 2Ki 3:25; 2Ch 26:14).

SLIP A cutting from a plant (Isa 17:10).

SLOTHFULNESS Characteristic of the sluggard (Pr 10:4-5, 26; 13:4; 15:19; 18:9; 19:15, 24; 20:4; 21:25; 22:13; 23:21; 24:30-34; 26:13-16; Isa 56:10).

Results in: poverty (Pr 10:4-5; 12:24, 27; 13:4; 15:19; 18:9; 19:15, 24; 20:4; 21:25; 23:21; 24:30-34; 26:13-16; Ecc 10:18), condemnation (Mt 25:26-27).

Condemned: The ant, an example against (Pr 6:6-11). Christians are not to be lazy (Ro 12:11; 2Th 3:10-12; Heb 6:12).

See Idleness; Industry.

SLOW TO ANGER (Ne 9:17; Ps 103:8; 145:8). *See God, Longsuffering; Longsuffering.*

SLUG Melting away (Ps 58:8). *See Animals.*

SLUGGARD *See Idleness; Laziness; Slothfulness.*

SMITH A worker in metals. Tubal-Cain (Ge 4:22). Bezalel (Ex 31:1-11). The Philistines (1Sa 13:19). Jewish, carried captive to Babylon (2Ki 24:14; Jer 24:1). The manufacturers of idols (Isa 41:7; 44:12). Genius of, from God (Ex 31:3-5; 35:30-35; Isa 54:16).

SMITING *See Assault and Battery.*

SMITING AND SCOURGING OF JESUS *See Flog, Flogging.*

SMOKE Rising from destruction (Ge 19:28; Jos 8:20; Rev 19:3). Figurative of God's presence (Ex 19:18; Isa 6:4; Rev 15:8), of short-lived humanity (Ps 37:20; 68:2; 102:3; Hos 13:3).

SMYRNA An ancient seaport on the W coast of Asia Minor forty miles N of Ephesus; the seat of an important Christian church (Rev 1:11; 2:8-11).

SNAIL NIV "skink" (Lev 11:30), "slug" (Ps 58:8). *See Animals.*

SNAKE *See Serpent.*

SNARE A device for catching birds and animals (Ps 124:7), also used figuratively (Ps 91:3).

SNIFF Smelling the wind (Jer 2:24). Showing contempt for God's sacrifices (Mal 1:13).

SNOUT Long projecting nose of a beast, as of a pig (Pr 11:22).

SNOW Falls in elevated areas of Israel in January and February, but soon melts; Mt. Hermon covered with snow even in summer; used for cooling purposes. Used figuratively for righteousness and purity (Isa 1:18; Ps 51:7; Mt 28:3; Rev 1:14).

SNUFF *See Sniff.*

SNUFFDISHES NIV "trays" for the lamps of the tabernacle and temple. *See Wick Trimmers.*

SNUFFERS *See Wick Trimmers.*

SO A king of Egypt with whom Hoshea, king of Israel, made an alliance, so bringing down the wrath of Assyria upon Israel (2Ki 17:4), possibly Oskoron.

SOAP In a modern sense was unknown in OT times, but launderers made a cleansing material compounded from vegetable alkali (Jer 2:22; Mal 3:2). *See Soda.*

SOBERMINDEDNESS Commanded (Ro 12:3; 1Pe 1:13; 4:7; 5:8), to women (1Ti 3:11; Tit 2:4-5), to men (Tit 2:2, 6), to ministers (1Ti 3:2; Tit 1:8).

SOBRIETY Commanded (1Pe 1:13; 5:8). The gospel designed to teach (Tit 2:12). With watchfulness (1Th 5:6). With prayer (1Pe 4:7). Required in ministers (1Ti 3:2-3; Tit 1:8), wives of ministers (1Ti 3:11), aged men (Tit 2:2), young men (Tit 2:6), young women (Tit 2:4), all saints (1Th 5:6, 8). Women should exhibit in dress (1Ti 2:9). We should estimate our character and talents with (Ro 12:3). We should live in (Tit 2:12). Motive for (1Pe 4:7; 5:8). *See Temperance; Drunkenness; Self-Control.*

SOCO (perhaps *thorny place*).
1. Son of Heber (1Ch 4:18).
2. A city in Judah, built by Rehoboam (2Ch 11:7; 28:18).

SOCOH (possibly *thorny place* IDB).
1. A town in Judah (Jos 15:35; 1Sa 17:1; 1Ki 4:10), NW of Adullam; identified with Khirbet Shuweikeh.
2. Another city by this name ten miles SW of Hebron (Jos 15:48).

SODA A mixture of washing and baking sodas found in deposits around alkali lakes of Egypt. Used to make soap (Job 9:30; Pr 25:20; Jer 2:22). *See Soap.*

SODI (*Yahweh confides*). The father of a Zebulun spy (Nu 13:10).

SODOM Situated in the plain of the Jordan (Ge 13:10). The southeastern limit of the Canaanites (Ge 10:19). Lot dwells at (Ge 13:12). The king of, joins other kings of the nations resisting the invasion of Kedorlaomer (Ge 14:1-12). Wickedness of the inhabitants of (Ge 13:13; 19:4-13; Dt 32:32; Isa 3:9; Jer 23:14; La 4:6; Eze 16:46, 48-49; Jude 7). Abraham's intercession for (Ge 18:16-33). Destroyed on account of the wickedness of the people (Ge 19:1-29; Dt 29:23; Isa 13:19; Jer 49:18; 50:40; La 4:6; Am 4:11; Zep 2:9; Mt 10:15; Lk 17:29; Ro 9:29; 2Pe 2:6). Figurative of wickedness (Dt 23:17; 32:32; Isa 1:10; Eze 16:46-56).

SODOMITES (*of Sodom*). Inhabitants of Sodom. Wickedness of (Ge 19:4-14). Destroyed by fire as a judgment (Ge 19:24-25). To be judged according to opportunity (Mt 11:24; Lk 10:12). *See Homosexual.*

SODOMY *See Homosexual.*

SOJOURNERS Temporary residents (Ge 12:10; 20:1; 21:34; 47:4; Lev 18:26; 20:2; 25:40; Nu 15:15; Dt 26:5; Jdg 17:7; Ru 1:1; Heb 11:9).

SOLDER *See Welding.*

SOLDIERS Military enrollment of Israel in the wilderness of Sinai (Nu 1; 2), in the plains of Moab (Nu 26). Levies of, in the ration of one man to ten subject to duty (Jdg 20:10). Dressed in scarlet (Na 2:3). Cowards, excused from duty as (Dt 20:8; Jdg 7:3). Others exempt from service (Dt 20:5-9; 24:5). Come to John (Lk 3:14). Mock Jesus (Mt 27:27-31; Mk 15:16-20; Lk 23:11, 36-37). Officers concerned in the betrayal of Jesus (Lk 22:4). Crucified Jesus (Mt 27:27, 31-37; Mk 15:16-24; Jn 19:23-24). Guard the tomb (Mt 27:65; 28:11-15). Guard prisoners (Ac 12:4-6; 28:16). Maintain the peace (Ac 21:31-35). Their duty as sentinels (Ac 12:19). Perform escort duty (Ac 21:31-33, 35; 22:24-28; 23:23, 31-33; 27:1, 31, 42-43; 28:16).

Figurative: Of the divine protection (Isa 59:16-17). Of the Christian (Eph 6:11-17; 2Ti 2:3). *See Armies.*

SOLOMON (*peace, well being*). Son of David by Bathsheba (2Sa 12:24; 1Ki 1:13, 17, 21). Named Jedidiah, by Nathan the prophet (2Sa 12:24-25). Ancestor of Joseph (Mt 1:6). Succeeds David to the throne of Israel (1Ki 1:11-48; 2:12; 1Ch 23:1; 28; Ecc 1:12). Anointed king a second time (1Ch 29:22). His prayer for wisdom and his vision (1Ki 3:5-14; 2Ch 1:7-12). Covenant renewed in a vision after the dedication of the temple (1Ki 9:1-9; 2Ch 7:12-22). His rigorous reign (1Ki 2).

Builds the temple (1Ki 5; 6; 9:10; 1Ch 6:10; 2Ch 2; 3; 4; 7:11; Jer 52:20; Ac 7:45-47). Dedicates the temple (1Ki 8; 2Ch 6). Renews the courses of the priests and Levites and the forms of service according to the regulations of David (2Ch 8:12-16; 35:4; Ne 12:45).

Builds his palace (1Ki 3:1; 7:1, 8; 9:10; 2Ch 7:11; 8:1; Ecc 2:4), his house of the forest of Lebanon (1Ki 7:2-7), for Pharaoh's daughter (1Ki 7:8-12; 9:24; 2Ch 8:11; Ecc 2:4). Ivory throne of (1Ki 7:7; 10:18-20). Porches of judgment (1Ki 7:7). Builds Millo, the wall of Jerusalem; the cities of Hazor, Megiddo, Gezer, Beth Horon, Baalath, Tadmor; store cities and cities for chariots and for cavalry (1Ki 9:15-19; 2Ch 9:25). Provides an armory (1Ki 10:16-17). Plants vineyards and orchards of all kinds of fruit trees; makes pools (Ecc 2:4-6), imports apes and baboons (1Ki 10:22). Drinking vessels of his houses (1Ki 10:21; 2Ch 9:20). Musicians and musical instruments of his court (1Ki 10:12; 2Ch 9:11; Ecc 2:8). The splendor of his court (1Ki 10:5-9, 12; 2Ch 9:3-8; Ecc 2:9; Mt 6:29; Lk 12:27).

Commerce of (1Ki 9:28; 10:11-12, 22, 28-29; 2Ch 1:16-17; 8:17-18; 9:13-22, 28). Presents received (1Ki 10:10; 2Ch 9:9, 23-24). Is visited by the queen of Sheba (1Ki 10:1-13; 2Ch 9:1-12). Wealth of (1Ki 9; 10:10, 14-15, 23, 27; 2Ch 1:15; 9:1, 9, 13, 24, 27; Ecc 1:16). Has seven hundred wives and three hundred concubines (1Ki 11:3; w Dt 17:17); their influence over him (1Ki 11:3). Marries one of Pharaoh's daughters (1Ki 3:1). Builds idolatrous temples (1Ki 11:1-8; 2Ki 23:13). His idolatry (1Ki 3:3-4; 2Ki 23:13; Ne 13:26).

Extent of his dominions (1Ki 4:21, 24; 8:65; 2Ch 7:8; 9:26). Receives tribute (1Ki 4:21; 9:21; 2Ch 8:8). Officers of (1Ki 2:35; 4:1-19; 2Ch 8:9-10). His suppliers (1Ki 4:7-19). Divides the kingdom into subsistence departments; the daily subsistence rate for his court (1Ki 4:7-23, 27-28).

Military equipment of (1Ki 4:26, 28; 10:16-17, 26, 28; 2Ch 1:14; 9:25, w Dt 17:15-16). Cedes certain cities to Hiram (1Ki 9:10-13; 2Ch 8:2). Wisdom and fame of (1Ki 4:29-34; 10:3-4, 8, 23-24; 1Ch 29:24-25; 2Ch 9:2-7, 22-23; Ecc 1:16; Mt 12:42). Piety of (1Ki 3:5-15; 4:29; 8). Beloved of God (2Sa 12:24). Justice

of, illustrated in his judgment of the two harlots (1Ki 3:16-28). Oppressions of (1Ki 12:4; 2Ch 10:4).

Reigns forty years (2Ch 9:30). Death of (2Ch 9:29-31). Prophecies concerning (2Sa 7:12-16; 1Ki 11:9-13; 1Ch 17:11-14; 28:6-7; Ps 132:11).

A type of Christ (Ps 45:2-17; 72).

SOLOMON, SONG OF *See Song of Solomon, Song of Songs.*

SOLOMON'S POOLS Three pools near Jerusalem from which water was brought by means of aqueducts to Jerusalem (Ecc 2:6). They are still in use.

SOLOMON'S PORCH Colonnade built by Solomon on the E side of the temple area (Jn 10:23; Ac 3:11; 5:12).

SOLOMON'S SERVANTS Slaves used by Solomon in his temple for menial tasks; their descendants returning from Babylon under Zerubbabel (Ezr 2:55, 58; Ne 7:57, 60; 11:3).

SOLOMON'S TEMPLE *See Temple.*

SON
1. A direct male offspring (Ge 4:25, 26).
2. A male descendant generations removed (Mt 1:1).
3. The member of a guild or profession (1Ki 20:35).
4. Spiritual son (1Ti 1:18).
5. Address to a younger man (1Sa 3:6).
6. Adopted son (Ex 2:10).
7. Native (La 4:2).
8. Possessor of a quality (Jn 12:36).
9. Used of Jesus in a unique sense. *See One and Only; Son of God; Son of Man.*

SON OF GOD A title of Jesus referring to his equality, eternity, and consubstantiality with the Father and the Spirit in the eternal Triune Godhead (Jn 5:18, 23, 36). Christ claimed to be eternal, equal and of the same substance as the Father. He is uniquely God's son. *See Jesus the Christ, Son of God; One and Only.*

SON OF MAN
1. A human being (Eze 2:1, 3, 8ff; Ps 8:4).
2. Used in a messianic sense (Da 7:13-14). Jesus applies the term to himself many times in the Gospels (Mt 8:20; 9:6; 10:23; 11:19; 12:8, etc). Sometimes he uses it in connection with his earthly mission, but he also uses it when describing his final triumph as Redeemer and Judge (Mt 16:27f; 19:28; 24:30; 25:31). The phrase identifies him with humanity (cf. Heb 2:14-18) and with the heavenly Son of Man (Da 7:13-14). *See Jesus the Christ, Son of Man.*

SONG Sung at the Passover (Mt 26:30; Mk 14:26). Didactic (Dt 32). *See Psalms, Topically Arranged.* Personification of the church (SS 1-8). Of Moses (Ex 15:1-19). Of Deborah and Barak (Jdg 5). Of Hannah (1Sa 2:1-10). Of David (2Sa 22:2-51; 23:1-7). Of Mary (Lk 1:46-55). Of Moses and the Lamb (Rev 15:3-4). New (Ps 33:3; 40:3). Prophetic. *See Psalms, Topically Arranged.* Spiritual, singing of, commanded (Eph 5:19; Col 3:16). Of praise. *See Poetry; Praise; Psalms, Topically Arranged; Thankfulness.* Of redemption (Rev 5:9-10). Of the redeemed (Rev 14:2-5). Of thanksgiving. *See Psalms, Topically Arranged; Thankfulness.* War (Ex 15:1-21; Nu 21:27-30; Jdg 5; 2Sa 1:19-27; 22). Solomon wrote one thousand and five (1Ki 4:32).

See Poetry; Praise; Psalms, Topically Arranged.

SONG OF DEGREES *See Ascents, Songs of; Music.*

SONG OF SOLOMON, SONG OF SONGS

Author: Verse 1 appears to ascribe authorship to Solomon

Date: In the tenth century B.C. during Solomon's reign

Outline:
I. Title (1:1).
II. First Meeting (1:2-2:7).
III. Second Meeting (2:8-3:5).
IV. Third Meeting (3:6-5:1).
V. Fourth Meeting (5:2-6:3).
VI. Fifth Meeting (6:4-8:4).
VII. Literary Climax (8:5-7).
VIII. Conclusion (8:8-14).

SONG OF THE THREE HEBREW CHILDREN An addition to the book of Daniel found in the OT Apocrypha. Anonymous; written before 100 B.C.

SON-IN-LAW Unjust, Jacob (Ge 30:37-42). Faithful, Peter (Mk 1:29-30; Lk 4:38).

SONS OF GOD, CHILDREN OF GOD Any personal creatures of God: angelic beings (Job 1:6; 2:1; 38:7), the entire human race (Ac 17:28), the regenerate as distinguished from the unregenerate (1Jn 3:10). The "sons of God" (Ge 6:1-4).

SONS OF THE PROPHETS NIV usually "company of the prophets." Members of prophetic guilds or schools; gathered around great prophets like Samuel and Elijah for common worship, united prayer, religious fellowship, and instruction of the people (1Sa 10:5, 10; 2Ki 4:38, 40). In the times of Elijah and Elisha they lived together at Bethel, Jericho, and Gilgal (2Ki 2:3, 5; 4:38). *See School.*

SOOTHSAYER, SOOTHSAYING One claiming power to foretell future events (Jos 13:22; Jer 27:9), interpret dreams (Da 4:7), and reveal secrets (Da 2:27).

SOOTHSAYERS' TREE A pagan shrine near Shechem (Jdg 9:37), possibly the great tree of Moreh (Ge 12:6).

SOP NIV "piece of bread" used to dip food from a common platter (Jn 13:26-27).

S

SOPATER (*saving one's father*). Berean Christian; companion of Paul (Ac 20:4).

SOPHERETH (*scribe*). A servant of Solomon, whose descendants returned from captivity to Jerusalem (Ne 7:57).
See Hassophereth.

SORCERY Divination by an alleged assistance of evil spirits. Forbidden (Lev 19:26-28, 31; 20:6; Dt 18:9-14). Denounced (Isa 8:19; Mal 3:5).
Practiced: By, the Egyptians (Isa 19:3, 11-12), the magicians (Ex 7:11, 22; 8:7, 18), Balaam (Nu 22:6; 23:23, w 22; 23), Jezebel (2Ki 9:22), the Ninevites (Na 3:4-5), the Babylonians (Isa 47:9-13; Eze 21:21-22; Da 2:2, 10, 27), Belshazzar (Da 5:7, 15), Simon the sorceror (Ac 8:9, 11), Elymas (Ac 13:8), the young woman at Philippi (Ac 16:16), vagabond Jews (Ac 19:13), sons of Sceva (Ac 19:14-15), astrologers (Jer 10:2; Mic 3:6-7), false prophets (Jer 14:14; 27:9; 29:8-9; Eze 13:6-9; 22:28; Mt 24:24).
To cease (Eze 12:23-24; 13:23; Mic 5:12).
Messages, of false (Eze 21:29; Zec 10:2; 2Th 2:9). Diviners shall be confounded (Mic 3:7). Belongs to the works of the flesh (Gal 5:20). Wickedness of (1Sa 15:23). Vainness of (Isa 44:25). Punishment for (Ex 22:18; Lev 20:27; Dt 13:5). Divining by familiar spirits (Lev 20:27; 1Ch 10:13; 2Ch 33:6; Isa 8:19; 19:3; 29:4), by entrails (Eze 21:21), by images (2Ki 23:24; Eze 21:21), by rods (Hos 4:12).
Saul consulted the medium of Endor (1Sa 28:7-25).
Books of, destroyed (Ac 19:19).

SORE Laws to determine whether clean or unclean (Lev 13). Festering sores disqualified from priesthood (Lev 21:20) or acceptable offering (Lev 22:22). Figurative of judgment for sin (Jer 30:13). See Disease.

SOREK, VALLEY OF (*[blood red grapes]*; hence, *choice vines*). A valley in the Philistine territory c. eight-and-a-half miles S of Joppa (Jdg 16:4).

SORROW God takes notice of Hagar's (Ge 21:17-20), Israelites (Ex 3:7-10).
For sin (2Co 7:10-11). See Repentance; Sin, Confession of.
No sorrow in heaven (Rev 21:4). "Sorrow and sighing will flee away" (Isa 35:10).
Of Hannah (1Sa 1:15). Of David for Absalom (2Sa 18:33; 19:1-8). Of Mary and Martha (Jn 11:19-40). Jeremiah (La 1:12). Jesus (Isa 53:11; Mt 26:37-44; Mk 14:34-42; Lk 22:42-44).
From bereavement: Of Jacob for Joseph (Ge 37:34-35), for Benjamin (Ge 43:14).
Of the lost (Mt 8:12; 13:42, 50; 22:13; 24:51; 25:30; Lk 13:28; 16:23). See Wicked, Punishment of.
See Affliction, Consolation Under; Suffering.

SOSIPATER (*saving ones father*). Kinsman of Paul (Ro 16:21).

SOSTHENES
1. Chief ruler of the synagogue in Corinth (Ac 18:17).
2. A Christian with whom Paul wrote the first letter to the Corinthians (1Co 1:1).

SOTAI A servant of Solomon whose descendants returned from captivity to Jerusalem (Ezr 2:55; Ne 7:57).

SOUL The immortal, nonmaterial part of a human being (Mt 10:28; Rev 6:9; 20:4). Can represent the whole person (Jdg 5:21) or one's life (Job 33:18; Ps 26:9). Used with heart to represent the will and emotions (Dt 4:29; 6:4). See Immortality; Mankind, A Spirit; Spirit.

SOUNDING In navigation (Ac 27:28).

SOUTH
1. A direction of the compass (Ge 13:14).
2. The Negev, an indefinite area lying between Israel and Egypt (Ge 12:9; 13:1; 1Sa 27:8-12; 2Ch 28:18).

SOVEREIGNTY OF GOD The supreme authority of God. He is not subject to any power or law which could be conceived as superior to or other than himself (Isa 45:9; Ro 9:20-21).
See God, Sovereign; Jesus the Christ, King.

SOWER Parable of the (Mt 13:3-8; Mk 4:3-20; Lk 8:5-8). Sowing (Ecc 11:4; Isa 28:25).
Figurative (Ps 126:5; Pr 11:18; Isa 32:20; Hos 8:7; 10:12; Gal 6:7-8).

SPAIN The westernmost peninsula of Europe. Paul hoped to visit this Roman province (Ro 15:24, 28).

SPAN About nine or ten inches (Ex 28:16; 39:9).

SPARROW Nests of (Ps 84:3). Two sold for a penny (Mt 10:29; Lk 12:6).

SPEAKING OR SPEECH
Evil:
(Ps 10:8; 52:2-4; Isa 32:6-7; Jer 20:10; Jude 8, 10). Causes strife (Pr 15:1; 16:27-28; 17:9; 25:23). Excludes from kingdom of heaven (1Co 6:10). Hated by God (Pr 6:16-19; 8:13).
Characteristic of mankind (Ro 1:29-30; 3:13-14). Not characteristic of a Christian (Eph 4:25, 29, 31; 5:4; Tit 3:2; Jas 1:26; 3:5-6, 8-10; 4:11; 1Pe 2:1; 3:9-10).
Forbidden (Ex 22:28; Ps 34:13; Pr 4:24; 6:16-19; Mt 5:22, 37; 12:34-37; Ac 23:5; Eph 4:25, 29, 31; Tit 3:2; Jas 1:26; 3:5-6, 8-10; 4:11; 1Pe 2:1; 3:9-10). Punishment for (Ps 12:3-4; 52:1-4).
Proverbs concerning (Pr 4:24; 6:16-19; 8:13; 10:11, 19, 31-32; 11:11; 12:5-6, 13, 17-19; 13:3; 14:25; 15:1, 4, 28; 16:27-28; 17:4, 9, 20; 18:8, 21, 23; 19:1, 22-23; 24:2; 25:23; 26:20-23, 28; Ecc 10:11, 20).
Prayers for deliverance from curse of (Ps 64:2-5; 70:3; 120:1-7). Self-accusation: Solomon (Ecc 7:22). Isaiah (Isa 6:5). Paul (Ac 23:5).

Instances of—
Against Job (Job 19:18). Against Lot, those of Sodom (2Pe 2:7-8, 10). Against Moses (Ps 106:33). Against the psalmists (Ps 35:21; 41:5-9; 69:12, 26; 102:8; 119:23). Against the church, those of the circumcision (Tit 1:10-11). False teachers (Jude 8, 10).
See Accusation, False; Blasphemy; Busybody; Falsehood; Flattery; Slander; Talebearer; Uncharitableness.

Foolish:
(Job 13:5; 16:3-4; 38:2). Accountable to God (Mt 12:36-37). Forbidden (Pr 30:18). Not characteristic of a Christian (Eph 5:4).
Proverbs concerning (Pr 10:14; 12:23; 13:3; 14:3; 15:2, 7, 14; 18:6-7, 13; 26:4, 7, 9; 29:11, 20; 30:10; Ecc 5:3, 5; 10:13-14).
See Fool.

Wise:
(Job 16:5; 27:4; Am 5:13; Zep 3:13; Zec 8:16; Rev 14:17). As good as nails (Ecc 12:11). Precious as jewels (Pr 20:16).
Edifying (Eph 4:29). Rewards of (Ps 15:1-3; 50:23; Pr 14:3; 22:11).
Of the noble woman (Pr 31:26).
Admonitions concerning, to believers (Eph 4:22, 25, 29; Php 1:27; Col 4:6; Jas 1:19, 26; 3:2, 13; 1Pe 2:12; 3:15-16). Christ's words concerning (Mt 12:35, 37; Lk 6:45).
Of psalmists (Ps 37:30; 39:1; 77:12; 119:13, 27, 46, 54, 172; 141:3; 145:5-7, 11-12).
Proverbs concerning (Pr 10:11, 13, 19-21, 31-32; 11:12-14; 12:6, 14, 16-20, 23; 13:2-3; 14:3; 15:1-2, 4, 7, 23, 26, 28; 16:21, 23-24; 17:7, 27-28; 18:4, 20; 19:1; 20:15; 21:23; 22:11; 24:6; 25:11, 15; 26:5; 29:11; 31:26; Ecc 3:7; 9:17; 10:12; 12:9-11).
Prayer concerning (Ps 141:3).
See Wisdom.

SPEAR Spears and javelins differed in weight and size but had similar uses.
An implement of war (2Ki 11:10; Ne 4:13). Goliath's (1Sa 17:7). Saul's (1Sa 18:10-11). Stored in the temple (2Ch 23:9). To be changed into pruning hooks (Isa 2:4; Mic 4:3). Pruning hooks to be beaten into (Joel 3:10). Thrust into Jesus' side (Zec 12:10; Jn 19:34; 20:27; Rev 1:7). For catching fish (Job 41:7, 26). See Armory.

SPECK Particle of dust or splinter of wood in one's eye, figurative of improper judgment (Mt 7:3-5; Lk 6:41-42). See Judgment.

SPECKLED Mottled in color (Ge 30:25-43). See Streaked.

SPELT A small grain grown in Egypt (Ex 9:32). Cultivated in Canaan (Isa 28:25). Used in bread (Eze 4:9).

SPERMATORRHEA A disease of the genitals (possibly Lev 15:16).

SPICES In the formula for the sacred oil (Ex 25:6; 35:8). Stores of (2Ki 20:13). Used in the temple (1Ch 9:29). Exported from Gilead (Ge 37:25). Sent as a present by Jacob to Joseph (Ge 43:11). Presented by the queen of Sheba to Solomon (1Ki 10:2, 10). Sold in the markets of Tyre (Eze 27:22). Used in the embalming of Asa (2Ch 16:14). Prepared for embalming the body of Jesus (Mk 16:1; Lk 23:56; 24:1; Jn 19:39-40).

SPIDER Web of, figurative of the hope of the hypocrite (Job 8:14; Isa 59:5).

SPIES (Ge 42:9). Sent to investigate Canaan (Nu 13), Jazer (Nu 21:32), Jericho (Jos 2:1). Used by David (1Sa 26:4), at the court of Absalom (2Sa 15:10; 17:1-17). Pharisees acted as (Lk 20:20). In the church of Galatia (Gal 2:4). See Reconnaissance.

SPIKENARD See Nard; Perfume, 2.

SPINDLE Implement used in spinning (Ex 35:24; Pr 31:19).

SPINNING By hand (Ex 35:25; Pr 31:19).

SPIRIT (*breath, wind, spirit*). The immortal, nonmaterial part of a human being, similar to the soul (Job 7:11). Represents one's lifeforce or strength (Ge 45:27; Jas 2:26), character (Nu 14:24; Dt 2:30; 1Pe 3:4), desire (2Sa 13:39), heart or emotions (Ps 73:21; 77:6). The self is often called "spirit" when the direct relationship of the individual to God is the point of emphasis (2Ti 4:22; Phm 25). See Ghost; Immortality; Mankind, A Spirit; Soul.

SPIRIT, HOLY See Holy Spirit.

SPIRITISTS Divination by means of communication with the spirit of the dead (necromancy) was known and practiced in the ancient Near East.
Consulting of:
Forbidden (Lev 19:31; 20:6, 27; Dt 18:10-11), vain (Isa 8:19; 19:3). Those who consulted, to be cut off (Lev 20:6, 27).
Instances of Consulting of:
Saul (1Sa 28:3-25; 1Ch 10:13-14). Manasseh (2Ki 21:6; 2Ch 33:6). A slave girl (Ac 16:16-18).
See Demons; Medium; Necromancer; Necromancy; Sorcery; Witchcraft.

SPIRITS IN PRISON Those who in the days of Noah refused his message (1Pe 3:18-20; 4:6). The exact interpretation of this passage is strongly debated.

SPIRITS See Demons.

SPIRITUAL ADOPTION See Adoption, Spiritual.

SPIRITUAL BLESSINGS See Blessings, Spiritual; Holy Spirit; Sanctification.

SPIRITUAL BLINDNESS Blindness, Spiritual.

SPIRITUAL BOASTING (Ro 11:18-21). Incompatible with faith (Ro 3:27; Eph 2:8-10), with humility (1Co 1:29, w

1:17-31; 4:6-7; 2Co 10:12-16). In the Lord, approved (Jer 9:24; 2Co 10:17-18; Gal 6:14).
See Boasting, Spiritual.

SPIRITUAL DEATH Alienation from the life of God; a state of condemnation (Ro 7:9, 11; 8:5-6, 13; Eph 4:18). Making alive from (Jn 5:24-26; Ro 5:12, 15; Eph 2:1, 5-6; 5:14; Col 2:13).
See Death, Physical; Second Death.

SPIRITUAL DESIRE See Desire, Spiritual.

SPIRITUAL DILIGENCE See Zeal.

SPIRITUAL GIFTS Extraordinary gifts of the Spirit given to Christians to equip them for the service of the Church (Ro 11:29; 12:6-8; 1Co 12:4-11, 28-30; Eph 4:7-11; 1Pe 4:10-11).
See Charism, Charisma, Charismata; Holy Spirit; Tongues, Gift of.

SPIRITUAL HUNGER See Hunger, Figurative.

SPIRITUAL PEACE (Isa 27:5; 54:1, 10, 13; 55:2, 12; 57:19; Eze 34:25; Lk 2:14, 29; Ro 5:1; 1Co 14:33). Christ's kingdom, a kingdom of (Isa 9:6; 11:6-9, 13; Mic 5:5; Lk 1:79; Ac 10:36).
See Peace, Spiritual.

SPIRITUAL PURIFICATION (Ps 65:3; 73:1; Pr 20:9; Jn 13:8-9). By corrective judgments (Isa 4:3-4). By mercy and truth (Pr 16:6). By the Holy Spirit (1Co 6:11; Tit 3:5-6). By the blood of Christ (Heb 1:3; 9:14; 2Pe 1:9; 1Jn 1:7; Rev 1:5; 7:14).
Of the Church (Eph 5:26).
Commanded (Isa 1:16; Mt 23:26; Ac 22:16; 1Co 5:7; 2Co 7:1; Heb 10:22; Jas 4:8).
Promised (Isa 1:18; Jer 33:8; Eze 36:25; Da 12:10; Zec 13:1; 1Jn 1:9). Prayer for (Ps 51:2, 7; 79:9).
See Purification; Sanctification.

SPIRITUAL UNDERSTANDING (Mt 13:23; Lk 10:21-22; Jn 7:17). Of apostles (Mt 13:16-17; Lk 8:10; 10:23-24). Of Peter (Mt 16:16-17). Of Mary (Lk 10:39, 42).
Lacking, in disciples (Mt 15:15-16; Lk 24:25), in Jews (Mt 13:11-16; Jn 6:26, 41, 52; 9:28-29, 39-41; 12:27-40; Ac 28:24-27).
Commanded:
Concerning, the importance of preaching (Mt 11:13-15), the importance of parables (Mt 13:9, 43; Lk 8:8), the character of the disciples of Jesus (Lk 14:33-35), the Holy Spirit's message to the churches (Rev 2:7).
See Wisdom, Spiritual.

SPIRITUALISM See Necromancer; Sorcery.

SPIRITUALITY Described as the great and enduring good (Lk 10:42), as love and devotion to God (Dt 6:5; Jos 22:5; 1Ki 8:23; Ps 1:2; 51:6).
Brings peace (Isa 26:3; Jer 33:6; Ro 8:6; 14:17), indifference to worldly good (1Co 7:29-31; Col 3:1-3), thirst for heavenly blessings (Mt 5:6; Jn 6:27).
Is produced by the indwelling of the Holy Spirit (Jn 14:16-17; Ro 8:4).

SPITTING In the face, as an indignity (Nu 12:14; Dt 25:9; Job 30:10; Mt 26:67; 27:30). Jesus used spittle in healing (Mk 7:33; 8:23).

SPOILS Of war (Ge 14:11-12; Nu 31:9-10; Dt 2:35). Divided between the combatants and noncombatants of the Israelites, including priests and Levites (Nu 31:25-54; 1Sa 30:24). Dedicated to the Lord (1Sa 15:15; 1Ch 26:27; 2Ch 15:11).

SPOKES Rods connecting the rim of a wheel with the hub. Basins for washing of sacrifices were set on bases moving upon wheels. The spokes were part of these wheels (1Ki 7:27-33).

SPONGE (Mt 27:48; Mk 15:36; Jn 19:29).

SPOONS Of the tabernacle (Ex 25:29; Nu 4:7; 7). Of the temple (1Ki 7:50; 2Ch 4:22).

SPOT Blemish, blot (SS 4:7; Job 11:15; Lev 24:19ff; Pr 9:7; Jude 23).

SPOUSE See Bride; Marriage.

SPREAD Scatter, disperse (Mt 21:8; Mk 1:28).

SPRING
1. Of water. Hot (Ge 36:24).
Figurative: muddied or salty (Pr 25:26; Jas 3:11).
See Wells.
2. Season of, promised annual return of (Ge 8:22). Described (Pr 27:25; SS 2:11-13).

SPRINKLING Of blood (Lev 14:7, 51; 16:14; Heb 9:13, 19, 21; 11:28; 1Pe 1:2). See Blood. Of water (Nu 8:7; Eze 36:25; Heb 9:19; 10:22).

STABILITY Of character (Ps 57:7; 108:1; 112:7).
Commanded (1Co 7:20; 15:58; 2Th 2:15; Heb 10:23; 13:9; Jas 1:23-25; Rev 22:11). Rewarded (Mt 10:22; 24:13; Mk 4:20; 2Th 3:3).
See Character; Decision; Perseverance.

STABLE See Pasture.

STACHYS (*head of grain*). A Christian in Rome (Ro 16:9).

STACTE See Gum Resin.

STADIA Plural of *stadion*, about 202 yards (Rev 14:20; 21:16).

STAFF Used as weapons (Mt 27:30; Mk 15:19).
Symbolic (Zec 11:7-14).

S

See Rod.

STAIRS Steps leading to an upper chamber (1Ki 6:8; Ac 21:40), or some other elevated place (Ne 9:4; Eze 40:6; 43:17). Jacob's vision of a stairway from earth to heaven (Ge 28:10-22). The sign to Hezekiah on the stairway of Ahaz (1Ki 20:1-12).

STAKE Tent pin or tent pole (Ex 27:19; Isa 33:20).

STALL A place for care of livestock or compartment in a stable for one animal (2Ch 32:28). Solomon's barns provided stalls for 4000 horses (2Ch 9:25).

STAMMERING (Isa 32:4; 33:19). Of Moses (Ex 4:10).

STANDARD An ensign used by each of the tribes of Israel in camp and march (Nu 1:52; 2:2). Banners used as (Ps 20:5; SS 6:4, 10). Used in war (Jer 4:21). Used to signal the route to defended cities (Jer 4:6), to call attention to news (Jer 50:2; 51:12).
See Armies; Banner; Ensign.
Figurative (Isa 49:22; 62:10; Jer 4:6).

STARS Created by God (Ge 1:16; Job 26:13; Ps 8:3; 33:6; 136:7, 9; Am 5:8). Differ in splendor (1Co 15:41). Worship of, forbidden (Dt 4:19). Worshiped (2Ki 17:16; 21:3; 23:5; Jer 19:13; Am 5:26; Zep 1:5; Ac 7:42-43). Constellations of (Isa 13:10), Orion (Job 9:9; Am 5:8), serpent (Job 26:13). Planets (2Ki 23:5), the morning star (Job 38:7; Rev 2:28; 22:16). Darkening of (Job 9:7; Ecc 12:2; Isa 13:10; 34:4; Joel 2:10; 3:15; Rev 8:11-12). Comets (Jude 13). Falling of (Da 8:10; 9:1; 12:4). Guides the wise men (Mt 2:2, 7, 9-10).

Figurative:
Of the deliverer (Nu 24:17). Seven stars of the seven churches (Rev 1:16, 20). Crown of twelve stars (Rev 12:1). Of Jesus (Rev 22:16).

STATE *See Church, The Body of Believers; State; Government.*

STATECRAFT Wisdom in (Pr 28:2). School in (Da 1:3-5). Skilled in.
Instances of: Joseph (Ge 47:15-26), Samuel (1Sa 11:12-15), Nathan (1Ki 1:11-14), Jeroboam (1Ki 12:26-33), Daniel. *See Daniel.*
See Government; Kings; Rulers.

STATURE Natural height of an animal body (2Sa 21:20; Isa 45:14; Lk 19:3).

STAVES *See Staff.*

STEADFASTNESS (Ps 57:7; 108:1; 112:7; Ro 14:4; 1Th 3:8; Col 1:23; Jas 1:25).
Commanded (1Co 7:20; 15:58; 16:13; Gal 6:1; Eph 6:11, 13-14; Php 1:27; 4:1; 1Th 5:21; 2Th 2:15; 3:13; Heb 10:23; 13:9; Jas 1:25; 1Pe 5:9).
Rewards of (Mt 10:22; 24:13; Mk 13:13; Rev 2:7, 10-11, 17, 25-28; 3:5, 11-12, 21; 21:17).
See Decision; Perseverance; Stability.

STEALING *See Theft.*

STEEL Steel is not mentioned in the Bible. *See Bronze.*

STELE (*erect block* or *shaft*). Narrow, upright slab of stone with an inscription cut on it to commemorate an event, mark a grave, or give a votive likeness of a deity. Prevalent especially in Egypt and Greece.

STEPHANAS (*victor's wreath*). A Christian in Corinth, whose household Paul baptized (1Co 1:16; 16:15, 17).

STEPHEN (*victor's wreath*). A Christian martyr. Appointed one of the committee of seven to oversee power of (Ac 6:5, 8-10). False charges against (Ac 6:11-15). Defense of (Ac 7). Stoned (Ac 7:54-60; 8:1; 22:20). Burial of (Ac 8:2). Gentle and forgiving spirit of (Ac 7:59-60).

STERILITY Of women. *See Barrenness.*

STEW Soup of vegetables and meat (Ge 25:29-30, 34; 2Ki 4:38-39).

STEWARD (Ge 15:2; 43:19; 1Ch 28:1; Lk 8:3). Must be faithful (1Co 4:1-2; Tit 1:7; 1Pe 4:10).
Figurative: The faithful steward described (Lk 12:35-38, 42). The unfaithful, described (Lk 16:1-8). The parable of the pounds (Lk 19:12-27), of the talents (Mt 25:14-30).

STEWARDSHIP Of the gospel (1Co 9:17; Gal 2:7; Col 1:25; 1Th 2:4; 1Ti 1:11; Tit 1:3).

STICKS Used as cymbals (Eze 37:16).

STIFF-NECKED *See Impenitence; Obduracy.*

STOCK
1. Wooden idol worshiped by apostate Israel (Isa 44:19; Jer 2:27).
2. Family (Lev 25:47; Isa 40:24; Ac 13:26; Php 3:5).
3. Instrument of punishment in which head, hands, and feet were fastened (2Ch 16:10; Jer 20:2; Job 13:27).

STOICISM A Grecian philosophy, inculcating doctrines of severe morality, self-denial, and inconvenient services.
Scripture analogies to: John the Baptist, wears camel's hair and subsists on locusts and wild honey (Mt 3:4), comes "neither eating nor drinking" (Mt 11:18; Lk 7:33). Jesus requires self-denial and crosses (Mt 10:38-39; 16:24; Mk 8:34-35; Lk 9:23-26; 14:27), the subordination of natural affection (Mt 10:37; Lk 14:26). Paul teaches that the "law of my mind" is at war with the "law of sin at work within my members" (Ro 7:23, w 7:14-24), that the body must be kept under (1Co 9:27), advises celibacy (1Co 7:1-9, 25-26, 32-33, 39-40).

School of, at Athens (Ac 17:18).
See Aratus; Asceticism; Cleanthes.

STOICS (*learners on the painted*] *porch*). *See Aratus; Asceticism; Cleanthes; Stoicism.*

STOMACHER NIV "fine clothing" (Isa 3:24).

STONES Commandments engraved upon (Ex 24:12; 31:18; 34:1-4; Dt 4:13; 5:22; 9:9-11; 10:1-3). The law of Moses written upon (Jos 8:32). Houses built of (Isa 9:10; Am 5:11). Temple built of (1Ki 5:17-18; 7:9-12; Mt 24:2; Lk 19:44; 21:5-6). Prepared in the quarries (1Ki 6:7). Hewn (Ex 34:1; Dt 10:1; 1Ki 5:17; 6:36; 7:9; 2Ki 12:12; 22:6; 1Ch 22:2; 2Ch 34:11; La 3:9). Sawn (1Ki 7:9). Stonemasons (1Ki 5:18; 2Ki 12:12; 1Ch 22:15).
City walls built of (Ne 4:3). Memorial pillars of (Ge 28:18-22; 31:45-52; Jos 4:2-9, 20-24; 24:25; 1Sa 7:12). Great, as landmarks, Abel (1Sa 6:18), Ezel (1Sa 20:19), Zoheleth (1Ki 1:9).
Cast upon accursed ground (2Ki 3:19, 25). Used in building altars (Jos 8:31), for weighing (Lev 19:36), for closing tombs (Mt 27:60; Mk 15:46; 16:3). Tombs cut in (Mt 27:60; Mk 15:46; 16:3). Idols made of (Dt 4:28; 28:36, 64; 29:17; 2Ki 19:18; Isa 37:19; Eze 20:32).
Great, in Solomon's temple (1Ki 5:17-18; 7:9-12). Magnificent, in Herod's (Mk 13:1). Skill in throwing (Jdg 20:16; 1Ch 12:2). *See Sling.*
See Adamant; Chalcedony; Marble; Onyx; Pillar. See below, Precious.

Figurative—
(Ge 49:24; Zec 3:9). Of temptation, "a stone that causes men to stumble" (Isa 8:14; Ro 9:33; 1Pe 2:8). Of Christ, "a tested stone, a precious cornerstone for a sure foundation" (Isa 28:16), of Christ's rejection, the rejected corner stone (Ps 118:22; Mt 21:42-44; Mk 12:10; Lk 20:17-18; Ac 4:11; 1Pe 2:4), the true foundation (Isa 28:16; Mt 16:18; 1Co 3:11; Eph 2:20; Rev 21:14). Of Christ, the source of spiritual water (1Co 10:4). Of the impenitent heart (Eze 36:26). Of the witness of the Spirit, the white stone (Rev 2:17).

Symbolic—
Of the kingdom of Christ (Da 2:34, 45).

Precious:
In the breastplate and ephod (Ex 28:9-21; 39:6-14). Voluntary offerings of, by the Israelites for the breastplate and ephod (Ex 35:27). Exported from Sheba (1Ki 10:2, 10; 2Ch 9:9-10; Eze 27:22), Ophir (1Ki 10:11). Partial catalog of (Eze 28:13). Seen in the foundation of the New Jerusalem in John's apocalyptic vision (Rev 21:19-20).
In kings' crowns (2Sa 12:30; 1Ch 20:2).
Figurative— (Isa 54:11-12).
See Adamant; Agate; Amber; Amethyst; Bdellium; Beryl; Carbuncle; Carnelian; Chalcedony; Chrysolite; Chrysoprase; Coral; Crystal; Diamond; Emerald; Flint; Glowing Metal; Hardest Stone; Jacinth; Jasper; Minerals of the Bible, 1; Onyx; Pearl; Ruby; Sapphire; Sardius; Sardonyx; Topaz; Turquoise.

STONING The ordinary form of capital punishment prescribed by Hebrew law (Lev 20:2) for blasphemy (Lev 24:16), idolatry (Dt 13:6-10), desecration of the Sabbath day (Ex 31:15; 35:2; Nu 15:32-36), human sacrifice (Lev 20:2), occultism (Lev 20:27).
Unlike unintentional sins, for which there are provisions of God's mercy, one who sets his hand defiantly to despise the word of God and to blaspheme his name must be punished. The one who sins defiantly (literally "with a high hand"), whether in the case of the willful blasphemer (Ex 20:7; 22:28; Lev 24:11-16), or the Sabbath-breaker (Ex 31:12-15; 35:2), was guilty of high-handed rebellion and was judged with death (Nu 15:30-31, 32-36).
Execution took place outside city (Lev 24:14; 1Ki 21:10, 13; Ac 7:58).
See Assault and Battery; Bruise(s); Flog, Flogging; Lashes; Scourging; Stripes.

STOOL
1. Delivery stool (Ex 1:16).
2. Footstool. Figurative: Of the earth (Isa 66:1; Mt 5:35; Ac 7:49), temple (1Ch 28:2; La 2:1), sanctuary (Ps 99:5; 132:7), enemies of Jesus (Ps 110:1; Mt 22:44; Mk 12:36; Lk 20:43; Ac 2:35; Heb 1:13). *See Footstool.*

STORE CITIES Supply depots for provisions and arms (1Ki 9:15-19; 2Ch 8:4-6; 16:4).

STOREHOUSE Place for keeping treasures, supplies, and equipment (Dt 28:8; 1Ch 29:16; 2Ch 31:10; Mal 3:10). *See Barn; Granary.*

STORK (*kindly, loyal one*). Forbidden as food (Lev 11:19). Nest of, in fir trees (Ps 104:17). Migratory (Jer 8:7).
Figurative (Zec 5:9).

STOVE Household stoves usually made of clay; were small and portable, burning charcoal; the well-to-do had metal stoves or braziers (Jer 36:22ff).

STRAIGHT Name of a street in Damascus (Ac 9:11).
Figurative of righteousness, "straight paths" (Isa 40:3-4; Mt 3:3; Heb 12:13).

STRAIT GATE *See Gates, Figurative.*

STRAKES Archaic word for:
1. "White stripes" (Ge 30:37). *See Stripes, 4.*
2. "Greenish or reddish depressions" (Lev 14:37).

STRANGERS Mosaic law relating to: Authorized bondservice of (Lev 25:44-45), usury of (Dt 15:3; 23:20), sale to, of flesh of animals that had died (Dt 14:21), forbid their being made kings over Israel (Dt 17:15), their eating the Passover (Ex 12:43, 48), their eating things offered in sacrifice (Ex 29:33; Lev 22:10, 12, 25), their blaspheming (Lev 24:16), their approaching the tabernacle (Nu 1:51), their eating blood (Lev 17:10), injustice to

forbidden to (Ex 12:49; Lev 24:22; Nu 9:14; Dt 1:16; Jer 22:3), oppression of, forbidden (Ex 22:21; Lev 23:9; Dt 24:14, 17; 27:19; Jer 22:3). Instances of oppression of (Eze 22:29; Mal 3:5).
Required to observe the Sabbath (Ex 20:10; 23:12). Might offer sacrifices (Lev 17:8; 22:18-19). Were buried in separate burial places (Mt 27:7).
Kindness to, required (Lev 19:33-34). Love of, commanded (Dt 10:18-19). Abhorrence of, forbidden (Dt 23:7). Marriage with, forbidden (Dt 25:5). Hospitality to. *See Hospitality.*
See Alms; Foreigner; Heathen; Proselyte.

STRANGLE To deprive of life by choking. Israelites were forbidden to eat flesh from strangled animals (Lev 17:12). At the Jerusalem council even Jewish Christians were forbidden to eat such meat (Ac 15:20).

STRATEGY In war (Jdg 14:14-15; 32:7-8; Jos 8:3-25; Jdg 7:16-23; 20:29-43; 2Sa 15:32-34, w 17:7-14; Ne 6; Isa 15:1; Jer 6:5).
See Ambush; Armies.

STRAW Used for feed (Ge 24:32; Isa 65:25), for brick (Ex 5:7).

STRAY Animals straying to be returned (Ex 23:4; Dt 22:1-3). Instances of animals straying, Kish's (1Sa 9).

STREAKED Mottled or blotchy of color, characterizing Laban's sheep (Ge 30:35; 31:8, 12). *See Speckled.*

STREAM OF EGYPT *See River of Egypt.*

STREETS (Pr 1:20; Na 2:4; Mk 6:56; Lk 14:21; Ac 9:11).

STRENGTH A title given Yahweh (1Sa 15:29). Spiritual. *See Power, Spiritual.*

STRIFE

General:
(Ps 55:9; 80:6). Domestic (Pr 19:13; 21:19; 25:24). Hated by God (Isa 58:4; Hab 1:3).
Christ brings (Mt 10:34-36; Lk 12:51-53, 58-59). Caused by: Busybodies (Pr 26:20). Perversity (Pr 16:28). Hatred (Pr 10:12). Lusts (Jas 4:1-2). Pride (Pr 13:10). Scornfulness (Pr 22:10). Wrath (Pr 15:18; 29:22; 30:33). Excessive indulgence in intoxicating drinks (Pr 23:29-30).
Destructive (Mt 12:25; Mk 3:24-25; Lk 11:17).

Exhortations against:
(Ge 13:8; 45:24; Ps 31:20; Pr 3:30; 17:14; 25:8; Mt 5:25, 39-41; Ro 12:18; 13:13; 14:1, 19, 21; 16:17-18; 1Co 4:6-7; 2Co 12:20; Gal 5:15, 20; Php 2:3, 14-15; 1Ti 3:2-3; 6:3-5, 20-21; 2Ti 2:14, 23-25; Tit 3:1-3, 9; Jas 3:14-16).
Punishment for (Isa 41:11-12; Ro 2:8-9). Correction of (Mt 18:15-17).
Abstinence from, honorable (Pr 20:3).
Prayers concerning (Ps 55:9; 1Ti 2:8).
Proverbs concerning (Pr 3:30; 6:12-14, 16-19; 10:12; 13:10; 15:18; 17:1, 14, 19; 18:6, 19; 19:13; 20:3; 21:19; 22:10; 23:29-30; 25:8, 24; 26:17, 20-21; 27:15; 28:25; 29:22; 30:33).
See Anger; Envy; Jealousy; Malice.

Instances of:
Between Abraham and Lot's herdsmen (Ge 13:6-7), Abimelech's (Ge 21:25), Isaac's and those of Gerar (Ge 26:20-22). Laban and Jacob (Ge 31:36). Israelites (Dt 1:12). Jephthah and his brothers (Jdg 11:2), and Ephraimites (Jdg 12:1-6). Israel and Judah, about David (2Sa 19:41-43).
Disciples, over who might be the greatest (Mk 9:34; Lk 22:24). Jews, concerning Jesus (Jn 10:19). Christians at Antioch, about circumcision (Ac 15:2). Paul and Barnabas, about Mark (Ac 15:38-39). Pharisees and Sadducees, concerning the Resurrection (Ac 23:7-10). Christians, at Corinth (1Co 1:10-12; 3:3-4; 6:1-7; 11:16-21). At Philippi (Php 1:15-17).

STRIKER
See Violence.

STRINGED INSTRUMENTS *See Music.*

STRIPES
1. Wounds inflicted by scourges for punishment (Ex 21:25). *See Bruise(s), 1.*
2. Authorized by Jewish law for certain offenses (Dt 25:2-3). *See Lashes, 1.*
3. Practiced also by Romans (Mt 27:26 & Jn 19:1, w Isa 53:5). Roman floggings were so brutal that sometimes the victim died before crucifixion. *See Flog, Flogging.*
4. The Hebrew terms for the words "poplar" and "white stripes" are puns on the name Laban. As Jacob had gotten the best of Esau (whose other name, Edom, means "red") by means of red stew (Ge 25:30), so he now tries to get the best of Laban (whose name means "white") by means of white branches (Ge 30:37). *See Strakes, 1. See also, Assault and Battery; Scourging; Stoning.*

STRIVING WITH GOD Folly of (Job 9:3; 33:13; 40:2; Isa 45:9; Ro 9:20).

STRONG DRINK *See Beer; Fermented Drink; Wine.*

STUBBLE Figurative of the wicked (Ex 15:7; Job 21:18; Ps 83:13; Isa 5:24; 40:24; 41:2; 47:14; Jer 13:24; Joel 2:5; Na 1:10; Mal 4:1).

STUBBORNNESS *See Obduracy.*

STUDENTS Poverty of (2Ki 4:1). In state school (Da 1). In schools of the prophets (1Sa 19:20; 1Ki 20:35; 2Ki 2:2-3, 5, 7, 15; 4:1). *See Instruction; School.*

STUMBLING Causes of (Ps 69:6). Stone of (Isa 8:14; Ro 9:32-33; 1Pe 2:8). Stumbling block (Lev 19:14; Ps 119:165; Isa

57:14; Jer 6:21; Eze 3:20; 7:19; 14:3-4, 7; Zep 1:3; Lk 11:52; Ro 11:9; 14:13; 1Co 1:23; 8:9-13; Rev 2:14).
See Temptation.

SUAH (possibly *offal, dung, viscera*). An Asherite. The son of Zophah (1Ch 7:36).

SUBJECTS See *Citizens; Government; Patriotism; Rulers.*

SUBMISSION To authority: Jesus an example of (Mt 26:39, 42; Mk 14:36; Lk 22:42; Heb 5:8).
Of Paul (1Co 16:7).
See Obedience.

SUBSTITUTION (Ge 22:13; Ex 28:38). The offering for the offerer (Lev 1:4; 16:21-22). The Levites for the firstborn of the Israelites (Nu 3:12, 41, 45; 8:18). The life of Ahab for that of Ben-Hadad (1Ki 20:42).
Of Christ for us (Isa 53:4-6; 1Co 5:7; 2Co 5:21; Gal 3:13; 1Pe 2:24).
See Suffering, Vicarious.

SUBURB See *Pasture.*

SUCATHITES One of three clans of scribes who lived at Jabez (1Ch 2:55).

SUCCESSION Of priests, irregularity in (Heb 7:1-28). *See Priest.* Of kings. *See Kings.*

SUCCOTH (*booths*).
1. A city probably east of the Jordan. Jacob builds a house in (Ge 33:17). Allotted to Gad (Jos 13:27). People of, punished by Gideon (Jdg 8:5-8, 14-16). Located near the Jordan (1Ki 7:46; 2Ch 4:17; Ps 60:6; 108:7).
2. First camping place of the Israelites on leaving Rameses (Ex 12:37; 13:20; Nu 33:5-6).

SUCCOTH BENOTH A pagan idol brought into Samaria after Assyria had captured it (2Ki 17:24-30).

SUCHATHITES See *Sucathites.*

SUDDEN EVENTS (Ecc 9:12; Mal 3:1; Mt 24:27; Mk 13:36; Lk 2:13; Ac 2:2; 9:3; 16:26).

SUETONIUS A Roman writer (c. A.D. 69-140), famous for his *Lives of the Caesars.*

SUFFERING
For Christ:
Promised by Christ (Mt 10:34-36; Lk 12:51-53, 58-59; Ac 9:16). Fellowship with Christ on account of (Php 3:10). Conditions of joint heirship with Christ (Ro 8:17-22, 26). A privilege (Php 1:29). Rejoicing in (Ac 5:41; Col 1:24).
Motives for patient enduring of: Future glory (Ro 8:17-18; 2Co 4:8-10; 2Co 4:11-12, 17-18; 1Pe 4:13-14). Reigning with Christ (2Ti 2:12; Rev 22:5).
Consolations in (2Co 1:7; Php 2:27-30; 2Ti 2:12; 1Pe 5:10). Patience in (1Co 4:11-13; 2Th 1:4-5; Jas 5:10; 1Pe 4:14).
See Affliction; Persecution.

Of Christ:
Purpose of his coming (Lk 24:46-47; Jn 6:51; 10:11, 15; 11:50-52). Reason for his coming (Ro 4:25; 5:6-8; 14:15; 1Co 1:17-18, 23-24; 15:3; 2Co 5:14-15; Gal 1:4; 2:20-21; Eph 5:2, 25; 1Th 5:9-10; Heb 2:9-10, 14, 18; 5:8-9; 9:15-16, 28; 10:10, 18-20; 1Pe 2:21, 24; 3:18; 4:1; 1Jn 3:16).
See Atonement; Jesus the Christ, Death of; Purpose of His Death; Sufferings of.

Vicarious:
(Ex 9:13-16; Jn 15:13; Ro 9:3; 1Pe 2:21-24; 1Jn 3:16).
See Jesus the Christ, Sufferings of; Penalty, Vicariously Assumed; above, Suffering, Of Christ.
Instance of: Goliath, for the Philistines (1Sa 17).

SUICIDE (Am 9:2; Rev 9:6). Temptation to, of Jesus (Mt 4:5-6; Lk 4:9-11). Of the Philippian jailer (Ac 16:27). *See Death, Physical, Desired.*
Instances of: Samson (Jdg 16:29-30). Saul and his armor-bearer (1Sa 31:4-5; 1Ch 10:4-5). Ahithophel (2Sa 17:23). Zimri (1Ki 16:18). Judas (Mt 27:5; Ac 1:18).

SUING (Mt 5:40). *See Creditor; Debtor.*

SUKKITES Mercenary soldiers, possibly Libyan, who joined Shishak in his invasion of Judah (2Ch 12:3).

SUKKOTH See *Succoth.*

SULFUR Fire and, rained upon Sodom (Ge 19:24; Lk 17:29). In Israel (Dt 29:23). Figurative of God's judgment (Job 18:15; Ps 11:6; Isa 30:33; Eze 38:22; Rev 9:17-18; 14:10; 19:20; 21:8). *See Minerals of the Bible.*

SUMER One of two political divisions, Sumer and Akkad, originally comprising Babylonia.

SUMMER Season of, promised while the earth remains (Ge 8:22). Cool rooms for (Jdg 3:20, 24; Am 3:15). Fruits of (2Sa 16:1-2; Isa 16:9; 28:4; Jer 40:10, 12; 48:32; Am 8:1-2; Mic 7:1). Drought of (Ps 32:4). Given by God (Ps 74:17). The time for labor and harvest (Pr 6:6-8; 10:5; 30:25; Jer 8:20). Snow in (Pr 26:1). Threshing in (Da 2:35). Approach of (Mt 24:32; Mk 13:28; Lk 21:30).
Figurative (Jer 8:20).

SUMMER HOUSE, SUMMER PALACE The wealthy had separate residences for hot and cold seasons. Called a "summer house" (Am 3:15), a "summer palace" (Jdg 3:20, ftn). *See Winter Apartment, Winter House.*

SUN Created (Ge 1:14-18; Ps 74:16; 136:7; Jer 31:35). Rising and setting of (Ecc 1:5). Diurnal motion of (Ps 19:4, 6). Worship of, forbidden (Dt 4:19; 17:3). Worshiped (Job 31:26-28; Jer 8:2; Eze 6:4, 6; 8:16). Kings of Judah dedicate horses to (2Ki 23:11).
Miracles concerning: Darkening of (Ex 10:21-23; Isa 5:30; 24:23; Eze 32:7; Joel 2:10, 31; 3:15; Am 8:9; Mic 3:6; Mt 24:29; 27:45; Mk 13:24; 15:33; Lk 21:25; 23:44-45; Ac 2:20; Rev 6:12; 8:12; 9:2; 16:8). Stands still (Jos 10:12-13; Hab 3:11). Shadow of, goes back on Ahaz's stairway (2Ki 20:11; Isa 38:8).
Light of, not needed in eternity (Rev 21:23).
Figurative (Ps 84:11; Mal 4:2; Jdg 5:31; Isa 30:26; 60:19-20; Jer 15:9; Rev 1:16; 12:1; 19:17).

SUN, WORSHIP OF Worship of the sun found varied forms in the ancient world. Even the Israelites at times worshiped sun images (Lev 26:30; Isa 17:8). Shamash was a great sun god of the ancient Middle East. Phoenicia worshiped a sun Baal, Baal Hamon. In Egypt the center of sun worship was On, or Heliopolis, where the sun was called Re.

SUNDAY The first day of the week, commemorating the resurrection of Jesus (Jn 20:1-25), and the Day of Pentecost (Ac 2:1-41). For a time after the Ascension of Jesus the Christians met on the seventh and the first days of the week, but as the Hebrew Christian churches declined in influence, the tendency to observe the Hebrew Sabbath slowly passed. The disciples at Troas worshiped on the first day (Ac 20:7). Paul admonished the Corinthians to lay by in store as God had prospered them, doing it week by week on the first day (1Co 16:2). The term "Lord's Day" occurs (Rev 1:10).

SUN-DIAL NIV "stairway" (2Ki 20:11; Isa 38:8). *See Stairs.*

SUNSTROKE (2Ki 4:19).

SUPER-APOSTLES Paul's critics (2Co 11:5; 12:11).

SUPEREROGATION The doctrine of excessive and meritorious righteousness (Eze 33:12-13; Lk 17:10).

SUPERSCRIPTION (*inscription*).
1. The wording on coins (Mt 22:20).
2. Words written on a board attached to the cross naming the crime of which the condemned was accused (Mk 15:26; Lk 23:38; Jn 19:19-20).
3. Titles of the Psalms. *See Music, Symbols Used in; Psalms.*

SUPERSTITION (Ac 25:19).
Instances of:
Israelites in supposing that their defeat in battle with the Philistines was due to their not having brought the ark of the covenant with them (1Sa 4:3, w 4:10-11), attributing their calamities to having stopped offering sacrifices to the Queen of Heaven (Jer 44:17-19). Philistines in refusing to step on the threshold where the image of Dagon had repeatedly fallen (1Sa 5:5).
The belief of the Syrians concerning the help of the gods (1Ki 20:23). Nebuchadnezzar in supposing that the spirit of the gods was upon Daniel (Da 4:8-9). The sailors who threw Jonah into the sea (Jnh 1:4-16). The disciples in supposing they saw a spirit when Jesus came walking upon the sea (Mt 14:26; Mk 6:49-50). Herod in imagining that John the Baptist had risen from the dead (Mk 6:14, 16).
The Gadarenes on account of Jesus casting demons out of the demoniac (Mt 8:34). The disciples who were frightened at the appearance of Peter (Ac 12:14-15). The Ephesians in their sorceries (Ac 19:13-19). The people of the island of Malta in imagining Paul to be a god (Ac 28:6).
See Idolatry; Sorcery.

SUPERSTITIOUS NIV "very religious" (Ac 17:22), could either commend or criticize the Athenians.

SUPH, SUPHAH (*reeds, rushes*). "The Red Sea" is used for these words (Nu 21:14; Dt 1:1). Suph is an unidentified region E of the Jordan; Suphah, is probably the region of the Red Sea.

SUPPER See *Feasts; Eucharist.*

SUPPER, LORD'S See *Lord's Supper.*

SUPPLICATION See *Prayer.*

SUPREME COMMANDER Commander-in-chief of the Assyrian army (Isa 20:1; 2Ki 18:17).

SUR The gate of the temple (2Ki 11:6).

SURETY See *Security, For Debt; Debt.*

SURFEITING Overindulgence of food or drink; dissipation (Lk 21:34).

SUSA
1. Capital of the Medo-Persian Empire (Est 1:2-3; 8:15).
2. King's palace at (Ne 1:1; Est 1:2, 5; 2:5, 8; 4:8, 16; 8:14-15; 9:11, 15).

SUSAH See *Hazar Susah.*

SUSANCHITES NIV "of Susa" (Ezr 4:9). *See Susa.*

SUSANNA (*lily*).
1. Woman who ministered to Christ (Lk 8:1-3).
2. Heroine of *The History of Susanna,* in the OT Apocrypha.

SUSI (*[my] horse*). A Manassite (Nu 13:11).

SUSIM See *Hazar Susah.*

SUSPICION See *Accusation, False.*

SWADDLING BAND Bands of cloth in which a newborn baby was wrapped (Lk 2:7, 12). Used figuratively (Job 38:9).

SWALLOW Builds its nest in the sanctuary (Ps 84:3). Chattering of, figurative of the mourning of the afflicted (Isa 38:14). Migration of (Jer 8:7).

SWAN See *White Owl.*

SWEARING See *Blasphemy; God, Name of; Oath.*

SWEAT (Ge 3:19). An offense in the sanctuary (Eze 44:18). Of blood (Lk 22:44).

SWEAT, BLOODY Physical manifestation of the agony of Jesus in Gethsemane (Lk 22:44). Christ's sweat most likely did not become bloody, but "his sweat was like great drops of blood falling to the ground" as if from an open wound.

SWEET INCENSE Made of spices (Ex 25:6). *See Incense.*

SWEET SAVOR See *Pleasing Aroma.*

SWELLING Usually "pride"; or means the flooding of the Jordan in the spring (Jer 12:5; 49:19; 50:44). It refers to the tumult of a stormy sea (Ps 46:3).

SWIFT An amphibious bird (Isa 38:14; Jer 8:7).

SWINE See *Animals; Pig.*

SWORD, THE Probable origin of (Ge 3:24). Was pointed (Eze 21:15). Frequently had two edges (Ps 149:6).

Described as:
Sharp (Ps 57:4). Bright (Na 3:3). Glittering (Dt 32:41; Job 20:25). Oppressive (Jer 46:16). Hurtful (Ps 144:10). Carried in a sheath or scabbard (1Ch 21:27; Jer 47:6; Eze 21:3-5). Suspended from the belt (1Sa 17:39; 2Sa 20:8; Ne 4:18; Ps 45:3).

Was Used:
By the patriarchs (Ge 34:25; 48:22). By the Jews (Jdg 7:22; 2Sa 24:9). By heathen nations (Jdg 7:22; 1Sa 15:33). For self-defense (Lk 22:36). For destruction of enemies (Nu 21:24; Jos 6:21). For punishing criminals (1Sa 15:33; Ac 12:2). Sometimes for self-destruction (1Sa 31:4-5; Ac 16:27). Hebrews early acquainted with making of (1Sa 13:19). In time of war, plowshares made into (Joel 3:10). In time of peace, made into plowshares (Isa 2:4; Mic 4:3). Sharpened and furbished before going to war (Ps 7:12; Eze 21:9). Was brandished over the head (Eze 32:10). Was thrust through enemies (Eze 16:40). Often threatened as a punishment (Lev 26:25, 33; Dt 32:25). Often sent as a punishment (Jer 9:7; Ps 78:62). Was one of God's four sore judgments (Eze 14:21). Those slain by, communicated ceremonial uncleanness (Nu 19:16).

Illustrative:
Of the Word of God (Eph 6:17, w Heb 4:12). Of the word of Christ (Isa 49:2, w Rev 1:16). Of the justice of God (Dt 32:41; Zec 13:7). Of the protection of God (Dt 33:29). Of war and contention (Mt 10:34). Of severe and heavy calamities (Eze 5:2, 17; 14:17; 21:9). Of deep mental affliction (Lk 2:35). Of the wicked (Ps 17:13). Of the tongue of the wicked (Ps 57:4; 64:3; Pr 12:18). Of persecuting spirit of the wicked (Ps 37:14). Of the end of the wicked (Pr 5:4). Of false witnesses (Pr 25:18). Of judicial authority (Ro 13:4). Drawing of illustrative of war and destruction (Lev 26:33; Eze 21:3-5). Putting into its sheath illustrative of peace and friendship (Jer 47:6). Living by illustrative of violence (Ge 27:40). Not departing from one's house illustrative of perpetual calamity (2Sa 12:10).

SYCAMINE NIV "mulberry tree" (Lk 17:6).

SYCAMORE-FIG A tree. Abundant in the land of Canaan (1Ki 10:27; 2Ch 1:15; 9:27; Isa 9:10). Groves of, cared for (1Ch 27:28). Destroyed by frost (Ps 78:47). Care of (Am 7:14). Zacchaeus climbs into (Lk 19:4).

SYCHAR A village one half mile N of Jacob's well, on the E slope of Mt. Ebal (Jn 4:5).

SYCHEM See *Shechem, 1.*

SYENE See *Aswan.*

SYMBOLS, AND SIMILITUDES
General
Almond tree branch (Jer 1:11). Altar split apart (1Ki 13:3, 5). Basket for measuring (Zec 5:6-11). Belt (Jer 13:1-7; Ac 21:11). Blood sprinkled (Ex 24:8). Book cast into Euphrates (Jer 51:63). Bow shot (1Sa 20:21-37; 2Ki 13:15-19). Bread (Mt 26:26; Mk 14:22; Lk 22:19). Breaking of clay jar (Jer 19). Change of residence (Eze 12:3-11). Childlike (Mt 18:3; Mk 10:14-15; Lk 18:16-17). Circumcision, of the covenant of Abraham (Ge 17:11; Ro 4:11). Cooking (Jer 1:13; Eze 4:9-15; 24:3-5). Curtain of the temple torn in two (Mt 27:51; Mk 15:38; Lk 23:45). Darkness (Ex 20:21; Lev 16:2; 1Ki 8:12; Ps 18:11; 97:2; Heb 12:18-19). Death [without mourning] (Eze 24:16-19). Deeds of land (Jer 32:11-16). Eating food with anxiety (Eze 12:17-20). Figs [basket of good and bad] (Jer 24). Fish [Jonah in the] (Mt 16:4; Lk 11:29-30; Isa 37:30). Fruit [basket of] (Jer 24:1-3; Am 8:1-2).
Handwriting on the wall (Da 5:5-6, 16-28). Harvest (2Ki 19:29). Invitation by enemy to approach (1Sa 14:8-12). Isaiah's children (Isa 8:18). Manna [in the desert] (Jn 6:31-58). Marrying a prostitute (Hos 1:2-9; 3:1-4). Men meeting Saul (1Sa 10:2-7). Mosaic rites [system of] (Heb 9:9-10, 18-23). Mute (Eze 3:26-27; 24:27; 29:21; 33:22; Lk 1:20-22, 62-64). Nakedness (Isa 20:2-4). Passover [of the sparing of the firstborn] (Ex 12:3-28). Passover [atonement made by Christ] (1Co 5:7). Pillar of cloud (Ex 13:21-22; 14:19-20; 19:9, 16). Plumb line (Am 7:7-8). Posture [lie on side] (Eze 4:4-8). Pot for cooking (Eze 24:1-5). Praying toward the temple (1Ki 8:29; Da 6:10). Rainbow (Ge 9:12-13).

S

Sacrificial animals (Ge 15:8-11; Jn 1:29, 36). Salt [gracious words] (Col 4:6). Salt, Covenant of (Nu 18:19). Scroll flying (Zec 5:2-4). Shadow on Ahaz's stairway (2Ki 20:8-11; Isa 38:7-8). Shaving head and beard (Eze 5:1-4). Siege (Eze 4:1-3). Snake of bronze [lifted up, of Christ] (Nu 21:8-9; Jn 3:14). Spiritual rest [Canaan] (Heb 3:11-12; 4:5). Star in the east (Mt 2:2). Sticks and staffs (Eze 37:16-17; Zec 11:7, 10-11, 14). Striken rock [of Christ] (Ex 17:6; 1Co 10:4). Tabernacle and sanctuary (Ps 15:1; Eze 37:27; Heb 8:2, 5; 9:1-12, 23-24). Thunder and lightning on Mount Sinai (Ex 19:9, 16). Thunder and rain (1Sa 12:16-18). Trees of life and knowledge (Ge 2:9, 17; 3:3, 24; Rev 22:2). Unclean food [preparing of] (Eze 4:9-17). Vine (Eze 15:2; 19:10-14). Water [lapping of] (Jdg 7:4-8). Water to drink [drawing of in hospitality of] (Ge 24:13-15, 42-44). Waving and ritual offering (Ex 29:24-28; Lev 8:27-29; 9:21). Wine (Jer 25:15-17; Isa 27:3, 6; 44:3-4; 51:17). Wine [of the atoning blood] (Mt 26:27-29; Mk 14:23-25; Lk 22:17-18, 20). Wineskins (Jer 13:12; 19:1-2, 10). Wounding (1Ki 20:35-40). Yokes (Jer 27:2-3; 28:10).

Of the Holy Spirit:

Water (Jn 3:5; 7:38-39): cleansing by (Eze 16:9; 36:25; Eph 5:26; Heb 10:22), making prosperous (Ps 1:3; Isa 27:3, 6; 44:3-4; 58:11).

Fire (Mt 3:11): refining (Isa 4:4; Mal 3:2-3), guiding (Ex 13:21; Ps 78:14), searching (Zep 1:12, w 1Co 2:10). Flame shaped like tongues (Ac 2:3, 6, 11).

Wind (SS 4:16): incomprehensible (Jn 3:8; 1Co 12:11), powerful (1Ki 19:11, w Ac 2:2), quiet but present (Jn 3:8), reviving, life giving (Eze 37:9-10, 14).

Oil (Ps 45:7): healing (Isa 1:6; Lk 10:34; Rev 18:13), joy causing (Isa 61:3; Heb 1:9), illuminating (Zec 4:2-3, 11-13; Mt 25:3-4; 1Jn 2:20, 27), consecrating (Ex 29:7; 30:30; Isa 61:1).

Rain and dew (Ps 72:6): enriching and fertilizing (Eze 34:26-27; Hos 6:3; 10:12; 14:5), refreshing (Ps 68:9; Isa 18:4), abundant (Ps 133:3), imperceptible (2Sa 17:12, w Mk 4:26-28).

Dove (Mt 3:16).

Voice (Isa 6:8): speaking (Mt 10:20), guiding (Isa 30:21, w Jn 16:13), warning (Heb 3:7-11).

Seal (Rev 7:2): impressing (Job 38:14, w 2Co 3:18), guarantee (Eph 1:13-14; 4:30; 2Co 1:22).

See Holy Spirit, Emblems of.

Washings, a symbol of purity. See Washings; Purification. For symbolisms of color, See Colors, Figurative and Symbolic.

See also, Allegory; Instruction, By Object Lessons; By Types; In Religion.

SYMEON See Simeon.

SYMPATHY (Ecc 7:2). Commanded (Ro 12:15; Jas 1:27; 1Pe 3:8). In Christ (Php 2:1-2).

Instances of:

David with Hanun (2Sa 10:2). The Jewish maid with Naaman (2Ki 5:1-4). Job's friends (Job 2:11-13), turned against Job (Job 6:14; 22:29). Ebed-Melech with Jeremiah (Jer 38:7-13). Nebuchadnezzar with Daniel (Da 6:18-23).

The four friends with the crippled man whom they took to Jesus (Mk 2:3-4). Others with the helpless whom they brought to Jesus (Mt 4:24). The good Samaritan with the man who fell among robbers (Lk 10:33-35). The Jews with Martha and Mary (Jn 11:19, 31, 33). The people of Malta with the shipwrecked mariners (Ac 28:1-2).

See Afflicted; Afflictions; Jesus the Christ, Compassion of; Kindness; Pity; Poor.

SYNAGOGUE (place of gathering).

1. Primarily an assembly (Ac 13:43; Jas 2:2). Constitutes a court of justice (Lk 12:11; Ac 9:2). Had powers of criminal courts (Mt 10:17; Mt 23:34; Ac 22:19; 26:11), of ecclesiastical courts (Jn 9:22, 34; 12:42; 16:2).

2. Place of assembly. Scriptures read and expounded in (Ne 8:1-8; 9:3, 5; Mt 4:23; 9:35; 13:54; Mk 1:39; 6:2; Lk 4:15-33; 13:10; Jn 18:20; Ac 9:20; 13:5-44; 14:1; 15:21; 17:2, 10; 18:4, 19, 26).

In Jerusalem (Ac 6:9), Damascus (Ac 9:2, 20), other cities (Ac 14:1; 17:1, 10; 18:4). Built by Jairus (Lk 7:5), Jesus performed healing in (Mt 12:9-13; Lk 13:11-14). Alms given in (Mt 6:2).

Of Satan (Rev 2:9; 3:9).

See Church, Place of Worship; Testaments, Time Between.

SYNAGOGUE, MEN OF THE GREAT Or of the Great Assembly, a college of learned men supposedly organized by Nehemiah after the return from exile (Ne 8-10), to which Jewish tradition attributed the origination and authoritative promulgation of many ordinances and regulations.

SYNOPTIC GOSPELS, THE

A careful comparison of the four Gospels reveals that Matthew, Mark, and Luke are noticeably similar, while John is quite different. The first three Gospels agree extensively in language, in the material they include, and in the order in which events and sayings from the life of Christ are recorded. (Chronological order does not appear to have been rigidly followed in any of the Gospels, however.) Because of this agreement, these three books are called the Synoptic Gospels (syn, "together with"; optic, "seeing"; thus "seeing together"). For an example of agreement in content see Mt 9:2-8; Mk 2:3-12; Lk 5:18-26. An instance of verbatim agreement is found in Mt 10:22a; Mk 13:13a; Lk 21:17. A mathematical comparison shows that 91 percent of Mark's Gospel is contained in Matthew, while 53 percent of Mark is found in Luke. Such agreement raises questions as to the origin of the Synoptic Gospels. Did the authors rely on a common source? Were they interdependent? Questions such as these constitute what is known as the Synoptic Problem. Several suggested solutions have been advanced:

1. The use of oral tradition. Some have thought that tradition had become so stereotyped that it provided a common source from which all the Gospel writers drew.

2. The use of an early Gospel. Some have postulated that the Synoptic authors all had access to an earlier Gospel, now lost.

3. The use of written fragments. Some have assumed that written fragments had been composed concerning various events

from the life of Christ and that these were used by the Synoptic authors.

4. Mutual dependence. Some have suggested that the Synoptic writers drew from each other with the result that what they wrote was often very similar.

5. The use of two major sources. The most common view currently is that the Gospel of Mark and a hypothetical document, called Quelle (German for "source") or Q, were used by Matthew and Luke as sources for most of the materials included in their Gospels.

6. The priority and use of Matthew. Another view suggests that the other two Synoptics drew from Matthew as their main source.

7. A combination of most of the above. This theory assumes that the authors of the Synoptic Gospels made use of oral tradition, written fragments, mutual dependence on other Synoptic writers or on their Gospels, and the testimony of eyewitnesses.

SYNTYCHE (coincidence, success). Christian woman at Philippi (Php 4:2).

SYRACUSE A city of Sicily. Paul visits (Ac 28:12).

SYRIA Highlands lying between the Euphrates river and the Mediterranean Sea. Called Aram, from the son of Shem (Ge 10:22-23; Nu 23:7; 1Ch 1:17; 2:23). In the time of Abraham it seems to have embraced the region between the rivers Tigris and Euphrates (Ge 24:10, w 25:20), including Paddan Aram (Ge 25:20, ftn; 28:5).

Minor kingdoms within the region: Aram Zobah, also called Zobah (1Sa 14:47; 2Sa 8:3; 10:6, 8; 1Ki 11:23; 1Ch 18:5, 9; 19:6; Ps 60, title), Geshur (2Sa 15:8), Aram Rehob, also called Beth Rehob (2Sa 10:6, 8), Damascus (2Sa 8:5-6; 1Ch 18:5-6), Hamath (2Sa 8:9-10).

Conquest of: By David (2Sa 8:3-13), by Jeroboam (2Ki 14:25, 28), by Tiglath-Pileser, king of Assyria (2Ki 16:7-9; 18:33-34). People of, colonized in Samaria by the king of Assyria (2Ki 17:24). Confederate with Nebuchadnezzar (2Ki 24:2; Jer 39:5).

The Roman province of, included the land of Canaan (Lk 2:2-3), and Phoenicia (Mk 7:26; Ac 21:3). The fame of Jesus extended over (Mt 4:24).

Paul goes to, with letters to apprehend the Christians; is converted and begins his evangelistic ministry (Ac 9:1-31). See Paul.

Paul preaches in (Ac 15:41; 18:18; 21:3; Gal 1:21). Damascus, the capital of. See Damascus.

Wars between, and the kingdoms of Judah and Israel. See Israel. Prophecies concerning (Isa 7:8-16; 8:4-7; 17:1-3; Jer 1:15; 49:23-27; Am 1:3-5; Zec 9:1).

SYRIAC See Aramaic.

SYRIAC VERSIONS See Texts and Versions.

SYRIA-MAACHAH See Aram Maacah.

SYRIAN The people of Syria (Lk 4:27). See Aram, 6; Aramaic; Syria.

SYRIAN PHOENICIAN The nationality of a woman whose daughter was cured by Jesus (Mt 15:21-28; Mk 7:24-30).

SYRTIS Banks of quicksand off the coast of Libya (Ac 27:17).

T

TAANACH A city conquered by Joshua (Jos 12:21). Allotted to Manasseh (Jos 17:11; 1Ch 7:29). Canaanites not driven from (Jos 17:12; Jdg 1:27). Assigned to the Levites (Jos 21:25). The scene of Barak's victory (Jdg 5:19). One of Solomon's district governors at (1Ki 4:12).

TAANATH SHILOH (possibly approach to Shiloh IDB). Town on the NE border of Ephraim (Jos 16:6), c. ten miles E of Shechem.

TABALIAH (Yahweh has dipped). The son of Hosah (1Ch 26:11).

TABBAOTH (/ornamental or signet/ ring). A family of temple servants who returned with Zerubbabel (Ezr 2:43; Ne 7:46).

TABBATH (possibly good). A place probably E of the Jordan between Jabesh Gilead and Succoth (Jdg 7:22).

TABEAL See Tabeel, 2.

TABEEL (God [El] is good).

1. A Persian official in Samaria (Ezr 4:7).

2. The father of one whom the kings of Syria and Israel sought to make king in Judah instead of Ahaz (Isa 7:6).

TABERAH (burning). An encampment of Israel in the wilderness where fire of the Lord consumed some complainers (Nu 11:1-3; Dt 9:22), the site is unidentified.

TABERNACLE One existed before Moses received the pattern authorized on Mount Sinai (Ex 33:7-11). The one instituted by Moses was called Sanctuary (Ex 25:8), Tent of Meeting (Ex 27:21; 33:7; 2Ch 5:5), Tabernacle of the Testimony (Ex 38:21; Nu 1:50),

Tent of the Testimony (Nu 17:7-8; 2Ch 24:6), Temple of the Lord (1Sa 1:9; 3:3), House of the Lord (Jos 6:24).

The pattern of, revealed to Moses (Ex 25:9; 26:30; 39:32; 42-43; Ac 7:44; Heb 8:5). Materials for, voluntarily offered (Ex 25:1-8; 35:4-29; 36:3-7). Value of the substance contributed for (Ex 38:24-31). Workmen who constructed it were inspired (Ex 31:1-11; 35:30-35).

Description of: Frame (Ex 26:15-37; 36:20-38). Outer covering (Ex 25:5; 26:7-14; 36:14-19). Second covering (Ex 25:5; 26:14; 35:7, 23; 36:19; 39:34). Curtains of (Ex 26:1-14, 31-37; 27:9-16; 35:15, 17; 36:8-19, 35, 37). Court of (Ex 27:9-17; 38:9-16, 18; 40:8, 33). Holy Place of (Ex 26:31-37; 40:22-26; Heb 9:2-6, 8). The Most Holy Place (Ex 26:33-35; 40:20-21; Heb 9:3-5, 7-8). See Altar; Ark; Atonement Cover; Bread, Consecrated; Lampstand; Cherubim.

Furniture of (Ex 25:10-40; 27:1-8, 19; 37; 38:1-8). See Altar; Ark; Atonement Cover; Bread, Consecrated; Lampstand; Cherubim.

Completed (Ex 39:32). Dedicated (Nu 7). Sanctified (Ex 29:43; 40:9-16; Nu 7:1). Anointed with holy oil (Ex 30:25-26; Lev 8:10; Nu 7:1). Sprinkled with blood (Lev 16:15-20; Heb 9:21, 23). Filled with the cloud of glory (Ex 40:34-38).

How prepared for removal during the travels of the Israelites (Nu 1:51; 4:5-15). How and by whom carried (Nu 4:5-33; 7:6-9). Strangers forbidden to enter (Nu 1:51). Duties of the Levites concerning. See Levites. Defilement of, punished (Lev 15:31; Nu 19:13, 20; Eze 5:11; 23:38). Duties of the priests in relation to. See Priest. Israelites worship at (Nu 10:3; 16:19, 42-43; 20:6; 25:6; 1Sa 2:22; Ps 27:4). Offerings brought to (Lev 17:4; Nu 31:54; Dt 12:5-6, 11-14).

Tribes encamped around, while in the wilderness (Nu 2). All males required to appear before, three times each year (Ex 23:17). Tabernacle tax (Ex 20:11-16).

Carried in front of the Israelites in the line of march (Nu 10:33-36; Jos 3:3-6). The Lord reveals himself at (Lev 1:1; Nu 1:1; 7:89; 12:4-10; Dt 31:14-15).

Pitched at Gilgal (Jos 4:18-19), at Shiloh (Jos 18:1; 19:51; Jdg 18:31; 20:18, 26-27; 21:19; 1Sa 2:14; 4:3-4; Jer 7:12, 14), at Nob (1Sa 21:1-6), at Gibeon (1Ch 21:29). Renewed by David and pitched on Mount Zion (1Ch 15:1; 16:1-2; 2Ch 1:4). Solomon offers sacrifice at (2Ch 1:3-6). Brought to the temple by Solomon (2Ch 5:5, w 1Ki 8:1, 4-5).

Symbol of spiritual things (Ps 15:1; Heb 8:2, 5; 9:1-12, 24). See Levites; Priest; Temple.

TABERNACLES, FEAST OF Also called the Feast of Ingathering. Instituted (Ex 23:16; 34:22; Lev 23:34-43; Nu 29:12-40; Dt 16:13-16). Design of (Lev 23:42-43). The law read in connection with, every seventh year (Dt 31:10-12; Ne 8:18). Observance of, after the captivity (Ezr 3:4; Ne 8:14-18), by Jesus (Jn 7:2, 14). Observance of, omitted (Ne 8:17). Penalty for not observing (Zec 14:16-19).

Jeroboam institutes an idolatrous feast to correspond to, in the eighth month (1Ki 12:32-33; 1Ch 27:11).

TABITHA (gazelle). A Christian woman in Joppa; befriended poor widows; raised from dead by Peter (Ac 9:36-43).

TABLE

1. Table for food (Jdg 1:7; 1Ki 2:7).

2. Lord's table = Lord's Supper (1Co 10:21).

3. "Wait on tables" (Ac 6:2) refers to distribution of food, etc., to the Christian poor.

4. Tabernacle and temple were provided with various tables (Ex 25:23-30).

TABLE OF CONSECRATED BREAD Twelve loaves of consecrated, unleavened bread were placed on a table in the Holy Place in the tabernacle and temple (Ex 25:30; Lev 24:5-9).

TABLET

1. Stone or clay tablets for writing (Ex 24:12; Eze 4:1; Lk 1:63). Metaphorical (2Co 3:3). See Tablets of the Law.

2. See Dress.

TABLETS OF THE LAW Stone tablets on which Moses wrote the Ten Commandments (Ex 31:18; 32:15-16; Dt 4:13; 5:22). See Commandments and Statutes, Of God.

TABOR

1. A mountain on the border of Issachar (Jos 19:22; Jdg 8:18; Ps 89:12; Jer 46:18; Hos 5:1). Assembling place of Barak's army (Jdg 4:6, 12, 14).

2. A plain located by the great tree of Tabor (1Sa 10:3).

3. A Levitical city in Zebulun (1Ch 6:77).

See Kisloth Tabor.

TABRET See Tambourine.

TABRIMMON (/pagan god/ Rimmon is good). The father of Ben-Hadad, king of Syria (1Ki 15:18).

TACHE See Clasp.

TACHMONITE See Tahkemonite.

TACKLE The masts and rigging of a ship (Isa 33:23; Ac 27:19).

TACT (Pr 15:1; 25:15). In preaching (1Co 9:19-22; 2Co 12:6). Of Gideon (Jdg 8:1-3). Of Saul, in managing malcontents (1Sa 10:27; 11:7, 12-15). Nabal's wife (1Sa 25:18-37). In David's popular methods: In mourning for Abner (2Sa 3:28-37), in organizing the temple music (1Ch 15:16-24), in securing popular consent to bringing the ark to Jerusalem (1Ch 13:1-4). Mephibosheth (2Sa 9:8). Joab's trick in obtaining David's consent to the return of Absalom (2Sa 14:1-22). The woman of Tekoa (2Sa 14:4-20). The wise woman of Abel (2Sa 20:16-22). Solomon, in arbitrating between the harlots (1Ki 3:24-28).

Mordecai, in concealing Esther's nationality (Est 2:10). Esther, in placating the king (Est 5-7). Paul, in circumcising Timothy (Ac 16:3), in turning the preaching of adversaries to account (Php 1:10-22), in stimulating benevolent giving (2Co 8:1-8; 9:1-5), in

arraying the two religious factions of the Jews against each other when he was in trouble (Ac 23:6-10). The town clerk of Ephesus (Ac 19:35-41). The church council at Jerusalem (Ac 21:20-25).

See Wisdom.

TACTICS See Armies; Strategy.

TADMOR (palm tree). A city in the desert NE of Damascus (1Ki 9:18; 2Ch 8:4), a fabulously rich trade metropolis later called Palmyra. Magnificent ruins have been excavated.

TAHAN, TAHANITE (possibly grace, favor).
1. The son of Ephraim and his clan (Nu 26:35).
2. A descendant of Ephraim (1Ch 7:25).

TAHAPANES See Tahpanhes.

TAHASH (a species of dolphin). The son of Nahor and Reumah (Ge 22:24).

TAHATH (compensation).
1. Camping place of the Israelites (Nu 33:26-27).
2. A Kohathite (1Ch 6:24, 37).
3. The name of two Ephraimites (1Ch 7:20).

TAHKEMONITE The family of David's chief captain (2Sa 23:8); also spelled Hacmonite (1Ch 11:11).

TAHPANHES (the fortress of Penhase [the Black Man]). A fortress city at the E edge of the Nile Delta to which Israelites fled after the fall of Jerusalem (Jer 2:16; 43:7-9; 44:1; 46:14; Eze 30:18).

TAHPENES (title wife of the king). A queen of Egypt (1Ki 11:19-20).

TAHREA (possibly clever one BDB). The grandson of Mephibosheth (1Ch 9:41); also spelled Tarea (1Ch 8:35).

TAHTIM HODSHI A place E of Jordan in the land of the Hittites (2Sa 24:6).

TAILORING (Ex 31:2-3, 6, 10; 39:1).

TALEBEARER (The vice of repeating damaging reports, either true or false). (Ps 15:1-3; Pr 11:13; 20:19).
Separates friends (Pr 16:28; 17:9). Causes strife (Pr 26:20), tension (Pr 18:8).
Is forbidden (Lev 19:16; 1Ti 5:11, 13).
See Busybody; Gossip; Slander; Speaking, Evil.
Instances of: Joseph (Ge 37:2). Israelites (2Sa 3:23). Tobiah (Ne 6).
See Backbiting; Slander.

TALENT A weight equal to sixty minas or about seventy-five pounds (1Ki 9:14, 28; 10:10, 14; Ex 25:39; 38:27). Parables of the (Mt 18:23-34; 25:15-30). See Measure.

TALES Avoid myths and old wives' tales (1Ti 4:7). See Myths.

TALITHA KOUM Aramaic for "Little girl, get up!" (Mk 5:41).

TALKING With God. See Communion.

TALMAI (possibly [my] furrow maker).
1. A son of Anak (Nu 13:22; Jos 15:14; Jdg 1:10).
2. King of Geshur (2Sa 3:3; 13:37; 1Ch 3:2).

TALMON (perhaps brightness). A gatekeeper of the temple (1Ch 9:17). Family of, returned from captivity with Zerubbabel (Ezr 2:42; Ne 7:45; 11:19; 12:25).

TALMUD (education, instruction). A collection of Jewish tradition of the early Christian centuries; The two forms: Palestinian and Babylonian.

TAMAH See Temah.

TAMAR (date palm).
1. The wife of Er, then of Onan; mother of Perez and Zerah (Ge 38; Mt 1:3).
2. Daughter of David; abused by her half brother Amon (2Sa 13:1-33).
3. The daughter of Absalom (2Sa 14:27).
4. Unidentified borderland site in restored Israel (Eze 47:19; 48:28).
5. A city in Syria, more commonly known as Tadmor, later Palmyra.

TAMARISK A tree (1Sa 22:6; 31:13), planted by Abraham (Ge 21:33). See Tree.

TAMBOURINE Used by Miriam (Ex 15:20), by Jephthah's daughter (Jdg 11:34). Used in religious service (2Sa 6:5; 1Ch 13:8; Ps 68:25; 81:2; 149:3; 150:4). Used in dances (Job 21:12). See Music, Instruments of.

TAMIR See Tadmor.

TAMMUZ
1. Month four in sacred sequence, month ten in civil sequence. Not mentioned by name in the Bible. Ezekiel called in the fourth month (Eze 1:1); Nebuchadnezzar breaks through the wall of Jerusalem (Jer 39:1). The time for tending vines (June-July). See Month, 4.
2. The fertility god worshiped in Mesopotamia, Syria, and Israel; corresponded to Osiris in Egypt and Adonis of the Greeks (Eze 8:14).

TANACH See Taanach.

TANHUMETH (comfort). The father of Seraiah (2Ki 25:23; Jer 40:8).

TANIS See Zoar.

TANNER, TANNING Tanning is the conversion of skin into leather by removing the hair and soaking it in tanning solution (Ex 25:5; 26:14; Ac 10:6).

TANTALIZING NIV "provoking" (1Sa 1:6-7); "taunt" (1Ki 18:27).

TAPESTRY (Pr 7:16; 31:22). Of the tabernacle (Ex 26:1-14, 31-37; 27:9-17; 36:8-18). Gold thread woven in (Ex 39:3). In palaces (Est 1:6; SS 1:5). In groves (2Ki 23:7). See Curtains; Embroidery; Veil.

TAPHATH (possibly little child). The daughter of Solomon (1Ki 4:11).

TAPPUAH (apple).
1. A city of Judah (Jos 12:17; 15:34).
2. A city in Ephraim (Jos 16:8; 17:8).
3. A city near Tirzah in Samaria (2Ki 15:16); a variant reading for Tiphsah. See Tiphsah, 2.
4. The son of Hebron (1Ch 2:43).

TAR A flammable substance, asphalt (Ge 14:10). Lumps of asphalt are often seen even today floating in the southern end of the Dead Sea. Used as mortar in building the Tower of Babel (Ge 11:3), and in setting the burnt brick which formed the outer layers of the ziggurat of Ur. It was used by Moses' mother to caulk the papyrus basket (Ex 2:3), as for the rafts and reed boats on the Euphrates.
See Caulkers; Pitch.

TARAH See Terah, 2.

TARALAH A city of Benjamin between Irpeel and Zelah (Jos 18:28).

TAREA A son of Micah (1Ch 8:35). Called Tahrea (1Ch 9:41).

TARES See Weeds, 2.

TARGET A defensive article of armor. Made of bronze (1Sa 17:6), of gold (1Ki 10:16; 2Ch 9:15). Used by spearmen (2Ch 14:8).
See Shield.

TARIFF See Duty, 1.

TARPELITES See Tripolis.

TARSHISH (possibly [precious stone] yellow jasper BDB; possibly greedy one IDB; foundry, refinery KB).
1. The son of Javan (Ge 10:4).
2. A place in the W Mediterranean, perhaps in Spain or Tunisia (2Ch 9:21; 20:36-37; Ps 72:10; Jn 1:3).
3. "Ships of Tarshish"; large, seagoing trade ships (1Ki 9:26; 10:22; 22:48; 2Ch 9:21).
4. Great-grandson of Benjamin (1Ch 7:10).
5. Persian prince (Est 1:14).

TARSUS Capital of Cilicia, in Asia Minor. Paul's birthplace (Ac 9:11; 21:39; 22:3). Paul sent to, from Jerusalem, to avoid assassination (Ac 9:30). Paul brought from, by Barnabas (Ac 11:25-26).

TARTAK A god worshiped by Avvites, colonists in Samaria (2Ki 17:31).

TARTAN See Supreme Commander.

TASKMASTER One who burdens another with labor: overseer (Ex 1:11; 3:7; 5:6, 10, 13).

TASSEL(S) Prescribed for garments worn by the Israelites, to remember God's commands (Nu 15:38-41; Dt 22:12). Made long by the Pharisees (Mt 23:5).

TASTE The sense of, lost (2Sa 19:35). Figurative (Job 27:2; Ps 34:8; 119:103; Heb 6:4-5; 1Pe 2:3); taste death (Mt 16:28; Mk 9:1; Lk 9:27; Jn 8:52; Heb 2:9). See Savor; Savory Meat.

TATTENAI The Persian governor ordered to assist the Jews in rebuilding the temple (Ezr 5:3, 6; 6:6, 13).

TATTLER See Gossip; Talebearer.

TATTOO Pagan custom; forbidden (Lev 19:28). See Mark.

TAVERNS, THREE A place, c. thirty-three miles SE of Rome where Paul met Roman Christians (Ac 28:15).

TAX Census (Ex 30:11-16; 38:26; Ne 10:32; Lk 2:1). Jesus pays (Mt 17:24-27).
Land (Ge 41:34, 48; 2Ki 23:35). Land mortgaged for (Ne 5:3-4). Priests exempted from (Ge 47:26; Ezr 7:24). Paid in grain (Am 5:11; 7:1), in provisions (1Ki 4:7-28).
Personal (1Ki 9:15; 2Ki 15:19-20; 23:35). Resisted by Israelites (1Ki 12:18; 2Ch 10:18). Worldwide, levied by Caesar.
Collectors of See Tax Collectors.

TAX COLLECTORS Disreputable (Isa 33:18; Da 11:20; Mt 5:46-47; 9:11; 11:19; 18:17; 21:31; Lk 18:11). Repent under the preaching of John the Baptist (Mt 21:32; Lk 3:12; 7:29). Matthew, the collector of Capernaum, becomes an apostle (Mt 9:9; 10:3; Mk 2:14; Lk 5:27). Parable concerning (Lk 18:9-14). Zacchaeus, chief among, receives Jesus into his house (Lk 19:2-10).

TEACHERS Samuel, head of school of the prophets (1Sa 19:20). Elisha, head of, at Gilgal (2Ki 4:38).
Itinerant (2Ch 17:7-9). Of public assemblies (Ne 8:1-8, 13, 18). Should receive compensation (Gal 6:6).
See Instruction; Jesus, Teacher; Minister, Duties of.

False:
Admonition against (Dt 13:1-3; Mt 5:19; 7:15; 15:2-20; 23:2-33; Lk 11:38-52).
See Heresy; Minister, False and Corrupt.

TEACHING See Instruction; Minister, Duties of.

TEAR See Rending.

TEARS (Ps 6:6; 39:12; 42:3). Wash Jesus' feet (Lk 7:38, 44). Observed by God (Ps 56:8; Isa 38:3-5). Wiped away (Rev 7:17). None in heaven (Rev 21:4). Figurative (Ps 80:5).

TEBAH (possibly one born at the time or place of slaughtering KB IDB).
1. The son of Nahor (Ge 22:24).
2. A city of Zobah, E of Anti-Lebanon Mountains (1Ch 18:7-9, ftn); a city belonging to Hadadezer, Hebrew Betah (2Sa 8:8, ftn).

TEBALIAH See Tabaliah.

TEBETH Month ten in sacred sequence, month four in civil sequence (December-January). Esther taken to King Xerxes (Est 2:16). See Month, 10.

TECHNICALITIES Legal (Mt 12:2, 10; Lk 6:2, 7).

TEETH (Pr 10:26). Gnashing of (Ps 112:10; La 2:16; Mt 8:12; 13:42, 50; 22:13; 24:51; 25:30; Mk 9:18; Lk 13:28).

TEHAPHNEHES See Tahpanhes.

TEHINNAH (supplication for favor). The son of Eshton (1Ch 4:12).

TEIL TREE See Terebinth.

TEKEL Weighed (Da 5:25, 27).

TEKOA, TEKOITE
1. The son of Ashhur (1Ch 2:24; 4:5). Some authorities interpret these passages to mean that Ashhur colonized the town of Tekoa.
2. A city in Judah (2Ch 11:6). Home of the woman who interceded for Absalom (2Sa 14:2, 4, 9). Rebuilt by Rehoboam (2Ch 11:6). Desert of (2Ch 20:20). People of, work on the new wall of Jerusalem (Ne 3:5, 27). Prophecy concerning (Jer 6:1). Home of Amos (Am 1:1).

TEKOAH See Tekoa, 2.

TEL A mound or hill that marks the site of an ancient city. Composed of accumulated debris, usually covering a number of archaeological or historical periods and showing numerous building levels or strata (Dt 13:16; Jer 30:18). In the following four place names.

TEL ABIB (mound of barley ISBE; Akkadian mound of storm tide KB; mound of flood IDB). A place on the Kebar River where Ezekiel lived (Eze 3:15).

TEL ASSAR (ruined city mound of Assar). A city or district conquered by the Assyrians (2Ki 19:12; Isa 37:12).

TEL HARSHA (the ruined city mound of the deaf mute). A place in Babylonia (Ezr 2:59; Ne 7:61).

TEL MELAH (ruined city and mound of salt). Babylonian town, probably not far N of Persian Gulf (Ezr 2:59; Ne 7:61).

TELAH (fissure, split, fracture). The son of Rephah (1Ch 7:25).

TELAIM (lambs). The place where Saul mustered an army against Amalek (1Sa 15:4), may be the same as Telem in Judah (Jos 15:24).

TELEM (brightness).
1. A city of Judah (Jos 15:24).
2. A gatekeeper who put away his Gentile wife (Ezr 10:24).

TELL EL AMARNA See Amarna, Tell El; Ras Shamra.

TEMA (on the right side, hence south country).
1. The son of Ishmael (Ge 25:15; 1Ch 1:30).
2. A people of Arabia, probably descended from Tema, Ishmael's son (Job 6:19; Isa 21:14; Jer 25:23).

TEMAH One of the temple servants (Ezr 2:53; Ne 7:55).

TEMAN (on the right side, hence south country).
1. The grandson of Esau (Ge 36:11).
2. Edomite chief (Ge 36:42).
3. A city in NE Edom (Jer 49:7).

TEMANI, TEMANITE(S) (on the right side, southern). Inhabitant of Teman (Ge 36:34). Of Eliphaz, one of Job's friends (Job 2:11; 4:1).

TEMENI (one from the right, hence southerner). The son of Ashhur (1Ch 4:6).

TEMPER See Anger; Malice; Self-Control.

TEMPERANCE (Php 4:5; Tit 1:8; 2Pe 1:6). In eating (Pr 23:1-3; 25:16). In the use of wine (1Ti 3:8; Tit 2:3).
Commanded (Ro 13:14; 1Th 5:6-8; 1Ti 3:2; Tit 2:2-3, 12; 2Pe 1:5-6).
Practiced: By athletes (1Co 9:25, 27). By Daniel (Da 1:8, 12-16).
See Abstinence; Drunkenness; Self-Control; Wine.

TEMPLE

Solomon's:

Described—
Also called Father's House (Jn 2:16). Glorious Temple (Isa 60:7). Holy Mountain (Isa 27:13). Holy and Glorious Temple (Isa 64:11). Holy Temple (Ps 79:1; 1Ch 29:3). House of Prayer (Isa 56:7; Mt 21:13). House of God (1Ch 29:2). House of the God of Jacob (Isa 2:3). House of the Lord (Jer 26:9). Mountain of the Lord's Temple (Isa 2:2). Palatial structure (1Ch 29:1, 19). Sanctuary (2Ch 20:8; 2Ch 36:17). Temple of the Lord (2Ki 11:10; 2Ch 23:9). Temple for Sacrifice (2Ch 7:12). Tent of the Testimony (2Ch 24:6). Zion (Ps 20:2; 48:12; 74:2; 87:2; Isa 2:3).
Greatness of (2Ch 2:5-6). Beauty of (Isa 64:11). Holiness of (1Ki 8:10; 9:3; La 1:10; Mt 23:17; Jn 2:14-16).

History—
David undertakes the building of (2Sa 7:2-3; 1Ch 22:7; 28:2; Ps 132:2-5; Ac 7:46), forbidden of God because he was a warrior (2Sa 7:4-12; 1Ki 5:3; 1Ch 22:8; 28:3). Not asked for by God (2Sa 7:7). The building of, committed to Solomon (2Sa 7:13). David makes preparations of (1Ch 22; 28:14-18; 29:1-5; 2Ch 3:1; 5:1).
Solomon builds (Ac 7:47; 2Sa 7:13). Solomon conscripts laborers for the building of (1Ki 5:13-16; 2Ch 2:2, 17-18). Materials for, furnished by Hiram (1Ki 5:8-18). Pattern and building of (1Ki 6; 7:13-51; 1Ch 28:11-19; 2Ch 3; 4; Ac 7:47). Time when begun (1Ki 6:1, 37; 2Ch 3:2), finished (1Ki 6:38). Site of (1Ch 21:28-30; 22:1; 2Ch 3:1), where Abraham offered Isaac (Ge 22:2, 4).
Materials prepared for (1Ki 5:17-18). No tools used on temple site (1Ki 6:7). Foundations of (1Ki 5:17-18; Lk 21:5).
Destroyed by Nebuchadnezzar, and the valuable contents carried to Babylon (2Ki 24:13; 25:9-17; 2Ch 36:7, 19; Ps 79:1; Isa 64:11; Jer 27:16, 19-22; 28:3; 52:13, 17-23; La 2:7; 4:1; Ezr 1:7). Vessels of, used by Belshazzar (Da 5:2-3). Destruction of, foretold (Isa 66:6; Jer 27:18-22; Eze 7:22, 25; Mt 24:2; Mk 13:2). Restoration of, ordered by Cyrus (Ezr 1:7-11).

Areas and Furnishings of—
Inner Sanctuary (1Ki 6:19-20; 8:6). Called the Most Holy Place (2Ch 3:8), innermost room (1Ki 6:27).
Most Holy Place: Description of (1Ki 6:16, 19-35; 2Ch 3:8-14; 4:22). Contents of the Most Holy Place: Ark (1Ki 6:19; 8:6; 2Ch 5:2-10), cherubim (1Ki 6:23-28; 2Ch 3:10-13; 5:7-8). Called Holy Place (1Ki 8:8, 10), the main hall (2Ch 3:5). Description of (1Ki 6:15-18; 2Ch 3:3, 5-7, 14-17). *See Ark; Atonement Cover; Cherubim; Curtains; Veil.*
Holy Place (1Ki 8:8, 10). Contents of the holy place: The Golden table of the Bread of Presence (1Ki 7:48; 2Ch 29:18). *See Bread, Consecrated.* Other tables of gold and silver (1Ch 28:16; 2Ch 4:18-19). Lampstands and their utensils (1Ki 7:49-50; 1Ch 28:15; 2Ch 4:7, 20-22). *See Lampstand.* Altar of incense and its furniture (1Ki 6:20; 7:48, 50; 1Ch 28:17-18; 2Ch 4:19, 22). *See Altar of Incense.*
Porch of, called Porch of the Lord (2Ch 15:8). Dimensions of (1Ki 6:3; 2Ch 3:4). Doors of (2Ch 29:7). Overlaid with gold (2Ch 3:4). Pillars of (1Ki 7:15-22; 2Ki 11:14; 23:3; 25:17; 2Ch 3:15-17; 4:12-13).
Structure around (1Ki 6:5-10; 2Ki 11:2-3). Offerings brought to (Ne 10:37-39). Treasuries in. *See Treasure.*
Courts of: Of the priests (2Ch 4:9), inner (1Ki 6:36), surrounded by rows of stones and cedar beams (1Ki 6:36; 7:12). Contents of the courts: Altar of burnt offering (2Ch 15:8). *See Altar.* The Sea of cast metal (1Ki 7:23-37, 44, 46; 2Ch 4:2-5, 10), ten basins (1Ki 7:38-46; 2Ch 4:6). Large court of (2Ch 4:9; Jer 19:14; 26:2).
Sabbath canopy and royal entryway (2Ki 16:18).
Gates of: Upper Gate (2Ch 15:35). New Gate (Jer 26:10; 36:10). Gate facing east (Eze 46:1, 12). Gifts received at (2Ch 24:8-11).

Uses of—
A dwelling place of the Lord (1Ki 8:10-11, 13; 9:3; 2Ki 21:7; 1Ch 29:1; 2Ch 5:13-14; 7:1-3, 16; Eze 10:3-4; Mic 1:2), to contain the ark of the covenant (1Ki 8:21), for the offering of fragrant incense (2Ch 2:4), for the regular offering of consecrated bread and the burnt offerings (2Ch 2:4), for prayer and worship (1Ki 8; 2Ki 19:14-15; 2Ch 30:27; Isa 27:13; 56:7; Jer 7:2; 26:2; Eze 46:2-3, 9; Zec 7:3; 8:21-22; Mk 11:17; Lk 1:10; 2:37; 18:10; Ac 3:1; 22:17), prayer made toward (1Ki 8:38; Da 6:10; Jnh 2:4), for weapon storage (2Ki 11:10; 2Ch 23:9-10), for refuge (2Ki 11:15; Ne 6:10-11).

Facts About—
Dedication of (1Ki 8; 2Ch 5-7), services in, organized by David (1Ch 15:16; 23:24). Sacking and pillaging by Shishak (1Ki 14:25-26), by Jehoash, king of Israel (2Ki 14:14). Repaired by Jehoash, king of Judah (2Ki 12:4-14; 2Ch 24:7-14), by Josiah (2Ki 22:3-7; 2Ch 34:8-13). Ahaz changes the detailed plans (2Ki 16:10-17). Purified by Hezekiah (2Ch 29:15-19). Converted into an idolatrous shrine by Manasseh (2Ki 21:4-7; 2Ch 33:4-7).
Treasures of, used in the purchase of peace: By Asa, from Ben-Hadad (1Ki 15:18), by Jehoash, king of Judah, from Hazael (2Ki 12:18), by Hezekiah, from the king of Assyria (2Ki 18:15-16). Jews swore by (Mt 23:16-22).

Ezekiel's Vision: (Eze 37:26, 28; 40-48).

The Second:

Rebuilt by Zerubbabel (Ezr 1; 2:68-69; 3:2-13; 4; 5:2-17; 6:3-5; Ne 7:70-72; Isa 44:28; Hag 2:3). Building of, suspended (Ezr 4), resumed (Ezr 4:24; 5; 6; Hag 1:2-9; 2:15; Zec 8:9), finished (Ezr 6:14-15), dedicated (Ezr 6:15-18). Artaxerxes' favorable action toward (Ezr 7:11-28; 8:25-34).
Prophecies of its restoration (Isa 44:28; Da 8:13-14; Hag 1; 2; Zec 1:16; 4:8-10; 6:12-15; 8:9-15; Mal 3:1).

Herod's:
Forty-six years in building (Jn 2:20). Massive and beautiful stones of (Mk 13:1; Lk 21:5). Magnificence of (Mt 24:1). Beautiful gate of (Ac 3:10). Solomon's Colonnade (Jn 10:23; Ac 3:11; 5:12). Treasury of (Mk 12:41-44). Zechariah receives promise of a son (Lk 1:5-23, w 1:57-64). Jesus the infant brought to, according to the law and custom (Lk 2:21-39), Simeon blesses Jesus in (Lk 2:25-35), Anna the prophetess never left (Lk 2:36-37).

Jesus in, when a youth (Lk 2:46), taken to the highest point of, in his temptation (Mt 4:5-7; Lk 4:9-12), teaches in (Mk 11:27-33; 12:35-44; 14:49; Jn 5:14-47; 7:14-28; 8; 10:23-38; 18:20), performs miracles in (Mt 21:14-15), drives money changers from (Mt 21:12-13; Mk 11:15-17; Lk 19:45-46; Jn 2:15-16).
Officer of temple guard (Lk 22:52; Ac 4:1; 5:24, 26). Judas threw the money into (Mt 27:5). Veil of, torn at the time of the crucifixion (Mt 27:51).
The disciples worship in, after the resurrection (Lk 24:53; Ac 2:46; 3:1). Peter heals the crippled man at the gate of (Ac 3:1-16). Disciples preach in (Ac 5:20-21, 42). Paul's vision in (Ac 22:17-21). Paul observes the rights of (Ac 21:26-30), is arrested in (Ac 21:33).
Prophecies concerning its destruction, by Daniel (Da 8:11-15; 11:30-31). Jesus predicts the destruction of (Mt 24; Mk 13:2; Lk 21:6).

Figurative:
Of the body of Jesus (Mt 26:61; 27:40; Jn 2:19). Of the indwelling of God (1Co 3:16-17; 2Co 6:16). Of the church (Eph 2:21; 2Th 2:4; Rev 3:12). Of the kingdom of Christ (Rev 11; 14:15, 17). Of Christ, the head of the church, sending forth the forces of righteousness against the powers of evil (Rev 15:5-8; 16:1-17).

Idolatrous:
Of Dagon, at Ashdod (1Sa 5:2), of the calves, at Bethel (1Ki 12:31, 33), of Rimmon, at Damascus (2Ki 5:18), of Baal, at Samaria (2Ki 10:21, 27), at Babylon (2Ch 36:7; Da 1:2), of Diana, at Ephesus (Ac 19:27).
Trophies stored in (1Sa 31:10; 1Ch 10:9-10; Da 1:2).
See Tabernacle.

TEMPLE SERVANTS Large group of servants who performed menial tasks in the temple (1Ch 9:2; Ezr 2:43-58; 8:17-20; Ne 7:46-56), probably descended from Midianites (Nu 31:47), Gibeonites (Jos 9:23), and other captives. Usually listed with the priests, Levites, singers, and gatekeepers (Ezr 2:70).

TEMPORAL BLESSINGS See Blessings.

TEMPTATION (*trial, proof*). Has two meanings: Any attempt to entice or tempt into evil; a testing which aims at an ultimate spiritual good.

Temptation to Evil:
(Pr 12:26; Ro 8:35-39). Called snares of death (Pr 13:14; 14:27). The way of escape from (1Co 10:13). Christ gives help in (Heb 2:18; 4:15; Rev 3:10). The Lord delivers from (2Pe 2:9).

Benefits of: (Jas 1:2-4, 12; 1Pe 1:6-7).

Leading into:
To be avoided (Mt 5:29-30; 6:9; Mk 9:42-48; Lk 17:1; Ro 14:13, 15, 21; 1Co 7:5; 8:9-13; 10:28-32). Prayer against being led into (Mt 6:13; 26:41; Mk 14:38; Lk 11:4; 22:40, 46). Not to lead others into (Ro 14:13-15, 21; 1Co 7:5; 8:9-13; 10:28-32).

Instances of—
Abraham, of Pharaoh (Ge 12:18-19), of Abimelech (Ge 20:9). Rebekah, of Jacob (Ge 27:6-14). Balak, of Balaam (Nu 22:5-7, 16-17; 23:11-13, 25-27). Eli's sons, of Israel (1Sa 2:24-25). Gideon, of Israel (Jdg 8:27). The old prophet of Bethel, of the prophet of Judah (1Ki 13:15-19). Jeroboam, of Israel (1Ki 15:30, 34).

Resistance to:
Commanded (Dt 7:25-26; Pr 1:10-19; 4:14-15; 5:3, 8; 19:27; Mt 24:42-44; 25:13; 26:41; Mk 13:21-22; 13:33-37; 14:37-38; Ro 6:12-14; 12:21; Eph 6:11, 13-17; Jas 4:7; 1Pe 5:8-9; 1Jn 4:4). Source of resistance (Ps 17:4; 73:2-25; 94:17-18).
Rewards to those who resist (Isa 33:15-16; Jas 1:12; Rev 3:10).

Instances of—
Joseph (Ge 39:7-12). Balaam (Nu 22:7-18, 38; 23:7-12, 18-24). David (2Sa 16:5-25). The prophet of Judah (1Ki 13:7-9). Micaiah (1Ki 22:13-28). The people of Jerusalem (Isa 18:30-36). Job (Job 1:6-21; 2:4-10; 31:1, 5-17, 19-34, 38-40). Recabites (Jer 35:5-9). Nehemiah (Ne 4:9).
Jesus (Mt 4:1-11; 26:38-42; Lk 4:1-3; Heb 4:15; 12:3-4).

Sources of:
Cherished pleasures (Mt 5:29-30; 18:7-9; Mk 9:43-45). Evil company (Ex 34:13-16; Pr 2:10-16). Adultery and sexual desires (Pr 5:1-20; 6:24-29; 7:1-27; 9:15-18; Ecc 7:26). Sinful desires (Ro 7:5; Gal 5:17; Jas 1:13-15; 2Pe 2:18; 1Jn 2:16-17). False teachers (Mt 18:6-7; Lk 17:1; 1Jn 2:26; 4:1-3; Rev 2:20). Persecutions (Jn 16:1-2). Prosperity (Dt 8:10-17; Lk 12:16-21). Riches (Mt 19:16-24; Mk 10:17-30; 1Ti 6:9-10). Cares, riches and pleasures (Mt 13:22; Lk 8:13-14; 21:34-38).
Satan (Ge 3:1-5; 1Ch 21:1; Mk 4:15, 17; Lk 22:3, 31-32; 2Co 2:11; 11:3, 14-15; 12:7; Gal 4:14; Eph 4:27; 6:11, 13-17; 1Th 3:5; 1Ti 5:15; Jas 4:7; 1Pe 5:8-9; Rev 12:10-11, 17). Wicked people (Pr 16:29; 28:10; Hos 7:5; Am 2:12; Mt 5:19; 2Ti 3:13).
See Demons; Faith, Trial of; Satan.

Warnings Against Yielding to:
(Ex 34:12-16; Dt 8:11-20; Pr 2:10-16; 5:1-21; 6:27-28; 7:1-27; 9:15-18; Ecc 7:26; Jer 2:25; Mt 26:31, 41; Mk 14:37-38; Lk 21:34-36; 22:40; 1Co 16:13; Eph 6:11, 13-17; Heb 12:3-4; 1Pe 4:7; 5:8-9; 2Pe 3:17; Rev 3:2-3).

Instances of—
Adam and Eve (Ge 3:1-19). Sarah, to lie (Ge 12:13; 18:13-15; 20:13). Isaac, to lie (Ge 26:7). Jacob to defraud Esau (Ge 27:6-13). Balaam (Nu 22:15-22; 2Pe 2:15). Achan (Jos 7:21). David, to commit adultery (2Sa 11:2-5), to number Israel (1Ch 21). Solomon, to become an idolater through the influences of his wives (1Ki 11:4; Ne 13:26). The prophet of Judah (1Ki 13:11-19). Hezekiah (2Ki 20:12-20; Isa 39:1-4, 6-7). Peter (Mt 26:69-74; Mk 14:66-71; Lk 22:55-60).

Of Jesus:
(Lk 22:28). In all points as we are (Heb 4:15). By the devil (Mt 4:1-11; Lk 4:1-13). Before his crucifixion (Mt 26:38-42).

Test of God:

Design of, a test (Ps 66:10-13; 119:101, 110; Da 12:10; Zec 13:9; 1Pe 1:6-7; 4:12). Of fidelity (Dt 13:1-3; 2Ch 32:31; Job 1:8-22; 2:3-10). Of obedience (Ge 22:1-14; Dt 8:2, 5; Heb 11:17). Benefits of (Jas 1:2-4, 12; 1Pe 1:6-7). Rewards of (Isa 33:15-16; Lk 12:35-38; Jas 1:12; 1Jn 4:4).
See Affliction; Afflictions; Faith, Trial of.

TEN Used for an indefinite number (Ge 31:7; Lev 26:26; Nu 14:22; Zec 8:23).

TEN COMMANDMENTS See *Commandments and Statutes, Of God; Decalogue.*

TENANTS Evicted (Mt 21:41; Mk 12:9; Lk 20:16).

TENONS NIV "projections" on tabernacle boards to hold the boards in place (Ex 26:17).

TENSION See *Anxiety.*

TENT Used for dwelling (Ge 4:20), by Noah (Ge 9:21), by Abraham (Ge 12:8; 13:18; 18:1), by Lot (Ge 13:5), by Moses (Ex 18:7), by Israelites (Nu 24:5-6; 2Sa 20:1; 1Ki 12:16), by the Midianites (Jdg 6:5), by Cushites (Hab 3:7), by Arabs (Isa 13:20), by shepherds (Isa 38:12; Jer 6:3). Women had tents apart from men (Ge 24:67; 31:33). Used for cattle (Ge 14:15). Manufacture of (Ac 18:3). Used as a place of worship. *See Tabernacle.*

TERAH
1. The son of Nahor (Ge 11:24-25), father of Abraham, Nahor, Haran (Ge 11:26), idolater (Jos 24:2), went as far as Haran with Abraham (Ge 11:24-32).
2. The encampment of the Israelites in wilderness (Nu 33:27-28).

TERAPHIM See *Household Gods; Idolatry.*

TEREBINTH A small tree (Isa 6:13; Hos 4:13).

TERESH (perhaps *desire*). A Persian eunuch. Plotted against Xerxes (Est 2:21-23; 6:2).

TERRACE Steps leading up to the temple (2Ch 9:11).

TERROR Extreme fear or dread; or sometimes the one who causes such agitation (Ge 35:5; Ps 55:4; 2Co 5:11).

TERTIUS (*third*). Paul's amanuensis in writing the book of Romans (Ro 16:22).

TERTULLUS (*third*). Diminutive of Tertius; lawyer employed by the Jews to state their case against Paul before Felix (Ac 24:1).

TESTAMENT
1. A covenant. See *Covenant.*
2. Testamentary disposition or will. See *Will, A Testament.*
3. Divisions of the English Bible. See *New Testament, Old Testament.*

TESTAMENTS OF THE TWELVE PROPHETS A pseudepigraphal document that claims to report the last words of the twelve sons of Jacob; probably written c. second century A.D.

TESTAMENTS, TIME BETWEEN A time of the realignment of traditional power blocs and the passing of a Near Eastern cultural tradition that had been dominant for almost 3000 years.
In biblical history, the approximately 400 years that separate the birth of Nehemiah from the birth of Christ are known as the intertestamental period (c. 432-5 B.C.). Sometimes called the "silent" years, they were anything but silent. The events, literature and social forces of these years would shape the world of the NT.

History:
With the Babylonian captivity, Israel ceased to be an independent nation and became a minor territory in a succession of larger empires. Very little is known about the latter years of Persian domination because the Jewish historian Josephus, our primary source for the intertestamental period, all but ignores them.
With Alexander the Great's acquisition of Israel (332 B.C.), a new and more insidious threat to Israel emerged. Alexander was committed to the creation of a world united by Greek language and culture, a policy followed by his successors. This policy, called Hellenization, had a dramatic impact on the Jews.
At Alexander's death (323 B.C.) the empire he won was divided among his generals. Two of them founded dynasties—the Ptolemies in Egypt and the Seleucids in Syria and Mesopotamia—that would contend for control of Israel for over a century.
The rule of the Ptolemies was considerate of Jewish religious sensitivities, but in 198 B.C. the Seleucids took control and paved the way for some of the most heroic periods in Jewish history.
The early Seleucid years were largely a continuation of the tolerant rule of the Ptolemies, but Antiochus IV Epiphanes (whose title means "God made manifest" who ruled 175-164 B.C.) changed that when he attempted to consolidate his fading empire through a policy of radical Hellenization. While a segment of the Jewish aristocracy had already adopted Greek ways, the majority of Jews were outraged.
Antiochus's atrocities were aimed at the eradication of Jewish religion. He prohibited some of the central elements of Jewish practice, attempted to destroy all copies of the Torah (the Pentateuch), and required offerings to the Greek god Zeus. His crowning outrage was the erection of a statue of Zeus and the sacrificing of a pig in the Jerusalem temple itself.
Opposition to Antiochus was led by Mattathias, an elderly villager from a priestly family, and his five sons: Judas (Maccabeus), Jonathan, Simon, John, and Eleazar. Mattathias destroyed a Greek altar established in his village, Modein, and killed Antiochus's emissary. This triggered the Maccabean revolt, a 24-year war

(166-142 B.C.) that resulted in the independence of Judah until the Romans took control in 63 B.C.

The victory of Mattathias's family was Pyrrhic, however. With the death of his last son, Simon, the Hasmonean dynasty that they founded soon evolved into an aristocratic, Hellenistic regime sometimes hard to distinguish from that of the Seleucids. During the reign of Simon's son, John Hyrcanus, the orthodox Jews who had supported the Maccabees fell out of favor. With only a few exceptions, the rest of the Hasmoneans supported the Jewish Hellenizers. The Pharisees were actually persecuted by Alexander Janneus (103-76 B.C.).

The Hasmonean dynasty ended when, in 63 B.C., an expanding Roman empire intervened in a dynastic clash between the two sons of Janneus, Aristobulus II and Hyrcanus II. Pompey, the general who subdued the East for Rome, took Jerusalem after a three-month siege of the temple area, massacring priests in the performance of their duties and entering the Most Holy Place. This sacrilege began Roman rule in a way that Jews could neither forgive nor forget.

Literature:
During these unhappy years of oppression and internal strife, the Jewish people produced a sizable body of literature that both recorded and addressed their era. Three of the most significant works are the Septuagint, the Apocrypha and the Dead Sea Scrolls.

Septuagint—
Jewish legend says that seventy-two scholars, under the sponsorship of Ptolemy Philadelphus (c. 250 B.C.), were brought together on the island of Pharos, near Alexandria, where they produced a Greek translation of the OT in seventy-two days. From this tradition the Latin word for seventy, "Septuagint," became the name attached to the translation. The Roman numeral for seventy, LXX, is used as an abbreviation for it.

Behind the legend lies the probability that at least the Torah (the five books of Moses) was translated into Greek c. 250 B.C. for the use of the Greek-speaking Jews of Alexandria. The rest of the OT and some noncanonical books were also included in the LXX before the dawning of the Christian era, though it is difficult to be certain when.

The Septuagint quickly became the Bible of the Jews outside Israel who, like the Alexandrians, no longer spoke Hebrew. It would be difficult to overestimate its influence. It made the Scriptures available both to the Jews who no longer spoke their ancestral language and to the entire Greek-speaking world. It later became the Bible of the early church. Also, its widespread popularity and use contributed to the retention of the Apocrypha by some branches of Christendom.

Apocrypha—
Derived from a Greek word that means "hidden," Apocrypha has acquired the meaning "false," but in a technical sense it describes a specific body of writings. This collection consists of a variety of books and additions to canonical books that, with the exception of 2 Esdras (c. A.D. 90), were written during the intertestamental period. Their recognition as authoritative in Roman and Eastern Christianity is the result of a complex historical process.

The canon of the OT accepted by Protestants today was very likely established by the dawn of the second century A.D., though after the fall of Jerusalem and the destruction of the temple in 70. The precise scope of the OT was discussed among the Jews until the Council of Jamnia (c. 90). This Hebrew canon was not accepted by the early church, which used the Septuagint. In spite of disagreements among some of the church fathers as to which books were canonical and which were not, the Apocryphal books continued in common use by most Christians until the Reformation. During this period most Protestants decided to follow the original Hebrew canon while Rome, at the Council of Trent (1546) and more recently at the First Vatican Council (1869-70), affirmed the larger "Alexandrian" canon that includes the Apocrypha.

The Apocryphal books have retained their place primarily through the weight of ecclesiastical authority, without which they would not commend themselves as canonical literature. There is no clear evidence that Jesus or the apostles ever quoted any Apocryphal works as Scripture (Jude 14). The Jewish community that produced them repudiated them, and the historical surveys in the apostolic sermons recorded in Acts completely ignore the period they cover. Even the sober, historical account of 1 Maccabees is tarnished by numerous errors and anachronisms.

There is nothing of theological value in the Apocryphal books that cannot be duplicated in canonical Scripture, and they contain much that runs counter to its teachings. Nonetheless, this body of literature does provide a valuable source of information for the study of the intertestamental period.

Dead Sea Scrolls—
In the spring of 1947 an Arab shepherd chanced upon a cave in the hills overlooking the southwestern shore of the Dead Sea that contained what has been called "the greatest manuscript discovery of modern times."

The documents and fragments of documents found in those caves, dubbed the "Dead Sea Scrolls," included OT books, a few books of the Apocrypha, apocalyptic works, pseudepigrapha (books that purport to be the work of ancient heroes of the faith), and a number of books peculiar to the sect that produced them.

Approximately a third of the documents are Biblical, with Psalms, Deuteronomy and Isaiah—the books quoted most often in the NT—occurring most frequently. One of the most remarkable finds was a complete 24-foot-long scroll of Isaiah.

The Scrolls have made a significant contribution to the quest for a form of the OT texts most accurately reflecting the original manuscripts; they provide copies a thousand years closer to the originals than were previously known. The understanding of Biblical Hebrew and Aramaic and knowledge of the development of Judaism between the Testaments have been increased significantly. Of great importance to readers of the Bible is the demonstration of the care with which OT texts were copied, thus providing objective evidence for the general reliability of those texts.

Social Developments:
The Judaism of Jesus' day is, to a large extent, the result of changes that came about in response to the pressures of the intertestamental period.

Diaspora—
The Diaspora (dispersion) of Israel begun in the Exile accelerated during these years until a writer of the day could say that Jews filled "every land and sea."

Jews outside Israel, cut off from the temple, concentrated their religious life in the study of the Torah and the life of the synagogue (see below). The missionaries of the early church began their Gentile ministries among the Diaspora, using their Greek translation of the OT.

Sadducees—
In Israel, the Greek world made its greatest impact through the party of the Sadducees. Made up of aristocrats, it became the temple party. Because of their position, the Sadducees had a vested interest in the status quo.

Relatively few in number, they wielded disproportionate political power and controlled the high priesthood. They rejected all religious writings except the Torah, as well as any doctrine (such as the Resurrection) not found in those five books.

Synagogue—
During the Exile, Israel was cut off from the temple, divested of nationhood and surrounded by pagan religious practices. Her faith was threatened with extinction. Under these circumstances, the exiles turned their religious focus from what they had lost to what they retained—the Torah and the belief that they were God's people. They concentrated on the law rather than nationhood, on personal piety rather than sacramental rectitude, and on prayer as an acceptable replacement for the sacrifices denied to them.

When they returned from the Exile, they brought with them this new form of religious expression, as well as the synagogue (its center), and Judaism became a faith that could be practiced wherever the Torah could be carried.

The emphases on personal piety and a relationship with God, which characterized synagogue worship, not only helped preserve Judaism but also prepared the way for the Christian gospel.

Pharisees—
As the party of the synagogue, the Pharisees strove to reinterpret the law. They built a "hedge" around it to enable Jews to live righteously before God in a world that had changed drastically since the days of Moses. Although they were comparatively few in number, the Pharisees enjoyed the support of the people and influenced popular opinion if not national policy. They were the only party to survive the destruction of the temple in A.D. 70 and were the spiritual progenitors of modern Judaism.

Essenes—
An almost forgotten Jewish sect until the discovery of the Dead Sea Scrolls, the Essenes were a small, separatist group that grew out of the conflicts of the Maccabean age. Like the Pharisees, they stressed strict legal observance, but they considered the temple priesthood corrupt and rejected much of the temple ritual and sacrificial system. Mentioned by several ancient writers, the precise nature of the Essenes is still not certain, though it is generally agreed that the Qumran community that produced the Dead Sea Scrolls was an Essene group.

Because they were convinced that they were the true remnant, these Qumran Essenes had separated themselves from Judaism at large and devoted themselves to personal purity and preparation for the final war between the "Sons of Light and the Sons of Darkness." They practiced an apocalyptic faith, looking back to the contributions of their "Teacher of Righteousness" and forward to the coming of two, and possibly three, Messiahs. The destruction of the temple in A.D. 70, however, seems to have delivered a death blow to their apocalyptic expectations.

Attempts have been made to equate aspects of the beliefs of the Qumran community with the origins of Christianity. Some have seen a prototype of Jesus in their "Teacher of Righteousness," and both John the Baptist and Jesus have been assigned membership in the sect. There is, however, only a superficial, speculative base for these conjectures.

TESTIMONY

Commandments:
Those revealed to Moses (Ex 25:16; Dt 4:44-45; 1Ki 2:3). Kept in the ark (Ex 25:16, 21). Engraved on tablets (Ex 31:18; 32:15; 38:21). Atonement cover was over (Ex 26:34; 30:6; 40:20).

Ark, called ark of (Ex 25:22; 26:34; 40:3, 5, 20-21). Tabernacle called tabernacle of (Nu 1:50, 53; 9:19; 10:11). *See Ark; Tabernacle.*

See Commandments and Statutes, Of God; Decalogue.

Legal: *See Evidence; Witness.*

Religious:
(Ps 18:49; 22:22; 26:12; 34:1-4, 8-9; 77:12; 119:13, 26-27, 46, 67, 71; Isa 43:10; 44:8; 45:24; 1Co 1:5-6; 12:3; 15:15).

Required of the righteous (1Ch 16:8-9; Ps 9:11; Isa 12:4-6; 43:10; 44:8; Jer 51:10; Mt 4:21; 5:15-16, 19-20; Mk 4:21; 5:19-20; Lk 8:16, 39; 24:48; Jn 15:27; Ac 1:8, 22; 3:15; 5:32; 13:31; Ro 10:9-10; Eph 5:19; 2Ti 1:8; 1Pe 3:15; 5:12).

Concerning God's, faithfulness (Ps 73:23-26, 28; 89:1), glory (Ps 145:11-12), merciful providence (Ps 40:1-3; 54:7; 91:2-13; Da 4:2-3; Ac 14:15-17), righteousness (Ps 35:28; 71:16), salvation (Ps 30:1-6; 40:1-3; 62:1-2; 66:16-20; 71:15, 18; Gal 2:20; Php 3:4-14; Tit 3:3-7; Heb 2:3, 12), words (Ps 119:172), works (Ps 71:17, 24; 145:4-7, 10-12; Jer 51:10; Ac 2:11).

Concerning confidence in God (Ps 16:5-9; 18:2-3, 35-36; 23:1-6; 26:6-7; 27:1-6, 13; 28:6-8; 30:1-6). Rewards of (Mt 10:32; Lk 12:8). Victory by (Rev 12:11).

Exemplified by:
Job (Job 19:25-27). The psalmist (Ps 35:28; 40:1-3, 9; 57:7-9; 116:1-19). Nebuchadnezzar (Da 4:34-37). The woman of Sychar (Jn 4:28-30, 39, 41-42). The blind man whom Jesus healed (Jn 9:17, 30-33). The apostles to the resurrection of Jesus (Ac 4:33; 1Jn 1:1-4). The disciples at Pentecost (Ac 2:4-11). Peter (Ac 4:18-20; 1Pe 5:1, 12; 2Pe 1:16). John (Ac 4:18-20; 1Jn 1:1-4).

Paul's conversion (Ac 22:1-16; 26:12-23), devotion to Christ (1Co 13:1; Php 3:4-14), confidence in Christ (2Co 4:13-14; 5:1; 2Ti 1:12), hope of the crown of righteousness (2Ti 4:7-8), hope of eternal life (Tit 1:1-2).

TETRARCH Ruler of a fourth part of a region (Mt 14:1; Lk 3:1; 9:7; Ac 13:1).

TEXTS, ANCIENT NEAR EASTERN NON-BIBLICAL TEXTS RELATING TO THE OLD TESTAMENT
Major representative examples of ancient Near Eastern non-biblical documents that provide parallels to or shed light on various OT passages.

Amarna Letters: [Canaanite Akkadian]—*fourteenth century B.C. Hundreds of letters, written primarily by Canaanite scribes, illuminate social, political and religious relationships between Canaan and Egypt during the reigns of Amenhotep III and Akhenaten.*

Amenemope's Wisdom: [Egyptian]—*early first millennium B.C. Thirty chapters of wisdom instruction are similar to Pr 22:17-24:22 and provide the closest external parallels to OT wisdom literature.*

Atrahasis Epic: [Akkadian]—*early second millennium B.C. A cosmological epic depicts Creation and early human history, including the Flood (cf. Ge 1-9).*

Babylonian Theodicy: [Akkadian]—*early first millennium B.C. A sufferer and his friend dialogue with each other (cf. Job).*

Cyrus Cylinder: [Akkadian]—*sixth century B.C. King Cyrus of Persia records the conquest of Babylon (cf. Da 5:30; 6:28) and boasts of his generous policies toward his new subjects and their gods.*

Dead Sea Scrolls: [Hebrew, Aramaic, Greek]—*third century B.C. to first century A.D. Several hundred scrolls and fragments include the oldest copies of OT books and passages.*

Ebal Tablets: [Sumerian, Eblaite]—*mid-third millennium B.C. Thousands of commercial, legal, literary, and epistolary texts describe the cultural vitality and political power of a prepatriarchal civilization in northern Syria.*

Elephantine Papyri: [Aramaic]—*late fifth century B.C. Contracts and letters document life among Israelites who fled to southern Egypt after Jerusalem was destroyed in 586 B.C.*

Enuma Elish: [Akkadian]—*early second millennium B.C. Marduk, the Babylonian god of cosmic order, is elevated to the supreme position in the pantheon. The seven-tablet epic contains an account of creation (cf. Ge 1-2).*

Gezer Calendar: [Hebrew]—*tenth century B.C. A schoolboy from west-central Israel describes the seasons, crops and farming activity of the agricultural year.*

Gilgamesh Epic: [Akkadian]—*early second millennium B.C. Gilgamesh, ruler of Uruk, experiences numerous adventures, including a meeting with Utnapishtim, the only survivor of a great deluge (cf. Ge 6-9).*

Hammurapi's Code: [Akkadian]—*eighteenth century B.C. Together with similar law codes that preceded and followed it, the Code of Hammurapi exhibits close parallels to numerous passages in the Mosaic laws of the OT.*

Hymn to the Aten: [Egyptian]—*fourteenth century B.C. The poem praises the beneficence and universality of the sun in language somewhat similar to that used in Ps 104.*

Ishtar's Descent: [Akkadian]—*first millennium B.C. The goddess Ishtar temporarily descends to the netherworld, which is pictured in terms reminiscent of OT descriptions of Sheol.*

Jehoiachin's Ration Dockets: [Akkadian]—*early sixth century B.C. Brief texts from the reign of Nebuchadnezzar II refer to rations allotted to Judah's exiled king Jehoiachin and his sons (cf. 2Ki 25:27-30).*

King Lists: [Sumerian]—*late third millennium B.C. The reigns of Sumerian kings before the Flood are described as lasting for thousands of years, reminding us of the longevity of the pre-Flood patriarchs in Ge 5.*

Lachish Letters: [Hebrew]—*early sixth century B.C. Inscriptions on pottery fragments vividly portray the desperate days preceding the Babylonian siege of Jerusalem in 588-586 B.C. (cf. Jer 34:7).*

Lamentation Over the Destruction of Ur: [Sumerian]—*early second millennium B.C. The poem mourns the destruction of the city of Ur at the hands of the Elamites (cf. the OT book of Lamentations).*

Ludlul Bel Nemeqi: [Akkadian]—*late second millennium B.C. A suffering Babylonian nobleman describes his distress in terms faintly reminiscent of the experience of Job.*

Mari Tablets: [Akkadian]—*eighteenth century B.C. Letters and administration texts provide detailed information regarding customs, language, and personal names that reflect the culture of the OT patriarchs.*

Merneptah Stele: [Egyptian]—*thirteenth century B.C. Pharaoh Merneptah figuratively describes his victory over various peoples in western Asia, including "Israel."*

Mesha Stele (Moabite Stone): [Moabite]—*ninth century B.C. Mesha, king of Moab (see 2Ki 3:4), rebels against a successor of Israel's king Omri.*

Murashu Tablets: [Akkadian]—*fifth century B.C. Commercial documents describe financial transactions engaged in by Murashu and Sons, a Babylonian firm that did business with Jews and other exiles.*

Mursilis's Treaty with Duppi-Tessub: [Hittite]—*mid-second millennium B.C. King Mursilis imposes a suzerainty treaty on King Duppi-Tessub. The literary outline of this*

and other Hittite treaties is strikingly paralleled in OT covenants established by God with his people.

Nabonidus Chronicle: [Akkadian]—*mid-sixth century* B.C. *The account describes the absence of King Nabonidus from Babylon. His son Belshazzar is therefore the regent in charge of the kingdom (cf. Da 5:29-30).*

Nebuchadnezzar Chronicle: [Akkadian]—*early sixth century* B.C. *A chronicle from the reign of Nebuchadnezzar II includes the Babylonian account of the siege of Jerusalem in 597 B.C. (2Ki 24:10-17).*

Nuzi Tablets: [Akkadian]—*mid-second millennium* B.C. *Adoption, birthright sale and other legal documents graphically illustrate OT patriarchal customs current centuries earlier.*

Pessimistic Dialogue: [Akkadian]—*early first millennium* B.C. *A master and his servant discuss the pros and cons of various activities (cf. Ecc 1-2).*

Ras Shamra Tablets: [Ugaritic]—*fifteenth century* B.C. *Canaanite deities and rulers experience adventures in epics that enrich our understanding of Canaanite mythology and religion and of OT poetry.*

Sargon Legend: [Akkadian]—*first millennium* B.C. *Sargon I (the Great), ruler of Akkad in the late third millennium* B.C. *claims to have been rescued as an infant from a reed basket found floating in a river (cf. Ex 2).*

Sargon's Display Inscription: [Akkadian]— *eighth century* B.C. *Sargon II takes credit for the conquest of Samaria in 722/721 B.C. and states that he captured and exiled 27, 290 Israelites.*

Sennacherib's Prism: [Akkadian]—*early seventh century* B.C. *Sennacherib vividly describes his siege of Jerusalem in 701 B.C., making Hezekiah a prisoner in his own royal city (but cf. 2Ki 19:35-37).*

Seven Lean Years Tradition: [Egyptian]—*second century* B.C. *Egypt experiences seven years of low Nile levels and famine, which, by a contractual agreement between Pharaoh Djoser (twenty-eighth century* B.C.*) and a god, will be followed by prosperity (cf. Ge 41).*

Shalmaneser's Black Obelisk: [Akkadian]—*ninth century* B.C. *Israel's king Jehu (or his servant) presents tribute to Assyria's king Shalmaneser III. Additional Assyrian and Babylonian texts refer to other kings of Israel and Judah.*

Shishak's Geographical List: [Egyptian]— *tenth century* B.C. *Pharaoh Shishak lists the cities that he captured or made tributary during his campaign in Judah and Israel (cf. 1Ki 14:25-26).*

Siloam Inscription: [Hebrew]—*late eighth century* B.C. *A Judahite workman describes the construction of an underground conduit to guarantee Jerusalem's water supply during Hezekiah's reign (cf. 2Ki 20:20; 2Ch 32:30).*

Sinuhe's Story: [Egyptian]—*twentieth to nineteenth centuries* B.C. *An Egyptian official of the twelfth dynasty goes into voluntary exile in Syria and Canaan during the OT patriarchal period.*

Tale of Two Brothers: [Egyptian]—*thirteenth century* B.C. *A young man rejects the amorous advances of his older brother's wife (cf. Ge 39).*

Wenamun's Journey: [Egyptian]—*eleventh century* B.C. *An official of the Temple of Amun at Thebes in Egypt is sent to Byblos in Canaan to buy lumber for the ceremonial barge of his god.*

TEXTS AND VERSIONS

Old Testament

Major Hebrew texts—
1. The oldest copies of the Hebrew OT are the famous Dead Sea Scrolls, dating from 250 B.C. to c. A.D. 70. *See Dead Sea Scrolls; Testaments, Time Between.*
2. Portions of the OT text include the Nash Papyrus (second century B.C.) and the Cairo Genizah fragments (sixth to ninth centuries A.D.).
3. The Masoretes preserved and standardized the Hebrew text between the sixth and tenth centuries A.D.. The oldest examples of this text type include the Cairo Codex of the Prophets (895), the Aleppo Codex (c. 900-925) and the Leningrad Codex (1008).
4. The Samaritan Pentateuch (eleventh century A.D.).

Major versions—
1. Greek: Septuagint (250-100 B.C.); second century A.D. versions by Aquila, Theodotion, and Symmachus; by Origen c. A.D. 240.
2. Aramaic (first to fifth century A.D.).
3. Syriac (second or third century A.D.).
4. Latin: Old Latin (second century A.D.), Jerome's Vulgate (383-405 A.D.).

New Testament:

Major Greek texts—
Greek manuscripts of portions or of the whole of the NT total nearly 5000. Of these, c. 70 are papyri, 250 uncials, 2, 500 minuscules, and 1800 lectionaries.
1. Fragments and books on papyrus date back to the second century A.D., such as Bodmer Papyrus p^{66} of John.
2. Codex Sinaiticus (fourth century) contains the entire NT.
3. Codicies Alexandrinus (fifth century) and Vaticanus are nearly complete.
4. Quotations from the early church fathers also provide an ancient witness to the NT.

Major versions—
1. Latin (second to fourth centuries).
2. Syriac (second to sixth centuries).
3. Coptic (second and third centuries).

THADDAEUS (*possibly breast nipple*). One of the twelve apostles (Mt 10:3; Mk 3:18). This name does not appear in (Lk 6:16; Ac 1:13), the name "Judas son of James" occurs instead. Little is known about him.
See Lebbaeus.

THAHASH *See Tahash.*

THAMAH *See Temah.*

THAMAR *See Tamar, 1.*

THANK OFFERINGS *See Offerings.*

THANKFULNESS

To God:
Commanded or required (Ge 35:1; Ex 12:14, 17, 42; 13:3, 8-10, 14-16; 16:32; 34:26; Lev 19:24; 23:14; Dt 12:18; 16:9-15; 26:10; Jdg 5:11; Ps 50:14-15). Commanded (Ps 48:11; 106:1; Pr 3:9-10; Ecc 7:14; Isa 48:20; Joel 2:26; Ro 2:4; 15:27; Eph 1:16; 5:4, 19-20; Php 4:6; Col 1:12; 2:7; 3:15-17; 4:2; 1Th 5:18; Heb 13:15; Jas 1:9). Exhorted (Ps 98:1; 105:1, 5, 42-45; 107:1-2, 15, 22, 42-43; 118:1, 4; Col 3:15; 1Ti 2:1; 4:3-5).
Jesus set an example of (Mt 11:25; 15:36; 26:27; Mk 8:6-7; 14:23; Lk 22:17, 19; Jn 6:11, 23; 11:41).

Should be Offered—
To God (Ps 30:4; 50:14; 75:1; 92:1; 97:12; 106:1; 118:1; 2Co 9:11; Eph 5:4, 19-20; Php 4:6; Col 1:12; 2:7; 3:15-17; 4:2; 1Th 5:18; 1Ti 2:1; Heb 13:15), through Christ (Ro 1:8; Col 3:17; Heb 13:15), in the name of Christ (Eph 5:20), in behalf of ministers (2Co 1:11), in private worship (Da 6:10), in public (1Ch 23:30; 25:3; Ne 11:17; Ps 35:18), in everything (1Th 5:18), upon the completion of great undertakings (Ne 12:31, 40), before taking food (Mt 14:19; Mk 8:9; Lk 24:30; Jn 6:11; Ac 27:35), always (Eph 1:16; 5:20; 1Th 1:2), as the remembrance of God's holiness (Ps 30:4; 97:12).

For—
The goodness and mercy of God (Ps 68:19; 79:13; 89:1; 100:4; 106:1; 107:1; 116:12-14, 17; 136:1-3; Isa 63:7), the gift of Christ (2Co 9:15), Christ's power and reign (Rev 11:17), the reception and effectual working of the word of God in others (1Th 2:13), deliverance, from adversity (Ps 31:7, 21; 35:9-10; 44:7-8; 54:6-7; 66:8-9, 12-16, 20; 98:1), through Christ, from indwelling sin (Ro 7:23-25), providential deliverance (Ps 105:1-45; 107:1-2, 15, 22, 42-43; Jdg 5:11; Ps 105:1-45; 107:1-2, 15, 22, 42-43; 136:1-26; Joel 2:26), victory over death and the grave (1Co 15:57), wisdom and might (Da 2:23), the triumph of the gospel (2Co 2:14), the conversion of others (Ro 6:17), faith exhibited by others (Ro 1:8; 2Th 1:3), love exhibited by others (2Th 1:3), the grace bestowed on others (1Co 1:4; Php 1:3-5; Col 1:3-6), the zeal exhibited by others (2Co 8:16), nearness of God's presence (Ps 75:1), appointment to the ministry (1Ti 1:12), willingness to offer our property for God's service (1Ch 29:6-14), the supply of our bodily wants (Ro 14:6-7; 1Ti 4:3-4), all men (1Ti 2:1), all things (2Co 9:11; Eph 5:20), temporal blessings (Ro 14:6-7; 1Ti 4:3-5).

By—
Ministers appointed to offer, in public (1Ch 16:4, 7; 23:30; 2Ch 31:2).
Saints, exhorted to (Ps 105:1; Col 3:15), resolve to offer (Ps 18:49; 30:12), habitually offer (Da 6:10), offer sacrifices of (Ps 116:17), abound in the faith with (Col 2:7), magnify God by (Ps 95:2), come before God with (Ps 95:2), should enter God's gates with (Ps 100:4). Of hypocrites, full of boasting (Lk 18:11). The wicked averse to (Ro 1:21).
The heavenly host (Rev 4:9; 7:11-12; 11:16-17).

Accompanied By—
Should be accompanied by intercession for others (1Ti 2:1; 2Ti 1:3; Phm 4). Should always accompany prayer (Ne 11:17; Php 4:6; Col 4:2). Should always accompany praise (Ps 92:1; Heb 13:15). Expressed in psalms (1Ch 16:7).
Cultivated, by the Feast of Tabernacles (Dt 16:9-15), by thank offerings (Ex 34:26; Lev 19:24; 23:14; Dt 12:18; 26:10; Pr 3:9-10), by songs (1Ch 16:7-36; Ps 95:2; 100).

Instances of—
Eve (Ge 4:1, 25). Noah (Ge 8:20). Melchizedek (Ge 14:20). Lot (Ge 19:19). Abraham (Ge 12:7). Sarah (Ge 21:6-7). Abraham's servant (Ge 24:27). Isaac (Ge 26:22). Leah (Ge 29:32-35). Rachel (Ge 30:6). Jacob (Ge 32:10; 35:3, 7; 48:11, 15-16). Joseph (Ge 41:51-52).
Moses (Ex 15:1-18). Miriam (Ex 15:19-21). Jethro (Ex 18:10). Israel (Ex 4:31; 15:1-18; Nu 21:17; 31:49-54; 1Ch 29:22). Deborah (Jdg 5). Hannah (1Sa 1:27-28; 2:1-10). Samuel (1Sa 7:12).
David (2Sa 6:21; 1Ch 29:13). Solomon (1Ki 8:15, 56; 2Ch 6:4). Queen of Sheba (1Ki 10:9). Hiram (2Ch 2:12). Jehoshaphat's army (2Ch 20:27-28). The psalmist (Ps 9:1-2, 4; 13:6; 22:23-25; 26:7; 28:7; 30:1, 3, 11-12; 31:7, 21; 35:9-10, 18; 40:2-3, 5; 41:11-12; 44:7-8; 54:6-7; 56:12-13; 59:16-17; 66:8-9, 12-16, 20; 68:19; 71:15, 23-24; 79:13; 89:1; 92:1-2, 4; 98:1; 100:4; 102:18-20; 104:1; 116:12-14, 17; 119:65, 108; 136).
Isaiah (Isa 63:7). Daniel (Da 2:23; 6:22). Nebuchadnezzar (Da 4:2, 34). The mariners (Jnh 1:16). Jonah (Jnh 2:9). Ezra (Ezr 7:27). The Levites (2Ch 5:12-13; Ne 9:4-38). The Jews (Ne 12:31, 40, 43).
The shepherds (Lk 2:20). Simeon (Lk 2:28). Anna (Lk 2:38).
Those whom Jesus healed: The paralyzed man (Lk 5:25), the demoniac (Lk 8:39), the woman bent with infirmity (Lk 13:13), one of the ten lepers (Lk 17:15-16), blind Bartimaeus (Lk 18:43), the centurion for his son (Jn 4:53).
The lame man healed by Peter (Ac 3:8). Early Christians (Ac 2:46-47). Paul (Ac 27:35; 28:15; Ro 1:8; 6:17; 1Co 1:4; 2Co 2:14; Php 1:3-5; Col 1:3-6; 2Th 1:3; 1Ti 1:12).
See Joy; Praise; Psalms; Worship.

Of Person to Person:
The Israelites, to Joshua (Jos 19:49-50). The spies, to Rahab (Jos 6:22-25). Saul, to the Kenites (1Sa 15:6). Naomi, to Boaz (Ru 2:19-20). David, to the men of Jabesh Gilead (2Sa 2:5-7), to Hanun (2Sa 10:2), to Barzillai (1Ki 2:7). Paul, to Phoebe (Ro 16:1-4), to Onesiphorus (2Ti 1:16-18). The people of Malta, to Paul (Ac 28:10).

THANKSGIVING By Jesus (Mt 11:25; 15:36; 26:27; Mk 8:6-7; 14:23; Lk 22:17, 19; Jn 6:11, 23; 11:41).
For food, commonly called "grace" (1Sa 9:13; Mt 14:19; 15:36; Mk 6:41; 8:6-7; Lk 9:16; 24:30; Jn 6:11, 23; Ac 27:35; Ro 14:6; 1Co 10:30-31; 1Ti 4:3-5).
Instances of: Jesus (Mt 14:19; Mk 8:6-7). Paul (Ac 27:35).
See Praise; Prayer; Thanksgiving; Thankfulness.

THARA *See Terah, 2.*

THARSHISH *See Trade and Travel; Tarshish, 2, 4.*

THEATER A place for dramatic and musical performances (Ac 19:29, 31).

THEBES (*town, village*). Capital of Egypt during the eighteenth dynasty (KJV "No"); on the E bank of the Nile; famous for temples; cult center of the god Amon (Jer 46:25), denounced by prophets (Jer 46:25; Eze 30:14-16).

THEBEZ A city in Ephraim about halfway between Beth Shan to Shechem; Abimelech, the son of Gideon, slain there (Jdg 9:50; 2Sa 11:21).

THEFT (Na 3:1; Mt 6:19-20; 15:19; Mk 7:21-22; Ro 2:21; Rev 9:21).

Forbidden:
(Ex 20:15; Lev 19:11, 13; Dt 5:19; 23:24-25; Ps 62:10; Mt 19:18; Lk 18:20; Ro 13:9; Eph 4:28; Tit 2:10; 1Pe 4:15). Penalty for (Ex 21:16; 22:1-4, 10-15; Lev 6:2-5; Pr 6:30-31; Zec 5:3; Mt 27:38, 44; Mk 15:27). Restitution for things stolen required of the penitent (Eze 33:15).

Instances of:
Rachel, of the household gods (Ge 31:19, 34-35). Achan (Jos 7:11). Micah (Jdg 17:2). The spies of Laish (Jdg 18:14-27). Israelites (Eze 22:29; Hos 4:1-2). Judas (Jn 12:6).
See Dishonesty; Robbery; Thief, Thieves.

THELASAR *See Tel Assar.*

THEOCRACY (*rule of God*). Established (Ex 19:8; 24:3, 7; Dt 5:25-29; 33:2-5; Jdg 8:23; 1Sa 12:12). Rejected by Israel (1Sa 8:7, 19; 10:19; 2Ch 13:8).
See God, Sovereign; Government.

THEOLOGY *See God.*

THEOPHANY (*appearance of God*). Visible appearance of God, generally in human form (Ge 3:8; 4; 28:10-17).

THEOPHILUS (*friend of God*). A man to whom the Gospel of Luke and Acts of the Apostles are addressed (Lk 1:3; Ac 1:1). Nothing is known of him.

THESSALONIANS, 1 and 2

1 Thessalonians:
Author: the apostle Paul
Date: c. A.D. 51
Outline:
I. The Thanksgiving for the Thessalonians (ch 1).
 A. The Grounds for the Thanksgiving (1:1-4).
 B. The Genuineness of the Grounds (1:5-10).
II. The Defense of the Apostolic Actions and Absence (chs. 2-3).
 A. The Defense of the Apostolic Actions (2:1-16).
 B. The Defense of the Apostolic Absence (2:17-3:10).
 C. The Prayer (3:11-13).
III. The Exhortations to the Thessalonians (4:1-5:22).
 A. Primarily Concerning Personal Life (4:1-12).
 B. Concerning the Coming of Christ (4:13-5:11).
 C. Primarily Concerning Church Life (5:12-22).
IV. The Concluding Prayer, Greetings and Benediction (5:23-28).

2 Thessalonians:
Author: the apostle Paul
Date: c. A.D. 51 or 52
Outline:
I. Introduction (ch. 1).
 A. Salutation (1:1-2).
 B. Thanksgiving for Their Faith, Love and Perseverance (1:3-10).
 C. Intercession for Their Spiritual Progress (1:11-12).
II. Instruction (ch. 2).
 A. Prophecy Regarding the Day of the Lord (2:1-12).
 B. Thanksgiving for Their Election and Calling (Their Position) (2:13-15).
 C. Prayer for Their Service and Testimony (Their Practice) (2:16-17).
III. Injunctions (ch. 3).
 A. Call to Prayer (3:1-3).
 B. Charge to Discipline for the Disorderly and Lazy (3:4-15).
 C. Conclusion, Greeting and Benediction (3:16-18).

THESSALONICA A city of Macedonia. Paul visits (Ac 17:1; Php 4:16). People of, accompany Paul (Ac 20:4; 27:2). Paul writes to Christians in (1Th 1:1; 2Th 1:1). Demas goes to (2Ti 4:10).

THEUDAS (*gift of God*). A Jew who led a rebellion against Rome (Ac 5:36-37).

THICKET (1Sa 13:6; Jer 4:7).

THIEF, THIEVES In Mosaic law, punishment of thieves was very severe (Ex 22:1-4).
Penalty for (Dt 24:7; Pr 6:30-31; Eze 18:10, 13; Zec 5:3; Mt 27:38, 44; Mk 15:27).
Collusion with (Ps 50:18). Excluded from the kingdom of God (1Co 6:10). Desecrated the temple (Mt 21:13; Mk 11:17; Lk 19:45-46). Disgraceful (Jer 2:26). Worship of, offensive to God (Jer 7:9-10).
Christ's coming again as unexpected as (Rev 3:3).

Figurative (Ob 5; Jn 10:1).
See Theft.

THIGH To put one's hand under the thigh of another was to enhance the sacredness of an oath (Ge 24:2, 9; 47:29).

THIMNATHAH *See Timnah.*

THIRST Figurative of the ardent desire of the devout mind (Ps 42:1-4; 63:1; 143:6; Isa 55:1; Am 8:11-13; Mt 5:6; Jn 4:14-15; 7:37; Rev 21:6; 22:17).
See Desire, Spiritual; Diligence; Hunger, Figurative; Zeal.

THISTLE Exists in many varieties in Israel. Used figuratively for trouble, desolation, judgment, wickedness (Nu 33:55; Pr 24:31; 15:19; Isa 5:6; 2Co 12:7).

THOMAS (*twin*). Called Didymus. One of the twelve apostles (Mt 10:3; Mk 3:18; Lk 6:15). Present at the raising of Lazarus (Jn 11:16). Asks Jesus the way to the Father's house (Jn 14:5). Absent when Jesus first appeared to the disciples after the Resurrection (Jn 20:24). Skepticism of (Jn 20:25). Sees Jesus after the Resurrection (Jn 20:26-29; 21:1-2). Lives with the other apostles in Jerusalem (Ac 1:13-14). Loyalty of, to Jesus (Jn 11:16; 20:28).

THOMAS, GOSPEL OF A Gnostic gospel consisting entirely of sayings attributed to Jesus; dated c. A.D. 140; found at Nag Hammadi in Egypt in 1945.

THONG Strap to fasten a sandal to the foot. Used figuratively of something small and insignificant (Ge 14:23; Isa 5:27). Untying of, an act of humble service (Mk 1:7; Lk 3:16).

THORN The ground cursed with (Ge 3:18). Used as an awl (Job 41:2), for fuel (Ps 58:9; 118:12; Ecc 7:6). Hedges formed of (Hos 2:6; Mic 7:4). Crown of, mockingly put on Jesus' head (Mt 27:29; Mk 15:17; Jn 19:2, 5).
Figurative:
Of afflictions (Nu 33:55; 2Co 12:7). Of the adversities of the wicked (Pr 22:5). Of the evils that spring from the heart to choke the truth (Mt 13:7, 22).

THORN IN THE FLESH Paul's description of a physical ailment from which he prayed to be relieved (2Co 12:7). What it was is not known.

THOUGHTS, GOD'S (Ps 40:5, 17; 139:17; Isa 55:9; Jer 29:11).

THOUSAND Often used symbolically in the Bible. In the OT sometimes means "many" (1Sa 21:11; 2Ch 15:11), "family" (Nu 10:4).

THOUSAND YEARS As a day to the Lord (Ps 90:4; 2Pe 3:8). Satan bound (Rev 20:1-3). The reign of Christ (Rev 20:4-6).
See Millennium.

THRACE Kingdom and later a Roman province, in SE Europe, E of Macedonia (2Mc 12:35).

THREAD (Ge 14:23; Jdg 16:21; SS 4:3).

THREATENINGS Of God against the wicked (Lev 26:16; Jos 23:15; 1Sa 12:25; 1Ki 9:7; Ps 7:12; Isa 14:23; 66:4; Mal 3:5).

THREE HOLY CHILDREN, SONG OF Apocryphal additions to the OT book of Daniel; probably written in the first century B.C.

THREE TAVERNS A town in Italy. Roman Christians meet Paul in (Ac 28:15).

THRESHING By beating (Ru 2:17), by treading (Dt 25:4; Isa 25:10; Hos 10:11; 1Co 9:9; 1Ti 5:18). With instruments of wood (2Sa 24:22), of iron (Am 1:3), with a cart wheel (Isa 28:27-28). Floors for (Ge 50:10-11; Jdg 6:37; Ru 3:2-14; 1Sa 23:1; 2Sa 6:6; Hos 9:2; Joel 2:24). Floor of Araunah bought by David for a place of sacrifice (2Sa 24:16-25). Floor for, in barns (2Ki 6:27).

THRESHING FLOOR A place where grain was threshed, usually clay soil packed to a hard, smooth surface (Dt 25:4; Isa 28:27; 1Co 9:9).

THRESHOLD A piece of wood or stone at the bottom of a door, which has to be crossed on entering the house.

THRONE (*judgment seat*). Of Pharaoh (Ge 41:40; Ex 11:5). Of David (1Ki 2:12, 24; Ps 132:11-12; Isa 9:7; Jer 13:13; 17:25; Lk 1:32). Of Solomon (1Ki 2:19; 2Ch 9:17-19). Of ivory (1Ki 10:18-20). Of Solomon, called the throne of the LORD (1Ch 29:23). Of Herod (Ac 12:21). Of Israel (1Ki 8:20; 10:9; 2Ch 6:10). Abdicated by David (1Ki 1:32-40).
Figurative:
Anthropomorphic use of: Of God (2Ch 18:18; Ps 9:4, 7; 11:4; 47:8; 89:14; 97:2; 103:19; Isa 6:1; 66:1; Mt 5:34; 23:22; Heb 8:1; 12:2; Rev 14:3, 5), of Christ (Mt 19:28; 25:31; Ac 2:30; Rev 1:4; 3:21; 4:2-10; 7:9-17; 19:4; 21:5; 22:3).

THRUSH A bird (Isa 38:14; Jer 8:7). *See Birds.*

THUMB Blood put on, in consecration (Ex 29:20; Lev 8:23), in purification (Lev 14:14, 25). Oil put on (Lev 14:17, 28). Of prisoners cut off (Jdg 1:6-7). *See Hand.*

THUMMIM *See Urim and Thummim.*

THUNDER Sent as a plague upon the Egyptians (Ex 9:3-24), the Philistines, in battle with the Israelites (1Sa 7:10). Sent as a judgment (Isa 29:6). On Sinai (Ex 19:16; Ps 77:18; Heb 12:18-19). A token of divine anger (1Sa 12:17-18). A manifestation of divine power (Job 26:14; Ps 77:18). Sons of Zebedee called sons of (Mk 3:17).

THUNDER, SONS OF A title given James and John by Jesus (Mk 3:17).

THUTMOSE (*[Egyptian god] Thoth is born*). The name of four kings of Egypt of the eighteenth dynasty, centering in Thebes. Under their rule, Egypt attained her greatest power. Thutmose III may have been the Pharaoh who enslaved the Hebrews (Ex 1:8).

THYATIRA A city in the Roman province of Asia; on the boundary of Lydia and Mysia; noted for weaving and dyeing (Ac 16:14; Rev 2:18-29).

THYINE *See Citron Wood.*

TIARAS (Isa 3:23). *See Crown; Jewel, Jewelry.*

TIBERIAS A city on the W shore of the Sea of Galilee; built by Herod Antipas and named for the emperor Tiberias; a famous health resort; after A.D. 70 it became a center of rabbinic learning. Modern Tabariya.

TIBERIAS, SEA OF *See Sea of Galilee.*

TIBERIUS The second Roman emperor (A.D. 14-37); reigning emperor at the time of Christ's death (Lk 3:1).

TIBHATH *See Tebah, 2.*

TIBNI The son of Ginath; unsuccessful competitor for the throne of Israel (1Ki 16:21).

TIDAL King of Goiim; confederate of Kedorlaomer (Ge 14:1-17).

TIGLATH-PILESER (*my trust is in the son of [the temple] Esharra*). A famous Assyrian king (745-727 B.C.); great conqueror; received tribute from King Azariah of Judah and King Menahem of Samaria (2Ki 15:19-20), Ahaz secured his help against Pekah of Israel and Rezin of Syria; deported Trans-Jordanian Israelites (1Ch 5:6, 26), Ahaz gave tribute to him (2Ch 28:20-21).

TIGRIS (*arrow*). One of the two great rivers of the Mesopotamian area; 1, 150 miles long (Ge 2:14; Da 10:4).

TIKVAH (*hope*).
1. Father-in-law of the prophetess Huldah (2Ki 22:14). *See Tokhath.*
2. Father of Jahzeiah (Ezr 10:15).

TILE Ceiling tiles (Lk 5:19).

TILGATH-PILNESER *See Tiglath-Pileser.*

TILON The son of Shimon (1Ch 4:20).

TIMAEUS (*precious, valuable*). The father of Bartimaeus (Mk 10:46).

TIMBREL *See Tambourine.*

TIME In the early biblical period, time was marked by sunrise and sunset, phases of the moon, seasons, and years (Ge 1:14). *See Calendar.*

Ancient people had no method of reckoning long periods of time. They dated from great and well-known events, like the Exodus, the Babylonian Exile, the earthquake (Am 1:1), and especially the reigns of kings (1Ki 15:1; Hag 1:1). The year was lunar (354 days, 8 hours, 38 seconds), divided into twelve lunar months, with seven intercalary months added over nineteen years. The Hebrew month began with the new moon. Early Hebrews gave the months names; later they used numbers; and after the Exile they used Babylonian names. *See Month.*

Months were divided by the Jews into weeks of seven days, ending with the Sabbath (Ex 20:11; Dt 5:14-15). Days were divided into twenty-four hours of sixty minutes of sixty seconds. The Roman day began at midnight and had twelve hours (Jn 11:9), the Hebrew day was reckoned from sunset. Night was divided into watches. At first the Hebrews had three watches; in the time of Christ there were four. *See Day; Watches of the Night.*

TIMES, OBSERVER OF A person who has a superstitious regard for days regarded as lucky or unlucky, as decided by astrology (Dt 18:8-14).

TIMNA (*lot, portion*).
1. Concubine of Eliphaz (Ge 36:12).
2. Sister of Lotan (Ge 36:22).
3. Chieftain of Edom (Ge 36:40).
4. Son of Eliphaz (1Ch 1:36).

TIMNAH (*lot, portion*).
1. A town about two-and-a-half miles west of Beth Shemesh (Ge 38:12-14; 2Ch 28:18).
2. A town on the border of Judah approximately three miles SW of Beth Shemesh (Jos 15:10), possibly modern Tell Batash.
3. A town in the hill country of Judah (Jos 15:57), possibly the same as 1.
4. A Philistine town (Jdg 14:1-5), possibly the same as 1.

TIMNATH *See Timnah.*

TIMNATH HERES (*place of the sun [worship]*). A city in the hill country of Ephraim (Jdg 2:9).

TIMNATH SERAH (*place of the sun [worship]*). Given to Joshua (Jos 19:50). Joshua buried in (Jos 24:30). Modern Khirbet Tibnah.

TIMNITE A native of Timnah (Jdg 15:3-6).

TIMON (*precious, valuable*). One of seven ministers (Ac 6:5).

TIMOTHEUS *See Timothy.*

TIMOTHY (*precious one of God*). Parentage of (Ac 16:1). Reputation and Christian faith of (Ac 16:2; 1Co 4:17; 16:10; 2Ti 1:5; 3:15). Circumcised; becomes Paul's companion (Ac 16:3; 1Th 3:2). Left by Paul at Berea (Ac 17:14). Rejoins Paul at Corinth (Ac 17:15; 18:5). Sent into Macedonia (Ac 19:22). Rejoined by Paul; accompanies Paul to Asia (Ac 20:1-4). Sent to the Corinthians (1Co 4:17; 16:10-11). Preaches to the Corinthians (2Co 1:19). Sent to the Philippians (Php 2:19, 23). Sent to the Thessalonians (1Th 3:2, 6). Sent by Paul in Ephesus (1Ti 1:3). Joins Paul in the Epistle to the Philippians (Php 1:1), to the Colossians (Col 1:1-2), to the Thessalonians (1Th 1:1; 2Th 1:1), to Philemon (Phm 1).

Zeal of (Php 2:19-22; 1Ti 6:12). Power of (1Ti 4:14; 2Ti 1:6). Paul's love for (1Co 4:17; Php 2:22; 1Ti 1:2, 18; 2Ti 1:2-4). Paul writes to (1Ti 1:1-2; 2Ti 1:1-2).

TIMOTHY, 1 and 2

1 Timothy:

Author: the apostle Paul

Date: c. A.D 63-65

Outline:
I. Salutation (1:1-2).
II. Warning Against False Teachers (1:3-11).
 A. The Nature of the Heresy (1:3-7).
 B. The Purpose of the Law (1:8-11).
III. The Lord's Grace to Paul (1:12-17).
IV. The Purpose of Paul's Instructions to Timothy (1:18-20).
V. Instructions Concerning the Administration of the Church (chs. 2-3).
 A. Public Worship (ch. 2).
 1. Prayer in public worship (2:1-8).
 2. Women in public worship (2:9-15).
 B. Qualifications for Church Officers (3:1-13).
 1. Overseers (3:1-7).
 2. Deacons (3:8-13).
 C. Purpose of These Instructions (3:14-16).
VI. Methods of Dealing With False Teaching (ch. 4).
 A. False Teaching Described (4:1-5).
 B. Methods of Dealing With It Explained (4:6-16).
VII. Methods of Dealing With Different Groups in the Church (5:1-6:2).
 A. The Older and Younger (5:1-2).
 B. Widows (5:3-16).
 C. Elders (5:17-25).
 D. Slaves (6:1-2).
VIII. Miscellaneous Matters (6:3-19).
 A. False Teachers (6:3-5).
 B. Love of Money (6:6-10).
 C. Charge to Timothy (6:11-16).
 D. The Rich (6:17-19).
IX. Concluding Appeal (6:20-21).

2 Timothy:

Author: the apostle Paul

Date: c. A.D. 66-67

Outline:
I. Introduction (1:1-4).
II. Paul's Concern for Timothy (1:5-14).
III. Paul's Situation (1:15-18).
IV. Special Instructions to Timothy (ch. 2).
 A. Call for Endurance (2:1-13).
 B. Warning About Foolish Controversies (2:14-26).
V. Warning About the Last Days (ch. 3).
 A. Terrible Times (3:1-9).
 B. Means of Combating Them (3:10-17).
VI. Paul's Departing Remarks (4:1-8).
 A. Charge to Preach the Word (4:1-5).
 B. Paul's Victorious Prospect (4:6-8).
VII. Final Requests and Greetings (4:9-22).
 See Church, The Body of Believers, Qualifications for Elders/Overseers and Deacons; Missionary Journeys of Paul; Pastoral Epistles.

TIN (Nu 31:22; Eze 22:18, 20; 27:12).

TINKLING The sound of small bells worn by women on chain fastened to anklets (Isa 3:16).

TIPHSAH
1. City on Euphrates (1Ki 4:24).
2. A town, apparently not far from Tirzah in Samaria (2Ki 15:16); some versions have Tappuah. *See Tappuah, 3.*

TIRAS The son of Japheth (Ge 10:2; 1Ch 1:5).

TIRATHITES A family of scribes in Jabez (1Ch 2:55).

TIRE (*headdress*). Ornamental headdress (Eze 24:17, 23; Isa 3:20; 61:10).

TIRHAKAH An Egyptian king, third of the twenty-fifth dynasty; defeated by Sennacherib (2Ki 19:9; Isa 37:9), and later by Esarhaddon and Ashurbanipal.

TIRHANAH The son of Caleb and Maacah (1Ch 2:48).

TIRIA The son of Jehallelel (1Ch 4:16).

TIRSHATHA *See Governor.*

TIRZAH (*pleasant one* or *compensation*).
1. A daughter of Zelophehad (Nu 26:33; 36:11; Jos 17:3). Special legislation in regard to the inheritance of (Nu 27:1-11; 36; Jos 17:3-4).
2. A city of Canaan. Captured by Joshua (Jos 12:24). Becomes the residence of the kings of Israel (1Ki 14:17; 15:21, 33; 16:6, 8-9, 15, 17, 23). Royal residence moved from (1Ki 16:23-24). Base of military operations of Menahem (2Ki 15:14, 16). Beauty of (SS 6:4).

T

TISHBE, TISHBITE The designation of Elijah (1Ki 17:1), probably to be identified with modern el-Istib, little W of Mahanaim.

TISHRI See Ethanim; Month, 7.

TITHES (a tenth). Paid by Abraham to Melchizedek (Ge 14:20; Heb 7:2-6). Jacob vows a tenth of all his property to God (Ge 28:22).

Mosaic laws instituting (Lev 27:30-33; Nu 18:21-24; Dt 12:6-7, 17, 19; 14:22-29; 26:12-15). Customs relating to (Ne 10:37-38; Am 4:4; Heb 7:5-9). Tithe of tithes for priests (Nu 18:26; Ne 10:38). Stored in the temple (Ne 10:38-39; 12:44; 13:5, 12; 2Ch 31:11-12; Mal 3:10).

Payment of, resumed in Hezekiah's reign (2Ch 31:5-10). Under Nehemiah (Ne 13:12). Withheld (Mal 3:8).

Customary in later times (Mt 23:23; Lk 11:42; 18:12). Observed by idolaters (Am 4:4-5).

See Alms; Beneficence; Giving; Liberality; Tax.

TITLE To real estate. See Land.

TITLES AND NAMES

Of God: See God, Names of.

Titles and Names of Christ:
Adam, Last (1Co 15:45). Almighty (Rev 1:8). Alpha and Omega (Rev 1:8; 22:13). Amen (Rev 3:14). Angel of his presence (Isa 63:9). Angel of the Lord (Ex 3:2; Jdg 13:15-18). Angel (Ge 48:16; Ex 23:20-21). Anointed One (Da 9:25; Jn 1:41). Apostle (Heb 3:1). Arm of the Lord (Isa 51:9; 53:1). Author of life (Ac 3:15). Author and Perfecter of our faith (Heb 2:10; 12:2).

Blessed and only Ruler (1Ti 6:15). Branch (Jer 23:5; Zec 3:8; 6:12). Bread of Life (Jn 6:35, 48).

Chief Shepherd (1Pe 5:4). Chief Cornerstone (Eph 2:20; 1Pe 2:6). Chosen One of God (Isa 42:1). Christ of God (Lk 9:20). Commander of the Lord's army (Jos 5:14-15). Commander (Isa 55:4). Consolation of Israel (Lk 2:25). Counselor (Isa 9:6).

David (Jer 30:9; Eze 34:23). Defender (1Jn 2:1). Deliverer (Ro 11:26). Door (Jn 10:7).

Eternal life (1Jn 1:2; 5:20). Everlasting Father (Isa 9:6).

Faithful witness (Rev 1:5; 3:14). First and Last (Rev 1:17; 2:8). Firstborn of the dead (Rev 1:5). Firstborn of all creation (Col 1:15).

Glory of the Lord (Isa 40:5). God over all (Ro 9:5). God (Isa 40:9; Jn 20:28). Good Shepherd (Jn 10:14). Great High Priest (Heb 4:14). Guarantee (Heb 7:22).

Head of the Church (Eph 5:23; Col 1:18). Heir of all things (Heb 1:2). Holy One of God (Mk 1:24). Holy One (Ps 16:10, w Ac 2:27, 31). Holy One of Israel (Isa 41:14). Horn of salvation (Lk 1:69).

I Am (Ex 3:14, w Rev 1:8; 22:13). Immanuel (Isa 7:14, w Mt 1:23). Israel's Ruler (Mic 5:1).

Jesus (Mt 1:21; 1Th 1:10).

King of the Jews (Mt 2:2). King of Israel (Jn 1:49). King of Kings (1Ti 6:15; Rev 17:14). King of the ages (Rev 15:3). King (Zec 9:9, w Mt 21:5).

Lamb of God (Jn 1:29, 36). Lamb (Rev 5:6, 12; 13:8; 21:22; 22:3). Lawgiver (Isa 33:22). Leader (Isa 55:4). Life (Jn 14:6; Col 3:4; 1Jn 1:2). Light of the world (Jn 8:12). Lion of the tribe of Judah (Rev 5:5). Lord of all (Ac 10:36). Lord of glory (1Co 2:8). Lord our righteousness (Jer 23:6). Lord God Almighty (Rev 15:3). Lord of the prophets (Rev 22:6).

Mediator (1Ti 2:5). Mighty One of Jacob (Isa 60:16). Mighty God (Isa 9:6). Morning Star (Rev 22:16).

Nazarene (Mt 2:23).

One and Only (Jn 1:14). One Before Us (Heb 6:20). Our Passover (1Co 5:7).

Prince of peace (Isa 9:6). Prophet (Lk 24:19; Jn 7:40).

Ransom (1Ti 2:6). Redeemer (Job 19:25; Isa 59:20; 60:16). Resurrection and life (Jn 11:25). Righteous One (Ac 7:52). Rock (1Co 10:4). Root of Jesse (Isa 11:10). Root of David (Rev 22:16). Root and Offspring of David (Rev 22:16). Ruler of the kings of the earth (Rev 1:5). Ruler of the creation of God (Rev 3:14). Ruler over Israel (Mic 5:2). Ruler (Mt 2:6).

Savior (2Pe 2:20; 3:18). Servant (Isa 42:1; 52:13). Shepherd and Overseer of Souls (1Pe 2:25). Son of the Most High (Lk 1:32). Son of man (Lk 22:67; 6:37). Son of David (Mt 9:27). Son of God (Lk 1:35; Jn 1:49). Son of the Blessed One (Mk 14:61). Star (Nu 24:17). Sun of righteousness (Mal 4:2).

The desired of all nations (Hag 2:7). True Light (Jn 1:9). True Vine (Jn 15:1). True God (1Jn 5:20). Truth (Jn 14:6).

Way (Jn 14:6). Wisdom (Pr 8:12). Witness (Isa 55:4). Wonderful (Isa 9:6). Word of Life (1Jn 1:1). Word (Jn 1:1; 1Jn 5:7). Word of God (Rev 19:13).

Titles and Names of the Church:
Assembly of the saints (Ps 89:7). Assembly of the saints (Ps 149:1). Body of Christ (1Co 12:27; Col 1:24). Bride of Christ (Rev 21:9). Church of the Firstborn (Heb 12:23). Church of the firstborn (Heb 12:23). Church of the Living God (1Ti 3:15). Church of God (Ac 20:28). City of the Living God (Heb 12:22). Council of the upright (Ps 111:1). Dwelling of God (Eph 2:22).

Family in heaven and on earth (Eph 3:15). Flock of God (Eze 34:15; 1Pe 5:2). Flock of Christ (Jn 10:16). God's field (1Co 3:9). God's inheritance (Joel 3:2; 1Pe 5:3). God's building (1Co 3:9). Golden lampstand (Rev 1:20). Holy City (Rev 21:2). House of the God of Jacob (Isa 2:3). House of Christ (Heb 3:6). House(hold) of God (1Ti 3:15; Heb 10:21; Eph 2:19). Inheritance (Dt 9:29; Isa 19:25). Israel of God (Gal 6:16). Lamb's bride (Rev 19:7; 21). Mount Zion (Ps 2:6; Heb 12:22). Mountain of the Lord's house (Isa 2:2).

New Jerusalem (Rev 21:2). Pillar and foundation of the truth (1Ti 3:15). Portion of the Lord (Dt 32:9). Princess (Ps 45:13). Sanctuary of God (Ps 114:2). Shoot of God's Planting (Isa 60:21). Sought After, the City no longer Deserted (Isa 62:12). Spiritual house (1Pe 2:5). Temple of the Living God (2Co 6:16). Temple of God (1Co 3:16-17). Vineyard (Jer 12:10; Mt 21:41).

Titles and Names of the Devil:
Abaddon (Rev 9:11). Accuser of our brothers (Rev 12:10). Ancient serpent (Rev 12:9; 20:2). Angel of the Abyss (Rev 9:11). Apollyon (Rev 9:11). Beelzebub (Mt 12:24). Belial (2Co 6:15).

Coiling serpent (Isa 27:1). Dominion of darkness (Col 1:13). Dragon (Isa 27:1; Rev 20:2). Enemy (Mt 13:39; 1Pe 5:8). Evil one (Mt 13:19, 38). Evil spirit (1Sa 16:14; Mt 12:43).

Father of lies (Jn 8:44). Gliding serpent (Isa 27:1). God of this age (2Co 4:4). Leviathan (Isa 27:1). Liar (Jn 8:44). Lying spirit (1Ki 22:22). Murderer (Jn 8:44). Powers of this dark world (Eph 6:12). Prince of demons (Mt 12:24). Prince of this world (Jn 14:30). Red dragon (Rev 12:3). Ruler of the kingdom of the air (Eph 2:2). Satan (1Ch 21:1; Job 1:6). Serpent (Ge 3:4, 14; 2Co 11:3). Spirit that works in those disobedient (Eph 2:2). Tempter (Mt 4:3; 1Th 3:5).

Titles and Names of the Holy Spirit:
Breath of the Almighty (Job 33:4). Counselor (Jn 14:16, 26; 15:26). Eternal Spirit (Heb 9:14). God (Ac 5:3-4). Good Spirit (Ne 9:20; Ps 143:10). Holy Spirit (Ps 51:11; Lk 11:13; Eph 1:13; 4:30). Power of the Most High (Lk 1:35).

Sevenfold Spirit (Rev 1:4 ftn). Spirit of fear of the Lord (Isa 11:2). Spirit of knowledge (Isa 11:2). Spirit of understanding (Isa 11:2). Spirit of power (Isa 11:2). Spirit of the Lord (Isa 11:2; 15:26). Spirit of holiness (Ro 1:4). Spirit of glory (1Pe 4:14). Spirit of fire (Isa 4:4). Spirit of judgment (Isa 4:4). Spirit of revelation (Eph 1:17). Spirit, The (Mt 4:1; Jn 3:6; 1Ti 4:1). Spirit of counsel (Isa 11:2). Spirit of Christ (Ro 8:9; 1Pe 1:11). Spirit of the Father (Mt 10:20). Spirit of God (Ge 1:2; 1Co 2:11; Job 33:4). Spirit of the Lord (Isa 11:2; Ac 5:9). Spirit of wisdom (Isa 11:2; Eph 1:17). Spirit of his Son (Gal 4:6). Spirit of sonship (Ro 8:15). Spirit of life (Ro 8:2). Spirit of prophecy (Rev 19:10). Spirit of grace (Zec 12:10; Heb 10:29). Willing Spirit (Ps 51:12).

Titles and Names of Ministers:
Administers of the grace of God (1Pe 4:10). Ambassadors for Christ (2Co 5:20). Apostles of Jesus Christ (Tit 1:1). Apostles (Lk 6:13; Eph 4:11; Rev 18:20). Deacons (Ac 6:1ff; 1Ti 3:8; Php 1:1). Elders (1Ti 5:17; 1Pe 5:1). Entrusted with the secrets of God (1Co 4:1). Entrusted with God's work (Tit 1:7). Evangelists (Eph 4:11; 2Ti 4:5). Fellow workers with God (2Co 6:1). Fishers of men (Mt 4:19; Mk 1:17). Messengers of the Church (Rev 1:20; 2:1 ftn). Messenger of the Lord Almighty (Mal 2:7).

Ministers of the New Covenant (2Co 3:6). Ministers in the sanctuary (Eze 45:4). Ministers of the Lord (Joel 2:17). Ministers of Christ (Ro 15:16; 1Co 4:1). Overseers (Ac 20:28; 1Pe 5:2; Tit 1:7; Tit 1:7). Pastors (Jer 3:15; Eph 4:11). Preachers (Ro 10:14; 1Ti 2:7). Representatives of the Church (2Co 8:23).

Servant of the Church (Col 1:24-25). Servant of this gospel (Eph 3:7; Col 1:23). Servants of the word (Lk 1:2). Servants of the Church (2Co 4:5). Servants of righteousness (2Co 11:15). Servants of God (2Co 6:4). Servants of God (Tit 1:1; Jas 1:1). Servants of the Lord (2Ti 2:24). Servants of Jesus Christ (Php 1:1; Jude 1). Shepherds (Jer 23:4). Soldiers of Christ (Php 2:25; 2Ti 2:3). Stars (Rev 1:20; 2:1). Teachers (Isa 30:20; Eph 4:11). Watchmen (Isa 62:6; Eze 33:7). Witnesses (Ac 1:8; 5:32; 26:16). Workers (Mt 9:38, w Phm 1; 1Th 2:2).

Titles and Names of Saints:
Believers (Ac 5:14; 1Ti 4:12). Blessed by the Father (Mt 25:34). Blessed by the Lord (Ge 24:31; 26:29). Brothers (Mt 23:8; Ac 22:17). Brothers of Christ (Lk 8:21; Jn 20:17). Called to belong to Jesus Christ (Ro 1:6).

Children of Abraham (Gal 3:7). Children (Jn 13:33; 1Jn 2:1). Children of the free woman (Gal 4:31). Children of promise (Ro 9:8; Gal 4:28). Children of the Lord (Dt 14:1). Children of the resurrection (Lk 20:36). Children of God (Jn 1:12; Php 2:15; 1Jn 3:1-2). Children of God (Jn 11:52; 1Jn 3:10). Chosen instrument (Ac 9:15). Chosen ones (1Ch 16:13). Chosen people (1Pe 2:9). Chosen of God (1Co 3:12; Tit 1:1). Christians (Ac 11:26; 26:28). co-heirs with Christ (Ro 8:17). Dear brothers (1Co 15:58; Jas 2:5). Dearly loved children (Eph 5:1). Disciples of Christ (Jn 8:31; 15:8).

Faithful brothers in Christ (Col 1:2). Faithful in the land, The (Ps 101:6). Faithful, The (Ps 12:1). Fellow citizens with God's people (Eph 2:19). Fellow servants (Rev 6:11). Freedman (1Co 7:22). Friends of God (2Ch 20:7; Jas 2:23). Friends of Christ (Jn 15:15). Glorious ones (Isa 16:3). Godly, The (Ps 4:3; 2Pe 2:9). Guests of the bridegroom (Mt 9:15). Heirs with you of the gracious gift of life (1Pe 3:7). Heirs of God (Ro 8:17; Gal 4:7). Heirs together with Israel (Eph 3:6). Heirs of promise (Heb 6:17; Gal 3:29). Holy brothers (Heb 3:1). Holy people (Dt 26:19; Isa 62:12). Holy nation (Ex 19:6; 1Pe 2:9). Holy priesthood (1Pe 2:5). Inheritors of salvation (Heb 1:14). Inheritors of the kingdom (Jas 2:5). Instrument for noble purposes (2Ti 2:21).

Kingdom of priests (Ex 19:6). Kings and priests to serve God (Rev 1:6). Lambs (Isa 40:11; Jn 21:15). Letter from Christ (2Co 3:3). Light of the world (Mt 5:14). Living stones (1Pe 2:5). Loved of God (Ro 1:7). Man of God (1Ti 6:11; 2Ti 3:17). Members of Christ (1Co 6:15; Eph 5:30). Oaks of righteousness (Isa 61:3). Obedient children (1Pe 1:14). Objects of mercy (Ro 9:23).

People close to God's heart (Ps 148:14). People of God (Heb 4:9; 1Pe 2:10). People saved by the Lord (Dt 33:29). People of Zion (Ps 149:2; Joel 2:23). Pillars in the temple of God (Rev 3:12). Ransomed of the Lord (Isa 35:10; Isa 51:11). Righteous, The (Hab 2:4). Royal priesthood (1Pe 2:9). Salt of the earth (Mt 5:13). Sheep of Christ (Jn 10:1-16; 21:16). Slaves of Christ (1Co 7:22; Eph 6:6). Slaves to Righteousness (Ro 6:18).

Sons of the Living God (Ro 9:26). Sons of Jacob (Ps 105:6). Sons of the Most High (Lk 6:35). Sons of light (Lk 16:8; Eph 5:8; 1Th 5:5). Sons of the day (1Th 5:5). Sons of the Father (Mt 5:45). Sons of the kingdom (Mt 13:38). Treasured possession (Ex 19:5; Dt 14:2; Tit 2:14; 1Pe 2:9). Witnesses for God (Isa 44:8).

Titles and Names of the Wicked:
Accursed brood (2Pe 2:14). Base and nameless brood (Job 30:8). Brood of rebels (Isa 57:4). Brood of evildoers (Isa 1:4; 14:20). Brood of vipers (Mt 3:7; 12:34). Child of the devil (Ac 13:10; 1Jn 3:10). Children unwilling to hear the Lord's instruction (Isa 30:9). Children unfaithful (Dt 32:20). Children given to corruption (Isa 1:4). Clasp hands with Pagans (Isa 2:6). Corrupt generation (Ac 2:40). Crooked and depraved generation (Php 2:15).

Deceitful children (Isa 30:9). Disobedient ones (Eph 2:2; Col 3:6). Enemies of God (Ps 37:20; Jas 4:4). Enemies of the cross of Christ (Php 3:18). Enemies of everything right (Ac 13:10). Evil men (Ps 37:1; Pr 4:14; 2Ti 3:13). Evil generation (Lk 11:35). Evildoer (Ps 101:8; Pr 17:4; Ps 28:3; 36:12). Evildoers (Hos 10:9). Failers of a test (2Co 13:5-7). Fools (Pr 1:7; Ro 1:22). Foreigners (Ps

144:7). God-haters (Ps 81:15; Ro 1:30). Hardened rebels (Jer 6:28). Invent ways of doing evil (Ro 1:30). Men of this world (Ps 17:14). Mockers (Ps 1:1). Natural children (Ro 9:8).

Objects of wrath (Ro 9:22; Eph 2:3). Obstinate children (Eze 2:4; Isa 30:1; 65:2). Offspring of liars (Isa 57:4). Offspring of the wicked (Ps 37:28; Isa 14:20). Opposers of the Lord (1Sa 2:10). People loaded with guilt (Isa 1:4). People of this world (Lk 16:8). Perverse generation (Dt 32:20; Mt 17:17). Proud, The (Job 41:34). Rebellious people (Isa 30:9). Rebellious house (Eze 2:5, 8; 12:2). Senseless children (Jer 4:22). Sinful generation (Mk 8:38). Sinners (Ps 26:9; Pr 1:10; Ps 37:38). Slaves to sin (Jn 8:34; Ro 6:20). Slaves of Depravity (2Pe 2:19). Snakes (Mt 23:33). Son of hell (Mt 23:15). Sons of the evil one (Mt 13:38). Stubborn and rebellious generation (Ps 78:8). Transgressors (Ps 51:13).

Warped and crooked generation (Dt 32:5). Wicked men (Dt 13:13; 2Ch 13:7). Wicked traitors (Ps 59:5). Wicked generation (Mt 12:45; 16:4). Wicked servants (Mt 25:26). Wicked and adulterous generation (Mt 12:39). Wicked of the earth (Ps 75:8). Wicked people (2Sa 7:10). Worthless servants (Mt 25:30). Wrongdoers (1Pe 2:14). See also Wicked, Compared With.

TITTLE NIV "the least stroke of a pen"; figurative of the smallest details of the law (Mt 5:18; Lk 16:17).

TITUS A Greek companion of Paul. Paul's love for (2Co 2:13; 7:6-7, 13-14; 8:23; Tit 1:4). With Paul in Macedonia (2Co 7:5-6). Affection of, for the Corinthians (2Co 7:15). Sent to Corinth (2Co 8:6, 16-22; 12:17-18). Character of (2Co 12:18). Accompanies Paul to Jerusalem (Gal 2:1-3, w Ac 15:1-29). Left by Paul in Crete (Tit 1:5), to rejoin him in Nicopolis (Tit 3:12). Paul writes to (Tit 1:1-4). With Paul in Rome; goes to Dalmatia (2Ti 4:10).

TITUS, EPISTLE TO

Author: the apostle Paul

Date: Probably between A.D. 63 and 65

Outline:
I. Salutation (1:1-4).
II. Concerning Elders (1:5-9).
 A. Reasons for Leaving Titus in Crete (1:5).
 B. Qualifications of Elders (1:6-9).
III. Concerning False Teachers (1:10-16).
IV. Concerning Various Groups in the Congregations (ch. 2).
 A. The Instructions to Different Groups (2:1-10).
 B. The Foundation for Christian Living (2:11-14).
 C. The Duty of Titus (2:15).
V. Concerning Believers in General (3:1-8).
 A. Obligations as Citizens (3:1-2).
 B. Motives for Godly Conduct (3:3-8).
VI. Concerning Response to Spiritual Error (3:9-11).
VII. Conclusion (3:12-15).
 See Church, The Body of Believers, Qualifications for Elders/Overseers and Deacons; Missionary Journeys of Paul; Pastoral Epistles.

TITUS, FLAVIUS VESPASIANUS A Roman emperor (A.D. 79-81); captured and destroyed Jerusalem in A.D. 70.

TITUS JUSTUS See Justus.

TIZITE The designation of Joha, one of David's soldiers (1Ch 11:45).

TOAH An ancestor of Samuel (1Ch 6:34), probably the same as "Nahath" (1Ch 6:26), and perhaps "Tohu" (1Sa 1:1). See Nahath, 2; Tohu.

TOB (good).
1. A district in Syria, extending NE from Gilead, to which Jephthah fled (Jdg 11:3, 5).
2. Place in Israel which supplied Ammonites with soldiers against David (2Sa 10:6, 8).

TOB-ADONIJAH (good is [my] lord Yahweh). A Levite sent by Jehoshaphat to instruct the people in the law (2Ch 17:8).

TOBIAH (Yahweh is good).
1. An ancestor of a family of Babylonian captives (Ezr 2:60; Ne 7:62).
2. An enemy of the Jews in the time of Nehemiah. Opposes the rebuilding of the wall of Jerusalem (Ne 2:10, 19; 4:3, 7-8). Conspires to injure and intimidate Nehemiah (Ne 6:1-14, 19). Subverts nobles of Judah (Ne 6:17-18). Allies himself with Eliashib, the priest (Ne 13:4-9).

TOBIJAH (Yahweh is good).
1. A Levite chosen by Jehoshaphat to instruct the people in the law (2Ch 17:8).
2. A captive in Babylon (Zec 6:10, 14).

TOBIT, BOOK OF See Apocrypha.

TOCHEN See Token, 2.

TOE Anointed in consecration (Ex 29:20; Lev 8:23-24), in purification (Lev 14:14, 17, 25, 28). Of prisoners of war cut off (Jdg 1:6-7). Six, on each foot (2Sa 21:20; 1Ch 20:6).

TOGARMAH Son of Gomer (Ge 10:3; 1Ch 1:6). Descendants of (Eze 27:14; 38:6).

TOHU An ancestor of Samuel (1Sa 1:1), probably the same as "Nahath" (1Ch 6:26), and perhaps "Toah" (1Ch 6:34). See Nahath, 2; Toah.

TOI See Tou.

TOKEN (measure).
1. A sign (Ge 3:12). Sun and moon for time and seasons (Ge 1:14). The mark of Cain (Ge 4:15). Rainbow, that the world might no more be destroyed by a flood (Ge 9:12-17). Circumcision, of the covenant of Abraham (Ge 17:11). Presents (Ge 21:27, 30).

Miracles of Moses, of the divine authority of his missions (Ex 4:1-9). Blood of the Passover lamb (Ex 12:13). The Passover (Ex 13:9). Consecration of the firstborn (Ex 13:14-16). The Sabbath (Ex 31:13, 17), a fringe (Nu 15:38-40). Scarlet thread (Jos 2:18, 21). Cover of the altar (Nu 16:38-40). Aaron's rod (Nu 17:10). Memorial stones (Jos 4:2-9). Dew on Gideon's fleece (Jdg 6:36-40). Prayer for tokens of mercy (Ps 86:17).
> See Miracles.
> 2. A city in Simeon (1Ch 4:32).

TOKHATH Father-in-law of Huldah the prophetess; also called Tokhath (2Ch 34:22, ftn). See Tikvah.

TOLA, TOLAITE (worm of scarlet).
1. The son of Issachar (Ge 46:13).
2. Judged Israel twenty-three years (Jdg 10:1-2).

TOLAD City of Simeon (1Ch 4:29).

TOLERANCE Religious (Mic 4:4-5; Mk 9:38-40; Lk 9:49-50; Ac 17:11; 28:31; Ro 14; 1Co 10:28-32). See Intolerance.

TOLL See Tribute; Tax.

TOMB A burial place. Most Hebrew burying sites were unmarked; some kings were buried in a vault in Jerusalem (2Sa 2:32; Ne 2:3). Tombs of NT times were natural or man-made caves, sealed with circular stones weighing from one to three tons (Lk 24:2; Jn 20:1). See Grave; Pillar; Tombstone.

TOMBSTONE At the tomb of the man of God from Judah (2Ki 23:17). A pillar at Rachel's grave (Ge 35:20). See Pillar.

TONGS Used to tend the lamps in the temple (1Ki 7:49). In Isaiah's vision (Isa 6:6). See Wick Trimmers.

TONGUE Language (Ge 10:5, 20; Isa 66:18; Rev 7:9). Confusion of (Ge 11:1-9). Gift of (Ac 2:1-18, 33; 10:46; 19:6; 1Co 12:10, 28, 30; 14).
> Chattering (Pr 10:8, 19). Restrained by wisdom (Pr 17:27; 21:23; Ecc 3:7). Hasty (Pr 29:20).
> An evil. See Speaking, Evil; Slander.

TONGUES, CONFUSION OF Punishment by God for arrogant attempt to build tower reaching to heaven (Ge 11:1-9).

TONGUES, GIFT OF A spiritual gift (Mk 16:17; Ac 2:1-13; 10:44-46; 19:6; 1Co 12; 14). The gift appeared on the day of Pentecost with the outpouring of the Holy Spirit on the assembled believers (Ac 2:1-13). The phenomenon appeared again in the home of Cornelius (Ac 10:44-11:17), and at Ephesus (Ac 19:6), and in the church at Corinth (1Co 12; 14). Instruction regarding the use of tongues in worship (1Co 12-14).

TONGUES OF FIRE One of the phenomena that occurred at the outpouring of the Holy Spirit on the Day of Pentecost. Symbolic of the Holy Spirit who came in power on the church (Ac 2:3).

TOOLS The following kinds are mentioned in the Bible: cutting, boring, forks and shovels, carpentry, drawing, measuring, tilling, metalworking, stoneworking.

TOOTH Both human and animal teeth are mentioned (Nu 11:33; Dt 32:24), figurative use is common: cleanness of teeth, famine (Am 4:6), gnashing of teeth, rage and despair (Job 16:9), oppression (Pr 30:14), plenty (Ge 49:12).

TOPAZ
1. A precious stone (Eze 28:13; Rev 21:20).
2. In the priestly breastplate (Ex 28:17; 39:10).
Figurative:
Topaz cannot compare to the price of wisdom (Job 28:19).
Symbolic:
Seen in the foundation of the Holy City, the New Jerusalem (Rev 21:20).
> See Minerals of the Bible, 1; Stones.

TOPHEL (cement). A place in the wilderness where Moses addressed the Israelites (Dt 1:1), possibly modern el-Tafila, fifteen miles SE of the Dead Sea.

TOPHETH A place in the valley of the sons of Hinnom or Ben Hinnom (2Ki 23:10). Israelite children burned in sacrifice to Molech there (2Ki 23:10; Jer 7:31-32; 19:6, 11-14; 32:35; cf. 2Ch 28:3; 33:6). Destroyed by Josiah (2Ki 23:10). Horror of (Isa 30:33).
> See Ben Hinnom; Hinnom, Valley of.

TOPOGRAPHY Of Canaan (Jos 13:15-33; 15; 18:9).

TORAH Divine law (Ex 13:9); instruction (Ex 16:4, 28); the Law of Moses (1Ki 2:3); the Book of the Law (Dt 28:61); the entire Jewish Scriptures (Jn 10:34). See Law.

TORCHES (Jdg 7:16; 15:4; Na 2:3; Jn 18:3).

TORMENTOR Conquerors of Israel (Ps 137:3; Isa 51:23). Abusive jailers (Mt 18:34).

TORMENTS Of the wicked (Lk 16:23-28; Rev 14:10-11).
> See Wicked, Punishment of.

TORTOISE See Lizard.

TOTAL ABSTINENCE See Abstinence.

TOU King of Hamath who congratulated David for victory over Hadadezer (2Sa 8:9-11; 1Ch 18:9-10).

TOW NIV "thong, tinder, wick." Short fibers of flax or hemp (Jdg 16:9; Isa 1:31; 43:17).

TOWEL A cloth for wiping and drying (Jn 13:4-5).

TOWER Of Babel (Ge 11:1-9). Of Eder (Ge 35:21). Peniel (Jdg 8:8-9, 17). Of Shechem (Jdg 9:46, 49). Of the Hundred (Ne 3:1; 12:39). Of Hananel (Ne 3:1; 12:39; Jer 31:38; Zec 14:10). Of David (SS 4:4). Of Aswan (Eze 29:10). Of Siloam (Lk 13:4). In the walls of Jerusalem (2Ch 26:9; 32:5; Ne 12:38-39). Of other cities (2Ch 14:7).
> In the desert (2Ch 26:10). For watchmen or sentinels (2Ki 9:17; 18:8). As fortress (Mt 21:33).
> Parable of (Lk 14:28-29).
> See Fortification; Ziggurat.
> Figurative of divine protection (2Sa 22:3, 51; Ps 18:2; 61:3; 144:2; Pr 18:10).

TOWN In ancient times, large cities had towns or villages surrounding them for protection (Nu 21:25, 32; Jos 15:45-47), sometimes it means an unwalled town (Dt 3:5; 1Sa 16:4).

TOWNCLERK See City Clerk.

TRACONITIS (rough, stony district). An area of c. 370 sq. miles S of Damascus; tetrarchy of Philip (Lk 3:1).

TRADE AND TRAVEL
Trade in the OT:
Ur of the Chaldeans a trading port; Egypt, from earliest times, a great trading nation (Ge 37:25). First organized commerce of Hebrew people was under Solomon, who formed a partnership with the great mercantile cities of Tyre and Sidon (1Ki 9:27-28; 10:11); after the death of Solomon, Israel again became an agricultural nation.
Trade in the NT:
Jewish trade and commerce have small place in the Gospels. Through the NT times, trade, in the wider sense of the word, was in the hands of Rome and of Italy.
Travel:
Motives for travel: Trade, colonization, exploration, migration, pilgrimage, preaching, courier service, exile. Travel had serious hazards (Ac 27-28; 2Co 11:25-27); was facilitated by wonderful Roman roads, some of which still are used. Regular passenger service by land or sea was unknown.

TRADE GUILDS Societies of tradesmen organized chiefly for the purpose of social interaction (Ac 19), not trade unions in the modern sense.

TRADERS See Commerce; Merchant.

TRADITION The decisions and minor precepts taught by Paul (1Co 11:2; 2Th 2:15; 3:6).
> Commandments of men (Mt 12:1-8; 15:2-6; Mk 7:3-9; Lk 6:1-11; Col 2:8; 1Pe 1:18). Not authoritative (Mt 15:3-20; 1Ti 1:4; 4:7). See Commandments and Statutes, of Men.

TRAFFIC Commerce suspended on the Sabbath (Ne 13:15-22).

TRAIN
1. Retinue of a monarch (Ps 68:18).
2. Skirt of a robe (Isa 6:1).
3. To educate or discipline (2Sa 22:35; Pr 22:6).

TRAITOR Judas (Mt 26:14-16, 46-50; Mk 14:10-11, 43-45; Lk 22:3-6, 21-23, 47-48; Jn 13:2, 27-30; 18:2-8, 13).
> See Treason.

TRAMP NIV "bandit" (Pr 6:11).

TRANCE (a throwing of the mind out of its normal state). A mental state in which the senses are partially or wholly suspended and the person is unconscious of his environment while he contemplates some extraordinary object (Ac 10:9-16; 22:17-21).

TRANS-EUPHRATES The region beyond the Euphrates; from the Persian perpective it included Israel and its neighbors (Ezr 4:10-20; 5:6; 6:6).

TRANSFIGURATION Of Moses (Ex 34:29-35). Of Jesus (Mt 17:2-9; Mk 9:2-10; Lk 9:29-36; 2Pe 1:16-18). Of Stephen (Ac 6:15). See Translation.

TRANSGRESSION Breaking of a law (Pr 17:19; Ro 4:15). See Sin.

TRANSJORDAN (beyond [East of] the Jordan). A large plateau E of Jordan, comprised in modern Hashemite Kingdom of Jordan; in the NT times, the Perea and the Decapolis; in OT times, Moab, Ammon, Gilead, and Bashan. Associated with Moses; Joshua; the tribes of Reuben, Gad, and Manasseh; David; Nabateans.

TRANSLATION Removal from earth to heaven. Of Enoch (Ge 5:24; Heb 11:5). Of Elijah (2Ki 2:1-12). Of Jesus (Mk 16:19; Lk 24:51; Ac 1:9-11). Desired by Paul (2Co 5:4).

TRANSLATIONS OF THE BIBLE Ancient: See Texts and Versions.

TRANSPORTATION In ancient times done chiefly by camels, donkeys, horses, and boats.

TRAP (Jos 23:13; Job 18:10; Jer 5:26).

TRAVAIL Pangs of childbirth (Ge 35:16; 38:27; 1Sa 4:19), trouble (Isa 23:4; 54:1), to be weak or sick (Jer 4:31), weariness (Ex 18:8).

TRAVEL See Trade and Travel.

TREACHERY (Jer 9:8). Of Rahab to her people (Jos 2). Of the man of Bethel (Jdg 1:24-25). Of Jael (Jdg 4:18-21). Of Shechemites (Jdg 9:23). Of Joab (2Sa 3:26-27). Of Baanah and Recab (2Sa 4:6).

Of David to Uriah (2Sa 11). Of Joab to Amasa (2Sa 20:9-10). Of Jehu (2Ki 10:18-28). Of the enemies of Nehemiah (Ne 6).
> See Conspiracy; Treason.

TREASON
Instances of:
Of Aaron and Miriam against Moses (Nu 12:1-11). Of Korah, Dathan, and Abiram against Moses and Aaron (Nu 16:1-33). Of Rahab against Jericho (Jos 2). Of the betrayer of Bethel (Jdg 1:24-25). Of the Shechemites against Abimelech (Jdg 9:22-25). Of the Ephraimites against Jephthah (Jdg 12:1-4). Of the Israelites against Saul (1Sa 10:27), against Rehoboam (1Ki 12:16-19). Of the Egyptian servant against the Amalekites (1Sa 30:15-16). Of Abner against Ish-Bosheth (2Sa 3:6-21). Of Jehoiada against Athaliah (2Ki 11:14-16). Of Absalom against his father. See Absalom.
> Death penalty for (Est 2:23).
> Jesus falsely accused of (Mt 27:11, 29-30; Lk 23:2-3, 38; Jn 19:12, 14-15, 19). Paul falsely accused of (Ac 17:7).
> David's amnesty of the traitors (2Sa 19:16-23), to Amasa (2Sa 19:13).
> See Conspiracy; Treachery.

TREASURE A thing of highly estimated value. Money (Ge 42:25, 27-28, 35; 43:23, w 43:18, 21-22). Valuables of the temple and royal residence (1Ki 14:26; 2Ki 20:13).
> Cannot save life (Job 20:20). Jesus forbids the hoarding of (Mt 6:19; 19:21; Lk 12:33). Hidden (Mt 13:44).
Figurative:
Of God's people (Ex 19:5; Dt 7:6). Of wisdom (Pr 2:4; 24:4; Col 2:3). Of spiritual understanding (Mt 13:52; Col 2:3), spiritual calling (2Co 4:6-7).
> Treasures in heaven (Mt 6:19-21; 19:21; Lk 12:33-34). Gospel called (2Co 4:7). Parables of (Mt 13:44, 52).

TREASURE CITIES NIV "store cities" for Pharaoh (Ex 1:11).

TREASURE HOUSE See Treasury.

TREASURER One trusted with charge of the treasury. See Treasury. Of the temple (2Ki 12:5, 7). Of Persia (Ezr 1:8; 7:21). Of Babylon (Da 3:2, 3).

TREASURY Of kings (2Ki 14:14; 2Ch 32:27-28; Ezr 1:7-8; Est 3:9). Records preserved in (Ezr 6:1). See Archives. Treasurer in charge of (Ezr 7:20-21). See Treasurer.
> Tabernacle used for (Jos 6:19, 24). Solomon's temple used for (1Ki 7:51; 2Ki 12:4-14, 18; 22:4-5; 1Ch 28:11-12; Mt 27:6; Mk 12:41, 43; Lk 21:1; Jn 8:20). Under the charge of the Levites (1Ch 26:20). Storerooms provided in the temple for various kinds of offerings (Ne 10:38-39; 13:5, 9, 12; Mal 3:10). Priests and Levites in charge of (1Ch 9:26; 26:20-28; Ne 12:44; 13:13). Pagan temples used for (Da 1:2).

TREATY Between nations: Israelites and Gibeonites (Jos 9:3-15), Judah and Syria (1Ki 15:19). Cession of territory by (1Ki 9:10-14; 20:34). Sacredness of (Jos 9:16-21, w 2:8-21).
> Reciprocity (1Ki 5:1-12). With idolatrous nations forbidden (Ex 34:12, 15).
> See Covenant.

TREE Israel in ancient times was far more wooded than today. Over 25 different kinds of trees have been identified as having grown in the Holy Land. Trees were venerated by heathen people; Hebrews forbidden to plant a tree near a sacred altar (Dt 16:21). Known by its fruit (Mt 7:17-19; Lk 6:43-44).
Specific Trees:
Acacia tree (Ex 25:10ff). Algum tree (2Ch 2:8; 9:11). Almond tree (Ge 30:37; Ex 25:33-36; Ecc 12:5; Jer 1:11). Almug tree (1Ki 10:11, 12; 2Ch 2:8, 9:10 ftn). Apple tree (SS 2:3; 8:5; Joel 1:12). Balsam trees (2Sa 5:23-24). Broom tree (1Ki 19:3-4; Job 30:4; Ps 120:4). Cedar Wood (Lev 14:4, 6, 49, 51, 52; 2Sa 5:11; 2Sa 7:2; 1Ki 4:33). Citron Wood (Rev 18:12). Cypress Wood (Ge 6:14; Isa 44:14, 60:13; Eze 27:6). Fig tree (Dt 8:7). Fir (Isa 41:19; 60:13; SS 1:17). Fruit trees (Ge 1:29; Lev 19:23). Incense tree (SS 4:14). Mulberry tree (Lk 17:6). Mustard tree (Mt 13:32; Lk 13:18). Myrtle tree (Ne 8:15). Nut trees (SS 6:11). Oak (Ge 35:4; Zec 11:2; Eze 6:13). Olive tree (Jdg 9:8; Job 15:33; Ps 52:8; Isa 17:6; Isa 41:19). Palm trees (Ex 15:27). Pine tree (1Ki 5:10; Ps 104:17 ;Isa 60:13). Pistachio (Ge 43:11). Plane tree (Ge 30:37; Eze 31:8). Pomegranate (Dt 8:8; 1Sa 14:2). Poplars (Ge 30:37; Lev 23:40; Job 40:22; Ps 137:2; Isa 15:7, 44:4). Sycamore-fig tree (Lk 19:4; 1Ki 10:27; 1Ch 27:28; 2Ch 1:15; Am 7:14; Lk 19:4). Tamarisk tree (Ge 21:33; 1Sa 22:6; 31:13). Terebinth (Isa 6:13; Hos 4:13).
Generic and Symbolic Trees:
Bad tree (Mt 7:18; 12:33; Lk 6:43). Eden trees (Eze 31:9, 18). Execution tree (Dt 21:23; Ac 5:30; 10:39; 13:29). Field trees (Isa 55:12). Forest trees (1Ch 16:33; Ps 96:12). Good tree (2Ki 3:19, 25; Mt 7:17, 12:33; Lk 6:43). Great trees (Ge 13:18; 14:13; Jos 19:33). Great tree (Ge 12:6). Green tree (Ps 37:35; Lk 23:30). Tree of Knowledge (Ge 2:9). Leafy tree (Eze 20:28). Tree of Life (Ge 3:22-24; Pr 3:18, 11:30, 13:12; 15:4; Rev 2:7; 22:2, 19). Lofty trees (Isa 10:33). Shade tree (Isa 8:15). Spreading tree (Dt 12:2; 1Ki 14:23; 2Ki 16:4, 17:10). Wild olive tree (Ro 11:24). Of Nebuchadnezzar (Da 4:1-27).
> See Plants of the Bible; Tree of Knowledge; Tree of Life.

TREE OF KNOWLEDGE A special tree in the garden of Eden, set apart by the Lord as an instrument to test the obedience of Adam and Eve (Ge 2:9, 17; 3:3-6, 11-12, 17).

TREE OF LIFE Another special tree in the Garden of Eden; its fruit conferred immortality on persons eating it (Ge 2:9; 3:22, 24; Rev 22:2).

TRENCH Rampart, entrenchment (2Sa 20:15; 1Sa 17:20; 26:5).

TRES TABERNAE See Three Taverns.

T

TRESPASS (Ex 22:9). Of an ox (Ex 21:28-36). Of a brother (Mt 18:15-18; Lk 17:3-4). Creditor shall not enter a debtor's house to take a pledge (Dt 24:10). *See Sin.*

TRESPASS OFFERING *See Guilt Offering; Offerings.*

TRIAL Before court (Lev 24:10-14). Right of (Jn 7:51; Ac 16:37-39; 22:25-30). *See Court, Of Law; Justice; Prisoners.*

TRIAL OF JESUS Betrayed by Judas into the hands of the Jewish religious leaders, Jesus was first brought before Annas, former high priest, and father-in-law of the current high priest Caiaphas, for a brief examination (Jn 18:13); then before dawn he appeared before the Sanhedrin in the palace of Caiaphas, where he was questioned and insulted (Mk 14:60-65; Lk 22:63-64); at dawn he appeared before the Sanhedrin again and was condemned to death (Lk 22:66-70); next he was brought by the Sanhedrin before Pilate, who after an examination pronounced him innocent (Jn 18:33-38), but the Jews would not hear of his being released.

Pilate therefore sent him to Herod Antipas, who was also present for the Passover, on the plea that he belonged to Herod's jurisdiction. Herod, however, merely mocked Jesus and returned him to Pilate uncondemned (Lk 23:2-12); Pilate then gave the Jews the opportunity of choosing for release either Barabbas or Jesus, and the Jews chose Barabbas; another attempt by Pilate to have Jesus released met with failure, for the Jews threatened him if he did not carry out their wishes; after the Roman soldiers flogged and mocked Jesus, he was crucified (Mk 15:16-20).

See Jesus, History of.

TRIBE, TRIBES The tribes of Israel were descended from the twelve sons of Jacob, with Joseph's sons, Ephraim and Manasseh forming two, while no tribal territory was allotted to Levi (Ge 48:5; Nu 26:5-51; Jos 13:7-33; 15-19). The leaders of the tribes are called by various names: princes, rulers, heads, chiefs (Ex 34:31; Nu 1:16; Ge 36:1ff); before the Israelites entered the promised land two tribes, Reuben and Gad, and half of Manasseh chose to settle on the E side of the Jordan (Nu 32:33). During the period of the Judges in Israel, the tribes were each one a law to themselves. When David became king over the whole land the 12 tribes were unified. He appointed a captain over each tribe (1Ch 27:16-22). The captivities wiped out tribal distinctions.

TRIBULATION, GREAT A period of suffering sent from God upon the earth at the end time because of its awful wickedness (Da 12:1; Mt 24:21).

TRIBUTE From conquered nations (Jos 16:10; Jdg 1:30-33; 2Ki 15:19; 23:35; Mt 17:24-27; 22:15-22; Lk 2:1-5). By Arabs to Solomon (2Ch 9:14), to Jehoshaphat (2Ch 17:11). *See Duty; Levy; Tax.*

TRIMMERS, WICK *See Wick Trimmers.*

TRINITY, HOLY (*triad, union of three*). The word "trinity" is not used in the Bible. Plurality in the unity of God is implied in the OT; Father, Son, and Spirit are all called "God" in the NT.

Implied in the Old Testament:
God speaks of self in the plural (Ge 1:26; 3:22; Isa 6:3, 8). LORD, Servant, and Spirit (Isa 11:2-3; 42:1 w Mt 12:48; Isa 48:16). Tri-holiness of God suggests (Isa 6:3; Rev 4:8).

Implied in the NT:
Father, Son, and Spirit (Mt 28:19; Lk 3:22 w Mt 3:16; Jn 3:34-35; 14:16-17, 26; 15:26; 16:7, 13-15; Ac 1:2, 4-5; 2:33; 10:36-38; Ro 1:3-4; 8:9-11, 26-27; 1Co 12:3-6; 2Co 1:21-22; 5:5; 13:14; Gal 4:4, 6; 2Ti 2:13-14, 16; 1Ti 3:16; Tit 3:4-6; Heb 9:14; 1Pe 1:2; 3:18; 1Jn 5:6-7). Tri-holiness of God suggests (Isa 6:3; Rev 4:8).

Relationships Within the Godhead:
The Father and the Son (Mt 11:27; Lk 9:26; Jn 3:35; 5:19-27; 6:27; 10:36; 17:1; Ac 13:33; Heb 1:5; 5:5; 2Pe 1:17; 1Jn 1:3; 2:22-24).
The Father and the Holy Spirit (Isa 42:1; 48:16; 63:9-10; 1Co 2:10-11; 6:19).
Jesus and the Holy Spirit (Isa 61:1-3; Lk 4:18; Mt 1:18, 20; 12:28; 28:19; Lk 1:35; 4:1, 14; Jn 1:32-33; 7:39; 20:22; 1Co 8:6; 2Co 3:17; Php 1:19; Col 2:2).
See Angel [of the Lord]; God; Holy Spirit; Jesus the Christ, Deity of.

TRIPOLIS People sent as colonists to Samaria by the Assyrians (Ezr 4:9-10).

TRIUMPH (*to lead in triumph*). In Roman times a magnificent procession in honor of a victorious general (2Co 2:14; Col 2:15).

TRIUMPHAL ENTRY OF JESUS Into Jerusalem (Ps 118:26; Zec 9:9; Mt 21:5, 8-10; Mk 11:7-11; Lk 19:35-38; Jn 12:12-13).

TROAS A chief city and port of the Roman Province of Asia, on the Aegean coast, c. ten miles from the ruins of ancient Troy; known as Alexandria Troas (Ac 16:8; 20:5; 2Co 2:12).

TROGYLLIUM A promontory thrusting SW from the Asian mainland N of Miletus, opposite the island of Samos (Ac 20:15, KJV).

TROPHIES Goliath's head and armor (1Sa 17:54; 21:9), Saul's (1Sa 31:8-10). Placed in temples. *See Temple.*

TROPHIMUS (*nourished [child]*). An Ephesian companion of Paul. Accompanies Paul from Greece to Asia (Ac 20:4). With Paul in Jerusalem; made the occasion of an attack on Paul (Ac 21:27-30). Left ill at Miletus (2Ti 4:20).

TROUBLE Being anxious, forbidden (Mt 6:25-34; Php 4:6). Remedy for anxiety (Ps 16:6-7; 1Pe 5:7).
See Affliction; Anxiety; Suffering.

Instances of:
Israelites at the Red Sea (Ex 14:10-12), about water (Ex 15:23-25; 17:2-3; Nu 20:1-13), food (Ex 16:2-3; Nu 11:4-33). When Moses remained on Mount Sinai (Ex 32:1). When the spies brought their adverse report (Nu 13:28-29, 31-33; 14:1-4, w 14:4-12). Elijah, under the broom tree and in the cave (1Ki 19:4-15). The disciples, as to how the multitude could be fed (Mt 14:15; Mk 6:37), in the tempest, when Jesus was asleep in the ship (Mt 8:23-26; Mk 4:36-39; Lk 8:22-24), when Jesus was crucified (Lk 24:4-9, 24-31, 36-40). Mary at the tomb (Jn 20:11-17). The people in the shipwreck (Ac 27:22-25, 30-36).

TRUCE In battle (2Sa 2:26-31).

TRUMPET Made of ram's horn (Jos 6:4-6, 8, 13), of silver (Nu 10:2).

Uses of:
Prescribed by Moses (Nu 10:1-10). Used in war (Job 39:24-25; Jer 4:19; 6:1, 17; 42:14; 51:27; Eze 7:14; Am 2:2; 3:6; Zep 1:16; 1Co 14:8). To summon soldiers, by Phinehas (Nu 31:6), by Ehud (Jdg 3:27), by Gideon (Jdg 6:34), by Saul (1Sa 13:3), by Joab (2Sa 2:28; 18:16; 20:22), by Absalom (2Sa 15:10), by Sheba (2Sa 20:1), by Nehemiah (Ne 4:18, 20). Gideon's soldiers (Jdg 7:8-22). In war, of Abijah (2Ch 13:12, 14). In the siege of Jericho (Jos 6:4-20).
Sounded in time of danger (Eze 33:3-6; Joel 2:1).
Used at Sinai (Ex 19:13-19; 20:18; Heb 12:19), on the Day of Atonement (Isa 27:13), at the Jubilee (Lev 25:9), at the bringing up of the ark (2Sa 6:5, 15; 1Ch 13:8; 15:28), the anointing of kings (1Ki 1:34, 39; 2Ki 9:13; 11:14), dedication of Solomon's temple (2Ch 5:12-13; 7:6), in worship (1Ch 15:24; 16:42; 25:5; Ps 81:3-4), at Jehoshaphat's triumph (2Ch 20:28), at the foundation of the second temple (Ezr 3:10-11), at the dedication of the wall (Ne 12:35, 41).

Figurative:
(Isa 27:13; Eze 33:3; Joel 2:1; Zec 9:14; Mt 6:2).

Symbolic:
(Mt 24:31; 1Co 15:52; 1Th 4:16; Rev 1:10; 4:1; 8; 9:1-14; 10:7; 11:15).
See Horn; Music, Instruments of.

TRUMPETS, FEAST OF When and how observed (Lev 23:24-25; Nu 29:1-6). Celebrated after the captivity with joy (Ne 8:2, 9-12).
See Feasts.

TRUST *See Faith.*

TRUSTEE Mosaic law concerning (Ex 22:7-13; Lev 6:2-7). The parable of the pounds (Mt 25:14-28; Lk 19:12-27).
See Steward.

TRUTH Truth and faithful(ness) are translated from the same Hebrew and Greek words. *See Faithfulness.*

Characteristics of:
(Ps 85:10-11). Precious (Pr 23:23). Preserves (Ps 46:11; 61:7; 91:4; Pr 20:28). Purifies (Pr 16:6; 1Pe 1:22). Sanctifies (Jn 17:17, 19; 2Th 2:13). Brings freedom (Jn 8:32).
Reaches to the clouds (Ps 57:10; 108:4). Endures forever (Ps 100:5; 117:2). Ways of the Lord in (Ps 25:10).
The foundation of which Christ is the cornerstone (Eph 2:20). Came by Jesus Christ (Jn 1:17; 8:45; 14:6; 18:37-38; Eph 2:20). Revealed to the righteous (Ps 57:3; 86:11).
Word of God called the word of (Jn 17:17; Eph 1:13; Col 1:5; 2Ti 2:15; Jas 1:18). Scripture of (Da 10:21).
Acceptance of, necessary to salvation (2Th 2:12-13; 1Ti 2:4; 2Ti 2:25; 3:7; Heb 10:26). Rejection of, brings condemnation (2Th 2:10-12; Tit 1:14).
To be taught by parents to children (Isa 38:19). Church is the pillar of (1Ti 3:15).
Believers should worship God in (Jn 4:24, w Ps 145:18), serve God in (Jos 24:14; 1Sa 12:24), walk before God in (1Ki 2:4; 2Ki 20:3), keep religious feasts with (1Co 5:8), value as inestimable (Pr 23:23), love (Zec 8:19), rejoice in (1Co 13:6), speak to one another (Zec 8:16; Eph 4:25), execute judgment with (Zec 8:16), meditate upon (Php 4:8), bind about the neck (Pr 3:3), write upon the tables of the heart (Pr 3:3).
The fruit of the light (Eph 5:9). They who speak, show righteousness (Pr 12:17), are the delight of God (Pr 12:22), will be established forever (Pr 2:1).
The wicked are destitute of truth (Isa 59:14-15; Da 9:13; Hos 4:1; 1Ti 6:5). The wicked resist (2Ti 3:8; 4:4), turn away from (2Ti 4:4), speak not (Jer 9:5), plead not for (Isa 59:4), are not valiant for (Jer 9:3), punished for lack of (Jer 9:5, 9; Hos 4:1, 3). *See Wicked.*

The Gospel As:
Came by Christ (Jn 1:17). Is in Christ (1Ti 2:7). John bore witness to (Jn 5:33). Is according to godliness (Tit 1:1). Is sanctifying (Jn 17:17, 19). Is purifying (1Pe 1:22). Is part of the Christian armor (Eph 6:14). Revealed abundantly to saints (Jer 33:6). Abides continually with saints (2Jn 2).
Should be acknowledged (2Ti 2:25). Should be believed (2Th 2:12-13; 1Ti 4:3). Should be obeyed (Ro 2:8; Gal 3:1). Should be loved (2Th 2:10). Should be manifested (2Co 4:2). Should be rightly divided (2Ti 2:15). The church is the pillar and ground of (1Ti 3:15).
The devil is devoid of (Jn 8:44).

Of the Gospel:
(2Ti 4:3-4; Tit 1:1, 14; 2:1; Jas 1:18, 21, 23, 25; 2:13; 5:19; 1Pe 1:22-25; 2:2, 8; 3:1; 5:12; 2Pe 1:12). *See God, Truth.*

Of God:
Is one of his attributes (Dt 32:4; Isa 65:16). Often linked with his mercy (Ps 85:10-11; 93:3; 100:5).
He keeps, forever (Ps 146:6), abundant (Ex 34:6), inviable (Nu 23:19; Tit 1:2), enduring to all generations (Ps 100:5). Exhibited in his ways (Rev 15:3), works (Ps 33:4; 111:7; Da 4:37), judicial statutes (Ps 19:9), word (Ps 119:160; Jn 17:17), fulfillment of promises in Christ (2Co 1:20), fulfillment of His covenant (Mic 7:20), dealings with saints (Ps 25:10), deliverance of saints (Ps

57:3), punishment of the wicked (Rev 16:7). Is a shield and buckler to saints (Ps 91:4).
Believers should confide in (Ps 31:5; Tit 1:2). Plead in prayer (Ps 89:49). Pray for its manifestation to ourselves (2Ch 6:17). Pray for its exhibition to others (2Sa 2:6). Make known, to others (Isa 38:19). Magnify (Ps 71:22; 138:2).
Is denied by the devil (Ge 3:4-5), the self-righteous (1Jn 1:10), unbelievers (1Jn 5:10).

Attribute:
Of God (Ex 34:6; Dt 32:4; Ps 31:5; 40:10-11; 71:22; 86:15; 89:14; 115:1; 117:2; 138:2; 146:6; Isa 25:1; 65:16; Jer 4:2; 5:3). Exhibited in His government (Ps 119:151), in His judgments (Ps 96:13; Ro 2:2), in His word (Jn 17:19), in His works (Ps 111:7-8; Da 4:37).
Of Christ (Jn 1:14; 14:6).
Of the Holy Spirit (Jn 14:17; 16:13; 1Jn 5:7-8).
Of the Righteous (Ps 51:6; Pr 3:3; Jn 3:21; 3Jn 3).
Righteous, should be prepared with (Eph 6:14), should know (1Ti 4:3; 1Jn 2:21; 3:19; 4:6), should love (Zec 8:19; 2Th 2:10), should rejoice in (1Co 13:6), should meditate upon (Php 4:8).

TRUTHFULNESS Commended (Pr 12:17, 19). Commanded (Zec 8:16; Eph 4:25; Col 3:9). Magistrates should be men of (Ex 18:21). Fearlessness in (2Co 12:6; Gal 4:16). Of Job (Job 27:4; 36:4).
Wicked, lack (Jer 9:5). Satan, devoid of (Jn 8:44). *See Satan; Wicked.*

TRYPHENA (*dainty*). A Christian woman friend of Paul's in Rome (Ro 16:12).

TRYPHOSA (*delicate*). A Christian woman friend of Paul's in Rome (Ro 16:12).

TUBAL The son of Japheth (Ge 10:2; 1Ch 1:5). Descendants of, become a nation (Isa 66:19; Eze 27:13; 32:26; 38:2-3; 39:1).

TUBAL-CAIN The son of Lamech and Zillah; worker in bronze and iron (Ge 4:22).

TUMBLEWEED Symbolic of wicked blown away in judgment (Ps 83:13; Isa 17:13). *See Plants of the Bible.*

TUMOR A disease with which the Philistines were afflicted (1Sa 5:6, 9, 12; 6:4-5, 11, 17). *See Disease; Hemorrhoids.*

TUNIC A shirtlike garment worn by men and women under other clothes in Bible times. Worn by priests (Ex 28:4, 39-40). Saul offers his to David (1Sa 17:38-39), as does Jonathan (1Sa 18:4). *See Dress.*

TURBAN Headcovering. Worn by the high priest (Ex 28:3, 37-39), by other priests (Eze 44:18), by royalty (Eze 21:26). *See Headbands.*

TURQUOISE In the high priest's breastpiece (Ex 28:18; 39:11), in the temple (1Ch 29:2). Commerce in (Eze 27:16). *See Minerals of the Bible; Stones.*

TURTLE, TURTLEDOVE *See Dove, Turtle.*

TUTOR (2Ki 10:1; Ac 22:3; Gal 4:1-2).

TWELVE, THE *See Apostles.*

TWILIGHT (1Sa 30:17; 2Ki 7:5; Job 3:9; Eze 12:6).

TWINS Jacob and Esau (Ge 25:24-26). Perez and Zerah (Ge 38:27-30). *See Castor and Pollux.*

TWO-AND-A-HALF TRIBES Reuben, Gad, and half of Manasseh settled in the Trans-Jordan (Jos 14:3).

TYCHICUS (*good fortune*). An Asian companion of Paul. Accompanies Paul from Greece to Asia (Ac 20:4). With Paul in Nicopolis (Tit 3:12), in Rome (Eph 6:21-22; Col 4:7-8). Sent to Ephesus (Eph 6:21-22; 2Ti 4:12), to Colosse (Col 4:7-8).

TYPES

Miscellaneous:
Bride, a type of the church (Rev 21:2, 9; 22:17). The sanctuary a type of the heavenly sanctuary (Ex 40:2-24; Heb 8:2, 5; 9:1-12). The saving of Noah and his family, of the salvation through the gospel (1Pe 3:20-21).
Defilement a type of sin. *See Defilement; Purification.* Leaven a type of sin. *See Leaven.* Washings a type of purification. *See Washings.*
See Allegory; Parable; Symbols and Similitudes.

Of Sin: *See Blemish; Defilement; Leaven.*

Of the Savior:
(Col 2:17; Heb 9:7-15, 18-28; 10:1-10). High priest, typical of the mediatorship (Ex 28:1, 12, 29-30, 38; Lev 16:15; Zec 6:12-13, w Heb 5; 8:2; 10:21). The institutions ordained by Moses (Mt 26:54; Lk 24:25-27, 44-47; Col 2:14-17; Heb 10:1-14). The sacrifices (Lev 4:2-3, 12; Heb 9:7-15, 18-25; 10:1-22, 29; 13:11-13; 1Pe 1:19; Rev 5:6). The morning and evening sacrifice (Jn 1:29, 36). The red heifer (Nu 19:2-6, w Heb 9:13-14). The Passover lamb (1Co 5:7). The bronze altar (Ex 27:1-2, w Heb 13:10). The bronze basin (Ex 30:18-20, w Zec 13:1; Eph 5:26-27). Atonement cover (Ex 25:17-22, w Heb 4:16). The veil (Ex 40:21; 2Ch 3:14, w Heb 10:20). Manna (Jn 6:32-35; 1Co 10:3). Cities of refuge (Nu 35:6, w Heb 6:18). Bronze snake (Nu 21:9; Jn 3:14-15). Tree of life (Ge 2:9, w Jn 1:4; Rev 22:2).
Adam (Ro 5:14; 1Co 15:45). Abel (Ge 4:8, 10, w Heb 12:24). Noah (Ge 5:29, w 2Co 1:5). Melchizedek (Heb 7:1-17). Moses (Dt 18:15, 18; Ac 3:20, 22; 7:37; Heb 3:2-6). David (2Sa 8:15; Ps 89:19-20; Eze 37:24; Php 2:9). Eliakim (Isa 22:20-22; Rev 3:7). Jonah (Jnh 1:17, w Mt 12:40).

TYRANNUS (*ruler*). A Greek teacher in whose school Paul preached after he was expelled from the synagogue (Ac 19:9).

T

TYRANNY (Pr 28:16; Isa 54:11-14). *See Government.*

TYRE, TYRIANS (*rocky place*).

1. Kingdom of; Hiram, king of (1Ki 5:1-2; 2Ch 2:3). Sends material to David for his palace (2Ch 2:3). Men and materials sent from, to Solomon, for the building of the temple and palaces (1Ki 5:1-11; 9:10-11; 2Ch 2:3-16).

See Hiram.

2. City of. Situated on the shore of the Mediterranean. On the northern boundary of Asher (Jos 19:29). Pleasant site of (Hos 9:13). Fortified (Jos 19:29; 2Sa 24:7). Commerce of (1Ki 9:26-28; 10:11; Isa 23; Eze 27; 28:1-19; Zec 9:2; Ac 21:3). Merchants of (Isa 23:8). Antiquity of (Isa 23:7). Riches of (Isa 23:8; Zec 9:3). Besieged by Nebuchadnezzar (Eze 26:7; 29:18).

Jesus goes to the coasts of (Mt 15:21). Heals the daughter of the Syrian Phoenician woman near (Mt 15:21-28; Mk 7:24-31). Multitudes from, come to hear Jesus and to be healed of their diseases (Mk 3:8; Lk 6:17). Herod's hostility toward (Ac 12:20-23). Paul visits (Ac 21:3-7).

To be judged according to its opportunity and privileges (Mt 11:21-22; Lk 10:13-14).

Prophecies relating to (Ps 45:12; 87:4; Isa 23; Jer 25:22; 27:1-11; 47:4; Eze 26-28; Joel 3:4-8; Am 1:9-10; Zec 9:2-4).

TYROPEON VALLEY (*valley of the cheese makers*).

A valley in Jerusalem separating W and E hills and joining Kidron and Hinnom valleys on the S.

U

UCAL (possibly *I am consumed,* or *I cease*). An obscure word; usually taken as son or pupil of Agur (Pr 30:1).

UEL (possibly *will of El [God]* BDB KB). An Israelite who divorced his Gentile wife (Ezr 10:34).

UGARIT *See Amarna, Tell El; Ras Shamra; Texts, Ancient Near Eastern Non-Biblical Texts Relating to the Old Testament.*

ULAI A river in Elam near Susa on whose bank Daniel saw a vision (Da 8:2, 16).

ULAM (*first, leader*).

1. The son of Sheresh (1Ch 7:16-17).
2. The son of Eshek (1Ch 8:39-40).

ULLA An Asherite (1Ch 7:39).

UMMAH A city of Asher (Jos 19:30).

UNBELIEF

Characteristics of:

Caused by spiritual blindness (Isa 6:9-10; Mt 13:13-15, 58; Lk 13:34; 19:41-42; Jn 12:37, 39-40, 47). Hardens the heart (Ps 95:8-11; Heb 3:12; 3:16-19; Ac 19:9). Rejects Christ (Isa 53:1-3; Jn 12:38; Mk 6:3, 6; Jn 1:11; 5:38, 40, 44, 46-47; 10:25-26). Displeases God (Ps 78:19-22; Heb 11:6). Makes God a liar (1Jn 5:10). Does not nullify God's faithfulness (Ro 3:3-4). Allows God to extend his mercy (Ro 11:20, 30-32). Characteristic of all mankind (Ro 11:20, 30-32; 2Th 3:2).

Illustrated (Ro 10:6-7, 16; 2Pe 3:4). Parable of (Mk 4:24-25; Lk 8:12, 18; 14:16-24).

At Christ's second coming (Lk 18:8). The spirit of the antichrist (1Jn 2:22-23; 4:3).

Used as an excuse by Moses (Ex 4:1).

Condemned:

Leads to: Defeat (Isa 7:9). Destruction (Ro 11:20; 2Th 2:12). Reproof (Jn 16:8-9). Condemnation (Ro 14:23). Rejection (1Pe 2:7-8). Instability (Jas 1:6-7).

Admonitions against (Ac 13:40-41; 2Co 6:14-16; Heb 3:12, 16-19; 4:1-3, 6, 11; 12:25).

UNBELIEVERS

Are spiritually blind (Jn 14:17; 1Co 2:14; 2Pe 3:4-7). Are impure (Tit 1:15). Make God a liar (1Jn 5:10). Will not be convinced (Lk 16:31; 22:67; Jn 4:48; 12:37-40). God's forbearance toward (Ro 10:16, 21). Shall be destroyed (Jer 5:12-14; Mt 10:14-15; Lk 12:46; Jn 8:24; 12:48; Ac 13:41; 1Co 1:18; 2Th 2:11-12; Jude 5-7; Rev 21:8). Tongues a sign to (1Co 14:22).

Instances of:

Eve (Ge 3:4-6). Moses (Nu 11:21-23) and Aaron (Nu 20:12). Israelites (Dt 9:23; 2Ki 17:14; Ps 78; 106:7, 24; Isa 58:3; Mal 1:2, 7). Naaman (2Ki 5:12). Samaritan lord (2Ki 7:2).

Disciples (Mt 17:17; Lk 24:11, 25). Zechariah (Lk 1:20). Chief priests (Mt 21:32; Lk 22:67). The Jews (Mt 11:16-19; Mk 1:45; 2:6-11; 8:11-12; 15:29-32; Lk 7:31-35; Jn 5:38, 40, 43, 46-47; Ac 22:18; 28:24). Disciples (Mt 17:20; Mk 4:38, 40; 16:14, 16; Lk 24:11, 21, 25-26, 36-45; Jn 6:36, 60-62, 64, 66, 70-71). The father of a child possessed with a spirit confesses (Mk 9:24). Brothers of Christ (Jn 7:5). Thomas (Jn 20:25). Jews of Iconium (Ac 14:2). Thessalonian Jews (Ac 17:5). Jews in Jerusalem (Ro 15:31). Ephesians (Ac 19:9). Saul (1Ti 1:13). People of Jericho (Heb 11:31).

UNBELIEVING ISRAELITES Destroyed (Nu 14:11, 13-39; 32:11; Dt 1:34-35; Ps 95:11; 106:26; 1Co 10:5, 10; Heb 3:17; Jude 5).

UNBLEMISHED Offerings must be (Ex 12:5; Lev 22:21; Eph 5:27; 1Pe 1:19).

UNCHARITABLENESS (Isa 29:21).

Admonitions Against:

(Mt 7:1-5; Lk 6:37-42; 12:57; Jn 7:24; 8:7; Ro 2:1; 14:1-15; 1Co 4:3-5, 7; 13:1-6). Forbidden (Jas 4:11-12).

See Accusation, False; Charitableness; Judgment; Slander; Speaking, Evil; Talebearer.

Instances of:

The Israelites toward Moses, charging him with having made them abhorred by the Egyptians (Ex 5:21), charging him with bringing them out of Egypt to die (Ex 14:11-12), in murmuring against Moses. *See Murmuring, Instances of.*

The tribes west of Jordan toward the two and a half tribes (Nu 32:1-33; Jos 22:11-31). Of Eli toward Hannah (1Sa 1:14-17).

Eliab toward David, charging him with presumption, when he offered to fight Goliath (1Sa 17:28). Princes of Ammon toward David, when he sent messengers to convey his sympathy to Hanun (2Sa 10:3). Bildad toward Job (Job 8). Eliphaz toward Job (Job 15; 22; 42:7-8). Zophar toward Job (Job 11:1-6; 20). Nathanael, when he said, "Can any good thing come out of Nazareth" (Jn 1:46). The Jews, charging Paul with teaching contrary to the law and against the temple (Ac 21:28).

UNCIAL LETTERS A style of handwriting that uses capitals for most letters. Early Greek manuscripts of the NT were written in uncials.

UNCIRCUMCISED

1. One who has not submitted to the Jewish rite of circumcision.
2. Gentiles (Ge 34:14; Jdg 14:3; Ro 4:9).
3. One whose heart is not open to God (Jer 4:4; 6:10; Ac 7:51).

UNCLE

1. Brother of one's father or mother (2Ki 24:17).
2. Any kinsman on father's side (Lev 10:4; Am 6:10).

UNCLEAN, UNCLEANNESS

1. Two kinds of uncleanness: Moral and ceremonial.
2. Foods regarded as unclean in the OT: Animals that did not chew the cud and have a split hoof; animals and birds that eat blood or carrion; anything strangled or that died of itself (Lev 11:1-8, 26-28); water creatures without scales and fins (Lev 11:9-12); insects without hind legs for jumping (Lev 11).
3. Other forms of ceremonial uncleanness; contact with the dead (Lev 11:24-40; 17:15; Nu 19:16-22), leprosy (Lev 13; 14; Nu 5:2), sexual discharge (Lev 15:16-33), childbirth (Lev 12:6-8). In Christianity uncleanness is moral, not ceremonial.

See Purification.

UNCLOTHED Figurative (Mt 22:11; 2Co 5:3; Rev 3:17; 16:15).

UNCTION *See Anointing.*

UNDEFILED Any person or thing not tainted with moral evil (Ps 119:1; Heb 7:26; 13:4; 1Pe 1:4).

UNDERGARMENTS For the priests (Ex 28:42; 39:28; Lev 6:10; 16:4; Eze 44:18). Of Jesus (Jn 19:23). *See Dress.*

UNDERSETTERS NIV "supports" for the movable stands in Solomon's temple (1Ki 7:30, 34).

UNFAITHFULNESS

Characteristics of:

Unfaithful in little, unfaithful in much (Lk 16:10). Brings spiritual bankruptcy (Mt 13:12; 25:29). Brings destruction (Jn 15:2). Brings condemnation (Lk 19:12-27; Mt 25:41-46). God deals with accordingly (Pr 24:11-12; Mt 25:8-13, 24-30, 41-46).

Denounced:

In the parables of the vineyard (Isa 5:1-7; Mt 21:33-43; Mk 12:1-9). In the parable of the empty vine (Hos 10:1-2). In the parable of the slothful servant (Mt 25:24-30; Lk 19:20-27).

Illustrated:

By the unfruitful tree (Mt 3:10; Mk 11:13-14). By the unfruitful branch (Jn 15:2, 4, 6). By blindness (2Pe 1:8-9).

See Sin, Fruits of; Unfruitfulness; also, Righteousness, Fruits of. Of friends: See Friends, False.

UNFRUITFULNESS Punished (Isa 5:1-10; Mt 3:10 w Lk 3:9; Mt 7:19; 13:3-7 w Mk 4:3-7, 14-19 & Lk 8:4-14; Mt 21:19-20; Mk 11:13; 13:9; 13:6-9; Jn 15:2, 4; 15:6).

See Sin, Fruits of; Unfaithfulness; also, Righteousness, Fruits of.

UNGODLY To be avoided (Ps 1:1). Seem to materially prosper (Ps 73:11). Judged (Ps 1:6; 3:7; 2Pe 3:7). Christ died for (Ro 5:6), therefore God justifies (Ro 4:5). Law made for (1Ti 1:9).

See Wicked.

UNICORN *See Wild Ox.*

UNION Advantages of (Pr 15:22; Ecc 4:9-12).

Of the righteous: *See Unity, Of the Righteous; Righteous, Union of, with Christ.*

UNITY

Of the Godhead: *See God, Unity of.*

Of the Righteous:

(Ps 133:1; Isa 52:8; Ac 4:32). Advantages of (Pr 15:22; Ecc 4:9-12). Fraternal (Mt 23:8).

Commanded among Christians (Ro 12:16; 14:19; 15:5-6; 1Co 1:10; 2Co 13:11; Eph 4:3; Php 1:27; 2:2; 3:16-17; 1Pe 3:8). Christ's prayer for, of the church (Jn 17:11, 21-23).

See Communion; Fellowship; One Another.

UNKNOWN GOD Inscription on an altar at Athens dedicated to an unknown god that worshipers did not want to overlook (Ac 17:23).

UNKNOWN TONGUE KJV "unknown" is a translator's insertion (in italics) for the term normally rendered simply "tongues" (1Co 14:2, 4, 13-14, 19, 27). *See Tongues, Gift of.*

UNLEARNED Illiterate (Ac 4:13; 2Pe 3:16), nonprofessional (1Co 14:16, 23f).

UNLEAVENED Unmixed with yeast (1Co 5:7-8).

UNLEAVENED BREAD Bread made without yeast (Ex 12:8).

UNLEAVENED BREAD, FEAST OF *See Feasts.*

UNNI (*Yahweh has answered*).

1. A Levite; musician (1Ch 15:18, 20).
2. A Levite; musician (Ne 12:9).

UNPARDONABLE SIN Blasphemy against the Holy Spirit (Mt 12:31-32; Mk 3:28-29; Lk 12:10); either attributing to Satan the work of the Holy Spirit through Jesus, or rejecting the testimony of the Holy Spirit regarding the person and work of Jesus Christ. Possibly the same as the sin that leads to death (1Jn 5:16-17).

Instances of unpardoned sin: Israel (Nu 14:26-45), Eli's house (1Sa 3:14).

UNSELFISHNESS

Commanded:

In the royal law (Jas 2:8). In the church (Ro 12:10; 15:1; 1Co 10:24; Gal 6:2; Php 2:3-4).

Inspired by:

Love (1Co 13:4-5). Jesus' love (2Co 5:14-15).

Instances of:

Abraham (Ge 13:9; 14:23-24). King of Sodom (Ge 14:21). Hittites (Ge 23:6, 11). Judah (Ge 44:33-34). Moses (Nu 11:29; 14:12-19). Gideon (Jdg 8:22-23). Saul (1Sa 11:12-13). Jonathan (1Sa 23:17-18). David (1Sa 24:17; 2Sa 15:19-20; 23:16-17; 1Ch 21:17; Ps 69:6). Araunah (2Sa 24:22-24). Nehemiah (Ne 5:14-18). Jews (Est 9:15). Daniel (Da 5:17). Jonah (Jnh 1:12-13).

Joseph (Mt 1:19). Jesus (Ro 15:3; 2Co 8:9). The disciples (Ac 4:34-35). Priscilla and Aquila (Ro 16:3-4). Paul (1Co 10:33; Php 1:18; 4:17; 2Th 3:8). Philemon (Phm 13-14). Onesiphorus (2Ti 1:16-18).

See Charitableness; Fellowship; Fraternity; Selfishness.

UNTEMPERED MORTAR *See Whitewash.*

UNWORTHINESS (Mt 10:37; 22:8; Ac 13:46).

UPHARSIN *See Parsin.*

UPHAZ A place where gold was obtained (Jer 10:9; Da 10:5), location unknown. Perhaps "Ophir" should be read. *See Ophir, 2.*

UPPER CHAMBER, UPPER ROOM A room built on the wall or roof of a house (1Ki 17:19; Ac 20:9); scene of the Lord's Last Supper (Mk 14:15; Lk 22:12).

UPPER EGYPT Pathros; southern Egypt. Israelite captives in (Isa 11:11, ftn; Jer 44:1, 15; Eze 29:14). Prophecy against (Eze 30:14). *See Egypt.*

UPRIGHTNESS *See Righteousness.*

UR (*flame, light*). Father of Eliphal (1Ch 11:35). Possibly same as Ahasbai (2Sa 23:34). *See Ahasbai.*

UR OF THE CHALDEANS A city in S Mesopotamia, c. 140 miles SE of old Babylon; the early home of Abraham (Ge 11:28, 31; 15:7; Ne 9:7).

URBANUS (*refined, elegant*). A Roman Christian (Ro 16:9).

URI (*Yahweh is [my] flame, light*).

1. The father of Bezalel (Ex 31:2; 35:20; 38:22; 1Ch 2:20; 2Ch 1:5).
2. The father of Geber (1Ki 4:19).
3. The temple gatekeeper who divorced his foreign wife (Ezr 10:24).

URIAH (*Yahweh is [my] flame, light*).

1. A Hittite; the husband of Bathsheba (2Sa 11:3).
2. High priest during the reign of Ahaz of Judah, for whom he built a pagan altar in the temple (2Ki 16:10-16).
3. A priest who aided Ezra (Ne 8:4).
4. The father of Meremoth (Ezr 8:33; Ne 3:4).
5. The son of Shemaiah, a prophet of Kiriath Jearim, in the time of Jehoiakim. Prophesies against Judah (Jer 26:20). Fled to Egypt; taken; slain by Jehoiakim (Jer 26:21-23).

URIEL (*God [El] is [my] flame, light*).

1. A Kohathite Levite (1Ch 6:24).
2. A chief of the Kohathites who assisted in bringing the ark from the house of Obed-Edom (1Ch 15:5, 11).
3. The father of Maacah, wife of Rehoboam (2Ch 13:2, ftn).

URIJAH *See Uriah.*

URIM AND THUMMIM (*lights and perfections*). Signifying light and perfection. In the breastplate (Ex 28:30; Lev 8:8). Eleazar to ask counsel for Joshua, after the judgment of (Nu 27:21). Priests only might interpret (Dt 33:8; Ezr 2:63; Ne 7:65). Israelites consult (Jdg 1:1; 20:18, 23). Withheld answer from King Saul (1Sa 28:6).

USURPATION

Of Political Functions:

By Absalom (2Sa 15:1-12). By Adonijah (1Ki 1:5-9). By Baasha (1Ki 15:27-28). By Zimri (1Ki 16:9-10). By Jehu (2Ki 9:11-37). By Athaliah (2Ki 11:1-16). By Shallum (2Ki 15:10). *See Rebellion.*

In Ecclesiastical Affairs:
By Saul, in assuming priestly functions (1Sa 13:8-14). By Solomon, in thrusting Abiathar out of the priesthood (1Ki 2:26-27). By Uzziah, in assuming priestly offices (2Ch 26:16-21). By Ahaz (2Ki 16:12-13).
See Church, The Body of Believers, State; Government, Ecclesiastical.

Of Executive Power:
In ordering Naboth's death and confiscation of his vineyard (1Ki 21:7-19). In the scheme of Joseph to dispossess the Egyptians of their real and personal property (Ge 47:13-26). Of Pharaoh, making bondservants of the Israelites (Ex 1:9-22). Moses accused of (Nu 16:3).

USURY Interest, not necessarily unreasonable exaction, but all income from loans. Forbidden (Ex 22:25; Lev 25:35-37; Dt 23:19; Ps 15:5; Pr 28:8; Jer 15:10; Eze 18:8, 13, 17; 22:12). Exaction of, rebuked (Ne 5:1-13). Authorized, of strangers (Dt 23:20). Exacted by the Jews (Eze 22:12). Just men innocent of the vice of requiring (Eze 18:8).
See Interest; Money.

UTHAI (possibly *superiority of Yahweh* IDB; possibly *[my] restoration* KB).
1. The son of Ammihud (1Ch 9:4).
2. A man who returned with Ezra (Ezr 8:14).

UZ
1. The son of Nahor (Ge 22:21).
2. The son of Aram (Ge 10:23; 1Ch 1:17).
3. The son of Dishan (Ge 36:28).
4. The country in which Job lived (Job 1:1); the site is uncertain.

UZAI (*Yahweh has given ear, listened*). Father of Palal (Ne 3:25).

UZAL
1. The son of Joktan (Ge 10:27; 1Ch 1:21).
2. A region, perhaps Yemen or the area between Haran and the Tigris (Eze 27:19).

UZZA (*strength*).
1. The son of Shimei (1Ch 6:29).
2. The son of Ehud (1Ch 8:7).
3. The owner or caretaker of a garden in which Manasseh and Amon were buried (2Ki 21:18, 26).
4. One whose children returned under Zerubbabel (Ezr 2:49; Ne 7:51).

UZZA, GARDEN OF A garden in which Manasseh and his son were buried (2Ki 21:18, 26).

UZZAH (*strong, fierce one*). The son of Abinadab; slain for touching the ark to steady it when the oxen carrying it stumbled (2Sa 6:3-8; 1Ch 13:6-11).

UZZEN SHEERAH (perhaps *ear of Sheerah*). A town built by Ephraim's daughter Sheerah (1Ch 7:24).

UZZI (*Yahweh is [my] strength*).
1. Descendant of Aaron (1Ch 6:5, 51; Ezr 7:4).
2. The grandson of Issachar (1Ch 7:2-3).
3. A Benjamite (1Ch 7:7).
4. The father of Elah (1Ch 9:8).
5. An overseer of the Levites (Ne 11:22).
6. A priest in the family of Jedaiah (Ne 12:19).

UZZIA (*[my] strength* or *Yahweh is [my] strength*). One of David's mighty men (1Ch 11:44).

UZZIAH (*Yahweh is [my] strength*).
1. Also called Azariah. The king of Judah (2Ki 14:21; 15:1-2; 2Ch 26:1, 3). Rebuilds Elath (2Ki 14:22; 2Ch 26:2). Reigns righteously (2Ki 15:3; 2Ch 26:4-5). Defeats the Philistines (2Ch 26:6-7). Takes tribute from the Ammonites; strengthens the kingdom (2Ch 26:8). Strengthens the fortifications of Jerusalem (2Ch 26:9). Promotes cattle raising and agriculture (2Ch 26:10). Military establishment of (2Ch 26:11-15). Is presumptuous in burning incense; stricken with leprosy; quarantined (2Ch 26:16-21; 2Ki 15:5). Jotham regent during quarantine of (2Ki 15:5; 2Ch 26:21). Death of (2Ki 15:7; 2Ch 26:23). History of, written by Isaiah (2Ch 26:22; Isa 1:1). Earthquake in the reign of (Am 1:1; Zec 14:5). An ancestor of Jesus and listed in Matthew's record of Jesus' genealogy (Mt 1:8-9).
2. The son of Uriel (1Ch 6:24).
3. The father of Jonathan (1Ch 27:25).
4. A priest who divorced his Gentile wife (Ezr 10:21).
5. The father of Athaiah (Ne 11:4).

UZZIEL, UZZIELITES (*God [El] is [my] strength*).
1. A Kohathite Levite (Ex 6:18, 22; Lev 10:4).
2. The son of Ishi; Simeonite (1Ch 4:42).
3. Head of Benjamite family (1Ch 7:7).
4. The son of Heman (1Ch 25:4), also known as Azarel (1Ch 25:18). *See Azarel, 2.*
5. A Levite who helped in cleansing the temple (2Ch 29:14-19).
6. The son of Harhaiah (Ne 3:8). Anyone descended from Uzziel, the Levite, was known as an Uzzielite (Nu 3:27; 1Ch 15:10; 26:23).

V

VAGABOND NIV "wanderer, wandering." A word used in a curse pronounced upon Cain (Ge 4:12, 14), in an imprecatory prayer of David (Ps 109:10), and of professional exorcists (Ac 19:13).

VAIL *See Curtains; Veil.*

VAIN REPETITIONS *See Babbling.*

VAIZATHA (possibly *given of the best one* BDB). The son of Haman (Est 9:9).

VALLEY Low-lying ground; plain, ravine, gorge, a wadi (Dt 34:6; Jos 10:40; Lk 3:5).

Mentioned in Scripture:
Achor (Jos 7:24; Isa 65:10; Hos 2:15). Aijalon (Jos 10:12). Baca (Ps 84:6). Beracah (2Ch 20:26). Bokim (Jdg 2:5). Craftsmen (1Ch 4:14, ftn). Elah (1Sa 17:2; 21:9). Emek Keziz (Jos 18:21). Eshcol (Nu 32:9; Dt 1:24). Gad (2Sa 24:5). Gerar (Ge 26:17). Gibeon (Isa 28:21). Hebron (Ge 37:14). Ben Hinnom or Tophet (Jos 15:8; 2Ki 23:10; 2Ch 28:3; Jer 7:32). Hamon Gog (Eze 39:11). Iphtah El (Jos 19:14, 27). Jehoshaphat or decision (Joel 3:2, 14). Jericho (Dt 34:3). Jezreel (Hos 1:5). King's Valley (Ge 14:17; 2Sa 18:18). Lebanon (Jos 11:17). Megiddo (2Ch 35:22; Zec 12:11). Moab, where Moses was buried (Dt 34:6). Rephaim (Jos 15:8; 18:16; 2Sa 5:18; Isa 17:5). Salt (2Sa 18:13; 2Ki 14:7). Shaveh (Ge 14:17; 2Sa 18:18). Shittim (Joel 3:18). Siddim (Ge 14:3, 8, 10). Sorek (Jdg 16:4). Succoth (Ps 60:6). Zeboim (1Sa 13:18; Ne 11:34). Zephathah (2Ch 14:10). Zered (Nu 21:12).

VALLEY GATE A gate in the Jerusalem walls (Ne 2:13; 3:13; 12:31, 38), location uncertain.

VALOR *See Courage.*

VANIAH (possibly *worthy of love* IDB). A man who divorced his foreign wife (Ezr 10:36).

VANITY
1. Archaic word meaning "temporary" or "meaningless":
"Temporary, a breath." Every human is but a breath (Ps 39:5, 11; 62:9; 144:4). Beauty is fleeting (Ps 39:11; Pr 31:30). Wealth acquired by lies (Pr 21:6).
"Futile, meaningless, in vain, worthless." A consequence of the Fall (Ro 8:20). Human life (Job 7:16; Ecc 6:12), youth and vigor (Ecc 11:10), thoughts (Ps 94:11), help (Ps 60:11; La 4:17). Worldly wisdom (Ecc 2:15, 21; 1Co 3:20), pleasure (Ecc 2:1-3, 10-11), activity (Ps 39:6; 127:2), achievement (Ecc 2:11; 4:4), possessions (Ecc 2:4-11). Accumulating wealth (Ecc 2:26; 4:8), love of wealth (Ecc 5:10; 6:2). Everything (Ecc 1:2). Foolish controversies (1Ti 1:6-7; 6:20; 2Ti 2:14, 16; Tit 3:9). The conduct of the ungodly (1Pe 1:18). The religion of hypocrites (Isa 1:13; Jas 1:26), pagans (Mt 6:7). Faith without works is (Jas 2:14).
The wicked, especially characterized by (Job 11:11). Fools follow those given to (Pr 12:11), leading to poverty (Pr 28:19). Saints hate the thoughts of (Ps 119:113), pray to be kept from (Ps 119:37; Pr 30:8), avoid (Ps 24:4), avoid those given to (Ps 26:4).
2. *See Pride.*

VASHNI KJV Samuel's firstborn (1Ch 6:28). NIV follows the LXX and supplies "Joel" as the firstborn (cf. 1Sa 6:33; 8:2; 15:17), rendering *vashni* as "the second." *See Joel, 1.*

VASHTI (*one beautiful, desired*). The wife of Xerxes; queen of Persia; divorced (Est 1:19).

VEDAN A place whose merchants traded with Tyre (Eze 27:19, NRSV). Translated as the Hebrew conjunction *vav* and the proper name Danites/Dan in the NIV and KJV. *See Dan, 2.*

VEGETARIANS Persons who eat no meat. Daniel chooses to eat only vegetables (Da 1:11-16). Christians are not to judge or be judged by diet (Ro 14).

VEGETATION Created the third day (Ge 1:11; 2:5). For food (Ge 1:29-30).

VEIL
1. Scarf used for concealment or for protection against the elements (Ge 24:65; 1Co 11:4-16). Worn by Rebekah (Ge 24:65), by Tamar (Ge 38:14, 19), by Moses, to screen his face when he descended from Mount Sinai (Ex 34:33, 35). Metaphoric of failing to understand the gospel (2Co 3:14-18; 4:3-4).
2. *See Curtains.*

VEIN NIV "mine" for silver (Job 28:1). *See Mines, Mining.*

VENERATION For parents (Ge 48:15-16). *See Old Age; Parents; Reverence.*

VENGEANCE Any punishment meted out in the sense of retribution (Jdg 15:7; Jer 11:20; 20:12). It belongs to God (Dt 32:35-36; Ps 94:1; Lk 18:7-8; Ro 12:19; 2Th 1:6; Heb 10:30; Rev 6:10).
Instance of: Sons of Jacob on Hamor and Shechem (Ge 34:20-31).
See Judgments; Revenge; Retaliation.

VENISON NIV "(wild) game," taken in hunting (Ge 25:28; 27:5-33).

VENTRILOQUISM Possibly a trick of mediums and spiritists (Isa 29:4).

VERDICT Against Jesus (Mt 26:66; 27:24-26; Mk 15:15; Lk 23:24; Jn 19:16). *See Court, Of Law.*

VERMILION *See Red.*

VERSIONS OF THE BIBLE Ancient: *See Texts and Versions.*

VESSEL Any material thing which may be used for any purpose, whether a tool, implement, weapon, or receptacle (Isa 22:24; 52:11; 66:20). A ship (Isa 2:16).
KJV "earthen vessels" is NIV "jars of clay" (2Co 4:7). *See Jar(s).* KJV "weaker vessel" is NIV "weaker partner" (1Pe 3:7). *See Women.*

VESTMENTS Of priests. *See Priest.*

VESTRY *See Wardrobe.*

VESTURE An archaic word for garments (Ge 41:42; Dt 22:12; Ps 22:18). Sometimes used metaphorically (Ps 102:26; Heb 1:12).
See Cloak; Clothing; Dress; Robe.

VIA DOLOROSA The traditional route which our Lord traveled on the day of his crucifixion from the judgment seat of Pilate to the place of his crucifixion (Mt 27:26, 31, 33).

VIAL *See Bowl.*

VICARIOUS DEATH The ram for Isaac (Ge 22:13). Jesus for sinners. *See Jesus the Christ, Death of; Mission of; Savior; Sufferings of; also, Atonement; Suffering, Vicarious.*

VICEGERENCY Imputed authority. Of Elisha, in miraculously rewarding the Shunammite (2Ki 4:16-17), in cursing Gehazi (2Ki 5:27). Of the apostles (Mt 16:19; 18:18; Jn 20:23).

VICTORIES In battle, from God (Ps 55:18; 76:5-6). Celebrated in song (Jdg 5; 2Sa 22), by women (1Sa 18:6-7; 2Sa 1:20).
See Armies; War.

VICTUAL Food.

VIGILANCE Instances of: The LORD in the Exodus (Ex 12:42). King of Jericho (Jos 2:1-3).
See Watchman.

VILLAGE Villages were usually grouped around a fortified town to which the people could flee in a time of war (2Ch 8:18).

VINE Degeneracy of (Jer 2:21). Fable of (Jdg 9:12-13). Pruned (Isa 5:6; Jn 15:1-5). Parables of (Ps 80:8-14; Eze 17:6-10; 19:10-14). *See Vineyards.*
Symbolic (Jn 15:1-5).

VINEGAR A sour wine. Forbidden to the Nazirites (Nu 6:3). Used with food (Ru 2:14; Ps 69:21; Pr 10:26; 25:20). Offered to Christ on the cross (Mt 27:34, 48; Jn 19:29, w Mk 15:23).

VINEYARDS Origin and antiquity of (Ge 9:20). The design of planting (Ps 107:37; 1Co 9:7). Frequently walled or fenced with hedges (Nu 22:24; Pr 24:31; Isa 5:2, 5). Cottages built in, for the keepers (Isa 1:8). Provided with the apparatus for making wine (Isa 5:2; Mt 21:33). The stones carefully gathered out of (Isa 5:2).

Laws Respecting:
Not to be planted with different kinds of seed (Dt 22:9). Not to be cultivated during the sabbatical year (Ex 23:11; Lev 25:4). The spontaneous fruit of, not to be gathered the sabbatical or jubilee year (Lev 25:5, 11). Compensation in kind to be made for injury done to (Ex 22:5). Strangers entering, allowed to eat the fruit of, but not to take any away (Dt 23:24).
The gleaning of, to be left for the poor (Lev 19:10; Dt 24:21). The fruit of new, not to be eaten for three years (Lev 19:23), to be holy to the Lord in the fourth year (Lev 19:24), to be eaten by the owners from the fifth year (Lev 19:25).
Planters of, not liable to military service till they had eaten of the fruit (Dt 20:6). Frequently rented out to tenant farmers (SS 8:11; Mt 21:33). Rent of, frequently paid by part of the fruit (Mt 21:34). Were often mortgaged (Ne 5:3-4). Estimated rent of (SS 8:11; Isa 7:23). Estimated profit arising from, to the cultivators (SS 8:12). The poor engaged in the culture of (2Ki 25:12; Isa 61:5). Members of the family often wrought in (SS 1:6; Mt 21:28-30). Mode of hiring and paying laborers for working in (Mt 20:1-2). Of the kings of Israel superintended by officers of state (1Ch 27:27).

The Vintage or Ingathering of:
Was a time of great rejoicing (Isa 16:10). Sometimes continued to the time of sowing seed (Lev 26:5). Failure in, occasioned great grief (Isa 16:9-10). Of red grapes particularly esteemed (Isa 27:2). The produce of, was frequently destroyed by enemies (Jer 48:32). The whole produce of, often destroyed by insects (Dt 28:39; Am 4:9). In unfavorable seasons produced but little wine (Isa 5:10; Hag 1:9, 11). The wicked judicially deprived of the enjoyment of (Am 5:11; Zep 1:13). The Recabites forbidden to plant (Jer 35:7-9). Of the slothful man neglected and laid waste (Pr 24:30-31).

Illustrative:
Of Israel (Isa 5:7; 27:2; Jer 12:10; Mt 21:23).

VINEYARDS, PLAIN OF THE *See Abel Keramim.*

VINTAGE (Lev 26:5; Jdg 8:2; Isa 16:10; 24:13; 32:10; Jer 48:32; Mic 7:1). *See Vine; Vineyards.*

VIOL *See Lyre; Music, Instruments of.*

VIOLENCE A cause of the Flood (Ge 6:11-13). Prayer for deliverance from (2Sa 22:49; Ps 7:9; Hab 1:2-3). Divorce (Mal 2:16). An overseer must not be (1Ti 3:3; Tit 1:7).

VIPER A poisonous snake (Dt 32:24; Isa 59:5). Fastens on Paul's hand (Ac 28:3).

Figurative (Ge 49:17; Ps 140:3; Pr 23:32; Mt 3:7; 23:33; Lk 3:7).

See Adder; Cobra; Serpent.

VIRGIN

General:

Proofs of (Dt 22:13-21). Dowry of (Ex 22:17). Character of, to be protected (Dt 22:17-21, 23-24). Betrothal of, a quasi-marriage (Dt 22:23-24). Distinguishing apparel of (2Sa 13:18). Priests might marry none but (Lev 21:14). Mourn in the temple (La 1:4; 2:10). Virginity of, bewailed (Jdg 11:37-39).

Parable of the wise and foolish (Mt 25:1-13). Advised by Paul not to marry (1Co 7).

Mother of Jesus (Isa 7:14; Mt 1:23; Lk 1:27). *See Virgin Birth.*

Figurative:

Of the Church (Isa 62:5; Jer 14:17; 31:4, 13; 2Co 11:2). Of personal purity (1Co 7:25, 37; Rev 14:4).

VIRGIN BIRTH The NT teaching that Jesus Christ became a human being without the mediation of an earthly father, not born by means of sexual intercourse, but as a result of the supernatural overshadowing of the Holy Spirit (Mt 1:18-25; Lk 1:26-2:7).

VIRGINITY *See Virgin.*

VIRTUE Positive character traits (Col 3:12-14). *See Character.*

VISION A mode of revelation (Nu 12:6; 1Sa 3:1; 2Ch 26:5; Ps 89:19; Pr 29:18; Jer 14:14; 23:16; Da 1:17; Hos 12:10; Joel 2:28; Ob 1; Hab 2:2; Ac 2:17).

Examples of:

Of Abraham, concerning his descendants (Ge 15:1-17). Of Jacob, of the stairway with ascending and descending angels (Ge 28:12), at Beersheba (Ge 46:2). Of Job, of a spirit (Job 4:12-16). Of Moses, of the burning bush (Ex 3:2), of the glory of God (Ex 24:9-11; 33:18-23). Of the Israelites, of the manifestation of the glory of God (Ex 24:10, 17; Heb 12:18-21). Of Balaam, in a trance. *See Balaam.* Of Joshua, of the captain of the Lord's host (Jos 5:13-15).

Of David, of the angel of the Lord by the threshing floor of Araunah (1Ch 21:15-18, ftn v.15). *See Araunah.* Of Elisha, at the translation of Elijah (2Ki 2:11). Of Elisha's servant, of the chariots of the Lord (2Ki 6:17). Of Micaiah, of the defeat of the Israelites; of the Lord on his throne; and of a lying spirit (1Ki 22:17-23; 2Ch 18:16-22).

Of Isaiah, of the Lord and his glory in the temple (Isa 6), of the valley of vision (Isa 22). Of Jeremiah, of an almond rod (Jer 1:11), of the boiling pot (Jer 1:13). Of Ezekiel, of the glory of God (Eze 1:3, 12-14; 3:23), of the scroll (Eze 2:9), of the man of fire (Eze 8:9), of the coals of fire (Eze 10:1-7), of the dry bones (Eze 37:1-14), of the city and temple (Eze 40-48), of the waters (Eze 47:1-12). Of Daniel, of the four beasts (Da 7), of the Ancient of Days (Da 7:9-27), of the ram and the goat (Da 8), of the angel (Da 10).

Of Amos, of grasshoppers (Am 7:1-2), of fire (Am 7:4), of a plumb line (Am 7:7-8), of summer fruit (Am 8:1-2), of the temple (Am 9:1). Of Zechariah, of horses (Zec 1:8-11), of horns and carpenters (Zec 1:18-21), of the high priest (Zec 3:1-5), of the golden lampstand (Zec 4), of the flying scroll (Zec 5:1-4), of the mountains and chariots (Zec 6:1-8).

Of Zechariah, in the temple (Lk 1:13-22). Of John the Baptist, at the baptism of Jesus (Mt 3:16; Mk 1:10; Lk 3:22; Jn 1:32-34). Peter, James, and John, of the transfiguration of Jesus and the appearance of Moses and Elijah (Mt 17:1-9; Lk 9:28-36). Of the people, of the tongues of fire at Pentecost (Ac 2:2-3). Of Stephen, of Christ (Ac 7:55-56).

Of Paul, of Christ, on the way to Damascus (Ac 9:3-6; 1Co 9:1), of Ananias (Ac 9:12), of a man of Macedonia, saying, "Come over to Macedonia and help us" (Ac 16:9), in Corinth (Ac 18:9-10), in a trance of paradise (2Co 12:1-4). Of Ananias, of Christ (Ac 9:10-12). Of Cornelius, the centurion, of an angel (Ac 10:3). Of Peter, of the sheet let down from heaven (Ac 10:9-18).

Of John on the Isle of Patmos—

Of Christ and the golden lampstands (Rev 1:10-20), the open door (Rev 4:1), a rainbow and throne (Rev 4:2-3), twenty-four elders (Rev 4:4), seven lamps (Rev 4:5), sea of glass (Rev 4:6), four living creatures (Rev 4:6-8), book with seven seals (Rev 5:1-5), golden bowls (Rev 5:8), of the six seals (Rev 6), four horses (Rev 6:2-8), earthquake and celestial phenomena (Rev 6:12-14).

Four angels (Rev 7:1), sealing of the 144, 00 (Rev 7:2-8), of the seventh seal and seven angels (Rev 8:11), of the censer (Rev 8:5), hail and fire (Rev 8:7), mountain cast into the sea (Rev 8:8-9), falling star (Rev 8:10-11; 9:1), the third part of sun and moon and stars darkened (Rev 8:12), bottomless pit (Rev 9:2), locusts (Rev 9:3-11), four angels loosed from the Euphrates (Rev 9:14), army of horsemen (Rev 9:16-19), angel having a book (Rev 10:1-10), seven thunders (Rev 10:3-4), measurement of the temple (Rev 11:1-2), two witnesses (Rev 11:3-12), court of the Gentiles (Rev 11:2), two olive trees and two lampstands (Rev 11:4), the beast out of the bottomless pit (Rev 11:7), fall of the city (Rev 11:13), second and third woes (Rev 11:14), a woman clothed with the sun and the birth of the male child (Rev 12), a red dragon (Rev 12:4-17), war in heaven (Rev 12:7-9), the beast rising out of the sea (Rev 13:1-10), the beast coming out of the earth (Rev 13:11-18).

The Lamb on Mount Zion (Rev 14:1-5), the angel having the everlasting gospel (Rev 14:6-7), the angel proclaiming the fall of Babylon (Rev 14:8-13), the Son of man with a sickle (Rev 14:14-16), an angel reaping the harvest (Rev 14:14-20), angel coming out of the temple (Rev 14:17-19), an angel having power over fire (Rev 14:18), the vine and the winepress (Rev 14:18-20), angels with the seven last plagues (Rev 15), sea of glass (Rev 15:2), temple opened (Rev 15:5), the plague upon the people who had the mark of the beast (Rev 16:2), sea turned into blood (Rev 16:3), the seven angels with the seven bowls of the wrath of God (Rev 16-17), destruction of Babylon (Rev 18), of the multitude praising (Rev 19:1-9), of him who is faithful and true riding a white horse (Rev 19:11-16), an angel in the sun (Rev 19:17-21).

Satan bound a thousand years (Rev 20:1-3), thrones of judgment, and the resurrection, and the freeing of Satan (Rev 20:1-10), the great white throne (Rev 20:11), opening of the Book of Life (Rev 20:12), death and hell (Rev 20:14), New Jerusalem (Rev 21), river of life (Rev 22:1), Tree of Life (Rev 22:2). *See Revelation, Book of.*

VISITATION A divine visit for purpose of rewarding or punishing people for their deeds (Jer 10:15; Lk 19:44; 1Pe 2:12).

VISITORS *See Guest.*

VOICE, OF GOD (Eze 1:24, 28; 10:5; Jn 5:37; 12:28-30; Ac 7:31; 9:4, 7; 26:14-15). *See Anthropomorphisms.*

VOLCANOES Smoking or flaming mountains symbolic of God's presence (Dt 4:11; 5:23; Jdg 5:5; Ps 97:5; 104:32; 144:5; Isa 34:9-10; 64:1-3; Jer 51:25; Mic 1:4; Na 1:5-6). *See Earthquakes; Mountain.*

VOLUPTUOUSNESS *See Lasciviousness; Sensuality.*

VOPHSI The father of Nahbi (Nu 13:14).

VOWS A part of Israel's worship (Ps 22:25; 61:8; 65:1). Heard by God (Ps 61:5). Obligatory (Nu 30:2; Dt 23:21-23; Job 22:27; Ps 50:14; 56:12; 66:13-14; 76:11; Ecc 5:4-5; Na 1:15). In affliction (Ps 116:14-19).

Mosaic Laws Concerning:

Must be voluntary (Lev 22:18-25; 23:37-38; Nu 15:2-16; 29:39).

Must be performed (Lev 5:4-13; Nu 30:2-16). *See above, Obligatory.* Estimation of the redemption price of things offered in vows, to be made by the priest, according to age and gender of the person making the offering (Lev 27:1-13). The redemptive price of the offering of real estate, to be valued by the priest (Lev 27:14-15), of a field (Lev 27:16-25).

Of women (Nu 30:3-16). Of Nazirites (Nu 6:1-21). Unintentional (Lev 5:4-5). Offerings devoted under (Lev 5:6-13; 7:16-18; 27:1-25; Nu 15:2-16). Things offered in, must be perfect (Lev 22:18-25).

Edible things offered in, to be eaten the same day they were offered (Lev 7:16-18). Things offered in, to be brought to the tabernacle or temple (Dt 12:6, 11, 17-18, 26), belonged to the priests (Nu 18:14).

Things forbidden to pay a vow (Dt 23:18).

Traditions that invalidate vows (Mk 7:11-13).

See Contract; Covenant.

Rash Vows:

(Pr 20:25; Ecc 5:6). By Jephthah (Jdg 11:29-40), by Israelites (Jdg 20:7-11).

Instances of:

Of Jacob (Ge 28:20-22). Of the mother of Micah, in the dedication of silver for the making of an idol (Jdg 17:2-3). Of Hannah, to consecrate to the Lord the child for which she prayed (1Sa 1:11, w 1:27-28). Of Elkanah (1Sa 1:21). Of Absalom (2Sa 15:7-8). Of Job, not to entertain thoughts of fornication (Job 31:1). Of David (Ps 132:2).

Of Jephthah, and of the Israelites. *See above, Rash Vows.*

Of Ananias and Sapphira, in the dedication of the proceeds of the sale of their land (Ac 5:1-11). Of the Jews, to kill Paul (Ac 23:12-15).

See Nazirite(s).

VULTURE The name given to several kinds of large birds of prey, usually feeding on carrion; unclean for food (Lev 11:13; Dt 14:12; Mic 1:16; Hab 1:8).

W

WADI (*ravine, valley*). A valley which forms the bed of a stream during the winter, but which dries up in the summer (Ge 26:19).

WADI OF EGYPT *See River of Egypt.*

WAFERS Thin cakes (Ex 16:31; 1Ch 23:29).

WAGES Of Jacob (Ge 29:15-30; 30:28-34; 31:7, 41).

Laborer entitled to (Dt 25:4; Mt 10:10; Lk 10:7; Ro 4:4). Must be just (Col 4:1). Must be paid promptly (Lev 19:13; Dt 24:15). Withholding of, denounced (Jer 22:13; Mal 3:5; Jas 5:4). Wasting of, denounced (Hag 1:6). Contentment with, commanded (Lk 3:14).

Parable concerning (Mt 20:1-15).

Figurative (Ro 6:23).

WAGON Used to carry supplies (Isa 66:20; Eze 23:24; 26:10). *See Cart(s).*

WAHEB If this is a proper noun then it is an unknown place in Moab. Its meaning is uncertain (Nu 21:14).

WAIL In ancient funeral processions wailing relatives and hired mourners and musicians preceded body to grave (Jer 9:17-21; Am 5:16; Mt 9:23). Of the wicked (Mt 13:42).

WAITING

Upon God:

As the God of providence (Jer 14:22), as the God of salvation (Ps 25:5), as the giver of all temporal blessings (Ps 104:27-28; 145:15-16).

Is good (Ps 52:9). God calls us to (Zep 3:8). Exhortations and encouragements to (Ps 27:14; 37:7; Hos 12:6).

For—

Mercy (Ps 123:2), pardon (Ps 39:7-8), the consolation of Israel (Lk 2:25), salvation (Ge 49:18; Ps 62:1-2), guidance and teaching (Ps 25:5), protection (Ps 33:20; 59:9-10), the fulfillment of his word (Hab 2:3), the fulfillment of his promises (Ac 1:4), hope of righteousness by faith (Gal 5:5), coming of Christ (1Co 1:7; 1Th 1:10).

Attitudes in Waiting—

Should be with the soul (Ps 62:1, 5), with earnest desire (Ps 130:6), with patience (Ps 37:7; 40:1), with resignation (La 3:26), with hope in his word (Ps 130:5), with full confidence (Mic 7:7), continually (Hos 12:6), all the day (Ps 25:5), specially in adversity (Ps 59:1-9; Isa 8:17), in the way of his judgments (Isa 26:8).

Those Who Wait Upon God—

They who engage in, wait upon him only (Ps 62:5), are heard (Ps 40:1), are blessed (Isa 30:18; Da 12:12), experience his goodness (La 3:24-26), shall not be ashamed (Ps 25:3; Isa 49:23), shall renew their strength (Isa 40:31), shall inherit the earth (Ps 37:9), shall be saved (Pr 20:22; Isa 25:9), shall rejoice in salvation (Isa 25:9), shall receive the glorious things prepared by God for them (Isa 64:4).

Saints resolve on (Ps 52:9; 59:9). Saints have expectation from (Ps 62:5). Saints plead, in prayer (Ps 25:21; Isa 33:2). The patience of saints often tried in (Ps 69:3).

Predicted of the Gentiles (Isa 42:4; 60:9). Illustrated (Ps 123:2; Lk 12:36; Jas 5:7).

Exemplified:

Jacob (Ge 49:18), David (Ps 39:7), Isaiah (Isa 8:17), Micah (Mic 7:7), Joseph (Mk 15:43).

Faith; Hope.

WALKING

With God—a Godly Lifestyle:

According to his commands (Dt 5:33; Ps 1; Jer 7:23); in his ways (Dt 28:9; Jos 22:5); in the old paths (Jer 6:16); as taught by him (1Ki 8:36; Isa 2:3; 30:21); uprightly (Pr 2:7); in his statutes and judgments (Eze 37:24); in newness of life (Ro 6:4); not after the flesh, but after the Spirit (Ro 8:1; Gal 5:16); honestly, as in the day (Ro 13:13); by faith, not by sight (2Co 5:7); in love, following Christ (Eph 5:2); worthy of the Lord (Col 1:10); in Christ (Col 2:6); by the gospel rule (Php 3:16); in the light, as God is (1Jn 1:7); in white clothing (Rev 3:4); in the light of heaven (Rev 21:24).

Instances of: Enoch (Ge 5:24), Noah (Ge 6:9).

WALLED CITIES Settlements were enclosed with walls for protection against invasion (Lev 25:29-31; 1Ki 4:13). *See Walls.*

WALLS Of the cities: Of Bashan, destroyed by the Israelites (Dt 3:5-6). Of Jericho (Jos 2:15; 6). Of Jerusalem. Of Babylon (Jer 51:44), broad (Jer 51:58). Of Beth Shan (1Sa 31:10). Of Rabbah (2Sa 11:20). Of Abel (2Sa 20:15, 21).

Houses upon (Jos 2:15). Double (2Ki 25:4; Isa 22:11). Sentinels on. *See Watchman.*

Figurative of the New Jerusalem (Rev 21:12, 14, 17-21).

WAR Divine approval of (2Sa 22:35). Civil (Jdg 12:1-6; 20; 2Sa 2:12-31; 3:1; 20; 1Ki 14:30; 16:21; Isa 19:2), forbidden (2Ch 11:4), averted (Jos 22:11-34). Enemy harangued by general of opposing side (2Ki 18:19-36; 2Ch 13:4-12). War of extermination (Nu 31:7-17; Dt 2:33-34; 3:6; 20:13-18; Jos 6:21, 24; 8:24-25; 10:2-40; 11:11-23; 1Sa 15:3-9; 27:8-11).

Tumult (Am 2:2). Slain in, neglected (Isa 14:19; 18:6). Evils of (2Sa 2:26; Ps 46:8; 79:1-3; 137:9; Isa 3:5, 25-26; 5:29-30; 6:11-12; 9:5, 19-21; 13:15-16; 15; 16:9-10; 18:6; 19:2-16; 32:13-14; 33:8-9; 34:7-15; Jer 4:19-31; 5:16-17; 6:24-26; 7:33-34; 8:16-17; 9:10-21; 10:20; 13:14; 14:18; 15:8-9; 19:7-9; 25:33; 46:3-12; 47:3; 48:28, 33; 51:30-58; La 1-5; Eze 33:27; 39:17-19; Hos 10:14; 13:16; Joel 2:2-10; Am 1:13; 6:9-10; 8:3; Na 2:10; 3:3, 10; Zec 14:2; Lk 21:20-26; Rev 19:17-18).

To cease (Ps 46:9; Isa 2:4; Mic 4:3).

Wars and rumors of (Mt 24:6; Mk 13:7; Lk 21:9).

God and War—

God in (Ex 14:13-14; Dt 1:30; 3:21-22; 7:17-24; 20:1, 4; 31:6-8, 23; 32:29-30; Jos 1:1, 5-7, 9; Jdg 1:2; 6:16; 7:9; 11:29; 1Sa 17:45-47; 19:5; 30:7-8; 2Sa 5:22-24; 22:18; 1Ki 20:28; Ps 18:34; 76:3; Jer 46:15; Am 5:8-9; Zec 10:5). God uses, as a judgment (Ex 23:24; Lev 26:17, 31-39; Dt 28:25-68; 32:30; Jdg 2:14; 2Ki 15:37; 1Ch 5:22, 26; 21:12; 2Ch 12:1-12; 15:6; 24:23-24; 33:11; 36; Job 19:29; Isa 44:9-16; 60:1-3; 105:25; Isa 5:1-8, 25-30; 9:8-12; 13:3-4, 9; 19:2; 34:2-6; 43:28; 45:7; Jer 12:7, 12; 46:15-17, 21; 47:6-7; 48:10; 49:5; 50:25; Eze 23:22-25; Am 3:6; 4:11; Zep 1:7-18; Zec 8:10; 14:2).

Repugnant to God (1Ch 22:8-9; Ps 68:30; 120:6-7; Rev 13:10). God sends panic in (Ex 15:14-16), threatens defeat in (Dt 32:25; 1Sa 2:10; 2Ch 18:12-16; Isa 30:15-17; Eze 15:6-8; 21:9-17), inflicts defeat in (Jos 7:12-13; 2Ch 12:5-8; 24:23-24; Ps 48:4-7; Pr 11:14; 20:18). Wisdom required in (Pr 21:22; 24:6; Ecc 9:14-18; Lk 14:31-32).

See Armies; Armor; Fort; Soldiers; Strategy; Tower; Watchman.

Figurative:

Warfare of Saints—

Is not after the flesh (2Co 10:3). Is a good warfare (1Ti 1:18-19). Called the good fight of faith (1Ti 6:12).

Is against the devil (Ge 3:15; 2Co 2:11; Eph 6:12; Jas 4:7; 1Pe 5:8; Rev 12:17), the flesh (Ro 7:23; 1Co 9:25-27; 2Co 12:7; Gal 5:17; 1Pe 2:11), enemies (Ps 38:19; 56:2; 59:3), the world (Jn 16:33; 1Jn 5:4-5), death (1Co 15:26, w Heb 2:14-15).

Often arises from the opposition of friends or relatives (Mic 7:6; Mt 10:35-36). To be carried on under Christ, as our Captain (Heb

2:10), under the Lord's banner (Ps 60:4), with faith (1Ti 1:18-19), with a good conscience (1Ti 1:18-19), with steadfastness in the faith (1Co 16:13; 1Pe 5:9, w Heb 10:23), with earnestness (Jude 3), with watchfulness (1Co 16:13; 1Pe 5:8), with sobriety (1Th 5:6; 1Pe 5:8), with endurance of hardness (2Ti 2:3, 10), with self-denial (1Co 9:25-27), with confidence in God (Ps 27:1-3), with prayer (Ps 35:1-3; Eph 6:18), without earthly entanglements (2Ti 2:4). Mere professors do not maintain (Jer 9:3).

Saints are all engaged in (Php 1:30), must stand firm in (Eph 6:13-14), exhorted to diligence in (1Ti 6:12; Jude 3). Encouraged in (Isa 41:11-12; 51:12; Mic 7:8; 1Jn 4:4), helped by God in (Ps 118:13; Isa 41:13-14), protected by God in (Ps 140:7), comforted by God in (2Co 7:5-6), strengthened by God in (Ps 20:2; 27:14; Isa 41:10), strengthened by Christ in (2Co 12:9; 2Ti 4:17), delivered by Christ in (2Ti 4:18), thank God for victory in (Ro 7:25; 1Co 15:57).

Armor for—
A belt of truth (Eph 6:14), the breastplate of righteousness (Eph 6:14), readiness from the gospel (Eph 6:15), shield of faith (Eph 6:16), helmet of salvation (Eph 6:17; 1Th 5:8), sword of the Spirit (Eph 6:17). Called armor of God (Eph 6:11), weapons of righteousness (2Co 6:7), armor of light (Ro 13:12), not weapons of the world (2Co 10:4). Mighty through God (2Co 10:4-5), the whole is required (Eph 6:13), must be put on for (Ro 13:12; Eph 6:11), to be on the right hand and the left (2Co 6:7).

Victory in—
Is from God (1Co 15:57; 2Co 2:14), through Christ (Ro 7:25; 1Co 15:57; 2Co 12:9; Rev 12:11), by faith (Heb 11:33-37; 1Jn 5:4-5), over the devil (Ro 16:20; 1Jn 2:14), over the flesh (Ro 7:24-25; Gal 5:24), over the world (1Jn 5:4-5), over all that exalts itself (2Co 10:5), over death and the grave (Isa 25:8; 26:19; Hos 13:14; 1Co 15:54-55), triumphant (Ro 8:37; 2Co 10:5).

They who overcome in, shall eat of the hidden manna (Rev 2:17), eat of the tree of life (Rev 2:7), be clothed in white garments (Rev 3:5), be pillars in the temple of God (Rev 3:12), sit with Christ in his throne (Rev 3:21), have a white stone and on it a new name written (Rev 2:17), have power over the nations (Rev 2:26), have the name of God written upon them by Christ (Rev 3:12), have God as their God (Rev 21:7), have the morning star (Rev 2:28), inherit all things (Rev 21:7), be confessed by Christ before God the Father (Rev 3:5), be sons of God (Rev 21:7), not be hurt by the second death (Rev 2:11), not have their names blotted out of the book of life (Rev 3:5).

Symbolized by a red horse (Rev 6:4).

In Heaven:
Symbolic (Rev 12:7).

WAR SONGS Celebrating the destruction of Pharaoh's army (Ex 15:1-21); victory over Sihon, king of the Amorites (Nu 21:24-30); victory over Sisera (Jdg 5); David's victories over his enemies and his deliverance from Saul (2Sa 22). David's lament over the defeat of Saul (2Sa 1:19-27).

WARDROBE Place where royal or ceremonial garments were kept (2Ki 10:22; 22:14; 34:22). *See Dress.*

WARFARE *See War, Figurative; In Heaven.*

WARNING *See Wicked, Warned.*

WARRIORS (Nu 32:17; Jos 4:13; 1Ch 8:40; 12:2, 8, 21; 2Ch 14:8; 17:18; 25:5; 26:13).

WARTS Unacceptable on a sacrificial animal (Lev 22:22).

WASHERMAN'S FIELD A field outside Jerusalem where fullers or launderers washed the cloth that they were processing (2Ki 18:17; Isa 7:3; 36:2).

WASHINGS (Ex 19:10, 14; Mt 15:2; Mk 7:2-5, 8-9; Lk 11:38; Heb 9:10).

General:
Of priests (Ex 29:4; 30:18-21; 40:12, 31-32; Lev 8:6; 16:4, 24, 26, 28; Nu 19:7-10, 19; 2Ch 4:6).
Of burnt offerings (Lev 1:9, 13; 9:14; 2Ch 4:6). Of the dead (Ac 9:37). Of infants (Eze 16:4). Of the face (Mt 6:17). Of feet (Ge 18:4; 19:2; 24:32; 43:24; Ex 30:19, 21; 40:31; Jdg 19:21; 2Sa 11:8; SS 5:3; Lk 7:38, 44; Jn 13:5; 1Ti 5:10). Of hands (Ex 30:18-21; 40:30-32), as a token of innocency (Dt 21:6; Ps 26:6; Mt 27:24).
For defilement of, lepers (Lev 14:8-9), those having bloody issue (Lev 15:5-13), those having eaten that which died (Lev 17:15-16). Traditions of, not observed by Jesus (Lk 11:38-39).

Figurative:
Of baptism (Ac 22:16). Of believers (1Co 6:11; Tit 3:5; Heb 1:3; 9:14; 2Pe 1:9; 1Jn 1:7, 9). Of bodies (Heb 10:22). Of the Church (Eph 5:26). Of conscience (Heb 9:14; 10:22). Of robes (Rev 7:14; 22:14). Of leaven (1Co 5:7). Of robes (Rev 7:14; 22:14). Of regeneration (Ps 51:7; Pr 30:12; Isa 1:16; 4:4; Zec 13:1; 1Co 6:11; Eph 5:26; Tit 3:5). Of sin: Corporate (Ps 79:9; Isa 1:16, 18; 4:3-4; Da 12:10; Zec 13:1; Jn 13:8; 2Co 7:1; Rev 1:5). General (Pr 16:6). Personal (Ps 51:2; 65:3; Pr 20:9; Jn 13:8; 2Pe 1:9; 1Jn 1:7, 9). By Christ, work and blood of (Eph 5:26; Tit 3:5-6; Heb 1:3; 9:14; 1Jn 1:7; Rev 1:5; 7:14).
See Defilement; Fuller; Purification; Regeneration; Soap.

WASTE PLACES Restored (Isa 35:1; 41:19; 44:26; 49:19; 51:3; 52:9; 58:12; 61:4; Eze 36:10).

WATCH A man or group of men set to guard a city, crops, etc. (Ne 4:9; Mt 27:62-66).

WATCHES OF THE NIGHT Divisions into which hours of the night were divided. Jews had a threefold division; Romans, fourfold (Jdg 7:19; Mk 6:48). *See Time.*

WATCHFULNESS (Ps 102:7; Hab 2:1; 1Co 9:27).

In Prayer:
(Ne 4:9; Mt 26:41; Mk 13:33; Eph 6:18; Col 4:2; 1Pe 4:7).

Commanded:
(Dt 4:15; 6:17; Jos 22:5; 23:11; 1Ki 2:3-4; 8:25; 2Ch 19:7; Job 36:18-21; Pr 8:34; 16:17; Na 2:1; Mt 18:10; 24:42-51; 25:13; Mk 4:24; 13:32-37; Lk 8:18; 11:35; 12:35-40; 17:3; 21:34-36; Ro 11:20; 1Co 10:12; 11:28; 16:13; Gal 6:1; Eph 5:15; Col 2:8; 1Th 5:4, 6, 21; Heb 2:1; 1Pe 5:8; 2Pe 1:19; 1Jn 5:18).
Upon: Israel (Dt 27:9). Young men (Ps 119:9; Pr 4:23-27). Married men (Mal 2:15). Ministers (Ac 20:28-31; 1Co 3:10; Col 4:2; 1Pe 4:5).
Over: Motives (Mt 6:1-5). Conscience (Lk 11:35). The heart (Pr 4:23; 28:26). The tongue (Ps 39:1; 141:3; Jas 3:5-8).
Against: Hypocrisy (Mt 16:6). Apostasy (2Jn 8). Lethargy (Ro 13:11; 1Pe 1:13, 17). Backsliding (Dt 4:9, 23; Heb 3:12; 12:15; Jude 20-21; Rev 3:2-3, 11). Worldliness (1Co 7:29-31). Covetousness (Mt 24:42-47; Mk 13:33-37; Lk 12:15, 35-40). Idolatry (Ex 23:13; Dt 4:23; 11:16; 12:13). Evil associations (Ex 34:12; Php 3:2; 2Pe 3:17). False teachers (Mt 7:15; Mk 13:22-23; Ac 20:28-31; 1Jn 4:1). Deceivers (Mt 24:4).
See Temptation.

WATCHMAN A sentinel. On the walls of cities (SS 3:3; 5:7), of Jerusalem (2Sa 13:34; 18:24-25; Ne 4:9; 7:3; Isa 52:8; 62:6), of Babylon (Jer 51:12). On towers (2Ki 9:17; 2Ch 20:24; Isa 21:5-12; Jer 31:6). At the gates of the temple (2Ki 11:6-7). Alarm of, given by trumpets (Eze 33:3-6). Unfaithfulness in the discharge of duty of, punished by death (Eze 33:6; Mt 28:14; Ac 12:19). *See Guard.*

WATER
General:
Creation of (Ps 148:4-5). Covered the whole earth (Ge 1:9). Daily allowance of (Eze 4:11). City waterworks (2Ki 20:20). Vision of, by Ezekiel (Eze 47:1-5). Of separation (Nu 19:2-22). Libation of (1Sa 7:6). Irrigation with. *See Irrigation.*
Miraculously supplied to the Israelites (Ex 17:1, 6; Nu 20:11), to Samson (Jdg 15:19), to Jehoshaphat's army (2Ki 3:16-20). Purified by Elisha (2Ki 2:19-22). Red Sea divided (Ex 14:21-22), the Jordan River (Jos 3:14-17; 2Ki 2:6-8, 14). Jesus walks on (Mt 14:25). Changed to wine (Jn 2:1-11), to blood (Rev 16:3-5).

Figurative:
Water of life (Jn 4:14; 7:37-39; Rev 21:6; 22:17). Of affliction (2Sa 22:17; Ps 69:1; Isa 30:20; 43:2). Of salvation (Isa 12:3; 49:10; 55:1; Eze 36:25; Jn 4:10; 7:38). Domestic love (Pr 5:15).

Symbolic:
(Isa 8:7; Rev 8:11; 12:15; 16:4; 17:1, 15).

WATER JAR Clay or stone jars for carrying or holding water (Ru 2:9; Jn 2:6-7; 4:28). *See Jar(s).*

WATER OF BITTERNESS Water mingled with dust which a woman suspected of unfaithfulness was expected to drink to prove her innocence (Nu 5:12-31).

WATER OF SEPARATION Water for removal of impurity (Nu 19:9, 13, 20-21; 31:23).

WATERSPOUT NIV "waterfalls" (Ps 42:7).

WATERWAY *See Aqueduct.*

WAVE OFFERING Sacrificial portion waved before the Lord (Ex 29:24-27; Lev 7:30; 8:27-29). *See Offerings.*

WAVES *See Sea, Waves of.*

WAX (Ps 22:14; 68:2; 97:5; Mic 1:4).

WAY
Figurative:
Of holiness (Ps 16:11; Isa 35:8-9; Jer 6:16; Hos 14:9). Of righteousness, narrow (Mt 7:14). Of sin, broad (Mt 7:13). Jesus the (Jn 14:6; Heb 9:8). Doctrines taught by Christ (Ac 9:2; 19:23; 22:4; 24:14, 22).

WAYFARING MAN Traveler (Jdg 19:17; 2Sa 12:4; Isa 33:8; 35:8).

WAYS OF GOD Perfect (Ps 18:30), righteous or just (Ps 145:17; Da 4:37; Hos 14:9; Rev 15:3), higher than human ways (Isa 55:9), eternal (Hab 3:6).

WEAK Duty of the strong to (Job 4:3-4; Isa 35:3-7; Mt 25:35, 40; Ro 14:1-23; 15:1-3; 1Co 8:7-13; 9:22; 2Co 11:29; Gal 6:1-2; Jas 5:19-20). *See Kindness.*

WEALTH Abundance of possessions, whether material, social, or spiritual. In early history of Israel, wealth consisted largely of flocks and herds, silver and gold, bronze, iron, and clothing (Jos 22:8). God taught Israel that he was the giver of their wealth (Dt 8:18), taught them to be generous (Pr 11:24). Jesus did not condemn wealth but stressed the difficulty of the rich in entering the kingdom of God (Mt 19:24; Lk 16:19-31).

WEANING To wean is to accustom a child to depend upon other food than its mother's milk; celebrated by a feast (Ge 21:8), and with an offering (1Sa 1:24).

WEAPONS *See Armor.*

WEASEL A small, carnivorous animal, allied to the ferret; for Israelites, unclean (Lev 11:29).

WEATHER There is no Hebrew word corresponding to "weather, " but the Israelites were keenly aware of weather phenomena. The great topographical diversity of Israel assures a variety of weather on a given day: on the top of Mt. Hermon (9, 232 feet above sea level) there is snow on the ground the year round; while at Jericho (800 feet below sea level) the heat is oppressive in summer, and the region around the Dead Sea (1, 290 feet below sea level) is intolerable in summer. On the coast even the hottest summer day is made bearable by refreshing breezes from the Mediterranean. Signs of (Mt 16:2-3). Sayings concerning (Job 37:9, 17, 22). *See Meteorology.*

WEAVING (Isa 19:9; 38:12). Bezalel skilled in (Ex 35:35). Wrought by women (2Ki 23:7). Of the ephod (Ex 28:32; 39:22). Of coats (Ex 39:27).
Weaver's shuttle (Job 7:6), beam (Jdg 16:14; 2Sa 21:19; 1Ch 11:23).

WEDDING A joyous occasion, celebrated with music, feasting, drinking of wine, joking; after the Exile written contracts were drawn up and sealed; bridegroom went to the bride's home with friends and escorted her to his own house (Mt 25:7); festive apparel expected of guests; festivities lasted one or two weeks (Ge 29:27; Jdg 14:12).

WEDGE A bar of gold (Jos 7:21, 24).

WEEDING (Mt 13:28).

WEEDS
1. A general term for obnoxious plants (Job 31:40).
2. Probably bearded darnel, a poisonous plant resembling wheat (Mt 13:25-30).

WEEK *See Calendar; Time.*

WEEKS, FEAST OF Pentecost, celebrated fifty days after the sheaf waving on the sixteenth of Nisan (Ex 34:18-26).
See Annual Feasts; Feasts; Pentecost.

WEEPING (Ro 12:15; 1Co 7:30). In perdition, the outer darkness (Mt 8:12; 22:13; 24:51; 25:30). None in heaven (Rev 7:17). Penitential (Jer 50:4; Joel 2:12).

Instances of Penitential:
The Israelites (Jdg 2:4-5). Peter (Mt 26:75; Mk 14:72; Lk 22:62). While doing good (Ps 126:5-6). For others (Jer 9:1). On account of tribulation (Jer 22:10; Am 5:16-17).

Instances of:
Of Abraham for Sarah (Ge 23:2). Of Esau (Ge 27:38). Of Jacob and Esau (Ge 33:4). Of Jacob (Ge 37:35). Of Joseph (Ge 42:24; 43:30; 45:2, 14; 46:29; 50:1, 17). Of Hannah (1Sa 1:7). Of Jonathan and David (1Sa 20:41). Of David (2Sa 1:17; 3:32; 13:36; 15:23, 30; 18:33). Of Hezekiah (2Ki 20:3; Isa 38:3). Of Jesus, over Jerusalem (Lk 19:41), at the grave of Lazarus (Jn 11:35). Of Mary, when she washed the feet of Jesus (Lk 7:38; Jn 11:2, 33). Of Mary Magdalene (Jn 20:11). Of Paul (Ac 20:19; Php 3:18).

WEIGHTS AND MEASURES Balances were used for scales (Lev 19:36; Pr 16:11), and stones for weights (Lev 19:36). For biblical weights and measures, *See Measure.*

WELDING A process used to join metals together (Isa 41:7).

WELLS The occasion of feuds: between Abraham and Abimelech (Ge 21:25-30), between Isaac and Abimelech (Ge 26:15-22, 32-33). Of Jacob (Jn 4:6). Of Solomon (Ecc 2:6). Of Uzziah (2Ch 26:10). Of Hezekiah. *See Gihon.* At Haran (Ge 24:16).
Figurative: Of salvation (Isa 12:3; Jn 4:14). Without water (Jer 15:18; 2Pe 2:17).
See Spring.

WEN *See Warts.*

WEST Used figuratively with "east" to denote great distance (Ps 103:12).

WHALE *See Fish; Sea Monster.*

WHEAT (Rev 6:6). Grown in Israel (1Ki 5:11; Ps 81:16; 147:14). Offerings of (Nu 18:12). Prophecy of the sale of a measure of, for a penny (Rev 6:6). Parables of (Mt 13:25; Lk 16:7). Winnowing of (Mt 3:12; Lk 3:17). Ground in a mortar (Pr 27:22). Chaff of (Jer 23:28; Mt 3:12; Lk 3:17). Growth of, figurative of vicarious death (Jn 12:24).
Figurative: Of God's mercy (Ps 81:16; 147:14). Of self-righteousness (Jer 12:13).

WHEEL Potter's (Jer 18:3).
Figurative (Pr 20:26; Ecc 12:6).
Symbolic (Eze 1:15-21; 3:13; 10:9-19; 11:22).

WHELP *See Cub.*

WHIP (1Ki 12:11; Pr 26:3; Na 3:2).

WHIRLWIND Destructive (Pr 1:27). From the south in the land of Uz (Job 37:9), in the valley of the Euphrates (Isa 21:1), in the land of Canaan (Zec 9:14). From the north (Eze 1:4). Elijah translated in (2Ki 2:1, 11). God answered Job in (Job 38:1).
See Meteorology.
Figurative:
Of the judgment of God (Jer 23:19; 30:23). Of the fruits of unrighteousness (Hos 8:7). Of divine judgments (Eze 1:4).

WHISPER *See Busybody; Slander; Talebearer.*

WHISPERER A slanderer (Ro 1:29; 2Co 12:20). *See Slander; Speaking, Evil.*

WHITE *See Colors, Figurative and Symbolic.*

WHITE OWL Forbidden as food (Lev 11:18; Dt 14:16). *See Owl.*

WHITEWASH Used to "repair" a flimsy wall (Eze 13:10-16). Whitewashed tomb or wall a picture of hypocrisy (Mt 23:27-28; Ac 23:3).

WHOEVER Of condemnation (Ex 32:33; Dt 18:19; Mt 5:22; Jn 8:34; Ro 2:1; 1Jn 2:23; 3:4, 10, 15; 2Jn 9).

Of salvation (Lk 12:8; Jn 4:14; Ac 10:43; 1Jn 5:1; Rev 22:17).

WHORE, WHOREDOM *See Adultery; Idolatry; Fornication; Prostitute.*

WHOREMONGER *See Adultery; Sensuality.*

WICK TRIMMERS Used to trim and adjust the wicks of the lamps in the temple and the tabernacle (Ex 37:23; Nu 4:9; 1Ki 7:50; 2Ki 12:13; 25:14; 2Ch 4:22; Jer 52:18).

WICKED

General:
God is angry with (Ps 5:5-6; 7:11; Ro 9:13; 1Co 10:5). Spirit of God withdrawn from (Ge 6:3; Hos 4:17-19; Ro 1:24, 26, 28). Hate the righteous (Mt 5:11-12; Lk 6:22-23). Worship of, offensive to God (Ps 50:16-17; Isa 1:10-15).

God's mercy to (Job 33:14-30), love for (Dt 5:29; 32:29; Mt 18:11-14; Jn 3:16-17; Ro 5:8; 1Jn 3:16; 4:9-10). Gospel invitation to, illustrated by the parables of the householder (Mt 20:1-16), and marriage supper (Mt 22:1-14).

Prosperity of (Job 5:3-5; 12:6; 15:21-23, 27, 29; 20:5, 22; 21:7-13; Ps 37:1, 35-36; 49:10-15; 73:3-22; Ecc 8:12-13; Jer 12:1-2; Hab 1:3-4; Mal 3:15). Hate reproof (1Ki 22:8; 2Ch 18:7). Dread God (Job 18:11).Temporal punishment of (Job 15:20-35; 18:5-21; 20:5-29; 21:7-33; 24:2-24; 27:13-23; Jer 5:25; Eze 11:10; 12:19-20; Zec 14:17-19). False hope in (Job 8:13-18). Warned (Jer 7:13-15, 23-25; 25:4-6; 26:2-7, 12-13; 29:17-19; Eze 33:8; Da 4:4-27; 5:4-29; Zep 2:1-2; Lk 3:7-9; 1Co 10:11; Jude 4-7; Rev 3:1-3, 16-19). Terrors of, at the judgment (Rev 1:7). Death of (Ps 49:14; 73:4).

Compared With:
Ashes under the feet (Mal 4:3), bad fish (Mt 13:48), bad trees (Lk 6:43), beasts (Ps 49:12; 2Pe 2:12), the blind (Zep 1:17; Mt 15:14), bronze and iron (Jer 6:28; Eze 22:18), briers and thorns (Isa 55:13; Eze 2:6), bulls of Bashan (Ps 22:12), burning thorns (Ps 118:12), bushes in the wastelands (Jer 17:6), chaff (Job 21:18; Ps 1:4; Mt 3:12).

Clouds without rain (Jude 12), corpses trampled underfoot (Isa 14:19), deaf cobras (Ps 58:4), dogs (Pr 26:11; Mt 7:6; 2Pe 2:22), dross (Eze 119:119; Eze 22:18-19), early dew that passes away (Hos 13:3), earthenware coated with glaze (Pr 26:23), fading leaves (Isa 1:30), fiery furnace (Ps 21:9; Hos 7:4), fools building upon sand (Mt 7:26), fuel for the fire (Isa 9:19).

Garden without water (Isa 1:30), goats (Mt 25:32), grass that withers (2Ki 19:26; Ps 37:2; 92:7), green plants that die away (Ps 37:2), horses charging into the battle (Jer 8:6), idols (Ps 115:8), lions hungry for prey (Ps 17:12), melting wax (Ps 68:2), morning mist (Hos 13:3), moth-eaten garments (Isa 50:9; 51:8), pigs (Mt 7:6), poor figs (Jer 24:8), rejected branches (Isa 14:19), rejected silver (Jer 6:30), rocky places (Mt 13:5).

Scorpions (Eze 2:6), serpents (Ps 58:4; Mt 23:33), smoke through a window (Hos 13:3), sows (2Pe 2:22), springs without water (2Pe 2:17), storms sweeping by (Pr 10:25), straw before the wind (Job 21:18), stubble (Mal 4:1), tossing sea (Isa 57:20), tumbleweeds (Ps 83:13), visions of the night (Job 20:8), wandering stars (Jude 13), wayward children (Mt 11:16), weeds (Mt 13:38), whitewashed tombs (Mt 23:27), wild waves of the sea (Jude 13), wild donkey's colts (Job 11:12).

See Base Fellows; Impenitence; Obduracy; Penitence; Reprobate; Reprobacy; Seekers; Sin, Confession of.

Contrasted With the Righteous:
(Ps 1:1-6; 11:5; 17:14-15; 32:10; 37:17-22, 37-38; 73:1-28; 75:10; 91:7-8; 107:33-38; 125:5; Pr 2:21-22; 3:32-33; 4:16-19; 10:3, 6, 9, 11, 16, 20-21, 23-25, 28-32; 11:3, 5-6, 8-11, 18-21, 23, 31; 12:2-3, 5-7, 10, 12-13, 21, 26; 13:5-6, 9, 17, 21-22, 25; 14:2, 11, 19, 22, 32; 15:6, 8-9, 28-29; 21:15, 18, 26, 29; 22:5, 8-9; 24:16; 28:1, 4-5, 13-14, 18; 29:2, 6-7, 27; Isa 32:1-8; 65:13-14; Mal 3:18; Ro 2:7-10; Eph 2:12-14; Php 2:15; 1Th 5:5-8; Tit 1:15; 1Pe 4:17-18; 1Jn 1:6-7; 3:3-17).

Present and future state of the wicked and righteous contrasted (Job 8; Ps 49). *See below.*

Described as:
(Job 8:13-17; 15:16, 20-35; Ps 10:4-11; 36:1-4; 73:4-12; Isa 59:2-8; Jer 2:22-25). Abomination (Pr 13:19; 15:9; Hos 9:10). Alienated (Col 1:21). Beasts (Ps 49:20). Dogs (Ps 59:6; 2Pe 2:22; Rev 22:15). Horse rushing into battle (Jer 8:6).

Blind (Eze 12:2). Carnal (Ro 8:5, 7-8; 9:8). Children of the devil (Jn 8:44; Ac 13:10; 1Jn 3:10). Perverse (Jer 9:6; Ro 1:21; 2:4-5; Php 2:15). Despising God (Job 21:14; Ro 11:28). Contentious (Ro 2:8). Corrupt (Ps 53:1; 73:8; Isa 59:3; Jer 2:22; Eze 16:47; 20:16; Mic 7:2-4; Tit 1:15). Loving darkness (Jn 3:19-20). Dead in sin (Eph 2:1-3; 1Jn 3:14). Delighting in lies (Ps 62:4), in perversity (Pr 2:13-19).

Defiled (Tit 1:15-16). Depraved (Isa 1:4-6; Jer 17:9; 30:12-15; Ro 1:20-32; 3:10-18; 1Ti 1:9-10; 2Ti 3:2-9, 13; Tit 3:2; 2Pe 2:10, 12-19; Jude 12-13). Destitute of faithfulness (Ps 5:9). Destitute of the love of God (Jn 5:42). Devilish (Jas 3:15). Devisers of evil (Ps 52:1-4; 64:3-6; Pr 4:16; 6:12-15; 10:23; Isa 32:6-7; Jer 4:22). Enemies (Ro 5:10; Col 1:21). Filthy (Ezr 9:11). Full of bitterness (Ac 8:23).

Uncircumcised (Isa 52:1; Jer 6:10; Eze 28:10; 31:18; 32:19-32). Uncircumcised of heart (Lev 26:41; Eze 44:7; Ac 7:51), of lips (Ex 6:12). Disobedient (Jer 11:8; Tit 1:16). Alienated from God (Col 1:21). Full of bitterness and venom (Dt 32:32-33; Ps 58:3-5). Grievous sinners (Ge 13:13; 18:20; Job 22:5; Isa 1:4-6). Hating: Correction (Ps 15:10; Am 5:10). Instruction (Ps 50:17; Pr 1:29-30). The light (Jn 3:20).

Being in moral darkness (Mt 4:16; 6:23; Lk 1:79; Eph 4:17-18). Not knowing the way of the Lord (Jer 5:4). Lewd (Jer 11:15). Lost (Lk 19:10). Loving wickedness (Ps 7:14; Jer 14:10; Hos 4:8; Mic 3:2). Malicious toward the righteous (Ps 37:12; 94:3-8; 140:9). Mocking sin (Pr 14:9). Obdurate (Ps 10:4, 11; Pr 1:29-30; Isa 26:10-11; Eze 3:7). Outsiders (Mk 4:11). Past feeling (Eph 4:19). Progressing in wickedness (Isa 30:1, 10-11; Jer 9:3; 2Ti 3:13). Rebellious (Dt 9:24).

Sensual (Php 3:19; Jude 19). Servants of sin (Jn 8:34). Shameful (Eph 5:11-12). Shameless (Jer 6:15; 8:12; Zep 3:5). Unscrupulous (Job 24:2-24; Ps 10:4-10; Isa 5:18-23; Jer 5:26-28; 9:2-6). Sold to work iniquity (1Ki 21:20). Stiff-necked (Dt 9:13; Ac 7:51). Under condemnation (Jn 3:18-19). Unclean (Ezr 9:11; Job 14:4; Hag 2:14). Ungodly (Ro 5:6), without strength (Ro 5:6). Vomit (Lev 18:25). Wretched, miserable, poor, blind, naked (Rev 3:17-18).

Happiness of:
Sensual (Isa 22:13; 56:12). Limited to this life (Lk 16:25). Ends suddenly (Job 21:12-13; Lk 12:19-20).

Hope of:
Shall perish (Job 8:13; 11:20; 27:8; Pr 10:28).

Prayers of:
Abominable to God (Pr 15:8, 29; 21:27; 28:9).

Not answered (Dt 1:45; 1Sa 28:6; 32a 22:42; Job 27:9; 35:12-13; Ps 18:41; 66:18; Pr 1:24-28; 21:13, 27; Isa 1:15; 59:2; Jer 11:11; 14:12; 18:17; La 3:8, 44; Eze 8:18; 20:3, 31; Hos 5:6; Mic 3:4; Zec 7:13; Mal 1:9; 2:11-13; Jn 9:31; Jas 1:6-7; 4:3; 1Pe 3:7).

On behalf of, not answered (Dt 3:26; Jer 15:11).

Prosperity of:
(Job 12:6; 21:7-13; Ps 73:3-12; Jer 12:1-2; Mal 3:15). Brief (Job 5:3-5; 15:21, 23, 27, 29; 20:5, 22-23; 21:17-18; 24:24; Ps 37:35-36; 49:10-14; 73:18-19; 92:7; Ecc 8:12-13).

Punishment of:
(Ge 4:7; Ex 20:5; 34:7; Nu 32:23; 1Sa 3:11-14; 2Sa 3:39; 7:14; 22:27-28; 23:6-7; 1Ki 21:20-21; Job 8:20, 22; 11:20; 18:5-21; 19:29; 21:7-33; 27:13-23; 36:12, 17; Ps 3:7; 5:5; 18:14, 26-27; 36:12; 37:1-2, 9-10, 17, 20, 22, 34-38; 64:7-8; 73:18-20, 27; 91:8; 97:3; 107:17, 33-34; 119:21, 118-119, 155; 129:4; 146:9; 147:6; Pr 3:33; 10:3, 6-8, 14, 24-25, 27-31; 11:3, 5-8, 19, 21, 23, 31; 13:2, 5-6, 9, 21, 13, 21, 12, 19, 32; 16:4-5; 22:5, 23; Ecc 8:12-13; Isa 3:11; 26:21; Jer 21:14; 36:31; La 3:39; Eze 3:18-20; 18:1-32; 33:7-20; Hos 14:9; Am 3:2; Mic 2:3; 6:13; Mt 15:13; Ro 1:18; 2:5, 8-9; Col 3:25; 1Th 1:10; 1Pe 2:3-9, 12-17; Jude 5-7; Rev 14:10-11).

By—
Chastisements (Ps 89:32; 1Co 5:5; 1Ti 1:20). Judgments (Ex 32:35; Lev 26:14-39; Dt 11:26-28; 28:15-68; 30:15, 18-19; Job 20:5-29; Ps 11:6; 21:9-10; 39:11; 75:8; 78:49-51; Isa 5:11-14, 24; 9:18; 10:3; 13:9, 11, 14-22; 24:17-18; 28:18-22; 65:12-15; Jer 5:25; 8:12-14, 20-22; 14:10, 12; 25:31; 44:2-14, 23-29; 49:10; La 3:39; 4:22; 5:16-17; Eze 5:4, 8-17; 9:5-7, 10; 20:8; 22:14, 20-21, 31; 24:13-14; Hos 2:9-13; 5:4-6, 9; 9:7, 9, 15; Joel 2:1-2; 3:13-16; Am 5:18-20; Lk 12:46; 1Co 10:5-11; 1Ti 5:24; Heb 10:26-31; 1Pe 4:17-18).

Sorrow (Ge 3:16-19; Job 15:20-24; Ps 32:10; Ecc 2:26; Isa 50:11). Trouble (Isa 48:22; 57:20-21). Being rejected of the Lord (1Ch 28:9; 2Ch 15:2; Mt 10:33; Mk 8:38; Lk 9:26; 13:27-28; Mt 7:23; Jn 8:21; 2Ti 2:12-13; Heb 6:8). Being excluded from the kingdom of heaven (1Co 6:9-10; Gal 5:19-21; Eph 5:5; Rev 21:27; 22:19). Being blotted from God's book (Ex 32:33).

Destruction (Ge 6:3, 7, 12-13; Nu 15:31; Dt 7:9-10; 1Sa 12:25; 1Ch 10:13-14; Job 4:8-9; 31:3; Ps 2:9; 7:11-13; 9:5, 17; 34:16, 21; 52:5; 55:19, 23; 92:7, 9; 94:13, 23; 101:8; 104:35; 106:18, 43; 145:20; Pr 2:22; 12:7; 21:12, 15-16; 24:20; Isa 11:4; 13:8; 64:5-7; Jer 13:14, 16, 22; Eze 25:7; Hos 7:12-13; Am 8:14; Na 1:2, 8-10; Zep 1:12-18; Zec 5:2-4; Mal 4:1; Mt 3:10, 12 w Lk 3:17; Mt 7:13, 19; 10:28 w Lk 12:4-5; Mt 21:41, 44 w Mk 12:1-9 & Lk 20:16, 18; Mt 24:50-51; Lk 9:24-25 w Mt 16:26 & Mk 8:36; Lk 19:27; Jn 5:29; Ac 3:23; Ro 2:12; 9:22; 1Co 3:17; Php 3:19; 1Th 5:3; 2Th 2:8-10). Sudden destruction (Pr 6:15; 24:22; 28:18; 29:1). Everlasting destruction (2Th 1:9). Everlasting contempt (Da 12:2). Everlasting fire (Isa 28:18-22; Mt 18:8-9; 25:41; Mk 9:43; Rev 20:15; 21:8).

Death (Ge 2:17; Pr 1:4-6; Pr 16:25; 19:16; Hos 13:1, 3; Am 9:1-5, 10; Ro 5:12, 21; 6:16, 21; 8:2, 6, 13; 1Co 15:21-22; 2Co 7:10; Gal 6:8; 1Jn 3:14-15; Jas 1:15; 5:20; Rev 2:22-23). The second death (Rev 21:8).

Condemnation to hell (Mt 23:33; Mk 16:16; Jn 3:15-16, 18, 36). Being cast into outer darkness (Mt 8:12; 22:13; 25:30). The last judgments (Rev 6:15-17; 9:4-6, 15, 18; 11:18; 16:2-21; 18:5; 19:15, 17-21; 20:10, 15; 21:8, 27; 22:19). Everlasting (Mt 25:46; Rev 14:10-11; 20:10). Degrees in (Mt 10:15; 11:22, 24; Mk 12:40). No escape from (Job 34:22; 1Th 5:3; Heb 2:3). God has no pleasure in the death of (Eze 18:23; 33:11).

Punishment Illustrated in Parables—
The weeds (Mt 13:24-30, 38-42, 49-50). The talents (Mt 25:14-30). The barren fig tree (Lk 13:6-9). The man who built his house on the sand (Mt 7:26-27; Lk 6:49). Lazarus and the rich man (Lk 16:22-28).

Woes Against the Wicked:
(Isa 5:8, 11, 18-23; Mt 26:24; Mk 14:21; Lk 11:52; 17:1-2; 22:22; Jude 11).

Warned:
(Jer 7:13-15, 23-25; 25:4-6; 26:2-7, 12-13; 29:17-19; Eze 33:8; Da 4:4-27; 5:4-29; Zep 2:1-2; Lk 3:7-9; 1Co 10:11; Rev 3:1-3, 16-19).

See Hell; Judgments; Punishment.

WIDOW

Mosaic Laws Concerning:
High priest forbidden to marry (Lev 21:14). Supported by father, when daughter of priest (Lev 22:13). Vows of, binding (Nu 30:9). Entitled to glean in the orchards and harvest fields (Dt 24:19-21). Levirate marriage of (Dt 25:5-10).

Care of commanded (Dt 14:28-29; 16:11, 14; Isa 1:17; Jer 7:6-7).

Widow's dowry. *See Dowry.*

In the Church:
Remarriage of, authorized (Ro 7:3; 1Co 7:39; 1Ti 5:14). Remarriage of, discouraged (1Co 7:8-9).

Qualifications for widows in 1Ti 5:3-16 may indicate a church office.

Kindness to:
Exemplified by Job (Job 29:13; 31:16, 22). God, the friend of (Dt 10:18; Ps 68:5; 146:9; Pr 15:25; Jer 49:11). Care of in the church (Ac 6:1; 1Ti 5:3-6, 9-12, 16; Jas 1:27).

Oppression of:
(Job 22:9; 24:3, 21; Ps 94:6; Isa 1:23; Eze 22:7; Mk 12:40; Lk 20:47).

Oppression of, forbidden (Ex 22:22-24; Dt 24:17; 27:19; Isa 10:2; Jer 22:3; Zec 7:10; Mal 3:5).

Instances of:
Naomi (Ru 1:3). Ruth (Ru 1-4). The widow of Zarephath, who sustained Elijah during a famine (1Ki 17). The woman whose sons Elisha saved from being sold for debt (2Ki 4:1-7). Anna (Lk 2:36-37). The woman who gave two mites in the temple (Mk 12:41-44; Lk 21:2), of Nain, whose only son Jesus raised from the dead (Lk 7:11-15).

See Levirate Marriage; Marriage; Women.

WIFE

Described:
Called a helper (Ge 2:18, 20), desire of the eyes (Eze 24:10). Compared to a fruitful vine (Ps 128:3).

Beloved, by Isaac (Ge 24:67), by Jacob (Ge 29:30). Hated (Ge 29:31-33).

Contentious (Pr 19:13; 21:9, 19; 25:24). Instances of: Zipporah (Ex 4:25), Peninnah (1Sa 1:6-7).

Loyal, Jacob's (Ge 31:14-16).

Unfaithful (Nu 5:12-31). Instances of: Potiphar's (Ge 39:7), Bathsheba (2Sa 11:2-5).

Prudent (Pr 19:14). Tactful: Abigail (1Sa 25:3, 14-34), Esther (Est 5:5-8; 7:1-4). Virtuous (Pr 12:4; 31:10-12). Incorruptible or strong-willed: Vashti (Est 1:10-12). Wise (Pr 14:1).

Marrying of:
Commended (Pr 18:22; 1Co 7:2; 1Ti 5:14).

Bought (Ge 29:18-30; 31:41; Ex 21:7-11; Ru 4:10). Obtained by kidnapping (Jdg 21:21). Procured (Ge 24; 34:4-10; 38:6).

Duty:
Husband to wife (1Co 7:2-5, 27; Eph 5:25, 28, 31, 33; Col 3:19; 1Pe 3:7).

Wife to husband: To be obedient (1Co 14:34-35; Eph 5:22, 24; Col 3:18; Tit 2:5; 1Pe 3:1, 6). To be affectionate (Tit 2:4). To be faithful (Tit 3:11).

Relation of, to the husband (Ge 2:18, 23-24; 1Co 7:2-5, 10-11, 13, 39; 11:3, 8-9, 11-12).

Domestic duties of (Ge 18:6; Pr 31:13-27).

Vows of (Nu 30:6-16). *See Vow.*

Instances of Evil Influence of:
Eve (Ge 3:6, 12). Solomon's wives (1Ki 11:1-8; Ne 13:26). Jezebel (1Ki 21:25; 2Ki 9:30-37). Haman's (Est 5:14). Herodias (Mt 14:3, 6-11; Mk 6:17, 24-28).

See Husband; Marriage; Parents; Widow; Women.

WILD OX A powerful animal (Nu 23:22; 24:8; Ps 92:9); two-horned (Dt 33:17); wild and difficult to catch (Job 39:9-12; Ps 29:6); KJV "unicorn." *See Animals.*

WILDERNESS Wandering of the Israelites in. *See Israel.* Typical of the sinner's state (Dt 32:10). Jesus' temptation in (Mt 4:1; Mk 1:12-13; Lk 4:1).

See Deserts.

WILL

The Mental Faculty:
Freedom of, recognized by God (Ge 4:6-10; Dt 5:29; 1Ki 20:42; Isa 1:18-20; 43:26; Jer 36:3, 7; Jn 7:17).

See Blessings, Spiritual, Contingent Upon Obedience; Choice; Contingencies.

Of God:
Defined: God's purpose (2Ti 1:9, w Eph 1:9), God's plan (1Co 12:11; 2Co 1:15; Jas 3:4), God's will (Ac 27:12; Eph 1:11).

The supreme rule of duty (Mt 6:10; 12:50 w Mk 3:35; Mt 26:39, 42; Mk 14:36; Lk 22:42; Jn 4:34; 5:30; 6:38-40; Ro 12:2; Eph 5:17). Plans of the righteous subject to (Ac 18:21; Ro 1:10; 15:32; 1Co 4:19; 16:7; Heb 6:3; Jas 4:15).

"Lord's prayer" concerns (Mt 6:10; Lk 11:2). *See Agency.*

Reasons for Wanting to Know—
Love for God (Jn 14:15, 21, 23-24), desire to please God (1Jn 3:22). Blessings in this life (1Pe 3:10-12), rewards in the future life (1Co 3:10-15; 2Ti 4:8; Heb 10:35). Avoid discipline (1Co 3:16-17; 11:31-32; 1Pe 4:17). Good example to other believers (1Co 4:16; 1Th 1:7; 2Th 3:9; Heb 13:7). Will not be ashamed at the Second Coming (1Jn 2:28). Glorify God (1Co 10:31; Col 3:17, 23; Heb 12:10; 2Pe 1:4). Obligation to know (Eph 5:15-17).

How God Reveals—
Through his Word (Ps 119:105; 2Ti 3:16-17). Through control of thoughts, indirectly (2Co 7:8-11; 12:7; 1Pe 1:6-7; 4:12-13; Jas 1:2-4), directly (Pr 16:1, 9; 21:1; Eph 2:13), through Satan (Job 1:12; 2:6). Through the control of circumstances (Pr 16:9; 20:24; Ac 2:23; 4:28; Eph 1:11). Until revelation is complete, through dreams (Ge 20:3, 6; 31:11, 24; 1Ki 3:5; Mt 2:12-13) and visions (Ge 15:1; Zec 1:7-8; Ac 10:10-11).

Prerequisites: Spiritual maturity (Isa 55:8-9; 1Co 2:7; Eph 4:14; Col 1:9; 1Ti 3:6; Heb 5:13-14; 13:21), through the teaching ministry of the Holy Spirit (Jn 16:13-14; 1Co 2:12-14; 1Jn 2:27), through application in testings (Php 3:15; Heb 5:14; 12:7, 11; Jas 1:2-5). Yieldedness or self-denial (Ro 6:13, 19; 12:1; 1Pe 2:9; Rev 1:6), discipleship (Mt 16:24; Mk 8:34; Lk 9:23). Desire to know God's will (Jn 7:17), to do it (Mk 4:24-25; Ac 10:22, 35, 44, 47; 1Jn 2:11). Willingness to obey daily (Mt 16:24; Mk 8:34; Lk 9:23; Ro 6:16; Php 2:13; 2Pe 2:19). Faith (Jer 37:5; Pr 3:5-6; Ro 14:23; 2Co 5:7; Php 2:13; Heb 11:17, 27). Patience (Ps 37:7; Jas 1:5-6). Common sense (Tit 2:12). Peace of God (Col 3:15). A clear conscience (Ro 14:23).

W

A Testament:
Of Abraham (Ge 25:5-6). Jacob (Ge 48:49). David (1Ki 2:1-9). Jehoshaphat (2Ch 21:3). May not be annulled (Gal 3:15). In force after death only (Heb 9:16-17). See Testament; Wills.

WILLFULNESS See Obduracy; Self-Will.

WILLOW A type of tree growing along the brook or near water; several species in Israel; symbol of joy (Lev 23:40; Job 40:22), sorrow (Ps 137:2).

WILLOWS, BROOK OF THE See Poplars, Ravine of.

WILLS
Statements, oral or written in a form, to which law courts give effect, by which property may be disposed of after death (Heb 9:16-17). See Covenant; Will, A Testament.

WIMPLE See Cloak.

WIND

Characterized:
Blasting (2Ki 19:7, 35).
East: Hot and blasting in Egypt (Ge 41:6), in the valley of the Euphrates (Eze 19:12), in Canaan (Hos 13:15; Lk 12:55), at Nineveh (Jnh 4:8), tempestuous in Uz (Job 27:21).
West: Took away the plague of locusts from the land of Egypt (Ex 10:19).
North: Free from humidity in Canaan (Pr 25:23).
South: Soothing (Job 37:17), tempestuous (Job 37:9), purifying (Job 37:21).

Figurative:
Hos 4:19). Of the judgments of God (Jer 22:22; Hos 13:15; Mt 7:25). Of the Spirit (Jn 3:8). Of heresy (Eph 4:14).

WINDOW An opening in a wall (Ge 6:16; 26:8; Jos 2:15, 21; 1Ki 6:4; Eze 40:16-36; Ac 20:9).

WINE

General
Made from grapes (Ge 49:11; Jer 40:10, 12), from pomegranates (SS 8:2). Kept in wineskins (Jos 9:4, 13; Job 32:19; Jer 13:12; Mt 9:17; Lk 5:37-38), in jars (Jer 48:12), in vats (1Ch 27:27), in buildings (2Ch 32:28). Commerce in (Rev 18:13). Banquets of (Est 5:6). Plentiful in Canaan (Dt 33:28; 2Ki 18:32).
Fermented (Lev 10:9; Nu 6:3; Dt 14:26; 29:6). New wine, a staple (Hos 2:8, 22; 7:14; Joel 2:24; Hag 1:11; Mk 2:22; Lk 5:37-39). Aged wine, a delicacy (Isa 25:6; Jer 48:11). Old wine (Lk 5:39).

Positive Use of:
Offered with sacrifices (Ex 29:40; Lev 23:13; Nu 15:5, 10; 18:12; 28:7, 14; Dt 14:23; Ne 10:39).
For enjoyment (Ps 4:7; 104:15; Pr 31:6-7; Ecc 2:3; Isa 25:6; Zec 9:17; 10:7).
Recommended by Paul to Timothy (1Ti 5:23).
Given by Melchizedek to Abraham (Ge 14:18). Used at meals (Mt 26:27-29; Mk 14:23). Made by Jesus at the marriage feast in Cana (Jn 2:9-10). Used in the Lord's Supper (Mt 26:27-29; Lk 22:17-20). Given to Jesus at the Crucifixion, possibly as a pain killer (Mt 27:48; Mk 15:23; Lk 23:36; Jn 19:29).

Negative Use of:
Drunkenness condemned (Pr 20:1; Isa 5:11, 22; 24:9; 28:1, 3, 7; 56:12; Jer 23:9; Hos 4:11; Joel 1:5; Am 6:6; Hab 2:5; Eph 5:18; 1Ti 3:8; Tit 2:3). Addiction and craving condemned (Pr 21:17; 23:29-32; Joel 1:5). Children sold for (Joel 3:3).

Instances of drunkenness:
Noah (Ge 9:21), Lot (Ge 19:32), Joseph and his brothers (Ge 43:34), Nabal (1Sa 25:36), Amnon (2Sa 13:28-29), Xerxes (Est 1:10), kings of Israel (Hos 7:5). Falsely charged against Jesus (Mt 11:19; Lk 7:34) and the disciples (Ac 2:13).

Abstinence From:
Required—
Of Levites while on duty (Lev 10:9; Eze 44:21). Of Nazirites during their vow (Nu 6:3). Of Samson's mother during her pregnancy (Jdg 13:4-5). See Nazirite(s). Required of kings and rulers (Pr 31:4-5). Of John the Baptist (Lk 1:15).

Chosen—
By Daniel to avoid defilement (Da 1:8-20), in mouring (Da 10:3). By the Recabites to honor a vow (Jer 35:6, 8, 14, 16). With bread, denied to the Israelites in the desert (Dt 29:6). Temperance allowed the quests at Xerxes' banquet (Est 1:8).
For the sake of the weaker brother (Ro 14:21). Possibly abstained from by Timothy (1Ti 5:23).

Figurative:
Of, the divine judgments (Ps 60:3; 75:8; Jer 51:7; Rev 14:10; 16:19), the joy of wisdom (Pr 9:2, 5), the joys of religion (Isa 25:6; 55:1; Joel 2:19), abominations (Rev 14:9; 17:2; 18:3).

Symbolic:
Of the blood of Jesus (Mt 26:28; Mk 14:23-24; Lk 22:20; Jn 6:53-56).
See Abstinence; Drunkenness; Vine; Vineyards.

WINEBIBBER See Drunkard; Drunkenness; Wine.

WINEPRESS (Nu 18:27, 30; Dt 15:14; Jdg 6:11). In vineyards (Isa 5:2; Mt 21:33; Mk 12:1).
Figurative: Treading the winepress of the judgments of God (Isa 63:2-3; La 1:15; Rev 14:19-20).

WINESKIN Made of tanned whole skins of animals (Mt 9:17). See Wine.

WING Often used figuratively (Ps 18:10; 55:6; 68:13; Pr 23:5; Mt 23:37).

WINNOWING Separating kernels of threshed grain from chaff; done by shaking bunches of grain into air so that the kernels

fall to the ground, while the chaff is blown away by the wind (Ru 3:2).
Figurative:
Of Israel in destroying its enemies (Isa 41:15-16). God's judgment separating evil people from good (Jer 15:7; 51:2; Mt 3:12; Lk 3:17). The character of a good king, not all kings (Pr 20:8; 20:26).

WINTER Annual return of, shall never cease (Ge 8:22). Plowing in, in Canaan (Pr 20:4). Rainy season in, in Canaan (SS 2:11). Shipping suspended in, on the Mediterranean Sea (Ac 27:12; 28:11). Paul remains for one, at Nicopolis (Tit 3:12). Summer and winter houses (Jer 36:22; Am 3:15).
See Meteorology.

WINTER APARTMENT, WINTER HOUSE The wealthy had separate residences for hot and cold seasons. Called a "winter apartment" (Jer 36:22), a "winter house" (Am 3:15).
See Summer House, Summer Palace.

WISDOM (Job 32:9; Ps 2:10; 90:12; Pr 2:1-20; 4:18-20; 7:4; 9:1-6; 10:13, 21, 23; 12:1, 8, 15; 13:14-16; 14:6-8, 16, 18, 33; 15:2, 7, 14, 33; 16:16, 20-24; 17:10, 24; 18:15; 19:8, 20; 21:11; Ecc 8:1, 5; 9:13-18; 10:12, 12:11; Isa 11:9; 29:24; Mt 11:19; Lk 1:17; 7:35; 21:15; Jas 1:5).

Spiritual:
(Dt 32:29; Job 5:27; 8:8, 10; 12:2-3, 7-13, 16-17, 22).
The fear of the Lord is the beginning of (Ps 111:10; Pr 1:7; 9:10; Isa 33:6). Is revealed to the obedient (Ps 107:43; Pr 28:5, 7; 29:3; Ecc 8:5; Da 12:3-4, 10; Hos 6:3, 6; 14:9; Mt 6:22-23; Lk 11:34-36; Jn 7:17; 10:4, 14; 1Co 2:6-10; 8:3; 1Jn 4:6). Exemplified (Ps 9:10; 76:1; Pr 1:5; 11:12; Mt 7:24-25; 25:1-13; Mk 12:32-34; Ac 6:10; Ro 15:14; 1Co 13:11; Php 3:7-8, 10; 1Th 5:4-5; Jas 3:13).

Commended—
(Pr 3:13-26; 24:3-7; Ecc 7:11-12, 19; 10:1, 12). Is above value (Job 28:12-19; Pr 3:13-15; 16:16). Exhortations to attain to (Pr 2:1-20; 4:4-13, 18-20; 22:17-21; 23:12, 19; 23:23; 24:13-14; Ro 16:19; 1Co 8:3; 14:20; 2Co 8:7; Eph 5:15-17; Col 3:10, 16; 2Pe 3:18).
Parable of (Mt 25:1-13).
Personified (Pr 1:20-33; 8; 9:1-18).
See Knowledge; Speaking or Speech, Wise.

From God—
(Ex 4:12; 8:4, 10; Dt 4:5-6, 35-36; 29:4; 1Ch 22:12; Ne 9:20; Job 4:3; 11:5-6; 22:21-22; 28:20-28; 32:7-8; 33:16; 35:10-11; 36:22; 38:36-37; Ps 16:7; 19:1-2; 25:8-9, 12, 14; 32:8; 36:9; 51:6; 71:17; 94:12; 112:4; 119:130; Pr 1:23; 2:6-7; 3:5-6; Ecc 2:26; Isa 2:3; 11:1-3; 30:21; 42:6-7, 16; 48:17; 54:13; Jer 9:23-24; 24:7; Da 1:17; 2:21-23; 11:32-33; Mt 11:25-27; 13:11; 16:16-17; Lk 1:76-79; 12:11-12; 21:15; 24:32, 45; Jn 1:1, 4-5, 7-9, 17; 6:45; 8:12, 31-32; 9:5, 39; 12:46; 14:7; 16:13-14; 17:3, 6-8, 25-26; 18:37; Ro 1:19-20; 1Co 1:30; 2:9, 11-14; 12:8; 2Co 3:15; 4:6; Gal 4:9; Eph 4:11-13; Php 3:15; Col 1:26-28; 1Ti 2:4; 2Ti 1:7; 3:15; Jas 3:17; 2Pe 1:2-5, 8, 12; 3:18; 1Jn 2:20, 27; 5:20). See God, Wisdom of.

Exemplified—
Of Joseph (Ge 41:16, 25-39; Ac 7:10). Of Moses (Ac 7:22). Of Bezalel (Ex 31:3-5; 35:31-35; 36:1). Of Oholiab (Ex 31:6; 35:34-35; 36:1), of other skilled artisans (Ex 36:2), of women (Ex 35:26). Of Hiram (1Ki 7:14; 2Ch 2:14). Of Solomon (1Ki 3:12, 16-28; 4:29-34; 5:12; 10:24). Of Ethan, Heman, Calcol, and Darda (1Ki 4:31). Of the princes of Issachar (1Ch 12:32). Of Ezra (Ezr 7:25). Of Daniel (Da 1:17; 5:14). Of Paul (2Pe 3:15). Of the Magi (Mt 2:1-12).
Prayer for (Nu 27:21; Jdg 20:18, 23, 26-28; 1Ki 3:7, 9; 8:36; 2Ch 1:10; Job 34:32; Ps 5:8; 25:4-5; 27:11; 31:3; 39:4; 43:3; 86:11; 90:12; 119:12, 18-19, 26-27, 33-34, 66, 68, 73, 80, 124-125, 135, 144, 169, 171; 139:24; Pr 1:16-19; 3:14-19; 6:18-20; Php 1:9; Col 1:9-10; 2:1-3; 4:2-4; 2Ti 2:7; Jas 1:5).
To be possessed in humility (Jer 9:23-24; Jas 3:13). See Desire, Spiritual. Solomon's prayer for. See Solomon.
Promised (Jn 8:22). Opportunity to obtain, forfeited (Pr 1:24-31). Shall become universal.

Worldly:
Condemned—
(Job 4:18-21; 5:13; 11:2, 12; 37:24). Desired by Eve (Ge 3:6-7). Misleading (Pr 21:30; Isa 47:10; Lk 9:25). Ending in death (Pr 16:25). Folly of (Ecc 2:1-26; 7:11-13, 16-25; 8:1, 16-17; Jer 8:7-9; 49:7; Mt 6:23; Ro 1:21-23). Increases sorrow (Ecc 1:18; Isa 47:10-11).
Denounced (2Co 1:12). Woe denounced against (Isa 5:21). Shall perish (Isa 29:14-16). Illustration of (Mt 7:24-27; Lk 16:8).
Admonitions against (Pr 3:7; Col 2:8; 1Ti 6:20-21). Admonitions against glorying in (Jer 9:23-24).
Heavenly things not discerned by (Mt 11:25; Lk 10:21). Gospel not to be preached with (1Co 1:17-26; 2:1-14). To be renounced in order to attain spiritual wisdom (1Co 3:18-20).

Commended—
Council of others commanded (Pr 15:22; 20:18; 24:3-7). Wise application of, profitable (Ecc 10:10; Isa 28:24-29).

Of God: See God, Wisdom of.

Of Jesus: See Jesus the Christ, Wisdom of.

WISDOM OF JESUS, SON OF SIRACH See Apocrypha.

WISDOM OF SOLOMON See Apocrypha.

WISE MEN
1. Men of understanding and skill in ordinary affairs (Pr 1:5; Job 15:2; Ps 49:10), came to be recognized as a distinct class, listed with priests and prophets (Jer 18:18), and also found outside Israel (Ge 41:8; Ex 7:11; Da 2:12-5:15).
2. The Magi (Mt 2:1-12), astrologers who came from the East. Their number and names are not given in Scripture. See Magi.

WITCH One (usually a woman) in league with evil spirits who practices witchcraft, sorcery, and divination; condemned by law (Ex 22:18; Dt 18:9-14; 1Sa 28:3, 9; 2Ki 23:24; Isa 8:19; 19:18-19). See Divination; Medium; Sorcery; Spiritists; Witchcraft.

WITCHCRAFT Detestable to God (Dt 18:9-13; 2Ki 9:22; 2Ch 33:6; Na 3:4; Gal 5:19). To be destroyed (Mic 5:12).
See Divination; Sorcery; Spiritists; Witch.

WITHE NIV "thong" (Jdg 16:7-9).

WITHERED HAND Hand wasted away through some form of atrophy (Mk 3:1-6).

WITNESS (Lev 5:1; Pr 18:17). Qualified by oath (Ex 22:11; Nu 5:19,21; 1Ki 8:31-32), by laying hands on the accused (Lev 24:14). Two necessary to establish a fact (Nu 35:30; Dt 17:6; 19:15; Mt 18:16; Jn 8:17; 2Co 13:1; 1Ti 5:19; Heb 10:28). Required to cast the first stone in executing sentence (Dt 13:9; 17:5-7; Ac 7:58).
To the transfer of land (Ge 21:25-30; 23:11, 16-18; Ru 4:1-9; Jer 32:9-12, 25, 44). To marriage (Ru 4:10-11; Isa 8:2-3). Incorruptible (Ps 15:4). Corrupted by money (Mt 28:11-15; Ac 6:11, 13).
Figurative of instruction in righteousness (Rev 11:3).
See Court, Of Law; Evidence; Falsehood; False Witness; Holy Spirit; Testimony, Religious.

WITNESS OF THE SPIRIT Direct, personal communication by the Holy Spirit that we are children of God (Ro 8:15-16), or some other truth (Ac 20:23; 1Ti 4:1).

WITNESSING FOR CHRIST (Lk 2:17, 38; 24:48; Ac 1:8; 10:39; 22:15; 23:11; 26:22). Of John the Baptist (Jn 1:15; 3:26). Of the apostles (Jn 15:27; 19:35; Ac 10:39-43; 1Jn 1:1-5), to his resurrection (Ac 1:22; 2:32; 3:15; 4:33; 5:32; 1Co 15:3-8).

WIZARD See Spiritists.

WOLF Ravenous (Ge 49:27; Jer 5:6; Eze 22:27; Zep 3:3; Jn 10:12).
Figurative: Of the enemies of the righteous (Mt 7:15; 10:16; Jn 10:12; Ac 20:29). Of the reconciling power of the gospel (Isa 11:6).

WOMEN

General:
Creation of (Ge 1:27; 2:21-22). Named (Ge 2:23). Fall and curse upon (Ge 3:1-16; 2Co 11:3; 1Ti 2:14). Promise to (Ge 3:15).
Took part in ancient worship (Ex 15:20-21; 38:8; 1Sa 2:22), in choir (1Ch 25:5-6; Ezr 2:65; Ne 7:67). Served at the entrance to the Tent of Meeting (Ex 38:8; 1Sa 2:22). Consecrated jewels to tabernacle (Ex 35:22), mirrors (Ex 38:8). Required to attend the reading of the law (Dt 31:12; Jos 8:35). Ministered in the tabernacle (Ex 38:8; 1Sa 2:22). Religious privileges of, among early Christians (Ac 1:14; 12:12-13; 1Co 11:5; 14:34; 1Ti 2:11).
Purifications of after menstruation (Lev 15:19-33; 2Sa 11:4), childbirth (Lev 12; Lk 2:22). Difference in ceremonies made between male and female children (Lev 12). Vows of (Nu 30:3-16).
Had their own tents (Ge 24:67; 31:33). Domestic duties of (Ge 18:6; Pr 31:15-19; Mt 24:41). Cooked (Ge 18:6). Spun (Ex 35:25-26; 1Sa 2:19; Pr 31:19-24). Embroidered (Pr 31:22). Made garments (1Sa 2:19; Ac 9:39). Gleaned (Ru 2:7-8, 15-23). Kept vineyards (SS 1:6). Tended flocks and herds (Ge 24:11, 13-14, 19-20; 29:9; Ex 2:16). Worked in fields (Ru 2:2-3, 6-8). Doorkeeper (Mt 26:69; Jn 18:16-17; Ac 12:13-14). Did not serve in army (Isa 19:16; Jer 50:37; 51:30; Na 3:13).
Veiled the face (Ge 24:65), See Veil. Forbidden to wear men's clothing (Dt 22:5). Ornaments of (Isa 3:16-23; Jer 3:32). Wore hair long (1Co 11:5-15). Commended for modesty in dress (1Ti 2:9-10; 1Pe 3:3-6).
Compassionate to her children (Isa 49:15), rejoice with dancing (Jdg 11:34; 21:21; Jer 31:13), courteous to strangers (Ge 24:17-20), wise (1Sa 25:3; 2Sa 20:16-22), weaker partner but co-heir (1Pe 3:7).
Property rights of: In inheritance (Nu 27:1-11; 36; Jos 17:3-6; Job 42:15), to sell real estate (Ru 4:3-9).
First to sin (Ge 3:6). Last at the cross (Mt 27:55-56; Mk 15:40-41). First at the tomb (Mk 15:46-47; 16:1-6; Lk 23:27-28, 49, 55-56; 24:1-10). First to whom the risen Lord appeared (Mk 16:9; Jn 20:14-18). Converted by preaching of Paul (Ac 16:14-15; 17:4, 12, 34).
Virtuous, held in high esteem (Ru 3:11; Pr 11:16, 22; 12:4; 14:1; 31:10-30). See below, Good.
Zealous in promoting superstition and idolatry (Jer 7:18; Eze 13:17, 23). Active in instigating iniquity (Nu 31:15-16; 1Ki 21:25; Ne 13:26). Guilty of lesbianism (Ro 1:26). See below, Wicked.
Could not marry without consent of parents, father (Ge 24:3-4; 34:6; Ex 22:17; Jos 3:16-17; 1Sa 17:25; 18:17-27). Not to be given in marriage considered a calamity (Jdg 11:37; Ps 78:63; Isa 4:1). When charged with infidelity, guilt or innocence was determined by trial (Nu 5:12-31). Sold for husband's debts (Mt 18:25). Taken captive (Nu 31:9, 15, 17-18, 35; La 1:18; Eze 30:17-18).
Punishment to be inflicted on men for seducing, when betrothed (Dt 22:23-27). Punishment for seducing, when not betrothed (Ex 22:16-17; Dt 22:28-29). Protected during menstruation (Lev 18:19; 20:18). Treated with cruelty in war (Dt 32:25; La 2:21; 5:11).

In Leadership:
Rulers of nations—
Deborah, judge and prophetess (Jdg 4:4); Athaliah, queen of Judah (2Ki 11:1-16; 2Ch 22:2-3, 10-12; 23:1-15); Jezebel, queen of Israel (1Ki 16:31); as rulers in Israel (Isa 3:12); Queen of Sheba (1Ki 10:1-13; 2Ch 9:1-9, 12); Esther, queen of Persia (Est 2:17); Candace, queen of Ethiopia (Ac 8:27).

Patriots—
Miriam (Ex 15:20), Deborah (Jdg 4:4-16; 5), women of Israel (1Sa 18:6), of Thebez (Jdg 9:50), of Abel (2Sa 20:16-22), Esther (Est 4:4-17; 5:1-8; 7:1-6; 8:1-8), of the Philistines (2Sa 1:20). Aid in defensive operations (Jdg 9:53).

W

Influential in public affairs—
The wise woman from Tekoa (2Sa 14:1-21), Bathsheba (1Ki 1:15-21), Jezebel (1Ki 21:7-15, 25), Athaliah (2Ki 11:1, 3; 2Ch 21:6; 22:3), Huldah (2Ki 22:14-20; 2Ch 34:22-28), the queen of Babylon (Da 5:9-13), Pilate's wife (Mt 27:19).
In business (1Ch 7:24; Pr 31:14-18, 24).

Poets—
Miriam (Ex 15:21), Deborah (Jdg 5), Hannah (1Sa 2:1-10), Elizabeth (Lk 1:42-45), Mary (Lk 1:46-55).

Prophets—
Miriam (Ex 15:20-21; Mic 6:4), Deborah (Jdg 4:4-5), Huldah (2Ki 22:14-20; 2Ch 34:22-28), Anna (Lk 2:36-38), Philip's daughters (Ac 21:9).

False prophets and mediums—
The medium at Endor (1Sa 28:7-25), false prophets (Eze 13:17-23), Noadiah the prophetess (Ne 6:14).

In the church—
Present at the selection of Matthias (Ac 1:13-26), present at Pentecost (Ac 2:1-18), churches met in women's homes (Ac 12:12; 16:40; Ro 16:3-5; 1Co 1:11; 16:19; Col 4:15; 2Jn), teachers (Ac 18:26; Tit 2:3-5), deaconesses or wives of deacons (Ro 16:1-2; 1Ti 3:11), and if Junias was a woman, apostles (Ro 16:7). Widow may have been a church office (1Ti 5:1-16).

Social Status of:
In Persia (Est 1:10-22; Da 5:1-12). In Roman empire (Ac 24:24; 25:13, 23; 26:30).
Paul's precepts concerning women in the church (Gal 3:28; 1Co 11:5-15; 14:34-35; Eph 5:22-24; Col 3:18; 1Ti 2:9-12; 3:11; 5:1-16; Tit 2:3-5).
See Widow; Wife. See also, Husbands; Parents.

Good:
Good wife, from the Lord (Pr 12:4; 18:22; 19:13-14; 31:10-31; 1Ti 2:9-10; 3:11; 5:3-16; Tit 2:3-5). Virtuous (Ru 3:11; Pr 11:16, 22; 12:4; 14:1). Affectionate (2Sa 1:26), to offspring (Isa 49:15). Illustrated by the five wise virgins (Mt 25:1-10).

Instances of—
Deborah, a judge, prophetess, and military leader (Jdg 4:5). Mother of Samson (Jdg 13:23). Naomi (Ru 1:2; 3:1; 4:14-17). Ruth (Ru 1:4, 14-22, & Ru 2-4). Hannah, the mother of Samuel (1Sa 1:9-18, 24-28). Widow of Zarephath, who fed Elijah during the famine (1Ki 17:8-24). The Shunammite, who gave hospitality to Elisha (2Ki 4:8-38). Vashti (Est 1:11-12). Esther (Est 4:15-17; 5:1-8; 7:1-6; 8:1-8).
Mary (Lk 1:26-38). Elizabeth (Lk 1:6, 41-45). Anna (Lk 2:37). The widow who cast her mite into the treasury (Mk 12:41-44; Lk 21:2-4). Mary and Martha (Lk 14:3-9; Lk 10:42; Jn 11:5). Mary Magdalene (Mk 16:1; Lk 8:2; Jn 20:1-2, 11-16). Pilate's wife (Mt 27:19). Dorcas (Ac 9:36). Lydia (Ac 16:14). Priscilla (Ac 18:26). Phoebe (Ro 16:1-2). Julia (Ro 16:15). Mary (Ro 16:6). Lois and Eunice (2Ti 1:5). Philippians (Php 4:3). The chosen lady (2Jn).

Figurative—
Of the church of Christ (Ps 45:2-15; Gal 4:26; Rev 12:1). Of saints (Mt 25:1-4; 2Co 11:2; Rev 14:4).

Wicked:
(2Ki 9:30-37; 23:7; Jer 44:15-19, 25; Eze 8:14; Ro 1:26). Zeal of, in licentious practices of idolatry (2Ki 23:7; Hos 4:13-14), in promoting superstition and idolatry (Jer 7:18; Eze 13:17, 23). Careless (Isa 32:9-11). Contentious (Pr 27:15-16). Fond of self-indulgence (Isa 32:9-11), of ornaments (Jer 2:32). Guilty of lesbianism (Ro 1:26). Subtle and deceitful (Pr 6:24-29, 32-35; 7:6-27; Ecc 7:26). Weak-willed (2Ti 3:6).
Active in instigating wickedness (Nu 31:15-16; 1Ki 21:25; Ne 13:26). Idolatrous (Nu 31:15-16; 2Ki 23:7; Ne 13:26; Jer 7:18). Gossips (1Ti 5:11-13). Haughty and vain (Isa 3:16). Odious (Pr 30:23). Guileful and licentious (Pr 2:16-19; 5:3-20; 6:24-29, 32-35; 7:6-27; Ecc 7:26; Eze 16:32; Ro 1:26). Commits forgery (1Ki 21:8). Subtle and deceitful (Pr 6:24-29, 32-35; 7:6-27; Ecc 7:26). Illustrated by the five foolish virgins (Mt 25:1-12).

Instances of Wicked—
Eve, in yielding to temptation and seducing her husband (Ge 3:6; 1Ti 2:14). Sarah, in her jealousy and malice toward Hagar (Ge 21:9-11, w 21:12-21). Lot's wife, in her rebellion against her situation, and against the destruction of Sodom (Ge 19:26; Lk 17:32). The daughters of Lot, in their incestuous lust (Ge 19:31-38). Rebekah, in her partiality for Jacob and her actions to secure for him Isaac's blessing (Ge 27:11-17). Rachel, in her jealousy of Leah (Ge 30:1), in stealing images (Ge 31:19, 34), Leah in her imitation of Rachel in the matter of children (Ge 30:9-18). Tamar, in her adultery (Ge 38:14-24). Potiphar's wife, in her lust and slander against Joseph (Ge 39:7-20).
Miriam, in her sedition with Aaron against Moses (Nu 12). Rahab, in her harlotry (Jos 2:1). Delilah, in her conspiracy against Samson (Jdg 16:4-20). Peninnah, the wife of Elkanah, in her jealous taunting of Hannah (1Sa 1:4-8). The Midianite woman in the camp of Israel, taken in adultery (Nu 25:6-8).
Michal, in her derision of David's religious zeal (2Sa 6:16, 20-23). Bathsheba, in her adultery and in becoming the wife of her husband's murderer (2Sa 11:4-5, 27; 12:9-10). Solomon's wives, in their idolatrous and wicked influence over Solomon (1Ki 11:1-11; Ne 13:26). Jezebel, in her persecution and destruction of the prophets of the Lord (1Ki 18:4, 13); in her persecution of Elijah (1Ki 19:2), ;in her conspiracy against Naboth to despoil him of his vineyard (1Ki 21:1-16); in her evil influence over Ahab (1Ki 21:25, w 21:17-27, & 2Ki 9:30-37). The cannibal mothers of Samaria (2Ki 6:28-29). Athaliah, in destroying the royal household and usurping the throne (2Ki 11:1-16; 2Ch 22:10, 12; 23:12-15).
Noadiah, a false prophetess, in troubling the Jews when they were restoring Jerusalem (Ne 6:14). Haman's wife, in counseling him to hang Mordecai (Est 5:14; 6:13). Job's wife, in counseling him to curse God (Job 2:9; 19:17). The idolatrous wife of Hosea (Hos 1:2-3; 3:1).
Herodias, in her incestuous marriage with Herod (Mt 14:3-4; Mk 6:17-19; Lk 3:19) and causing the death of John the Baptist (Mt 14:6-11; Mk 6:24-28). The daughter of Herodias, in her complicity with her mother in causing the death of John the Baptist

(Mt 14:8; Mk 6:18-28). Sapphira, in her blasphemous falsehood (Ac 5:2-10).

Figurative—
Of backsliding (Jer 6:2; Rev 17:4, 18). Of the wicked (Isa 32:9, 11; Mt 25:1-13).

Symbolic—
Of wickedness (Zec 5:7-8; Rev 17; 19:2).
See Widow; Wife.

WONDERFUL The acts of God (1Ch 16:9; Ps 26:7; 107:8, 15, 21, 24, 31). The name of God is (Jdg 13:18, ftn). A name of the Messiah (Isa 9:6).
See Jesus the Christ, Names of; Titles and Names.

WOOL Used for clothing (Lev 13:47-52, 59; Pr 31:13; Eze 34:3; 44:17). Prohibited in the priest's temple dress (Eze 44:17). Mixing of, with other fabrics forbidden (Lev 19:19; Dt 22:11). Fleece of (Jdg 6:37). First fleece of, belonged to the priests (Dt 18:4).

WORD A title of Jesus (Jn 1:1, 14; 1Jn 5:7; Rev 19:13). *See Jesus the Christ, Names of; Logos.*

WORD OF GOD
Written Word; the Bible:
Psalms of (Ps 19; 119).

Called—
Book (Ps 40:7; Rev 22:19). Book of the Lord (Isa 34:16). Book of the Law (Ne 8:3; Gal 3:10). Holy Scriptures (Ro 1:2; 2Ti 3:15). Law of the Lord (Ps 1:2; Isa 30:9). Oracles (Zec 9:1; 12:1; Mal 1:1). Scriptures (1Co 15:3). Scriptures of Truth (Da 10:21). Sword of the Spirit (Eph 6:17).
The Word (Jas 1:21-23; 1Pe 2:2). Word of God (Lk 11:28; Heb 4:12). Good Word of God (Heb 6:5). Word of Christ (Col 3:16). Word of Life (Php 2:16). Word of Truth (Pr 22:21; Eph 1:13; 2Ti 2:15; Jas 1:18).

Compared to—
A lamp (Ps 119:105; Pr 6:23). Fire (Jer 23:29). Seed (Mt 13:38, 18-23, 37-38; Mk 4:3-20, 26-32; Lk 8:5-15). To a two-edged sword (Heb 4:12).

To Be—
Publicly read (Ex 24:7; Dt 31:11-13; Jos 8:33-35; 2Ki 23:2; 2Ch 17:7-9; Ne 8:1-8, 13, 18; Isa 2:3; Jer 36:6; Ac 13:15, 27; Col 4:16; 1Th 5:27). Instruction of, to be desired (Ps 119:18-19). The people stood and responded saying "Amen" (Ex 24:7; Dt 27:12-26; Ne 8:5-6).
Publicly expounded (Ne 8:8), by Jesus (Lk 4:16-27; 24:27, 45; Jn 2:22), by the apostles (Ac 2:16-47; 8:32, 35; 17:2; 28:23). Searched (Ac 17:11). Searching of, commanded (Isa 34:16; Jn 5:39; 7:52). To be studied (2Ti 2:15; 1Pe 2:2-3). Various portions to be compared (2Pe 2:20). Studied by rulers (Dt 17:18-19; Jos 1:8). Taught to children (Dt 6:7; 11:19; 21:12-13; Ps 78:5).
Obeyed (Dt 4:5-6; 29:29; Ps 78:1, 7; Isa 34:16; Eze 44:5; Hab 2:2; Mt 7:24-25; Lk 6:47-48; 11:28; Ro 16:26; 1Co 11:2; 1Th 4:1-2; 2Th 2:14-15; Heb 2:1-3; Jas 1:25; 2Pe 3:1-2; Jude 3, 17; Rev 1:3). Believed (Mk 1:15; Jn 5:11, 13). Longed for (Ps 119:20, 131; Am 8:11-13). Walked after (Ps 119:30).
In the heart (Dt 30:11-14; Job 22:22; Ps 37:31; 40:8; 119:11; Pr 6:20-21; Isa 51:7; Eze 3:10; Ro 10:6-8). Meditated upon (Jos 1:8; Ps 1:2; 119:15, 23, 48, 78, 97, 99, 148). Worn on the hand and forehead (Ex 13:9; Dt 6:8; 11:18). Written on the doorframes (Dt 6:9; 11:20). In public places (Dt 27:2-3, 8; Jos 8:32). Placed inside of the ark of the covenant (Ex 40:20), beside the ark (Dt 31:26), read in public assemblies (Dt 31:11), *See above, In Public Places.* Taught in the Psalms (Dt 31:19, 21; Ps 119:54). Used for teaching and admonishing one another (1Co 10:11; Col 3:16). Instruction (2Ti 3:16-17).

Not To Be—
Added to nor taken from (Dt 4:2; 12:32; Pr 30:6; Rev 22:18-19). Handled deceitfully (2Co 4:2). Broken (Jn 10:35).

Nature of—
Comforting (Ps 119:28, 50, 52, 76, 83, 92). Delight of the righteous (Job 23:12; Ps 1:2; 119:16, 24, 35, 77, 103, 143, 162, 174). Desired more than gold (Ps 119:72, 127). Edifying (Ps 119:98, 99, 104, 130; Ac 20:32; Ro 4:23-24; 15:4; 1Ti 4:6; 1Jn 2:7-8, 12, 14, 21). Effective (Isa 55:11). Enduring forever (Ps 119:89, 138, 152; Isa 40:8; Mk 13:31; Lk 16:17; 1Pe 1:23-25). Full of hope (Ps 119:81; Col 1:5). Full of joy (Jer 15:16; 1Jn 1:4).
Inspired (Ex 19:7; 20:1; 24:3-4, 12; 31:18; 32:16; 34:27, 32; Lev 26:46; Dt 4:5, 10, 14; 2Ki 17:13; 2Ch 33:18; Ps 99:7; 147:19; Isa 34:16; 59:21; Jer 30:2; 36:1-2, 27-28, 32, 59-64; Eze 11:25; Da 10:21; Hos 8:12; Zec 7:12; Ac 1:16; 28:25; Ro 3:1-2; 1Co 2:12-13; 14:37; Eph 6:17; 1Th 2:13; 2Ti 3:16-17; Heb 1:1-2; 3:7-8; 4:12; 2Pe 1:21; 3:2; Rev 1:1-2, 11, 17-19; 2:7; 22:6-8). Life giving (Ps 119:25, 93; Jas 1:18; 1Pe 1:23). Living (Heb 4:12). Loved (Ps 119:47-48, 70, 97, 111, 113, 119, 159, 163, 167). Part of the Christian armor (Eph 6:17). Perfect (Ps 19:7; Jas 1:24). Powerful (Lk 1:37; Heb 4:12). Praiseworthy (Ps 56:4). Pure (Ps 12:6; 19:8; 119:140; Pr 30:5). Restraining (Ps 17:4; 119:11). Revered (Ps 119:161; 138:2).
Sanctifying (Jn 15:3; 17:17, 19; Eph 5:26; 1Ti 4:5). Spirit and life (Jn 6:63). Spiritual food, bread (Dt 8:3; Mt 4:4). Standard of righteous (Ps 119:138, 144, 172; Isa 8:20). Trustworthy (Ps 19:7, 9; 33:4, 6; 93:5; 111:7-8; 119:86). Truth (Ps 119:142, 151, 160; 1Th 2:13; Jas 1:18). Wonderful (Ps 119:129).
Bears the test of criticism and experience (2Sa 22:31; Ps 18:30). Cleanses life of youth (Ps 119:9). Convicts of sin (2Ki 22:9-13; 2Ch 17:7-10; 34:14-33). Gives peace (Ps 119:165). Inspires faith (Ro 10:17; Heb 11:3). Makes free (Ps 119:45; Jn 8:32). Makes wise (Ps 119:99; 2Ti 3:15). Rejoices the heart (Ps 119:111; Jer 15:16). Spirit of, gives life (2Co 3:6). Standard of judgment, the world to be judged by (Jn 12:48; Ro 2:16; Rev 20:12; 1Th 2:13; 1Pe 1:23).
Fulfilled by Jesus (Mt 5:17; Lk 24:27; Jn 19:24). Testify of Jesus (Jn 5:39; 20:31; Ac 10:43; 18:28; 1Co 15:3; Heb 10:7). *See Jesus the Christ, Prophecies Concerning.*

Ignorance of—
(Mt 22:29; Mk 12:24).
Disbelief in (Lk 16:31; 24:25; Jn 5:46-47; 8:37; 2Ti 4:3-4; 1Pe 2:8; 2Pe 3:15-16).
Rejected by the wicked (Ps 50:16-17; Pr 1:29; 13:13; Isa 5:24; 28:9-14; 30:9-11; 53:1; Jer 6:10; 8:9; Hos 8:12; Am 2:12; Mic 2:6; Mk 7:9, 13; Lk 16:31; 24:25; Jn 3:20; 5:46-47; 8:37, 45; Ac 13:46; 1Co 1:18; 2:2-3; 2Ti 4:3-4; 1Pe 2:8; 2Pe 3:15-16; Rev 22:19).
See Commandments and Statutes, Of God.

Jesus, the Living Word:
(Jn 1:1, 14; 1Jn 5:7; Rev 19:13). *See Jesus the Christ, Names of; Logos.*

WORDS
Of Jesus:
Gracious (Lk 4:22), spirit and life (Jn 6:63), eternal life (Jn 6:68), shall judge (Jn 12:47-48).

Of the Wise:
As goads, and as nails well fastened (Ecc 12:11), gracious (Ecc 10:12). Spoken in season (Pr 15:23; Isa 50:4). Fitly spoken, like apples of gold in settings of silver (Pr 25:11). Of the perfect man, gentle (Jas 3:2). Of the teacher, should be plain (1Co 14:9, 19). Should be acceptable to God (Ps 19:14).

Unwise:
Unprofitable, to be avoided (2Ti 2:14). Unspeakable, heard by Paul in paradise (2Co 12:4). Vain, not to be regarded (Ex 5:9; Eph 5:6), like a tempest (Job 8:2). Without knowledge, darken counsel (Job 38:2). Idle, account must be given for in the day of judgment (Mt 12:36-37).
Hasty, folly of (Pr 29:20). In a multitude of, is sin (Pr 10:19). Fool known by the multitude of (Ecc 5:3), will swallow himself (Ecc 10:12-14). Seditious, deceive the simple (Ro 16:18). Deceitful, are a snare to him who utters them (Pr 6:2). Of the hypocrite, softer than oil (Ps 55:21). Of the talebearer, wounds to the soul (Pr 18:8).
See Busybody; Slander; Speaking, Evil; Talebearer.

WORK *See Industry; Labor.*

WORKS, GOOD
General:
(2Co 9:8; Eph 2:10; Php 2:13; Col 1:10; 1Th 1:3, 7-8; 2Th 2:17, 21; Jas 1:22-27; 3:17-18).
Under the Law (Lev 18:5; Eze 20:11, 13, 20; Lk 10:28; Ro 10:5; Gal 3:12). In humanitarian service (Eze 18:7-8; Mt 10:42; 25:35-46; Jas 1:27). Hypocritical (Mt 6:1-4).
Jesus an example of (Jn 10:32; Ac 10:38). Ministers should be patterns of (Tit 2:7). Ministers should manifest (1Ti 6:17-18; Tit 3:1, 8, 14). Holy women should manifest (1Ti 2:10; 5:10). Manifest faith (Ps 37:3; Mt 19:16-21; Ro 2:13; Gal 6:4; Jas 2:14-26). Scriptures given for (Tit 2:14).
God is glorified by (Mt 25:34-46; Jn 15:2-8, 14; 1Co 3:6-9; Php 1:11; Heb 13:21). Designed to lead others to glorify God (Mt 5:16; 1Pe 2:12). A blessing attends (Jas 1:25). God remembers (Pr 6:25; 24:13; Ps 106:30-31; Jer 22:15-16; Eze 18:5-9; Mt 6:1-4; 18:5; 25:34-36; Jn 15:2-8, 14; Ac 10:14, 38; Heb 6:9-10; Rev 14:13; 22:14).
Of the righteous, are manifest (1Ti 5:25). God remembers (Ne 13:14; Heb 6:9-10). Shall be brought into judgment (Ecc 12:14, w 2Co 5:10). In the judgment, will be an evidence of faith (Mt 25:34-40, w Jas 2:14-20).
Parables relating to: The talents and pounds (Mt 25:14-29; Lk 19:12-27), the laborers in the vineyard (Mt 20:11-15), the two sons (Mt 21:28-31), the barren fig tree (Lk 13:6-9).

Commanded:
(Ps 37:3; Mt 3:8; Jn 14:2-8, 14) To ministers (Tit 2:7), women professing godliness (1Ti 2:10), widows (1Ti 5:10). To Christians (Mt 5:16; Col 3:13; Tit 3:1-2, 8, 14; Heb 10:24; Jas 1:22-27; 3:13; 1Pe 2:12). To the rich (1Ti 6:18). To be done without a show (Mt 6:1-4). Following the example of the faithful (Heb 10-14). Zeal in (Tit 2:14).

Insufficient for Salvation:
(Ps 49:7-8; 127:1-2; Ecc 1:14; Isa 13:14; 57:12; 64:6; Eze 7:19; 33:12-19; Da 9:18; Mt 5:20; Lk 17:7-10; 18:9-14; Ac 13:39; Ro 3:20-21; 4:1-25; 8:3; 9:16, 31-32; 11:6; 1Co 13:1-3; Gal 2:16, 21; 3:10-12, 21; 4:9-11; 5:2, 4, 6, 18; 6:15; Eph 2:8-9; Php 3:3-9; Col 2:20-23; 2Ti 1:9; Tit 3:4-5; Heb 4:3-10; 6:1-2; 9:1-14; Jas 2:10-11).

WORKS OF GOD In creation (Job 9:8-9; Ps 8:3-5; 89:11; 136:5-9; 139:13-14; 148:4-5; Ecc 3:11; Jer 10:12), good (Ge 1:10, 18, 21, 25). Faithful (Ps 33:4). Wonderful (Ps 26:7; 40:5). Incomparable (Ps 86:8). In his overruling providence in human affairs (Ps 26:7; 40:5; 66:3; 75:1; 111:2, 4, 6; 118:17; 145:4-17).
See also, God, Works of.

WORLD
1. Universe (Jn 1:10).
2. Human race (Ps 9:8; 96:13; Ac 17:31).
3. Unregenerate humanity (Jn 15:18; 1Jn 2:15).
4. Roman Empire (Lk 2:1).

WORLDLINESS
Described:
(Ecc 1:8; 8:15; Isa 56:12; Jn 15:19; Tit 3:3; 2Pe 2:12-15, 18-19). Proverbial theme (Ecc 1:8; Lk 12:19; 1Co 15:32). Tends to poverty (Pr 21:17; Hag 1:6). Fatal to spirituality (Gal 6:8; Php 3:19; 1Ti 5:6). Chokes the Word (Mt 13:22; Mk 4:19; Lk 8:14).
Leads to: the rejection of the gospel (Mt 22:2-6; Lk 14:17-24). The rejection of Christ (Jn 5:44; 12:43). Moral insensibility (Isa 22:13; 32:9-11; 47:7-9). Death (Pr 14:12-13).
Prosperity is short-lived (Job 20:4-29; 21:11-15; Ps 49:16-18; Isa 24:11; 28:4). Vanity of (Ecc 1:2-6; 6:11-12).
Prayer regarding (Ps 73:2-22). Parables of (Lk 16:1-13, 19-25).

Admonitions Against:
(Pr 23:20-21; 27:1, 7; Ecc 7:2-4; 11:9-10; Hos 9:1, 11, 13; Am 6:3-7; 8:10; Mic 2:10; 6:14, 19, 24; Mt 6:25-34; 16:26; 24:28;

Mk 8:36-37; Lk 17:26-29, 33; 21:34; Jn 12:25; Ro 12:2; 1Co 7:29-31; 10:6; Col 3:2, 5; 2Ti 2:4, 22; 3:2-9; Tit 2:12; Jas 2:1-4; 4:4, 9; 5:5; 1Pe 1:14, 24; 2:11; 4:1-4; 1Jn 2:15-17). Denounced (Isa 5:11-12; 47:8-9; Jude 11-13, 16, 19).
Moses' choice against (Heb 11:24-26).

Instances of:
Antediluvians (Mt 24:38-39; Lk 17:26-27). Sodomites (Lk 17:28-29). Esau (Ge 25:31-34; Heb 12:16). Jacob (Ge 25:31-34; 27:36; 30:37-43). Judah (Ge 37:26-27). Israelites (1Sa 8:19-20). Balaam (2Pe 2:15; Jude 11, w Nu 22; 23; 24). Eli's sons (1Sa 2:12-17). Gehazi (2Ki 5:20-27).
Herod (Mt 14:6-7). The disciples (Mt 18:1-4; Mk 9:34; Lk 9:46-48). The rich fool (Lk 12:16-21). Dives (Lk 16:19-25). The worldly steward (Lk 16:1-13). Cretans (Tit 1:12).
See Worldly Pleasure.

WORLDLY CARE *See Anxiety.*

WORLDLY PLEASURE (Job 20:12; Ecc 7:4; Isa 22:13; 2Ti 3:4; Tit 3:3). To be rejected by the righteous (1Pe 4:3-4). Brings poverty (Pr 21:17). Chokes righteousness (Lk 8:14). Leads to suffering (Isa 47:8-9; 2Pe 3:13), spiritual death (1Ti 5:6). Denounced (Isa 5:11-12; Jas 5:5). Folly of (Ecc 1:17; 2:1-13).
See Worldliness.

WORLDLY WISDOM Desired by Eve (Ge 3:6-7). Misleading (Isa 47:10). Increases sorrow (Ecc 1:18). Shall perish (Isa 29:14). Heavenly things not discerned by (Mt 11:25; Lk 10:21). Gospel not to be preached with (1Co 1:17-26; 2:1-14). To be renounced in order to attain spiritual wisdom (1Co 3:18-20). Admonitions against (Col 2:8; 1Ti 6:20-21). Admonitions against glorying in (Jer 9:23-24).
See Wisdom.

WORM Low form of life (Ex 16:24; Isa 51:8; Ac 12:23), used metaphorically of mankind's insignificance (Job 25:6; Isa 41:14).

WORMWOOD Bitter plant that grows in wastelands; name of a star that turns water bitter (Rev 8:11).

WORSHIP
General:
To be rendered to God only (Ex 20:3; Dt 5:7; 6:13; Mt 4:10; Lk 4:8; Ac 10:26; 14:15; Col 2:18; Rev 19:10; 22:8). Not needed by God (Ac 17:24-25).
Divine presence in (Ex 29:42-43; 40:34-35; Lev 19:30; Nu 17:4; 1Ki 8:3-11; 2Ch 5:13-14; Ps 77:13; 84:4; Isa 56:7; Mt 18:20; Ac 2:1-4; Heb 10:25).
Origin of (Ge 4:26). Of Jesus. *See Jesus the Christ, Worship of.* Acceptable to God (Ge 4:4; 8:21). Of the wicked, rejected (Ge 4:5, 7). *See Prayer, of the Wicked.* "Iniquity of the holy things" (Ex 28:38).
Sanctuary instituted for (Ex 25:8, 22; 29:43; 40:34-35; Nu 17:4).
Attitudes in: Bowing (Ex 34:8; 2Ch 20:18). Prostration (Ge 17:3; Mk 3:11).
Prayer in. *See Prayer.*
Benedictions pronounced. *See Benedictions.*
With music (2Ch 5:13-14; Ezr 3:10-11; Ps 100:1-2; 126:1-3; Isa 30:29; 38:20). Rendering praise (Ps 22:22; 138:2; 149:1). Thanksgiving (Ps 35:18; 100:4; 116:17).
In spirit and in truth (Jn 4:23-24; 1Co 14:15; Php 3:3). Renews strength (Isa 40:31). Loved by God's people (Ps 27:4; 84:1-4; 84:10; Zec 8:21). Reward of (Ps 65:4; 92:13-14; 122:1).
Preparation for (Ex 19:10-13, 21-24; 20:24-25; 30:19, 21; Lev 10:3; Ps 26:6; Isa 56:6-7; Zep 3:18; Mal 3:3-4). Requirements of (Ps 24:3-6; 51:18-19).
Proprieties in (Ecc 5:1-2; 1Co 11:13, 20-22; 14:2-19). Reverence in (Ex 3:5; 19:10-12, 21-24; 24:1-2; Ecc 5:1; Hab 2:20). Private (Mt 6:6; 14:23; Lk 6:12).
At night (Isa 30:29; Ac 16:25). Jesus prays at night (Lk 6:12). In the temple (Jer 26:2; Lk 18:10; 24:53; Ac 3:1). In the heavenly temple (Rev 11:1). In private homes (Ac 1:13-14; 5:42; 12:12; 20:7-9; Ro 16:5; 1Co 16:19; Col 4:15; Phm 2). Anywhere (Jn 4:21-24). To become universal (Isa 45:23; Ro 14:11; Php 2:10).
Of hypocrites, despised by God (Isa 1:11-15; 29:13-16; Hos 6:6; Am 5:21-24). Of the wicked, rejected (Ge 4:5, 7).
Commanded:
(Ge 35:1; Ex 15:1; 23:17-18; 34:23; Dt 12:5-7, 11-12; 16:6-8; 31:11-13; 33:19; 2Ki 17:36; 1Ch 16:29; Ne 10:39; Ps 29:2; 45:11; 76:11; 96:8-9; 97:7; 99:5; Isa 12:5-6; 49:13; 52:9; Jer 31:11-12; Joel 1:14-15; 2:15-17; Na 1:15; Hag 1:8; Zec 14:16-18; Mt 8:4; Mk 1:44; Lk 4:8; 5:14; 1Ti 2:8; Heb 10:25; 12:28; Rev 14:7; 19:10).
Summons to (Ps 95:6; Isa 2:3; Mic 4:2).
Family:
(Dt 16:11, 14). Of Abraham (Ge 12:7-8; 13:4, 18). Of Jacob (Ge 35:2-3). Of Job (Job 1:5). Of the Philippian jailer (Ac 16:34).
National:
(Rev 15:4). The whole nation required to assemble for, including men, women, children, servants, and strangers (Dt 16:11; 31:11-13), in Mount Gerizim and Mount Ebal (Jos 8:32-35). The word of God read in public assemblies (Ex 24:7; Dt 27:12-26; 31:11-13; Jos 8:33-35; 2Ki 23:1-3; Ne 8:1-8, 13-18; Mt 21:23; Lk 4:16-17).
See Affliction, Prayer Under; Blasphemy; Children; Church, The Body of Believers; Consecration; Dedication; Idolatry; Instruction, in Religion; Levites; Minister; Music; Offerings; Praise; Prayer; Preaching; Priest; Psalms; Religion; Sacrilege; Servant; Strangers; Tabernacle; Temple; Thanksgiving; Women; Word of God; Young Men.
Instances of:
Israel (Ex 15:1-2; Ps 107:6-8, 32). Moses (Ex 34:8). Solomon (2Ch 7:1). Priests and Levites (2Ch 30:27). Psalmists (Ps 5:7; 42:4; 48:9; 55:14; 63:1-2; 66:4, 13-14; 89:7; 93:5; 103:1-4; 116:12-14, 17; 119:108; 132:7, 13-14). Isaiah (Isa 49:13; 52:9).

WORSHIPERS Examples of (Ge 22:5; 24:26; Ex 34:8; Jos 5:14; Jdg 7:15; 1Sa 1:28; 2Sa 12:20; 2Ch 7:3; Ne 8:6; Job 1:20; Rev 4:10; 7:11; 11:16).

WOUNDS Treatment of (Pr 20:30; Isa 1:6; Lk 10:34). By Jesus' wounds we are healed (Isa 53:5; 1Pe 2:24).

WRATH
1. Anger of people (Ge 30:2; 1Sa 17:28), may be evil (2Co 12:20), or a reaction to evil (1Sa 20:34), or a work of the flesh (Gal 5:20). *See Anger.*
2. Anger of God—reaction of a righteous God against sinful people and in all forms (Dt 9:7; Isa 13:9; Ro 1:18; Eph 5:6; Rev 14:10, 19). *See Anger of God.*

WREATHS Decorating the tabernacle and temple (Ex 28:14; 1Ki 7:17; 2Ch 4:12).

WRESTLE To contend by grappling with an opponent (Ge 32:24-25), used figuratively (Eph 6:12).

WRITING Discovered to be in use in Mesopotamia as early as 3200 B.C., its development credited to the Sumerians. They had a primitive, nonalphabetic linear writing, not phonetic but pictographic, ideas being recorded by means of pictures of sense-symbols, rather than by sounds-symbols. The next stage in the history of writing was the introduction of the phonogram, or the type of sign which indicates a sound, and afterward came alphabetic scripts. The Egyptians first developed an alphabetic system of writing. Hebrews derived their alphabet from Phoenicians. Semitic writing dating between 1900 and 1500 B.C. has been found at Serabit el-Khadim in Sinai. Greeks received their alphabet from Phoenicians and Arameans.
Writing mentioned in Bible (Ex 17:14). Ten Commandments written with the finger of God (Ex 31:18; 32:15-16). Ancient writing materials: clay, wax, wood, metal, plaster (Dt 27:2-3; Jos 8:32; Lk 1:63), later, parchment (2Ti 4:13), and papyrus (2Jn 12). Instruments of writing: reed on papyrus and parchment; stylus on hard material (Ex 32:4).
See Book; Engraving; Ink; Letters; Pen; Tablet, 1.

WRITING KIT
In Ezekiel's vision (Eze 9:2-3, 11).

X

XERXES
1. Xerxes is a transliteration of the Greek form of the Persian name Khshayarshan; KJV Ahasuerus. The king of Persia mentioned in the book of Esther and Ezr 4:6. Xerxes succeeded his father Darius I the Great and reigned from 486 to 465 B.C.
2. Father of Darius the Mede (Da 9:1).

Y

YAHWEH (*He who is [I am]* or *He who causes to be*). The Hebrew personal name for God, Yahweh, is translated in the KJV and NIV as LORD, and sometimes also in the KJV as GOD. God revealed his name as "I AM WHO I AM," his eternal covenant name implying self-existence and saving presence (Ex 3:14-17). YHWH is often called the "tetragrammaton," referring to the "four letters" or consonants of Yahweh.
See God, Names of; Yahweh; Jehovah.

YARMUK, WADI EL Stream six miles SE of Sea of Galilee flowing into Jordan, marked S boundary of Bashan.

YARN
1. Blue, purple, and scarlet yarn used to embroider the tabernacle and priestly garments (Ex 25:4; 26:1; 28:5), in the temple (1Ch 2:7, 14; 3:14). Used in cleansing sacrifices (Lev 14:4, 6, 49, 51-52).
2. *See Kue.*

YAUDI A place in N Aram or the same as Judah (2Ki 14:28, ftn).

YEAR (Ge 1:14). Divided into months (Ex 12:2; Nu 10:10; 28:11). *See Month.*
Annual feasts (Lev 25:5). *See Feasts.*
Redemption of houses sold, limited to one (Lev 25:29-30). Land to rest one, in seven (Lev 25:5). Of release (Dt 15:9).
Age computed by: of Abraham (Ge 25:7), of Jacob (Ge 47:9). *See Longevity.*
A thousand, with the Lord as one day (Ps 90:4; 2Pe 3:8). Satan to be bound a thousand (Rev 20:2-4, 7).
See Jubilee; Millennium; Time.

YEAST *See Leaven.*

YHWH *See Lord; Yahweh.*

YOKE Wooden frame for joining two draft animals; a wooden bar held on neck by thongs around neck (Nu 19:2; Dt 21:3). Yoke of oxen is a pair (1Sa 14:14; Lk 14:19).
Figurative of:
Oppression (Lev 26:13; 1Ki 12:4; 2Ch 10:4, 9-11; Isa 9:4; 10:27; Jer 28:2, 4, 10; 30:8), the bondage of sin (La 1:14), burdensome ordinances (Ac 15:10; Gal 5:1), discipleship to Christ (Mt 11:29-30), discipline (La 3:27).
Removal of, figurative of deliverance (Ge 27:40; Jer 2:20; Mt 11:29-30).

YOKEFELLOW (*yoked together*). Person united to another by close bonds, as in marriage or labor (Php 4:3, ftn).

YOM KIPPUR Hebrew for "Day of Atonement." *See Feasts.*

YOUNG MEN, WOMEN Note: In the proverbs throughout this entry, "son" can be read as an inclusive term for both male and female children.
Wise and Foolish:
Wise, exemplified in Moses' wise choice (Ex 24:3-5; Heb 11:24-26). A comfort to parents (Pr 10:1; 15:20; 29:3). Glory of (Pr 20:29).
Foolish, a sorrow to parents (Pr 10:1; 17:25; 19:13, 26; 28:7). Wise and foolish, contrasted (Pr 10:1; 13:1; 15:20). *See below, Folly of.*
Admonitions to:
(Pr 3:1-5; 4:20-27; 6:1-5, 20-25; 19:27; 23:15-26; 24:1-12, 15-34; 27:11). Against lust (2Ti 2:22-23). Against drunkenness (Pr 23:20-21; 23:29-35). Against loving the world (1Jn 2:13-17). Against the snares of the adulteress (Pr 5:3-14; 6:24-35; 7:1-27; 23:27-28; 31:1-3). Against the enticements of sinners (Pr 1:10-16). Against evil companions (Pr 2:12-15; 4:14-15; 24:1-2).
Exhortations to:
Be sober-minded (Tit 2:6). Be an example of piety (1Ti 4:12). Keep the heart with all diligence (Pr 4:23). Paying attention to God's word (Ps 119:9). Seek wisdom (Pr 2:1-8; 3:13-23; 4:5-13; 24:13-14). Obey parents (Pr 6:20-23; 23:22-26). Obey the Lord (Pr 3:5-12). Praise the Lord (Ps 148:12-13).
Instances of Religious: *See Joseph, 1; Joshua; Samuel; David; Solomon; Uriah.*
Foolish, Exemplified:
Esau (Ge 25:31-34; Heb 12:16-17), Rehoboam's counselors (1Ki 12:8-11). Rehoboam (1Ki 12:13-14). The rich young ruler (Mt 19:16-22; Mk 10:17-22; Lk 18:18-23). The prodigal son (Lk 15:11-32).
See also, Children; Parents.

Z

ZAANAIM *See Zaanannim.*

ZAANAN A place of uncertain location (Mic 1:11).

ZAANANNIM A plain near Kedesh (Jos 19:33; Jdg 4:11).

ZAAVAN (possibly *trembling, terror*). A son of Ezer (Ge 36:27; 1Ch 1:42).

ZABAD (*he bestows*).
1. Son of Nathan (1Ch 2:36-37).
2. An Ephraimite (1Ch 7:21).
3. One of David's valiant men (1Ch 11:41).
4. An assassin of King Joash (2Ch 24:26). Also called Jozabad (2Ki 12:21). *See Jozabad, 1.*
5. Three Israelites who divorced their Gentile wives (Ezr 10:27, 33, 43).

ZABBAI (perhaps *God has given*).
1. Son of Bebai (Ezr 10:28).
2. Father of Baruch (Ne 3:20).

ZABBUD *See Zaccur, 5.*

ZABDI (*Yahweh bestows*).
1. Father of Carmi (Jos 7:1, 17-18, ftn). *See Zimri, 3.*
2. A Benjamite (1Ch 8:19).
3. A Shiphmite in charge of David's wine vats (1Ch 27:27).
4. Son of Asaph (Ne 11:17).

ZABDIEL (*God [El] bestows*).
1. Father of Jashobeam (1Ch 27:2).
2. An chief officer of 128 able men who lived in Jerusalem (Ne 11:14).

ZABUD (*[he has] bestowed upon*). A chief officer of Solomon (1Ki 4:5).

ZABULON *See Zebulun.*

ZACCAI (*Yahweh has remembered*, or perhaps *Yahweh remember*). A Jew whose descendants returned from the Exile (Ezr 2:9; Ne 7:14).

ZACCHAEUS (*righteous, pure one*). Chief tax collector; climbed sycamore tree to see Jesus and became his disciple (Lk 19:8).

ZACCUR (remembering).
1. Father of Reubenite spy, Shammua (Nu 13:4).
2. Simeonite (1Ch 4:26).
3. Son of Merari (1Ch 24:27).
4. Son of Asaph; musician (1Ch 25:1-2; Ne 12:35).
5. A returned exile (Ezr 8:14).
6. Son of Imri who helped rebuild walls of Jerusalem (Ne 3:2).
7. Man who sealed covenant with Nehemiah (Ne 10:12).
8. Father of Hanan (Ne 13:13).

ZACHARIAH See Zechariah, 1 & 15.

ZACHARIAS See Zechariah, 30 & 31.

ZACHER See Zeker.

ZADOC See Zadok, 10.

ZADOK (righteous one).
1. High priest in time of David's reign (2Sa 19:11; 20:25; 1Ch 15:11; 16:39). Removes the ark from Jerusalem at the time of Absalom's usurpation; returns with it at David's command (2Sa 15:24-36; 17:15, 17-21). Stands aloof from Adonijah at the time of his attempted usurpation (1Ki 1:32-40, 44-45). Summoned by David to anoint Solomon (1Ki 1:32-40, 44-45). Performs the function of high priest after Abiathar was deposed by Solomon (1Ki 2:35; 1Ch 29:22).
2. Father of Jerusha (2Ki 15:33; 2Ch 27:1).
3. Son of Ahitub (1Ch 6:12).
4. A man of valor (1Ch 12:28).
5. Son of Baana (Ne 3:4).
6. A priest (Ne 3:29).
7. A returned exile (Ne 10:21).
8. Son of Meraioth (Ne 11:11).
9. A treasurer of the temple (Ne 13:13).
10. Descendant of Zerubbabel and an ancestor of Jesus (Mt 1:14).

ZAHAM (putrid, loathsome). Grandson of Solomon (2Ch 11:19).

ZAHAR An area NW of Damascus (Eze 27:18); modern Sahra.

ZAIR (small, insignificant, hence narrow pass). Village E of Dead Sea where Jehoram NIV, broke through the lines of the Edomites (2Ki 8:21).

ZALAPH (low, prickly shrub [caper plant]). Father of man who helped Nehemiah repair walls (Ne 3:30).

ZALMON (in his image, a copy; black hill).
1. Forest near Shechem (Jdg 9:48).
2. One of David's mighty men (2Sa 23:28), called "Ilai the Ahohite" (1Ch 11:29).

ZALMONAH (dark, gloomy, shaded place). Encampment of Israelites in wilderness, SE of Edom (Nu 33:41-42).

ZALMUNNA (protection refused). King of Midian (Jdg 8:5-21; Ps 83:11).

ZAMZUMMITES (babblers). Ammonite name for Rephaites (Dt 2:20), lived E of Jordan. May be same as Zuzites (Ge 14:5). See Rephaites; Zuzites.

ZANOAH (rejected).
1. A city of W Judah (Jos 15:34; Ne 3:13; 11:30).
2. A city of E Judah (Jos 15:56).
3. A descendant of Caleb (1Ch 4:18).

ZAPHENATH-PANEAH (the [pagan] god speaks and he [the newborn] lives). Name given to Joseph by Pharaoh (Ge 41:45).

ZAPHON (possibly North or [proper name of a god], Zephon). Territory E of Jordan assigned to Gad (Jos 13:27); possibly modern Amateh.

ZARA, ZARAH See Zerah.

ZAREAH A city of Judah (Ne 11:29). See Zorah.

ZAREATHITES See Zorathites.

ZARED See Zered.

ZAREDA See Zeredah.

ZAREPHATH (possibly smelting place BDB; place of pigmenting, staining KB). A city between Tyre and Sidon. Elijah performs two miracles in (1Ki 17:8-24; Lk 4:26).

ZARETHAN Place in Ephraim or Manasseh near Beth Shan and Adam (Jos 3:16; 1Ki 4:12), and near Succoth (1Ki 7:46; 2Ch 4:17). Exact site not known.

ZARETH-SHAHAR See Zereth Shahar.

ZARHITES See Zerahite(s).

ZARTANAH, ZARTHAN See Zarethan.

ZATTU
1. One whose descendants returned with Zerubbabel (Ezr 2:8; 10:27; Ne 7:13).
2. One who sealed the covenant with Nehemiah (Ne 10:14). Probably the same as 1.

ZAVAN See Zaavan.

ZAZA (a form of a shortened nickname; term of endearment). Son of Jonathan (1Ch 2:33).

ZEAL (zeal, jealousy).

General:
Without love, unprofitable (1Co 13:3). Without knowledge (Nu 11:27-28; Jdg 11:30-31, 34-35; Ecc 7:16; Mt 8:19-20; Lk 9:57-58; Jn 16:2; Ac 21:20; Ro 10:2-3; Gal 1:13-14).
Wisdom of (Pr 11:30).
Required (Isa 62:6-7; Mt 5:13-16; Mk 4:21-22; Lk 8:16-17; Ac 10:42; 1Co 15:58; Tit 2:14; 3:1). Commanded (Jos 24:15-16; Ezr 7:23; Ps 60:4; 96:2; Ecc 9:10; Isa 60:1; Hag 2:4; Ro 12:11; 1Co 7:29-35; Gal 6:9; Eph 5:15-16; 6:10-20; Php 1:27; Col 4:5; 2Th 3:13; Heb 12:1-2; 13:13-15; 1Pe 2:2; 2Pe 1:10-11; 3:14; Jude 3, 22-23; Rev 3:19).
Expected (Hab 2:2; Zec 14:20-21; 2Co 4:8-10, 13, 16-18; Gal 4:18; Php 2:15).
Rewards of (Da 12:3; Mt 25:21, 23; Lk 19:17-19; Jas 5:20).

Exemplified in:
Moses (Ex 2:12; 11:8; 32:19-20, 31-32; Nu 10:29; 11:29; Dt 9:18-19). Phinehas (Nu 25:7-13; Ps 106:30). Joshua (Nu 11:27-28; Jos 7:6; 24:14-16). Gideon (Jdg 6:11-32). Jephthah (Jdg 11:30-31, 34-39). Samuel (1Sa 12:23; 15:11, 35; 16:1).
David (1Sa 22:3; 2Sa 6; 7:2; 8:11-12; 24:24; 1Ch 29:17; Ps 40:8-10; 42:1-2; 51:13; 69:7-9; 71:17-18). Solomon (1Ki 8:31-53; 2Ch 6:22-42). Elijah (1Ki 19:10). Obadiah (1Ki 18:3-4). Micaiah (1Ki 22:14). Jehu (2Ki 9:10). Jehoiada (2Ki 11:4-17; 2Ch 23:1-17). Asa (1Ki 15:11-15; 2Ch 14:1-5, 15). Israelites (2Ch 15:15; Eze 9:4). Jehoshaphat (2Ch 17:3-10, 19).
Isaiah (Isa 6:8; 62:1). Hezekiah (Isa 37:1). Josiah (2Ki 22:11-13; 2Ch 34:3-7, 29-33). Priests (Eze 44:15). Ezra (Ezr 7:10; 9:10; Ne 8:1-6, 13, 18). Nehemiah (Ne 4; 5; 13:7-9, 15-28). Job (Job 16:19). Psalmist (Ps 119:53, 126, 136, 139, 158). Jeremiah (Jer 9:1-3; 13:17; 18:20; 20:9; 25:3-4; 26:12-15). Three Hebrews (Da 3:17-18). Habakkuk (Hab 1:2-4). Old Testament faithful (Heb 11).
Jesus (Mt 23:27; Lk 19:41; Jn 4:34-35; 9:4). Anna (Lk 2:38). Andrew and Philip (Jn 1:41-46). Apostles (Mk 16:20; Ac 4:31, 33; 5:21, 25, 29-32, 41-42; 8:4, 25, 30, 35, 40; 11:19-20, 24, 26). Two blind men proclaiming the miracle of healing, contrary to the injunction of Jesus (Mt 9:30-31). The restored leper (Mk 1:44-45). Man delivered of demons (Mk 5:19-20).
Peter (Mt 16:22; Mk 14:29-31; Lk 22:33; Ac 2:14-40; 3:12-26; 4:2, 8-12, 18-20; 5:29-32; 2Pe 1:12-15). Samaritan woman (Jn 4:28-30, 39).
Paul and Barnabas (Ac 14:14-15).
Timothy (Php 2:22). Phoebe (Ro 16:1-2). Epaphroditus (Php 2:26, 30). Corinthians (1Co 14:12; 2Co 7:11; 9:2). Thessalonians (1Th 1:2-8). Ephesians (Rev 2:2-3, 6). Christian Jews (Heb 10:34). John (Ac 4:8-13, 18-20; 3Jn 4; Rev 5:4).

Paul—
For the evangelization of the Jews (Ro 9:1-3; 10:1; 11:14).
In his ministry (Ac 9:21-29; 14:1-28; 15:25-26; 17:16-17, 22-31; 19:8-10; 20:18-24, 26-27, 31, 33-34; 21:13; 24:14-25; 26:1-18; Ac 26:19-29; 28:23, 30-31; Ro 1:1, 8-9, 14-32; 1Co 4:1-21; 9:12-27; 2Co 1:12, 17-19; 5:9, 11, 13-14, 20; 6:3-11; 11:16-33; 12:10-21; Gal 1:15-16; 2:2; 4:19; Eph 6:20; Php 1:18, 20, 24-25, 27; 2:16-17; 3:4-16; Col 1:28-29; 2:1, 5; 1Th 1:5-6; 2:2-11; 2Th 3:7-9; 2Ti 1:3, 7, 11-13).
In his piety (1Co 4:12; 10:33; 15:31; 2Co 4:8-18; 11:22-33; 12:10; Php 3:4-16; 4:11-12, 17; 2Ti 3:10-11).
In providing self-support (Ac 20:33-34; 1Co 4:12; 2Co 11:7-12; 2Th 3:7-9).
In suffering for Christ (Ac 21:13; 2Co 6:4-5, 8-10; 11:22-33; 12:10, 14-15, 21; 2Ti 2:9-10; 3:10-11).

In Punishing the Wicked:
Moses and Levites (Ex 32:20, 26-29). Phinehas (Nu 25:11-13; Ps 106:30-31). Israelites (Jos 22:11-20; Jdg 20). Samuel (1Sa 15:33). David (2Sa 1:14; 4:9-12). Elijah (1Ki 18:40). Jehu (2Ki 10:15-28). Jehoiada (2Ki 11:18). Josiah (2Ki 23:20).

In Reproving Iniquity: See Reproof, Faithfulness in.

ZEALOT Member of Jewish patriotic party started to resist Roman rule over Israel; violent; fanatical.

ZEALOT, SIMON THE An apostle (Mt 10:4; Mk 3:18; Lk 6:15; Ac 1:13), was known either for religious zeal or for membership in the party of the Zealots. See Simon, 2; Zealot.

ZEBADIAH (Yahweh bestows).
1. Benjamite (1Ch 8:15).
2. Another Benjamite (1Ch 8:17).
3. Ambidextrous Benjamite soldier of David (1Ch 12:1-2, 7).
4. Korahite gatekeeper (1Ch 26:2).
5. Son of Asahel (1Ch 27:7).
6. Levite sent by Jehoshaphat to teach law to residents of Judah (2Ch 17:8).
7. Son of Ishmael; head of Jehoshaphat's affairs (2Ch 19:11).
8. Son of Michael; returned with Ezra (Ezr 8:8).
9. Son of Immer; priest who divorced foreign wife (Ezr 10:20).

ZEBAH (sacrifice). King of Midian defeated and slain by Gideon (Jdg 8:10, 12, 18, 21; Ps 83:11).

ZEBAIM See Pokereth-Hazzebaim.

ZEBEDEE (Yahweh bestows). Father of James and John (Mt 4:21; 20:20; 27:56; Mk 1:20).

ZEBIDAH (given). Wife of Josiah, king of Judah (2Ki 23:36).

ZEBINA (one bought, purchased). Son of Nebo (Ezr 10:43).

ZEBOIIM, ZEBOIM (hyenas).
1. Called Zeboiim: One of the cities in the valley of Siddim (Ge 10:19; 14:2, 8; Dt 29:23; Hos 11:8).
2. Called Zeboim: A city and valley in Benjamin (1Sa 13:18; Ne 11:34).

ZEBUDAH See Zebidah.

ZEBUL (elevation, height, lofty [temple]). An officer of Abimelech (Jdg 9:28-41).

ZEBULONITES See Zebulun.

ZEBULUN, ZEBULUNITE (honor Ge. 30:20 ISBE).
1. Son of Jacob and Leah (Ge 30:20; 35:23; 46:14; 49:13; Ex 1:3; 1Ch 2:1). Descendants of (Ge 46:14; Nu 26:26-27).
2. Tribe of. Place of, in march and camp (Nu 2:3, 7; 10:14, 16). Territory awarded to (Ge 49:13; Jos 19:10-16; Mt 4:13). Aboriginal inhabitants of the territory of, not expelled (Jdg 1:30). Levitical cities of (Jos 21:34-35; 1Ch 6:77). Moses' benediction upon (Dt 33:18-19).
Loyalty of, in resisting the enemies of Israel: With Barak against Sisera (Jdg 4:6, 10; 5:14, 18), with Gideon against the Midianites (Jdg 6:35), with David when made king over Israel (1Ch 12:33, 38-40). Joins with Hezekiah in renewing the Passover (2Ch 30:11, 18). Conquest of, by Tiglath-Pileser; carried to Assyria into captivity (2Ki 15:29; Isa 9:1). Jesus lived in the land of (Mt 4:15). Twelve thousand sealed (Rev 7:8).
See Israel.

ZECHARIAH (Yahweh remembers).
1. Son of Jeroboam II, and last of the house of Jehu, whose reign lasted six months (2Ki 10:30; 14:29; 15:8-12).
2. Reubenite chief (1Ch 5:7).
3. Korahite, son of Meshelemiah (1Ch 9:21; 26:2, 14).
4. Benjamite (1Ch 9:37).
5. Levite; musician (1Ch 15:20; 16:5).
6. Priest; trumpeter (1Ch 15:24).
7. Levite (1Ch 24:25).
8. Merarite Levite (1Ch 26:11).
9. Manassite chief; father of Iddo (1Ch 27:21).
10. Prince who taught in cities of Judah (2Ch 17:7).
11. Father of prophet Jahaziel (2Ch 20:14).
12. Son of Jehoshaphat; killed by Jehoram (2Ch 21:2-4).
13. Son of Jehoiada, the high priest; stoned (2Ch 24:20-22).
14. Prophet in reign of Uzziah (2Ch 26:5).
15. Grandfather of Hezekiah and father of Abijah, wife of Ahaz (2Ki 18:2; 2Ch 29:1).
16. Levite; son of Asaph (2Ch 29:13).
17. Kohathite who assisted in repair of temple in days of Josiah (2Ch 34:12).
18. Temple ruler (2Ch 35:8).
19. Man who returned with Ezra (Ezr 8:3).
20. Another man who returned with Ezra (Ezr 8:11).
21. Adviser of Ezra (Ne 8:4; Ezr 8:15-16).
22. Man who divorced foreign wife (Ezr 10:26).
23. Judahite (Ne 11:4).
24. Another Judahite (Ne 11:5).
25. Son of Pashhur; aided rebuilding of walls (Ne 11:12).
26. Son of Iddo; priest (Ne 12:16).
27. Priest; son of Jonathan; trumpeter (Ne 12:35, 41).
28. Son of Jeberekiah (Isa 8:2).
29. Prophet; son of Berekiah and grandson of Iddo (Zec 1:1), returned with Zerubbabel; contemporary with Haggai.
30. Father of John the Baptist (Lk 1:5), righteous priest; angel announced to him he would have a son (Lk 1:5-80).
31. Son of Berekiah; slain between altar and temple (Mt 23:35; Lk 11:51).

ZECHARIAH, BOOK OF

Author: Zechariah son of Berekiah

Dates (correlated with Haggai and Ezra):
1. Haggai's first message (Hag 1:1-11; Ezr 5:1): Aug. 29, 520 B.C.
2. Resumption of the building of the temple (Hag 1:12-15; Ezr 5:2): Sept. 21, 520
3. Haggai's second message (Hag 2:1-9): Oct. 17, 520
4. Beginning of Zechariah's preaching (1:1-6): Oct./Nov., 520
5. Haggai's third message (Hag 2:10-19): Dec. 18, 520
6. Haggai's fourth message (Hag 2:20-23): Dec. 18, 520
7. Tattenai's letter to Darius concerning the rebuilding of the temple (Ezr 5:3-6:14).: 519-518
8. Zechariah's eight night visions (1:7-6:8): Feb 15, 519
9. Joshua crowned (6:9-15): Feb 16 (?), 519
10. Repentance urged, blessings promised (chs. 7-8): Dec. 7, 518
11. Dedication of the temple (Ezr 6:15-18): Mar. 12, 516
12. Zechariah's final prophecy (chs. 9-14): After 480 (?)

Outline:

Part I (chs. 1-8):
I. Introduction (1:1-6).
 A. The Date and the Author's Name (1:1).
 B. A Call to Repentance (1:2-6).
II. A Series of Eight Night Visions (1:7-6:8).
 A. The Horseman among the Myrtle Trees (1:7-17).
 B. The Four Horns and the Four Craftsmen (1:18-21).
 C. A Man with a Measuring Line (ch. 2).
 D. Clean Garments for the High Priest (ch. 3).
 E. The Gold Lampstand and the Two Olive Trees (ch. 4).
 F. The Flying Scroll (5:1-4).
 G. The Woman in a Basket (5:5-11).
 H. The Four Chariots (6:1-8).
III. The Symbolic Crowning of Joshua the High Priest (6:9-15).
IV. The Problem of Fasting and the Promise of the Future (chs. 7-8).
 A. The Question by the Delegation from Bethel (7:1-3).
 B. The Rebuke by the Lord (7:4-7).
 C. The Command to Repent (7:8-14).
 D. The Restoration of Israel to God's Favor (8:1-17).
 E. Kingdom Joy and Jewish Favor (8:18-23).

Part II (chs. 9-14):
V. Two Prophetic Oracles: The Great Messianic Future and the Full Realization of God's Kingdom (chs. 9-14).
 A. The First Oracle: The Advent and Rejection of the Messiah (chs. 9-11).
 1. The advent of the Messianic King (chs. 9-10).
 2. The rejection of the Messianic Shepherd-King (ch. 11).
 B. The Second Oracle: The Advent and Reception of the Messiah (chs. 12-14).
 1. The deliverance and conversion of Israel (chs. 12-13).
 2. The Messiah's coming and his kingdom (ch. 14).
See Prophets, The Minor.

Z

ZEDAD (*a siding*). A place near Hamath (Nu 34:8; Eze 47:15).

ZEDEKIAH (*Yahweh is [my] righteousness*).
1. Made king of Judah by Nebuchadnezzar (2Ki 24:17-18; 1Ch 3:15; 2Ch 36:10; Jer 37:1). Breaks his allegiance to Nebuchadnezzar (2Ki 24:20; 2Ch 36:13; Jer 52:3; Eze 17:12-21). Forms an alliance with the king of Egypt (Eze 17:11-18). The allegiance denounced by Jeremiah (2Ch 36:12; Jer 21; 24:8-10; 27:12-22; 32:3-5; 34; 37:7-10, 17; 38:14-28), by Ezekiel (Eze 12:10-16; 17:12-21). Imprisons Jeremiah on account of his denunciations (Jer 32:2-3; 37:15-21; 38:5-28). Seeks the intercession of Jeremiah with God in his behalf (Jer 21:1-3; 37:3; 28:14-27). Wicked reign of (2Ki 24:19-20; 2Ch 36:12-13; Jer 37:2; 38:5, 19, 24-26; 52:2). Nebuchadnezzar destroys the city and temple, makes him captive to Babylon, blinds his eyes, slays his sons (2Ki 25:1-10; 2Ch 36:17-20; Jer 1:3; 32:1-2; 39:1-10; 51:59; 52:4-30).
2. Grandson of Jehoiakim (1Ch 3:16).
3. A chief prince of the exiles who returned to Jerusalem (Ne 10:1).
4. A false prophet (Jer 29:21-23).
5. A prince of Judah (Jer 36:12).
6. A false prophet. Prophesies to Ahab victory over the Syrians, instead of defeat (1Ki 22:11; 2Ch 18:10). Smites Micaiah, the true prophet (1Ki 22:24; 2Ch 18:23).

ZEEB (*wolf*). A prince of Midian (Jdg 7:25; 8:3; Ps 83:11).

ZEKER (*memorial*). Son of Jeiel (1Ch 8:31), called Zechariah (1Ch 9:37). See Zechariah, 4.

ZELA (*side, slope*). Saul buried in (2Sa 21:14).

ZELAH (*side, slope*). A city in Benjamin (Jos 18:28).

ZELEK (*cry aloud* KB). An Ammonite (2Sa 23:37; 1Ch 11:39).

ZELOPHEHAD (*shadow of dread, terror* [i.e., *protection from dread and terror*]). Grandson of Gilead. His daughters petition for his inheritance (Nu 27:1-11; 36; Jos 17:3-6; 1Ch 7:15).

ZELOTES See Zealot.

ZELZAH A city of Benjamin (1Sa 10:2).

ZEMARAIM (possibly *double peak* KB).
1. Town c. four miles N of Jericho assigned to tribe of Benjamin (Jos 18:22).
2. Mountain in Ephraim upon which King Abijah rebuked King Jeroboam (2Ch 13:4).

ZEMARITES (*[snow, wool] white*; possibly *peak, height*). A tribe descended from Canaan (Ge 10:18; 1Ch 1:16).

ZEMIRAH (possibly *song [with instrumental accompaniment]* KB; possibly *Yahweh has helped* IDB). Grandson of Benjamin (1Ch 7:8).

ZENAN (*place of flocks*). A city of Judah (Jos 15:37).

ZENAS (*gift of Zeus*). A Christian believer and lawyer (Tit 3:13).

ZEPHANIAH (*Yahweh has hidden [to shelter]* or *Yahweh has hidden [as a treasure]*).
1. Ancestor of prophet Samuel (1Ch 6:36).
2. Author of book of Zephaniah (Zep 1:1), of royal descent; principal work done in Josiah's reign; contemporaries were Nahum and Habakkuk.
3. Priest, son of Maaseiah (2Ki 25:18-21; Jer 21:1).
4. Father of a Josiah to whom God sent the prophet Zechariah (Zec 6:10).

ZEPHANIAH, BOOK OF

Author: The prophet Zephaniah

Date: Probably between 640 and 627 B.C.

Outline:
I. Introduction (1:1-3).
 A. Title: The Prophet Identified (1:1).
 B. Prologue: Double Announcement of Total Judgment (1:2-3).
II. The Day of the Lord Coming on Judah and the Nations (1:4-18).
 A. Judgment on the Idolaters in Judah (1:4-9).
 B. Wailing throughout Jerusalem (1:10-13).
 C. The Inescapable Day of the Lord's Wrath (1:14-18).
III. God's Judgment on the Nations (2:1-3:8).
 A. Call to Repentance (2:1-3).
 B. Judgment on Philistia (2:4-7).
 C. Judgment on Moab and Ammon (2:8-11).
 D. Judgment on Cush (2:12).
 E. Judgment on Assyria (2:13-15).
 F. Judgment on Jerusalem (3:1-5).
 G. Jerusalem's Refusal to Repent (3:6-8).
IV. Redemption of the Remnant (3:9-20).
 A. The Nations Purified, the Remnant Restored, Jerusalem Purged (3:9-13).
 B. Rejoicing in the City (3:14-17).
 C. The Nation Restored (3:18-20).
See Prophets, The Minor.

ZEPHATH (*watchtower* IDB). A Canaanite city c. twenty-two miles SW of S end of Dead Sea; destroyed by tribes of Judah and Simeon and renamed "Hormah" (Jdg 1:17, ftn).

ZEPHATHAH (*watchtower* IDB). Valley near Mareshah in W part of Judah (2Ch 14:10).

ZEPHI See Zepho.

ZEPHO (possibly *gaze* BDB ISBE). The grandson of Esau (Ge 36:11, 15; 1Ch 1:36).

ZEPHON, ZEPHONITE (possibly *gaze* BDB; possibly *look out [tower], watch* KB). A son of Gad and his descendants (Ge 46:16; Nu 26:15).

ZER A city in Naphtali (Jos 19:35).

ZERAH (*dawning, shining,* or *flashing [red or scarlet] light* KB).
1. Son of Reuel (Ge 36:13, 17; 1Ch 1:37).
2. Father of Jobab (Ge 36:33; 1Ch 1:44).
3. Son of Judah and Tamar (Ge 38:30; 46:12; Nu 26:20; 1Ch 2:4, 6).
4. Son of Simeon (Nu 26:13; 1Ch 4:24).
5. A Gershonite (1Ch 6:21).
6. A Levite (1Ch 6:41).
7. King of Ethiopia, possibly Pharaoh Osorkon I (2Ch 14:9-15).

ZERAHIAH (*Yahweh shines brightly [red or scarlet]*; *Yahweh has risen [like the sun]* BDB).
1. Levite in ancestry of Ezra (1Ch 6:6, 51).
2. Leader of 200 who returned with Ezra (Ezr 8:4).

ZERAHITE(S) (*those who shine*).
1. Descendants of Zerah, son of Judah (Nu 26:20; Jos 7:17; 1Ch 27:11, 13).
2. Descendants of Zerah, son of Simeon (Nu 26:13).

ZERED, VALLEY OF, BROOK OF (*valley of [some kind of] plant*). Valley between Moab and Edom; encampment of Israel in wilderness wanderings (Nu 21:12; Dt 2:13-14).

ZEREDAH A city or district on the N of Mount Ephraim, but in Manasseh, and the birthplace of Jeroboam (1Ki 11:26).

ZEREDATHAH See Zarethan.

ZERERAH Part of Valley of Jezreel to which Midianites fled from Gideon (Jdg 7:22).

ZERESH (possibly *[pagan goddess] Kirisha* BDB IDB; *gold* ISBE; *mop-head* KB). Wife of Haman the Agagite (Est 5:10, 14; 6:13).

ZERETH (*splendor*). Son of Ashhur (1Ch 4:7).

ZERETH SHAHAR (*the glory of dawn*). A city in Reuben (Jos 13:19).

ZERI (*balsam* IDB). The son of Jeduthun (1Ch 25:3).

ZEROR (*money bag, pouch,* or possibly *pebbles* KB). Benjamite; great-grandfather of King Saul (1Sa 9:1).

ZERQA See Jabbok.

ZERUAH (*one with skin disease*). Mother of Jeroboam (1Ki 11:26).

ZERUBBABEL (*offspring [seed] of Babylon* BDB ISBE KB; *scion* i.e., *one grafted into the [plant] of Babylon* IDB). Directs the rebuilding of the altar and temple after his return from captivity in Babylon (Ezr 3:2-8; 4:2-3; 5:2; Hag 1:12-14). Leads the freed Jews back from Babylon (Ezr 2; Ne 12). Appoints the Levites to inaugurate the rebuilding of the temple (Ezr 3:2-8). Prophecies relating to (Hag 2:2; Zec 4:6-10). In the genealogy of Joseph (Mt 1:12; Lk 3:27).
 Possibly the same as Sheshbazzar (Ezr 1:8, 11; 5:14, 16). See Sheshbazzar.

ZERUIAH (*perfumed resin* IDB KB). Sister of David (1Ch 2:16). Mother of three of David's great soldiers (1Ch 2:16; 2Sa 2:18; 3:39; 16:9-11; 17:25).

ZETHAM (possibly *olive tree*). A son of Ladan (1Ch 23:8; 26:22).

ZETHAN (*olive tree* or *one who deals in olives*). Son of Bilhan (1Ch 7:10).

ZETHAR (possibly *conqueror* BDB; *slayer* KB). Chamberlain of Xerxes (Est 1:10).

ZEUS (*shine, bright*). Chief of Greek gods, corresponding to Roman Jupiter (Ac 14:12-13).

ZIA (possibly *trembler* IDB). A Gadite (1Ch 5:13).

ZIBA (*gazelle*). Member of Saul's household staff (2Sa 9:2), appointed by David to work for Mephibosheth; slandered Mephibosheth (2Sa 19:24-30).

ZIBEON (*hyena*).
1. A Hivite (Ge 36:2, 14).
2. Son of Seir (Ge 36:20, 24, 29; 1Ch 1:38, 40).

ZIBIA (*gazelle*). Early descendant of Benjamin (1Ch 8:9).

ZIBIAH (*gazelle*). Woman of Beersheba who married King Ahaziah; mother of King Joash (2Ki 12:1; 2Ch 24:1).

ZICRI (*Yahweh remembers* IDB).
1. A Levite; son of Izhar, cousin of Aaron and Moses (Ex 6:21).
2. Three Benjamites (1Ch 8:19, 23, 27).
3. A Levite; ancestor of Mattaniah who returned from captivity (1Ch 9:15), "Zabdi" (Ne 11:17).
4. Two chiefs in the days of David; a descendant of Eliezer (1Ch 26:25), father of Eliezer, a Reubenite (1Ch 27:16).
5. Father of Amasiah; a soldier (2Ch 17:16).
6. Father of Elishaphat (2Ch 23:1).
7. An Ephraimite; killed the son of Ahaz (2Ch 28:7).
8. Father of Joel, the overseer of the Benjamites (Ne 11:9).
9. A descendant of Abijah; a priest (Ne 12:17).

ZIDDIM (*place on the sides or flanks [of the hill]*). A city in Naphtali (Jos 19:35).

ZIDKIJAH See Zedekiah, 3.

ZIDON See Sidon.

ZIDONIANS See Sidon.

ZIF See Ziv.

ZIGGURAT (*pinnacle*). Temple tower of the Babylonians, consisting of a lofty structure in the form of a pyramid, built in successive stages, with staircases on the outside and a shrine at the top. The tower of Babel may have been a ziggurat (Ge 11:1-9). See Pyramids; Tower.

ZIHA
1. Head of family of temple servants that returned with Zerubbabel (Ezr 2:43; Ne 7:46).
2. Leader of the temple servants (Ne 11:21).

ZIKLAG A city within the territory allotted to the tribe of Judah (Jos 15:31). Reallotted to the tribe of Simeon (Jos 19:5). David lives at (1Sa 27:5-6; 2Sa 1:1; 1Ch 12:1). Amalekites destroy (1Sa 30). Inhabited by the returned exiles of Judah (Ne 11:28).

ZIKRI See Zicri.

ZILLAH (*[God is my] shadow* [i.e., *protection*]). Wife of Lamech (Ge 4:19, 22-23).

ZILLETHAI (*shadow of Yahweh*).
1. A Benjamite (1Ch 8:20).
2. A captain of Manasseh (1Ch 12:20).

ZILPAH (*short-nosed person* KB). Leah's handmaid (Ge 29:24). Mother of Gad and Asher by Jacob (Ge 30:9-13; 35:26; 37:2; 46:18).

ZIMMAH (*consider, plan* ISBE).
1. A son of Jahath (1Ch 6:20).
2. Two Gershonites (1Ch 6:42; 2Ch 29:12).

ZIMRAN (*wild goats, sheep* ISBE). Son of Abraham (Ge 25:2; 1Ch 1:32).

ZIMRI (*wild goats, sheep* ISBE; possibly *awe of Yahweh* IDB).
1. Prince of Simeon; slain by Phinehas, grandson of Aaron, for committing adultery with Midianite woman (Nu 25:14).
2. The fifth king of N kingdom; murdered King Elah; ruled seven days (c. 885 B.C.); overthrown by Omri (1Ki 16:8-20).
3. Son of Zerah; grandson of Judah (1Ch 2:6). See Zabdi, 1.
4. Benjamite; father of Moza (1Ch 8:36; 9:42).
5. Unknown tribe in East (Jer 25:25).

ZIN A desert S of Judah (Nu 13:21; 20:1; 27:14; 33:36; 34:3-4; Dt 32:51; Jos 15:1, 3).

ZINA (possibly *dry place*). See Ziza.

ZION (*citadel*). Taken from the Jebusites by David (2Sa 5:6-9; 1Ch 11:5-7). Called thereafter "the city of David" (2Sa 5:7, 9; 6:12, 16; 1Ki 11:5, 7; 15:1, 7; Isa 22:9). Ark of the covenant placed in (2Sa 6:12, 16; 1Ki 8:1; 1Ch 15:1, 29; 2Ch 5:2). Removed from to Solomon's temple on Mount Moriah (1Ki 8:1; 2Ch 5:2, w 2Ch 3:1).
 Collectively, the place, the forms, and the assemblies of Israelite worship (Ps 129:1, 31; Ps 9:11; 48:2, 11-12; 74:2; 132:13; 137:1; Isa 35:10; 40:9; 49:14; 51:16; 52:1-2, 7-8; 60:14; 62:1, 11; Jer 31:6; 50:5; La 1:4; Joel 2:1, 15; Mt 21:5; Jn 12:15; Ro 9:33; 11:26; 1Pe 2:6). Name of, applied to Jerusalem (Ps 87:2, 5; 149:2; SS 3:11; Isa 33:14, 20; Jer 9:19; 30:17; Zec 9:13). Called the city of God (Ps 87:2-3; Isa 60:14). Restoration of, promised (Isa 51:3, 11, 16; 52:1-2, 7-8; 59:20; 60:14; Ob 17, 21; Zep 3:14, 16; Zec 1:14, 17; 2:7, 10; 8:2-3; 9:9, 13). Name of, applied to the city of the redeemed (Heb 12:22; Rev 14:1).
 See Church, Place of Worship; Jerusalem.

ZIOR (*small, insignificant*). Town in S Judah probably near Hebron (Jos 15:54).

ZIPH
1. City in Negev, probably c. four miles S by E from Hebron (Jos 15:55).
2. Wilderness named from above city where David hid (1Sa 23:14-24; 26:1-2).
3. City in W Judah (2Ch 11:8).
4. Calebite family name (1Ch 2:42).
5. Judahite (1Ch 4:16).

ZIPHAH A son of Jehallelel (1Ch 4:16).

ZIPHIMS See Ziphites.

ZIPHION (possibly *gaze* BDB ISBE; possibly *place of the lookout, tower* KB). See Zephon.

ZIPHITES Inhabitants of Ziph (1Sa 23:19; 26:1-5; Ps 54:T).

ZIPHRON A place in the N of Israel (Nu 34:9).

ZIPPOR (*bird, swallow*). Father of Balak (Nu 22:2, 4, 10, 16; 23:18; Jos 24:9).

ZIPPORAH (*bird, swallow*). Wife of Moses (Ex 2:16-22). Reproaches Moses (Ex 4:25-26). Separates from Moses, is brought again to him by her father (Ex 18:2-6). May have been a Cushite (Nu 12:1).

ZITHER A stringed instrument (Da 3:5, 7, 10, 15). See Music, Instruments of.

ZITHRI See Sithri.

Z

ZIV (*bright [as in colorful flowers]*). Month two in sacred sequence, month eight in civil sequence. Also called Iyyar (not in the Bible). Time of the barley harvest (April-May); the dry season begins. Solomon begins building the temple (1Ki 6:1, 37). The later Passover is celebrated (Nu 9:10-11). *See Month, 2.*

ZIZ (possibly *ascent where the flowers grow*). Cliff near W side of Red Sea on way from En Gedi to Tekoa (2Ch 20:16).

ZIZA (a childish duplicated abbreviation, like "mama, " as a name of endearment, IDB ISBE).
1. Simeonite; son of Shiphi (1Ch 4:37-41).
2. Son of Rehoboam and brother of Abijah, kings of Judah (2Ch 11:20).
3. A son of Shimei (1Ch 23:10-11, ftn).

ZIZAH *See Ziza, 3.*

ZOAN A city in Egypt. Built seven years after Hebron in the land of Canaan (Nu 13:22). Prophecies concerning (Eze 30:14). Wise men from, were counselors of Pharaoh (Isa 19:11, 13). Princes of (Isa 30:4).

ZOAR (*small, insignificant*). A city of the Moabites near the Jordan (Ge 13:10). Territory of (Dt 34:3; Isa 15:5; Jer 48:34). King of, fought against Kedorlaomer (Ge 14:2, 8). Not destroyed with Sodom and Gomorrah (Ge 19:20-23, 30).

ZOBAH Also called Aram Zobah; Hamath Zobah. A kingdom in the N of Israel (1Sa 14:47). Conquest of, by David (2Sa 8:3-8, 12; 1Ki 11:23-24; 1Ch 18:2-9). Its inhabitants mercenaries of the Ammonites against David (2Sa 10:6-19; 1Ch 19:6-19). David

writes a psalm after the conquest of (Ps 60, title). Invaded by Solomon (2Ch 8:3).
 See Aram Maacah; Aram Naharaim.

ZOBEBAH (*one who slithers [like a lizard]* or *one born in a covered wagon*). *See Hazzobebah.*

ZODIAC *See Constellations; Mazzaroth.*

ZOHAR (*one yellowish red, tawny*).
1. Hittite; father of Ephron from whom Abraham purchased field of Machpelah (Ge 23:8; 25:9).
2. Son of Simeon, second son of Jacob (Ge 46:10; Ex 6:15); "Zerah" (Nu 26:13; 1Ch 4:24).
3. A son of Helah, wife of Ashhur (1Ch 4:7).

ZOHELETH (*serpent*). Stone or ledge by En Rogel (1Ki 1:9).

ZOHETH (*proud*). Son of Ishi (1Ch 4:20).

ZOPHAH (*bellied jug*). Son of Helem (1Ch 7:35-36).

ZOPHAI (*[dripping, full] honeycomb*). Ancestor of Samuel the prophet (1Ch 6:26), also called Zuph (1Ch 6:35).

ZOPHAR (possibly *peep, twitter [as a bird]* KB). One of Job's three friends (Job 2:11; 11; 20; 42:7-9).

ZOPHIM (*watchers, lookouts*).
1. A place on the top of Pisgah (Nu 23:14).
2. A city on Mount Ephraim (1Sa 1:1).

ZORAH A city of Dan or Judah (Jos 15:33; 19:41). The city of Samson (Jdg 13:2, 24-25; 16:31). Representatives of the tribe of

Dan sent from, to spy out the land with a view to its conquest (Jdg 18). Fortified by Rehoboam (2Ch 11:10). Repopulated after the Captivity (Ne 11:29).

ZORATHITES Inhabitants of Zorah (1Ch 2:53).

ZOREAH *See Zorah.*

ZORITES Judahite family, descendants of Salma (1Ch 2:54).

ZOROBABEL *See Zerubbabel.*

ZUAR (*little one*). Father of Nethanel (Nu 1:8; 2:5; 7:18, 23; 10:15).

ZUPH, ZUPHITE (*honeycomb*).
1. Ancestor of the prophet Samuel (1Sa 1:1; 1Ch 6:35), also called Zophai (1Ch 6:26).
2. District in Benjamin, near N border (1Sa 9:5), Location unknown.

ZUR (*rock*).
1. King of Midian slain by Israel (Nu 25:15; 31:8).
2. Son of Jeiel (1Ch 8:29, ftn; 8:30).

ZURIEL (*God [El] is [my] rock*). Son of Abihail, prince of Merarite Levites in wilderness (Nu 3:35).

ZURISHADDAI (*Shaddai is [my] rock*). Father of Shelumiel (Nu 1:6; 2:12; 7:36, 41; 10:19).

ZUZITES (*strong nations* ISBE; *babblers* KB). A people defeated by Kedorlaomer and his allies (Ge 14:5). May be the same as Zamzummites. *See Rephaites; Zamzummites.*

Z

ADDITIONAL FEATURES

ADDITIONAL FEATURES

MAJOR SOCIAL CONCERNS IN THE MOSAIC COVENANT

1. Personhood
Everyone's person is to be secure (Ex 20:13; Dt 5:17; Ex 21:16-21,26-31; Lev 19:14; Deut 24:7; 27:18).

2. False Accusation
Everyone is to be secure against slander and false accusation (Ex 20:16; Deut 5:20; Ex 23:1-3; Lev 19:16; Deut 19:15-21).

3. Woman
No woman is to be taken advantage of within her subordinate status in society (Ex 21:7-11,20,26-32; 22:16-17; Deut 21:10-14; 22:13-30; 24:1-5).

4. Punishment
Punishment for wrongdoing shall not be excessive so that the culprit is dehumanized (Deut 25:1-5).

5. Dignity
Every Israelite's dignity and right to be God's freedman and servant are to be honored and safeguarded (Ex 21:2,5-6; Lev 25; Deut 15:12-18).

6. Inheritance
Every Israelite's inheritance in the promised land is to be secure (Lev 25; Num 27:5-7; 36:1-9; Deut 25:5-10).

7. Property
Everyone's property is to be secure (Ex 20:15; Deut 5:19; Ex 21:33-36; 22:1-15; 23:4-5; Lev 19:35-36; Deut 22:1-4; 25:13-15).

8. Fruit of Labor
Everyone is to receive the fruit of his labors (Lev 19:13; Deut 24:14; 25:4).

9. Fruit of the Ground
Everyone is to share the fruit of the ground (Ex 23:10-11; Lev 19:9-10; 23:22; 25:3-55; Deut 14:28-29; 24:19-21).

10. Rest on Sabbath
Everyone, down to the humblest servant and the resident alien, is to share in the weekly rest of God's sabbath (Ex 20:8-11; Deut 5:12-15; Ex 23:12).

11. Marriage
The marriage relationship is to be kept inviolate (Ex 20:14; Deut 5:18; see also Lev 18:6-23; 20:10-21; Deut 22:13-30).

12. Exploitation
No one, however disabled, impoverished or powerless, is to be oppressed or exploited (Ex 22:21-27; Lev 19:14,33-34; 25:35-36; Deut 23:19; 24:6,12-15,17; 27:18).

13. Fair Trial
Everyone is to have free access to the courts and is to be afforded a fair trial (Ex 23:6,8; Lev 19:15; Deut 1:17; 10:17-18; 16:18-20; 17:8-13; 19:15-21).

14. Social Order
Every person's God-given place in the social order is to be honored (Ex 20:12; Deut 5:16; Ex 21:15,17; 22:28; Lev 19:3,32; 20:9; Deut 17:8-13; 21:15-21; 27:16).

15. Law
No one shall be above the law, not even the king (Deut 17:18-20).

16. Animals
Concern for the welfare of other creatures is to be extended to the animal world (Ex 23:5,11; Lev 25:7; Deut 22:4,6-7; 25:4).

OLD TESTAMENT SACRIFICES

Sacrifice	OT References	Elements	Purpose
Burnt Offering	Lev 1; 6:8–13; 8:18–21; 16:24	Bull, ram or male bird (dove or young pigeon for the poor); wholly consumed; no defect	Voluntary act of worship; atonement for unintentional sin in general; expression of devotion, commitment and complete surrender to God
Grain Offering	Lev 2; 6:14–23	Grain, fine flour, olive oil, incense, baked bread (cakes or wafers), salt; no yeast or honey; accompanied burnt offering and peace offering (along with drink offering)	Voluntary act of worship; recognition of God's goodness and provisions; devotion to God
Peace Offering	Lev 3; 7:11–34	Any animal without defect from herd or flock; variety of breads	Voluntary act of worship; thanksgiving and fellowship (it included a communal meal)
Sin Offering	Lev 4:1—5:13; 6:24–30; 8:14–17; 16:3–22	1. Young bull: for high priest and congregation 2. Male goat: for leader 3. Female goat or lamb: for common person 4. Turtledove or pigeon: for the poor 5. Tenth of an ephah of fine flour: for the very poor	Mandatory atonement for specific unintentional sin; confession of sin; forgiveness of sin; cleansing from defilement
Guilt Offering	Lev 5:14—6:7; 7:1–6	Ram or lamb	Mandatory atonement for unintentional sin requiring restitution; cleansing from defilement; make restitution; pay 20% fine

When more than one kind of offering was presented (as in Num 7:16,17), the procedure was usually as follows: (1) sin offering or guilt offering, (2) burnt offering, (3) peace offering and grain offering (along with a drink offering). This sequence furnishes part of the spiritual significance of the sacrificial system. First, sin had to be dealt with (sin offering or guilt offering). Second, the worshiper committed himself completely to God (burnt offering and grain offering). Third, fellowship or communion between the Lord, the priest and the worshiper (peace offering) was established. To state it another way, there were sacrifices of expiation (sin offerings and guilt offerings), consecration (burnt offerings and grain offerings) and communion (peace offerings—these included vow offerings, thank offerings and freewill offerings).

HEBREW CALENDAR AND SELECTED EVENTS

NUMBER OF MONTH		HEBREW NAME	MODERN EQUIVALENT	BIBLICAL REFERENCES	AGRICULTURE	FEASTS
1 Sacred sequence begins	7	Abib; Nisan	March–April	Ex 12:2; 13:4; 23:15; 34:18; Dt 16:1; Ne 2:1; Est 3:7	Spring (later) rains; barley and flax harvest begins	Passover; Unleavened Bread; Firstfruits
2	8	Ziv (Iyyar)*	April–May	1Ki 6:1, 37	Barley harvest, dry season	
3	9	Sivan	May–June	Est 8:9	Wheat harvest	Pentecost (Weeks)
4	10	(Tammuz)*	June–July		Tending vines	
5	11	(Ab)*	July–August		Ripening of grapes, figs and olives	
6	12	Elul	August–September	Ne 6:15	Processing grapes, figs and olives	
7 Civil sequence	1	Ethanim (Tishri)*	September–October	1Ki 8:2	Autumn (early) rains begin; plowing	Trumpets; Atonement Tabernacles (Booths)
8	2	Bul (Marcheshvan)*	October–November	1Ki 6:38	Sowing of wheat and barley	
9	3	Kislev	November–December	Ne 1:1; Zec 7:1	Winter rains begin (snow in some areas)	Hanukkah ("Dedication")
10	4	Tebeth	December–January	Est 2:16		
11	5	Shebat	January–February	Zec 1:7		
12	6	Adar	February–March	Ezr 6:15; Est 3:7, 13; 8:12; 9:1, 15, 17, 19, 21	Almond trees bloom; citrus fruit harvest	Purim
		(Adar Sheni)* Second Adar	This intercalary month was added about every three years so the lunar calendar would correspond to the solar year.			

Names in parentheses are not in the Bible.

OLD TESTAMENT FEASTS AND OTHER SACRED DAYS

Name	Old Testament References	OT Time	Modern Time
Sabbath	Ex 20:8–11; 31:12–17; Lev 23:3; Dt 5:12–15	7th day	Same
Sabbath Year	Ex 23:10–11; Lev 25:1–7	7th year	Same
Year of Jubilee	Lev 25:8–55; 27:17–24; Nu 36:4	50th year	Same
Passover	Ex 12:1–14; Lev 23:5; Nu 9:1–14; 28:16; Dt 16:1–3a, 4b–7	1st month (Abib) 14	Mar.–Apr.
Unleavened Bread	Ex 12:15–20; 13:3–10; 23:15; 34:18; Lev 23:6–8; Nu 28:17–25; Dt 16:3b, 4a, 8	1st month (Abib) 15–21	Mar.–Apr.
First fruits	Lev 23:9–14	1st month (Abib) 16	Mar.–Apr.
Weeks (Pentecost) (Harvest)	Ex 23:16a; 34:22a; Lev 23:15–21; Nu 28:26–31; Dt 16:9–12	3rd month (Sivan) 6	May–June
Trumpets (Later: Rosh Hashanah)	Lev 23:23–25; Nu 29:1–6	7th month (Tishri) 1	Sept.–Oct.
Day of Atonement (Yom Kippur)	Lev 16; 23:26–32; Nu 29:7–11	7th month (Tishri) 10	Sept.–Oct.
Booths (Tabernacles) (Ingathering)	Ex 23:16b; 34:22b; Lev 23:33–36a, 39–43; Nu 29:12–34; Dt 16:13–15; Zec 14:16–19	7th month (Tishri) 15–21	Sept.–Oct.
Holy Convocation	Lev 23:36b; Nu 29:35–38	7th month (Tishri) 22	Sept.–Oct.
Purim	Est 9:18–32	12th month (Adar) 14, 15	Feb.–Mar.

On Kislev 25 (mid-December) Hanukkah, the feast of dedication or festival of lights, commemorated the purification of the temple and altar in the Maccabean period (165/4 B.C.). This feast is mentioned in John 10:22.

Description	Purpose	New Testament References
Day of rest; no work	Rest for people and animals	Mt 12:1–14; 28:1; Lk 4:16; Jn 5:9; Ac 13:42; Col 2:16; Heb 4:1–11
Year of rest; fallow fields	Rest for land	
Canceled debts; liberation of slaves and indentured servants; land returned to original family owners	Help for poor; stabilize society	
Slaying and eating a lamb, together with bitter herbs and bread made without yeast, in every household	Remember Israel's deliverance from Egypt	Mt 26:17; Mk 14:12–26; Jn 2:13; 11:55; 1Co 5:7; Heb 11:28
Eating bread made without yeast; holding several assemblies; making designated offerings	Remember how the Lord brought the Israelites out of Egypt in haste	Mk 14:1; Ac 12:3; 1Co 5:6–8
Presenting a sheaf of the first of the barley harvest as a wave offering; making a burnt offering and a grain offering	Recognize the Lord's bounty in the land	Ro 8:23; 1Co 15:20–23
A festival of joy; mandatory and voluntary offerings, including the first fruits of the wheat harvest	Show joy and thankfulness for the Lord's blessing of harvest	Ac 2:1–4; 20:16; 1Co 16:8
An assembly on a day of rest commemorated with trumpet blasts and sacrifices	Present Israel before the Lord for his favor	
A day of rest, fasting and sacrifices of atonement for priests and people and atonement for the tabernacle and altar	Cleanse priests and people from their sins and purify the holy place	Ro 3:24–26; Heb 9:7; 10:3, 19–22
A week of celebration for the harvest; living in booths and offering sacrifices	Memorialize the journey from Egypt to Canaan; give thanks for the productivity of Canaan	Jn 7:2, 37
A day of convocation, rest and offering sacrifices	Commemorate the closing of the cycle of feasts	
A day of joy and feasting and giving presents	Remind the Israelites of their national deliverance in the time of Esther	

In addition, new moons were often special feast days (Nu 10:10; 1Ch 23:31; Ezr 3:5; Ne 10:33; Ps 81:3; Isa 1:13-14; 66:23; Hos 5:7; Am 8:5; Col 2:16).

WEIGHTS, LENGTHS AND MEASURES OF THE BIBLE

	Biblical Unit	Approximate American Equivalent	Approximate Metric Equivalent
Weights	talent (60 minas)	75 pounds	34 kilograms
	mina (50 shekels)	1 1/4 pounds	0.6 kilogram
	shekel (2 bekas)	2/5 ounce	11.5 grams
	pim (2/3 shekel)	1/3 ounce	1/3 ounce
	beka (10 gerahs)	1/5 ounce	5.5 grams
	gerah	1/50 ounce	0.6 gram
Length	cubit	18 inches	0.5 meter
	span	9 inches	23 centimeters
	handbreadth	3 inches	8 centimeters
Capacity			
Dry Measure	cor [homer] (10 ephahs)	6 bushels	220 liters
	lethek (5 ephahs)	3 bushels	110 liters
	ephah (10 omers)	3/5 bushel	22 liters
	seah (1/3 ephah)	7 quarts	7.3 liters
	omer (1/10 ephah)	2 quarts	2 liters
	cab (1/18 ephah)	1 quart	1 liter
Liquid Measure	bath (1 ephah)	6 gallons	22 liters
	hin (1/6 bath)	4 quarts	4 liters
	log (1/72 bath)	1/3 quart	0.3 liter

The figures of the table are calculated on the basis of a shekel equaling 11.5 grams, a cubit equaling 18 inches and an ephah equaling 22 liters. The quart referred to is either a dry quart (slightly larger than a liter) or a liquid quart (slightly smaller than a liter), whichever is applicable. The ton referred to in the footnotes is the American ton of 2,000 pounds.

This table is based upon the best available information, but it is not intended to be mathematically precise; it merely gives approximate amounts and distances. Weights and measures differed somewhat at various times and places in the ancient world. There is uncertainty particularly about the ephah and the bath; further discoveries may shed more light on these units of capacity.

THE KINGS OF THE UNITED KINGDOM

	Name	Ruled	Dates B.C.	Biblical References
1.	Saul	40 years	1050–1010	1Sa 11:15,31; 1Ch 10
2.	David	40 years	1010–970	2Sa 2:4; 1Ki 2:11; 1Ch 11–29
3.	Solomon	40 years	970–930	1Ki 1:39; 11:43; 2Ch 1–9

THE KINGS (AND QUEEN) OF JUDAH

	Name	Ruled	Dates B.C.	Biblical References
1.	Rehoboam	17 years	930–913	1Ki 12:1–24; 14:21–31; 2Ch 10:1–17; 12
2.	Abijah	3 years	913–910	1Ki 15:1–8; 2Ch 13
3.	Asa	41 years	910–869	1Ki 15:9–24; 2Ch 14; 16:14
4.	Jehoshaphat	25 years	872–848	1Ki 22:41–50; 2Ch 17; 21:1
5.	Jehoram	8 years	848–841	2Ki 8:16–24; 21
6.	Ahaziah	1 year	841	2Ki 8:25–29; 9:16–29; 2Ch 22:1–9
7.	Queen Athaliah	6 years	841–835	2Ki 11:1–3; 2Ch 22:10–12
8.	Joash	40 years	835–796	2Ki 11:4; 12; 2Ch 23–24
9.	Amaziah	29 years	796–767	2Ki 14:1–20; 2Ch 25
10.	Uzziah / Azariah	52 years	792–740	2Ki 14:21–22; 15:1–7; 2Ch 26
11.	Jotham	16 years	750–735	2Ki 15:32–38; 2Ch 27
12.	Ahaz	16 years	732–715	2Ki 16; 2Ch 28
13.	Hezekiah	29 years	715–686	2Ki 18–20; 2Ch 29–32
14.	Manasseh	55 years	697–642	2Ki 21:1–18; 2Ch 33:1–20
15.	Amon	2 years	642–640	2Ki 21:19–26; 2Ch 33:21–25
16.	Josiah	31 years	640–609	2Ki 22; 23:1–30; 2Ch 34–35
17.	Jehoahaz	3 months	609	2Ki 23:31–33; 2Ch 36:1–4
18.	Jehoiakim	11 years	609–598	2Ki 23:34–37; 24:1–6; 2Ch 36:5–8
19.	Jehoiachin	3 months	598–597	2Ki 24:8–16; 2Ch 36:9–10
20.	Zedekiah / Mattaniah	11 years	597–586	2Ki 24:17–20; 25:1–7; 2Ch 36:11–21

THE KINGS OF ISRAEL

1.	Jeroboam I	22 years	930–909	1Ki 12:20,25; 14:20
2.	Nadab	2 years	909–908	1Ki 15:25–27,31
3.	Baasha	24 years	908–886	1Ki 15:28–34; 16:1–7
4.	Elah	2 years	886–885	1Ki 16:8–14
5.	Zimri	7 days	885	1Ki 16:11–12,15–20
6.	Omri	12 years	885–874	1Ki 16:23–28
7.	Ahab	22 years	874–853	1Ki 16:29–22:40
8.	Ahaziah	2 years	853–852	1Ki 22:51–53; 2Ki 1
9.	Joram	12 years	852–841	2Ki 3–9:26
10.	Jehu	28 years	841–814	2Ki 9:3–10; 36
11.	Jehoahaz	17 years	814–798	2Ki 13:1–9
12.	Jehoash	16 years	798–782	2Ki 13:10–25; 14:8–16
13.	Jeroboam II	41 years	793–753	2Ki 14:23–29
14.	Zechariah	6 months	753	2Ki 15:8–12
15.	Shallum	1 month	752	2Ki 15:13–15
16.	Menahem	10 years	752–742	2Ki 15:16–22
17.	Pekahiah	2 years	742–740	2Ki 15:23–26
18.	Pekah	20 years	752–732	2Ki 15:27–31; 16:5
19.	Hoshea	9 years	732–722	2Ki 17:1–6

Note: Some kings, such as Jehoash and Jeroboam II, had overlapping reigns.

A HARMONY OF THE GOSPELS

	MATTHEW	MARK	LUKE	JOHN
A Preview of Who Jesus Is				
Luke's purpose in writing a gospel			1:1–4	
John's prologue: Jesus Christ, the preexistent Word incarnate				1:1–18
Jesus' legal lineage through Joseph and natural lineage through Mary	1:1–17		3:23b–38	
The Early Years of John the Baptist				
John's birth foretold to Zacharias			1:5–25	
Jesus' birth foretold to Mary			1:26–38	
Mary's visit to Elizabeth and Elizabeth's song			1:39–45	
Mary's song of joy			1:46–56	
John's birth			1:57–66	
Zacharias's prophetic song			1:67–79	
John's growth and early life			1:80	
The Early Years of Jesus Christ				
Circumstances of Jesus' birth explained to Joseph	1:18–25			
Birth of Jesus			2:1–7	
Praise of the angels and witness of the shepherds			2:8–20	
Circumcision of Jesus			2:21	
Jesus presented in the temple with the homage of Simeon and Anna			2:22–38	
Visit of the magi	2:1–12			
Escape into Egypt and murder of boys in Bethlehem	2:13–18			
Return to Nazareth	2:19–23			
Growth and early life of Jesus			2:40	
Jesus' first Passover in Jerusalem			2:41–50	
Jesus' growth to adulthood			2:51–52	
The Public Ministry of John the Baptist				
His ministry launched			3:1–2	
His person, proclamation, and baptism	3:1–6	1:2–6	3:3–6	
His messages to the Pharisees, Sadducees, crowds, tax collectors, and soldiers	3:7–10		3:7–14	
His description of Christ	3:11–12	1:7–8	3:15–18	
The End of John's Ministry and the Beginning of Christ's Public Ministry				
Jesus' baptism by John	3:13–17	1:9–11	3:21–23a	
Jesus' temptation in the wilderness	4:1–11	1:12–13	4:1–13	
John's testimony about himself to the priests and Levites				1:19–28
John's testimony to Jesus as the Son of God				1:29–34
Jesus' first followers				1:35–51
Jesus' first miracle: water becomes wine				2:1–11
Jesus' first stay in Capernaum with His relatives and early disciples				2:12
First cleansing of the temple at the Passover				2:13–22
Early response to Jesus' miracles				2:23–25
Nicodemus's interview with Jesus				3:1–21
John superseded by Jesus				3:22–36
Jesus' departure from Judea	4:12	1:14a	3:19–20; 4:14a	4:1–4
Discussion with a Samaritan woman				4:5–26
Challenge of a spiritual harvest				4:27–38
Evangelization of Sychar				4:39–42
Arrival in Galilee				4:43–45

	MATTHEW	MARK	LUKE	JOHN
The Ministry of Christ in Galilee				
Opposition at Home and a New Headquarters				
Nature of the Galilean ministry	4:17	1:14b-15	4:14b-15	
Child at Capernaum healed by Jesus while at Cana				4:46–54
Ministry and rejection at Nazareth			4:16–31a	
Move to Capernaum	4:13–16			
Disciples Called and Ministry Throughout Galilee				
Call of the four	4:18–22	1:16–20	5:1–11	
Teaching in the synagogue of Capernaum authenticated by healing a demoniac		1:21–28	4:31b-37	
Peter's mother-in-law and others healed	8:14–17	1:29–34	4:38–41	
Tour of Galilee with Simon and others	4:23–25	1:35–39	4:42–44	
Cleansing of a man with leprosy, followed by much publicity	8:2–4	1:40–45	5:12–16	
Forgiving and healing of a paralytic	9:1–8	2:1–12	5:17–26	
Call of Matthew	9:9	2:13–14	5:27–28	
Banquet at Matthew's house	9:10–13	2:15–17	5:29–32	
Jesus defends His disciples for feasting instead of fasting with three parables	9:14–17	2:18–22	5:33–39	
Sabbath Controversies and Withdrawals				
Jesus heals an invalid on the Sabbath				5:1–9
Effort to kill Jesus for breaking the Sabbath and saying He was equal with God				5:10–18
Discourse demonstrating the Son's equality with the Father				5:19–47
Controversy over disciples' picking grain on the Sabbath	12:1–8	2:23–28	6:1–5	
Healing of a man's withered hand on the Sabbath	12:9–14	3:1–6	6:6–11	
Withdrawal to the Sea of Galilee with large crowds from many places	12:15–21	3:7–12		
Appointment of the twelve and Sermon on the Mount				
Twelve apostles chosen		3:13–19	6:12–16	
Setting of the Sermon	5:1–2		6:17–19	
Blessings of those who inherit the kingdom and woes to those who do not	5:3–12		6:20–26	
Responsibility while awaiting the kingdom	5:13–16			
Law, righteousness, and the kingdom	5:17–20			
Six contrasts in interpreting the law	5:21–48		6:27–30, 32–36	
Three hypocritical "acts of righteousness" to be avoided	6:1–18			
Three prohibitions against avarice, harsh judgment, and unwise exposure of sacred things	6:19–7:6		6:37–42	
Application and conclusion	7:7–27		6:31, 43–49	
Reaction of the crowds	7:28–8:1			
Growing Fame and Emphasis on Repentance				
A centurion's faith and the healing of his servant	8:5–13		7:1–10	
A widow's son raised at Nain			7:11–17	
John the Baptist's relationship to the kingdom	11:2–19		7:18–35	
Woes upon Chorazin and Bethsaida for failure to repent	11:20–30			
Christ's feet anointed by a sinful but contrite woman			7:36–50	
First Public Rejection by Jewish Leaders				
A tour with the twelve and other followers			8:1–3	
Blasphemous accusation by the scribes and Pharisees	12:22–37	3:20–30		
Request for a sign refused	12:38–45			
Announcement of new spiritual kinship	12:46–50	3:31–35	8:19–21	
Secrets About the Kingdom Given in Parables				
To the Crowds by the Sea				
The setting of the parables	13:1–3a	4:1–2	8:4	
The parable of the soils	13:3b-23	4:3–25	8:5–18	
The parable of the seed's spontaneous growth		4:26–29		
The parable of the tares	13:24–30			

	MATTHEW	MARK	LUKE	JOHN
The parable of the mustard tree	13:31–32	4:30–32		
The parable of the leavened loaf	13:33–35	4:33–34		
To the Disciples in the House				
The parable of the tares explained	13:36–43			
The parable of the hidden treasure	13:44			
The parable of the valuable pearl	13:45–46			
The parable of the dragnet	13:47–50			
The parable of the head of a household	13:51–53			
Continuing Opposition				
Crossing the lake and calming the storm	8:18, 23–27	4:35–41	8:22–25	
Healing the Gerasene demoniacs and resultant opposition	8:28–34	5:1–20	8:26–39	
Return to Galilee, healing of a woman who touched Jesus' garment, and raising of Jairus's daughter	9:18–26	5:21–43	8:40–56	
Three miracles of healing and another blasphemous accusation	9:27–34			
Final visit to unbelieving Nazareth	13:54–58	6:1–6a		
Final Galilean Campaign				
Shortage of workers	9:35–38	6:6b		
Commissioning of the twelve	10:1–42	6:7–11	9:1–5	
Workers sent out	11:1	6:12–13	9:6	
Antipas's mistaken identification of Jesus	14:1–2	6:14–16	9:7–9	
Earlier imprisonment and beheading of John the Baptist	14:3–12	6:17–29		

The Ministry of Christ Around Galilee

Lesson on the Bread of Life
	MATTHEW	MARK	LUKE	JOHN
Return of the workers		6:30	9:10a	
Withdrawal from Galilee	14:13–14	6:31–34	9:10b-11	6:1–3
Feeding the five thousand	14:15–21	6:35–44	9:12–17	6:4–13
A premature attempt to make Jesus king blocked	14:22–23	6:45–46		6:14–15
Walking on the water during a storm on the lake	14:24–33	6:47–52		6:16–21
Healings at Gennesaret	14:34–36	6:53–56		
Discourse on the true bread of life				6:22–59
Defection among the disciples				6:60–71

Lesson on the Leaven of the Pharisees, Sadducees, and Herodians
	MATTHEW	MARK	LUKE	JOHN
Conflict over the tradition of ceremonial uncleanness	15:1–3a, 7–9b, 3b–6, 10–20	7:1–23		7:1
Ministry to a believing Greek woman in Tyre and Sidon	15:21–28	7:24–30		
Healings in Decapolis	15:29–31	7:31–37		
Feeding the four thousand in Decapolis	15:32–38	8:1–9a		
Return to Galilee and encounter with the Pharisees and Sadducees	15:39–16:4	8:9b-12		
Warning about the error of the Pharisees, Sadducees, and Herodians	16:5–12	8:13–21		
Healing a blind man at Bethsaida		8:22–26		

Lesson of Messiahship Learned and Confirmed
	MATTHEW	MARK	LUKE	JOHN
Peter's identification of Jesus as the Christ and first prophecy of the church	16:13–20	8:27–30	9:18–21	
First direct prediction of the rejection, crucifixion, and resurrection	16:21–26	8:31–37	9:22–25	
Coming of the Son of Man and judgment	16:27–28	8:38–9:1	9:26–27	
Transfiguration of Jesus	17:1–8	9:2–8	9:28–36a	
Discussion of resurrection, Elijah, and John the Baptist	17:9–13	9:9–13	9:36b	

Lessons on Responsibility to Others
	MATTHEW	MARK	LUKE	JOHN
Healing of demoniac boy and unbelief rebuked	17:14–20	9:14–29	9:37–43a	
Second prediction of Jesus' death and resurrection	17:22–23	9:30–32	9:43b-45	
Payment of temple tax	17:24–27			
Rivalry over greatness in the kingdom	18:1–5	9:33–37	9:46–48	
Warning against causing believers to sin	18:6–14	9:38–50	9:49–50	
Treatment and forgiveness of a sinning brother	18:15–35			

	MATTHEW	MARK	LUKE	JOHN
Journey to Jerusalem for the Feast of Booths				
Complete commitment required of followers	8:19–22		9:57–62	
Ridicule by Jesus' half-brothers				7:2–9
Journey through Samaria			9:51–56	7:10

The Later Judean Ministry of Christ
Ministry Beginning at the Feast of Booths

	MATTHEW	MARK	LUKE	JOHN
Mixed reaction to Jesus' teaching and miracles				7:11–31
Frustrated attempt to arrest Jesus				7:32–52
Jesus' forgiveness of a woman caught in adultery				7:53–8:11
Conflict over Jesus' claim to be the light of the world				8:12–20
Jesus' relationship to God the Father				8:21–30
Jesus' relationship to Abraham, and attempted stoning				8:31–59
Healing of a man born blind				9:1–7
Response of the blind man's neighbors				9:8–12
Examination and excommunication of the blind man by the Pharisees				9:13–34
Jesus' identification of Himself to the blind man				9:35–38
Spiritual blindness of the Pharisees				9:39–41
Allegory of the good shepherd and the thief				10:1–18
Further division among the Jews				10:19–21

Private Lessons on Loving Service and Prayer

	MATTHEW	MARK	LUKE	JOHN
Commissioning of the seventy			10:1–16	
Return of the seventy			10:17–24	
Story of the good Samaritan			10:25–37	
Jesus' visit with Mary and Martha			10:38–42	
Lesson on how to pray and parable of the bold friend			11:1–13	

Second Debate with the Scribes and the Pharisees

	MATTHEW	MARK	LUKE	JOHN
A third blasphemous accusation and a second debate			11:14–36	
Woes to the Pharisees and the scribes while eating with a Pharisee			11:37–54	
Warning the disciples about hypocrisy			12:1–12	
Warning about greed and trust in wealth			12:13–34	
Warning against being unprepared for the Son of Man's coming			12:35–48	
Warning about the coming division			12:49–53	
Warning against failing to discern the present time			12:54–59	
Two alternatives: repent or perish			13:1–9	
Opposition from a synagogue ruler for healing a woman on the Sabbath			13:10–21	
Another attempt to stone or arrest Jesus for blasphemy at the Feast of Dedication				10:22–39

The Ministry of Christ in and Around Perea
Principles of Discipleship

	MATTHEW	MARK	LUKE	JOHN
From Jerusalem to Perea				10:40–42
Question about salvation and entering the kingdom			13:22–30	
Anticipation of Jesus' coming death and His sorrow over Jerusalem			13:31–35	
Healing of a man with dropsy while eating with a prominent Pharisee on the Sabbath, and three parables suggested by the occasion			14:1–24	
Cost of discipleship			14:25–35	
Parables in defense of association with sinners			15:1–32	
Parable to teach the proper use of money			16:1–13	
Story to teach the danger of wealth			16:14–31	
Four lessons on discipleship			17:1–10	
Sickness and death of Lazarus				11:1–16
Lazarus raised from the dead				11:17–44
Decision of the Sanhedrin to put Jesus to death				11:45–54

Teaching While on Final Journey to Jerusalem

	MATTHEW	MARK	LUKE	JOHN
Healing of ten lepers while passing through Samaria and Galilee			17:11–21	

	MATTHEW	MARK	LUKE	JOHN
Instructions regarding the Son of Man's coming			17:22–37	
Two parables on prayer: the persistent widow, and the Pharisee and the tax collector			18:1–14	
Conflict with Pharisaic teaching on divorce	19:1–12	10:1–12		
Example of little children in relation to the kingdom	19:13–15	10:13–16	18:15–17	
Riches and the kingdom	19:16–30	10:17–31	18:18–30	
Parable of the landowner's sovereignty	20:1–16			
Third prediction of Jesus' death and resurrection	20:17–19	10:32–34	18:31–34	
Warning against ambitious pride	20:20–28	10:35–45		
Healing of blind Bartimaeus and his companion	20:29–34	10:46–52	18:35–43	
Salvation of Zacchaeus			19:1–10	
Parable to teach responsibility while the kingdom is delayed			19:11–28	

The Formal Presentation of Christ to Israel and the Resulting Conflict

Triumphal Entry and the Fig Tree

	MATTHEW	MARK	LUKE	JOHN
Arrival at Bethany				11:55–12:1, 9–11
Triumphal entry into Jerusalem	21:1–3, 6–7, 4–5, 8–11, 14–17	11:1–11	19:29–44	12:12–19
Cursing of the fig tree having leaves but no figs	21:18–19a	11:12–14		
Second cleansing of the temple	21:12–13	11:15–18	19:45–48	
Request of some Greeks to see Jesus and necessity of the Son of Man's being lifted up				12:20–36a
Different responses to Jesus and Jesus' response to the crowds				12:36b-50
Withered fig tree and the lesson on faith	21:19b-22	11:19–25	21:37–38	

Official Challenge to Christ's Authority

	MATTHEW	MARK	LUKE	JOHN
Questioning of Jesus' authority by the chief priests, teachers of the law, and elders	21:23–27	11:27–33	20:1–8	
Jesus' response with His own question and three parables	21:28–22:14	12:1–12	20:9–19	
Attempts by Pharisees and Herodians to trap Jesus with a question about paying taxes to Caesar	22:15–22	12:13–17	20:20–26	
Sadducees' puzzling question about the resurrection	22:23–33	12:18–27	20:27–40	
A Pharisee's legal question	22:34–40	12:28–34		

Christ's Response to His Enemies' Challenges

	MATTHEW	MARK	LUKE	JOHN
Christ's relationship to David as son and Lord	22:41–46	12:35–37	20:41–44	
Seven woes against the scribes and Pharisees	23:1–36	12:38–40	20:45–47	
Jesus' sorrow over Jerusalem	23:37–39			
A poor widow's gift of all she had		12:41–44	21:1–4	

Prophecies in Preparation for the Death of Christ

The Olivet Discourse: Jesus Speaks Prophetically About the Temple and His Own Second Coming

	MATTHEW	MARK	LUKE	JOHN
Setting of the discourse	24:1–3	13:1–4	21:5–7	
Beginning of birth pains	24:4–14	13:5–13	21:8–19	
Abomination of desolation and subsequent distress	24:15–28	13:14–23	21:20–24	
Coming of the Son of Man	24:29–31	13:24–27	21:25–27	
Signs of nearness but unknown time	24:32–41	13:28–32	21:28–33	
Five parables to teach watchfulness and faithfulness	24:42–25:30	13:33–37	21:34–36	
Judgment at the Son of Man's coming	25:31–46			

Arrangements for Betrayal

	MATTHEW	MARK	LUKE	JOHN
Plot by the Sanhedrin to arrest and kill Jesus	26:1–5	14:1–2	22:1–2	
Mary's anointing of Jesus for burial	26:6–13	14:3–9		12:2–8
Judas's agreement to betray Jesus	26:14–16	14:10–11	22:3–6	

The Last Supper

	MATTHEW	MARK	LUKE	JOHN
Preparation for the Passover meal	26:17–19	14:12–16	22:7–13	

	MATTHEW	MARK	LUKE	JOHN
Beginning of the Passover meal and dissension among the disciples over greatness	26:20	14:17	22:14–16, 24–30	
Washing the disciples' feet				13:1–20
Identification of the betrayer	26:21–25	14:18–21	22:21–23	13:21–30
Prediction of Peter's denial	26:31–35	14:27–31	22:31–38	13:31–38
Conclusion of the meal and the Lord's Supper instituted (1Co 11:23–26)	26:26–29	14:22–25	22:17–20	

Discourse and Prayers from the Upper Room to Gethsemane

	MATTHEW	MARK	LUKE	JOHN
Questions about His destination, the Father, and the Holy Spirit answered				14:1–31
The vine and the branches				15:1–17
Opposition from the world				15:18–16:4
Coming and ministry of the Spirit				16:5–15
Prediction of joy over His resurrection				16:16–22
Promise of answered prayer and peace				16:23–33
Jesus' prayer for His disciples and all who believe				17:1–26
Jesus' three agonizing prayers in Gethsemane	26:30, 36–46	14:26, 32–42	22:39–46	18:1

The Death of Christ

Betrayal and Arrest

	MATTHEW	MARK	LUKE	JOHN
Jesus betrayed, arrested, and forsaken	26:47–56	14:43–52	22:47–53	18:2–12

Trial

	MATTHEW	MARK	LUKE	JOHN
First Jewish phase, before Annas				18:13–14, 19–23
Second Jewish phase, before Caiaphas and the Sanhedrin	26:57, 59–68	14:53, 55–65	22:54a, 63–65	18:24
Peter's denials	26:58, 69–75	14:54, 66–72	22:54b-62	18:15–18, 25–27
Third Jewish phase, before the Sanhedrin	27:1	15:1a	22:66–71	
Remorse and suicide of Judas Iscariot (Ac 1:18–19)	27:3–10			
First Roman phase, before Pilate	27:2, 11–14	15:1b-5	23:1–5	18:28–38
Second Roman phase, before Herod Antipas			23:6–12	
Third Roman phase, before Pilate	27:15–26	15:6–15	23:13–25	18:39–19:16a

Crucifixion

	MATTHEW	MARK	LUKE	JOHN
Mockery by the Roman soldiers	27:27–30	15:16–19		
Journey to Golgotha	27:31–34	15:20–23	23:26–33a	19:16b-17
First three hours of crucifixion	27:35–44	15:24–32	23:33b-43	19:18, 23–24, 19–22, 25–27
Last three hours of crucifixion	27:45–50	15:33–37	23:44–45a, 46	19:28–30
Witness of Jesus' death	27:51–56	15:38–41	23:45b, 47–49	

Burial

	MATTHEW	MARK	LUKE	JOHN
Certification of Jesus' death and procurement of His body	27:57–58	15:42–45	23:50–52	19:31–38
Jesus' body placed in a tomb	27:59–60	15:46	23:53–54	19:39–42
The tomb watched by the women and guarded by the soldiers	27:61–66	15:47	23:55–56	

The Resurrection and Ascension of Christ

The Empty Tomb

	MATTHEW	MARK	LUKE	JOHN
The tomb visited by the women	28:1	16:1		
The stone rolled away	28:2–4			
The tomb found to be empty by the women	28:5–8	16:2–8	24:1–8	20:1
The tomb found to be empty by Peter and John			24:9–12	20:2–10

The Post Resurrection Appearances

	MATTHEW	MARK	LUKE	JOHN
Appearance to Mary Magdalene		16:9–11		20:11–18
Appearance to the other women	28:9–10			
Report of the soldiers to the Jewish authorities	28:11–15			
Appearance to the two disciples traveling to Emmaus		16:12–13	24:13–32	
Report of the two disciples to the rest (1Co. 15:5a)			24:33–35	
Appearance to the ten assembled disciples		16:14	24:36–43	20:19–25
Appearance to the eleven assembled disciples (1Co. 15:5b)				20:26–31

	MATTHEW	MARK	LUKE	JOHN
Appearance to the seven disciples while fishing				21:1–25
Appearance to the Eleven in Galilee (1Co. 15:6)	28:16–20	16:15–18		
Appearance to James, Jesus' brother (1Co. 15:7)				
Appearance to the disciples in Jerusalem (Ac 1:3–8)			24:44–49	

The Ascension

	MATTHEW	MARK	LUKE	JOHN
Christ's parting blessing and departure (Ac 1:9–12)		16:19–20	24:50–53	

PROPHECIES OF THE MESSIAH FULFILLED IN JESUS

OT Text	NT Text	Subject
Ge 3:15	Lk 22:53	Satan against Jesus
Ge 3:15	Heb 2:14; 1Jn 3:8	Jesus' victory over Satan
Ge 12:3	Ac 3:25; Gal 3:8	Gentiles blessed through Christ as the offspring of Abraham
Ge 13:15	Gal 3:15–16, 19	Messiah as the seed of Abraham
Ge 14:18–20	Heb 7	Jesus' priesthood according to the likeness of Melchizedek
Ge 18:18	Ac 3:25; Gal 3:8	Gentiles blessed through Christ as the offspring of Abraham
Ge 22:18	Ac 3:25; Gal 3:8	Gentiles blessed through Christ as the offspring of Abraham
Ge 49:10	Lk 1:32–33	Coming ruler from Judah
Ex 12:1–14, 46	Jn 19:31–36; 1Co 5:7; 1Pe 1:19	The Messiah as the Passover Lamb
Ex 16:4	Jn 6:31–33	Messiah to give true bread from heaven
Ex 24:8	Heb 9:11–28	The Messiah's blood to be shed as sacrifice
Lev 15:15–17	Ro 3:25; Heb 9:1–14, 24; 1Jn 2:2	Atoning sacrifice of blood
Nu 21:8–9	Jn 3:14–15	Life through looking at one on a cross
Nu 24:17	Lk 1:32–33	Coming ruler from Jacob
Nu 24:17	Rev 22:16	Coming star out of Jacob
Dt 18:17	Jn 6:14; 12:49–50; Ac 3:22–23	Coming prophet sent from God
Dt 21:23	Gal 3:13	Messiah cursed for hanging on a tree
Dt 30:12–14	Ro 10:6–8	Jesus is God's word near to us
2Sa 7:14	Heb 1:5	Messiah to be God's Son
2Sa 7:16	Lk 1:32–33; Rev 19:11–16	David's Son as eternal king
1Ch 17:13	Heb 1:5	Messiah to be God's Son
1Ch 17:14	Lk 1:32–33; Rev 19:11–16	David's Son as eternal king
Ps 2:7	Mt 3:17; 17:5; Mk 1:11; 9:7; Lk 3:22; 9:35; Ac 13:33; Heb 1:5	God's address to his Son
Ps 2:9	Rev 2:27	Messiah to rule the nations with power
Ps 8:2	Mt 21:16	Children to praise God's Son
Ps 8:4–5	Heb 2:6–9	Jesus lower than the angels

OT Text	NT Text	Subject
Ps 8:6	1Co 15:27–28; Eph 1:22	Everything subject to God's Son
Ps 16:8–11	Ac 2:25–32; 13:35–37	David's Son to be raised from the dead
Ps 22:1	Mt 27:46; Mk 15:34	God–forsaken cry by the Messiah
Ps 22:7–8	Mt 27:29, 41–44; Mk 15:18, 29–32; Lk 23:35–39	Messiah mocked by a crowd
Ps 22:18	Mt 27:35; Mk 15:24; Lk 23:34; Jn 19:24	Casting lots for Jesus' clothes
Ps 22:22	Heb 2:12	Jesus to declare his name in the church
Ps 31:5	Lk 23:46	Messiah to commit his spirit to God
Ps 34:20	Jn 19:31–36	Messiah to have no broken bones
Ps 35:19	Jn 15:25	Messiah experiencing hatred for no reason
Ps 40:6–8	Jn 6:38; Heb 10:5–9	Messiah to do God's perfect will
Ps 41:9	Jn 13:18	The Messiah's betrayal by a friend
Ps 45:6–7	Heb 1:8–9	Characteristics of the coming King
Ps 68:18	Eph 4:7–11	Ascension and giving gifts to humans
Ps 69:4	Jn 15:25	Messiah experiencing hatred for no reason
Ps 69:9	Jn 2:14–22	The Messiah's zeal for God's house
Ps 69:21	Jn 19:29	The thirst of the suffering Messiah
Ps 69:25	Ac 1:20	Judgment on the Messiah's persecutor
Ps 78:2	Mt 13:34–35	Messiah to speak in parables
Ps 102:25–27	Heb 1:10–12	Characteristics of the coming King
Ps 110:1	Ac 2:34–35; 1Co 15:25; Eph 1:20–22; Heb 1:13; 10:12–13	Jesus exalted in power at God's right hand
Ps 110:1	Mt 22:41–45; Mk 12:35–37; Lk 20:41–44	Jesus as Son and Lord of David
Ps 110:4	Heb 5:6; 7:11–22	Jesus' priesthood after Melchizedek
Ps 118:22–23	Mt 21:42–44; Mk 12:10; Lk 20:17–19; Ac 4:10–11; 1Pe 2:7–8	Rejected stone to become capstone
Ps 118:26	Mt 21:9; Mk 11:9; Lk 19:38; Jn 12:13	Messiah to come in the name of the Lord
Isa 6:9–10	Mt 13:14–15; Mk 4:12; Lk 8:10; Jn 12:37–41	Hearts to be closed to the gospel
Isa 7:14	Mt 1:18–23; Lk 1:26–35	Virgin birth of the Messiah

OT Text	NT Text	Subject
Isa 8:14	Ro 9:32–33; 1 Pe 2:7–8	A stone over which people stumble
Isa 9:1–2	Mt 4:13–16; Mk 1:14–15; Lk 4:14–15	Ministry to begin in Galilee
Isa 9:6–7	Lk 1:32–33	David's Son as eternal king
Isa 9:7	Jn 1:1, 18	The Messiah to be God
Isa 9:7	Eph 2:14–17	The Messiah to be a man of peace
Isa 11:1–2	Mt 3:16; Mk 1:16; Lk 3:21–22	Branch of Jesse (David) to receive the Spirit)
Isa 11:10	Lk 1:32–33	Root of Jesse (David) as coming ruler
Isa 11:10	Ro 15:12	Salvation to be available for Gentiles
Isa 22:22	Rev 3:7	Jesus to receive the key of David
Isa 25:8	1Co 15:54	Death to be swallowed up in victory
Isa 28:16	Ro 9:32–33; 1Pe 2:6	Messiah to be the chief cornerstone
Isa 35:5–6	Mt 11:4–6; Lk 7:22	Messiah to be a mighty worker of miracles
Isa 40:3–5	Mt 3:3; Mk 1:3; Lk 3:4; Jn 1:23	Jesus' forerunner, a voice in the desert
Isa 42:1–4	Mt 12:15–21	Messiah as the chosen servant of the Lord
Isa 45:23	Ro 14:11; Php 2:10	Every knee to bow before the Messiah
Isa 49:6	Ac 13:46–47	Messiah as a light to the Gentiles
Isa 50:6	Mt 27:26–30; Mk 14:65; 15:15, 19; Lk 22:63; Jn 19:1, 3	Beating God's servant
Isa 50:6	Mt 26:67; Mk 14:65	Spitting on God's servant
Isa 53:1	Jn 12:38; Ro 10:16	Israel not to believe in the Messiah
Isa 53:3	Jn 1:11	Messiah to be rejected by his own people
Isa 53:4–5	Mt 8:16–17; Mk 1:32–34; Lk 4:40–41; 1Pe 2:24	Healing ministry of God's servant
Isa 53:7–8	Jn 1:29, 36; Ac 8:30–35; 1Pe 1:19; Rev 5:6, 12	Suffering Lamb of God
Isa 53:9	Heb 4:15; 1Pe 2:22	The sinless servant of God
Isa 53:9	Mt 27:57–60	Messiah to be buried in a rich man's grave
Isa 53:12	Mt 27:38; Mk 15:27–28; Lk 22:37; 23:33; Jn 19:18	God's servant numbered with transgressors
Isa 55:3	Lk 22:20; 1Co 11:25	Everlasting covenant through the Messiah
Isa 55:3	Ac 13:33	Blessings of David given to the Messiah

OT Text	NT Text	Subject
Isa 59:20–21	Ro 11:26–27	Israel's Deliverer to come from Zion
Isa 60:1–3	Mt 2:11; Ro 15:8–12	Gentiles coming to worship the Messiah
Isa 61:1–2	Mt 4:16; Mk 1:10; Lk 4:18–21	The Messiah anointed by the Holy Spirit
Isa 65:1	Ro 10:20	Gentiles would believe in the Messiah
Isa 65:2	Ro 10:21	Israel would reject the Messiah
Jer 23:5	Lk 1:32–33	David's Son to be a great King
Jer 23:6	Mt 1:21	David's Son to be Savior
Jer 23:6	1Co 1:30	Messiah to be named "Our Righteousness"
Jer 31:15	Mt 2:16–18	Rachel weeping when God's Son is born
Jer 31:31–34	Lk 22:20; 1Co 11:25; Heb 8:8–12; 10:15–18	Jesus and the new covenant
Jer 32:40	Lk 22:20; 1Co 11:25	Everlasting covenant through the Messiah
Jer 33:15	Lk 1:32–33	David's Son to be a great King
Jer 33:16	Mt 1:21	David's Son to be Savior
Jer 33:16	1Co 1:30	Messiah to be named "Our Righteousness"
Eze 21:26–27	Lk 1:32–33	A rightful crown for the Messiah
Eze 34:23–24	Jn 10:11, 14, 16; Heb 13:20; 1Pe 5:4	The coming good shepherd
Eze 37:24–25	Lk 1:32–33	Messiah to be David's son and a king
Eze 37:24–25	Jn 10:11, 14, 16; Heb 13:20; 1Pe 5:4	The coming good shepherd
Eze 37:26	Lk 22:20; 1Co 11:25	Messiah's everlasting covenant of peace
Da 7:13–14	Mt 24:30; 26:64; Mk 13:26; 14:62; Lk 21:27; Rev 1:13; 14:14	The coming of the Son of Man
Da 7:27	Rev 11:15	The coming everlasting kingdom of the Messiah
Da 9:24–26	Gal 4:4	Timetable for the Messiah's coming
Hos 11:1	Mt 2:14–15	Jesus to return from Egypt
Joel 2:28–32	Ac 2:14–21	God's Spirit to be poured out
Am 9:11–12	Ac 15:13–18	Gentiles would believe in the Messiah
Jnh 1:17	Mt 12:39–40	Messiah to be three days and nights in grave
Mic 5:2	Mt 2:1–6	The Messiah to be born in Bethlehem
Mic 5:2	Lk 1:32–33	The Messiah as an eternal king

OT Text	NT Text	Subject
Mic 5:4	Jn 10:11, 14	The coming shepherd of God's flock
Mic 5:5	Eph 2:14–17	The Messiah to be a man of peace
Zec 9:9	Mt 21:1–9; Mk 11:1–10; Lk 19:28–38; Jn 12:12–16	The coming ruler on a donkey
Zec 11:12–13	Mt 27:1–10	Thirty pieces of silver for a potter's field
Zec 12:10	Jn 19:37; Rev 1:7	Looking on the pierced Messiah
Zec 13:7	Mt 26:31; 26:55–56; Mk 14:27; 14:48–50	Striking the coming shepherd; the sheep flee
Mal 3:1	Mt 11:7–10; Mk 1:2–4; Lk 7:24–27	The forerunner to the Messiah
Mal 4:5–6	Mt 11:14; 17:11–13; Mk 9:11–13; Mk 9:11–13; Lk 1:16–17	The forerunner as Elijah returned

PARABLES OF JESUS

Parable	Matthew	Mark	Luke
Lamp under a basket	5:14–15	4:21–22	8:16; 11:33
Wise and foolish builders	7:24–27		6:47–49
New cloth on an old garment	9:16	2:21	5:36
New wine in old wineskins	9:17	2:22	5:37–38
Sower and the soils	13:3–8, 18–23	4:3–8, 14–20	8:5–8, 11–15
Tares	13:24–30, 36–43		
Mustard seed	13:31–32	4:30–32	13:18–19
Leaven	13:33		13:20–21
Hidden treasure	13:44		
Valuable pearl	13:45–46		
Dragnet	13:47–50		
Head of a household	13:52		
Lost sheep	18:12–14		15:4–7
Unmerciful slave	18:23–34		
Laborers in the vineyard	20:1–16		
Two sons	21:28–32		
Vine–growers	21:33–44	12:1–11	20:9–18
Wedding feast	22:2–14		
Fig tree	24:32–35	13:28–29	21:29–31
Faithful and sensible slave	24:45–51		12:42–48
Ten virgins	25:1–13		
Talents (minas)	25:14–30		19:12–27
Sheep and goats	25:31–46		
Growing seed		4:26–29	

Parable	Matthew	Mark	Luke
Watchful slaves		13:35–37	12:35–40
Moneylender			7:41–43
Good Samaritan			10:30–37
Friend in need			11:5–8
Rich fool			12:16–21
Unfruitful fig tree			13:6–9
Lowest seat at the feast			14:7–14
Big dinner			14:16–24
Cost of discipleship			14:28–33
Lost coin			15:8–10
Lost (prodigal) son			15:11–32
Shrewd manager			16:1–8
Rich man and Lazarus			16:19–31
Master and his slave			17:7–10
Persistent widow			18:2–8
Pharisee and tax collector			18:10–14

MIRACLES OF JESUS

Healing Miracles	Matthew	Mark	Luke	John
Man with leprosy	8:2–4	1:40–42	5:12–13	
Roman centurion's servant	8:5–13		7:1–10	
Peter's mother–in–law	8:14–15	1:30–31	4:38–35	
Two men from Gadara	8:28–34	5:1–15	8:27–35	
Paralyzed man	9:2–7	2:3–12	5:18–25	
Woman with bleeding	9:20–22	5:25–29	8:43–48	
Two blind men	9:27–31			
Mute, demon–possessed man	9:32–33			
Man with a withered hand	12:10–13	3:1–5	6:6–10	
Blind, mute, demon–possessed man	12:22		11:14	
Canaanite woman's daughter	15:21–28	7:24–30		
Boy with a demon	17:14–18	9:17–29	9:38–43	
Two blind men (including Bartimaeus)	20:29–34	10:46–52	18:35–43	
Deaf mute		7:31–37		
Possessed man in synagogue		1:23–26	4:33–35	
Blind man at Bethsaida		8:22–26		
Crippled woman			13:11–13	
Man with dropsy			14:1–4	
Ten men with leprosy			17:11–19	
The high priest's servant			22:50–51	
Official's son at Capernaum				4:46–54
Sick man at pool of Bethesda				5:1–9
Man born blind				9:1–7

Miracles showing power over nature	Matthew	Mark	Luke	John
Calming the storm	8:23–27	4:37–41	8:22–25	
Walking on water	14:25	6:48–51		6:19–21
Feeding of the 5,,000	14:15–21	6:35–44	9:12–17	6:6–13
Feeding of the 4,,000	15:32–38	8:1–9		
Coin in fish	17:24–27			
Fig tree withered	21:18–22	11:12–14, 20–25		
Large catch of fish			5:4–11	
Water turned into wine				2:1–11
Another large catch of fish				21:1–11
Miracles of raising the dead				
Jairus's daughter	9:18–19, 23–25	5:22–24, 38–42	8:41–42, 49–56	
Widow's son at Nain			7:11–15	
Lazarus				11:1–44

OLD TESTAMENT CHRONOLOGY (FROM ABRAHAM)

Abram born	2166 B.C.
Abraham dies	1991
Jacob and family in Egypt	1876
Moses born	1526
The Exodus	1446
Moses dies; Israelites enter Canaan	1406
The Judges	1375–1050
Saul as king	1050–1010
David as king	1010–970
Solomon as king	970–930
Northern kingdom of Israel	930–722
Southern kingdom of Judah	930–586
Exile	586–538
First return under Zerubbabel	538
Temple rebuilt	536–516
Second return under Ezra	458
Wall of Jerusalem rebuilt	445
Third return under Nehemiah	432
Close of OT history and prophecy	c. 400

NEW TESTAMENT CHRONOLOGY

Birth of Jesus	7–5 B.C.
Baptism of Jesus	A.D. 26
Crucifixion of Jesus	30
Conversion of Saul	34/35
Death of Herod Agrippa I	44
James written	before 50 (?)
First Missionary Journey	46–48
Galatians written	48/49
Jerusalem Conference	49/50
Second Missionary Journey	50–52
Paul at Corinth	50–52
1 and 2 Thessalonians written	51

Arrival of Gallio as Proconsul	52
Third Missionary Journey	53–57
Paul at Ephesus	54–57
1 and 2 Corinthians written	55
Romans written	57
Paul's Arrest in Jerusalem	57
Imprisonment at Caesarea	57–59
On Island of Malta	59
Arrival at Rome	59
Roman Imprisonment	59–61/62
Colossians, Philemon, Ephesians written	60
Philippians written	61
Paul's Release and Further Work	62–67
1 Timothy and Titus written	63–65
Synoptic Gospels and Acts written	before 67
1 and 2 Peter written	67/68
Peter's Death at Rome	67/68
Paul's Second Roman Imprisonment	67/68
2 Timothy written	67/68
Paul's Death at Rome	67/68
Jude written	c. 65–80
Writings of John	c. 90–100
Death of John	c. 100

TABLE OF NATIONS

Tiras?

Gomer

Javan

Javan

LUD?

Meshech

Tubal

▲ *Mt. Ararat*

ASSHUR

Madai

ARPACHSHAD

ARAM

Tigris R.

ELAM

Euphrates R.

CANAAN

PUT?

MIZRAIM

Nile R.

CUSH

Descendants of Noah (Ge 10)

HAM *SHEM* Japheth

Miles	0		200		400		600
Kms	0	300		600		900	

THE EXODUS

CITIES OF REFUGE

DAVID'S JERUSALEM

SOLOMON'S JERUSALEM

THE DIVIDED KINGDOM

JERUSALEM OF THE PROPHETS

EXILE OF THE NORTHERN KINGDOM

EXILE OF THE SOUTHERN KINGDOM

RETURN FROM EXILE

JERUSALEM OF THE RETURNED EXILES

THE KINGDOM OF HEROD

Legend:
- ⛊ Fortress cities of Herod
- General location of boundaries of Herod's kingdom
- Indefinite boundary (desert, etc.)
- ▲ Mountain

Labels on map: ITUREA, ABILENE, Abana R., Damascus, Sidon, Leontes R., Mt. Hermon, Phar par R., TRACHONITIS, Tyre, Caesarea Philippi, Lake Semechonitis, Mt. Meiron, GAULANITIS, BATANEA, PHOENICIA, Acco (Ptolemais), Chorazin, Capernaum, Bethsaida, Raphana, Tiberias, Sea of Galilee, Dion, Mt. Carmel, GALILEE, Nazareth, Mt. Tabor, AURANITIS, Dor, Nain, Yarmuk R., Caesarea, Scythopolis, DECAPOLIS, ARABIA, Pella, The Great Sea (Mediterranean), SAMARIA, Samaria, Mt. Ebal, Sychar, Mt. Gerizim, Jabbok R., Antipatris, Alexandrium, Joppa, Phaselis, Philadelphia, Arimathea, Ephraim, Ramah, Lydda, Jericho, Jamnia, PEREA, Jordan R., Ashdod, JUDEA, Azotus, Jerusalem, Ashkelon, Bethlehem, Qumran, Mt. Nebo, Herodium, Gaza, Hebron, Machaerus, Arnon R., IDUMEA, Masada, Dead Sea, Beersheba, NABATEAN KINGDOM, ARABIA

Miles / Kms scale

JERUSALEM IN THE TIME OF JESUS

Labels: Hippodrome, Psephinus Tower, NORTH, Tyropoeon Street, Present Damascus Gate, "Garden Tomb" (alternate crucifixion site) †††, Maximum city growth within walls by A.D. 70, Bridge over valley ("Wilson's Arch"), Xystus (Greek exercise hall), Antonia Fortress (later Praetorium?), Hasmonean Palace, BEZETHA ("New City"), Pool of Bethesda, Traditional Crucifixion Site †††, Herod's Towers, Herod's Royal Palace, MT. ZION ("Upper City"), TEMPLE, Gentiles Court, HINNOM VALLEY, FIRST WALL, Essene Gate, FIRST WALL, Huldah Gates and Stairways, Traditional Upper Room?, Gihon Spring, HINNOM VALLEY, SOUTH, Ashpot Gate/ Tekoa Gate, KIDRON VALLEY, CITY OF DAVID "Lower City", MOUNT OF OLIVES, Pool of Siloam, Theater

GALILEE IN THE TIME OF JESUS

Labels: Lake Semechonitis, Mediterranean Sea, Ptolemais, Chorazin, Bethsaida, Capernaum, Mt. Carmel, Magdala, Sea of Galilee, Tiberias, Kishon R., Cana, Nazareth, Mt. Tabor, Nain, Yarmuk R., Jordan R., Caesarea, Scythopolis

Miles / Kms scale

SAMARIA-JUDEA IN THE TIME OF JESUS

Labels: Ptolemais, Capernaum, Mediterranean Sea, GALILEE, Sea of Galilee, Cana, Tiberias, Nazareth, Mt. Tabor, Yarmuk R., Nain, Caesarea, Scythopolis, Pella, SAMARIA, Salim, Aenon, Samaria, Sychar, Mt. Gerizim, Jabbok R., PEREA, Jordan R., JUDEA, Jericho, Emmaus, Jerusalem, Bethany, Bethlehem, Dead Sea, Machaerus, Arnon R.

Miles / Kms scale

PAUL'S FIRST MISSIONARY JOURNEY PAUL'S SECOND MISSIONARY JOURNEY

PAUL'S THIRD MISSIONARY JOURNEY PAUL'S JOURNEY TO ROME

PAUL'S FOURTH MISSIONARY JOURNEY

THE SEVEN CHURCHES OF REVELATION

★ Pergamum

★ Thyatira

ASIA

EUBOEA

CHIOS

★ Sardis

★ Philadelphia

Antioch

★ Smyrna

Aegean Sea

ANDROS

SAMOS

★ Ephesus

★ Laodicea

TINOS

Miletus

NAXOS

PATMOS

COS

PAMPHYLIA

LYCIA

MILOS

Cnidus

Attalia

Rhodes

Patara Myra

RHODES

Miles 0 50 100

Kms 0 50 100 150 200